# GARDNER'S
# ART through the AGES

GARDNER'S

FRED S. KLEINER

# ART through the AGES

A GLOBAL HISTORY

FOURTEENTH EDITION

WADSWORTH
CENGAGE Learning

Australia • Brazil • Japan • Korea • Mexico • Singapore • Spain • United Kingdom • United States

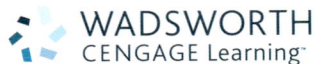
**WADSWORTH**
CENGAGE Learning™

**Gardner's Art through the Ages:
A Global History, Fourteenth Edition**
**Fred S. Kleiner**

Publisher: Clark Baxter

Senior Development Editor: Sharon Adams Poore

Assistant Editor: Ashley Bargende

Editorial Assistant: Elizabeth Newell

Associate Media Editor: Kimberly Apfelbaum

Senior Marketing Manager: Jeanne Heston

Marketing Coordinator: Klaira Markenzon

Senior Marketing Communications Manager: Heather Baxley

Senior Content Project Manager: Lianne Ames

Senior Art Director: Cate Rickard Barr

Senior Print Buyer: Mary Beth Hennebury

Rights Acquisition Specialist, Images: Mandy Groszko

Production Service & Layout: Joan Keyes, Dovetail Publishing Services

Text Designer: tani hasegawa

Cover Designer: tani hasegawa

Cover Image: © Estate of Joan Mitchell. Photograph: © Butler Institute of American Art, Youngstown, OH, USA/Gift of Marilynn Meeker, 1986 Courtesy of the Joan Mitchell Foundation, NYC/The Bridgeman Art Library International

Compositor: Thompson Type, Inc.

For product information and technology assistance, contact us at **Cengage Learning Customer & Sales Support, 1-800-354-9706**

For permission to use material from this text or product, submit all requests online at **www.cengage.com/permissions.** Further permissions questions can be emailed to **permissionrequest@cengage.com.**

Library of Congress Control Number: 2011931486

Student Edition:
ISBN-13: 978-0-495-91542-3
ISBN-10: 0-495-91542-4

**Wadsworth**
20 Channel Center Street
Boston, MA 02210
USA

Cengage Learning is a leading provider of customized learning solutions with office locations around the globe, including Singapore, the United Kingdom, Australia, Mexico, Brazil and Japan. Locate your local office at **international.cengage.com/region**

Cengage Learning products are represented in Canada by Nelson Education, Ltd.

For your course and learning solutions, visit **www.cengage.com.** Purchase any of our products at your local college store or at our preferred online store **www.cengagebrain.com.**

**Instructors:** Please visit **login.cengage.com** and log in to access instructor-specific resources.

Printed in the United States of America
1 2 3 4 5 6 7 15 14 13 12 11

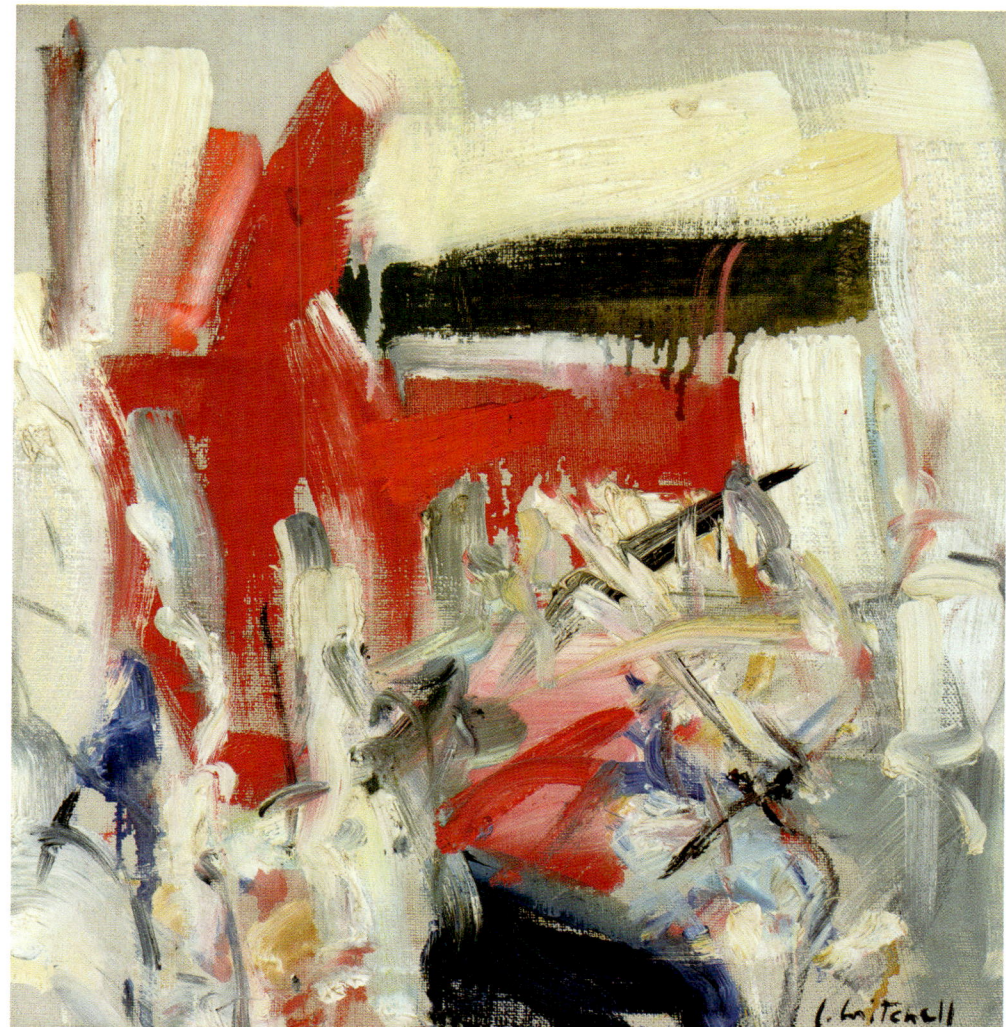

JOAN MITCHELL, *Untitled,* ca. 1953–1954. Oil on canvas, 1′ 5″ × 1′ 4″. Butler Institute of American Art, Youngstown (gift of Marilynn Meekder, 1986).

The first major American art movement to emerge in the years following World War II was Abstract Expressionism. The Abstract Expressionists built on the innovations of earlier 20th-century masters, but went even further in rejecting the illusionism that had dominated Western art since the Renaissance. As the name suggests, the Abstract Expressionists produced paintings that are abstract but express the artist's state of mind, with the goal also of striking emotional chords in the viewer. Abstract Expressionist paintings often feature vigorous application of pigment to the canvas—sometimes literally flung from the brush or dripped onto the canvas—hence the name "action painting" often applied to this movement.

JOAN MITCHELL (1925–1992) was the most prominent woman to embrace action painting, an art form widely regarded as violent, heroic, and distinctly masculine. Indeed, Mitchell took offense at the very notion of a "woman painter" as opposed to a painter who was a woman. Illustrated here is one of Mitchell's early and characteristically untitled canvases. It features broad intersecting bands of red, black, and white, mixed with shorter, narrower, curving brushstrokes that fill almost the entire surface of the canvas. In contrast to most works in the Western tradition, both figural and abstract, the focus of attention in this composition is off-center at the upper left.

Mitchell's intensely personal approach to painting characterizes the art of the modern era in general, but it is not typical of many periods of art history when artists toiled in anonymity to fulfill the wishes of their patrons, whether Egyptian pharaohs, Roman emperors, or medieval monks. *Art through the Ages* surveys the art of all periods from prehistory to the present, and worldwide, and examines how artworks of all kinds have always reflected the historical contexts in which they were created.

# BRIEF CONTENTS

# CONTENTS

# CHAPTER 27

## ROMANTICISM, REALISM, PHOTOGRAPHY: EUROPE AND AMERICA, 1800 TO 1870  754

FRAMING THE ERA | Napoleon at Jaffa  755

# CHAPTER 28

## IMPRESSIONISM, POST-IMPRESSIONISM, SYMBOLISM: EUROPE AND AMERICA, 1870 TO 1900  798

FRAMING THE ERA | Impressions of Modern Life  799

# CHAPTER 29

## MODERNISM IN EUROPE AND AMERICA, 1900 TO 1945  834

FRAMING THE ERA | Global War, Anarchy, and Dada  835

# PREFACE

## THE GARDNER LEGACY IN THE 21ST CENTURY

I take great pleasure in introducing the extensively revised and expanded 14th edition of *Gardner's Art through the Ages: A Global History,* which, like the enhanced 13th edition, is a hybrid art history textbook—the first, and still the only, introductory survey of the history of art of its kind. This innovative new kind of "Gardner" retains all of the best features of traditional books on paper while harnessing 21st-century technology to increase by 25% the number of works examined—without increasing the size or weight of the book itself and at very low additional cost to students compared to a larger book.

When Helen Gardner published the first edition of *Art through the Ages* in 1926, she could not have imagined that more than 85 years later instructors all over the world would still be using her textbook in their classrooms. Indeed, if she were alive today, she would not recognize the book that, even in its traditional form, long ago became—and remains—the most widely read introduction to the history of art and architecture in the English language. During the past half-century, successive authors have constantly reinvented Helen Gardner's groundbreaking global survey, always keeping it fresh and current, and setting an ever-higher standard with each new edition. I am deeply gratified that both professors and students seem to agree that the 13th edition, released in 2008, lived up to that venerable tradition, for they made it the number-one choice for art history survey courses. I hope they will find the 14th edition of this best-selling book exceeds their high expectations.

In addition to the host of new features (enumerated below) in the book proper, the 14th edition follows the enhanced 13th edition in incorporating an innovative new online component. All new copies of the 14th edition are packaged with an access code to a web site with *bonus essays* and *bonus images* (with zoom capability) of more than 300 additional important paintings, sculptures, buildings, and other art forms of all eras, from prehistory to the present and worldwide. The selection includes virtually all of the works professors have told me they wished had been in the 13th edition, but were not included for lack of space. I am extremely grateful to Cengage Learning/Wadsworth for the considerable investment of time and resources that has made this remarkable hybrid textbook possible.

In contrast to the enhanced 13th edition, the online component is now fully integrated into the 14th edition. Every one of the more than 300 bonus images is cited in the text of the traditional book and a thumbnail image of each work, with abbreviated caption, is inset into the text column where the work is mentioned. The integration extends also to the maps, index, glossary, and chapter summaries, which seamlessly merge the printed and online information. The 14th edition is in every way a unified, comprehensive history of art and architecture, even though the text is divided into paper and digital components.

## KEY FEATURES OF THE 14TH EDITION

In this new edition, I have added several important features while retaining the basic format and scope of the previous edition. Once again, the hybrid Gardner boasts roughly 1,700 photographs, plans, and drawings, nearly all in color and reproduced according to the highest standards of clarity and color fidelity, including hundreds of new images, among them a new series of superb photos taken by Jonathan Poore exclusively for *Art through the Ages* during three photographic campaigns in France and Italy in 2009, 2010, and 2011. The online component also includes custom videos made at each site by Sharon Adams Poore. This extraordinary new archive of visual material ranges from ancient Roman ruins in southern France to Romanesque and Gothic churches in France and Tuscany to Le Corbusier's modernist chapel at Ronchamp and the postmodern Pompidou Center and the Louvre Pyramide in Paris. The 14th edition also features the highly acclaimed architectural drawings of John Burge. Together, these exclusive photographs, videos, and drawings provide readers with a visual feast unavailable anywhere else.

The captions accompanying those illustrations contain, as before, a wealth of information, including the name of the artist or architect, if known; the formal title (printed in italics), if assigned, description of the work, or name of the building; the provenance or place of production of the object or location of the building; the date; the material(s) used; the size; and the present location if the work is in a museum or private collection. Scales accompany not only all architectural plans, as is the norm, but also appear next to each photograph of a painting, statue, or other artwork—another unique feature of the Gardner text. The works discussed in the 14th edition of *Art through the Ages* vary enormously in size, from colossal sculptures carved into mountain cliffs and paintings that cover entire walls or ceilings to tiny figurines, coins, and jewelry that one can hold in the hand. Although the captions contain the pertinent dimensions, it is difficult for students who have never seen the paintings or statues in person to translate those dimensions into an appreciation of the real size of the objects. The scales provide an effective and direct way to visualize how big or how small a given artwork is and its relative size compared with other objects in the same chapter and throughout the book.

Also retained in this edition are the Quick-Review Captions introduced in the 13th edition. Students have overwhelmingly reported that they found these brief synopses of the most significant aspects of each artwork or building illustrated invaluable when preparing for examinations. These extended captions accompany not only every image in the printed book but also all the digital images in the online supplement. Another popular tool introduced in the 13th edition to aid students in reviewing and mastering the material reappears in the 14th edition. Each chapter ends with a full-page feature called *The Big Picture,* which sets forth in bullet-point format the most important characteristics of each period or artistic movement discussed in the chapter. Small illustrations of characteristic works accompany the summary of major points. The 14th edition, however, introduces two new features in every chapter: a timeline summarizing the major developments during the era treated (again in bullet-point format for easy review) and a chapter-opening essay on a characteristic painting, sculpture, or building. Called *Framing the Era,* these in-depth essays are accompanied by a general view and four enlarged details of the work discussed.

The 14th edition of *Art through the Ages* is available in several different traditional paper formats—a single hardcover volume; two paperback volumes designed for use in the fall and spring semesters of a yearlong survey course; a six-volume "backpack" set; and an interactive e-book version. Another pedagogical tool not found in any other introductory art history textbook is the *Before 1300* section that appears at the beginning of the second volume of the paperbound version of the book and at the beginning of Book D of the backpack edition. Because many students taking the second half of a survey course will not have access to Volume I or to Books A, B, and C, I have provided a special set of concise primers on architectural terminology and construction methods in the ancient and medieval worlds, and on mythology and religion—information that is essential for understanding the history of art after 1300, both in the West and the East. The subjects of these special boxes are Greco-Roman Temple Design and the Classical Orders; Arches and Vaults; Basilican Churches; Central-Plan Churches; The Gods and Goddesses of Mount Olympus; The Life of Jesus in Art; Buddhism and Buddhist Iconography; and Hinduism and Hindu Iconography.

Boxed essays once again appear throughout the book as well. This popular feature first appeared in the 11th edition of *Art through the Ages,* which in 2001 won both the Texty and McGuffey Prizes of the Text and Academic Authors Association for a college textbook in the humanities and social sciences. In this edition the essays are more closely tied to the main text than ever before. Consistent with that greater integration, almost all boxes now incorporate photographs of important artworks discussed in the text proper that also illustrate the theme treated in the boxed essays. These essays fall under six broad categories:

*Architectural Basics* boxes provide students with a sound foundation for the understanding of architecture. These discussions are concise explanations, with drawings and diagrams, of the major aspects of design and construction. The information included is essential to an understanding of architectural technology and terminology. The boxes address questions of how and why various forms developed, the problems architects confronted, and the solutions they used to resolve them. Topics discussed include how the Egyptians built the pyramids; the orders of classical architecture; Roman concrete construction; and the design and terminology of mosques, stupas, and Gothic cathedrals.

*Materials and Techniques* essays explain the various media artists employed from prehistoric to modern times. Since materials and techniques often influence the character of artworks, these discussions contain essential information on why many monuments appear as they do. Hollow-casting bronze statues; fresco painting; Chinese silk; Andean weaving; Islamic tilework; embroidery and tapestry; engraving, etching, and lithography; and daguerreotype and calotype photography are among the many subjects treated.

*Religion and Mythology* boxes introduce students to the principal elements of the world's great religions, past and present, and to the representation of religious and mythological themes in painting and sculpture of all periods and places. These discussions of belief systems and iconography give readers a richer understanding of some of the greatest artworks ever created. The topics include the gods and goddesses of Egypt, Mesopotamia, Greece, and Rome; the life of Jesus in art; Buddha and Buddhism; Muhammad and Islam; and Aztec religion.

*Art and Society* essays treat the historical, social, political, cultural, and religious context of art and architecture. In some instances, specific monuments are the basis for a discussion of broader themes, as when the Hegeso stele serves as the springboard for an exploration of the role of women in ancient Greek society. Another essay discusses how people's evaluation today of artworks can differ from those of the society that produced them by examining the problems created by the contemporary market for undocumented archaeological finds. Other subjects include Egyptian mummification; Etruscan women; Byzantine icons and iconoclasm; artistic training in Renaissance Italy; 19th-century academic salons and independent art exhibitions; the Mesoamerican ball game; Japanese court culture; and art and leadership in Africa.

*Written Sources* present and discuss key historical documents illuminating important monuments of art and architecture throughout the world. The passages quoted permit voices from the past to speak directly to the reader, providing vivid and unique insights into the creation of artworks in all media. Examples include Bernard of Clairvaux's treatise on sculpture in medieval churches; Giovanni Pietro Bellori's biographies of Annibale Carracci and Caravaggio; Jean François Marmontel's account of 18th-century salon culture; as well as texts that bring the past to life, such as eyewitness accounts of the volcanic eruption that buried Roman Pompeii and of the fire that destroyed Canterbury Cathedral in medieval England.

Finally, in the *Artists on Art* boxes, artists and architects throughout history discuss both their theories and individual works. Examples include Sinan the Great discussing the mosque he designed for Selim II; Leonardo da Vinci and Michelangelo debating the relative merits of painting and sculpture; Artemisia Gentileschi talking about the special problems she confronted as a woman artist; Jacques-Louis David on Neoclassicism; Gustave Courbet on Realism; Henri Matisse on color; Pablo Picasso on Cubism; Diego Rivera on art for the people; and Judy Chicago on her seminal work *The Dinner Party.*

For every new edition of *Art through the Ages,* I also reevaluate the basic organization of the book. In the 14th edition, the unfolding narrative of the history of art in Europe and America is no longer interrupted with "excursions" to Asia, Africa, and Oceania. Those chapters are now grouped together at the end of Volumes I and II and in backpack Books D and F. And the treatment of the art of the later 20th century and the opening decade of the 21st century has been significantly reconfigured. There are now separate chapters on the art and architecture of the period from 1945 to 1980 and from 1980 to the present. Moreover, the second chapter (Chapter 31, "Contemporary Art Worldwide") is no longer confined to Western art but presents the art and architecture of the past three decades as a multifaceted global phenomenon. Furthermore, some chapters now appear in more than one of the paperbound versions of the book in order to provide enhanced flexibility to instructors who divide the global history of art into two or three semester-long courses. Chapter 14—on Italian art from 1200 to 1400—appears in both Volumes I and II and in backpack Books B and D. The Islamic and contemporary art chapters appear in both the Western and non-Western backpack subdivisions of the full global text.

Rounding out the features in the book itself is a greatly expanded Bibliography of books in English with several hundred new entries, including both general works and a chapter-by-chapter list of more focused studies; a Glossary containing definitions of all italicized terms introduced in both the printed and online texts; and, for the first time, a complete museum index listing all illustrated artworks by their present location .

The 14th edition of *Art through the Ages* also features a host of state-of-the-art online resources (enumerated on page xxix).

## WRITING AND TEACHING THE HISTORY OF ART

Nonetheless, some things have not changed in this new edition, including the fundamental belief that guided Helen Gardner so many years ago—that the primary goal of an introductory art history textbook should be to foster an appreciation and understanding of historically significant works of art of all kinds from all periods and from all parts of the globe. Because of the longevity and diversity of the history of art, it is tempting to assign responsibility for telling its story to a large team of specialists. The original publisher of *Art through the Ages* took this approach for the first edition prepared after Helen Gardner's death, and it has now become the norm for introductory art history surveys. But students overwhelmingly say the very complexity of the global history of art makes it all the more important for the story to be told with a consistent voice if they are to master so much diverse material. I think Helen Gardner would be pleased to know that *Art through the Ages* once again has a single storyteller—aided in no small part by invaluable advice from well over a hundred reviewers and other consultants whose assistance I gladly acknowledge at the end of this Preface.

I continue to believe that the most effective way to tell the story of art through the ages, especially to anyone studying art history for the first time, is to organize the vast array of artistic monuments according to the civilizations that produced them and to consider each work in roughly chronological order. This approach has not merely stood the test of time. It is the most appropriate way to narrate the *history* of art. The principle underlying my approach to every period of art history is that the enormous variation in the form and meaning of the paintings, sculptures, buildings, and other artworks men and women have produced over the past 30,000 years is largely the result of the constantly changing contexts in which

artists and architects worked. A historically based narrative is therefore best suited for a global history of art because it enables the author to situate each work discussed in its historical, social, economic, religious, and cultural context. That is, after all, what distinguishes art history from art appreciation.

In the 1926 edition of *Art through the Ages*, Helen Gardner discussed Henri Matisse and Pablo Picasso in a chapter entitled "Contemporary Art in Europe and America." Since then many other artists have emerged on the international scene, and the story of art through the ages has grown longer and even more complex. As already noted, that is reflected in the addition of a new chapter at the end of the book on contemporary art in which developments on all continents are treated together for the first time. Perhaps even more important than the new directions artists and architects have taken during the past several decades is that the discipline of art history has also changed markedly—and so too has Helen Gardner's book. The 14th edition fully reflects the latest art historical research emphases while maintaining the traditional strengths that have made previous editions of *Art through the Ages* so popular. While sustaining attention to style, chronology, iconography, and technique, I also ensure that issues of patronage, function, and context loom large in every chapter. I treat artworks not as isolated objects in sterile 21st-century museum settings but with a view toward their purpose and meaning in the society that produced them at the time they were produced. I examine not only the role of the artist or architect in the creation of a work of art or a building, but also the role of the individuals or groups who paid the artists and influenced the shape the monuments took. Further, in this expanded hybrid edition, I devote more space than ever before to the role of women and women artists in societies worldwide over time. In every chapter, I have tried to choose artworks and buildings that reflect the increasingly wide range of interests of scholars today, while not rejecting the traditional list of "great" works or the very notion of a "canon." Indeed, the expanded hybrid nature of the 14th edition has made it possible to illustrate and discuss scores of works not traditionally treated in art history survey texts without reducing the space devoted to canonical works.

## CHAPTER-BY-CHAPTER CHANGES IN THE 14TH EDITION

All chapters feature many new photographs, revised maps, revised Big Picture chapter-ending summaries, and changes to the text reflecting new research and discoveries.

**Introduction:** What is Art History?  New painting by Ogata Korin added.

**1: Art before History.**  New Framing the Era essay "The Dawn of Art" and new timeline. Göbekli Tepe added.

**2: Mesopotamia and Persia.**  New Framing the Era essay "The Cradle of Civilization" and new timeline.

**3: Egypt under the Pharaohs.**  New Framing the Era essay "Divine Kingship on the Nile" and new timeline. Hatshepsut's expedition to Punt added.

**4: The Prehistoric Aegean.**  New Framing the Era essay "Greece in the Age of Heroes" and new timeline. Mycenean ivory goddesses added.

**5: Ancient Greece.** New Framing the Era essay "The Perfect Temple" and new timeline. Euphronios *Death of Sarpedon* and Olympia Apollo added.

**6: The Etruscans.** New Framing the Era essay "The Rediscovery of Etruscan Art" and new timeline. Tomb of the Augurs added.

**7: The Roman Empire.** New Framing the Era essay "The Ancient World's Greatest Empire" and new timeline. New box on "Roman Ancestor Portraits" added. Column of Trajan frieze and new portrait of Caracalla added.

**8: Late Antiquity.** New Framing the Era essay "Romans, Jews, and Christians" and new timeline. Villa Torlonia Jewish catacomb and Mildenhall treasure added.

**9: Byzantium.** New Framing the Era essay "Church and State United" and new timeline. Revised discussion of iconoclasm and of Byzantine women. New box on "Born to the Purple: Empress Zoe."

**10: The Islamic World.** New Framing the Era essay "The Rise and Spread of Islam" and new timeline. Muqarnas tilework of Imam Mosque, Isfahan, added.

**11: Early Medieval Europe.** New Framing the Era essay "Missionaries and the Spread of Christian Art" and new timeline. Detail photos of Book of Kells added.

**12: Romanesque Europe.** New Framing the Era essay "The Rebirth of Monumental Sculpture" and new timeline. New photos of newly cleaned Autun tympanum and many other French churches. Revised boxes on "Pilgrimage Roads in France and Spain" and "The Veneration of Relics." Reliquary of St. Foy added.

**13: Gothic Europe.** New Framing the Era essay "The Age of the Great Cathedrals" and new timeline. Extensive new photographic documentation of French churches and portal sculpture. Expanded treatment of German Gothic art and architecture.

**14: Late Medieval Italy.** New Framing the Era essay "Late Medieval or Proto-Renaissance?" and new timeline. New series of photos of architecture and sculpture in Florence, Orvieto, Pisa, and Siena. Andrea Pisano Baptistery doors added.

**15: South and Southeast Asia before 1200.** New Framing the Era essay "The Life of the Buddha" and new timeline. New series of photos of Buddhist and Hindu monuments.

**16: China and Korea to 1279.** New Framing the Era essay "Chinese Silk for the Afterlife" and new timeline. Flying horse of Governor-General Zhang and Korean statuette of bodhisattva Maitreya added.

**17: Japan before 1333.** New Framing the Era essay "Buddhism Spreads to Japan" and new timeline. Kosho's portrait of the priest Kuya added.

**18: Native Arts of the Americas before 1300.** New Framing the Era essay "Ancient Cities in a New World" and new timeline. Expanded discussions of Teotihuacán and Chichén Itzá.

**19: Africa before 1800.** New Framing the Era essay "Sacred Kingship in Benin" and new timeline. Seated statue of a man from Tada added.

**20: Late Medieval and Early Renaissance Northern Europe.** New Framing the Era essay "The Virgin in a Flemish Home" and new timeline. New section of the *Nuremberg Chronicle* illustrated. Diptych of Martin van Nieuwenhove added.

**21: The Renaissance in Quattrocento Italy.** New Framing the Era essay "Medici Patronage and Classical Learning" and new timeline. Expanded discussion of Botticelli and Neo-Platonism. Revised boxes on linear and atmospheric perspective and on Cennino Cennini. Tomb of Leonardo Bruni and *Resurrection* by Piero della Francesca added.

**22: Renaissance and Mannerism in Cinquecento Italy.** New Framing the Era essay "Michelangelo in the Service of Julius II" and new timeline. Michelangelo's late *Pietà* and Parmigianino's self-portrait added. Revised box on "Palma il Giovane and Titian." Series of new photos of Florence, Rome, and Venice.

**23: High Renaissance and Mannerism in Northern Europe and Spain.** New Framing the Era essay "Earthly Delights in the Netherlands" and new timeline. Dürer's self-portrait and *Melencolia I* and El Greco's *View of Toledo* added.

**24: The Baroque in Italy and Spain.** New Framing the Era essay "Baroque Art and Spectacle" and new timeline. Bernini's Four Rivers Fountain and Gentileschi's self-portrait added.

**25: The Baroque in Northern Europe.** New Framing the Era essay "Still-Life Painting in the Dutch Republic" and new timeline. Expanded discussion of Dutch mercantilism. Vermeer's *Woman Holding a Balance* added.

**26: Rococo to Neoclassicism: The 18th Century in Europe and America.** New Framing the Era essay "Art and Science in the Era of Enlightenment" and new timeline. Expanded discussion of Diderot as art critic. Adelaide Labille-Guiard added.

**27: Romanticism, Realism, Photography: Europe & America, 1800 to 1870.** New Framing the Era essay "Napoleon at Jaffa" and new timeline. Friedrich's *Wanderer above a Sea of Mist* and Altes Museum, Berlin, added.

**28: Impressionism, Post-Impressionism, Symbolism: Europe and America, 1870 to 1900.** New Framing the Era essay "Impressions of Modern Life" and new timeline. New discussion of Manet and Monet. Rodin's *Gates of Hell* and James Ensor added.

**29: Modernism in Europe and America, 1900 to 1945.** New Framing the Era essay "Global War, Anarchy, and Dada" and new timeline. New box on "Walter Gropius and the Bauhaus." Grosz's *Eclipse of the Sun,* de Chirico's *Song of Love,* Arthur Dove, Egon Schiele, Adolf Loos, and Margaret Bourke-White added.

**30: Modernism and Postmodernism in Europe and America, 1945 to 1980.** Former 1945–Present chapter significantly expanded and divided into two chapters. New Framing the Era essay "Art and Consumer Culture" and new timeline. Arshile Gorky, Lee Krasner, Franz Kline, Robert Motherwell, Joan Mitchell, Bridget Riley, Isamu Noguchi, George Segal, Niki de Saint-Phalle, Lucian Freud, Diane Arbus, Minor White, and Vanna Venturi house added.

**31: Contemporary Art Worldwide.** Former 1945–Present chapter significantly expanded and divided into two chapters. This chapter also now includes contemporary non-Western art. New Framing the Era essay "Art as Socio-Political Message" and new timeline. Robert Mapplethorpe, Shahzia Sikander, Carrie Mae Weems, Jean-

Michel Basquiat, Kehinde Wiley, Shirin Neshat, Edward Burtynksy, Wu Guanzhong, Emily Kame Kngwarreye, Tara Donovan, Jenny Saville, Marisol, Rachel Whiteread, Andy Goldsworthy, Keith Haring, Andreas Gursky, Zaha Hadid, I.M. Pei, Daniel Libeskind, and green architecture added.

**32: South and Southeast Asia, 1200 to 1980.** New Framing the Era essay "Painting at the Mughal Imperial Court" and new timeline. Sahifa Banu, Abdul Hasan, and Manohar added.

**33: China and Korea, 1279 to 1980.** New Framing the Era essay "The Forbidden City" and new timeline. Zhao Mengfu and Ni Zan added.

**34: Japan, 1336 to 1980.** New Framing the Era essay "Famous Views of Edo" and new timeline. White Heron Castle, Tawaraya Sotatsu, Ando Hiroshige, Kitagawa Utamaro, and Kano Hogai added.

**35: Native Arts of the Americas, 1300 to 1980.** New Framing the Era essay "The Founding of Tenochtitlán" and new timeline. Expanded discussion of Aztec religion and of the Templo Mayor in Mexico City with recently discovered relief of Tlaltecuhtli. New box on Inka technology. *Codex Mendoza* and Mandan buffalo-hide robe added.

**36: Oceania before 1980.** New Framing the Era essay "Maori Men's Meetinghouses" and new timeline. *Ambum Stone* and Austral Islands Rurutu added. Expanded discussion of Hawaiian art with new illustrations.

**37: Africa, 1800 to 1980.** New Framing the Era essay "Kalabari Ijaw Ancestral Screens" and new timeline. Chokwe art and Olowe of Ise's Ikere palace doors added.

Go to the online instructor companion site or PowerLecture for a more detailed list of chapter-by-chapter changes and the Image Transition Guide.

# ACKNOWLEDGMENTS

A work as extensive as a global history of art could not be undertaken or completed without the counsel of experts in all areas of world art. As with previous editions, Cengage Learning/Wadsxworth has enlisted more than a hundred art historians to review every chapter of *Art through the Ages* in order to ensure that the text lives up to the Gardner reputation for accuracy as well as readability. I take great pleasure in acknowledging here the important contributions to the 14th edition made by the following : Michael Jay Adamek, Ozarks Technical Community College; Charles M. Adelman, University of Northern Iowa; Christine Zitrides Atiyeh, Kutztown University; Gisele Atterberry, Joliet Junior College; Roann Barris, Radford University; Philip Betancourt, Temple University; Karen Blough, SUNY Plattsburgh; Elena N. Boeck, DePaul University; Betty Ann Brown, California State University Northridge; Alexandra A. Carpino, Northern Arizona University; Anne Walke Cassidy, Carthage College; Harold D. Cole, Baldwin Wallace College; Sarah Cormack, Webster University, Vienna; Jodi Cranston, Boston University; Nancy de Grummond, Florida State University; Kelley Helmstutler Di Dio, University of Vermont; Owen Doonan, California State University Northridge; Marilyn Dunn, Loyola University Chicago; Tom Estlack, Pittsburgh Cultural Trust; Lois Fichner-Rathus, The College of New Jersey; Arne R. Flaten, Coastal Carolina University; Ken Friedman, Swinburne University of Technology; Rosemary Gallick, Northern Virginia Community College; William V. Ganis, Wells College; Marc Gerstein, University of Toledo; Clive F. Getty, Miami University; Michael Grillo, University of Maine; Amanda Hamilton, Northwest Nazarene University; Martina Hesser, Heather Jensen, Brigham Young University; Grossmont College; Mark Johnson, Brigham Young University; Jacqueline E. Jung, Yale University; John F. Kenfield, Rutgers University; Asen Kirin, University of Georgia; Joanne Klein, Boise State University; Yu Bong Ko, Tappan Zee High School; Rob Leith, Buckingham Browne & Nichols School; Adele H. Lewis, Arizona State University; Kate Alexandra Lingley, University of Hawaii–Manoa; Ellen Longsworth, Merrimack College; Matthew Looper, California State University–Chico; Nuria Lledó Tarradell, Universidad Complutense, Madrid; Anne McClanan, Portland State University; Mark Magleby, Brigham Young University; Gina Miceli-Hoffman, Moraine Valley Community College; William Mierse, University of Vermont; Amy Morris, Southeastern Louisiana University; Charles R. Morscheck, Drexel University; Johanna D. Movassat, San Jose State University; Carola Naumer, Truckee Meadows Community College; Irene Nero, Southeastern Louisiana University; Robin O'Bryan, Harrisburg Area Community College; Laurent Odde, Kutztown University of Pennsylvania; E. Suzanne Owens, Lorain County Community College; Catherine Pagani, The University of Alabama; Martha Peacock, Brigham Young University; Mabi Ponce de Leon, Bexley High School; Curtis Runnels, Boston University; Malia E. F. Serrano, Grossmont College; Molly Skjei, Normandale Community College; James Swensen, Brigham Young University; John Szostak, University of Hawaii–Manoa; Fred T. Smith, Kent State University; Thomas F. Strasser, Providence College; Katherine H. Tachau, University of Iowa; Debra Thompson, Glendale Community College; Alice Y. Tseng, Boston University; Carol Ventura, Tennessee Technological University; Marc Vincent, Baldwin Wallace College; Deborah Waite, University of Hawaii–Manoa; Lawrence Waldron, Saint John's University; Victoria Weaver, Millersville University; and Margaret Ann Zaho, University of Central Florida.

I am especially indebted to the following for creating the instructor and student materials for the 14th edition: William J. Allen, Arkansas State University; Ivy Cooper, Southern Illinois University Edwardsville; Patricia D. Cosper, The University of Alabama at Birmingham; Anne McClanan, Portland State University; and Amy M. Morris, Southeastern Louisiana University. I also thank the members of the Wadsworth Media Advisory Board for their input: Frances Altvater, University of Hartford; Roann Barris, Radford University; Bill Christy, Ohio University-Zanesville; Annette Cohen, Great Bay Community College; Jeff Davis, The Art Institute of Pittsburgh–Online Division; Owen Doonan, California State University-Northridge; Arne R. Flaten, Coastal Carolina University; Carol Heft, Muhlenberg College; William Mierse, University of Vermont; Eleanor F. Moseman, Colorado State University; and Malia E. F. Serrano, Grossmont College.

I am also happy to have this opportunity to express my gratitude to the extraordinary group of people at Cengage Learning/Wadsworth involved with the editing, production, and distribution of *Art through the Ages*. Some of them I have now worked with on various projects for nearly two decades and feel privileged to count among my friends. The success of the Gardner series in all of its various permutations depends in no small part on the expertise and unflagging commitment of these dedicated professionals, especially Clark Baxter, publisher; Sharon Adams Poore, senior development editor (as well as videographer extraordinaire); Lianne Ames, senior content project manager; Mandy Groszko, rights acquisitions specialist; Kimberly Apfelbaum, associate media editor; Robert White, product manager; Ashley Bargende, assistant editor; Elizabeth Newell, editorial assistant; Amy Bither and Jessica Jackson, editorial interns; Cate Rickard Barr, senior art director; Jeanne M. Heston, senior marketing manager, Heather Baxley, senior marketing communications manager, and the incomparable group of local sales representatives who have passed on to me the welcome advice offered by the hundreds of instructors they speak to daily during their visits to college campuses throughout North America.

I am also deeply grateful to the following out-of-house contributors to the 14th edition: the peerless and tireless Joan Keyes, Dovetail Publishing Services; Helen Triller-Yambert, development editor; Ida May Norton, copy editor; Do Mi Stauber and Michael Brackney, indexers; Susan Gall, proofreader; tani hasegawa, designer; Catherine Schnurr, Mary-Lise Nazaire, Lauren McFalls, and Corey Geissler, PreMediaGlobal, photo researchers; Alma Bell, Scott Paul, John Pierce, and Lori Shranko, Thompson Type; Jay and John Crowley, Jay's Publishing Services; Mary Ann Lidrbauch, art manuscript preparer; Kim Meyer, image consulting; and, of course, Jonathan Poore and John Burge, for their superb photos and architectural drawings.

Finally, I owe thanks to my former co-author, Christin J. Mamiya of the University of Nebraska–Lincoln, for her friendship and advice, especially with regard to the expanded contemporary art section of the 14th edition, as well as to my colleagues at Boston University and to the thousands of students and the scores of teaching fellows in my art history courses since I began teaching in 1975. From them I have learned much that has helped determine the form and content of *Art through the Ages* and made it a much better book than it otherwise might have been.

*Fred S. Kleiner*

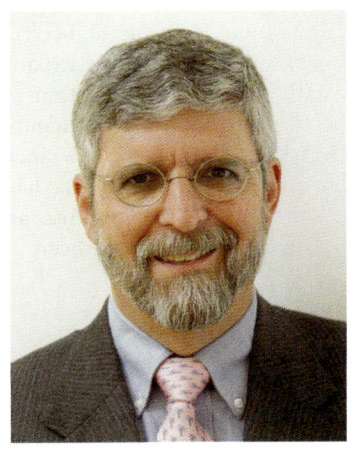

FRED S. KLEINER (Ph.D., Columbia University) is the author or co-author of the 10th, 11th, 12th, and 13th editions of *Art through the Ages: A Global History,* as well as the 1st, 2nd, and 3rd editions of *Art through the Ages: A Concise History,* and more than a hundred publications on Greek and Roman art and architecture, including *A History of Roman Art,* also published by Wadsworth, a part of Cengage Learning. He has taught the art history survey course for more than three decades, first at the University of Virginia and, since 1978, at Boston University, where he is currently Professor of Art History and Archaeology and Chair of the Department of History of Art and Architecture. From 1985 to 1998, he was Editor-in-Chief of the *American Journal of Archaeology.* Long acclaimed for his inspiring lectures and dedication to students, Professor Kleiner won Boston University's Metcalf Award for Excellence in Teaching as well as the College Prize for Undergraduate Advising in the Humanities in 2002, and he is a two-time winner of the Distinguished Teaching Prize in the College of Arts and Sciences Honors Program. In 2007, he was elected a Fellow of the Society of Antiquaries of London, and, in 2009, in recognition of lifetime achievement in publication and teaching, a Fellow of the Text and Academic Authors Association.

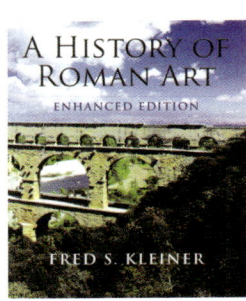

Also by Fred Kleiner: *A History of Roman Art, Enhanced Edition* (Wadsworth/Cengage Learning 2010; ISBN 9780495909873), winner of the 2007 Texty Prize for a new college textbook in the humanities and social sciences. In this authoritative and lavishly illustrated volume, Professor Kleiner traces the development of Roman art and architecture from Romulus's foundation of Rome in the eighth century BCE to the death of Constantine in the fourth century CE, with special chapters devoted to Pompeii and Herculaneum, Ostia, funerary and provincial art and architecture, and the earliest Christian art. The enhanced edition also includes a new introductory chapter on the art and architecture of the Etruscans and of the Greeks of South Italy and Sicily.

# RESOURCES

## FOR FACULTY

### PowerLecture with Digital Image Library

This flashdrive is an all-in-one lecture and class presentation tool that makes it easy to assemble, edit, and present customized lectures for your course using Microsoft® PowerPoint®. The Digital Image Library provides high-resolution images (maps, diagrams, and most of the fine art images from the text, including the over 300 new images) for lecture presentations, either in PowerPoint format, or in individual file formats compatible with other image-viewing software. A zoom feature allows you to magnify selected portions of an image for more detailed display in class, or you can display images side by side for comparison. You can easily add your own images to those from the text. The Google Earth™ application allows you to zoom in on an entire city, as well as key monuments and buildings. There are links to specific figures for every chapter in the book. PowerLecture also includes an Image Transition Guide, an electronic Instructor's Manual and a Test Bank with multiple-choice, matching, short-answer, and essay questions in ExamView® computerized format. The text-specific Microsoft® PowerPoint® slides are created for use with JoinIn™, software for classroom personal response systems (clickers).

### WebTutor™ with eBook on WebCT® and Blackboard®

WebTutor™ enables you to assign preformatted, text-specific content that is available as soon as you log on. You can also customize the WebTutor™ environment in any way you choose. Content includes the Interactive ebook, Test Bank, Practice Quizzes, Video Study Tools, and CourseMate™.

**To order, contact your Cengage Learning representative.**

## FOR STUDENTS

### CourseMate™ with eBook

Make the most of your study time by accessing everything you need to succeed in one place. Open the interactive eBook, take notes, review image and audio flashcards, watch videos, and take practice quizzes online with CourseMate™. You will find hundreds of zoomable, high-resolution bonus images (represented by thumbnail images in the text) along with discussion of the images, videos created specifically to enhanced your reading comprehension, audio chapter summaries, compare-and-contrast activities, Guide to Studying, and more.

### Slide Guides

The Slide Guide is a lecture companion that allows you to take notes alongside thumbnails of the same art images that are shown in class. This handy booklet includes reproductions of the images from the book with full captions, page numbers, and space for note taking. It also includes Google Earth™ exercises for key cities, monuments, and buildings that will take you to these locations to better understand the works you are studying.

**To order, go to www.cengagebrain.com**

# GARDNER'S
## ART through the AGES

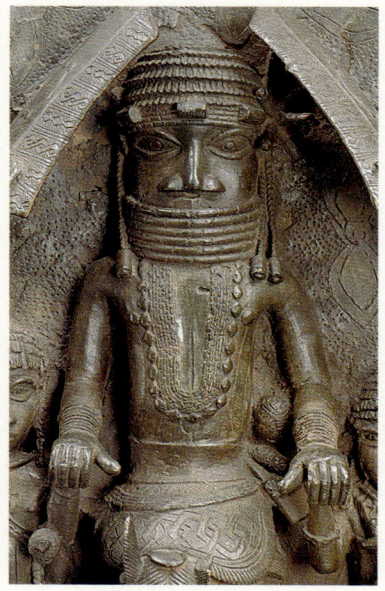

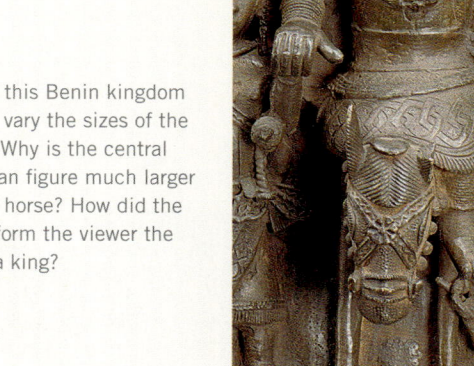

Why did this Benin kingdom sculptor vary the sizes of the figures? Why is the central equestrian figure much larger than his horse? How did the artist inform the viewer the rider is a king?

Art historians seek to understand not only why individual artworks appear as they do but also why those works exist at all. Who paid this African artist to make this bronze plaque? Why?

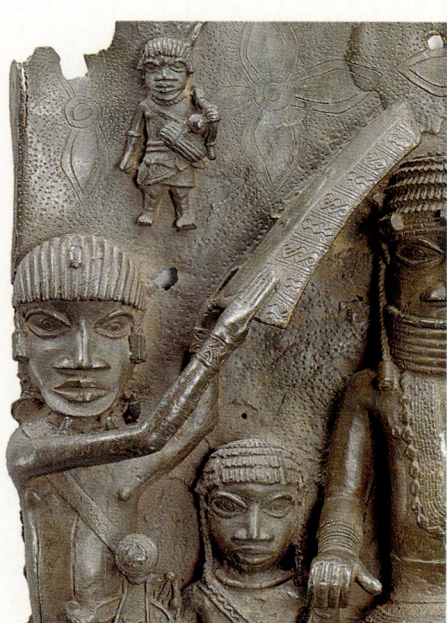

Dating and signing artworks are relatively recent practices. How can art historians determine when an unlabeled work such as this one was made, and by whom? Style, technique, and subject are clues.

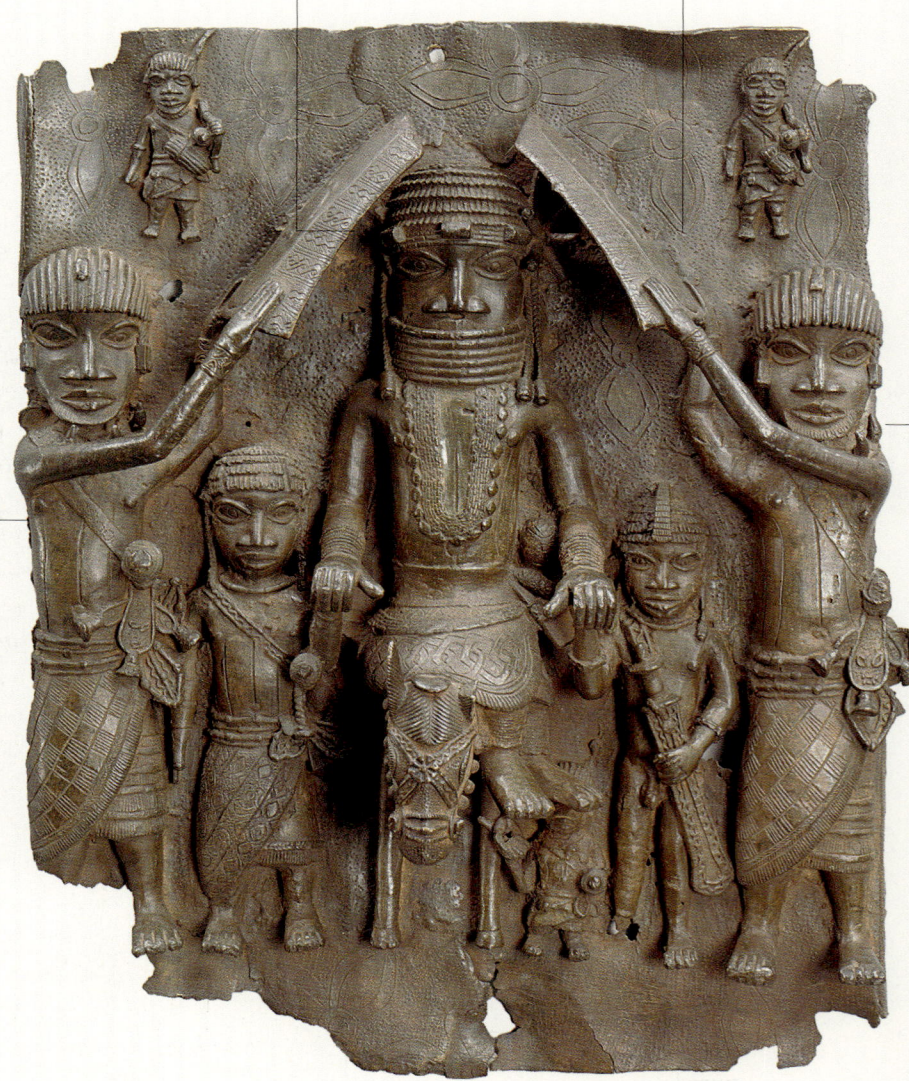

1 in.

I-1 King on horseback with attendants, from Benin, Nigeria, ca. 1550–1680. Bronze, 1′ 7½″ high. Metropolitan Museum of Art, New York (Michael C. Rockefeller Memorial Collection, gift of Nelson A. Rockefeller).

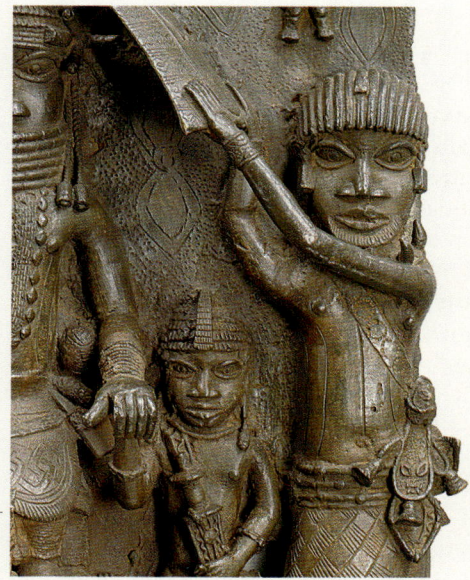

What tools and techniques did the African sculptor employ to transform molten bronze into this plaque representing a king and his attendants projecting in high relief from the background plane?

# Introduction

# WHAT IS ART HISTORY?

**W**hat is art history? Except when referring to the modern academic discipline, people do not often juxtapose the words *art* and *history*. They tend to think of history as the record and interpretation of past human actions, particularly social and political actions. In contrast, most think of art, quite correctly, as part of the present—as something people can see and touch. Of course, people cannot see or touch history's vanished human events, but a visible, tangible artwork is a kind of persisting event. One or more artists made it at a certain time and in a specific place, even if no one now knows who, when, where, or why. Although created in the past, an artwork continues to exist in the present, long surviving its times. The first painters and sculptors died 30,000 years ago, but their works remain, some of them exhibited in glass cases in museums built only a few years ago.

Modern museum visitors can admire these objects from the remote past—and countless others humankind has produced over the millennia, whether small bronze sculptures from Africa (FIG. I-1) or large paintings on canvas by American artists (FIG. I-2)—without any knowledge of the circumstances leading to the creation of those works. The beauty or sheer size of an object can impress people, the artist's virtuosity in the handling of ordinary or costly materials can dazzle them, or the subject depicted can move them emotionally. Viewers can react to what they see, interpret the work in the light of their own experience, and judge it a success or a failure. These are all valid responses to a work of art. But the enjoyment and appreciation of artworks in museum settings are relatively recent phenomena, as is the creation of artworks solely for museum-going audiences to view.

Today, it is common for artists to work in private studios and to create paintings, sculptures, and other objects commercial art galleries will offer for sale. This is what American painter CLYFFORD STILL (1904–1980) did when he created large canvases (FIG. I-2) of pure color titled simply with the year of their creation. Usually, someone the artist has never met will purchase the artwork and display it in a setting the artist has never seen. This practice is not a new phenomenon in the history of art—an ancient potter decorating a vase for sale at a village market stall probably did not know who would buy the pot or where it would be housed—but it is not at all typical. In fact, it is exceptional. Throughout history, most artists created paintings, sculptures, and other objects for specific patrons and settings and to fulfill a specific purpose, even if today no one knows the original contexts of those artworks. Museum visitors can appreciate the visual and tactile qualities of these objects, but they cannot understand why they were made or why they appear as they do without knowing the circumstances of their creation. Art *appreciation* does not require knowledge of the historical context of an artwork (or a building). Art *history* does.

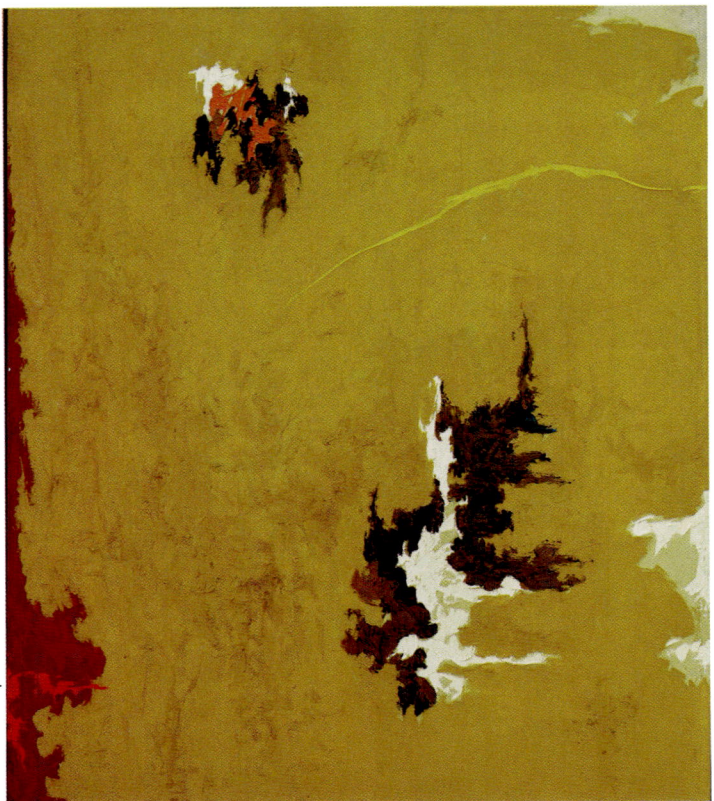

1 ft.

**I-2** CLYFFORD STILL, *1948-C,* 1948. Oil on canvas, 6′ 8⅞″ × 5′ 8¾″. Hirshhorn Museum and Sculpture Garden, Smithsonian Institution, Washington, D.C. (purchased with funds of Joseph H. Hirshhorn, 1992).

Clyfford Still painted this abstract composition without knowing who would purchase it or where it would be displayed, but throughout history, most artists created works for specific patrons and settings.

Thus, a central aim of art history is to determine the original context of artworks. Art historians seek to achieve a full understanding not only of why these "persisting events" of human history look the way they do but also of why the artistic events happened at all. What unique set of circumstances gave rise to the construction of a particular building or led an individual patron to commission a certain artist to fashion a singular artwork for a specific place? The study of history is therefore vital to art history. And art history is often indispensable for a thorough understanding of history. Art objects and buildings are historical documents that can shed light on the peoples who made them and on the times of their creation in ways other historical documents may not. Furthermore, artists and architects can affect history by reinforcing or challenging cultural values and practices through the objects they create and the structures they build. Thus, the history of art and architecture is inseparable from the study of history, although the two disciplines are not the same.

The following pages introduce some of the distinctive subjects art historians address and the kinds of questions they ask, and explain some of the basic terminology they use when answering these questions. Readers armed with this arsenal of questions and terms will be ready to explore the multifaceted world of art through the ages.

# ART HISTORY IN THE 21ST CENTURY

Art historians study the visual and tangible objects humans make and the structures humans build. Scholars traditionally have classified these works as architecture, sculpture, the pictorial arts (painting, drawing, printmaking, and photography), and the craft arts, or arts of design. The craft arts comprise utilitarian objects, such as ceramics, metalwork, textiles, jewelry, and similar accessories of ordinary living. Artists of every age have blurred the boundaries among these categories, but this is especially true today, when multimedia works abound.

Beginning with the earliest Greco-Roman art critics, scholars have studied objects their makers consciously manufactured as "art" and to which the artists assigned formal titles. But today's art historians also study a multitude of objects their creators and owners almost certainly did not consider to be "works of art." Few ancient Romans, for example, would have regarded a coin bearing their emperor's portrait as anything but money. Today, an art museum may exhibit that coin in a locked case in a climate-controlled room, and scholars may subject it to the same kind of art historical analysis as a portrait by an acclaimed Renaissance or modern sculptor or painter.

The range of objects art historians study is constantly expanding and now includes, for example, computer-generated images, whereas in the past almost anything produced using a machine would not have been regarded as art. Most people still consider the performing arts—music, drama, and dance—as outside art history's realm because these arts are fleeting, impermanent media. But during the past few decades, even this distinction between "fine art" and "performance art" has become blurred. Art historians, however, generally ask the same kinds of questions about what they study, whether they employ a restrictive or expansive definition of art.

## The Questions Art Historians Ask

**HOW OLD IS IT?** Before art historians can write a history of art, they must be sure they know the date of each work they study. Thus, an indispensable subject of art historical inquiry is *chronology,* the dating of art objects and buildings. If researchers cannot determine a monument's age, they cannot place the work in its historical context. Art historians have developed many ways to establish, or at least approximate, the date of an artwork.

*Physical evidence* often reliably indicates an object's age. The material used for a statue or painting—bronze, plastic, or oil-based pigment, to name only a few—may not have been invented before a certain time, indicating the earliest possible date (the *terminus post quem:* Latin "point after which") someone could have fashioned the work. Or artists may have ceased using certain materials—such as specific kinds of inks and papers for drawings—at a known time, providing the latest possible date (the *terminus ante quem:* Latin "point before which") for objects made of those materials. Sometimes the material (or the manufacturing technique) of an object or a building can establish a very precise date of production or construction. The study of tree rings, for instance, usually can determine within a narrow range the date of a wood statue or a timber roof beam.

*Documentary evidence* can help pinpoint the date of an object or building when a dated written document mentions the work. For example, official records may note when church officials commissioned a new altarpiece—and how much they paid to which artist.

*Internal evidence* can play a significant role in dating an artwork. A painter might have depicted an identifiable person or a kind of hairstyle, clothing, or furniture fashionable only at a certain time. If so, the art historian can assign a more accurate date to that painting.

*Stylistic evidence* is also very important. The analysis of *style*—an artist's distinctive manner of producing an object—is the art historian's special sphere. Unfortunately, because it is a subjective assessment, stylistic evidence is by far the most unreliable chronological criterion. Still, art historians find style a very useful tool for establishing chronology.

**WHAT IS ITS STYLE?** Defining artistic style is one of the key elements of art historical inquiry, although the analysis of artworks solely in terms of style no longer dominates the field the way it once did. Art historians speak of several different kinds of artistic styles.

*Period style* refers to the characteristic artistic manner of a specific era or span of years, usually within a distinct culture, such as "Archaic Greek" or "High Renaissance." But many periods do not display any stylistic unity at all. How would someone define the artistic style of the second decade of the new millennium in North America? Far too many crosscurrents exist in contemporary art for anyone to describe a period style of the early 21st century—even in a single city such as New York.

*Regional style* is the term art historians use to describe variations in style tied to geography. Like an object's date, its *provenance,* or place of origin, can significantly determine its character. Very often two artworks from the same place made centuries apart are more similar than contemporaneous works from two different regions. To cite one example, usually only an expert can distinguish between an Egyptian statue carved in 2500 BCE and one made in 500 BCE. But no one would mistake an Egyptian statue of 500 BCE for one of the same date made in Greece or Mexico.

Considerable variations in a given area's style are possible, however, even during a single historical period. In late medieval Europe, French architecture differed significantly from Italian architecture. The interiors of Beauvais Cathedral (FIG. I-3) and the church of Santa Croce (FIG. I-4) in Florence typify the architectural styles of France and Italy, respectively, at the end of the 13th century. The rebuilding of the east end of Beauvais Cathedral began in 1284. Construction commenced on Santa Croce only 10 years later. Both structures employ the *pointed arch* characteristic of this era, yet the two churches differ strikingly. The French church has towering stone ceilings and large expanses of colored windows, whereas the Italian building has a low timber roof and small, widely separated windows. Because the

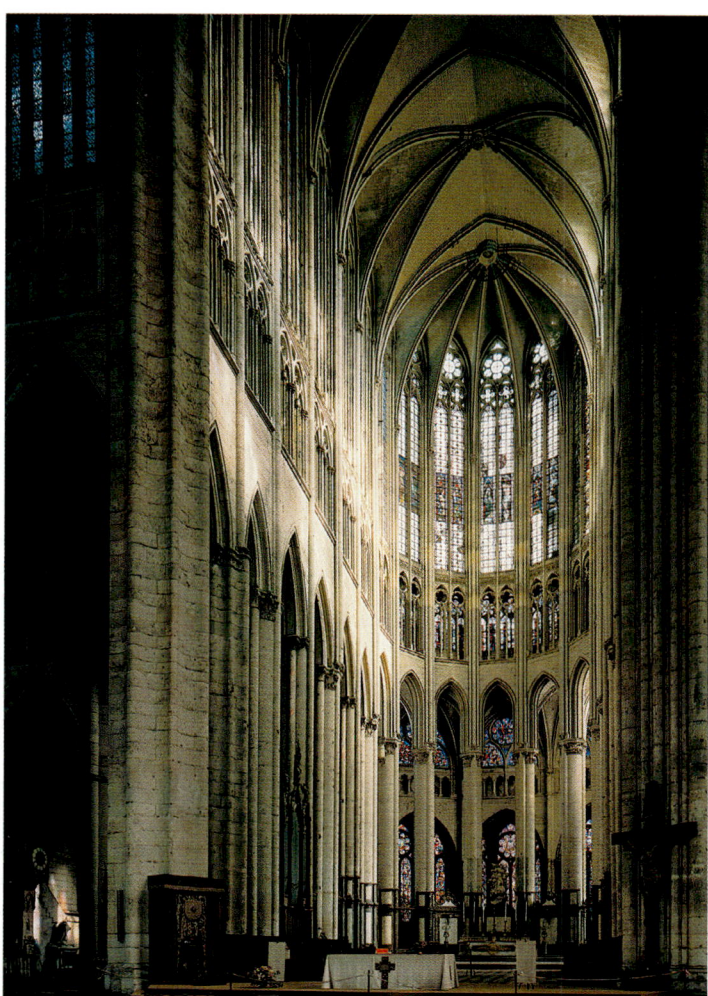

I-3 **Choir of Beauvais Cathedral (looking east), Beauvais, France, rebuilt after 1284.**

The style of an object or building often varies from region to region. This cathedral has towering stone vaults and large stained-glass windows typical of 13th-century French architecture.

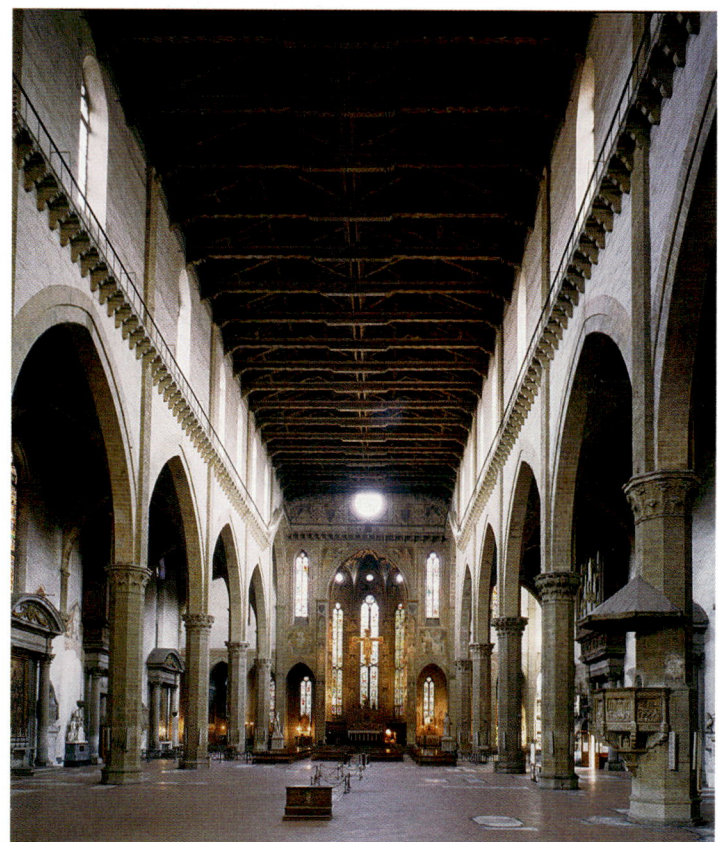

I-4 **Interior of Santa Croce (looking east), Florence, Italy, begun 1294.**

In contrast to Beauvais Cathedral (FIG. I-3), this contemporaneous Florentine church conforms to the quite different regional style of Italy. The building has a low timber roof and small windows.

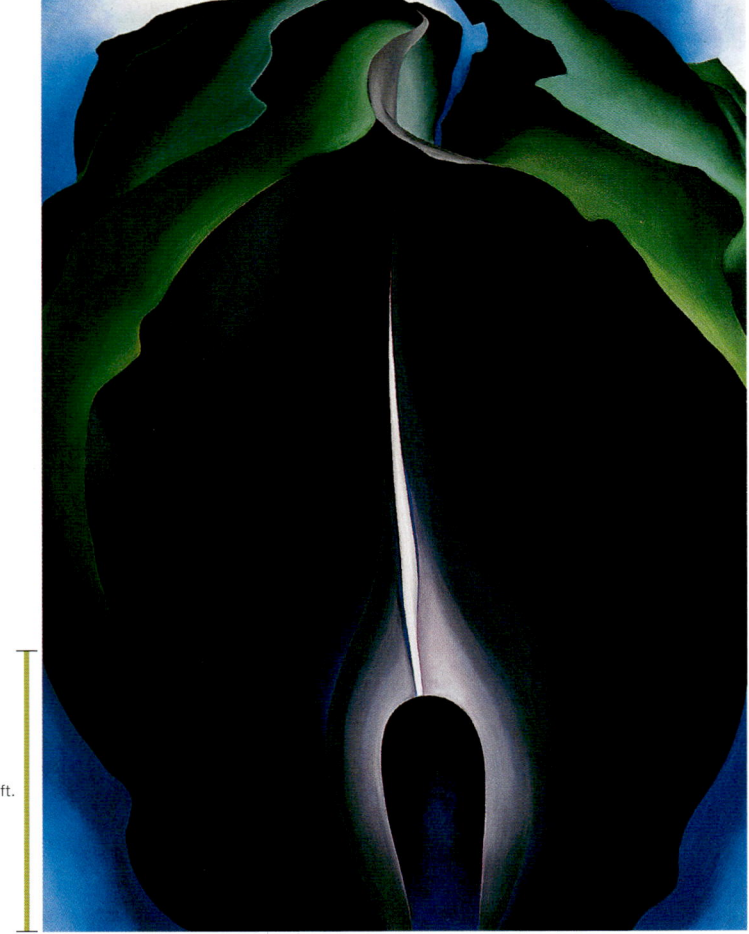

1 ft.

**I-5** GEORGIA O'KEEFFE, *Jack-in-the-Pulpit No. 4*, 1930. Oil on canvas, 3′ 4″ × 2′ 6″. National Gallery of Art, Washington (Alfred Stieglitz Collection, bequest of Georgia O'Keeffe).

O'Keeffe's paintings feature close-up views of petals and leaves in which the organic forms become powerful abstract compositions. This approach to painting typifies the artist's distinctive personal style.

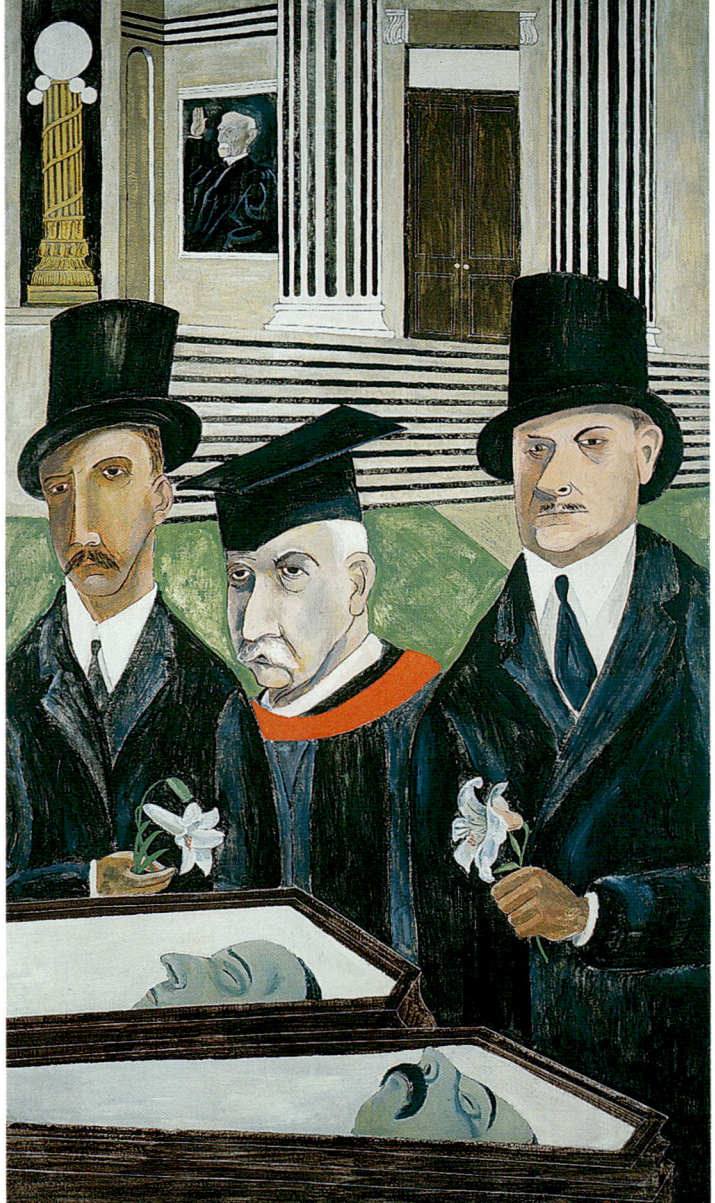

1 ft.

**I-6** BEN SHAHN, *The Passion of Sacco and Vanzetti,* 1931–1932. Tempera on canvas, 7′ $\frac{1}{2}$″ × 4′. Whitney Museum of American Art, New York (gift of Edith and Milton Lowenthal in memory of Juliana Force).

O'Keeffe's contemporary, Shahn developed a style markedly different from hers. His paintings are often social commentaries on recent events and incorporate readily identifiable people.

two contemporaneous churches served similar purposes, regional style mainly explains their differing appearance.

*Personal style,* the distinctive manner of individual artists or architects, often decisively explains stylistic discrepancies among monuments of the same time and place. In 1930 the American painter GEORGIA O'KEEFFE (1887–1986) produced a series of paintings of flowering plants. One of them—*Jack-in-the-Pulpit No. 4* (FIG. **I-5**)—is a sharply focused close-up view of petals and leaves. O'Keeffe captured the growing plant's slow, controlled motion while converting the plant into a powerful abstract composition of lines, forms, and colors (see the discussion of art historical vocabulary in the next section). Only a year later, another American artist, BEN SHAHN (1898–1969), painted *The Passion of Sacco and Vanzetti* (FIG. **I-6**), a stinging commentary on social injustice inspired by the trial and execution of two Italian anarchists, Nicola Sacco and Bartolomeo Vanzetti. Many people believed Sacco and Vanzetti had been unjustly convicted of killing two men in a robbery in 1920. Shahn's painting compresses time in a symbolic representation of the trial and its aftermath. The two executed men lie in their coffins. Presiding over them are the three members of the commission (headed by a college president wearing academic cap and gown) who declared the original trial fair and cleared the way for the

executions. Behind, on the wall of a stately government building, hangs the framed portrait of the judge who pronounced the initial sentence. Personal style, not period or regional style, sets Shahn's canvas apart from O'Keeffe's. The contrast is extreme here because of the very different subjects the artists chose. But even when two artists depict the same subject, the results can vary widely. The *way* O'Keeffe painted flowers and the *way* Shahn painted faces are distinctive and unlike the styles of their contemporaries. (See the "Who Made It?" discussion on page 6.)

The different kinds of artistic styles are not mutually exclusive. For example, an artist's personal style may change dramatically during a long career. Art historians then must distinguish among

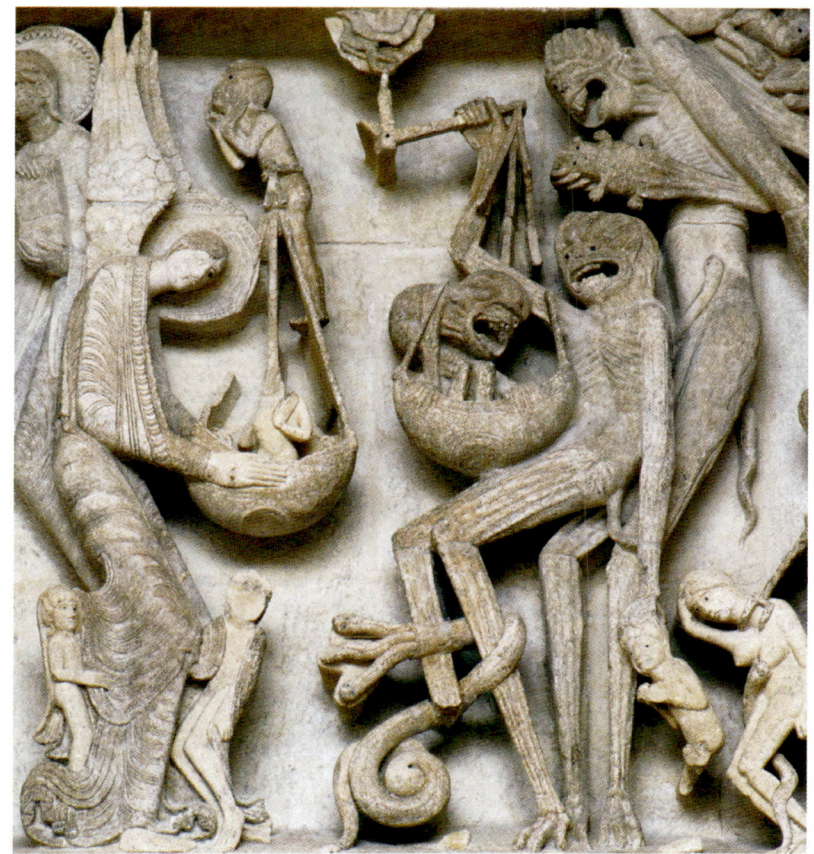

In this high relief portraying the weighing of souls on judgment day, Gislebertus used disproportion and distortion to dehumanize the devilish figure yanking on the scales of justice.

the different period styles of a particular artist, such as the "Rose Period" and the "Cubist Period" of the prolific 20th-century artist Pablo Picasso.

**WHAT IS ITS SUBJECT?** Another major concern of art historians is, of course, subject matter, encompassing the story, or narrative; the scene presented; the action's time and place; the persons involved; and the environment and its details. Some artworks, such as modern *abstract* paintings (FIG. I-2), have no subject, not even a setting. The "subject" is the artwork itself—its colors, textures, composition, and size. But when artists represent people, places, or actions, viewers must identify these features to achieve complete understanding of the work. Art historians traditionally separate pictorial subjects into various categories, such as religious, historical, mythological, *genre* (daily life), portraiture, *landscape* (a depiction of a place), *still life* (an arrangement of inanimate objects), and their numerous subdivisions and combinations.

*Iconography*—literally, the "writing of images"—refers both to the content, or subject, of an artwork, and to the study of content in art. By extension, it also includes the study of *symbols*, images that stand for other images or encapsulate ideas. In Christian art, two intersecting lines of unequal length or a simple geometric cross can serve as an emblem of the religion as a whole, symbolizing the cross of Jesus Christ's crucifixion. A symbol also can be a familiar object the artist imbued with greater meaning. A balance or scale, for example, may symbolize justice or the weighing of souls on judgment day (FIG. **I-7**).

Artists may depict figures with unique *attributes* identifying them. In Christian art, for example, each of the authors of the biblical gospel books, the four evangelists (FIG. **I-8**), has a distinctive attribute. People can recognize Saint John by the eagle associated with him, Luke by the ox, Mark by the lion, and Matthew by the winged man.

Throughout the history of art, artists have used *personifications*—abstract ideas codified in human form. Worldwide, people visualize Liberty as a robed woman wearing a rayed crown and holding a torch because of the fame of the colossal statue set up in New York City's harbor in 1886.

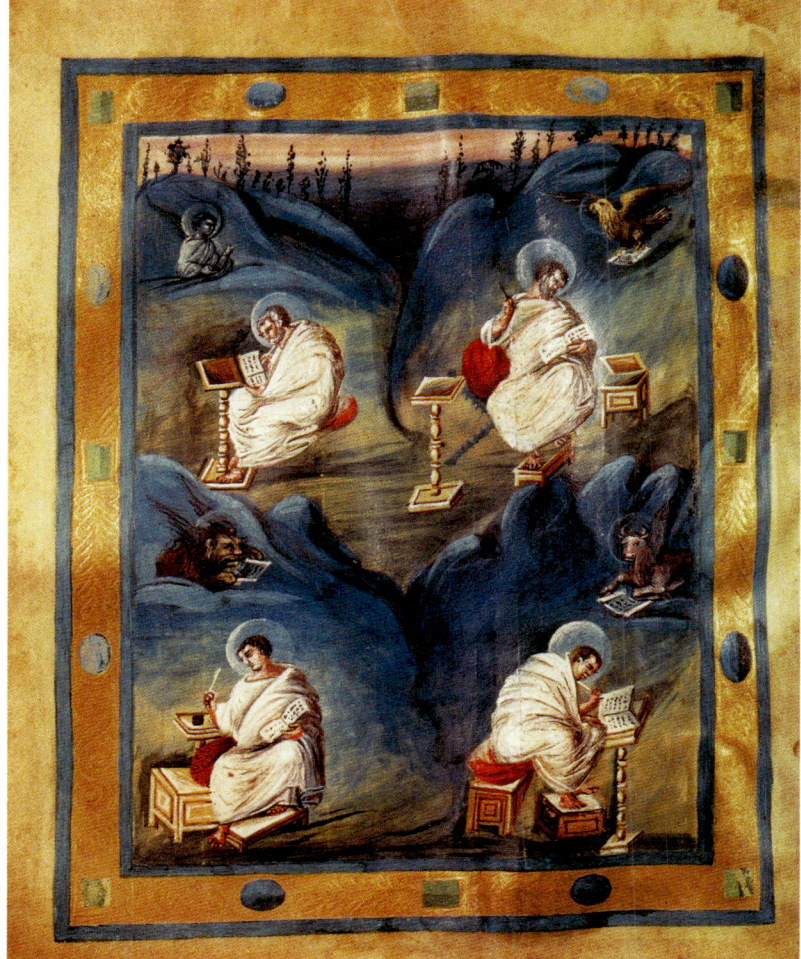

1 in.

**I-8** The four evangelists, folio 14 verso of the *Aachen Gospels,* ca. 810. Ink and tempera on vellum, $1' \times 9\frac{1}{2}''$. Domschatzkammer, Aachen.

Artists depict figures with attributes in order to identify them for viewers. The authors of the four gospels have distinctive attributes—eagle (John), ox (Luke), lion (Mark), and winged man (Matthew).

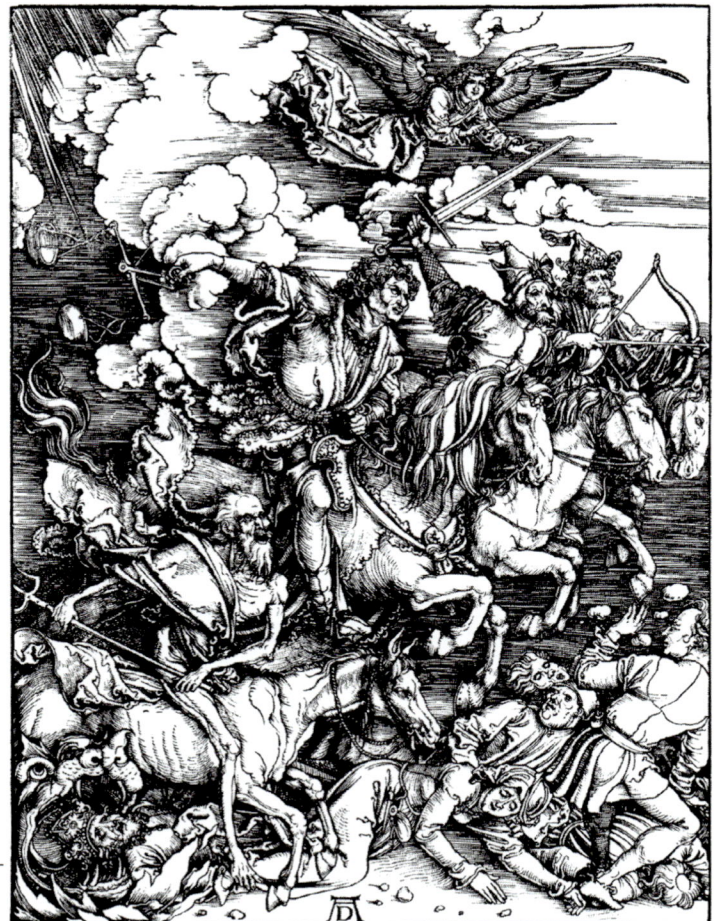

**I-9** ALBRECHT DÜRER, *The Four Horsemen of the Apocalypse*, ca. 1498. Woodcut, 1′ 3¼″ × 11″. Metropolitan Museum of Art, New York (gift of Junius S. Morgan, 1919).

Personifications are abstract ideas codified in human form. Here, Albrecht Dürer represented Death, Famine, War, and Pestilence as four men on charging horses, each one carrying an identifying attribute.

*The Four Horsemen of the Apocalypse* (FIG. I-9) is a terrifying late-15th-century depiction of the fateful day at the end of time when, according to the Bible's last book, Death, Famine, War, and Pestilence will annihilate the human race. German artist ALBRECHT DÜRER (1471–1528) personified Death as an emaciated old man with a pitchfork. Dürer's Famine swings the scales for weighing human souls (compare FIG. I-7), War wields a sword, and Pestilence draws a bow.

Even without considering style and without knowing a work's maker, informed viewers can determine much about the work's period and provenance by iconographical and subject analysis alone. In *The Passion of Sacco and Vanzetti* (FIG. I-6), for example, the two coffins, the trio headed by an academic, and the robed judge in the background are all pictorial clues revealing the painting's subject. The work's date must be after the trial and execution, probably while the event was still newsworthy. And because the two men's deaths caused the greatest outrage in the United States, the painter–social critic was probably American.

**WHO MADE IT?** If Ben Shahn had not signed his painting of Sacco and Vanzetti, an art historian could still assign, or *attribute* (make an *attribution* of), the work to him based on knowledge of

the artist's personal style. Although signing (and dating) works is quite common (but by no means universal) today, in the history of art countless works exist whose artists remain unknown. Because personal style can play a major role in determining the character of an artwork, art historians often try to attribute anonymous works to known artists. Sometimes they assemble a group of works all thought to be by the same person, even though none of the objects in the group is the known work of an artist with a recorded name. Art historians thus reconstruct the careers of artists such as "the Achilles Painter," the anonymous ancient Greek artist whose masterwork is a depiction of the hero Achilles. Scholars base their attributions on internal evidence, such as the distinctive way an artist draws or carves drapery folds, earlobes, or flowers. It requires a keen, highly trained eye and long experience to become a *connoisseur*, an expert in assigning artworks to "the hand" of one artist rather than another. Attribution is subjective, of course, and ever open to doubt. At present, for example, international debate rages over attributions to the famous 17th-century Dutch painter Rembrandt van Rijn.

Sometimes a group of artists works in the same style at the same time and place. Art historians designate such a group as a *school. School* does not mean an educational institution or art academy. The term connotes only shared chronology, style, and geography. Art historians speak, for example, of the Dutch school of the 17th century and, within it, of subschools such as those of the cities of Haarlem, Utrecht, and Leyden.

**WHO PAID FOR IT?** The interest many art historians show in attribution reflects their conviction that the identity of an artwork's maker is the major reason the object looks the way it does. For them, personal style is of paramount importance. But in many times and places, artists had little to say about what form their work would take. They toiled in obscurity, doing the bidding of their *patrons*, those who paid them to make individual works or employed them on a continuing basis. The role of patrons in dictating the content and shaping the form of artworks is also an important subject of art historical inquiry.

In the art of portraiture, to name only one category of painting and sculpture, the patron has often played a dominant role in deciding how the artist represented the subject, whether that person was the patron or another individual, such as a spouse, son, or mother. Many Egyptian pharaohs and some Roman emperors, for example, insisted artists depict them with unlined faces and perfect youthful bodies no matter how old they were when portrayed. In these cases, the state employed the sculptors and painters, and the artists had no choice but to portray their patrons in the officially approved manner. This is why Augustus, who lived to age 76, looks so young in his portraits (FIG. I-10). Although Roman emperor for more than 40 years, Augustus demanded artists always represent him as a young, godlike head of state.

All modes of artistic production reveal the impact of patronage. Learned monks provided the themes for the sculptural decoration of medieval church portals (FIG. I-7). Renaissance princes and popes dictated the subject, size, and materials of artworks destined for display in buildings also constructed according to their specifications. An art historian could make a very long list of commissioned works, and it would indicate patrons have had diverse tastes and needs throughout the history of art and consequently have demanded different kinds of art. Whenever a patron contracts an artist or architect to paint, sculpt, or build in a prescribed manner, personal style often becomes a very minor factor in the ultimate

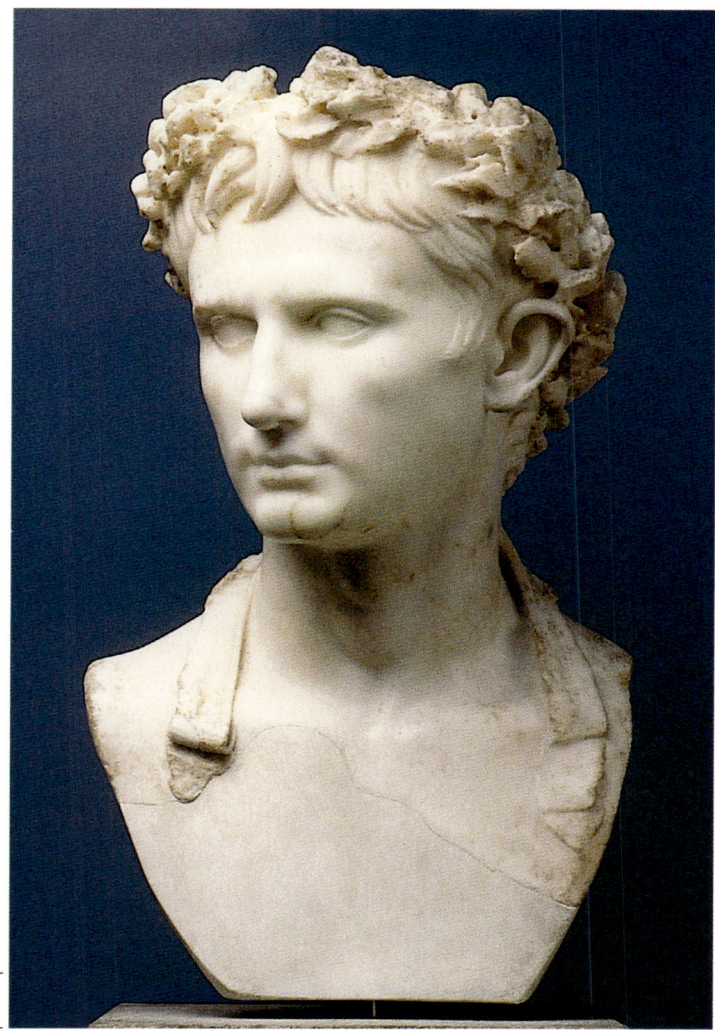

1 in.

**I-10** Bust of Augustus wearing the corona civica, early first century CE. Marble, 1′ 5″ high. Glyptothek, Munich.

Patrons frequently dictate the form their portraits will take. The Roman emperor Augustus demanded he always be portrayed as a young, godlike head of state even though he lived to age 76.

appearance of the painting, statue, or building. In these cases, the identity of the patron reveals more to art historians than does the identity of the artist or school. The portrait of Augustus illustrated here (FIG. I-10)—showing the emperor wearing a *corona civica,* or civic crown—was the work of a virtuoso sculptor, a master wielder of hammer and chisel. But scores of similar portraits of this Roman emperor also exist today. They differ in quality but not in kind from this one. The patron, not the artist, determined the character of these artworks. Augustus's public image never varied.

## The Words Art Historians Use

As in all fields of study, art history has its own specialized vocabulary consisting of hundreds of words, but certain basic terms are indispensable for describing artworks and buildings of any time and place. They make up the essential vocabulary of *formal analysis,* the visual analysis of artistic form. Definitions and discussions of the most important art historical terms follow.

**FORM AND COMPOSITION** *Form* refers to an object's shape and structure, either in two dimensions (for example, a figure painted on a canvas) or in three dimensions (such as a statue carved from a marble block). Two forms may take the same shape but may differ in their color, texture, and other qualities. *Composition* refers to how an artist *composes* (organizes) forms in an artwork, either by placing shapes on a flat surface or by arranging forms in space.

**MATERIAL AND TECHNIQUE** To create art forms, artists shape materials (pigment, clay, marble, gold, and many more) with tools (pens, brushes, chisels, and so forth). Each of the materials and tools available has its own potentialities and limitations. Part of all artists' creative activity is to select the *medium* and instrument most suitable to the purpose—or to develop new media and tools, such as bronze and concrete in antiquity and cameras and computers in modern times. The processes artists employ, such as applying paint to canvas with a brush, and the distinctive, personal ways they handle materials constitute their *technique.* Form, material, and technique interrelate and are central to analyzing any work of art.

**LINE** Among the most important elements defining an artwork's shape or form is *line.* A line can be understood as the path of a point moving in space, an invisible line of sight. More commonly, however, artists and architects make a line visible by drawing (or chiseling) it on a *plane,* a flat surface. A line may be very thin, wirelike, and delicate. It may be thick and heavy. Or it may alternate quickly from broad to narrow, the strokes jagged or the outline broken. When a continuous line defines an object's outer shape, art historians call it a *contour line.* All of these line qualities are present in Dürer's *The Four Horsemen of the Apocalypse* (FIG. I-9). Contour lines define the basic shapes of clouds, human and animal limbs, and weapons. Within the forms, series of short broken lines create shadows and textures. An overall pattern of long parallel strokes suggests the dark sky on the frightening day when the world is about to end.

**COLOR** Light reveals all *colors.* Light in the world of the painter and other artists differs from natural light. Natural light, or sunlight, is whole or *additive light.* As the sum of all the wavelengths composing the visible *spectrum,* it may be disassembled or fragmented into the individual colors of the spectral band. The painter's light in art—the light reflected from pigments and objects—is *subtractive light.* Paint pigments produce their individual colors by reflecting a segment of the spectrum while absorbing all the rest. Green pigment, for example, subtracts or absorbs all the light in the spectrum except that seen as green.

*Hue* is the property giving a color its name. Although the spectrum colors merge into each other, artists usually conceive of their hues as distinct from one another. Color has two basic variables—the apparent amount of light reflected and the apparent purity. A change in one must produce a change in the other. Some terms for these variables are *value,* or *tonality* (the degree of lightness or darkness), and *intensity,* or *saturation* (the purity of a color, its brightness or dullness).

Artists call the three basic colors—red, yellow, and blue—the *primary colors.* The *secondary colors* result from mixing pairs of primaries: orange (red and yellow), purple (red and blue), and green (yellow and blue). *Complementary colors* represent the pairing of a primary color and the secondary color created from mixing the two other primary colors—red and green, yellow and purple, and blue and orange. They "complement," or complete, each other, one absorbing colors the other reflects.

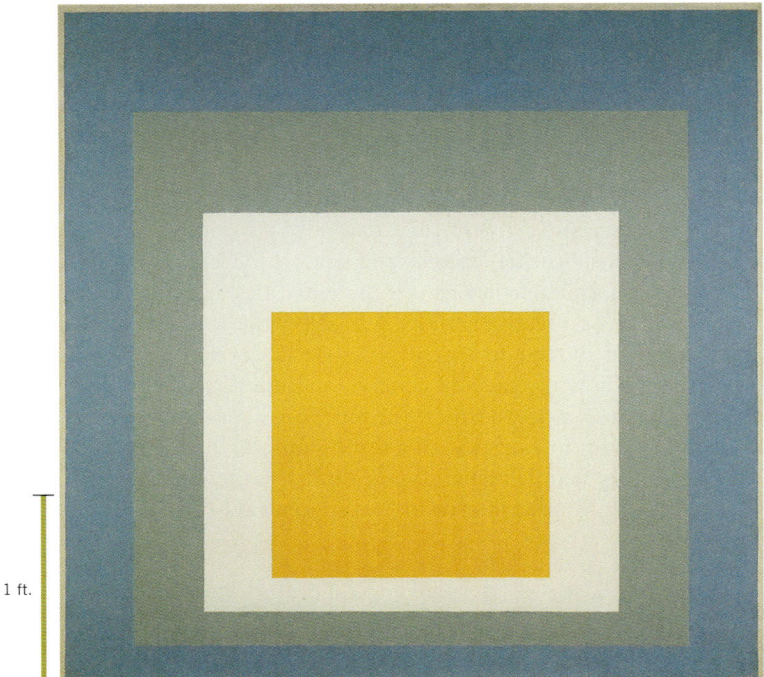

1 ft.

**I-11** JOSEF ALBERS, *Homage to the Square: "Ascending,"* 1953. Oil on composition board, 3′ 7½″ × 3′ 7½″. Whitney Museum of American Art, New York.

Albers painted hundreds of canvases using the same composition but employing variations in hue, saturation, and value in order to reveal the relativity and instability of color perception.

Artists can manipulate the appearance of colors, however. One artist who made a systematic investigation of the formal aspects of art, especially color, was JOSEF ALBERS (1888–1976), a German-born artist who emigrated to the United States in 1933. In connection with his studies, Albers created the series *Homage to the Square*—hundreds of paintings, most of which are color variations on the same composition of concentric squares, as in the illustrated example (FIG. **I-11**). The series reflected Albers's belief that art originates in "the discrepancy between physical fact and psychic effect."[1] Because the composition in most of these paintings remains constant, the works succeed in revealing the relativity and instability of color perception. Albers varied the hue, saturation, and value of each square in the paintings in this series. As a result, the sizes of the squares from painting to painting appear to vary (although they remain the same), and the sensations emanating from the paintings range from clashing dissonance to delicate serenity. Albers explained his motivation for focusing on color juxtapositions:

> They [the colors] are juxtaposed for various and changing visual effects. . . . Such action, reaction, interaction . . . is sought in order to make obvious how colors influence and change each other; that the same color, for instance—with different grounds or neighbors—looks different. . . . Such color deceptions prove that we see colors almost never unrelated to each other.[2]

**TEXTURE** The term *texture* refers to the quality of a surface, such as rough or shiny. Art historians distinguish between true texture, that is, the tactile quality of the surface, and represented texture, as when painters depict an object as having a certain tex-

ture even though the pigment is the true texture. Sometimes artists combine different materials of different textures on a single surface, juxtaposing paint with pieces of wood, newspaper, fabric, and so forth. Art historians refer to this mixed-media technique as *collage*. Texture is, of course, a key determinant of any sculpture's character. People's first impulse is usually to handle a work of sculpture—even though museum signs often warn "Do not touch!" Sculptors plan for this natural human response, using surfaces varying in texture from rugged coarseness to polished smoothness. Textures are often intrinsic to a material, influencing the type of stone, wood, plastic, clay, or metal sculptors select.

**SPACE, MASS, AND VOLUME** *Space* is the bounded or boundless "container" of objects. For art historians, space can be the real three-dimensional space occupied by a statue or a vase or contained within a room or courtyard. Or space can be *illusionistic*, as when painters depict an image (or illusion) of the three-dimensional spatial world on a two-dimensional surface.

*Mass* and *volume* describe three-dimensional objects and space. In both architecture and sculpture, mass is the bulk, density, and weight of matter in space. Yet the mass need not be solid. It can be the exterior form of enclosed space. Mass can apply to a solid Egyptian pyramid or stone statue, to a church, synagogue, or mosque—architectural shells enclosing sometimes vast spaces—and to a hollow metal statue or baked clay pot. Volume is the space that mass organizes, divides, or encloses. It may be a building's interior spaces, the intervals between a structure's masses, or the amount of space occupied by three-dimensional objects such as a statue, pot, or chair. Volume and mass describe both the exterior and interior forms of a work of art—the forms of the matter of which it is composed and the spaces immediately around the work and interacting with it.

**PERSPECTIVE AND FORESHORTENING** *Perspective* is one of the most important pictorial devices for organizing forms in space. Throughout history, artists have used various types of perspective to create an illusion of depth or space on a two-dimensional surface. The French painter CLAUDE LORRAIN (1600–1682) employed several perspective devices in *Embarkation of the Queen of Sheba* (FIG. **I-12**), a painting of a biblical episode set in a 17th-century European harbor with a Roman ruin in the left foreground. For example, the figures and boats on the shoreline are much larger than those in the distance. Decreasing the size of an object makes it appear farther away. Also, the top and bottom of the port building at the painting's right side are not parallel horizontal lines, as they are in a real building. Instead, the lines converge beyond the structure, leading the viewer's eye toward the hazy, indistinct sun on the horizon. These perspective devices—the reduction of figure size, the convergence of diagonal lines, and the blurring of distant forms—have been familiar features of Western art since the ancient Greeks. But it is important to note at the outset that all kinds of perspective are only pictorial conventions, even when one or more types of perspective may be so common in a given culture that people accept them as "natural" or as "true" means of representing the natural world.

In *Waves at Matsushima* (FIG. **I-13**), a Japanese seascape painting on a six-part folding screen, OGATA KORIN (1658–1716) ignored these Western perspective conventions. A Western viewer might interpret the left half of Korin's composition as depicting the distant horizon, as in Claude's painting, but the sky is a flat, unnatural gold, and in five of the six sections of the composition, waves fill the

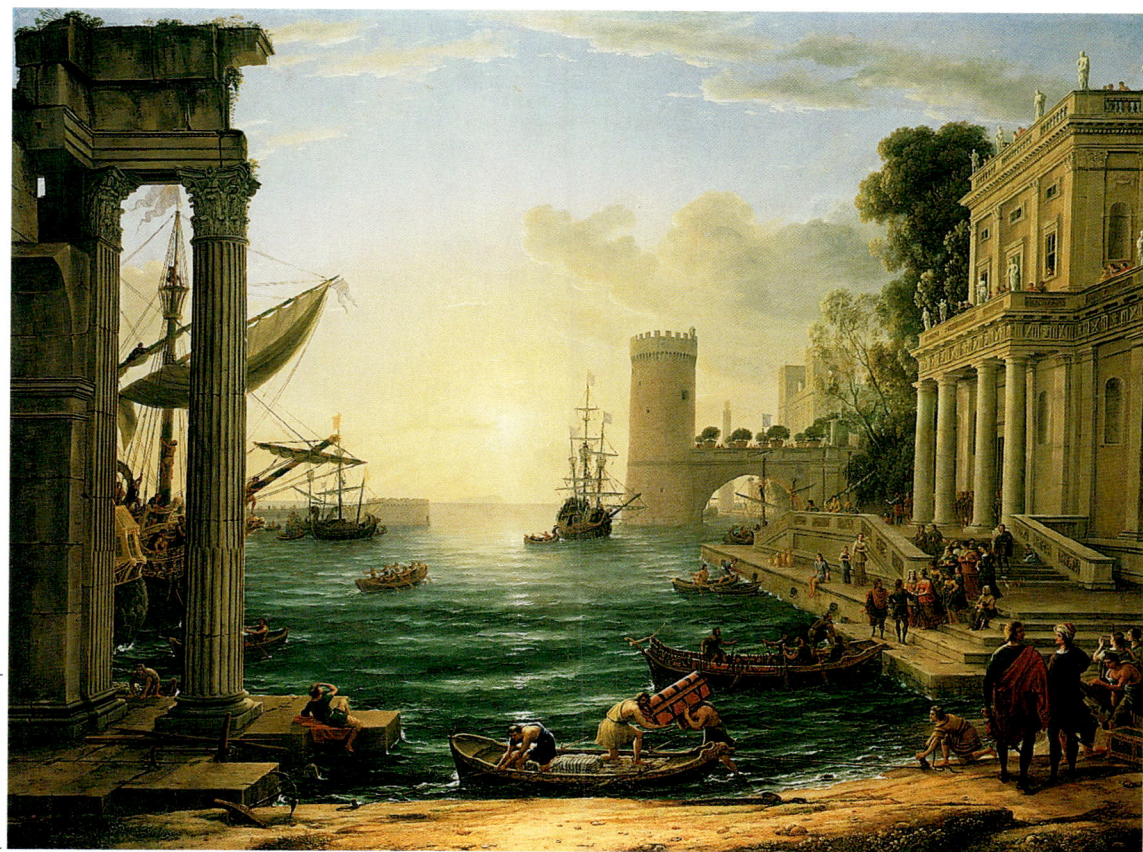

I-12 CLAUDE LORRAIN, *Embarkation of the Queen of Sheba,* 1648. Oil on canvas, 4′ 10″ × 6′ 4″. National Gallery, London.

To create the illusion of a deep landscape, Claude Lorrain employed perspective, reducing the size of and blurring the most distant forms. Also, all diagonal lines converge on a single point.

1 ft.

full height of the screen. The rocky outcroppings decrease in size with distance, but all are in sharp focus, and there are no shadows. The Japanese artist was less concerned with locating the boulders and waves in space than with composing shapes on a surface, playing the water's swelling curves against the jagged contours of the rocks. Neither the French nor the Japanese painting can be said to project "correctly" what viewers "in fact" see. One painting is not a "better" picture of the world than the other. The European and Asian artists simply approached the problem of picture-making differently.

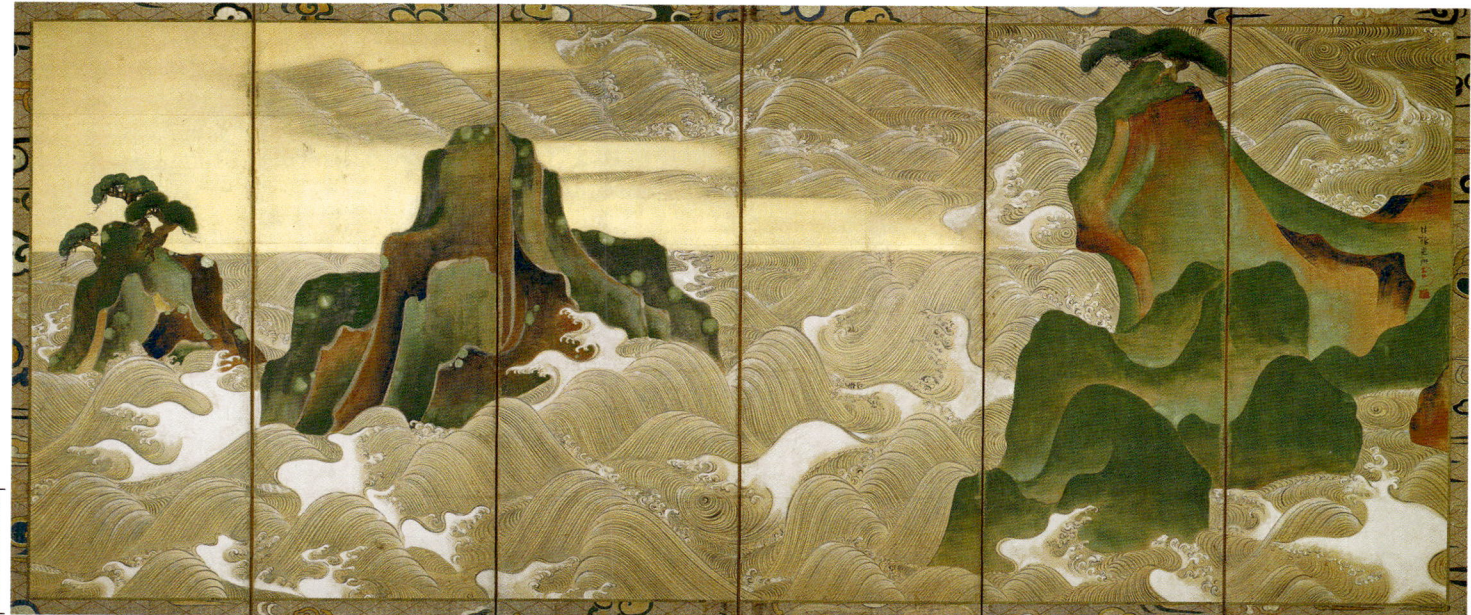

1 ft.

I-13 OGATA KORIN, *Waves at Matsushima,* Edo period, ca. 1700–1716. Six-panel folding screen, ink, color, and gold leaf on paper, 4′ 11⅛″ × 12′ ⅞″. Museum of Fine Arts, Boston (Fenollosa-Weld Collection).

Korin was more concerned with creating an intriguing composition of shapes on a surface than with locating boulders and waves in space. Asian artists rarely employed Western perspective.

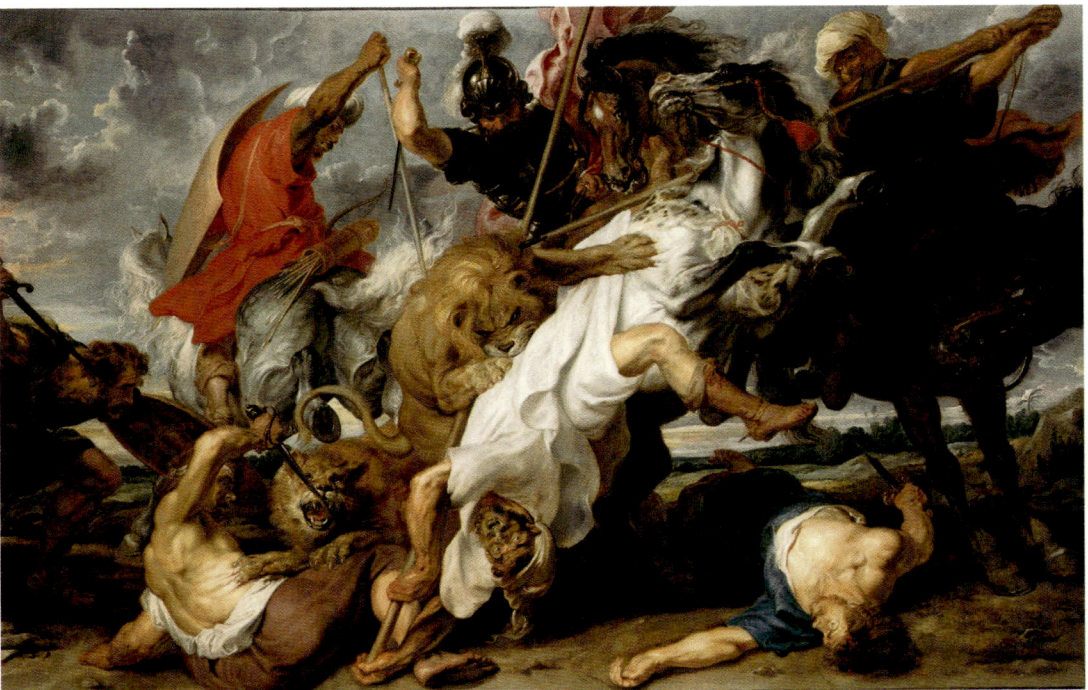

I-14 PETER PAUL RUBENS, *Lion Hunt*, 1617–1618. Oil on canvas, 8′ 2″ × 12′ 5″. Alte Pinakothek, Munich.

Foreshortening—the representation of a figure or object at an angle to the picture plane—is a common device in Western art for creating the illusion of depth. Foreshortening is a type of perspective.

1 ft.

Artists also represent single figures in space in varying ways. When Flemish artist PETER PAUL RUBENS (1577–1640) painted *Lion Hunt* (FIG. I-14), he used *foreshortening* for all the hunters and animals—that is, he represented their bodies at angles to the picture plane. When in life one views a figure at an angle, the body appears to contract as it extends back in space. Foreshortening is a kind of perspective. It produces the illusion that one part of the body is farther away than another, even though all the forms are on the same surface. Especially noteworthy in *Lion Hunt* are the gray horse at the left, seen from behind with the bottom of its left rear hoof facing viewers and most of its head hidden

by its rider's shield, and the fallen hunter at the painting's lower right corner, whose barely visible legs and feet recede into the distance.

The artist who carved the portrait of the ancient Egyptian official Hesire (FIG. I-15) did not employ foreshortening. That artist's purpose was to present the various human body parts as clearly as possible, without overlapping. The lower part of Hesire's body is in profile to give the most complete view of the legs, with both the heels and toes of the foot visible. The frontal torso, however, allows viewers to see its full shape, including both shoulders, equal in size, as in nature. (Compare the shoulders of the hunter on the gray horse or those of the fallen hunter in *Lion Hunt*'s left foreground.) The result—an "unnatural" 90-degree twist at the waist—provides a precise picture of human body parts. Rubens and the Egyptian sculptor used very different means of depicting forms in space. Once again, neither is the "correct" manner.

**PROPORTION AND SCALE** *Proportion* concerns the relationships (in terms of size) of the parts of persons, buildings, or objects. People can judge "correct proportions" intuitively ("that statue's head seems the right size for the body"). Or proportion can be a mathematical relationship between the size of one part of an artwork or building and the other parts within the work. Proportion in art implies using a *module,* or basic unit of measure. When an artist or architect uses a formal system of proportions, all parts of a building, body, or other entity will be fractions or multiples of the module. A module might be a *column*'s diameter, the height of a human head, or any other component whose dimensions can be multiplied or divided to determine the size of the work's other parts.

In certain times and places, artists have devised *canons,* or systems, of "correct" or "ideal" proportions for representing human figures, constituent parts of buildings, and so forth. In ancient Greece, many sculptors formulated canons of proportions so strict and all-encompassing that they calculated the size of every body part in advance, even the fingers and toes, according to mathematical ratios.

Proportional systems can differ sharply from period to period, culture to culture, and artist to artist. Part of the task art history

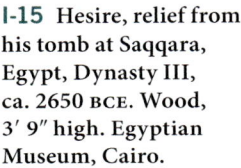

I-15 Hesire, relief from his tomb at Saqqara, Egypt, Dynasty III, ca. 2650 BCE. Wood, 3′ 9″ high. Egyptian Museum, Cairo.

Egyptian artists combined frontal and profile views to give a precise picture of the parts of the human body, as opposed to depicting how an individual body appears from a specific viewpoint.

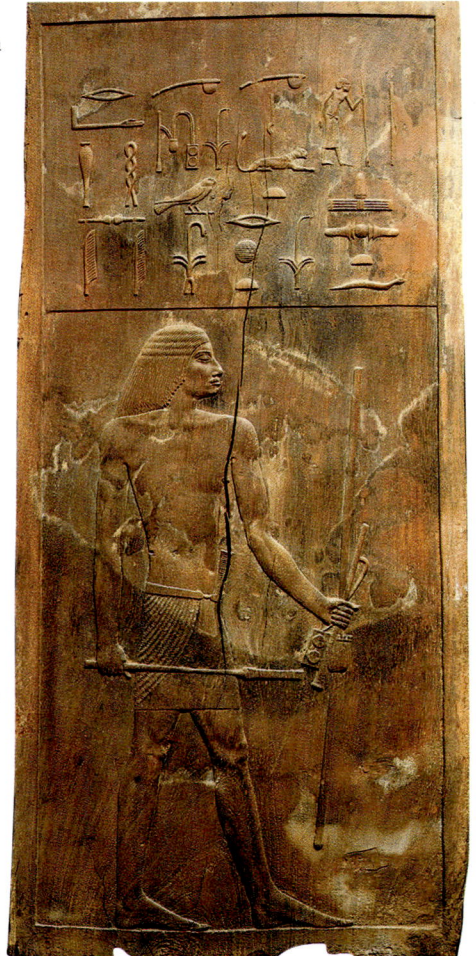

1 ft.

students face is to perceive and adjust to these differences. In fact, many artists have used disproportion and distortion deliberately for expressive effect. In the medieval French depiction of the weighing of souls on judgment day (FIG. I-7), the devilish figure yanking down on the scale has distorted facial features and stretched, lined limbs with animal-like paws for feet. Disproportion and distortion make him appear "inhuman," precisely as the sculptor intended.

In other cases, artists have used disproportion to focus attention on one body part (often the head) or to single out a group member (usually the leader). These intentional "unnatural" discrepancies in proportion constitute what art historians call *hierarchy of scale,* the enlarging of elements considered the most important. On the bronze plaque from Benin, Nigeria, illustrated here (FIG. I-1), the sculptor enlarged all the heads for emphasis and also varied the size of each figure according to the person's social status. Central, largest, and therefore most important is the Benin king, mounted on horseback. The horse has been a symbol of power and wealth in many societies from prehistory to the present. That the Benin king is disproportionately larger than his horse, contrary to nature, further aggrandizes him. Two large attendants fan the king. Other figures of smaller size and status at the Benin court stand on the king's left and right and in the plaque's upper corners. One tiny figure next to the horse is almost hidden from view beneath the king's feet.

One problem students of art history—and professional art historians too—confront when studying illustrations in art history books is that although the relative sizes of figures and objects in a painting or sculpture are easy to discern, it is impossible to determine the absolute size of the work reproduced because they all appear at approximately the same size on the page. Readers of *Art through the Ages* can learn the exact size of all artworks from the dimensions given in the captions and, more intuitively, from the scales positioned at the lower left or right corner of each illustration.

**I-16** MICHELANGELO BUONARROTI, unfinished statue, 1527–1528. Marble, 8′ 7½″ high. Galleria dell'Accademia, Florence.

Carving a freestanding figure from stone or wood is a subtractive process. Michelangelo thought of sculpture as a process of "liberating" the statue within the block of marble.

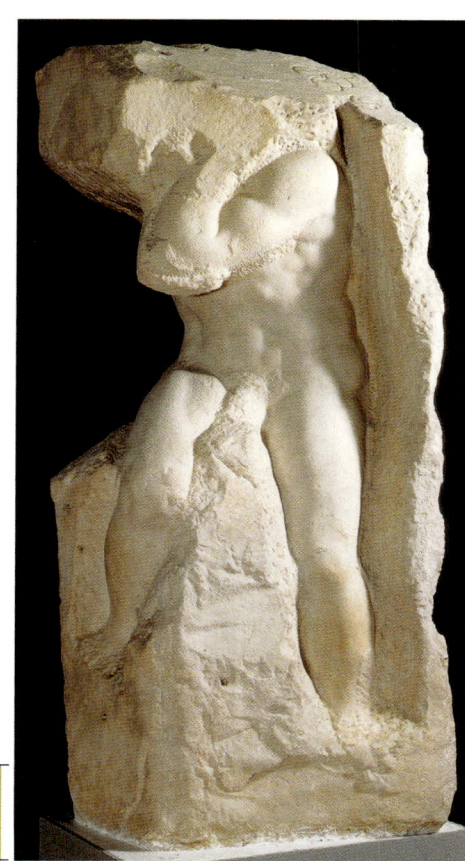

1 ft.

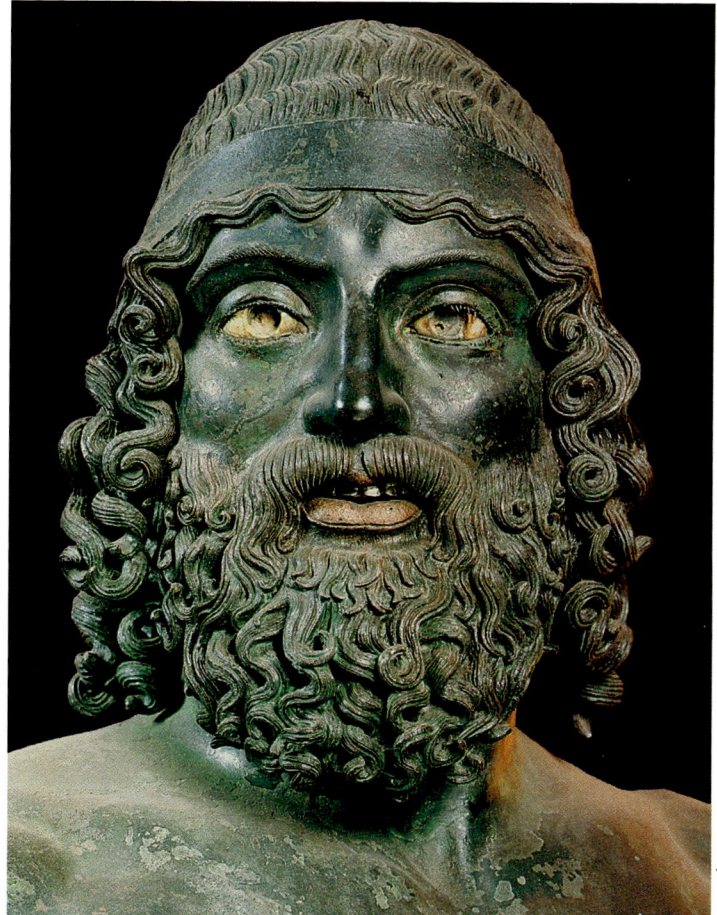

1 in.

**I-17** **Head of a warrior, detail of a statue** (FIG. 5-35) **from the sea off Riace, Italy, ca. 460–450 BCE. Bronze, full statue 6′ 6″ high. Museo Nazionale della Magna Grecia, Reggio Calabria.**

The sculptor of this life-size statue of a bearded Greek warrior cast the head, limbs, torso, hands, and feet in separate molds, then welded the pieces together and added the eyes in a different material.

**CARVING AND CASTING** Sculptural technique falls into two basic categories, *subtractive* and *additive. Carving* is a subtractive technique. The final form is a reduction of the original mass of a block of stone, a piece of wood, or another material. Wood statues were once tree trunks, and stone statues began as blocks pried from mountains. The unfinished marble statue illustrated here (FIG. **I-16**) by renowned Italian artist MICHELANGELO BUONARROTI (1475–1564) clearly reveals the original shape of the stone block. Michelangelo thought of sculpture as a process of "liberating" the statue within the block. All sculptors of stone or wood cut away (subtract) "excess material." When they finish, they "leave behind" the statue—in this example, a twisting nude male form whose head Michelangelo never freed from the stone block.

In additive sculpture, the artist builds up (*models*) the forms, usually in clay around a framework, or *armature.* Or a sculptor may fashion a *mold,* a hollow form for shaping, or *casting,* a fluid substance such as bronze or plaster. The ancient Greek sculptor who made the bronze statue of a warrior found in the sea near Riace, Italy, cast the head (FIG. **I-17**) as well as the limbs, torso, hands, and feet (FIG. 5-35) in separate molds and then *welded* them together (joined them by heating). Finally, the artist added features, such as the pupils of the eyes (now missing), in other materials. The warrior's teeth are silver, and his lower lip is copper.

**RELIEF SCULPTURE** *Statues* and *busts* (head, shoulders, and chest) that exist independent of any architectural frame or setting and that viewers can walk around are *freestanding* sculptures, or *sculptures in the round,* whether the artist produced the piece by carving (FIG. I-10) or casting (FIG. I-17). In *relief* sculpture, the subjects project from the background but remain part of it. In *high-relief* sculpture, the images project boldly. In some cases, such as the medieval weighing-of-souls scene (FIG. I-7), the relief is so high the forms not only cast shadows on the background, but some parts are even in the round, which explains why some pieces, for example, the arms of the scales, broke off centuries ago. In *low-relief,* or *bas-relief, sculpture,* such as the portrait of Hesire (FIG. I-15), the projection is slight. Artists can produce relief sculptures, as they do sculptures in the round, either by carving or casting. The plaque from Benin (FIG. I-1) is an example of bronze-casting in high relief.

**ARCHITECTURAL DRAWINGS** Buildings are groupings of enclosed spaces and enclosing masses. People experience architecture both visually and by moving through and around it, so they perceive architectural space and mass together. These spaces and masses can be represented graphically in several ways, including as plans, sections, elevations, and cutaway drawings.

A *plan,* essentially a map of a floor, shows the placement of a structure's masses and, therefore, the spaces they circumscribe and enclose. A *section,* a kind of vertical plan, depicts the placement of the masses as if someone cut through the building along a plane. Drawings showing a theoretical slice across a structure's width are *lateral sections.* Those cutting through a building's length are *longitudinal sections.* Illustrated here are the plan and lateral section of Beauvais Cathedral (FIG. I-18), which readers can compare with the photograph of the church's *choir* (FIG. I-3). The plan shows the choir's shape and the location of the *piers* dividing the *aisles* and supporting the *vaults* above, as well as the pattern of the crisscrossing vault *ribs.* The lateral section shows not only the interior of the choir with its vaults and tall *stained-glass* windows but also the structure of the roof and the form of the exterior *flying buttresses* holding the vaults in place.

Other types of architectural drawings appear throughout this book. An *elevation* drawing is a head-on view of an external or internal wall. A *cutaway* combines in a single drawing an exterior view with an interior view of part of a building.

This overview of the art historian's vocabulary is not exhaustive, nor have artists used only painting, drawing, sculpture, and architecture as media over the millennia. Ceramics, jewelry, textiles, photography, and computer graphics are just some of the numerous other arts. All of them involve highly specialized techniques described in distinct vocabularies. As in this introductory chapter, new terms are in *italics* when they first appear. The comprehensive Glossary at the end of the book contains definitions of all italicized terms.

## Art History and Other Disciplines

By its very nature, the work of art historians intersects with the work of others in many fields of knowledge, not only in the humanities but also in the social and natural sciences. Today, art historians must go beyond the boundaries of what the public and even professional art historians of previous generations traditionally considered the specialized discipline of art history. In short, art historical research in the 21st century is typically interdisciplinary in nature. To cite one example, in an effort to unlock the secrets of a particular statue, an art historian might conduct archival research hoping to uncover new documents shedding light on who paid for the work and why, who made it and when, where it originally stood, how its contemporaries viewed it, and a host of other questions. Realizing, however, that the authors of the written documents often were not objective recorders of fact but observers with their own biases and agendas, the art historian may also use methodologies developed in fields such as literary criticism, philosophy, sociology, and gender studies to weigh the evidence the documents provide.

At other times, rather than attempting to master many disciplines at once, art historians band together with other specialists in multidisciplinary inquiries. Art historians might call in chemists

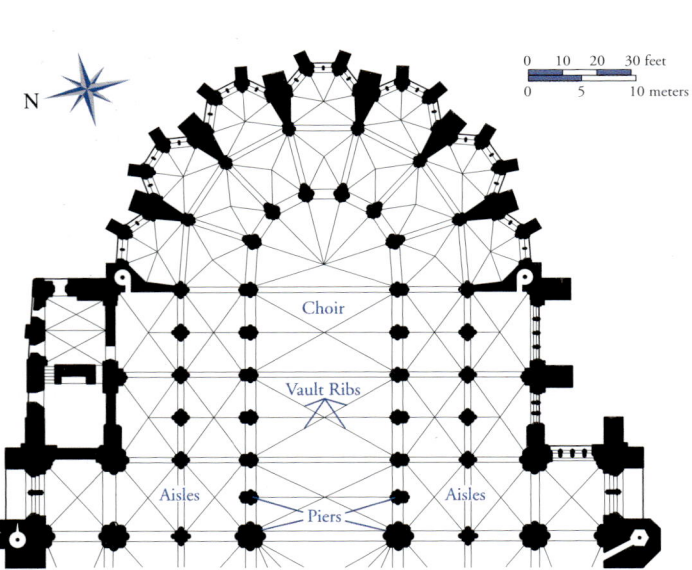

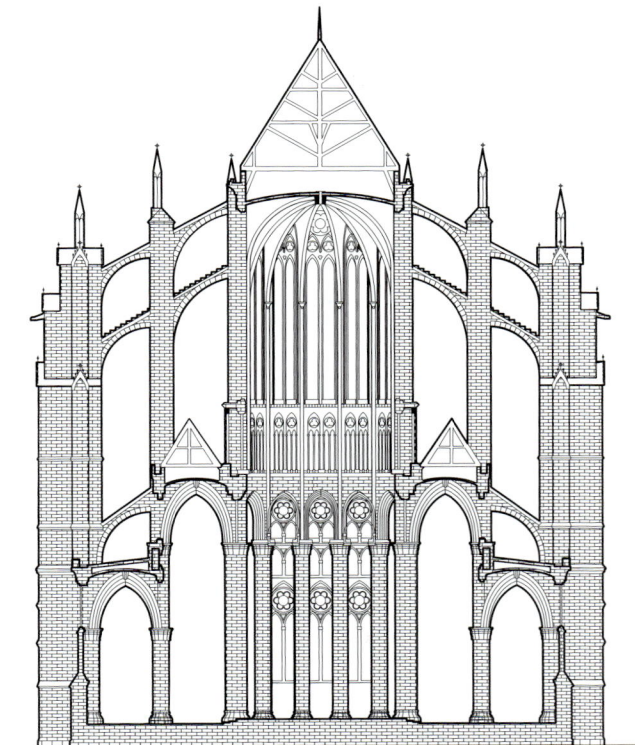

**I-18** Plan (*left*) and lateral section (*right*) of Beauvais Cathedral, Beauvais, France, rebuilt after 1284.

Architectural drawings are indispensable aids for the analysis of buildings. Plans are maps of floors, recording the structure's masses. Sections are vertical "slices" across either a building's width or length.

to date an artwork based on the composition of the materials used, or might ask geologists to determine which quarry furnished the stone for a particular statue. X-ray technicians might be enlisted in an attempt to establish whether a painting is a forgery. Of course, art historians often reciprocate by contributing their expertise to the solution of problems in other disciplines. A historian, for example, might ask an art historian to determine—based on style, material, iconography, and other criteria—if any of the portraits of a certain king date after his death. Such information would help establish the ruler's continuing prestige during the reigns of his successors. (Some portraits of Augustus [FIG. I-10], the founder of the Roman Empire, postdate his death by decades, even centuries.)

## DIFFERENT WAYS OF SEEING

The history of art can be a history of artists and their works, of styles and stylistic change, of materials and techniques, of images and themes and their meanings, and of contexts and cultures and patrons. The best art historians analyze artworks from many viewpoints. But no art historian (or scholar in any other field), no matter how broad-minded in approach and no matter how experienced, can be truly objective. As were the artists who made the works illustrated and discussed in this book, art historians are members of a society, participants in its culture. How can scholars (and museum visitors and travelers to foreign locales) comprehend cultures unlike their own? They can try to reconstruct the original cultural contexts of artworks, but they are limited by their distance from the thought patterns of the cultures they study and by the obstructions to understanding—the assumptions, presuppositions, and prejudices peculiar to their own culture—their own thought patterns raise. Art historians may reconstruct a distorted picture of the past because of culture-bound blindness.

A single instance underscores how differently people of diverse cultures view the world and how various ways of seeing can result in sharp differences in how artists depict the world. Illustrated here are two contemporaneous portraits of a 19th-century Maori chieftain (FIG. I-19)—one by an Englishman, JOHN HENRY SYLVESTER (active early 19th century), and the other by the New Zealand chieftain himself, TE PEHI KUPE (d. 1829). Both reproduce the chieftain's facial tattooing. The European artist (FIG. I-19, *left*) included the head and shoulders and downplayed the tattooing. The tattoo pattern is one aspect of the likeness among many, no more or less important than the chieftain's European attire. Sylvester also recorded his subject's momentary glance toward the right and the play of light on his hair, fleeting aspects having nothing to do with the figure's identity.

In contrast, Te Pehi Kupe's self-portrait (FIG. I-19, *right*)—made during a trip to Liverpool, England, to obtain European arms to take back to New Zealand—is not a picture of a man situated in space and bathed in light. Rather, it is the chieftain's statement of the supreme importance of the tattoo design announcing his rank among his people. Remarkably, Te Pehi Kupe created the tattoo patterns from memory, without the aid of a mirror. The splendidly composed insignia, presented as a flat design separated from the body and even from the head, is Te Pehi Kupe's image of himself. Only by understanding the cultural context of each portrait can art historians hope to understand why either representation appears as it does.

As noted at the outset, the study of the context of artworks and buildings is one of the central concerns of art historians. *Art through the Ages* seeks to present a history of art and architecture that will help readers to understand not only the subjects, styles, and techniques of paintings, sculptures, buildings, and other art forms created in all parts of the world during 30 millennia but also their cultural and historical contexts. That story now begins.

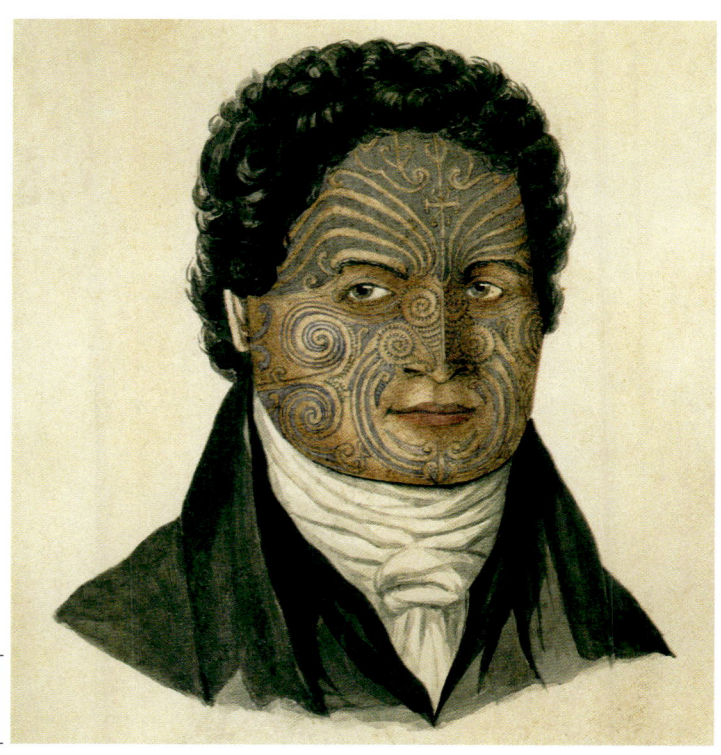

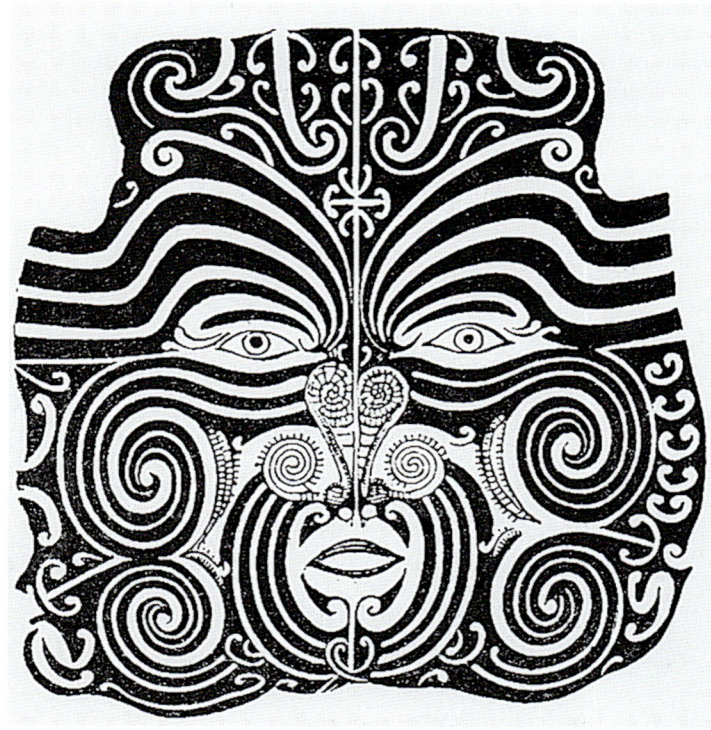

1 in.

**I-19** *Left:* JOHN HENRY SYLVESTER, *Portrait of Te Pehi Kupe,* 1826. Watercolor, $8\frac{1}{4}'' \times 6\frac{1}{4}''$. National Library of Australia, Canberra (Rex Nan Kivell Collection). *Right:* TE PEHI KUPE, *Self-Portrait,* 1826. From Leo Frobenius, *The Childhood of Man* (New York: J. B. Lippincott, 1909).

These strikingly different portraits of the same Maori chief reveal the different ways of seeing by a European artist and an Oceanic one. Understanding the cultural context of artworks is vital to art history.

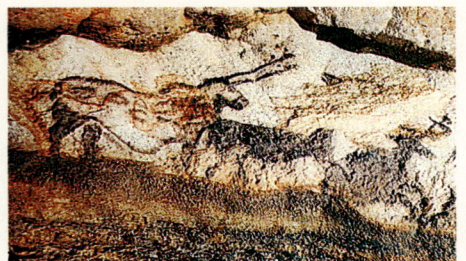

The species of animals depicted in the cave paintings of France and Spain are not among those Paleolithic humans typically consumed as food. The meaning of these paintings remains an enigma.

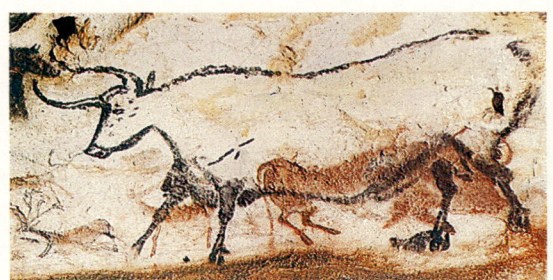

Prehistoric painters consistently represented animals in strict profile, the only view showing the head, body, tail, and all four legs. But at Lascaux, both horns are included to give a complete picture of the bull.

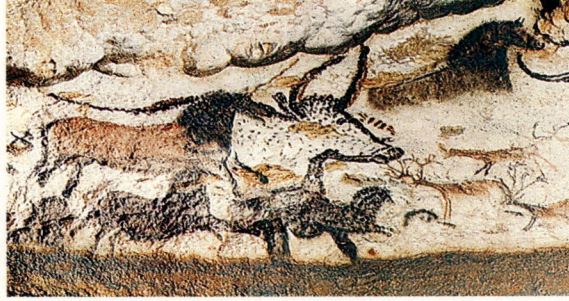

The Lascaux animals are inconsistent in size and move in different directions. Some are colored silhouettes; others are outline drawings. They were probably made at different times by different painters.

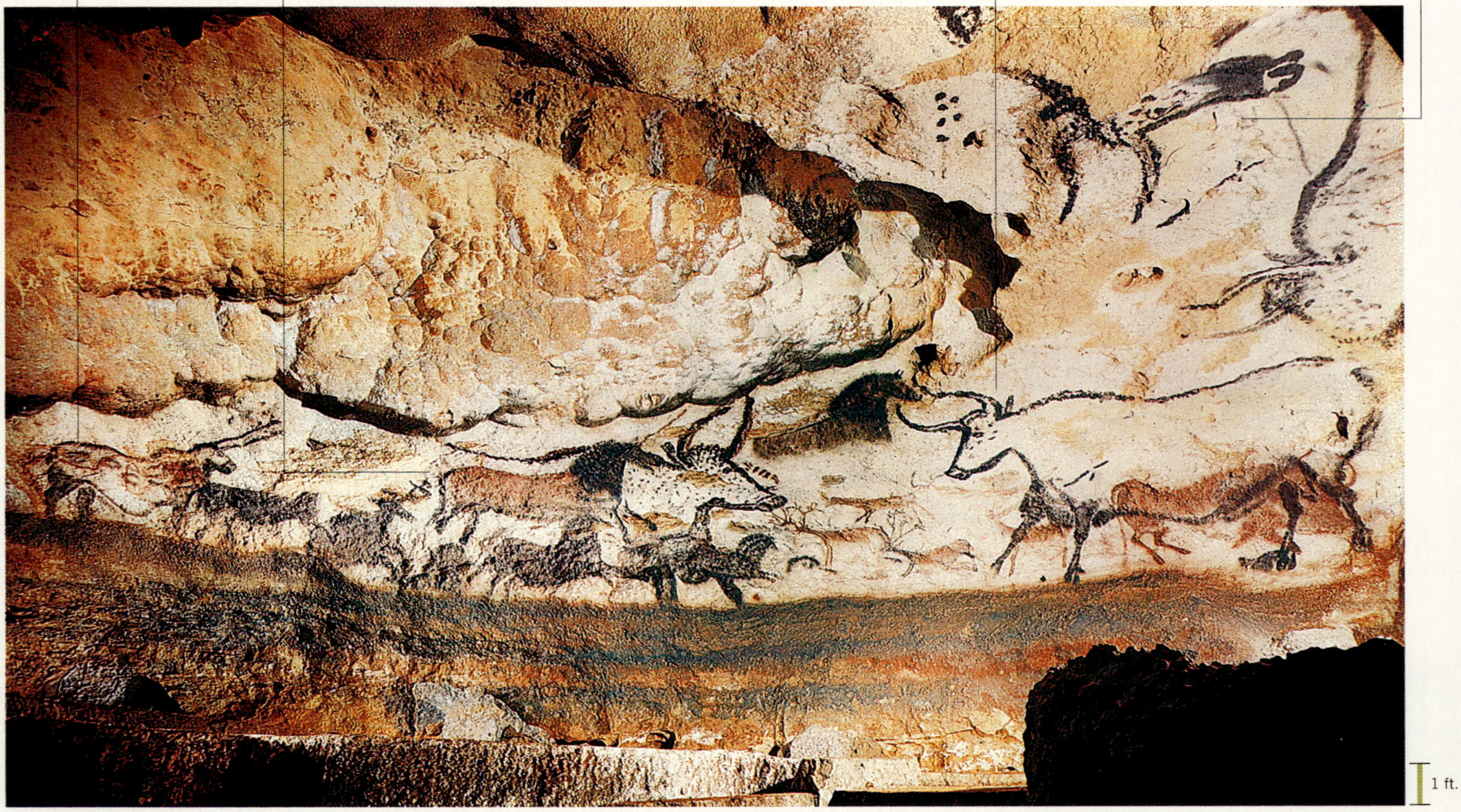

1 ft.

**1-1** Left wall of the Hall of the Bulls in the cave at Lascaux, France, ca. 16,000–14,000 BCE. Largest bull 11′ 6″ long. ◼◀

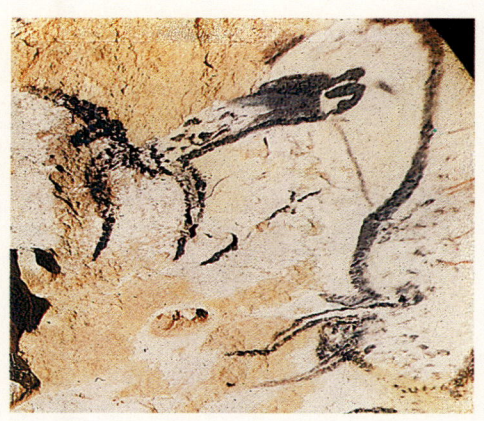

Most of the animals painted on prehistoric cave walls do not stand on a common ground line, nor do they share a common orientation. Paleolithic paintings have no background and no indication of place.

# ART BEFORE HISTORY

## THE DAWN OF ART

The Old Stone Age, which began around 30,000 BCE, was arguably the most important era in the entire history of art. It was then that humans invented the concept of recording the world around them in pictures, often painted on or carved into the walls of caves.

The oldest and best known painted caves are in southern France, and the cave at Lascaux is the most famous of them all. More than 17,000 years ago, prehistoric painters covered many of the walls of the cave with images of animals. The main chamber (FIG. 1-1), nicknamed the Hall of the Bulls, is an unusually large space and easily accessible, but many of the paintings at Lascaux and in other caves are almost impossible to reach. Even the Hall of the Bulls is far from the cave entrance, and its paintings could only have been seen with the flickering light of a primitive lamp. The representations of animals cannot have been merely decorative, but what meaning they carried for those who made and viewed them remains an enigma. Bulls and horses, the most commonly depicted species, were not diet staples in the Old Stone Age. Why, then, did the painters choose to represent these particular animals? In the absence of written records, no one will ever know.

Art historians can, however, learn a great deal about the working methods and conceptual principles of the world's first artists by closely studying the Lascaux paintings and others like them. The immediate impression a modern viewer gets of a rapidly moving herd is almost certainly false. The "herd" consists of several different kinds of animals of various sizes moving in different directions. Also, two fundamentally different approaches to picture making are on display. Many of the animals are colored silhouettes, whereas others are outline drawings. These differences in style and technique suggest different painters created the images in the Hall of the Bulls at different times, perhaps over the course of generations.

Nonetheless, all prehistoric representations of animals for thousands of years depict the beasts in the same way—in strict profile, the only view of an animal wherein the head, body, tail, and all four legs are visible. The Lascaux painters, however, showed the bulls' horns from the front, not in profile, because two horns are part of the concept "bull." Only much later in the history of art did painters become concerned with how to depict animals and people from a fixed viewpoint or develop an interest in recording the environment around the figures. The paintings created at the dawn of art are in many ways markedly different in kind from all that followed.

# PALEOLITHIC ART

Humankind originated in Africa in the very remote past. From that great continent also has come the earliest evidence of human recognition of abstract images in the natural environment, if not the first examples of what people generally call "art." In 1925, explorers of a cave at Makapansgat in South Africa (MAP 19-1) discovered bones of *Australopithecus,* a predecessor of modern humans who lived some three million years ago. Associated with the bones was a waterworn, reddish-brown jasperite pebble (FIG. **1-2**) that bears an uncanny resemblance to a human face. The nearest known source of this variety of ironstone is 20 miles from the cave. Perhaps an early human who took refuge in the rock shelter at Makapansgat noticed the pebble in a streambed and, awestruck by the "face" on the stone, carried it back for safekeeping.

Is the Makapansgat pebble "art"? In modern times, many artists have created works critics universally consider art by removing objects from their normal contexts, altering them, and then labeling them. In 1917, for example, Marcel Duchamp chose a ceramic urinal, set it on its side, called it *Fountain* (FIG. 29-27), and declared his "readymade" worthy of exhibition among more conventional artworks. But the artistic environment of the past century cannot be projected into the remote past. For art historians to classify as an "artwork" a found object such as the Makapansgat pebble, it must have been modified by human intervention beyond mere selection—and it was not. In fact, evidence indicates that, with few exceptions, it was not until three million years later, around 30,000 BCE, when large parts of northern Europe were still covered with glaciers during the Ice Age, that humans intentionally manufactured sculptures and paintings. Only then does the story of art through the ages really begin.

The several millennia following 30,000 BCE brought a powerful outburst of creativity. The works produced by the peoples of the Old Stone Age, or *Paleolithic* period (from the Greek *paleo,* "old," and *lithos,* "stone"), are of an astonishing variety. They range from simple shell necklaces to human and animal forms in ivory, clay, and stone to monumental paintings, engravings, and relief sculptures covering the huge wall surfaces of caves. During the Paleolithic period, humankind went beyond the *recognition* of human and animal forms in the natural environment to the *representation* (literally, the presenting again—in different and substitute form—of something observed) of humans and animals. The immensity of this achievement cannot be overstated.

## Africa

Some of the earliest paintings yet discovered come from Africa, and, like the treasured pebble resembling a face found at Makapansgat, the oldest African paintings were portable objects.

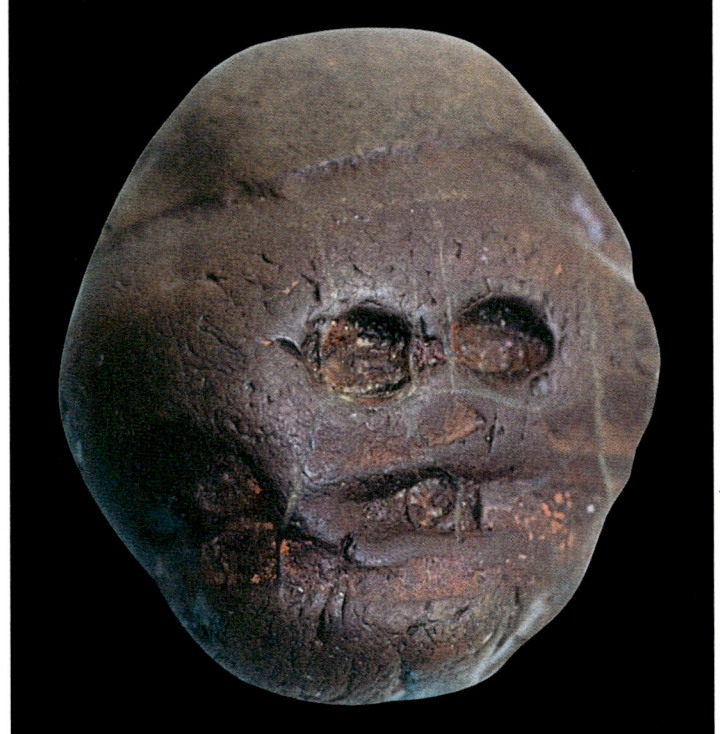

**1-2** Waterworn pebble resembling a human face, from Makapansgat, South Africa, ca. 3,000,000 BCE. Reddish-brown jasperite, $2\frac{3}{8}''$ wide. Natural History Museum, London.

Three million years ago, someone recognized a face in this pebble and brought it to a rock shelter for safekeeping, but the stone is not an artwork because it was neither manufactured nor modified.

**APOLLO 11 CAVE** Between 1969 and 1972, scientists working in the Apollo 11 Cave in Namibia (MAP 19-1) found seven fragments of stone plaques with paint on them, including four or five recognizable images of animals. In most cases, including the example illustrated here (FIG. **1-3**), the species is uncertain, but the painters always rendered the forms with care. One plaque depicts a striped beast, possibly a zebra. The approximate date of the charcoal from the archaeological layer containing the Namibian plaques is 23,000 BCE.

As has every artist in every age in every medium, the painter of the Apollo 11 plaque had to answer two questions before beginning work: *What* shall be my subject? *How* shall I represent it? In Paleolithic art, the almost universal answer to the first question was an animal—bison, horse, mammoth, and ibex are the most common. In fact, Paleolithic painters and sculptors depicted humans infrequently, and men almost never. In equally stark contrast to today's world, there was also agreement on the best answer to the second question. Artists represented virtually every animal in every Paleolithic, *Mesolithic* (Middle Stone Age), and *Neolithic* (New Stone Age) painting in the same manner—in strict profile. The profile is the only view of an animal wherein the head, body, tail, and all four legs are visible. The frontal view conceals most of the body, and a three-quarter view

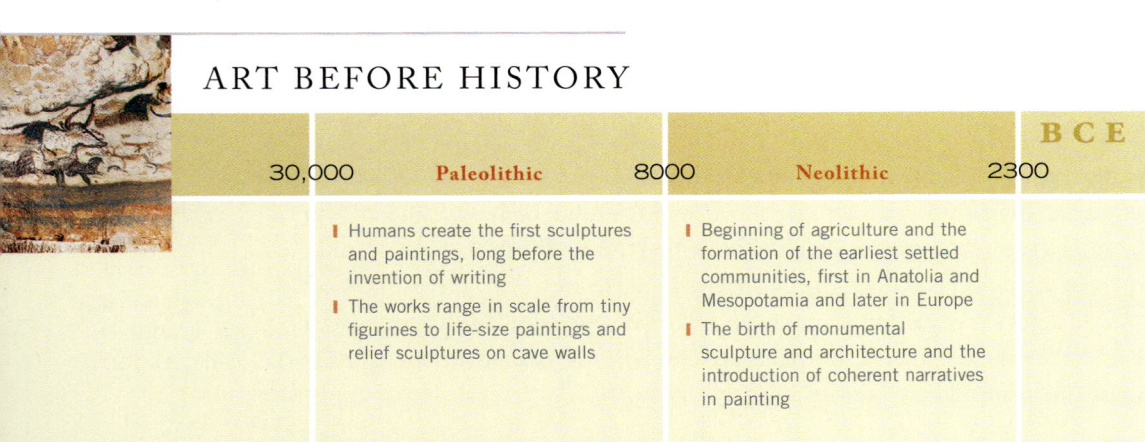

## ART BEFORE HISTORY

| | 30,000 | Paleolithic | 8000 | Neolithic | 2300 | **B C E** |
|---|---|---|---|---|---|---|
| | | ▮ Humans create the first sculptures and paintings, long before the invention of writing<br>▮ The works range in scale from tiny figurines to life-size paintings and relief sculptures on cave walls | | ▮ Beginning of agriculture and the formation of the earliest settled communities, first in Anatolia and Mesopotamia and later in Europe<br>▮ The birth of monumental sculpture and architecture and the introduction of coherent narratives in painting | | |

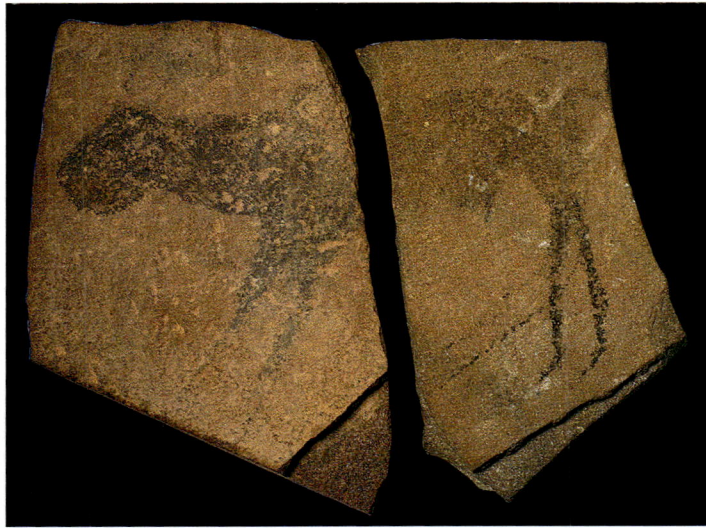

**1-3** Animal facing left, from the Apollo 11 Cave, Namibia, ca. 23,000 BCE. Charcoal on stone, $4\frac{1}{4}'' \times 5''$. State Museum of Namibia, Windhoek.

Like most other paintings for thousands of years, this very early example from Africa represents an animal in strict profile so that the head, body, tail, and all four legs are clearly visible.

shows neither the front nor side fully. Only the profile view is completely informative about the animal's shape, and that is why Stone Age painters universally chose it. A very long time passed before artists placed any premium on "variety" or "originality," either in subject choice or in representational manner. These are quite modern notions in the history of art. The aim of the earliest painters was to create a convincing image of their subject, a kind of pictorial definition of the animal capturing its very essence, and only the profile view met their needs.

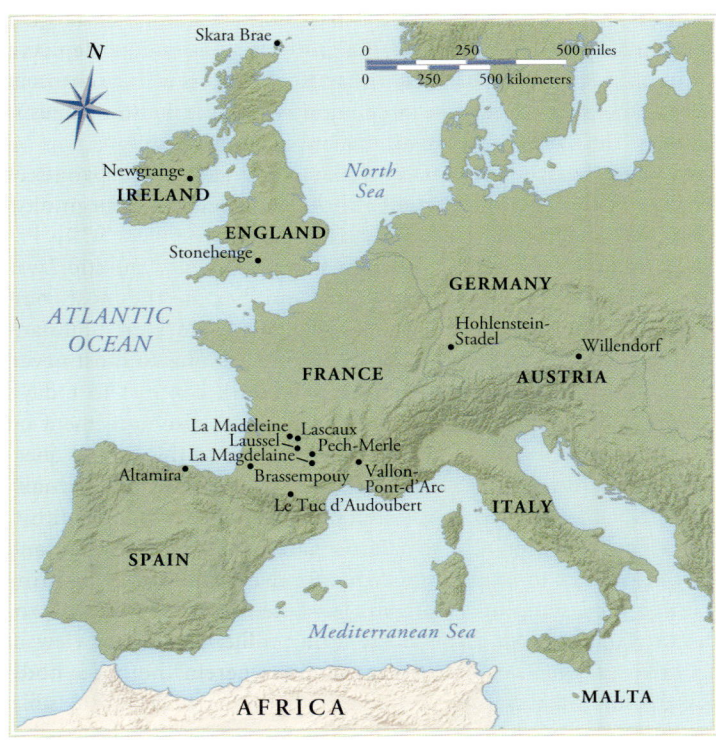

**MAP 1-1** Prehistoric sites in Europe.

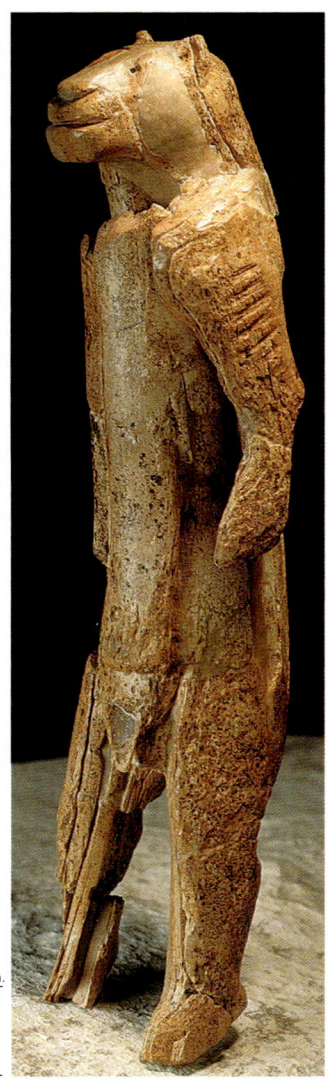

**1-4** Human with feline head, from Hohlenstein-Stadel, Germany, ca. 30,000–28,000 BCE. Mammoth ivory, $11\frac{5}{8}''$ high. Ulmer Museum, Ulm.

One of the oldest known sculptures is this large ivory figure of a human with a feline head. It is uncertain whether the work depicts a composite creature or a human wearing an animal mask.

## Western Europe

Even older than the Namibian painted plaques are some of the first sculptures and paintings of western Europe (MAP **1-1**), although examples of still greater antiquity may yet be found in Africa, bridging the gap between the Makapansgat pebble and the Apollo 11 Cave painted plaques.

### HOHLENSTEIN-STADEL

One of the earliest sculptures discovered yet is an extraordinary ivory statuette (FIG. **1-4**), which may date back as far as 30,000 BCE. Found in fragments inside a cave at Hohlenstein-Stadel in Germany and meticulously restored, the statuette is mammoth ivory and nearly a foot tall—a truly huge image for its era. It represents something that existed only in the vivid imagination of the Paleolithic sculptor who conceived it. It is a human (whether male or female cannot be determined) with a feline head. Composite creatures with animal heads and human bodies (and vice versa) are familiar in the art of ancient Mesopotamia and Egypt (compare, for example, FIGS. 2-10 and 3-36). In those civilizations, surviving texts usually enable historians to name the figures and describe their role in religion and mythology. But for Stone Age representations, no one knows what their makers had in mind. Some scholars identify the animal-headed humans as sorcerers, whereas others describe them as magicians wearing masks. Similarly, Paleolithic human-headed animals have been interpreted as humans dressed up as animals. In the absence of any contemporaneous written explanations—this was a time before writing, before (or pre-) history—researchers can only speculate on the purpose and function of statuettes like the one from Hohlenstein-Stadel.

Art historians are certain, however, that these sculptures were important to those who created them, because manufacturing an ivory figure, especially one a foot tall, was a complicated process. First, the hunter or the sculptor had to remove the tusk from the dead animal by cutting into the ivory where it joined the head. Then the sculptor cut the tusk to the desired size and rubbed it into its approximate final shape with sandstone. Finally, the carver used a sharp stone blade to shape the body, limbs, and head, and a stone burin (a pointed engraving tool) to incise (scratch) lines into the surfaces, as on the Hohlenstein-Stadel creature's arms. All this probably required at least several days of skilled work.

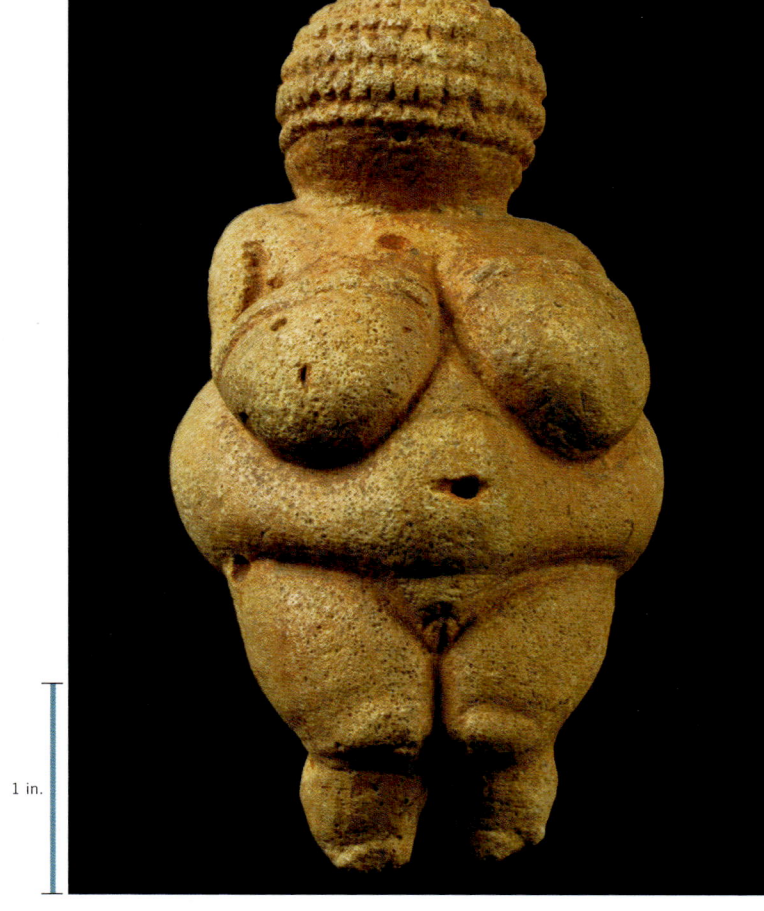

**1-5** Nude woman (*Venus of Willendorf*), from Willendorf, Austria, ca. 28,000–25,000 BCE. Limestone, 4¼″ high. Naturhistorisches Museum, Vienna. ◼◀

The anatomical exaggerations in this tiny figurine from Willendorf are typical of Paleolithic representations of women, whose child-bearing capabilities ensured the survival of the species.

**WILLENDORF** The composite feline-human from Germany is exceptional for the Stone Age. The vast majority of prehistoric sculptures depict either animals or humans. In the earliest art, humankind consists almost exclusively of women as opposed to men, and Paleolithic painters and sculptors almost invariably showed them nude, although historians generally assume that during the Ice Age both women and men wore garments covering parts of their bodies. When archaeologists first encountered Stone Age statuettes of women, they dubbed them "Venuses," after the Greco-Roman goddess of beauty and love, whom later artists usually depicted nude. The nickname is inappropriate and misleading. Indeed, it is doubtful the Paleolithic figurines represent deities of any kind.

One of the oldest and most famous prehistoric female images is the tiny limestone figurine of a woman that long ago became known as the *Venus of Willendorf* (FIG. **1-5**) after its *findspot* (place of discovery) in Austria. Its cluster of almost ball-like shapes is unusual, the result in part of the sculptor's response to the natural shape of the stone selected for carving. The anatomical exaggeration has suggested to many observers that this and similar statuettes served as fertility images. But other Paleolithic stone women of far more slender proportions exist, and the meaning of these images is as elusive as everything else about Paleolithic art. Yet the preponderance of female over male figures in the Old Stone Age seems to indicate a preoccupation with women, whose child-bearing capabilities ensured the survival of the species.

One thing at least is clear: The *Venus of Willendorf* sculptor did not aim for naturalism in shape and proportion. As with most Paleolithic figures, the sculptor did not carve any facial features. A similar but even smaller ivory figurine found in 2008 in a cave at Hohle Fels, near Ulm, Germany, contemporaneous with or perhaps even several thousand years older than the Hohlenstein-Stadel statuette, lacks any head at all. The ivory head (FIG. **1-5A**) of a woman from Brassempouy, France, is a notable exception. The carver of the Willendorf figurine suggested only a mass of curly hair or, as some researchers have argued, a hat woven from plant fibers—evidence for the art of textile manufacture at a very early date. In either case, the emphasis is on female anatomy. The breasts of the Willendorf woman are enormous, far larger in proportion than the tiny forearms and hands that rest upon them. The carver also took pains to scratch into the stone the outline of the pubic triangle. Sculptors often omitted this detail in other early figurines, leading some scholars to question the nature of these figures as fertility images. Whatever the purpose of these statuettes, the makers' intent seems to have been to represent not a specific woman but the female form.

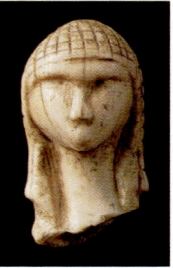

**1-5A** Head of a woman, Brassempouy, ca. 25,000–20,000 BCE.

**LAUSSEL** Probably later in date than the *Venus of Willendorf* is a female figure (FIG. **1-6**) from Laussel in France. The Willendorf and Hohlenstein-Stadel figures are *sculptures in the round* (*freestanding sculptures*). The Laussel woman is one of the earliest *relief sculptures* known. The sculptor employed a stone *chisel* to cut into the relatively flat surface of a large rock in order to create an image that projects from the background. Today, the Laussel relief is on display in a museum, divorced from its original context, a detached piece of what once was a much more imposing monument. When discovered, the Laussel woman (who is about 1½ feet tall, more than four times larger than the Willendorf statuette) was part of a great stone block that measured about 140 cubic feet. The carved block stood in the open air in front of a Paleolithic rock shelter. Rock shelters were a common type of dwelling for early humans, along with huts and the mouths of caves. The Laussel relief is one of many examples of open-air art in the Old Stone Age. The popular notions that early humans dwelled exclusively in caves and that all Paleolithic art comes from mysterious dark caverns are false. Reliefs depicting nude women do, however, occur inside Old Stone Age caves. Perhaps the most interesting is the reclining nude woman (FIG. **1-6A**) on the wall of a corridor in a cave at La Magdeleine, France. She has a counterpart in the relief on the opposite wall (not shown).

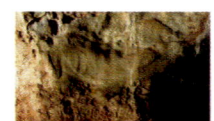

**1-6A** Reclining woman, La Magdeleine, ca. 12,000 BCE.

After chiseling out the female form and incising the details with a sharp burin, the Laussel sculptor applied red ocher, a naturally colored mineral, to the body. (Traces of red ocher coloration also remain on parts of the *Venus of Willendorf*.) Contrary to modern misconceptions, ancient artists usually painted stone sculptures (compare FIG. 5-63A). The Laussel woman has the same bulbous forms as the earlier Willendorf figurine, with a similar exaggeration of the breasts, abdomen, and hips. The head is once again featureless, but the arms have taken on greater importance. The left arm draws attention to the midsection and pubic

1 in.

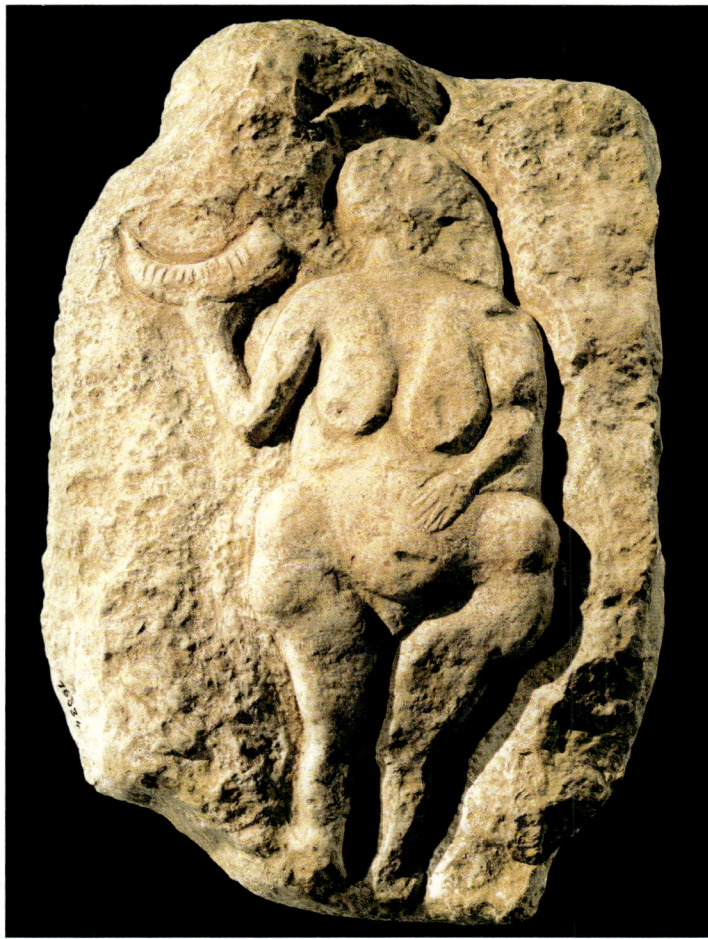

1 in.

**1-6** Woman holding a bison horn, from Laussel, France, ca. 25,000–20,000 BCE. Painted limestone, 1′ 6″ high. Musée d'Aquitaine, Bordeaux.

One of the oldest known relief sculptures depicts a woman who holds a bison horn and whose left arm draws attention to her belly. Scholars continue to debate the meaning of the gesture and the horn.

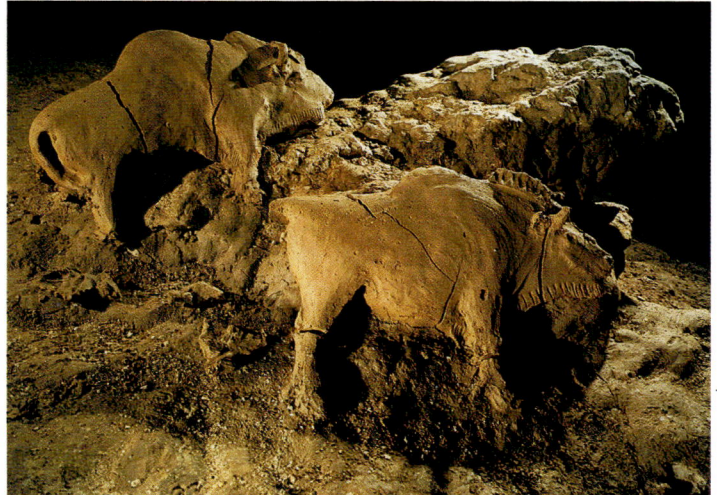

1 ft.

**1-7** Two bison, reliefs in the cave at Le Tuc d'Audoubert, France, ca. 15,000–10,000 BCE. Clay, right bison 2′ $\frac{7}{8}$″ long.

Representations of animals are far more common than those of humans in Paleolithic art. The sculptor built up these clay bison using a stone spatula-like smoothing tool and fingers to shape the details.

area, and the raised right hand holds what most scholars identify as a bison horn with 13 parallel incised lines. Scholars continue to debate the meaning of the horn as well as the gesture of the left hand.

**LE TUC D'AUDOUBERT** Paleolithic sculptors sometimes created reliefs by building up forms out of clay rather than by cutting into stone blocks or cave walls. Sometime 12,000 to 17,000 years ago in the low-ceilinged circular space at the end of a succession of cave chambers at Le Tuc d'Audoubert, a master sculptor modeled a pair of bison (FIG. **1-7**) in clay against a large, irregular freestanding rock. The two bison, like the much older painted animal (FIG. 1-3) from the Apollo 11 Cave, are in strict profile. Each is about 2 feet long. They are among the largest Paleolithic sculptures known. The sculptor brought the clay from elsewhere in the cave complex and used both hands to form the overall shape of the animals. The artist then smoothed the surfaces with a spatula-like tool and finally used fingers to shape the eyes, nostrils, mouths, and manes. The cracks in the two reliefs resulted from the drying process and probably appeared within days of the sculptures' completion.

**LA MADELEINE** As already noted, sculptors fashioned ivory mammoth tusks into human (FIG. 1-5A), animal, and composite human-animal (FIG. 1-4) forms from very early times. Prehistoric

carvers also used antlers as a sculptural medium. The broken spear-thrower carved from a reindeer antler in the form of a bison (FIG. **1-8**) found at La Madeleine in France is only 4 inches long. The sculptor incised lines into the bison's mane using a sharp burin. Compared with the bison at Le Tuc d'Audoubert, the engraving is much more detailed and extends to the horns, eye, ear, nostrils, mouth, tongue, and the hair on the face. Especially interesting is the engraver's decision to represent the bison with its head turned and licking its flank. The small size and irregular shape of the reindeer horn may have been the primary motivation for this space-saving device rather than a desire to record a characteristic anecdotal activity. Whatever the reason, it is noteworthy that the sculptor turned the neck a full 180 degrees to maintain the strict profile Paleolithic sculptors and painters insisted on for the sake of clarity and completeness.

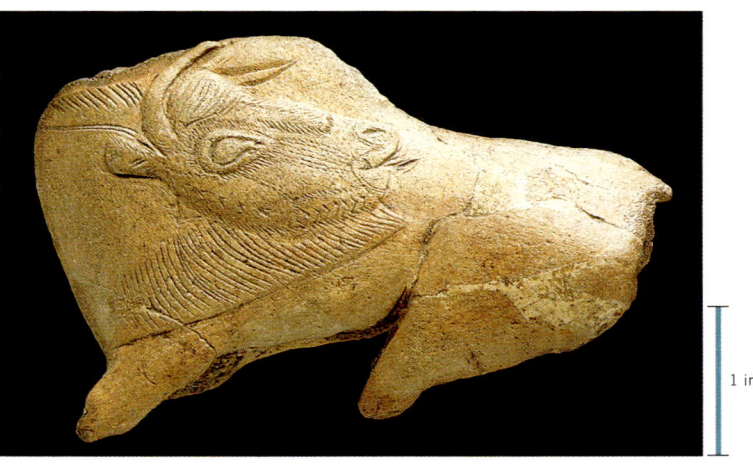

1 in.

**1-8** Bison licking its flank, fragmentary spear-thrower, from La Madeleine, France, ca. 12,000 BCE. Reindeer horn, 4$\frac{1}{8}$″ long. Musée d'Archéologie Nationale, Saint-Germain-en-Laye.

This fragment of a spear-thrower was carved from a reindeer antler. The sculptor turned the bison's head a full 180 degrees to maintain the profile view and incised the details with a stone burin.

# Paleolithic Cave Painting

The caves of Altamira (FIG. 1-9), Lascaux (FIGS. 1-1, 1-12, and 1-12A), and other sites in prehistoric Europe are a few hundred to several thousand feet long. They are often choked, sometimes almost impassably, by mineral deposits, such as stalactites and stalagmites. Far inside these caverns, well removed from the cave mouths early humans often chose for habitation, painters sometimes made pictures on the walls and ceilings. Examples of Paleolithic painting now have been found at more than 200 sites, but art historians still regard painted caves as rare occurrences because the images in them, even if they number in the hundreds, were created over a period of some 10,000 to 20,000 years.

To illuminate the surfaces while working, Paleolithic painters used stone lamps filled with marrow or fat, with a wick, perhaps of moss. For drawing, they used chunks of red and yellow ocher. For painting, they ground these same ochers into powders they mixed with water before applying. Analyses of the pigments used show that Paleolithic painters employed many different minerals, attesting to a technical sophistication surprising at so early a date.

Large flat stones served as *palettes*. The painters made brushes from reeds, bristles, or twigs and may have used a blowpipe of reeds or hollow bones to spray pigments on out-of-reach surfaces. Some caves have natural ledges on the rock walls upon which the painters could have stood in order to reach the upper surfaces of the naturally formed chambers and corridors. One Lascaux gallery wall has holes that once probably anchored a scaffold made of saplings lashed together. Despite the difficulty of making the tools and pigments, modern attempts at replicating the techniques of Paleolithic painting have demonstrated that skilled workers could cover large surfaces with images in less than a day.

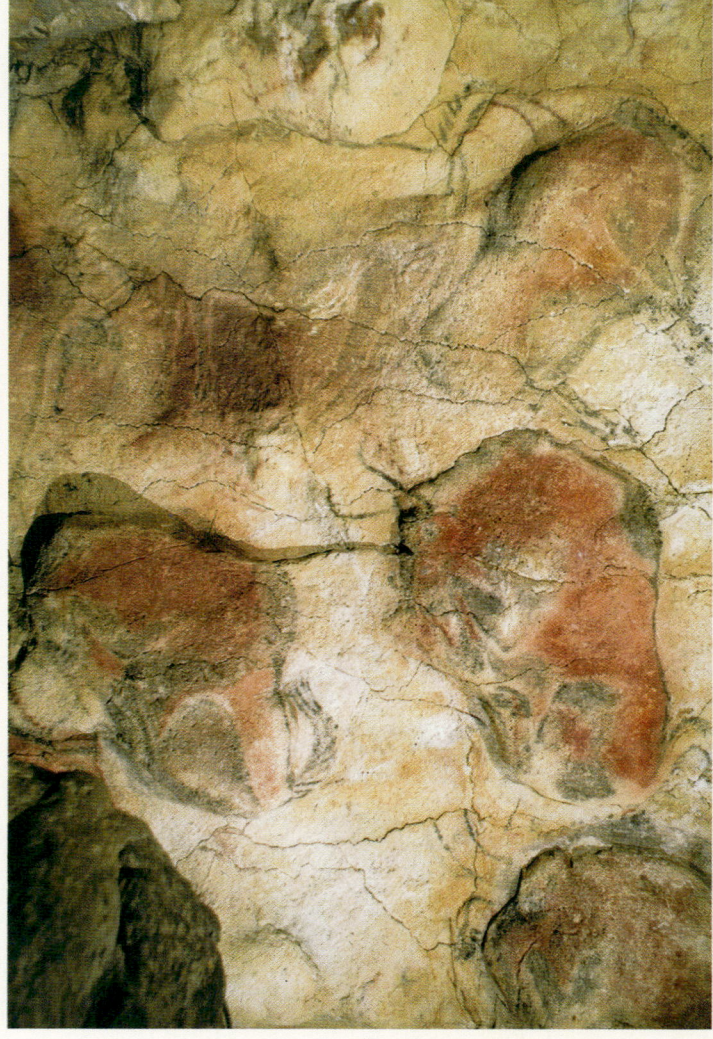

**1-9** Bison, detail of a painted ceiling in the cave at Altamira, Spain, ca. 13,000–11,000 BCE. Standing bison 5′ 2½″ long.

As in other Paleolithic caves, the painted ceiling at Altamira has no ground line or indication of setting. The artist's sole concern was to represent the animals, not to locate them in a specific place.

1 ft.

**ALTAMIRA** The works examined here thus far, whether portable or fixed to rocky outcroppings or cave walls, are all small, with the exception of the Lascaux Hall of the Bulls (FIG. 1-1). The Lascaux animals dwarf all the other illustrated examples, as do the other "herds" of painted animals that roam the walls and ceilings of other caves in southern France and northern Spain, where some of the most spectacular examples of prehistoric art have been discovered (see "Paleolithic Cave Painting," above). An amateur archaeologist accidentally found the first examples of Stone Age mural painting at Altamira, Spain, in 1879. Don Marcelino Sanz de Sautuola was exploring a cave on his estate where he had previously collected specimens of flint and carved bone. His little daughter Maria was with him when they reached a chamber some 85 feet from the cave's entrance. Because it was dark and the ceiling of the debris-filled cavern was only a few inches above the father's head, the child was the first to discern, from her lower vantage point, the shadowy forms of painted beasts on the cave roof (FIG. **1-9**, a detail of a much larger painting approximately 60 feet long). Sanz de Sautuola was certain the bison painted on the ceiling of the cave dated to prehistoric times. Professional archaeologists, however, doubted the authenticity of these works, and at the Lisbon Congress on Prehistoric Archaeology in 1880, they officially dismissed the paintings as forgeries. But by the close of the century, other caves had been discovered with painted walls partially covered by mineral deposits that would have taken thousands of years to accumulate. This finding finally persuaded skeptics that the world's oldest paintings were of an age far more remote than anyone had ever dreamed.

The bison at Altamira are 13,000 to 14,000 years old, but the painters of Paleolithic Spain approached the problem of representing an animal in essentially the same way as the painter of the Namibian stone plaque (FIG. 1-3), who worked in Africa more than 10,000 years earlier. Every one of the Altamira bison is in profile, whether alive and standing or curled up on the ground—probably dead, although this is disputed. (One suggestion is that these bison are giving birth.) To maintain the profile in the latter case, the painter had to adopt a viewpoint above the animal, looking down, rather than the view of a person standing on the ground.

Modern critics often refer to the Altamira animals as a "group" of bison, but that is very likely a misnomer. The several bison in FIG. 1-9 do not stand on a common *ground line* (a painted or carved

## Art in the Old Stone Age

Ever since the discovery in 1879 of the first cave paintings, scholars have wondered why the hunters of the Old Stone Age decided to cover the surfaces of dark caverns with animal images such as those found at Lascaux (FIG. 1-1), Altamira (FIG. 1-9), and Pech-Merle (FIG. 1-10). Researchers have proposed various theories, including that the painted and engraved animals were mere decoration, but this explanation cannot account for the inaccessibility of many of the representations. In fact, the remote locations of many images, and indications the caves were used for centuries, are precisely why many experts have suggested the prehistoric hunters attributed magical properties to the images they painted and sculpted. According to this argument, by confining animals to the surfaces of their cave walls, the Paleolithic hunters believed they were bringing the beasts under their control. Some prehistorians have even hypothesized that rituals or dances were performed in front of the images and that these rites served to improve the hunters' luck. Still other scholars have suggested the animal representations may have served as teaching tools to instruct new hunters about the character of the various species they would encounter or even to serve as targets for spears.

In contrast, some prehistorians have argued that the magical purpose of the paintings and reliefs was not to facilitate the *destruc-*tion of bison and other species. Instead, they believe prehistoric painters and sculptors created animal images to assure the *survival* of the herds on which Paleolithic peoples depended for their food supply and for their clothing. A central problem for both the hunting-magic and food-creation theories is that Old Stone Age diet staples do not include the animals most frequently portrayed. For example, faunal remains show that the Altamirans ate red deer, not bison.

Other scholars have sought to reconstruct an elaborate mythology based on the cave paintings and sculptures, suggesting that Paleolithic humans believed they had animal ancestors. Some researchers have equated certain species with men and others with women and postulated various meanings for the abstract signs that sometimes accompany the images. Almost all of these theories have been discredited over time, and most prehistorians admit that no one knows the intent of these representations. In fact, a single explanation for all Paleolithic animal images, even ones similar in subject, style, and *composition* (how the motifs are arranged on the surface), is unlikely to apply universally. The works remain an enigma—and always will, because before the invention of writing, no contemporaneous explanations could be recorded.

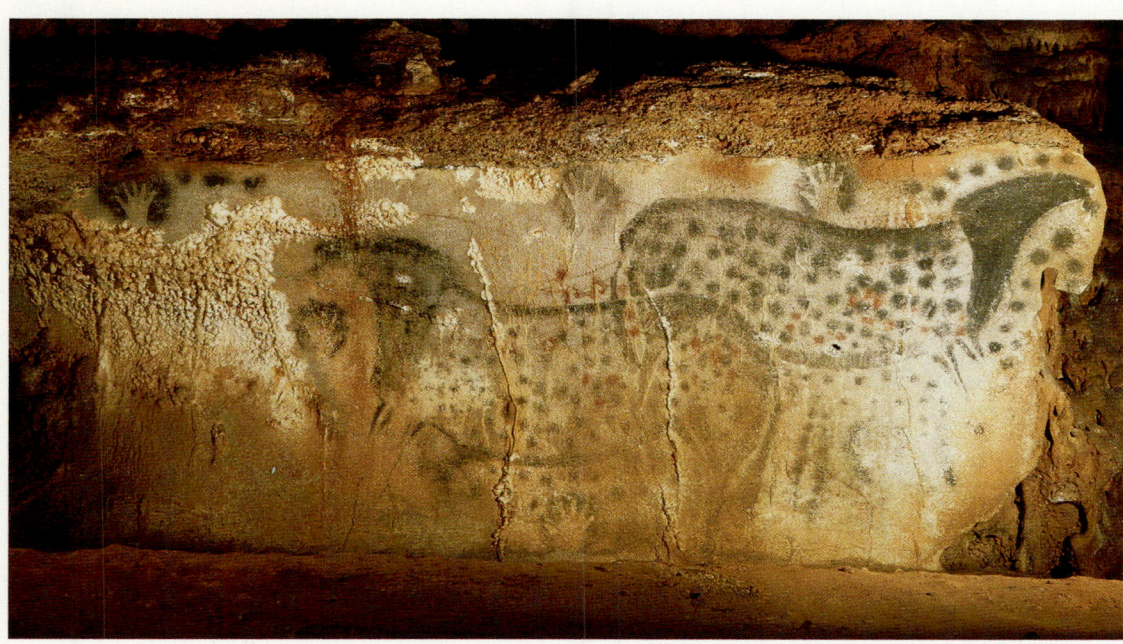

**1-10** Spotted horses and negative hand imprints, wall painting in the cave at Pech-Merle, France, ca. 23,000–22,000 BCE. 11′ 2″ long.

The purpose and meaning of Paleolithic art are unknown. Some researchers think the painted hands near the Pech-Merle horses are "signatures" of community members or of individual painters.

1 ft.

baseline on which figures appear to stand in paintings and reliefs), nor do they share a common orientation. They seem almost to float above viewers' heads, like clouds in the sky. And the dead(?) bison are seen in an "aerial view," whereas the others are seen from a position on the ground. The painting has no setting, no background, no indication of place. *Where* the animals are or how they relate to one another, if at all, was of no concern to the Paleolithic painter. Instead, several *separate* images of a bison adorn the ceiling, perhaps painted at different times spanning generations, and each is as complete and informative as possible—even if their meaning remains a mystery (see "Art in the Old Stone Age," above).

**PECH-MERLE** That the paintings did have meaning to the Paleolithic peoples who made and observed them cannot, however, be doubted. In fact, signs consisting of checks, dots, squares, or other arrangements of lines often accompany the pictures of animals. Representations of human hands also are common. At Pech-Merle (FIG. 1-10) in France, painted hands accompany representations of spotted horses. (The "spots" also surround the horses and may not be spots at all but stones or abstract signs.) Most of the painted hands in Paleolithic caves are "negative," that is, the painter placed one hand against the wall and then brushed or blew or spat pigment around it. Occasionally, the painter dipped a hand in the

# The World's Oldest Paintings?

One of the most spectacular archaeological finds of the past century came to light in December 1994 at Vallon-Pont-d'Arc, France. Unlike some other recent "finds" of prehistoric art that proved to be forgeries, the paintings in the Chauvet Cave (named after the leader of the exploration team, Jean-Marie Chauvet) seemed to be authentic. But no one, including Chauvet and his colleagues, guessed at the time of their discovery that *radiocarbon dating* (a measure of the rate of degeneration of carbon 14 in organic materials) of the paintings would establish the murals in the cave as thousands of years older than any previously discovered. Tests conducted by French scientists revealed that the Chauvet Cave paintings date between 30,000 and 28,000 BCE.

This unexpectedly early date immediately caused scholars to reevaluate the scheme of "stylistic development" from simple to more complex forms that art historians had almost universally accepted for decades. In the Chauvet Cave, in contrast to the Lascaux Cave (FIG. 1-1), the Paleolithic painters depicted the horns of the aurochs (extinct long-horned wild oxen) naturalistically, one be-

hind the other, not in the twisted perspective normally used in Old Stone Age art. Moreover, the two rhinoceroses at the lower right of FIG. 1-11 appear to attack each other, suggesting that the painter intended a narrative, another "first" in either painting or sculpture. If the paintings are twice as old as those of Lascaux and Altamira (FIG. 1-9) and almost 10,000 years earlier than the Pech-Merle murals (FIG. 1-10), the assumption that Paleolithic art "evolved" from simple to more sophisticated representations is wrong.

Much research remains to be conducted in the Chauvet Cave, but already the paintings have become the subject of intense controversy. Recently, some archaeologists have contested the early dating of the Chauvet paintings on the grounds the tested samples were contaminated. If the Chauvet animals are later than those at Lascaux, their advanced stylistic features can be more easily explained. The dispute exemplifies the frustration—and the excitement—of studying the art of an age so remote that almost nothing remains and almost every new find causes art historians to reevaluate what they had previously taken for granted.

**1-11** Aurochs, horses, and rhinoceroses, wall painting in the Chauvet Cave, Vallon-Pont-d'Arc, France, ca. 30,000–28,000 or ca. 15,000–13,000 BCE. Right rhinoceros 3′ 4″ long. ◼◀

The date of the Chauvet Cave paintings is the subject of much controversy. If the murals are the oldest paintings known, they exhibit surprisingly advanced features, such as overlapping animal horns.

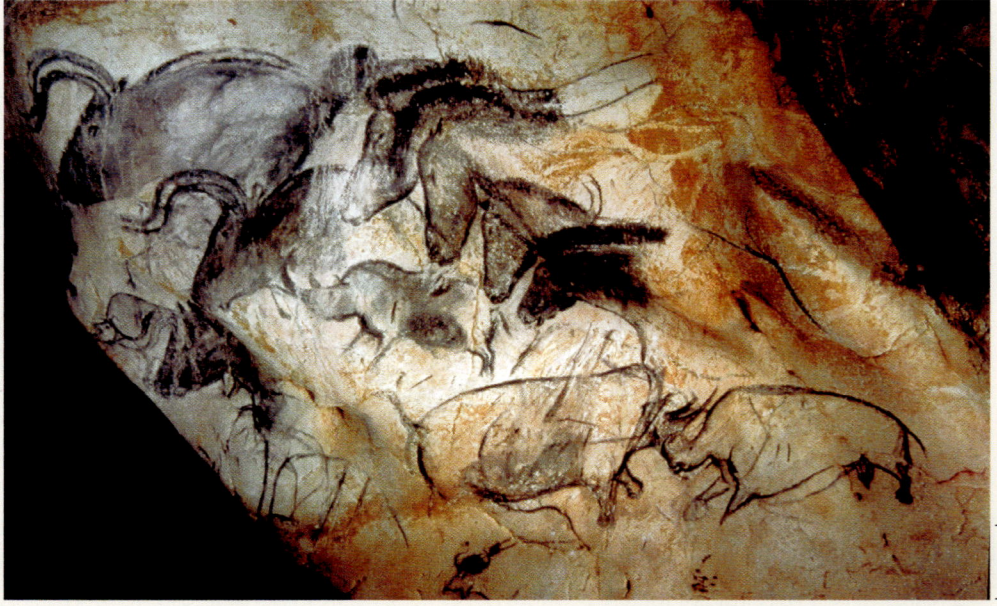

1 ft.

pigment and then pressed it against the wall, leaving a "positive" imprint. These handprints, too, must have served a purpose. Some researchers have considered them "signatures" of cult or community members or, less likely, of individual painters. But like so much in Paleolithic art, their meaning is unknown.

The *mural* (wall) paintings at Pech-Merle also furnish some insight into the reasons Paleolithic peoples chose subjects for specific places in a cave. One of the horses (at the right in FIG. 1-10) may have been inspired by the rock formation in the wall surface resembling a horse's head and neck. Old Stone Age painters and sculptors frequently and skillfully used the naturally irregular surfaces of caves to help give the illusion of real presence to their forms, as they did at La Magdeleine (FIG. 1-6A) and at Altamira (FIG. 1-9), where many of the bison paintings cover bulging rock surfaces. In fact, prehistori-

ans have observed that bison and cattle appear almost exclusively on convex surfaces, whereas nearly all horses and hands are painted on concave surfaces. What this signifies has yet to be determined.

**LASCAUX** Perhaps the most impressive collection of Paleolithic animal paintings is in the Hall of the Bulls (FIG. 1-1) at Lascaux. The large chamber, far from the cave entrance and mysteriously dark, has good acoustics, and would have provided an excellent setting for the kinds of rituals that many archaeologists assume took place in front of the paintings. One noteworthy aspect of the Lascaux murals is that they exhibit, side by side, the two basic approaches to drawing and painting found repeatedly in the history of art—silhouettes and outlines—indicating that different painters created these pictures, probably at different times. The Lascaux

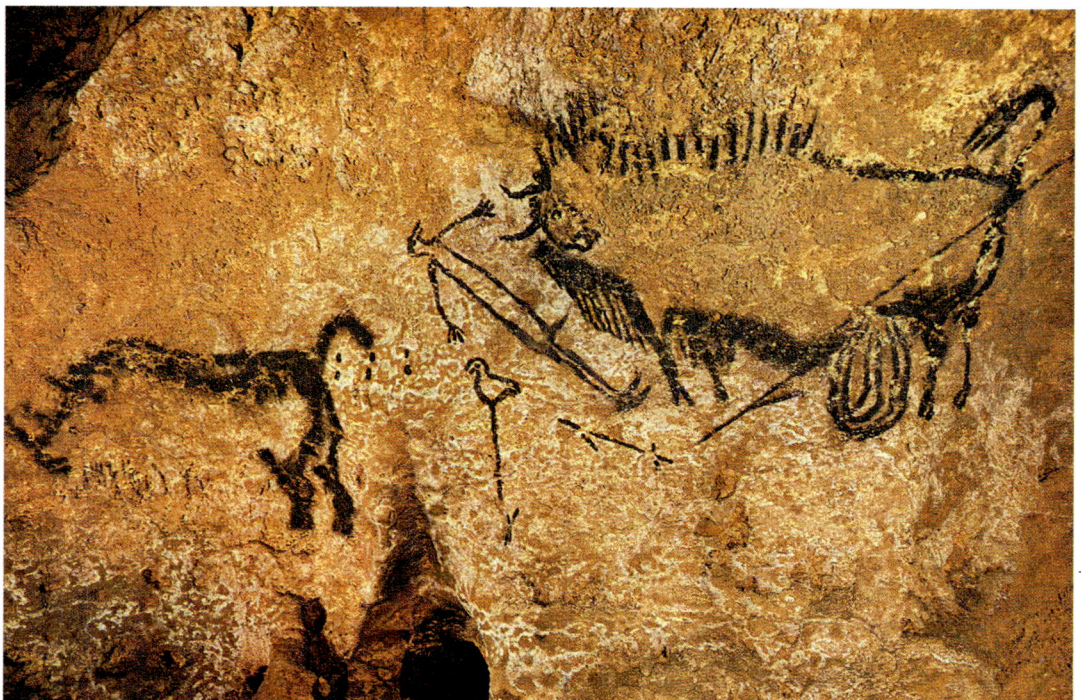

**1-12** Rhinoceros, wounded man, and disemboweled bison, painting in the well of the cave at Lascaux, France, ca. 16,000–14,000 BCE. Bison 3′ 4½″ long. ■◀

If these paintings of two animals and a bird-faced (masked?) man deep in a Lascaux well shaft depict a hunting scene, they constitute the earliest example of narrative art ever discovered.

1 ft.

bulls also show a convention of representing horns that art historians call *twisted perspective,* or *composite view,* because viewers see the heads in profile but the horns from the front. Thus, the painter's approach is not strictly or consistently optical (seen from a fixed viewpoint). Rather, the approach is descriptive of the fact that cattle have two horns. Two horns are part of the concept "bull." In strict optical-perspective profile, only one horn would be visible, but to paint the animal in that way would amount to an incomplete definition of it. This kind of twisted perspective was the norm in prehistoric painting, but it was not universal. In fact, the 1994 discovery of Paleolithic paintings in the Chauvet Cave (FIG. **1-11**) at Vallon-Pont-d'Arc in France, where the painters represented horns in a more natural way, has caused art historians to rethink many of the assumptions they had made about Paleolithic art (see "The World's Oldest Paintings?" page 22).

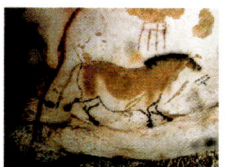

**1-12A** "Chinese horse," Lascaux, ca. 16,000–14,000 BCE.

Paintings of animals appear throughout the cave complex at Lascaux, including in the so-called Axial Gallery, which features a representation of a running, possibly pregnant horse (FIG. **1-12A**) surrounded by what may be arrows or traps. But the most perplexing painting at Lascaux and perhaps in all Paleolithic art is the one (FIG. **1-12**) deep in a well shaft, where man (as opposed to woman) makes one of his earliest appearances in prehistoric art. At the left, and moving to the left, is a rhinoceros. Beneath its tail are two rows of three dots of uncertain significance. At the right is a bison, also facing left but with less realistic proportions, probably the work of someone else. The second painter nonetheless successfully suggested the bristling rage of the animal, whose bowels are hanging from it in a heavy coil. Between the two beasts is a bird-faced (masked?) man (compare the feline-headed human, FIG. 1-4, from Hohlenstein-Stadel) with outstretched arms and hands having only four fingers. The man is depicted with far less care and detail than either animal, but the painter made the hunter's gender explicit by the prominent penis. The position of the man is ambiguous. Is he wounded or dead or merely tilted back and

unharmed? Do the staff(?) with the bird on top and the spear belong to him? Is it he or the rhinoceros who has gravely wounded the bison—or neither? Which animal, if either, has knocked the man down, if indeed he is on the ground? Are these three images related at all? Modern viewers can be sure of nothing, but if the painters placed the figures beside each other to tell a story, this is evidence for the creation of complex narrative compositions involving humans and animals at a much earlier date than anyone had imagined only a few generations ago. Yet it is important to remember that even if the artists intended to tell a story, very few people would have been able to "read" it. The painting, in a deep shaft, is very difficult to reach and could have been viewed only in flickering lamplight. Like all Paleolithic art, the scene in the Lascaux well shaft remains enigmatic.

# NEOLITHIC ART

Around 9000 BCE, the ice that covered much of northern Europe during the Paleolithic period melted as the climate warmed. The sea level rose more than 300 feet, separating England from continental Europe, and Spain from Africa. The reindeer migrated north, and the woolly mammoth disappeared. The Paleolithic gave way to a transitional period, the Mesolithic, and then, for several thousand years at different times in different parts of the globe, a great new age, the Neolithic, dawned.* Human beings began to domesticate plants and animals and to settle in fixed abodes. Their food supply assured, many groups changed from hunters to herders to farmers and finally to townspeople. Wandering hunters settled down to organized community living in villages surrounded by cultivated fields.

The basis for the conventional division of prehistory into the Paleolithic, Mesolithic, and Neolithic periods is the development of

---

*This chapter treats the Neolithic art of Europe, Anatolia, and Mesopotamia only. For the Neolithic art of Africa, see Chapter 19; for Asia, see Chapters 15 to 17.

stone implements. However, a different kind of distinction may be made between an age of food gathering and an age of food production. In this scheme, the Paleolithic period corresponds roughly to the age of food gathering. Intensified food gathering and the taming of the dog are the hallmarks of the Mesolithic period. In the Neolithic period, agriculture and stock raising became humankind's major food sources. The transition to the Neolithic occurred first in Anatolia and Mesopotamia.

## Anatolia and Mesopotamia

The remains of the oldest known settled communities lie in the grassy foothills of the Antilebanon, Taurus, and Zagros mountains in present-day Turkey, Syria, Iraq, and Iran (MAP **1-2**). These regions provided the necessary preconditions for the development of agriculture. Species of native plants, such as wild wheat and barley, were plentiful, as were herds of animals (goats, sheep, and pigs) that could be domesticated. Sufficient rain occurred for the raising of crops. When village farming life was well developed, some settlers, attracted by the greater fertility of the soil and perhaps also by the need to find more land for their rapidly growing populations, moved into the valleys and deltas of the Tigris and Euphrates rivers.

In addition to systematic agriculture, the new sedentary societies of the Neolithic age originated weaving, metalworking, pottery, and counting and recording with clay tokens. These innovations spread with remarkable speed throughout Anatolia (roughly equivalent to present-day Turkey) and Mesopotamia (primarily present-day Syria and Iraq). Village farming communities such as Jarmo in Iraq and Çatal Höyük in southern Anatolia date to the midseventh millennium BCE. The remarkable fortified town of Jericho, before whose walls the biblical Joshua appeared thousands of years later, is even older. Archaeologists are constantly uncovering surprises, and the discovery and exploration of new sites each year are

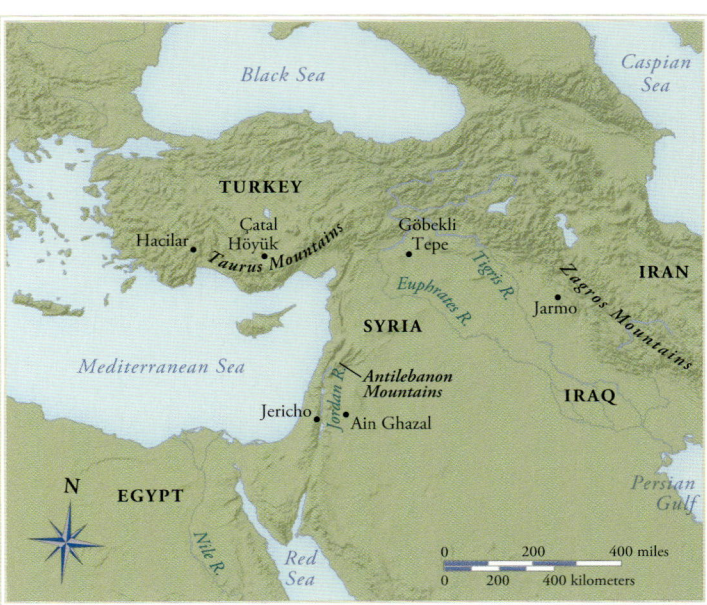

MAP **1-2** Neolithic sites in Anatolia and Mesopotamia.

compelling them to revise their views about the emergence of Neolithic society. Especially noteworthy are the ongoing excavations at Göbekli Tepe in southeastern Turkey, where German archaeologists have uncovered the remains of what appears to be the world's oldest stone temple, dating around 9000 BCE, with animal reliefs on T-shaped pillars. If the dating and the interpretation are correct, Göbekli Tepe overturns one of the most basic assumptions about prehistoric societies. It now appears possible that hunter-gatherers erected stone temples long before sedentary farmers established permanent village communities. Of those sites known for some time, Jericho, Ain Ghazal, and Çatal Höyük together probably offer the most complete picture of the rapid and exciting transformation of human society and of art during the Neolithic period.

**JERICHO** By 7000 BCE, agriculture was well established from Anatolia to ancient Palestine and Iran. Its advanced state by this date presupposes a long development. Indeed, the very existence of a major settlement such as Jericho gives strong support to this assumption. Jericho, situated on a plateau in the Jordan River valley with an unfailing spring, was the site of a small village as early as the ninth millennium BCE. This village underwent spectacular development around 8000 BCE, when the inhabitants established a new Neolithic settlement covering about 10 acres. Its mud-brick houses sat on round or oval stone foundations and had roofs of branches covered with earth.

As Jericho's wealth grew, the need for protection against marauding nomads resulted in the first known permanent stone fortifications. By 7500 BCE, a wide rock-cut ditch and a 5-foot-thick wall surrounded the town, which probably had a population exceeding 2,000. Set into the circuit wall, which has been preserved to a height of almost 13 feet, was a 30-foot-tall circular tower (FIG. **1-13**) constructed of roughly shaped stones laid without mortar. Almost 33 feet in diameter at the base, the tower has an inner stairway leading to its summit. (Today, a grate covers the entrance to the stairway.) Not enough of the site has been excavated to determine whether this tower was solitary or one of several similar towers that formed a complete defense system. In either case, a stone structure as large as the Jericho tower was a tremendous technological achievement and a testimony to the builders' ability to organize a significant workforce.

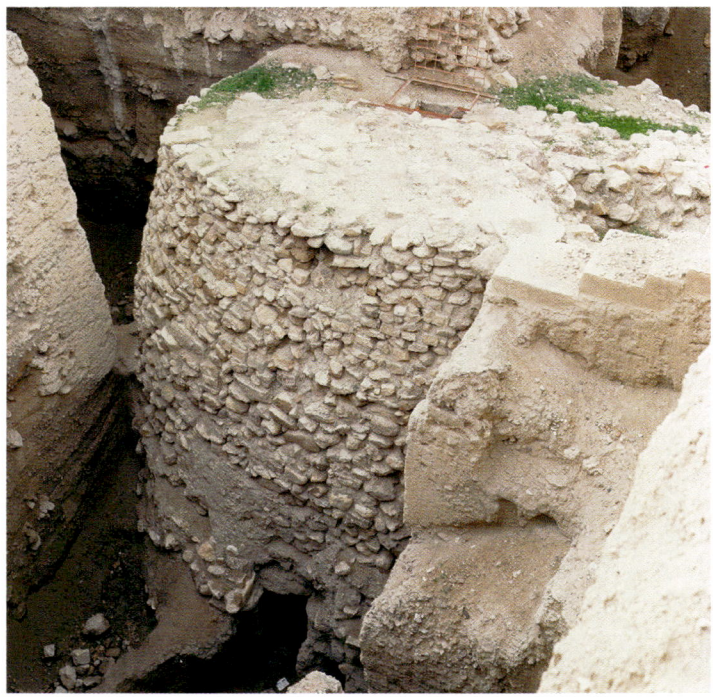

**1-13** Stone tower built into the settlement wall, Jericho, ca. 8000–7000 BCE.

Protecting Neolithic Jericho were 5-foot-thick walls and at least one tower 30 feet high and 33 feet in diameter constructed of stone laid without mortar—an outstanding technological achievement.

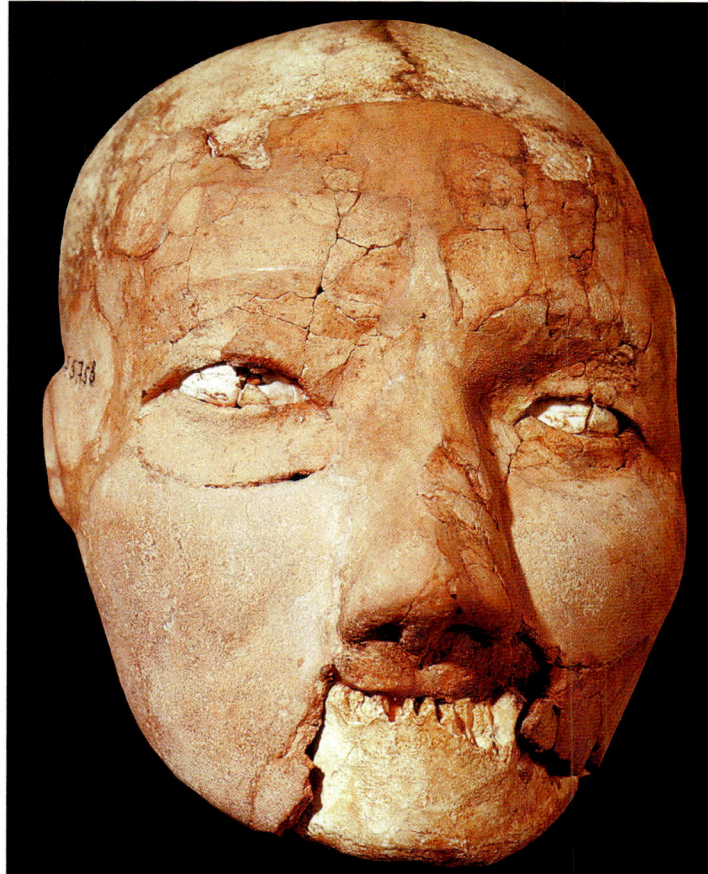

1 in.

**1-14** Human skull with restored features, from Jericho, ca. 7200–6700 BCE. Features modeled in plaster, painted, and inlaid with seashells. Life-size. Archaeological Museum, Amman.

The Neolithic farmers of Jericho removed the skulls of their dead before burial, modeled them in plaster, and inlaid the eyes to create lifelike "portraits" of their ancestors, whom they may have worshiped.

Sometime around 7000 BCE, Jericho's inhabitants abandoned their fortified site, but new settlers arrived in the early seventh millennium and established a new farming community of rectangular mud-brick houses on stone foundations with plastered and painted floors and walls. Several of the excavated buildings contained statuettes of animals and women and seem to have served as shrines. The new villagers buried their dead beneath the floors of their houses with the craniums detached from their skeletons and their features reconstructed in plaster. Subtly modeled with inlaid seashells for eyes and painted hair, the appearance of these reconstructed heads is strikingly lifelike. One head (FIG. **1-14**) features a painted mustache, distinguishing it from the others. The Jericho skulls constitute the world's earliest known "portrait gallery," but the artists' intention was certainly not portraiture in the modern sense. The plastered skulls must have served a ritualistic purpose. The community of several hundred Neolithic farmers who occupied Jericho at this time honored and perhaps worshiped their ancestors as intercessors between the living and the world beyond. They may have believed that the dead could exert power over the living and that they had to offer sacrifices to their ancestors to receive favorable treatment. These skulls were probably the focus of rites in honor of those ancestors.

**AIN GHAZAL** A second important Neolithic settlement in ancient Palestine was Ain Ghazal, near the modern Jordanian capi-

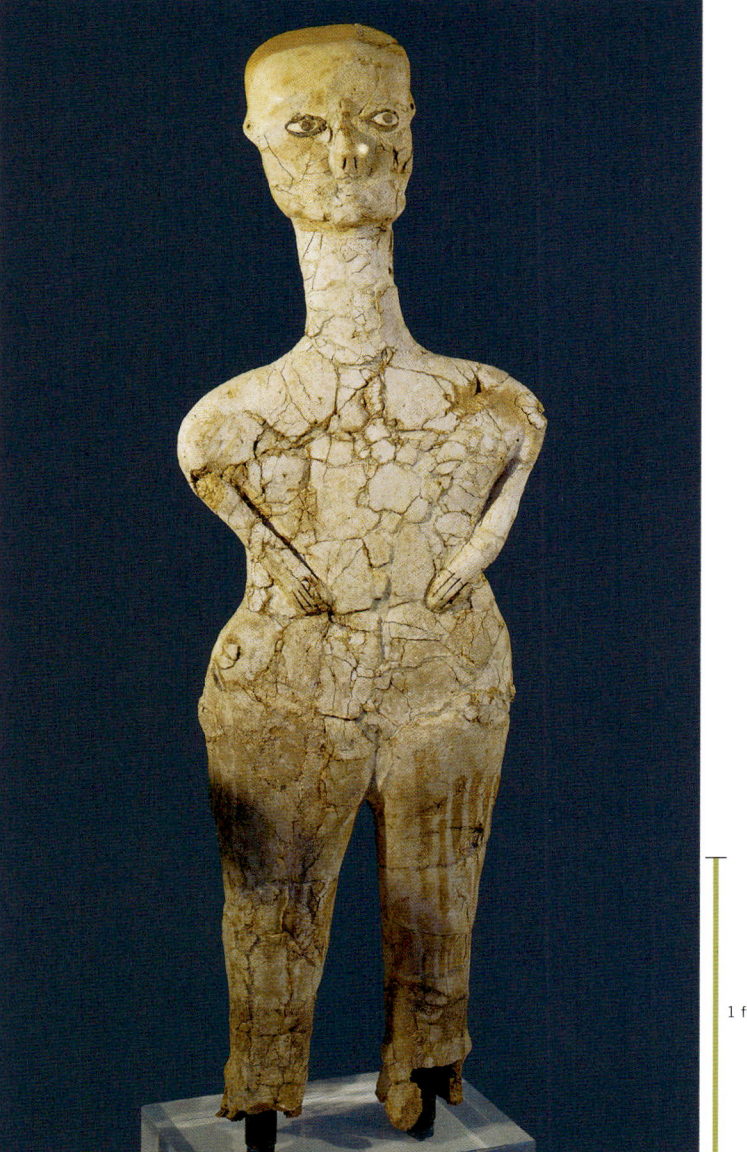

1 ft.

**1-15** Human figure, from Ain Ghazal, Jordan, ca. 6750–6250 BCE. Plaster, painted and inlaid with bitumen, 3′ 5⅜″ high. Musée du Louvre, Paris.

The dozens of large white plaster statuettes (some with two heads and with details added in paint or inlaid with bitumen) found at Ain Ghazal are the earliest large-scale sculptures known.

tal of Amman. Occupied from around 7200 to 5000 BCE, the site featured houses of irregularly shaped stones with plastered floors and walls painted red. The most striking finds, however, are two caches containing three dozen plaster statuettes (FIG. **1-15**) and busts, some with two heads, datable to ca. 6500 BCE. The sculptures, which appear to have been ritually buried, are white plaster built up over a core of reeds and twine, with black bitumen, a tarlike substance, for the pupils of the eyes. Some of the figures have painted clothing. Only rarely did the sculptors indicate the gender of the figures. Whatever their purpose, by their size (as much as three feet tall) and sophisticated technique, the Ain Ghazal statuettes and busts tower over Paleolithic figurines such as the tiny *Venus of Willendorf* (FIG. 1-5) and even the foot-tall Hohlenstein-Stadel ivory statuette (FIG. 1-4). They mark the beginning of monumental sculpture in Mesopotamia.

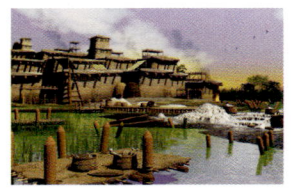

1-16A Restored view of Çatal Höyük, ca. 6000–5900 BCE.

**ÇATAL HÖYÜK** During the past half century, archaeologists also have made remarkable discoveries in Turkey, not only at Göbekli Tepe but also at Hacilar and especially Çatal Höyük (FIG. 1-16A), the site of a flourishing Neolithic culture on the central Anatolian plain between 6500 and 5700 BCE. Although animal husbandry was well established, hunting continued to play an important part in the early Neolithic economy of Çatal Höyük. The importance of hunting as a food source is reflected in the wall paintings of the site's older decorated rooms, where hunting scenes predominate. In style and concept, however, the deer hunt mural (FIG. 1-16) at Çatal Höyük is worlds apart from the wall paintings the hunters of the Paleolithic period produced. Perhaps what is most strikingly new about the Çatal Höyük painting and other Neolithic examples like it is the regular appearance of the human figure—not only singly but also in large, coherent groups with a wide variety of poses, subjects, and settings. As noted earlier, humans were unusual in Paleolithic cave paintings, and pictorial narratives are almost unknown. Even the "hunting scene" (FIG. 1-12) in the well at Lascaux is doubtful as a narrative. In contrast, human themes and concerns and action scenes with humans dominating animals are central subjects of Neolithic paintings.

In the Çatal Höyük hunt, the group of hunters—and no one doubts it is, indeed, an organized hunting party, not a series of individual figures—is a rhythmic repetition of basic shapes, but the painter took care to distinguish important descriptive details—for example, bows, arrows, and garments—and the heads have clearly defined noses, mouths, chins, and hair. The Neolithic painter placed all the heads in profile for the same reason Paleolithic painters universally chose the profile view for representations of animals. Only the side view of the human head shows all its shapes clearly. However, at Çatal Höyük the painter presented the torsos from the front—again, the most informative viewpoint—whereas the profile view was the choice for the legs and arms. This composite view of the human body is highly artificial—the human body cannot make an abrupt 90-degree shift at the hips—but it well describes what a human body is, as opposed to how it appears from a particular viewpoint. The technique of painting also changed dramatically from the Paleolithic to the Neolithic. The Çatal Höyük painters used brushes to apply their pigments to a background of dry white plaster. The careful preparation of the wall surface is in striking contrast to the direct application of pigment to the irregularly shaped walls and ceilings of Old Stone Age caves.

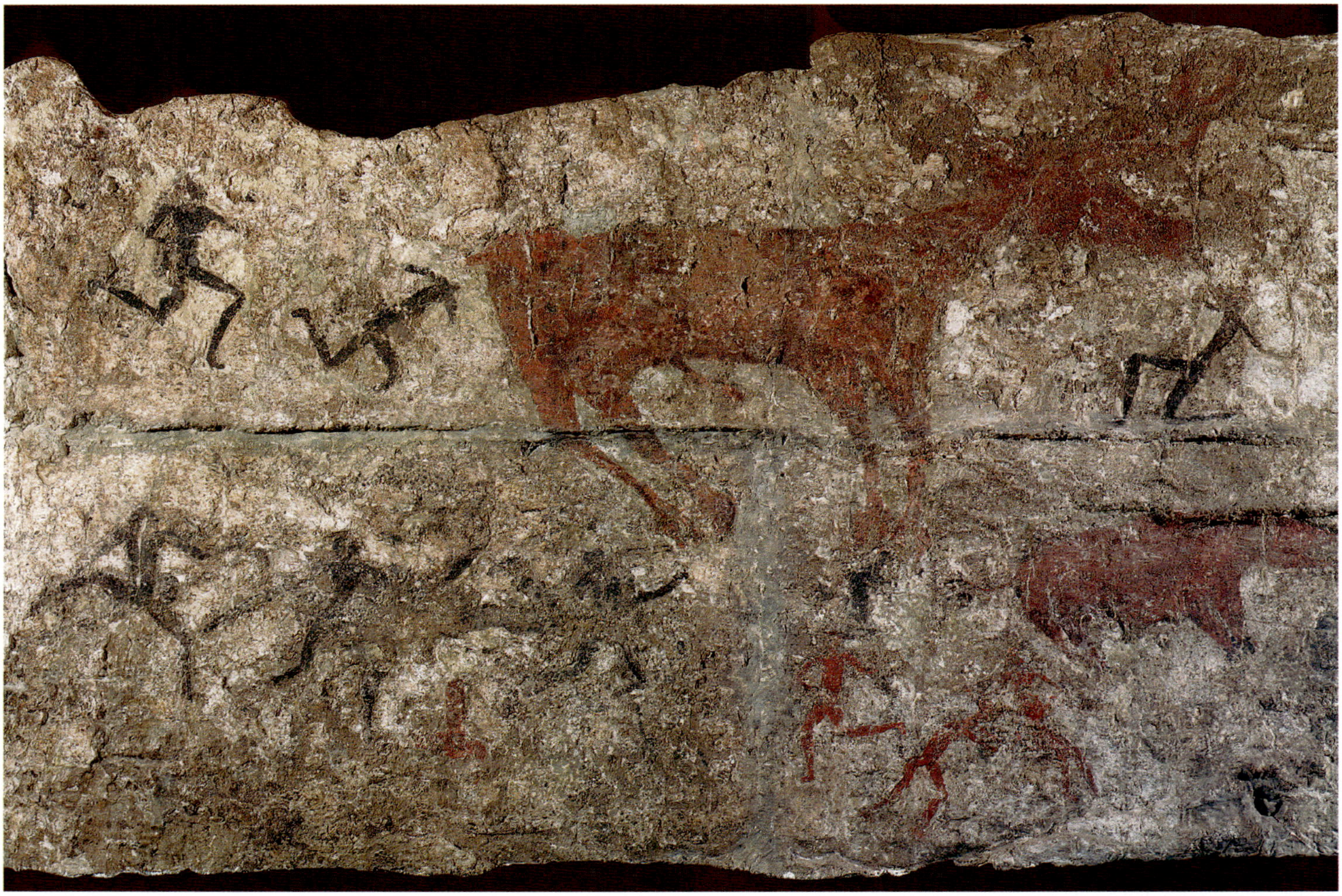

**1-16** Deer hunt, detail of a wall painting from level III, Çatal Höyük, Turkey, ca. 5750 BCE. Museum of Anatolian Civilization, Ankara.

This Neolithic painter depicted human figures as a composite of frontal and profile views, the most descriptive picture of the shape of the human body. This format would become the rule for millennia.

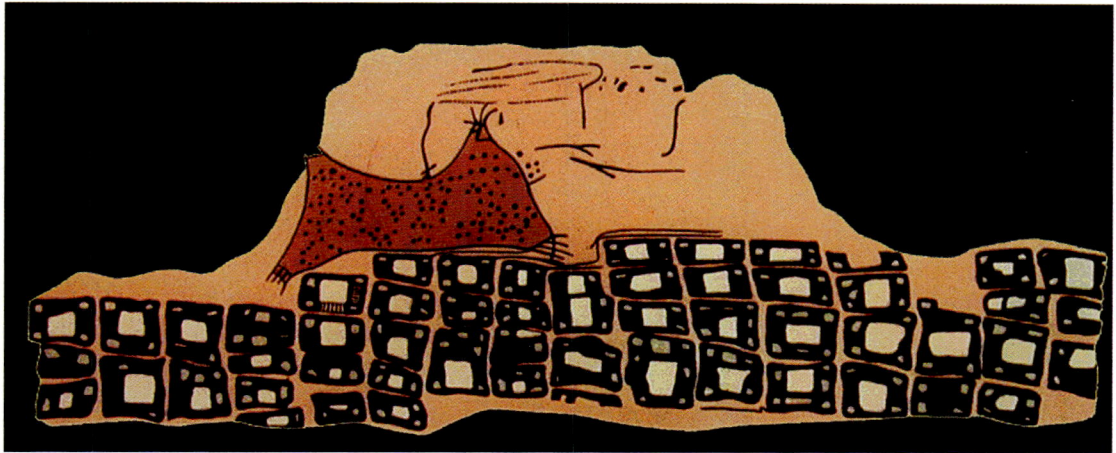

More remarkable still is a painting (FIG. **1-17** is a watercolor copy) in one of the older rooms at Çatal Höyük. Art historians generally have acclaimed this mural as the world's first *landscape* (a picture of a natural setting in its own right, without any narrative content). As such, it remained unique for thousands of years. According to radiocarbon analysis, the painting dates to around 6150 BCE. Scholars interpret the foreground as a town with rectangular houses neatly laid out side by side, probably representing Çatal Höyük itself. Behind the town appears a mountain with two peaks. Many archaeologists think the dots and lines issuing from the higher of the two cones represent a volcanic eruption, and have suggested that the mountain is the 10,600-foot-high Hasan Dağ, which is within view of Çatal Höyük and is the only twin-peaked volcano in central Anatolia. The conjectured volcanic eruption shown in the mural does not necessarily depict a specific historical event. If, however, the Çatal Höyük painting relates a story, even a recurring one, then it cannot be considered a pure landscape. Nonetheless, this mural is the first depiction of a setting devoid of both humans and animals.

## Western Europe

In western Europe, where Paleolithic paintings and sculptures abound, no comparably developed towns of the time of Çatal Höyük have been found. However, in succeeding millennia, perhaps as early as 4000 BCE, the local Neolithic populations in several areas developed a monumental architecture employing massive rough-cut stones. The very dimensions of the stones, some as high as 17 feet and weighing as much as 50 tons, have prompted historians to call them *megaliths* (great stones) and to designate Neolithic architecture employing them as *megalithic*.

**NEWGRANGE** One of the most impressive megalithic monuments in Europe is also one of the oldest. The megalithic tomb at Newgrange in Ireland, north of Dublin, may date to as early as 3200 BCE and is one of the oldest burial monuments in Europe. It takes the form of a *passage grave,* that is, a tomb with a long stone corridor leading to a dome-covered burial chamber (FIG. **1-18**) beneath a great *tumulus* (earthen burial mound). Some mounds contain more than one passage grave. Similar graves have been found also in England, France, Spain, and Scandinavia. All attest to the importance of honoring the dead in Neolithic society. The Newgrange tumulus is 280 feet in diameter and 44 feet tall. Its passageway is 62 feet long, and it and the primitive dome over

the main chamber are early examples of *corbel vaulting* (FIGS. 4-16 and 4-17*b*). At Newgrange, the huge megaliths forming the vaulted passage and the dome are held in place by their own weight, each stone countering the thrust of neighboring stones. Decorating some of the megaliths are incised spirals and other abstract motifs (not visible in FIG. 1-18). A special feature of the Newgrange tomb is that at the winter solstice the sun illuminates the passageway and the burial chamber.

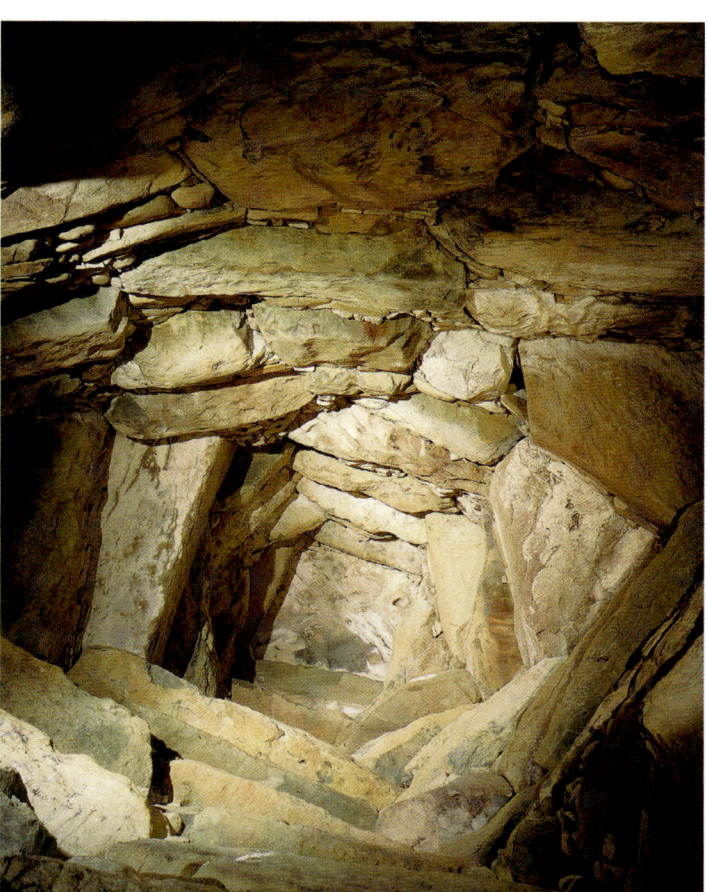

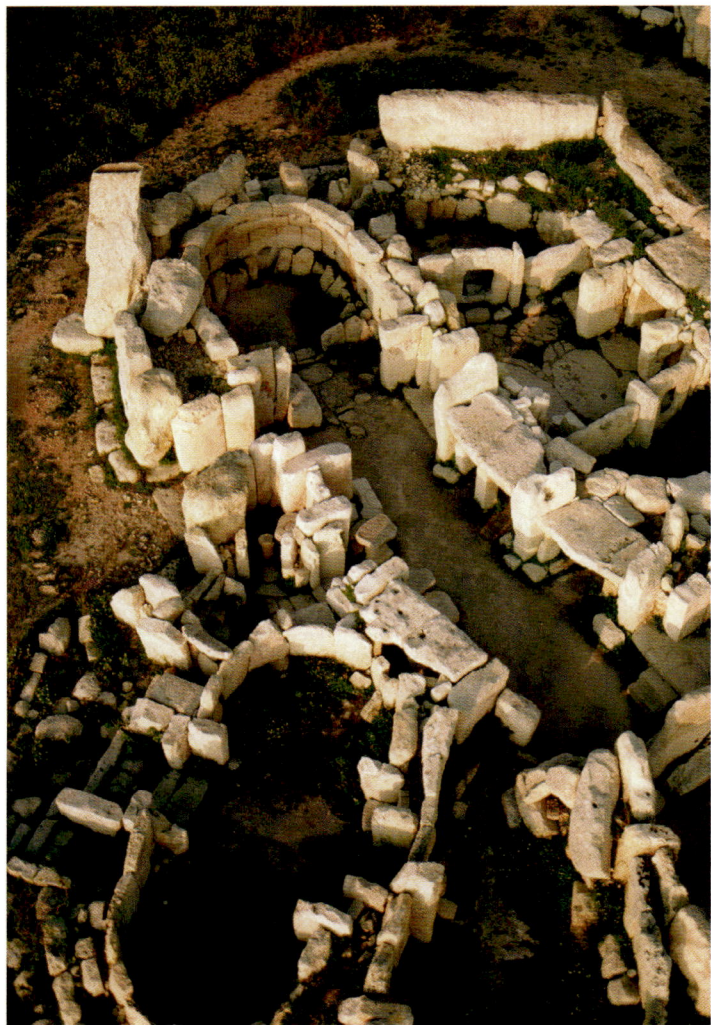

**1-19** Aerial view of the ruins of Hagar Qim (looking east), Malta, ca. 3200–2500 BCE.

The 5,000-year-old stone temple at Hagar Qim on the remote island of Malta is remarkably sophisticated for its date, especially in the way the Neolithic builders incorporated both rectilinear and curved forms.

**HAGAR QIM** By the end of the fourth millennium BCE, Neolithic civilization had spread to the most remote parts of Europe, including, in the far north, Skara Brae (FIG. **1-19A**) in the Orkney Islands, and, in the far south, Malta. The megalithic temple (FIG. **1-19**)

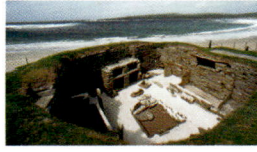

**1-19A** House 1, Skara Brae, ca. 3100–2500 BCE.

of Hagar Qim is one of many constructed on Malta between 3200 and 2500 BCE. The Maltese builders erected their temples by piling carefully cut stone blocks in *courses* (stacked horizontal rows). To construct the doorways at Hagar Qim, the builders employed the *post-and-lintel* system (FIG. 4-17a) in which two upright stones (posts) support a horizontal beam (lintel). The layout of this and other Neolithic Maltese temples is especially noteworthy for the combination of rectilinear and curved forms, including multiple *apses* (semicircular recesses). Inside the Hagar Qim temple, archaeologists found altars (hence the identification of the structure as a religious shrine) and several stone statues of headless nude women, one standing, the others seated. The level of architectural and sculptural sophistication seen on this isolated island at so early a date is extraordinary.

**STONEHENGE** The most famous megalithic monument in Europe is Stonehenge (FIG. **1-20**) on the Salisbury Plain in southern England. A *henge* is an arrangement of megalithic stones in a circle, often surrounded by a ditch. The type is almost entirely limited to Britain. Stonehenge is a complex of rough-cut sarsen (a form of sandstone) stones and smaller "bluestones" (various volcanic rocks) built in several stages over hundreds of years. The final henge took the form of concentric post-and-lintel circles. The outer ring, almost 100 feet in diameter, consists of huge sarsen megaliths. Inside is a ring of bluestones, and this ring, in turn, encircles a horseshoe (open end facing east) of *trilithons* (three-stone constructions)—five lintel-topped pairs of the largest sarsens, each weighing 45 to 50 tons. Standing apart and to the east (outside the aerial view in FIG. 1-20) is the "heel stone," which, for a person looking outward from the center of the complex, would have marked the point where the sun rose at the summer solstice. Stonehenge, perhaps originally a funerary site where Neolithic peoples cremated their dead, seems in its latest phase to have been a kind of astronomical observatory and a remarkably accurate solar calendar. According to a recent theory, it also served as a center of healing that attracted the sick and dying from throughout the region.

Whatever role they played in society, the megalithic tombs, temples, houses, and henges of Europe are enduring testaments to the rapidly developing intellectual powers of Neolithic humans as well as to their capacity for heroic physical effort.

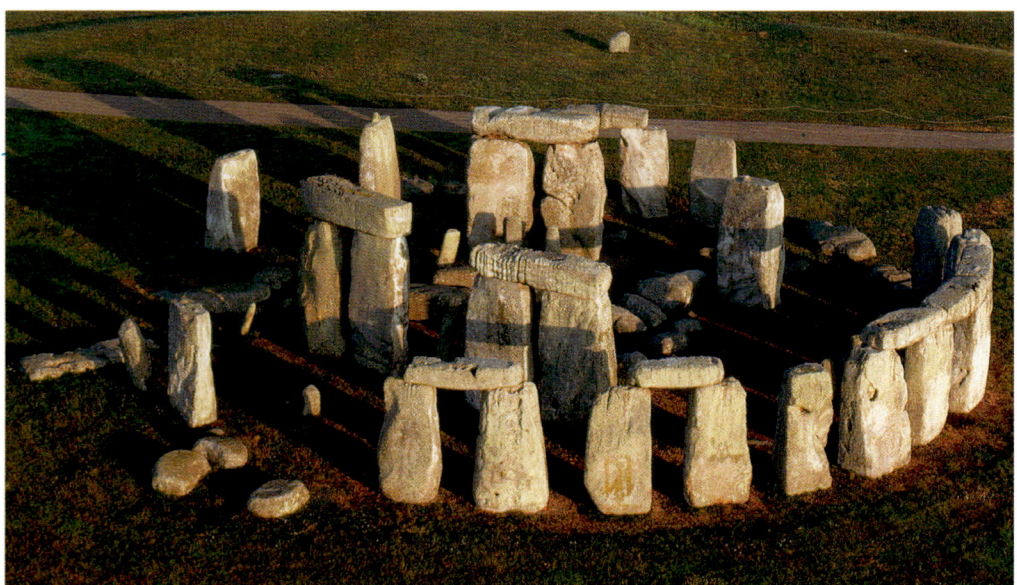

**1-20** Aerial view of Stonehenge (looking northwest), Salisbury Plain, Wiltshire, England, ca. 2550–1600 BCE. Circle 97′ in diameter; trilithons 24′ high.

The circles of trilithons at Stonehenge probably functioned as an astronomical observatory and solar calendar. The sun rises over its "heel stone" at the summer solstice. Some of the megaliths weigh 50 tons.

# ART BEFORE HISTORY

## PALEOLITHIC (OLD STONE AGE) ART  ca. 30,000–9000 BCE

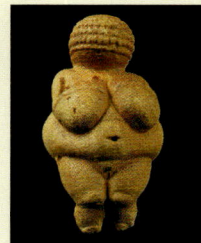

Nude woman (*Venus of Willendorf*), ca. 28,000–25,000 BCE

▌ The first sculptures and paintings antedate the invention of writing by tens of thousands of years. Paleolithic humans' decision to represent the world around them initiated an intellectual revolution of enormous consequences.

▌ No one knows why humans began to paint and carve images or what role those images played in the lives of Paleolithic hunters. Women were far more common subjects than men, but animals, not humans, dominate Paleolithic art.

▌ The works created range in size from tiny portable figurines, such as the so-called *Venus of Willendorf,* to large, sometimes over-life-size, carved and painted representations of animals, as in the caves of Lascaux, Pech-Merle, Altamira, and elsewhere in southern France and northern Spain.

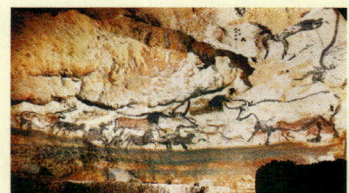

Hall of the Bulls, Lascaux, ca. 16,000–14,000 BCE

▌ Paleolithic artists regularly depicted animals in profile in order to present a complete picture of each beast, including its head, body, tail, and all four legs. This format persisted for millennia.

## NEOLITHIC (NEW STONE AGE) ART  ca. 8000–2300 BCE

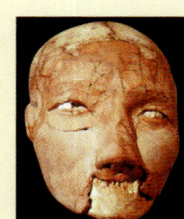

Skull with restored features, Jericho, ca. 7200–6700 BCE

▌ Around 9000 BCE, the ice that had covered much of northern Europe for millennia receded. After a transitional period, the Neolithic Age began in Anatolia and Mesopotamia and spread gradually to Europe, where it continued longer in remote places like Stonehenge in England.

▌ The Neolithic Age revolutionized human life with the beginning of agriculture and the formation of the first settled communities, such as that at Çatal Höyük in Anatolia, where archaeologists have uncovered an extensive town with numerous shrines. Some Neolithic towns also had fortified stone circuit walls, like those at Jericho.

▌ In art, the Neolithic period brought the birth of monumental sculpture, notably the painted plaster figurines from Ain Ghazal and the restored life-size skulls from Jericho.

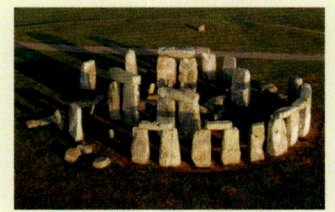

Stonehenge, Salisbury Plain, ca. 2550–1600 BCE

▌ In painting, coherent narratives became common, and artists began to represent human figures as composites of frontal and profile views—another formula that would remain universal for a very long time.

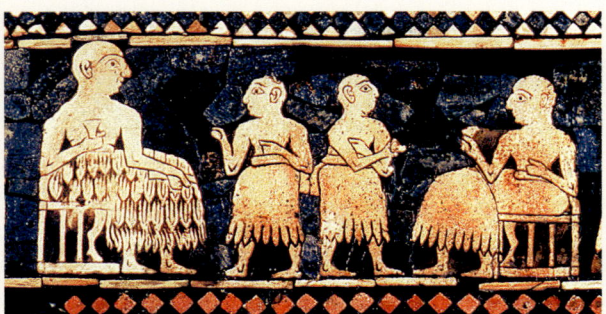

The human figures in Sumerian art are a composite of frontal and profile views. Artists used hierarchy of scale to distinguish the most important (largest) figures from those of lesser rank in society.

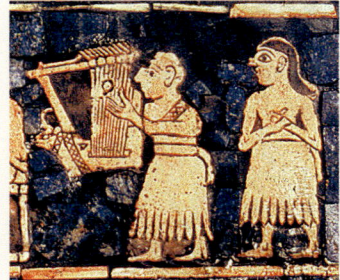

The entertainers at this banquet of Sumerian nobility include a musician playing a bull-headed harp of a type found in royal graves at Ur. The long-haired, bare-chested singer is a court eunuch.

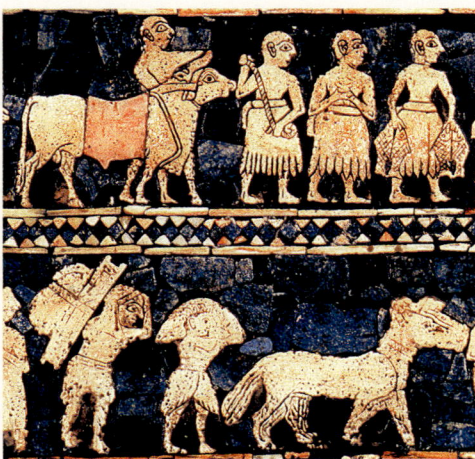

The Sumerians may have been the first culture to use pictures to tell coherent stories. Sumerian artists divided the pictorial field into a series of registers with figures on a common ground line.

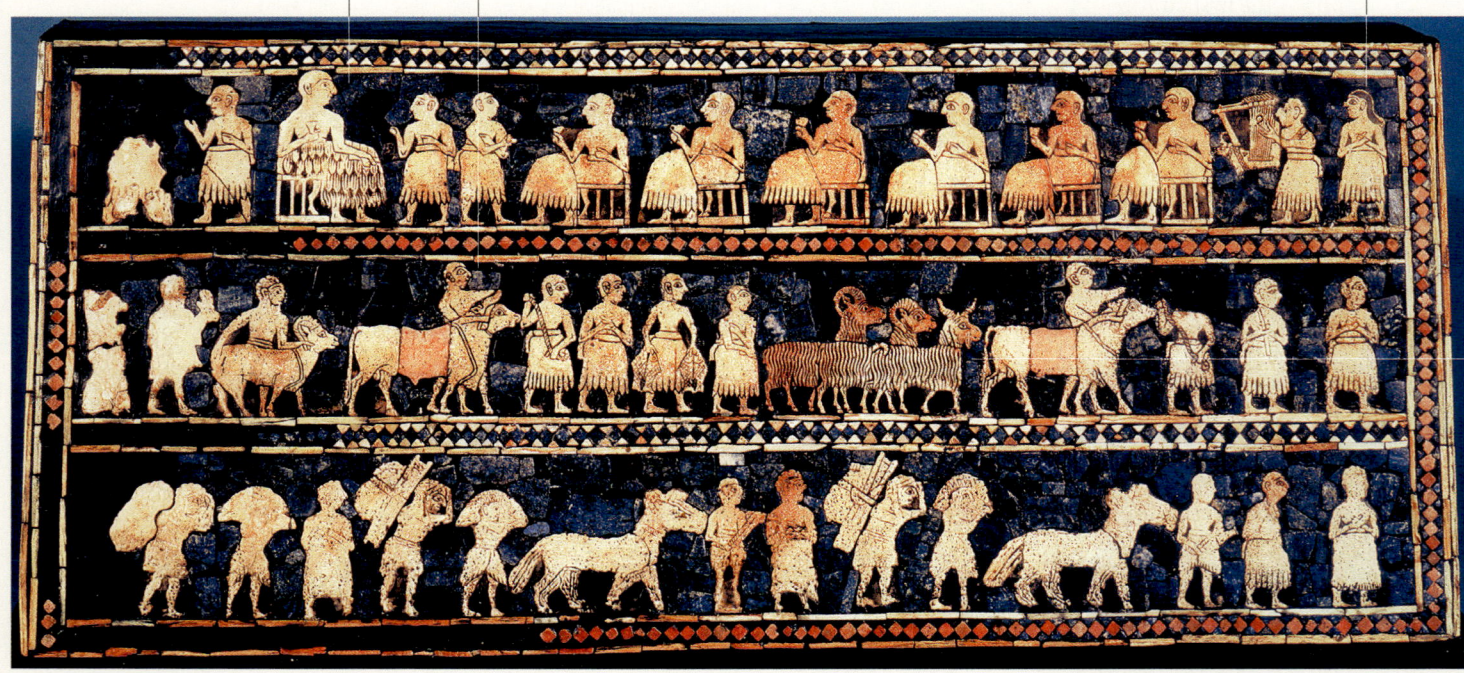

1 in.

**2-1** Peace side of the *Standard of Ur,* from tomb 779, Royal Cemetery, Ur (modern Tell Muqayyar), Iraq, ca. 2600–2400 BCE. Wood, lapis lazuli, shell, and red limestone, 8″ × 1′ 7″. British Museum, London. ◼◀

# MESOPOTAMIA AND PERSIA

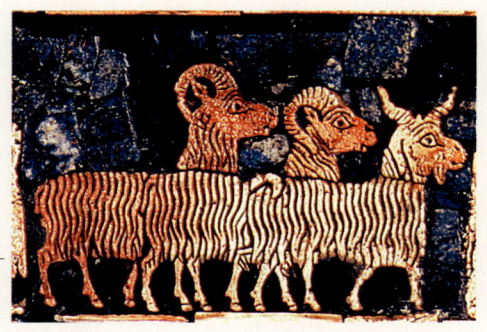

As in prehistoric art, representations of animals in Mesopotamian art are always strict profile views, save for the animals' eyes, which are seen from the front, as are also sometimes an animal's two horns.

**FRAMING THE ERA**

## THE CRADLE OF CIVILIZATION

Mesopotamia, the core of the region often called the Fertile Crescent and the presumed locale of the biblical Garden of Eden (Gen. 2:10–15), was where humans first learned how to use the wheel and plow and how to control floods and construct irrigation canals. In the fourth millennium BCE, the inhabitants of ancient Sumer, the first great Mesopotamian civilization, also established the earliest complex urban societies, called *city-states,* and invented writing. They may also have been the first culture to use pictures to tell coherent stories, far surpassing Stone Age artists' tentative efforts at pictorial narration.

The so-called *Standard of Ur* (FIG. **2-1**), from the Sumerian city that was home to the biblical Abraham, is one of the earliest extant works incorporating all of the pictorial conventions that would dominate ancient narrative art for more than 2,000 years. The artist divided the pictorial field into three successive bands (called *registers,* or *friezes*) and placed all the figures on a common *ground line,* a compositional format that marks a significant break with the haphazard figure placement of Stone Age art. The Sumerians also pioneered the use of *hierarchy of scale,* a highly effective way of distinguishing the most important (largest) figure from those of lesser rank. This pictorial convention would also have a long future in the history of art.

In FIG. 2-1, the narrative reads from left to right and bottom to top. In the lowest band, men carry provisions on their backs. Above, attendants transport a variety of animals and fish for the great banquet depicted in the uppermost register. There, seated dignitaries and a larger-than-life personage—probably a king (third from the left)—feast, while a harp player and singer entertain the group. Some art historians have interpreted the scene as a celebration after the victory in warfare represented on the other side of the wooden box (FIG. 2-8). But the two sides may be independent narratives illustrating the two principal roles of a Sumerian ruler—the mighty warrior who defeats enemies of his city-state, and the chief administrator who, with the blessing of the gods, assures the bountifulness of the land in peacetime. The absence of an inscription prevents connecting the scenes with a specific occasion or person, but the *Standard of Ur* is undoubtedly among the world's oldest depictions of contemporaneous events—another of the many seminal innovations of the Sumerians.

# MESOPOTAMIA

When humans first gave up the dangerous and uncertain life of the hunter and gatherer for the more predictable and stable life of the farmer and herder, the change in human society was so significant that historians justly have dubbed it the Neolithic Revolution (see Chapter 1). This fundamental change in the nature of daily life first occurred in Mesopotamia—a Greek word that means "the land between the [Tigris and Euphrates] rivers."

Mesopotamia, the land mass that forms a huge arc from the mountainous border between Turkey and Syria through Iraq to Iran's Zagros Mountains (MAP 2-1), is the region that gave birth to three of the world's great modern faiths—Judaism, Christianity, and Islam—and consequently has long been of interest to historians. Not until the 19th century, however, did systematic excavation open the public's eyes to the extraordinary art and architecture of this ancient land between the rivers. After the first discoveries in Syria and Iraq, the great museums of Europe and North America began avidly to collect Mesopotamian art. The most popular 19th-century acquisitions were the stone reliefs depicting warfare and hunting (FIGS. 2-22 and 2-23) and the colossal statues of monstrous man-headed bulls (FIG. 2-20) from the palaces of the Assyrians, rulers of a northern Mesopotamian empire during the ninth to the seventh centuries BCE. But nothing archaeologists extracted from the earth garnered as much attention as the treasure of gold objects, jewelry, artworks, and musical instruments (FIGS. 2-1 and 2-8 to 2-11) that British archaeologist Leonard Woolley (1880–1960) discovered in the 1920s at the Royal Cemetery at Ur in southern Iraq. The interest in the lavish third-millennium Sumerian cemetery he excavated rivaled the fascination with the 1922 discovery of the second-millennium tomb of the Egyptian boy-king Tutankhamen (see Chapter 3).

## Sumer

The discovery of the treasures of ancient Ur put the Sumerians once again in a prominent position on the world stage, from which they had been absent for more than 4,000 years. The Sumerians were the people who in the fourth millennium BCE transformed the vast and previously sparsely inhabited valley between the Tigris and Euphrates into the Fertile Crescent of the ancient world. Ancient Sumer, which roughly corresponds to southern Iraq today, was not a unified nation, however. Rather, it comprised a dozen or so independent city-states under the protection of different Mesopotamian deities (see "The Gods and Goddesses of Mesopotamia," page 34).

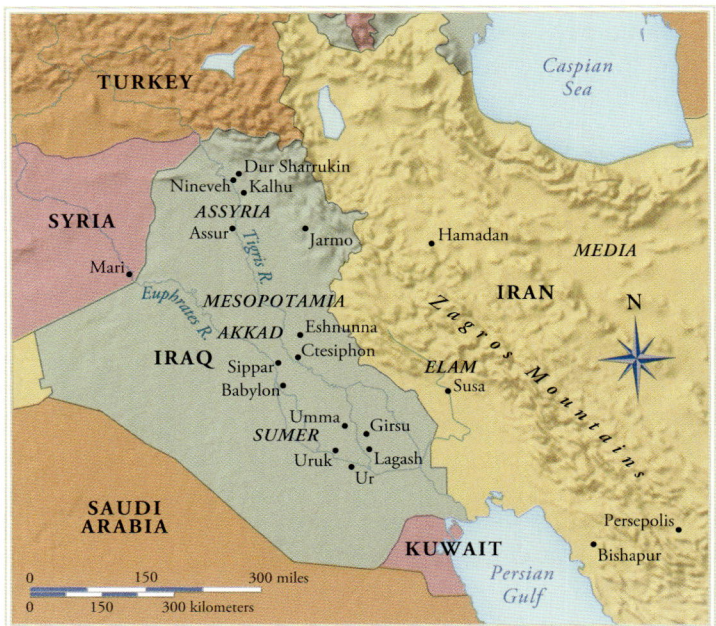

MAP 2-1 Mesopotamia and Persia.

The Sumerian rulers were the gods' representatives on earth and the stewards of their earthly treasure.

The rulers and priests directed all communal activities, including canal construction, crop collection, and food distribution. Because the Sumerians developed agriculture to such an extent that only a portion of the population had to produce food, some members of the community were free to specialize in other activities, including manufacturing, trade, and administration. Specialization of labor is the hallmark of the first complex urban societies. In the city-states of ancient Sumer, activities that once had been individually initiated became institutionalized for the first time. The community, rather than the family, assumed functions such as defense against enemies and the caprices of nature. Whether ruled by a single person or a council chosen from among the leading families, these communities gained permanent identities as discrete cities. The city-state was one of the great Sumerian inventions.

Another was writing. The oldest written documents known are Sumerian records of administrative acts and commercial transactions. At first, around 3400 to 3200 BCE, the Sumerians made inventories of cattle, food, and other items by scratching *pictographs*

---

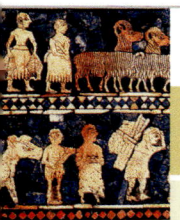

## MESOPOTAMIA AND PERSIA

| | 3500 | Sumerian | 2332 | Akkadian | 2150 | Neo-Sumerian and Babylonian | 1600 | Hittite and Assyrian | 612 | Neo-Babylonian and Achaeminid | 559 | | 330 | Greco-Roman and Sasanian | 636 | BCE | CE |
|---|---|---|---|---|---|---|---|---|---|---|---|---|---|---|---|---|---|

- ▌ World's first city-states founded and writing invented
- ▌ Construction of oldest temples on ziggurats
- ▌ Artists present narratives in register format

- ▌ First Mesopotamian rulers to call themselves kings
- ▌ Earliest preserved hollow-cast bronze statuary

- ▌ Largest extant ziggurat erected at Ur
- ▌ Gudea rebuilds temples and commissions portraits
- ▌ Hammurabi sets up a stele recording his laws

- ▌ Hittites sack Babylon and fortify their capital at Hattusa
- ▌ Assyrians rule a vast empire from citadels guarded by lamassu
- ▌ Extensive relief cycles celebrate Assyrian military campaigns

- ▌ Nebuchadnezzar II rebuilds Babylon, which boasts two of the Seven Wonders of the ancient world
- ▌ Persians build an immense palace complex at Persepolis

- ▌ After conquest by Alexander the Great, Mesopotamia and Persia are absorbed into the Greco-Roman world
- ▌ New Persian Empire challenges Rome from Ctesiphon

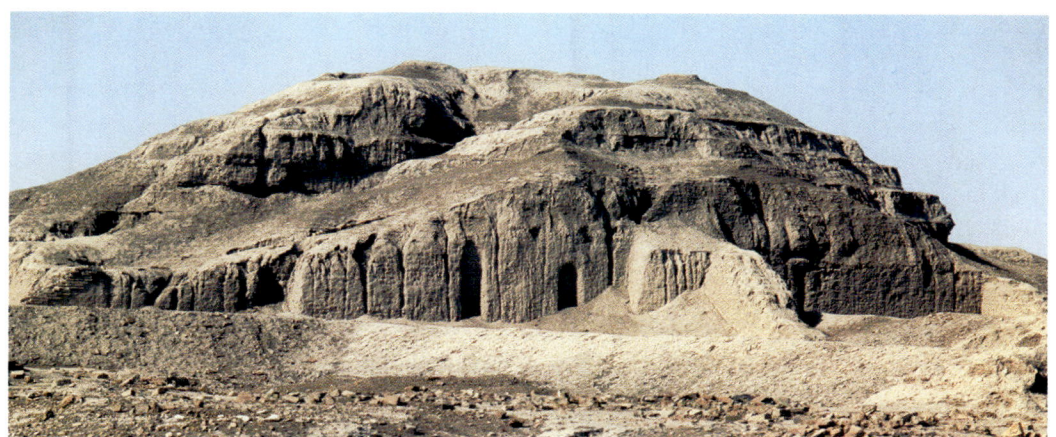

Using only mud bricks, the Sumerians erected temple platforms called ziggurats several centuries before the Egyptians built stone pyramids. The most famous ziggurat was the biblical Tower of Babel.

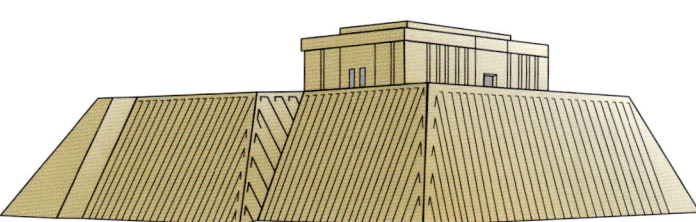

2-3 Restored view of the White Temple and ziggurat, Uruk (modern Warka), Iraq, ca. 3200–3000 BCE.

The White Temple at Uruk was probably dedicated to Anu, the sky god. It had a central hall (cella) with a stepped altar. There, the Sumerian priests would await the apparition of the deity.

(simplified pictures standing for words) into soft clay with a sharp tool, or *stylus*. The clay plaques hardened into breakable, yet nearly indestructible, tablets. Thousands of these plaques dating back nearly five millennia exist today. The Sumerians wrote their pictorial signs from the top down and arranged them in boxes they read from right to left. By 3000 to 2900 BCE, they had further simplified the pictographic signs by reducing them to a group of wedge-shaped (*cuneiform*) signs (FIGS. 2-7 and 2-11 are early examples; see also FIGS. 2-13, 2-16, and 2-18). The development of cuneiform marked the beginning of writing, as historians strictly define it. The surviving cuneiform tablets testify to the far-flung network of Sumerian contacts reaching from southern Mesopotamia eastward to the Iranian plateau, northward to Assyria, and westward to Syria. Trade was essential for the Sumerians, because despite its fertile soil, Sumeria was poor in such vital natural resources as metal, stone, and wood.

The Sumerians also produced great literature. Their most famous work, known from fragmentary cuneiform texts, is the late-third-millennium *Epic of Gilgamesh,* which antedates the Greek poet Homer's *Iliad* and *Odyssey* by some 1,500 years. It recounts the heroic story of Gilgamesh, legendary king of Uruk and slayer of the monster Huwawa. Translations of the Sumerian epic into several other ancient languages attest to the fame of the original version.

**WHITE TEMPLE, URUK** The layout of Sumerian cities reflected the central role of the gods in daily life. The main temple to each state's chief god formed the city's monumental nucleus. In fact, the temple complex was a kind of city within a city, where a staff of priests and scribes carried on official administrative and commercial business as well as oversaw all religious functions.

The outstanding preserved example of early Sumerian temple architecture is the 5,000-year-old White Temple (FIG. 2-2) at Uruk, a city that in the late fourth millennium BCE had a population of about 40,000. Usually, only the foundations of early Mesopotamian temples remain. The White Temple is a rare exception. Sumerian builders did not have access to stone quarries and instead formed mud bricks for the superstructures of their temples and other buildings. Almost all these structures have eroded over the course of time. The fragile nature of the building materials did not, however, prevent the Sumerians from erecting towering works, such as the Uruk temple, several centuries before the Egyptians built their famous stone pyramids. The construction of monumental shrines without stone says a great deal about the Sumerians' desire to provide grandiose settings for the worship of their deities.

Enough of the White Temple at Uruk remains to permit a fairly reliable reconstruction (FIG. 2-3). The temple (whose white-washed walls suggested its modern nickname) stands atop a high platform, or *ziggurat,* 40 feet above street level in the city center. A stairway on one side leads to the top but does not end in front of any of the temple doorways, necessitating two or three angular changes in direction. This *bent-axis plan* is the standard arrangement for Sumerian temples, a striking contrast to the linear approach the Egyptians preferred for their temples and tombs (see Chapter 3).

As in other Sumerian temples, the corners of the White Temple are oriented to the cardinal points of the compass. The building, probably dedicated to Anu, the sky god, is of modest proportions (61 by 16 feet). By design, it did not accommodate large throngs of worshipers but only a select few, the priests and perhaps the leading community members. The temple had several chambers. The central hall, or *cella,* was the divinity's room and housed a stepped altar. The Sumerians referred to their temples as "waiting rooms," a reflection of their belief the deity would descend from the heavens to appear before the priests in the cella. Whether the Uruk temple had a roof, and if it did, what kind, are uncertain.

The Sumerian notion of the gods residing above the world of humans is central to most of the world's religions. Moses ascended Mount Sinai to receive the Ten Commandments from the Hebrew God, and the Greeks placed the home of their gods and goddesses on Mount Olympus. The elevated placement of Mesopotamian temples on giant platforms reaching toward the sky is consistent with this widespread religious concept. Eroded ziggurats still dominate most of the ruined cities of Sumer. The loftiness of the great temple platforms made a profound impression on the peoples of

## The Gods and Goddesses of Mesopotamia

The Sumerians and their successors in Mesopotamia worshiped numerous deities, mostly nature gods. Listed here are the Mesopotamian gods and goddesses discussed in this chapter.

▎ *Anu.* The chief deity of the Sumerians. Anu was the god of the sky and of the city of Uruk. One of the earliest Sumerian temples (FIGS. 2-2 and 2-3) may have been dedicated to his worship.

▎ *Enlil.* Anu's son. Enlil was the lord of the winds and the earth. He eventually replaced his father as king of the gods.

▎ *Inanna.* The Sumerian goddess of love and war, later known as *Ishtar.* Inanna was the most important female deity in all periods of Mesopotamian history. As early as the fourth millennium BCE, the Sumerians constructed a sanctuary to Inanna at Uruk. Amid the ruins, excavators uncovered statues and reliefs (FIGS. 2-4 and 2-5) connected with her worship.

▎ *Nanna.* The moon god, also known as *Sin.* Nanna was the chief deity of Ur, where the Sumerians erected his most important shrine.

▎ *Utu.* The sun god, later known as *Shamash.* Utu was especially revered at Sippar. On a Babylonian stele (FIG. 2-18) of ca. 1780 BCE, King Hammurabi presents his laws to Shamash, whom the sculptor depicted as a bearded god wearing a horned headdress. Flames radiate from the sun god's shoulders.

▎ *Marduk, Nabu,* and *Adad.* Marduk was the chief god of the Babylonians. His son Nabu was the god of writing and wisdom. Adad was the Babylonian god of storms. Marduk and Nabu's dragon and Adad's sacred bull adorn the sixth-century BCE Ishtar Gate (FIG. 2-24) at Babylon.

▎ *Ningirsu.* The local god of Lagash and Girsu. Ningirsu helped Eannatum, one of the early rulers of Lagash, defeat an enemy army. The *Stele of the Vultures* (FIG. 2-7) of ca. 2600–2500 BCE records Ningirsu's role in the victory. Gudea (FIGS. 2-16 and 2-17), one of Eannatum's Neo-Sumerian successors, built a great temple around 2100 BCE in honor of Ningirsu after the god instructed him to do so in a dream.

▎ *Ashur.* The local deity of Assur, the city that took his name. Ashur became the king of the Assyrian gods. He sometimes is identified with Enlil.

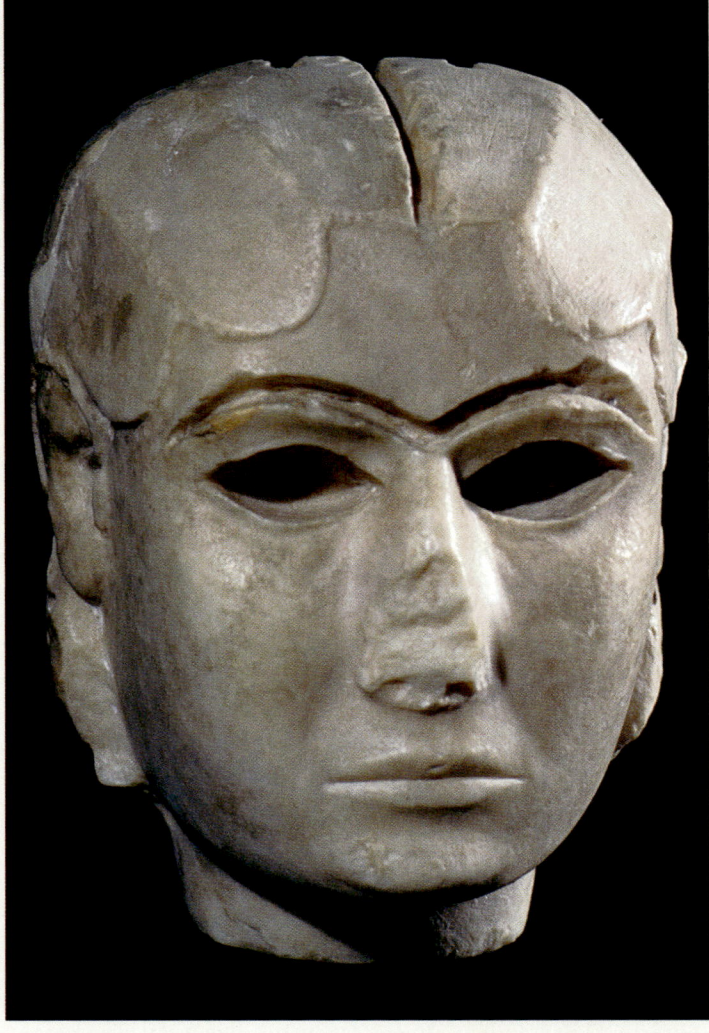

1 in.

**2-4** Female head (Inanna?), from Uruk (modern Warka), Iraq, ca. 3200–3000 BCE. Marble, 8″ high. National Museum of Iraq, Baghdad.

The Sumerians imported the marble for this head at great cost. It may represent the goddess Inanna and originally had inlaid colored shell or stone eyes and brows, and a wig, probably of gold leaf.

ancient Mesopotamia. The tallest ziggurat of all, at Babylon, was about 270 feet high. Known to the Hebrews as the Tower of Babel, it became the centerpiece of a biblical story about the insolent pride of humans (see "Babylon, City of Wonders," page 49).

**INANNA** A fragmentary white marble female head (FIG. **2-4**) from Uruk is also an extraordinary achievement at so early a date. The head, one of the treasures of the recently reopened National Museum of Iraq in Baghdad, disappeared during the Iraq war of 2003, but was later recovered, along with other priceless items (FIGS. 2-5 and 2-12). The Sumerians lacked a ready source of fine stones suitable for carving sculptures, and consequently used stone sparingly. The lustrous hard stone selected for this head had to be

brought to Uruk at great cost. In fact, the "head" is really only a face with a flat back. It has drilled holes for attachment to the rest of the head and the body, which may have been of much less costly wood. Although found in the sacred precinct of the goddess Inanna, the subject is unknown. Many have suggested that the face is an image of Inanna, but it may instead portray a mortal woman, perhaps a priestess.

Often the present condition of an artwork can be very misleading, and this female head from Uruk is a dramatic example. Its original appearance would have been much more vibrant than the pure white fragment preserved today. Colored shell or stone filled the deep recesses for the eyebrows and the large eyes. The deep groove at the top of the head anchored a wig, probably made of gold leaf.

The hair strands engraved in the metal fell in waves over the forehead and sides of the face. The bright coloration of the eyes, brows, and hair likely overshadowed the soft modeling of the cheeks and mouth. The missing body was probably clothed in expensive fabrics and bedecked with jewels.

*WARKA VASE* As noted in the discussion of the *Standard of Ur* (FIG. 2-1), the Sumerians, pioneers in so many areas, were the first masters of pictorial narration. The so-called *Warka Vase* (FIG. **2-5**)

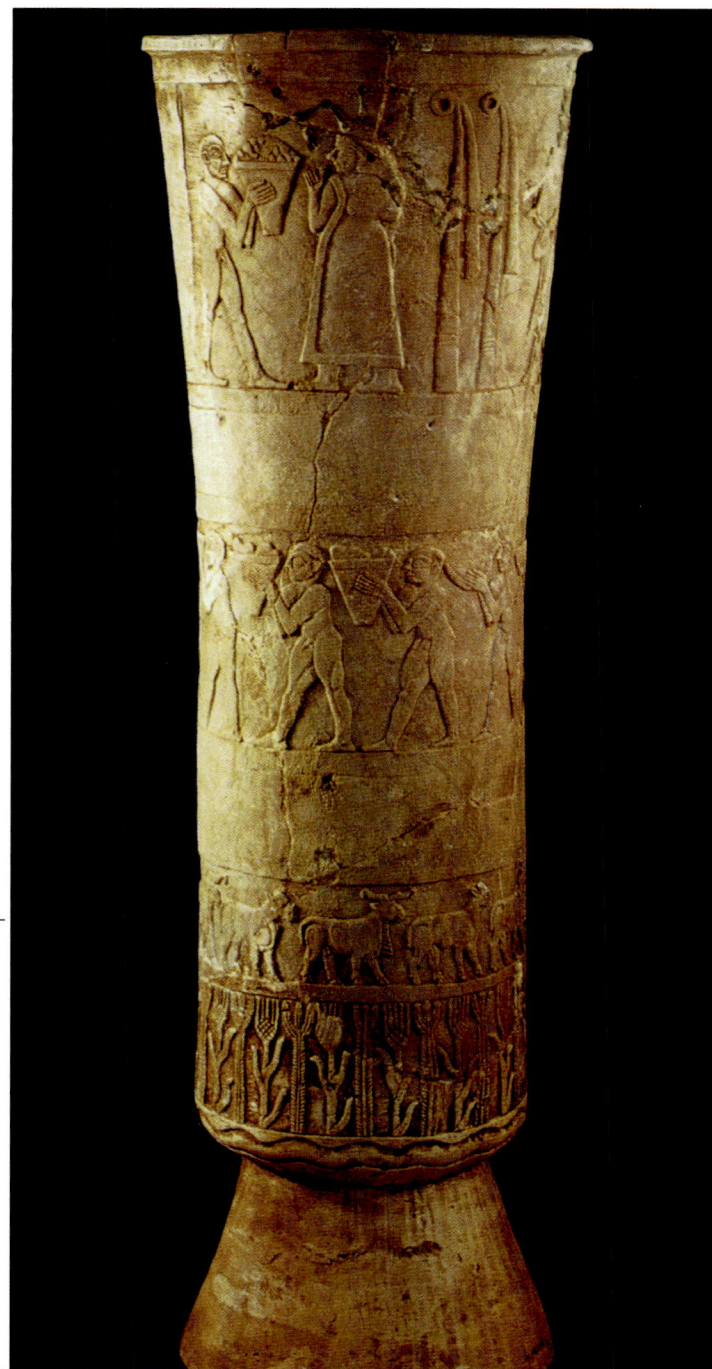

1 ft.

**2-5** Presentation of offerings to Inanna (*Warka Vase*), from Uruk (modern Warka), Iraq, ca. 3200–3000 BCE. Alabaster, 3′ $\frac{1}{4}$″ high. National Museum of Iraq, Baghdad.

In this oldest known example of Sumerian narrative art, the sculptor divided the tall stone vase's reliefs into registers, a significant break with the haphazard figure placement found in earlier art.

from Uruk (modern Warka), several hundred years older than the *Standard of Ur,* is the first great work of narrative relief sculpture known. Found within the Inanna temple complex, it depicts a religious festival in honor of the goddess.

The division of the vase's surface into registers with figures standing on a common ground line—a compositional device still used today in comic strips—contrasts starkly with the haphazard arrangement of figures found in earlier paintings and reliefs. This Sumerian formula remained the norm for narrative art in Mesopotamia, Persia, Egypt, and Greece for millennia. The lowest band on the *Warka Vase* shows wheat and other crops above a wavy line representing water. Then comes a register with ewes and rams moving from left to right in strict profile, consistent with an approach to representing animals that was then some 20,000 years old. Agriculture and animal husbandry were the staples of the Sumerian economy, but the produce and the alternating female and male animals are also symbols of fertility. They underscore that Inanna had blessed Uruk's inhabitants with good crops and increased herds.

A procession of naked men moving in the opposite direction of the animals fills the band at the center of the vase. The men carry baskets and jars overflowing with the earth's abundance. They will present their bounty to the goddess as a *votive offering* (gift of gratitude to a deity usually made in fulfillment of a vow) and will deposit it in her temple. The spacing of each figure involves no overlapping. The Uruk men, like the Neolithic deer hunters (FIG. 1-16) at Çatal Höyük, are a composite of frontal and profile views, with large staring frontal eyes in profile heads. The artist depicted those human body parts necessary to communicate the human form and avoided positions, attitudes, or views that would conceal the characterizing parts. For example, if the figures were in strict profile, an arm and perhaps a leg would be hidden. The body would appear to have only half its breadth. And the eye would not "read" as an eye at all, because it would not have its distinctive oval shape. Art historians call this characteristic early approach to representation *conceptual representation* (as opposed to *optical representation*— the portrayal of people and objects seen from a fixed point) because artists who used it did not seek to record the immediate, fleeting aspect of figures. Instead, they rendered the human body's distinguishing and fixed properties. The fundamental forms of figures, not their accidental appearance, dictated the artist's selection of the composite view as the best way to represent the human body.

In the uppermost (and tallest) band of the *Warka Vase* is a female figure with a tall horned headdress next to two large poles that are the sign of the goddess Inanna. (Some scholars think the woman is a priestess and not the goddess herself.) A nude male figure brings a large vessel brimming with offerings to be deposited in the goddess's shrine. At the far right and barely visible in FIG. 2-5 is an only partially preserved clothed man. Near him is the early pictograph for the Sumerian official that scholars usually, if ambiguously, refer to as a "priest-king," that is, both a religious and secular leader. The greater height of the priest-king and Inanna compared with the offering bearers indicates their greater importance. Some art historians interpret the scene as a symbolic marriage between the priest-king and the goddess, ensuring her continued goodwill—and reaffirming the leader's exalted position in society.

**ESHNUNNA STATUETTES** Further insight into Sumerian religious beliefs and rituals comes from a cache of sculptures reverently buried beneath the floor of a temple at Eshnunna

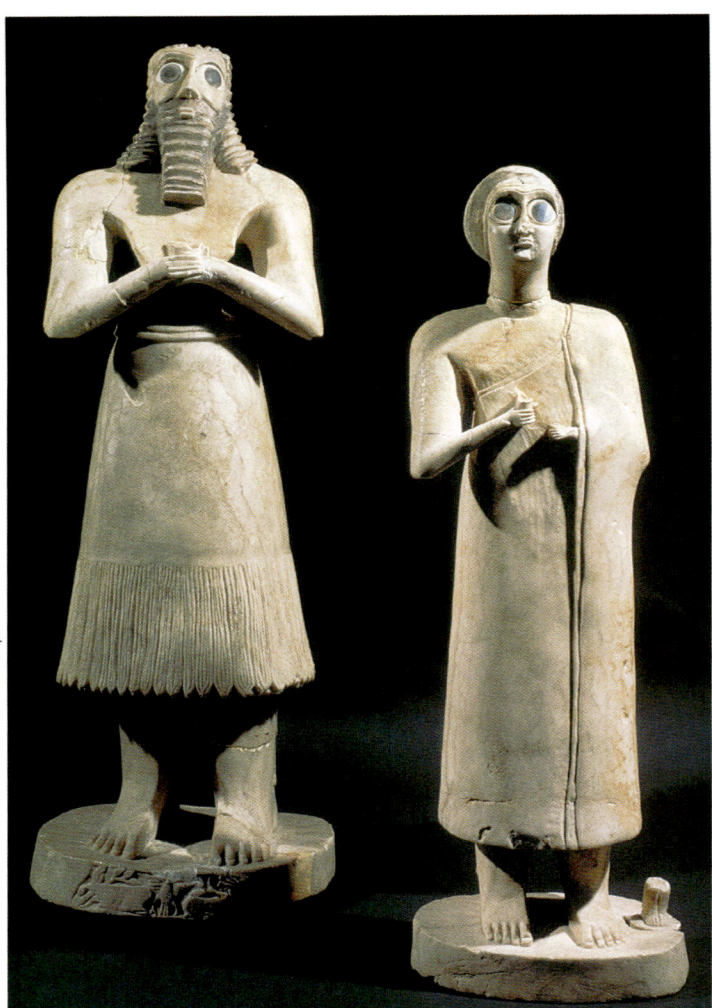

**2-6** Statuettes of two worshipers, from the Square Temple at Eshnunna (modern Tell Asmar), Iraq, ca. 2700 BCE. Gypsum, shell, and black limestone, man 2′ 4¼″ high, woman 1′ 11¼″ high. National Museum of Iraq, Baghdad.

The oversized eyes probably symbolize the perpetual wakefulness of these substitute worshipers offering prayers to the deity. The beakers the figures hold were used to pour libations for the gods.

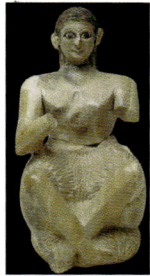

**2-6A** Urnanshe, from Mari, ca. 2600–2500 BCE.

the name of the donor or the god. The texts inscribed on some statuettes are specific prayers to the deity on the owner's behalf. With their heads tilted upward, the figures represented in these statuettes wait in the Sumerian "waiting room" for the divinity to appear.

The Sumerian sculptors employed simple forms, primarily cones and cylinders, for the figures. The statuettes, even those bearing the names of individuals (for example, Urnanshe), are not portraits in the strict sense of the word, but the sculptors did distinguish physical types. At Eshnunna, the sculptors portrayed at least one child, because next to the woman in FIG. 2-6 are the remains of two small legs. Most striking is the disproportionate relationship between the inlaid oversized eyes and the tiny hands. Scholars have explained the exaggeration of the eye size in various ways. But because the purpose of these votive figures was to offer constant prayers to the gods on their donors' behalf, the open-eyed stares most likely symbolize the eternal wakefulness necessary to fulfill their duty.

***STELE OF THE VULTURES*** The city-states of ancient Sumer were often at war with one another, and warfare is the theme of the so-called *Stele of the Vultures* (FIG. **2-7**) from Girsu. A *stele* is a carved stone slab set up to commemorate a historical event or, in some cultures, to mark a grave. The Girsu stele presents a labeled historical narrative with cuneiform inscriptions filling almost every blank space. (It is not, however, the first historical representation in the history of art. That honor belongs—at the moment—to an Egyptian relief [FIG. 3-1] carved more than three centuries earlier.) The inscriptions reveal that the *Stele of the Vultures* celebrates the victory of Eannatum, the *ensi* (ruler; king?) of Lagash, over the neighboring city-state of Umma. The stele has reliefs on both sides and takes its modern name from a fragment depicting a gruesome scene of vultures carrying off the severed heads and arms of the defeated enemy soldiers. Another fragment shows the giant figure of the local god Ningirsu holding tiny enemies in a net and beating one of them on the head with a mace.

The fragment in FIG. 2-7 depicts Eannatum leading an infantry battalion into battle (*above*) and attacking from a war chariot (*below*). The foot soldiers protect themselves by forming a wall of shields—there are far more hands and spears than heads and feet—and trample naked enemies as they advance. (The fragment representing vultures devouring corpses belongs just to the right in the same register.) Both on foot and in a chariot, Eannatum is larger than anyone else, except Ningirsu on the other side of the stele. The artist presented the ensi as the fearless general who paves the way for his army. Many Girsu attackers nonetheless lost their lives, and Eannatum himself sustained wounds in the campaign. Still, the outcome was never in doubt, because Ningirsu fought with the men of Lagash.

Despite its fragmentary state, the *Stele of the Vultures* is an extraordinary find, not only as a very early effort to record historical events in relief but also for the insight it yields about Sumerian society. Through both words and pictures, it provides information about warfare and the special nature of the Sumerian ruler. Eannatum was greater in stature than other men, and Ningirsu watched over him. According to the text, the ensi was born from the god Enlil's semen, which Ningirsu implanted in the womb. When Eannatum incurred injuries in battle, the god shed tears for him. The inscription also says it was Ningirsu who chose Eannatum to rule Lagash and preside over all aspects of the city-state, both in war and in peace. This also seems to have been the role of the ensi in the other Sumerian city-states.

(modern Tell Asmar) during remodeling of the structure. Carved of soft gypsum and inlaid with shell and black limestone, the statuettes range in size from well under a foot to about 30 inches tall. FIG. **2-6** shows the two largest figures. All of the statuettes represent mortals, rather than deities, with their hands folded in front of their chests in a gesture of prayer, usually holding the small beakers the Sumerians used for *libations* (ritual pouring of liquid) in honor of the gods. (Archaeologists found hundreds of these goblets in the temple complex at Eshnunna.) The men wear belts and fringed skirts. Most have beards and shoulder-length hair. The women wear long robes, with the right shoulder bare. Similar figurines have been unearthed at other sites. Some stand, as do the Eshnunna statuettes. Others are seated, for example, the figurine portraying Urnanshe (FIG. **2-6A**) from the Ishtar temple at Mari in Syria. Many bear inscriptions giving valuable information, such as

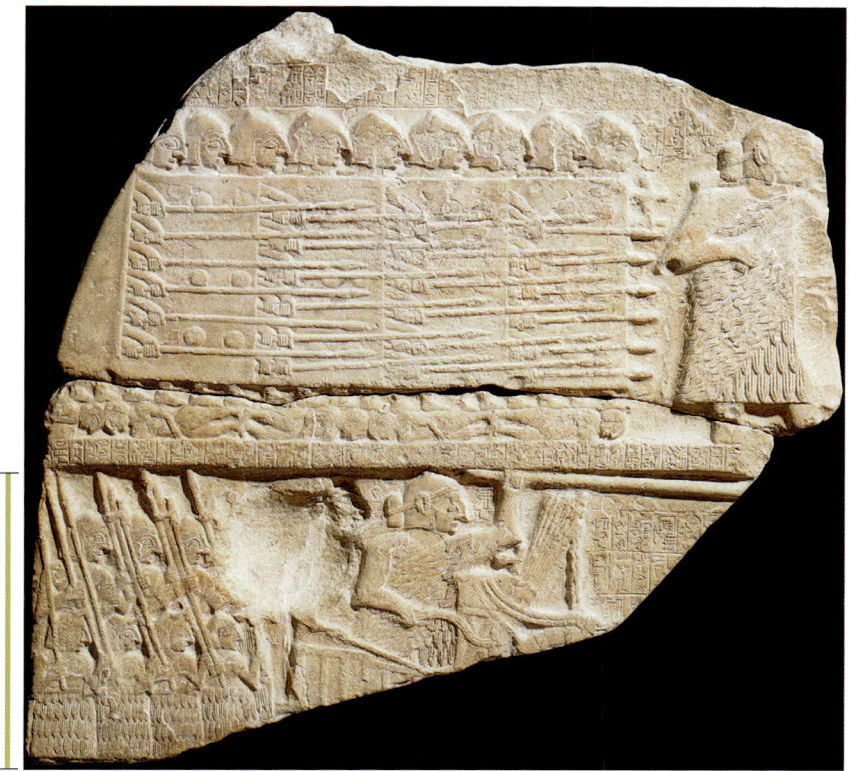

2-7 Battle scenes, fragment of the victory stele of Eannatum (*Stele of the Vultures*), from Girsu (modern Telloh), Iraq, ca. 2600–2500 BCE. Limestone, fragment 2′ 6″ high; full stele 5′ 11″ high. Musée du Louvre, Paris.

Cuneiform inscriptions on this stele describe Eannatum's victory over the city of Umma with the aid of the god Ningirsu. This fragment shows Eannatum, at gigantic size, leading his troops into battle.

1 ft.

still debate whether these deceased individuals were true kings and queens or simply aristocrats, priests, and priestesses, but the Sumerians laid them to rest in regal fashion. Archaeologists exploring the Ur cemetery uncovered gold helmets and daggers with handles of lapis lazuli (a rich azure-blue stone imported from Afghanistan), golden beakers and bowls, jewelry of gold and lapis, musical instruments, chariots, and other luxurious items. The excavators also found dozens of bodies in the richest tombs—a retinue of musicians, servants, and soldiers ritually sacrificed in order to accompany the "kings and queens" into the afterlife. (Comparable rituals occurred in other societies, for example, in ancient America; see Chapter 18.)

Not the costliest object found in the "royal" graves, but probably the most significant from the viewpoint of the history of art, is the *Standard of Ur* (FIGS. 2-1 and 2-8), discussed briefly at the beginning of this chapter. This wooden box inlaid with lapis lazuli, shell, and red limestone has broad rectangular faces and narrow trapezoidal ends. It is of uncertain function. The excavator, Leonard Woolley, thought the object was originally mounted on a pole, and he considered it a kind of military standard—hence its nickname.

**STANDARD OF UR** Agriculture and trade brought considerable wealth to some of the city-states of ancient Sumer. Nowhere is this more evident than in what the excavators dubbed the Royal Cemetery at Ur. In the third millennium BCE, the leading families of Ur buried their dead in vaulted chambers beneath the earth. Scholars

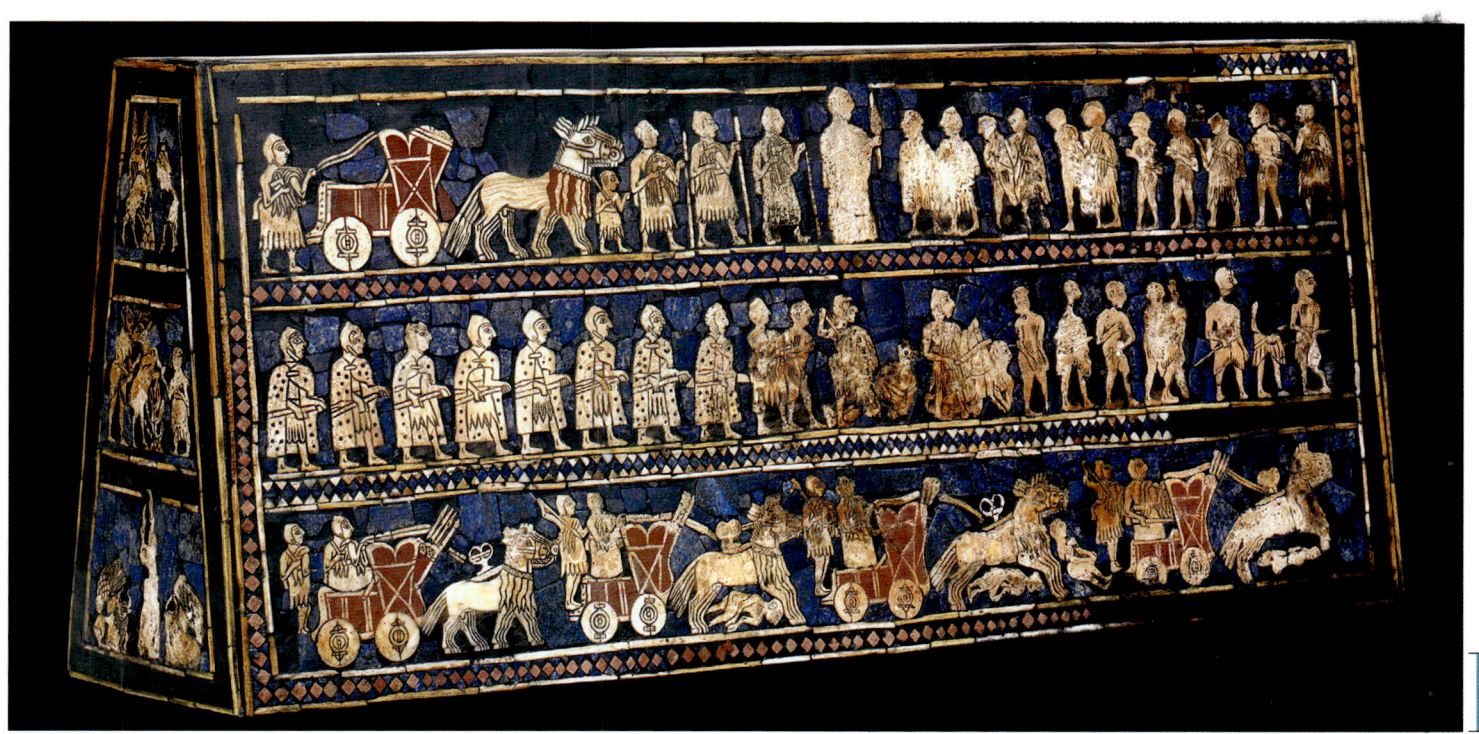

1 in.

2-8 War side of the *Standard of Ur,* from tomb 779, Royal Cemetery, Ur (modern Tell Muqayyar), Iraq, ca. 2600–2400 BCE. Wood, lapis lazuli, shell, and red limestone, 8″ × 1′ 7″. British Museum, London. ■◀

Using a mosaic-like technique, this Sumerian artist depicted a battlefield victory in three registers. The narrative reads from bottom to top, and the size of the figures varies with their importance in society.

Art historians usually refer to the two long sides of the box as the "war side" and "peace side," which celebrate the two principal roles of a Sumerian ruler, but the two sides may represent the first and second parts of a single narrative. The artist divided each side into three horizontal bands. The narrative reads from left to right and bottom to top. On the war side (FIG. 2-8), four ass-drawn, four-wheeled war chariots crush enemies, whose bodies appear on the ground in front of and beneath the animals. The gait of the asses accelerates along the band from left to right. Above, foot soldiers gather up and lead away captured foes. In the uppermost register, soldiers bring bound captives (whom the victors have stripped naked to degrade them) to a kinglike figure, who has stepped out of his chariot. His central place in the composition and his greater stature (his head breaks through the border at the top) set him apart from all the other figures.

**BULL-HEADED HARPS** On the peace side of the *Standard of Ur,* the head of the largest figure also interrupts the upper border. The "king" presides over a banquet at which a musician plays a harp

and a long-haired eunuch (compare FIG. 2-6A) sings (FIG. 2-1, *top right*). From the tomb of "Queen" Pu-abi (many historians prefer to designate her more conservatively and ambiguously as "Lady" Pu-abi) comes a fragmentary harp that, as reconstructed (FIG. 2-9), resembles the instrument depicted on the *Standard of Ur.* A magnificent bull's head fashioned of gold leaf over a wooden core caps the harp's sound box. The hair and beard of the bull are of lapis lazuli, as is the inlaid background of the sound box, which features figures of shell and red limestone.

The excavators unearthed a similar harp in the adjacent "King's Grave." It too has a costly inlaid sound box (FIG. 2-10). In the uppermost of the four panels is a heroic figure embracing two man-bulls in a *heraldic composition* (symmetrical on either side of a central figure). The hero's body and that of the scorpion-man in the lowest panel are in composite view. The animals are, equally characteristically, solely in profile: the dog wearing a dagger and carrying a laden table, the lion bringing in the beverage service, the ass playing the harp, the jackal playing the zither, the bear steadying the harp

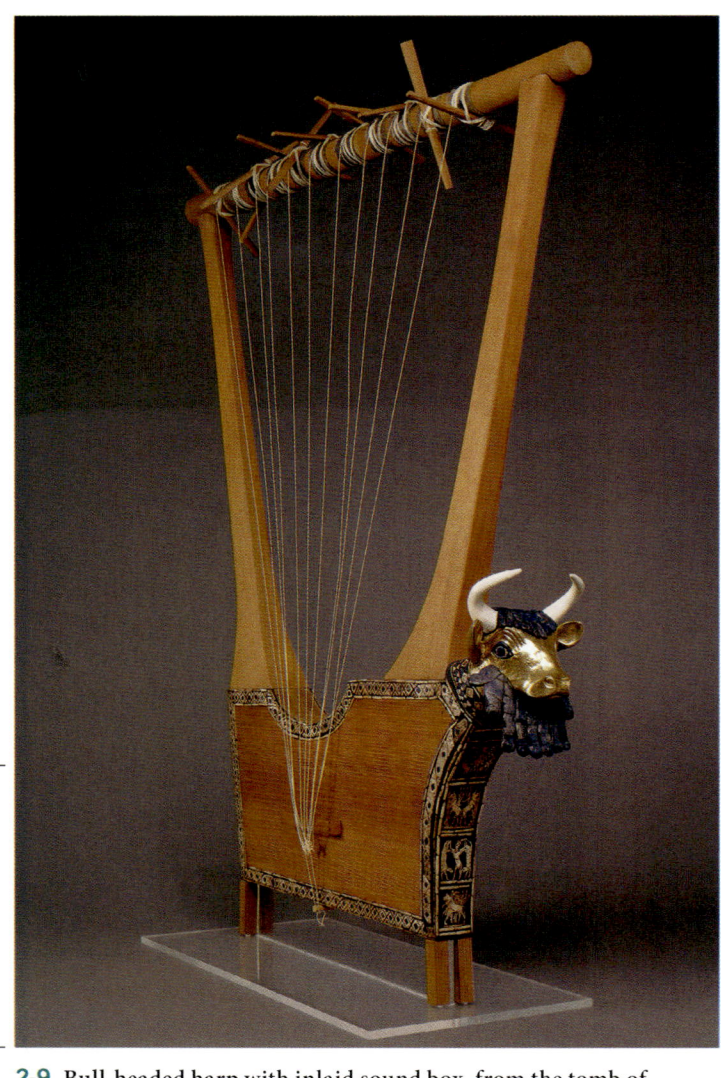

**2-9** Bull-headed harp with inlaid sound box, from the tomb of Pu-abi (tomb 800), Royal Cemetery, Ur (modern Tell Muqayyar), Iraq, ca. 2600–2400 BCE. Wood, gold, lapis lazuli, red limestone, and shell, 3′ 8⅛″ high. British Museum, London.

A bearded bull's head fashioned of gold leaf and lapis lazuli over a wooden core adorns this harp from the tomb of "Queen" Pu-abi of Ur. The inlaid sound box features four narrative scenes.

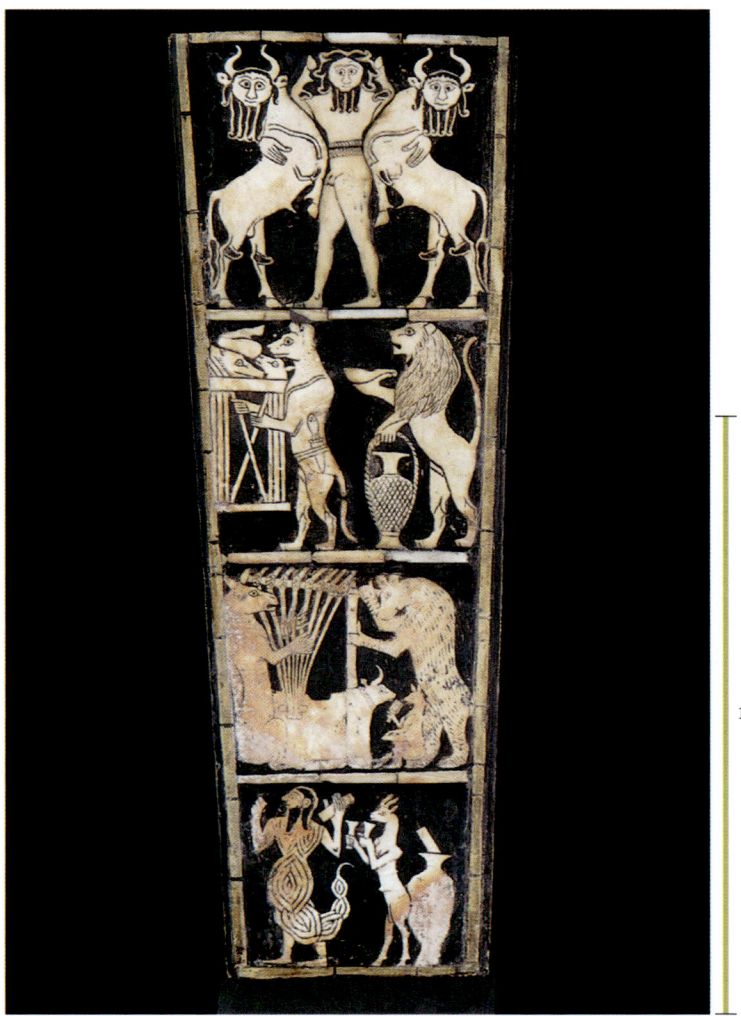

**2-10** Sound box of the bull-headed harp from tomb 789 ("King's Grave"), Royal Cemetery, Ur (modern Tell Muqayyar), Iraq, ca. 2600–2400 BCE. Wood, lapis lazuli, and shell, 1′ 7″ high. University of Pennsylvania Museum of Archaeology and Anthropology, Philadelphia.

The four inlaid panels on the sound box of the harp found in the "King's Grave" at Ur represent a Gilgamesh-like hero between man-bulls and animals acting out scenes of uncertain significance.

## Mesopotamian Seals

Archaeologists (and farmers and treasure hunters) have unearthed seals in great numbers at sites throughout Mesopotamia. Generally made of stone, seals of ivory, glass, and other materials also survive. The seals take two forms: flat *stamp seals* and *cylinder seals.* The latter have a hole drilled lengthwise through the center of the cylinder so that they could be strung and worn around the neck or suspended from the wrist. Cylinder seals (FIG. 2-11) were prized possessions, signifying high positions in society, and when their owners died, they frequently carried the seals with them into the afterlife.

The primary function of cylinder seals, however, like the earlier stamp seals, was not to serve as items of adornment. The Sumerians (and other ancient Mesopotamian peoples) used both stamp and cylinder seals to identify their documents and protect storage jars and doors against unauthorized opening. The oldest seals predated the invention of writing and conveyed their messages with pictographs that ratified ownership. Later seals often bore long cuneiform inscriptions and recorded the names and titles of rulers, bureaucrats, and deities. Although sealing is increasingly rare, the tradition lives on today whenever someone seals an envelope with a lump of wax and then stamps it with a monogram or other identifying mark. Customs officials often still seal packages and sacks with official stamps when goods cross national borders.

In Mesopotamia, artists decorated both stamp and cylinder seals with incised designs, producing a raised pattern when the owner pressed the seal into soft clay. (Cylinder seals largely displaced stamp seals because they could be rolled over the clay and could thus cover a greater area more quickly.) Illustrated here are a cylinder seal with the name of Queen Pu-abi from the Royal Cemetery at Ur and a modern impression made from it. Note how cracks in the stone cylinder become raised lines in the impression and how the engraved figures, chairs, and cuneiform characters appear in relief. Continuous rolling of the seal over a clay strip results in a repeating design, as the impression also demonstrates at the edges.

The miniature reliefs the seals produce are a priceless source of information about Mesopotamian religion and society. Without them, archaeologists would know much less about how Mesopotamians dressed and dined; what their shrines looked like; how they depicted their gods, rulers, and mythological figures; how they fought wars; and what role women played in society. Clay seal impressions excavated in architectural contexts shed a welcome light on the administration and organization of Mesopotamian city-states. Finally, Mesopotamian seals are an invaluable resource for art historians, providing them with thousands of miniature examples of relief sculpture spanning three millennia.

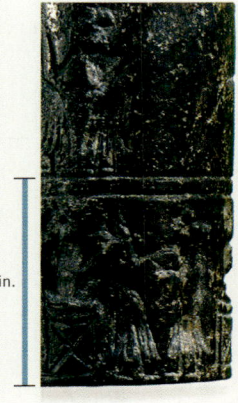

1 in.

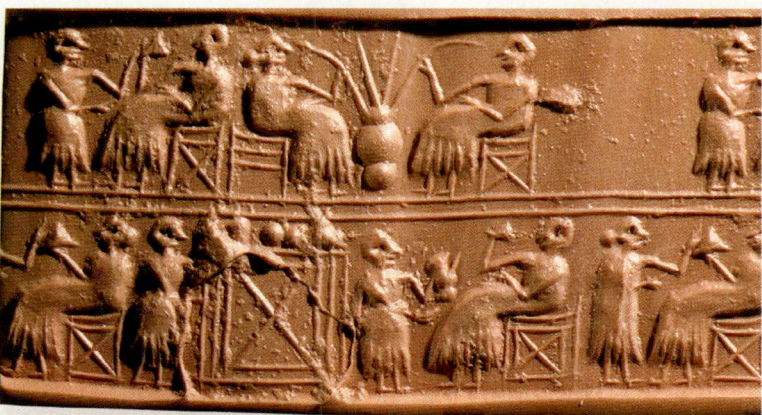

**2-11** Banquet scene, cylinder seal (*left*) and its modern impression (*right*), from the tomb of Pu-abi (tomb 800), Royal Cemetery, Ur (modern Tell Muqayyar), Iraq, ca. 2600–2400 BCE. Lapis lazuli, $1\frac{7}{8}''$ high, $1''$ diameter. British Museum, London.

The Mesopotamians used seals to identify and secure goods. Artists incised designs into stone cylinders and then rolled them over clay to produce miniature artworks such as this banquet scene.

(or perhaps dancing), and the gazelle bearing goblets. The banquet animals almost seem to be burlesquing the kind of regal feast reproduced on the *Standard of Ur.* The meaning of the sound box scenes is unclear. Some scholars have suggested, for example, that the creatures inhabit the land of the dead and that the narrative has a funerary significance. In any event, the sound box is a very early specimen of the recurring theme in both literature and art of animals acting as people. Later examples include Aesop's fables in ancient Greece, medieval bestiaries, and Walt Disney's cartoon animal actors.

**CYLINDER SEALS** The excavators of the Ur cemetery found Pu-abi's remains on a bier in her tomb, wearing an elaborate headdress and jewelry of gold, silver, lapis lazuli, carnelian, and agate.

Near her body were pins to fasten her garment and three *cylinder seals,* one of which (FIG. **2-11**) gives her name in cuneiform script. The seal is typical of the period, consisting of a cylindrical piece of stone engraved to produce a raised impression when rolled over clay (see "Mesopotamian Seals," above). In the upper zone, a woman, probably Pu-abi, and a man sit and drink from beakers, attended by servants. Below, male attendants serve two more seated men. Even in miniature and in a medium very different from that of the *Standard of Ur* (FIG. 2-1), the Sumerian artist employed the same figure types and followed the same compositional rules to depict a banquet. All the figures are in composite views with large frontal eyes in profile heads, and the seated dignitaries are larger in scale to underscore their elevated position in the social hierarchy.

## Akkad

In 2332 BCE, the loosely linked group of cities known as Sumer came under the domination of a great ruler, Sargon of Akkad (r. 2332–2279 BCE). Archaeologists have yet to locate the specific site of the city of Akkad, but it was in the vicinity of Babylon. The Akkadians were Semitic in origin—that is, they were a Mesopotamian people who spoke a language related to Hebrew and Arabic. Their language, Akkadian, was entirely different from the language of Sumer, but they used the Sumerians' cuneiform characters for their written documents. Under Sargon (whose name means "true king") and his followers, the Akkadians introduced a new concept of royal power based on unswerving loyalty to the king rather than to the city-state. Naram-Sin (r. 2254–2218 BCE), Sargon's grandson, regarded the governors of his cities as mere royal servants, and called himself "King of the Four Quarters"—in effect, ruler of the earth, akin to a god.

**AKKADIAN PORTRAITURE** A magnificent copper head (FIG. **2-12**) found at Nineveh that portrays an Akkadian king em-

bodies this new concept of absolute monarchy. The head is all that survives of a statue knocked over in antiquity, perhaps when the Medes, a people that occupied the land south of the Caspian Sea (MAP 2-1), sacked Nineveh in 612 BCE. But the damage to the portrait was not the result solely of the statue's toppling. There are also signs of deliberate mutilation. To make a political statement, the attackers gouged out the eyes (once inlaid with precious or semiprecious stones), broke off the lower part of the beard, and slashed the ears of the royal portrait. Later parallels for this kind of political vandalism abound, for example—in the same region—the destruction of images of Saddam Hussein after the Iraqi ruler's downfall in 2003. Even in its mutilated state, however, the Akkadian portrait conveys the king's majestic serenity, dignity, and authority. The portrait is also remarkable for the masterful way the sculptor balanced naturalism and abstract patterning. The artist carefully observed and recorded the Akkadian's distinctive features—the profile of the nose and the long, curly beard—and brilliantly communicated the differing textures of flesh and hair, even the contrasting textures of the mustache, beard, and braided hair on the top of the head. The

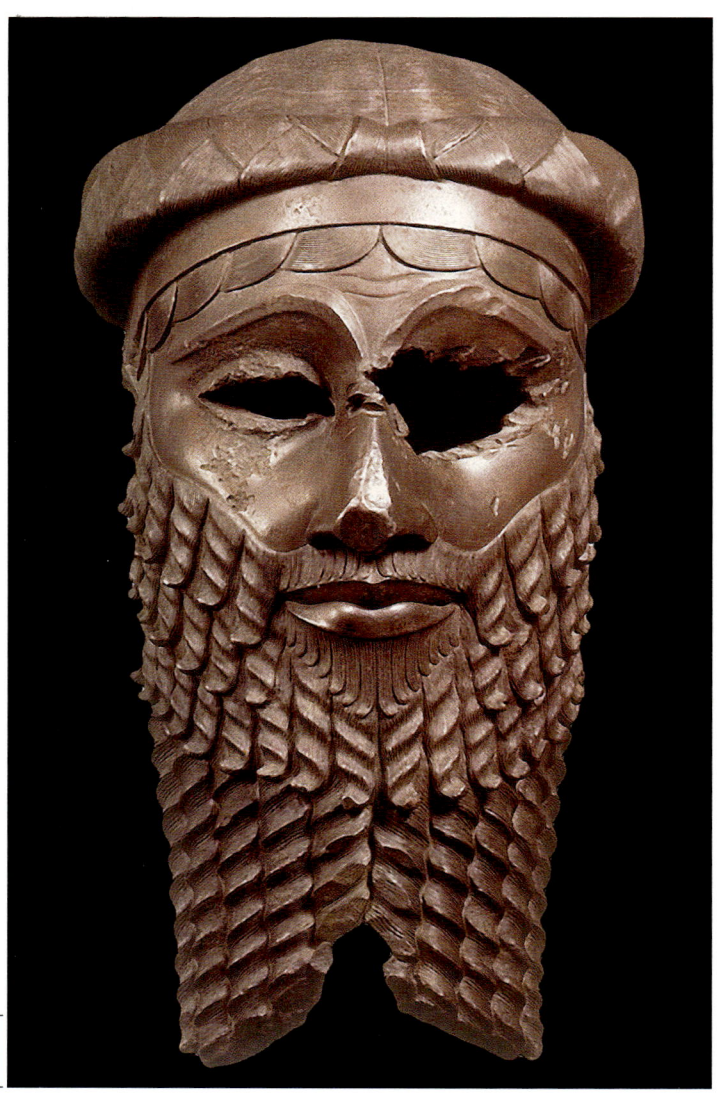

1 in.

**2-12** Head of an Akkadian ruler, from Nineveh (modern Kuyunjik), Iraq, ca. 2250–2200 BCE. Copper, 1′ 2⅜″ high. National Museum of Iraq, Baghdad.

The sculptor of this oldest known life-size hollow-cast head captured the distinctive features of the ruler while also displaying a keen sense of abstract pattern. Vandals damaged the head in antiquity.

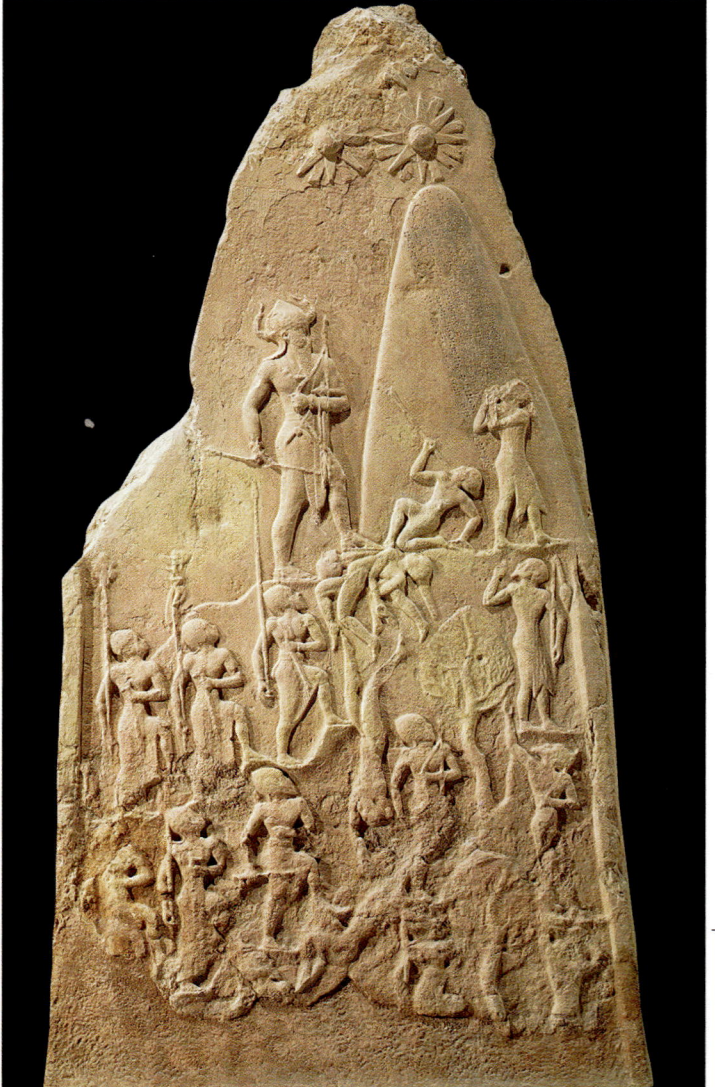

1 ft.

**2-13** Victory stele of Naram-Sin, from Susa, Iran, 2254–2218 BCE. Pink sandstone, 6′ 7″ high. Musée du Louvre, Paris.

To commemorate his conquest of the Lullubi, Naram-Sin set up this stele showing him leading his army up a mountain. The sculptor staggered the figures, abandoning the traditional register format.

## Enheduanna, Priestess and Poet

In the man's world of ancient Akkad, one woman stands out prominently—Enheduanna, daughter of King Sargon and priestess of the moon god Nanna at Ur. Her name appears in several inscriptions, and she was the author of a series of hymns in honor of the goddess Inanna. Enheduanna's is the oldest recorded name of a poet, male or female—indeed, the earliest known name of the author of any literary work in world history.

The most important surviving object associated with Enheduanna is the alabaster disk (FIG. 2-14) found in several fragments in the residence of the priestess of Nanna at Ur. The reverse bears a cuneiform inscription identifying Enheduanna as the "wife of Nanna" and "daughter of Sargon, king of the world." It also credits Enheduanna with erecting an altar to Nanna in his temple. The dedication of the relief to the moon god explains its unusual round format, which corresponds to the shape of the full moon. The front of the disk shows four figures approaching a four-story ziggurat. The first figure is a nude man who is either a priest or Enheduanna's assistant. He pours a libation into a plant stand. The second figure, taller than the rest and wearing the headgear of a priestess, is Enheduanna herself. She raises her right hand in a gesture of greeting and respect for the god. Two figures, probably female attendants, follow her.

Artworks created to honor women are rare in Mesopotamia and in the ancient world in general, but they are by no means unknown. The Sumerians, for example, buried Pu-abi of Ur in her own tomb filled with a treasure of jewelry, metal vessels, and musical instruments (FIG. 2-9), accompanied by 10 female retainers to attend her in the afterlife. The works created in honor of Pu-abi and Enheduanna are among the oldest known, but they pale in comparison with the monuments erected in the mid-second millennium BCE in honor of Queen Hatshepsut of Egypt (see "Hatshepsut," Chapter 3, page 69).

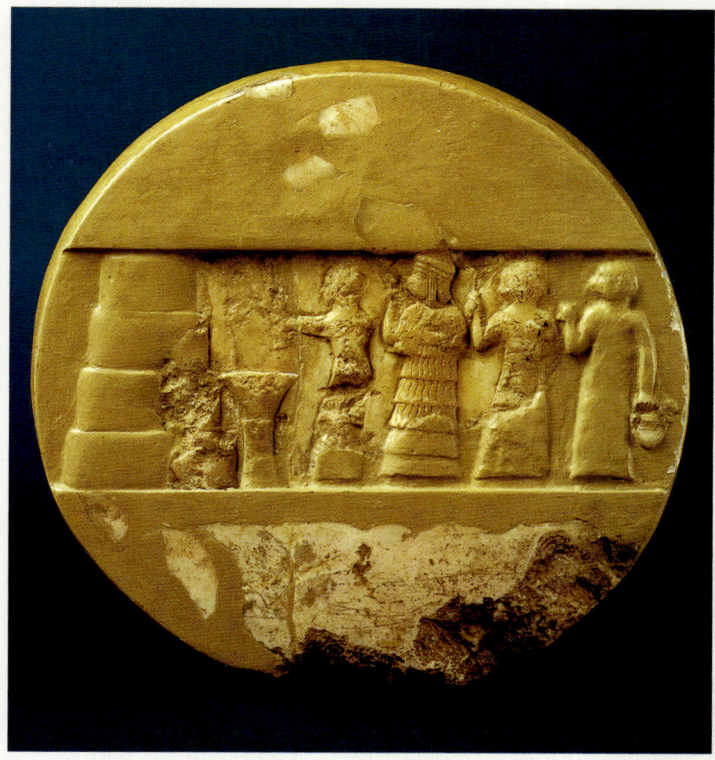

1 in.

**2-14** Votive disk of Enheduanna, from Ur (modern Tell Muqayyar), Iraq, ca. 2300–2275 BCE. Alabaster, diameter 10″. University of Pennsylvania Museum of Archaeology and Anthropology, Philadelphia.

Enheduanna, daughter of Sargon of Akkad and priestess of Nanna at Ur, is the first author whose name is known. She is the tallest figure on this votive disk, which she dedicated to the moon god.

---

coiffure's triangles, lozenges, and overlapping disks of hair and the great arching eyebrows that give such character to the portrait reveal the sculptor was also sensitive to formal pattern.

No less remarkable is the fact this is a life-size, hollow-cast metal sculpture (see "Hollow-Casting Life-Size Bronze Statues," Chapter 5, page 130), one of the earliest known. The head demonstrates the bronze-worker's sophisticated skill in casting and polishing copper and in engraving the details. The portrait is the oldest known monumental work of hollow-cast sculpture.

**NARAM-SIN STELE** The godlike sovereignty the kings of Akkad claimed is also evident in the victory stele (FIG. **2-13**) Naram-Sin set up at Sippar. The stele commemorates the Akkadian ruler's defeat of the Lullubi, a people of the Iranian mountains to the east. It carries two inscriptions, one in honor of Naram-Sin and one naming the Elamite king who captured Sippar in 1157 BCE and took the stele as booty back to Susa in southwestern Iran (MAP 2-1), the stele's findspot. The sculptor depicted Naram-Sin leading his army up the slopes of a wooded mountain. His routed enemies fall, flee, die, or beg for mercy. The king stands alone, far taller than his men, treading on the bodies of two of the fallen Lullubi. He wears the

horned helmet signifying divinity—the first time a king appears as a god in Mesopotamian art. At least three favorable stars (the stele is damaged at the top) shine on his triumph.

By storming the mountain, Naram-Sin seems also to be scaling the ladder to the heavens, the same conceit that lies behind the great Mesopotamian ziggurats. His troops march up the mountain behind him in orderly files, suggesting the discipline and organization of the king's forces. In contrast, his enemies are in disarray, depicted in a great variety of postures. One falls headlong down the mountainside. The Akkadian artist adhered to older conventions in many details, especially by portraying the king and his soldiers in composite views and by placing a frontal two-horned helmet on Naram-Sin's profile head. But the sculptor showed daring innovation in creating a landscape setting for the story and placing the figures on successive tiers within that landscape. For the first time, an artist rejected the standard Mesopotamian format of telling a story in a series of horizontal registers, the compositional formula that had been the rule for a millennium. The traditional frieze format was the choice, however, for an alabaster disk (FIG. **2-14**) that is in other respects an equally unique find (see "Enheduanna, Priestess and Poet," above).

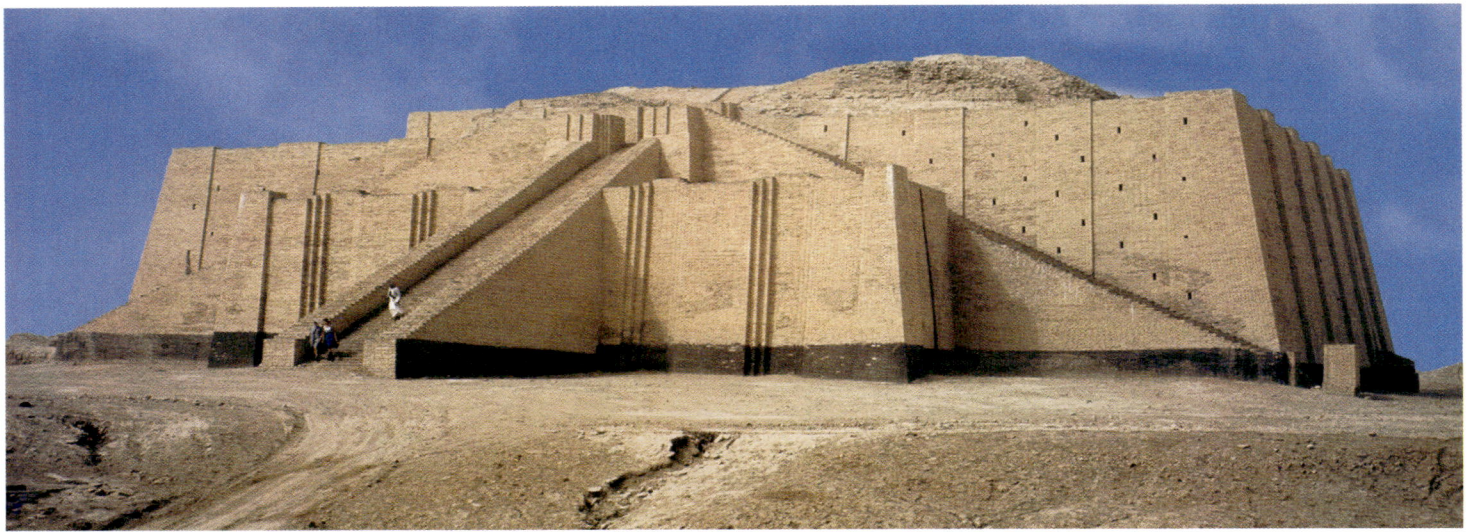

**2-15** Ziggurat (looking southwest), Ur (modern Tell Muqayyar), Iraq, ca. 2100 BCE.

The Ur ziggurat is one of the largest in Mesopotamia. It has three (restored) ramplike stairways of a hundred steps each that originally ended at a gateway to a brick temple, which does not survive.

## Third Dynasty of Ur

Around 2150 BCE, a mountain people, the Gutians, brought an end to Akkadian power. The cities of Sumer, however, soon united in response to the alien presence, drove the Gutians out of Mesopotamia, and established a Neo-Sumerian state ruled by the kings of Ur. Historians call this period the Neo-Sumerian age or the Third Dynasty of Ur.

**ZIGGURAT, UR** The most imposing extant Neo-Sumerian monument is the ziggurat (FIG. **2-15**) at Ur. One of the largest ever erected, with a massive mud-brick base 50 feet high, it is about a millennium later than Uruk's more modest White Temple (FIGS. 2-2 and 2-3). The Neo-Sumerian builders used baked bricks laid in bitumen, an asphaltlike substance, for the facing of the entire monument. (Today, most of the bricks are part of a modern reconstruction.) Three ramplike stairways of a hundred steps each converge on a tower-flanked gateway. From there another flight of steps (not restored) probably led to the temple proper, which does not survive.

**GUDEA OF LAGASH** Of all the preserved sculptures of the Third Dynasty of Ur, the most conspicuous are those portraying Gudea, the ensi of Lagash around 2100 BCE (see "The Piety of Gudea," page 43). His statues show him seated (FIG. **2-16**) or standing (FIG. **2-17**), hands usually tightly clasped, head shaven, sometimes wearing a brimmed sheepskin hat, and always dressed in a long garment that leaves one shoulder and arm exposed. He has a youthful face with large, arching, herringbone-patterned eyebrows framing wide-open eyes. Gudea was zealous in granting the gods their due, and the numerous statues he commissioned are an enduring testimony to his piety—and to his wealth and pride. All his portraits are of polished diorite, a rare and costly dark stone that had to be imported from present-day Oman. Diorite is also extremely hard and difficult to carve. Underscoring the prestige of the material—which in turn lent prestige to Gudea's portraits—is an inscription on one of his statues: "This statue has not been made from silver nor from lapis lazuli, nor from copper nor from lead, nor yet from bronze; it is made of diorite."

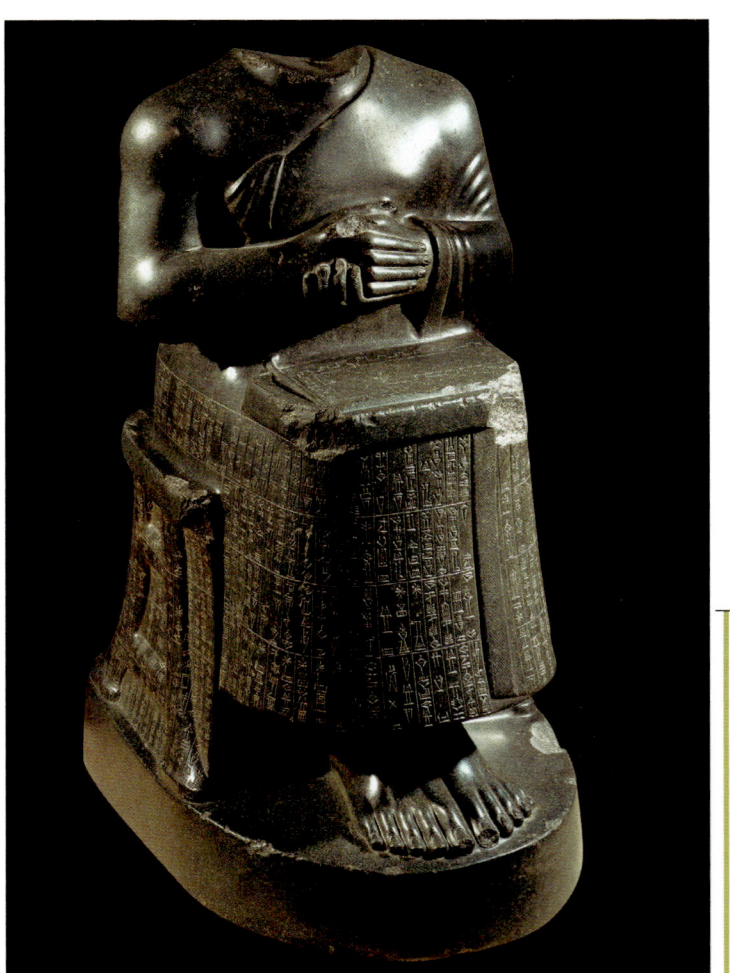

1 ft.

**2-16** Gudea seated, holding the plan of a temple, from Girsu (modern Telloh), Iraq, ca. 2100 BCE. Diorite, 2′ 5″ high. Musée du Louvre, Paris.

Gudea built or rebuilt many temples and placed statues of himself in all of them. The inscription on this seated portrait states that Gudea has on his lap a plan of the new temple he erected to Ningirsu.

# The Piety of Gudea

A central figure of the Neo-Sumerian age was Gudea of Lagash. Nearly two dozen portraits of him survive. All stood in temples where they could render perpetual service to the gods and intercede with the divine powers on his behalf. Although a powerful ruler, Gudea rejected the regal trappings of Sargon of Akkad and his successors, as well as their pretensions of divinity, in favor of a return to the Sumerian model of the ruler as the agent of the gods in the service of his people. Gudea's portraits follow the votive tradition of the Eshnunna (FIG. 2-6) and Mari (FIG. 2-6A) statuettes. Like the earlier examples, many of his statues bear inscriptions with messages to the gods of Sumer. One from Girsu says, "I am the shepherd loved by my king [Ningirsu, the god of Girsu]; may my life be prolonged." Another, also from Girsu, as if in answer to the first, says, "Gudea, the builder of the temple, has been given life." Some of the inscriptions clarify why Gudea was portrayed as he was. For example, his large chest is a sign the gods have given him fullness of life, and his muscular arms reveal his god-given strength. Other inscriptions explain that his large eyes signify that his gaze is perpetually fixed on the gods (compare FIG. 2-6).

Gudea built or rebuilt, at great cost, all the temples in which he placed his statues. One characteristic portrait (FIG. 2-16) depicts the pious ruler of Lagash seated with his hands clasped in front of him in a gesture of prayer. But the statue is unique because Gudea has a temple plan drawn on a tablet on his lap. It is the plan for a new temple dedicated to Ningirsu. Gudea buried accounts of his building enterprises in the temple foundations. The surviving texts describe how the Neo-Sumerians prepared and purified the sites, obtained the materials, and dedicated the completed temples. They also record Gudea's dreams of the gods asking him to erect temples in their honor, promising him prosperity if he fulfilled his duty. In one of these dreams, Ningirsu addresses Gudea:

> When, O faithful shepherd Gudea, thou shalt have started work for me on Erinnu, my royal abode [Ningirsu's new temple], I will call up in heaven a humid wind. It shall bring the abundance from on high. . . . All the great fields will bear for thee; dykes and canals will swell for thee; . . . good weight of wool will be given in thy time.*

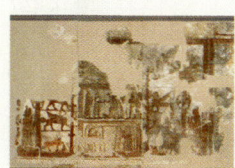

2-17A Investiture of Zimri-Lim, Mari, ca. 1775–1760 BCE.

One of Gudea's portraits (FIG. 2-17) differs from the rest in depicting the ensi holding a jar from which water flows freely in two streams, one running down each side of his cloak. Fish swim in the coursing water. In Mesopotamian art, gods and goddesses often hold similar overflowing vessels (FIG. 2-17A), which symbolize the prosperity they bring to their people. This small statue (less than half life-size) is the only known instance in which a Mesopotamian ruler appears as the source of the prosperity. For that reason and because the statue is made of calcite instead of the costly imported diorite used for Gudea's other portraits (FIG. 2-16), some scholars have questioned the authenticity of this piece. But the cuneiform inscription, which states that Gudea dedicated the statue in the temple he built in honor of the goddess Geshtinanna, the divine interpreter of dreams, is genuine, and so too must be the statue.

*Translated by Thorkild Jacobsen, in Henri Frankfort, *The Art and Architecture of the Ancient Orient,* 5th ed. (New Haven, Conn.: Yale University Press, 1996), 98.

2-17 Gudea standing, holding an overflowing water jar, from the Temple of Geshtinanna, Girsu (modern Telloh), Iraq, ca. 2100 BCE. Calcite, 2′ 3/8″ high. Musée du Louvre, Paris.

The overflowing water jar that Gudea holds symbolizes the prosperity he brings to the people of Lagash. In Mesopotamian art, normally only gods and goddesses are the sources of life-giving water.

1 ft.

## Babylon

The resurgence of Sumer was short-lived. The last of the kings of the Third Dynasty of Ur fell at the hands of the Elamites, who ruled the territory east of the Tigris River. In the following two centuries, the traditional Mesopotamian political pattern of several independent city-states existing side by side reemerged.

HAMMURABI Babylon was one of those city-states until its most powerful king, Hammurabi (r. 1792–1750 BCE), reestablished a centralized government in southern Mesopotamia in the area known as Babylonia, after its chief city. Perhaps the most renowned king in Mesopotamian history, Hammurabi was famous for his conquests. But he is best known today for his laws (FIG. 2-18),

# Hammurabi's Laws

In the early 18th century BCE, the Babylonian king Hammurabi formulated a set of nearly 300 laws for his people. At the time, parts of Europe were still in the Stone Age. Even in Greece, it was more than a thousand years later that Draco provided Athens with its first comprehensive law code. Two earlier sets of Sumerian laws survive in part, but Hammurabi's laws are the only ones known in great detail, thanks to the chance survival of a tall black-basalt stele (FIG. 2-18) that the Elamites carried off as booty to Susa in 1157 BCE, together with the Naram-Sin stele (FIG. 2-13). At the top is a representation in high relief of Hammurabi in the presence of Shamash, the flame-shouldered sun god. The king raises his hand in respect. The god extends to Hammurabi the rod and ring that symbolize authority. (Ishtar presents Hammurabi's contemporary, Zimri-Lim, with the same emblems of power in a mural painting [FIG. 2-18A] in that king's palace at Mari.) The symbols are builders' tools—measuring rods and coiled rope—and connote the ruler's capacity to build the social order and to measure people's lives, that is, to render judgments and enforce the laws spelled out on the stele. The collection of Hammurabi's judicial pronouncements is inscribed on the Susa stele in Akkadian in 3,500 lines of cuneiform characters. Hammurabi's laws governed all aspects of Babylonian life, from commerce and property to murder and theft to marital infidelity, inheritances, and the treatment of slaves.

Here is a small sample of the infractions described and the penalties imposed, which vary with the person's standing in society and notably deal with the rights and crimes of women as well as men:

▌ If a man puts out the eye of another man, his eye shall be put out.

▌ If he kills a man's slave, he shall pay one-third of a *mina*.

▌ If someone steals property from a temple, he will be put to death, as will the person who receives the stolen goods.

▌ If a married woman dies before bearing any sons, her dowry shall be repaid to her father, but if she gave birth to sons, the dowry shall belong to them.

▌ If a man strikes a freeborn woman so that she loses her unborn child, he shall pay ten *shekels* for her loss. If the woman dies, his daughter shall be put to death.

▌ If a man is guilty of incest with his daughter, he shall be exiled.

Hammurabi's stele is noteworthy artistically as well. The sculptor depicted Shamash in the familiar convention of combined front and side views but with two important exceptions. His great headdress with its four pairs of horns is in true profile so that only four, not all eight, of the horns are visible. Also, the artist seems to have tentatively explored the notion of *foreshortening*—a device for suggesting depth by representing a figure or object at an angle, instead of frontally or in profile. Shamash's beard is a series of diagonal rather than horizontal lines, suggesting its recession from the picture plane. The sculptor also depicted the god's throne at an angle.

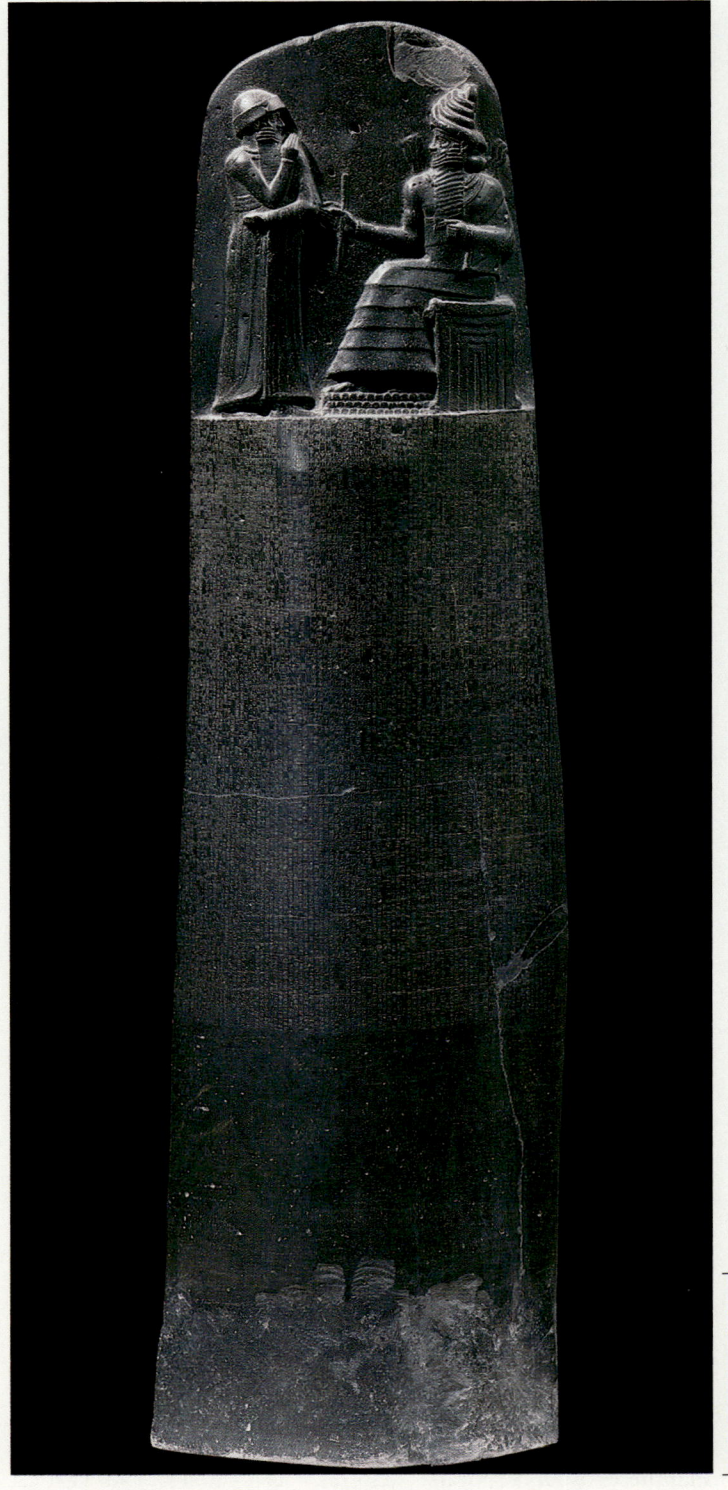

**2-18** Stele with the laws of Hammurabi, from Susa, Iran, ca. 1780 BCE. Basalt, 7′ 4″ high. Musée du Louvre, Paris. ◼◀

Crowning the stele recording Hammurabi's laws is a representation of the flame-shouldered sun god Shamash extending to the Babylonian king the symbols of his authority to govern and judge.

which prescribed penalties for everything from adultery and murder to the cutting down of a neighbor's trees (see "Hammurabi's Laws," page 44).

## Elam

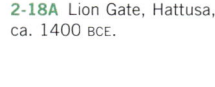

2-18A Lion Gate, Hattusa, ca. 1400 BCE.

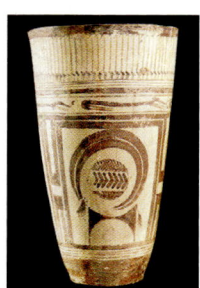

2-19A Beaker with animal decoration, Susa, ca. 4000 BCE.

The Babylonian Empire toppled in the face of an onslaught by the Hittites, an Anatolian people whose heavily fortified capital was at Hattusa (FIG. **2-18A**) near modern Boghazköy, Turkey. After sacking Babylon around 1595 BCE, the Hittites abandoned Mesopotamia and returned to their homeland, leaving Babylon in the hands of the Kassites. To the east of Babylon was Elam, which appears in the Bible as early as Genesis 10:22. Archaeologists have discovered painted pottery (FIG. **2-19A**) at the Elamite capital of Susa in present-day Iran dating as far back as the Neolithic period. Elam reached the height of its political and military power during the second half of the second millennium BCE. At that time the Elamites were strong enough to plunder Babylonia and to carry off the stelae of Naram-Sin (FIG. 2-13) and Hammurabi (FIG. 2-18) and display them as war booty in Susa.

**NAPIR-ASU** In the ruins of Susa, archaeologists discovered a life-size bronze-and-copper statue (FIG. **2-19**) of Queen Napir-Asu, wife of one of the most powerful Elamite kings, Untash-Napirisha (r. ca. 1345–ca. 1305 BCE). The statue weighs 3,760 pounds even in its fragmentary and mutilated state, because the sculptor, incredibly, cast the statue with a solid bronze core inside a hollow-cast copper shell. The bronze core increased the cost of the statue enormously, but the queen wished her portrait to be a permanent, immovable votive offering in the temple where archaeologists found it. In fact, the Elamite inscription on the queen's skirt explicitly asks the gods to protect the statue:

> He who would seize my statue, who would smash it, who would destroy its inscription, who would erase my name, may he be smitten by the curse of [the gods], that his name shall become extinct, that his offspring be barren. . . . This is Napir-Asu's offering.[1]

Napir-Asu's portrait thus falls within the votive tradition dating back to the third-millennium BCE Eshnunna (FIG. 2-6) and Mari (FIG. 2-6A) figurines. In the Elamite statue, the Mesopotamian instinct for cylindrical volume is again evident. The tight silhouette, strict frontality, and firmly crossed hands held close to the body are all enduring characteristics common to the Sumerian statuettes. Yet within these rigid conventions of form and pose, the Elamite artist incorporated features based on close observation. The sculptor conveyed the feminine softness of arm and bust, the grace and elegance of the long-fingered hands, the supple bend of the wrist, the ring and bracelets, and the gown's patterned fabric. The loss of the head is especially unfortunate. The figure presents a portrait of the ideal queen. The hands crossed over the belly may allude to fertility and the queen's role in assuring peaceful dynastic succession.

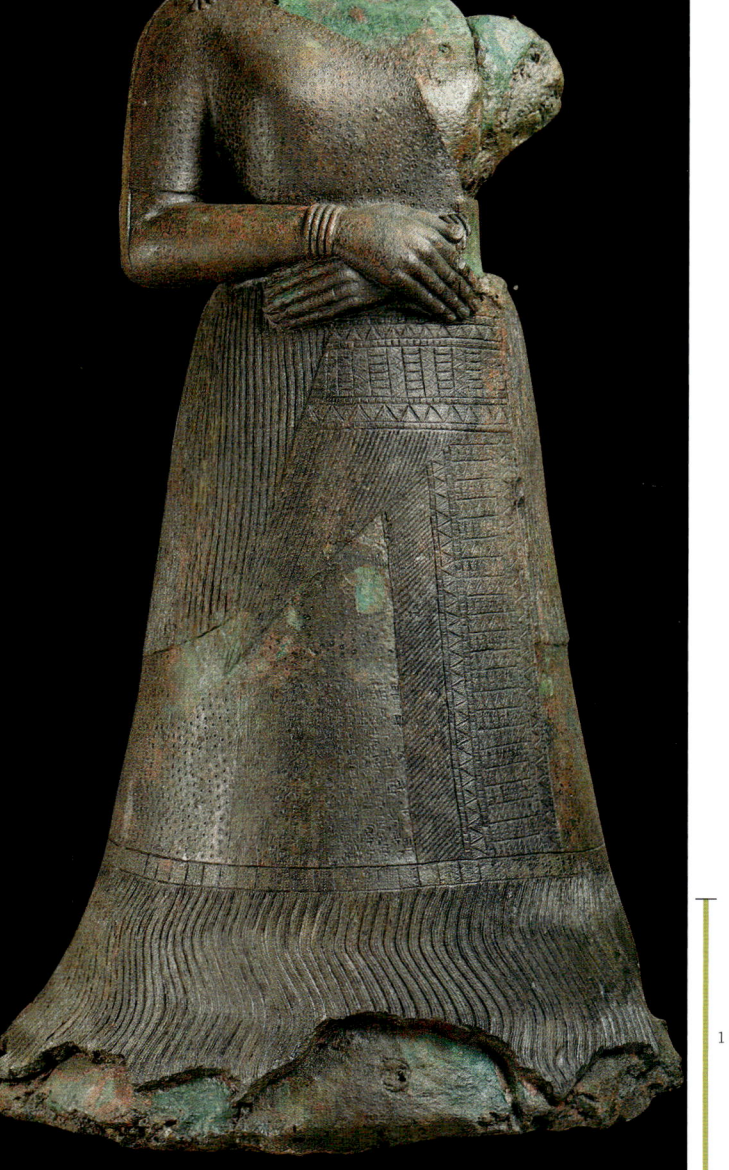

1 ft.

**2-19** Statue of Queen Napir-Asu, from Susa, Iran, ca. 1350–1300 BCE. Bronze and copper, 4′ 2¾″ high. Musée du Louvre, Paris.

This life-size bronze-and-copper statue of the wife of a powerful Elamite king weighs 3,760 pounds. The queen wanted her portrait to stand in a temple at Susa as an immovable votive offering to the deity.

## Assyria

During the first half of the first millennium BCE, the fearsome Assyrians vanquished the various warfaring peoples that succeeded the Babylonians and Hittites, including the Elamites, whose capital of Susa they sacked in 641 BCE. The Assyrians took their name from Assur, the city on the Tigris River in northern Iraq dedicated to the god Ashur. At the height of their power, the Assyrians ruled an empire that extended from the Tigris River to the Nile and from the Persian Gulf to Asia Minor.

**PALACE OF SARGON II** The Assyrian kings cultivated an image of themselves as merciless to anyone who dared oppose them but forgiving to those who submitted to their will. Ever mindful of

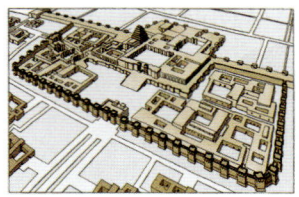

possible attack, the Assyrians constructed their palaces as fortified citadels. A reconstruction on paper of the palace that Sargon II (r. 721–705 BCE) built at Dur Sharrukin (FIG. 2-20A) gives a good idea of the original appearance of Assyrian royal citadels.

Guarding the gate to Sargon's palace were colossal limestone monsters (FIG. 2-20), which the Assyrians probably called *lamassu*. These winged, man-headed bulls served to ward off the king's enemies. The task of moving and installing these immense stone sculptures was so daunting that several reliefs in the palace of Sargon's successor celebrate the feat, showing scores of men dragging lamassu figures with the aid of ropes and sledges. The Assyrian lamassu sculptures are partly in the round, but the sculptor nonetheless conceived them as high reliefs on adjacent sides of a corner. They combine the front view of the animal at rest with the side view of it in motion. Seeking to present a complete picture of the lamassu from both the front and the side, the sculptor gave the monster five legs—two seen from the front, four seen from the side. This sculpture, then, is yet another case of early artists' providing a conceptual picture of an animal or person and of all its important parts, as opposed to an optical view of the lamassu as it would really stand in space.

## PALACE OF ASHURNASIRPAL II

For their palace walls, the Assyrian kings commissioned extensive series of mural paintings and narrative reliefs exalting royal power. Unfortunately, few Assyrian paintings exist today. A notable exception is the depiction (FIG. 2-21) of King Ashurnasirpal II (r. 883–859 BCE) and his retinue paying homage to the gods. It comes from the northwest palace at Kalhu. The painting medium is glazed brick, a much more durable format than direct painting on plastered mud-brick walls, the technique used a millennium earlier in Zimri-Lim's palace at Mari (FIG. 2-17A). The Assyrian painter first applied lines and colors to a clay panel and then baked the clay in a kiln, fusing the colors to the clay.

The Kalhu panel shows Ashurnasirpal—his name means "Ashur guards the heir"—delicately holding a cup. With it, he will make a libation in honor of the protective Assyrian gods. The artist represented the king as taller than everyone else, befitting his rank, and rendered the figures in outline, lavishing much attention on the patterns of the rich fabrics they wear. The color palette is limited to yellow and brown. The king and the attendant behind him are in consistent profile view, but the painter adhered to the convention of showing the eye from the front in a profile head. Painted scenes such as this hint at the original appearance (before the color disappeared) of the stone reliefs (FIGS. 2-21 to 2-23) in Assyrian palaces, although the reliefs would have featured a wider range of hues than those available to the ceramic painter.

The degree of documentary detail in the Assyrian reliefs is without parallel in the ancient world before the Roman Empire (see Chapter 7). Ashurnasirpal's Kalhu palace also boasts one of the earliest and most extensive cycles of Assyrian relief sculptures. The painted gypsum reliefs sheathed the lower parts of the mud-brick palace walls below brightly colored plaster. Rich textiles on the floors contributed to the luxurious ambience. Every relief bore an inscription naming Ashurnasirpal and describing his accomplishments.

The relief illustrated here (FIG. 2-22) probably depicts an episode that occurred in 878 BCE when Ashurnasirpal drove his enemy's forces into the Euphrates River. Two Assyrian archers shoot arrows at the fleeing foe. Three enemy soldiers are in the water. One swims with an arrow in his back. The other two attempt to float to safety by inflating animal skins. Their destination is a fort where their compatriots await them. The artist showed the fort as if it were in the middle of the river, but it was, of course, on land, perhaps at some distance from where the escapees entered the water. The artist's purpose was to tell the story clearly and

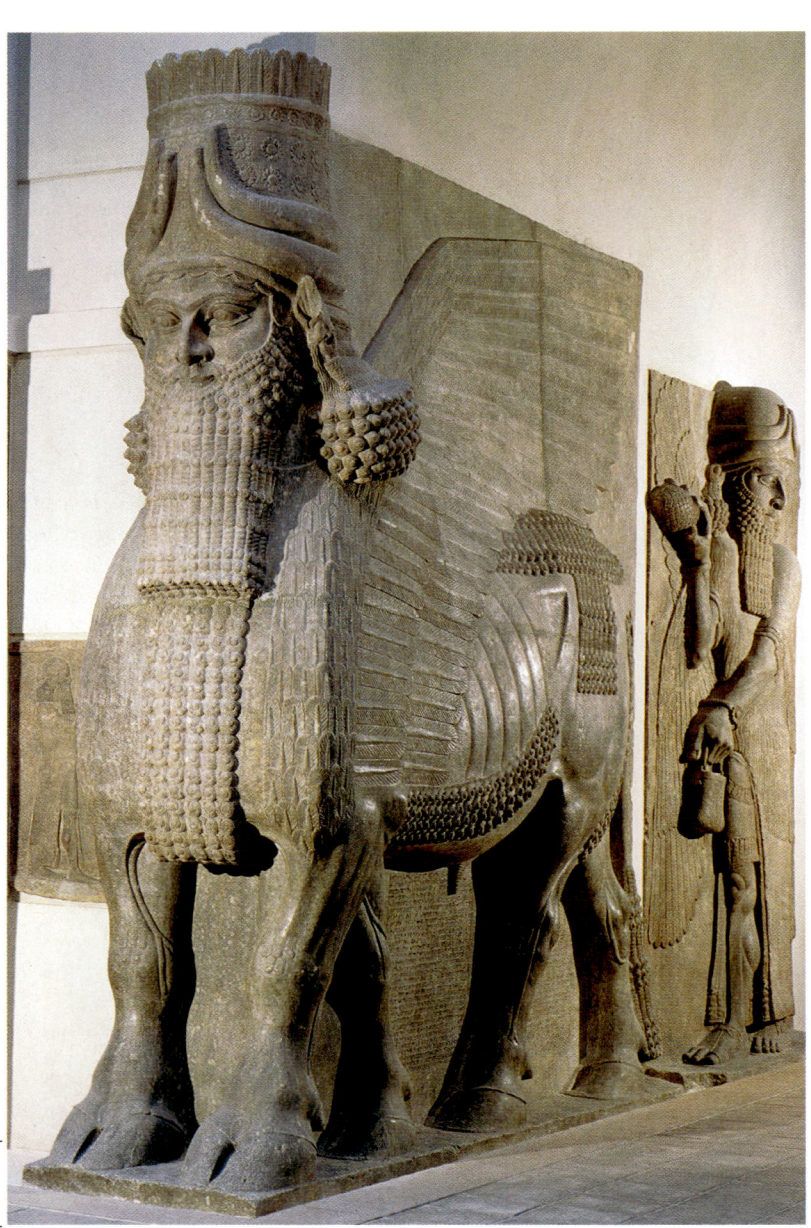

1 ft.

**2-20** Lamassu (man-headed winged bull), from the citadel of Sargon II, Dur Sharrukin (modern Khorsabad), Iraq, ca. 720–705 BCE. Limestone, 13′ 10″ high. Musée du Louvre, Paris.

Ancient sculptors insisted on complete views of animals. This four-legged composite monster that guarded an Assyrian palace has five legs—two when seen from the front and four in profile view.

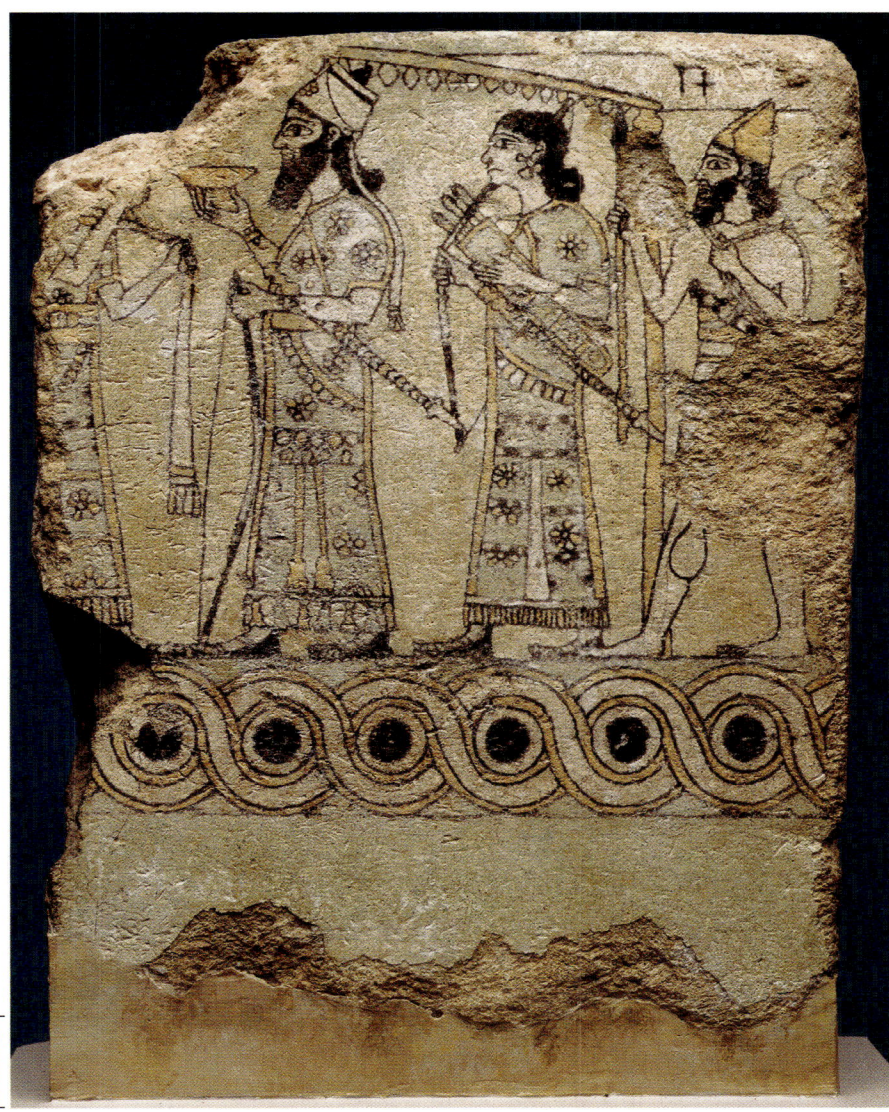

**2-21** Ashurnasirpal II with attendants and soldier, from the northwest palace of Ashurnasirpal II, Kalhu (modern Nimrud), Iraq, ca. 875–860 BCE. Glazed brick, 11¾″ high. British Museum, London.

Paintings on glazed bricks adorned the walls of Assyrian palaces. This rare example shows Ashurnasirpal II paying homage to the gods. The artist represented the king as taller than his attendants.

economically. Ancient sculptors and painters often compressed distances and enlarged the human actors so they would stand out from their environment. Literally interpreted, the defenders of the fort are too tall to walk through its archway. (Compare Naram-Sin and his men scaling a mountain, FIG. 2-13.) The sculptor also combined different viewpoints in the same frame, just as the figures are composites of frontal and profile views. The spectator views the river from above, and the men, trees, and fort from the side. The artist also made other adjustments for clarity. The archers' bowstrings are in front of their bodies but behind their heads in order not to hide their faces. (The men will snare their heads in their bows when they launch their arrows.) All these liberties with optical reality, however, result in a vivid and easily legible retelling of a decisive moment in the king's victorious campaign. That was the artist's primary goal.

**PALACE OF ASHURBANIPAL** Two centuries later, sculptors carved hunting reliefs for the Nineveh palace of the conqueror of Elamite Susa, Ashurbanipal (r. 668–627 BCE), whose name means "Ashur is creator of the son." The Greeks called him Sardanapalus, and the French painter Eugène Delacroix immortalized the Assyrian king in the 19th

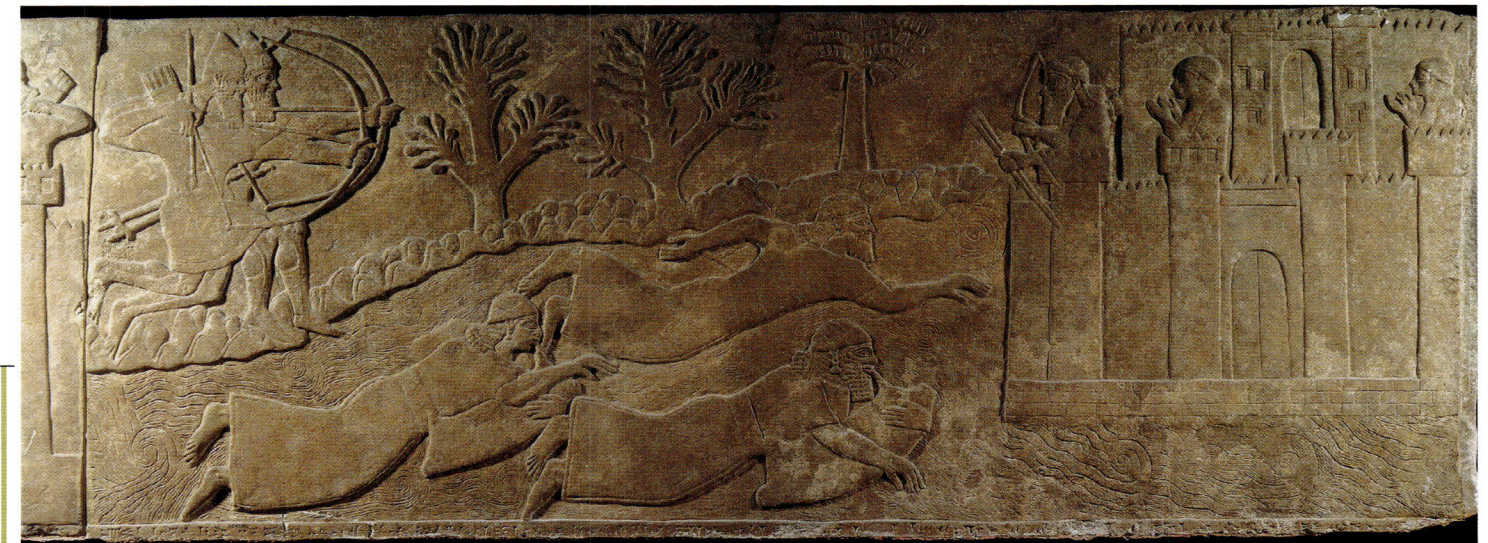

**2-22** Assyrian archers pursuing enemies, relief from the northwest palace of Ashurnasirpal II, Kalhu (modern Nimrud), Iraq, ca. 875–860 BCE. Gypsum, 2′ 10⅝″ high. British Museum, London.

Extensive reliefs exalting the king and recounting his great deeds have been found in several Assyrian palaces. This one depicts Ashurnasirpal II's archers driving the enemy into the Euphrates River.

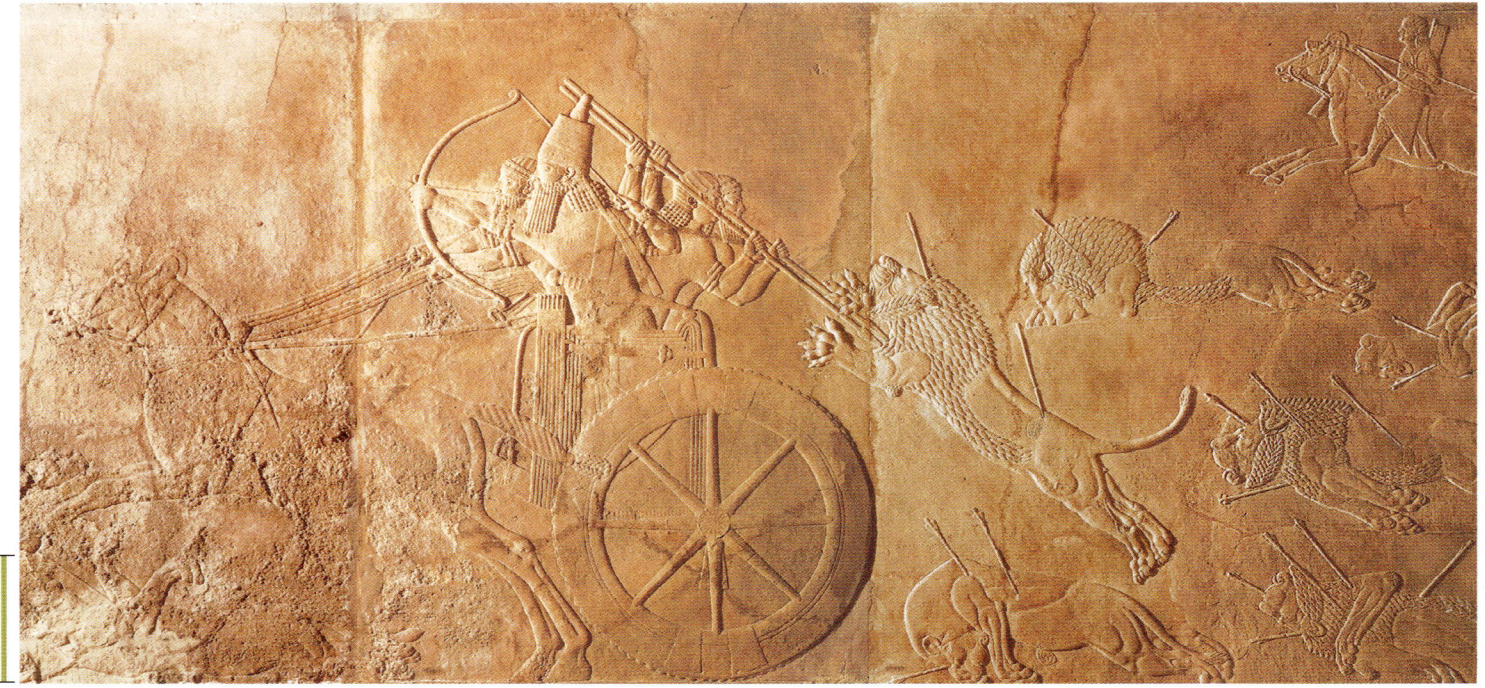

**2-23** Ashurbanipal hunting lions, relief from the north palace of Ashurbanipal, Nineveh (modern Kuyunjik), Iraq, ca. 645–640 BCE. Gypsum, 5′ 4″ high. British Museum, London.

In addition to ceremonial and battle scenes, the hunt was a common subject of Assyrian palace reliefs. The Assyrians viewed hunting and killing lions as manly royal virtues on a par with victory in warfare.

century in one of the most dramatic canvases (FIG. 27-15) of the Romantic era in Europe. The Assyrians, like many other societies before and after, regarded prowess in hunting as a manly virtue on a par with success in warfare. The royal hunt did not take place in the wild, however, but in a controlled environment, ensuring the king's safety and success. In FIG. **2-23**, lions released from cages in a large enclosed arena charge the king, who, in his chariot and protected by his attendants, thrusts a spear into a savage lion. The animal leaps at the king even though it already has two arrows in its body. All around the royal chariot is a pathetic trail of dead and dying animals, pierced by what appear to be far more arrows than needed to kill them. Blood streams from some of the lions, but they refuse to die. The artist brilliantly depicted the straining muscles, the swelling veins, the muzzles' wrinkled skin, and the flattened ears of the powerful and defiant beasts. Modern sympathies make this scene of carnage a kind of heroic tragedy, with the lions as protagonists. It is unlikely, however, that the king's artists had any intention other than to glorify their ruler by showing the king of men pitted against and repeatedly besting the king of beasts. Portraying Ashurbanipal's beastly foes as possessing courage and nobility as well as the power to kill made the king's accomplishments that much grander.

The Assyrian Empire was never very secure, and most of its kings had to fight revolts throughout Mesopotamia. Assyria's conquest of Elam in the seventh century BCE and frequent rebellions in Babylonia apparently overextended its resources. During the last years of Ashurbanipal's reign, the empire began to disintegrate. Under his successors, it collapsed from the simultaneous onslaught of the Medes from the east and the resurgent Babylonians from the south. Neo-Babylonian kings held sway over the former Assyrian Empire until the Persian conquest.

## Neo-Babylonia

The most renowned of the Neo-Babylonian kings was Nebuchadnezzar II (r. 605–562 BCE), whose exploits the biblical book of Daniel recounts. Nebuchadnezzar restored Babylon to its rank as one of the great cities of antiquity. The city's famous hanging gardens were counted among the Seven Wonders of the ancient world, and the Bible (Gen. 11:1–9) immortalized its enormous ziggurat as the Tower of Babel (see "Babylon, City of Wonders," page 49).

**ISHTAR GATE** Nebuchadnezzar's Babylon was a mud-brick city, but dazzling blue-glazed bricks faced the most important monuments, such as the Ishtar Gate (FIG. **2-24**), really a pair of gates, one of which has been restored and installed in a German museum. The Ishtar Gate consists of a large *arcuated* (*arch*-shaped) opening flanked by towers, and features glazed bricks with reliefs of animals, real and imaginary. The Babylonian builders molded and glazed each brick separately, then set them in proper sequence on the wall. On the Ishtar Gate, profile figures of Marduk and Nabu's dragon and Adad's bull alternate. Lining the processional way leading up to the gate were reliefs of Ishtar's sacred lion, glazed in yellow, brown, and red against a blue ground.

## PERSIA

Although Nebuchadnezzar—the "king of kings" in the book of Daniel (2:37)—had boasted in an inscription that he "caused a mighty wall to circumscribe Babylon . . . so that the enemy who would do evil would not threaten," Cyrus of Persia (r. 559–529 BCE) captured the city in the sixth century. Cyrus, who may have been descended from an Elamite line, was the founder of the Achaemenid dynasty and traced his ancestry back to a mythical King Achaemenes.

# Babylon, City of Wonders

The uncontested list of the Seven Wonders of the ancient world was not codified until the 16th century. But already in the second century BCE, Antipater of Sidon, a Greek poet, compiled a roster of seven must-see monuments, including six of the seven later Wonders. All of the Wonders were of colossal size and constructed at great expense. The oldest were of great antiquity, nearly 2,500 years old in Antipater's day: the pyramids of Gizeh (FIG. 3-7), which he described as "man-made mountains." Only one site on Antipater's list could boast two Wonders: Babylon, with its "hanging gardens" and "impregnable walls." Later list makers preferred to distribute the Seven Wonders among seven different cities. Most of these Wonders date to Greek times—the Temple of Artemis at Ephesos, with its 60-foot-tall columns; Phidias's colossal gold-and-ivory statue of Zeus at Olympia; the "Mausoleum" at Halikarnassos, the gigantic tomb (FIG. 5-64B) of the fourth-century BCE ruler Mausolus; the Colossus of Rhodes, a bronze statue of the Greek sun god 110 feet tall; and the lighthouse at Alexandria, perhaps the tallest building in the ancient world. The Babylonian gardens were the only Wonder in the category of "landscape architecture."

Several ancient texts describe Babylon's wondrous gardens. Quintus Curtius Rufus reported in the mid-first century CE:

On the top of the citadel are the hanging gardens, a wonder celebrated in the tales of the Greeks. . . . Columns of stone were set up to sustain the whole work, and on these was laid a floor of squared blocks, strong enough to hold the earth which is thrown upon it to a great depth, as well as the water with which they irrigate the soil; and the structure supports trees of such great size that the thickness of their trunks equals a measure of eight cubits [about twelve feet]. They tower to a height of fifty feet, and they yield as much

fruit as if they were growing in their native soil. . . . To those who look upon [the trees] from a distance, real woods seem to be overhanging their native mountains.*

Not qualifying as a Wonder, but in some ways no less impressive, was Babylon's Marduk ziggurat, the biblical Tower of Babel, erected by King Nebuchadnezzar, who also constructed Babylon's Ishtar Gate (FIG. 2-24). According to the Bible, humankind's arrogant desire to build a tower to Heaven angered God. The Lord put an end to it by causing the workers to speak different languages, preventing them from communicating with one another. The fifth-century BCE Greek historian Herodotus described the Babylonian temple complex:

In the middle of the sanctuary [of Marduk] has been built a solid tower . . . which supports another tower, which in turn supports another, and so on: there are eight towers in all. A stairway has been constructed to wind its way up the outside of all the towers; halfway up the stairway there is a shelter with benches to rest on, where people making the ascent can sit and catch their breath. In the last tower there is a huge temple. The temple contains a large couch, which is adorned with fine coverings and has a golden table standing beside it, but there are no statues at all standing there. . . . [The Babylonians] say that the god comes in person to the temple [compare the Sumerian notion of the temple as a "waiting room"] and rests on the couch; I do not believe this story myself.†

*Quintus Curtius 5.1.31–35. Translated by John C. Rolfe, *Quintus Curtius I* (Cambridge: Harvard University Press, 1971), 337–339.
† Herodotus 1.181–182. Translated by Robin Waterfield, *Herodotus: The Histories* (New York: Oxford University Press, 1998), 79–80.

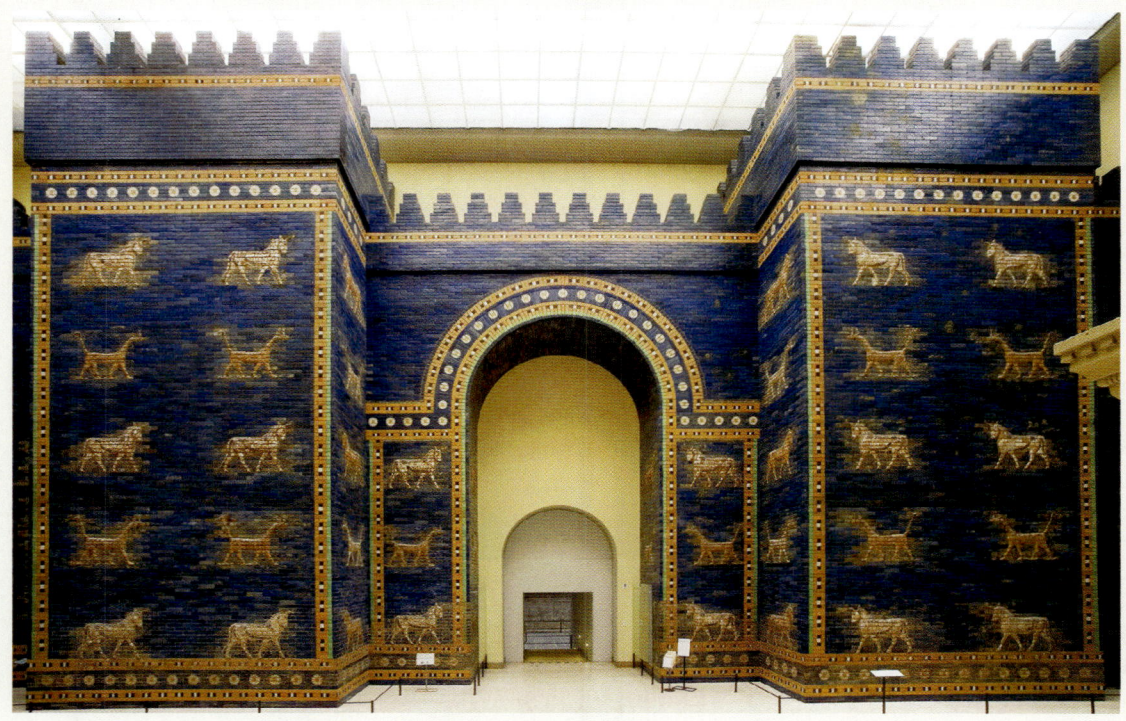

**2-24** Ishtar Gate (restored), Babylon, Iraq, ca. 575 BCE. Vorderasiatisches Museum, Staatliche Museen zu Berlin, Berlin.

Nebuchadnezzar II's Babylon was one of the ancient world's greatest cities and boasted two of the Seven Wonders. Its Ishtar Gate featured glazed-brick reliefs of Marduk and Nabu's dragon and Adad's bull.

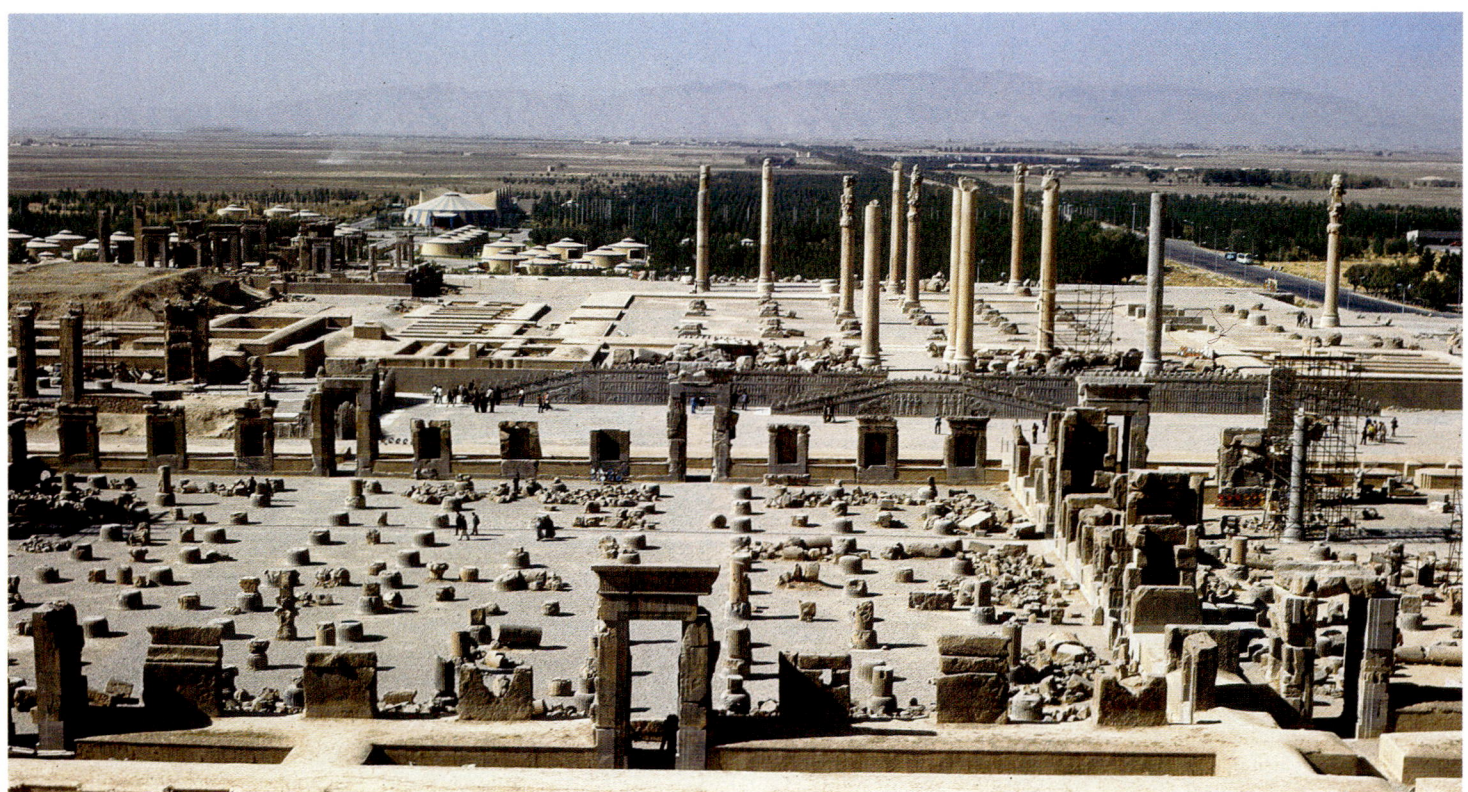

**2-25** Aerial view of Persepolis (looking west with the apadana in the background), Iran, ca. 521–465 BCE.

The heavily fortified complex of Persian royal buildings on a high plateau at Persepolis included a royal audience hall, or apadana, with 36 colossal columns topped by animal protomes (FIG. 2-26).

## Achaemenid Empire

Babylon was but one of the Achaemenids' conquests. Egypt fell to them in 525 BCE, and by 480 BCE they boasted the largest empire the world had yet known, extending from the Indus River in South Asia to the Danube River in northeastern Europe. If the Greeks had not succeeded in turning back the Persians in 479 BCE, they would have taken control of southeastern Europe as well. The Achaemenid line ended with the death of Darius III in 330 BCE, after his defeat at the hands of Alexander the Great (FIG. 5-70).

**PERSEPOLIS** The most important source of knowledge about Persian art and architecture is the ceremonial and administrative complex on the citadel at Persepolis (FIG. **2-25**), which the successors of Cyrus, Darius I (r. 522–486 BCE) and Xerxes (r. 486–465 BCE), built between 521 and 465 BCE. Situated on a high plateau, the heavily fortified complex of royal buildings stood on a wide platform overlooking the plain. Alexander the Great razed the site in a gesture symbolizing the destruction of Persian imperial power. Some said it was an act of revenge for the Persian sack of the Athenian Acropolis in 480 BCE (see Chapter 5). Nevertheless, even in ruins, the Persepolis citadel is impressive.

The approach to the citadel led through a monumental gateway called the Gate of All Lands, a reference to the harmony among the

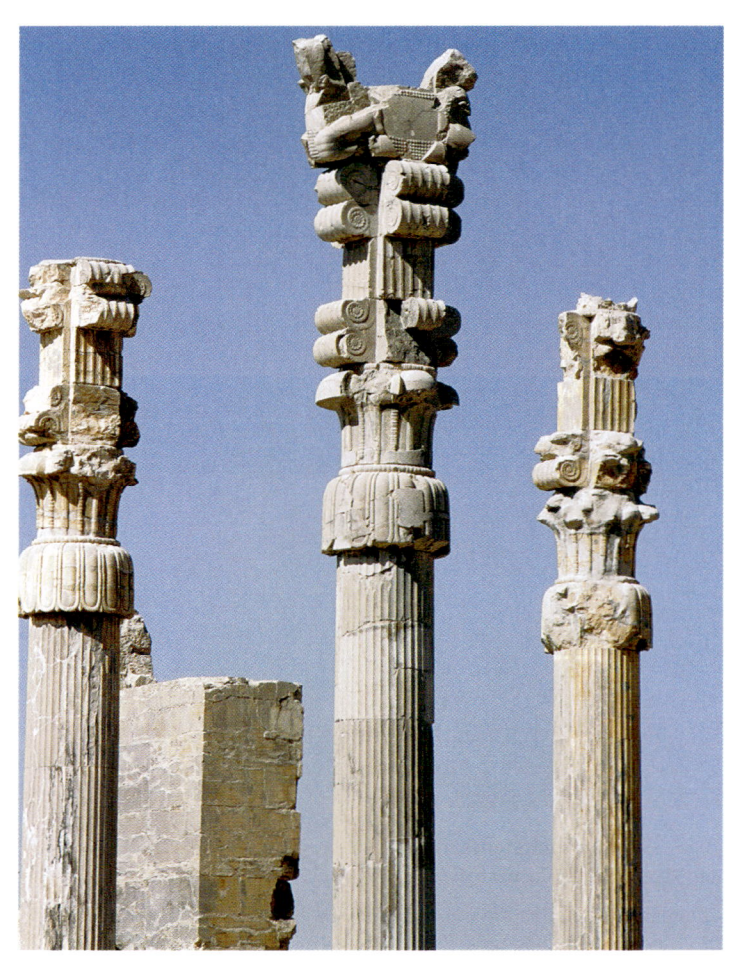

**2-26** Columns with animal protomes, from the apadana of the palace (FIG. 2-25), Persepolis, Iran, ca. 521–465 BCE.

The 64-foot columns of the Persepolis apadana drew on Greek, Egyptian, and Mesopotamian models but are unique in form. The back-to-back protomes of the capitals supported gigantic wood beams.

peoples of the vast Persian Empire. Assyrian-inspired colossal man-headed winged bulls flanked the great entrance. Broad ceremonial stairways provided access to the platform and the immense royal audience hall, or *apadana,* in which at least 10,000 guests could stand at one time. Although the hall had mud-brick walls, the floors were paved in stone or brick, and the apadana's chief feature—its forest of 36 colossal *columns* (FIG. 2-26)—was entirely of stone. The columns consisted of tall *bases* with a ring of palm leaves, *fluted* 57-foot *shafts,* and enormous *capitals* composed of double vertical *volutes* (see "Doric and Ionic Orders," Chapter 5, page 116, for the architectural terminology) topped by polished and painted back-to-back animal *protomes* (the head, forelegs, and part of the body). The columns are unique in form, but the designers drew on Greek, Egyptian, and Mesopotamian traditions.

The capitals with animal protomes in the Persepolis apadana are nearly 7 feet tall, bringing the total height of the columns to almost 64 feet. The animals—*griffins* (eagle-headed winged lions), bulls, lions, and composite man-headed bulls—vary from capital to capital. The Persepolis architect must have wanted to suggest that the Persian king had captured the fiercest animals and monsters to hold up the roof of his palace. The paired protomes form a U-shaped socket that held massive cedar beams (imported from Lebanon), which in turn supported a timber roof sealed with mud plaster. Animal protomes were also popular motifs for the luxurious tableware used to serve the Achaemenid king and his of-ficial guests. A preserved gold *rhyton* (conical pouring vessel) in the form of a winged lion (FIG. 2-26A) suggests the ostentatious wealth on display in Persian palaces.

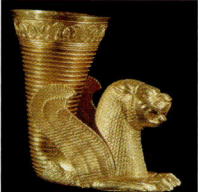

2-26A Gold rhyton, Hamadan, fifth to third century BCE.

The reliefs (FIG. 2-27) decorating the walls of the terrace and staircases leading to the apadana represent processions of royal guards, Persian nobles and dignitaries, and representatives from 23 subject nations, including Medes, Elamites, Babylonians, Egyptians, and Nubians, bringing tribute to the king. Every emissary wears a characteristic costume and carries a typical regional gift for the conqueror. The section of the procession reproduced here represents Persian nobles (in pleated skirts) and Medes wearing their distinctive round caps, knee-length tunics, and trousers. The carving of the Persepolis reliefs is technically superb, with subtly modeled surfaces and crisply chiseled details. Traces of color prove the reliefs were painted, and the original effect surely was more striking than it is today.

Although the Assyrian palace reliefs may have inspired those at Persepolis, the Persian sculptures differ in style. The forms are more rounded, and they project more from the background. Some of the details, notably the treatment of drapery folds, echo forms characteristic of Archaic Greek sculpture (compare FIG. 5-11), and Greek influence seems to be one of the many ingredients of Achaemenid style.

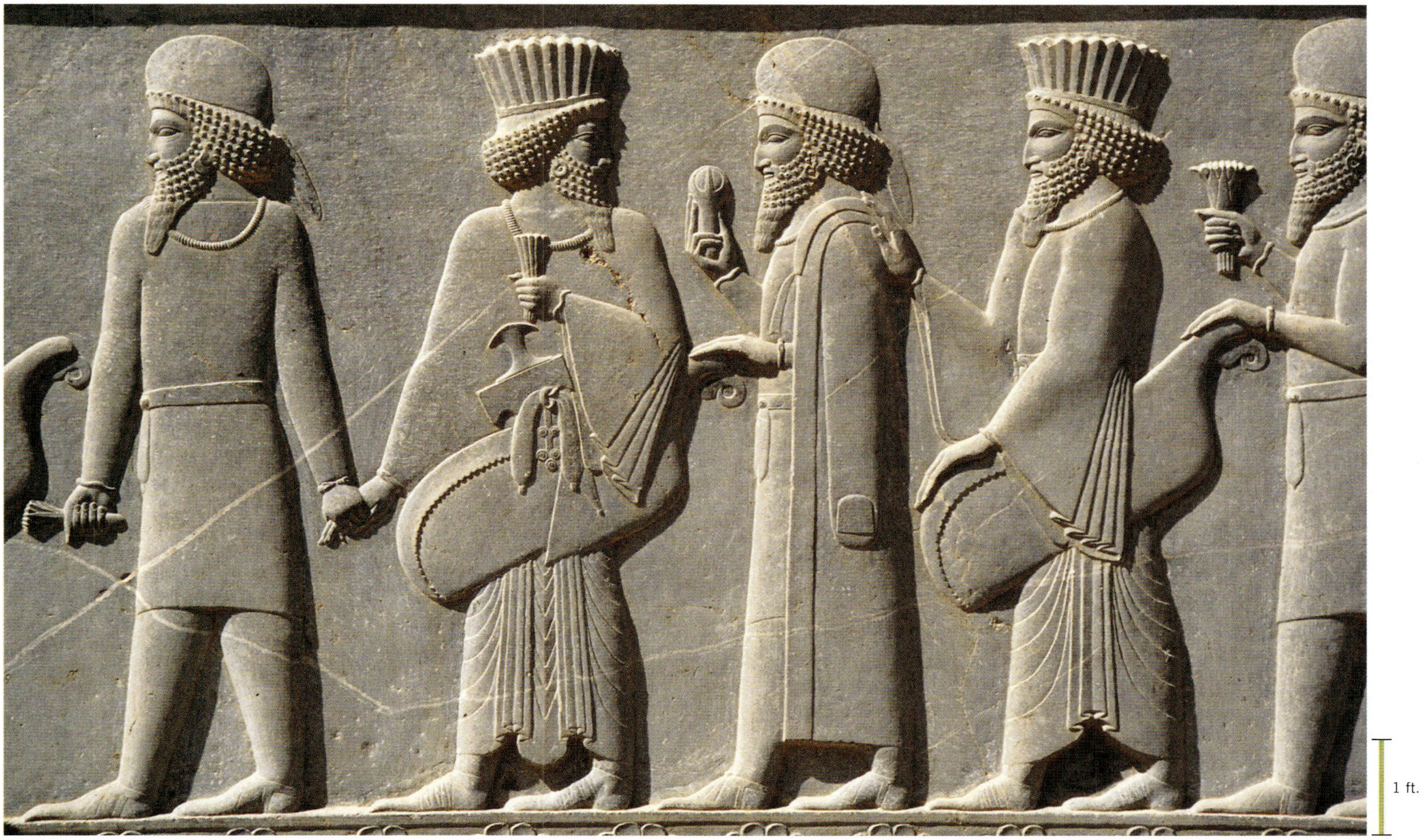

2-27 **Persians and Medes, detail of the processional frieze on the east side of the terrace of the apadana of the palace** (FIG. 2-25), **Persepolis, Iran, ca. 521–465 BCE. Limestone, 8′ 4″ high.**

The reliefs decorating the walls of the terrace and staircases leading up to the Persepolis apadana (FIG. 2-25) included depictions of representatives of 23 nations bringing tribute to the Persian king.

1 ft.

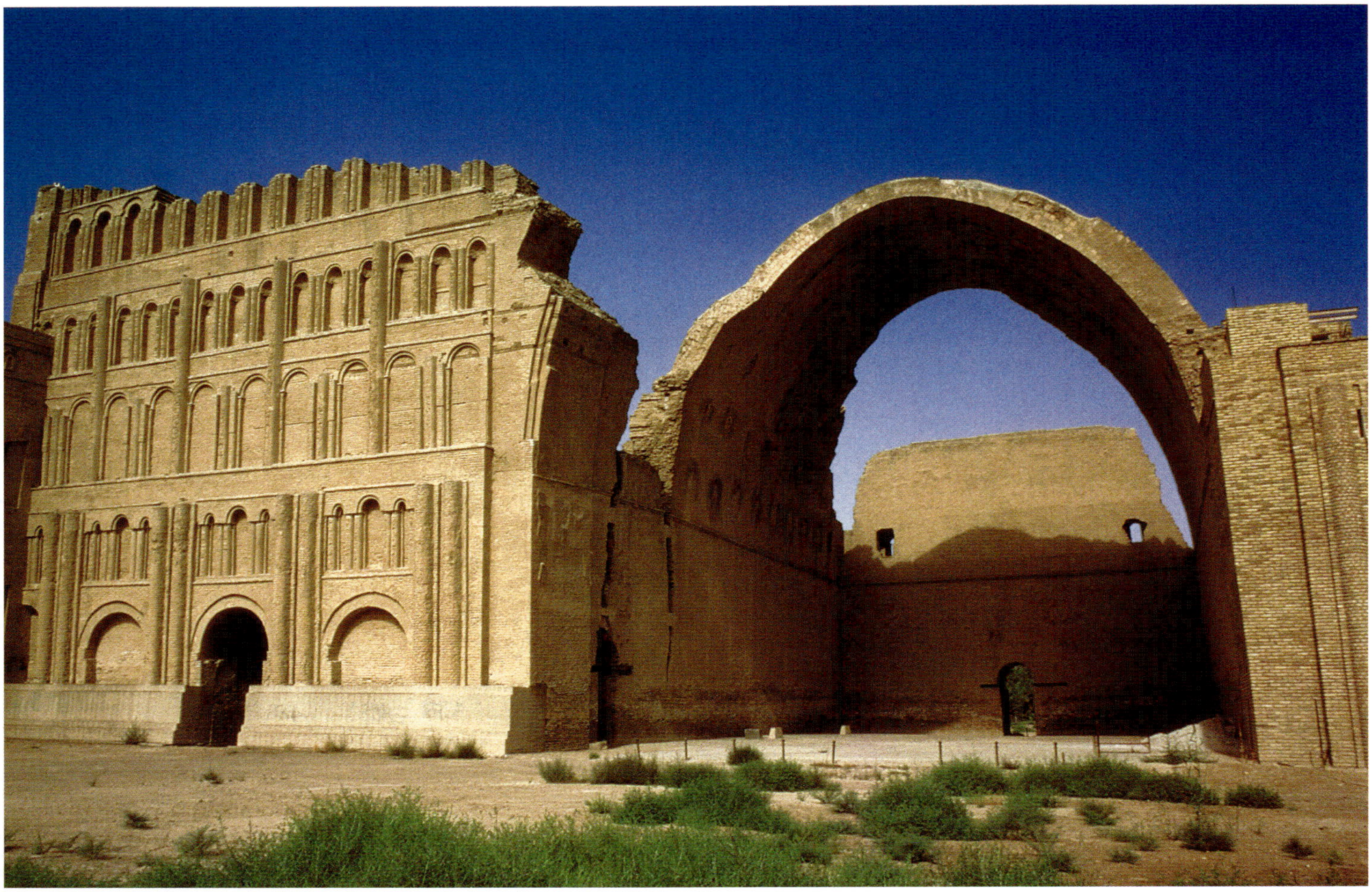

**2-28** Palace of Shapur I, Ctesiphon, Iraq, ca. 250 CE.

The last great pre-Islamic civilization of Mesopotamia was that of the Sasanians. Their palace at Ctesiphon, near Baghdad, features a brick audience hall (iwan) covered by an enormous pointed vault.

Persian art testifies to the active exchange of ideas and artists among all the civilizations of the Mediterranean, Mesopotamia, and Persia at this date. In an inscription at Susa, for example, Darius I boasted of the diverse origin of the stonemasons, carpenters, and sculptors who constructed and decorated his palace. He names Ionian Greeks, Medes, Egyptians, and Babylonians. This heterogeneous workforce created a new and coherent style that perfectly suited the expression of Persian imperial ambitions.

## Sasanian Empire

Alexander the Great's conquest of the Achaemenid Empire in 330 BCE marked the beginning of a long period of first Greek and then Roman rule of large parts of Mesopotamia and Persia, beginning with one of Alexander's former generals, Seleucus I (r. 312–281 BCE), founder of the Seleucid dynasty. In the third century CE, however, a new power rose up in Persia that challenged the Romans and sought to force them out of Asia. The new rulers called themselves Sasanians. They traced their lineage to a legendary figure named Sasan, said to be a direct descendant of the Achaemenid kings. The first Sasanian king, Artaxerxes I (r. 211–241 CE), founded the New Persian Empire in 224 CE after he defeated the Parthians (another of Rome's eastern enemies).

**SHAPUR I** The son and successor of Artaxerxes, Shapur I (r. 241–272 CE), built a great palace (FIG. **2-28**) at Ctesiphon, the capital his father had established near modern Baghdad in Iraq. The central feature of Shapur's palace was the monumental *iwan*, or brick audience hall, covered by a *vault* (here, a deep arch over an oblong space)

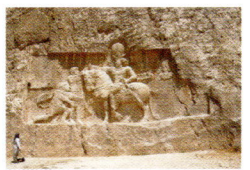

**2-28A** Triumph of Shapur I, Bishapur, ca. 260 CE.

that came almost to a point more than 100 feet above the ground. A series of horizontal bands made up of *blind arcades* (a series of arches without openings, applied as wall decoration) divide the *facade* to the left and right of the iwan. Shapur was also an accomplished general who further extended Sasanian territory. In 260 CE, he even captured the Roman emperor Valerian—a singular feat, which he immortalized in a series of reliefs (FIG. **2-28A**) at Bishapur, Iran.

The New Persian Empire endured more than 400 years, until the Arabs drove the Sasanians out of Mesopotamia in 636 CE, just four years after the death of Muhammad. But the prestige of Sasanian art and architecture long outlasted the empire. A thousand years after Shapur I built his palace at Ctesiphon, Islamic architects still considered its soaring iwan as the standard for judging their own engineering feats (see Chapter 10).

# MESOPOTAMIA AND PERSIA

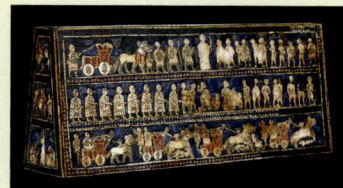

*Standard of Ur*, ca. 2600–2400 BCE

### SUMERIAN ART ca. 3500–2332 BCE

▌ The Sumerians founded the world's first city-states in the valley between the Tigris and Euphrates rivers and invented writing in the fourth millennium BCE.

▌ They were also the first to build towering temple platforms, called ziggurats, and to place figures in registers to tell coherent stories.

### AKKADIAN ART ca. 2332–2150 BCE

▌ The Akkadians were the first Mesopotamian rulers to call themselves kings of the world and to assume divine attributes. The earliest recorded name of an author is the Akkadian priestess Enheduanna.

▌ Akkadian artists may have been the first to cast hollow life-size bronze sculptures and to place figures at different levels in a landscape setting.

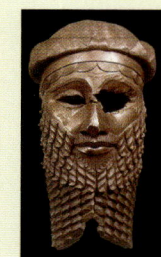

Portrait of an Akkadian king, ca. 2250–2200 BCE

### NEO-SUMERIAN AND BABYLONIAN ART ca. 2150–1600 BCE

▌ During the Third Dynasty of Ur, the Sumerians rose again to power and constructed one of the largest ziggurats in Mesopotamia at Ur.

▌ Gudea of Lagash (r. ca. 2100 BCE) built numerous temples and placed diorite portraits of himself in all of them as votive offerings to the gods.

▌ Babylon's greatest king, Hammurabi (r. 1792–1750 BCE), formulated wide-ranging laws for the empire he ruled. Babylonian artists were among the first to experiment with foreshortening.

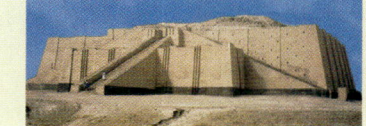

Ziggurat, Ur, ca. 2100 BCE

### ASSYRIAN AND NEO-BABYLONIAN ART ca. 900–539 BCE

▌ At the height of their power, the Assyrians ruled an empire that extended from the Persian Gulf to the Nile and Asia Minor.

▌ Assyrian palaces were fortified citadels with gates guarded by monstrous lamassu sculptures. Paintings and reliefs depicting official ceremonies and the king in battle and hunting lions decorated the walls of the ceremonial halls.

▌ In the sixth century BCE, the Babylonians constructed two of the Seven Wonders of the ancient world. The Ishtar Gate, with its colorful glazed brick reliefs, gives an idea of Babylon's magnificence under Nebuchadnezzar II (r. 605–562 BCE).

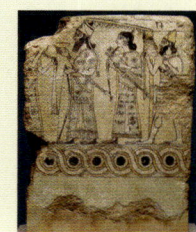

Ashurnasirpal II with attendants, ca. 875–860 BCE

### ACHAEMENID AND SASANIAN ART ca. 559–330 BCE and 224–636 CE

▌ The capital of the Achaemenid Persians was at Persepolis, where Darius I (r. 522–486 BCE) and Xerxes (r. 486–465 BCE) built a huge palace complex with an audience hall that could accommodate 10,000 guests. Painted reliefs of subject nations bringing tribute adorned the terraces.

▌ The Sasanians, enemies of Rome, ruled the New Persian Empire from their palace at Ctesiphon until the Arabs defeated them four years after the death of Muhammad.

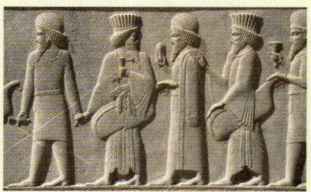

Apadana, Persepolis, ca. 521–465 BCE

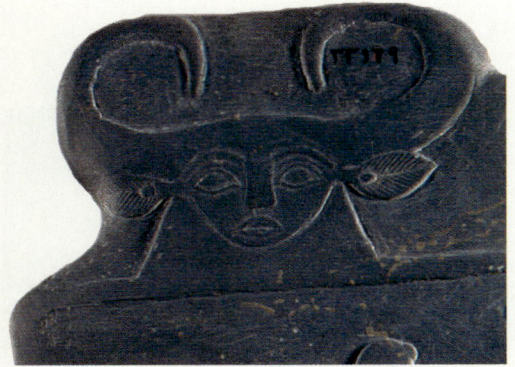

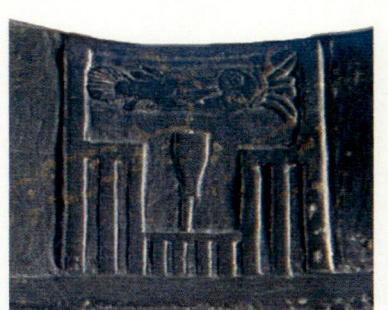

The head of a cow with a woman's face appears twice on each side of Narmer's palette. She is probably the goddess Hathor, whom the Egyptians believed was the divine mother of the pharaoh.

King Narmer's palette is the earliest surviving labeled work of historical art. This hieroglyph gives his name (catfish = *nar*; chisel = *mer*) within a frame representing the royal palace.

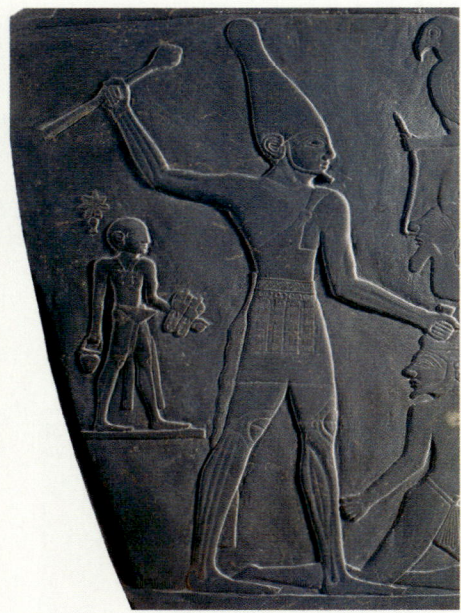

Narmer, the largest figure in the composition, shown in a composite of frontal and profile views, effortlessly slays an enemy as the attendant carrying the pharaoh's sandals looks on.

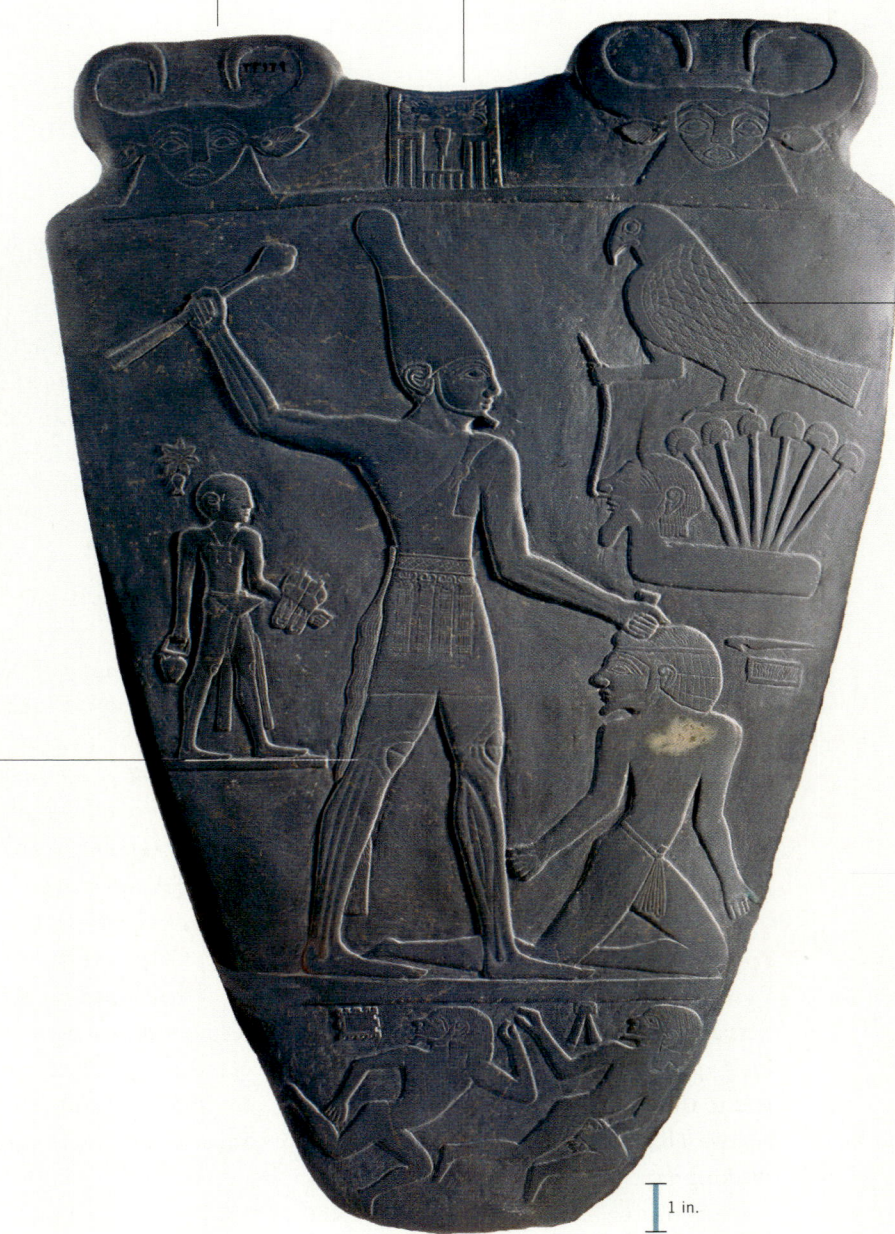

1 in.

**3-1** Back of the palette of King Narmer (compare FIG. 3-2), from Hierakonpolis, Egypt, Predynastic, ca. 3000–2920 BCE. Slate, 2′ 1″ high. Egyptian Museum, Cairo.

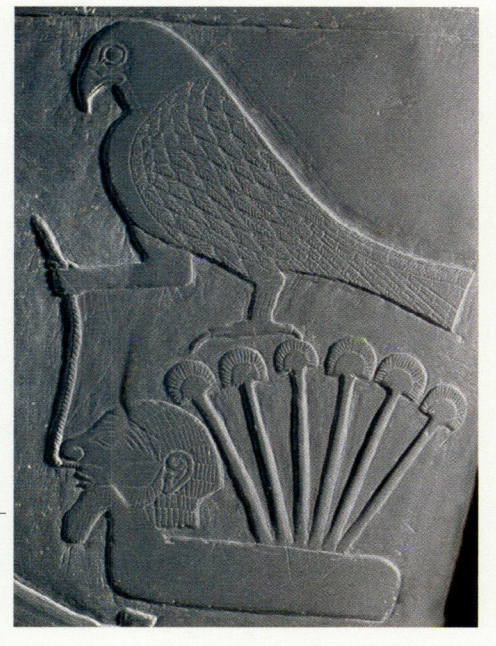

3

# EGYPT UNDER THE PHARAOHS

The falcon with human arms is the god Horus, the pharaoh's protector, who takes captive a man-headed hieroglyph with a papyrus plant growing from it that stands for defeated Lower Egypt.

FRAMING THE ERA

## DIVINE KINGSHIP ON THE NILE

Blessed with ample sources of stone of different hues suitable for carving statues and fashioning building blocks, the Egyptians left to posterity a profusion of spectacular monuments spanning three millennia. Many of them glorify the kings whom they called *pharaohs* and believed to be divine. Indeed, the Egyptians devoted enormous resources to erecting countless monuments and statues to honor the pharaohs during their lifetimes and to constructing and furnishing magnificent tombs to serve as their god-kings' eternal homes in the afterlife.

It is not surprising, then, that the earliest preserved artwork labeled with the name of a ruler is Egyptian—the two-foot-tall slate *palette* (stone slab with a circular depression—FIG. **3-1**; compare FIG. 3-2) portraying Narmer, a pharaoh of the first of Egypt's 31 dynasties, and commemorating the unification of the two previously independent kingdoms of Upper and Lower Egypt. At the top of the 5,000-year-old palette are two heads of a cow with a woman's face, whom scholars usually identify as the goddess Hathor, the divine mother of all pharaohs, but who may be the sky goddess Bat. Between the heads is a *hieroglyph* giving Narmer's name (catfish = *nar;* chisel = *mer*) within a frame representing the pharaoh's royal palace.

At the center and dominating the palette is Narmer, whom the sculptor depicted as larger than everyone else, appropriate for his divine status. The pharaoh wears the high, white, bowling-pin-shaped crown of Upper Egypt. Accompanying the king is an official who carries his sandals. The representation of the pharaoh (and of the attendant) combines profile views of the head, legs, and arms with front views of the eye and torso, the same composite view of the human figure found in Mesopotamian and Persian art. Narmer effortlessly slays an unarmed foe, a motif that became a standard pictorial formula in Egyptian art signifying the inevitable triumph of the Egyptian god-kings over their enemies. Above and to the right, the falcon with human arms is the god Horus, the king's protector. The deity takes captive a hieroglyph of the land of Lower Egypt consisting of a man's head and a papyrus plant. Below the king are two fallen enemies.

Furnishing anecdotal details of a specific event was not the goal of this Egyptian artist. Rather, the objective was to characterize the pharaoh as supreme and protected by the gods, isolated from and larger than all ordinary men, and solely responsible for the triumph over the enemy. The Narmer palette set the standard for narrative art in Egypt for 3,000 years.

# EGYPT AND EGYPTOLOGY

The backbone of Egypt was, and still is, the Nile River, which, through its annual floods, supported all life in that ancient land (MAP 3-1). Even more so than the Tigris and the Euphrates rivers of Mesopotamia (MAP 2-1), the Nile defined the cultures that developed along its banks. Originating deep in Africa, the world's longest river flows through regions that may not receive a single drop of rainfall in a decade. Yet crops thrive from the rich soil the Nile brings thousands of miles from the African hills. In antiquity, the land bordering the Nile consisted of marshes dotted with island ridges. Amphibious animals swarmed in the marshes, where the Egyptians hunted them through tall forests of *papyrus* and rushes (FIGS. 3-14 and 3-28). The fertility of Egypt was famous. When the Kingdom of the Nile became a province of the Roman Empire after the death of Queen Cleopatra (r. 51–30 BCE), it served as the granary of the Mediterranean world.

During the Middle Ages, the detailed knowledge the Romans possessed about the Egyptians and their gods (see "The Gods and Goddesses of Egypt," page 57) was largely forgotten. With the Enlightenment of the 18th century (see Chapter 26), scholars began to piece together Egypt's history from references in the Old Testament, from the fifth-century BCE Greek historian Herodotus and other Greco-Roman authors, and from preserved portions of a third-century BCE history of Egypt written in Greek by Manetho, an Egyptian high priest. Manetho described the succession of pharaohs, dividing them into the still-useful groups called dynasties, but his chronology was inaccurate, and today historians still do not agree on the absolute dates of the pharaohs. The chronologies scholars have proposed for the earliest Egyptian dynasties can vary by as much as two centuries. Exact years cannot be assigned to the reigns of individual pharaohs until 664 BCE (26th Dynasty).[1]

The European rediscovery of ancient Egypt and the modern discipline of Egyptology date to the late 18th century, when archaeological exploration of the land of the Nile began. In 1799, on a military expedition to Egypt, Napoleon Bonaparte (1769–1821) took with him a small troop of scholars, linguists, antiquarians, and artists. Their chance discovery of the famed *Rosetta Stone,* now in the British Museum, provided the key to deciphering Egyptian hieroglyphic writing. The stone bears an inscription in three sections: one in Greek, which Napoleon's team easily read; one in *demotic* (Late Egyptian); and one in formal hieroglyphic. On the assumption the text was the same in all three sections, scholars attempted to decipher the two non-Greek sections. Eventually, Jean-François Champollion (1790–1832) deduced the hieroglyphs were not simply pictographs, but the signs of a once-spoken language whose traces survived in Coptic, the language of Christian Egypt. The ability to read hieroglyphic inscriptions revolutionized the study of Egyptian civilization and art.

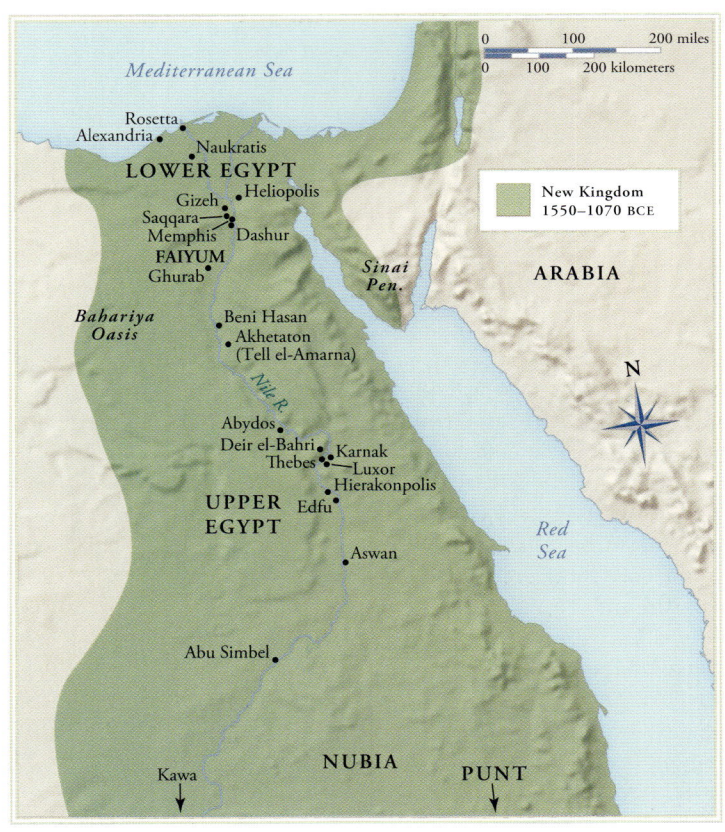

MAP 3-1 Ancient Egypt.

# PREDYNASTIC AND EARLY DYNASTIC PERIODS

The Predynastic, or prehistoric, beginnings of Egyptian civilization are obscure. Nevertheless, tantalizing remains of tombs, paintings, pottery, and other artifacts attest to the existence of a sophisticated culture on the banks of the Nile around 3500 BCE.

## Painting and Sculpture

In Predynastic times, Egypt was divided geographically and politically into Upper Egypt (the southern, upstream part of the Nile Valley), a narrow tract of grassland that encouraged hunting, and Lower (northern) Egypt, where the rich soil of the Nile Delta islands promoted agriculture and animal husbandry. The major finds of Predynastic art come from Upper Egypt, especially Hierakonpolis, where archaeologists discovered not only the Narmer palette (FIG. 3-1) but also the most extensive series of early

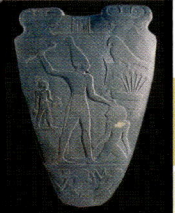

# EGYPT UNDER THE PHARAOHS

| | Predynastic and Early Dynastic | | Old Kingdom | | Middle Kingdom | | New Kingdom | | First Millennium | BCE | CE |
|---|---|---|---|---|---|---|---|---|---|---|---|
| 3500 | | 2575 | | 2040 | | 1550 | | 1070 | | 30 | |
| | ❚ Earliest Egyptian narrative reliefs and paintings  ❚ Imhotep, first recorded artist's name | | ❚ Statuary types expressing the eternal nature of pharaonic kingship  ❚ Construction of the Great Pyramids at Gizeh | | ❚ Rock-cut tombs become the preferred Egyptian burial sites | | ❚ Construction of grandiose pylon temples  ❚ Akhenaton introduces a new religion and new art forms | | ❚ Egyptian artistic traditions continue under foreign rule | | |

## The Gods and Goddesses of Egypt

The worldview of the Egyptians was distinct from the outlook of their neighbors in the ancient Mediterranean, Mesopotamian, and Persian worlds. Egyptians believed that before the beginning of time the primeval waters, called *Nun,* existed alone in the darkness. At the moment of creation, a mound rose out of the limitless waters—just as muddy mounds emerge from the Nile after the annual flood recedes. On this mound the creator god appeared and brought light to the world. In later times, the Egyptians symbolized the original mound as a pyramidal stone called the *ben-ben,* which supported the supreme god, *Amen,* the god of the sun (*Re*).

The supreme god also created the first of the other gods and goddesses of Egypt. According to one version of the myth, the creator masturbated and produced *Shu* and *Tefnut,* the primary male and female forces in the universe. They coupled to give birth to *Geb* (Earth) and *Nut* (Sky), who bore Osiris, Seth, Isis, and Nephthys. The eldest, *Osiris,* was the god of order, whom the Egyptians revered as the king who brought civilization to the Nile valley. His brother, *Seth,* was his evil opposite, the god of chaos. Seth murdered Osiris and cut him into pieces, which he scattered across Egypt. *Isis,* the sister and consort of Osiris, with the help of Seth's wife, *Nephthys,* succeeded in collecting Osiris's body parts, and with her powerful magic brought him back to life. The resurrected Osiris fathered a son with Isis—*Horus,* who avenged his father's death and displaced Seth as king of Egypt. Osiris then became the lord of the Underworld. Horus appears in art either as a falcon, considered the noblest bird of the sky, or as a falcon-headed man. The Egyptians identified all their living pharaohs with Horus, then with Osiris after they died.

Other Egyptian deities include *Mut,* the consort of the sun god Amen, and *Khonsu,* the moon god, who was their son. *Thoth,* another lunar deity and the god of knowledge and writing, appears in art as an ibis, a baboon, or an ibis-headed man crowned with the crescent moon and the moon disk. When Seth tore out Horus's falcon-eye (*wedjat*), Thoth restored it. The Egyptians associated Thoth too with rebirth and the afterlife. *Hathor,* daughter of Re, was a divine mother of the pharaoh, nourishing him with her milk. Egyptian artists represented her as a cow-headed woman or as a woman with a cow's horns. *Anubis,* a jackal or jackal-headed deity, was the god of the dead and of mummification. *Maat,* another daughter of Re, was the goddess of truth and justice. Her feather was used to measure the weight of the deceased's heart on Anubis's scales to determine if the *ka* (life force) would be blessed in the afterlife.

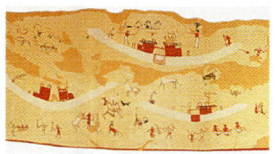

3-1A Tomb 100, Hierakonpolis, ca. 3500–3200 BCE.

Egyptian mural paintings (FIG. **3-1A**) on the walls of a tomb dating between 3500 and 3200 BCE.

### PALETTE OF KING NARMER

The Predynastic period ended with the unification of Upper and Lower Egypt, which until recently historians thought occurred during the rule of the First Dynasty pharaoh Menes. Many Egyptologists have identified Menes with King Narmer, the larger-than-life victor named on the ceremonial palette (FIG. 3-1) already discussed (see "Divine Kingship on the Nile," page 55). Scholars still debate exactly what event or events the reliefs on the two sides of Narmer's palette depict. No longer regarded as commemorating the founding of the first of Egypt's 31 dynasties around 2920 BCE (the last ended in 332 BCE), the scenes probably record the unification of the two kingdoms. Egyptologists now believe this unification occurred over several centuries, but the palette presents the creation of the "Kingdom of the Two Lands" as a single great event.

Narmer's palette is an elaborate, formalized version of a utilitarian object commonly used in the Predynastic period to prepare eye makeup, which Egyptians used to protect their eyes against irritation and the glare of the sun. On the front (FIG. **3-2**), the elongated necks of two felines form the circular depression that would

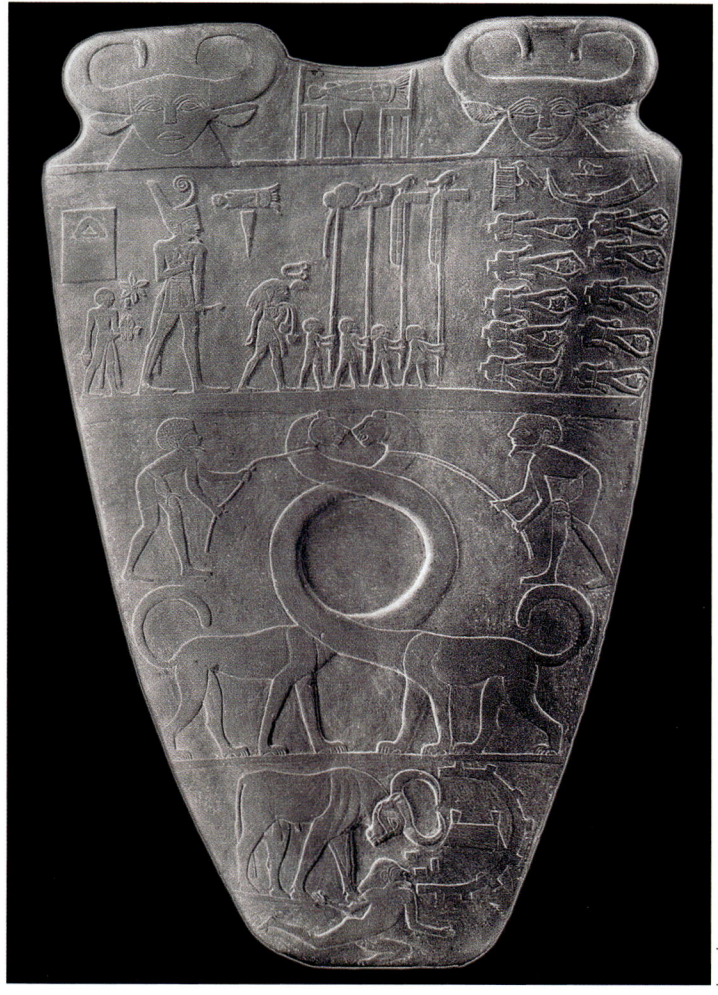

**3-2** Front of the palette of King Narmer (compare FIG. 3-1), from Hierakonpolis, Egypt, Predynastic, ca. 3000–2920 BCE. Slate, 2′ 1″ high. Egyptian Museum, Cairo.

Narmer, king of Upper Egypt, wears the crown of Lower Egypt as he reviews the beheaded enemy bodies. Below, the intertwined animal necks may symbolize the unification of the two kingdoms.

1 in.

have held eye makeup in an ordinary palette not made for display. The intertwined necks of the animals (a motif common in Mesopotamian art) may be a pictorial reference to Egypt's unification. In the uppermost register, Narmer, wearing the red crown of Lower Egypt, reviews the beheaded bodies of the enemy. The dead are seen from above, a perspective reminiscent of the Paleolithic paintings (FIG. 1-9) on the ceiling of the Altamira cave in Spain representing bison lying on the ground. The Egyptian artist depicted each body with its severed head neatly placed between its legs. By virtue of his superior rank, the king, on both sides of the palette, performs his ritual task alone and towers over his men and the enemy. The king's superhuman strength is symbolized in the lowest band by a great bull knocking down a rebellious city whose fortress walls also are seen in an "aerial view."

As in Mesopotamian art (see Chapter 2), the Egyptian artist's portrayal of Narmer combines profile views of his head, legs, and arms with front views of his eye and torso. Although the proportions of the human figure changed, this composite representation of the body's parts became standard in Egyptian art as well. In the Hierakonpolis painting (FIG. 3-1A), the artist scattered the figures across the wall more or less haphazardly. On Narmer's palette, the sculptor subdivided the surface into registers and inserted the pictorial elements into their organized setting in a neat and orderly way. The horizontal lines separating the narratives also define the ground supporting the figures. This too was the preferred mode for narrative art in Mesopotamia. Narmer's palette established this compositional scheme as the norm in Egypt for millennia. Egyptian artists who departed from this convention did so deliberately, usually to express the absence of order, as in a chaotic battle scene (FIG. 3-36).

## Architecture

Narmer's palette is exceptional among surviving Egyptian artworks because it is commemorative rather than funerary in nature. Far more typical is the Predynastic mural (FIG. 3-1A) from tomb 100 at Hierakonpolis. In fact, Egyptian tombs provide the principal, if not the exclusive, evidence for the historical reconstruction of Egyptian civilization. The majority of monuments the Egyptians left behind were dedicated to ensuring safety and happiness in the next life (see "Mummification and Immortality," page 61).

**MASTABAS** The standard tomb type in early Egypt was the *mastaba* (Arabic for "bench"), a rectangular brick or stone structure with sloping sides erected over an underground burial chamber (FIG. **3-3**). The form probably developed from earthen mounds that had covered even earlier tombs. Although mastabas originally housed single burials, as in FIG. 3-3, they later became increasingly complex in order to accommodate multiple family burials. The main feature of these tombs, other than the burial chamber itself, was the chapel, which had a false door through which the ka could join the world of the living and partake in the meals placed on an offering table. Some mastabas also had a *serdab*, a small room housing a statue of the deceased.

**IMHOTEP AND DJOSER** One of the most renowned figures in Egyptian history was IMHOTEP, master builder for King Djoser (r. 2630–2611 BCE) of the Third Dynasty. Imhotep's is the first recorded name of an artist anywhere in the world. A man of legendary talent, Imhotep also served as the pharaoh's official seal bearer and as high priest of the sun god Re. After his death, the Egyptians deified Imhotep as the son of the god Ptah and in time probably inflated the list of his achievements, but architectural historians accept Manetho's attribution to Imhotep of the stepped pyramid (FIG. **3-4**)

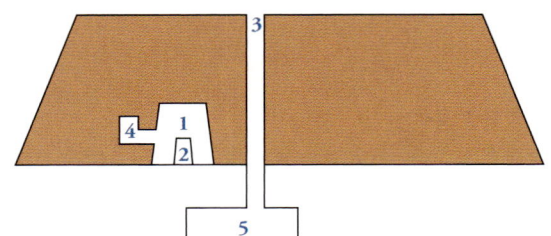

1. Chapel
2. False door
3. Shaft into burial chamber
4. Serdab (chamber for statue of deceased)
5. Burial chamber

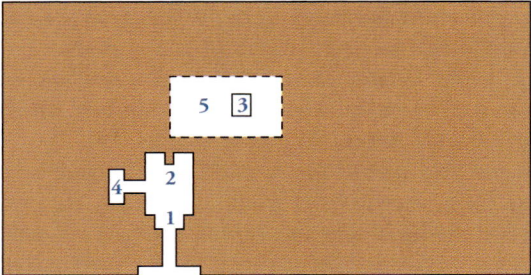

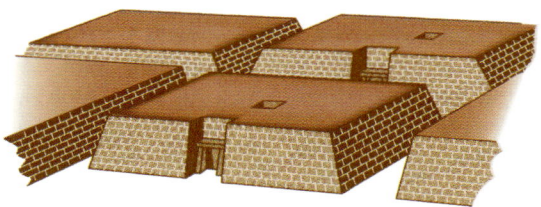

**3-3** Section (*top*), plan (*center*), and restored view (*bottom*) of typical Egyptian mastaba tombs.

Egyptian mastabas had underground chambers containing the mummified body, portrait statues, and offerings to the deceased. Scenes of daily life often decorated the interior walls.

of Djoser at Saqqara. Saqqara was the ancient *necropolis* (Greek for "city of the dead") of Memphis, Egypt's capital at the time. Built before 2600 BCE, Djoser's pyramid is one of the oldest stone structures in Egypt and, in its final form, the first truly grandiose royal tomb. Begun as a large mastaba with each of its faces oriented toward one of the cardinal points of the compass, the tomb was enlarged at least twice before assuming its ultimate shape. About 200 feet high, the stepped pyramid seems to be composed of a series of mastabas of diminishing size, stacked one atop another to form a structure that resembles the great Mesopotamian ziggurats (FIGS. 2-15 and 2-20A). Unlike a ziggurat, however, Djoser's pyramid is a tomb, not a temple platform, and its dual function was to protect the mummified king and his possessions and to symbolize, by its gigantic presence, his absolute and godlike power. Beneath the pyramid was a network of several hundred underground rooms and galleries cut out of the Saqqara bedrock. The vast subterranean complex resembles a palace. It was to be Djoser's home in the afterlife.

Djoser's pyramid stands near the center of an immense (37-acre) rectangular enclosure (FIG. **3-5**) surrounded by a wall of white limestone 34 feet high and 5,400 feet long. The huge precinct, with its protective walls and tightly regulated access (FIGS. 3-5, no. 5, and **3-5A**), stands in sharp contrast to the roughly contemporaneous Sumerian Royal Cemetery at Ur, where no

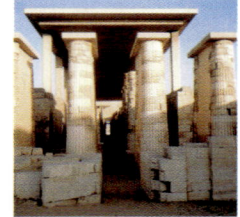

**3-5A** Entrance hall, Djoser precinct, Saqqara, ca. 2630–2611 BCE.

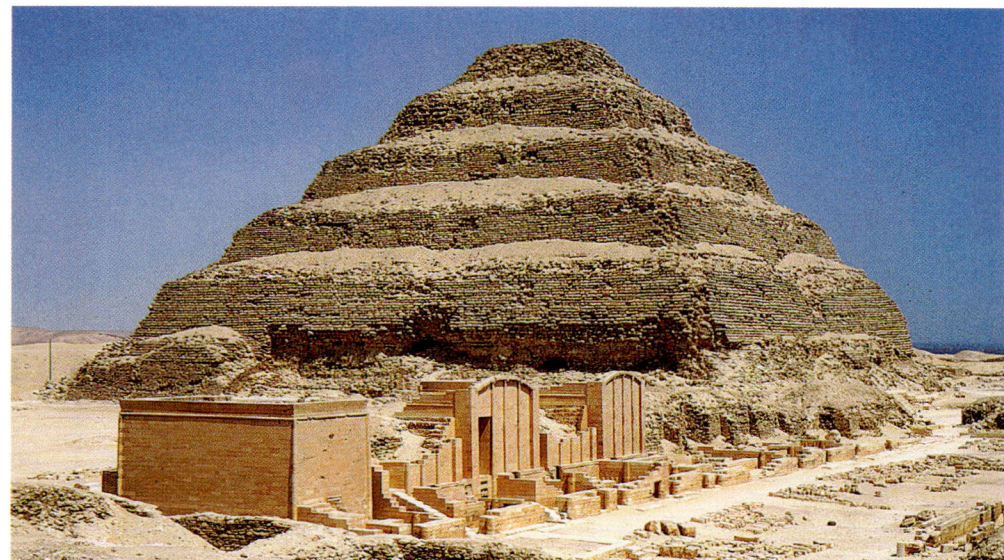

Imhotep, the first artist whose name is recorded, built the first pyramid during the Third Dynasty for King Djoser. The pharaoh's pyramid resembles a series of stacked mastabas of diminishing size.

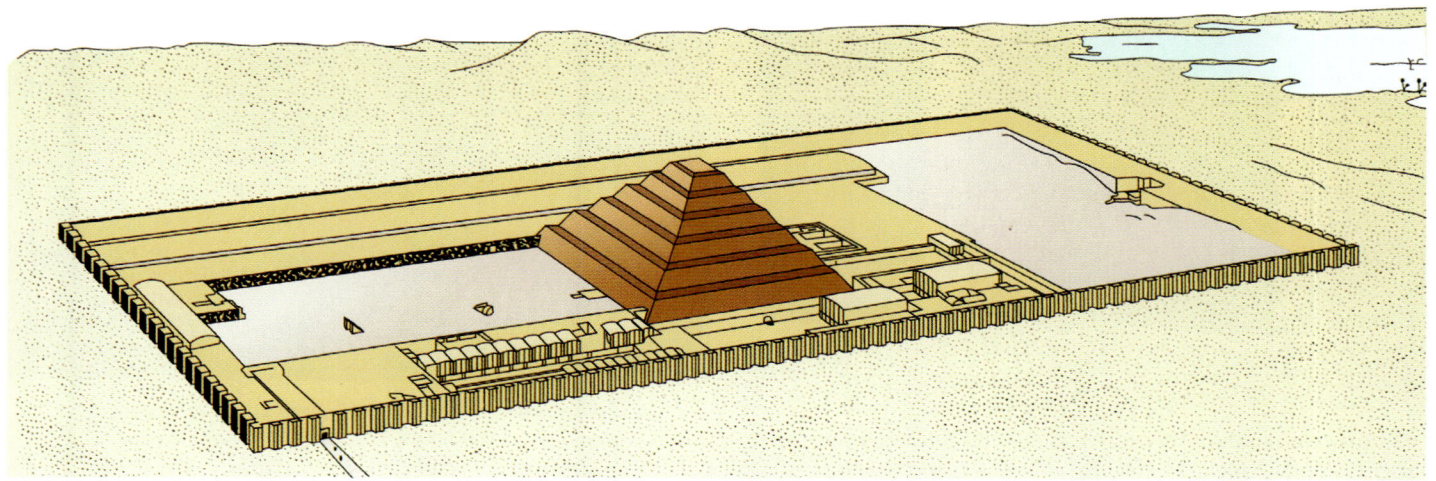

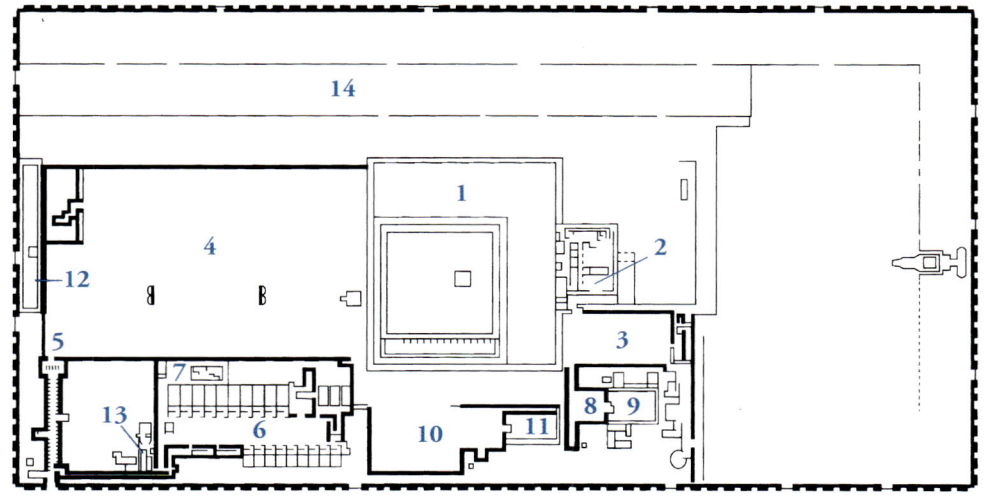

1. Stepped pyramid
2. Funerary temple of Djoser
3. Court with serdab
4. Large court with altar
5. Entrance portico
6. Heb-Sed court and sham chapels
7. Small temple
8. Court before North Palace
9. North Palace
10. Court before South Palace
11. South Palace
12. South tomb
13. Royal Pavilion
14. Magazines

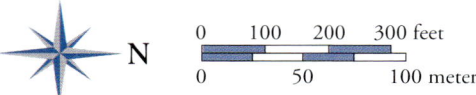

N

```
0    100   200   300 feet
0       50      100 meters
```

**3-5** Restored view (*top*) and plan (*bottom*) of the mortuary precinct of Djoser, Saqqara, Egypt, Third Dynasty, ca. 2630–2611 BCE.

Djoser's pyramid was the centerpiece of an immense funerary complex that included a mortuary temple, other buildings, and courtyards. A network of underground galleries resembled a palace.

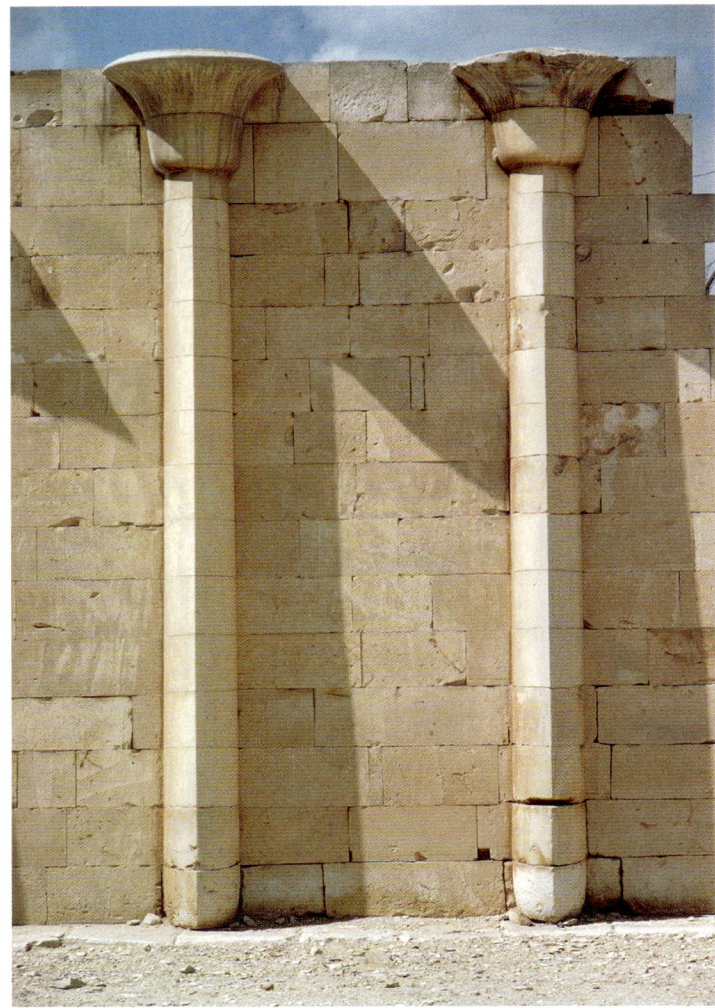

**3-6** Detail of the facade of the north palace of the mortuary precinct of Djoser (FIG. 3-5), Saqqara, Egypt, Third Dynasty, ca. 2630–2611 BCE.

The earliest known stone columns are in Djoser's funerary precinct. Those on the north palace facade are engaged (attached) to the walls and have shafts and capitals resembling papyrus plants.

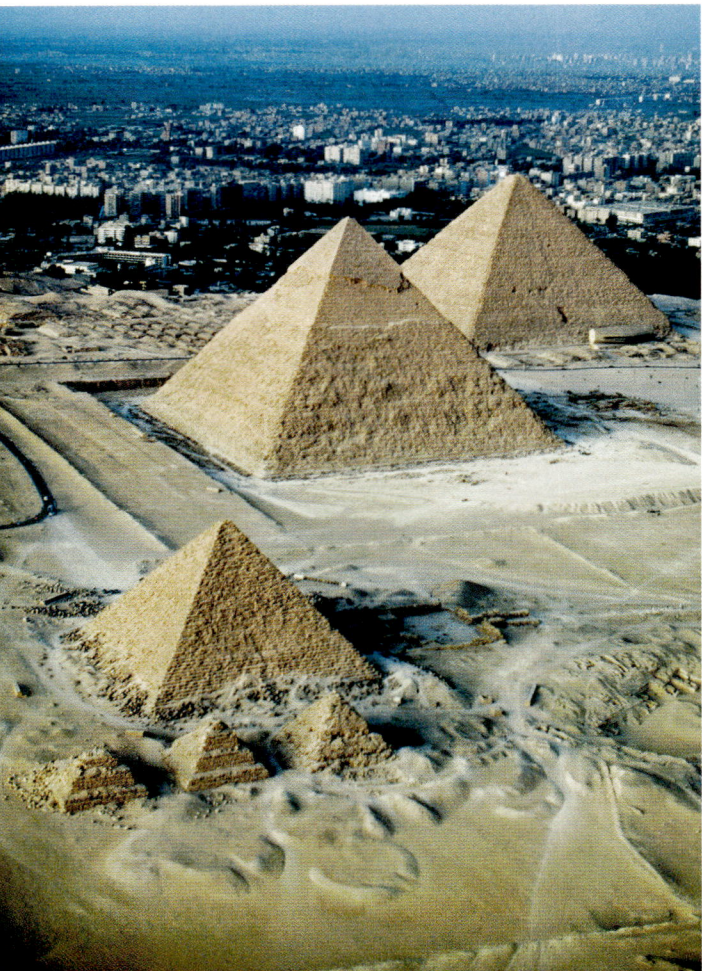

**3-7** Great Pyramids, Gizeh, Egypt, Fourth Dynasty. *From bottom:* pyramids of Menkaure, ca. 2490–2472 BCE; Khafre, ca. 2520–2494 BCE; and Khufu, ca. 2551–2528 BCE. ◼◀

The Great Pyramids of Gizeh took the shape of the ben-ben, the emblem of the sun, Re. The sun's rays were the ramp the Egyptian pharaohs used to ascend to the heavens after their death and rebirth.

barriers kept people away from the burial area. Nor did the Mesopotamian cemetery have a temple for the worship of the deified dead. At Saqqara, a funerary temple stands against the northern face of Djoser's pyramid (FIG. 3-5, no. 2). Priests performed daily rituals at the temple in celebration of the divine pharaoh.

Djoser's funerary temple was but one of many buildings arranged around several courts. Most of the others were dummy structures (FIG. 3-5, no. 6) with stone walls enclosing fills of rubble, sand, or gravel. The buildings imitated in stone various types of temporary structures made of plant stems and mats erected in Upper and Lower Egypt to celebrate the Jubilee Festival, which perpetually reaffirmed the royal existence in the hereafter. The translation into stone of structural forms previously made out of plants may be seen in the columns (FIG. **3-6**) of the north palace (FIG. 3-5, no. 9) of Djoser's funerary precinct. The columns end in *capitals* ("heads") that take the form of the papyrus blossoms of Lower Egypt. The column shafts resemble papyrus stalks. Djoser's columns are not freestanding, as are most later columns. They are *engaged* (attached) to walls, but are nonetheless the earliest known stone columns in the history of architecture.

# OLD KINGDOM

The Old Kingdom is the first of the three great periods of Egyptian history, called the Old, Middle, and New Kingdoms, respectively. Many Egyptologists now begin the Old Kingdom with the first pharaoh of the Fourth Dynasty, Sneferu (r. 2575–2551 BCE), although the traditional division of kingdoms places Djoser and the Third Dynasty in the Old Kingdom. It ended with the demise of the Eighth Dynasty around 2134 BCE.

## Architecture

The pharaohs of the Old Kingdom amassed great wealth and expended it on grandiose architectural projects, of which the most spectacular were the Great Pyramids of Gizeh, the oldest of the Seven Wonders of the ancient world (see "Babylon, City of Wonders," Chapter 2, page 49). The prerequisites for membership in this elite club were colossal size and enormous cost.

**GIZEH** The Egyptians constructed the three pyramids (FIG. **3-7**) at Gizeh in the course of about 75 years (see "Building the Great

# Mummification and Immortality

The Egyptians did not make the sharp distinction between body and soul that is basic to many religions. Rather, they believed that from birth a person possessed a kind of other self, the *ka* or life force, which, on the death of the body, could inhabit the corpse and live on. For the ka to live securely, however, the body had to remain as nearly intact as possible. To ensure that it did, the Egyptians developed the technique of embalming (*mummification*) to a high art. Although they believed the god Anubis invented embalming to preserve the body of the murdered Osiris (see "The Gods and Goddesses of Egypt," page 57), Egyptians did not practice mummification systematically until the Fourth Dynasty, when they also buried their dead in underground chambers beneath monumental brick or stone tombs (FIG. 3-3).

The first step in the 70-day process was the surgical removal of the lungs, liver, stomach, and intestines through an incision in the left flank. The Egyptians thought these organs were most subject to decay, and wrapped them individually and placed them in four containers known as *canopic jars* for eventual deposit in the burial chamber with the corpse. (The jars take their name from the port of Canopus, where the Egyptians worshiped human-headed jars as personifications of Osiris. These jars were not, however, used in embalming.) Egyptian surgeons extracted the brain through the nostrils and then discarded it because they did not attach any special significance to that organ. But they left in place the heart, necessary for life and also regarded as the seat of intelligence.

Next, the body was treated for 40 days with natron, a naturally occurring salt compound that dehydrated the body. Then the embalmers filled the corpse with resin-soaked linens, and closed and covered the incision with a representation of the *wedjat* eye of Horus, a powerful *amulet* (a device to ward off evil and promote rebirth). Finally, they treated the body with lotions and resins and wrapped it tightly with hundreds of yards of linen bandages to maintain its shape. The Egyptians often placed other amulets within the bandages or on the corpse. The most important were heart *scarabs* (gems in the shape of beetles). Spells written on them ensured that the heart would be returned to its owner if lost. Between the legs of the deceased the embalmers often put a scroll copy of the *Book of the Dead* (FIG. 3-37), which contained some 200 spells intended to protect the mummy and the ka in the afterlife. Masks (FIG. 3-35) covered the faces of the wealthy.

The Egyptian practice of mummification endured for thousands of years, even under Greek and Roman rule. Roman mummies with painted portraits (FIGS. 7-62 to 7-62B) have been popular attractions in museums worldwide for a long time, but the discovery in 1996 of a cemetery at Bahariya Oasis in the desert southwest of Cairo greatly expanded their number. The site, which archaeologists call the Valley of the Golden Mummies, extends for at least four square miles. The largest tomb found to date contained 32 mummies, but another held 43, some stacked on top of others because the tomb was used for generations and space ran out.

The care with which families laid their dead to rest in the Bahariya cemetery varied markedly with social position and wealth. The bodies of the poorer members of the community were carelessly wrapped in linen and have almost completely decayed. The 60 most elaborate mummies, probably those of successful merchants and their families, have gilded stucco masks. Some also have gilded chest plates with reliefs depicting Egyptian deities, including Thoth holding Maat's feather (compare the weighing scene in FIG. 3-37). Others have painted decoration (compare FIG. 7-62A), and some have eyes of white marble with black obsidian irises and copper eyelashes. The excavators believe the cemetery was still in use as late as the fourth or fifth century CE.

Preserving the deceased's body by mummification was only the first requirement for immortality in ancient Egypt. Food and drink also had to be provided, as did clothing, utensils, and furniture. Nothing that had been enjoyed on earth was to be lacking. The Egyptians also placed statuettes called *ushabtis* (answerers) in the tomb. These figurines performed any labor required of the deceased in the afterlife, answering whenever his or her name was called.

Beginning in the third millennium BCE, the Egyptians also set up statues of the dead (for example, FIGS. 3-11 to 3-13) in their tombs. The statues were meant to guarantee the permanence of the person's identity by providing substitute dwelling places for the ka in case the mummy disintegrated. Wall paintings and reliefs (for example, FIGS. 3-14 and 3-15) recorded the recurring round of human activities. The Egyptians hoped and expected that the images and inventory of life, collected and set up within the protective stone walls of the tomb, would ensure immortality.

Pyramids," page 62) to serve as the tombs of the Fourth Dynasty pharaohs Khufu (r. 2551–2528 BCE; FIG. **3-8**), Khafre (r. 2520–2494 BCE), and Menkaure (r. 2490–2472 BCE). They represent the culmination of an architectural evolution that began with the mastaba (FIG. 3-3), but the classic pyramid form is not simply a refinement of the stepped pyramid (FIG. 3-4). The new tomb shape probably reflects the influence of Heliopolis, the seat of the powerful cult of Re, whose emblem was a pyramidal stone, the *ben-ben* (see "The Gods and Goddesses of Egypt," page 57). The Great Pyramids are symbols of the sun. The Pyramid Texts, inscribed on the burial chamber walls of many royal tombs beginning with the Fifth Dynasty pyramid of Unas (r. 2356–2323 BCE), refer to the sun's rays as the ladder the pharaoh uses to ascend to the heavens.

Ho, Unas! You have not gone away dead: You have gone away alive.[2]

So, you shall go forth, Unas, to the sky and step up on it in this its identity of the ladder.[3]

[Unas] has flown . . . to the sky amidst his brothers the gods. . . . Unas's seat is with you, Sun.[4]

The pyramids were where Egyptian kings were reborn in the afterlife, just as the sun is reborn each day at dawn.

Imhotep may have conceived Djoser's stepped pyramid as a giant stairway. As with the Saqqara pyramid, the four sides of each of the Great Pyramids are oriented to the cardinal points of the compass. But the funerary temples associated with the three Gizeh

# Building the Great Pyramids

The Great Pyramids (FIG. 3-7) across the Nile from modern Cairo attest to the extraordinary engineering and mathematical expertise of the Egyptians of the mid-third millennium BCE. The structures also are testaments to the Old Kingdom builders' mastery of masonry construction and ability to mobilize, direct, house, and feed a huge workforce engaged in one of the most labor-intensive enterprises ever undertaken. Like all building projects of this type, the process of erecting the pyramids began with the quarrying of stone, in this case primarily the limestone of the Gizeh plateau itself. Teams of skilled workers had to cut into the rock and remove large blocks of roughly equal size using stone or copper chisels and wooden mallets and wedges. Often, the artisans had to cut deep tunnels to find high-quality stone free of cracks and other flaws. To remove a block, the workers cut channels on all sides and partly underneath. Then they pried the stones free from the bedrock with wooden levers. New tools for this difficult work had to be manufactured constantly because the chisels and mallets broke or became dull very quickly.

After workers liberated the stones, the rough blocks had to be transported to the building site and *dressed* (shaped to the exact dimensions required, with smooth faces for a perfect fit). Small blocks could be carried on a man's shoulders or on the back of a donkey, but the Egyptians moved the massive blocks for the Great Pyramids using wooden rollers and sleds. The artisans dressed the blocks by chiseling and pounding the surfaces and, in the last stage, by rubbing and grinding the surfaces with fine polishing stones. Architectural historians call this kind of construction *ashlar masonry*—carefully cut and regularly shaped blocks of stone piled in successive rows, or *courses*.

To set the ashlar blocks in place, workers under the direction of master builders such as Hemiunu (FIG. 3-13B), who supervised the construction of Khufu's pyramid, erected great rubble ramps against the core of the pyramid. They adjusted the ramps' size and slope as work progressed and the tomb grew in height. Scholars debate whether the Egyptians used simple linear ramps inclined at a right angle to one face of the pyramid or zigzag or spiral ramps akin to staircases. Linear ramps would have had the advantage of simplicity and would have left three sides of the pyramid unobstructed. But zigzag ramps placed against one side of the structure or spiral ramps winding around the pyramid would have greatly reduced the slope of the incline and would have made the dragging of the blocks easier. Some scholars also have suggested a combination of straight and spiral ramps, and one recent theory posits a system of spiral ramps within, instead of outside, the pyramid.

The Egyptians used ropes, pulleys, and levers both to lift and to lower the stones, guiding each block into its designated place.

Finally, the pyramid received a casing of white limestone blocks (FIG. 3-8, no. 1), cut so precisely that the eye could scarcely detect the joints. The reflection of sunlight on the facing would have been dazzling, underscoring the pyramid's solar symbolism. A few casing stones still can be seen in the cap that covers the pyramid of Khafre (FIGS. 3-7, *center*, and 3-10, *left*).

Of the three Fourth Dynasty pyramids at Gizeh, the tomb of Khufu (FIGS. 3-8 and 3-9, no. 7) is the oldest and largest. Except for the galleries and burial chamber, it is an almost solid mass of limestone masonry. Some dimensions will suggest the immensity of the Gizeh pyramids: At the base, the length of one side of Khufu's tomb is approximately 775 feet, and its area is some 13 acres. Its present height is about 450 feet (originally 480 feet). The structure contains roughly 2.3 million blocks of stone, each weighing an average of 2.5 tons. Some of the stones at the base weigh about 15 tons. Napoleon's scholars calculated that the blocks in the three Great Pyramids were sufficient to build a wall 1 foot wide and 10 feet high around France.

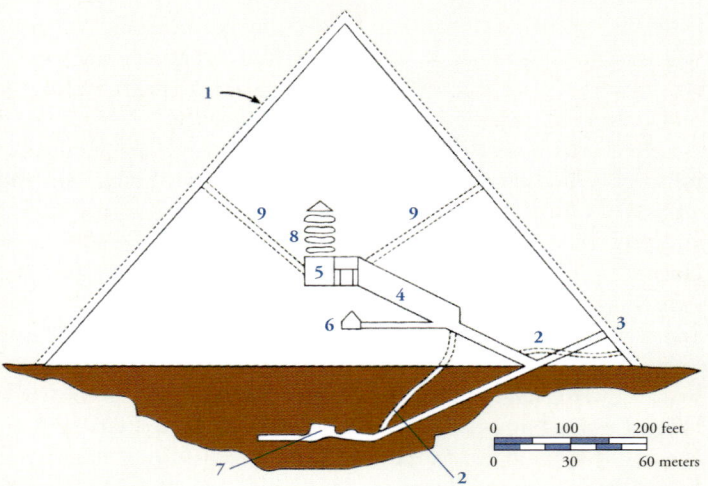

1. Silhouette with original facing stone
2. Thieves' tunnels
3. Entrance
4. Grand gallery
5. King's chamber
6. So-called Queen's chamber
7. False tomb chamber
8. Relieving blocks
9. Air shafts(?)

**3-8** Section of the pyramid of Khufu, Gizeh, Egypt, Fourth Dynasty, ca. 2551–2528 BCE.

Khufu's pyramid is the largest at Gizeh. Constructed of roughly 2.3 million blocks of stone weighing an average of 2.5 tons, the structure is an almost solid mass of stone quarried from the Gizeh plateau itself.

pyramids are not on the north side, facing the stars of the northern sky, as was Djoser's temple. The temples are on the east side, facing the rising sun and underscoring their connection with Re.

From the remains surrounding the pyramid of Khafre at Gizeh, archaeologists have been able to reconstruct an entire funerary complex (FIG. 3-9). The complex included the pyramid itself with the pha-

raoh's burial chamber; the *mortuary temple* adjoining the pyramid on the east side, where priests made offerings to the god-king and stored cloth, food, and ceremonial vessels; the roofed causeway leading to the mortuary temple; and the *valley temple* at the edge of the floodplain. Many Egyptologists believe the complex served not only as the king's tomb and temple but also as his palace in the afterlife.

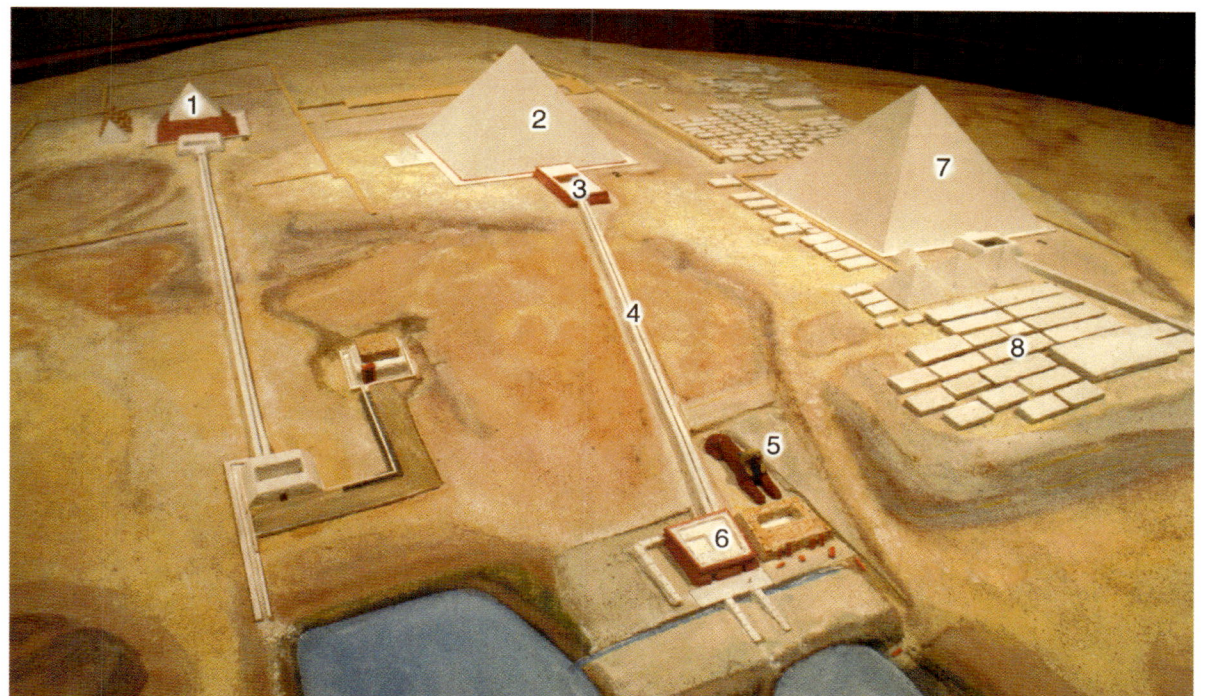

**3-9** Model of the pyramid complex, Gizeh, Egypt. Harvard University Semitic Museum, Cambridge. (1) pyramid of Menkaure, (2) pyramid of Khafre, (3) mortuary temple of Khafre, (4) causeway, (5) Great Sphinx, (6) valley temple of Khafre, (7) pyramid of Khufu, (8) pyramids of the royal family and mastabas of nobles. ◼◀

Like Djoser's pyramid (FIG. 3-4), the Great Pyramids were not isolated tombs but parts of funerary complexes with a valley temple, a covered causeway, and a mortuary temple adjoining the pyramid.

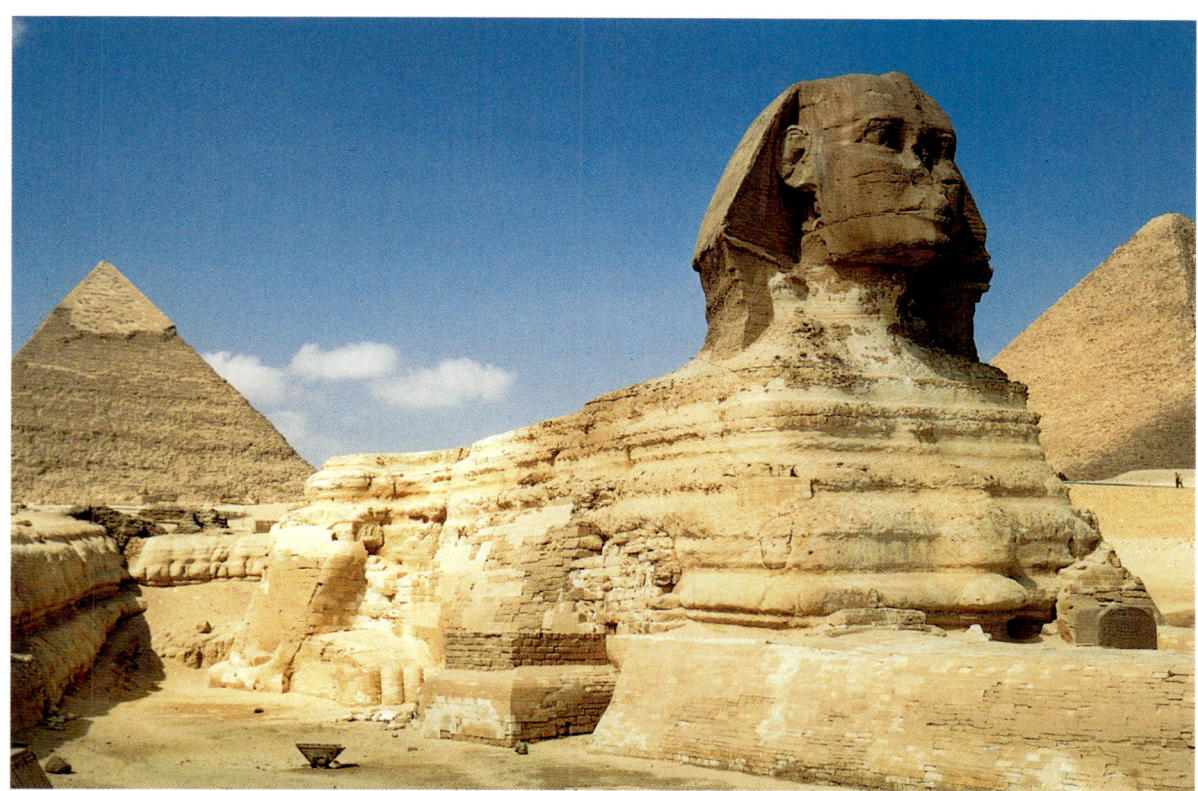

**3-10** Great Sphinx (with pyramid of Khafre in the background at left), Gizeh, Egypt, Fourth Dynasty, ca. 2520–2494 BCE. Sandstone, 65′ × 240′.

Carved out of the Gizeh stone quarry, the Great Sphinx is of colossal size. The sphinx has the body of a lion and the head of a pharaoh (probably Khafre) and is associated with the sun god.

**GREAT SPHINX** Beside the causeway and dominating the valley temple of Khafre rises the Great Sphinx (FIG. **3-10**). Carved from a spur of rock in an ancient quarry, the colossal statue—the largest in Egypt, Mesopotamia, or Persia—is probably an image of Khafre (originally complete with the pharaoh's ceremonial beard and *uraeus* cobra headdress), although some scholars think it portrays Khufu and predates the construction of Khafre's complex. Whichever king it portrays, the *sphinx*—a lion with a human head—was associated with the sun god and therefore was an appropriate image for a pharaoh. The composite form suggests that the pharaoh combines human intelligence with the fearsome strength and authority of the king of beasts.

# Sculpture

Old Kingdom statues survive in significant numbers because they fulfilled an important function in Egyptian tombs as substitute abodes for the ka (see "Mummification and Immortality," page 61). Although Egyptian sculptors worked with wood, clay, and other materials, mostly for images of individuals not of the royal or noble classes, the primary material for funerary statuary was stone.

**KHAFRE ENTHRONED** The seated statue of Khafre (FIG. 3-11) is one of a series of similar statues carved for the pharaoh's valley temple (FIG. 3-9, no. 6) near the Great Sphinx. The stone is diorite, an exceptionally hard dark stone brought some 400 miles down the Nile from royal quarries in the south. (The Neo-Sumerian ruler Gudea [FIG. 2-16] so admired diorite that he imported it to faraway Girsu.) Khafre wears a simple kilt and sits rigidly upright on a throne formed of two stylized lions' bodies. Intertwined lotus and papyrus plants—symbolic of the united Egypt—appear between the throne's legs. The falcon-god Horus (compare FIG. 3-1) extends his protective wings to shelter the pharaoh's head. Khafre has the royal false beard fastened to his chin and wears the royal linen *nemes* headdress with the uraeus cobra of kingship on the front. The headdress covers his forehead and falls in pleated folds over his shoulders. (The head of the Great Sphinx is similarly attired.) As befitting a divine ruler, the sculptor portrayed Khafre with a well-developed, flawless body and a perfect face, regardless of his real age and appearance. Because Egyptians considered ideal proportions appropriate for representing their god-kings, the statue of Khafre is not a true likeness and was not intended to be. The purpose of pharaonic portraiture was not to record individual features or the distinctive shapes of bodies, but rather to proclaim the divine nature of Egyptian kingship.

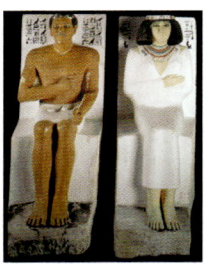

3-11A Rahotep and Nofret, Maidum, ca. 2575–2550 BCE.

The enthroned Khafre radiates serenity. The sculptor created this effect, common to Egyptian royal statues (compare FIG. 3-11A), in part by giving the figure great compactness and solidity, with few projecting, breakable parts. The form manifests the purpose: to last for eternity. Khafre's body is one with the unarticulated slab that forms the back of the king's throne. His arms follow the bend of his body and rest on his thighs, and his legs are close together. Part of the original stone block still connects the king's legs to his chair. Khafre's pose is frontal, rigid, and *bilaterally symmetrical* (the same on either side of an axis, in this case the vertical axis). The sculptor suppressed all movement and with it the notion of time, creating an aura of eternal stillness.

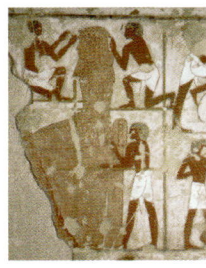

3-11B Sculptors at work, Thebes, ca. 1425 BCE.

Some extant reliefs and paintings (FIG. 3-11B) show Egyptian sculptors at work and provide detailed information about the successive stages of carving a statue. To produce the statue, the artist first drew the front, back, and two profile views of the pharaoh on the four vertical faces of the stone block. Next, apprentices chiseled away the excess stone on each side, working inward until the planes met at right angles. Finally, the master sculpted the parts of Khafre's body, the falcon, and so forth. The polished surface was achieved by *abrasion* (rubbing or grinding). This *subtractive* method of

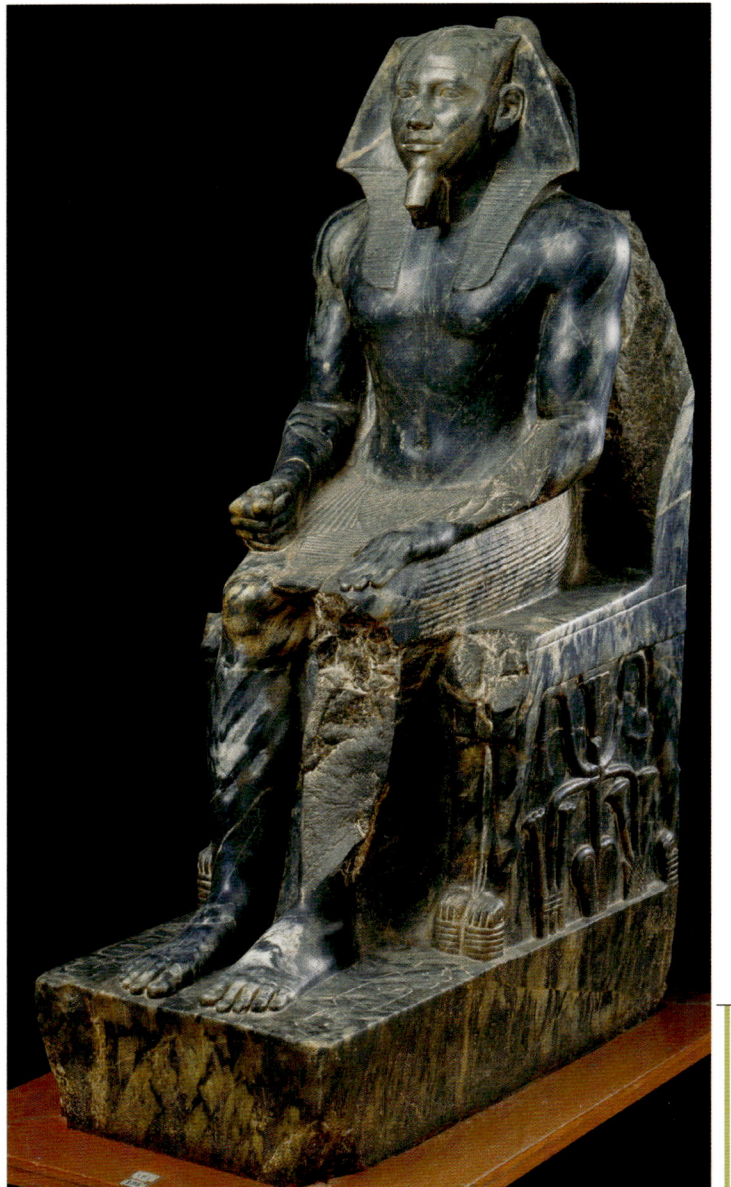

3-11 **Khafre enthroned, from Gizeh, Egypt, Fourth Dynasty, ca. 2520–2494 BCE. Diorite, 5′ 6″ high. Egyptian Museum, Cairo.** ◼◀

This portrait from his pyramid complex depicts Khafre as an enthroned divine ruler with a perfect body. The rigidity of the pose creates an aura of eternal stillness, appropriate for the timeless afterlife.

creating statuary accounts in large part for the blocklike look of the standard Egyptian statue. Nevertheless, other sculptors, both ancient and modern, with different aims, have transformed stone blocks into dynamic, twisting human forms (for example, FIGS. I-15 and 5-84).

**MENKAURE AND KHAMERERNEBTY** The seated statue is one of only a small number of basic formulaic types Old Kingdom sculptors employed to represent the human figure. Another is the image of a person or deity standing, either alone or in a group, for example the double portrait (FIG. 3-12) of Menkaure and one of his wives, probably the queen Khamerernebty. The statue once stood in the valley temple of Menkaure's pyramid complex at Gizeh. Here, too, the figures remain wedded to the stone

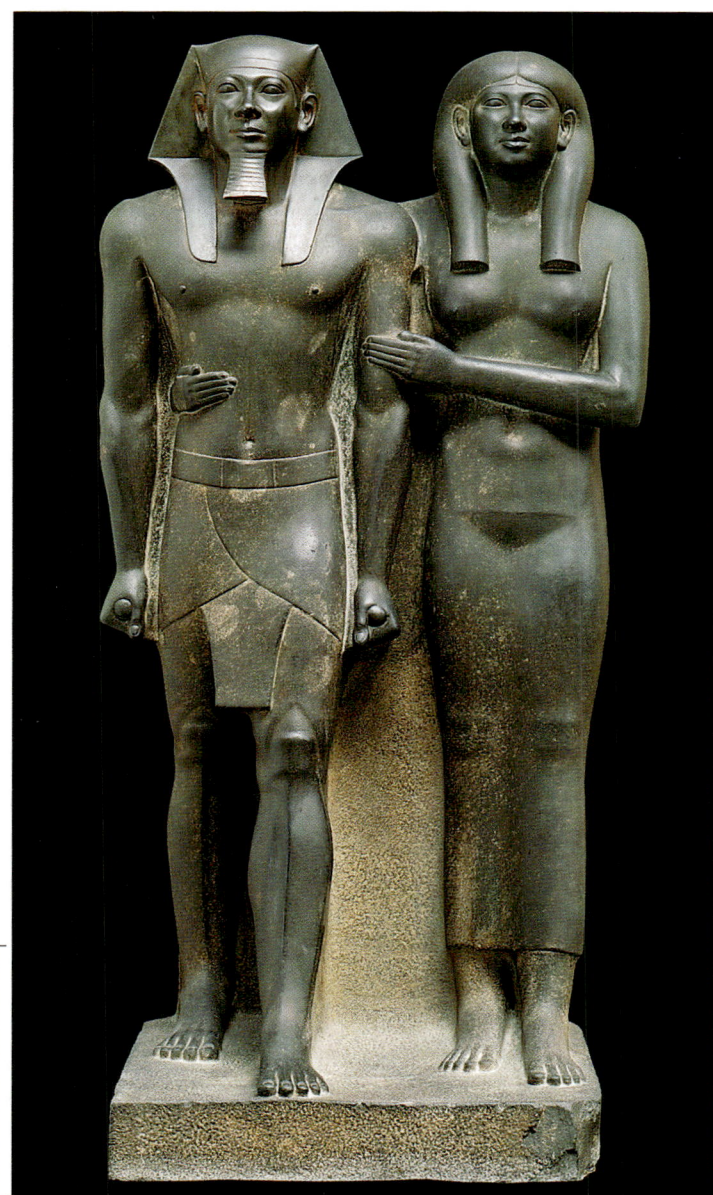

1 ft.

**3-12** Menkaure and Khamerernebty(?), from Gizeh, Egypt, Fourth Dynasty, ca. 2490–2472 BCE. Graywacke, 4′ 6½″ high. Museum of Fine Arts, Boston. ◼◣

The double portrait of Menkaure and his wife displays the conventional postures used for statues designed as substitute homes for the ka. The frozen gestures signify the couple are married.

block. In fact, the statue could be classified as a *high-relief* sculpture. Menkaure's pose—duplicated in countless other Egyptian statues—is rigidly frontal with the arms hanging straight down and close to his well-built body. He clenches his hands into fists with the thumbs forward and advances his left leg slightly. But no shift occurs in the angle of the hips to correspond to the uneven distribution of weight. Khamerernebty stands in a similar position. Her right arm, however, circles around the king's waist, and her left hand gently rests on his left arm. This frozen stereotypical gesture indicates their marital status. The husband and wife show no other sign of affection or emotion and look not at each other but out into space. The artist's aim was not to portray living figures, but to suggest the timeless nature of the stone statue that might have to serve as an eternal substitute home for the ka.

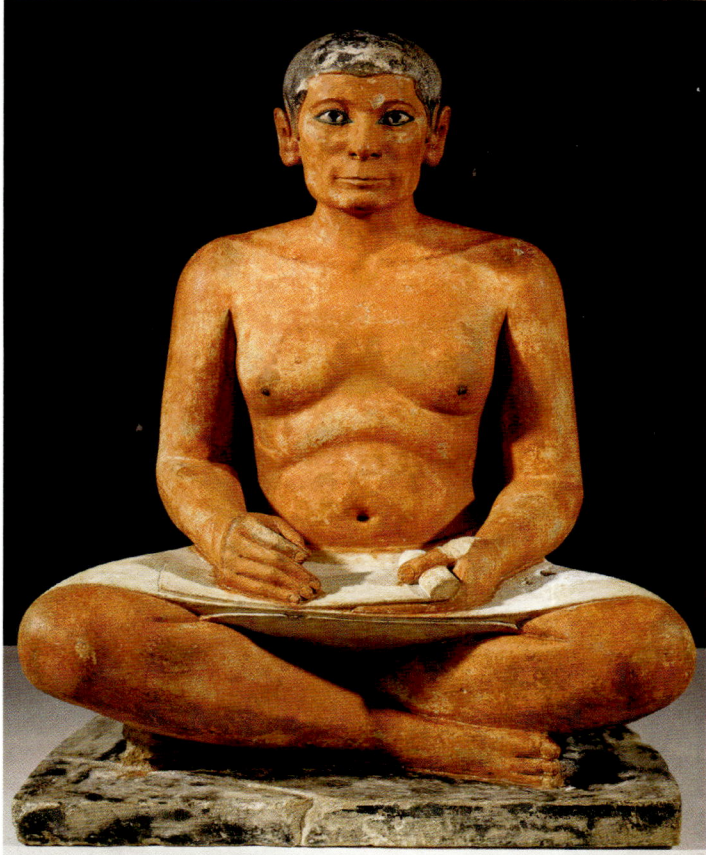

1 in.

**3-13** Seated scribe, from Saqqara, Egypt, Fourth Dynasty, ca. 2500 BCE. Painted limestone, 1′ 9″ high. Musée du Louvre, Paris.

The idealism that characterizes the portraiture of the Egyptian god-kings did not extend to the portrayal of nonelite individuals. This more realistic painted depiction of a scribe shows clear signs of aging.

**SEATED SCRIBE** Traces of paint remain on the portraits of Menkaure and Khamerernebty. Egyptian artists painted most of their statues, although sometimes sculptors left the natural color of the stone exposed, enhancing the sense of abstraction and timelessness. Striking examples of painted sculpture are the seated statues of Rahotep and Nofret (FIG. 3-11A) and the statue found at Saqqara portraying a Fourth Dynasty scribe (FIG. **3-13**). Despite the stiff upright postures of all these statues and the frontality of head and body, the coloration lends a lifelike quality to the stone images.

The head of the Saqqara scribe displays an extraordinary sensitivity. The sculptor conveyed the personality of a sharply intelligent and alert individual with a penetration and sympathy seldom achieved at this early date. The scribe sits directly on the ground, not on a throne or even on a chair. Although he occupied a position of honor in a largely illiterate society, the scribe was a much lower figure in the Egyptian hierarchy than the pharaoh, whose divinity made him superhuman. In the history of art, especially portraiture, it is almost a rule that as a person's importance decreases, formality is relaxed and realism increases. It is telling that the sculptor reproduced the scribe's sagging chest muscles and protruding belly. These signs of age would have been disrespectful and wholly inappropriate in a depiction of an Egyptian god-king or members of his family. But the statue of the scribe is not a true portrait either. Rather, it is a composite of conventional types. Obesity, for example, characterizes many nonroyal Old Kingdom male portraits (for

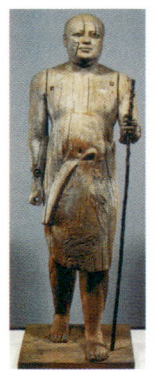

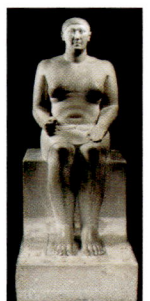

example, FIGS. 3-13A and especially 3-13B), perhaps because it attested to the comfortable life of the person represented and his relatively high position in society.

**TOMB OF TI** In Old Kingdom tombs, images of the deceased also frequently appear in relief sculpture and in mural painting, sometimes singly (FIG. I-15) and sometimes in a narrative context. The painted limestone relief scenes that decorate the walls of the mastaba of a Fifth Dynasty official named Ti typify the subjects Old Kingdom patrons favored for the adornment of their final resting places. Depictions of agriculture and hunting fill Ti's tomb. The Egyptians associated these activities with the provisioning of the ka in the hereafter, but the subjects also had powerful symbolic overtones. In ancient Egypt, success in the hunt, for example, was a metaphor for triumph over the forces of evil.

On one wall (FIG. 3-14) of his tomb, Ti, his men, and his boats move slowly through the marshes, hunting hippopotami and birds in a dense growth of towering papyrus. The sculptor delineated the reedy stems of the plants with repeated fine grooves that fan out gracefully at the top into a commotion of frightened birds and stalking foxes. The water beneath the boats, signified by a pattern of wavy lines, is crowded with hippopotami and fish. Ti's men seem frantically busy with their spears, whereas Ti, depicted twice their size, stands aloof. The basic conventions of Egyptian figure representation—used a half millennium earlier for the palette of King Narmer (FIG. 3-1)—appear again here. As in the Predynastic work, the artist exaggerated the size of Ti to announce his rank, and combined frontal and profile views of Ti's body to show its most characteristic parts clearly. This approach to representation was well suited for Egyptian funerary art because it emphasizes the essential nature of the deceased, not his accidental appearance. Ti's conventional pose contrasts with the realistically rendered activities of his tiny servants and with the naturalistically carved and painted birds and animals among the papyrus buds. Ti's immobility suggests that he is not an actor in the hunt. He does not *do* anything. He simply *is,* a figure apart from time and an impassive observer of life, like his ka.

The idealized and stiff image of Ti is typical of Egyptian relief sculpture. Egyptian artists regularly ignored the endless variations in body types of real human beings. Painters and sculptors did not sketch their subjects from life but applied a strict *canon,* or system of proportions, to the human figure. They first drew a grid on the wall. Then they placed various human body parts at specific points on the network of squares. The height of a figure, for example, was a fixed number of squares, and the head, shoulders, waist, knees, and other parts of the body also had a predetermined size and place within the scheme. This approach to design lasted for more than 2,500 years. Specific proportions

might vary from workshop to workshop and change over time, but the principle of the canon persisted.

On another wall (FIG. 3-15) of Ti's mastaba, goats tread in seeds in the upper register and, below, cattle ford a canal in the Nile. Once again, the scenes may be interpreted on a symbolic as well as a literal level. The fording of the Nile, for example, was a metaphor for the deceased's passage from life to the hereafter. Ti is absent from the scenes, and all the men and animals participate in the narrative. Despite the sculptor's repeated use of similar poses for most of the human and animal figures, the reliefs are full of anecdotal details. Especially charming is the group at the lower right. A youth, depicted in a complex unconventional posture, carries a calf on his back. The animal, not a little afraid, turns its head back a full 180 degrees (compare FIG. 1-8) to seek reassurance from its mother, who returns the calf's gaze. Scenes such as this demonstrate that Egyptian artists could be close observers of daily life. The suppression of the anecdotal (that is, of the time-bound) from their representations of the deceased both in relief and in the round was a deliberate choice. Their primary purpose was to suggest the deceased's eternal existence in the afterlife, not to portray his activities while alive.

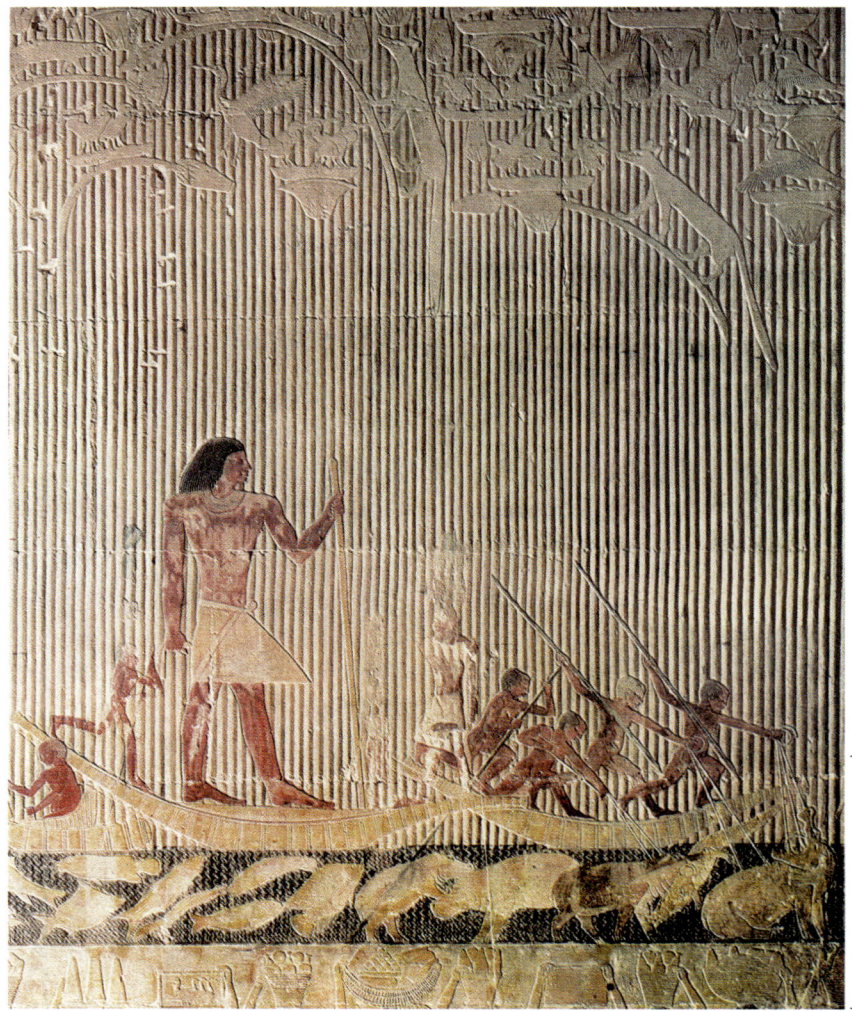

1 ft.

**3-14** Ti watching a hippopotamus hunt, relief in the mastaba of Ti, Saqqara, Egypt, Fifth Dynasty, ca. 2450–2350 BCE. Painted limestone, 4′ high.

In Egypt, a successful hunt was a metaphor for triumph over evil. In this painted tomb relief, the deceased stands aloof from the hunters busily spearing hippopotami. Ti's size reflects his high rank.

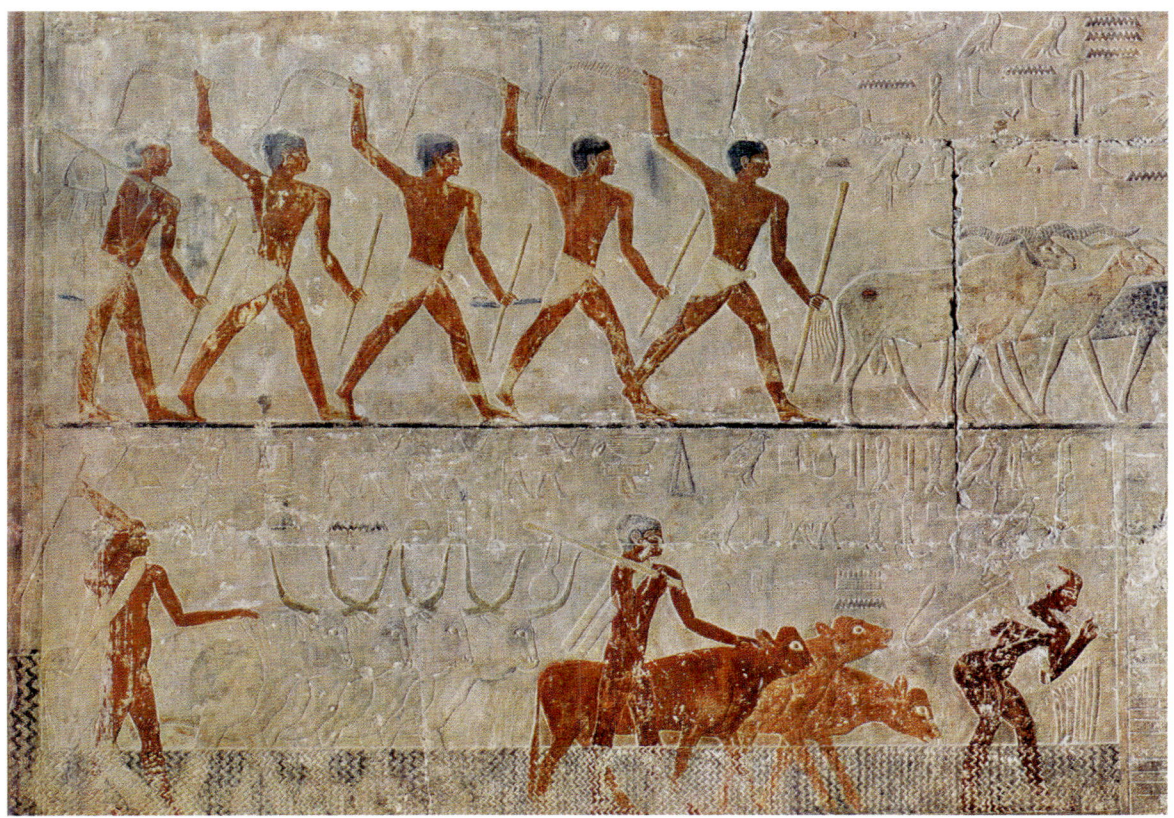

**3-15** Goats treading seed and cattle fording a canal, reliefs in the mastaba of Ti, Saqqara, Egypt, Fifth Dynasty, ca. 2450–2350 BCE. Painted limestone.

The fording of the Nile was a metaphor for the passage to the afterlife. These reliefs combine stereotypical poses for humans and animals with unconventional postures and anecdotal details.

# MIDDLE KINGDOM

About 2150 BCE, the Egyptians challenged the pharaohs' power, and for more than a century the land was in a state of civil unrest and near anarchy. But in 2040 BCE, the pharaoh of Upper Egypt, Mentuhotep II (r. 2050–1998 BCE), managed to unite Egypt again under the rule of a single king and established the Middle Kingdom (11th to 14th Dynasties), which lasted 400 years.

## Sculpture

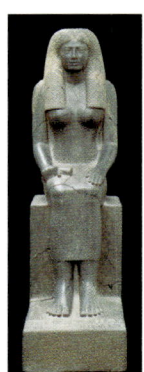

**3-15A** Lady Sennuwy, Kerma, 1960–1916 BCE.

Although in most respects Middle Kingdom sculptors adhered to the conventions established during the Old Kingdom, portraying both men and women in the familiar seated (FIG. **3-15A**) and standing poses, there were some notable innovations.

**SENUSRET III** One of Mentuhotep II's successors was Senusret III (r. 1878–1859 BCE), who fought four brutal military campaigns in Nubia (MAP 3-1). Although Egyptian armies devastated the land and poisoned the wells, Senusret never fully achieved secure control over the Nubians. In Egypt itself, he attempted, with greater success, to establish a more powerful central government. His portraits (FIG. **3-16**) are of special interest because they represent a sharp break from Old Kingdom practice. Although the king's preserved statues have idealized bodies, the sculptors brought a stunning and unprecedented realism to the rendition of Senusret's features. His pessimistic expression reflects the dominant mood of the time, echoed in Middle Kingdom literature. The strong mouth, the drooping lines about the nose and eyes, and the shadowy brows show a determined

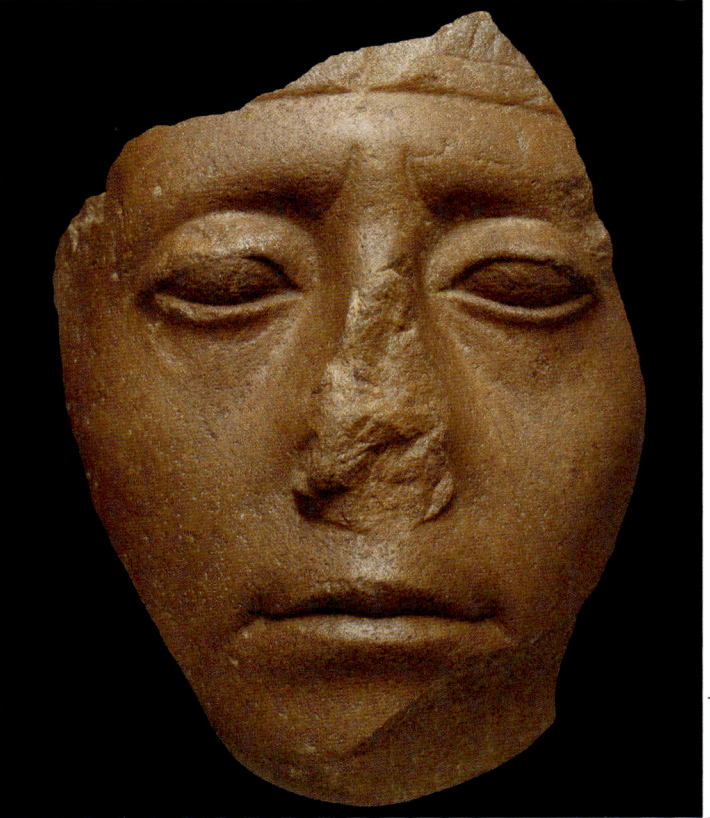

1 in.

**3-16** Fragmentary head of Senusret III, 12th Dynasty, ca. 1860 BCE. Red quartzite, $6\frac{1}{2}''$ high. Metropolitan Museum of Art, New York.

Senusret III's portraits exhibit an unprecedented realism. The king's brooding expression reflects the mood of the time and contrasts sharply with the impassive faces of Old Kingdom pharaohs.

ruler who had also shared in the cares of the world, sunk in brooding meditation. The portrait is different in kind from the typically impassive faces of the Old Kingdom. It is personal, almost intimate, in its revelation of the mark of anxiety that a troubled age might leave on the soul of a king.

## Architecture

Senusret III's tomb, at Dashur, is a mud-brick pyramid, but the most characteristic burials of the Middle Kingdom are rock-cut tombs. This kind of tomb, documented also in the Old Kingdom, became especially popular during the Middle Kingdom and largely replaced the mastaba as the standard Egyptian tomb type.

**BENI HASAN** Some of the best preserved Middle Kingdom tombs are at Beni Hasan (FIG. **3-17**). Hollowed out of the cliffs, the typical tomb there has a shallow columnar porch, which leads into a columned hall and then into a burial chamber featuring statues of the deceased in niches and paintings and painted reliefs on the walls. In the 12th Dynasty tomb of Amenemhet, the columns in the hall (FIG. **3-18**) serve no supporting function because, like the porch columns, they are continuous parts of the rock fabric. (Note the broken column in the rear suspended from the ceiling like a stalactite.) The column shafts are *fluted,* like those in the entrance corridor (FIG. 3-5A) of Djoser's mortuary precinct at Saqqara. The Beni Hasan columns are more formalized versions of Imhotep's earlier columns, which still look like bundles of reeds. The Middle Kingdom columns closely resemble later Greek columns of the Doric order (FIG. 5-13, *left*), and there is no doubt the Greeks knew about and emulated many aspects of Egyptian architecture (see Chapter 5). Archaeologists believe the kind of *fluting* used for the Beni Hasan column shafts derived from the dressing of softwood trunks with the rounded cutting edge of the adze.

**3-17** Rock-cut tombs BH 3 to 5, Beni Hasan, Egypt, 12th Dynasty, ca. 1950–1900 BCE.

The tombs of Beni Hasan are characteristic of the Middle Kingdom. Hollowed out of the cliffs, these tombs often have a shallow columnar porch, which leads into a columned hall and burial chamber.

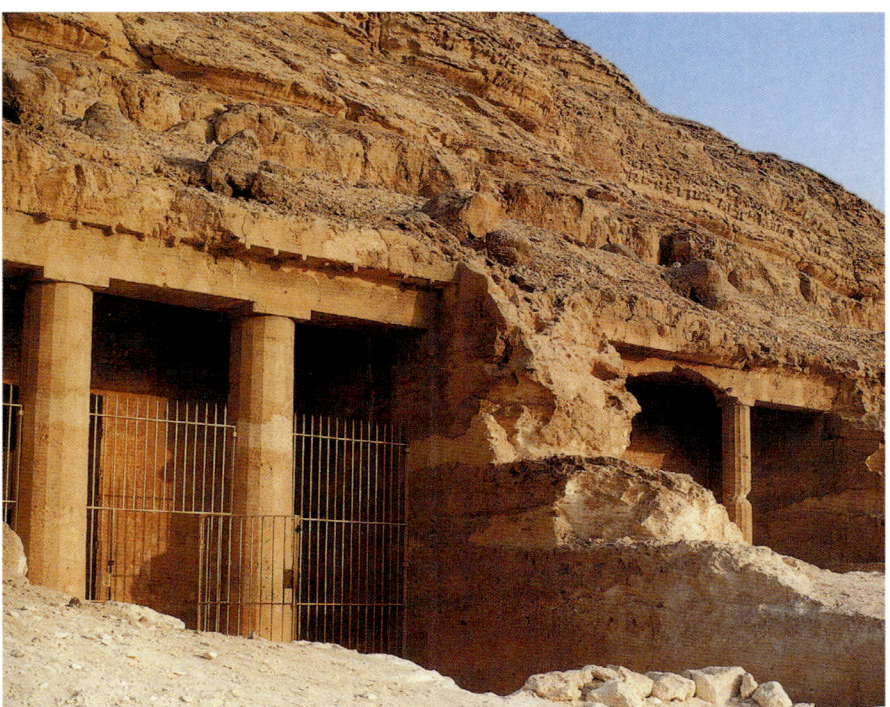

**3-18** Interior hall of the rock-cut tomb of Amenemhet (tomb BH 2), Beni Hasan, Egypt, 12th Dynasty, ca. 1950–1900 BCE.

Stonemasons carved the columnar hall of Amenemhet's tomb out of the living rock, which explains the suspended broken column at the rear. The shafts have flutes, a form Greek architects later emulated.

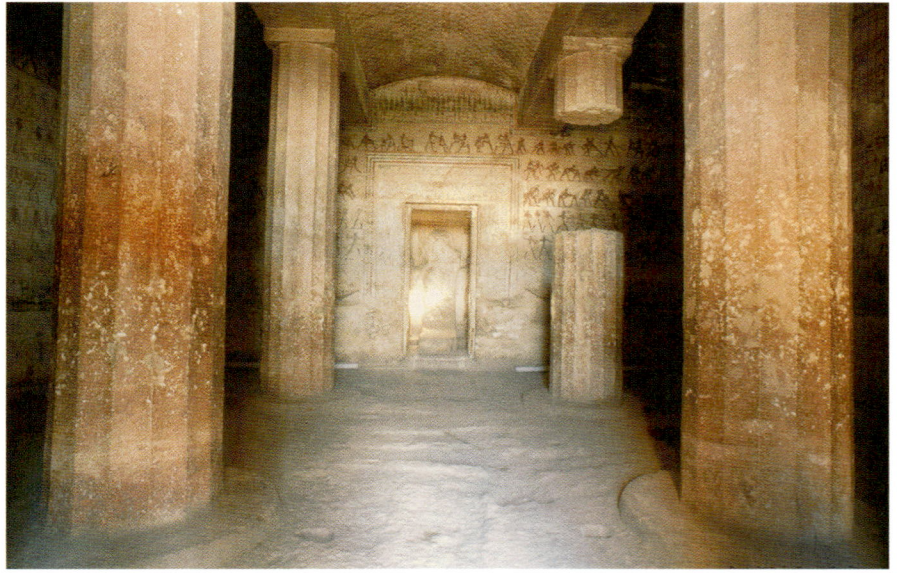

# Hatshepsut, the Woman Who Would Be King

In 1479 BCE, Thutmose II, the fourth pharaoh of the 18th Dynasty (r. 1492–1479 BCE), died. His principal wife (and half sister), Queen Hatshepsut (r. 1473–1458 BCE), had not given birth to any sons who survived, so the title of king went to Thutmose III, son of Thutmose II by a minor wife. Hatshepsut became regent for the boy-king. Within a few years, however, the queen proclaimed herself pharaoh and insisted her father, Thutmose I, had chosen her as his successor during his lifetime. Underscoring her claim, one of the reliefs decorating Hatshepsut's enormous funerary complex (FIG. 3-19) depicts Thutmose I crowning his daughter as king in the presence of the Egyptian gods.

Hatshepsut is the first great female monarch whose name has been recorded. (In the 12th Dynasty, Sobekneferu was crowned king of Egypt, but she reigned as pharaoh for only a few years.)

Hatshepsut boasted of having made the "two Lands to labor with bowed back" for her, and for two decades she ruled what was then the most powerful and prosperous empire in the world.

Hatshepsut commissioned numerous building projects, and sculptors produced portraits of the female pharaoh in great numbers for display in those complexes. Unfortunately, Thutmose III (r. 1458–1425 BCE), for reasons still not fully understood, late in his reign ordered Hatshepsut's portraits destroyed. In her surviving portraits, Hatshepsut uniformly wears the costume of the male pharaohs, with royal headdress and kilt, and in some cases (FIG. 3-21) even a false ceremonial beard. (Many inscriptions refer to Hatshepsut as "*His* Majesty.") In other statues, however, Hatshepsut has delicate features, a slender frame, and breasts, leaving no doubt artists also represented her as a woman.

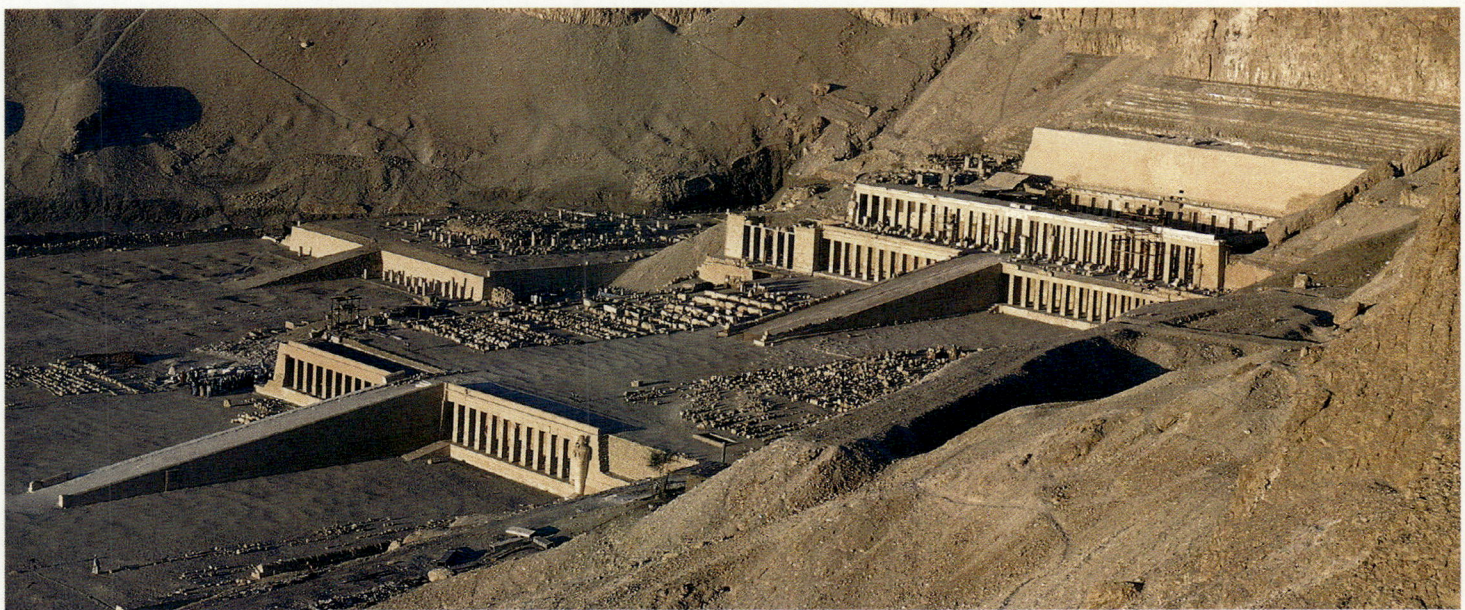

**3-19** Mortuary temple of Hatshepsut (looking southwest), Deir el-Bahri, Egypt, 18th Dynasty, ca. 1473–1458 BCE.

Hatshepsut was the first great female monarch whose name is recorded. Her immense funerary temple incorporated shrines to Amen, whom she claimed was her father, and to Hathor and Anubis.

# NEW KINGDOM

The Middle Kingdom disintegrated when the Hyksos descended on Egypt from the Syrian and Mesopotamian uplands. They ruled the Nile Delta and Lower Egypt during what historians call the Second Intermediate Period until, in the mid-16th century, native Egyptian kings of the 17th Dynasty rose up in revolt. Ahmose I (r. 1550–1525 BCE), final conqueror of the Hyksos and first king of the 18th Dynasty, ushered in the New Kingdom, the most glorious period in Egypt's long history. At this time, Egypt extended its borders by conquest from the Euphrates River in the east deep into Nubia to the south (MAP 3-1). A new capital—Thebes, in Upper Egypt—became a great metropolis with magnificent palaces, tombs, and temples along both banks of the Nile.

# Architecture

If the most impressive monuments of the Old Kingdom are its pyramids, those of the New Kingdom are its grandiose temples, built to honor pharaohs and queens as well as gods. Great pharaonic mortuary temples arose along the Nile in the Thebes district. These shrines provided the rulers with a place for worshiping their patron gods during their lifetimes and then served as temples in their own honor after their death.

**DEIR EL-BAHRI** The most majestic of these royal mortuary temples (FIG. 3-19) is at Deir el-Bahri, erected by and for the female pharaoh Hatshepsut, one of the most remarkable women of the ancient world (see "Hatshepsut, the Woman Who Would Be King," above). Some Egyptologists attribute the temple to SENMUT

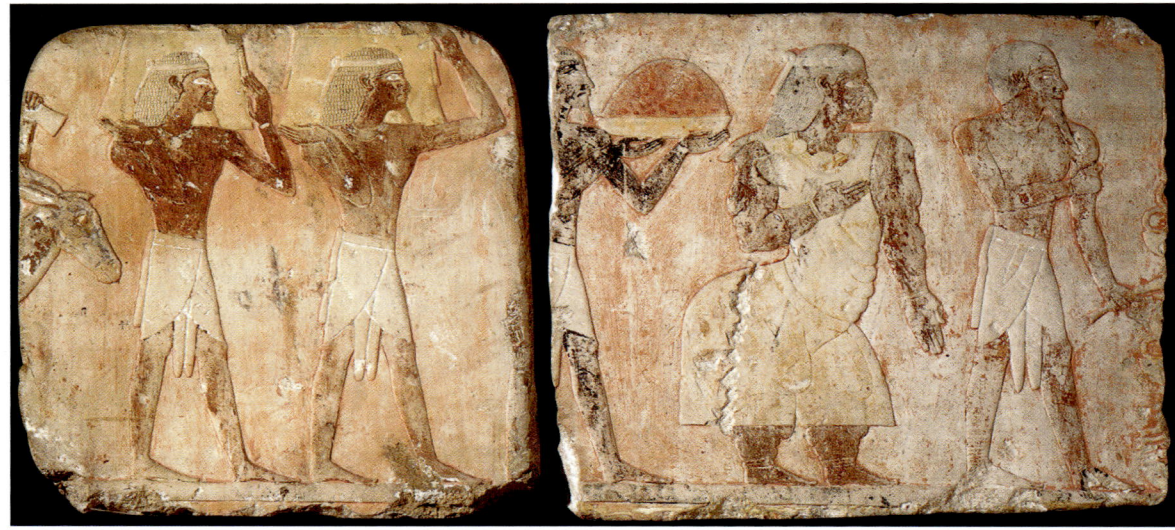

**3-20** King and queen of Punt and attendants, relief from the mortuary temple of Hatshepsut, Deir el-Bahri, Egypt, 18th Dynasty, ca. 1473–1458 BCE. Painted limestone, 1′ 3″ high. Egyptian Museum, Cairo.

Painted limestone reliefs throughout Hatshepsut's mortuary temple complex celebrated her reign, her divine birth, and her successful expedition to the kingdom of Punt on the Red Sea.

1 in.

(FIG. 3-27), Hatshepsut's chancellor and possible lover, described in two inscriptions as the queen's architect. His association with this project is uncertain, however. Hatshepsut's temple rises from the valley floor in three colonnaded terraces connected by ramps on the central axis. It is striking how visually well suited the structure is to its natural setting. The long horizontals and verticals of the *colonnades* and their rhythm of light and dark repeat the pattern of the limestone cliffs above.

As imposing as it is today, Hatshepsut's mortuary temple was once part of an even larger complex with a causeway connecting it to a now-lost valley temple. The multi-level funerary temple proper incorporated shrines to Amen, Hathor, and Anubis as well as to Hatshepsut and her father, Thutmose I. Statues portraying the queen and reliefs glorifying her and her reign were on display throughout the vast complex. Together the statues and reliefs constitute the first great tribute to a woman's achievements in the history of art. In the middle colonnade of the second level, for example, painted limestone reliefs commemorated Hatshepsut's divine birth. Hatshepsut claimed to be the daughter of Amen, who had assumed the form of the pharaoh Thutmose I in order to impregnate her mother, the king's principal wife. Other reliefs depicted the impressive engineering feat of transporting huge granite obelisks from the Aswan quarries to the temple of Amen-Re (FIG. 3-24) at Karnak.

The relief illustrated here (FIG. **3-20**) is one of those documenting Hatshepsut's successful expedition to Punt, famed for its gold, myrrh, and other exotic natural resources. The reliefs record the sea journey, the precious cargo of gold ingots and frankincense trees the Egyptians brought back with them, and the people, animals, and houses the Egyptians found in Punt. In this detail, bare-chested men carry the local goods that the Egyptians will load onto their ships. Leading the procession are two figures that art historians traditionally identify as the king and queen of Punt. The Egyptian sculptor depicted the queen as an obese and misshapen woman. Scholars debate whether this is an accurate portrayal or an exaggeration designed to underscore the foreignness of the Punt queen.

As many as 200 statues in the round depicting Hatshepsut in various guises complemented the extensive relief program. On the lowest terrace, to either side of the processional way, statues repeatedly portrayed Hatshepsut as a sphinx. On the uppermost level, the royal sculptors represented the female pharaoh standing, seated, and in the form of a mummy. At least eight colossal kneeling statues in red granite lined the way to the entrance of the Amen-Re sanctuary. The statue reproduced here (FIG. **3-21**) suffered the same fate as most of Hatshepsut's portraits during the reign of Thutmose III. Vandals smashed it and threw the pieces in a dump, but conservators have skillfully reassembled the portrait. Hatshepsut holds a globular offering jar in each hand as she takes part in a ritual in honor of the sun god. (A king kneeled only before a god, never a mortal.) She wears the royal male nemes headdress and the pharaoh's ceremonial beard (compare FIGS. 3-10 to 3-12 and 3-35). The agents of Thutmose III hacked off the uraeus cobra that once adorned the

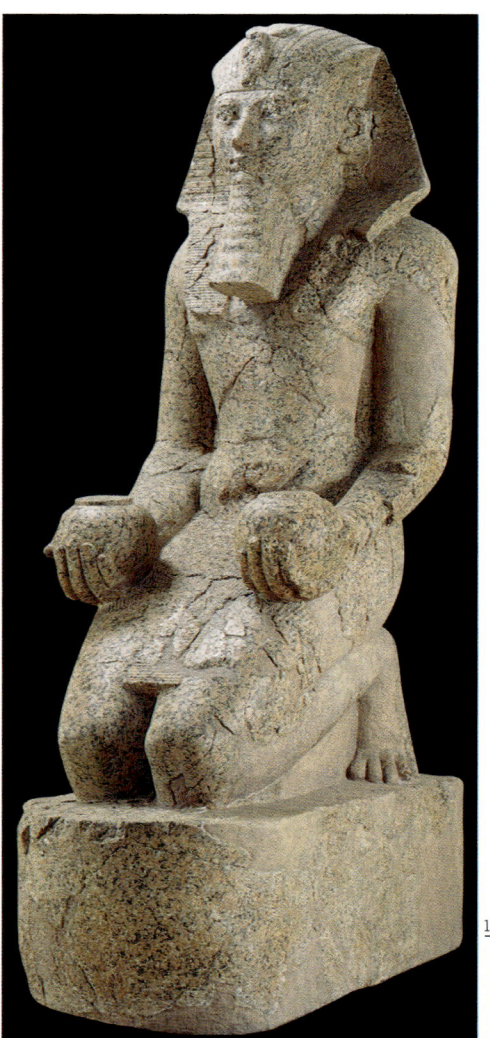

**3-21** Hatshepsut with offering jars, from the upper court of her mortuary temple, Deir el-Bahri, Egypt, 18th Dynasty, ca. 1473–1458 BCE. Red granite, 8′ 6″ high. Metropolitan Museum of Art, New York.

1 ft.

Her successor destroyed many of Hatshepsut's portraits. Conservators reassembled this one, which depicts the queen as a male pharaoh, consistent with inscriptions calling her "His Majesty."

front of the headdress. The figure is also anatomically male, although other surviving portraits of Hatshepsut represent her with a woman's breasts. The male imagery, however, is consistent with the queen's formal assumption of the title of king and with the many inscriptions that address her as a man.

**ABU SIMBEL** The sheer size of Hatshepsut's mortuary temple never fails to impress visitors, and this is no less true of the rock-cut temple (FIG. **3-22**) of Ramses II (r. 1290–1224 BCE) at Abu Simbel. In 1968, engineers moved the immense Nubian temple nearly 700 feet—an amazing achievement in its own right—to save it from submersion in the Aswan High Dam reservoir. Ramses, Egypt's last great warrior pharaoh, ruled for two-thirds of a century, an extraordinary accomplishment even in peacetime in an era when life expectancy was far shorter than it is today. The pharaoh, proud of his many campaigns to restore the empire, proclaimed his greatness by placing four colossal images of himself on the temple facade. The portraits are 65 feet tall—almost a dozen times the height of an ancient Egyptian, even though the pharaoh is seated. Spectacular as they are, the rock-cut statues nonetheless lack the refinement of earlier periods, because the sculptors sacrificed detailed carving to overwhelming size. This trade-off is characteristic of colossal statuary of every period and every place (compare FIG. 16-14).

The rock-cut interior (FIG. **3-23**) of the Abu Simbel temple is also of colossal size. The distance from the facade to the back wall is an astounding 206 feet. In the main gallery stand 32-foot-tall figures of the king in the guise of Osiris, carved as one with the *pillars,* facing each other across the narrow corridor. The pillars,

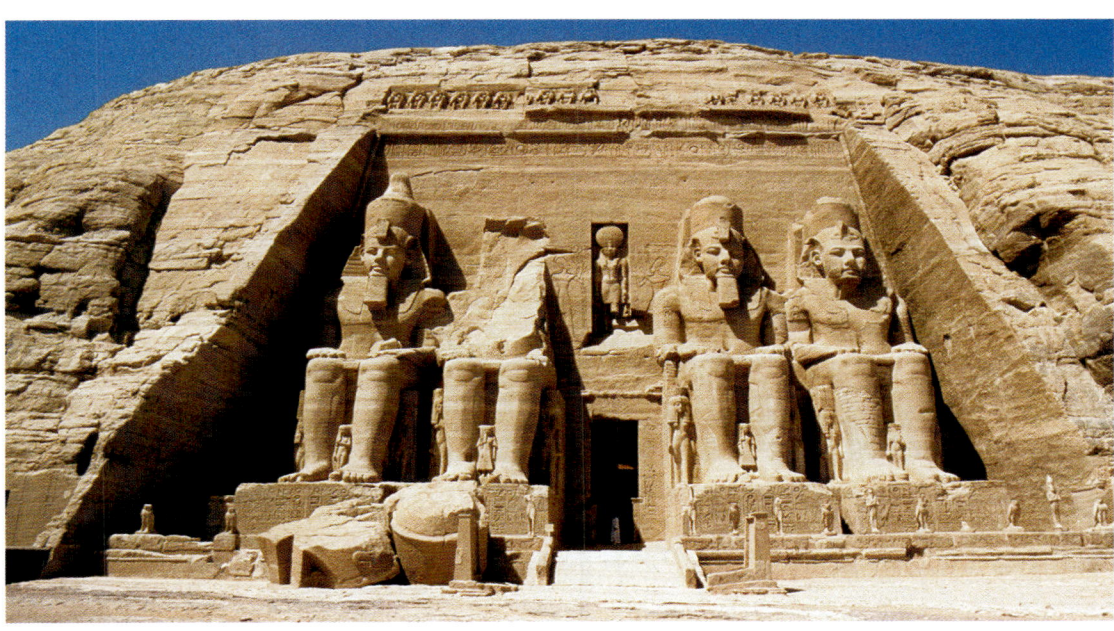

**3-22** Facade of the temple of Ramses II, Abu Simbel, Egypt, 19th Dynasty, ca. 1290–1224 BCE. Sandstone, colossi 65′ high.

Four rock-cut images of Ramses II dominate the facade of his mortuary temple at Abu Simbel in Nubia. The colossal portraits are a dozen times the height of a man, even though the pharaoh is seated.

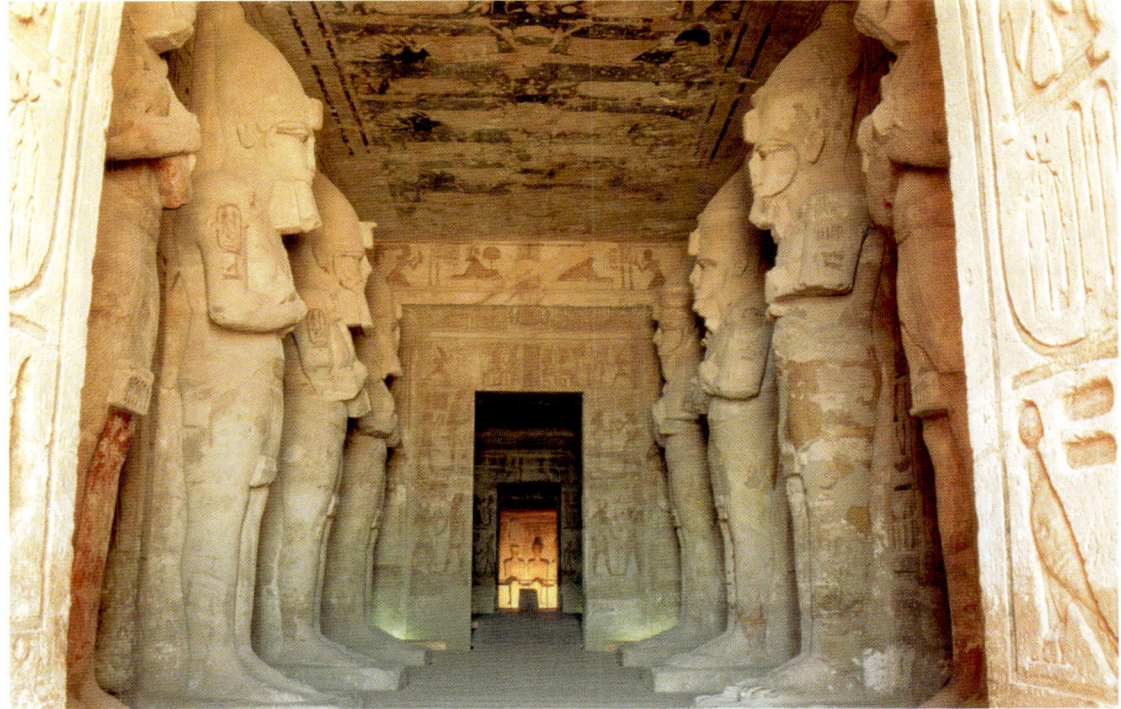

**3-23** Interior of the temple of Ramses II, Abu Simbel, Egypt, 19th Dynasty, ca. 1290–1224 BCE. Sandstone, pillar statues 32′ high.

Inside Ramses II's mortuary temple are colossal statues of the long-reigning pharaoh in the guise of Osiris, carved as one with the pillars, facing each other across the narrow corridor.

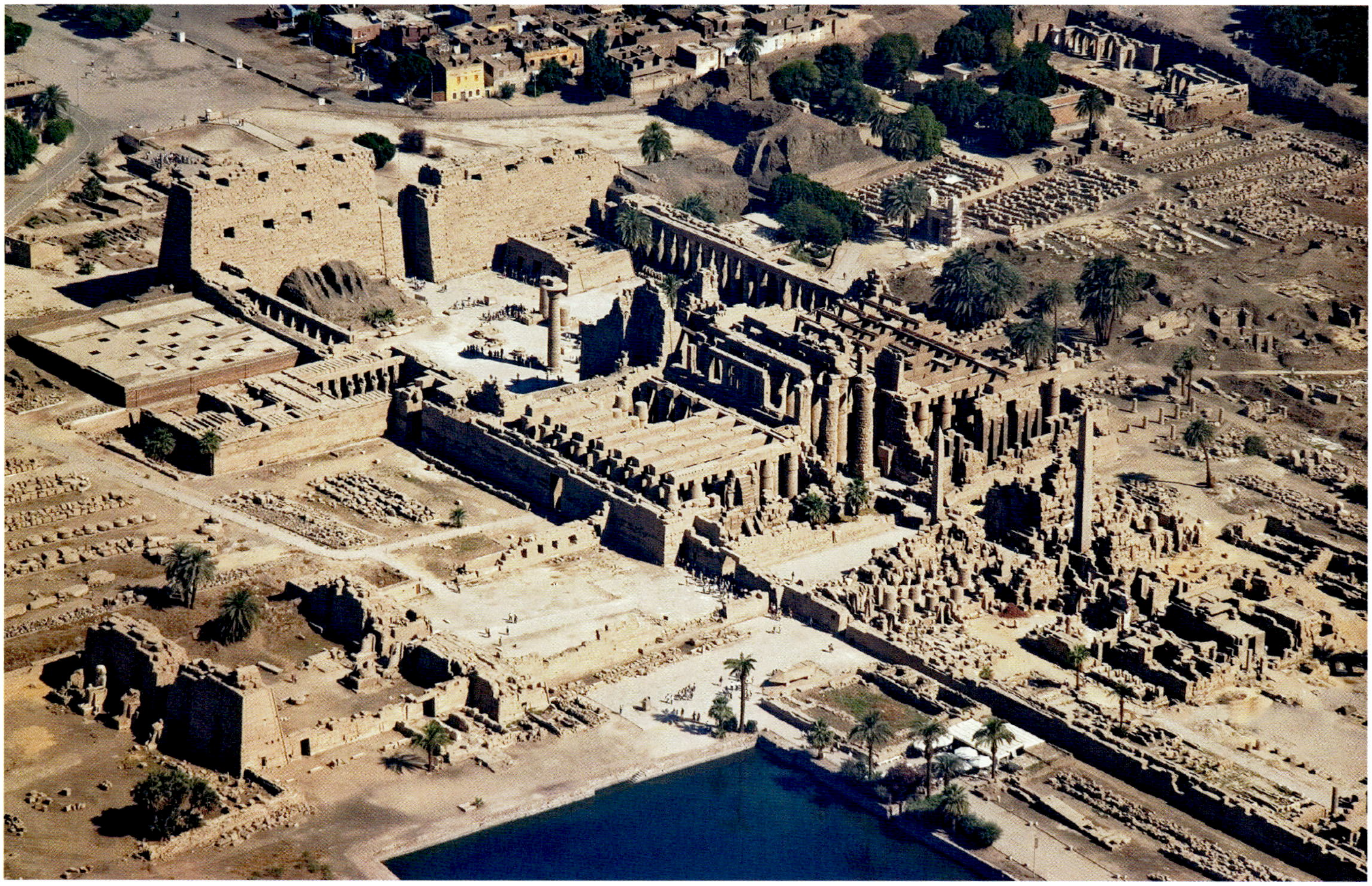

**3-24** Aerial view of the temple of Amen-Re (looking north), Karnak, Egypt, begun 15th century BCE.

The vast Karnak temple complex contains an artificial lake associated with the primeval waters of the Egyptian creation myth and a pylon temple with a bilaterally symmetrical axial plan.

carved from the cliff like the pharaoh's facade portraits, have no load-bearing function. In this respect, they resemble the columns in the tombs at Beni Hasan (FIG. 3-18). The statue-column, in its male (*atlantid*) or female (*caryatid*) variants, reappears throughout the history of art. Often, as here, the human figure is attached to a column or *pier*. At other times the figure replaces the architectural member and forms the sole source of support (FIG. 5-54).

Ramses, like other pharaohs, had many wives, and he fathered scores of sons. The pharaoh honored the most important members of his family with immense monuments of their own. At Abu Simbel, for example, north of his temple, Ramses ordered the construction of a grand temple for his principal wife, Nefertari. Huge rock-cut statues—four standing images of the king and two of the queen—dominate the temple's facade. For his sons, Ramses constructed a huge underground tomb complex in the Valley of the Kings at Thebes, which an American team rediscovered in 1987. Robbers looted the tomb within a half century of its construction, but archaeologists have yet to find the royal burial chambers in the complex, so the tomb may one day yield important artworks.

**KARNAK** Distinct from the New Kingdom temples honoring pharaohs and queens are the edifices built to honor one or more of the gods. Successive kings often added to them until they reached gigantic size. The temple of Amen-Re (FIG. 3-24) at Karnak, for ex-

ample, was largely the work of the 18th Dynasty pharaohs, including Thutmose I and III and Hatshepsut, but Ramses II (19th Dynasty) also contributed sections, and other pharaohs added chapels to the complex as late as the 26th Dynasty. Enclosing the 247-acre complex and shutting it off from the outside world was a perimeter wall 39 feet high and 26 feet thick. Inside, next to the temple proper, was an artificial sacred lake (FIG. 3-24, *bottom*)—a reference to the primeval waters before creation (see "The Gods and Goddesses of Egypt," page 57). The temple of Amen-Re rises from the earth as the original sacred mound rose from the waters at the beginning of time.

The Karnak temple and similar New Kingdom temples such as the equally huge one at nearby Luxor (FIG. **3-24A**) all had similar *axial plans*. A typical *pylon temple* (the name derives from the sanctuaries' simple and massive gateways, or *pylons,* with sloping walls) is bilaterally symmetrical along a single axis

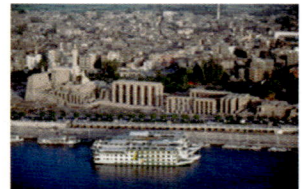

**3-24A** Temple of Amen-Re, Luxor, begun early 14th century BCE.

that runs from an approaching avenue through a colonnaded court and hall into a dimly lit sanctuary. Axial plans are characteristic of much of Egyptian architecture. Narrow corridors on the longitudinal axis are also the approaches to the Great Pyramids (FIG. 3-9)

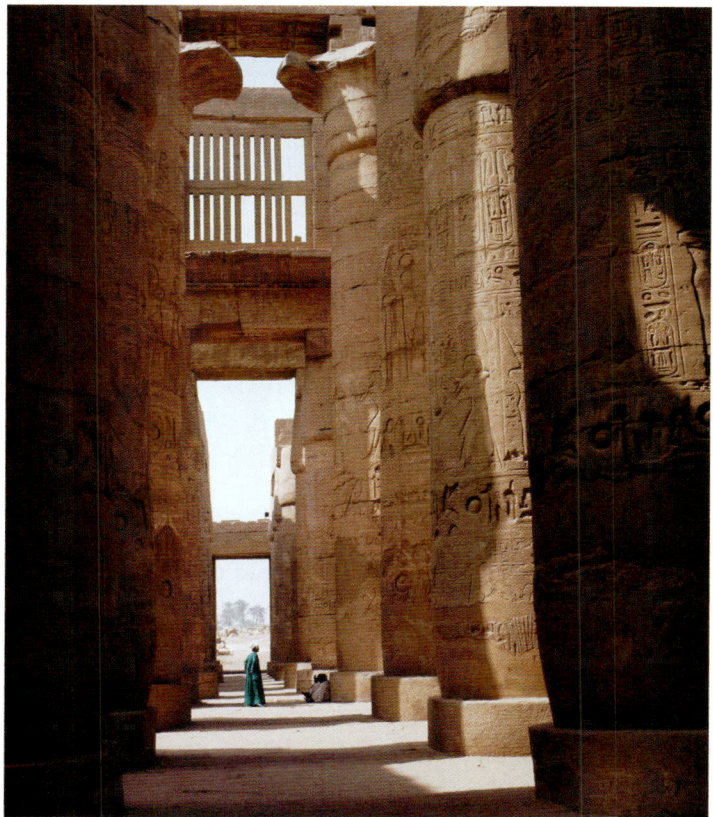

**3-25** Hypostyle hall of the temple of Amen-Re, Karnak, Egypt, 19th Dynasty, ca. 1290–1224 BCE.

Columns crowd the hypostyle hall of the Amen-Re temple. The tallest are 66 feet high and have capitals that are 22 feet in diameter. The columns support a roof of stone slabs carried on lintels.

and to Hatshepsut's multilevel mortuary temple (FIG. 3-19). Marking the end of the statuary-lined approach to a New Kingdom temple was the monumental facade of the pylon (FIG. 3-24, *top left*), which Egyptian sculptors routinely covered with reliefs glorifying their rulers (FIG. 3-40). Inside was an open court with columns on two or more sides, followed by a hall (FIG. 3-24, *center*) between

the court and sanctuary, its long axis placed at right angles to the corridor of the entire building complex. Only the pharaohs and the priests could enter the sanctuary. A chosen few were admitted to the great columnar *hypostyle hall* (a hall with a roof resting on columns). The majority of the people could proceed only as far as the open court.

Filling Karnak's gigantic (58,000 square feet) hypostyle hall were massive columns, which supported a roof of stone slabs carried on *lintels* (FIGS. **3-25** and **3-26**). The 134 sandstone columns have bud-cluster or bell-shaped capitals resembling lotus or papyrus, the plants of Upper and Lower Egypt. The 12 central columns are 75 feet high, and the capitals are 22 feet in diameter at the top, large enough to hold a hundred people. The Egyptians, who used no cement, depended on precise cutting of the joints and the weight of the huge stone blocks to hold the columns in place. The two central rows of columns are taller than those at the sides. Raising the roof's central section created a *clerestory*. Openings in the clerestory permitted sunlight to filter into the interior, although the stone grilles (FIG. 3-25) would have blocked much of the light. This method of construction appeared in primitive form in the Old Kingdom valley temple of Khafre at Gizeh. The clerestory is evidently an Egyptian innovation, and its significance cannot be overstated. Before the invention of the electric light bulb, illuminating a building's interior was always a challenge for architects. The clerestory played a key role in the history of architecture until very recently.

In the hypostyle hall at Karnak, the columns are indispensable structurally, unlike the rock-cut columns of the tombs at Beni Hasan (FIGS. 3-17 and 3-18) and Abu Simbel (FIG. 3-23). But horizontal bands of painted *sunken relief* sculpture almost hide their function as vertical supports. To create these reliefs, the New Kingdom sculptors chiseled deep outlines below the stone's surface, rather than cut back the stone around the figures to make the figures project from the surface. Sunken reliefs have the advantage of preserving the contours of the columns they adorn. Otherwise, the columns would have an irregular, wavy profile. Despite this effort to maintain sharp architectural lines, the overwhelming of the surfaces with reliefs indicates the Egyptian architects' intention was not to emphasize the functional role of the columns. Instead, they used columns as image- and message-bearing surfaces.

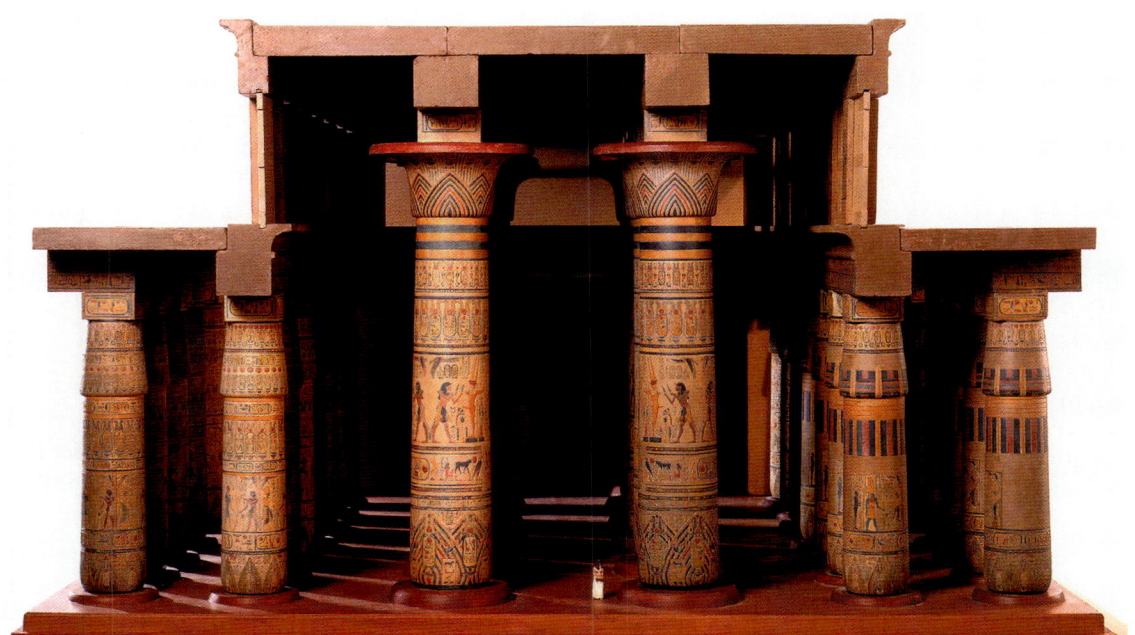

**3-26** Model of the hypostyle hall, temple of Amen-Re, Karnak, Egypt, 19th Dynasty, ca. 1290–1224 BCE. Metropolitan Museum of Art, New York.

The two central rows of columns of Karnak's hypostyle hall are taller than the rest. Raising the roof's central section created a clerestory that admitted light through windows with stone grilles.

# Sculpture and Painting

Although the Egyptians lavishly decorated the great temple complexes of the New Kingdom with statues and painted reliefs, many of the finest examples of statuary and mural painting adorned tombs, as in the Old and Middle Kingdoms.

**SENMUT AND NEFRURA** *Block statues* were popular during the New Kingdom. In these works Egyptian sculptors expressed the idea that the ka could find an eternal home in the cubic stone image of the deceased in an even more radical simplification of form than was common in Old Kingdom statuary. In the statue illustrated here (FIG. **3-27**) depicting Hatshepsut's chancellor Senmut and her daughter Nefrura, the streamlined design

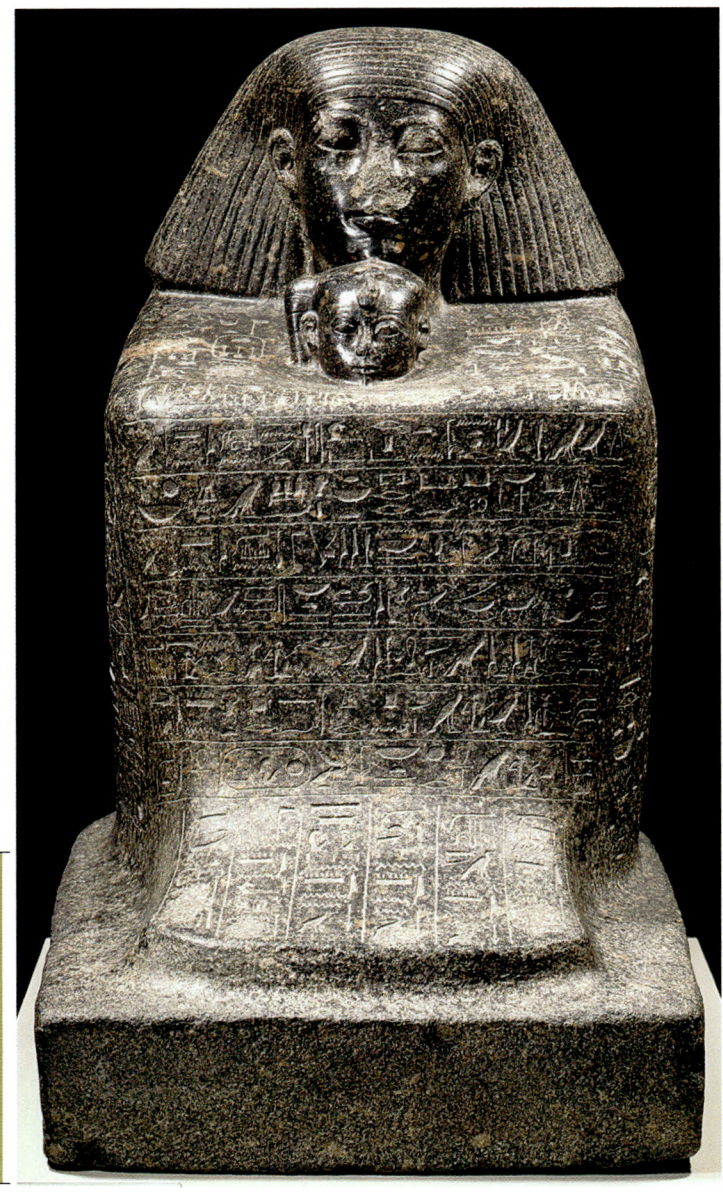

1 ft.

**3-27** Senmut with Princess Nefrura, from Thebes, Egypt, 18th Dynasty, ca. 1470–1460 BCE. Granite, 3′ ½″ high. Ägyptisches Museum, Berlin.

Hatshepsut's chancellor holds the queen's daughter in his "lap" and envelops her in his cloak. New Kingdom block statues exhibit a more radical simplification of form than do Old Kingdom statues.

concentrates attention on the heads. The sculptor treated the two bodies as a single cubic block, given over to inscriptions. Senmut holds the pharaoh's daughter by Thutmose II in his "lap" and envelops the girl in his cloak. The polished stone shape has its own simple beauty, with the surfaces turning subtly about smoothly rounded corners. The work—one of many surviving statues depicting Senmut with the princess—is also a reflection of the power of Egypt's queen. The frequent depiction of Senmut with Nefrura enhanced the chancellor's stature through his association with the pharaoh's daughter (he was her tutor) and, by implication, with Hatshepsut herself.

**TOMB OF NEBAMUN** Some of the best preserved mural paintings of the New Kingdom come from the Theban tomb of Nebamun, whose official titles were "scribe and counter of grain." On one wall (FIG. **3-28**), the painter depicted Nebamun standing in his boat, flushing birds from a papyrus swamp. The hieroglyphic text beneath his left arm says that Nebamun is enjoying recreation in his eternal afterlife. (Here, as elsewhere in Egyptian art, the accompanying text amplifies the message of the picture—and vice versa.) In contrast to the static pose of Ti watching others hunt hippopotami (FIG. 3-14), Nebamun strides forward and vigorously swings his throwing stick. In his right hand, he holds three birds he has caught. A wild cat, impossibly perched on a papyrus stem just in front of and below him, has caught two more in its claws and is holding the wings of a third in its teeth. Nebamun's wife and daughter accompany him on this hunt and hold the lotuses they have gathered. The artist scaled down the figures in proportion to their rank, as did Old Kingdom artists. As in Ti's tomb, the painter depicted the animals naturalistically, based on careful observation.

The painting technique, also employed in earlier Egyptian tombs, is *fresco secco* (dry fresco), in which artists let the plaster dry before painting on it. This procedure, in contrast to true fresco painting on wet plaster (see "Fresco Painting," Chapter 14, page 408), permitted slower and more meticulous work than painting on fresh plaster, which had to be completed before the plaster dried. Fresco secco, however, is not as durable as true fresco painting, because the colors do not fuse with the wall surface.

Another fresco fragment (FIG. **3-29**) from Nebamun's tomb shows a funerary banquet in which four noblewomen (*lower left*) watch and apparently participate in a musical performance in which two nimble and almost nude girls dance in front of the guests at a banquet. When his family buried Nebamun, they must have eaten the customary ceremonial meal at his tomb. His relatives would have returned one day each year to partake in a commemorative banquet during which the living communed with the dead. This fresco represents one of these feasts, with an ample supply of wine jars at the right. It also shows that New Kingdom artists did not always adhere to the old norms for figural representation. This painter carefully recorded the dancers' overlapping figures, their facing in opposite directions, and their rather complicated gyrations, producing a pleasing intertwined motif at the same time. The profile view of the dancers is consistent with their lower stature in the Egyptian hierarchy. The New Kingdom artist reserved the composite view for Nebamun and his family. Of the four seated women, the painter represented the two at the left conventionally, but the other two face the observer in what is a rarely attempted frontal pose. They clap and beat time to the dance, while one of them plays the reeds. The painter took careful note of the soles of their feet as they sit cross-legged and suggested the movement of the women's heads by the loose arrangement

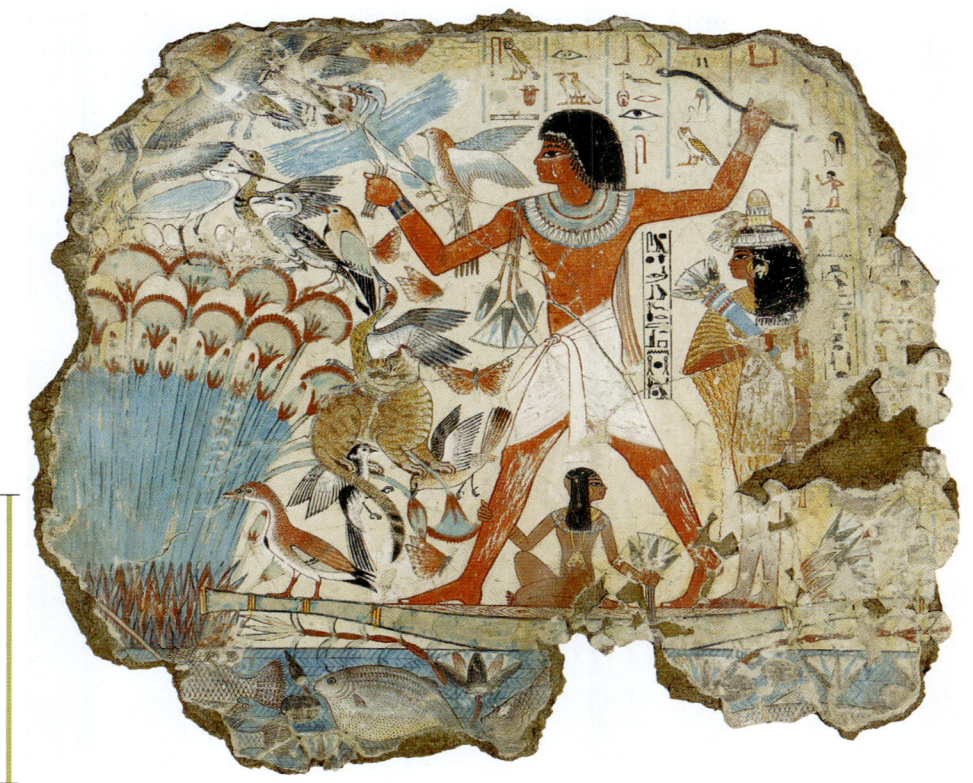

Nebamun's wife and daughter—depicted smaller than the deceased—accompany him on his hunt for fowl. An inscription states that Nebamun is enjoying recreation in his eternal afterlife.

lithe dancers, and leisure time to hunt and fish in the marshes. Still, as in the earlier tomb of Ti, the scenes should be read both literally and allegorically. Although Nebamun enjoys himself in the afterlife, the artist symbolically asked viewers to recall how he got there. Hunting scenes reminded Egyptians of Horus, the son of Osiris, hunting down his father's murderer, Seth, the god of disorder (see "The Gods and Goddesses of Egypt," page 57). Successful hunts were metaphors for triumphing over death and disorder, ensuring a happy existence in the afterlife. Music and dance were sacred to Hathor, who aided the dead in their passage to the other world. The sensual women at the banquet are a reference to fertility, rebirth, and regeneration.

of their hair strands. This informality constitutes a relaxation of the Old Kingdom's stiff rules of representation.

The frescoes in Nebamun's tomb testify to the luxurious life of the Egyptian nobility, filled with good food and drink, fine musicians,

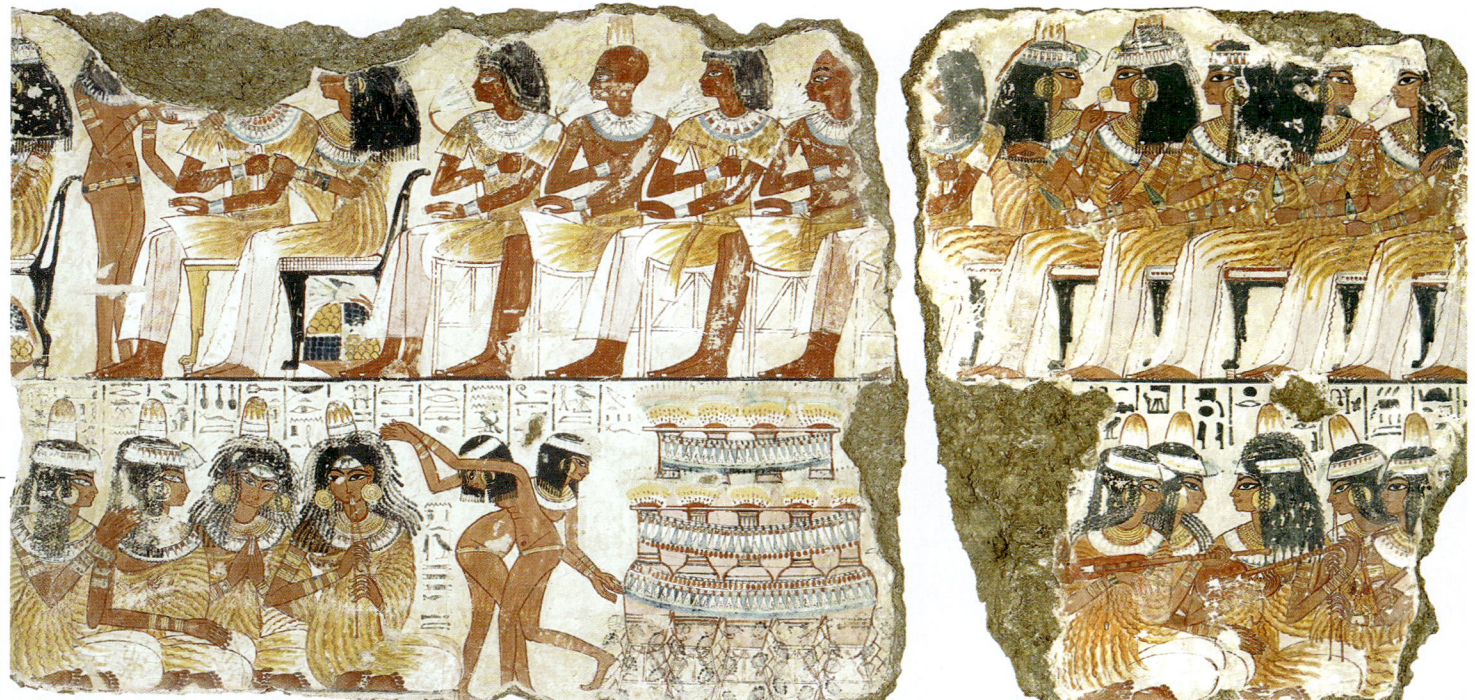

3-29 Funerary banquet, from the tomb of Nebamun, Thebes, Egypt, 18th Dynasty, ca. 1400–1350 BCE. Fresco secco, 2′ 10⅝″ × 3′ 10⅞″. British Museum, London.

A second fresco in Nebamun's tomb represents a funerary banquet in which the artist experimented with frontal views of faces and bodies—a relaxation of the Old Kingdom's stiff rules of representation.

New Kingdom    75

## Akhenaton and the Amarna Period

Not long after his family laid Nebamun to rest in his tomb at Thebes, a revolution occurred in Egyptian society and religion. In the mid-14th century BCE, Amenhotep IV, later known as Akhenaton (r. 1353–1335 BCE), abandoned the worship of most of the Egyptian gods in favor of Aton, identified with the sun disk, whom the pharaoh declared to be the universal and only god. Akhenaton deleted the name of Amen from all inscriptions and even from his own name and that of his father, Amenhotep III. He emptied the great temples, enraged the priests, and moved his capital downriver from Thebes to present-day Amarna, a site he named Akhetaton (after his new god). The pharaoh claimed to be both the son and sole prophet of Aton. To him alone could the god make revelation. Moreover, in stark contrast to earlier practice, painters and sculptors represented Akhenaton's god neither in animal nor in human form but simply as the sun disk emitting life-giving rays. The pharaohs who followed Akhenaton reestablished the Theban cult and priesthood of Amen at Karnak (FIG. 3-24) and elsewhere and restored Amen's temples and inscriptions. Akhenaton's brief religious revolution was soon undone, and his new city largely abandoned.

During the brief heretical episode of Akhenaton, profound changes also occurred in Egyptian art. A colossal statue (FIG. **3-30**) of Akhenaton from Karnak, toppled and buried after his death, retains the standard frontal pose of canonical pharaonic portraits. But the effeminate body, with its curving contours, and the long face with full lips and heavy-lidded eyes are a far cry indeed from the heroically proportioned figures of the pharaoh's predecessors (compare FIG. 3-12). Akhenaton's body is curiously misshapen, with weak arms, a narrow waist, protruding belly, wide hips, and fatty thighs. Modern physicians have tried to explain his physique by attributing a variety of illnesses to the pharaoh. They cannot agree on a diagnosis, and their premise—that the statue is an accurate depiction of a physical deformity—is probably faulty. Some art historians think Akhenaton's portrait is a deliberate artistic reaction against the established style, paralleling the suppression of traditional religion. They argue that Akhenaton's artists tried to formulate a new androgynous image of the pharaoh as the manifestation of Aton, the sexless sun disk. But no consensus exists other than that the style was revolutionary and short-lived.

**NEFERTITI AND TIYE** A painted limestone bust (FIG. **3-31**) of Akhenaton's queen, Nefertiti (her name means "the beautiful one has come"), also breaks with the past. The portrait exhibits an expression of entranced musing and an almost mannered sensitivity and delicacy of curving contour. Excavators discovered the bust in the Amarna workshop of the sculptor THUTMOSE. Although one scholar has recently questioned its authenticity, art historians still consider the portrait to be a genuine work, a deliberately unfinished model very likely by the master's own hand. The left eye socket still lacks the inlaid eyeball, making the face a kind of before-and-after demonstration piece. With this elegant bust, Thutmose may have been alluding to a heavy flower on its slender stalk by exaggerating

**3-30** Akhenaton, from the temple of Aton, Karnak, Egypt, 18th Dynasty, ca. 1353–1335 BCE. Sandstone, 13′ high. Egyptian Museum, Cairo.

Akhenaton initiated both religious and artistic revolutions. This androgynous figure is a deliberate reaction against tradition. It may be an attempt to portray the pharaoh as Aton, the sexless sun disk.

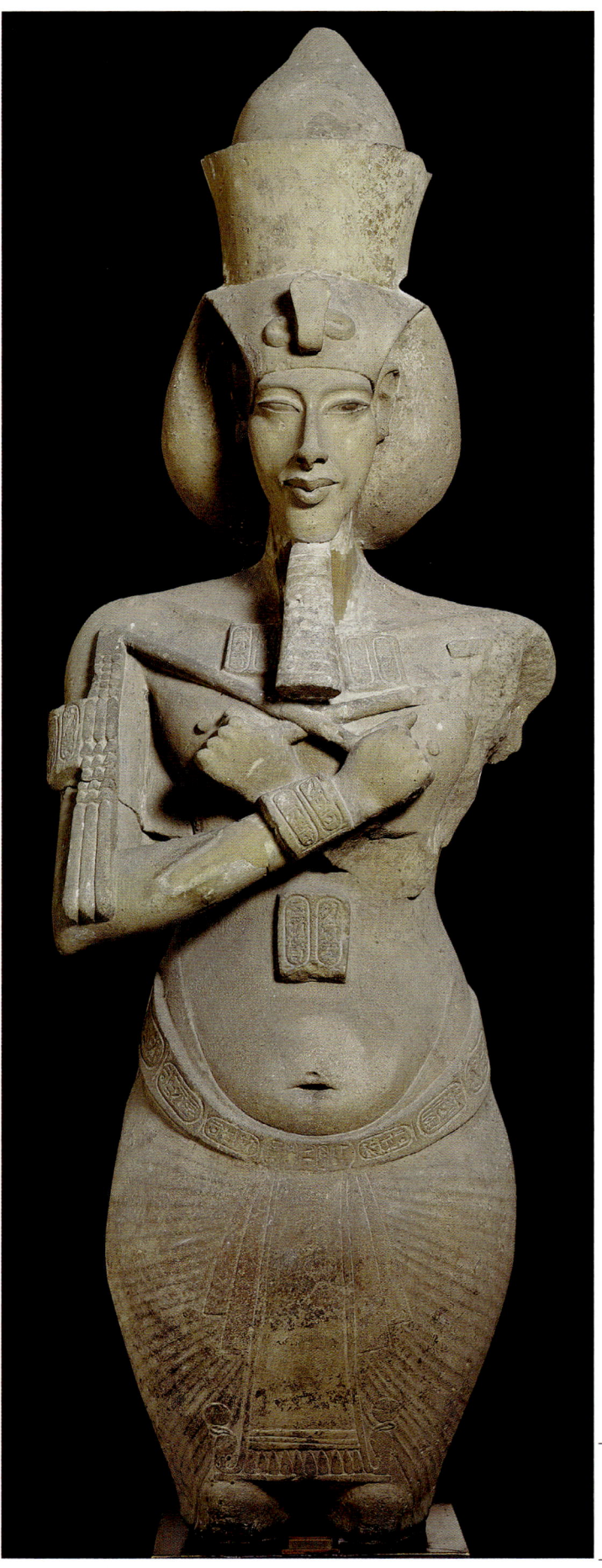

1 ft.

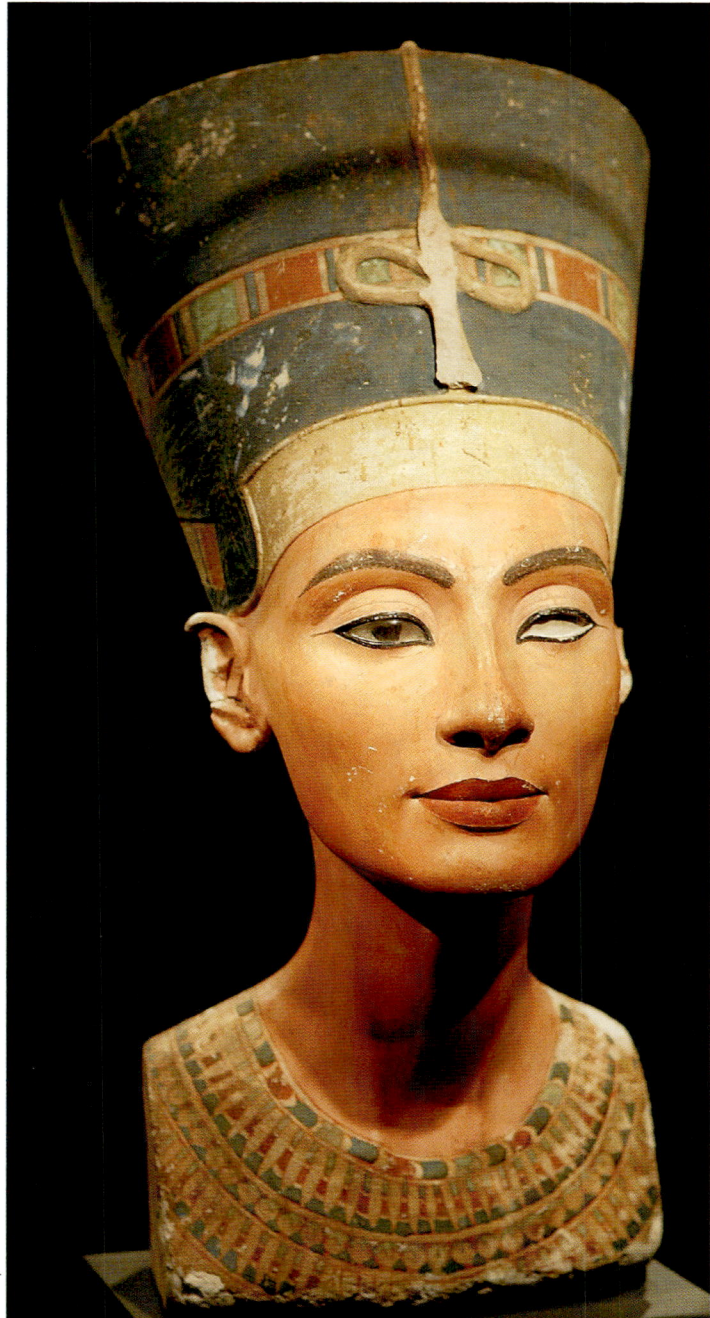

1 in.

**3-31** Thutmose, Nefertiti, from Amarna, Egypt, 18th Dynasty, ca. 1353–1335 BCE. Painted limestone, 1′ 8″ high. Ägyptisches Museum, Berlin.

Found in the sculptor's workshop, Thutmose's bust of Nefertiti portrays Akhenaton's influential wife as an elegant beauty with a pensive expression and a long, delicately curved neck.

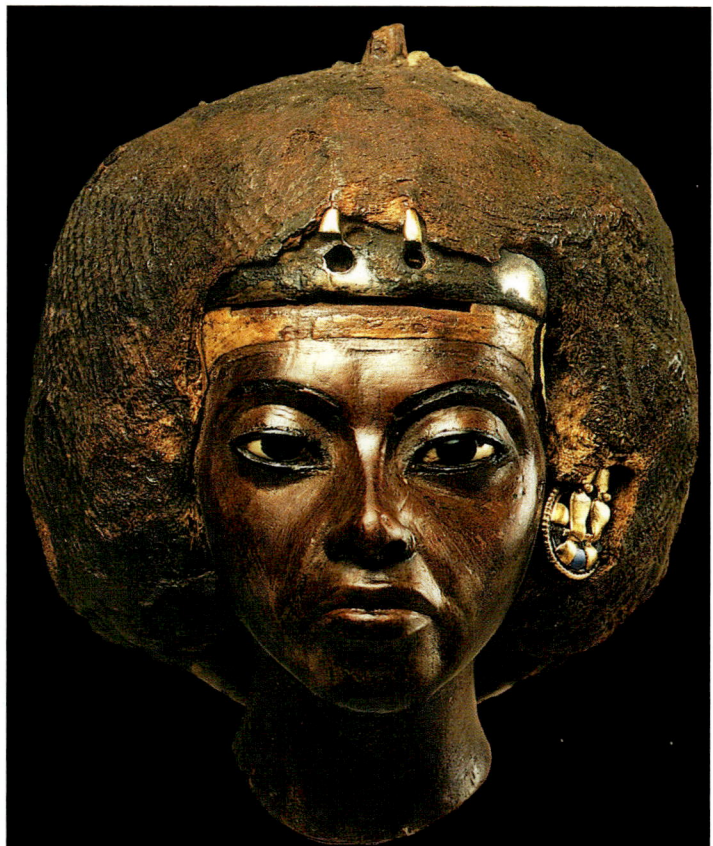

1 in.

**3-32** Tiye, from Ghurab, Egypt, 18th Dynasty, ca. 1353–1335 BCE. Wood, with gold, silver, alabaster, and lapis lazuli, $3\frac{3}{4}$″ high. Ägyptisches Museum, Berlin.

This portrait of Akhenaton's mother is carved of dark yew wood, possibly to match the queen's complexion. The head was remodeled during her son's reign to remove all references to traditional deities.

her portrait, carved of dark yew wood (possibly to match her complexion), at Ghurab with other objects connected with the funerary cult of Amenhotep III. A sculptor probably remodeled the portrait during her son's reign to eliminate all reference to deities of the old religion. That is when the head acquired the present wig of plaster and linen with small blue beads. Tiye appears as an older woman with lines and furrows, consistent with the new relaxation of artistic rules in the Amarna age. The sculptor inlaid her heavy-lidded slanting eyes with alabaster and ebony, and painted the lips red. The earrings (one is hidden by the later wig) are of gold and lapis lazuli. The wig covers what was originally a silver-foil headdress. A gold band still adorns the forehead. Luxurious materials such as these were common for royal portraits.

Both Nefertiti and Tiye figured prominently in the art and life of the Amarna age. Tiye, for example, regularly appeared in art beside her husband during his reign, and she apparently played an important role in his administration as well as her son's. Letters survive from foreign rulers advising the young Akhenaton to seek his mother's counsel in the conduct of international affairs. Nefertiti, too, was an influential woman. She frequently appears in the decoration of the Aton temple at Karnak, and she not only equals her husband in size but also sometimes wears pharaonic headgear.

the weight of the crowned head and the length of the almost serpentine neck. The sculptor seems to have adjusted the likeness of his subject to meet the era's standard of spiritual beauty.

In contrast, the miniature head (FIG. **3-32**) of Queen Tiye, mother of Akhenaton, is a moving portrait of old age. Although not of royal birth, Tiye was the daughter of a high-ranking official and became the chief wife of Amenhotep III. Archaeologists unearthed

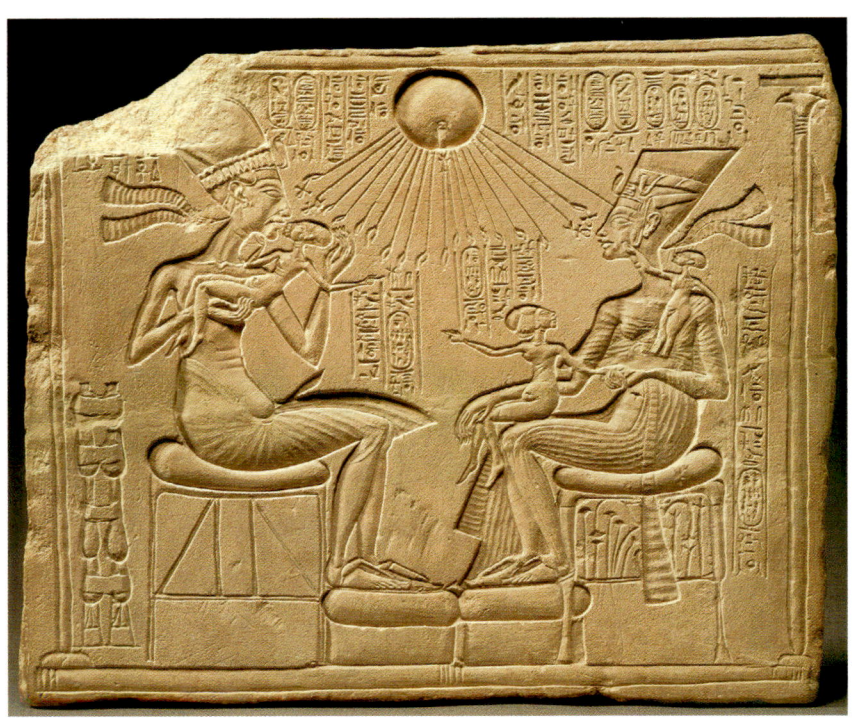

**3-33** Akhenaton, Nefertiti, and three daughters, from Amarna, Egypt, 18th Dynasty, ca. 1353–1335 BCE. Limestone, 1' ¼" high. Ägyptisches Museum, Berlin.

In this sunken relief, the Amarna artist provided a rare intimate look at the royal family in a domestic setting. Akhenaton, Nefertiti, and three of their daughters bask in the life-giving rays of Aton, the sun disk.

1 in.

**FAMILY OF AKHENATON** A sunken relief stele (FIG. **3-33**), perhaps from a private shrine, provides a rare look at this royal family. The style is familiar from the colossus of Akhenaton (FIG. 3-30) and the portrait head of Nefertiti (FIG. 3-31). Undulating curves have replaced rigid lines, and the figures possess the prominent bellies that characterize figures of the Amarna period. The pharaoh, his wife, and three of their daughters bask in the life-giving rays of Aton, the sun disk. The mood is informal and anecdotal. Akhenaton lifts one of his daughters in order to kiss her. Another daughter sits on Nefertiti's lap and gestures toward her father, while the youngest daughter reaches out to touch a pendant on her mother's crown. This kind of intimate portrayal of the pharaoh and his family is unprecedented in Egyptian art. Matching the political and religious revolution under Akhenaton was an equally radical upheaval in art.

## The Tomb of Tutankhamen and the Post-Amarna Period

The most famous figure of the Post-Amarna period is Tutankhamen (r. 1333–1323 BCE), who was probably Akhenaton's son by a minor wife. Tutankhamen ruled for a decade and died at age 18. (Although some have speculated foul play, examination of the king's mummy in 2005 ruled out murder.) Tutankhamen was a very minor figure in Egyptian history, however. The public remembers him today solely because in 1922 Howard Carter (1874–1939), a British archaeologist, discovered the boy-king's tomb with its fabulously rich treasure of sculpture, furniture, and jewelry largely intact.

**TUTANKHAMEN'S MUMMY** The principal item Carter found in Tutankhamen's tomb was the enshrined body of the pharaoh himself. The royal mummy reposed in the innermost of three coffins, nested one within the other. The innermost coffin (FIG. **3-34**) was the most luxurious of the three. Made of beaten gold (about a quarter ton of it) and inlaid with semiprecious stones such as lapis lazuli, turquoise, and carnelian, it is a supreme monument to the sculptor's and goldsmith's crafts. The portrait mask (FIG. **3-35**), which covered the king's face, is also made of gold with inlaid semiprecious stones. It is a sensitive portrayal of the serene adolescent king dressed in his official regalia, including the nemes headdress and false beard. The general effect of the mask and the tomb treasures as a whole is one of grandeur and richness expressive of Egyptian power, pride, and affluence.

**TUTANKHAMEN AT WAR** Although Tutankhamen probably was too young to fight, his position as king required that artists represent him as a conqueror, and he appears as a victorious general in the panels of a painted chest (FIG. **3-36**) deposited in

his tomb. The lid panel shows the king as a successful hunter pursuing droves of fleeing animals in the desert. On the side panel, the pharaoh, larger than all other figures on the chest, rides in a war chariot pulled by spirited, plumed horses. He draws his bow against a cluster of bearded Asian enemies, who fall in confusion before him. (The absence of a ground line in an Egyptian painting or relief implies chaos and death.) Tutankhamen slays the enemy, like game, in great numbers. Behind him are three tiers of undersized war chariots, which serve to magnify the king's figure and to increase the count of his warriors. The themes are traditional, but the fluid, curvilinear forms are features reminiscent of the Amarna style.

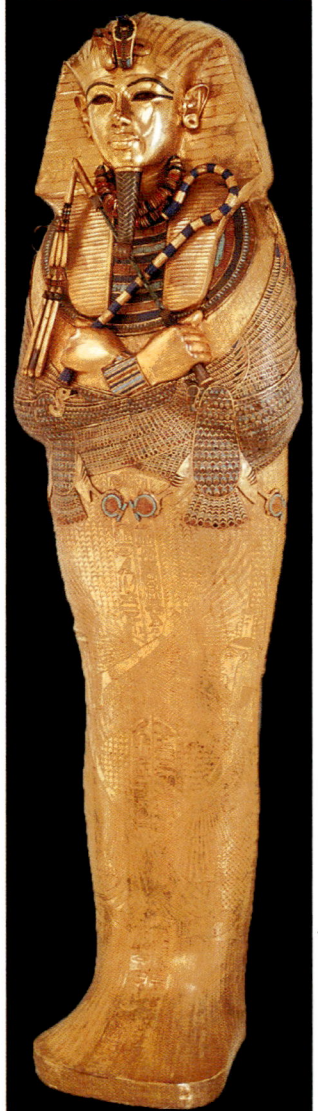

**3-34** Innermost coffin of Tutankhamen, from his tomb at Thebes, Egypt, 18th Dynasty, ca. 1323 BCE. Gold with inlay of enamel and semiprecious stones, 6' 1" long. Egyptian Museum, Cairo.

The boy-king Tutankhamen owes his fame today to his treasure-laden tomb. His mummy was encased in three nested coffins. The innermost one, made of gold, portrays the pharaoh as Osiris.

1 ft.

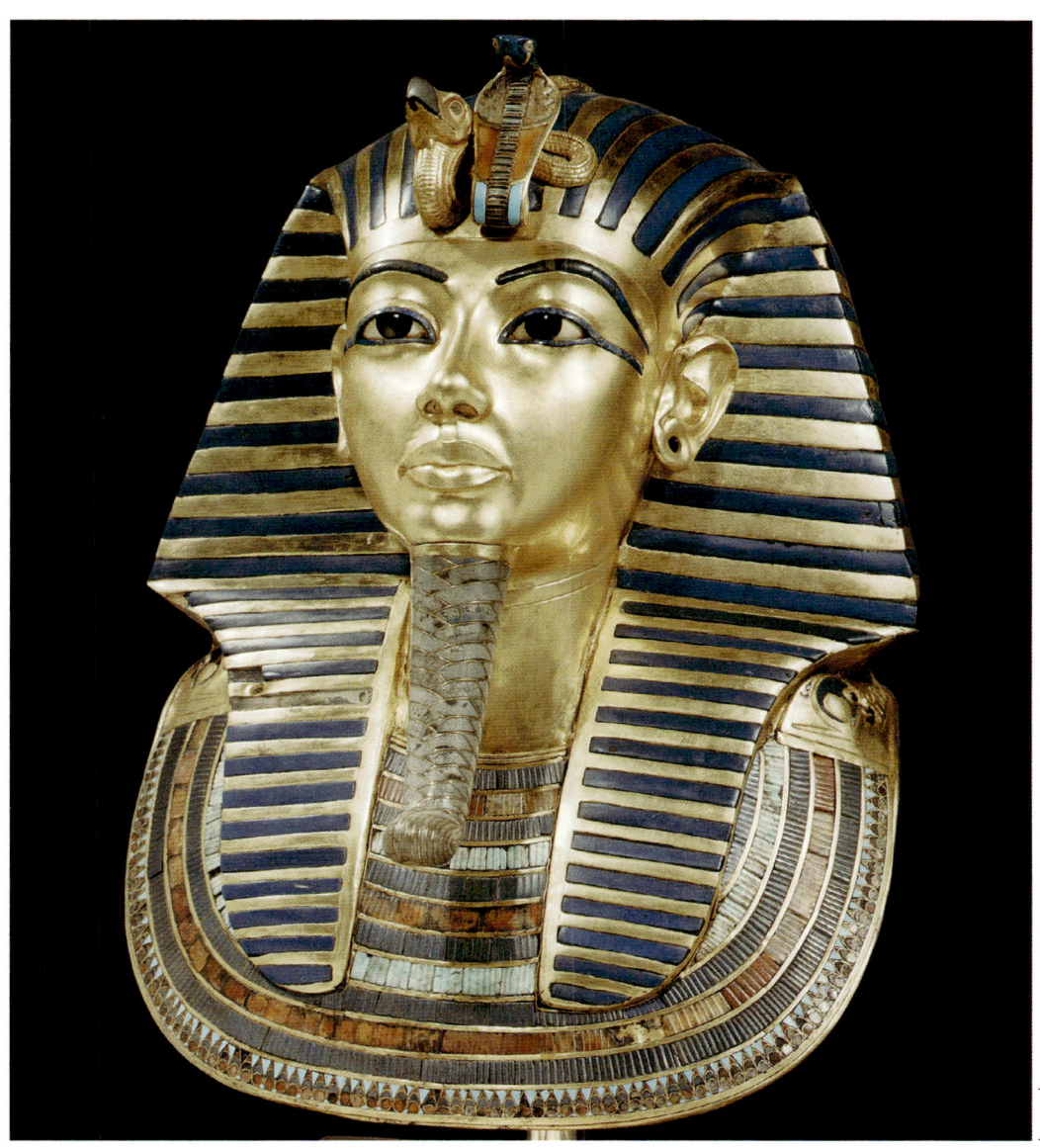

**3-35** Death mask of Tutankhamen, from the innermost coffin in his tomb at Thebes, Egypt, 18th Dynasty, ca. 1323 BCE. Gold with inlay of semiprecious stones, 1′ 9¼″ high. Egyptian Museum, Cairo.

The treasures in Tutankhamen's tomb include this mummy mask portraying the teenaged pharaoh with idealized features and wearing the traditional false beard and uraeus cobra headdress.

⊤ 1 in.

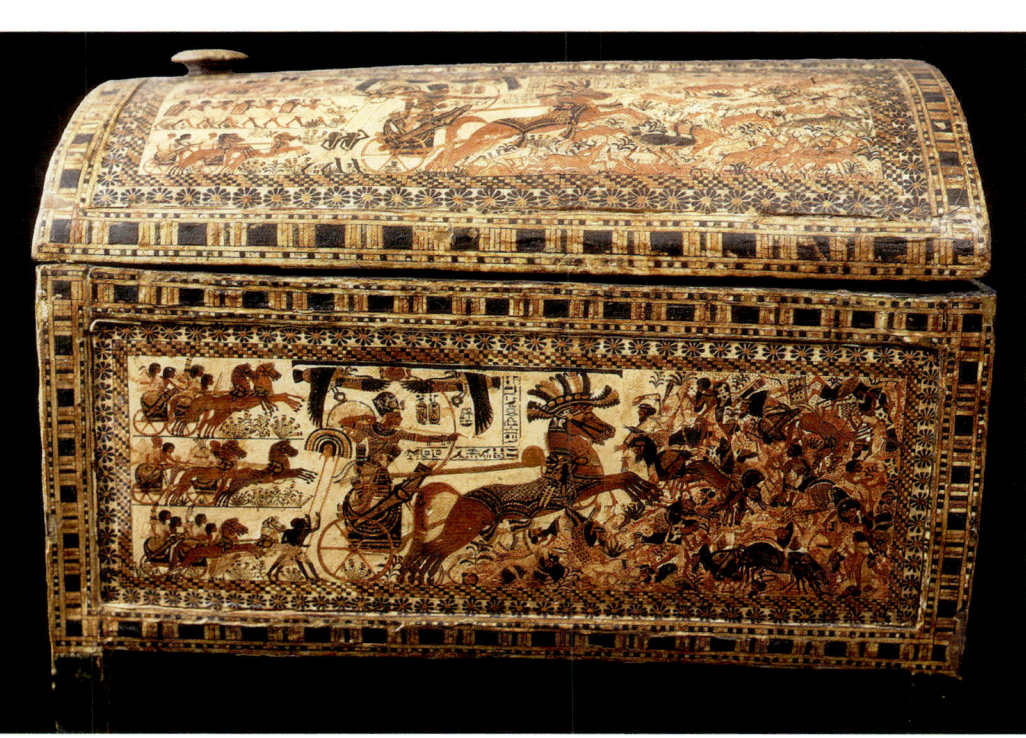

**3-36** Painted chest, from the tomb of Tutankhamen, Thebes, Egypt, 18th Dynasty, ca. 1333–1323 BCE. Wood, 1′ 8″ long. Egyptian Museum, Cairo.

In this representation of Tutankhamen triumphing over Asian enemies, the artist contrasted the orderly registers of Egyptian chariots with the chaotic pile of foreign soldiers who fall before the king.

⊤ 1 in.

New Kingdom 79

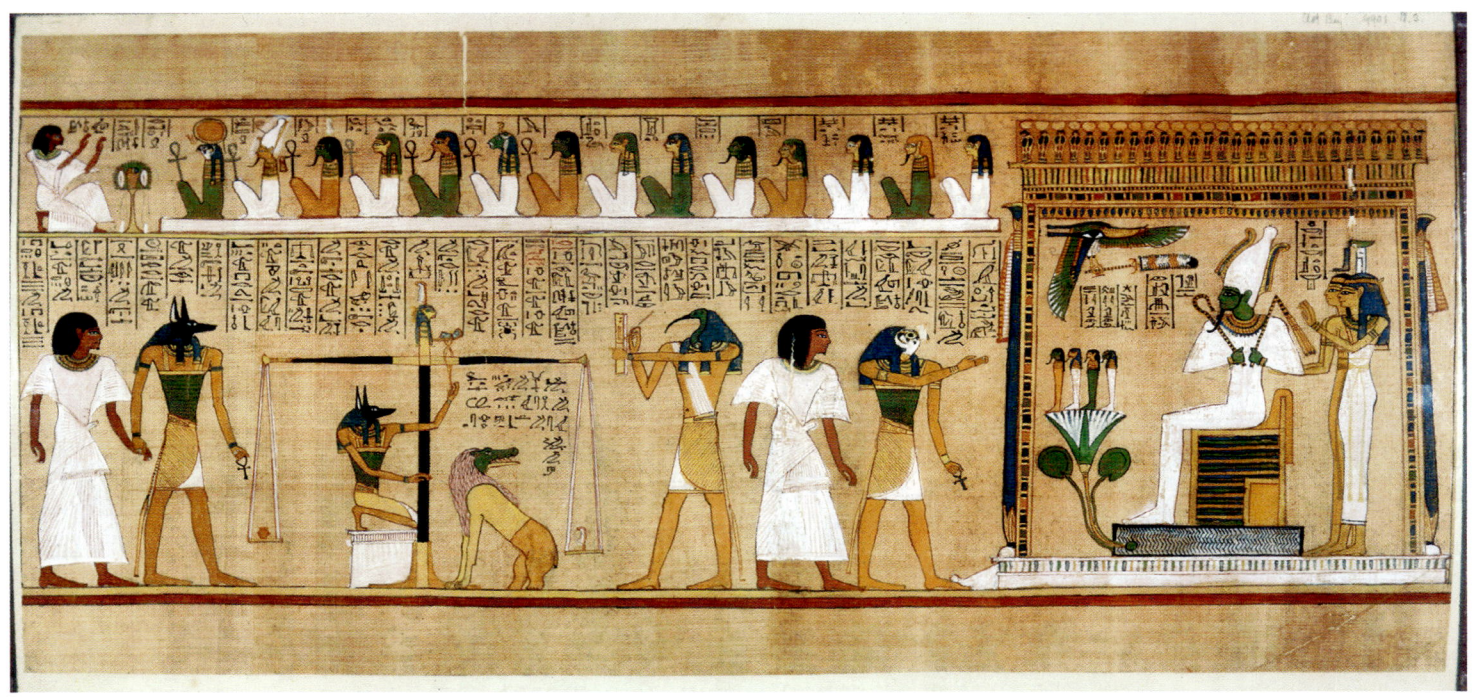

**3-37** Last judgment of Hunefer, from his tomb at Thebes, Egypt, 19th Dynasty, ca. 1300–1290 BCE. Painted papyrus scroll, 1′ 6″ high. British Museum, London.

The Book of the Dead contained spells and prayers. This scroll depicts the weighing of Hunefer's heart against Maat's feather before the deceased can be presented to Osiris, god of the Underworld.

**SCROLL OF HUNEFER** Tutankhamen's mummy case (FIG. 3-34) shows the boy-king in the guise of Osiris, god of the dead and king of the Underworld, as well as giver of eternal life. The so-called *Book of the Dead,* a collection of spells and prayers, records the ritual of the cult of Osiris. Illustrated papyrus scrolls (some are 70 feet long) containing these texts were essential items accompanying well-to-do persons into the afterlife (see "Mummification and Immortality," page 61). One surviving scroll (FIG. **3-37**) represents the final judgment of the deceased. It comes from the Theban tomb of Hunefer, the royal scribe and steward of Seti I (r. 1306–1290 BCE), the father of Ramses II. At the left of the section reproduced here, Anubis, the jackal-headed god of embalming, leads Hunefer into the hall of judgment. The god then adjusts the scales to weigh the dead man's heart against the feather of the goddess Maat, protectress of truth and right. A hybrid crocodile-hippopotamus-lion monster, Ammit, devourer of the sinful, awaits the decision of the scales. If the weighing had been unfavorable to the deceased, the monster would have eaten his heart. The ibis-headed god Thoth records the proceedings. Above, the gods of the Egyptian pantheon sit in a row as witnesses, while Hunefer kneels in adoration before them. Having been justified by the scales, Hunefer is brought by Osiris's son, the falcon-headed Horus, into the presence of the green-faced Osiris and his sisters Isis and Nephthys to receive the award of eternal life.

In Hunefer's scroll, the figures have all the formality of stance, shape, and attitude of traditional Egyptian art. Abstract figures and hieroglyphs alike are aligned rigidly, and the flexible, curvilinear style suggestive of movement that characterized the art of Amarna and Tutankhamen has disappeared. The return to conservatism is unmistakable.

# FIRST MILLENNIUM BCE

During the first millennium BCE, Egypt lost the commanding role it once had played in the ancient world. The empire dwindled away, and foreign powers invaded and occupied the land until, beginning in the fourth century BCE, Alexander the Great of Macedon and his Greek successors and, eventually, the emperors of Rome replaced the pharaohs as rulers of the Kingdom of the Nile.

## Thebes

One of those foreign powers was Assyria (see Chapter 2), which sacked Thebes in 660 BCE. A rich and powerful man named Mentuemhet had the misfortune to be mayor of Thebes during the Assyrian invasion of his city.

**MENTUEMHET** In addition to serving as mayor, Mentuemhet was the Fourth Prophet (priest) of Amen, and according to the inscriptions on works he commissioned, he was responsible for restoring the temples the Assyrians had razed. He placed portrait statues of himself in those temples and also in the tomb he constructed in a prominent place in the Theban necropolis. More than a dozen of his portraits survive, including the somewhat under life-size granite statue illustrated here (FIG. **3-38**).

Mentuemhet's portrait statues exemplify Egyptian sculpture at about the time the Greeks first encountered the art of the Nile region (see Chapter 5). The pose is traditional, as is his costume of kilt and wig, but the face, with its frank portrayal of the mayor's advanced age, is much more realistic than most earlier representations of elite men. In fact, almost all of Mentuemhet's portraits have idealized features. This one is an exception, but even here the

**3-38** Portrait statue of Mentuemhet, from Karnak, Egypt, 26th Dynasty, ca. 660–650 BCE. Granite, 4′ 5″ high. Egyptian Museum, Cairo.

Mentuemhet's portrait combines a realistic face with an idealized body. The costume and pose, however, recall Old Kingdom statuary, a testimony to the longevity of stylistic modes in Egypt.

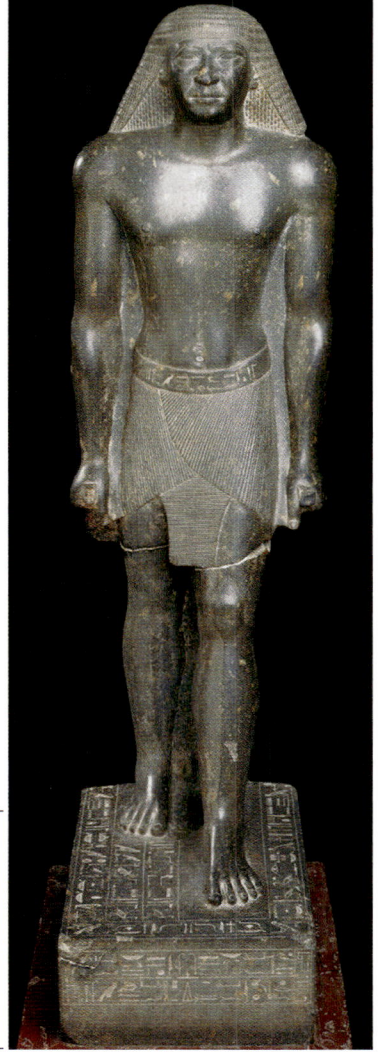

1 ft.

trim, muscular body is that of a young man in the tradition of Old Kingdom royal portraits (FIG. 3-12). The sculptor removed the slab of stone that forms a backdrop to most earlier pharaonic portraits, but left the stone block intact between the arms and the torso and between the legs, an artistic decision that contributes significantly to the rigid look of the statue, so appropriate for a timeless image of the deceased in his eternal afterlife. The stylistic similarity between Egyptian statues created 2,000 years apart is without parallel in the history of art.

## Kingdom of Kush

Another foreign power that occupied the Nile valley during the first millennium BCE was Egypt's gold-rich neighbor to the south, the kingdom of Kush, part of which is in present-day Sudan. Called Nubia by the Romans, perhaps from the Egyptian word for gold, Kush appears in Egyptian texts as early as the Old Kingdom. During the New Kingdom, the pharaohs colonized Nubia and appointed a viceroy of Kush to administer the Kushite kingdom, which included Abu Simbel (FIG. 3-22) and controlled the major trade route between Egypt and sub-Saharan Africa. But in the eighth century BCE, the Nubians conquered Egypt and established themselves as the 25th Dynasty.

**TAHARQO**  Around 680 BCE, the Kushite pharaoh Taharqo (r. 690–664 BCE) constructed a temple at Kawa and placed a portrait of himself in it. Emulating traditional Egyptian types, the sculptor portrayed Taharqo as a sphinx (FIG. 3-39; compare FIG. 3-10) with the ears, mane, and body of a lion but with a human face and a headdress featuring two uraeus cobras. The king's name is inscribed on his chest, and his features are distinctly African, although, as in all pharaonic portraiture, they are generic and idealized rather than a specific likeness.

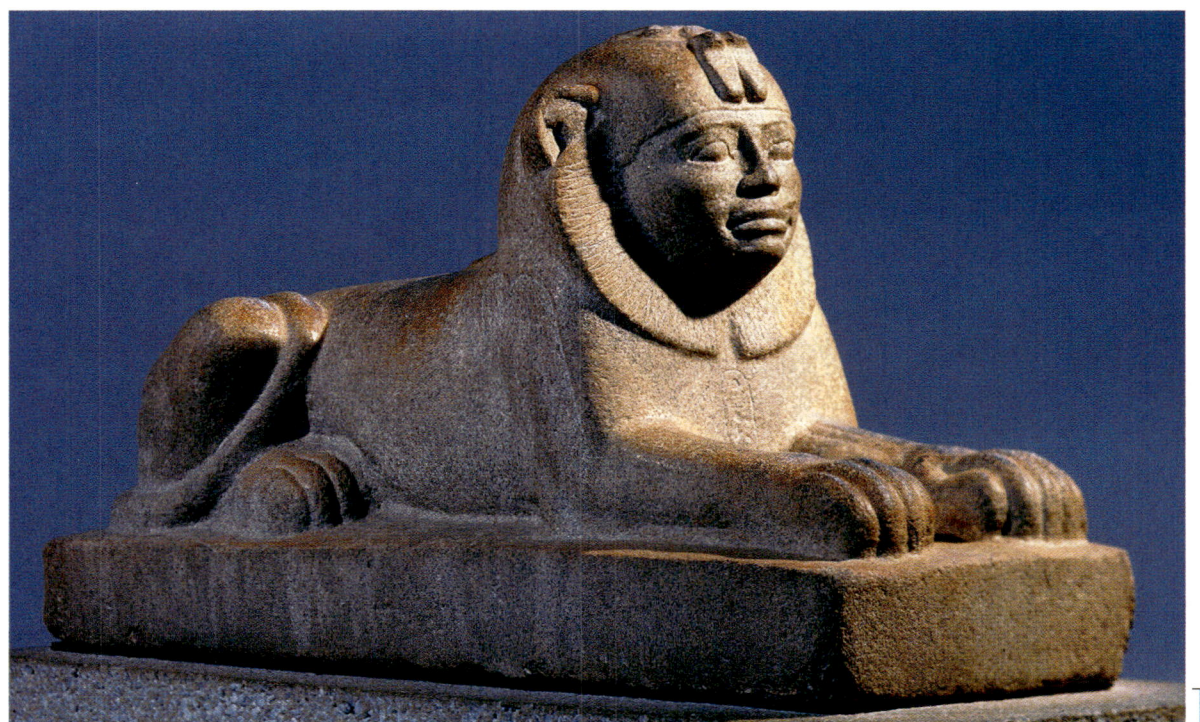

**3-39** Taharqo as a sphinx, from temple T, Kawa, Sudan, 25th Dynasty, ca. 680 BCE. Granite, 1′ 4″ × 2′ 4¾″. British Museum, London.

The Nubian kings who ruled Egypt during the 25th Dynasty adopted traditional Egyptian statuary types, such as the sphinx, but sculptors incorporated the Kushite pharaohs' distinctly African features.

1 in.

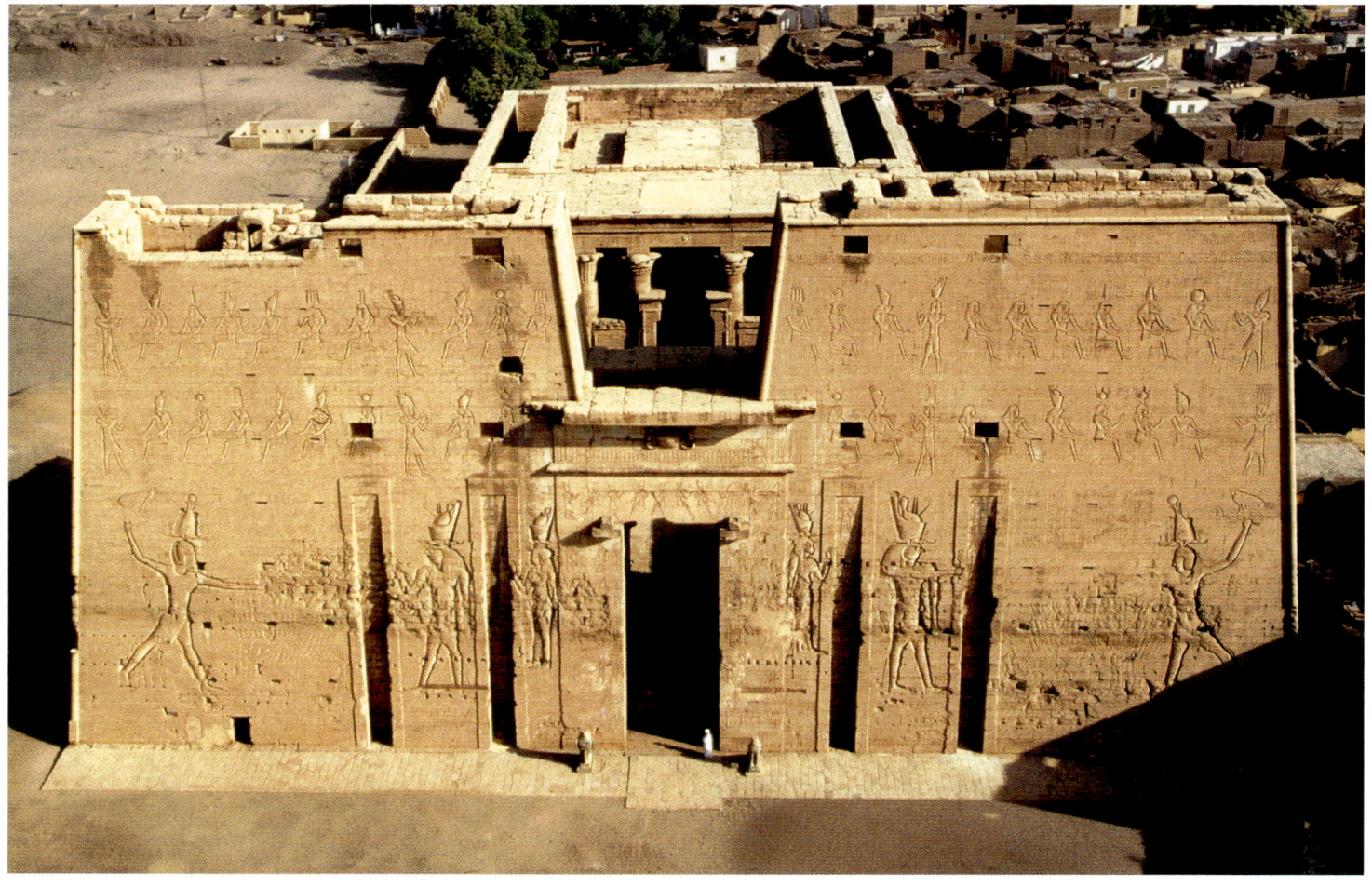

**3-40** Temple of Horus (looking east), Edfu, Egypt, ca. 237–47 BCE.

The pylon temple at Edfu is more than a thousand years later than that at Karnak (FIG. 3-24), but it adheres to the same basic architectural scheme. Egyptian artistic forms tended to have very long lives.

## After Alexander

Once formulated, Egyptian traditions tended to have very long lives, in architecture as in the other arts—even after Alexander the Great brought Greek rule and Greek culture to the Kingdom of the Nile.

**TEMPLE OF HORUS, EDFU** The temple of Horus (FIG. **3-40**) at Edfu, built during the third, second, and first centuries BCE, still follows the basic pylon temple scheme architects worked out more than a thousand years before (compare the New Kingdom temples at Karnak, FIG. 3-24, and Luxor, FIG. 3-24A). The great entrance pylon at Edfu is especially impressive. The broad surface of its massive facade, with its sloping walls, is broken only

by the doorway with its overshadowing *moldings* at the top and sides, deep channels to hold great flagstaffs, and sunken reliefs. The reliefs depict Horus and Hathor witnessing an oversized King Ptolemy XIII (r. 51–47 BCE) smiting undersized enemies—a motif first used in Egyptian reliefs and paintings in Predynastic times (FIGS. 3-1 and 3-1A). The Edfu temple is eloquent testimony to the persistence of Egyptian architectural and pictorial types even under Greek rule.

Indeed, the exceptional longevity of formal traditions in Egypt is one of the marvels of the history of art. It attests to the invention of an artistic style so satisfactory that it endured in Egypt for millennia. Everywhere else in the ancient Mediterranean, stylistic change was the only common denominator.

# EGYPT UNDER THE PHARAOHS

## PREDYNASTIC AND EARLY DYNASTIC PERIODS ca. 3500–2575 BCE

▌ The unification of Upper and Lower Egypt into a single kingdom under the rule of a divine pharaoh occurred around 3000–2920 BCE. The earliest labeled work of narrative art, the palette of King Narmer, commemorates the event. The Narmer palette also established the basic principles of Egyptian representational art for 3,000 years.

▌ Imhotep, the first artist in history whose name is known, was the earliest master of monumental stone architecture. He designed the funerary complex and stepped pyramid of King Djoser (r. 2630–2611 BCE) at Saqqara.

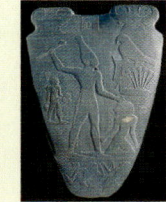

Palette of King Narmer,
ca. 3000–2920 BCE

## OLD KINGDOM ca. 2575–2134 BCE

▌ The Old Kingdom was the first golden age of Egyptian art and architecture, the time when three pharaohs of the Fourth Dynasty erected the Great Pyramids at Gizeh, the oldest of the Seven Wonders of the ancient world. The pyramids were emblems of the sun on whose rays the pharaohs ascended to the heavens when they died.

▌ Old Kingdom sculptors created seated and standing statuary types in which all movement was suppressed in order to express the eternal nature of pharaonic kingship. These types would dominate Egyptian art for 2,000 years.

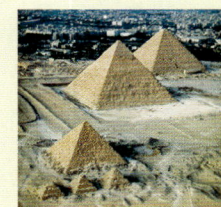

Great Pyramids, Gizeh,
ca. 2551–2472 BCE

## MIDDLE KINGDOM ca. 2040–1640 BCE

▌ After an intermediate period of civil war, Mentuhotep II (r. 2050–1998 BCE) reestablished central rule and founded the Middle Kingdom.

▌ The major artistic innovation of this period was the rock-cut tomb in which sculptors hewed both the facade and interior chambers out of the living rock. The fluted columns in Middle Kingdom tombs closely resemble the columns later used in Greek temples.

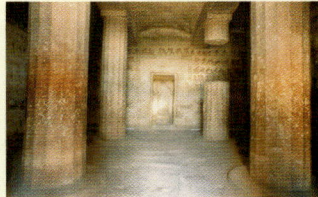

Tomb of Amenemhet, Beni Hasan,
ca. 1950–1900 BCE

## NEW KINGDOM ca. 1550–1070 BCE

▌ During the New Kingdom, Egypt extended its borders to the Euphrates River in the east and deep into Nubia in the south.

▌ The most significant architectural innovation of this period was the axially planned pylon temple incorporating an immense gateway, columnar courtyards, and a hypostyle hall with clerestory lighting.

▌ Powerful pharaohs such as Hatshepsut (r. 1473–1458 BCE) and Ramses II (r. 1290–1224 BCE) built gigantic temples in honor of their patron gods and, after their deaths, for their own worship.

▌ Akhenaton (r. 1353–1335 BCE) abandoned the traditional Egyptian religion in favor of Aton, the sun disk, and initiated a short-lived artistic revolution in which undulating curves and anecdotal content replaced the cubic forms and impassive stillness of earlier Egyptian art.

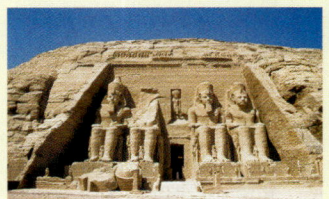

Temple of Ramses II, Abu Simbel,
ca. 1290–1224 BCE

## FIRST MILLENNIUM BCE 1000–30 BCE

▌ After the demise of the New Kingdom, Egypt's power in the ancient world declined, and the Nile came under the control of foreigners. These included the Kushite kings of Nubia and, after 332 BCE, Alexander the Great and his Greek successors. In 30 BCE, Egypt became a province of the Roman Empire.

▌ The traditional forms of Egyptian art and architecture lived on even under foreign rule, for example, in the pylon temple erected at Edfu in honor of Horus.

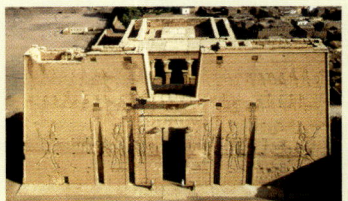

Temple of Horus, Edfu,
ca. 237–47 BCE

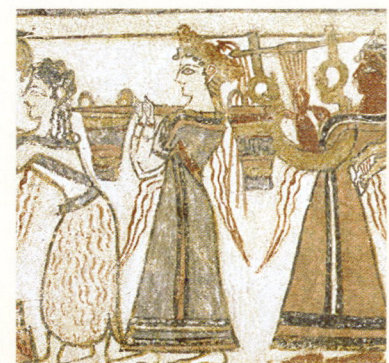

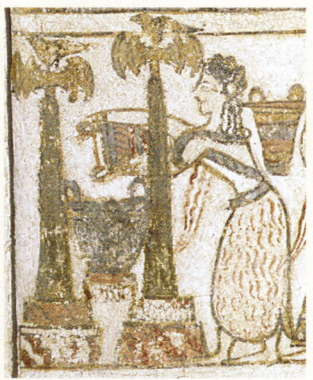

Next to a woman who may be
pouring ox blood from a jar into
a vessel between two double axes
is a second woman, also with fair
skin, and a male (dark-skinned)
harp player.

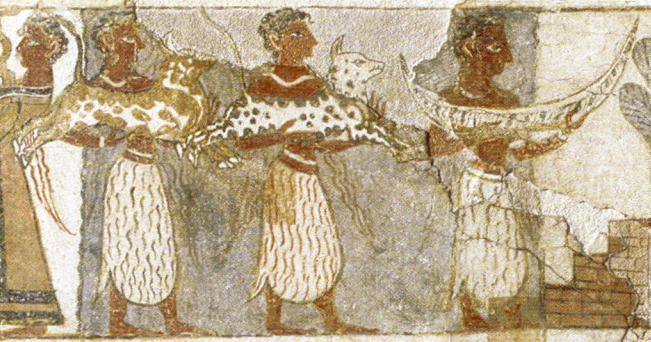

Archaeologists have not
yet deciphered Minoan
inscriptions, but the scenes
on this sarcophagus from
Hagia Triada in southern
Crete provide information
about Minoan funerary
rituals.

Three men moving in the opposite direction carry sculptures
of two sacrificial animals and a model of a boat, offerings to
the deceased man whose remains this sarcophagus housed.

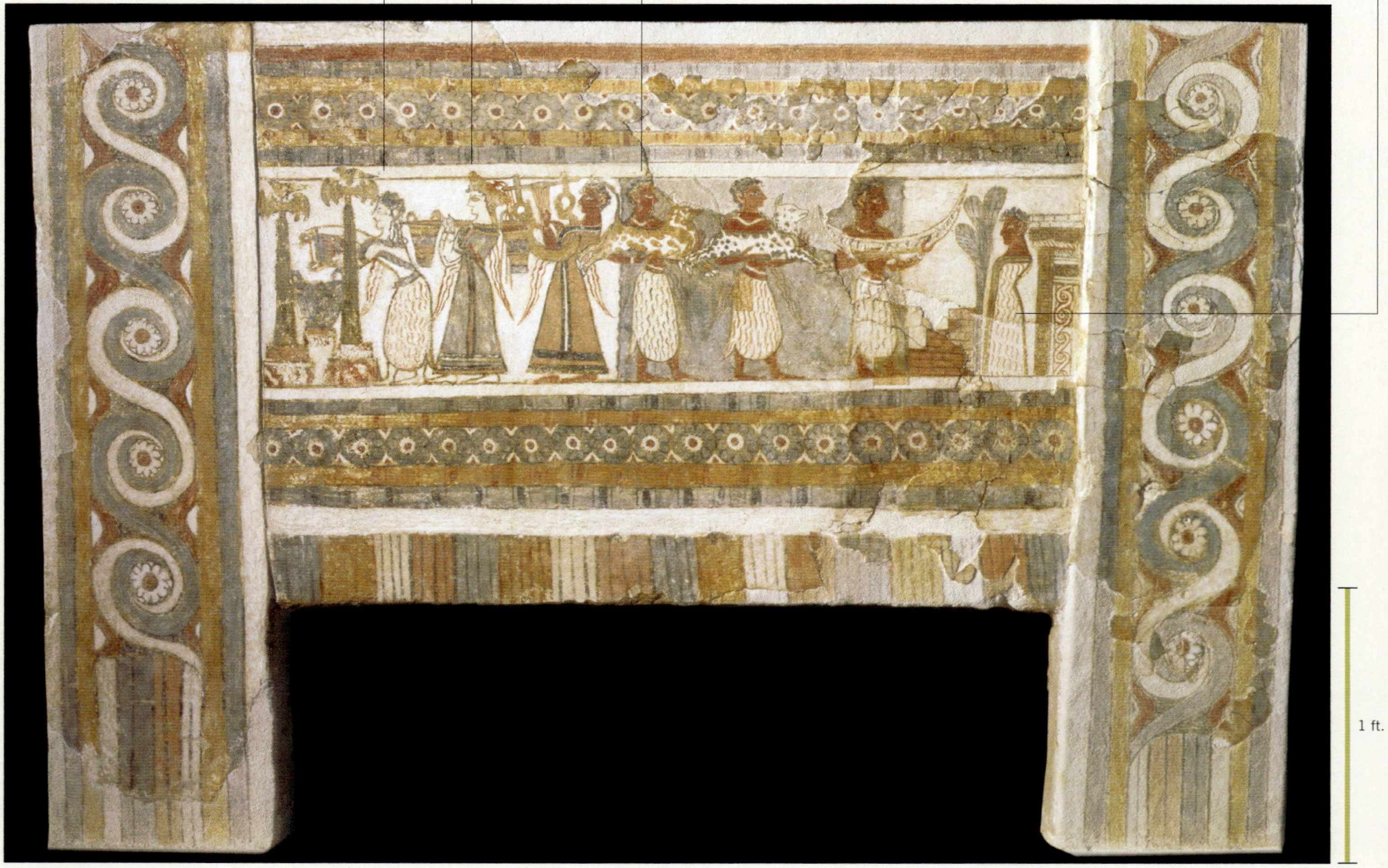

1 ft.

**4-1** Sarcophagus, from Hagia Triada (Crete), Greece, ca. 1450–1400 BCE. Painted limestone, 4′ 6″ long. Archaeological Museum, Herakleion.

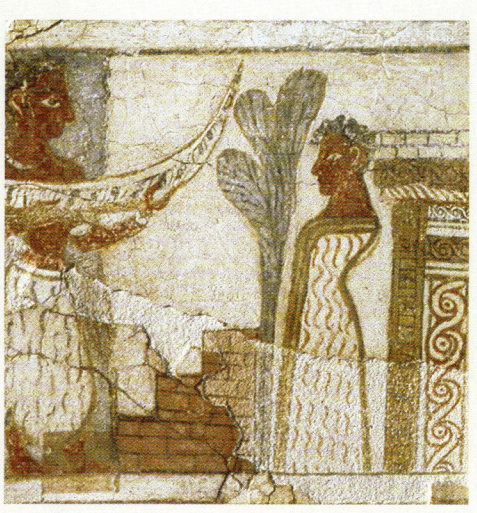

The Minoan painter included the deceased himself in this depiction of the funerary rites in his honor. He stands in front of his tomb facing the three men presenting him with gifts.

# THE PREHISTORIC AEGEAN

## GREECE IN THE AGE OF HEROES

When, in the eighth century BCE, Homer immortalized in the *Iliad* and the *Odyssey* the great war between the Greeks and the Trojans and the subsequent adventures of Odysseus on his tortuous journey home, the epic poet was describing a time long before his own—a golden age of larger-than-life heroes. Since the late 19th century, archaeologists have gradually uncovered impressive remains of that heroic age, including the palaces of the legendary King Minos at Knossos (FIGS. 4-4 to 4-6) on Crete and of King Agamemnon at Mycenae (FIGS. 4-19 and 4-22A) on the Greek mainland. But they have also recovered thousands of less glamorous objects and inscriptions that provide a contemporaneous view of life in the prehistoric Aegean unfiltered by the romantic lens of Homer and later writers.

One of the most intriguing finds to date is the painted Minoan (named after King Minos) sarcophagus (FIG. 4-1) from Hagia Triada on the southern coast of Crete. The paintings adorning the sides of the small coffin are closely related in technique, color scheme, and figure style to the more monumental frescoes on the walls of Minoan palaces, but the subject is foreign to the royal repertoire. The paintings illustrate the funerary rites in honor of the dead. They furnish welcome information about Minoan religion, which still remains obscure despite more than a century of excavation on Crete.

On one long side (not shown) of the sarcophagus, four women and a male double-flute player take part in a ritual centered on an ox tied up on a table. One of the women makes an offering at an altar. In contrast to this unified narrative, the painter divided the side illustrated in FIG. 4-1 into two scenes. At the left, a woman pours liquid (perhaps the blood of the ox on the other side) from a jar into a large vessel on a stand between two double axes. Behind her, a second woman carries two more jars, and a male figure plays the harp. In conformance with the common convention in many ancient cultures, the women have light skin and the men dark skin (compare FIG. 3-11A). To their right, three men carry two sculpted sacrificial animals and a model of a boat to offer to a dead man, whom the painter represented as standing in front of his tomb, just as the biblical Lazarus later appears in medieval art.

The precise meaning of the sarcophagus paintings is uncertain, but there is no doubt that they document well-established Minoan rites in honor of the dead, which included the sacrifice of animals accompanied by music and the deposit of gifts in the tomb. Until scholars can decipher the written language of the Minoans, artworks such as the Hagia Triada sarcophagus will be the primary tools for reconstructing life on Crete, and in Greece as a whole, during the two millennia before the birth of Homer.

# GREECE BEFORE HOMER

In the *Iliad,* Homer describes the might and splendor of the Greek armies poised before the walls of Troy.

> Clan after clan poured out from the ships and huts onto the plain . . . innumerable as the leaves and blossoms in their season . . . the Athenians . . . the men of Argos and Tiryns of the Great Walls . . . troops from the great stronghold of Mycenae, from wealthy Corinth . . . from Knossos . . . Phaistos . . . and the other troops that had their homes in Crete of the Hundred Towns.[1]

The Greeks had come from far and wide, from the mainland and the islands (MAP 4-1), to seek revenge against Paris, the Trojan prince who had abducted Helen, wife of King Menelaus of Sparta. The *Iliad,* composed around 750 BCE, is the first great work of Greek literature. Until about 1870, the world regarded Homer's epic poem as pure fiction. Scholars paid little heed to the bard as a historian, instead attributing the profusion of names and places in his writings to the rich abundance of his imagination. The prehistory of Greece remained shadowy and lost in an impenetrable world of myth.

**TROY AND MYCENAE**  In the late 1800s, however, Heinrich Schliemann (1822–1890), a wealthy German businessman turned archaeologist, proved that scholars had not given Homer his due. Between 1870 and his death 20 years later, Schliemann (whose methods later archaeologists have harshly criticized) uncovered some of the very cities Homer named. In 1870, he began work at Hissarlik on the northwestern coast of Turkey, which a British archaeologist, Frank Calvert (1828–1908), had postulated was the site of Homer's Troy. Schliemann dug into a vast mound and found a number of fortified cities built on the remains of one another. Fire had destroyed one of them in the 13th century BCE. This, scholars now generally agree, was the Troy of King Priam and his son Paris.

Schliemann continued his excavations at Mycenae on the Greek mainland, where, he believed, King Agamemnon, Menelaus's brother, had once ruled. Here his finds were even more startling, among them a massive fortress-palace with a monumental gateway (FIGS. 4-19 and 4-22A); tombs with lofty stone domes beneath earthen mounds (FIGS. 4-20 and 4-21); quantities of gold jewelry, masks (FIG. 4-22), and cups; and inlaid bronze weapons (FIG. 4-23). Schliemann's discoveries revealed a magnificent civilization far older than the famous vestiges of Classical Greece that had remained visible in Athens and elsewhere. Subsequent excavations proved that Mycenae had not been the only center of this fabulous civilization.

**MINOAN CRETE**  Another legendary figure was Minos, the king of Knossos on the island of Crete, who exacted from Athens a tribute of youths and maidens to be fed to the *Minotaur,* a creature half bull and half man that inhabited a vast labyrinth. In 1900, an Englishman, Arthur Evans (1851–1941), began work at Knossos, where he uncovered a palace (FIGS. 4-4 to 4-6) that resembled a maze. Evans named the people who had constructed it the Minoans after their mythological king. Other archaeologists soon discovered further evidence of the Minoans at Phaistos, Hagia Triada (FIG. 4-1), and other sites, including Gournia, which Harriet Boyd Hawes (1871–1945), an American archaeologist (and one of the first women of any nationality to direct a major excavation), explored between 1901 and 1904.

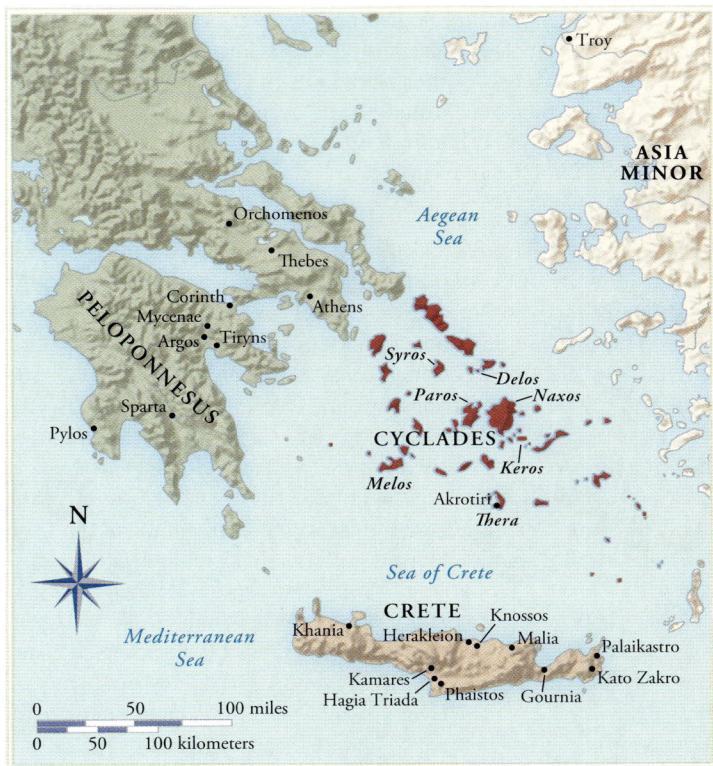

MAP 4-1  The prehistoric Aegean.

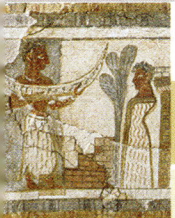

## THE PREHISTORIC AEGEAN

| | | | | BCE |
|---|---|---|---|---|
| **3000** | **2000** | **1600** | **1400** | **1200** |
| ❙ Early Cycladic sculptors create marble figurines for placement in graves to accompany the dead into the afterlife | ❙ Minoans construct major palaces on Crete and adorn the walls with frescoes focusing on palace rituals and nature<br><br>❙ Cretan ceramists produce Kamares painted pottery<br><br>❙ Volcanic eruption destroys Thera, ca. 1628 BCE | ❙ Minoan potters manufacture Marine Style vases, and sculptors carve small-scale images of gods and goddesses<br><br>❙ Mycenaeans bury their dead in deep shaft graves with gold funerary masks, ornately inlaid daggers, and gold cups<br><br>❙ Mycenaeans occupy Crete | ❙ Mycenaeans erect fortification walls around their citadels at Mycenae, Tiryns, and elsewhere, and build tombs featuring corbeled domes<br><br>❙ Mycenaeans fashion the oldest known monumental sculptures in Greece<br><br>❙ Destruction of the Mycenaean palaces, ca. 1200 BCE | |

More recently, archaeologists have excavated important Minoan remains at many other locations on Crete, and have explored contemporaneous sites on other islands in the Aegean, most notably miThera. Together, the Minoan and Mycenaean buildings, paintings, sculptures, and other finds attest to the wealth and sophistication of the people who occupied Greece and the Aegean Islands in that once-obscure heroic age celebrated in later Greek mythology.

**AEGEAN ARCHAEOLOGY TODAY** Arguably more important for the understanding of Aegean society than the art objects tourists flock to see in the museums of Athens and Herakleion (near Knossos) are the many documents archaeologists have found written in scripts conventionally called Linear A and Linear B. The progress made during the past several decades in deciphering these texts has provided a welcome corrective to the romantic treasure-hunting approach of Schliemann and Evans. Scholars now regard Linear B as an early form of Greek, and they have begun to reconstruct Aegean civilization by referring to records made at the time and not just to Homer's heroic account. Archaeologists now also know that humans inhabited Greece as far back as the early Paleolithic period and that village life was firmly established in Greece and on Crete in Neolithic times. The heyday of the ancient Aegean, however, did not arrive until the second millennium BCE, well after the emergence of the river valley civilizations of Mesopotamia, Egypt, and South Asia (see Chapters 2, 3, and 15).

The prehistoric Aegean has three geographic areas, and each has its own distinctive artistic identity. *Cycladic* art is the art of the Cyclades Islands (so named because they "circle" around Delos), as well as of the adjacent islands in the Aegean, excluding Crete. *Minoan* art encompasses the art of Crete. *Helladic* art is the art of the Greek mainland (*Hellas* in Greek). Scholars subdivide each area chronologically into early, middle, and late periods, designating the art of the Late Helladic period Mycenaean after Agamemnon's great citadel of Mycenae.

# CYCLADIC ART

Marble was abundantly available in the superb quarries of the Aegean Islands, especially on Naxos, which the sculptors of the Early Cycladic period used to produce statuettes (FIGS. 4-2 and 4-3) that collectors revere today (see "Archaeology, Art History, and the Art Market," page 88) because of their striking abstract forms, which call to mind some modern sculptures (FIGS. 29-20 and 29-61A).

**SYROS WOMAN** Most of the Cycladic sculptures, like many of their Stone Age predecessors in the Aegean, Anatolia, Mesopotamia, and western Europe (FIG. 1-5), represent nude women. The Cycladic examples often are women with their arms folded across their abdomens. The sculptures, which excavators have found both in graves and in settlements, vary in height from a few inches to almost life-size. The statuette illustrated here (FIG. **4-2**) is about a foot and a half tall—but only about a half inch thick—and comes from a grave on the island of Syros. The sculptor rendered the human body in a highly schematic manner. Large simple triangles dominate the form—the head, the body itself (which tapers from exceptionally broad shoulders to tiny feet), and the incised triangular pubis. The feet have the toes pointed downward, so the figurine cannot stand upright and must have been placed on its back in the grave—lying down, like the deceased. Archaeologists speculate whether the Syros statuette and the many other similar Cycladic figurines known today represent dead women or fertility figures or goddesses. In any

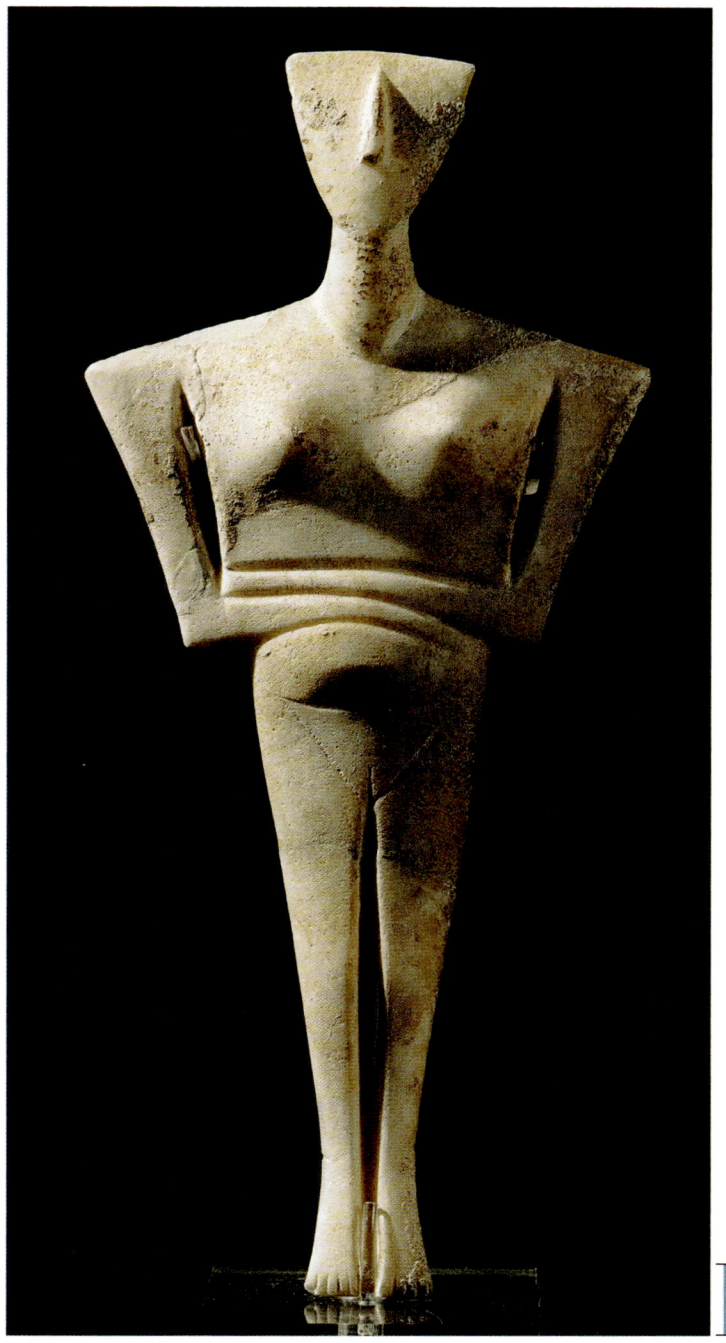

**4-2** Figurine of a woman, from Syros (Cyclades), Greece, ca. 2600–2300 BCE. Marble, 1′ 6″ high. National Archaeological Museum, Athens.

Most Cycladic statuettes depict nude women. This one comes from a grave, but whether it represents the deceased is uncertain. The sculptor rendered the female body schematically as a series of triangles.

1 in.

case, the sculptors took pains to emphasize the breasts as well as the pubic area. In the Syros statuette, a slight swelling of the belly may suggest pregnancy. Traces of paint found on some of the Cycladic figurines indicate that at least parts of these sculptures were colored. The now almost featureless faces would have had painted eyes and mouths in addition to the sculpted noses. Red and blue necklaces and bracelets, as well as painted dots on the cheeks and necks, characterize a number of the surviving figurines.

# Archaeology, Art History, and the Art Market

One way the ancient world is fundamentally different from the world today is that ancient art is largely anonymous and undated. The systematic signing and dating of artworks—a commonplace feature in the contemporary art world—has no equivalent in antiquity. That is why the role of archaeology in the study of ancient art is so important. Only the scientific excavation of ancient monuments can establish their context. Exquisite and strikingly "modern" sculptures, such as the marble Cycladic figurines illustrated in FIGS. 4-2 and 4-3, may be appreciated as masterpieces when displayed in splendid isolation in glass cases in museums or private homes. But to understand the role these or any other artworks played in ancient society—in many cases, even to determine the date of an object—the art historian must learn the provenance of the piece. Only when the context of an artwork is known can anyone go beyond an appreciation of its formal qualities and begin to analyze its place in art history—and in the society that produced it.

The extraordinary popularity of Cycladic figurines in recent decades has had unfortunate consequences. Clandestine treasure hunters, anxious to meet the insatiable demands of collectors, have plundered many sites and smuggled their finds out of Greece to sell to the highest bidder on the international art market. Such looting has destroyed entire prehistoric cemeteries and towns because of the high esteem the marketplace has established for these sculptures. Two British scholars have calculated that only about 10 percent of the known Cycladic marble statuettes come from secure archaeological contexts. Many of the rest could be forgeries produced after World War II when developments in modern art fostered a new appreciation of these abstract renditions of human anatomy and created a boom in demand for "Cycladica" among collectors. For some categories of Cycladic sculptures—those of unusual type or size—not a single piece with a documented provenance exists. Those groups may be 20th-century inventions designed to fetch even higher prices due to their rarity. Consequently, most of the conclusions art historians have drawn about chronology, attribution to different workshops, range of types, and how the figurines were used are purely speculative. The importance of the information the original contexts would have provided cannot be overestimated. That information, however, can probably never be recovered.

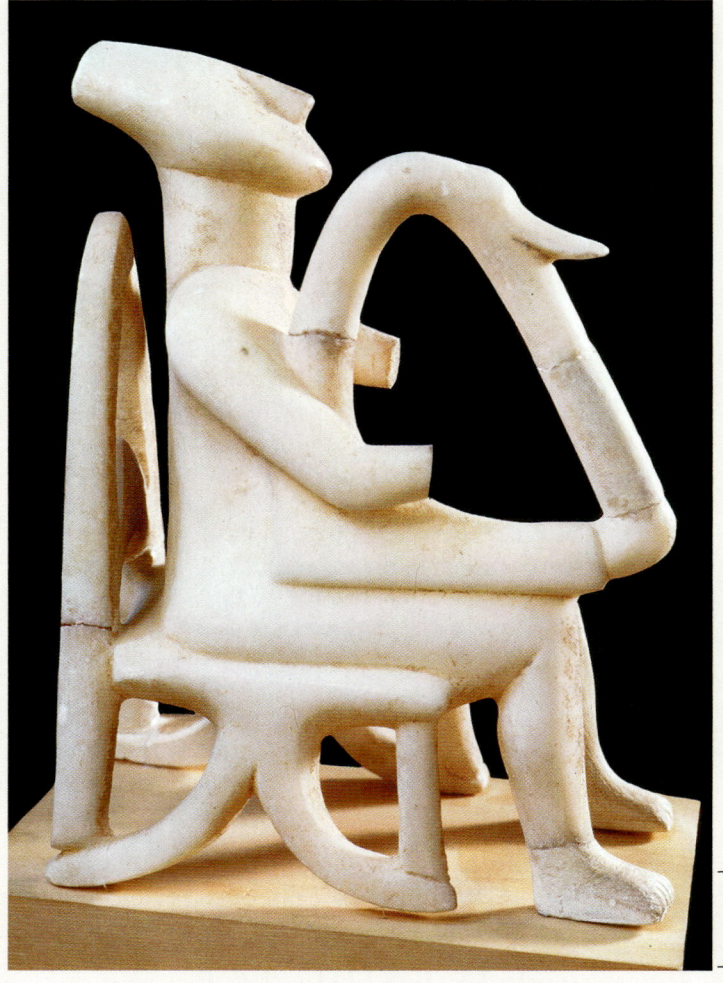

4-3 Male harp player, from Keros (Cyclades), Greece, ca. 2600–2300 BCE. Marble, 9″ high. National Archaeological Museum, Athens.

The meaning of all Cycladic figurines is elusive, but this musician may be playing for the deceased in the afterlife. The statuette displays simple geometric shapes and flat planes, as in FIG. 4-2.

**KEROS MUSICIAN** Cycladic sculptors also represented men. The most elaborate figurines portray seated musicians, such as the harp player (FIG. 4-3) from Keros. Wedged between the echoing shapes of chair and instrument, he may be playing for the deceased in the afterlife, although, again, the meaning of these statuettes remains elusive. The harpist reflects the same preference for simple geometric shapes and large flat planes as do the female figures. Still, the artist showed a keen interest in recording the elegant shape of what must have been a prized possession: the harp with a duck-bill or swan-head ornament. (Compare the form of Sumerian harps, FIGS. 2-1, *top*, 2-9, and 2-10.)

One woman's grave contained figurines of both a musician and a reclining woman. The burial of a male figure together with

the body of a woman suggests that the harp players are not images of dead men, but it does not prove that the female figurines represent dead women. The musician might be entertaining the deceased herself, not her image, or be engaged in commemorative rites honoring the dead. (The harp player on the Hagia Triada sarcophagus, FIG. 4-1, may indicate some continuity in funerary customs and beliefs from the Cycladic to the Minoan period in the Aegean.) Given the absence of written documents in Greece at this date, as everywhere else in prehistoric times, and the lack of information about the provenance of most Cycladic sculptures, art historians cannot be sure of the meaning of these statuettes. It is likely, in fact, that the same form took on different meanings in different contexts.

# MINOAN ART

During the third millennium BCE, both on the Aegean Islands and on the Greek mainland, most settlements were small and consisted only of simple buildings. Rarely were the dead buried with costly offerings such as the Cycladic statuettes just examined. In contrast, the hallmark of the opening centuries of the second millennium BCE (the Middle Minoan period on Crete) is the construction of large palaces.

## Architecture

The first, or Old Palace, period ended abruptly around 1600 BCE, when fire destroyed these grand structures, probably following an earthquake. Rebuilding began almost immediately, and archaeologists consider the ensuing Late Minoan (New Palace) period the golden age of Crete, an era when the first great Western civilization emerged. The rebuilt palaces were large, comfortable, and handsome, with residential suites for the king and his family and courtyards for pageants, ceremonies, and games. They also had storerooms, offices, and shrines, which enabled these huge complexes to serve as the key administrative, commercial, and religious centers of Minoan life. The principal palace sites on Crete are at Knossos, Phaistos, Malia, Kato Zakro, and Khania. The Minoans laid out all of these complexes along similar lines. The size and number of the palaces, as well as the rich finds they have yielded, attest to the power and prosperity of the Minoans.

**KNOSSOS** The largest Cretan palace—at Knossos (FIGS. 4-4 and 4-5)—was the legendary home of King Minos. Here, the hero Theseus hunted the bull-man Minotaur in his labyrinth. According to the myth, after defeating the monster, Theseus found his way out of the mazelike complex only with the aid of the king's daughter,

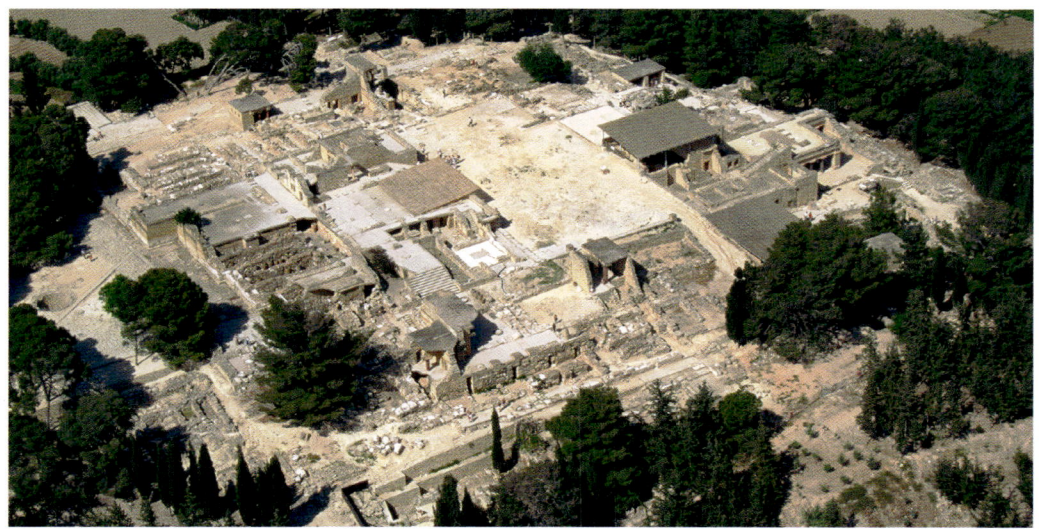

**4-4** Aerial view of the palace (looking northeast), Knossos (Crete), Greece, ca. 1700–1370 BCE. ◼◀

The Knossos palace, the largest on Crete, was the legendary home of King Minos. Its layout features a large central court surrounded by scores of residential and administrative units.

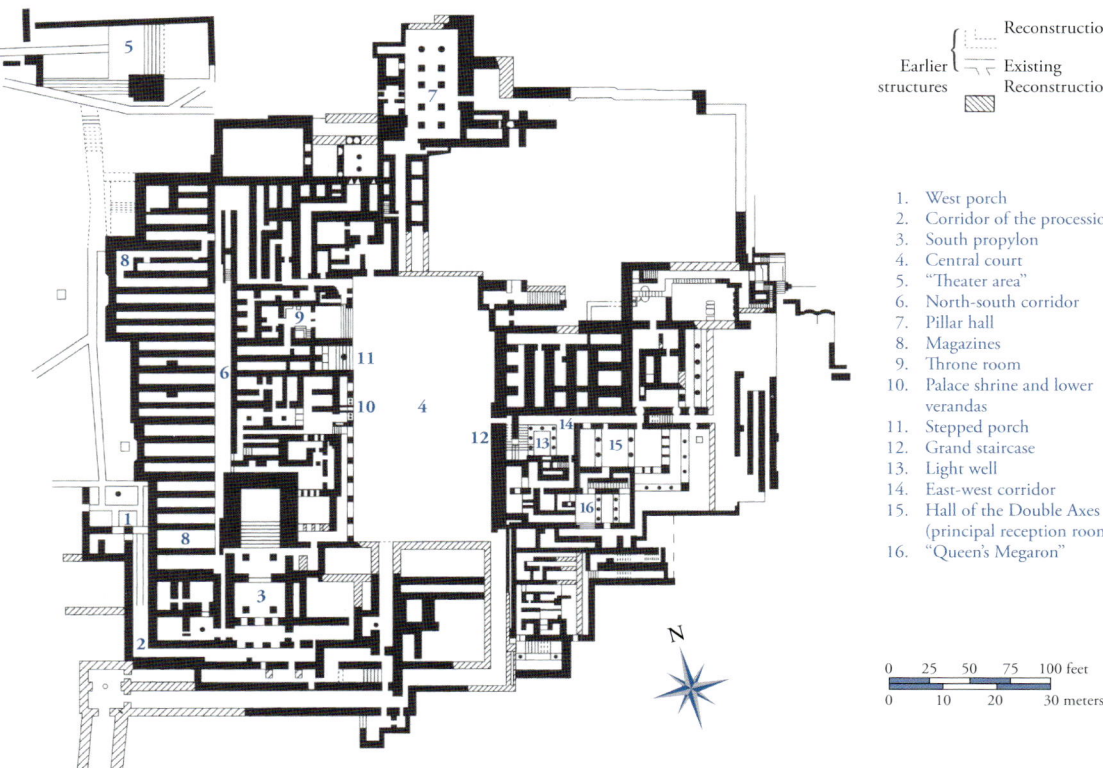

Reconstruction

Earlier { Existing
structures { Reconstruction

1. West porch
2. Corridor of the procession
3. South propylon
4. Central court
5. "Theater area"
6. North-south corridor
7. Pillar hall
8. Magazines
9. Throne room
10. Palace shrine and lower verandas
11. Stepped porch
12. Grand staircase
13. Light well
14. East-west corridor
15. Hall of the Double Axes (principal reception room)
16. "Queen's Megaron"

0   25   50   75   100 feet
0   10   20   30 meters

**4-5** Plan of the palace, Knossos (Crete), Greece, ca. 1700–1370 BCE.

The mazelike plan of the Knossos palace gave rise to the Greek myth of the Cretan labyrinth inhabited by the Minotaur, a half-man half-bull monster that King Theseus of Athens slew.

Ariadne. She had given Theseus a spindle of thread to mark his path through the labyrinth and safely find his way out again. In fact, the English word labyrinth derives from the intricate plan and scores of rooms of the Knossos palace. *Labrys* ("double ax") serves as a recurring motif in the Minoan palace and in Minoan art generally (FIG. 4-1, *left*), referring to sacrificial slaughter. The *labyrinth* was the "House of the Double Ax."

The Knossos palace was a rambling structure built against the upper slopes and across the top of a low hill that rises from a fertile plain (FIG. 4-4). All around the palace proper were mansions and villas of the Minoan elite. The central feature of the palace was its great rectangular court (FIG. 4-5, no. 4). The builders carefully planned the structure with clusters of rooms of similar function grouped around this primary space. A secondary organization of the palace plan involves two long corridors. On the west side of the court, a north-south corridor (FIG. 4-5, no. 6) separates official and ceremonial rooms from the magazines (no. 8), where the Minoans stored wine, grain, oil, and honey in large jars. On the east side of the court, a smaller east-west corridor (no. 14) separates the administrative areas (to the south) from the workrooms (to the north). At the northwest corner of the palace is a theater-like area (no. 5) with steps on two sides that may have served as seats. This arrangement is a possible forerunner of the later Greek theater (FIG. 5-71). Its purpose is unknown, but the feature also appears in the Phaistos palace.

The Knossos palace was complex in elevation as well as plan. It had as many as three stories around the central court and even more on the south and east sides where the terrain sloped off sharply. Interior light and air wells with staircases (FIG. 4-6) provided necessary illumination and ventilation. The Minoans also addressed practical issues such as drainage of rainwater. At Knossos, a remarkably efficient system of *terracotta* (baked clay) pipes underlies the enormous building.

The Cretan palaces were sturdy structures, with thick walls composed of rough, unshaped fieldstones embedded in clay. For corners and around door and window openings, the builders used large ashlar blocks. The painted wooden columns (which Evans restored in cement at Knossos) have distinctive capitals and shafts (FIG. 4-6). The bulbous, cushionlike Minoan capitals resemble those of the later Greek Doric order (FIG. 5-13, *left*), but the column shafts—essentially stylized inverted tree trunks—taper from a wide top to a narrower base, the opposite of both Egyptian and later Greek columns.

## Painting

Mural paintings liberally adorned the palace at Knossos, constituting one of its most striking features. The brightly painted walls and the red shafts and black capitals of the wooden columns produced an extraordinarily rich effect. The paintings depict many aspects of Minoan life (bull-leaping, processions, and ceremonies) and of nature (birds, animals, flowers, and marine life).

**LA PARISIENNE** From a ceremonial scene of uncertain significance comes the fragment (FIG. 4-7) dubbed *La Parisienne* (The Parisian Woman) on its discovery because of the elegant dress, elaborate coiffure, and full rouged lips of the young woman depicted. Some have identified her as a priestess taking part in a religious ritual, but because the figure has no arms, it is most likely a statue of a goddess. Although the representation is still convention-bound (note especially the oversized frontal eye in the profile head), the charm and freshness of the mural are undeniable. Unlike the Egyptians, who painted in fresco secco (dry fresco), the Minoans

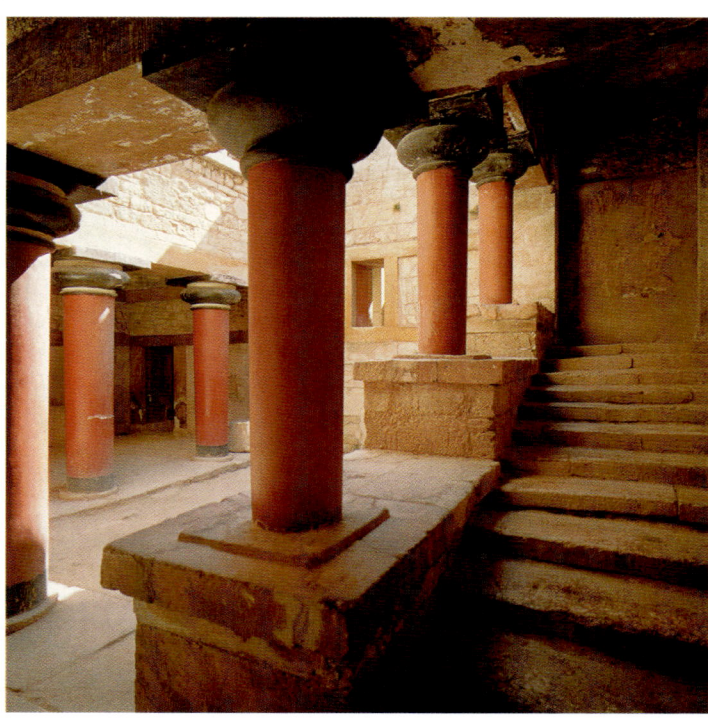

**4-6** Stairwell in the residential quarter of the palace, Knossos (Crete), Greece, ca. 1700–1370 BCE. ◼◀

The Knossos palace was complex in elevation as well as plan. It had at least three stories on all sides of the court. Minoan columns taper from top to bottom, the opposite of Egyptian and Greek columns.

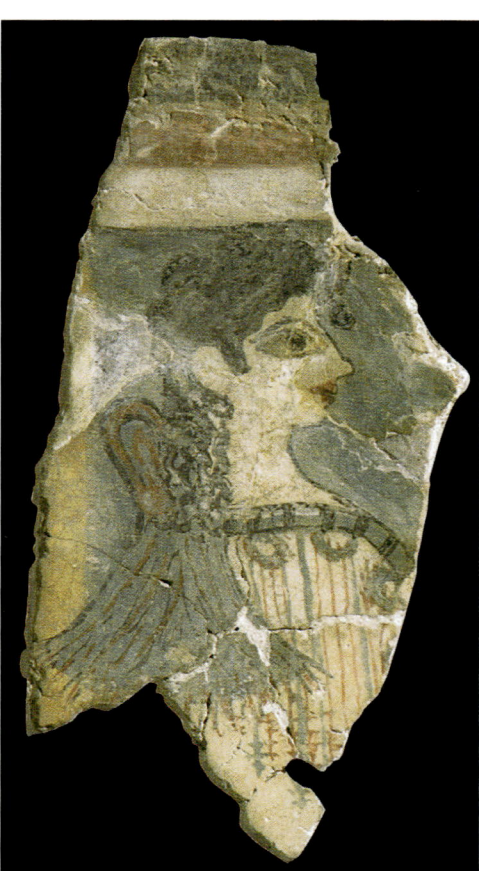

**4-7** Minoan woman or goddess (*La Parisienne*), from the palace, Knossos (Crete), Greece, ca. 1400–1370 BCE. Fragment of a fresco, 10″ high. Archaeological Museum, Herakleion. ◼◀

Frescoes decorated the Knossos palace walls. This fragment depicts a woman or a goddess—perhaps a statue—with a large frontal eye in her profile head, as in Mesopotamian and Egyptian art.

1 in.

coated the rough fabric of their rubble walls with a fine white lime plaster and used a true (wet) fresco method in which the painter applies the pigments while the walls are still wet. The color consequently becomes chemically bonded to the plaster after it dries (see "Fresco Painting," Chapter 14, page 408). The Minoan painters therefore had to execute their work rapidly, in contrast to Egyptian practice, which permitted slower, more deliberate work.

**BULL-LEAPING** Another fresco (FIG. **4-8**) from the palace at Knossos depicts the Minoan ceremony of bull-leaping, in which young men grasped the horns of a bull and vaulted onto its back—a perilous and extremely difficult acrobatic maneuver. Excavators recovered only fragments of the full composition (the dark patches are original; the rest is a modern restoration). The Minoan artist provided no setting, instead focusing all attention on the three protagonists and the fearsome bull. The young women have fair skin and the leaping youth has dark skin in accord with the widely accepted ancient convention for distinguishing male and female, as on the Hagia Triada sarcophagus (FIG. 4-1; compare FIG. 3-11A). The painter brilliantly suggested the powerful charge of the bull by elongating the animal's shape and using sweeping lines to form a funnel of energy, beginning at the very narrow hindquarters of the bull and culminating in its large, sharp horns and galloping fore-

legs. The highly animated human figures also have stylized shapes, with typically Minoan pinched waists. Although the profile pose with the full-view eye was a familiar convention in Egypt and Mesopotamia, the elegance of the Cretan figures, with their long, curly hair and proud and self-confident bearing, distinguishes them from all other early figure styles. In contrast to the angularity of the figures in Egyptian wall paintings, the curving lines the Minoan artist employed suggest the elasticity of living and moving beings.

**THERA** Much better preserved than the Knossos frescoes are the mural paintings Greek archaeologists discovered in their ongoing excavations at Akrotiri on the volcanic island of Thera in the Cyclades, some 60 miles north of Crete. In the Late Cycladic period, Thera was artistically (and possibly also politically) within the Minoan orbit. The Akrotiri murals are invaluable additions to the fragmentary and frequently misrestored frescoes from Crete. The excellent condition of the Theran paintings is due to an enormous seismic explosion on the island that buried Akrotiri in volcanic pumice and ash, making it a kind of Pompeii of the prehistoric Aegean (see "The Theran Eruption and the Chronology of Aegean Art," page 92). The Akrotiri frescoes decorated the walls of houses, not the walls of a great palace like Minos's at Knossos, and therefore the number of painted walls from the site is especially impressive.

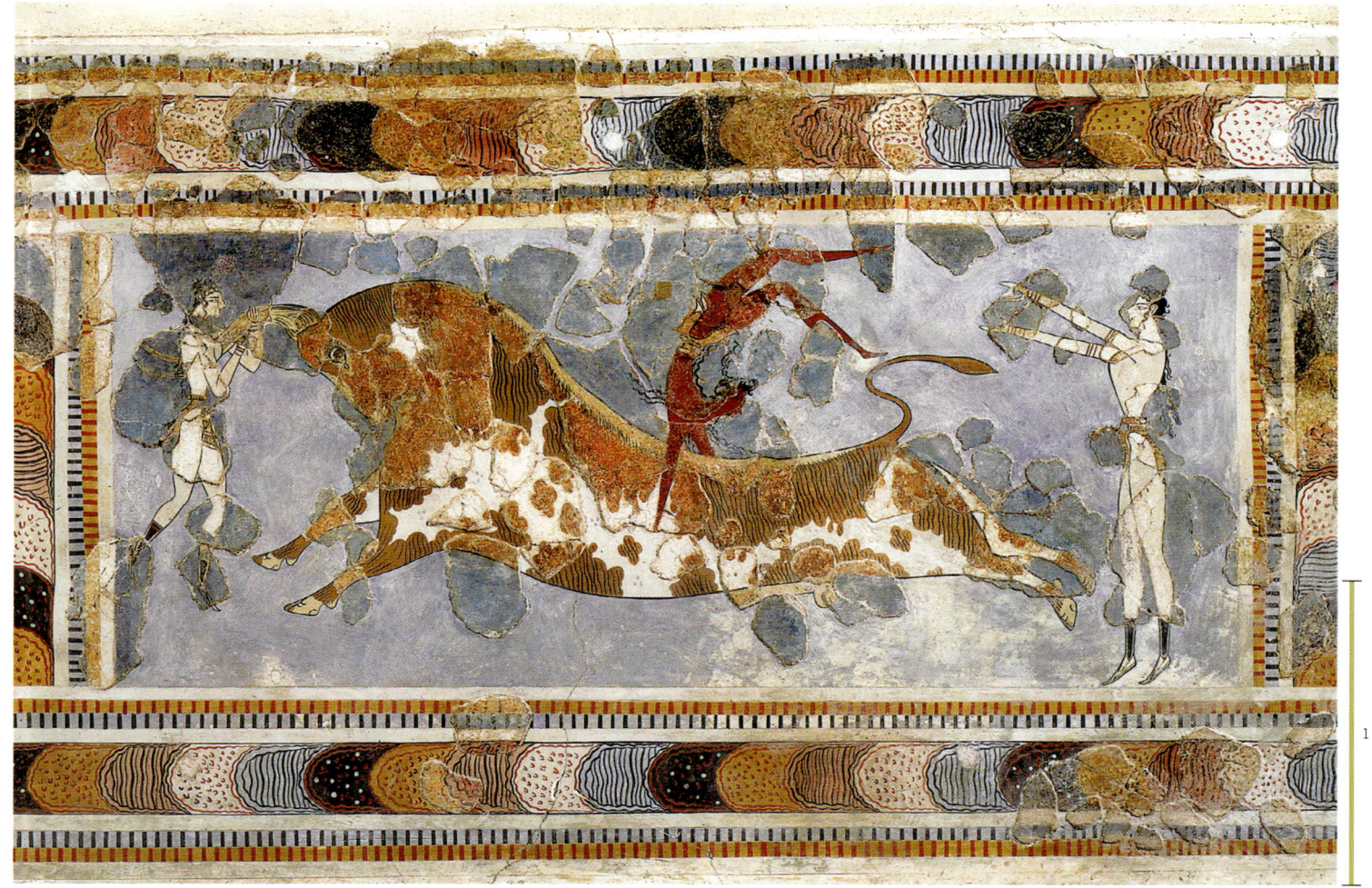

**4-8** Bull-leaping, from the palace, Knossos (Crete), Greece, ca. 1400–1370 BCE. Fresco, 2′ 8″ high, including border. Archaeological Museum, Herakleion. ◼◄

The subjects of the Knossos frescoes are often ceremonial scenes, such as this one of bull-leaping. The women have fair skin and the man has dark skin, a common convention in ancient painting.

## The Theran Eruption and the Chronology of Aegean Art

Today, ships bound for the beautiful Greek island of Thera, with its picture-postcard white houses, churches, shops, and restaurants, weigh anchor in a bay beneath steep cliffs. Until about 20,000 BCE, however, Thera had gentler slopes. Then, suddenly, a volcanic eruption blew out the center of the island, leaving behind the crescent-shaped main island and several lesser islands grouped around a bay that roughly corresponds to the shape of the gigantic ancient volcano. The volcano erupted again, thousands of years later, during the zenith of Aegean civilization.

The site of Akrotiri, which Greek excavators have been gradually uncovering for a half century, was buried in that later explosion by a layer of pumice more than a yard deep in some areas and by an even larger volume of volcanic ash (*tephra*) that often exceeds five yards in depth, even after nearly 37 centuries of erosion. Tephra filled whole rooms, and boulders the volcano spewed forth pelted the walls of some houses. Closer to the volcano's cone, the tephra is almost 60 yards deep in places. In fact, the force of the eruption was so powerful that sea currents carried the pumice and wind blew the ash throughout much of the eastern Mediterranean, not only to Crete, Rhodes, and Cyprus but also as far away as Anatolia, Egypt, Syria, and Israel.

A generation ago, most scholars embraced the theory formulated by Spyridon Marinatos (1901–1974), an eminent Greek archae-

ologist, that the otherwise unexplained demise of Minoan civilization on Crete around 1500 BCE was the by-product of the volcanic eruption on Thera. According to Marinatos, devastating famine followed the rain of ash that fell on Crete. But archaeologists now know that after the eruption, life went on in Crete, if not on Thera.

Teams of researchers, working closely in an impressive and most welcome interdisciplinary effort, have determined that a major climatic event occurred during the last third of the 17th century BCE. In addition to collecting evidence from Thera, they have studied tree rings at sites in Europe and in North America for evidence of retarded growth and have examined ice cores in Greenland for peak acidity layers. The scientific data pinpoint a significant disruption in weather patterns in 1628 BCE. Most scholars now believe the cause of this disruption was the cataclysmic volcanic eruption on Thera. The date of the Aegean catastrophe remains the subject of much debate, however, and many archaeologists favor placing the eruption in the 16th century BCE. In either case, the date of Thera's destruction has profound consequences for determining the chronology of Aegean art. If the Akrotiri frescoes (FIGS. 4-9 to 4-9B) date between 1650 and 1625 BCE, they are at least 150 years older than scholars thought not long ago, and are much older than the Knossos palace murals (FIGS. 4-7 and 4-8).

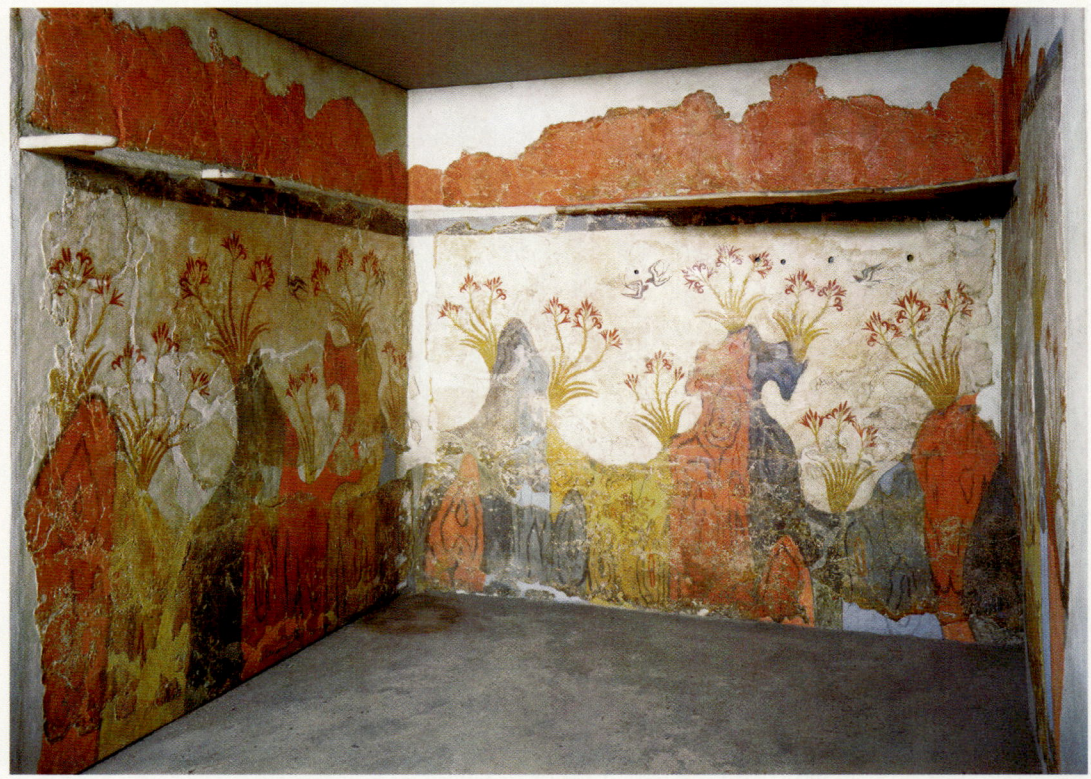

**4-9** Landscape with swallows (*Spring Fresco*) from room Delta 2, Akrotiri, Thera (Cyclades), Greece, ca. 1650–1625 BCE. Fresco, 7′ 6″ high. National Archaeological Museum, Athens.

Aegean muralists painted in wet fresco, which required rapid execution. In this wraparound landscape, the painter used vivid colors and undulating lines to capture the essence of nature.

The almost perfectly preserved mural painting from Akrotiri known as the *Spring Fresco* (FIG. 4-9) is the largest and most complete prehistoric example of a pure landscape painting (compare FIG. 1-17). Landscapes—and seascapes—are key elements of many

of the mural paintings found at Akrotiri (FIGS. 4-9A and 4-9B). In each case, however, the artist's aim was not to render the rocky island terrain realistically but rather to capture its essence. In FIG. 4-9, the irrationally undulating and vividly colored rocks, the graceful

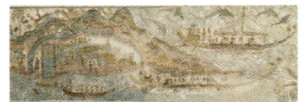

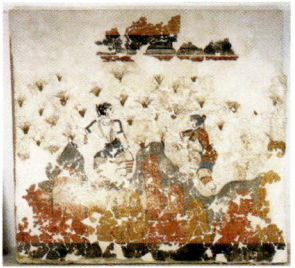

lilies swaying in the cool island breezes, and the darting swallows express the vigor of growth, the delicacy of flowering, and the lightness of birdsong and flight. In the lyrical language of curving line, the artist celebrated the rhythms of nature. The *Spring Fresco* represents the polar opposite of the first efforts at mural painting in the caves of Paleolithic Europe (see Chapter 1), where animals (and occasionally humans) appeared as isolated figures with no indication of setting.

**MINOAN POTTERY** The love of nature manifested itself in Crete on the surfaces of painted vases even before the period of the new palaces. During the Middle Minoan period, Cretan potters fashioned sophisticated shapes using newly introduced potters' wheels, and decorated their vases in a distinctive and fully polychromatic style. These Kamares Ware vessels, named for the cave on the slope of Mount Ida where they were first discovered, have been found in quantity at Phaistos and Knossos. Some examples come from as far away as Egypt. On the jar in FIG. 4-10, as on other Kamares vases, the painter applied creamy white and reddish-brown decoration to a rich black ground. The central motif is a great leaping fish and perhaps a fishnet surrounded by a host of curvilinear abstract patterns including waves and spirals. The swirling lines evoke life in the sea, and both the abstract and the natural forms beautifully complement the shape of the vessel.

The sea and the creatures that inhabit it also inspired the Late Minoan Marine Style octopus flask (FIG. 4-11) from Palaikastro. The tentacles of the octopus reach out over the curving surfaces of the vessel, embracing the piece and emphasizing its volume. The flask is a masterful realization of the relationship between the vessel's decoration and its shape, always a problem for the vase painter. This later jar, which is contemporaneous with the new palaces at Knossos and elsewhere, differs markedly from its Kamares Ware predecessor in color. Not only is the octopus vase more muted in tone, but the Late Minoan artist also reversed the earlier scheme and placed dark silhouettes on a light ground. Dark-on-light coloration remained the norm for about a millennium in Greece, until about 530 BCE when, albeit in a very different form, light figures on a dark ground emerged once again as the preferred manner (FIG. 5-21).

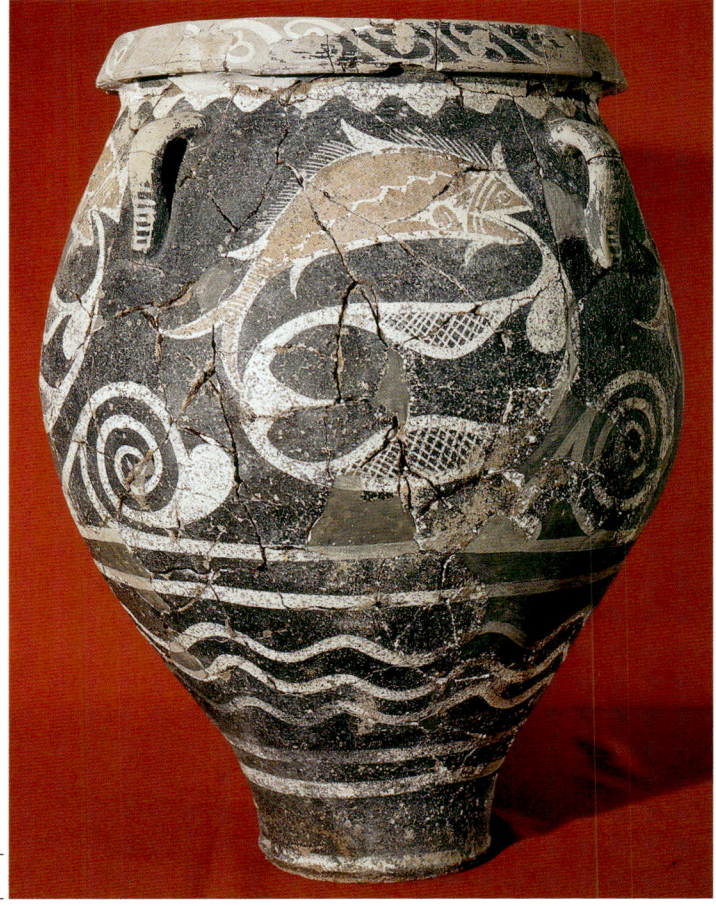

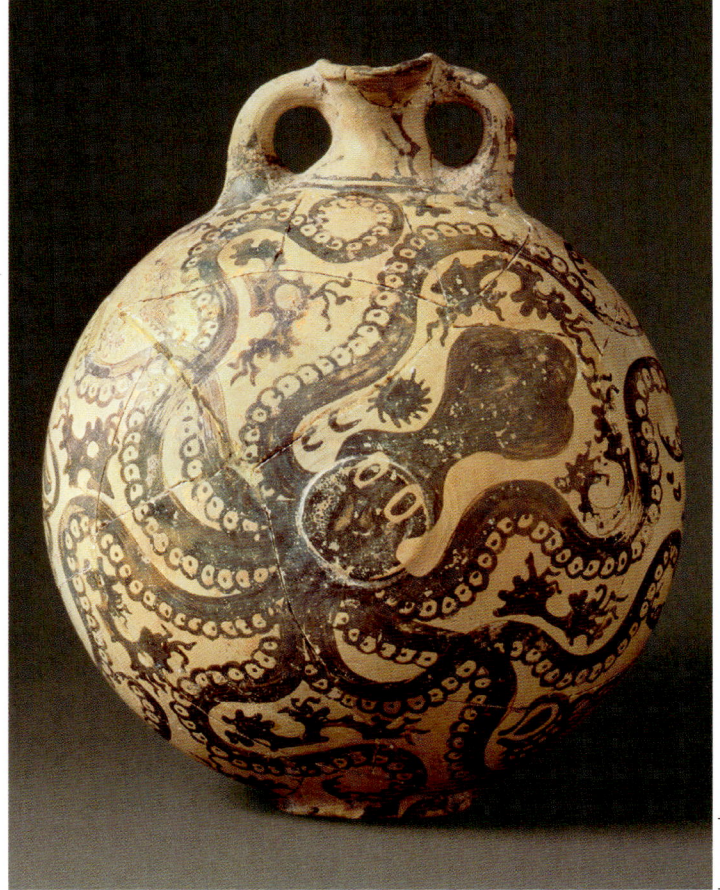

1 in.

1 in.

**4-10** Kamares Ware jar, from Phaistos (Crete), Greece, ca. 1800–1700 BCE. 1′ 8″ high. Archaeological Museum, Herakleion.

Kamares vases have creamy white and reddish-brown decoration on a black background. This jar combines a fish (and a net?) with curvilinear abstract patterns including spirals and waves.

**4-11** Marine Style octopus flask, from Palaikastro (Crete), Greece, ca. 1450 BCE. 11″ high. Archaeological Museum, Herakleion.

Marine Style vases have dark figures on a light ground. On this octopus flask, the tentacles of the sea creature reach out over the curving surface of the vessel to fill the shape perfectly.

# Sculpture

In contrast to Mesopotamia and Egypt, Minoan Crete has yielded no trace of temples or monumental statues of gods, kings, or monsters. Large wooden images may once have existed—*La Parisienne* (FIG. 4-7) perhaps is a depiction of one of them—but what remains of Minoan sculpture is uniformly small in scale.

*SNAKE GODDESS* One of the most striking finds from the palace at Knossos is the *faience* (low-fired opaque glasslike silicate) statuette popularly known as the *Snake Goddess* (FIG. 4-12). Reconstructed from many pieces, it is one of several similar figurines that some scholars believe may represent mortal priestesses rather than a deity, although the prominently exposed breasts suggest that these figurines stand in the long line of prehistoric fertility images usually considered divinities. The Knossos woman holds snakes in her hands and supports a tamed leopardlike feline on her

head. This implied power over the animal world also seems appropriate for a deity. The frontality of the figure is reminiscent of Egyptian and Mesopotamian statuary, but the costume, with its open bodice and flounced skirt, is distinctly Minoan. If the statuette represents a goddess, as seems likely, it is yet another example of how human beings fashion their gods in their own image.

**PALAIKASTRO YOUTH** British excavations at Palaikastro between 1987 and 1990 yielded fragments of one of the most remarkable objects ever found on Crete. It is a statuette (FIG. 4-13) nearly 20 inches tall, fashioned from hippopotamus-tusk ivory, gold, serpentine, and rock crystal. The figurine is a very early example of *chryselephantine* (gold-and-ivory) sculpture, a technique the Greeks would later use for their largest and costliest cult images (FIG. 5-46). The Minoans probably imported the ivory and gold from Egypt, the source also of the pose with left foot advanced

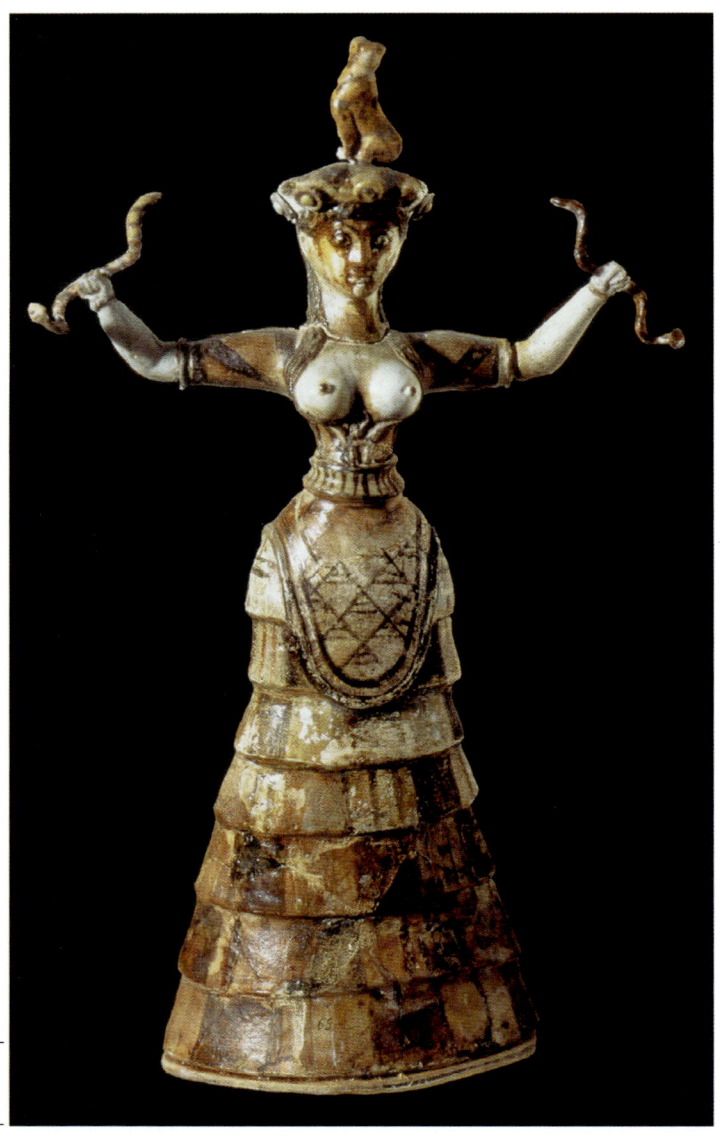

1 in.

4-12 *Snake Goddess,* from the palace, Knossos (Crete), Greece, ca. 1600 BCE. Faience, 1′ 1½″ high. Archaeological Museum, Herakleion.

This figurine may represent a priestess, but it is more likely a bare-breasted goddess. The snakes in her hands and the feline on her head imply that she has power over the animal world.

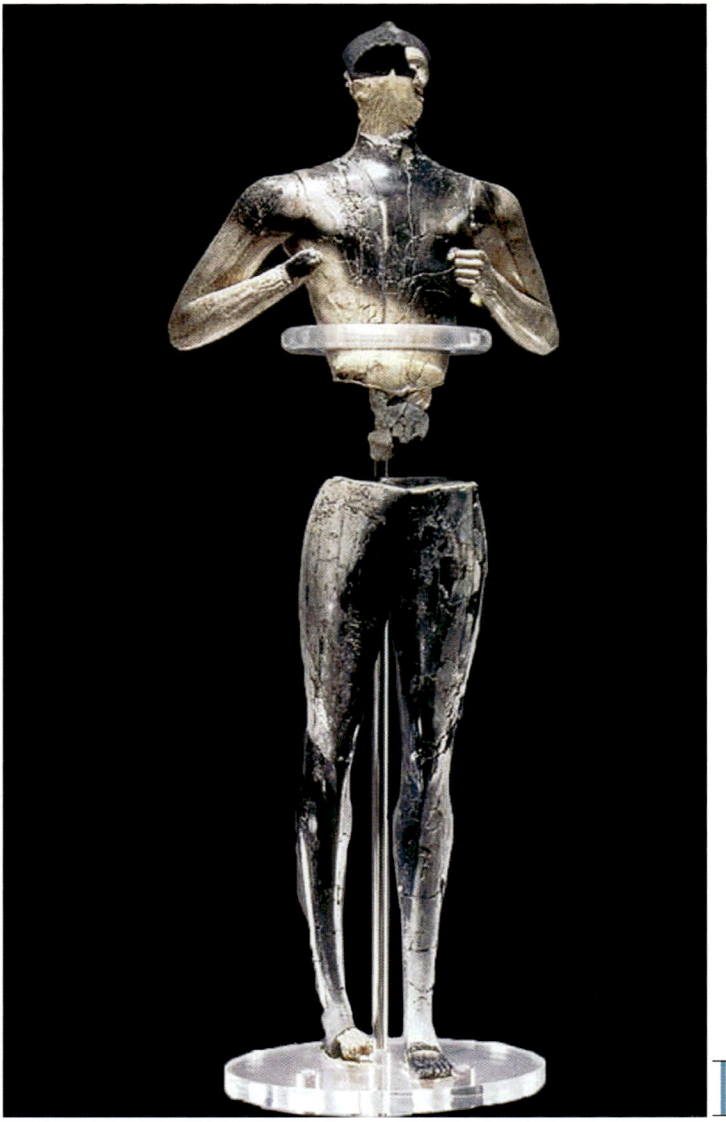

1 in.

4-13 Young god(?), from Palaikastro (Crete), Greece, ca. 1500–1450 BCE. Ivory, gold, serpentine, and rock crystal, restored height 1′ 7½″. Archaeological Museum, Siteia.

This statuette, probably representing a young god, is a very early example of chryselephantine (gold-and-ivory) sculpture, a technique later used for the largest and costliest Greek cult statues.

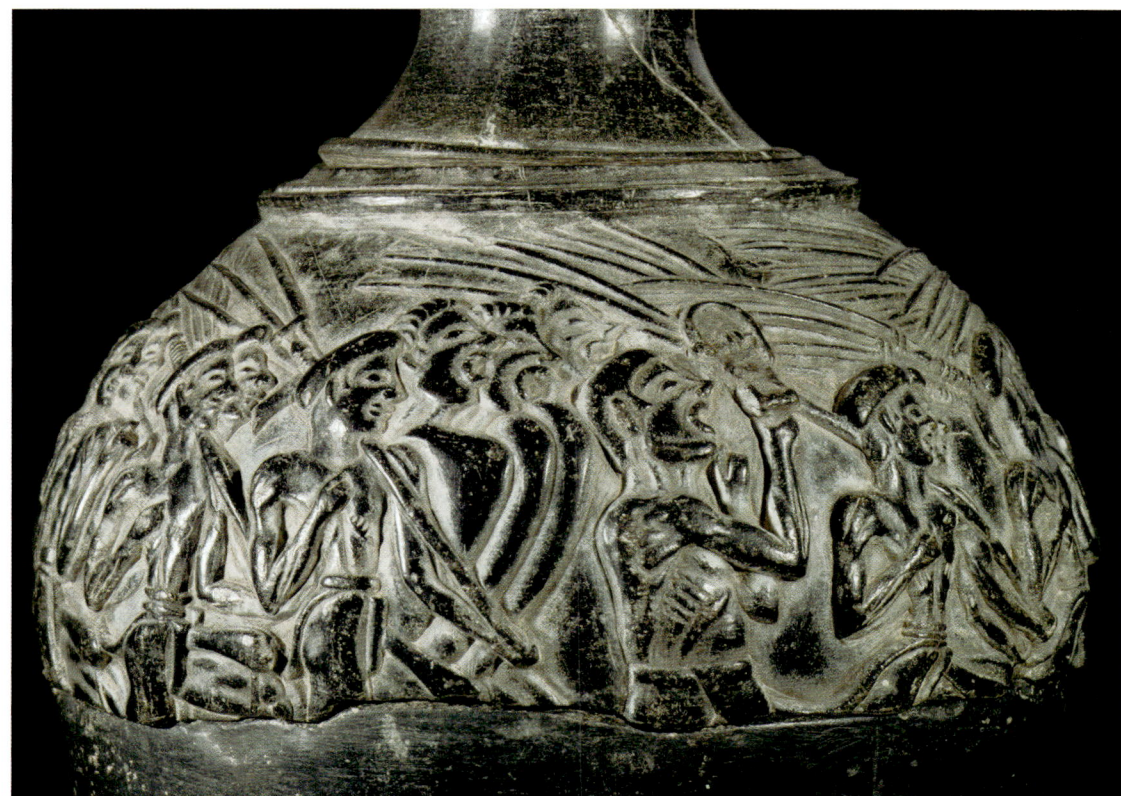

The relief sculptor of the singing harvesters on this small stone vase was one of the first artists in history to represent the underlying muscular and skeletal structure of the human body.

1 in.

(FIG. 3-12), but the style and iconography are unmistakably Cretan. The work is the creation of a sculptor of extraordinary ability who delighted in rendering minute details of muscles and veins. The Palaikastro youth (his coiffure, with shaved head save for a central braid, indicates his age) stood alone in a shrine and therefore seems to have been a god rather than a mortal. The excavators found the statuette in scattered and blackened fragments, suggesting fire following a willful destruction of the sacred image in the 15th century BCE.

***HARVESTERS VASE*** The finest surviving example of Minoan relief sculpture is the so-called *Harvesters Vase* (FIG. **4-14**) from Hagia Triada. Only the upper half of the egg-shaped body and neck of the vessel remain. Missing are the lower parts of the harvesters (or, as some think, sowers) and the ground on which they stand as well as the gold leaf that originally covered the relief figures. Formulaic scenes of sowing and harvesting were staples of Egyptian funerary art (FIG. 3-15), but the Minoan artist shunned static repetition in favor of a composition bursting with the energy of its individually characterized figures. The relief shows a riotous crowd singing and shouting as they go to or return from the fields. The artist vividly captured the forward movement and lusty exuberance of the youths.

Although most of the figures conform to the age-old convention of combined profile and frontal views, the relief sculptor singled out one figure (FIG. 4-14, *right of center*) from his companions. He shakes a *sistrum* (an Egyptian percussion instrument or rattle) to beat time, and the artist depicted him in full profile with his lungs so inflated with air that his ribs show. This is one of the first instances in the history of art of a sculptor showing a keen interest in the underlying muscular and skeletal structure of the human body. The Minoan artist's painstaking study of human anatomy is a singular achievement, especially given the size of the *Harvesters*

*Vase,* barely five inches at its greatest diameter. Equally noteworthy is how the sculptor recorded the tension and relaxation of facial muscles with astonishing exactitude, not only for this figure but for his nearest companions as well. This degree of animation of the human face is without precedent in ancient art.

**MINOAN DECLINE** Scholars dispute the circumstances ending the Minoan civilization, although most now believe Mycenaeans had already moved onto Crete and established themselves at Knossos at the end of the New Palace period. From the palace at Knossos, these intruders appear to have ruled the island for at least a half century, perhaps much longer. Parts of the palace continued to be occupied until its final destruction around 1200 BCE, but its importance as a cultural center faded soon after 1400 BCE, as the focus of Aegean civilization shifted to the Greek mainland.

# MYCENAEAN ART

The origin of the Mycenaeans is also the subject of continuing debate among archaeologists and historians. The only certainty is the presence of these forerunners of the Greeks on the mainland about the time of the construction of the old palaces on Crete—that is, about the beginning of the second millennium BCE. Doubtless, Cretan civilization influenced these people even then, and some scholars believe the mainland was a Minoan economic dependency for a long time. In any case, Mycenaean power developed in the north in the days of the new palaces on Crete, and by 1500 BCE a distinctive Mycenaean culture was flourishing in Greece. Several centuries later, Homer described Mycenae as "rich in gold." The dramatic discoveries of Schliemann and his successors have fully justified this characterization, even if today's archaeologists no longer view the Mycenaeans solely through the eyes of Homer.

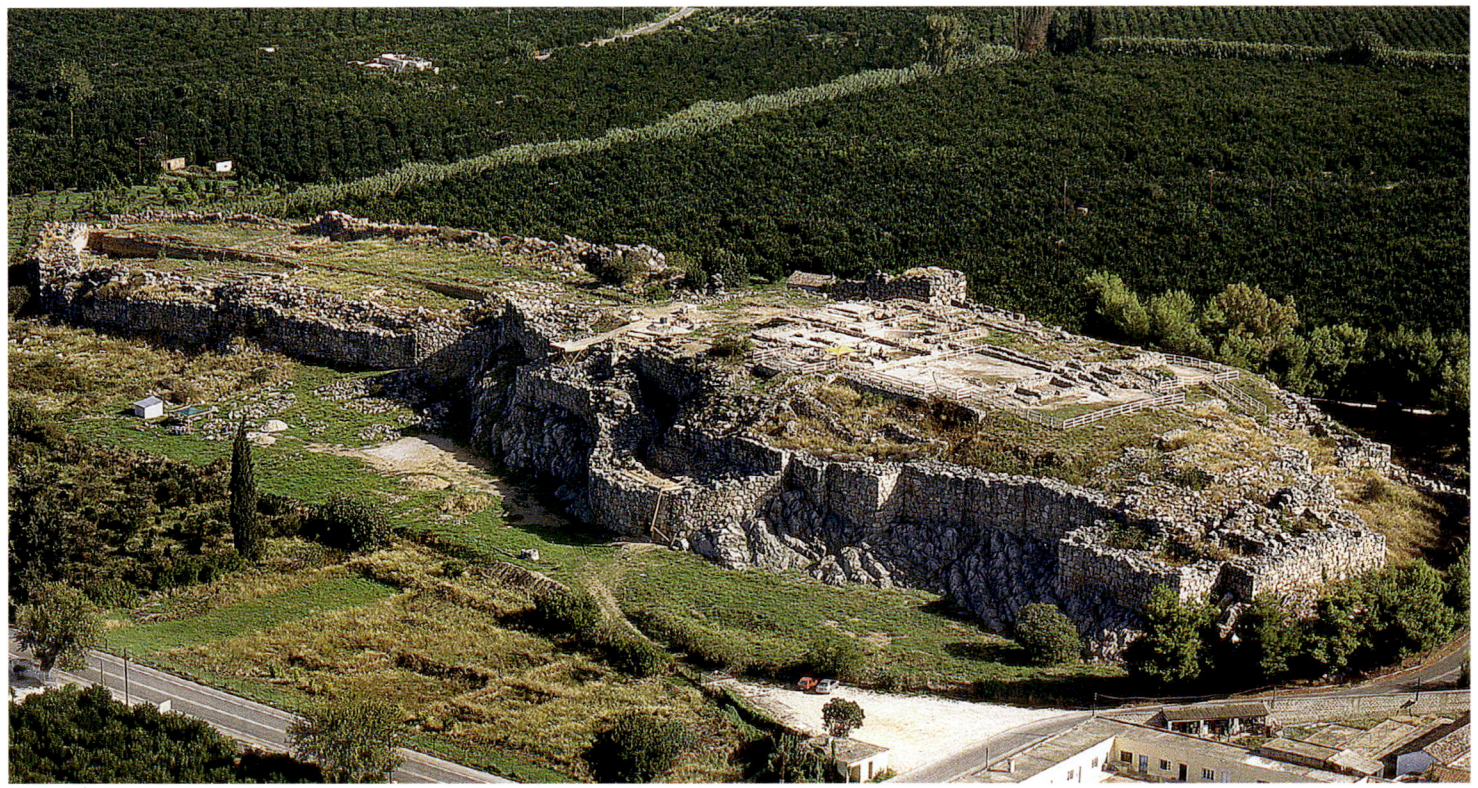

**4-15** Aerial view of the citadel (looking east), Tiryns, Greece, ca. 1400–1200 BCE.

In the *Iliad,* Homer called the fortified citadel of Tiryns the city "of the great walls." Its huge, roughly cut stone blocks are examples of Cyclopean masonry, named after the mythical one-eyed giants.

## Architecture

The destruction of the Cretan palaces left the mainland culture supreme. Although historians usually refer to this Late Helladic civilization as Mycenaean, Mycenae was but one of several large palace complexes. Archaeologists have also unearthed Mycenaean remains at Tiryns, Orchomenos, Pylos, and elsewhere, and a section of a Mycenaean fortification wall is still in place on the Acropolis of Athens. The best-preserved and most impressive Mycenaean remains are those of the fortified palaces at Tiryns and Mycenae. Construction of both citadels began about 1400 BCE. Both palaces burned (along with all the others) between 1250 and 1200 BCE when northern invaders overran the Mycenaeans or they fell victim to internal warfare.

**TIRYNS** Homer knew the citadel of Tiryns (FIG. **4-15**), located about 10 miles from Mycenae, as "Tiryns of the Great Walls." In the second century CE, when Pausanias, author of an invaluable guidebook to Greece, visited the long-abandoned site, he marveled at the towering fortifications and considered the walls of Tiryns as spectacular as the pyramids of Egypt. Indeed, the Greeks of the historical age believed mere humans could not have built these enormous edifices. They attributed the construction of the great Mycenaean

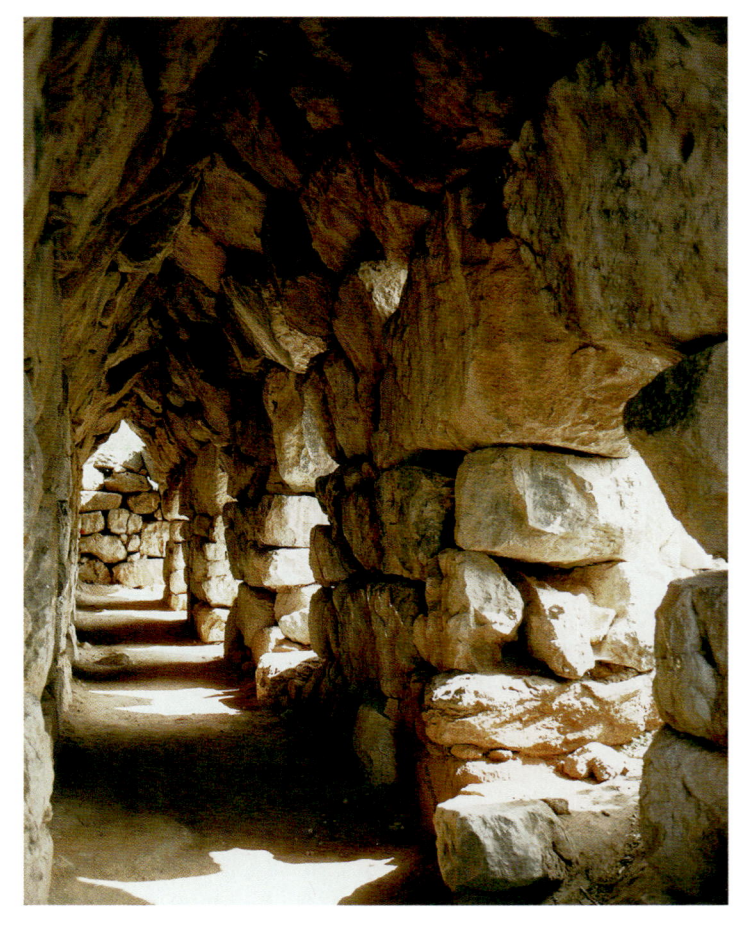

**4-16** Corbel-vaulted gallery in the circuit wall of the citadel, Tiryns, Greece, ca. 1400–1200 BCE.

In this long gallery within the circuit wall of Tiryns, the Mycenaeans piled irregular Cyclopean blocks in horizontal courses and then cantilevered them until the two walls met in a pointed arch.

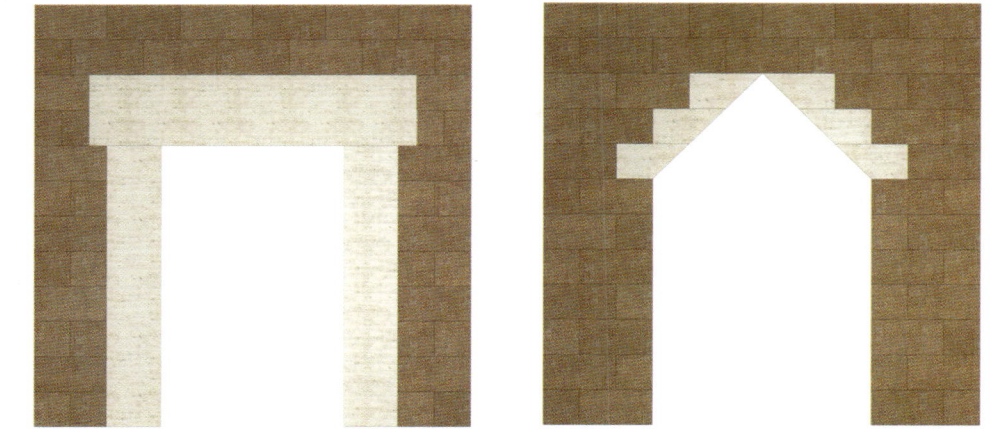

(a)          (b)          (c)

**4-17** Three methods of spanning a passageway: **(a)** post and lintel, **(b)** corbeled arch, **(c)** arch (John Burge).

Post-and-lintel construction **(a)** was the norm in ancient Greece, but the Mycenaeans also used corbeled arches **(b)**. The round arch **(c)**, used already in Mesopotamia, was popular later in Rome.

citadels to the mythical *Cyclopes,* a race of one-eyed giants. Architectural historians still employ the term *Cyclopean masonry* to refer to the huge, roughly cut stone blocks forming the massive fortification walls of Tiryns and other Mycenaean sites.

The heavy walls of Tiryns and Mycenae contrast sharply with the open Cretan palaces (FIG. 4-4) and clearly reveal their defensive character. Those of Tiryns average about 20 feet in thickness, and in one section they incorporate a long gallery (FIG. 4-16) covered by corbeled vaults (FIG. 4-17*b*) similar to those constructed long before at Neolithic sites such as Newgrange (FIG. 1-18). At Tiryns, the builders piled the large, irregular Cyclopean blocks in horizontal courses and then cantilevered them inward until the two walls met in a pointed arch. The builders used no mortar. The vault is held in place only by the weight of the blocks (often several tons each), by the smaller stones used as wedges, and by the clay that fills some of the empty spaces. This primitive but effective vaulting scheme possesses an earthy monumentality. It is easy to see how a later age came to believe that the uncouth Cyclopes were responsible for these massive but unsophisticated fortifications.

The Mycenaean engineers who designed the circuit wall of Tiryns compelled would-be attackers to approach the palace (FIG. 4-18) within the walls via a long ramp that forced the soldiers (usually right-handed; compare FIG. 4-26) to expose their unshielded sides to the Mycenaean defenders above. Then—if they got that far—the enemy forces had to pass through a series of narrow gates that also could be defended easily. Inside, at Tiryns as elsewhere, the most important element in the palace plan was the *megaron,* or reception hall and throne room, of the king. The main room of the megaron had a throne against the right wall and a central hearth bordered by four Minoan-style wooden columns serving as supports for the roof. A vestibule with a columnar facade preceded the throne room. The remains of the megaron at Tiryns are scant, but at Pylos, home of Homer's King Nestor, archaeologists found sufficient evidence to permit a reconstruction (FIG. 4-18A) of the original appearance of that palace's megaron, complete with mural and ceiling paintings.

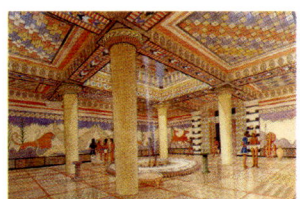

**4-18A** Megaron, Palace of Nestor, Pylos, ca. 1300 BCE.

Approach ramp

Main gate

Megaron

Citadel walls

Citadel walls

Outer propylon

N

0  25  50  75  100 feet
0  10  20  30 meters

**4-18** Plan of the palace and southern part of the citadel, Tiryns, Greece, ca. 1400–1200 BCE.

The king's reception room, or megaron, was the main feature of a Mycenaean palace. It had a columnar porch leading to a hall containing the throne and a central hearth bordered by four columns.

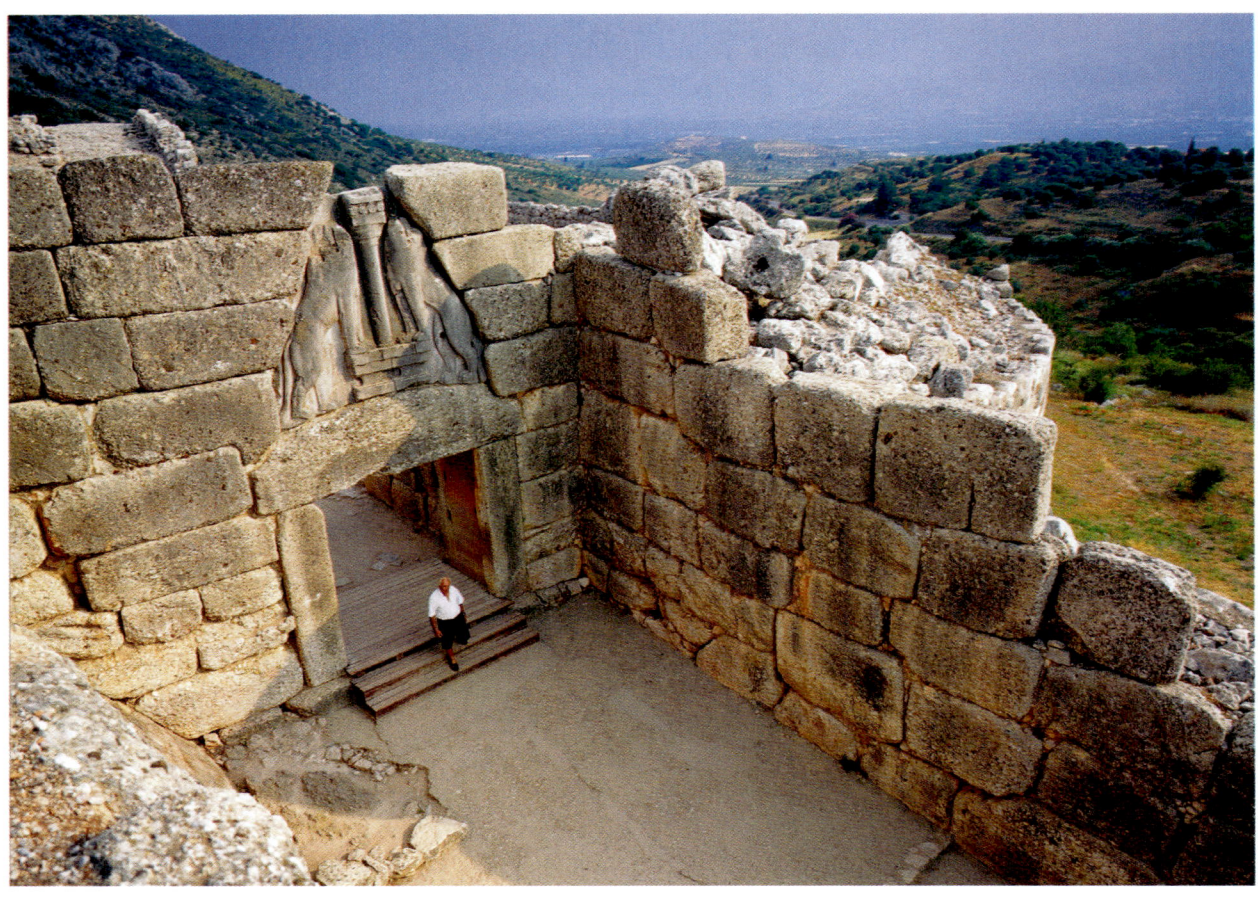

**4-19** Lion Gate (looking southeast), Mycenae, Greece, ca. 1300–1250 BCE. Limestone, relief panel 9′ 6″ high. ◼◀

The largest sculpture in the prehistoric Aegean is the relief of confronting lions that fills the relieving triangle of Mycenae's main gate. The gate itself consists of two great monoliths and a huge lintel.

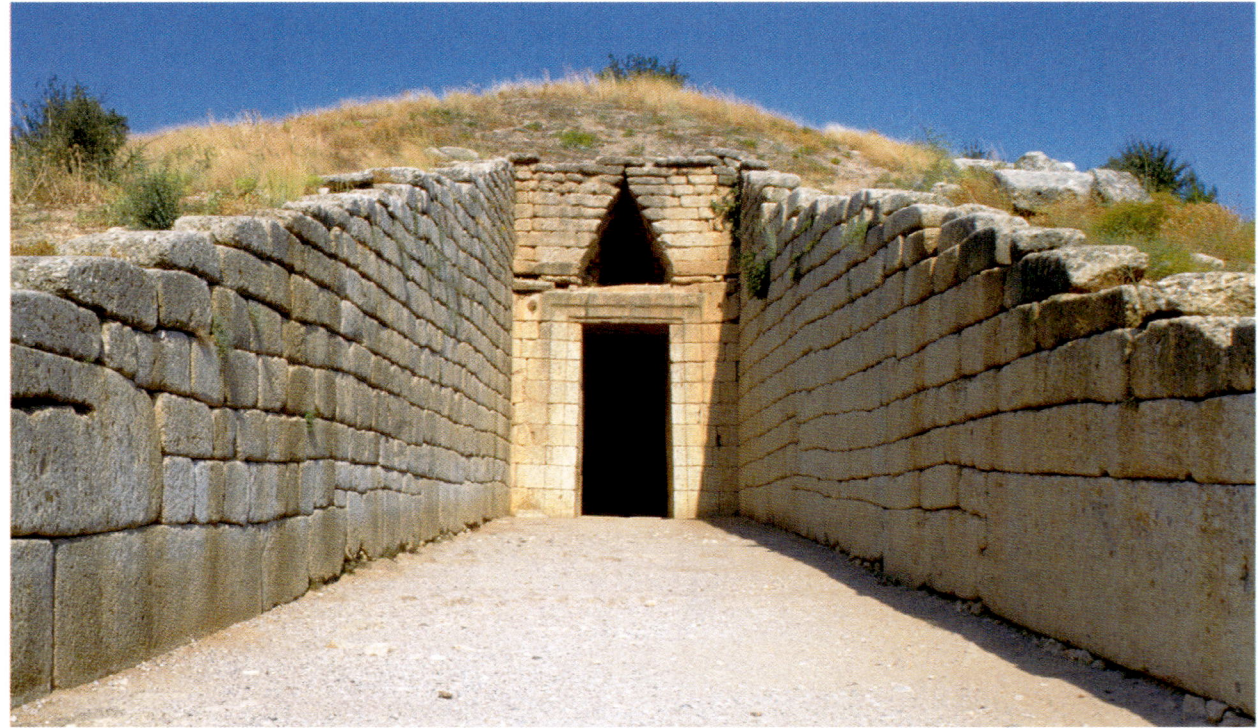

**4-20** Treasury of Atreus, Mycenae, Greece, ca. 1300–1250 BCE. ◼◀

The best-preserved Mycenaean tholos tomb is named after Homer's King Atreus. An earthen mound covers the burial chamber, reached through a doorway at the end of a long passageway.

**LION GATE, MYCENAE** Although frescoed walls were commonplace in the Mycenaean fortress-palaces, as in the Cretan palaces, monumental sculpture was rare. Agamemnon's Mycenae was the exception. The so-called Lion Gate (FIG. **4-19**) is the outer gateway of the stronghold at Mycenae. It is protected on the left by a wall built on a natural rock outcropping and on the right by a projecting bastion of large blocks. Any approaching enemies would have had to enter this 20-foot-wide channel and face Mycenaean defenders above them on both sides. The gate itself consists of two great upright monoliths (*posts*) capped with a huge horizontal *lintel* (FIG. 4-17*a*). Above the lintel, the masonry courses form a *corbeled arch* (FIG. 4-17*b*), leaving an opening that lightens the weight the lintel carries. Filling this *relieving triangle* is a great limestone slab with two lions in high relief facing a central Minoan-type column. The whole design admirably matches its triangular shape, harmonizing in dignity, strength, and scale with the massive stones that form the walls and gate. Similar groups appear in miniature on Cretan seals, but the concept of placing monstrous guardian figures at the entrances to palaces, tombs, and sacred places has its origin in Mesopotamia and Egypt (FIGS. 2-18A, 2-20, and 3-10). At Mycenae, the sculptors fashioned the animals' heads separately. Because those heads are lost, some scholars have speculated that the "lions" perhaps were composite beasts, possibly sphinxes or *griffins* (winged lions with eagles' heads).

**TREASURY OF ATREUS** The Mycenaeans erected the Lion Gate and the towering fortification wall of which it formed a part a few generations before the presumed date of the Trojan War. At that time, elite families buried their dead outside the citadel walls in beehive-shaped tombs covered by enormous earthen mounds. Nine such tombs remain at Mycenae and scores more at other sites. The best preserved of these *tholos tombs* is Mycenae's so-called Treasury of Atreus (FIG. **4-20**), which already in antiquity people mistakenly believed was the repository of the treasure of Atreus, father of Agamemnon and Menelaus. A long passageway (*dromos*) leads to a doorway surmounted by a relieving triangle similar to that in the roughly contemporaneous Lion Gate, but without figural ornamentation. Both the doorway and the relieving triangle, however, once had engaged columns on each side, preserved in fragments today. The burial chamber, or *tholos* (FIG. **4-21**), consists of a series of stone corbeled courses laid on a circular base to form a lofty *dome*. The builders probably constructed the vault using rough-hewn blocks. After they set the stones in place, the masons had to finish the surfaces with great precision to make them conform to both the horizontal and vertical curvature of the wall. The principle involved is no different from that of the corbeled gallery (FIG. 4-16) of Tiryns. But the problem of constructing a complete dome is far more complicated, and the execution of the vault in the Treasury of Atreus is much more sophisticated than that of the vaulted gallery at Tiryns. About 43 feet high, this Mycenaean dome was at the time the largest vaulted space without interior supports that had ever been built. The achievement was not surpassed until the Romans constructed the Pantheon (FIG. 7-51) almost 1,500 years later using a new technology—concrete construction—unknown to the Mycenaeans.

## Metalwork, Sculpture, and Painting

The Treasury of Atreus was thoroughly looted long before its modern rediscovery, but archaeologists have unearthed spectacular grave goods elsewhere at Mycenae. Just inside the Lion Gate, Schliemann uncovered what archaeologists call Grave Circle A (FIG. **4-22A**). It predates the Lion Gate and the walls of Mycenae by some three centuries, and encloses six deep shafts that served as tombs for the kings and their families. The Mycenaeans lowered the royal corpses into their deep graves with masks covering the men's faces, recalling the Egyptian funerary practice (see "Mummification and Immortality," Chapter 3, page 61). Jewelry adorned the bodies of the women, and weapons and golden cups accompanied the men into the afterlife.

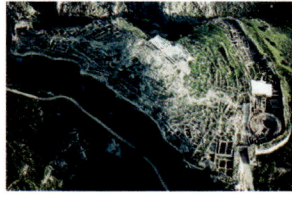

**4-22A** Grave Circle A, Mycenae, ca. 1600 BCE.

**4-21** Interior of the Treasury of Atreus, Mycenae, Greece, ca. 1300–1250 BCE. ◼◀

The beehive-shaped tholos of the Treasury of Atreus consists of corbeled courses of stone blocks laid on a circular base. The 43-foot-high dome was the largest in the world for almost 1,500 years.

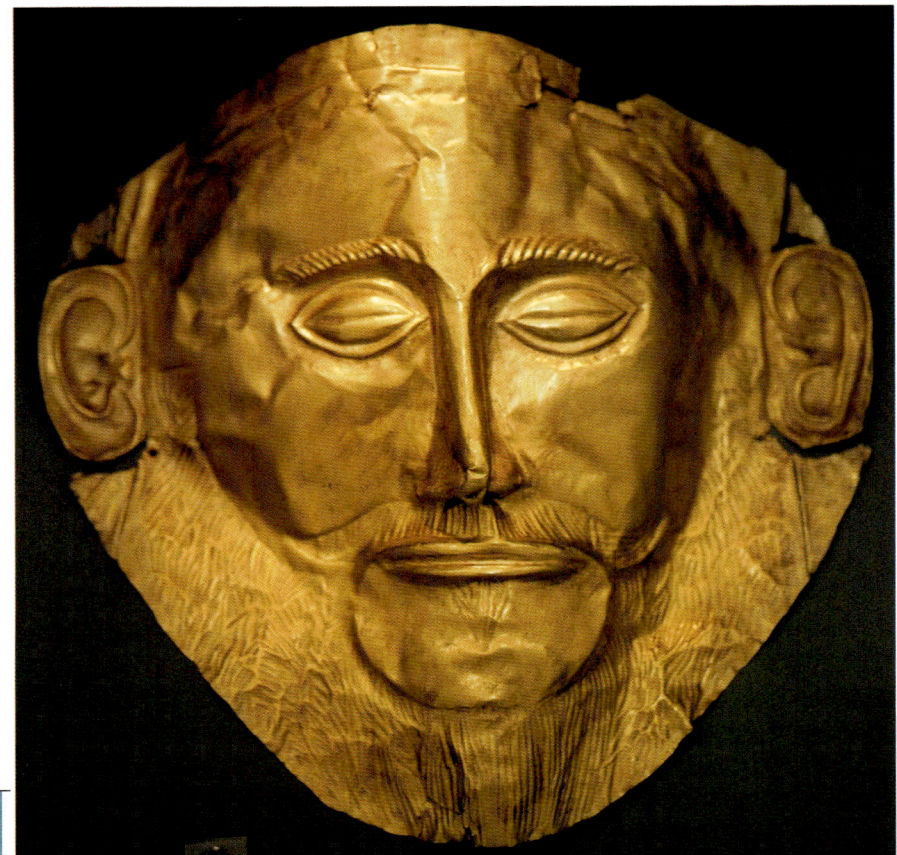

**4-22** Funerary mask, from Grave Circle A, Mycenae, Greece, ca. 1600–1500 BCE. Beaten gold, 1' high. National Archaeological Museum, Athens. ◼◄

Homer described the Mycenaeans as "rich in gold." This beaten (repoussé) gold mask of a bearded man comes from a royal shaft grave. It is one of the first attempts at life-size sculpture in Greece.

**MASKS AND DAGGERS** The Mycenaeans used the *repoussé* technique to fashion the masks Schliemann found—that is, goldsmiths hammered the shape of each mask from a single sheet of metal and pushed the features out from behind. Art historians have often compared the mask illustrated here (FIG. **4-22**) to Tutankhamen's gold mummy mask (FIG. 3-35), but it is important to remember that the Mycenaean metalworker was one of the first

in Greece to produce a sculpted image of the human face at life-size. Tutankhamen's mask stands in a long line of monumental Egyptian sculptures going back more than a millennium. No one knows whether the Mycenaean masks were intended as portraits, but the artists recorded different physical types with care. The masks found in Grave Circle A portray youthful faces as well as mature ones. The mask in FIG. 4-22, with its full beard, must depict a mature man, perhaps a king—although not Agamemnon, as Schliemann wished. If Agamemnon was a real king, he lived some 300 years after the death of the man who wore this mask. Clearly, the Mycenaeans were "rich in gold" long before Homer's heroes fought at Troy.

Also found in Grave Circle A were several magnificent bronze dagger blades inlaid with gold, silver, and *niello* (a black metallic alloy), again attesting to the wealth of the Mycenaean kings as well as to their warlike nature. The largest and most elaborate of the group features on one side (FIG. **4-23**) a scene of four hunters attacking a lion that has struck down a fifth hunter, while two other lions flee. The other side (not illustrated) depicts lions attacking deer. The slim-waisted, long-haired figures are Minoan in style, but the artist borrowed the subject from the repertoire of Egypt and Mesopotamia. It is likely that a Minoan metalworker made the dagger for a Mycenaean patron who admired Minoan art but whose tastes in subject matter differed from those of his Cretan counterparts. Excavations at other Mycenaean sites have produced other luxurious objects decorated with Minoan-style figures. Chief among them is the pair of gold drinking cups (FIG. **4-23A**) from a tholos tomb at Vapheio.

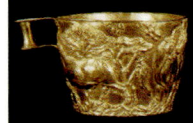

**4-23A** Gold drinking cup, Vapheio, ca. 1600–1500 BCE.

**IVORY GODDESSES** Gold was not the only opulent material elite Mycenaean patrons demanded for the objects they commissioned. For a shrine within the palace at Mycenae, a master sculptor carved an intricately detailed group of two women and a

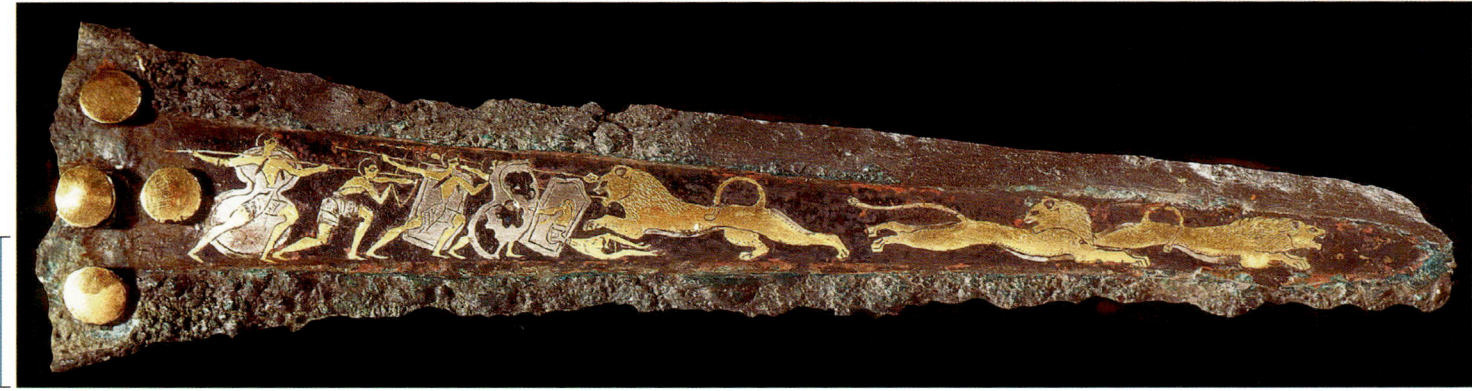

**4-23** Inlaid dagger blade with lion hunt, from Grave Circle A, Mycenae, Greece, ca. 1600–1500 BCE. Bronze, inlaid with gold, silver, and niello, 9″ long. National Archaeological Museum, Athens.

The burial goods in Grave Circle A included costly weapons. The lion hunters on this bronze dagger are Minoan in style, but the metalworker borrowed the subject from Egypt and Mesopotamia.

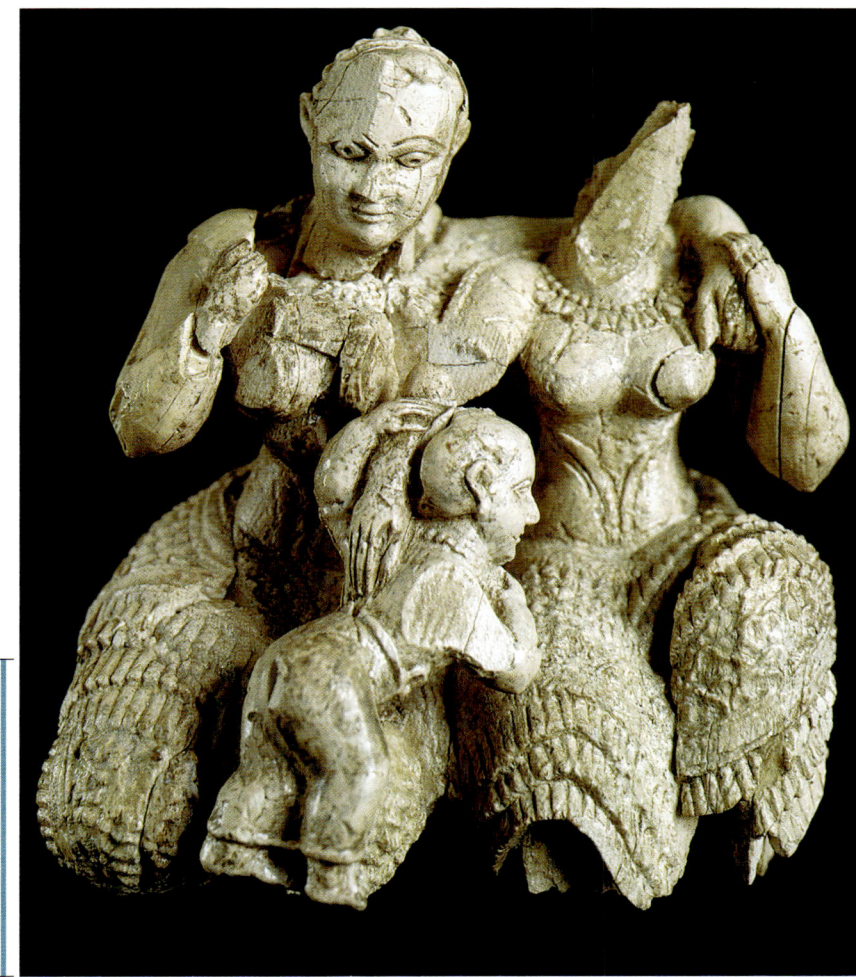

**4-24** Two goddesses(?) and a child, from Mycenae, Greece, ca. 1400–1250 BCE. Ivory, $2\frac{3}{4}''$ high. National Archaeological Museum, Athens.

Made of rare imported ivory, perhaps by a Cretan artist, this statuette may represent deities later paralleled in Greek mythology, but their identity and even the gender of the child are uncertain.

child (FIG. **4-24**) from a single piece of costly imported ivory. The women's costumes with breasts exposed have the closest parallels in Minoan art, and this statuette is probably of Cretan manufacture. The intimate and tender theme also is foreign to the known Mycenaean repertoire, in which scenes of hunting and warfare dominate.

The identity of the three figures remains a mystery. Some scholars have suggested that the two women are the "two queens" mentioned in inscriptions found in the excavation of the Mycenaean palace at Pylos (FIG. 4-18A). Others have speculated that the two women are deities, Mycenaean forerunners of the Greek agricultural goddesses Demeter and Persephone (see "The Gods and Goddesses of Mount Olympus," Chapter 5, page 107) and that the child is Triptolemos, the hero who spread the gift of agriculture to the Greeks. That myth, however, probably postdates the Mycenaean era.

**MONUMENTAL STATUARY** Large-scale figural art is very rare on the Greek mainland, as on Crete, other than the paintings that once adorned the walls of Mycenaean palaces (FIG. 4-18A). The triangular relief of the Lion Gate at Mycenae is exceptional, as is the painted plaster head (FIG. **4-25**) of a woman, goddess, or, perhaps, sphinx found at Mycenae. The white flesh tone indicates the head is female. The hair and eyes are dark blue, almost black, and the lips, ears, and headband are red. The artist decorated the cheeks and chin with red circles surrounded by a ring of red dots, recalling the facial paint or tattoos recorded on Early Cycladic figurines of women. Although the large staring eyes give the face a menacing, if not terrifying, expression appropriate for a guardian figure such as a sphinx, the closest parallels to this work in the prehistoric Aegean are terracotta images of goddesses. This head may therefore be a fragment of a very early monumental cult statue in Greece, many times the size of the Palaikastro youth (FIG. 4-13).

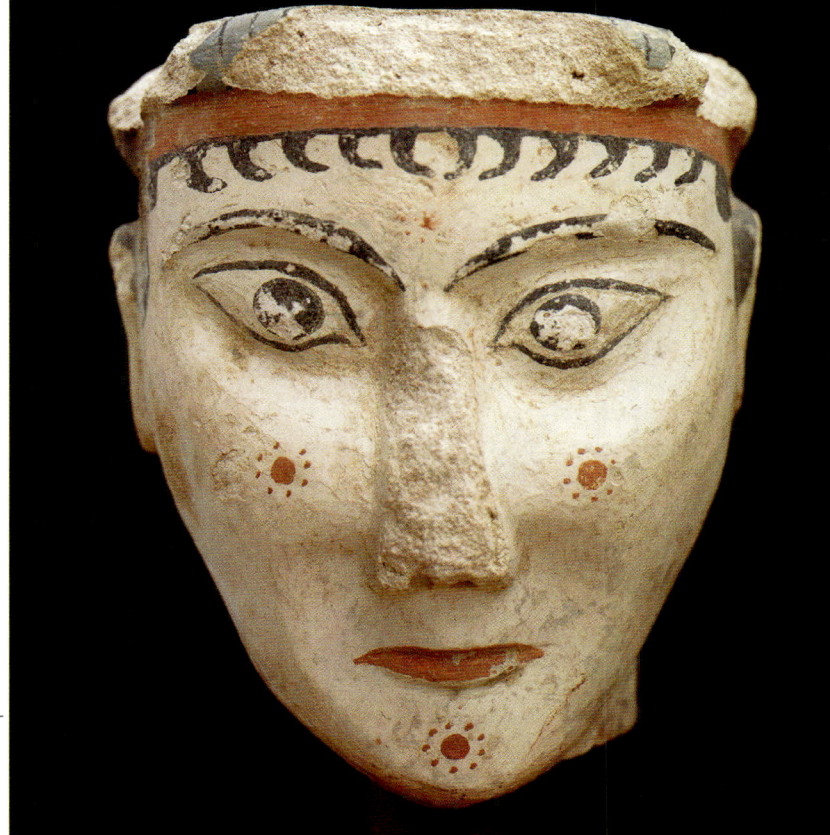

**4-25** Female head, from Mycenae, Greece, ca. 1300–1250 BCE. Painted plaster, $6\frac{1}{2}''$ high. National Archaeological Museum, Athens.

This painted white plaster head of a woman with staring eyes may be a fragment of a very early monumental statue of a goddess in Greece, but some scholars think it is the head of a sphinx.

Mycenaean Art **101**

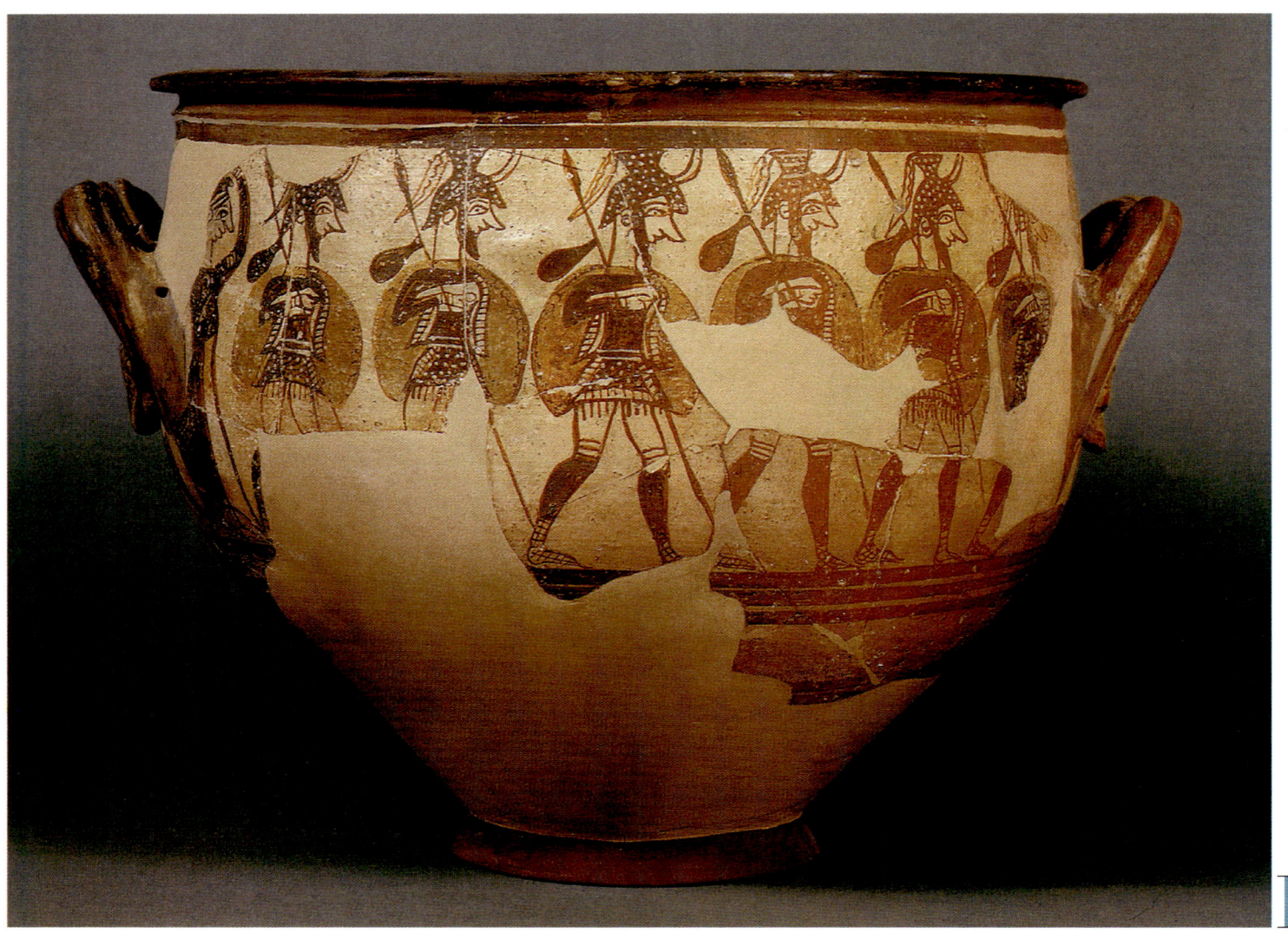

**4-26** *Warrior Vase* (krater), from Mycenae, Greece, ca. 1200 BCE. 1′ 4″ high. National Archaeological Museum, Athens.

This mixing bowl shows a woman bidding farewell to a column of heavily armed Mycenaean warriors depicted using both silhouette and outline and a combination of frontal and profile views.

Were it not for this plaster head and a few other exceptional pieces, art historians might have concluded, wrongly, that the Mycenaeans had no monumental freestanding statuary—a reminder that it is always dangerous to generalize from the chance remains of an ancient civilization. Nonetheless, life-size Aegean statuary must have been rare. After the collapse of Mycenaean civilization and for the next several hundred years, no attempts at monumental statuary are evident until, after the waning of the Dark Ages, Greek sculptors became exposed to the great sculptural tradition of Egypt (see Chapter 5).

**WARRIOR VASE** An art form that did continue throughout the period after the downfall of the Mycenaean palaces was vase painting. One of the latest examples of Mycenaean painting is the *krater* (bowl for mixing wine and water) commonly called the *Warrior Vase* (FIG. 4-26) after its prominent frieze of soldiers

marching off to war. At the left a woman bids farewell to the column of heavily armed warriors moving away from her. The painting on this vase has no indication of setting and lacks the landscape elements that commonly appear in earlier Minoan and Mycenaean art. All the soldiers repeat the same pattern, a far cry from the variety and anecdotal detail of the lively procession shown on the Minoan *Harvesters Vase* (FIG. 4-14).

This simplification of narrative has parallels in the increasingly schematic and abstract treatment of marine life on other painted vases. The octopus, for example, eventually became a stylized motif composed of concentric circles and spirals that are almost unrecognizable as a sea creature. By Homer's time, the apogee of Aegean civilization was but a distant memory, and the men and women of Crete and Mycenae—Minos and Ariadne, Agamemnon and Helen—had assumed the stature of heroes from a lost golden age.

# THE PREHISTORIC AEGEAN

## EARLY CYCLADIC ART ca. 3000–2000 BCE

▌ Marble statuettes are the major surviving artworks of the Cyclades Islands during the third millennium BCE, but little is known about their function.

▌ Many of the Cycladic figurines come from graves and may represent the deceased, but others, for example, musicians, almost certainly do not. Whatever their meaning, these statuettes mark the beginning of the long history of marble sculpture in Greece.

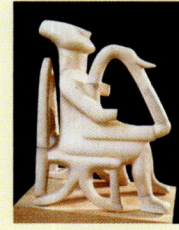

Harp player, Keros,
ca. 2600–2300 BCE

## LATE MINOAN ART ca. 1600–1200 BCE

▌ The Old Palace period (ca. 2000–1600 BCE) on Crete brought the construction of the first palaces on the island, but the golden age of Crete was the Late Minoan period.

▌ The greatest Late Minoan palace was at Knossos. A vast multistory structure arranged around a central court, the Knossos palace was so complex in plan that it gave rise to the myth of the Minotaur in the labyrinth of King Minos.

▌ The largest art form in the Minoan world was fresco painting. The murals depicted rituals (such as bull-leaping), landscapes, seascapes, and other subjects.

▌ Vase painting also flourished. Sea motifs—the octopus, for example—were popular subjects.

▌ Surviving examples of Minoan sculpture are of small scale. They include statuettes of "snake goddesses" and reliefs on stone vases.

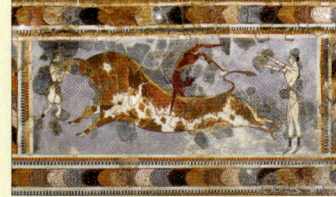

Bull-leaping fresco, Knossos,
ca. 1400–1370 BCE

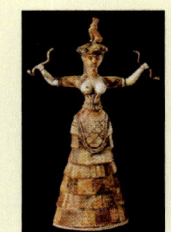

*Snake Goddess,* Knossos,
ca. 1600 BCE

## MYCENAEAN (LATE HELLADIC) ART ca. 1600–1200 BCE

▌ The Mycenaeans, who with their Greek allies later waged war on Troy, were already by 1600–1500 BCE burying their kings in deep shaft graves with gold funerary masks and bronze daggers inlaid with gold and silver.

▌ By 1450 BCE, the Mycenaeans had occupied Crete, and between 1400 and 1200 BCE, they constructed great citadels on the mainland at Mycenae, Tiryns, and elsewhere with "Cyclopean" walls of huge, irregularly shaped stone blocks.

▌ Masters of corbel vaulting, the Mycenaeans also built beehive-shaped tholos tombs covered by earthen mounds. One example is the Treasury of Atreus at Mycenae, which boasted the largest dome in the pre-Roman world.

▌ The oldest preserved monumental sculptures in Greece, most notably Mycenae's Lion Gate, date to the end of the Mycenaean period.

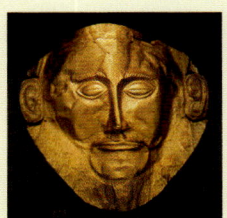

Gold funerary mask, Mycenae,
ca. 1600–1500 BCE

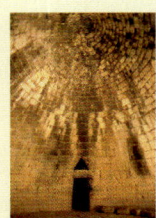

Treasury of Atreus, Mycenae,
ca. 1300–1250 BCE

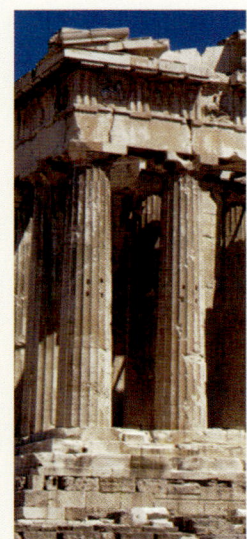

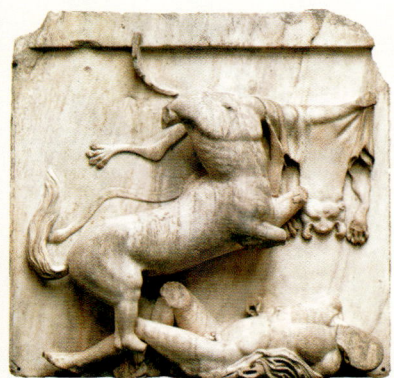

The reliefs depicting Greeks battling semihuman centaurs are allegories of the triumph of civilization and rational order over barbarism and chaos—and of the Greek defeat of the Persians in 479 BCE.

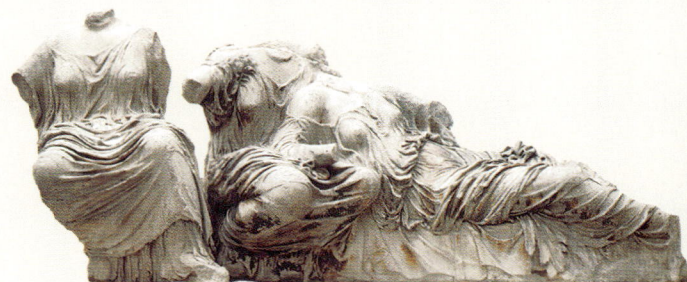

The statues in the two pediments of the Parthenon depicted important events in the life of Athena, the patron goddess of Athens. The east pediment represented Athena's birth from the head of Zeus.

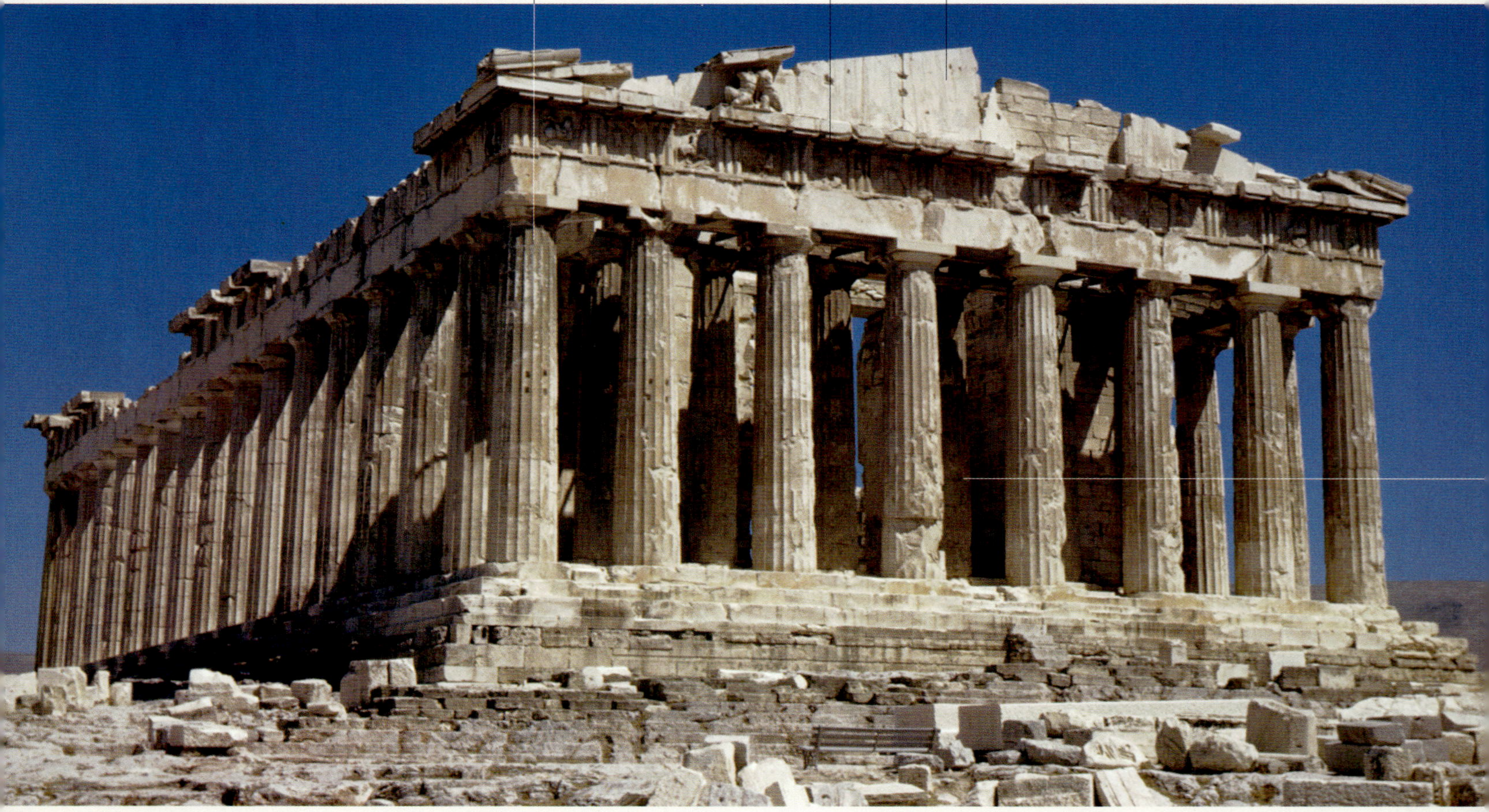

The architects of the Parthenon calculated the dimensions of every part of the temple using harmonic numerical ratios, which determined, for example, the height and diameter of each column.

**5-1** IKTINOS and KALLIKRATES, Parthenon (Temple of Athena Parthenos; looking southeast), Acropolis, Athens, Greece, 447–438 BCE. ∎◀

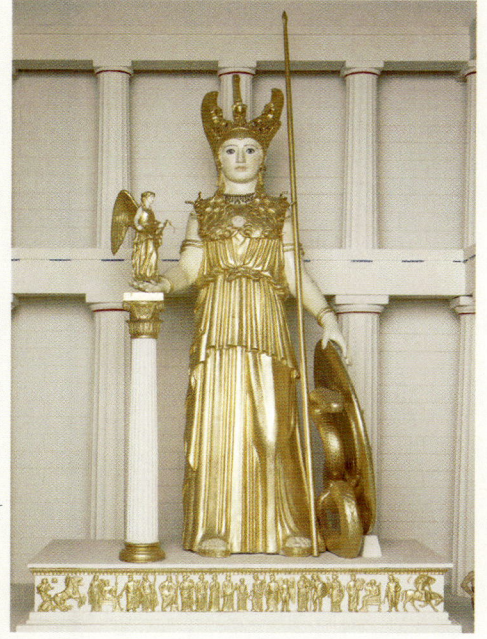

The costliest part of the Parthenon's lavish sculptural program was inside the temple—Phidias's colossal gold-and-ivory statue depicting Athena presenting the personification of Victory to Athens.

# 5

# ANCIENT GREECE

## THE PERFECT TEMPLE

Although the Greeks borrowed many ideas from Egypt and Mesopotamia, they quickly developed an independent artistic identity. Their many innovations in painting, sculpture, and architecture became the foundation of the Western tradition. Indeed, no building type has ever had a longer and more profound impact on the later history of architecture than the Greek temple, which was itself a multimedia monument, richly adorned with painted statues and reliefs.

The greatest Greek temple was the Parthenon (FIG. **5-1**), erected on the Acropolis of Athens in the mid-fifth century BCE. It represents the culmination of a century-long effort by Greek architects to build a temple having perfect proportions. Consistent with the thinking of the influential philosopher Pythagoras of Samos, who believed that beauty resided in harmonic numerical ratios, the architect IKTINOS calculated the dimensions of every part of the Parthenon in terms of a fixed proportional scheme. Thus, the ratio of the length to the width of the building, the number of columns on the long versus the short sides, even the relationship between the diameter of a column and the space between neighboring columns, conformed to an all-encompassing mathematical formula. The result was a "perfect temple."

The Athenians did not, however, construct the Parthenon to solve a purely formal problem of architectural design. Nor was this perfect temple, dedicated to Athena Parthenos (the Virgin), a shrine honoring the goddess alone. The temple also celebrated the Athenian people, who a generation earlier had led the Greeks in their successful effort to defeat the Persians after they had sacked the Acropolis in 480 BCE. Under the direction of PHIDIAS, a team of gifted sculptors lavishly decorated the building with statues and reliefs that in many cases alluded to the victory over the Persians. For example, the sculptural program included a series of reliefs depicting nude Greek warriors battling with the part-horse part-human *centaurs*—an allegory of the triumph of civilization (that is, Greek civilization) over barbarism (in this case, the Persians). The statues in one of the *pediments* (the triangular area above the columns beneath the roof) told the story of the birth of Athena, who emerged from the head of her father Zeus, king of the gods, fully armed and ready to protect her people. The costliest sculpture, and most prestigious of all, however, Phidias reserved for himself: the colossal gold-and-ivory statue of Athena inside the temple in which the warrior goddess presented the Athenians with the winged personification of Victory—an unmistakable reference to the Greek victory over the Persians.

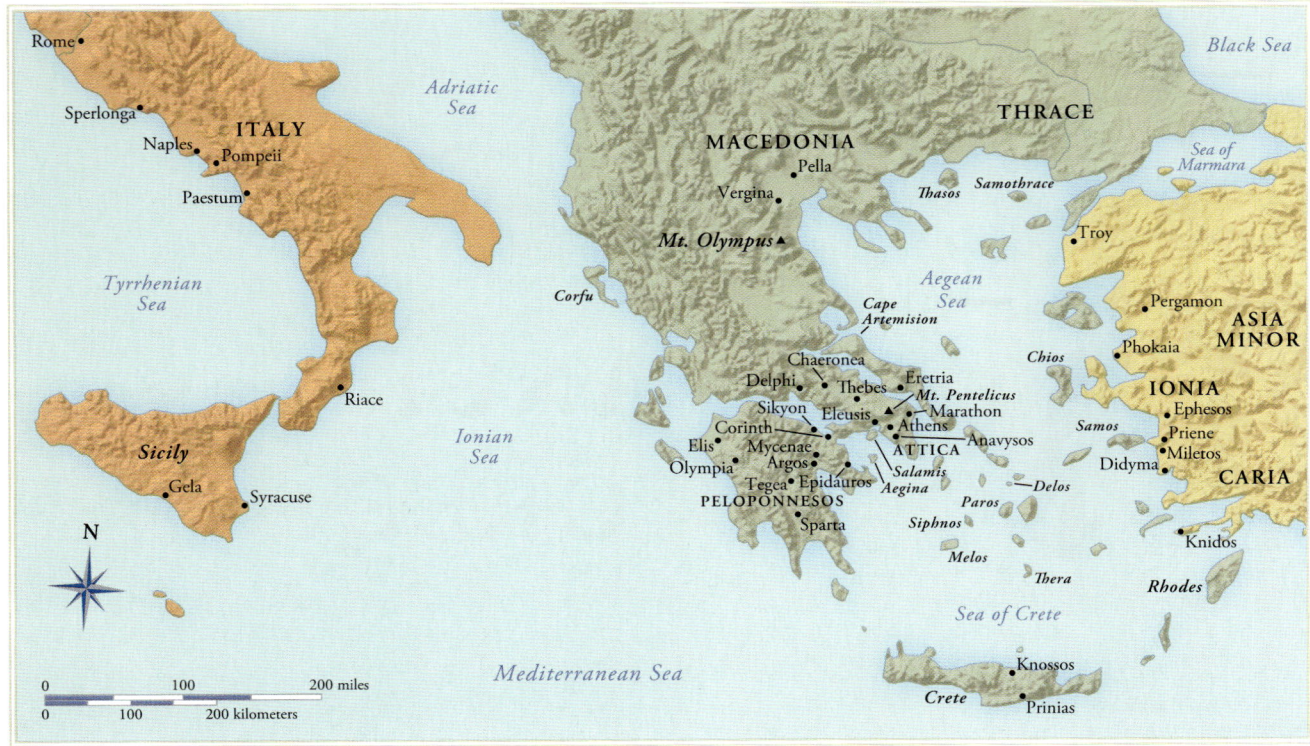

**MAP 5-1** The Greek world.

# THE GREEKS AND THEIR GODS

Ancient Greek art occupies a special place in the history of art through the ages. Many of the cultural values of the Greeks, especially the exaltation of humanity as the "measure of all things," remain today fundamental tenets of Western civilization. This humanistic worldview led the Greeks to create the concept of democracy (rule by the *demos*, the people) and to make groundbreaking contributions in the fields of art, literature, and science. Ancient Greek ideas are so completely part of modern Western habits of mind that most people are scarcely aware the concepts originated in Greece 2,500 years ago.

The Greeks, or *Hellenes*, as they called themselves, were the product of an intermingling of Aegean and Indo-European peoples who established independent city-states, or *poleis* (singular, *polis*). The Dorians of the north, who many believe brought an end to Mycenaean civilization, settled in the Peloponnesos (MAP 5-1). The Ionians settled the western coast of Asia Minor (modern Turkey) and the islands of the Aegean Sea, possibly because the northern invaders

forced them out of Greece. But the Ionians may have been native to Asia Minor, developing out of a mixed stock of settlers between the 11th and 8th centuries BCE. Whatever the origins of the various regional populations, in 776 BCE the separate Greek-speaking states held their first athletic games in common at Olympia. From then on, despite their differences and rivalries, the Greeks regarded themselves as citizens of *Hellas,* distinct from the surrounding "barbarians" who did not speak Greek.

Even the gods of the Greeks (see "The Gods and Goddesses of Mount Olympus," page 107) differed in kind from those of neighboring civilizations. Unlike Egyptian and Mesopotamian deities, the Greek gods and goddesses differed from human beings only in being immortal. The Greeks made their gods into humans and their humans into gods. The perfect individual became the Greek ideal—and the portrayal of beautiful humans became the focus of many of the greatest Greek artists.

The sculptures, paintings, and buildings discussed in this chapter come from cities all over Greece and their many colonies abroad (MAP 5-1), but Athens, where the plays of Aeschylus, Sophocles,

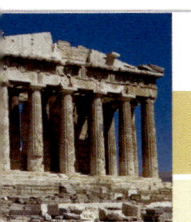

## ANCIENT GREECE

| 900 | Geometric and Orientalizing | 600 | Archaic | 480 | Early and High Classical | 400 | Late Classical | 323 | Hellenistic | 30 | BCE |
|---|---|---|---|---|---|---|---|---|---|---|---|

- Revival of figure painting in Greece during the Geometric period
- Eastern motifs enter Greek art during the Orientalizing period

- Construction of the oldest peripteral Doric and Ionic temples
- First Greek life-size stone statues with "Archaic smiles"
- Innovations in black- and red-figure vase painting

- Contrapposto introduced in Greek statuary
- Polykleitos formulates his canon of proportions
- Pericles rebuilds the Athenian Acropolis after the Persian sack

- Sculptors humanize the Greek gods and goddesses
- Corinthian capitals introduced in Greek architecture
- Lysippos appointed the official court artist of Alexander the Great

- Hellenistic kingdoms replace Athens as leading cultural centers
- Artists explore new subjects in sculpture and painting
- Architects break the rules of the Classical orders

# The Gods and Goddesses of Mount Olympus

The names of scores of Greek gods and goddesses appear as early as the eighth century BCE in Homer's epic tales of the war against Troy (*Iliad*) and of the adventures of the Greek hero Odysseus on his long and tortuous journey home (*Odyssey*). The poet Hesiod enumerated even more names, especially in his *Theogony* (*Genealogy of the Gods*), composed around 700 BCE.

The Greek deities most often represented in art are all ultimately the offspring of the two key elements of the Greek universe: Earth (*Gaia/Ge*; all names are given in their Greek and Latin forms respectively) and Heaven (*Ouranos/Uranus*). Earth and Heaven mated to produce 12 Titans, including Ocean (*Okeanos/Oceanus*) and his youngest brother *Kronos* (*Saturn*). Kronos castrated his father in order to rule in his place, married his sister *Rhea*, and then swallowed all his children as they were born, lest one of them seek in turn to usurp him. When *Zeus* (*Jupiter*) was born, Rhea deceived Kronos by feeding him a stone wrapped in clothes in place of the infant. After growing to manhood, Zeus forced Kronos to vomit up Zeus's siblings. Together they overthrew their father and the other Titans and ruled the world from their home on Mount Olympus, Greece's highest peak.

This cruel and bloody tale of the origin of the Greek gods has parallels in Mesopotamian mythology and is clearly pre-Greek in origin, one of many Greek borrowings from the East. The Greek version of the creation myth, however, appears infrequently in painting and sculpture. Instead, the later 12 Olympian gods and goddesses figure most prominently in art—not only in antiquity but also in the Middle Ages, the Renaissance, and up to the present.

- **Zeus (Jupiter)** King of the gods, Zeus ruled the sky and allotted the sea to his brother Poseidon and the Underworld to his other brother Hades. His weapon was the thunderbolt, and with it he led the other gods to victory over the giants, who had challenged the Olympians for control of the world.
- **Hera (Juno)** Wife and sister of Zeus, Hera was the goddess of marriage.
- **Poseidon (Neptune)** Poseidon, one of the three sons of Kronos and Rhea, was lord of the sea. He controlled waves, storms, and earthquakes with his three-pronged pitchfork (*trident*).
- **Hestia (Vesta)** Sister of Zeus, Poseidon, and Hera, Hestia was goddess of the hearth.
- **Demeter (Ceres)** Third sister of Zeus, Demeter was the goddess of grain and agriculture.
- **Ares (Mars)** God of war, Ares was the son of Zeus and Hera and the lover of Aphrodite. His Roman counterpart, Mars, was the father of the twin founders of Rome, Romulus and Remus.

- **Athena (Minerva)** Goddess of wisdom and warfare, Athena was a virgin (*parthenos* in Greek), born not from a woman's womb but from the head of her father, Zeus.
- **Hephaistos (Vulcan)** God of fire and of metalworking, Hephaistos, son of Zeus and Hera, fashioned the armor Achilles wore in battle against Troy. He also provided Zeus his scepter and Poseidon his trident, and was the "surgeon" who split open Zeus's head to facilitate the birth of Athena. Hephaistos was born lame and, uncharacteristically for a god, ugly. His wife Aphrodite was unfaithful to him.
- **Apollo (Apollo)** God of light and music, Apollo was the son of Zeus with **Leto/Latona,** daughter of one of the Titans. His epithet, *Phoibos,* means "radiant," and the young, beautiful Apollo was sometimes identified with the sun (**Helios/Sol**).
- **Artemis (Diana)** Sister of Apollo, Artemis was goddess of the hunt and of wild animals. As Apollo's twin, she was occasionally regarded as the moon (**Selene/Luna**).
- **Aphrodite (Venus)** Daughter of Zeus and **Dione** (daughter of Okeanos and one of the *nymphs*—the goddesses of springs, caves, and woods), Aphrodite was the goddess of love and beauty. In one version of her myth, she was born from the foam (*aphros* in Greek) of the sea. She was the mother of Eros by Ares and of the Trojan hero Aeneas by a mortal named Anchises.
- **Hermes (Mercury)** Son of Zeus and another nymph, Hermes was the fleet-footed messenger of the gods and possessed winged sandals. He was also the guide of travelers, including the dead journeying to the Underworld. He carried the *caduceus,* a magical herald's rod, and wore a winged traveler's hat.

Several non-Olympian deities also appear frequently in Greek art.

- *Hades* (*Pluto*) One of the children of Kronos who fought with his brothers against the Titans, Hades was equal in stature to the Olympians but never resided on Mount Olympus. He was the god of the dead and lord of the Underworld (also called Hades).
- *Dionysos* (*Bacchus*) The son of Zeus and a mortal woman, Dionysos was the god of wine.
- *Eros* (*Amor* or *Cupid*) The son of Aphrodite and Ares, Eros was the winged child-god of love.
- *Asklepios* (*Aesculapius*) The son of Apollo and a mortal woman, Asklepios was the Greek god of healing, whose serpent-entwined staff is the emblem of modern medicine.

and Euripides were first performed, and where many of the most famous artists and architects worked, has justifiably become the symbol of ancient Greek culture. There, Socrates engaged his fellow citizens in philosophical argument, and Plato formulated his prescription for the ideal form of government in his *Republic*. Complementing the rich intellectual life of Athens was a strong interest in athletic exercise. The Athenian aim of achieving a balance of intellectual and physical discipline, an ideal of humanistic educa-

tion, is well expressed in the familiar phrase "a sound mind in a sound body."

The distinctiveness and originality of Greek contributions to art, science, and politics should not, however, obscure the enormous debt the Greeks owed to the cultures of Egypt and Mesopotamia. The ancient Greeks themselves readily acknowledged borrowing ideas, motifs, conventions, and skills from those older civilizations. Nor should a high estimation of Greek art and culture blind anyone to the realities of Hellenic life and society. Even Athenian "democracy" was a political reality for only one segment of the demos. Slavery was a universal institution among the Greeks, and Greek women were in no way the equals of Greek men. Women normally remained secluded in their homes, emerging usually only for weddings, funerals, and religious festivals. They played little part in public or political life. Despite the fame of the poet Sappho, only a handful of female artists' names are known, and none of their works survive. The existence of slavery and the exclusion of women from public life are both reflected in Greek art. Freeborn men and women often appear with their slaves in monumental sculpture. The *symposium* (a dinner party only men and prostitutes attended) is a popular subject on painted vases.

# GEOMETRIC AND ORIENTALIZING PERIODS

The destruction of the Mycenaean palaces brought with it the disintegration of the Bronze Age social order. The disappearance of powerful kings and their retinues led to the loss of the knowledge of how to cut masonry, to construct citadels and tombs, to paint frescoes, and to sculpt in stone. Depopulation, poverty, and an almost total loss of contact with the outside world characterized the succeeding centuries, sometimes called the Dark Age of Greece. Only in the eighth century BCE did economic conditions improve and the population begin to grow again. This era was in its own way a heroic age, when the Greeks established the Olympic Games and wrote down Homer's epic poems, formerly passed orally from bard to bard. During the eighth century BCE, the Greeks broke free of their isolation and once again began to trade with cities in both the east and the west.

## Geometric Art

The eighth century also brought the return of the human figure to Greek art—not in monumental statuary, which was exceedingly rare even in Bronze Age Greece, but in small bronze figurines and in paintings on ceramic pots.

**DIPYLON KRATER** One of the earliest examples of Greek figure painting is a huge krater (FIG. **5-2**) that marked the grave of a man buried around 740 BCE in the Dipylon cemetery of Athens. At well over three feet tall, this vase is a considerable technical achievement and a testament both to the potter's skill and to the wealth and position of the deceased's family in the community. The bottom of the great vessel is open, perhaps to permit visitors to the grave to pour libations in honor of the dead, perhaps simply to provide a drain for rainwater, or both.

The artist covered much of the krater's surface with precisely painted abstract angular motifs in horizontal bands. Especially prominent is the *meander,* or key, pattern around the rim of the krater. The decoration of most early Greek vases consists exclusively of abstract motifs—hence the designation of this formative phase of Greek art as the *Geometric* period. On this krater, however, Geometric ornament does not dominate. Instead, the painter reserved the widest part of the vase for two bands of human figures and horse-drawn chariots rather than for geometric ornament. Befitting the vase's function, the scenes depict the mourning for a man laid out on his bier and the grand chariot procession in his honor, scenes that appear frequently on other large Geometric vessels that served as grave markers, for example, the namepiece of the DIPYLON PAINTER, a five-foot-tall vase (FIG. **5-2A**) that also stood in the Dipylon cemetery. The painter of the krater filled every empty space around the

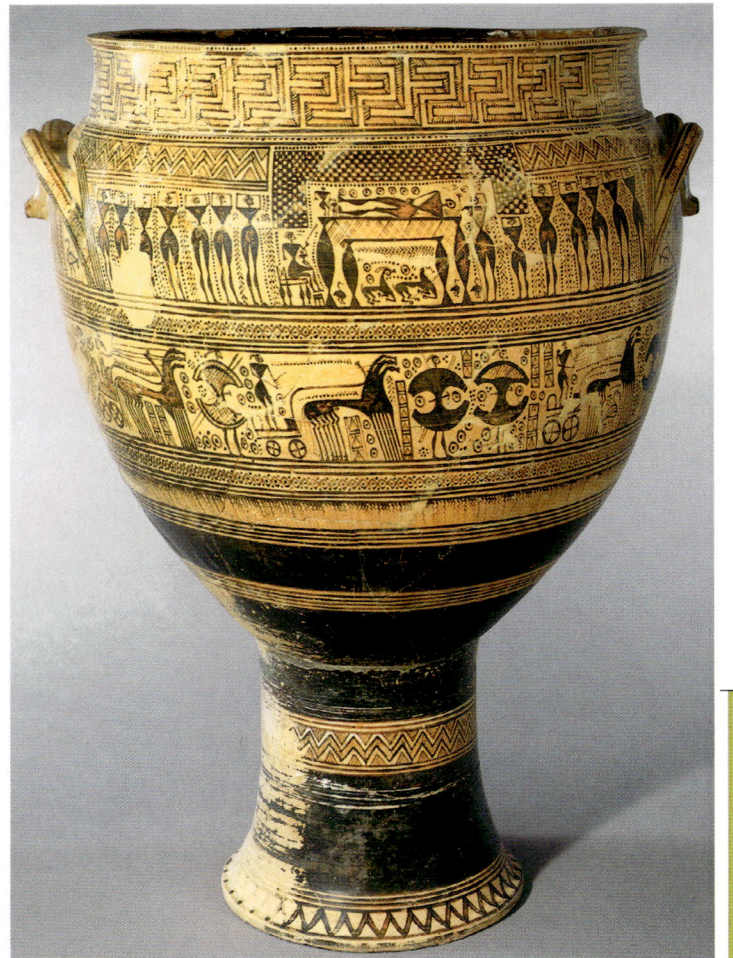

**5-2** Geometric krater, from the Dipylon cemetery, Athens, Greece, ca. 740 BCE. 3′ 4½″ high. Metropolitan Museum of Art, New York.

Figure painting returned to Greek art in the Geometric period, named for the abstract motifs on vessels such as this funerary krater featuring a mourning scene and procession in honor of the deceased.

figures with circles and M-shaped ornaments, negating any sense that the mourners or soldiers inhabit open space. The human figures, animals, and furniture are as two-dimensional as the geometric shapes elsewhere on the vessel. In the upper band, the shroud, raised to reveal the corpse, is an abstract checkerboard-like backdrop. The figures are silhouettes constructed of triangular (frontal) torsos with attached profile arms, legs, and heads (with a single large frontal eye in the center), following the age-old convention. To distinguish male from female, the painter added a penis growing out of one of the deceased's thighs. The mourning women, who tear their hair out in grief, have breasts emerging beneath their armpits. In both cases the artist's concern was specifying gender, not anatomical accuracy. Below, the warriors look like walking shields and, in the old conceptual manner, the two wheels of the chariots appear side by side. The horses have the correct number of heads and legs but seem to share a common body, so that there is no sense of overlapping or depth. Despite the highly stylized and conventional manner of representation, vessels like this one and the Dipylon Painter's funerary vase (FIG. 5-2A) mark a significant turning point

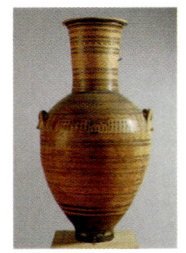

**5-2A** DIPYLON PAINTER, Geometric funerary amphora, ca. 750 BCE.

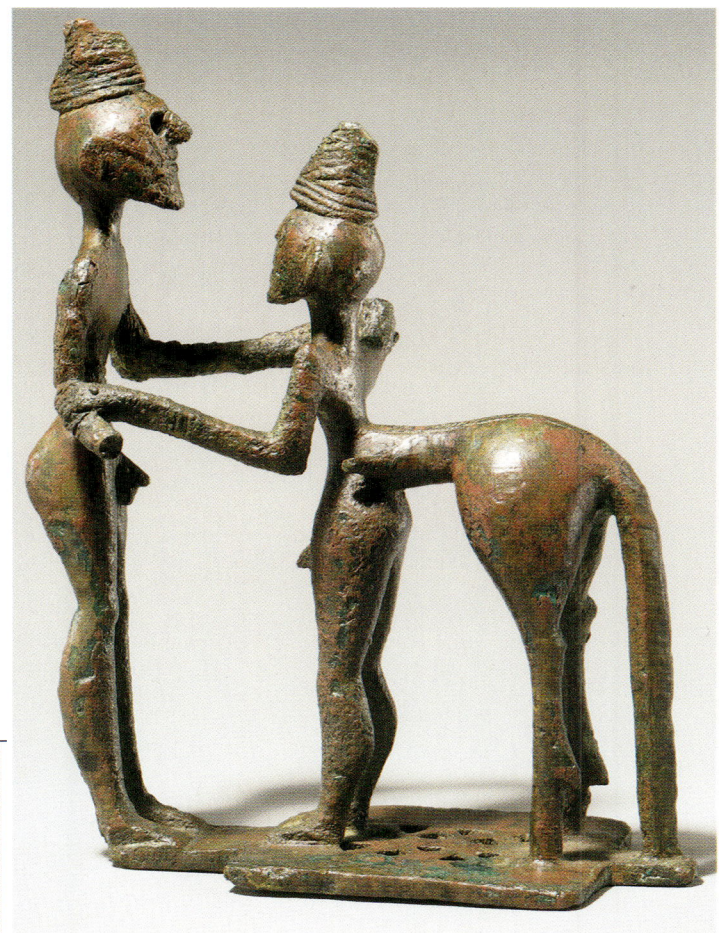

1 in.

**5-3** Hero and centaur (Herakles and Nessos?), from Olympia, Greece, ca. 750–730 BCE. Bronze, 4½″ high. Metropolitan Museum of Art, New York (gift of J. Pierpont).

Sculpture of the Geometric period is small in scale, and the figures have simple stylized shapes. This statuette depicts a hero battling a centaur—an early example of mythological narrative.

in the history of Greek art. Not only did the human figure reenter the painter's repertoire, but the Geometric artists also revived the art of storytelling in pictures.

**HERAKLES AND NESSOS** One of the most impressive surviving Geometric sculptures is a characteristically small solid-cast bronze group (FIG. **5-3**) made up of two schematic figures locked in a hand-to-hand struggle. The man is a hero, probably Herakles (see "Herakles," page 128). His opponent is a centaur, possibly Nessos, who had volunteered to carry the hero's bride across a river and then assaulted her. Whether or not the hero is Herakles and the centaur is Nessos, the mythological nature of the group is certain. The repertoire of the Geometric artist was not limited to scenes inspired by daily life (and death). Composite monsters were enormously popular in Mesopotamia and Egypt, and renewed contact with foreign cultures may have inspired the human-animal monsters of Geometric Greece. The centaur, however, is a purely Greek invention—and one that posed a problem for the artist, who had, of course, never seen such a creature. The Geometric artist conceived the centaur as a man in front and a horse in back, a rather unhappy and unconvincing configuration in which the fore-legs and hind legs belong to different species. In this example, the

sculptor rendered the figure of the hero and the human part of the centaur in a similar fashion. Both have beards and wear helmets, but (contradictory to nature) the man is larger than the horse to indicate that he will be the victor. Like other Geometric male figures, both painted and sculpted, this hero is nude, in contrast to the Mesopotamian statuettes that might have inspired the Greek works. Here, at the very beginning of Greek figural art, the Hellenic instinct for the natural beauty of the human figure is evident. Greek athletes exercised without their clothes and even competed nude in the Olympic Games from very early times.

## Orientalizing Art

During the seventh century BCE, the pace and scope of Greek trade and colonization accelerated and Greek artists became exposed more than ever before to Eastern artworks, especially small portable objects such as Syrian ivory carvings. The closer contact had a profound effect on the development of Greek art. Indeed, so many motifs borrowed from or inspired by Egyptian and Mesopotamian art entered the Greek pictorial vocabulary at this time that art historians have dubbed the seventh century BCE the *Orientalizing* period.

*MANTIKLOS APOLLO* One of the masterworks of the early seventh century BCE is the *Mantiklos Apollo* (FIG. **5-4**), a small bronze statuette dedicated to Apollo by an otherwise unknown man named Mantiklos. Scratched into the thighs of the figure is a message to the deity: "Mantiklos dedicated me as a tithe to the far-shooting Lord of the Silver Bow; you, Phoibos [Apollo], might give some pleasing favor in return." Because the Greeks conceived their gods in human form, it is uncertain whether the figure represents the youthful Apollo or Mantiklos (or neither). But if the left hand at one time held a bow, the statuette is certainly an image of the deity. In any case, the purpose of the votive offering is clear. Equally apparent is the increased interest Greek artists at this time had in reproducing details of human anatomy, such as the long hair framing the unnaturally elongated neck, and the pectoral and abdominal muscles, which define the stylized triangular

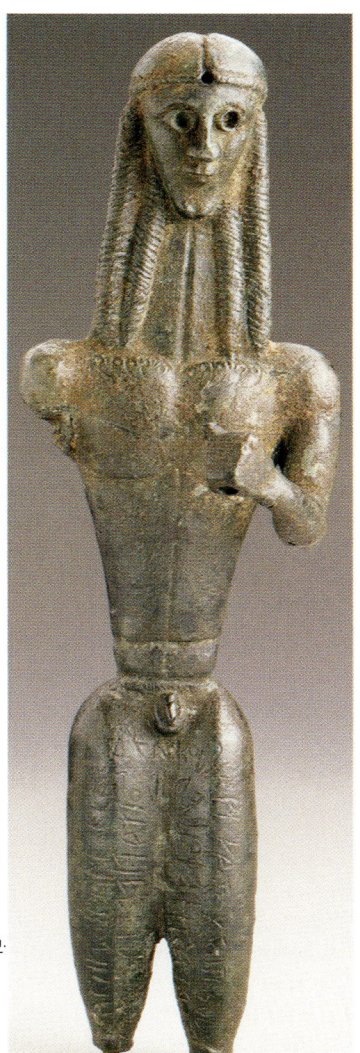

1 in.

**5-4** *Mantiklos Apollo,* statuette of a youth dedicated by Mantiklos to Apollo, from Thebes, Greece, ca. 700–680 BCE. Bronze, 8″ high. Museum of Fine Arts, Boston.

Mantiklos dedicated this statuette to Apollo, and it probably represents the god. The treatment of the body reveals the interest seventh-century BCE Greek artists had in representing human anatomy.

# Greek Vase Painting

The techniques Greek ceramists used to shape and decorate fine vases required great skill, acquired over many years as apprentices in the workshops of master potters. During the Archaic and Classical periods, when the art of vase painting was at its zenith in Greece, both potters and painters frequently signed their work. These signatures reveal the pride of the artists. In the ancient world, the Greeks were unique in celebrating individual artists as creative geniuses and in systematically recording artists' names for posterity. Many artists achieved great renown even during their lifetimes. No earlier civilization held artists in such high esteem (Egypt's deification of Imhotep was exceptional)—nor would any later culture bestow such high regard on painters, sculptors, and other artisans until the Renaissance in Italy 2,000 years later.

The signatures on Greek vases also might have functioned as "brand names" for a large export market. The products of the workshops in Corinth and Athens in particular were highly prized and have been found all over the Mediterranean world. The Corinthian Orientalizing amphora shown here (FIG. 5-5) was found on Rhodes, an island at the opposite side of the Aegean from mainland Corinth (MAP 5-1). The Etruscans of central Italy (MAP 6-1) were especially good customers. Athenian vases were staples in Etruscan tombs, and all of the illustrated sixth-century BCE examples (FIGS. 5-19 to 5-23A) came from Etruscan sites. Other painted Athenian pots have been found as far away as France, Russia, and the Sudan.

The first step in manufacturing a Greek vase was to remove any impurities found in the natural clay and then to knead it, like dough, to remove air bubbles and make it flexible. The Greeks used dozens of different kinds and shapes of pots, and produced most of them in several parts. Potters formed the vessel's body by placing the clay on a rotating horizontal wheel. While an apprentice turned the wheel by hand, the potter pulled up the clay with the fingers until achieving the desired shape. The master or the apprentice shaped the handles separately and attached them to the vase body by applying *slip* (liquefied clay) to the joints.

Painting was usually the job of a specialist, although many potters decorated their own work. (Today most people tend to regard painters as more elevated artists than potters, but in Greece the potters owned the shops and employed the painters.) Art historians customarily refer to the "pigment" the painter applied to the clay surface as *glaze*, but the black areas on Greek pots are neither pigment nor glaze but a slip of finely sifted clay that originally was of the same rich red-orange color as the clay of the pot. In the three-phase firing process Greek ceramists used, the first (*oxidizing*) phase turned both pot and slip red. During the second (*reducing*) phase, the potter shut off the oxygen supply into the kiln, and both pot and slip turned black. In the final (*reoxidizing*) phase, the pot's coarser material reabsorbed oxygen and became red again, while

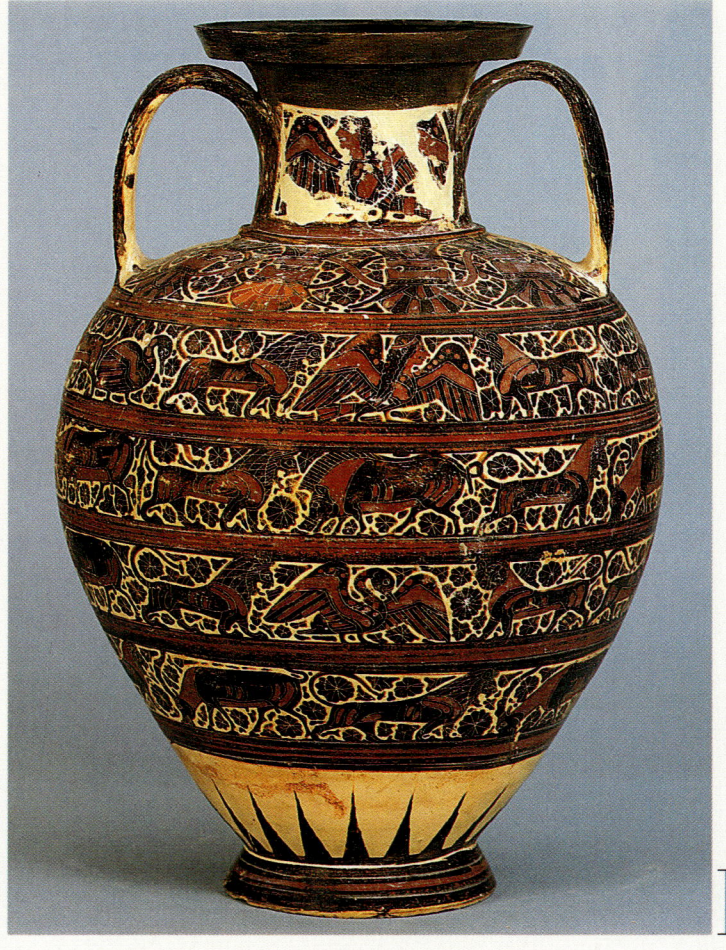

**5-5** Corinthian black-figure amphora with animal friezes, from Rhodes, Greece, ca. 625–600 BCE. 1′ 2″ high. British Museum, London.

The Corinthians invented the black-figure technique of vase painting in which artists incised linear details into black-glaze silhouettes. This early example features Orientalizing animals.

the smoother, silica-laden slip did not and remained black. After long experimentation, Greek ceramists developed a velvety jet-black "glaze" of this kind, produced in kilns heated to temperatures as high as 950° Celsius (about 1,742° Fahrenheit). The firing process was the same whether the painter worked in black-figure or in red-figure. In fact, sometimes Greek vase painters employed both manners on the same vessel (FIG. 5-21).

torso. The triangular face once had inlaid eyes, and the figure may have worn a separately fashioned helmet.

**ORIENTALIZING AMPHORA** An elaborate Corinthian *amphora* (FIG. 5-5), or two-handled storage jar, typifies the new

Greek fascination with the Orient. In a series of bands recalling the organization of Geometric painted vases, animals such as the native boar appear beside exotic lions and panthers and composite creatures inspired by Eastern monsters such as the sphinx and lamassu—in this instance the *siren* (part bird, part woman) prominently

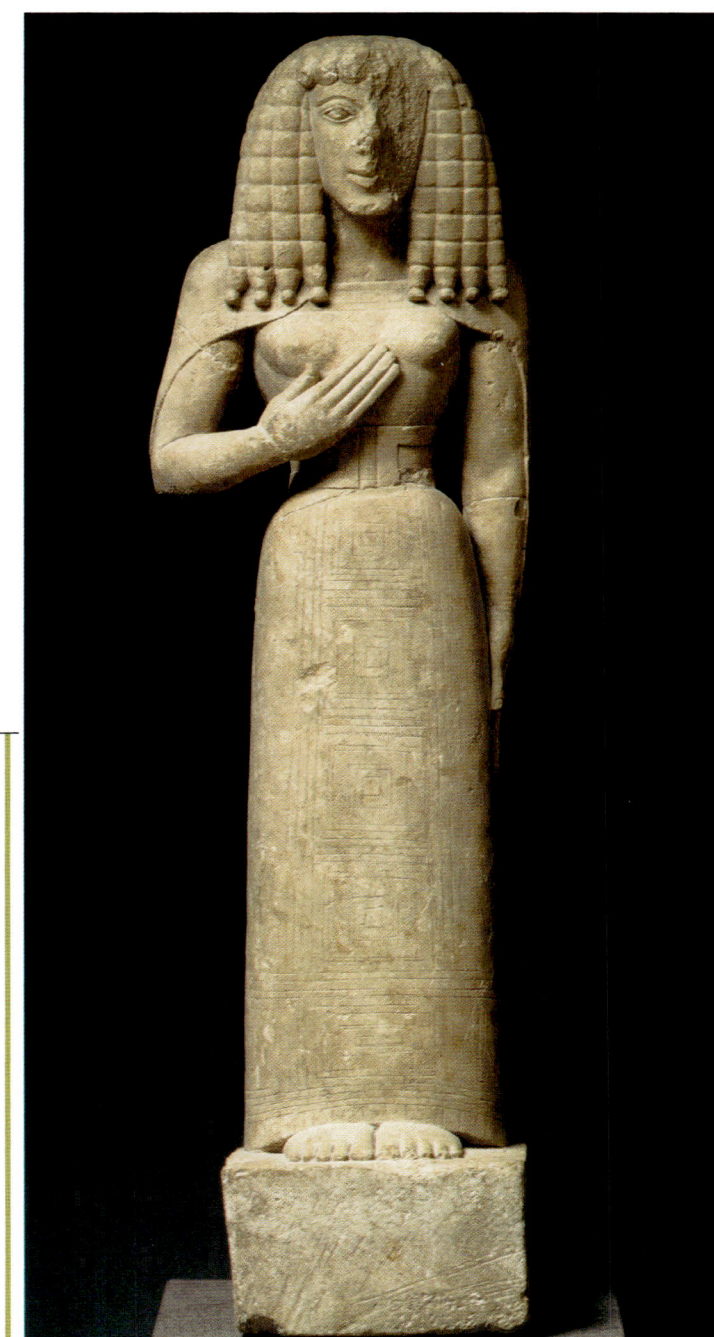

1 ft.

**5-6** *Lady of Auxerre,* ca. 650–625 BCE. Limestone, 2′ 1½″ high. Musée du Louvre, Paris.

Probably from Crete, this kore (maiden) typifies the Daedalic sculptural style of the seventh century BCE with its triangular face and hair and lingering Geometric fondness for abstract pattern.

displayed on the amphora's neck. The wide appeal of these vases was due not solely to their Orientalizing animal friezes but also to a new ceramic technique the Corinthians invented. Art historians call this type of vase decoration *black-figure painting* (see "Greek Vase Painting," page 110). The black-figure painter first put down black silhouettes on the clay surface, as in Geometric times, but then used a sharp pointed instrument to incise linear details within the forms, usually adding highlights in white or purplish red over the black figures before firing the vase. The combination of the weighty black silhouettes with the delicate detailing and the bright

polychrome overlay proved to be irresistible, and Athenian painters soon copied the technique the Corinthians pioneered.

**DAEDALIC ART** The founding of the Greek trading colony of Naukratis in Egypt (MAP 3-1) before 630 BCE brought the Greeks into direct contact with the monumental stone architecture of the Egyptians. Soon after, Greek builders be-

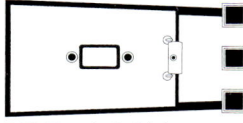

**5-6A** Temple A, Prinias, ca. 625 BCE.

gan to erect the first stone edifices since the fall of the Mycenaean kingdoms. One of the oldest is Temple A (FIG. **5-6A**) at Prinias on Crete. That island, once the center of Minoan civilization (see Chapter 4), is probably also where an early Greek sculptor carved the limestone statuette of a goddess or maiden (*kore;* plural, *korai*) popularly known as the *Lady of Auxerre* (FIG. **5-6**) after the French town that is her oldest recorded location. The *Lady of Auxerre* is the masterpiece of the style usually referred to as *Daedalic,* after the legendary artist Daedalus, whose name means "the skillful one." In addition to his status as a great sculptor, Daedalus reputedly built the labyrinth in Crete to house the Minotaur and also designed a temple at Memphis in Egypt. The historical Greeks attributed to him almost all the great achievements in early sculpture and architecture.

As with the figure Mantiklos dedicated (FIG. 5-4), it is uncertain whether the Auxerre "lady" is a mortal or a deity. She is clothed, as are all Greek goddesses and women of this period, but she does not wear a headdress, as do the contemporaneous

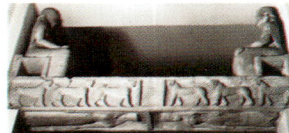

**5-6B** Lintel of Temple A, Prinias, ca. 625 BCE.

goddesses (FIG. **5-6B**) of Temple A at Prinias. Moreover, the placement of the right hand across the chest is probably a gesture of prayer, also indicating that this is a kore. The style is much more naturalistic than in Geometric times, but the love of abstract shapes is still evident. Note, for example, the triangular flat-topped head framed by long strands of hair that form triangles complementary to the shape of the face, and the decoration of the long skirt with its incised concentric squares, once brightly painted, as were all Greek stone statues. The modern notion that Greco-Roman statuary was pure white is mistaken. The Greeks did not, however, color their statues garishly. They left the flesh in the natural color of the stone, which they waxed and polished, and painted the eyes, lips, hair, and drapery in *encaustic* (see "Iaia of Cyzicus and the Art of Encaustic Painting," Chapter 7, page 218, and FIG. 5-63A). In this technique, the painter mixed the pigment with hot wax and applied it to the statue to produce a durable coloration.

# ARCHAIC PERIOD

The legend that Daedalus worked in Egypt reflects the enormous influence of Egyptian art and architecture on the Greeks not only during the Orientalizing age of the seventh century BCE but also in the succeeding *Archaic* period, which lasted from 600 to 480 BCE.

## Statuary

According to the first-century BCE Greek historian Diodorus Siculus, Daedalus used the same compositional patterns for his statues as the Egyptians used for their own.[1] The earliest surviving truly monumental stone statues of the Greeks do, in fact, follow very closely the standard Egyptian format.

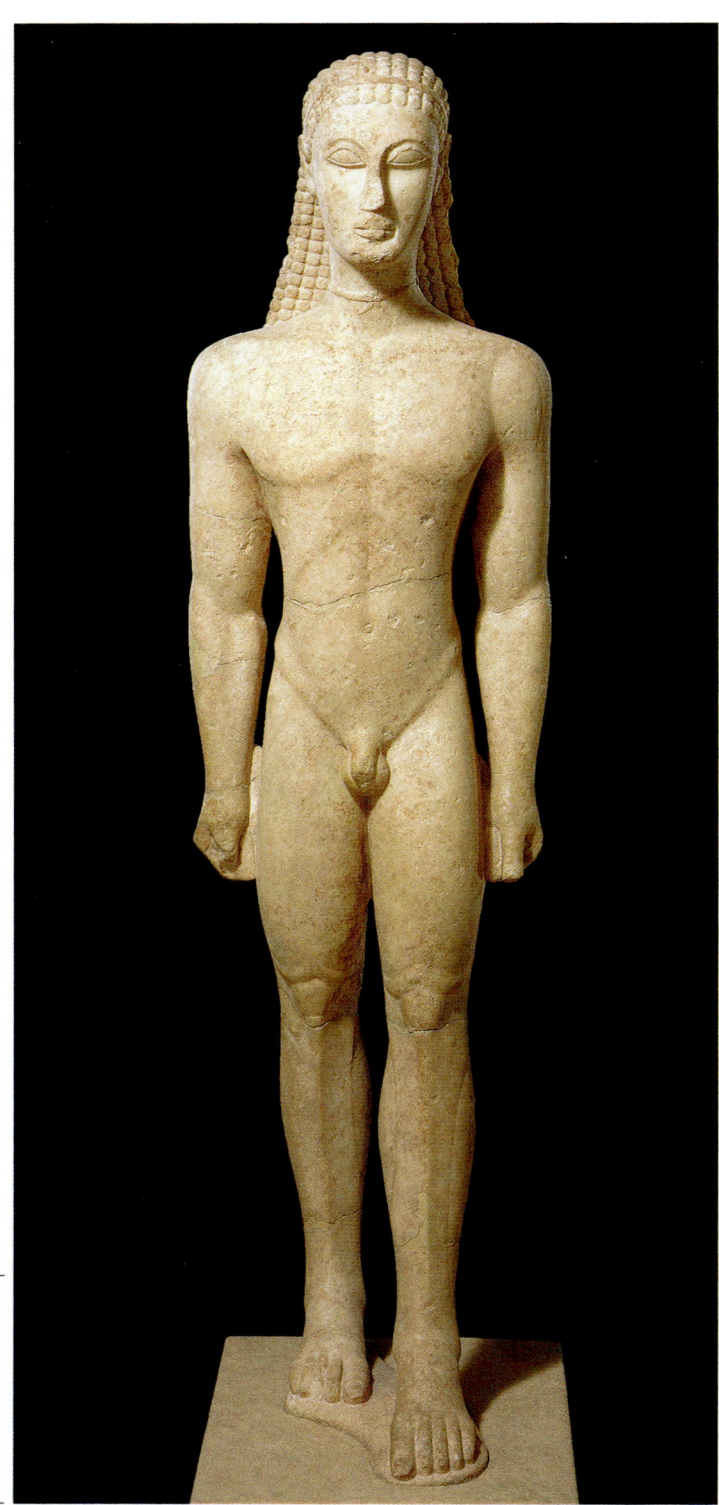

1 ft.

**5-7** Kouros, from Attica, Greece, ca. 600 BCE. Marble, 6′ ½″ high. Metropolitan Museum of Art, New York. ◼◀

The sculptors of the earliest life-size statues of kouroi (young men) adopted the Egyptian pose for standing figures (FIG. 3-12), but the kouroi are nude and liberated from the stone block.

**NEW YORK KOUROS** One of the earliest Greek examples of life-size statuary (FIG. **5-7**) is the marble *kouros* ("youth"; plural, *kouroi*) now in New York, which emulates the stance of Egyptian statues (FIG. 3-12). In both Egypt and Greece, the figure is rigidly frontal with the left foot advanced slightly. The arms are held

beside the body, and the fists are clenched with the thumbs forward. Like most Egyptian statues, the New York kouros was a funerary statue. It stood over a grave in the countryside of Attica, the region around Athens. Statues such as this one replaced the huge vases (FIGS. 5-2 and 5-2A) of Geometric times as the preferred form of grave marker in the sixth century BCE. The Greeks also used kouroi as votive offerings in sanctuaries. The kouros type, because of its generic quality, could be employed in several different contexts.

Despite the adherence to Egyptian prototypes, Greek kouros statues differ from their models in two important ways. First, the Greek sculptors liberated the figures from the stone block. The Egyptian obsession with permanence was alien to the Greeks, who were preoccupied with finding ways to represent motion rather than stability in their sculpted figures. Second, the kouroi are nude, and in the absence of identifying attributes, they, like Mantiklos's bronze statuette (FIG. 5-4), are formally indistinguishable from Greek images of deities with their perfect bodies exposed for all to see.

The New York kouros shares many traits with the *Mantiklos Apollo* and other Orientalizing works such as the *Lady of Auxerre,* especially the triangular shape of head and hair and the flatness of the face—the hallmarks of the Daedalic style. Eyes, nose, and mouth all sit on the front of the head, and the ears on the sides. The long hair forms a flat backdrop behind the head. The placement of the various anatomical parts is the result of the sculptor's having drawn these features on four independent sides of the marble block, following the same workshop procedure used in Egypt for millennia. The New York kouros also has the slim waist of earlier Greek statues and exhibits the same love of pattern. The pointed arch of the rib cage, for example, echoes the V-shaped ridge of the hips, which suggests but does not accurately reproduce the rounded flesh and muscle of the human body.

**CALF BEARER** A generation later than the New York kouros is the statue of a *moschophoros* (FIG. **5-8**), or calf bearer, found in fragments on the Athenian Acropolis. Its inscribed base (not visible in the photograph) states that a man named Rhonbos dedicated the statue to Athena in thanksgiving for his prosperity. Rhonbos is almost certainly the calf bearer himself, bringing an offering to the goddess. He stands in the left-foot-forward manner of the kouroi, but he is bearded and therefore no longer a youth. He wears a thin cloak (once painted to set it off from the otherwise nude body). No one dressed in this way in ancient Athens. The sculptor adhered to the artistic convention of male nudity and attributed to the calf bearer the noble perfection nudity imparts but nevertheless indicated that this mature gentleman is clothed, as any respectable citizen would be in this context. The Archaic sculptor's love of pattern is evident once again in the handling of the difficult problem of representing man and animal together. The calf's legs and the moschophoros's arms form a bold X that unites the two bodies both physically and formally.

The calf bearer's face differs markedly from those of earlier Greek statues (and those of Egypt and Mesopotamia) in one notable way. The man smiles—or at least seems to. From this time on, Archaic Greek statues always smile, even in the most inappropriate contexts (see, for example, FIG. 5-27, where a dying warrior with an arrow in his chest grins broadly). Art historians have interpreted this so-called *Archaic smile* in various ways, but the smile should not be taken literally. Rather, the Archaic smile seems to be the sculptor's way of indicating that the person portrayed is alive. By adopting this convention, Greek artists signaled a very different intention from their Egyptian counterparts.

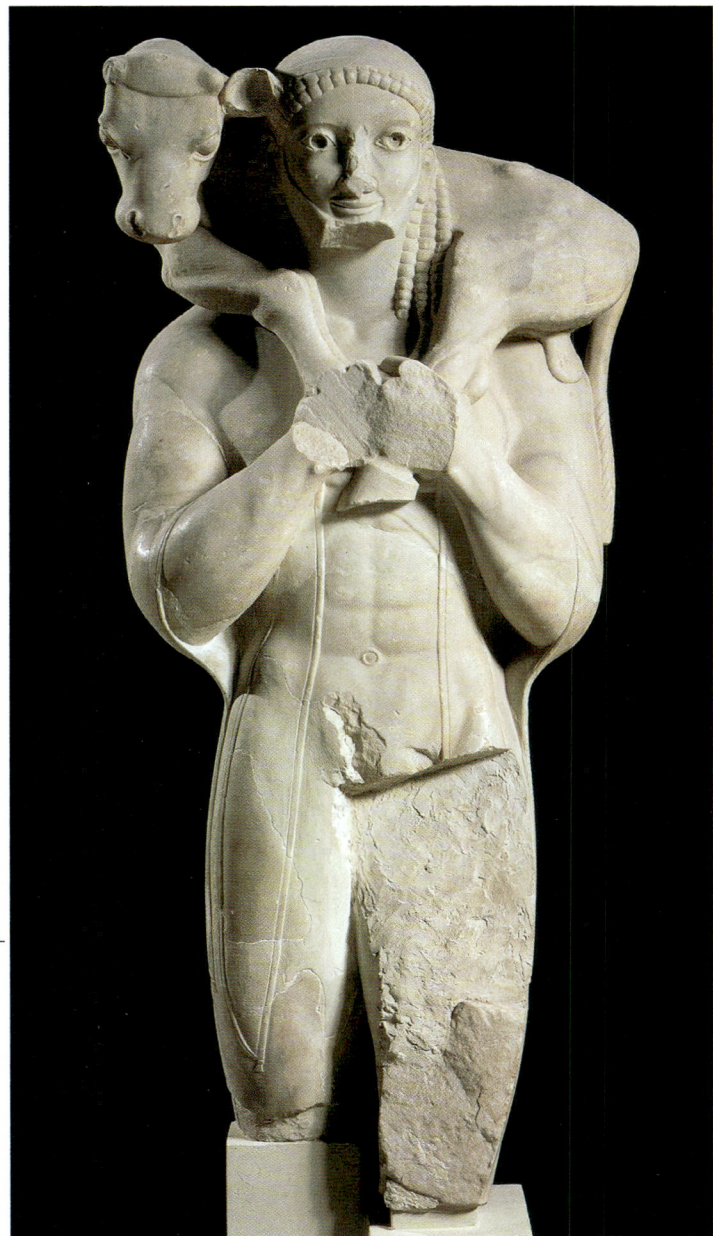

1 ft.

**5-8** Calf bearer, dedicated by Rhonbos on the Acropolis, Athens, Greece, ca. 560 BCE. Marble, restored height 5′ 5″; fragment 3′ 11½″ high. Acropolis Museum, Athens.

This statue of a bearded man bringing a calf to sacrifice to Athena is one of the first to employ the so-called Archaic smile—the Greek sculptor's way of indicating a person is alive.

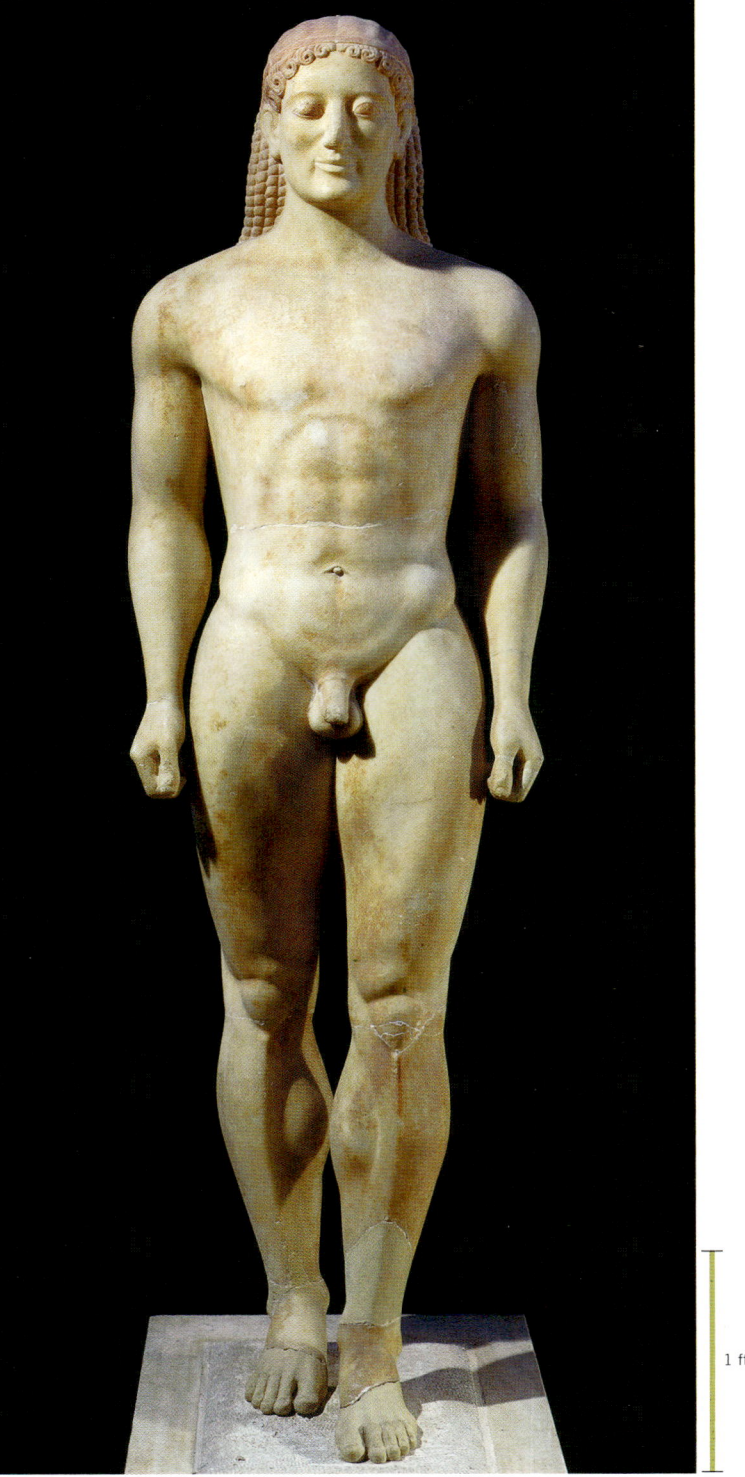

1 ft.

**5-9** Kroisos, from Anavysos, Greece, ca. 530 BCE. Marble, 6′ 4″ high. National Archaeological Museum, Athens. ◼◀

This later kouros stood over the grave of Kroisos, a young man who died in battle. The statue displays more naturalistic proportions and more rounded modeling of face, torso, and limbs.

**ANAVYSOS KOUROS** Sometime around 530 BCE, a young man named Kroisos died a hero's death in battle, and his family erected a kouros statue (FIG. **5-9**) over his grave at Anavysos, not far from Athens. Fortunately, some of the paint remains, giving a better sense of the statue's original appearance. The inscribed base invites visitors to "stay and mourn at the tomb of dead Kroisos, whom raging Ares destroyed one day as he fought in the foremost ranks." The smiling statue is no more a portrait of a specific youth than is the New York kouros. But two generations later, without rejecting the Egyptian stance, the Greek sculptor rendered the human body in a far more naturalistic manner. The head is no longer too large

for the body, and the face is more rounded, with swelling cheeks replacing the flat planes of the earlier work. The long hair does not form a stiff backdrop to the head but falls naturally over the back. The V-shaped ridges of the New York kouros have become rounded, fleshy hips.

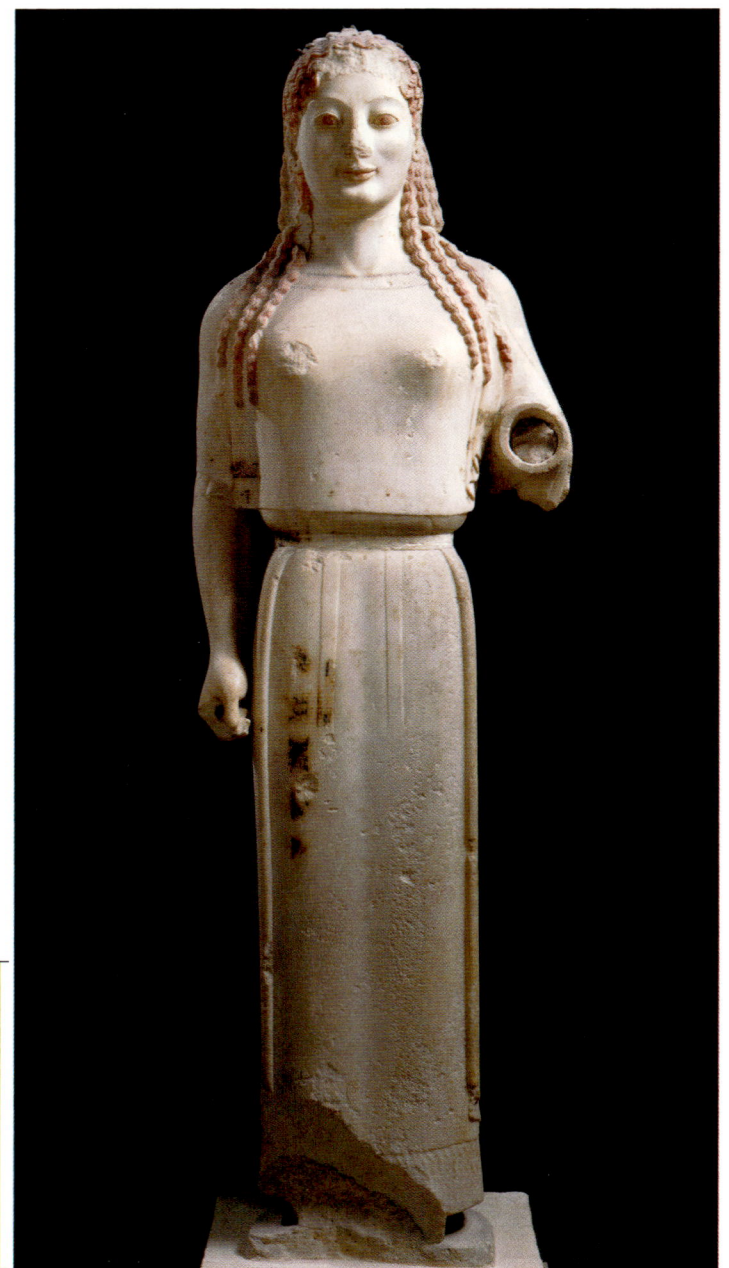

1 ft.

**5-10** *Peplos Kore,* from the Acropolis, Athens, Greece, ca. 530 BCE. Marble, 4′ high. Acropolis Museum, Athens.

Unlike men, women are always clothed in Archaic statuary. This kore is a votive statue of a goddess wearing four garments. She held her identifying attribute in her missing left hand.

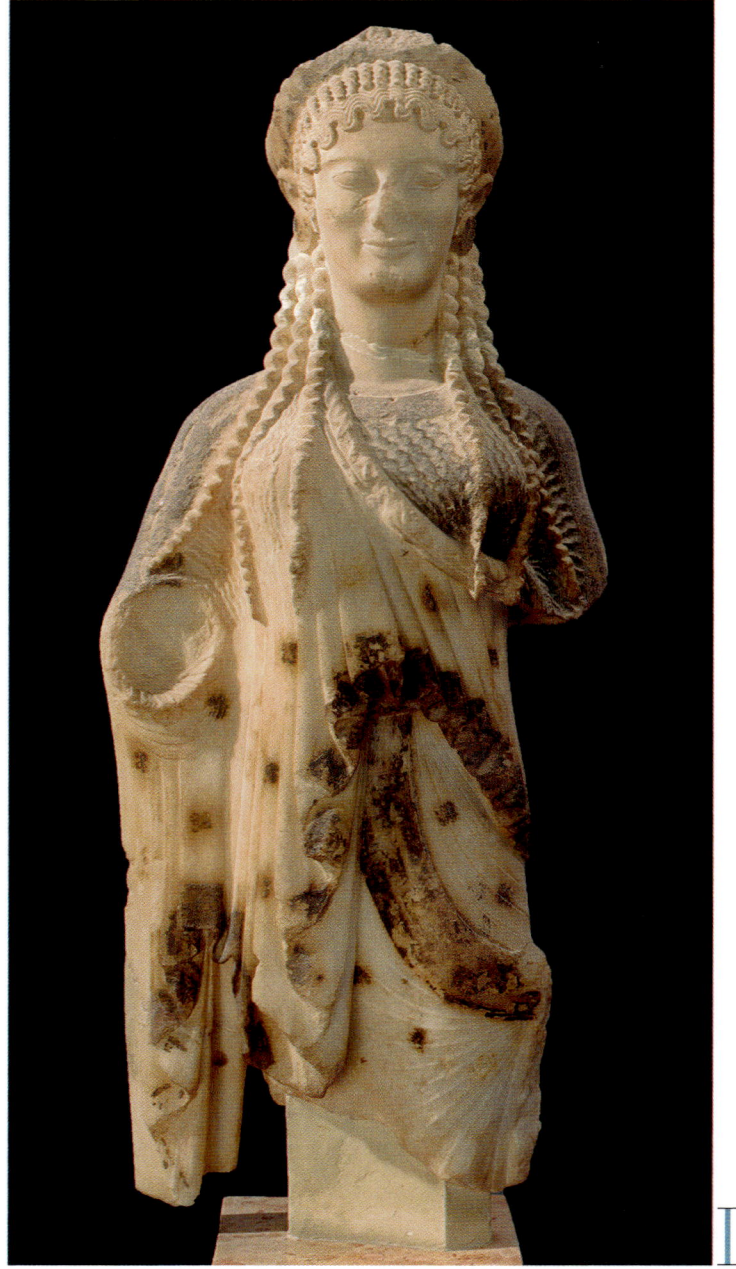

1 in.

**5-11** Kore in Ionian dress, from the Acropolis, Athens, Greece, ca. 520–510 BCE. Marble, 1′ 9″ high. Acropolis Museum, Athens.

Archaic sculptors delighted in rendering the intricate asymmetrical patterns created by the cascading folds of garments such as the Ionian chiton and himation worn by this smiling Acropolis kore.

***PEPLOS KORE*** A stylistic "sister" to the Anavysos kouros is the statue of a woman traditionally known as the *Peplos Kore* (FIG. **5-10**) because until recently scholars thought this kore wore a peplos. A *peplos* is a simple, long, woolen belted garment. Careful examination of the statue has revealed, however, that she wears four different garments, one of which only goddesses wore. The attribute the goddess held in her missing left hand would immediately have identified her. Whichever goddess she is, the contrast with the *Lady of Auxerre* (FIG. 5-6) is striking. Although in both cases the drapery conceals the entire body save for head, arms, and feet, the sixth-century BCE sculptor rendered the soft female form much more naturally. This

softer treatment of the flesh also sharply differentiates later korai from kouroi, which have hard, muscular bodies.

Traces of paint remain on the *Peplos Kore* because the statue lay buried for more than two millennia, which protected the painted surface from the destructive effects of exposure to the atmosphere and bad weather. The Persians had knocked over this statue, Rhonbos's (FIG. 5-8), and many other votive offerings in Athena's sanctuary during their sack of the Acropolis in 480 BCE. Shortly thereafter, the Athenians buried all the damaged Archaic sculptures, which accounts for the preservation of the coloration today.

## Greek Temple Plans

The core of an ancient Greek temple plan (FIG. 5-12) was the *naos,* or *cella,* a windowless room that usually housed the cult statue of the deity. In front of the naos was a *pronaos,* or porch, often with two columns between the *antae,* or extended walls (columns *in antis*). A smaller second room might be placed behind the cella (FIG. 5-15), but in its canonical form, the Greek temple had a porch at the rear (*opisthodomos*) set against the blank back wall of the cella. The second porch served only a decorative purpose: It satisfied the Greek passion for balance and symmetry.

Around this core, Greek builders might erect a colonnade across the front of the temple (*prostyle;* FIG. 5-52), across both front and back (*amphiprostyle;* FIG. 5-55), or, more commonly, all around the cella and its porch(es) to form a *peristyle,* as in FIG. 5-12 (compare FIGS. 5-1 and 5-14). Single (*peripteral*) colonnades were the norm, but double (*dipteral*) colonnades were features of especially elaborate temples (FIG. 5-75).

The Greeks' insistence on proportional order guided their experiments with the proportions of temple plans. The earliest temples tended to be long and narrow, with the proportion of the ends to the sides roughly expressible as 1:3. From the sixth century BCE on, plans approached but rarely had a proportion of exactly 1:2.

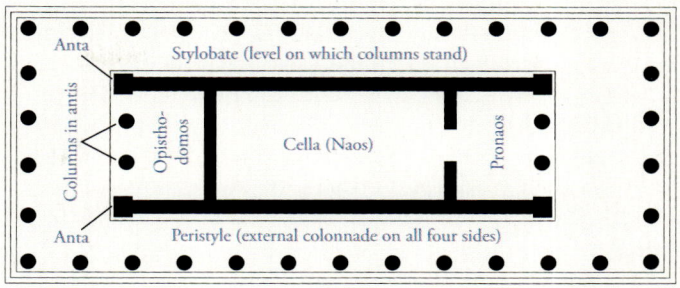

**5-12** Plan of a typical Greek peripteral temple.

The basic form of the canonical Greek temple derives from that of the Mycenaean megaron (FIG. 4-18), but Greek temples housed statues of deities, and most were surrounded by columns.

Classical temples tended to be a little longer than twice their width. To the Greek mind, proportion in architecture and sculpture was comparable to harmony in music—reflections and embodiments of the cosmic order.

**KORE IN IONIAN DRESS** By the late sixth century BCE, the light linen Ionian *chiton,* worn in conjunction with a heavier *himation* (mantle), was the garment of choice for fashionable women. Archaic sculptors of korai in Ionian dress (FIG. **5-11**) delighted in rendering the intricate patterns created by the cascading folds of thin, soft material. The asymmetry of the folds greatly relieves the stiff frontality of the body and makes the figure appear much more lifelike than the typical kouros. The sculptor achieved added variety by showing the kore grasping part of her chiton in her left hand (unfortunately broken off) to lift it off the ground in order to take a step forward. This is the equivalent of the advanced left foot of the kouroi and became standard for statues of korai. Despite the varied surface treatment of brightly colored garments on the korai, the kore postures are as fixed as those of their male counterparts.

## Architecture and Architectural Sculpture

The earliest Greek temples do not survive because their builders constructed them of wood and mud brick. Pausanias noted in his second-century CE guidebook to Greece that in the even-then-ancient Temple of Hera at Olympia, one oak column was still in place.[2] (Stone columns had replaced the others.) For Archaic and later Greek temples, however, Greek builders used more permanent materials—limestone or, where it was available, marble, which was more impressive and durable (and more expensive). In Greece proper, if not in its western colonies, marble was readily at hand. Bluish-white marble came from Mount Hymettus, just east of Athens, and glittering white marble from Mount Pentelicus, northeast of the city, and from the Aegean Islands, especially Paros.

Already in the Orientalizing seventh century BCE, at Prinias, the Greeks had built a stone temple (FIG. 5-6A) embellished with

stone sculptures, but the Cretan temple resembled the megaron of a Mycenaean palace more than anything Greek traders had seen in their travels overseas. In the Archaic age of the sixth century BCE, with the model of Egyptian columnar halls such as those at Luxor (FIG. 3-24A) and Karnak (FIGS. 3-25 and 3-26) before them, Greek architects began to build the columnar stone temples that have become synonymous with Greek architecture and influenced countless later structures in the Western world.

**THE CANONICAL GREEK TEMPLE** Greek temples differed in function from most later religious shrines. The altar lay outside the temple—at the east end, facing the rising sun—and the Greeks gathered outside, not inside, the building to worship. The temple proper housed the so-called *cult statue* of the deity, the grandest of all votive offerings. Both in its early and mature manifestations, the Greek temple was the house of the god or goddess, not of his or her followers.

In basic plan (see "Greek Temple Plans," above, and FIG. **5-12**), the Greek temple still discloses a close affinity with the Mycenaean megaron (FIG. 4-18), and even in its most elaborate form, it retains the megaron's basic simplicity. In all cases, the remarkable order, compactness, and symmetry of the Greek scheme strike the eye first, reflecting the Greeks' sense of proportion and their effort to achieve ideal forms in terms of regular numerical relationships and geometric rules (see "The Perfect Temple," page 105).

Figural sculpture played a major role in the exterior program of the Greek temple from early times, partly to embellish the god's shrine, partly to tell something about the deity represented within, and partly to serve as a votive offering. But Greek architects also conceived the building itself, with its finely carved capitals and moldings, as sculpture, abstract in form and possessing the power

# Doric and Ionic Orders

Architectural historians describe the elevation (FIG. 5-13) of a Greek temple in terms of the platform, the colonnade, and the superstructure (*entablature*). In the Archaic period, two basic systems, or *orders,* evolved for articulating the three units. The Greek architectural orders differ both in the nature of the details and in the relative proportions of the parts. The names of the orders derive from the Greek regions where they were most commonly employed. The *Doric,* formulated on the mainland, remained the preferred manner there and in Greece's western colonies. The *Ionic* was the order of choice in the Aegean Islands and on the western coast of Asia Minor. The geographical distinctions are by no means absolute. The Ionic order, for example, was often used in Athens (where, according to some ancient authors, the Athenians considered themselves Ionians who never migrated).

In both orders, the columns rest on the *stylobate,* the uppermost course of the platform. Metal clamps held together the stone blocks in each horizontal course, and metal dowels joined vertically the blocks of different courses. The columns have two or three parts, depending on the order: the *shaft,* usually marked with vertical channels (*flutes*); the *capital;* and, in the Ionic order, the *base.* Greek column shafts, in contrast to their Minoan and Mycenaean forebears, taper gradually from bottom to top. They usually are composed of separate *drums* joined by metal dowels to pre-

vent turning as well as shifting, although occasionally the Greeks erected *monolithic* (single-piece) columns.

Greek column capitals have two elements. The lower part (the *echinus*) varies with the order. In the Doric, it is convex and cushionlike, similar to the echinus of Minoan (FIG. 4-6) and Mycenaean (FIG. 4-18A) capitals. In the Ionic, it is small and supports a bolster ending in scroll-like spirals (the *volutes*). The upper element, present in both orders, is a flat, square block (the *abacus*) that provides the immediate support for the entablature.

The entablature has three parts: the *architrave,* the main weight-bearing and weight-distributing element; the *frieze;* and the *cornice,* a molded horizontal projection that together with two sloping (*raking*) cornices forms a triangle that frames the *pediment.* In the Ionic order, the architrave is usually subdivided into three horizontal bands. Doric architects subdivided the frieze into *triglyphs* and *metopes,* whereas Ionic builders left the frieze open to provide a continuous field for relief sculpture.

The Doric order is massive in appearance, its sturdy columns firmly planted on the stylobate. Compared with the weighty and severe Doric, the Ionic order seems light, airy, and much more decorative. Its columns are more slender and rise from molded bases. The most obvious differences between the two orders are, of course, the capitals—the Doric, severely plain, and the Ionic, highly ornamental.

DORIC ORDER

IONIC ORDER

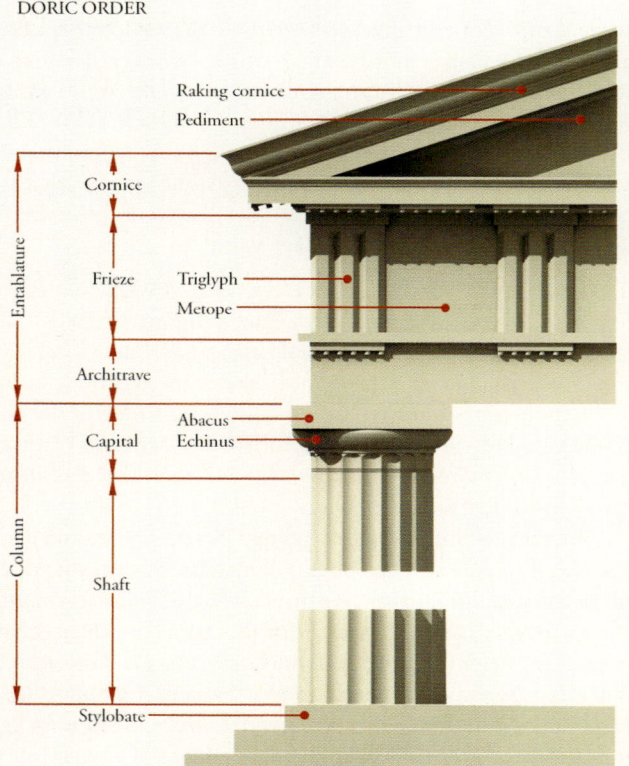
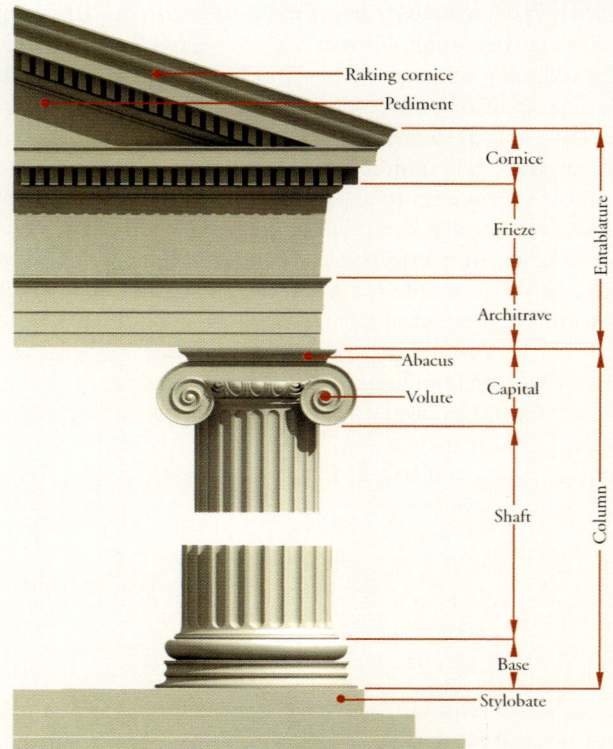

**5-13** Elevations of the Doric and Ionic orders (John Burge).

The major differences between the Doric and Ionic orders are the form of the capitals and the treatment of the frieze. The Doric frieze is subdivided into triglyphs and metopes.

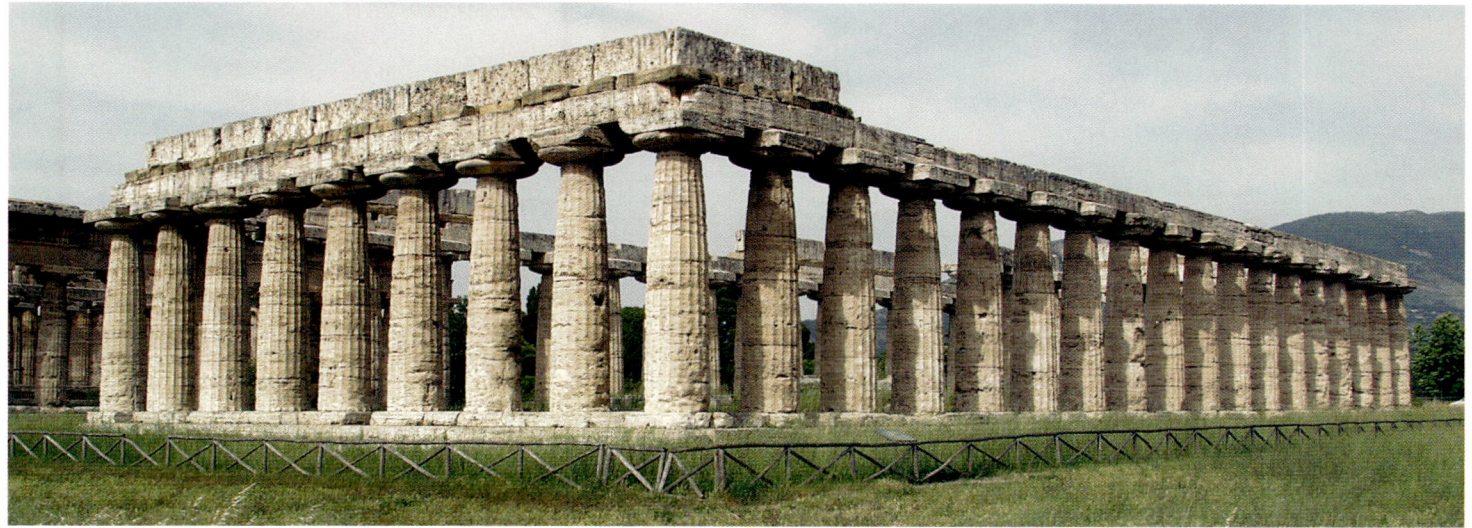

**5-14** Temple of Hera I ("Basilica," looking northeast), Paestum, Italy, ca. 550 BCE.

The peristyle of this huge early Doric temple consists of heavy, closely spaced, cigar-shaped columns with bulky, pancakelike capitals, characteristic features of Archaic Greek architecture.

of sculpture to evoke human responses. To underscore the commanding importance of the sculptured temple and its inspiring function in public life, the Greeks usually erected their temples on elevated sites, often on a hill above the city (*acropolis* means "high city").

Most of the sculptural ornament was on the upper part of the building, in the frieze and pediments (see "Doric and Ionic Orders," page 116). The Greeks painted their architectural sculptures (FIG. 5-26), as they did their freestanding statues, and usually placed sculpture only in the building parts that had no structural function. This is true particularly of the Doric order (FIG. **5-13**, *left*), in which decorative sculpture appears only in the "voids" of the metopes and pediments. Ionic (FIG. 5-13, *right*) builders were willing to decorate the entire frieze and sometimes even the lower column drums. Occasionally, Ionic architects replaced columns with female figures (*caryatids;* FIGS. 5-17 and 5-54). Designers also painted capitals, decorative moldings, and other architectural elements, which enabled architects to bring out more clearly the relationships of the structural parts and soften the stone's glitter at specific points, as well as provide a background to set off the figures.

Although the Greeks used color for emphasis and to relieve what might have seemed too bare, Greek architecture primarily depended on clarity and balance. To the Greeks, it was unthinkable to use surfaces in the way the Egyptians used their gigantic columns—as fields for complicated ornamentation (FIG. 3-25). The history of Greek temple architecture is the history of Greek architects' unflagging efforts to find the most satisfactory (that is, what they believed were perfect) proportions for each part of the building and for the structure as a whole.

**BASILICA, PAESTUM** The premier example of early Greek efforts at Doric temple design is not in Greece but in Italy, south of Naples, at Paestum (Greek Poseidonia). The huge (80 by 170 feet) Archaic temple (FIG. **5-14**) erected there around 550 BCE retains its entire peripteral colonnade, but most of the entablature, including the frieze, pediment, and all of the roof, has vanished. Called the "Basilica" after the Roman columnar hall building type (see Chapter 7) that early investigators felt it resembled, the structure was a shrine to the goddess Hera—known as the Temple of Hera I to dis-

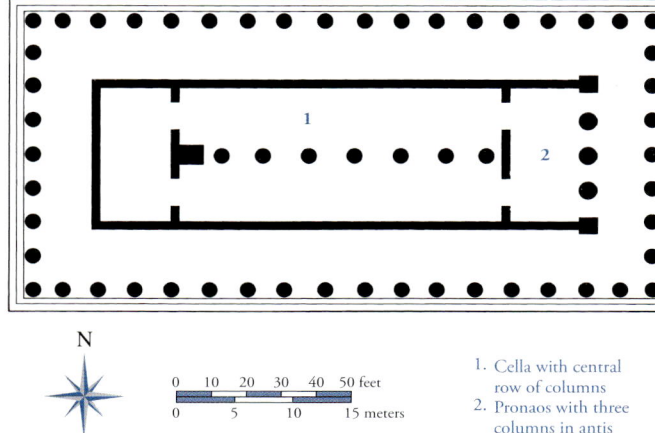

**5-15** Plan of the Temple of Hera I, Paestum, Italy, ca. 550 BCE.

The Hera temple's plan also reveals its early date. The building has an odd number of columns on the facade and a single row of columns in the cella, leaving no place for a central cult statue.

1. Cella with central row of columns
2. Pronaos with three columns in antis

tinguish it from its neighbor, the later Temple of Hera II (FIG. 5-29). The misnomer is partly due to the building's plan (FIG. **5-15**), which differs from that of most other Greek temples. The unusual feature, found only in early Archaic temples, is the central row of columns dividing the cella into two aisles. Placing columns underneath the *ridgepole* (the timber beam running the length of the building below the peak of the gabled roof) might seem the logical way to provide interior support for the roof structure, but it had several disadvantages. The cella columns allowed no place for a central cult statue. Further, in order to correspond with the interior, the temple's facade required an odd number of columns (nine in this case). At Paestum, there are also three columns in antis instead of the standard two, which in turn ruled out a central doorway for viewing the statue. (This design, however, was well suited for two statues, perhaps of Zeus and Hera.) In any case, the architect still achieved a simple 1:2 ratio of facade and flank columns by placing 18 columns on each side of the temple.

Another early aspect of the Paestum temple is the shape of its heavy, closely spaced columns (FIG. 5-14) with their large, bulky, pancakelike Doric capitals, which seem compressed by the overbearing weight of what probably was a high, massive entablature. The columns have a pronounced swelling (*entasis*) at the middle of the shafts, giving them a profile akin to that of a cigar. The columns and capitals thus express in a vivid manner their weight-bearing function. One structural reason, perhaps, for the heaviness of the design and the narrowness of the spans between the columns might be that the Archaic builders were afraid thinner and more widely spaced columns would result in the superstructure's collapse. In later Doric temples (FIGS. 5-1, 5-24, 5-29, and 5-44), the builders placed the columns farther apart and refined the forms. The shafts became more slender, the entasis subtler, the capitals smaller, and the entablature lighter. Greek architects sought the ideal proportional relationship among the parts of their buildings. The sculptors of Archaic kouroi and korai grappled with similar problems. Architecture and sculpture developed in a parallel manner in the sixth century BCE.

**TEMPLE OF ARTEMIS, CORFU** In fact, architects and sculptors frequently worked together, as at Corfu (ancient Corcyra), where, soon after 600 BCE, the Greeks constructed a large Doric temple in honor of Artemis. Corfu is an island off the western coast of Greece and was an important stop on the trade route between the mainland and the Greek settlements in Italy (MAP 5-1). Prosperity made possible one of the earliest stone peripteral temples in Greece, one also lavishly embellished with sculpture. Sculptors decorated the metopes with reliefs (unfortunately very fragmentary today) and filled both pediments with huge high-relief sculptures (more than 9 feet high at the center). It appears the pediments on both ends of the temple were decorated in an identical manner. The west pediment (FIG. 5-16) is better preserved.

Designing figural decoration for a pediment was never an easy task for the Greek sculptor because of the pediment's awkward triangular shape. The central figures had to be of great size. In contrast, as the pediment tapered toward the corners, the available area became increasingly cramped. At the center of the Corfu pediment is the *gorgon* Medusa, a demon with a woman's body and a bird's wings. Medusa also had a hideous face and snake hair, and anyone who gazed at her turned into stone. The Corfu sculptor depicted her in the conventional Archaic bent-leg, bent-arm, pinwheel-like posture that signifies running or, for a winged creature, flying.

To her left and right are two great felines. Together they serve as temple guardians, repulsing all enemies from the sanctuary of the goddess. Similar panthers stood sentinel on the lintel (FIG. 5-6B) of the seventh-century BCE temple at Prinias. The Corfu felines are in the tradition of the guardian lions of Mycenae (FIG. 4-19) and the beasts that stood guard at the entrances to Hittite and Assyrian palaces (FIGS. 2-18B and 2-20). Medusa herself is also an *apotropaic* figure that protects the temple and wards off evil spirits. The triad of Medusa and the felines recalls as well Mesopotamian heraldic human-and-animal compositions (FIG. 2-10). The Corfu figures are, in short, still further examples of the Orientalizing manner in early Greek sculpture.

Between Medusa and the two felines are two smaller figures—the human Chrysaor at her left and the winged horse Pegasus at her right (only the rear legs remain, next to Medusa's right foot). Chrysaor and Pegasus were Medusa's children. According to legend, they sprang from her head when the Greek hero Perseus severed it with his sword. Their presence here on either side of the living Medusa is therefore a chronological impossibility. The Archaic artist was not interested in telling a coherent story but in identifying the central figure by depicting her offspring. Narration was, however, the purpose of the much smaller groups situated in the pediment corners. To the viewer's right is Zeus, brandishing his thunderbolt and slaying a kneeling giant. In the extreme corner (not preserved) was a dead giant. The *gigantomachy* (battle of gods and giants) was a popular theme in Greek art from Archaic through Hellenistic times and was a metaphor for the triumph of reason and order over chaos. In the pediment's left corner is one of the Trojan War's climactic events: Achilles' son Neoptolemos kills the enthroned King Priam. The fallen figure to the left of this group may be a dead Trojan.

The master responsible for the Corfu pediments was a pioneer, and the composition shows all the signs of experimentation. The lack of narrative unity in the Corfu pediment and the figures' extraordinary diversity of scale eventually gave way to pedimental designs with freestanding figures in place of reliefs all acting out a single event and appearing the same size. But the Corfu designer already had shown the way. That sculptor realized, for example, the area beneath the raking cornice could be filled with gods and heroes of similar size by employing a combination of standing, leaning, kneeling, seated, and prostrate figures. The Corfu master also discovered that animals could be very useful space fillers because, unlike humans, they have one end taller than the other.

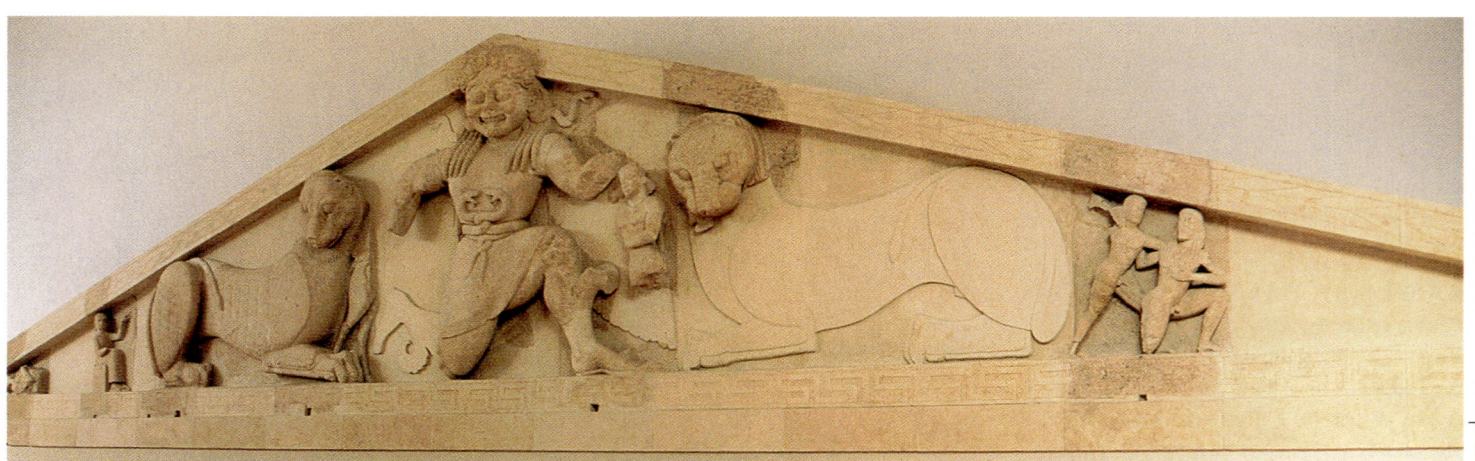

1 ft.

**5-16** West pediment, Temple of Artemis, Corfu, Greece, ca. 600–580 BCE. Limestone, greatest height 9′ 4″. Archaeological Museum, Corfu.

The hideous Medusa and two panthers at the center of this early pediment served as temple guardians. To either side, and much smaller, are scenes from the Trojan War and the battle of gods and giants.

**SIPHNIAN TREASURY, DELPHI** With the sixth century BCE also came the construction of grandiose Ionic temples on the Aegean Islands and the west coast of Asia Minor. The gem of Archaic Ionic architecture and architectural sculpture is, however, not a temple but a treasury (FIG. 5-17) erected by the city of Siphnos in the Sanctuary of Apollo (FIG. 5-17A) at Delphi. Greek *treasuries* were small buildings set up for the safe storage of votive offerings. At Delphi many poleis expressed their civic pride by erecting these templelike but nonperipteral structures. Athens built one with Doric columns in the porch and sculptured metopes in the frieze. The Siphnians equally characteristically employed the Ionic order for their Delphic treasury. Based on the surviving fragments now on display in the Delphi museum, archaeologists have been able to reconstruct the treasury's original appearance (FIG. 5-17). Wealth from the island's gold and silver mines made such a luxurious building possible. In the porch, where one would expect to find fluted Ionic columns, far more elaborate caryatids were employed instead. Caryatids are rare, even in Ionic architecture, but they are unknown in Doric architecture, where they would have been discordant elements in that much more severe order. The Siphnian statue-columns resemble contemporary korai dressed in Ionian chitons and himations (FIG. 5-11).

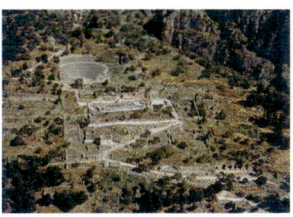

5-17A Sanctuary of Apollo, Delphi (looking north).

Another Ionic feature of the Siphnian Treasury is the continuous sculptured frieze on all four sides of the building. The north frieze represents the popular theme of the gigantomachy, but it is a much more detailed rendition than that in the corner of the Corfu pediment (FIG. 5-16). In the section reproduced here (FIG. 5-18), Apollo and Artemis pursue a fleeing giant at the right, while behind them one of the lions pulling a goddess's chariot attacks a

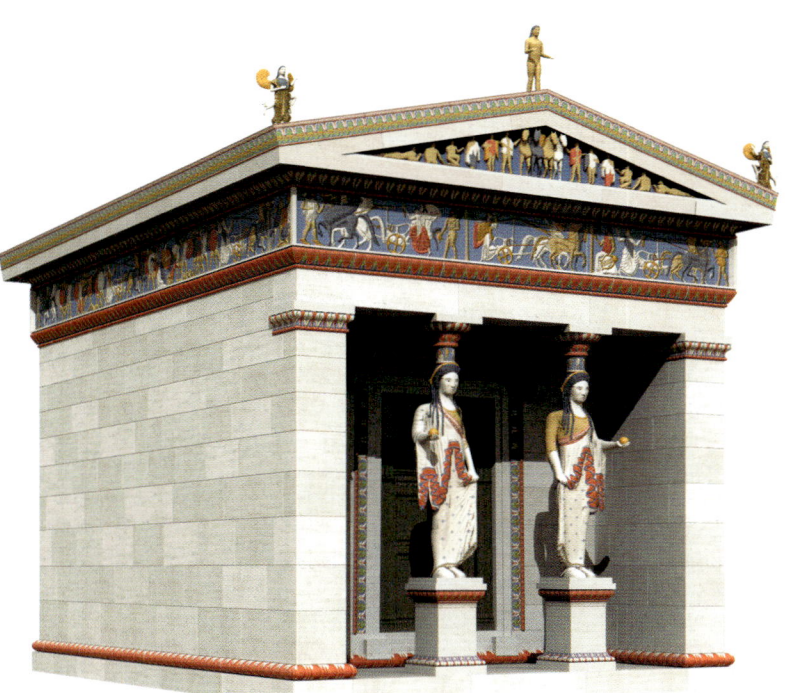

**5-17** Restored view of the Siphnian Treasury, Sanctuary of Apollo, Delphi, Greece, ca. 530 BCE (John Burge).

Treasuries were storehouses for a city's votive offerings. The Ionic treasury the Siphnians erected in Apollo's sanctuary had caryatids in the porch and sculptures in the pediment and frieze.

giant and bites into his midsection. Paint originally enlivened the crowded composition, and painted labels identified the various protagonists, as they do on Archaic black-figure vases (FIGS. 5-19 and 5-20). Some figures had metal weapons. The effect must have been dazzling. On one of the shields the sculptor inscribed his name (unfortunately lost), a clear indication of pride in accomplishment.

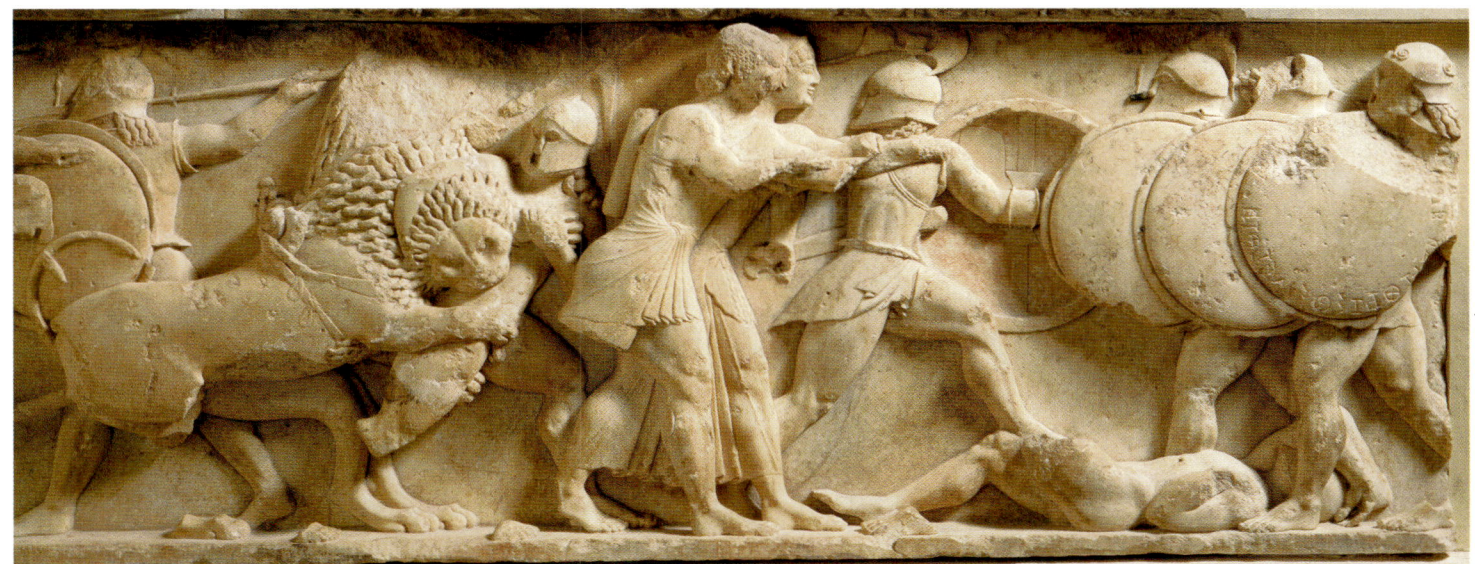

**5-18** Gigantomachy, detail of the north frieze of the Siphnian Treasury, Delphi, Greece, ca. 530 BCE. Marble, 2′ 1″ high. Archaeological Museum, Delphi.

Greek friezes were brightly painted (FIG. 5-17). As in Archaic vase painting, the Siphnian frieze also had painted labels identifying the various gods and giants. Some of the figures held metal weapons.

## Vase Painting

By the mid-sixth century BCE, the Athenians, having learned the black-figure technique from the Corinthians (FIG. 5-5), had taken over the export market for fine painted ceramics (see "Greek Vase Painting," page 110).

**FRANÇOIS VASE** The masterpiece of early Athenian black-figure painting is the *François Vase* (FIG. **5-19**), named for the excavator who discovered it (in hundreds of fragments) in an Etruscan tomb at Chiusi. The vase is a new kind of krater with volute-shaped handles, probably inspired by costly metal prototypes. The signatures of both its painter ("KLEITIAS painted me") and potter ("ERGOTIMOS made me") appear twice among the more than 200 figures in five registers. Labels abound, naming humans and animals alike, even some inanimate objects. The painter devoted only the lowest band to the Orientalizing repertoire of animals and sphinxes. The rest constitute a selective encyclopedia of Greek mythology, focusing on the exploits of Peleus and his son Achilles, the great hero of Homer's *Iliad*, and of Theseus, the legendary king of Athens.

In the detail of the *centauromachy* shown here (FIG. 5-19, *bottom*), Lapiths (a northern Greek tribe) and centaurs battle after a wedding celebration at which the man-beasts, who were invited guests, got drunk and attempted to abduct the Lapith maidens and young boys. Theseus, also on the guest list, was prominent among the centaurs' Greek adversaries. Kleitias did not fill the spaces between his figures with decorative ornament, as did his Geometric predecessors (FIGS. 5-2 and 5-2A). But his heroes still conform to the age-old composite type (profile heads with frontal eyes, frontal torsos, and profile legs and arms). His centaurs, however, are much more believable than their Geometric counterparts (FIG. 5-3). The man-horse combination is top/bottom rather than front/back. The lower (horse) portion has four legs of uniform type, and the upper part of the monster is fully human. In characteristic fashion, Kleitias painted the animal section of the centaur in strict profile, whereas the human head and torso are a composite of frontal and profile views. (He used a consistent profile for the more adventurous detail of the collapsed centaur at the right.)

**EXEKIAS** The acknowledged master of the black-figure technique was an Athenian named EXEKIAS, whose vases were not only widely exported but copied as well. Perhaps his greatest work is an amphora (FIG. **5-20**), found in an Etruscan tomb at Vulci, which Exekias signed as both painter and potter. Unlike Kleitias, Exekias did not divide the surface of the vase into a series of horizontal bands. Instead, he placed figures of monumental stature in a single large framed panel. At the left is Achilles, fully armed, the mightiest Greek soldier in the war against Troy. He appears again on another of Exekias's amphoras (FIG. **5-20A**) battling Penthesilea, queen of the Amazons. On the Vulti amphora Achilles plays a dice game with his comrade Ajax during a lull in the Trojan conflict. Out of the lips of Achilles comes the word *tesara* (four). Ajax calls out *tria* (three). Although Ajax has taken off his helmet, both men hold their spears. Their shields are nearby. Each man is ready for action at a moment's notice. This depiction of "the calm before the storm" is the antithesis of the Archaic preference for dramatic action. The gravity and tension that will characterize much Classical Greek art of the next century, but that are generally absent in Archaic art, already may be seen in this vase.

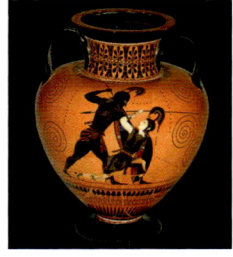

5-20A EXEKIAS, Achilles killing Penthesilea, ca. 540–530 BCE.

Exekias had no equal as a black-figure painter. This is evident in details such as the extraordinarily intricate engraving of the patterns on the heroes' cloaks (highlighted with delicate touches of white) and in the brilliant composition. The arch formed by the

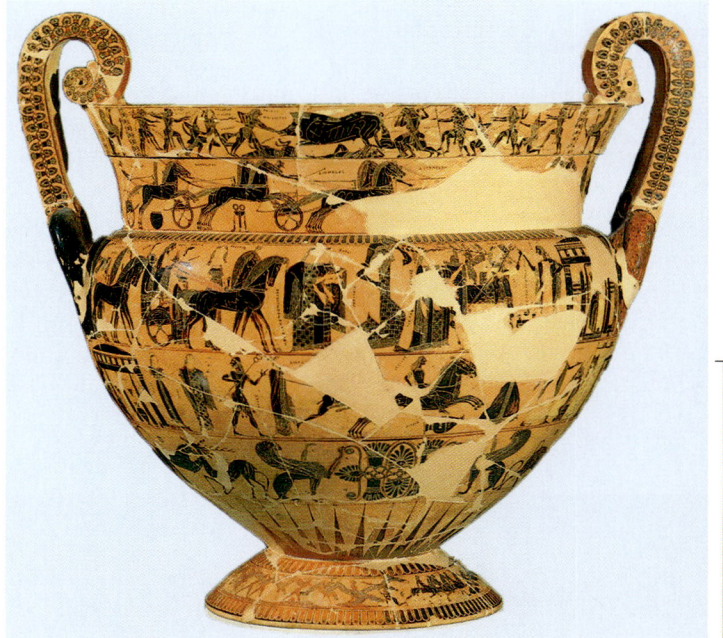

1 ft.

**5-19** KLEITIAS and ERGOTIMOS, *François Vase* (Athenian black-figure volute krater), from Chiusi, Italy, ca. 570 BCE. General view (*top*) and detail of the centauromachy on the other side of vase (*bottom*). Krater 2′ 2″ high; detail 3″ high. Museo Archeologico Nazionale, Florence. ◼

The painter and potter both signed this huge krater found in an Etruscan tomb. The vase has more than 200 mythological figures in five registers, the same format as on Geometric and Orientalizing vases.

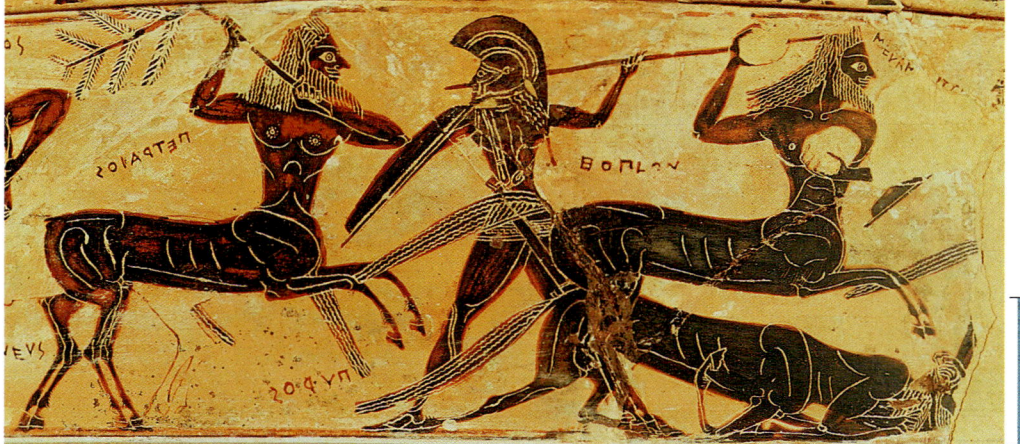

1 in.

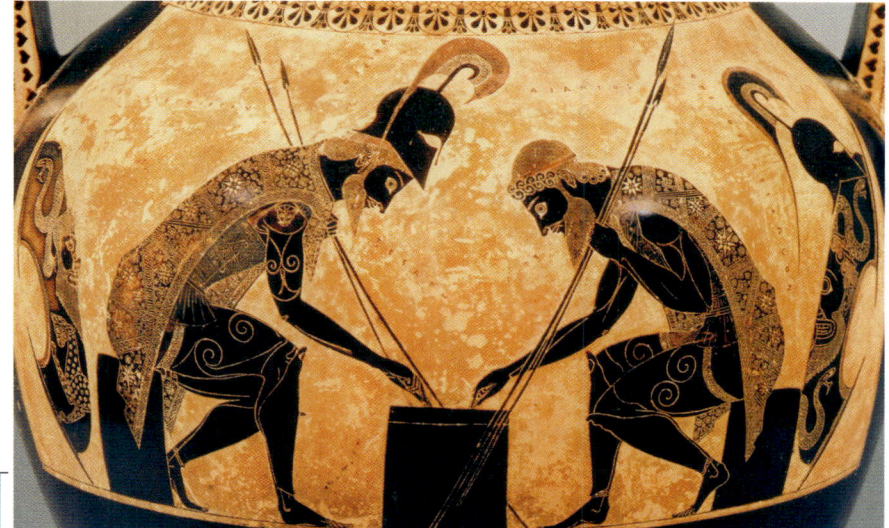

**5-20** Exekias, *Achilles and Ajax playing a dice game* (detail of an Athenian black-figure amphora), from Vulci, Italy, ca. 540–530 BCE. Amphora 2′ high; detail 8½″ high. Musei Vaticani, Rome. ◼◀

The dramatic tension, coordination of figural poses and vase shape, and intricacy of the engraved patterns of the cloaks are hallmarks of Exekias, the greatest master of black-figure painting.

1 in.

backs of the two warriors echoes the shape of the rounded shoulders of the amphora. The shape of the vessel (compare FIGS. 5-20A and 5-21) is echoed again in the void between the heads and spears of Achilles and Ajax. Exekias also used the spears to lead the viewer's eyes toward the thrown dice, where the heroes' eyes are fixed. Of course, those eyes do not really look down at the table but stare out from the profile heads in the old manner. For all his brilliance, Exekias was still wedded to many of the old conventions. Real innovation in figure drawing would have to await the invention of a new ceramic painting technique of greater versatility than black-figure, with its dark silhouettes and incised details.

**BILINGUAL PAINTING** The birth of this new technique occurred around 530 BCE, and art historians refer to the person responsible as the ANDOKIDES PAINTER, that is, the anonymous painter who decorated the vases signed by the potter ANDOKIDES. The differences between the two techniques can best be studied on a series of experimental vases with the same composition painted on both sides, once in black-figure and once in the new technique, *red-figure*. The Athenians produced these so-called *bilingual vases* for only a short time. An especially interesting example is an amphora (FIG. 5-21) by the Andokides Painter that features copies of the Achilles and Ajax panel by Exekias, his teacher.

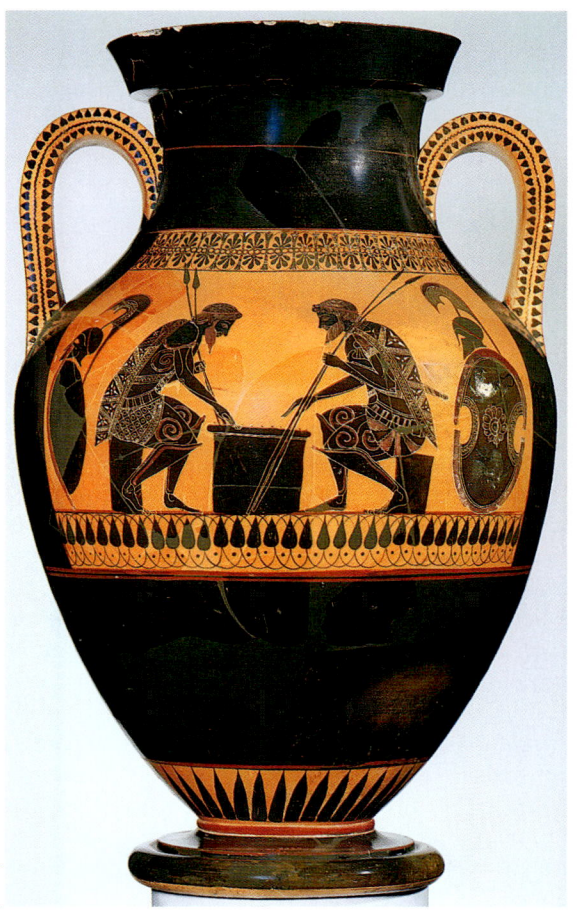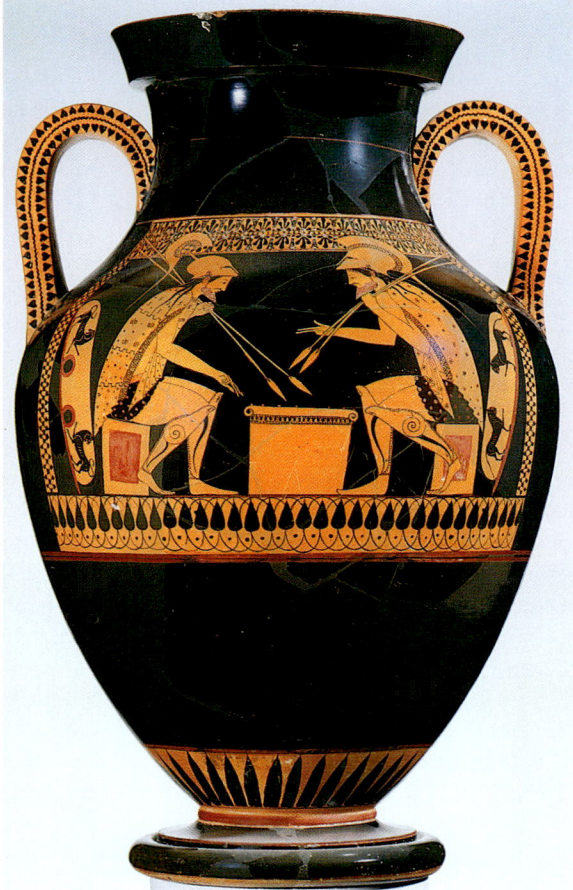

**5-21** ANDOKIDES PAINTER, *Achilles and Ajax playing a dice game* (Athenian bilingual amphora), from Orvieto, Italy, ca. 525–520 BCE. Black-figure side (*left*) and red-figure side (*right*). 1′ 9″ high. Museum of Fine Arts, Boston. ◼◀

Around 530 BCE, the Andokides Painter invented the red-figure technique. Some of his early vases are "bilingual," that is, they have the same scene on both sides, one in black-figure and one in red-figure.

1 in.

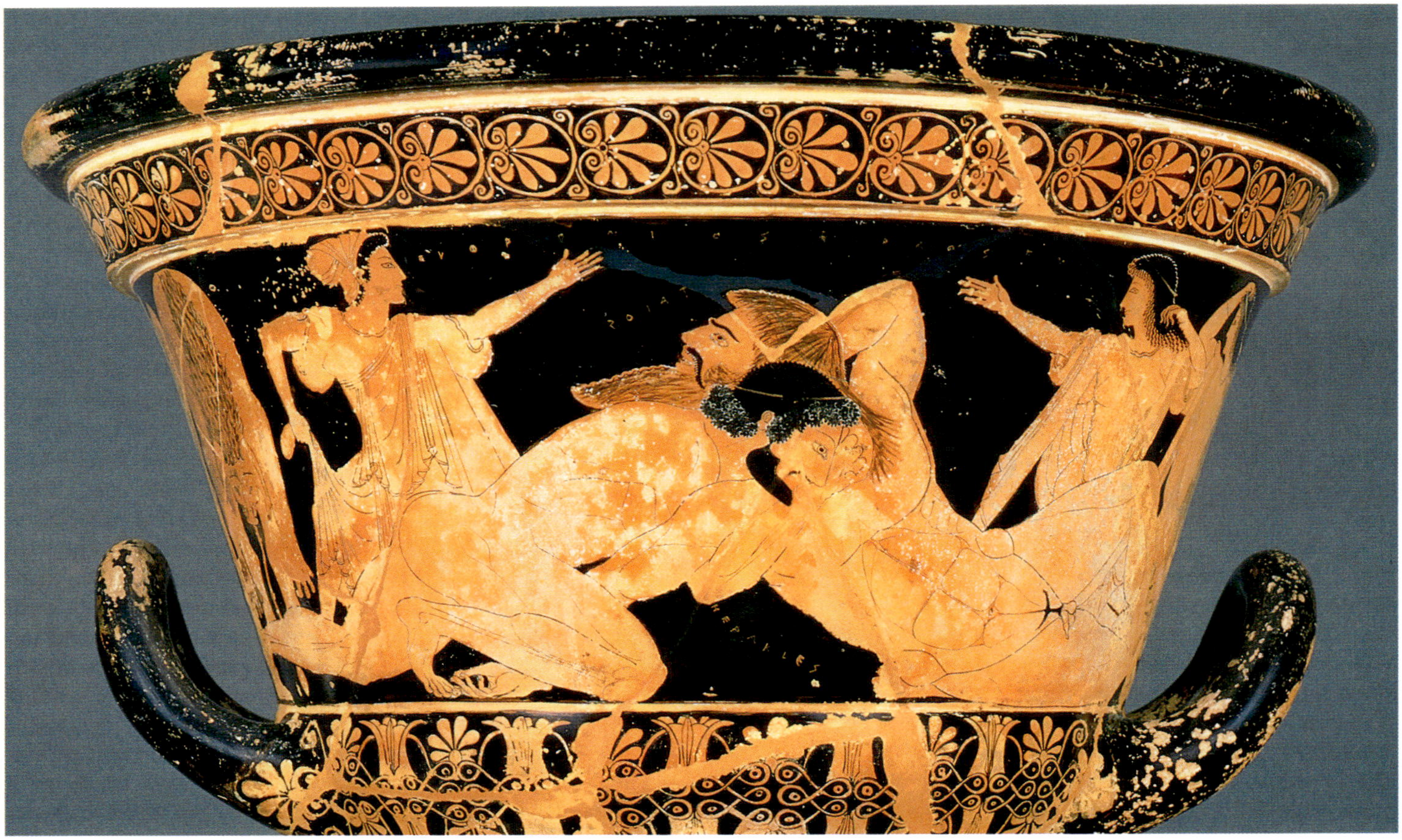

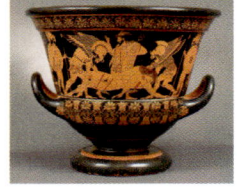

**5-22** EUPHRONIOS, Herakles wrestling Antaios (detail of an Athenian red-figure calyx krater), from Cerveteri, Italy, ca. 510 BCE. Krater 1′ 7″ high; detail 7¾″ high. Musée du Louvre, Paris.

Euphronios rejected the age-old composite view for his depiction of Herakles and the giant Antaios and instead attempted to reproduce the way the human body appears from a specific viewpoint.

In neither black-figure nor red-figure did the Andokides Painter capture the intensity of the model, and the treatment of details is decidedly inferior. Yet the new red-figure technique had obvious advantages over the old black-figure manner. Red-figure is the opposite of black-figure. What was previously black became red, and vice versa. The artist used the same black glaze for the figures, but instead of using the glaze to create silhouettes, the painter outlined the figures and then colored the background black. The ceramist reserved the red clay for the figures themselves and used a soft brush instead of a stiff metal graver to draw the interior details. This gave the red-figure painter much greater flexibility. The artist could vary the thickness of the lines and even build up the glaze to give relief to curly hair or dilute it to create brown shades, thereby expanding the chromatic range of the Greek vase painter's craft. The Andokides Painter—very likely the potter Andokides himself—did not yet appreciate the full potential of his own invention. Still, he created a technique that, in the hands of other, more skilled artists, helped revolutionize the art of drawing.

**EUPHRONIOS** One of those younger and more adventurous painters was EUPHRONIOS, whose krater depicting the struggle between Herakles and Antaios (FIG. **5-22**) reveals the exciting possibilities of the new red-figure technique. Antaios was a Libyan giant, a son of Earth, and he derived his power from contact with the ground. To defeat him, Herakles had to lift him into the air and strangle him while no part of the giant's body touched the earth. In Euphronios's representation of the myth, the two wrestle on the

ground, and Antaios still possesses enormous strength. Nonetheless, Herakles has the upper hand. The giant's face is a mask of pain. His eyes roll and his teeth are bared. His right arm is paralyzed, with the fingers limp.

On this krater, as on his other signed masterworks, including the most expensive vase ever purchased (FIG. **5-22A**), Euphronios used the new red-figure technique brilliantly. For example, he took advantage of the ability to dilute the glaze and produced a golden brown hue for Antaios's hair—intentionally contrasting the giant's unkempt hair with the neat coiffure and

**5-22A** EUPHRONIOS, Death of Sarpedon, ca. 515 BCE.

carefully trimmed beard of the emotionless Greek hero. The artist also used thinned glaze to delineate the muscles of both figures. But rendering human anatomy convincingly was not his only interest. Euphronios also wished to show that his figures occupy space. He deliberately rejected the conventional composite posture for the human figure, which communicates so well the individual parts of the human body, and attempted instead to reproduce how a particular human body is *seen*. He presented, for example, not only Antaios's torso but also his right thigh from the front. The lower leg disappears behind the giant, and only part of the right foot is visible. The viewer must mentally make the connection between the upper leg and the foot. Euphronios did not create a two-dimensional panel filled with figures in stereotypical postures, as his Archaic and pre-Greek predecessors always did. His panel is a window onto a mythological

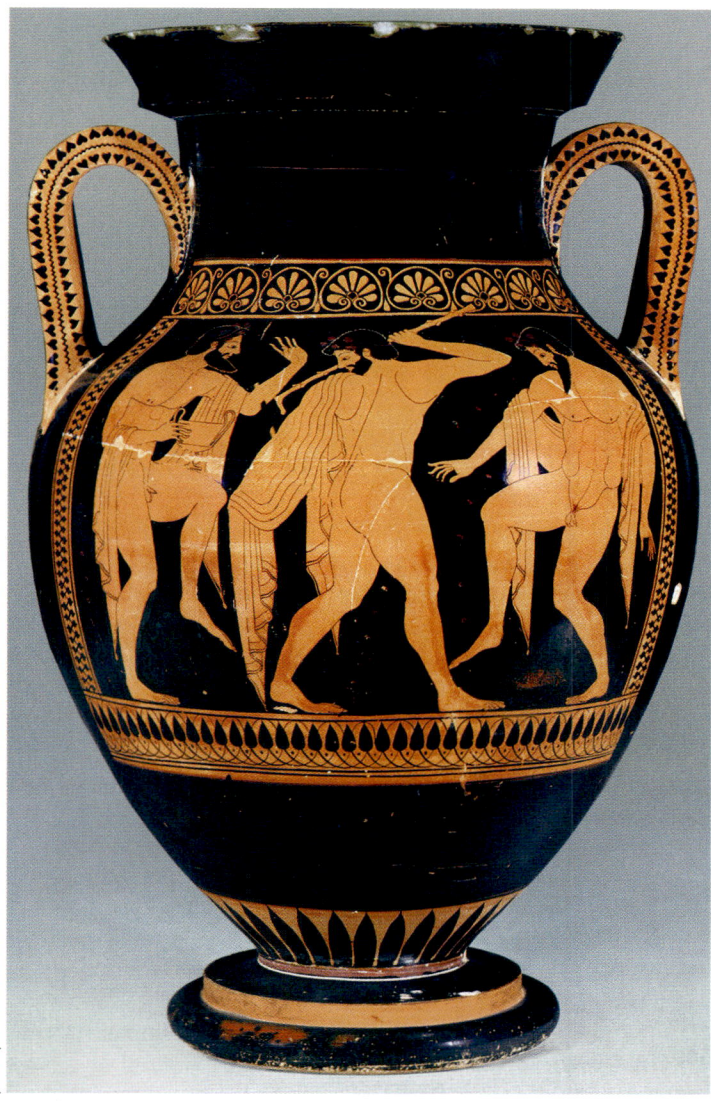

**5-23** Euthymides, Three revelers (Athenian red-figure amphora), from Vulci, Italy, ca. 510 BCE. 2′ high. Staatliche Antikensammlungen, Munich. ◼◀

Euthymides chose this theme as an excuse to represent bodies in unusual positions, including a foreshortened three-quarter rear view. He claimed to have surpassed Euphronios as a draftsman.

are incomplete views but also do not show the "main" side of the human body. For Euthymides, however, the challenge of drawing a figure from this unusual viewpoint was a reward in itself. With understandable pride he proclaimed his achievement by adding to the formulaic signature "Euthymides painted me" the phrase "as never Euphronios [could do!]" Other vase painters also challenged themselves to outdo their

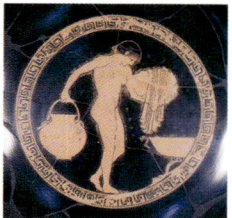

contemporaries in representing the human form. ONESIMOS, for example, successfully drew a young woman's nude torso from a three-quarter view (FIG. **5-23A**).

## Aegina and the Transition to the Classical Period

The years just before and after 500 BCE were also a time of dynamic transition in architecture and architectural sculpture. Some of the changes were evolutionary in nature, others revolutionary. Both kinds are evident in the Doric temple at Aegina dedicated to Aphaia, a local nymph.

**TEMPLE OF APHAIA, AEGINA** The temple (FIG. **5-24**) sits on a prominent ridge with dramatic views out to the sea. The peripteral colonnade consists of 6 Doric columns on the facade and 12 on the flanks. This is a much more compact structure than the impressive but ungainly Archaic temple (FIG. 5-14) at Paestum, even though the ratio of width to length is similar. Doric architects had learned a great deal in the half century that elapsed between construction of the two temples. The columns of the Aegina temple are more widely spaced and more slender. The capitals create a smooth transition from the vertical shafts below to the horizontal architrave above. Gone are the Archaic flattened echinuses and bulging shafts of the Paestum columns. The Aegina architect also refined the internal elevation and plan (FIG. **5-25**). In place of a

world with protagonists moving in three-dimensional space—a revolutionary new conception of what a picture is supposed to be.

**EUTHYMIDES** A preoccupation with the art of drawing per se is evident in a remarkable amphora (FIG. **5-23**) painted by EUTHYMIDES, a rival of Euphronios's. The subject is appropriate for a wine storage jar—three tipsy revelers. But the theme was little more than an excuse for the artist to experiment with the representation of unusual positions of the human form. It is no coincidence that the bodies do not overlap, for each is an independent figure study. Euthymides cast aside the conventional frontal and profile composite views. Instead, he painted torsos that are not two-dimensional surface patterns but are *foreshortened,* that is, drawn in a three-quarter view with some parts of the figures closer to the viewer and others farther away. Most noteworthy is the central figure, shown from the rear with a twisting spinal column and buttocks in three-quarter view. Earlier artists had no interest in attempting to depict figures seen from behind and at an angle because those postures not only

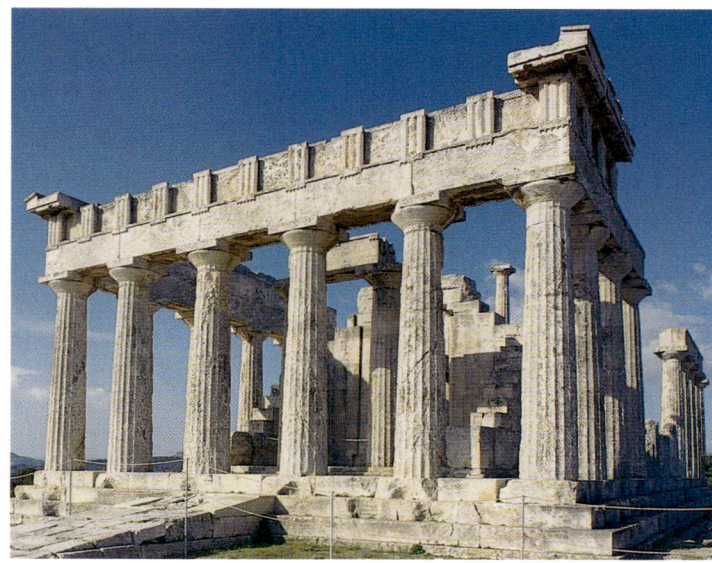

**5-24** Temple of Aphaia (looking southwest), Aegina, Greece, ca. 500–490 BCE.

In this refined early-fifth-century BCE Doric design (compare FIG. 5-14), the columns are more slender and widely spaced, and there are only 6 columns on the facade and 12 on the flanks.

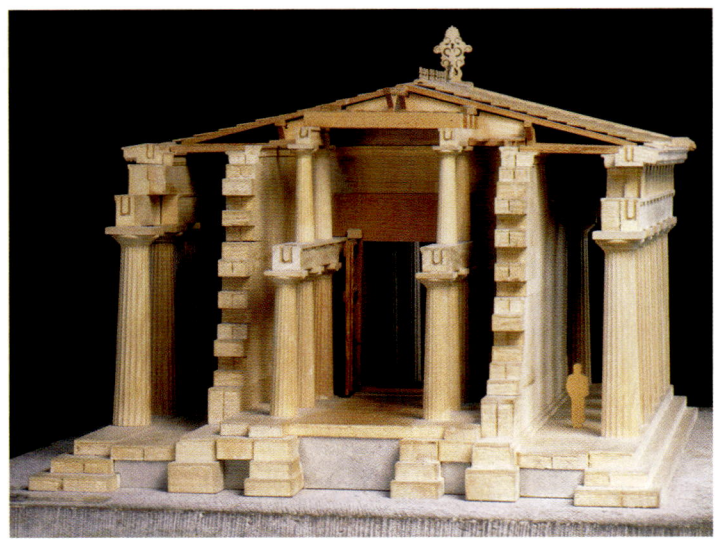

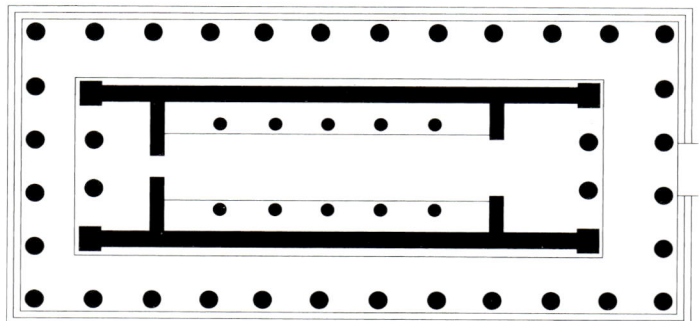

**5-25** Model showing internal elevation (*top*) and plan (*bottom*) of the Temple of Aphaia, Aegina, Greece, ca. 500–490 BCE. Model: Glyptothek, Munich.

Later Doric architects also modified the plan of their temples (compare FIG. 5-15). The Aegina temple's cella has two colonnades, each of two stories (originally with a statue of the deity between them).

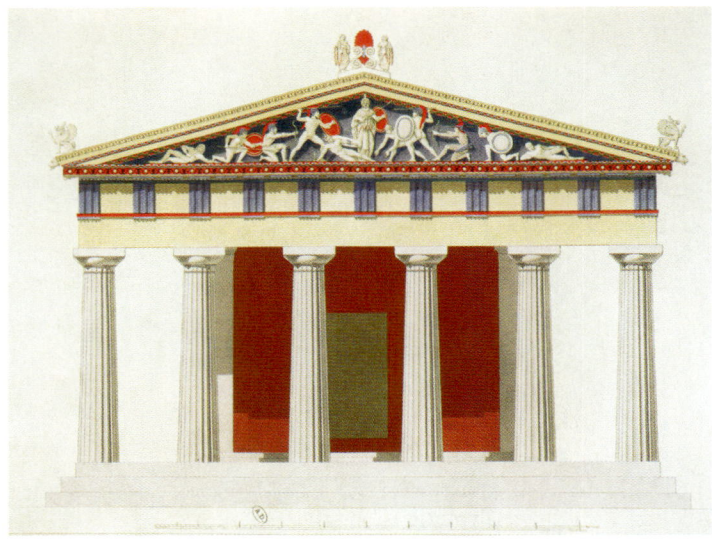

**5-26** GUILLAUME-ABEL BLOUET, restored view (1828) of the facade of the Temple of Aphaia, Aegina, Greece, ca. 500–490 BCE.

The restored view suggests how colorful Greek temples were. The designer solved the problem of composing figures in a pediment by using the whole range of body postures from upright to prostrate.

single row of columns down the center of the cella is a double colonnade—and each row has two stories. This arrangement allowed a statue to be placed on the central axis and also gave worshipers gathered in front of the building an unobstructed view through the pair of columns in the pronaos.

Painted life-size statuary (FIG. **5-26**) filled both pediments, in contrast to the high reliefs characteristic of most Archaic temple pediments. The theme of both statuary groups was the battle of Greeks and Trojans, but the sculptors depicted different episodes. The compositions were nonetheless almost identical, with Athena at the center of the bloody combat. She is larger than all the other figures because she is superhuman, but all the mortal heroes are the same size, regardless of the statue's position in the pediment. Unlike the experimental design at Corfu (FIG. **5-16**), the Aegina pediments feature a unified theme and consistent scale. The designer was able to keep the size of the figures constant by using the whole range of body postures from upright (Athena) to leaning, falling, kneeling, and lying (Greeks and Trojans).

The Aegina sculptors set the pedimental statues in place around 490 BCE, as soon as construction of the temple concluded. Many scholars believe the statues at the eastern end were damaged and replaced with a new group a decade or two later, although some think both groups date after 480 BCE. In either case, it is instructive to

compare the eastern and western figures. The sculptor of the west pediment's dying warrior (FIG. **5-27**) still conceived the statue in the Archaic mode. The warrior's torso is rigidly frontal, and he looks out directly at the spectator—with his face set in an Archaic smile despite the bronze arrow that punctures his chest. He is like a mannequin in a store window whose arms and legs have been arranged by someone else for effective display. There is no sense whatsoever of a thinking and feeling human being.

The comparable figure (FIG. **5-28**) in the east pediment is radically different. This warrior's posture is more natural and more complex, with the torso placed at an angle to the viewer (compare FIG. 5-22). Moreover, he reacts to his wound as a flesh-and-blood human would. He knows that death is inevitable, but he still struggles to rise once again, using his shield for support. He does not look out at the spectator. This dying warrior is concerned with his plight, not with the viewer. No more than a decade separates the two statues, but they belong to different eras. The eastern warrior is not a creation of the Archaic world, when sculptors imposed anatomical patterns (and smiles) on statues. This statue belongs to the Classical world, where statues move as humans move and possess the self-consciousness of real men and women. This constitutes a radical change in the conception of the nature of statuary. In sculpture, as in painting, the Classical revolution had occurred.

## EARLY AND HIGH CLASSICAL PERIODS

Art historians date the beginning of the Classical* age from a historical event: the defeat of the Persian invaders of Greece by the allied Hellenic city-states. Shortly after the Persians occupied and

*Note: In *Art through the Ages,* the adjective "Classical," with uppercase *C,* refers specifically to the Classical period of ancient Greece, 480–323 BCE. Lowercase "classical" refers to Greco-Roman antiquity in general, that is, the period treated in Chapters 5, 6, and 7.

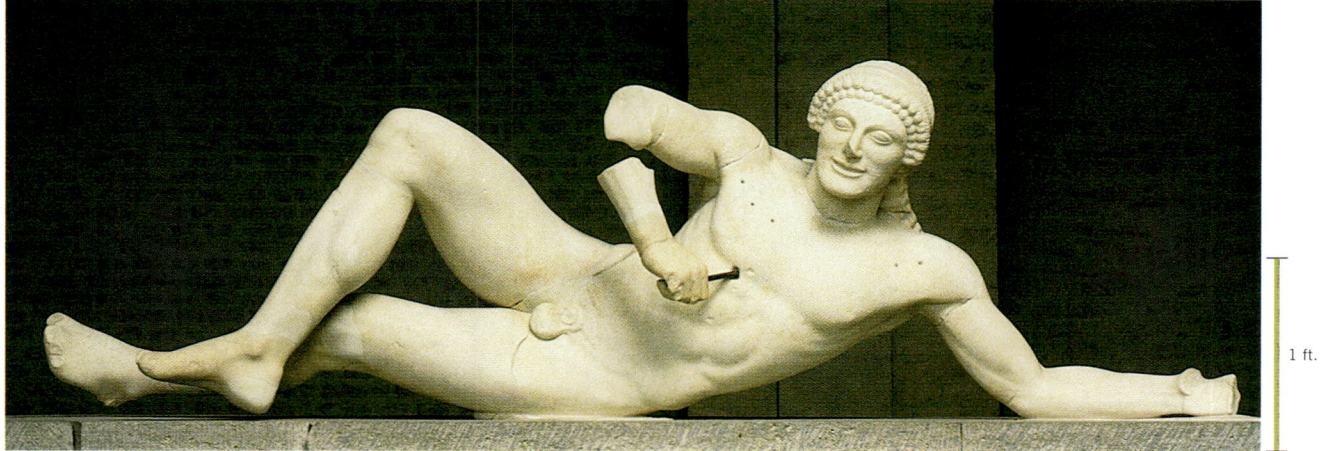

**5-27** Dying warrior, from the west pediment of the Temple of Aphaia, Aegina, Greece, ca. 490 BCE. Marble, 5′ 2½″ long. Glyptothek, Munich.

The statues of the west pediment of the early-fifth-century BCE temple at Aegina exhibit Archaic features. This fallen warrior still has a rigidly frontal torso and an Archaic smile.

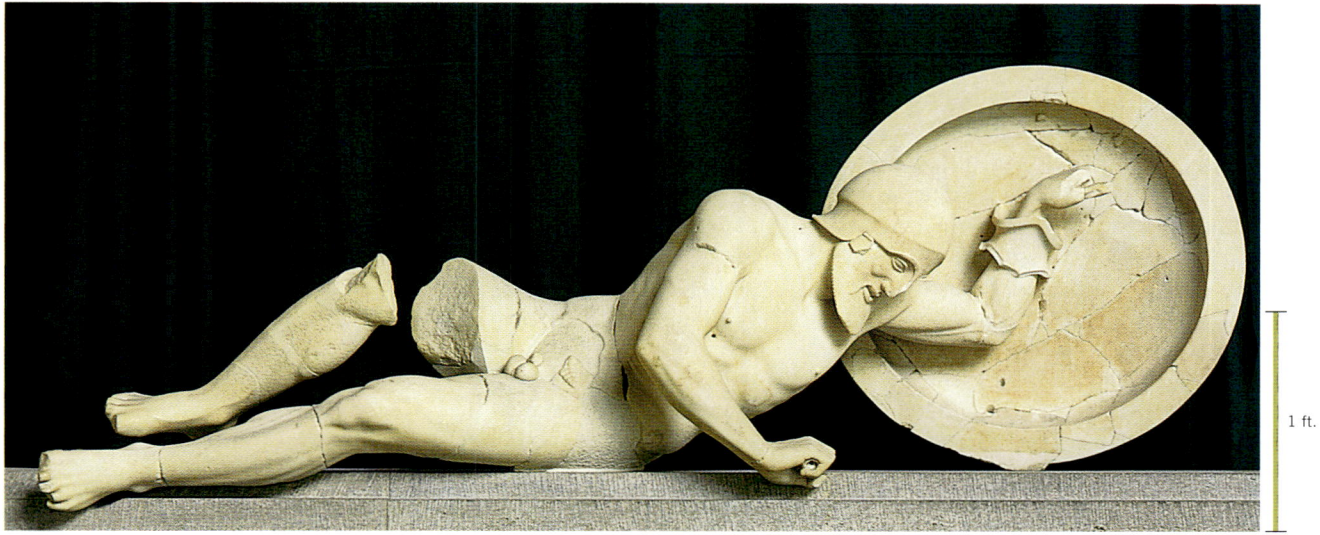

**5-28** Dying warrior, from the east pediment of the Temple of Aphaia, Aegina, Greece, ca. 480 BCE. Marble, 6′ 1″ long. Glyptothek, Munich.

The eastern dying warrior already belongs to the Classical era. His posture is more natural, and he exhibits a new self-consciousness. Concerned with his own pain, he does not face the viewer.

sacked Athens in 480 BCE, the Greeks won a decisive naval victory over the Persians at Salamis. It had been a difficult war, and at times it appeared Asia would swallow up Greece and the Persian king Xerxes (see Chapter 2) would rule over all. When the Persians destroyed the Greek city Miletos in 494 BCE, they killed the male inhabitants and sold the women and children into slavery. The narrow escape of the Greeks from domination by Asian "barbarians" nurtured a sense of Hellenic identity so strong that from then on the history of European civilization would be distinct from the civilization of Asia, even though they continued to interact. Typical of the time were the views of the great dramatist Aeschylus, who celebrated, in his *Oresteia* trilogy, the triumph of reason and law over barbarous crimes, blood feuds, and mad vengeance. As a veteran himself of the epic battle of Marathon, Aeschylus repudiated in majestic verse all the slavish and inhuman traits of nature the Greeks at that time of crisis associated with the Persians.

## Architecture and Architectural Sculpture

The decades following the removal of the Persian threat are universally considered the high point of Greek civilization. This is the era of the dramatists Sophocles and Euripides, as well as Aeschylus; the historian Herodotus; the statesman Pericles; the philosopher Socrates; and many of the most famous Greek architects, sculptors, and painters.

**TEMPLE OF ZEUS, OLYMPIA** The first great monument of Classical art and architecture is the Temple of Zeus at Olympia, site of the Olympic Games. The architect was LIBON OF ELIS, who began work on the temple about 470 BCE and completed it by 457 BCE. Today, the structure is in ruins, its picturesque tumbled column drums an eloquent reminder of the effect of the passage of time on even the grandest monuments humans have built. A good idea of its original appearance can be gleaned, however,

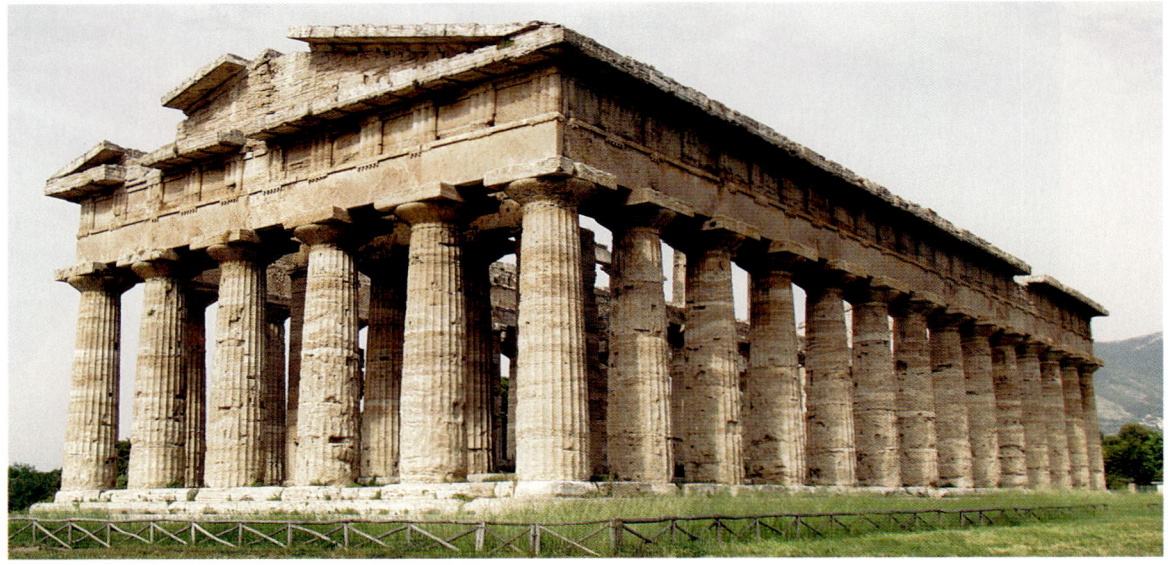

The model for the second Hera(?) temple at Paestum was Libon's Zeus temple at Olympia. The Paestum temple reflects the Olympia design but lacks the pedimental sculpture of its model.

from a slightly later Doric temple (FIG. 5-29) modeled closely on the Olympian shrine of Zeus—the temple usually identified as the second Temple of Hera at Paestum but possibly a temple dedicated to Apollo. The plans and elevations of both temples follow the pattern of the Temple of Aphaia (FIG. 5-25) at Aegina: an even number of columns (six) on the short ends, two columns in antis, and two rows of columns in two stories inside the cella. But the Temple of Zeus was more lavishly decorated than even the Aphaia temple. Statues filled both pediments, and narrative reliefs adorned the six metopes over the doorway in the pronaos and the matching six of the opisthodomos.

The subject of the Temple of Zeus's east pediment (FIG. 5-30) is the chariot race between Pelops (from whom the Peloponnesos region takes its name) and King Oinomaos. The story, which had deep local significance, is a sinister one. Oinomaos had one daughter, Hippodameia, and a prophecy foretold that he would die if she married. Consequently, Oinomaos challenged any suitor who wished to make Hippodameia his bride to a chariot race from Olympia to Corinth. If the suitor won, he also won the hand of the king's daughter. But if he lost, Oinomaos killed him. The outcome of each race was predetermined, because Oinomaos possessed the divine horses of his father Ares. To ensure his victory when all others had failed, Pelops resorted to bribing the king's groom, Myrtilos, to rig the royal chariot so that it would collapse during the race. Oinomaos was killed and Pelops won his bride, but he drowned

Myrtilos rather than pay his debt to him. Before he died, Myrtilos brought a curse on Pelops and his descendants. This curse led to the murder of Pelops's son Atreus and to events that figure prominently in some of the greatest Greek tragedies of the Classical era, Aeschylus's three plays known collectively as the *Oresteia*: the sacrifice by Atreus's son Agamemnon of his daughter Iphigeneia; the slaying of Agamemnon by Aegisthus, lover of Agamemnon's wife Clytaemnestra; and the murder of Aegisthus and Clytaemnestra by Orestes, the son of Agamemnon and Clytaemnestra.

Indeed, the pedimental statues (FIG. 5-30), which faced toward the starting point of all Olympic chariot races, are posed as if actors on a stage—Zeus in the center, Oinomaos and his wife on one side, Pelops and Hippodameia on the other, and their respective chariots to each side. All are quiet. The horrible events known to every spectator have yet to occur. Only one man reacts—a seer (FIG. 5-31) who knows the future. He is a remarkable figure. Unlike the gods, heroes, and noble youths and maidens who are the almost exclusive subjects of Archaic and Classical Greek statuary, this seer is a rare depiction of old age. He has a balding, wrinkled head and sagging musculature—and a shocked expression on his face. This is a true show of emotion, unlike the stereotypical Archaic smile, without precedent in earlier Greek sculpture and not a regular feature of Greek art until the Hellenistic age.

In the west pediment, Apollo (FIG. 5-32), the central figure, is also at rest, but all around him is a chaotic scene of Greeks battling

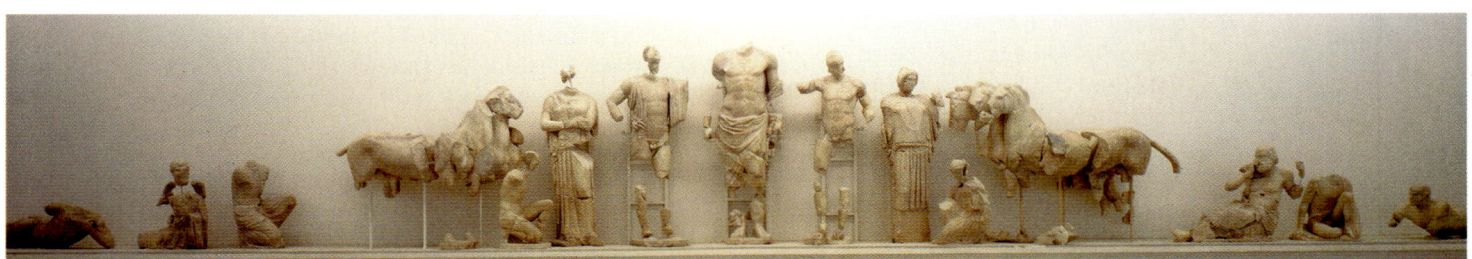

10 ft.

**5-30** Chariot race of Pelops and Oinomaos, east pediment, Temple of Zeus, Olympia, Greece, ca. 470–456 BCE. Marble, 87′ wide. Archaeological Museum, Olympia.

The east pediment of the Zeus temple depicts the legendary chariot race across the Peloponnesos from Olympia to Corinth. The actors in the pediment faced the starting point of Olympic chariot races.

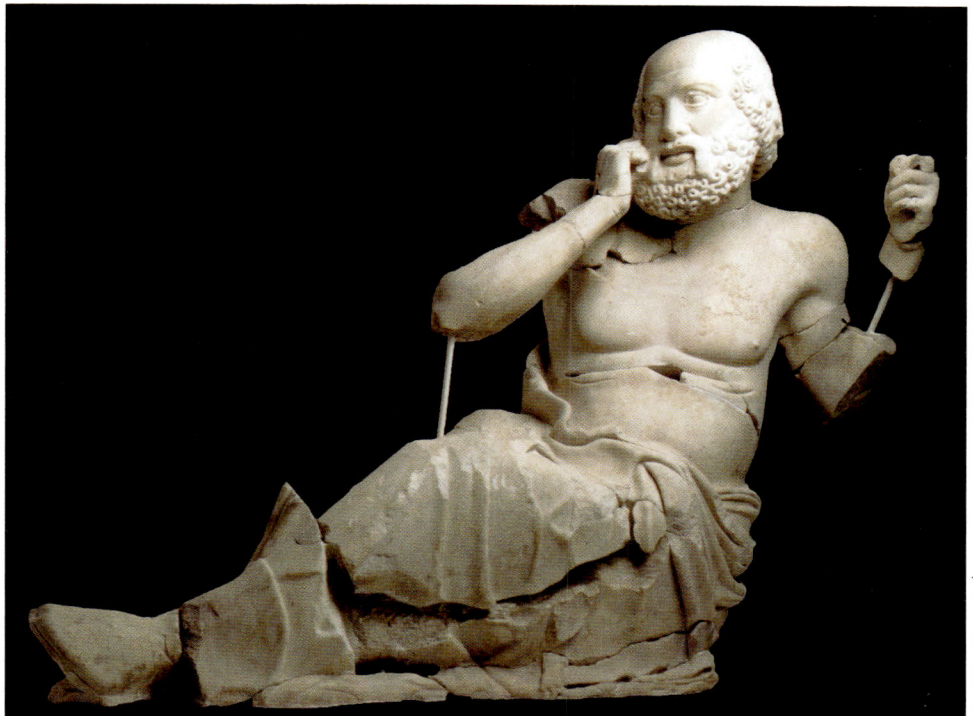

**5-31** Seer, from the east pediment (FIG. 5-30) of the Temple of Zeus, Olympia, Greece, ca. 470–456 BCE. Marble, 4′ 6″ high. Archaeological Museum, Olympia.

The balding seer in the Olympia east pediment is a rare depiction of old age in Classical sculpture. He has a shocked expression because he foresees the tragic outcome of the chariot race.

1 ft.

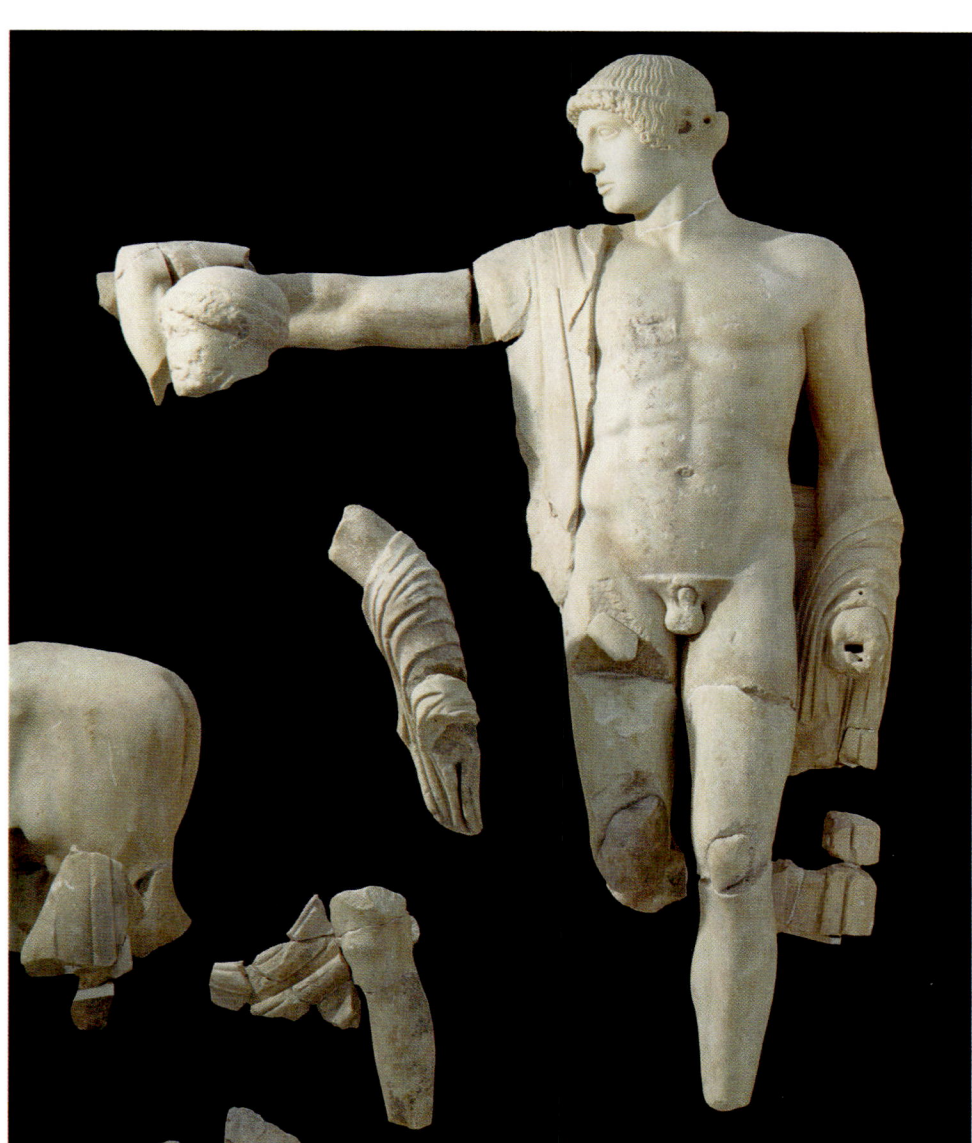

**5-32** Apollo, from the west pediment (FIG. 5-32A) of the Temple of Zeus, Olympia, Greece, ca. 470–456 BCE. Marble, restored height 10′ 8″. Archaeological Museum, Olympia.

The epitome of calm rationality, Apollo, with a commanding gesture of his right hand, attempts to bring order out of the chaotic struggle all around him between the Lapiths and the beastly centaurs.

1 ft.

Early and High Classical Periods     **127**

## Herakles, Greatest of Greek Heroes

Greek heroes were a class of mortals intermediate between ordinary humans and the immortal gods. Most often the children of gods, some were great warriors, such as Achilles and Ajax (FIG. 5-20) and others who fought at Troy and were celebrated in Homer's epic poems. Some heroes went from one fabulous adventure to another, ridding the world of monsters and generally benefiting humankind. Perseus, for example, was the slayer of the hideous Medusa (FIG. 5-16). Bellerophon killed the chimera (FIG. 6-12), a composite lion-goat-serpent beast. Many heroes were worshiped after their deaths, especially in the cities with which they were most closely associated.

The greatest Greek hero was Herakles (the Roman Hercules), who may be the subject of one of the earliest preserved works of Greek narrative art—the bronze figure (FIG. 5-3) depicting a hero battling a centaur. Born in Thebes, Herakles was the son of Zeus and Alkmene, a mortal woman. Zeus's jealous wife Hera hated Herakles and sent two serpents to attack him in his cradle, but the infant strangled them. Later, Hera caused the hero to go mad and to kill his wife and children. As punishment, he was condemned to perform 12 great labors. In the first, he defeated the legendary lion of Nemea and ever after wore its pelt. The lion's skin and his weapon, a club, are Herakles' distinctive attributes (FIGS. 5-63A and 5-66). His last task was to obtain the golden apples the goddess Gaia gave to Hera at her marriage (FIG. 5-33). They grew from a tree in the garden of the Hesperides at the western edge of the ocean, where a dragon guarded them. After completion of the 12 seemingly impossible tasks, Herakles was awarded immortality. Athena, who had watched over him carefully throughout his life and assisted him in performing the labors, introduced him into the realm of the gods on Mount Olympus.

The legendary strongman was the model for many Greek athletes. In fact, the Greeks believed Herakles was the founder of the Olympic Games.

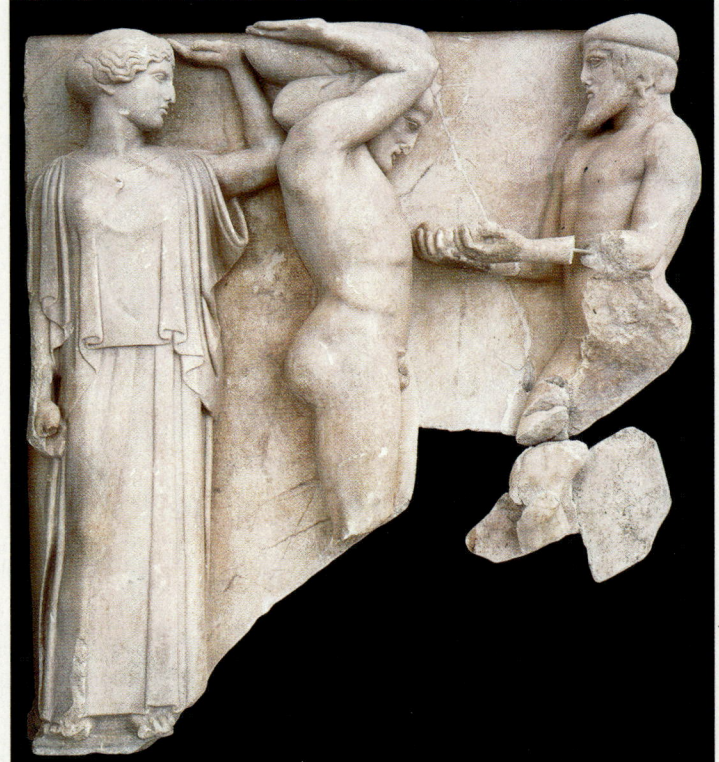

**5-33** Athena, Herakles, and Atlas with the apples of the Hesperides, metope from the Temple of Zeus, Olympia, Greece, ca. 470–456 BCE. Marble, 5' 3" high. Archaeological Museum, Olympia.

Herakles founded the Olympic Games, and his 12 labors were the subjects of the 12 metopes of the Zeus temple. This one shows the hero holding up the world (with Athena's aid) for Atlas.

1 ft.

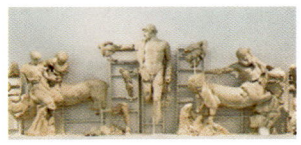

**5-32A** West pediment, Temple of Zeus, Olympia, ca. 470–456 BCE.

centaurs (FIG. 5-32A). A mixture of calm, even pensive, figures and others involved in violent action also characterizes the narrative reliefs of the 12 metopes of the Zeus temple. They are thematically connected with Olympia, for they depict the 12 labors of Herakles (see "Herakles, Greatest of Greek Heroes," above), the legendary founder of the Olympic Games. In the metope illustrated here (FIG. 5-33), Herakles holds up the sky (with the aid of the goddess Athena—and a cushion) in place of Atlas, who had undertaken the dangerous journey to fetch the golden apples of the Hesperides for the hero. Herakles will soon transfer the load back to Atlas (at the right, still holding the apples), but now each of the very high relief figures in the metope stands quietly with the same serene dignity as the statues in the east pediment (FIG. 5-30) and Apollo (FIG. 5-32) in the west pediment. In both attitude and dress (simple Doric peploi for the women), these Olympia figures display a severity that contrasts sharply with the smiling and elaborately clad fig-

ures of the Late Archaic period. Consequently, many art historians call this Early Classical phase of Greek art the *Severe Style*.

## Statuary

The hallmark of Early Classical statuary is the abandonment of the rigid and unnatural Egyptian-inspired pose of Archaic statues. The figures in the Olympia pediments exemplify this radical break with earlier practice, but the change occurred even earlier—at the very moment Greece was under attack by the Persians.

**KRITIOS BOY** Although it is well under life-size, the marble statue known as the *Kritios Boy* (FIG. 5-34)—because art historians once thought it was the work of the sculptor Kritios—is one of the most important statues in the history of art. Never before had a sculptor been concerned with portraying how a human being (as opposed to a stone image) truly stands. Real people do not stand in the stiff-legged pose of the kouroi and korai or their Egyptian predecessors. Humans shift their weight and the position of the torso around the vertical (but flexible) axis of the spine. When

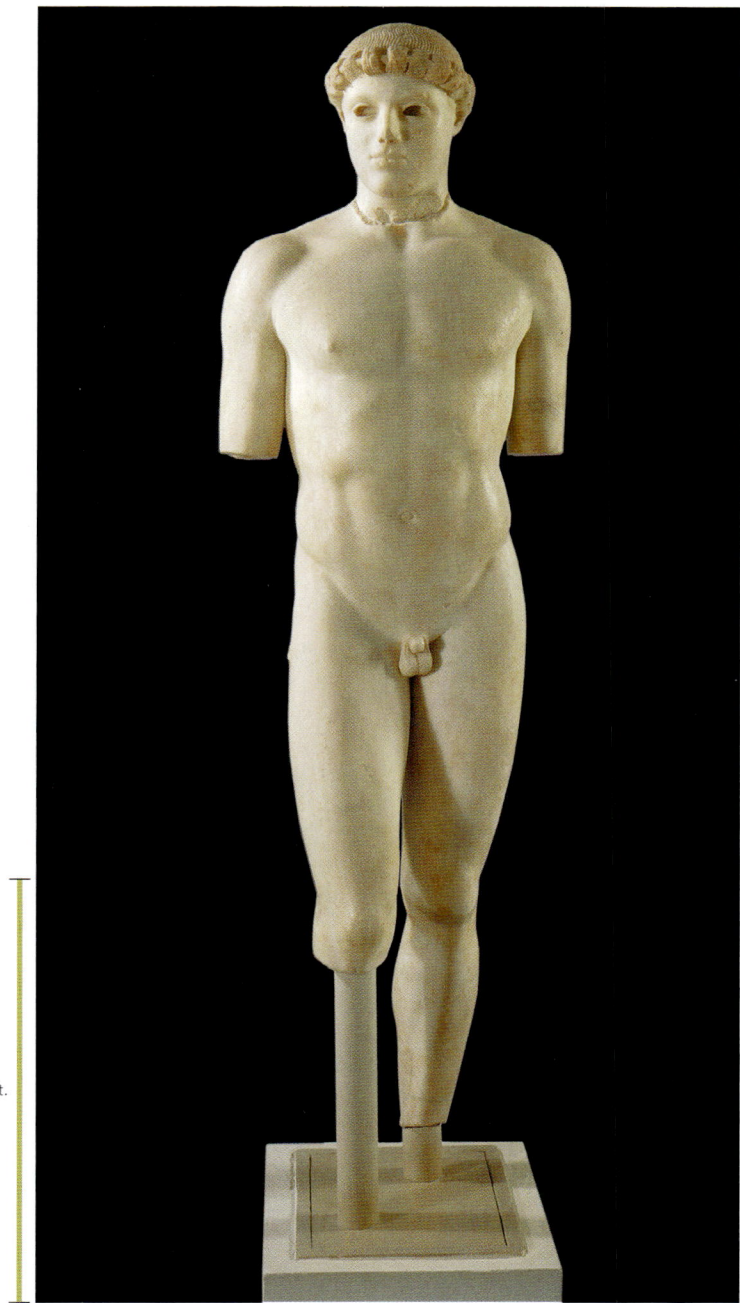

1 ft.

**5-34** *Kritios Boy,* from the Acropolis, Athens, Greece, ca. 480 BCE. Marble, 2′ 10″ high. Acropolis Museum, Athens.

This is the first statue to show how a person naturally stands. The sculptor depicted the weight shift from one leg to the other (contrapposto). The head turns slightly, and the Archaic smile is gone.

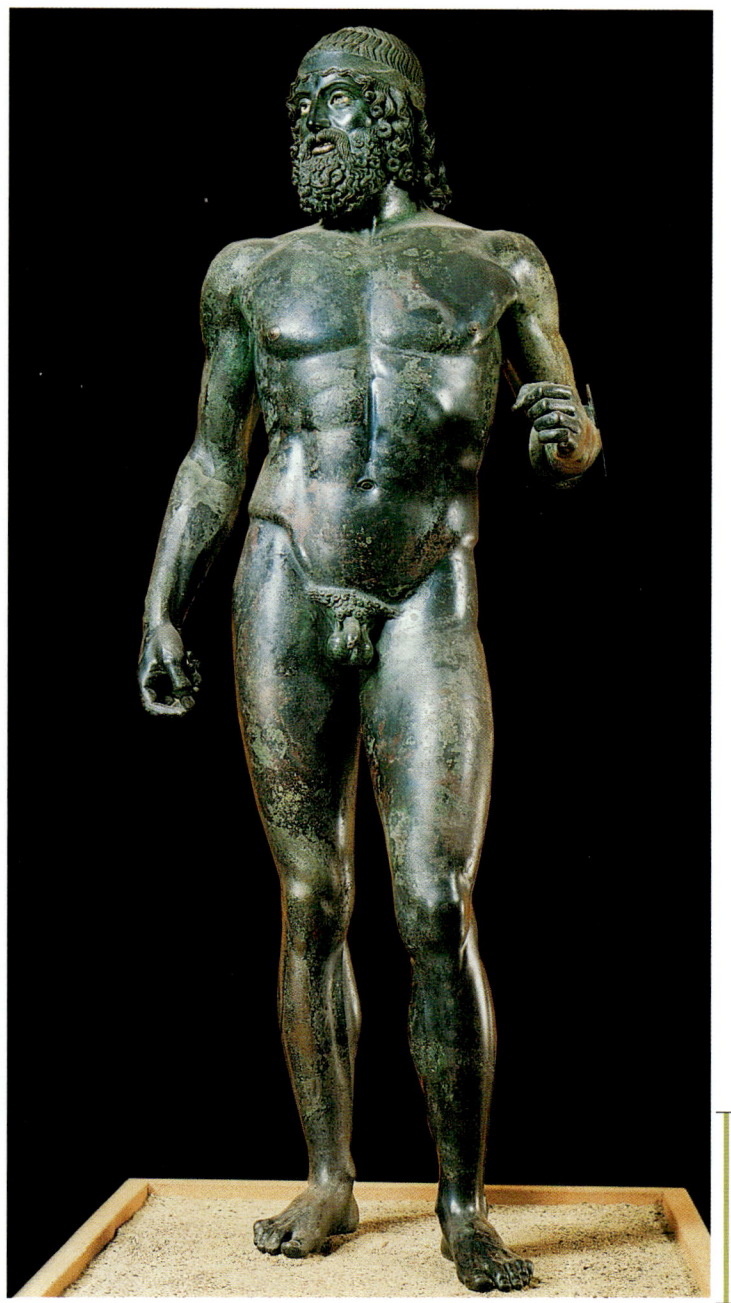

1 ft.

**5-35** Warrior, from the sea off Riace, Italy, ca. 460–450 BCE. Bronze, 6′ 6″ high. Museo Archeologico Nazionale, Reggio Calabria.

The bronze Riace warrior statue has inlaid eyes, silver teeth and eyelashes, and copper lips and nipples (FIG. I-17). The contrapposto is more pronounced than in the *Kritios Boy* (FIG. 5-34).

humans move, the body's elastic musculoskeletal structure dictates a harmonious, smooth motion of all its parts. The sculptor of the *Kritios Boy* was the first, or one of the first, to grasp this anatomical fact and to represent it in statuary. The youth has a slight dip to the right hip, indicating the shifting of weight onto his left leg. His right leg is bent, at ease. The head also turns slightly to the right and tilts, breaking the unwritten rule of frontality dictating the form of virtually all earlier statues. This weight shift, which art historians describe as *contrapposto* (counterbalance), separates Classical from Archaic Greek statuary.

**RIACE WARRIOR** An unknown sculptor carried the innovations of the *Kritios Boy* even further in the bronze statue (FIG. **5-35**) of a warrior found in the sea near Riace at the "toe" of the Italian "boot." It is one of a pair of statues divers accidentally discovered in the cargo of a ship that sank in antiquity on its way from Greece probably to Rome, where Greek sculpture was much admired. Known as the Riace Bronzes, the two statues had to undergo several years of cleaning and restoration after nearly two millennia of submersion in salt water, but they are nearly intact. The statue shown here lacks only its shield, spear, and helmet. It is a masterpiece of

Early and High Classical Periods **129**

## Hollow-Casting Life-Size Bronze Statues

Monumental bronze statues such as the Riace warrior (FIG. 5-35), the Delphi charioteer (FIG. 5-37), and the Artemision god (FIG. 5-38) required great technical skill to produce. They could not be manufactured using a single simple mold of the sort Geometric and Archaic sculptors used for their small-scale figures (FIGS. 5-3 and 5-4). Weight, cost, and the tendency of large masses of bronze to distort when cooling made life-size castings in solid bronze impractical, if not impossible. Instead, the Greeks hollow-cast large statues by the *cire perdue* (*lost-wax*) method. The lost-wax process entailed several steps and had to be repeated many times, because sculptors typically cast monumental statues in parts—head, arms, hands, torso, and so forth.

First the sculptor fashioned a full-size clay model of the intended statue. Then an assistant formed a clay master mold around the model and removed the mold in sections. When dry, the various pieces of the master mold were reassembled for each separate body part. Next, assistants applied a layer of beeswax to the inside of each mold. When the wax cooled, the sculptor removed the mold, revealing a hollow wax model in the shape of the original clay model. The artist could then correct or refine details—for example, engrave fingernails on the wax hands or individual locks of hair on the head.

In the next stage, an assistant applied a final clay mold (*investment*) to the exterior of the wax model and poured liquid clay inside the model. Apprentices then hammered metal pins (*chaplets*)

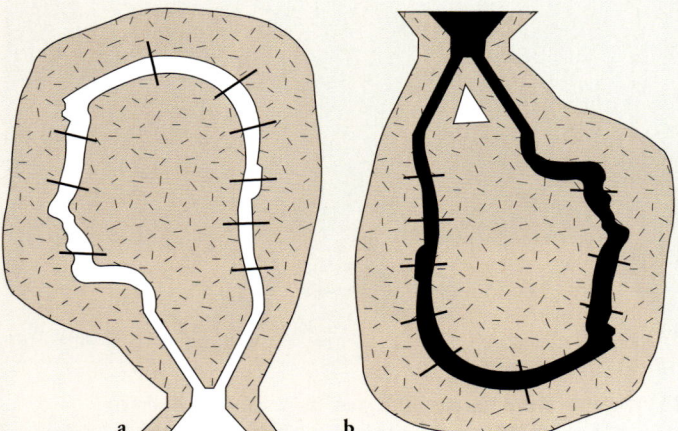

**5-36** Two stages of the lost-wax method of bronze casting (after Sean A. Hemingway).

Drawing *a* shows a clay mold (investment), wax model, and clay core connected by chaplets. Drawing *b* shows the wax melted out and the molten bronze poured into the mold to form the cast bronze head.

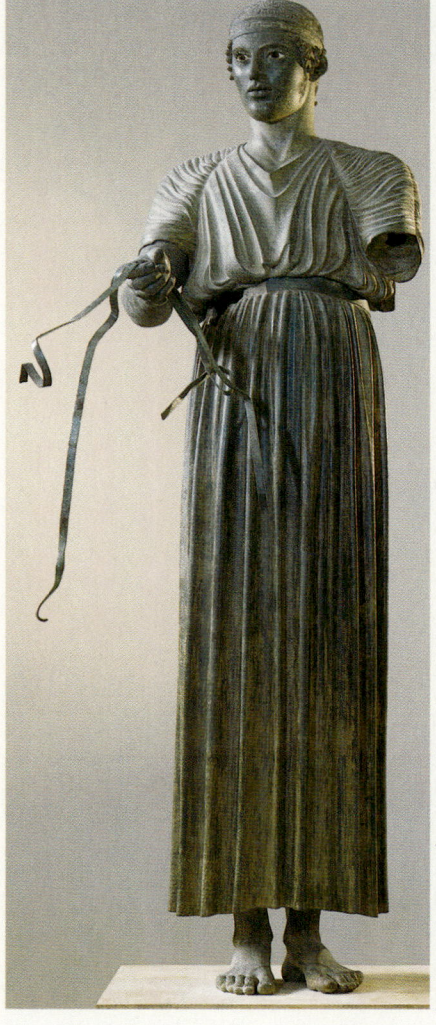

**5-37** Charioteer, from a group dedicated by Polyzalos of Gela in the Sanctuary of Apollo (FIG. 5-17A), Delphi, Greece, ca. 470 BCE. Bronze, 5′ 11″ high. Archaeological Museum, Delphi.

The charioteer was part of a large bronze group that also included a chariot, a team of horses, and a groom. The assemblage required hundreds of individually cast pieces soldered together.

1 ft.

through the new mold to connect the investment with the clay core (FIG. 5-36*a*). Next, the wax was melted out ("lost") and molten bronze poured into the mold in its place (FIG. 5-36*b*). When the bronze hardened and assumed the shape of the wax model, the bronze-caster removed the investment and as much of the core as possible, completing the hollow-casting process. The last step was to fit together and solder the individually cast pieces, smooth the joins and any surface imperfections, inlay the eyes, and add teeth, eyelashes, and accessories such as spears and wreaths. Life-size bronze statues produced in this way were very costly but highly prized.

hollow-casting (see "Hollow-Casting Life-Size Bronze Statues," above, and FIG. **5-36**), with inlaid eyes, silver teeth and eyelashes, and copper lips and nipples (FIG. I-17). The weight shift is more pronounced than in the *Kritios Boy*. The warrior's head turns more forcefully to the right, his shoulders tilt, his hips swing more markedly, and his arms have been freed from the body. Natural motion in space has replaced Archaic frontality and rigidity.

**CHARIOTEER OF DELPHI** A bronze statuary group that equals or exceeds the Riace warrior in technical quality is the chariot group set up a decade or two earlier by the tyrant Polyzalos of Gela (Sicily) to commemorate his victory in the Pythian Games at Delphi (FIG. 5-17A). Almost all that remains of the large group composed of Polyzalos's driver, the chariot, the team of horses, and a young groom is the bronze charioteer (FIG. **5-37**). He stands in an almost Archaic

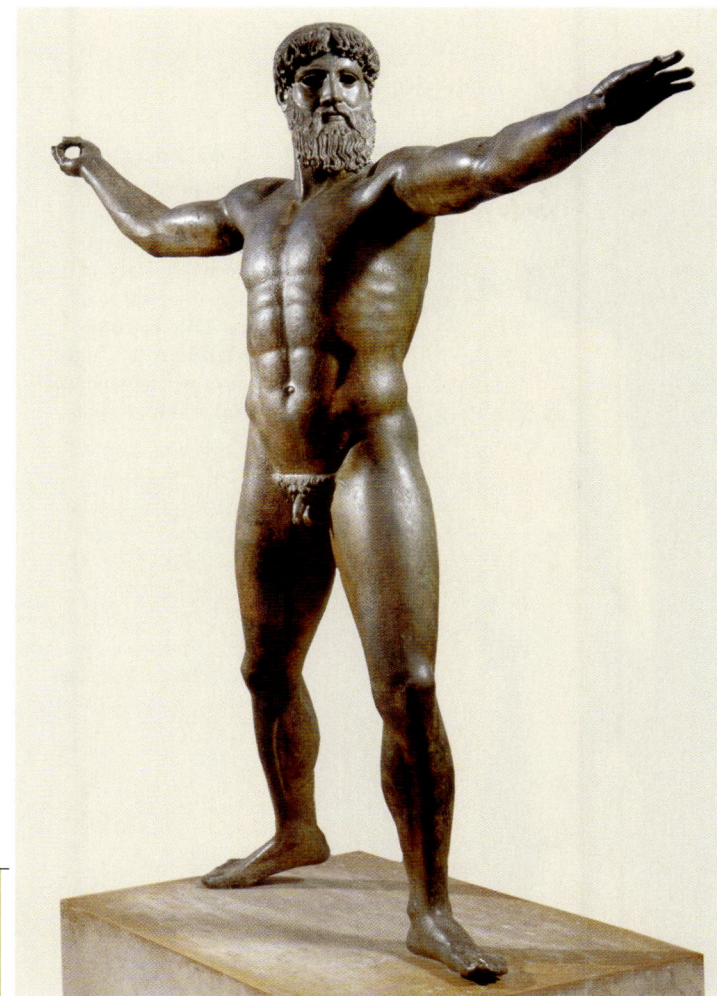

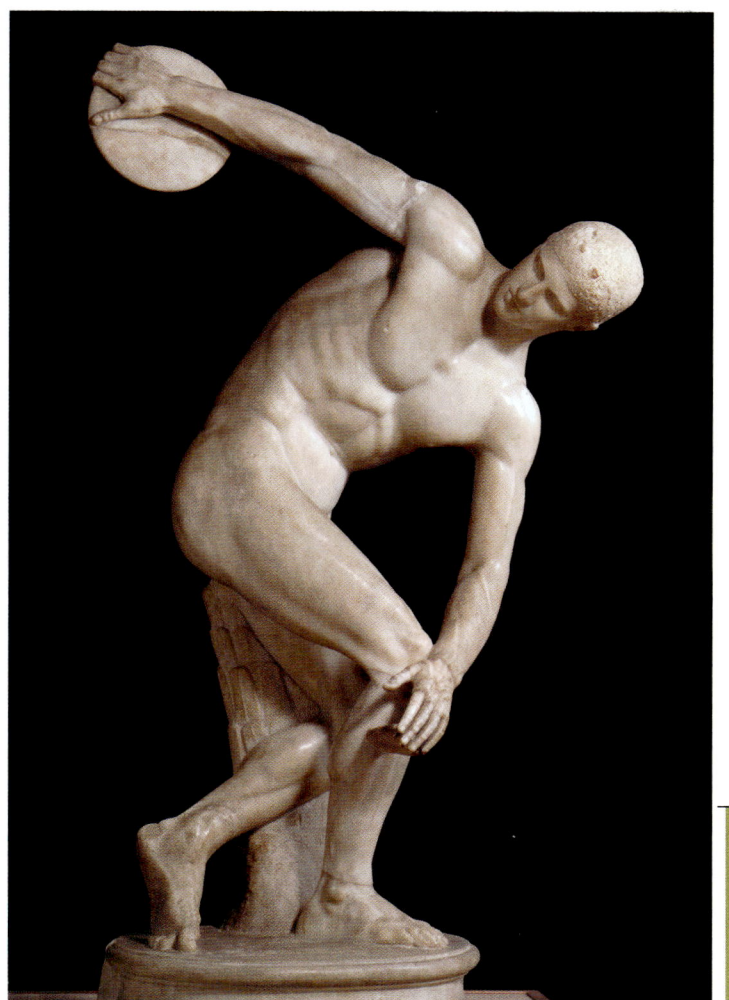

1 ft.

1 ft.

**5-38** Zeus (or Poseidon?), from the sea off Cape Artemision, Greece, ca. 460–450 BCE. Bronze, 6′ 10″ high. National Archaeological Museum, Athens.

In this statue, the god—probably Zeus hurling a thunderbolt—boldly extends both arms and raises his right heel off the ground, underscoring the lightness and stability of hollow-cast bronze statues.

**5-39** MYRON, *Diskobolos* (*Discus Thrower*). Roman copy of a bronze statue of ca. 450 BCE. Marble, 5′ 1″ high. Museo Nazionale Romano—Palazzo Massimo alle Terme.

This marble copy of Myron's lost bronze statue captures how the sculptor froze the action of discus throwing and arranged the nude athlete's body and limbs so they form two intersecting arcs.

pose, but the turn of the head and feet in opposite directions as well as a slight twist at the waist are in keeping with the Severe Style. The moment the sculptor chose for depiction was not during the frenetic race but after, when the driver modestly held his horses quietly in the winner's circle. The charioteer grasps the reins in his outstretched right hand (the lower left arm, cast separately, is missing), and he wears the standard charioteer's garment, girdled high and held in at the shoulders and the back to keep it from flapping. The folds emphasize both the verticality and calm of the figure and recall the flutes of a Greek column. The fillet that holds the charioteer's hair in place is inlaid with silver. The eyes are glass paste, shaded by delicate bronze lashes individually cut from a sheet of bronze and soldered to the head.

**ARTEMISION ZEUS** The male human form in motion is, in contrast, the subject of another Early Classical bronze statue (FIG. **5-38**), which, like the Riace warrior, divers found in an ancient shipwreck, this time off the coast of Greece itself at Cape Artemision. The bearded god once hurled a weapon held in his right hand, probably a thunderbolt, in which case he is Zeus. A less likely suggestion is that this is Poseidon with his trident (see "Gods and Goddesses," page 107). The pose could be employed equally well for

a javelin thrower. Both arms are boldly extended, and the right heel is raised off the ground, underscoring the lightness and stability of hollow-cast monumental statues.

**MYRON, *DISKOBOLOS*** A bronze statue similar to the Artemision Zeus was the renowned *Diskobolos* (*Discus Thrower*) by the Early Classical master MYRON. The original is lost. Only marble copies (FIG. **5-39**) survive, made in Roman times, when demand so far exceeded the supply of Greek statues that a veritable industry was born to meet the call for Greek statuary to display in public places and private villas alike. Usually, the copies were of less costly painted marble, which presented a very different appearance from shiny bronze. In most cases, the copyist also had to add an intrusive tree trunk to support the great weight of the stone statue and to place struts between arms and body to strengthen weak points. The copies rarely approach the quality of the originals, and the Roman sculptors sometimes took liberties with their models according to their own tastes and needs. Occasionally, for example, sculptors created a mirror image of the original for a specific setting. Nevertheless, the copies are indispensable today. Without them it would be impossible to reconstruct the history of Greek sculpture after the Archaic period.

# Polykleitos's Prescription for the Perfect Statue

One of the most influential philosophers of the ancient world was Pythagoras of Samos, who lived during the latter part of the sixth century BCE. A famous geometric theorem still bears his name. Pythagoras also is said to have discovered that harmonic chords in music are produced on the strings of a lyre at regular intervals that may be expressed as ratios of whole numbers—for example, 2:1, 3:2, 4:3. He and his followers, the Pythagoreans, believed more generally that underlying harmonic proportions could be found in all of nature, determining the form of the cosmos as well as of things on earth, and that beauty resided in harmonious numerical ratios.

By this reasoning, a perfect statue would be one constructed according to an all-encompassing mathematical formula. In the mid-fifth century BCE, the sculptor Polykleitos of Argos set out to make just such a statue (FIG. 5-40). He recorded the principles he followed and the proportions he used in a treatise titled the *Canon*, that is, the standard of perfection. His treatise is unfortunately lost, but Galen, a physician who lived during the second century CE, summarized the sculptor's philosophy as follows:

> [Beauty arises from] the commensurability [*symmetria*] of the parts, such as that of finger to finger, and of all the fingers to the palm and the wrist, and of these to the forearm, and of the forearm to the upper arm, and, in fact, of everything to everything else, just as it is written in the *Canon* of Polykleitos. . . . Polykleitos supported his treatise [by making] a statue according to the tenets of his treatise, and called the statue, like the work, the *Canon*.*

This is why Pliny the Elder, whose first-century CE multivolume *Natural History* is one of the most important sources for the history of Greek art, maintained that Polykleitos "alone of men is deemed to have rendered art itself [that is, the theoretical basis of art] in a work of art."†

Polykleitos's belief that a successful statue resulted from the precise application of abstract principles is reflected in an anecdote (probably a later invention) told by the Roman historian Aelian:

> Polykleitos made two statues at the same time, one which would be pleasing to the crowd and the other according to the principles of his art. In accordance with the opinion of each person who came into his workshop, he altered something and changed its form, submitting to the advice of each. Then he put both statues on display. The one was marvelled at by everyone, and the other was laughed at. Thereupon Polykleitos said, "But the one that you find fault with, you made yourselves; while the one that you marvel at, I made."‡

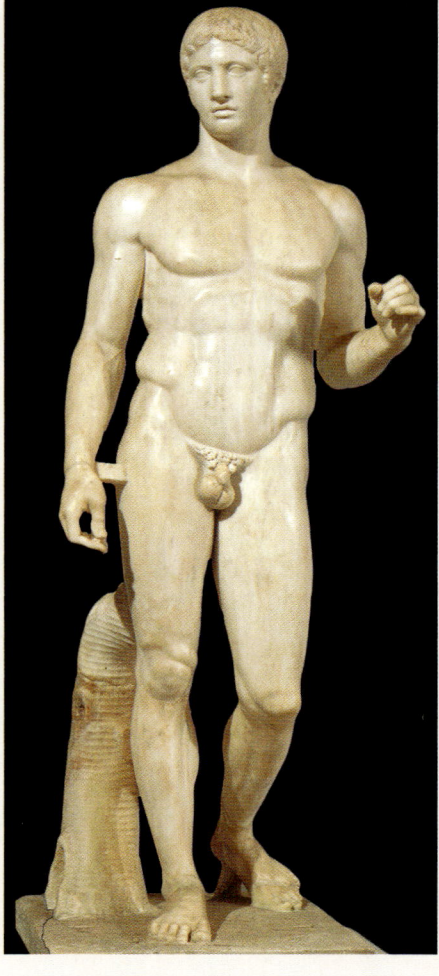

**5-40** POLYKLEITOS, *Doryphoros* (*Spear Bearer*). Roman copy from the palaestra, Pompeii, Italy, of a bronze statue of ca. 450–440 BCE. Marble, 6′ 11″ high. Museo Archeologico Nazionale, Naples.

Polykleitos sought to portray the perfect man and to impose order on human movement. He achieved his goals through harmonic proportions and a system of cross balance for all parts of the body. ◼

1 ft.

Galen, Pliny, and Aelian are only three of the many Greek and Roman authors who wrote about Greek art and artists. Although none of those writers was an art historian in the modern sense, the existence in the Greco-Roman world of theoretical treatises by artists and of a tradition of art criticism is noteworthy and without parallel in antiquity or during the Middle Ages.

*Galen, *De placitis Hippocratis et Platonis*, 5. Translated by J. J. Pollitt, *The Art of Ancient Greece: Sources and Documents* (New York: Cambridge University Press, 1990), 76.
†Pliny the Elder, *Natural History*, 34.55. Translated by Pollitt, 75.
‡Aelian, *Varia historia*, 14.8. Translated by Pollitt, 79.

---

Myron's *Discus Thrower* is a vigorous action statue, like the Artemision Zeus, but the sculptor posed the body in an almost Archaic manner, with profile limbs and a nearly frontal chest, suggesting the tension of a coiled spring. Like the arm of a pendulum clock, the right arm of the *Diskobolos* has reached the apex of its arc but has not yet begun to swing down again. Myron froze the action and arranged the body and limbs to form two intersecting arcs (one from the discus to the left hand, one from the head to the right knee), creating the impression of a tightly stretched bow a moment

before the archer releases the string. This tension, however, is not mirrored in the athlete's face, which remains expressionless. Once again, as in the warrior statue (FIG. 5-28) from the Aegina east pediment, the head is turned away from the spectator. In contrast to Archaic athlete statues, the Classical *Diskobolos* does not perform for the spectator but concentrates on the task at hand.

**POLYKLEITOS, *DORYPHOROS*** One of the most frequently copied Greek statues was the *Doryphoros* (*Spear Bearer*) by

POLYKLEITOS, the sculptor whose work epitomizes the intellectual rigor of Classical art. The best marble replica (FIG. 5-40) stood in a *palaestra* (gymnasium) at Pompeii, where it served as a model for Roman athletes. The *Doryphoros* was the embodiment of Polykleitos's vision of the ideal statue of a nude male athlete or warrior. (The *Spear Bearer* may also have held a shield.) In fact, the sculptor made it as a demonstration piece to accompany a treatise on the subject. *Spear Bearer* is a modern descriptive title for the statue. The name Polykleitos assigned to it was *Canon* (see "Polykleitos's Prescription for the Perfect Statue," page 132).

The *Doryphoros* is the culmination of the evolution in Greek statuary from the Archaic kouros to the *Kritios Boy* to the *Riace* warrior. The contrapposto is more pronounced than ever before in a standing statue, but Polykleitos was not content with simply rendering a figure that stands naturally. His aim was to impose order on human movement, to make it "beautiful," to "perfect" it. He achieved this through a system of cross balance. What appears at first to be a casually natural pose is, in fact, the result of an extremely complex and subtle organization of the figure's various parts. Note, for instance, how the straight-hanging arm echoes the rigid supporting leg, providing the figure's right side with the columnar stability needed to anchor the left side's dynamically flexed limbs. If read anatomically, however, the tensed and relaxed limbs may be seen to oppose each other diagonally—the right arm and the left leg are relaxed, and the tensed supporting leg opposes the flexed arm, which held a spear. In like manner, the head turns to the right while the hips twist slightly to the left. And although the *Doryphoros* seems to take a step forward, he does not move. This dynamic asymmetrical balance, this motion while at rest, and the resulting harmony of opposites are the essence of the Polykleitan style.

## The Athenian Acropolis

While Polykleitos was formulating his *Canon* in Argos, the Athenians, under the leadership of Pericles, were at work on one of the most ambitious building projects ever undertaken, the reconstruction of the Acropolis after the Persian sack. In September 480 BCE, the Athenian commander Themistocles decisively defeated the Persian navy off the island of Salamis, southwest of Athens, and forced it to retreat to Asia. Athens, despite the damage it suffered at the hands of the army of Xerxes, emerged from the war with enormous power and prestige. Less than two years later, in 478 BCE, the Greeks formed an alliance for mutual protection against any renewed threat from the East. The new confederacy came to be known as the Delian League, because its headquarters were on the sacred island of Delos, midway between the Greek mainland and the coast of Asia Minor. Although at the outset each league member had an equal vote, Athens was "first among equals," providing the allied fleet commander and determining which cities were to furnish ships and which were instead to pay an annual tribute to the treasury at Delos.

Continued fighting against the Persians kept the Delian alliance intact, but Athens gradually assumed a dominant role. In 454 BCE, the league's treasury was transferred to Athens, ostensibly for security reasons. Pericles, who was only in his teens when the Persians laid waste to the Acropolis, was by mid-century the recognized leader of the Athenians, and he succeeded in converting the alliance into an Athenian empire. Tribute continued to be paid, but the Athenians did not spend the surplus reserves for the common good of the allied Greek states. Instead, Pericles expropriated the money to pay the enormous cost of executing his grand plan to embellish the Acropolis of Athens.

The reaction of the allies—in reality the subjects of Athens—was predictable. Plutarch, who wrote a biography of Pericles in the early second century CE, reported not only the wrath the Greek victims of Athenian tyranny felt but also the protest voiced against Pericles' decision even in the Athenian assembly. Greece, Pericles' enemies said, had been dealt "a terrible, wanton insult" when Athens used the funds contributed out of necessity for a common war effort to "gild and embellish itself with images and extravagant temples, like some pretentious woman decked out with precious stones."[3] That the Delian League was the source of the funds used for the Acropolis building program is important to keep in mind when examining those great and universally admired buildings erected to realize Pericles' vision of his polis reborn from the ashes of the Persian sack. They are not the glorious fruits of Athenian democracy but are instead the by-products of tyranny and the abuse of power. Too often art and architectural historians do not ask how patrons, whether public or private, paid for the monuments they commissioned. The answer can be very revealing—and very embarrassing.

**PORTRAIT OF PERICLES** A number of extant Roman marble sculptures are copies of a famous bronze portrait statue of Pericles by KRESILAS, who was born on Crete but worked in Athens. The Athenians set up the portrait on the Acropolis, probably immediately after their leader's death in 429 BCE. Kresilas depicted Pericles in heroic nudity, and his portrait must have resembled the Riace warrior (FIG. 5-35). The copies reproduce the head only, sometimes, as in FIG. 5-41, in the form of a *herm* (a bust on a square pillar). The inscription on the herm reads "Pericles, son of Xanthippos, the Athenian." Pericles wears the helmet of a *strategos* (general), the elective position he held 15 times. The Athenian leader was said to have had an abnormally elongated skull, and Kresilas recorded this feature (while also concealing it) by providing a glimpse through the helmet's eye slots of the hair at the top of the head. This, together with the unblemished features of Pericles' aloof face and, no doubt, his body's perfect physique, led Pliny to assert that

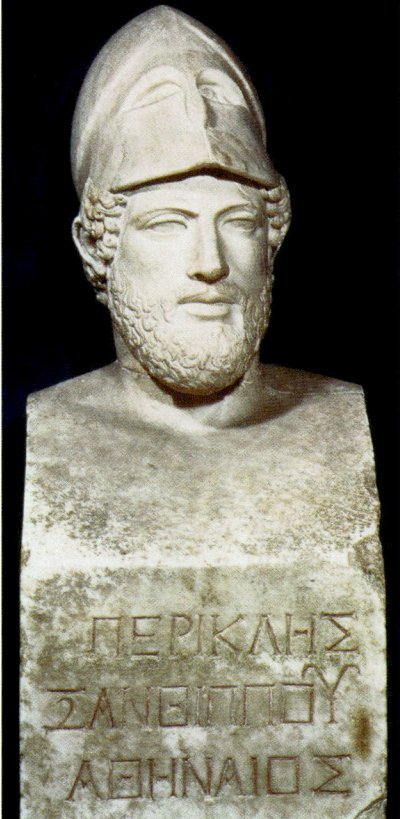

1 ft.

**5-41** KRESILAS, *Pericles.* Roman herm copy of the head of a bronze statue of ca. 429 BCE. Marble, full herm 6′ high; detail 4′ 6½″ high. Musei Vaticani, Rome.

In his portrait of Pericles, Kresilas was said to have made a noble man appear even nobler. Classical Greek portraits were not likenesses but idealized images in which humans appeared godlike.

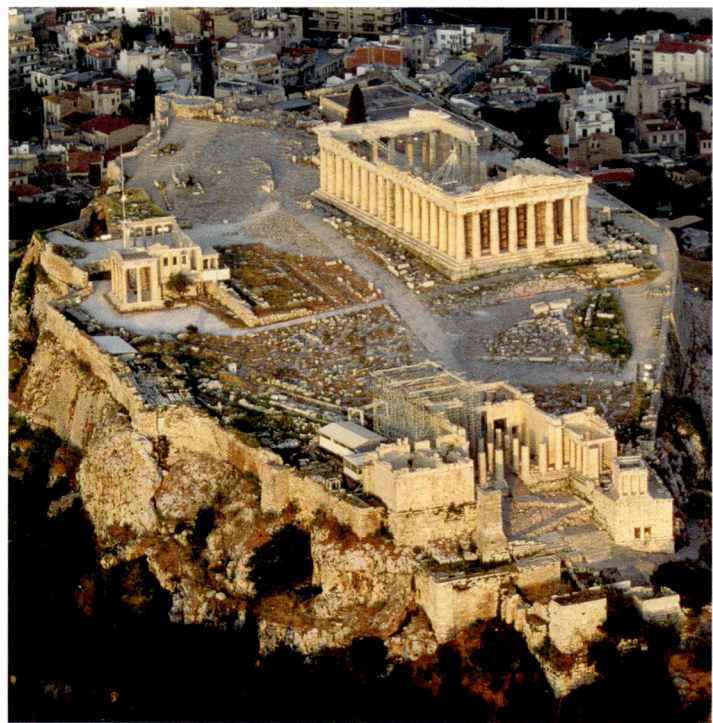

5-42 **Aerial view of the Acropolis (looking southeast), Athens, Greece.** ◼◀

Under the leadership of Pericles, the Athenians undertook the costly project of reconstructing the Acropolis after the Persian sack of 480 BCE. The funds came from the Delian League treasury.

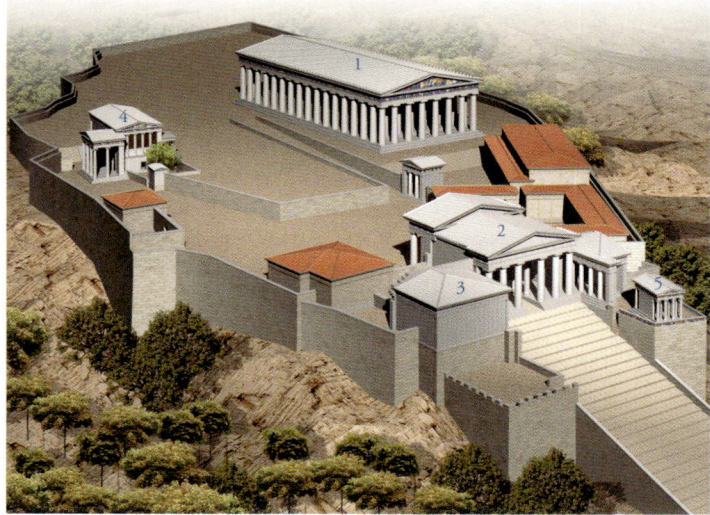

5-43 **Restored view of the Acropolis, Athens, Greece (John Burge). (1) Parthenon, (2) Propylaia, (3) pinakotheke, (4) Erechtheion, (5) Temple of Athena Nike.**

Of the four main fifth-century BCE buildings on the Acropolis, the first to be erected was the Parthenon, followed by the Propylaia, the Erechtheion, and the Temple of Athena Nike.

Kresilas had the ability to make noble men appear even more noble in their portraits. This praise was apt because the Acropolis statue was not a portrait in the modern sense of a record of specific features, but an image of an individual that conformed to the Classical ideal of beauty. Pliny refers to Kresilas's "portrait" as "the Olympian Pericles," because the statue made Pericles appear almost godlike.[4]

**PERICLEAN ACROPOLIS** The centerpiece of the Periclean building program on the Acropolis (FIG. **5-42**) was the Parthenon (FIGS. 5-1 and **5-43,** no. 1), dedicated to Athena Parthenos, and erected in the remarkably short period between 447 and 438 BCE. (Work on the temple's ambitious sculptural ornamentation continued until 432 BCE.) As soon as the Athenian builders completed work on the Parthenon, construction commenced on the Propylaia (FIG. 5-43, no. 2), the grand new western gateway to the Acropolis (the only accessible side of the natural plateau). Begun in 437 BCE, work stopped in 431 at the outbreak of the Peloponnesian War between Athens and Sparta and never resumed. Two later temples, the Erechtheion (FIG. 5-43, no. 4) and the Temple of Athena Nike (FIG. 5-43, no. 5), built after Pericles died, were probably also part of the original project. The greatest Athenian architects and sculptors of the Classical period focused their attention on the construction and decoration of these four buildings.

That these ancient buildings exist at all today is something of a miracle. In the Middle Ages, the Parthenon, for example, became a Byzantine and later a Roman Catholic church and then, after the Ottoman conquest of Greece, a mosque. With each rededication, religious officials remodeled the building. The Christians early on removed the colossal statue of Athena inside. The churches had a great curved *apse* at the east end housing the altar. The Ottomans added a *minaret* (tower used to call Muslims to prayer). In 1687,

the Venetians besieged the Acropolis. One of their rockets scored a direct hit on the ammunition depot the Ottomans had installed in part of the Parthenon. The resultant explosion blew out the building's center. To make matters worse, the Venetians subsequently tried to remove some of the statues from the Parthenon's pediments. In more than one case, the workmen dropped the statues, which smashed on the ground. From 1801 to 1803, Thomas Bruce (1766–1841), Lord Elgin, brought most of the surviving sculptures to England. For the past two centuries, they have been on exhibit in the British Museum (FIGS. 5-47 to 5-50), although Greece has appealed many times for the return of the "Elgin Marbles" and built a new museum near the Acropolis to house them. Today, a uniquely modern blight threatens the Parthenon and the other buildings of the Periclean age. The corrosive emissions of factories and automobiles are decomposing the ancient marbles. A comprehensive campaign has been under way for some time to protect the columns and walls from further deterioration. What little original sculpture remained in place when modern restoration began is now in the new museum's climate-controlled rooms.

**PARTHENON: ARCHITECTURE** Despite the ravages of time and humanity, most of the Parthenon's peripteral colonnade (FIG. 5-1) is still standing (or has been reerected), and art historians know a great deal about the building and its sculptural program. The architect was Iktinos, assisted, according to some sources, by KALLIKRATES. The statue of Athena (FIG. 5-46) in the cella was the work of Phidias, who was also the overseer of the temple's sculptural decoration. In fact, Plutarch stated that Phidias was in charge of the entire Acropolis project.

Just as the contemporaneous *Doryphoros* (FIG. 5-40) may be seen as the culmination of nearly two centuries of searching for the ideal proportions of the various human body parts, so, too, the Parthenon may be viewed as the ideal solution to the Greek architect's quest for perfect proportions in Doric temple design (see "The Perfect Temple," page 105). Its well-spaced columns (FIG. **5-44**), with their slender shafts, and the capitals, with their straight-sided conical echinuses,

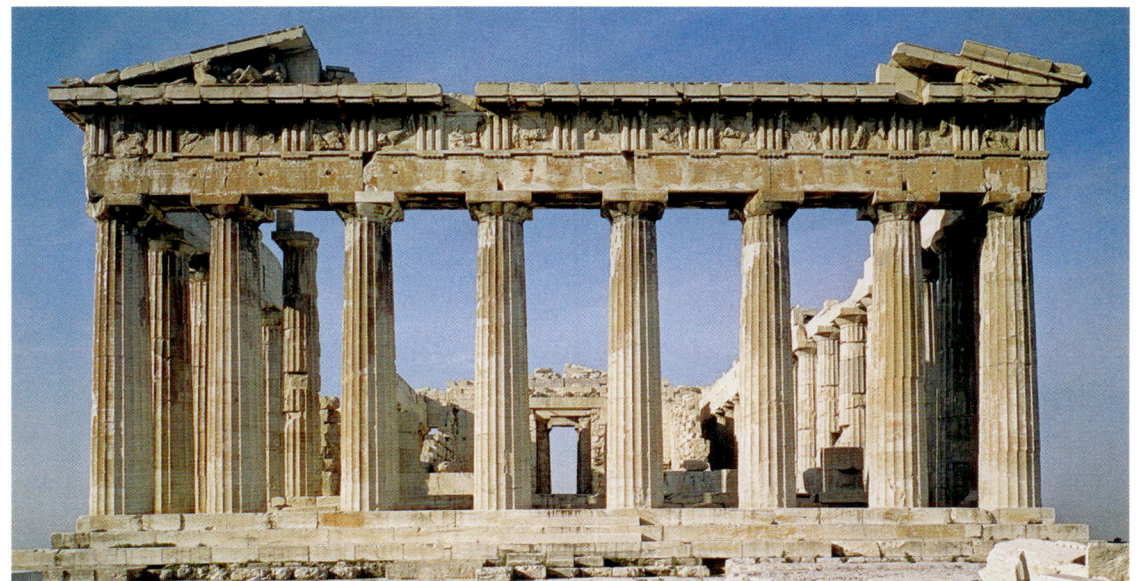

5-44 IKTINOS and KALLIKRATES, east facade of the Parthenon, Acropolis, Athens, Greece, 447–438 BCE. ◼◄

Iktinos believed harmonic proportions produced beautiful buildings. In the Parthenon, the ratio of larger and smaller parts is $x = 2y + 1$ (8 columns on the facade, 17 on the side).

are the ultimate refinement of the bulging and squat Doric columns and compressed capitals of the Archaic Hera temple (FIG. 5-14) at Paestum. The Parthenon architects and Polykleitos were kindred spirits in their belief that beautiful proportions resulted from strict adherence to harmonic numerical ratios, whether in a temple more than 200 feet long or a life-size statue of a nude man. For the Parthenon, the controlling ratio for the *symmetria* of the parts may be expressed algebraically as $x = 2y + 1$. Thus, for example, the temple's plan (FIG. 5-45) called for 8 columns on the short ends and 17 on the long sides, because $17 = (2 \times 8) + 1$. The stylobate's ratio of length to width is 9:4, because $9 = (2 \times 4) + 1$. This ratio also characterizes the cella's proportion of length to width, the distance between the centers of two adjacent column drums (the *interaxial*) in proportion to the columns' diameter, and so forth.

The Parthenon's harmonious design and the mathematical precision of the sizes of its constituent elements tend to obscure the fact that this temple, as actually constructed, is quite irregular in shape. Throughout the building are pronounced deviations from the strictly horizontal and vertical lines assumed to be the basis of all Greek post-and-lintel structures. The stylobate, for example, curves upward at the center on the sides and both facades, forming a kind of shallow dome, and this curvature carries up into the entablature. Moreover, the peristyle columns (FIGS. 5-1 and 5-44) lean inward slightly. Those at the corners have a diagonal inclination and are also about 2 inches thicker than the rest. If their lines continued, they would meet about 1.5 miles above the temple. These deviations from the norm meant that virtually every Parthenon block and drum had to be carved according to the special set of specifications dictated by its unique place in the structure. This was obviously a daunting task, and the builders must have had a reason for introducing these so-called refinements in the Parthenon. Some modern observers note, for example, how the curving of horizontal lines and the tilting of vertical ones create a dynamic balance in the building—a kind of architectural contrapposto—and give it a greater sense of life. The oldest recorded explanation, however, may be the most likely. Vitruvius, a Roman architect of the late first century BCE who claims to have had access to Iktinos's treatise on the Parthenon (again, note the kinship with the *Canon* of Polykleitos), maintained that these adjustments were made to compensate for optical illusions. Vitruvius noted, for example, that if a stylobate is laid out on a level surface, it will appear to sag at the center. He also recommended that the corner columns of a building should be thicker because they are surrounded by light and would otherwise appear thinner than their neighbors.

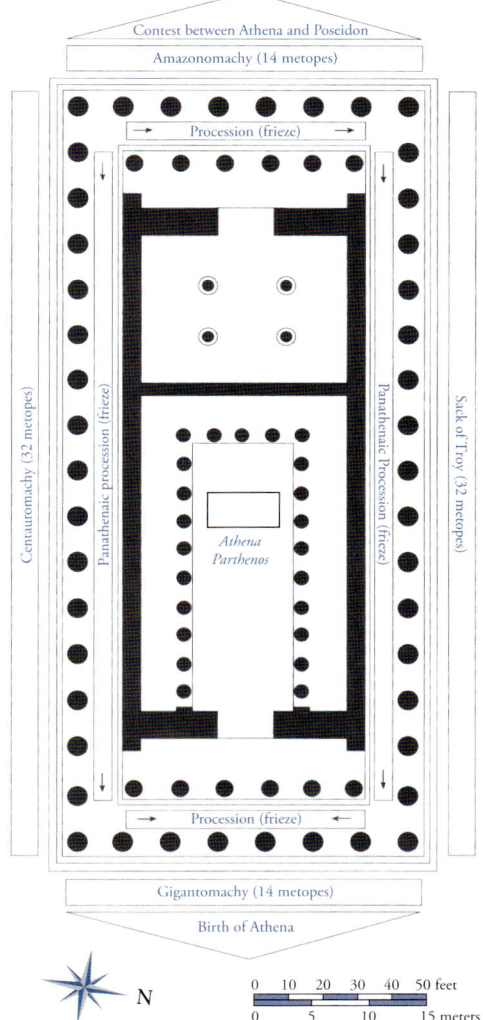

**5-45** Plan of the Parthenon, Acropolis, Athens, Greece, with diagram of the sculptural program (after Andrew Stewart), 447–432 BCE.

A team of sculptors directed by Phidias lavishly decorated the Parthenon with statues in both pediments, figural reliefs in all 92 Doric metopes, and an inner 524-foot sculptured Ionic frieze.

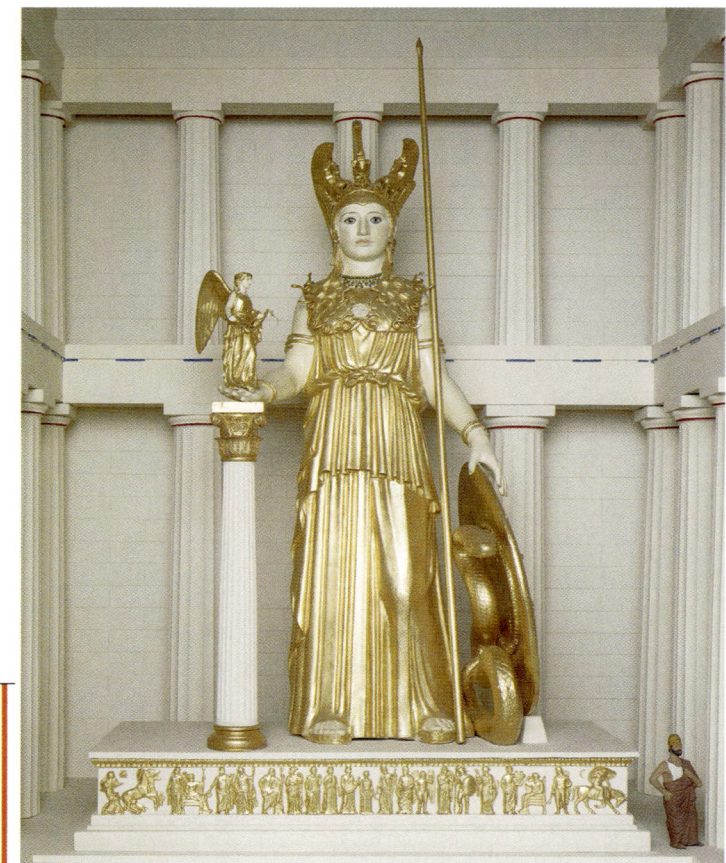

**5-46** PHIDIAS, *Athena Parthenos,* in the cella of the Parthenon, Acropolis, Athens, Greece, ca. 438 BCE. Model of the lost chryselephantine statue. Royal Ontario Museum, Toronto.

Inside the cella of the Parthenon stood Phidias's 38-foot-tall gold-and-ivory *Athena Parthenos* (the Virgin). The goddess is fully armed and holds Nike (Victory) in her extended right hand.

The Parthenon is "irregular" in other ways as well. One of the ironies of this most famous of all Doric temples is that it is "contaminated" by Ionic elements. Although the cella (FIG. 5-46) had a two-story Doric colonnade, the back room (which housed the goddess's treasury and the tribute collected from the Delian League) had four tall and slender Ionic columns as sole supports for the superstructure (FIG. 5-45). And whereas the temple's exterior had a standard Doric frieze (FIG. 5-44), the inner frieze (FIG. 5-50) that ran around the top of the cella wall was Ionic. Perhaps this fusion of Doric and Ionic elements reflects the Athenians' belief that the Ionians of the Aegean Islands and Asia Minor were descendants of Athenian settlers and were therefore their kin. Or it may be Pericles and Iktinos's way of suggesting that Athens was the leader of *all* the Greeks. In any case, a mix of Doric and Ionic features characterizes the fifth-century BCE buildings of the Acropolis as a whole.

*ATHENA PARTHENOS* The costly decision to incorporate two sculptured friezes in the Parthenon's design is symptomatic. This Pentelic-marble temple was more lavishly adorned than any Greek temple before it, Doric or Ionic. A mythological scene appears in every one of the 92 Doric metopes, and every inch of the 524-foot-long Ionic frieze depicts a procession and cavalcade. Dozens of larger-than-life-size statues filled both pediments. And inside was the most expensive item of all—Phidias's *Athena Parthenos,* a colossal gold-and-ivory (chryselephantine) statue of the virgin goddess. Art historians know a great deal about Phidias's lost statue from descriptions by Greek and Latin authors and from Roman copies. A model (FIG. 5-46) gives a good idea of its appearance and setting. Athena stood 38 feet tall, and to a large extent Iktinos designed the Parthenon around her. To accommodate the statue's huge size, the cella had to be wider than usual. This, in turn, dictated the width of the facade—eight columns at a time when six columns were the norm (FIGS. 5-25 and 5-29).

Athena was fully armed with shield, spear, and helmet, and she held Nike (the winged female personification of Victory) in her extended right hand. No one doubts that this Nike referred to the victory of 479 BCE. The memory of the Persian sack of the Acropolis was still vivid, and the Athenians were intensely conscious that by driving back the Persians, they had saved their civilization from the Eastern "barbarians" who had committed atrocities at Miletos. In fact, Phidias's *Athena Parthenos* incorporated multiple allusions to the Persian defeat. On the thick soles of Athena's sandals was a representation of a centauromachy. High reliefs depicting the battle of Greeks and Amazons (*Amazonomachy*), in which Theseus drove the Amazons out of Athens, emblazoned the exterior of her shield. On the shield's interior, Phidias painted a gigantomachy. Each of these mythological contests was a metaphor for the triumph of order over chaos, of civilization over barbarism, and of Athens over Persia.

**PARTHENON: METOPES** Phidias took up these same themes again in the Parthenon's metopes (FIG. 5-45). The best-preserved metopes—although the paint on these and all the other Parthenon marbles long ago disappeared—are those of the south side,

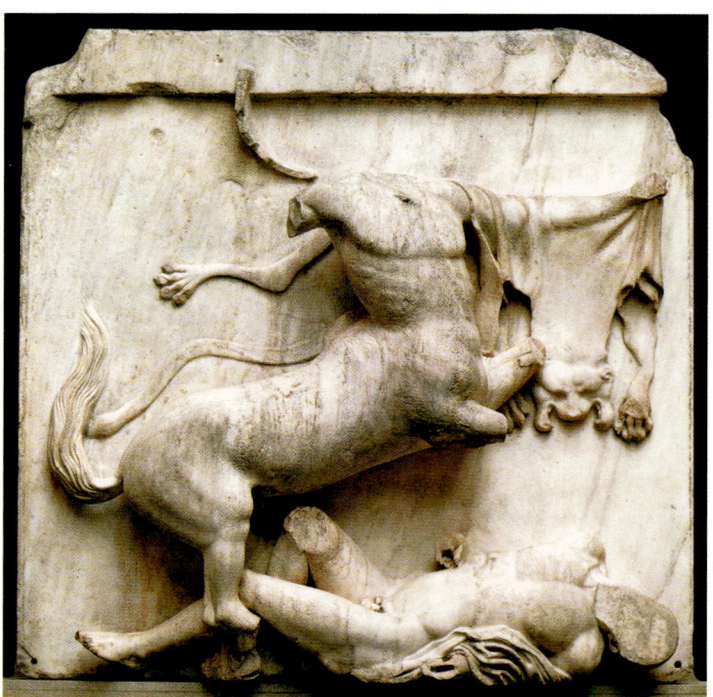

**5-47** Centauromachy, metope from the south side of the Parthenon, Acropolis, Athens, Greece, ca. 447–438 BCE. Marble, 4′ 8″ high. British Museum, London. ◼◀

The Parthenon's centauromachy metopes allude to the Greek defeat of the Persians. Here, the sculptor brilliantly distinguished the vibrant living centaur from the lifeless Greek corpse.

which depicted the battle of Lapiths and centaurs, a combat in which Theseus played a major role. On one extraordinary slab (FIG. 5-47), a triumphant centaur rises up on its hind legs, exulting over the crumpled body of the Greek it has defeated. The relief is so high that parts are fully in the round. Some have broken off. The sculptor brilliantly distinguished the vibrant, powerful form of the living beast from the lifeless corpse on the ground. In other metopes, the Greeks have the upper hand, but the full set suggests that the battle was a difficult one against a dangerous enemy and that losses as well as victories occurred. The same was true of the war against the Persians, and the centauromachy metopes—and also the gigantomachy, Amazonomachy, and Trojan War metopes—are allegories for the Greek-Persian conflict of the early fifth century BCE.

**PARTHENON: PEDIMENTS** The subjects of the two pediments were especially appropriate for a temple that celebrated Athena—and the Athenians. The east pediment depicted the birth of the goddess. At the west was the contest between Athena and Poseidon to determine which one would become the city's patron deity. Athena won, giving her name to the polis and its citizens. It is significant that in the story and in the pediment the Athenians are the judges of the relative merits of the two gods. The selection of this theme for the temple reflects the same arrogance that led to the use of Delian League funds to adorn the Acropolis.

The Christians removed the center of the east pediment when they added an apse to the Parthenon at the time of its conversion into a church. What remains are the spectators to the left and the right who witnessed Athena's birth on Mount Olympus. At the far left (FIG. 5-48) are part of the head and arms of Helios (the Sun) and his chariot horses rising from the pediment floor (FIG. 5-44). Next to them is a powerful male figure usually identified as Dionysos or possibly Herakles, who entered the realm of the gods on completion of his 12 labors (see "Herakles," page 128). At the right (FIG. 5-49) are three goddesses, probably Hestia, Dione, and Aphrodite (see "Gods and Goddesses," page 107), and either Selene (the Moon) or Nyx (Night) and more horses, this time sinking below the pediment's floor. Here, Phidias, who must have designed the composition even if his assistants executed it, discovered an entirely new way to deal with the awkward triangular frame of the pediment. Its floor is now the horizon line, and charioteers and their horses move through it effortlessly. The individual figures, even the animals, are brilliantly characterized. The horses of the Sun, at the beginning of the day, are energetic. Those of the Moon or Night, having labored until dawn, are weary. The reclining figures fill the space beneath the raking cornice beautifully. Dionysos/Herakles and Aphrodite in the lap of her mother Dione are monumental Olympian presences yet totally relaxed organic forms. The Athenian sculptors fully understood not only the surface appearance of human anatomy, both male and female, but also the mechanics of how muscles and bones make the body move. The Phidian workshop mastered the rendition of clothed forms as well. In the Dione-Aphrodite group, the thin and heavy folds of the garments alternately reveal and conceal the main and lesser body masses while swirling in a compositional tide that subtly unifies the two figures. The articulation and integration of the bodies produce a wonderful variation of surface and play of light and shade.

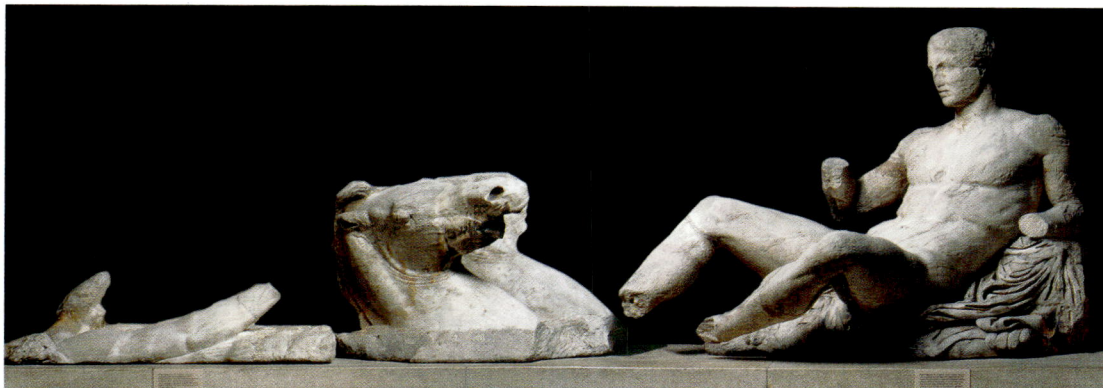

**5-48** Helios and his horses, and Dionysos (Herakles?), from the east pediment of the Parthenon, Acropolis, Athens, Greece, ca. 438–432 BCE. Marble, greatest height 4′ 3″. British Museum, London.

The east pediment of the Parthenon depicts the birth of Athena. At the left, Helios and his horses emerge from the pediment's floor, suggesting the sun rising above the horizon at dawn.

1 ft.

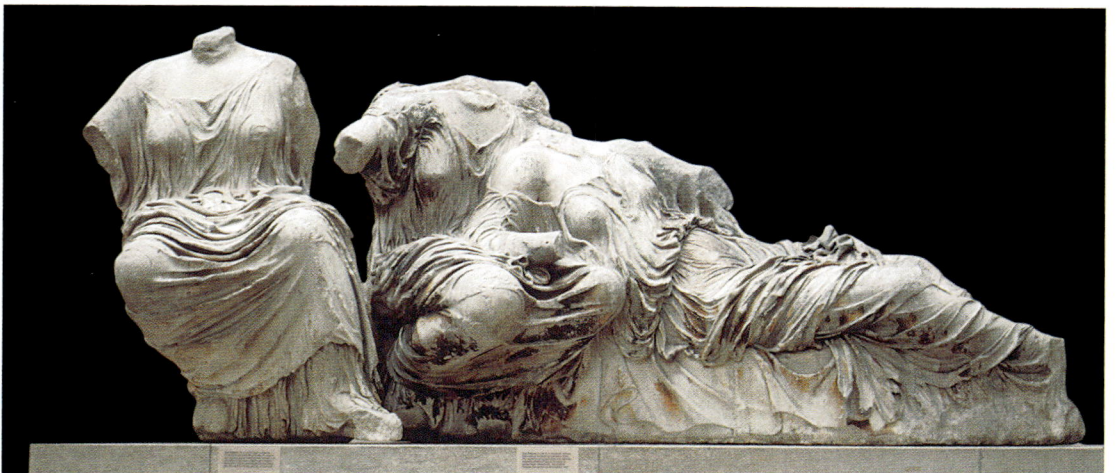

**5-49** Three goddesses (Hestia, Dione, and Aphrodite?), from the east pediment of the Parthenon, Acropolis, Athens, Greece, ca. 438–432 BCE. Marble, greatest height 4′ 5″. British Museum, London.

The statues of Hestia, Dione, and Aphrodite conform perfectly to the sloping right side of the Parthenon's east pediment. The thin and heavy folds of the garments alternately reveal and conceal the body forms.

1 ft.

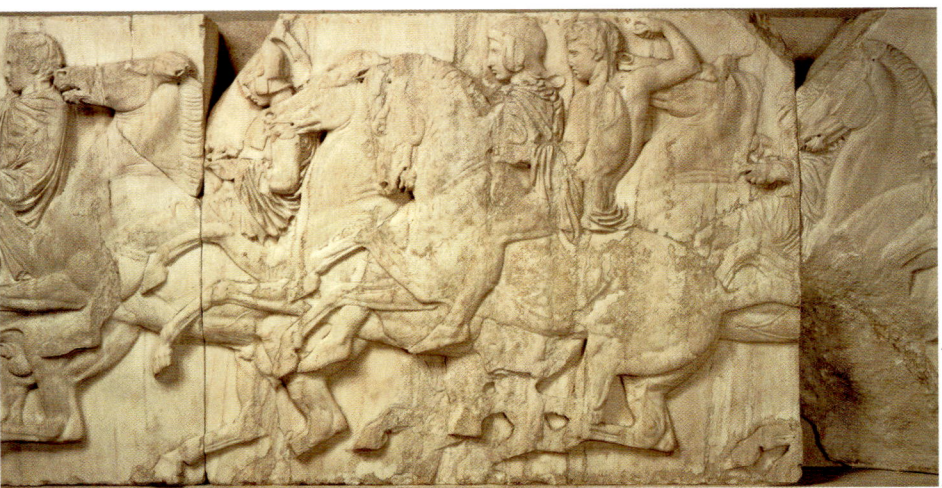

**5-50** Three details of the Panathenaic Festival procession frieze, from the Parthenon, Acropolis, Athens, Greece, ca. 447–438 BCE. Marble, 3′ 6″ high. *Top:* horsemen (north frieze), British Museum, London. *Center:* Poseidon, Apollo, Artemis, Aphrodite, and Eros (east frieze), Acropolis Museum, Athens. *Bottom:* elders and maidens (east frieze), Musée du Louvre, Paris. ◼

The Parthenon's Ionic frieze represents the Panathenaic procession of citizens on horseback and on foot under the gods' watchful eyes. The temple celebrated the Athenians as much as Athena.

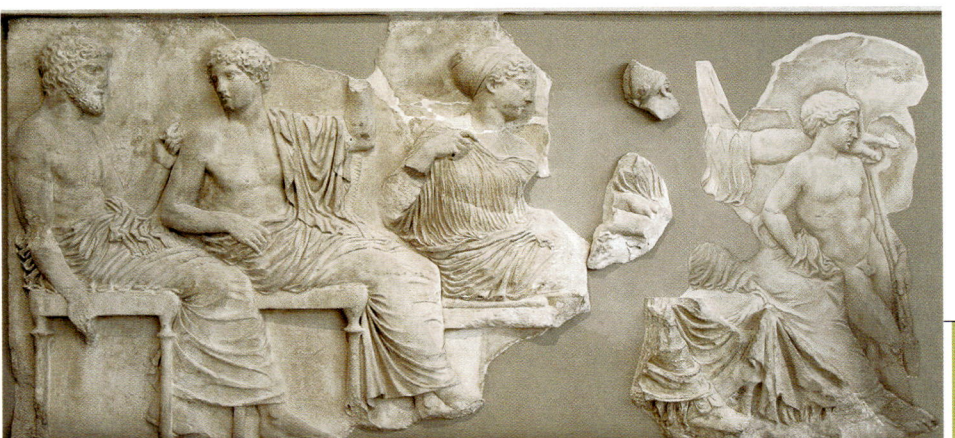

1 ft.

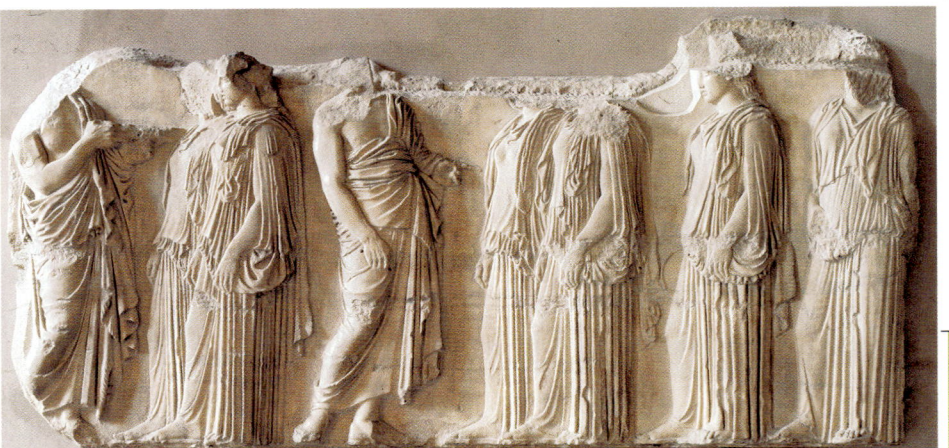

1 ft.

1 ft.

**PARTHENON: IONIC FRIEZE** In many ways the most remarkable part of the Parthenon's sculptural program is the inner Ionic frieze (FIG. **5-50**). Scholars still debate its subject, but most agree it represents the Panathenaic Festival procession that took place every four years in Athens. If this identification is correct, the Athenians judged themselves fit for inclusion in the temple's sculptural decoration—the first instance in Greek art of the depiction of a human event on a temple. It is another example of the Athenians' extraordinarily high sense of self-worth.

The procession began at the Dipylon Gate, passed through the *agora* (central square), and ended on the Acropolis, where the Athenians placed a new peplos on an ancient wooden statue of Athena. That statue (probably similar in general appearance to the *Lady of Auxerre,* FIG. 5-6) had been housed in the Archaic temple the Persians razed in 480 BCE, but the Athenians removed it before the attack for security reasons and eventually installed it in the Erechtheion (FIG. 5-53, no. 1). On the Parthenon frieze the procession begins on the west, that is, at the temple's rear, the side facing the gateway to the Acropolis. It then moves in parallel lines down the long north and south sides of the building and ends at the center of the east frieze, over the doorway to the cella housing Phidias's statue (FIG. 5-45). It is noteworthy that the upper part of the frieze is in higher relief than the lower part so that the more distant and more shaded upper zone is as legible from the ground as the lower part of the frieze. This is another instance of how the Parthenon's designers took optical effects into consideration.

The frieze vividly communicates the procession's acceleration and deceleration. At the outset, on the west side, marshals gather and youths mount their horses. On the north (FIG. 5-50, *top*) and south, the momentum picks up as the cavalcade moves from the lower town to the Acropolis, accompanied by chariots, musicians, jar carriers, and animals destined for sacrifice. On the east, seated gods and goddesses (FIG. 5-50, *center*), the invited guests, watch the procession slow almost to a halt (FIG. 5-50, *bottom*) as it nears its goal at the shrine of Athena's ancient wooden idol. Most remarkable of all is the role assigned to the Olympian deities. They do not take part in the festival or determine its outcome but are merely spectators. Aphrodite, in fact, extends her left arm to draw her son Eros's attention to the Athenians, just as today a parent at a parade would point out important people to a child. Indeed, the Athenian people *were* important—self-important, one might say. They were the masters of an empire, and in Pericles' famous funeral oration, he painted a picture of Athens that elevated its citizens almost to the stature of gods. The Parthenon celebrated the greatness of Athens and the Athenians as much as it honored Athena.

**PROPYLAIA** Even before all the sculptures were in place on the Parthenon, work began on a new monumental entrance to the Acropolis, the Propylaia (FIG. **5-51**). The architect entrusted with

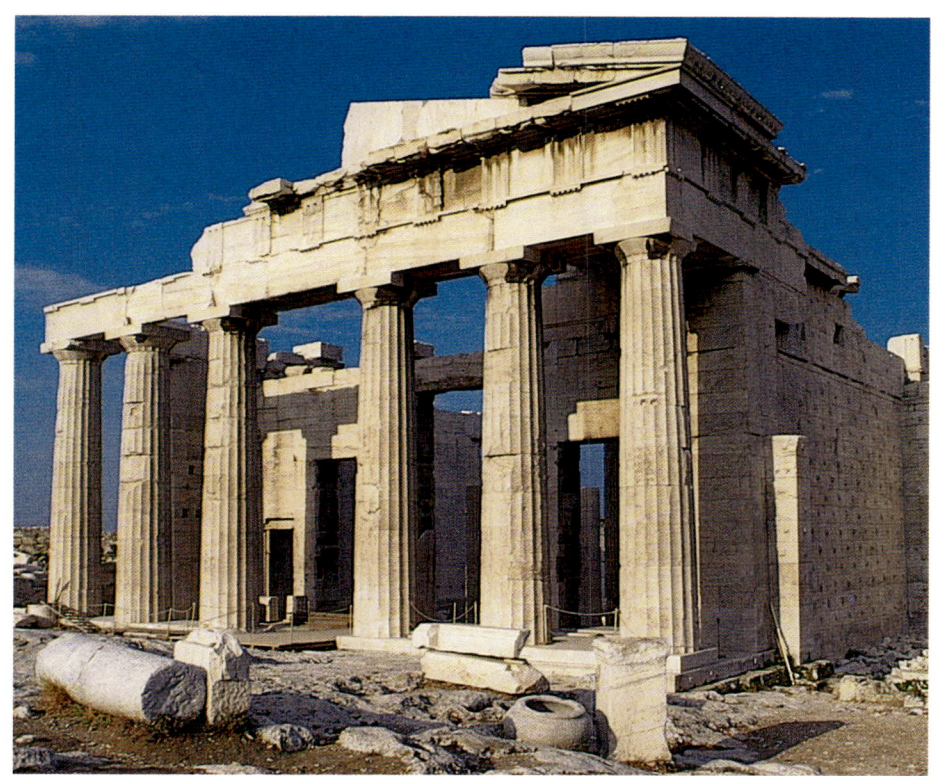

ther side of the central ramp were stairs for pedestrian traffic. Inside, tall, slender Ionic columns supported the split-level roof. Once again an Athenian architect mixed the two orders on the Acropolis. But as with the Parthenon, the Doric order was the choice for the stately exterior.

Mnesikles' full plan for the Propylaia was never executed because of the change in the fortunes of Athens after the outbreak of the Peloponnesian War in 431 BCE. Of the side wings that were part of the original project, only the northwest one (FIG. 5-43, no. 3) was completed. That wing is of special importance in the history of art. In Roman times it housed a *pinakotheke* (picture gallery). In it were displayed paintings on wood panels by some of the major artists of the fifth century BCE. It is uncertain whether this was the wing's original function. If it was, the Propylaia's pinakotheke is the first recorded structure built for the specific purpose of displaying paintings, and it is the forerunner of modern museums.

this important commission was MNESIKLES. The site was a difficult one, on a steep slope, but Mnesikles succeeded in disguising the change in ground level by splitting the building into eastern and western sections (FIG. 5-43, no. 2), each one resembling a Doric temple facade. Practical considerations dictated that the space between the central pair of columns on each side be enlarged. This was the path the chariots and animals of the Panathenaic Festival procession took, and they required a wide ramped causeway. To ei-

**ERECHTHEION** In 421 BCE, work finally began on the temple that was to replace the Archaic Athena temple the Persians had destroyed. The new structure, the Erechtheion (FIGS. **5-52** and

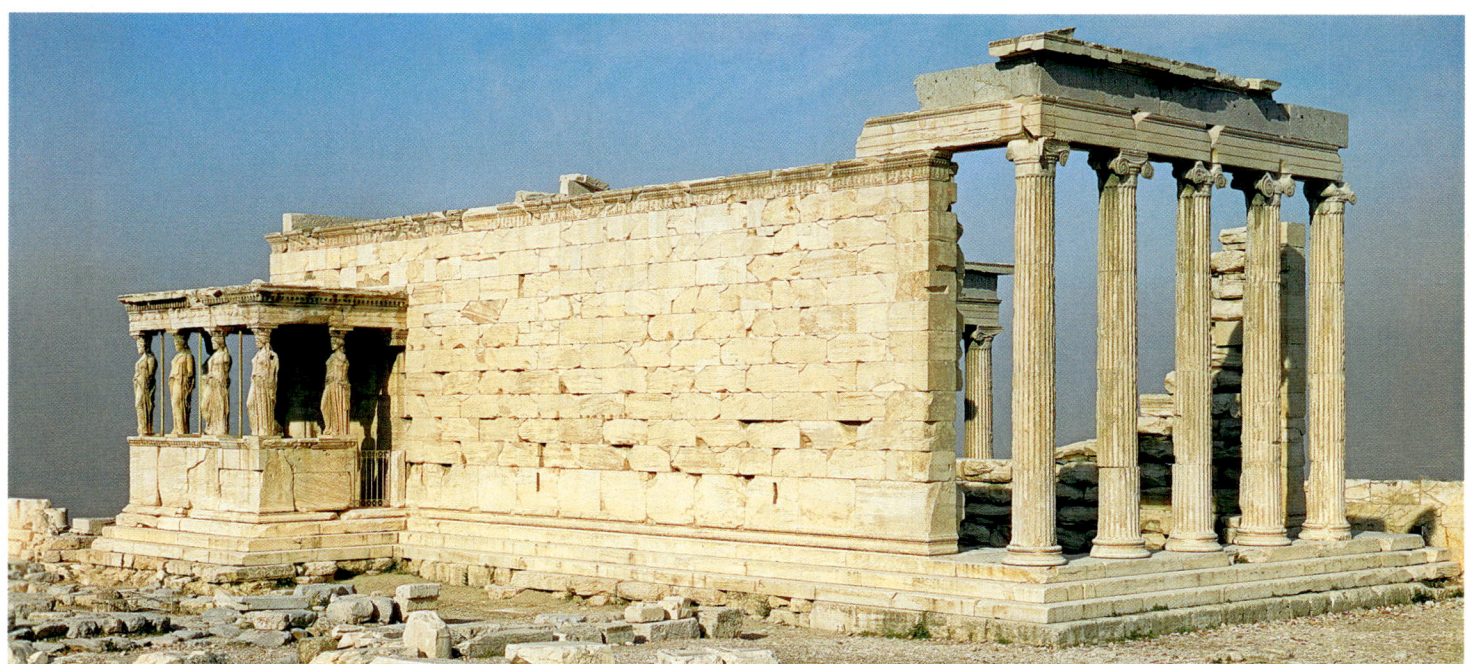

5-52 Erechtheion (looking northwest), Acropolis, Athens, Greece, ca. 421–405 BCE.

The Erechtheion is in many ways the antithesis of the Doric Parthenon directly across from it. An Ionic temple, it has some of the finest decorative details of any ancient Greek building.

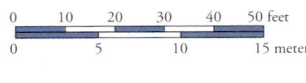

1. Shrine housing wooden image of Athena
2. Athena's olive tree
3. Poseidon's trident mark
4. Ruins of Archaic temple

N

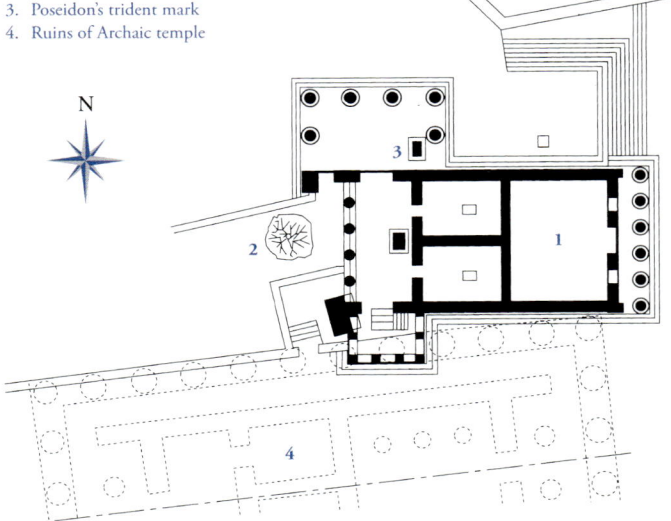

**5-53** Plan of the Erechtheion, Acropolis, Athens, Greece, ca. 421–405 BCE.

The asymmetrical form of the Erechtheion is unique for a Greek temple. It reflects the need to incorporate preexisting shrines into the plan, including those of the kings Erechtheus and Kekrops.

**5-53**), built to the north of the old temple's remains, was to be a multiple shrine, however. It honored Athena and housed the ancient wood image of the goddess that was the goal of the Panathenaic Festival procession. But it also incorporated shrines to a host of other gods and demigods who loomed large in the city's legendary past. Among these were Erechtheus, an early king of Athens, during whose reign the ancient idol of Athena was said to have fallen from the heavens, and Kekrops, another king of Athens, who served as judge of the contest between Athena and Poseidon. In fact, the site chosen for the new temple was the very spot where that contest occurred. Poseidon had staked his claim to Athens by striking the Acropolis rock with his trident and producing a salt-water spring. The imprint of his trident remained for Athenians of the historical period to see. Nearby, Athena had miraculously caused an olive tree to grow. This tree still stood as a constant reminder of her victory over Poseidon.

The asymmetrical plan (FIG. 5-53) of the Ionic Erechtheion is unique for a Greek temple and the antithesis of the simple and harmoniously balanced plan of the Doric Parthenon across the way. Its irregular form reflected the need to incorporate the tomb of King Kekrops and other preexisting shrines, the trident mark, and the olive tree into a single complex. The unknown architect responsible for the building also had to struggle with the problem of uneven terrain. The area could not be leveled by terracing because that would disturb the ancient sacred sites. As a result, the Erechtheion has four sides of very different character, and each side rests on a different ground level.

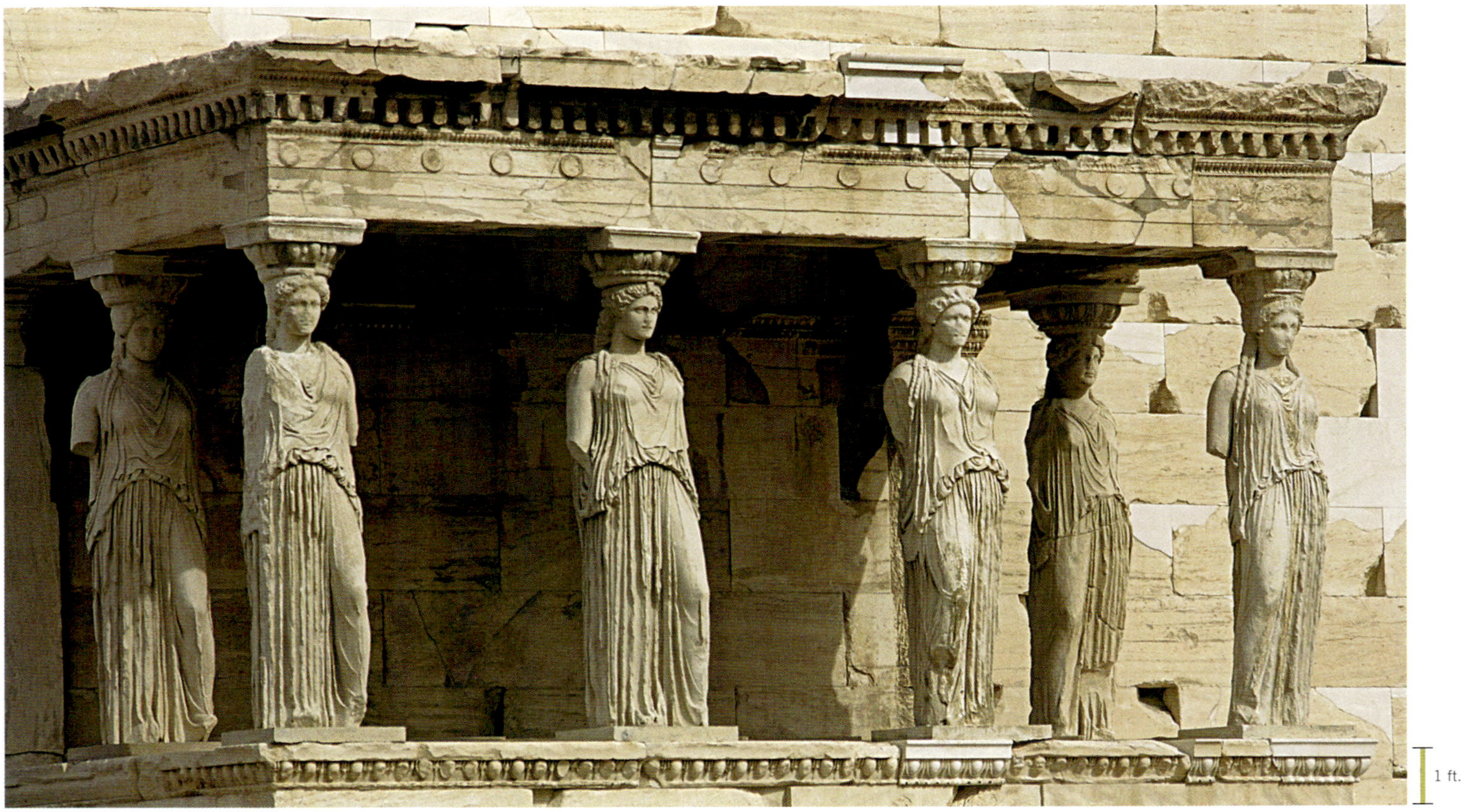

**5-54** Caryatids of the south porch of the Erechtheion, Acropolis, Athens, Greece, ca. 421–405 BCE. Marble, 7' 7" high.

The south porch of the Erechtheion features caryatids with contrapposto stances. They are updated versions of the Archaic caryatids of the porch of the Siphnian Treasury (FIG. 5-17) at Delphi.

1 ft.

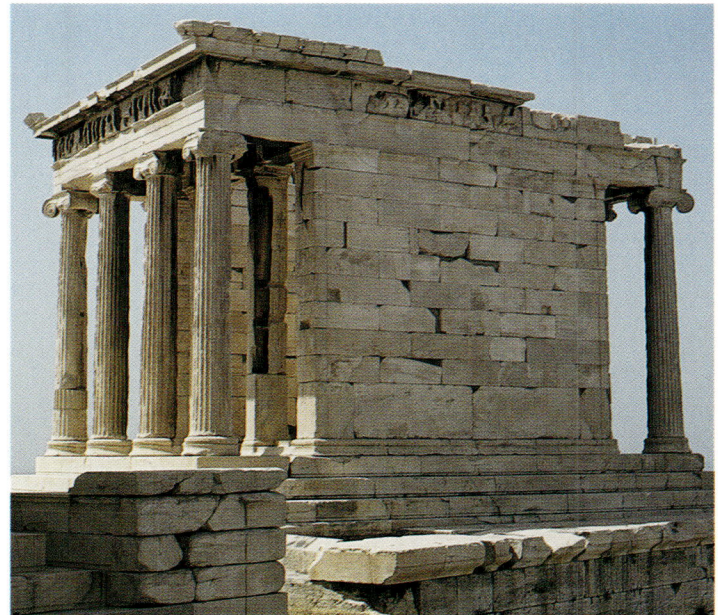

**5-55** KALLIKRATES, Temple of Athena Nike (looking southwest), Acropolis, Athens, Greece, ca. 427–424 BCE.

The Ionic temple at the entrance to the Acropolis is an unusual amphiprostyle building. It celebrates Athena as bringer of victory, and one of the friezes depicts the defeat of the Persians at Marathon.

Perhaps to compensate for the awkward character of the building as a whole, the architect took great care with the Erechtheion's decorative details. The Ionic capitals were inlaid with gold, rock crystal, and colored glass, and the frieze received special treatment. The stone chosen was the dark-blue limestone of Eleusis to contrast with the white Pentelic marble of the walls and columns and the marble relief figures attached to the dark frieze.

The Erechtheion's most striking and famous feature is its south porch (FIG. 5-54), where the architect replaced Ionic columns with caryatids, as on the Ionic Siphnian Treasury (FIG. 5-17) at Delphi. The Archaic caryatids resemble sixth-century BCE korai, and their Classical counterparts equally characteristically look like Phidian-era statues. Although the caryatids exhibit the weight shift that was standard for the fifth century BCE, the flutelike drapery folds concealing their stiff, weight-bearing legs underscores their role as architectural supports. The figures have enough rigidity to suggest the structural column and just the degree of flexibility needed to suggest the living body.

**TEMPLE OF ATHENA NIKE** Another Ionic building on the Athenian Acropolis is the small Temple of Athena Nike (FIG. 5-55), designed by Kallikrates, who designed the Parthenon with Iktinos and may have been responsible for that temple's Ionic elements. The Athena Nike temple is amphiprostyle (see "Greek Temple Plans," page 115) with four columns on both the east and west facades. It stands on what used to be a Mycenaean bastion near the Propylaia and greets all visitors entering Athena's great sanctuary. Like the Parthenon, this temple commemorated the victory over the Persians—and not just in its name. The sculptors devoted part of the frieze to a representation of the decisive battle at Marathon, which turned the tide against the Persians—a human event, as in the Parthenon's Panathenaic Festival procession frieze. But on the Athena Nike temple, the Athenians chronicled a specific occasion, not a recurring event involving anonymous citizens.

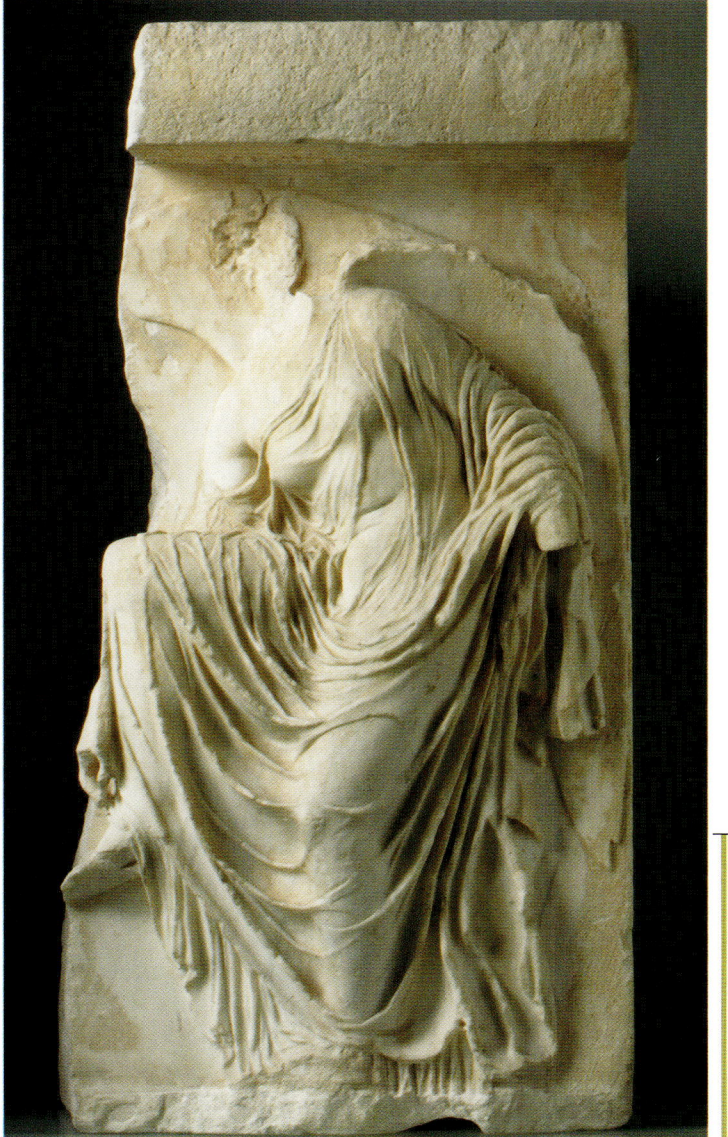

1 ft.

**5-56** Nike adjusting her sandal, from the south side of the parapet of the Temple of Athena Nike, Acropolis, Athens, Greece, ca. 410 BCE. Marble, 3′ 6″ high. Acropolis Museum, Athens.

Dozens of images of winged Victory adorned the parapet on three sides of the Athena Nike temple. The sculptor carved this Nike with garments that appear almost transparent.

Around the building, at the bastion's edge, was a *parapet* decorated with exquisite reliefs. The theme of the balustrade matched that of the temple proper—victory. Dozens of images of Nike adorn the parapet, always in different attitudes. Sometimes she erects trophies bedecked with Persian spoils. Other times she brings forward sacrificial bulls for Athena. One relief (FIG. 5-56) shows Nike adjusting her sandal—an awkward posture that the sculptor rendered elegant and graceful. The artist carried the style of the Parthenon pediments (FIG. 5-49) even further and created a figure whose garments cling so tightly to the body that they seem almost transparent, as if drenched with water. The sculptor was, however, interested in much more than revealing the supple beauty of the young female body. The drapery folds form intricate linear patterns unrelated to the body's anatomical structure and have a life of their own as abstract designs.

# The Hegeso Stele

In Geometric times, huge painted vases (FIGS. 5-2 and 5-2A) marked the graves of wealthy Athenians. In the Archaic period, the Greeks placed kouroi (FIGS. 5-7 and 5-9) and, to a lesser extent, korai, or stelae ornamented with relief depictions of the deceased over their graves. The stele (FIG. 5-57) erected in the Dipylon cemetery at the end of the fifth or beginning of the fourth century BCE to commemorate the death of Hegeso, daughter of Proxenos, is in this tradition. An inscription giving the names of the daughter and father is on the cornice of the pediment that crowns the stele. Antae at left and right complete the architectural framework.

Hegeso is the well-dressed woman seated on an elegant chair (with footstool). She examines a piece of jewelry (once rendered in paint, not now visible) selected from a box a servant girl brings to her. The maid's simple unbelted chiton contrasts sharply with the more elaborate attire of her mistress. The garments of both women reveal the body forms beneath them. The faces are serene, without a trace of sadness. Indeed, the sculptor depicted both mistress and maid during a characteristic shared moment out of daily life. Only the epitaph reveals that Hegeso is the one who has departed.

The simplicity of the scene on the Hegeso stele is deceptive, however. This is not merely a bittersweet scene of tranquil domestic life before an untimely death. The setting itself is significant—the secluded women's quarters of a Greek house, from which Hegeso rarely would have emerged. Contemporaneous grave stelae of men regularly show them in the public domain, often as warriors. The servant girl is not so much the faithful companion of the deceased in life as she is Hegeso's possession, like the jewelry box. The slave girl may look solicitously at her mistress, but Hegeso has eyes only for her ornaments. Both slave and jewelry attest to the wealth of Hegeso's father, unseen but prominently cited in the epitaph. (It is noteworthy that there is no mention of the mother's name.) Indeed, even the jewelry box carries a deeper significance, for it probably represents the dowry Proxenos would have provided to his daughter's husband when she left her father's home to enter her husband's home. In the patriarchal society of ancient Greece, the dominant position of men is manifest even when only women are depicted.

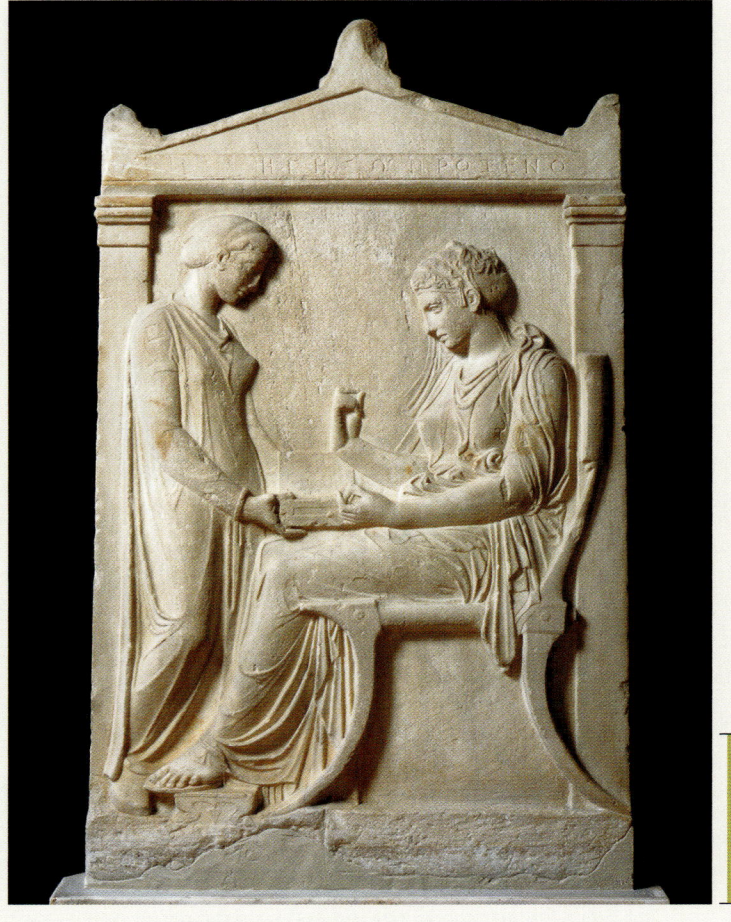

**5-57** Grave stele of Hegeso, from the Dipylon cemetery, Athens, Greece, ca. 400 BCE. Marble, 5′ 2″ high. National Archaeological Museum, Athens.

On her tombstone, Hegeso examines jewelry from a box her servant girl holds. Mistress and maid share a serene moment out of daily life. Only the epitaph reveals that Hegeso is the one who died.

**HEGESO STELE** Although the decoration of the great building projects on the Acropolis must have occupied most of the finest sculptors of Athens in the second half of the fifth century BCE, other commissions were available in the city, notably in the Dipylon cemetery. There, around 400 BCE, a beautiful and touching grave stele (FIG. 5-57) in the style of the Temple of Athena Nike parapet reliefs was set up in memory of a woman named Hegeso. Its subject—a young woman in her home, attended by her maid (see "The Hegeso Stele," above)—and its composition have close parallels in Classical vase painting.

## Painting

In the Classical period, some of the most renowned artists were the painters of monumental wood panels displayed in public buildings, both secular and religious. Those works were by nature perishable, and all of the great panels of the masters are unfortunately lost.

Nonetheless, one can get some idea of the polychrome nature of Classical panel paintings by studying Greek vases, especially those painted using the *white-ground* technique, which takes its name from the chalky-white slip used to provide a background for the painted figures. Experiments with white-ground painting date back to the Andokides Painter, but the method became popular only toward the middle of the fifth century BCE.

**ACHILLES PAINTER** One of the masters of white-ground painting was the so-called ACHILLES PAINTER, who decorated the *lekythos* (flask to hold perfumed oil) in FIG. 5-58. White-ground is essentially a variation of the red-figure technique. First the painter covered the pot with a slip of very fine white clay, then applied black glaze to outline the figures, and diluted brown, purple, red, and white to color them. The artist could use other colors—for example, the yellow the Achilles Painter chose for the garments of

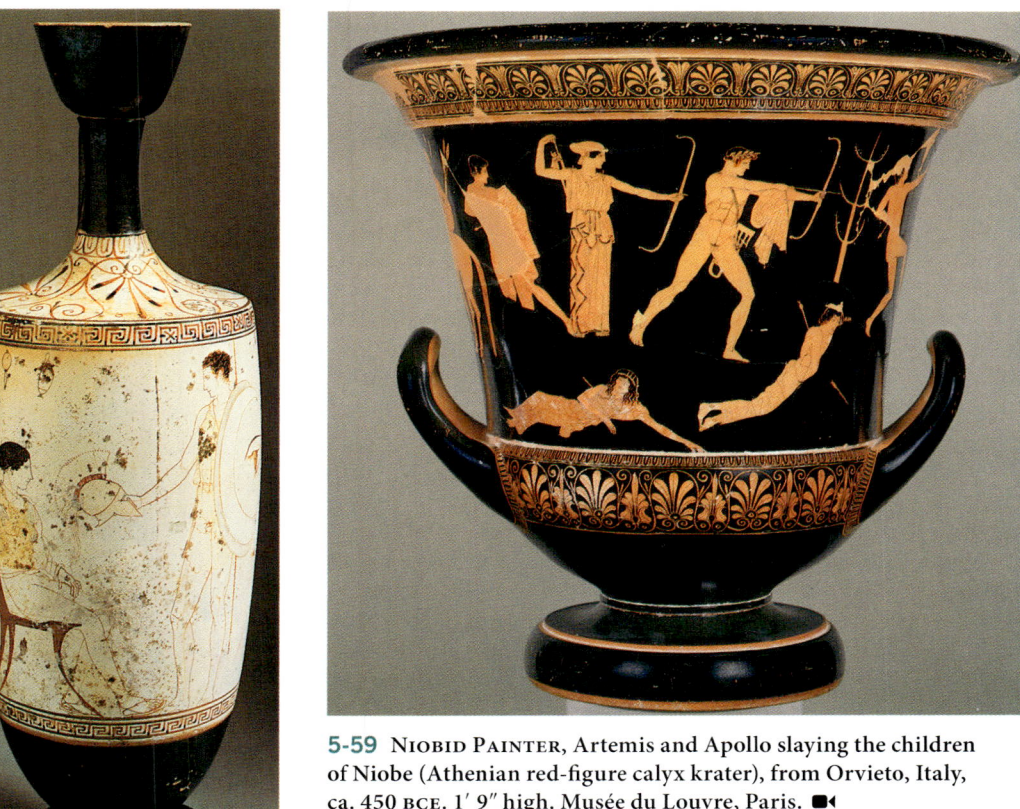

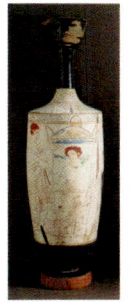

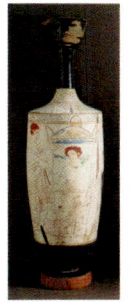

**5-58** Achilles Painter, Warrior taking leave of his wife (Athenian white-ground lekythos), from Eretria, Greece, ca. 440 BCE. 1′ 5″ high. National Archaeological Museum, Athens. ◀

White-ground painters applied the colors after firing because most colored glazes could not withstand the kiln's heat. The Achilles Painter here displayed his mastery at drawing an eye in profile.

both figures on this lekythos— but these had to be applied after firing because the Greeks did not know how to make them withstand the heat of the kiln. Despite the obvious attractions of the technique, the impermanence of the expanded range of colors discouraged white-ground painting on everyday vessels, such as drinking cups and kraters. In fact, Greek artists explored the full polychrome possibilities of the white-ground technique almost exclusively on lekythoi, which families commonly placed in graves as offerings to the deceased. For vessels designed for short-term use, the fragile nature of white-ground painting was of little concern.

The Achilles Painter, like the Reed Painter (FIG. 5-58A) later in the century, selected a scene appropriate for the funerary purpose of a lekythos. A youthful warrior takes leave of his wife. The red scarf, mirror, and jug hanging on the wall behind the woman indicate that the setting is the interior of their home. The motif of the seated woman is strikingly similar to that of Hegeso on her grave stele (FIG. 5-57), but here the woman is the survivor. It is her husband, preparing to go to war with helmet, shield, and spear, who will depart, never to return. On his shield is a large painted eye, roughly life-size. Greek shields often bore decorative devices such as the horrific face of Medusa, intended to ward off evil spirits and frighten the enemy (compare FIG. 5-16). This eye undoubtedly recalls this tradition, but for the Achilles Painter it was little more than an excuse to display superior drawing skills. Since the late sixth century BCE, Greek painters had abandoned the Archaic habit of placing frontal eyes on profile faces and attempted to render the eyes in profile. The Achilles Painter's mastery of this difficult problem in foreshortening is on exhibit here.

**5-58A** Reed Painter, Warrior seated at his tomb, ca. 410–400 BCE.

**POLYGNOTOS** The leading panel painter of the first half of the fifth century BCE was Polygnotos of Thasos, whose works adorned important buildings both in Athens and Delphi. One of these was the pinakotheke of Mnesikles' Propylaia, but the most famous was a portico in the Athenian marketplace that came to

**5-59** Niobid Painter, Artemis and Apollo slaying the children of Niobe (Athenian red-figure calyx krater), from Orvieto, Italy, ca. 450 BCE. 1′ 9″ high. Musée du Louvre, Paris. ◀

The placement of figures on different levels in a landscape on this red-figure krater depicting the massacre of the Niobids reflects the compositions of the panel paintings of Polygnotos of Thasos.

be called the Stoa Poikile (Painted Stoa). Descriptions of Polygnotos's paintings make clear that he introduced a revolutionary compositional format. Before Polygnotos, figures stood on a common ground line at the bottom of the picture plane, whether they appeared in horizontal bands or single panels. Polygnotos placed his figures on different levels, staggered in tiers in the manner of Ashurbanipal's lion hunt relief (FIG. 2-23) of two centuries before. He also incorporated landscape elements into his paintings, making his pictures true windows onto the world and not simply surface designs peopled with foreshortened figures. Polygnotos's abandonment of a single ground line was as momentous a break from the past as Early Classical Greek sculptors' rejection of frontality in statuary.

**NIOBID PAINTER** Polygnotos's influence is evident on a red-figure krater (FIG. 5-59) painted around the middle of the fifth century BCE by the Niobid Painter—so named because one side of this krater depicts the massacre of the Niobids, the children of Niobe. Niobe, who had at least a dozen children, had boasted that she was superior to the goddess Leto, who had only two offspring, Apollo and Artemis. To punish her *hubris* (arrogance) and teach the lesson that no mortal could be superior to a god or goddess, Leto sent her two children to slay all of Niobe's many sons and daughters. On the Niobid Painter's krater, the horrible slaughter occurs in a schematic landscape setting of rocks and trees. The painter disposed the figures on several levels, and they actively interact with their setting. One slain son, for example, not only has fallen upon a rocky outcropping but is partially hidden by it. The Niobid Painter also drew the son's face in a three-quarter view, something that even Euphronios and Euthymides had not attempted.

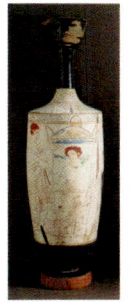

Early and High Classical Periods **143**

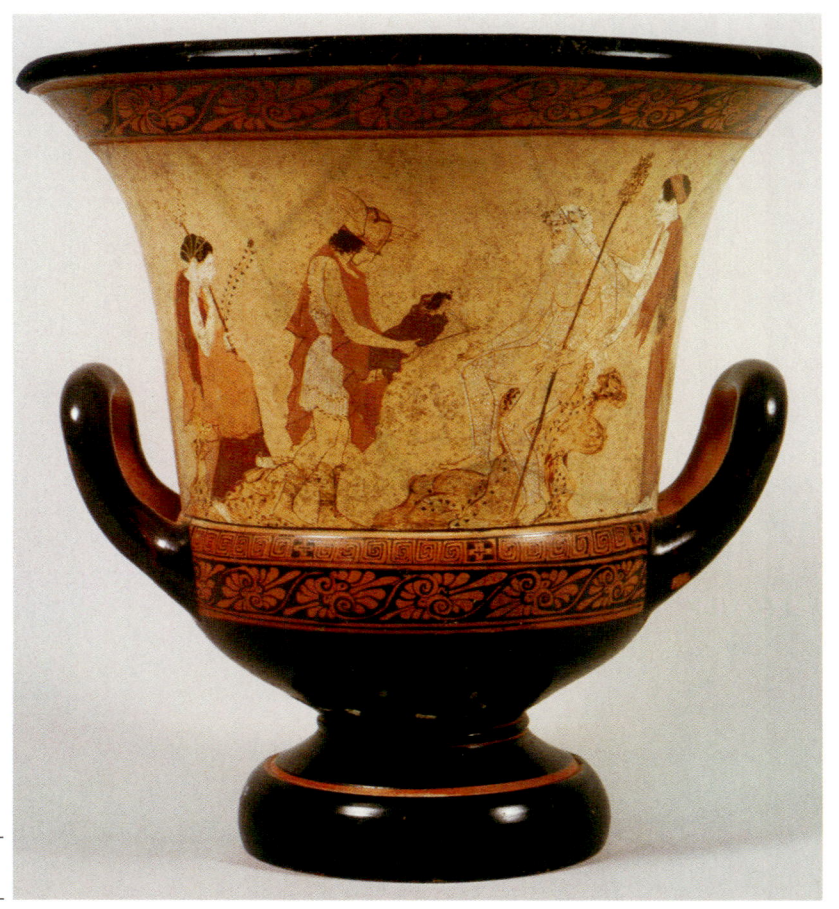

**5-60** PHIALE PAINTER, Hermes bringing the infant
Dionysos to Papposilenos (Athenian white-ground calyx
krater), from Vulci, Italy, ca. 440–435 BCE. 1′ 2″ high.
Musei Vaticani, Rome.

In the Phiale Painter's white-ground representation of Hermes
and the infant Dionysos at Nysa, the use of diluted brown to color
and shade the rocks may also reflect the work of Polygnotos.

that could survive the heat of a Greek kiln—red, brown,
purple, and a special snowy white reserved for the flesh of
the nymphs and for the hair, beard, and shaggy body of
Papposilenos. The use of diluted brown wash to color and
shade the rocks may reflect the coloration of Polygnotos's
landscapes. This vase and the Niobid krater together provide a shadowy idea of the character of Polygnotos's lost
paintings.

**TOMB OF THE DIVER, PAESTUM** Although
all of the panel paintings of the masters disappeared long
ago, some Greek mural paintings survive. An early example is in the Tomb of the Diver at Paestum. Covering
the four walls of this small, coffinlike tomb are banquet
scenes of the kind that appear regularly on Greek vases.
On the tomb's cover slab (FIG. **5-61**), a youth dives from a
stone platform into a body of water. The scene most likely
symbolizes the plunge from this life into the next. Trees
resembling those of the Niobid krater are included within
the decorative frame.

**PHIALE PAINTER** Further insight into the appearance of
monumental panel paintings of the fifth century BCE comes from
a white-ground krater (FIG. **5-60**) by the PHIALE PAINTER. The
subject is Hermes handing over his half brother, the infant Dionysos, to Papposilenos ("grandpa-satyr"). The other figures represent the nymphs in the shady glens of Nysa, where Zeus had sent
Dionysos, one of his numerous natural sons, to be raised, safe from
the possible wrath of his wife, Hera. Unlike the decorators of funerary lekythoi, the Phiale Painter used for this krater only colors

# LATE CLASSICAL PERIOD

The Peloponnesian War, which began in 431 BCE, ended in 404 BCE
with the complete defeat of a plague-weakened Athens. The victor,
Sparta, and then Thebes undertook the leadership of Greece, both
unsuccessfully. In the middle of the fourth century BCE, a threat
from without caused the rival Greek states to put aside their animosi-
ties and unite for their common defense, as they had earlier against
the Persians. But at the battle of Chaeronea in 338 BCE, the Greek
cities suffered a devastating loss and had to relinquish their indepen-

**5-61** Youth diving, cover slab of
the Tomb of the Diver, Tempe del
Prete necropolis, Paestum, Italy,
ca. 480–470 BCE. Fresco, 3′ 4″ high.
Museo Archeologico Nazionale,
Paestum. ▪◀

This tomb in Italy is a rare example
of Classical mural painting. The
diving scene most likely symbolizes
the deceased's plunge into the
Underworld. The trees resemble those
on the Niobid krater (FIG. 5-59).

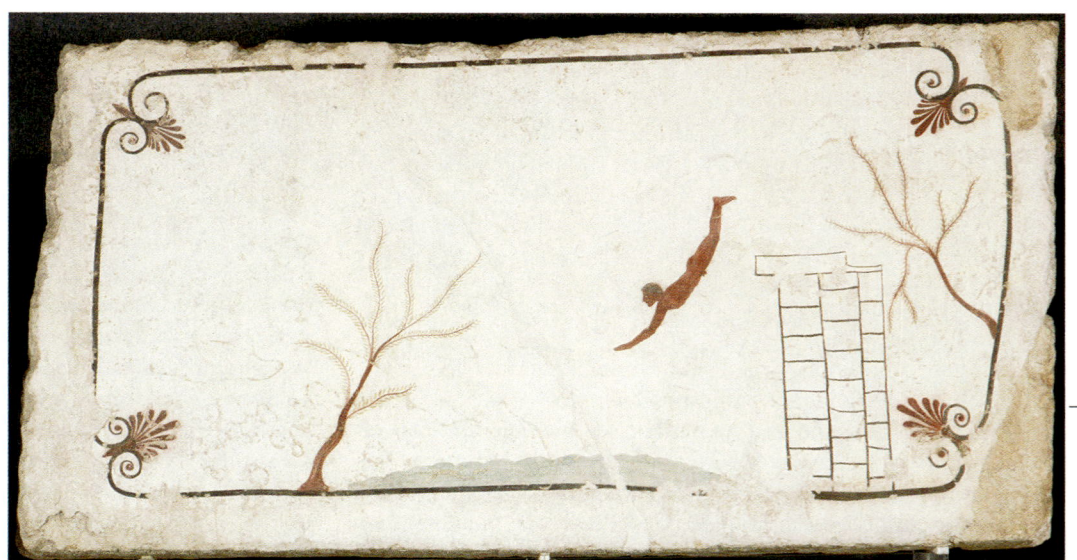

dence to the Macedonian king, Philip II (r. 359–336 BCE). Philip was assassinated in 336, and his son, Alexander III (r. 336–323 BCE), better known simply as Alexander the Great, succeeded him. Alexander led a powerful army on an extraordinary campaign that overthrew the Persian Empire (the ultimate revenge for the Persian invasion of Greece in the early fifth century), wrested control of Egypt, and even reached India (see Chapter 15).

## Sculpture

The fourth century BCE in Greece was thus a time of political upheaval, which had a profound impact on the psyche of the Greeks and on the art they produced. In the fifth century BCE, Greeks had generally believed that rational human beings could impose order on their environment, create "perfect" statues such as the *Canon* of Polykleitos, and discover the "correct" mathematical formulas for constructing temples such as the Parthenon. The Parthenon frieze celebrated the Athenians as a community of citizens with shared values. The Peloponnesian War and the unceasing strife of the fourth century BCE brought an end to the serene idealism of the previous century. Disillusionment and alienation followed. Greek thought and Greek art began to focus more on the individual and on the real world of appearances instead of on the community and the ideal world of perfect beings and perfect buildings.

**PRAXITELES** The new approach to art is immediately apparent in the work of PRAXITELES, one of the great masters of the fourth century BCE. Praxiteles did not reject the favored sculptural themes of the High Classical period, and his Olympian gods and goddesses retained their superhuman beauty. But in his hands, those deities lost some of their solemn grandeur and took on a worldly sensuousness. Nowhere is this new humanizing spirit plainer than in the statue of Aphrodite (FIG. **5-62**) that Praxiteles sold to the Knidians after another city had rejected it. The lost original, carved from Parian marble, is known only through copies of Roman date, but Pliny considered it "superior to all the works, not only of Praxiteles, but indeed in the whole world." It made Knidos famous, and many people sailed there just to see the statue in its round temple (compare FIG. 5-72), where "it was possible to view the image of the goddess from every side." According to Pliny, some visitors were "overcome with love for the statue."[5]

The *Aphrodite of Knidos* caused such a sensation in its time because Praxiteles took the unprecedented step of representing the goddess of love completely nude. Female nudity was rare in earlier Greek art and had been confined almost exclusively to paintings on vases designed for household use. The women so depicted also were usually not noblewomen or goddesses but courtesans or slave girls, like the one Onesimos depicted on a red-figure drinking cup (FIG. 5-23A). No one had ever dared place inside a temple a statue of a goddess wearing no clothes. Moreover, Praxiteles' Aphrodite is not a cold and remote image. In fact, the goddess engages in a trivial act out of everyday life. She has removed her garment, draped it over a large *hydria* (water pitcher), and is about to step into the bath.

Although shocking in its day, the *Aphrodite of Knidos* is not openly erotic (the goddess modestly shields her pelvis with her right hand), but she is quite sensuous. Lucian, writing in the second century CE, noted that she had a "welcoming look" and a "slight smile" and that Praxiteles was renowned for his ability to transform marble into soft and radiant flesh. Lucian mentioned, for example, the "dewy quality of Aphrodite's eyes."[6] Unfortunately, the rather

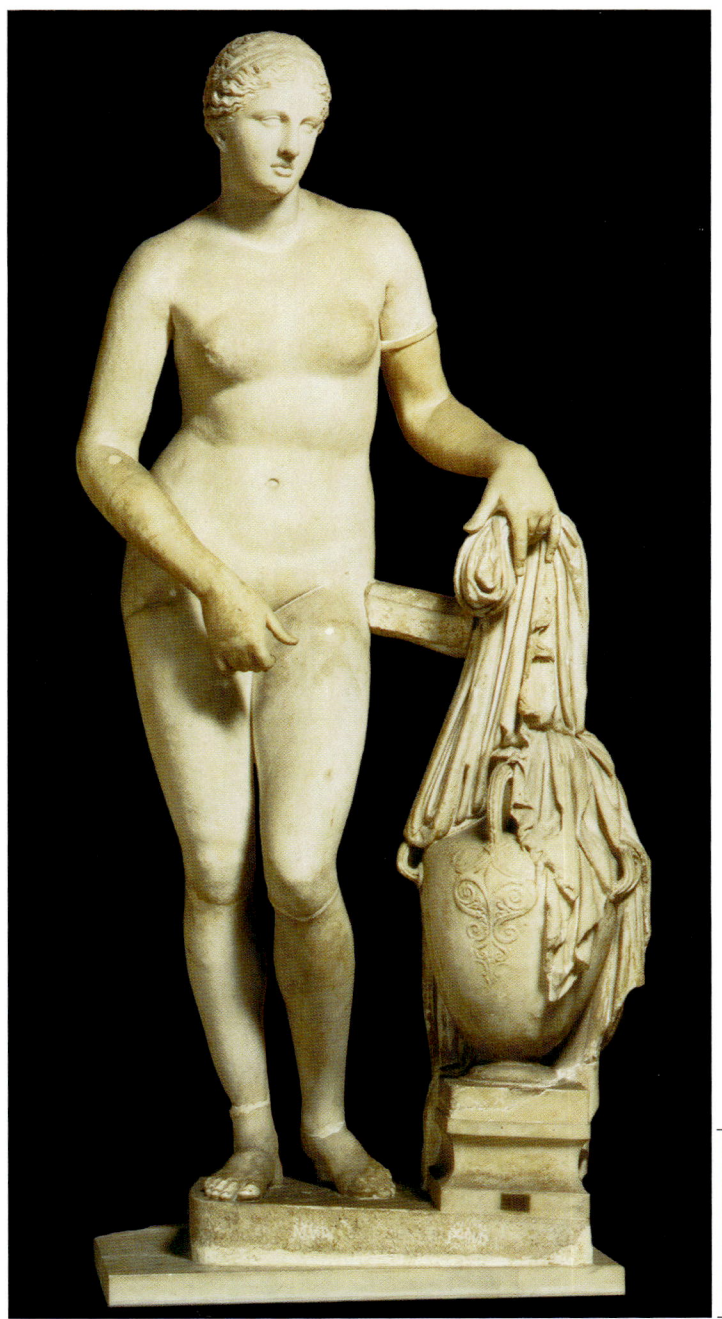

**5-62** PRAXITELES, *Aphrodite of Knidos.* Roman copy of a marble statue of ca. 350–340 BCE. Marble, 6′ 8″ high. Musei Vaticani, Rome. 🎥

This first nude statue of a Greek goddess caused a sensation. But Praxiteles was also famous for his ability to transform marble into soft and radiant flesh. His Aphrodite had "dewy eyes."

mechanical Roman copies do not capture the quality of Praxiteles' modeling of the stone, but some originals of the period do—for example, a female head (FIG. **5-62A**) from Chios.

The Praxitelean "touch" is also evident in a statue once thought to be by the hand of the master himself but now generally considered either a copy of the highest quality or an original work by a son or grandson of

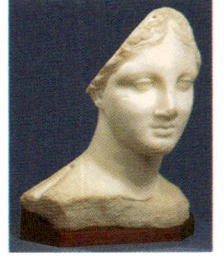

**5-62A** Head of a woman, Chios, ca. 320–300 BCE.

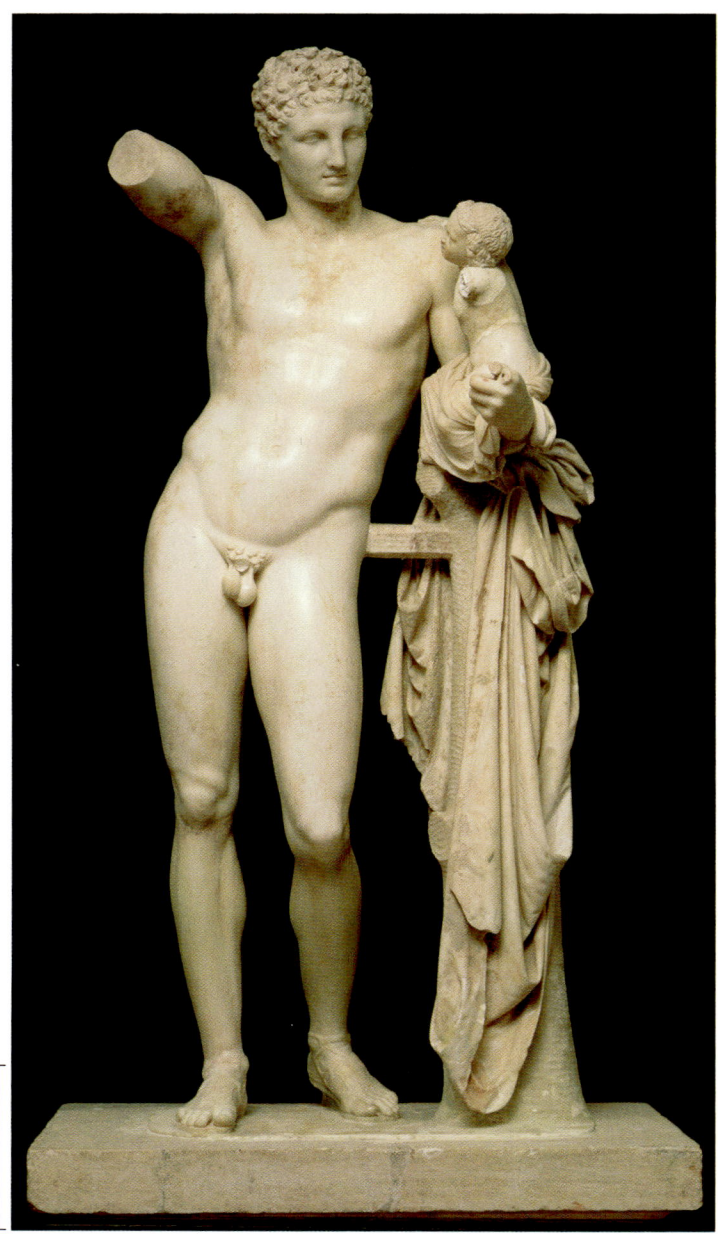

**5-63** PRAXITELES(?), Hermes and the infant Dionysos, from the Temple of Hera, Olympia, Greece. Copy of a marble statue by Praxiteles of ca. 340 BCE or an original work of ca. 330–270 BCE by a son or grandson. Marble, 7′ 1″ high. Archaeological Museum, Olympia.

Praxiteles humanized the Olympian deities. This Hermes is as sensuous as the sculptor's Aphrodite. The god gazes dreamily into space while he dangles grapes as temptation for the infant wine god.

the master with the same name. The statue of Hermes and the infant Dionysos (FIG. 5-63) found in the Temple of Hera at Olympia brings to the realm of monumental statuary the theme the Phiale Painter had chosen for a white-ground krater (FIG. 5-60) a century earlier. Hermes has stopped to rest in a forest on his journey to Nysa to entrust the upbringing of Dionysos to Papposilenos and the nymphs. Hermes leans on a tree trunk (here it is an integral part of the composition and not a copyist's addition), and his slender body forms a sinuous, shallow S-curve that is the hallmark of many of Praxiteles' statues. He gazes dreamily into space while he dangles a bunch of grapes (now missing) as a temptation for the

infant, who is to become the Greek god of the vine. This is the kind of tender and very human interaction between an adult and a child that one encounters frequently in real life but that had been absent from Greek statuary before the fourth century BCE.

The quality of the carving is superb. The modeling is deliberately smooth and subtle, producing soft shadows that follow the planes as they flow almost imperceptibly one into another. All that is missing to give a complete sense of the "look" of a Praxitelean statue is the original paint, which a specialist, not the sculptor, applied to the statue (compare FIG. 5-63A). The delicacy of the marble facial features stands in sharp contrast to the metallic precision of Polykleitos's bronze *Doryphoros*

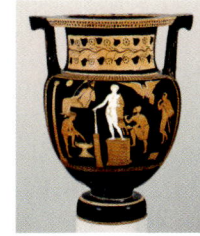

**5-63A** Artist painting a statue of Herakles, ca. 350–320 BCE.

(FIG. 5-40). The High Classical sculptor even subjected the *Spear Bearer*'s locks of hair to the laws of symmetry, and the hair does not violate the skull's perfect curve. The comparison of these two statues reveals the sweeping change in artistic attitude and intent that took place from the fifth to the fourth century BCE. In the statues of Praxiteles, the deities of Mount Olympus still possess a beauty mortals can aspire to, although not achieve, but they are no longer aloof. Praxiteles' gods have stepped off their pedestals and entered the world of human experience.

**SKOPAS** In the Archaic period and throughout most of the Early and High Classical periods, Greek sculptors generally shared common goals, but in the Late Classical period of the fourth century BCE, distinctive individual styles emerged. The dreamy, beautiful divinities of Praxiteles had enormous appeal, and the master had many followers (FIG. 5-62A). Other sculptors, however, pursued very different interests. One of these was SKOPAS OF PAROS, an architect as well as a sculptor, who designed a temple at Tegea (fragments of the pedimental sculptures remain; FIG. 5-64A) and contributed to the decoration of one of the Seven Wonders of the ancient world, the Mausoleum (FIG. 5-64B) at Halikarnassos (see "Wonders," Chapter 2, page 49). Although his sculptures reflect the general Late Classical trend toward the humanization of the Greek gods and heroes, Skopas's hallmark was intense emotionalism. None of his statues survives, but a grave

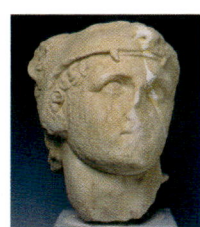

**5-64A** Herakles, Temple of Athena Alea, Tegea, ca. 340 BCE.

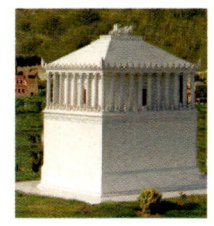

**5-64B** Mausoleum, Halikarnassos, ca. 353–340 BCE.

stele (FIG. 5-64) found near the Ilissos River in Athens exhibits the psychological tension for which the master's works were famous.

The Ilissos stele was originally set into an architectural frame similar to that of the earlier Hegeso stele (FIG. 5-57). A comparison of the two works is revealing. In the later stele the relief is much higher, with parts of the figures carved fully in the round. The major difference, however, is the pronounced change in mood, which reflects Skopas's innovations. The Late Classical work makes a clear distinction between the living and the dead and depicts overt mourning. The deceased is a young hunter who has the large, deeply set eyes and fleshy overhanging brows that characterized Skopas's sculpted figures (compare FIG. 5-64A). At his feet a small boy, either his servant or perhaps a younger brother, sobs openly. The hunter's dog also droops its head in sorrow. Beside the youth, an old man, undoubtedly his father, leans on a walking stick and, in a gesture

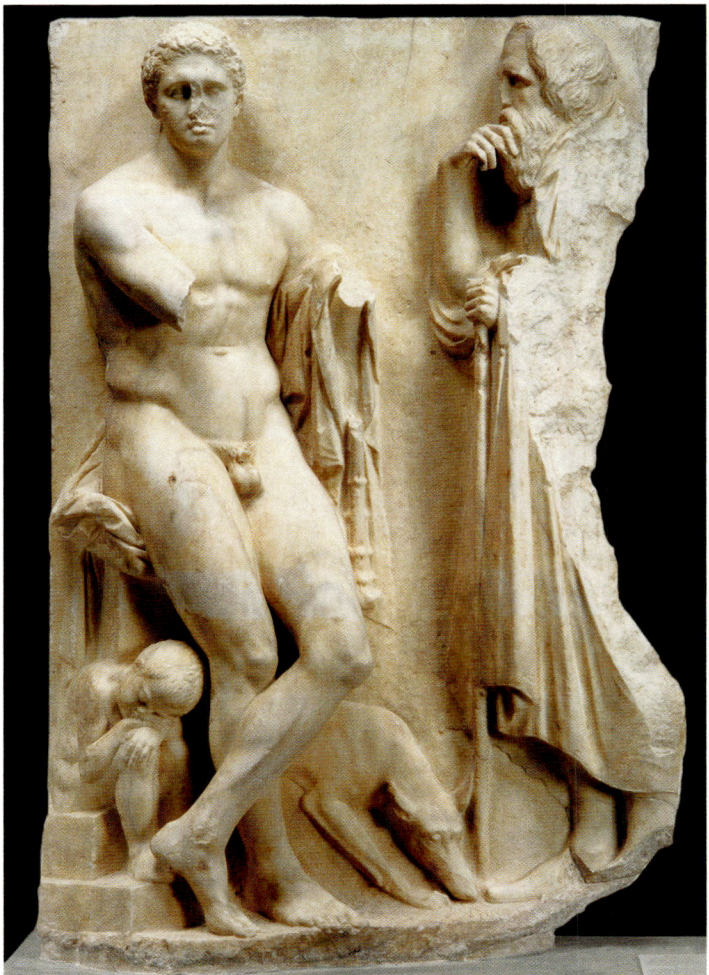

**5-64** Grave stele of a young hunter, found near the Ilissos River, Athens, Greece, ca. 340–330 BCE. Marble, 5′ 6″ high. National Archaeological Museum, Athens.

The emotional intensity of this stele representing an old man mourning the loss of his son and the figures' large, deeply set eyes with fleshy overhanging brows reflect the style of Skopas of Paros.

reminiscent of that of the Olympia seer (FIG. 5-31), ponders the irony of fate that has taken the life of his powerful son yet preserved him, the father, in his frail old age. Most remarkable of all, the hunter himself looks out at the viewer, inviting sympathy and creating an emotional bridge between the spectator and the artwork that was inconceivable in the art of the High Classical period.

**LYSIPPOS** The third great Late Classical sculptor, LYSIPPOS OF SIKYON, won such renown that Alexander the Great selected him to create his official portrait. (Alexander could afford to employ the best because the Macedonian kingdom enjoyed vast wealth. King Philip was able to hire the leading thinker of his age, Aristotle, as the young Alexander's tutor.) Lysippos introduced a new canon of proportions in which the bodies were more slender than those of Polykleitos and the heads roughly one-eighth the height of the body rather than one-seventh, as in the previous century. One of Lysippos's most famous works, a bronze statue of an *apoxyomenos* (an athlete scraping oil from his body after exercising)—known, as usual, only from Roman copies in marble (FIG. **5-65**)—exhibits the new proportions. A comparison with Polykleitos's *Doryphoros* (FIG. 5-40) reveals more than a change in physique, however. A nervous energy, lacking in the bal-

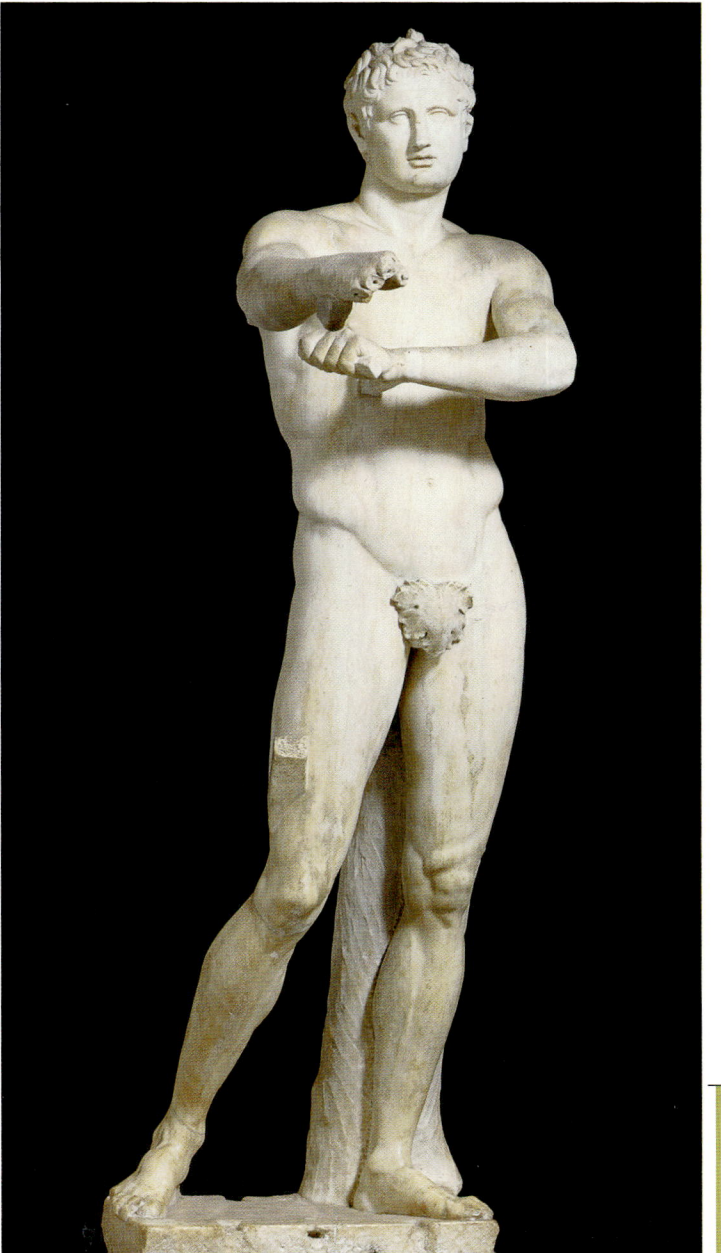

**5-65** LYSIPPOS, *Apoxyomenos* (*Scraper*). Roman copy of a bronze statue of ca. 330 BCE. Marble, 6′ 9″ high. Musei Vaticani, Rome. ◼◀

Lysippos introduced a new canon of proportions and a nervous energy to his statues. He also broke down the dominance of the frontal view and encouraged viewing his statues from multiple angles.

anced form of the *Doryphoros*, runs through Lysippos's *Apoxyomenos*. The *strigil* (scraper) is about to reach the end of the right arm, and at any moment the athlete will switch it to the other hand so that he can scrape his left arm. At the same time, he will shift his weight and reverse the positions of his legs. Lysippos also began to break down the dominance of the frontal view in statuary and encouraged the observer to view his athlete from multiple angles. Because Lysippos represented the apoxyomenos with his right arm boldly thrust forward, the figure breaks out of the shallow rectangular box that defined the boundaries of earlier statues. To comprehend the action, the observer must move to the side and view Lysippos's work at a three-quarter angle or in full profile.

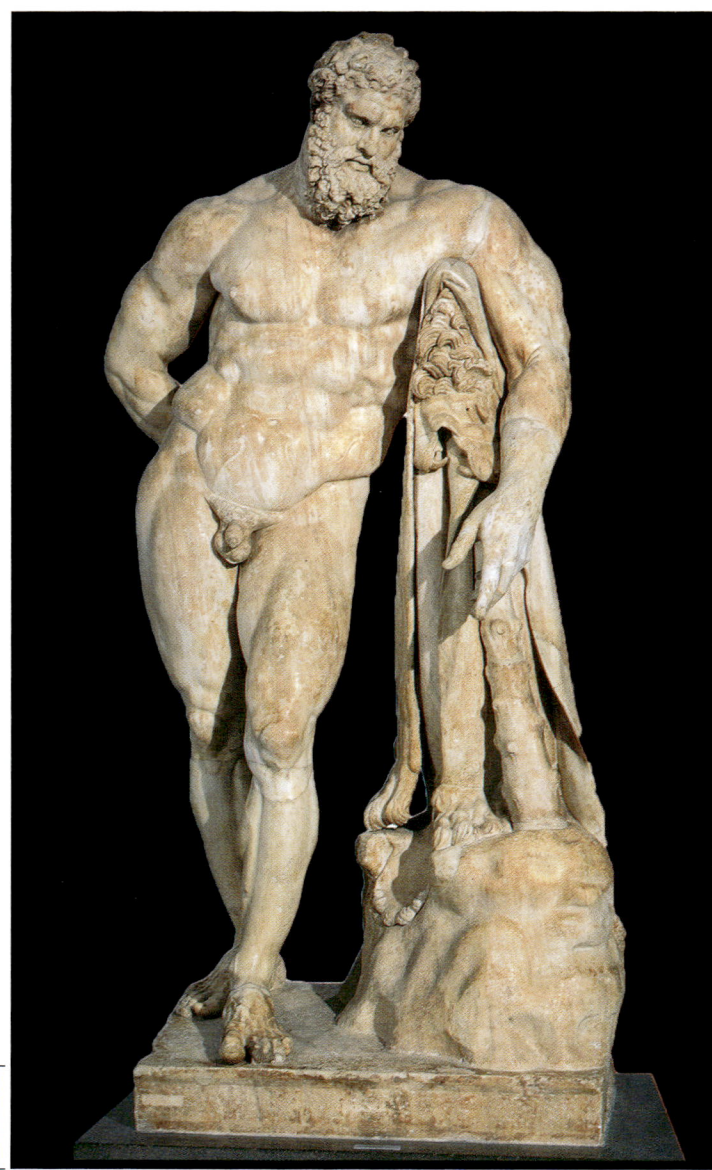

**5-66** LYSIPPOS, Weary Herakles (*Farnese Hercules*). Roman statue from the Baths of Caracalla (FIG. 7-66), Rome, Italy, signed by GLYKON OF ATHENS, based on a bronze statue of ca. 320 BCE. Marble, 10′ 5″ high. Museo Archeologico Nazionale, Naples.

Lysippos's portrayal of Herakles after the hero obtained the golden apples of the Hesperides ironically shows the muscle-bound hero as so weary that he must lean on his club for support.

To grasp the full meaning of another of Lysippos's works, a colossal statue (FIG. 5-66) depicting a weary Herakles, the viewer must walk around it. Once again, the original is lost. The most impressive of the surviving statues based on the Lysippan original is nearly twice life-size. It stood in the Baths of Caracalla in Rome, where, like the marble copy of Polykleitos's *Doryphoros* (FIG. 5-40) from the Roman palaestra at Pompeii, Lysippos's muscle-bound Greek hero provided inspiration for Romans who came to the baths to exercise. (The Roman sculptor, GLYKON OF ATHENS, signed the statue, but did not mention Lysippos. The educated Roman public needed no label to identify the famous work.) The exaggerated muscular development of Herakles is poignantly ironic, however. Lysippos depicted the hero as so weary that he must lean on his club for support. Without that prop, Herakles would topple over. Lysippos and other fourth-century BCE artists rejected stability and balance as worthy goals for statuary.

Herakles holds the golden apples of the Hesperides in his right hand behind his back—unseen unless the viewer walks around the statue. Lysippos's subject is thus the same as that of the metope (FIG. 5-33) of the Early Classical Temple of Zeus at Olympia, but the fourth-century BCE Herakles is no longer serene. Instead of expressing joy, or at least satisfaction, at having completed 1 of the impossible 12 labors, he is almost dejected. Exhausted by his physical efforts, he can think only of his pain and weariness. Lysippos's portrayal of Herakles in this statue is an eloquent testimony to Late Classical sculptors' interest in humanizing the Greek gods and heroes. In this respect, despite their divergent styles, Praxiteles, Skopas, and Lysippos followed a common path.

## Alexander the Great and Macedonian Court Art

Alexander the Great's favorite book was the *Iliad,* and his own life very much resembled an epic saga, full of heroic battles, exotic locales, and unceasing drama. Alexander was a man of singular character, an inspired leader with boundless energy and an almost foolhardy courage. He personally led his army into battle on the back of Bucephalus (FIG. 5-70), the wild and mighty steed only he could tame and ride.

**ALEXANDER'S PORTRAITS** Ancient sources reveal that Alexander believed only Lysippos had captured his essence in a portrait, and thus only he was authorized to sculpt the king's image. Lysippos's most famous portrait of the Macedonian king was a full-length, heroically nude bronze statue of Alexander holding a lance

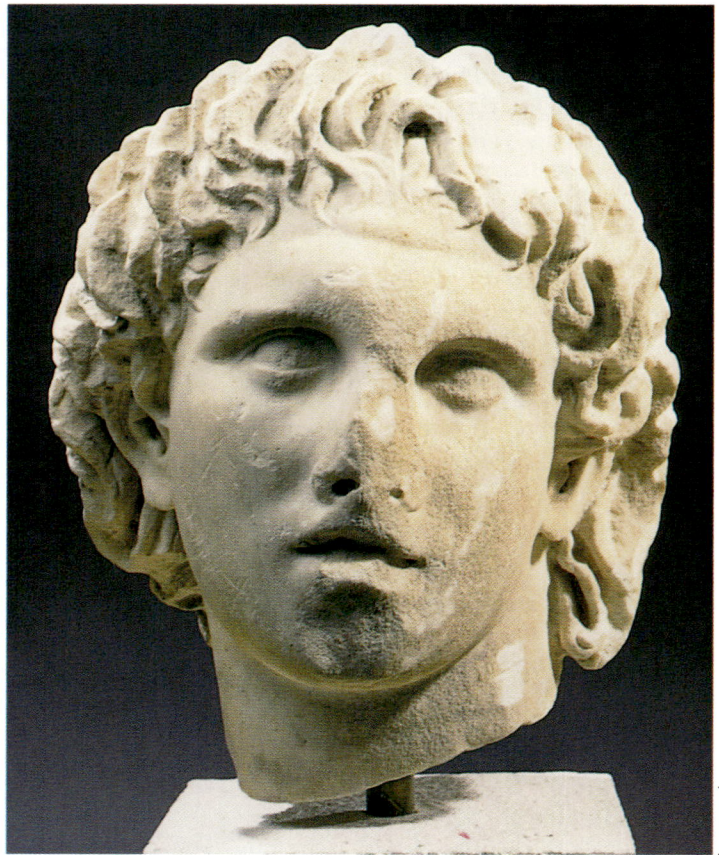

**5-67** Head of Alexander the Great, from Pella, Greece, third century BCE. Marble, 1′ high. Archaeological Museum, Pella.

Lysippos was the official portrait sculptor of Alexander the Great. This third-century BCE sculpture has the sharp turn of the head and thick mane of hair of Lysippos's statue of Alexander with a lance.

and turning his head toward the sky. According to Plutarch, an epigram inscribed on the base stated the statue depicted Alexander gazing at Zeus and proclaiming, "I place the earth under my sway; you, O Zeus, keep Olympus." Plutarch also reported that Lysippos's portrait immortalized Alexander's "leonine" hair and "melting glance."[7] The Lysippan original is lost, and because Alexander was portrayed so many times, and long after his death, it is very difficult to determine which of the many surviving images is most faithful to the fourth-century BCE portrait. A leading candidate is a third-century BCE marble head (FIG. 5-67) from Pella, the capital of Macedonia and Alexander's birthplace. It has the sharp turn of the head and thick mane of hair that were key ingredients of Lysippos's portrait. The Pella sculptor's treatment of the features also is consistent with the style of the later fourth century BCE. The deep-set eyes and parted lips recall the manner of Skopas (FIG. 5-64A), and the delicate handling of the flesh brings to mind the faces of Praxitelean statues (FIG. 5-63). Although not a copy, this head very likely approximates the young king's official portrait and provides insight into Alexander's personality as well as Lysippos's art.

**PELLA MOSAICS** Alexander's palace has not been excavated, but the sumptuous life of the Macedonian aristocracy is evident from the costly objects found in Macedonian graves and from the abundance of mosaics uncovered in houses at Pella. The Macedonian mosaics are *pebble mosaics* (see "Mosaics," Chapter 8, page 245). The floors consist of small stones of various colors collected from beaches and riverbanks and set into a thick coat of cement. The finest pebble mosaic yet to come to light from the Pella excavations has a stag hunt (FIG. 5-68) as its *emblema* (central framed panel), bordered in turn by an intricate floral pattern and a stylized wave motif (not shown in the illustration). The artist signed his work in the same manner as proud Greek vase painters and potters did: "GNOSIS made it." This is the earliest mosaicist's signature known,

and its prominence in the design undoubtedly attests to the artist's reputation. The home's owner wanted guests to know that Gnosis himself, not an imitator, had laid this floor.

The Pella stag hunt, with its light figures against a dark ground, has much in common with red-figure painting. In the pebble mosaic, however, thin strips of lead or terracotta define most of the contour lines and some of the interior details. Subtle gradations of yellow, brown, and red, as well as black, white, and gray pebbles, suggest the interior volumes. Gnosis used shading to model the musculature of the hunters, their billowing cloaks, and the animals' bodies. The use of light and dark to suggest volume is rare on Greek painted vases, although examples do exist. Monumental painters, however, commonly used shading, the Greek term for which was *skiagraphia* (literally, "shadow painting"). The Greeks attributed the invention of shading to an Athenian painter of the fifth century BCE named Apollodoros. Gnosis's emblema, with its sparse landscape setting, probably reflects contemporaneous panel painting.

**HADES AND PERSEPHONE** Excavations at Vergina have provided valuable additional information about Macedonian art and about Greek mural painting. One of the most important finds was a painted tomb with a representation of Hades, lord of the Underworld, abducting Persephone, the daughter of Demeter, the goddess of grain. The mural (FIG. 5-69) is remarkable for its intense drama and for the painter's use of foreshortening and

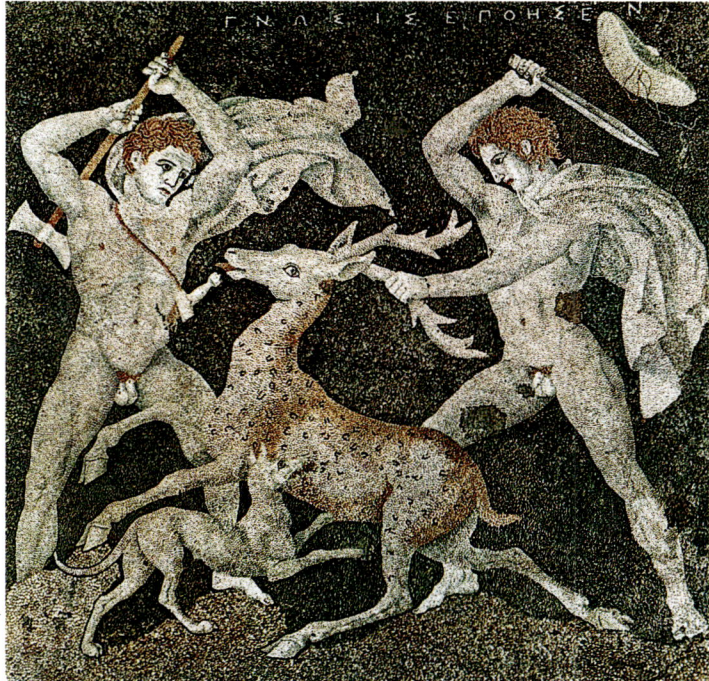

1 ft.

**5-68** GNOSIS, Stag hunt, from Pella, Greece, ca. 300 BCE. Pebble mosaic, figural panel 10′ 2″ high. Archaeological Museum, Pella.

The floor mosaics at the Macedonian capital of Pella are of the early type made with pebbles of various natural colors. This stag hunt by Gnosis bears the earliest known signature of a mosaicist.

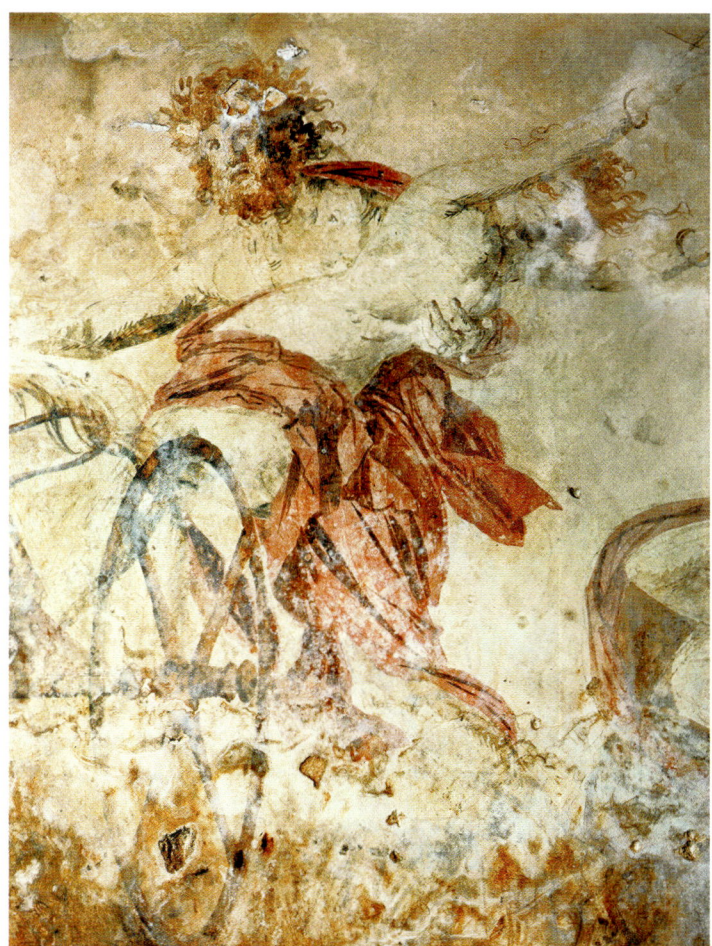

1 ft.

**5-69** Hades abducting Persephone, detail of a wall painting in tomb 1, Vergina, Greece, mid-fourth century BCE. Fresco, detail 3′ 3½″ high.

The intense drama, three-quarter views, and shading in this representation of the lord of the Underworld kidnapping Demeter's daughter are characteristics of mural painting at the time of Alexander.

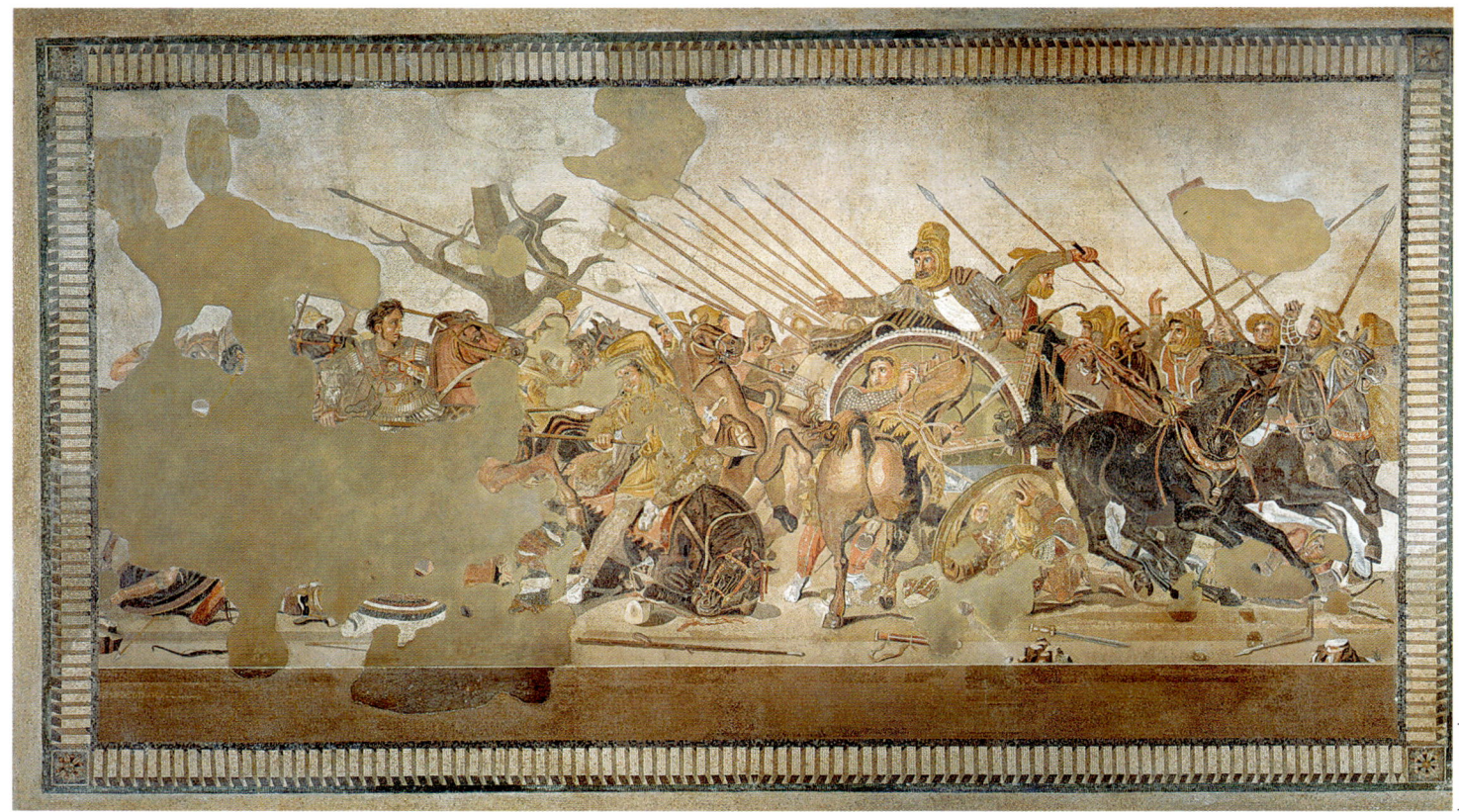

**5-70** PHILOXENOS OF ERETRIA, *Battle of Issus*, ca. 310 BCE. Roman copy (*Alexander Mosaic*) from the House of the Faun, Pompeii, Italy, late second or early first century BCE. Tessera mosaic, 8′ 10″ × 16′ 9″. Museo Archeologico Nazionale, Naples. ◼◀

*Battle of Issus* reveals Philoxenos's mastery of foreshortening, of modeling figures in color, and of depicting reflections and shadows, as well as his ability to capture the psychological intensity of warfare.

shading. Hades holds the terrified seminude Persephone in his left arm and steers his racing chariot with his right as Persephone's garments and hair blow in the wind. The artist depicted the heads of both figures and even the chariot's wheels in three-quarter views. The chariot, in fact, seems to be bursting into the viewer's space. Especially noteworthy is the way the painter used short, dark brushstrokes to suggest shading on the underside of Hades' right arm, on Persephone's torso, and elsewhere. Although fragmentary, the Vergina mural is a precious document of the almost totally lost art of monumental painting in ancient Greece.

**BATTLE OF ISSUS** Further insight into developments in painting at the time of Alexander comes from a large mosaic (FIG. **5-70**) that decorated the floor of a room in a lavishly appointed Roman house at Pompeii. The mosaicist employed *tesserae* (cubical pieces of glass or tiny stones cut to the desired size and shape) instead of pebbles (see "Mosaics," Chapter 8, page 245). The subject is a great battle between the armies of Alexander the Great and the Achaemenid Persian king Darius III (r. 336–330 BCE), probably the battle of Issus in southeastern Turkey, when Darius fled in his chariot in humiliating defeat. The mosaic dates to the late second or early first century BCE. Most art historians believe it is a reasonably faithful copy of *Battle of Issus,* a famous panel painting of about 310 BCE made by PHILOXENOS OF ERETRIA for King Cassander, one of Alexander's successors. Some scholars have proposed, however, that the *Alexander Mosaic,* as it is commonly called, is a copy of a painting by one of the few Greek woman artists whose name is known, Helen of Egypt.

*Battle of Issus* is notable for the artist's technical mastery of problems that had long fascinated Greek painters. Even Euthymides would have marveled at the fourth-century BCE painter's depiction of the rearing horse seen in a three-quarter rear view below Darius. The subtle modulation of the horse's rump through shading in browns and yellows is much more accomplished than the comparable attempts at shading in the Pella mosaic (FIG. 5-68) or the Vergina mural (FIG. 5-69). Other details are even more impressive. The Persian to the right of the rearing horse has fallen to the ground and raises, backward, a dropped Macedonian shield to protect himself from being trampled. Philoxenos recorded the reflection of the man's terrified face on the polished surface of the shield. Everywhere in the scene, men, animals, and weapons cast shadows on the ground. This interest in the reflection of insubstantial light on a shiny surface, and in the absence of light (shadows), stands in sharp contrast to earlier painters' preoccupation with the clear presentation of weighty figures seen against a blank background. Philoxenos here truly opened a window into a world filled not only with figures, trees, and sky but also with light. This new, distinctly Greek notion of what a painting should be characterizes most of the history of art in the Western world from the Renaissance on.

Most impressive about *Battle of Issus,* however, is the psychological intensity of the drama unfolding before the viewer's eyes. Alexander, riding Bucephalus, leads his army into battle, recklessly one might say, without even a helmet to protect him. He drives his spear through one of Darius's trusted "Immortals," who swore to guard the king's life, while the Persian's horse collapses beneath him. The Macedonian king is only a few yards away from Darius,

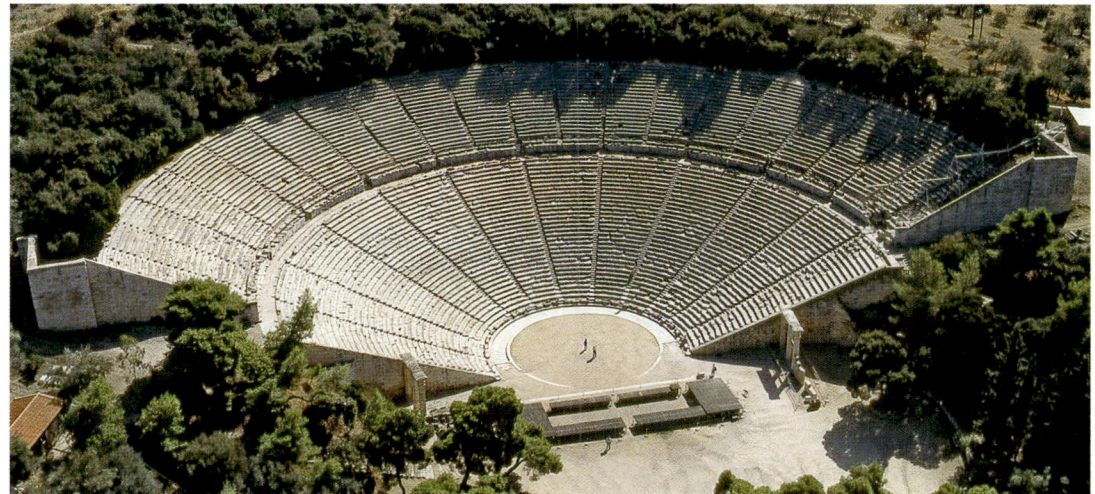

and Alexander directs his gaze at the Persian king, not at the man impaled on his now-useless spear. Darius has called for retreat. In fact, his charioteer is already whipping the horses and speeding the king to safety. Before he escapes, Darius looks back at Alexander and in a pathetic gesture reaches out toward his brash foe. But the victory has slipped from his hands. In Pliny's opinion, Philoxenos's painting of the battle between Alexander and Darius was "inferior to none."[8] It is easy to see why he reached that conclusion.

## Architecture

In architecture, as in sculpture and painting, the Late Classical period was a time of innovation and experimentation.

**THEATER OF EPIDAUROS** In ancient Greece, actors did not perform plays repeatedly over months or years as they do today, but only during sacred festivals. Greek drama was closely associated with religious rites and was not pure entertainment. In the fifth century BCE, for example, the Athenians staged performances of the tragedies of Aeschylus, Sophocles, and Euripides during the Dionysos festival in the theater dedicated to the god on the southern slope of the Acropolis. Yet it is Epidauros, in the Peloponnesos, that boasts the finest theater (FIG. 5-71) in Greece. Constructed shortly after the birth of Alexander, the theater is still the setting for performances of ancient Greek dramas. The architect was POLYKLEITOS THE YOUNGER, possibly a nephew of the famous fifth-century BCE sculptor.

The precursor of the formal Greek theater was a circular patch of earth where actors performed sacred rites, songs, and dances. This circular hard and level surface later became the orchestra of the theater. *Orchestra* literally means "dancing place." The actors and the chorus performed there, and at Epidauros an altar to Dionysos stood at the center of the circle. The spectators sat on a slope overlooking the orchestra—the *theatron,* or "place for seeing." When the Greek theater took architectural shape, the builders always situated the auditorium (*cavea,* Latin for "hollow place, cavity") on a hillside. The cavea at Epidauros, composed of wedge-shaped sections (*cunei,* singular *cuneus*) of stone benches separated by stairs, is somewhat greater than a semicircle in plan. The auditorium is 387 feet in diameter, and its 55 rows of seats accommodated about 12,000 spectators. They entered the theater via a passageway between the seating area and the scene building (*skene*), which housed dressing rooms for the actors and also formed a backdrop for the plays. The design is simple but perfectly suited to its function. Even in antiquity, the Epidauros theater was famous for the harmony of its proportions. Although spectators sitting in some of the seats would have had a poor view of the skene, all had unobstructed views of the orchestra. Because of the open-air cavea's excellent acoustics, everyone could hear the actors and chorus.

**CORINTHIAN CAPITALS** The theater at Epidauros is about 500 yards southeast of the sanctuary of Asklepios, and Polykleitos the Younger worked there as well. He was the architect of the *tholos,* the circular shrine that probably housed the sacred snakes of the healing god. That building lies in ruins today, its architectural fragments removed to the local museum, but one can get an approximate idea of its original appearance from the somewhat earlier and partially reconstructed tholos (FIG. 5-72) at Delphi that THEODOROS OF PHOKAIA designed. Both tholoi had an exterior colonnade of Doric columns, but the interior columns had bases and *Corinthian capitals*

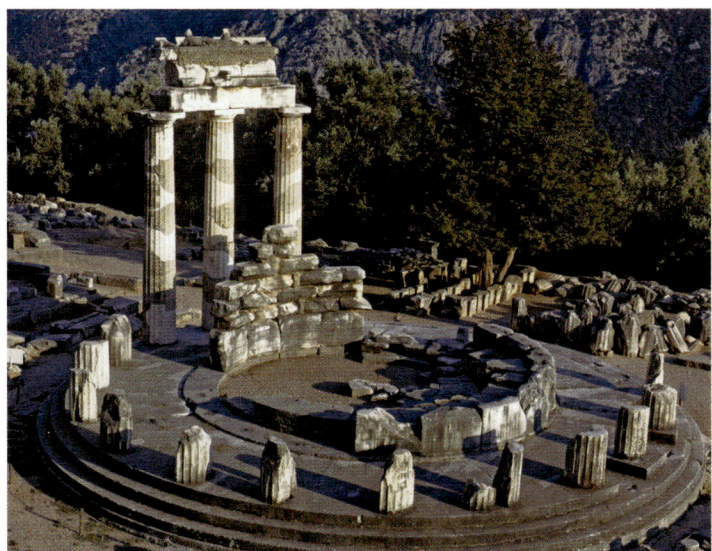

5-72 THEODOROS OF PHOKAIA, Tholos, Delphi, Greece, ca. 375 BCE.

## The Corinthian Capital

The Corinthian capital (FIG. 5-73) is more ornate than either the Doric or Ionic (FIG. 5-13). It consists of a double row of acanthus leaves, from which tendrils and flowers emerge, wrapped around a bell-shaped echinus. Although architectural historians often cite this capital as the distinguishing feature of the Corinthian order, strictly speaking no Corinthian order exists. The new capital type was simply a substitute for the Ionic order's volute capital.

The sculptor Kallimachos invented the Corinthian capital during the second half of the fifth century BCE. Vitruvius recorded the circumstances that supposedly led to its creation:

> A maiden who was a citizen of Corinth . . . died. After her funeral, her nurse collected the goblets in which the maiden had taken delight while she was alive, and after putting them together in a basket, she took them to the grave monument and put them on top of it. In order that they should remain in place for a long time, she covered them with a tile. Now it happened that this basket was placed over the root of an acanthus. As time went on the acanthus root, pressed down in the middle by the weight, sent forth, when it was about springtime, leaves and stalks; its stalks growing up along the sides of the basket and being pressed out from the angles because of the weight of the tile, were forced to form volute-like curves at their extremities. At this point, Kallimachos happened to be going by and noticed the basket with this gentle growth of leaves around it. Delighted with the order and the novelty of the form, he made columns using it as his model and established a canon of proportions for it.*

Kallimachos worked on the Acropolis in Pericles' great building program. Many scholars believe a Corinthian column supported the outstretched right hand of Phidias's *Athena Parthenos* (FIG. 5-46) because one appears in some of the Roman copies of the lost statue. In any case, the earliest preserved Corinthian capital dates to the time of Kallimachos. The new type was rarely used before the mid-fourth century BCE, however, and did not become popular until Hellenistic and especially Roman times. Later architects favored the Corinthian capital because of its ornate character and because it eliminated certain problems of both the Doric and Ionic orders (see "Doric and Ionic Orders," page 116, and FIG. 5-13).

The Ionic capital, unlike the Doric, has two distinct profiles—the front and back (with the volutes) and the sides. The volutes always faced outward on a Greek temple, but architects met with a vexing problem at the corners of their buildings, which had two adjacent "fronts." They solved the problem by placing volutes on both outer faces of the corner capitals (as on the Erechtheion, FIG. 5-52, and the Temple of Athena Nike, FIG. 5-55), but that was an awkward solution.

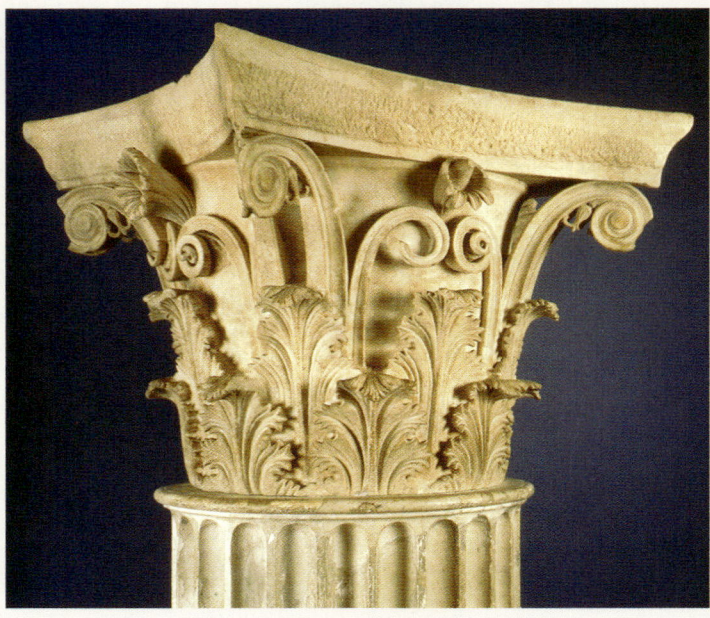

**5-73** POLYKLEITOS THE YOUNGER, Corinthian capital, from the tholos, Epidauros, Greece, ca. 350 BCE. Archaeological Museum, Epidauros.

Corinthian capitals, invented by the fifth-century BCE sculptor Kallimachos, are more ornate than Doric and Ionic capitals. They feature a double row of acanthus leaves with tendrils and flowers.

Doric design rules also presented problems for Greek architects at the corners of buildings. Doric friezes had to satisfy three supposedly inflexible rules:

▎ A triglyph must be exactly over the center of each column

▎ A triglyph must be over the center of each *intercolumniation* (the space between two columns)

▎ Triglyphs at the corners of the frieze must meet so that no space is left over

These rules are contradictory, however. If the corner triglyphs must meet, then they cannot be placed over the center of the corner column (FIGS. 5-1, 5-25, 5-30, and 5-44).

The Corinthian capital eliminated both problems. Because the capital's four sides have a similar appearance, corner Corinthian capitals do not have to be modified, as do corner Ionic capitals. And because the Corinthian "order" incorporates an Ionic frieze, architects do not have to contend with corner triglyphs.

*Vitruvius, *De architectura,* 4.1.8–10. Translated by J. J. Pollitt, *The Art of Ancient Greece: Sources and Documents* (New York: Cambridge University Press, 1990), 193–194.

(FIG. **5-73;** see "The Corinthian Capital," above), an invention of the second half of the fifth century BCE.

Consistent with the extremely conservative nature of Greek temple design, architects did not readily embrace the Corinthian capital. Until the second century BCE, Greek architects used Corinthian capitals only for the interiors of sacred buildings, as at Delphi and Epidauros. The earliest instance of a Corinthian capital on the exterior of a Greek building is the Choragic Monument of Lysikrates (FIG. **5-74**), which is not really a building at all. Lysikrates had sponsored a chorus in a theatrical contest in 334 BCE, and

**5-74** Choragic Monument of Lysikrates, Athens, Greece, 334 BCE.

The first known use of Corinthian capitals on the exterior of a building is on the monument Lysikrates erected in Athens to commemorate the victory his chorus won in a theatrical contest.

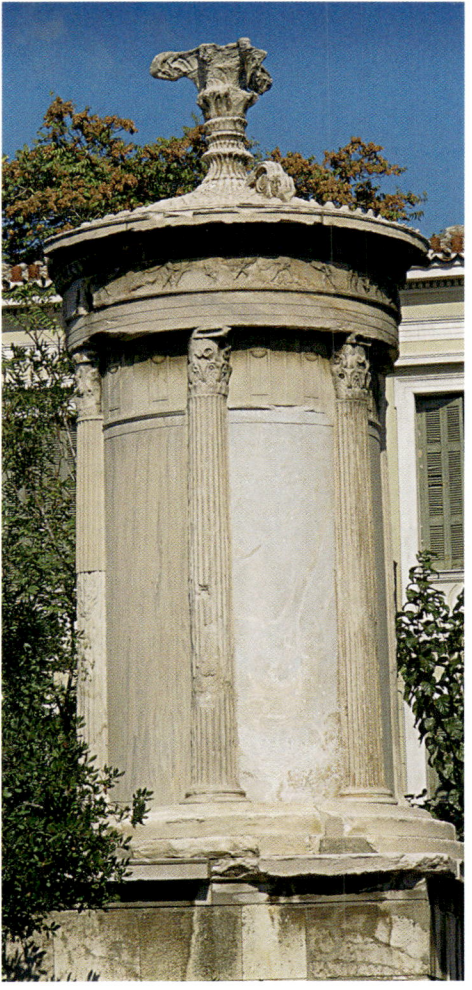

Alexander the Great's conquest of the Near East and Egypt ushered in a new cultural age that historians and art historians alike call *Hellenistic*. The Hellenistic period opened with the death of Alexander in 323 BCE and lasted nearly three centuries, until the double suicide of Queen Cleopatra of Egypt and her Roman consort Mark Antony in 30 BCE after their decisive defeat at the battle of Actium by Antony's rival Augustus (see page 197). That year, Augustus made Egypt a province of the Roman Empire.

The cultural centers of the Hellenistic period were the court cities of the Greek kings who succeeded Alexander and divided his far-flung empire among themselves. Chief among them were Antioch in Syria, Alexandria in Egypt (named after Alexander and the site of his tomb), and Pergamon in Asia Minor (MAP 5-1). An international culture united the Hellenistic world, and its language was Greek. Hellenistic kings became enormously rich on the spoils of the East, priding themselves on their libraries, art collections, scientific enterprises, and skills as critics and connoisseurs, as well as on the learned men they could assemble at their courts. The world of the small, austere, and heroic city-state passed away, as did the power and prestige of its center, Athens. A cosmopolitan ("citizen of the world," in Greek) civilization, much like today's, replaced it.

## Architecture

The greater variety, complexity, and sophistication of Hellenistic culture called for an architecture on an imperial scale and of wide diversity, something far beyond the requirements of the Classical polis, even beyond that of Athens at the height of its power. Building activity shifted from the old centers on the Greek mainland to the opulent cities of the Hellenistic monarchs in the East.

**TEMPLE OF APOLLO, DIDYMA** Great scale, a theatrical element of surprise, and a willingness to break the traditional rules of Greek temple design characterize one of the most ambitious projects of the Hellenistic period, the Temple of Apollo (FIG. **5-75**) at Didyma. The Hellenistic temple replaced the Archaic temple at the site the Persians burned in 494 BCE when they sacked nearby Miletos. Construction began in 313 BCE under the direction of two architects native to the area, PAIONIOS OF EPHESOS and DAPHNIS OF MILETOS. So vast was

after he won, he erected a monument to commemorate his victory. The monument consists of a cylindrical drum resembling a tholos on a square base. Engaged Corinthian columns adorn the drum of Lysikrates' monument, and a huge Corinthian capital sits atop the roof. The freestanding capital once supported the victor's trophy, a bronze tripod.

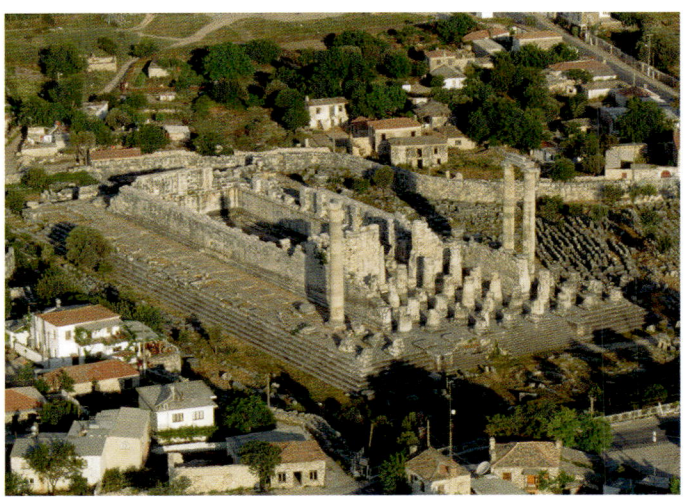

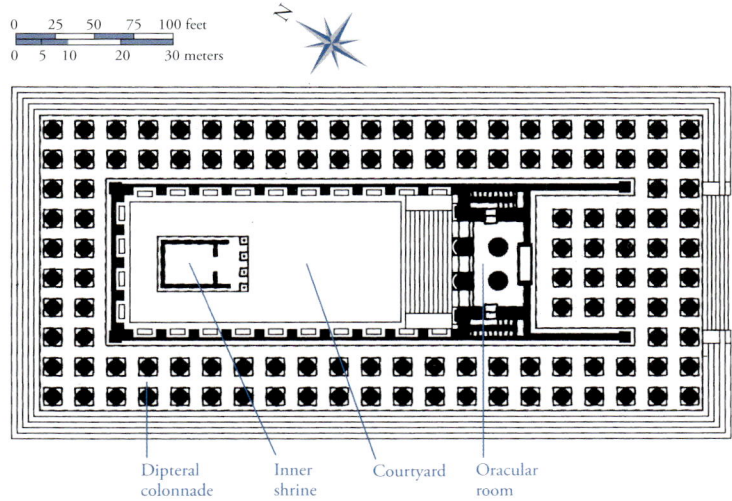

Dipteral colonnade · Inner shrine · Courtyard · Oracular room

**5-75** PAIONIOS OF EPHESOS and DAPHNIS OF MILETOS, aerial view (*left*, looking east) and plan (*right*) of the Temple of Apollo, Didyma, Turkey, begun 313 BCE.

This unusual Hellenistic temple was hypaethral (open to the sky) and featured a dipteral (double peripteral) colonnade framing an interior courtyard with a smaller shrine to Apollo.

the undertaking, however, that work on the temple continued off and on for more than 500 years—and still the project was never completed.

The temple was dipteral in plan and had an unusually broad facade of 10 Ionic columns almost 65 feet tall. The sides had 21 columns, consistent with the Classical formula for perfect proportions used for the Parthenon (21 = [2 × 10] + 1), but nothing else about the design is Classical. One anomaly immediately apparent to anyone who approached the building was that it had no pediment and no roof—it was *hypaethral,* or open to the sky. Also, the grand doorway to what should have been the temple's cella was nearly 5 feet off the ground and could not be entered. The explanation for the peculiar elevated doorway is that it served as a kind of stage where the oracle of Apollo could be announced to those assembled in front of the temple. Further, the unroofed dipteral colonnade did not surround a traditional cella. The columns were instead an elaborate frame for a central courtyard in which was a small prostyle shrine that housed a statue of Apollo. Entrance to the interior court was through two smaller doorways to the left and right of the great portal and down two narrow vaulted tunnels that could accommodate only a single file of people. From these dark and mysterious lateral passageways, worshipers emerged into the clear light of the courtyard, which also had a sacred spring and laurel trees in honor of Apollo. Opposite Apollo's inner temple, a stairway some 50 feet wide rose majestically toward three portals leading into the oracular room that also opened onto the front of the temple. This complex spatial planning marked a sharp departure from Classical Greek architecture, which stressed a building's exterior almost as a work of sculpture and left its interior relatively undeveloped.

**HIPPODAMOS OF MILETOS** When the Greeks finally expelled the Persians from Asia Minor in 479 BCE, they returned to cities in near ruin. Reconstruction of Miletos began after 466 BCE, according to a plan laid out by Hippodamos of Miletos, whom Aristotle singled out as the father of rational city planning. Hippodamos imposed a strict grid plan on the site, regardless of the terrain, so that all streets met at right angles. In fact, such *orthogonal plans* predate Hippodamos, not only in Archaic Greece and Etruscan Italy but also in the ancient Near East and Egypt. Still, Hippodamos was so famous that his name has ever since been synonymous with this kind of urban plan. The so-called *Hippodamian plan* also designated separate quarters for public, private, and religious functions. A "Hippodamian city" was logically as well as regularly planned. This desire to impose order on nature and to assign a proper place in the whole to each of the city's constituent parts was very much in keeping with the philosophical tenets of the fifth century BCE. Hippodamos's formula for the ideal city was another manifestation of the same outlook that produced Polykleitos's *Canon* and the Parthenon.

**PRIENE** Hippodamian planning was still the norm in Late Classical and Hellenistic Greece. The city of Priene (FIG. **5-76**), also in Asia Minor, was laid out during the fourth century BCE. It had fewer than 5,000 inhabitants (Hippodamos thought 10,000 was the ideal number). Situated on sloping ground, many of its narrow north-south streets were little more than long stairways. Uniformly sized city blocks, the standard planning unit, were nonetheless imposed on the irregular terrain. More than one unit was reserved for major structures such as the Temple of Athena and the theater. The central agora occupied six blocks.

**STOA OF ATTALOS, ATHENS** Framing each side of Priene's agora was a *stoa.* These covered colonnades, or *porticos,* which often housed shops and civic offices, were ideal vehicles for shaping urban spaces, and they were staples of Hellenistic cities. Even the agora of Athens, an ancient city notable for its haphazard, unplanned development, was eventually framed to the east and south by stoas placed at right angles to one another. These new porticos joined the famous Painted Stoa (see page 143), where the Hellenistic philosopher Zeno and his successors taught. The *Stoic* school of Greek philosophy took its name from that building.

The finest of the new Athenian stoas was the Stoa of Attalos II (FIG. **5-77**), a gift to the city by a grateful alumnus, the king of Pergamon (r. 159–138 BCE), who had studied at Athens in his youth. The stoa was meticulously reconstructed under the direction of the American School of Classical Studies at Athens and today has a second life as a museum housing more than seven decades of finds from the Athenian agora, as well as the offices of the American excavation

**5-76** Restored view of Priene, Turkey, fourth century BCE and later (John Burge).

Despite its irregular terrain, Priene had a strict grid plan conforming to the principles of Hippodamos of Miletos, whom Aristotle singled out as the father of rational city planning.

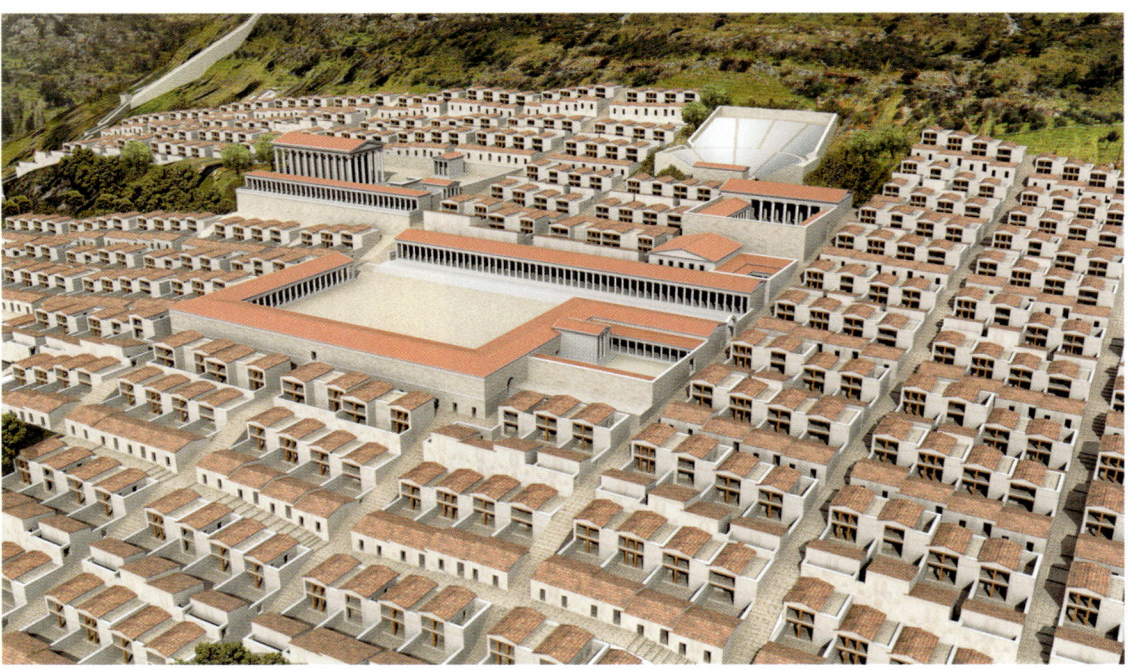

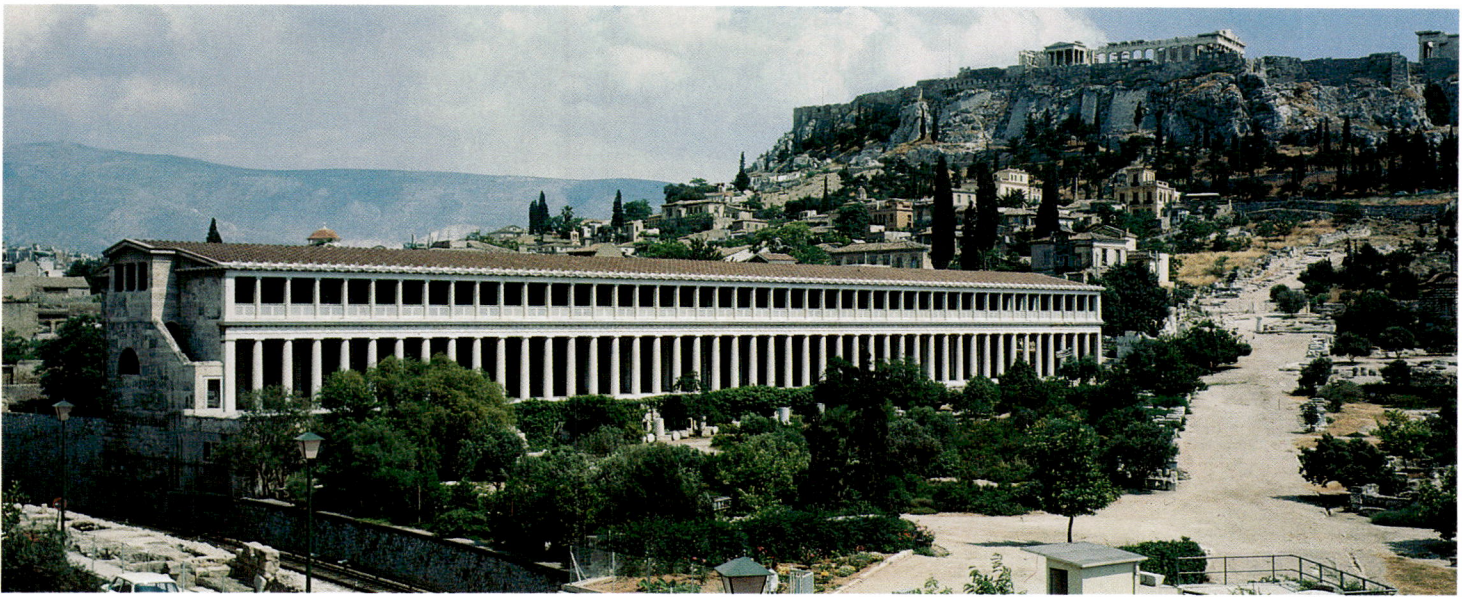

**5-77** Stoa of Attalos II (looking southeast with the Acropolis in the background), Agora, Athens, Greece, ca. 150 BCE.

The Stoa of Attalos II in the Athenian agora has been meticulously restored. Greek stoas were covered colonnades that housed shops and civic offices. They were also ideal vehicles for shaping urban spaces.

team. The stoa has two stories, each with 21 shops opening onto the colonnade. The facade columns are Doric on the ground level and Ionic on the second story. The mixing of the two orders on a single facade had occurred even in the Late Classical period. But it became increasingly common in the Hellenistic period, when respect for the old rules of Greek architecture was greatly diminished and a desire for variety and decorative effects often prevailed. Practical considerations also governed the form of the Stoa of Attalos. The columns are far more widely spaced than in Greek temple architecture, to allow for easy access. Also, the builders left the lower third of every Doric column shaft unfluted to guard against damage from constant traffic.

## Pergamon

Pergamon, the kingdom of Attalos II, was born in the early third century BCE after the breakup of Alexander's empire. Founded by Philetairos (r. 282–263 BCE), the Pergamene kingdom embraced almost all of western and southern Asia Minor. Upon the death in 133 BCE of its last king, Attalos III (r. 138–133 BCE), Pergamon was bequeathed to Rome, which by then was the greatest power in the Mediterranean world. The Attalids enjoyed immense wealth and expended much of it on the embellishment of their capital city, especially its acropolis. Located there were the royal palace, an arsenal and barracks, a great library and theater, an agora, and the sacred precincts of Athena and Zeus.

**ALTAR OF ZEUS, PERGAMON** The Altar of Zeus at Pergamon, erected about 175 BCE, is the most famous Hellenistic sculptural ensemble. The monument's west front (FIG. 5-78) has been reconstructed in Berlin. The altar proper was on an elevated platform, framed by an Ionic stoalike colonnade with projecting

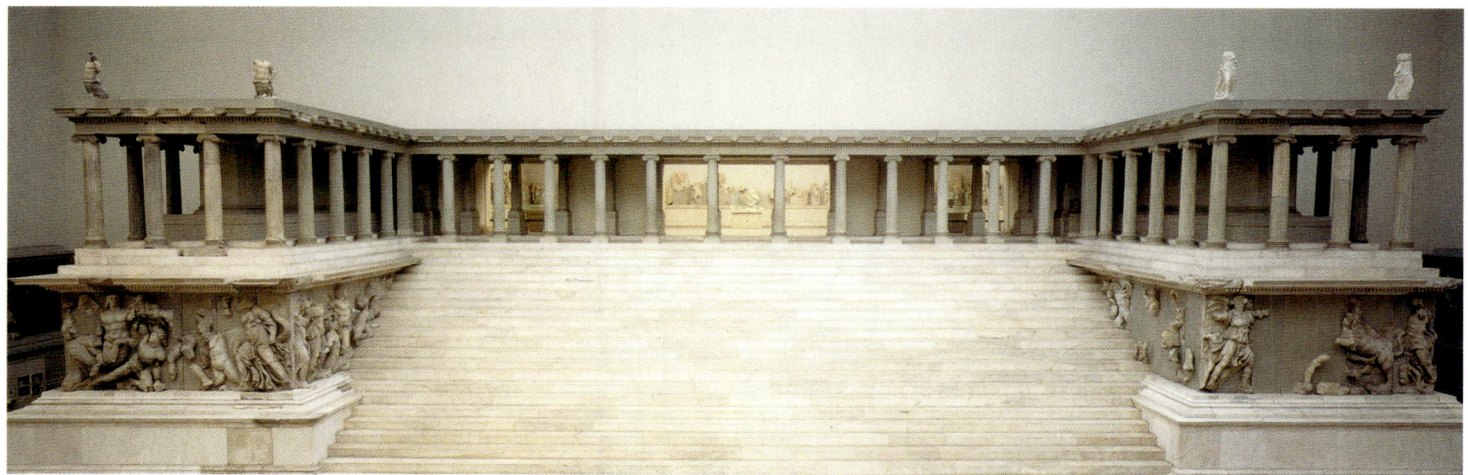

**5-78** Reconstructed west front of the Altar of Zeus, Pergamon, Turkey, ca. 175 BCE. Staatliche Museen zu Berlin, Berlin.

The gigantomachy frieze of Pergamon's monumental Altar of Zeus is almost 400 feet long. The battle of gods and giants alluded to the victory of King Attalos I over the Gauls of Asia Minor.

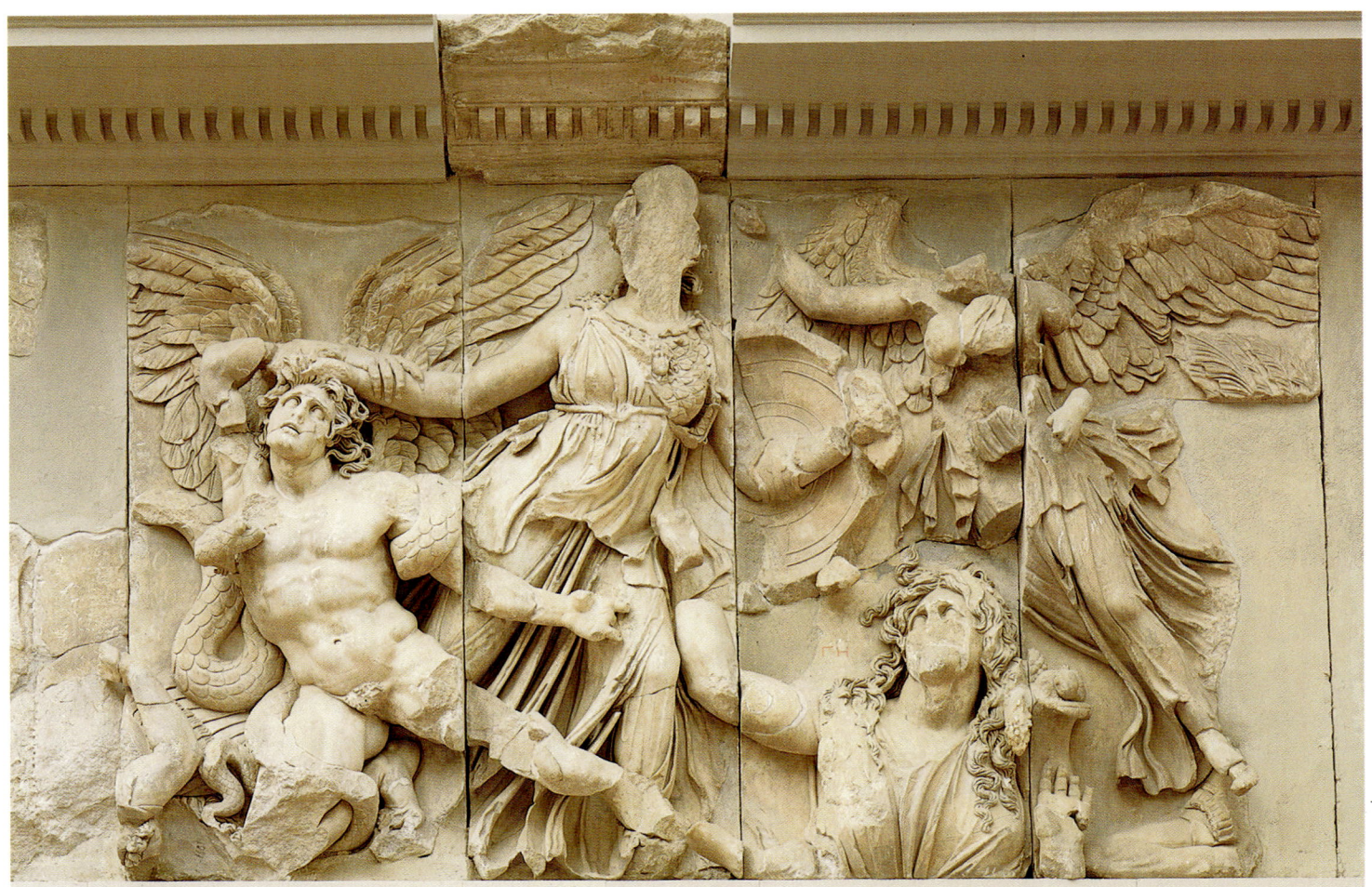

**5-79** Athena battling Alkyoneos, detail of the gigantomachy frieze, Altar of Zeus, Pergamon, Turkey, ca. 175 BCE. Marble, 7′ 6″ high. Staatliche Museen zu Berlin, Berlin.

The tumultuous battle scenes of the Pergamon altar have an emotional power unparalleled in earlier Greek art. Violent movement, swirling draperies, and vivid depictions of suffering fill the frieze.

1 ft.

wings on either side of a broad central staircase. All around the altar platform was a sculpted frieze almost 400 feet long, populated by about a hundred larger-than-life-size figures. The subject is the battle of Zeus and the gods against the giants. It is the most extensive representation Greek artists ever attempted of that epic conflict for control of the world. The gigantomachy also appeared on the shield of Phidias's *Athena Parthenos* and on some of the Parthenon metopes, because the Athenians wished to draw a parallel between the defeat of the giants and the defeat of the Persians. In the third century BCE, King Attalos I (r. 241–197 BCE) had successfully turned back an invasion of the Gauls in Asia Minor. The gigantomachy of the Altar of Zeus alluded to that Attalid victory over those barbarians. The Pergamene designers also used the gigantomachy frieze to establish a connection with Athens, whose earlier defeat of the Persians was by then legendary, and with the Parthenon, which the Hellenistic Greeks already recognized as a Classical monument—in both senses of the word. The figure of Athena (FIG. 5-79), for example, closely resembles the Athena from the Parthenon's east pediment. While Gaia, the earth goddess and mother of all the giants, emerges from the ground and looks on with horror, Athena grabs the hair of the giant Alkyoneos as Nike flies in to crown her. Zeus himself (not illustrated) was based on the Poseidon of the west pediment.

The Pergamene frieze, however, is not a dry series of borrowed motifs. On the contrary, its tumultuous narrative has an emotional intensity without parallel in earlier sculpture. The battle rages everywhere, even up and down the steps used to reach Zeus's altar (FIG. 5-78). Violent movement, swirling draperies, and vivid depictions of death and suffering fill the frieze. Wounded figures writhe in pain, and their faces reveal their anguish. Deep carving creates dark shadows. The figures project from the background like bursts of light. Art historians have justly described these features as "baroque," borrowing the term from 17th-century European sculpture (see Chapter 24). Indeed, there perhaps can be no greater contrast than between the Pergamene gigantomachy frieze and the comparable frieze (FIG. 5-18) of the Archaic Siphnian Treasury at Delphi.

**DYING GAULS** On the Altar of Zeus, Pergamene sculptors presented the victory of Attalos I over the Gauls in mythological disguise. An earlier Pergamene statuary group explicitly depicted the defeat of the barbarians. Roman copies of some of these figures reveal that the Hellenistic sculptors carefully studied and reproduced the distinctive features of the foreign Gauls, most notably their long, bushy hair and mustaches and the *torques* (neck bands) they frequently wore. The Pergamene victors were apparently not

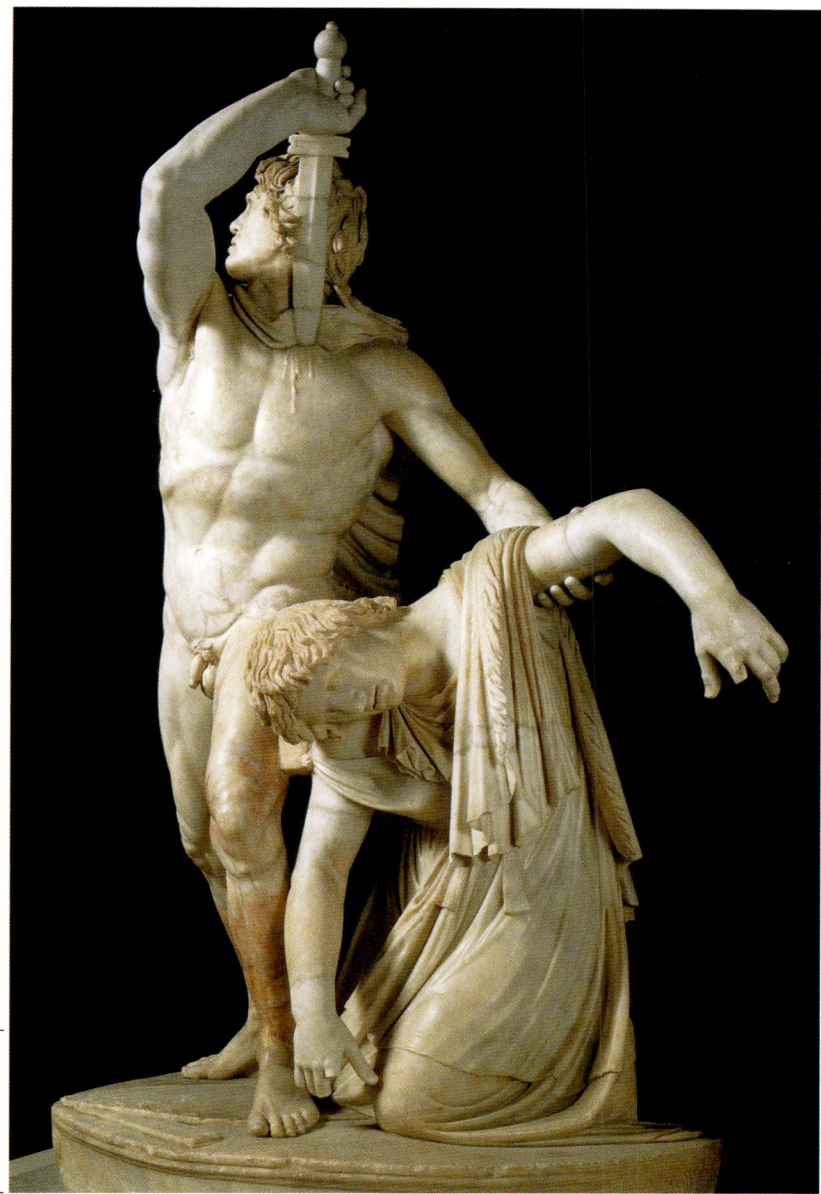

1 ft.

The defeat of the Gauls was also the subject of Pergamene statuary groups. The centerpiece of one group was a Gallic chieftain committing suicide after taking his wife's life. He preferred death to surrender.

part of this group. The viewer saw only their Gallic foes and their noble and moving response to defeat.

In what was probably the centerpiece of the group, a heroic Gallic chieftain (FIG. **5-80**) defiantly drives a sword into his own chest just below the collarbone, preferring suicide to surrender. He already has taken the life of his wife, who, if captured, would have been sold as a slave. In the best Lysippan tradition, the group can be fully appreciated only by walking around it. From one side, the observer sees the Gaul's intensely expressive face, from another his powerful torso, and from a third the woman's limp, lifeless body. The man's twisting posture, the almost theatrical gestures, and the emotional intensity of the suicidal act are hallmarks of the Pergamene baroque style and have close parallels in the later frieze of Zeus's altar.

The third Gaul from this group is a trumpeter (FIG. **5-81**) who collapses upon his large oval shield as blood pours from the gash in his chest. He stares at the ground with a pained expression. The Hellenistic figure recalls the dying warrior (FIG. 5-28) from the east pediment of the Temple of Aphaia at Aegina, but the pathos and drama of the suffering Gaul are far more pronounced. As in the suicide group and the gigantomachy frieze, the sculptor rendered the male musculature in an exaggerated manner. Note the tautness of the chest and the bulging veins of the left leg—implying that the unseen Pergamene warrior who has struck down this noble and savage foe must have been an extraordinarily powerful man. If this figure is the *tubicen* (trumpeter) Pliny mentioned as the work of the Pergamene master EPIGONOS, then Epigonos may be the sculptor of the entire group and the creator of the dynamic Hellenistic baroque style.[9]

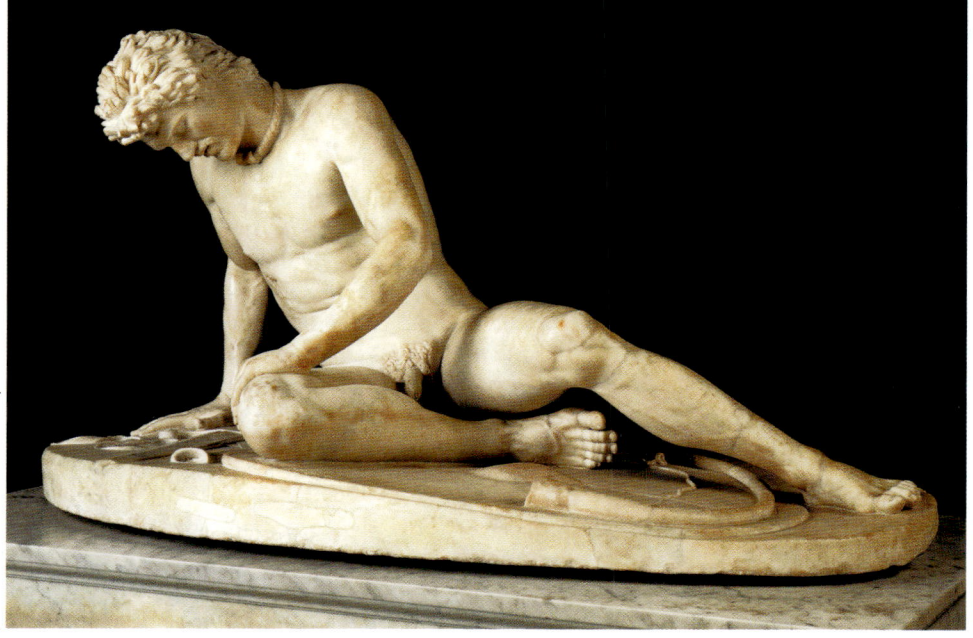

1 ft.

A Pergamene sculptor depicted this defeated Gallic trumpeter and the other Gauls as barbarians with bushy hair, mustaches, and neck bands, but also as noble foes who fought to the death.

## Sculpture

In different ways, Praxiteles, Skopas, and Lysippos had already taken bold steps in redefining the nature of Greek statuary. Still, Hellenistic sculptors went further, both in terms of style and in expanding the range of subjects considered suitable for monumental sculpture.

*NIKE OF SAMOTHRACE* One of the masterpieces of Hellenistic baroque sculpture is the statue of winged Victory set up in the Sanctuary of the Great Gods on the island of Samothrace. The *Nike of Samothrace* (FIG. 5-82) has just alighted on the prow of a Greek warship. She raises her (missing) right arm to crown the naval victor, just as Nike places a wreath on Athena's head on the Altar of Zeus (FIG. 5-79). But the Pergamene relief figure seems calm by comparison. The Samothracian Nike's wings still beat, and the wind sweeps her drapery. Her himation bunches in thick folds around her right leg, and her chiton is pulled tightly across her abdomen and left leg.

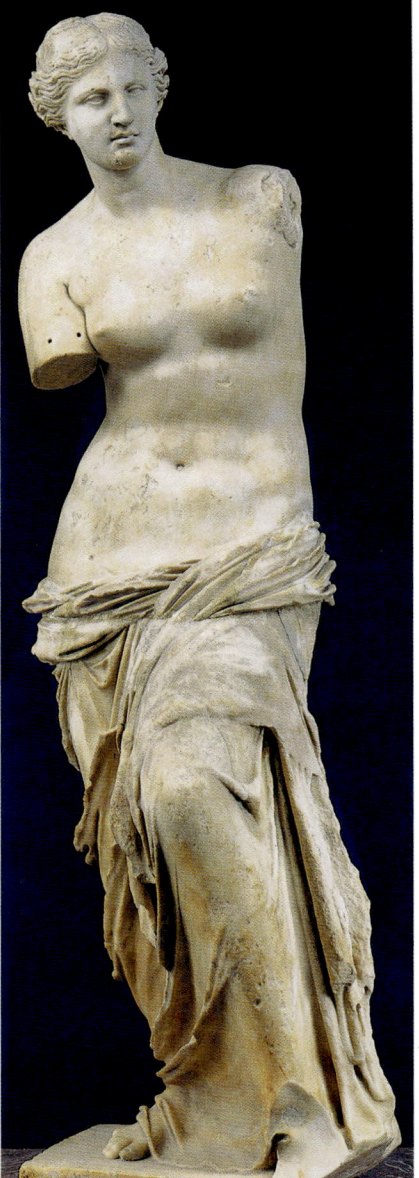

**5-83** ALEXANDROS OF ANTIOCH-ON-THE-MEANDER, Aphrodite (*Venus de Milo*), from Melos, Greece, ca. 150–125 BCE. Marble, 6′ 7″ high. Musée du Louvre, Paris.

Displaying the eroticism of many Hellenistic statues, this Aphrodite is more overtly sexual than the Knidian Aphrodite (FIG. 5-62). The goddess's slipping garment teases the spectator.

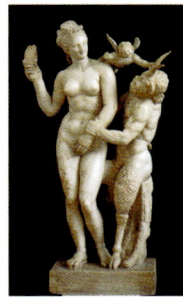

**5-83A** Aphrodite, Eros, and Pan, Delos, ca. 100 BCE.

1 ft.

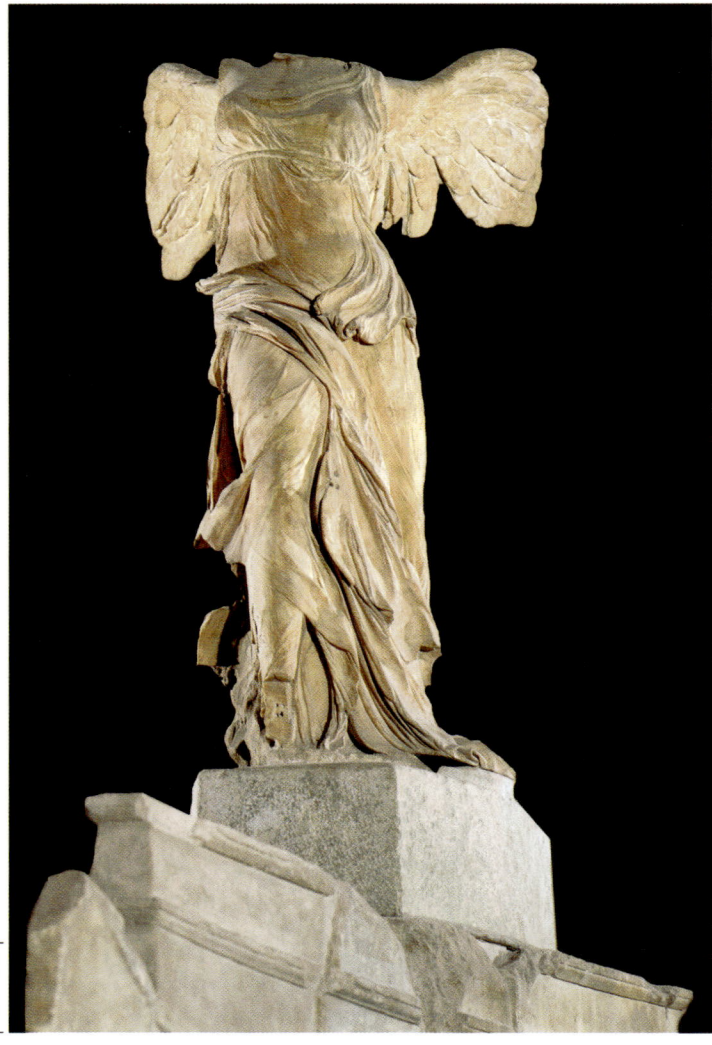

1 ft.

**5-82** Nike alighting on a warship (*Nike of Samothrace*), from Samothrace, Greece, ca. 190 BCE. Marble, Nike 8′ 1″ high. Musée du Louvre, Paris. ◼◀

Victory lands on a ship's prow to crown a naval victor. Her wings still beat, and the wind sweeps her drapery. The statue's placement in a fountain of splashing water heightened the dramatic visual effect.

The statue's setting amplified this theatrical effect. The sculptor set the war galley in the upper basin of a two-tiered fountain. In the lower basin were large boulders. The fountain's flowing water created the illusion of rushing waves hitting the prow of the ship. The statue's reflection in the shimmering water below accentuated the sense of lightness and movement. The sound of splashing water added an aural dimension to the visual drama. Art and nature combined here to create one of the most successful sculptures ever fashioned. In the *Nike of Samothrace* and other works in the Hellenistic baroque manner, sculptors resoundingly rejected the Polykleitan conception of a statue as an ideally proportioned, self-contained entity on a bare pedestal. The Hellenistic statues interact with their environment and appear as living, breathing, and intensely emotive human (or divine) presences.

*VENUS DE MILO* In the Hellenistic period, sculptors regularly followed Praxiteles' lead in undressing Aphrodite, but they also openly explored the eroticism of the nude female form. The famous *Venus de Milo* (FIG. 5-83) is a larger-than-life-size marble

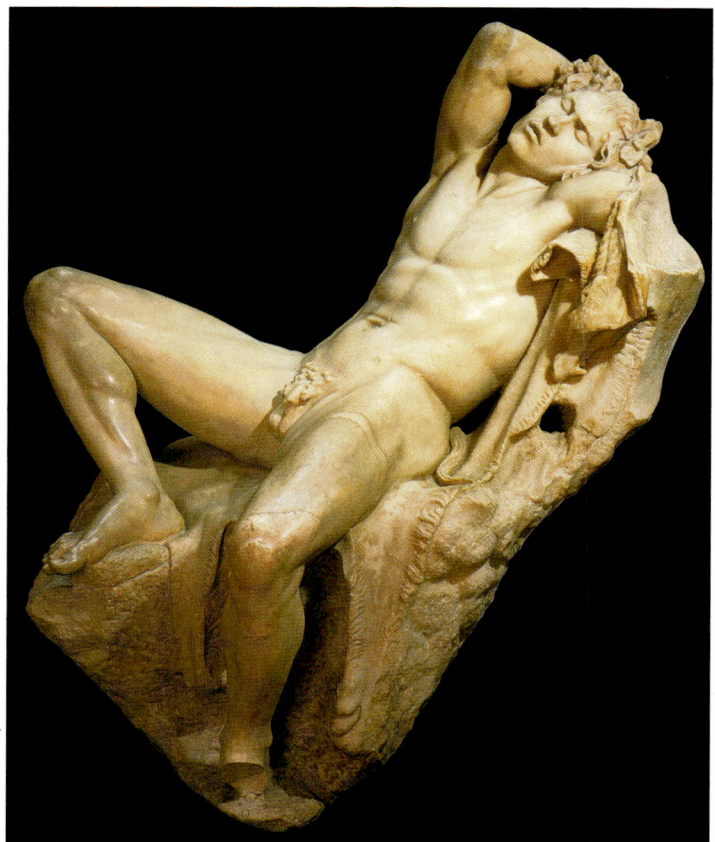

**5-84** Sleeping satyr (*Barberini Faun*), from Rome, Italy, ca. 230–200 BCE. Marble, 7′ 1″ high. Glyptothek, Munich.

Here, a Hellenistic sculptor represented a restlessly sleeping, drunken satyr, a semihuman in a suspended state of consciousness—the antithesis of the Classical ideals of rationality and discipline.

statue of Aphrodite found on Melos together with its inscribed base (now lost) signed by the sculptor ALEXANDROS OF ANTIOCH-ON-THE-MEANDER. In this statue, the goddess of love is more modestly draped than the *Aphrodite of Knidos* (FIG. 5-62) but is more overtly sexual. Her left hand (separately preserved) holds the apple Paris awarded her when he judged her the most beautiful goddess. Her right hand may have lightly grasped the edge of her drapery near the left hip in a halfhearted attempt to keep it from slipping farther down her body. The sculptor intentionally designed the work to tease the spectator, instilling this partially draped Aphrodite with a sexuality absent from Praxiteles' entirely nude image of the goddess. Other Hellenistic sculptors (FIG. 5-83A), especially when creating works for private patrons, went even further in depicting the goddess of love as an object of sexual desire.

*BARBERINI FAUN* Archaic statues smile at the viewer, and even when Classical statues look away, they are always awake and alert. Hellenistic sculptors often portrayed sleep. The suspension of consciousness and the entrance into the fantasy world of dreams—the antithesis of the Classical ideals of rationality and discipline—had great appeal for them. This newfound interest is evident in a marble statue (FIG. 5-84) of a drunken, restlessly sleeping *satyr* (a semihuman follower of Dionysos) known as the *Barberini Faun,* after Cardinal Barberini, who acquired the statue when it was unearthed in Rome in the 17th century. Barberini hired Gianlorenzo Bernini, the great Italian Baroque sculptor (FIGS. 24-6 to 24-8), to

restore the statue. Bernini no doubt felt that this dynamic statue in the Pergamene manner was the work of a kindred spirit. The satyr has consumed too much wine and has thrown down his panther skin on a convenient rock, then fallen into a disturbed, intoxicated sleep. His brows are furrowed, and one can almost hear him snore.

Eroticism also comes to the fore in this statue. Although men had been represented naked in Greek art for hundreds of years, Archaic kouroi and Classical athletes and gods do not exude sexuality. Sensuality surfaced in the works of Praxiteles and his followers in the fourth century BCE. But the dreamy and supremely beautiful Hermes playfully dangling grapes before the infant Dionysos (FIG. 5-63) has nothing of the blatant sexuality of the *Barberini Faun,* whose wantonly spread legs focus attention on his genitals. Homosexuality was common in the male world of ancient Greece. It is not surprising that when Hellenistic sculptors began to explore the sexuality of the human body, they turned their attention to both men and women.

**SLEEPING EROS** Another Hellenistic depiction of sleep, but one radically different in character, is the bronze statue (FIG. **5-85**) from Rhodes portraying Eros sleeping on a rock. Before the Hellenistic age, artists usually represented the winged child-god of love as an adolescent (FIG. 5-50, *center*). Here, as in the group of *Aphrodite, Eros, and Pan* (FIG. 5-83A), he is the pudgy winged infant Cupid, the form he takes in art from this point up to the present. The Hellenistic representations of Eros are noteworthy because throughout history, artists frequently painted and sculpted babies as miniature adults—often with adult personalities to match their mature bodies. Hellenistic sculptors were masters at reproducing the soft flesh and muscles of infants and portraying the spirit of young children in memorable statues. This representation of Eros differs from the contemporaneous group from Delos in one important respect. The winged child does not participate in any action. Rather, like the *Barberini Faun* (FIG. 5-84), he is asleep, one wing folded beneath him, one foot barely touching the ground, his right arm hanging limply, and his mouth open as he breathes. Eros enjoys the peaceful sleep of an infant free of the worries of the world.

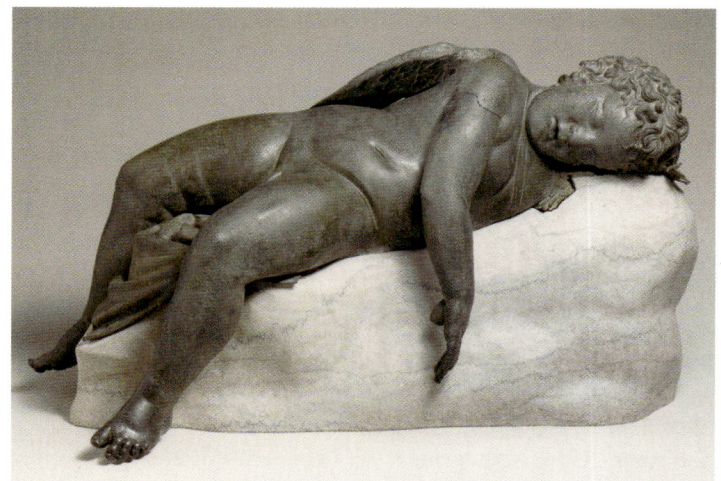

**5-85** Sleeping Eros, from Rhodes, ca. 150–100 BCE. Bronze, 2′ 9½″ long. Metropolitan Museum of Art, New York (Rogers Fund, 1943).

Eros, an adolescent in earlier Greek art, appears here as a pudgy winged infant sleeping on a rock. The Hellenistic sculptor skillfully represented the anatomy and personality of infants.

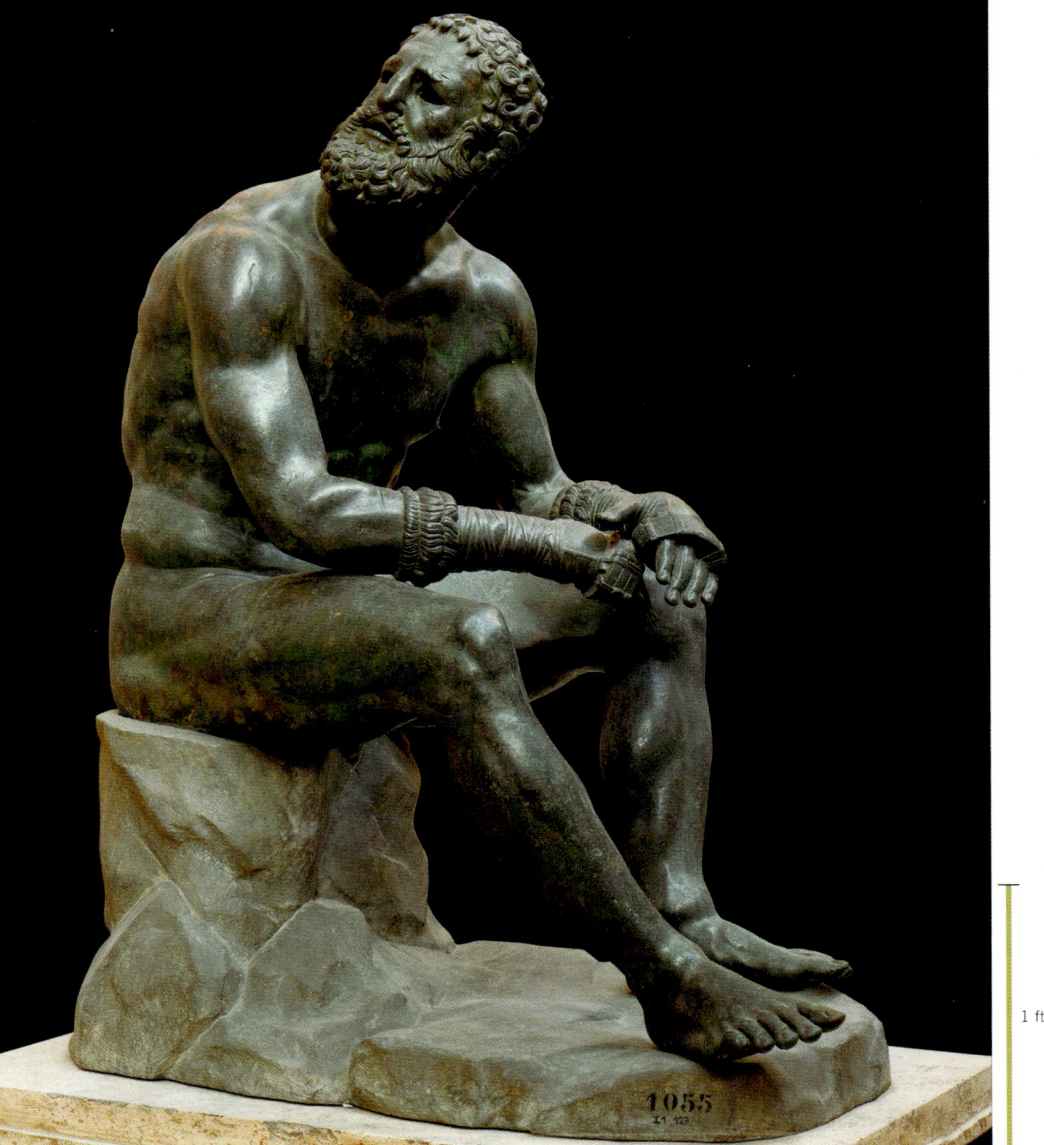

**5-86** Seated boxer, from Rome, Italy, ca. 100–50 BCE. Bronze, 4′ 2″ high. Museo Nazionale Romano—Palazzo Massimo alle Terme, Rome.

Even when Hellenistic artists treated traditional themes, they approached them in novel ways. This bronze statue depicts an older, defeated boxer with a broken nose and battered ears.

**DEFEATED BOXER** Although Hellenistic sculptors tackled an expanded range of subjects, they did not abandon such traditional themes as the Greek athlete. Nevertheless, they often treated the old subjects in novel ways. This is certainly true of the magnificent bronze statue (FIG. 5-86) of a seated boxer, a Hellenistic original found in Rome and perhaps at one time part of a group. The boxer is not a victorious young athlete with a perfect face and body but a heavily battered, defeated veteran whose upward gaze may have been directed at the man who had just beaten him. Too many punches from powerful hands wrapped in leather thongs—Greek boxers did not use the modern sport's cushioned gloves—have distorted the boxer's face. His nose is broken, as are his teeth. He has smashed "cauliflower" ears. Inlaid copper blood drips from the cuts on his forehead, nose, and cheeks. How different is this rendition of a powerful bearded man from that of the noble Riace warrior (FIGS. 5-35 and I-17) of the Early Classical period. The Hellenistic sculptor appealed not to the intellect but to the emotions when striving to evoke compassion for the pounded hulk of a once-mighty fighter.

**OLD MARKET WOMAN** The realistic bent of much Hellenistic sculpture—the very opposite of the Classical period's idealism—is evident above all in a series of statues of old men and women from the lowest rungs of the social order. Shepherds, fishermen, and drunken beggars are common—the kinds of people pictured earlier on red-figure vases but never before thought worthy of monumental statuary. One of the finest preserved statues of this type depicts a haggard old woman (FIG. 5-87) bringing chickens and a basket of fruits and vegetables to sell in the market. Her face is wrinkled, her body bent with age, and her spirit broken by a lifetime of poverty. She carries on because she must, not because she derives any pleasure from life. No one knows the purpose of these statues, but they attest to an interest in social realism absent in earlier Greek statuary.

Statues of the aged and the ugly are, of course, the polar opposites of the images of the young and the beautiful that dominated Greek art until the Hellenistic age, but they are consistent with the period's changed character. The Hellenistic world was a cosmopolitan place, and the highborn could not help but encounter the poor and a growing number of foreigners (non-Greek "barbarians") on a daily basis. Hellenistic art reflects this different social climate in the depiction of a much wider variety of physical types, including different ethnicities. The sensitive portrayal of Gallic warriors with their shaggy hair, strange mustaches, and golden torques (FIGS. 5-80 and 5-81) has already been noted. Africans, Scythians, and others, formerly only the occasional subject of vase painters, also entered the realm of monumental sculpture in Hellenistic art.

**DEMOSTHENES** These sculptures of foreigners and the urban poor, however realistic, are not portraits. Rather, they are sensitive studies of physical types. But the growing interest in the individual beginning in the Late Classical period did lead in the Hellenistic era to the production of true likenesses of specific persons. In fact, one of the great achievements of Hellenistic artists was the redefinition of portraiture. In the Classical period, Kresilas won fame for having made the noble Pericles appear even nobler in his portrait (FIG. 5-41). In contrast, in Hellenistic times, sculptors sought not only to record the true appearance of their subjects in bronze and stone but also to capture the essence of their personalities in likenesses both accurate and moving.

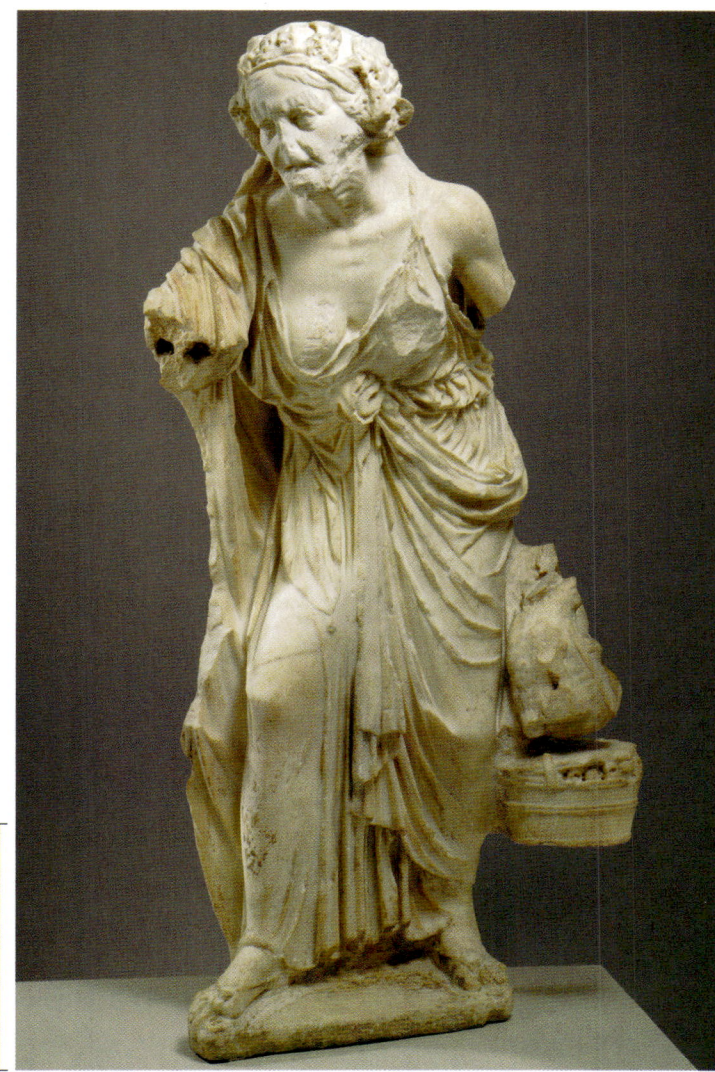

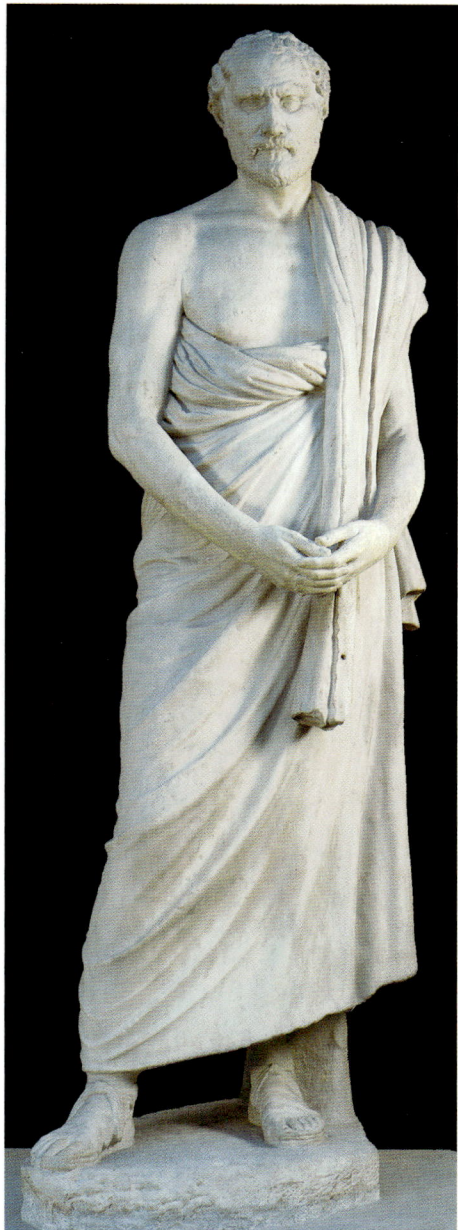

**5-88** POLYEUKTOS, Demosthenes. Roman copy of a bronze original of ca. 280 BCE. Marble, 6′ 7½″ high. Ny Carlsberg Glyptotek, Copenhagen.

One of the earliest Hellenistic portraits, frequently copied, was Polyeuktos's representation of the great orator Demosthenes as a frail man who possessed great courage and moral conviction.

**5-87** Old market woman. Roman copy(?) of a marble statue of ca. 150–100 BCE. Marble, 4′ 1⅝″ high. Metropolitan Museum of Art, New York.

Consistent with the realism of much Hellenistic art, many statues portray the elderly of the lowest rungs of society. Earlier Greek artists did not consider them suitable subjects for statuary.

One of the earliest of these, perhaps the finest of the Hellenistic age and frequently copied in Roman times, was a bronze portrait statue of Demosthenes (FIG. **5-88**) by POLYEUKTOS. The original, commissioned in 280 BCE, 42 years after the great orator's death, stood in the Athenian agora. Demosthenes was a frail man and in his youth even suffered from a speech impediment, but he had enormous courage and great moral conviction. A veteran of the disastrous battle against Philip II at Chaeronea, he repeatedly tried to rally opposition to Macedonian imperialism, both before and after Alexander's death. In the end, when it was clear the Macedonians would capture him, he took his own life by drinking poison.

Polyeuktos rejected Kresilas's and Lysippos's notions of the purpose of portraiture and did not attempt to portray a supremely confident leader with a magnificent physique. His Demosthenes has an aged and slightly stooped body. The orator clasps his hands nervously in front of him as he looks downward, deep in thought. His face is lined, his hair is receding, and his expression is one of great sadness. Whatever physical discomfort Demosthenes felt is

here joined by an inner pain, his deep sorrow over the tragic demise of democracy at the hands of the Macedonian conquerors.

## Hellenistic Art under Roman Patronage

In the opening years of the second century BCE, the Roman general Flamininus defeated the Macedonian army and declared the old poleis of Classical Greece free once again. The city-states never regained their former glory, however. Greece became a Roman province in 146 BCE. When Athens 60 years later sided with King Mithridates VI of Pontus (r. 120–63 BCE) in his war against Rome, the general Sulla crushed the Athenians. Thereafter, although Athens retained some of its earlier prestige as a center of culture and learning, politically it was merely another city in the ever-expanding Roman Empire. Nonetheless, Greek artists continued to be in great demand, both to furnish the Romans with an endless stream of copies of Classical and Hellenistic masterpieces and to create new statues in Greek style for Roman patrons.

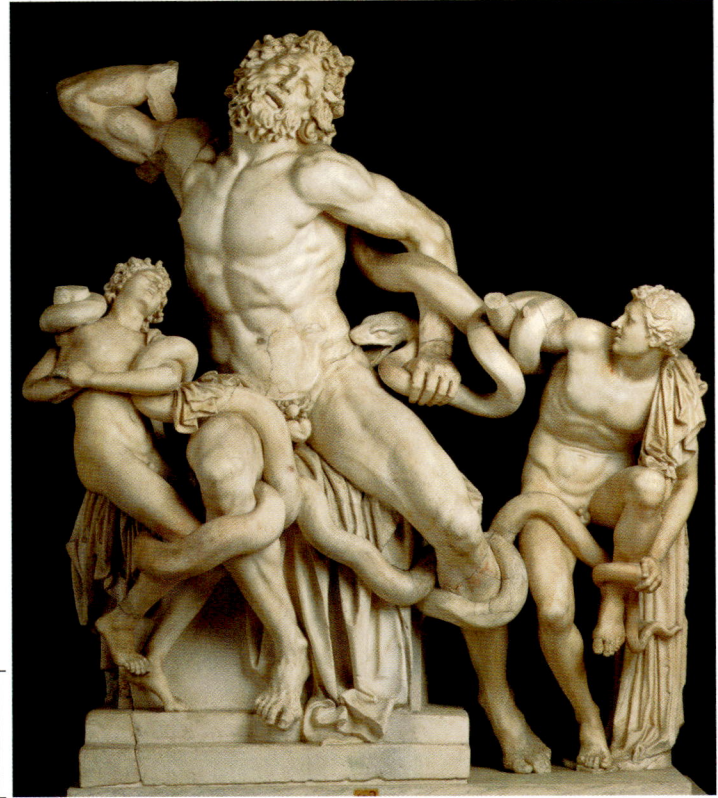

1 ft.

**5-89** ATHANADOROS, HAGESANDROS, and POLYDOROS OF RHODES, *Laocoön and his sons*, from Rome, Italy, early first century CE. Marble, 7′ 10½″ high. Musei Vaticani, Rome.

Hellenistic style lived on in Rome. Although stylistically akin to Pergamene sculpture, this statue of sea serpents attacking Laocoön and his two sons matches the account given only in the *Aeneid*.

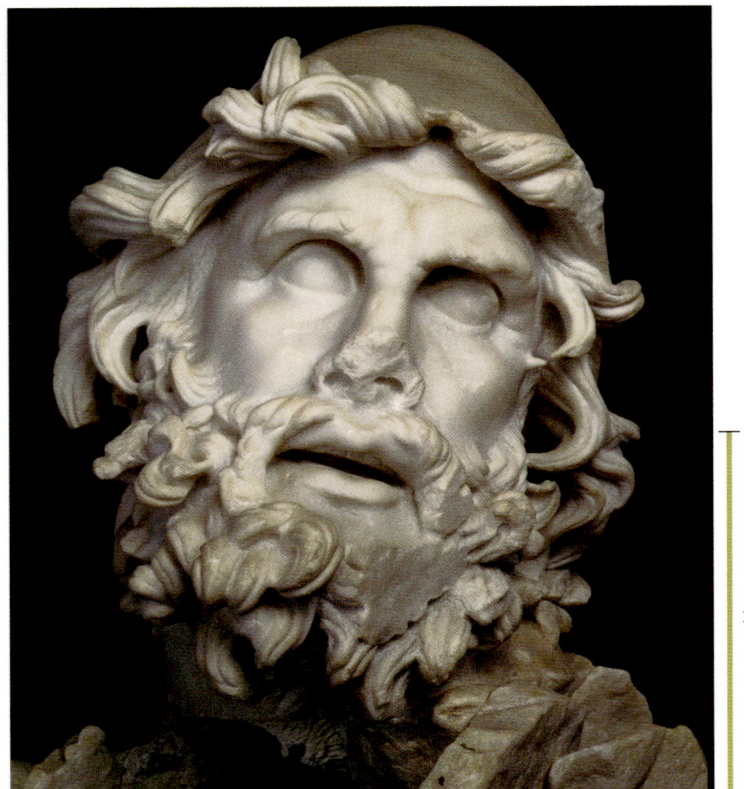

1 ft.

**5-90** ATHANADOROS, HAGESANDROS, and POLYDOROS OF RHODES, *head of Odysseus*, from the villa of Tiberius, Sperlonga, Italy, early first century CE. Marble, 2′ 1¼″ high. Museo Archeologico, Sperlonga.

This emotionally charged depiction of Odysseus was part of a mythological statuary group the three Laocoön sculptors made for a grotto at the emperor Tiberius's seaside villa at Sperlonga.

**LAOCOÖN** One work of this type is the famous group (FIG. **5-89**) of the Trojan priest Laocoön and his sons, unearthed in Rome in 1506 in the presence of the great Italian Renaissance artist Michelangelo (see Chapter 22). The marble group, long believed an original of the second century BCE, was found in the remains of the palace of the emperor Titus (r. 79–81 CE), exactly where Pliny had seen it more than 14 centuries before. Pliny attributed the statue to three sculptors—ATHANADOROS, HAGESANDROS, and POLYDOROS OF RHODES—who art historians now generally think worked in the early first century CE. These artists probably based their group on a Hellenistic masterpiece depicting Laocoön and only one son. Their variation on the original added the son at Laocoön's left (note the greater compositional integration of the other two figures) to conform with the Roman poet Vergil's account in the *Aeneid*. Vergil vividly described the strangling of Laocoön and his *two* sons by sea serpents while sacrificing at an altar. The gods who favored the Greeks in the war against Troy had sent the serpents to punish Laocoön, who had tried to warn his compatriots about the danger of bringing the Greeks' wooden horse within the walls of their city.

In Vergil's graphic account, Laocoön suffered in terrible agony. Athanadoros and his colleagues communicated the torment of the priest and his sons in spectacular fashion in the marble group. The three Trojans writhe in pain as they struggle to free themselves from the death grip of the serpents. One bites into Laocoön's left hip as the priest lets out a ferocious cry. The serpent-entwined figures recall the suffering giants of the great frieze of the Altar of Zeus at Pergamon, and Laocoön himself is strikingly similar to Alkyoneos (FIG. **5-79**), Athena's opponent. In fact, many scholars

believe that a Pergamene statuary group of the second century BCE was the inspiration for the three Rhodian sculptors.

**SPERLONGA** That the work seen by Pliny was made for Romans rather than Greeks was confirmed in 1957 by the discovery of fragments of several Hellenistic-style groups illustrating scenes from Homer's *Odyssey*. Archaeologists found the sculptures in a grotto that served as the summer banquet hall of the seaside villa of the Roman emperor Tiberius (r. 14–37 CE) at Sperlonga. One of these groups—depicting the monster Scylla attacking Odysseus's ship—bears the signatures of the same three sculptors Pliny cited as the creators of the Laocoön group. Another group, installed around a central pool in the grotto, depicted the blinding of the Cyclops Polyphemos by Odysseus and his comrades, an incident also set in a cave in the Homeric epic. The figure of Odysseus (FIG. **5-90**) from this theatrical group is one of the finest sculptures of antiquity. The hero's cap can barely contain his swirling locks of hair. Even Odysseus's beard seems to be swept up in the emotional intensity of the moment. The parted lips and the deep shadows produced by sharp undercutting add drama to the head, which complemented Odysseus's agitated body.

The baroque school of Hellenistic sculpture thus lived on long after Greece ceased to be a political force. When Rome inherited the Pergamene kingdom from the last of the Attalids in 133 BCE, it also became heir to the Greek artistic legacy. What Rome adopted from Greece it passed on to the medieval and modern worlds. If Greece was peculiarly the inventor of the European spirit, Rome (see Chapter 7) was its propagator and amplifier.

# ANCIENT GREECE

## GEOMETRIC AND ORIENTALIZING ART ca. 900–600 BCE

▎ Homer lived during the eighth century BCE, the era when the city-states of Classical Greece took shape, the Olympic Games were founded (776 BCE), and the Greeks began to trade with their neighbors to both east and west. At the same time, the human figure returned to Greek art in the form of bronze statuettes and simple silhouettes amid other abstract motifs on Geometric vases.

▎ Increasing contact with the civilizations of Egypt and Mesopotamia precipitated the so-called Orientalizing phase (ca. 700–600 BCE) of Greek art, when Eastern monsters began to appear on black-figure vases.

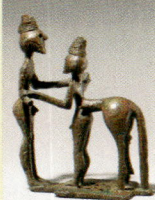

Hero and centaur,
ca. 750–730 BCE

## ARCHAIC ART ca. 600–480 BCE

▎ Around 600 BCE, the first life-size stone statues appeared in Greece. The earliest kouroi emulated the frontal poses of Egyptian statues, but artists depicted the young men nude, the way Greek athletes competed at Olympia. During the course of the sixth century BCE, Greek sculptors refined the proportions and added "Archaic smiles" to the faces of their statues to make them seem more lifelike.

▎ The Archaic age also brought the construction of the first stone temples with peripteral colonnades and the codification of the Doric and Ionic orders.

▎ The Andokides Painter invented red-figure vase painting around 530 BCE. Euphronios and Euthymides rejected the age-old composite view for the human figure and experimented with foreshortening.

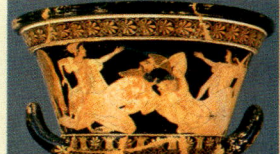

Euphronios, Herakles and Antaios,
ca. 510 BCE

## EARLY AND HIGH CLASSICAL ART ca. 480–400 BCE

▎ The Classical period opened with the Persian sack of the Athenian Acropolis in 480 BCE and the Greek victory a year later. During the Early Classical period (480–450 BCE), sculptors revolutionized statuary by introducing contrapposto (weight shift) to their figures.

▎ In the High Classical period (450–400 BCE), Polykleitos developed a canon of proportions for the perfect statue. Iktinos similarly applied mathematical formulas to temple design in the belief that beauty resulted from the use of harmonic numbers. Under the patronage of Pericles and the artistic directorship of Phidias, the Athenians rebuilt the Acropolis after 447 BCE. The Parthenon, Phidias's statue of Athena Parthenos, and the works of Polykleitos have defined what it means to be "Classical" ever since.

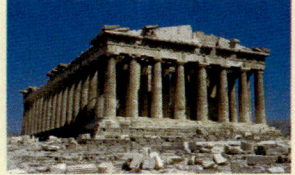

Parthenon, Acropolis, Athens,
447–438 BCE

## LATE CLASSICAL ART ca. 400–323 BCE

▎ In the aftermath of the Peloponnesian War, which ended in 404 BCE, Greek artists, though still adhering to the philosophy that humanity was the "measure of all things," began to focus more on the real world of appearances than on the ideal world of perfect beings. Late Classical sculptors humanized the remote deities, athletes, and heroes of the fifth century BCE. Praxiteles, for example, caused a sensation when he portrayed Aphrodite undressed. Lysippos depicted Herakles as muscle-bound but so weary that he needed to lean on his club for support.

▎ In architecture, the ornate Corinthian capital became increasingly popular, breaking the monopoly of the Doric and Ionic orders.

▎ The period closed with Alexander the Great, who transformed the Mediterranean world politically and ushered in a new artistic age as well.

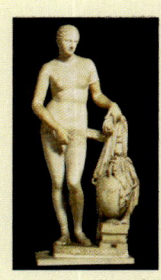

Praxiteles, *Aphrodite of Knidos*,
ca. 350–340 BCE

## HELLENISTIC ART ca. 323–30 BCE

▎ The Hellenistic age extends from the death of Alexander until the death of Cleopatra, when Egypt became a province of the Roman Empire.

▎ In art, both architects and sculptors broke most of the rules of Classical design. At Didyma, for example, the Temple of Apollo had no roof and contained a smaller temple within it. Hellenistic sculptors explored new subjects—Gauls with strange mustaches and necklaces, impoverished old women—and treated traditional subjects in new ways—athletes with battered bodies and faces, openly erotic goddesses. Artists delighted in depicting violent movement and unbridled emotion.

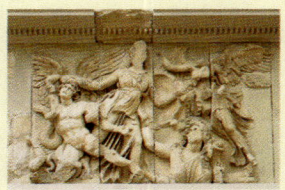

Altar of Zeus, Pergamon,
ca. 175 BCE

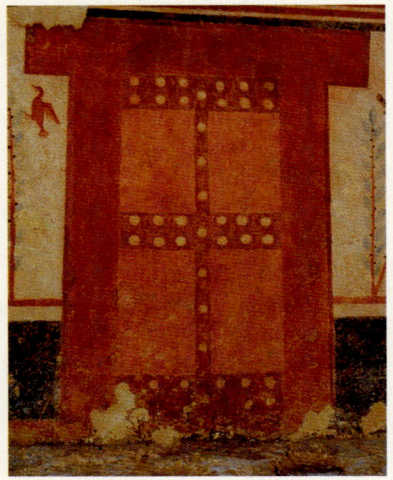

The Tomb of the Augurs is one of the oldest tombs at Tarquinia to have frescoes on all four walls. Dominating the rear wall is a large door, probably the symbolic entrance to the Underworld.

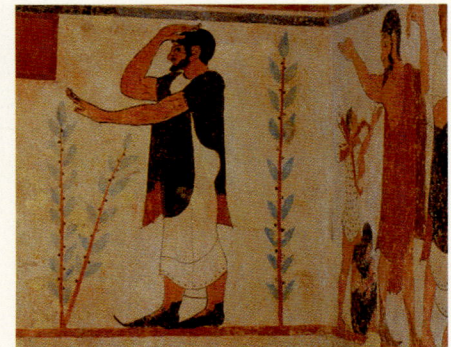

Two men extend one arm toward the door and place one hand against the forehead in a double gesture signifying salute and mourning. The deceased may be the purple-robed official to the right.

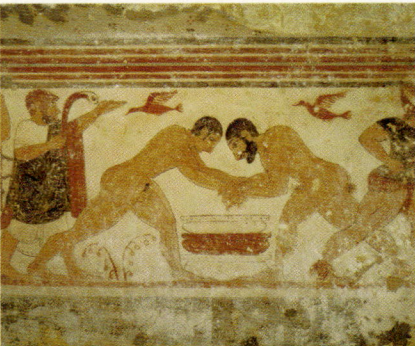

On the right wall, the Etruscan painter depicted the funerary games in honor of the deceased. The man with a curved staff is not a Roman augur with a lituus but is the umpire at a wrestling match.

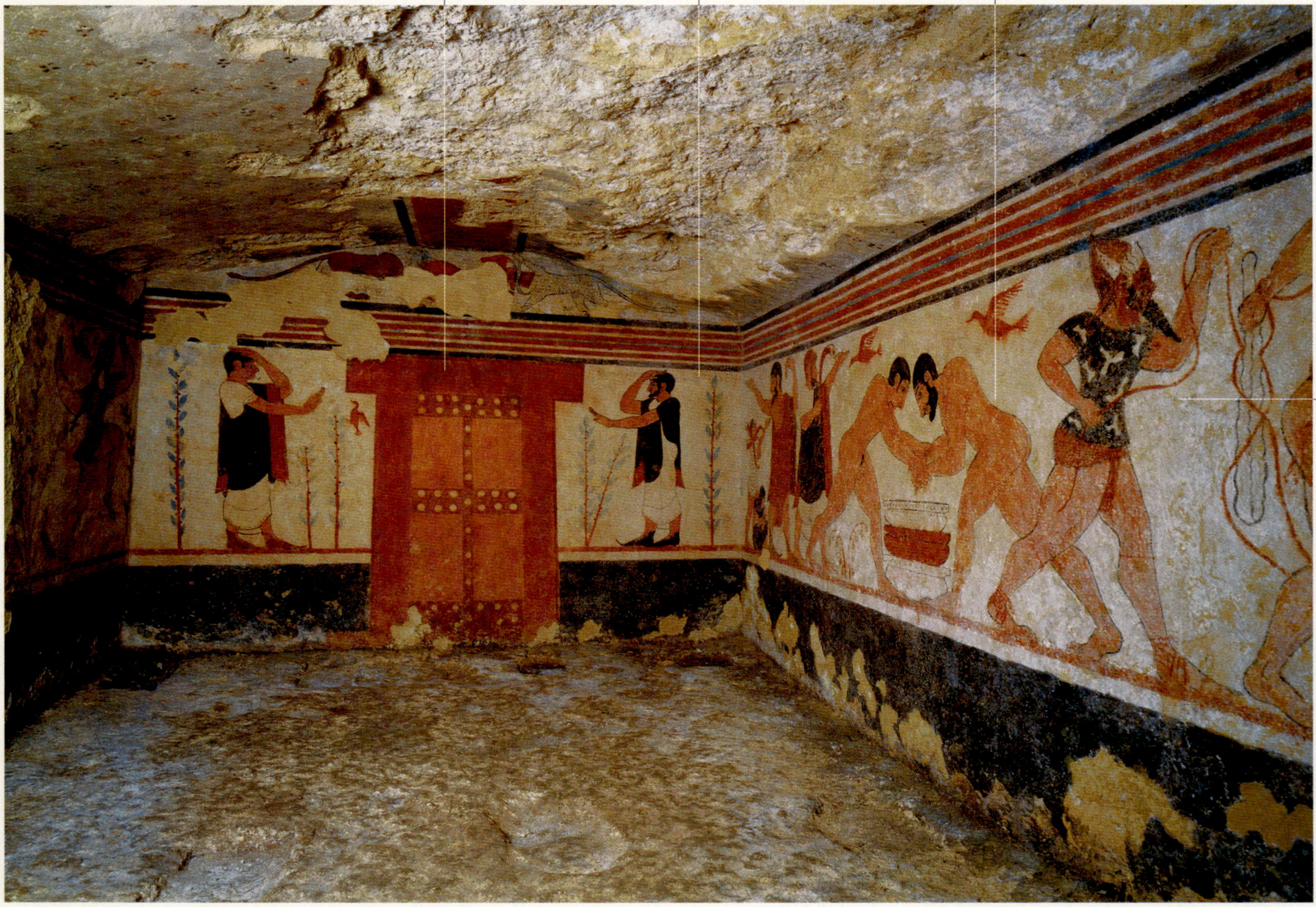

**6-1** Interior of the Tomb of the Augurs, Monterozzi necropolis, Tarquinia, ca. 520 BCE.

# 6

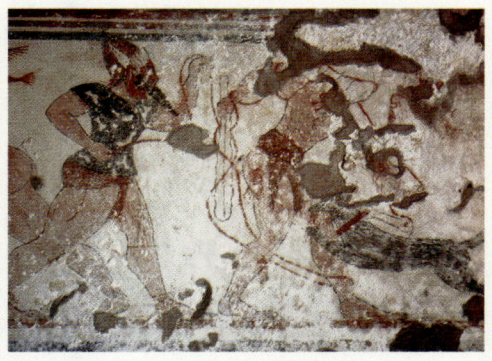

A masked phersu, unique to Etruria, oversees a gruesome contest between a club-wielding man whose head is covered by a sack and a fearsome dog—perhaps a precursor of Roman gladiatorial games.

# THE ETRUSCANS

FRAMING THE ERA

## THE REDISCOVERY OF ETRUSCAN ART

"The Etruscans, as everyone knows, were the people who occupied the middle of Italy in early Roman days, and whom the Romans, in their usual neighborly fashion, wiped out entirely." So opens D. H. Lawrence's witty and sensitive *Etruscan Places* (1929), one of the earliest modern essays to place a high value on Etruscan art and treat it as much more than a debased form of Greek art. ("Most people despise everything B.C. that isn't Greek, for the good reason that it ought to be Greek if it isn't," Lawrence quipped.) Fortunately, scholars and the public at large soon also came to admire the Etruscans, and it has been a long time since anyone had to argue for the importance and originality of Etruscan art. Indeed, although influenced by Greek art, Etruscan art differs in many fundamental ways.

The Tomb of the Augurs (FIG. **6-1**), datable around 520 BCE, makes that point forcefully. It is one of thousands of underground tombs, laboriously carved out of the bedrock at the important Etruscan city of Tarquinia, at a time when the Greeks still buried their dead in simple earth graves. The tomb also has fresco paintings—an art form virtually unknown in sixth-century BCE Greece—on all four walls, and although the artists adhered to many Greek conventions, the subjects they depicted are distinctly Etruscan.

At the center of the rear wall is a large door, probably the symbolic portal to the Underworld. To either side of it, two men extend one arm toward the door and place one hand against the forehead in a double gesture signifying salute and mourning. At the far end of the right wall is a man in a purple robe, a mark of his elevated stature, and two attendants. One carries a chair, the official seat of the man's high office. The other sleeps, or more likely weeps, crouched on the ground. The official is likely the one who has died. The rest of the right wall as well as the left and front walls depict the funerary games in honor of the dead man. To the right of the official and his attendants is a man with a curved staff similar to the *lituus* of the Roman priests called *augurs*, hence the modern name of the tomb. But the Etruscan "augur" is really an umpire at a wrestling match. To the right, a masked man labeled *phersu* (another phersu is at the far end of the left wall) controls a fearsome dog on a leash. The phersu's leash also entangles and restrains the legs of a club-wielding man. A sack covers his head, rendering him an almost helpless victim of the dog, which has already drawn blood. Some historians regard this gruesome contest as a direct precursor of Roman gladiatorial shows. In any case, Etruscan art and architecture unquestionably provided the models for the earliest Roman painters, sculptors, and architects.

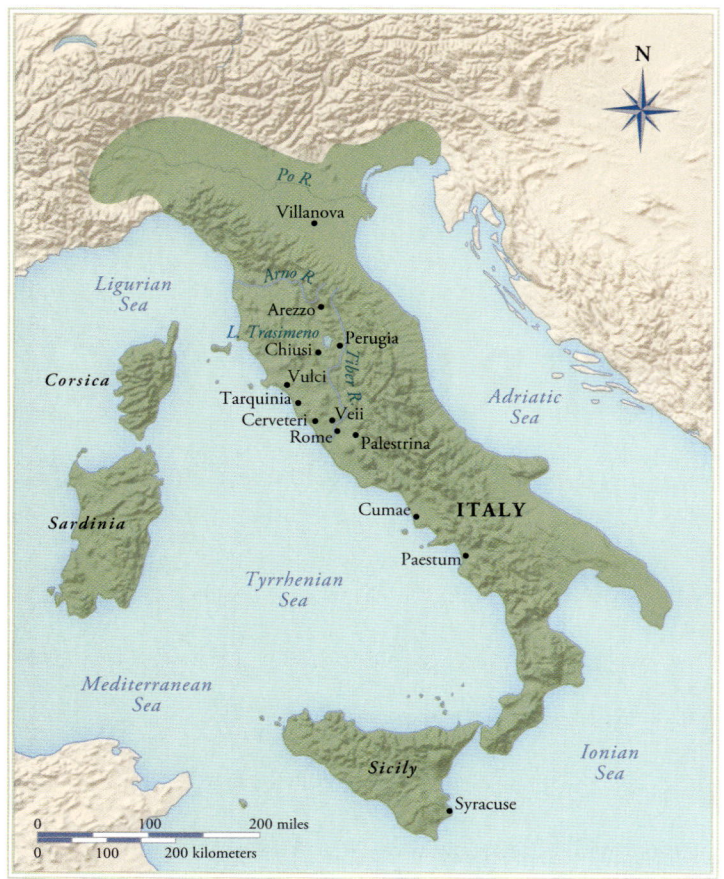

**MAP 6-1** Italy in Etruscan times.

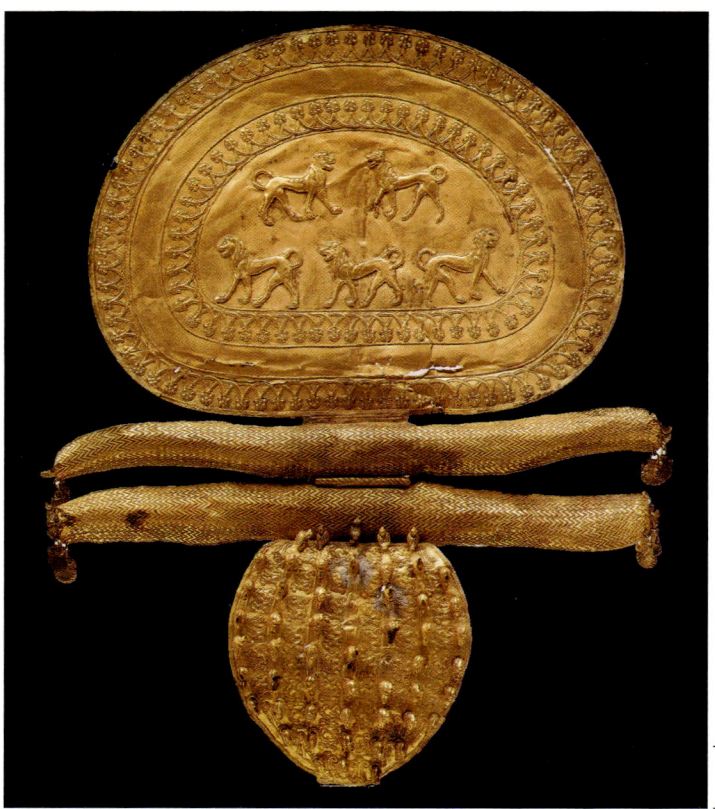

**6-2** Fibula with Orientalizing lions, from the Regolini-Galassi Tomb, Sorbo necropolis, Cerveteri, Italy, ca. 650–640 BCE. Gold, 1′ ½″ high. Musei Vaticani, Rome.

This huge gold pin found with other Orientalizing jewelry in a Cerveteri tomb combines repoussé and granulation and is the work of an Etruscan artist, but the lions are Egyptian and Mesopotamian motifs.

# ETRURIA AND THE ETRUSCANS

The heartland of the Etruscans (who called themselves Rasenna) was the territory between the Arno and Tiber rivers of central Italy (MAP 6-1). The lush green hills still bear their name—Tuscany, the land of the people the Romans called Etrusci or Tusci, the region centered on Florence. So, too, do the blue waters that splash against the western coastline of the Italian peninsula, for the Greeks referred to the Etruscans as Tyrsenoi or Tyrrhenoi and gave their name to the Tyrrhenian Sea. Both ancient and modern commentators have debated whether the Etruscans were an indigenous people or immigrants. Their language, although written in a Greek-derived script, is unrelated to the Indo-European linguistic family and remains largely undeciphered. The fifth-century BCE Greek historian Herodotus claimed the Etruscans came from Lydia in Asia Minor

and that Tyrsenos was their king—hence their Greek name. But Dionysius of Halicarnassus, a first-century BCE Greek historian, maintained the Etrusci were native Italians. Some modern researchers have theorized the Etruscans descended from the north into Italy. No doubt some truth exists in each theory. The Etruscan people of historical times—the Rasenna—were very likely the result of a gradual fusion of native and immigrant populations. This mixing of peoples occurred in the early first millennium BCE during the so-called Villanovan period, named for an archaeological site near present-day Bologna. At that time—contemporaneous with the Geometric period in Greece—the Etruscans emerged as a people with an art-producing culture related to but distinct from those of other Italic peoples and from the civilizations of Greece and the Orient.

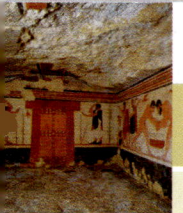

## THE ETRUSCANS

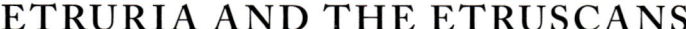

| 700 | Orientalizing | 600 | Archaic | 480 | Classical and Hellenistic | 89 | BCE |
|---|---|---|---|---|---|---|---|

▌ The Etruscans emerge as a distinct artistic culture during the Villanovan period (ca. 900–700 BCE)

▌ During the seventh century BCE, trade with Mesopotamia inspires the incorporation of monsters and other Orientalizing motifs in Etruscan funerary goods

▌ The Etruscans construct temples of mud brick and wood with columns and stairs only on the front and terracotta statuary on the roof

▌ At Cerveteri, the Etruscans bury their dead beneath huge earthen tumuli in multichambered tombs resembling houses

▌ Tarquinian tombs feature fresco paintings depicting funerary games and banquets

▌ Etruscan sculptors excel in bronze casting, engraving mirrors and cistae, and carving stone sarcophagi

▌ Etruscan architects construct arcuated gateways, often with columns framing the arched passageway

During the eighth and seventh centuries BCE, the Etruscans, as highly skilled seafarers, enriched themselves through trade abroad. By the sixth century BCE, they controlled most of northern and central Italy. Their most powerful cities included Tarquinia, Cerveteri, Vulci, and Veii. These and the other Etruscan cities never united to form a state, however, so it is inaccurate to speak of an Etruscan "nation" or "kingdom," but only of Etruria, the territory the Etruscans occupied. Any semblance of unity among the independent Etruscan cities was based primarily on common linguistic ties and religious beliefs and practices.

# EARLY ETRUSCAN ART

Although art historians now universally acknowledge the distinctive character of Etruscan painting, sculpture, and architecture, they still usually divide the history of Etruscan art into periods mirroring those of Greek art. The seventh century BCE is the Orientalizing period of Etruscan art (followed by the Archaic, Classical, and Hellenistic periods).

## Orientalizing Art

During the Orientalizing period, the Etruscans successfully mined iron, tin, copper, and silver, creating great wealth and, in the process, transforming Etruscan society. Villages with agriculturally based economies gave way in the seventh century BCE to prosperous cities engaged in international commerce. Wealthy families could afford to acquire foreign goods, and the Etruscan elite quickly developed a taste for luxury objects incorporating Eastern motifs. To satisfy the demand, local artisans, inspired by imported goods, produced magnificent objects for both homes and tombs. As in Greece at the same time, the locally manufactured Orientalizing artifacts cannot be mistaken for their foreign models.

REGOLINI-GALASSI TOMB About 650–640 BCE, a wealthy Etruscan family in Cerveteri stocked the Regolini-Galassi Tomb (named for its excavators) with bronze cauldrons and gold jewelry produced in Etruria but of Orientalizing style. The most spectacular of the many luxurious objects in the tomb is a gold *fibula* (clasp or safety pin; FIG. 6-2) of unique shape used to fasten a woman's gown at the shoulder. The gigantic disk-shaped fibula is in the Italic tradition, but the five lions striding across its surface are motifs originating in the Orient. The technique, also emulating Eastern imports, is masterful, combining repoussé and *granulation* (the fusing of tiny metal balls, or granules, to a metal surface). The Regolini-Galassi fibula equals or exceeds in quality anything that might have served as a model.

The jewelry from the Regolini-Galassi Tomb also includes a gold *pectoral* that covered a deceased woman's chest, and two gold circlets that may be earrings, although they are large enough to be bracelets. A taste for this kind of ostentatious display is frequently the hallmark of newly acquired wealth, and this was certainly the case in seventh-century BCE Etruria.

## Archaic Art and Architecture

The art and architecture of Greece also impressed Etruscan artists looking eastward for inspiration. Still, however eager those artists may have been to emulate Greek works, their distinctive Etruscan temperament always manifested itself.

ETRUSCAN TEMPLES In religious architecture, for example, the differences between temples honoring the Etruscan gods (see "Etruscan Counterparts of Greco-Roman Gods and Heroes," above) and their Greek prototypes far outweigh the similarities. Because of the materials Etruscan architects employed, usually only the foundations of their temples have survived. These are nonetheless sufficient to reveal the plans of the edifices. Supplementing the archaeological record is the Roman architect Vitruvius's treatise on architecture written near the end of the first century BCE. In it, Vitruvius provided an invaluable chapter on Etruscan temple design.

Archaeologists have constructed a model (FIG. 6-3) of a typical Archaic Etruscan temple based on Vitruvius's account. The sixth-century BCE Etruscan temple resembled contemporaneous Greek stone gable-roofed temples, but it had wood columns, a tile-covered wood roof, and walls of sun-dried mud brick. Entrance was possible only via a narrow staircase at the center of the front of the temple, which sat on a high podium, the only part of the building made of stone. The proportions also differed markedly. Greek temples were about twice as long as wide. Vitruvius reported the typical ratio for Etruscan temples was 6:5. Greek and Etruscan architects

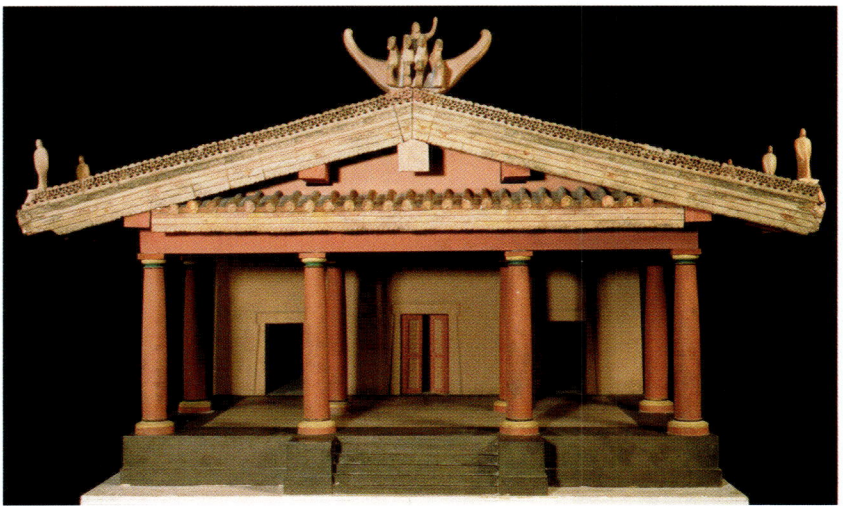

**6-3** Model of a typical Etruscan temple of the sixth century BCE, as described by Vitruvius. Istituto di Etruscologia e di Antichità Italiche, Università di Roma, Rome. ◼◀

Etruscan temples resembled Greek temples but had widely spaced, unfluted wood columns only at the front, walls of sun-dried mud brick, and a narrow staircase at the center of the facade.

## Etruscan Artists in Rome

In 616 BCE, according to the traditional chronology, Tarquinius Priscus of Tarquinia became Rome's first Etruscan king. He ruled for almost 40 years. His grandson, Tarquinius Superbus ("the Arrogant"), was Rome's last king. Outraged by his tyrannical behavior, the Romans drove him from power in 509 BCE. Before his expulsion, however, Tarquinius Superbus embarked on a grand program to embellish the city he ruled.

The king's most ambitious undertaking was the construction of a magnificent temple on the Capitoline Hill for the joint worship of Jupiter, Juno, and Minerva. For this great commission, he summoned architects, sculptors, and workers from all over Etruria. Rome's first great religious shrine was therefore Etruscan in patronage, manufacture, and form. The architect's name is unknown, but several sources preserve the identity of the Etruscan sculptor brought in to adorn the temple—Vulca of Veii, who may also have made a statue of the god Apulu (FIG. 6-4) for his native city. Pliny the Elder described Vulca's works as "the finest images of deities of that era . . . more admired than gold."* The Romans entrusted Vulca with creating the statue of Jupiter that stood in the central cella (one for each of the three deities) in the Capitoline temple. He also fashioned the enormous terracotta statuary group of Jupiter in a four-horse chariot, which he mounted on the roof at the highest point directly over the center of the temple facade. The fame of Vulca's red-faced (painted terracotta) portrayal of Jupiter was so great Roman generals would paint their faces red in emulation of the ancient statue when they paraded in triumph through Rome after a battlefield victory. (The model of a typical three-cella Etruscan temple in FIG. 6-3 also serves to give an approximate idea of the appearance of the Capitoline Jupiter temple and of Vulca's roof statue.)

Vulca is the only Etruscan artist any ancient writer named, but the signatures of other Etruscan artists appear on extant artworks. One of these is Novios Plautios (FIG. 6-13), who also worked in Rome, although a few centuries later. By then the Etruscan kings of Rome were a distant memory, and the Romans had captured Veii and annexed its territory.

*Pliny, *Natural History*, 35.157.

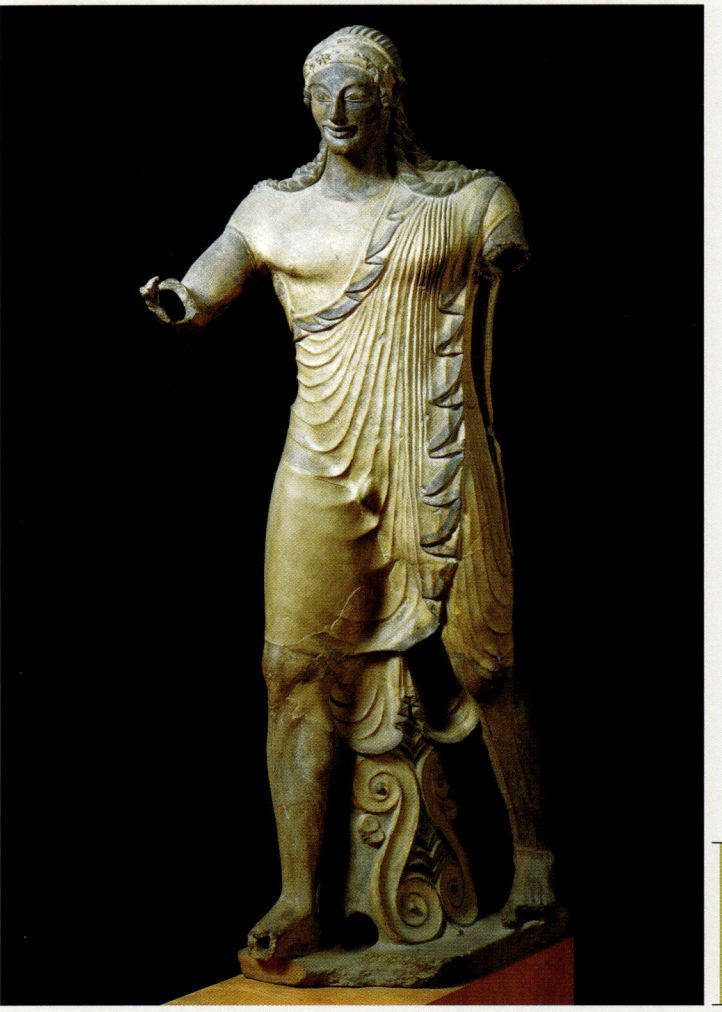

1 ft.

**6-4** Apulu (*Apollo of Veii*), from the roof of the Portonaccio temple, Veii, Italy, ca. 510–500 BCE. Painted terracotta, 5′ 11″ high. Museo Nazionale di Villa Giulia, Rome.

The statue of Apulu was part of a group depicting a Greek myth. Distinctly Etruscan, however, are the god's vigorous motion and gesticulating arms and the placement of the statue on a temple roof.

also arranged the columns in distinct ways. The columns in Etruscan temples were usually all at the front of the building, creating a deep porch occupying roughly half the podium and setting off one side of the structure as the main side. In contrast, the front and rear of Greek temples were indistinguishable, and builders placed steps and columns on all sides (FIG. 5-12). The Etruscan temple was not meant to be seen as a sculptural mass from all directions, as Greek temples were.

Furthermore, although the columns of Etruscan temples resembled Greek Doric columns (FIG. 5-13, *left*), *Tuscan columns* were made of wood, were unfluted, and had bases. Also, because of the lightness of the superstructure, fewer, more widely spaced columns were the rule in Etruscan temples. Unlike their Greek counterparts, Etruscan temples also frequently had three cellas—one for each of their chief

gods, Tinia, Uni, and Menrva. Pedimental statuary was also rare in Etruria. The Etruscans normally placed life-size narrative statuary—in terracotta instead of stone—on the roofs of their temples.

***APOLLO OF VEII*** The finest surviving Etruscan temple statue is the life-size image of Apulu (FIG. **6-4**), which displays the energy and excitement that characterize Archaic Etruscan art in general. The statue comes from the rooftop of a temple in the Portonaccio sanctuary at Veii. Popularly known as the *Apollo of Veii*, it is but one of a group of at least four painted terracotta figures that adorned the temple's ridgepole. The statues depicted one of the 12 labors of Herakles (see "Herakles," Chapter 5, page 128). Apulu confronted Hercle for possession of the hind of Ceryneia, a wondrous gold-horned beast sacred to the god's sister Artumes. The

# The "Audacity" of Etruscan Women

At the instigation of the emperor Augustus at the end of the first century BCE, Titus Livy wrote a history of Rome from its legendary founding in 753 BCE to his own day. In the first book of his great work, Livy recounted the tale of Tullia, daughter of Servius Tullius, an Etruscan king of Rome in the sixth century BCE. The princess had married the less ambitious of two brothers of the royal Tarquinius family, while her sister had married the bolder of the two princes. Together, Tullia and her brother-in-law, Tarquinius Superbus (see "Etruscan Artists in Rome," page 168), arranged for the murder of their spouses. They then married each other and plotted the overthrow and death of Tullia's father. After the king's murder, Tullia ostentatiously drove her carriage over her father's corpse, spraying herself with his blood. (The Romans still call the road where the evil deed occurred the Street of Infamy.) Livy, though condemning Tullia's actions, placed them in the context of the famous "audacity" of Etruscan women.

The independent spirit and relative freedom women enjoyed in Etruscan society similarly horrified (and threatened) other Greco-Roman male authors. The stories the fourth-century BCE Greek historian Theopompus heard about the debauchery of Etruscan women appalled him. Etruscan women epitomized immorality for Theopompus, but much of what he reported is untrue. Etruscan women did not, for example, exercise naked alongside Etruscan men. But archaeological evidence confirms the accuracy of at least one of his "slurs": Etruscan women did attend banquets and recline with their husbands on a common couch (FIGS. 6-5 and 6-9). Aristotle also remarked on this custom. It was so foreign to the Greeks it both shocked and frightened them. Only men, boys, slave girls, and prostitutes attended Greek symposiums. The wives remained at home, excluded from most aspects of public life. In Etruscan Italy, in striking contrast to Greece, women also regularly attended sporting events with men. Etruscan paintings and reliefs document this as well.

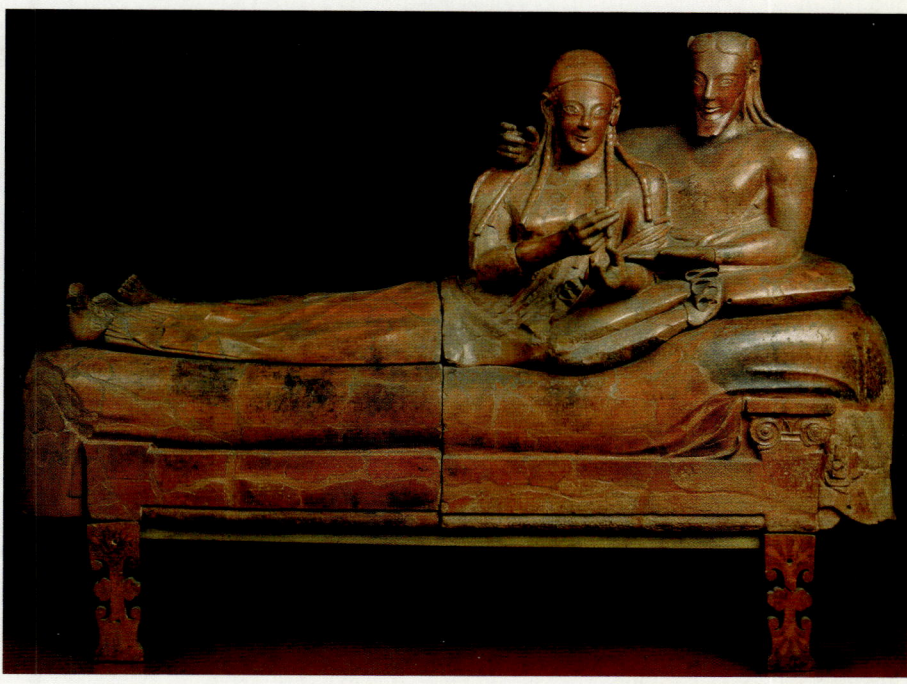

**6-5** Sarcophagus with reclining couple, from the Banditaccia necropolis, Cerveteri, Italy, ca. 520 BCE. Painted terracotta, 3′ 9½″ × 6′ 7″. Museo Nazionale di Villa Giulia, Rome. ◼◀

Sarcophagi in the form of a husband and wife on a dining couch have no parallels in Greece. The artist's focus on the upper half of the figures and the emphatic gestures are Etruscan hallmarks.

Etruscan inscriptions also reflect the higher status of women in Etruria as compared with Greece. They often give the names of both the father and mother of the person commemorated (for example, the inscribed portrait of Aule Metele, FIG. 6-16), a practice unheard of in Greece (witness the grave stele of "Hegeso, daughter of Proxenos," FIG. 5-57). Etruscan women, moreover, retained their own names (Ramtha Visnai, FIG. 6-15A) and could legally own property independently of their husbands. The frequent use of inscriptions on Etruscan mirrors and other toiletry items (FIG. 6-13) buried with women seems to attest to a high degree of female literacy as well.

bright paint and the rippling folds of Apulu's garment call to mind Archaic Greek korai in Ionian garb (FIG. 5-11). But Apulu's vigorous striding motion, gesticulating arms, fanlike calf muscles, rippling drapery, and animated face are distinctly Etruscan. Some scholars have attributed the Apulu statue to VULCA OF VEII, the most famous Etruscan sculptor of the time (see "Etruscan Artists in Rome," page 168). The statue's discovery in 1916 was instrumental in prompting a reevaluation of the originality of Etruscan art.

**CERVETERI SARCOPHAGUS** Although the Greeks produced statues in terracotta, Etruscan sculptors especially favored that medium. Another Archaic Etruscan terracotta masterwork is the sarcophagus (FIG. 6-5) from a Cerveteri tomb in the form of a husband and wife reclining on a banqueting couch. The sarcopha-

gus, which was once brightly painted, consists of four separately cast and fired sections. Although the man and woman on the couch are life-size, the sarcophagus contained only the ashes of the husband or wife, or perhaps both. Cremation was the most common means of disposing of the dead in Archaic Italy. This kind of funerary monument had no parallel at this date in Greece, where there were no monumental tombs that could house large sarcophagi. The Greeks buried their dead in simple graves marked by a stele or a statue. Moreover, although banquets were common subjects on Greek vases (which, by the late sixth century BCE, the Etruscans imported in great quantities and regularly deposited in their tombs), only men dined at Greek symposiums. The image of a husband and wife sharing the same banqueting couch is uniquely Etruscan (see "The 'Audacity' of Etruscan Women," above).

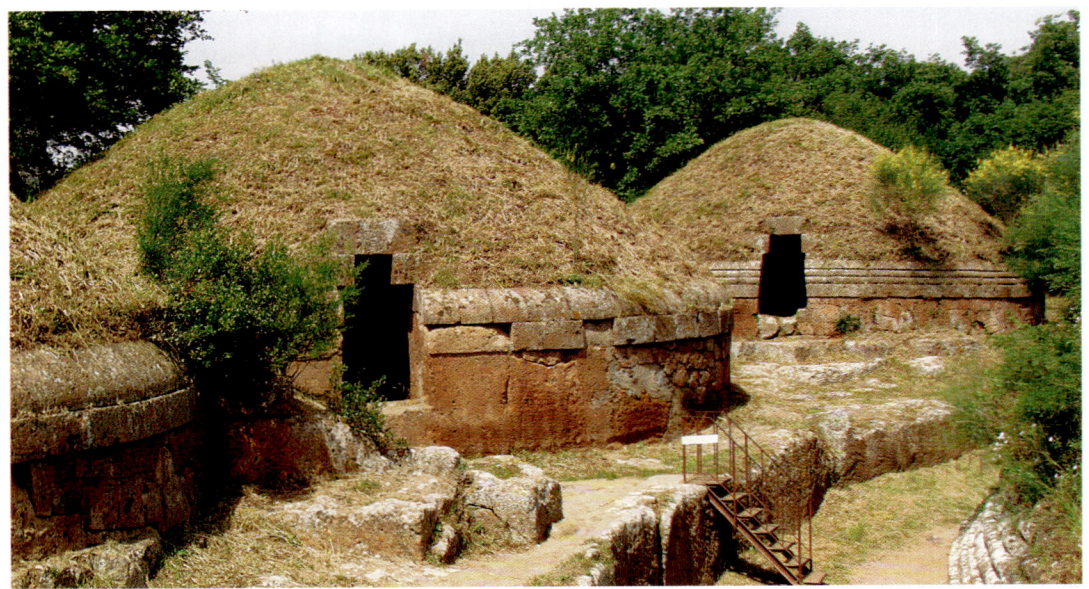

**6-6** Tumuli in the Banditaccia necropolis, Cerveteri, Italy, seventh to second centuries BCE. ◼◣

In the Banditaccia necropolis at Cerveteri, the Etruscans buried several generations of families in multichambered rock-cut underground tombs covered by great earthen mounds (tumuli).

The man and woman on the Cerveteri sarcophagus are as animated as the *Apollo of Veii* (FIG. 6-4), even though they are at rest. The woman may have held a perfume flask and a pomegranate in her hands, the man an egg (compare FIG. 6-9). They are the antithesis of the stiff and formal figures encountered in Egyptian funerary sculpture (compare FIG. 3-12). Also typically Etruscan, and in sharp contrast to contemporaneous Greek statues with their emphasis on proportion and balance, is the manner in which the Cerveteri sculptor rendered the upper and lower parts of each body. The artist shaped the legs only summarily, and the transition to the torso at the waist is unnatural. The sculptor's interest focused on the upper half of the figures, especially on the vibrant faces and gesticulating arms. The Cerveteri banqueters and the Veii Apulu speak to the viewer in a way Greek statues of similar date, with their closed contours and calm demeanor, never do.

**BANDITACCIA NECROPOLIS** The exact findspot of the Cerveteri sarcophagus is unrecorded, but it came from the Banditaccia necropolis, where, beginning in the seventh century BCE, wealthy Etruscan families constructed enormous tombs (FIG. 6-6) in the form of a mound, or *tumulus*, not unlike the Mycenaean Treasury of Atreus (FIG. 4-20). But whereas the Mycenaeans built their tholos tombs with masonry blocks and then covered the burial chambers with an earthen mound, each Etruscan tumulus stood over one or more subterranean multichambered tombs cut out of the dark local limestone called tufa. The largest burial

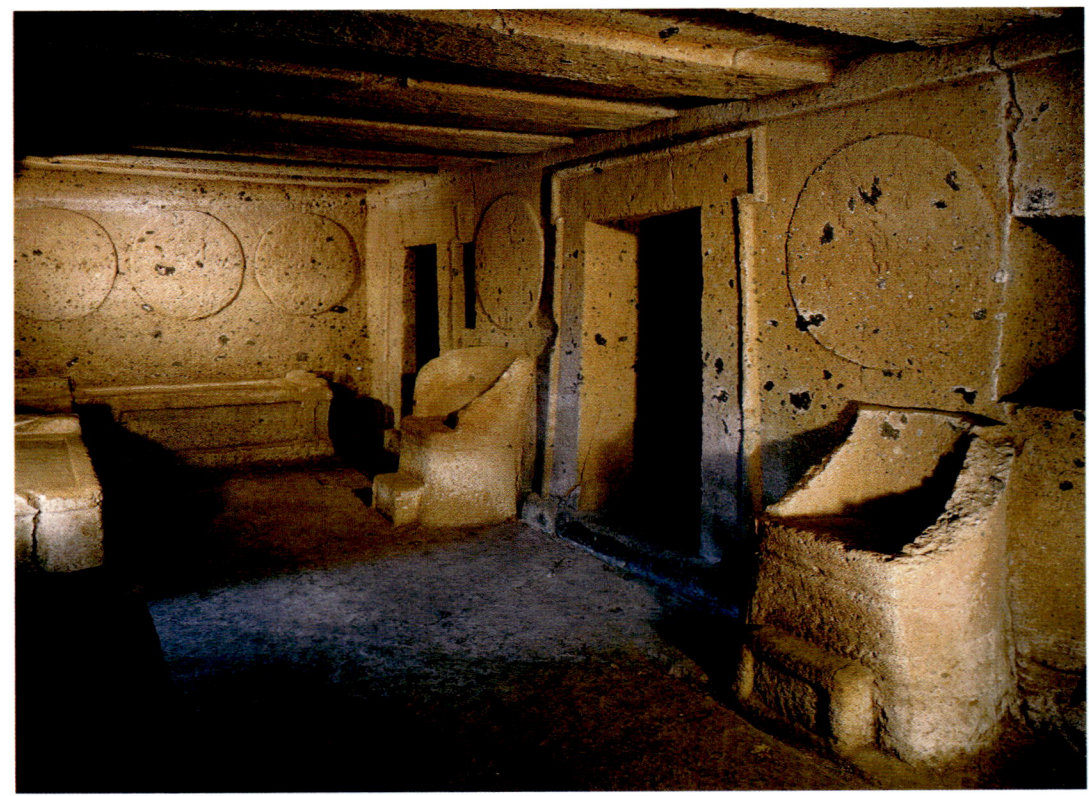

**6-7** Interior of the Tomb of the Shields and Chairs, Banditaccia necropolis, Cerveteri, Italy, ca. 550–500 BCE.

Terracotta statues of the deceased probably "sat" in the chairs cut out of the bedrock of this subterranean tomb chamber. The tomb's plan (FIG. 6-7A) follows that of a typical Etruscan house.

mounds at Cerveteri are truly of colossal size, exceeding 130 feet in diameter and reaching nearly 50 feet in height. Arranged in an orderly manner along a network of streets spread over 200 acres, the Banditaccia tombs constitute a veritable city of the dead—the literal meaning of the Greek word *necropolis*.

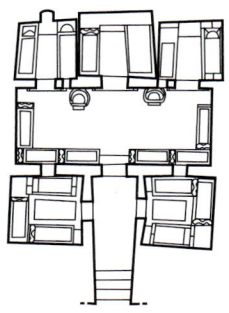

6-7A Tomb of the Shields and Chairs, Cerveteri, ca. 550–500 BCE.

### TOMB OF THE SHIELDS AND CHAIRS

The aptly named Tomb of the Shields and Chairs (FIGS. **6-7** and **6-7A**) is one of the most elaborate in the Banditaccia necropolis. Sculptors carved out of the tufa bedrock six beds and two high-backed chairs with footstools, as well as door frames and ceiling beams, in imitation of the wooden furniture and timber architecture of Archaic Etruscan homes. Based on evidence from other tombs, the Etruscans probably placed terracotta figures of the deceased on the chairs. Reliefs of 14 shields adorn the walls. The technique recalls that of rock-cut Egyptian tombs such as Amenemhet's (FIG. 3-18) at Beni Hasan and highlights the very different values of the Etruscans and the Greeks. The Etruscans' temples no longer stand because they constructed them of wood and mud brick, but their grand subterranean tombs are as permanent as the bedrock itself. The Greeks employed stone for the shrines of their gods but only rarely built monumental tombs for their dead.

### TOMB OF THE RELIEFS

The most elaborate Cerveteri tomb, in decoration if not in plan, is the Tomb of the Reliefs (FIG. **6-8**). Like the much earlier Tomb of the Shields and Chairs, it accommodated several generations of a single family. The Etruscans, as usual, gouged the burial chamber out of the tufa bedrock, but in this instance they covered the sculpted walls and piers with painted stucco reliefs, hence the tomb's modern name. The stools, mirrors, drinking cups, pitchers, and knives effectively suggest a domestic context, underscoring the connection between Etruscan houses of the dead and those of the living. Other reliefs—for example, the helmet and shields over the main funerary couch (the pillows are also shallow reliefs)—are signs of the elite status of this Cerveteri family. The three-headed dog beneath the same couch is Cerberus, guardian of the gate to the Underworld, a reference to the passage from this life to the next.

### TARQUINIA

Large underground burial chambers hewn out of the natural rock were also the norm in the Monterozzi necropolis at Tarquinia. Earthen mounds may once have covered the Tarquinia tombs too, but the tumuli no longer exist. In contrast to Cerveteri, the subterranean rooms at Tarquinia lack carvings imitating the appearance of Etruscan houses. In around 200 tombs, however, paintings decorate the walls, as in the Tomb of the Augurs (FIG. 6-1). Painted tombs are nonetheless statistically rare, the privilege of only the wealthiest Tarquinian families. Archaeologists have succeeded in locating so many of them by using periscopes to explore tomb interiors from the surface before considering time-consuming and costly excavation. Consequently, art historians have an almost unbroken record of monumental painting in Etruria from Archaic to Hellenistic times.

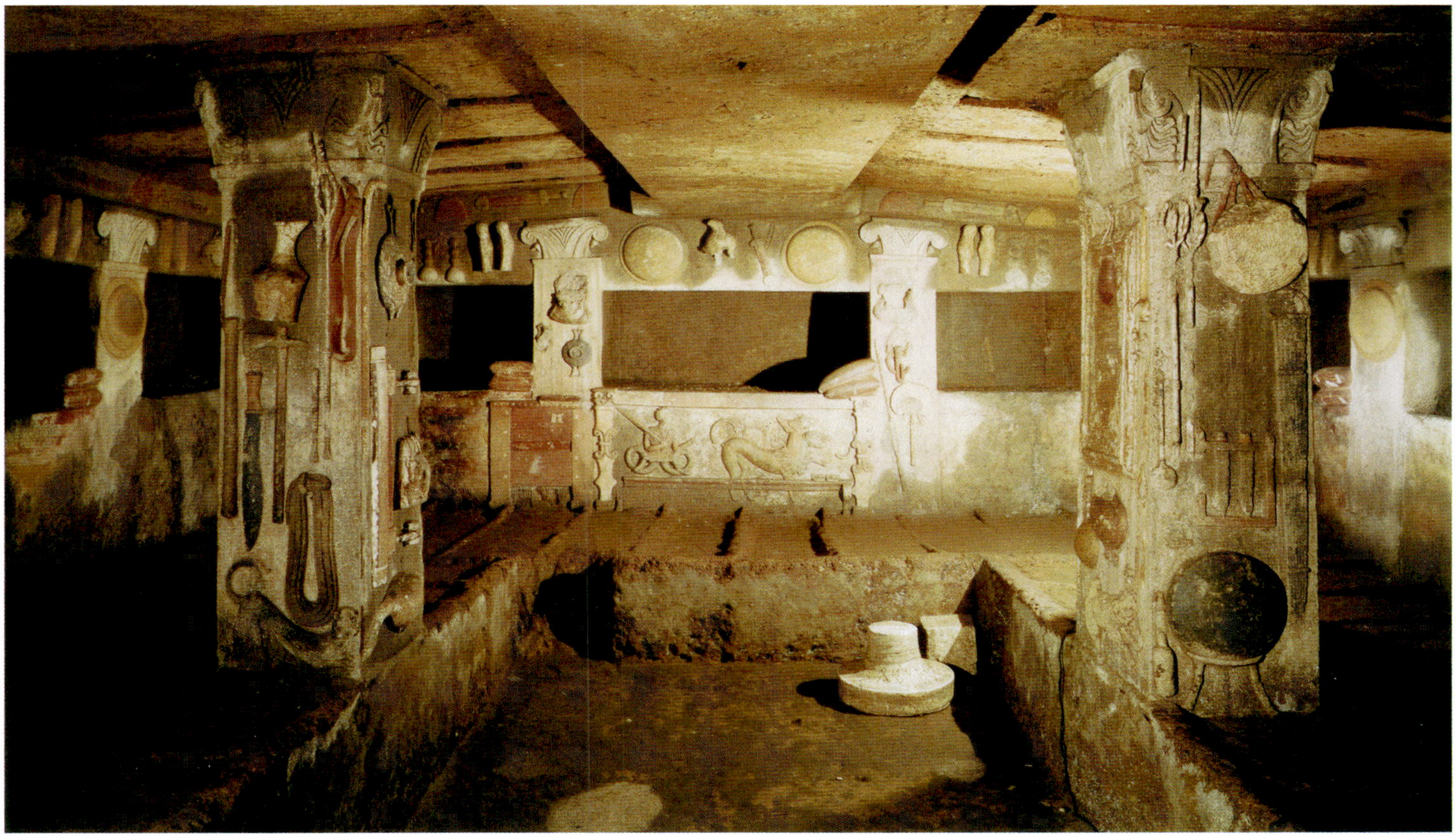

**6-8** Interior of the Tomb of the Reliefs, Banditaccia necropolis, Cerveteri, Italy, late fourth or early third century BCE. ◼◀

The Tomb of the Reliefs takes its name from the painted stucco reliefs covering its walls and piers. The stools, mirrors, drinking cups, and other items are reminders of the houses of the living.

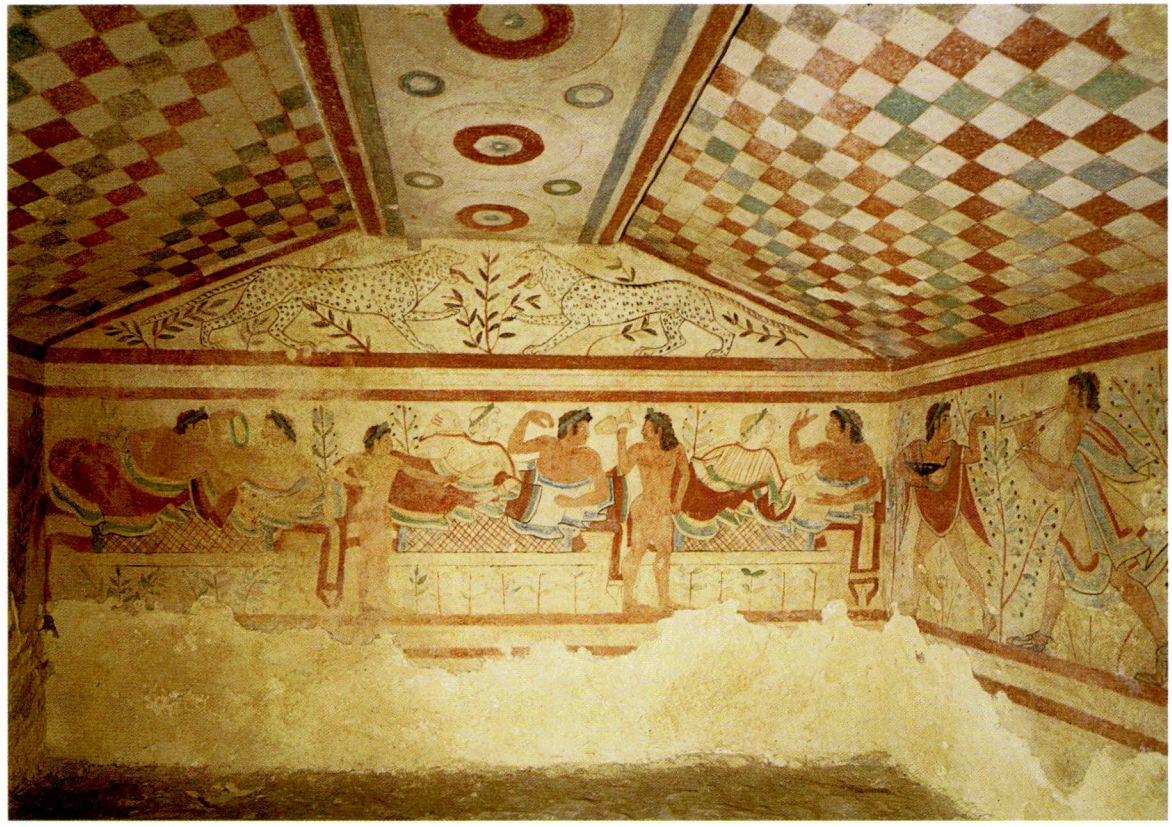

**6-9** Interior of the Tomb of the Leopards, Monterozzi necropolis, Tarquinia, Italy, ca. 480–470 BCE. ◀◣

The paintings in the Tomb of the Leopards, named after the guardian beasts in the rear pediment, depict banqueting couples, servants, and musicians. The men have dark skin, the women fair skin.

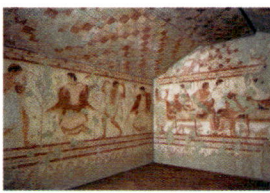

**6-9A** Tomb of the Triclinium, Tarquinia, ca. 480–470 BCE.

## TOMB OF THE LEOPARDS

Two important tombs—the Tomb of the Leopards (FIG. 6-9) and the Tomb of the Triclinium (FIG. 6-9A) are about 40 years later than the Tomb of the Augurs. The Leopards tomb takes its name from the beasts that guard the burial chamber from their perch within the pediment of the rear wall. The leopards are reminiscent of the panthers on each side of Medusa in the pediment (FIG. 5-16) of the temple of Artemis at Corfu. But mythological figures, whether Greek or Etruscan, are uncommon in Tarquinian murals, and neither the Augurs nor the Leopards tomb includes any. In the later tomb, banqueting couples (the men with dark skin, the women with light skin, in conformity with the age-old convention; compare FIGS. 3-11A and 5-20A) adorn the walls—painted versions of the terracotta sarcophagus (FIG. 6-5) from Cerveteri. Pitcher- and cup-bearers serve the guests, and musicians entertain them. The banquet takes place in the open air or perhaps in a tent set up for the occasion. In characteristic Etruscan fashion, the banqueters, servants, and entertainers all make exaggerated gestures with unnaturally enlarged hands. The man on the couch at the far right on the rear wall holds up an egg, the symbol of regeneration. The tone is joyful, rather than a somber contemplation of death—a celebration of the good life of the privileged Etruscan elite.

In stylistic terms, the Etruscan figures are comparable to those on sixth-century BCE Greek vases before Late Archaic painters became preoccupied with the problem of foreshortening. Etruscan painters were somewhat backward in this respect, but in other ways they outpaced their counterparts in Greece, especially in their interest in rendering nature. In the Tomb of the Leopards, the "landscape" is but a few trees and shrubs placed between the entertainers (and leopards) and behind the banqueting couches. But in at least one Tarquinian tomb, the natural environment was the painters' chief interest.

**TOMB OF HUNTING AND FISHING** In the Tomb of Hunting and Fishing, scenes of Etruscans enjoying the pleasures of nature decorate all the walls of the main chamber. In the detail reproduced here (FIG. 6-10), a youth dives off a rocky promontory, while others fish from a boat and birds fill the sky all around. On another wall, youthful hunters aim their slingshots at the brightly painted birds. The scenes of hunting and fishing recall the paintings in Egyptian tombs (FIGS. 3-15 and 3-28) and may indicate knowledge of that Eastern funerary tradition. The multicolored rocks evoke those of the Theran Spring Fresco (FIG. 4-9), but art historians know of nothing similar in contemporaneous Greek art save the Tomb of the Diver (FIG. 5-61) at Paestum. That exceptional Greek work, however, is from a Greek tomb in Italy about a half century later than the Tarquinian tomb. In fact, the Paestum painter probably emulated older Etruscan designs, undermining the outdated art historical judgment that Etruscan art was merely derivative and that Etruscan artists never set the standard for Greek artists.

## LATER ETRUSCAN ART

The fifth century BCE was a golden age in Greece but not in Etruria. In 509 BCE the Romans expelled the last of their Etruscan kings, Tarquinius Superbus (see "Etruscan Artists in Rome," page 168), and replaced the monarchy with a republican form of government. In 474 BCE the allied Greek forces of Cumae and Syracuse won a victory over the Etruscan fleet off Cumae, effectively ending Etruscan dominance of the seas—and with it Etruscan prosperity.

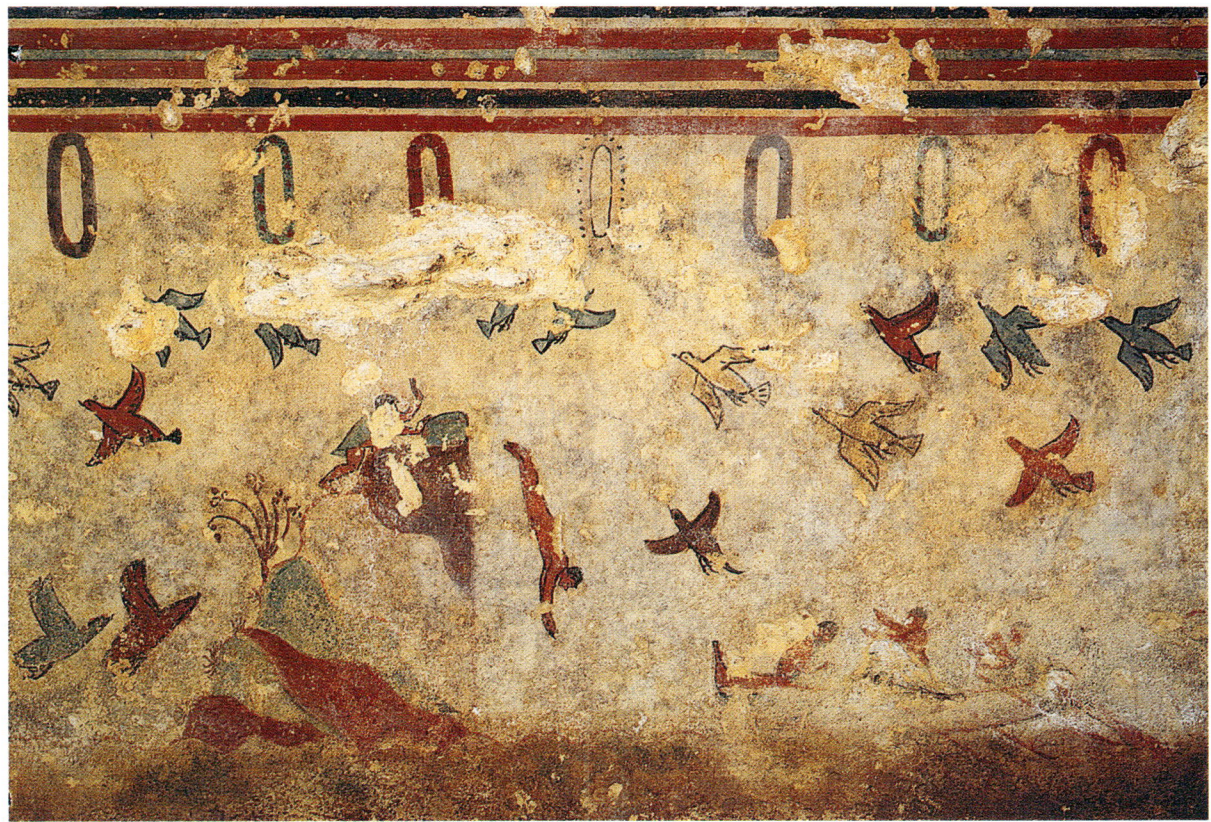

1 ft.

## Classical Art

These events had important consequences in the world of art and architecture. The number of grandiose Etruscan tombs, for example, decreased sharply, and the quality of the furnishings declined markedly. No longer did the Etruscan elite fill their tombs with gold jewelry and imported Greek vases or decorate the walls with paintings of the first rank. But art did not cease in Etruria. Indeed, in the areas in which Etruscan artists excelled, especially the casting of statues in bronze and terracotta, they continued to produce impressive works, even though fewer in number.

*CAPITOLINE WOLF* The best-known Etruscan statue of the Classical period is the *Capitoline Wolf* (FIG. **6-11**), one of the most memorable portrayals of an animal in the history of world art. The statue is a somewhat larger than life-size hollow-cast bronze image of the she-wolf that, according to legend, nursed Romulus and Remus after they were abandoned as infants. When the twins grew to adulthood, they quarreled, and Romulus killed his brother. On April 21, 753 BCE, Romulus founded Rome and became the city's king. The statue of the she-wolf seems to have been made for the new Roman Republic after the expulsion of

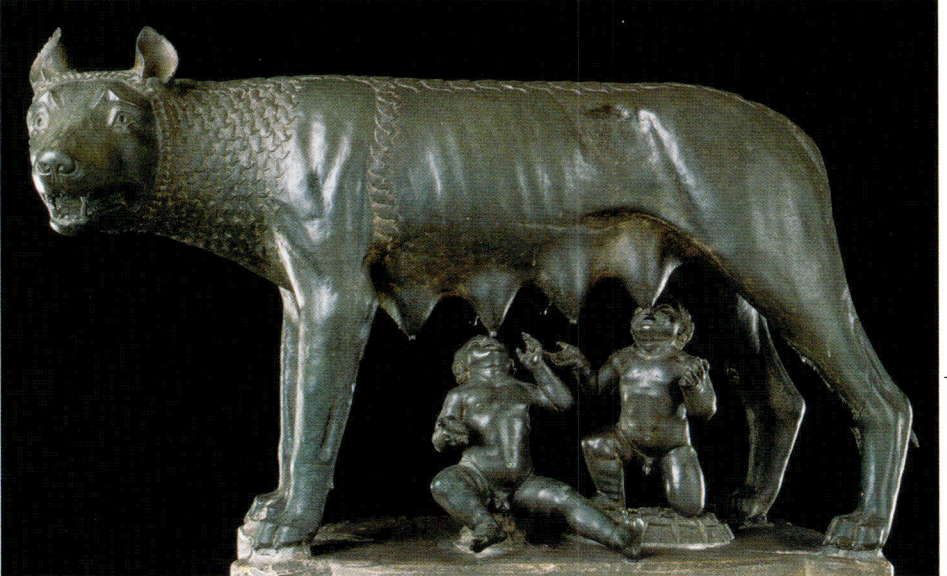

**6-11** *Capitoline Wolf,* from Rome, Italy, ca. 500–480 BCE. Bronze, 2′ 7½″ high. Musei Capitolini, Rome.

An Etruscan sculptor cast this bronze statue of the she-wolf that nursed the infants Romulus and Remus, founders of Rome. The animal has a tense, gaunt body and an unforgettable psychic intensity.

1 ft.

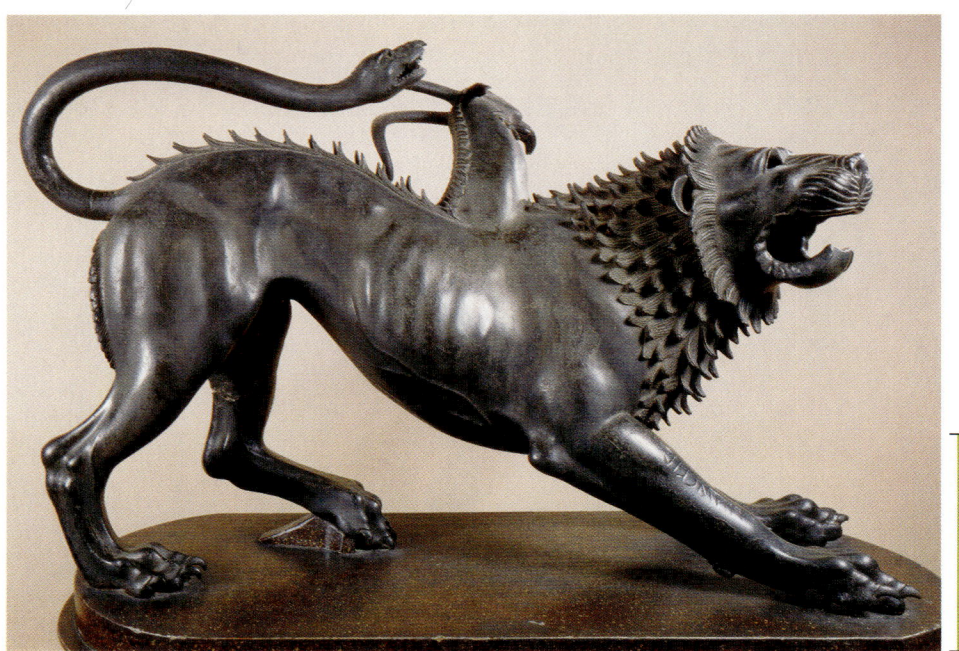

**6-12** *Chimera of Arezzo,* from Arezzo, Italy, first half of fourth century BCE. Bronze, 2′ 7½″ high. Museo Archeologico Nazionale, Florence.

The chimera was a composite monster, which the Greek hero Bellerophon slew. In this Etruscan statue, the artist depicted the wounded beast poised to attack and growling ferociously.

Tarquinius Superbus. It became the new government's totem. The appropriately defiant image has remained the emblem of Rome to this day.

The *Capitoline Wolf* is not, however, a work of Roman art, which had not yet developed a distinct identity, nor is it a medieval sculpture, as one scholar has argued. It is the product of an Etruscan workshop. (The suckling infants are Renaissance additions.) The sculptor brilliantly characterized the she-wolf physically and psychologically. The body is tense, with spare flanks, gaunt ribs, and taut, powerful legs. The lowered neck and head, alert ears, glaring eyes, and ferocious muzzle capture the psychic intensity of the fierce and protective beast as danger approaches. Not even the great animal reliefs of Assyria (FIG. 2-23) match this profound characterization of animal temperament.

**CHIMERA OF AREZZO** Another masterpiece of Etruscan bronze-casting is the Late Classical *Chimera of Arezzo* (FIG. **6-12**), found at Arezzo in 1553 and inscribed *tinscvil* (Etruscan, "gift"), indicating the chimera was a votive offering in a sanctuary. The *chimera* is a monster of Greek invention with a lion's head and body and a serpent's tail (restored in this case). A second head, that of a goat, grows out of the lion's left side. The goat's neck bears the wound the Greek hero Bellerophon inflicted when he hunted and slew the composite beast. As rendered by the Etruscan sculptor, the chimera, although injured and bleeding, refuses to surrender. Like the earlier *Capitoline Wolf,* the bronze chimera has muscles stretched tightly over its rib cage. The monster prepares to attack, and a ferocious cry emanates from its open jaws. Some scholars have postulated the statue was part of a group originally including Bellerophon, but the chimera could have just as well stood alone. The menacing gaze upward toward an unseen adversary need not have been answered. In this respect, too, the chimera is in the tradition of the *Capitoline Wolf.*

## Etruscan Art and the Rise of Rome

At about the time an Etruscan sculptor cast the *Chimera of Arezzo,* Rome began to appropriate Etruscan territory. Veii fell to the Romans in 396 BCE after a terrible 10-year siege. The Tarquinians

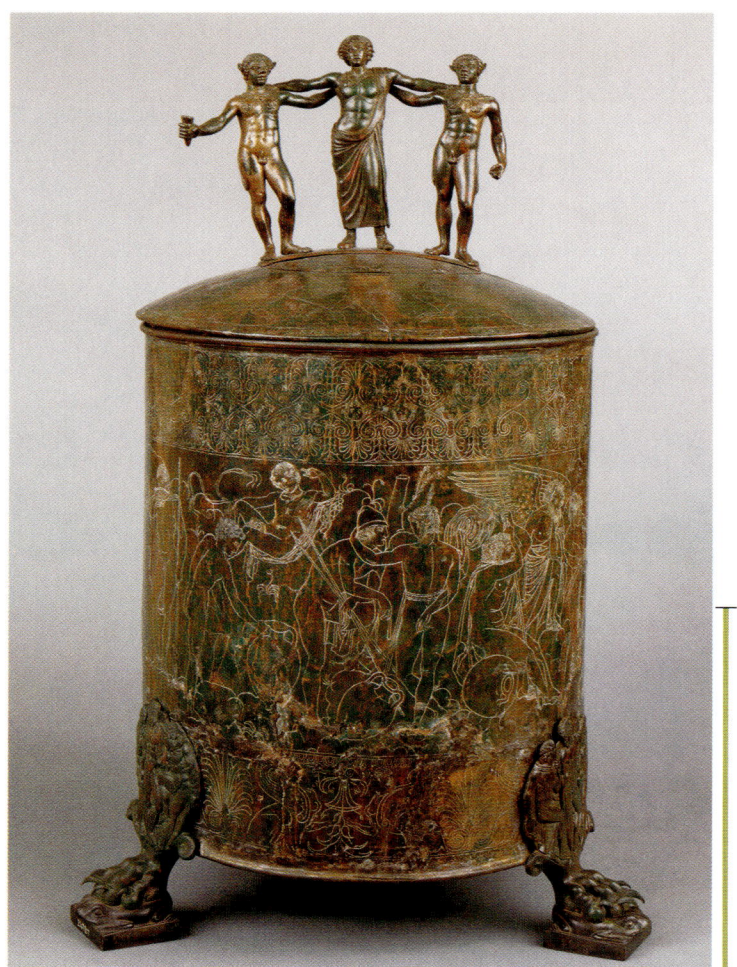

**6-13** NOVIOS PLAUTIOS, *Ficoroni Cista,* from Palestrina, Italy, late fourth century BCE. Bronze, 2′ 6″ high. Museo Nazionale di Villa Giulia, Rome.

Novios Plautios made this container for a woman's toiletry articles in Rome and engraved it with the Greek myth of the Argonauts. The composition is probably an adaptation of a Greek painting.

forged a peace treaty with the Romans in 351, but by the beginning of the next century, Rome had annexed Tarquinia too, and in 273 BCE the Romans conquered Cerveteri.

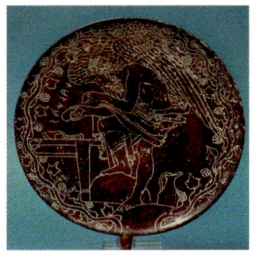

**6-13A** Chalchas examining a liver, ca. 400–375 BCE.

**FICORONI CISTA** An inscription on the *Ficoroni Cista* (FIG. **6-13**) reflects Rome's growing power in central Italy. In the fourth century BCE, Etruscan artists began to produce large numbers of *cistae* (cylindrical containers for a woman's toiletry articles) made of sheet bronze with cast handles and feet and elaborately engraved bodies. Along with engraved bronze mirrors (FIG. **6-13A**), they were popular gifts for both the living and the dead. The center of the Etruscan bronze cista industry was Palestrina, where Francesco de' Ficoroni acquired the cista that still bears his name. The inscription on the cista's handle states that Dindia Macolnia, a local noblewoman, gave the cista (the largest found to date) to her daughter and that the artist was NOVIOS PLAUTIOS. According to the inscription, his workshop was not in Palestrina but in Rome, which by this date was becoming an important Italian cultural, as well as political, center.

The engraved frieze of the *Ficoroni Cista* depicts an episode from the Greek story of the expedition of the Argonauts (the crew of the ship *Argo*) in search of the Golden Fleece. Art historians generally agree the composition is an adaptation of a lost Greek panel painting, perhaps one on display in Rome—another testimony to the burgeoning wealth and prestige of the city Etruscan kings once ruled. The Greek source for Novios Plautios's engraving is evident in the figures seen entirely from behind or in three-quarter view

and in the placement of the protagonists on several levels in the Polygnotan manner (FIG. 5-59).

**PORTA MARZIA** In the third century BCE, the Etruscans of Perugia formed an alliance with Rome and were spared the destruction Veii, Cerveteri, and other Etruscan cities suffered. Portions of Perugia's ancient walls still stand, as do some of its gates. One of these, the so-called Porta Marzia (Gate of Mars), was dismantled during the Renaissance, but the upper part of the gate (FIG. **6-14**) is preserved, embedded in a later wall. A series of trapezoidal stone *voussoirs* held in place by being pressed against each other (FIG. 4-17c) form the archway. Arches of similar construction have been documented earlier in Greece as well as in Mesopotamia (FIG. 2-24), but Italy, first under the Etruscans and later under the Romans, is where *arcuated* (arch-shaped) gateways and freestanding ("triumphal") arches became a major architectural type.

The use of Hellenic-inspired *pilasters* (flat columns) to frame the rounded opening of the Porta Marzia typifies the Etruscan adaptation of Greek motifs. Arches bracketed by engaged columns or pilasters have a long and distinguished history in Roman and later times. In the Porta Marzia, sculpted half-figures of Jupiter and his sons Castor and Pollux and their steeds look out from between the fluted pilasters. The divine twins had appeared miraculously on a battlefield in 484 BCE to turn the tide in favor of the Romans. The presence of these three deities at the apex of the Porta Marzia may reflect the new Roman practice of erecting triumphal arches with gilded bronze statues on top.

**SARCOPHAGUS OF LARS PULENA** In Hellenistic Etruria, the descendants of the magnificent Archaic terracotta sarcophagus (FIG. 6-5) from Cerveteri were coffins of local stone. The leading production center was Tarquinia, and that is where,

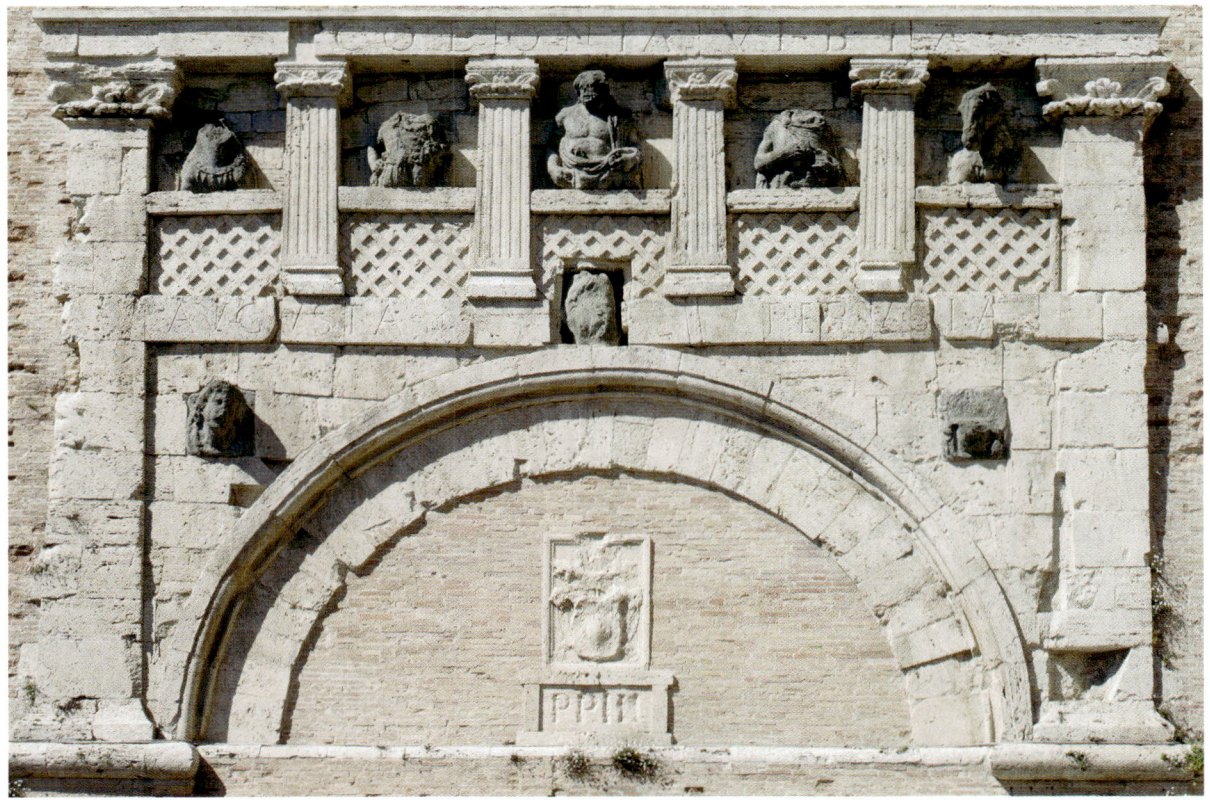

**6-14** Porta Marzia, Perugia, Italy, second century BCE. ◼◀

The Porta Marzia was one of the gates in Perugia's walls. The use of fluted pilasters or engaged columns to frame arches typifies Etruscan builders' adaptation of Greek architectural motifs.

**6-15** Sarcophagus of Lars Pulena, from Tarquinia, Italy, late third or early second century BCE. Tufa, 6′ 6″ long. Museo Archeologico Nazionale, Tarquinia.

Images of the deceased on late Etruscan sarcophagi are more somber than those on Archaic examples (FIG. 6-5), but Lars Pulena proudly displays a list of his life's achievements on an open scroll.

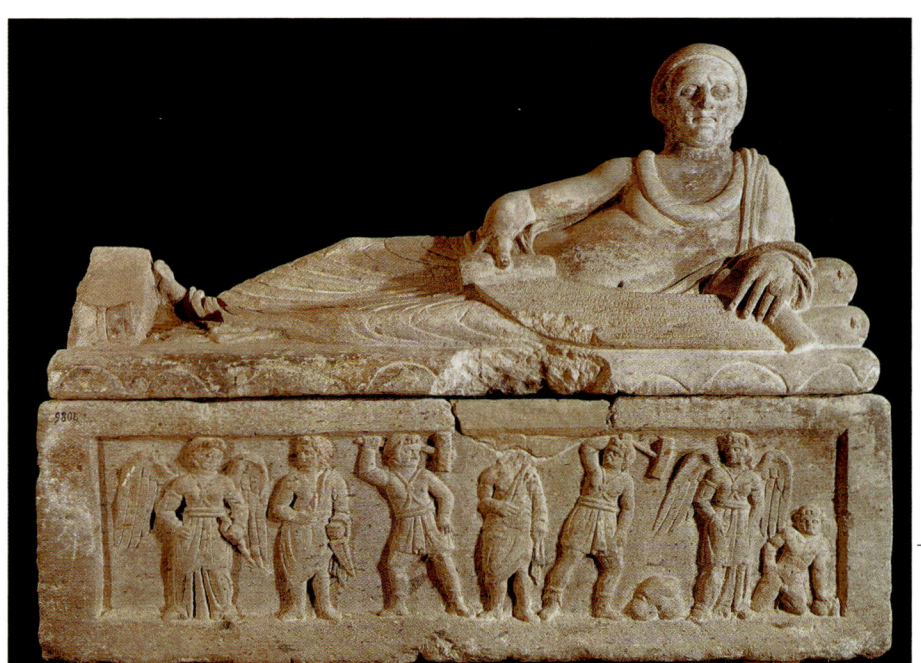

during the late third or early second century BCE, an Etruscan sculptor carved the sarcophagus (FIG. **6-15**) containing the remains of Lars Pulena. The scene sculpted on the front of the coffin shows the deceased in the Underworld between two *charuns* (Etruscan death demons) swinging hammers. Two *vanths* (winged female demons) stand to the left and right. The representation signifies that Lars Pulena has successfully made the journey to the afterlife. Above, the deceased reclines on a couch, as do the couple on the Cerveteri sarcophagus, but he is not at a festive banquet, and his wife is not present. The somber expression on his middle-aged face contrasts sharply with the smiling, confident faces of the Archaic era when Etruria enjoyed its greatest prosperity. Similar heads—realistic but generic types, not true portraits—can be found on most later Etruscan sarcophagi (FIG. **6-15A**) and in tomb paintings. They are symptomatic of the economic and political decline of the once-mighty Etruscan city-states. Nonetheless, Lars Pulena was a proud man. He wears a fillet on his head and a wreath around his neck, and he displays a partially unfurled scroll inscribed with his name and those of his ancestors as well as a record of his life's accomplishments.

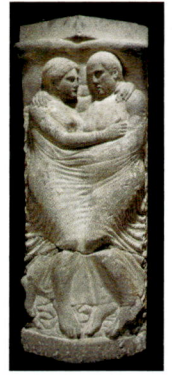

**6-15A** Sarcophagus of Ramtha Visnai and Arnth Tetnies, ca. 350–300 BCE.

**AULE METELE** An even later Etruscan portrait is the bronze statue (FIG. **6-16**) representing the magistrate Aule Metele raising his arm to address an assembly—hence his modern nickname *Arringatore* (*Orator*). This life-size statue, which dates to the early first century BCE, proves that Etruscan artists continued to be experts at bronze-casting long after the heyday of Etruscan prosperity. The time coincides with the Roman achievement of total hegemony over the Etruscans. The so-called Social War ended in 89 BCE with the conferring of Roman citizenship on all of Italy's inhabitants. In fact, Aule Metele—identifiable because the sculptor inscribed the magistrate's Etruscan name and those of his father and mother on the hem of his garment—wears the short *toga* and high laced boots of a Roman magistrate. His head, with its close-cropped hair and signs of age in the face, resembles portraits produced in Rome at the same time. This orator is Etruscan in name only. If the origin of the Etruscans remains the subject of debate, the question of their demise has a ready answer. Aule Metele and his compatriots became Roman citizens, and Etruscan art became Roman art.

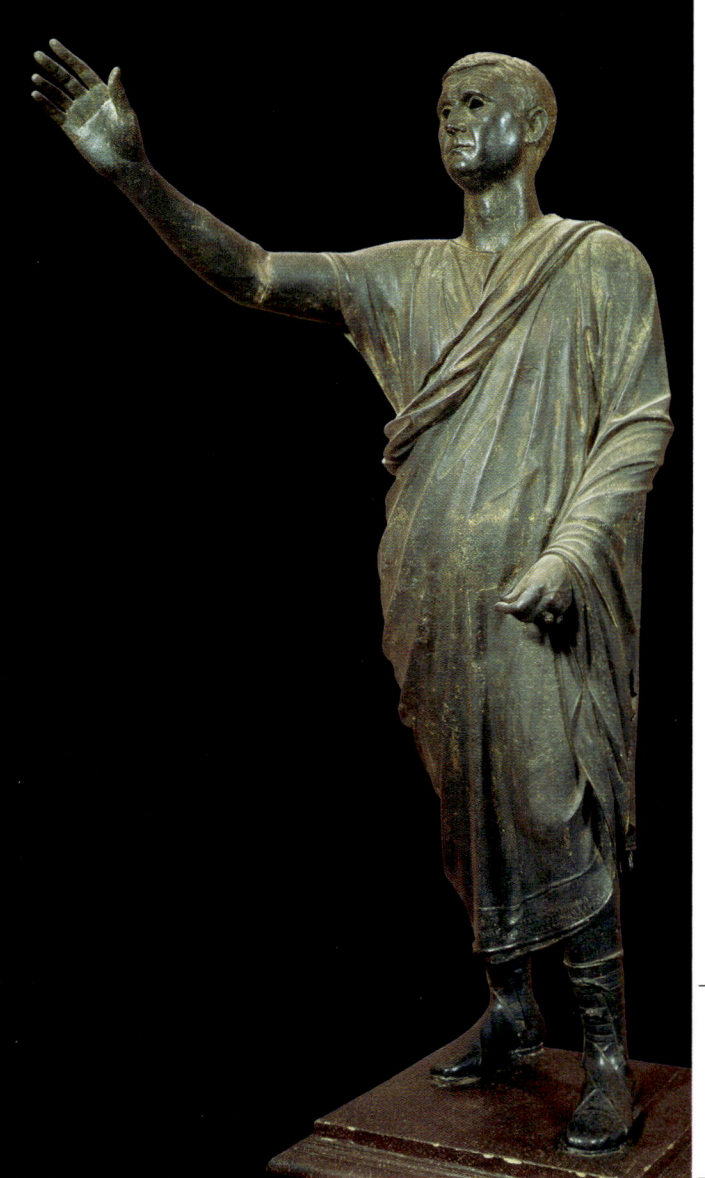

**6-16** Aule Metele (*Arringatore*), from Cortona, Italy, early first century BCE. Bronze, 5′ 7″ high. Museo Archeologico Nazionale, Florence.

The life-size bronze statue portraying Aule Metele is Etruscan in name only. The orator wears the short toga and high boots of a Roman magistrate, and the portrait style is Roman as well.

# THE ETRUSCANS

## ORIENTALIZING ART ca. 700–600 BCE

❙ During the Villanovan period of the early first millennium BCE, the Etruscans emerged as a people with a culture distinct from those of other Italic peoples and the Greeks. Their language, although written in a Greek-derived script, is unrelated to the Indo-European linguistic family.

❙ In the seventh century BCE, the Etruscans traded metals from their mines for foreign goods and began to produce jewelry and other luxury objects decorated with motifs modeled on those found on imports from Mesopotamia. The Regolini-Galassi Tomb at Cerveteri contained a treasure trove of Orientalizing Etruscan jewelry.

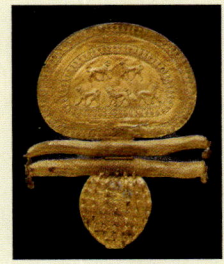

Regolini-Galassi fibula, Cerveteri, ca. 650–640 BCE

## ARCHAIC ART ca. 600–480 BCE

❙ The sixth century BCE was the apex of Etruscan power in Italy. Etruscan kings even ruled Rome until 509 BCE.

❙ The Etruscans admired Greek art and architecture but did not copy Greek works. They constructed their temples of wood and mud brick instead of stone and placed the columns and stairs only at the front. Terracotta statuary decorated the roof.

❙ Most surviving Etruscan artworks come from underground tomb chambers. At Cerveteri, great earthen mounds (tumuli) covered tombs with interiors sculptured to imitate the houses of the living.

❙ At Tarquinia, painters covered the tomb walls with monumental frescoes, often depicting funerary games, as in the Tomb of the Augurs, or banquets attended by both men and women.

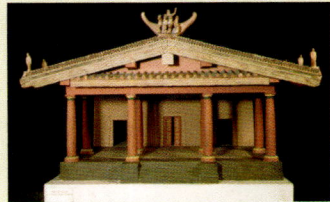

Model of a typical Etruscan temple, sixth century BCE

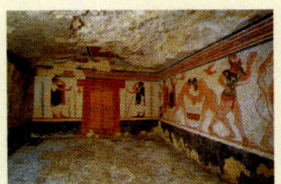

Tomb of the Augurs, Tarquinia, ca. 520 BCE

## CLASSICAL AND HELLENISTIC ART ca. 480–89 BCE

❙ The Greek victory over the Etruscan fleet off Cumae in 474 BCE ended Etruscan domination of the sea and marked the beginning of the decline of Etruria. Rome destroyed Veii in 396 BCE and conquered Cerveteri in 273 BCE. All of Italy became Romanized by 89 BCE.

❙ A very different, more somber mood pervades Etruscan art during the fifth through first centuries BCE, as seen, for example, in the sarcophagus of Lars Pulena.

❙ Later Etruscan architecture is noteworthy for the widespread use of the stone arch, often framed with Greek pilasters or engaged columns, as on the Porta Marzia at Perugia.

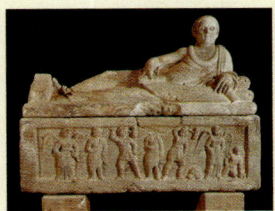

Sarcophagus of Lars Pulena, ca. 200 BCE

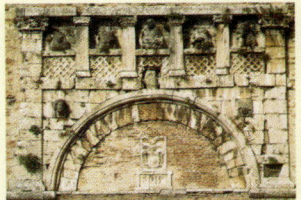

Porta Marzia, Perugia, second century BCE

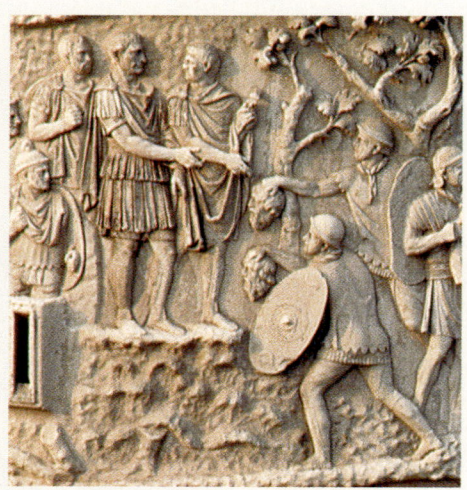

The spiral frieze of the Column of Trajan recounts the emperor's two military campaigns in Dacia (present-day Romania). Here, Roman soldiers present severed Dacian heads to Trajan.

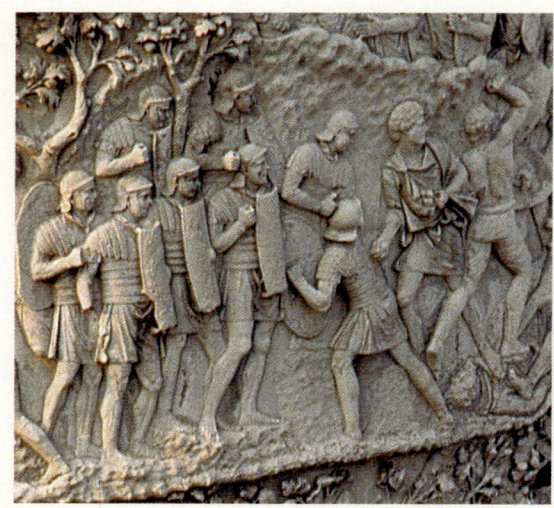

The campaign against the Dacians had few interludes. As soon as one skirmish ended, the Romans moved on and launched another attack. On Trajan's Column, each scene merges with the next.

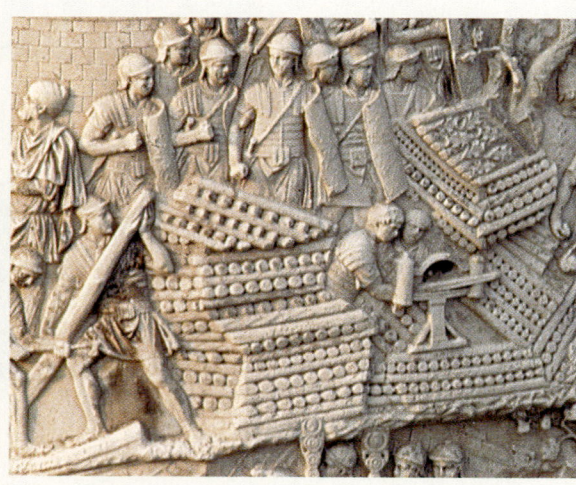

The sculptors of the frieze of Trajan's Column depicted not only combat but all aspects of warfare. Here, Roman soldiers pile up logs to be transported for use at the next battle site.

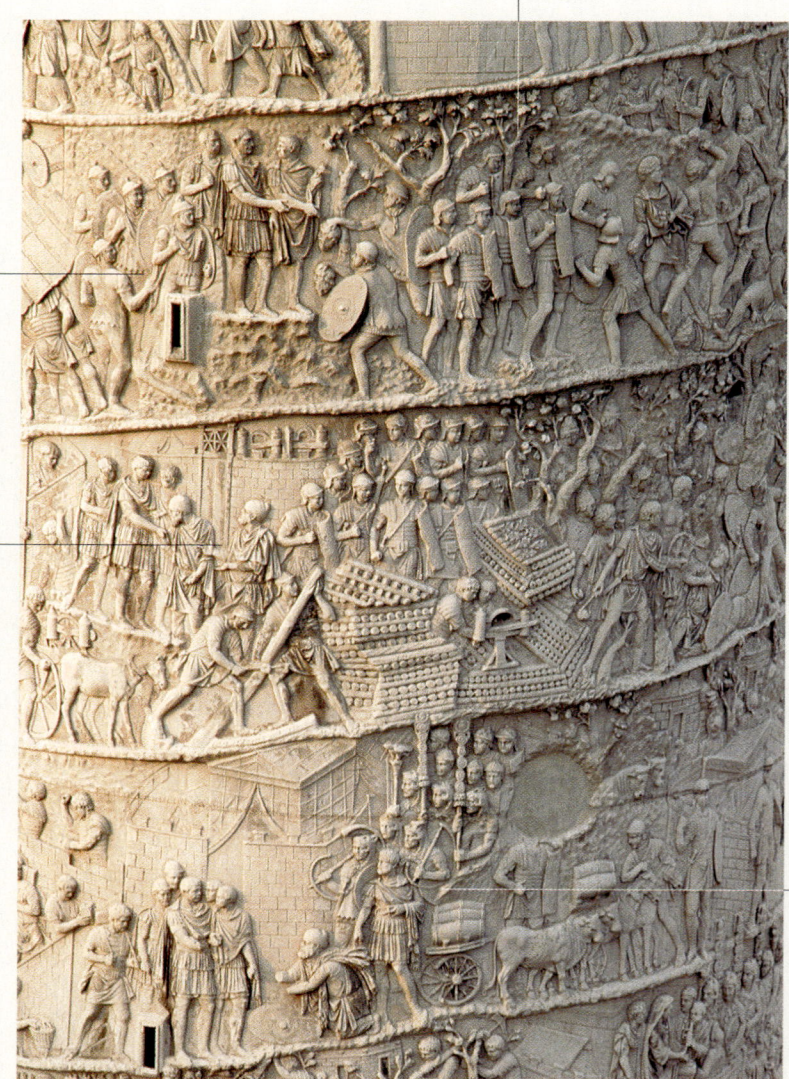

7-1 Detail of three bands of the spiral frieze of the Column of Trajan (FIG. 7-45), Forum of Trajan, Rome, Italy, dedicated 112 CE. ◼◀

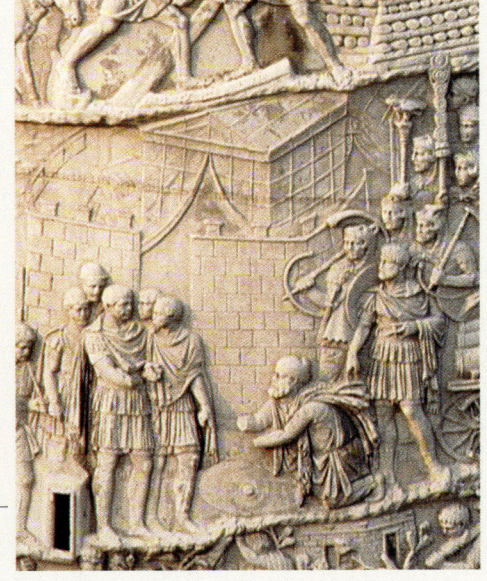

After losing a battle, a Dacian
chieftain kneels before Trajan
and seeks mercy. The war does
not end, however, until, at the
end of the frieze, the Dacian king
Decebalus commits suicide.

# 7

# THE ROMAN EMPIRE

## THE ANCIENT WORLD'S GREATEST EMPIRE

At the death of the emperor Trajan in 117 CE, for the first time in history a single government ruled an empire that extended from the Nile to the Strait of Gibraltar, from the Tigris and Euphrates to the Rhone, Danube, Thames, and beyond (MAP 7-1). No government, before or after, used art more effectively as a political tool. Trajan, perhaps Rome's greatest general, had led the imperial army to victory in both the East and West, bringing vast new territories under Roman dominion. To celebrate his successes in Dacia (roughly equivalent to present-day Romania), Trajan erected a 128-foot-tall column (FIG. 7-45) in Rome. Although frequently imitated, the Column of Trajan was the first of its kind. Its distinguishing new feature was the 625-foot frieze winding around the shaft 23 times from bottom to top. It recounts the emperor's two campaigns against the Dacians.

Illustrated here (FIG. 7-1) are three of the bands midway up the column. Carving the frieze was a complex process. First, the stonemasons had to fashion enormous marble column drums, hollowed out to accommodate the internal spiral staircase running the entire length of the column shaft. The sculptors carved the figures and buildings after the drums were in place to ensure they lined up perfectly. (Note the horizontal line through the lowest frieze in the photograph corresponding to the junction between two column drums.) The sculptors carved the last scenes in the narrative first, working from the top to the bottom of the shaft so that falling marble chips or a dropped chisel would not damage the reliefs below.

At the top left of the section shown, a group of Roman soldiers storms a Dacian fortress with their shields raised and joined to form a protective turtle-shell. To the right, the battle won, Trajan, flanked by two lieutenants, views the severed Dacian heads his soldiers have brought to him as evidence of the successful completion of their mission. Further to the right, another battle begins. In the middle band, Trajan, again with an officer at each side, accepts the surrender of two Dacians. But, as before, there are still more enemies to pursue and conquer, so the Roman army cuts down more trees and piles up the logs to be transported for use at the next battle site. Another scene of surrender, this time with a Dacian kneeling before the emperor, is the subject of the lowest band, coupled with the loading of carts as the army moves on.

The repetition of standard motifs such as these characterizes the frieze as a whole. From every vantage point, Trajan could be seen directing the military operation. His personal involvement in all aspects of the Dacian campaigns—and in expanding Rome's empire on all fronts—was one of the central messages of the Column of Trajan.

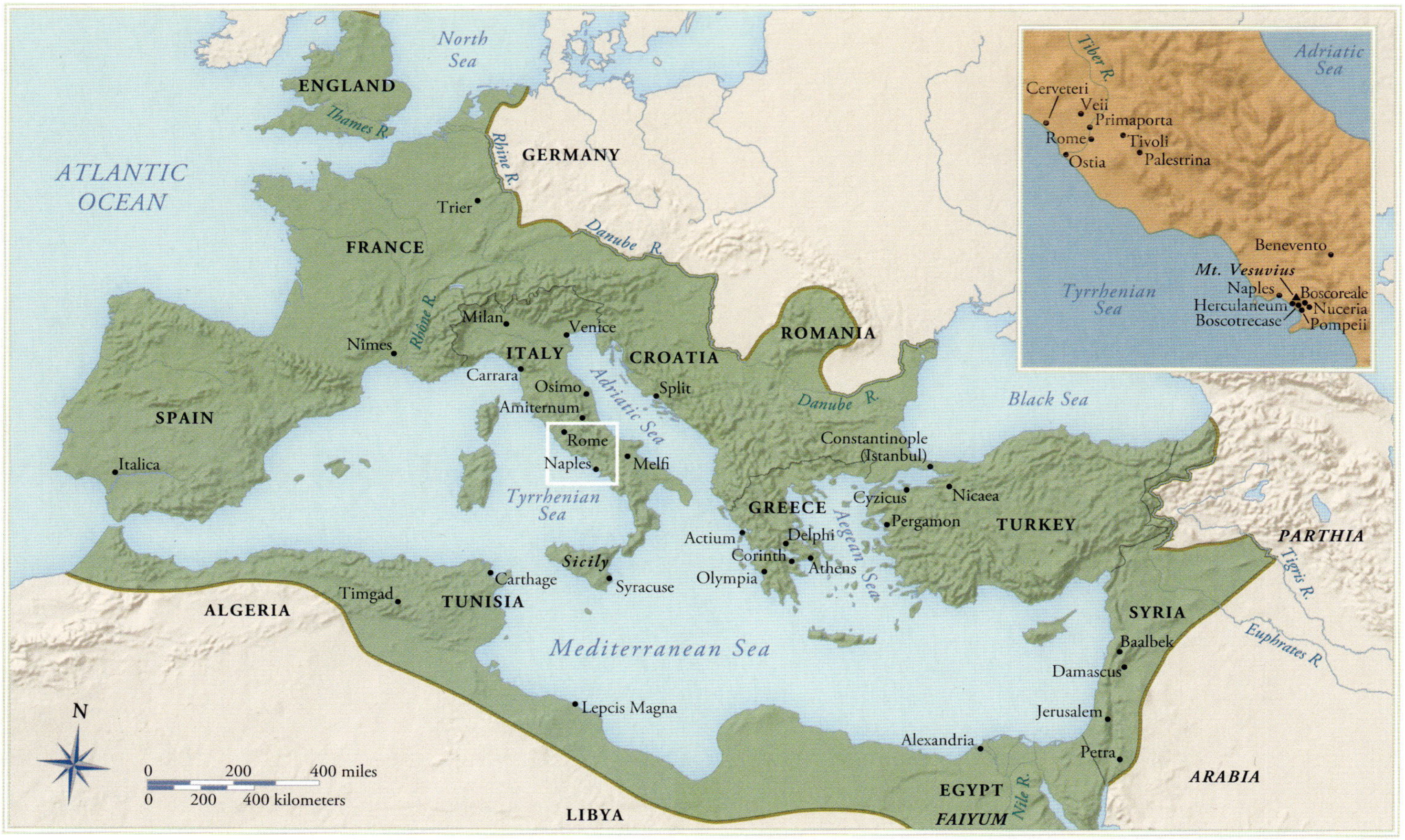

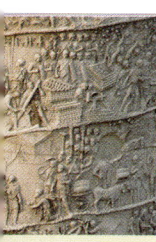

**MAP 7-1** The Roman Empire at the death of Trajan in 117 CE.

# ROME, *CAPUT MUNDI*

The Roman Empire spanned three continents. Within its borders (MAP 7-1) lived millions of people of numerous races, religions, languages, and cultures: Britons and Gauls, Greeks and Egyptians, Africans and Syrians, Jews and Christians, to name but a few. Of all the ancient civilizations, the Roman most closely approximated today's world in its multicultural character.

Roman monuments of art and architecture are the most conspicuous and numerous remains of any ancient civilization. In Europe, the Middle East, and Africa today, Roman temples and basilicas have an afterlife as churches. The powerful concrete vaults of ancient Roman buildings form the cores of modern houses, stores, restaurants, factories, and museums. Bullfights, sports events, operas, and rock concerts are staged in Roman amphitheaters. Ships dock in what were once Roman ports, and Western Europe's highway system still closely follows the routes of Roman roads.

Ancient Rome also lives on in the Western world in concepts of law and government, in languages, in the calendar—even in the coins used daily. Roman art speaks in a language almost every Western viewer can readily understand. Its diversity and eclecticism foreshadowed the modern world. The Roman use of art, especially portraits and narrative reliefs (FIG. 7-1), to manipulate public opinion is similar to the carefully crafted imagery of contemporary political campaigns. And the Roman mastery of concrete construction began an architectural revolution still felt today.

The center of the far-flung Roman Empire was the city on the Tiber River that, according to legend, Romulus and his twin brother Remus founded on April 21, 753 BCE. Hundreds of years later, it would become the *caput mundi,* the "head (capital) of the world," but in the eighth century BCE, Rome consisted only of small huts clustered together on the Palatine Hill (FIG. 7-2, no. 3) overlooking what was then uninhabited marshland. In the Archaic period,

# THE ROMAN EMPIRE

| | Monarchy and Republic | | Early Empire | | High Empire | | Late Empire | |
|---|---|---|---|---|---|---|---|---|
| 753 | | 27 | | 96 | | 192 | | 337 |

BCE | CE

- Hellenization of Etruscan architecture
- Republican veristic (superrealistic) portraiture
- First and Second Styles of Pompeian painting

- Augustan revival of Classical style in art and architecture
- Third Style of Pompeian painting

- Architects realize the full potential of concrete construction
- Fourth Style of Pompeian painting

- Trajan extends the Empire and builds a new forum in Rome
- Hadrian makes beards fashionable and builds the Pantheon
- Domination of Classical style erodes under the Antonines

- Late Antique style takes root under the Severans
- Portraits of soldier emperors reveal insecurity of the age
- Constantine founds a New Rome at Constantinople

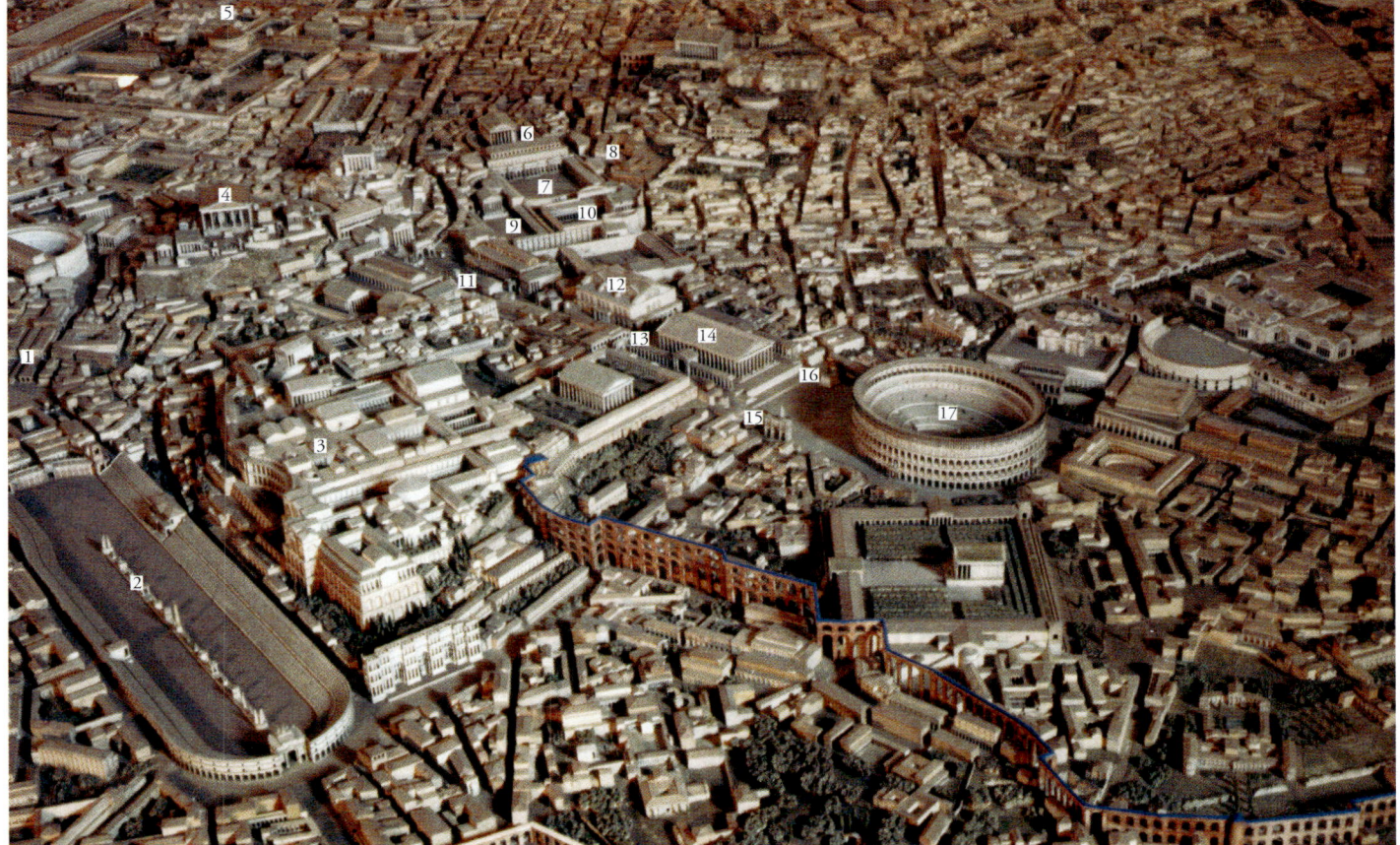

**7-2** Model of the city of Rome during the early fourth century CE. Museo della Civiltà Romana, Rome. (1) Temple of Portunus, (2) Circus Maximus, (3) Palatine Hill, (4) Temple of Jupiter Capitolinus, (5) Pantheon, (6) Column of Trajan, (7) Forum of Trajan, (8) Markets of Trajan, (9) Forum of Julius Caesar, (10) Forum of Augustus, (11) Forum Romanum, (12) Basilica Nova, (13) Arch of Titus, (14) Temple of Venus and Roma, (15) Arch of Constantine, (16) Colossus of Nero, (17) Colosseum.

By the time of Constantine, the city of Rome was densely packed with temples, forums, triumphal arches, theaters, baths, racetracks, aqueducts, markets, private homes, and apartment houses.

Rome was essentially an Etruscan city, both politically and culturally. Its greatest shrine, the Temple of Jupiter Optimus Maximus (Best and Greatest) on the Capitoline Hill, was built by an Etruscan king, designed by an Etruscan architect, made of wood and mud brick in the Etruscan manner, and decorated with terracotta statuary fashioned by an Etruscan sculptor (see "Etruscan Artists in Rome," Chapter 6, page 168).

# REPUBLIC

In 509 BCE, the Romans overthrew Tarquinius Superbus, the last of Rome's Etruscan kings, and established a constitutional government (see "An Outline of Roman History," page 182). The new Roman Republic vested power mainly in a *senate* (literally, "a council of elders," *senior* citizens) and in two elected *consuls*. Under extraordinary circumstances, a *dictator* could be appointed for a limited time and specific purpose, such as commanding the army during a crisis. All leaders came originally from among the wealthy landowners, or *patricians,* but later also from the *plebeian* class of small farmers, merchants, and freed slaves.

Before long, the descendants of Romulus conquered Rome's neighbors one by one: the Etruscans and the Gauls to the north, the Samnites and the Greek colonists to the south. Even the Carthaginians of North Africa, who under Hannibal's dynamic leadership had annihilated some of Rome's legions and almost brought down the Republic, fell before the mighty Roman armies.

# Architecture

The year 211 BCE was a turning point both for Rome and for Roman art. Breaking with precedent, Marcellus, conqueror of the fabulously wealthy Sicilian Greek city of Syracuse, brought back to Rome not only the usual spoils of war—captured arms and armor, gold and silver coins, and the like—but also the city's artistic patrimony. Thus began, in the words of the historian Livy, "the craze for works of Greek art."[1] Exposure to Greek sculpture and painting and to the splendid marble temples of the Greek gods increased as the Romans expanded their conquests beyond Italy. Greece became a Roman province in 146 BCE, and in 133 BCE the last king of Pergamon willed his kingdom to Rome (see page 162). Nevertheless, although the Romans developed a virtually insatiable taste for Greek "antiques," the influence of Etruscan art and architecture persisted. The artists and architects of the Roman Republic drew on both Greek and Etruscan traditions.

## An Outline of Roman History

### MONARCHY (753–509 BCE)

Latin and Etruscan kings ruled Rome from the city's founding by Romulus and Remus until the revolt against Tarquinius Superbus (exact dates of rule unreliable).

### REPUBLIC (509–27 BCE)

The Republic lasted from the expulsion of Tarquinius Superbus until the bestowing of the title of Augustus on Octavian, the grand-nephew of Julius Caesar and victor over Mark Antony in the civil war that ended the Republic. Some major figures were

- Marcellus, b. 268(?), d. 208 BCE; consul
- Marius, b. 157, d. 86 BCE; consul
- Sulla, b. 138, d. 79 BCE; consul and dictator
- Pompey, b. 106, d. 48 BCE; consul
- Julius Caesar, b. 100, d. 44 BCE; consul and dictator
- Mark Antony, b. 83, d. 30 BCE; consul

### EARLY EMPIRE (27 BCE–96 CE)

The Early Empire began with the rule of Augustus and his Julio-Claudian successors and continued until the end of the Flavian dynasty. Selected emperors and their dates of rule (with names of the most influential empresses in parentheses) were

- Augustus (Livia), r. 27 BCE–14 CE
- Tiberius, r. 14–37
- Caligula, r. 37–41
- Claudius (Agrippina the Younger), r. 41–54
- Nero, r. 54–68
- Vespasian, r. 69–79

- Titus, r. 79–81
- Domitian, r. 81–96

### HIGH EMPIRE (96–192 CE)

The High Empire began with the rule of Nerva and the Spanish emperors, Trajan and Hadrian, and ended with the last emperor of the Antonine dynasty. The emperors (and empresses) of this period were

- Nerva, r. 96–98
- Trajan (Plotina), r. 98–117
- Hadrian (Sabina), r. 117–138
- Antoninus Pius (Faustina the Elder), r. 138–161
- Marcus Aurelius (Faustina the Younger), r. 161–180
- Lucius Verus, coemperor with Marcus Aurelius, r. 161–169
- Commodus, r. 180–192

### LATE EMPIRE (193–337 CE)

The Late Empire began with the Severan dynasty and included the so-called soldier emperors of the third century, the tetrarchs, and Constantine, the first Christian emperor. Selected emperors (and empresses) were

- Septimius Severus (Julia Domna), r. 193–211
- Caracalla (Plautilla), r. 211–217
- Severus Alexander, r. 222–235
- Philip the Arabian, r. 244–249
- Trajan Decius, r. 249–251
- Trebonianus Gallus, r. 251–253
- Diocletian, r. 284–305
- Constantine I, r. 306–337

**TEMPLE OF PORTUNUS** The mixing of Greek and Etruscan forms is the primary characteristic of the Republican-era Temple of Portunus (FIGS. 7-2, no. 1, and 7-3), the Roman god of harbors. Popularly known as the Temple of Fortuna Virilis, its plan follows the Etruscan pattern with a high podium and a flight of steps only at the front (FIG. 6-3). The six freestanding columns are all in the deep porch. The structure is stone (local tufa and travertine), overlaid originally with *stucco* in imitation of Greek marble. The columns are not Tuscan but Ionic, complete with flutes and bases, and there is a matching Ionic frieze. Moreover, in an effort to approximate a peripteral Greek temple yet maintain the basic Etruscan plan, the architect added a series of engaged Ionic half columns to the sides and back of the cella. The result was a *pseudoperipteral* temple. Although the design combines Etruscan and Greek elements, the resultant mix is uniquely Roman.

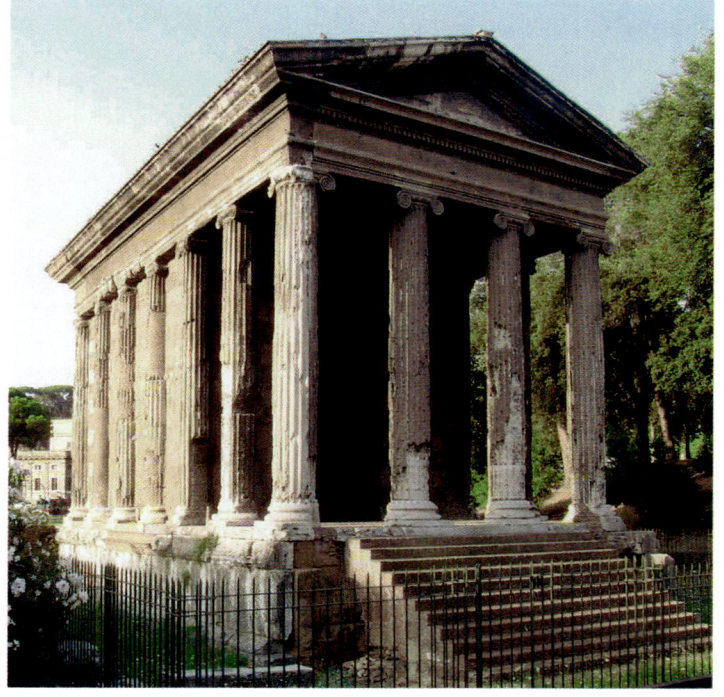

**7-3** Temple of Portunus (Temple of Fortuna Virilis), Rome, Italy, ca. 75 BCE. ◼◀

Republican temples combined Etruscan plans and Greek elevations. This pseudoperipteral stone temple employs the Ionic order, but it has a staircase and freestanding columns only at the front.

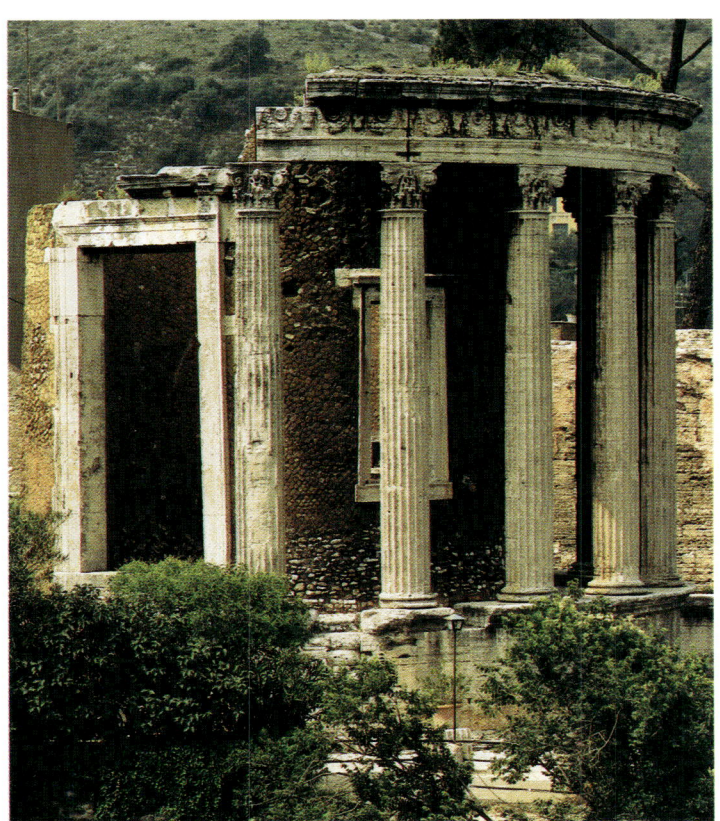

**7-4** Temple of Vesta(?), Tivoli, Italy, early first century BCE.

The round temple type is unknown in Etruria. The models for the Tivoli temple's builders were Greek tholoi (FIG. 5-72), but the Roman building has a frontal orientation and a concrete cella.

## TEMPLE OF VESTA

The Romans' admiration for the Greek temples they encountered in their conquests also led to the importation into Republican Italy of a temple type unknown in Etruscan architecture—the round, or tholos, temple. At Tivoli, on a dramatic site overlooking a deep gorge, a Republican architect built a Greek-inspired round temple (FIG. **7-4**) early in the first century BCE. The circular plan is standard for shrines of Vesta, and she is probably the deity honored here. The temple has travertine Corinthian columns and a frieze carved with garlands held up by ox heads, also in emulation of Greek models. But the high podium can be reached only via a narrow stairway leading to the cella door. This arrangement introduced an axial alignment not found in Greek tholoi (FIG. 5-72), where, as in Greek rectangular temples, steps continue all around the structure. Also in contrast with the Greeks, the Roman builders did not construct the cella wall using masonry blocks but a new material of recent invention: concrete.

## SANCTUARY OF FORTUNA

The most impressive and innovative use of concrete during the Republic was in the Sanctuary of Fortuna Primigenia (FIG. **7-5**), the goddess of good fortune, at Palestrina. Spread out over several terraces leading up the hillside to a tholos at the peak of an ascending triangle, the layout reflects

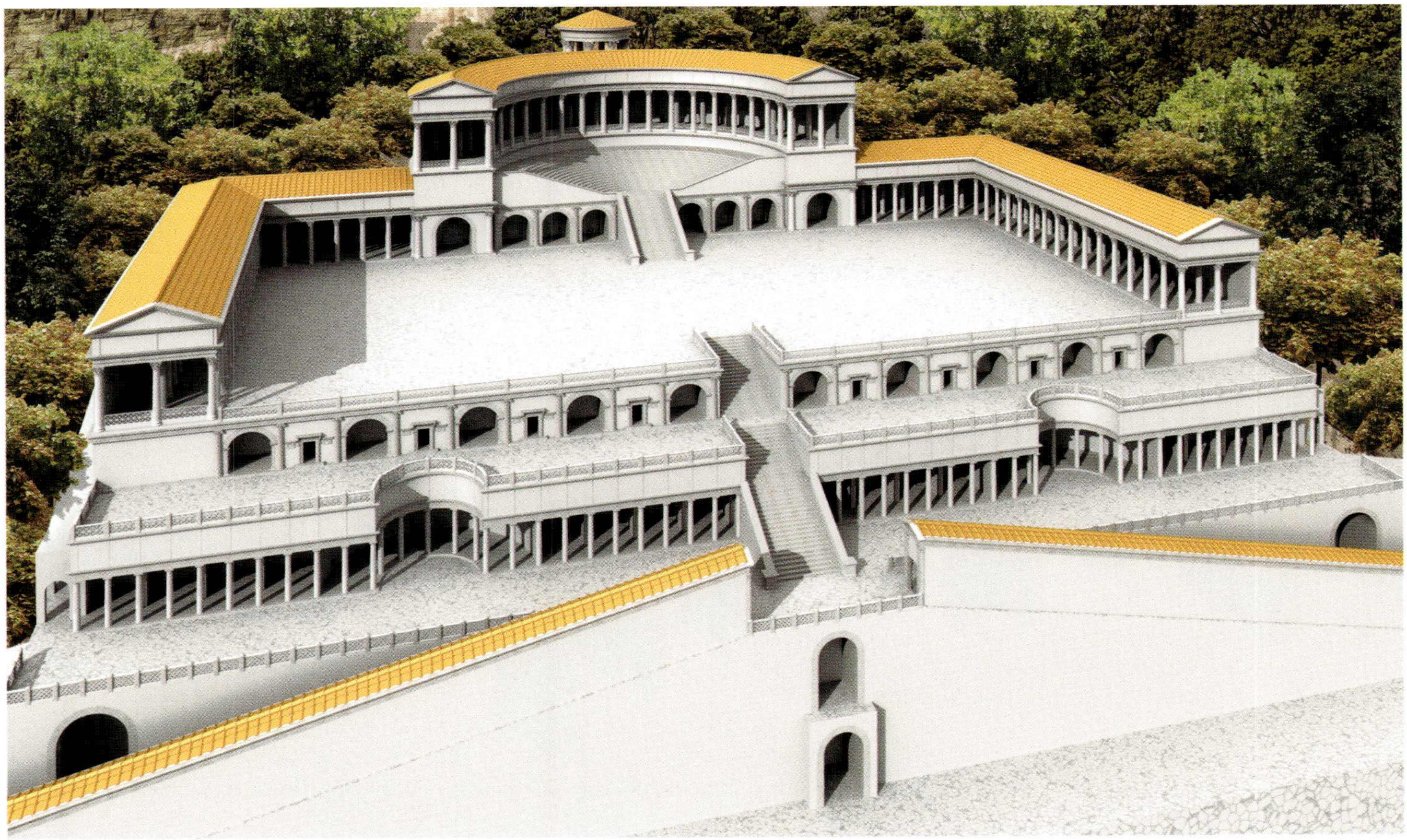

**7-5** Restored view of the Sanctuary of Fortuna Primigenia, Palestrina, Italy, late second century BCE (John Burge). ◼◀

Concrete construction made possible Fortuna's hillside sanctuary at Palestrina with its terraces, ramps, shops, and porticos spread out over several levels. A tholos temple crowned the complex.

## Roman Concrete Construction

The history of Roman architecture would be very different had the Romans been content to use the same building materials the Greeks, Etruscans, and other ancient peoples did. Instead, the Romans developed concrete construction, which revolutionized architectural design. Roman builders mixed *concrete* according to a changing recipe of lime mortar, volcanic sand, water, and small stones (*caementa,* from which the English word *cement* derives). After mixing the concrete, the builders poured it into wooden frames and left it to dry. When the concrete hardened completely, they removed the wooden molds, revealing a solid mass of great strength, though rough in appearance. The Romans often covered the rough concrete with stucco or with marble *revetment* (facing). Despite this lengthy procedure, concrete walls were much less costly to construct than walls of imported Greek marble or even local tufa and travertine.

The advantages of concrete went well beyond cost, however. It was possible to fashion concrete shapes unachievable in masonry construction, especially huge vaulted and domed rooms without internal supports. The new medium became a vehicle for shaping architectural space and enabled Roman architects to design buildings in revolutionary ways.

The most common types of Roman concrete vaults and domes are

**Barrel Vaults** Also called the *tunnel vault,* the *barrel vault* (FIG. 7-6a) is an extension of a simple arch, creating a semi-cylindrical ceiling over parallel walls. Pre-Roman builders constructed barrel vaults using traditional ashlar masonry (FIG. 2-24), but those earlier vaults were less stable than concrete barrel vaults. If even a single block of a cut-stone vault comes loose, the whole vault may collapse. Also, masonry barrel vaults can be illuminated only by light entering at either end of the tunnel. Using concrete, Roman builders could place windows at any point in a barrel vault, because once the concrete hardened, it formed a seamless sheet of "artificial stone" in which the openings did not lessen the vault's structural integrity. Whether made of stone or concrete, barrel vaults require *buttressing* (lateral support) of the walls below the vaults to counteract their downward and outward *thrust.*

**Groin Vaults** A *groin* (or *cross*) *vault* (FIG. 7-6b) is formed by the intersection at right angles of two barrel vaults of equal size. Besides appearing lighter than the barrel vault, the groin vault needs less buttressing. Whereas the barrel vault's thrust is continuous along the entire length of the supporting wall, the groin vault's thrust is concentrated along the groins, the lines at the juncture of the two barrel vaults. Buttressing is needed only at the points where the groins meet the vault's vertical supports, usually *piers.* The system leaves the area between the piers open, permitting light to enter. Builders can construct groin vaults as well as barrel vaults, using stone blocks, but stone groin vaults have the same structural limitations when compared with concrete vaults.

When a series of groin vaults covers an interior hall (FIG. 7-6c; compare FIG. 7-47), the open lateral arches of the vaults form the equivalent of a *clerestory* of a traditional timber-roofed structure (for example, FIG. 8-10). A *fenestrated* (with openings or windows) sequence of groin vaults has a major advantage over a wooden clerestory. Concrete vaults are relatively fireproof, always an important consideration because fires were common occurrences (see "Timber Roofs and Stone Vaults," Chapter 12, page 339).

**Hemispherical Domes** The largest domed space in the ancient world for more than a millennium was the corbeled, beehive-shaped tholos (FIG. 4-21) of the Treasury of Atreus at Mycenae. The Romans were able to surpass the Mycenaeans by using concrete to construct hemispherical *domes* (FIG. 7-6d), which usually rested on concrete cylindrical *drums.* If a barrel vault is a round arch extended in a line, then a hemispherical dome is a round arch rotated around the full circumference of a circle. Masonry domes, like masonry vaults, cannot accommodate windows without threat to their stability. Concrete domes can be opened up even at their apex with a circular *oculus* ("eye"), allowing light to reach the vast spaces beneath (FIGS. 7-35 and 7-51).

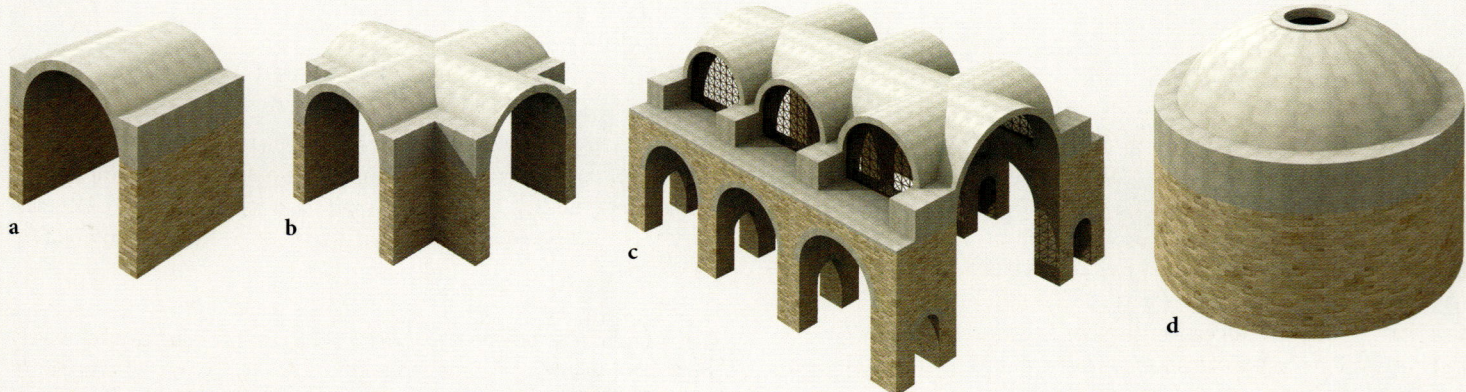

**7-6** Roman concrete construction. (a) barrel vault, (b) groin vault, (c) fenestrated sequence of groin vaults, (d) hemispherical dome with oculus (John Burge).

Concrete domes and vaults of varying designs enabled Roman builders to revolutionize the history of architecture by shaping spaces in novel ways.

## Roman Ancestor Portraits

In Republican Rome, ancestor portraits separated the old patrician families not only from the plebeian middle and lower classes of working citizens and former slaves but also from the newly wealthy and powerful of more modest origins. The case of Marius, a renowned Republican general who lacked a long and distinguished genealogy, is instructive. When his patrician colleagues in the Senate ridiculed him as a man who had no *imagines* (portrait masks) in his home, he defended himself by saying that his battle scars were his masks, the proof of his nobility.

Patrician pride in genealogy was unquestionably the motivation for a unique portrait statue (FIG. 7-7), datable to the late first century BCE, in which a man wearing a toga, the badge of Roman citizenship, holds in each hand a bust of one of his male forebears. The head of the man is ancient but unfortunately does not belong to this statue. The two heads he holds, which are probably likenesses of his father and grandfather, are characteristic examples of Republican portraiture of the first century BCE. The heads may be reproductions of wax or terracotta portraits. Marble or bronze heads would have been too heavy to carry. They are not, however, wax *imagines,* because they are sculptures in the round, not masks. The statue nonetheless would have had the same effect on the observer as the spectacle of parading ancestral portraits at a patrician funeral.

Polybius, a Greek author who wrote a history of Rome in the middle of the second century BCE, described these patrician funerals in detail:

> For whenever one of the leading men amongst [the Romans] dies . . . they place a likeness of the dead man in the most public part of the house, keeping it in a small wooden shrine. The likeness is a mask especially made for a close resemblance . . . And whenever a leading member of the family dies, they introduce [the wax masks] into the funeral procession, putting them on men who seem most like them in height and as regards the rest of their general appearance. . . . It is not easy for an ambitious and high-minded young man to see a finer spectacle than this. For who would not be won over at the sight of all the masks together of those men who had been extolled for virtue as if they were alive and breathing?*

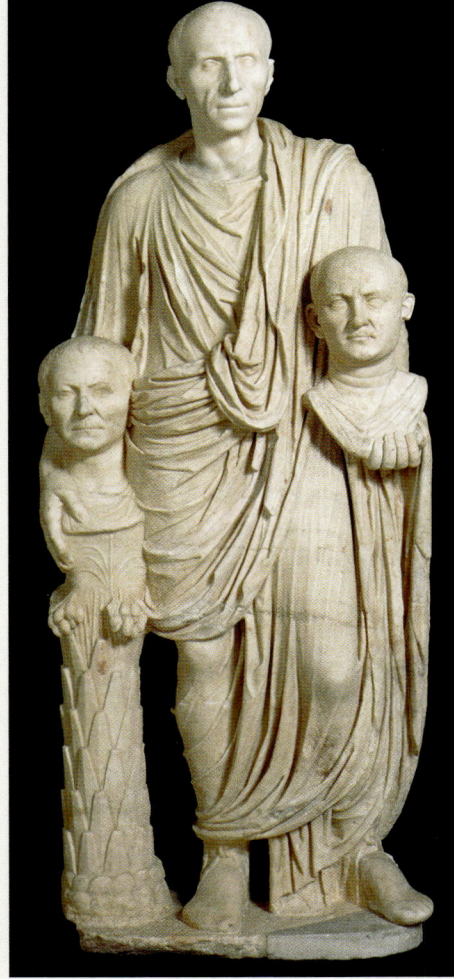

**7-7** Man with portrait busts of his ancestors, from Rome, late first century BCE. Marble, 5′ 5″ high. Musei Capitolini–Centro Montemartini, Rome.

Reflecting the importance patricians placed on genealogy, this toga-clad man proudly displays the portrait busts of his father and grandfather. Both are characteristically realistic likenesses.

1 ft.

*Polybius, *History of Rome,* 6.5. Translated by Harriet I. Fowler, *Ancestor Masks and Aristocratic Power in Roman Culture* (Oxford: Clarendon Press, 1996), 309.

the new Republican familiarity with the terraced sanctuaries of the Hellenistic East. The construction method, however, was distinctly Roman. The builders used concrete barrel vaults (see "Roman Concrete Construction," page 184, and FIG. 7-6a) of enormous strength to support the imposing terraces and to cover the great ramps leading to the grand central staircase, as well as to give shape to the shops selling food, souvenirs, and the like, aligned on two levels. In this way, Roman engineers transformed the entire hillside, subjecting nature itself to human will and rational order.

## Sculpture

The patrons of Republican temples and sanctuaries were in almost all cases men from old and distinguished families. Often they were victorious generals who used the spoils of war to finance public works. These aristocratic patricians were fiercely proud of their lineage. They kept likenesses of their ancestors in wooden cupboards in their homes and paraded them at the funerals of prominent relatives (see "Roman Ancestor Portraits," above, and FIG. 7-7). Portraiture was one way the patrician class celebrated its elevated position in society.

**VERISM** The subjects of these portraits were almost exclusively men (and to a lesser extent women) of advanced age, for generally only elders held power in the Republic. These patricians did not ask sculptors to make them appear nobler than they were, as Kresilas portrayed Pericles (FIG. 5-41). Instead, they requested brutally realistic images with their distinctive features, in the tradition of the treasured household *imagines.* One of the most striking of these

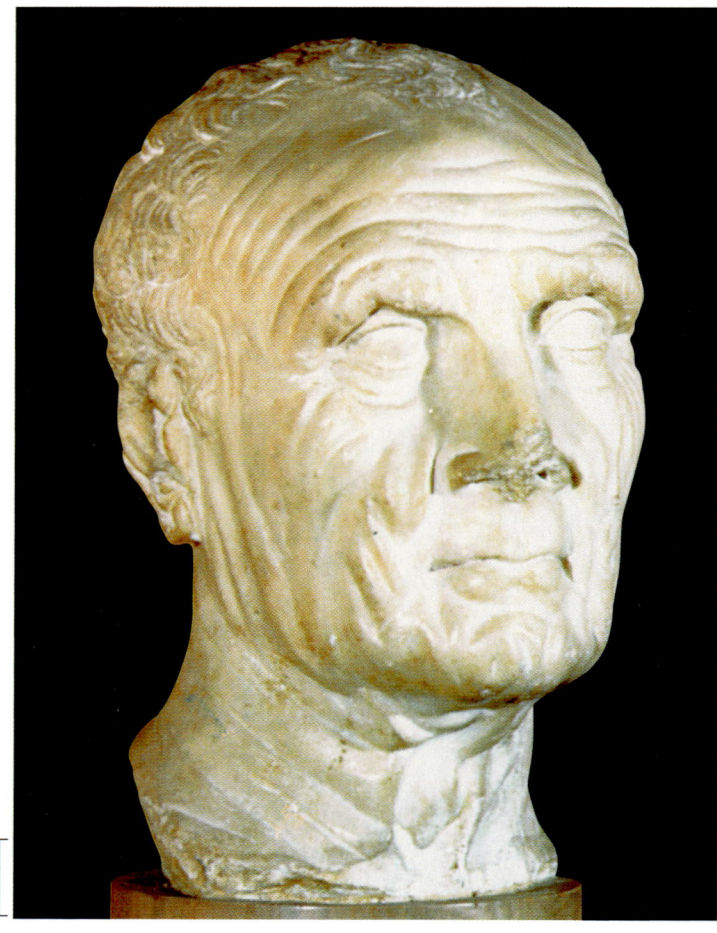

1 in.

**7-8** Head of an old man, from Osimo, mid-first century BCE. Marble, life-size. Palazzo del Municipio, Osimo.

Veristic (superrealistic) portraits of old men from distinguished families were the norm during the Republic. The sculptor of this head painstakingly recorded every detail of the elderly man's face.

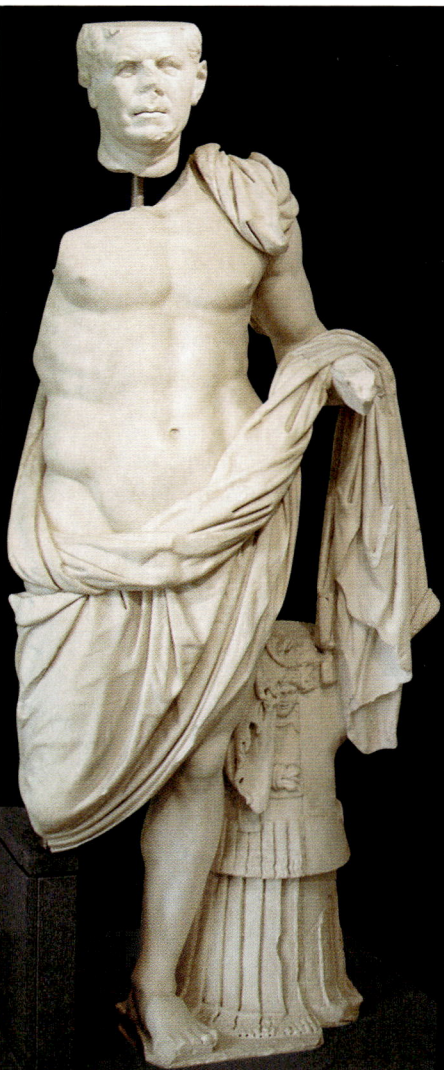

**7-9** Portrait of a Roman general, from the Sanctuary of Hercules, Tivoli, Italy, ca. 75–50 BCE. Marble, 6′ 2″ high. Museo Nazionale Romano—Palazzo Massimo alle Terme, Rome.

The sculptor based this life-size portrait of a general on idealized Greek statues of heroes and athletes, but the man's head is a veristic likeness. The combination is typical of Republican portraiture.

1 ft.

so-called *veristic* (superrealistic) portraits is the head (FIG. **7-8**) of an unidentified patrician from Osimo. The sculptor painstakingly recorded each rise and fall, each bulge and fold, of the facial surface, like a mapmaker who did not want to miss the slightest detail of surface change. Scholars debate whether Republican veristic portraits were truly blunt records of individual features or exaggerated types designed to make a statement about personality: serious, experienced, determined, loyal to family and state—the most admired virtues during the Republic.

**TIVOLI GENERAL** The Osimo head illustrates that the Romans believed the head or bust alone (FIGS. 7-7 and 7-11) was enough to constitute a portrait. The Greeks, in contrast, believed head and body were inseparable parts of an integral whole, so their portraits were always full length (FIG. 5-87), although Roman copies often reproduced only the head (FIG. 5-41). In fact, Republican sculptors often, if incongruously, placed veristic heads on bodies to which they could not possibly belong, as in the curious and discordant seminude portrait statue (FIG. **7-9**) from Tivoli representing a Republican general. The *cuirass* (leather breastplate) at his side, which acts as a prop for the heavy marble statue, is the emblem of his rank. But the general does not appear as he would in life. Although he has a typically Republican stern and lined face, the head sits atop a powerful youthful body. The sculptor modeled the portrait on the

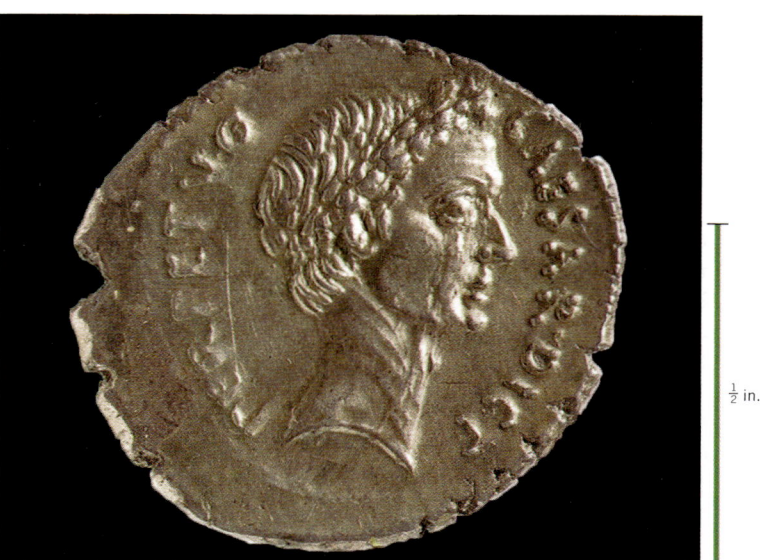

½ in.

**7-10** Denarius with portrait of Julius Caesar, 44 BCE. Silver, diameter ¾″. American Numismatic Society, New York.

Julius Caesar was the first to place his own portrait on Roman coinage during his lifetime. This denarius, issued just before his assassination, shows the dictator with a deeply lined face and neck.

# Art for Former Slaves

Historians and art historians alike tend to focus on the lives and monuments of famous individuals, but some of the most interesting remains of ancient Roman civilization are the artworks ordinary people commissioned, especially former slaves—*freedmen* and *freedwomen*. Slavery was common in the Roman world. Indeed, at the end of the Republic, there were approximately two million slaves in Italy—roughly one slave for every three citizens. The very rich might own hundreds of slaves, but slaves could be found in all but the poorest households. The practice was so much a part of Roman society that even slaves often became slave owners when their former masters freed them. Some gained freedom in return for meritorious service, others as bequests in their masters' wills. Most slaves died as slaves in service to their original or new owners.

The most noteworthy artworks Roman freedmen and freedwomen commissioned are the stone reliefs that regularly adorned their tomb facades. One of these reliefs (FIG. 7-11) depicts two men and a woman, all named Gessius. At the left is Gessia Fausta and at the right Gessius Primus. Both are the freed slaves of Publius Gessius, the freeborn citizen in the center, shown wearing a general's cuirass and portrayed in the standard Republican superrealistic fashion (FIGS. 7-7 and 7-8). As slaves this couple had no legal standing. They were the property of Publius Gessius. According to Roman law, however, after gaining freedom the ex-slaves became people. These stern frontal portraits proclaim their new status as members of Roman society—and their gratitude to Publius Gessius for granting them that status.

As was the custom, the ex-slaves bear their patron's name, but whether they are sister and brother, wife and husband, or unrelated is unclear. The inscriptions on the relief explicitly state Gessius Primus provided the funds for the monument in his will and Gessia Fausta, the only survivor of the three, directed the work. The relief thus depicts the living and the dead side by side, indistinguishable without the accompanying inscriptions. This theme is common in Roman art and proclaims that death does not break the bonds formed in life.

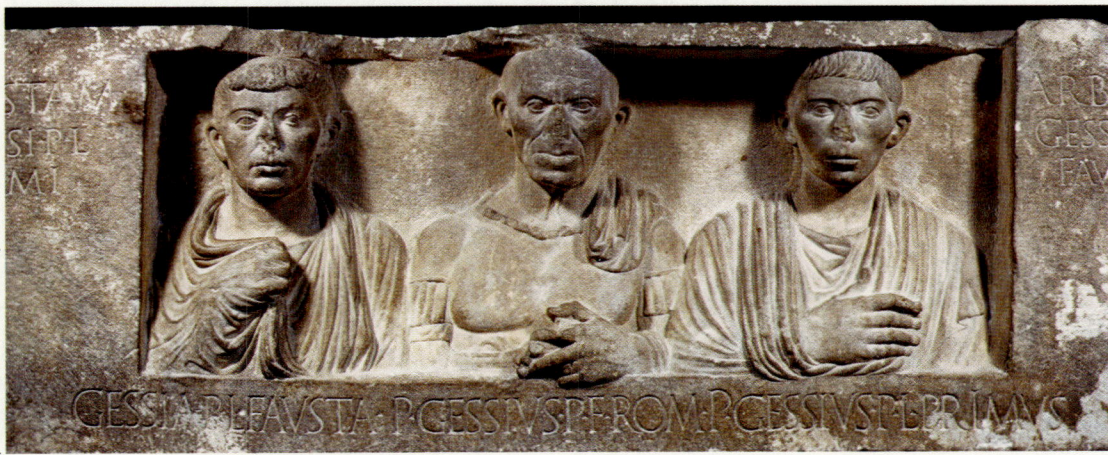

**7-11** Funerary relief with portraits of the Gessii, from Rome(?), Italy, ca. 30 BCE. Marble, 2′ 1½″ high. Museum of Fine Arts, Boston.

Roman freedmen often placed reliefs depicting themselves and their former owners on the facades of their tombs. The portraits and inscriptions celebrated their freedom and new status as citizens.

1 ft.

---

statues of Greek athletes and heroes the Romans admired so much and often copied. The incorporation of references to Greek art in these portrait statues evoked the notion of patrician cultural superiority. To be portrayed nude also suggested the person possessed a heroic character.

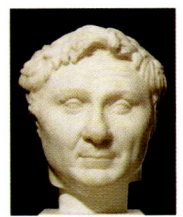

**7-10A** Pompey the Great, ca. 55–50 BCE.

**JULIUS CAESAR** Beginning early in the first century BCE, the Roman desire to advertise distinguished ancestry led to the placement of portraits of illustrious forebears on Republican coins. These ancestral portraits supplanted the earlier Roman tradition (based on Greek convention) of using images of divinities on coins. No Roman, however, not even Pompey "the Great" (FIG. 7-10A), who likened himself to Alexander, dared to place his own likeness on a coin until 44 BCE, when Julius Caesar, shortly before his assassination on the Ides of March, issued coins featuring his portrait and his newly acquired title, *dictator perpetuo* (dictator for life). The *denarius* (the standard Roman silver coin, from which the word *penny* ultimately derives) illustrated here (FIG. 7-10) records Caesar's aging face and receding hairline in conformity with the Republican veristic tradition. But placing the likeness of a living person on a coin violated all the norms of Republican propriety. Henceforth, Roman coins, which circulated throughout the vast territories under Roman control, would be used to mold public opinion in favor of the ruler by announcing his achievements—both real and fictional.

## NONELITE PORTRAITURE

In stark contrast to the patrician tradition of displaying portraits in homes and public places, slaves and former slaves could not possess any family portraits, because, under Ro-

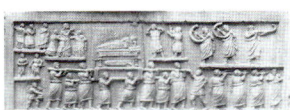

**7-11A** Funerary procession, Amiternum, ca. 50–1 BCE.

man law, their parents and grandparents were not people but property. Freed slaves, however, often ordered portrait (FIG. 7-11) and narrative (FIG. 7-11A) reliefs for their tombs to commemorate their new status as Roman citizens (see "Art for Former Slaves," above).

## An Eyewitness Account of the Eruption of Mount Vesuvius

**7-12** Aerial view of the forum (looking northeast), Pompeii, Italy, second century BCE and later. (1) forum, (2) Temple of Jupiter (Capitolium), (3) basilica.

Before the eruption of Mount Vesuvius, the forum was the center of civic life at Pompeii. At the north end was the city's main temple, the Capitolium, and at the southwest corner, the basilica (law court).

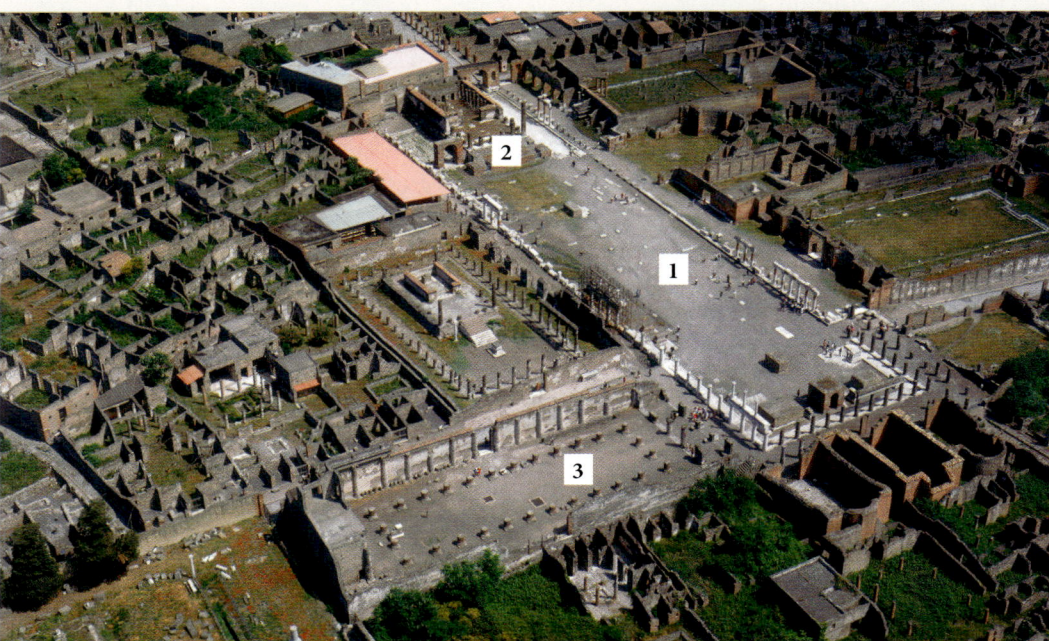

Pliny the Elder, whose *Natural History* is one of the most important sources for the history of Greek art, was among those who tried to rescue others from danger when Mount Vesuvius erupted. Overcome by the volcano's fumes, he died. His nephew, Pliny the Younger (ca. 61–ca. 112 CE), a government official under the emperor Trajan, left an account of the eruption and his uncle's demise:

> [The volcanic cloud's] general appearance can best be expressed as being like a pine . . . for it rose to a great height on a sort of trunk and then split off into branches. . . . Sometimes it looked white, sometimes blotched and dirty, according to the amount of soil and ashes it carried with it. . . . The buildings were now shaking with violent shocks, and seemed to be swaying to and fro as if they were torn from their foundations. Outside, on the other hand, there was the danger of falling pumice-stones, even though these were light and porous. . . . Elsewhere there was daylight, [but around Vesuvius, people] were still in darkness, blacker and denser than any night that ever was. . . . When daylight returned on the 26th—two days after the last day [my uncle] had been seen—his body was found intact and uninjured, still fully clothed and looking more like sleep than death.*

*Betty Radice, trans., *Pliny the Younger: Letters and Panegyricus,* vol. 1 (Cambridge, Mass.: Harvard University Press, 1969), 427–433.

## POMPEII AND THE CITIES OF VESUVIUS

On August 24, 79 CE, Mount Vesuvius, a long-dormant volcano, suddenly erupted (see "An Eyewitness Account of the Eruption of Mount Vesuvius," above). Many prosperous towns around the Bay of Naples (the ancient Greek city of Neapolis), among them Pompeii, were buried in a single day. The eruption was a catastrophe for the inhabitants of the Vesuvian cities but a boon for archaeologists and art historians. When researchers first explored the buried cities in the 18th century, the ruins had lain undisturbed for nearly 1,700 years, permitting a reconstruction of the art and life of Roman towns of the Late Republic and Early Empire to a degree impossible anywhere else.

The Oscans, one of the many early Italic population groups, were the first to settle at Pompeii, but toward the end of the fifth century BCE, the Samnites took over the town. Under the influence of their Greek neighbors, the Samnites greatly expanded the original settlement and gave monumental shape to the city center (FIG. **7-12**). Pompeii fought with other Italian cities on the losing side against Rome in the so-called Social War that ended in 89 BCE, and in 80 BCE Sulla founded a new Roman colony on the site, with Latin as its official language. The colony's population had grown to between 10,000 and 20,000 when, in February 62 CE, an earthquake shook the city, causing extensive damage. When Mount Vesuvius erupted 17 years later, repairs were still in progress.

### Architecture

Walking through Pompeii today is an unforgettable experience. The streets, with their heavy flagstone pavements and sidewalks, are still there, as are the stepping stones pedestrians used to cross the streets without having to step in puddles. Ingeniously, the city planners placed these stones in such a way that vehicle wheels could straddle them, enabling supplies to be brought directly to the shops, taverns, and bakeries. Tourists still can visit the impressive concrete-vaulted rooms of Pompeii's public baths, sit in the seats of its theater and amphitheater, enter the painted bedrooms and statue-filled gardens of private homes, even walk among the tombs outside the city's walls. Pompeii has been called the living city of the dead for good reason.

**FORUM** The center of civic life in any Roman town was its *forum,* or public square. Usually located at the city's geographic center at the intersection of the main north-south street, the *cardo,* and the main east-west avenue, the *decumanus* (FIG. 7-43), the forum was nevertheless generally closed to all but pedestrian traffic. Pompeii's forum (FIG. 7-12) lies in the southwest corner of the expanded Roman city but at the heart of the original town. The forum probably took on monumental form in the second century BCE when the Samnites, inspired by Hellenistic architecture, constructed two-story colonnades on three sides of the long and narrow plaza. At the north end they built a temple of Jupiter (FIG. 7-12, no. 2). When Pompeii became a Roman colony in 80 BCE, the Romans converted the temple into a *Capitolium*—a triple shrine of Jupiter, Juno, and Minerva, the chief Roman gods. The temple is of standard Republican type, constructed of tufa covered with fine white stucco and combining an Etruscan plan with Corinthian columns. It faces into the civic square, dominating the area. This contrasts with the siting of Greek temples (FIGS. 5-42 and 5-43), which stood in isolation and could be approached and viewed from all sides, like colossal statues on giant stepped pedestals. The Roman forum, like the Etrusco-Roman temple, had a chief side, a focus of attention.

The area within the porticos of the forum at Pompeii was empty, except for statues portraying local dignitaries and, later, Roman emperors. This is where the citizens conducted daily commerce and held festivities. All around the square, behind the colonnades, were secular and religious structures, including the town's administrative offices. Most important was the *basilica* (FIG. 7-12, no. 3) at the southwest corner. It is the earliest well-preserved building of its kind. Constructed during the late second century BCE, the basilica was Pompeii's law court and chief administrative building. In plan it resembled the forum itself: long and narrow, with two stories of internal columns dividing the space into a central *nave* and flanking *aisles.* This scheme had a long afterlife in architectural history and will be familiar to anyone who has ever entered a church.

**AMPHITHEATER** Shortly after the Romans took control of Pompeii, two of the town's wealthiest officials, Quinctius Valgus and Marcus Porcius, used their own funds to build a large amphitheater (FIG. 7-13) at the southeastern end of town. The earliest amphitheater known, it could seat some 20,000 spectators—more than the entire population of the town even a century and a half after its construction. The donors would have had choice reserved seats in the new entertainment center. In fact, seating was by civic and military rank. The Roman social hierarchy was therefore on display at every event.

The word *amphitheater* means "double theater," and Roman amphitheaters resemble two Greek theaters put together. Greek theaters were always on natural hillsides (FIG. 5-71), but supporting an amphitheater's continuous elliptical *cavea* (seating area) required building an artificial mountain. Only concrete, unknown to the Greeks, could easily meet that challenge. In the Pompeii amphitheater, shallow concrete barrel vaults form a giant retaining wall holding up the earthen mound and stone seats. Barrel vaults running all the way through the elliptical mountain of earth form the tunnels leading to the *arena,* the central area where the Pompeians staged bloody gladiatorial combats and wild animal hunts (see "Spectacles in the Colosseum," page 203). (*Arena* is Latin for "sand," which soaked up the blood of the wounded and killed.) Roman amphitheaters stand in sharp contrast, both architecturally and functionally, to Greco-Roman theaters, where actors performed comedies and tragedies.

A painting (FIG. 7-14) found in one of Pompeii's houses records a brawl in the amphitheater between the Pompeians and their neighbors, the Nucerians, during a gladiatorial contest in 59 CE. The fighting left many seriously wounded and led to the closing of

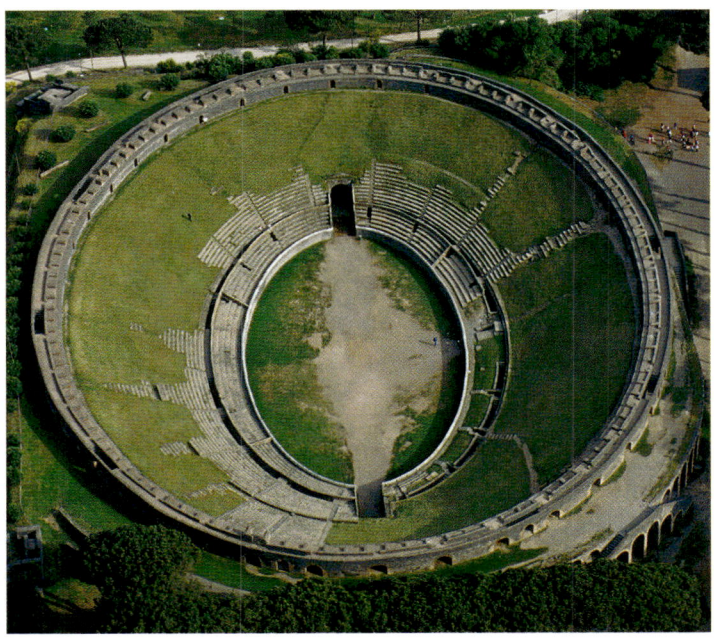

**7-13** Aerial view of the amphitheater (looking southeast), Pompeii, Italy, ca. 70 BCE.

Pompeii's amphitheater is the oldest known and an early example of Roman concrete technology. In the arena, bloody gladiatorial combats and wild animal hunts took place before 20,000 spectators.

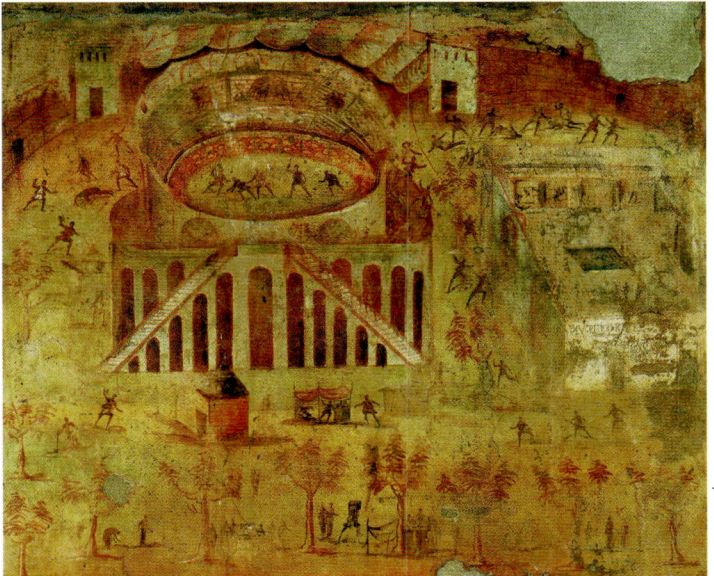

1 ft.

**7-14** Brawl in the Pompeii amphitheater, wall painting from House I,3,23, Pompeii, Italy, ca. 60–79 CE. Fresco, 5′ 7″ × 6′ 1″. Museo Archeologico Nazionale, Naples.

This wall painting records a brawl that broke out in the Pompeii amphitheater in 59 CE. The painter included the awning (velarium) that could be rolled down to shield the audience from sun and rain.

# The Roman House

The Roman house (FIG. 7-15) was not only a place to live. It played an important role in societal rituals. In the Roman world, individuals were frequently bound to others in a patron-client relationship whereby a wealthier, better-educated, and more powerful *patronus* would protect the interests of a *cliens*, sometimes large numbers of them. The size of a patron's clientele was one measure of his standing in society. Being seen in public accompanied by a crowd of clients was a badge of honor. In this system, a plebeian might be bound to a patrician, a freed slave to a former owner, or even one patrician to another. Regardless of rank, all clients were obligated to support their patron in political campaigns and to perform specific services on request, as well as to call on and salute the patron at the patron's home.

A client calling on a patron would enter the typical Roman *domus* (private house) through a narrow foyer (*fauces*, the "jaws" of the house), which led to a large central reception area, the *atrium*. The rooms flanking the fauces could open onto the atrium, as in FIG. 7-15, or onto the street, in which case the owner could use or rent them as shops. The roof over the atrium was partially open to the sky, not only to admit light but also to channel rainwater into a basin (*impluvium*) below to be stored in cisterns for household use. Opening onto the atrium were small bedrooms called *cubicula* (cubicles). At the back were two recessed areas (*alae*, wings) and the patron's *tablinum* or "home office," a dining room (*triclinium*), a kitchen, and sometimes a small garden.

Extant houses display endless variations of the same basic plan, dictated by the owners' personal tastes and means, the size and shape of the lot, and so forth, but all Roman houses of this type were inward-looking in nature. The design shut off the street's noise and dust, and all internal activity focused on the brightly illuminated atrium at the center of the residence. This basic module (only the front half of the typical house in FIG. 7-15) resembles the plan of the typical Etruscan house as reflected in the tombs of Cerveteri (FIGS. 6-7 and 6-7A). The early Roman house, like the early Roman temple, grew out of the Etruscan tradition.

During the second century BCE, when Roman architects were beginning to construct stone temples with Greek columns, the Roman house also took on Greek airs. Builders added a *peristyle* garden (FIG. 7-16A) behind the Etruscan-style house, providing a second internal source of illumination as well as a pleasant setting for meals served in a summer triclinium. The axial symmetry of the plan meant that on entering the fauces of the house, a visitor had a view through the atrium directly into the peristyle garden (as in FIG. 7-16), which often boasted a fountain or pool, marble statuary, mural paintings, and mosaic floors (FIG. 5-70).

Private houses of this type were typical of Pompeii and other Italian towns, but they were very rare in cities such as Rome, where the masses lived instead in multistory apartment houses (FIG. 7-54).

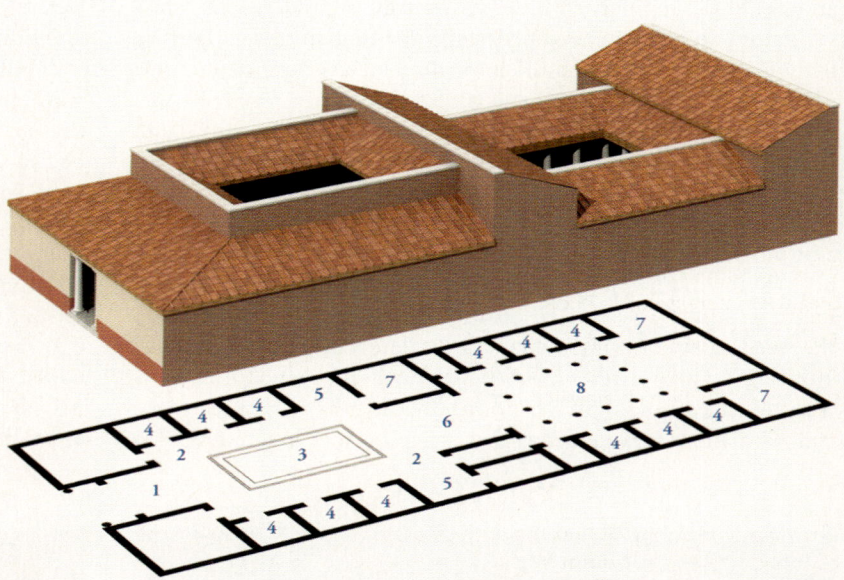

**7-15** Restored view and plan of a typical Roman house of the Late Republic and Early Empire (John Burge). (1) fauces, (2) atrium, (3) impluvium, (4) cubiculum, (5) ala, (6) tablinum, (7) triclinium, (8) peristyle.

Older Roman houses closely followed Etruscan models and had atriums and small gardens, but during the Late Republic and Early Empire, peristyles with Greek columns became common.

the amphitheater for a decade. The painting shows the cloth awning (*velarium*) that could be rolled down from the top of the cavea to shield spectators from sun and rain as well as the distinctive external double staircases (FIG. 7-13, *lower right*) that enabled large numbers of people to enter and exit the cavea in an orderly fashion.

**HOUSE OF THE VETTII** The evidence from Pompeii regarding Roman domestic architecture (see "The Roman House," above, and FIG. 7-15) is unparalleled anywhere else and is the most precious by-product of the volcanic eruption of 79 CE. One of the best-preserved houses at Pompeii, partially rebuilt by Italian excavators, is the House of the Vettii, an old second-century BCE house remodeled and repainted after the earthquake of 62 CE. A photograph

(FIG. 7-16) taken in the *fauces* shows the *impluvium* in the center of the *atrium*, the opening in the roof above, and, in the background, the *peristyle* garden (FIG. 7-16A) with its marble tables and splendid mural paintings dating to the last years of the Vesuvian city. At that time, two brothers, Aulus Vettius Restitutus and Aulus Vettius Conviva, owned

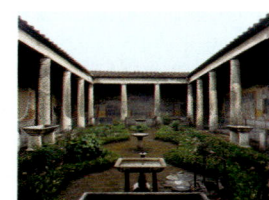

7-16A Peristyle, House of the Vettii, second century BCE.

the house. They were freedmen who probably made their fortune as merchants. Their wealth enabled them to purchase and furnish the kind of fashionable townhouse that in an earlier era only patricians could have acquired.

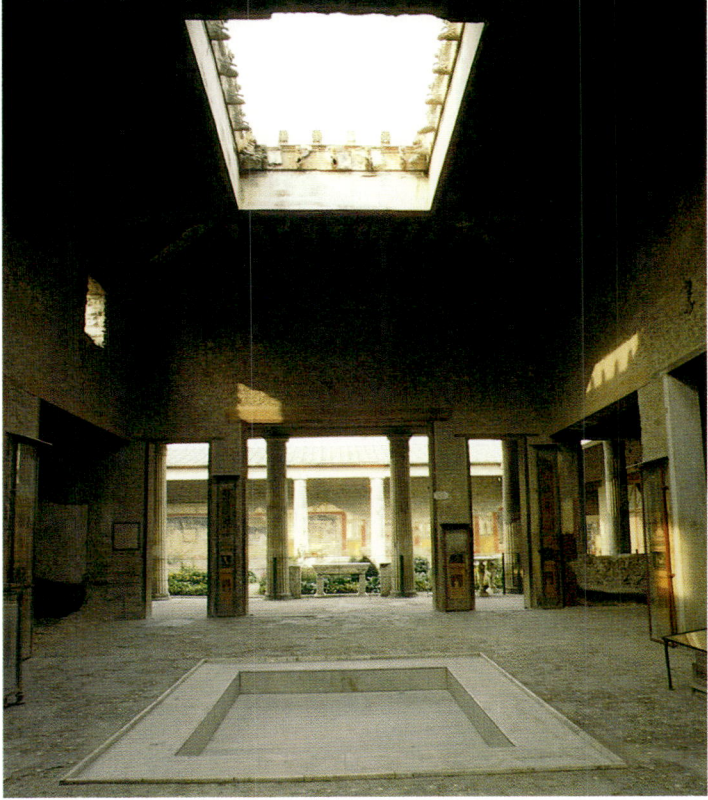

**7-16** Atrium of the House of the Vettii, Pompeii, Italy, second century BCE, rebuilt 62–79 CE.

The house of the Vettius brothers was of the later Hellenized type with a peristyle garden (FIG. 7-16A) behind the atrium. The impluvium below the open roof collected rainwater for domestic use.

## Painting

The houses of Pompeii and neighboring cities and the villas in the countryside around Mount Vesuvius have yielded a treasure trove of mural paintings—the most complete record of the changing fashions in interior decoration found anywhere in the ancient world. The sheer quantity of these paintings tells a great deal about both the prosperity and the tastes of the times. How many homes today, even of the very wealthy, have custom-painted murals in nearly every room? Roman wall paintings were true frescoes (see "Fresco Painting," Chapter 14, page 408), with the colors applied while the plaster was still damp. The process was painstaking. First, the painter prepared the wall by using a trowel to apply several layers of plaster (mixed with marble dust if the patron could afford it). Only then could painting begin. Finally, when the painter completed work and the surface dried, an assistant polished the wall to achieve a marblelike finish.

In the early years of exploration at Pompeii and nearby Herculaneum, excavators focused almost exclusively on the figural panels that formed part of the overall mural designs, especially those depicting Greek myths. Workers cut the panels out of the walls and transferred them to the Naples Archaeological Museum. In time, more enlightened archaeologists put an end to the practice of cutting pieces out of the walls, and began to give serious attention to the mural designs as a whole. Toward the end of the 19th century, August Mau (1840–1909), a German art historian, divided the various mural painting schemes into four "Pompeian Styles." Mau's classification system, although later refined and modified in detail, still serves as the basis for the study of Roman painting.

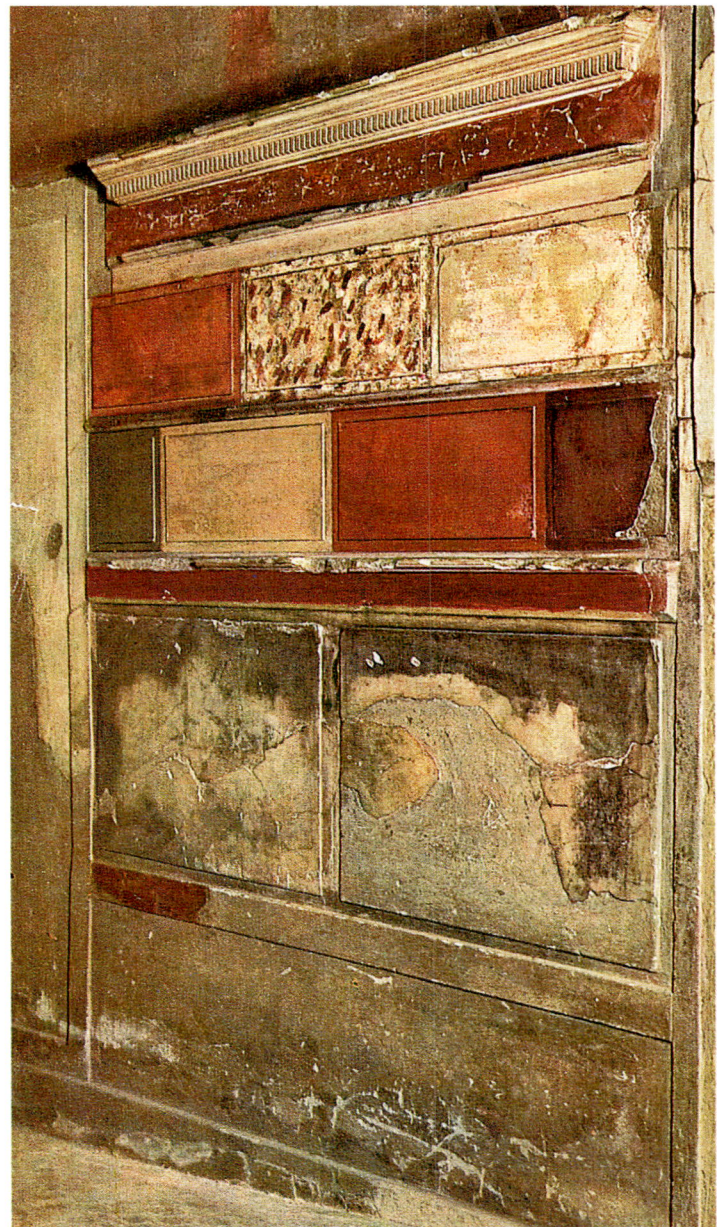

**7-17** First Style wall painting in the fauces of the Samnite House, Herculaneum, Italy, late second century BCE.

In First Style murals, the aim was to imitate costly marble panels using painted stucco relief. The style is Greek in origin and another example of the Hellenization of Republican architecture.

**FIRST STYLE** In the *First Style,* or Masonry Style, the decorator's aim was to imitate costly marble panels using painted stucco relief. The fauces (FIG. 7-17) of an old mansion at Herculaneum, the so-called Samnite House, greets visitors with a stunning illusion of walls faced with marbles imported from quarries throughout the Mediterranean. This approach to wall decoration is comparable to the modern practice, employed in private libraries and corporate meeting rooms alike, of using cheaper manufactured materials to approximate the look and shape of genuine wood paneling. The practice is not, however, uniquely Roman. First Style walls are well documented in Greece from the late fourth century BCE on. The use of the First Style in Italian houses is yet another example of the Hellenization of Republican architecture.

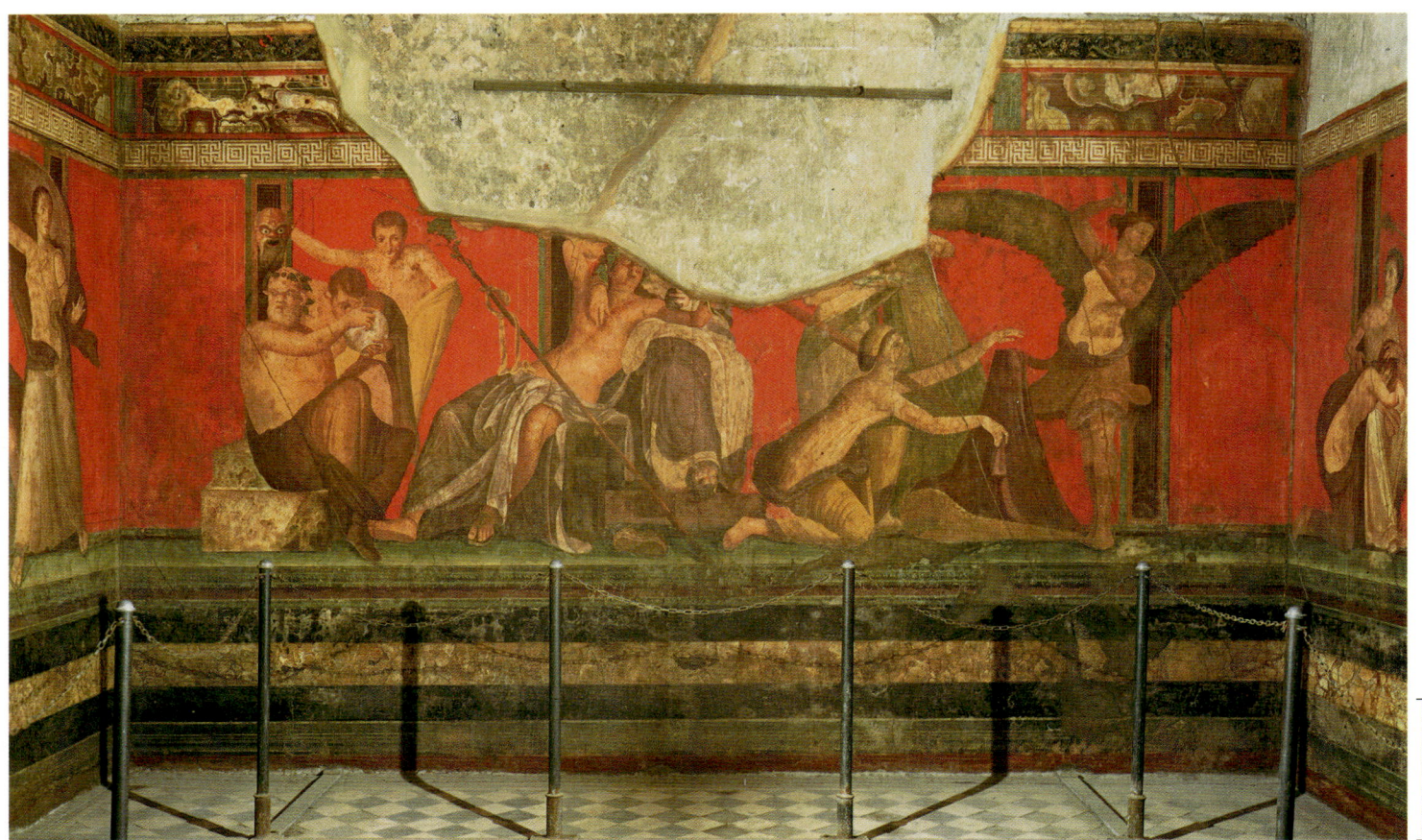

1 ft.

**7-18** Dionysiac mystery frieze, Second Style wall paintings in room 5 of the Villa of the Mysteries, Pompeii, Italy, ca. 60–50 BCE. Fresco, frieze 5′ 4″ high.

Second Style painters created the illusion of an imaginary three-dimensional world on the walls of Roman houses. The figures in this room are acting out the initiation rites of the Dionysiac mysteries.

**SECOND STYLE** The First Style never went completely out of fashion, but after 80 BCE a new approach to mural design became more popular. The *Second Style* is in most respects the antithesis of the First Style. Some scholars have argued that the Second Style also has precedents in Greece, but most believe it is a Roman invention. Certainly, the Second Style evolved in Italy, where it was the preferred manner until around 15 BCE, when Roman painters introduced the Third Style. Second Style painters did not aim to create the illusion of an elegant marble wall, as First Style painters sought to do. Rather, they wanted to dissolve a room's confining walls and replace them with the illusion of an imaginary three-dimensional world.

**VILLA OF THE MYSTERIES** An early example of the new style is the room (FIG. **7-18**) that gives its name to the Villa of the Mysteries at Pompeii. Many archaeologists believe this chamber was used to celebrate, in private, the rites of the Greek god Dionysos (Roman Bacchus). Dionysos was the focus of an unofficial mystery religion popular among women in Italy at this time. The precise nature of the Dionysiac rites is unknown, but the figural cycle in the Villa of the Mysteries, illustrating mortals (all female save for one boy) interacting with mythological figures, probably provides some evidence for the cult's initiation rites. In these rites young women, emulating Ariadne, daughter of King Minos (see page 89), united in marriage with Dionysos.

The backdrop for the nearly life-size figures is a series of painted panels imitating marble revetment, just as in the First Style but without the modeling in relief. In front of this painted marble wall, the artist created the illusion of a shallow ledge on which the human and divine actors move around the room. Especially striking is the way some of the figures interact across the corners of the room. For example, a seminude winged woman at the far right of the rear wall lashes out with her whip across the space of the room at a kneeling woman with a bare back (the initiate and bride-to-be of Dionysos) on the left end of the right wall. Nothing comparable to this room existed in Hellenistic Greece. Despite the presence of Dionysos, satyrs, and other Greek mythological figures, this is a Roman design.

**BOSCOREALE** In the early Second Style Dionysiac mystery frieze, the spatial illusionism is confined to the painted platform that projects into the room. But in mature Second Style designs, Roman painters created a three-dimensional setting that also extends beyond the wall, as in a cubiculum (FIG. **7-19**) from the Villa of Publius Fannius Synistor at Boscoreale, near Pompeii. The excavators removed the frescoes soon after their discovery, and today they are on display in a replica of the Roman room in New York's Metropolitan Museum of Art. All around the cubiculum the Second Style painter opened up the walls with vistas of Italian towns, marble temples, and colonnaded courtyards. Painted doors (FIG. 7-19, *left,* near the far right corner of the room; compare FIG. 6-1) and gates (FIG. 7-19, *right*) invite the viewer to walk through the wall into the magnificent world the painter created.

Although the Boscoreale painter was inconsistent in applying it, this Roman artist, like many others around the Bay of Naples, demonstrated familiarity with *linear perspective,* often incorrectly said to be an innovation of Italian Renaissance artists (see "Linear and Atmospheric Perspective," Chapter 21, page 567). In this kind of perspective, all the receding lines in a composition converge on

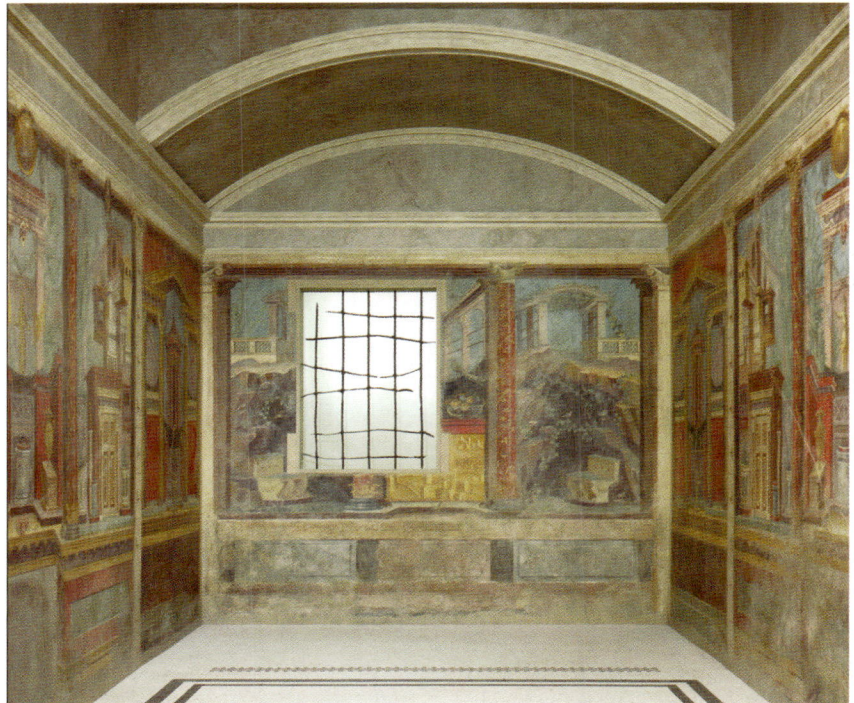 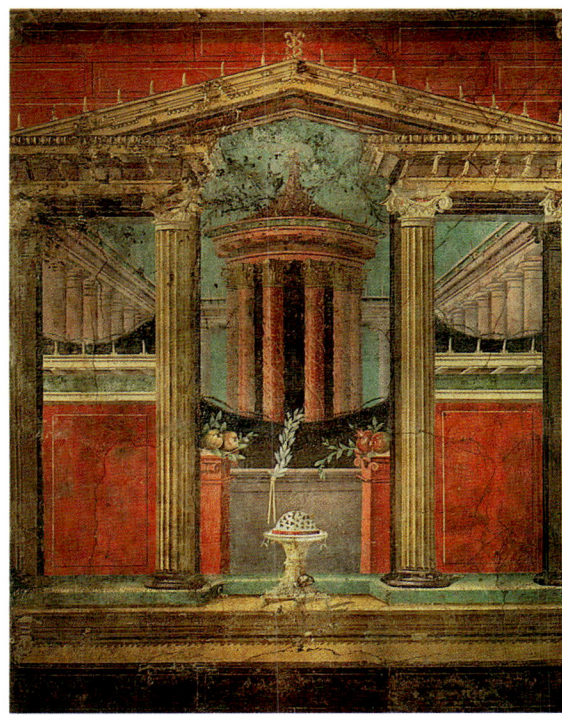

1 ft.

**7-19** Second Style wall paintings (general view, *left,* and detail of tholos, *right*), from cubiculum M of the Villa of Publius Fannius Synistor, Boscoreale, Italy, ca. 50–40 BCE. Fresco, 8′ 9″ high. Metropolitan Museum of Art, New York.

In this Second Style bedroom, the painter opened up the walls with vistas of towns, temples, and colonnaded courtyards. The convincing illusionism is due in part to the use of linear perspective.

a single point along the painting's central axis to show depth and distance. Ancient writers state that Greek painters of the fifth century BCE first used linear perspective for the design of Athenian stage sets (hence its Greek name, *skenographia,* "scene painting"). In the Boscoreale cubiculum, the painter most successfully employed skenographia in the far corners, where a low gate leads to a peristyle framing a tholos temple (FIG. 7-19, *right*). Linear perspective was a

favored tool of Second Style painters seeking to transform the usually windowless walls of Roman houses into "picture-window" vistas that expanded the apparent space of the rooms.

**PRIMAPORTA** The ultimate example of a Second Style picture-window mural (FIG. **7-20**) comes from the villa of the emperor Augustus's wife Livia (FIG. 7-28) at Primaporta, just north of Rome.

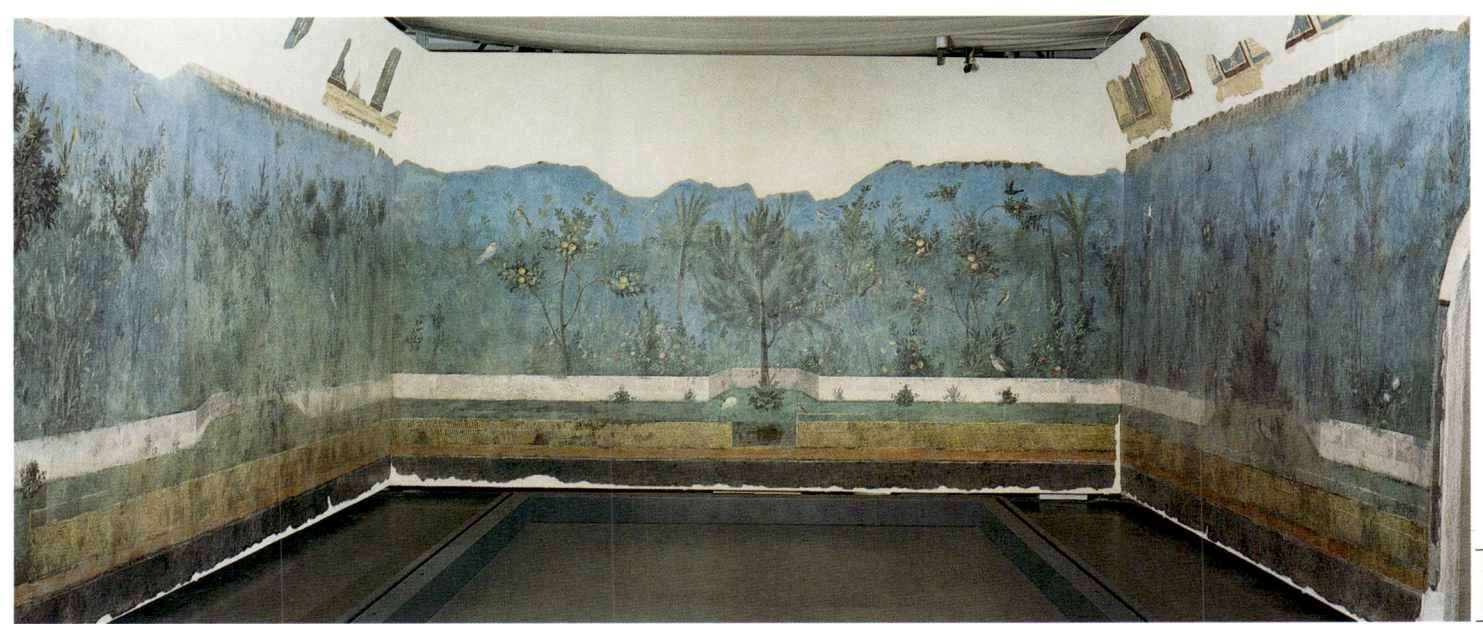

1 ft.

**7-20** Gardenscape, Second Style wall paintings, from the Villa of Livia, Primaporta, Italy, ca. 30–20 BCE. Fresco, 6′ 7″ high. Museo Nazionale Romano—Palazzo Massimo alle Terme, Rome.

The ultimate example of a Second Style "picture window" wall is Livia's gardenscape. To suggest recession, the painter used atmospheric perspective, intentionally blurring the most distant forms.

Pompeii and the Cities of Vesuvius **193**

There, imperial painters decorated all the walls of a vaulted room with lush gardenscapes. The only architectural element is the flimsy fence of the garden itself. To suggest recession, the painter mastered another kind of perspective, *atmospheric perspective,* indicating depth by the increasingly blurred appearance of objects in the distance (see "Linear and Atmospheric Perspective," Chapter 21, page 567). At Primaporta, the artist precisely painted the fence, trees, and birds in the foreground, whereas the details of the dense foliage in the background are indistinct. Among the wall paintings examined so far, only the landscape fresco (FIG. 4-9) from Thera offers a similar wraparound view of nature. But the Aegean fresco's white sky and red, yellow, and blue rock formations do not create a successful illusion of a world filled with air and light just a few steps away.

**THIRD STYLE** The Primaporta gardenscape is the polar opposite of First Style designs, which reinforce, rather than deny, the heavy presence of confining walls. But tastes changed rapidly in the Roman world, as in society today. Not long after Livia decorated her villa, Roman patrons began to favor mural designs that reasserted the primacy of the wall surface. In the *Third Style* of Pompeian painting, artists no longer attempted to replace the walls with three-dimensional worlds of their own creation. Nor did they seek to imitate the appearance of the marble walls of Hellenistic kings. Instead they adorned walls with delicate linear fantasies sketched on predominantly *monochromatic* (one-color) backgrounds.

**BOSCOTRECASE** One of the earliest examples of the Third Style—dating around 10 BCE—is a cubiculum (FIG. **7-21**) in the Villa of Agrippa Postumus at Boscotrecase. Nowhere did the artist use illusionistic painting to penetrate the wall. In place of the stately columns of the Second Style are insubstantial and impossibly thin *colonnettes* supporting featherweight canopies barely reminiscent of pediments. In the center of this delicate and elegant architectural frame is a tiny floating landscape painted directly on the jet black ground. It is hard to imagine a sharper contrast with the panoramic gardenscape at Livia's villa. On other Third Style walls, landscapes and mythological scenes appear in frames, like modern easel paintings hung on walls. Never could these framed panels be mistaken for windows opening onto a world beyond the room.

**FOURTH STYLE** In the *Fourth Style,* however, a taste for illusionism returned once again. This style became popular in the 50s CE, and it was the preferred manner of mural decoration at Pompeii when the eruption of Vesuvius buried the town in volcanic ash in 79. Some examples of the new style, such as room 78 (FIG. **7-22**) in the emperor Nero's Golden House (see page 202), display a kinship with the Third Style. All the walls are an austere creamy white. In some areas the artist painted sea creatures, birds, and other motifs directly on the monochromatic background, much like the Boscotrecase landscape (FIG. 7-21). Landscapes appear in Nero's palace too—as framed paintings in the center of each large white subdivision of the wall. Views through the wall are also part of the design, but the Fourth Style architectural vistas are irrational

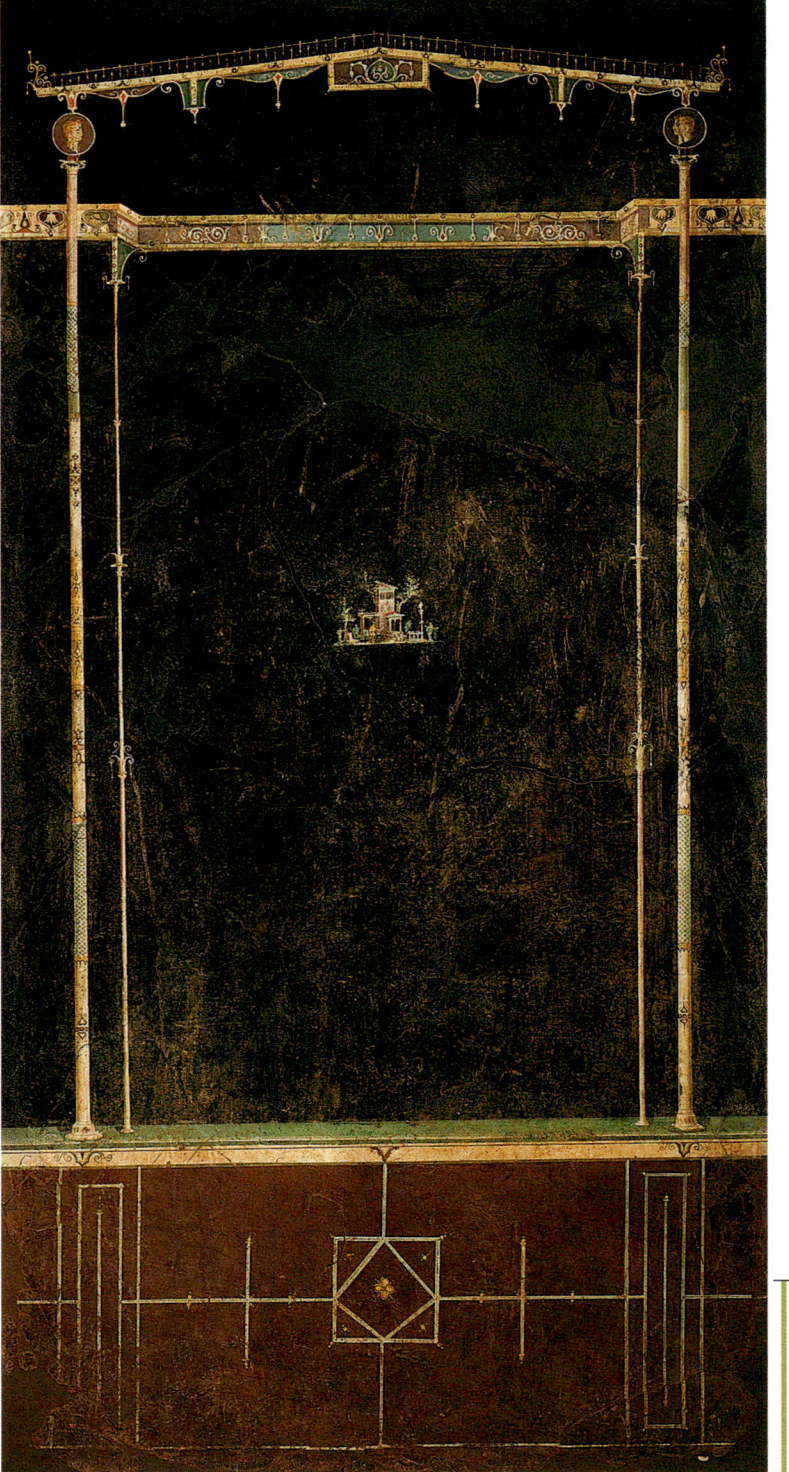

**7-21** Detail of a Third Style wall painting, from cubiculum 15 of the Villa of Agrippa Postumus, Boscotrecase, Italy, ca. 10 BCE. Fresco, 7′ 8″ high. Metropolitan Museum of Art, New York.

In the Third Style, Roman painters decorated walls with delicate linear fantasies sketched on monochromatic backgrounds. Here, a tiny floating landscape on a black ground is the central motif.

1 ft.

fantasies. The viewer looks out not on cityscapes or round temples set in peristyles but at fragments of buildings—columns supporting half-pediments, double stories of columns supporting nothing at all—painted on the same white ground as the rest of the wall. In the Fourth Style, architecture became just another motif in the Roman painter's ornamental repertoire.

**IXION ROOM** In the latest Fourth Style designs, painters rejected the quiet elegance of the Third Style and early Fourth Style in favor of crowded and confused compositions and sometimes garish color combinations. The Vettius brothers hired painters to decorate the Ixion Room (FIG. **7-23**)—a triclinium opening onto

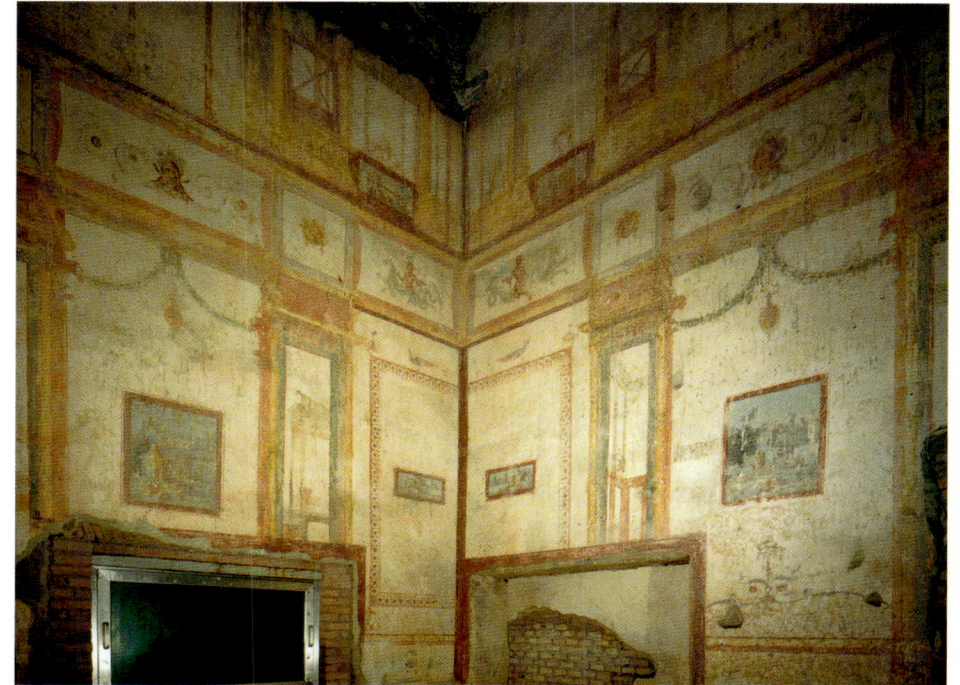

**7-22** Fourth Style wall paintings in room 78 of the Domus Aurea (Golden House, FIG. 7-35) of Nero, Rome, Italy, 64–68 CE.

The creamy white walls of this Neronian room display a kinship with the Third Style, but views through the wall reveal the irrational architectural vistas that characterize the new Fourth Style.

the peristyle (FIG. 7-16A) of their Pompeian house—in this manner just before the eruption of Mount Vesuvius. The decor of the dining room is a kind of summation of all the previous mural schemes, another instance of the mixing of styles noted earlier as characteristic of Roman art in general. The lowest zone, for example, is one of the most successful imitations anywhere of costly multicolored imported marbles, despite the fact the painter created the illusion without recourse to relief, as in the First Style. The large white panels in the corners of the room, with their delicate floral frames and floating central motifs, would fit naturally into the most elegant Third Style design. Unmistakably Fourth Style, however, are the fragmentary architectural vistas of the central and upper zones of the walls. They are unrelated to one another, do not constitute a unified cityscape beyond the wall, and the figures depicted would tumble into the room if they took a single step forward.

The Ixion Room takes its name from the mythological panel painting at the center of the rear wall. Ixion had attempted to seduce Hera, and Zeus punished him by binding him to a perpetually spinning wheel. The panels on the two side walls also have Greek myths as subjects. The Ixion Room is a kind of private art gallery. Many art historians believe lost Greek panel paintings were the models for the many mythological paintings on Third and Fourth Style walls. The mythological paintings on Pompeian walls attest to the Romans' continuing admiration for Greek artworks three centuries after Marcellus brought the treasures of Syracuse to Rome. Still, few, if any, of these mythological paintings can be described as true copies of famous Greek works. Unlike the replicas of Greek statues that have been found throughout the Roman world, including Pompeii (FIG. 5-40), these panels seem to be merely variations on standard compositions.

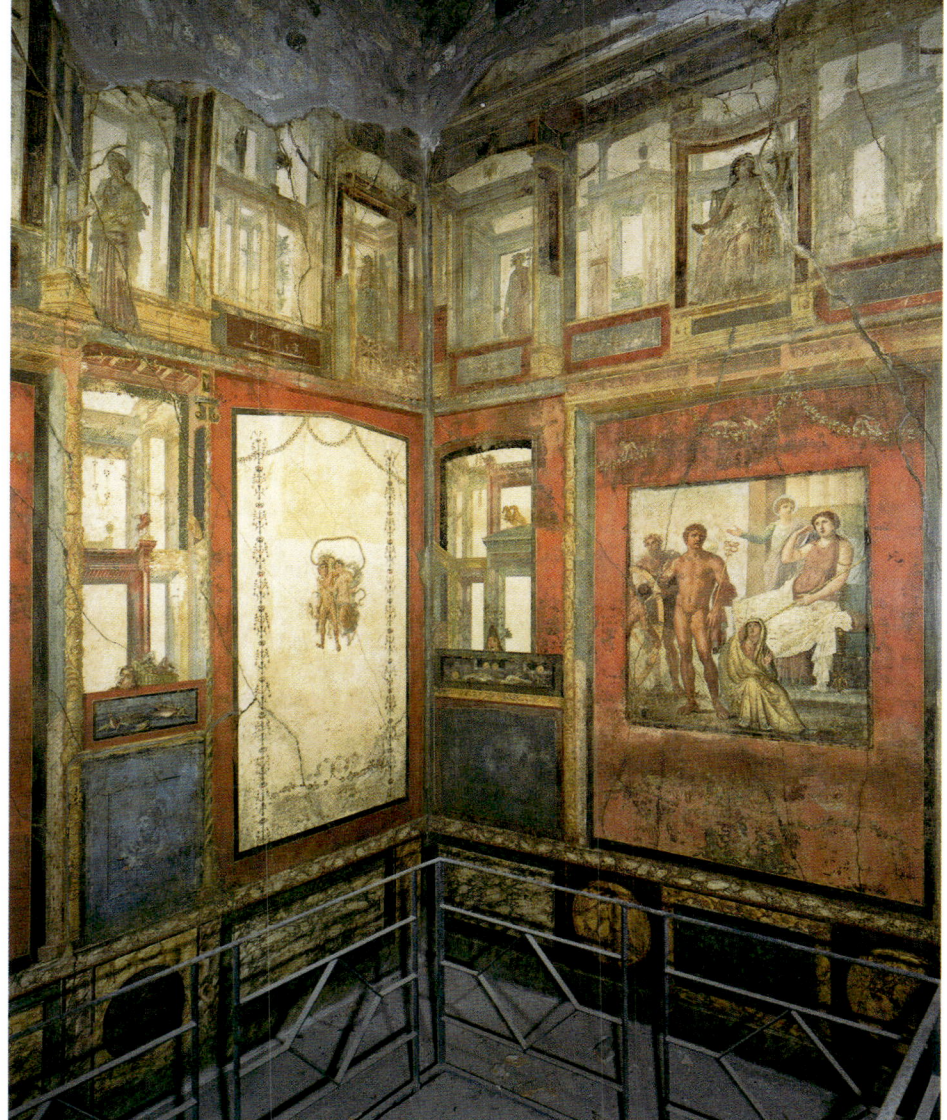

**7-23** Fourth Style wall paintings in the Ixion Room (triclinium P) of the House of the Vettii (FIG. 7-16), Pompeii, Italy, ca. 70–79 CE.

Late Fourth Style murals are often garishly colored, crowded, and confused compositions with a mixture of architectural views, framed mythological panels, and First and Third Style motifs.

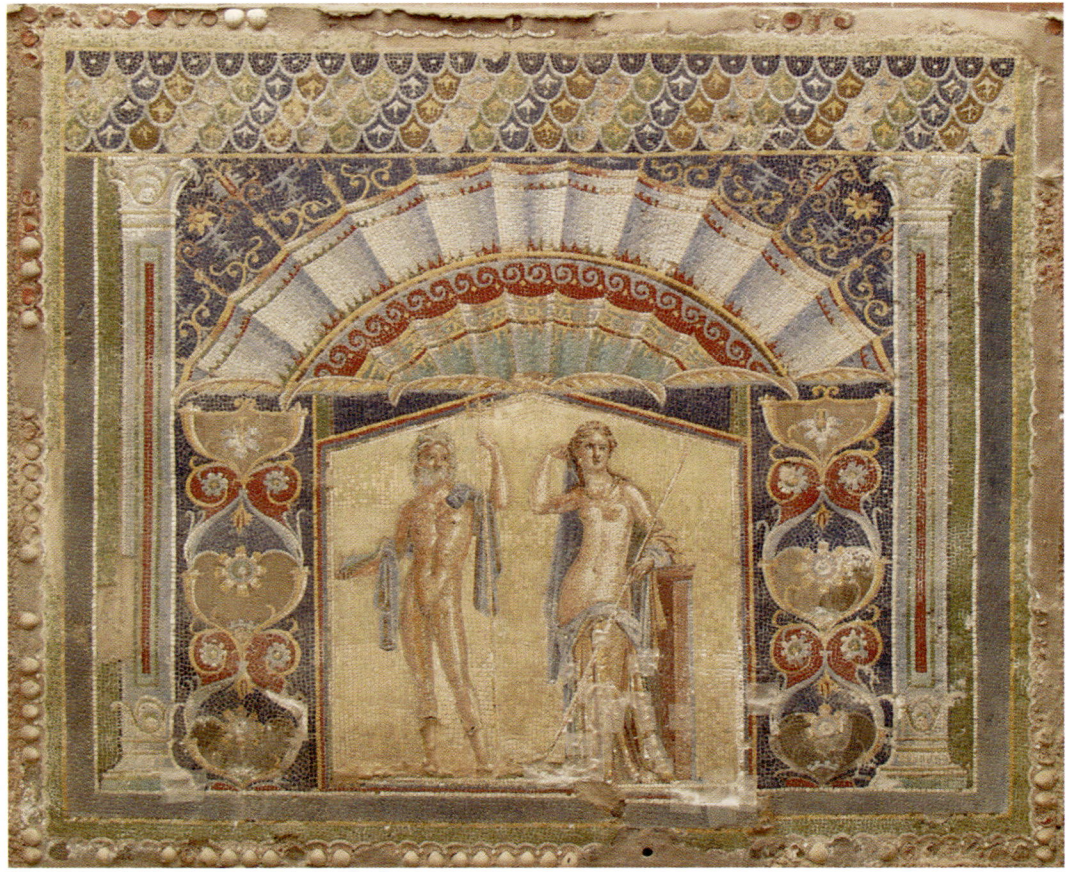

**7-24** Neptune and Amphitrite, wall mosaic in the summer triclinium of the House of Neptune and Amphitrite, Herculaneum, Italy, ca. 62–79 CE.

In the ancient world, mosaics usually decorated floors, but this example adorns a wall. The sea deities Neptune and Amphitrite fittingly overlook an elaborate fountain in a private home.

**WALL MOSAICS** Mythological themes were on occasion also the subject of Roman mosaics. In the ancient world, mosaics usually covered floors. For example, the *Alexander Mosaic* (FIG. 5-70) was the floor of an *exedra* (recessed area) opening onto a peristyle in the largest house at Pompeii. But occasionally Roman mosaics decorated walls and even ceilings, foreshadowing the extensive use of wall and vault mosaics in the Middle Ages (see "Mosaics," Chapter 8, page 245). An early example of a wall mosaic (FIG. **7-24**) is in the House of Neptune and Amphitrite at Herculaneum. The statuesque figures of the sea god and his wife appropriately presided over the flowing water of the fountain in the courtyard in front of them, where the house's owners and guests enjoyed outdoor dining in warm weather.

**PRIVATE PORTRAITS** The themes chosen for Roman wall paintings and mosaics were diverse. Although mythological compositions were immensely popular, Roman patrons commissioned a vast range of other subjects for the walls of their homes. As noted, landscape paintings frequently appear on Second, Third, and Fourth Style walls. Paintings and mosaics depicting scenes from history include the *Alexander Mosaic* (FIG. 5-70) and the brawl in the Pompeii amphitheater (FIG. 7-14). Given the Roman custom of keeping *imagines* of illustrious ancestors in atriums, it is not surprising painted portraits also appear in Pompeian houses. The double portrait of a husband and wife illustrated here (FIG. **7-25**) originally formed part of a Fourth Style wall of an exedra opening onto the atrium of a Pompeian house. The man, who may be the lawyer Terentius Neo, holds a scroll and the woman holds a *stylus* (writing instrument) and wax writing tablet, standard attributes in Roman marriage portraits (FIG. **7-25A**). The scroll and stylus suggest the fine education of those depicted—even if, as was sometimes true, the individuals were uneducated or even illiterate. These portraits were the Roman equivalent of modern wedding photographs of a bride and groom posing in rented formal garments never worn by them before or afterward. In contrast, the heads are not standard types but sensitive studies of the couple's individual faces. This is another instance of a realistic portrait placed on a conventional figure type (compare FIG. 7-9), a recurring phenomenon in Roman portraiture (see "Role Playing in Roman Portraiture," page 198).

Rarer on Pompeian walls are portraits of famous men and women of earlier eras, but several examples survive, including a full-length seated portrait of the Greek poet Menander (FIG. **7-25B**).

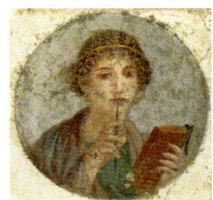

**7-25A** Woman with stylus, Pompeii, ca. 55–70 CE.

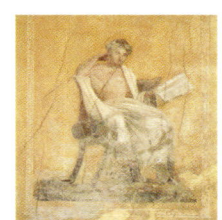

**7-25B** Menander, Pompeii, ca. 62–79 CE.

**STILL-LIFE PAINTING** Another genre Roman mural painters explored was *still-life* paintings (the representation of inanimate objects, artfully arranged). A still life with peaches and a carafe (FIG. **7-26**), a detail of a Fourth Style wall from a house in Herculaneum, is one of the finest extant examples. The painter was a master of illusionism and devoted as much attention to the shadows and highlights on the fruit, the stem and leaves, and the glass jar as to the objects themselves. Roman still lifes of this type are without precedent and have few successors until the 17th-century Dutch studies of food and other inanimate objects (FIGS. 25-1, 25-22, and 25-23).

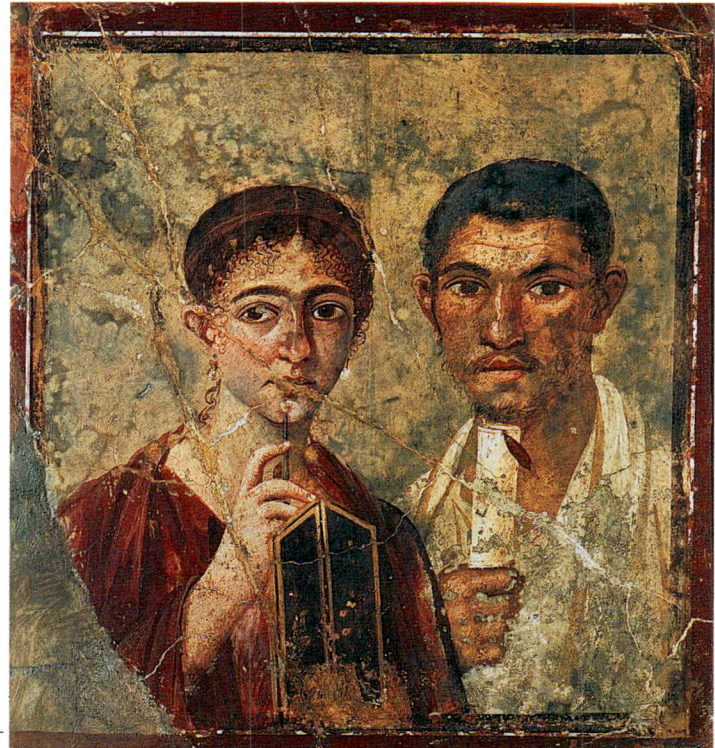

1 in.

**7-25** Portrait of a husband and wife, wall painting from House VII,2,6, Pompeii, Italy, ca. 70–79 CE. Fresco, 1′ 11″ × 1′ 8½″. Museo Archeologico Nazionale, Naples.

This husband and wife wished to present themselves to their guests as thoughtful and well-read. The portraits are individualized likenesses, but the poses and attributes are conventional.

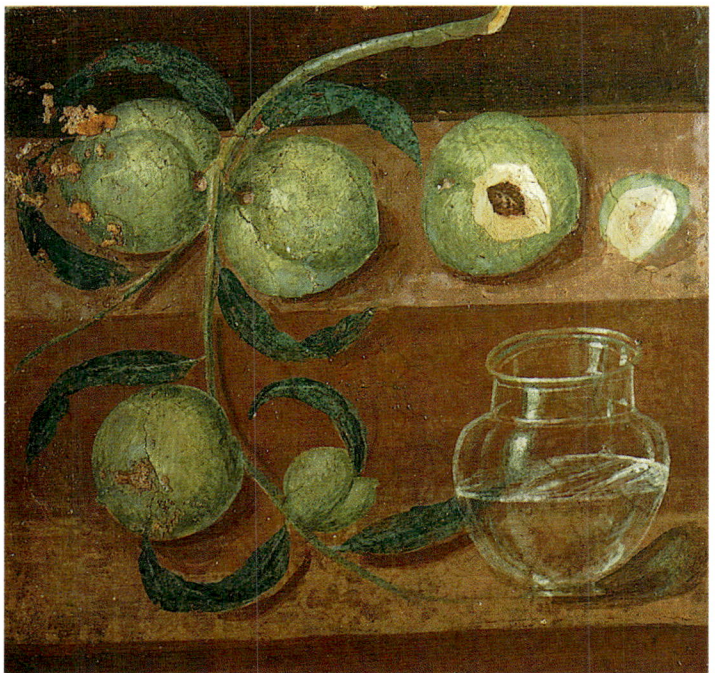

1 in.

**7-26** Still life with peaches, detail of a Fourth Style wall painting, from Herculaneum, Italy, ca. 62–79 CE. Fresco, 1′ 2″ × 1′ 1½″. Museo Archeologico Nazionale, Naples.

The Roman interest in illusionism explains the popularity of still-life paintings. This painter paid scrupulous attention to the play of light and shadow on different shapes and textures.

# EARLY EMPIRE

The murder of Julius Caesar on the Ides of March, 44 BCE, plunged the Roman world into a bloody civil war. The fighting lasted until 31 BCE when Octavian, Caesar's grandnephew and adopted son, crushed the naval forces of Mark Antony and Queen Cleopatra of Egypt at Actium in northwestern Greece. Antony and Cleopatra committed suicide, and in 30 BCE, Egypt, once the wealthiest and most powerful kingdom of the ancient world, became another province in the ever-expanding Roman Empire.

Historians mark the passage from the Roman Republic to the Roman Empire from the day in 27 BCE when the Senate conferred the title of Augustus (the Majestic, or Exalted, One; r. 27 BCE–14 CE) on Octavian. The Empire was ostensibly a continuation of the Republic, with the same constitutional offices, but in fact Augustus, whom the Senate recognized as *princeps* (first citizen), occupied all the key positions. He was consul and *imperator* (commander in chief; root of the word *emperor*) and even, after 12 BCE, *pontifex maximus* (chief priest of the state religion). These offices gave Augustus control of all aspects of Roman public life.

**PAX ROMANA** With powerful armies keeping order on the Empire's frontiers and no opposition at home, Augustus brought peace and prosperity to a war-weary Mediterranean world. Known in his day as the *Pax Augusta* (Augustan Peace), the peace Augustus established prevailed for two centuries. It came to be called simply the *Pax Romana*. During this time the emperors commissioned a huge number of public works throughout the Empire: roads and bridges, theaters, amphitheaters, and bathing complexes, all on an unprecedented scale. The erection of imperial portrait statues and monuments covered with inscriptions and reliefs recounting the rulers' great deeds reminded people everywhere that the emperors were the source of peace and prosperity. These portraits and reliefs, however, often presented a picture of the emperors and their achievements bearing little resemblance to historical fact. Their purpose was not to provide an objective record but to mold public opinion. The Roman emperors and the artists they employed have had few equals in the effective use of art and architecture for propagandistic ends.

## Augustus and the Julio-Claudians

When Augustus vanquished Antony and Cleopatra at Actium and became undisputed master of the Mediterranean world, he was not yet 32 years old. The rule by elders that had characterized the Roman Republic for nearly 500 years came to an abrupt end. Suddenly, Roman portraitists had to produce images of a youthful head of state. But Augustus was not merely young. The Senate had declared Caesar a god after his death, and Augustus, though never claiming to be a god himself, widely advertised himself as the son of a god. His portraits were designed to present the image of a godlike leader who miraculously never aged. Although Augustus lived until 14 CE, even official portraits made near the end of his life show him as a handsome youth (FIG. I-10). Such fictional likenesses might seem ridiculous today, when everyone can easily view photographs of world leaders as they truly appear, but in antiquity few people ever saw the emperor. His official image was all most knew. It therefore could be manipulated at will.

**AUGUSTUS AS GENERAL** The portraits of Augustus depict him in his many different roles in the Roman state (see "Role Playing in Roman Portraiture," page 198), but the models for many

# Role Playing in Roman Portraiture

In every town throughout the vast Roman Empire, portraits of the emperors and empresses and their families were on display—in forums, basilicas, baths, and markets; in front of temples; atop triumphal arches—anywhere a statue could be placed. The rulers' heads varied little from Britain to Syria. All were replicas of official images, either imported or scrupulously copied by local artists. But the imperial sculptors combined portrait heads with many different statuary types. The type chosen depended on the position the person held in Roman society or the various fictitious guises members of the imperial family assumed. Portraits of Augustus, for example, show him not only as armed general (FIG. 7-27) but also as recipient of the civic crown for saving the lives of fellow citizens (FIG. I-10), hooded priest, toga-clad magistrate, traveling commander on horseback, heroically nude warrior, and various Roman gods, including Jupiter, Apollo, and Mercury.

Role playing was not the exclusive prerogative of emperors and princes but extended to their wives, daughters, sisters, and mothers. Portraits of Livia (FIG. 7-28) depict her as many goddesses, including Ceres, Juno, Venus, and Vesta. She also appears as the personification of Health, Justice, and Piety. In fact, it was common for imperial women to appear on Roman coins as goddesses or as embodiments of feminine virtue. Faustina the Younger, for example, the wife of Marcus Aurelius and mother of 13 children, appears as Venus and Fecundity, among many other roles. Julia Domna (FIG. 7-63), Septimius Severus's wife, is Juno, Venus, Peace, or Victory in some portraits.

Ordinary citizens also engaged in role playing. Many assumed literary pretensions in the painted portraits (FIGS. 7-25 and 7-25A) they commissioned for the walls of their homes. Others equated themselves with Greek heroes (FIG. 7-60) or Roman deities (FIG. 7-61) on their coffins. The common people followed the lead of the emperors and empresses.

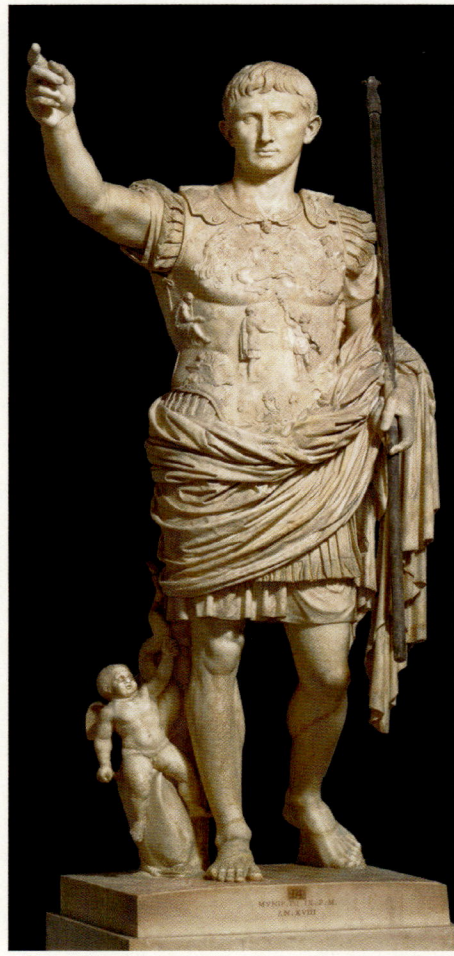

**7-27** Portrait of Augustus as general, from Primaporta, Italy, early-first-century CE copy of a bronze original of ca. 20 BCE. Marble, 6' 8" high. Musei Vaticani, Rome. ◼)

The models for Augustus's idealized portraits, which depict him as a never-aging god, were Classical Greek statues (FIG. 5-40). This portrait presents the emperor in armor in his role as general.

of them were Classical Greek statues. The portrait (FIG. **7-27**) of the emperor found at his wife Livia's villa at Primaporta (FIG. 7-20) portrays Augustus as general, standing like Polykleitos's *Doryphoros* (FIG. 5-40) but with his right arm raised to address his troops in the manner of the orator Aule Metele (FIG. 6-16). Augustus's head, although depicting a recognizable individual, also emulates the idealized Polykleitan youth's head in its overall shape, the sharp ridges of the brows, and the tight cap of layered hair. Augustus is not nude, however, and the details of the statue carry political messages. The reliefs on his cuirass advertise an important diplomatic victory—the return of the Roman military standards the Parthians had captured from a Republican general—and the Cupid at Augustus's feet proclaims his divine descent. Caesar's family, the Julians, traced their ancestry back to Venus. Cupid was the goddess's son.

**LIVIA** A marble portrait (FIG. **7-28**) of Livia shows the imperial women of the Augustan age shared the emperor's eternal youthfulness. Although the empress sports the latest Roman coiffure, with the hair rolled over the forehead and knotted at the nape of the neck, her blemish-free skin and sharply defined features derive from images of Classical Greek goddesses. Livia outlived Augustus by 15 years, dying at age 87. In her portraits, the coiffure changed

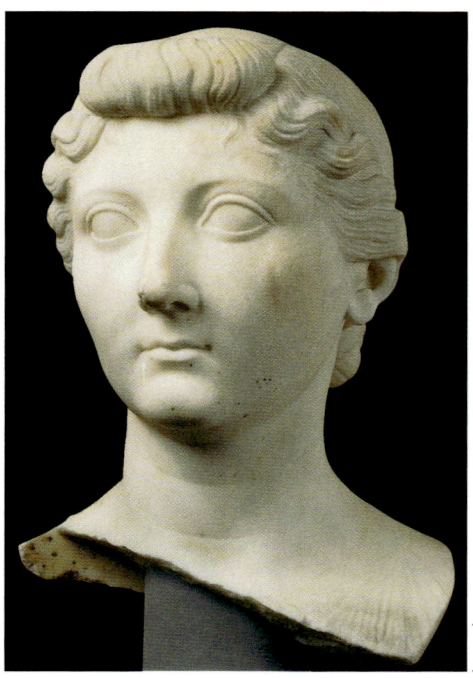

**7-28** Portrait bust of Livia, from Arsinoe, Egypt, early first century CE. Marble, 1' 1½" high. Ny Carlsberg Glyptotek, Copenhagen.

Although Livia sports the latest Roman coiffure, her youthful appearance and sharply defined features derive from images of Greek goddesses. She died at 87, but never aged in her portraits.

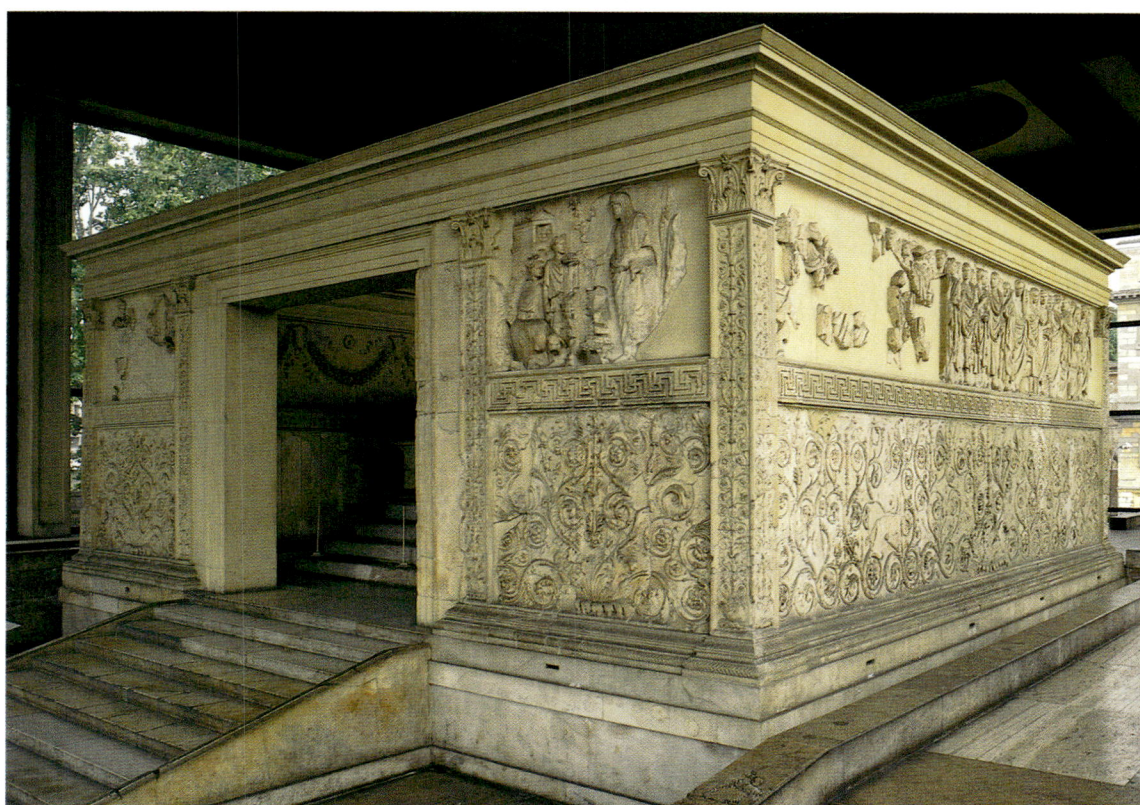

**7-29** Ara Pacis Augustae (Altar of Augustan Peace, looking northeast), Rome, Italy, 13–9 BCE. ◼◀

Augustus sought to present his new order as a Golden Age equaling that of Athens under Pericles. The Ara Pacis celebrates the emperor's most important achievement, the establishment of peace.

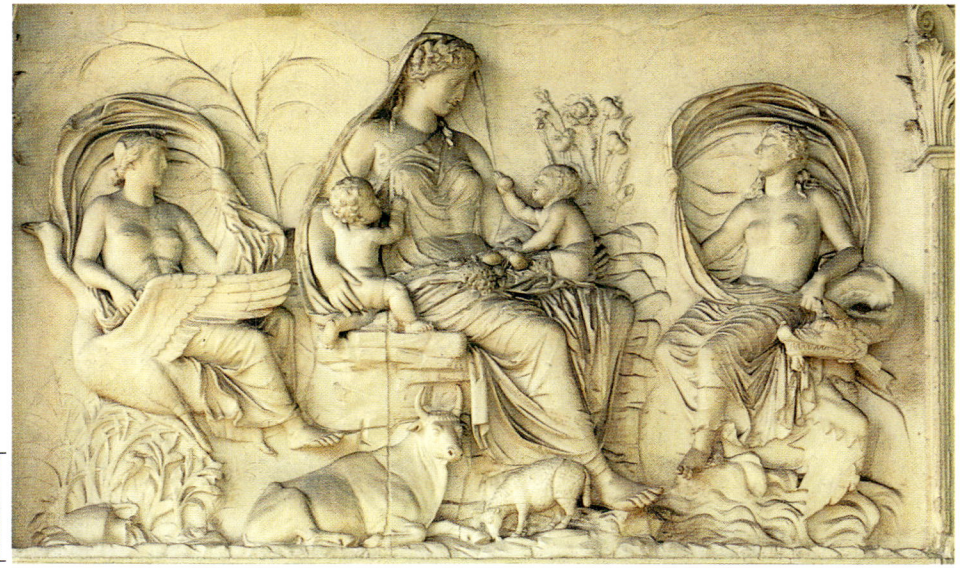

1 ft.

**7-30** Female personification (Tellus?), panel on the east facade of the Ara Pacis Augustae, Rome, Italy, 13–9 BCE. Marble, 5′ 3″ high. ◼◀

This female personification with two babies on her lap embodies the fruits of the Pax Augusta. All around her the bountiful earth is in bloom, and animals of different species live together peacefully.

with the introduction of each new fashion, but her face remained ever young, befitting her exalted position in the Roman state.

**ARA PACIS AUGUSTAE** On Livia's birthday in 9 BCE, Augustus dedicated the Ara Pacis Augustae (Altar of the Pax Augusta, the Augustan Peace; FIG. **7-29**), the monument celebrating his most significant achievement, the establishment of peace. Figural reliefs and acanthus tendrils adorn the altar's marble precinct walls. Four panels on the east and west ends depict carefully selected mythological subjects, including a relief of Aeneas making a sacrifice (FIG. 7-29, *right*). Aeneas was the son of Venus and one of Augustus's forefathers. The connection between the emperor and Aeneas was a key element of Augustus's political ideology for his new Golden Age. It is no coincidence Vergil wrote the *Aeneid* during the rule of Augustus. Vergil's epic poem glorified the young emperor by celebrating the founder of the Julian line.

A second panel (FIG. **7-30**), on the other end of the altar enclosure, depicts a seated matron with two lively babies on her lap. Her identity is uncertain. Art historians usually call her Tellus (Mother Earth), although some scholars have identified her as Pax (Peace), Ceres (goddess of grain), or even Venus. Whoever she is, she embodies the fruits of the Pax Augusta. All around her the bountiful earth is in bloom, and animals of different species live peacefully side by side. Personifications of refreshing breezes (note their windblown drapery) flank her. One rides a bird, the other a sea creature. Earth, sky, and water are all elements of this picture of peace and fertility in the Augustan cosmos.

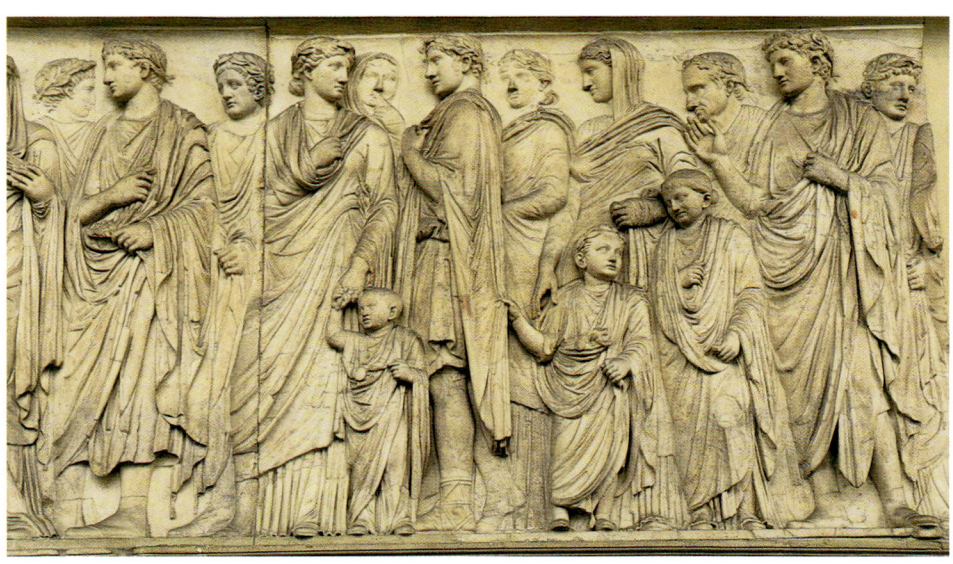

**7-31** Procession of the imperial family, detail of the south frieze of the Ara Pacis Augustae, Rome, Italy, 13–9 BCE. Marble, 5′ 3″ high. ■◀

Although inspired by the frieze (FIG. 5-50) of the Parthenon, the Ara Pacis processions depict recognizable individuals, including children. Augustus promoted marriage and childbearing.

1 ft.

Processions of the imperial family (FIG. **7-31**) and other important dignitaries appear on the long north and south sides of the Ara Pacis. The inspiration for these parallel friezes was very likely the Panathenaic procession frieze (FIG. 5-50, *bottom*) of the Parthenon. Augustus sought to present his new order as a Golden Age equaling that of Athens under Pericles. The emulation of Classical models thus made a political as well as an artistic statement.

Even so, the Roman procession is very different in character from its presumed Greek model. On the Parthenon, anonymous figures act out an event that recurred every four years. The frieze stands for all Panathenaic Festival processions. The Ara Pacis depicts a specific event—probably the inaugural ceremony of 13 BCE when work on the altar began—and recognizable historical figures. Among those portrayed are children, who restlessly tug on their elders' garments and talk to one another when they should be quiet on a solemn occasion—in short, children who act like children and not like miniature adults, as they frequently do in the history of art. Their presence lends a great deal of charm to the procession, but that is not why the imperial sculptors included children on the Ara Pacis when they had never before appeared on any Greek or Roman state monument. Augustus was concerned about a decline in the birthrate among the Roman nobility, and he enacted a series of laws designed to promote marriage, marital fidelity, and raising children. The portrayal of men with their families on the Altar of Peace served as a moral exemplar. The emperor used relief sculpture as well as portraiture to further his political and social agendas.

**FORUM OF AUGUSTUS** Augustus's most ambitious project in the capital was the construction of a new forum (FIG. 7-2, no. 10) next to Julius Caesar's forum (FIG. 7-2, no. 9), which Augustus completed. The temples and porticos in both forums were white marble from Carrara. Prior to the opening of those quarries in the second half of the first century BCE, marble had to be imported at great cost from abroad, and the Romans used it sparingly. The ready availability of Italian marble under Augustus made possible the emperor's famous boast that he found Rome a city of brick and transformed it into a city of marble.

The extensive use of Carrara marble for public monuments (including the Ara Pacis) must be seen as part of Augustus's larger program to make his city the equal of Periclean Athens. In fact, the Forum of Augustus incorporated several explicit references to Classical Athens and to the Acropolis in particular, most notably copies of the caryatids (FIG. 5-54) of the Erechtheion in the upper story of the porticos. The forum also evoked Roman history. The porticos contained dozens of portrait statues, including images of all the major figures of the Julian family going back to Aeneas. Augustus's forum became a kind of public atrium filled with *imagines*. His family history thus became part of the Roman state's official history.

**NÎMES** The Forum of Augustus is in ruins today, but many scholars believe some of the stonemasons from that project also constructed the so-called Maison Carrée (Square House; FIG. **7-32**)

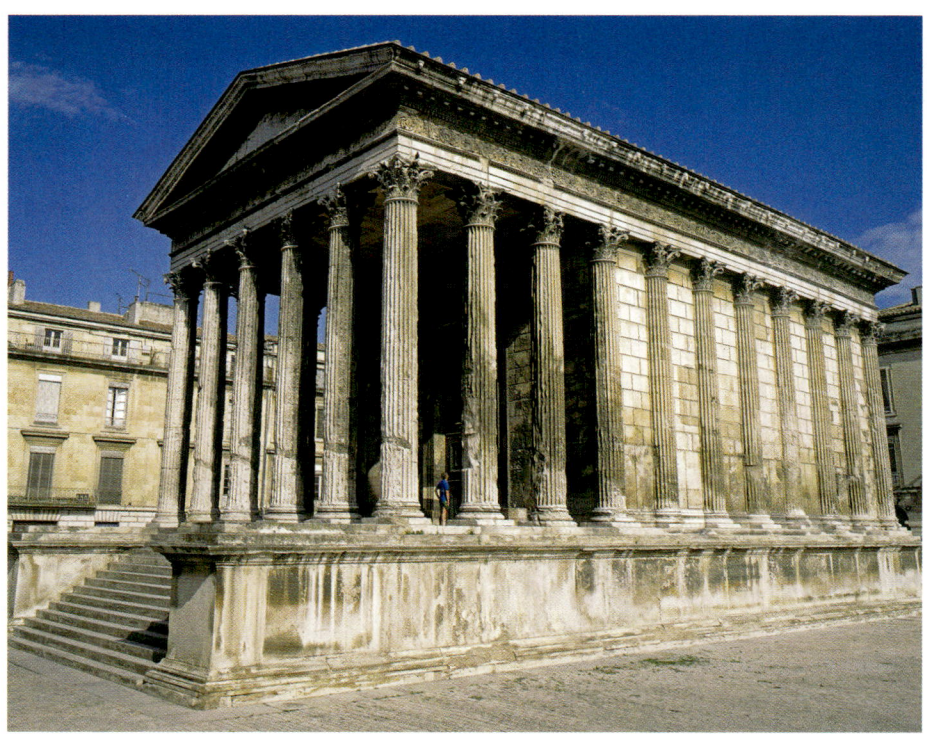

**7-32** Maison Carrée, Nîmes, France, ca. 1–10 CE. ■◀

This well-preserved Corinthian pseudoperipteral temple in France, modeled on the temple in the Forum of Augustus in Rome, exemplifies the conservative Neo-Classical Augustan architectural style.

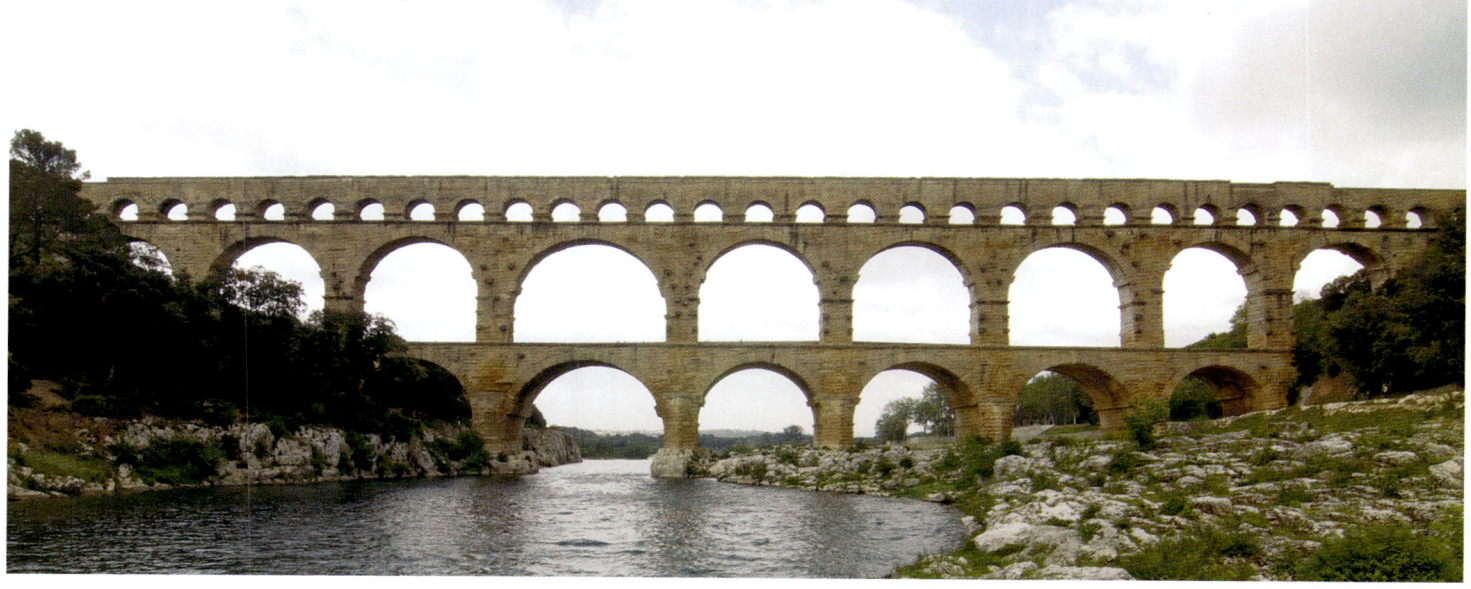

**7-33** Pont-du-Gard, Nîmes, France, ca. 16 BCE. ◼◄

Roman engineers constructed roads and bridges throughout the Empire. This aqueduct bridge brought water from a distant mountain spring to Nîmes— about 100 gallons a day for each inhabitant.

at Nîmes in southern France (Roman Gaul). This exceptionally well-preserved Corinthian pseudoperipteral temple, which dates to the opening years of the first century CE, is the best surviving example of the Augustan Neo-Classical architectural style.

An earlier Augustan project at Nîmes was the construction of the great aqueduct-bridge known today as the Pont-du-Gard (FIG. **7-33**). In the fourth century BCE, the Romans began to build aqueducts to carry water from mountain sources to their city on the Tiber River. As Rome's power spread through the Mediterranean world, its engineers constructed aqueducts, roads, and bridges to serve colonies throughout the far-flung empire. The Nîmes aqueduct provided about 100 gallons of water a day for each inhabitant from a source some 30 miles away. The water flowed over the considerable distance by gravity alone, which required channels built with a continuous gradual decline over the entire route from source to city. The three-story Pont-du-Gard maintained the height of the water channel where the water crossed

the Gard River. Each large arch spans some 82 feet and consists of blocks weighing up to two tons each. The bridge's uppermost level is a row of smaller arches, three above each of the large openings below. They carry the water channel itself. The harmonious proportional relationship between the larger and smaller arches reveals the Roman hydraulic engineer who designed the aqueduct bridge also had a keen aesthetic sense.

**PORTA MAGGIORE** The demand for water in the capital required the construction of many aqueducts. The emperor Claudius (r. 41–54 CE) erected a grandiose gate, the Porta Maggiore (FIG. **7-34**), at the point where two of Rome's water lines (and two major intercity roads) converged. Its huge *attic* (uppermost story) bears a lengthy dedicatory inscription concealing the stacked conduits of both aqueducts. The gate is the outstanding example of the Roman *rusticated* (rough) masonry style. Instead of using the precisely shaped blocks Greek and Augustan architects preferred, the designer of the Porta Maggiore combined smooth and rusticated surfaces. These created an exciting, if eccentric, facade with crisply carved pediments resting on engaged columns composed of rusticated drums.

**NERO'S GOLDEN HOUSE** In 64 CE, when Nero (r. 54–68 CE), stepson and successor of Claudius, was emperor, a great fire destroyed large sections of Rome. Afterward, Nero enacted a new building code requiring greater fireproofing, resulting in the widespread use of concrete and more opportunities for Roman architects to explore the possibilities opened up by the still relatively new material. The fire also enabled the emperor

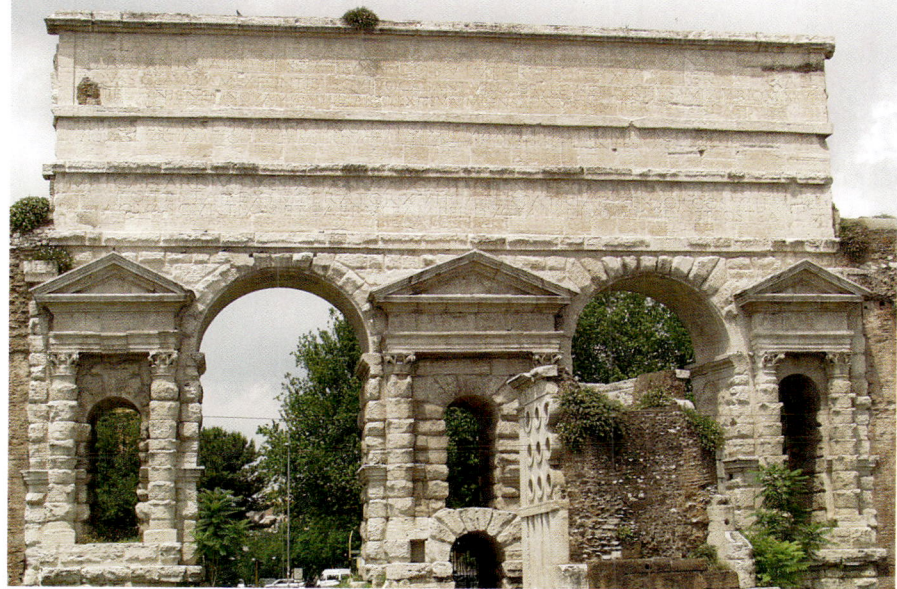

**7-34** Porta Maggiore, Rome, Italy, ca. 50 CE.

This double gateway, which supports the water channels of two important aqueducts, is the outstanding example of Roman rusticated (rough) masonry, which was especially popular under Claudius.

## The Golden House of Nero

Nero's Domus Aurea, or Golden House, was a vast and notoriously extravagant country villa in the heart of Rome. The second-century CE Roman biographer Suetonius described it vividly:

The entrance-hall was large enough to contain a huge statue [of Nero in the guise of Sol, the sun god; FIG. 7-2, no. 16], 120 feet high; and the pillared arcade ran for a whole mile. An enormous pool, like a sea, was surrounded by buildings made to resemble cities, and by a landscape garden consisting of ploughed fields, vineyards, pastures, and woodlands—where every variety of domestic and wild animal roamed about. Parts of the house were overlaid with gold and studded with precious stones and mother-of-pearl. All the dining-rooms had ceilings of fretted ivory, the panels of which could slide back and let a rain of flowers, or of perfume from hidden sprinklers, shower upon [Nero's] guests. The main dining-room was circular, and its roof revolved, day and night, in time with the sky. Sea water, or sulphur water, was always on tap in the baths. When the palace had been decorated throughout in this lavish style, Nero dedicated it, and condescended to remark: "Good, now I can at last begin to live like a human being!"*

Suetonius's description is a welcome reminder that the Roman ruins tourists flock to see are but a dim reflection of the magnificence of the original structures. Only in rare instances, such as the Pantheon, with its marble-faced walls and floors (FIG. 7-51), can visitors experience anything approaching the architects' intended effects. Even there, much of the marble paneling is of later date, and the gilding is missing from the dome.

*Suetonius, *Nero*, 31. Translated by Robert Graves, *Suetonius: The Twelve Caesars* (New York: Penguin, 1957; illustrated edition, 1980), 197–198.

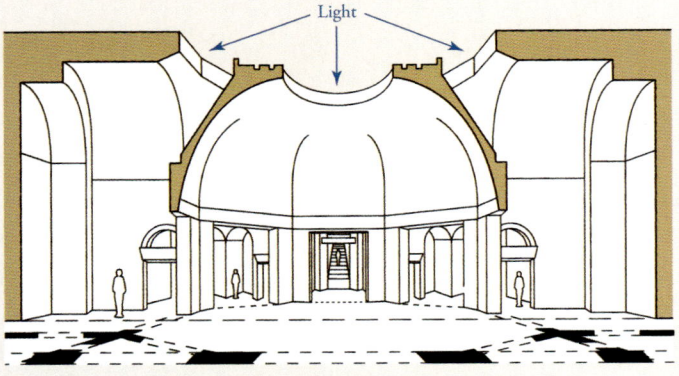

**7-35** SEVERUS and CELER, section *(left)* and plan *(right)* of the octagonal hall of the Domus Aurea of Nero, Rome, Italy, 64–68 CE.

Nero's architects illuminated this octagonal room by placing an oculus in its concrete dome, and ingeniously lit the rooms around it by leaving spaces between their vaults and the dome's exterior.

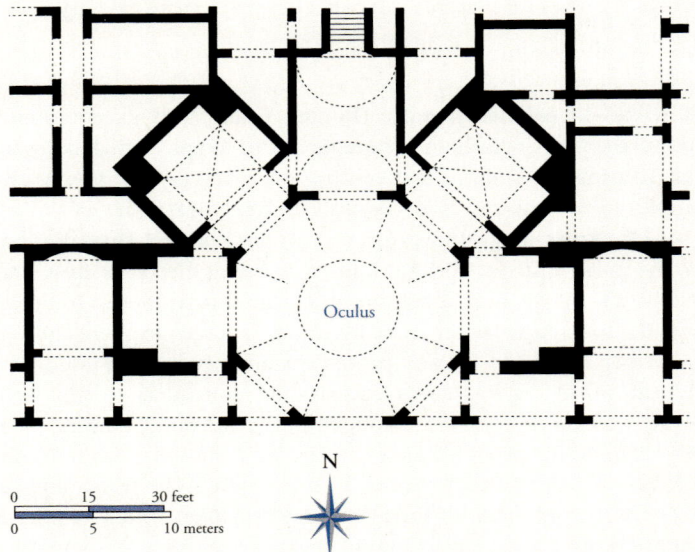

to build a luxurious new palace on a huge confiscated plot of fire-ravaged land near the Forum Romanum. Nero chose two brilliant architect-engineers, SEVERUS and CELER, to design and construct his new home (see "The Golden House of Nero," above). The palace they built for the emperor had scores of rooms, many adorned with frescoes (FIG. 7-22) in the Fourth Style, others with marble paneling or painted and gilded stucco reliefs. Structurally, most of these rooms, although built of concrete, are unremarkable. One octagonal hall (FIG. **7-35**), however, stands apart from the rest and testifies to Severus and Celer's bold new approach to architectural design.

The ceiling of the octagonal room is a dome that modulates from an eight-sided to a hemispherical form as it rises toward the *oculus*—the circular opening that admitted light to the room. Radiating outward from the five inner sides (the other three, directly or indirectly, face the outside) are smaller, rectangular rooms, three covered by barrel vaults, two others (marked by a broken-line X on the plan; FIG. 7-35, *right*) by the earliest known concrete groin

vaults. Severus and Celer ingeniously lit these satellite rooms by leaving spaces between their vaulted ceilings and the central dome's exterior. But the most significant aspect of the design is that here, for the first time, the architects appear to have thought of the walls and vaults not as limiting space but as shaping it.

Today, the octagonal hall is deprived of its stucco decoration and marble *incrustation* (veneer). The concrete shell stands bare, but this serves to focus the visitor's attention on the design's spatial complexity. Anyone walking into the domed hall perceives that the space is defined not by walls but by eight angled piers. The wide square openings between the piers are so large the rooms beyond look like extensions of the central hall. The grouping of spatial units of different sizes and proportions under a variety of vaults creates a dynamic three-dimensional composition that is both complex and unified. Nero's architects were not only inventive but also progressive in their recognition of the malleable nature of concrete, a material not limited to the rectilinear forms of traditional architecture.

## Spectacles in the Colosseum

A favorite pastime throughout the Roman Empire was going to the amphitheater to see two immensely popular kinds of spectacles: gladiatorial combats and animal hunts.

*Gladiators* were professional fighters, usually slaves who had been purchased to train in gladiatorial schools as hand-to-hand combatants. Their owners, seeking to turn a profit, rented them out for performances. Beginning with Domitian, however, all gladiators who competed in Rome were state-owned to ensure they could not be used as a private army to overthrow the government. Although every gladiator faced death each time he entered the arena, some had long careers and achieved considerable fame. Others, for example, criminals or captured enemies, entered the amphitheater without any training and without any defensive weapons. Those "gladiatorial games" were a form of capital punishment coupled with entertainment for the masses.

The participants in wild animal hunts (*venationes*) were also professionals, but often the hunts, like the gladiatorial games, were executions in thin disguise involving helpless prisoners who were easy prey for the animals. Sometimes no one entered the arena with the animals. Instead, skilled archers in the stands shot the beasts with arrows. Other times animals would be pitted against other animals—bears versus bulls, lions versus elephants, and the like—to the delight of the crowds.

The Colosseum (FIGS. 7-36 and 7-37) was the largest and most important amphitheater in the world, and the kinds of spectacles staged there were costlier and more impressive than those held anywhere else. Some ancient accounts even mention the flooding of the Colosseum so naval battles could be staged in the arena. Many scholars, however, doubt that the arena could be made watertight or that ships could maneuver in the space available. The games celebrating Titus's inauguration of the Colosseum in 80 were especially lavish. In the early third century, the historian Dio Cassius described them:

> There was a battle between cranes and also between four elephants; animals both tame and wild were slain to the number of nine thousand; and women . . . took part in despatching them. As for the men, several fought in single combat and several groups contended together both in infantry and naval battles. For Titus suddenly filled [the arena] with water and brought in horses and bulls and some other domesticated animals that had been taught to behave in the liquid element just as on land. He also brought in people on ships, who engaged in a sea-fight there. . . . On the first

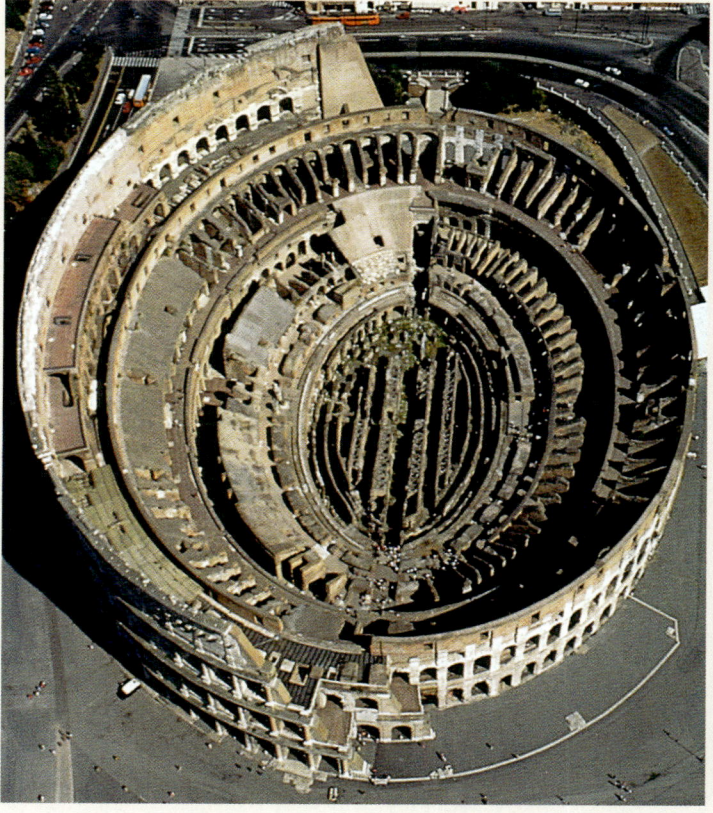

**7-36** Aerial view of the Colosseum (Flavian Amphitheater, looking east), Rome, Italy, ca. 70–80 CE. ◼◀

A complex system of concrete barrel vaults once held up the seats in the world's largest amphitheater, where 50,000 spectators could watch gladiatorial combats and wild animal hunts.

> day there was a gladiatorial exhibition and wild-beast hunt. . . . On the second day there was a horse-race, and on the third day a naval battle between three thousand men, followed by an infantry battle. . . . These were the spectacles that were offered, and they continued for a hundred days.*

*Dio Cassius, *Roman History*, 66.25. Translated by Earnest Cary, *Dio's Roman History*, vol. 8 (Cambridge, Mass.: Harvard University Press, 1925), 311, 313.

## The Flavians

Because of his outrageous behavior, Nero faced certain assassination in 68 CE and committed suicide, bringing the Julio-Claudian dynasty to an end. A year of renewed civil strife followed. The man who emerged triumphant in this brief but bloody conflict was Vespasian (r. 69–79 CE), a general who had served under Claudius and Nero. Vespasian, whose family name was Flavius, had two sons, Titus (r. 79–81 CE) and Domitian (r. 81–96 CE). Both became emperor in turn after their father's death. The Flavian dynasty ruled Rome for more than a quarter century.

**COLOSSEUM** The Flavians left their mark on the capital in many ways, not the least being the construction of the Colosseum (FIGS. 7-2, no. 17, and **7-36**), the monument that, for most people, still represents Rome more than any other building. The Flavian Amphitheater, as it was then known, was one of Vespasian's first undertakings after becoming emperor. The decision to build the Colosseum was politically shrewd. The site chosen was the artificial lake on the grounds of Nero's Domus Aurea, which engineers drained for the purpose. By building the new amphitheater there, Vespasian reclaimed for the public the land Nero had confiscated for

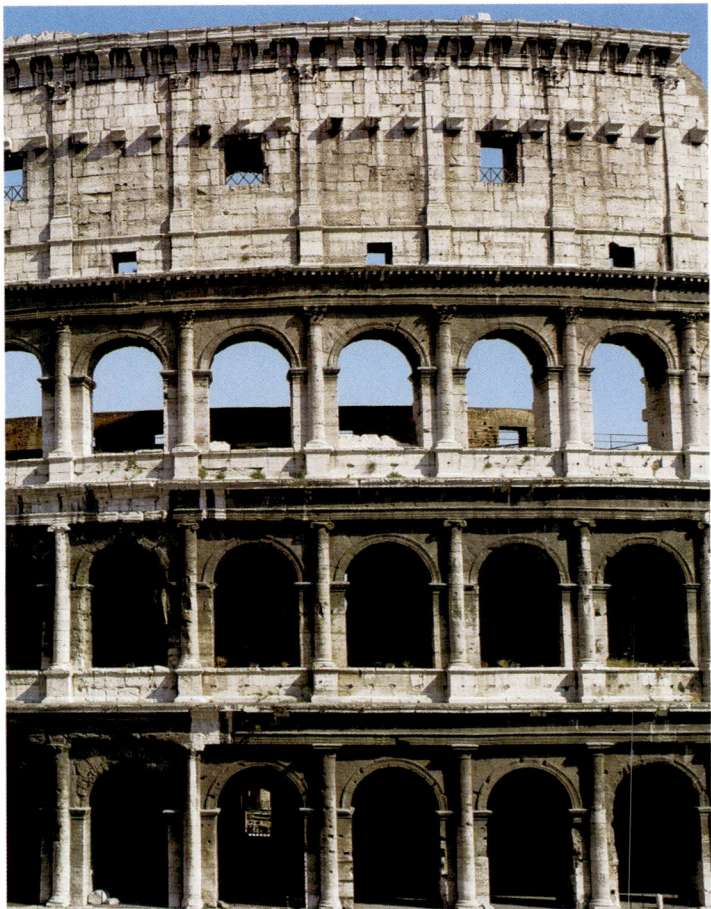

**7-37** Detail of the facade of the Colosseum (Flavian Amphitheater), Rome, Italy, ca. 70–80 CE. ■◄

For the facade of the Colosseum, an unknown architect mixed Roman arches and Greek columns—Tuscan on the lowest story, then Ionic and Corinthian. Wooden poles held up an awning over the cavea.

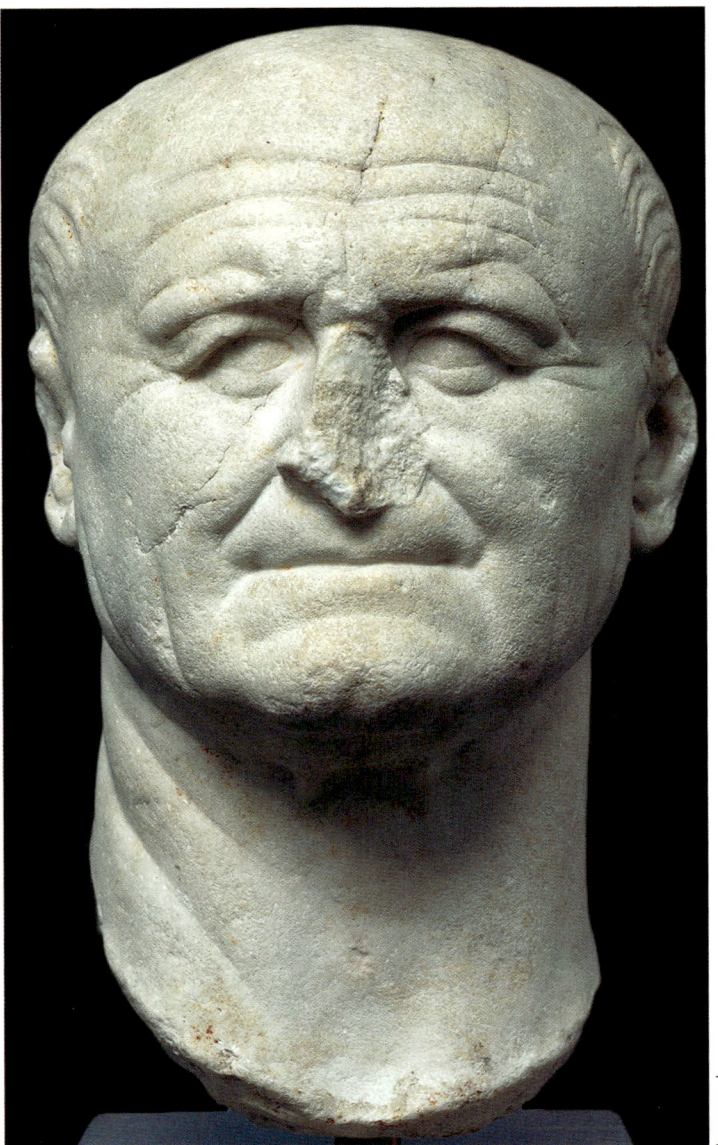

1 in.

**7-38** Portrait of Vespasian, ca. 75–79 CE. Marble, 1′ 4″ high. Ny Carlsberg Glyptotek, Copenhagen.

Vespasian's sculptors revived the veristic tradition of the Republic to underscore the elderly new emperor's Republican values in contrast to Nero's self-indulgence and extravagance.

his private pleasure and provided Romans with the largest arena for gladiatorial combats and other lavish spectacles ever constructed. The Colosseum takes its name, however, not from its size—it could hold more than 50,000 spectators—but from its location beside the Colossus of Nero (FIG. 7-2, no. 16), the 120-foot-tall statue at the entrance to his urban villa. Vespasian did not live to see the Colosseum in use. Titus completed and formally dedicated the amphitheater in the year 80 with great fanfare (see "Spectacles in the Colosseum," page 203).

The Colosseum, like the much earlier Pompeian amphitheater (FIG. 7-13), could not have been built without concrete. A complex system of barrel-vaulted corridors held up the enormous oval seating area. This concrete "skeleton" is exposed today because in the centuries following the fall of Rome, the Colosseum served as a convenient quarry for ready-made building materials. Almost all its marble seats were hauled away, revealing the network of vaults below (FIG. 7-36). Also visible today but hidden in antiquity are the arena substructures, which in their present form date to the third century CE. They housed waiting rooms for the gladiators, animal cages, and machinery for raising and lowering stage sets as well as animals and humans. Cleverly designed lifting devices brought beasts from their dark dens into the arena's bright light. Above the seats a great velarium, as at Pompeii (FIG. 7-14), once shielded the spectators.

The exterior travertine shell (FIG. **7-37**) is approximately 160 feet high, the height of a modern 16-story building. In antiquity, 76 numbered gateways provided efficient entrance and exit paths leading to and from the cavea, where the spectators sat according to their place in the social hierarchy. The decor of the exterior, however, had nothing to do with function. The architect divided the facade into four bands, with large arched openings piercing the lower three. Ornamental Greek orders frame the arches in the standard Roman sequence for multistoried buildings: from the ground up, Tuscan, Ionic, and then Corinthian. The diverse proportions of the orders formed the basis for this progression, with the Tuscan viewed as capable of supporting the heaviest load. Corinthian pilasters (and between them the brackets for the wooden poles that held up the velarium) circle the uppermost story.

The use of engaged columns and a lintel to frame the openings in the Colosseum's facade is a variation of the scheme used

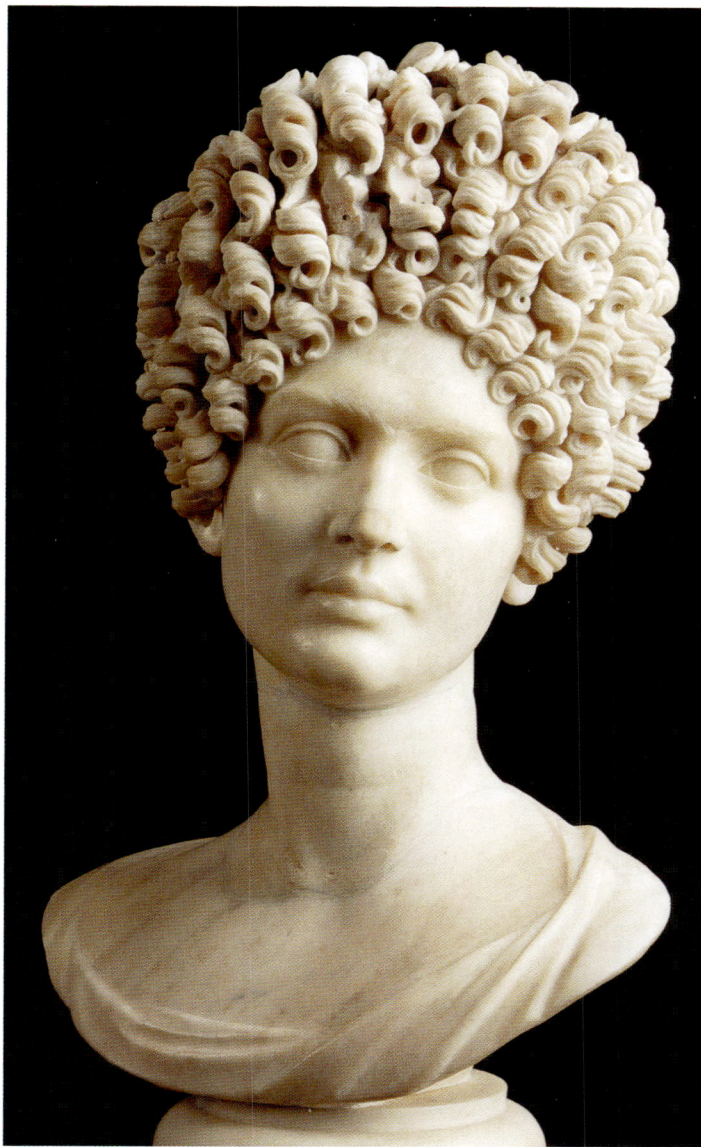

1 in.

**7-39** Portrait bust of a Flavian woman, from Rome, Italy, ca. 90 CE. Marble, 2′ 1″ high. Museo Capitolino, Rome.

The Flavian sculptor reproduced the elaborate coiffure of this elegant woman by drilling deep holes for the corkscrew curls, and carved the rest of the hair and the face with hammer and chisel.

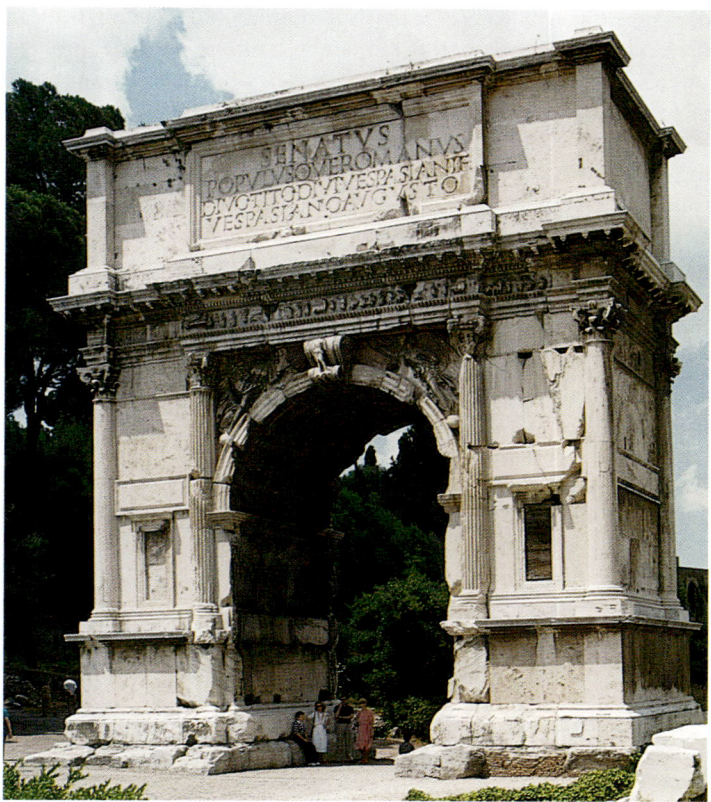

**7-40** West facade of the Arch of Titus, Rome, Italy, after 81 CE. ◼◀

Domitian built this arch on the road leading into the Roman Forum to honor his brother, the emperor Titus, who became a god after his death. Victories fill the spandrels of the arcuated passageway.

on the Etruscan Porta Marzia (FIG. 6-14) at Perugia. The Romans commonly used this scheme from Late Republican times on, for example, at Palestrina (FIG. 7-5). Like the pseudoperipteral temple, which combines Greek orders with an Etruscan plan, this manner of decorating a building's facade mixed Greek orders with an architectural form foreign to Greek post-and-lintel architecture, namely the arch. The Roman practice of framing an arch with an applied Greek order had no structural purpose, but it added variety to the surface. In the Colosseum, it also unified a multistoried facade by casting a net of verticals and horizontals over it.

**FLAVIAN PORTRAITURE** Vespasian was an unpretentious career army officer who desired to distance himself from Nero's extravagant misrule. His portraits (FIG. 7-38) reflect his much simpler tastes. They also made an important political statement. Breaking with the tradition Augustus established of depicting the

Roman emperor as an eternally youthful god on earth, Vespasian's sculptors resuscitated the veristic tradition of the Republic, possibly at his specific direction. Although not as brutally descriptive as many Republican likenesses (FIG. 7-8), Vespasian's portraits frankly recorded his receding hairline and aging, leathery skin—proclaiming his traditional Republican values in contrast to Nero's.

Portraits of people of all ages survive from the Flavian period, in contrast to the Republic, when only elders were deemed worthy of depiction. A portrait bust (FIG. **7-39**) of a young woman is a case in point. Its purpose was not to project Republican virtues but rather idealized beauty—through current fashion rather than by reference to images of Greek goddesses. The portrait is notable for its elegance and delicacy and for the virtuoso way the sculptor rendered the differing textures of hair and flesh. The elaborate Flavian coiffure, with its corkscrew curls punched out using a drill instead of a chisel, is a dense mass of light and shadow set off boldly from the softly modeled and highly polished skin of the face and swan-like neck. The drill played an increasing role in Roman sculpture in succeeding periods, and when much longer hair and full beards became fashionable for men, sculptors used drills for their portraits as well (for example, FIG. 7-59A).

**ARCH OF TITUS** When Titus died in 81 CE, only two years after becoming emperor, his younger brother, Domitian, succeeded him. Domitian erected an arch (FIGS. 7-2, no. 13, and **7-40**) in Titus's honor on the Sacred Way leading into the Republican Forum Romanum (FIG. 7-2, no. 11). This type of freestanding arch, the so-called *triumphal arch,* has a long history in Roman art and architecture, beginning in the second century BCE. The term is something of a misnomer, however, because Roman arches celebrated more than merely military victories. Usually crowned by gilded bronze statues, they commemorated a wide variety of events, ranging from victories abroad to the building of roads and bridges at home.

The Arch of Titus is a typical early triumphal arch in having only one passageway. As on the Colosseum, engaged columns frame the *arcuated* (curved or arched) opening. The capitals are not Greek, however, but Roman *Composite capitals,* an ornate combination of Ionic volutes and Corinthian acanthus leaves. The new type became popular at about the same time as the Fourth Style in Roman painting. Reliefs depicting personified Victories (winged women, as in Greek art) fill the *spandrels* (the area between the arch's curve and the framing columns and entablature). A dedica-

tory inscription stating the Senate erected the arch to honor the god Titus, son of the god Vespasian, dominates the attic. In the vault of the passageway is a relief (FIG. **7-40A**) showing Titus's ascent to Heaven (*apotheosis*). The Senate normally proclaimed Roman emperors gods after they died, unless they ran afoul of the senators and were damned. The statues of those who suffered *damnatio memoriae* were torn down, and their names erased from public inscriptions. This was Nero's fate.

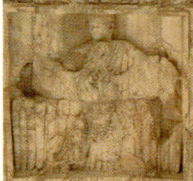

7-40A Apotheosis of Titus, after 81 CE.

Inside the passageway of the Arch of Titus are two great relief panels. They represent the triumphal parade of Titus down the

**7-41** Spoils of Jerusalem, relief panel in the passageway of the Arch of Titus, Rome, Italy, after 81 CE. Marble, 7′ 10″ high.

The reliefs inside the bay of the Arch of Titus commemorate the emperor's conquest of Judaea. Here, Roman soldiers carry in triumph the spoils taken from the Jewish temple in Jerusalem.

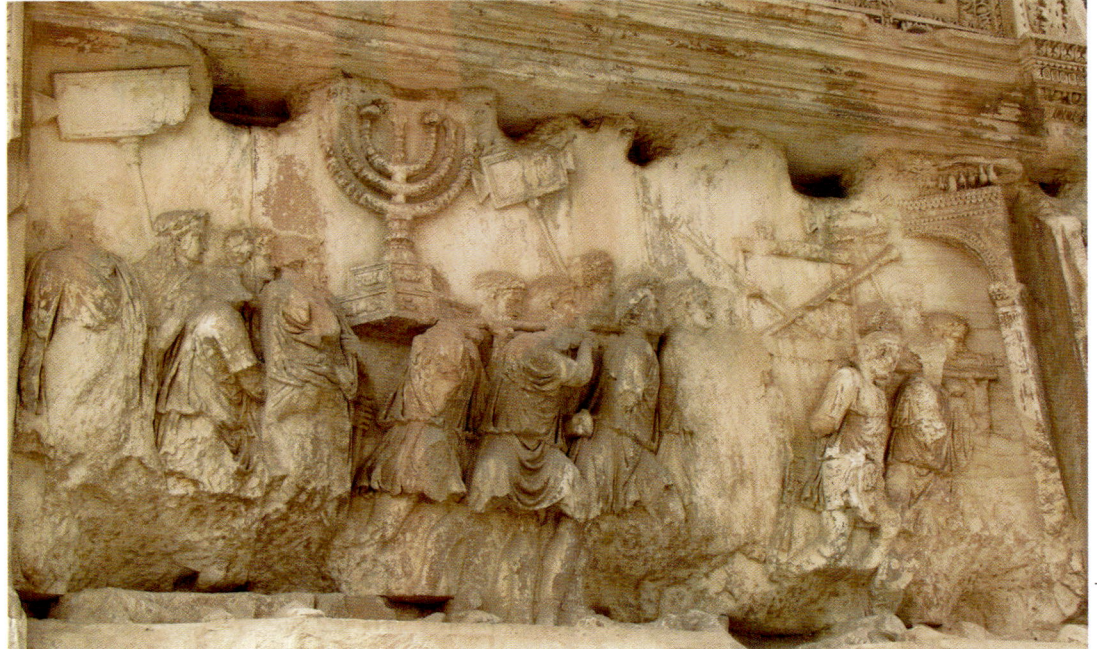

1 ft.

**7-42** Triumph of Titus, relief panel in the passageway of the Arch of Titus, Rome, Italy, after 81 CE. Marble, 7′ 10″ high.

Victory crowns Titus in his triumphal chariot. Also present are personifications of Honor and Valor in this first known instance of the intermingling of human and divine figures in a Roman historical relief.

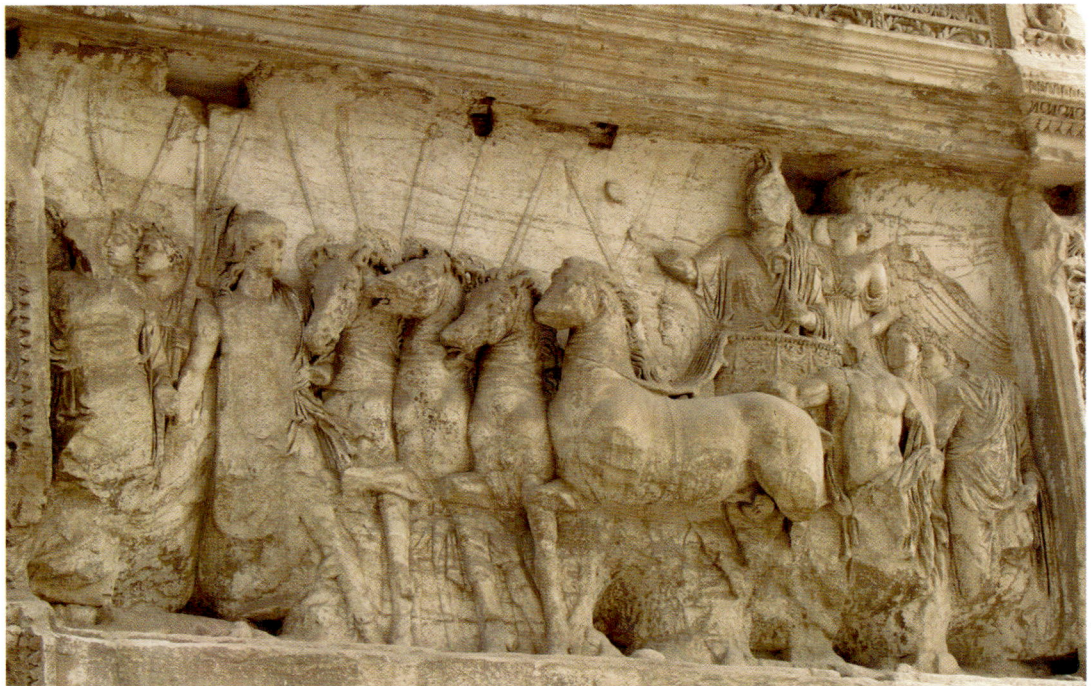

1 ft.

Sacred Way after his return from the conquest of Judaea at the end of the Jewish wars in 70 CE. One of the reliefs (FIG. **7-41**) depicts Roman soldiers carrying the spoils—including the sacred seven-branched candelabrum, the *menorah*—from the Jewish temple in Jerusalem. Despite considerable damage to the relief, the illusion of movement is convincing. The parade emerges from the left background into the center foreground and disappears through the obliquely placed arch in the right background. The energy and swing of the column of soldiers suggest a rapid march. The sculptor rejected the Classical low-relief style of the Ara Pacis (FIG. 7-31) in favor of extremely deep carving, which produces strong shadows. The heads of the forward figures have broken off because they stood free from the block. Their high relief emphasized their different placement in space compared with the heads in low relief, which are intact. The play of light and shadow across the protruding foreground and receding background figures enhances the sense of movement.

On the other side of the passageway, the panel (FIG. **7-42**) shows Titus in his triumphal chariot. The seeming historical accuracy of the spoils panel—it closely corresponds to the Jewish historian Josephus's contemporaneous description of Titus's triumph—gave way in this panel to allegory. Victory rides with Titus in the four-horse chariot and places a wreath on his head. Below her is a bare-chested youth who is probably a personification of Honor (*Honos*). A female personification of Valor (*Virtus*) leads the horses. These allegorical figures transform the relief from a record of Titus's battlefield success into a celebration of imperial virtues. A comparable intermingling of divine and human figures characterized the Dionysiac frieze (FIG. 7-18) of the Villa of the Mysteries at Pompeii, but the Arch of Titus panel is the first known instance of divine beings interacting with humans on an official Roman historical relief. (On the Ara Pacis, FIG. 7-29, Aeneas and "Tellus" appear in separate framed panels, carefully segregated from the procession of living Romans.) The Arch of Titus, however, honors the god Titus, not the living emperor. Soon afterward, however, this kind of interaction between mortals and immortals became a staple of Roman narrative relief sculpture, even on monuments set up while the emperor was alive.

# HIGH EMPIRE

In the second century CE, under Trajan, Hadrian, and the Antonines, the Roman Empire reached its greatest geographic extent (MAP 7-1) and the height of its power. Rome's might was unchallenged in the Mediterranean world, although the Germanic peoples in Europe, the Berbers in Africa, and the Parthians and Persians in the East constantly applied pressure. Within the Empire's secure boundaries, the Pax Romana meant unprecedented prosperity for all who came under Roman rule.

## Trajan

Domitian's extravagant lifestyle and ego resembled Nero's. He demanded to be addressed as *dominus et deus* (lord and god), and so angered the senators that he was assassinated in 96 CE. The Senate chose the elderly Nerva (r. 96–98 CE), one of its own, as emperor. Nerva ruled for only 16 months, but before he died he established a pattern of succession by adoption that lasted for almost a century. Nerva picked Trajan, a capable and popular general born in Italica, Spain, as the next emperor—the first non-Italian to rule Rome. Under Trajan, imperial armies brought Roman rule to ever more distant areas (MAP 7-1), and the imperial government took on ever greater responsibility for its people's welfare by instituting a num-

ber of farsighted social programs. Trajan was so popular the Senate granted him the title *Optimus* (the Best), an epithet he shared with Jupiter (who was said to have instructed Nerva to choose Trajan as his successor). In time, Trajan, along with Augustus, became the yardsticks for measuring the success of later emperors, who strove to be *felicior Augusto, melior Traiano* (luckier than Augustus, better than Trajan).

**TIMGAD** In 100 CE, as part of his program to extend and strengthen Roman rule on three continents, Trajan founded a new colony for army veterans at Timgad (FIG. **7-43**) in what is today Algeria. Like other colonies, Timgad became the physical embodiment of Roman authority and civilization for the local population. Roman engineers laid out the town with great precision, on the pattern of a Roman military encampment, or *castrum,* although some scholars think the castrum plan followed the scheme of Roman colonies, not vice versa. Unlike the sprawling unplanned cities of Rome and Pompeii, Timgad is a square divided into equal quarters by its two colonnaded main streets, the cardo and the decumanus, which cross at right angles. The forum is at the point where the two avenues intersect, and monumental gates marked the ends of both streets. The quarters are subdivided into square blocks, and the forum and public buildings, such as the theater and baths, occupy areas sized as multiples of these blocks. The Roman plan is a modification of the Hippodamian plan of Greek cities (FIG. 5-76), though more rigidly ordered. The Romans laid out most of their new settlements in the same manner, regardless of whether they were in North Africa, Mesopotamia, or England. This uniformity expresses concretely the centralized power of the Roman Empire at its height. But even the Romans could not regulate human behavior completely. As the satellite view reveals, when the population of Timgad grew sevenfold and burst through the Trajanic colony's walls, the colonists abandoned rational planning, and the city and its streets branched out haphazardly.

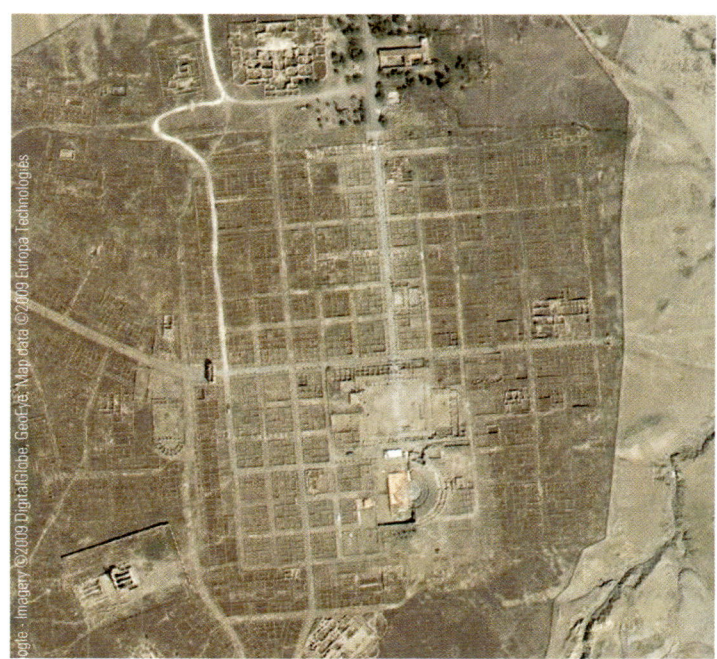

**7-43** Satellite view of Timgad, Algeria, founded 100 CE.

The plan of Trajan's new colony of Timgad in North Africa features a strict grid scheme with the forum at the intersection of the two main thoroughfares, the cardo and the decumanus.

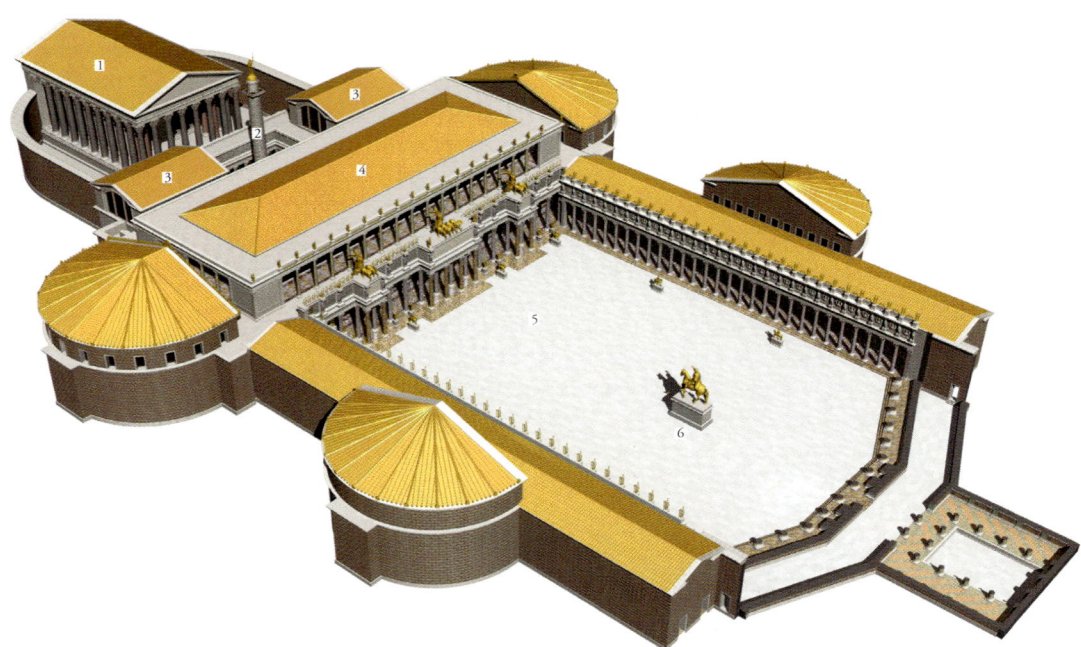

**7-44** Apollodorus of Damascus, Forum of Trajan (restored view), Rome, Italy, dedicated 112 CE (James E. Packer and John Burge). (1) Temple of Trajan, (2) Column of Trajan, (3) libraries, (4) Basilica Ulpia, (5) forum, (6) equestrian statue of Trajan.

Funded by the spoils from two Dacian wars, Rome's largest forum featured a basilica with clerestory lighting, two libraries, a commemorative column (FIG. 7-45), and a temple of the deified Trajan.

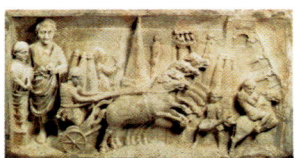

**7-44A** Funerary relief of a circus official, ca. 110–130 CE.

**FORUM OF TRAJAN** Trajan completed several major building projects in Rome, including the re-modeling of the Circus Maximus (FIGS. 7-2, no. 2, and **7-44A**), Rome's giant chariot-racing stadium, and the construction of a vast new bathing complex near the Colosseum constructed on top of Nero's Golden House. His most important undertaking, however, was a huge new forum (FIGS. 7-2, no. 7, and **7-44**), roughly twice the size of the century-old Forum of Augustus (FIG. 7-2, no. 10)—even excluding the enormous adjoining market complex. The new forum glorified Trajan's victories in his two wars against the Dacians (FIG. 7-1), the spoils of which paid for Trajan's building program in the capital. The architect was APOLLODORUS OF DAMASCUS, Trajan's chief military engineer during the Dacian wars. Apollodorus's plan incorporated the main features of most early forums (FIG. 7-12), except a huge basilica, not a temple, dominated the colonnaded open square. The temple (completed after the emperor's death and dedicated to the newest god in the Roman pantheon, Trajan himself) stood instead behind the basilica facing two libraries and a giant commemorative column. Entry to Trajan's forum was through an impressive gateway

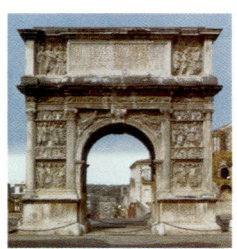

**7-44B** Arch of Trajan, Benevento, ca. 114–118 CE.

resembling a triumphal arch. (Trajan also erected freestanding triumphal arches in Rome and elsewhere in Italy, for example, at Benevento [FIG. **7-44B**], northeast of Naples.) Inside the forum were other reminders of Trajan's military prowess. A larger-than-life-size gilded bronze equestrian statue of the emperor stood at the center of the great court in front of the basilica. Statues of captive Dacians stood above the columns of the forum porticos.

The Basilica Ulpia (Trajan's family name was Ulpius) was a much larger and far more ornate version of the basilica in the forum of Pompeii (FIG. 7-12, no. 3). As shown in FIG. 7-44, no. 4, it had *apses,* or semicircular recesses, on each short end. Two aisles flanked the nave on each side. In contrast to the Pompeian basilica, the entrances were on the long side facing the forum. The building was

vast: about 400 feet long (without the apses) and 200 feet wide. Light entered through clerestory windows, made possible by elevating the timber-roofed nave above the colonnaded aisles. In the Republican basilica at Pompeii, light reached the nave only indirectly through aisle windows. The clerestory (used more than a thousand years before at Karnak in Egypt; FIG. 3-26) was a much better solution.

**COLUMN OF TRAJAN** The Column of Trajan (FIG. **7-45**) was probably also the brainchild of Apollodorus of Damascus. The idea of covering the shaft of a colossal freestanding column with a continuous spiral narrative frieze (FIG. 7-1) seems to have been invented here, but it was often copied in antiquity, during the Middle Ages (FIG. 11-24A), the Enlightenment (FIG. 26-3A), and the 19th century. The 128-foot-tall column once had a heroically nude statue of the emperor at the top. (The present statue of Saint Peter dates to the 16th century.) The tall pedestal, decorated with captured Dacian arms and armor, served as Trajan's tomb.

Art historians have likened the 625-foot band winding around the column to an illustrated scroll (FIG. 3-37) of the type housed in the neighboring libraries. The reliefs recount Trajan's two successful campaigns against the Dacians in more than 150 episodes in which some 2,500 figures appear. The band increases in width as it winds to the top of the column, in order to make the upper portions easier to see. Throughout, the relief is very low so as not to distort the contours of the shaft. Paint enhanced the legibility of the figures, but it still would have been very difficult for anyone to follow the narrative from beginning to end.

Easily recognizable compositions like those found on coin reverses and on historical relief panels—Trajan addressing his troops, sacrificing to the gods, and so on—fill most of the frieze. The narrative is not a reliable chronological account of the Dacian wars, as once thought. The sculptors nonetheless accurately recorded the general character of the campaigns. Notably, battle scenes take up only about a quarter of the frieze (FIG. 7-1). As is true of modern military operations, the Romans spent more time constructing forts, transporting men and equipment, and preparing for battle than fighting. The focus is always on the emperor, who appears repeatedly in the frieze, but the enemy is not belittled. The Romans won because of their superior organization and more powerful army, not because they were inherently superior beings.

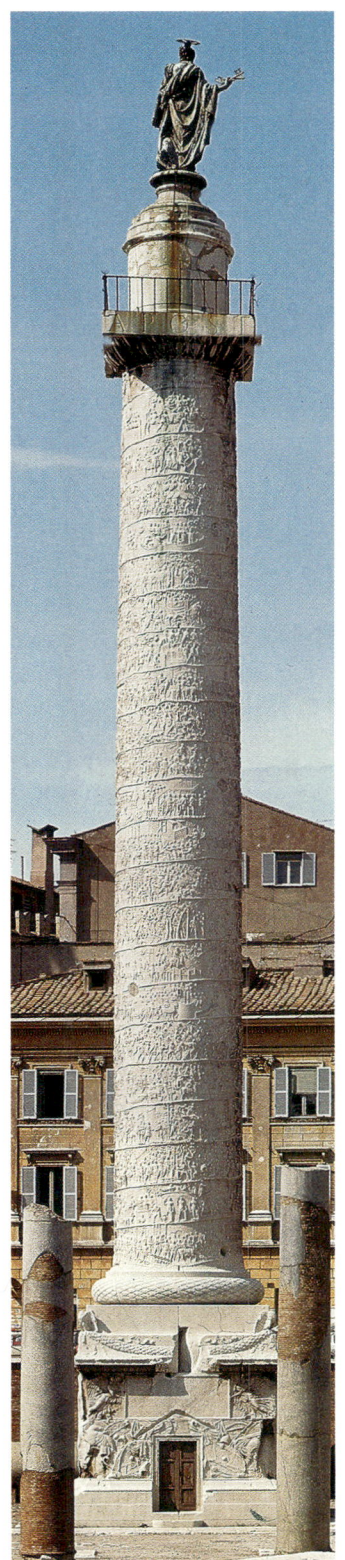

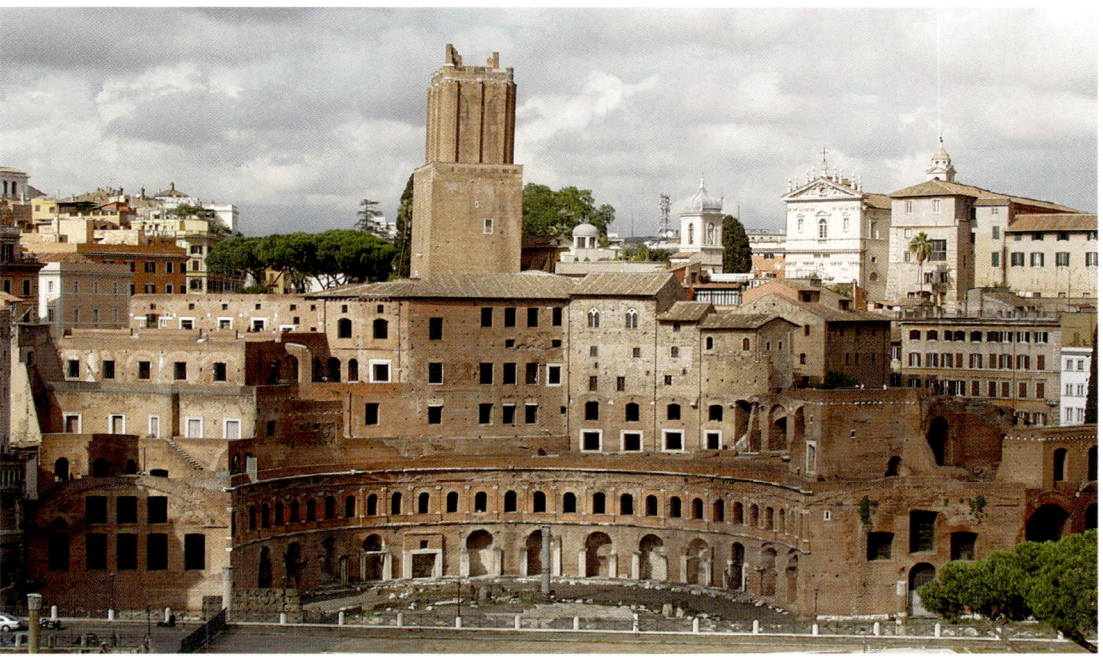

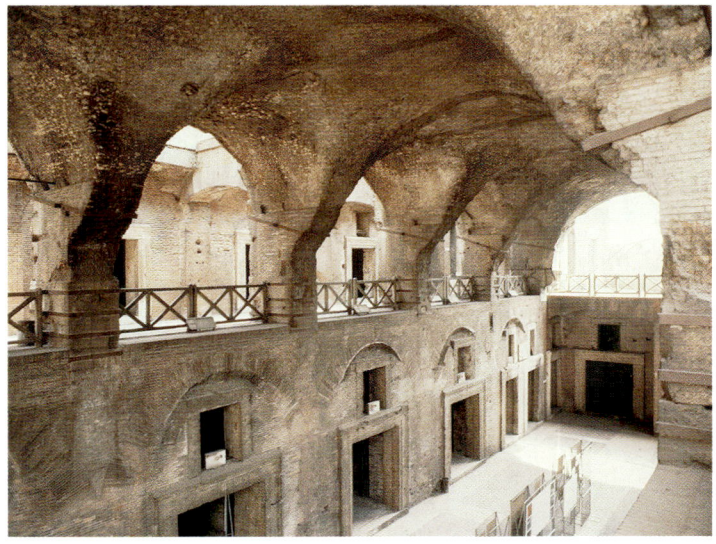

**7-45** Column of Trajan, Forum of Trajan, Rome, Italy, dedicated 112 CE. ◼◀

The spiral frieze of Trajan's Column tells the story of the Dacian wars in 150 episodes. The reliefs depicted all aspects of the campaigns, from battles to sacrifices to road and fort construction.

**7-46** APOLLODORUS OF DAMASCUS, Markets of Trajan (looking northeast), Rome, Italy, ca. 100–112 CE.

Apollodorus of Damascus used brick-faced concrete to transform the Quirinal Hill overlooking Trajan's Forum into a vast multilevel complex of barrel-vaulted shops and administrative offices.

**7-47** APOLLODORUS OF DAMASCUS, interior of the great hall, Markets of Trajan, Rome, Italy, ca. 100–112 CE.

The great hall of Trajan's Markets resembles a modern shopping mall. It housed two floors of shops, with the upper ones set back and lit by skylights. Concrete groin vaults cover the central space.

**MARKETS OF TRAJAN** On the Quirinal Hill overlooking the forum, Apollodorus built the Markets of Trajan (FIGS. 7-2, no. 8, **7-46, a**nd **7-47**) to house both shops and administrative offices. As earlier at Palestrina (FIG. 7-5), concrete made possible the transformation of a natural slope into a multilevel complex. Trajan's architect was a master of this modern medium as well as of the traditional stone-and-timber post-and lintel architecture of the forum below. The basic unit was the *taberna,* a single-room shop covered by a barrel vault. Each taberna had a wide doorway, usually with a window above it through which light entered a wooden inner attic used for storage. The shops were on several levels. They opened either onto a hemicyclical facade winding around one of the great exedras of Trajan's forum, onto a paved street farther up the hill, or onto a great indoor market hall (FIG. 7-47) resembling a modern shopping mall. The hall housed two floors of shops, with the upper shops set back on each side and lit by skylights. Light from the same sources reached the ground-floor shops through arches beneath the great umbrella-like groin vaults (FIG. 7-6c) covering the hall.

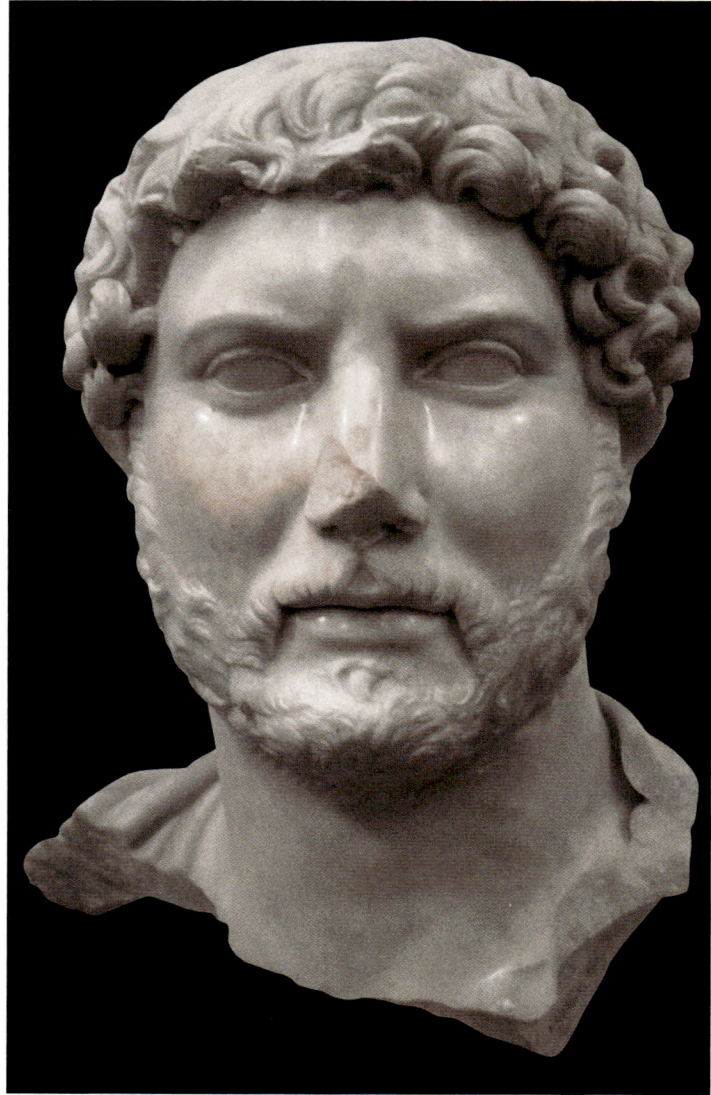

1 in.

**7-48** Portrait bust of Hadrian, from Rome, ca. 117–120 CE. Marble, 1′ 4¾″ high. Museo Nazionale Romano—Palazzo Massimo alle Terme, Rome.

Hadrian, a lover of all things Greek, was the first Roman emperor to wear a beard. His artists modeled his idealized official portraits on Classical Greek statues such as Kresilas's Pericles (FIG. 5-41).

## Hadrian

Hadrian (FIG. 7-48), Trajan's chosen successor and fellow Spaniard, was a connoisseur and lover of all the arts, as well as an author, architect, and hunter (FIG. 7-48A). He greatly admired Greek cul-

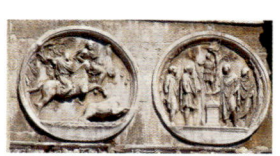

**7-48A** Hadrianic hunting tondi, ca. 130–138 CE.

ture and traveled widely as emperor, often in the Greek East. Everywhere he went, local officials set up statues and arches in his honor. That is why more portraits of Hadrian exist today than of any other emperor except Augustus. Hadrian, who was 41 years old at the time of Trajan's death and who ruled for more than two decades, always appears as a mature man, but one who never ages. His likenesses more closely resemble Kresilas's portrait of Pericles (FIG. 5-41) than those of any Roman emperor before him. Fifth-century BCE statues also provided the prototypes for the idealizing official portraits of Augustus, but the Augus-

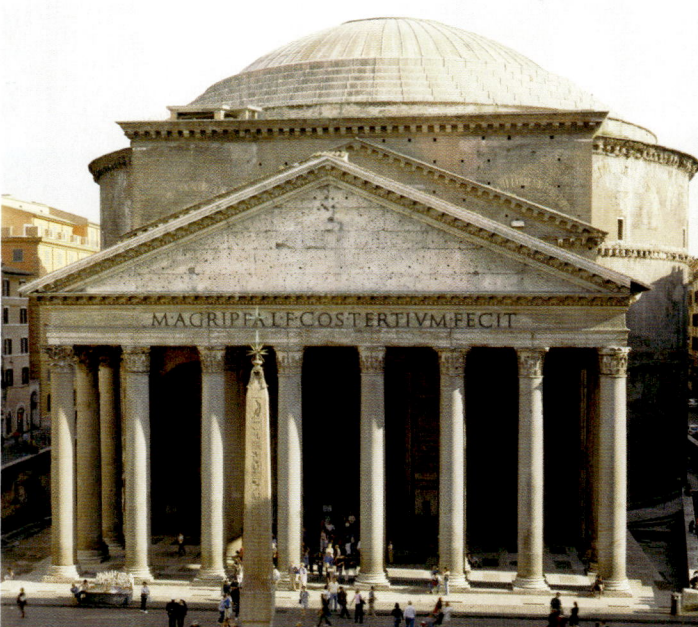

**7-49** Pantheon (looking south), Rome, Italy, 118–125 CE. ◼️◀

The Pantheon's traditional facade masked its revolutionary cylindrical drum and its huge hemispherical dome. The interior symbolized both the orb of the earth and the vault of the heavens.

tan models were Greek images of young athletes. The models for Hadrian's artists were Classical statues of bearded men. Hadrian's beard was a Greek affectation at the time, but thereafter beards became the norm for all Roman emperors for more than a century and a half.

**PANTHEON** Soon after Hadrian became emperor, work began on the Pantheon (FIGS. 7-2, no. 5, and 7-49), the temple of all the gods, one of the best-preserved buildings of antiquity. It also has been one of the most influential designs in architectural history. In the Pantheon, an unknown architect revealed the full potential of concrete, both as a building material and as a means for shaping architectural space. The original approach to the temple was from a columnar courtyard, and, like temples in Roman forums, the Pantheon stood at one narrow end of the enclosure (FIG. 7-50, *left*). Its facade of eight Corinthian columns—almost all that could be seen from ground level in antiquity—was a bow to tradition. Everything else about the Pantheon was revolutionary. Behind the columnar porch is an immense concrete cylinder covered by a huge hemispherical dome 142 feet in diameter. The dome's top is also 142 feet from the floor (FIG. 7-50, *right*). The design is thus based on the intersection of two circles (one horizontal, the other vertical). The interior space can be imagined as the orb of the earth and the dome as the vault of the heavens.

If the Pantheon's design is simplicity itself, executing that design took all the ingenuity of Hadrian's engineers. The builders constructed the cylindrical drum level by level using concrete of varied composition. Extremely hard and durable basalt went into the mix for the foundations, and the recipe gradually changed until, at the top of the dome, featherweight pumice replaced stones to lighten the load. The dome's thickness also decreases as it nears the oculus, the circular opening 30 feet in diameter that is the only light source for the interior (FIG. 7-51). The use of *coffers* (sunken

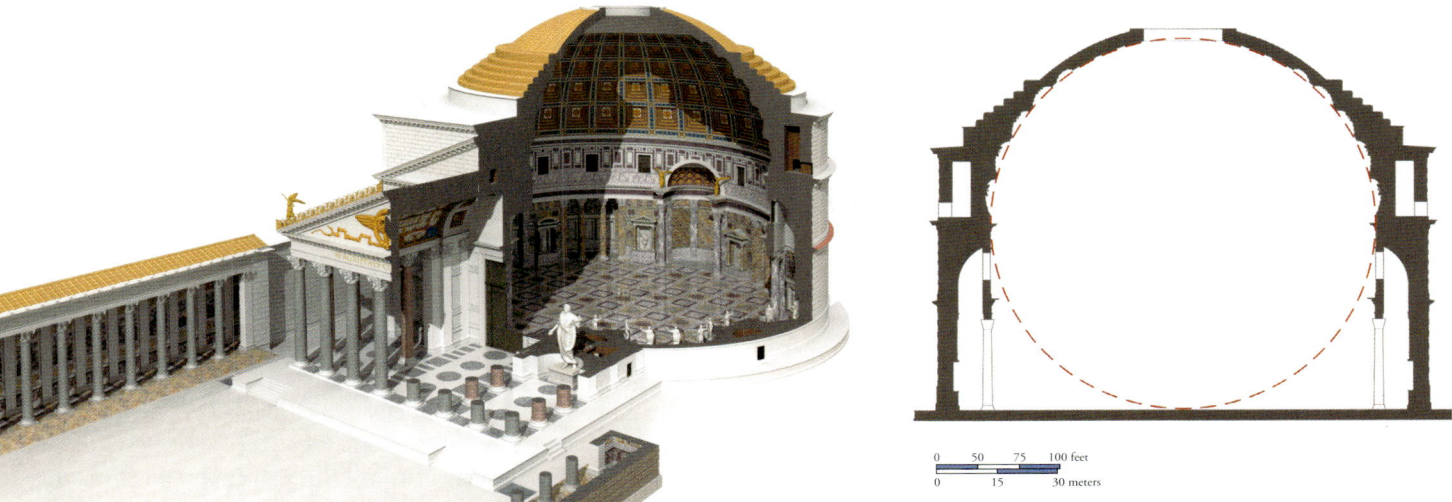

**7-50** Restored cutaway view (*left*) and lateral section (*right*) of the Pantheon, Rome, Italy, 118–125 CE (John Burge).

Originally, the approach to Hadrian's "temple of all gods" was from a columnar courtyard. Like a temple in a Roman forum (FIG. 7-12), the Pantheon stood at one narrow end of the enclosure.

decorative panels) lessened the dome's weight without weakening its structure, further reduced its mass, and even provided a handsome pattern of squares within the vast circle. Renaissance drawings suggest each coffer once had a glistening gilded-bronze rosette at its center, enhancing the symbolism of the dome as the starry heavens.

Below the dome, much of the original marble veneer of the walls, niches, and floor has survived. In the Pantheon, visitors can appreciate, as almost nowhere else (compare FIG. 7-67), how magnificent the interiors of Roman concrete buildings could be. But despite the luxurious skin of the Pantheon's interior, on first entering the structure, visitors do not sense the weight of the enclosing walls but the vastness of the space they enclose. In pre-Roman architecture, the form of the enclosed space was determined by the placement of the solids, which did not so much shape space as interrupt it. Roman architects were the first to conceive of architecture in terms of units of space that could be shaped by the enclosures. The Pantheon's interior is a single unified, self-sufficient whole, uninterrupted by supporting solids. It encloses people without imprisoning them, opening through the oculus to the drifting clouds, the blue sky, the sun, and the gods. In this space, the architect used light not merely to illuminate the darkness but to create drama and underscore the symbolism of the building's shape. On a sunny day, the light passing through the oculus forms a circular beam, a disk of light that moves across the coffered dome in the course of the day as the sun moves across the sky itself. Escaping from the noise and heat of a Roman summer day into the Pantheon's cool, calm, and mystical immensity is an experience not to be missed.

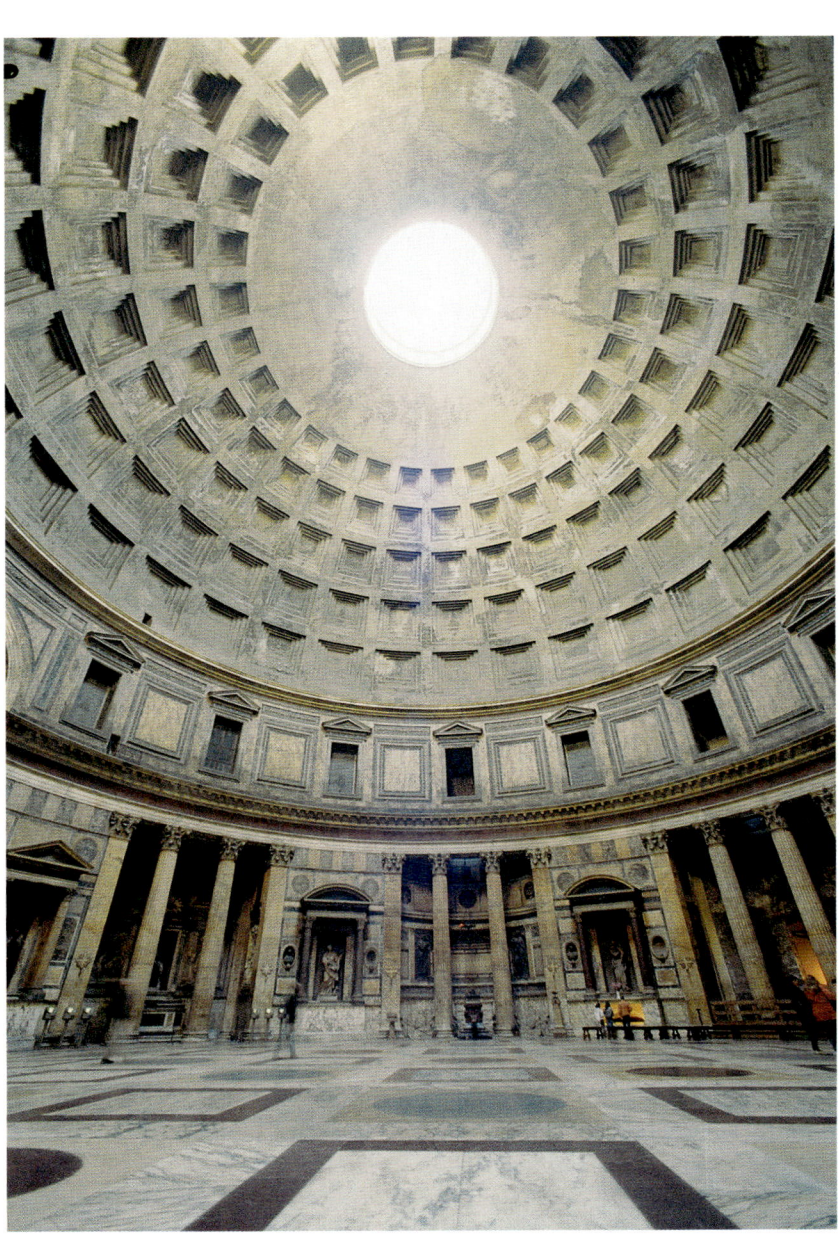

**7-51** Interior of the Pantheon, Rome, Italy, 118–125 CE.

The coffered dome of the Pantheon is 142 feet in diameter and 142 feet high. Light entering through its oculus forms a circular beam that moves across the dome as the sun moves across the sky.

## Hadrian and Apollodorus of Damascus

Dio Cassius, a third-century CE senator who wrote a history of Rome from its founding to his day, recounted a revealing anecdote about Hadrian and Apollodorus of Damascus, architect of the Forum of Trajan (FIG. 7-44):

> Hadrian first drove into exile and then put to death the architect Apollodorus who had carried out several of Trajan's building projects. . . . When Trajan was at one time consulting with Apollodorus about a certain problem connected with his buildings, the architect said to Hadrian, who had interrupted them with some advice, "Go away and draw your pumpkins. You know nothing about these problems." For it so happened that Hadrian was at that time priding himself on some sort of drawing. When he became emperor he remembered this insult and refused to put up with Apollodorus's outspokenness. He sent him [his own] plan for the temple of Venus and Roma [FIG. 7-2, no. 14], in order to demonstrate that it was possible for a great work to be conceived without his [Apollodorus's] help, and asked him if he thought the building

was well designed. Apollodorus sent a [very critical] reply. . . . [The emperor did not] attempt to restrain his anger or hide his pain; on the contrary, he had the man slain.*

The story says a great deal both about the absolute power Roman emperors wielded and about how seriously Hadrian took his architectural designs. But perhaps the most interesting detail is the description of Hadrian's drawings of "pumpkins." These must have been drawings of concrete domes similar to the one in the Serapeum (FIG. 7-52) at Hadrian's Tivoli villa. Such vaults were too adventurous for Apollodorus, or at least for a public building in Trajanic Rome, and Hadrian had to try them out later at home at his own expense.

*Dio Cassius, *Roman History*, 69.4.1–5. Translated by J. J. Pollitt, *The Art of Rome, c. 753 B.C.–A.D. 337: Sources and Documents* (New York: Cambridge University Press, 1983), 175–176.

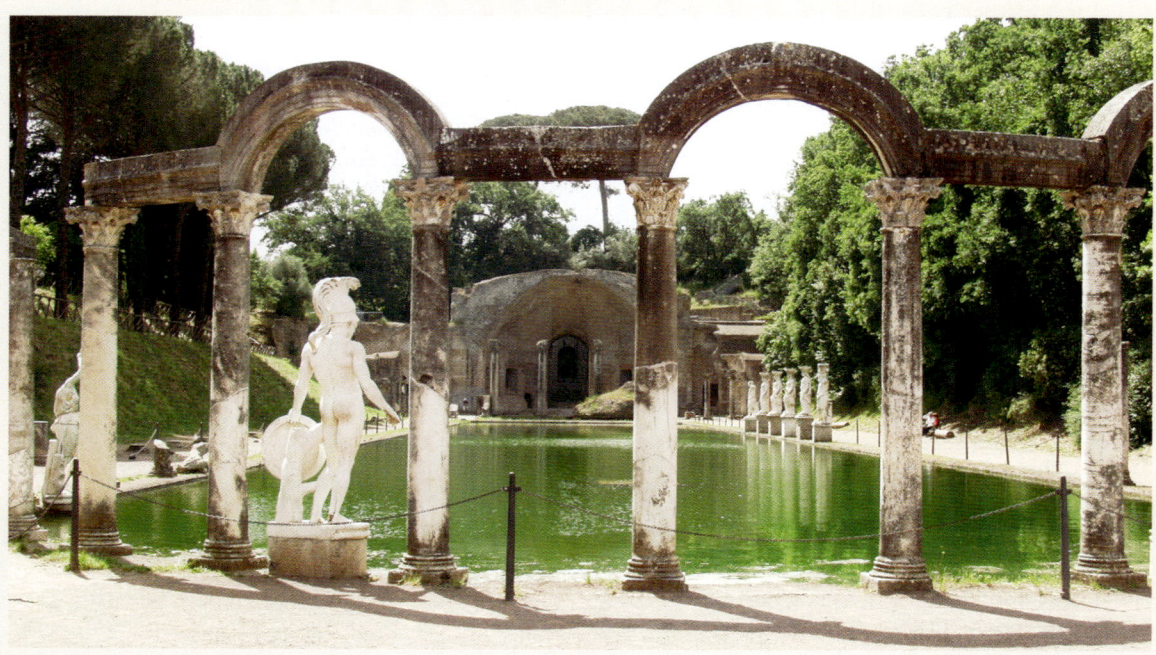

**7-52** Canopus and Serapeum, Hadrian's Villa, Tivoli, Italy, ca. 125–128 CE.

Hadrian was an architect and may have personally designed some buildings at his private villa at Tivoli. The Serapeum features the kind of pumpkin-shaped concrete dome the emperor favored.

**HADRIAN'S VILLA** Hadrian, the amateur architect, was not the designer of the Pantheon, but the emperor became deeply involved with the development of the country villa he owned at Tivoli. One of his projects there was the construction of a pool and an artificial grotto, called the Canopus and Serapeum (FIG. **7-52**), respectively. Canopus was an Egyptian city connected to Alexandria by a canal. Its most famous temple was dedicated to the god Serapis. Nothing about the Tivoli design, however, derives from Egyptian architecture. The grotto at the end of the pool is made of

concrete and has an unusual pumpkin-shaped dome Hadrian probably designed himself (see "Hadrian and Apollodorus of Damascus," above). Yet, in keeping with the persistent mixing of styles in Roman art and architecture as well as Hadrian's love of Greek art, traditional Greek columns and marble copies of famous Greek statues, including the Erechtheion caryatids (FIG. 5-54), lined the pool. The Corinthian colonnade at the curved end of the pool is, however, of a type unknown in Classical Greek architecture. The colonnade not only lacks a superstructure but has arcuated lintels, as

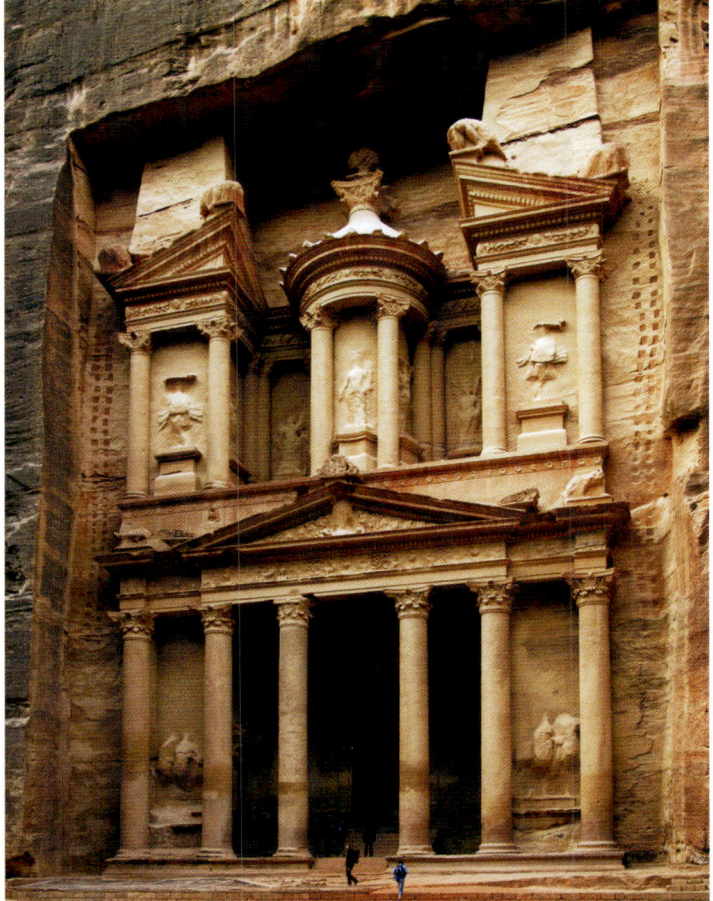

**7-53** Al-Khazneh (Treasury), Petra, Jordan, second century CE.

This rock-cut tomb facade is a prime example of Roman "baroque" architecture. The designer used Greek architectural elements in a purely ornamental fashion and with a studied disregard for Classical rules.

second-century CE tomb nicknamed Al-Khazneh, the "Treasury" (FIG. **7-53**), at Petra, Jordan. It is one of the most elaborate of many tomb facades cut into the sheer rock faces of the local rose-colored mountains. As at Hadrian's villa, the architect used Greek architectural elements in a purely ornamental fashion and with a studied disregard for Classical rules.

The Treasury's facade is more than 130 feet high and consists of two stories. The lower story resembles a temple facade with six columns, but the columns are unevenly spaced and the pediment is only wide enough to cover the four central columns. On the upper level, a temple-within-a-temple sits atop the lower temple. Here the facade and roof split in half to make room for a central tholoslike cylinder, which contrasts sharply with the rectangles and triangles of the rest of the design. On both levels, the rhythmic alternation of deep projection and indentation creates dynamic patterns of light and shadow. At Petra, as at Tivoli, the architect used the vocabulary of Greek architecture, but the syntax is new and distinctively Roman. In fact, the design recalls some of the architectural fantasies painted on the walls of Roman houses—for example, the tholos seen through columns surmounted by a broken pediment (FIG. 7-19, *right*) in the Second Style cubiculum from Boscoreale.

## Ostia

The average Roman, of course, did not own a luxurious country villa and was not buried in a grand tomb. About 90 percent of Rome's population of close to one million lived in multistory apartment blocks (*insulae*). After the great fire of 64 CE, these were brick-faced concrete buildings. The rents were not inexpensive, as the law of supply and demand in real estate was just as valid in antiquity as it is today. Juvenal, a Roman satirist of the early second century CE, commented that people willing to give up chariot races and the other diversions Rome had to offer could purchase a fine home in the countryside "for a year's rent in a dark hovel" in a city so noisy "the sick die mostly from lack of sleep."[2] Conditions were much the same for the inhabitants of Ostia, Rome's harbor city. After its new port opened under Trajan, Ostia's prosperity increased dramatically and so did its population. A burst of building activity began under Trajan and continued under Hadrian and throughout the second century CE.

**APARTMENT HOUSES** Ostia had many multistory insulae (FIG. **7-54**). Shops occupied the ground floors. Above were up to four floors of apartments. Although many of the apartments were large and had frescoed walls and ceilings, as in the aptly named

opposed to traditional Greek horizontal lintels, between alternating pairs of columns. This simultaneous respect for Greek architecture and willingness to break the rules of Greek design typifies much Roman architecture of the High and Late Empire.

**AL-KHAZNEH** An even more extreme example of what many have called Roman "baroque" architecture (because of the striking parallels with 17th-century Italian buildings; see Chapter 24) is the

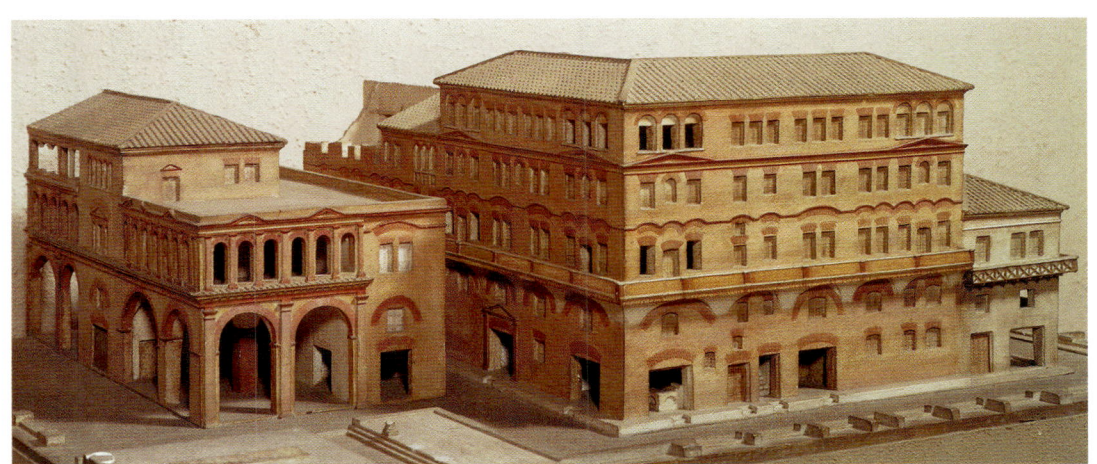

**7-54** Model of an insula, Ostia, Italy, second century CE. Museo della Civiltà Romana, Rome.

Rome and Ostia were densely populated cities, and most Romans lived in multistory brick-faced concrete insulae (apartment houses) with shops on the ground floor. Private toilet facilities were rare.

**7-55** Neptune and creatures of the sea, detail of a floor mosaic in the Baths of Neptune, Ostia, Italy, ca. 140 CE.

Black-and-white floor mosaics were popular during the second and third centuries CE. The artists conceived them as surface decorations, not as illusionistic compositions meant to rival paintings.

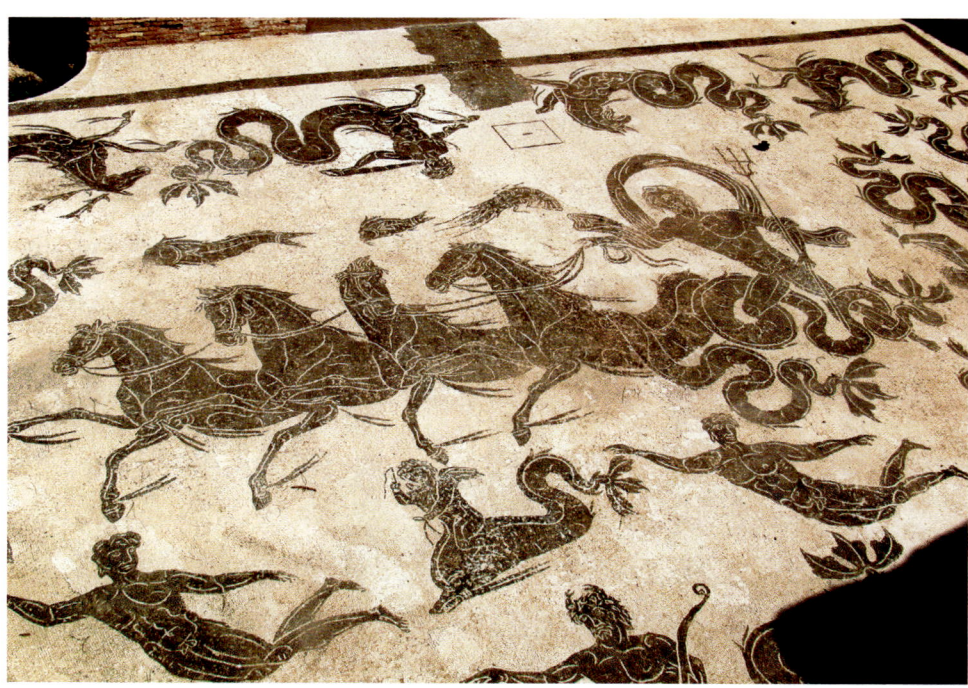

Insula of the Painted Vaults (FIG. 7-54A), they had neither the space nor the light of the typical Pompeian private domus (see "The Roman House," page 190). In place of peristyles, insulae had only narrow light wells or small courtyards. Consequently, instead of looking inward, large numbers of windows faced the city's noisy streets. The residents cooked their food in the hallways. Only deluxe apartments

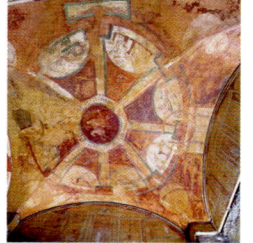

**7-54A** Insula of the Painted Vaults, Ostia, ca. 200–220 CE.

had private toilets. Others shared latrines, often on a different floor from their apartments. Still, these insulae were quite similar to modern apartment houses, which also sometimes have shops on the ground floor.

Another strikingly modern feature of these multifamily residences is their brick facades, which were not concealed by stucco or marble veneers. When builders desired to incorporate a Classical motif, they added brick pilasters or engaged columns but always left the brick exposed. Ostia and Rome have many examples of apartment houses, warehouses, and tombs with intricate moldings and contrasting colors of brick. In the second century CE, brick came to be appreciated as attractive in its own right.

**BATHS OF NEPTUNE** Although the decoration of Ostian insulae tended to be more modest than that of the private houses of Pompeii, the finer apartments had mosaic floors as well as painted walls and ceilings (FIG. 7-54A). The most popular choice for elegant pavements at Ostia in both private and public edifices was the black-and-white mosaic. One of the largest and best-preserved examples is in the Baths of Neptune, named for the grand mosaic floor (FIG. 7-55) showing four seahorses pulling the Roman god of the sea across the waves. Neptune needs no chariot to support him as he speeds along, his mantle blowing in the strong wind. All about the god are other sea denizens, positioned so that wherever a visitor enters the room, some figures appear right side up. The second-century artist rejected the complex polychrome modeling of figures seen in Pompeian mosaics such as the *Battle of Issus* (FIG. 5-70) and used simple black silhouettes enlivened by white interior lines—an approach to pictorial representation akin in many respects to Greek black-figure vase painting (FIG. 5-19, *bottom*). Like the Archaic Greek decorators of pots, the Roman mosaicists conceived their black-and-white designs as surface decorations, not as illusionistic windows onto a three-dimensional world, and thus they were especially appropriate for floors.

**ISOLA SACRA** The tombs in Ostia's Isola Sacra cemetery were not the final resting places of the very wealthy but communal houses

of the dead. Constructed of brick-faced concrete, these middle-class tombs resembled the multifamily insulae of the living. Small painted terracotta plaques immortalizing the activities of merchants and professional people frequently adorned the facades. A characteristic example (FIG. 7-56) depicts a vegetable seller behind a counter. The

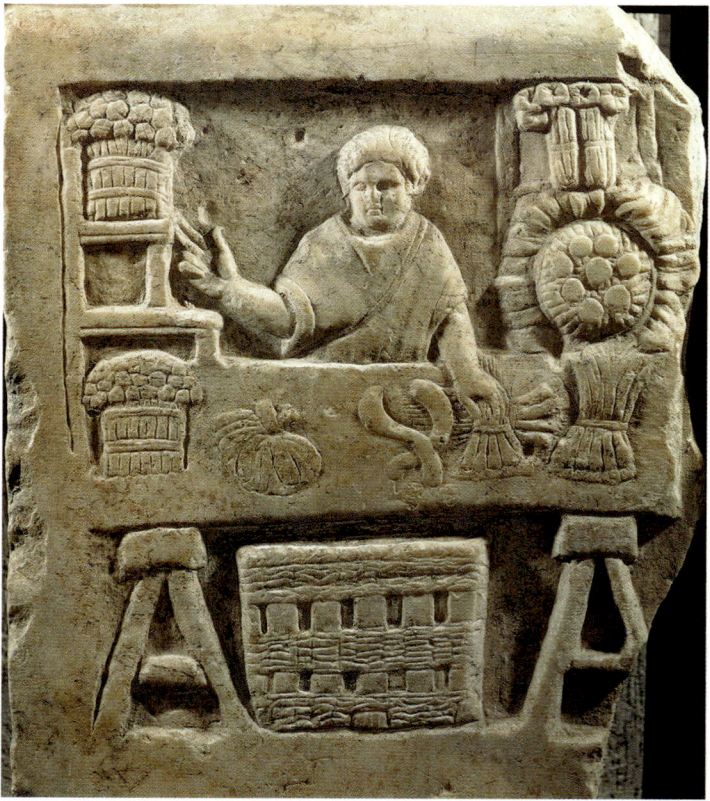

1 in.

**7-56** Funerary relief of a vegetable vendor, from Ostia, Italy, second half of second century CE. Painted terracotta, 1′ 5″ high. Museo Ostiense, Ostia.

Terracotta plaques illustrating the activities of middle-class merchants frequently adorned Ostian tomb facades. In this relief of a vegetable seller, the artist tilted the counter to display the produce clearly.

artist had little interest in the Classical-revival style the emperors favored and tilted the counter forward so the observer could see the produce clearly. Comparable scenes of daily life appear on Roman funerary reliefs throughout Europe. They were as much a part of the Roman artistic legacy to the later history of Western art as the emperors' monuments, which until recently were the almost exclusive interest of art historians.

## The Antonines

Early in 138 CE, Hadrian adopted the 51-year-old Antoninus Pius (r. 138–161 CE). At the same time, he required Antoninus to adopt Marcus Aurelius (r. 161–180 CE) and Lucius Verus (r. 161–169 CE),

thereby assuring a peaceful succession for at least another generation. When Hadrian died later in the year, the Senate proclaimed him a god, and Antoninus Pius became emperor. Antoninus ruled the Roman world with distinction for 23 years. After his death and deification, Marcus Aurelius and Lucius Verus became the Roman Empire's first coemperors.

**COLUMN OF ANTONINUS PIUS** Shortly after Antoninus Pius's death, Marcus and Lucius set up a memorial column in his honor. Its pedestal has a relief on one side illustrating the apotheosis of Antoninus and his wife, Faustina the Elder (FIG. **7-57**). On the adjacent sides are two identical representations of the *decursio* (FIG. **7-58**), or ritual circling of the imperial funerary pyre.

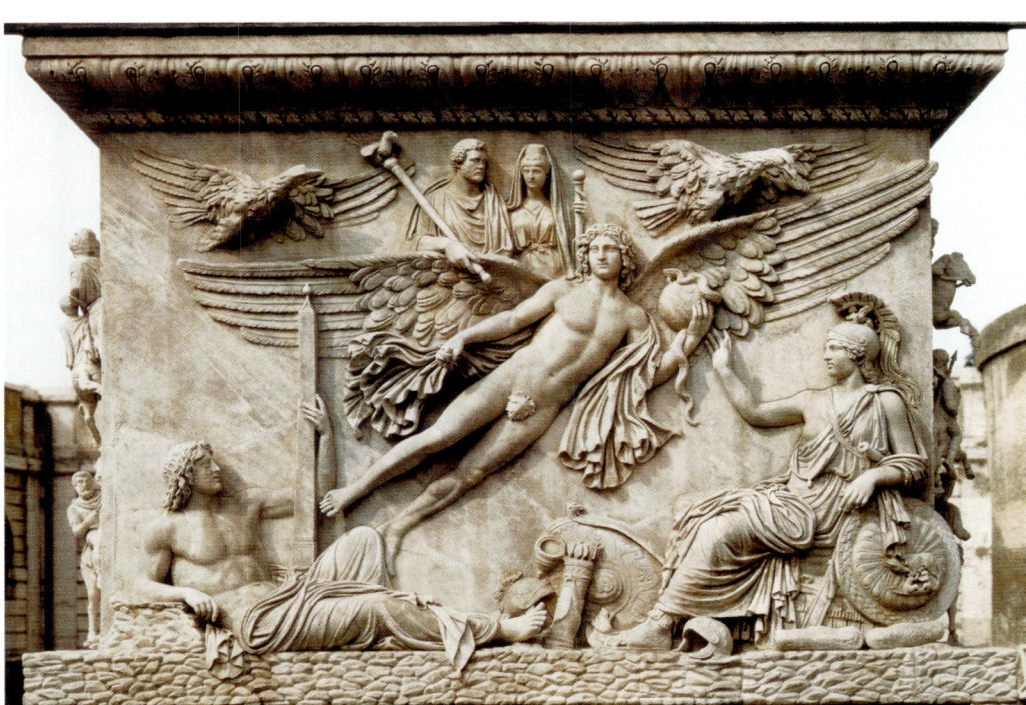

1 ft.

**7-57** Apotheosis of Antoninus Pius and Faustina, pedestal of the Column of Antoninus Pius, Rome, Italy, ca. 161 CE. Marble, 8′ 1½″ high. Musei Vaticani, Rome.

This representation of the joint apotheosis of Antoninus Pius and Faustina is firmly in the Classical tradition with its elegant, well-proportioned figures, personifications, and single ground line.

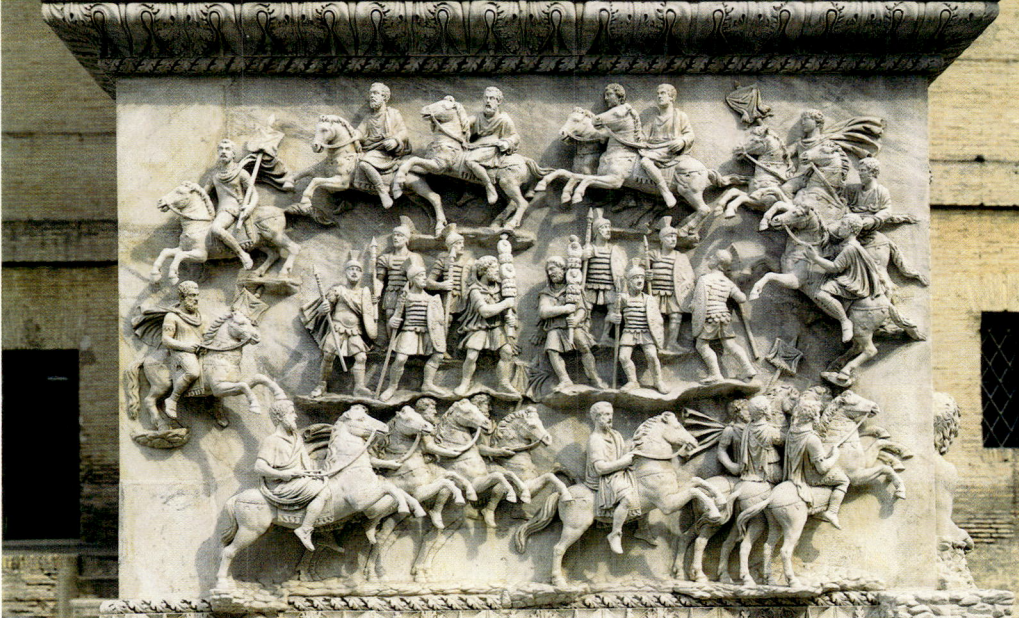

1 ft.

**7-58** Decursio, pedestal of the Column of Antoninus Pius, Rome, Italy, ca. 161 CE. Marble, 8′ 1½″ high. Musei Vaticani, Rome.

In contrast to FIG. 7-57, the Antonine decursio reliefs break sharply with Classical art conventions. The ground is the whole surface of the relief, and the figures stand on floating patches of earth.

The two figural compositions are very different. The apotheosis relief remains firmly in the Classical tradition with its elegant, well-proportioned figures, personifications, and single ground line corresponding to the panel's lower edge. The Campus Martius (Field of Mars), personified as a youth holding the Egyptian obelisk that stood in that area of Rome, reclines at the lower left corner. Roma (Rome personified) leans on a shield decorated with the she-wolf suckling Romulus and Remus (compare FIG. 6-11). Roma bids farewell to the couple being lifted into the realm of the gods on the wings of a personification of uncertain identity. Scenes of apotheosis (FIG. 7-40A) had been standard in imperial art since Augustus. New to the pictorial repertoire, however, was the fusion of time the joint apotheosis represents. Faustina had died 20 years before Antoninus Pius. By depicting the two as ascending together, the artist wished to suggest Antoninus had been faithful to his wife for two decades and now they would be reunited in the afterlife—a common conceit in Roman middle-class funerary art (FIG. 7-44A).

The decursio reliefs (FIG. 7-58) break even more strongly with Classical convention. The figures are much stockier than those in the apotheosis relief, and the sculptor did not conceive the panel as a window onto the world. The ground is the whole surface of the relief, and marching soldiers and galloping horses alike stand on floating patches of earth. This, too, had not occurred before in imperial art, only in the art of freedmen (FIG. 7-11A). After centuries of following the rules of Classical design, elite Roman artists and patrons finally became dissatisfied with them. When seeking a new direction, they adopted some of the non-Classical conventions of the art of freedmen.

**MARCUS AURELIUS** Another break with the past occurred in the official portraits of Marcus Aurelius, although his images retain the pompous trappings of imperial iconography. In a larger-than-life-size gilded-bronze equestrian statue (FIG. **7-59**), the emperor possesses a superhuman grandeur and is much larger than any normal human would be in relation to his horse. Marcus stretches out his right arm in a gesture that is both a greeting and an offer of clemency. Beneath the horse's raised right foreleg, an enemy once cowered, begging the emperor for mercy. The statue is a rare example of an imperial equestrian portrait, but the type was common in antiquity. For example, an equestrian statue of Trajan stood in the middle of his forum (FIG. 7-44, no. 6). Marcus's portrait survived the wholesale melting down of ancient bronze statues during the Middle Ages because it was mistakenly thought to portray Constantine, the first Christian emperor of Rome. Perhaps more than any other statuary type, the equestrian portrait expresses the Roman emperor's majesty and authority.

This message of supreme confidence is not, however, conveyed by the portrait head of Marcus's equestrian statue or any of the other portraits of the emperor in the years just before his death. Portraits of aged emperors were not new (FIG. 7-38), but Marcus's were the first ones in which a Roman emperor appeared weary, saddened, and even worried. For the first time, the strain of constant warfare on the frontiers and the burden of ruling a worldwide empire show in the emperor's face. The Antonine sculptor ventured beyond Republican verism, exposing the ruler's character, his thoughts, and his soul for all to see, as Marcus revealed them himself in his *Meditations,* a deeply moving philosophical treatise setting forth the emperor's personal worldview. This was a major turning point in the history of ancient art, and, coming as it did when relief sculptors were also challenging the Classical style (FIG. 7-58), it marked the beginning of the end of Classical art's domination in the Greco-Roman world.

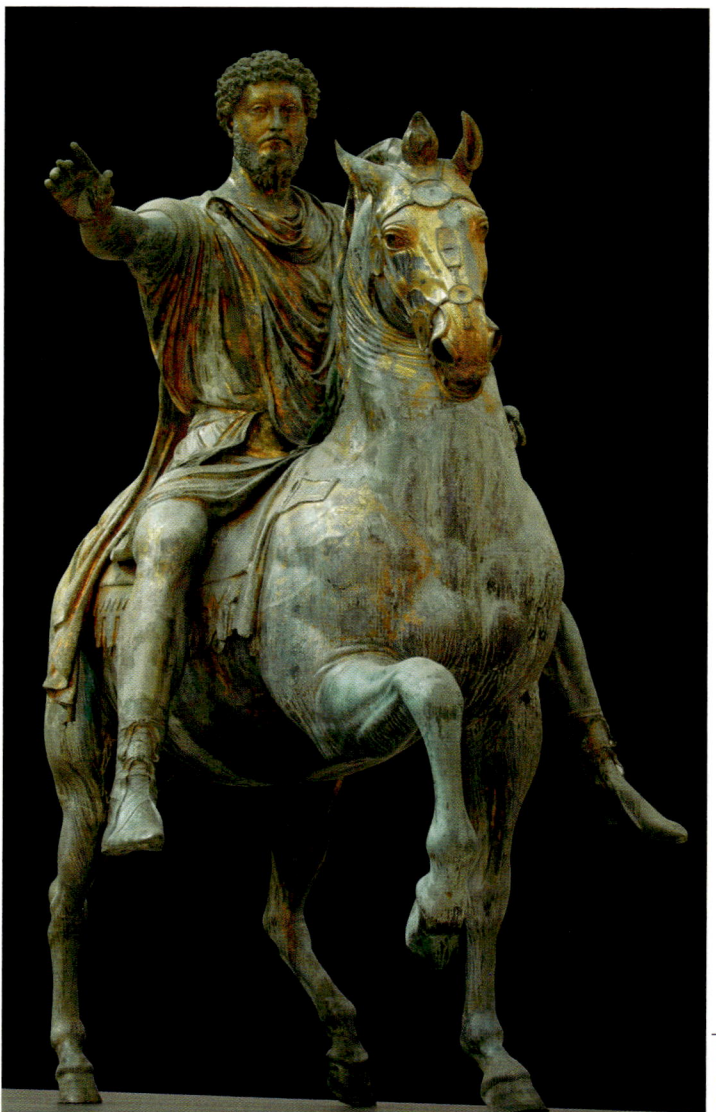

**7-59** Equestrian statue of Marcus Aurelius, from Rome, Italy, ca. 175 CE. Bronze, 11′ 6″ high. Musei Capitolini–Palazzo dei Conservatori, Rome. ◼◀

In this equestrian portrait of Marcus Aurelius as omnipotent conqueror, the emperor stretches out his arm in a gesture of clemency. An enemy once cowered beneath the horse's raised foreleg.

**FROM CREMATION TO BURIAL** Other profound changes were taking place in Roman art and society at this time. Under Trajan and Hadrian and especially during the rule of the Antonines, Romans began to favor burial over cremation. This reversal of funerary practices may reflect the influence of Christianity and other Eastern religions, whose adherents believed in an afterlife for the human body. Although the emperors themselves continued to be cremated in the traditional Roman manner, many private citizens opted for burial. Thus they required larger containers for their remains than the ash urns that were the norm until the second century CE. This in turn led to a sudden demand for sarcophagi, which are more similar to modern coffins than any other ancient type of burial container.

**ORESTES SARCOPHAGUS** Greek mythology was one of the most popular subjects for the decoration of these sarcophagi. In many cases, especially in the late second and third centuries CE, Roman men and women identified themselves on their coffins with

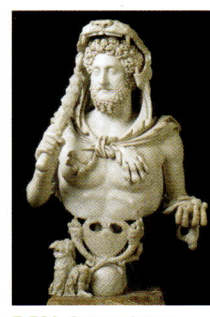

Greek heroes and heroines, whose heads often were portraits of the deceased. These private patrons were following the model of imperial portraiture, in which emperors and empresses frequently masqueraded as gods and goddesses and heroes and heroines (see "Role Playing in Roman Portraiture," page 198, and FIG. 7-59A, a portrait of Commodus, son and successor of Marcus Aurelius, in the guise of Hercules). An early example of the type (although it lacks any portraits) is a sarcophagus (FIG. 7-60) now in Cleveland, one of many decorated with the story of the tragic Greek hero Orestes. All the examples of this type use the same basic composition. Orestes appears more than once in every case. At the center of the Cleveland sarcophagus, Orestes slays his mother, Clytaemnestra, and her lover, Aegisthus, to avenge their murder of his father, Agamemnon, and then, at the right, takes refuge at Apollo's sanctuary at Delphi (symbolized by the god's tripod).

The repetition of sarcophagus compositions indicates Roman sculptors had access to pattern books. In fact, sarcophagus production was a major industry during the High and Late Empire. Several important regional manufacturing centers existed. The sarcophagi produced in the Latin West, such as the Cleveland Orestes sarcophagus, differ in format from those made in the Greek-speaking East. Western sarcophagi have reliefs only on the front and sides, because they were placed in floor-level niches inside Roman tombs. Eastern sarcophagi have reliefs on all four sides and stood in the center of the burial chamber. This contrast parallels the essential difference between the Etrusco-Roman and the Greek temple. The former was set against the wall of a forum or sanctuary and approached from the front, whereas the latter could be reached (and viewed) from every side.

**MELFI SARCOPHAGUS** An elaborate sarcophagus (FIG. 7-61) of the Eastern type found at Rapolla, near Melfi in southern Italy, but manufactured in Asia Minor, attests to the vibrant export market for these luxury items in Antonine times. The distinctively Asiatic decoration of all four sides of the marble box consists of statuesque images of Greek gods and heroes in architectural frames. The figures portrayed include Venus and the legendary beauty, Helen of Troy. The lid portrait, which carries on the tradition of Etruscan sarcophagi (FIGS. 6-5, 6-15, and 6-15A), is also a feature of the most expensive Western Roman coffins. Here, the deceased woman reclines on a *kline* (bed). With her are her faithful little dog (only its forepaws remain at the left end of the lid) and

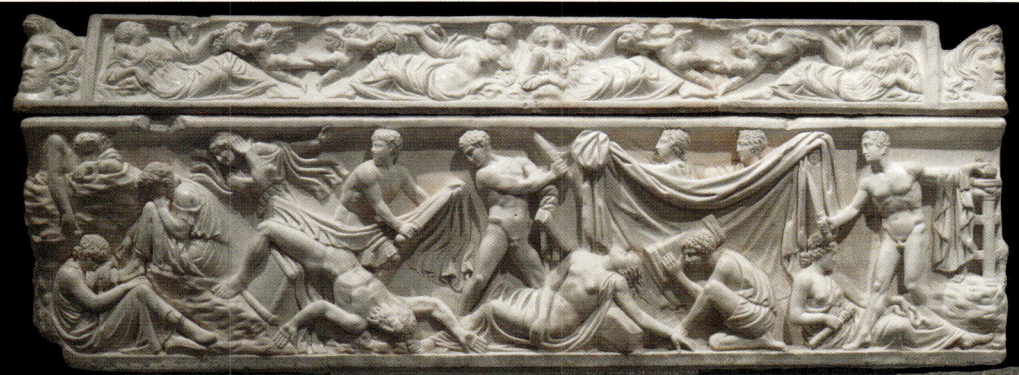

**7-60** Sarcophagus with the myth of Orestes, ca. 140–150 CE. Marble, 2′ 7½″ high. Cleveland Museum of Art, Cleveland.

Under the Antonines, Romans began to favor burial over cremation, and sarcophagi became very popular. Themes from Greek mythology, like the tragic saga of Orestes, were common subjects.

1 ft.

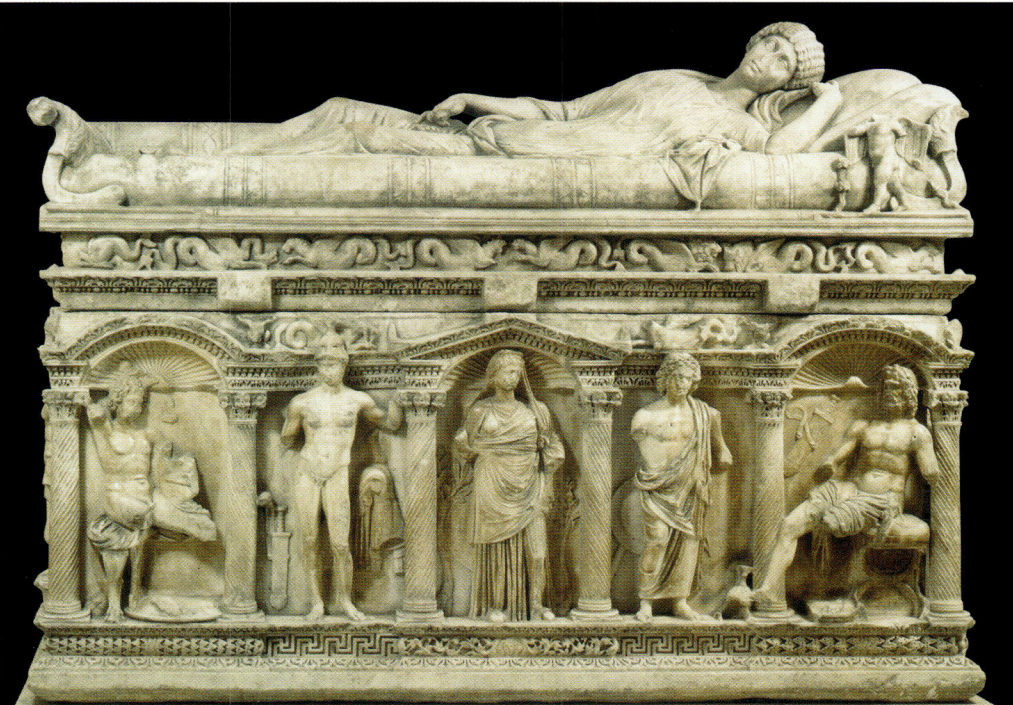

**7-61** Asiatic sarcophagus with kline portrait of a woman, from Rapolla, near Melfi, Italy, ca. 165–170 CE. Marble, 5′ 7″ high. Museo Nazionale Archeologico del Melfese, Melfi.

The Romans produced sarcophagi in several regions. Western sarcophagi have carvings only on the front. Eastern sarcophagi, such as this one with a woman's portrait on the lid, feature reliefs on all four sides.

1 ft.

## Iaia of Cyzicus and the Art of Encaustic Painting

The names of very few Roman artists survive. Those that do tend to be names of artists and architects who directed major imperial building projects (Severus and Celer, Domus Aurea; Apollodorus of Damascus, Forum of Trajan), worked on a gigantic scale (Zenodorus, Colossus of Nero), or made precious objects for famous patrons (Dioscurides, gem cutter for Augustus).

An interesting exception to this rule is IAIA OF CYZICUS. Pliny the Elder reported the following about this renowned painter from Asia Minor who worked in Italy during the Republic:

> Iaia of Cyzicus, who remained a virgin all her life, painted at Rome during the time when M. Varro [116–27 BCE; a renowned Republican scholar and author] was a youth, both with a brush and with a cestrum on ivory, specializing mainly in portraits of women; she also painted a large panel in Naples representing an old woman and a portrait of herself done with a mirror. Her hand was quicker than that of any other painter, and her artistry was of such high quality that she commanded much higher prices than the most celebrated painters of the same period.*

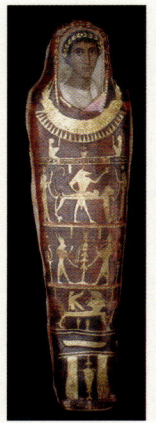

7-62A Mummy of Artemidorus, ca. 100–120 CE.

The *cestrum* Pliny mentioned is a small spatula used in *encaustic* painting, a technique of mixing colors with hot wax and then applying them to the surface. Pliny knew of encaustic paintings of considerable antiquity, including those of Polygnotos of Thasos (see page 143). The best evidence for the technique comes, however, from Roman Egypt, where mummy cases (FIG. 7-62A) routinely incorporated encaustic portraits on wood panels (FIGS. 7-62 and 7-62B).

Artists applied encaustic to marble (FIG. 5-63A) as well as to wood. According to Pliny, when Praxiteles was asked which of his statues he preferred, the fourth-century BCE Greek artist, perhaps the ancient world's greatest marble sculptor, replied: "Those that Nikias painted."† This anecdote underscores the importance of coloration in ancient statuary.

*Pliny the Elder, *Natural History*, 35.147–148. Translated by J. J. Pollitt, *The Art of Rome, c. 753 B.C.–A.D. 337: Sources and Documents* (New York: Cambridge University Press, 1983), 87.
†Pliny the Elder, *Natural History*, 35.133.

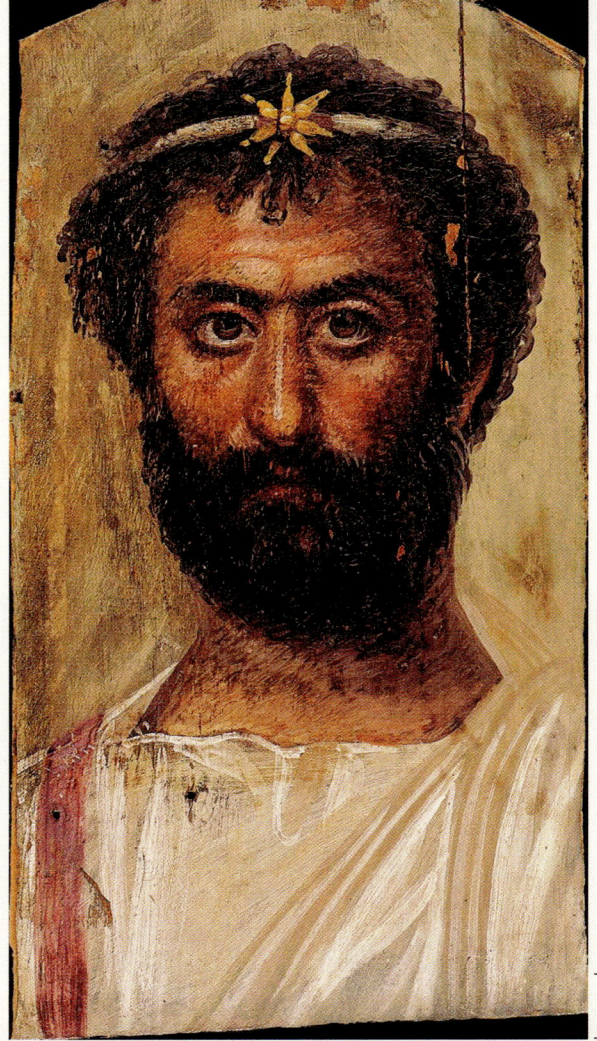

1 in.

**7-62** Mummy portrait of a priest of Serapis, from Hawara (Faiyum), Egypt, ca. 140–160 CE. Encaustic on wood, 1′ 4¾″ × 8¾″. British Museum, London.

In Roman times, the Egyptians continued to bury their dead in mummy cases, but painted portraits replaced the traditional masks. The painting medium is encaustic—colors mixed with hot wax.

---

Cupid (at the right). The winged infant god mournfully holds a downturned torch, a reference to the death of a woman whose beauty rivaled that of his mother, Venus, and of Homer's Helen.

**MUMMY PORTRAITS** In Egypt, burial had been practiced for millennia. Even after Augustus reduced the Kingdom of the Nile to a Roman province in 30 BCE, Egyptians continued to bury their dead in mummy cases (see "Mummification," Chapter 3, page 61). In Roman times, however, painted portraits on wood often replaced the traditional stylized portrait masks (see "Iaia of Cyzicus and the Art of Encaustic Painting," above). Hundreds of Roman mummy portraits (FIGS. **7-62, 7-62A,** and **7-62B**) have been unearthed in the cemeteries of the Faiyum district. One example

(FIG. 7-62) depicts a priest of the Egyptian god Serapis. His curly hair and beard closely emulate the Antonine fashion in Rome, but the corkscrew curls of hair on the forehead are distinctive to images of Serapis and his followers. The priest's portrait exhibits the painter's refined use of the brush and spatula, mastery of the depiction of varied textures and of the play of light over the soft and delicately modeled face, and sensitive portrayal of the deceased's calm demeanor. The Faiyum mummies enable art historians to trace the evolution of portrait painting (FIGS. 7-25 and 7-25A) after Mount Vesuvius erupted in 79 CE.

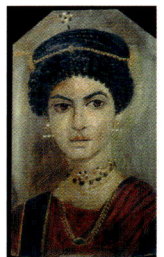

**7-62B** Young woman, Hawara, ca. 110–120 CE.

# LATE EMPIRE

By the time of Marcus Aurelius, two centuries after Augustus established the Pax Romana, Roman power was beginning to erode. It was increasingly difficult to keep order on the frontiers, and even within the Empire many challenged the authority of Rome. The assassination of Marcus's son Commodus (FIG. 7-59A) in 192 CE brought the Antonine dynasty to an end. The economy was in decline, and the efficient imperial bureaucracy was disintegrating. Even the official state religion was losing ground to Eastern cults, Christianity among them. The Late Empire was a pivotal era in world history during which the pagan ancient world gradually gave way to the Christian Middle Ages.

## The Severans

Civil conflict followed Commodus's death. When it ended, an African-born general named Septimius Severus (r. 193–211 CE) was master of the Roman world. He succeeded in establishing a new dynasty that ruled the Empire for nearly a half century.

SEVERAN PORTRAITURE Anxious to establish his legitimacy after the civil war, Septimius Severus adopted himself into the Antonine dynasty, declaring he was Marcus Aurelius's son. It is not surprising, then, that official portraits of the emperor in bronze and marble depict him with the long hair and beard of his Antonine "father"—whatever Severus's actual appearance may have been. That is also how he appears in the only preserved painted portrait (FIG. 7-63) of an emperor. Discovered in Egypt and painted in *tempera* (pigments in egg yolk) on wood (as were many of the mummy portraits from Faiyum), the portrait is of *tondo* (circular) format. It shows Severus with his wife, Julia Domna, the daughter of a Syrian priest, and their two sons, Caracalla and Geta. Painted likenesses of

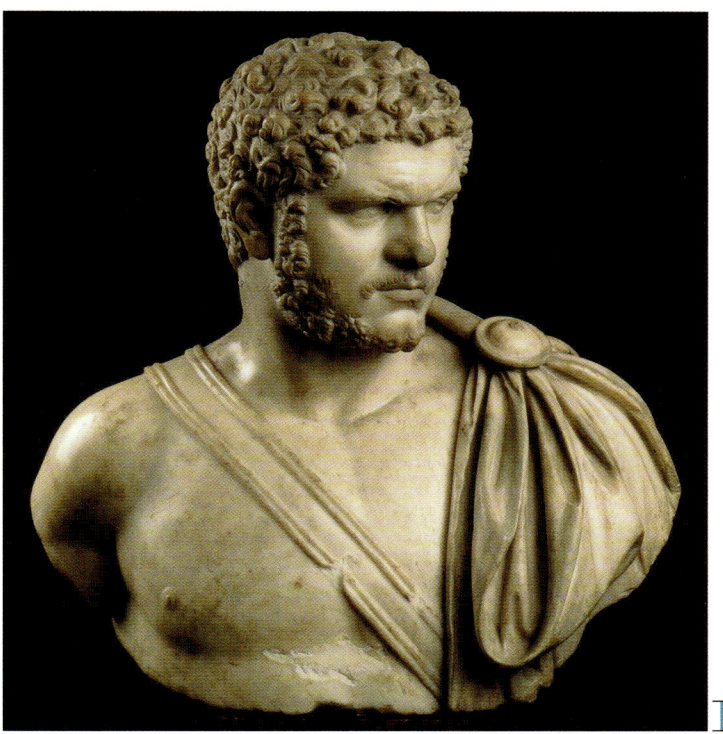

**7-64** Bust of Caracalla, ca. 211–217. Marble, 1′ 10¾″ high. Staatliche Museen, Antikensammlung, Berlin.

Caracalla's portraits introduced a new fashion in male coiffure but are more remarkable for the dramatic turn of the emperor's head and the moving characterization of his personality.

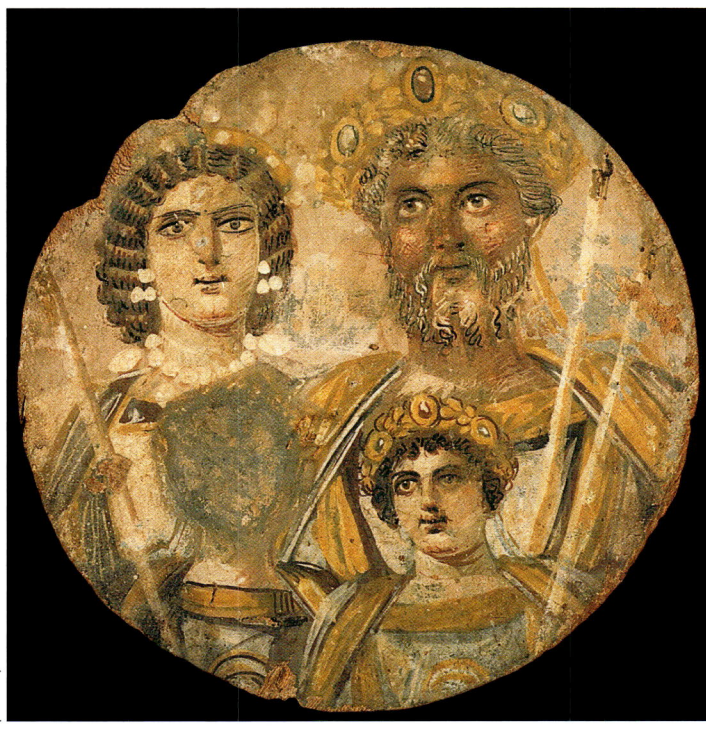

1 in.

**7-63** Painted portrait of Septimius Severus and his family, from Egypt, ca. 200 CE. Tempera on wood, 1′ 2″ diameter. Staatliche Museen, Berlin.

The only known painted portrait of an emperor shows Septimius Severus with gray hair. With him are his wife, Julia Domna, and their two sons, but Geta's head was removed after his damnatio memoriae.

the imperial family must have been quite common in Italy and the provinces, but their perishable nature explains their almost total loss.

The Severan family portrait is of special interest for two reasons beyond its survival. Severus's hair is tinged with gray, suggesting his marble portraits—which, like all marble sculptures in antiquity, were painted—also may have revealed his advancing age in this way. (The same was very likely true of the marble likenesses of the elderly Marcus Aurelius.) The group portrait is also notable because of the erasure of Geta's face. When Caracalla (r. 211–217 CE) succeeded his father as emperor, he had his younger brother murdered and ordered the Senate to damn Geta's memory. (Caracalla also ordered the death of his wife, Plautilla.) The Severan family portrait is an eloquent testimony to that *damnatio memoriae* and to the long arm of Roman authority, which reached all the way to Egypt in this case. This kind of defacement of a rival's image is not unique to ancient Rome, but the Roman government employed damnatio memoriae as a political tool more often and more systematically than any other civilization.

CARACALLA In the Severan painted tondo, the artist portrayed Caracalla as a boy with long, curly Antonine hair. The portraits of Caracalla as emperor are very different. In a bust (FIG. 7-64) in Berlin, Caracalla appears in heroic nudity save for a mantle over one shoulder and a sword sheath across his chest. His hair and beard, although still curly, are much shorter (compare FIG. 7-64A)—initiating a new fashion in male coiffure during the third century CE. More remarkable, however, is the moving characterization of Caracalla's personality, a further development from the groundbreaking introspection of the portraits of Marcus Aurelius. Caracalla's brow is knotted, and he abruptly turns his head over his

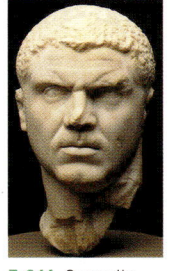

**7-64A** Caracalla, ca. 211–217 CE.

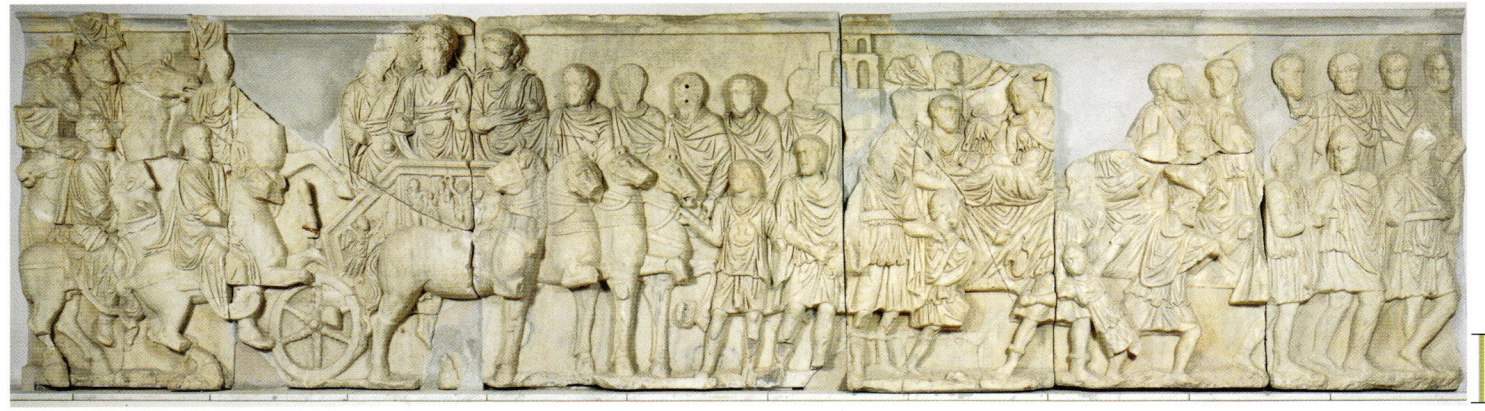

**7-65** Chariot procession of Septimius Severus, relief from the attic of the Arch of Septimius Severus, Lepcis Magna, Libya, 203 CE. Marble, 5′ 6″ high. Castle Museum, Tripoli.

A new non-naturalistic aesthetic emerged in later Roman art. In this relief from a triumphal arch, Septimius Severus and his two sons face the viewer even though their chariot is moving to the right.

left shoulder. The sculptor probably intended the facial expression and the dramatic movement to suggest energy and strength, but it appears to the viewer as if Caracalla suspects danger from behind. The emperor had reason to be fearful. An assassin's dagger felled him in the sixth year of his rule. Assassination would be the fate of many Roman emperors during the turbulent third century CE.

**LEPCIS MAGNA** The hometown of the Severans was Lepcis Magna, on the coast of what is now Libya. In the late second and early third centuries CE, the Severans constructed a modern harbor there, as well as a new forum, basilica, arch, and other monuments. The rebuilt Arch of Septimius Severus has friezes on the attic on all four sides. One (FIG. **7-65**) depicts the chariot procession of the emperor and his two sons on the occasion of their homecoming in 203. Unlike the triumph panel (FIG. 7-42) on the Arch of Titus in Rome, this relief gives no sense of rushing motion. Rather, it has a stately stillness. The chariot and the horsemen behind it move forward, but the emperor and his sons are frozen in place and face the viewer. Also different is the way the figures in the second row, whether on horseback or on foot, have no connection with the ground. The sculptor elevated them above the heads of those in the first row so they could be seen more clearly.

Both the frontality and the floating figures were new to official Roman art in Antonine and Severan times, but both appeared long before in the private art of freed slaves (FIGS. 7-11 and 7-11A). Once sculptors in the emperor's employ embraced these non-Classical elements, they had a long afterlife, largely (although never totally) displacing the Classical style the Romans adopted from Greece. As is often true in the history of art, the emergence of a new aesthetic was a by-product of a period of social, political, and economic upheaval. Art historians call this new non-naturalistic, more abstract style the Late Antique style.

**BATHS OF CARACALLA** The Severans were also active builders in the capital. The Baths of Caracalla (FIG. **7-66**) in Rome were the greatest in a long line of bathing and recreational complexes constructed with imperial funds to win the public's favor. Caracalla's baths dwarfed the typical baths of cities and towns such as Ostia and Pompeii. All the rooms had thick brick-faced concrete walls up to 140 feet high covered by enormous concrete vaults. The design was symmetrical along a central axis, facilitating the Roman custom of taking sequential plunges in warm-, hot-, and cold-water

baths in, respectively, the *tepidarium, caldarium,* and *frigidarium.* The caldarium (FIG. 7-66, no. 4) was a huge circular chamber with a concrete drum even taller than the Pantheon's (FIGS. 7-49 to 7-51) and a dome almost as large. Caracalla's Baths also had landscaped gardens, lecture halls, libraries, colonnaded exercise courts (*palaestras*), and a giant swimming pool (*natatio*). The entire complex covered an area of almost 50 acres. Archaeologists estimate that up to 1,600 bathers at a time could enjoy this Roman equivalent of a modern health spa. A branch of one of the city's major aqueducts supplied water, and furnaces circulated hot air through hollow floors and walls throughout the bathing rooms.

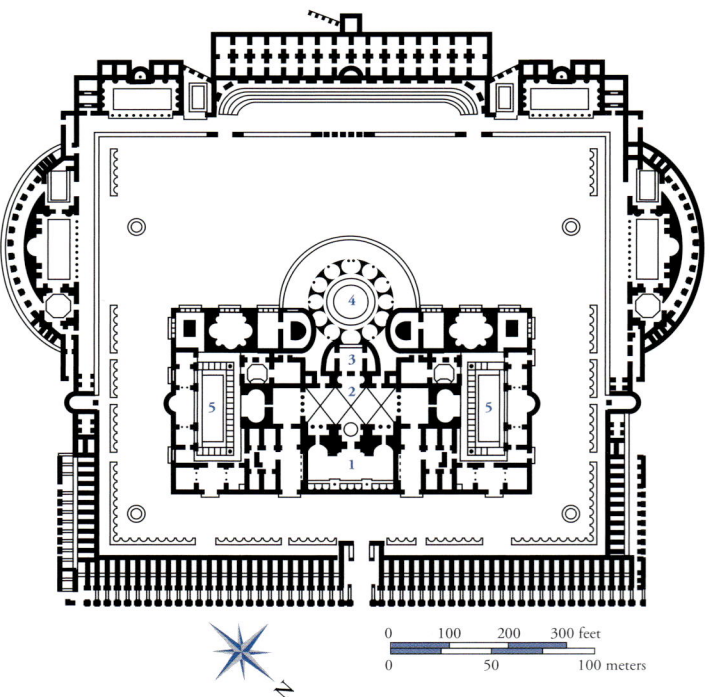

**7-66** Plan of the Baths of Caracalla, Rome, Italy, 212–216 CE. (1) natatio, (2) frigidarium, (3) tepidarium, (4) caldarium, (5) palaestra.

Caracalla's baths could accommodate 1,600 bathers. They resembled a modern health spa and included libraries, lecture halls, and exercise courts in addition to bathing rooms and a swimming pool.

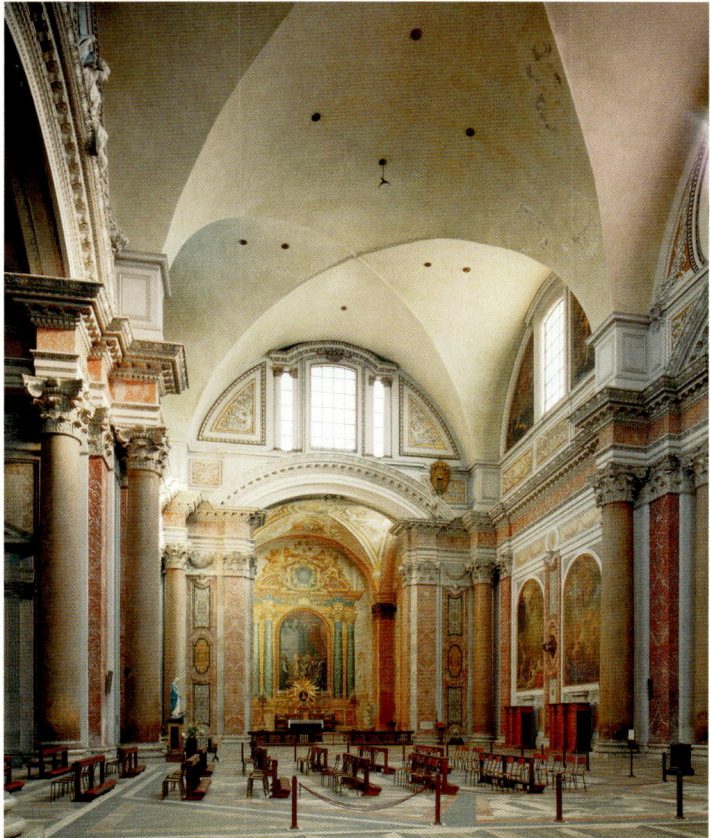

**7-67** Frigidarium, Baths of Diocletian, Rome, ca. 298–306 (remodeled by MICHELANGELO BUONARROTI as the nave of Santa Maria degli Angeli, 1563).

The groin-vaulted nave of the church of Santa Maria degli Angeli in Rome was once the frigidarium of the Baths of Diocletian. It gives an idea of the lavish adornment of imperial Roman baths.

The Baths of Caracalla also featured stuccoed vaults, mosaic floors (both black-and-white and polychrome), marble-faced walls, and marble statuary. One of the statues on display was the 10-foot-tall marble version of Lysippos's Herakles (FIG. 5-66), whose muscular body must have inspired Romans to exercise vigorously. The concrete vaults of the Baths of Caracalla collapsed long ago, but visitors can approximate the original appearance of the central bathing hall, the frigidarium, by entering the nave (FIG. 7-67) of the church of Santa Maria degli Angeli in Rome, which was once the frigidarium of the later Baths of Diocletian. The Renaissance interior (remodeled in the 18th century) of that church has, of course, many features foreign to a Roman bath, including a painted altarpiece. The ancient mosaics and marble revetment are long gone, but the present-day interior with its rich wall treatment, colossal columns with Composite capitals, immense groin vaults, and clerestory lighting provides a better sense of what it was like to be in a Roman imperial bathing complex than does any other building in the world. It takes a powerful imagination to visualize the original appearance of Roman concrete buildings from the pathetic ruins of brick-faced walls and fallen vaults at ancient sites today, but Santa Maria degli Angeli makes the task much easier.

## The Soldier Emperors

The Severan dynasty ended with the murder of Severus Alexander (r. 222–235 CE). The next half century was one of almost continuous civil war. The Roman legions declared one general after another emperor, only to have each murdered in turn by another general a few years or even a few months later. (In the year 238, two coemperors selected by the Senate were dragged from the imperial palace and murdered in public after only three months in office.) In such unstable times, no emperor could begin ambitious architectural projects. The only significant building activity in Rome during the era of the "soldier emperors" occurred under Aurelian (r. 270–275 CE). He constructed a new defensive circuit wall for the capital—a military necessity and a poignant commentary on the decay of Roman power.

**TRAJAN DECIUS** If architects went hungry in third-century Rome, engravers and sculptors had much to do. The mint produced great quantities of coins (in debased metal) so that the troops could be paid with money stamped with the current emperor's portrait and not with the likeness of his predecessor or rival. Each new ruler set up portrait statues and busts everywhere to assert his authority. The sculpted portraits of the third century CE are among the most moving ever made, as notable for their emotional content as they are for their technical virtuosity. Portraits of Trajan Decius (r. 249–251 CE), such as the marble bust illustrated here (FIG. 7-68), show

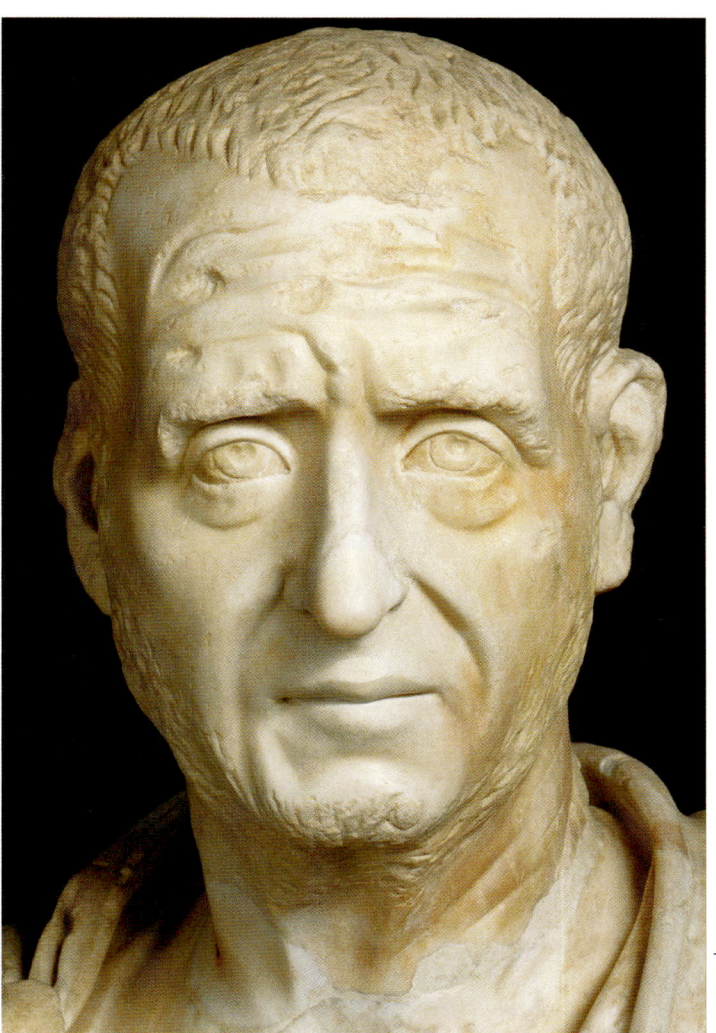

1 in.

**7-68** Portrait bust of Trajan Decius, 249–251 CE. Marble, full bust 2′ 7″ high. Museo Capitolino, Rome.

This portrait of a short-lived soldier emperor depicts an older man with bags under his eyes and a sad expression. The eyes glance away nervously, reflecting the anxiety of an insecure ruler.

the emperor—best known for persecuting Christians—as an old man with bags under his eyes and a sad expression. The eyes glance away nervously rather than engage the viewer directly, revealing the anxiety of a man who knows he can do little to restore order to an out-of-control world. The sculptor modeled the marble as if it were pliant clay, compressing the sides of the head at the level of the eyes, etching the hair and beard into the stone, and chiseling deep lines in the forehead and around the mouth. The portrait reveals the anguished soul of the man—and of the times.

**TREBONIANUS GALLUS** Portraits of Decius's short-lived predecessor, Philip the Arabian (r. 244–249 CE), and successor, Trebonianus Gallus (r. 251–253 CE), also have survived. Philip's busts (FIG. **7-68A**) are marble and typical of the era, but the portrait of Trebonianus illustrated here (FIG. **7-69**) is a larger-than-life-size bronze statue. Trebonianus appears in heroic nudity, as had so many emperors and generals before him. His physique, however, is not that of the strong but graceful Greek athletes Augustus and his successors admired so much. Instead, his is a wrestler's body with massive legs and a swollen trunk. The heavyset body dwarfs the head, with its nervous expression. In this portrait, the Greek ideal of the keen mind in the harmoniously proportioned body gave way to an image of brute force—an image well suited to the age of the soldier emperors.

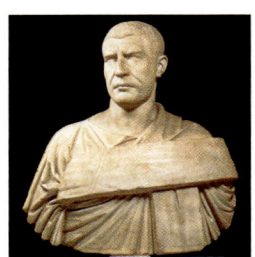

7-68A Philip the Arabian, 244–249 CE.

*LUDOVISI BATTLE SARCOPHAGUS* By the third century, burial of the dead had become so widespread that even the imperial family practiced it in place of cremation. Sarcophagi were more popular than ever. An unusually large sarcophagus (FIG. **7-70**), discovered in Rome in 1621 and purchased by Cardinal Ludovisi, is decorated on the front with a chaotic scene of battle between Romans and one of their northern foes, probably the Goths. The sculptor spread the writhing and highly emotive figures evenly across the entire relief, with no illusion of space behind them. This piling of figures is an even more extreme rejection of Classical perspective than was the use of floating ground lines in the decursio panel (FIG. 7-58) of the Column of Antoninus Pius. It underscores the increasing dissatisfaction of Late Antique artists with the Classical style.

Within this dense mass of intertwined bodies, the central horseman stands out vividly. He wears no helmet and thrusts out his open right hand to demonstrate he holds no weapon. Several scholars have identified him as one of the sons of Trajan Decius. In an age when the Roman army was far from invincible and Roman emperors were constantly felled by other Romans, the young general on the *Ludovisi Battle Sarcophagus* boasts that he is a fearless commander assured of victory. His self-assurance may stem from his having embraced one of the increasingly popular Oriental mystery religions. On the youth's forehead, the sculptor carved the emblem of Mithras, the Persian god of light, truth, and victory over death.

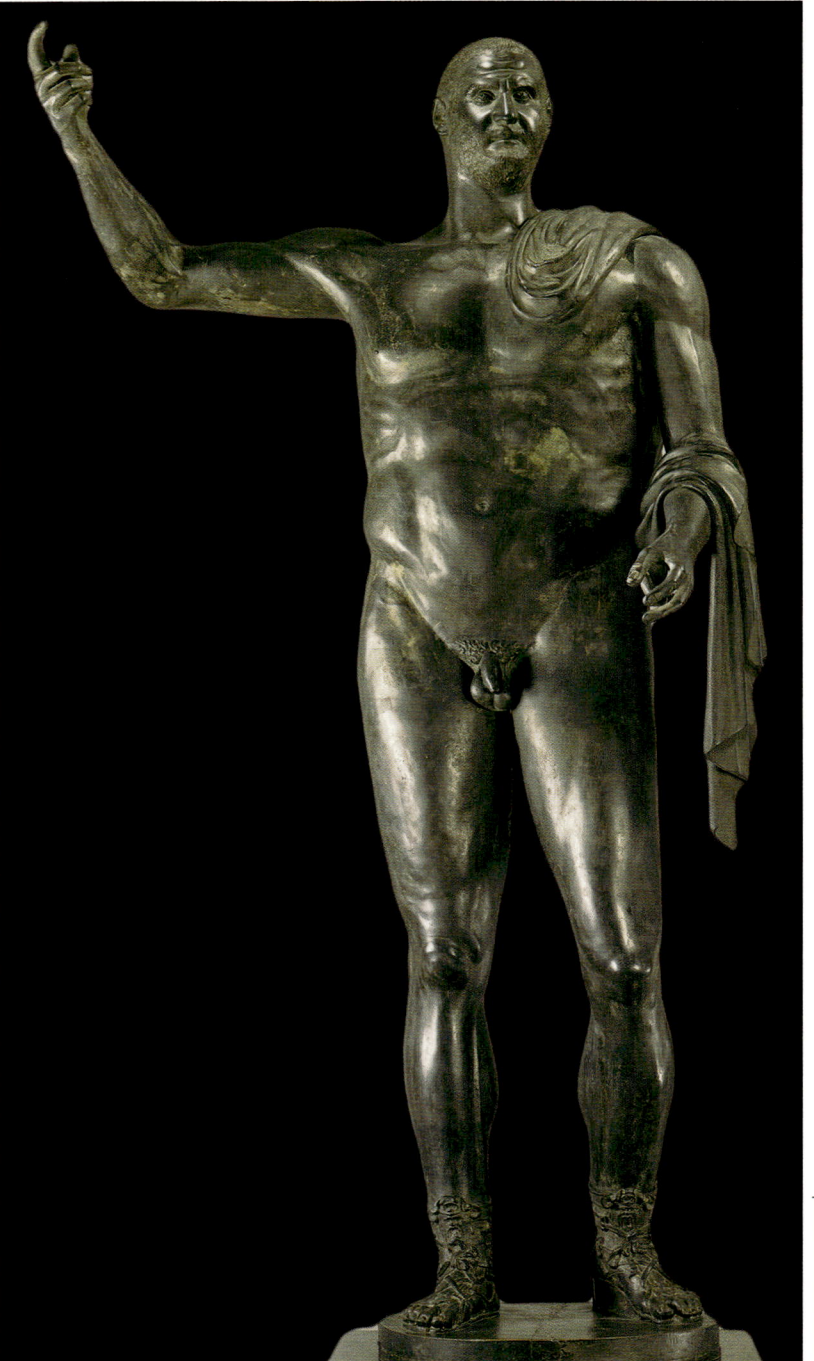

**7-69** Heroic portrait of Trebonianus Gallus, from Rome, Italy, 251–253 CE. Bronze, 7′ 11″ high. Metropolitan Museum of Art, New York.

In this over-life-size heroically nude statue, Trebonianus Gallus projects an image of brute force. He has the massive physique of a powerful wrestler, but his face expresses nervousness.

**PHILOSOPHER SARCOPHAGUS** The insecurity of the times led some Romans to seek solace in philosophy. On many third-century sarcophagi, the deceased assumed the role of the learned intellectual. One especially large example depicts a seated Roman philosopher holding a scroll (FIG. **7-71**). Two standing women (also with portrait features) gaze at him from left and right, confirming his importance. In the background are other philosophers, students or colleagues of the central deceased teacher. The two women may be the deceased's wife and daughter, two sisters,

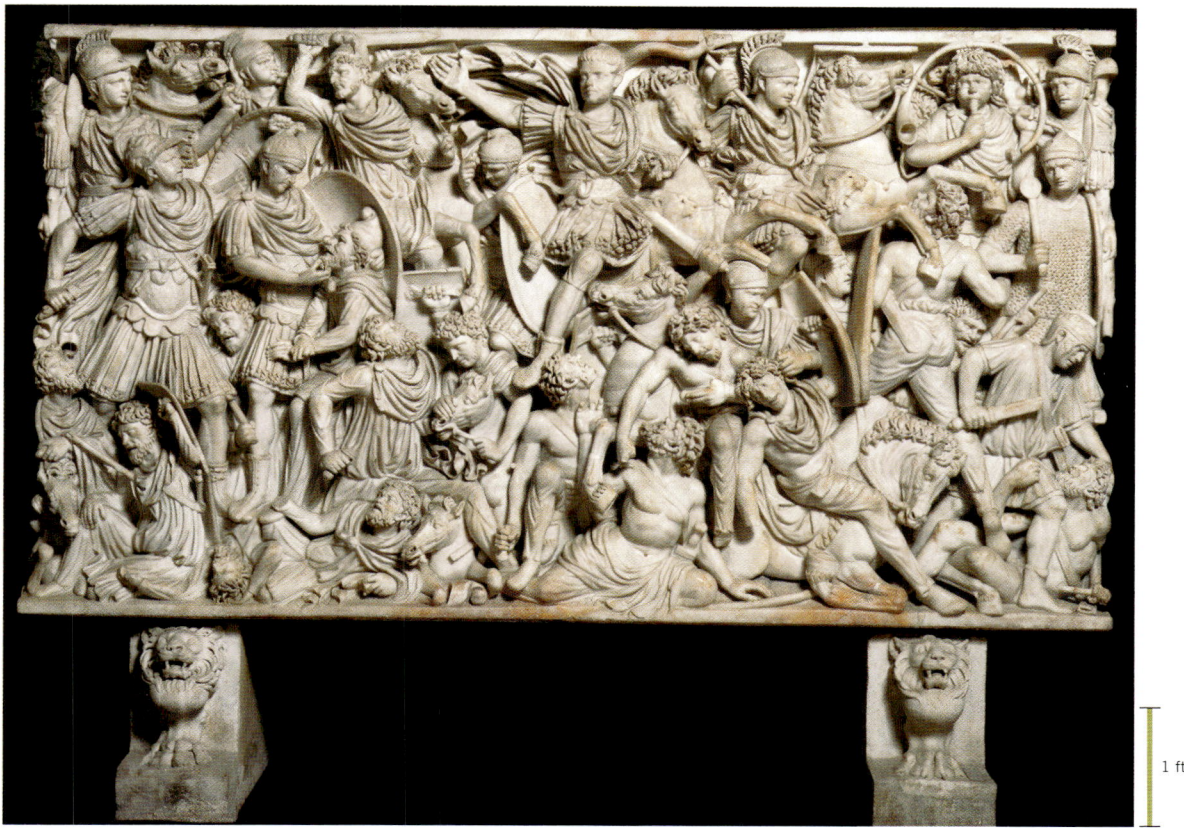

**7-70** Battle of Romans and barbarians (*Ludovisi Battle Sarcophagus*), from Rome, Italy, ca. 250–260 CE. Marble, 5′ high. Museo Nazionale Romano—Palazzo Altemps, Rome.

A chaotic scene of battle between Romans and barbarians decorates the front of this sarcophagus. The sculptor piled up the writhing, emotive figures in an emphatic rejection of Classical perspective.

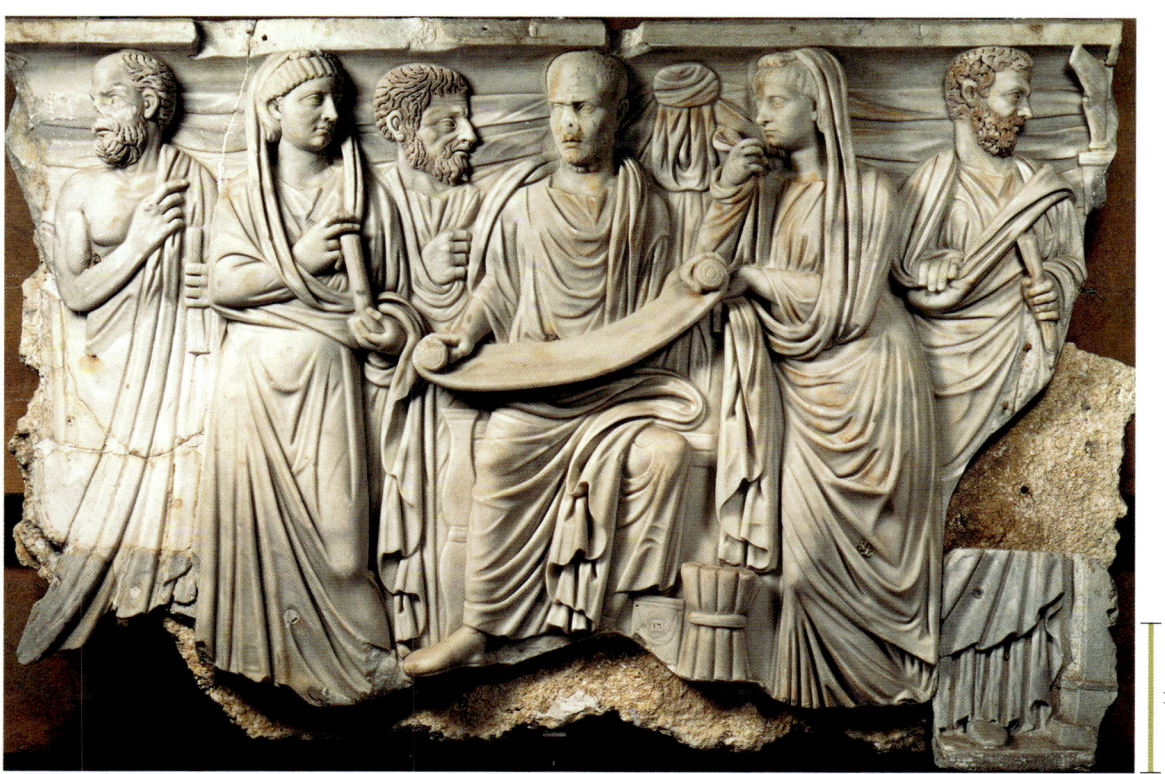

**7-71** Sarcophagus of a philosopher, ca. 270–280 CE. Marble, 4′ 11″ high. Musei Vaticani, Rome.

On many third-century CE sarcophagi, the deceased appears as a learned intellectual. Here, the seated philosopher is the central frontal figure. His two female muses also have portrait features.

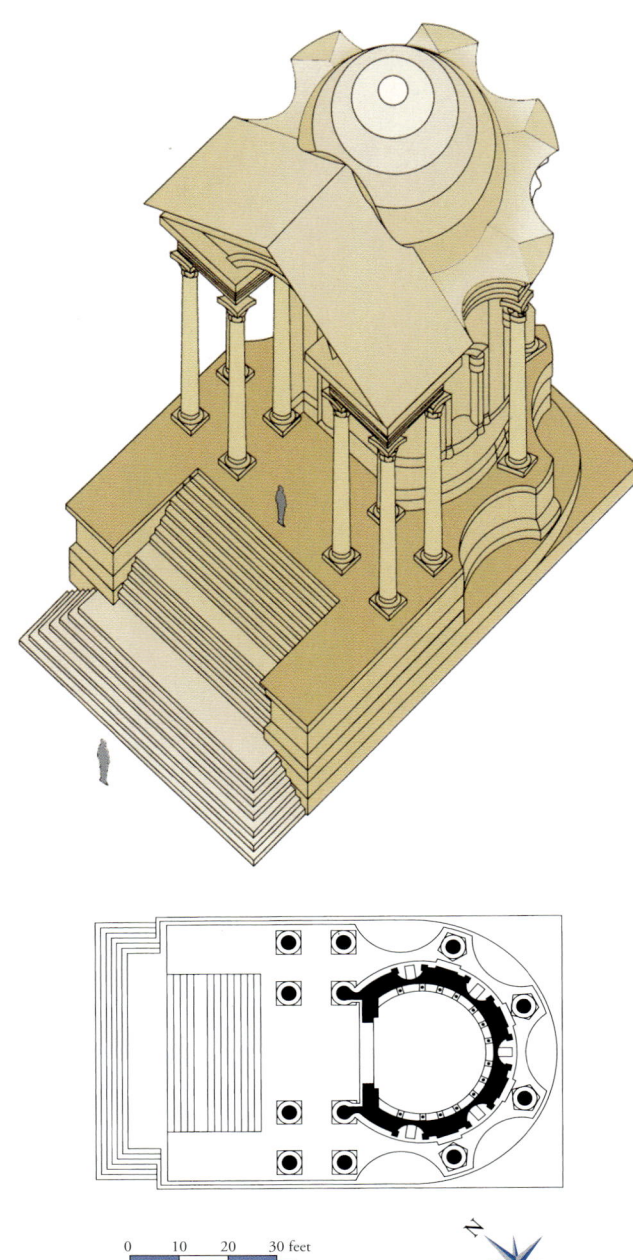

every rule of Classical design. Although made of stone, the building, with its circular domed cella set behind a gabled columnar facade, is in many ways a critique of the concrete Pantheon (FIG. 7-49), which by then had achieved the status of a "classic." Many features of the Baalbek temple intentionally depart from the norm. The platform, for example, is scalloped all around the cella. The columns—the only known instance of five-sided Corinthian capitals with corresponding pentagonal bases—support a matching scalloped entablature (which serves to buttress the shallow stone dome). These concave forms and those of the niches in the cella walls play off against the cella's convex shape. Even the "traditional" facade of the Baalbek temple is eccentric. The unknown architect inserted an arch within the triangular pediment.

## Diocletian and the Tetrarchy

In an attempt to restore order to the Roman Empire, Diocletian (r. 284–305 CE), whose troops proclaimed him emperor, decided to share power with his potential rivals. In 293, he established the *tetrarchy* (rule by four) and adopted the title of Augustus of the East. The other three *tetrarchs* were a corresponding Augustus of the West, and Eastern and Western Caesars (whose allegiance to the two Augusti was cemented by marriage to their daughters). Together, the four emperors ruled without strife until Diocletian retired in 305. Without his leadership, the tetrarchic form of government collapsed, and renewed civil war followed. The division of the Roman Empire into eastern and western spheres persisted throughout the Middle Ages, however, setting the Byzantine East apart from the Latin West.

**GROUP PORTRAITS** In art, if not in life, the four tetrarchs often appeared together, both on coins and in statues. Artists did not try to capture their individual appearances and personalities but sought instead to represent the nature of the tetrarchy itself—that is, to portray four equal partners in power. In the two pairs of porphyry (purple marble) tetrarchic portraits (FIG. **7-73**) in Venice, it is impossible to name the rulers. Each of the four emperors has lost his identity as an individual and been subsumed into the larger entity of the tetrarchy. All the tetrarchs are identically clad in cuirass and cloak. Each grasps a sheathed sword in his left hand. With their right arms they embrace one another in an overt display of concord. The figures, like those on the decursio relief (FIG. 7-58) of the Column of Antoninus Pius, have large cubical heads and squat bodies. The drapery is schematic, the bodies are shapeless, and the faces are emotionless masks, distinguished only by the beards of two of the tetrarchs (probably the older Augusti, differentiating them from the younger Caesars). Nonetheless, each pair is as alike as freehand carving can achieve. In this group portrait, carved eight centuries after Greek sculptors first freed the human form from the formal rigidity of the Egyptian-inspired kouros stance, an artist once again conceived the human figure in iconic terms. Idealism, naturalism, individuality, and personality have disappeared.

**PALACE OF DIOCLETIAN** When Diocletian abdicated in 305, he returned to his birthplace, Dalmatia (roughly the former Yugoslavia), where he built a palace (FIG. **7-74**) at Split on the Adriatic coast. Just as Aurelian had felt it necessary to girdle Rome with fortress walls, Diocletian instructed his architects to provide him with a walled suburban palace. The fortified complex, which covers about 10 acres, has the layout of a Roman *castrum*, complete with watchtowers flanking the gates. It gave the emperor a sense of security in the most insecure of times.

**7-72** Restored view (*top*) and plan (*bottom*) of the Temple of Venus, Baalbek, Lebanon, third century CE.

This "baroque" temple violates almost every rule of Classical design. It has a scalloped platform and entablature, five-sided Corinthian capitals, and a facade with an arch inside the pediment.

or some other combination of family members. The composition, with a frontal central figure and two subordinate flanking figures, is typical of the Late Antique style. This type of sarcophagus became popular for Christian burials. Sculptors used the wise-man motif to portray not only the deceased (FIG. 8-7) but also Christ flanked by saints (FIG. 8-1).

**BAALBEK** The decline in respect for Classical art also is evident in third-century architecture. At Baalbek in present-day Lebanon, the architect of the Temple of Venus (FIG. **7-72**), following in the "baroque" tradition of the Petra Treasury (FIG. 7-53), ignored almost

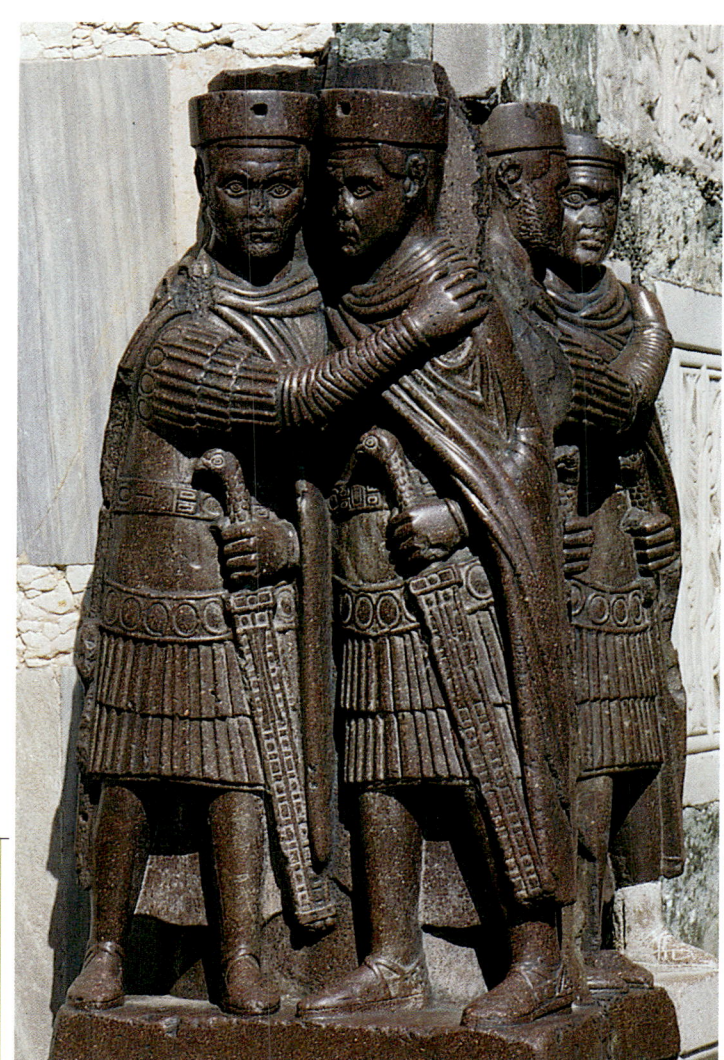

**7-73** Portraits of the four tetrarchs, from Constantinople, ca. 305 CE. Porphyry, 4′ 3″ high. Saint Mark's, Venice.

Diocletian established the tetrarchy to bring order to the Roman world. In group portraits, artists always depicted the four corulers as nearly identical partners in power, not as distinct individuals.

1 ft.

Within the high walls, two avenues (comparable to the cardo and decumanus of a Roman city; FIG. 7-43) intersected at the palace's center. Where a city's forum would have been situated, Diocletian's palace had a colonnaded court leading to the entrance to the imperial residence, which had a templelike facade with an arch within its pediment, as in Baalbek's Temple of Venus (FIG. 7-72). Diocletian presented himself as if he were a god in his temple when he appeared before those who gathered in the court to pay homage to him. On one side of the court was a Temple of Jupiter. On the other side was Diocletian's domed octagonal *mausoleum* (FIG. 7-74, *center right*), which towered above all the other structures in the complex. Domed tombs of this type became very popular in Late Antiquity not only for mausoleums but eventually also for churches, especially in the Byzantine East (see Chapters 8 and 9). In fact, Diocletian's mausoleum is a church today.

## Constantine

An all-too-familiar period of conflict followed the short-lived concord among the tetrarchs that ended with Diocletian's abdication. This latest war among rival Roman armies lasted two decades. The eventual victor was Constantine I, son of Constantius Chlorus, Diocletian's Caesar of the West. After the death of his father, Constantine (r. 306–337 CE), called the Great, invaded Italy. In 312 CE, in a decisive battle at Rome's Milvian Bridge, he defeated and killed Maxentius and took control of the capital. Constantine attributed his victory to the aid of the Christian god. The next year, he and

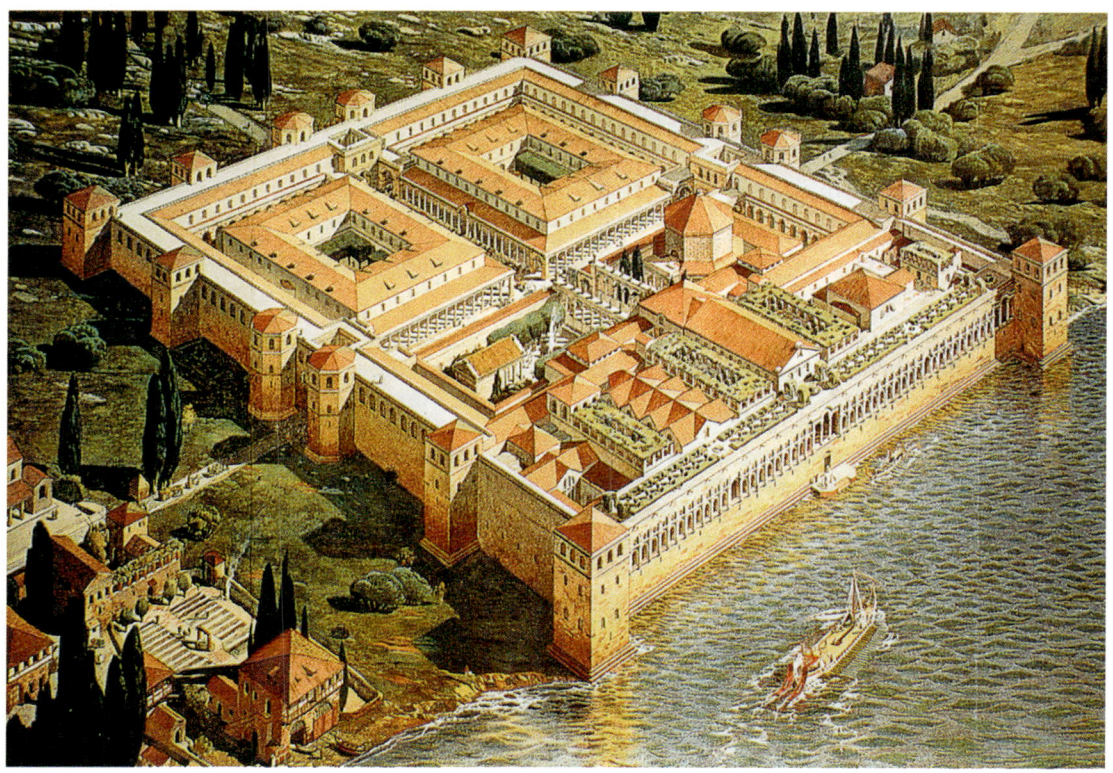

**7-74** Restored view of the palace of Diocletian, Split, Croatia, ca. 298–306.

Diocletian's palace resembled a fortified Roman city (compare FIG. 7-43). Within its high walls, two avenues intersected at the forumlike colonnaded courtyard leading to the emperor's residential quarters.

Licinius, Constantine's coemperor in the East, issued the Edict of Milan, ending the persecution of Christians.

In time, Constantine and Licinius became foes, and in 324 Constantine defeated and executed Licinius near Byzantium (modern Istanbul, Turkey). Constantine, now unchallenged ruler of the whole Roman Empire, founded a "New Rome" at Byzantium and named it Constantinople (City of Constantine). In 325, at the Council of Nicaea, Christianity became the de facto official religion of the Roman Empire. From this point on, the ancient cults declined rapidly. Constantine dedicated Constantinople on May 11, 330, "by the commandment of God," and in 337 the emperor was baptized on his deathbed. For many scholars, the transfer of the seat of power from Rome to Constantinople and the recognition of Christianity mark the end of antiquity and the beginning of the Middle Ages.

Constantinian art is a mirror of this transition from the ancient to the medieval world. In Rome, for example, Constantine was a builder in the grand tradition of the emperors of the first, second, and early third centuries, erecting public baths, a basilica on the road leading into the Roman Forum, and a triumphal arch. But he was also the patron of the city's first churches (see Chapter 8).

**ARCH OF CONSTANTINE** Between 312 and 315, Constantine erected a great triple-passageway arch (FIGS. 7-2, no. 15, and 7-75) next to the Colosseum to commemorate his defeat of Maxentius. The arch was the largest set up in Rome since the end of the Severan dynasty. The builders, however, took much of the sculptural decoration from earlier monuments of Trajan, Hadrian (FIG. 7-48A), and Marcus Aurelius, and all of the columns and other architectural elements date to an earlier era. Constantine's sculptors refashioned the second-century reliefs to honor him by recutting the heads of the earlier emperors with his features. They also added labels to the old reliefs, such as *Liberator Urbis* (Liberator of the City) and *Fundator Quietus* (Bringer of Peace), references to the downfall of Maxentius and the end of civil war. Art historians have often cited this reuse of statues and reliefs as evidence of a decline in creativity and technical skill in the Late Roman Empire. Although such a judgment is in part deserved, it ignores the fact that the reused sculptures were carefully selected to associate Constantine with the "good emperors" of the second century. One of the arch's few Constantinian reliefs underscores that message. It shows Constantine on the speaker's platform in the Roman Forum between statues of Hadrian and Marcus Aurelius.

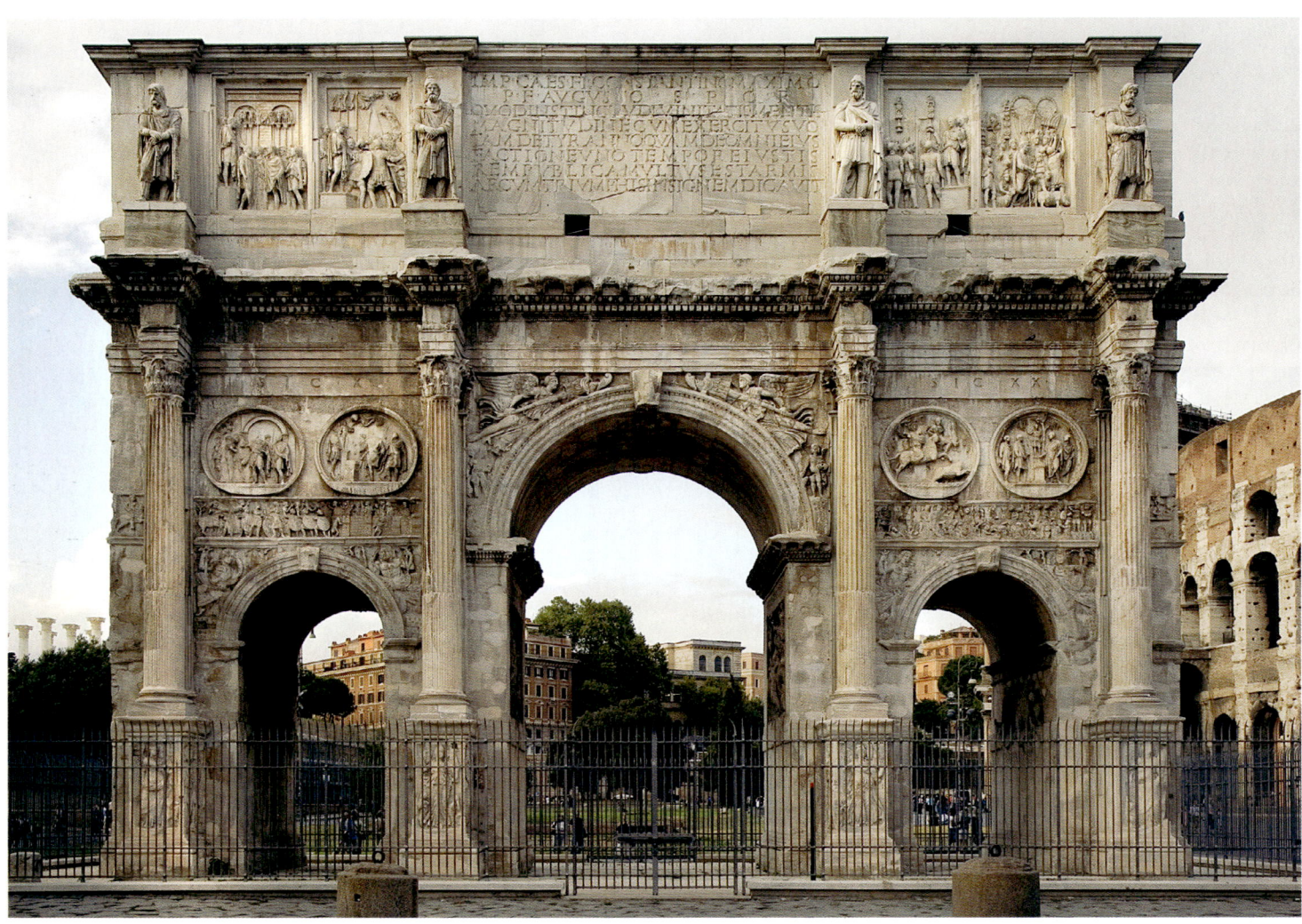

**7-75** South facade of the Arch of Constantine, Rome, Italy, 312–315 CE. ◼◀

Much of the sculptural decoration of Constantine's arch came from monuments of Trajan, Hadrian, and Marcus Aurelius. Sculptors recut the heads of the earlier emperors to substitute Constantine's features.

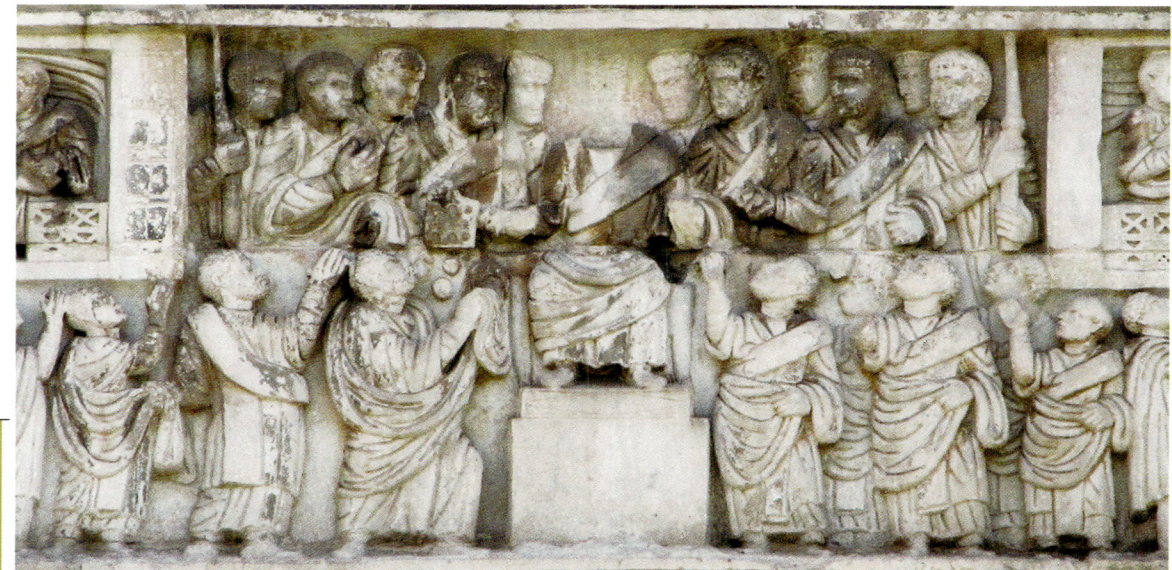

In another Constantinian relief (FIG. 7-76), the emperor distributes largesse to grateful citizens who approach him from right and left. Constantine is a frontal and majestic presence, elevated on a throne above the recipients of his munificence. The figures are squat in proportion, like the tetrarchs (FIG. 7-73). They do not move according to any Classical principle of naturalistic movement but, rather, with the mechanical and repeated stances and gestures of puppets. The relief is very shallow, the forms are not fully modeled, and the details are incised. The frieze is less a narrative of action than a picture of actors frozen in time so that the viewer can distinguish instantly the all-important imperial donor (at the center on a throne) from his attendants (to the left and right above) and the recipients of the largesse (below and of smaller stature).

An eminent art historian once characterized this approach to pictorial narrative as a "decline of form," and when judged by the standards of Classical art, it was. But the composition's rigid formality, determined by the rank of those portrayed, was consistent with a new set of values. It soon became the preferred mode, supplanting the Classical notion that a picture is a window onto a world of anecdotal action. Comparing this Constantinian relief with a Byzantine icon (FIG. 9-18) reveals that the compositional principles of the Late Antique style became those of medieval art. They were very different from, but not "better" or "worse" than, those of Greco-Roman art. The Arch of Constantine is the quintessential monument of its era, exhibiting a respect for the past in its reuse of second-century sculptures while rejecting the norms of Classical design in its frieze and thereby paving the way for the iconic art of the Middle Ages.

**COLOSSUS OF CONSTANTINE** After Constantine's victory over Maxentius, his official portraits broke with tetrarchic tradition as well as with the style of the soldier emperors, and resuscitated the Augustan image of an eternally youthful head of state. The most impressive of Constantine's preserved portraits is an eight and-one-half-foot-tall head (FIG. 7-77), one of several fragments of a colossal enthroned statue of the emperor composed of a brick core, a wooden torso covered with bronze, and a head and limbs of

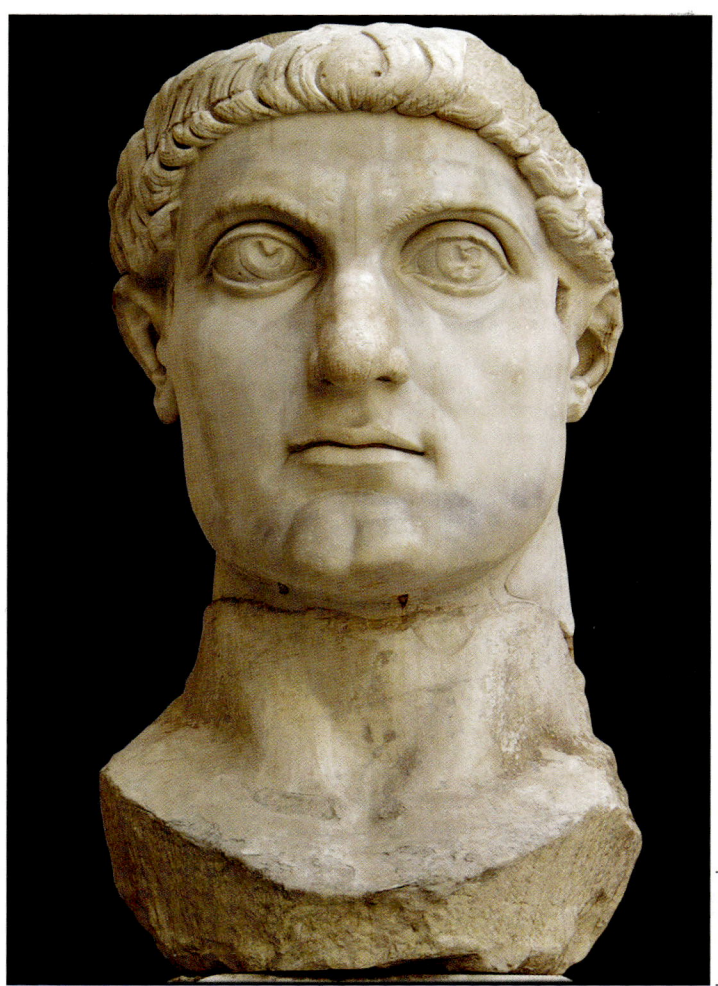

**7-77** Colossal head of Constantine, from the Basilica Nova, Rome, Italy, ca. 315–330 CE. Marble, 8′ 6″ high. Musei Capitolini–Palazzo dei Conservatori, Rome. ◼◀

marble. Constantine's artist modeled the seminude seated portrait on Roman images of Jupiter. The emperor held an orb (possibly surmounted by the cross of Christ), the symbol of global power, in his extended left hand. The nervous glance of third-century portraits is absent, replaced by a frontal mask with enormous eyes set into the broad and simple planes of the head. The emperor's personality is lost in this immense image of eternal authority. The colossal size, the likening of the emperor to Jupiter, the eyes directed at no person or thing of this world—all combine to produce a formula of overwhelming power appropriate to Constantine's exalted position as absolute ruler.

**BASILICA NOVA** Constantine's gigantic portrait sat in the western apse of the Basilica Nova (New Basilica) in Rome (FIGS. 7-2, no. 12, and **7-78**), a project Maxentius had begun and Constantine completed. From its position in the apse, the emperor's image dominated the interior of the basilica in much the same way enthroned statues of Greco-Roman divinities loomed over awestruck mortals in temple cellas (compare FIG. 5-46).

The Basilica Nova ruins never fail to impress tourists with their size and mass. The original structure was 300 feet long and 215 feet wide. Brick-faced concrete walls 20 feet thick supported coffered barrel vaults in the aisles. These vaults also buttressed the groin vaults of the nave, which was 115 feet high. Marble slabs and stuccoes covered the walls and floors. The reconstruction in FIG. 7-78 effectively suggests the immensity of the interior, where the great vaults dwarf even the emperor's colossal portrait. The drawing

also clearly reveals the fenestration of the groin vaults (FIG. 7-6*c*), a lighting system akin to the clerestory of a traditional stone-and-timber basilica. The architect here applied to basilica design the lessons learned in the design and construction of buildings such as Trajan's great market hall (FIG. 7-46) and the Baths of Caracalla and Diocletian (FIG. 7-67).

**AULA PALATINA** Few architects, however, followed suit. At Trier on the Moselle River in Germany, the imperial seat of Constantius Chlorus as Caesar of the West, Constantine built a traditional basilica-like audience hall, the Aula Palatina (FIG. **7-79**), as part of his new palace complex. The Trier basilica measures about 190 feet long and 95 feet wide and has an austere brick exterior, enlivened somewhat by highlighting in grayish-white stucco. The use of lead-framed panes of glass for the windows enabled the builders to give life and movement to the blank exterior surfaces.

Inside (FIG. **7-80**), the audience hall was also very simple. Its flat, coffered wood ceiling is some 95 feet above the floor. The interior has no aisles, only a wide space with two stories of large windows that provide ample light. At the narrow north end, a *chancel arch* divides the main hall from the semicircular apse (which also has a flat ceiling). The Aula Palatina's interior is quite severe, although mosaics and marble plaques originally covered the arch and apse to provide a magnificent frame for the enthroned emperor. The design of both the interior and exterior has close parallels in many Early Christian churches (see Chapter 8).

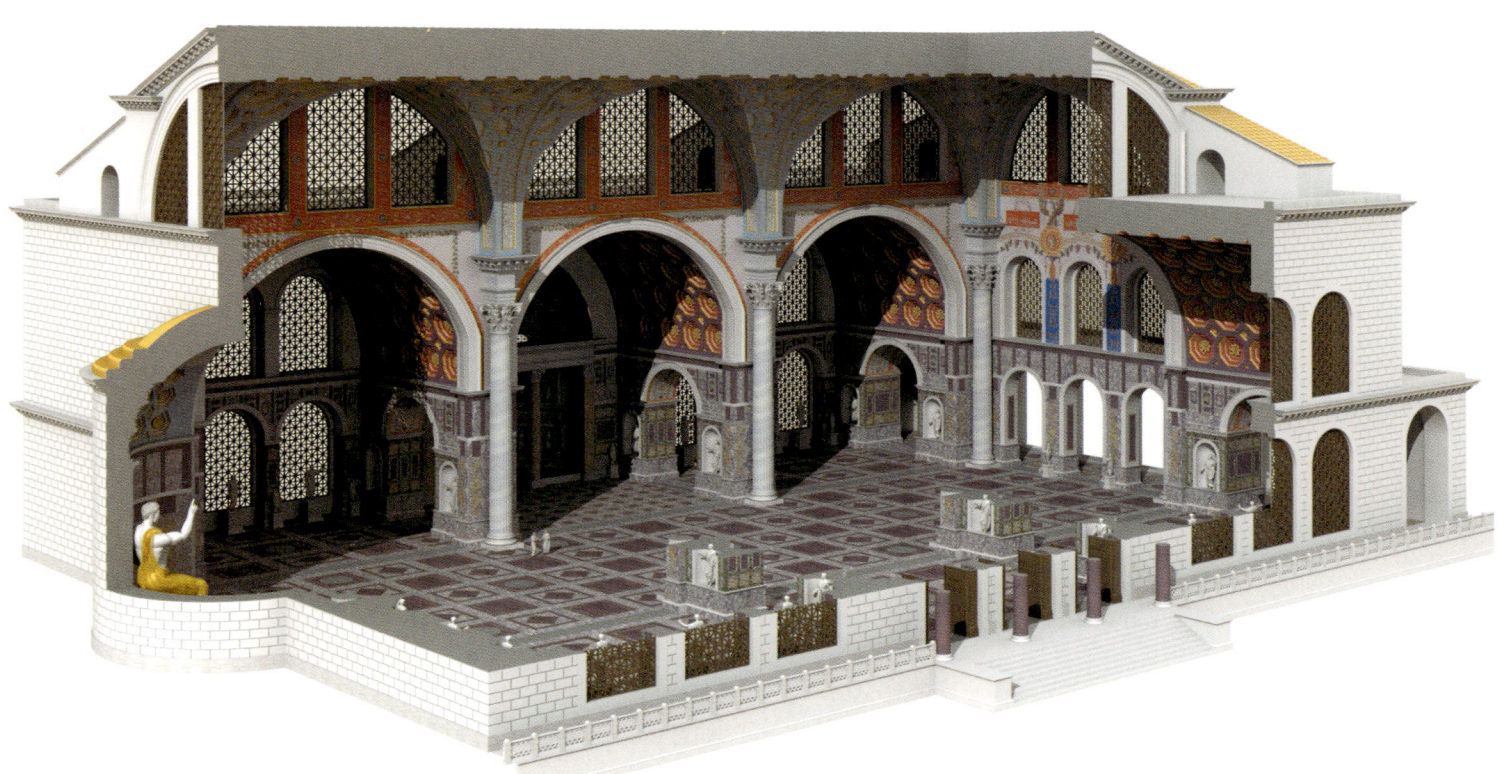

**7-78** Restored cutaway view of the Basilica Nova, Rome, Italy, ca. 306–312 CE (John Burge).

Roman builders applied the lessons learned constructing baths and market halls to the Basilica Nova, where fenestrated concrete groin vaults replaced the clerestory of a stone-and-timber basilica.

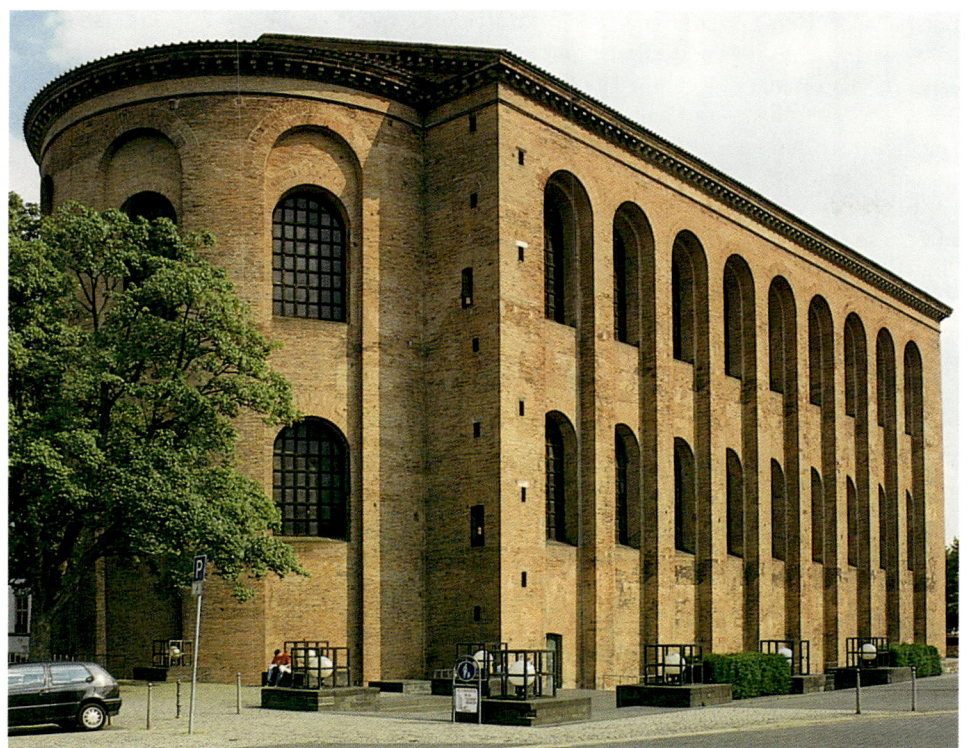

**7-79** Exterior of the Aula Palatina (looking southeast), Trier, Germany, early fourth century CE. ◀

The austere brick exterior of Constantine's Aula Palatina at Trier is typical of later Roman architecture. Two stories of windows with lead-framed panes of glass take up most of the surface area.

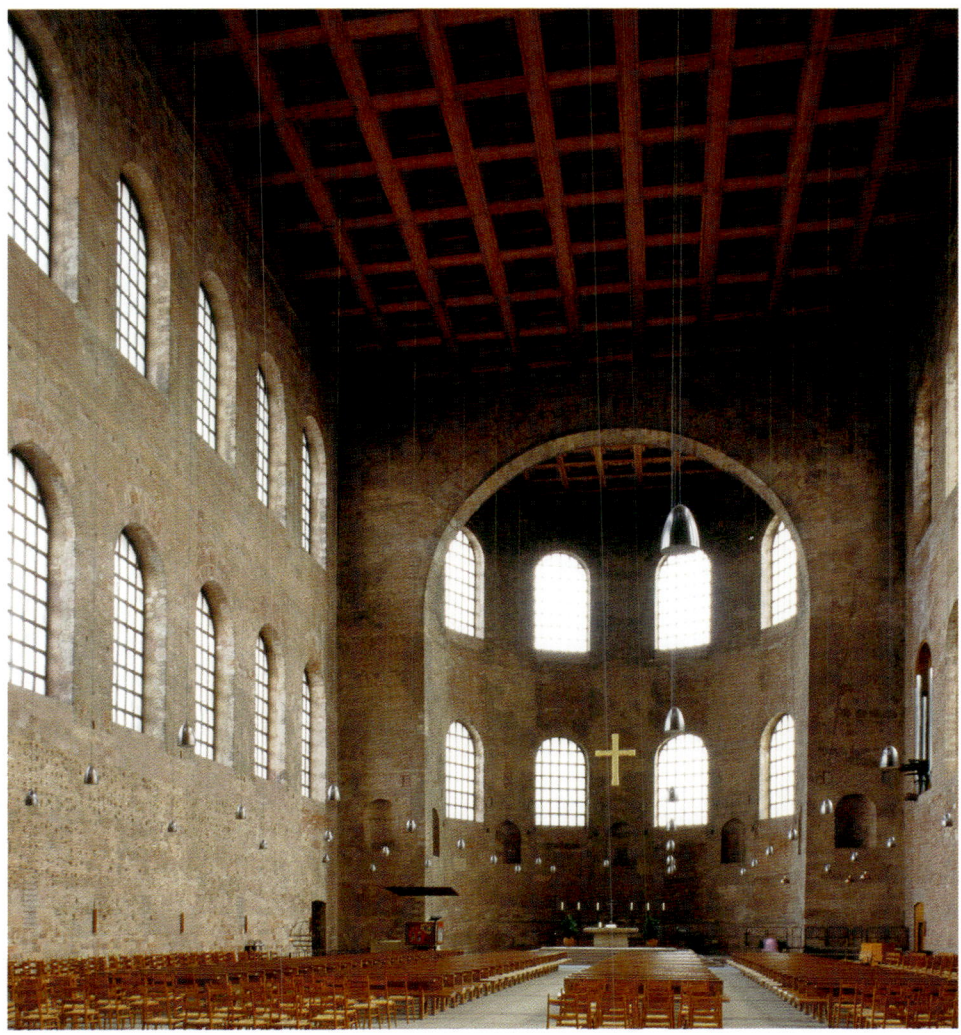

**7-80** Interior of the Aula Palatina (looking north), Trier, Germany, early fourth century CE. ◀

The interior of the audience hall of Constantine's palace in Germany resembles a timber-roofed basilica with an apse at one end, but it has no aisles. The large windows provided ample illumination.

**CONSTANTINIAN COINS** The two portraits of Constantine on the coins in FIG. **7-81** reveal both the essential character of Roman imperial portraiture and the special nature of Constantinian art.

The first (FIG. 7-81, *left*) dates shortly after the death of Constantine's father, when Constantine was in his early 20s and his position was still insecure. Here, in his official portrait, he appears considerably older, because he adopted the imagery of the tetrarchs. Indeed, were it not for the accompanying label identifying this Caesar as Constantine, it would be impossible to know whom the coin engraver portrayed.

Eight years later (FIG. 7-81, *right*)—after the defeat of Maxentius and the Edict of Milan—Constantine, now the unchallenged Augustus of the West, is clean-shaven and looks his real age, having rejected the mature tetrarchic look in favor of youth. These two coins should dispel any uncertainty about the often fictive nature of imperial portraiture and the ability of Roman emperors to choose any of-

ficial image that suited their needs. In Roman art, "portrait" is often not synonymous with "likeness."

The later coin is also an eloquent testimony to the dual nature of Constantinian rule. The emperor appears in his important role as imperator, dressed in armor, wearing an ornate helmet, and carrying a shield bearing the enduring emblem of the Roman state— the she-wolf nursing Romulus and Remus (compare FIG. 6-11 and Roma's shield in FIG. 7-57). Yet he does not carry the traditional eagle-topped scepter of the Roman emperor. Rather, he holds a cross crowned by an orb. At the crest of his helmet, at the front, just below the grand plume, is a disk containing the *Christogram,* the monogram ☧ made up of *chi* (X), *rho* (P), and *iota* (I), the initial letters of Christ's name in Greek (compare the shield a soldier holds in FIG. 9-13). The artist portrayed Constantine as both Roman emperor and soldier in the army of the Lord. The coin, like Constantinian art in general, belongs both to the ancient and to the medieval worlds.

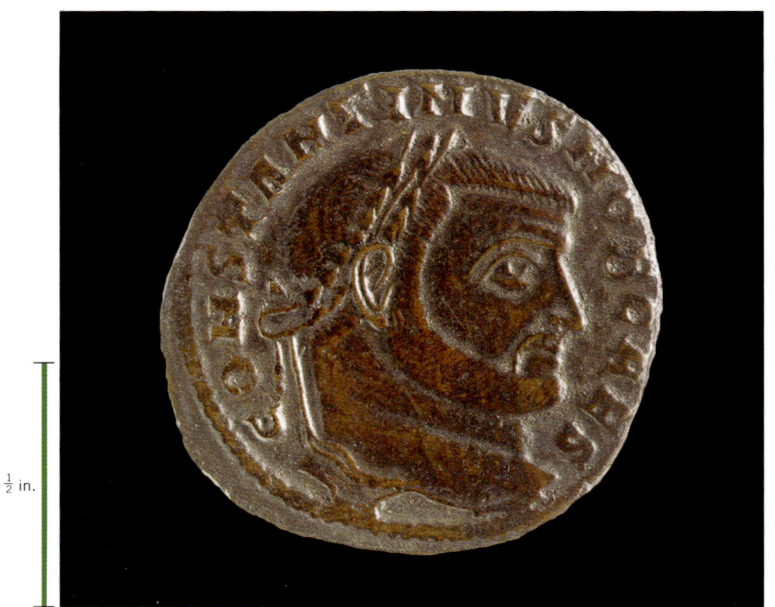 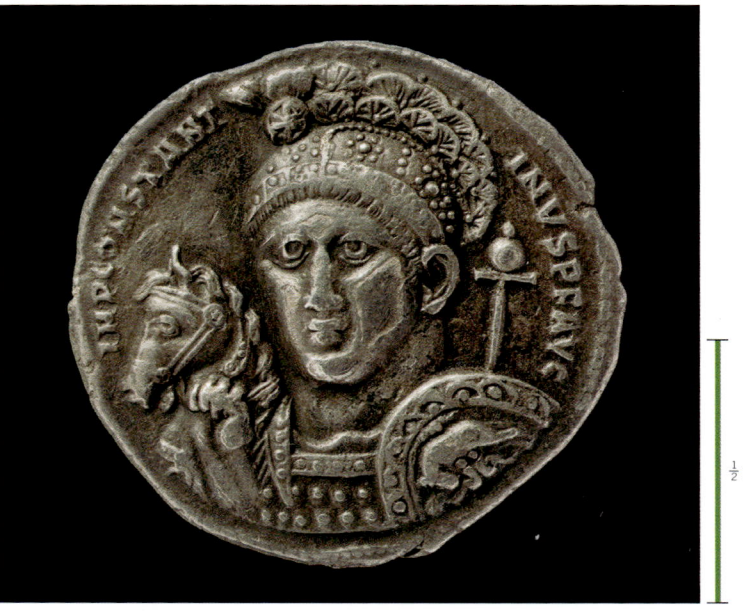

½ in.      ½ in.

**7-81** Two coins with portraits of Constantine. *Left:* nummus, 307 CE. Billon, diameter 1″. American Numismatic Society, New York. *Right:* medallion, ca. 315 CE. Silver, diameter 1″. Staatliche Münzsammlung, Munich.

These two coins underscore that portraits of Roman emperors were rarely true likenesses. On the earlier coin, Constantine appears as a bearded tetrarch. On the later coin, he appears eternally youthful.

# THE ROMAN EMPIRE

## MONARCHY AND REPUBLIC 753–27 BCE

▎ According to legend, Romulus and Remus founded Rome in 753 BCE. In the sixth century BCE, Etruscan kings ruled the city, and Roman art was Etruscan in character.

▎ In the centuries following the establishment of the Republic in 509 BCE, Rome conquered its neighbors in Italy and then moved into Greece, bringing exposure to Greek art and architecture.

▎ Republican temples combined Etruscan plans with the Greek orders, and houses had peristyles with Greek columns. The Romans, however, pioneered the use of concrete as a building material.

▎ The First Style of mural painting derived from Greece, but the illusionism of the Second Style is distinctly Roman.

▎ Republican portraits were usually superrealistic likenesses of elderly patricians and celebrated traditional Roman values.

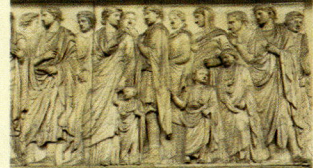

Man with ancestor busts, late first century BCE

## EARLY EMPIRE 27 BCE–96 CE

▎ Augustus (r. 27 BCE–14 CE) defeated Mark Antony and Cleopatra at Actium in 31 BCE and became the first Roman emperor.

▎ Augustan art revived the Classical style with frequent references to Periclean Athens. Augustus's ambitious building program made lavish use of marble, and his portraits always depicted him as an idealized youth.

▎ Under the Julio-Claudians (r. 14–68 CE), builders began to realize the full potential of concrete in buildings such as the Golden House of Nero.

▎ The Flavian emperors (r. 68-96 CE) built the Colosseum, the largest Roman amphitheater, and arches and other monuments celebrating their victory in Judaea.

▎ The eruption of Mount Vesuvius in 79 CE buried Pompeii and Herculaneum. During the quarter century before the disaster, painters decorated the walls of houses in the Third and Fourth Styles.

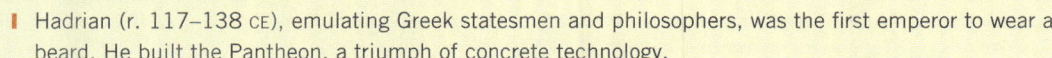

Ara Pacis Augustae, Rome, 13–9 BCE

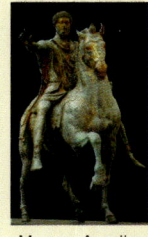

Colosseum, Rome, ca. 70–80 CE

## HIGH EMPIRE 96–192 CE

▎ The Roman Empire reached its greatest extent under Trajan (r. 98–117 CE). The emperor's new forum and markets transformed the civic center of Rome. Trajan's Column commemorated his two campaigns in Dacia in a spiral frieze with thousands of figures.

▎ Hadrian (r. 117–138 CE), emulating Greek statesmen and philosophers, was the first emperor to wear a beard. He built the Pantheon, a triumph of concrete technology.

▎ Under the Antonines (r. 138–192 CE), the dominance of Classical art began to erode, and imperial artists introduced new compositional schemes in relief sculpture and a psychological element in portraiture.

Marcus Aurelius, ca. 175 CE

## LATE EMPIRE 192–337 CE

▎ In the art of the Severans (r. 193–235 CE), the non-Classical Late Antique style took root. Artists represented the emperor as a central frontal figure disengaged from the action around him.

▎ During the chaotic era of the soldier emperors (r. 235–284 CE), artists revealed the anxiety and insecurity of the emperors in moving portraits.

▎ Diocletian (r. 284–305 CE) reestablished order by sharing power. Statues of the tetrarchs portray the four emperors as identical and equal rulers, not as individuals.

▎ Constantine (r. 306–336 CE) restored one-man rule, ended persecution of Christians, and transferred the capital of the Empire from Rome to Constantinople in 330. The abstract formality of Constantinian art paved the way for the iconic art of the Middle Ages.

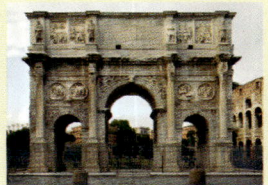

Arch of Constantine, Rome, 312–315 CE

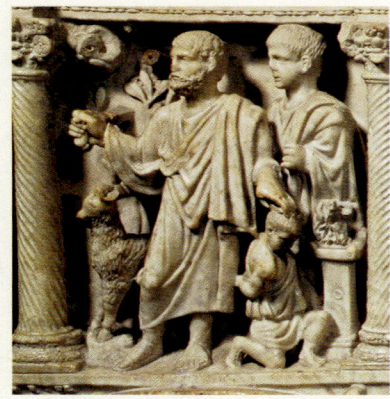

Episodes from the Hebrew scriptures, including Abraham's sacrifice of Isaac, appear side by side with scenes from the life of Jesus on this sarcophagus of a recent convert to Christianity.

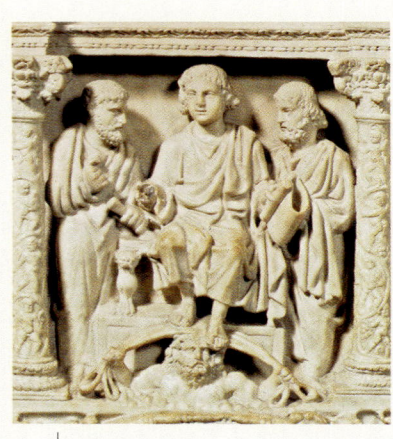

Christ, long-haired and youthful in the Early Christian tradition, sits above a personification of the Roman sky god. Flanking the new ruler of the universe are Saints Peter and Paul.

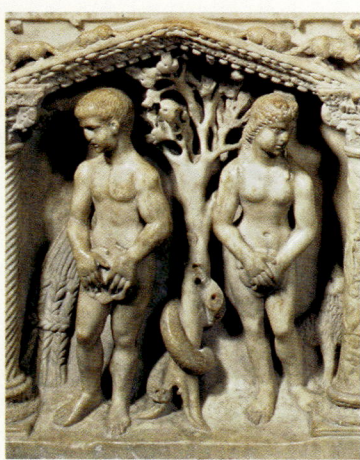

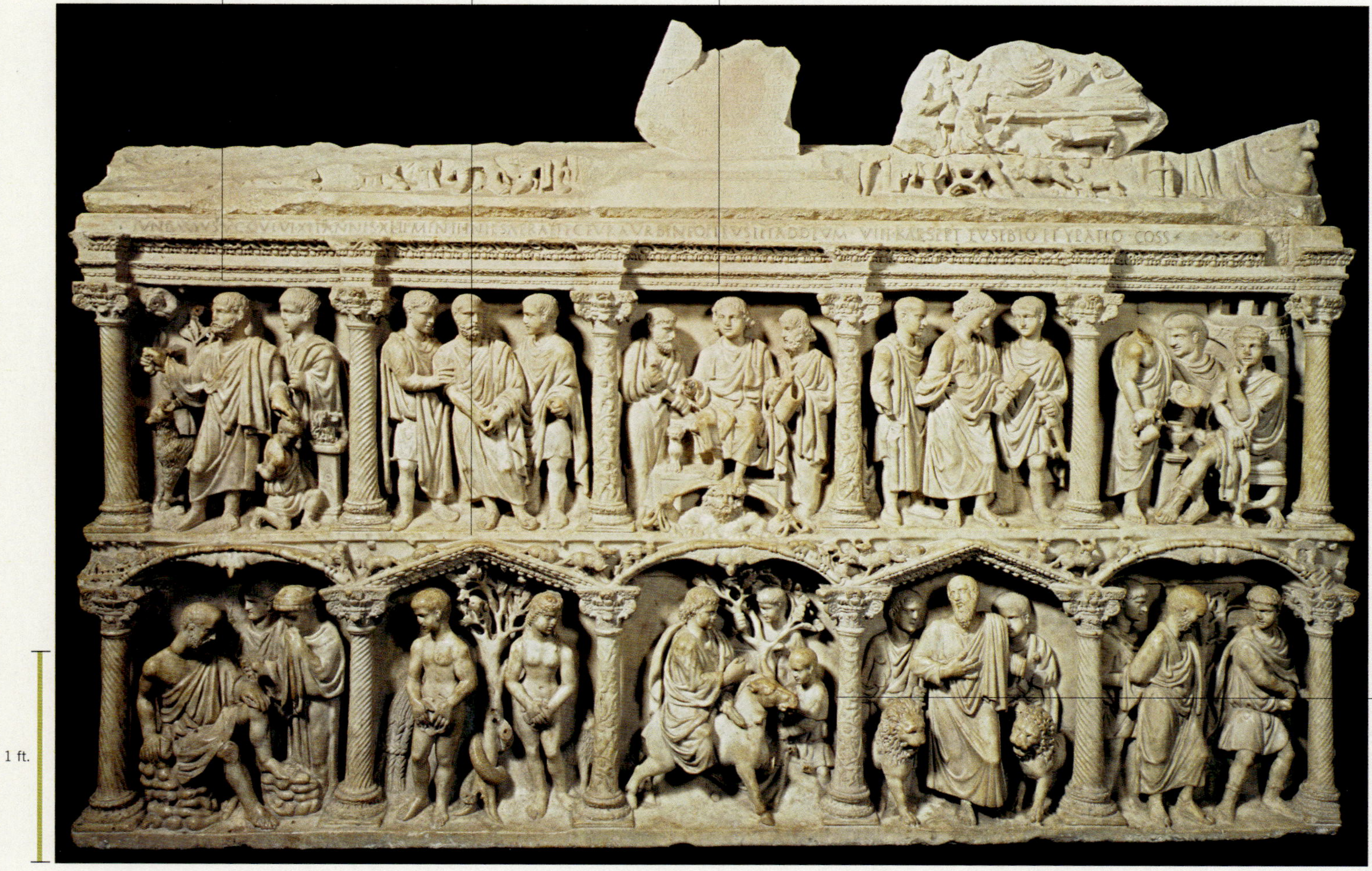

The Jewish scenes on Junius Bassus's sarcophagus had special significance for Christians. Adam and Eve's original sin of eating the apple in the Garden of Eden necessitated Christ's sacrifice.

1 ft.

**8-1** Sarcophagus of Junius Bassus, from Rome, Italy, ca. 359. Marble, 3′ 10½″ × 8′. Museo Storico del Tesoro della Basilica di San Pietro, Rome.

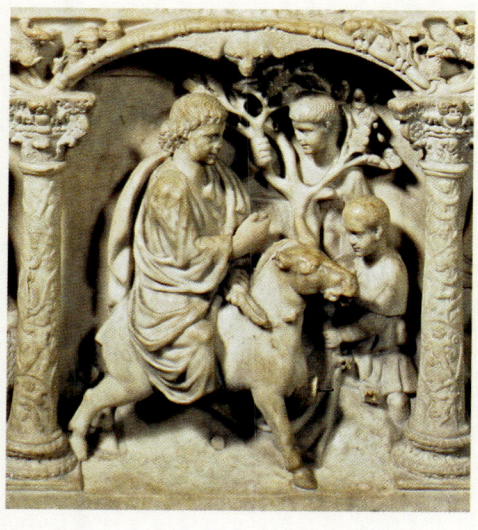

The compositions of many Early Christian reliefs derive from Greco-Roman art. The scene of Jesus entering Jerusalem on a donkey recalls portrayals of Roman emperors entering conquered cities.

# LATE ANTIQUITY

## ROMANS, JEWS, AND CHRISTIANS

During the third and fourth centuries, a rapidly growing number of Romans rejected polytheism (belief in multiple gods) in favor of monotheism (the worship of a single all-powerful god)—but they did not stop commissioning works of art. A prominent example is Junius Bassus, the mid-fourth-century city prefect of Rome who converted to Christianity and, according to the inscription on his sarcophagus (FIG. 8-1), was baptized just before his death in 359. He grew up immersed in traditional Roman culture and initially paid homage to the old Roman gods, but when he died, he chose to be buried in a sarcophagus decorated with episodes from the Hebrew scriptures and the life of Jesus.

The sculptor of Junius Bassus's sarcophagus decorated it with reliefs only on the front and two short sides in the western Roman manner (see Chapter 7). The front has 10 figural scenes in two registers of five compartments, each framed by columns in the tradition of Asiatic sarcophagi (FIG. 7-61). The deceased does not appear in any of those compartments. Instead, Jewish and Christian biblical stories fill the niches. Jesus has pride of place and appears in the central compartment of each register: as a teacher enthroned between Saints Peter and Paul (top niche), and entering Jerusalem on a donkey (bottom niche). Both compositions owe a great deal to official Roman art. In the upper zone, Christ, like an enthroned Roman emperor, sits above a personification of the sky god holding a billowing mantle over his head, indicating Christ is ruler of the universe. The scene below derives in part from portrayals of Roman emperors entering conquered cities on horseback, but Jesus' steed and the absence of imperial attributes contrast sharply with the imperial models the sculptor used as compositional sources.

The Jewish scenes on the Junius Bassus sarcophagus include the stories of Adam and Eve and Abraham and Isaac, which took on added significance for Christians as foretelling events in the life of their Savior. Christians believe Adam and Eve's original sin of eating the apple in the Garden of Eden ultimately necessitated Christ's sacrifice for the salvation of humankind. At the upper left, Abraham is about to sacrifice Isaac. Christians view this Genesis story as a prefiguration of God's sacrifice of his son, Jesus.

The crucifixion, however, does not appear on the sarcophagus and was rare in Early Christian art. Artists emphasized Christ's divinity and exemplary life as teacher and miracle worker, not his suffering and death at the hands of the Romans. This sculptor, however, alluded to the crucifixion in the scenes at the upper right showing Jesus led before Pontius Pilate for judgment. The Romans condemned Jesus to death, but he triumphantly overcame it. Junius Bassus hoped for a similar salvation.

# THE LATE ANTIQUE WORLD

The Roman Empire was home to an extraordinarily diverse population. In Rome alone on any given day, someone walking through the city's various quarters would have encountered people of an astonishing range of social, ethnic, racial, linguistic, and religious backgrounds. This multicultural character of Roman society became only more pronounced as the Romans expanded their territories throughout Europe, Africa, and Mesopotamia (MAP 7-1). Chapter 7 focused on the public and private art and architecture of Romans through the time of Constantine, who worshiped the traditional gods and embraced the values of the classical world.* This chapter treats primarily Late Antique Jewish and Christian artworks, created both before and after Constantine. These sculptures, paintings, mosaics, and other art forms are no less Roman than imperial

*Note: In *Art through the Ages,* the adjective "Classical," with uppercase *C,* refers specifically to the Classical period of ancient Greece, 480–323 BCE. Lowercase "classical" refers to Greco-Roman antiquity in general, that is, the period treated in Chapters 5, 6, and 7.

portraits, statues of gods and heroes, or sarcophagi with mythological scenes. Indeed, the artists may in some cases have been the same. But although they are Roman in style and technique, the Jewish and Christian sculptures, paintings, and buildings of Late Antiquity differ significantly in subject and often in function from contemporaneous Roman secular and religious art and architecture. For that reason, and because these Late Antique artworks and sacred buildings formed the foundation of the art and architecture of the Middle Ages, they are the subject of a separate chapter.

# DURA-EUROPOS AND JEWISH ART

The powerful religious crosscurrents of Late Antiquity may be seen in microcosm in a distant outpost of the Roman Empire on a promontory overlooking the Euphrates River in Syria (MAP 8-1). Called Europos by the Greeks and Dura by the Romans, the town probably was founded shortly after the death of Alexander the Great by one of his successors. By the end of the second century BCE, Dura-Europos was in the hands of the Parthians. Trajan captured the city

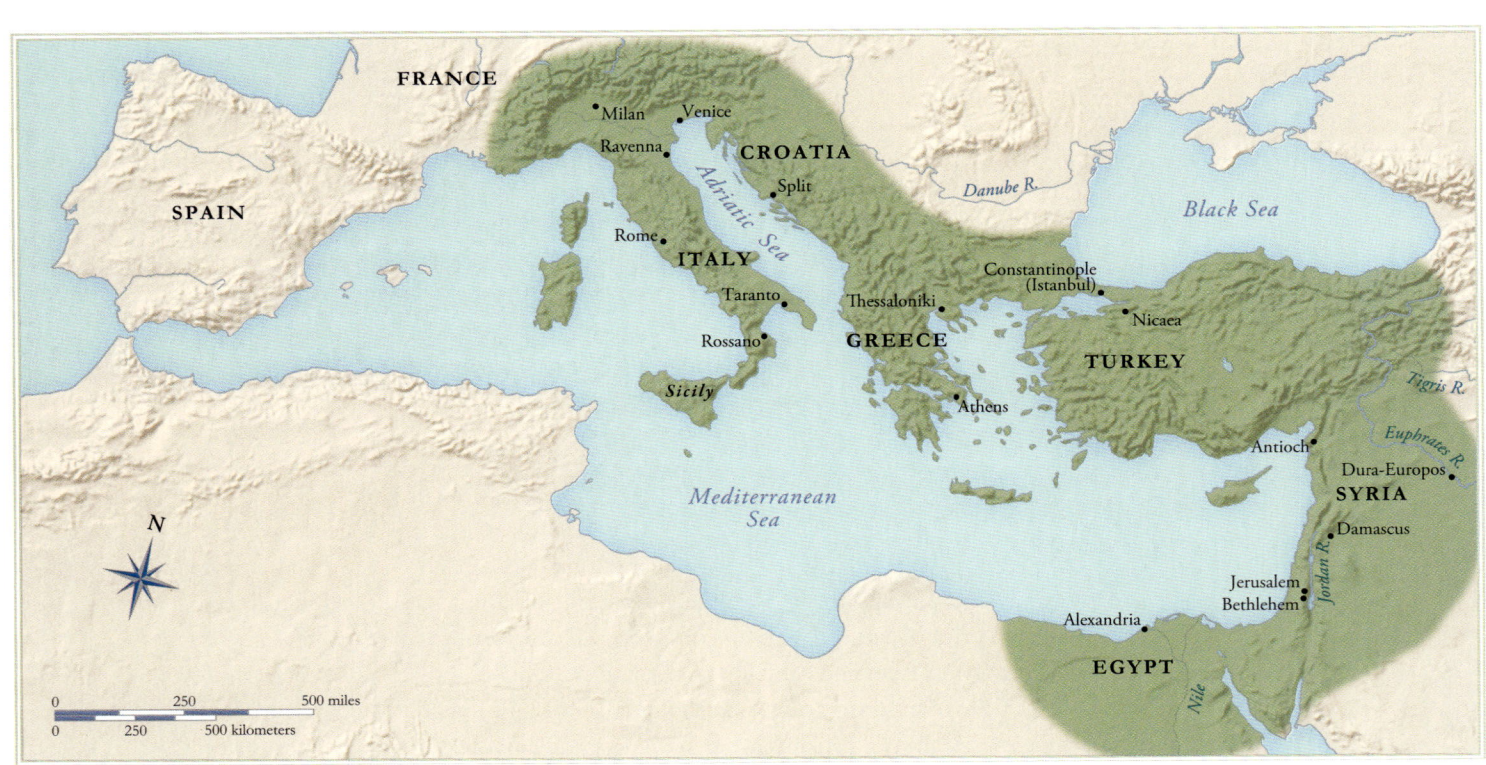

MAP 8-1 The Mediterranean world in late antiquity.

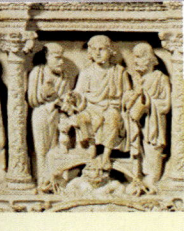

# LATE ANTIQUITY

| | 192 | Pre-Constantinian | 306 | Constantine | 337 | Sons of Constantine to Justinian | 526 |
|---|---|---|---|---|---|---|---|
| | | ▪ Biblical murals in the Dura-Europos synagogue<br>▪ Earliest Christian sarcophagi and catacomb paintings | | ▪ Construction of the first churches in Rome, including Old Saint Peter's<br>▪ Dedication of Constantinople as the New Rome | | ▪ Capital of Western Roman Empire moved to Ravenna<br>▪ Mosaics become the primary medium for church decoration<br>▪ Earliest preserved illustrated manuscripts with biblical themes | |

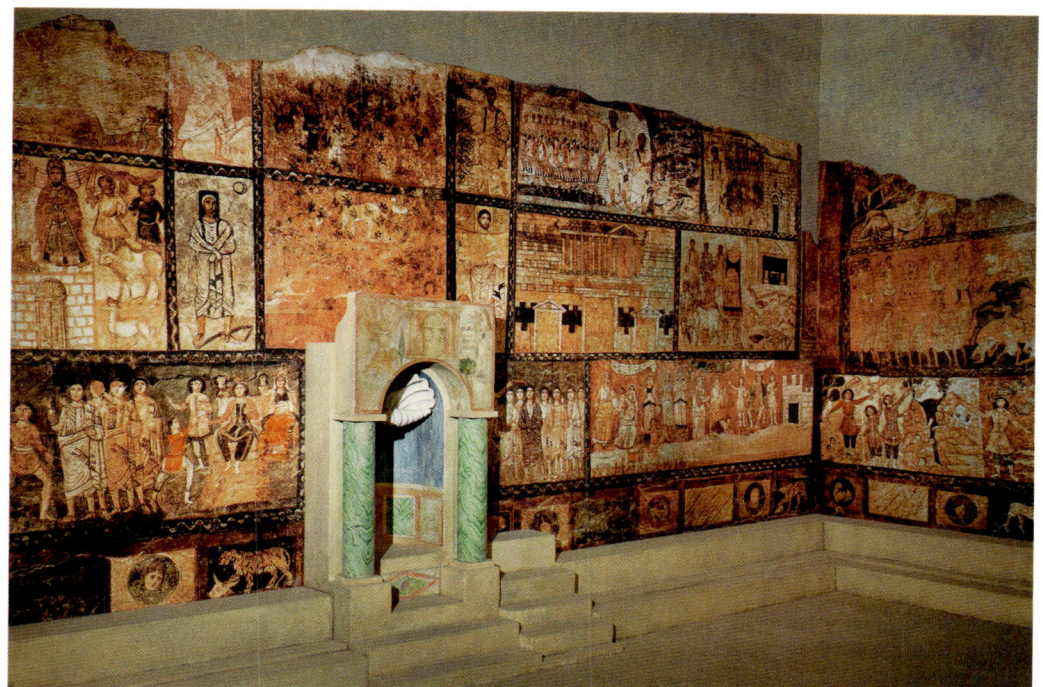

stylized gestures, and the figures, which have expressionless features and, in most of the panels, lack both volume and shadow, tend to stand in frontal rows. The painting from the book of Samuel in which *Samuel Anoints David* (FIG. **8-3**) exemplifies this Late Antique style, also seen in the friezes of the Arch of Septimius Severus (FIG. 7-65) at Lepcis Magna and the Arch of Constantine (FIG. 7-76) in Rome. The episode is on the main wall just to the right of the Torah niche. The prophet anoints the future king of Israel, as David's six older brothers look on. The painter drew attention to Samuel by depicting him larger than all the rest, a familiar convention of Late Antique art. David and his brothers are frontal figures looking out at the viewer. They seem almost weightless, and their bodies do not even have enough feet. The painter distinguished David from his brothers by the purple toga he wears. Purple was the color associated with the Roman emperor, and the Dura artist borrowed the imperial toga to signify David's royalty.

in 115,[†] but Dura reverted to Parthian control shortly thereafter. In 165, under Marcus Aurelius, the Romans retook the city and placed a permanent garrison there. Dura-Europos fell in 256 to Rome's new enemy in the East, the Sasanians, heirs to the Parthian Empire (see Chapter 2). The Sasanian siege of Dura is an important fixed point in the chronology of Late Antiquity because the inhabitants evacuated the town, leaving its buildings largely intact. This "Pompeii of the desert" has revealed the remains of more than a dozen different cult buildings, including many shrines of the polytheistic religions of the Mediterranean and Mesopotamia. But the excavators also discovered places of worship for the monotheistic creeds of Judaism and Christianity.

**SYNAGOGUE PAINTINGS** Dura-Europos's synagogue is remarkable not only for its very existence in a Roman garrison town but also for its extensive cycle of mural paintings depicting episodes from the sacred Jewish *Torah* (the scroll containing the *Pentateuch,* the first five books of the Hebrew scriptures). The Jews of Dura-Europos converted a private house with a central courtyard into a synagogue during the latter part of the second century. The main room (FIG. **8-2**) has a niche for the Torah at the center of one long wall. The paintings cover all the remaining wall surfaces. The discovery of an elaborate mural cycle in a Jewish temple initially surprised scholars because they had assumed the Second Commandment (Exodus 20:4–6) prohibiting Jews from worshiping images precluded the decoration of synagogues with figural scenes. Narrative scenes like those at Dura must have appeared in many Late Antique synagogues as well as in Jewish manuscripts, although no illustrated Bible of this period survives (see "Medieval Manuscript Illumination," page 249). God (YHWH, or Yahweh in the Torah), however, never appears in the Dura paintings, except as a hand emerging from the top of the framed panels.

The Dura murals are mostly devoid of action, even when the subject is a narrative theme. The artists told the stories through

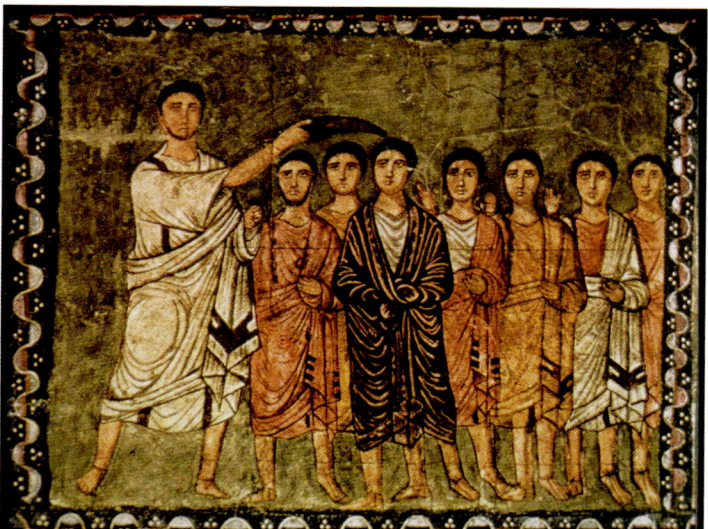

1 ft.

**8-3** *Samuel Anoints David,* detail of main interior wall of the synagogue, Dura-Europos, Syria, ca. 245–256. Tempera on plaster, 4′ 7″ high.

The figures in this scene from the book of Samuel lack volume, stand in frontal rows, and exhibit stylized gestures, features characteristic of Late Antique art, regardless of subject matter.

[†]In this chapter, all dates are CE unless otherwise indicated.

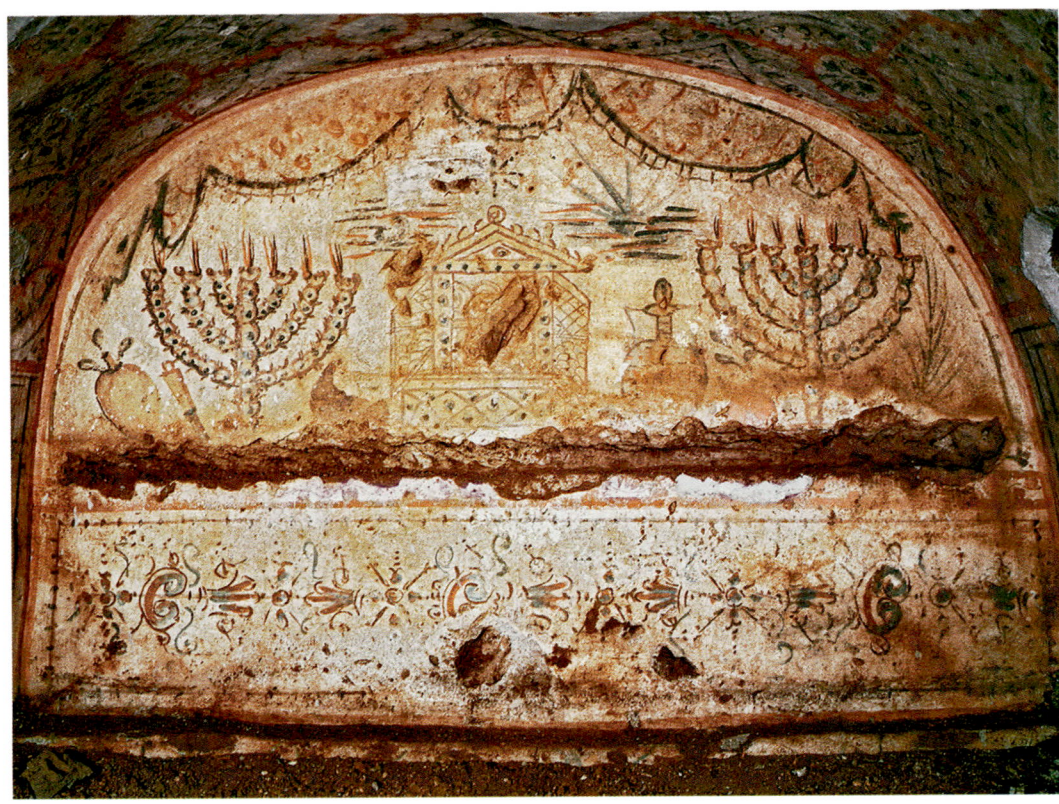

**8-4** Ark of the Covenant and two menorahs, painted wall in a Jewish catacomb, Villa Torlonia, Rome, Italy, third century. Fresco, 3′ 11″ high.

Some of the oldest catacombs in Rome were Jewish burial places. This example features mural paintings that include depictions of the sacred Ark of the Covenant and two menorahs.

**VILLA TORLONIA** Mural paintings of similar date depicting Jewish themes have also been found in Rome, most notably in underground chambers on the grounds of the present Villa Torlonia, where Jewish families buried their dead beginning in the second century. Perhaps the finest of the Torlonia paintings (FIG. **8-4**) depicts two seven-branched menorahs, modest versions of the sumptuous menorah (FIG. 7-41) Roman soldiers brought back from Jerusalem after Titus sacked the great Hebrew temple there. At the center is the Ark of the Covenant of the Jerusalem temple, which contained the sacred stone tablets of Moses with the Ten Commandments. These important emblems of their faith appropriately decorated one wall of the tomb in which these Roman Jews were laid to rest.

**CHRISTIAN COMMUNITY HOUSE** The Christian community at Dura-Europos also had a place to gather for worship and to conduct important ceremonies. As was the synagogue, the Christian meeting house (FIG. **8-5**) was a remodeled private residence with a central courtyard (FIG. 8-5, no. 1). Its meeting hall (no. 2)—created by breaking down the partition between two rooms on the court's south side—could accommodate no more than about 70 people at a time. It had a raised platform at one end where the leader of the congregation sat or stood. Another room (no. 3), on the opposite side of the courtyard, had a font for *baptismal* rites, the all-important ceremony initiating a new convert into the Christian community.

Although the *baptistery* had mural paintings (poorly preserved), the place where Christians gathered to worship at Dura, as elsewhere in the Roman Empire, was a modest secondhand house, in striking contrast to the grand temples of the Roman gods. Without the approval of the state, Christian as well as Jewish communities remained small in number. Nonetheless, the emperor Diocletian (FIG. 7-73) was so concerned by the growing popularity of Christianity in the Roman army ranks that he ordered a fresh round of persecutions in 303 to 305, a half century after the last great persecutions under Trajan Decius (FIG. 7-68). As Christianity's appeal grew, so too did the Roman state's fear of weakening imperial authority, because the Christians refused to pay even token homage to the Roman state's official gods (which included deified emperors as well as the traditional pantheon of gods and goddesses). Persecution ended only in 311, when Galerius issued an edict of toleration,

and especially in 313, when Constantine (FIG. 7-77), who believed the Christian God was the source of his power rather than a threat to it (see pages 225–226), issued the Edict of Milan, which established Christianity as a legal religion with equal or superior standing to the traditional Roman cults.

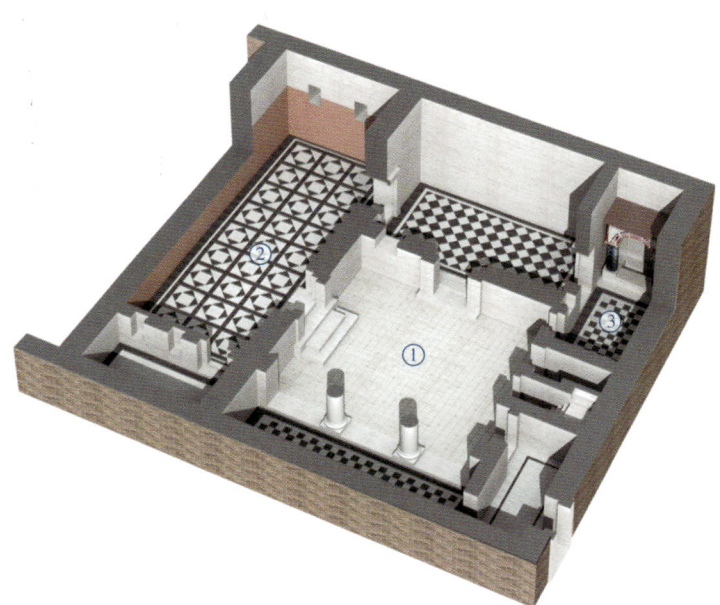

**8-5** Restored cutaway view of the Christian community house, Dura-Europos, Syria, ca. 240–256 (John Burge). (1) former courtyard of private house, (2) meeting hall, (3) baptistery.

The Christian community at Dura-Europos met in a remodeled private home that could accommodate only about 70 people. The house had a central courtyard, a meeting hall, and a baptistery.

# THE CATACOMBS AND FUNERARY ART

Very little is known about the art of the first Christians. When art historians speak about "Early Christian art," they are referring to the earliest preserved artworks with Christian subjects, not the art of Christians at the time of Jesus. Most Early Christian art in Rome dates to the third and fourth centuries and is found in the *catacombs*—vast subterranean networks of galleries (passageways) and chambers designed as cemeteries for burying Christians and, to a lesser extent, Jews (FIG. 8-4) and others. The name derives from the Latin *ad catacumbas,* which means "in the hollows." The Christian and Jewish communities tunneled the catacombs out of the tufa bedrock, much as the Etruscans created the underground tomb chambers (FIGS. 6-7 and 6-8) in the Cerveteri necropolis. The catacombs are less elaborate than the Etruscan tombs but much more extensive. The known catacombs in Rome (others exist elsewhere), which ring the outskirts of the city, comprise galleries estimated to run for 60 to 90 miles. From the second through the fourth centuries, these burial complexes were in constant use, accommodating as many as four million bodies.

In accordance with Roman custom, the dead had to be buried outside a city's walls on private property. Christian families often pooled funds in a burial association, or *confraternity.* Each of the now-labyrinthine catacombs was initially of modest extent. First, the workers dug a gallery three to four feet wide around the perimeter of the burial ground at a convenient level below the surface. In the walls of these galleries, they cut *loculi* (openings to receive the bodies of the dead, one above another, like shelves). Often, small rooms carved out of the rock, called *cubicula* (as in Roman houses of the living), served as mortuary chapels. Once the original perimeter galleries were full of loculi and cubicula, the excavators cut other galleries at right angles to them. This process continued as long as lateral space permitted, at which point the confraternities opened lower levels connected by staircases to those above. Some Roman catacomb systems extend as deep as five levels. When adjacent burial areas belonged to members of the same confraternity, or by gift or purchase fell into the same hands, the owners opened passageways between the respective cemeteries. The galleries thus spread laterally and gradually acquired a vast extent.

After Christianity received official approval under Constantine, churches rose on the land above the catacombs so the pious could worship openly at the burial sites of some of the earliest Christian *martyrs* (men and women who chose to die rather than deny their religious beliefs), whom the Church had declared *saints.*

## Painting

As already noted, Late Antique Jewish and Christian works of art do not differ from contemporaneous secular Roman artworks in style or technique, only in content. Some catacomb paintings, including many of those in the fourth-century Via Dino Compagni Catacomb (FIG. **8-5A**) on the Via Latina in Rome, even depict traditional Greco-Roman myths. It is not surprising, therefore, that the painted ceiling (FIG. **8-6**) of a cubiculum in the Catacomb of Saints Peter and Marcellinus in Rome, for example, is similar in format to the painted vaults (FIG. 7-54A) of some third-century apartment houses at Ostia that have a circular frame with a central medallion and *lunettes* (semicircular frames) around the circumference. The lunettes in the Early Christian cubiculum illustrated here (FIG. 8-6) contain the key episodes from the biblical story of Jonah. Sailors throw him from his ship on the left. He emerges on the right from the "whale." (The Greek word is *ketos,* or sea dragon, and that is how the artist represented the monstrous marine creature that swallowed Jonah; compare the sea dragon, FIG. 7-30, *right*.) At the bottom, safe on land,

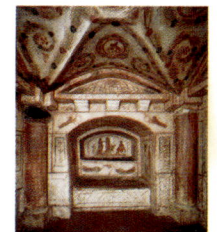

8-5A Via Dino Compagni Catacomb, Rome, ca. 320–360.

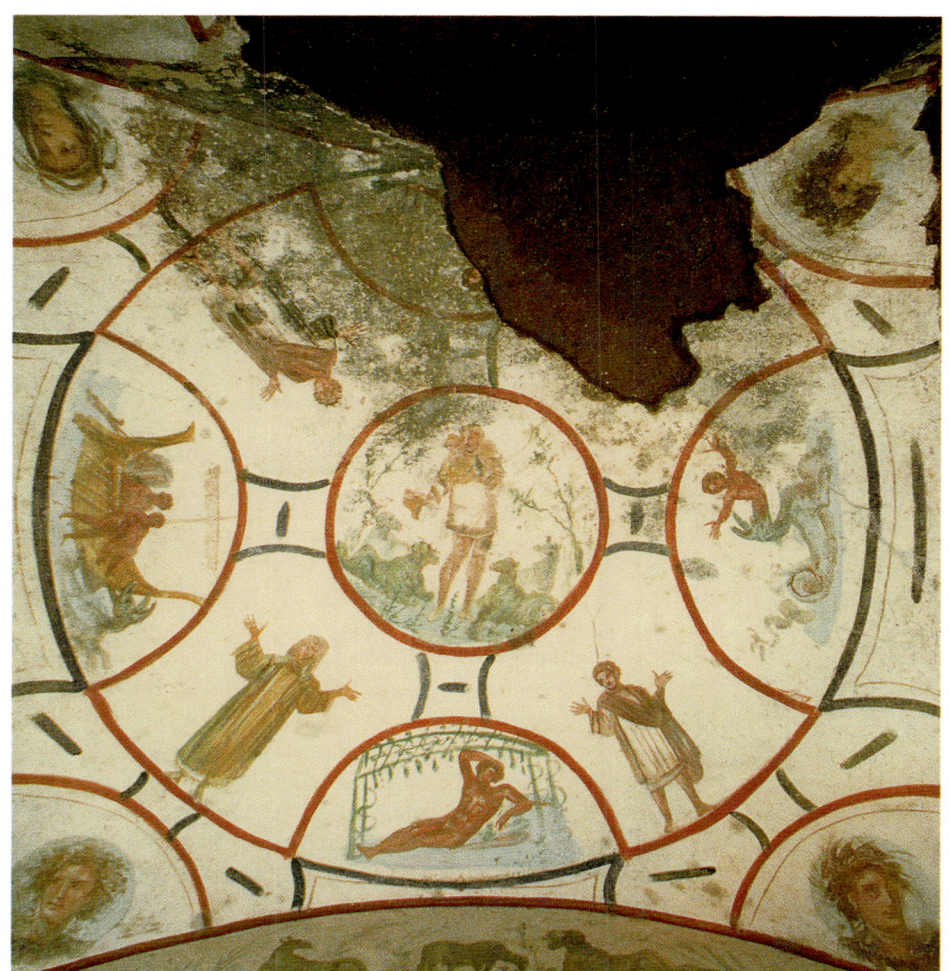

**8-6** The Good Shepherd, the story of Jonah, and orants, frescoed ceiling of a cubiculum in the Catacomb of Saints Peter and Marcellinus, Rome, Italy, early fourth century.

This ceiling in a Roman catacomb is similar in format to the painted vaults of some Ostian apartment houses, but the subjects come from the Hebrew scriptures and the New Testament.

## Jewish Subjects in Christian Art

When the Christians codified the Bible in its familiar form, they incorporated the Hebrew Torah and other writings, and designated the Jewish books as the "Old Testament" in contrast to the Christian books of the "New Testament." From the beginning, the Hebrew scriptures played an important role in Christian life and Christian art, in part because Jesus was a Jew and so many of the first Christians were converted Jews, but also because Christians came to view many of the persons and events of the Old Testament as prefigurations of New Testament persons and events. Christ himself established the pattern for this kind of biblical interpretation, called *typology*, when he compared Jonah's spending three days in the belly of the sea dragon (usually translated as "whale" in English) to the comparable time he would be entombed in the earth before his resurrection (Matt. 12:40). In the fourth century, Saint Augustine (354–430) confirmed the validity of this typological approach to the Old Testament when he stated that "the New Testament is hidden in the Old; the Old is clarified by the New."* Thus the Hebrew scriptures figured prominently in Early Christian art in all media. Biblical tales of Jewish faith and salvation were especially common in funerary contexts but appeared also in churches and on household objects.

*Augustine, *City of God*, 16.26.

The following are three of the most popular Jewish biblical stories depicted in Early Christian art:

▌ *Adam and Eve.* Eve, the first woman, tempted by a serpent, ate the forbidden fruit of the tree of knowledge, and fed some to Adam, the first man. As punishment, God expelled Adam and Eve from Paradise. This "original sin" ultimately led to Christ's sacrifice on the cross so that all humankind could be saved. Christian theologians often consider Christ the new Adam and his mother, Mary, the new Eve.

▌ *Sacrifice of Isaac.* God instructed Abraham, the father of the Hebrew nation, to sacrifice Isaac, his only son with his wife Sarah, as proof of his faith. (The mother of Abraham's first son, Ishmael, was Sarah's handmaiden.) When it became clear that Abraham would obey, the Lord sent an angel to restrain him and provided a ram for sacrifice in Isaac's place. Christians view this episode as a prefiguration of the sacrifice of God's only son, Jesus.

▌ *Jonah.* The Old Testament prophet Jonah had disobeyed God's command. In his wrath, the Lord caused a storm while Jonah was at sea. Jonah asked the sailors to throw him overboard, and the storm subsided. A sea dragon then swallowed Jonah, but God answered his prayers, and the monster spat out Jonah after three days, foretelling Christ's resurrection.

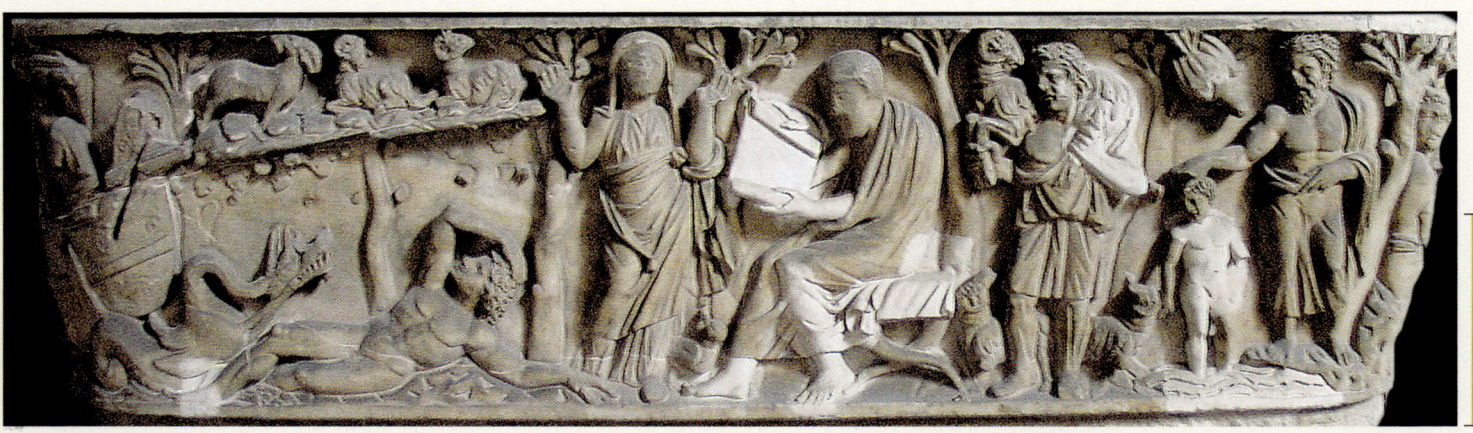

1 ft.

**8-7** Sarcophagus with philosopher, orant, and Old and New Testament scenes, ca. 270. Marble, 1′ 11¼″ × 7′ 2″. Santa Maria Antiqua, Rome.

Early Christian sarcophagi often mixed Old and New Testament themes. Jonah was a popular subject because he emerged safely from a sea monster after three days, prefiguring Christ's resurrection.

Jonah contemplates the miracle of his salvation and the mercy of God. Jonah was a popular figure in Early Christian painting and sculpture, especially in funerary contexts. The Christians honored him as a *prefiguration* (prophetic forerunner) of Christ, who rose from death as Jonah had been delivered from the belly of the *ketos*, also after three days. Hebrew miracles prefiguring Christ's resurrection abound in the catacombs and in Early Christian art in general (see "Jewish Subjects in Christian Art," above).

A man, a woman, and at least one child occupy the compartments between the Jonah lunettes. They are *orants* (praying figures), raising their arms in the ancient attitude of prayer. Together they make up a cross-section of the Christian family seeking a heavenly afterlife, although they may be generic portraits of the owners of the cubiculum. The central medallion shows Christ as the Good Shepherd, whose powers of salvation the painter underscored by placing the four episodes of the Jonah story around him. The motif of the Good Shepherd can be traced back to Archaic Greek art, but there the calf bearer (FIG. 5-8) was a bearded man offering his animal in sacrifice to Athena. In Early Christian art, Christ is the youthful and loyal protector of the Christian flock, who said to his disciples, "I am the good shepherd; the good shepherd gives his life for the sheep" (John 10:11). In the Christian motif, the sheep on Christ's shoulders is not a sacrificial offering.

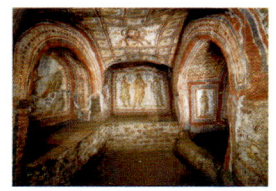

8-6A Catacomb of Commodilla, Rome, ca. 370–385.

It is one of the lost sheep Christ has retrieved, symbolizing a sinner who has strayed and been rescued. Early Christian artists almost invariably represented Christ either as the Good Shepherd or as a teacher. Only after Christianity became the Roman Empire's official religion in 380 did Christ take on in art such imperial attributes as the halo, the purple robe, and the throne, which denoted rulership. Eventually, artists depicted Christ with the beard of a mature adult—as in the late-fourth-century Catacomb of Commodilla in Rome (FIG. 8-6A)—which has been the standard form for centuries, supplanting the youthful imagery of most Early Christian portrayals of the Savior.

## Sculpture

Most Christians rejected cremation because they believed in the resurrection of the body, and the wealthiest Christian faithful, as other well-to-do Romans, favored impressive marble sarcophagi. Many of these coffins have survived in the catacombs and elsewhere. As expected, the most common themes painted on the walls and vaults of the Roman subterranean cemeteries were also the subjects that appeared on Early Christian sarcophagi. Often, the decoration of the marble coffins was a collection of significant Jewish and Christian themes, just as on the painted ceiling (FIG. 8-6) in the Catacomb of Saints Peter and Marcellinus.

**SANTA MARIA ANTIQUA SARCOPHAGUS** On the front of a sarcophagus (FIG. 8-7) in Santa Maria Antiqua in Rome, the story of Jonah occupies the left third. At the center are an orant and a seated philosopher, the latter a motif borrowed directly from Roman sarcophagi (FIG. 7-71) and popular also in Roman painting (FIG. 7-25B) and statuary. The heads of both the praying woman and the seated man reading from a scroll are unfinished. Roman workshops often produced sarcophagi before knowing who would purchase them. The sculptors added the portraits at the time of burial, if they added them at all. This practice underscores the universal appeal of the themes chosen.

At the right are two different, yet linked, representations of Jesus—as the Good Shepherd and as a child receiving baptism in the Jordan River, though he really was baptized at age 30 (see "The Life of Jesus in Art," pages 240–241). In the early centuries of Christianity, baptism was usually delayed almost to the moment of death because it cleansed the Christian of all sin. One of those who was baptized on his deathbed was the emperor Constantine. On this sarcophagus, the newly baptized child Jesus turns his head toward the Good Shepherd and places his right hand on one of the sheep—perhaps the sculptor's way of suggesting Jesus' future ministry.

**GOOD SHEPHERD STATUETTE** Apart from the reliefs on privately commissioned sarcophagi such as the Santa Maria Antiqua sarcophagus and that of the city prefect Junius Bassus (FIG. 8-1), monumental sculpture became increasingly uncommon in the fourth century. Roman emperors and other officials continued to set up portraits, and sculptors still carved and cast statues of Greco-Roman gods and mythological figures, but the number of freestanding sculptures decreased sharply. In his *Apologia,* Justin Martyr, a second-century philosopher who converted to Christianity, condemned the traditional Greco-Roman practice of worshiping statues as gods, which the Second Commandment prohibited. Christians tended to suspect the freestanding statue, linking it with the false gods of the Romans, so Early Christian houses of worship, like Late

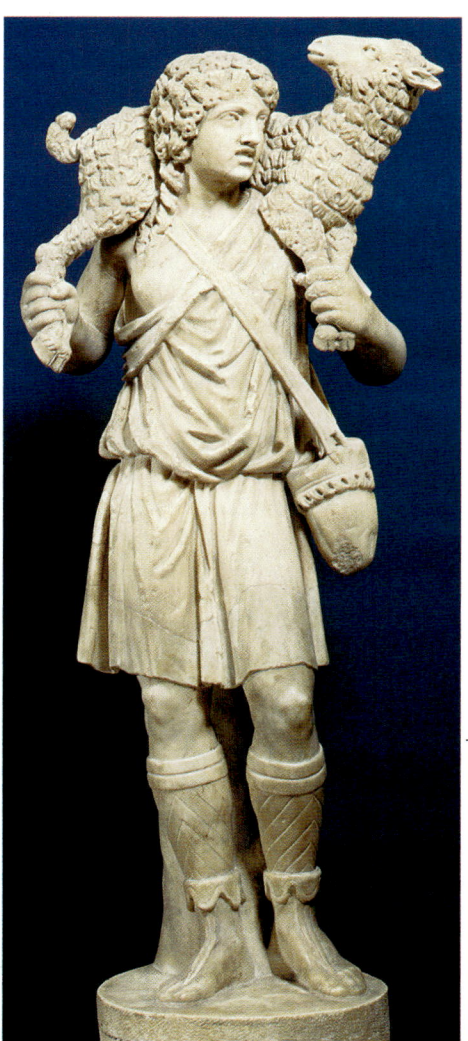

8-8 **Christ as the Good Shepherd,** ca. 300–350. Marble, 3′ ¼″ high. Musei Vaticani, Rome.

Although freestanding images of Christ were uncommon in Late Antiquity, several statuettes exist representing the Good Shepherd. The patrons were probably recent converts to Christianity.

1 ft.

Antique synagogues (FIG. 8-2), had no cult statues. Nor did churches or synagogues have any equivalent of the pedimental statues and relief friezes of Greco-Roman temples.

The Greco-Roman experience, however, was still a living part of the Mediterranean mentality, and many recently converted Christians retained some of the traditional values of the Greco-Roman world. This may account for those rare instances of freestanding Early Christian sculptures, such as the fourth-century statuettes representing Christ as the Good Shepherd (FIG. 8-8) or as a seated philosopher (FIG. 8-8A). As in Early

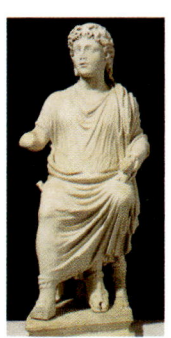

8-8A Christ seated, ca. 350–375.

Christian catacomb paintings (FIG. 8-6) and sarcophagi (FIG. 8-7), Christ is a long-haired young man dressed in a simple tunic. In the Good Shepherd statuette, he stands in a classical contrapposto stance with his right hip outthrust and his left leg bent. Several other marble statuettes of Christ bearing a sheep on his shoulders have been found, including one now in the Cleveland Museum of Art. It was part of a cache of sculptures from Turkey that included portraits and four marble statuettes illustrating episodes of the story of Jonah. Like the Good Shepherd statues, the Jonah figures are freestanding versions of the narrative scenes popular on Early Christian sarcophagi.

# The Life of Jesus in Art

Christians believe Jesus of Nazareth is the son of God, the *Messiah* (Savior, *Christ*) of the Jews prophesied in the Hebrew scriptures. His life—his miraculous birth from the womb of a virgin mother, his preaching and miracle working, his execution by the Romans and subsequent ascent to Heaven—has been the subject of countless artworks from Roman times through the present day. The primary literary sources for these representations are the Gospels of the New Testament attributed to the four evangelists, Saints Matthew, Mark, Luke, and John (see "The Four Evangelists," Chapter 11, page 314); later apocryphal works; and medieval theologians' commentaries on these texts.

The life of Jesus dominated the subject matter of Christian art to a far greater extent than Greco-Roman religion and mythology ever did classical art. Whereas images of athletes, portraits of statesmen and philosophers, narratives of war and peace, genre scenes, and other secular subjects were staples of the classical tradition, Christian iconography held a near monopoly in the art of the Western world in the Middle Ages.

Although during certain periods artists rarely, if ever, depicted many of the events of Jesus' life, the cycle as a whole has been one of the most frequent subjects of Western art, even after the widespread revival of classical and secular themes during the Renaissance. Thus it is useful to summarize at the outset the entire cycle of events as they usually appear in artworks.

## INCARNATION AND CHILDHOOD

The first "cycle" of the life of Jesus consists of the events of his conception (incarnation), birth, infancy, and childhood.

- *Annunciation to Mary.* The archangel Gabriel announces to the Virgin Mary that she will miraculously conceive and give birth to God's son Jesus. Artists sometimes indicated God's presence at the incarnation by a dove, the symbol of the Holy Spirit, the third "person" of the *Trinity* with God the Father and Jesus.

- *Visitation.* The pregnant Mary visits Elizabeth, her older cousin, who is pregnant with the future Saint John the Baptist. Elizabeth is the first to recognize that the baby Mary is bearing is the son of God, and they rejoice.

- *Nativity, Annunciation to the Shepherds, and Adoration of the Shepherds.* Jesus is born at night in Bethlehem and placed in a basket. Mary and her husband, Joseph, marvel at the newborn in a stable or, in Byzantine art, in a cave. An angel announces the birth of the Savior to shepherds in the field, who rush to adore the infant Jesus.

- *Adoration of the Magi.* A bright star alerts three wise men (*magi*) in the East that the king of the Jews has been born. They travel 12 days to find the holy family and present precious gifts to the infant Jesus.

- *Presentation in the Temple.* In accordance with Jewish tradition, Mary and Joseph bring their firstborn son to the temple in Jerusalem, where the aged Simeon, who God said would not die until he had seen the Messiah, recognizes Jesus as the prophesied savior of humankind.

- *Massacre of the Innocents and Flight into Egypt.* King Herod, fearful a rival king has been born, orders the massacre of all infants in Bethlehem, but an angel warns the holy family and they escape to Egypt.

- *Dispute in the Temple.* Joseph and Mary travel to Jerusalem for the feast of *Passover* (the celebration of the release of the Jews from bondage to the pharaohs of Egypt). Jesus, only 12 years old at the time, engages in learned debate with astonished Jewish scholars in the temple, foretelling his ministry.

## PUBLIC MINISTRY

The public-ministry cycle comprises the teachings of Jesus and the miracles he performed.

- *Baptism.* Jesus' public ministry begins with his baptism at age 30 by John the Baptist in the Jordan River, where the dove of the Holy Spirit appears and God's voice is heard proclaiming Jesus as his son.

- *Calling of Matthew.* Jesus summons Matthew, a tax collector, to follow him, and Matthew becomes one of his 12 disciples, or *apostles* (from the Greek for "messenger"), and later the author of one of the four Gospels of the New Testament.

- *Miracles.* In the course of his teaching and travels, Jesus performs many miracles, revealing his divine nature. These include acts of healing and raising the dead, turning water into wine, walking on water and calming storms, and creating wondrous quantities of food. In the miracle of loaves and fishes, for example, Jesus transforms a few loaves of bread and a handful of fishes into enough food to feed several thousand people.

- *Delivery of the Keys to Peter.* The fisherman Peter was one of the first men Jesus summoned as a disciple. Jesus chooses Peter (whose name means "rock") as his successor. He declares Peter is the rock on which his church will be built, and symbolically delivers to Peter the keys to the kingdom of Heaven.

- *Transfiguration.* Jesus scales a high mountain and, in the presence of Peter and two other disciples, James and John the Evangelist, transforms into radiant light. God, speaking from a cloud, discloses Jesus is his son.

- *Cleansing of the Temple.* Jesus returns to Jerusalem, where he finds money changers and merchants conducting business in the temple. He rebukes them and drives them out of the sacred precinct.

## PASSION

The passion (from Latin *passio*, "suffering") cycle includes the episodes leading to Jesus' trial, execution, resurrection, and ascent to Heaven.

■ *Entry into Jerusalem.* On the Sunday before his crucifixion (Palm Sunday), Jesus rides into Jerusalem on a donkey, accompanied by disciples. Crowds of people enthusiastically greet Jesus and place palm fronds in his path.

■ *Last Supper and Washing of the Disciples' Feet.* In Jerusalem, Jesus celebrates Passover with his disciples. During this last supper, Jesus foretells his imminent betrayal, arrest, and death and invites the disciples to remember him when they eat unleavened bread (symbol of his body) and drink wine (his blood). This ritual became the celebration of *Mass* (*Eucharist*) in Christian liturgy. At the same meal, Jesus sets an example of humility for his apostles by washing their feet.

■ *Agony in the Garden.* Jesus goes to the Mount of Olives in the Garden of Gethsemane, where he struggles to overcome his human fear of death by praying for divine strength. The apostles who accompanied him there fall asleep despite his request they stay awake with him while he prays.

■ *Betrayal and Arrest.* One of the disciples, Judas Iscariot, agrees to betray Jesus to the Jewish authorities in return for 30 pieces of silver. Judas leads the soldiers to Jesus and identifies the "king of the Jews" by kissing him, whereupon the soldiers arrest Jesus. Later, a remorseful Judas hangs himself from a tree.

■ *Trials of Jesus and Denial of Peter.* The soldiers bring Jesus before Caiaphas, the Jewish high priest, who interrogates Jesus about his claim to be the Messiah. Meanwhile, the disciple Peter thrice denies knowing Jesus, as Jesus predicted he would. Jesus is then brought before the Roman governor of Judaea, Pontius Pilate, on the charge of treason because he had proclaimed himself as the Jews' king. Pilate asks the crowd to choose between freeing Jesus or Barabbas, a murderer. The people choose Barabbas, and the judge condemns Jesus to death. Pilate then washes his hands, symbolically relieving himself of responsibility for the mob's decision.

■ *Flagellation and Mocking.* The Roman soldiers who hold Jesus captive tie him up, whip (flagellate) him, and mock him by dressing him as king of the Jews and placing a crown of thorns on his head.

■ *Carrying of the Cross, Raising of the Cross, and Crucifixion.* The Romans force Jesus to carry the cross on which he will be crucified from Jerusalem to Mount Calvary (Golgotha, the "place of the skull," Adam's burial place). Jesus falls three times, and his robe is stripped along the way. Soldiers erect the cross—often labeled in art *INRI* (the initial letters of "Jesus of Nazareth, King of the Jews" in Latin)—and nail his hands and feet to it. Jesus' mother, John the Evangelist, and Mary Magdalene mourn at the foot of the cross, while the Roman soldiers torment Jesus. One of them (the centurion Longinus) stabs Jesus in the side with a spear. After suffering great pain, Jesus dies. The crucifixion occurred on a Friday, and Christians celebrate the day each year as Good Friday.

■ *Deposition, Lamentation, and Entombment.* Two disciples, Joseph of Arimathea and Nicodemus, remove Jesus' body from the cross (the deposition). Sometimes those present at the crucifixion look on. His mother and his followers take Jesus to the tomb Joseph had purchased for himself, and Joseph, Nicodemus, the Virgin Mary, Saint John the Evangelist, and Mary Magdalene mourn over the dead Jesus (the lamentation). (When in art the isolated figure of the Virgin Mary cradles her dead son in her lap, it is called a *Pietà*—Italian for "pity.") In portrayals of the entombment, his followers lower Jesus into a sarcophagus in the tomb.

■ *Descent into Limbo.* During the three days he spends in the tomb, Jesus (after death, Christ) descends into Hell, or Limbo, and triumphantly frees the souls of the righteous, including Adam, Eve, Moses, David, Solomon, and John the Baptist. In Byzantine art, the label *Anastasis* (Greek, "resurrection") often identifies this episode, although the event precedes Christ's emergence from the tomb and reappearance on earth.

■ *Resurrection and Three Marys at the Tomb.* On the third day after his burial (Easter Sunday), Christ rises from the dead and leaves the tomb while the Roman guards sleep. The Virgin Mary, Mary Magdalene, and Mary, the mother of James, visit the tomb but find it empty. An angel informs them Christ has been resurrected.

■ *Noli Me Tangere, Supper at Emmaus, and Doubting of Thomas.* During the 40 days between Christ's resurrection and his ascent to Heaven, he appears on several occasions to his followers. When he encounters Mary Magdalene weeping at his tomb, Christ warns her with the words "Don't touch me" (*Noli me tangere* in Latin), but he tells her to inform the apostles of his return. At Emmaus he eats supper with two of his astonished disciples. Later, Christ invites Thomas, who cannot believe Jesus has risen, to touch the wound in his side that he received at his crucifixion.

■ *Ascension.* On the 40th day, on the Mount of Olives, with his mother and apostles as witnesses, Christ gloriously ascends to Heaven in a cloud.

# ARCHITECTURE AND MOSAICS

Although the Christians conducted some ceremonies in the catacombs, regular services took place in private community houses of the type found at Dura-Europos (FIG. 8-5). Once Christianity achieved imperial sponsorship under Constantine, an urgent need suddenly arose to construct churches. The new buildings had to meet the requirements of Christian *liturgy* (the official ritual of public worship), provide a suitably monumental setting for the celebration of the Christian faith, and accommodate the rapidly growing numbers of worshipers.

Constantine believed the Christian god had guided him to victory over Maxentius, and in lifelong gratitude he protected and advanced Christianity throughout the Empire. As emperor, he was, of course, obliged to safeguard the ancient Roman religion, traditions, and monuments, and he was (for his time) a builder on a grand scale in the heart of the city (FIGS. 7-75 and 7-78). But Constantine, eager to provide buildings to house the Christian rituals and venerated burial places, especially the memorials of founding saints, also was the first major patron of Christian architecture. He constructed elaborate basilicas, memorials, and mausoleums not only in Rome but also in Constantinople, his "New Rome" in the East, and at sites sacred to Christianity, most notably Bethlehem, the birthplace of Jesus, and Jerusalem, the site of the crucifixion.

## Rome

The major Constantinian churches in Rome stood on sites associated with the graves of Christian martyrs, which, in keeping with Roman burial practice, were all on the city's outskirts. The decision to erect churches at those sites also enabled Constantine to keep the new Christian shrines out of the city center and avoid any confrontation between Rome's Christians and those who continued to worship the old gods.

**OLD SAINT PETER'S** The greatest of Constantine's churches in Rome was Old Saint Peter's (FIG. 8-9), probably begun as early as 319. The present-day church (FIGS. 24-3 and 24-4), one of the master-

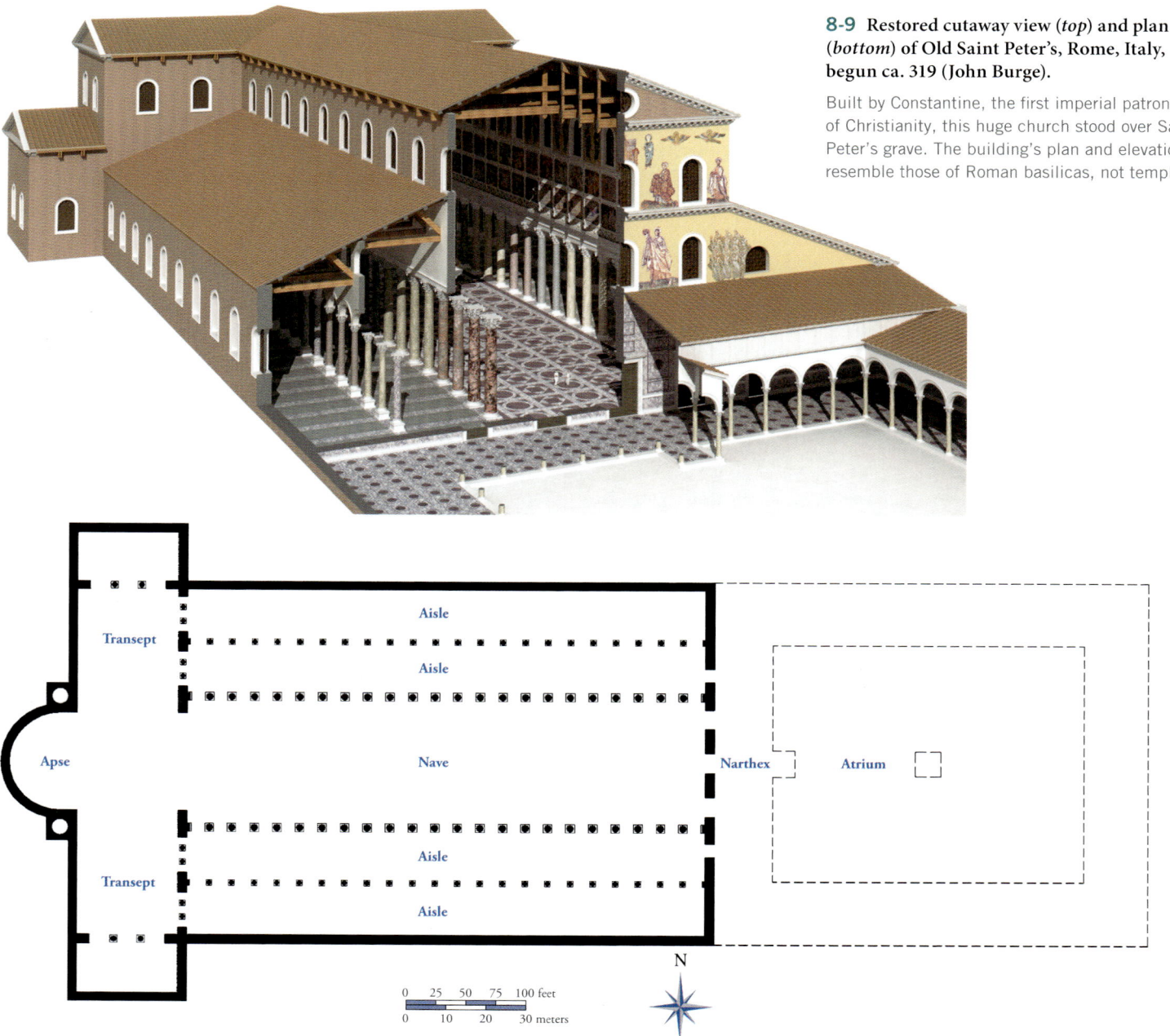

**8-9** Restored cutaway view (*top*) and plan (*bottom*) of Old Saint Peter's, Rome, Italy, begun ca. 319 (John Burge).

Built by Constantine, the first imperial patron of Christianity, this huge church stood over Saint Peter's grave. The building's plan and elevation resemble those of Roman basilicas, not temples.

pieces of Italian Renaissance and Baroque architecture, is a replacement for the Constantinian structure. Old Saint Peter's stood on the western side of the Tiber River on a terrace on the irregular slope of the Vatican Hill over the ancient cemetery in which Constantine and Pope Sylvester (r. 314–335) believed Peter, the founder of the Christian community in Rome, had been buried. Excavations in the Roman cemetery beneath the church have in fact revealed a second-century memorial erected in honor of the Christian martyr at his reputed grave. Capable of housing 3,000 to 4,000 worshipers at one time, the immense church enshrined Peter's tomb, one of the most hallowed sites in Christendom, second only to the Holy Sepulcher in Jerusalem, the site of Christ's resurrection. The project also fulfilled the figurative words of Christ himself, when he said, "Thou art Peter, and upon this rock I will build my church" (Matt. 16:18). Peter was Rome's first bishop and the head of the long line of popes extending to the present.

The plan and elevation (FIG. 8-9) of Old Saint Peter's resemble those of Roman basilicas and audience halls, such as the Basilica Ulpia (FIG. 7-44, no. 4) in the Forum of Trajan and Constantine's own Aula Palatina (FIGS. 7-79 and 7-80) at Trier, rather than the design of any Greco-Roman temple. The Christians, understandably, did not want their houses of worship to mimic the form of polytheistic shrines, but practical considerations also contributed to their shunning the classical temple type. Greco-Roman temples housed only the cult statue of the deity. All rituals took place outside at open-air altars. Therefore, architects would have found it difficult to adapt the classical temple as a building accommodating large numbers of people within it. The Roman basilica, in contrast, was ideally suited as a place for congregation.

Like most Roman basilicas, Old Saint Peter's had a wide central *nave* (FIG. 8-9, *bottom*) with flanking *aisles* and an *apse* at the end. But unlike Roman basilicas, which sometimes had doorways on one long side opening onto an aisle (FIG. 7-44, no. 4), Early Christian basilicas all had a pronounced *longitudinal* axis. Worshipers entered the basilica through a *narthex,* or vestibule. When they emerged in Saint Peter's 300-foot-long nave, they had an unobstructed view of the altar in the apse, framed by the *chancel arch* dividing the nave from the transept. The *transept,* or transverse aisle, an area perpendicular to the nave between the nave and apse, was a special feature of this Constantinian church. It housed Saint Peter's *relics,* which attracted hordes of pilgrims. (Relics are body parts, clothing, or objects associated with a saint or Christ himself; see "The Veneration of Relics," Chapter 12, page 336.) The transept became a standard element of church design in the West only much later, when it also took on, with the nave and apse, the symbolism of the Christian cross. Saint Peter's basilica also had a colonnaded courtyard in front of the narthex, very much like the forum proper in the Forum of Trajan (FIG. 7-44, no. 5) but called an *atrium,* like the central room in a Roman private house (FIG. 7-15).

Compared with Roman temples, which usually displayed statuary in pediments on their facades, most Early Christian basilicas were quite austere on the exterior. Inside, however, were frescoes and mosaics, marble columns (taken from older Roman buildings, as was customary at the time), and costly ornaments. The *Liber pontificalis,* or *Book of the Pontiffs* (*Popes*), compiled by an anonymous sixth-century author, lists Constantine's gifts to Old Saint Peter's. They included altars, chandeliers, candlesticks, pitchers, goblets, and plates fashioned of gold and silver and sometimes embellished with jewels and pearls, as well as jeweled altar cloths for use in the Mass and gold foil to sheathe the vault of the apse.[1] A huge marble *baldacchino* (domical canopy over an altar), supported by four spiral porphyry columns, marked the spot of Saint Peter's tomb.

**SANTA SABINA** Some idea of the character of the timber-roofed interior of Old Saint Peter's can be gleaned from the interior (FIG. **8-10**) of Santa Sabina in Rome. Santa Sabina, built a century later, is a basilican church of much more modest proportions than Constantine's immense Vatican basilica, but it still retains its Early Christian character, as well as its original carved wooden doors (FIG. **8-10A**). The Corinthian columns of its nave *arcade* produce a steady rhythm that focuses all attention on the chancel arch and the apse, which frame the altar. In Santa Sabina,

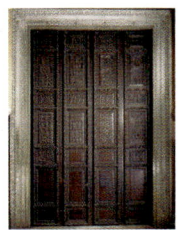

8-10A West doors, Santa Sabina, Rome, ca. 432.

as in Old Saint Peter's, light drenched the nave from the *clerestory* windows piercing the thin upper wall beneath the timber roof. The same light would have illuminated the frescoes and mosaics that commonly adorned the nave and apse of Early Christian churches. Outside, Santa Sabina has plain brick walls. They closely resemble the exterior of Trier's Aula Palatina (FIG. 7-79).

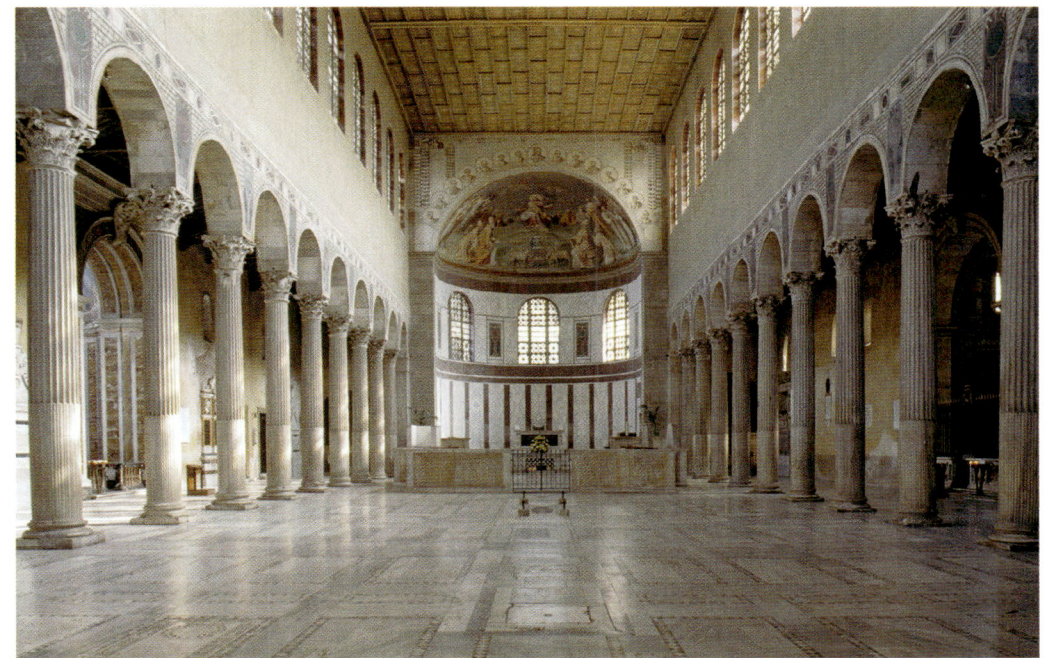

**8-10** Interior of Santa Sabina (looking northeast), Rome, Italy, 422–432. ◼◀

Santa Sabina and other Early Christian basilican churches were timber-roofed and illuminated by clerestory windows. The nave arcade focused attention on the apse, which framed the altar.

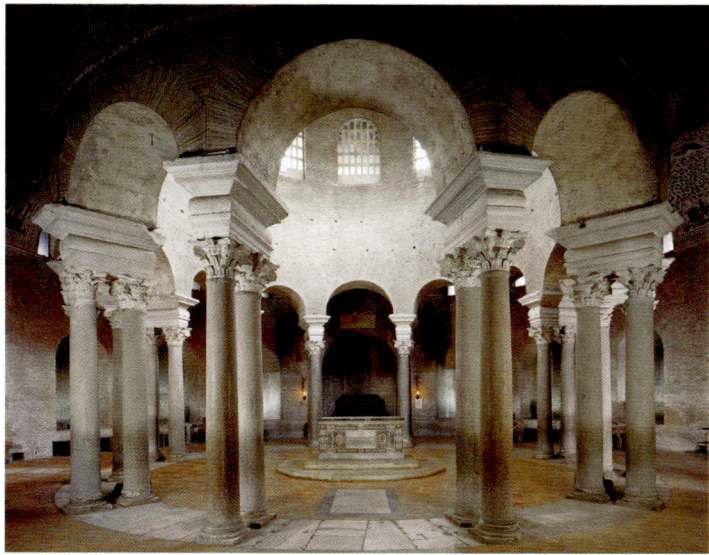

**8-11** Interior of Santa Costanza (looking southwest), Rome, Italy, ca. 337–351. ◼◂

Possibly built as the mausoleum of Constantine's daughter, Santa Costanza later became a church. Its central plan, featuring a domed interior, would become the preferred form for Byzantine churches.

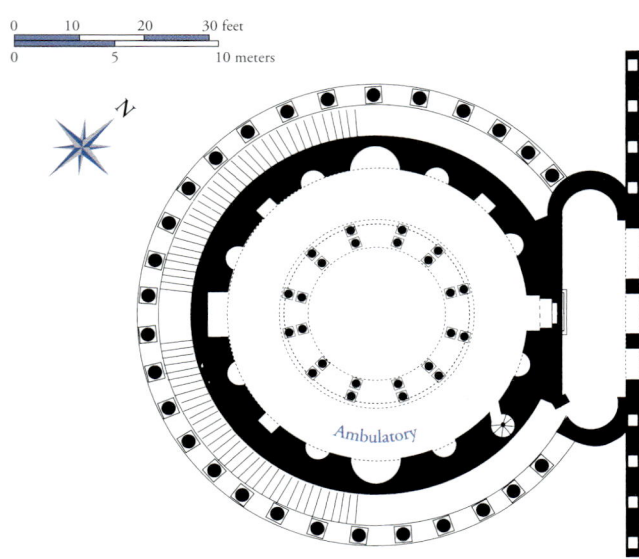

**8-12** Plan of Santa Costanza, Rome, Italy, ca. 337–351.

Santa Costanza has antecedents in the domed temples (FIG. 7-51) and mausoleums (FIG. 7-74) of the Romans, but its plan, with 12 pairs of columns and a vaulted ambulatory, is unique.

**SANTA COSTANZA** The rectangular basilican church design was long the favorite of the Western Christian world. But Early Christian architects also adopted another classical architectural type: the *central-plan* building, in which the parts are of equal or almost equal dimensions around the center. Roman central-plan buildings were usually round or polygonal domed structures. Byzantine architects developed this form to monumental proportions and amplified its theme in numerous ingenious variations (see Chapter 9). In the West, builders generally used the central plan for structures adjacent to the main basilicas, such as mausoleums, baptisteries, and private chapels, rather than for churches, as in the East.

A highly refined example of the central-plan design is Santa Costanza (FIGS. **8-11** and **8-12**), built on the northern outskirts of Rome in the mid-fourth century, possibly as the mausoleum for Constantina, the emperor Constantine's daughter. Recent excavations have called the traditional identification into question, but the building housed Constantina's monumental porphyry sarcophagus, even if the structure was not originally her tomb. The mausoleum, later converted into a church, stood next to the basilican church of Saint Agnes, who was buried in a nearby catacomb. Santa Costanza's antecedents are traceable to the tholos tombs (FIGS. 4-20 and 4-21) of the Mycenaeans, but its immediate predecessors were the domed structures of the Romans, such as the Pantheon (FIGS. 7-49 to 7-51) and especially imperial mausoleums such as Diocletian's (FIG. 7-74, *right*) at Split. At Santa Costanza, the architect modified the interior design of those Roman buildings to accommodate an *ambulatory,* a ringlike barrel-vaulted corridor separated from the central domed cylinder by a dozen pairs of columns.

Like most Early Christian basilicas, Santa Costanza has a severe brick exterior. Its interior was once richly adorned with mosaics, although most are lost. Old and New Testament themes appeared side by side, as in the catacombs and on Early Christian sarcophagi. The Santa Costanza mosaic program, however, also included subjects

**8-13** Detail of the mosaic in the ambulatory vault of Santa Costanza, Rome, Italy, ca. 337–351. ◼◂

The ambulatory mosaics of Santa Costanza depict putti harvesting grapes and making wine, motifs associated with Bacchus, but for a Christian, the scenes evoked the Eucharist and Christ's blood.

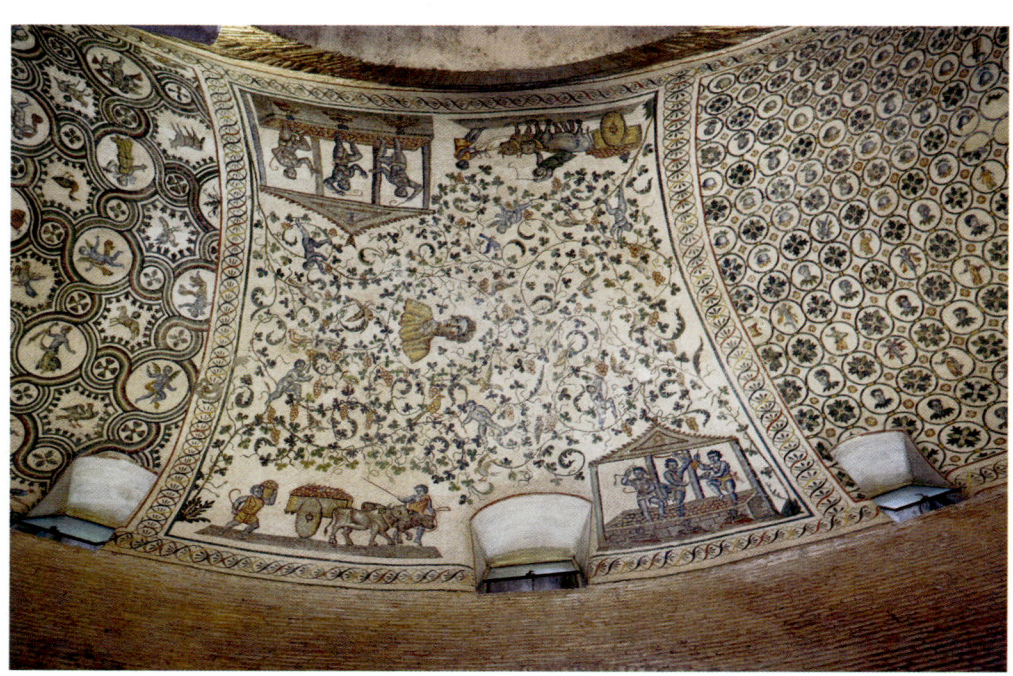

## Mosaics

As an art form, *mosaic* had a rather simple and utilitarian beginning, seemingly invented primarily to provide an inexpensive and durable flooring. Originally, mosaicists set small beach pebbles, unaltered from their natural form and color, into a thick coat of cement. Artisans soon discovered, however, that the stones could be arranged in decorative patterns. At first, these *pebble mosaics* were uncomplicated and confined to geometric shapes. Generally, the artists used only black and white stones. Examples of this type, dating to the eighth century BCE, have been found at Gordion in Asia Minor. Eventually, artists arranged the stones to form more complex pictorial designs, and by the fourth century BCE the technique had developed to a high level of sophistication. Mosaicists depicted elaborate figural scenes using a broad range of colors—red, yellow, and brown in addition to black, white, and gray—and shaded the figures, clothing, and setting to suggest volume. Thin strips of lead provided linear definition (FIG. 5-68).

By the middle of the third century BCE, artists had invented a new kind of mosaic that enabled the best mosaicists to create designs more closely approximating true paintings. The new technique employed *tesserae* (Latin for "cubes" or "dice"). These tiny cut stones gave artists much greater flexibility because they could adjust the size and shape of the tesserae, eliminating the need for lead strips to indicate contours and interior details. More gradual gradations of color also became possible (FIG. 5-70), and mosaicists finally could aspire to rival the achievements of painters.

In Early Christian mosaics (FIGS. 8-13, 8-13A, 8-14, and 8-16 to 8-19A), the tesserae are usually made of glass, which reflects light and makes the surfaces sparkle. Ancient mosaicists occasionally used glass tesserae, but the Romans preferred opaque marble pieces. Mosaics quickly became the standard means of decorating walls and vaults in Early Christian buildings, although mural paintings were also popular. The mosaics caught the light flooding through the windows in vibrant reflection, producing sharp contrasts and concentrations of color that could focus attention on a composition's central, most relevant features. Early Christian mosaics were not meant to incorporate the subtle tonal changes a naturalistic painter's approach would require. Artists "placed," rather than blended, colors. Bright, hard, glittering texture, set within a rigorously simplified pattern, became the rule. For mosaics situated high in an apse or ambulatory vault or over the nave colonnade, far above the observer's head, the painstaking use of tiny tesserae seen in Roman floor and wall mosaics (FIGS. 5-70 and 7-24) would be meaningless. Early Christian mosaics, designed to be seen from a distance, employed larger tesserae. The mosaicists also set the tesserae unevenly so that their surfaces could catch and reflect the light. Artists favored simple designs for optimal legibility. For several centuries, mosaic, in the service of Christian theology, was the medium of some of the supreme masterpieces of medieval art.

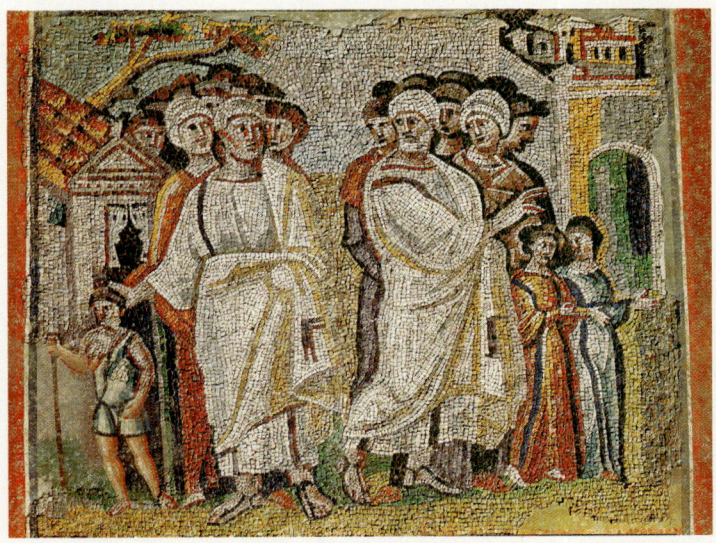

**8-14** *The Parting of Abraham and Lot,* mosaic in the nave of Santa Maria Maggiore, Rome, Italy, 432–440.

In this Early Christian glass-tessera mosaic depicting *The Parting of Abraham and Lot,* the artist included the yet-unborn Isaac because of his importance as a prefiguration of Christ.

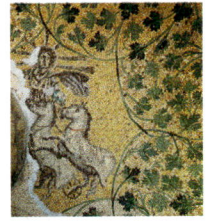

**8-13A** Christ as Sol Invictus, late third century.

common in Roman funerary art, although they were susceptible to a Christian interpretation. In one section (FIG. 8-13) of the mosaic in the ambulatory vault, for example, are scenes of putti harvesting grapes and making wine. (Similar scenes decorate Constantina's sarcophagus.) A portrait bust is at the center of a rich vine scroll. A second bust appears in another section of the mosaic vault, but both are heavily restored, and the identification of the pair as Constantina and her husband is uncertain. In the Roman world, wine was primarily associated with Bacchus, but for a Christian, the vineyards brought to mind the wine of the Eucharist and the blood of Christ. Already in the third century, however, mosaics of explicitly Christian content had been used in tombs, for example, in the Mausoleum of the Julii (FIG. 8-13A) in the ancient cemetery beneath Saint Peter's in Rome.

**SANTA MARIA MAGGIORE** Mosaic decoration (see "Mosaics," above) played an important role in the interiors of Early Christian buildings of all types. In churches, mosaics not only provided a beautiful setting for the Christian liturgy, but also were vehicles for instructing the congregation about biblical stories and Christian dogma. Old Testament themes are the focus of the extensive fifth-century mosaic cycle in the nave of the basilican church of Santa Maria Maggiore in Rome, the first major church in the West dedicated to the Virgin Mary. Construction of the church began in 432, the year after the Council of Ephesus officially designated Mary as the Mother of God (*Theotokos,* "bearer of god" in Greek). The council, convened to debate whether Mary had given birth to the man Jesus or to God as man, ruled that the divine and human coexisted in Christ and that Mary was indeed the Mother of God.

One mosaic panel (FIG. 8-14) dramatically represents *The Parting of Abraham and Lot,* as set forth in Genesis, the Bible's opening book. Agreeing to disagree, Abraham's nephew Lot leads his family and followers to the right, toward the city of Sodom, while Abraham heads for Canaan, moving toward a basilica-like building (perhaps symbolizing the Church) on the left. Lot's is the evil choice, and the instruments of the evil (his two daughters) stand in front of him. The figure of the yet-unborn Isaac, the instrument of good (and, as noted earlier, a prefiguration of Christ), stands before his father, Abraham.

The cleavage of the two groups is emphatic, and the mosaicist represented each group using a shorthand device called a *head cluster,* which had precedents in antiquity and a long history in Christian art. The figures engage in a sharp dialogue of glance and gesture. The wide eyes turn in their sockets, and the enlarged hands make broad gestures. This kind of simplified motion, which is characteristic of Late Antique narrative art of Roman, Jewish, and Christian subject matter alike, has great power to communicate without ambiguity. But the Abraham and Lot mosaic also reveals the heritage of classical art. The town in the background of the Abraham and Lot mosaic would not be out of place in a Roman mural (FIG. 7-19, *left*) or on the Column of Trajan (FIG. 7-1), and the figures themselves are modeled in light and dark, cast shadows, and still loom with massive solidity. Another century had to pass before Western Christian mosaicists portrayed figures as flat images, rather than as three-dimensional bodies, finally rejecting the norms of classical art in favor of a style better suited for a focus on the spiritual instead of the natural world. Early Christian art, like Late Antique Roman art in general, vacillates between these two stylistic poles.

## Ravenna

In the decades after the 324 founding of Constantinople, the New Rome in the East, and the death of Constantine in 337, the pace of Christianization of the Roman Empire quickened. In 380 the emperor Theodosius I (r. 379–395) issued an edict finally establishing Christianity as the state religion. In 391 he enacted a ban against worship of the old Roman gods, and in 394 he abolished the Olympic Games, the enduring symbol of the classical world and its values.

Theodosius died in 395, and imperial power passed to his two sons, Arcadius (r. 395–408), who became Emperor of the East, and

Honorius (r. 395–423), Emperor of the West. In 404, when the Visigoths, under their king, Alaric (r. 395–410), threatened to overrun Italy from the northwest, Honorius moved his capital from Milan to Ravenna, an ancient Roman city (perhaps founded by the Etruscans) near Italy's Adriatic coast, some 80 miles south of Venice. In 410, Alaric captured Rome, and in 476, Ravenna fell to Odoacer (r. 476–493), the first Germanic king of Italy. Odoacer was overthrown in turn by Theodoric (r. 471–526), king of the Ostrogoths, who established his capital at Ravenna in 493. Ravenna fell to the Byzantine emperor Justinian in 539, and the subsequent history of the city belongs with that of Byzantium (see Chapter 9).

**MAUSOLEUM OF GALLA PLACIDIA** The so-called Mausoleum of Galla Placidia, Honorius's half-sister, is a rather small *cruciform* (cross-shaped) structure (FIG. 8-15) with barrel-vaulted arms and a tower at the *crossing*. Built shortly after 425, almost a quarter century before Galla Placidia's death in 450, it was probably originally a chapel to the martyred Saint Lawrence. The building was once thought to be Galla Placidia's tomb, however, hence its name today. The chapel adjoined the narthex of the now greatly altered palace-church of Santa Croce (Holy Cross), which was also cruciform in plan. The chapel's cross arms are of unequal length, so that the building has a longitudinal orientation, unlike the centrally planned Santa Costanza (FIGS. 8-11 and 8-12), but because all four arms are very short, the emphasis is on the tall *crossing tower* with

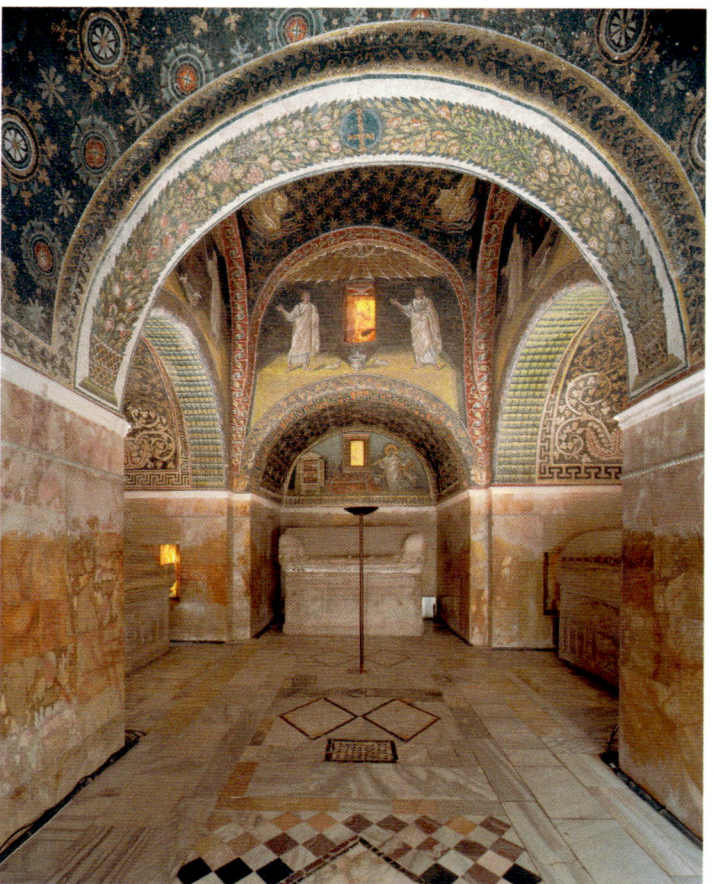

**8-16** Interior of the Mausoleum of Galla Placidia, Ravenna, Italy, ca. 425.

Before Late Antiquity, mosaics were usually confined to floors. Inside the so-called Mausoleum of Galla Placidia, mosaics cover every square inch of the interior above the marble-faced walls.

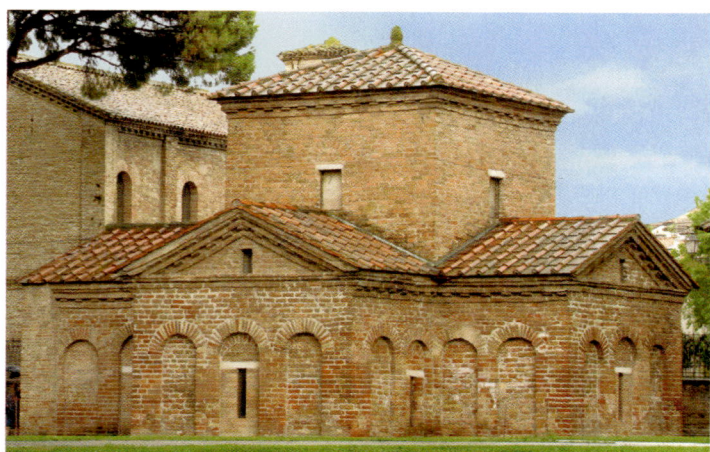

**8-15** Mausoleum of Galla Placidia, Ravenna, Italy, ca. 425. ◼◀

This cruciform chapel with a domed crossing is an early example of the combination of central and longitudinal plans. The unadorned brick shell encloses a rich ensemble of mosaics.

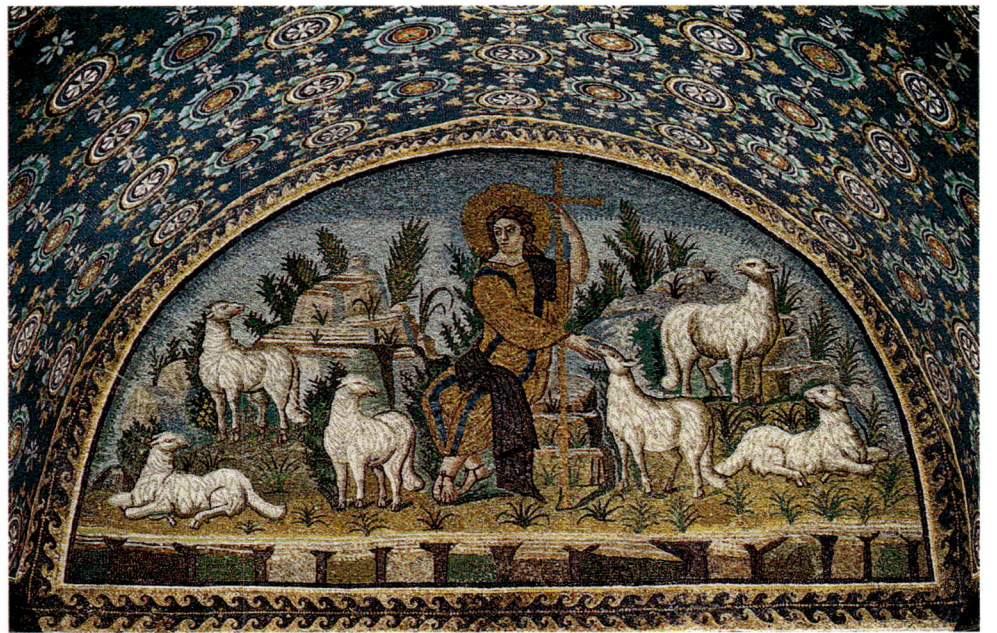

8-17 *Christ as Good Shepherd,* mosaic from the entrance wall of the Mausoleum of Galla Placidia, Ravenna, Italy, ca. 425. ◼◂

Jesus sits among his flock, haloed and robed in gold and purple. The landscape and the figures, with their cast shadows, are the work of a mosaicist still rooted in the naturalistic classical tradition.

Christ as Good Shepherd is the subject of the lunette (FIG. 8-17) above the entrance. No earlier version of the Good Shepherd is as regal as this one. Instead of carrying a lamb on his shoulders (FIGS. 8-6 to 8-8), Jesus sits among his flock, haloed and robed in gold and purple. To his left and right, the sheep are distributed evenly in groups of three. But their arrangement is rather loose and informal, and they occupy a carefully described landscape extending from foreground to background beneath a blue sky. As at Santa Maria Maggiore (FIG. 8-14), all

its vault resembling a dome. This small, unassuming building thus represents one of the earliest successful fusions of the two basic Late Antique plans—the longitudinal, used for basilican churches, and the central, used primarily for baptisteries and mausoleums. It introduced, on a small scale, a building type that was to have a long history in church architecture: the longitudinally planned building with a vaulted or domed crossing.

the forms have three-dimensional bulk and are still deeply rooted in the classical tradition.

**SANT'APOLLINARE NUOVO** Ravenna is famous for its treasure trove of Early Christian and Byzantine mosaics. About 30 years later than the Galla Placidia mosaics are those of Ravenna's Orthodox Baptistery (FIG. 8-17A). An especially large cycle of mosaics adorns the palace-church Theodoric built in 504, soon after he settled in Ravenna. A three-aisled basilica originally dedicated to "Our Lord Jesus Christ," the church was rededicated in the ninth century as Sant'Apollinare Nuovo, when it acquired the relics of Saint Apollinaris. The rich mosaic decoration of the nave walls (FIG. 8-18) fills three zones. Only the upper two date from Theodoric's time. Hebrew patriarchs

The chapel's unadorned brick shell encloses one of the richest mosaic ensembles (FIG. 8-16) in Early Christian art. Mosaics cover every square inch of the interior surfaces above the marble-faced walls. Garlands and decorative medallions resembling snowflakes on a dark blue ground adorn the barrel vaults of the nave and cross arms. The tower has a large golden cross set against a star-studded sky. Representations of saints and apostles cover the other surfaces. At the end of the nave is a mosaic representing Saint Lawrence next to the gridiron on which he was tortured. The martyred saint carries a cross, suggesting faith in Christ led to his salvation.

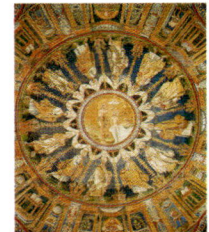

8-17A Orthodox Baptistery, Ravenna, ca. 458.

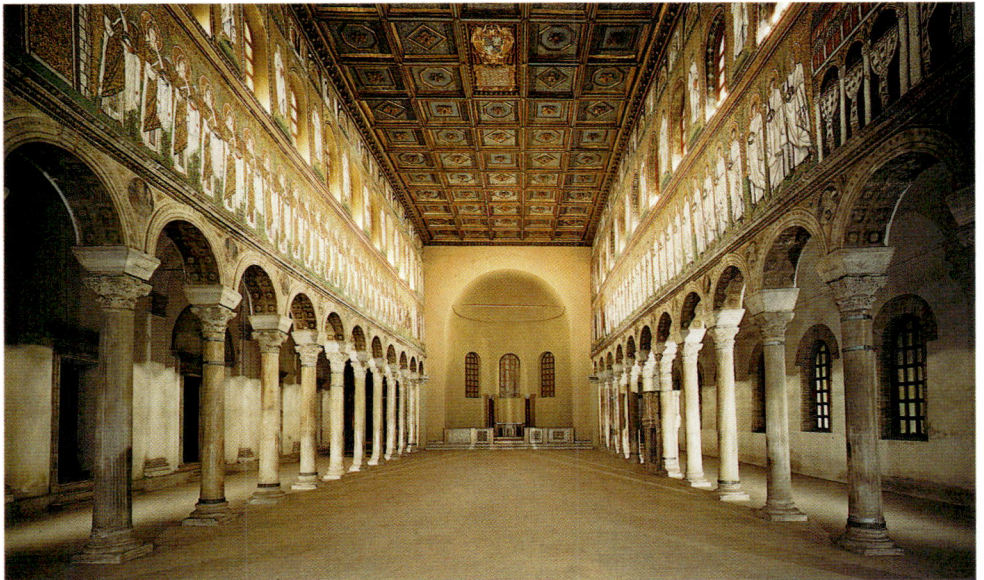

8-18 Interior of Sant'Apollinare Nuovo (looking east), Ravenna, Italy, dedicated 504. ◼◂

Theodoric, king of the Ostrogoths, established his capital at Ravenna in 493. His palace-church features an extensive series of mosaics depicting Hebrew prophets and scenes from the life of Christ.

**8-19** *Miracle of the Loaves and Fishes,* mosaic from the top register of the nave wall (above the clerestory windows in FIG. 8-18) of Sant'Apollinare Nuovo, Ravenna, Italy, ca. 504.

In contrast to FIG. 8-17, Jesus here faces directly toward the viewer. Blue sky has given way to the otherworldly splendor of heavenly gold, the standard background color for medieval mosaics.

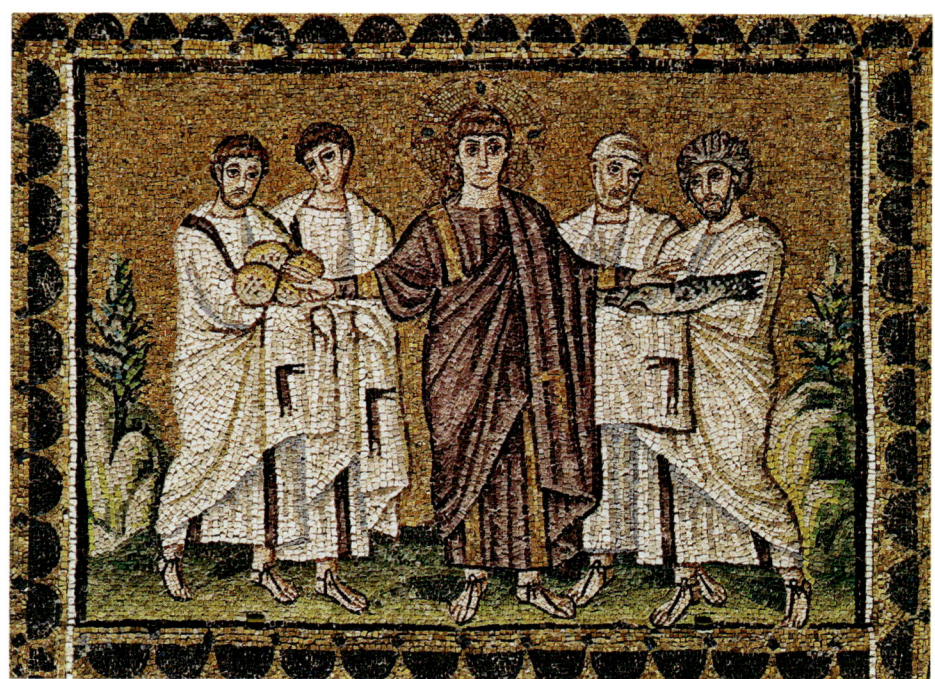

and prophets stand between the clerestory windows. Above them, scenes from Christ's life alternate with decorative panels.

The *Miracle of the Loaves and Fishes* mosaic (FIG. 8-19) stands in sharp contrast to the 80-year-earlier mosaics of the Mausoleum of Galla Placidia. Jesus, beardless, in the imperial dress of gold and purple, and now distinguished by the cross-inscribed *nimbus* (halo) that signifies his divinity, faces directly toward the viewer. With extended arms he directs his disciples to distribute to the great crowd the miraculously increased supply of bread and fish he has produced. The mosaicist told the story with the least number of figures necessary to make its meaning explicit, aligning the figures laterally, moving them close to the foreground, and placing them in a shallow picture box. The composition, so different from those in the lunettes of the Mausoleum of Galla Placidia, is similar to that of the *Samuel and David* mural (FIG. 8-3) in the Dura-Europos synagogue two and a half centuries earlier as well as

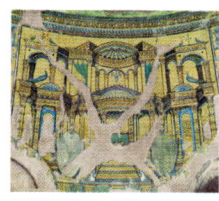

**8-19A** Hagios Georgios, Thessaloniki, ca. 390–450.

the late-fourth-century mosaics (FIG. 8-19A) in Hagios Georgios in Thessaloniki, Greece, illustrating once again that Early Christian artists inherited both classical naturalism and Late Antique abstraction from Roman art. But the Sant'Apollinare Nuovo mosaic, like those in Hagios Georgios, differs from the Dura murals as well as the Galla Placidia mosaics in having a golden background, which lifts the mosaic out of time and space and emphasizes the spiritual over the physical. The landscape setting, which the artist who decorated the Mausoleum of Galla Placidia so explicitly described (FIG. 8-17), is here merely a few rocks and bushes enclosing the figure group like parentheses. The blue sky of the physical world has given way to the otherworldly splendor of heavenly gold. The ethereal golden background as well as the weightless figures with their flat, curtainlike garments would soon become the norm in Byzantine art, although even in Byzantium echoes of classical naturalism persisted (see Chapter 9).

# LUXURY ARTS

Throughout history, artists have produced so-called "minor arts"—jewelry, metalwork, cameos, ivories, among other crafts—alongside the "major arts" of sculpture and painting. Although the terminology seems to suggest a difference in importance or quality, "minor" refers only to size. Indeed, the artists who fashioned jewelry, carved ivories and cameos, and produced gold and silver vessels by casting or hammering (*repoussé*) employed the costliest materials known. Some of them, for example, Dioscurides, official gem cutter of the emperor Augustus, are among the few Roman artists whose names survive. In Late Antiquity and the Middle Ages, the minor arts—

more appropriately called "luxury arts"—enjoyed high status, and they figure prominently in the history of art through the ages.

## Illuminated Manuscripts

Although few examples survive, illustrated books were common in public and private libraries in the ancient world. The long tradition of placing pictures in manuscripts began in pharaonic Egypt (FIG. 3-37) and continued in Greek and Roman times.

***VATICAN VERGIL*** The oldest preserved painted Greek or Latin manuscript is the *Vatican Vergil,* which dates from the early fifth century and is among the earliest preserved illustrated medieval books (see "Medieval Manuscript Illumination," page 249). It originally contained more than 200 pictures illustrating all of Vergil's works. Today, only 50 painted *folios* (leaves or pages) of the *Aeneid* and *Georgics* survive. The manuscript is important not only because of its age. The *Vatican Vergil* is a prime example of traditional Roman iconography and of the classical style long after Theodosius banned worship of the old gods.

The page illustrated here (FIG. 8-20) includes a section of text from the *Georgics* at the top and a framed illustration below. Vergil recounts his visit to a modest farm near Taranto in southern Italy belonging to an old man from Corycus in Asia Minor. In the illustration, the old farmer sits at the left. His rustic farmhouse is in the background, rendered in three-quarter view. The farmer speaks about the pleasures of the simple life in the country—a recurrent theme in Latin poetry—and on his methods of gardening. His audience is two laborers and, at the far right, Vergil himself in the guise of a farmhand. The style is reminiscent of Pompeian landscapes, with quick touches that suggest space and atmosphere. In fact, the heavy, dark frame has close parallels in the late Pompeian styles of mural painting (FIG. 7-22).

***VIENNA GENESIS*** The oldest well-preserved painted manuscript containing biblical scenes is the early-sixth-century *Vienna Genesis,* so called because of its present location. The book is sumptuous. The pages are fine calfskin dyed with rich purple, the same dye used to give imperial cloth its distinctive color. The Greek text is in silver ink.

# Medieval Manuscript Illumination

Rare as medieval books are, they are far more numerous than their ancient predecessors. An important invention during the Early Roman Empire was the *codex,* which greatly aided the dissemination of manuscripts as well as their preservation. A codex is much like a modern book, composed of separate leaves (*folios*) enclosed within a cover and bound together at one side. The new format superseded the long manuscript scroll (*rotulus*) of the Egyptians, Greeks, Etruscans, and Romans. (The Etruscan magistrate Lars Pulena, FIG. 6-15; the philosophers on Roman and Early Christian sarcophagi, FIGS. 7-71 and 8-7; and Christ himself in his role as teacher, FIGS. 8-1 and 8-8A, all hold rotuli in their hands.) Much more durable *vellum* (calfskin) and *parchment* (lambskin), which provided better surfaces for painting, also replaced the comparatively brittle *papyrus* used for ancient scrolls. As a result, luxuriousness of ornamentation became increasingly typical of sacred books in the Middle Ages, and at times the material beauty of the pages

and their illustrations overwhelm or usurp the spiritual beauty of the text. Art historians refer to the luxurious painted books produced before the invention of the printing press as *illuminated manuscripts,* from the Latin *illuminare,* meaning "to adorn, ornament, or brighten." The oldest preserved examples (FIGS. 8-20 to 8-22) date to the fifth and sixth centuries.

Illuminated books were costly to produce and involved many steps. Numerous artisans performed very specialized tasks, beginning with the curing and cutting (and sometimes the dyeing; FIGS. 8-21, 8-21A, and 8-22) of the animal skin, followed by the sketching of lines to guide the scribe and to set aside spaces for illumination, the lettering of the text, the addition of paintings, and finally the binding of the pages and attachment of covers, buckles, and clasps. The covers could be even more sumptuous than the book itself. Many preserved covers are fashioned of gold and decorated with jewels, ivory carvings, and repoussé reliefs (FIG. 11-16).

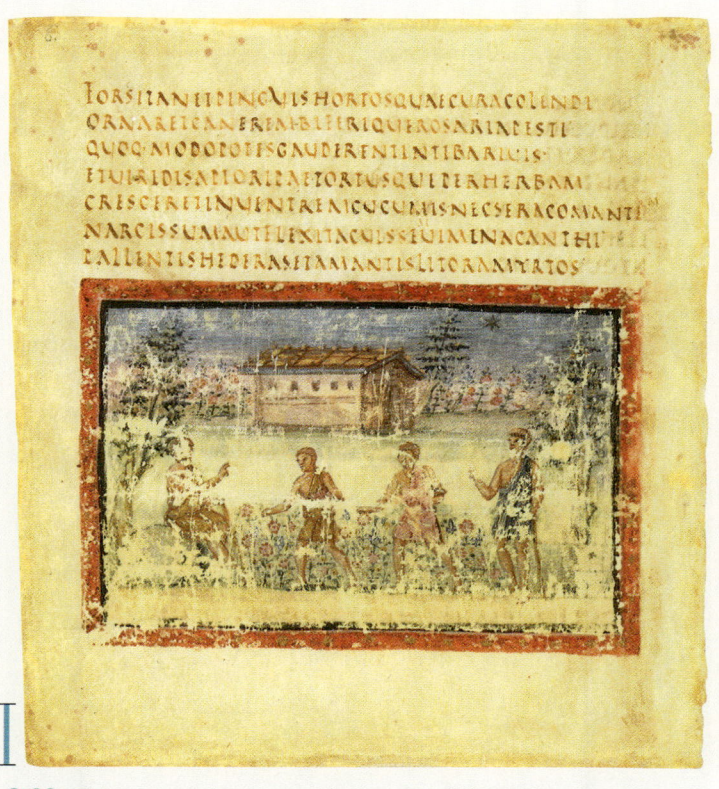

**8-20** *Old Farmer of Corycus,* folio 7 verso of the *Vatican Vergil,* ca. 400–420. Tempera on parchment, 1′ ½″ × 1′. Biblioteca Apostolica Vaticana, Rome.

The earliest surviving painted Latin manuscript is a collection of the poet Vergil's works. This page includes part of the text of the *Georgics* and a pastoral scene reminiscent of Roman landscape murals.

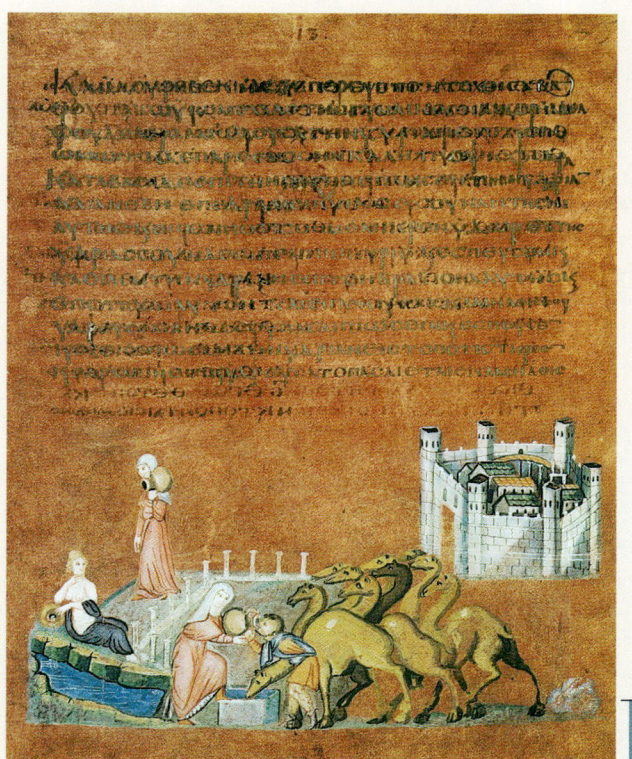

**8-21** *Rebecca and Eliezer at the Well,* folio 7 recto of the *Vienna Genesis,* early sixth century. Tempera, gold, and silver on purple vellum, 1′ ¼″ × 9¼″. Österreichische Nationalbibliothek, Vienna.

This sumptuously painted book of Genesis is the oldest well-preserved manuscript containing biblical scenes. Two episodes of the Rebecca story appear in a single setting filled with classical motifs.

Folio 7 (FIG. 8-21) of the *Vienna Genesis* illustrates *Rebecca and Eliezer at the Well* (Gen. 24:15–61). When Isaac, Abraham's son, was 40 years old, his parents sent their servant Eliezer to find a wife for him. Eliezer chose Rebecca, because when he stopped at a well, she was the first woman to draw water for him and his camels. As elsewhere in the manuscript (FIG. 8-21A), the painter presented

more than one episode of the story within a single frame, employing an ancient manner of pictorial storytelling called *continuous narration* (compare FIG. 7-44A). In the first episode, at the left, Rebecca leaves the city of Nahor to fetch water from the well.

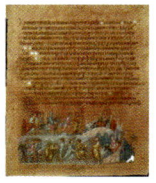
**8-21A** Story of Jacob, *Vienna Genesis,* early sixth century.

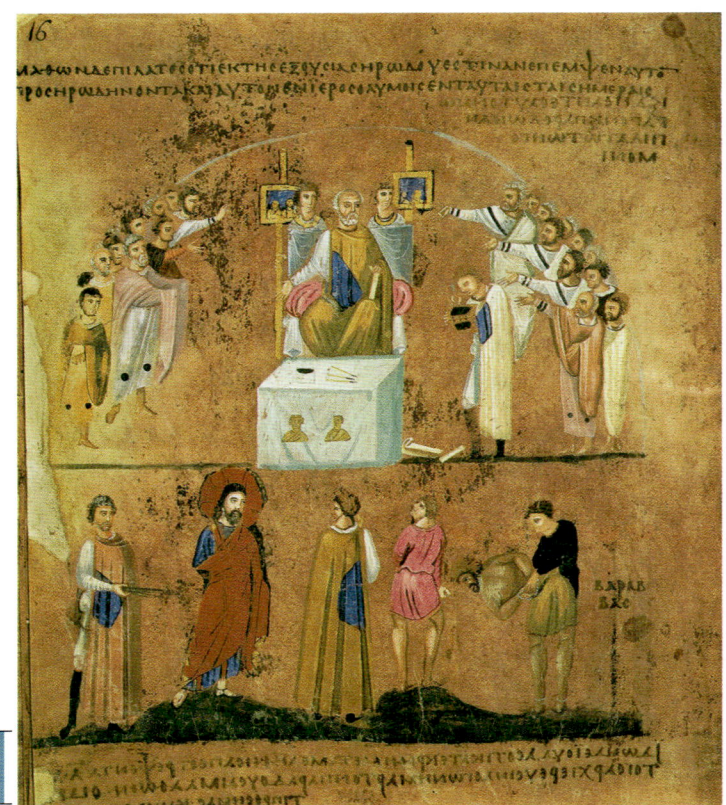

**8-22** *Christ before Pilate,* folio 8 verso of the *Rossano Gospels,* early sixth century. Tempera on purple vellum, 11″ × 10¼″. Museo Diocesano d'Arte Sacra, Rossano.

The sources for medieval manuscript illustrations were diverse. The way the people form an arch around Pilate on this page suggests the composition derives from a painting in an apse.

In the second episode, she offers water to Eliezer and his camels, while one of them already laps water from the well. The artist painted Nahor as a walled city seen from above, like the cityscapes in the Santa Maria Maggiore mosaics (FIG. 8-14), the Column of Trajan (FIG. 7-1), and innumerable earlier Roman representations of cities in painting and relief sculpture. Rebecca walks to the well along the colonnaded avenue of a Roman city. A seminude female personification of a spring is the source of the well water. These are further reminders of the persistence of classical motifs and stylistic modes in Early Christian art.

Contemporaneous with, but radically different from, the mosaic panels (FIG. 8-19) of Sant'Apollinare Nuovo, the *Vienna Genesis* incorporates many anecdotal details, such as the drinking camel and Rebecca bracing herself with her raised left foot on the rim of the well as she tips up her jug for Eliezer. Nonetheless, the illuminator placed the figures in a blank landscape except for the miniature city and the road to the well. As at Ravenna, only those elements necessary to tell the story and set the scene are present, nothing else.

***ROSSANO GOSPELS*** Closely related to the *Vienna Genesis* is another early-sixth-century Greek manuscript, the *Rossano Gospels,* the earliest preserved illuminated book containing illustrations of the New Testament. By this time a canon of New Testament iconography had been fairly well established. As in the *Vienna Genesis,* the text of the *Rossano Gospels* is in silver ink on purple-dyed vellum. The Rossano artist, however, attempted with considerable success to harmonize the colors with the purple

background. The subject of folio 8 (FIG. **8-22**) is the appearance of Jesus before Pilate, who asks the Jews to choose between Jesus and Barabbas (Matt. 27:2–26). The vividly gesturing figures are on two levels separated by a simple ground line, which not only separates the figures spatially but also temporally. In the upper level, Pilate presides over the tribunal. He sits indoors on an elevated dais, following a long-established pattern in Roman art (FIG. 7-76). The people form an arch around Pilate. (The artist may have based the composition on a painting in an apse—an appropriate setting for a seated magistrate.) They demand the death of Jesus, while a court scribe records the proceedings. Below, and outdoors, are Jesus (here a bearded adult, as soon became the norm for medieval and later depictions of Christ; compare FIG. 8-6A) and the bound Barabbas. The painter explicitly labeled Barabbas to avoid any possible confusion and make the picture as readable as the text. Neither the haloed Christ nor Pilate on his magistrate's dais, flanked by painted imperial portraits, needed any further identification.

## Metalwork

Especially prized in antiquity and throughout the Middle Ages were items of tableware fashioned out of precious metals, for example, the gold Achaemenid rhyton (FIG. 2-26A) from Hamadan and the Mycenaean drinking cups (FIG. 4-23A) from Vapheio, discussed earlier.

**MILDENHALL TREASURE** In 1942, a farmer plowing his fields near Mildenhall, England, discovered a hoard of silver tableware dating to the mid-fourth century CE. The "Mildenhall Treasure" must have been the proud possession of a wealthy local family. The hoard consists of 34 silver pieces, including bowls, platters, ladles, and spoons. The most spectacular item is a large platter known as the "Great Dish" (FIG. **8-23**). At the center is the bearded head of the god Oceanus, framed by a ring of Nereids (sea nymphs).

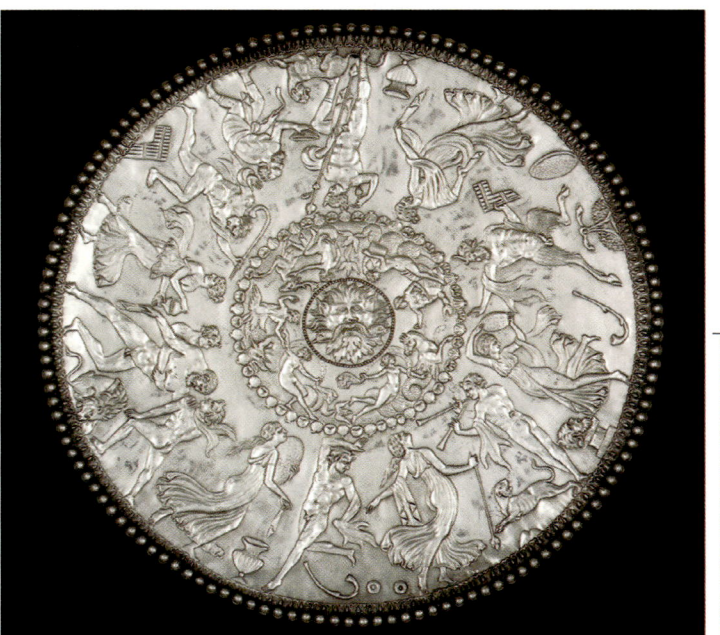

**8-23** Oceanus and Nereids, and drinking contest between Bacchus and Hercules, "Great Dish," from Mildenhall, England, mid-fourth century CE. Silver, 1′ 11¾″ diameter. British Museum, London.

Part of a hoard of silver tableware owned by a Christian family, this large platter nonetheless features sea deities and a drinking contest between Bacchus, the Roman god of wine, and Hercules.

## Ivory Carving

Ivory has been prized since the earliest times, when sculptors fashioned the tusks of Ice Age European mammoths into pendants, beads, and other items for body adornment, and, occasionally, statuettes (FIGS. 1-4 and 1-5A). The primary ivory sources in the historical period have been the elephants of India and especially Africa, where the species is larger than the Asian counterpart and the tusks longer, heavier, and of finer grain. African elephant tusks 5 to 6 feet in length and weighing 10 pounds are common, but tusks of male elephants can be 10 feet long or more and weigh well over 100 pounds. Carved ivories are familiar, if precious, finds at Mesopotamian and Egyptian sites, and ivory objects were also coveted in the prehistoric Aegean (FIG. 4-24) and throughout the classical world. Most frequently employed then for household objects, small votive offerings, and gifts to the deceased, ivory also could be used for grandiose statues such as Phidias's *Athena Parthenos* (FIG. 5-46).

In the Greco-Roman world, people admired ivory both for its beauty and because of its exotic origin. Elephant tusks were costly imports, and Roman generals proudly displayed them in triumphal processions when they paraded the spoils of war before the people. (In FIG. 9-4, a barbarian brings tribute to a Byzantine emperor in the form of an ivory tusk.) Adding to the expense of the material itself was that only highly skilled artisans were capable of working in ivory. The tusks were very hard and of irregular shape, and the ivory workers needed a full toolbox of saws, chisels, knives, files, and gravers close at hand to cut the tusks into blocks for statuettes or thin plaques decorated with relief figures and ornamentation.

In Late Antiquity and the early medieval period, artists chose ivory most frequently for book covers, chests and boxes (FIG. 8-24),

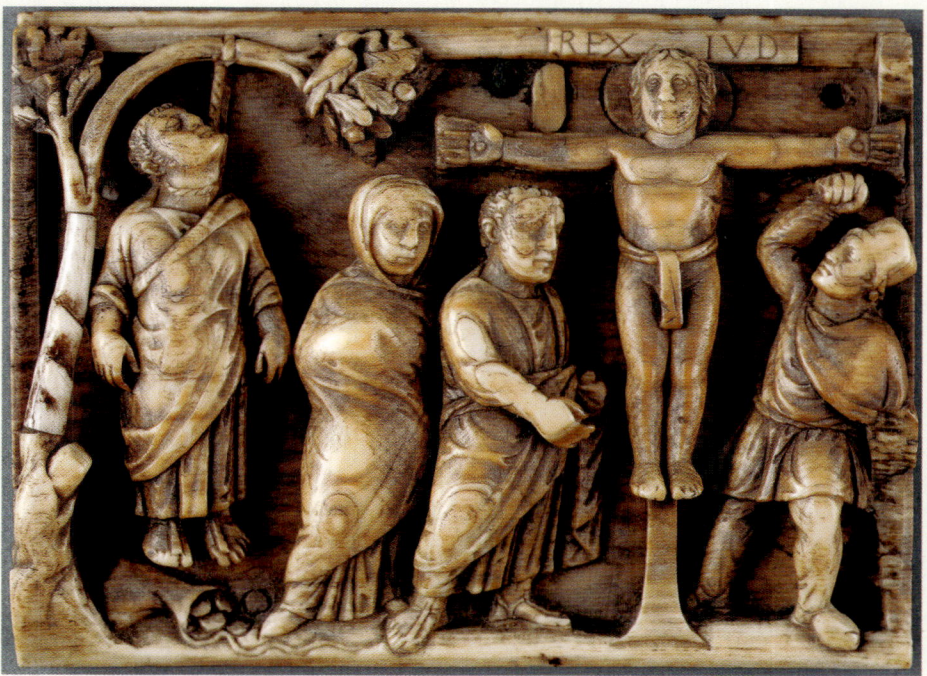

**8-24** *Suicide of Judas* and *Crucifixion,* plaque from a box, ca. 420. Ivory, $3'' \times 3\frac{7}{8}''$. British Museum, London. ◼◀

This plaque from a luxurious ivory box is the first known representation of the *Crucifixion of Christ,* shown here as a beardless youth who experiences no pain. At the left, Judas, his betrayer, hangs himself.

and diptychs (FIGS. 8-25 and 9-2). A *diptych* is a pair of hinged tablets, usually of wood, with a wax layer on the inner sides for writing letters and other documents. (The court scribe recording Jesus' trial in the *Rossano Gospels,* FIG. 8-22, and the women in two painted portraits from Pompeii, FIGS. 7-25 and 7-25A, both hold wooden diptychs.) Diptychs fashioned from ivory generally were reserved for ceremonial and official purposes—for example, to announce the election of a consul or a marriage between two wealthy families or to commemorate the death of an elevated member of society.

A larger outer band celebrates the consumption of wine and features a drinking contest between Bacchus (with his left foot resting on a panther) and Hercules, who is so drunk two satyrs struggle to support him. Three of the spoons bear the Greek letters *chi, rho, alpha,* and *omega*—explicit references to Christ (FIG. 8-6A)—but the figural decoration of all the items in the treasure illustrates classical mythology. The hoard attests to the survival of the Roman gods and of classical iconography during the Late Antique period even in Christian contexts.

## Ivory Carving

Among the other important luxury arts of Late Antiquity was ivory carving, which has an even longer history in the ancient world than does metalwork (see "Ivory Carving," above).

*SUICIDE OF JUDAS* **AND** *CRUCIFIXION* A century before a manuscript painter illuminated the pages of the *Rossano Gospels* (FIG. 8-22) with scenes from the passion cycle, a Roman or northern Italian sculptor produced a series of ivory plaques for a small box that dramatically recount the suffering and triumph of Christ. The narrative on the box begins with Pilate washing his hands, Jesus carrying the cross on the road to Calvary, and the denial of Peter, all compressed into a single panel. The plaque illustrated here, *Suicide of Judas* (FIG. **8-24**), is the next in the sequence and shows, at the left, Judas hanging from a tree with his open bag of silver dumped on the ground beneath his feet. The *Crucifixion* is at the right. The Virgin Mary and Joseph of Arimathea are to the left of the cross. On the other side, Longinus thrusts his spear into the side of the "king of the Jews" (the inscribed letters *REX IVD* appear above Jesus' head).

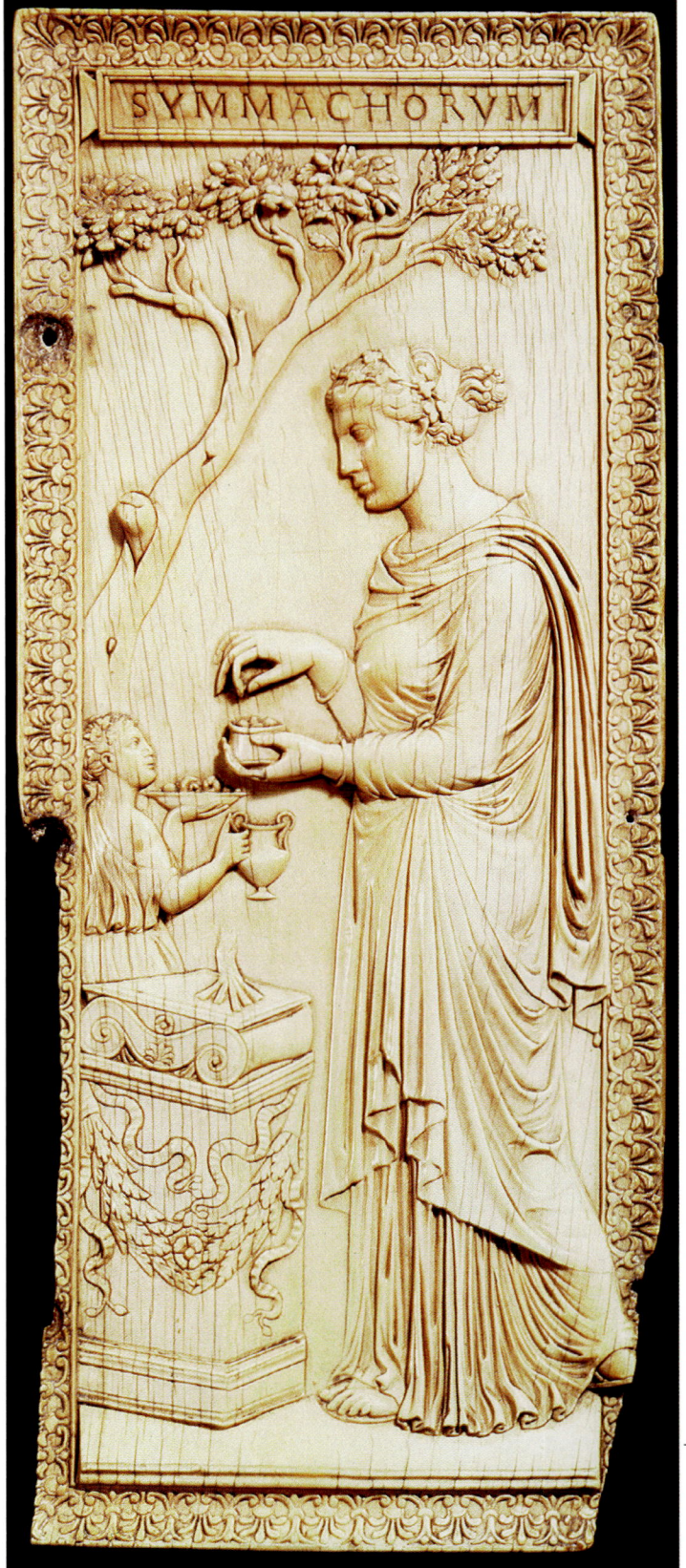

**8-25** Woman sacrificing at an altar, right leaf of the diptych of the Nicomachi and the Symmachi, ca. 400. Ivory, 11¾″ × 5½″. Victoria & Albert Museum, London.

Even after Theodosius banned all pagan cults in 391, some Roman families still practiced the ancient rites. The sculptor who carved this ivory plaque also carried on the classical artistic style.

The two remaining panels show two Marys and two soldiers at the open doors of a tomb with an empty coffin within and the doubting Thomas touching the wound of the risen Christ.

The series is one of the oldest cycles of passion scenes preserved today. It dates to the period when artists were beginning to establish the standard iconographical types for medieval narratives of Christ's life. On these plaques, Jesus always appears as a beardless youth. In the *Crucifixion* scene (FIG. 8-24, *right*), the earliest known rendition of the subject in the history of art, Jesus exhibits a superhuman imperviousness to pain. He is a muscular, nearly nude, heroic figure who appears virtually weightless. Jesus does not *hang* from the cross. He is *displayed* on it—a divine being with open eyes who has conquered death. The striking contrast between the powerful frontal unsuffering Jesus on the cross and the limp hanging body of his betrayer with his snapped neck is highly effective, both visually and symbolically.

**DIPTYCH OF THE SYMMACHI** Although Constantine endorsed Christianity and dedicated his New Rome in the East to the Christian God, not everyone converted to the new religion, even after Theodosius banned all ancient cults and closed all temples in 391. An ivory plaque (FIG. **8-25**), probably produced in Rome around 400, strikingly exhibits the endurance of the traditional Roman gods and of the classical style on the eve of Alaric's sack of the "eternal city." The ivory, one of a pair of leaves of a diptych, may commemorate either the marriage of members of two powerful Roman families of the senatorial class, the Nicomachi and the Symmachi, or the passing within a decade of two prominent male members of the two families. Whether or not the diptych refers to any specific event(s), the Nicomachi and the Symmachi here ostentatiously reaffirmed their faith in the old gods. Certainly, they favored the aesthetic ideals of the classical past, as exemplified by the stately processional friezes of the Greek Parthenon (FIG. 5-50, *bottom*) and the Roman Ara Pacis (FIG. 7-31).

The leaf inscribed "of the Symmachi" (FIG. 8-25) represents a woman sacrificing at an altar in front of a tree. She wears ivy in her hair and seems to be celebrating the rites of Bacchus—the same wine god featured on the Mildenhall silver platter (FIG. 8-23). Some scholars dispute the identity of the divinity honored, but no one questions that the deity is one of the Roman gods whose worship had been banned. The other diptych panel, inscribed "of the Nicomachi," also shows a woman at an open-air altar. On both panels, the precise yet fluent and graceful line, the relaxed poses, and the mood of spiritual serenity reveal an artist who practiced within a still-vital classical tradition that idealized human beauty as its central focus. The great senatorial magnates of Rome, who resisted the Empire-wide imposition of the Christian faith at the end of the fourth century, probably deliberately sustained the classical tradition. Despite the widespread adoption during the third and fourth centuries of the new non-naturalistic Late Antique aesthetic featuring wafer-thin frontal figures, the classical tradition in art lived on and was never fully extinguished in the Middle Ages. Classical art survived in intermittent revivals, renovations, and restorations side by side and in contrast with the opposing nonclassical medieval styles until it rose to dominance once again in the Renaissance.

# LATE ANTIQUITY

## PRE-CONSTANTINIAN 192–306

▌ The Second Commandment prohibition against worshiping images once led scholars to think the Jews of the Roman Empire had no figural art, but the synagogue at Dura-Europos contains an extensive series of mural paintings illustrating episodes from the Hebrew scriptures. The Dura synagogue, like the Christian community house at the same site, was a remodeled private home.

▌ Christ was crucified ca. 33, but very little Christian art or architecture survives from the first centuries of Christianity. "Early Christian art" means the earliest art of Christian content, not the art of Christians at the time of Jesus, and comes primarily from the catacombs of Rome.

▌ During the second half of the third century, Christian sarcophagi adorned with a mixture of Old and New Testament scenes began to appear.

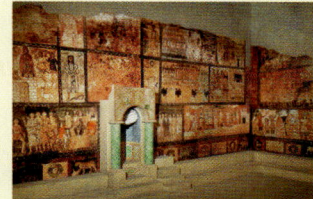

Synagogue, Dura-Europos, ca. 245–256

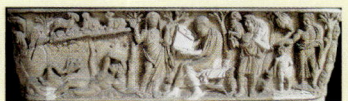

Santa Maria Antiqua sarophagus, ca. 270

## CONSTANTINE 306–337

▌ Constantine's Edict of Milan of 313 granted Christianity legal status equal or superior to the cults of the traditional gods. The emperor was the first great patron of Christian art and built the first churches in Rome, including Old Saint Peter's.

▌ In a Christian ceremony, Constantine dedicated Constantinople as the new capital of the Roman Empire in 330. He was baptized on his deathbed in 337.

▌ Early Christian artists profusely decorated the walls and ceilings of the catacombs with frescoes. Popular themes were Christ as Good Shepherd and the salvation of Jonah.

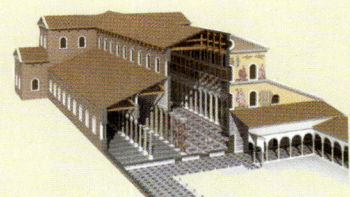

Old Saint Peter's, Rome, begun ca. 319

## SONS OF CONSTANTINE TO JUSTINIAN 337–526

▌ The emperor Theodosius I (r. 379–395) proclaimed Christianity the official religion of the Roman Empire in 380 and banned worship of the old Roman gods in 391.

▌ Honorius (r. 395–423) moved the capital of his Western Roman Empire to Ravenna in 404. Rome fell to the Visigothic king Alaric in 410.

▌ Mosaics became a major vehicle for the depiction of Christian themes in churches. Extensive mosaic cycles are preserved in the nave of Santa Maria Maggiore in Rome and especially in Sant'Apollinare Nuovo in Ravenna.

▌ The earliest preserved manuscripts featuring illustrations of the Old and New Testaments date to the early sixth century. Illuminated manuscripts, such as the *Vienna Genesis*, would become one of the major art forms of the Middle Ages.

▌ Late Antique artists excelled in producing luxurious items for domestic use in silver and ivory, such as tableware, boxes, and diptychs, and decorated them with reliefs depicting both Christian and traditional Roman themes.

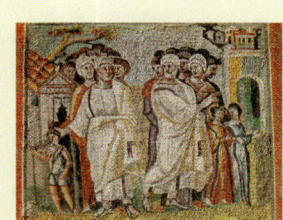

Santa Maria Maggiore, Rome, 432–440

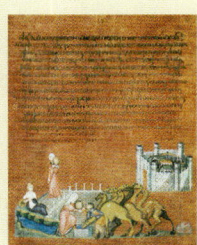

*Vienna Genesis,* early sixth century

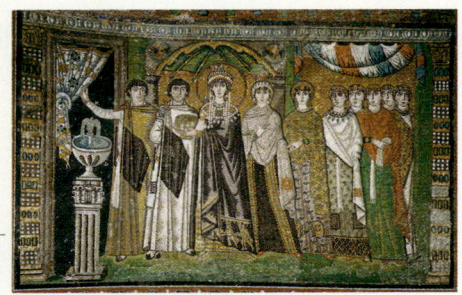

The Byzantine empress Theodora holds the golden cup of wine for the Eucharist as her husband carries the platter of bread. But neither she nor Justinian was ever in Ravenna.

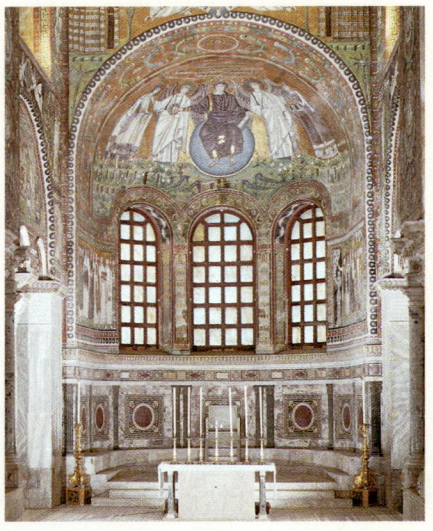

The apse mosaics celebrate Justinian's right to rule on earth. Christ, dressed in the purple robe worn by Byzantine emperors, sits on the orb of the world at the time of his second coming.

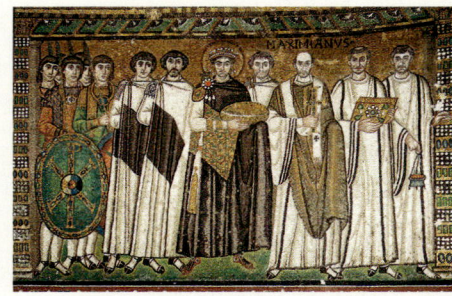

The emperor Justinian and Maximianus, the bishop who dedicated the church, appear in the apse. The mosaic program of San Vitale underscores the Byzantine emperor's dual political and religious roles.

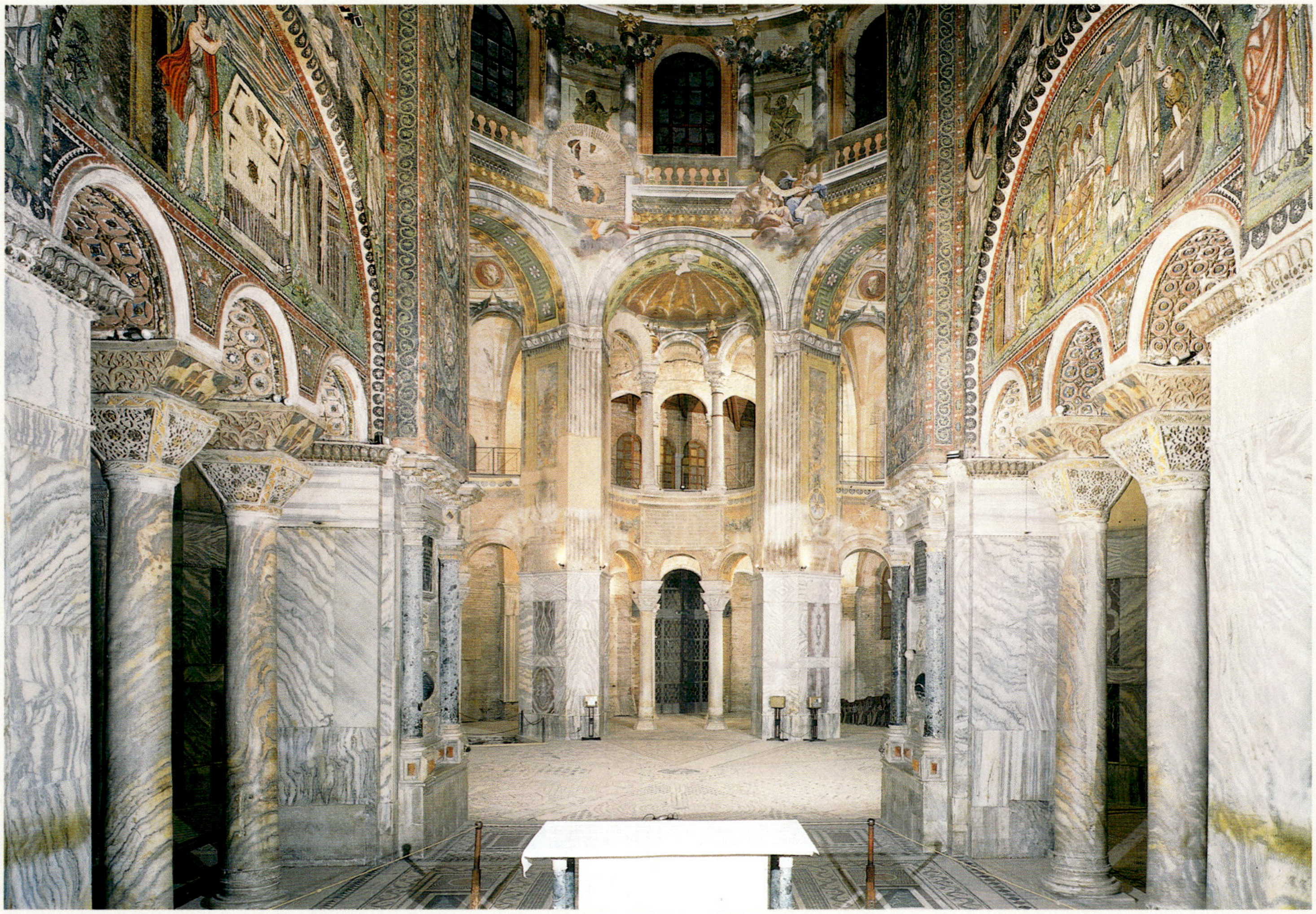

**9-1** Interior of San Vitale (looking from the apse into the choir), Ravenna, Italy, 526–547. ◼️📹

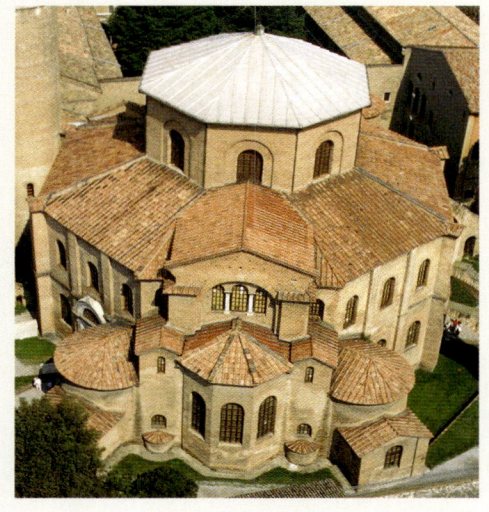

San Vitale is a central-plan church with an octagonal plan modeled on churches in Constantinople. Its austere facade gives no hint of its sumptuous marble- and mosaic-covered interior.

# BYZANTIUM

## CHURCH AND STATE UNITED

San Vitale (FIG. 9-1), dedicated by Bishop Maximianus in 547 in honor of Saint Vitalis, who died a martyr at the hands of the Romans at Ravenna in the second century, is the most spectacular building in that northern Italian outpost of the Byzantine Empire. The church is an unforgettable experience for all who have entered it and marveled at its intricate design and magnificent mosaics.

The exterior's octagonal regularity is not readily apparent inside the centrally planned church. The design features two concentric octagons. The dome-covered inner octagon rises above the surrounding octagon to provide the interior with clerestory lighting. Eight large rectilinear piers alternate with curved, columned exedrae, pushing outward into the surrounding two-story ambulatory. A rich diversity of ever-changing perspectives greets visitors walking through the building. Arches looping over arches, curving and flattened spaces, and wall and vault shapes all seem to change constantly with the viewer's position. Light filtered through alabaster-paned windows plays over the glittering mosaics and glowing marbles covering the building's complex surfaces, producing a sumptuous effect.

The mosaics in San Vitale's choir and apse, like the building itself, must be regarded as one of the greatest achievements of Byzantine art. Completed less than a decade after the Ostrogoths surrendered Ravenna (see Chapter 8), the apse and choir decorations form a unified composition, whose theme is the holy ratification of the emperor Justinian's right to rule. In the apse vault, Christ sits on the orb of the world at the time of his second coming. On the choir wall to the left of the apse mosaic appears Justinian. He stands on the Savior's right side. The two are united visually and symbolically by the imperial purple they wear and by their haloes. A dozen attendants accompany Justinian, paralleling Christ's 12 apostles. Thus, the mosaic program underscores the dual political and religious roles of the Byzantine emperor. The laws of the Church and the laws of the state, united in the laws of God, manifest themselves in the person of the emperor, whose right to rule was God-given.

Justinian's counterpart on the opposite wall of the apse is his empress, Theodora, with her corresponding retinue. Both processions move into the apse, Justinian proceeding from left to right and Theodora from right to left, in order to take part in the Eucharist. Justinian carries the paten containing the bread, and Theodora the golden cup with the wine. Neither she nor Justinian ever visited Ravenna, however. Their participation in the liturgy at San Vitale is pictorial fiction. The mosaics are proxies for the absent sovereigns. Justinian is present because he was the head of the Byzantine state, and his appearance in the mosaic underscores that his authority extends over his territories in Italy.

# THE CHRISTIAN ROMAN EMPIRE

In 324, when Constantine I founded Constantinople (Greek, "Constantine's city") on the site of ancient Byzantium, he legitimately could claim to be ruler of a united Roman Empire. But when Theodosius I (r. 379–395) died, he divided the Empire between his sons. Arcadius, the elder brother, became Emperor of the East, and Honorius, Emperor of the West. Arcadius ruled from Constantinople. After the sack of Rome in 410, Honorius moved the Western capital to Milan and later to Ravenna. Though not formally codified, Theodosius's division of the Empire (which paralleled Diocletian's century-earlier division of administrative responsibility) became permanent. Centralized government soon disintegrated in the Western half and gave way to warring kingdoms (see Chapter 11).

The Eastern half of the Roman Empire, only loosely connected by religion to the West and with only minor territorial holdings there, had a long and complex history of its own. Centered at Constantinople—dubbed the New Rome—the Eastern Christian Empire remained a cultural and political entity for a millennium, until the last of a long line of Eastern Roman emperors, ironically named Constantine XI, died at Constantinople in 1453, defending the city in vain against the Ottoman Turks.

Historians refer to that Eastern Christian Roman Empire as Byzantium (MAP **9-1**), employing Constantinople's original name, and use the term *Byzantine* to identify whatever pertains to Byzantium—its territory, its history, and its culture. The Byzantine emperors, however, did not use the term to define themselves. They called their empire Rome and themselves Romans. Though they spoke Greek and not Latin, the Eastern Roman emperors never

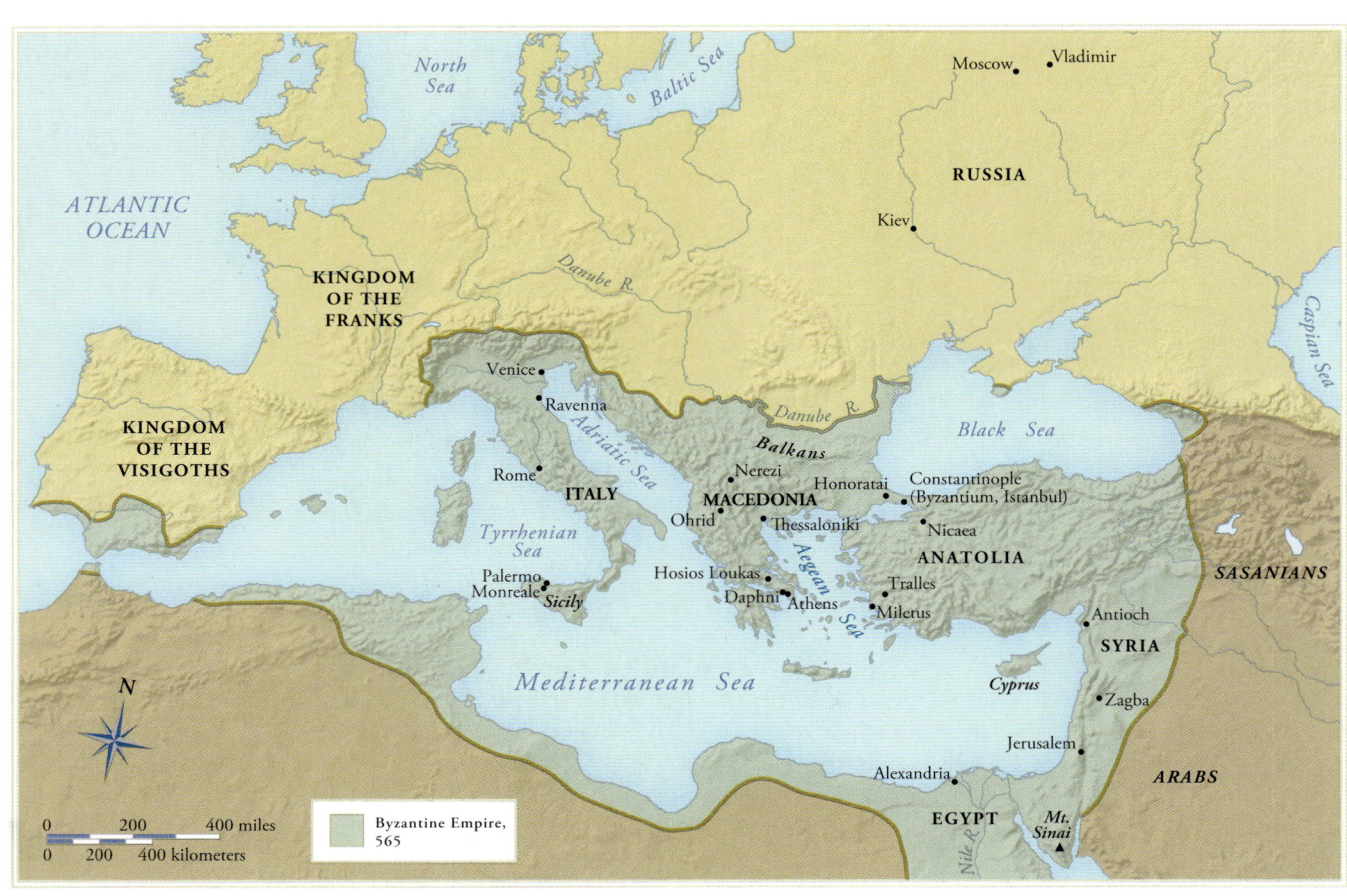

**MAP 9-1** The Byzantine Empire at the death of Justinian in 565.

# BYZANTIUM

| 324 | Early Byzantine | 726 | 843 | Middle Byzantine | 1204 | 1261 | Late Byzantine | 1453 |
|---|---|---|---|---|---|---|---|---|

- Constantine founds Constantinople, 324
- Justinian builds Hagia Sophia with a 180-foot-high dome resting on pendentives, 532–537
- Dedication of San Vitale at Ravenna with its rich mosaic program, 547
- Icon painting flourishes at Mount Sinai until Leo III bans picturing the divine in 726

- Theodora repeals iconoclasm, 843
- Churches feature exterior walls with decorative patterning, Greek-cross plans, and domes on drums resting on pendentives or squinches
- Ivory triptychs for personal prayer become popular

- Michael VIII recaptures Constantinople after the Crusader sack of 1204
- Revival of mural and icon painting
- Fall of Constantinople to the Ottoman Turks, 1453

relinquished their claim as the legitimate successors to the ancient Roman emperors (see "The Emperors of New Rome," page 259). During the long course of its history, Byzantium was the Christian buffer against the expansion of Islam into central and northern Europe, and its cultural influence was felt repeatedly in Europe throughout the Middle Ages. Byzantium Christianized the Slavic peoples of the Balkans and of Russia, giving them its Orthodox religion and alphabet, its literary culture, and its art and architecture. Byzantium's collapse in 1453 brought the Ottoman Empire into Europe as far as the Danube River, but Constantinople's fall had an impact even farther to the west. The westward flight of Byzantine scholars from the Rome of the East introduced the study of classical Greek to Italy and helped inspire there the new consciousness of antiquity historians call the Renaissance (see Chapter 14).

Art historians divide the history of Byzantine art into three periods. The first, Early Byzantine, extends from the founding of Constantinople in 324 to the onset of *iconoclasm* (the destruction of images used in religious worship) in 726 under Leo III. The Middle Byzantine period begins with the renunciation of iconoclasm in 843 and ends with the Western Crusaders' occupation of Constantinople in 1204. Late Byzantine corresponds to the two centuries after the Byzantines recaptured Constantinople in 1261 until its final loss in 1453 to the Ottoman Turks and the conversion of many churches to mosques (see Chapter 10).

# EARLY BYZANTINE ART

The golden age of Early Byzantine art began with the accession of Justinian in 537, but important Byzantine artworks survive from the century before Justinian's reign, especially ivories and illuminated manuscripts—costly, treasured objects, as in the Late Antique West (see Chapter 8).

## Before Justinian

**ARCHANGEL MICHAEL** In the early sixth century, a master carver, probably working in Constantinople, produced the largest extant Byzantine ivory panel (FIG. 9-2). It is probably the right half of a hinged diptych and depicts Saint Michael the Archangel. The inscription opens with the words "Receive these gifts." The dedication is perhaps a reference to the cross-surmounted orb of power the archangel once offered to a Byzantine emperor depicted on the missing diptych leaf. The prototype of Michael must have been a classical winged Victory, although Victory was personified as a woman in Greco-Roman art and usually carried the palm branch of victory, as she does on a somewhat later Byzantine ivory (FIG. 9-4). The Christian artist here ingeniously adapted a classical personification and imbued it with new meaning.

The archangel's flowing drapery, which reveals the body's shape, the delicately incised wings, and the facial type and coiffure are other indications the artist who carved this ivory was still working in the classical tradition. Nonetheless, the Byzantine sculptor had little concern for the rules of naturalistic representation. The archangel dwarfs the architectural setting. Michael's feet rest on three steps at once, and his upper body, wings, and arms are in front of the column shafts, whereas his lower body is behind the column bases at the top of the receding staircase. These spatial ambiguities do not detract from the figure's striking beauty, but they do signify the emergence in Byzantium of the same aesthetic already noted in the Late Antique mosaics of Thessaloniki (FIG. 8-19A). Here, as there, the Byzantine artist rejected the goal

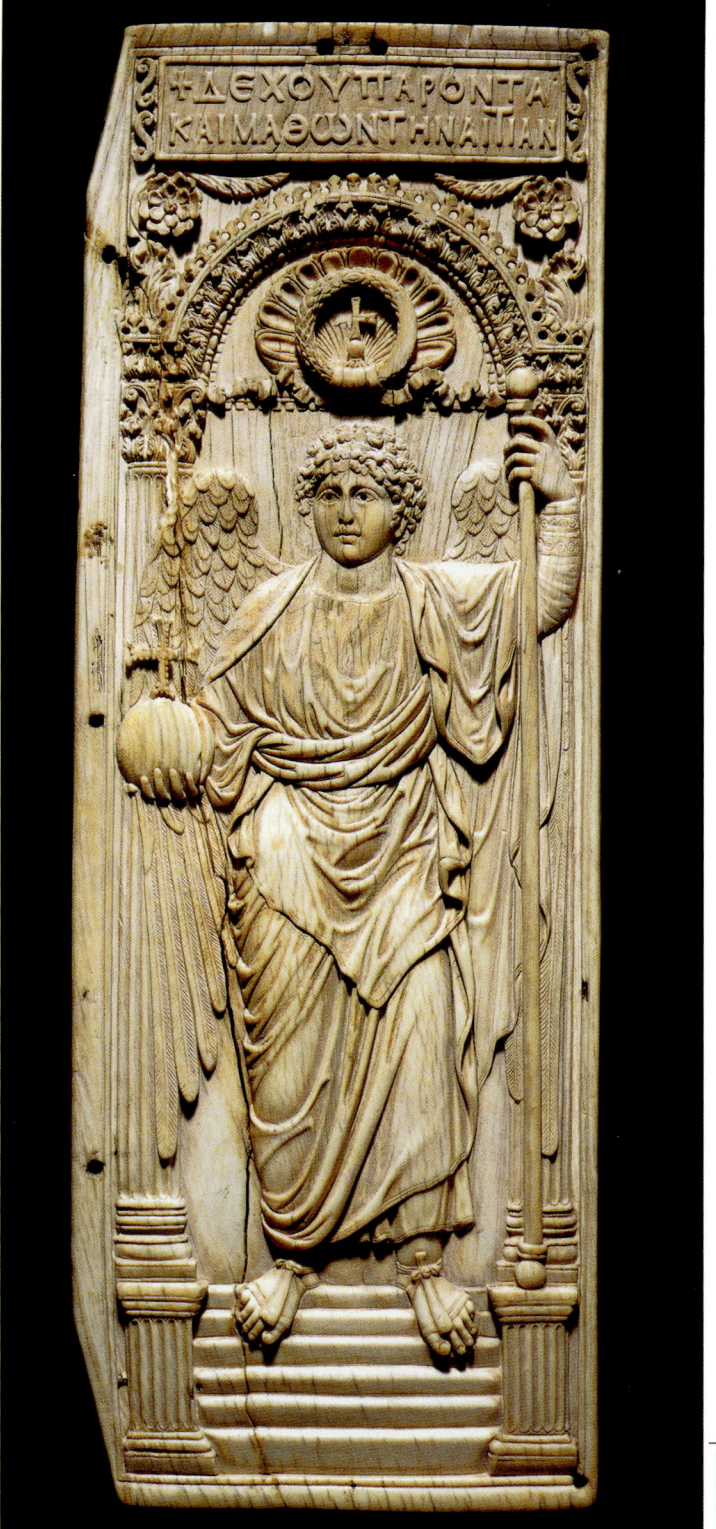

1 in.

**9-2** Saint Michael the Archangel, right leaf of a diptych, early sixth century. Ivory, 1′ 5″ × 5½″. British Museum, London.

The sculptor who carved this largest extant Byzantine ivory panel modeled Saint Michael on a classical winged Victory, but the archangel seems to float in front of the architecture rather than stand in it.

of most classical artists: to render the three-dimensional world in convincing and consistent fashion and to people that world with fully modeled figures firmly rooted on the ground. Michael seems more to float in front of the architecture than to stand in it.

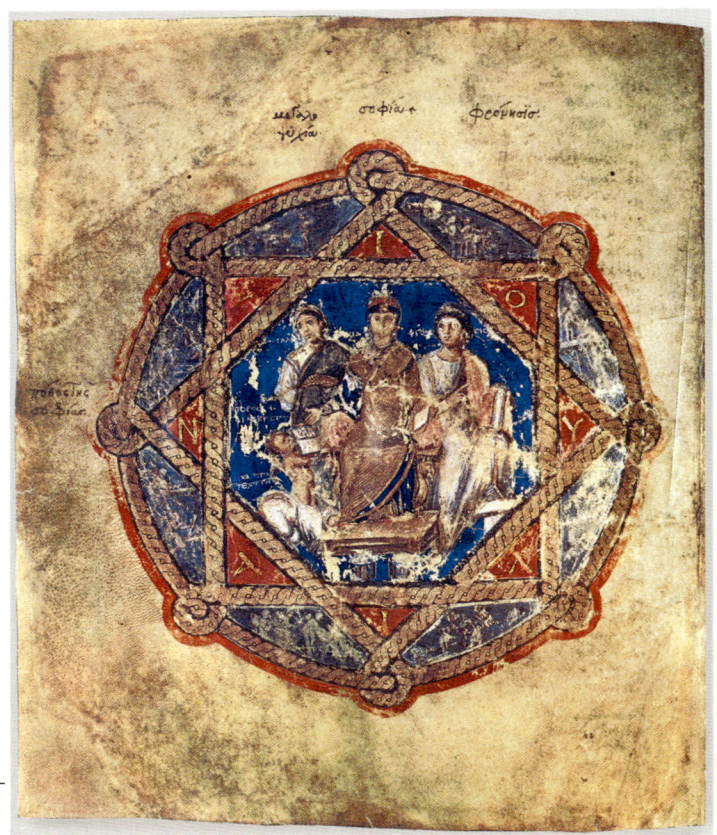

**9-3** Anicia Juliana between Magnanimity and Prudence, folio 6 verso of the *Vienna Dioskorides,* from Honoratai, near Constantinople (Istanbul), Turkey, ca. 512. Tempera on vellum, 1′ 3″ × 1′ 11″. Österreichische Nationalbibliothek, Vienna.

In gratitude for her generosity, the people of Honoratai presented Anicia Juliana, a great art patron, with a book in which she appears enthroned with personifications of Magnanimity and Prudence.

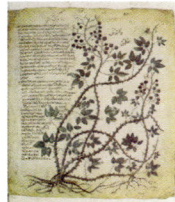

**9-3A** Blackberry bush, *Vienna Dioskorides,* 512.

***VIENNA DIOSKORIDES*** The physical world was, however, the focus of one of the rare surviving early medieval secular books. In the mid-first century, a Greek physician named Dioskorides compiled an encyclopedia of medicinal herbs called *De materia medica.* An early-sixth-century copy (FIGS. **9-3** and **9-3A**) of this medical manual, nearly a thousand pages in length, is in the Austrian National Library. The so-called *Vienna Dioskorides* was a gift from the people of Honoratai, near Constantinople, to Anicia Juliana, daughter of the short-lived Emperor of the West, Anicias Olybrias (r. 472). Anicia Juliana was a leading patron of the arts and had built a church dedicated to the Virgin Mary at Honoratai in 512. She also provided the funds to construct Saint Polyeuktos in Constantinople between 524 and 527. The excavated ruins of that church indicate it was a domed basilica—an important forerunner of the pioneering design of Justinian's Hagia Sophia (FIGS. 9-5 to 9-8).

The *Vienna Dioskorides* contains 498 illustrations, almost all images of plants (FIG. 9-3A) rendered with a scientific fidelity to nature that stands in stark contrast to contemporaneous Byzantine paintings and mosaics of religious subjects. It is likely the *Vienna Dioskorides* painters copied the illustrations as well as the text of a classical manuscript. One page, however, cannot be a copy—the dedication page (FIG. 9-3) featuring a portrait of Anicia Juliana in an eight-pointed star and circle frame. This earliest known illustrated dedication page shows Anicia Juliana enthroned between personifications of Magnanimity and Prudence, with a kneeling figure labeled Gratitude of the Arts at her feet. The princess holds a book in her left hand, probably this *De material medica.* The shading and modeling of the figures, the heads seen at oblique angles, the rendering of the throne's footstool in perspective, and the use of personifications establish that the painter still worked in the classical tradition most other Byzantine artists had by then rejected.

## Justinianic Art and Architecture

Historians and art historians alike regard the reign of the emperor Justinian (r. 527–565) as Byzantium's first golden age, during which the Christian Roman Empire briefly rivaled the old Roman Empire in power and extent (MAP 9-1). Justinian's generals, Belisarius and Narses, drove the Ostrogoths out of Italy, expelled the Vandals from the African provinces, beat back the Bulgars on the northern frontier, and held the Sasanians at bay on the eastern borders. At home, the emperor put down a dangerous rebellion in 532 of political and religious factions in the city (the Nika revolt) and supervised the codification of Roman law in a great work known as the *Corpus juris civilis* (*Code of Civil Law*), which became the foundation of the law systems of many modern European nations. Justinian could claim, with considerable justification, to have revived the glory of Old Rome in New Rome.

At the beginning of the fourth century, Constantine recognized Christianity and became its first imperial sponsor. By the end of the century, Theodosius had established Christianity as the Roman Empire's official religion. It was Justinian, however, who proclaimed Christianity the Empire's only lawful religion, specifically the Orthodox Christian doctrine. In Orthodox Christianity, the central article of faith is the equality of the three aspects of the Trinity of Father, Son, and Holy Spirit (as stated in Roman Catholic, Protestant, and Eastern Orthodox creeds today). All other versions of Christianity were heresies, especially the Arian, which asserted that the Father and Son were distinct entities and that the Father created the Son. Therefore, Christ was not equal to God. Also classified as a heresy was the Monophysite view that Christ had only one nature, which was divine, contrary to both the Orthodox and Arian belief that Christ had a dual divine-human nature. Justinian considered it his first duty not only to stamp out the few surviving polytheistic cults but also to crush all those who professed any Christian doctrine other than the Orthodox.

***BARBERINI IVORY*** Justinianic art, like Late Antique art, was both religious and secular. A masterwork of political art is the ivory plaque known today as the *Barberini Ivory* (FIG. **9-4**) because it was once part of the 17th-century collection of Cardinal Barberini in Rome. Carved in five parts (one is lost), the panel shows at the center an emperor, usually identified as Justinian, riding triumphantly on a rearing horse, while a startled, half-hidden barbarian recoils in fear behind him. The dynamic twisting postures of both horse and rider and the motif of the spear-thrusting equestrian emperor are familiar motifs in Roman imperial works (see "The Emperors of New Rome," page 259), as are the personifications of bountiful Earth (below the horse) and palm-bearing Victory (flying in to crown the conqueror). Also borrowed from the art of Old Rome are the barbarians at the bottom of the plaque bearing tribute and seeking clemency. Accompanying them are a lion, elephant, and tiger—exotic animals native to Africa and Asia, sites of Justinianic

# The Emperors of New Rome

The emperors of Byzantium, the New Rome on the Bosporus, considered themselves the direct successors of the emperors of the Old Rome on the Tiber. Although they proclaimed Orthodox Christianity as the official state religion and suppressed all of Old Rome's polytheistic cults, the political imagery of Byzantine art displays a striking continuity between ancient Rome and medieval Byzantium. Artists continued to portray emperors sitting on thrones holding the orb of the earth in their hands, battling foes while riding on mighty horses, and receiving tribute from defeated enemies. In the Early Byzantine period, official portraits continued to be set up in great numbers throughout the territories Byzantium controlled. But, as was true of the classical world, much of imperial Byzantine statuary is forever lost. Nonetheless, some of the lost portraits of the Byzantine emperors can be visualized from miniature versions of them on ivory reliefs such as the *Barberini Ivory* (FIG. 9-4) and from descriptions in surviving texts.

One especially impressive portrait in the Roman imperial tradition, melted down long ago, depicted the emperor Justinian on horseback atop a grandiose column. Cast in glittering bronze, like the equestrian statue of Marcus Aurelius (FIG. 7-59) set up nearly 400 years earlier, it attested to the continuity between the art of Old and New Rome, where pompous imperial images were commonly displayed at the apex of freestanding columns. (Compare FIG. 7-45, where a statue of Saint Peter has replaced a lost statue of the emperor Trajan.) Procopius, the historian of Justinian's reign, described the equestrian portrait:

Finest bronze, cast into panels and wreaths, encompasses the stones [of the column] on all sides, both binding them securely together and covering them with adornment. . . . This bronze is in color softer than pure gold, while in value it does not fall much short of an equal weight of silver. At the summit of the column stands a huge bronze horse turned towards the east, a most noteworthy sight. . . . Upon this horse is mounted a bronze image of the Emperor like a colossus. . . . He wears a cuirass in heroic fashion and his head is covered with a helmet . . . and a kind of radiance flashes forth from there. . . . He gazes towards the rising sun, steering his course, I suppose, against the Persians. In his left hand he holds a globe, by which the sculptor has signified that the whole earth and sea were subject to him, yet he carries neither sword nor spear nor any other weapon, but a cross surmounts his globe, by virtue of which alone he has won the kingship and victory in war. Stretching forth his right hand towards the regions of the East and spreading out his fingers, he commands the barbarians that dwell there to remain at home and not to advance any further.*

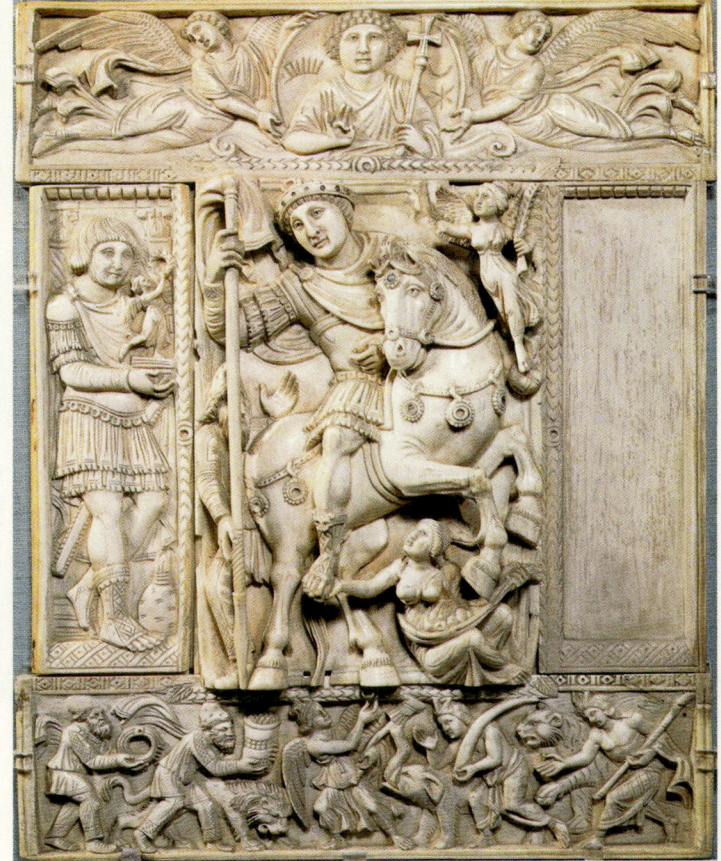

**9-4** Justinian as world conqueror (*Barberini Ivory*), mid-sixth century. Ivory, 1′ 1½″ × 10½″. Musée du Louvre, Paris.

Classical style and motifs lived on in Byzantine art in ivories such as this one. Justinian rides a rearing horse accompanied by personifications of Victory and Earth. Above, Christ blesses the emperor.

1 in.

Statues such as this one are the missing links in an imperial tradition that never really died and that lived on also in the Holy Roman Empire (FIG. 11-12) and in Renaissance Italy (FIGS. 21-16 and 21-17).

*Cyril Mango, trans., *The Art of the Byzantine Empire, 312–1453: Sources and Documents* (reprint of 1972 ed., Toronto: Toronto University Press, 1986), 110–111.

conquest. At the left, a Roman soldier carries a statuette of another Victory, reinforcing the central panel's message. The source of the emperor's strength, however, comes not from his earthly armies but from God. The uppermost panel depicts two angels holding aloft a youthful image of Christ carrying a cross in his left hand. Christ blesses Justinian with a gesture of his right hand, indicating approval of the emperor's rule.

**HAGIA SOPHIA** Like the emperors of Old Rome, Justinian was an ambitious builder. In Constantinople alone, he built or restored more than 30 churches of the Orthodox faith. The historian Procopius of Caesarea (ca. 500–ca. 565) declared the emperor's extravagant building program was an obsession that cost his subjects dearly in taxation. But Justinian's monuments defined the Byzantine style in architecture forever after.

**9-5** ANTHEMIUS OF TRALLES and ISIDORUS OF MILETUS, aerial view of Hagia Sophia (looking north), Constantinople (Istanbul), Turkey, 532–537. ◼◀

Justinian's reign was the first golden age of Byzantine art and architecture. Hagia Sophia was the most magnificent of the more than 30 churches Justinian built or restored in Constantinople alone.

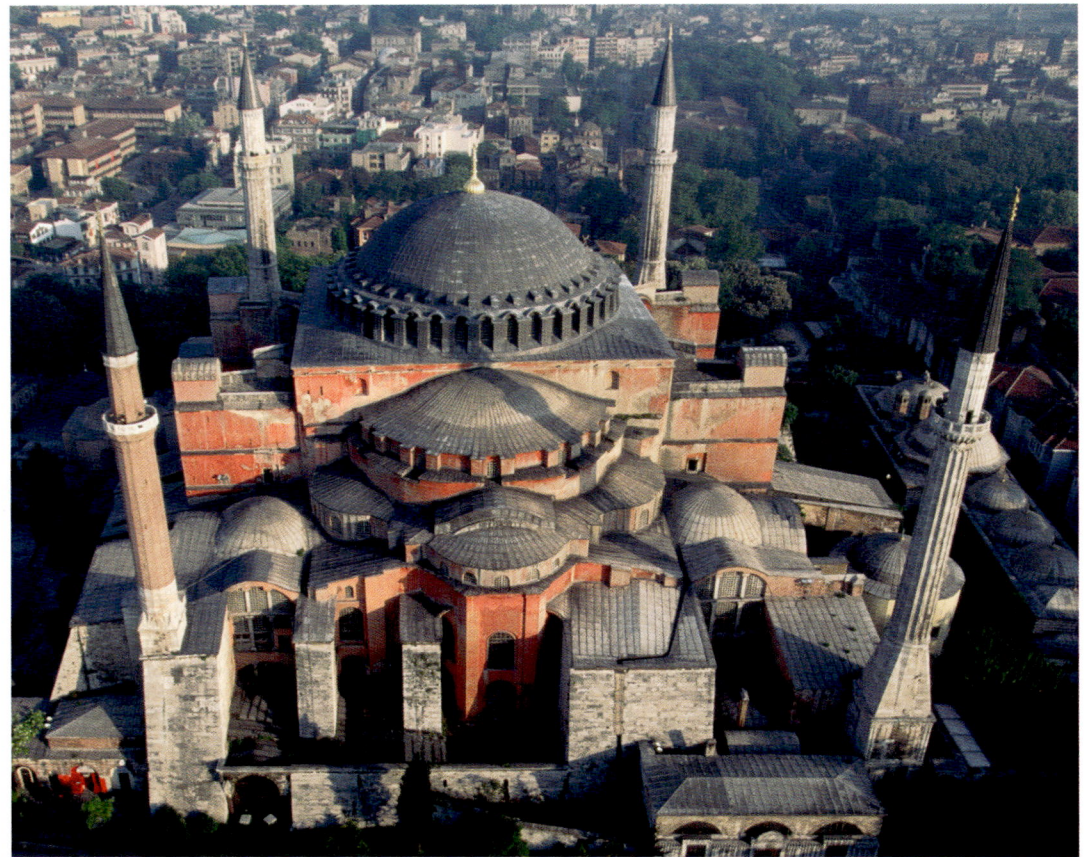

**9-6** ANTHEMIUS OF TRALLES and ISIDORUS OF MILETUS, restored cutaway view of Hagia Sophia, Constantinople (Istanbul), Turkey, 532–537 (John Burge). ◼◀

Hagia Sophia is a domed basilica. Buttressing the great dome are eastern and western half-domes whose thrusts descend, in turn, into smaller half-domes surmounting columned exedrae.

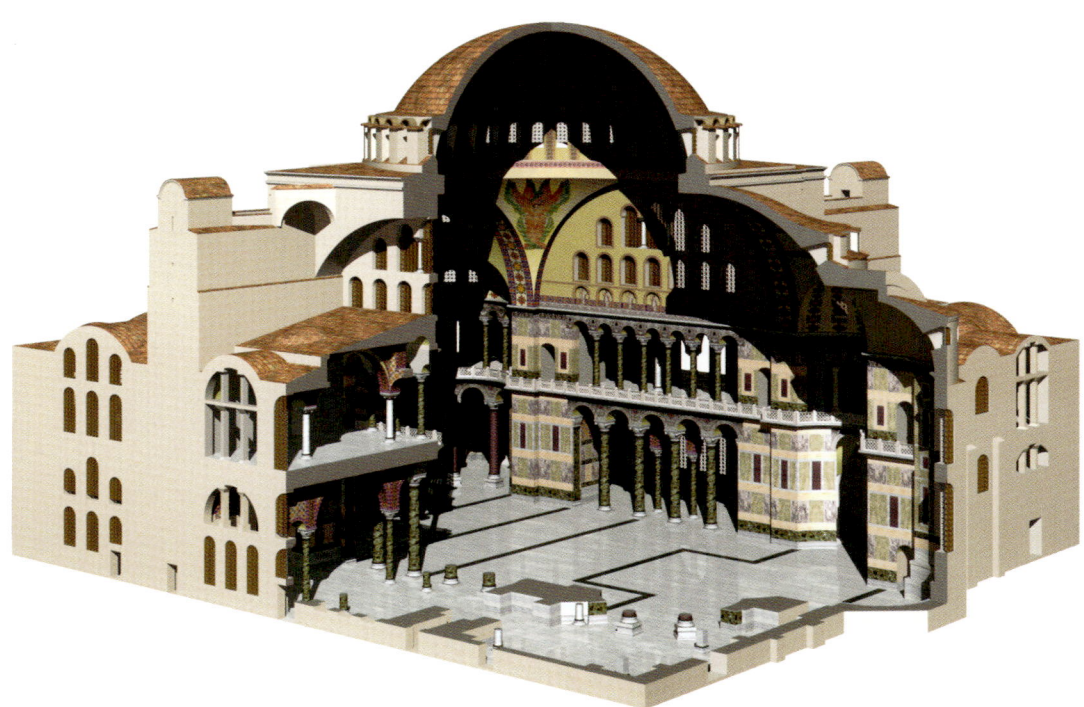

The emperor's most important project was the construction of Hagia Sophia (FIGS. **9-5** and **9-6**), the church of Holy Wisdom, in Constantinople. ANTHEMIUS OF TRALLES and ISIDORUS OF MILETUS, a mathematician and a physicist (neither man an architect in the modern sense of the word), designed and built the church for Justinian between 532 and 537. They began work immediately after fire destroyed an earlier church on the site during the Nika riot in January 532. Justinian intended the new church to rival all other churches ever built and even to surpass in scale and magnificence the Temple of Solomon in Jerusalem. The result was Byzantium's grandest building and one of the supreme accomplishments of world architecture.

Hagia Sophia's dimensions are formidable for any structure not made of steel. In plan (FIG. **9-7**), it is about 270 feet long and

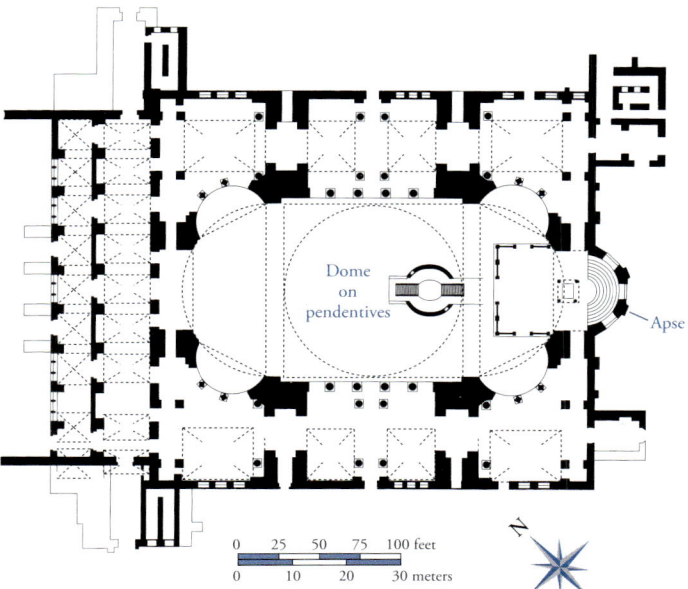

**9-7** ANTHEMIUS OF TRALLES and ISIDORUS OF MILETUS, plan of Hagia Sophia, Constantinople (Istanbul), Turkey, 532–537 (John Burge).

In Hagia Sophia, Justinian's architects succeeded in fusing two previously independent architectural traditions: the vertically oriented central-plan building and the longitudinally oriented basilica.

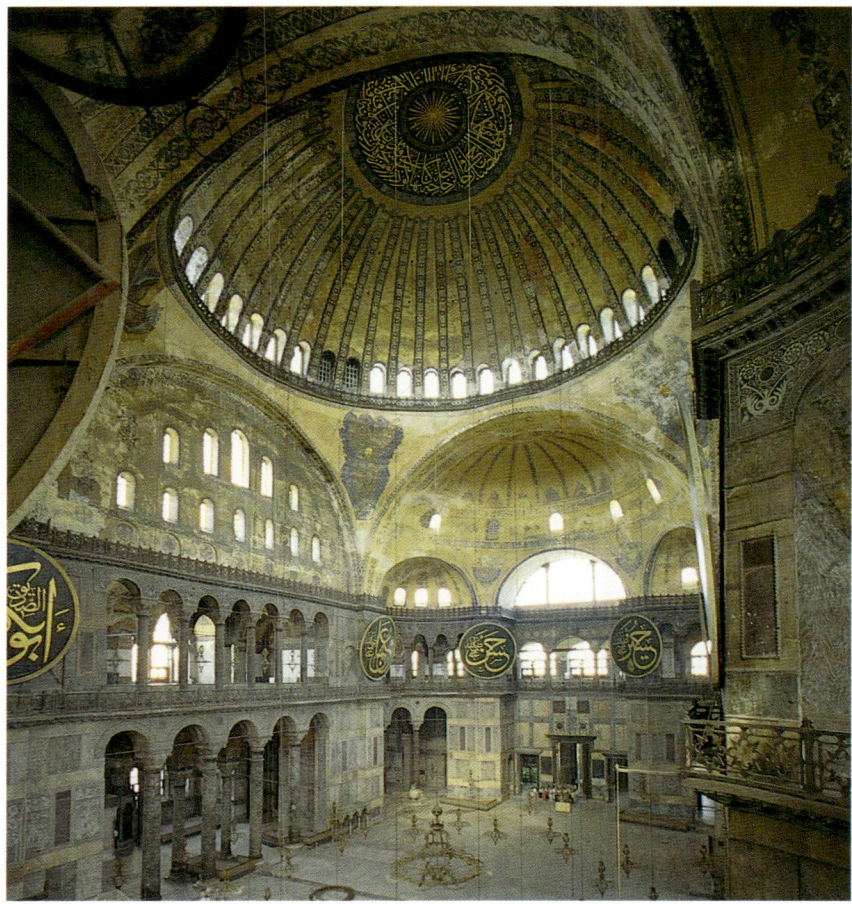

**9-8** ANTHEMIUS OF TRALLES and ISIDORUS OF MILETUS, interior of Hagia Sophia (looking southwest), Constantinople (Istanbul), Turkey, 532–537. ◼◀

Pendentive construction made possible Hagia Sophia's lofty dome, which seems to ride on a halo of light. A contemporary said the dome seemed to be suspended by "a golden chain from Heaven."

240 feet wide. The dome is 108 feet in diameter, and its crown rises some 180 feet above the pavement (FIG. **9-8**). (The first dome collapsed in 558. Its replacement required repair in the 9th and 14th centuries. The present dome is steeper and more stable than the original.) In scale, Hagia Sophia rivals the architectural wonders of Rome: the Pantheon, the Baths of Caracalla, and the Basilica of Constantine (see Chapter 7). In exterior view (FIG. 9-5), the great dome dominates the structure, but the building's external aspects today are much changed from their original appearance. The huge buttresses are later additions to the Justinianic design, and after the Ottoman conquest of 1453, when Hagia Sophia became a *mosque*, the Turks constructed four towering *minarets* (see Chapter 10) at the corners of the former church. The building is now a museum.

The characteristic Byzantine plainness and unpretentiousness of the exterior scarcely prepare visitors for the building's interior (FIG. 9-8). A poet and *silentiary* (an usher responsible for maintaining silence in the palace) at Justinian's court, Paul Silentiarius, vividly described the original magnificence of Hagia Sophia's interior:

Who . . . shall sing the marble meadows gathered upon the mighty walls and spreading pavement. . . . [There is stone] from the green flanks of Carystus [and] the speckled Phrygian stone, sometimes rosy mixed with white, sometimes gleaming with purple and silver flowers. There is a wealth of porphyry stone, too, besprinkled with little bright stars. . . . You may see the bright green stone of Laconia and the glittering marble with wavy veins found in the deep gullies of the Iasian peaks, exhibiting slanting streaks of blood-red and livid white; the pale yellow with swirling red from the Lydian headland; the glittering crocus-like golden stone [of Libya]; . . . glittering [Celtic] black [with] here and there an abundance of milk; the pale onyx with glint of precious metal; and [Thessalian marble] in parts vivid green not unlike emerald. . . . It has spots resembling snow next to flashes of black so that in one stone various beauties mingle.[1]

The feature that distinguishes Hagia Sophia from equally lavishly revetted Roman buildings such as the Pantheon (FIG. 7-51) is the special mystical quality of the light flooding the interior. The soaring canopy-like dome that dominates the inside as well as the outside of the church rides on a halo of light from windows in the dome's base. Visitors to Hagia Sophia from Justinian's time to today have been struck by the light within the church and its effect on the human spirit. The 40 windows at the base of the dome create the illusion the dome rests on the light pouring through them.

Procopius observed that the dome looked as if it were suspended by "a golden chain from Heaven" and that "the space is not illuminated by the sun from the outside, but that the radiance is generated within, so great an abundance of light bathes this shrine all around."[2] Paul the Silentiary compared the dome to "the firmament which rests on air" and described the vaulting as covered with "gilded tesserae from which a glittering stream of golden rays pours abundantly and strikes men's eyes with irresistible force. It is as if one were gazing at the midday sun in spring."[3] Thus, Hagia Sophia has a vastness of space shot through with light, and a central dome that appears to be supported by the light it admits. Light is the mystic element—light that

## Pendentives and Squinches

Perhaps the most characteristic feature of Byzantine architecture is the placement of a dome, which is circular at its base, over a square, as in the Justinianic church of Hagia Sophia (FIGS. 9-6 to 9-8) and countless later structures (for example, FIGS. 9-21, 9-22, and 9-26). Two structural devices that are hallmarks of Byzantine engineering made this feat possible: *pendentives* and *squinches*.

In pendentive construction (from the Latin *pendere*, "to hang"), a dome rests on what is, in effect, a second, larger dome (FIG. 9-9, *left*). The builders omit the top portion and four segments around the rim of the larger dome, producing four curved triangles, or pendentives. The pendentives join to form a ring and four arches whose planes bound a square. The pendentives and arches transfer the weight of the dome not to the walls but to the four piers from which the arches spring. The first use of pendentives on a monumental scale was in Hagia Sophia (FIGS. 9-6 and 9-8) in the mid-sixth century, although Mesopotamian architects had experimented with them earlier. In Roman and Early Christian central-plan buildings, such as the Pantheon (FIGS. 7-50 and 7-51) and Santa Costanza (FIG. 8-11), the domes spring directly from the circular top of a cylinder (FIG. 7-6*d*).

The pendentive system is a dynamic solution to the problem of setting a round dome over a square, making possible a union of centralized and longitudinal or basilican structures. A similar effect can be achieved using squinches (FIG. 9-9, *right*)—arches, corbels, or lintels—that bridge the corners of the supporting walls and form an octagon inscribed within a square. To achieve even greater height, a builder can rest a dome on a cylindrical drum that in turn rests on either pendentives or squinches (FIG. 9-22), but the principle of supporting a dome over a square is the same.

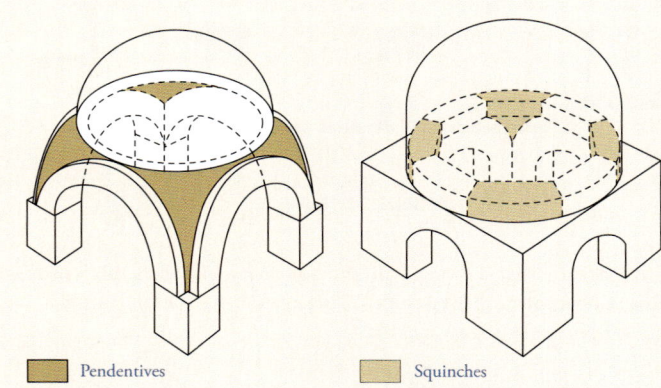

Pendentives    Squinches

**9-9** Dome on pendentives (*left*) and on squinches (*right*).

Pendentives (triangular sections of a sphere) make it possible to place a dome on a ring over a square. Squinches achieve the same goal by bridging the corners of the square to form an octagonal base.

glitters in the mosaics, shines forth from the marbles, and pervades and defines spaces that escape definition. Light seems to dissolve material substance and transform it into an abstract spiritual vision. Pseudo-Dionysius, perhaps the most influential mystic philosopher of the age, wrote in *The Divine Names:* "Light comes from the Good and . . . light is the visual image of God."[4]

**PENDENTIVES** To achieve this illusion of a floating "dome of Heaven," Anthemius and Isidorus used *pendentives* (see "Pendentives and Squinches," above) to transfer the weight from the great dome to the piers beneath rather than to the walls. With pendentives (FIG. 9-9, *left*), not only could the space beneath the dome be unobstructed but scores of windows also could puncture the walls. The pendentives created the impression of a dome suspended above, not held up by, walls. Experts today can explain the technical virtuosity of Justinian's builders, but it remained a mystery to their contemporaries. Procopius communicated the sense of wonderment experienced by those who entered Justinian's great church: "No matter how much they concentrate their attention on this and that, and examine everything with contracted eyebrows, they are unable to understand the craftsmanship and always depart from there amazed by the perplexing spectacle."[5]

By placing a hemispherical dome on a square base instead of on a circular base, as in the Pantheon (FIGS. 7-50 and 7-51), Anthemius and Isidorus succeeded in fusing two previously independent and seemingly mutually exclusive architectural traditions: the vertically oriented central-plan building and the longitudinally oriented

basilica. Hagia Sophia is, in essence, a domed basilica (FIG. 9-6)—a uniquely successful conclusion to several centuries of experimentation in Christian church architecture. However, the thrusts of the pendentive construction at Hagia Sophia made external buttresses necessary, as well as huge internal northern and southern wall piers and eastern and western half-domes (FIG. 9-5). The semidomes' thrusts descend, in turn, into still smaller half-domes surmounting columned exedrae (FIG. 9-8) that give a curving flow to the design.

The diverse vistas and screenlike ornamented surfaces mask the structural lines. The columnar arcades of the nave and second-story galleries have no real structural function. Like the walls they pierce, they are only part of a fragile "fill" between the huge piers. Structurally, although Hagia Sophia may seem Roman in its great scale and majesty, the organization of its masses is not Roman. The very fact the "walls" in Hagia Sophia are concealed (and barely adequate) piers indicates the architects sought Roman monumentality as an *effect* and did not design the building according to Roman principles. Using brick in place of concrete was a further departure from Roman practice and marks Byzantine architecture as a distinctive structural style. Hagia Sophia's eight great supporting piers are ashlar masonry, but the screen walls are brick, as are the vaults of the aisles and galleries and the dome and semicircular half-domes.

The ingenious design of Hagia Sophia provided the illumination and the setting for the solemn liturgy of the Orthodox faith. The large windows along the rim of the great dome poured light down upon the interior's jeweled splendor, where priests staged the sacred spectacle. Sung by clerical choirs, the Orthodox equivalent of the Latin Mass celebrated the sacrament of the Eucharist at the altar in the apsidal sanctuary, in spiritual reenactment of Jesus' crucifixion. Processions of chanting priests, accompanying the patriarch (archbishop) of Constantinople, moved slowly to and from the sanctuary and the vast nave. The gorgeous array of their vestments (compare FIG. 9-35A) rivaled the interior's polychrome marbles, complementing the interior's finely wrought, gleaming candlesticks and candelabra; the illuminated books bound in gold or ivory and inlaid with jewels and enamels; and the crosses, sacred vessels, and processional banners. Each, with its great richness of texture and color, glowing in shafts of light from the dome, contributed to the majestic ambience of Justinian's great church.

The nave of Hagia Sophia was reserved for the clergy, not the congregation. The laity, segregated by sex, had only partial views of the brilliant ceremony from the shadows of the aisles and galleries, restrained in most places by marble parapets. The emperor was the only layperson privileged to enter the sanctuary. When he participated with the patriarch in the liturgical drama, standing at the pulpit beneath the great dome, his rule was again sanctified and his person exalted. Church and state were symbolically made one (see "Church and State United," page 255). The church building was then the earthly image of the court of Heaven, its light the image of God and God's holy wisdom.

At Hagia Sophia, the intricate logic of Greek theology, the ambitious scale of Rome, the vaulting tradition of Mesopotamia, and the mysticism of Eastern Christianity combined to create a monument that is at once a summation of antiquity and a positive assertion of the triumph of Christian faith.

**RAVENNA** In 493, Theodoric, the Ostrogoths' greatest king, chose Ravenna, an Etruscan and later a Roman city near the Adriatic coast of Italy south of Venice, as the capital of his kingdom, which encompassed much of the Balkans and all of Italy (see Chapter 8). During the short history of Theodoric's unfortunate successors, Ravenna's importance declined. But in 539, Justinian's general Belisarius captured the city, initiating an important new chapter in its history. Ravenna remained the Eastern Empire's foothold in Italy for two centuries, until the Lombards and then the Franks overtook it. During Justinian's reign, Ravenna enjoyed great prosperity at a time when repeated sieges, conquests, and sackings threatened the "eternal city" of Rome with extinction. As the seat of Byzantine dominion in Italy, Ravenna and its culture became an extension of Constantinople. Its art, even more than that of the Byzantine capital (where relatively little outside of architecture has survived), clearly reveals the transition from the Early Christian to the Byzantine style.

**SAN VITALE** Construction of Ravenna's greatest shrine, San Vitale (FIGS. 9-1, **9-10**, and **9-11**), began under Bishop Ecclesius (r. 522–532) shortly after Theodoric's death in 526. A wealthy citizen, Julianus Argentarius (Julian the Banker), provided the enormous sum of 26,000 *solidi* (gold coins weighing in excess of 350 pounds) required to proceed with the work. San Vitale is unlike any of the Early Christian churches (FIG. 8-18) of Ravenna. It is not a basilica. Rather, it is centrally planned, like Justinian's churches in Constantinople, and it seems, in fact, to have been loosely modeled on the earlier Church of Saints Sergius and Bacchus there.

As already discussed (FIG. 9-1), San Vitale's design features a dome-covered clerestory-lit central space defined by piers alternating with curved, columned exedrae, creating an intricate eight-leafed plan (FIG. 9-11). The exedrae closely integrate the inner and

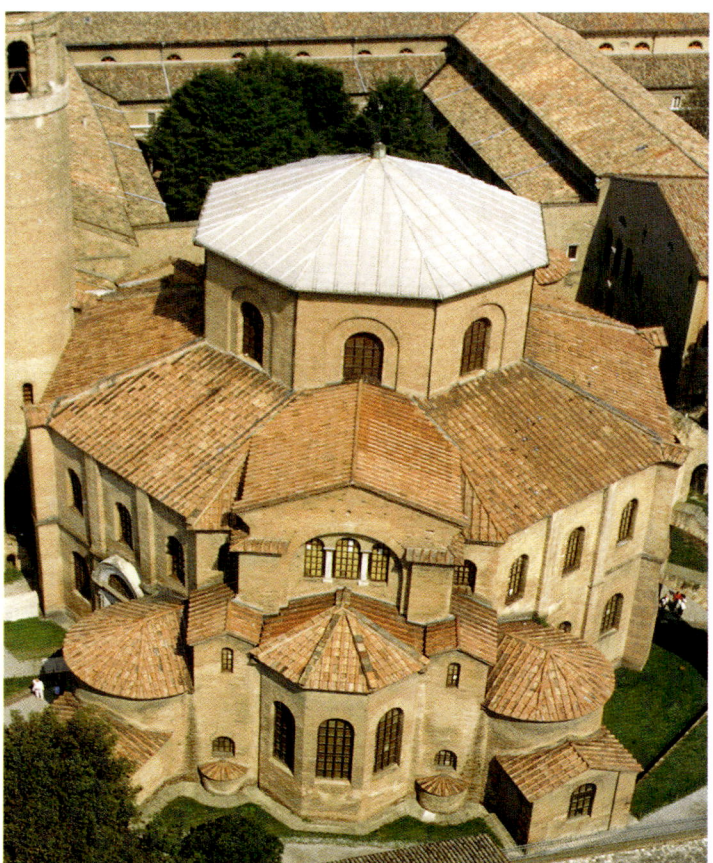

**9-10** Aerial view of San Vitale (looking northwest), Ravenna, Italy, 526–547. ◼◀

Justinian's general Belisarius captured Ravenna from the Ostrogoths. The city became the seat of Byzantine dominion in Italy. San Vitale honored Saint Vitalis, a second-century Ravenna martyr.

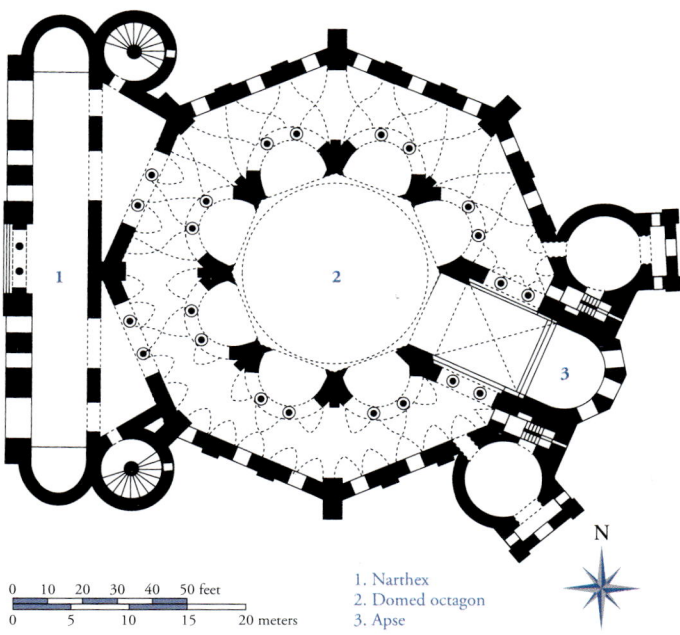

0  10  20  30  40  50 feet
0     5      10      15      20 meters

1. Narthex
2. Domed octagon
3. Apse

**9-11** Plan of San Vitale, Ravenna, Italy, 526–547.

Centrally planned like Justinian's churches in Constantinople, San Vitale has a design featuring an off-axis narthex and two concentric octagons. A dome crowns the taller, inner octagon.

youthful in the Early Christian tradition, sits atop the world and holds a scroll with seven seals (Rev. 5:1). The four rivers of Paradise flow beneath him, and rainbow-hued clouds float above. Christ extends the golden martyr's wreath to Vitalis, the patron saint of the church, whom an angel introduces. At Christ's left, another angel presents Bishop Ecclesius, who offers a model of San Vitale to Christ. The arrangement recalls Christ's prophecy of the last days of the world: "And then shall they see the Son of Man coming in the clouds with great power and glory. And then shall he send his angels, and shall gather together his elect from the four winds, from the uttermost part of Heaven" (Mark 13:26–27).

Images and symbols covering the entire sanctuary express the single idea of Christ's redemption of humanity and the reenactment of it in the Eucharist. For example, the lunette mosaic over the two columns on the northern side of the choir depicts the story of Abraham and the three angels. Sarah, Abraham's wife, was 90 years old and childless when three angels visited Abraham. They announced Sarah would bear a son, and she later miraculously gave birth to Isaac. Christians believe the Old Testament angels symbolize the Holy Trinity. Immediately to the right in the lunette is the sacrifice of Isaac, a prefiguration of Christ's crucifixion (see "Jewish Subjects in Christian Art," Chapter 8, page 238).

**JUSTINIAN AND THEODORA** The most distinctive elements of the mosaic program of San Vitale are the facing panels in the choir depicting Justinian (FIG. **9-13**) and Theodora (FIG. **9-14**). The positions of the figures are all-important. They express the formulas of precedence and rank. In the Justinian mosaic, the emperor is at the center, distinguished from the other dignitaries by his purple robe and halo, which connect him with the Savior in the vault above.

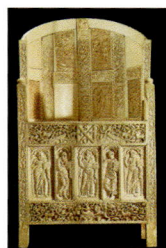

9-14A Throne of Maximianus, ca. 546–556.

At Justinian's left (at right in the mosaic) is Bishop Maximianus (r. 546–556), the man responsible for San Vitale's completion. (His magnificent ivory throne [FIG. **9-14A**] is on display today in one of Ravenna's museums.) The mosaicist stressed the bishop's importance by labeling his figure with the only identifying inscription in the composition. (Some scholars think Maximianus added the inscription and the bishop represented was originally Ecclesius.)

The artist divided the figures into three groups: the emperor and his staff; the clergy; and the imperial guard, bearing a shield with the *chi-rho-iota* (☧) monogram of Christ. Each group has a leader whose feet precede (by one foot overlapping) the feet of those who follow. The positions of Justinian and Maximianus are curiously ambiguous. Although the emperor appears to be slightly behind the bishop, the golden *paten* (large shallow bowl or plate for the Eucharist bread) he carries overlaps the bishop's arm. Thus, symbolized by place and gesture, the imperial and churchly powers are in balance. The emperor's paten, the bishop's cross, and the attendant clerics' book and censer produce a slow forward movement that strikingly modifies the scene's rigid formality. The artist placed nothing in the background, wishing the observer to understand the procession as taking place in this very sanctuary. Thus, the emperor appears forever as a participant in the sacred rites and as the proprietor of this royal church and the ruler of the Western Empire.

The procession at San Vitale recalls but contrasts with that of Augustus and his entourage (FIG. 7-31) on the Ara Pacis, built more than a half millennium earlier in Rome. There, the fully modeled marble figures have their feet planted firmly on the ground. The

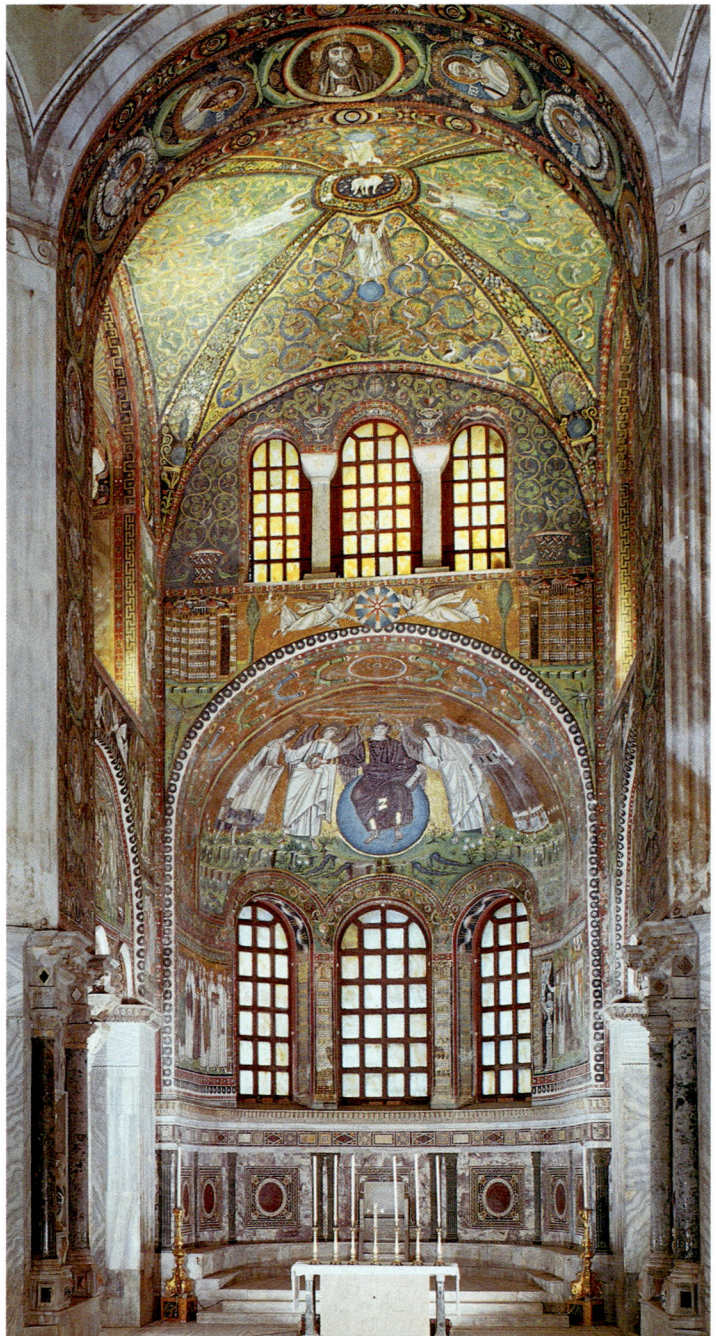

**9-12** Choir and apse of San Vitale with mosaic of Christ between two angels, Saint Vitalis, and Bishop Ecclesius, Ravenna, Italy, 526–547. ◼️

In the apse vault, a youthful Christ, seated on the orb of the world at the time of his second coming, extends the gold martyr's wreath to Saint Vitalis. Bishop Ecclesius offers Christ a model of San Vitale.

outer spaces that otherwise would have existed simply side by side as independent units. A cross-vaulted *choir* (FIG. **9-12**) preceding the apse interrupts the ambulatory and gives the plan some axial stability. Weakening this effect, however, is the off-axis placement of the narthex, whose odd angle never has been explained fully. (The atrium, which no longer exists, may have paralleled a street running in the same direction as the angle of the narthex.)

The mosaic-clad walls and vaults of San Vitale's interior are dazzling. In the apse vault is a vision of the second coming. Christ,

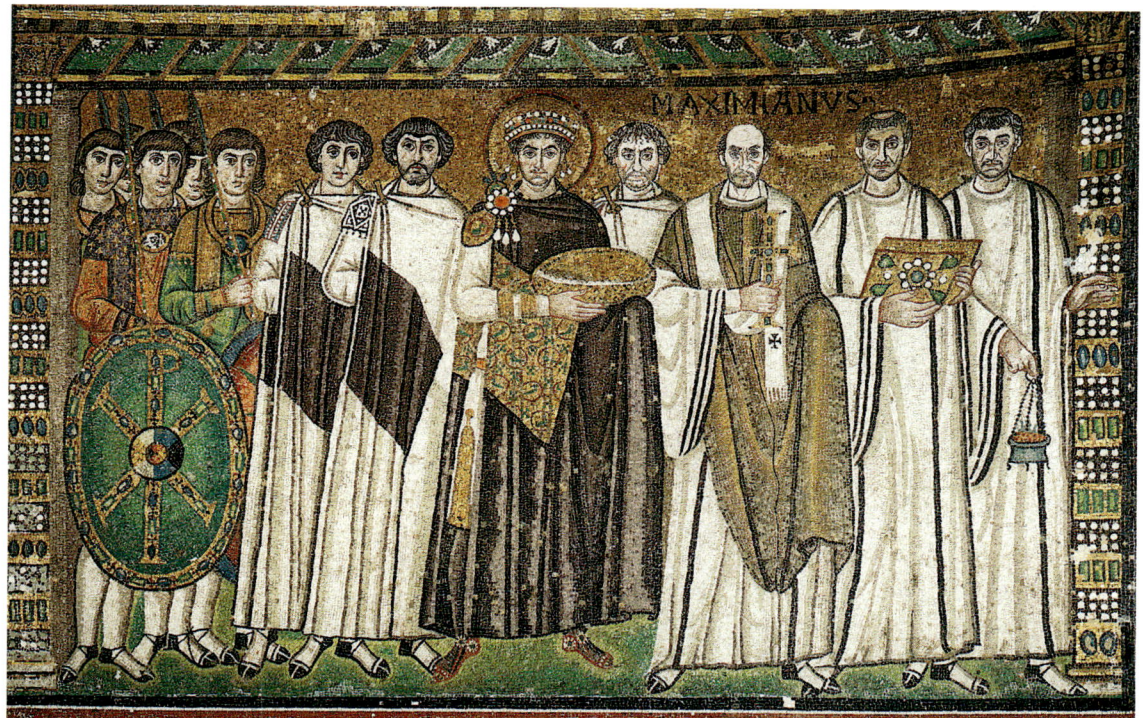

**9-13** Justinian, Bishop Maximianus, and attendants, mosaic on the north wall of the apse, San Vitale, Ravenna, Italy, ca. 547. ■◀

San Vitale's mosaics reveal the new Byzantine aesthetic. Justinian is foremost among the weightless and speechless frontal figures hovering before the viewer, their positions in space uncertain.

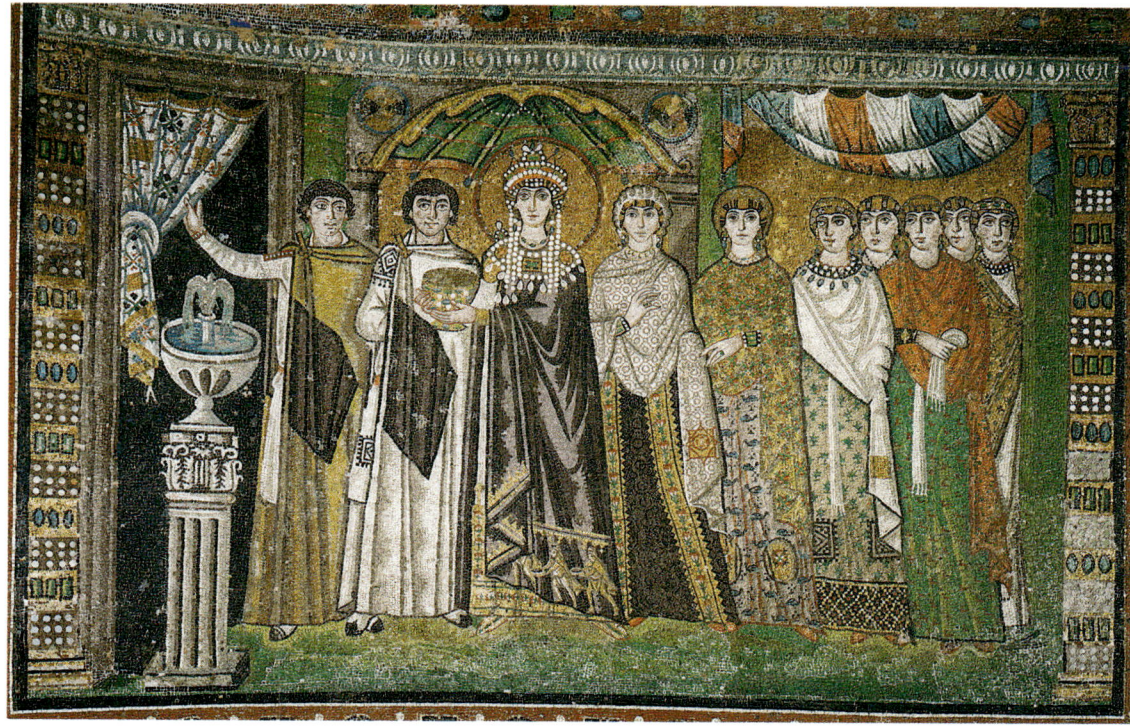

**9-14** Theodora and attendants, mosaic on the south wall of the apse, San Vitale, Ravenna, Italy, ca. 547. ■◀

Justinian's counterpart on the opposite wall is the powerful Empress Theodora. Neither she nor Justinian ever visited Ravenna. San Vitale's mosaics are proxies for the absent sovereigns.

Romans talk among themselves, unaware of the viewer's presence. All is anecdote, all very human and of this world, even if the figures themselves conform to a classical ideal of beauty that cannot be achieved in reality. The frontal figures of the Byzantine mosaic hover before viewers, weightless and speechless, their positions in space uncertain. Tall, spare, angular, and elegant, they have lost the rather squat proportions characteristic of much Early Christian figural art. The garments fall straight, stiff, and thin from the narrow shoulders. The organic body has dematerialized, and, except for the heads, some of which seem to be true portraits, viewers see a procession of solemn spirits gliding silently in the presence of the sacrament. Indeed, the theological basis for this approach to representation was the idea that the divine was invisible and that the purpose of religious art was to stimulate spiritual seeing. Theodulf of Orleans summed up this idea around 790: "God is beheld not with the eyes of the flesh but only with the eye of the mind."[6] The mosaics of San Vitale reveal this new Byzantine aesthetic, one very different from that of the classical world but equally compelling. Byzantine art disparages matter and material values. It is an art in which blue sky has given way to heavenly gold, an art without solid bodies or cast shadows, and with the perspective of Paradise, which is nowhere and everywhere.

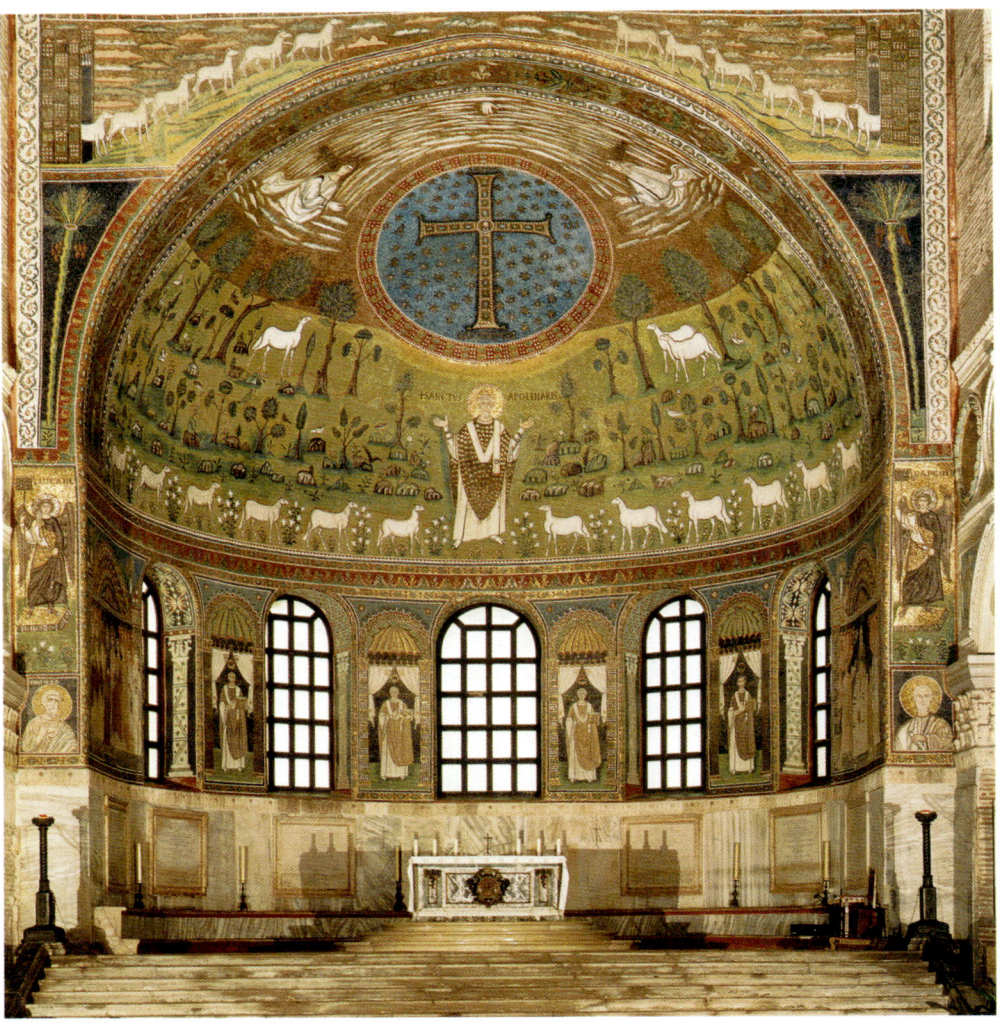

The figures in the Theodora mosaic (FIG. 9-14) exhibit the same stylistic traits as those in the Justinian mosaic, but the artist represented the women within a definite architecture, perhaps the atrium of San Vitale. The empress stands in state beneath an imperial canopy, waiting to follow the emperor's procession. An attendant beckons her to pass through the curtained doorway. The fact she is outside the sanctuary in a courtyard with a fountain and only about to enter attests that, in the ceremonial protocol, her rank was not quite equal to her consort's. But the very presence of Theodora at San Vitale is significant. She, like many other Byzantine empresses (see "Zoe," page 273), wielded enormous influence in the Byzantine state. Of humble origin, Theodora, who was 15 years younger than Justinian, initially attracted his attention because of her beauty, but she soon became his most trusted adviser. John the Lydian, a civil servant at Constantinople at the time, described her as "surpassing in intelligence all men who ever lived." For example, during the Nika revolt in Constantinople in 532, when all of her husband's ministers counseled flight from the city, Theodora, by the sheer force of her personality, persuaded Justinian and his generals to hold their ground—and they succeeded in suppressing the uprising. In the mosaic, the artist underscored Theodora's elevated rank by decorating the border of her garment with a representation of the three magi, suggesting the empress belongs in the company of the three monarchs bearing gifts who approached the newborn Jesus.

**SANT'APOLLINARE IN CLASSE** Until the ninth century, the Church of Sant'Apollinare in Classe housed the body of Saint Apollinaris, who suffered his martyrdom in Classe, Ravenna's port. The church itself is Early Christian in type, a basilica with a nave and flanking aisles, like Theodoric's palace-church (FIG. 8-18) dedicated to the same saint in Ravenna. As in the earlier church, the Justinianic building's exterior is plain and unadorned, but inside sumptuous mosaics fill the apse (FIG. **9-15**). The mosaic decorating the semidome above the apse was probably in place by the time of the church's dedication in 549. The mosaics of the framing arch are of later date.

Against a gold ground, a large medallion with a jeweled cross dominates the composition. This may represent the cross Constantine erected on the hill of Calvary to commemorate the martyrdom of Jesus. Visible just above the cross is the hand of God. On either side of the medallion, in the clouds, are the Old Testament prophets Moses and Elijah, who appeared before Jesus during his Transfiguration (FIG. 9-16). Below these two figures are three sheep, symbols of the disciples John, Peter, and James, who accompanied Jesus to the foot of the mountain he ascended in order to converse with the prophets. Beneath, amid green fields with trees, flowers, and birds, stands the church's patron saint, Apollinaris. The mosaicist portrayed him in the Early Christian manner as an orant with uplifted arms. Accompanying Apollinaris are 12 sheep, perhaps representing the Christian congregation under the saint's protection, and forming, as they march in regular file across the apse, a wonderfully decorative base.

Comparison of the Early Byzantine Sant'Apollinare in Classe mosaic with the Galla Placidia mosaic (FIG. 8-17) from the Early Christian period at Ravenna shows how the style and artists' approach to the subject changed during the course of a century. Both mosaics portray a human figure and some sheep in a landscape. But in Classe, in the mid-sixth century, the artist did not try to represent voluminous figures in a naturalistic setting, but instead treated the saint, the animals, and the plants as flat symbols, lined up side by side. The mosaicist carefully avoided overlapping in what must have been an intentional effort to omit all reference to the three-

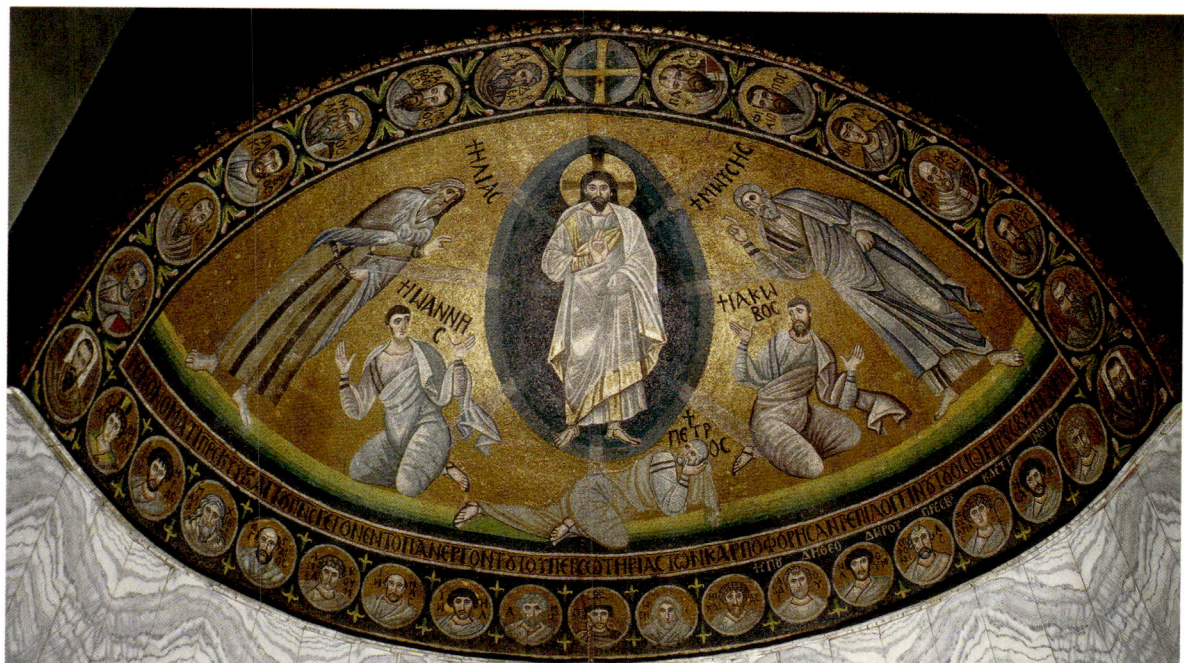

**9-16** *Transfiguration of Jesus,* apse mosaic, Church of the Virgin, monastery of Saint Catherine, Mount Sinai, Egypt, ca. 548–565.

In this apse mosaic, unlike FIG. 9-15, the artist swept away all traces of landscape for a depthless field of gold. The prophets and disciples cast no shadows even though bathed in divine light.

dimensional space of the material world and physical reality. Shapes have lost the volume seen in the earlier mosaic and instead are flat silhouettes with linear details. The effect is that of an extremely rich, flat tapestry without illusionistic devices. This new Byzantine style became the ideal vehicle for conveying the extremely complex symbolism of the fully developed Christian dogma.

Indeed, the Classe apse mosaic is much richer in meaning than first meets the eye. The cross symbolizes not only Christ's own death, with its redeeming consequences, but also the death of his martyrs (in this case, Saint Apollinaris). The lamb, also a symbol of martyrdom, appropriately represents the martyred apostles. The whole scene expands above the altar, where the priests celebrated the sacrament of the Eucharist—the miraculous recurrence of the supreme redemptive act. The altars of Christian churches were, from early times, sanctified by the bones and relics of martyrs (see "The Veneration of Relics," Chapter 12, page 336). Thus, the mystery and the martyrdom joined in one concept. The death of the martyr, in imitation of Christ, is a triumph over death that leads to eternal life. The images above the altar present an inspiring vision, delivered with overwhelming force, to the eyes of believers. Looming above their eyes is the apparition of a great mystery, ordered to make perfectly simple and clear that humankind's duty is to seek salvation. Even the illiterate, who might not grasp the details of the complex theological program, could understand that the way of the martyr is open to the Christian faithful and that the reward of eternal life is within their reach.

**MOUNT SINAI** During Justinian's reign, almost continuous building took place, not only in Constantinople and Ravenna but throughout the Byzantine Empire. At about the time mosaicists in Ravenna were completing their work at San Vitale and Sant'Apollinare in Classe, Justinian's builders were rebuilding an important early *monastery* (an enclosed compound for monks) at Mount Sinai in Egypt where Moses received the Ten Commandments from God. Now called Saint Catherine's, the monastery marked the spot at the foot of the mountain where the Bible says God first spoke to the Hebrew prophet from a burning bush.

*Monasticism* began in Egypt in the third century and spread rapidly to Palestine and Syria in the East and as far as Ireland in the West (see Chapter 11). It began as a migration to the wilderness by those who sought a more spiritual way of life, far from the burdens, distractions, and temptations of town and city. In desert places, these refuge seekers lived austerely as hermits, in contemplative isolation, cultivating the soul's perfection. So many thousands fled the cities that the authorities became alarmed—noting the effect on the tax base, military recruitment, and business in general.

The origins of the monastic movement are associated with Saints Anthony and Pachomius in Egypt in the fourth century. By the fifth century, many of the formerly isolated monks had begun to live together within a common enclosure and formulate regulations governing communal life under the direction of an abbot (see "Medieval Monasteries and Benedictine Rule," Chapter 11, page 322). The monks typically lived in a walled monastery, an architectural complex that included the monks' residence (an alignment of single cells), an oratory (monastic church), a *refectory* (dining hall), a kitchen, storage and service quarters, and a guest house for pilgrims (FIG. 11-19).

Justinian rebuilt the monastery at Mount Sinai between 548 and 565 and constructed imposing walls around it. The site had been an important pilgrimage destination since the fourth century, and Justinian's fortress protected not only the monks but also the lay pilgrims during their visits. The Mount Sinai church was dedicated to the Virgin Mary, whom the Orthodox Church had officially recognized in the mid-fifth century as the Mother of God (*Theotokos,* "she who bore God" in Greek), putting to rest a controversy about the divine nature of Christ.

In the church's apse is the *Transfiguration of Jesus* mosaic (FIG. **9-16**). (Other mosaics in the church depict Moses receiving the Law and standing before the burning bush.) Jesus appears in a deep-blue almond-shaped *mandorla* (almond-shaped aureole of light). At his feet are John, Peter, and James. At the left and right are Elijah and Moses. Portrait busts of saints and prophets in medallions frame the whole scene. The artist stressed the intense

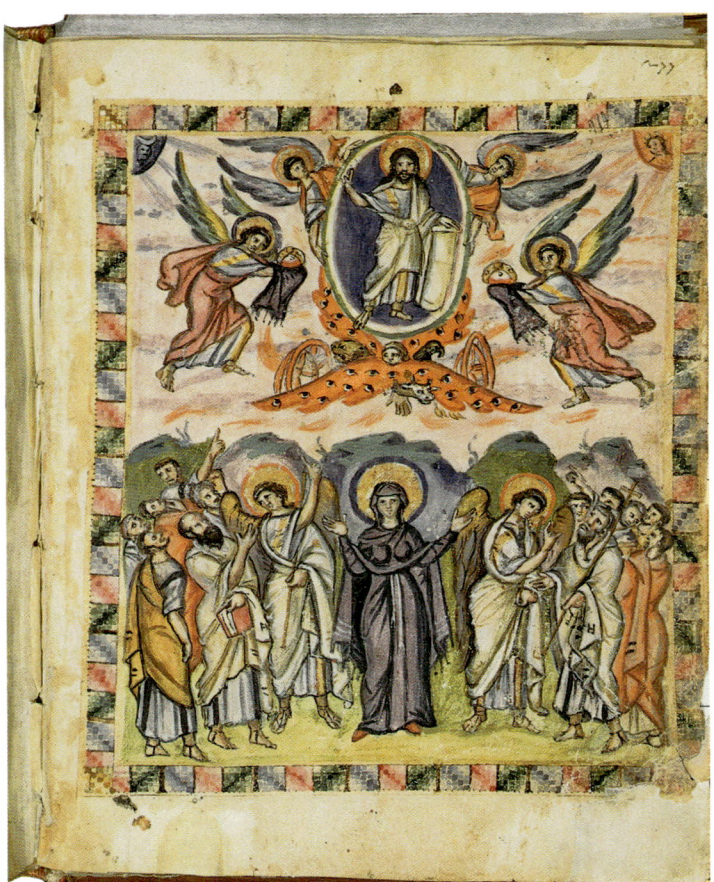

**9-17** *Ascension of Christ,* folio 13 verso of the *Rabbula Gospels,* from Zagba, Syria, 586. Tempera on parchment, 1′ 1″ × 10½″. Biblioteca Medicea-Laurenziana, Florence.

The Gospels do not mention the Virgin as a witness of Christ's Ascension. Her prominent position in the *Rabbula Gospels* is an early example of the important role Mary played in medieval art.

whiteness of Jesus' transfigured, spiritualized form, from which rays stream down on the disciples. The stately figures of the prophets and the static frontality of Jesus set off the frantic terror and astonishment of the gesticulating disciples. These distinctions dramatically contrast the eternal composure of heavenly beings with the distraught responses of the earthbound. At Mount Sinai, the mosaicist swept away all traces of landscape and architectural setting for a depthless field of gold, fixing the figures and their labels in isolation from one another. A rainbow band of colors graduating from yellow to blue bounds the golden field at its base. The relationship of the figures to this multicolor ground line is ambiguous. The artist placed some figures behind it, whereas others overlap it. The bodies cast no shadows, even though supernatural light streams over them. This is not the natural world Jesus and his disciples inhabited. It is a world of mystical vision. The mosaicist subtracted all substance that might suggest the passage of time or motion through physical space, enabling the devout to contemplate the eternal and motionless world of religious truth.

## Manuscript and Icon Painting

As in the Early Christian period, manuscript painting was an important art form during the Early Byzantine era. This period also marked the beginning of another Byzantine pictorial tradition with a long and distinguished history—icon painting.

**RABBULA GOSPELS** One of the essential Christian beliefs is that following his execution at the hands of the Romans, Christ rose from his tomb after three days and, on the 40th day, ascended from the Mount of Olives to Heaven. The *Crucifixion, Resurrection,* and *Ascension* are all subjects of full-page paintings (FIGS. **9-17** and **9-17A**) in a manuscript known as the *Rabbula Gospels.* Written in Syriac by the monk Rabbula at the monastery of Saint John the Evangelist at Zagba in Syria, it dates to 586. The page depicting the *Ascension of Christ* (FIG. 9-17) shows Christ, bearded and surrounded by a mandorla, as in the Mount Sinai *Transfiguration* (FIG. 9-16), but here angels bear the mandorla aloft. Below, Mary, other angels, and various apostles look on. The artist set the figures into a mosaic-like frame (compare FIGS. 9-13 and 9-14), and many art historians think the model for the manuscript page was a mural painting or mosaic in a Byzantine church somewhere in the Eastern Empire.

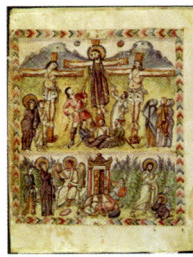

**9-17A** *Crucifixion* and *Resurrection, Rabbula Gospels,* 586.

The account of Christ ascending to Heaven is not part of the accompanying text of the *Rabbula Gospels* but comes from the book of Acts. In the latter, the Virgin is not present at the miraculous event. In the *Rabbula Gospels* representation, however, the Theotokos occupies a prominent position, central and directly beneath Christ. It is an early example of the important role the Mother of God played in medieval art, both in the East and in the West. Frontal, with a nimbus, and posed as an orant, Mary stands apart from the commotion all about her and looks out at the viewer. Other details also depart from the Gospel texts. Christ, for example, does not rise in a cloud. Rather, as in the vision of Ezekiel in the book of Revelation, he ascends in a mandorla above a fiery winged chariot. The chariot carries the symbols of the four evangelists—the man, lion, ox, and eagle (see "The Four Evangelists," Chapter 11, page 314). This page therefore does not illustrate the Gospels. Rather, its purpose is to present one of the central tenets of Christian faith. Similar compositions appear on pilgrims' flasks from Palestine that were souvenir items reproducing important monuments visited. They reinforce the theory that the Byzantine painter based the *Ascension of Christ* in the *Rabbula Gospels* on a lost painting or mosaic in a major church.

**ICONS** Gospel books such as the *Rabbula Gospels* played an important role in monastic religious life. So, too, did *icons,* which also figured prominently in private devotion (see "Icons and Iconoclasm," page 269). Unfortunately, few early icons survive. Two of the finest examples come from Saint Catherine's monastery at Mount Sinai. One represents the enthroned Theotokos (FIG. **9-18**), and the other (FIG. **9-18A**) Christ blessing the viewer of the icon. The medium used for both icons is encaustic on wood, continuing a tradition of panel painting in Egypt that, like so much else in the Byzantine world, dates to the Roman Empire (FIGS. 7-62, 7-62A, 7-62B, and 7-63).

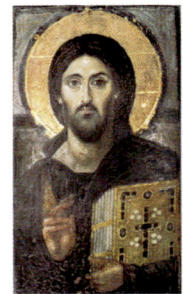

**9-18A** *Christ blessing,* Mount Sinai, sixth century.

The smaller of the two illustrated icons (FIG. 9-18) is more ambitious in the number of figures depicted. In a composition reminiscent of the portrait of Anicia Juliana (FIG. 9-3) in the *Vienna Dioskorides,* the Sinai icon painter represented the enthroned Theotokos and Child with Saints Theodore and George. The two guardian saints intercede with the Virgin on the viewer's behalf. Behind

# Icons and Iconoclasm

*I*cons ("images" in Greek) are small portable paintings depicting Christ, the Virgin, or saints (or a combination of all three, as in FIG. 9-18). Icons survive from as early as the fourth century. From the sixth century on, they became enormously popular in Byzantine worship, both public and private. Eastern Christians considered icons a personal, intimate, and indispensable medium for spiritual transaction with holy figures. Some icons (for example, FIG. 9-31) came to be regarded as wonder-working, and believers ascribed miracles and healing powers to them.

Icons, however, were by no means universally accepted. From the beginning, many Christians were deeply suspicious of the practice of imaging the divine, whether on portable panels, on the walls of churches, or especially as statues that reminded them of ancient idols. The opponents of Christian figural art had in mind the Old Testament prohibition of images the Lord dictated to Moses in the Second Commandment: "Thou shalt not make unto thee any graven image or any likeness of anything that is in heaven above, or that is in the earth beneath, or that is in the water under the earth. Thou shalt not bow down thyself to them, nor serve them" (Exod. 20:4, 5). For example, early in the fourth century, Constantia, sister of the emperor Constantine, requested an image of Christ from Eusebius of Caesarea (ca. 263–339), the first great historian of the Church. He rebuked her, referring to the Second Commandment:

> Can it be that you have forgotten that passage in which God lays down the law that no likeness should be made of what is in heaven or in the earth beneath? . . . Are not such things banished and excluded from churches all over the world, and is it not common knowledge that such practices are not permitted to us . . . lest we appear, like idol worshipers, to carry our God around in an image?*

Opposition to icons became especially strong in the eighth century, when the faithful often burned incense and knelt before the icons in prayer to seek protection or a cure for illness. Although their purpose was only to evoke the presence of the holy figures addressed in prayer, in the minds of many, icons became identified with the personages represented. Icon veneration became confused with idol worship, and this brought about an imperial ban not only on the making of icons but of all sacred images as well as edicts ordering the destruction of existing images (*iconoclasm*). The *iconoclasts* (breakers of images) and the *iconophiles* (lovers of images) became bitter and irreconcilable enemies. The anguish of the latter is evident in the following graphic description of the deeds of the iconoclasts, written in about 754:

> In every village and town one could witness the weeping and lamentation of the pious, whereas, on the part of the impious, [one saw] sacred things trodden upon, [liturgical] vessels turned to other use, churches scraped down and smeared with ashes because they contained holy images. And wherever there were venerable images of Christ or the Mother of God or the saints, these were consigned to the flames or were gouged out or smeared over.†

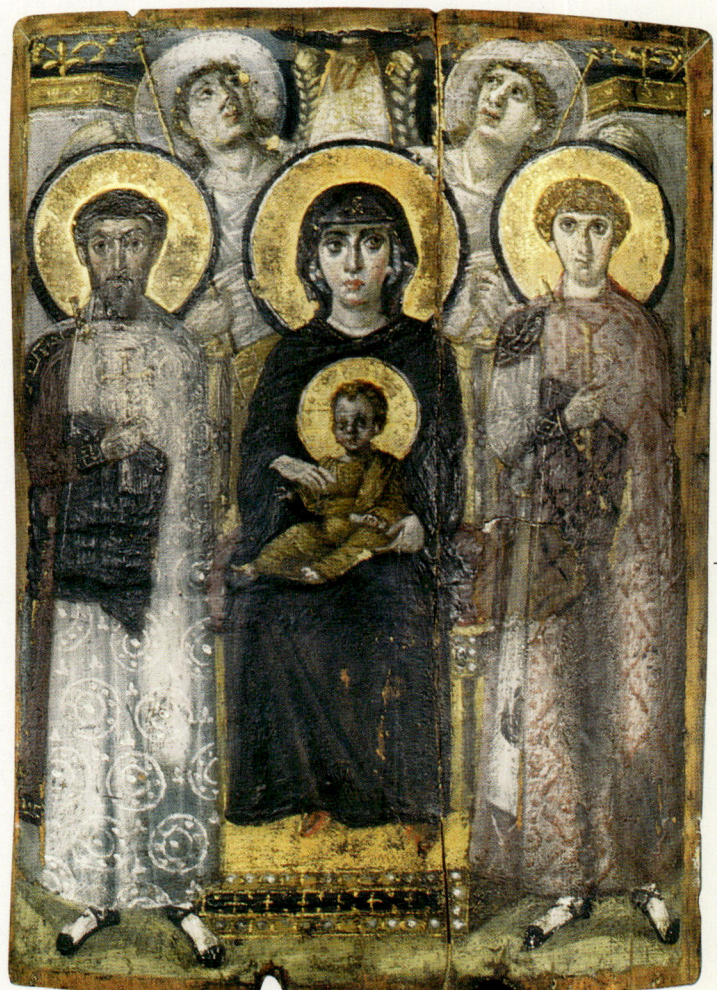

**9-18** Virgin (Theotokos) and Child between Saints Theodore and George, icon, sixth or early seventh century. Encaustic on wood, 2′ 3″ × 1′ 7¾″. Monastery of Saint Catherine, Mount Sinai, Egypt.

Byzantine icons are the heirs to the Roman tradition of portrait painting on small wood panels, but their Christian subjects and function as devotional objects broke sharply from classical models.

The consequences of iconoclasm for the early history of Byzantine art are difficult to overstate. For more than a century, not only did the portrayal of Christ, the Virgin, and the saints cease, but the iconoclasts also destroyed countless works from the first several centuries of Christendom. For this reason, writing a history of Early Byzantine art presents a great challenge to art historians.

*Cyril Mango, trans., *The Art of the Byzantine Empire, 312–1453: Sources and Documents* (reprint of 1972 ed., Toronto: University of Toronto Press, 1986), 17–18.
†Mango, 152.

them, two angels gaze upward to a shaft of light where the hand of God appears. The foreground figures are strictly frontal and have a solemn demeanor. Background details are few and suppressed. The shallow forward plane of the picture dominates. Traces of the Greco-Roman illusionism noted in the Anicia Juliana portrait remain in the Virgin's rather personalized features, in her sideways glance, and in the posing of the angels' heads. But the painter rendered the saints' bodies in the new Byzantine manner.

**ICONOCLASM** The preservation of the Early Byzantine icons at the Mount Sinai monastery is fortuitous but ironic, for opposition to icon worship was especially prominent in the Monophysite provinces of Syria and Egypt. There, in the seventh century, a series of calamities erupted, indirectly causing an imperial ban on images. The Sasanians (see Chapter 2), chronically at war with Rome, swept into the Eastern provinces, and between 611 and 617 they captured the great cities of Antioch, Jerusalem, and Alexandria. The Byzantine emperor Heraclius (r. 610–641) had hardly defeated them in 627 when a new and overwhelming power appeared unexpectedly on the stage of history. The Arabs, under the banner of the new Islamic religion, conquered not only Byzantium's Eastern provinces but also Persia itself, replacing the Sasanians in the age-old balance of power with the Christian West (see Chapter 10). In a few years the Arabs were launching attacks on Constantinople, and Byzantium was fighting for its life.

These were catastrophic years for the Eastern Roman Empire. They terminated once and for all the long story of imperial Rome, closed the Early Byzantine period, and inaugurated the medieval era of Byzantine history. The Byzantine Empire lost almost two-thirds of its territory—many cities and much of its population, wealth, and material resources. The shock of these events may have persuaded the emperor Leo III (r. 717–741) that God was punishing the Christian Roman Empire for its idolatrous worship of icons by setting upon it the merciless armies of the infidel—an enemy that, moreover, shunned the representation not only of God but of all living things in holy places (see Chapter 10). Some scholars believe another motivation for Leo's 726 ban on picturing the divine was to assert the authority of the state over the Church. In any case, for more than a century, Byzantine artists produced little new religious figurative art. In place of images of holy figures, the iconoclasts used symbolic forms already familiar in Early Christian art, for example, the cross (FIG. 9-12).

# MIDDLE BYZANTINE ART

In the late eighth and ninth centuries, a powerful reaction against iconoclasm set in. The case in favor of icons had been made forcefully earlier in the eighth century by Saint John of Damascus (ca. 675–ca. 749), who argued that the invisible God the Father had made an image of himself in the son Jesus and in humankind in general and that although icons were likenesses of holy figures, they were not identical to their prototypes. To oppose making images of holy figures was contrary to the actions of God. Two female regents in particular led the movement to restore image-making in the Byzantine Empire: the empresses Irene in 780 and Theodora in 843, after the death of her husband Theophilos (r. 829–842). Unlike Irene's short-lived repeal of the prohibition against icons, Theodora's opposition proved to be definitive and permanent and led to the condemnation of iconoclasm as a heresy.

Shortly thereafter, a new line of emperors, the Macedonian dynasty, resuscitated the Early Byzantine tradition of lavish imperial patronage of religious art and architecture and the making of images of Christ, the Virgin, and saints. Basil I (r. 867–886), head

of the new dynasty, regarded himself as the restorer of the Roman Empire. He denounced as usurpers the Carolingian monarchs of the West (see Chapter 11) who, since 800, had claimed the title "Roman Empire" for their realm. Basil bluntly reminded their emissary that the only true emperor of Rome reigned in Constantinople. They were not Roman emperors but merely "kings of the Germans." Iconoclasm had forced Byzantine artists westward, where doubtless they found employment at the courts of these Germanic kings (see "Theophanu, a Byzantine Princess in Ottonian Germany," Chapter 11, page 328). These Byzantine "refugees" strongly influenced the character of Western European art.

## Architecture and Mosaics

The triumph of the iconophiles over the iconoclasts meant Byzantine mural painters, mosaicists, book illuminators, ivory carvers, and metalworkers once again received plentiful commissions. Basil I and his successors also undertook the laborious and costly task of refurbishing the churches the iconoclasts defaced and neglected.

**THEOTOKOS, HAGIA SOPHIA** In 867, the Macedonian dynasty dedicated a new mosaic (FIG. 9-19) depicting the enthroned Virgin with the Christ Child in her lap in the apse of the Justinianic church of Hagia Sophia. In the vast space beneath the dome of the great church, the figures look undersized, but the seated Theotokos is more than 16 feet tall. An accompanying inscription, now fragmentary, announced "pious emperors" (the Macedonians) had commissioned the mosaic to replace one the "impostors" (the

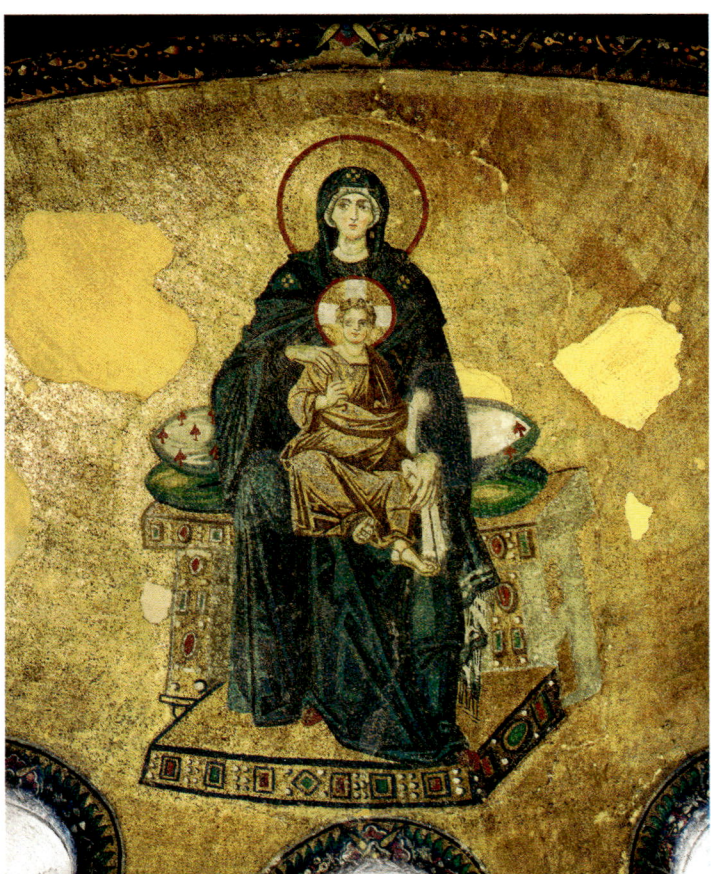

**9-19** Virgin (Theotokos) and Child enthroned, apse mosaic, Hagia Sophia, Constantinople (Istanbul), Turkey, dedicated 867. ◼◀

After the repeal of iconoclasm, Basil I dedicated a huge new mosaic in the apse of Hagia Sophia depicting the Virgin and Child enthroned. An inscription says it replaced one the iconoclasts destroyed.

iconoclasts) had destroyed. The declaration may be purely rhetorical, however. There was probably no comparable image of the Virgin and Child in the sixth-century apse.

The ninth-century mosaic echoes the style and composition of the Early Byzantine Mount Sinai icon (FIG. 9-18) of the Theotokos, Christ, and saints. Here, however, the angular placement of the throne and footstool alleviate the strict frontality of Mother and (much older) Child. The mosaicist rendered the furnishings in a perspective that, although imperfect, recalls once more the Greco-Roman roots of Byzantine art. The treatment of the folds of Christ's robes is, by contrast, even more schematic and flatter than in earlier mosaics. These seemingly contradictory stylistic features are not uncommon in Byzantine paintings and mosaics.

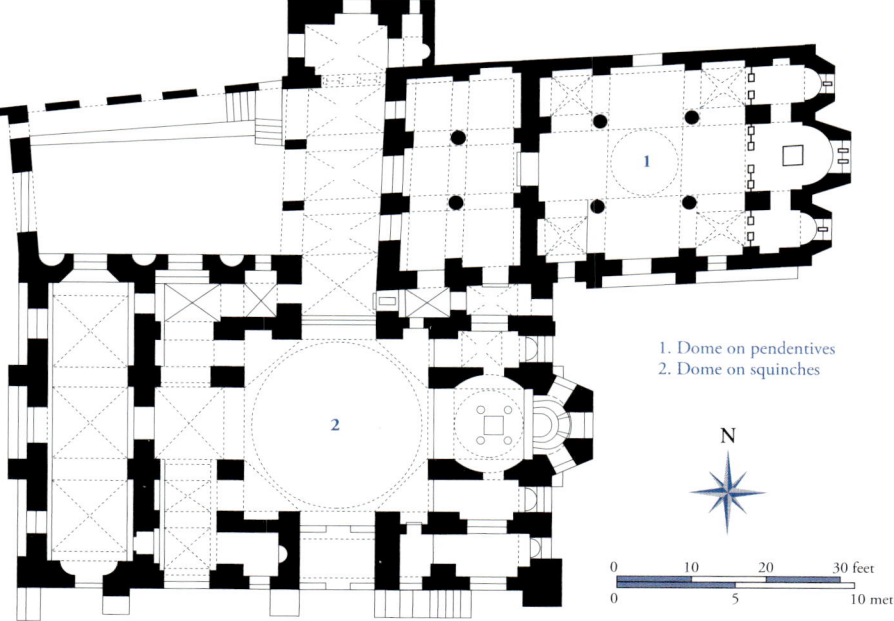

**9-20** Katholikon (looking northeast), Hosios Loukas, Greece, first quarter of 11th century.

Middle Byzantine churches typically are small and high-shouldered, with a central dome on a drum and exterior wall surfaces with decorative patterns, probably reflecting Islamic architecture.

1. Dome on pendentives
2. Dome on squinches

N

0    10    20    30 feet
0         5         10 meters

Most significant about the images in the Hagia Sophia apse is their very existence, marking the end of iconoclasm in the Byzantine Empire.

**HOSIOS LOUKAS** Although the new emperors did not wait long to redecorate the churches of their predecessors, they undertook little new church construction in the decades after the renunciation of iconoclasm in 843. But in the 10th century and through the 12th, a number of monastic churches arose that are the flowers of Middle Byzantine architecture. They feature a brilliant series of variations on the domed central plan. From the exterior, the typical later Byzantine church building is a domed cube, with the dome rising above the square on a kind of cylinder or *drum*. The churches are small, vertical, high-shouldered, and, unlike earlier Byzantine buildings, have exterior wall surfaces decorated with vivid patterns, probably reflecting Islamic architecture.

The Katholikon (FIGS. **9-20** and **9-21,** *bottom*) at Hosios Loukas (Saint Luke) in Greece, near ancient Delphi, dates to the early 11th century. One of two churches at the site—the other is the Church of the Theotokos (FIG. 9-21, *top*) built during the second half of the 10th century—the Katholikon exemplifies church design during this second golden age of Byzantine art and architecture. Light stones framed by dark red bricks—the so-called *cloisonné* technique, a term borrowed from enamel work (FIG. 11-3)—make up the walls. The interplay of arcuated windows, projecting apses, and varying roof lines further enhances this surface dynamism. The plans of both Hosios Loukas churches show the form of a domed cross in a square with four equal-length, vaulted cross arms (the *Greek cross*). The dome of the smaller Church of the Theotokos rests on pendentives. In the larger and later Katholikon, the architect placed the dome over an octagon inscribed within a square. The octagon was formed by squinches (FIG. 9-9, *right*), which play the same role as pendentives in making the transition from a square base to a round dome but create a different visual effect on the interior. This arrangement departs from the older designs, such as Santa Costanza's circular plan (FIG. 8-12), San Vitale's octagonal plan (FIG. 9-11), and Hagia Sophia's dome on pendentives rising from a square (FIGS. 9-6 to 9-8). The Katholikon's complex core lies within two rectangles, the outermost one forming the exterior walls. Thus, in plan from the center out, a circle-octagon-square-oblong series exhibits an intricate interrelationship that is at once complex and unified.

**9-21** Plan of the Church of the Theotokos (*top*) and the Katholikon (*bottom*), Hosios Loukas, Greece, second half of 10th and first quarter of 11th century respectively.

The plans of the pair of monastic churches at Hosios Loukas in Greece take the form of a domed square at the center of a cross with four equal-length vaulted arms (the Greek cross).

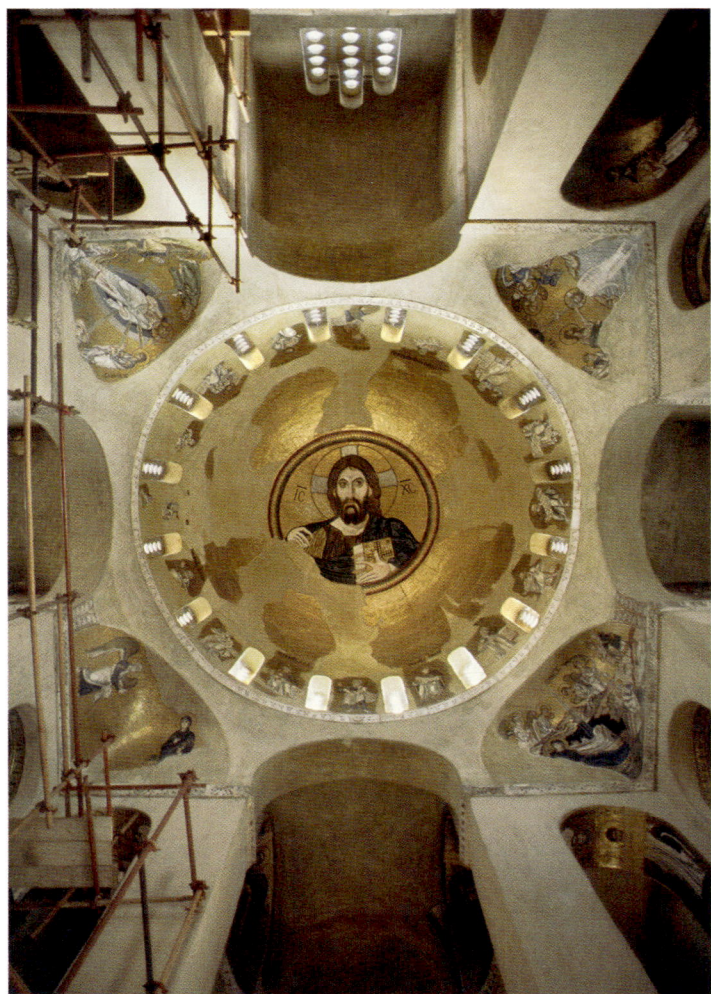

**9-22** Interior of the Church of the Dormition (looking into the dome), Daphni, Greece, ca. 1090–1100.

The Daphni dome rests on an octagon formed by squinches, which play the same role as pendentives in making the transition from a square base to a round dome but create a different visual effect.

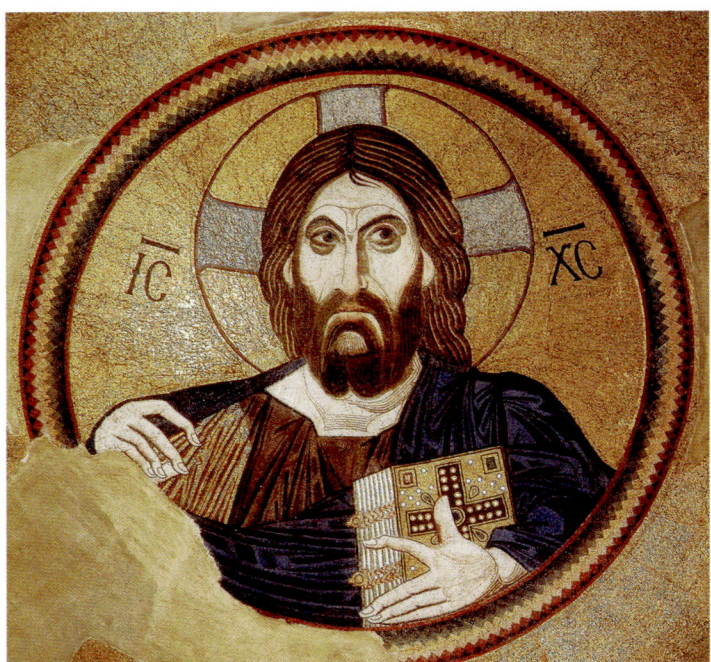

**9-23** *Christ as Pantokrator,* dome mosaic in the Church of the Dormition, Daphni, Greece, ca. 1090–1100.

The mosaic of Christ as last judge in the Daphni dome is like a gigantic icon hovering dramatically in space, connecting the awestruck worshiper below with Heaven through Christ.

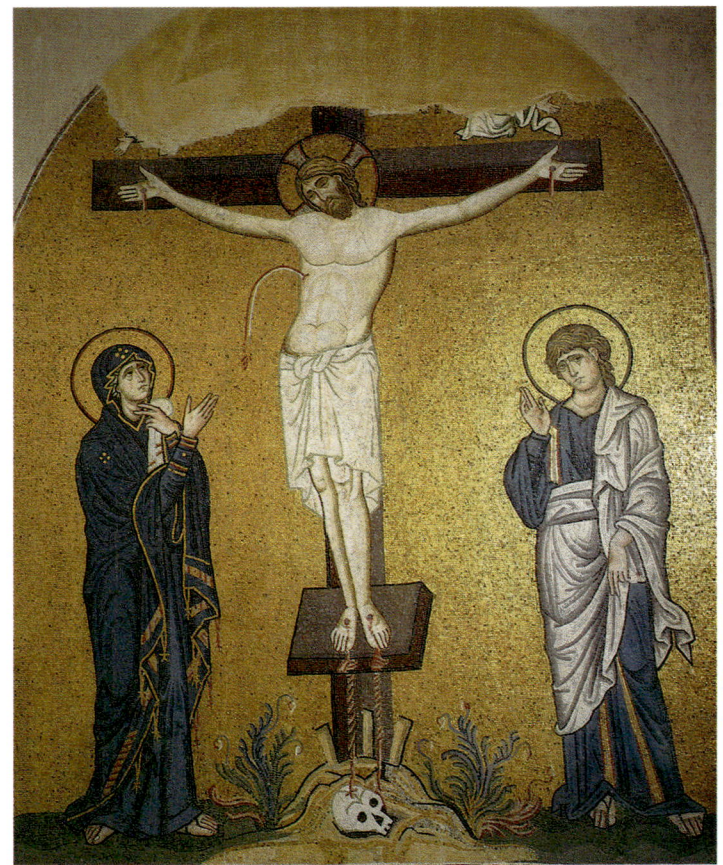

**9-24** *Crucifixion,* mosaic in the north arm of the east wall of the Church of the Dormition, Daphni, Greece, ca. 1090–1100.

The Daphni *Crucifixion* is a subtle blend of Hellenistic style and the more abstract Byzantine manner. The Virgin Mary and Saint John point to Christ on the cross as if to a devotional object.

**DAPHNI** Similar in general design to the Katholikon, but constructed at the end of the 11th century, is the monastic Church of the Dormition (from the Latin for "sleep," referring to the ascension of the Virgin Mary to Heaven at the moment of her death) at Daphni, near Athens. Like the Katholikon, the church's interior (FIG. **9-22**) creates a mystery out of space, surface, light, and dark. High and narrow, the design forces the viewer's gaze to rise and revolve. The eye is drawn upward toward the dome, but much can distract it in the interplay of flat walls and concave recesses; wide and narrow openings; groin and barrel vaults; and illuminated and dark spaces. Middle Byzantine architects aimed for the creation of complex interior spaces with dramatically shifting perspectives.

At Daphni, the main elements of the late-11th-century pictorial program are intact, although the mosaics underwent restoration in the 19th century. Gazing down from on high in the dome is the fearsome image (FIG. **9-23**) of Christ as *Pantokrator* (literally "ruler of all" in Greek but usually applied to Christ in his role as last judge of humankind). The dome mosaic is the climax of an elaborate hierarchical mosaic program including several New Testament episodes below. The Daphni Pantokrator is like a gigantic icon hovering dramatically in space. The image serves to connect the awestruck worshiper in the church below with Heaven through Christ.

## Born to the Purple: Empress Zoe

Although rarely rulers in their own right, Byzantine empresses often wielded great power and influence. Theodora (ca. 500–548) was Justinian's most trusted adviser. In 780, Irene (ca. 755–802) became regent for her 10-year-old son, Constantine VI (r. 780–797), and briefly repealed the imperial ban against icons. In 843, another empress, Theodora (ca. 815–867), convened a religious council, which permanently put an end to iconoclasm. Theodora achieved sainthood as a result.

The most influential Byzantine empress of the 11th century was Zoe Porphyrogenita ("born to the purple"), the elder daughter of Constantine VIII (r. 1025–1028). Born around 978, Zoe was not permitted to marry until just before her father's death, and she remained childless throughout her life. In 1028, Zoe married Romanos III Argyros (r. 1028–1034), Constantine's chosen successor, but she soon fell in love with another member of the court, with whom she may have plotted the drowning of Romanos in his bath. In any case, Zoe married Michael IV (r. 1034–1041) the same day, even though by law widows were supposed to wait a full year before remarrying. Toward the end of Michael's reign, the couple adopted a son, Michael V (r. 1042), who succeeded his father and banished his adoptive mother to a convent. With the support of her subjects, Zoe returned to Constantinople, deposed the emperor, and ruled briefly in 1042 in her own name before marrying Constantine IX Monomachos (r. 1042–1054), who outlived her by four years. Thus, four successive emperors of Byzantium owed their coronations to Zoe.

A mosaic portrait of Zoe and her last husband flanking the enthroned Christ (FIG. 9-25) adorns the east wall of the south gallery of Hagia Sophia. The emperor holds a purse, signifying the generous donation Constantine made to the church. Zoe holds a scroll, also a reference to her gifts to the church. Inscriptions next to the portraits describe Constantine as "pious emperor and king of the Romans" and Zoe as "pious empress." Many scholars believe that the mosaic

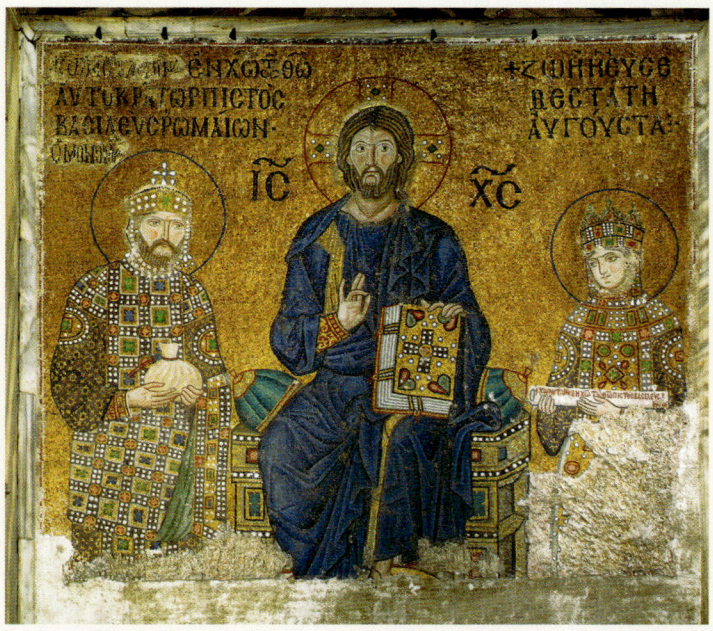

**9-25** Christ between Constantine IX Monomachus and the empress Zoe, mosaic on the east wall of the south gallery, Hagia Sophia, Constantinople (Istanbul), Turkey, ca. 1028–1035.

Zoe, who was the wife of three emperors, here appears with the enthroned Christ and her third husband. Constantine IX's portrait may have replaced successive portraits of Zoe's previous two husbands.

dates to the reign of Romanos and bore his portrait, and that Zoe twice asked the imperial artists to update the mosaic with new portraits and labels upon each of her subsequent marriages.

---

The Pantokrator theme was a common one in churches throughout the Byzantine Empire. A mosaic of the Pantokrator also once adorned the dome of the Hosios Loukas Katholikon.

Below the Daphni dome, on the wall beneath the barrel vault of one arm of the Greek cross, is the *Crucifixion* mosaic (FIG. **9-24**) in a pictorial style characteristic of the posticonoclastic Middle Byzantine period. Like the Pantokrator mosaic in the dome, the Daphni *Crucifixion* is a subtle blend of the painterly naturalistic style of Late Antiquity and the later, more abstract and formalistic Byzantine style. The Byzantine artist fully assimilated classicism's simplicity, dignity, and grace into a perfect synthesis with Byzantine piety and pathos. The figures have regained the classical organic structure to a surprising degree, particularly compared with figures from the Justinianic period (compare FIGS. 9-13 and 9-14). The style is a masterful adaptation of classical statuesque qualities to the linear Byzantine manner.

In quiet sorrow and resignation, the Virgin and Saint John flank the crucified Christ. A skull at the foot of the cross indicates Golgotha, the "place of skulls." The artist needed nothing else to set the scene. Symmetry and closed space combine to produce an effect of the motionless and unchanging aspect of the deepest mystery of

the Christian religion, as recalled in the ceremony of the Eucharist. The picture is not a narrative of the historical event of Jesus' execution, the approach taken by the carver of the Early Christian ivory panel (FIG. 8-24) examined in the previous chapter. Nor is Christ a triumphant, beardless youth, oblivious to pain and defiant of the laws of gravity. Rather, he has a tilted head and sagging body, and although the Savior is not overtly in pain, blood and water spurt from the wound Longinus inflicted on him, as recounted in Saint John's Gospel. The Virgin and John point to the figure on the cross as if to a devotional object. They act as intercessors between the viewer below and Christ, who, in the dome, appears as the last judge of all humans. The mosaic decoration of the church is the perfect complement to Christian liturgy.

**EMPRESS ZOE** As in the Early Byzantine period, Middle Byzantine mosaicists also produced portraits of their imperial patrons for church interiors. Several such portraits grace the interior walls of Hagia Sophia (FIG. 9-8) in Constantinople. Perhaps the finest of these is on the east wall of the south gallery. It depicts Constantine IX and Zoe (see "Born to the Purple: Empress Zoe," above) flanking the enthroned Christ (FIG. **9-25**). Like the much earlier imperial portraits (FIGS. 9-13 and 9-14) in San Vitale at Ravenna, the emperor and empress are haloed, but no longer is there a separation between the human and the divine, as in the sixth-century apse. Other Middle Byzantine mosaics depict the imperial couple flanking the Virgin.

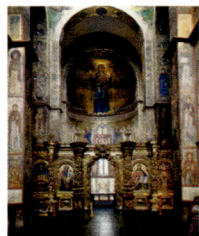

**SAINT MARK'S, VENICE** The Middle Byzantine revival of church building and of figural mosaics extended beyond the Greek-speaking East in the 10th to 12th centuries. The marriage of Anna, the sister of Basil II (r. 976–1025), to the Russian prince Vladimir (r. 980–1015) in 989, marked the introduction of Orthodox Christianity to Russia. Construction of the vast five-apse, 13-dome Cathedral of Saint Sophia (FIG. 9-25A) at Kiev followed within a half century. A resurgence of religious architecture and of the mosaicist's art also occurred in areas of the former Western Roman Empire where the ties with Constantinople were the strongest. In the Early Byzantine period, Venice, about 80 miles north of Ravenna on the eastern coast of Italy, was a dependency of that Byzantine stronghold. In 751, Ravenna fell to the Lombards, who wrested control of most of northern Italy from Constantinople. Venice, however, became an independent power. Its *doges* (dukes) enriched themselves and the city through seaborne commerce, serving as the crucial link between Byzantium and the West.

Venice had obtained the relics of Saint Mark from Alexandria in Egypt in 829, and the doges constructed the first Venetian shrine dedicated to the evangelist—a palace chapel and *martyrium* (martyr's shrine)—shortly thereafter. Fire destroyed the ninth-century chapel in 976. The Venetians then built a second shrine on the site, but a grandiose new Saint Mark's (FIG. 9-26) begun in 1063 by Doge Domenico Contarini (r. 1043–1071) replaced it. The model for Contarini's church was the Church of the Holy Apostles at Constantinople, built in Justinian's time. That shrine no longer exists, but its key elements were a cruciform plan with a central dome over the crossing and four other domes over the four equal arms of the Greek cross, as at Saint Mark's. Because of its importance to the city, the doges furnished the church's interior with costly altarpieces, such as the *Pala d'Oro* (FIG. 9-26A), and other liturgical objects and deposited there many of the treasures, including icons (FIG. 9-26B), they brought back as booty from the sack of Constantinople in 1204.

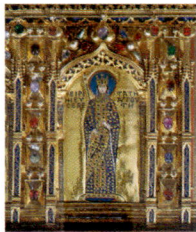

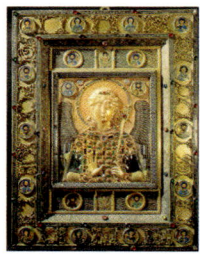

The interior (FIG. 9-26) of Saint Mark's is, like its plan, Byzantine in effect. Light enters through a row of windows at the bases of all five domes, vividly illuminating a rich cycle of mosaics. Both Byzantine and local artists worked on Saint Mark's mosaics over the course of several centuries. Most of the mosaics date to the 12th and 13th centuries. Cleaning and restoration on a grand scale have returned the mosaics to their original splendor, enabling visitors to experience the full radiance of 40,000 square feet of mosaics covering all the walls, arches, vaults, and domes like a gold-brocaded figured fabric.

In the vast central dome, 80 feet above the floor and 42 feet in diameter, Christ ascends to Heaven in the presence of the Virgin Mary and the 12 apostles. In the great arch framing the church crossing are mosaics of the *Crucifixion* and *Resurrection* and Christ's liberation from death (*Anastasis*) of Adam and Eve, Saint John the Baptist, and other biblical figures. The mosaics have explanatory labels in both Latin and Greek, reflecting Venice's position as the key link between Eastern and Western Christendom in the later Middle Ages. The insubstantial figures on the walls, vaults, and domes appear weightless, and they project no farther from their flat field than do the elegant Latin and Greek letters above them. Nothing here reflects on the world of matter, of solids, of light and shade, of perspective space. Rather, the mosaics reveal the mysteries of the Christian faith.

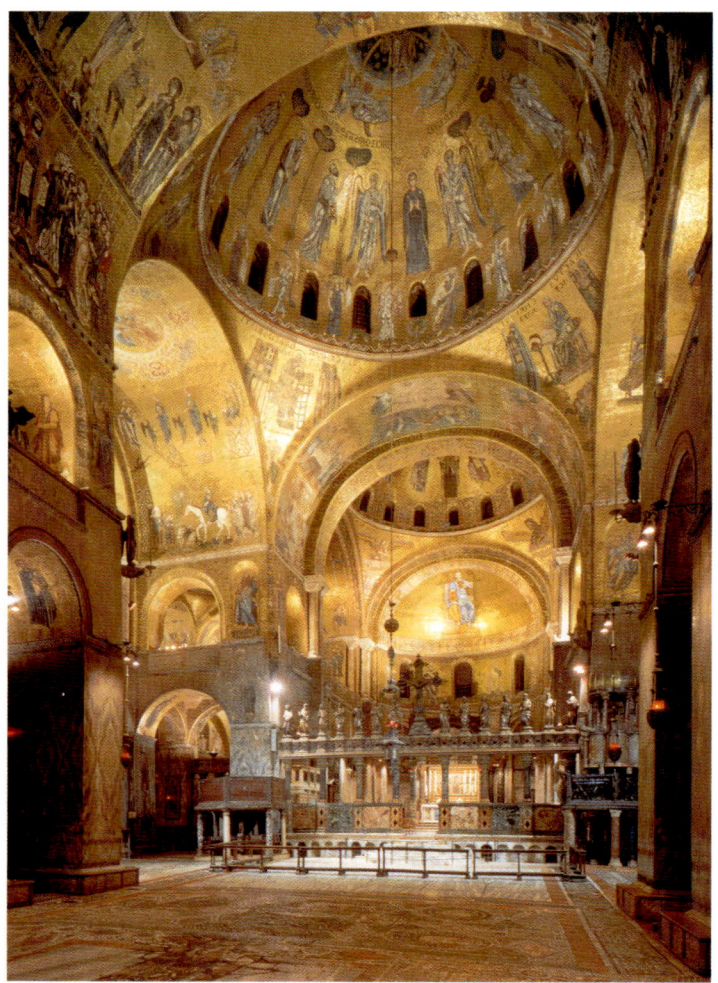

**9-26** Interior of Saint Mark's (looking east), Venice, Italy, begun 1063.

Modeled on a church in Constantinople, Saint Mark's has a central dome over the crossing, four other domes over the arms of the Greek cross, and 40,000 square feet of Byzantine-style mosaics.

**NORMAN SICILY** Matching Venetian success in the western Mediterranean were the Normans, the northern French descendants of the Vikings who, having driven the Arabs from Sicily, set up a powerful kingdom there. Though they were the enemies of Byzantium, the Normans, like the Venetians, assimilated Byzantine culture and even employed Byzantine artisans. They also incorporated in their monuments elements of the Islamic art of the Arabs they had defeated. The Normans' Palatine (palace) Chapel (FIG. 9-27A) at Palermo with its prismatic (*muqarnas*) ceiling, a characteristic Muslim form (see

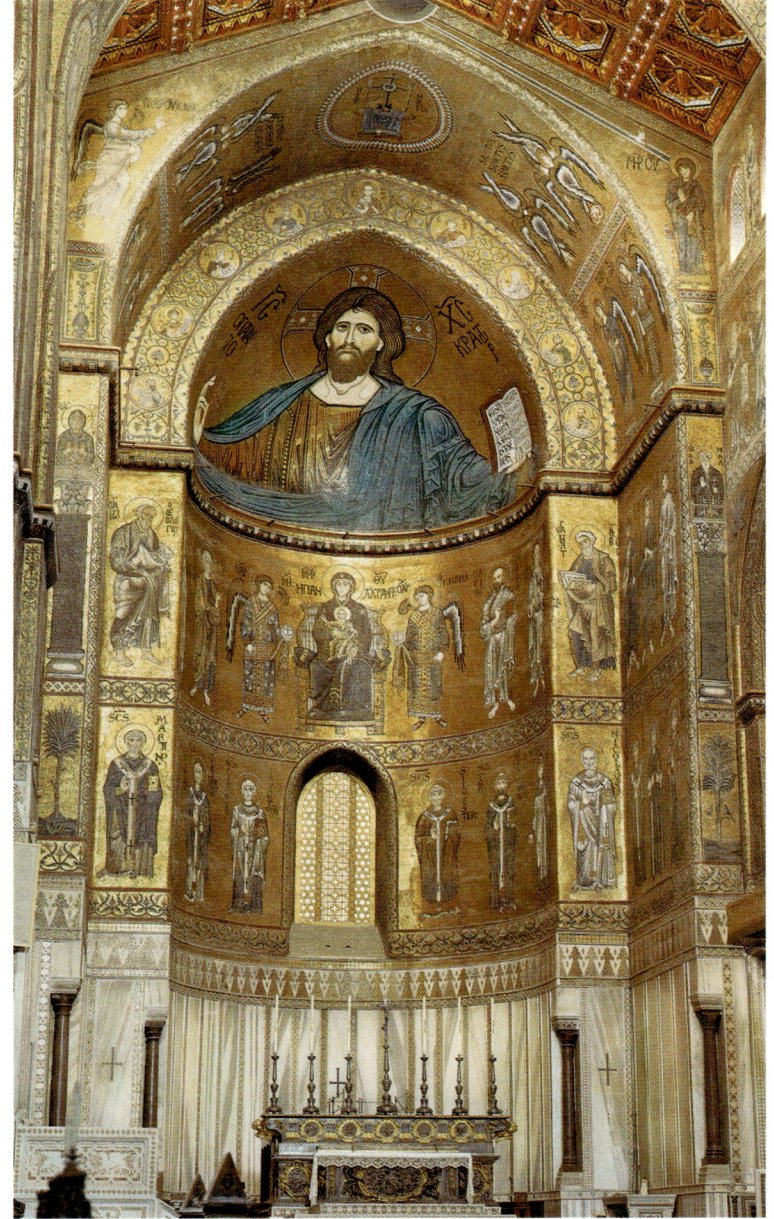

In centrally planned Byzantine churches, the image of the Pantokrator usually appears in the main dome, but Monreale's cathedral is a longitudinal basilica. The semidome of the apse is its only vault.

Chapter 10), is one example of the rich interplay of Western Christian, Byzantine, and Islamic cultures in Norman Sicily.

The mosaics of the great basilican church of Monreale (FIG. 9-27), not far from Palermo, are striking evidence of Byzantine influence. They rival those of Saint Mark's in both quality and extent. One scholar has estimated the Monreale mosaics required more than 100 million glass and stone tesserae. The Norman king William II (r. 1087–1100) paid for the mosaics, and the artists portrayed him twice in the church, continuing the theme of royal presence and patronage of the much earlier Ravenna portraits of Justinian and Theodora (FIGS. 9-13 and 9-14) at San Vitale and the Middle Byzantine portraits of Constantine IX and Zoe (FIG. 9-25) in Hagia Sophia in Constantinople. In one panel, William stands next to the enthroned Christ, who places his hand on William's crown. In the second, the king kneels before the Virgin and presents her with a model of the Monreale church.

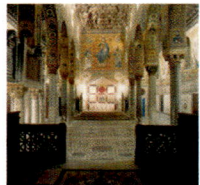

9-27A Cappella Palatina, Palermo, begun 1142.

The apse mosaics (FIG. 9-27) are especially impressive. The image of Christ as Pantokrator is in the vault. In Byzantium, the Pantokrator's image usually appears in the main dome (FIGS. 9-22 and 9-23). But the Monreale church is a basilica, longitudinally planned in the Western tradition. The semidome of the apse, the only vault in the building and its architectural focus, was the logical choice for the most important element of the pictorial program. Below the Pantokrator in rank and dignity is the enthroned Theotokos, flanked by archangels and the 12 apostles, symmetrically arranged in balanced groups. Lower on the wall (and less elevated in the church hierarchy) are popes, bishops, and other saints. The artists observed the stern formalities of Byzantine style here, far from Constantinople. The Monreale mosaics, like those at Saint Mark's (FIG. 9-26) in Venice and in the Palatine Chapel (FIG. 9-27A) in Palermo, testify to the stature of Byzantium and of Byzantine art in medieval Italy.

## Ivory Carving and Painting

Middle Byzantine artists also produced costly carved ivories in large numbers. The three-part *triptych* replaced the earlier diptych as the standard format for ivory panels.

*HARBAVILLE TRIPTYCH* One example of this type is the *Harbaville Triptych* (FIG. 9-28), a portable shrine with hinged wings used for private devotion. Ivory triptychs were very popular—among those who could afford such luxurious items—and they often replaced icons for use in personal prayer. Carved on

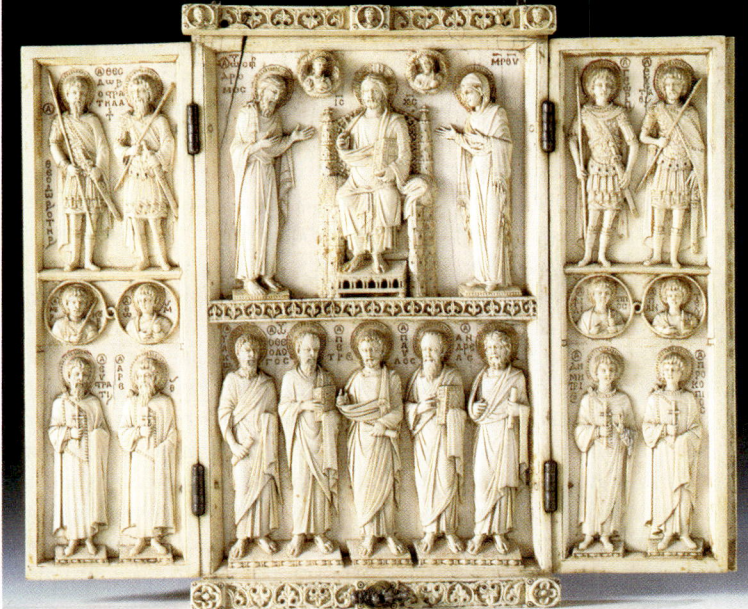

1 in.

9-28 Christ enthroned with saints (*Harbaville Triptych*), ca. 950. Ivory, central panel $9\frac{1}{2}'' \times 5\frac{1}{2}''$. Musée du Louvre, Paris.

In this small three-part shrine with hinged wings used for private devotion, the ivory carver depicted the figures with looser classical stances, in contrast to the frontal poses of most Byzantine figures.

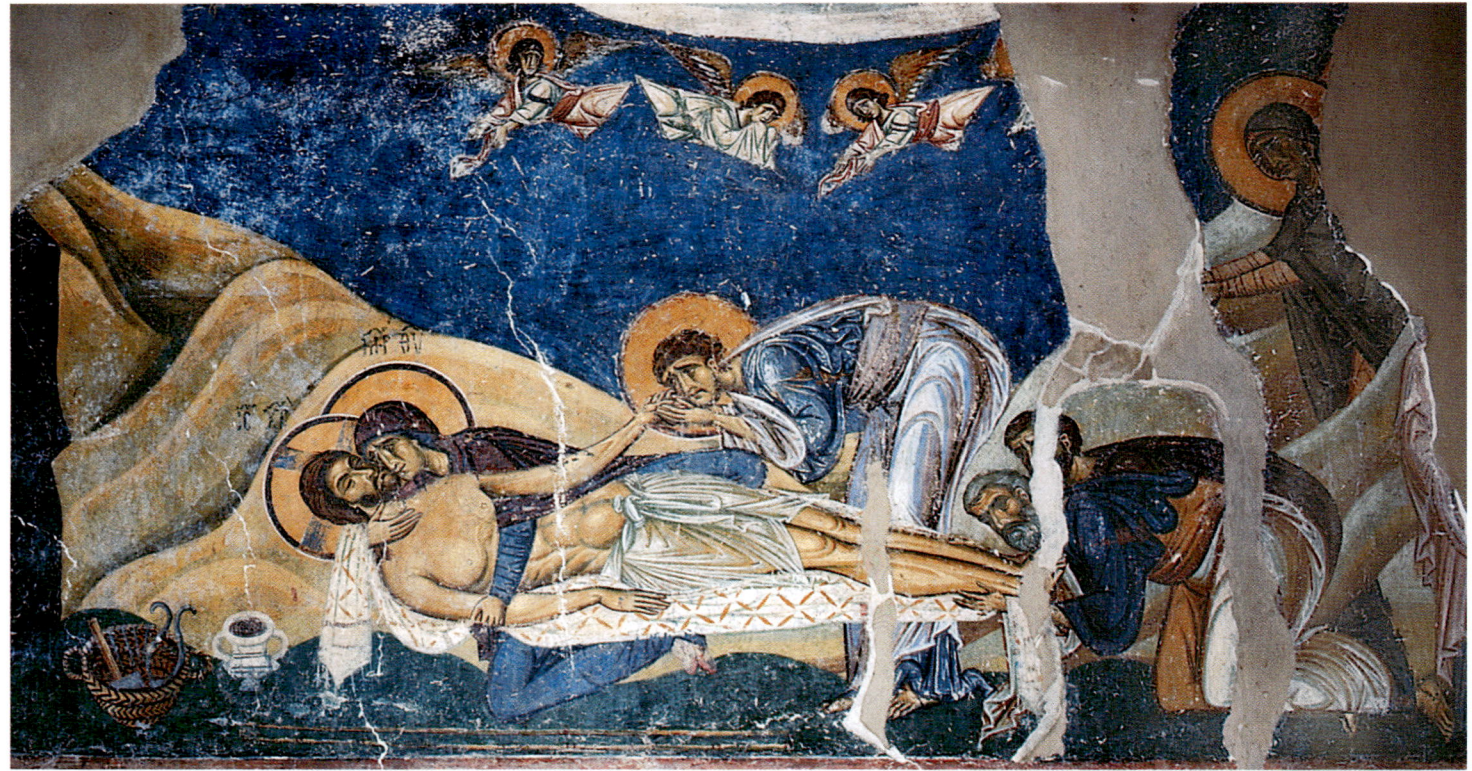

**9-29** *Lamentation,* wall painting, Saint Pantaleimon, Nerezi, Macedonia, 1164.

Working in the Balkans in an alternate Byzantine mode, this painter staged the emotional scene of the *Lamentation* in a hilly landscape below a blue sky and peopled it with fully modeled figures.

the wings of the *Harbaville Triptych,* both inside and out, are four pairs of full-length figures and two pairs of medallions depicting saints. A cross dominates the central panel on the back of the triptych (not illustrated). On the inside is a scene of *Deësis* (supplication). Saint John the Baptist and the Theotokos appear as intercessors, praying on behalf of the viewer to the enthroned Savior. Below them are five apostles.

The formality and solemnity usually associated with Byzantine art, visible in the mosaics of Ravenna and Monreale, yielded here to a softer, more fluid technique. The figures may lack true classical contrapposto, but the looser stances (most stand on bases, like freestanding statues) and three-quarter views of many of the heads relieve the hard austerity of the customary frontal pose. This more natural, classical spirit was a second, equally important stylistic current of the Middle Byzantine period. It also surfaced in mural painting and book illumination.

**NEREZI** When the emperors lifted the ban against religious images and again encouraged religious painting at Constantinople, the impact was felt far and wide. The style varied from region to region, but a renewed enthusiasm for picturing the key New Testament figures and events was universal. In 1164, at Nerezi in Macedonia, Byzantine painters embellished the church of Saint Pantaleimon with murals of great emotional power. One of these, *Lamentation* (FIG. **9-29**), is an image of passionate grief over the dead Christ. The artist captured Christ's followers in attitudes, expressions, and gestures of quite human bereavement. Joseph of Arimathea and the disciple Nicodemus kneel at his feet. Mary presses her cheek against her dead son's face. Saint John clings to Christ's left hand. In the Gospels, neither Mary nor John was present at the entombment of Christ. Their inclusion here, as elsewhere in Middle Byzantine art, intensified for the viewer the emotional impact of Christ's death. These

representations parallel the development of liturgical hymns recounting the Virgin lamenting her son's death on the cross.

At Nerezi, the painter set the scene in a hilly landscape below a blue sky—a striking contrast to the abstract golden world of the mosaics favored for church walls elsewhere in the Byzantine Empire. This Balkan artist strove to make utterly convincing an emotionally charged realization of the theme by staging the *Lamentation* in a more natural setting and peopling it with fully modeled actors. This alternate representational mode is no less Byzantine than the frontal, flatter figures at Constantinople and Ravenna. In time, this more naturalistic style would also be emulated in Italy (FIG. 14-8).

***PARIS PSALTER*** Another example of this classical-revival style is a page from a book of the Psalms of David. The so-called *Paris Psalter* (FIG. **9-30**) reasserts the artistic values of the Greco-Roman past with astonishing authority. Art historians believe the manuscript dates from the mid-10th century—the so-called Macedonian Renaissance, a time of enthusiastic and careful study of the language and literature of ancient Greece, and of humanistic reverence for the classical past. It is not surprising that artists would once again draw inspiration from the Hellenistic naturalism of the pre-Christian Mediterranean world.

David, the psalmist, surrounded by sheep, goats, and his faithful dog, plays his harp in a rocky landscape with a town in the background. Similar settings appeared frequently in Pompeian murals. Befitting an ancient depiction of Orpheus, the Greek hero who could charm even inanimate objects with his music, allegorical figures accompany the Old Testament harpist. Melody looks over his shoulder, and Echo peers from behind a column. A reclining male figure points to a Greek inscription identifying him as representing the mountain of Bethlehem. These allegorical figures do not appear in the Bible. They are the stock population of Greco-Roman painting.

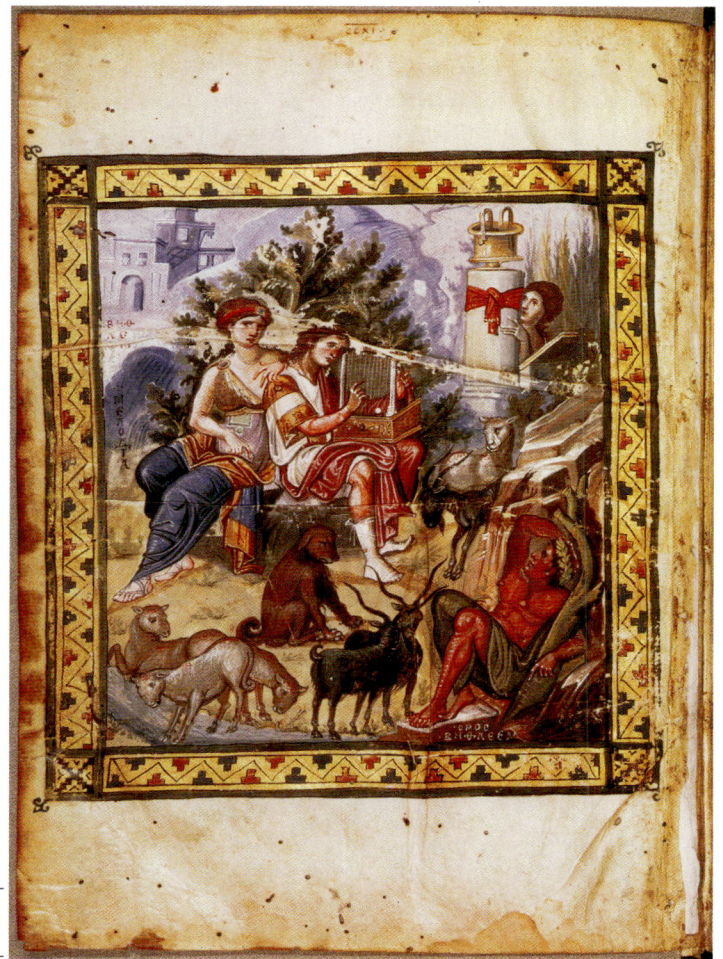

1 in.

**9-30** *David Composing the Psalms,* folio 1 verso of the *Paris Psalter,* ca. 950–970. Tempera on vellum, 1′ 2⅛″ × 10¼″. Bibliothèque Nationale, Paris.

During the Macedonian Renaissance, Byzantine artists revived the classical style. This painter portrayed David as if a Greek hero, accompanied by personifications of Melody, Echo, and Bethlehem.

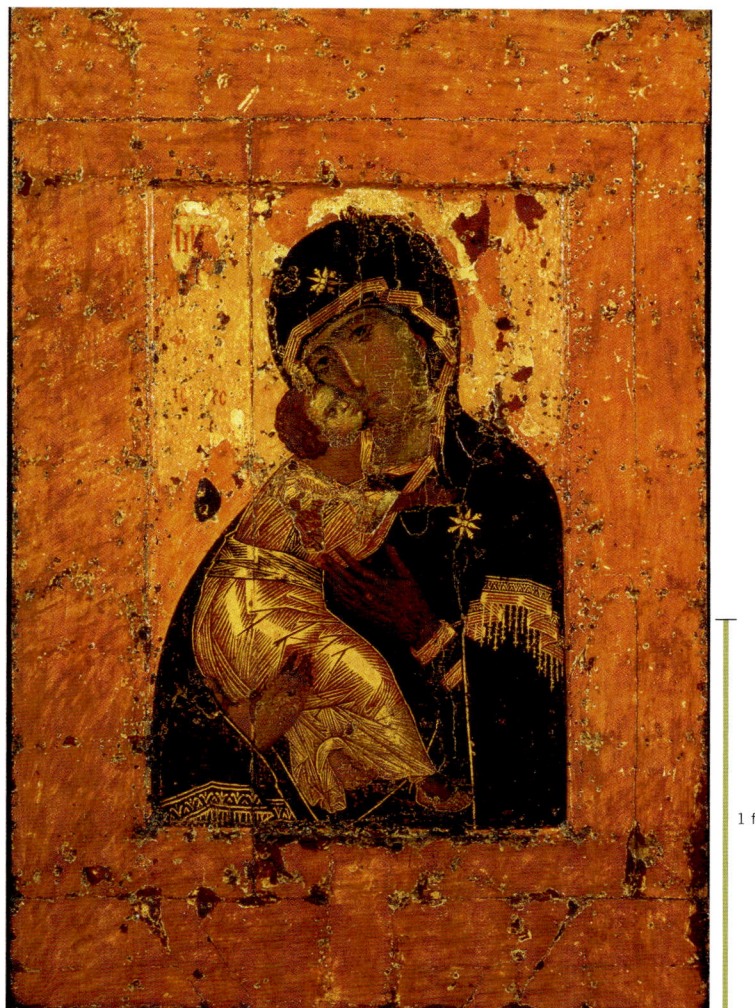

1 ft.

**9-31** Virgin of Compassion icon (*Vladimir Virgin*), late 11th or early 12th century, with later repainting. Tempera on wood, 2′ 6½″ × 1′ 9″. Tretyakov Gallery, Moscow.

In this icon, the artist depicted Mary as the Virgin of Compassion, who presses her cheek against her son's as she contemplates his future. The reverse side shows the instruments of Christ's passion.

Apparently, the artist had seen a work from Late Antiquity or perhaps earlier and partly translated it into a Byzantine pictorial idiom. In works such as this, Byzantine artists kept the classical style alive in the Middle Ages.

***VLADIMIR VIRGIN*** Nothing in Middle Byzantine art better demonstrates the rejection of the iconoclastic viewpoint than the painted icon's return to prominence. After the restoration of images, such icons multiplied by the thousands to meet public and private demand. In the 11th century, the clergy began to display icons in hierarchical order (Christ, the Theotokos, John the Baptist, and then other saints, as on the *Harbaville Triptych*) in tiers on the *templon,* the low columnar screen separating the sanctuary from the main body of a Byzantine church.

The *Vladimir Virgin* (FIG. **9-31**) is the most renowned Middle Byzantine icon produced in Russia. Unfortunately, the revered image has been repainted many times, and only traces of the original surface remain. Descended from works such as the Mount Sinai icon (FIG. 9-18), the *Vladimir Virgin* clearly reveals the stylized abstraction resulting from centuries of working and reworking the conventional image. Probably the work of a painter from Constantinople, the *Vladimir Virgin* displays all the characteristic traits of the Byzantine icon of the Virgin and Child: the Virgin's long,

straight nose and small mouth; the golden rays in the infant's drapery; the decorative sweep of the unbroken contour that encloses the two figures; and the flat silhouette against the golden ground. But this is a much more tender and personalized image of the Virgin than that in the Mount Sinai icon. Here Mary is the Virgin of Compassion, who presses her cheek against her son's in an intimate portrayal of Mother and Child. A deep pathos infuses the image as Mary contemplates the future sacrifice of her son. (The back of the icon bears images of the instruments of Christ's Passion.)

The icon of Vladimir, like most icons, has seen hard service. Placed before or above altars in churches or private chapels, the icon became blackened by the incense and smoke from candles that burned before or below it. It was taken to Kiev (Ukraine) in 1131, then to Vladimir (Russia) in 1155 (hence its name), and in 1395, as a wonder-working image, to Moscow to protect that city from Timur (Tamerlane) and his Mongol armies (see Chapter 10). The Russians believed the sacred picture saved the city of Kazan from later Tartar invasions and all of Russia from the Poles in the 17th century. The *Vladimir Virgin* is a historical symbol of Byzantium's religious and cultural mission to the Slavic world.

# LATE BYZANTINE ART

When rule passed from the Macedonian to the Comnenian dynasty in the later 11th and 12th centuries, three events of fateful significance changed Byzantium's fortunes for the worse. The Seljuk Turks conquered most of Anatolia. The Byzantine Orthodox Church broke finally with the Church of Rome. And the Crusades brought the Latins (a generic term for the peoples of the West) into Byzantine lands on their way to fight for the Christian cross against the Saracens (Muslims) in the Holy Land (see "The Crusades," Chapter 12, page 346).

Crusaders had passed through Constantinople many times en route to "smite the infidel" and had marveled at its wealth and magnificence. Envy, greed, religious fanaticism (the Latins called the Greeks "heretics"), and even ethnic enmity motivated the Crusaders when, during the Fourth Crusade in 1203 and 1204, the Venetians persuaded them to divert their expedition against the Muslims in Palestine and to attack Constantinople instead. They took the city and sacked it. Nicetas Choniates, a contemporaneous historian, expressed the feelings of the Byzantines toward the Crusaders: "The accursed Latins would plunder our wealth and wipe out our race. . . . Between us there can be only an unbridgeable gulf of hatred. . . . They bear the Cross of Christ on their shoulders, but even the Saracens are kinder."[7]

The Latins set up kingdoms within Byzantium, notably in Constantinople itself. What remained of Byzantium split into three small states. The Palaeologans ruled one of these, the kingdom of Nicaea. In 1261, Michael VIII Palaeologus (r. 1259–1282) succeeded in recapturing Constantinople. One of the gems of Late Byzantine architecture—the church dedicated to Saint Catherine (FIG. **9-32A**) in Constantinople—dates to his reign. But Michael's empire was no more than a fragment, and even that disintegrated during the next two centuries. Isolated from the Christian West by Muslim conquests in the Balkans and besieged by Muslim Turks to the East, Byzantium sought help from the West. It was not forthcoming. In 1453, the Ottoman Turks, then a formidable power, took Constantinople and brought to an end the long history of Byzantium (see Chapter 10). But despite the state's grim political condition under the Palaeologan dynasty, the arts flourished well into the 14th century.

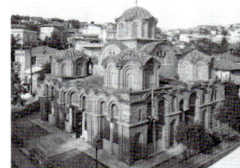

**9-32A** Saint Catherine, Thessaloniki, ca. 1280.

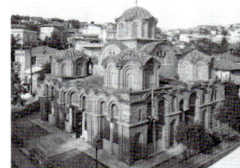

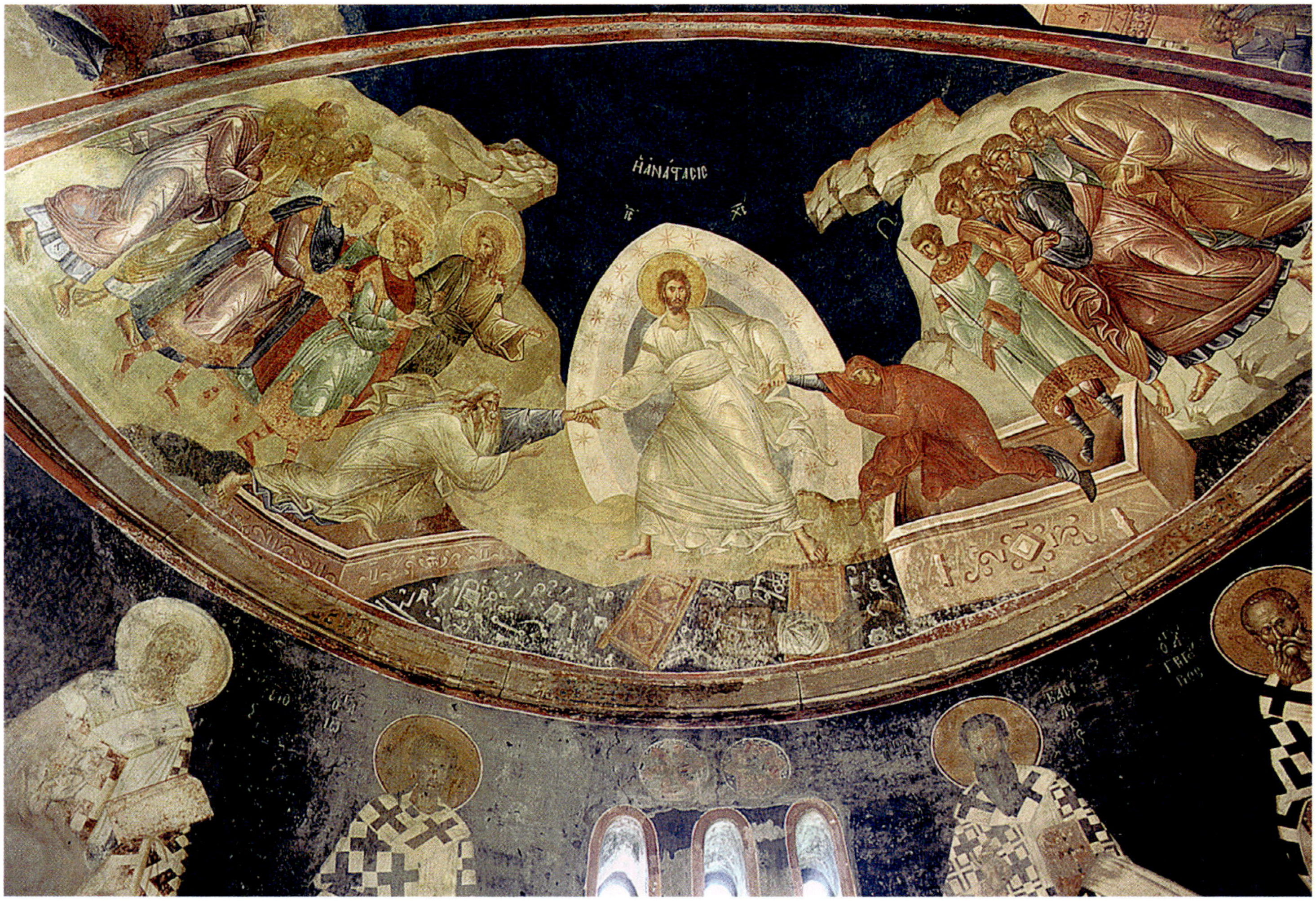

**9-32** *Anastasis,* fresco in the apse of the parekklesion of the Church of Christ in Chora (now the Kariye Museum), Constantinople (Istanbul), Turkey, ca. 1310–1320. ◼◀

In this Late Byzantine funerary chapel, Christ, a white apparition surrounded by a luminous mandorla, raises Adam and Eve from their tombs as John the Baptist and Kings David and Solomon look on.

# Painting

During the 14th and 15th centuries, artists throughout the Byzantine world produced masterpieces of mural and icon painting rivaling those of the earlier periods. Four characteristic examples from the old capital of Constantinople and as far away as Russia illustrate the range and quality of painting during the Late Byzantine period.

**CHRIST IN CHORA** A fresco of the *Anastasis* (FIG. **9-32**) is in the apse of the *parekklesion* (side chapel, in this instance a funerary chapel) of the Church of Christ in Chora in Constantinople. One of many subsidiary subjects that made up the complex mosaic program of Saint Mark's (FIG. 9-26) in Venice, the *Anastasis* is here central to a cycle of pictures portraying the themes of human mortality and redemption by Christ and of the intercession of the Virgin, both appropriate for a funerary chapel. Christ, trampling Satan and all the locks and keys of his prison house of Hell, raises Adam and Eve from their tombs. Looking on are John the Baptist, King David, and King Solomon on the left, and various martyr saints on the right. Christ, central and in a luminous mandorla, reaches out equally to Adam and Eve. The action is swift and smooth, the

supple motions executed with the grace of a ballet. The figures float in a spiritual atmosphere, spaceless and without material mass or shadow-casting volume. This same smoothness and lightness also characterize the modeling of the figures and the subtly nuanced coloration. The jagged abstractions of drapery found in many earlier Byzantine frescoes and mosaics are gone in a return to the fluid delineation of drapery characteristic of the long tradition of classical illusionism.

Throughout the centuries, Byzantine artists looked back to Greco-Roman illusionism. But unlike classical artists, Byzantine painters and mosaicists did not believe the systematic observation of material nature should be the source of their representations of the eternal. They drew their images from a persistent and conventionalized vision of a spiritual world unsusceptible to change. That consistent vision is what unites works as distant in time as the sixth-century apse mosaic (FIG. 9-16) at Mount Sinai and the 14th-century fresco in the Church of Christ in Chora.

**OHRID ICONS** Icon painting may most intensely reveal Byzantine spirituality. In the Late Byzantine period, the Early Byzantine templon developed into an *iconostasis* (icon stand), a high screen with doors. As its name implies, the iconostasis supported tiers of painted devotional images, which began to be produced again in large numbers, both in Constantinople and throughout the diminished Byzantine Empire.

One example (FIG. **9-33**), notable for the lavish use of finely etched silver foil to frame the painted figure of Christ as Savior of Souls, dates to the beginning of the 14th century. It comes from the church of Saint Clement at Ohrid in Macedonia, where many Late Byzantine icons imported from the capital have been preserved. The painter of the Ohrid Christ, in a manner consistent with Byzantine art's conservative nature, adhered to an iconographical and stylistic tradition dating to the earliest icons from the monastery at Mount Sinai. As elsewhere (FIGS. 9-18A, 9-23, and 9-25), the Savior holds a bejeweled Bible in his left hand while he blesses the faithful with his right hand. The mixture of styles is typical of Byzantine painting. Note especially the juxtaposition of Christ's fully modeled head and neck, which reveal the Byzantine artist's Greco-Roman heritage, with the schematic linear folds of Christ's garment, which do not envelop the figure but rather seem to be placed in front of it.

Late Byzantine icons often have paintings on two sides because they were carried in processions. When the clergy brought the icons into the church, they did not mount them on the iconostasis but exhibited them on stands so they could be viewed from both sides. The Ohrid icon of Christ has a painting of the *Crucifixion* on its reverse. Another double icon

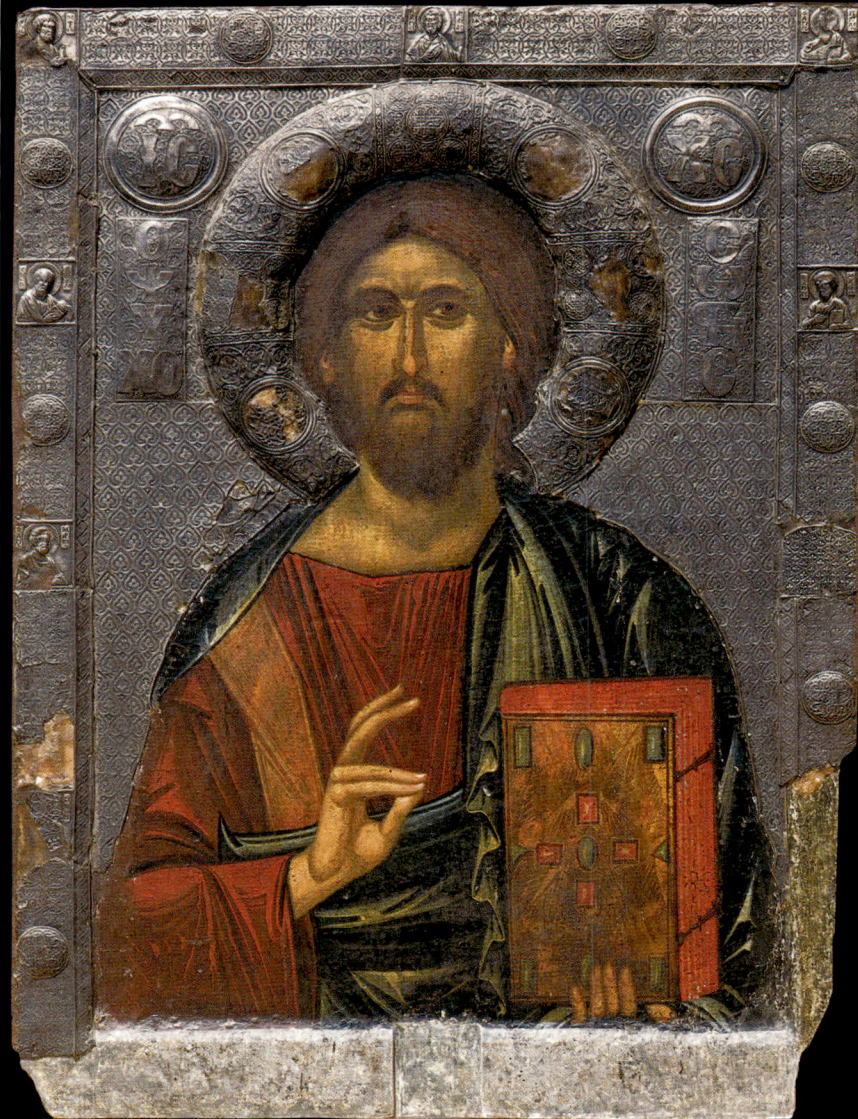

1 ft.

**9-33** **Christ as Savior of Souls**, icon from Saint Clement, Ohrid, Macedonia, early 14th century. Tempera, linen, and silver on wood, 3′ $\frac{1}{4}$″ × 2′ 2$\frac{1}{2}$″. Icon Gallery of Saint Clement, Ohrid. ▰◀

Notable for the lavish use of finely etched silver foil, this icon typifies Byzantine stylistic complexity. Christ's fully modeled head and neck contrast with the schematic linear folds of his garment.

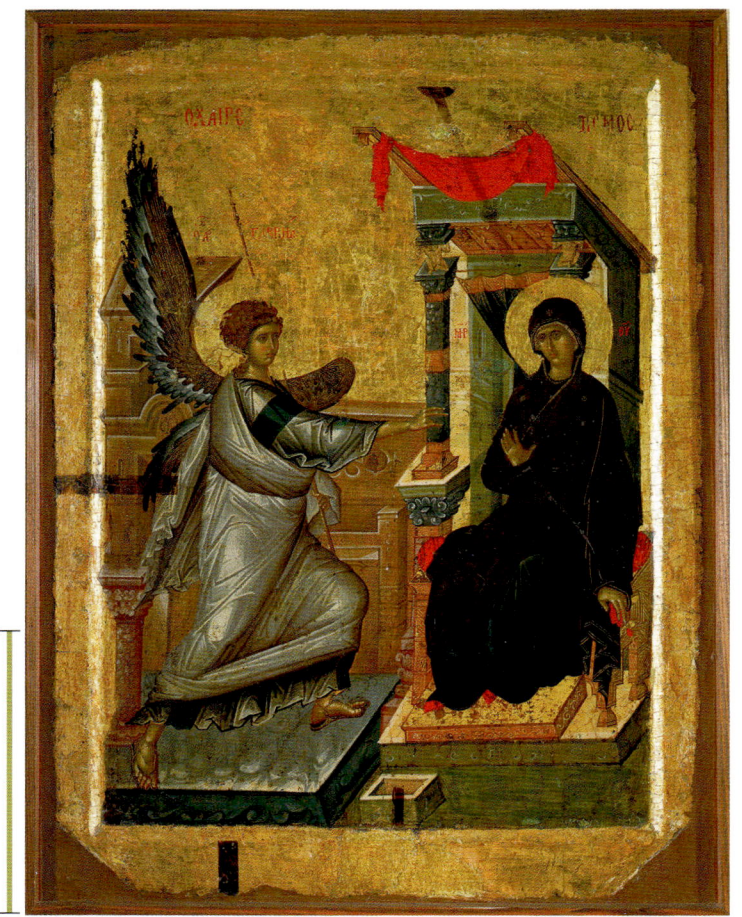

**9-34** *Annunciation,* reverse of two-sided icon from the Church of the Virgin Peribleptos, Ohrid, Macedonia, early 14th century. Tempera and linen on wood, 3′ $\frac{5}{8}$″ × 2′ 2$\frac{3}{4}$″. Icon Gallery of Saint Clement, Ohrid.

Late Byzantine icons often have two painted sides because they were carried in processions. On this icon the Virgin Mary appears on the front and this *Annunciation* scene on the back.

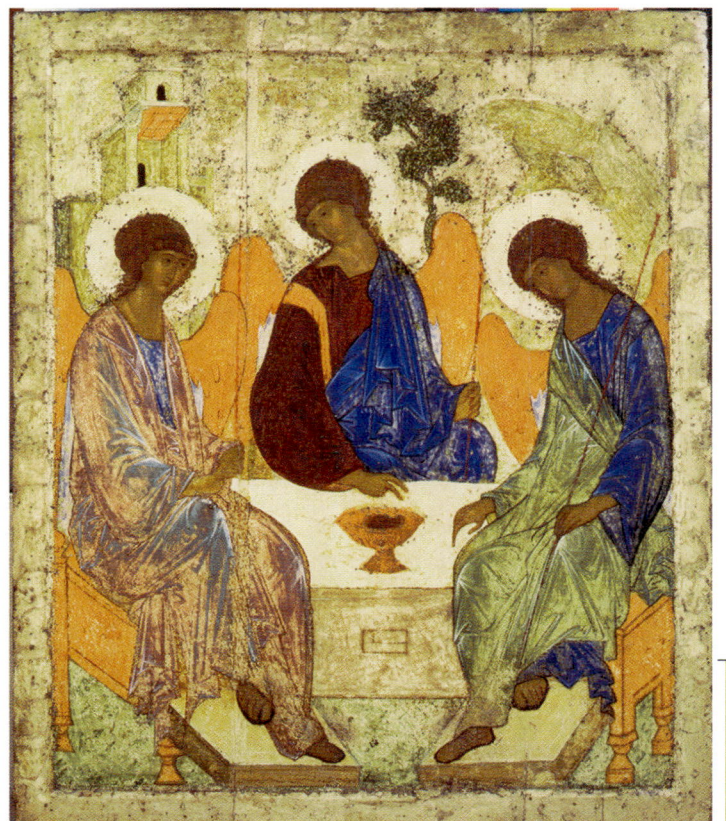

**9-35** ANDREI RUBLYEV, *Three Angels* (Old Testament Trinity), ca. 1410. Tempera on wood, 4′ 8″ × 3′ 9″. Tretyakov Gallery, Moscow. ◼◀

This exceptionally large icon featuring subtle line and vivid colors is one of the masterworks of Russian painting. It depicts the three angels who appeared to Abraham, prefiguring the Trinity.

from Ohrid, also imported from Constantinople, represents the Virgin on the front as Christ's counterpart as Savior of Souls. The *Annunciation* (FIG. **9-34**) is the subject of the reverse. With a commanding gesture of heavenly authority, the angel Gabriel announces to Mary that she is to be the Mother of God. She responds with a simple gesture conveying both astonishment and acceptance. The gestures and attitudes of the figures are again conventional, as are the highly simplified architectural props. The painter rendered the latter in inconsistent perspective derived from classical prototypes, but set the sturdy three-dimensional forms against an otherworldly golden sky, suggesting the sacred space in which the narrative unfolds. This icon therefore also exemplifies the diversity of stylistic sources that characterizes Byzantine art throughout its long history.

**ANDREI RUBLYEV** Icon painting flourished also in Russia. Russian icons usually have strong patterns, firm lines, and intense contrasting colors, which serve to heighten the legibility of the icons in the wavering candlelight and clouds of incense worshipers encountered in church interiors. For many art historians, Russian painting reached a climax in the work of ANDREI RUBLYEV (ca. 1370–1430). His nearly five-foot-tall panel (FIG. **9-35**) depicting the three Old Testament angels who appeared to Abraham is a work of great spiritual power. Painted during the tenure of Photius as Metropolitan (Orthodox archbishop) of Russia (FIG. **9-35A**), it is

an unsurpassed example of subtle line in union with what once were intensely vivid colors, now faded. The angels sit about a table, each framed with a halo and sweeping wings, three nearly identical figures distinguished primarily by their garment colors. The light linear play of the draperies sets off the tranquil demeanor of the figures. Juxtapositions of complementary hues add intensity to the coloration. The blue and green folds of the central figure's

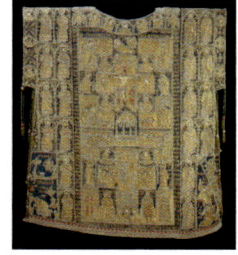

**9-35A** Large sakkos of Photius, ca. 1417.

cloak, for example, stand out starkly against the deep-red robe and the gilded orange of the wings. In the figure on the left, the highlights of the orange cloak are an opalescent blue-green. The unmodulated saturation, brilliance, and purity of the color harmonies are the hallmark of Rublyev's style.

**THE THIRD ROME** With the fall of Constantinople in 1453, Russia became Byzantium's self-appointed heir, defending Christendom against the infidel. The court of the tsar (derived from Caesar) declared: "Because the Old Rome has fallen, and because the Second Rome, which is Constantinople, is now in the hands of the godless Turks, thy kingdom, O pious Tsar, is the Third Rome. . . . Two Romes have fallen, but the Third stands, and there shall be no more."[8] Rome, Byzantium, Russia—Old Rome, New Rome, and Third Rome—were a continuum, spanning two and a half millennia during which artists and architects produced many of the most significant paintings, sculptures, and buildings in the long history of art through the ages.

# BYZANTIUM

## EARLY BYZANTINE ART 324–726

▌ Constantine founded Constantinople on the site of the ancient Greek city of Byzantium in 324 and dedicated this "New Rome" to the Christian God in 330.

▌ The first golden age of Byzantine art was the result of the lavish patronage of Justinian (r. 527–565). In Constantinople alone, Justinian built or restored more than 30 churches. The greatest was Hagia Sophia, which rivaled the architectural wonders of Old Rome. A brilliant fusion of central and longitudinal plans, its 180-foot-high dome rests on pendentives but seemed to contemporaries to be suspended "by a golden chain from Heaven."

▌ The seat of Byzantine power in Italy was Ravenna, which also prospered under Justinian. San Vitale is Ravenna's greatest church. Its mosaics, with their weightless, hovering, frontal figures against a gold background, reveal the new Byzantine aesthetic.

▌ Justinian also rebuilt the monastery at Mount Sinai in Egypt. The preserved Sinai icons—portable devotional paintings depicting Christ, the Virgin, and saints—are the finest of the Early Byzantine period.

▌ In 726, Leo III (r. 717–741) enacted a ban against picturing the divine, initiating the era of iconoclasm (726–843) and the destruction of countless Early Byzantine artworks.

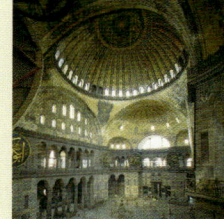

Hagia Sophia, Constantinople, 532–537

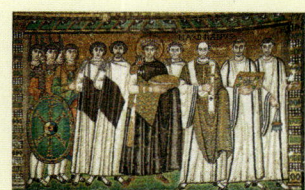

San Vitale, Ravenna, 526–547

## MIDDLE BYZANTINE ART 843–1204

▌ Empress Theodora repealed iconoclasm in 843, and in 867, Basil I (r. 867–886) dedicated a new mosaic depicting the Theotokos (Mother of God) in Hagia Sophia. It marked the triumph of the iconophiles over the iconoclasts.

▌ Ivory carving and manuscript painting flourished during the Middle Byzantine period, as during the preceding era. Hinged ivory shrines, such as the *Harbaville Triptych*, were popular for use in private prayer. The *Paris Psalter* is noteworthy for the conscious revival of classical naturalism.

▌ Middle Byzantine churches, such as those at Hosios Loukas and Daphni, have highly decorative exterior walls and feature domes that rest on drums above the center of a Greek cross. The climax of the interior mosaic programs was often an image of Christ as Pantokrator in the dome.

*Paris Psalter,* ca. 950–970

Church of the Dormition, Daphni, ca. 1090–1100

## LATE BYZANTINE ART 1261–1453

▌ In 1204, Latin Crusaders sacked Constantinople, bringing to an end the Middle Byzantine era. In 1261, Michael VIII Palaeologus (r. 1259–1282) succeeded in recapturing the city. Constantinople remained in Byzantine hands until its capture by the Ottoman Turks in 1453.

▌ Important mural paintings of the Late Byzantine period are in the Church of Christ in Chora. An extensive picture cycle portrays Christ as redeemer. In the apse, he raises Adam and Eve from their tombs.

▌ Late Byzantine icons were displayed in tiers on an iconostasis or on individual stands so that the paintings on both sides could be seen. Christ or the Virgin usually appeared on the front. The reverse depicted a narrative scene from the life of Christ.

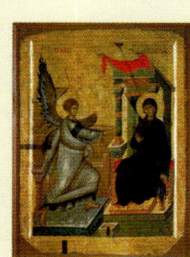

*Annunciation,* Ohrid, early 14th century

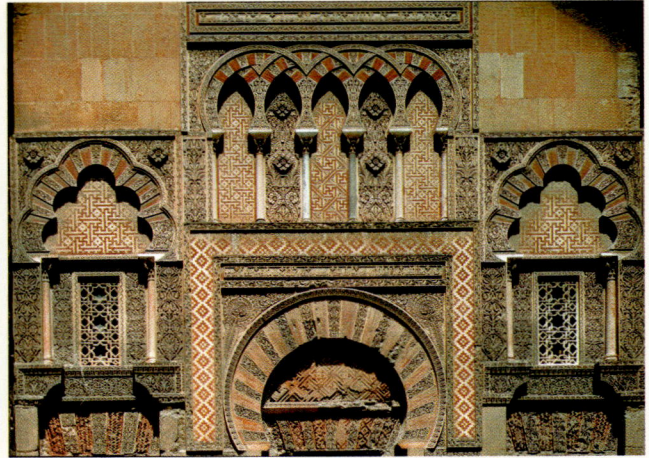

The horseshoe and multilobed arches of the gates to the Mezquita at Córdoba were part of the expansion and remodeling of the mosque carried out by the Umayyad caliph al-Hakam II.

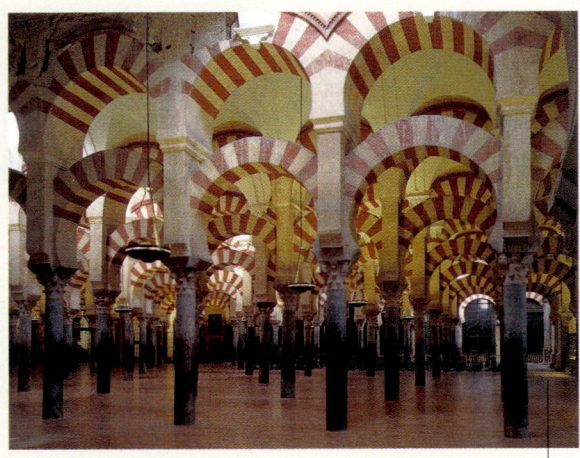

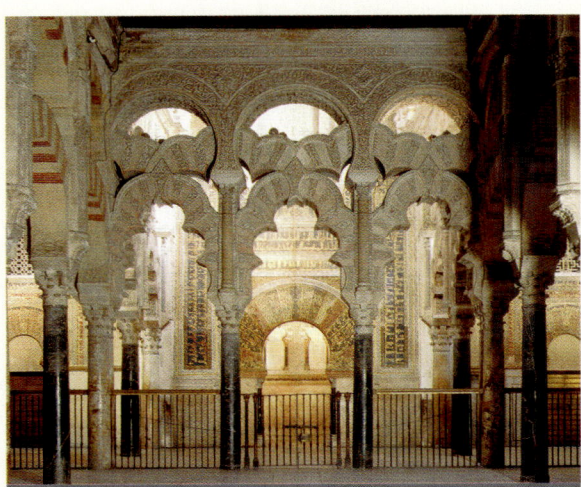

Islamic architecture draws on diverse sources. The horseshoe arches of the Córdoba mosque's prayer hall may derive from Visigothic architecture. The Arabs overthrew that Christian kingdom in 711.

In the 10th century, al-Hakam II also added a maqsura to the Córdoba Mezquita. The hall highlights Muslim architects' bold experimentation with curvilinear shapes and different kinds of arches.

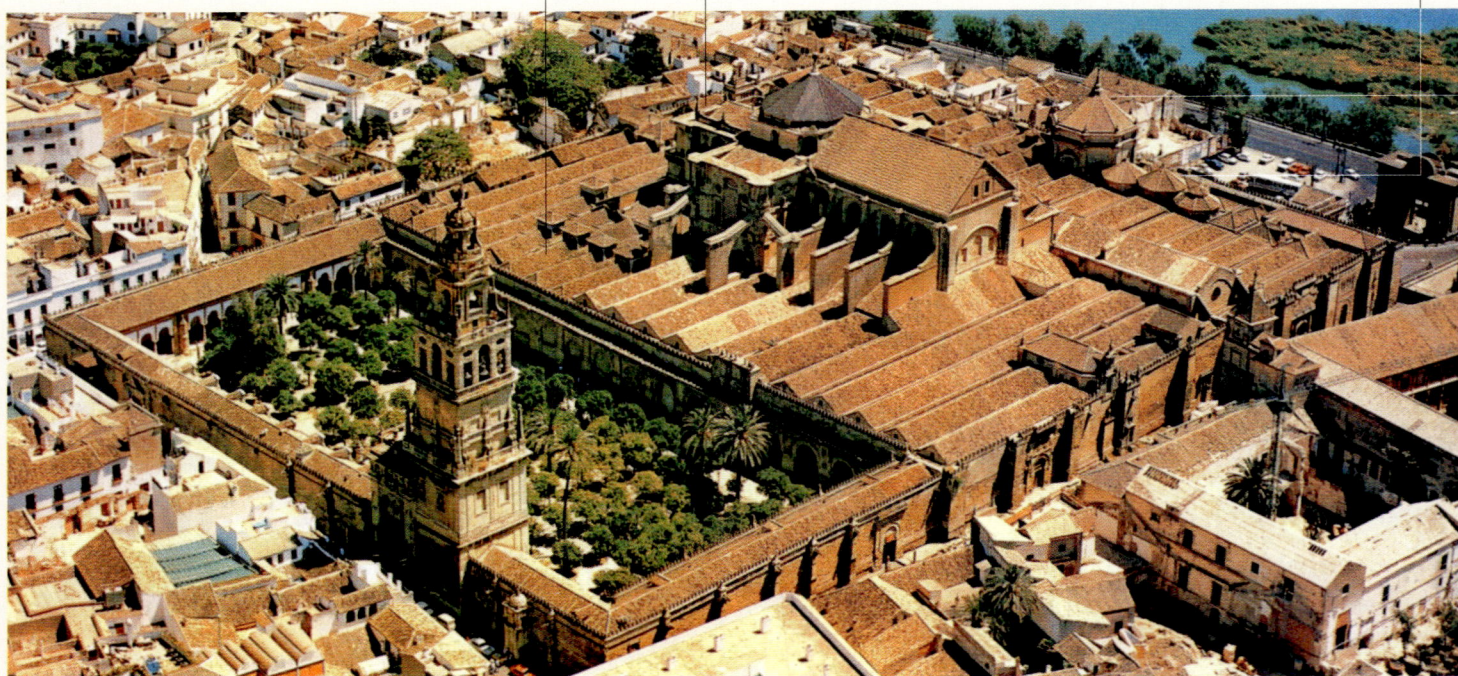

**10-1** Aerial view of the Mezquita (Great Mosque), Córdoba, Spain, 8th to 10th centuries; rededicated as the Cathedral of Saint Mary, 1236.

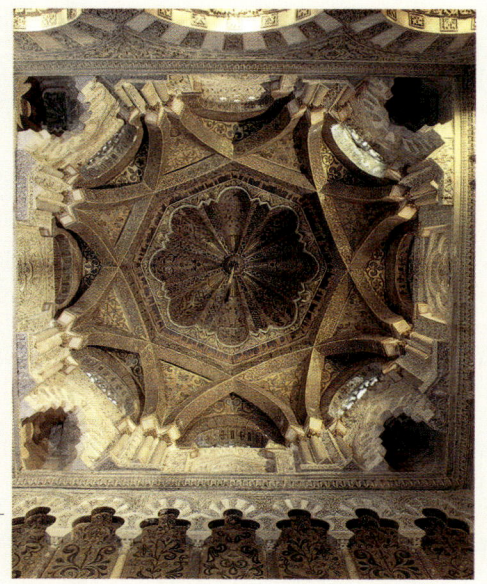

Byzantine artists installed the mosaics in the mihrab dome in the Córdoba mosque, but the decorative patterns formed by the crisscrossing ribs and the multilobed arches are distinctly Islamic.

# THE ISLAMIC WORLD

## THE RISE AND SPREAD OF ISLAM

At the time of Muhammad's birth around 570, the Arabian peninsula was peripheral to the Byzantine and Sasanian empires. The Arabs, nomadic herders and caravan merchants who worshiped many gods, resisted the Prophet's teachings of Islam, an Arabic word meaning "submission to the one God (Allah in Arabic)." Within a decade of Muhammad's death in 632, however, Muslims ("those who submit") ruled Arabia, Palestine, Syria, Iraq, and northern Egypt. From there, the new religion spread rapidly both eastward and westward.

With the rise of Islam also came the birth of a compelling new worldwide tradition of art and architecture. In the Middle East and North Africa, Islamic art largely replaced Late Antique art. In India, the establishment of Muslim rule at Delhi in the early 13th century brought Islamic art and architecture to South Asia (see Chapter 32). In fact, perhaps the most famous building in Asia, the Taj Mahal (FIG. 32-6) at Agra, is an Islamic mausoleum. At the opposite end of the then-known world, Abd al-Rahman I (r. 756–788) founded a Spanish Muslim dynasty at Córdoba, which became the center of a brilliant court culture that profoundly influenced medieval Europe.

The jewel of the capital at Córdoba was its Great Mosque (FIG. 10-1), begun in 784 and enlarged several times during the 9th and 10th centuries until it eventually became one of the largest mosques in the Islamic West. In 1236, the Christians rededicated and remodeled the shrine as a church (the tallest part of the complex, at the center of the aerial view, is Córdoba's cathedral) after they recaptured the city from the Muslims.

A visual feast greets all visitors to the mosque. Its Muslim designers used overlapping horseshoe-shaped arches (which became synonymous with Islamic architecture in Europe) in the uppermost zone of the eastern and western gates to the complex. Double rows of arches surmount the more than 500 columns in the mosque's huge prayer hall. Even more elaborate multilobed arches on slender columns form dazzling frames for other areas of the mosque, especially in the *maqsura,* the hall reserved for the ruler, which at Córdoba connects the mosque to the palace. Crisscrossing ribs form intricate decorative patterns in the complex's largest dome.

The Córdoba Mezquita (Spanish, "mosque") typifies Islamic architecture both in its conformity to the basic principles of mosque design and in its incorporation of distinctive regional forms.

# EARLY ISLAMIC ART

The religion of Islam arose in Arabia early in the seventh century, after the Prophet Muhammad began to receive God's revelations (see "Muhammad and Islam," page 285). At that time, the Arabs were not major players on the world stage. Yet within little more than a century, the eastern Mediterranean, which Byzantium once ringed and ruled, had become an Islamic lake, and the armies of Muhammad's successors had subdued the Middle East, long the seat of Persian dominance and influence. The swiftness of the Islamic advance is among the wonders of history. By 640, Muslims ruled Syria, Palestine, and Iraq. In 642, the Byzantine army abandoned Alexandria, marking the Muslim conquest of Lower (northern) Egypt. In 651, Islamic forces ended more than 400 years of Sasanian rule in Iran (see Chapter 2). All of North Africa was under Muslim control by 710. A victory at Jerez de la Frontera in southern Spain in 711 seemed to open all of western Europe to the Muslims. By 732, they had advanced north to Poitiers in France. There, however, an army of Franks under Charles Martel (r. 714–741), the grandfather of Charlemagne, opposed them successfully (see Chapter 11), halting Islamic expansion at the Pyrenees. In Spain, in contrast, the Muslim rulers of Córdoba (FIG. 10-1) flourished until 1031, and not until 1492 did

Islamic influence and power end in Iberia. That year the army of King Ferdinand II of Aragon (r. 1479–1516) and Queen Isabella, the sponsors of Columbus's voyage to the New World, overthrew the caliphs of Granada. In the East, the Muslims reached the Indus River by 751 (see Chapter 32). Only in Anatolia did stubborn Byzantine resistance slow their advance. Relentless Muslim pressure against the shrinking Byzantine Empire eventually brought about its collapse in 1453, when the Ottoman Turks entered Constantinople (see Chapter 9).

Military might alone cannot, however, account for the irresistible and far-ranging sweep of Islam from Arabia to India to North Africa and Spain (MAP 10-1). That Islam endured in the lands Muhammad's successors conquered can be explained only by the nature of the Islamic faith and its appeal to millions of converts. Islam remains today one of the world's great religions, with adherents on all continents. Its sophisticated culture has had a major influence around the globe. Arab scholars laid the foundations of arithmetic and algebra and made significant contributions to astronomy, medicine, and the natural sciences. During the 12th and 13th centuries, Christian scholars in the West eagerly studied Arabic translations of Aristotle and other ancient Greek writers. Arabic love lyrics and poetic descriptions of nature inspired the early French troubadours.

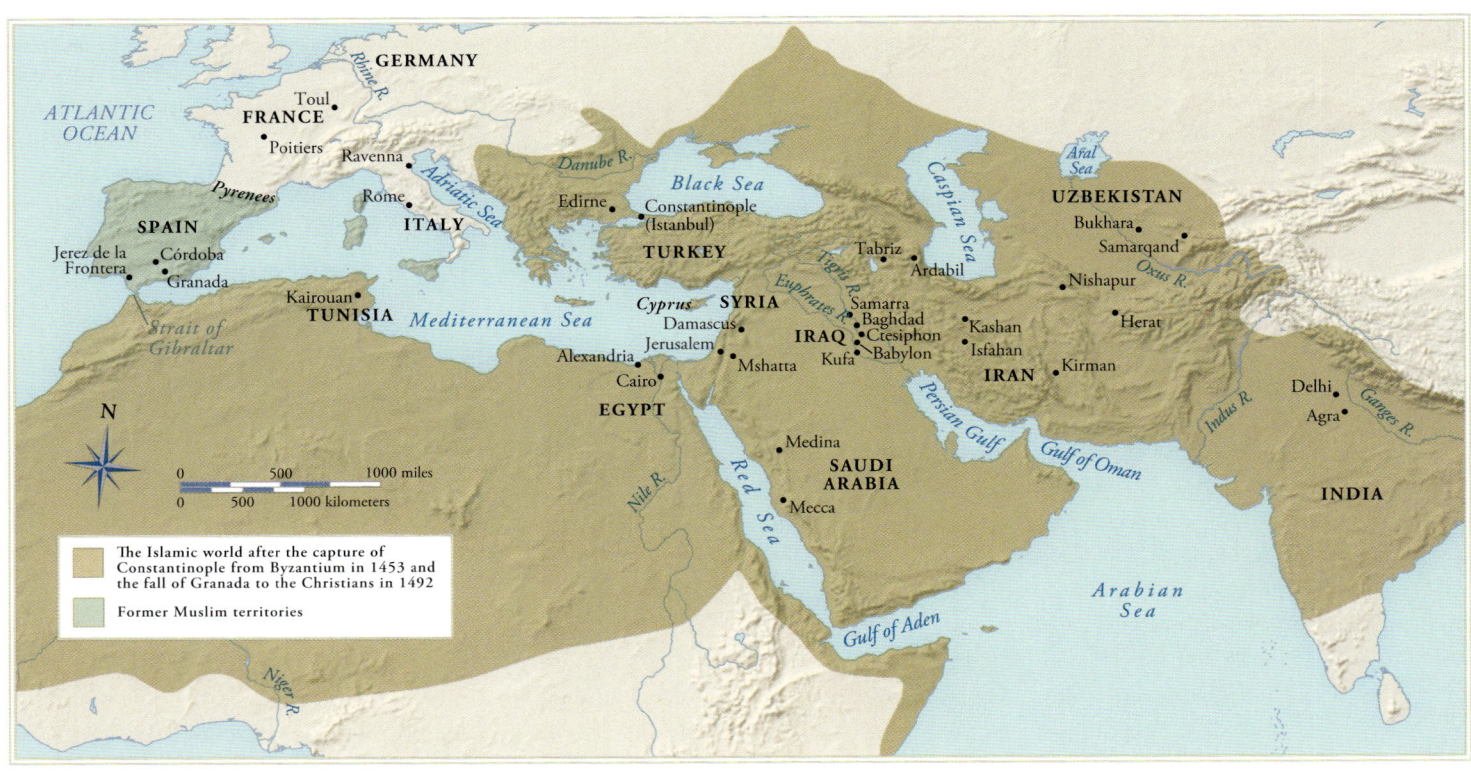

MAP 10-1  The Islamic world around 1500.

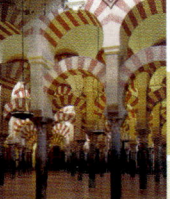

## THE ISLAMIC WORLD

| 622 | 756 | 1453 | 1924 |
|---|---|---|---|
| ▌ Muhammad abandons Mecca for Medina, 622 <br> ▌ Umayyads (r. 661–750), the first Islamic dynasty, build Dome of the Rock in Jerusalem and Great Mosque in Damascus | ▌ Abbasids produce earliest Korans with Kufic calligraphy <br> ▌ Spanish Umayyad dynasty builds Great Mosque in capital of Córdoba <br> ▌ Nasrids embellish Alhambra with magnificent palaces <br> ▌ Fatimid, Ayyubid, and Mamluk dynasties in Egypt are lavish art patrons | ▌ Ottomans capture Byzantine Constantinople in 1453 and develop the domed central-plan mosque <br> ▌ Flowering of Timurid book illumination under Shah Tahmasp <br> ▌ Safavid artisans perfect the manufacture of cuerda seca and mosaic tiles | |

# Muhammad and Islam

Muhammad, revered by Muslims as the Final Prophet in the line including Abraham, Moses, and Jesus, was a native of Mecca on the west coast of Arabia. Born around 570 into a family of merchants in the great Arabian caravan trade, Muhammad was critical of the polytheistic religion of his fellow Arabs. In 610, he began to receive the revelations of God through the archangel Gabriel. Opposition to Muhammad's message among the Arabs was strong and led to persecution. In 622, the Prophet and his followers abandoned Mecca for a desert oasis eventually called Medina ("City of the Prophet"). Islam dates its beginnings from this flight, known as the *Hijra* (emigration).* Barely eight years later, in 630, Muhammad returned to Mecca with 10,000 soldiers. He took control of the city, converted the population to Islam, and destroyed all the idols. But he preserved as the Islamic world's symbolic center the small cubical building that had housed the idols, the *Kaaba* (from the Arabic for "cube"). The Arabs associated the Kaaba with the era of Abraham and Ishmael, the common ancestors of Jews and Arabs. Muhammad died in Medina in 632.

The essential tenet of Islam is acceptance of and submission to God's will. Muslims must live according to the rules laid down in the collected revelations communicated through Muhammad during his lifetime. The *Koran,* Islam's sacred book, codified by the Muslim ruler Uthman (r. 644–656), records Mohammad's revelations. The word "Koran" means "recitations"—a reference to Gabriel's instructions to Muhammad in 610 to "recite in the name of God." The Koran is composed of 114 *surahs* (chapters) divided into verses.

The profession of faith in the one God is the first of five obligations binding all Muslims. In addition, the faithful must worship five times daily facing Mecca, give alms to the poor, fast during the month of Ramadan, and once in a lifetime—if possible—make a pilgrimage to Mecca. The revelations in the Koran are not the only guide for Muslims. Muhammad's words and exemplary ways and customs, the *Hadith,* recorded in the *Sunnah,* offer models to all Muslims on ethical problems of everyday life. The reward for the faithful is Paradise.

Islam has much in common with Judaism and Christianity. Muslims think of their religion as a continuation, a completion, and in some sense a reformation of those other great monotheisms. Islam, for example, incorporates many Old Testament teachings, with their sober ethical standards and rejection of idol worship. But, unlike Jesus in the New Testament Gospels, Muhammad did not claim to be divine. Rather, he was God's messenger, the Final Prophet, who purified and perfected the common faith of Jews, Christians, and Muslims in one God. Islam also differs from Judaism and Christianity in its simpler organization. Muslims worship God directly, without a hierarchy of rabbis, priests, or saints acting as intermediaries.

In Islam, as Muhammad defined it, the union of religious and secular authority was even more complete than in Byzantium. Muhammad established a new social order, replacing the Arabs' old decentralized tribal one, and took complete charge of his community's temporal as well as spiritual affairs. After Muhammad's death, the *caliphs* (from the Arabic for "successor") continued this practice of uniting religious and political leadership in one ruler.

*Muslims date events beginning with the Hijra in the same way Christians reckon events from Christ's birth and the Romans before them began their calendar with Rome's founding by Romulus and Remus in 753 BCE. The Muslim year is, however, a 354-day year of 12 lunar months, and thus dates cannot be converted by simply adding 622 to Christian-era dates.

## Architecture

During the early centuries of Islamic history, the Muslim world's political and cultural center was the Fertile Crescent of ancient Mesopotamia. The caliphs of Damascus (capital of modern Syria) and Baghdad (capital of Iraq) appointed provincial governors to rule the vast territories they controlled. These governors eventually gained relative independence by setting up dynasties in various territories and provinces, including the Umayyads in Syria (661–750) and in Spain (756–1031), the Abbasids in Iraq (750–1258, largely nominal after 945), the Samanids in Uzbekistan (819–1005), the Fatimids in Egypt (909–1171), and others.

Like other potentates before and after, the Muslim caliphs were builders on a grand scale. The first Islamic buildings, both religious and secular, are in the Middle East, but important early examples of Islamic architecture still stand also in North Africa, Spain, and Central Asia.

**DOME OF THE ROCK** The first great Islamic building was the Dome of the Rock (FIG. **10-2**) in Jerusalem. The Muslims had taken the city from the Byzantines in 638, and the Umayyad caliph Abd al-Malik (r. 685–705) erected the monumental shrine between 687 and 692 as an architectural tribute to the triumph of Islam. The Dome of the Rock marked the coming of the new religion to the city that had been, and still is, sacred to both Jews and

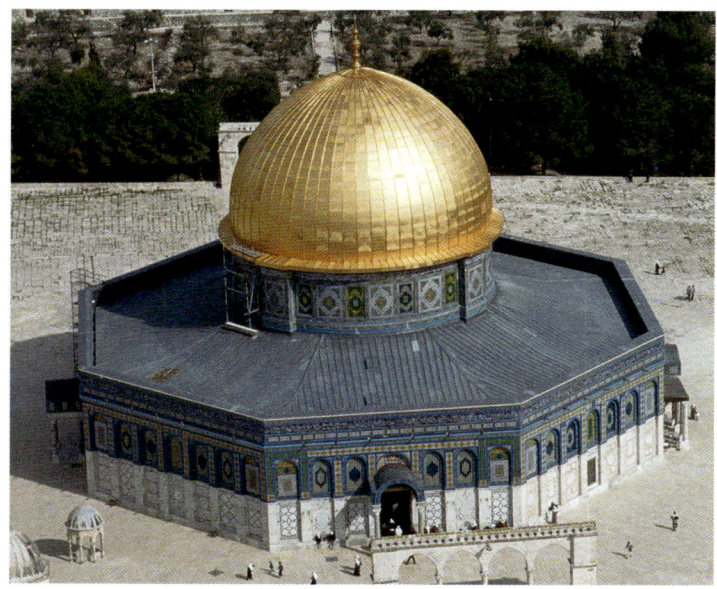

**10-2** Aerial view (looking southwest) of the Dome of the Rock, Jerusalem, 687–692.

Abd al-Malik built the Dome of the Rock to mark the triumph of Islam in Jerusalem on a site sacred to Muslims, Christians, and Jews. The shrine takes the form of an octagon with a towering dome.

Early Islamic Art    **285**

**10-3** Interior of the Dome of the Rock, Jerusalem, 687–692.

On the interior of the Dome of the Rock, the original mosaics are largely intact. At the center of the rotunda is the rocky outcropping later associated with Adam, Abraham, and Muhammad.

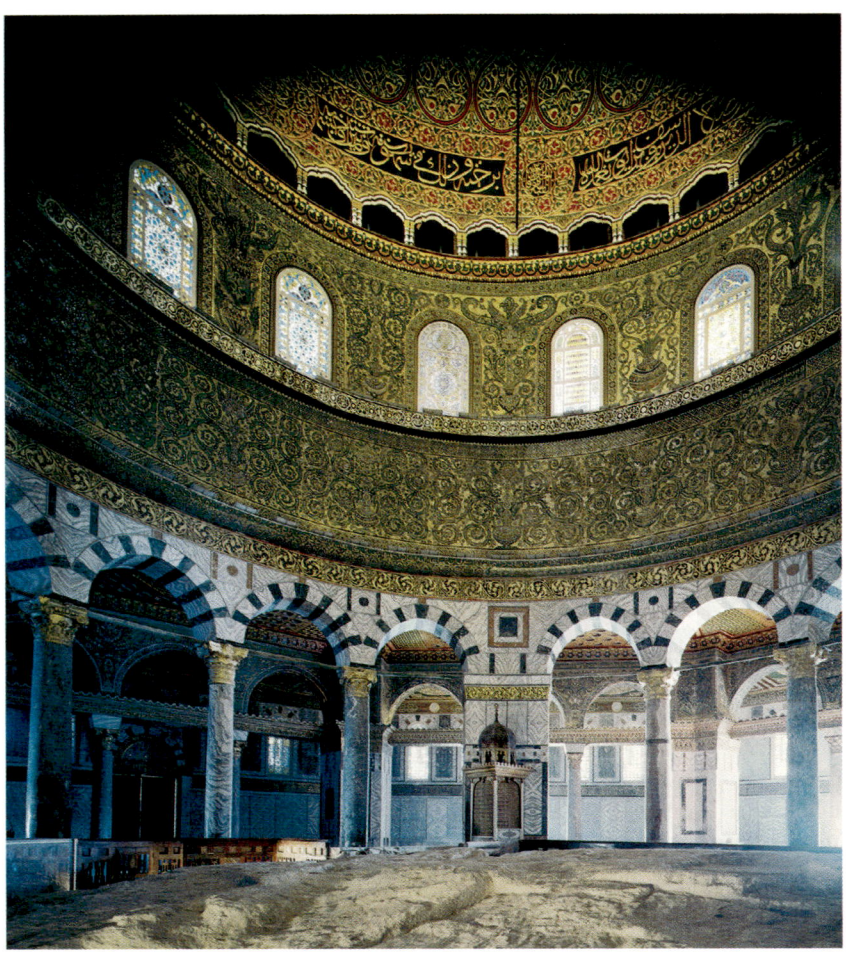

Christians. The structure rises from a huge platform known as the Noble Enclosure, where in ancient times the Hebrews built the Temple of Solomon that the Roman emperor Titus destroyed in the year 70 (see Chapter 7). In time, the site acquired additional significance as the reputed location of Adam's grave and the spot where Abraham prepared to sacrifice Isaac. The rock (FIG. 10-3) that gives the building its name also later came to be identified with the place where Muhammad began his miraculous journey to Heaven (the *Miraj*) and then, in the same night, returned to his home in Mecca.

In its form, construction, and decoration, the Dome of the Rock is firmly in the Late Antique tradition of the Mediterranean world. It is a domed central-plan structure descended from the Pantheon (FIG. 7-49) in Rome and Hagia Sophia (FIG. 9-5) in Constantinople, but it more closely resembles the octagonal San Vitale (FIG. 9-10) in Ravenna. In all likelihood, a neighboring Christian monument, Constantine's Church of the Holy Sepulcher, inspired the Dome of the Rock's designers. That fourth-century domed rotunda bore a family resemblance to the roughly contemporaneous Constantinian mausoleum later rededicated as Santa Costanza (FIGS. 8-11 and 8-12) in Rome. Crowning the Islamic shrine is a 75-foot-tall double-shelled

**10-4** Aerial view (looking southeast) of the Great Mosque, Damascus, Syria, 706–715. ◼◀

The Umayyads constructed Damascus's Great Mosque after they transferred their capital from Mecca in 661. The mosque owes a debt to Late Antique architecture in its plan and decoration.

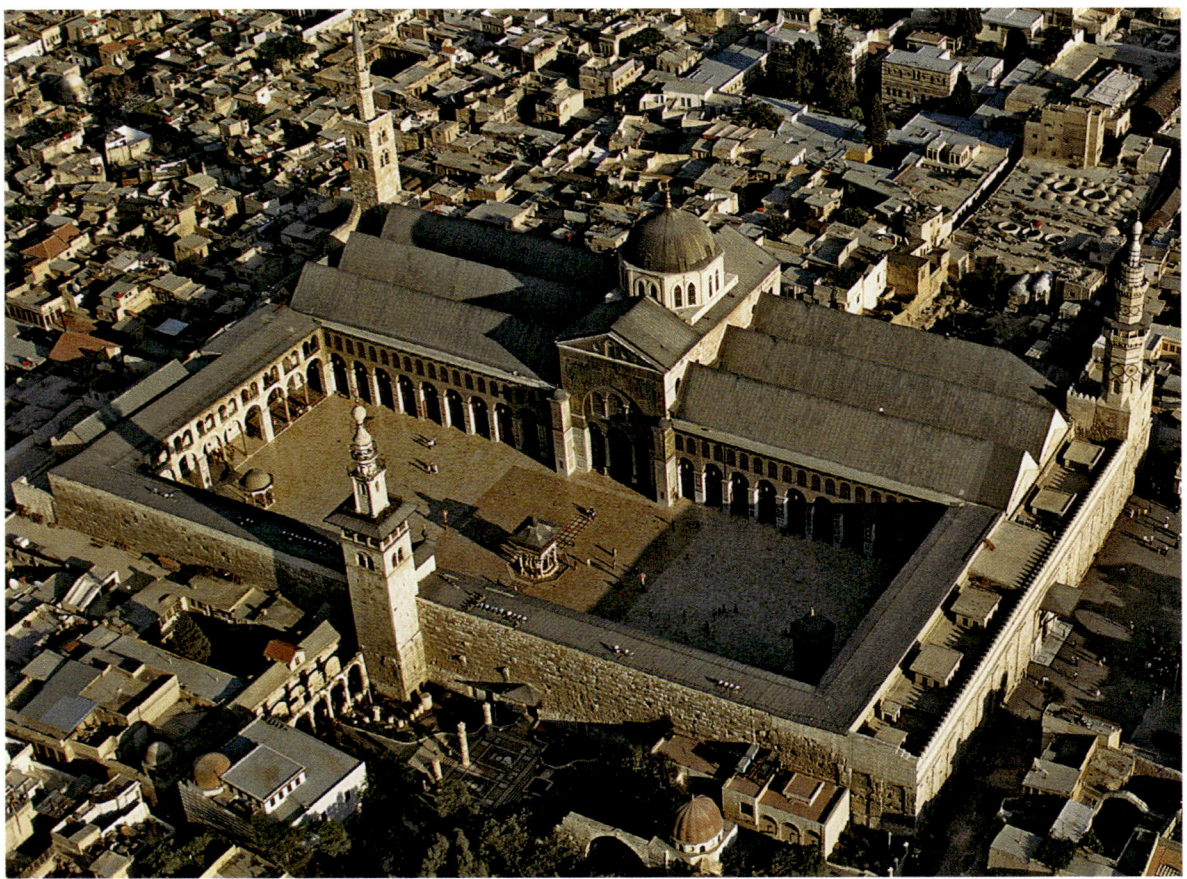

wooden dome, which so dominates the elevation as to reduce the octagon to function merely as its base. This soaring, majestic unit creates a decidedly more commanding effect than that of similar Late Antique and Byzantine domical structures (FIGS. 9-5 and 9-10). The silhouettes of those domes are comparatively insignificant when seen from the outside.

The building's exterior has been much restored. Tiling from the 16th century and later has replaced the original mosaic. Yet the vivid, colorful patterning wrapping the walls like a textile is typical of Islamic ornamentation. It contrasts markedly with Byzantine brickwork and Greco-Roman sculptured decoration. The interior's rich mosaic ornamentation (FIG. 10-3) is largely intact and suggests the original appearance of the exterior walls. Against a lush vegetal background, Abd al-Malik's mosaicists depicted crowns, jewels, chalices, and other royal motifs—probably a reference to the triumph of Islam over the Byzantine and Persian empires. Inscriptions, mostly from the Koran, underscore Islam as the superior new monotheism, superseding both Judaism and Christianity in Jerusalem. (Curiously, no inscription refers to the rock within the shrine.)

**GREAT MOSQUE, DAMASCUS** The Umayyads transferred their capital from Mecca to Damascus in 661. There, Abd al-Malik's son, the caliph al-Walid (r. 705–715), purchased a Byzantine church dedicated to John the Baptist (formerly a Roman temple of Jupiter) and built an imposing new mosque for the expanding Muslim population (see "The Mosque," page 288). The Umayyads demolished the church, but they used the Roman precinct walls as a foundation for their construction. Like the Dome of the Rock, Damascus's Great Mosque (FIG. 10-4) owes much to Roman and Early Christian archi-

tecture. The Islamic builders incorporated stone blocks, columns, and capitals salvaged from the earlier structures on the land acquired by al-Walid. Pier *arcades* reminiscent of Roman aqueducts (FIG. 7-33) frame the courtyard. The *minarets,* two at the southern corners and one at the northern side of the enclosure—the earliest in the Islamic world—are modifications of the preexisting Roman square towers. The grand prayer hall, taller than the rest of the complex, is on the south side of the courtyard (facing Mecca). The hall's facade, with its pediment and arches, recalls Roman and Byzantine models and faces into the courtyard, like a temple in a Roman forum (FIG. 7-12), a plan maintained throughout the long history of mosque architecture. The Damascus mosque synthesizes elements received from other cultures into a novel architectural unity, which includes the distinctive Islamic elements of *mihrab,* mihrab dome, *minbar,* and minaret.

An extensive cycle of glass mosaics once covered the walls of the Great Mosque. In one of the surviving sections (FIG. 10-5), a conch-shell niche "supports" an arcaded pavilion with a flowering rooftop flanked by structures shown in perspective. Like the architectural design, the mosaics owe much to Roman, Early Christian, and Byzantine art. Indeed, some evidence indicates they were the work of Byzantine mosaicists. Characteristically, temples, clusters of houses, trees, and rivers compose the pictorial fields, bounded by stylized vegetal designs also found in Roman, Early Christian, and Byzantine ornamentation. No zoomorphic forms, human or animal, appear either in the pictorial or ornamental spaces. This is true of all the mosaics in the Great Mosque as well as the mosaics in the earlier Dome of the Rock (FIG. 10-3). Although there is no prohibition against figural art in the Koran, Islamic tradition, based on the Hadith, shuns the representation of fauna of any kind in sacred places. Accompanying (but now lost) inscriptions explained the world shown in the Damascus mosaics, suspended miragelike in a featureless field of gold, as an image of Paradise. The imagery is consistent with many passages from the Koran describing the gorgeous places of Paradise awaiting the faithful—gardens, groves of trees, flowing streams, and "lofty chambers."

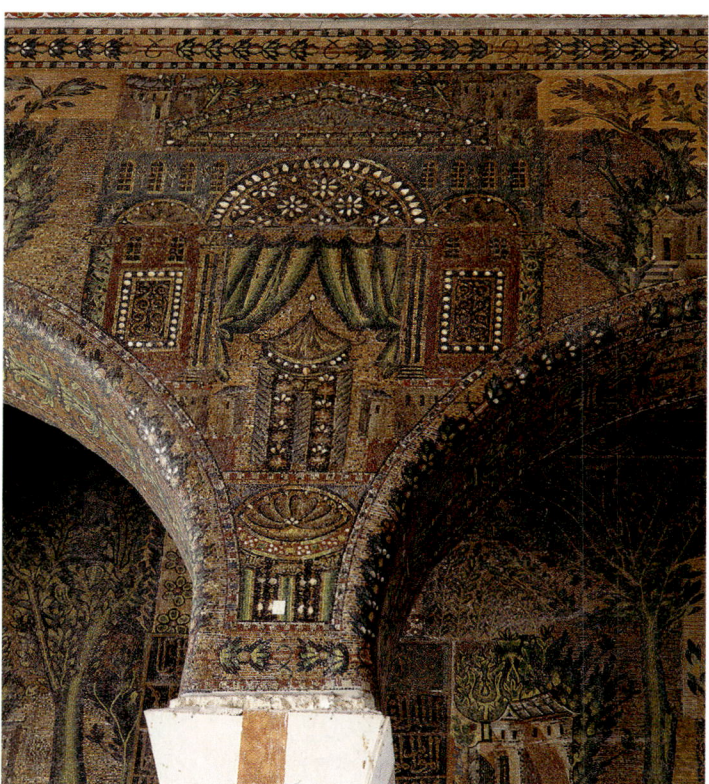

**10-5** Detail of a mosaic in the courtyard arcade of the Great Mosque, Damascus, Syria, 706–715.

The mosaics of the Great Mosque at Damascus are probably the work of Byzantine artists and include buildings and landscapes, though not zoomorphic forms, common in Late Antique art.

**BAGHDAD** The Umayyad caliphs maintained power for nearly a century, during which they constructed numerous palatial residences throughout their domains. Perhaps the most impressive was the palace (FIGS. 10-5A and 10-5B) at Mshatta in Jordan datable just before 750 when, after years of civil war, the Abbasids, who claimed descent from Abbas, an uncle of Muhammad, overthrew the Umayyad caliphs. The new rulers moved the capital from Damascus to a site in Iraq near the old Sasanian capital of Ctesiphon (FIG. 2-28). There the caliph al-Mansur (r. 754–775) established a new capital, Baghdad, which he called Madina al-Salam, the City of Peace. Laid out in 762 at a time astrologers determined was favor-

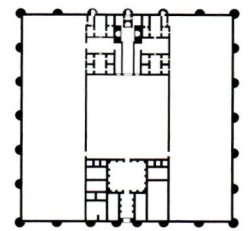

**10-5A** Plan, Umayyad palace, Mshatta, 740–750.

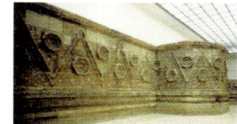

**10-5B** Frieze, Umayyad palace, Mshatta, 740–750.

able, Baghdad had a circular plan, about a mile and a half in diameter. The shape, which had precedents in ancient Assyria, Parthia, and Persia, signified the new capital was the center of the universe. The city had a moat and four gates oriented to the four compass points. At the center was the caliph's palace. No traces of al-Mansur's Round City remain today, but for almost 300 years, Baghdad was the hub of Arab power and of a brilliant Islamic culture. The Abbasid caliphs amassed great wealth and established diplomatic relations

# The Mosque

Islamic religious architecture is closely related to Muslim prayer, an obligation laid down in the Koran for all Muslims. In Islam, worshiping can be a private act and requires neither prescribed ceremony nor a special locale. Only the *qibla*—the direction (toward Mecca) Muslims face while praying—is important. But worship also became a communal act when the first Muslim community established a simple ritual for it. To celebrate the Muslim sabbath, which occurs on Friday, the community convened each Friday at noon, probably in the Prophet's house in Medina. The main feature of Muhammad's house was a large square court with rows of palm trunks supporting thatched roofs along the north and south sides. The southern side, which faced Mecca, was wider and had a double row of trunks. After the prayer, the *imam,* or leader of collective worship, stood on a stepped pulpit, or *minbar,* set up in front of the southern (qibla) wall, and preached the sermon.

These features became standard in the Islamic house of worship, the *mosque* (from Arabic "masjid," a place of prostration), where the faithful gather for the five daily prayers. The *congregational mosque* (also called the *Friday mosque* or *great mosque*) was ideally large enough to accommodate a community's entire population for the Friday noon prayer. An important feature both of ordinary mosques and of congregational mosques is the *mihrab* (FIG. 10-6, no. 2), a semicircular niche usually set into the qibla wall. Often a dome over the bay in front of the mihrab marked its position (FIGS. 10-4 and 10-6, no. 3). The niche was a familiar Greco-Roman architectural feature, generally enclosing a statue. Scholars still debate its origin, purpose, and meaning in Islamic architecture. The mihrab originally may have honored the place where the Prophet stood in his house at Medina when he led communal worship.

In some mosques, a *maqsura* precedes the mihrab. The maqsura, the area generally reserved for the ruler or his representative, can be quite elaborate in form (FIG. 10-11). Many mosques also have one or more *minarets* (FIGS. 10-4, 10-7, and 10-23), towers used to call the faithful to worship. When the Muslims converted buildings of other faiths into mosques, they clearly signaled the change on the exterior by the construction of minarets (FIG. 9-5). *Hypostyle halls,* communal worship halls with roofs held up by a multitude of columns (FIGS. 10-6, no. 4, and 10-10), are characteristic features of early mosques. Later variations include mosques with four *iwans* (vaulted rectangular recesses), one on each side of the courtyard (FIGS. 10-13 and 10-14), and *central-plan* mosques with a single large dome-covered interior space (FIGS. 10-23 and 10-24), as in Byzantine churches, some of which later became mosques (FIG. 9-8).

Today, despite many variations in design and detail (see, for example, the adobe-and-wood mosque in Mali, FIG. 19-9) and the employment of building techniques and materials unknown in Muhammad's day, the mosque's essential features remain unchanged. The orientation of all mosques everywhere, whatever their plan, is Mecca, and the faithful worship facing the qibla wall.

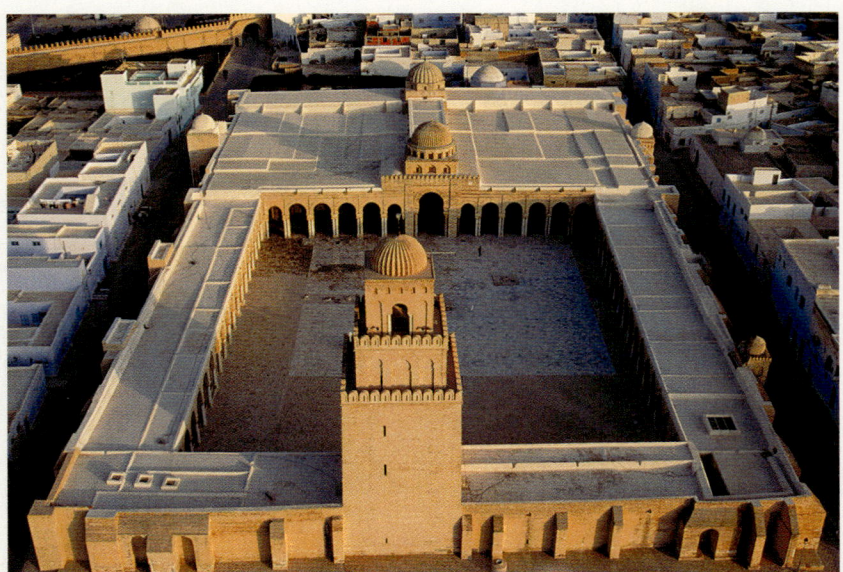

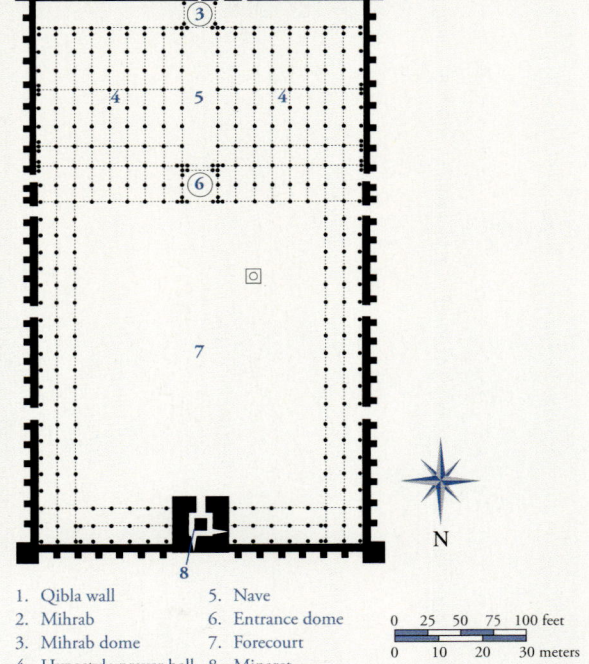

**10-6** Aerial view (looking south; *left*) and plan (*right*) of the Great Mosque, Kairouan, Tunisia, ca. 836–875. ◼◀

Kairouan's Great Mosque is a hypostyle mosque with forecourt and columnar prayer hall. The plan most closely resembles the layout of Muhammad's house in Medina.

1. Qibla wall
2. Mihrab
3. Mihrab dome
4. Hypostyle prayer hall
5. Nave
6. Entrance dome
7. Forecourt
8. Minaret

throughout the world, even with Charlemagne in Germany. They spent lavishly on art, literature, and science and were responsible for the translation of numerous Greek texts that otherwise would have been lost. In fact, many of these ancient works first became known in medieval Europe through their Arabic versions.

**GREAT MOSQUE, KAIROUAN** Several decades after the founding of Baghdad, the Abbasids constructed at Kairouan in Tunisia one of the best preserved early mosques (FIG. **10-6**). Of *hypostyle* design, it most closely reflects the mosque's supposed precursor, Muhammad's house in Medina (see "The Mosque," page 288). Still in use today, the Kairouan mosque retains its carved wooden minbar of 862, the oldest known. The precinct takes the form of a slightly askew parallelogram of huge scale, some 450 by 260 feet. Built of stone, its walls have sturdy buttresses, square in profile. Lateral entrances on the east and west lead to an arcaded forecourt (FIG. 10-6, no. 7) resembling a Roman forum (FIG. 7-44), oriented north-south on axis with the mosque's impressive minaret (no. 8) and the two domes of the hypostyle prayer hall (no. 4). The first dome (no. 6) is over the entrance bay, the second (no. 3) over the bay that fronts the mihrab (no. 2) set into the *qibla* wall (no. 1). A raised nave (no. 5) connects the domed spaces and prolongs the north-south axis of the minaret and courtyard. Eight columned aisles flank the nave on either side, providing space for a large congregation.

**MALWIYA MINARET, SAMARRA** The three-story minaret of the Kairouan mosque is square in plan and believed to be a near-copy of a Roman lighthouse, but minarets take a variety of forms. Perhaps the most striking and novel is the minaret of the immense (more than 45,000 square yards) Great Mosque at Samarra, Iraq, on the east bank of the Tigris River north of Baghdad. Samarra was the capital of the Abbasid caliph al-Mutawakkil (r. 847–861), who built the mosque between 848 and 852. At the time of its construction the Samarra mosque was the largest in the world. Known as the Malwiya ("snail shell" in Arabic) Minaret (FIG. **10-7**), it is more than 165 feet tall. Although it now stands alone, originally a bridge linked the minaret to the mosque. The distinguishing feature of the brick tower is its stepped spiral ramp, which increases in slope from bottom to top. Once thought to be an ancient Mesopotamian *ziggurat*, the Samarra minaret inspired some European depictions of the biblical Tower of Babel (Babylon's ziggurat; see "Babylon, City of Wonders," Chapter 2, page 49). Because it is too tall to have been used to call Muslims to prayer, the Abbasids probably intended the Malwiya Minaret, visible from a considerable distance in the flat plain around Samarra, to announce the presence of Islam in the Tigris Valley. Unfortunately, since 2005 the minaret has suffered damage at the hands of various parties during the continuing unrest in Iraq.

**SAMANID MAUSOLEUM, BUKHARA** Dynasties of governors who exercised considerable independence while recognizing the ultimate authority of the Baghdad caliphs oversaw the eastern realms of the Abbasid Empire. One of these dynasties, the Samanids (r. 819–1005), presided over the eastern frontier beyond the Oxus River (Transoxiana) on the border with India. In the early 10th century, the Samanids erected an impressive domed brick mausoleum (FIG. **10-8**) at Bukhara in modern Uzbekistan. Monumental tombs were virtually unknown in the early Islamic period. Muhammad had been opposed to elaborate burials and instructed his followers to bury him in a simple unmarked grave. In time, however, the

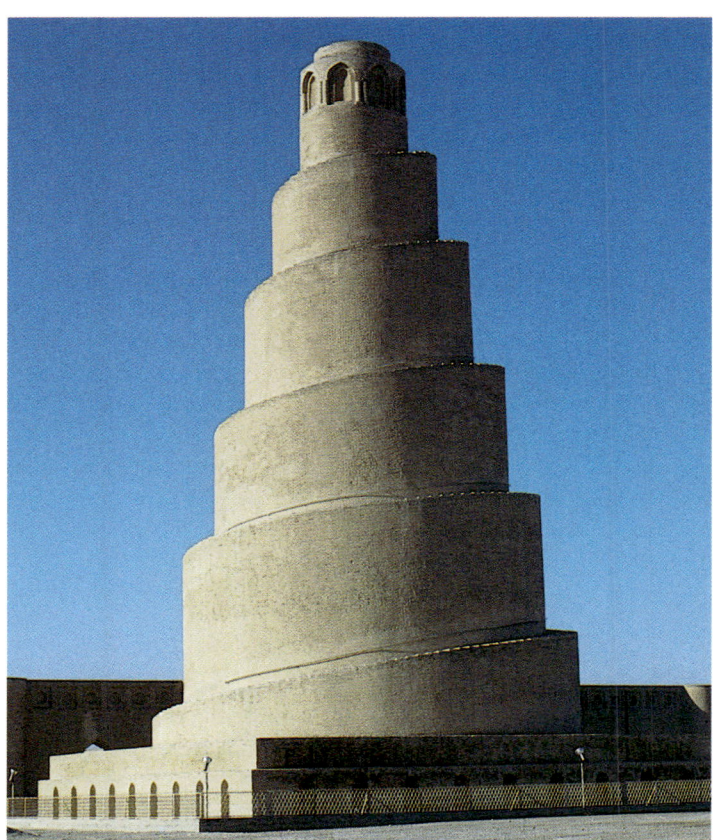

**10-7** Malwiya Minaret, Great Mosque, Samarra, Iraq, 848–852.

The unique spiral Malwiya (snail shell) Minaret of Samarra's Great Mosque is more than 165 feet tall and can be seen from afar. It served to announce the presence of Islam in the Tigris Valley.

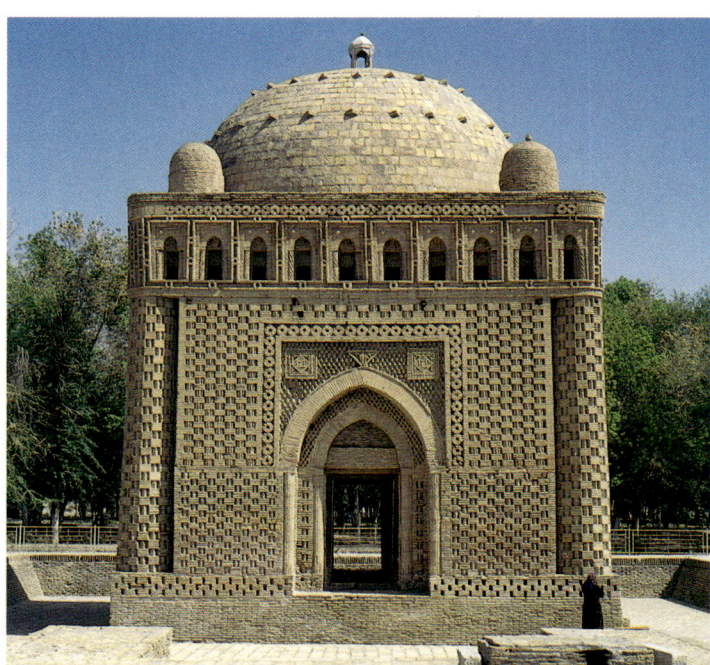

**10-8** Mausoleum of the Samanids, Bukhara, Uzbekistan, early 10th century.

Monumental tombs were almost unknown in the early Islamic period. The Samanid mausoleum at Bukhara is one of the oldest. Its dome-on-cube form had a long afterlife in Islamic funerary architecture.

**10-9** Prayer hall of the Mezquita (Great Mosque), Córdoba, Spain, 8th to 10th centuries.

Córdoba was the capital of the Spanish Umayyad dynasty. In the Great Mosque's hypostyle prayer hall, 36 piers and 514 columns support a unique series of double-tiered horseshoe-shaped arches.

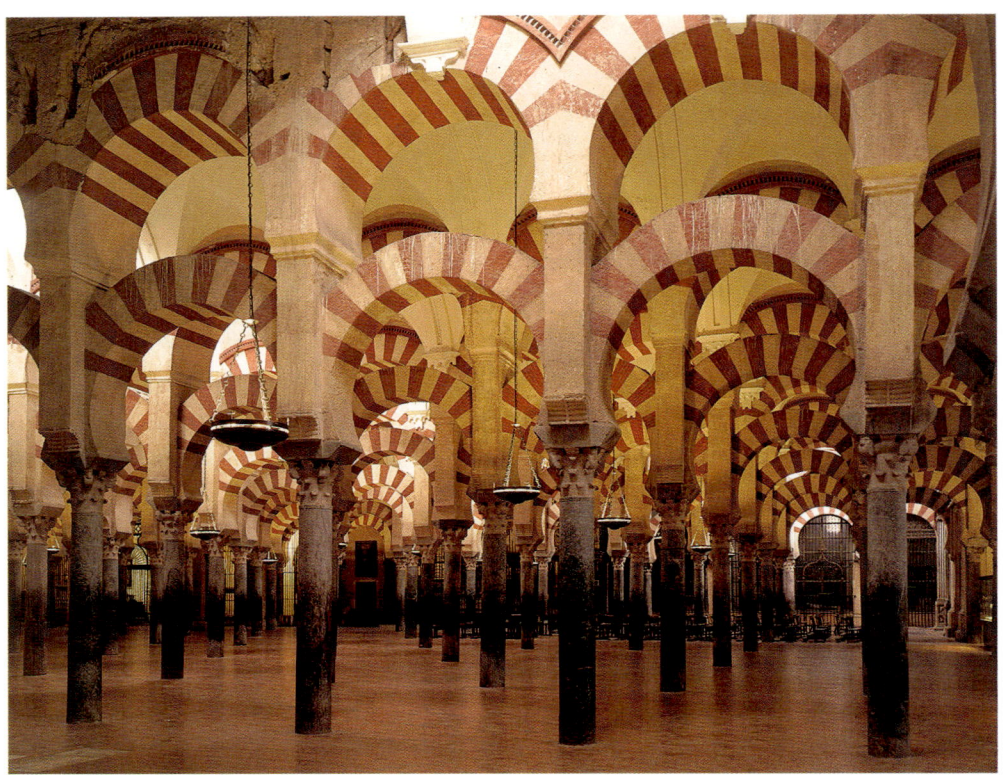

Prophet's resting place in Medina acquired a wooden screen and a dome. By the ninth century, Abbasid caliphs were laid to rest in dynastic mausoleums.

The Samanid mausoleum at Bukhara is one of the earliest preserved tombs in the Islamic world. Constructed of baked bricks, it takes the form of a dome-capped cube with slightly sloping sides. With exceptional skill, the builders painstakingly shaped the bricks to create a vivid and varied surface pattern. Some of the bricks form *engaged columns* (half-round, attached columns) at the corners. A brick *blind arcade* (a series of arches in relief, with blocked openings) runs around all four sides. Inside, the walls are as elaborate as the exterior. The brick dome rests on arcuated brick squinches (see "Pendentives and Squinches," Chapter 9, page 262) framed by engaged *colonnettes* (thin columns). The dome-on-cube form had a long and distinguished future in Islamic funerary architecture (FIGS. 10-22 and 32-6).

**GREAT MOSQUE, CÓRDOBA** At the opposite end of the Muslim world, Abd al-Rahman I (r. 756–788), the only Umayyad notable to escape the Abbasid massacre of his clan in Syria, fled to Spain in 750. There, the Arabs had overthrown the Christian kingdom of the Visigoths in 711 (see Chapter 11). The Arab military governors accepted the fugitive as their overlord, and he founded the Spanish Umayyad dynasty, which lasted nearly three centuries. The capital of the Spanish Umayyads was Córdoba, which became the center of a brilliant culture rivaling that of the Abbasids at Baghdad and exerting major influence on the civilization of the Christian West.

The jewel of the capital at Córdoba was its Great Mosque (FIG. 10-1), begun in 784 by Abd al-Rahman I and enlarged

several times during the 9th and 10th centuries. Córdoba's Mezquita eventually became one of the largest mosques in the Islamic West. The hypostyle prayer hall (FIG. 10-9) has 36 piers and 514 columns topped by a unique system of double-tiered arches that carried a wooden roof (later replaced by vaults). The two-story system was the builders' response to the need to raise the roof to an acceptable height using short columns that had been employed earlier in other structures. The lower arches are horseshoe-shaped, a form perhaps adapted from earlier Mesopotamian architecture or

**10-10** Detail of the upper zones of the east gate of the Mezquita (Great Mosque), Córdoba, Spain, 961–965.

The caliph al-Hakam II expanded and renovated Córdoba's Mezquita. The new gates to the complex feature intricate surface patterns of overlapping horseshoe-shaped and multilobed arches.

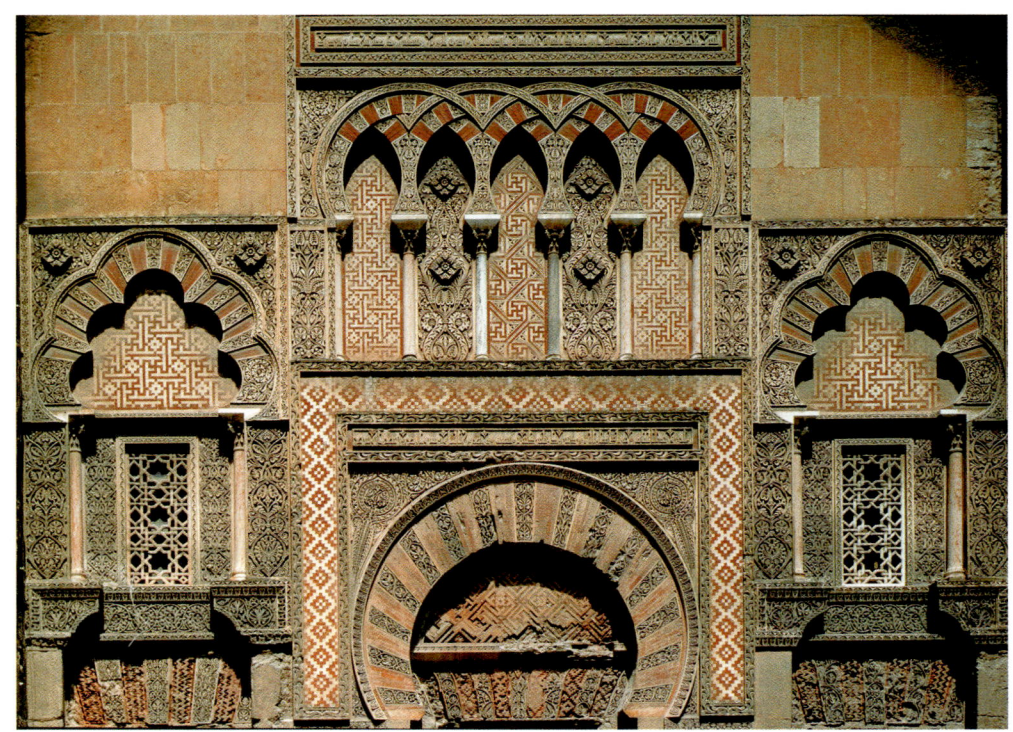

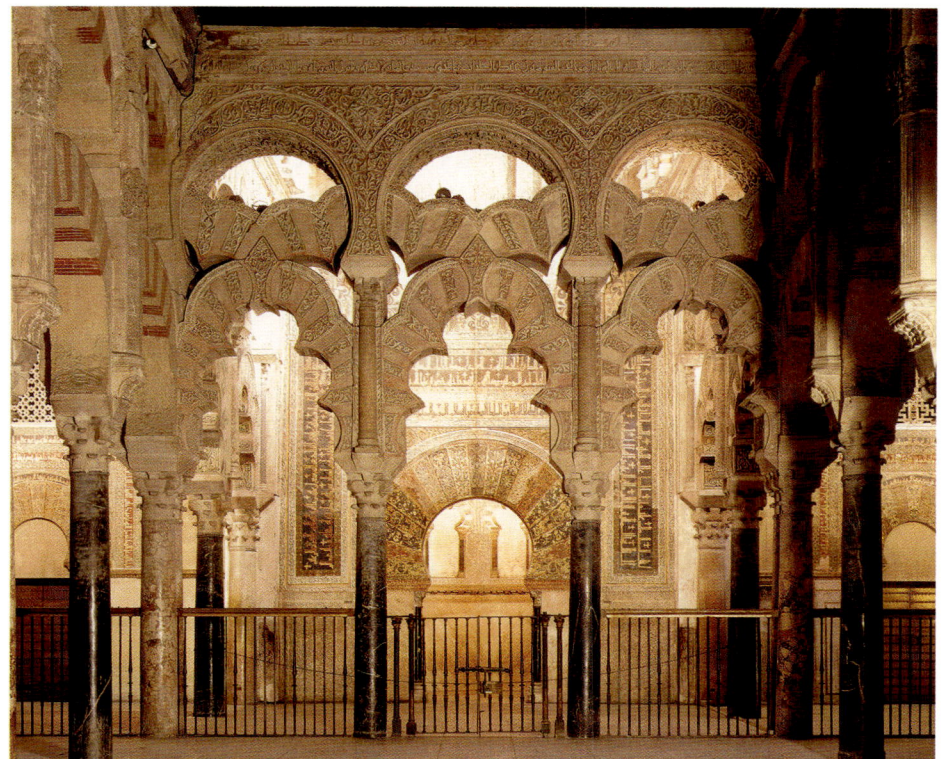

Reserved for the caliph, the maqsura of the Córdoba mosque connected the mosque to his palace. It is a prime example of Islamic experimentation with highly decorative multilobed arches.

of Visigothic origin (FIG. 11-10). In the West, the horseshoe arch quickly became closely associated with Muslim architecture. Visually, these arches seem to billow out like windblown sails, and they contribute greatly to the light and airy effect of the Córdoba mosque's interior.

In 961, al-Hakam II (r. 961–976) became caliph. A learned man who amassed a library of 400,000 volumes, he immediately undertook major renovations to the mosque. His builders expanded the prayer hall, added a series of domes, and constructed monumental gates on the complex's eastern (FIG. 10-10) and western facades. The gates are noteworthy for their colorful masonry and intricate surface patterns, especially in the uppermost zone, with its series of overlapping horseshoe-shaped arches springing from delicate colonnettes.

Also dating to the caliphate of al-Hakam II is the mosque's extraordinary maqsura (FIG. 10-11), the area reserved for the caliph and connected to his palace by a corridor in the qibla wall. The Córdoba maqsura is a prime example of Islamic experimentation with highly decorative multilobed arches (which are subsidiary motifs in the contemporaneous gate, FIG. 10-10). The Muslim builders created rich and varied abstract patterns and further enhanced the magnificent effect of the complex arches by sheathing the walls with marbles and mosaics. Al-Hakam II wished to emulate the great mosaic-clad monuments his Umayyad predecessors had erected in Jerusalem (FIG. 10-3) and Damascus (FIG. 10-5), and he brought the mosaicists and even the *tesserae* (cubical pieces) to Córdoba from Constantinople.

The same desire for decorative effect also inspired the design of the dome (FIG. 10-12) covering the area in front of the mihrab, one of the four domes built during the 10th century to emphasize the axis leading to the mihrab. The dome rests on an octagonal base of arcuated squinches. Crisscrossing ribs form an intricate pattern centered on two squares set at 45-degree angles to each other. The mosaics are the work of the same Byzantine artists responsible for the maqsura's decoration.

**FRIDAY MOSQUE, ISFAHAN** Muslim rulers built mosques of the hypostyle type throughout their realms during the early centuries of the new religion, but other mosque plans gradually gained favor in certain regions (see "The Mosque," page 288). At Isfahan, the third-largest city in Iran today, the Abbasids constructed the first mosque

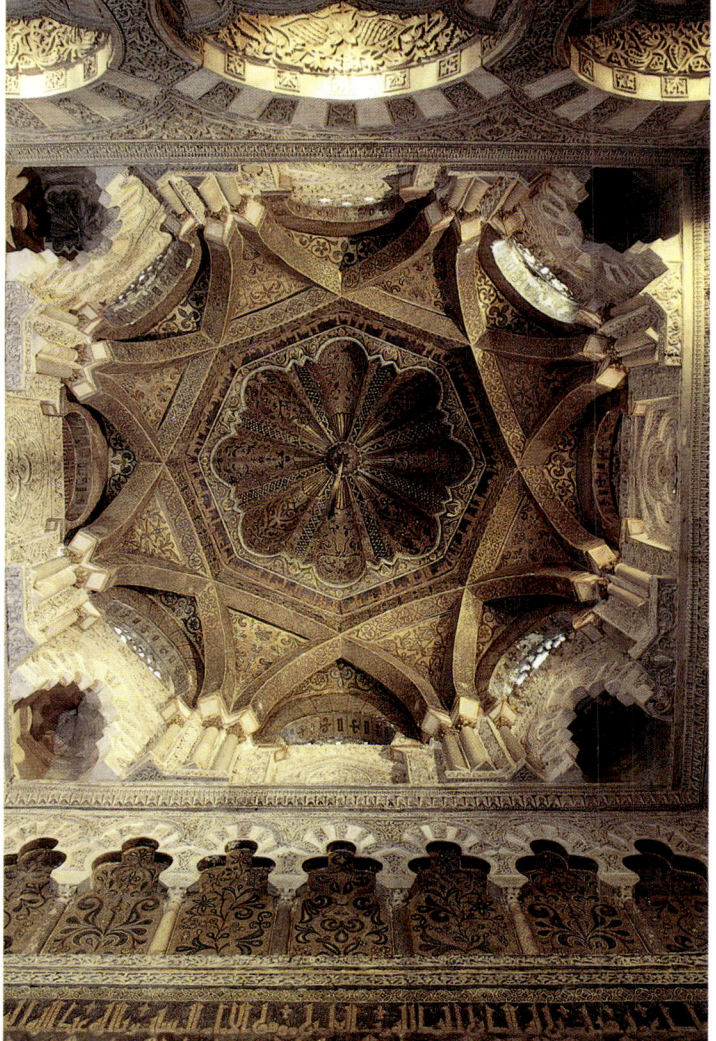

10-12 Dome in front of the mihrab of the Mezquita (Great Mosque), Córdoba, Spain, 961–965.

The dome in front of the Córdoba mihrab rests on an octagonal base of arcuated squinches. Crisscrossing ribs form an intricate decorative pattern. Byzantine artists fashioned the mosaic ornamentation.

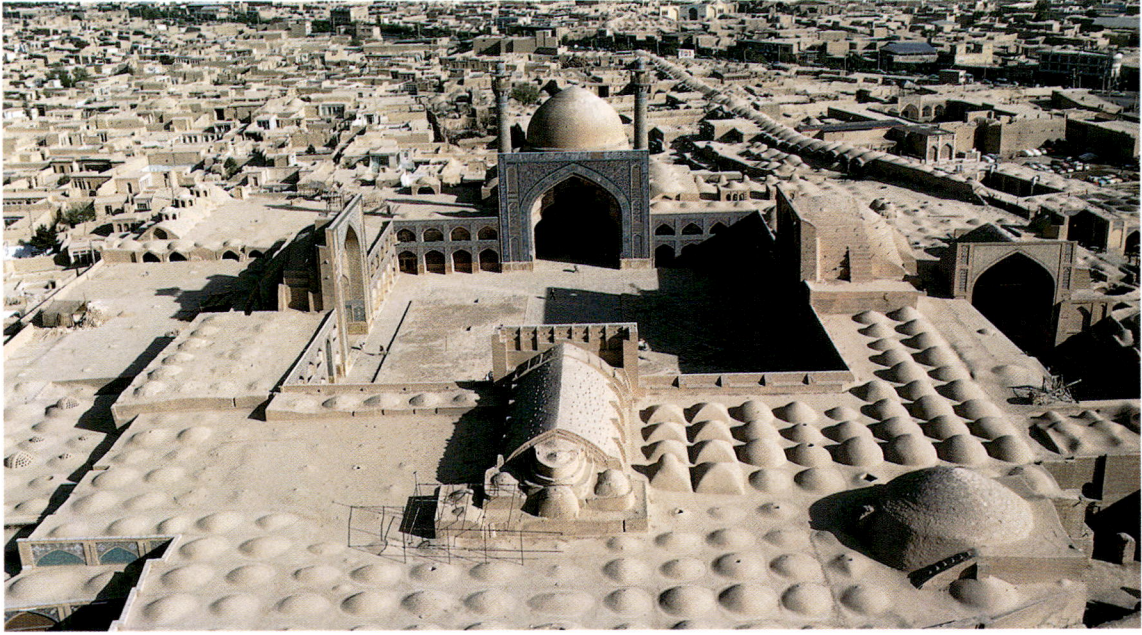

**10-13** Aerial view (looking southwest) of the Friday Mosque, Isfahan, Iran, 11th to 17th centuries. ◼◀

The typical Iranian mosque plan with four vaulted iwans and a courtyard was perhaps first used in the mosque Sultan Malik Shah I built in the late 11th century at his capital of Isfahan.

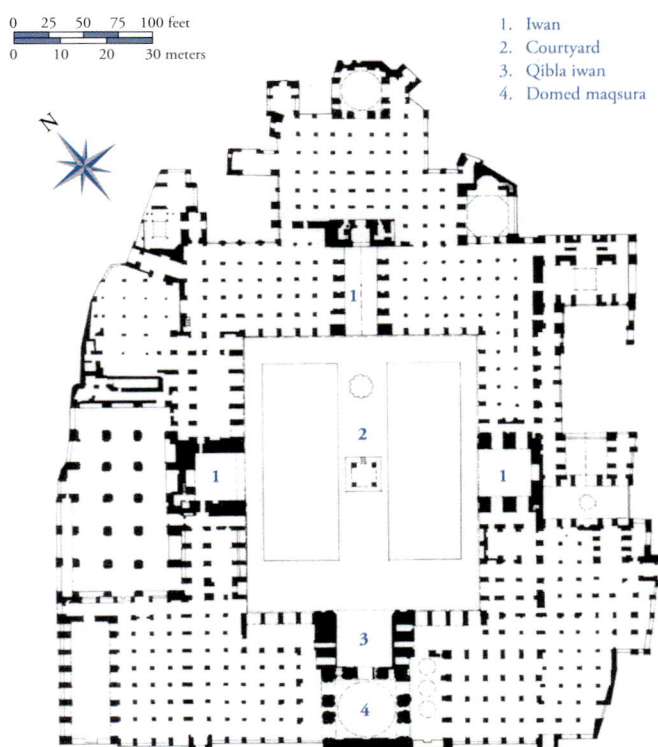

| | |
|---|---|
| 0   25   50   75   100 feet | 1. Iwan |
| 0    10    20    30 meters | 2. Courtyard |
| | 3. Qibla iwan |
| | 4. Domed maqsura |

**10-14** Plan of the Friday Mosque, Isfahan, Iran, 11th to 17th centuries.

In Isfahan's Friday Mosque, as in other four-iwan mosques, the qibla iwan is the largest. Its size and the dome-covered maqsura in front of it indicated the proper direction to face for Muslim prayer.

of hypostyle design in that formerly Sasanian city during the eighth century. In the 11th century, the Seljuks, a Turkic people who had converted to Islam, built an extensive, although short-lived empire that stretched eastward from Anatolia and included Iran. At that time, the Seljuk *sultan* (ruler) Malik Shah I (r. 1072–1092) made Isfahan his capital and transformed the Abbasid mosque in stages.

The Seljuk Friday Mosque (FIGS. **10-13** and **10-14**) underwent further modification over subsequent centuries, but still retains its basic 11th-century plan, consisting of a large courtyard bordered by a two-story arcade on each side. Four vaulted iwans open onto the courtyard, one at the center of each side. The southwestern iwan (FIG. 10-14, no. 3) leads into a dome-covered room (no. 4) in front of the mihrab that functioned as a maqsura reserved for the sultan and his attendants. It is uncertain whether Isfahan's Friday Mosque is the earliest example of a four-iwan mosque, but that plan became standard in Iranian religious architecture. In this type of mosque, the qibla iwan is always the largest. Its size (and the dome that often accompanied it) immediately indicated to worshipers the proper direction for prayer.

## Luxury Arts

The furnishings of Islamic mosques and palaces reflect a love of sumptuous materials and rich decorative patterns. Muslim artisans artfully worked ivory (FIG. 10-15), metal, wood, and glass into a great variety of objects for sacred spaces or the home. They used colored glass with striking effect in mosque lamps (FIG. 10-28) and produced ceramics (FIG. 10-18) of high quality in large numbers. Muslim metalworkers created elaborate ewers (FIG. 10-16), basins (FIG. 10-31), jewel cases, writing boxes, and other portable items (FIG. 10-32) made of bronze or brass, engraved, and inlaid with silver. Weavers employed silk (FIGS. **10-14A** and 10-26A) and wool (FIG. 10-27) to fashion textiles featuring both abstract and pictorial motifs. Because wood is scarce in most of the Islamic world, the kinds of furniture used in the West—beds, tables, and chairs—are rare in Muslim buildings. Movable furnishings, therefore, do not define Islamic architectural spaces. A room's function (eating or sleeping, for example) can change simply by rearranging the carpets and cushions.

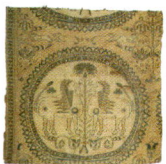

**10-14A** Silk textile, from Zandana, eighth century.

**IVORY** The centers of production for these luxurious art forms were usually the courts of the Muslim caliphs and sultans. One

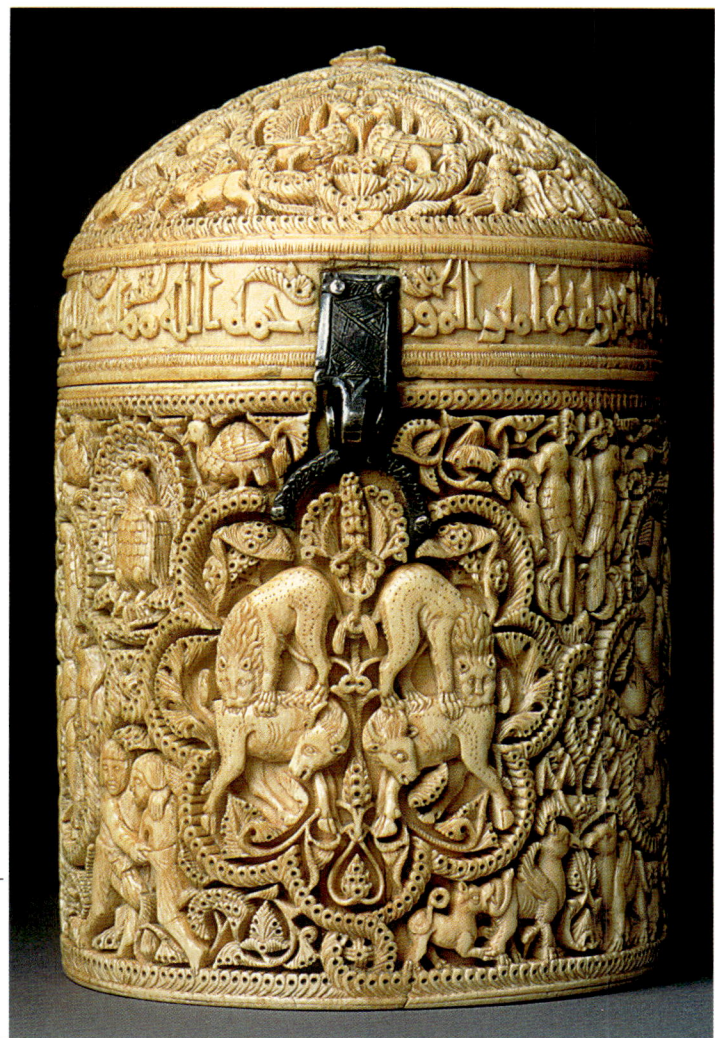

1 in.

**10-15** Pyxis of al-Mughira, from Medina al-Zahra, near Córdoba, Spain, 968. Ivory, $5\frac{7}{8}''$ high. Musée du Louvre, Paris.

The royal workshops of Abd al-Rahman III produced luxurious objects such as this ivory pyxis decorated with hunting motifs and vine scrolls. It belonged to al-Mughira, the caliph's younger son.

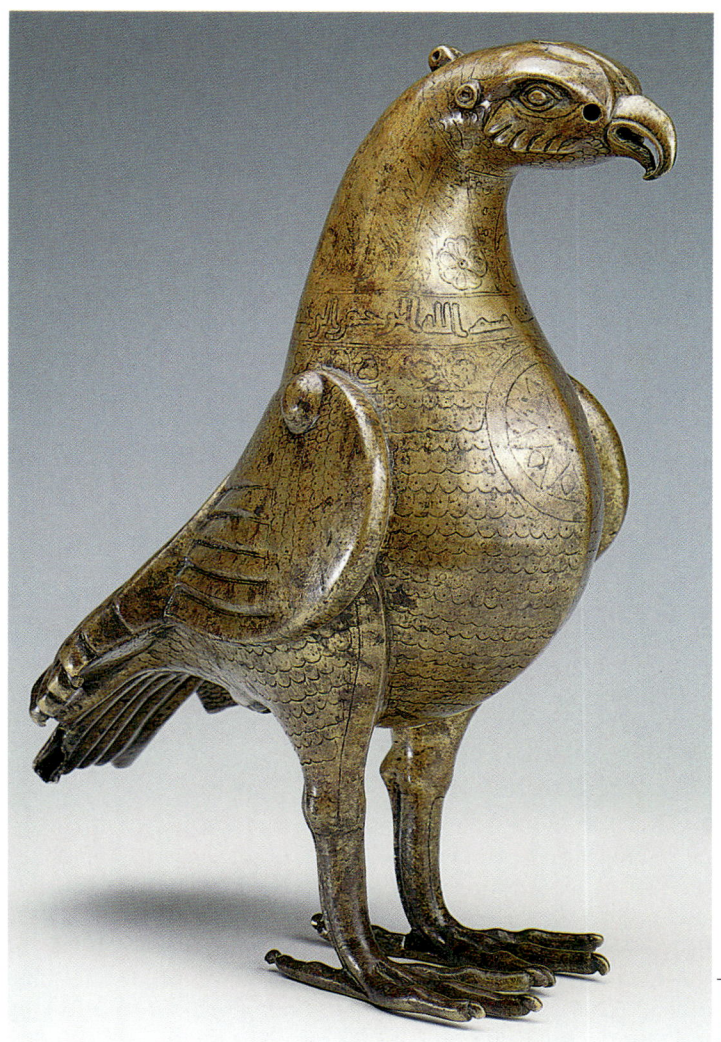

1 in.

**10-16** SULAYMAN, Ewer in the form of a bird, 796. Brass with silver and copper inlay, 1′ 3″ high. Hermitage, Saint Petersburg.

Signed and dated by its maker, this bird ewer resembles a freestanding statuette. The engraved decoration of the body combines natural feathers with abstract motifs and Arabic calligraphy.

was Córdoba (FIGS. 10-1 and 10-9 to 10-12). Abd al-Rahman III (r. 912–961), a descendant of the founder of the Umayyad dynasty in Spain, became *emir* (ruler) when he was 22. In 929, he declared himself caliph, a title previously restricted to the Muslim rulers who controlled the holy cities of Mecca and Medina. During his nearly 50-year reign, he constructed a lavish new palace for himself and his successors at Medina al-Zahra, about five miles from Córdoba. The palace complex housed royal workshops for the production of luxury items for the caliph's family and for use as diplomatic gifts, including richly carved ivory boxes (FIG. 10-15). Befitting their prospective owners, Spanish Umayyad ivory *pyxides* (singular, *pyxis;* a cylindrical box with a hemispherical lid) usually featured motifs symbolic of royal power and privilege, including hunting scenes and musical entertainments.

The pyxis shown here (FIG. 10-15) belonged to al-Mughira, the younger son of Abd al-Rahman III. The inscription carved at the base of the lid is a prayer for the 18-year-old prince's well-being: "God's blessing, favors, and happiness to al-Mughira, son of the commander of the faithful, may God have mercy upon him,

in the year 357 [968 CE]." The anonymous ivory carver decorated the pyxis with a rich array of animals and hunters amid lush vine scrolls surrounding four eight-lobed figural medallions. In one medallion, lions attack bulls. In another (not visible in FIG. 10-15), the prince himself appears, serenaded by a lutenist.

**METALWORK** One striking example of early Islamic metalwork is the cast brass ewer (FIG. 10-16) in the form of a bird signed by SULAYMAN and dated 796. Some 15 inches tall, the ewer is nothing less than a freestanding statuette, although the holes between the eyes and beak function as a spout and betray its utilitarian purpose. The decoration on the body, which bears traces of silver and copper inlay, takes a variety of forms. In places, the incised lines seem to suggest natural feathers, but the rosettes on the neck, the large medallions on the breast, and the inscribed collar have no basis in anatomy. Similar motifs appear in Islamic textiles, pottery, and architectural tiles. The ready adaptability of motifs to various scales and to various techniques illustrates both the flexibility of Islamic design and its relative independence from its carrier.

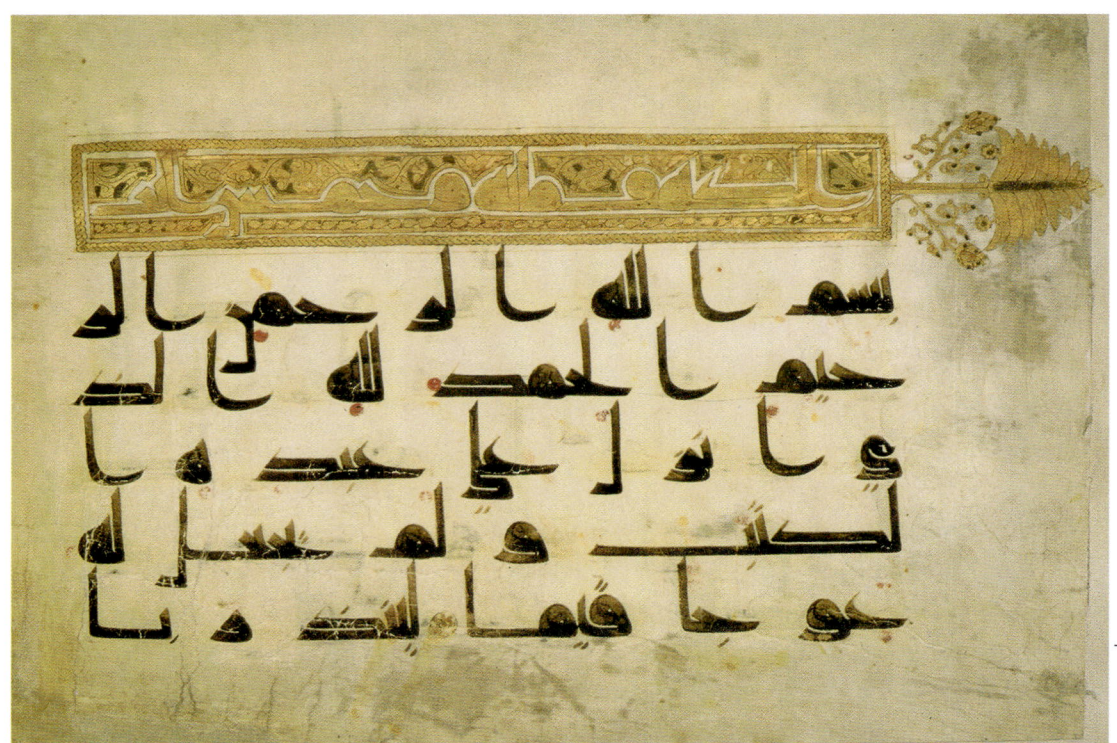

**10-17** Koran page with beginning of surah 18, 9th or early 10th century. Ink and gold on vellum, $7\frac{1}{4}'' \times 10\frac{1}{4}''$. Chester Beatty Library and Oriental Art Gallery, Dublin.

The script used in the oldest-known Korans is the stately rectilinear Kufic. This page has five text lines and a palm-tree finial but characteristically does not include depictions of animals or humans.

1 in.

**KORANS** In the Islamic world, the art of *calligraphy*, ornamental writing, held a place of honor. The faithful wanted to reproduce the Koran's sacred words in a script as beautiful as human hands could contrive. Passages from the Koran adorned not only the fragile pages of books but also the walls of buildings—for example, in the mosaic band above the outer ring of columns inside the Dome of the Rock (FIG. 10-3). The practice of calligraphy was itself a holy task and required long, arduous training. The scribe had to possess exceptional spiritual refinement. An ancient Arabic proverb proclaims, "Purity of writing is purity of soul." Only in China does calligraphy hold as elevated a position among the arts (see "Calligraphy and Inscriptions on Chinese Paintings," Chapter 33, page 997).

Arabic script predates Islam. It is written from right to left with certain characters connected by a baseline. Although the codification of the chief Islamic book, the sacred Koran, occurred in the mid-seventh century, the earliest preserved Korans date to the ninth century. Koran pages were either bound into books or stored as loose sheets in boxes. Most of the early examples feature texts written in the script form called *Kufic*, after the city of Kufa, one of the renowned centers of Arabic calligraphy. Kufic script—used also for the inscription on al-Mughira's 10th-century pyxis (FIG. 10-15)—is quite angular, with the uprights forming almost right angles with the baseline. As with Hebrew and other Semitic languages, the usual practice was to write in consonants only. But to facilitate recitation of the Koran, scribes often indicated vowels by red or yellow symbols above or below the line.

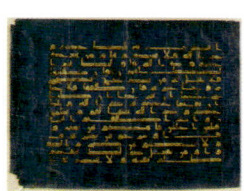

**10-17A** *Blue Koran,* from Kairouan, 9th to mid-10th century.

All of these features are present in a 9th- or early-10th-century Koran page (FIG. **10-17**) now in Dublin and in the blue-dyed page (FIG. **10-17A**) of a contemporaneous Koran now at Harvard University. The Dublin page carries the heading and opening lines of surah 18 of the Koran. The five text lines are in black ink with red vowels below a decorative band incorporating the chapter title in gold and ending in a palm-tree *finial* (a crowning ornament). This approach to page design has parallels at the extreme northwestern corner of the then-known world—in the early medieval manuscripts of Britain and Ireland, where text and ornamentation are similarly united (FIG. 11-1). But the stylized human and animal forms that populate those Christian books never appear in Korans.

**CERAMICS** Around the same time, potters in Nishapur in Iran and in Samarqand in Uzbekistan developed a simple but elegant type of glazed dish with calligraphic decoration. One of the best-preserved examples of *Samarqand ware* is a large dish (FIG. **10-18**) from the Nishapur region in Khurasan province of northeastern Iran. To produce dishes such as this, the ceramists formed the shape from the local dark pink clay and then immersed the dish in a tub of white slip. When the slip dried, a painter-calligrapher wrote a Kufic text in black or brown paint around the flat rim of the dish, usually, as here, extending the angular letters both horizontally and vertically to create a circular border and to fill the full width of the rim. A transparent glaze, applied last, sealed the decoration and, after firing, gave the dish an attractive sheen.

The text on this dish is an Arabic proverb, which reads: "Knowledge is bitter-tasting at first, but in the end it is sweeter than honey. Good health [to the owner of this dish]." Because the Arabic words are so similar, recently some scholars have translated "knowledge" as "magnanimity." In either case, this and similar proverbs with practical advice for secular life would have appealed to cultured individuals such as successful merchants. The proverb's reference to food is, of course, highly appropriate for the decoration of tableware.

## LATER ISLAMIC ART

In 1192, a Muslim army under the command of Muhammad of Ghor won a decisive battle at Tarain, which led to the formation in 1206 of an Islamic sultanate at Delhi and eventually to the greatest Muslim

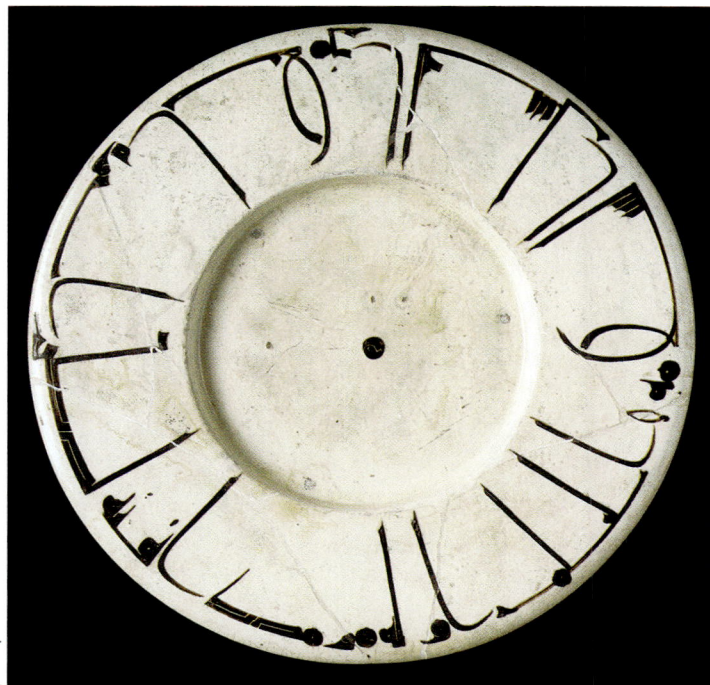

1 in.

**10-18** Dish with Arabic proverb, from Nishapur, Iran, 10th century. Painted and glazed earthenware, 1′ 2½″ diameter. Musée du Louvre, Paris.

An Arabic proverb in Kufic calligraphy is the sole decoration of this dish made for a cultured owner. It states that knowledge, although bitter at first taste, is ultimately sweeter than honey.

empire in Asia, the Mughal Empire. But no sooner did the Muslims establish a permanent presence in South Asia than the Mongols, who had invaded northern China in 1210 (see Chapter 33), overthrew the Abbasid caliphs in Central Asia and Persia. Isfahan fell to the Mongols in 1236, Baghdad in 1258, and Damascus in 1260. Islamic art continued to flourish, however, and important new regional artistic centers emerged. The rest of this chapter treats the art and architecture of the Nasrids (1232–1492) in Spain, the Ayyubids (1171–1250) and Mamluks (1250–1517) in Egypt, the Timurids (1370–1501) and Safavids (1501–1732) in Iran, and the Ottomans (1281–1924) in Turkey. For Islamic art in South Asia, see Chapter 32.

## Architecture

In the early years of the 11th century, the Umayyad caliphs' power in Spain unraveled, and their palaces fell prey to Berber soldiers from North Africa. The Berbers ruled southern Spain for several generations but could not resist the pressure of Christian forces from the north. Córdoba fell to the Christians in 1236, the same year the Mongols captured Isfahan. From then until the final Christian triumph in 1492, the Nasrids, an Arab dynasty that had established its capital at Granada in 1232, ruled the remaining Muslim territories in Spain.

**ALHAMBRA** On a rocky spur at Granada, the Nasrids constructed a huge palace-fortress called the Alhambra ("the Red" in Arabic), named for the rose color of the stone used for its walls and 23 towers. By the end of the 14th century, the complex had a population of 40,000 and included at least a half dozen royal residences. Only two of these fared well over the centuries. Paradoxically, they owe their preservation to the Christian victors, who maintained a few of the buildings as trophies commemorating the expulsion of the Nasrids. The two palaces present a vivid picture of court life in Islamic Spain before the Christian reconquest.

The Palace of the Lions takes its name from its courtyard (FIG. **10-19**), which contains a fountain with 12 marble lions carrying a water basin on their backs. Colonnaded courtyards with fountains and statues have a long history in the Mediterranean world, especially in the houses and villas of the Roman Empire (FIG. 7-16A). The Alhambra's lion fountain is an unusual instance of freestanding stone sculpture in the Islamic world, unthinkable in a sacred setting. But the design of the courtyard is distinctly Islamic and features many multilobed pointed arches and lavish stuccoed walls with interwoven abstract motifs and Arabic calligraphy. The palace was the residence of Muhammad V (r. 1354–1391), and its courtyards, lush gardens, and luxurious carpets and other furnishings served to conjure the image of Paradise.

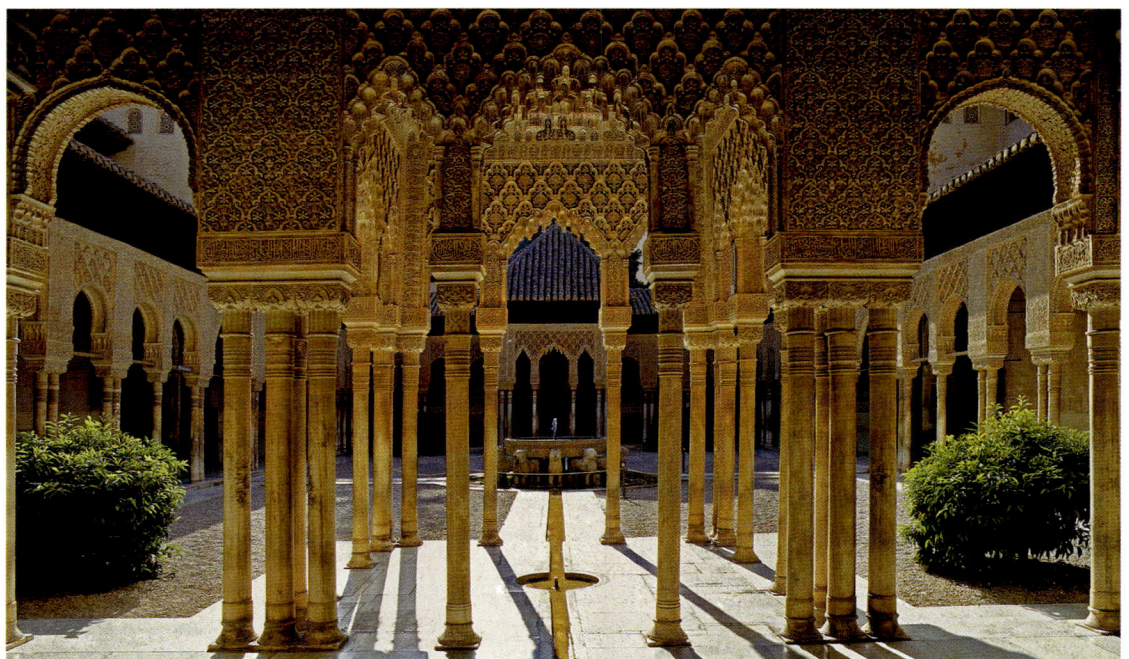

**10-19** Court of the Lions (looking east), Palace of the Lions, Alhambra, Granada, Spain, 1354–1391.

The Nasrid Palace of the Lions takes its name from the fountain in this courtyard, a rare Islamic example of stone sculpture. Interwoven abstract ornamentation and Arabic calligraphy cover the stucco walls.

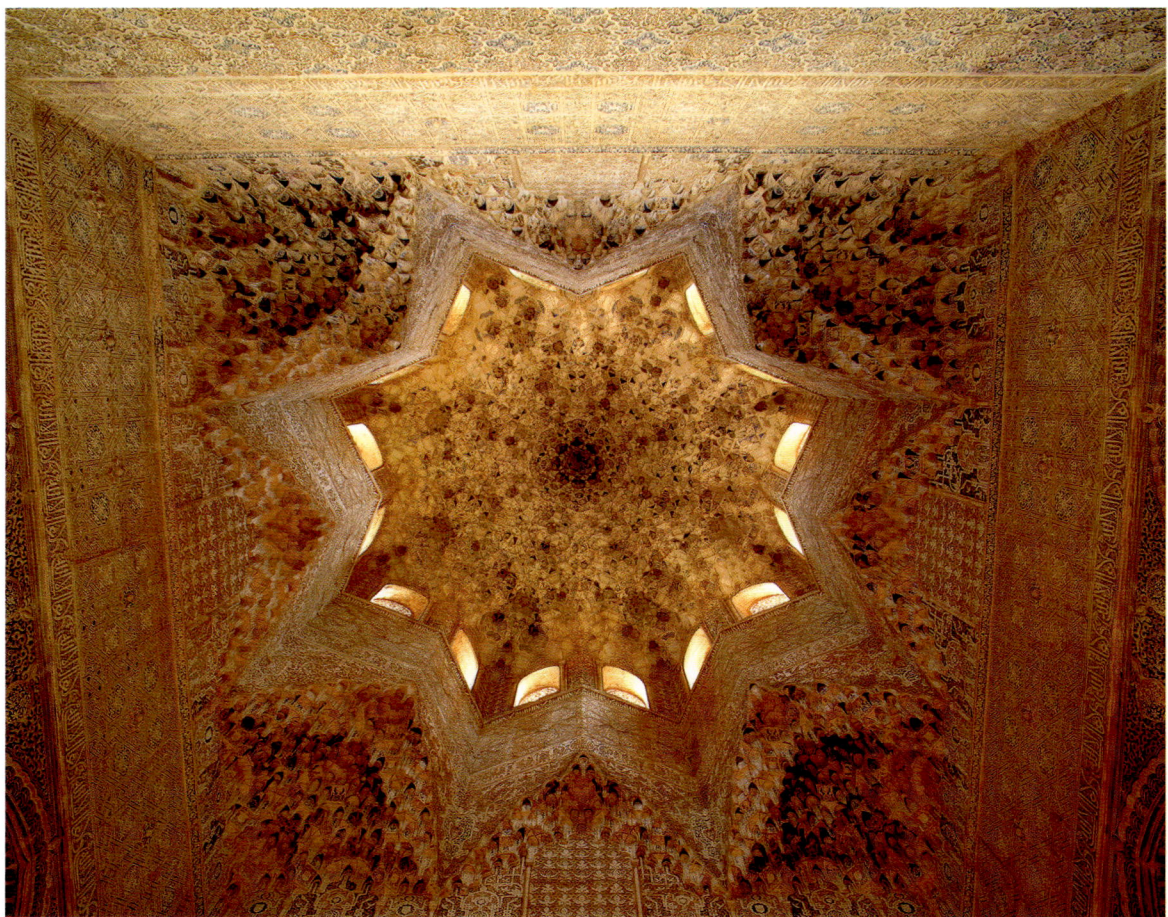

**10-20** Muqarnas dome, Hall of the Abencerrajes, Palace of the Lions, Alhambra, Granada, Spain, 1354–1391.

The structure of this dome on an octagonal drum is difficult to discern because of the intricately carved stucco muqarnas. The prismatic forms reflect sunlight, creating the effect of a starry sky.

The Palace of the Lions is noteworthy also for its elaborate stucco ceilings. A spectacular example is the dome (FIG. **10-20**) of the Hall of the Abencerrajes (a leading Spanish family). The dome rests on an octagonal drum supported by squinches and pierced by eight pairs of windows, but its structure is difficult to discern because of the intricate carved stucco decoration. Some 5,000 *muqarnas*—tier after tier of stalactite-like prismatic forms that seem aimed at denying the structure's solidity—cover the ceiling. The muqarnas catch and reflect sunlight as well as form beautiful abstract patterns. The lofty vault in this hall and others in the palace symbolize the dome of Heaven. The flickering light and shadows create the effect of a starry sky as the sun's rays glide from window to window during the day. To underscore the symbolism, the palace walls bear inscriptions with verses by the court poet Ibn Zamrak (1333–1393), who compared the Alhambra's lacelike muqarnas ceilings to "the heavenly spheres whose orbits revolve."

**MAUSOLEUM OF SULTAN HASAN** After the Mongol conquests, the center of Islamic power moved from Baghdad to Egypt. The lords of Egypt at the time were former Turkish slaves ("mamluks" in Arabic) who converted to Islam. The capital of the Mamluk sultans was Cairo, which became the largest Muslim city of the late Middle Ages. The Mamluks were prolific builders, and Sultan Hasan, although not an important figure in Islamic history, was the most ambitious of all. He ruled briefly as a child and was deposed but regained the sultanate from 1354 until his assassination in 1361.

Hasan's major building project in Cairo was a huge madrasa complex (FIGS. **10-21** and **10-22**) on a plot of land about 8,000 square yards in area. A *madrasa* ("place of study" in Arabic) is a theological college devoted to the teaching of Islamic law. Hasan's complex was so large it housed not only four madrasas for the study of the four major schools of Islamic law but also a mosque, mausoleum, orphanage, and hospital, as well as shops and baths. Like all Islamic building complexes incorporating religious, educational, and charitable functions, this one depended on an endowment funded by rental properties. The income from these paid the salaries of attendants and faculty, provided furnishings and supplies such as oil for the lamps or free food for the poor, and supported scholarships for needy students.

The grandiose structure has a large central courtyard (FIG. 10-21, no. 5) with a monumental fountain in the center and four vaulted iwans opening onto it, as in Iranian mosques (FIG. 10-14). In each corner of the main courtyard, between the iwans (FIG. 10-21, no. 3), is a madrasa (no. 4) with its own courtyard and four or five stories of rooms for the students. The largest iwan (no. 2) in the complex, on the southern side, served as a mosque. Contemporaries believed the soaring vault that covered this iwan was taller than the arch of the Sasanian palace (FIG. 2-28) at Ctesiphon, which was then one of the most admired engineering feats in the world. Behind the qibla wall stands the sultan's mausoleum (FIGS. 10-21, no. 1, and 10-22), a gigantic version of the Samanid tomb (FIG. 10-8) at Bukhara but with two flanking minarets. The builders intentionally placed the dome-covered cube south of the mosque so that the prayers of the faithful facing Mecca would be directed toward Hasan's tomb. (The tomb houses only the bodies of the sultan's two sons, however. They could not recover their father's remains after his assassination.)

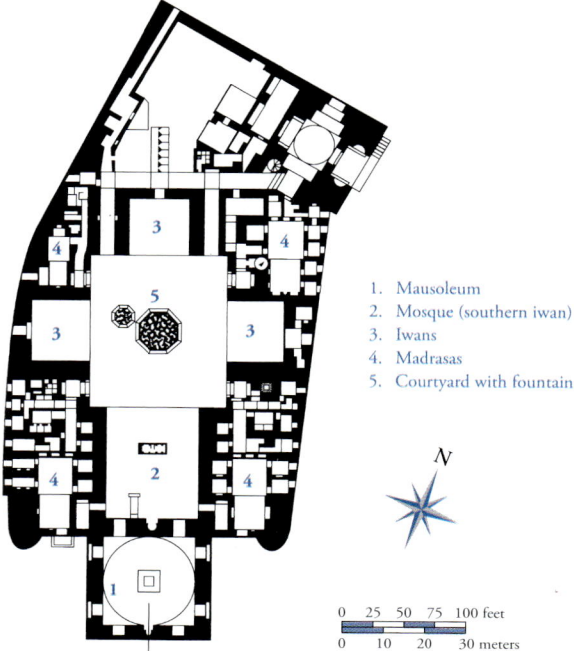

**10-21** Plan of the madrasa-mosque-mausoleum complex of Sultan Hasan, Cairo, Egypt, begun 1356.

1. Mausoleum
2. Mosque (southern iwan)
3. Iwans
4. Madrasas
5. Courtyard with fountain

Sultan Hasan's complex included his tomb, four madrasas, and a mosque. The plan with four iwans opening onto a central courtyard derives from Iranian mosques (FIG. 10-14).

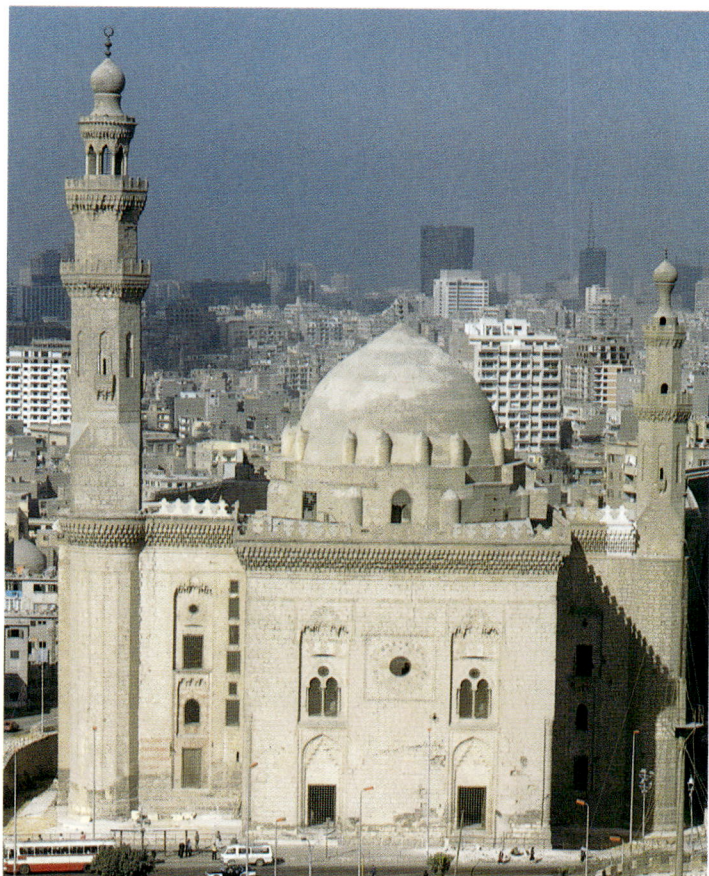

**10-22** Madrasa-mosque-mausoleum complex of Sultan Hasan (looking northwest with the mausoleum in the foreground), Cairo, Egypt, begun 1356.

Hasan's mausoleum is a gigantic version of the earlier Samanid mausoleum (FIG. 10-8). Because of its location south of the complex's mosque, praying Muslims faced the Mamluk sultan's tomb.

A muqarnas cornice crowns the exterior walls of Hasan's complex, and marble plaques of several colors cover the mihrab in the mosque and the walls of the mausoleum. The complex as a whole is relatively austere, however. Its massiveness and geometric clarity present a striking contrast to the filigreed elegance of the contemporaneous Alhambra (FIGS. 10-19 and 10-20) and testify to the diversity of regional styles within the Islamic world, especially after the end of the Umayyad and Abbasid dynasties.

**OTTOMAN EMPIRE** After the downfall of the Seljuks (FIGS. 10-13 and 10-14), several local dynasties established themselves in Anatolia, among them the Ottomans, founded by Osman I (r. 1281–1326). Under Osman's successors, the Ottoman state expanded throughout vast areas of Asia, Europe, and North Africa. By the middle of the 15th century, the Ottoman Empire had become one of the great world powers.

The Ottoman emperors were lavish patrons of architecture, and the builders in their employ developed a new type of mosque, the core of which was a dome-covered square prayer hall. The combination of dome and square had an appealing geometric clarity and became the nucleus of all Ottoman architecture. At first used singly, the domed units came to be used in multiples, the distinctive feature of later Ottoman architecture.

After the Ottoman Turks conquered Constantinople (Istanbul) in 1453, they firmly established their architectural code. Hagia Sophia (FIGS. 9-5 to 9-8) especially impressed the new lords of Constantinople. In some respects, Justinian's great church conformed to their own ideals, and they converted the Byzantine church into a mosque with minarets. But the longitudinal orientation of Hagia Sophia's interior never satisfied Ottoman builders, and Anatolian development moved instead toward the central-plan mosque.

**SINAN THE GREAT** The first Ottoman central-plan mosques date to the 1520s, but the finest examples are the designs of the most famous Ottoman architect, SINAN (ca. 1491–1588), who worked for one of the greatest Ottoman sultans, Suleyman the Magnificent (r. 1520–1566; FIG. 10-22A). Sinan perfected the Ottoman architectural style. By his time, Ottoman

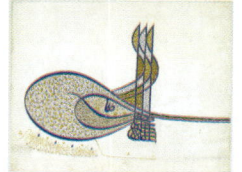

**10-22A** Tughra of Suleyman the Magnificent, ca. 1555–1560.

builders almost universally employed the basic domed unit, which could be multiplied, enlarged, or contracted as needed, and almost any number of units could be combined. Thus, the typical 16th-century Ottoman mosque was a creative assemblage of domical units and artfully juxtaposed geometric spaces. Architects usually designed domes with an extravagant margin of structural safety that has since served them well in earthquake-prone Istanbul and other Turkish cities. (Vivid demonstration of the sound construction of the Ottoman mosques came in August 1999 when a powerful earthquake centered 65 miles east of Istanbul toppled hundreds of modern buildings and killed thousands of people but caused no damage to the centuries-old mosques.) Working within this architectural tradition, Sinan searched for solutions to the problems of unifying the additive elements and of creating a monumental centralized space with harmonious proportions.

# Sinan the Great and the Mosque of Selim II

Sinan, called "the Great," was truly the greatest Ottoman architect. Born a Christian around 1491, he converted to Islam, served in the Ottoman government, and trained in engineering and the art of building while in the Ottoman army. Officials quickly recognized Sinan's talent and entrusted him with increasing responsibility until, in 1538, he became chief court architect for Suleyman the Magnificent, a generous patron of art and architecture. He retained that position for a half century. Tradition associates Sinan with hundreds of building projects, both sacred and secular, although he could not have been involved with all of them.

The capstone of Sinan's distinguished career was the Edirne mosque (FIGS. 10-23 and 10-24) of Suleyman's son, Selim II, which Sinan designed when he was almost 80 years old. In it, he sought to surpass the greatest achievements of Byzantine architects, just as Sultan Hasan's builders in Cairo (FIG. 10-22) attempted to rival and exceed the Sasanian architects of antiquity. Sa'i Mustafa Çelebi, Sinan's biographer, recorded the architect's accomplishment in his own words:

> Sultan Selim Khan ordered the erection of a mosque in Edirne. . . . His humble servant [I, Sinan] prepared for him a drawing depicting, on a dominating site in the city, four minarets on the four corners of a dome. . . . Those who consider themselves architects among Christians say that in the realm of Islam no dome can equal that of the Hagia Sophia; they claim that no Muslim architect would be able to build such a large dome. In this mosque, with the help of God and the support of Sultan Selim Khan, I erected a dome six cubits higher and four cubits wider than the dome of the Hagia Sophia.*

The Edirne dome is, in fact, higher than Hagia Sophia's (FIG. 9-8) when measured from its base, but its crown is not as far above the pavement as that of the dome of Justinian's church. Nonetheless, Sinan's feat won universal acclaim as a triumph. The Ottomans considered the Mosque of Selim II proof they finally had outshone the Christian emperors of Byzantium in the realm of architecture.

*Aptullah Kuran, *Sinan: The Grand Old Master of Ottoman Architecture* (Washington, D.C.: Institute of Turkish Studies, 1987), 168–169.

**10-23** SINAN, Mosque of Selim II, Edirne, Turkey, 1568–1575. ◼◀

The Ottomans developed a new type of mosque with a dome-covered square prayer hall. The dome of Sinan's Mosque of Selim II is taller than Hagia Sophia's (FIG. 9-8) and is an engineering triumph.

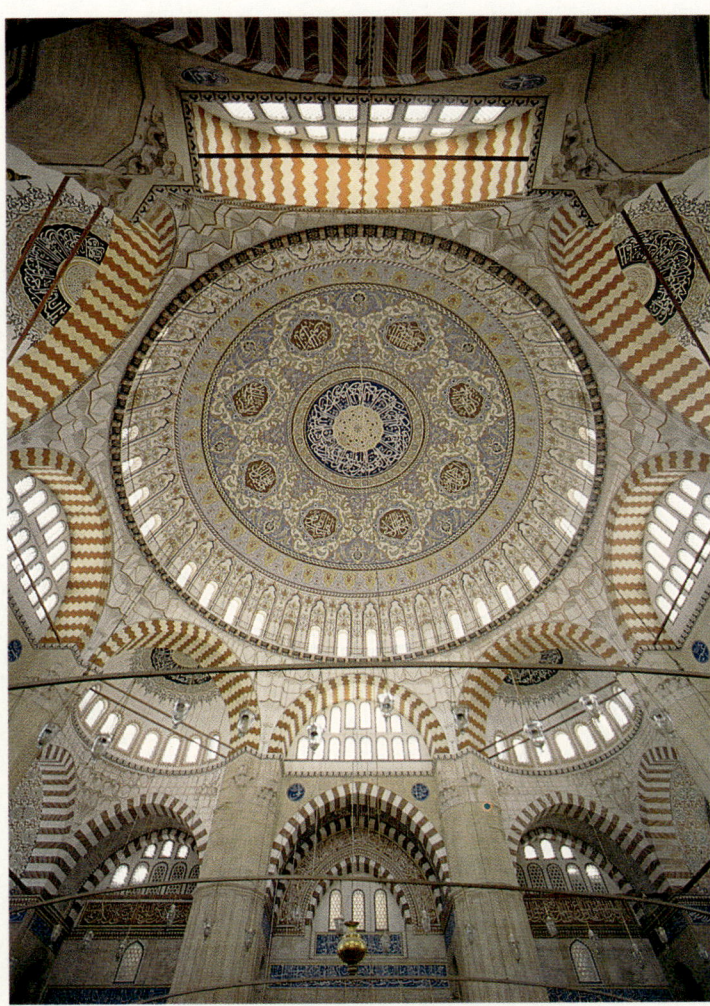

**10-24** SINAN, interior of the Mosque of Selim II, Edirne, Turkey, 1568–1575. ◼◀

The interior of Sinan's Edirne mosque is a fusion of an octagon and a dome-covered square with four half-domes at the corners. The plan features geometric clarity and precise numerical ratios.

## Islamic Tilework

From the Dome of the Rock (FIGS. 10-2 and 10-3), the earliest major Islamic building, to the present day, Muslim builders have used mosaics or ceramic tiles to decorate the walls and vaults of mosques, madrasas, palaces, and tombs. The golden age of Islamic tilework was the 16th and 17th centuries. At that time, artists used two basic techniques to enliven building interiors with brightly colored tiled walls and to sheathe their exteriors with gleaming tiles that reflected the sun's rays.

In *mosaic tilework* (for example, FIG. 10-26), potters fire large ceramic panels of single colors in the kiln and then cut them into smaller pieces and set the pieces in plaster in a manner similar to the laying of mosaic *tesserae* of stone or glass (see "Mosaics," Chapter 8, page 245).

*Cuerda seca* (dry cord) tilework was introduced in Umayyad Spain during the 10th century—hence its Spanish name even in Middle Eastern and Central Asian contexts. Cuerda seca tiles (for example, FIG. 10-25) are polychrome and can more easily bear complex geometric and vegetal patterns as well as Arabic script than can mosaic tiles. They are also more economical to use because vast surfaces can be covered with large tiles much more quickly than they can with thousands of smaller mosaic tiles. But when builders use cuerda seca tiles to sheathe curved surfaces (vaults, domes, minarets), the ceramists must fire the tiles in the exact shape required—a daunting challenge. Polychrome tiles have other drawbacks. Because the ceramists fire all the glazes at the same temperature, cuerda seca tiles are not as brilliant in color as mosaic tiles and do not reflect light the way the more irregular surfaces of tile

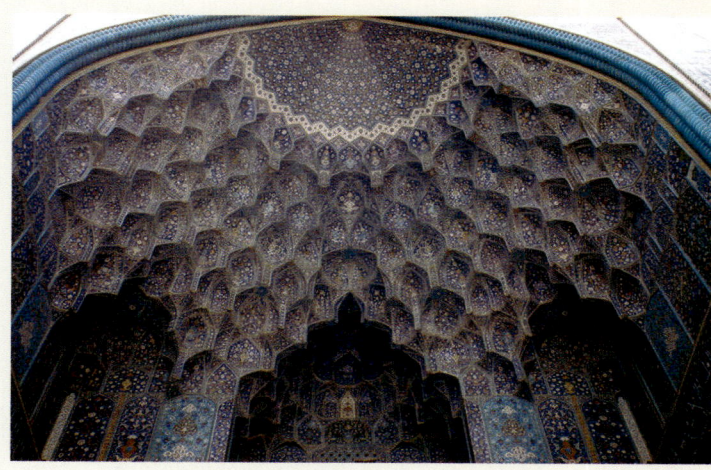

**10-25** Muqarnas tilework of the entrance portal of the Imam (Shah) Mosque, Isfahan, Iran, 1611–1638. ◼◀

The ceramists who produced the cuerda seca tiles of the muqarnas-filled portal to the Imam mosque had to manufacture a wide variety of shapes with curved surfaces to cover the prismatic, pointed half dome.

mosaics do. The preparation of the multicolored tiles also requires greater care. To prevent the colors from running together during firing, the potters outline the motifs on cuerda seca tiles with cords containing manganese, which leaves a matte black line between the colors after firing.

Sinan's vision found ultimate expression in the Mosque of Selim II (FIGS. **10-23** and **10-24**) at Edirne, which had been the capital of the Ottoman Empire from 1367 to 1472 and where Selim II (r. 1566–1574) maintained a palace. There, Sinan designed a mosque with a massive dome set off by four slender pencil-shaped minarets (each more than 200 feet high, among the tallest ever constructed). The dome's height surpasses that of Hagia Sophia's dome (see "Sinan the Great and the Mosque of Selim II," page 298). But it is the organization of the Edirne mosque's interior space that reveals Sinan's genius. The mihrab is recessed into an apselike alcove deep enough to permit window illumination from three sides, making the brilliantly colored tile panels of its lower walls sparkle as if with their own glowing light. The plan of the main hall is an ingenious fusion of an octagon with the dome-covered square. The octagon, formed by the eight massive dome supports, is pierced by the four half-dome-covered corners of the square. The result is a fluid interpenetration of several geometric volumes that represents the culminating solution to Sinan's lifelong search for a monumental, unified interior space. Sinan's forms are clear and legible, like mathematical equations. Height, width, and masses relate to one another in a simple but effective ratio of 1:2, and precise numerical ratios similarly characterize the complex as a whole. The forecourt

of the building, for example, covers an area equal to that of the mosque proper. Most architectural historians regard the Mosque of Selim II as the climax of Ottoman architecture. Sinan proudly proclaimed it his masterpiece.

**IMAM MOSQUE, ISFAHAN** While the Ottomans held sway in Turkey, the Safavids (r. 1501–1732) ruled the ancient Persian domains formerly under the control of the Abbasids, Seljuks, and Timurids (FIG. 10-29). The Safavids installed the ceramic-tile revetment on the walls and vaults of the Seljuks' Friday Mosque (FIG. 10-13) at Isfahan and built the Imam Mosque (formerly the Shah, or Royal, Mosque) in the early 17th century, which boasts some of the finest examples of Iranian tilework (FIG. **10-25**). The use of glazed tiles has a long history in the Middle East. Even in ancient Mesopotamia, builders sometimes covered walls and gates with colorful baked bricks (FIG. 2-24).

In the Islamic world, the art of ceramic tilework reached its peak in the 16th and 17th centuries in Iran and Turkey (see "Islamic Tilework," above), when, for example, the Ottomans replaced the exterior mosaics of the Dome of the Rock (FIG. 10-2) in Jerusalem with glazed tiles. In the Imam Mosque in Isfahan, Safavid tiles cover almost every surface. For the entrance portal (FIG. 10-25), the cera-

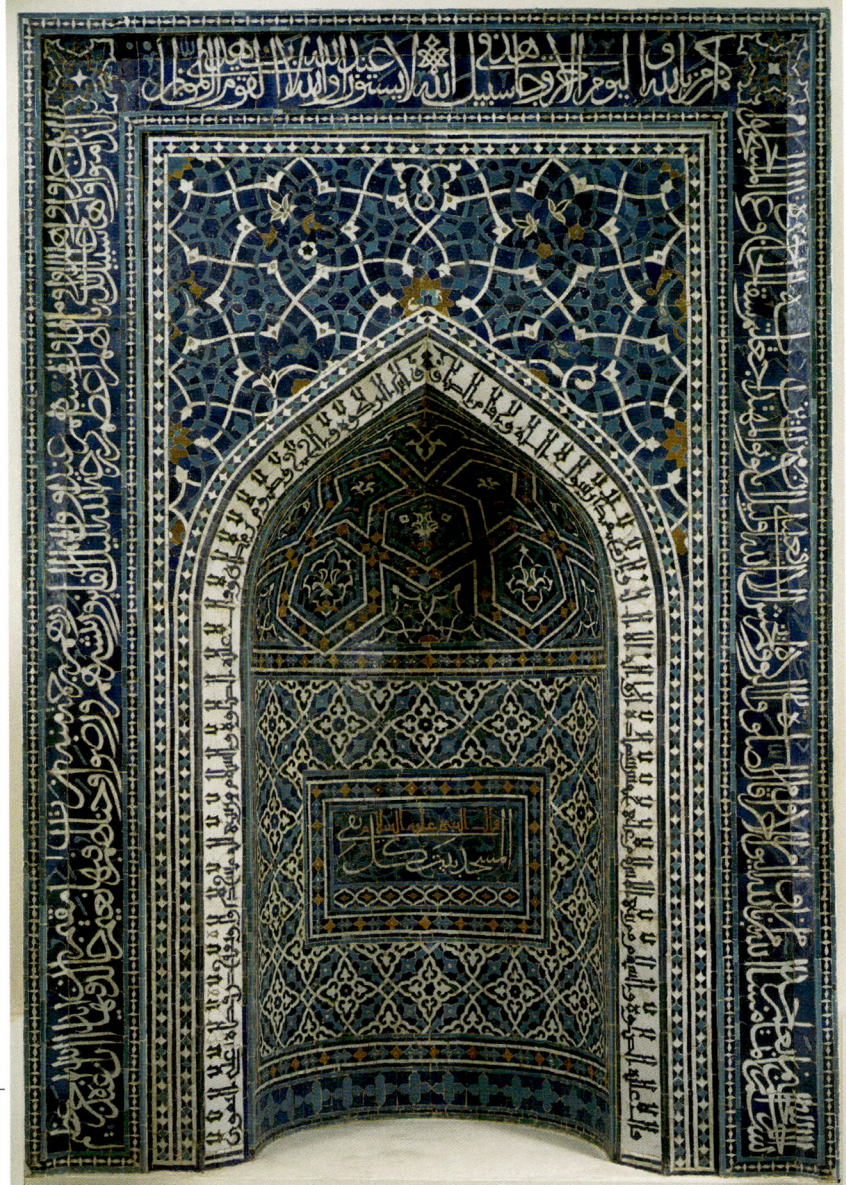

**10-26** Mihrab, from the Madrasa Imami, Isfahan, Iran, ca. 1354. Glazed mosaic tilework, 11′ 3″ × 7′ 6″. Metropolitan Museum of Art, New York. ◼◀

This Iranian mihrab is a masterpiece of mosaic tilework. Every piece had to be cut to fit its specific place in the design. It exemplifies the perfect aesthetic union of Islamic calligraphy and ornamentation.

1 ft.

from the Koran in Kufic, the stately rectilinear script employed for the earliest Korans (FIGS. 10-17 and 10-17A). Many supple cursive styles also make up the repertoire of Islamic calligraphy. One of these styles, known as *Muhaqqaq,* fills the mihrab's outer rectangular frame. The mosaic tile decoration on the curving surface of the niche and the area above the pointed arch consists of tighter and looser networks of geometric and abstract floral motifs. The mosaic technique is masterful. Every piece had to be cut to fit its specific place in the mihrab—even the tile inscriptions. The ceramist smoothly integrated the subtly varied decorative patterns with the framed inscription in the center of the niche—proclaiming that the mosque is the domicile of the pious believer. The mihrab's outermost inscription—detailing the five pillars of Islamic faith (see "Muhammad and Islam," page 285)—serves as a fringelike extension, as well as a boundary, for the entire design. The unification of calligraphic and geometric elements is so complete that only the practiced eye can distinguish them. The artist transformed the architectural surface into a textile surface—the three-dimensional wall into a two-dimensional hanging—weaving the calligraphy into it as another cluster of motifs within the total pattern.

## Luxury Arts

The tile-covered mosques of Isfahan, Sultan Hasan's madrasa complex in Cairo, and the architecture of Sinan the Great in Edirne are enduring testaments to the brilliant artistic culture of the Safavid, Mamluk, and Ottoman rulers of the Muslim world. Still, these are but some of the most conspicuous public manifestations of the greatness of later Islamic art and architecture (see Chapter 32 for the achievements of the Muslim rulers of India). In the smaller-scale, and often private, realm of the luxury arts, Muslim artists also excelled. From the vast array of manuscript paintings, ceramics, and metalwork, the six masterpieces illustrated here (FIGS. 10-27 to 10-32) suggest both the range and the quality of the inappropriately dubbed Islamic "minor arts" of the 13th to 16th centuries.

**ARDABIL CARPETS** The first of these artworks (FIG. **10-27**) is by far the largest, one of a pair of carpets from Ardabil in Iran. The carpets come from the funerary mosque of Shaykh Safi al-Din (1252–1334), the founder of the Safavid line, but they date to 1540, two centuries after the construction of the mosque, during the reign of Shah Tahmasp (r. 1524–1576). Tahmasp elevated carpet weaving to a national industry and set up royal factories at Isfahan, Kashan, Kirman, and Tabriz. The name MAQSUD OF KASHAN appears as part of the design of the carpet illustrated here. Maqsud must have been the artist who supplied the master pattern to two teams of royal weavers (one for each of the two carpets). The carpet, almost 35 by 18 feet, consists of roughly 25 million knots, some 340 to the square inch. (Its twin has even more knots.)

The design consists of a central sunburst medallion, representing the inside of a dome, surrounded by 16 pendants. Mosque lamps (appropriate motifs for the Ardabil funerary mosque) hang from two pendants on the long axis of the carpet. The lamps are

mists had to manufacture a wide variety of shapes with curved surfaces to sheathe the complex forms of the muqarnas-filled, pointed half dome. The result was a technological triumph as well as a dazzling display of abstract decoration.

**MADRASA IMAMI, ISFAHAN** As already noted, verses from the Koran appeared in the mosaics of the Dome of the Rock (FIG. 10-3) in Jerusalem and in mosaics and other media on the walls of countless later Islamic structures. Indeed, some of the masterworks of Arabic calligraphy are not in manuscripts but on walls. A 14th-century mihrab (FIG. **10-26**) from the Madrasa Imami in Isfahan exemplifies the perfect aesthetic union between the Islamic calligrapher's art and abstract ornamentation. The pointed arch framing the mihrab niche bears an inscription

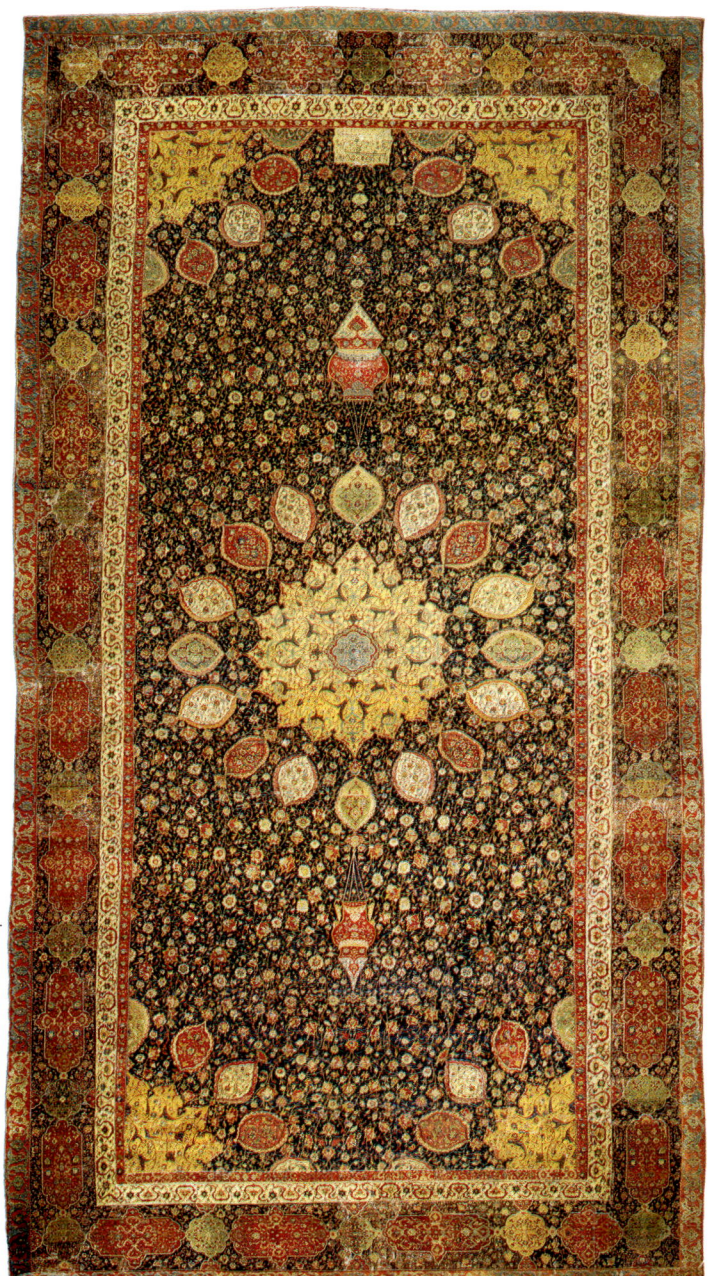

10 ft.

**10-27** MAQSUD OF KASHAN, carpet from the funerary mosque of Shaykh Safi al-Din, Ardabil, Iran, 1540. Wool and silk, 34′ 6″ × 17′ 7″. Victoria & Albert Museum, London.

Maqsud of Kashan's enormous Ardabil carpet required roughly 25 million knots. It presents the illusion of a heavenly dome with mosque lamps reflected in a pool of water filled with floating lotus blossoms.

of different sizes. This may be an optical device to make the two appear equal in size when viewed from the end of the carpet at the room's threshold (the bottom end in FIG. 10-27). Covering the rich, dark blue background are leaves and flowers attached to delicate stems that spread over the whole field. The entire composition presents the illusion of a heavenly dome with lamps reflected in a pool of water full of floating lotus blossoms. No human or animal figures appear, as befits a carpet intended for a mosque, although they can be found on other Islamic textiles used in secular contexts, both earlier (FIG. 10-15A) and later.

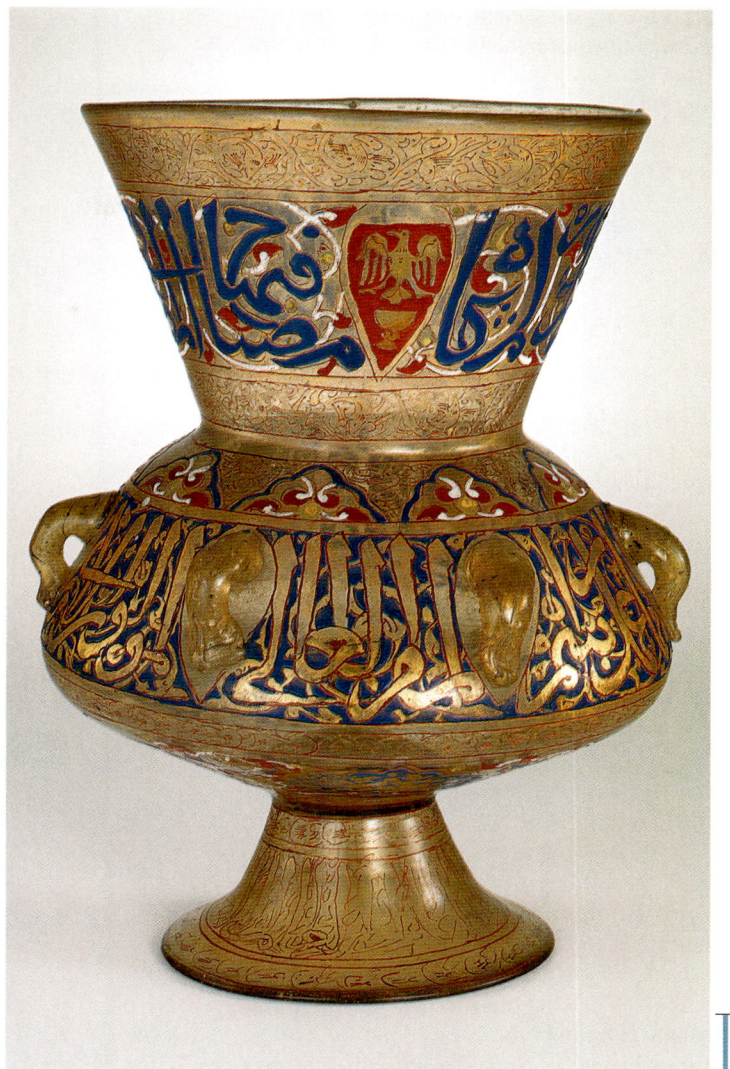

1 in.

**10-28** Mosque lamp of Sayf al-Din Tuquztimur, from Egypt, 1340. Glass with enamel decoration, 1′ 1″ high. British Museum, London.

The enamel decoration of this glass mosque lamp includes a quotation from the Koran comparing God's light with the light in a lamp. The burning wick dramatically illuminated the sacred verse.

**MOSQUE LAMPS** The kind of mosque lamps depicted on the Ardabil carpets were usually made of glass and lavishly decorated. Islamic artists perfected this art form, and fortunately, despite their exceptionally fragile nature, many examples survive, in large part because those who handled them did so with reverence and care. One of the finest is the mosque lamp (FIG. 10-28) made for Sayf al-Din Tuquztimur (d. 1345), an official in the court of the Mamluk sultan al-Nasir Muhammad (r. 1309–1341). The glass lamps hung on chains from mosque ceilings. The shape of Tuquztimur's lamp is typical of the period, consisting of a conical neck, a wide body with six vertical handles, and a tall foot. Inside, a small glass container held the oil and wick. The *enamel* (colors fused to the surfaces) decoration includes Tuquztimur's emblem—an eagle over a cup (Tuquztimur served as the sultan's cup-bearer)—and cursive Arabic calligraphy giving the official's name and titles as well as a quotation of the Koranic verse (24:35) that compares God's light with the light in a lamp. The lamplight dramatically illuminated that verse (and Tuquztimur's name).

BIHZAD, *Seduction of Yusuf,* folio 52 verso of the *Bustan* of Sultan Husayn Mayqara, from Herat, Afghanistan, 1488. Ink and color on paper, $11\frac{7}{8}'' \times 8\frac{5}{8}''$. National Library, Cairo.

The most famous Timurid manuscript painter was Bihzad. This page displays vivid color, intricate decorative detailing, and a brilliant balance between two-dimensional patterning and perspective.

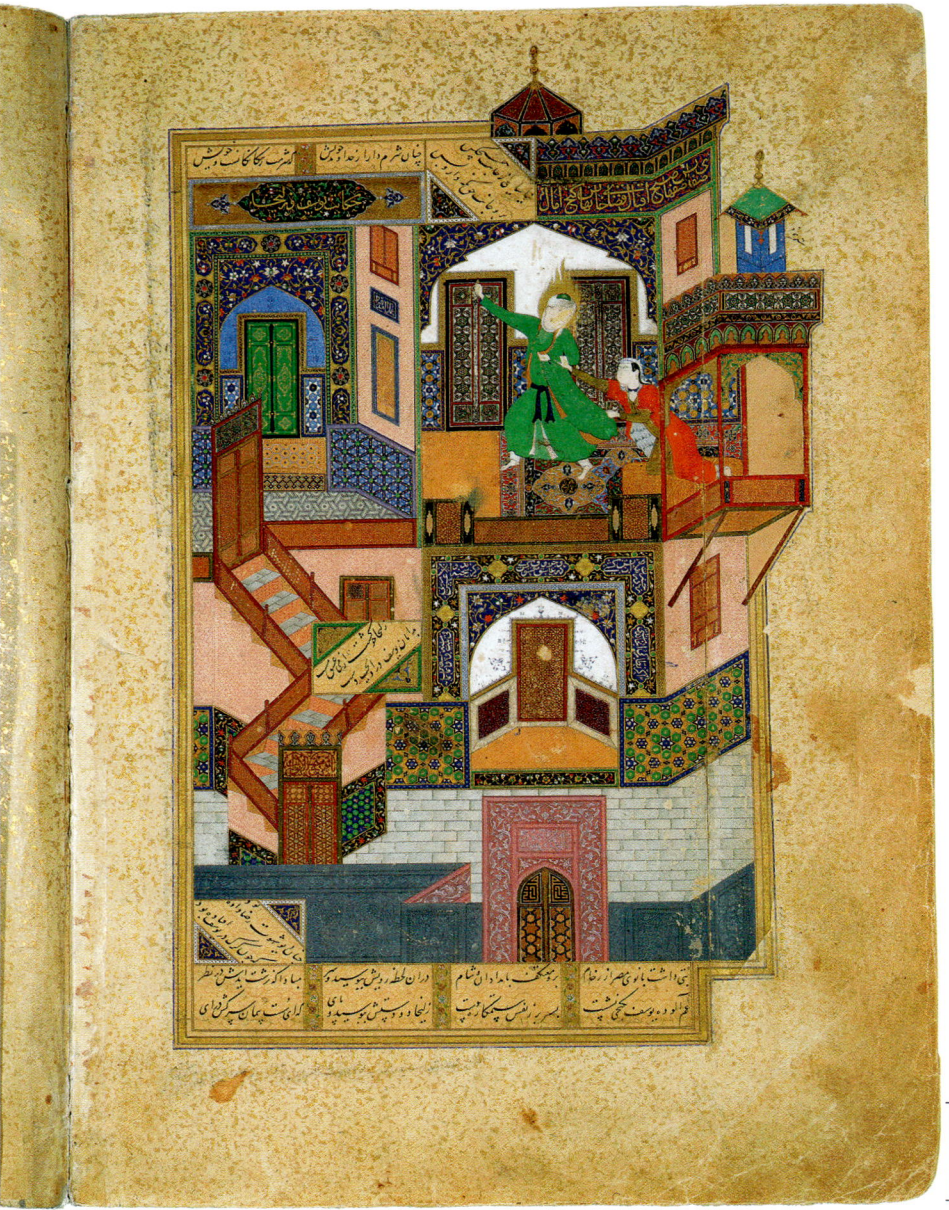

**TIMURID *BUSTAN*** In the late 14th century, a new Islamic empire arose in Central Asia under the leadership of Timur (r. 1370–1405), known in the Western world as Tamerlane. Timur, a successor of the Mongol conqueror Genghis Khan, quickly extended his dominions to include Iran and parts of Anatolia. The Timurids, who ruled until 1501, were great patrons of art and architecture in Herat, Bukhara, Samarqand, and other cities. Herat in particular became a leading center for the production of luxurious books under the patronage of the Timurid sultan Husayn Mayqara (r. 1470–1506).

The most famous Persian painter of his age was BIHZAD, who worked at the Herat court before migrating to Tabriz. At Herat, he illustrated the sultan's copy of *Bustan* (*The Orchard*) by the Persian poet Sadi (ca. 1209–1292). One page (FIG. **10-29**) represents a story in both the Bible and the Koran— the seduction of Yusuf (Joseph) by Potiphar's wife, Zulayhka. Bihzad dispersed Sadi's text throughout the page in elegant Arabic script in a series of beige panels. According to the tale as told by Jami (1414–1492), an influential mystic theologian and poet whose Persian text appears in blue in the white pointed arch of the composition's lower center, Zulaykha lured Yusuf into her palace and led him through seven rooms, locking each door behind him. In the last room she threw herself at Yusuf, but he resisted and was able to flee when the seven doors opened miraculously. Bihzad's painting of the story highlights all the stylistic elements that brought him great renown: vivid color, intricate decorative detailing suggesting luxurious textiles and tiled walls, and a brilliant balance between two-dimensional patterning and perspective depictions of balconies and staircases. Bizhad's apprentices later worked for the Mughal court in India and introduced his distinctive style to South Asia (see Chapter 32).

**SAFAVID *SHAHNAMA*** The successors of the Timurids in Iran were the Safavids. Shah Tahmasp (FIG. 32-5), the Safavid ruler who commissioned the Ardabil carpets (FIG. 10-27), was also a great patron of books. Around 1525, he commissioned an ambitious decade-long project to produce an illustrated 742-page copy of the *Shahnama* (*Book of Kings*). The *Shahnama,* the Persian national epic poem by Firdawsi (940–1025), recounts the history of

Iran from creation until the Muslim conquest. Tahmasp's *Shahnama* contains 258 illustrations by many artists, including some of the most admired painters of the day. It was eventually presented as a gift to Selim II, the Ottoman sultan who was the patron of Sinan's mosque (FIGS. 10-23 and 10-24) at Edirne. The manuscript later entered a private collection in the West and ultimately was auctioned as a series of individual pages, destroying its integrity but underscoring that Western collectors viewed each page as an independent masterpiece.

The page reproduced here (FIG. **10-30**) is the work of SULTAN-MUHAMMAD and depicts Gayumars, the legendary first king of Iran, and his court. According to tradition, Gayumars ruled from a mountaintop when humans first learned to cook food and clothe themselves in leopard skins. In Sultan-Muhammad's representation of the story, Gayumars presides over his court (all the figures wear leopard skins) from his mountain throne. The king is surrounded by light amid a golden sky. His son and grandson perch on multicolored rocky outcroppings to the viewer's left and right, respectively.

1 in.

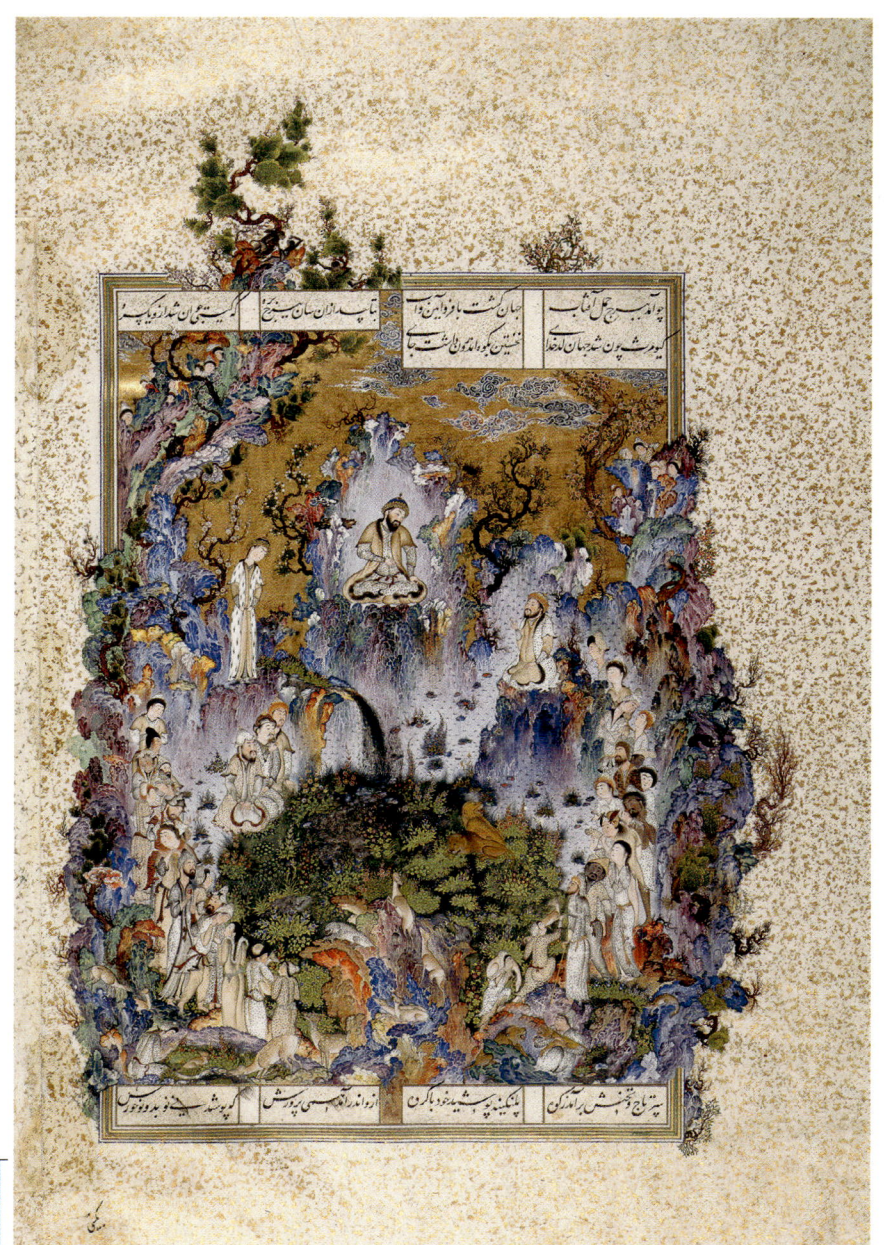

**10-30** Sultan-Muhammad, *Court of Gayumars,* folio 20 verso of the *Shahnama* of Shah Tahmasp, from Tabriz, Iran, ca. 1525–1535. Ink, watercolor, and gold on paper, 1′ 1″ × 9″. Prince Sadruddin Aga Khan Collection, Geneva.

Sultan-Muhammad painted the legend of King Gayumars for the Safavid ruler Shah Tahmasp. The off-center placement on the page enhances the sense of lightness that permeates the painting.

The court encircles the ruler and his heirs. Dozens of human faces appear within the rocks, and many species of animals populate the lush landscape. According to the *Shahnama,* wild beasts became instantly tame in the presence of Gayumars. Sultan-Muhammad rendered the figures, animals, trees, rocks, and sky with an extraordinarily delicate touch. The sense of lightness and airiness that permeates the painting is enhanced by its placement on the page—floating, off center, on a speckled background of gold leaf. The painter gave his royal patron a singular vision of Iran's fabled past.

*BAPTISTÈRE DE SAINT LOUIS* Metalwork was another early Islamic art form (FIG. 10-16) that continued to play an important role in the later period. An example of the highest quality is a brass basin (FIG. **10-31**) from Egypt inlaid with gold and silver and signed—six times—by the Mamluk artist Muhammad ibn al-Zayn. The basin, used for washing hands at official ceremonies, must have been fashioned for a specific Mamluk patron. Some scholars think a court official named Salar ordered the piece as a gift for his sultan, but no inscription identifies him. The central band depicts Mamluk hunters and Mongol enemies. Running animals fill the friezes above and below. Stylized vegetal forms of inlaid silver fill the background of all the bands and roundels.

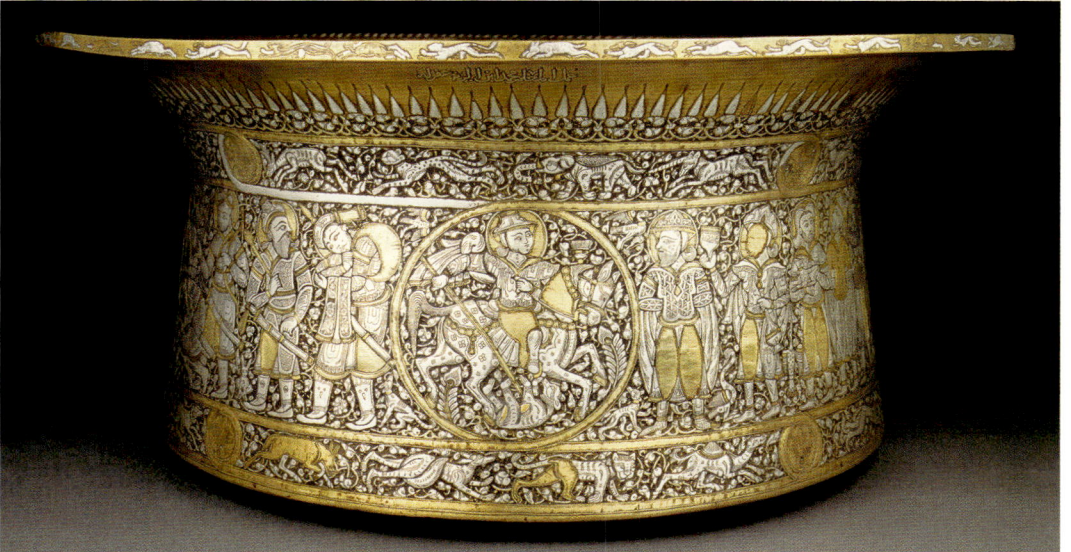

**10-31** Muhammad ibn al-Zayn, basin (*Baptistère de Saint Louis*), from Egypt, ca. 1300. Brass, inlaid with gold and silver, $8\frac{3}{4}$″ high. Musée du Louvre, Paris.

Muhammad ibn al-Zayn proudly signed (six times) this basin used for washing hands at official ceremonies. The central band, inlaid with gold and silver, depicts Mamluk hunters and Mongol enemies.

1 in.

1 in.

# Christian Patronage of Islamic Art

During the 11th through 13th centuries, large numbers of Christians traveled to Islamic lands, especially to the Christian holy sites in Jerusalem and Bethlehem, either as pilgrims or as Crusaders (see "Pilgrimages" and "The Crusades," Chapter 12, pages 335 and 346). Many returned with mementos of their journey, usually in the form of inexpensive mass-produced souvenirs. But some wealthy individuals commissioned local Muslim artists to produce custom-made pieces using costly materials.

A unique brass canteen (FIG. 10-32) inlaid with silver and decorated with scenes of the life of Jesus appears to be the work of a 13th-century Ayyubid metalsmith in the employ of a Christian patron. The canteen is a luxurious version of the "pilgrim flasks" Christian visitors to the Holy Land often carried back to Europe. Four inscriptions in Arabic promise eternal glory, secure life, perfect prosperity, and increasing good luck to the canteen's unnamed owner, who must have been a Christian, not only because of the type of object but especially the choice of scenes engraved into the canteen. The Madonna and Christ Child appear enthroned in the central medallion, and three panels depicting New Testament events (see "The Life of Jesus in Art," Chapter 8, pages 240–241) fill most of the band around the medallion. The narrative unfolds in a counterclockwise sequence (Arabic is read from right to left), beginning with the *Nativity* (at 2 o'clock) and continuing with the *Presentation in the Temple* (10 o'clock) and Jesus' *Entry into Jerusalem* (6 o'clock). The scenes may have been chosen because the patron had visited their locales (Bethlehem and Jerusalem). Most scholars believe the artist used Syrian Christian manuscripts as the source for the canteen's Christian iconography. Many of the decorative details, however, are common in contemporaneous Islamic metalwork inscribed with the names of Muslim patrons. Whoever the owner was, the canteen testifies to the fruitful artistic interaction between Christians and Muslims in 13th-century Syria.

**10-32** Canteen with episodes from the life of Jesus, from Syria, ca. 1240–1250. Brass, inlaid with silver, 1' 2½" high. Freer Gallery of Art, Washington, D.C.

This unique canteen is the work of an Ayyubid metalsmith in the employ of a Christian pilgrim to the Holy Land. The three scenes from the life of Jesus appear in counterclockwise sequence.

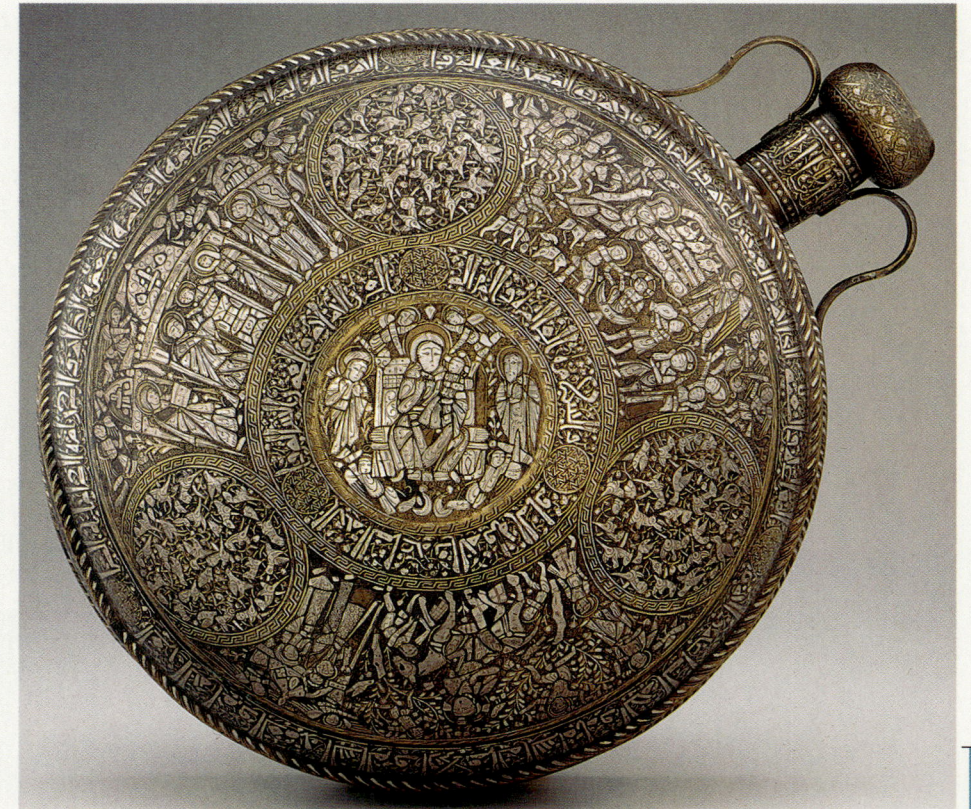

1 in.

Figures and animals also decorate the inside and underside of the basin, which has long been known as the *Baptistère de Saint Louis.* The association with the famous French king (see "Louis IX, the Saintly King," Chapter 13, page 385) is a myth, however. Louis died before Muhammad ibn al-Zayn made the piece. Nonetheless, the *Baptistère,* taken to France long ago, was used in the baptismal rites of newborns of the French royal family as early as the 17th century. Like the Zandana silk (FIG. 10-14A) in Toul Cathedral and a canteen (FIG. **10-32**) featuring scenes of the life of Christ (see "Christian Patronage of Islamic Art," above), the *Baptistère de Saint Louis* testifies to the prestige of Islamic art well beyond the boundaries of the Islamic world.

# THE ISLAMIC WORLD

## UMAYYAD SYRIA AND ABBASID IRAQ 661–1258

▮ The Umayyads (r. 661–750) were the first Islamic dynasty. They ruled from their capital at Damascus (Syria) until the Abbasids (r. 750–1258) overthrew them and established a new capital at Baghdad (Iraq).

▮ The first great Islamic building was the Dome of the Rock, a domed octagon commemorating the triumph of Islam in Jerusalem, which the Muslims captured from the Byzantines in 638.

▮ Umayyad and Abbasid mosques, for example those in Damascus and Kairouan (Tunisia), are of the hypostyle-hall type and incorporate arcaded courtyards and minarets. The mosaic decoration of early mosques was often the work of Byzantine artists but excluded zoomorphic forms.

▮ The earliest preserved Korans date to the ninth century and feature Kufic calligraphy and decorative motifs but no figural illustrations.

Dome of the Rock, Jerusalem, 687–692

## ISLAMIC SPAIN 756–1492

▮ Abd-al-Rahman I established the Umayyad dynasty (r. 756–1031) in Spain when he escaped the Abbasid massacre of his clan in 750.

▮ The Umayyad capital was at Córdoba, where the caliphs constructed and expanded the Great Mosque between the 8th and 10th centuries. The mosque features horseshoe and multilobed arches and mosaic-clad domes resting on arcuated squinches.

▮ The last Spanish Muslim dynasty was the Nasrid (r. 1232–1492), whose capital was at Granada. The Alhambra is the best surviving example of Islamic palace architecture. It is famous for its stuccoed walls and arches and its muqarnas decoration on vaults and domes.

Great Mosque, Córdoba, 8th to 10th centuries

## ISLAMIC EGYPT 909–1517

▮ The Fatimids (r. 909–1171) established their caliphate at Cairo (Egypt) in 909. Their successors were the Ayyubids (r. 1171–1250) and the Mamluks (r. 1250–1517).

▮ The most ambitious Mamluk builder was Sultan Hasan, whose madrasa-mosque-mausoleum complex in Cairo derives from Iranian four-iwan mosque designs.

▮ Egyptian artists excelled in glassmaking, metalwork, and other luxury arts and produced magnificent mosque lamps and engraved basins.

Mosque lamp of Sayf al-Din Tuquztimur, 1340

## TIMURID AND SAFAVID IRAN AND CENTRAL ASIA 1370–1732

▮ The Timurid (r. 1370–1501) and Safavid (r. 1501–1732) dynasties, which ruled Iran and Central Asia for almost four centuries, were great patrons of art and architecture.

▮ The Timurid court at Herat (Afghanistan) employed the most skilled painters of the day, who specialized in illustrating books. The most famous was Bihzad.

▮ Persian painting also flourished in Safavid Iran under Shah Tahmasp (r. 1524–1576), who in addition set up royal carpet factories in several cities.

▮ The art of tilework reached its peak under the patronage of the Safavid dynasty. Builders of the time frequently used cuerda seca and mosaic tiles to cover the walls, vaults, and domes of mosques, madrasas, palaces, and tombs.

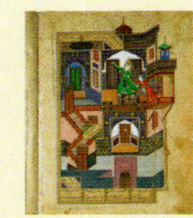

Bihzad, *Seduction of Yusuf,* 1488

## OTTOMAN TURKEY 1281–1924

▮ Osman I (r. 1281–1326) founded the Ottoman dynasty in Turkey. By the middle of the 15th century, the Ottomans had become a fearsome power and captured Byzantine Constantinople in 1453.

▮ The greatest Ottoman architect was Sinan (ca. 1491–1588), who perfected the design of the domed central-plan mosque. His Mosque of Selim II at Edirne is also an engineering triumph. Its dome is taller than Hagia Sophia's.

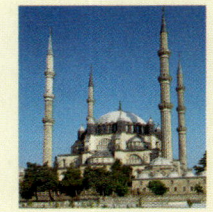

Sinan, Mosque of Selim II, Edirne, 1568–1575

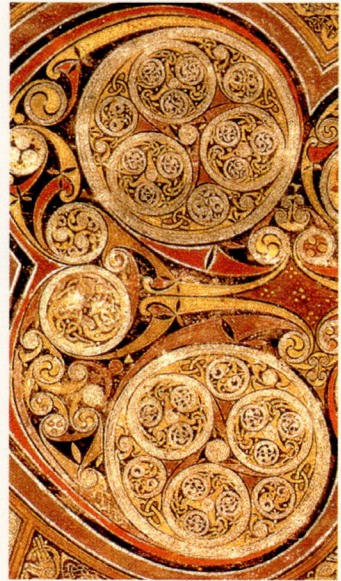

In this opening page to the Gospel of Saint Matthew, the painter transformed the biblical text into abstract pattern, literally making God's words beautiful. The intricate design recalls early medieval metalwork.

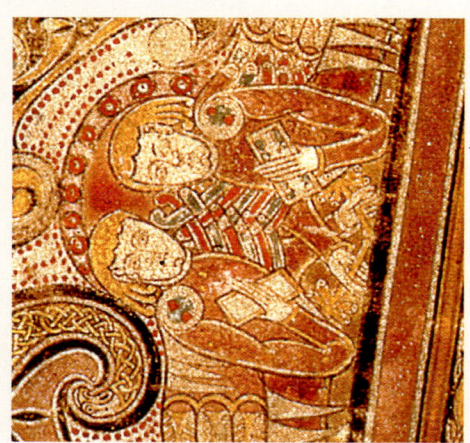

The *chi-rho-iota* (XPI) page is not purely embellished script and abstract pattern. Half-figures of winged angels appear to the left of *chi,* accompanying the monogram as if accompanying Christ himself.

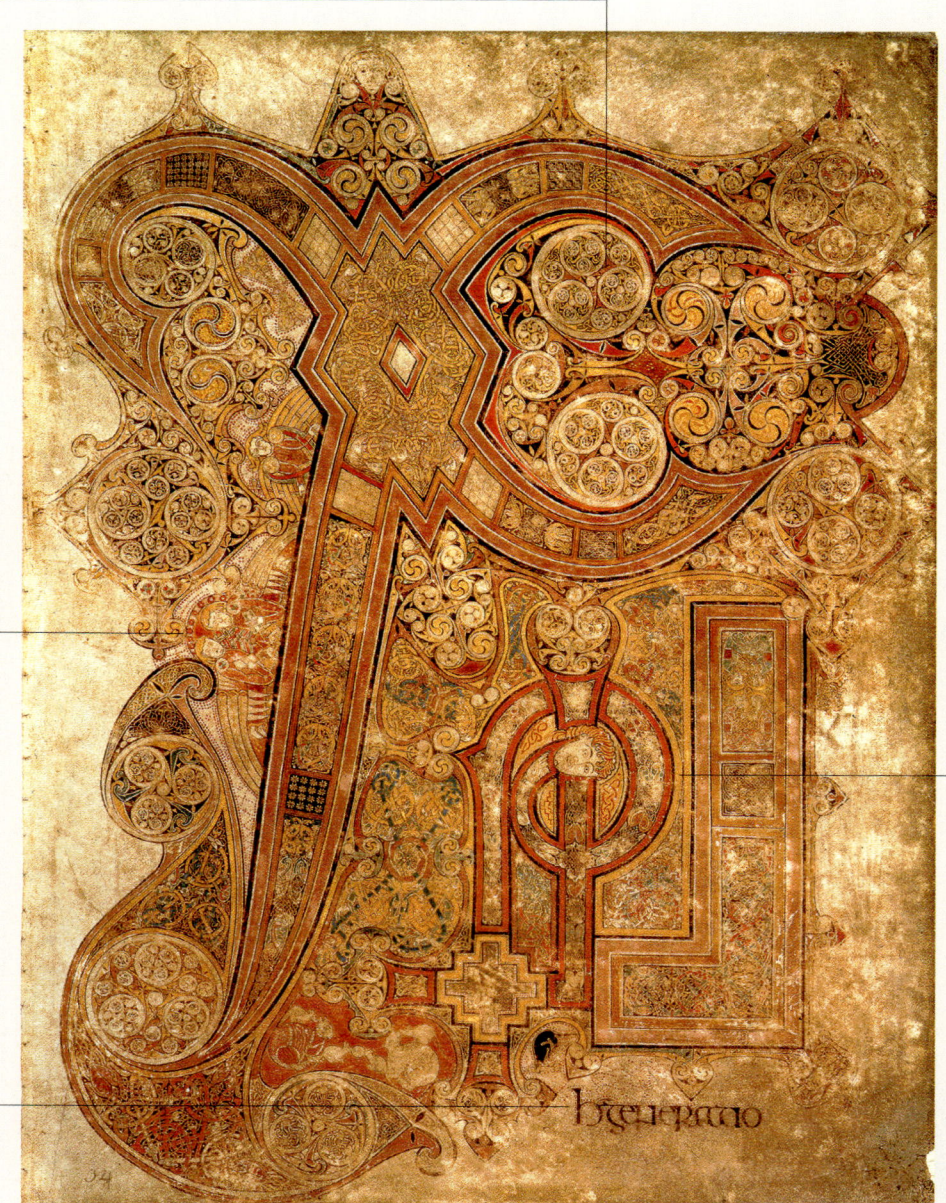

1 in.

**11-1** Chi-rho-iota (**XPI**) page, folio 34 recto of the *Book of Kells,* probably from Iona, Scotland, late eighth or early ninth century. Tempera on vellum, 1′ 1″ × 9½″. Trinity College Library, Dublin.

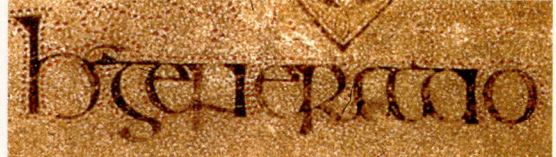

The only unadorned letters in the opening of the passage read on Christmas Eve are the two words *autem* (abbreviated simply as *h*) and *generatio:* "Now this is how the birth of Christ came about."

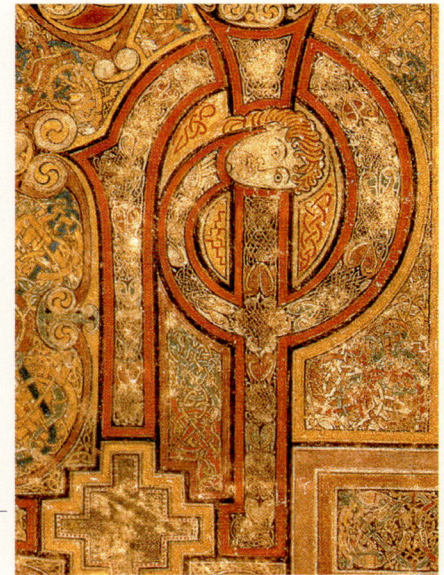

The other figural elements on this page of the *Book of Kells* include a male head growing out of the end of the curve in the letter *rho*. Animals are at the base of *rho* to the left of *h generatio*.

# EARLY MEDIEVAL EUROPE

## MISSIONARIES SPREAD CHRISTIAN ART

The half millennium between 500 and 1000 was the great formative period of western medieval art, a time of great innovation. The patrons of many of these works were Christian missionaries, who brought to the non-Christian peoples of the former northwestern provinces of the Roman Empire not only the Gospel but the culture of the Late Antique Mediterranean world as well.

In Ireland, the most distant European outpost, the Christianization of the Celts began in the fifth century. By the end of the seventh century, monks at several Irish monasteries were producing magnificent illuminated books for use by the clergy and for impressing the illiterate with the beauty of God's words. The greatest early medieval Irish book is the *Book of Kells,* which one commentator described in the *Annals of Ulster* for 1003 as "the chief relic of the western world." The manuscript was probably the work of scribes and illuminators at the monastery at Iona. The monks kept the book in an elaborate metalwork box, as befitted a greatly revered "relic," and likely displayed it on the church altar.

The page reproduced here (FIG. **11-1**) opens the account of the nativity of Jesus in the Gospel of Saint Matthew. The initial letters of Christ in Greek (XPI, *chi-rho-iota*) occupy nearly the entire page, although two words—*autem* (abbreviated simply as *h*) and *generatio*—appear at the lower right. Together they read: "Now this is how the birth of Christ came about." The page corresponds to the opening of Matthew's Gospel, the passage read in church on Christmas Eve. The illuminator transformed the holy words into extraordinarily intricate, abstract designs recalling metalwork (FIG. 11-3), but the page is not purely embellished script and abstract pattern. The letter *rho*, for example, ends in a male head, and animals are at the base of *rho* to the left of *h generatio.* Half-figures of winged angels appear to the left of *chi.* Close observation reveals many other figures, human and animal. When the priest Giraldus Cambrensis visited Ireland in 1185, he described a manuscript he saw that, if not the *Book of Kells* itself, must have been very much like it:

> Fine craftsmanship is all about you, but you might not notice it. Look more keenly at it and you . . . will make out intricacies, so delicate and subtle, so exact and compact, so full of knots and links, with colors so fresh and vivid, that you might say that all this was the work of an angel, and not of a man. For my part, the oftener I see the book, the more carefully I study it, the more I am lost in ever fresh amazement, and I see more and more wonders in the book.[1]

In the early Middle Ages, the monasteries of northern Europe were both the repositories of knowledge in the midst of an almost wholly illiterate population and the greatest centers of art production.

# ART OF THE WARRIOR LORDS

Early medieval art* in western Europe (MAP 11-1) was the result of a unique tripartite fusion of the classical heritage of Rome's northwestern provinces, the cultures of the non-Roman peoples north of the Alps, and Christianity. Although the Romans called everyone who lived beyond their empire's frontiers "barbarians," many northerners had risen to prominent positions within the Roman army and government during Late Antiquity. Others established their own areas of rule, sometimes with Rome's approval, sometimes in opposition to imperial authority. Over the centuries the various population groups merged, and a new order gradually replaced what had been the Roman Empire, resulting eventually in today's European nations.

As Rome's power waned, armed conflicts and competition for political authority became commonplace among the Huns, Vandals, Merovingians, Franks, Goths, and other non-Roman peoples of Europe. Once one group established itself in Italy or in one of Rome's European provinces, another often pressed in behind and compelled the first one to move on. The Visigoths, for example, who at one time controlled part of Italy and formed a kingdom in what is today southern France, were forced southward into Spain under pressure from the Franks, who had crossed the lower Rhine River and established themselves firmly in France, Switzerland, the Netherlands, and parts of

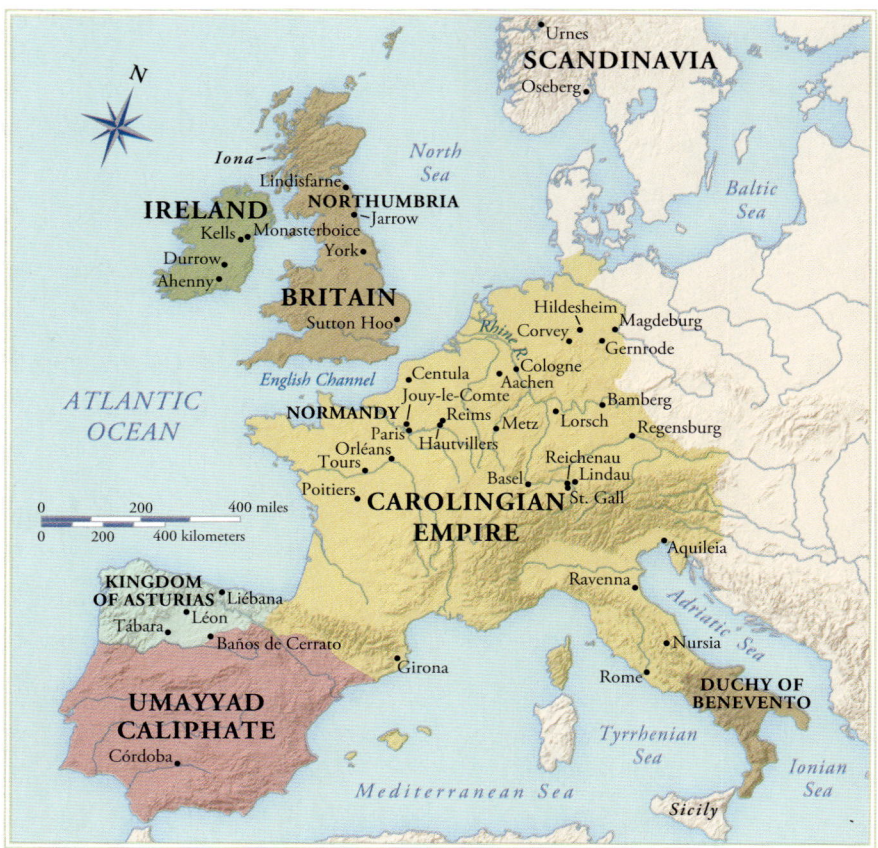

**MAP 11-1** The Carolingian Empire at the death of Charlemagne in 814.

Germany. The Ostrogoths moved from Pannonia (at the junction of modern Hungary, Austria, and the former Yugoslavia) to Italy. Under Theodoric (see page 246), they established their kingdom there, only to have it fall less than a century later to the Lombards, the last of the early Germanic powers to occupy land within the limits of the old Roman Empire. Anglo-Saxons controlled what had been Roman Britain. Celts inhabited France and parts of the British Isles, including Ireland. In Scandinavia, the seafaring Vikings held sway.

Art historians do not know the full range of art and architecture these non-Roman cultures produced. What has survived is

probably not fully representative and consists almost exclusively of small portable "status symbols"—weapons and items of personal adornment such as bracelets, pendants, and belt buckles that archaeologists have discovered in lavish burials. Earlier scholars, who viewed medieval art through a Renaissance lens, ignored these "minor arts" because of their small scale, seemingly utilitarian nature, and abstract ornamentation, and because their makers rejected the classical idea that naturalistic representation should be the focus of artistic endeavor. In the early Middle Ages, people regarded these objects, which often display a high degree of technical and stylistic

*The adjective *medieval* and the noun *Middle Ages* are very old terms stemming from an outmoded view of the roughly 1,000 years between the adoption of Christianity as the Roman Empire's official religion and the rebirth (Renaissance) of interest in classical antiquity. Earlier historians, following the lead of the humanist scholars of Renaissance

Italy, viewed this period as a long and artistically crude interval between—in the middle of—two great civilizations. The force of tradition dictates the retention of both terms to describe this period and its art, although scholars long ago ceased judging medieval art as unsophisticated or inferior.

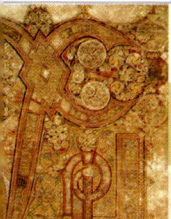

## EARLY MEDIEVAL EUROPE

| 410 | Warrior Lords | 768 | Hiberno-Saxon and Carolingian | 919 | Ottonian | 1024 |
|---|---|---|---|---|---|---|
| | ❙ After the fall of Rome, artists produce portable items of personal adornment featuring cloisonné ornamentation and intertwined animal and interlace patterns | | ❙ Christian missionaries commission sumptuous illuminated manuscripts featuring full pages devoted to embellishing the Word of God ❙ Charlemagne and his Carolingian successors (768–877) initiate a conscious revival of the art and culture of Early Christian Rome ❙ Carolingian architects introduce the twin-tower westwork and modular plans for basilican churches | | ❙ Ottonian painters and sculptors produce illuminated manuscripts and ivory reliefs inspired by Late Antique and Byzantine sources ❙ Ottonian architects introduce the alternate-support system and galleries into the naves of churches | |

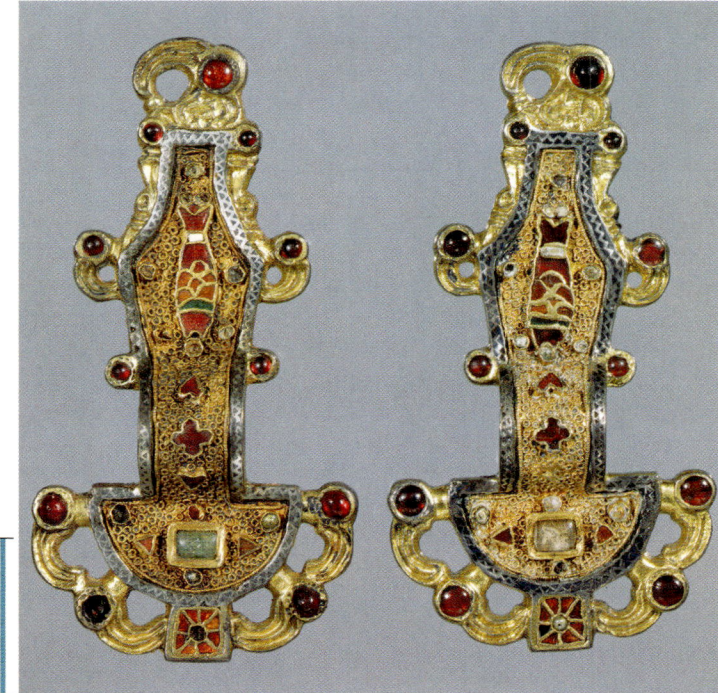

1 in.

**11-2** Pair of Merovingian looped fibulae, from Jouy-le-Comte, France, mid-sixth century. Silver gilt worked in filigree, with inlays of garnets and other stones, 4″ high. Musée d'Archéologie Nationale, Saint-Germain-en-Laye.

Jeweled fibulae were status symbols among early medieval warlords. This pair, probably owned by a Merovingian woman, features eagle heads and fish integrated into a highly decorative design.

**MEROVINGIAN FIBULAE** Most characteristic, perhaps, of the prestige adornments of the early medieval period was the *fibula*, a decorative pin the Romans wore (and the Etruscans before them; FIG. 6-2). Men and women alike used fibulae to fasten their garments. Made of bronze, silver, or gold, these pins often featured profuse decoration, sometimes incorporating inlaid precious or semi-precious stones. The pair of fibulae illustrated here (FIG. **11-2**) formed part of a find of jewelry of the mid-sixth century, when Merovingian kings (r. 482–751) ruled large parts of what is now France. The pins, probably once the proud possession of a wealthy Merovingian woman, accompanied their owner into the afterlife. They resemble, in general form, the roughly contemporaneous but plain fibulae used to fasten the outer garments of some of the attendants flanking the Byzantine emperor Justinian in the apse mosaic (FIG. 9-13) of San Vitale in Ravenna. (Note how much more elaborate is the emperor's clasp. In Rome, Byzantium, and early medieval Europe alike, these fibulae were emblems of office and of prestige.)

Covering almost the entire surface of each of the Merovingian fibulae are decorative patterns adjusted carefully to the basic shape of the object. They thus describe and amplify the fibula's form and structure, becoming an organic part of the pin itself. Often the early medieval metalworkers so successfully integrated zoomorphic elements into this type of highly disciplined, abstract decorative design that the animal forms became almost unrecognizable. For example, the fibulae in FIG. 11-2 incorporate a fish just below the center of each pin. The looped forms around the edges are stylized eagles' heads with red garnets forming the eyes.

**SUTTON HOO SHIP BURIAL** The *Beowulf* saga also recounts the funeral of the warrior lord Scyld, whom his comrades laid to rest in a ship overflowing with arms and armor and costly adornments set adrift in the North Sea.

sophistication, as treasures. The objects enhanced their owners' prestige and testified to the stature of those buried with them. In the great early (possibly seventh-century) Anglo-Saxon epic *Beowulf,* after Beowulf dies, his comrades cremate the hero and place his ashes in a huge *tumulus* (burial mound) overlooking the sea. As an everlasting tribute to Beowulf's greatness, they "buried rings and brooches in the barrow, all those adornments that brave men had brought out from the hoard after Beowulf died. They bequeathed the gleaming gold, treasure of men, to the earth."[2]

> They laid their dear lord, the giver of rings, deep within the ship by the mast in majesty; many treasures and adornments from far and wide were gathered there. I have never heard of a ship equipped more handsomely with weapons and war-gear, swords and corselets; on his breast lay countless treasures that were to travel far with him into the waves' domain.[3]

In 1939, archaeologists uncovered a treasure-laden ship in a burial mound at Sutton Hoo, near the sea, in Suffolk, England. Although the Sutton Hoo ship never set out to sea, it epitomizes the early medieval tradition of burying great lords in ships with rich furnishings, as recorded in *Beowulf.* Among the many precious finds were a purse cover (FIG. **11-3**) with gold, glass, and garnet ornamentation, a gold belt

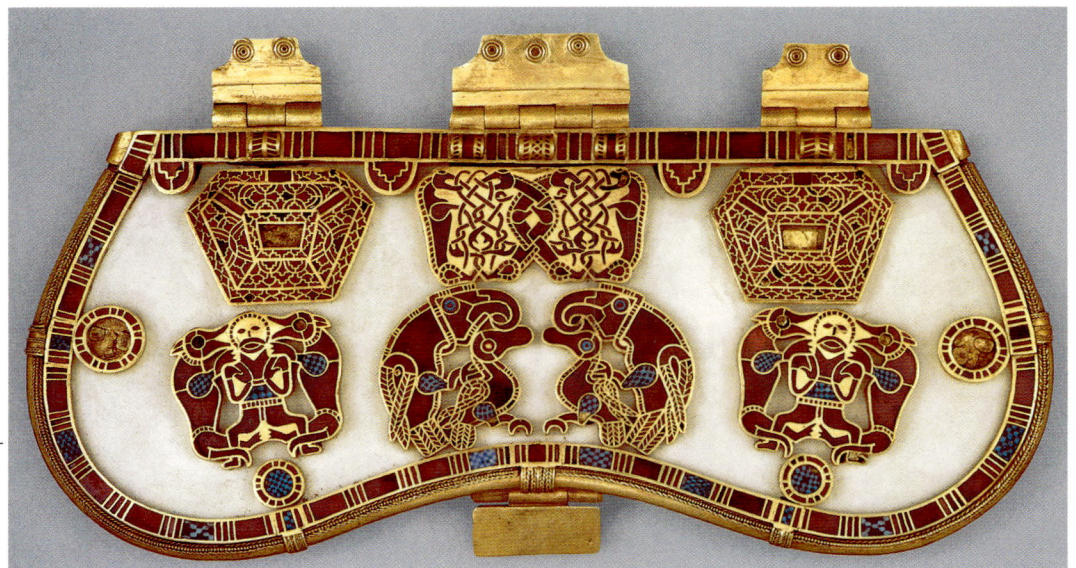

1 in.

**11-3** Purse cover, from the Sutton Hoo ship burial in Suffolk, England, ca. 625. Gold, glass, and cloisonné garnets, $7\frac{1}{2}$″ long. British Museum, London (gift of Mrs. E. M. Pretty). ◼◀

This purse cover comes from a treasure-laden royal burial ship. The combination of abstract interlace ornamentation with animal figures is the hallmark of the art of the early Middle Ages in western Europe.

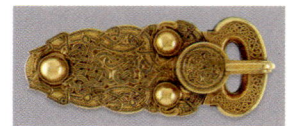

buckle (FIG. 11-3A), 10 silver bowls, a silver plate with the imperial stamp of the Byzantine emperor Anastasius I (r. 491–518), and 40 gold coins (perhaps to pay the 40 oarsmen who would row the deceased across the sea on his final voyage). Also placed in the ship were two silver spoons inscribed "Saulos" and "Paulos," Saint Paul's names in Greek before and after his baptism. They may allude to a conversion to Christianity. Some historians have associated the ship with the East Anglian king Raedwald (r. 599?–625), who was baptized a Christian before his death in 625, but the identity of the king buried at Sutton Hoo is uncertain.

The most extraordinary item found in the Sutton Hoo ship is the purse cover (FIG. 11-3). The decoration consists of seven *cloisonné* plaques within a cloisonné border. The cloisonné technique, a favorite of the early medieval "treasure givers," dates at least as early as the New Kingdom in Egypt. Metalworkers produced cloisonné jewelry by soldering small metal strips, or *cloisons* (French for "partitions"), edge up, to a metal background, and then filling the compartments with semiprecious stones, pieces of colored glass, or glass paste fired to resemble sparkling jewels. The edges of the cloisons are an important part of the design. Cloisonné is a cross between mosaic and stained glass (see "Mosaics," Chapter 8, page 245, and "Stained-Glass Windows," Chapter 13, page 375), but medieval artists used it only on a miniature scale.

On the Sutton Hoo purse cover, four symmetrically arranged groups of figures make up the lower row. The end groups consist of a man standing between two beasts. He faces front, and they appear in profile. This heraldic type of grouping has a venerable heritage in the ancient world (FIG. 2-10) but must have delivered a powerful contemporary message. It is a pictorial parallel to the epic sagas of the era in which heroes such as Beowulf battle and conquer horrific monsters. The two center groups represent eagles attacking ducks. The metalworker ingeniously composed the animal figures. For example, the convex beaks of the eagles (compare the Merovingian fibulae, FIG. 11-2) fit against the concave beaks of the ducks. The two figures fit together so snugly they seem at first to be a single dense abstract design. This is true also of the man-animals motif.

Above these figures are three geometric designs. The outer ones are purely linear, although they also rely on color contrasts for their effect. The central design is an interlace pattern in which the interlacements evolve into writhing animal figures. Elaborate intertwining linear patterns are characteristic of many times and places, notably in the art of the Islamic world (see Chapter 10). But the combination of interlace with animal figures was uncommon outside the realm of the early medieval warlords. In fact, metalcraft with interlace patterns and other motifs beautifully integrated with the animal form was, without doubt, the premier art of the early Middle Ages in northwestern Europe. Interest in it was so great that artists imitated the colorful effects of jewelry designs in the painted decorations of manuscripts (FIG. 11-1), in the masonry of churches, and in sculpture in stone and in wood, the last an especially important medium of Viking art.

**VIKINGS** In 793, the pre-Christian traders and pirates of Scandinavia known as Vikings (named after the *viks*—coves or "trading places"—of the Norwegian shoreline) landed in the British Isles. They destroyed the Christian monastic community on Lindisfarne Island off the Northumbrian (northeastern) coast of England. Shortly after, these Norsemen (North men) attacked the monastery

at Jarrow in England as well as that on Iona Island, off the west coast of Scotland. From then until the mid-11th century, the Vikings were the terror of western Europe. From their great ships they seasonally harried and plundered harbors and river settlements. Their fast, seaworthy longboats took them on wide-ranging voyages, from Ireland eastward to Russia and westward to Iceland and Greenland and even, briefly, to Newfoundland in North America, long before Columbus arrived in the New World.

The Vikings were intent not merely on a hit-and-run strategy of destruction but also on colonizing the lands they occupied by conquest. Their exceptional talent for organization and administration, as well as for war, enabled them to conquer and govern large territories in Ireland, England, and France, as well as in the Baltic regions and Russia. For a while, in the early 11th century, the whole of England was part of a Danish empire. When Vikings settled in northern France in the early 10th century, their territory came to be called Normandy—home of the Norsemen who became Normans. (Later, a Norman duke, William the Conqueror, sailed across the English Channel and invaded and became the master of Anglo-Saxon England; FIG. 12-38.)

**OSEBERG SHIP BURIAL** Much of the preserved art of the Viking sea-rovers consists of decoration of their great wooden ships (FIGS. 11-4 and 11-4A). Striking examples of Viking woodcarving come from a ship burial near the sea at Oseberg, Norway. The ship, discovered beneath an

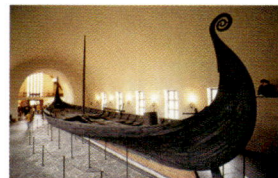

earthen mound as was the earlier Sutton Hoo burial, is more than 70 feet long. The vessel contained the remains of two women. The size of the burial alone and the lavishly carved wooden ornamentation of the sleek ship attest to the importance of those laid to rest

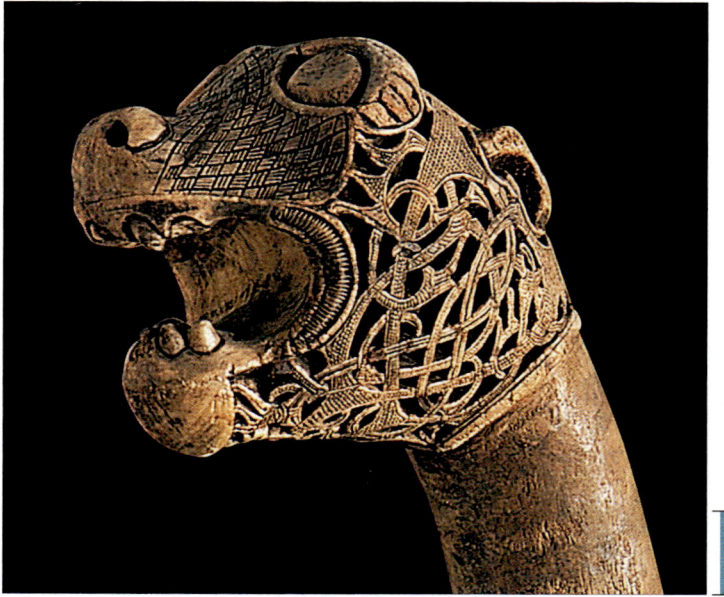

1 in.

**11-4 Animal-head post, from the Viking ship burial, Oseberg, Norway, ca. 825. Wood, head 5″ high. Viking Ship Museum, University of Oslo, Bygdoy.**

The Vikings were master wood-carvers. This Viking ship post combines in one composition the head of a roaring beast with surface ornamentation in the form of tightly interwoven writhing animals.

there. The vessel also once must have carried many precious objects robbers stole long before its modern discovery.

An animal-head post (FIG. 11-4) is characteristic of the masterfully carved decoration of the Oseberg ship. It combines in one composition the image of a roaring beast with protruding eyes and flaring nostrils and the complex, controlled pattern of tightly interwoven animals that writhe, gripping and snapping, in serpentine fashion. The Oseberg animal head is a powerfully expressive example of the union of two fundamental motifs of the warrior lords' art—the animal form and the interlace pattern.

**STAVE CHURCH, URNES** By the 11th century, much of Scandinavia had become Christian, but Viking artistic traditions persisted. Nowhere is this more evident than in the decoration of the portal (FIG. 11-5) of the stave church (*staves* are wedge-shaped timbers placed vertically) at Urnes, Norway. The portal and a few staves are almost all that remain from the mid-11th century church. Builders later incorporated these fragments into the walls of the 12th-century church. Gracefully elongated animal forms intertwine with flexible plant stalks and tendrils in spiraling rhythm. The effect of natural growth is astonishing, yet the designer subjected the organic forms to a highly refined abstract sensibility. This intricate Urnes style was the culmination of three centuries of Viking inventiveness.

# HIBERNO-SAXON ART

At the same time that powerful Merovingian, Anglo-Saxon, and Scandinavian warlords were amassing artworks dominated by abstract and animal motifs, Christian missionaries were establishing monasteries in northern Europe and sponsoring artworks of Christian content. The early medieval art of these monasteries, however, differs dramatically from contemporaneous works produced in Italy and the Byzantine Empire. These Christian artworks are among the most distinctive ever created and testify to the fruitful fusion of native and imported artistic traditions.

In Ireland, in part because of their isolation, the Celts who converted to Christianity, although nominally subject to the Roman popes, quickly developed a form of monastic organization that differed from the Church of Rome's. The monks often selected inaccessible and inhospitable places where they could carry on their duties far from worldly temptations and distractions. Before long, Irish monks, filled with missionary zeal, set up monastic establishments in Britain and Scotland. In 563, Saint Columba founded an important monastery on the Scottish island of Iona, where he successfully converted the native Picts to Christianity. Iona monks established the monastery at Lindisfarne off the northern coast of Britain in 635 and around 800 produced the extraordinary *Book of Kells* (FIG. 11-1).

The *Book of Kells* (named after the abbey in central Ireland that once owned it) is the outstanding example of the style art historians have named *Hiberno-Saxon* (Hibernia was the Roman name of Ireland) or *Insular* to denote the monastic art of the Irish-English islands. The most distinctive products of the Hiberno-Saxon monasteries were illuminated Christian books (see "Medieval Books," page 312). Books were the primary vehicles in the effort to Christianize Britain, Scotland, and Ireland. Indeed, they brought the word of God to a predominantly illiterate population who regarded the monks' sumptuous volumes with awe. Books were scarce and jealously guarded treasures of the libraries and *scriptoria* (writing studios) of monasteries and major churches. Illuminated books are the most important extant monuments of the brilliant artistic culture that flourished in Ireland and Northumbria during the seventh and eighth centuries.

***BOOK OF DURROW*** Among the earliest Hiberno-Saxon illuminated manuscripts is the *Book of Durrow,* a Gospel book that may have been written and decorated in the monastic scriptorium at Iona, although it has no documented provenance. In the late Middle Ages, it was in the monastery in Durrow, Ireland—hence its modern name. The Durrow Gospels already display one of the most characteristic features of Insular book illumination—full pages devoted neither to text nor to illustration but to pure embellishment. The Hiberno-Saxon painters must have felt beautiful decoration lent prestige to books just as ornamental jewelry lent status to those who wore it. Interspersed between the Durrow text pages are so-called *carpet pages,* resembling textiles, made up of decorative panels of abstract and zoomorphic forms (compare FIG. 11-7). The *Book of Durrow* also contains pages where the illuminator enormously enlarged the initial letters of an important passage of sacred text and transformed those letters into elaborate decorative patterns (compare FIG. 11-1). Such manuscript pages have no precedents in Greco-Roman books. They reveal the striking independence of Insular artists from the classical tradition.

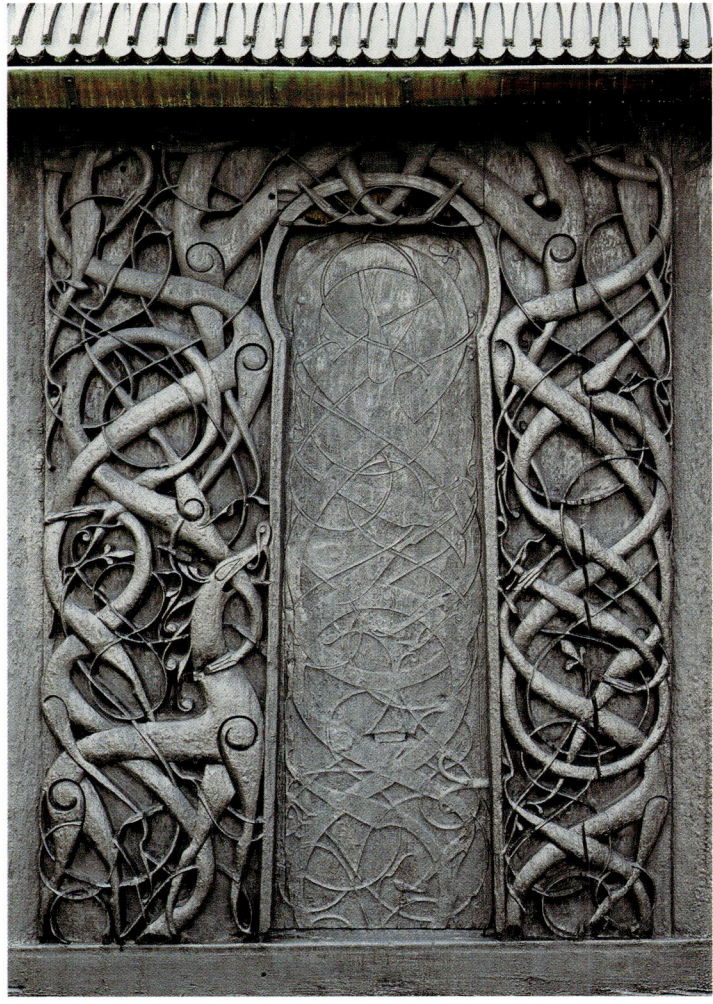

**11-5** Wooden portal of the stave church at Urnes, Norway, ca. 1050–1070.

By the 11th century, Scandinavia had become mostly Christian, but Viking artistic traditions persisted, as in the intertwining animal-and-plant decoration of this Norwegian church portal.

# Medieval Books

The central role books played in the medieval Church led to the development of a large number of specialized types for priests, monks and nuns, and laypersons.

The primary sacred text came to be called the Bible ("the Book"), consisting of the Hebrew scriptures (the "Old Testament") and the Christian "New Testament," written in Greek. In the late fourth century, Saint Jerome produced the canonical Latin, or *Vulgate* (vulgar, or common tongue), version of the Bible, which incorporates 46 Old and 27 New Testament books. Before the invention of the printing press in the 15th century, all books were handwritten ("manuscripts," from the Latin *manu scriptus*). Bibles were major undertakings, and few early medieval monasteries possessed a complete Bible. Instead, scribes usually produced separate volumes containing several biblical books.

The *Pentateuch* contains the five books of the Jewish Torah, beginning with the story of Adam and Eve (Genesis). The *Gospels* ("good news") are the New Testament works of Saints Matthew, Mark, Luke, and John (see "The Four Evangelists," page 314) and tell the story of the life of Christ (see "The Life of Jesus in Art," Chapter 8, pages 240–241). Medieval Gospel books often contained *canon tables*—a concordance, or matching, of the corresponding passages of the four Gospels, which Eusebius of Caesarea compiled in the fourth century. *Psalters* collected the 150 psalms of King David, written in Hebrew and translated into both Greek and Latin.

The Church also frequently employed other types of books. The *lectionary* contains passages from the Gospels reordered to appear in the sequence that priests read them during the celebration of Mass throughout the year. *Breviaries* include the texts required for monks' daily recitations. *Sacramentaries* incorporate the prayers priests recite during Mass. *Benedictionals* contain bishops' blessings. In the later Middle Ages, scribes developed books for the private devotions of the laity, patterned after monks' readers. The

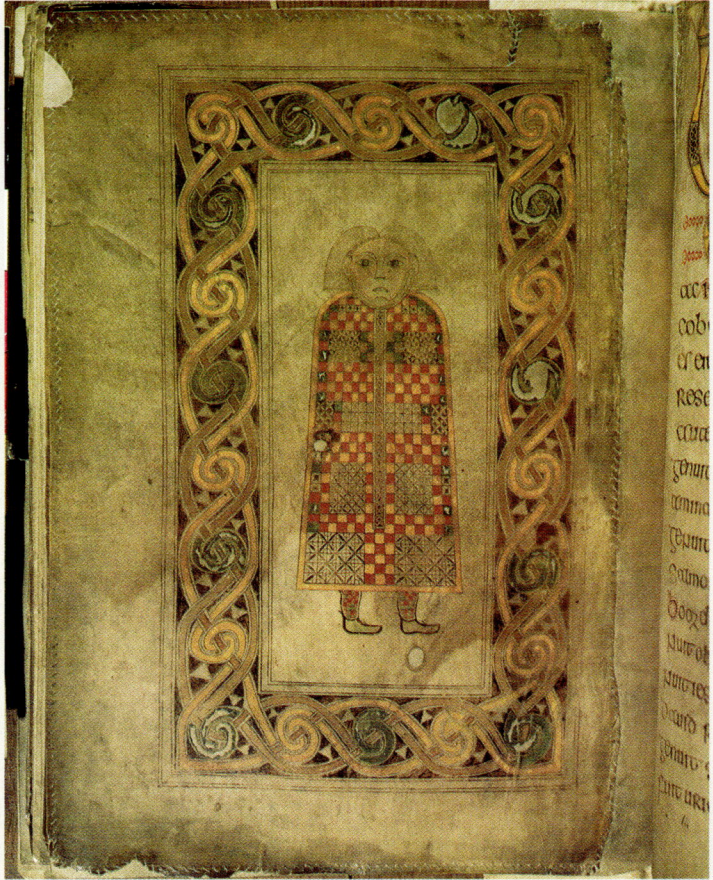

**11-6** Man (symbol of Saint Matthew), folio 21 verso of the *Book of Durrow*, possibly from Iona, Scotland, ca. 660–680. Ink and tempera on parchment, $9\frac{5}{8}'' \times 6\frac{1}{8}''$. Trinity College Library, Dublin.

This early Hiberno-Saxon Gospel book has four pages devoted to the symbols of the four evangelists. The cloak of Saint Matthew's man resembles a cloisonné brooch filled with abstract ornamentation.

1 in.

most popular was the *Book of Hours,* so called because it contains the prayers to be read at specified times of the day.

Medieval scribes produced many other types of books—compilations of saints' lives (*passionals*), theological treatises, secular texts on history and science, and even some classics of Greco-Roman literature—but these contained illustrations less frequently than did the various sacred texts.

---

In the *Book of Durrow,* each of the four Gospel books has a carpet page facing a page dedicated to the symbol of the evangelist who wrote that Gospel. An elaborate interlace design similar to those found on contemporaneous belt buckles and brooches frames each symbol. These pages served to highlight the major divisions of the text. The symbol of Saint Matthew (FIG. **11-6**) is a man (more commonly represented later as winged; see "The Four Evangelists," page 314), but the only human parts the artist—a seventh-century monk—chose to render are a schematic frontal head and two profile feet. A cloak of yellow, red, and green squares—resembling cloisons filled with intricate abstract designs and outlined in dark brown or black—envelops the rest of the "body." The *Book of Durrow* weds the abstraction of northern European early medieval personal

adornment with the Christian pictorial imagery of Italy and Byzantium. The vehicle for the transmission of those Mediterranean forms was the illustrated book itself, which Christian missionaries brought to Ireland.

***LINDISFARNE GOSPELS*** The marriage between Christian imagery and the animal-interlace style of the northern warlords is evident in the cross-inscribed carpet page (FIG. **11-7**) of the *Lindisfarne Gospels.* Produced in the Northumbrian monastery on Lindisfarne Island, the book contains several ornamental pages and exemplifies Hiberno-Saxon art at its best. According to a later *colophon* (an inscription, usually on the last page, providing information regarding a book's manufacture), Eadfrith, bishop of Lindisfarne

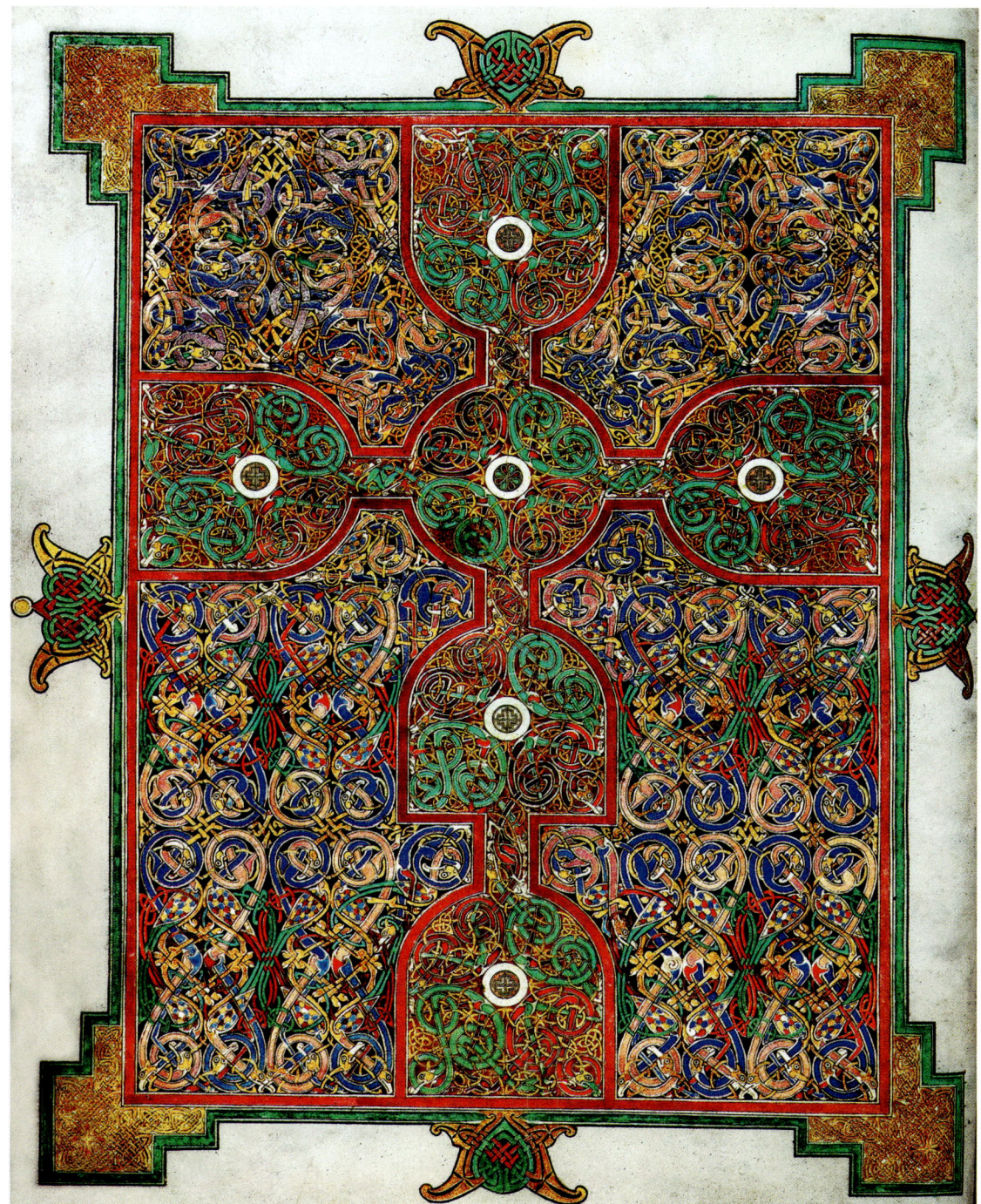

**11-7** Cross-inscribed carpet page, folio 26 verso of the *Lindisfarne Gospels,* from Northumbria, England, ca. 698–721. Tempera on vellum, 1' 1$\frac{1}{2}$" × 9$\frac{1}{4}$". British Library, London.

The cross-inscribed carpet page of the *Lindisfarne Gospels* exemplifies the way Hiberno-Saxon illuminators married Christian imagery and the animal-interlace style of the early medieval warlords.

1 in.

between 698 and his death in 721, wrote the *Lindisfarne Gospels* "for God and Saint Cuthbert." Cuthbert's relics recently had been deposited in the Lindisfarne church (see "The Veneration of Relics," Chapter 12, page 336).

The patterning and detail of this Lindisfarne ornamental page are much more intricate than the *Book of Durrow* pages. Serpentine interlacements of fantastic animals devour each other, curling over and returning on their writhing, elastic shapes. The rhythm of expanding and contracting forms produces a vivid effect of motion and change, but the painter held it in check by the regularity of the design and by the dominating motif of the inscribed cross. The cross—the all-important symbol of the imported religion—stabilizes the rhythms of the serpentines and, perhaps by contrast with

its heavy immobility, seems to heighten the effect of motion. The illuminator placed the motifs in detailed symmetries, with inversions, reversals, and repetitions the viewer must study closely to appreciate not only their variety but also their mazelike complexity. The zoomorphic forms intermingle with clusters and knots of line, and the whole design vibrates with energy. The color is rich yet cool. The painter adroitly adjusted shape and color to achieve a smooth and perfectly even surface.

Like most Hiberno-Saxon artworks, the Lindisfarne cross page displays the artist's preference for small, infinitely complex, and painstaking designs. Even the Matthew symbol (FIG. 11-6) in the *Book of Durrow* reveals the illuminator's concern was abstract design, not the depiction of the natural world. But exceptions exist. In some

# The Four Evangelists

*E*vangelist derives from the Greek word for "one who announces good news," namely the Gospel of Christ. The authors of the Gospels, the first four books of the New Testament, are Saints Matthew, Mark, Luke, and John, collectively known as the four evangelists. The Gospel books provide the authoritative account of the life of Jesus, differing in some details but together constituting the literary basis for the iconography of Christian art (see "The Life of Jesus in Art," Chapter 8, pages 240–241). Each evangelist has a unique symbol derived from passages in Ezekiel (1:5–14) and the Apocalypse (4:6–8).

**11-8** Saint Matthew, folio 25 verso of the *Lindisfarne Gospels*, from Northumbria, England, ca. 698–721. Tempera on vellum, 1' $\frac{1}{2}$" × 9$\frac{1}{4}$". British Library, London. ◼◄

Portraits of the four evangelists frequently appeared in Gospel books. A Mediterranean book probably inspired this Hiberno-Saxon depiction of Saint Matthew with his symbol, a winged man.

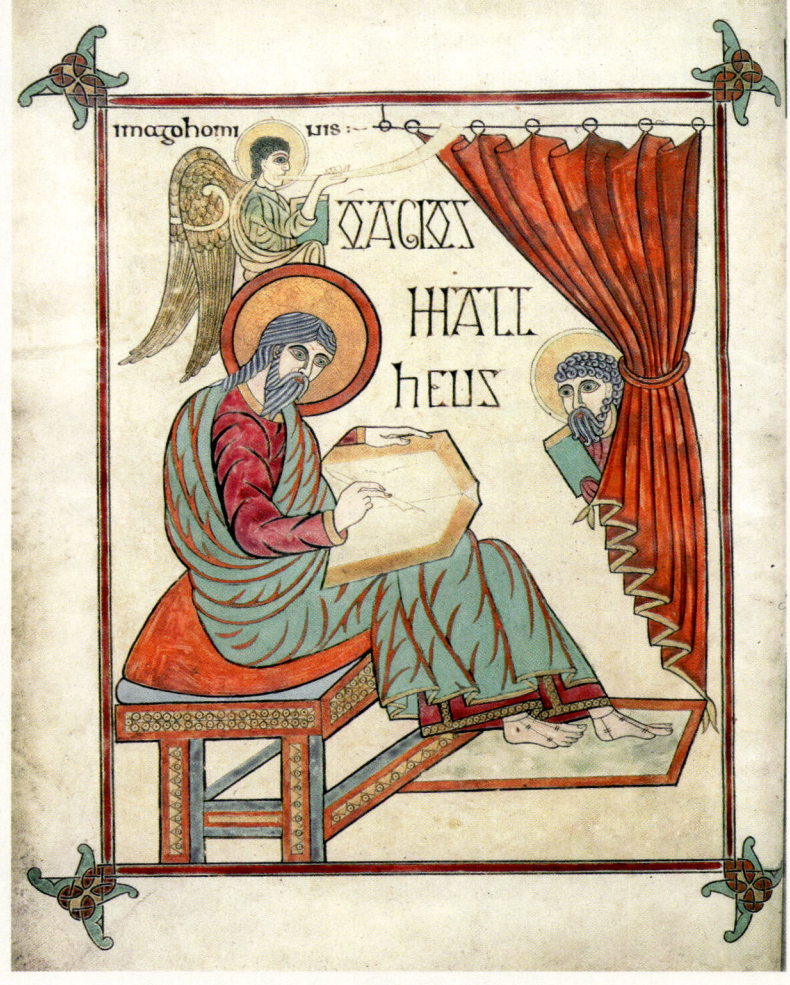

1 in.

- **Matthew** was a tax collector in Capernaum before Jesus called him to become an apostle. Little else is known about him, and accounts differ as to how he became a martyr. Matthew's symbol is the winged man or angel, because his Gospel opens with a description of the human ancestry of Christ.

- **Mark** was the first bishop of Alexandria in Egypt, where he suffered martyrdom. He was a companion of both Saint Peter and Saint Paul. One tradition says Peter dictated the Gospel to Mark, or at least inspired him to write it. Because Mark's Gospel begins with a voice crying in the wilderness, his symbol is the lion, the king of the desert.

- **Luke** was a disciple of Saint Paul, who refers to Luke as a physician. A later tradition says Luke painted a portrait of the Virgin Mary and the Christ Child. Consequently, late medieval painters' guilds often chose Luke as their patron saint. Luke's symbol is the ox, because his Gospel opens with a description of the priest Zacharias sacrificing an ox.

- **John** was one of the most important apostles. He sat next to Jesus at the last supper and was present at the crucifixion, lamentation, and transfiguration. John was also the author of the Apocalypse, the last book of the New Testament, which he wrote in exile on the Greek island of Patmos. The Apocalypse records John's visions of the end of the world, the last judgment, and the second

coming. John's symbol is the eagle, the soaring bird connected with his apocalyptic visions.

The four evangelists appear frequently in medieval art, especially in illuminated Gospel books where they regularly serve as frontispieces to their respective Gospels. Often, artists represented them as seated authors, with or without their symbols (FIGS. I-8, 11-8, 11-13, and 11-14). In some instances, all four evangelists appear together (FIG. I-8). Frequently, both in painting and in sculpture, artists represented only the symbols (FIGS. 9-14A, 11-6, 12-1, 12-8, 12-18, and 13-6).

Insular manuscripts, the artists based their compositions on classical pictures in imported Mediterranean books. This is the case with the author portrait of Saint Matthew (FIG. 11-8) in the *Lindisfarne Gospels*. The Hiberno-Saxon illuminator's model probably was an illustrated Gospel book a Christian missionary brought from Italy to England. Author portraits were familiar features of Greek and Latin books, and similar representations of seated philosophers or poets

writing or reading (FIGS. 7-25B, 7-71, and 8-7) abound in ancient art. The Lindisfarne Matthew sits in his study composing his account of the life of Christ. A curtain sets the scene indoors, as in classical art (FIG. 5-58), and Matthew's seat is at an angle, which also suggests a Mediterranean model employing classical perspective. The painter (or the scribe) labeled Matthew in a curious combination of Greek (*O Agios,* "saint"—written, however, using Latin rather than Greek

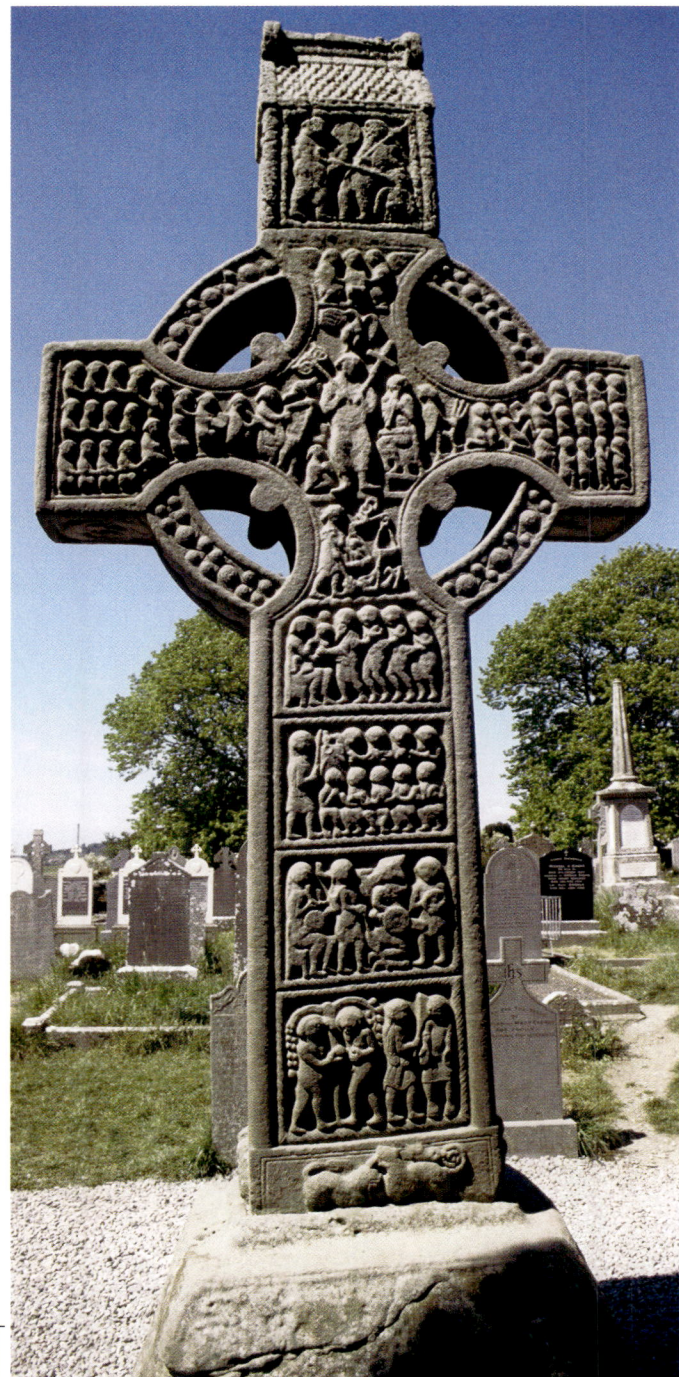

**11-9** *High Cross of Muiredach* (east face), Monasterboice, Ireland, 923. Sandstone, 18′ high.

Early medieval Irish high crosses are exceptional in size. The cross marking Muiredach's grave bears reliefs depicting the *Crucifixion* and *Last Judgment,* themes suited to a Christian burial.

in contrast with the open book of Matthew's New Testament, a common juxtaposition in medieval Christian art and thought.

Although a Mediterranean manuscript inspired the Lindisfarne composition, the Northumbrian painter's goal was not to copy the model faithfully. Instead, uninterested in the emphasis on volume, shading, and perspective that are the hallmarks of the pictorial illusionism of Greco-Roman painting, the Lindisfarne illuminator conceived the subject exclusively in terms of line and color. In the Hiberno-Saxon manuscript, the drapery folds are a series of sharp, regularly spaced, curving lines filled in with flat colors. The painter converted fully modeled forms bathed in light into the linear idiom of Insular art. The result is a vivid new vision of Saint Matthew.

**HIGH CROSSES** Surpassing the *Lindisfarne Gospels* in richness is the *Book of Kells,* which boasts an unprecedented number of full-page illuminations, including carpet pages, evangelist symbols, portrayals of the Virgin Mary and of Christ, New Testament narrative scenes, canon tables, and several instances (for example, FIG. 11-1, already discussed) of monumentalized and embellished words from the Bible. The *Book of Kells* is a relatively small object, however, designed for display on an altar. In the Hiberno-Saxon world, the high crosses of Ireland and northern England, set up between the 8th and 10th centuries, are exceptional in their mass and scale. These majestic monuments, some more than 20 feet in height, preside over burial grounds adjoining monasteries. Freestanding and unattached to any architectural fabric, the high crosses have the imposing unity, weight, and presence of both building and statue—architecture and sculpture combined.

The *High Cross of Muiredach* (FIG. **11-9**) at Monasterboice and the *South Cross* (FIG. **11-9A**) at Ahenny are two of the largest and finest early medieval high crosses. The Monasterboice cross is larger and more unusual because of its extensive narrative relief decoration. An inscription on the bottom of the west face of the shaft asks a prayer for a man named Muiredach. Most scholars identify him as the influential Irish cleric of the same name who was abbot of Monasterboice and died in 923. The monastery he headed was one of Ireland's oldest, founded in the late fifth century. The cross probably marked the abbot's grave. Four

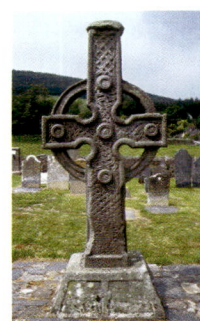

**11-9A** *South Cross,* Ahenny, late eighth century.

arcs forming a circle loop the concave arms, which expand into squared terminals (compare FIG. 11-7). The circle intersecting the cross identifies the type as Celtic. At the center of the west side of Muiredach's cross is a depiction of the crucified Christ. On the east side (FIG. 11-9), the risen Christ stands as judge of the world, the hope of the dead. Below him is a depiction of the weighing of souls on scales—a theme that two centuries later sculptors of church portals (FIG. 12-1) pursued with extraordinary force.

letters) and Latin (*Mattheus*), perhaps to lend the page the prestige of two classical languages. The former was the language of the New Testament, the latter that of the Church of Rome. Accompanying Matthew is his symbol, the winged man, labeled *imago hominis,* "image of the man" (see "The Four Evangelists," page 314). The identity of the figure—represented as a disembodied head and shoulders—behind the curtain is uncertain. Among the possibilities are Christ, Saint Cuthbert, and Moses holding the closed book of the Old Testament

# VISIGOTHIC AND MOZARABIC ART

The Romans never ruled Ireland, but Spain was a province of the Roman Empire for hundreds of years. The Roman conquest brought new roads to the Iberian peninsula and new cities with Roman temples, forums, theaters, and aqueducts. But in the early fifth century, the Roman cities fell to Germanic invaders, most notably the Visigoths, who had converted to Christianity. Many of the stone churches the Visigoths built in the sixth and seventh centuries still stand.

This three-aisled basilican church dedicated to Saint John the Baptist is typical of Visigothic architecture in Spain. It features three square apses and an entrance portal crowned by a horseshoe arch.

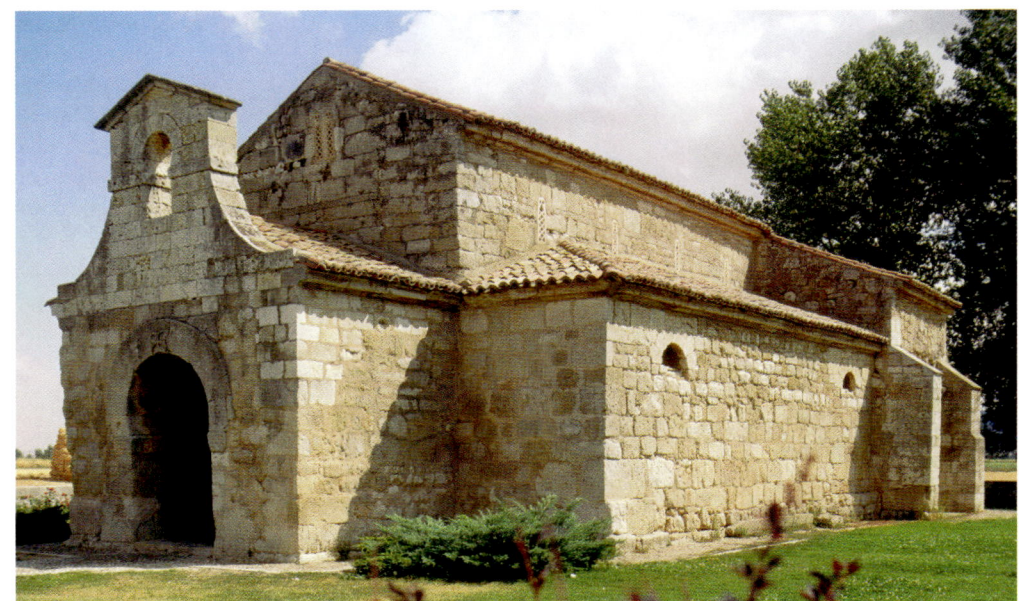

**BAÑOS DE CERRATO** An outstanding example is the church of San Juan Bautista (Saint John the Baptist, FIG. 11-10) at Baños de Cerrato, which the Visigothic king Recceswinth (r. 649–672) constructed in 661 in thanksgiving for a cure after bathing in the waters there. The Visigothic churches are basilican in form but often have multiple square apses. (The Baños de Cerrato church has three.) They also regularly incorporate horseshoe arches, a form usually associated with Islamic architecture (FIGS. 10-9 and 10-10) but that in Spain predates the Muslim conquest of 711.

**TÁBARA** Although the Islamic caliphs of Córdoba swept the Visigoths away (see Chapter 10), they never succeeded in gaining control of the northernmost parts of the peninsula. There, the Christian culture called *Mozarabic* (referring to Christians living in Arab territories) continued to flourish, as did some Jewish communities. One northern Spanish monk, Beatus (ca. 730–798), abbot of San Martín at Liébana, wrote *Commentary on the Apocalypse* around 776. This influential work was widely copied and illustrated in the monastic scriptoria of medieval Europe. One copy was produced at the monastery of San Salvador at Tábara in the kingdom of Léon in 970. The colophon (FIG. 11-11) to the illustrated *Commentary* presents the earliest known depiction of a medieval scriptorium. Because the artist provided a composite of exterior and interior views of the building, it is especially informative.

At the left is a great bell tower with a monk on the ground floor ringing the bells. The painter carefully recorded the Islamic-style glazed-tile walls of the tower, its interior ladders, and its elegant windows with their horseshoe arches, the legacy of the Visigoths. To the right, in the scriptorium proper, three monks perform their respective specialized duties. The colophon identifies the two monks in the main room as the scribe Senior and the painter EMETERIUS. To the right, a third monk uses shears to cut sheets of parchment. The colophon also pays tribute to Magius, "the worthy master painter. . . . May he deserve to be crowned with Christ,"[4] who died before he could complete his work on the book. His pupil Emeterius took his place and brought the project to fruition. He probably was the painter of the colophon.

The colophon of another Beatus manuscript, dated 975 and today in Girona Cathedral, also names Emeterius as coilluminator with the nun Ende, a "painter and servant of God." Ende's is one of the few recorded names of a woman artist in the Middle Ages, a rarity also in the ancient world (see "Iaia of Cyzicus," Chapter 7, page 218).

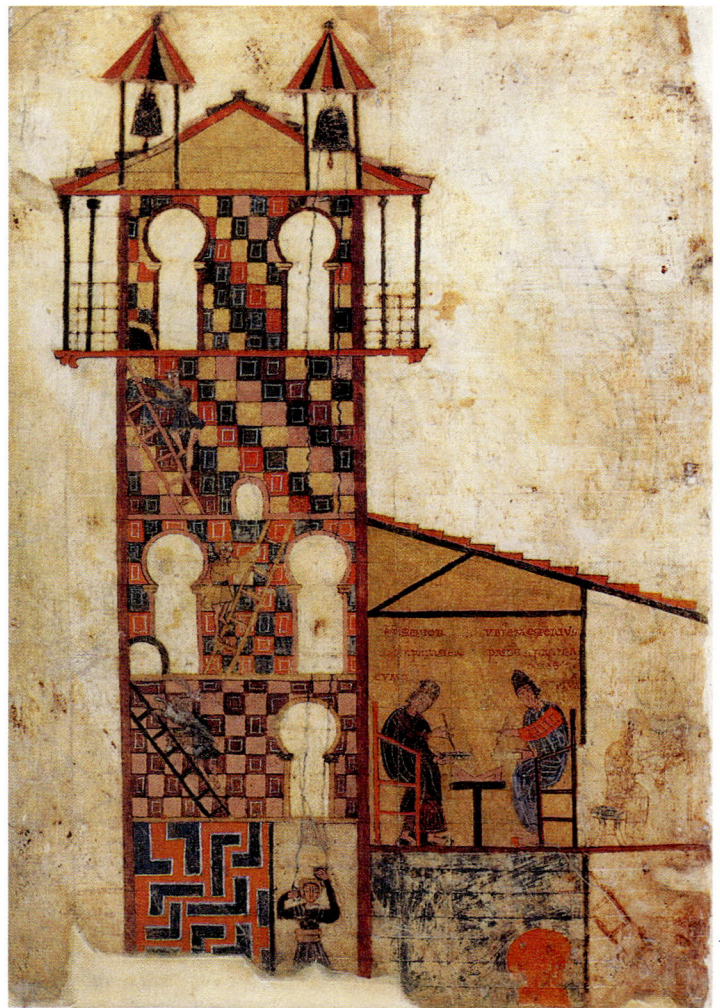

1 in.

**11-11** EMETERIUS, the tower and scriptorium of San Salvador de Tábara, colophon (folio 168) of the *Commentary on the Apocalypse* by Beatus, from Tábara, Spain, 970. Tempera on parchment, $1' 2\frac{1}{8}'' \times 10''$. Archivo Histórico Nacional, Madrid.

In this earliest known depiction of a medieval scriptorium, the painter carefully recorded the tower's Islamic-style glazed-tile walls and elegant windows with horseshoe arches, a Visigothic legacy.

## Charlemagne's *Renovatio Imperii Romani*

Charlemagne's official seal bore the phrase *renovatio imperii Romani* (renewal of the Roman Empire). As the pope's designated Roman emperor, Charlemagne sought to revive the glory of Early Christian Rome. He accomplished this in part through artistic patronage, commissioning imperial portrait statues (FIG. 11-12) and large numbers of illustrated manuscripts (FIGS. 11-12A and 11-13), and by fostering a general revival of learning.

To make his empire as splendid as Rome's, Charlemagne invited to his court at Aachen the best minds and the finest artisans of western Europe and the Byzantine East. Among them were Theodulf of Orléans (d. 821), Paulinus of Aquileia (d. 802), and Alcuin (d. 804), master of the cathedral school at York, the center of Northumbrian learning. Alcuin brought Anglo-Saxon scholarship to the Carolingian court.

Charlemagne himself, according to Einhard (d. 840), his biographer, could read and speak Latin fluently, in addition to Frankish, his native tongue. He also could understand Greek, and he studied rhetoric and mathematics with the learned men he gathered around him. But he never learned to write properly. That was a task best left to professional scribes. In fact, one of Charlemagne's dearest projects was the recovery of the true text of the Bible, which, through centuries of errors in copying, had become quite corrupted. Various scholars undertook the great project, but Alcuin of York's revision of the Bible, prepared at the new monastery at Tours, became the most widely used.

Charlemagne's scribes also were responsible for the development of a new, more compact, and more easily written and legible version of Latin script called *Caroline minuscule*. The letters on this page are descendants of the alphabet Carolingian scribes perfected. Later generations also owe to Charlemagne's patronage the restoration and copying of important classical texts. The earliest known manuscripts of many Greek and Roman authors are Carolingian in date.

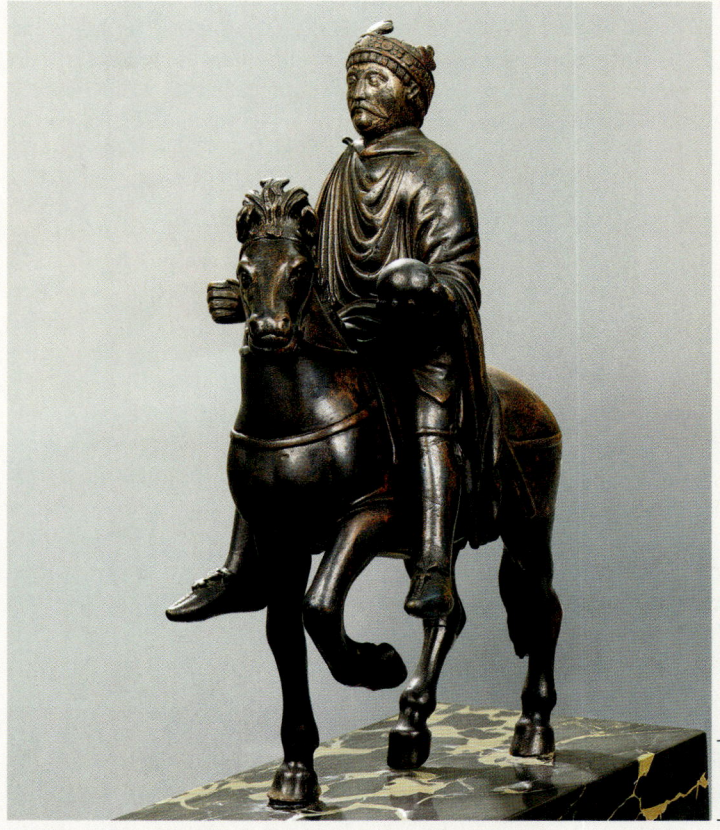

**11-12** Equestrian portrait of Charlemagne or Charles the Bald, from Metz, France, ninth century. Bronze, originally gilt, 9½″ high. Musée du Louvre, Paris.

The Carolingian emperors sought to revive the glory and imagery of the Roman Empire. This equestrian portrait depicts a crowned emperor holding a globe, the symbol of world dominion.

# CAROLINGIAN ART

On Christmas Day of the year 800, Pope Leo III (r. 795–816) crowned Charles the Great (Charlemagne), king of the Franks since 768, as emperor of Rome (r. 800–814). In time, Charlemagne came to be seen as the first Holy (that is, Christian) Roman Emperor, a title his successors did not formally adopt until the 12th century. The setting for Charlemagne's coronation, fittingly, was Saint Peter's basilica (FIG. 8-9) in Rome, built by Constantine, the first Roman emperor to embrace Christianity. Born in 742, when northern Europe was still in chaos, Charlemagne consolidated the Frankish kingdom his father and grandfather bequeathed him, defeated the Lombards in Italy (MAP 11-1), and laid claim to reviving the glory of the Roman Empire. He gave his name (Carolus Magnus in Latin) to an entire era, the *Carolingian* period.

The "Carolingian Renaissance" was a remarkable historical phenomenon, an energetic, brilliant emulation of the art, culture, and political ideals of Early Christian Rome (see "Charlemagne's *Renovatio Imperii Romani*," above). Charlemagne's (Holy) Roman Empire, waxing and waning for a thousand years and with many hiatuses, existed in central Europe until Napoleon destroyed it in 1806.

## Sculpture and Painting

When Charlemagne returned home from his coronation in Rome, he ordered the transfer of an equestrian statue of the Ostrogothic king Theodoric from Ravenna to the Carolingian palace complex at Aachen. That portrait is lost, as is the grand gilded-bronze statue of the Byzantine emperor Justinian that once crowned a column in Constantinople (see "The Emperors of New Rome," Chapter 9, page 259). But in the early Middle Ages, both statues stood as reminders of ancient Rome's glory and of the pretensions and aspirations of the medieval successors of Rome's Christian emperors.

**EQUESTRIAN STATUETTE** The portrait of Theodoric may have been the inspiration for a ninth-century bronze statuette (FIG. **11-12**) of a Carolingian emperor on horseback. Charlemagne greatly admired Theodoric, the first Germanic ruler of Rome. Many scholars have identified the small bronze figure as Charlemagne himself, although others think it portrays his grandson, Charles the Bald (r. 840–877). The ultimate model for the statuette was the equestrian portrait (FIG. 7-59) of Marcus Aurelius in Rome. In the Middle Ages, people mistakenly thought the bronze statue represented Constantine, another revered predecessor of Charlemagne and his Carolingian successors. Both the Roman and the medieval sculptors portrayed their emperor as overly large so that the ruler, not the horse, is the center of attention. But unlike Marcus Aurelius, who extends his right arm in a gesture of clemency to a foe who once cowered beneath the raised foreleg of his horse, Charlemagne (or Charles the Bald) is on parade. He wears imperial robes rather than a general's cloak, although his sheathed sword is visible. On his head is a crown, and in his outstretched left hand he holds a globe, symbol of world dominion. The portrait proclaimed the *renovatio* of the Roman Empire's power and trappings.

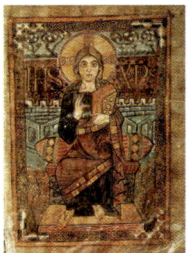

**11-12A** Christ enthroned, *Godesalc Lectionary*, 781–783.

***CORONATION GOSPELS*** Charlemagne was a sincere admirer of learning, the arts, and classical culture, even before his coronation as emperor of Rome. He placed high value on books, both sacred and secular, importing many and producing far more. One of the earliest is the *Godesalc Lectionary* (FIG. 11-12A), securely dated to 781 to 783, but the most famous is the early-ninth-century purple vellum *Coronation Gospels* (also known as the *Gospel Book of Charlemagne*), which has a text written in handsome gold letters. The major full-page illuminations, which show the four Gospel authors at work, reveal that Carolingian manuscript painters

brought a radically different stylistic sensibility to their work compared with their Hiberno-Saxon counterparts. For example, for the page depicting Saint Matthew (FIG. 11-13), the *Coronation Gospels* painter, in contrast to the Northumbrian illuminator who painted the portrait of the same evangelist in the *Lindisfarne Gospels* (FIG. 11-8), used color and modulation of light and shade, not line, to create shapes, and deft, illusionistic brushwork to define the massive drapery folds wrapped around Matthew's body. The cross-legged chair, the lectern, and the saint's toga are familiar Roman accessories. In fact, this Carolingian evangelist portrait closely follows the format and style of Greco-Roman author portraits, as exemplified by the seated Menander (FIG. 7-25B) at Pompeii. The *Coronation Gospels* landscape background also has many parallels in Roman painting, and the frame consists of the kind of acanthus leaves found in Roman temple capitals and friezes (FIG. 7-32). Almost nothing is known in the Hiberno-Saxon or Frankish world that could have prepared the way for this portrayal of Saint Matthew. If a Frankish, rather than an Italian or a Byzantine, artist painted the evangelist portraits of the *Coronation Gospels,* the Carolingian artist had fully absorbed the classical manner. Classical painting style was one of the many components of Charlemagne's program to establish Aachen as the capital of a renewed Christian Roman Empire.

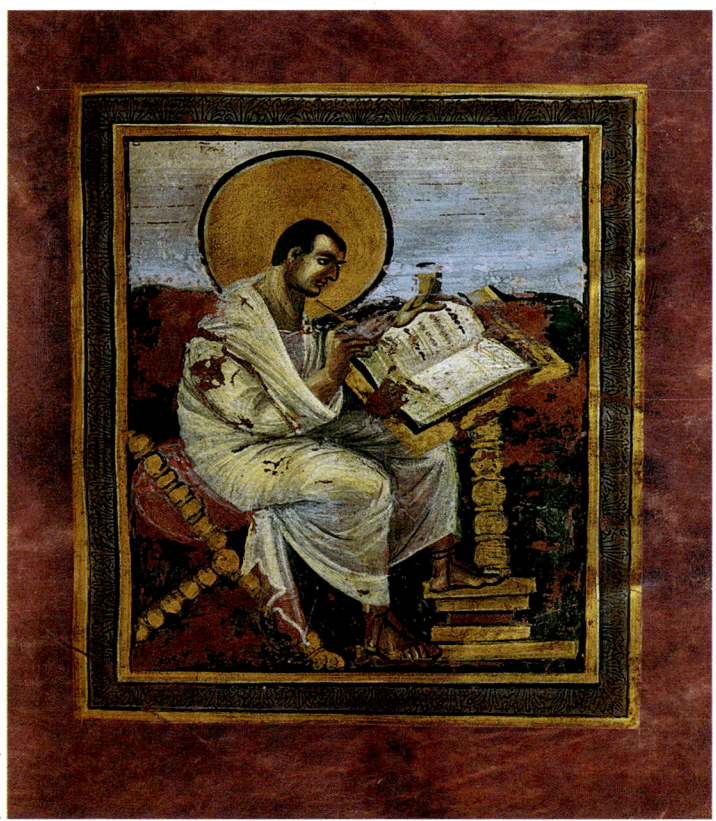

**11-13** Saint Matthew, folio 15 recto of the *Coronation Gospels* (*Gospel Book of Charlemagne*), from Aachen, Germany, ca. 800–810. Ink and tempera on vellum, 1' ¾" × 10". Schatzkammer, Kunsthistorisches Museum, Vienna. ◼◀

The books produced for Charlemagne's court reveal the legacy of classical art (FIG. 7-25B). The Carolingian painter used light, shade, and perspective to create the illusion of three-dimensional form.

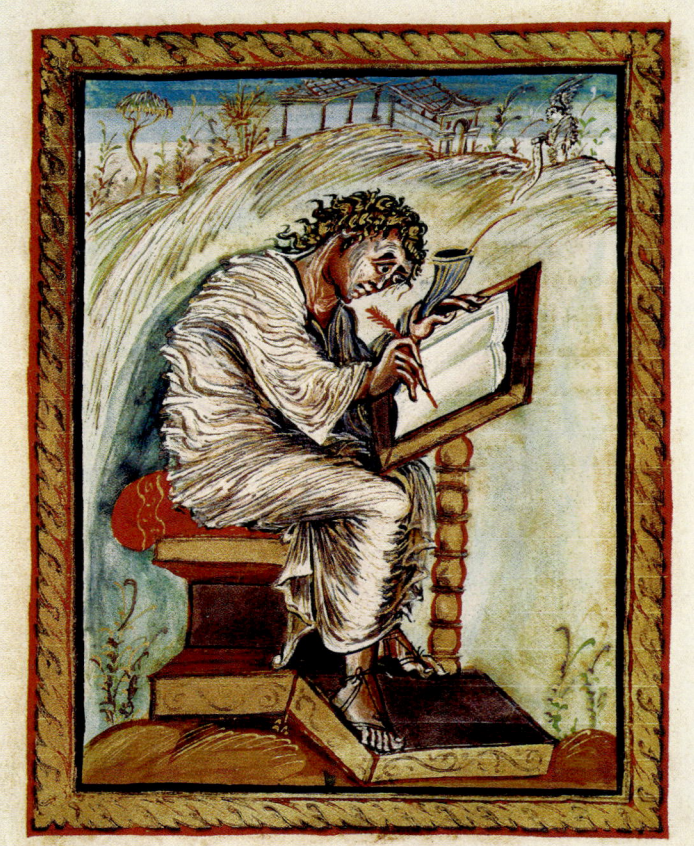

**11-14** Saint Matthew, folio 18 verso of the *Ebbo Gospels* (*Gospel Book of Archbishop Ebbo of Reims*), from Hautvillers, France, ca. 816–835. Ink and tempera on vellum, 10¼" × 8¾". Bibliothèque Municipale, Épernay. ◼◀

Saint Matthew writes frantically, and the folds of his drapery writhe and vibrate. Even the landscape rears up alive. The painter merged classical illusionism with the northern European linear tradition.

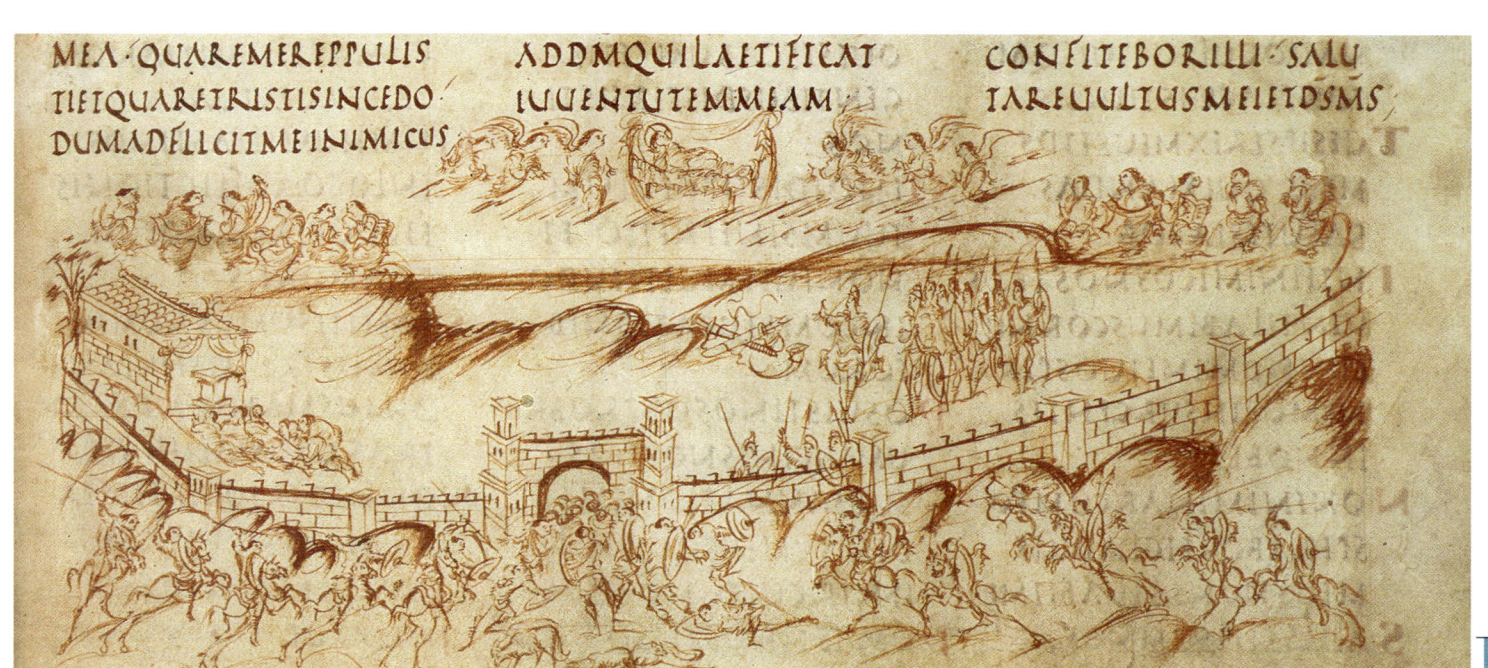

MEA·QUAREMEREPPULIS ADDMQUILAETIFICAT CONFITEBORILLI·SALU
TIETQUARETRISTISINCEDO IUUENTUTEMMEAM TAREUULTUSMEIETDSMS
DUMADELICITMEINIMICUS

1 in.

**11-15** Psalm 44, detail of folio 25 recto of the *Utrecht Psalter,* from Hautvillers, France, ca. 820–835. Ink on vellum, full page, 1′ 1″ × 9⅞″; detail, 4½″ high. University Library, Utrecht.

The drawings in the *Utrecht Psalter* are rich in anecdotal detail and show figures acting out—literally—King David's psalms. The vivid animation resembles that of the *Ebbo Gospels* Matthew (FIG. 11-14).

**EBBO GOSPELS** The classical-revival style evident in the *Coronation Gospels* was by no means the only one that appeared suddenly in the Carolingian world. Court school and monastic scriptoria employed a wide variety of styles derived from Late Antique prototypes. Another Saint Matthew (FIG. **11-14**), in a Gospel book made for Archbishop Ebbo of Reims, France, may be an interpretation of an author portrait very similar to the one the *Coronation Gospels* master used as a model. The *Ebbo Gospels* illuminator, however, replaced the classical calm and solidity of the *Coronation Gospels* evangelist with an energy approaching frenzy. Matthew (the winged man in the upper right corner identifies him) writes in frantic haste. His hair stands on end, his eyes open wide, the folds of his drapery writhe and vibrate, the landscape behind him rears up alive. The painter even set the page's leaf border in motion. Matthew's face, hands, inkhorn, pen, and book are the focus of the composition. This presentation contrasts strongly with the settled pose of the Saint Matthew of the *Coronation Gospels* with its even stress so that no part of the composition jumps out at viewers to seize their attention. Just as the painter of the *Lindisfarne Gospels* Matthew (FIG. 11-8) transformed an imported model into an original Hiberno-Saxon idiom, so the *Ebbo Gospels* artist translated a classical prototype into a new Carolingian vernacular. This master painter brilliantly merged classical illusionism and the northern linear tradition.

**UTRECHT PSALTER** One of the most extraordinary medieval manuscripts is the *Utrecht Psalter* (FIG. **11-15**). The text reproduces the psalms of David in three columns of Latin capital letters (FIG. **11-15A**) in emulation of the script and page organization of ancient books. The artist illustrated each psalm with a pen-and-ink drawing stretching across the entire width of the page. Some scholars have argued that the costumes and other details indicate the artist followed one or more manuscripts created 400 years before. Even if

the *Utrecht Psalter* is not a copy, the artist's intention was to evoke earlier artworks and to make the book appear ancient.

The painter of the *Utrecht Psalter* displayed a genius for anecdotal detail throughout the manuscript. On one page (FIG. 11-15), the figures act out—literally—Psalm 44 (Psalm 43 of the Vulgate text of the Carolingian era), in which the psalmist laments the plight of the oppressed Israelites. For example, the artist drew some slain sheep fallen to the ground ("We are counted

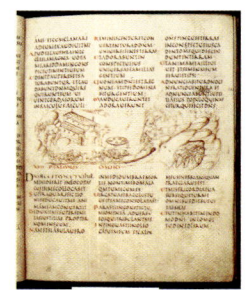

**11-15A** Psalm 23, *Utrecht Psalter,* ca. 820–835.

as sheep for slaughter") in front of a walled city reminiscent of cities on the Column of Trajan (FIG. 7-1) in Rome and in Early Christian mosaics (FIG. 8-14) and manuscripts (FIG. 8-21). At the left, the faithful grovel on the ground before a temple ("Our soul is bowed down to the dust; our belly cleaveth unto the earth"). In response to the six pleading angels ("Awake, why sleepest thou, O Lord?"), the artist depicted the Lord reclining in a canopied bed overlooking the slaughter below. But "the Lord" is Jesus, complete with cruciform halo, instead of David's Hebrew God. The drawing shows a vivid animation of much the same kind as the *Ebbo Gospels* Saint Matthew (FIG. 11-14). The bodies of the *Utrecht Psalter* figures are tense, with shoulders hunched and heads thrust forward. As in the *Ebbo Gospels,* even the earth heaves up around the figures. The rapid, sketchy techniques used to render the figures convey the same nervous vitality as found in the *Ebbo* evangelists.

**LINDAU GOSPELS** The taste for sumptuously wrought and portable objects, the hallmark of the art of the early medieval warlords, persisted under Charlemagne and his successors. The Carolingians commissioned numerous works employing costly materials, including book covers made of gold and jewels and sometimes

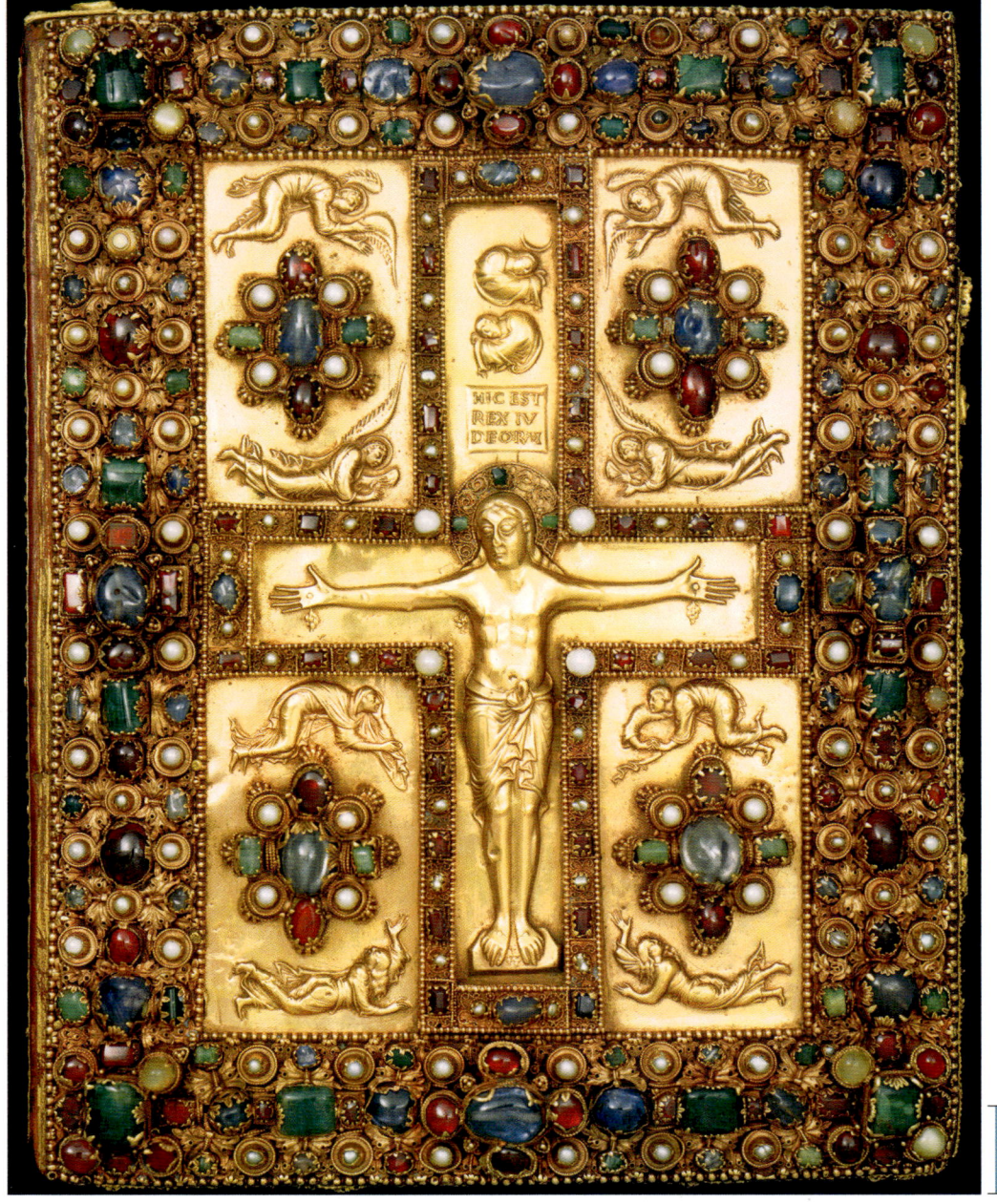

**11-16** *Crucifixion,* front cover of the *Lindau Gospels,* from Saint Gall, Switzerland, ca. 870. Gold, precious stones, and pearls, $1' 1\frac{3}{8}'' \times 10\frac{3}{8}''$. Pierpont Morgan Library, New York. ◼◂

This sumptuous Carolingian book cover revives the Early Christian imagery of the youthful Christ (FIG. 8-24). The statuesque, crucified Christ, heedless of pain, is classical in conception and execution.

1 in.

also ivory or pearls. Gold and gems not only glorified the word of God but also evoked the heavenly Jerusalem. One of the most luxurious Carolingian book covers (FIG. **11-16**) is the one later added to the *Lindau Gospels.* The gold cover, fashioned in one of the workshops of Charles the Bald's court, is monumental in conception. A youthful Christ in the Early Christian tradition, nailed to the cross, is the central motif. Surrounding Christ are pearls and jewels (raised on golden claw feet so they can catch and reflect the light even more brilliantly and protect the delicate metal relief from denting). The statuesque open-eyed figure, rendered in *repoussé* (hammered or pressed relief), recalls the beardless, unsuffering Christ of a fifth-century ivory plaque (FIG. 8-24) from Italy. In contrast, the four angels and the personifications of the Moon and the Sun above and the crouching figures of the Virgin Mary and Saint John (and two other figures of uncertain identity) in the quadrants below display the vivacity and nervous energy of the *Utrecht Psalter* figures (FIGS. 11-15 and 11-15A). The *Lindau Gospels* cover highlights the stylistic diversity of early medieval art in Europe. Here, however, the trans-

lated figural style of the Mediterranean prevailed, in keeping with the classical tastes and imperial aspirations of the Frankish emperors of Rome.

## Architecture

In his eagerness to reestablish the imperial past, Charlemagne also encouraged the use of Roman building techniques. In architecture, as in sculpture and painting, innovations made in the reinterpretation of earlier Roman Christian sources became fundamental to the subsequent development of northern European architecture. For his models, Charlemagne looked to Rome and Ravenna. One was the former heart of the Roman Empire, which he wanted to renew. The other was the long-term western outpost of Byzantine might and splendor, which he wanted to emulate in his own capital at Aachen, a site chosen because of its renowned hot springs.

**AACHEN** Charlemagne often visited Ravenna, and the equestrian statue of Theodoric he brought from there to display in his

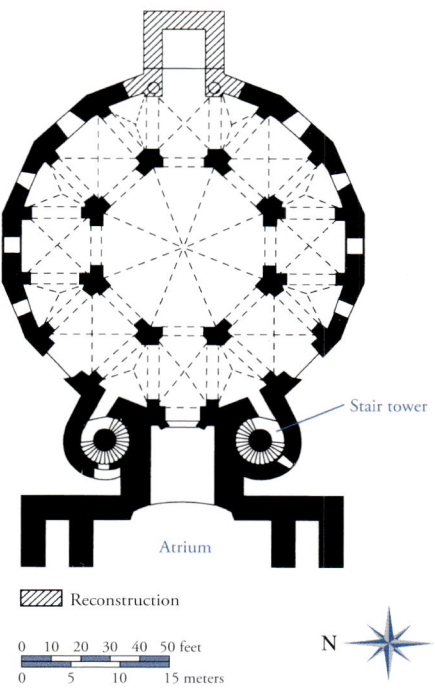

**11-17** Restored plan (*left*) and west facade (*right*) of the Palatine Chapel of Charlemagne, Aachen, Germany, 792–805.

Charlemagne sought to emulate Byzantine splendor in Germany. The plan of his Aachen palace chapel is based on that of San Vitale (FIG. 9-11) at Ravenna, but the west facade is distinctly Carolingian.

Stair tower

Atrium

Reconstruction

0 10 20 30 40 50 feet
0 5 10 15 meters

N

palace complex at Aachen served as a model for Carolingian equestrian portraits (FIG. 11-12). Charlemagne also imported porphyry (purple marble) columns from Ravenna to adorn his Palatine Chapel, and historians long have thought he chose one of Ravenna's churches as the model for the new structure. The plan (FIG. **11-17**, *left*) of the Aachen chapel resembles that of San Vitale (FIG. 9-11), and a direct relationship very likely exists between the two.

A comparison between the Carolingian chapel, the first vaulted structure of the Middle Ages north of the Alps, and its southern counterpart is instructive. The Aachen plan is simpler. The architect omitted San Vitale's apselike extensions reaching from the central octagon into the ambulatory. At Aachen, the two main units stand in greater independence of each other. This solution may lack the subtle sophistication of the Byzantine building, but the Palatine Chapel gains geometric clarity. A view of its interior (FIG. **11-18**) shows that Charlemagne's builders converted the "floating" quality of San Vitale (FIG. 9-1) into massive geometric form.

The Carolingian conversion of a complex and subtle Byzantine prototype into a building that expresses robust strength and clear structural articulation foreshadows the architecture of the 11th and 12th centuries and the style called Romanesque (see Chapter 12). So, too, does the treatment of the Palatine Chapel's exterior, where two cylindrical towers with spiral staircases flank the entrance portal (FIG. 11-17, *right*). This was a first step toward the great dual-tower facades of western European churches from the 10th century to the present. Above the portal, Charlemagne could appear in a large framing arch and be seen by those gathered in the atrium in front of the chapel. (The plan includes only part of the atrium.) Directly behind that second-story arch was Charlemagne's marble throne. From there he could peer down at the altar in the apse. Charlemagne's imperial gallery followed the model of the imperial gallery at Hagia Sophia (FIGS. 9-6 to 9-8) in Constantinople. The Palatine Chapel was in every sense a royal chapel. The coronation of Charlemagne's son, Louis the Pious (r. 814–840), took place there when he succeeded his father as emperor.

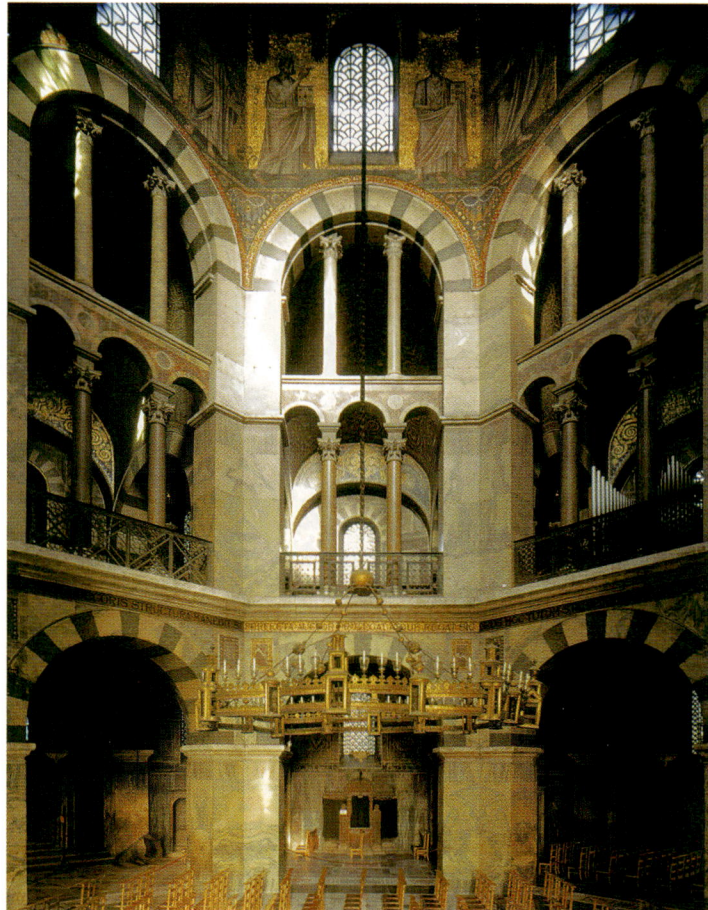

**11-18** Interior of the Palatine Chapel of Charlemagne (looking east), Aachen, Germany, 792–805.

Charlemagne's chapel is the first vaulted medieval structure north of the Alps. The architect transformed the complex, glittering interior of San Vitale (FIG. 9-1) into simple, massive geometric form.

## Medieval Monasteries and Benedictine Rule

Since Early Christian times, monks who established monasteries also made the rules that governed communal life. The most significant of these monks was Benedict of Nursia (Saint Benedict, ca. 480–547), who founded the Benedictine Order in 529. By the ninth century, the "Rule" Benedict wrote (*Regula Sancti Benedicti*) had become standard for all western European monastic communities, in part because Charlemagne had encouraged its adoption throughout the Frankish territories.

Saint Benedict believed the corruption of the clergy that accompanied the increasing worldliness of the Church had its roots in the lack of firm organization and regulation. As he saw it, idleness and selfishness had led to neglect of the commandments of God and of the Church. The cure for this was communal association in an *abbey* under the absolute rule of an *abbot* the monks elected (or an *abbess* the nuns chose), who would ensure the clergy spent each hour of the day in useful work and in sacred reading. The emphasis on work and study and not on meditation and austerity is of great historical significance. Since antiquity, manual labor had been considered unseemly, the business of the lowborn or of slaves. Benedict raised it to the dignity of religion. The core idea of what many people today call the "work ethic" found early expression in Benedictine monasteries as an essential feature of spiritual life. By thus exalting the virtue of manual labor, Benedict not only rescued it from its age-old association with slavery but also recognized it as the way to self-sufficiency for the entire religious community.

Whereas some of Saint Benedict's followers emphasized spiritual "work" over manual labor, others, most notably the Cistercians (see "Bernard of Clairvaux," Chapter 12, page 342), put Benedictine teachings about the value of physical work into practice. These monks reached into their surroundings and helped reduce the vast areas of daunting wilderness of early medieval Europe. They cleared dense forest teeming with wolves, bear, and wild boar, drained swamps, cultivated wastelands, and built roads, bridges, and dams, as well as monastic churches and their associated living and service quarters.

The ideal monastery (FIG. 11-19) provided all the facilities necessary for the conduct of daily life—a mill, bakery, infirmary, vegetable garden, and even a brewery—so the monks would feel no need to wander outside its protective walls. These religious communities were centrally important to the revival of learning. The clergy, who were also often scribes and scholars, had a monopoly on the skills of reading and writing in an age of almost universal illiteracy. The monastic libraries and scriptoria (FIG. 11-11), where the monks and nuns read, copied, illuminated, and bound books with ornamented covers, became centers of study. Monasteries were almost the sole

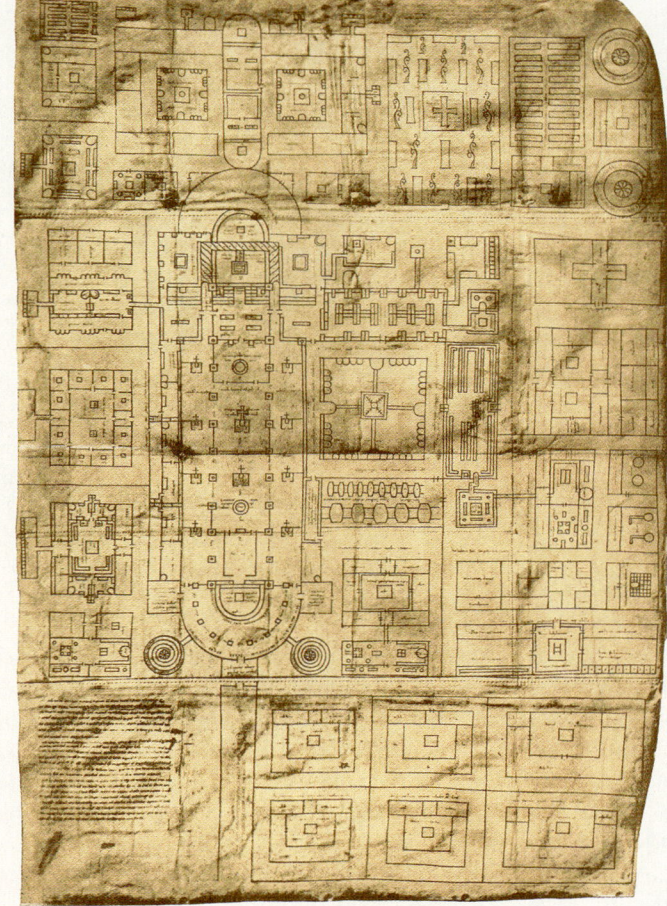

**11-19** Schematic plan for a monastery, from Saint Gall, Switzerland, ca. 819. Red ink on parchment, 2′ 4″ × 3′ 8⅛″. Stiftsbibliothek, Saint Gall.

The purpose of this plan for an ideal, self-sufficient Benedictine monastery was to separate the monks from the laity. Near the center is the church with its cloister, the monks' earthly paradise.

repositories of what remained of the literary culture of the Greco-Roman world and early Christianity. Saint Benedict's requirements of manual labor and sacred reading came to include writing and copying books, studying music for chanting daily prayers, and—of great significance—teaching. The monasteries were the schools of the early Middle Ages as well as self-sufficient communities and production centers.

**SAINT GALL** The emperor was not the only important builder of the Carolingian age. With prosperity also came the construction and expansion of many monasteries. A unique document, the ideal plan (FIG. 11-19) for a Benedictine monastery (see "Medieval Monasteries and Benedictine Rule," above) at Saint Gall in Switzerland, provides precious information about the design of Carolingian monastic communities. Haito, the abbot of Reichenau and bishop of Basel, ordered the preparation of the plan and sent it to the abbot of Saint Gall around 819 as a guide for the rebuilding of the Saint Gall

monastery. The design's fundamental purpose was to separate the monks from the laity (nonclergy) who also inhabited the community. Variations of the scheme may be seen in later monasteries all across western Europe. Near the center, dominating everything, was the church (*oratory*) with its *cloister*, a colonnaded courtyard not unlike the Early Christian atrium (FIG. 8-9) but situated to the side of the church instead of in front of its main portal. Reserved for the monks alone, the cloister was a kind of earthly paradise removed from the world at large. The Saint Gall cloister is an early example. Clustered

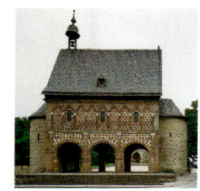

**11-19A** Torhalle, Lorsch, late eighth or ninth century.

around the cloister were the most essential buildings: dormitory, refectory, kitchen, and storage rooms. Other structures, including an infirmary, school, guest house, bakery, brewery, and workshops, filled the areas around this central core of church and cloister. In at least one Carolingian monastery, at Lorsch in Germany, a monumental freestanding gateway (FIG. **11-19A**) stood in front of the church.

Haito invited the abbot of Saint Gall to adapt the plan as he saw fit, and indeed, the Saint Gall builders did not follow the Reichenau model precisely. Nonetheless, had the abbot wished, Haito's plan could have served as a practical guide for the Saint Gall masons because it was laid out using a *module* (standard unit) of 2.5 feet. The designer consistently employed that module, or multiples or fractions of it, for all elements of the plan. For example, the nave's width, indicated on the plan as 40 feet, is equal to 16 modules. Each monk's bed is 2.5 modules long, and the paths in the vegetable garden are 1.25 modules wide.

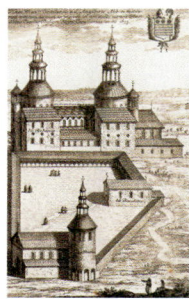

**11-19B** Saint-Riquier, Centula, 790–799.

The prototypes carrying the greatest authority for Charlemagne and his builders were those from the Christian phase of the Late Roman Empire. The widespread adoption of the Early Christian basilica, at Saint Gall and elsewhere, rather than the domed central plan of Byzantine churches, was crucial to the subsequent development of western European church architecture. Unfortunately, no Carolingian basilica has survived in its original form. Nevertheless, it is possible to reconstruct the appearance of some of them with fair accuracy, for example, the abbey of Saint-Riquier (FIG. **11-19B**) at Centula, France, which an 11th-century illuminator reproduced in a now-lost manuscript. Some Carolingian structures followed their Early Christian models quite closely. But in other instances, the ninth-century builders significantly modified the basilica plan, converting it into a much more complex form. The monastery church at Saint Gall, for example, was essentially a traditional basilica, but it had features not found in any Early Christian church. Most obvious is the addition of a second apse on the west end of the building, perhaps to accommodate additional altars and to display relics (see "The Veneration of Relics," Chapter 12, page 336). Whatever its purpose, this feature remained a characteristic regional element of German churches until the 11th century.

Not quite as evident but much more important to the subsequent development of church architecture in northern Europe was the presence of a transept at Saint Gall, a very rare feature but one that characterized the two greatest Early Christian basilicas in Rome, Saint Peter's (FIG. 8-9) and Saint Paul's, as well as the main church at the Centula abbey (FIG. 11-19B). The Saint Gall transept is as wide as the nave on the plan and was probably the same height. Early Christian builders had not been concerned with proportional relationships. On the Saint Gall plan, however, the various parts of the building relate to one another by a geometric scheme that ties them together into a tight and cohesive unit. Equalizing the widths of nave and transept automatically makes the area where they cross (the *crossing*) a square. Most Carolingian churches shared this feature. But Haito's planner also used the *crossing square* as the unit of measurement for the remainder of the church plan. The transept arms are equal to one crossing square, the distance between transept and apse is one crossing square, and the nave is 4.5 crossing squares long. In addition, the two aisles are half as wide as the nave, integrating all parts of the church in a rational and orderly plan.

The Saint Gall plan also reveals another important feature of many Carolingian basilicas, including Saint-Riquier (FIG. 11-19B) at Centula: towers framing the end(s) of the church. Haito's plan shows only two towers, both cylindrical and on the west side of the church, as at Charlemagne's Palatine Chapel (FIG. 11-17), but they stand apart from the church facade. If a tower existed above the crossing, the silhouette of Saint Gall would have shown three towers, altering the horizontal profile of the traditional basilica and identifying the church even from afar. Saint-Riquier had six towers.

**CORVEY** Other Carolingian basilicas had towers incorporated in the fabric of the west end of the building, thereby creating a unified monumental facade greeting all those who entered the church. Architectural historians call this feature of Carolingian and some later churches the *westwork* (from the German *Westwerk,* "western entrance structure"). Early medieval writers referred to it as a *castellum* (Latin, "castle" or "fortress") or *turris* ("tower"). The sole surviving example is the abbey church (FIG. **11-20**) at Corvey. The uppermost parts are 12th-century additions (easily distinguishable from

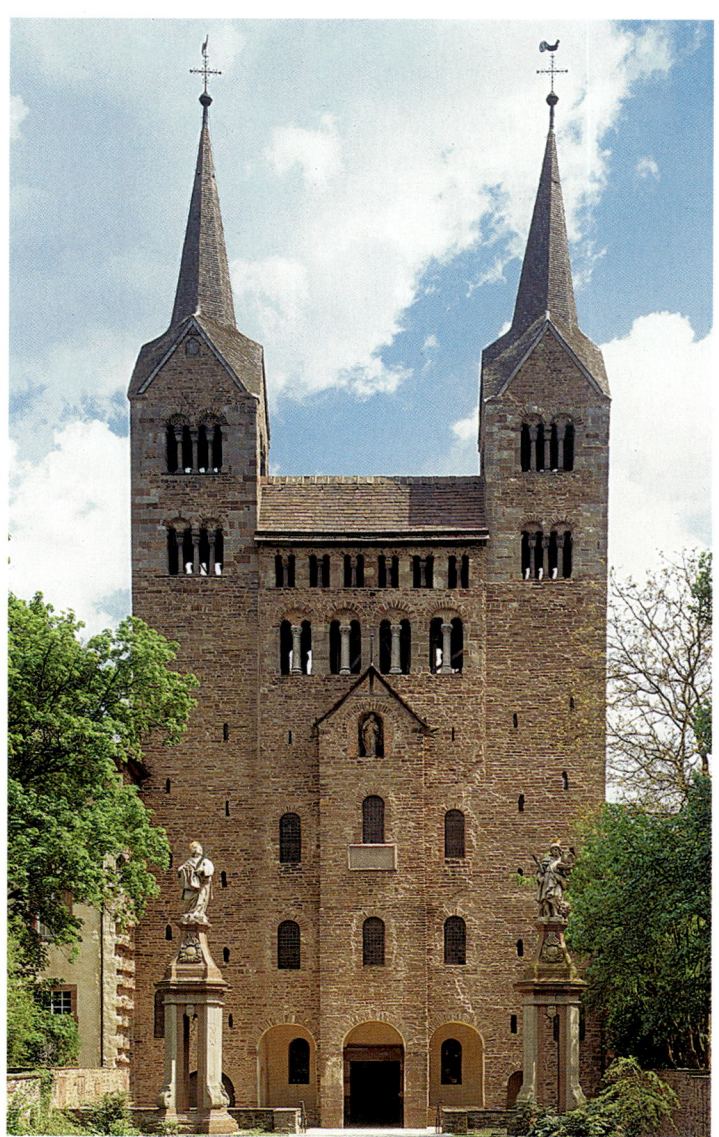

**11-20** Westwork of the abbey church, Corvey, Germany, 873–885.

An important new feature of Carolingian church architecture was the westwork, a monumental western facade incorporating two towers. The sole surviving example is the abbey church at Corvey.

the original westwork by the differing masonry technique). Stairs in each tower provided access to the upper stories of the westwork. On the second floor was a two-story chapel with an aisle and a gallery on three sides. As at Aachen, the chapel opened onto the nave, and from it the visiting emperor and his entourage could watch and participate in the service below. Not all Carolingian westworks, however, served as seats reserved for the emperor. They also functioned as churches within churches, housing a second altar for special celebrations on major feast days. Boys' choirs stationed in the westwork chapel participated from above in the services conducted in the church's nave.

# OTTONIAN ART

Louis the Pious laid Charlemagne to rest in the Palatine Chapel at Aachen in 814. Charlemagne had ruled for 46 years, but his empire survived him by fewer than 30. When Louis died in 840, his three sons—Charles the Bald, Lothair, and Louis the German—divided the Carolingian Empire among themselves. After bloody conflicts, the brothers signed a treaty at Verdun in 843 partitioning the Frankish lands into western, central, and eastern areas, very roughly foreshadowing the later nations of France and Germany and a third realm corresponding to a long strip of land stretching from the Netherlands and Belgium to Rome. Intensified Viking incursions in the west helped bring about the collapse of the Carolingians. The empire's breakup into weak kingdoms, ineffectual against the invasions, brought a time of confusion to Europe. Complementing the Viking scourge in the west were the invasions of the Magyars in the east and the plundering and piracy of the Saracens (Muslims) in the Mediterranean.

Only in the mid-10th century did the eastern part of the former empire consolidate under the rule of a new Saxon line of German emperors called, after the names of the three most illustrious family members, the *Ottonians*. The pope crowned the first Otto (r. 936–973) in Rome in 962, and Otto assumed the title "Emperor of Rome" that Charlemagne's weak successors held during most of the previous century. The Ottonian emperors made headway against the eastern invaders, remained free from Viking attacks, and not only preserved but also enriched the culture and tradition of the Carolingian period. The Church, which had become corrupt and disorganized, recovered in the 10th century under the influence of a great monastic reform the Ottonians encouraged and sanctioned. The new German emperors also cemented ties with Italy and the papacy as well as with Byzantium (see "Theophanu," page 328). The Ottonian line ended in the early 11th century with the death of Henry II (r. 1002–1024).

## Architecture

Ottonian architects followed the course of their Carolingian predecessors, building basilican churches with towering spires and imposing westworks, but they also introduced new features that would have a long future in Western church architecture.

**GERNRODE** The best-preserved 10th-century Ottonian basilica is Saint Cyriakus at Gernrode, begun in 961 and completed in 973. In the 12th century, a large apse replaced the western entrance, but the upper parts of the westwork, including the two cylindrical towers, are intact. The interior (FIG. **11-21**), although heavily restored in the 19th century, retains its 10th-century character. Saint Cyriakus reveals how Ottonian architects enriched the Early Christian and Carolingian basilica. The church has a transept at the east with a square choir in front of the apse. The nave is one of the first in western Europe to incorporate a gallery between the

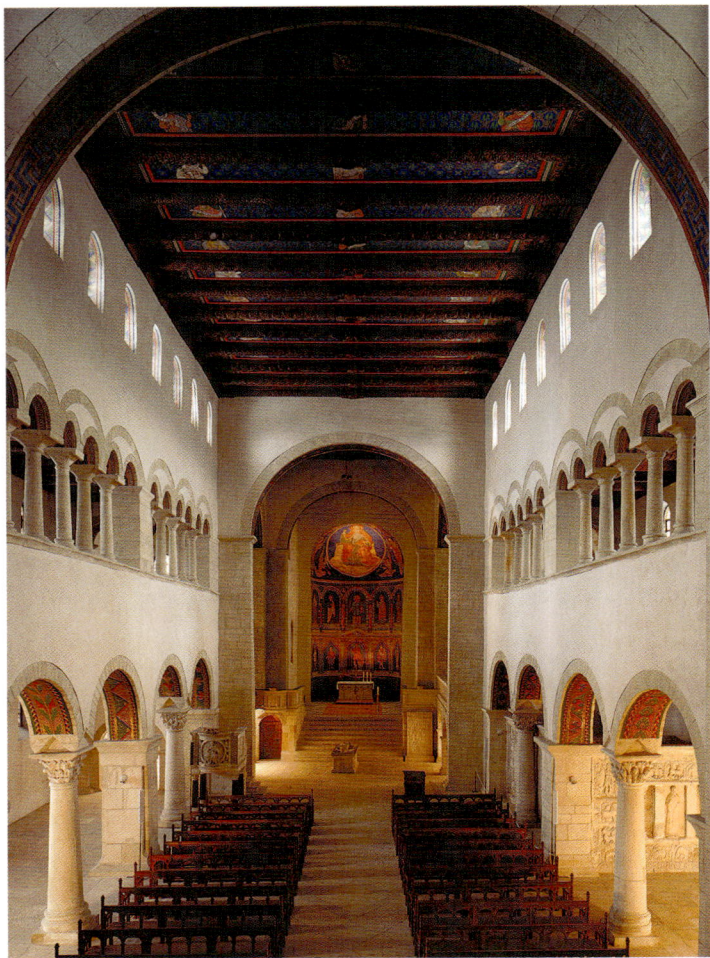

**11-21** Nave of the church of Saint Cyriakus (looking east), Gernrode, Germany, 961–973.

Ottonian builders modified the interior elevation of Early Christian basilicas. The Gernrode designer added a gallery above the nave arcade and adopted an alternate-support system of piers and columns.

ground-floor arcade and the clerestory, a design that became very popular in the succeeding Romanesque era (see Chapter 12). Scholars have reached no consensus on the function of these galleries in Ottonian churches. They cannot have been reserved for women, as some think they were in Byzantium, because Saint Cyriakus is the centerpiece of a convent exclusively for nuns, founded the same year construction of the church began. The galleries may have housed additional altars, as in the westwork at Corvey, or the singers in the church's choir. The Gernrode builders also transformed the nave arcade itself by adopting the *alternate-support system,* in which heavy square piers alternate with columns, dividing the nave into vertical units. The division continues into the gallery level, breaking the smooth rhythm of the all-column arcades of Early Christian and Carolingian basilicas and leading the eye upward. Later architects would carry this verticalization of the basilican nave much further (FIG. 13-19).

**HILDESHEIM** A great patron of Ottonian art and architecture was Bishop Bernward (r. 993–1022) of Hildesheim, Germany. He was the tutor of Otto III (r. 983–1002) and builder of the abbey church of Saint Michael (FIGS. **11-22** and **11-23**) at Hildesheim. Bernward, who made Hildesheim a center of learning, was an eager scholar, a lover of the arts, and, according to Thangmar of

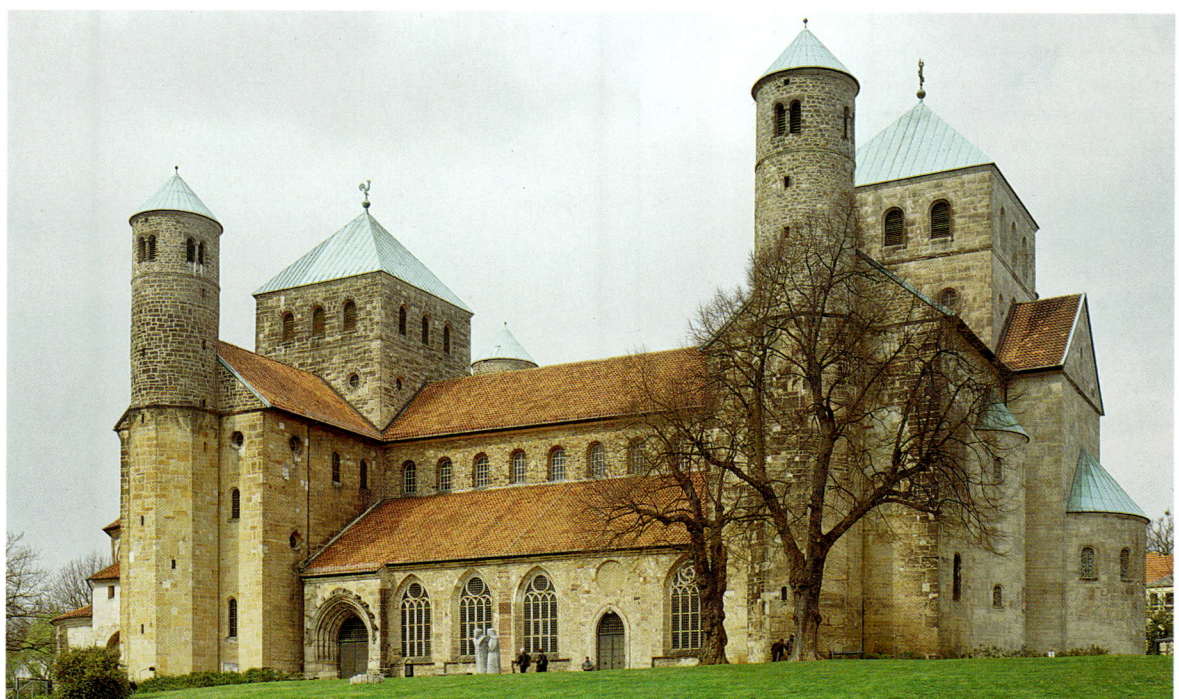

**11-22** Saint Michael's (looking northwest), Hildesheim, Germany, 1001–1031. ◼◀

Built by Bishop Bernward, a great art patron, Saint Michael's is a masterpiece of Ottonian basilica design. The church's two apses, two transepts, and multiple towers give it a distinctive profile.

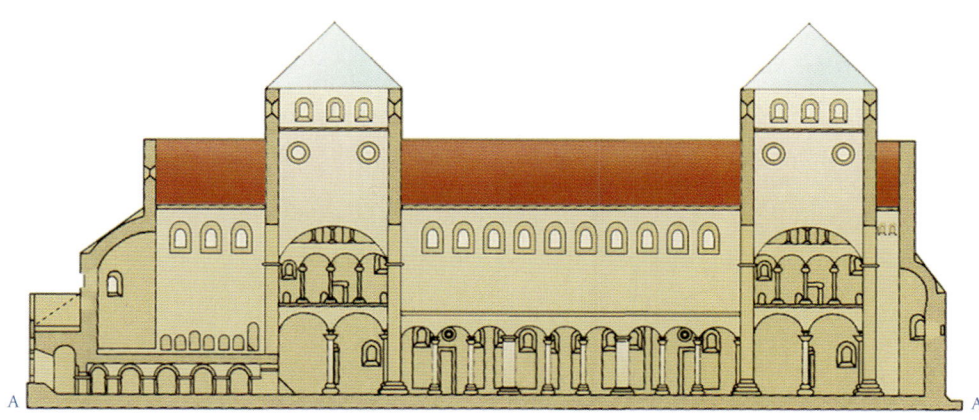

**11-23** Longitudinal section (*top*) and plan (*bottom*) of the abbey church of Saint Michael's, Hildesheim, Germany, 1001–1031.

Saint Michael's entrances are on the side. Alternating piers and columns divide the space in the nave into vertical units. These features transformed the tunnel-like horizontality of Early Christian basilicas.

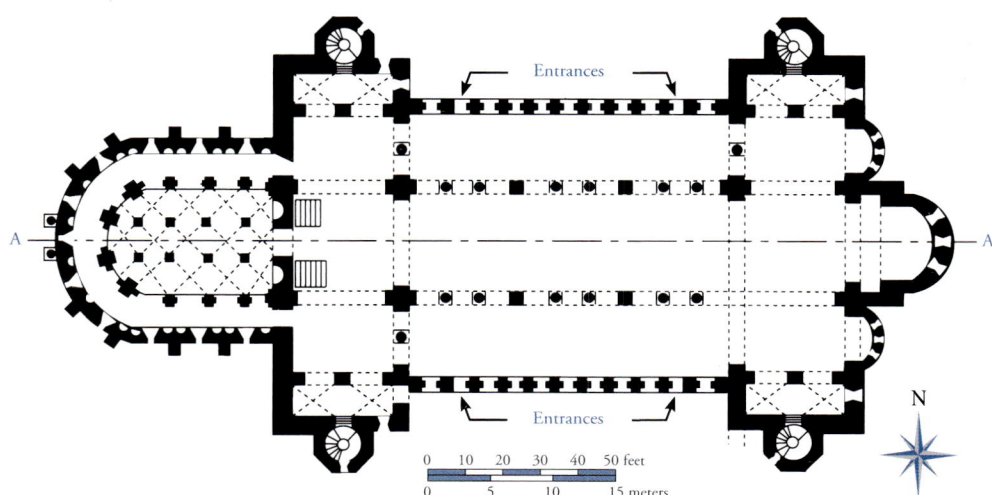

Heidelberg, his biographer, an expert craftsman and bronze-caster. In 1001, Bernward traveled to Rome as the guest of Otto III. During this stay, he studied at first hand the monuments of the ancient empire the Carolingian and Ottonian emperors revered.

Constructed between 1001 and 1031 (and rebuilt after a bombing raid during World War II), Saint Michael's has a double-transept plan (FIG. 11-23, *bottom*), six towers, and a westwork. The two transepts create eastern and western centers of gravity. The nave

Ottonian Art    **325**

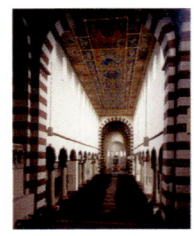

11-23A Nave, Saint Michael's, Hildesheim, 1001–1031.

(FIG. **11-23A**) merely seems to be a hall connecting them. Lateral entrances leading into the aisles from the north and south additionally make for an almost complete loss of the traditional basilican orientation toward the east. Some ancient Roman basilicas, such as the Basilica Ulpia (FIG. 7-44, no. 4) in Trajan's Forum, also had two apses and entrances on the side, and Bernward probably was familiar with this variant basilican plan.

At Hildesheim, as in the plan of the monastery at Saint Gall (FIG. 11-19), the builders adopted a modular approach. The crossing squares, for example, are the basis for the nave's dimensions—three crossing squares long and one square wide. The placement of heavy piers at the corners of each square gives visual emphasis to the three units. These piers alternate with pairs of columns (FIG. 11-23A) as wall supports in a design similar to that of Saint Cyriakus (FIG. 11-21) at Gernrode.

## Sculpture and Painting

In 1001, when Bishop Bernward was in Rome visiting the young Otto III, he resided in Otto's palace on the Aventine Hill in the neighborhood of Santa Sabina, an Early Christian church renowned for its carved wooden doors (FIG. 8-10A). Those doors, decorated with episodes from both the Old and New Testaments, may have inspired the remarkable bronze doors the bishop had cast for his new church in Germany.

**HILDESHEIM DOORS** The doors (FIG. **11-24**) to Saint Michael's, dated by inscription to 1015, are more than 15 feet tall. They are technological marvels, because the Ottonian metalworkers cast each giant door in a single piece with the figural sculpture. Carolingian sculpture, like most sculpture since Late Antiquity, consisted primarily of small-scale art executed in ivory and precious metals, often for book covers (FIG. 11-16). The Hildesheim doors are huge in comparison, but the 16 individual panels stem from this tradition.

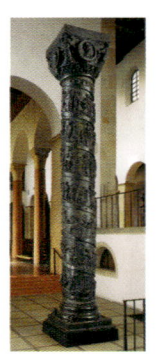

11-24A Column, Saint Michael's, Hildesheim, ca. 1015–1022. ◼◀

Bernward placed the bronze doors in the portal to Saint Michael's from the cloister, where the monks would see them each time they entered the church. The panels of the left door illustrate highlights from Genesis, beginning with the *Creation of Eve* (at the top) and ending with the murder of Adam and Eve's son Abel by his brother, Cain (at the bottom). The right door recounts the life of Jesus (reading from the bottom up), starting with the *Annunciation* and terminating with the appearance to Mary Magdalene of Christ after his resurrection (see "The Life of Jesus in Art," Chapter 8, pages 240–241). Together, the doors tell the story of original sin and ultimate redemption, showing the expulsion from the Garden of Eden and the path back to Paradise through the Church. (Reliefs depicting additional episodes from Jesus' life decorate a bronze column [FIG. **11-24A**] that Bernward also commissioned for Saint Michael's.) As in Early Christian times, the Ottonian clergy interpreted the Hebrew scriptures as prefiguring the New Testament (see "Jewish Subjects in Christian Art," Chapter 8, page 238). For example, the Hildesheim designer juxtaposed the panel depicting the *Fall of Adam and Eve* on the left door with the *Crucifixion* on the right door. Eve nursing the infant Cain is opposite Mary with the Christ Child in her lap.

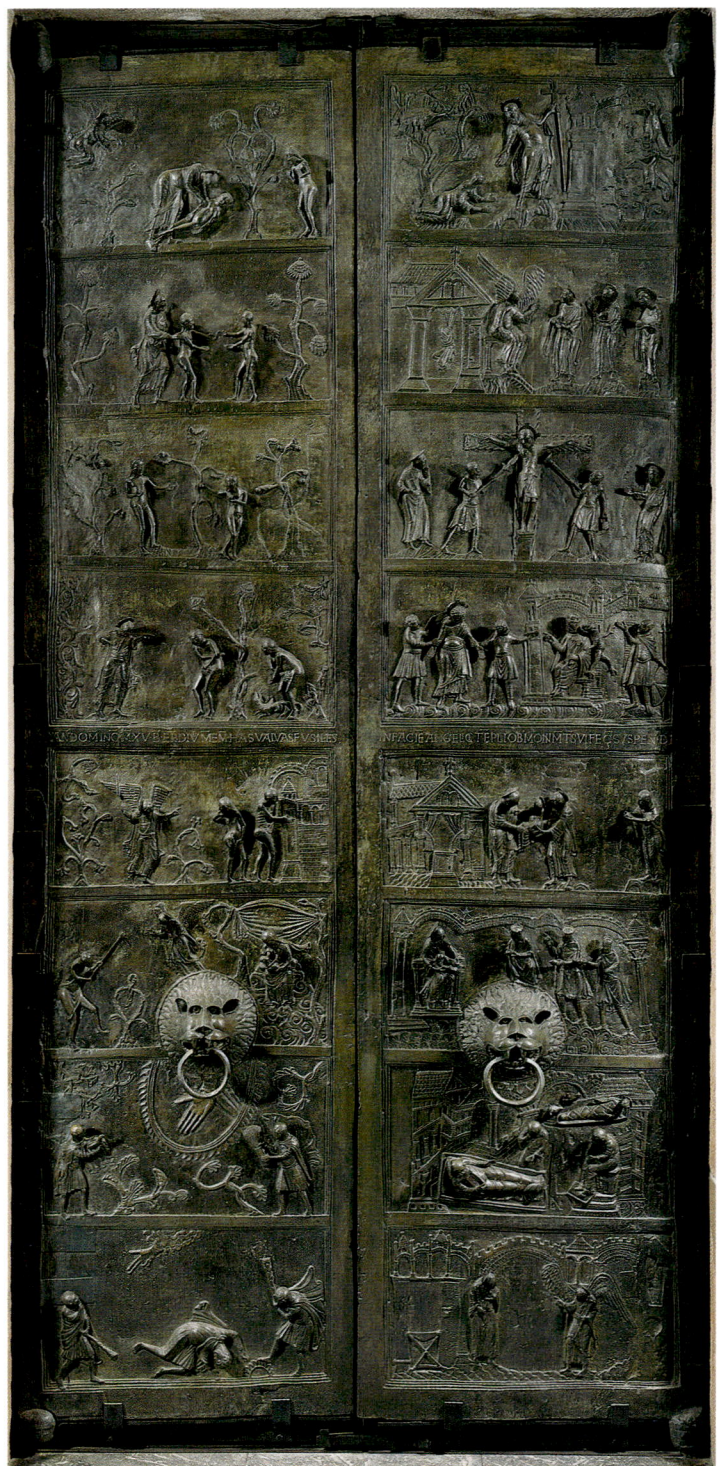

**11-24** Doors with relief panels (Genesis, left door; life of Christ, right door), commissioned by Bishop Bernward for Saint Michael's, Hildesheim, Germany, 1015. Bronze, 15′ 5¾″ high. Dom-Museum, Hildesheim. ◼◀

Bernward's doors tell the story of original sin and redemption, and draw parallels between the Old and New Testaments, as in the expulsion from Paradise and the infancy and suffering of Christ.

The composition of many of the scenes on the doors derives from Carolingian manuscript illumination, and the style of the figures has an expressive strength that brings to mind the illustrations in the *Utrecht Psalter* (FIGS. 11-15 and 11-15A). For example, in the fourth panel (FIG. **11-25**) from the top on the left door, God,

1 ft.

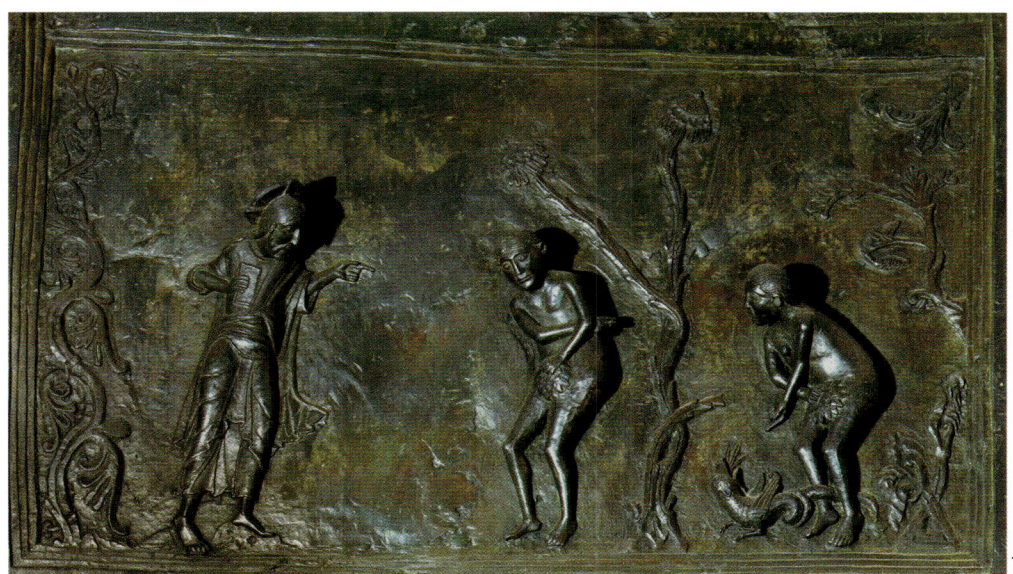

The Hildesheim bronze-caster recounted the story of original sin with a flair for anecdote. With vivid gestures, God accuses Adam, who passes the blame to Eve, who points in turn to the serpent.

1 in.

portrayed as a man, accuses Adam and Eve after their fall from grace. He jabs his finger at them with the force of his whole body. The force is concentrated in the gesture, which becomes the psychic focus of the entire composition. The frightened pair crouch, not only to hide their shame but also to escape the lightning bolt of divine wrath. Each passes the blame—Adam pointing backward to Eve and Eve pointing downward to the deceitful serpent. The starkly flat setting throws into relief the gestures and attitudes of rage, accusation, guilt, and fear. The sculptor presented the story with simplicity, although with great emotional impact, as well as a flair for anecdotal detail. Adam and Eve both struggle to point with one arm while attempting to shield their bodies from view with the other. With an instinct for expressive pose and gesture, the artist brilliantly communicated their newfound embarrassment at their nakedness and their unconvincing denials of wrongdoing.

**MAGDEBURG IVORIES** The figural panels of the bronze doors of Saint Michael's at Hildesheim constitute a unique ensemble, but they are not the only series of small-scale narrative relief panels made for display in an Ottonian church. Sixteen ivory plaques remain from a set of perhaps as many as 50 that once decorated the altar, pulpit, or another important item of church furniture in Magdeburg Cathedral. The cathedral housed the relics of Saint Mauritius (Maurice), a Christian army commander from Africa whom the Romans executed in Gaul during the third century when he refused to sacrifice to the old gods. Otto transferred the saint's relics from France to Magdeburg in 960. A former monastic community on the eastern frontier of the Ottonian Empire, Magdeburg became an archbishopric in 968, the year Otto I dedicated the city's new cathedral. The 10th-century church burned down in 1207. The present cathedral is a Gothic replacement.

Most of the plaques depict scenes from the life of Jesus. The one illustrated here (FIG. 11-26), however, features Otto I presenting Magdeburg Cathedral to Christ, who sits on a large wreath and extends his right hand to the emperor to indicate he welcomes the gift. Ottonian representations of the emperor usually depict him as the central figure and of large stature (FIG. 11-29), but the artist here represented the bearded and crowned Otto to one side and as the size of a child. The age-old principle of hierarchy of scale dictated that the artist depict the only mortal as the smallest figure.

Christ is largest, and the saints are intermediate in size. The two most prominent are Saint Peter, at the right holding the key to the kingdom of Heaven, and Saint Mauritius, who introduces the emperor to Christ. Art historians believe the plaques are the work of Milanese ivory carvers. Lombardy was part of Otto I's empire.

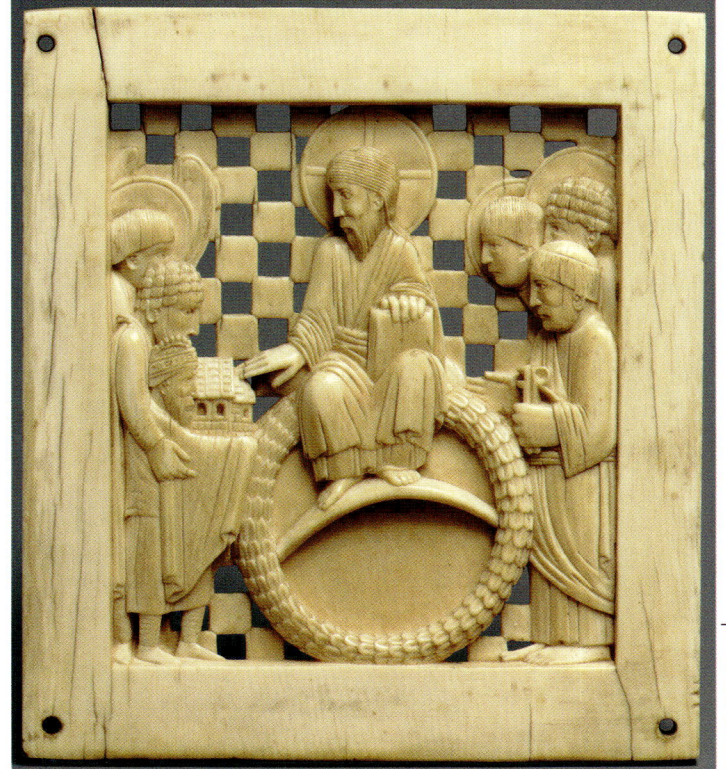

**11-26** Otto I presenting Magdeburg Cathedral to Christ, from an altar or pulpit in Magdeburg Cathedral, Magdeburg, Germany, 962–968. Ivory, 5″ × 4½″. Metropolitan Museum of Art, New York (gift of George Blumenthal, 1941).

This ivory panel from an altar or pulpit Otto I dedicated in Magdeburg Cathedral shows Saint Mauritius introducing the emperor to Christ, whom Otto presents with the new church.

1 in.

# Theophanu, a Byzantine Princess in Ottonian Germany

The bishop of Mainz crowned Otto I king of the Saxons at Aachen in 936, but it was not until 962 that Pope John XII (r. 955–964) conferred the title of Emperor of Rome upon him in Saint Peter's basilica. Otto, known as the Great, had ambitions to restore the glory of Charlemagne's Christian Roman Empire and to enlarge the territory under his rule. In 951, he defeated a Roman noble who had taken prisoner Adelaide, the widow of the Lombard king Lothar. Otto then married Adelaide, assumed the title of King of the Lombards, and extended his power south of the Alps. Looking eastward, in 972 he arranged the marriage of his son (and co-emperor since 967), Otto II, to Theophanu (ca. 955–991), probably the niece of Emperor Nikephoros II Phokas (r. 963–969). Otto was 17 years old, his bride 16. They wed in Saint Peter's in Rome, with Pope John XIII (r. 965–972) presiding. When Otto the Great died the next year, Otto II became sole emperor (r. 973–983). The second Otto died in Italy a decade later and was buried in the atrium of Saint Peter's. His son, Otto III, only three years old at the time, nominally became king, but it was his mother, Theophanu, coregent with Adelaide until 985 and sole regent thereafter, who wielded power in the Ottonian Empire until her death in 991. Adelaide then served as regent until Otto III was old enough to rule on his own. He became Roman emperor in 996 and died six years later.

Theophanu brought the prestige of Byzantium to Germany. Artistic ties between the Ottonian court and Constantinople became even stronger, and the Ottonians imported Byzantine luxury goods, including ivory plaques, in great quantities. One surviving ivory panel (FIG. 11-27) commemorates the marriage between Otto II and Theophanu. It shows Christ, central and the largest figure, extending both arms to bless the crowned emperor and his empress. (Otto appears much older than 17, consistent with his imperial stature.) The artist depicted all three standing rigidly and looking directly at the viewer. The frontality of the figures, the tripartite composition, and the style of carving suggest the work is an import from Constantinople, as does the lengthy Greek dedicatory inscription. A few words are in Latin, however, and the inscription also identifies the donor—the tiny bowing figure clinging to Christ's stool—as an Italian bishop. Some art historians therefore think the artist may have been an Ottonian ivory carver in Lombardy. Nonetheless, the iconography is distinctively Byzantine because the imagery declares that Otto's authority to rule comes directly

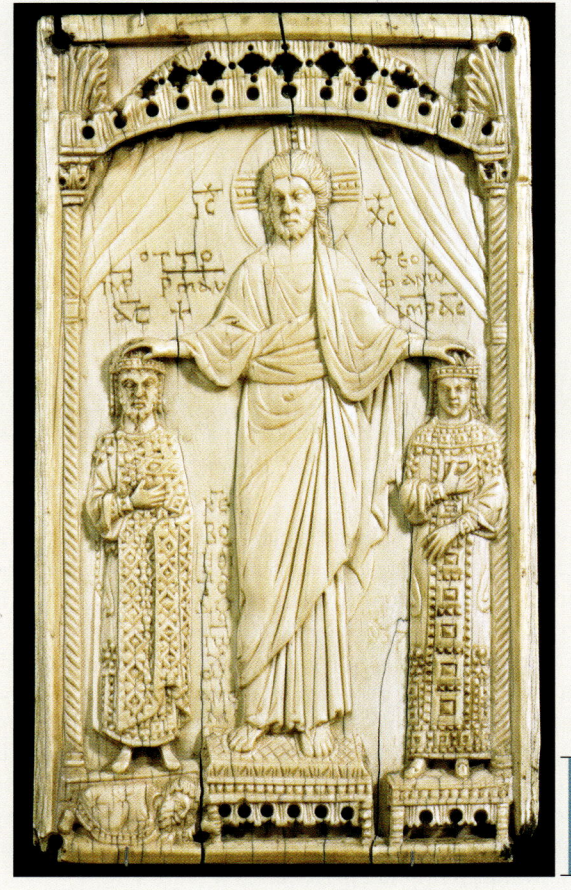

**11-27** Christ blessing Otto II and Theophanu, 972–973. Ivory, $7\frac{1}{8}'' \times 4''$. Musée National du Moyen Age, Paris.

Commemorating the marriage of Otto II and Theophanu, this ivory plaque is Byzantine in style and iconography. The princess promoted Byzantine art and culture at the Ottonian court.

from Christ, not from the pope. Whether of Byzantine or Ottonian manufacture, the ivory is an Ottonian commission in Byzantine style. The influence of Byzantine art is also evident in Ottonian manuscript painting (FIGS. 11-29A and 11-30).

**OTTO II AND THEOPHANU** On April 14, 972, Otto I arranged the marriage of his son Otto II to the Byzantine princess Theophanu (see "Theophanu, a Byzantine Princess in Ottonian Germany," above). The wedding secured the important political alliance between the Ottonian and Byzantine empires. Because the couple married in Rome with the pope administering the vows, the wedding simultaneously reaffirmed the close relationship between the Ottonians and the papacy. The marriage, commemorated on a unique ivory plaque (FIG. 11-27), also enhanced the already strong artistic and cultural ties between Germany and Constantinople.

**GERO CRUCIFIX** During the Ottonian period, interest in freestanding statuary, which had been exceedingly rare for the pre-

ceding half millennium, also revived. The outstanding example of Ottonian monumental sculpture is the crucifix (FIG. **11-28**) Archbishop Gero (r. 969–976) commissioned and presented to Cologne Cathedral in 970. Carved in oak, then painted and gilded, the 6-foot-tall image of Christ nailed to the cross is both statue and *reliquary* (a shrine for sacred relics; see "The Veneration of Relics," Chapter 12, page 336). A compartment in the back of the head held bread for the Eucharist. According to one story, a crack developed in the wood of Gero's crucifix but miraculously healed. Similar tales of miracles surround many sacred Christian objects, for example, some Byzantine icons (see "Icons," Chapter 9, page 269).

The Gero crucifix presents a dramatically different conception of Christ from that seen on the *Lindau Gospels* cover (FIG. 11-16),

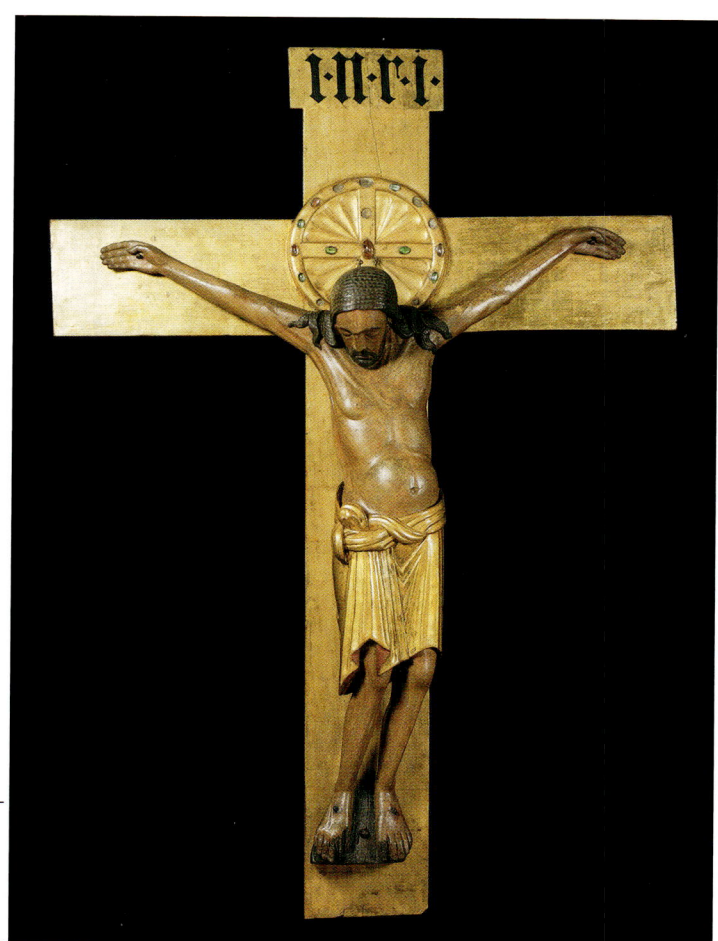

**11-28** Crucifix commissioned by Archbishop Gero for Cologne Cathedral, Cologne, Germany, ca. 970. Painted wood, height of figure 6′ 2″. Cathedral, Cologne. ◼

In this early example of the revival of monumental sculpture in the Middle Ages, an Ottonian sculptor depicted with unprecedented emotional power the intense agony of Christ's ordeal on the cross.

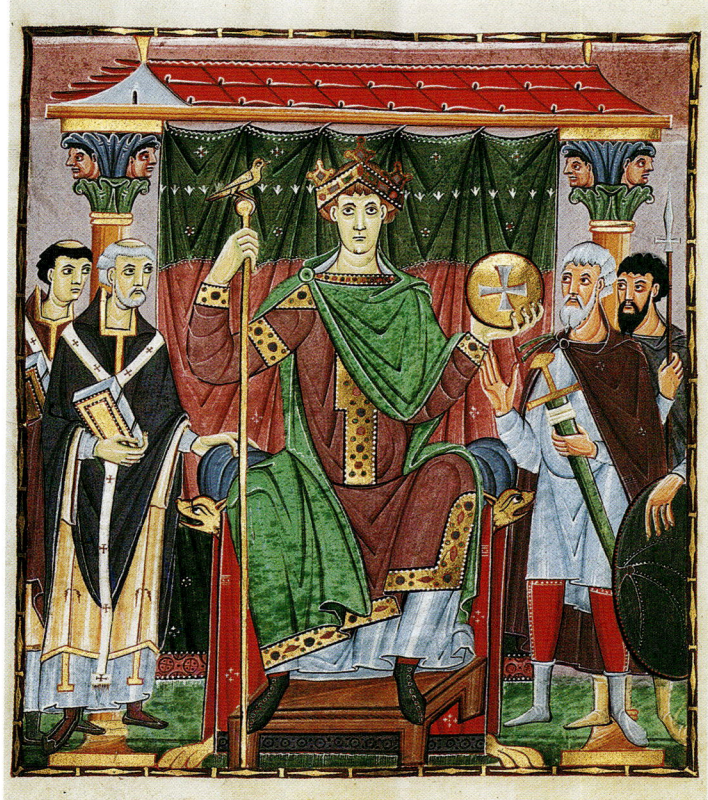

**11-29** Otto III enthroned, folio 24 recto of the *Gospel Book of Otto III,* from Reichenau, Germany, 997–1000. Tempera on vellum, 1′ 1″ × 9$\frac{3}{8}$″. Bayerische Staatsbibliothek, Munich.

Emperor Otto III, descended from both German and Byzantine imperial lines, appears in this Gospel book enthroned and holding the scepter and cross-inscribed orb signifying his universal authority.

with its Early Christian imagery of the youthful Christ triumphant over death. Consistent with the strong Byzantine element in Ottonian art, the bearded Christ of the Cologne crucifix is more akin to Byzantine representations (FIG. 9-24) of the suffering Jesus, but the emotional power of the Ottonian work is greater still. The sculptor depicted Christ as an all-too-human martyr. Blood streaks down his forehead from the (missing) crown of thorns. His eyelids are closed, his face is contorted in pain, and his body sags under its weight. The muscles stretch to their limit—those of the right shoulder and chest seem almost to rip apart. The halo behind Christ's head may foretell his subsequent resurrection, but the worshiper can sense only his pain. Gero's crucifix is the most powerful characterization of intense agony of the early Middle Ages.

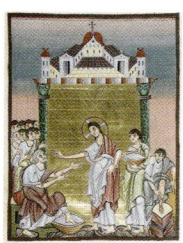

**11-29A** Jesus and Peter, *Gospel Book of Otto III,* 997–1000.

***GOSPEL BOOK OF OTTO III*** In a Gospel book containing some of the finest early medieval paintings of the life of Jesus (for example, FIG. **11-29A**), one full-page representation (FIG. **11-29**) stands apart from the rest. The page shows Otto III, son of Otto II and Theophanu, enthroned and holding the scepter and cross-inscribed orb that signify his universal authority, conforming to a Christian impe-

rial iconographic tradition that began with Constantine (FIG. 7-81, *right*). At the emperor's sides are the clergy and the barons (the Church and the state), both aligned in his support. On the facing page (not illustrated), also derived from ancient Roman sources, female personifications of Slavinia, Germany, Gaul, and Rome—the provinces of the Ottonian Empire—bring tribute to the young emperor.

Of the three Ottos, the last most fervently dreamed of a revived Christian Roman Empire. Indeed, it was his life's obsession. The boy-emperor was keenly aware of his descent from both German and Byzantine imperial lines, but he apparently was prouder of his Constantinopolitan than his German roots. He moved his court, with its Byzantine rituals, to Rome and there set up theatrically the symbols and trappings of Roman imperialism. Otto's romantic dream of imperial unity for Europe, the conceit behind his self-aggrandizing portrayal in the *Gospel Book of Otto III,* never materialized, however. He died prematurely, at age 21, and, at his request, was buried beside Charlemagne at Aachen.

***LECTIONARY OF HENRY II*** Otto III's successor, Henry II, was the last Ottonian emperor. Of the artworks produced during his reign, the *Lectionary of Henry II* is the most noteworthy. A product of the leading Ottonian scriptorium at Reichenau, as was Otto III's Gospel book, Henry's lectionary (a book of Gospel readings for the Mass; see "Medieval Books," page 312) was a gift to Bamberg Cathedral. In the full-page illumination of the announcement of Christ's

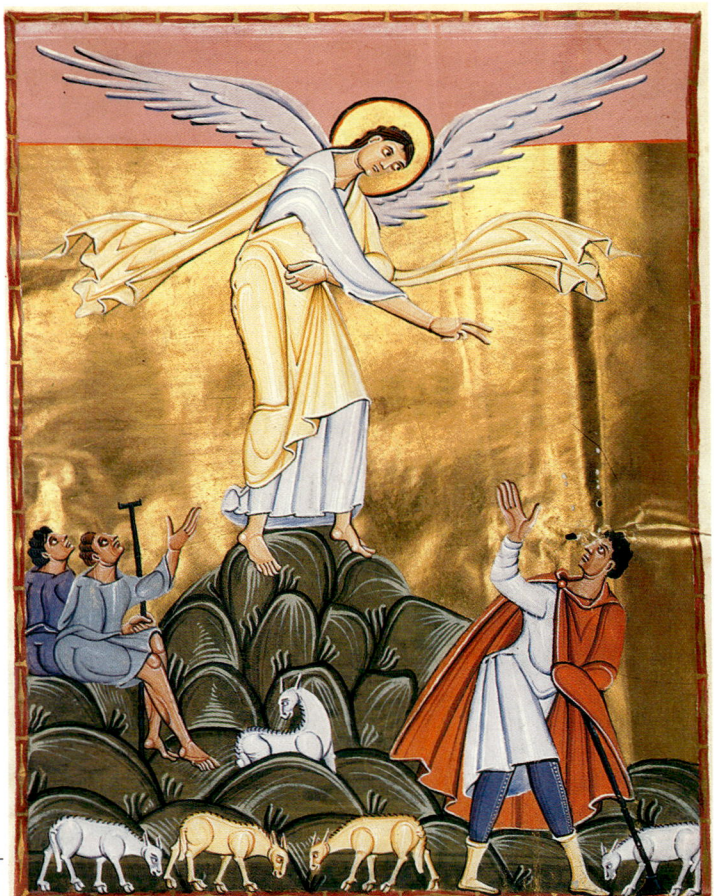

**11-30** *Annunciation to the Shepherds,* folio in the *Lectionary of Henry II,* from Reichenau, Germany, 1002–1014. Tempera on vellum, 1′ 5″ × 1′ 1″. Bayerische Staatsbibliothek, Munich.

The full-page illuminations in the *Lectionary of Henry II* fuse elements of Late Antique landscapes, the Carolingian-Ottonian anecdotal narrative tradition, and the golden background of Byzantine art.

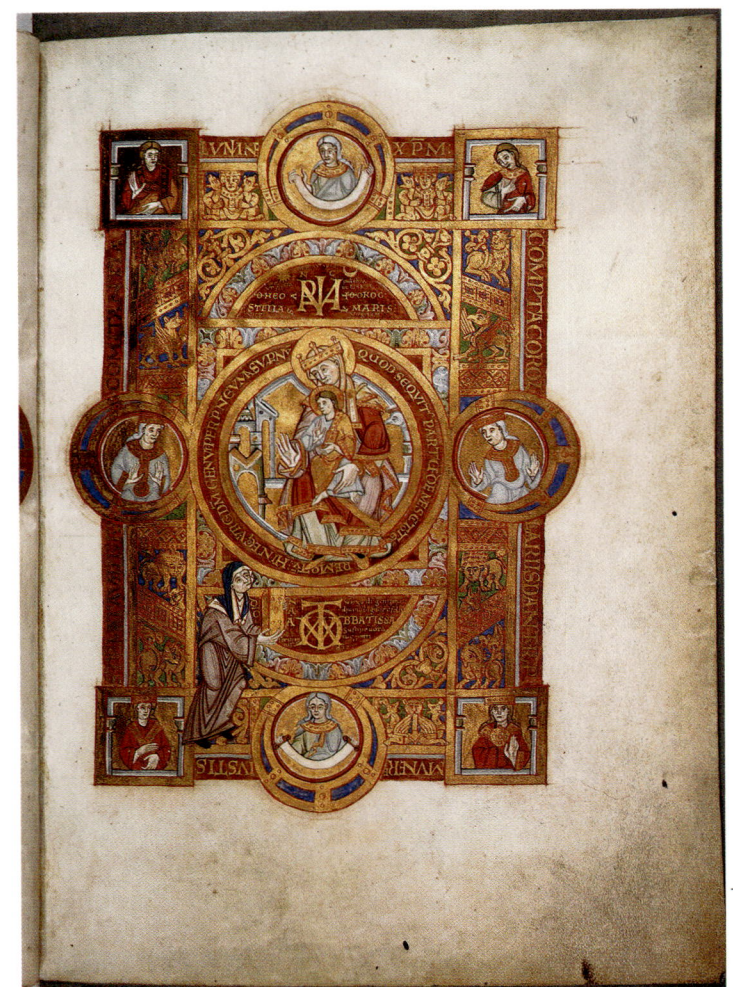

**11-31** Abbess Uta dedicating her codex to the Virgin, folio 2 recto of the *Uta Codex,* from Regensburg, Germany, ca. 1025. Tempera on parchment, 9⅝″ × 5⅛″. Bayerische Staatsbibliothek, Munich.

The *Uta Codex* illustrates the important role women played both in religious life and as patrons of the arts. The dedicatory page shows Abbess Uta presenting her codex to the Virgin Mary.

birth to the shepherds (FIG. **11-30**), the angel has just alighted on a hill, his still-beating wings agitating his draperies. The angel looms immense above the startled and terrified shepherds, filling the golden sky. He extends his hand in a gesture of authority and instruction. Emphasized more than the message itself are the power and majesty of God's authority. The painting is a summation of the stylistic complexity of Ottonian art. It is a highly successful fusion of the Carolingian-Ottonian anecdotal narrative tradition, elements derived from Late Antique painting—for example, the rocky landscape setting with grazing animals (FIG. 8-17)—and the golden background of Byzantine book illumination and mosaic decoration.

*UTA CODEX* Another lectionary (FIG. **11-31**), one of the finest Ottonian books produced for the clergy, as opposed to the imperial court, was the work of scribes and illuminators at Regensburg. Their patron was Uta, abbess of Niedermünster from 1003 to 1025, a leading nun well known in royal circles. Uta was instrumental in bringing Benedictine reforms to the Niedermünster convent, whose nuns were usually the daughters of the local nobility. Near the end of her life, she presented the nunnery with a sumptuous manuscript containing many full-page illuminations interspersed with Gospel readings, the so-called *Uta Codex.* The lectionary's gold-jewel-and-enamel case also survives, underscoring the nature

of medieval books as sacred objects to be venerated in their own right as well as embodiments of the eternal word of God.

The dedicatory page (FIG. **11-31**) at the front of the *Uta Codex* depicts the Virgin Mary with the Christ Child in her lap in the central medallion. Labeled *Virgo Virginum,* Virgin of Virgins, Mary is the model for Uta and the Niedermünster nuns. Uta is the full-length figure presenting a new book—this book—to the Virgin. An inscription accompanies the dedicatory image: "Virgin Mother of God, happy because of the divine Child, receive the votive offerings of your Uta of ready service."[5] The artist painted Uta last, superimposing her figure upon the design and carefully placing it so that Uta's head touches the Virgin's medallion but does not penetrate it, suggesting the interplay between, but also the separation of, the divine and human realms.

In many respects, the *Uta Codex* is more typical of the Middle Ages than are the artworks and buildings commissioned by the Carolingian and Ottonian emperors. The Roman Empire, in revived form, may have lived on to 1002 at Otto III's court in Rome, but after Henry II's death in 1024, a new age began, and Rome's influence waned. Romanesque Europe instead found unity in a common religious fervor (see Chapter 12).

# EARLY MEDIEVAL EUROPE

## ART OF THE WARRIOR LORDS  5th to 10th Centuries

▌ After the fall of Rome in 410, the Huns, Vandals, Merovingians, Franks, Goths, Vikings, and other non-Roman peoples competed for power and territory in the former northwestern provinces of the Roman Empire.

▌ Other than the ornamentation of ships used for burials, the surviving artworks of this period are almost exclusively small-scale status symbols, especially items of personal adornment such as bracelets, pins, purses, and belt buckles, often featuring cloisonné decoration. A mixture of abstract and zoomorphic motifs appears on these portable treasures. Especially characteristic are intertwined animal and interlace patterns.

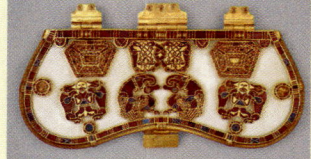

Sutton Hoo purse cover,
ca. 625

## HIBERNO-SAXON ART  6th to 10th Centuries

▌ Art historians call the Christian art of the early medieval Britain and Ireland Hiberno-Saxon or Insular. The most important extant artworks are the illuminated manuscripts produced in the monastic scriptoria of Ireland and Northumbria.

▌ These Insular books feature folios devoted neither to text nor to illustration but to pure embellishment. "Carpet pages" consist of decorative panels of abstract and zoomorphic motifs. Some books also have full pages depicting the four evangelists or their symbols. Text pages often present the initial letters of important passages enlarged and transformed into elaborate decorative patterns.

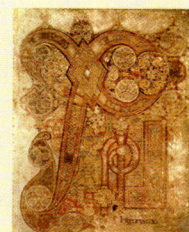

*Book of Kells,* late eighth
or early ninth century

## CAROLINGIAN ART  768–877

▌ Charlemagne, king of the Franks since 768, expanded the territories he inherited from his father, and in 800, Pope Leo III crowned him emperor of Rome (r. 800–814). Charlemagne and his successors initiated a conscious revival of the art and culture of Early Christian Rome.

▌ Carolingian sculptors revived the imperial Roman tradition of portraying rulers on horseback and the Early Christian tradition of depicting Christ as a statuesque youth. Artists merged the illusionism of classical painting with the northern European linear tradition, replacing the calm and solid figures of those models with figures that leap from the page with frenzied energy.

▌ Carolingian architects looked to Ravenna and Early Christian Rome for models but transformed their sources, introducing, for example, the twin-tower western facade for basilicas and employing strict modular plans for entire monasteries as well as individual churches.

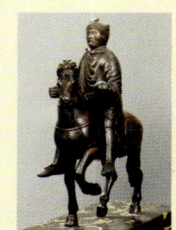

Charlemagne or Charles
the Bald, ninth century

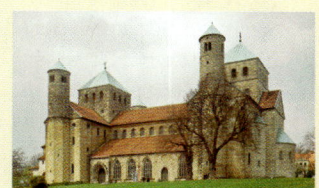

*Utrecht Psalter,* ca. 820–835

## OTTONIAN ART  919–1024

▌ In the mid-10th century, a new line of emperors, the Ottonians, consolidated the eastern part of Charlemagne's former empire and sought to preserve the culture and tradition of the Carolingian period.

▌ Ottonian artists, like other early medieval artists, excelled in producing sumptuous small-scale artworks, especially ivory plaques with narrative reliefs, often influenced by Byzantine art. But Ottonian sculptors also revived the art of monumental sculpture in works such as the *Gero Crucifix* and the colossal bronze doors of Saint Michael's at Hildesheim. Ottonian painting combines motifs and landscape elements from Late Antique art with the golden backgrounds of Byzantine art.

▌ Ottonian architects built basilican churches incorporating the towers and westworks of their Carolingian models but introduced the alternate-support system and galleries into the interior nave elevation.

Saint Michael's, Hildesheim,
1001–1031

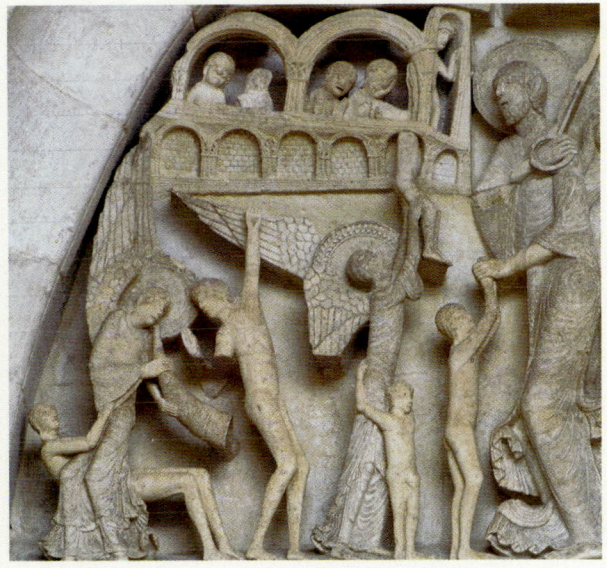

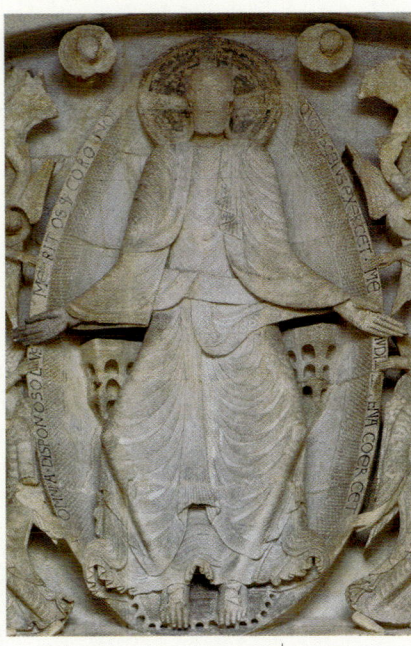

Christ presides over the separation of the blessed from the damned in Gislebertus's dramatic vision of the *Last Judgment,* designed to terrify those guilty of sin and beckon them into the church.

Above Autun Cathedral's portal, at the far left, a trumpet-blowing angel announces the second coming. Another obliging angel boosts one of the blessed over the fortified walls of Heaven.

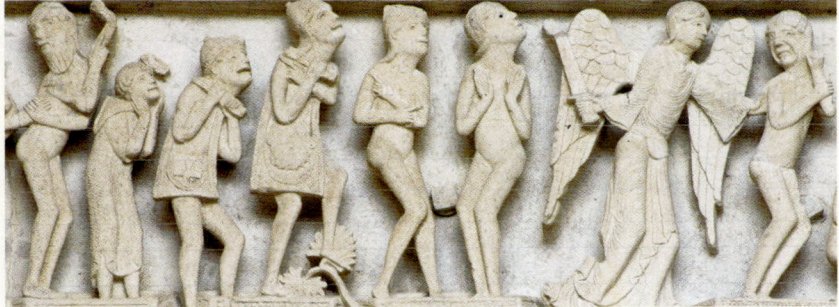

Below, the souls of the dead line up to await their fate. Two men whose travel bags identify them as pilgrims to Jerusalem and Santiago de Compostela can expect to be judged favorably.

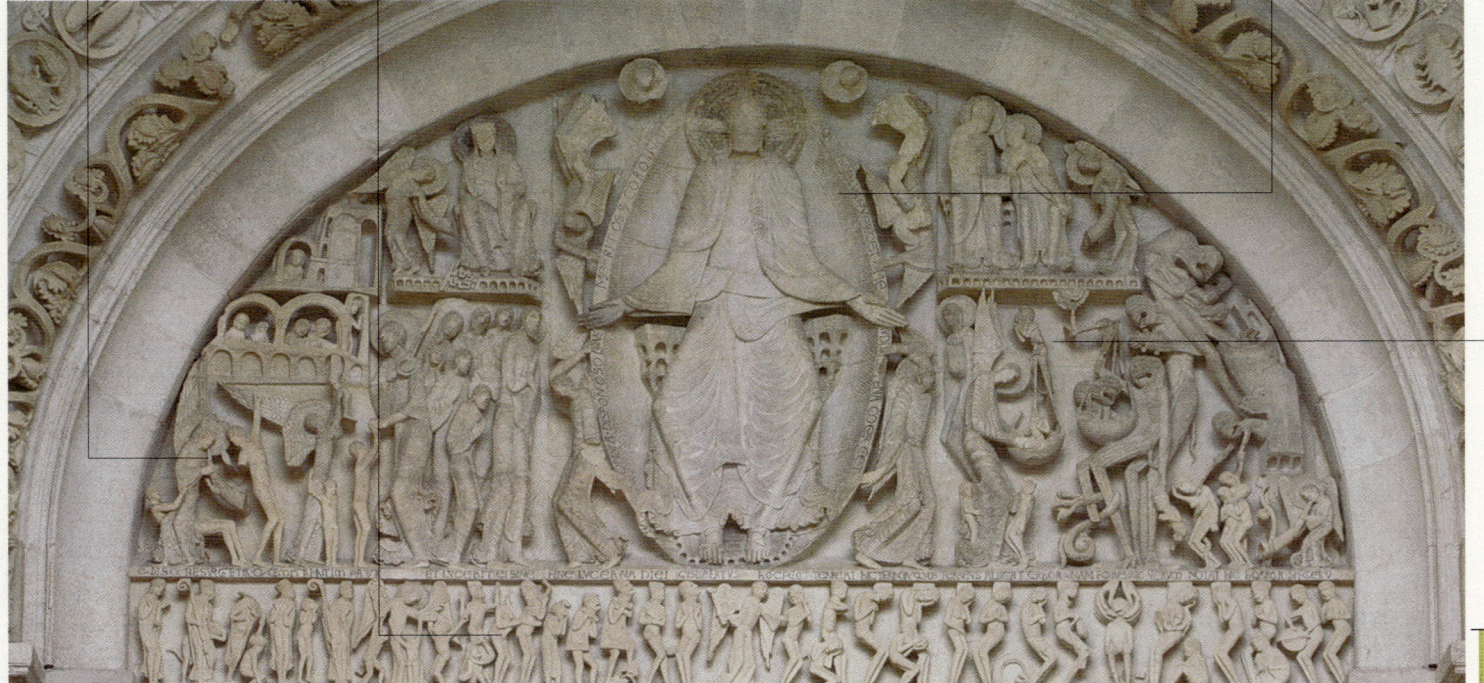

**12-1** GISLEBERTUS, *Last Judgment,* west tympanum of Saint-Lazare, Autun, France, ca. 1120–1135. Marble, 21′ wide at base. ◼◀

1 ft.

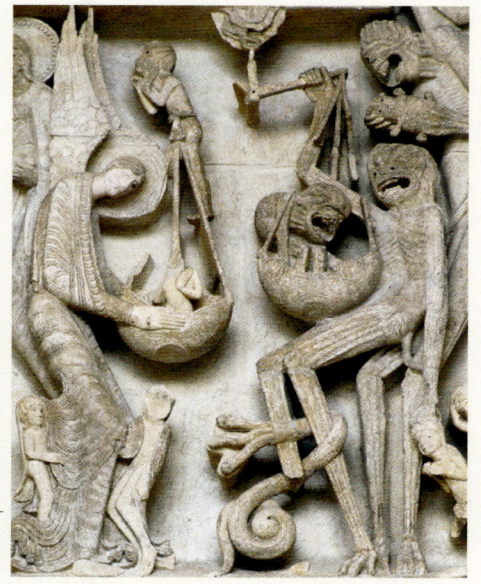

# ROMANESQUE EUROPE

In Gislebertus's unforgettable rendition of the weighing of souls on judgment day, angels and the Devil's agents contest at the scales, each trying to tip the balance for or against a soul.

## THE REBIRTH OF MONUMENTAL SCULPTURE

As worshipers entered the western portal of Saint-Lazare (Saint Lazarus) at Autun, they passed under a dramatic representation of the *Last Judgment* (FIG. **12-1**) by the sculptor GISLEBERTUS. A renowned artist, he inscribed his name in the stone relief and added this admonition: "May this terror terrify those whom earthly error binds, for the horror of these images here in this manner truly depicts what will be."[1] The warning echoes the sentiment expressed in a mid-10th-century copy of Beatus of Liébana's *Commentary on the Apocalypse.* There, the painter Magius (teacher of Emeterius; see FIG. 11-11) explained the purpose of his work: "I have painted a series of pictures for the wonderful words of [the Apocalypse's] stories, so that the wise may fear the coming of the future judgment of the world's end."[2]

Few people in 12th-century France other than the clergy could read Gislebertus's message, but even the illiterate could, in the words of Saint Bernard of Clairvaux, "read in the marble" (see "Bernard of Clairvaux on Cloister Sculpture," page 342). Indeed, in the entire history of art, there is probably no more terrifying visualization of what awaits sinners than the *Last Judgment* at Autun. Four trumpet-blowing angels announce the second coming of Christ, enthroned at the center, far larger than any other figure. He dispassionately presides over the separation of the blessed from the damned. At the left, an obliging angel boosts one of the saved into the heavenly city. Below, the souls of the dead line up to await their fate. Two of the men near the center of the lintel carry bags emblazoned with a cross and a shell. These are the symbols of pilgrims to Jerusalem and Santiago de Compostela, respectively (see "Pilgrimage Roads in France and Spain," page 335, and MAP **12-1**). Those who had made the difficult journey would be judged favorably. To their right, three small figures beg an angel to intercede on their behalf. The angel responds by pointing to the judge above. On the right side are those who will be condemned to Hell. Giant hands pluck one poor soul from the earth. Directly above is Gislebertus's unforgettable rendition of the weighing of souls (compare FIG. 11-9). Angels and the Devil's agents try to manipulate the balance for or against a soul. Hideous demons guffaw and roar. Their gaunt, lined bodies, with legs ending in sharp claws, writhe and bend like long, loathsome insects. A devilish creature, leaning from the dragon mouth of Hell, drags souls in, while above him, a howling demon crams the damned headfirst into a furnace.

The Autun *Last Judgment* is one of the earliest examples of the rebirth of the art of monumental sculpture in the Middle Ages, one hallmark of the age art historians have dubbed *Romanesque* because of the extensive use of stone sculpture and stone vaulting in ecclesiastical architecture.

# EUROPEAN CULTURE IN THE NEW MILLENNIUM

The Romanesque era is the first since Archaic and Classical Greece to take its name from an artistic style rather than from politics or geography. Unlike Carolingian and Ottonian art, named for emperors, or Hiberno-Saxon art, a regional term, *Romanesque* is a title art historians invented to describe medieval art that appeared "Roman-like." Architectural historians first employed the adjective in the early 19th century to describe European architecture of the 11th and 12th centuries. They noted that certain architectural elements of this period, principally barrel and groin vaults based on the round arch, resembled those of ancient Roman architecture. Thus, the word distinguished most Romanesque buildings from earlier medieval timber-roofed structures, as well as from later Gothic churches with vaults resting on pointed arches (see Chapter 13). Scholars in other fields quickly borrowed the term. Today "Romanesque" broadly designates the history and culture of western Europe between about 1050 and 1200.

**TOWNS AND CHURCHES** In the early Middle Ages, the focus of life was the *manor,* or estate, of a landholding *liege lord,* who might grant rights to a portion of his land to *vassals.* The vassals swore allegiance to their liege and rendered him military service in return for use of the land and the promise of protection. But in the Romanesque period, a sharp increase in trade encouraged the growth of towns and cities, gradually displacing *feudalism* as the governing political, social, and economic system of late medieval Europe. Feudal lords granted independence to the new towns in the form of charters, which enumerated the communities' rights, privileges, immunities, and exemptions beyond the feudal obligations the vassals owed the lords. Often located on navigable rivers, the new urban centers naturally became the nuclei of networks of maritime and overland commerce.

Separated by design from the busy secular life of Romanesque towns were the monasteries (see "Medieval Monasteries," Chapter 11, page 322) and their churches. During the 11th and 12th centuries, thousands of ecclesiastical buildings were remodeled or newly constructed. This immense building enterprise was in part a natural by-product of the rise of independent cities and the prosperity they enjoyed. But it also was an expression of the widely felt relief and thanksgiving that the conclusion of the first Christian millennium in the year 1000 had not brought an end to the world, as many had feared. In the Romanesque age, the construction of churches became almost an obsession. Raoul Glaber (ca. 985–ca. 1046), a monk who witnessed the coming of the new millennium, noted the beginning of it:

> [After the] year of the millennium, which is now about three years past, there occurred, throughout the world, especially in Italy and Gaul, a rebuilding of church basilicas. Notwithstanding, the greater number were already well established and not in the least in need, nevertheless each Christian people strove against the others to erect nobler ones. It was as if the whole earth, having cast off the old by shaking itself, were clothing itself everywhere in the white robe of the church.[3]

**PILGRIMS AND RELICS** The enormous investment in ecclesiastical buildings and furnishings also reflected a significant increase in pilgrimage traffic in Romanesque Europe (see "Pilgrimage Roads in France and Spain," page 335, and MAP 12-1). Pilgrims, along with wealthy landowners, were important sources of funding for those monasteries that possessed the *relics* of venerated saints (see "The Veneration of Relics," page 336). The monks of Sainte-Foy (FIG. 12-7A) at Conques, for example, used pilgrims' donations to pay for a magnificent cameo-and-jewel-encrusted gold-and-silver *reliquary* (FIG. **12-2**) to house the skull of Saint Faith. In fact, the clergy of the various monasteries vied with one another to provide the most magnificent settings for the display of their unique relics. They found justification for their lavish expenditures on buildings and furnishings in the Bible itself, for example, in Psalm 26:8, "Lord, I have loved the beauty of your house, and the place where your glory dwells." Traveling pilgrims fostered the growth of towns as well as monasteries. Pilgrimages were a major economic as well as conceptual catalyst for the art and architecture of the Romanesque period.

# FRANCE AND NORTHERN SPAIN

Although art historians use the adjective "Romanesque" to describe 11th- and 12th-century art and architecture throughout Europe, pronounced regional differences exist. This chapter examines in turn Romanesque France and Spain; the Holy Roman Empire; Italy; and Normandy and England. To a certain extent, Romanesque art and architecture can be compared with the European Romance languages, which vary regionally but have a common core in Latin, the language of the Romans.

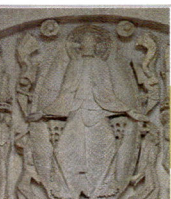

## ROMANESQUE EUROPE

| 1000 | 1100 | 1200 |
|---|---|---|
| ▌ Romanesque architects replace the timber roofs of churches with barrel vaults in the nave and groin vaults in the aisles<br><br>▌ Builders also add radiating chapels to ambulatories for the display of relics<br><br>▌ Sculptors revive the art of monumental stone relief carving | ▌ Architects introduce groin vaulting in church naves in conjunction with a three-story elevation (arcade-tribune-clerestory)<br><br>▌ Relief sculpture becomes commonplace on church facades, usually greeting worshipers with a vision of Christ as last judge<br><br>▌ Manuscript illumination flourishes in the scriptoria of Cluniac monasteries | |

## Pilgrimage Roads in France and Spain

In the Romanesque era, pilgrimage was the most conspicuous feature of public religious devotion, proclaiming pilgrims' faith in the power of saints and hope for their special favor. The major shrines—Saint Peter's and Saint Paul's in Rome and the Church of the Holy Sepulcher in Jerusalem—drew pilgrims from all over Europe, just as Muslims journeyed from afar to Mecca (see "Muhammad and Islam," Chapter 10, page 285). The pilgrims braved bad roads and hostile wildernesses infested with robbers who preyed on innocent travelers—all for the sake of salvation. The journeys could take more than a year to complete—when they were successful. People often undertook pilgrimage as an act of repentance or as a last resort in their search for a cure for some physical disability. Hardship and austerity were means of increasing pilgrims' chances for the remission of sin or of disease. The distance and peril of the pilgrimage were measures of pilgrims' sincerity of repentance or of the reward they sought.

For those with insufficient time or money to make a pilgrimage to Rome or Jerusalem (in short, most people in Europe), holy destinations could be found closer to home. In France, for example, the church at Vézelay (FIG. 12-14) housed the bones of Mary Magdalene. Pilgrims could also view Saint Lazarus's remains at Autun (FIG. 12-1), Saint Saturninus's at Toulouse (FIG. 12-5), Saint Faith's at Conques (FIGS. 12-2 and 12-7A), and Saint Martin's at Tours (see "The Veneration of Relics," page 336). Each of these great shrines was also an important way station en route to the most venerated shrine in western Europe, the tomb of Saint James at Santiago de Compostela (FIG. 12-7B) in northwestern Spain.

Large crowds of pilgrims paying homage to saints placed a great burden on the churches possessing their relics and led to changes in church design, principally longer and wider naves and aisles, transepts and ambulatories with additional chapels (FIG. 12-6), and second-story galleries (FIGS. 12-7 and 12-7B). Pilgrim traffic also established the routes that later became the major avenues of commerce and communication in western Europe. The popularity of pilgrimages gave rise to travel guides that, like modern guidebooks, provided pilgrims with information not only about saints and shrines but also about roads, accommodations, food, and drink. How widely circulated these handwritten books were remains a matter of scholarly debate, but the information they provide is invaluable.

The most famous Romanesque guidebook described the four roads leading to Santiago de Compostela through Arles and Tou-

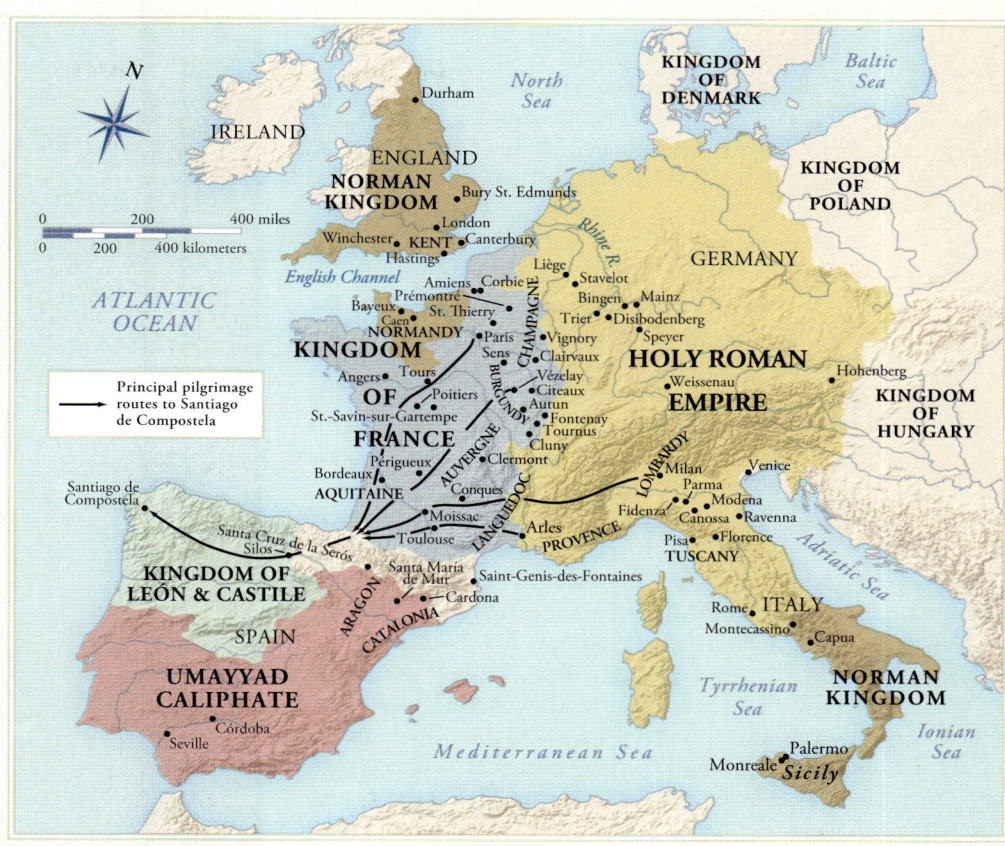

MAP 12-1  Western Europe around 1100.

louse, Conques and Moissac, Vézelay and Périgueux, and Tours and Bordeaux in France (MAP 12-1). Saint James was the symbol of Christian resistance to Muslim expansion in western Europe, and his relics, discovered in the ninth century, drew pilgrims to Santiago de Compostela from far and wide. The guidebook's anonymous 12th-century author, possibly Aimery Picaud, a Cluniac monk, was himself a well-traveled pilgrim. The text states the author wrote the guide "in Rome, in the lands of Jerusalem, in France, in Italy, in Germany, in Frisia and mainly in Cluny."* Pilgrims reading the guidebook learned about the saints and their shrines at each stop along the way to Spain. Saint Saturninus of Toulouse, for example, endured a martyr's death at the hands of the Romans when he

> was tied to some furious and wild bulls and then precipitated from the height of the citadel. . . . His head crushed, his brains knocked out, his whole body torn to pieces, he rendered his worthy soul to Christ. He is buried in an excellent location close to the city of Toulouse where a large basilica [FIGS. 12-5 to 12-7] was erected by the faithful in his honor.†

*William Melczer, *The Pilgrim's Guide to Santiago de Compostela* (New York: Italica Press, 1993), 133.
† Ibid., 103.

# The Veneration of Relics

The cult of *relics* was not new in the Romanesque era. For centuries, Christians had traveled to sacred shrines housing the body parts of, or objects associated with, the holy family or the saints. The faithful had long believed bones, clothing, instruments of martyrdom, and the like had the power to heal body and soul. The veneration of relics, however, reached a high point in the 11th and 12th centuries, prompting the devout to undertake often dangerous pilgrimages to hallowed shrines in Jerusalem, Rome, and throughout western Europe (see "Pilgrimage Roads in France and Spain," page 335). Churches vied with one another not only for the possession of relics but also in the magnificence of the containers (*reliquaries*) that preserved and protected them.

The case of the relics of Saint Faith (Sainte-Foy, in French), an early-fourth-century child martyr who refused to pay homage to the Roman gods, is a telling example. A monk from the abbey church at Conques (FIG. 12-7A) stole the saint's skull from the nearby abbey of Agen around 880. The monks justified the act as *furta sacra* (holy theft), claiming Saint Faith herself wished to move. The reliquary (FIG. 12-2) they provided to house the saint's remains is one of the most sumptuous ever produced. It takes the form of an enthroned statuette of the martyr. Fashioned of gold leaf and silver gilt over a wooden core, the reliquary prominently features inset jewels and cameos of various dates—the accumulated donations of pilgrims and church patrons over many years. The saint's oversize head is a reworked ancient Roman *parade helmet*—a masklike helmet worn by soldiers on special ceremonial occasions and not part of standard battle dress. The monks added a martyr's crown to the ancient helmet. The rear of the throne bears a *Crucifixion* image engraved in rock crystal, establishing a parallel between Christ's martyrdom and Saint Faith's.

Reflecting the Romanesque passion for relics, *The Song of Roland,* an 11th-century epic poem recounting a historical battle of 778 between Charlemagne's rear-guard and the Saracens, describes Durendal, the extraordinary sword the hero Roland wielded, as follows:

> Ah, Durendal, fair, hallowed, and devote,
> What store of relics lie in thy hilt of gold!
> St Peter's tooth, St Basil's blood, it holds,
> Hair of my lord St Denis, there enclosed,
> Likewise a piece of Blessed Mary's robe.*

Given the competition among Romanesque monasteries and cities for the possession of saints' relics, the 11th-century *Pilgrim's Guide to Santiago de Compostela* included comments on authenticity. For example, about Saint James's tomb, the anonymous author stated:

> May therefore the imitators from beyond the mountains blush who claim to possess some portion of him or even his entire relic. In fact, the body of the Apostle is here in its entirety, divinely lit by paradisiacal carbuncles, incessantly honored with immaculate and soft perfumes, decorated with dazzling celestial candles, and diligently worshipped by attentive angels.†

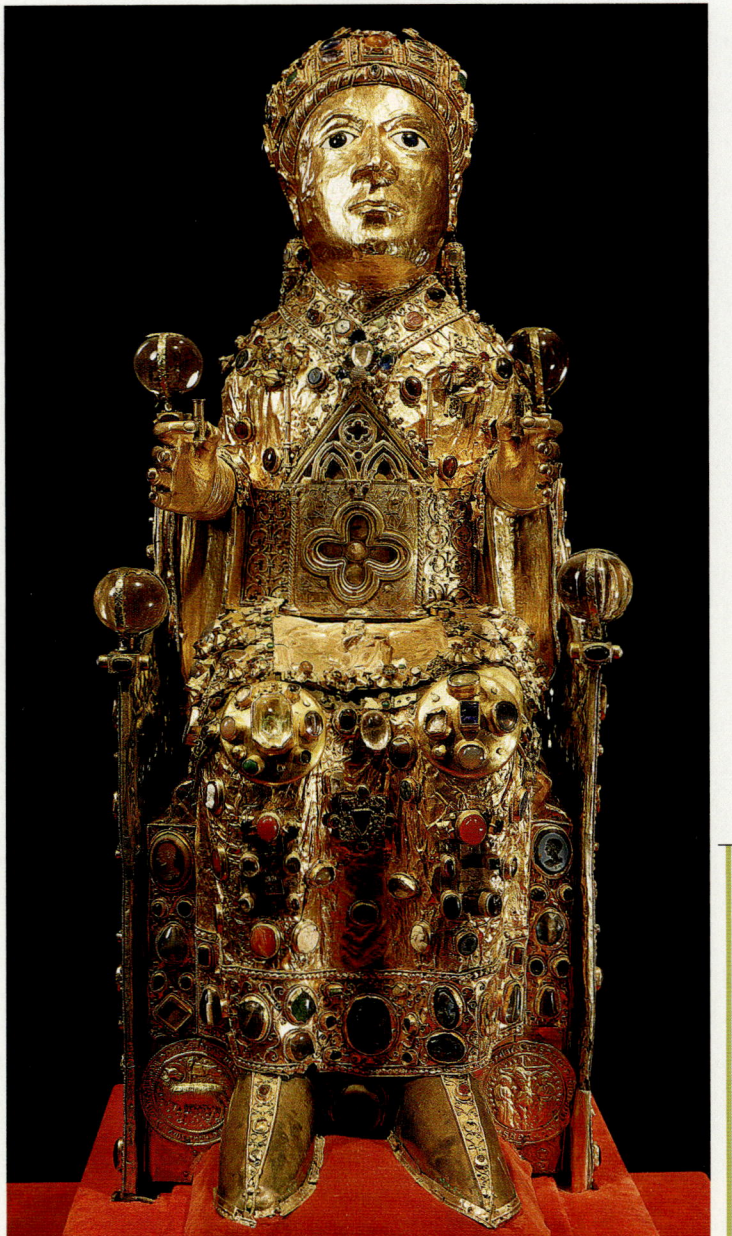

1 ft.

**12-2** Reliquary statue of Sainte-Foy (Saint Faith), late 10th to early 11th century with later additions. Gold, silver gilt, jewels, and cameos over a wooden core, 2′ 9½″ high. Treasury, Sainte-Foy, Conques.

This enthroned image containing the skull of Saint Faith is one of the most lavish Romanesque reliquaries. The head is an ancient Roman parade helmet, and the cameos are donations from pilgrims.

*173.2344–2348. Translated by Dorothy L. Sayers, *The Song of Roland* (New York: Penguin, 1957), 141.
†William Melczer, *The Pilgrim's Guide to Santiago de Compostela* (New York: Italica Press, 1993), 127.

## Architecture and Architectural Sculpture

The regional diversity of the Romanesque period is particularly evident in architecture. For example, some Romanesque churches, especially in Italy, retained the wooden roofs of their Early Christian predecessors long after stone vaulting had become commonplace elsewhere. Even in France and northern Spain, home of many of the most innovative instances of stone vaulting, some Romanesque architects continued to build timber-roofed churches.

**VIGNORY** The mid-11th-century church of Saint-Étienne (Saint Stephen) at Vignory in the Champagne region of central France has strong ties to Carolingian-Ottonian architecture but already incorporates features that became common only in later Romanesque buildings. The interior (FIG. **12-3**) reveals a kinship with the three-story wooden-roofed churches of the Ottonian era, for example, Saint Cyriakus (FIG. 11-21) at Gernrode. At Vignory, however, the second story is not a true *tribune* (gallery over the aisle opening onto the nave) but rather a screen with alternating piers

and columns opening onto very tall flanking aisles. The east end of the church, in contrast, has an innovative plan (FIG. **12-4**) with an ambulatory around the choir and three semicircular chapels opening onto it. These *radiating chapels* probably housed the church's relics, which the faithful could view without having to enter the choir where the main altar stood.

Although other 11th-century churches, for example, Sant Vicenç (FIG. **12-4A**) at Cardona, Spain, and Saint-Philibert (FIG. **12-4B**) at Tournus, France, are noteworthy as early Romanesque examples of stone vaulting, Saint-Étienne at Vignory is one of the first examples of the introduction of stone sculpture into Romanesque ecclesiastical architecture, one of the period's defining features. At Vignory, however, the only sculpture is the relief decoration of the capitals of the ambulatory and false tribunes where abstract and vegetal ornamentation, lions, and other quadrupeds are the exclusive motifs.

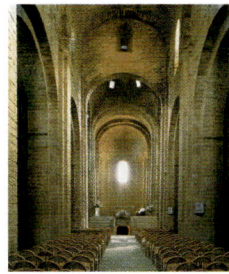

**12-4A** Sant Vicenç, Cardona, ca. 1029–1040.

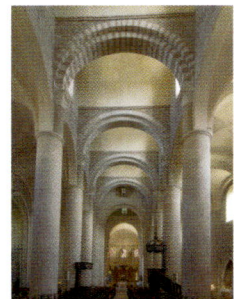

**12-4B** Saint-Philibert, Tournus, ca. 1060. ◼◂

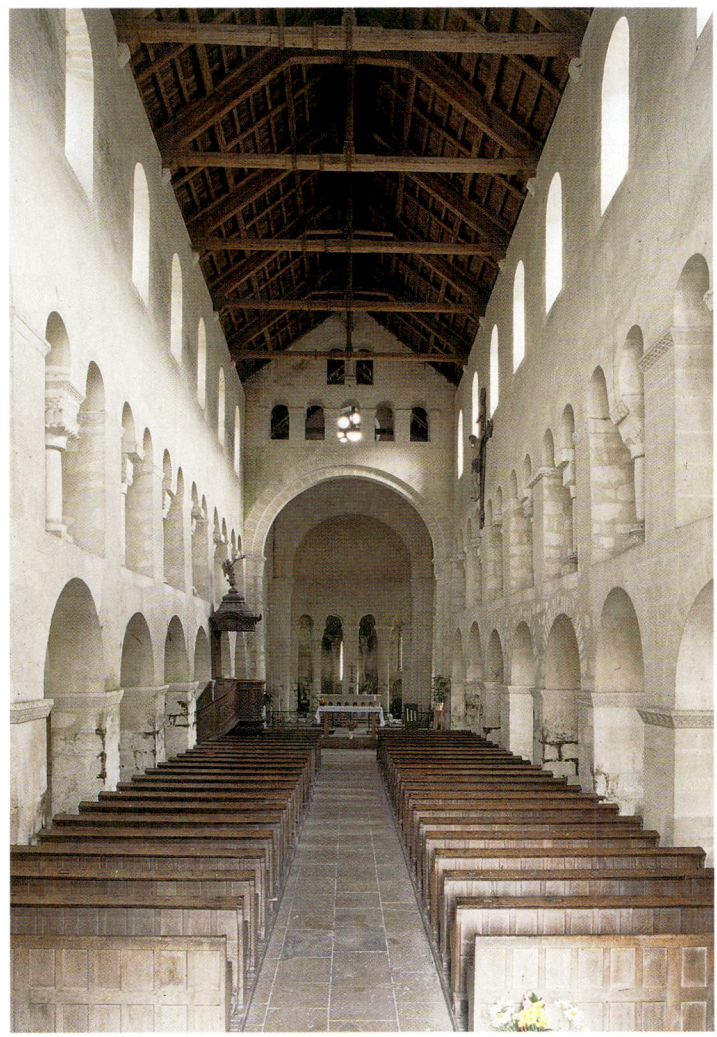

**12-3** Interior of Saint-Étienne (looking east), Vignory, France, 1050–1057. ◼◂

The timber-roofed abbey church at Vignory reveals a kinship with the three-story naves of Ottonian churches (FIG. 11-21), which also feature an alternate-support system of piers and columns.

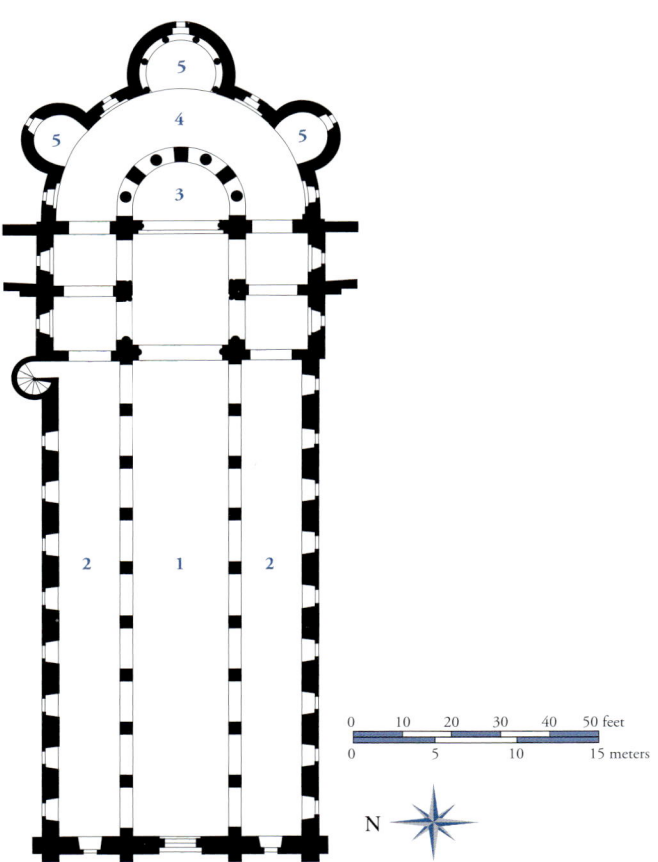

**12-4** Plan of Saint-Étienne, Vignory, France, 1050–1057. (1) nave, (2) aisles, (3) choir, (4) ambulatory, (5) radiating chapels.

The innovative plan of the east end of the abbey church of Saint Stephen features an ambulatory around the choir and three semicircular radiating chapels opening onto it for the display of relics.

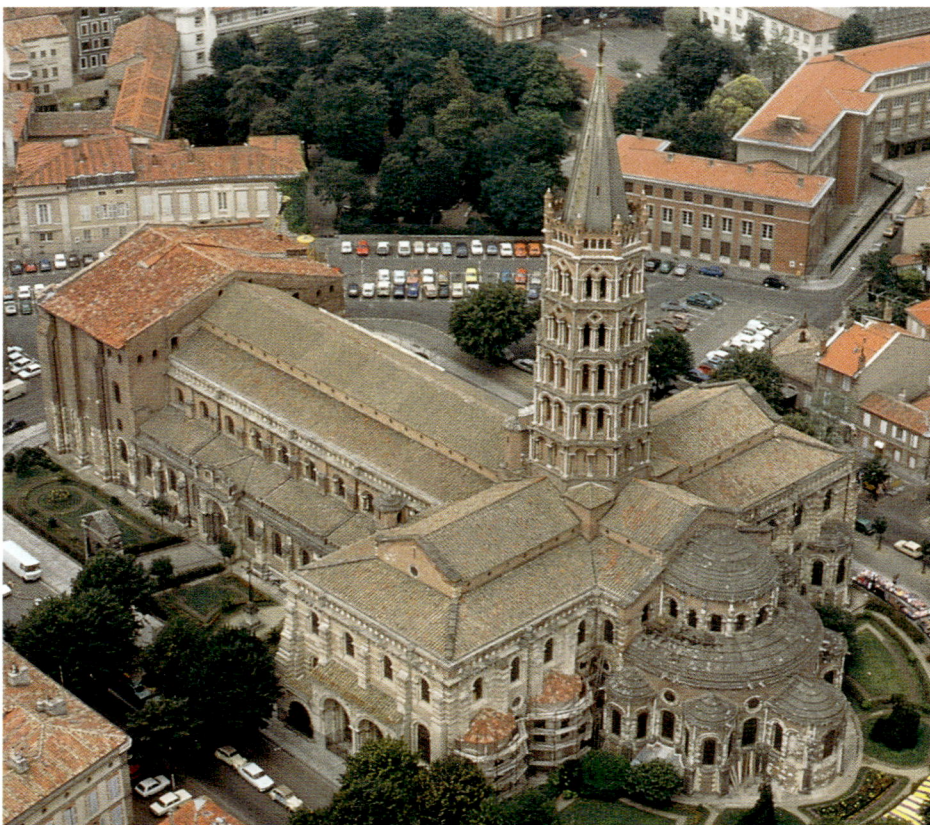

**TOULOUSE** Dwarfing the Vignory, Cardona, and Tournus churches is the immense stone-vaulted basilica of Saint-Sernin (Saint Saturninus; FIGS. **12-5** to **12-7**) at Toulouse. Construction began around 1070 to honor the city's first bishop, a martyr saint of the middle of the third century. Toulouse was an important stop on the pilgrimage road through southwestern France to Santiago de Compostela (see "Pilgrimage Roads," page 335). Large congregations gathered at the shrines along the major pilgrimage routes, and the unknown architect designed Saint-Sernin to accommo-

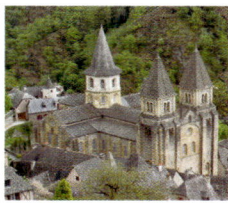

12-7A Sainte-Foy, Conques, mid-11th to early 12th century. ◼◀

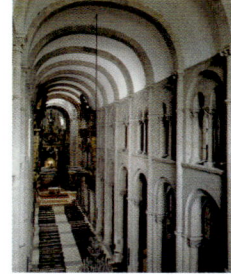

12-7B Saint James, Santiago de Compostela, ca. 1075–1120.

date them. The grand scale of the building is apparent in the aerial view (FIG. 12-5), which includes automobiles, trucks, and nearly invisible pedestrians. The church's 12th-century exterior is still largely intact, although the two towers of the western facade (at the left in FIG. 12-5) were never completed, and the prominent crossing tower dates to the Gothic and later periods. Saint-Sernin's plan (FIG. 12-6) closely resembles those of the churches of Saint Faith (FIG. **12-7A**) at Conques, Saint James (FIG. **12-7B**) at Santiago de Compostela, and Saint Martin at Tours, and exemplifies what has come to be called the "pilgrimage church" type. At Toulouse, the builders increased the length of the nave, doubled the side aisles, and added a transept, ambulatory, and radiating chapels to provide additional space for pilgrims and the clergy. Radiating chapels opening onto an ambulatory already were a feature of Vignory's abbey church (FIG. 12-4), but at Toulouse the chapels are greater in number and open onto the transept as well as the ambulatory.

The Saint-Sernin plan is extremely regular and geometrically precise. The crossing square, flanked by massive piers and marked off by heavy arches, served as the module for the entire church. Each nave bay, for example, measures exactly one-half of the crossing square, and each aisle bay measures exactly one-quarter. The builders employed similar simple ratios throughout the church. The first suggestion of this kind of planning scheme in medieval Europe was the Saint Gall monastery plan (FIG. 11-19), almost three

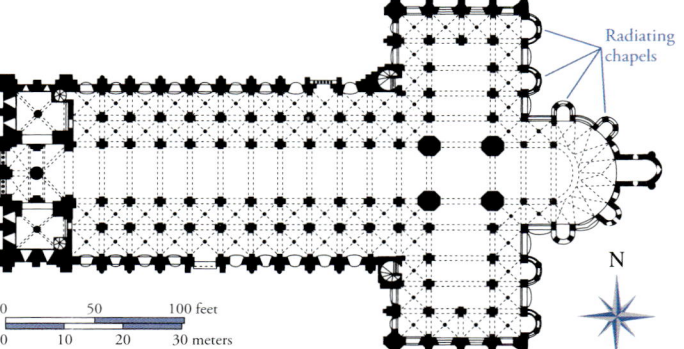

**12-6** Plan of Saint-Sernin, Toulouse, France, ca. 1070–1120 (after Kenneth John Conant).

Increased traffic led to changes in church design. "Pilgrimage churches" have longer and wider naves and aisles, as well as transepts and ambulatories with radiating chapels for viewing relics.

centuries earlier. The Toulouse solution was a crisply rational and highly refined realization of an idea first seen in Carolingian architecture. This approach to design became increasingly common in the Romanesque period.

Another telling feature of Saint-Sernin's design is the insertion of tribunes opening onto the nave over the inner aisles (FIG. 12-7), a feature also of the nave (FIG. 12-7B) of the church of Saint James at Santiago de Compostela. These galleries housed overflow crowds on special occasions and also played an important role in buttressing the nave's continuous semicircular cut-stone *barrel vault*, in contrast to the timber roof over the nave (FIG. 12-3) of the smaller abbey church at Vignory (see "Timber Roofs and Stone Vaults," page 339).

## Timber Roofs and Stone Vaults

The perils of wooden construction were the subject of frequent commentary among chroniclers of medieval ecclesiastical history. In some cases, churches burned over and over again in the course of a single century and repeatedly had to be extensively repaired or completely rebuilt. In September 1174, for example, Canterbury Cathedral, which had been dedicated only 44 years earlier, was accidentally set ablaze and destroyed. Gervase of Canterbury (1141–1210), who entered the monastery there in 1163 and wrote a history of the archbishopric from 1100 to 1199, provided a vivid eyewitness account of the disastrous fire in his *Chronica*:

> [D]uring an extraordinarily violent south wind, a fire broke out before the gate of the church, and outside the walls of the monastery, by which three cottages were half destroyed. From thence, while the citizens were assembling and subduing the fire, cinders and sparks carried aloft by the high wind were deposited upon the church, and being driven by the fury of the wind between the joints of the lead, remained there amongst the half-rotten planks, and shortly glowing with increased heat, set fire to the rotten rafters; from these the fire was communicated to the larger beams and their braces, no one yet perceiving or helping. For the well-painted ceiling below, and the sheet-lead covering above, concealed between them the fire that had arisen within. . . . But beams and braces burning, the flames arose to the slopes of the roof; and the sheets of lead yielded to the increasing heat and began to melt. Thus the raging wind, finding a freer entrance, increased the fury of the fire. . . . And now that the fire had loosened the beams from the pegs that bound them together, the half-burnt timbers fell into the choir below upon the seats of the monks; the seats, consisting of a great mass of woodwork, caught fire, and thus the mischief grew worse and worse. And it was marvellous, though sad, to behold how that glorious choir itself fed and assisted the fire that was destroying it. For the flames multiplied by this mass of timber, and extending upwards full fifteen cubits [about twenty-five feet], scorched and burnt the walls, and more especially injured the columns of the church. . . . In this manner the house of God, hitherto delightful as a paradise of pleasures, was now made a despicable heap of ashes, reduced to a dreary wilderness.*

After the fire, the Canterbury monks summoned a master builder from Sens, a French city 75 miles southeast of Paris, to supervise the construction of their new church. Gervase reported that the first task William of Sens tackled was "the procuring of stone from beyond the sea."

A quest for fireproof structures, however, apparently was not the primary rationale for stone vaulting. Although protec-

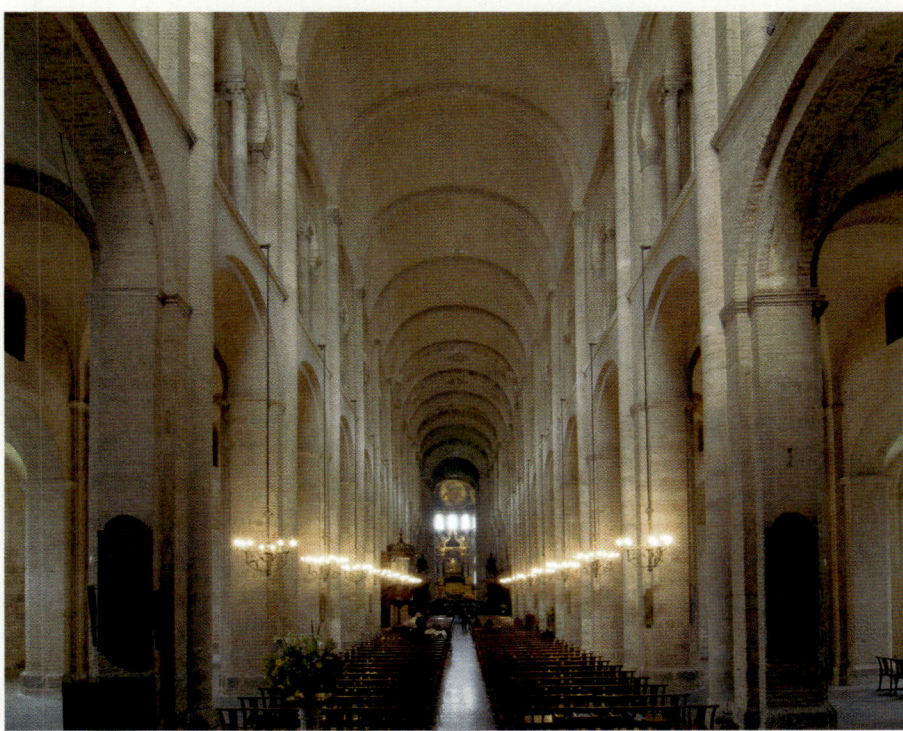

**12-7** Interior of Saint-Sernin (looking east), Toulouse, France, ca. 1070–1120. ◼◖

Saint-Sernin's stone vaults helped retard fire. The groin-vaulted tribune galleries also buttressed the nave's barrel vault whose transverse arches continue the lines of the compound piers.

tion from devastating conflagrations was no doubt one of the attractions of constructing masonry vaults in an age when candles and lamps provided interior illumination, other factors probably played a greater role in the decision to make the enormous investment of time and funds required. The rapid spread of stone vaulting throughout Romanesque Europe—beginning in the 11th century at Cardona (FIG. 12-4A), Tournus (FIG. 12-4B), Toulouse (FIG. 12-7), Santiago de Compostela (FIG. 12-7B), Speyer (FIG. 12-20), and Milan (FIG. 12-22)—was most likely the result of a desire to provide a suitably majestic setting for the display of relics as well as enhanced acoustics for the Christian liturgy and the music accompanying it. Some contemporaneous texts, in fact, comment on the visual impact of costly stone vaults. For example, in 1150 at Angers in northwestern France, a church chronicler explained what the bishop sought to achieve by replacing the timber roof of his cathedral with stone vaults: "[He] took down the timber beams of the nave of the church, threatening to fall from sheer old age, and began to build stone vaults of wondrous effect."†

*Translated by Robert Willis. Quoted in Elizabeth Gilmore Holt, *A Documentary History of Art,* 2d ed. (Princeton, N.J.: Princeton University Press, 1981), 1:52–54.

†Translated by John Hooper Harvey, *The Medieval Architect* (London: Waylan, 1972), 39.

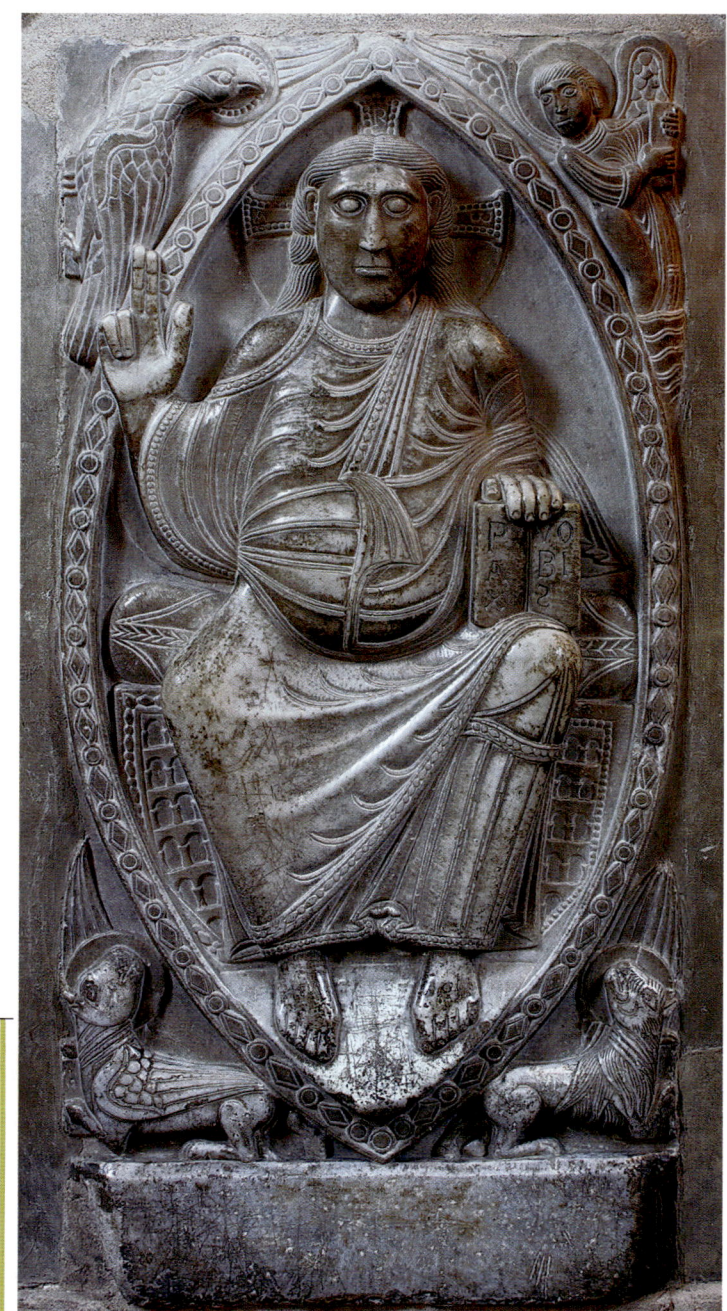

**12-8** BERNARDUS GELDUINUS, *Christ in Majesty,* relief in the ambulatory of Saint-Sernin, Toulouse, France, ca. 1096. Marble, 4′ 2″ high.

One of the earliest series of large Romanesque figural reliefs decorated the pilgrimage church of Saint-Sernin. The models were probably metal or ivory Carolingian and Ottonian book covers.

1 ft.

piers marking the corners of the bays, fully reflects the church's geometric floor plan (FIG. 12-6). Architectural historians refer to piers with columns or pilasters attached to their rectangular cores as *compound piers*. At Saint-Sernin, the engaged columns rise from the bottom of the compound piers to the vault's *springing* (the lowest stone of an arch) and continue across the nave as *transverse arches*. As a result, the Saint-Sernin nave gives the impression of being numerous identical vertical volumes of space placed one behind the other, marching down the building's length in orderly procession. Saint-Sernin's spatial organization corresponds to and renders visually the plan's geometric organization. The articulation of the building's exterior walls (FIG. 12-5), where buttresses frame each bay, also reflects the segmentation of the nave. This rationally integrated scheme, with repeated units decorated and separated by moldings, would have a long future in later European church architecture.

Saint-Sernin also boasts one of the earliest precisely dated series of large Romanesque figural reliefs—a group of seven marble slabs representing Christ, angels, and apostles. An inscription on the altar states the reliefs date to the year 1096 and identifies the artist as BERNARDUS GELDUINUS. Today, the plaques adorn the church's ambulatory wall, but their original location is uncertain. In the view of some scholars, the reliefs once formed part of a shrine dedicated to Saint Saturninus that stood in the *crypt* (a vaulted underground chamber) of the grand pilgrimage church. Others believe the plaques once decorated a choir screen or an exterior portal. The relief illustrated here (FIG. **12-8**), *Christ in Majesty,* is the centerpiece of the group. Christ sits in a mandorla, his right hand raised in blessing, his left hand resting on an open book inscribed *Pax vobis* ("Peace unto you"). The signs of the four evangelists (see "The Four Evangelists," Chapter 11, page 314) occupy the corners of the slab. Art historians debate the sources of Bernardus's style, but the composition could have been used earlier for a Carolingian or Ottonian work in metal or ivory, perhaps a book cover. The polished marble has the gloss of both materials, and the sharply incised lines and ornamentation of Christ's aureole are characteristic of pre-Romanesque metalwork.

Stone sculpture, with some notable exceptions, such as the Irish high crosses (FIGS. 11-9 and 11-9A), had almost disappeared from the art of western Europe during the early Middle Ages. The revival of stonecarving in the 11th century at Toulouse and Saint-Genis-des-Fontaines (FIG. **12-8A**) in southern France and Silos (FIG. **12-8B**) in northern Spain is a hallmark of the Romanesque age—and one reason the period is aptly named. The inspiration for stone sculpture no doubt came, at least in part, from the abundant remains of ancient statues and reliefs throughout Rome's northwestern provinces. Yet these models had been available for centuries, and they cannot explain the sudden proliferation of stone sculpture in Romanesque churches. Many art historians have noted that the reemergence of monumental stone sculpture coincided with the introduction of stone vaulting. But medieval builders had erected stone-walled churches and monumental westworks for centuries, even if the structures bore timber ceilings and roofs. The earliest Romanesque sculptures, in fact, appear in timber-roofed churches, such as Saint-Étienne (FIG. 12-3) at Vignory. Therefore, the addition of stone vaults to basilican churches cannot

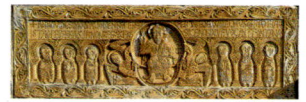

**12-8A** Saint-Genis-des-Fontaines, 1019–1020.

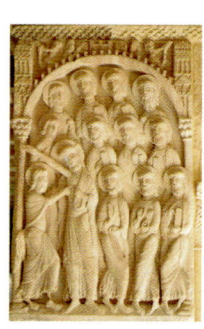

**12-8B** Santo Domingo, Silos, ca. 1090–1100.

*Groin vaults* (indicated by Xs on the plan, FIG. 12-6; compare FIG. 7-6*b*) in the tribunes as well as in the ground-floor aisles absorbed the pressure exerted by the barrel vault along the entire length of the nave and transferred the main thrust to the thick outer walls.

The builders of Saint-Sernin were not content merely to buttress the massive nave vault. They also carefully coordinated the design of the vault with that of the nave arcade below and with the modular plan of the building as a whole. The nave elevation (FIG. 12-7), which features *engaged columns* (attached half-columns) embellishing the

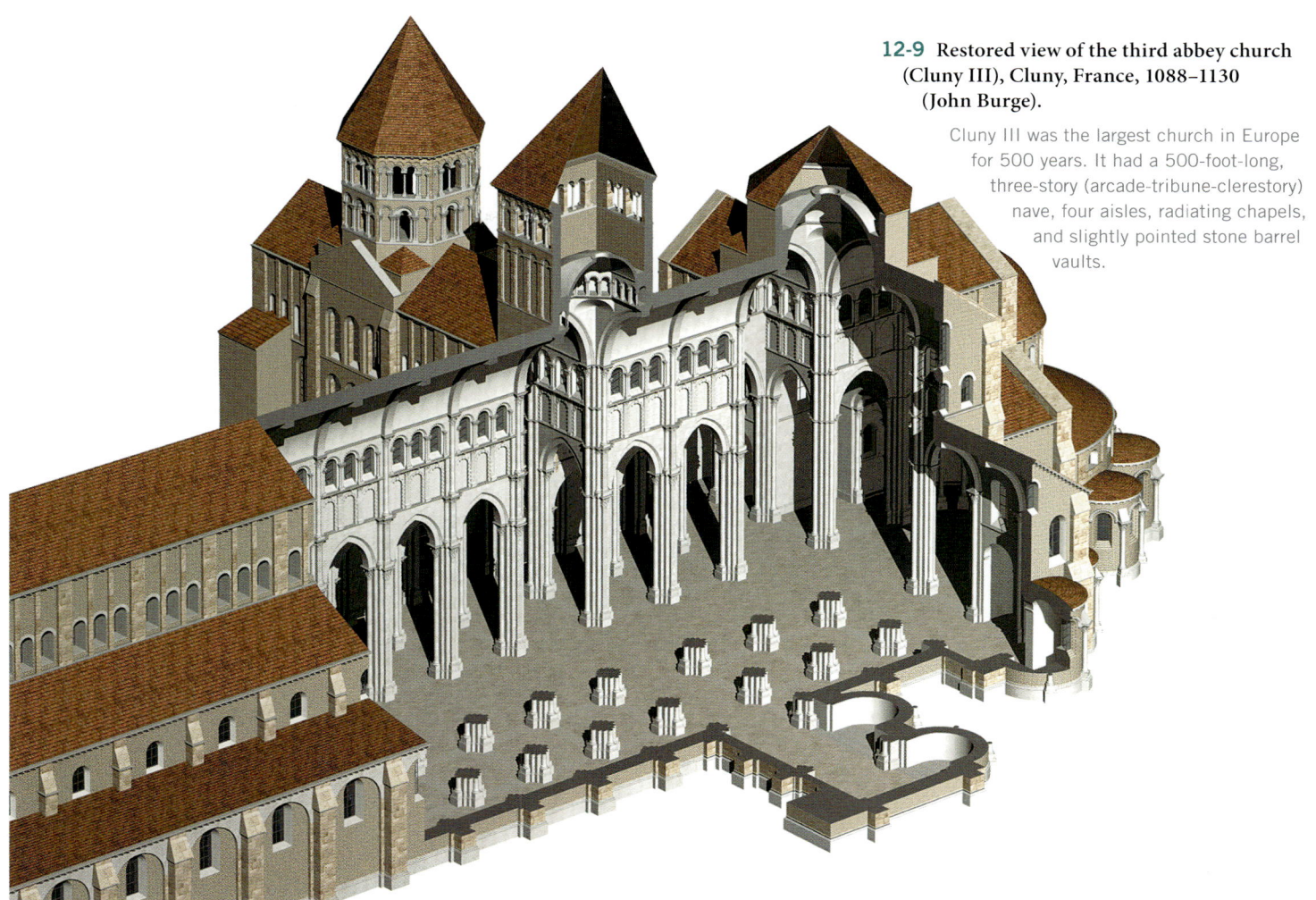

**12-9** Restored view of the third abbey church (Cluny III), Cluny, France, 1088–1130 (John Burge).

Cluny III was the largest church in Europe for 500 years. It had a 500-foot-long, three-story (arcade-tribune-clerestory) nave, four aisles, radiating chapels, and slightly pointed stone barrel vaults.

account for the resurgence of stonecarving in the Romanesque period. But just as stone vaulting reflects the greater prosperity of the age, so too does the decoration of churches with large-scale sculptures. Both are consistent with the widespread desire in the Romanesque period to beautify the house of God and make it, in the words of Gervase of Canterbury, "a paradise of pleasures."

The popularity of stone sculpture in the 12th century also reflects the changing role of many churches in western Europe. In the early Middle Ages, most churches served small monastic communities, and the worshipers were primarily or exclusively clergy. With the rise of towns in the Romanesque period, churches, especially those on the major pilgrimage routes, increasingly served the lay public. The display of sculpture both inside and outside Romanesque churches was a means of impressing—and educating—a new and largely illiterate audience.

**CLUNY** The primary patrons of Romanesque sculpture were the monks of the Cluniac order. In 909, William the Pious, duke of Aquitaine (r. 893–918), donated land near Cluny in Burgundy to a community of reform-minded Benedictine monks under the leadership of Berno of Baume (d. 927). Because William waived his feudal rights to the land, the abbot of Cluny was obligated only to the pope in Rome, a unique privilege. Berno founded a new order at Cluny according to the rules of Saint Benedict (see "Medieval Monasteries and Benedictine Rule," Chapter 11, page 322). Under Berno's successors, the Cluniac monks became famous for their scholarship, music, and art. Their influence and wealth grew

rapidly, and they built a series of ever more elaborate monastic churches at Cluny.

Abbot Hugh of Semur (1024–1109) began construction of the third church at Cluny in 1088. Called Cluny III by architectural historians, the building is, unfortunately, largely destroyed today but can be reconstructed in a computer drawing (FIG. **12-9**). When work concluded in 1130, Cluny III was the largest church in Europe, and it retained that distinction for almost 500 years until the completion of the new Saint Peter's (FIG. 24-4) in Rome in the early 17th century. Contemporaries considered Cluny III a place worthy for angels to dwell if they lived on earth. The church had a bold and influential design, with a barrel-vaulted nave, four aisles, and radiating chapels, as at Saint-Sernin, but with a three-story nave elevation (arcade-tribune-clerestory) and slightly pointed nave vaults. With a nave more than 500 feet long and more than 100 feet high (both dimensions are about 50 percent greater than at Saint-Sernin), it epitomized the grandiose scale of the new stone-vaulted Romanesque churches and was a symbol of the power and prestige of the Cluniac order.

**MOISSAC** An important stop in southwestern France along the pilgrimage route to Saint James's tomb at Santiago de Compostela was Moissac, which boasts the most extensive preserved ensemble of early Romanesque sculpture. The monks of the Moissac abbey had joined the Cluniac order in 1047. Enriched by the gifts of pilgrims and noble benefactors, they adorned their church with an elaborate series of relief sculptures. The oldest are in the *cloister* (from the Latin word *claustrum,* an enclosed place), which

# Bernard of Clairvaux on Cloister Sculpture

The most influential theologian of the Romanesque era was Bernard of Clairvaux (1090–1153). A Cistercian monk and abbot of the monastery he founded at Clairvaux in northern Burgundy, he embodied not only the reforming spirit of the Cistercian order but also the new religious fervor awakening throughout Europe. Bernard's impassioned eloquence made him a celebrity and drew him into the stormy politics of the 12th century. He intervened in high ecclesiastical and secular matters, defended and sheltered embattled popes, counseled kings, denounced heretics, and preached Crusades against the Muslims (see "The Crusades," page 346)—all in defense of papal Christianity and spiritual values. The Church declared Bernard a saint in 1174, barely two decades after his death.

In a letter Bernard wrote in 1127 to William, abbot of Saint-Thierry, he complained about the rich outfitting of non-Cistercian churches in general, and in particular, the sculptural adornment of monastic cloisters, such as those at Silos (FIG. 12-8B) and Moissac (FIG. 12-10).

> I will overlook the immense heights of the places of prayer, their immoderate lengths, their superfluous widths, the costly refinements, and painstaking representations which deflect the attention . . . of those who pray and thus hinder their devotion. . . . But so be it, let these things be made for the honor of God . . . [But] in the cloisters, before the eyes of the brothers while they read—

what . . . are the filthy apes doing there? The fierce lions? The monstrous centaurs? The creatures, part man and part beast? . . . You may see many bodies under one head, and conversely many heads on one body. On one side the tail of a serpent is seen on a quadruped, on the other side the head of a quadruped is on the body of a fish. Over there an animal has a horse for the front half and a goat for the back . . . Everywhere so plentiful and astonishing a variety of contradictory forms is seen that one would rather read in the marble than in books, and spend the whole day wondering at every single one of them than in meditating on the law of God. Good God! If one is not ashamed of the absurdity, why is one not at least troubled at the expense?*

*Apologia* 12.28–29. Translated by Conrad Rudolph, *The "Things of Greater Importance": Bernard of Clairvaux's* Apologia *and the Medieval Attitude toward Art* (Philadelphia: University of Pennsylvania Press, 1990), 279, 283.

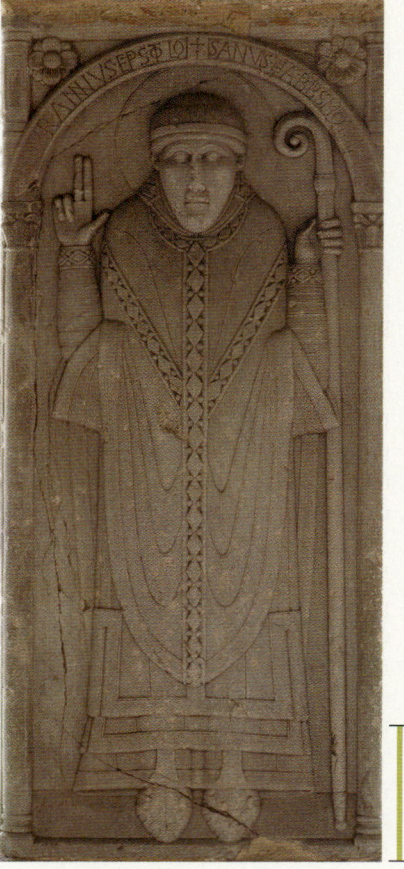

1 ft.

**12-10** General view of the cloister (*left;* looking southeast) and detail of the pier with the relief of Abbot Durandus (*right*), Saint-Pierre, Moissac, France, ca. 1100–1115. Relief: limestone, 6′ high. ◧◁

The revived tradition of stonecarving probably began with historiated capitals. The most extensive preserved ensemble of sculptured early Romanesque capitals is in the Moissac cloister.

connotes being shut away from the world. Architecturally, the medieval church cloister expressed the seclusion of the spiritual life, the *vita contemplativa*. At Moissac, as elsewhere, the cloister provided the monks (and nuns) with a foretaste of Paradise. In its garden or the timber-roofed columnar walkway framing the garden (FIG. 12-10, *left*), they could read their devotions, pray, meditate,

and carry on other activites in a beautiful and centrally located space. The cloisters of the 12th century are monuments to the vitality, popularity, and influence of monasticism at its peak.

Moissac's cloister sculpture program consists of large figural reliefs on the piers as well as *historiated* (ornamented with figures) capitals on the columns. The pier reliefs portray the 12 apostles and the monastery's first Cluniac abbot (FIG. 12-10, *right*), Durandus (1047–1072), whom the monks buried in the cloister. The Durandus relief is not a portrait in the modern sense of the word but a generic, bilaterally symmetrical image of the abbot holding his staff in his left hand and raising his right hand in a gesture of blessing. The carving is very shallow—an exercise in two-dimensional design rather than an attempt at representing a fully modeled figure in space. The feet, for example, which point downward, do not rest on the ground and cannot support the abbot's weight (compare FIG. 9-2).

The 76 capitals alternately crown single and paired column shafts. They are variously decorated, some with abstract patterns, many with biblical scenes or the lives of saints, others with fantastic monsters of all sorts—basilisks, griffins, lizards, gargoyles, and more. *Bestiaries*—collections of illustrations of real and imaginary animals—became very popular in the Romanesque age. The monstrous forms were reminders of the chaos and deformity of a world without God's order. Medieval artists delighted in inventing composite multiheaded beasts and other fantastic creations. Historiated capitals were also a feature of Moissac's mother church, Cluny III, and were common in Cluniac monasteries.

Not everyone shared the Cluniac monks' enthusiasm for stone sculpture. One group of Benedictine monks founded a new order at Cîteaux in eastern France in 1098. The Cistercians (from the Latin name for Cîteaux) split from the Cluniac order to return to the strict observance of the rules of Saint Benedict (see "Medieval Monasteries and Benedictine Rule," Chapter 11, page 322), changing the color of their habits from Cluniac black to unbleached white. These White Monks emphasized productive manual labor, and their systematic farming techniques stimulated the agricultural transformation of Europe. The Cistercian movement expanded with astonishing rapidity. Within a half century, the White Monks had established more than 500 monasteries. Their churches, such as Notre-Dame at Fontenay (FIG. **12-10A**), are uniformly austere. The Cistercians rejected figural sculpture as a

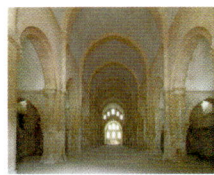

12-10A Notre-Dame, Fontenay, 1139–1147. ◼◀

distraction from their devotions. The most outspoken Cistercian critic of church sculpture was Abbot Bernard of Clairvaux (see "Bernard of Clairvaux on Cloister Sculpture," page 342).

Bernard directed his tirade against figural sculpture primarily at monks who allowed the carvings to distract them from their meditations. But at Moissac (FIG. **12-11**) and other Cluniac churches, the most extensive sculptural

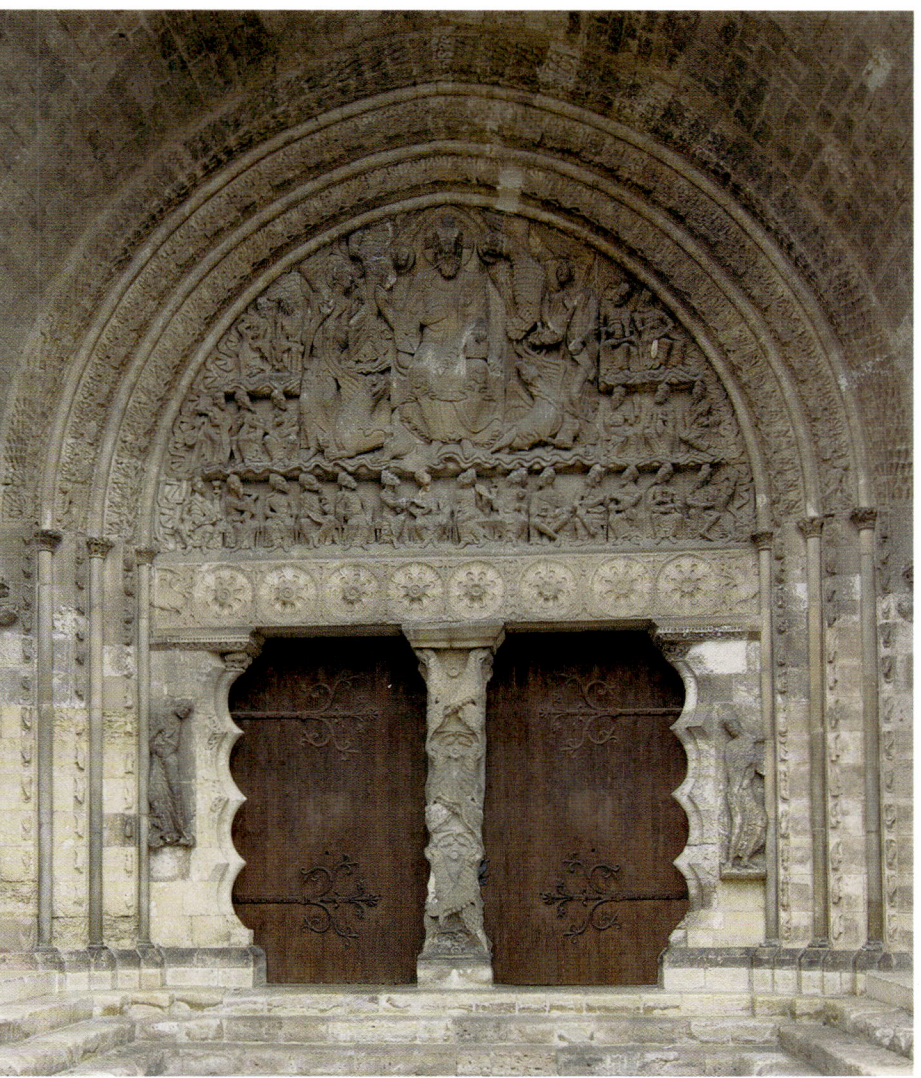

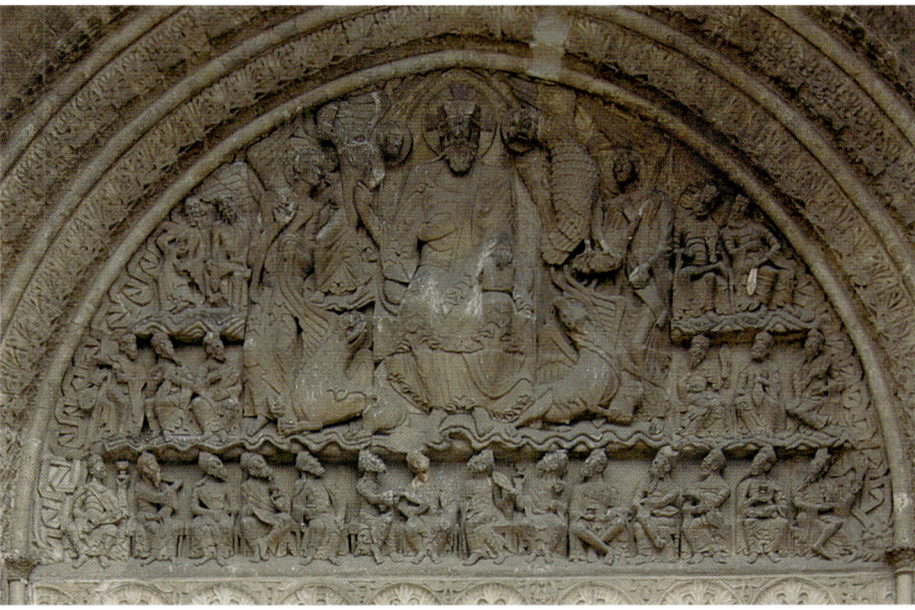

**12-11** South portal of Saint-Pierre, Moissac, France, ca. 1115–1135. *Top:* general view. *Bottom:* detail of tympanum with *Second Coming of Christ.* ◼◀

A vision of the second coming of Christ on judgment day greets worshipers entering Saint-Pierre at Moissac. The sculptural program reflects the belief that Christ is the door to salvation.

## The Romanesque Church Portal

One of the most significant and distinctive features of Romanesque art is the revival of monumental sculpture in stone. Large-scale carved biblical figures were extremely rare in Christian art before the year 1000. But in the late 11th and early 12th centuries, rich ensembles of figural reliefs began to appear again, most often in the grand stone portals (FIGS. 12-11 and 12-14A) through which the faithful had to pass. Sculpture had been employed in church doorways before. For example, carved wooden doors (FIG. 8-10A) greeted Early Christian worshipers as they entered Santa Sabina in Rome, and Ottonian bronze doors (FIG. 11-24) decorated with Old and New Testament scenes marked the entrance from the cloister to Saint Michael's at Hildesheim. But these were exceptions, and in the Romanesque era (and during the Gothic period that followed), sculpture usually appeared in the area *around,* rather than *on,* the doors.

Shown in FIG. 12-12 are the parts of church portals Romanesque sculptors regularly decorated with figural reliefs:

▌ *Tympanum* (FIGS. 12-1, 12-11, 12-14, and 12-14A), the prominent semicircular *lunette* above the doorway proper, comparable in importance to the triangular pediment of a Greco-Roman temple.

▌ *Voussoirs* (FIG. 12-14), the wedge-shaped blocks that together form the *archivolts* of the arch framing the tympanum.

▌ *Lintel* (FIGS. 12-8A, 12-11, 12-13B, and 12-14), the horizontal beam above the doorway.

▌ *Trumeau* (FIGS. 12-11 and 12-13), the center post supporting the lintel in the middle of the doorway.

▌ *Jambs* (FIG. 12-11), the side posts of the doorway.

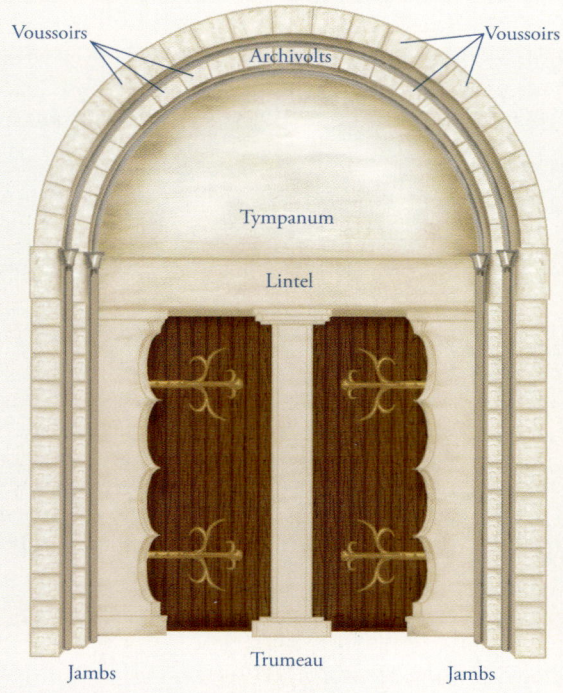

**12-12** The Romanesque church portal.

The clergy considered the church doorway the beginning of the path to salvation through Christ. Many Romanesque churches feature didactic sculptural reliefs above and beside the entrance portals.

ensembles adorned those parts of the church open to the laity, especially the facade—for example, that of Notre-Dame-la-Grande (FIG. 12-11A) at Poitiers. Saint-Pierre's richly decorated south portal faces the town square, and features figural and decorative reliefs in its *tympanum, voussoirs, lintel, trumeau,* and *jambs* (see "The Romanesque Church Portal," *left,* and FIG. 12-12). The tympanum depicts the *Second Coming* of Christ as

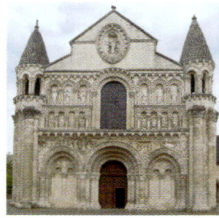

**12-11A** Notre-Dame-la-Grande, Poitiers, ca. 1130–1150. ◼◀

king and judge of the world in its last days. As befits his majesty, the enthroned Christ is at the center, reflecting a compositional rule followed since Early Christian times. Flanking him are the signs of the four evangelists and attendant angels holding scrolls to record human deeds for judgment. The figures of crowned musicians, which complete the design, are the 24 elders who accompany Christ as the kings of this world and make music in his praise. Each turns to face the enthroned judge, much as would the courtiers of a Romanesque monarch in attendance on their lord. Two courses of wavy lines symbolizing the clouds of Heaven divide the elders into three tiers.

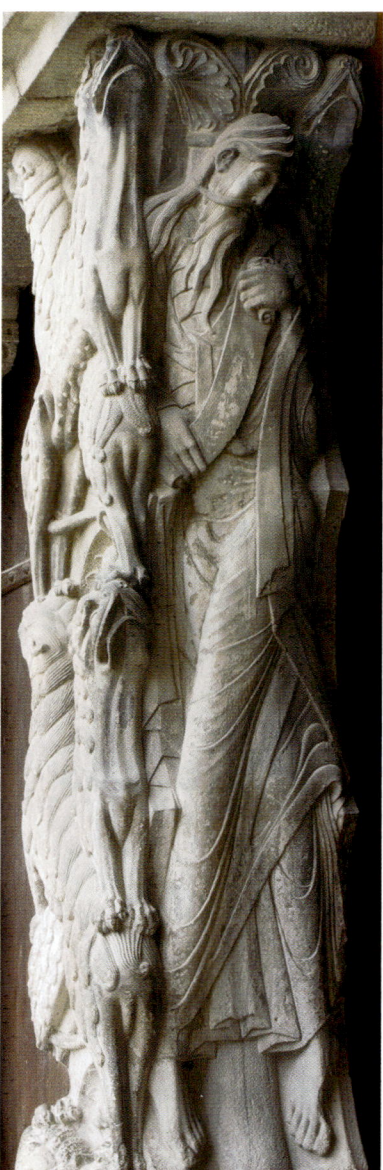

**12-13** Old Testament prophet (Jeremiah or Isaiah?), right side of the trumeau of the south portal of Saint-Pierre, Moissac, France, ca. 1115–1130. ◼◀

This animated prophet displays the scroll recounting his vision. His position below the apparition of Christ as last judge is in keeping with the tradition of pairing Old and New Testament themes.

Most sculptured Romanesque church portals present a larger-than-life Christ as the central motif. These facades reflect the belief, dating to Early Christian times, that Christ is the door to salvation ("I am the door; who enters through me will be saved"—John 10:9). An inscription on the tympanum of the late-11th-century monastic church of Santa Cruz de la Serós in Spain made this message explicit: "I am the eternal door. Pass through me faithful. I am the source of life."[4]

Many variations exist within the general style of Romanesque sculpture, as within Romanesque architecture. The figures of the Moissac tympanum contrast sharply with those of the earlier Saint-Sernin ambulatory reliefs (FIG. 12-8) and the Silos pier reliefs (FIG. 12-8B), as well as the contemporaneous *Last Judgment* tympanum (FIG. 12-1) at Autun and even the pier reliefs (FIG. 12-10, *right*) of the Moissac cloister. The extremely elongated bodies of the angels recording each soul's fate, the cross-legged dancing pose of Saint Matthew's angel, and the jerky, hinged movement of the elders' heads are characteristic of the nameless Moissac master's style of representing the human figure. The zigzag and dovetail lines of the draperies, the bandlike folds of the torsos, the bending back of the hands against the body, and the wide cheekbones are also common features of this distinctive style. The animation of the individual figures, however, contrasts with the stately monumentality of the composition as a whole, producing a dynamic tension in the tympanum.

The jambs and trumeau (FIG. **12-13**) of the Moissac portal have scalloped contours (FIG. 12-11), a borrowing from Spanish Islamic architecture (FIGS. 10-10 and 10-11). Six roaring interlaced lions on the front of the trumeau greet worshipers as they enter the church. The animal world was never far from the medieval mind, and people often associated the fiercest beasts with kings and barons—for example, Richard the Lionhearted, Henry the Lion, and Henry the Bear. Lions were the church's ideal protectors. In the Middle Ages, people believed lions slept with their eyes open. But the notion of placing fearsome images at the gateways to important places is of very ancient origin. Ancestors of the Moissac lions include the lions and composite monsters that guarded the palaces of Hittite, Assyrian, and Mycenaean kings (FIGS. 2-18A, 2-20, and 4-19) and the panthers and leopards in Greek temple pediments (FIG. 5-16) and Etruscan tombs (FIG. 6-9).

On the trumeau's right face is a prophet—identified by some scholars as Jeremiah, as Isaiah by others—who displays a scroll bearing his prophetic vision. His position below the apparition of Christ as the apocalyptic judge is yet another instance of the pairing of Old and New Testament themes, in keeping with an iconographic tradition established in Early Christian times (see "Jewish Subjects in Christian Art," Chapter 8, page 238). The prophet's figure is very tall and thin, in the manner of the tympanum angels, and like Matthew's angel, he executes a cross-legged step. The animation of the body reveals the passionate nature of the soul within. The flowing lines of the drapery folds ultimately derive from manuscript illumination (compare FIG. 12-15A) and here play gracefully around the elegant figure. The long, serpentine locks of hair and beard frame an arresting image of the dreaming mystic. The prophet seems entranced by his vision of what is to come, the light of ordinary day unseen by his wide eyes.

**VÉZELAY** At the same time sculptors were adorning Saint-Pierre at Moissac, Gislebertus and his assistants were at work on Saint-Lazare at Autun, decorating not only the west tympanum (FIG. 12-1) but also the nave (FIG. **12-13A**) and the north portal (FIG. **12-13B**). A team of stonecarvers also worked nearby at the church of La Madeleine (Mary Magdalene) at Vézelay. Vézelay is more closely associated with the Crusades (see "The Crusades," page 346) than is any other church in Europe. Pope Urban II had intended to preach the launching of the First Crusade at Vézelay in 1095, although he delivered the sermon at Clermont instead. In 1147, Bernard of Clairvaux called for the

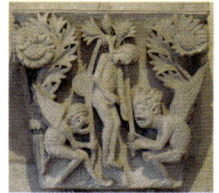

12-13A GISLEBERTUS, *Suicide of Judas*, Autun, ca. 1120–1135. 🎬

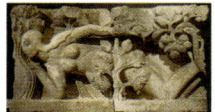

12-13B GISLEBERTUS, *Eve*, Autun, ca. 1120–1135. 🎬

Second Crusade at Vézelay, and King Louis VII of France took up the cross there. The Magdalene church at Vézelay was also where, in 1190, King Richard the Lionhearted of England and King Philip Augustus of France set out on the Third Crusade.

The major element of the sculptural program of La Madeleine at Vézelay is the tympanum (FIG. **12-14**) of the central portal of the

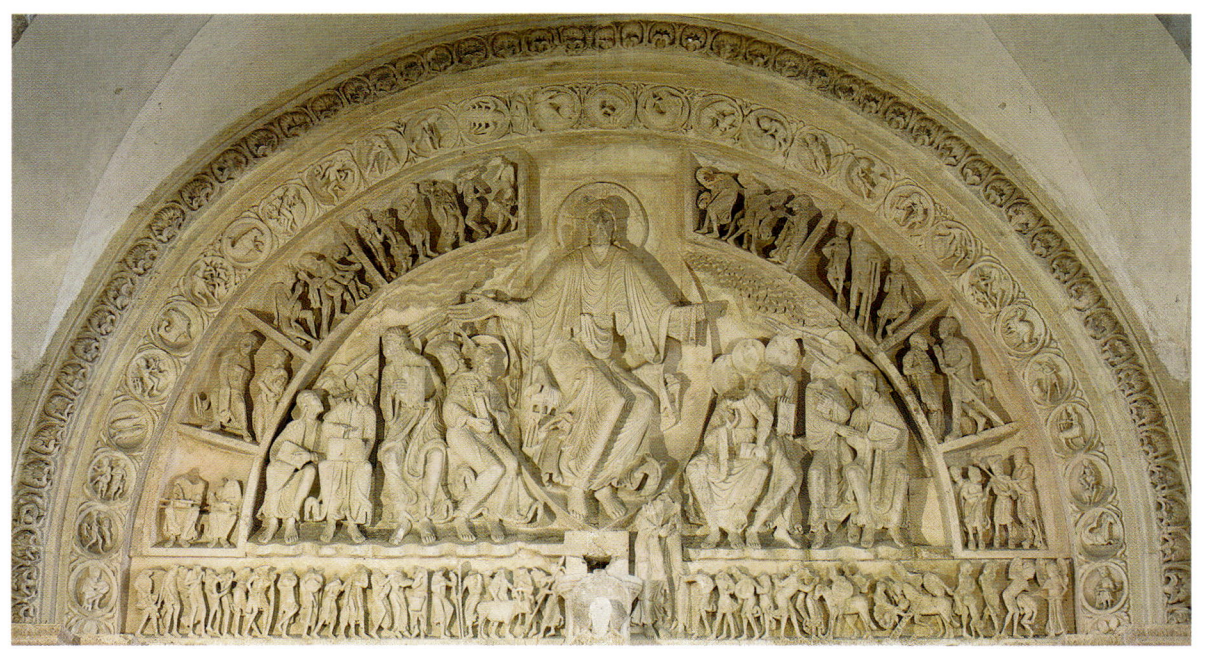

**12-14** *Pentecost* and *Mission of the Apostles*, tympanum of the center portal of the narthex of La Madeleine, Vézelay, France, 1120–1132. 🎬

In the tympanum of the church most closely associated with the Crusades, light rays emanating from Christ's hands instill the Holy Spirit in the apostles, whose mission is to convert the world's heathens.

## The Crusades

In 1095, Pope Urban II (r. 1088–1099) delivered a stirring sermon at the Council of Clermont in which he called for an assault on the Holy Land:

> [Y]our brethren who live in the East are in urgent need of your help . . . [because] the Turks and Arabs have attacked them. . . . They have killed and captured many, and have destroyed the churches . . . I, or rather the Lord, beseech you as Christ's heralds . . . to persuade all people of whatever rank, foot-soldiers and knights, poor and rich, to carry aid promptly to those Christians and to destroy that vile race from the lands of our friends. . . . All who die by the way . . . shall have immediate remission of sins. . . . Let those who go not put off the journey, but rent their lands and collect money for their expenses . . . [and] eagerly set out on the way with God as their guide.*

Between 1095 and 1190, Christians launched three great Crusades from France. The *Crusades* ("taking of the Cross") were mass armed pilgrimages whose stated purpose was to wrest the Christian shrines of the Holy Land from Muslim control. Similar vows bound Crusaders and pilgrims. They hoped not only to atone for sins and win salvation but also to glorify God and extend the power of the Church. The joint action of the papacy and the mostly French feudal lords in this type of holy war strengthened papal authority over the long run and created an image of Christian solidarity.

The symbolic embodiment of the joining of religious and secular forces in the Crusades was the Christian warrior, the fighting priest, or the priestly fighter. From the early medieval warrior evolved the Christian knight, who fought for the honor of God rather than in defense of his chieftain. The first and most typical of the crusading knights were the Knights Templar. After the Christian conquest of Jerusalem in 1099, they stationed themselves next to the Dome of the Rock (FIGS. 10-2 and 10-3), that is, on the site of Solomon's Temple, the source of their name. Their mission was to protect pilgrims visiting the recovered Christian shrines. Formally founded in 1118, the Knights Templar order received the blessing of Bernard of Clairvaux, who gave them a rule of organization based on that of his own Cistercians. Bernard justified their militancy by declaring "the knight of Christ" is "glorified in slaying the infidel . . . because thereby Christ is glorified," and the Christian knight then wins salvation. The Cistercian abbot saw the Crusades as part of the general reform of the Church and as the defense of the supremacy of Christendom. He himself called for the Second Crusade in 1147 at Vézelay (FIG. 12-14). For the Muslims, however, the Crusaders were nothing more than violent invaders who slaughtered the population of Jerusalem (Jewish as well as Muslim) when they took the city in July 1099.

In the end, the Muslims expelled the Christian armies, and the Crusaders failed miserably in their attempt to regain the Holy Land. But in western Europe, the Crusades had a much greater impact by increasing the power and prestige of the towns. Italian port cities such as Pisa (FIG. 12-26) thrived on the commercial opportunities presented by the transportation of Crusaders overseas. Many communities purchased their charters from the barons who owned their land when the latter needed to finance their campaigns in the Holy Land. This gave rise to a middle class of merchants and artisans to rival the power of the feudal lords and the great monasteries—an economic and societal change of enormous consequence for the later history of Europe.

*As recorded by Fulcher of Chartres (1059–ca. 1127). Translated by O. J. Thatcher and E. H. McNeal, quoted in Roberta Anderson and Dominic Aidan Bellenger, eds., *Medieval Worlds: A Sourcebook* (New York: Routledge, 2003), 88–90.

---

church's narthex. It depicts the *Pentecost* and the *Mission of the Apostles*. As related in Acts 1:4–9, Christ foretold the 12 apostles would receive the power of the Holy Spirit and become witnesses of the truth of the Gospels throughout the world. The light rays emanating from Christ's hands represent the instilling of the Holy Spirit in the apostles (Acts 2:1–42) at the Pentecost (the seventh Sunday after Easter). The apostles, holding the Gospel books, receive their spiritual assignment to preach the Gospel to all nations. The Christ figure is a splendid calligraphic design. The drapery lines shoot out in rays, break into quick zigzag rhythms, and spin into whorls, wonderfully conveying the spiritual light and energy flowing from Christ over and into the equally animated apostles. The overall composition, as well as the detailed treatment of the figures, contrasts with the much more sedate representation of the second coming (FIG. 12-11) at Moissac, where a grid of horizontal and vertical lines contains almost all the figures. The sharp differences between the two tympana once again highlight the regional diversity of Romanesque art.

The world's heathen, the objects of the apostles' mission, appear on the Vézelay lintel below and in eight compartments around the tympanum. The portrayals of the yet-to-be-converted constitute a medieval anthropological encyclopedia. Present are the legendary giant-eared Panotii of India, Pygmies (who require ladders to mount horses), and a host of other races, some characterized by a dog's head, others by a pig's snout, and still others by flaming hair. The assembly of agitated figures also includes hunchbacks, mutes, blind men, and lame men. Humanity, still suffering, awaits the salvation to come. As at Autun

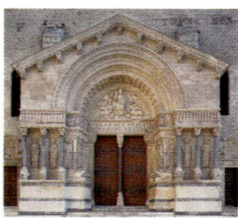

12-14A Saint-Trophîme, Arles, mid-12th century.

(FIG. 12-1) and Moissac (FIG. 12-11), and also at Saint-Trophîme (FIG. **12-14A**) in Arles, as worshipers passed through the portal, the tympanum established God's omnipotence and presented the Church as the road to salvation.

## Painting and Other Arts

Unlike the practices of placing vaults over naves and aisles and decorating building facades with monumental stone reliefs, the art of painting needed no "revival" in the Romanesque period. Monasteries produced illuminated manuscripts in large numbers in the early Middle Ages, and even the Roman tradition of mural painting had never died. But the quantity of preserved frescoes and illustrated books from the Romanesque era is unprecedented.

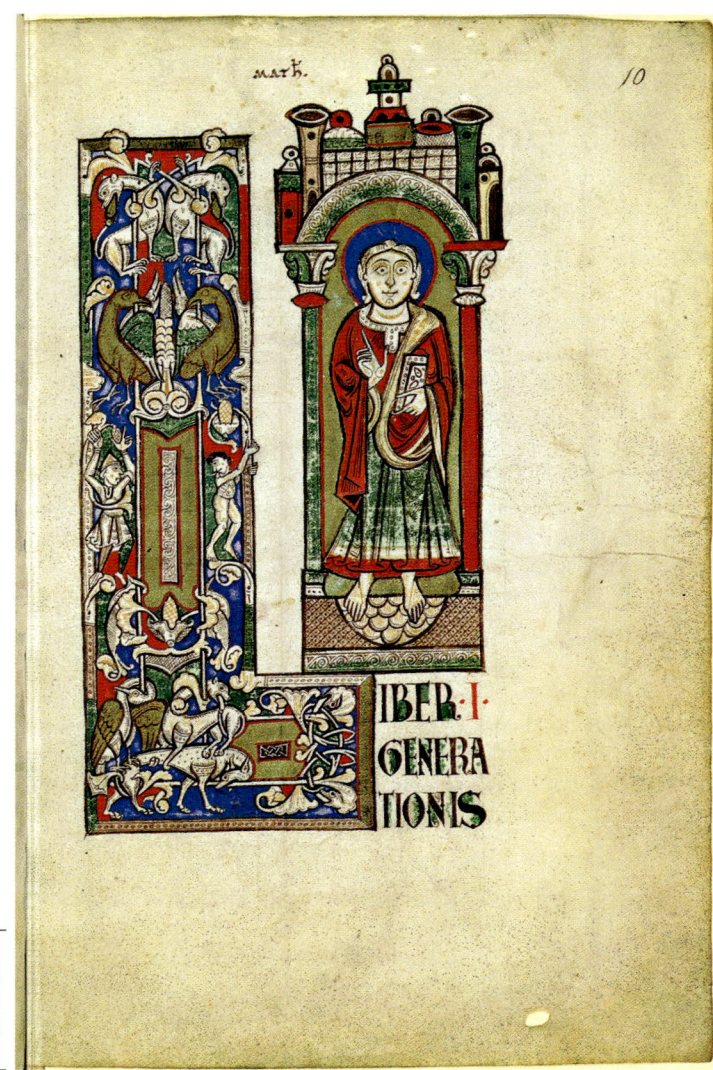

**12-15** Initial *L* and Saint Matthew, folio 10 recto of the *Codex Colbertinus,* probably from Moissac, France, ca. 1100. Tempera on vellum, $7\frac{1}{2}'' \times 4''$. Bibliothèque Nationale, Paris.

Probably produced in the Moissac scriptorium, the *Codex Colbertinus* illuminations are stylistically similar to the contemporaneous cloister sculptures (FIG. 12-10) of that Cluniac monastery.

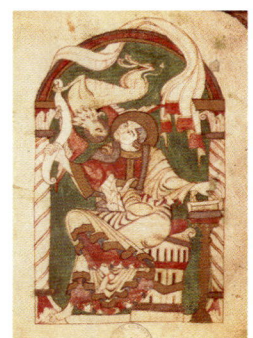

**12-15A** *Corbie Gospels,* ca. 1120.

***CODEX COLBERTINUS*** In addition to sponsoring the costliest sculptural programs of the Romanesque age, Cluniac monasteries produced many of the finest and most ornate illuminated manuscripts, including the *Codex Colbertinus* (FIG. **12-15**) and the *Corbie Gospels* (FIG. **12-15A**), both of which are closely related stylistically to the relief sculptures of Saint-Pierre at Moissac.

The *Codex Colbertinus* is, in fact, probably the work of scribes and painters in the Moissac scriptorium, and it is contemporaneous with the column capitals and pier reliefs of Saint-Pierre's cloister (FIG. 12-10). The major illuminations in the manuscript are the full pages featuring historiated initials and evangelist portraits. The opening page (FIG. 12-15) of the Gospel according to Saint Matthew includes both the large initial letter *L* of *Liber* (book)

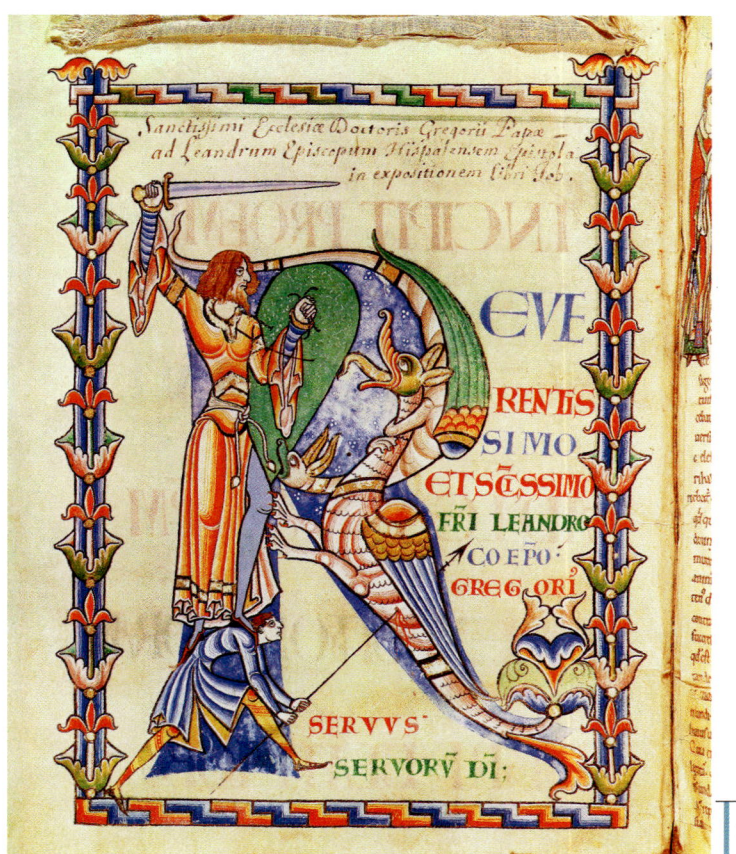

**12-16** Initial *R* with knight fighting dragons, folio 4 verso of the *Moralia in Job,* from Cîteaux, France, ca. 1115–1125. Ink and tempera on vellum, $1' \, 1\frac{3}{4}'' \times 9\frac{1}{4}''$. Bibliothèque Municipale, Dijon.

Ornamented initials date to the Hiberno-Saxon era (FIG. 11-1), but this artist translated the theme into Romanesque terms. The duel between knight and dragons symbolized a monk's spiritual struggle.

and a "portrait" of the author. Matthew holds a book in his left hand and raises his right hand in a gesture of blessing. He stands frontally between a pair of columns supporting an arch, just as does Abbot Durandus (FIG. 12-10, *right*) on one of the Moissac cloister piers. The two figures are similar in other respects as well. For example, both artists depicted the robed men with dangling feet.

The letter *L* has no equivalent in the Moissac sculptures, but the real and imaginary animals and birds with long, twisted necks that inhabit the initial have parallels in Saint-Pierre's cloister capitals (FIG. 12-10, *left*). The intertwining forms attest to the long afterlife of the animal-interlace style of the illuminated books (FIG. 11-7) of the Hiberno-Saxon period.

***MORALIA IN JOB*** Another major Romanesque scriptorium was at the abbey of Cîteaux, mother church of the Cistercian order. Just before Bernard of Clairvaux joined the monastery in 1112, the monks completed work on an illuminated copy of Saint Gregory's *Moralia in Job.* It is an example of Cistercian illumination before Bernard's passionate opposition to monastic figural art led in 1134 to a Cistercian ban on elaborate paintings in manuscripts as well as sculptural ornamentation in monasteries. After 1134, in sharp contrast to Cluniac Moissac, the Cistercian order prohibited full-page illustrations, and even initial letters had to be nonfigurative and of a single color.

The historiated initial illustrated here (FIG. **12-16**) clearly would have been in violation of Bernard's ban had it not been

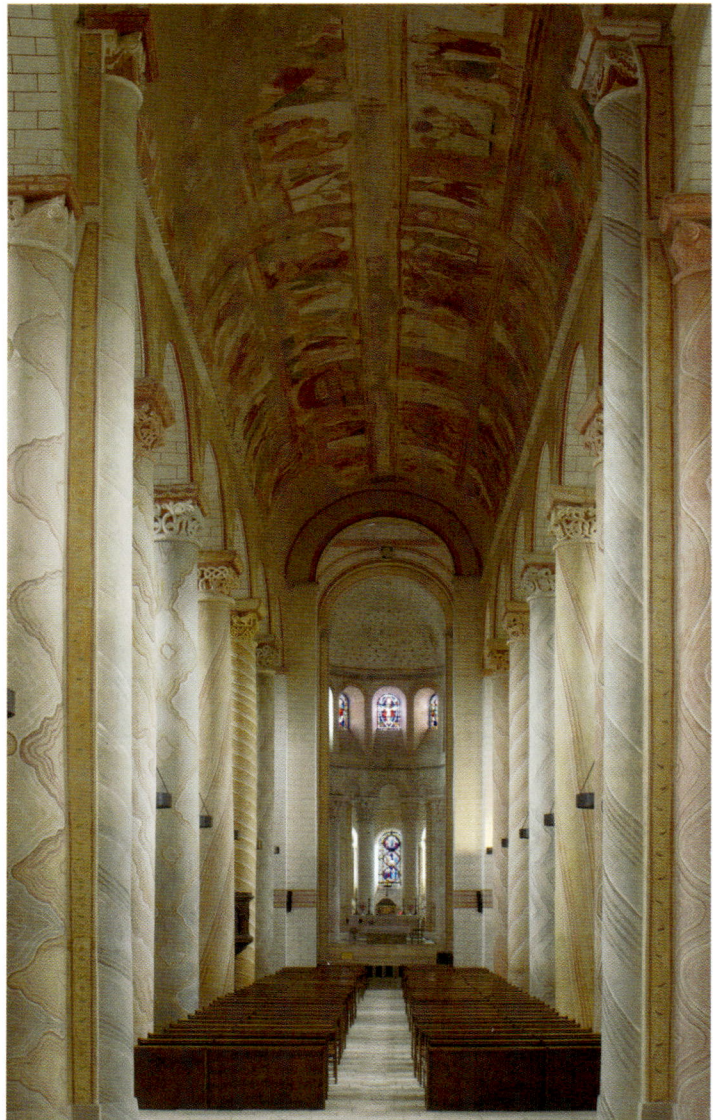

**12-17** Nave of the abbey church (looking east) of Saint-Savin, Saint-Savin-sur-Gartempe, France, ca. 1100. ◼◀

Saint-Savin is a hall church with aisles approximately the same height as the nave. The tall aisle windows provide ample illumination for the biblical paintings on the nave's barrel vault.

painted before his prohibitions took effect. A knight, his squire, and two roaring dragons form an intricate letter *R,* the initial letter of the salutation *Reverentissimo.* This page is the opening of Gregory's letter to "the very reverent" Leandro, bishop of Seville, Spain. The knight is a slender, regal figure who raises his shield and sword against the dragons, while the squire, crouching beneath him, runs a lance through one of the monsters. Although the clergy viewed the duel between knight and dragons as an allegory of the spiritual struggle of monks against the Devil for the salvation of souls, Bernard opposed this kind of illumination, just as he condemned carvings of monstrous creatures and "fighting knights" on cloister capitals (see "Bernard of Clairvaux," page 342).

Ornamented initials date to the Hiberno-Saxon period (FIG. 11-1), but in the *Moralia in Job,* the artist translated the theme into Romanesque terms. The page with the initial *R* may be a reliable picture of a medieval baron's costume. The typically French Romanesque band-

ing of the torso and partitioning of the folds are evident (compare FIG. 12-13), but the master painter deftly avoided stiffness and angularity. The partitioning here accentuates the knight's verticality and elegance and the thrusting action of his servant. The flowing sleeves add a spirited flourish to the swordsman's gesture. The knight, handsomely garbed, cavalierly wears no armor and calmly aims a single stroke, unmoved by the ferocious dragons lunging at him.

**SAINT-SAVIN-SUR-GARTEMPE** Although the art of fresco painting never died in early medieval Europe, the murals (not true frescoes, however) of the Benedictine abbey church of Saint-Savin-sur-Gartempe have no Carolingian or Ottonian parallels, because the paintings decorate the stone barrel vault of the church's nave (FIG. **12-17**). Saint-Savin is a *hall* church—a church where the aisles are approximately the same height as the nave. The tall windows in the aisles provided more illumination to the nave than in churches having low aisles and tribunes. The abundant light streaming into the church may explain why the monks chose to decorate the nave's barrel vault with paintings. (They also painted the nave piers to imitate rich veined marble.) The subjects of Saint-Savin's nave paintings all come from the Pentateuch, but New Testament themes appear in the transept, ambulatory, and chapels, where the painters also depicted the lives of Saint Savin and another local saint. The elongated, agitated, cross-legged figures have stylistic affinities both to the reliefs of southern French portals and to illuminated manuscripts such as the *Corbie Gospels* (FIG. 12-15A) and the *Moralia in Job* (FIG. 12-16).

**SANTA MARÍA DE MUR** In the Romanesque period, northern Spain, home to the great pilgrimage church of Saint James at Santiago de Compostela, was one of the most important regional artistic centers. In fact, Catalonia in northeastern Spain boasts more Romanesque mural paintings today than anywhere else. Especially impressive is the *Christ in Majesty* fresco (FIG. **12-18**), now in Boston, that once filled the apse of Santa María de Mur, a monastery church not far from Lérida. The formality, symmetry, and placement of the figures are Byzantine (compare FIGS. 9-16 and 9-27). But the Spanish artist rejected Byzantine mosaic in favor of direct painting on plaster-coated walls.

The iconographic scheme in the semidome of the apse echoes the themes of the sculpted tympana of contemporaneous French (FIGS. 12-11 and 12-14A) and Spanish Romanesque church portals. The signs of the four evangelists flank Christ in a star-strewn mandorla—the Apocalypse theme that so fascinated the Romanesque imagination. Seven lamps between Christ and the evangelists' signs symbolize the seven Christian communities where Saint John addressed his revelation (the Apocalypse) at the beginning of his book (Rev. 1:4, 12, 20). Below stand apostles, paired off in formal frontality, as in the Monreale Cathedral apse (FIG. 9-27). The Spanish painter rendered the principal figures with partitioning of the drapery into volumes, here and there made tubular by local shading, and stiffened the irregular shapes of pliable cloth into geometric patterns. The overall effect is one of simple, strong, and even blunt directness of statement, reinforced by harsh, bright color, appropriate for a powerful icon.

***MORGAN MADONNA*** Despite the widespread use of stone relief sculptures to adorn church portals, resistance to the creation of statues in the round—in any material—continued in the Romanesque period. The avoidance of anything that might be construed as an idol was still the rule, in keeping with the Second Commandment. Two centuries after Archbishop Gero commissioned a monumen-

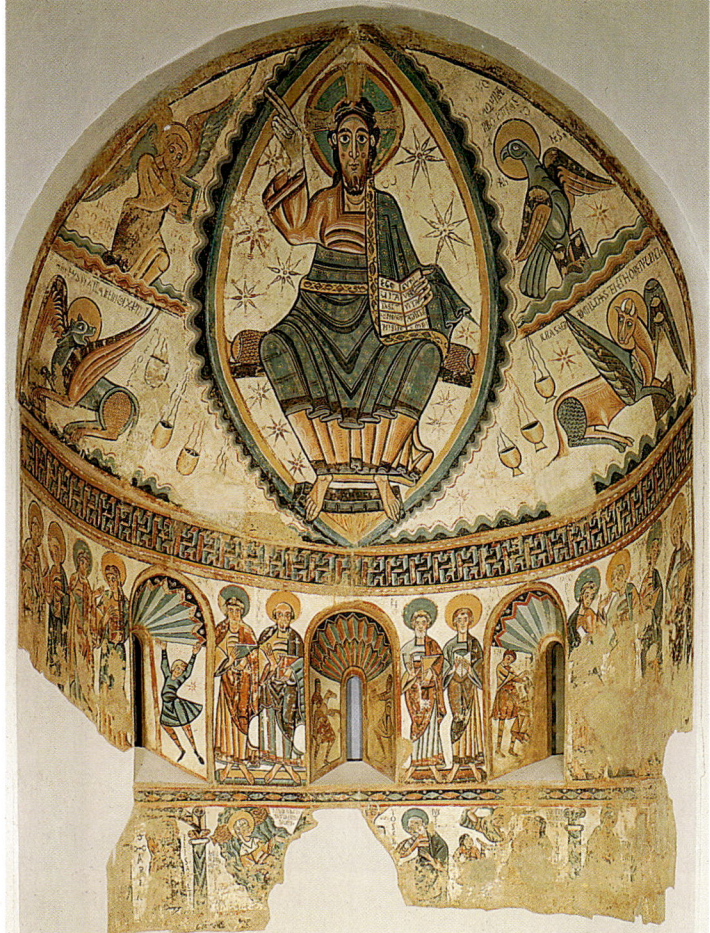

**12-18** *Christ in Majesty,* apse, Santa María de Mur, near Lérida, Spain, mid-12th century. Fresco, 24′ high. Museum of Fine Arts, Boston.

In this fresco, formerly in the apse of Santa María de Mur, Christ appears in a mandorla between the four evangelists' signs. The fresco resembles French and Spanish Romanesque tympanum reliefs.

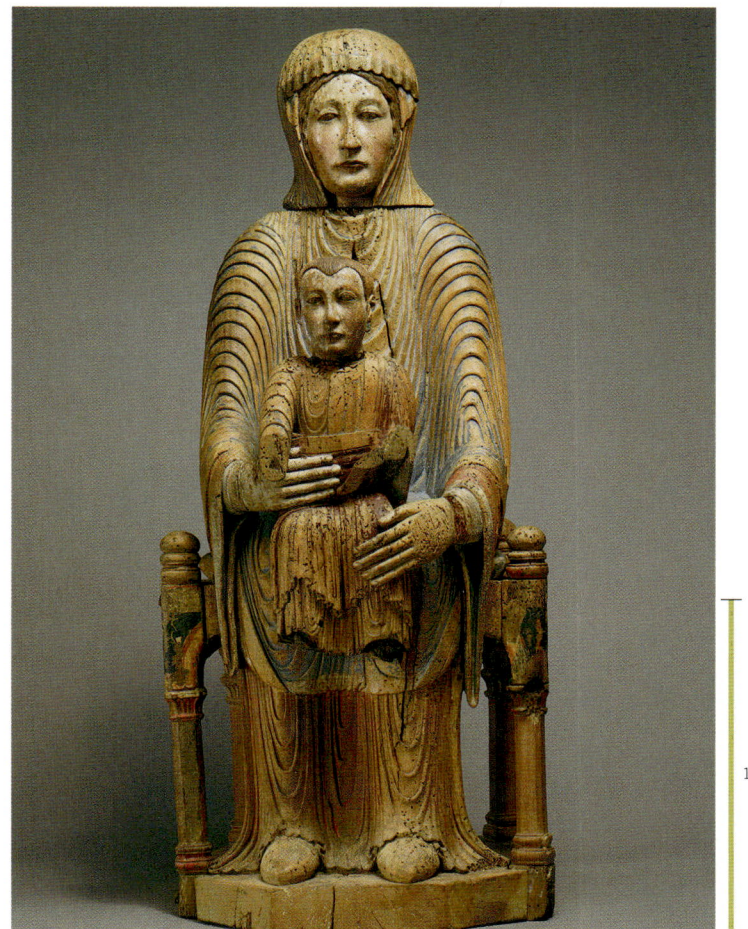

**12-19** Virgin and Child (*Morgan Madonna*), from Auvergne, France, second half of 12th century. Painted wood, 2′ 7″ high. Metropolitan Museum of Art, New York (gift of J. Pierpont Morgan, 1916).

The veneration of relics created a demand for small-scale images of the holy family and saints to be placed on chapel altars. This wooden statuette depicts the Virgin as the "throne of wisdom."

tal wooden image of the crucified Christ (FIG. 11-28) for Cologne Cathedral, freestanding statues of Christ, the Virgin Mary, and the saints were still quite rare. The veneration of relics, however, brought with it a demand for small-scale images of the holy family and saints to be placed on the chapel altars of the churches along the pilgrimage roads. Reliquaries in the form of saints (FIG. 12-2) or parts of saints (FIG. 12-25), tabletop crucifixes, and small wooden devotional images began to be produced in great numbers.

One popular type, a specialty of the workshops of Auvergne, France, was a wooden statuette depicting the Virgin Mary with the Christ Child in her lap. The *Morgan Madonna* (FIG. **12-19**), so named because it once belonged to the American financier and collector J. Pierpont Morgan, is one example. The type, known as the "throne of wisdom" (*sedes sapientiae* in Latin), is a western European freestanding version of the Byzantine Theotokos theme popular in icons and mosaics (FIGS. 9-18 and 9-19). Christ holds a Bible in his left hand and raises his right arm in blessing (both hands are broken off). He is the embodiment of the divine wisdom contained in the holy scriptures. His mother, seated on a wooden chair, is in turn the throne of wisdom because her lap is the Christ Child's throne. As in Byzantine art, both Mother and Child sit

rigidly upright and are strictly frontal, emotionless figures. But the intimate scale, the gesture of benediction, the once-bright coloring of the garments, and the soft modeling of the Virgin's face make the group seem much less remote than its Byzantine counterparts.

# HOLY ROMAN EMPIRE

The Romanesque successors of the Ottonians were the Salians (r. 1027–1125), a dynasty of Franks. They ruled an empire corresponding roughly to present-day Germany and the Lombard region of northern Italy (MAP 12-1). Like their predecessors, the Salian emperors were important patrons of art and architecture, although, as elsewhere in Romanesque Europe, the monasteries remained great centers of artistic production.

## Architecture

The barrel-vaulted naves of Saint-Sernin (FIG. 12-7) at Toulouse, Saint James at Santiago de Compostela (FIG. 12-7B), Cluny III (FIG. 12-9), and Notre-Dame (FIG. 12-10A) at Fontenay admirably met French and Spanish Romanesque architects' goals of making the house of the Lord beautiful and providing excellent acoustics for church services. In addition, they were relatively fireproof compared with timber-roofed structures such as Saint-Étienne (FIG. 12-3) at Vignory. But the barrel vaults often failed in one critical requirement—lighting. Due to the great outward thrust barrel vaults exert along their full length, even when pointed (FIGS. 12-9 and 12-10A) instead of semicircular, a clerestory is difficult to construct. (The Toulouse, Santiago de Compostela, and Fontenay designers did not even attempt to introduce a clerestory, although their counterparts at Cluny III succeeded.) Structurally, the central aim of Romanesque architects in the Holy Roman Empire (and in Normandy and England; see page 357) was to develop a masonry vault system that admitted light and was aesthetically pleasing.

Covering the nave with groin vaults instead of barrel vaults became the solution. Ancient Roman builders had used the groin vault widely, because they realized its concentration of thrusts at four supporting points enabled them to introduce clerestory windows (FIGS. 7-6c, 7-67, and 7-78). Concrete, which could be poured into forms, where it solidified into a homogeneous mass (see "Roman Concrete Construction," Chapter 7, page 184), made the gigantic Roman groin vaults possible. But the technique of mixing concrete had not survived into the Middle Ages. The technical problems of building groin vaults of cut stone and heavy rubble, which had very little cohesive quality, at first limited their use to the covering of small areas, such as the individual bays of the aisles of the pilgrimage churches at Toulouse and Santiago de Compostela (FIGS. 12-7 and 12-7B). During the 11th century, however, masons in the Holy Roman Empire, using cut-stone blocks held together with mortar, developed a groin vault of monumental dimensions.

**SPEYER** Construction of Speyer Cathedral (FIG. **12-20**) in the German Rhineland, far from the pilgrimage routes of southern France and northern Spain, began in 1030. The church was the burial place of the Holy Roman emperors until the beginning of the 12th century, and funding for the building campaign came from imperial patrons, not traveling pilgrims and local landowners. Like all *cathedrals,* Speyer was also the seat (*cathedra* in Latin) of the powerful local bishop. In its earliest form, the church was a timber-roofed structure. When Henry IV (r. 1056–1105) rebuilt the cathedral between 1082 and 1105, his masons covered the nave with stone groin vaults. The large clerestory windows above the nave arcade provided ample light to the interior. Architectural historians disagree about where the first comprehensive use of groin vaulting occurred in Romanesque times, and nationalistic concerns sometimes color the debate. But no one doubts that the large groin vaults covering the nave of Speyer Cathedral represent one of the most daring and successful engineering experiments of the time. The nave is 45 feet wide, and the crowns of the vaults are 107 feet above the floor.

Speyer Cathedral employs an alternate-support system in the nave, as in the Ottonian churches of Saint Cyriakus (FIG. 11-21) at Gernrode and Saint Michael's (FIGS. 11-23 and 11-23A) at Hildesheim. At Speyer, however, the alternation continues all the way up into the vaults, with the nave's more richly molded compound piers marking the corners of the groin vaults. Speyer's interior shows the same striving for height and the same compartmentalized effect seen at Toulouse and Santiago de Compostela (FIGS. 12-7 and 12-7B), but by virtue of the alternate-support system, the rhythm of the Speyer nave is a little more complex. Because each compartment has its own vault, the impression of a sequence of vertical spatial blocks is even more convincing.

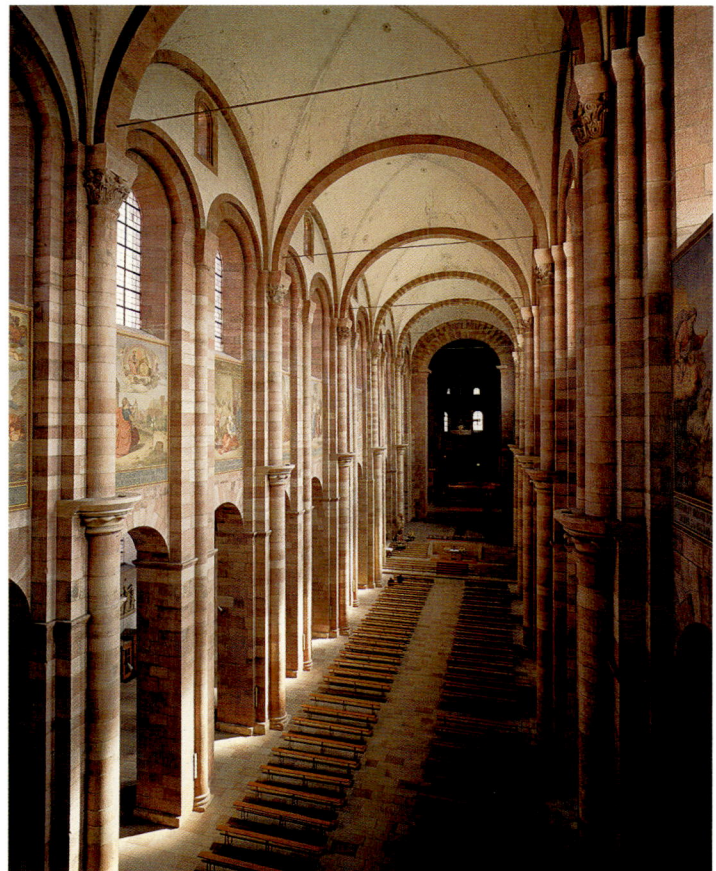

**12-20** Interior of Speyer Cathedral (looking east), Speyer, Germany, begun 1030; nave vaults, ca. 1082–1105.

The imperial cathedral at Speyer is one of the earliest examples of the use of groin vaulting in a nave. Groin vaults made possible the insertion of large clerestory windows above the nave arcade.

**MILAN** After Charlemagne crushed the Lombards in 773, German kings held sway over Lombardy, and the Rhineland and northern Italy cross-fertilized each other artistically. No scholarly agreement exists as to which source of artistic influence was dominant in the Romanesque age, the German or the Lombard. The question, no doubt, will remain the subject of controversy until the construction date of Sant'Ambrogio (FIG. **12-21**) in Milan can be established unequivocally. The church, erected in honor of Saint Ambrose (d. 397), Milan's first bishop, is the central monument of Lombard Romanesque architecture. Some scholars think the church was a prototype for Speyer Cathedral, but Sant'Ambrogio is a remarkable building even if it was not a model for Speyer's builders. The Milanese church has an atrium in the Early Christian tradition (FIG. 8-9)—one of the last to be built—and a two-story narthex pierced by arches on both levels. Two *campaniles* (Italian, "bell towers") join the building on the west. The shorter one dates to the 10th century, and the taller north campanile is a 12th-century addition. Over the nave's east end is an octagonal tower that recalls the crossing towers of Ottonian churches (FIG. 11-22).

Sant'Ambrogio has a nave (FIG. **12-22**) and two aisles but no transept. Each bay consists of a full square in the nave flanked by two small squares in each aisle, all covered with groin vaults. The main vaults are slightly domical, rising higher than the transverse arches. The

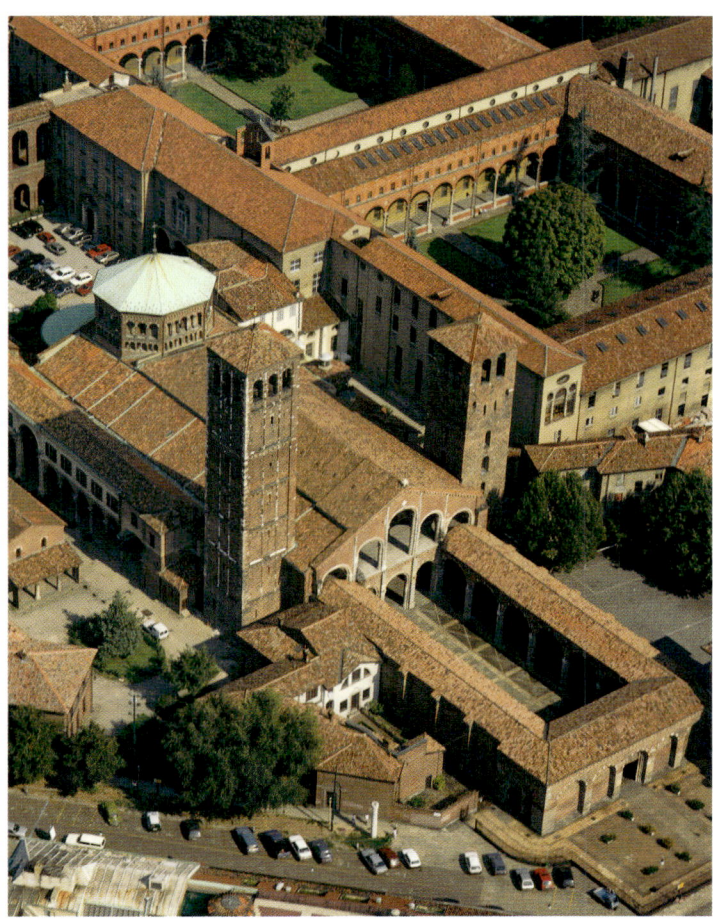

**12-21** Aerial view of Sant'Ambrogio (looking southeast), Milan, Italy, late 11th to early 12th century.

With its atrium and low, broad proportions, Sant'Ambrogio recalls Early Christian basilicas. Over the nave's east end, however, is an octagonal tower resembling Ottonian crossing towers.

windows in the octagonal dome over the last bay—probably here, as elsewhere, a reference to the dome of Heaven—provide the major light source for the otherwise rather dark interior. (The building lacks a clerestory.) The emphatic alternate-support system perfectly reflects the geometric regularity of the plan. The lightest pier moldings stop at the gallery level, and the heavier ones rise to support the main vaults. At Sant'Ambrogio, the compound piers even continue into the ponderous vaults, which have supporting arches, or *ribs*, along their groins. Sant'Ambrogio is one of the first instances of *rib vaulting*, a salient characteristic of mature Romanesque and of later Gothic architecture (see "The Gothic Rib Vault," Chapter 13, page 368).

The regional diversity of Romanesque architecture quickly becomes evident by comparing the proportions of Sant'Ambrogio with those of Speyer Cathedral (FIG. 12-20) and of Saint-Sernin (FIGS. 12-5 to 12-7) at Toulouse and Saint James (FIG. 12-7B) at Santiago de Compostela. The Milanese building does not aspire to the soaring height of the French, Spanish, and German churches. Save for the later of the two towers, Sant'Ambrogio's proportions are low and broad and remain close to those of Early Christian basilicas. Italian architects, even those working within the orbit of the Holy Roman Empire, had firm roots in the venerable Early Christian style and never sought the verticality found in northern European architecture, not even during the Gothic period.

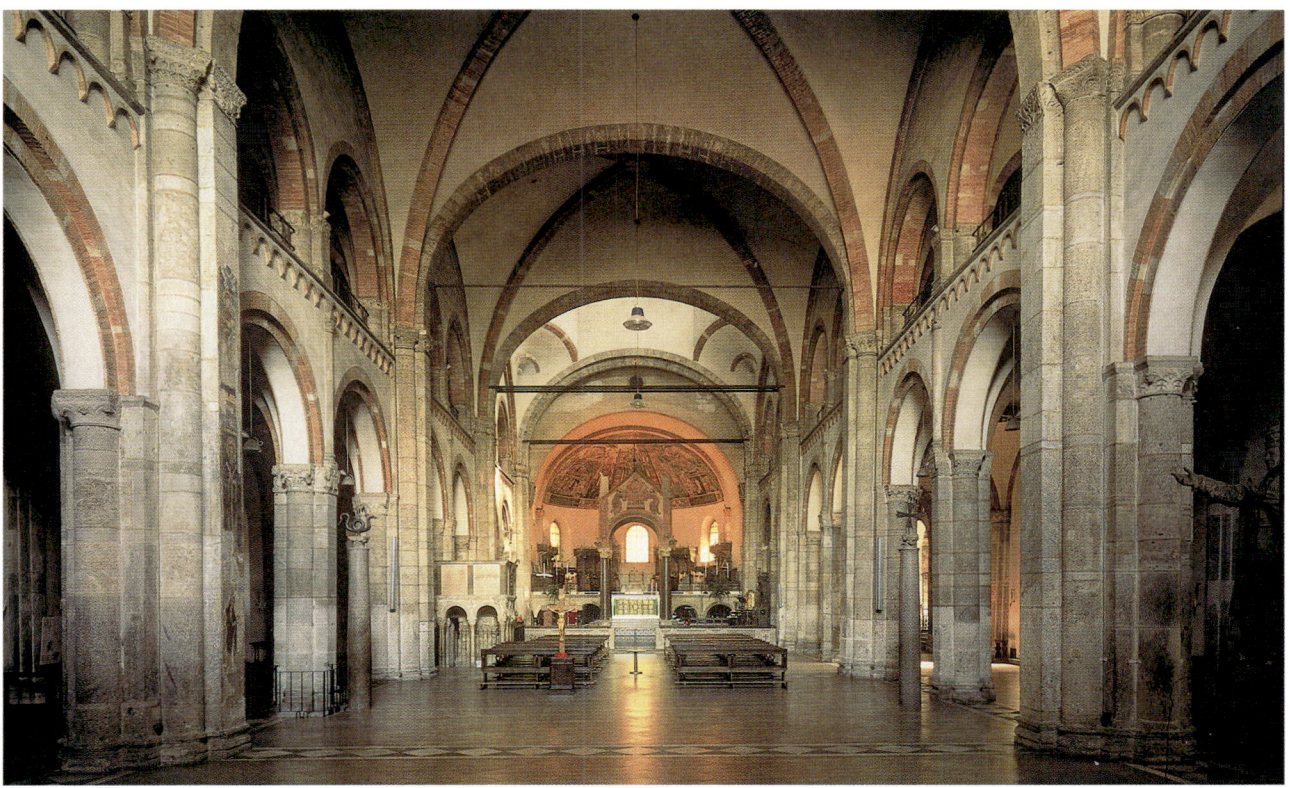

**12-22** Interior of Sant'Ambrogio (looking east), Milan, Italy, late 11th to early 12th century.

Sant'Ambrogio reveals the transalpine ties of Lombard architecture. Each groin-vaulted nave bay corresponds to two aisle bays. The alternate-support system complements this modular plan.

# Romanesque Countesses, Queens, and Nuns

Romanesque Europe was still a man's world, but women could and did have power and influence. Countess Matilda of Canossa (1046–1115), who ruled Tuscany after 1069, was sole heiress of vast holdings in northern Italy. She was a key figure in the political struggle between the popes and the German emperors who controlled Lombardy. With unflagging resolution, she defended the reforms of Pope Gregory VII (r. 1073–1085) and at her death willed most of her lands to the papacy.

More famous and more powerful was Eleanor of Aquitaine (1122–1204), wife of Henry II of England. She married Henry after the annulment of her marriage to Louis VII, king of France. She was queen of France for 15 years and queen of England for 35 years. During that time she bore three daughters and five sons. Two became kings—Richard I (the Lionhearted) and John. She prompted her sons to rebel against their father, for which Henry imprisoned her. Released at Henry's death, she lived on as dowager queen, managing England's government and King John's holdings in France.

Of quite different stamp was Hildegard of Bingen (1098–1179), the most prominent nun of the 12th century and one of the greatest religious figures of the Middle Ages. Hildegard was born into an aristocratic family that owned large estates in the German Rhineland. At a very early age she began to have visions. When she was eight, her parents placed her in the Benedictine *double monastery* (for monks and nuns) at Disibodenberg. She became a nun at 15. In 1141, God instructed Hildegard to disclose her visions to the world. Before then she had revealed them only to close confidants at the monastery. One of them was the monk Volmar, and Hildegard chose to dictate her visions to him for posterity (FIG. 12-23). No less a figure than Bernard of Clairvaux certified in 1147 that her visions were authentic, and Archbishop Heinrich of Mainz joined in the endorsement. In 1148, the Cistercian pope Eugenius III (r. 1145–1153) formally authorized Hildegard "in the name of Christ and Saint Peter to publish all that she had learned from the Holy Spirit." At this time Hildegard became the abbess of a new convent built for her near Bingen. As reports of Hildegard's visions spread, kings, popes, barons, and prelates sought her counsel. All of them were attracted by her spiritual insight into the Christian faith. In addition to her visionary works—the most important is the *Scivias* (FIG. 12-23)—Hildegard wrote two scientific

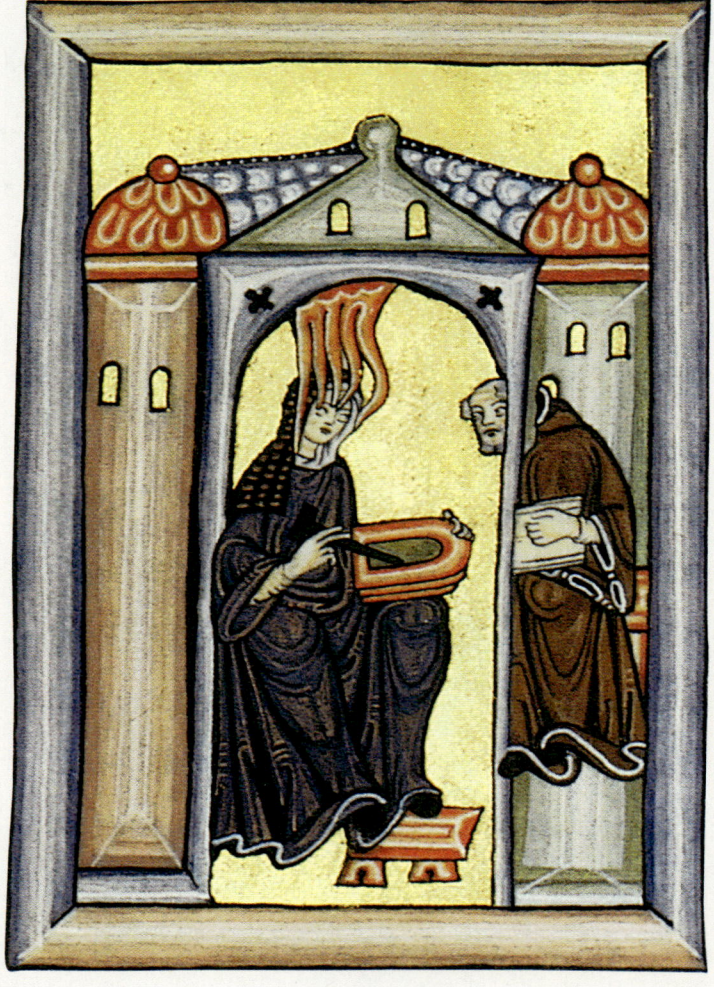

**12-23** Hildegard reveals her visions, detail of a facsimile of a lost folio in the Rupertsberger *Scivias* by Hildegard of Bingen, from Trier or Bingen, Germany, ca. 1050–1079. Abbey of St. Hildegard, Rüdesheim/Eibingen.

Hildegard of Bingen, the most prominent nun of her time, experienced divine visions, shown here as five tongues of fire entering her brain. She also composed music and wrote scientific treatises.

treatises. *Physica* is a study of the natural world, and *Causae et curae* (*Causes and Cures*) is a medical encyclopedia. Hildegard also composed the music and wrote the lyrics of 77 songs, which appeared under the title *Symphonia*.

Hildegard was the most famous Romanesque nun, but she was by no means the only learned woman of her age. A younger contemporary, Herrad (d. 1195), abbess of Hohenberg, Austria, was also the author of an important medieval encyclopedia. Herrad's *Hortus deliciarum* (*Garden of Delights*) is a history of the world intended for instructing the nuns under her supervision, but it reached a much wider audience.

## Painting and Other Arts

The number and variety of illuminated manuscripts dating to the Romanesque era attest to the great demand for illustrated religious tomes in the abbeys of western Europe. The extraordinarily productive scribes and painters who created these books were almost exclusively monks and nuns working in the scriptoria of those same isolated religious communities.

**HILDEGARD OF BINGEN** Among the most interesting German religious manuscripts is the *Scivias* (*Know the Ways [Scite vias] of God*) of Hildegard of Bingen. Hildegard was a nun who eventually became the abbess of the convent at Disibodenberg in the Rhineland (see "Romanesque Countesses, Queens, and Nuns," above). The manuscript, lost in 1945, exists today only in a facsimile. The original probably was written and illuminated at the monastery of Saint Matthias at Trier between 1150 and Hildegard's death in 1179, but it is possible Hildegard supervised production of the book at Bingen. The *Scivias* contains a record of Hildegard's vision of the divine order of the cosmos and of humankind's place in it. The vision came to her as a fiery light pouring into her brain from the open vault of Heaven.

On the opening page (FIG. **12-23**) of the Trier manuscript, Hildegard sits within the monastery walls, her feet resting on a footstool, in much the same way the painters of the *Coronation* and *Ebbo Gospels* (FIGS. 11-13 and 11-14) represented the evangelists. The *Scivias* page is a link in a chain of author portraits with roots in classical antiquity (FIG. 7-25B). The artist showed Hildegard experiencing her divine vision by depicting five long tongues of fire emanating from above and entering her brain, just as she describes the experience in the accompanying text. Hildegard immediately sets down what has been revealed to her on a wax tablet resting on her left knee. Nearby, the monk Volmar, Hildegard's confessor, copies into a book all she has written. Here, in a singularly dramatic context, is a picture of the essential nature of ancient and medie-

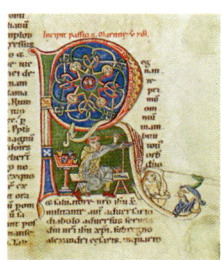

12-23A RUFILLUS, Initial *R*, ca. 1170–1200.

val book manufacture—individual scribes copying and recopying texts by hand (compare FIG. 11-11). The most labor-intensive and costliest texts, such as Hildegard's *Scivias,* also were illuminated (see "Medieval Manuscript Illumination," Chapter 8, page 249). They required the collaboration of skilled painters, for example, the Weissenau monk RUFILLUS, who placed a portrait of himself at work (FIG. **12-23A**) in a *passional* (book of saints' lives).

**RAINER OF HUY** The names of some Romanesque sculptors in the Holy Roman Empire are also known. One of them is RAINER OF HUY, a bronzeworker from the Meuse River valley in Belgium, an area renowned for its metalwork. Art historians have attributed an 1118 bronze baptismal font (FIG. **12-24**) to him. Made for Notre-Dame-des-Fonts in Liège, the bronze basin rests on the foreparts of a dozen oxen. The oxen refer to the "molten sea . . . on twelve oxen" cast in bronze for King Solomon's temple (1 Kings 7:23–25). The Old Testament story prefigured Christ's baptism (medieval scholars equated the oxen with the 12 apostles), which is the central scene on the Romanesque font. Rainer's work, as that of so many earlier artists in the Holy Roman Empire beginning in Carolingian times, revived the classical style and the classical spirit. The figures are softly rounded, with idealized bodies and faces and heavy clinging drapery. Rainer even represented one figure (at the left in FIG. 12-24) in a three-quarter view from the rear, a popular motif in classical art, and some of the figures, including Christ himself, are naked. Nudity is very rare in the art of the Middle Ages. Adam and Eve (FIGS. 8-1, 11-24A, 12-13B, and 12-28) are exceptions, but medieval artists usually depicted the first man and woman as embarrassed by their nudity, the opposite of the high value the classical world placed on the beauty of the human body.

**SAINT ALEXANDER** The reliquaries of Saint Faith (FIG. 12-2) and of Saint Alexander (FIG. **12-25**), a hallowed pope (Alexander II, r. 1061–1073), are among the most sumptuous of the Romanesque

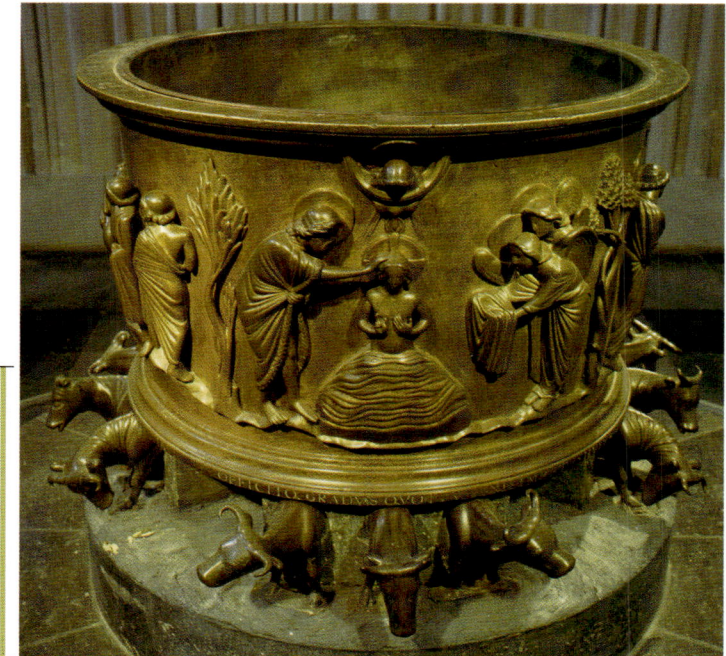

**12-24** RAINER OF HUY, *Baptism of Christ,* baptismal font from Notre-Dame-des-Fonts, Liège, Belgium, 1118. Bronze, 2′ 1″ high. Saint-Barthélémy, Liège.

In the work of Rainer of Huy, the classical style and the classical spirit lived on in the Holy Roman Empire. His Liège baptismal font features idealized figures and even a nude representation of Christ.

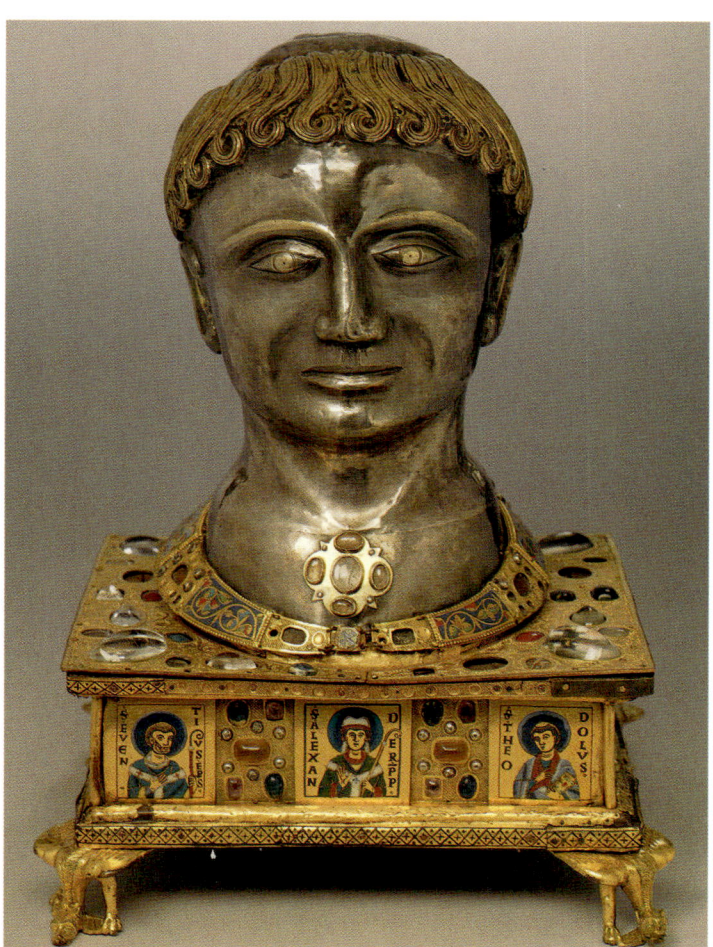

**12-25** Head reliquary of Saint Alexander, from the abbey church, Stavelot, Belgium, 1145. Silver repoussé (partly gilt), gilt bronze, gems, pearls, and enamel, 1′ 5½″ high. Musées Royaux d'Art et d'Histoire, Brussels.

The Stavelot reliquary is typical in the use of costly materials. The combination of an idealized classical head with Byzantine-style enamels underscores the stylistic diversity of Romanesque art.

age, a time when churches vied to possess the most important relics and often expended large sums on their containers (see "Relics," page 336). Made in 1145 for Abbot Wibald of Stavelot in Belgium, Saint Alexander's reliquary takes the form of an almost life-size head, fashioned in beaten (*repoussé*) silver with bronze gilding for the hair. The idealized head resembles portraits of youthful Roman emperors such as Augustus (FIG. I-10) and Constantine (FIG. 7-77), and the Romanesque metalworker may have used an ancient sculpture as a model. The saint wears a collar of jewels and enamel plaques around his neck. Enamels and gems also adorn the box on which the head is mounted. The reliquary rests on four bronze dragons—mythical animals of the kind populating Romanesque cloister capitals. Not surprisingly, Bernard of Clairvaux was as critical of lavish church furnishings like the reliquaries of Saints Faith and Alexander as he was of Romanesque cloister sculpture:

> [Men's] eyes are fixed on relics covered with gold and purses are opened. The thoroughly beautiful image of some male or female saint is exhibited and that saint is believed to be the more holy the more highly colored the image is. People rush to kiss it, they are invited to donate, and they admire the beautiful more than they venerate the sacred. . . . O vanity of vanities, but no more vain than insane! The Church . . . dresses its stones in gold and it abandons its children naked. It serves the eyes of the rich at the expense of the poor.[5]

The central plaque on the front of the Stavelot reliquary depicts the *canonized* (declared a saint) pope. Saints Eventius and Theodolus flank him. The nine plaques on the other three sides represent female allegorical figures—Wisdom, Piety, and Humility among them. Although a local artist produced these enamels in the Meuse River region, the models were surely Byzantine. Saint Alexander's reliquary underscores the multiple sources of Romanesque art, as well as its stylistic diversity. Not since antiquity had people journeyed as extensively as they did in the Romanesque period, and artists regularly saw works of wide geographic origin. Abbot Wibald himself epitomizes the well-traveled 12th-century clergyman. He was abbot of Montecassino in southern Italy and took part in the Second Crusade. Frederick Barbarossa (Holy Roman emperor, r. 1152–1190) sent him to Constantinople to arrange Frederick's

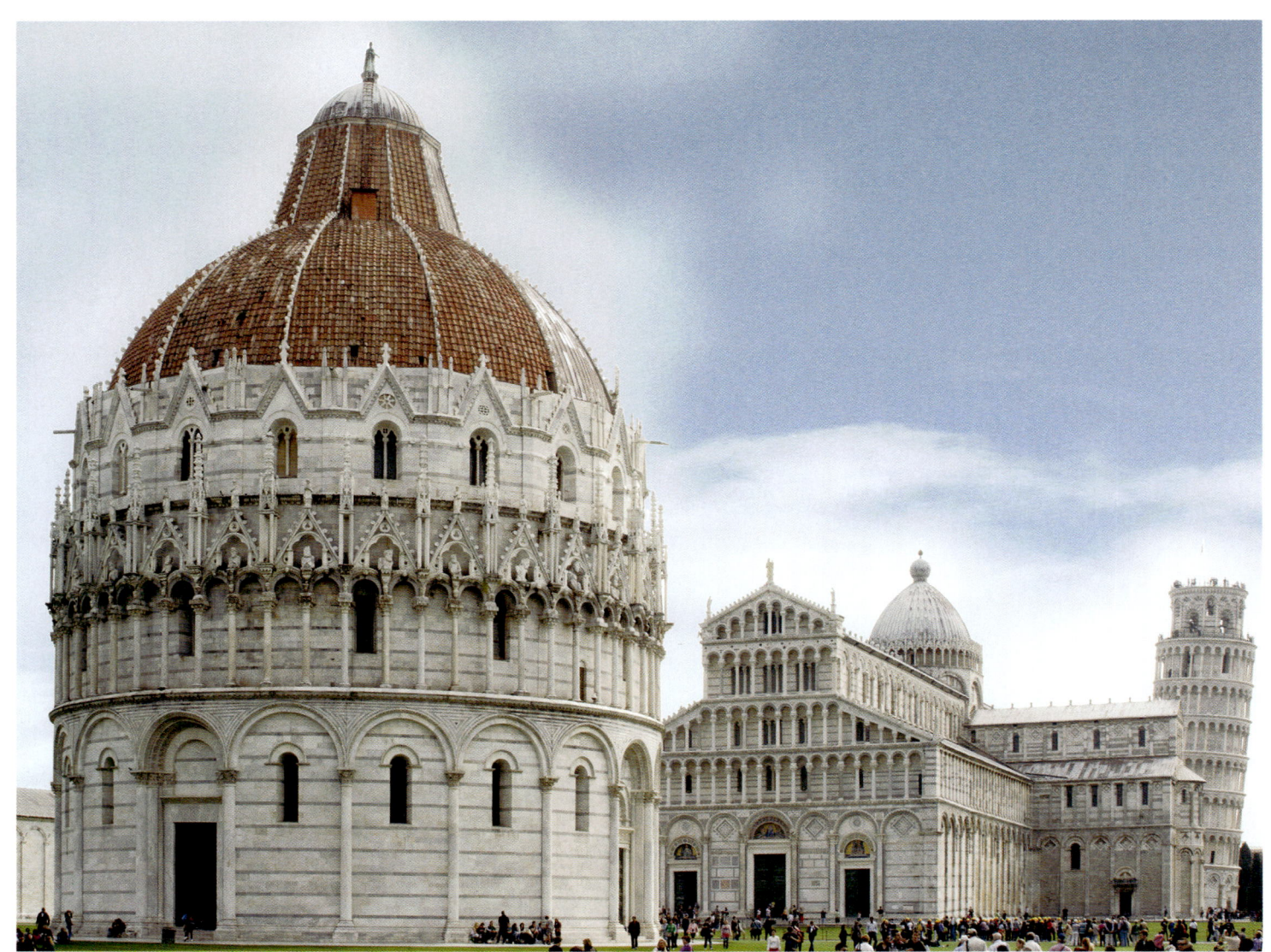

**12-26** Cathedral complex (looking northeast), Pisa, Italy; cathedral begun 1063; baptistery begun 1153; campanile begun 1174. ◼◀

Pisa's cathedral more closely resembles Early Christian basilicas than structurally more experimental French and German Romanesque churches. Separate bell towers and baptisteries are Italian features.

wedding to the niece of the Byzantine emperor Manuel Comnenus. (Two centuries before, another German emperor, Otto II, married the Byzantine princess Theophanu, which also served to promote Byzantine style in the Holy Roman Empire; see "Theophanu," Chapter 11, page 328.)

# ITALY

Nowhere is the regional diversity of Romanesque art and architecture more readily apparent than in Italy, where the ancient Roman and Early Christian heritage was strongest. Although Tuscany, the ancient Etruscan heartland (see Chapter 6), and other regions south of Lombardy were part of the territory of the Salian emperors, Italy south of Milan represented a distinct artistic zone during the Romanesque period.

## Architecture and Architectural Sculpture

Italian Romanesque architects designed buildings that were for the most part structurally less experimental than those erected in Germany and Lombardy. Italian builders adhered closely to the Early Christian basilican type of church.

**12-27** Baptistery of San Giovanni (looking northwest), Florence, Italy, begun 1059. ■◄

The Florentine baptistery is a domed octagon descended from Roman and Early Christian central-plan buildings. The distinctive Tuscan Romanesque marble paneling stems from Roman wall designs.

**PISA** The cathedral complex (FIG. **12-26**) at Pisa dramatically testifies to the prosperity that busy maritime city enjoyed. The spoils of a naval victory over the Muslims off Palermo in Sicily in 1062 provided the funds for the Pisan building program. The cathedral, its freestanding bell tower, and the baptistery, where infants and converts were initiated into the Christian community, present a rare opportunity to study a coherent group of three Romanesque buildings. Save for the upper portion of the baptistery, with its remodeled Gothic exterior, the three structures are stylistically homogeneous.

Construction of Pisa Cathedral began first—in 1063, the same year work began on Saint Mark's (FIG. 9-26) in Venice, another powerful maritime city. The cathedral is large, with a nave and four aisles, and is one of the most impressive and majestic Romanesque churches. The Pisans, according to a document of the time, wanted their bishop's church not only to be a monument to the glory of God but also to bring credit to the city. At first glance, Pisa Cathedral resembles an Early Christian basilica with a timber roof, columnar arcade, and clerestory. But the broadly projecting transept with apses, the crossing dome, and the facade's multiple arcaded galleries distinguish it as Romanesque. So too does the rich marble *incrustation* (wall decoration consisting of bright panels of different colors, as in the Pantheon's interior, FIG. 7-51). The cathedral's campanile, detached in the standard Italian fashion, is Pisa's famous Leaning Tower (FIG. 12-26, *right*). Graceful arcaded galleries mark the tower's stages and repeat the cathedral facade's motif, effectively relating the round campanile to its mother building. The tilted vertical axis of the tower is the result of a settling foundation. The tower began to "lean" even while under construction, and by the late 20th century had inclined some 5.5 degrees (about 15 feet) out of plumb at the top. In 1999, an international team of scientists began a daring project to remove soil from beneath the north side of the tower. The soil extraction has already moved the tower more than an inch closer to vertical and ensured the stability of the structure for at least 300 years. (Because of the touristic appeal of the Leaning Tower, there are no plans to restore the campanile to its original upright position.)

**FLORENCE** The public understandably thinks of Florence as a Renaissance city (MAP 21-1), but it was already an important independent city-state in the Romanesque period. The gem of Florentine Romanesque architecture is the baptistery (FIG. **12-27**) of San Giovanni (Saint John), the city's patron saint. Pope Nicholas II (r. 1059–1061) dedicated the building in 1059. It thus predates Pisa's baptistery (FIG. 12-26, *left*), but construction of the Florentine baptistery continued into the next century. Both baptisteries face their city's cathedral. Freestanding baptisteries are unusual, and these Tuscan examples reflect the great significance the Florentines and Pisans attached to baptismal rites. On the day of a newborn child's anointment, the citizenry gathered in the baptistery to welcome a new member into their community. Baptisteries therefore were important civic, as well as religious, structures. Some of the most renowned artists of the late Middle Ages and the Renaissance provided the Florentine and Pisan baptisteries with pulpits (FIG. 14-2), bronze doors (FIGS. 14-19, 21-2, 21-3, 21-9, and 21-10), and mosaics.

The simple and serene classicism of San Giovanni's design recalls ancient Roman architecture. The baptistery stands in a direct line of descent from the Pantheon (FIG. 7-49), imperial mausoleums (such as Diocletian's; FIG. 7-74), the Early Christian Santa Costanza (FIG. 8-11), the Byzantine San Vitale (FIG. 9-10),

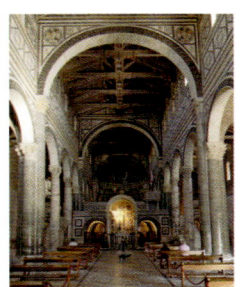

**12-27A** San Miniato al Monte, Florence, ca. 1062–1090. ▪◀

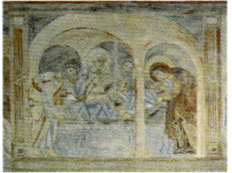

**12-27B** Sant'Angelo in Formis, near Capua, ca. 1085.

and other Roman and Christian central-plan structures, including Charlemagne's Palatine Chapel (FIGS. 11-17 and 11-18) at Aachen. The distinctive Tuscan Romanesque marble incrustation patterning the walls of Florence's baptistery and the slightly later church of San Miniato al Monte (FIG. **12-27A**) stems ultimately from Roman wall designs (FIGS. 7-17 and 7-51). (The ancient tradition of decorating walls with frescoes also survived in Romanesque Italy, for example, at Sant'Angelo in Formis, FIG. **12-27B**.) The simple oblong and arcuated panels of the baptistery assert the building's structural lines and its elevation levels. In plan, San Giovanni is a domed octagon, wrapped on the exterior by an elegant arcade, three arches to a bay. It has three entrances, one each on the north, south, and east sides. On the west side an oblong sanctuary replaces the original semicircular apse. The domical vault is some 90 feet in diameter, its construction a feat remarkable for its time.

**MODENA** Despite the pronounced structural differences between Italian Romanesque churches and those of France, Spain, and the Holy Roman Empire, Italian church officials also frequently employed sculptors to adorn the facades of their buildings. In fact, one of the first examples of fully developed narrative relief sculpture in Romanesque art is the marble frieze (FIG. **12-28**) on the facade of Modena Cathedral in northern Italy. Carved around 1110, it represents scenes from Genesis set against an architectural backdrop of a type common on Roman and Early Christian sarcophagi, which were plentiful in the region. The segment in FIG. 12-28, *Creation and Temptation of Adam and Eve* (Gen. 2, 3:1–8), repeats the theme employed almost exactly a century earlier on Bishop Bernward's bronze doors (FIGS. 11-24 and 11-25) at Hildesheim. At Modena, as at Saint Michael's, the faithful entered the Lord's house with a reminder of original sin and the suggestion that the only path to salvation is through Christ.

On the Modena frieze, Christ is at the far left, framed by a mandorla held up by angels—a variation on the motif of the Saint-Sernin ambulatory relief (FIG. 12-8). The creation of Adam, then Eve, and the serpent's temptation of Eve are to the right. The relief carving is high, and some parts are almost entirely in the round. The frieze is the work of a master craftsman whose name, WILIGELMO, appears in an inscription on another relief on the facade. There he boasts, "Among sculptors, your work shines forth, Wiligelmo." The inscription is also an indication of how proud Wiligelmo's patrons were to obtain the services of such an accomplished sculptor for their city's cathedral.

**FIDENZA** The reawakening of interest in stone sculpture in the round also is evident in northern Italy, where the sculptor

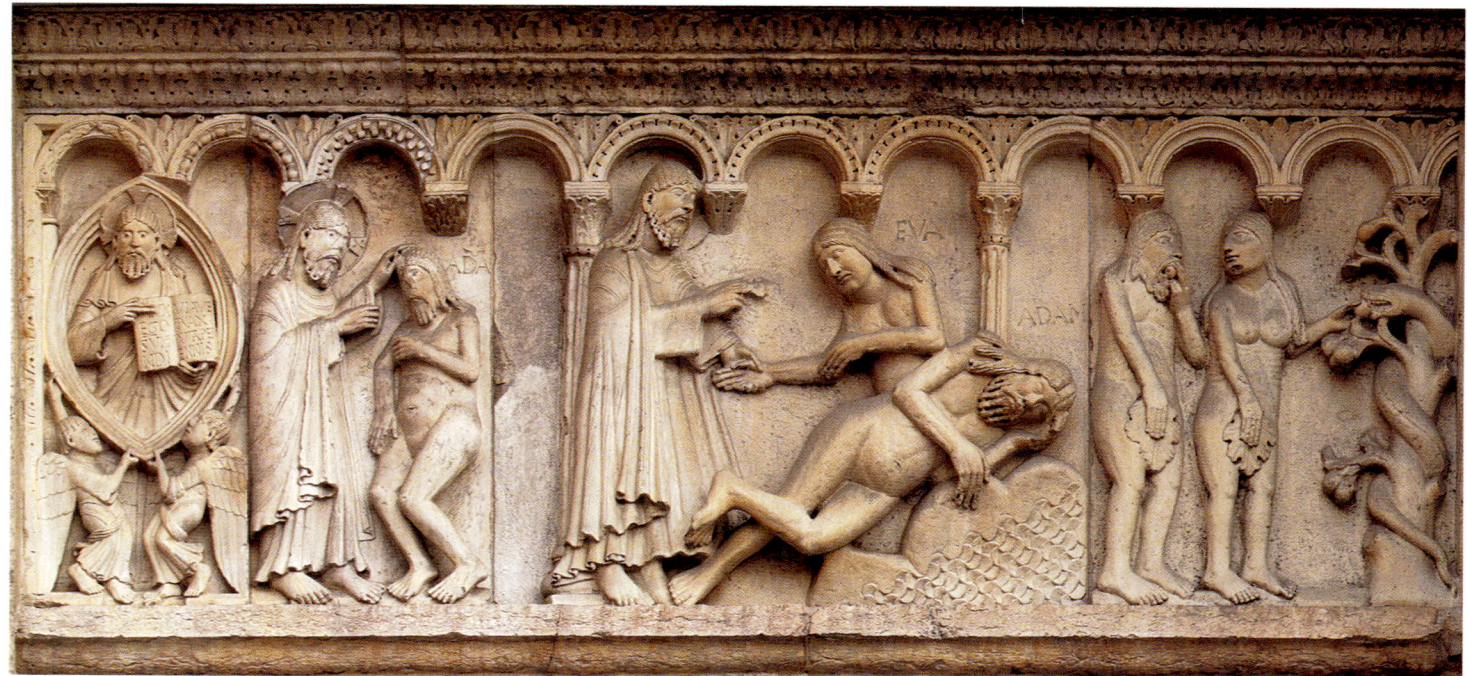

**12-28** WILIGELMO, *Creation and Temptation of Adam and Eve,* detail of the frieze on the west facade, Modena Cathedral, Modena, Italy, ca. 1110. Marble, 3′ high.

For Modena's cathedral, Wiligelmo represented scenes from Genesis against an architectural backdrop of a type common on Roman and Early Christian sarcophagi, which were plentiful in the area.

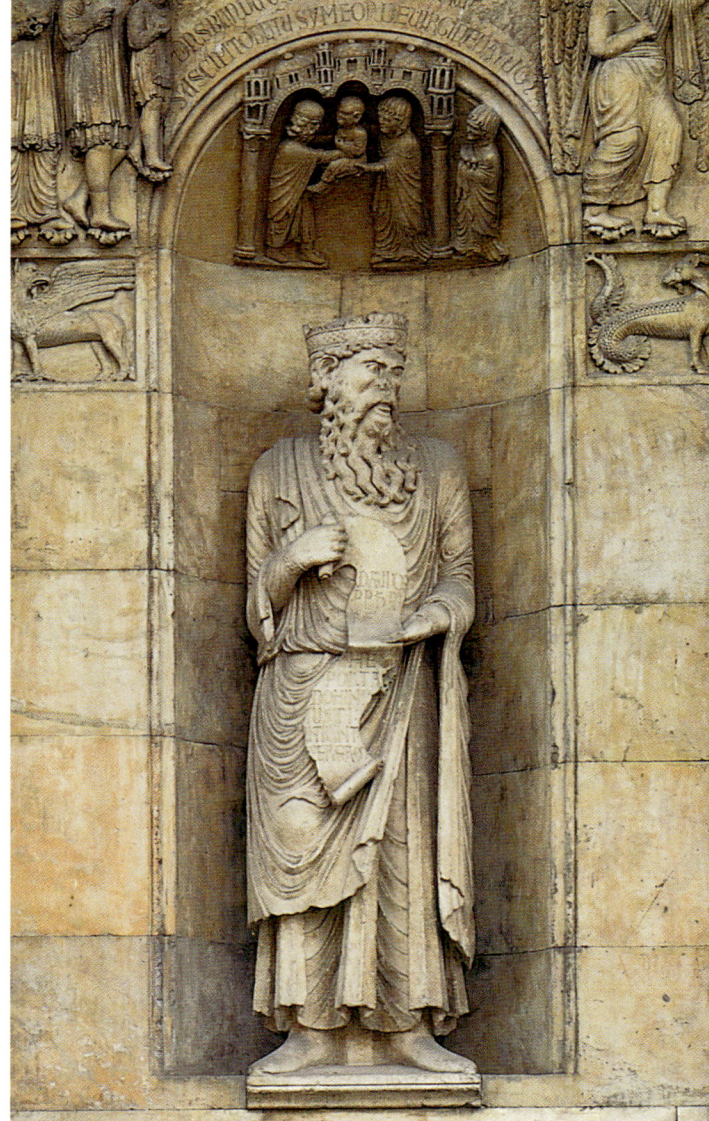

**12-29** BENEDETTO ANTELAMI, *King David*, statue in a niche on the west facade of Fidenza Cathedral, Fidenza, Italy, ca. 1180–1190.

Benedetto Antelami's King David on the facade of Fidenza Cathedral is a rare example of life-size freestanding statuary in the Romanesque period. The style is unmistakably rooted in Greco-Roman art.

BENEDETTO ANTELAMI was active in the last quarter of the 12th century. Several reliefs by his hand exist, including Parma Cathedral's pulpit and the portals of that city's baptistery. But his most unusual works are the two monumental marble statues of biblical figures he carved for the west facade of Fidenza Cathedral. Benedetto's *King David* (FIG. **12-29**) seems confined within his niche. His elbows are kept close to his body. Absent is the weight shift that is the hallmark of classical statuary. Yet the sculptor's conception of this prophet is unmistakably rooted in Greco-Roman art. Comparison of the Fidenza David with the prophet on the Moissac trumeau (FIG. 12-13), who also displays an unfurled scroll, reveals how much the Italian sculptor freed his figure from its architectural setting. Other sculptors did not immediately emulate Antelami's classical approach to portraying figures in stone. But the idea of placing freestanding statues in niches would be taken up again in Italy by Early Renaissance sculptors (FIGS. 21-4 to 21-6).

# NORMANDY AND ENGLAND

After their conversion to Christianity in the early 10th century, the Vikings (see Chapter 11) settled on the northern coast of France in present-day Normandy. Almost at once, they proved themselves not only aggressive warriors but also skilled administrators and builders, active in Sicily (FIG. 9-27) as well as in northern Europe.

## Architecture

The Normans quickly developed a distinctive Romanesque architectural style that became the major source of French Gothic architecture.

**CAEN** Most critics consider the abbey church of Saint-Étienne at Caen the masterpiece of Norman Romanesque architecture. Begun by William of Normandy (William the Conqueror; see page 361) in 1067, work must have advanced rapidly, because the Normans buried the duke in the church in 1087. Saint-Étienne's west facade (FIG. **12-30**) is a striking design rooted in the tradition of

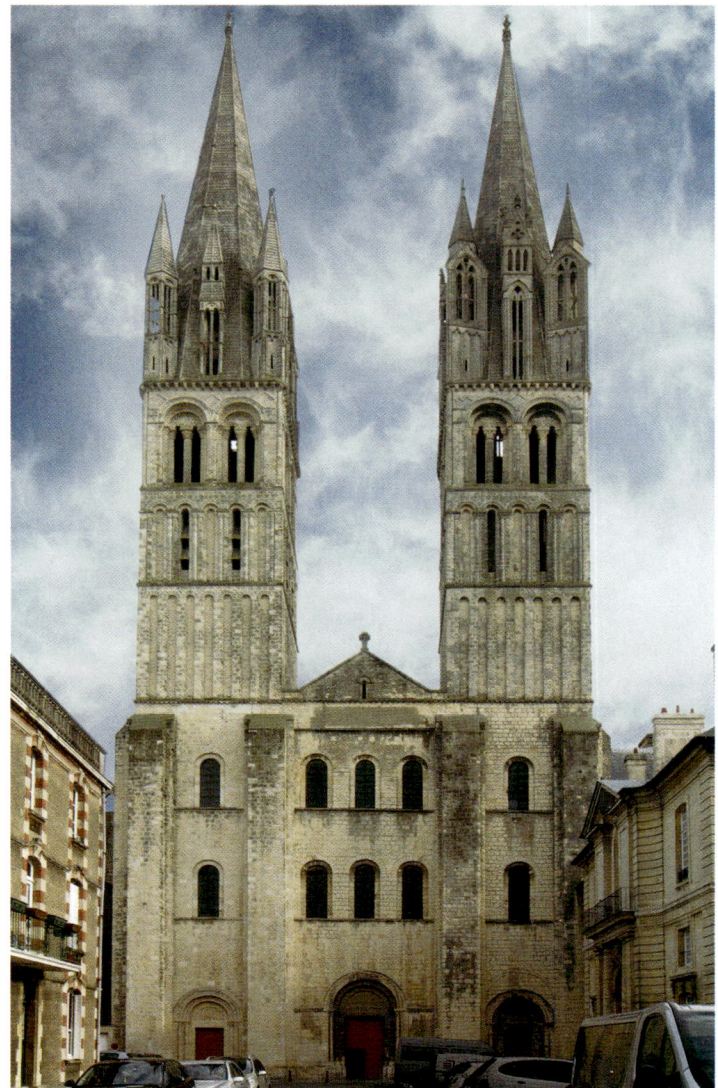

**12-30** West facade of Saint-Étienne, Caen, France, begun 1067. ◼◀

The division of Saint-Étienne's facade into three parts corresponding to the nave and aisles reflects the methodical planning of the entire structure. The towers also have a tripartite design.

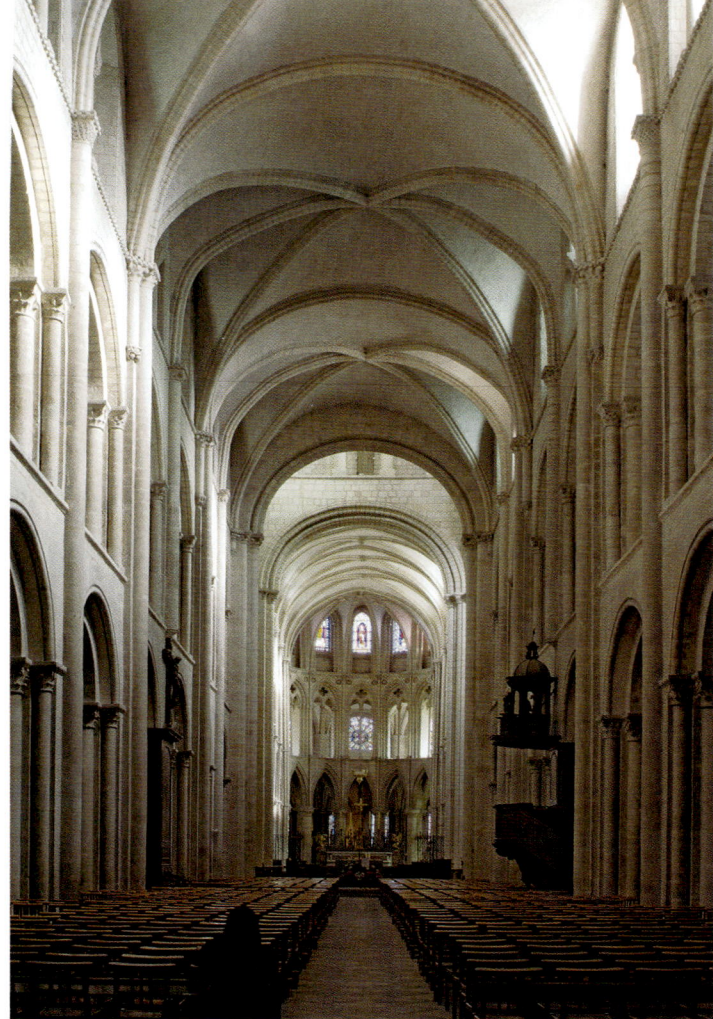

**12-31** Interior of Saint-Étienne (looking east), Caen, France, vaulted ca. 1115–1120. ◼◣

The groin vaults of Saint-Étienne made clerestory windows possible. The three-story elevation with its large arched openings provides ample light and makes the nave appear taller than it is.

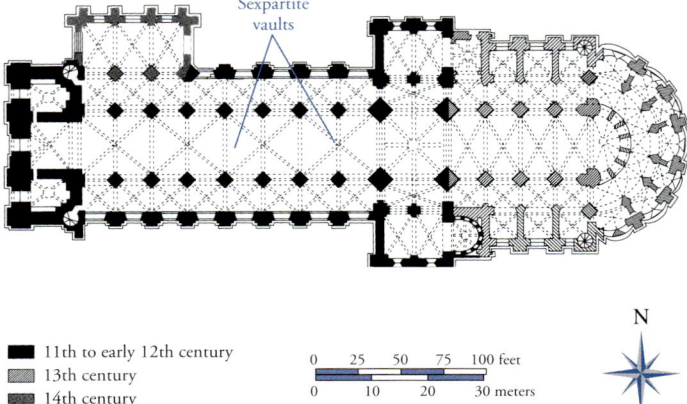

**12-32** Plan of Saint-Étienne, Caen, France.

The early-12th-century nave vaults of Saint-Étienne spring from compound piers with alternating half-columns and pilasters. The diagonal and transverse ribs divide the vaults into six compartments.

Carolingian and Ottonian westworks, but it reveals a new unified organizational scheme. Four large buttresses divide the facade into three bays corresponding to the nave and aisles. Above the buttresses, the towers also display a triple division and a progressively greater piercing of their walls from lower to upper stages. (The culminating spires are a Gothic addition.) The tripartite division extends throughout the facade, both vertically and horizontally, organizing it into a close-knit, well-integrated composition consistent with the careful and methodical planning of the entire structure.

The original design of Saint-Étienne called for a wooden roof, as originally at Speyer Cathedral. But the Caen nave (FIG. **12-31**) had compound piers with simple engaged half-columns alternating with piers with half-columns attached to pilasters. When the Normans decided to install groin vaults around 1115, the existing alternating compound piers in the nave proved a good match. Those piers soar all the way to the vaults' springing. Their branching ribs divide the large square-vault compartments into six sections—a *sexpartite vault* (FIG. **12-32**). The vaults rise high enough to provide room for clerestory windows. The resulting three-story elevation,

with its large arched openings, allows ample light to reach the interior. It also makes the nave appear taller than it is. As in the Milanese church of Sant'Ambrogio (FIG. 12-22), the Norman building has rib vaults. The diagonal and transverse ribs form a structural skeleton that partially supports the still fairly massive paneling between them. But despite the heavy masonry, the large windows and reduced interior wall surface give Saint-Étienne's nave a light and airy quality unusual in the Romanesque period.

**DURHAM** William of Normandy's conquest of Anglo-Saxon England in 1066 began a new epoch in English history. In architecture, it signaled the importation of Norman Romanesque building and design methods. Durham Cathedral (FIGS. **12-33** and **12-34**) sits majestically on a cliff overlooking the Wear River in northern England, the centerpiece of a monastery, church, and fortified-castle complex on the Scottish frontier. Unlike Speyer Cathedral and Saint-Étienne, Durham Cathedral, begun around 1093—before the remodeling of the Caen church—was a vaulted structure from the beginning. Consequently, the pattern of the ribs of the nave's groin vaults corresponds perfectly to the design of the arcade below. Each seven-part nave vault covers two bays. Large, simple pillars ornamented with abstract designs (diamond, chevron, and cable patterns, all originally painted) alternate with compound piers that carry the transverse arches of the vaults. The pier-vault relationship scarcely could be more visible or the building's structural rationale better expressed.

The bold surface patterning of the pillars in the Durham nave is a reminder that the raising of imposing stone edifices such as the Romanesque churches of England and Normandy required more than just the talents of master designers. A corps of expert masons had to transform rough stone blocks into the precise shapes necessary for their specific place in the church's fabric. Although thousands of simple quadrangular blocks make up the great walls of these buildings, the stonecutters also had to produce large numbers of blocks of far more complex shapes. To cover the nave and aisles, the masons had to carve blocks with concave faces to conform to the curve of the vault. Also required were blocks with projecting moldings for the ribs, blocks with convex surfaces for the pillars or with multiple profiles for the compound piers, and so forth. It was an immense undertaking, and it is no wonder medieval building campaigns often lasted for decades.

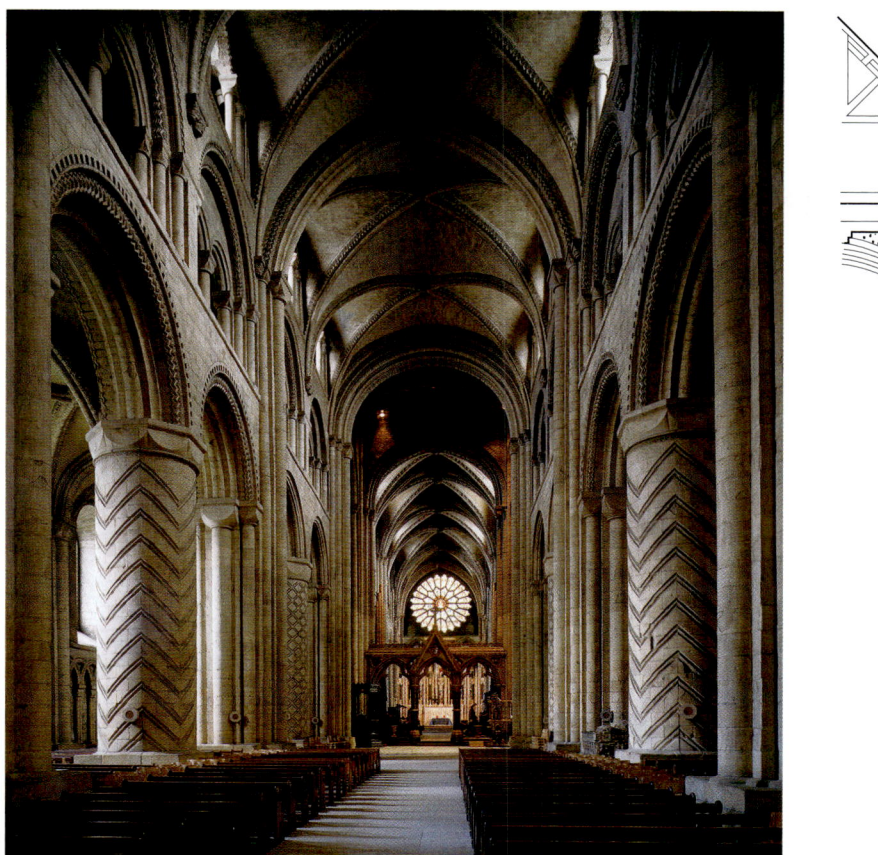

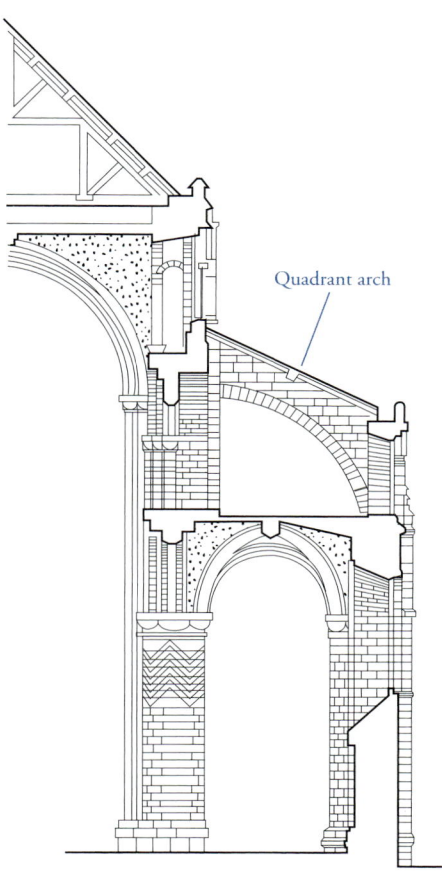

Quadrant arch

**12-33** Interior (*left;* looking east) and lateral section (*right*) of Durham Cathedral, Durham, England, begun ca. 1093.

Durham Cathedral is the first example of a rib groin vault placed over a three-story nave. Quadrant arches replaced groin vaults in the tribune as buttresses of the nave vaults.

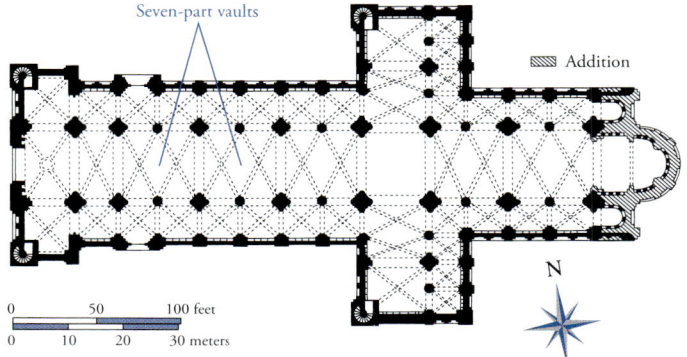

Seven-part vaults

Addition

0    50    100 feet
0  10  20  30 meters

N

**12-34** **Plan of Durham Cathedral, Durham, England (after Kenneth John Conant).**

Durham Cathedral is typically English in its long, slender proportions. In the nave, simple pillars alternate with compound piers that support the transverse arches of the seven-part groin vaults.

Durham Cathedral's plan (FIG. 12-34) is typically English with its long, slender proportions. It does not employ the modular scheme with the same care and logic seen at Caen. But in other ways, this English church is even more innovative than the French church. It is the earliest example known of a rib groin vault placed over a three-story nave. In the nave's western parts, completed before 1130, the rib vaults have slightly pointed arches, bringing together for the first time two key elements that determined the structural evolu-

tion of Gothic architecture (see "The Gothic Rib Vault," Chapter 13, page 368). Also of great significance is the way the English builders buttressed the nave vaults. The lateral section (FIG. 12-33, *right*) exposes the simple *quadrant arches* (arches whose curve extends for one-quarter of a circle's circumference) that take the place of groin vaults in the Durham tribune. The structural descendants of these quadrant arches are the flying buttresses that epitomize the mature Gothic solution to church construction (see "The Gothic Cathedral," Chapter 13, page 373, and FIG. 13-12).

## Painting and Other Arts

Many of the finest illustrated manuscripts of the Romanesque age were the work of monks in English scriptoria, following in the tradition of Hiberno-Saxon book production (see Chapter 11).

**BURY BIBLE** The *Bury Bible* (FIG. **12-35**), produced at the Bury Saint Edmunds abbey in England around 1135, exemplifies the sumptuous illumination common to the large Bibles produced in wealthy Romanesque abbeys not subject to the Cistercian restrictions on painted manuscripts. These costly books lent prestige to monasteries that could afford them (see "Medieval Books," Chapter 11, page 312). The artist responsible for the *Bury Bible* is known: MASTER HUGO, who was also a sculptor and metalworker. With Gislebertus (FIGS. 12-1, 12-13A, and 12-13B), Bernardus Gelduinus (FIG. 12-8), Rufillus (FIG. 12-23A), Rainer of Huy (FIG. 12-24), Wiligelmo (FIG. 12-28), and Benedetto Antelami (FIG. 12-29), Hugo was one of the small but growing number of Romanesque

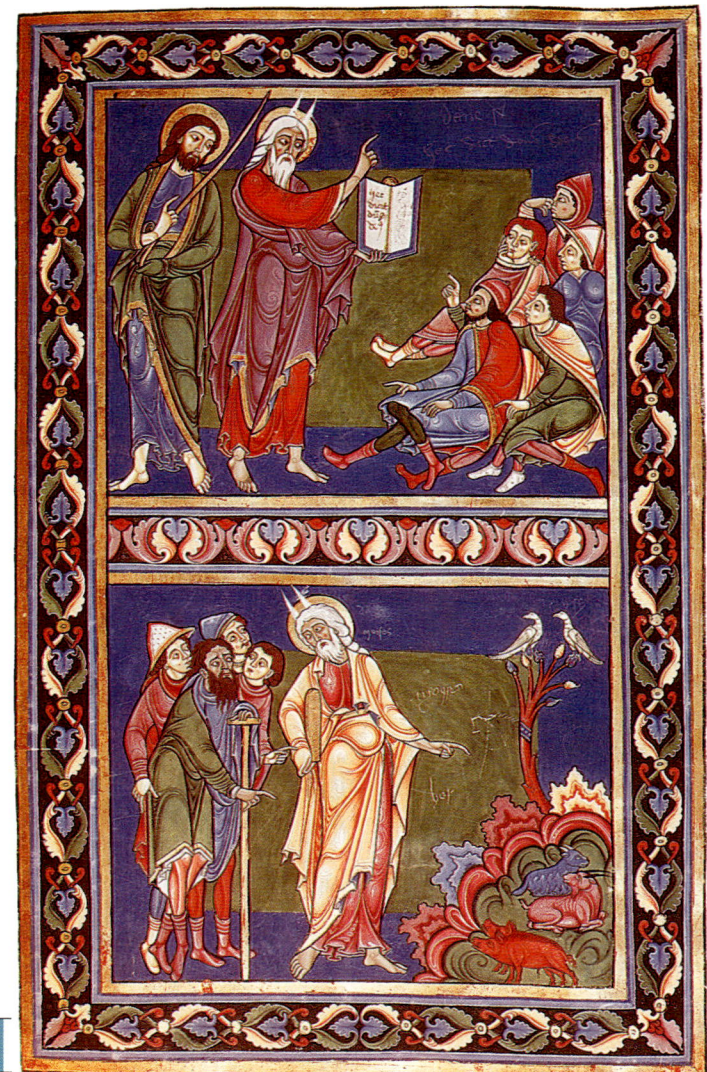

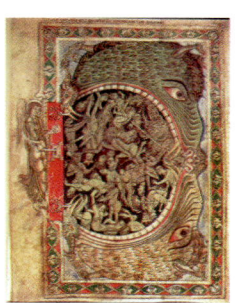

**12-35A** *Winchester Psalter,* ca. 1145–1155.

**12-35** MASTER HUGO, *Moses Expounding the Law,* folio 94 recto of the *Bury Bible,* from Bury Saint Edmunds, England, ca. 1135. Ink and tempera on vellum, 1′ 8″ × 1′ 2″. Corpus Christi College, Cambridge.

Master Hugo was a rare Romanesque lay artist, one of the emerging class of professional artists and artisans who depended for their livelihood on commissions from wealthy monasteries.

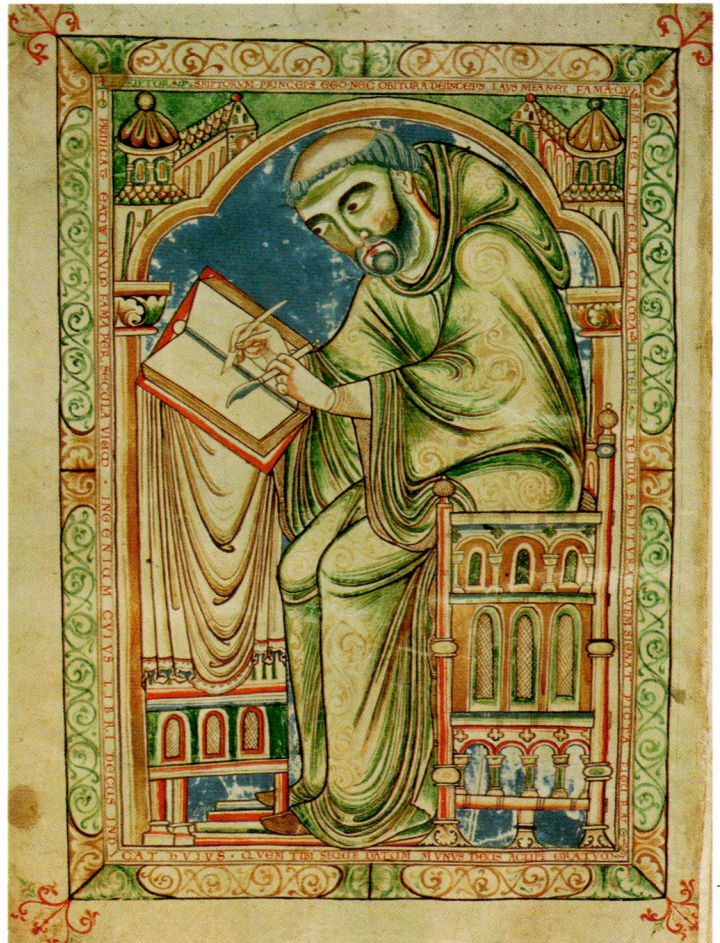

**12-36** EADWINE THE SCRIBE(?), Eadwine the Scribe at work, folio 283 verso of the *Eadwine Psalter,* ca. 1160–1170. Ink and tempera on vellum, 1′ 3$\frac{1}{2}$″ × 11$\frac{5}{8}$″. Trinity College, Cambridge. ◼

Although he humbly offered his book as a gift to God, the English monk Eadwine added an inscription to his portrait declaring himself a "prince among scribes" whose fame would endure forever.

artists who signed their works or whose names were recorded. In the 12th century, artists, illuminators as well as sculptors, increasingly began to identify themselves. Although most medieval artists remained anonymous, the contrast of the Romanesque period with the early Middle Ages is striking. Hugo apparently was a secular artist, one of the emerging class of professional artists and artisans who depended for their livelihood on commissions from well-endowed monasteries. These artists resided in towns rather than within secluded abbey walls, and they traveled frequently to find work. They were the exception, however, and most Romanesque scribes and illuminators continued to be monks and nuns working anonymously in the service of God. The Benedictine rule, for example, specified that "artisans in the monastery . . . are to practice their craft with all humility, but only with the abbot's permission."[6] Some monks, however, produced illuminated volumes not for use in the abbey but on royal commission, for example, the *Winchester Psalter* (FIG. **12-35A**).

One page (FIG. 12-35) of the *Bury Bible* shows two scenes from Deuteronomy framed by symmetrical leaf motifs in softly glowing harmonized colors. In the upper register, Master Hugo painted *Moses Expounding the Law,* in which he represented the prophet with horns, consistent with Saint Jerome's translation of the Hebrew word that also means "rays" (compare Michelangelo's similar conception of the Hebrew prophet, FIG. 22-14). The lower panel portrays Moses pointing out the clean and unclean beasts. The gestures are slow and gentle and have quiet dignity. The figures of Moses and Aaron seem to glide. This presentation is quite different from the abrupt emphasis and spastic movement seen in earlier Romanesque paintings. The movements of the figures appear more integrated and smooth. Yet patterning remains in the multiple divisions of the draped limbs, the lightly shaded volumes connected with sinuous lines and ladderlike folds. Hugo still thought of the drapery and body as somehow the same. The frame has a quite definite limiting function, and the painter carefully fit the figures within it.

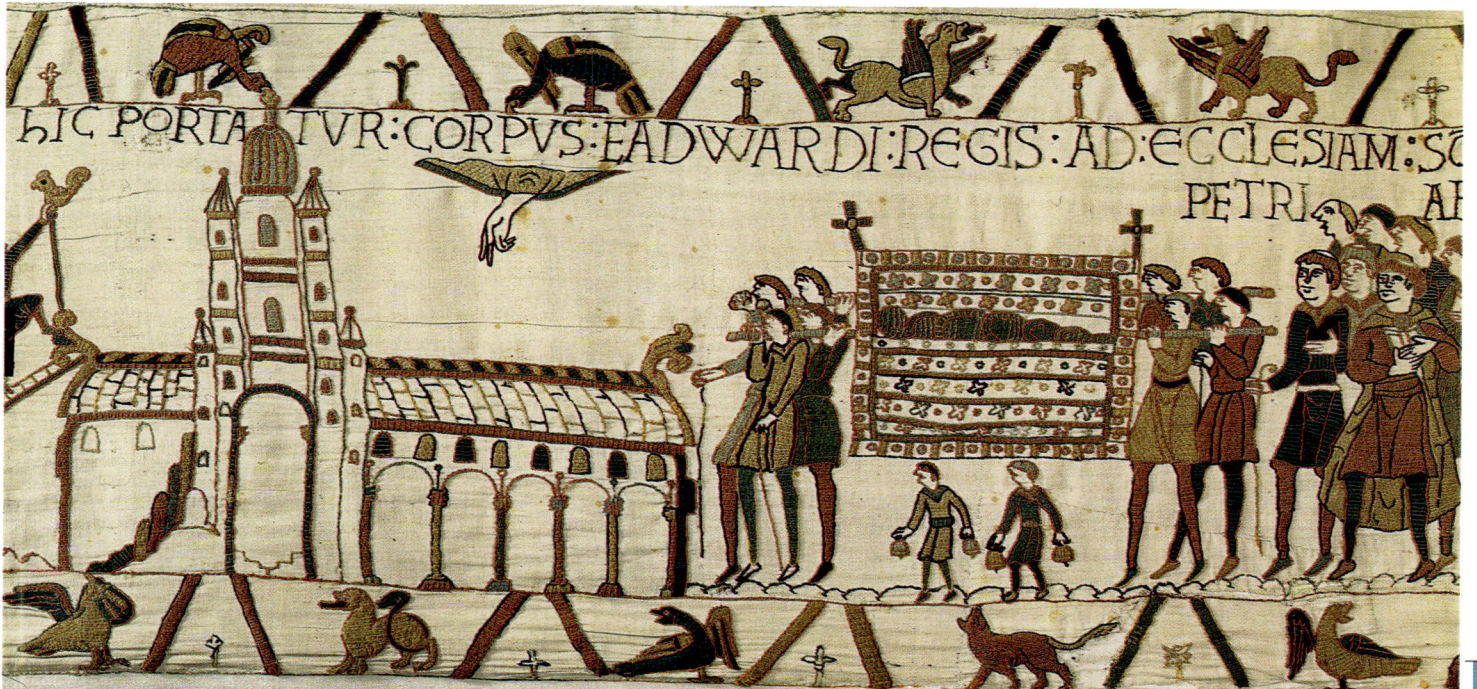

**12-37** Funeral procession to Westminster Abbey, detail of the *Bayeux Tapestry,* from Bayeux Cathedral, Bayeux, France, ca. 1070–1080. Embroidered wool on linen, 1′ 8″ high (entire length of fabric 229′ 8″). Centre Guillaume le Conquérant, Bayeux. ◼◄

The *Bayeux Tapestry* is unique in medieval art. Like historical narratives in Roman art, it depicts contemporaneous events in full detail, as in the scroll-like frieze of Trajan's Column (FIG. 7-1).

**EADWINE PSALTER** The *Eadwine Psalter* is the masterpiece of an English monk known as EADWINE THE SCRIBE. It contains 166 illustrations, many of them variations of those in the Carolingian *Utrecht Psalter* (FIGS. 11-15 and 11-15A). The last page (FIG. **12-36**), however, presents a rare picture of a Romanesque artist at work (compare FIG. 12-23A). The style of the Eadwine portrait resembles that of the *Bury Bible,* but although the patterning is still firm (notably in the cowl and the thigh), the drapery falls more softly and follows the movements of the body beneath it. Here, the abstract patterning of many Romanesque painted and sculpted garments yielded slightly, but clearly, to the requirements of more naturalistic representation. The Romanesque artist's instinct for decorating the surface remained, as is apparent in the gown's whorls and spirals. Significantly, however, the artist painted those interior lines very lightly so that they would not conflict with the functional lines containing them.

The "portrait" of Eadwine—it is probably a generic type and not a specific likeness—is in the long tradition of author portraits in ancient and medieval manuscripts (FIGS. 11-8, 11-13, 11-14, and 12-23; compare FIG. 7-25B), although the true author of the *Eadwine Psalter* is King David. Eadwine exaggerated his importance by likening himself to an evangelist writing his Gospel and by including an inscription within the inner frame identifying himself and proclaiming that he is a "prince among scribes." He declares the excellence of his work will cause his fame to endure forever, and consequently he can offer his book as an acceptable gift to God. Eadwine, like other Romanesque sculptors and painters who signed their works, may have been concerned for his fame, but these artists, whether clergy or laity, were as yet unaware of the concepts of fine art and fine artist. To them, their work existed not for its own sake but for God's. Nonetheless, works such as this one are an early sign of a new attitude toward the role of the artist in society that presages the reemergence in the Renaissance of the classical notion of individual artistic genius.

**BAYEUX TAPESTRY** The most famous work of English Romanesque art is neither a book nor Christian in subject. The so-called *Bayeux Tapestry* (FIGS. **12-37** and **12-38**) is unique in medieval art. It is an embroidered fabric—not, in fact, a woven tapestry—made of wool sewn on linen (see "Embroidery and Tapestry," page 362). Closely related to Romanesque manuscript illumination, its borders contain the kinds of real and imaginary animals found in contemporaneous books, and an explanatory Latin text sewn in thread accompanies many of the pictures. Some 20 inches high and about 230 feet long, the *Bayeux Tapestry* is a continuous, friezelike, pictorial narrative of a crucial moment in England's history and of the events leading up to it. The Norman defeat of the Anglo-Saxons at Hastings in 1066 brought England under the control of the Normans, uniting all of England and much of France under one rule. The dukes of Normandy became the kings of England. Commissioned by Bishop Odo, the half brother of the conquering Duke William, the embroidery may have been sewn by women at the Norman court. Many art historians, however, believe it was the work of English stitchers in Kent, where Odo was earl after the Norman conquest. Odo donated the work to Bayeux Cathedral (hence its nickname), but it is uncertain whether it was originally intended for display in the church's nave, where the theme would have been a curious choice.

The events that precipitated the Norman invasion of England are well documented. In 1066, Edward the Confessor (r. 1042–1066), the Anglo-Saxon king of England, died. The Normans believed Edward had recognized William of Normandy as his rightful heir. But the crown went to Harold, earl of Wessex, the king's Anglo-Saxon brother-in-law, who had sworn an oath of allegiance to William. The betrayed Normans, descendants of the seafaring Vikings, boarded their ships, crossed the English Channel, and crushed Harold's forces.

## Embroidery and Tapestry

The most famous embroidery of the Middle Ages is, ironically, known as the *Bayeux Tapestry* (FIGS. 12-37 and 12-38). Embroidery and tapestry are related—but different—means of decorating textiles. *Tapestry* designs are woven on a loom as part of the fabric. *Embroidery* patterns are sewn onto fabrics with threads.

The needleworkers who fashioned the *Bayeux Tapestry* were either Norman or English women. They employed eight colors of dyed wool yarn—two varieties of blue, three shades of green, yellow, buff, and terracotta red—and two kinds of stitches. In *stem stitching,* short overlapping strands of thread form jagged lines. *Laid-and-couched work* creates solid blocks of color. In the latter technique, the needleworker first lays down a series of parallel and then a series of cross stitches. Finally, the stitcher tacks down the cross-hatched threads using couching (knotting).

On the *Bayeux Tapestry,* the embroiderers left the natural linen color exposed for the background, human flesh, building walls, and other "colorless" design elements. Stem stitches define the contours of figures and buildings and delineate interior details, such as facial features, body armor, and roof tiles. The clothing, animal bodies, and other solid areas are laid-and-couched work.

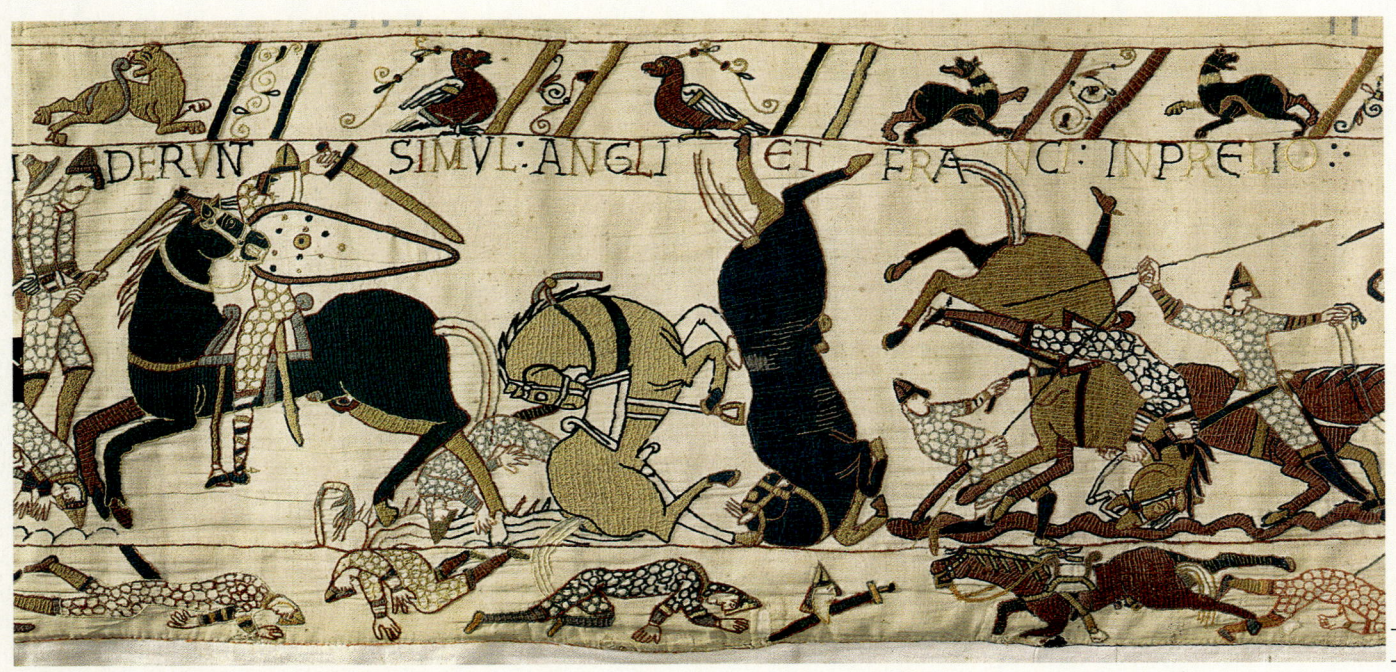

**12-38** Battle of Hastings, detail of the *Bayeux Tapestry,* from Bayeux Cathedral, Bayeux, France, ca. 1070–1080. Embroidered wool on linen, 1′ 8″ high (entire length of fabric 229′ 8″). Centre Guillaume le Conquérant, Bayeux. ◼️◀

The *Bayeux Tapestry* is really an embroidery. The needleworkers employed eight colors of dyed wool yarn and sewed the threads onto linen using both stem stitching and laid-and-couched work.

Illustrated here are two episodes of the epic tale as represented in the *Bayeux Tapestry*. The first detail (FIG. 12-37) depicts King Edward's funeral procession. The hand of God points the way to the church in London where he was buried—Westminster Abbey, consecrated on December 28, 1065, just a few days before Edward's death. The church was one of the first Romanesque buildings erected in England, and the embroiderers took pains to record its main features, including the imposing crossing tower and the long nave with tribunes. Here William was crowned king of England on Christmas Day, 1066. (The coronation of every English monarch since then also has occurred in Westminster Abbey.) The second detail (FIG. 12-38) shows the Battle of Hastings in progress. The Norman cavalry cuts down the English defenders. Filling the lower border are the dead and wounded, although the upper register continues the animal motifs of the rest of the embroidery. The Romanesque artists co-opted some of the characteristic motifs of Greco-Roman battle scenes, for example, the horses with twisted necks and contorted bodies (compare FIG. 5-70), but rendered the figures in the Romanesque manner. Linear patterning and flat color replaced classical three-dimensional volume and modeling in light and dark hues.

The *Bayeux Tapestry* stands apart from all other Romanesque artworks in depicting in full detail an event at a time shortly after it occurred, recalling the historical narratives of ancient Roman art. Art historians have often likened the Norman embroidery to the scroll-like frieze of the Column of Trajan (FIGS. 7-1 and 7-45). Like the Roman account, the story told on the textile is the conqueror's version of history, a proclamation of national pride. As in the ancient frieze, the narrative is not confined to battlefield successes. It is a complete chronicle of events. Included are the preparations for war, with scenes depicting the felling and splitting of trees for ship construction, the loading of equipment onto the vessels, the cooking and serving of meals, and so forth. In this respect, the *Bayeux Tapestry* is the most *Roman*-esque work of Romanesque art.

# ROMANESQUE EUROPE

## FRANCE AND NORTHERN SPAIN

▌ *Romanesque* takes its name from the Roman-like barrel and groin vaults based on round arches employed in many European churches built between 1050 and 1200. Romanesque vaults, however, are made of stone, not concrete.

▌ Numerous churches sprang up along the pilgrimage roads leading to the shrine of Saint James at Santiago de Compostela. These churches were large enough to accommodate crowds of pilgrims who came to view the relics displayed in radiating chapels off the ambulatory and transept.

▌ The Romanesque period also brought the revival of monumental stone relief sculpture in cloisters and especially in church portals, where scenes of Christ as last judge often greeted the faithful as they entered the doorway to the road to salvation.

▌ The leading patrons of Romanesque sculpture and painting were the monks of the Cluniac order. In contrast, the Cistercians, under the leadership of Bernard of Clairvaux, condemned figural art in churches and religious books.

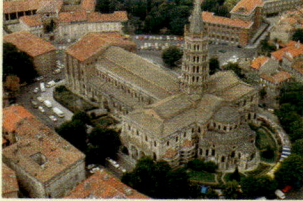

Saint-Sernin, Toulouse, ca. 1070–1120

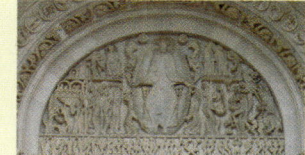

Saint-Lazare, Autun,
ca. 1120–1135

## HOLY ROMAN EMPIRE

▌ In the Romanesque period, the Salian dynasty (r. 1027–1125) ruled an empire corresponding roughly to present-day Germany and northern Italy.

▌ Architects in the Holy Roman Empire built structurally innovative churches. Speyer Cathedral and Sant'Ambrogio in Milan are two of the earliest examples of the use of groin vaults in naves.

▌ In Belgium, sculptors excelled in metalwork, producing costly reliquaries of silver, jewels, and enamel, such as that containing the remains of Pope Alexander II. Rainer of Huy, one of several Romanesque artists whose name is known, cast a bronze baptismal font in a single piece.

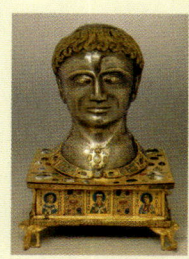

Reliquary of
Saint Alexander, 1145

## ITALY

▌ The regional diversity of Romanesque art and architecture is especially evident in Italy, where the heritage of ancient Rome and Early Christianity was strongest.

▌ Romanesque churches in Pisa and Florence have timber roofs in contrast to the vaulted interiors of northern European buildings. The exteriors often feature marble paneling of different colors. Church campaniles were usually freestanding, as were baptisteries, which took the form of independent central-plan buildings facing the cathedral.

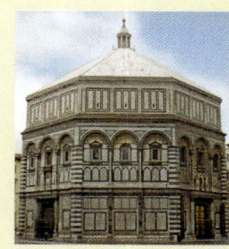

Baptistery of San Giovanni,
Florence, begun 1059

## NORMANDY AND ENGLAND

▌ After their conversion to Christianity in the early 10th century, the Vikings settled on the northern coast of France. From there, Duke William of Normandy crossed the channel and conquered England in 1066. The *Bayeux Tapestry* chronicles that war—a unique example of contemporaneous historical narrative art in the Middle Ages.

▌ Norman and English Romanesque architects introduced new features to church design that later greatly influenced French Gothic architecture. Saint-Étienne at Caen and Durham Cathedral are the earliest examples of the use of rib groin vaults over a three-story (arcade-tribune-clerestory) nave. The Durham builders also experimented with quadrant arches in the tribune to buttress the nave vaults.

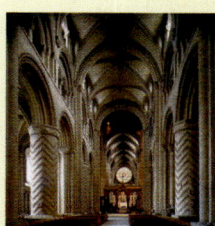

Durham Cathedral,
begun ca. 1093

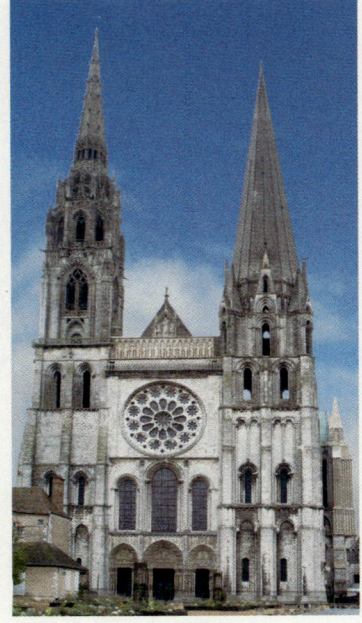

Chartres Cathedral is the key monument of both Early and High Gothic architecture. The west facade still has much in common with Romanesque designs but features statues on the door jambs.

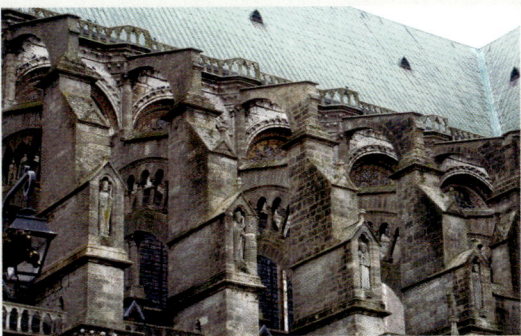

Architectural historians consider the rebuilt Chartres Cathedral the first great monument of High Gothic architecture. It is the first church planned from the beginning to have flying buttresses.

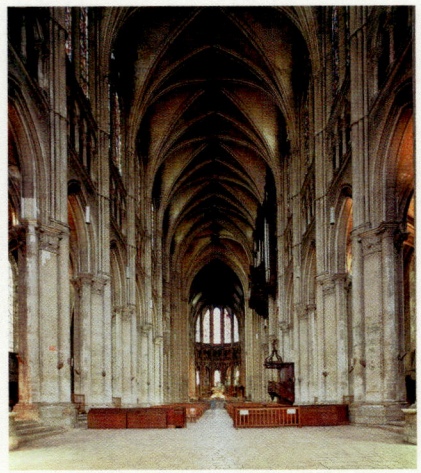

Chartres set the pattern for High Gothic cathedrals in the use of four-part rib vaults springing from pointed arches and in the introduction of a three-story nave elevation (arcade, triforium, clerestory).

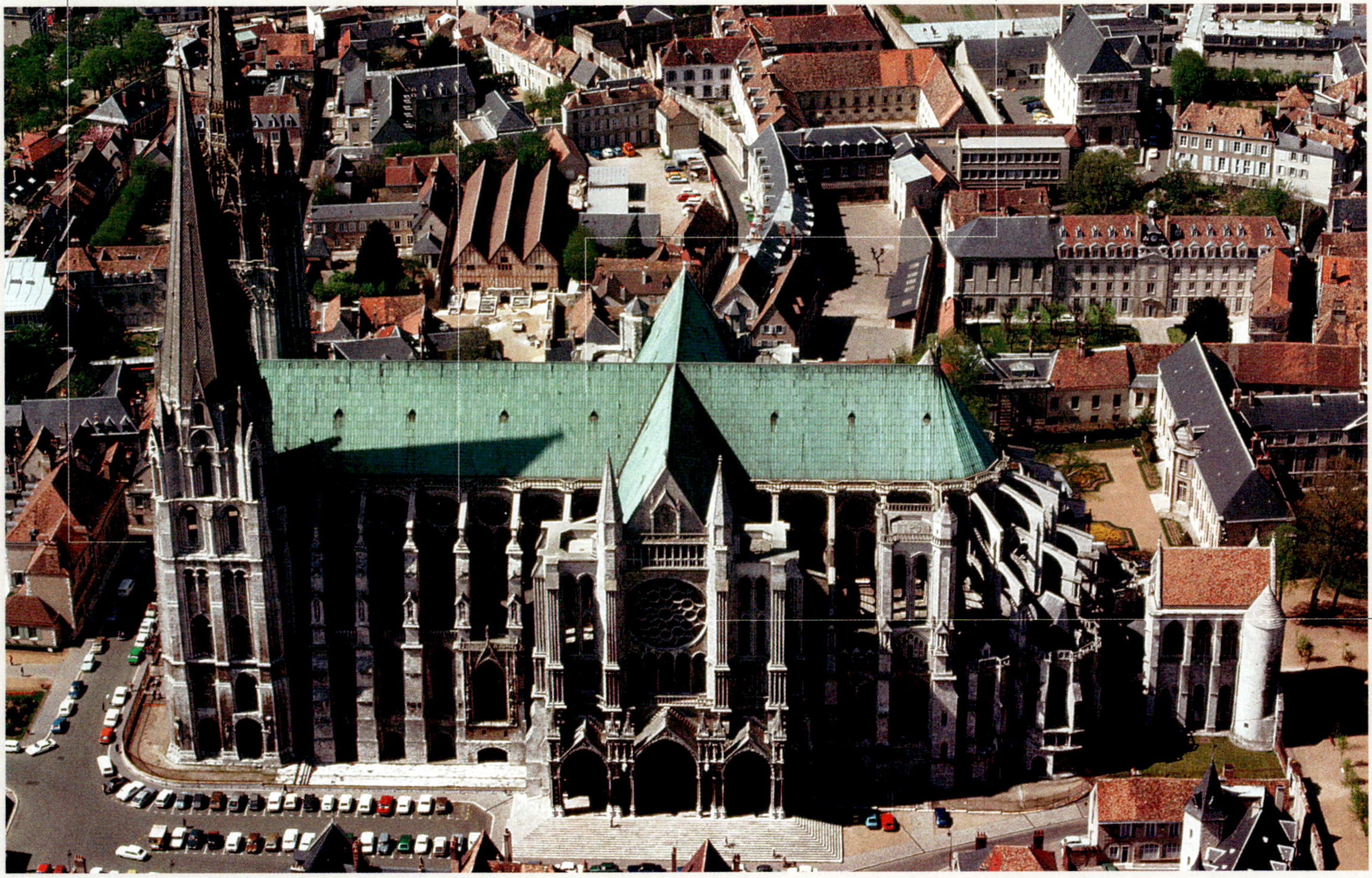

**13-1** Aerial view of Chartres Cathedral (looking north), Chartres, France, as rebuilt after 1194. ◼▶

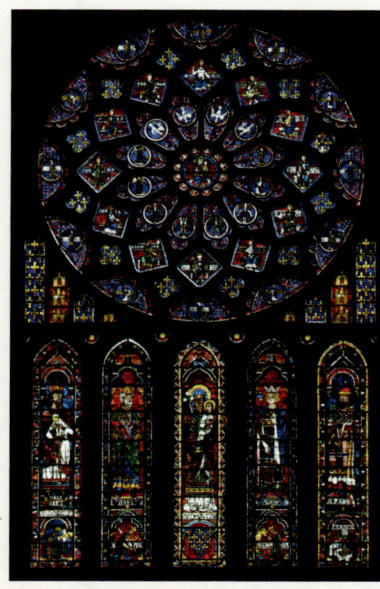

# 13

# GOTHIC EUROPE

Flying buttresses made possible the replacement of heavy masonry walls with immense stained-glass windows, which transformed natural sunlight into divine light of various hues.

FRAMING THE ERA

## THE AGE OF THE GREAT CATHEDRALS

In 1550, Giorgio Vasari (1511–1574) first used *Gothic* as a term of ridicule to describe late medieval art and architecture, which he attributed to the Goths and regarded as "monstrous and barbarous."[1] With the publication that year of his influential *Introduction to the Three Arts of Design,* Vasari codified for all time the notion the early Renaissance artist Lorenzo Ghiberti (1378–1455) had already advanced in his *Commentarii,* namely that the Middle Ages was a period of decline. The Italian humanists, who regarded Greco-Roman art as the standard of excellence, believed the uncouth Goths were responsible both for the downfall of Rome and for the decline of the classical style in art and architecture. They regarded "Gothic" art with contempt and considered it ugly and crude.

In the 13th and 14th centuries, however, Chartres Cathedral (FIG. **13-1**) and similar French buildings set the standard throughout most of Europe. For the clergy and the lay public alike, the great cathedrals towering over their towns were not distortions of the classical style but *opus modernum* ("modern work"), glorious images of the City of God, the Heavenly Jerusalem, which they were privileged to build on earth.

The Gothic cathedral was the unique product of an era of peace and widespread economic prosperity, deep spirituality, and extraordinary technological innovation. The essential ingredients of these towering holy structures were lofty masonry rib vaults on pointed arches invisibly held in place by external ("flying") buttresses, and interiors illuminated with mystical light streaming through huge colored-glass windows (see "The Gothic Cathedral," page 373).

The key monument of this exciting new style is Chartres Cathedral, discussed in detail later. Begun around 1145, the church dedicated to Our Lady (Notre Dame), the Virgin Mary, housed her mantle, a precious relic. The lower parts of the massive west towers and the portals between them are all that remain of that Early Gothic cathedral destroyed by fire in 1194 before it had been completed. Reconstruction of the church began immediately but in the High Gothic style with flying buttresses, rib vaults on pointed arches, and immense stained-glass windows. Chartres Cathedral is therefore a singularly instructive composite of a 12th-century facade and a 13th-century nave and transept, and documents the early and mature stages of the development of Gothic architecture in the place of its birth, the region around Paris called the Île-de-France.

# FRANCE

As in the Romanesque period, the great artistic innovations of the Gothic age were in large part the outgrowth of widespread prosperity. This was a time of profound change in European society. The focus of both intellectual and religious life shifted definitively from monasteries in the countryside to rapidly expanding secular cities. In these new urban centers, prosperous merchants made their homes and formed *guilds* (professional associations), scholars founded the first modern universities, and vernacular literature, especially courtly romances, exploded in popularity. Although the papacy was at the height of its power, and Christian knights still waged Crusades against the Muslims, the independent secular nations of modern Europe were beginning to take shape. Foremost among them was France, and that is where, around 1140, the Gothic style first appeared.

By the 13th century, the opus modernum of the region around Paris had spread throughout western Europe (MAP 13-1), and in the next century reached farther still. Saint Vitus Cathedral in Prague (Czech Republic), for example, begun in 1344, closely emulates French Gothic architecture. In fact, some late medieval writers referred to Gothic buildings anywhere in Europe as *opus francigenum* ("French work"). Nevertheless, many regional variants existed within European Gothic, just as distinct regional styles characterized the Romanesque period (see Chapter 12). Therefore, this chapter deals with contemporaneous developments in the major regions—France, England, and the Holy Roman Empire—in separate sections. The art and architecture of 13th- and 14th-century Italy are the subject of Chapter 14.

## Architecture, Sculpture, and Stained Glass

Art historians generally agree Saint-Denis, a few miles north of Paris, was the birthplace of Gothic architecture. Dionysius (Denis in French) was the legendary saint who brought Christianity to Gaul and who died a martyr's death there in the third century. The Benedictine order founded the abbey at Saint-Denis in the seventh century on the site of the saint's burial. (According to legend, after

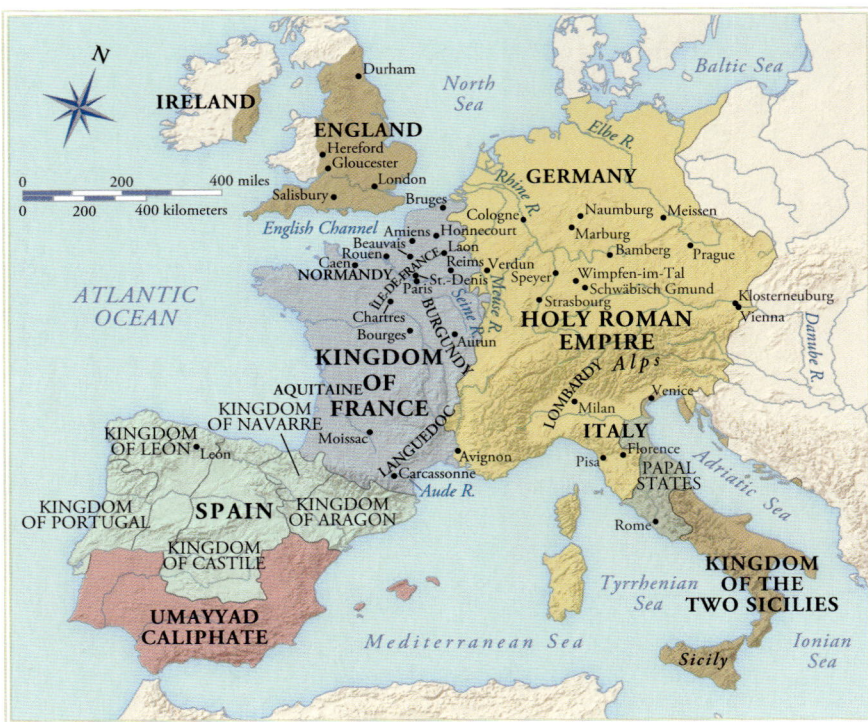

**MAP 13-1** Europe around 1200.

his execution, Dionysius miraculously stood up and marched to his grave carrying his severed head in his hands.) In the ninth century, the monks constructed a basilica at Saint-Denis, which housed the saint's tomb and those of nearly all the French kings dating back to the sixth century, as well as the crimson military banner that reputedly belonged to Charlemagne. The Carolingian basilica became France's royal church, the very symbol of the monarchy—just as Speyer Cathedral (FIG. 12-20) was the burial place of the German rulers of the Holy Roman Empire.

**SUGER AND SAINT-DENIS** By 1122, when a monk named Suger (ca. 1081–1151) became abbot of Saint-Denis, the old church was in disrepair and had become too small to accommodate the growing number of pilgrims. Suger also believed the basilica was of insufficient grandeur to serve as the official church of the French kings (see "Abbot Suger and the Rebuilding of Saint-Denis," page 367). In 1135, Suger began to rebuild the church (FIGS. 13-2 and 13-3) by

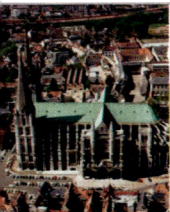

# GOTHIC EUROPE

| 1140 | Early Gothic | 1194 | High Gothic | 1300 | Late Gothic | 1500 |
|---|---|---|---|---|---|---|

**Early Gothic**
- Abbot Suger begins rebuilding the French royal abbey church at Saint-Denis with rib vaults on pointed arches and stained-glass windows
- As at Saint-Denis, sculpted jamb figures adorn all three portals of the west facade of Chartres Cathedral
- The builders of Laon Cathedral insert a triforium as the fourth story in the nave elevation

**High Gothic**
- The rebuilt Chartres Cathedral sets the pattern for High Gothic churches: four-part nave vaults braced by external flying buttresses, three-story elevation (arcade, triforium, clerestory), and stained-glass windows in place of heavy masonry
- At Chartres and Reims in France, at Naumburg in Germany, and elsewhere, statues become more independent of their architectural setting
- Manuscript illumination moves from monastic scriptoria to urban lay workshops, especially in Paris

**Late Gothic**
- The Flamboyant style in France and the Perpendicular style in England emphasize surface embellishment over structural clarity. Characteristic features are delicate webs of flamelike tracery and fan vaults with pendants resembling stalactites
- The humanization of holy figures in statuary continues, especially in Germany, where sculptors dramatically record the suffering of Jesus

## Abbot Suger and the Rebuilding of Saint-Denis

Abbot Suger of Saint-Denis (1081–1151) rose from humble parentage to become the right-hand man of both Louis VI (r. 1108–1137) and Louis VII (r. 1137–1180). When the latter, accompanied by his queen, Eleanor of Aquitaine, left to join the Second Crusade (1147–1149), Suger served as regent of France. From his youth, Suger wrote, he had dreamed of the possibility of embellishing the church in which most French monarchs since Merovingian times had been buried. Within 15 years of becoming abbot of Saint-Denis, Suger began rebuilding its Carolingian basilica. In his time, the French monarchy's power, except for scattered holdings, extended over an area not much larger than the Île-de-France, the region centered on Paris. But the kings had pretensions to rule all of France. Suger aimed to increase the prestige both of his abbey and of the monarchy by rebuilding France's royal church in grand fashion.

Suger wrote three detailed treatises about his activities as abbot, recording how he summoned masons and artists from many regions to help design and construct his new church. In one important passage, he described the special qualities of the new east end (FIGS. 13-2 and 13-3) dedicated in 1144:

> [I]t was cunningly provided that—through the upper columns and central arches which were to be placed upon the lower ones built in the crypt—the central nave of the old [Carolingian church] should be equalized, by means of geometrical and arithmetical instruments, with the central nave of the new addition; and, likewise, that the dimensions of the old side-aisles should be equalized with the dimensions of the new side-aisles, except for that elegant and praiseworthy extension in [the form of] a circular string of chapels, by virtue of which the whole [church] would shine with the wonderful and uninterrupted light of most sacred windows, pervading the interior beauty.*

The abbot's brief discussion of Sain-Denis's new ambulatory and chapels is key to understanding Early Gothic architecture. Suger wrote at much greater length, however, about his church's glorious golden and gem-studded furnishings. Here, for example, is his description of the *altar frontal* (the decorated panel on the front of the altar) in the choir:

> Into this panel, which stands in front of [Saint-Denis's] most sacred body, we have put . . . about forty-two marks of gold [and] a multifarious wealth of precious gems, hyacinths, rubies, sapphires, emeralds and topazes, and also an array of different large pearls.†

The costly furnishings and the light-filled space caused Suger to "delight in the beauty of the house of God" and "called [him] away from external cares." The new church made him feel as if he were "dwelling . . . in some strange region of the universe which neither exists entirely in the slime of the earth nor entirely in the purity of Heaven." In Suger's eyes, his splendid new church, permeated with light and outfitted with gold and precious gems, was a way station on the road to Paradise, which "transported [him] from this inferior to that higher world."‡ He regarded a lavish investment in art as a spiritual aid, not as an undesirable distraction for the pious monk, as did Bernard of Clairvaux (see "Bernard of Clairvaux," Chapter 12, page 342). Suger's forceful justification of art in the church set the stage for the proliferation of costly stained-glass windows and sculptures in the cathedrals of the Gothic age.

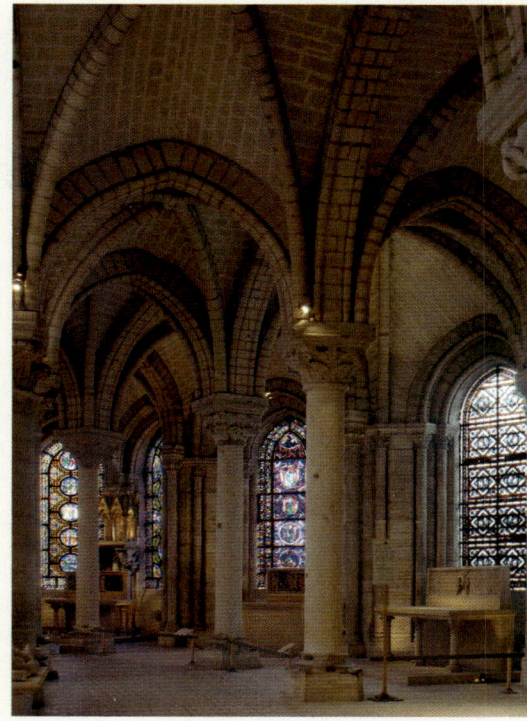

**13-2** Ambulatory and radiating chapels (looking northeast), abbey church, Saint-Denis, France, 1140–1144. ◼◂

Abbot Suger's remodeling of Saint-Denis marked the beginning of Gothic architecture. Rib vaults with pointed arches spring from slender columns. Stained-glass windows admit lux nova.

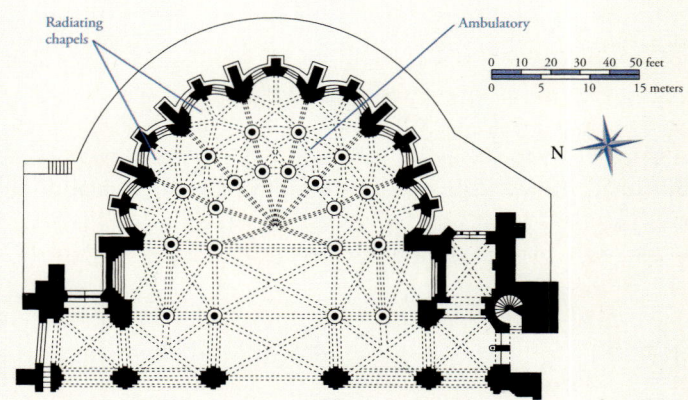

**13-3** Plan of the east end, abbey church, Saint-Denis, France, 1140–1144 (after Sumner Crosby).

The innovative plan of the east end of Saint-Denis dates to Abbot Suger's lifetime. By using very light rib vaults, the builders were able to eliminate the walls between the radiating chapels.

*Translated by Erwin Panofsky, *Abbot Suger on the Abbey Church of Saint-Denis and Its Art Treasures,* 2d ed. (Princeton: Princeton University Press, 1979), 101.
†Ibid., 55.
‡Ibid., 65.

# The Gothic Rib Vault

The ancestors of the Gothic *rib vault* are the Romanesque vaults found at Caen (FIG. 12-31), Durham (FIG. 12-33), and elsewhere. The rib vault's distinguishing feature is the crossed, or diagonal, arches under its groins, as seen in the Saint-Denis ambulatory and chapels (FIG. 13-2; compare FIG. 13-21). These arches form the *armature*, or skeletal framework, for constructing the vault. Gothic vaults generally have more thinly vaulted *webs* (the masonry between the ribs) than found in Romanesque vaults. But the chief difference between the two types of vaults is the *pointed arch*, an integral part of the Gothic skeletal armature. The first wide use of pointed (or *ogival*) arches was in Sasanian architecture (FIG. 2-28), and Islamic builders later adopted them. French Romanesque architects (FIGS. 12-10A and 12-11) borrowed the form from Muslim Spain and passed it to their Gothic successors. Pointed arches enabled Gothic builders to make the crowns of all the vault's arches approximately the same level, regardless of the space to be vaulted. Romanesque architects could not achieve this with their semicircular arches.

The drawings in FIG. 13-4 illustrate this key difference. In FIG. 13-4*a*, the rectangle *ABCD* is an oblong nave bay to be vaulted. *AC* and *DB* are the diagonal ribs; *AB* and *DC,* the transverse arches; and *AD* and *BC,* the nave arcade's arches. If the architect uses semi-circular arches (*AFB, BJC,* and *DHC*), their radii and, therefore, their heights (*EF, IJ,* and *GH*), will be different, because the width of a semicircular arch determines its height. The result will be a vault (FIG. 13-4*b*) with higher transverse arches (*DHC*) than the arcade's arches (*CJB*). The vault's crown (*F*) will be still higher. If the builder uses pointed arches (FIG. 13-4*c*), the transverse (*DLC*) and arcade (*BKC*) arches can have the same heights (*GL* and *IK* in FIG. 13-4*a*). The result will be a Gothic rib vault where the points of the arches (*L* and *K*) are at the same level as the vault's crown (*F*).

A major advantage of the Gothic vault is its flexibility, which permits the vaulting of compartments of varying shapes, as at Saint-Denis (FIG. 13-3). Pointed arches also channel the weight of the vaults more directly downward than do semicircular arches. The vaults therefore require less buttressing to hold them in place, in turn permitting the stonemasons to open up the walls and place large windows beneath the arches. Because pointed arches also lead the eye upward, they make the vaults appear taller than they are. In FIG. 13-4, the crown (*F*) of both the Romanesque (*b*) and Gothic (*c*) vaults is the same height from the pavement, but the Gothic vault seems taller. Both the physical and visual properties of rib vaults with pointed arches aided Gothic builders in their quest for soaring height in church interiors (FIG. 13-10).

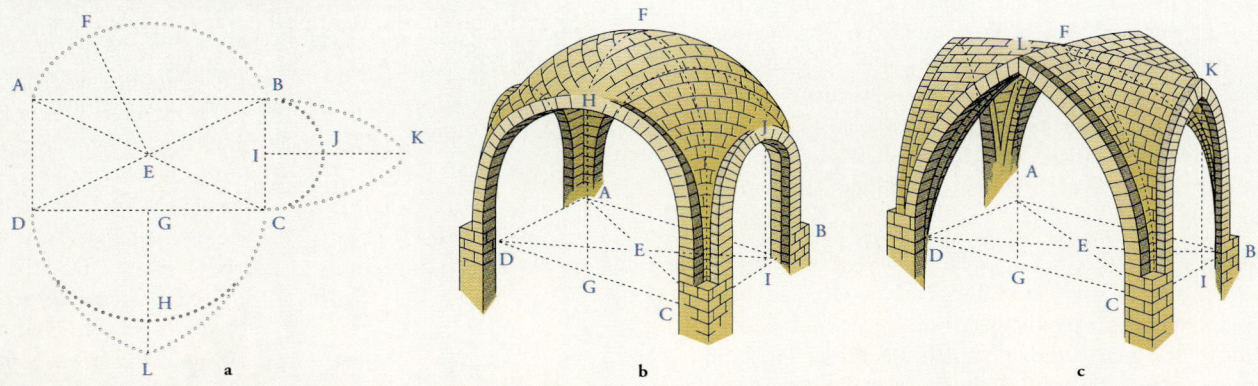

**13-4** Diagram (a) and drawings of rib vaults with semicircular (b) and pointed (c) arches.

Pointed arches channel the weight of the rib vaults more directly downward than do semicircular arches, requiring less buttressing. Pointed arches also make the vaults appear taller than they are.

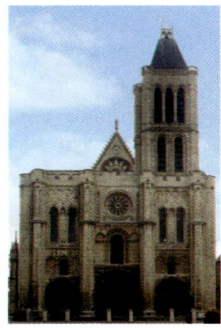

**13-3A** West facade, Saint-Denis, 1135–1140. ◼◀

erecting a new west facade (FIG. **13-3A**) with sculptured portals. Work began on the east end (FIGS. 13-2 and 13-3) in 1140. Suger died before he could remodel the nave, but he attended the dedication of the new choir, ambulatory, and radiating chapels on June 11, 1144. Also in attendance were King Louis VII of France, Queen Eleanor of Aquitaine (see "Romanesque Countesses, Queens, and Nuns," Chapter 12, page 352), and five archbishops. Because the French considered the old church a relic in its own right, the new east end had to conform to the dimensions of the crypt below it. Nevertheless, the remodeled portion of Saint-Denis represented a sharp break from past practice. Innovative rib vaults resting on pointed arches (see "The Gothic Rib Vault," above, and FIG. **13-4c**) cover the ambulatory and chapels (FIGS. 13-2 and 13-3). These pioneering, exceptionally lightweight vaults spring from slender columns in the ambulatory and from the thin masonry walls framing the chapels. The lightness of the vaults enabled the builders to eliminate the walls between the chapels and open up the outer walls and fill them with stained-glass windows (see "Stained-Glass Windows," page 375). Suger and his contemporaries marveled at the "wonderful and uninterrupted light" pouring in through the

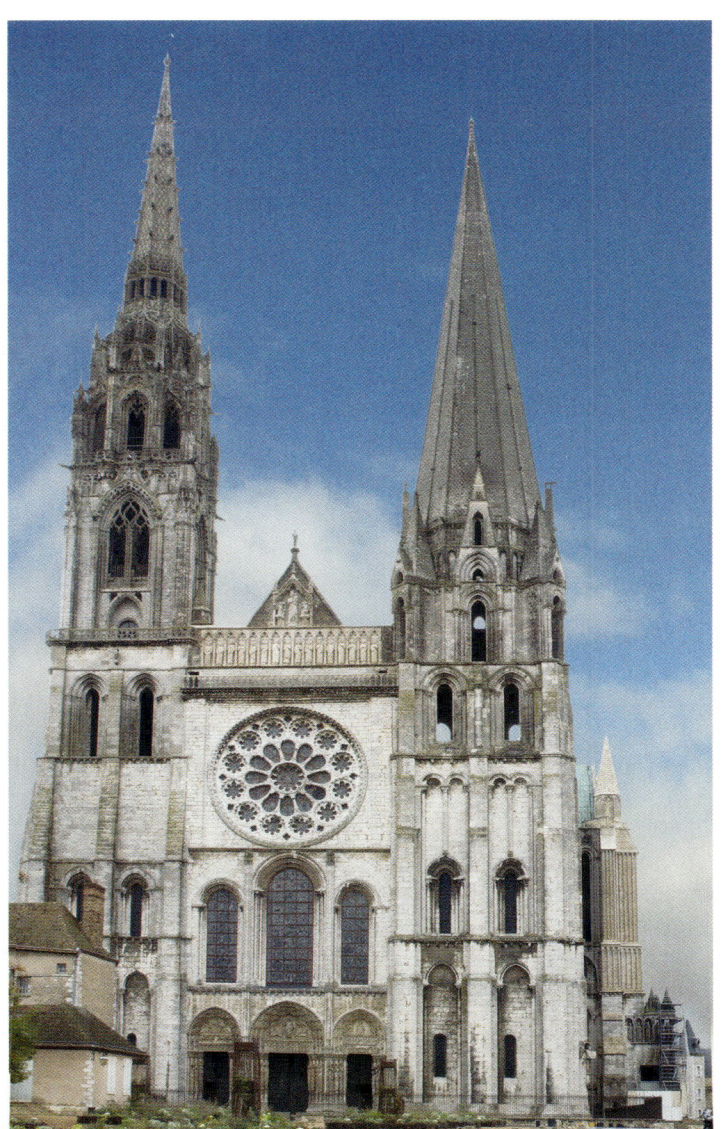

**13-5** West facade, Chartres Cathedral, Chartres, France, ca. 1145–1155. ◼◀

The Early Gothic west facade was all that remained of Chartres Cathedral after the 1194 fire. The design still has much in common with Romanesque facades. The rose window is an example of plate tracery.

"most sacred windows." The abbot called the colored light *lux nova* ("new light"). Both the new type of vaulting and the use of stained glass became hallmarks of French Gothic architecture.

Saint-Denis is also the key monument of Early Gothic sculpture. Little of the sculpture Suger commissioned for the west facade (FIG. 13-3A) of the abbey church survived the French Revolution of the late 18th century (see Chapter 26). Old engravings reveal Suger carried on the artistic heritage of Romanesque Burgundy (see Chapter 12) by filling all three portals with sculpture, but Suger's sculptors also introduced figures of Old Testament kings, queens, and prophets attached to columns on the jambs of all three doorways.

**ROYAL PORTAL, CHARTRES** This innovative treatment of the Saint-Denis portals appeared immediately afterward at the Cathedral of Notre Dame (FIG. 13-1) at Chartres, also in the Île-de-France. Work on the west facade (FIG. **13-5**) began around 1145. The west entrance, the Royal Portal (FIG. **13-6**)—so named because of the figures of kings and queens flanking its three doorways, as at Saint-Denis—constitutes the most complete surviving ensemble of Early Gothic sculpture. Thierry of Chartres, chancellor of the Cathedral School of Chartres from 1141 until his death 10 years later, may have conceived the complex iconographical program. The archivolts of the right portal, for example, depict the seven female personifications of the liberal arts with the learned men of antiquity at their feet. The figures celebrate the revival of classical scholarship in the 12th century and symbolize human knowledge, which Thierry and other leading intellectuals of the era believed led to true faith (see "Paris, Schoolmen, and Scholasticism" page 372).

The sculptures of the Royal Portal (FIG. 13-6) proclaim the majesty and power of Christ. To unite the three doorways iconographically and visually, the sculptors carved episodes from the lives of the Virgin (Notre Dame) and Christ on the capitals, which form a kind of frieze linking one entrance to the next. Christ's *Ascension* into Heaven appears in the tympanum of the left portal. All around, in the archivolts, are the signs of the zodiac and scenes representing the various labors of the months of the year. They are symbols of the cosmic and earthly worlds. The *Second Coming* is the subject of the central tympanum, as at Moissac

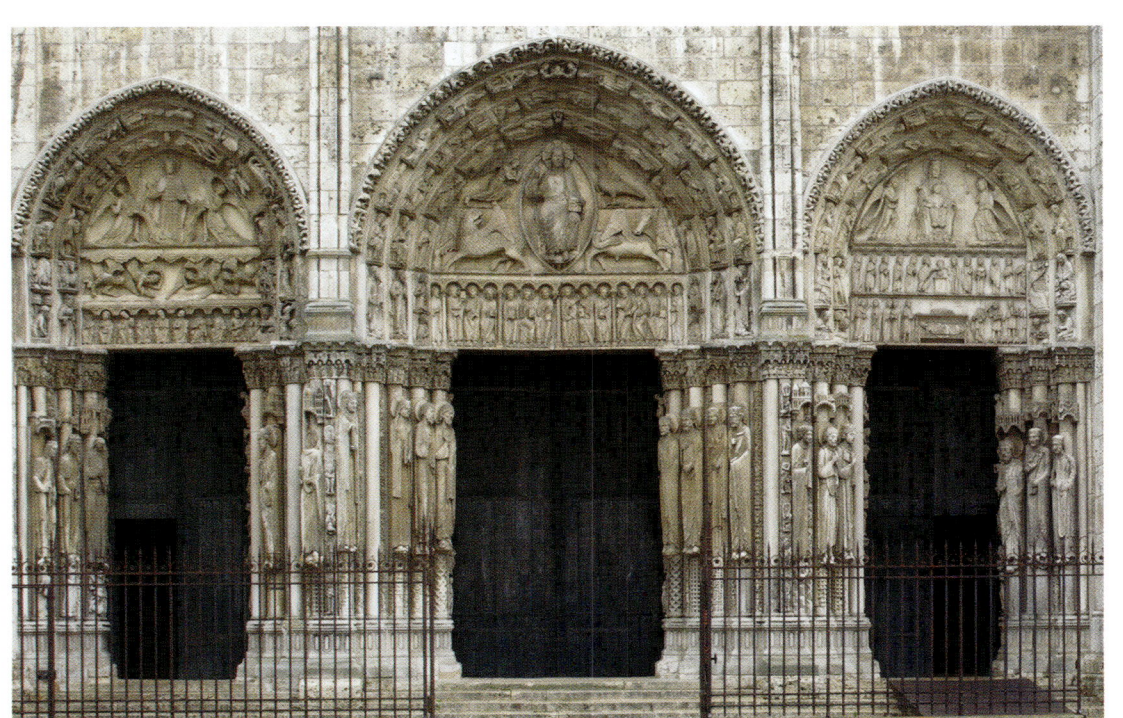

**13-6** Royal Portal, west facade, Chartres Cathedral, Chartres, France, ca. 1145–1155. ◼◀

The sculptures of the Royal Portal proclaim the majesty and power of Christ. The tympana depict, from left to right, Christ's *Ascension,* the *Second Coming,* and Jesus in the lap of the Virgin Mary.

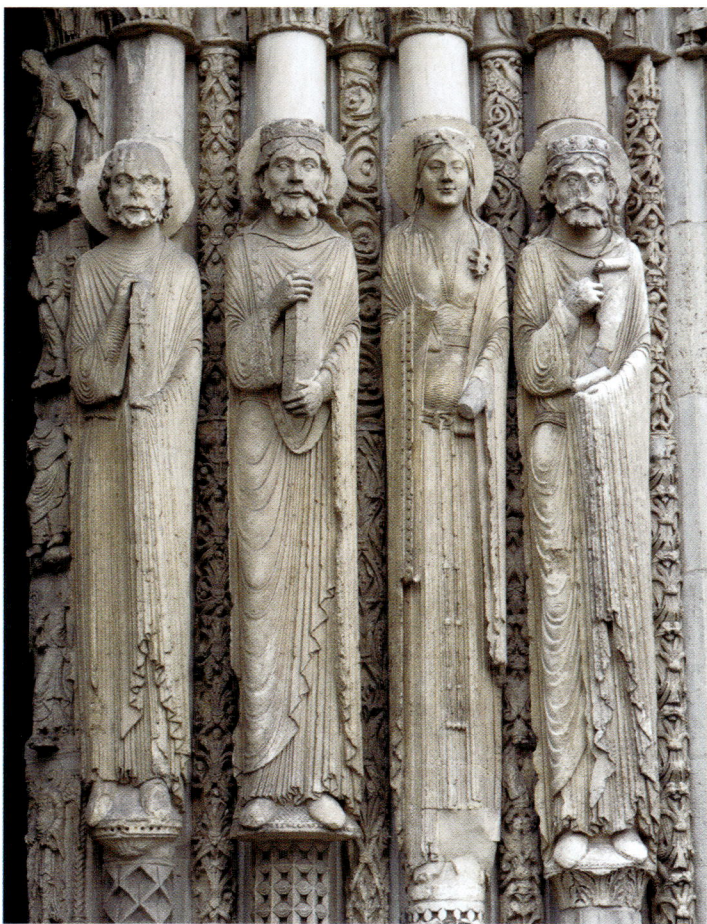

**13-7** Old Testament kings and queen, jamb statues, right side of the central doorway of the Royal Portal, Chartres Cathedral, Chartres, France, ca. 1145–1155. ■◀

The biblical kings and queens of the Royal Portal are the royal ancestors of Christ. These Early Gothic jamb figures display the first signs of a new naturalism in European sculpture.

(FIG. 12-11). The signs of the four evangelists, the 24 elders of the Apocalypse, and the 12 apostles appear around Christ or on the lintel. In the tympanum of the right portal, Christ appears in the lap of the Virgin Mary. Scenes of the Savior's childhood fill the lintel below, where Jesus appears on an altar, connecting the sculptures at the entrance to the church with the symbolic sacrifice of the Eucharist within.

The depiction of Mary in the right tympanum recalls Byzantine representations of the Theotokos (FIGS. 9-18 and 9-19), as well as the Romanesque "throne of wisdom" (FIG. 12-19). But the Virgin's prominence on the Chartres facade has no parallel in the sculptural programs of Romanesque church portals. At Chartres, Mary assumes a central role, a position she maintained throughout the Gothic period, during which time her cult reached a high point. As the Mother of Christ, she stood compassionately between the last judge and the horrors of Hell, interceding for all her faithful (compare FIG. 13-38B). Worshipers in the later 12th and 13th centuries sang hymns to the Virgin and dedicated great cathedrals to her. Soldiers carried her image into battle on banners, and Mary's name joined Saint Denis's as part of the French king's battle cry. The Virgin ("Our Lady") became the spiritual lady of chivalry, and the Christian knight dedicated his life to her. The severity of Romanesque themes stressing the last judgment yielded to the gentleness of Gothic art, in which Mary is the kindly queen of Heaven.

**JAMB STATUES** Statues of Old Testament kings and queens occupy the jambs flanking each doorway of the Royal Portal (FIGS. 13-6 and 13-7). They are the royal ancestors of Christ and, both figuratively and literally, support the New Testament figures above the doorways. They wear 12th-century clothes, and medieval observers may have regarded them as images of the kings and queens of France. (This was the motivation for vandalizing the comparable figures at Saint-Denis during the French Revolution.) The figures stand rigidly upright with their elbows held close against their hips. The linear folds of their garments—inherited from the Romanesque style, along with the elongated proportions—generally echo the vertical lines of the columns behind them. (In this respect, Gothic jamb statues differ significantly from classical caryatids; FIG. 5-54. The Gothic figures are *attached* to columns. The classical statues *replaced* the columns.) Yet, within and despite this architectural straitjacket, the statues display the first signs of a new naturalism. Although technically high reliefs, the kings and queens stand out from the plane of the wall, and, consistent with medieval (and ancient) practice, artists originally painted the statues in vivid colors, enhancing their lifelike appearance. The new naturalism is noticeable particularly in the statues' heads, where kindly human faces replace the masklike features of most Romanesque figures. At Chartres, a personalization of appearance began that led first to idealized portraits of the perfect Christian and finally, by 1400, to the portraiture of specific individuals. The sculptors of the Royal Portal figures initiated an era of artistic concern with personality and individuality.

**LAON CATHEDRAL** Both Chartres Cathedral and the abbey church of Saint-Denis had lengthy construction histories, and only small portions of the structures date to the Early Gothic period. Laon Cathedral (FIGS. 13-8 and 13-9), however, begun about 1160 and finished shortly after 1200, provides a comprehensive picture of French church architecture of the second half of the 12th century. Although the Laon builders retained many Romanesque features in their design, they combined them with the rib vault resting on pointed arches, the essential element of Early Gothic architecture.

Among the Laon plan's Romanesque features are the nave bays with their large sexpartite rib vaults, flanked by two small groin-vaulted squares in each aisle. The vaulting system (except for the pointed arches), as well as the vaulted gallery above the aisles, derived from Norman Romanesque churches such as Saint-Étienne (FIG. 12-31) at Caen. The Laon architect also employed the Romanesque alternate-support system in the nave arcade. Above the piers, alternating bundles of three and five shafts frame the aisle bays. A new feature found in the Laon interior, however, is the *triforium,* the band of arcades below the clerestory (FIGS. 13-9 and 13-10a). The triforium occupies the space corresponding to the exterior strip of wall covered by the sloping timber roof above the galleries. The insertion of the triforium into the Romanesque three-story nave elevation reflected a growing desire to break up all continuous wall surfaces. The new horizontal zone produced the characteristic four-story Early Gothic interior elevation: nave arcade, vaulted gallery, triforium, and clerestory with single *lancets* (tall, narrow windows ending in pointed arches).

Laon Cathedral's west facade (FIG. 13-8) signals an even more pronounced departure from the Romanesque style still lingering at Saint-Denis (FIG. 13-3A) and Chartres (FIG. 13-5). Typically Gothic are the huge central rose window, the deep porches in front of the doorways, and the open structure of the towers. A comparison of the facades of Laon Cathedral and Saint-Étienne (FIG. 12-30) at Caen reveals a much deeper penetration of the wall mass in the later building. At Laon, as in Gothic architecture generally, the

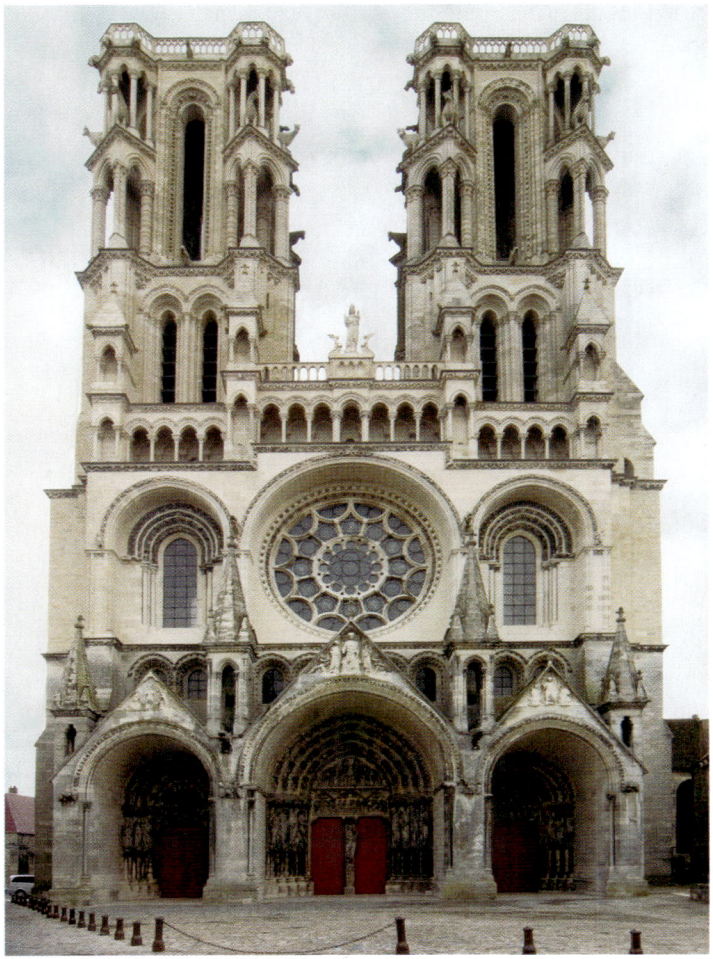

**13-8** West facade of Laon Cathedral, Laon, France, begun ca. 1190. ◼◀

The huge central rose window, the deep porches in front of the doorways, and the open structure of the towers distinguish Laon's Early Gothic facade from Romanesque church facades.

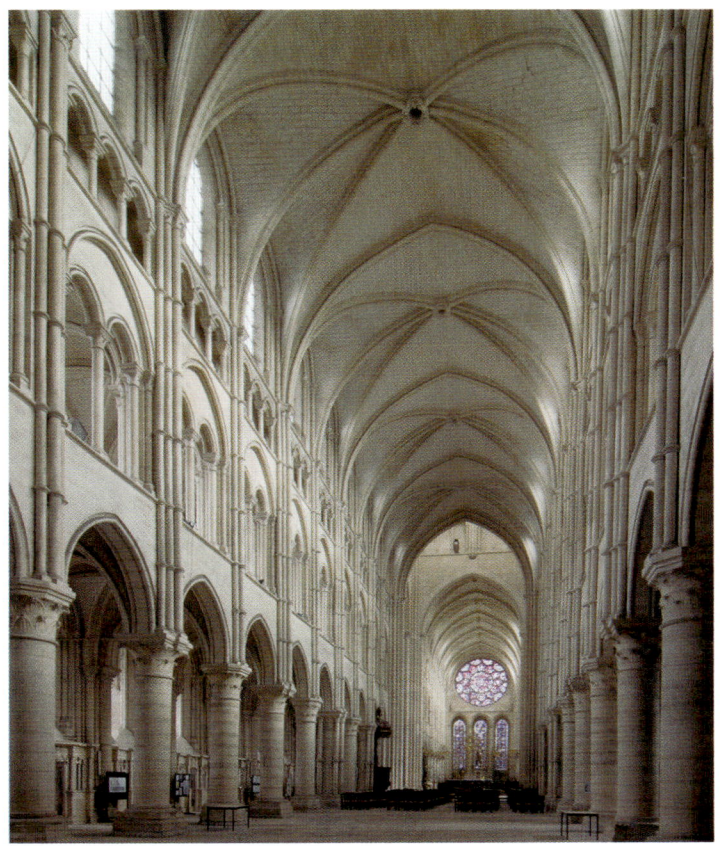

**13-9** Interior of Laon Cathedral (looking northeast), Laon, France, begun ca. 1190. ◼◀

The insertion of a triforium at Laon broke up the nave wall and produced the characteristic four-story Early Gothic interior elevation: nave arcade, vaulted gallery, triforium, and clerestory.

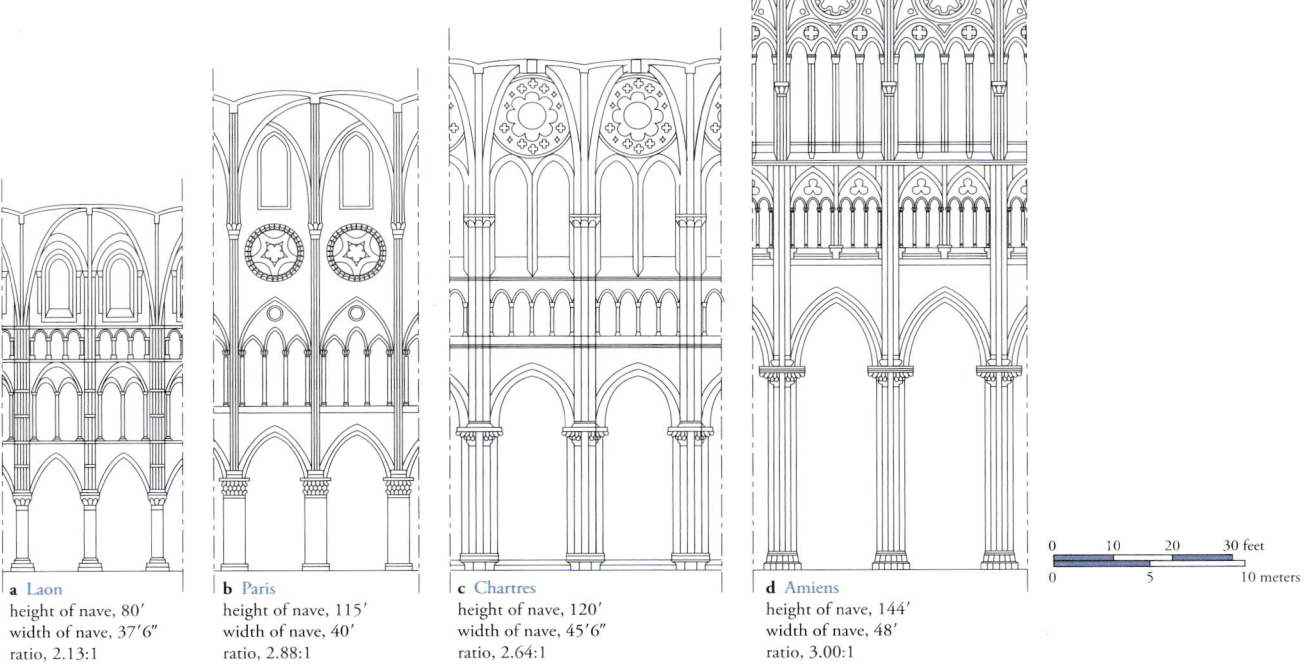

| **a** Laon | **b** Paris | **c** Chartres | **d** Amiens |
|---|---|---|---|
| height of nave, 80′ | height of nave, 115′ | height of nave, 120′ | height of nave, 144′ |
| width of nave, 37′6″ | width of nave, 40′ | width of nave, 45′6″ | width of nave, 48′ |
| ratio, 2.13:1 | ratio, 2.88:1 | ratio, 2.64:1 | ratio, 3.00:1 |

**13-10** Nave elevations of four French Gothic cathedrals at the same scale (after Louis Grodecki).

Gothic naves evolved from a four-story elevation (arcade, tribune gallery, triforium, clerestory) to a three-story elevation (without tribune). The height of the vaults also increased dramatically.

## Paris, Schoolmen, and Scholasticism

A few years before the formal consecration of the altar of the Cathedral of Notre-Dame (FIG. 13-11) in Paris, Philip II Augustus (r. 1180–1223) succeeded to the throne. Philip brought the feudal barons under his control and expanded the royal domains to include Normandy in the north and most of Languedoc in the south, laying the foundations for the modern nation of France. Renowned as "the maker of Paris," he gave the city its walls, paved its streets, and built the palace of the Louvre (now one of the world's great museums) to house the royal family. Although Rome remained the religious center of Western Christendom, the Île-de-France and Paris in particular became its intellectual capital as well as the leading artistic center of the Gothic world. The University of Paris attracted the best minds from all over Europe. Virtually every thinker of note in the Gothic age at some point studied or taught at Paris.

Even in the Romanesque period, Paris was a center of learning. Its Cathedral School professors, known as Schoolmen, developed the philosophy called *Scholasticism*. The greatest of the early Schoolmen was Peter Abelard (1079–1142), a champion of logical reasoning. Abelard and his contemporaries had been introduced to the writings of the Greek philosopher Aristotle through the Arabic scholars of Islamic Spain. Abelard applied Aristotle's system of rational inquiry to the interpretation of religious belief. Until the 12th century, both clergy and laymen considered truth the exclusive property of divine revelation as given in the holy scriptures. But the Schoolmen, using Aristotle's method, sought to demonstrate reason alone could lead to certain truths. Their goal was to prove the central articles of Christian faith by argument (*disputatio*). In Scholastic argument, Schoolmen state a possibility, then cite an authoritative view in objection, next reconcile the positions, and, finally, offer a reply to each of the rejected original arguments.

One of Abelard's greatest critics was Bernard of Clairvaux (see "Bernard of Clairvaux," Chapter 12, page 342), who believed Scholasticism

was equivalent to questioning Christian dogma. Although Bernard succeeded in 1140 in having the Church officially condemn Abelard's doctrines, the Schoolmen's philosophy developed systematically until it became the dominant Western philosophy of the late Middle Ages. By the 13th century, the Schoolmen of Paris already had organized as a professional guild of master scholars, separate from the numerous Church schools the bishop of Paris oversaw. The structure of the Parisian guild served as the model for many other European universities.

The greatest advocate of Abelard's Scholasticism was Thomas Aquinas (1225–1274), an Italian monk who became a saint in 1323. Aquinas settled in Paris in 1244. There, the German theologian Albertus Magnus (d. 1280) instructed him in Aristotelian philosophy. Aquinas went on to become an influential teacher at the University of Paris. His most famous work, *Summa Theologica* (left unfinished at his death), is a model of the Scholastic approach to knowledge. Aquinas divided his treatise into books, the books into questions, the questions into articles, each article into objections with contradictions and responses, and, finally, answers to the objections. He set forth five ways to prove the existence of God by rational argument. Aquinas's work remains the foundation of contemporary Catholic teaching.

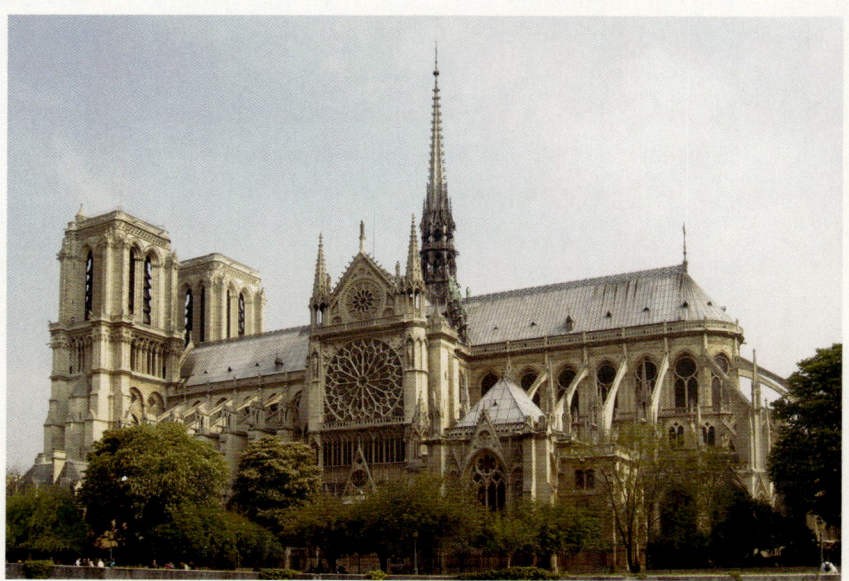

**13-11** Notre-Dame (looking north), Paris, France, begun 1163; nave and flying buttresses, ca. 1180–1200; remodeled after 1225. ◼◀

King Philip II initiated a building boom in Paris, which quickly became the intellectual capital of Europe. Notre-Dame in Paris was the first great cathedral built using flying buttresses.

operating principle was to reduce sheer mass and replace it with intricately framed voids.

**NOTRE-DAME, PARIS** About 1130, Louis VI moved his official residence to Paris, spurring much commercial activity and a great building boom. Paris soon became the leading city and intellectual capital of France, indeed of all northern Europe (see "Paris, Schoolmen, and Scholasticism," above). A new cathedral became a necessity. Notre-Dame (FIG. 13-11) occupies a picturesque site on an island in the Seine River called the Île-de-la-Cité. The Gothic church (see "The Gothic Cathedral," page 373), which replaced a large Merovingian basilica, has a complicated building

history. The choir and transept were completed by 1182, the nave by about 1225, and the facade not until 1250 to 1260. Sexpartite vaults cover the nave, as at Laon. The original elevation (the builders modified the design as work progressed) had four stories, but the scheme (FIG. 13-10b) differed from Laon's (FIG. 13-10a). In each bay, in place of the triforium over the gallery, was a stained-glass *oculus* (small round window), opening up the wall below the clerestory lancet. As a result, windows filled two of the four stories, further reducing the masonry area.

To hold the much thinner—and taller (compare FIGS. 13-10a and 13-10b)—walls of Notre-Dame in place, the unknown architect introduced *flying buttresses* that spring from the lower roofs over the

# The Gothic Cathedral

The great cathedrals erected throughout Europe in the later 12th and 13th centuries are the enduring symbols of the Gothic age. They are eloquent testimonies to the extraordinary skill of the architects, engineers, carpenters, masons, sculptors, glassworkers, and metalsmiths who constructed and embellished them. Most of the architectural components of Gothic cathedrals had appeared in earlier structures, but Gothic architects combined the elements in new ways. The essential ingredients of their formula for constructing churches in the *opus modernum* style were rib vaults with pointed arches (see "The Gothic Rib Vault," page 368), flying buttresses, and huge colored-glass windows (see "Stained-Glass Windows," page 375). These three features and other important terms used in describing Gothic buildings are listed and defined here and illustrated in FIG. 13-12.

▌ *Pinnacle* (FIG. 13-12, no. 1) A sharply pointed ornament capping the piers or flying buttresses; also used on cathedral facades.

▌ *Flying buttresses* (2) Masonry struts that transfer the thrust of the nave vaults across the roofs of the side aisles and ambulatory to a tall pier rising above the church's exterior wall.

▌ *Vaulting web* (3) The masonry blocks filling the area between the ribs of a groin vault.

▌ *Diagonal rib* (4) In plan, one of the ribs forming the X of a groin vault. In FIG. 13-4, the diagonal ribs are the lines AC and DB.

▌ *Transverse rib* (5) A rib crossing the nave or aisle at a 90-degree angle (lines *AB* and *DC* in FIG. 13-4).

▌ *Springing* (6) The lowest stone of an arch; in Gothic vaulting, the lowest stone of a diagonal or transverse rib.

▌ *Clerestory* (7) The windows below the vaults in the nave elevation's uppermost level. By using flying buttresses and rib vaults on pointed arches, Gothic architects could build huge clerestory windows and fill them with *stained glass* held in place by ornamental stonework called *tracery*.

▌ *Oculus* (8) A small, round window.

▌ *Lancet* (9) A tall, narrow window crowned by a pointed arch.

▌ *Triforium* (10) The story in the nave elevation consisting of arcades, usually blind arcades but occasionally filled with stained glass.

▌ *Nave arcade* (11) The series of arches supported by piers separating the nave from the side aisles.

▌ *Compound pier (cluster pier) with shafts (responds)* (12) A pier with a group, or cluster, of attached shafts, or responds, extending to the springing of the vaults.

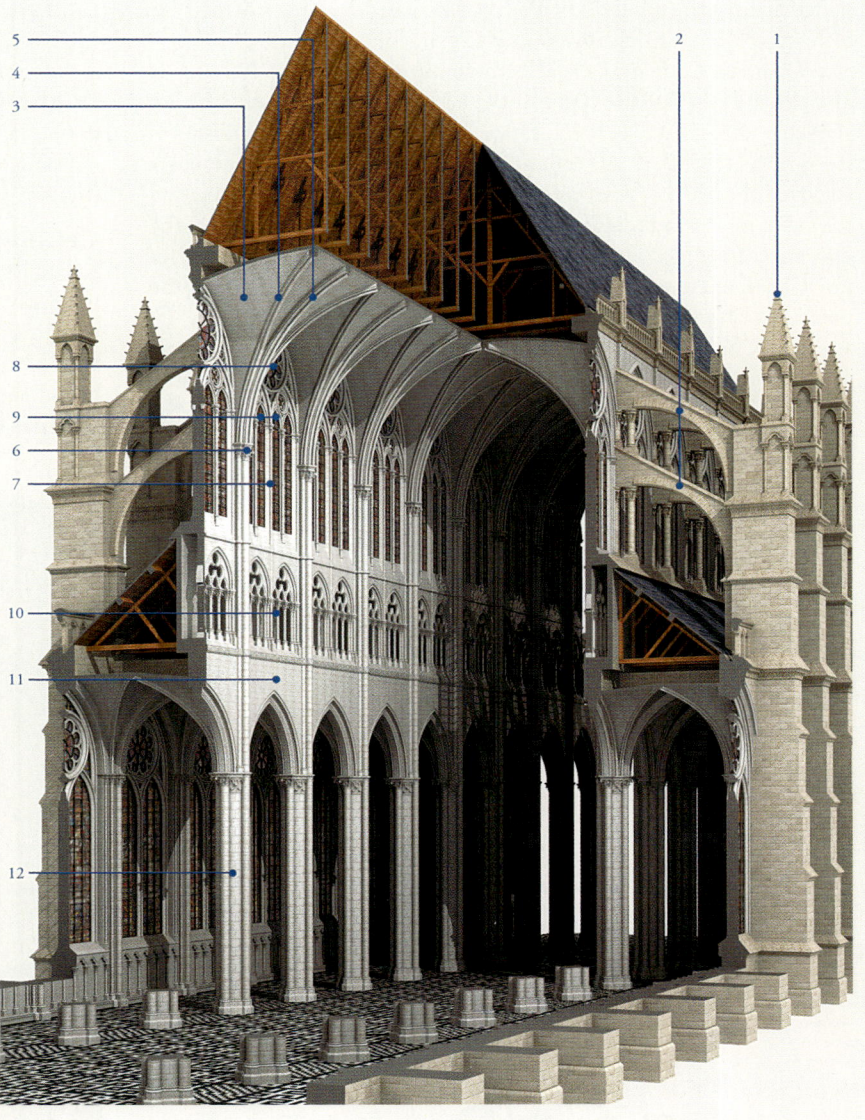

**13-12** Cutaway view of a typical French Gothic cathedral (John Burge). ■◀

The major elements of the Gothic formula for constructing a church in the *opus modernum* style were rib vaults with pointed arches, flying buttresses, and stained-glass windows.

aisles and ambulatory (FIG. 13-11; compare FIG. 13-12) and counter the outward thrust of the nave vaults. Gothic builders introduced flying buttresses as early as 1150 in a few smaller churches, but at Notre-Dame in Paris they circle a great urban cathedral. The internal quadrant arches (FIG. 12-33, *right*) beneath the aisle roofs at Durham, also employed at Laon, perform a similar function and may be regarded as precedents for exposed Gothic flying buttresses. The combination of precisely positioned flying buttresses and rib vaults with pointed arches was the ideal solution to the problem of constructing lofty naves with huge windows. The flying buttresses, which function as extended fingers holding up the walls, are key components of the distinctive "look" of Gothic cathedrals (FIG. 13-12).

**CHARTRES AFTER 1194** Churches burned frequently in the Middle Ages (see "Timber Roofs," Chapter 12, page 339), and church officials often had to raise money unexpectedly for new building campaigns. In contrast to monastic churches, which usually were small and often could be completed quickly, the construction histories of urban cathedrals frequently extended over decades and sometimes over centuries. Their financing depended largely on collections and public contributions (not always voluntary), and a lack of funds often interrupted building programs. Unforeseen events, such as wars, famines, or plagues, or friction between the town and cathedral authorities would also often halt construction, which then might not resume for years. At Reims (FIG. 13-23), the clergy offered *indulgences* (pardons for sins committed) to those who helped underwrite the enormous cost of erecting the cathedral. The rebuilding of Chartres Cathedral (FIG. 13-1) after the devastating fire of 1194 took a relatively short 27 years, but at one point the townspeople revolted against the prospect of a heavier tax burden. They stormed the bishop's residence and drove him into exile for four years.

Chartres Cathedral's mid-12th-century west facade (FIG. 13-5) and the masonry of the crypt to the east were the only sections left standing after the 1194 conflagration. The crypt housed the most precious relic of Chartres—the mantle of the Virgin, which miraculously survived the fire. For reasons of piety and economy, the builders used the crypt for the foundation of the new structure. The retention of the crypt and west facade determined the new church's dimensions but not its plan or elevation. Architectural historians usually consider the post-1194 Chartres Cathedral the first High Gothic building.

The Chartres plan (FIG. **13-13**) reveals a new kind of organization. Rectangular nave bays replaced the square bays with sexpartite vaults and the alternate-support system, still present in Early Gothic churches such as Laon Cathedral (FIG. 13-9). The new system, in which a single square in each aisle (rather than two, as before) flanks a single rectangular unit in the nave, became the High Gothic norm. A change in vault design and the abandonment of the alternate-support system usually accompanied this new bay arrangement. The High Gothic nave vault, which covered only one bay and therefore could be braced more easily than its Early Gothic predecessor, had only four parts. The visual effect of these changes was to unify the interior (FIG. 13-14), because the nave now consisted of a sequence of identical units. The level crowns of the successive nave vaults, which pointed arches made possible, enhanced this effect.

The 1194 Chartres Cathedral was also the first church planned from its inception to have flying buttresses, another key High Gothic feature. The flying buttresses enabled the builders to eliminate the tribune above the aisle, which had partially braced Romanesque and Early Gothic naves (compare FIG. 13-10c with FIGS. 13-10a and 13-10b). The new High Gothic tripartite nave elevation consisted of arcade, triforium, and clerestory with greatly enlarged windows. The Chartres windows are almost as tall as the main arcade and consist of double lancets with a single crowning oculus. The strategic placement of flying buttresses made possible the construction of nave walls with so many voids that heavy masonry played merely a minor role.

**CHARTRES STAINED GLASS** Despite the vastly increased size of its clerestory windows, the Chartres nave (FIG. 13-14) is relatively dark. This seeming contradiction is the result of using light-muffling colored glass for the windows instead of clear glass. The purpose of the Chartres windows was not to illuminate the interior with bright sunlight but to transform natural light into Suger's mystical *lux nova* (see "Stained-Glass Windows," page 375, and FIG. **13-15**).

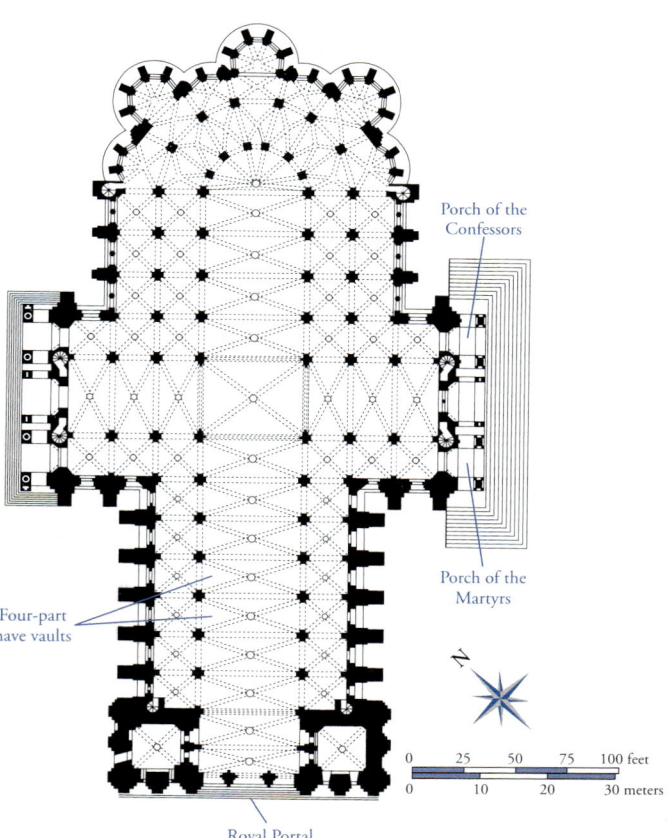

**13-13** Plan of Chartres Cathedral, Chartres, France, as rebuilt after the 1194 fire (after Paul Frankl).

The Chartres plan, in which one square (instead of two) in each aisle flanks a single rectangular unit in the nave with a four-part vault, became the norm for High Gothic church architecture.

Porch of the Confessors

Porch of the Martyrs

N

Four-part nave vaults

0   25   50   75   100 feet
0   10   20   30 meters

Royal Portal

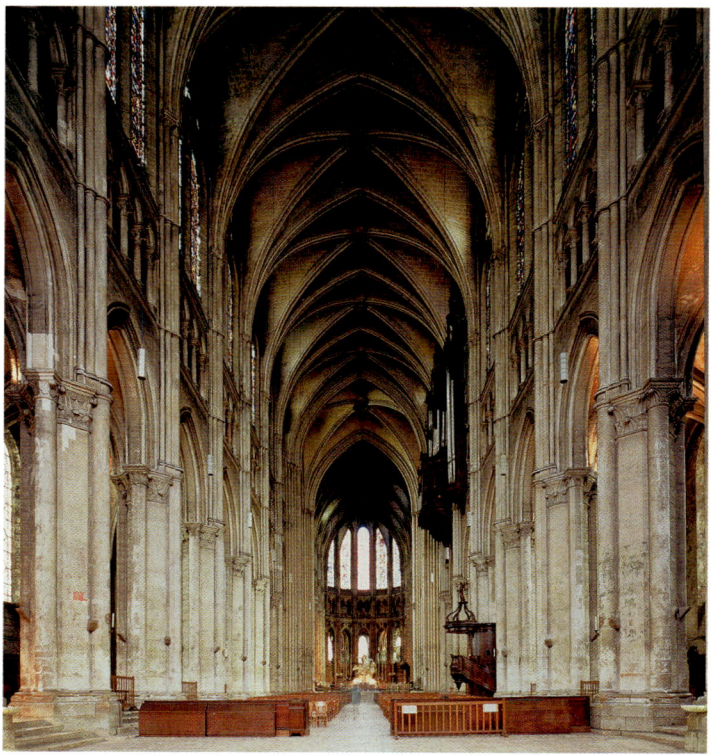

**13-14** Interior of Chartres Cathedral (looking east), Chartres, France, begun 1194. ◼◀

Chartres Cathedral established the High Gothic model also in its tripartite elevation consisting of nave arcade, triforium, and clerestory with stained-glass windows almost as tall as the main arcade.

## Stained-Glass Windows

Stained-glass windows, although not a Gothic invention, are almost synonymous with Gothic architecture. No other age produced windows of such rich color and beauty. The technology of manufacturing colored glass is very old, however. Egyptian artists excelled at fashioning colorful glass objects for both home and tomb, and archaeologists have uncovered thousands of colored-glass artifacts at classical sites. But Gothic artists used stained glass in new ways. In earlier eras, the clergy introduced color and religious iconography into church interiors mainly with mural paintings and mosaics, often with magnificent effect. Stained-glass windows differ from those techniques in one all-important respect. They do not conceal walls. They replace them. Moreover, they transmit rather than reflect light, filtering and transforming the natural sunlight.

Abbot Suger called this colored light *lux nova* (see "Abbot Suger," page 367). Suger's contemporary, Hugh of Saint-Victor (1096–1142), a prominent Parisian theologian, also commented on the special mystical quality of stained-glass windows: "Stained-glass windows are the Holy Scriptures . . . and since their brilliance lets the splendor of the True Light pass into the church, they enlighten those inside."* William Durandus (ca. 1237–1296), bishop of Mende (southern France), expressed a similar sentiment at the end of the 13th century: "The glass windows in a church are Holy Scriptures, which expel the wind and the rain, that is, all things hurtful, but transmit the light of the True Sun, that is, God, into the hearts of the faithful."†

According to Suger, the 12th-century stained-glass windows of Saint-Denis (FIG. 13-2) were "painted by the exquisite hands of many masters from different regions," proving the art was well established at that time. ‡ In fact, colored windows appeared in some churches as early as the fourth century, and several sophisticated Romanesque examples of figural stained-glass windows survive. The manufacture of these windows was costly and labor-intensive. A German Benedictine monk named Theophilus recorded the full process around 1100. First, the master designer drew the exact composition of the planned window on a wooden panel, indicating all the linear details and noting the colors for each section. Glassblowers provided flat sheets of glass of different colors to *glaziers* (glassworkers), who cut the windowpanes to the required size and shape with special iron shears. Glaziers produced an even greater range of colors by *flashing* (fusing one layer of colored glass to another). Next, painters added details such as faces, hands, hair, and clothing in enamel by tracing the master design on the wood panel through the colored glass. Then they heated the painted glass to fuse the enamel to the surface. Next the glaziers "leaded" the various fragments of glass—that is, they joined them by strips of lead called *cames*. The *leading* not only held the pieces together but also separated the colors to heighten the effect of the design as a whole. The distinctive character of Gothic stained-glass windows is largely the result of this combination of fine linear details with broad flat expanses of color framed by black lead. Finally, the glassworkers strengthened the completed window with an armature of iron bands, which in the 12th century formed a grid over the entire design (FIG. 13-16). In the 13th century, the bands followed the outlines of the medallions and of the surrounding areas (FIGS. 13-15, 13-17, and 13-25).

The form of the stone frames for the stained-glass windows also evolved. At Saint-Denis (FIG. 13-3A), Laon (FIG. 13-8), and on Chartres Cathedral's 12th-century west facade (FIG. 13-5), *plate tracery* holds the rose window in place. The glass fills only the "punched holes" in the heavy ornamental stonework. *Bar tracery,* a later development, is much more slender. The stained-glass windows of the Chartres transepts (FIG. 13-17) and on the facades of Amiens (FIG. 13-21) and Reims (FIG. 13-23) cathedrals fill almost the entire opening, and the stonework is unobtrusive, resembling delicate leading more than masonry wall.

*Hugh of Saint-Victor, *Speculum de mysteriis ecclesiae,* sermon 2.
†William Durandus, *Rationale divinorum officiorum,* 1.1.24. Translated by John Mason Neale and Benjamin Webb, *The Symbolism of Churches and Church Ornaments* (Leeds: T. W. Green, 1843), 28.
‡Translated by Erwin Panofsky, *Abbot Suger,* 73.

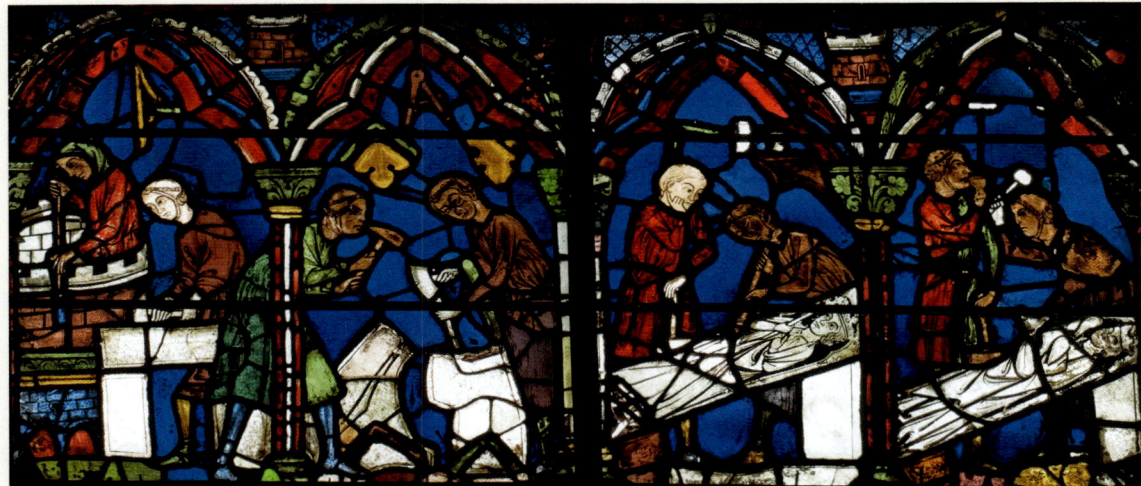

**13-15** Stonemasons and sculptors, detail of a stained-glass window in the northernmost radiating chapel in the ambulatory, Chartres Cathedral, Chartres, France, ca. 1200–1220. ◼◀

Glaziers made stained-glass windows by fusing layers of colored glass, joining the pieces with lead strips, and painting the details in enamel. The windows transformed natural light into divine light.

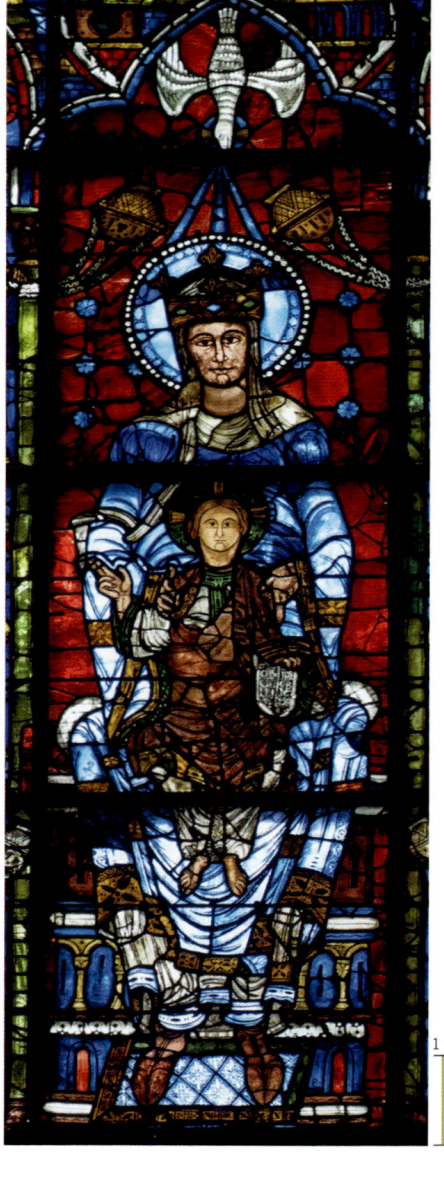

**13-16** Virgin and Child and angels (*Notre Dame de la Belle Verrière*), detail of a window in the choir of Chartres Cathedral, Chartres, France, ca. 1170, with 13th-century side panels. Stained glass, 12′ 9″ high. ◼◀

This stained-glass window miraculously survived the devastating Chartres fire of 1194. It has an armature of iron bands forming a grid over the entire design, an Early Gothic characteristic.

Chartres Cathedral retains almost the full complement of its original stained glass, paid for by workers' guilds (FIG. 13-15) and royalty (FIG. 13-17) alike. Although the tinted windows have a dimming effect, they transform the character of the church's interior in dramatic fashion. Gothic buildings that no longer have their original stained-glass windows give a false impression of what their designers intended.

1 ft.

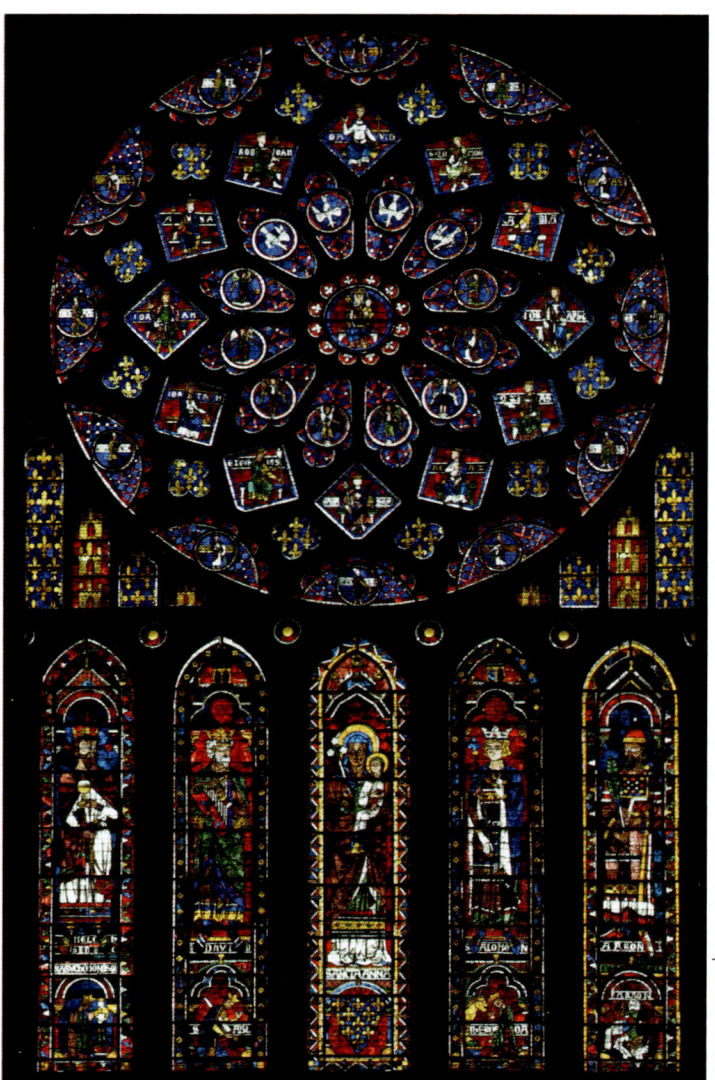

**13-17** Rose window and lancets, north transept, Chartres Cathedral, Chartres, France, ca. 1220. Stained glass, rose window 43′ in diameter. ◼◀

Immense stained-glass rose and lancet windows, held in place by an intricate armature of bar tracery, fill almost the entire facade wall of the High Gothic north transept of Chartres Cathedral.

10 ft.

One Chartres window that survived the fire of 1194 is the tall single lancet called *Notre Dame de la Belle Verrière* (Our Lady of the Beautiful Window, FIG. 13-16). The central section with a red background, which depicts the Virgin Mary enthroned with the Christ Child in her lap, dates to about 1170. High Gothic glaziers added framing angels seen against a blue ground when they reinstalled the window in the south aisle of the 13th-century choir. Mary is here the beautiful young queen of Heaven, haloed, crowned, and accompanied by the dove of the Holy Spirit. Comparing this Virgin and Child with the enthroned Theotokos and Child (FIG. 9-19) of Hagia Sophia highlights not only the greater severity and aloofness of the Byzantine image but also the sharp difference between the light-reflecting mosaic medium and Gothic light-filtering stained glass. Gothic and Byzantine builders used light to transform the material world into the spiritual, but in opposite ways. In Gothic architecture, light entered from outside the building through a screen of stone-set colored glass. In Byzantine architecture, light reflected off myriad glass tesserae set into the thick masonry wall.

Chartres's 13th-century Gothic windows are even more spectacular than the *Belle Verrière* because the introduction of flying buttresses made it possible for builders to plan from the outset on filling entire walls with stained glass. The immense rose window (approx-

imately 43 feet in diameter) and tall lancets of the north transept (FIG. 13-17) were the gift of Queen Blanche of Castile, around 1220. The royal motifs of yellow castles on a red ground and yellow *fleurs-de-lis*—three-petaled iris flowers (compare FIG. 25-24), France's royal floral emblem—on a blue ground fill the eight narrow windows in the rose's lower spandrels. The iconography is also fitting for a queen. The enthroned Virgin and Child appear in the roundel at the center of the rose, which resembles a gem-studded book cover or cloisonné brooch. Around her are four doves of the Holy Spirit and eight angels. Twelve square panels contain images of Old Testament kings, including David and Solomon (at the 12 and 1 o'clock positions respectively). These are the royal ancestors of Christ. Isaiah (11:1–3) had prophesied the Messiah would come from the family of the patriarch Jesse, father of David. The genealogical "tree of Jesse" is a familiar motif in medieval art. Below, in the lancets, are Saint Anne and the baby Virgin. Flanking them are four of Christ's Old Testament ancestors, Melchizedek, David, Solomon, and Aaron, echoing the royal genealogy of the rose

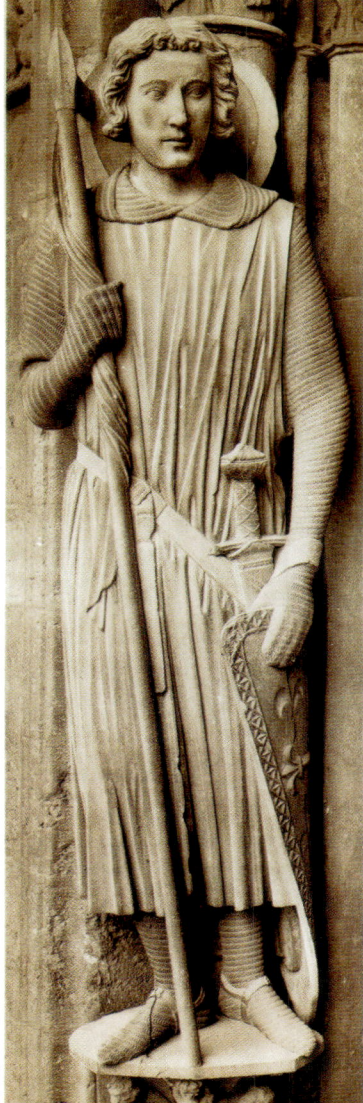

**13-18** Saint Theodore, jamb statue, left portal, Porch of the Martyrs, south transept, Chartres Cathedral, Chartres, France, ca. 1230.

Although the statue of Theodore is still attached to a column, the setting no longer determines its pose. The High Gothic sculptor portrayed the saint in a contrapposto stance, as in classical statuary.

but at a larger scale. Many Gothic stained-glass windows also present narrative scenes, and their iconographical programs are often more complex than those of the sculptured church portals. (The representation of masons and sculptors at work in FIG. 13-15, for example, is the lowest section of a lancet dedicated to the life of Caraunus—Chéron in French—a legendary local sixth-century martyr who was probably the patron saint of the Chartres stonemasons' guild.)

The rose and lancets change in hue and intensity with the hours, turning solid architecture into a floating vision of the celestial heavens. Almost the entire mass of wall opens up into stained glass, held in place by an intricate stone armature of bar tracery. Here, the Gothic passion for luminous colored light led to a most daring and successful attempt to subtract all superfluous material bulk just short of destabilizing the structure. That this vast, complex fabric of stone-set glass has maintained its structural integrity for almost 800 years attests to the Gothic builders' engineering genius.

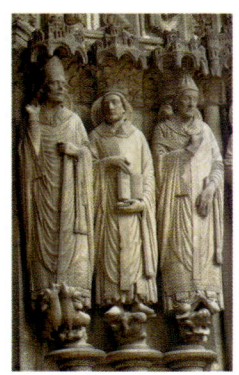

**13-18A** Porch of the Confessors, Chartres, ca. 1220–1230. ◼◀

## CHARTRES SOUTH TRANSEPT

The sculptures adorning the portals of the two Chartres transepts erected after the 1194 fire are also prime examples of the new High Gothic spirit. As at Laon (FIG. 13-8) and Paris (FIG. 13-11) cathedrals, the Chartres transept portals project more forcefully from the church than do the Early Gothic portals of its west facade (compare FIGS. 13-1 and 13-5). Similarly, the statues of saints (FIGS. **13-18** and **13-18A**) on the portal jambs, which date from 1220 to 1230, are more independent from the architectural framework. Although the figures

are still attached to columns, the architectural setting does not determine their poses as much as it did on the west portals (FIG. 13-7).

The masterpiece of the south transept is the figure of Saint Theodore (FIG. 13-18), the martyred warrior on the left jamb of the left portal (the Porch of the Martyrs). It reveals the great changes Gothic sculpture had undergone since the Royal Portal statues of the mid-12th century. The High Gothic sculptor portrayed Theodore as the ideal Christian knight, clothing him in the cloak and chain-mail armor of 13th-century Crusaders. The handsome, long-haired youth holds his spear firmly in his right hand and rests his left hand on his shield. He turns his head to the left and swings out his hip to the right. The body's resulting torsion and pronounced sway recall ancient Greek statuary, especially the contrapposto stance of Polykleitos's *Spear Bearer* (FIG. 5-40). The changes that occurred in 13th-century Gothic sculpture echo the revolutionary developments in ancient Greek sculpture during the transition from the Archaic to the Classical style (see Chapter 5) and could appropriately be described as a second "Classical revolution."

**AMIENS CATHEDRAL** Chartres Cathedral was one of the most influential buildings in the history of architecture. Its builders set a pattern many other Gothic architects followed, even if they refined the details. Construction of Amiens Cathedral (FIG. **13-19**) began in 1220 while work was still in progress at Chartres. The architects were ROBERT DE LUZARCHES, THOMAS DE CORMONT, and RENAUD

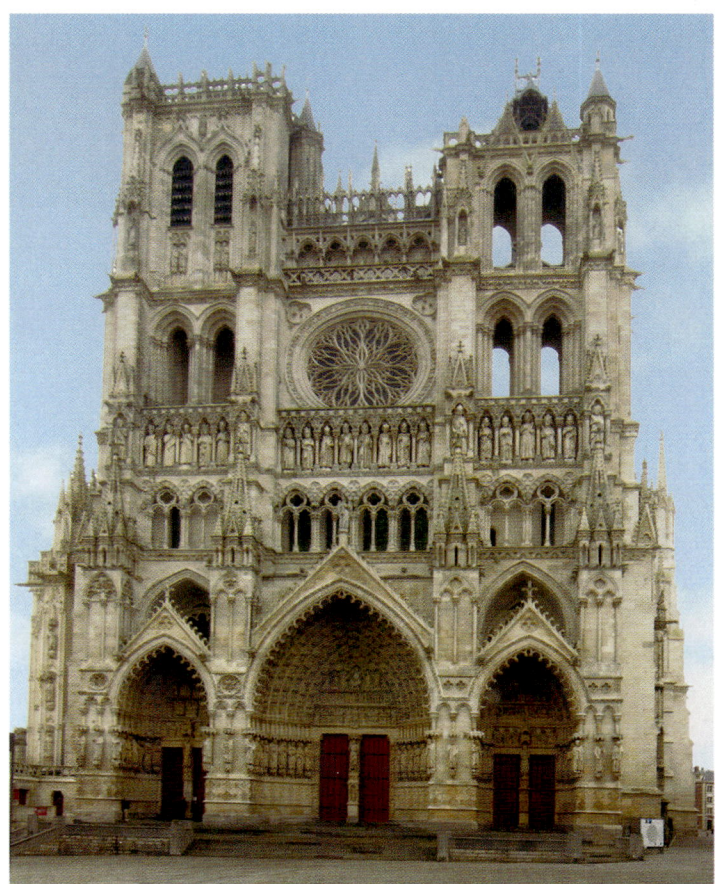

**13-19** ROBERT DE LUZARCHES, THOMAS DE CORMONT, and RENAUD DE CORMONT, west facade of Amiens Cathedral, Amiens, France, begun 1220. ◼◀

The deep piercing of the Amiens facade left few surfaces for decoration, but sculptors covered the remaining ones with colonnettes, pinnacles, and rosettes that nearly dissolve the structure's masonry.

France　377

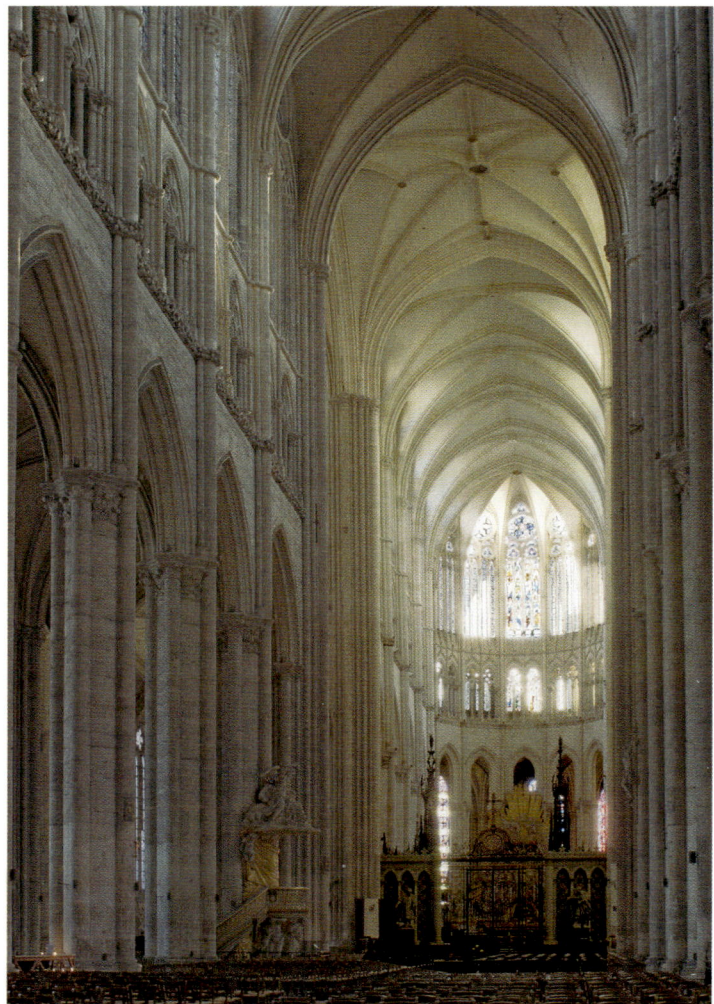

13-20 ROBERT DE LUZARCHES, THOMAS DE CORMONT, and RENAUD DE CORMONT, interior of Amiens Cathedral (looking east), Amiens, France, begun 1220. ◼◀

The concept of a self-sustaining skeletal architecture reached full maturity at Amiens Cathedral. The four-part vaults on pointed arches rise an astounding 144 feet above the nave floor.

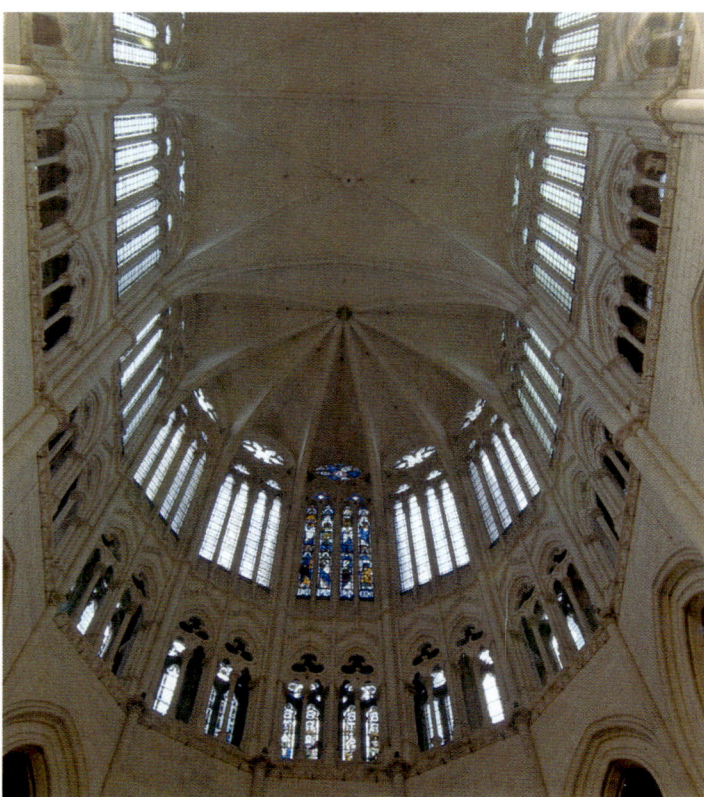

13-21 ROBERT DE LUZARCHES, THOMAS DE CORMONT, and RENAUD DE CORMONT, vaults, clerestory, and triforium of the choir of Amiens Cathedral, Amiens, France, begun 1220. ◼◀

The Amiens choir vaults resemble a canopy on bundled masts. The light entering from the clerestory and triforium creates a buoyant lightness not normally associated with stone architecture.

DE CORMONT. The builders finished the nave (FIG. **13-20**) by 1236 and the radiating chapels by 1247, but work on the choir (FIG. **13-21**) continued until almost 1270. The Amiens elevation (FIG. 13-10d) derived from the High Gothic formula of Chartres (FIG. 13-10c). But Amiens Cathedral's proportions are more slender, and the number and complexity of the lancet windows in both its clerestory and triforium are greater. The whole design reflects the builders' confident use of the complete High Gothic structural vocabulary: the rectangular-bay system, the four-part rib vault, and a buttressing system that made possible the almost complete elimination of heavy masses and thick weight-bearing walls. At Amiens, the concept of a self-sustaining skeletal architecture reached full maturity. The remaining stretches of wall seem to serve no purpose other than to provide a weather screen for the interior.

Amiens Cathedral is one of the most impressive examples of the French Gothic obsession with constructing ever-taller cathedrals. Using their new skeletal frames of stone, French builders attempted goals almost beyond limit, pushing to new heights with increasingly slender supports. The nave vaults at Laon rise to a

height of about 80 feet, at Paris 115 feet, and at Chartres 120 feet. Those at Amiens are 144 feet above the floor (FIG. 13-10). The most daring quest for exceptional height occurred at Beauvais (FIG. I-2), where the choir vaults are 157 feet high—but the builders never completed the cathedral. The Beauvais vaults are unstable and require additional buttressing today.

At Amiens, the lines of the vault ribs converge to the colonnettes and speed down the shell-like walls to the compound piers (FIG. 13-20). Almost every part of the superstructure has its corresponding element below. The overall effect is of effortless strength, of a buoyant lightness not normally associated with stone architecture. Viewed directly from below, the choir vaults (FIG. 13-21) resemble a canopy, tentlike and suspended from bundled masts. The light flooding in from the clerestory makes the vaults seem even more insubstantial. The effect recalls another great building, one utterly different from Amiens but where light also plays a defining role: Hagia Sophia (FIG. 9-8) in Constantinople. At Amiens, the designers also reduced the building's physical mass by structural ingenuity and daring, and light further dematerializes what remains. If Hagia Sophia is the perfect expression of Byzantine spirituality in architecture, Amiens, with its soaring vaults and giant windows admitting divine colored light, is its Gothic counterpart.

Work began on the Amiens west facade (FIG. 13-19) at the same time as the nave (1220). Its lower parts reflect the influence of Laon Cathedral (FIG. 13-8) in the spacing of the funnel-like and gable-covered portals. But the Amiens builders punctured the upper parts

**13-22** Christ (*Beau Dieu*), trumeau statue of the central doorway of the west facade, Amiens Cathedral, Amiens, France, ca. 1220–1235. ◼◀

The *Beau Dieu* blesses all who enter Amiens Cathedral. He tramples a lion and dragon symbolizing the evil forces in the world. This benevolent Gothic Christ gives humankind hope in salvation.

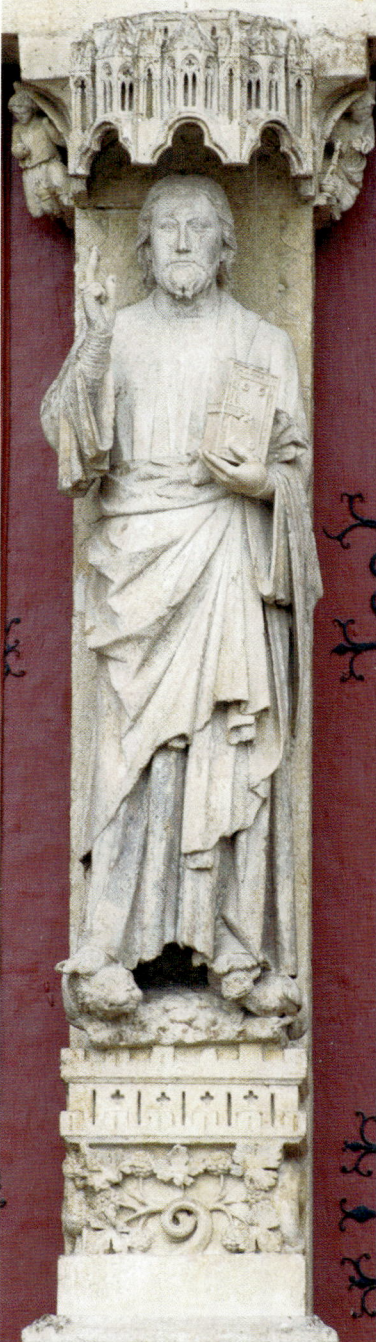

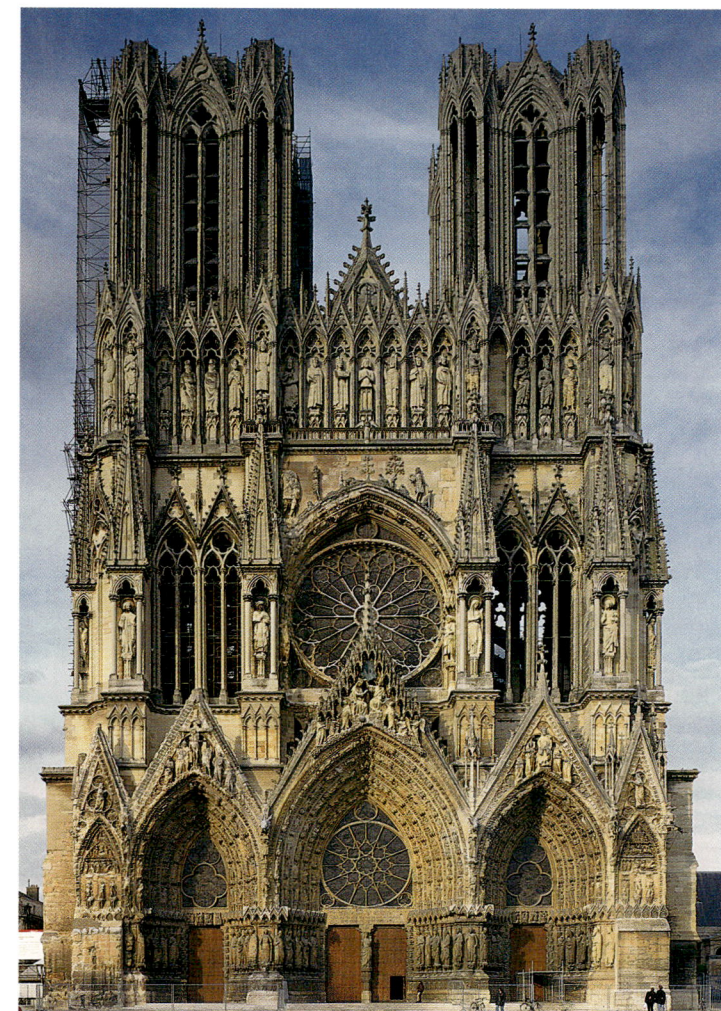

**13-23** GAUCHER DE REIMS and BERNARD DE SOISSONS, west facade of Reims Cathedral, Reims, France, ca. 1225–1290.

Reims Cathedral's facade reveals the High Gothic architect's desire to replace heavy masonry with intricately framed voids. Stained-glass windows, not stone reliefs, fill the three tympana.

of the facade to an even greater degree than did the Laon designer. The deep piercing of walls and towers at Amiens left few areas for decoration, but sculptors covered the remaining surfaces with a network of colonnettes, arches, pinnacles, rosettes, and other decorative stonework that visually screens and nearly dissolves the structure's solid core. Sculpture also extends to the areas above the portals, especially the band of statues (the so-called kings' gallery) running the full width of the facade directly below the rose window (with 15th-century tracery). The uneven towers were later additions. The shorter one dates from the 14th century, the taller one from the 15th century.

***BEAU DIEU*** Greeting worshipers as they enter the cathedral is the statue the French call *Beau Dieu* (Beautiful God; FIG. **13-22**) on the central doorway's trumeau. The High Gothic sculptor fully modeled Christ's figure, enveloping his body with massive drapery folds cascading from his waist. Compared with the kings and queens (FIG. 13-7) of the Royal Portal, the *Beau Dieu* is almost independent of its architectural setting. Nonetheless, the statue is still attached to the trumeau, and the sculptor placed an architectural canopy over Christ's head. The canopy mimics the east end of a 13th-century cathedral with a series of radiating chapels boasting elegant lancet windows in the latest Gothic style. Above the *Beau Dieu* is the great central tympanum with the representation of Christ as last judge. The trumeau Christ does not strike terror into sinners, however. Instead he blesses those who enter the church and tramples a lion and a dragon symbolizing the evil forces in the world. This image of Christ gives humankind hope in salvation. The *Beau*

*Dieu* epitomizes the bearded, benevolent Gothic image of Christ that replaced the youthful Early Christian Christ (FIG. 8-8) and the stern Byzantine Pantocrator (FIG. 9-23) as the preferred representation of the Savior in later European art. The handsome figure's quiet grace and grandeur also contrast sharply with the emotional intensity of the twisting Romanesque prophet (FIG. 12-13) carved in relief on the Moissac trumeau.

**REIMS CATHEDRAL** Construction of Reims Cathedral, for centuries the site of all French kings' coronations, began only a few years after work commenced at Amiens. GAUCHER DE REIMS and BERNARD DE SOISSONS, who were primarily responsible for the west facade (FIG. **13-23**), carried the High Gothic style of Amiens still further, both architecturally and sculpturally. The Amiens and Reims facades, although similar, display some significant differences. The *kings' gallery* of statues at Reims is *above* the great rose window, and the figures stand in taller and more ornate frames. In fact, the builders "stretched" every detail of the facade. The openings in the towers and those to the left and right of the rose window are taller, narrower, and more intricately decorated, and they more closely

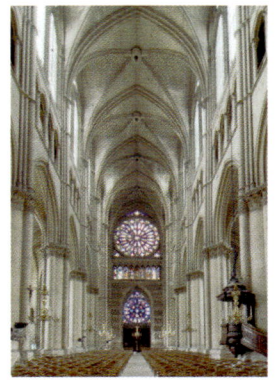

13-23A Interior of Reims Cathedral, begun 1211. ◼◀

resemble the elegant lancets of the clerestory within (FIG. 13-23A). A pointed arch also frames the rose window itself, and the pinnacles over the portals are taller and more elaborate than those at Amiens. Most striking, however, is the treatment of the tympana over the doorways, where stained-glass windows replaced the stone relief sculpture of earlier facades. The contrast with Romanesque heavy masonry construction (FIG. 12-30) is extreme. No less noteworthy, however, is the rapid transformation of the Gothic facade since the 12th-century designs of Saint-Denis (FIG. 13-3A) and Chartres (FIG. 13-5) and even Laon (FIG. 13-8).

Reims Cathedral is also a prime example of the High Gothic style in sculpture. The statues and reliefs of the west facade celebrate the Virgin Mary. Above the central gable, Mary is crowned as queen of Heaven. On the trumeau, she is the youthful Mother of God above reliefs depicting original sin. (Many medieval theologians considered Mary the new Eve.) The jamb statues to her left and right relate episodes from the infancy cycle (see "The Life of Jesus in Art," Chapter 8, pages 240–241), including *Annunciation* and *Visitation* (FIG. 13-24). The statues appear completely detached from their architectural background because the sculptors shrank the supporting columns into insignificance. The columns in no way restrict the free and easy movements of the full-bodied figures. These 13th-century jamb statues contrast strikingly with those of the Early Gothic Royal Portal (FIG. 13-7), where the background columns occupy a volume equal to that of the figures.

The Reims statues also vividly illustrate how long it frequently took to complete the sculptural ornamentation of a large Gothic cathedral. Sculptural projects of this magnitude normally required decades to complete and entailed hiring many sculptors often working in diverse styles. Art historians believe three different sculptors carved the four statues in FIG. 13-24 at different times during the quarter century from 1230 to 1255. The *Visitation* group (FIG. 13-24, *right*) is the work of one of the many artists of the era—in Germany and Italy as well as France—who must have studied classical statuary. Reims was an ancient Roman city. The heads of both Mary and Saint Elizabeth resemble Roman portraits, and the rich folds of the garments they wear also recall Roman statuary (FIG. 7-61). The Gothic statues closely approximate the classical naturalistic style and feature contrapposto postures in which the swaying of the hips is much more pronounced than in the Chartres's Saint Theodore (FIG. 13-18). The right legs of the Reims figures bend, and the knees press through the rippling folds of the garments. The sculptor also set the holy figures' arms in motion. Mary and Elizabeth turn their faces toward each other, and they converse through gestures. In the Reims *Visitation* group, the formerly isolated Gothic jamb statues became actors in a biblical narrative.

The statues in the *Annunciation* group (FIG. 13-24, *left*) also stand free from their architectural setting, but they are products of different workshops. Mary is a slender figure with severe drapery. This artist preferred broad expanses of fabric to the multiplicity of folds of the *Visitation* Mary. The angel Gabriel, the latest of the four statues, exhibits the elegant style of the Parisian court at the middle of the 13th century. Gabriel has a much more elongated body and is far more animated than his neighbors. He pivots gracefully, almost as if dancing, and smiles broadly. Like a courtier, Gabriel exudes charm. Mary, in contrast, is serious and introspective and does not respond overtly to the news the angel has brought.

**SAINTE-CHAPELLE, PARIS** The stained-glass windows inserted into the portal tympana of Reims Cathedral exemplify the wall-dissolving High Gothic architectural style. The architect of Sainte-Chapelle (FIG. 13-25) in Paris extended this style to an entire building. Louis IX built Sainte-Chapelle, joined to the royal palace, as a repository for the crown of thorns and other relics of Christ's

13-24 *Annunciation* and *Visitation*, jamb statues on the right side of the central doorway of the west facade, Reims Cathedral, Reims, France, ca. 1230–1255. ◼◀

Several sculptors working in diverse styles carved the Reims jamb statues, but all the figures resemble freestanding statues with bodies and arms in motion. The biblical figures converse through gestures.

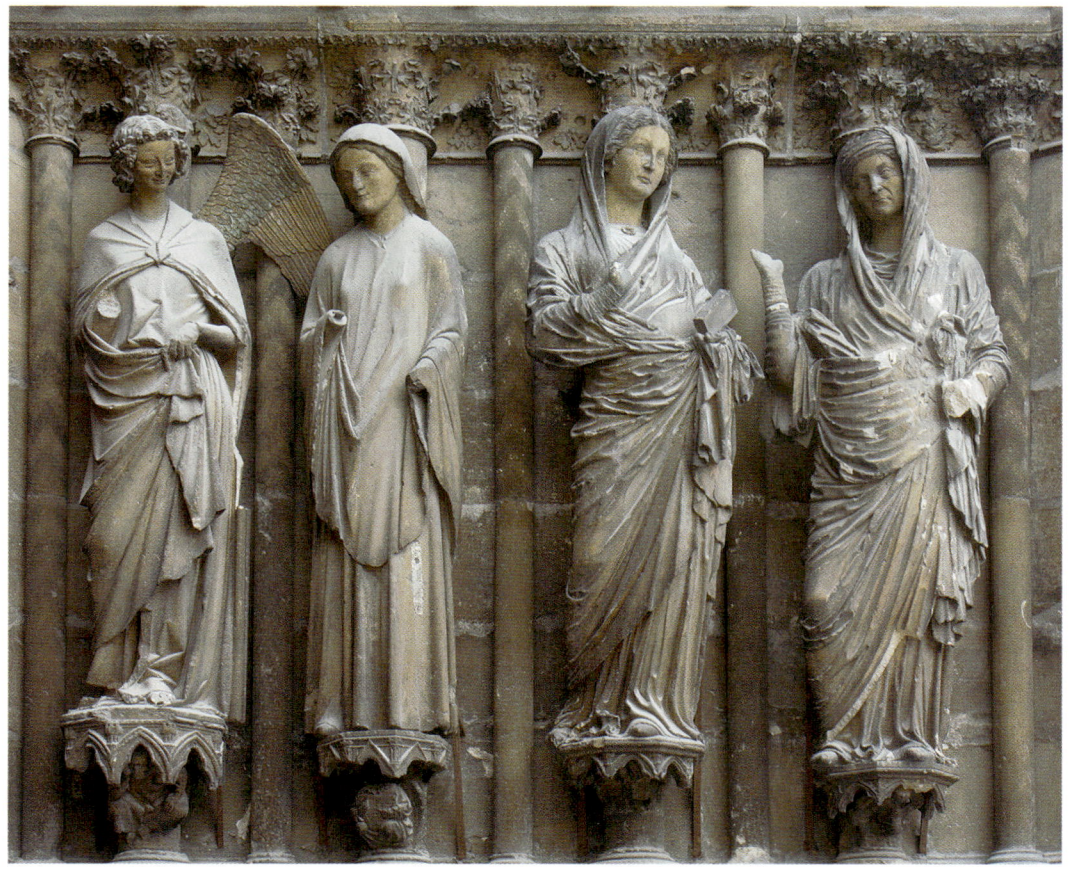

passion he had purchased in 1239 from his cousin Baldwin II (r. 1228–1261), the Latin emperor of Constantinople. The chapel is a masterpiece of the so-called *Rayonnant* (radiant) style of the High Gothic age, which dominated the second half of the 13th century. It was the preferred style of the Parisian court of Saint Louis (see "Louis IX," page 385). Sainte-Chapelle's architect carried the dissolution of walls and the reduction of the bulk of the supports to the point that some 6,450 square feet of stained glass make up more than three-quarters of the structure. The supporting elements are hardly more than large *mullions,* or vertical stone bars. The emphasis is on the extreme slenderness of the architectural forms and on linearity in general. Although the chapel required restoration in the 19th century (after suffering damage during the French Revolution), it retains most of its original 13th-century stained glass. Sainte-Chapelle's enormous windows filter the light and fill the interior with an unearthly rose-violet atmosphere. Approximately 49 feet high and 15 feet wide, they were the largest stained-glass windows designed up to their time.

***VIRGIN OF PARIS*** The "court style" of Sainte-Chapelle has its pictorial parallel in the mannered elegance of the roughly contemporaneous Gabriel of the Reims *Annunciation* group (FIG. 13-24,

*left*), but the style long outlived Saint Louis and his royal artists and architects. An example of the court style in Late Gothic sculpture is the early-14th-century statue nicknamed the *Virgin of Paris* (FIG. 13-26) because of its location in the Parisian Cathedral of Notre-Dame. The sculptor portrayed Mary in an exaggerated S-curve posture typical of Late Gothic sculpture. She is a worldly queen and wears a heavy gem-encrusted crown. The princely Christ Child reaches toward his young mother. The tender, anecdotal characterization of mother and son seen here is a later manifestation of the humanization of the portrayal of religious figures in Gothic sculpture that began at Chartres and developed especially in Germany (FIGS. 13-48 to 13-50). Late Gothic statuary is very different in tone from the solemnity of most High Gothic figures, just as Late Classical Greek statues of the Olympian gods differ from High Classical depictions (compare FIG. 13-26 with FIG. 5-63).

**SAINT-MACLOU, ROUEN** Late French Gothic architecture also represents a departure from the norms of High Gothic. The change from Rayonnant architecture to the *Flamboyant* style (named for the flamelike appearance of its pointed bar tracery) occurred in the 14th century. The new manner reached its florid maturity nearly a century later in Rouen, the capital of Normandy,

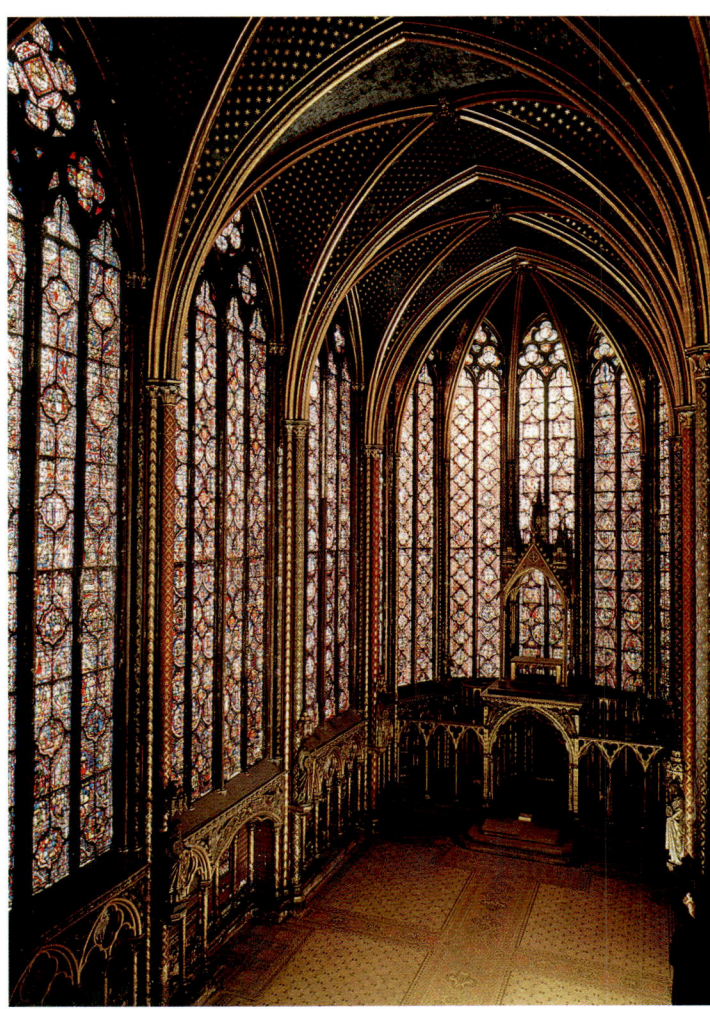

**13-25** Interior of the upper chapel (looking northeast), Sainte-Chapelle, Paris, France, 1243–1248. ◼◀

At Louis IX's Sainte-Chapelle, the architect succeeded in dissolving the walls to such an extent that 6,450 square feet of stained glass account for more than three-quarters of the Rayonnant Gothic structure.

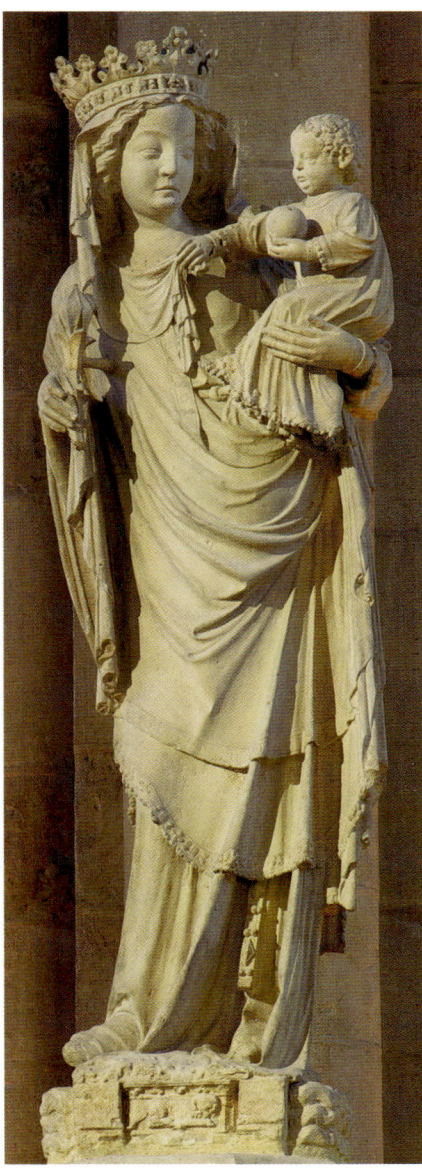

**13-26** Virgin and Child (***Virgin of Paris***), Notre-Dame, Paris, France, early 14th century. ◼◀

Late Gothic sculpture is elegant and mannered. Here, the solemnity of Early and High Gothic religious figures gave way to a tender, anecdotal portrayal of Mary and Jesus as royal mother and son.

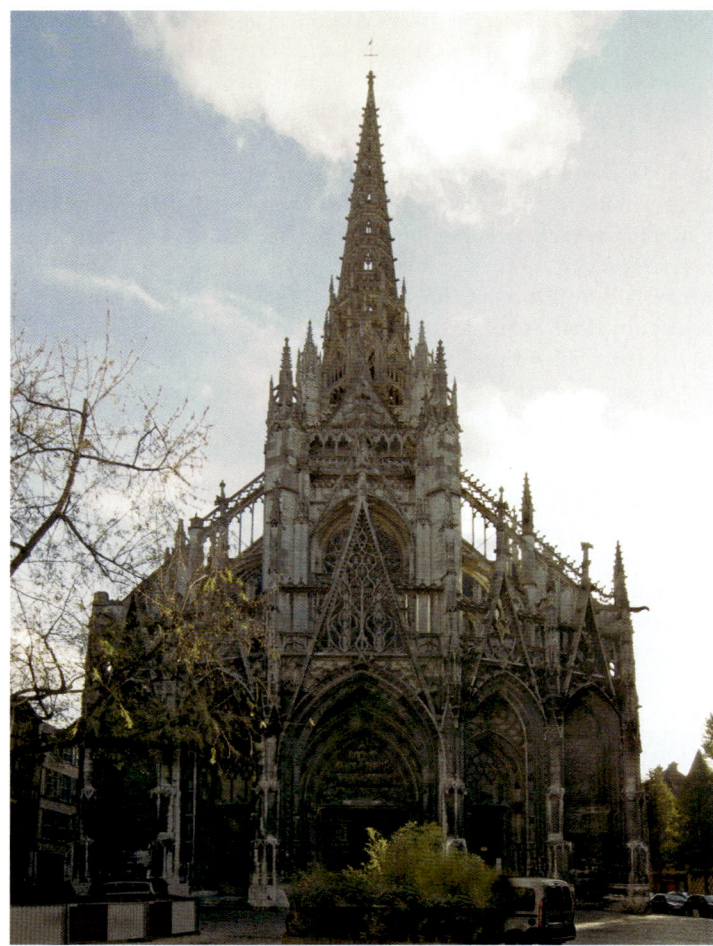

**13-27** West facade of Saint-Maclou, Rouen, France, ca. 1500–1514. ■◀

Saint-Maclou is the masterpiece of Late Gothic Flamboyant architecture. Its ornate tracery of curves and countercurves forms brittle decorative webs masking the building's structure.

in the church of Saint-Maclou (FIG. **13-27**). The shrine is tiny (only about 75 feet high and 180 feet long) compared with 13th-century cathedrals, and its facade breaks sharply from the High Gothic style (FIGS. 13-21 and 13-23). The five portals (two of them false doors) bend outward in an arc. Ornate gables crown the doorways, pierced through and filled with wiry, "flickering" Flamboyant tracery. Made up of curves and countercurves forming brittle decorative webs, the ornate Late Gothic tracery masks the building's structure. The transparency of the pinnacles over the doorways enables visitors to see the central rose window and the flying buttresses, even though they are set well back from the facade. The overlapping of all features, pierced as they are, confuses the structural lines and produces a bewildering complexity of views that is the hallmark of the Flamboyant style.

**CARCASSONNE** The Gothic period may have been the age of the great cathedrals, but widespread prosperity also stimulated the construction of major secular buildings such as town halls, palaces, and private residences. In a time of frequent warfare, the feudal barons often had constructed fortified castles in places enemies could not easily reach. Sometimes thick defensive wall circuits or *ramparts* enclosed entire towns. In time, however, purely defensive wars became obsolete due to the invention of artillery and improvements in siege craft. The fortress era gradually passed, and throughout Europe once-mighty ramparts fell into ruin.

Carcassonne (FIG. **13-28**) in Languedoc in southern France, once the regional center of resistance to the northern forces of royal France, is the best-preserved example of a Gothic fortified town. Restored in the 19th century by EUGÈNE VIOLLET-LE-DUC (1814–1879), Carcassonne occupies a site on a hill bounded by the Aude River. Fortified since Roman times, it has Visigothic walls dating from the 6th century, reinforced in the 12th century. *Battlements* (low parapets) with *crenellations* (composed of alternating solid *merlons* and open *crenels*) protected guards patrolling the stone ring surrounding the town. Carcassonne might be forced to surrender but could not easily be taken by storm. Within the town's double

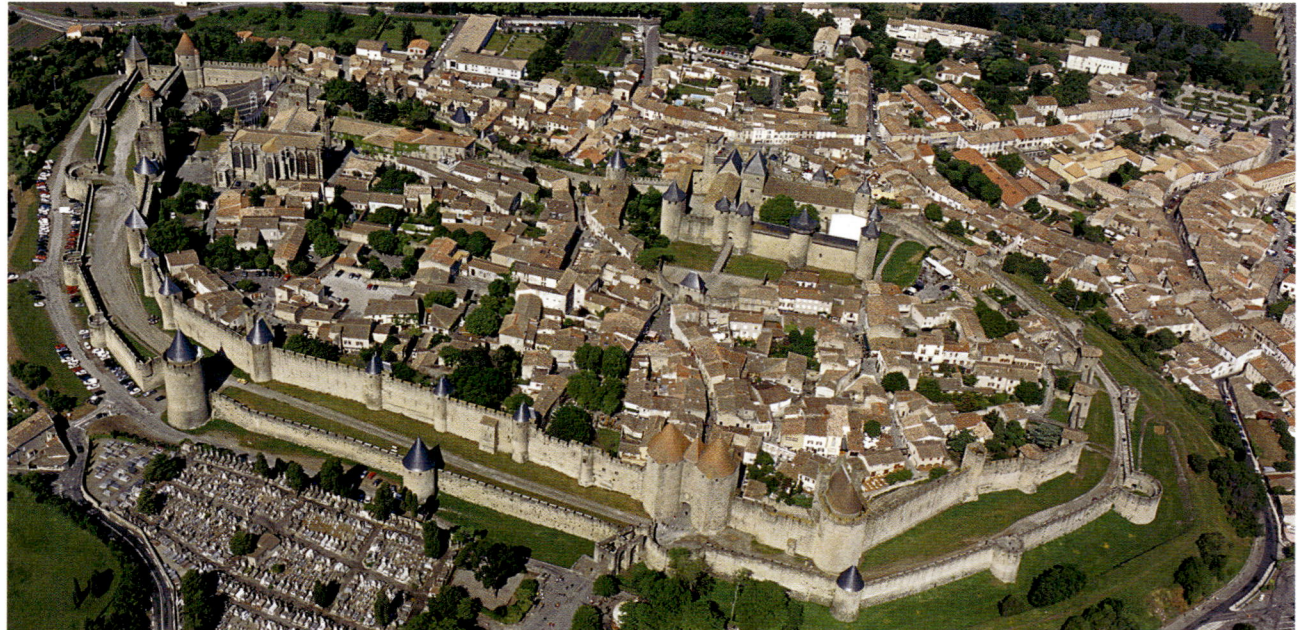

**13-28** Aerial view of the fortified town of Carcassonne (looking west), France. Bastions and towers, 12th–13th centuries, restored by EUGÈNE VIOLLET-LE-DUC in the 19th century.

Carcassonne provides a rare glimpse of what was once a familiar sight in Gothic France: a tight complex of castle, cathedral, and town with a crenellated and towered wall circuit for defense.

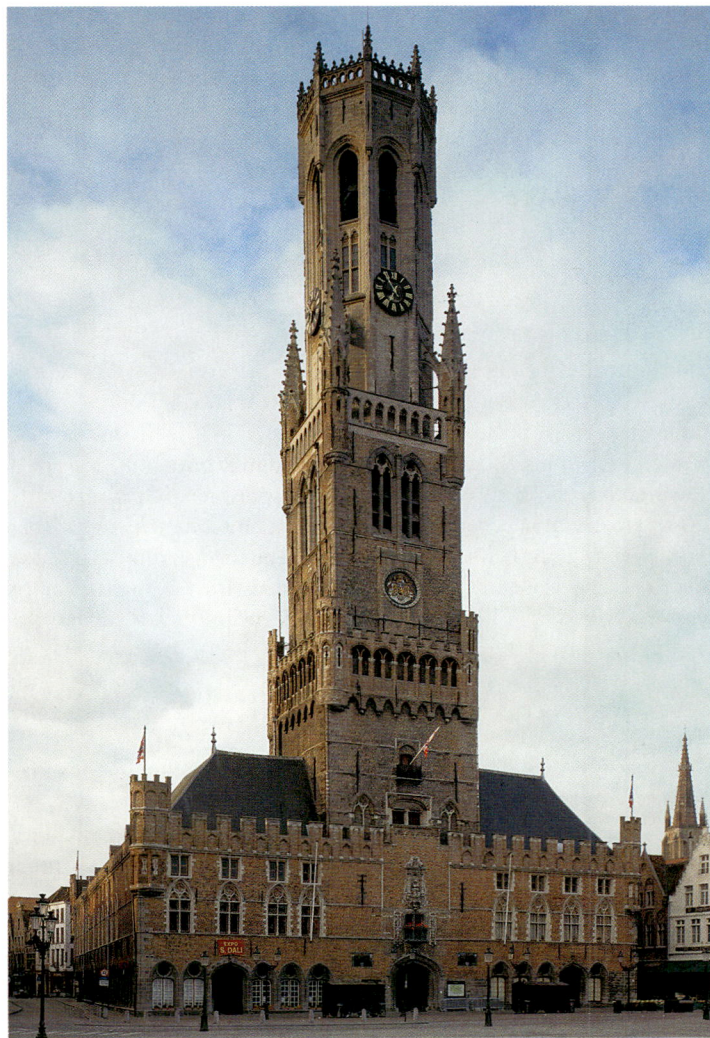

**13-29** Hall of the cloth guild, Bruges, Belgium, begun 1230.

The Bruges cloth guild's meeting hall is an early example of a new type of secular architecture in the late Middle Ages. Its lofty tower competed for attention with the towers of the cathedral.

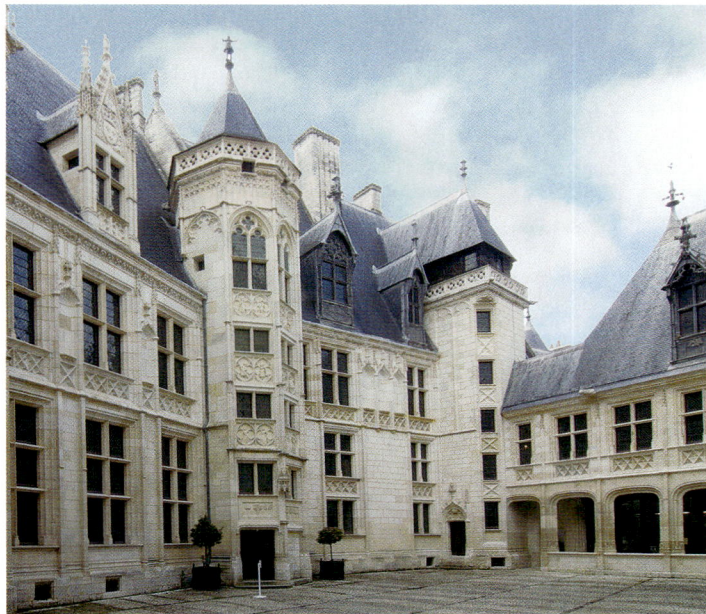

**13-30** Inner facade and courtyard of the house of Jacques Coeur, Bourges, France, 1443–1451. ◼◀

The townhouse of the wealthy Bourges financier Jacques Coeur is both a splendid example of Late Gothic architecture with elaborate tracery and a symbol of the period's new secular spirit.

walls was a fortified castle (FIG. 13-28, *right*) with a massive attached *keep*, a secure tower that could serve as a place of last refuge. Balancing that center of secular power was the bishop's seat, the cathedral of Saint-Nazaire (FIG. 13-28, *left*). The small church, built between 1269 and 1329, may have been the work of an architect brought in from northern France. In any case, Saint-Nazaire's builders were certainly familiar with the latest developments in architecture in the Île-de-France. Today, Carcassonne provides a rare glimpse of what was once a familiar sight in Gothic France: a tightly contained complex of castle, cathedral, and town within towered walls.

**GUILD HALL, BRUGES** One of the many signs of the growing secularization of urban life in the late Middle Ages was the erection of monumental meeting halls and warehouses for the increasing number of craft guilds being formed throughout Europe. An early example is the imposing market and guild hall (FIG. **13-29**) of the clothmakers of Bruges, begun in 1230. Situated in the city's major square, it testifies to the important role of artisans and merchants in Gothic Europe. The design combines features of military construction (the corner watchtowers with their crenellations) and ecclesiastical architecture (lancet windows with crowning oculi). The uppermost, octagonal portion of the tower with its flying buttresses and pinnacles dates to the 15th century, but even the original two-story

tower is taller than the rest of the hall. Lofty towers, a common feature of late medieval guild and town halls (compare FIGS. 14-15 and 14-18B), were designed to compete for attention and prestige with the towers of city cathedrals.

**HOUSE OF JACQUES COEUR** The new class of wealthy merchants who rose to prominence throughout Europe in the late Middle Ages may not have accumulated fortunes equaling those of the hereditary royalty, but they still wielded enormous power and influence. The career of the French financier Jacques Coeur (1395–1456) illustrates how enterprising private citizens could win—and quickly lose—wealth and power. Coeur had banking houses in every major city of France and many cities abroad. He employed more than 300 agents and competed with the great trading republics of Italy. His merchant ships filled the Mediterranean, and with the papacy's permission, he imported spices and textiles from Muslim lands to the east. He was the treasurer of King Charles VII (r. 1422–1461) of France and a friend of Pope Nicholas V (r. 1447–1455). In 1451, however, his enemies framed him on an absurd charge of having poisoned Agnes Sorel (1421–1450), the king's mistress. The judges who sentenced Coeur to prison and confiscated his vast wealth and property were among those who owed him money. Coeur escaped in 1454 and made his way to Rome, where the pope warmly received him. He died of fever while leading a fleet of papal war galleys in the eastern Mediterranean.

Jacques Coeur's great townhouse still stands in his native city of Bourges. Built between 1443 and 1451 (with special permission to encroach upon the town ramparts), it is the best-preserved example of Late Gothic domestic architecture. The house's plan is irregular, with the units arranged around an open courtyard (FIG. **13-30**). The service areas (maintenance shops, storage rooms, servants' quarters, and baths—a rare luxury anywhere until the 20th century) occupy the ground level. The upper stories house the great hall and auxiliary rooms used for offices and family living rooms. Over the main entrance is a private chapel. One of the towers served as a treasury. The exterior and interior facades have steep pyramidal roofs of different heights. Decorative details include Flamboyant tracery and large pointed-arch stained-glass windows. An elegant canopied niche facing the street once housed a royal equestrian statue. A comparable statue of Coeur on horseback dominated the facade opening onto the interior courtyard. Jacques Coeur's house is both a splendid example of Late Gothic architecture and a monumental symbol of the period's new secular spirit.

## Book Illumination and Luxury Arts

Paris's claim as the intellectual center of Gothic Europe (see "Paris," page 372) did not rest solely on the stature of its university faculty and the reputation of its architects, masons, sculptors, and stained-glass makers. The city was also a renowned center for the production of fine books. Dante Alighieri (1265–1321), the famous Florentine poet, in fact, referred to Paris in his *Divine Comedy* (ca. 1310–1320) as the city famed for the art of illumination.[2] During the Gothic period, bookmaking shifted from monastic scriptoria shut off from the world to urban workshops of professional artists—and Paris boasted the most and best workshops. The owners of these new for-profit secular businesses sold their products to the royal family, scholars, and prosperous merchants. The Parisian shops were the forerunners of modern publishing houses.

**VILLARD DE HONNECOURT** One of the most intriguing Parisian manuscripts preserved today was not, however, a book for sale but a personal sketchbook. Compiled by VILLARD DE HONNECOURT, an early-13th-century master mason, its pages contain plans of choirs with radiating chapels and drawings of church towers, lifting devices, a sawmill, stained-glass windows, and other subjects of obvious interest to architects and masons. But also sprinkled liberally throughout the pages are pictures of religious and worldly figures as well as animals, some realistic and others purely fantastic. On the page reproduced here (FIG. **13-31**), Villard demonstrated the value of the *ars de geometria* (art of geometry) to artists, showing how both natural forms and buildings are based on simple geometric shapes such as the square, circle, and triangle. Even when he claimed he drew his animals from nature, he composed his figures around a skeleton not of bones but of abstract geometric forms. Geometry was, in Villard's words, "strong help in drawing figures."

***GOD AS CREATOR*** Geometry also played a symbolic role in Gothic art and architecture. Gothic artists, architects, and theolo-

1 in.

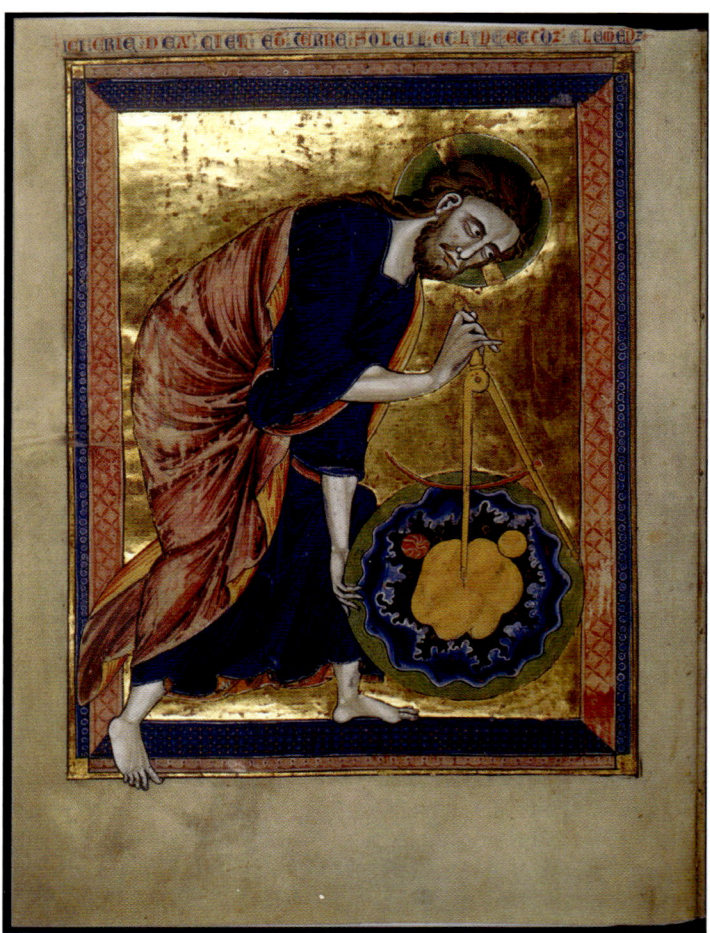

1 in.

**13-31** VILLARD DE HONNECOURT, figures based on geometric shapes, folio 18 verso of a sketchbook, from Paris, France, ca. 1220–1235. Ink on vellum, $9\frac{1}{4}'' \times 6''$. Bibliothèque Nationale, Paris.

On this page from his private sketchbook, the master mason Villard de Honnecourt sought to demonstrate how simple geometric shapes are the basis of both natural forms and buildings.

**13-32** *God as Creator of the World,* folio 1 verso of a moralized Bible, from Paris, France, ca. 1220–1230. Ink, tempera, and gold leaf on vellum, $1' 1\frac{1}{2}'' \times 8\frac{1}{4}''$. Österreichische Nationalbibliothek, Vienna.

Paris boasted renowned workshops for the production of illuminated manuscripts. In this book, the artist portrayed God in the process of creating the universe using a Gothic builder's compass.

## Louis IX, the Saintly King

The royal patron behind the Parisian Rayonnant court style of Gothic art and architecture was King Louis IX (1215–1270; r. 1226–1270), grandson of Philip Augustus. Louis inherited the throne when he was only 12 years old, so until he reached adulthood 6 years later, his mother, Blanche of Castile (FIG. 13-33), granddaughter of Eleanor of Aquitaine (see "Romanesque Countesses, Queens, and Nuns," Chapter 12, page 352), served as France's regent.

The French regarded Louis as the ideal king. In 1297, only 27 years after Louis's death, Pope Boniface VIII (r. 1294–1303) declared the king a saint. In his own time, Louis was revered for his piety, justice, truthfulness, and charity. His almsgiving and his donations to religious foundations were extravagant. He especially favored the *mendicant* (begging) orders, the Dominicans and Franciscans (see "Mendicant Orders," Chapter 14, page 404), as he admired their poverty, piety, and self-sacrificing disregard of material things.

Louis launched two unsuccessful Crusades (see "Crusades," Chapter 12, page 346), the Seventh (1248–1254, when, in her son's absence, Blanche was again French regent) and the Eighth (1270). He died in Tunisia during the latter. As a crusading knight who lost his life in the service of the Church, Louis personified the chivalric virtues of courage, loyalty, and self-sacrifice. Saint Louis united in his person the best qualities of the Christian knight, the benevolent monarch, and the holy man. He became the model of medieval Christian kingship.

Louis's political accomplishments were also noteworthy. He subdued the unruly French barons, and between 1243 and 1314 no one seriously challenged the crown. He negotiated a treaty with Henry III (r. 1216–1272), king of France's traditional enemy, Eng-

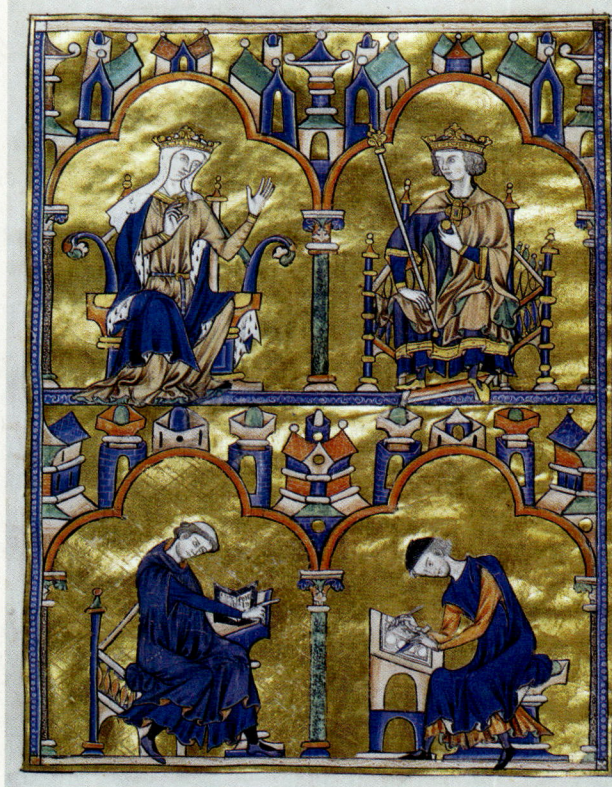

**13-33** Blanche of Castile, Louis IX, and two monks, dedication page (folio 8 recto) of a moralized Bible, from Paris, France, 1226–1234. Ink, tempera, and gold leaf on vellum, 1′ 3″ × 10½″. Pierpont Morgan Library, New York.

The dedication page of this royal book depicts Saint Louis, his mother and French regent Blanche of Castile, a monk, and a lay scribe at work on the paired illustrations of a moralized Bible.

1 in.

land. Such was his reputation for integrity and just dealing that he served as arbiter in at least a dozen international disputes. So successful was he as peacekeeper that despite civil wars through most of the 13th century, international peace prevailed. Under Saint Louis, medieval France was at its most prosperous, and its art and architecture were admired and imitated throughout Europe.

gians alike thought the triangle, for example, embodied the Trinity of God the Father, Christ, and the Holy Spirit. The circle, which has neither a beginning nor an end, symbolized the eternity of the one God. The book of Revelation (21.12–21) describes the Heavenly Jerusalem as a walled city in the form of a perfect square with 12 gates. When Gothic architects based their designs on the art of geometry, building their forms out of abstract shapes laden with symbolic meaning, they believed they were working according to the divinely established laws of nature.

A vivid illustration of this concept appears as the frontispiece (FIG. 13-32) of a moralized Bible produced in Paris during the 1220s. *Moralized Bibles* are heavily illustrated, each page pairing paintings of Old and New Testament episodes with explanations of their moral significance. The page reproduced here does not conform to this formula because it is the introduction to all that follows. Above the illustration, the scribe wrote (in French rather than Latin): "Here God creates heaven and earth, the sun and moon, and all the elements." The painter depicted God in the process of creating the world, shaping the universe with the aid of a compass. Within the perfect circle already created are the spherical sun and

moon and the unformed matter that will become the earth once God applies the same geometric principles to it. In contrast to the biblical account of creation, in which God created the sun, moon, and stars after the earth had been formed, and made the world by sheer force of will and a simple "Let there be" command, the Gothic artist portrayed God as systematically creating the universe with what Villard would describe as "the strong help of geometry."

**BLANCHE OF CASTILE** Not surprisingly, some of the finest Gothic books known today belonged to the French monarchy. Saint Louis in particular was an avid collector of both secular and religious books (see "Louis IX, the Saintly King," above). He and his royal predecessors and successors formed a vast library that eventually became the core of France's national library, the Bibliothèque Nationale.

One book the royal family commissioned is a moralized Bible now in the collection of New York's Pierpont Morgan Library. Louis's mother, Blanche of Castile, ordered the Bible during her regency (1226–1234) for her teenage son. The dedication page (FIG. 13-33) has a costly gold background and depicts Blanche and Louis enthroned beneath triple-lobed arches and miniature cityscapes. The latter are comparable to the architectural canopies above the heads of contemporaneous French portal statues (FIGS. 13-18 and 13-22). With vivid gestures, Blanche instructs the young Louis, underscoring her superior position. (The prominence of Mary as queen of Heaven in Gothic art parallels the rising influence of secular queens in Gothic Europe.) Below Blanche and Louis, in similar architectural frames, are a monk and a professional lay scribe. The older clergyman instructs the scribe, who already has divided his page into two columns of four roundels each, a format often used for the paired illustrations of moralized Bibles. The inspirations for such pages filled with circular frames were probably the roundels of Gothic stained-glass windows (compare the windows of Louis's own later Sainte-Chapelle, FIG. 13-25, in Paris).

The picture of Gothic book production on the dedication page of Blanche of Castile's moralized Bible is a very abbreviated one, as was the view of a monastic scriptorium discussed earlier (FIG. 11-11). Indeed, the manufacturing processes used in the workshops of 13th-century Paris and 10th-century Tábara did not differ significantly. Bookmaking involved many steps and numerous specialized artists, scribes, and assistants of varying skill levels. The Benedictine abbot Johannes Trithemius (1462–1516) described the way books were still made in his day in his treatise *In Praise of Scribes*:

> If you do not know how to write, you still can assist the scribes in various ways. One of you can correct what another has written. Another can add the rubrics [headings] to the corrected text. A third can add initials and signs of division. Still another can arrange the leaves and attach the binding. Another of you can prepare the covers, the leather, the buckles and clasps. All sorts of assistance can be offered the scribe to help him pursue his work without interruption. He needs many things which can be prepared by others: parchment cut, flattened and ruled for script, ready ink and pens. You will always find something with which to help the scribe.[3]

Preparation of the illuminated pages also involved several hands. Some artists, for example, specialized in painting borders or initials. Only the workshop head or one of the most advanced assistants would paint the main figural scenes. Given this division of labor and the assembly-line nature of Gothic book production, it is astonishing how uniform the style is on a single page, as well as from page to page, in most illuminated manuscripts.

**PSALTER OF SAINT LOUIS** The golden background of Blanche's Bible is unusual and has no parallel in Gothic windows. But the radiance of stained glass probably inspired the glowing color of other 13th-century Parisian illuminated manuscripts. In some cases, masters in the same urban workshop produced both glass and books. Many art historians believe the *Psalter of Saint Louis* (FIG. **13-34**) is one of several books produced in Paris for Louis IX by artists associated with those who made the stained glass for his Sainte-Chapelle. Certainly, the painted architectural setting in Louis's book of Psalms reflects the pierced screenlike lightness and transparency of royal Rayonnant buildings such as Sainte-Chapelle. The intense colors, especially the blues, emulate stained glass, and the lines in the borders resemble leading. The gables, pierced by rose windows with bar tracery, are standard Rayonnant architectural features.

On the page from the *Psalter of Saint Louis* shown here (FIG. 13-34), the illuminator represented *Abraham and the Three*

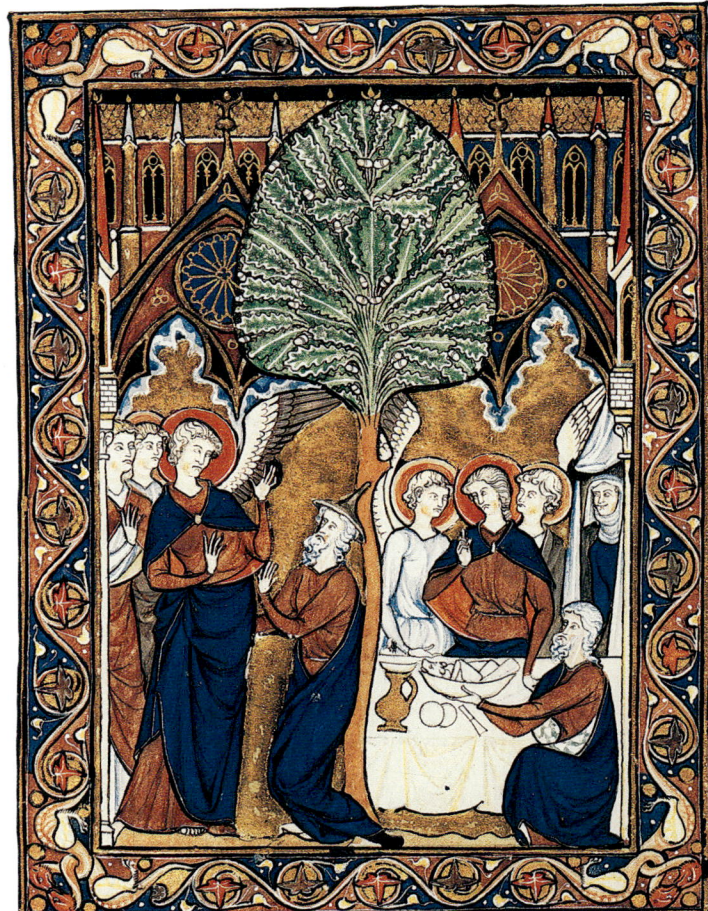

**13-34** *Abraham and the Three Angels,* folio 7 verso of the *Psalter of Saint Louis,* from Paris, France, 1253–1270. Ink, tempera, and gold leaf on vellum, $5'' \times 3\frac{1}{2}''$. Bibliothèque Nationale, Paris.

The architectural settings in the *Psalter of Saint Louis* reflect the lightness and transparency of Parisian royal buildings, such as Sainte-Chapelle (FIG. 13-25). The colors emulate stained glass.

*Angels,* the Old Testament story Christians believed prefigured the Trinity (see "Jewish Subjects in Christian Art," Chapter 8, page 238). Two episodes appear on the same page, separated by the tree of Mamre mentioned in the Bible. At the left, Abraham greets the three angels. In the other scene, he entertains them while his wife, Sarah, peers at them from a tent. The figures' delicate features and the linear wavy strands of their hair have parallels in Blanche of Castile's moralized Bible, as well as in Parisian stained glass. The elegant proportions, facial expressions, theatrical gestures, and swaying poses are characteristic of the Parisian court style admired throughout Europe. Compare, for example, the angel in the left foreground with the Gabriel statue (FIG. 13-24, *left*) of the Reims *Annunciation* group.

**BREVIARY OF PHILIPPE LE BEL** As in the Romanesque period, some Gothic manuscript illuminators signed their work. The names of others appear in royal accounts of payments made and similar official documents. One of the artists who produced books for the French court was MASTER HONORÉ, whose Parisian workshop was on the street known today as rue Boutebrie. Honoré illuminated a *breviary* (see "Medieval Books," Chapter 11, page 312) for Philippe le Bel (Philip the Fair, r. 1285–1314) in 1296. On the page illustrated here (FIG. **13-35**), Honoré painted two Old Testament scenes involving David. In the upper panel, Samuel

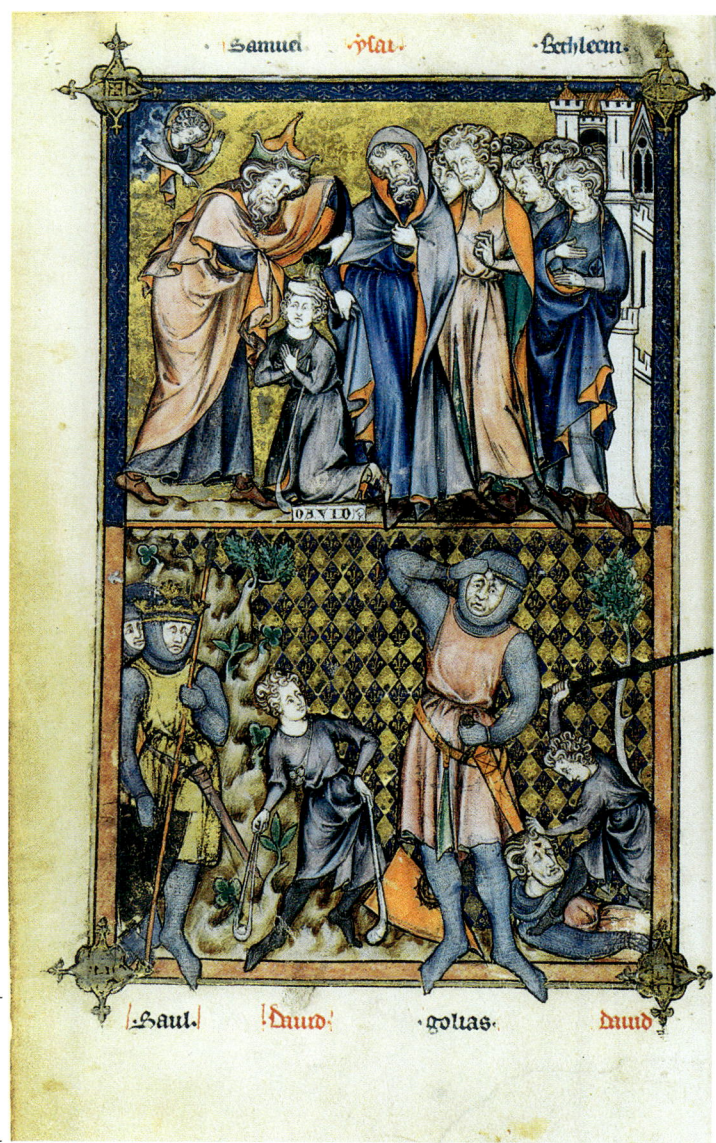

**13-35** MASTER HONORÉ, *Samuel Anointing David* and *Battle of David and Goliath,* folio 7 verso of the *Breviary of Philippe le Bel,* from Paris, France, 1296. Ink and tempera on vellum, $7\frac{7}{8}'' \times 4\frac{7}{8}''$. Bibliothèque Nationale, Paris.

Master Honoré was one of the Parisian lay artists who produced books for the French monarchy. His figures are noteworthy for their sculptural volume and the play of light and shade on their bodies.

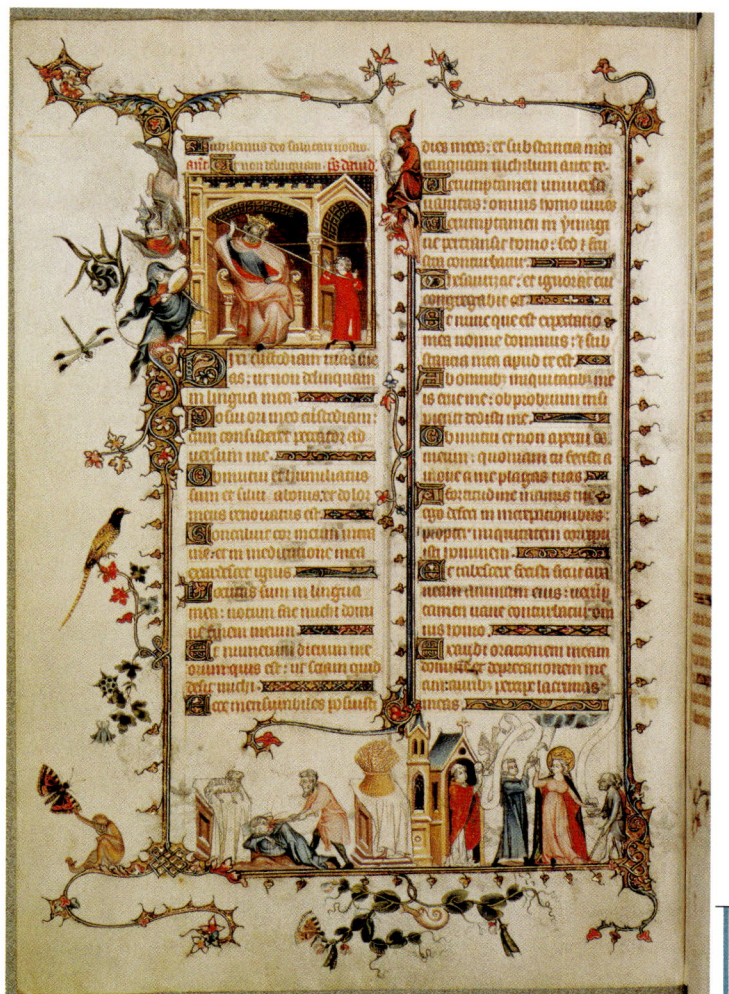

**13-36** JEAN PUCELLE, *David before Saul,* folio 24 verso of the *Belleville Breviary,* from Paris, France, ca. 1325. Ink and tempera on vellum, $9\frac{1}{2}'' \times 6\frac{3}{4}''$. Bibliothèque Nationale, Paris.

Pucelle's fully modeled figures in architectural settings rendered in convincing perspective reveal his study of contemporaneous painting in Italy. He was also a close observer of plants and fauna.

anoints the youthful David. Below, while King Saul looks on, David prepares to aim his slingshot at his most famous opponent, the giant Goliath (who already touches the wound on his forehead). Immediately to the right, David slays Goliath with his sword.

Master Honoré's linear treatment of hair, his figures' delicate hands and gestures, and their elegant swaying postures are typical of Parisian painting of the time. But this painter was much more interested than most of his colleagues in giving his figures sculptural volume and showing the play of light on their bodies. Honoré showed little concern for locating his figures in space, however. The Goliath panel in Philippe's breviary has a textilelike decorative background, and the feet of the artist's figures frequently overlap the border. Compared with his contemporaries, Master Honoré pioneered naturalism in figure painting. Still, he approached the art of book illumination as a decorator of two-dimensional pages.

He did not embrace the classical notion that a painting should be an illusionistic window into a three-dimensional world.

***BELLEVILLE BREVIARY*** David and Saul also are the subjects of a miniature painting at the top left of an elaborately decorated text page (FIG. 13-36) in the *Belleville Breviary,* which JEAN PUCELLE of Paris painted around 1325. In this manuscript and the Book of Hours (FIG. 13-36A) which he illuminated for Queen Jeanne d'Evreux, wife of Charles IV (r. 1322–1328), Pucelle outdid Honoré and other French artists by placing his fully modeled figures in three-dimensional architectural settings rendered in convincing perspective.

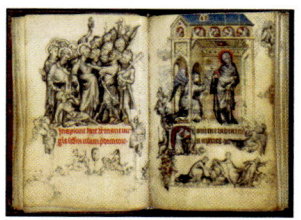

**13-36A** PUCELLE, *Hours of Jeanne d'Evreux,* ca. 1325–1328.

For example, he painted Saul as a weighty figure seated on a throne seen in three-quarter view, and he meticulously depicted the receding coffers of the barrel vault over the young David's head. Similar "stage sets" already had become commonplace in Italian painting, and art historians believe Pucelle visited Italy and studied Duccio di Buoninsegna's work (FIGS. 14-9 to 14-11) in Siena. Pucelle's (or an assistant's) renditions of plants, a bird, butterflies, a dragonfly, a fish, a snail, and a monkey also reveal a keen interest in and close observation of the natural world. Nonetheless, in the *Belleville Breviary,* the text still dominates the page, and the artist (and his patron) delighted in ornamental flourishes, fancy initial letters, and abstract patterns. In that respect, comparisons with panel paintings such as Duccio's are inappropriate. Pucelle's breviary remains firmly in the tradition of book illumination.

The *Belleville Breviary* is of special interest because Pucelle's name and those of some of his assistants appear at the end of the book, in a memorandum recording the payment they received for their work. Inscriptions in other Gothic illuminated books regularly state the production costs—the prices paid for materials, especially gold, and for the execution of initials, figures, flowery script, and other embellishments. By this time, illuminators were professional guild members, and their personal reputation guaranteed the quality of their work. Although the cost of materials was still the major factor determining a book's price, individual skill and "brand name" increasingly decided the value of the illuminator's services. The centuries-old monopoly of the Church in book production had ended.

***VIRGIN OF JEANNE D'EVREUX*** The royal family also patronized goldsmiths, silversmiths, and other artists specializing in the production of luxury works in metal and enamel for churches, palaces, and private homes. Especially popular were statuettes of sacred figures, which the wealthy purchased either for private devotion or as gifts to churches. The Virgin Mary was a favored subject, reflecting her new prominence in the iconography of Gothic portal sculpture.

Perhaps the finest of these costly statuettes is the large silver-gilt figurine known as the *Virgin of Jeanne d'Evreux* (FIG. **13-37**). The French queen donated the image of the Virgin and Child to the royal abbey church of Saint-Denis in 1339. Mary stands on a rectangular base decorated with enamel scenes of Christ's passion. (Some art historians think the enamels are Jean Pucelle's work.) But no hint of grief appears in the beautiful young Mary's face. The Christ Child, also without a care in the world, playfully reaches for his mother. The elegant proportions of the two figures, Mary's emphatic swaying posture, the heavy drapery folds, and the intimate human characterization of mother and son are also features of the roughly contemporaneous *Virgin of Paris* (FIG. 13-26). The sculptor of large stone statues and the royal silversmith working at small scale approached the representation of the Virgin and Child in a similar fashion. In both instances, Mary appears not only as the Mother of Christ but also as the queen of Heaven. The Saint-Denis Mary originally had a crown on her head, and the scepter she holds is in the form of the *fleur-de-lis* (compare FIG. 13-17). The statuette also served as a reliquary. The Virgin's scepter contained hairs believed to come from Mary's head.

**THE CASTLE OF LOVE** Gothic artists produced luxurious objects for secular as well as religious contexts. Sometimes they decorated these costly pieces with stories of courtly love inspired by the romantic literature of the day, such as the account of Lancelot and Queen Guinevere, wife of King Arthur of Camelot. The French poet Chrétien de Troyes recorded their love affair in the late 12th century.

An interesting object of this type is a woman's jewelry box adorned with ivory relief panels. The theme of the panel illustrated here (FIG. **13-38**) is related to the allegorical poem *Romance of the*

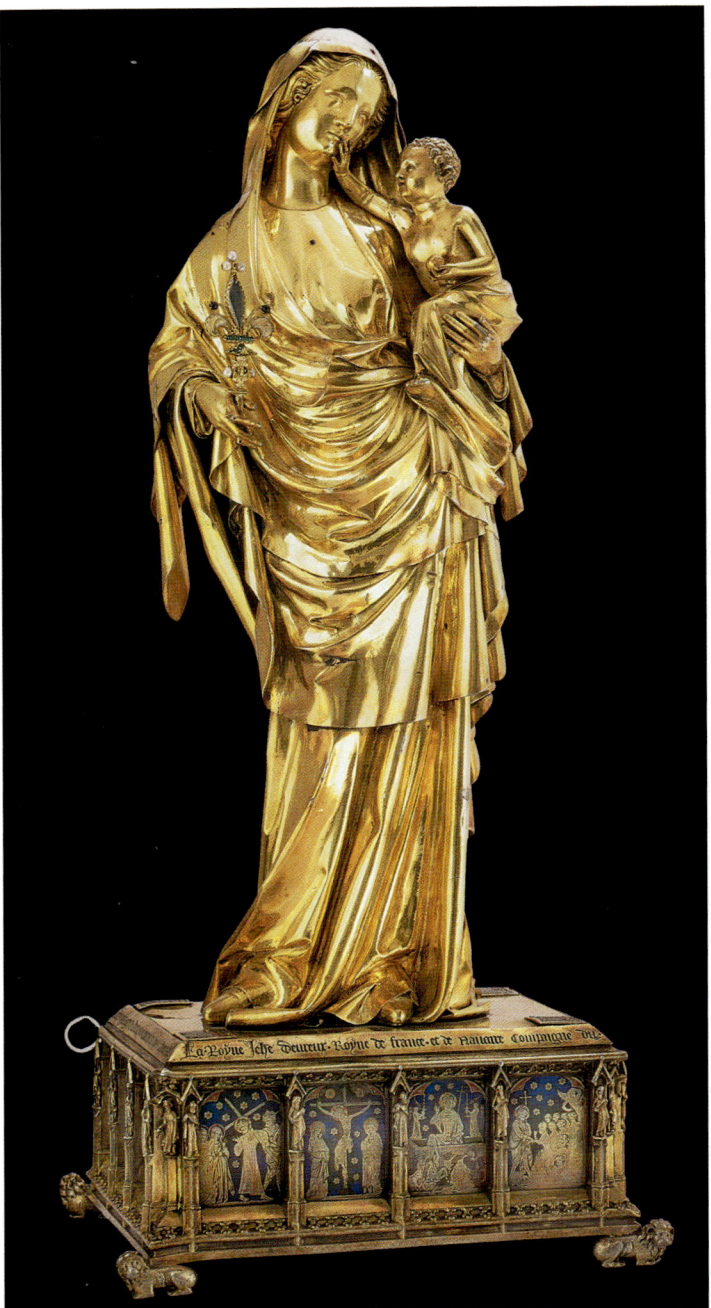

1 in.

**13-37** *Virgin of Jeanne d'Evreux,* from the abbey church of Saint-Denis, France, 1339. Silver gilt and enamel, 2′ 3½″ high. Musée du Louvre, Paris. ◼◀

Queen Jeanne d'Evreux donated this sumptuous reliquary-statuette to the royal abbey of Saint-Denis. It shares with the *Virgin of Paris* (FIG. 13-26) the intimate human characterization of the holy figures.

*Rose* by Guillaume de Lorris, written around 1225 to 1235 and completed by Jean de Meung between 1275 and 1280. At the left, the sculptor carved the allegory of the siege of the Castle of Love. Gothic knights attempt to capture love's fortress by shooting flowers from their bows and hurling baskets of roses over the walls from catapults. Among the castle's defenders is Cupid, who aims his arrow at one of the knights while a comrade scales the walls on a ladder. In the lid's central sections, two knights joust on horseback. Several maidens survey the contest from a balcony and cheer the knights on as trumpets blare. A youth in the crowd holds a hunting falcon. The

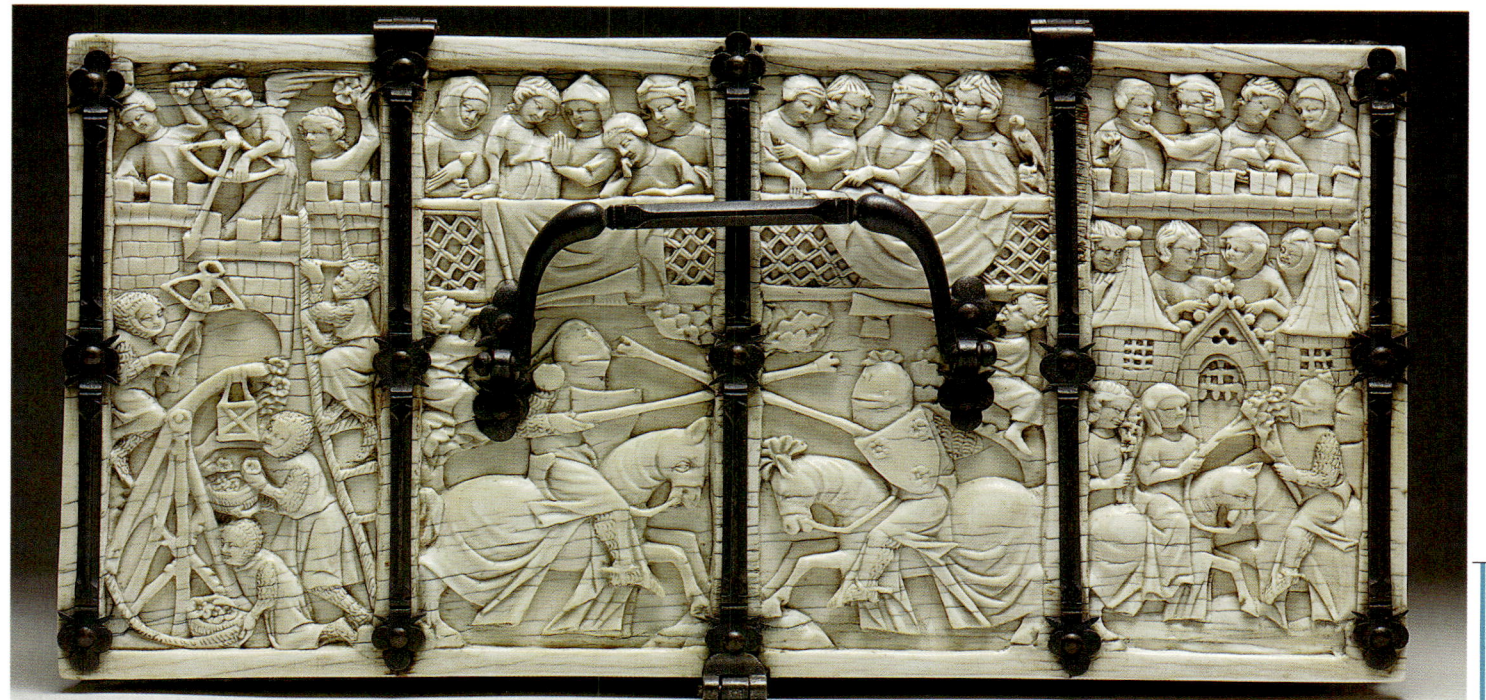

**13-38** *Castle of Love,* lid of a jewelry box, from Paris, France, ca. 1330–1350. Ivory and iron, $4\frac{1}{2}'' \times 9\frac{3}{4}''$. Walters Art Museum, Baltimore.

French Gothic artists also created luxurious objects for homes. Adorning this jewelry casket are ivory reliefs inspired by the romantic literature of the day. Knights joust and storm the Castle of Love.

1 in.

sport was a favorite pastime of the leisure class in the late Middle Ages. At the right, the victorious knight receives his prize (a bouquet of roses) from a chastely dressed maiden on horseback. The scenes on the sides of the box include the legend of the unicorn—a white horse with a single ivory horn, a medieval allegory of female virtue. Only a virgin could attract the rare animal, and any woman who could do so thereby demonstrated her moral purity. Although religious themes monopolized artistic production for churches in the Gothic age, secular themes figured prominently in private contexts. Unfortunately, very few examples of the latter survive.

# ENGLAND

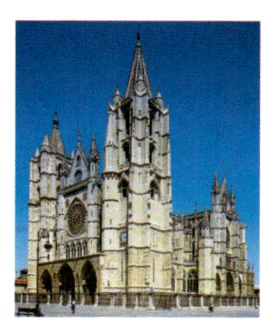

**13-38A** Santa María, Léon, begun 1254.

In 1269, the prior (deputy abbot) of the church of Saint Peter at Wimpfen-im-Tal in the German Rhineland hired "a very experienced architect who had recently come from the city of Paris" to rebuild his monastery church.[4] The architect reconstructed the church *opere francigeno* (in the French manner)—that is, in the Gothic style, the *opus modernum* of the Île-de-France. A French architect may also have designed the Cathedral of Santa María (FIG. **13-38A**) at Léon in northern Spain, begun in 1254. The spread of the Parisian Gothic style had begun even earlier, but in the second half of the 13th century, the new style became dominant throughout the Continent. European architecture did not, however, turn Gothic all at once or even uniformly. Almost everywhere, patrons and builders modified the court style of the Île-de-France according to local preferences. Because the old Romanesque traditions lingered on in many places, each area,

marrying its local Romanesque design to the new style, developed its own brand of Gothic architecture.

Beginning with the Norman conquest in 1066 (see Chapter 12), French artistic and architectural styles quickly had an influence in England, but in the Gothic period, as in the Romanesque, English artworks (for example, RICHARD DE BELLO's *mappamundi* in Hereford Cathedral, FIG. **13-38B**) have a distinctive character.

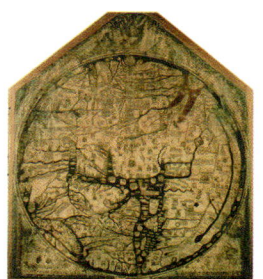

**13-38B** *Mappamundi* of Henry III, ca. 1277–1289.

**SALISBURY CATHEDRAL** English Gothic churches cannot be mistaken for French ones. The English Gothic style reflects an aesthetic sensibility quite different from French Gothic in emphasizing linear pattern and horizontality instead of structural logic and verticality. Salisbury Cathedral (FIGS. **13-39** to **13-41**), begun in 1220—the same year work started on Amiens Cathedral (FIGS. 13-19 to 13-21)—embodies these essential characteristics. The building campaign lasted about 40 years. The two cathedrals thus are almost exactly contemporaneous, and the differences between them are instructive. Although Salisbury's facade incorporates some of the superficial motifs of French Gothic architecture—for example, lancet windows and blind arcades with pointed arches as well as statuary—it presents a striking contrast to French High Gothic designs (FIGS. 13-21 and 13-23). The English facade is a squat screen in front of the nave, wider than the building behind it. The architect did not seek to match the soaring height of French facades or try to make the facade correspond to the three-part division of the interior (nave and two aisles). Different, too, is the emphasis on the great crossing tower (added around 1320–1330), which

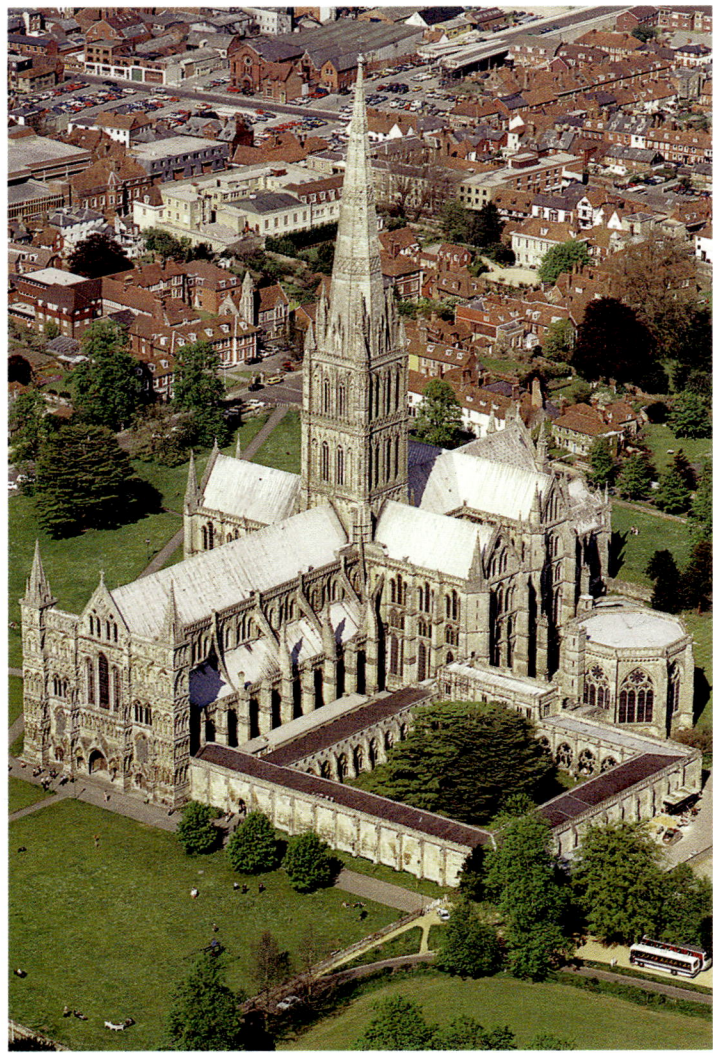

**13-39** Aerial view of Salisbury Cathedral (looking northeast), Salisbury, England, 1220–1258; west facade completed 1265; spire ca. 1320–1330. ◼◀

Exhibiting the distinctive regional features of English Gothic architecture, Salisbury Cathedral has a squat facade that is wider than the building behind it. The architects used flying buttresses sparingly.

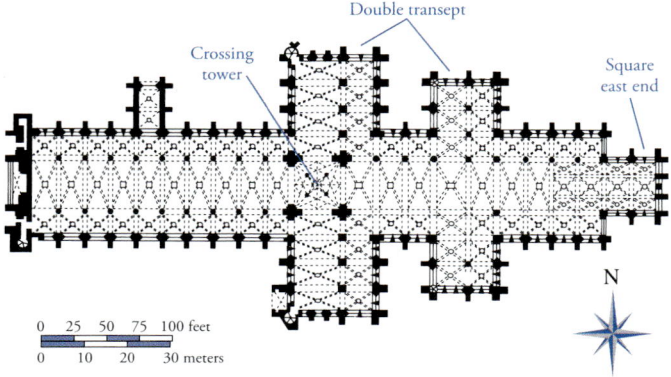

**13-40** Plan of Salisbury Cathedral, Salisbury, England, 1220–1258.

The long rectilinear plan of Salisbury Cathedral, with its double transept and flat eastern end, is typically English. The four-part rib vaults of the nave follow the Chartres model (FIG. 13-13).

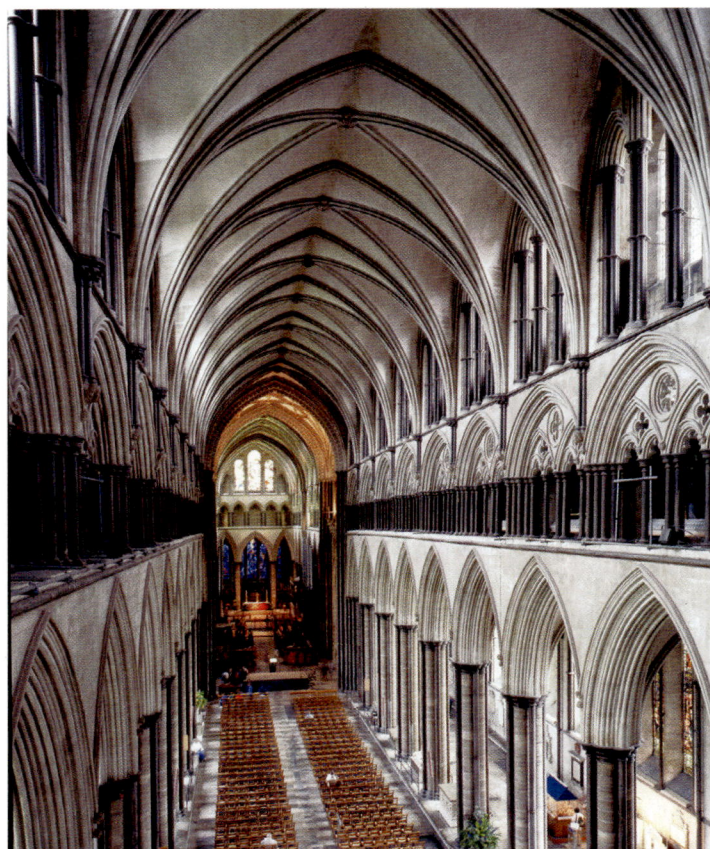

**13-41** Interior of Salisbury Cathedral (looking east), Salisbury, England, 1220–1258.

Salisbury Cathedral's interior differs from contemporaneous French Gothic designs in the strong horizontal emphasis of its three-story elevation and the use of dark Purbeck marble for moldings.

dominates the silhouette. Salisbury's height is modest compared with that of Amiens and Reims. Because height is not a decisive factor in the English building, the architect used the flying buttress sparingly.

Equally distinctive is Salisbury Cathedral's long rectilinear plan (FIG. 13-40), with its double transept and flat eastern end. The latter feature was characteristic of Cistercian (FIG. 12-10A) and English churches since Romanesque times. The interior (FIG. 13-41), although Gothic in its three-story elevation, pointed arches, four-part rib vaults, compound piers, and the tracery of the triforium, conspicuously departs from the French Gothic style. The pier colonnettes stop at the springing of the nave arches and do not connect with the vault ribs (compare FIGS. 13-19, 13-20, and 13-23A). Instead, the vault ribs rise from corbels in the triforium, producing a strong horizontal emphasis. Underscoring this horizontality is the rich color contrast between the light stone of the walls and vaults and the dark marble (from the Isle of Purbeck in southeastern England) used for the triforium moldings and corbels, compound pier responds, and other details. In short, French Gothic architecture may have inspired the design of Salisbury Cathedral, but its builders transformed the French style in accordance with English taste.

**GLOUCESTER CATHEDRAL** The elaboration of architectural pattern for its own sake had long been a distinguishing feature of English architecture. The decorative motifs on the Romanesque piers

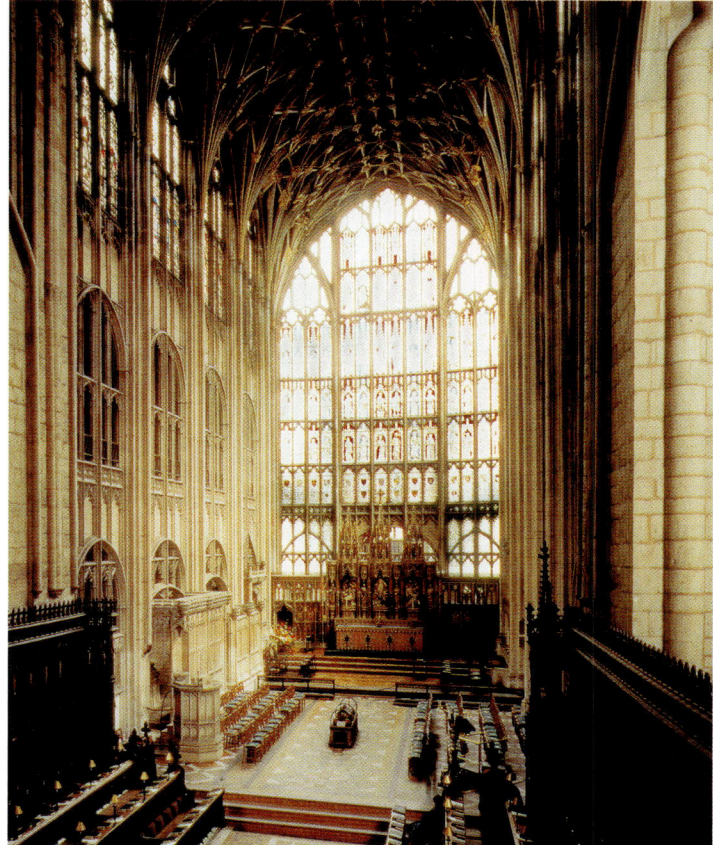

**13-42** Choir of Gloucester Cathedral (looking east), Gloucester, England, 1332–1357.

The Perpendicular style of Late English Gothic architecture takes its name from the pronounced verticality of its linear details. The multiplication of ribs in the vaults is also a characteristic feature.

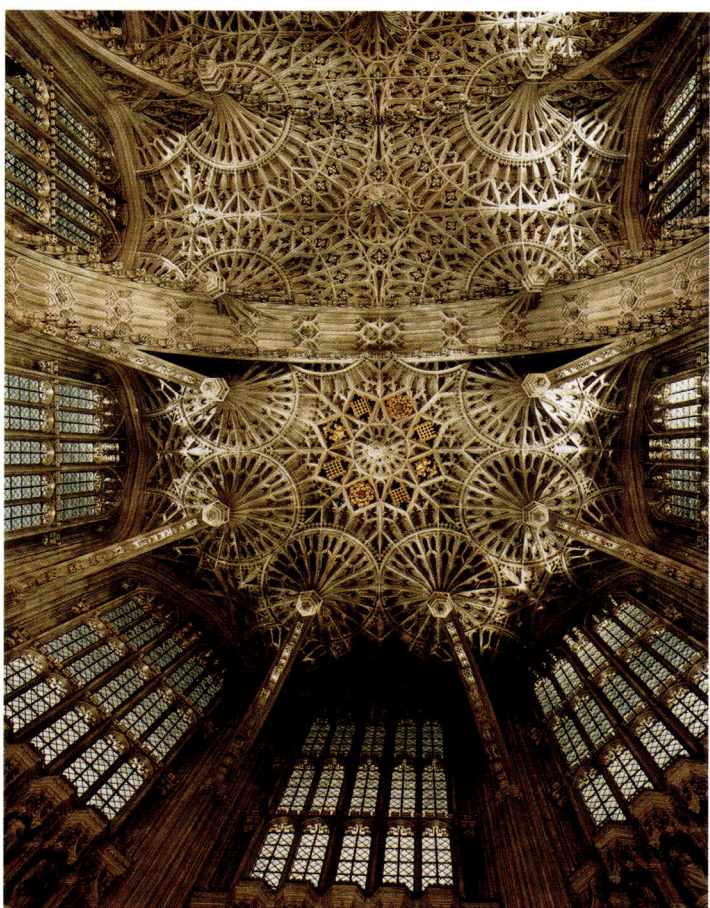

**13-43** ROBERT and WILLIAM VERTUE, fan vaults of the chapel of Henry VII, Westminster Abbey, London, England, 1503–1519. ◼◀

The chapel of Henry VII epitomizes the decorative and structure-disguising qualities of the Perpendicular style in the use of fan vaults with lacelike tracery and pendants resembling stalactites.

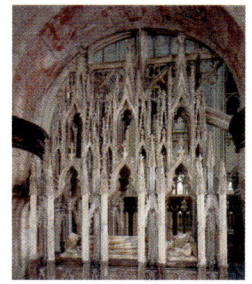

**13-42A** Tomb of Edward II, Gloucester, ca. 1330–1335.

of Durham Cathedral (FIG. 12-33, *left*) are an early example. The pier, wall, and vault elements, still relatively simple at Salisbury, became increasingly complex and decorative in the 14th century, culminating in what architectural historians call the *Perpendicular* style. This Late English Gothic style is on display in the choir (FIG. **13-42**) of Gloucester Cathedral, remodeled about a century after Salisbury under Edward III (r. 1327–1357), who also installed a Perpendicular style tomb (FIG. **13-42A**) in the church in honor of his father, Edward II (r. 1307–1327). The Perpendicular style takes its name from the pronounced verticality of its decorative details, in contrast to the horizontal emphasis of Salisbury and Early English Gothic.

A single enormous window divided into tiers of small windows of similar shape and proportion fills the characteristically flat east end of Gloucester Cathedral. At the top, two slender lancets flank a wider central section that also ends in a pointed arch. The design has much in common with the screen facade of Salisbury, but the proportions are different. Vertical, as opposed to horizontal, lines dominate. In the choir wall, the architect also erased Salisbury's strong horizontal accents, as the vertical wall elements lift directly from the floor to the vaulting, unifying the walls with the vaults in the French

manner. The vault ribs, which designers had begun to multiply soon after Salisbury, are at Gloucester a dense thicket of entirely ornamental strands serving no structural purpose. The choir, in fact, does not have any rib vaults at all but a continuous Romanesque barrel vault with applied Gothic ornamentation. In the Gloucester choir, the taste for decorative surfaces triumphed over structural clarity.

**CHAPEL OF HENRY VII** The decorative, structure-disguising qualities of the Perpendicular style became even more pronounced in its late phases. A primary example is the early-16th-century ceiling (FIG. **13-43**) of the chapel of Henry VII adjoining Westminster Abbey in London. Here, ROBERT and WILLIAM VERTUE turned the earlier English linear play of ribs into a kind of architectural embroidery. The architects pulled the ribs into uniquely English *fan vaults* (vaults with radiating ribs forming a fanlike pattern) with large hanging *pendants* resembling stalactites. The vault looks as if it had been some organic mass hardened in the process of melting. Intricate tracery resembling lace overwhelms the cones hanging from the ceiling. The chapel represents the dissolution of structural Gothic into decorative fancy. The architects released the Gothic style's original lines from their function and multiplied them into the uninhibited architectural virtuosity and theatrics of the Perpendicular style. A parallel phenomenon in France is the Flamboyant style of Saint-Maclou (FIG. 13-27) at Rouen.

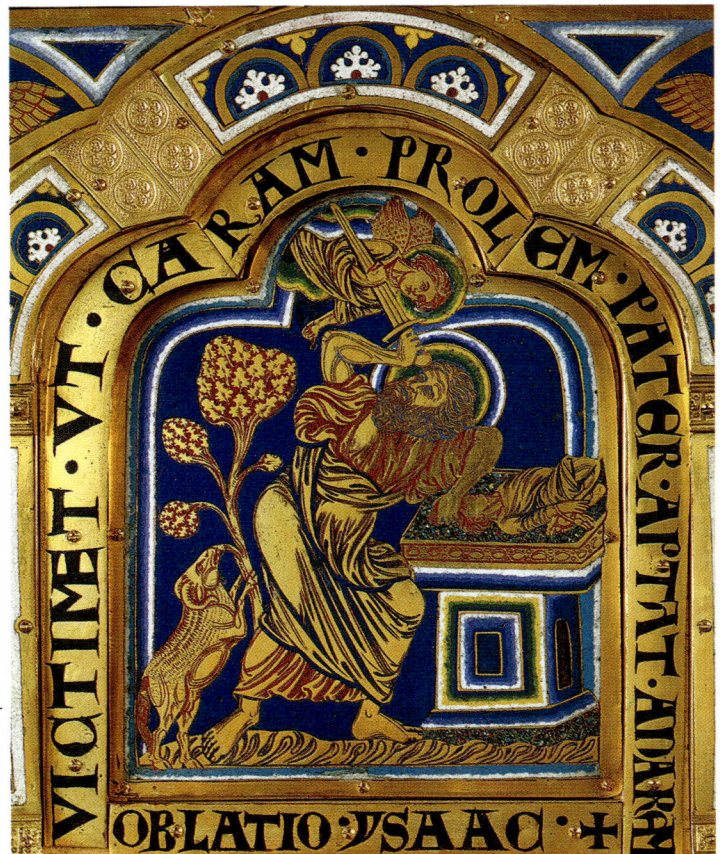

**13-44** NICHOLAS OF VERDUN, *Sacrifice of Isaac,* detail of the *Klosterneuburg Altar,* from the abbey church at Klosterneuburg, Austria, 1181. Gilded copper and enamel, 5½″ high. Stiftsmuseum, Klosterneuburg.

Nicholas of Verdun was the leading artist of the Meuse valley region, renowned for its enamel- and metalwork. His gold figures twist and turn and stand out vividly from the blue enamel background.

# HOLY ROMAN EMPIRE

As part of his plan to make his new church at Saint-Denis an earthly introduction to the splendors of Paradise (see "Abbot Suger," page 367), Suger selected artists from the Meuse River valley in present-day Belgium to fashion for the choir a magnificent crucifix on a sumptuous base decorated with 68 enamel scenes pairing Old and New Testament episodes. The Mosan region long had been famous for the quality of its metalworkers and enamelers (FIGS. 12-24 and 12-25). Indeed, as Suger's treatises demonstrate, in the Middle Ages the artists who worked at small scale with precious metals, ivory, and jewels produced the most admired objects in a church, far more important in the eyes of contemporaries than the jamb figures and tympanum reliefs that form the core of modern histories of medieval art.

**NICHOLAS OF VERDUN** The leading Mosan artist of the late 12th and early 13th centuries was NICHOLAS OF VERDUN. In 1181, Nicholas completed work on a gilded-copper and enamel *ambo* (a pulpit for biblical readings) for the Benedictine abbey church at Klosterneuburg, near Vienna in Austria. After a fire damaged the pulpit in 1330, the church hired artists to convert the pulpit into an *altarpiece.* The pulpit's sides became the wings of a *triptych* (three-part altarpiece). The 14th-century artists also

added six scenes to Nicholas's original 45. The *Klosterneuburg Altar* in its final form (FIG. **13-44A**) has a central row of enamels depicting New Testament episodes, beginning with the *Annunciation,* and bearing the label *sub gracia,* or the world "under grace," that is, after the coming of Christ. The upper and lower registers contain Old Testament scenes labeled, respectively, *ante legem,* "before the law" Moses received on Mount Sinai, and *sub lege,* "under the law" of the Ten Commandments. In this scheme, prophetic Old Testament events appear above and below the New Testament episodes they prefigure. For example, framing the *Annunciation* to Mary of the coming birth of Jesus are enamels of angels announcing the births of Isaac and Samson. In the central section of the triptych, the Old Testament counterpart of Christ's *Crucifixion* is Abraham's *Sacrifice of Isaac* (FIG. **13-44**), a parallel already established in Early Christian times (see "Jewish Subjects in Christian Art," Chapter 8, page 238, and FIG. 8-1). Here, the angel flies in at the last moment to grab the blade of Abraham's sword before he can slay the bound Isaac on the altar.

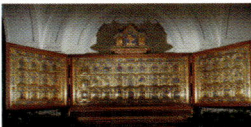

**13-44A** *Klosterneuburg Altar,* refashioned after 1330.

Nicholas of Verdun's Klosterneuburg enamels may give an idea of the appearance of the Old and New Testament enamels on the lost Saint-Denis crucifix. Universally admired, Mosan enamels and metalwork were instrumental in the development of the French Gothic figural style. The gold figures stand out vividly from the blue enamel background. The biblical actors twist and turn, make emphatic gestures, and wear garments almost overwhelmed by the intricate linear patterns of their folds.

Sculpted versions of the Klosterneuburg figures appear on the *Shrine of the Three Kings* (FIG. **13-45**) in Cologne Cathedral. Nicholas of Verdun probably began work on the huge reliquary (six feet long and almost as tall) in 1190. Philip von Heinsberg, archbishop of Cologne from 1167 to 1191, commissioned the shrine to contain relics of the three magi. Holy Roman Emperor Frederick Barbarossa (r. 1155–1190) acquired them in the conquest of Milan in 1164 and donated them to the German cathedral. Possession of the magi's relics gave the Cologne archbishops the right to crown German kings. Nicholas's reliquary, made of silver and bronze with ornamentation in enamel and gemstones, is one of the most luxurious ever fashioned, especially considering its size. The shape resembles that of a basilican church. Repoussé figures of the Virgin Mary, the three magi, Old Testament prophets, and New Testament apostles in arcuated frames are variations of those on the Klosterneuburg pulpit. The deep channels and tight bunches of drapery folds are hallmarks of Nicholas's style.

The *Klosterneuburg Altar* and *Shrine of the Three Kings,* together with Suger's treatises on the furnishings of Saint-Denis, are welcome reminders of how magnificently outfitted medieval church interiors were. The sumptuous small-scale objects exhibited in the choir and chapels, which also housed the church's most precious relics, played a defining role in creating a special otherworldly atmosphere for Christian ritual. These Gothic examples continued a tradition dating to the Roman emperor Constantine and the first imperial patronage of Christianity (see Chapter 8).

**STRASBOURG CATHEDRAL** About the time Nicholas of Verdun was at work on the *Klosterneuburg Altar,* construction began on a new cathedral for Strasbourg in present-day France, then an important city in the German Rhineland ruled by the successors of the Ottonian dynasty. The apse, choir, and transepts, begun in

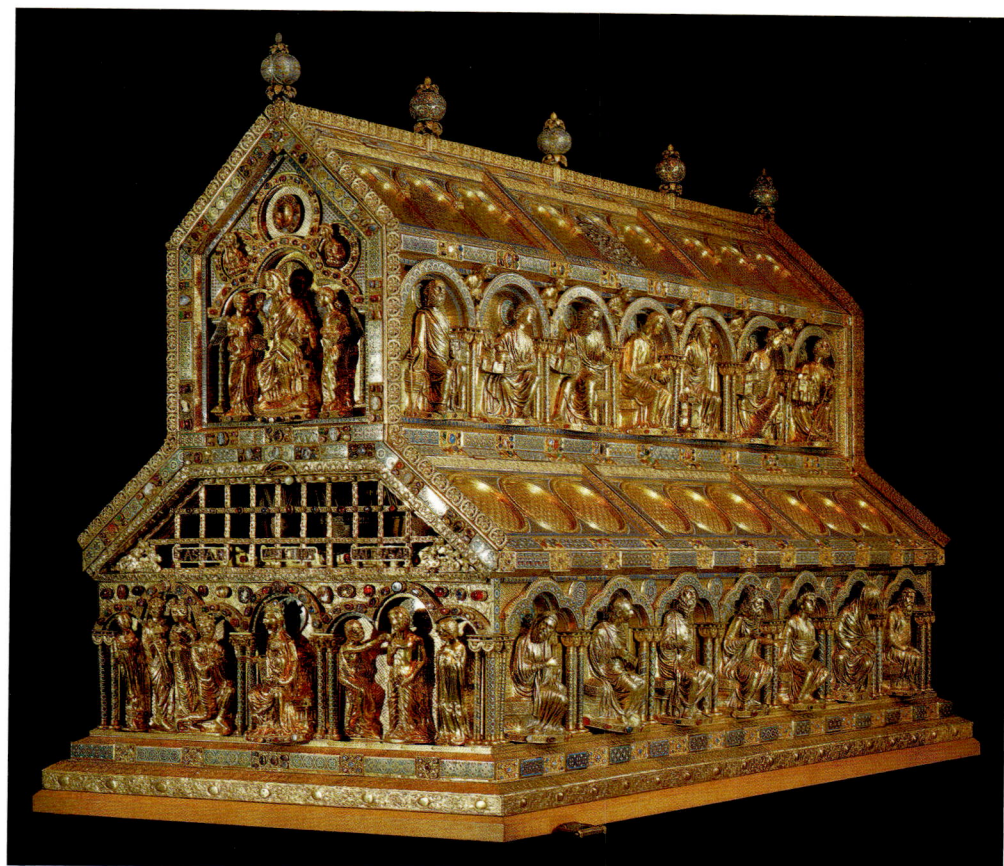

13-45 NICHOLAS OF VERDUN, *Shrine of the Three Kings,* from Cologne Cathedral, Cologne, Germany, begun ca. 1190. Silver, bronze, enamel, and gemstones, 5′ 8″ × 6′ × 3′ 8″. Dom Schatzkammer, Cologne.

Cologne's archbishop commissioned this huge reliquary in the shape of a church to house relics of the three magi. The deep channels of drapery folds are hallmarks of Nicholas's influential style.

1 ft.

1176, were in place by around 1230. Stylistically, these sections of Strasbourg Cathedral are Romanesque. But the reliefs of the two south-transept portals are fully Gothic and reveal the same interest in the antique style as in contemporaneous French sculpture, especially that of Reims, as well as in the earlier work of Nicholas of Verdun. By the mid-13th century, artists throughout Europe were producing antique-looking statuary and relief sculpture.

The left tympanum (FIG. 13-46) presents *Death of the Virgin.* A comparison of the Strasbourg Mary on her deathbed with the Mary of the Reims *Visitation* group (FIG. 13-24, *right*) shows the stylistic kinship of the Strasbourg and Reims masters. The 12 apostles gather around the Virgin, forming an arc of mourners well suited to the semicircular frame. The sculptor adjusted the heights of the figures to fit the available space (the apostles at the right are the shortest)

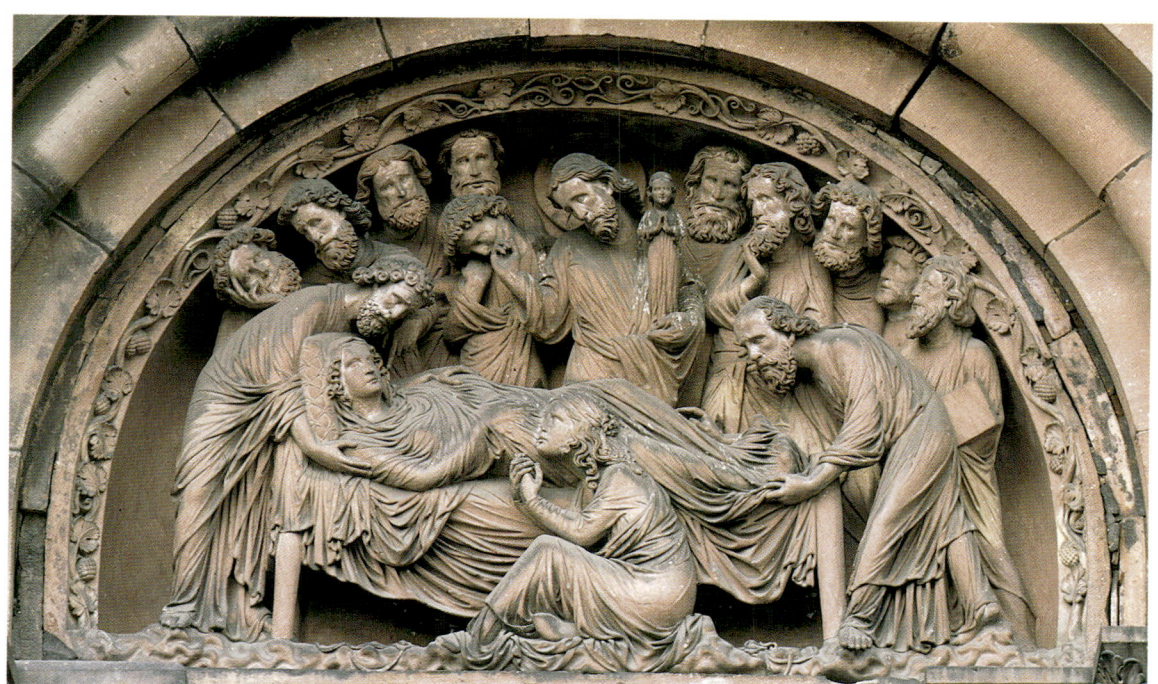

13-46 *Death of the Virgin,* tympanum of the left doorway of the south transept, Strasbourg Cathedral, Strasbourg, France, ca. 1230.

Stylistically akin to the *Visitation* group (FIG. 13-24, *right*) of Reims Cathedral, the figures in Strasbourg's south-transept tympanum express profound sorrow through dramatic poses and gestures.

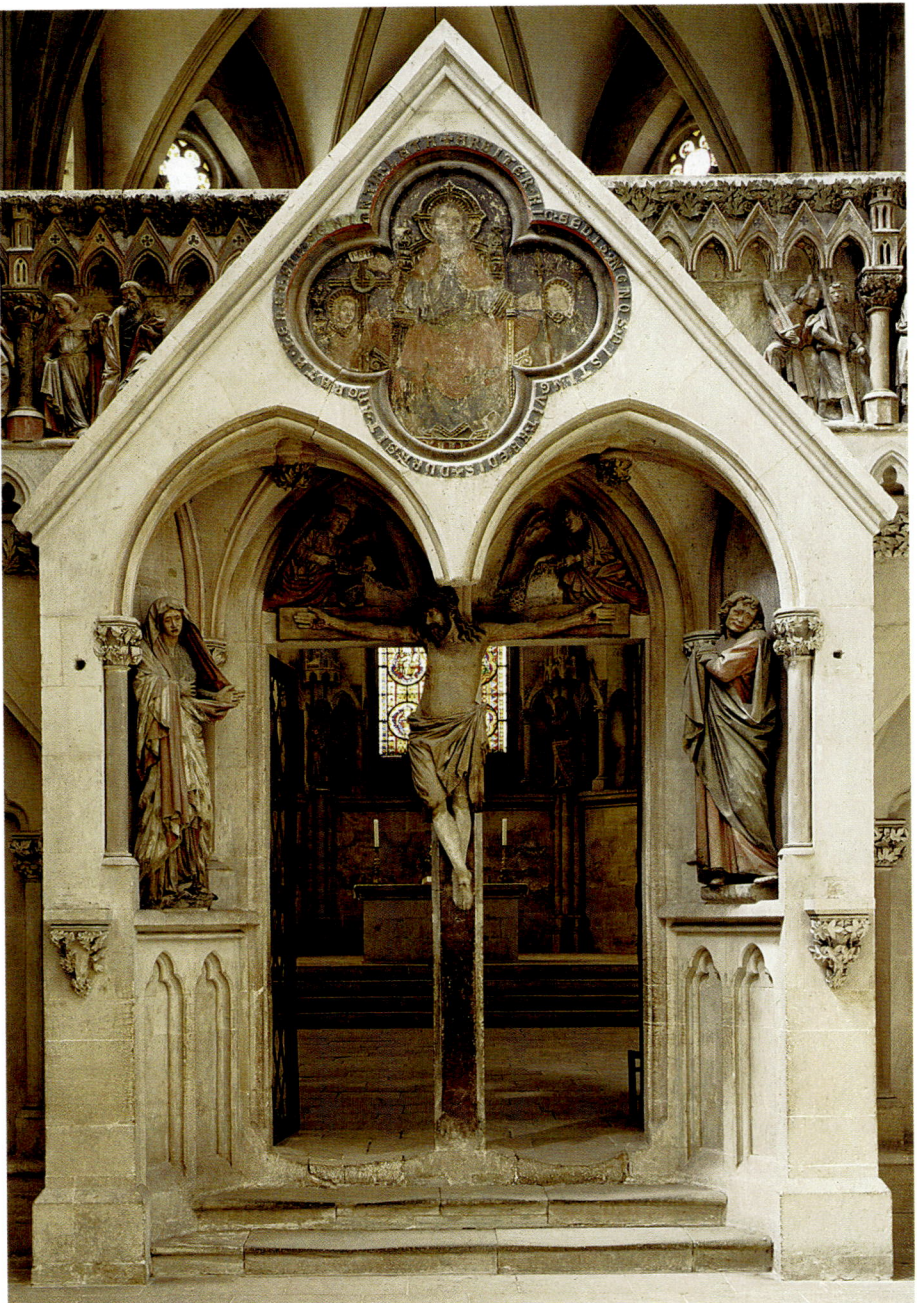

**13-47** NAUMBURG MASTER, *Crucifixion*, west choir screen of Naumburg Cathedral, Naumburg, Germany, ca. 1249–1255. Painted limestone statues, life size.

The emotional pathos of the crucified Christ and the mourning Virgin and Saint John are characteristic of German medieval sculpture. The choir screen is also notable for its preserved coloration.

and, as in many depictions of crowds in the history of art, some of the figures have no legs or feet. At the center, Christ receives his mother's soul (the doll-like figure he holds in his left hand). Mary Magdalene, wringing her hands in grief, crouches beside the deathbed. The sorrowing figures express emotion in varying degrees of intensity, from serene resignation to gesturing agitation. The sculptor organized the group both by dramatic pose and gesture and by the rippling flow of deeply incised drapery passing among them like a rhythmic electric pulse. The sculptor's objective was to imbue the sacred figures with human emotions and to stir emotional responses in observers. In Gothic France, as already noted, art became increasingly humanized and natural. In the Holy Roman Empire, artists carried this humanizing trend even further by emphasizing passionate drama.

**NAUMBURG CATHEDRAL** During his tenure as bishop (1244–1272), Dietrich II of Wettin completed the rebuilding of the Romanesque cathedral at Naumburg in northern Germany. The church had two choirs, and the western choir, which Dietrich commissioned, was the most distinctive aspect of the project. The bishop built the choir as a memorial to 12 donors of the original 11th-century church. The artist who oversaw this project, known as the NAUMBURG MASTER, directed the team of sculptors responsible for the monumental screen (FIG. **13-47**) that functioned as a portal to the western choir. Based loosely on contemporaneous church portals having statues on the trumeau and jambs, the Naumburg screen includes life-size figures of Christ on the cross and of the distraught Virgin Mary and John the Evangelist. John, openly crying, turns his head away, unable to look at the suffering Christ. Mary also does not look at her son, but she faces and gestures toward the approaching worshipers, suggesting she can intercede on their behalf at the last judgment (compare FIG. 13-38B).

The heightened emotionalism of the Naumburg statues had been a persistent characteristic of German medieval art since the Ottonian era. Indeed, the crucified Christ in the Naumburg choir is the direct descendant of the Christ of the *Gero Crucifix* (FIG. 11-28). Like that earlier statue, these indoor sculptures have retained their color, whereas almost all the statues on church exteriors, exposed to sun and rain for centuries, have lost their original paint. The Naumburg choir screen gives modern viewers an excellent idea of the original appearance of portal sculptures of Romanesque and Gothic churches.

**EKKEHARD AND UTA** Within the choir, the same workshop carved the statues of the 12 original donors, some of whom were the bishop's ancestors. Two of the figures (FIG. **13-48**) stand out from the group of solemn men and women because of their exceptional quality. They represent the margrave (military governor) Ekkehard II of Meissen and his wife, Uta. The statues are attached to columns and stand beneath architectural canopies, following the pattern of French Gothic portal statuary, but they project from the architecture more forcefully and move more freely than contemporaneous French jamb figures. The period costumes and the individualized features and personalities of the margrave and his wife give the impression they posed for their own portraits, although

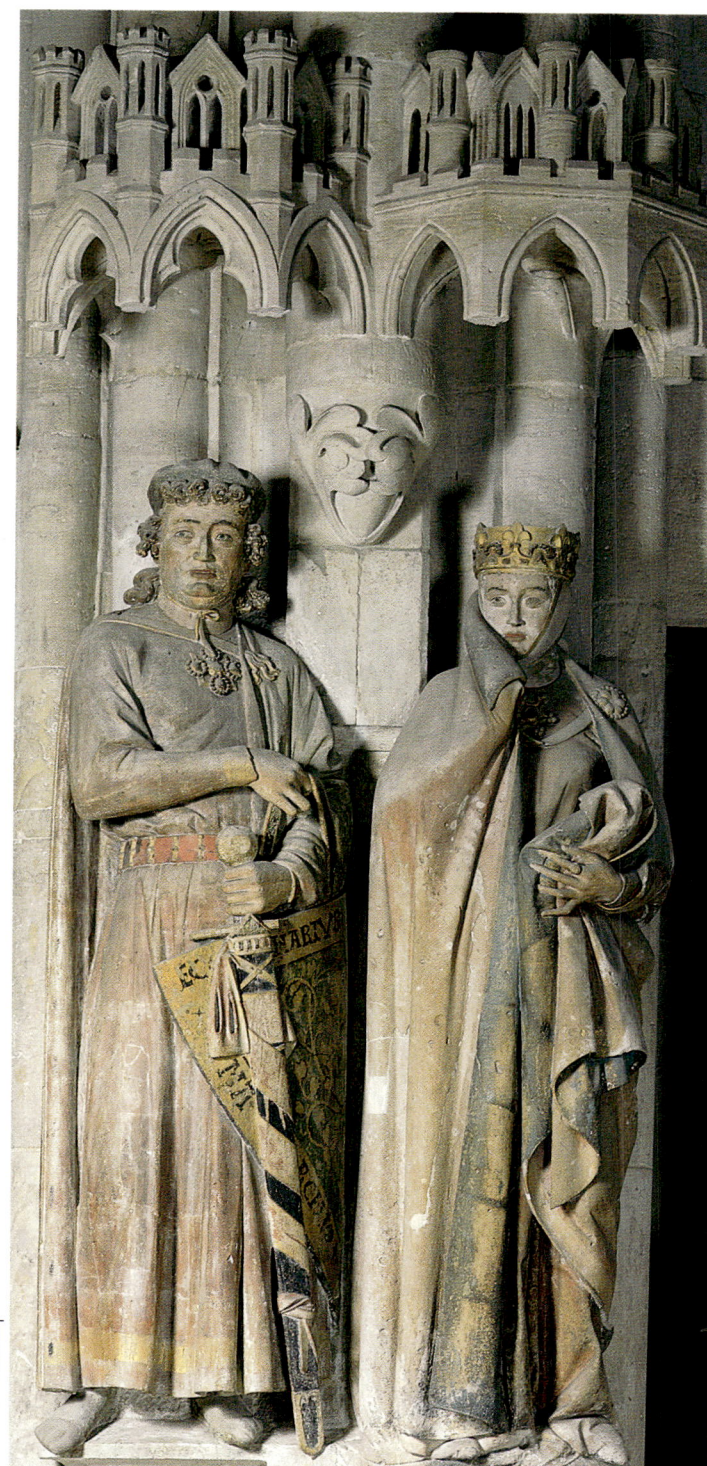

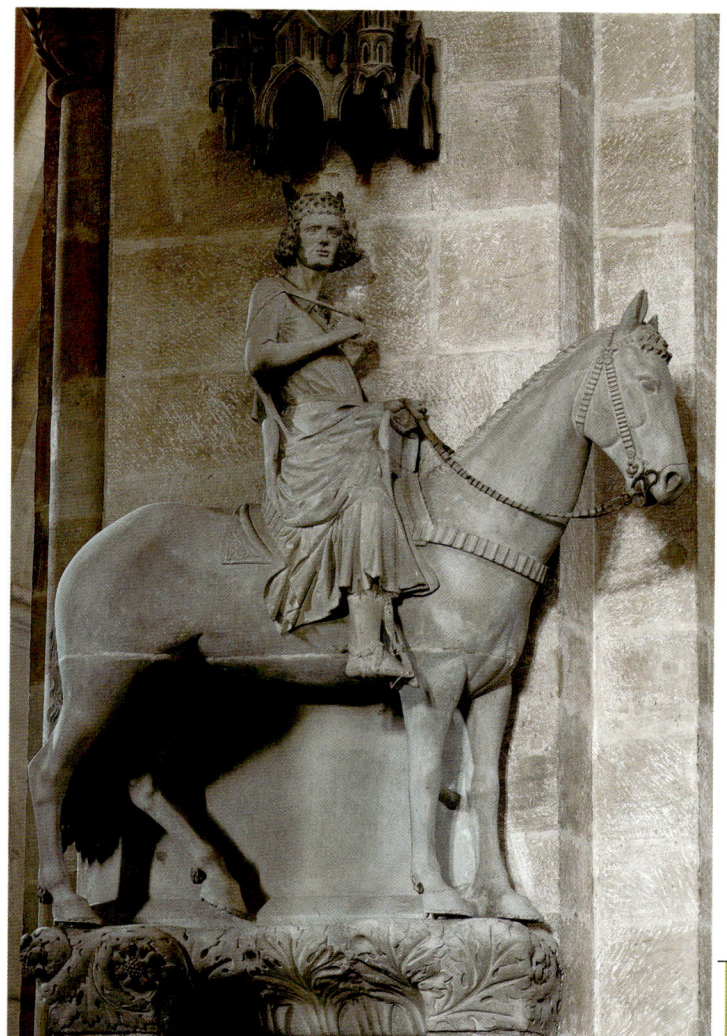

**13-49** Equestrian portrait (*Bamberg Rider*), statue in the east choir, Bamberg Cathedral, Germany, ca. 1235–1240. Sandstone, 7′ 9″ high.

Probably a portrait of a German emperor, perhaps Frederick II, the *Bamberg Rider* revives the imagery of the Carolingian Empire. The French-style architectural canopy cannot contain the statue.

1 ft.

1 ft.

**13-48** NAUMBURG MASTER, Ekkehard and Uta, statues in the west choir, Naumburg Cathedral, Naumburg, Germany, ca. 1249–1255. Painted limestone, Ekkehard 6′ 2″ high.

The period costumes and individualized features of these donor portraits give the impression Ekkehard and Uta posed for their statues, but they lived long before the Naumburg Master's time.

the subjects lived well before the Naumburg Master's time. Ekkehard, the intense knight, contrasts with the beautiful and aloof Uta. With a wonderfully graceful gesture, she draws the collar of her cloak partly across her face while she gathers up a soft fold of drapery with a jeweled, delicate hand. The sculptor subtly revealed the

shape of Uta's right arm beneath her cloak and rendered the fall of drapery folds with an accuracy suggesting the sculptor used a living model. The two statues are arresting images of real people, even if they bear the names of aristocrats the artist never met. By the mid-13th century, in the Holy Roman Empire as well as in England (FIG. 13-42A) and elsewhere, life-size images of secular personages had found their way into churches.

***BAMBERG RIDER*** Somewhat earlier in date than the Naumburg donor figures is the *Bamberg Rider* (FIG. **13-49**), the earliest preserved large-scale equestrian statue of the Middle Ages. For centuries, this statue has been mounted against a pier in Bamberg Cathedral beneath an architectural canopy that frames the rider's body but not his horse. Scholars debate whether the statue was made for this location or moved there, perhaps from the church's exterior. Whatever the statue's original location, it revives the imperial imagery of Byzantium (see "The Emperors of New Rome," Chapter 9, page 259) and the Carolingian Empire (FIG. 11-12), derived in turn from ancient Roman statuary (FIG. 7-59).

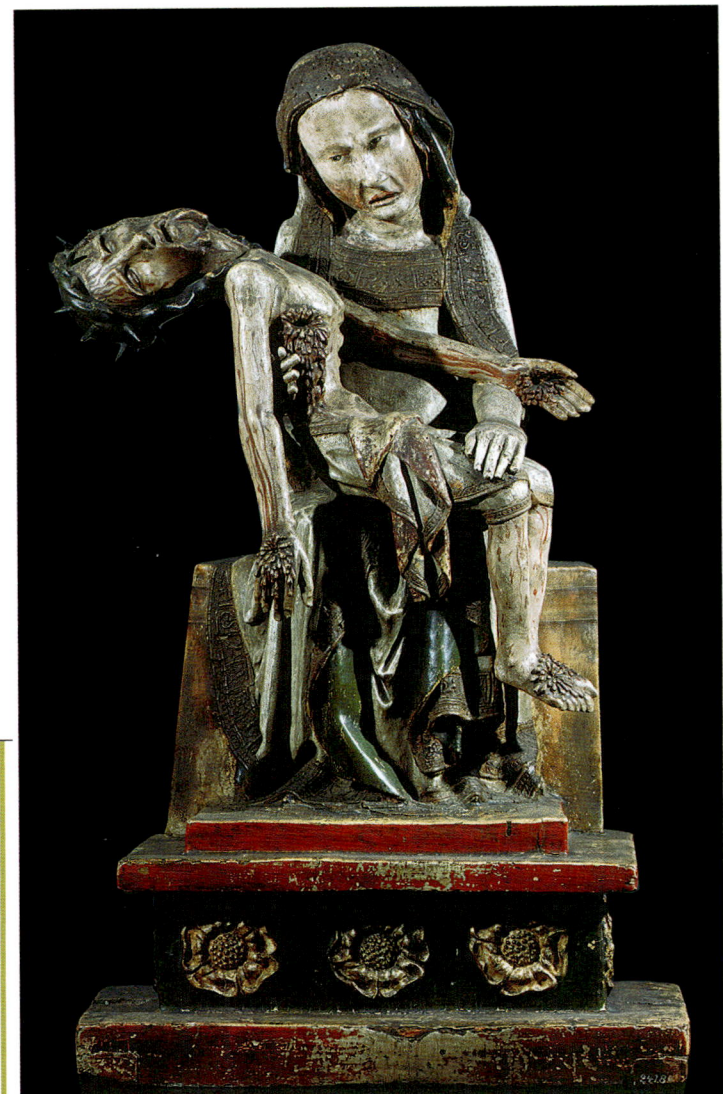

1 ft.

**13-50** *Röttgen Pietà,* from the Rhineland, Germany, ca. 1300–1325. Painted wood, 2′ 10½″ high. Rheinisches Landemuseum, Bonn. ◼◀

This statuette of the Virgin grieving over the distorted dead body of Christ in her lap reflects the increased interest in the 13th and 14th centuries in Jesus' suffering and the Virgin's grief.

Unlike Ekkehard and Uta, the *Bamberg Rider* seems to be a true portrait of a living person. Some art historians believe it represents a Holy Roman emperor, perhaps Frederick II (r. 1220– 1250), who was a benefactor of Bamberg Cathedral. The many other identifications include Saint George and one of the three magi, but a historical personality is most likely the subject. The placement of a portrait of a Holy Roman emperor in the cathedral would have underscored the unity of church and state in 13th-century Germany. The artist carefully represented the rider's costume, the high saddle, and the horse's trappings. The *Bamberg Rider* turns toward the observer, as if presiding at a review of troops. The torsion of this figure reflects the same impatience with subordination to architecture found in the sculptures of Naumburg Cathedral (FIGS. 13-47 and 13-48).

**RÖTTGEN PIETÀ** The confident 13th-century portraits at Naumburg and Bamberg stand in marked contrast to a haunting

14th-century German painted wooden statuette (FIG. **13-50**) of the Virgin Mary holding the dead Christ in her lap. Like the *Crucifixion* (FIG. 13-47) of Naumburg's west choir, this *Pietà* (Italian, "pity" or "compassion") reflects the increased interest during the 13th and 14th centuries in humanizing biblical figures and in the suffering of Jesus and grief of his mother and followers. This expressed emotionalism accompanied the shift toward representation of the human body in motion. As the figures of the church portals began to twist on their columns, then move within their niches, and then stand independently, their details became more outwardly related to the human audience as indicators of recognizable human emotions.

The sculptor of the *Röttgen Pietà* (named after a collector) portrayed Christ as a stunted, distorted human wreck, stiffened in death and covered with streams of blood gushing from a huge wound. The Virgin, who cradles him as if he were a child in her lap, is the very image of maternal anguish, her oversized face twisted in an expression of unbearable grief. This statue expresses nothing of the serenity of Romanesque and earlier Gothic depictions of Mary (FIGS. 12-19 and 13-16). Nor does it have anything in common with the aloof, iconic images of the Theotokos with the infant Jesus in her lap common in Byzantine art (FIGS. 9-18 and 9-19). Here the artist forcibly confronts the devout with an appalling icon of agony, death, and sorrow. The work calls out to the horrified believer, "What is your suffering compared to this?"

**COLOGNE CATHEDRAL** The architecture of the Holy Roman Empire remained conservatively Romanesque well into the 13th century. In many German churches, the only Gothic feature was the rib vault, buttressed solely by the heavy masonry of the walls. By mid-century, though, the French Gothic style began to have a profound influence.

Cologne Cathedral (FIG. **13-51**), begun in 1248 under the direction of GERHARD OF COLOGNE, was not completed until more than 600 years later, making it one of the longest construction projects on record. Work halted entirely from the mid-16th to the mid-19th century, when church officials unexpectedly discovered the 14th-century design for the facade. *Gothic Revival* architects then completed the building according to the original plans, adding the nave, towers, and facade to the east end, which had stood alone for several centuries. The Gothic/Gothic Revival structure is the largest cathedral in northern Europe and boasts a giant (422-foot-long) nave (FIG. **13-52**) with two aisles on each side.

The 150-foot-high 14th-century choir is a skillful variation of the Amiens Cathedral choir (FIGS. 13-20 and 13-21) design, with double lancets in the triforium and tall, slender single windows in the clerestory above and choir arcade below. Completed four decades after Gerhard's death but according to his plans, the choir expresses the Gothic quest for height even more emphatically than do many French Gothic buildings. Despite the cathedral's seeming lack of substance, proof of its stability came during World War II, when the city of Cologne suffered extremely heavy aerial bombardments. The church survived the war by virtue of its Gothic skeletal design. Once the first few bomb blasts blew out all of its windows, subsequent explosions had no adverse effects, and the skeleton remained intact and structurally sound.

**SAINT ELIZABETH, MARBURG** A different type of design, also probably of French origin (FIG. 12-17) but developed especially in Germany, is the *Hallenkirche* (hall church), in which the height of the aisles is the same as the height of the nave. Hall

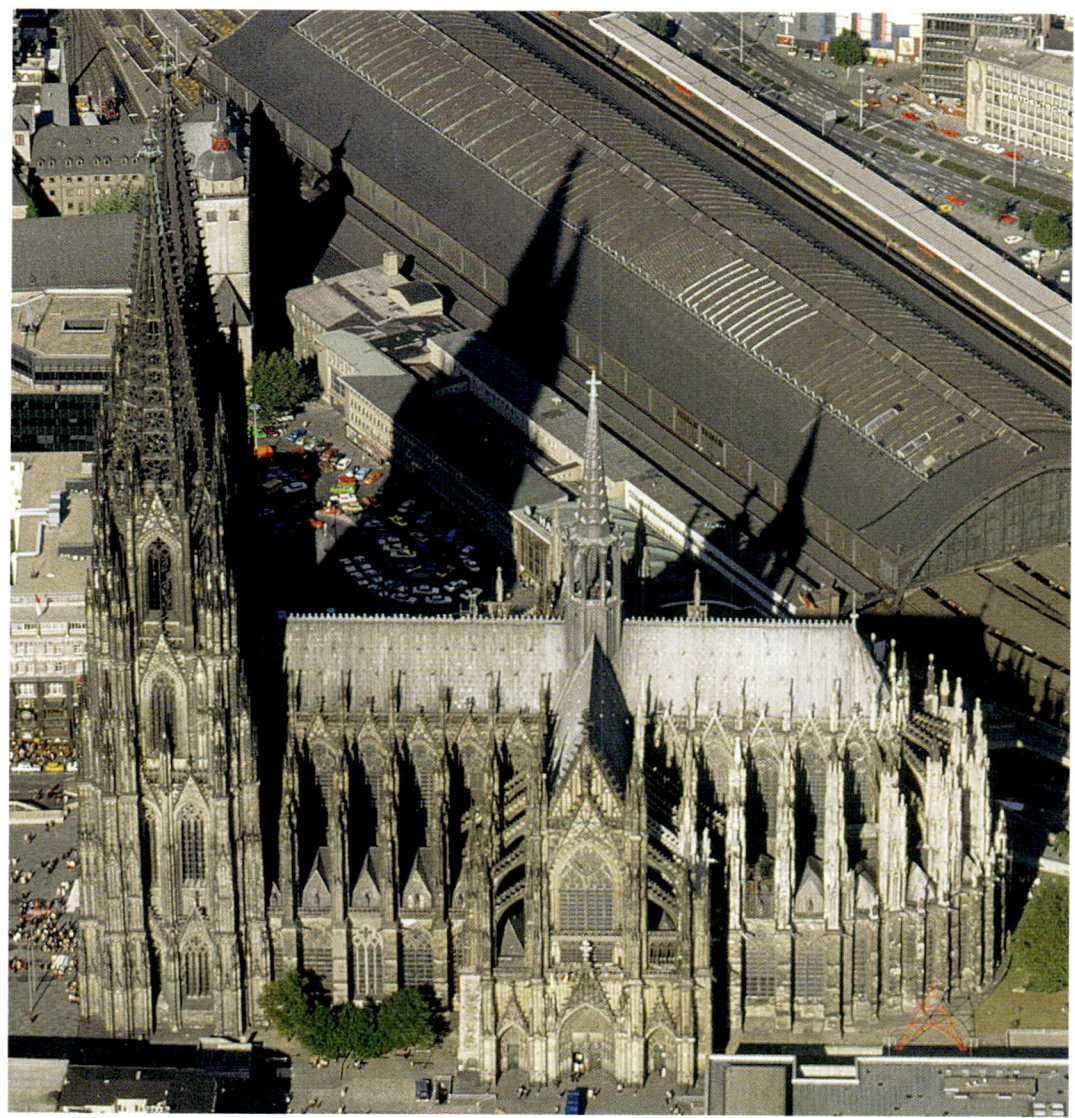

Cologne Cathedral, the largest church in northern Europe, took more than 600 years to build. Only the east end dates to the 13th century. The 19th-century portions follow the original Gothic plans.

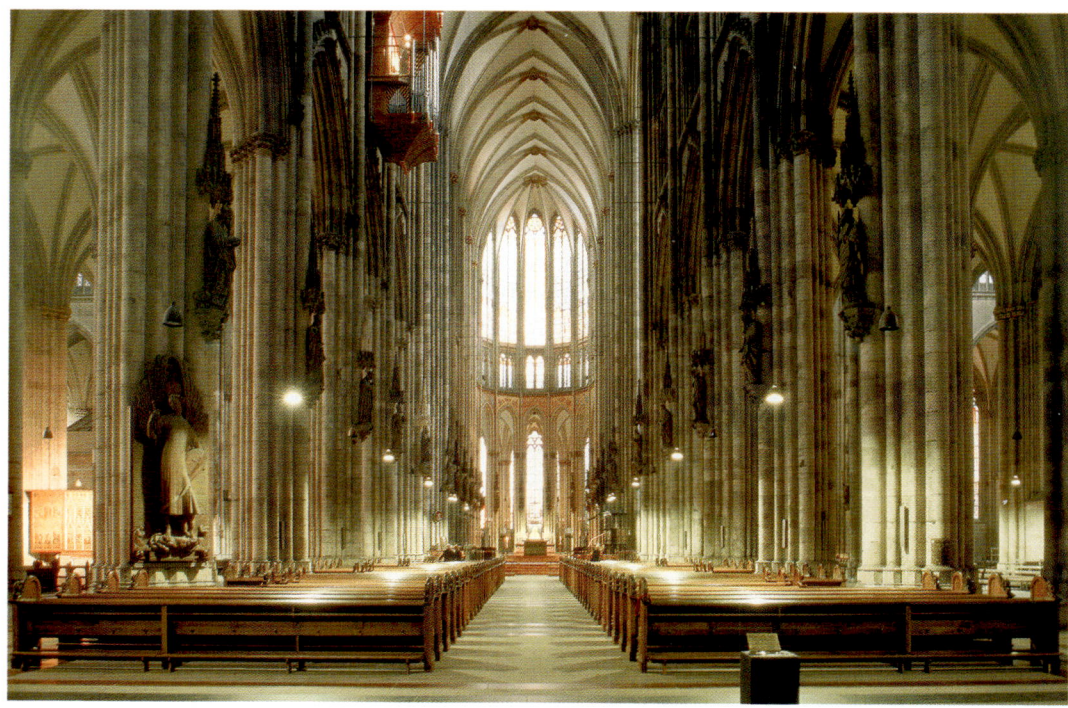

13-52 GERHARD OF COLOGNE, interior of Cologne Cathedral (looking east), Cologne, Germany. Choir completed 1322.

Cologne Cathedral's nave is 422 feet long. The 150-foot-high choir, a taller variation on the Amiens Cathedral choir (FIGS. 13-20 and 13-21), is a prime example of Gothic architects' quest for height.

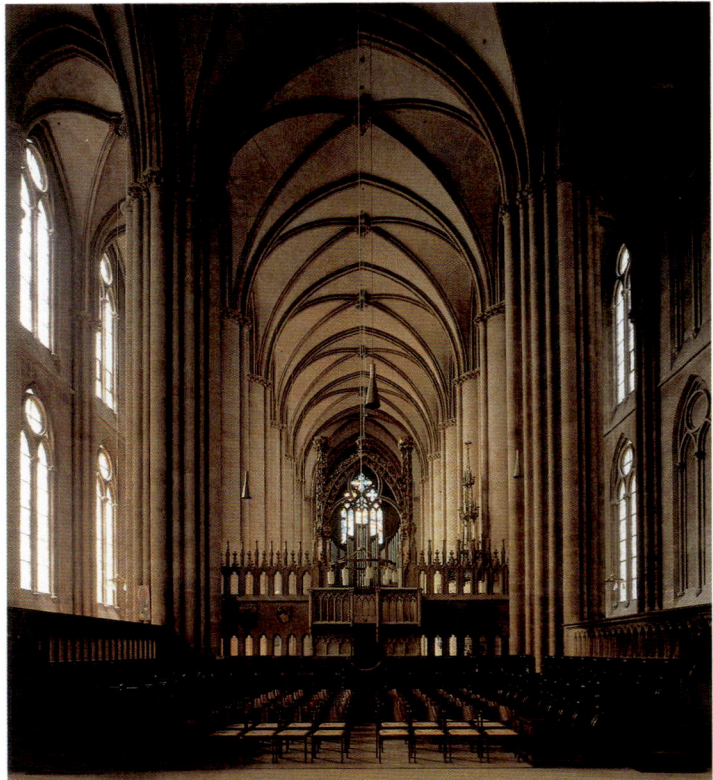

**13-53** Interior of Saint Elizabeth (looking west), Marburg, Germany, 1235–1283.

This German church is an early example of a Hallenkirche, in which the aisles are the same height as the nave. Because of the tall windows in the aisle walls, sunlight brightly illuminates the interior.

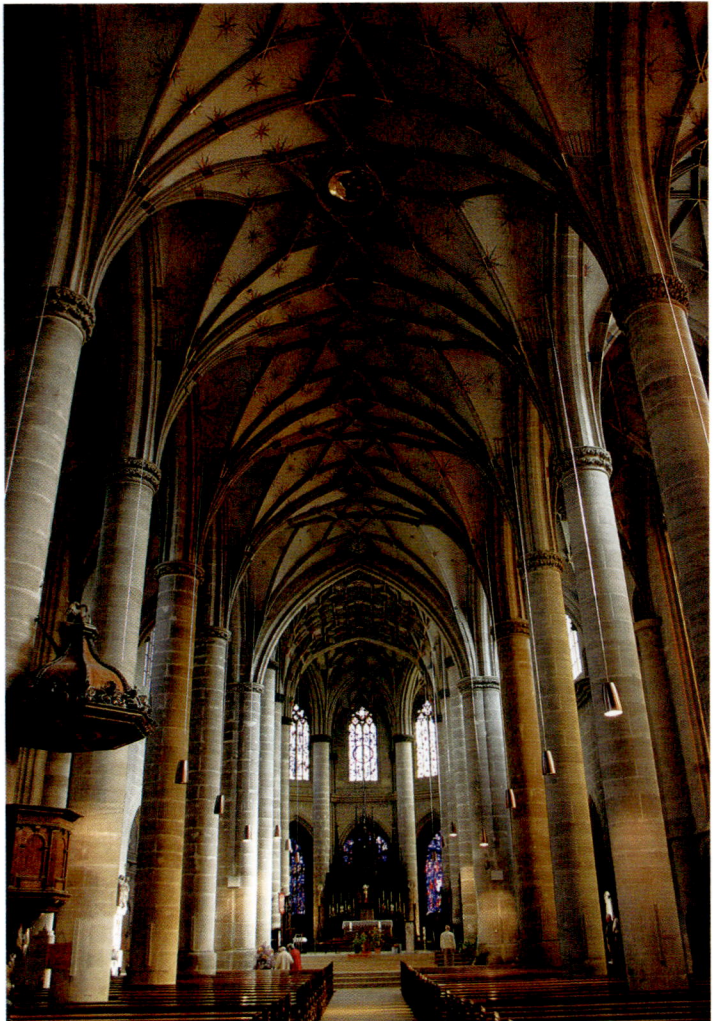

**13-54** PETER PARLER, interior (looking east) of Heiligkreuzkirche (Church of the Holy Cross), Schwäbisch Gmünd, Germany, begun 1351.

As in the Gloucester choir (FIG. 13-42), the vaults of this German church are structurally simple but visually complex. The multiplication of ribs characterizes Late Gothic architecture throughout Europe.

churches, consequently, have no tribune, triforium, or clerestory. An early German example of this type is the church of Saint Elizabeth (FIG. 13-53) at Marburg, built between 1235 and 1283. It incorporates French-inspired rib vaults with pointed arches and tall lancet windows. The facade has two spire-capped towers in the French manner but no tracery arcades or portal sculpture. Because the aisles provide much of the bracing for the nave vaults, the exterior of Saint Elizabeth is without the dramatic parade of flying buttresses typically circling French Gothic churches. But the Marburg interior, lighted by double rows of tall windows in the aisle walls, is more unified and free flowing, less narrow and divided, and more brightly illuminated than the interiors of most French and English Gothic churches.

**HEINRICH AND PETER PARLER** A later German hall church is the Heiligkreuzkirche (Church of the Holy Cross) at Schwäbisch Gmünd, begun in 1317 by HEINRICH PARLER (ca. 1290–ca. 1360). Heinrich was the founder of a family of architects who worked in Germany and later in northern Italy. His name first surfaces in the early 14th century, when he played a role in supervising the construction of Cologne Cathedral (FIGS. 13-51 and 13-52). Work continued on the Schwäbisch Gmünd church into the 16th century, but the nave was substantially complete when one of his sons, PETER PARLER (1330–1399), began work on the choir (FIG. 13-54) in 1351.

As in the nave of the church, the choir aisles are as tall as the central space. The light entering the choir through the large win-

dows in the aisle walls and in the chapels ringing the choir provides ample illumination for the clergy conducting services. It also enables worshipers to admire the elaborate patterns of the vault ribs. The multiplication of ribs in this German church is consistent with 14th-century taste throughout Europe and has parallels in the Flamboyant style of France and especially the Perpendicular style of England. As in the choir (FIG. 13-42) of Gloucester Cathedral, begun two decades before, the choir vaults at Schwäbisch Gmünd are structurally simple but visually complex. Parler's vaults form an elegant canopy for the severe columnar piers from which they spring, creating a very effective contrast.

One of Peter Parler's brothers, named Heinrich after their father, was also an architect. He was among those who formed a committee in 1386 to advise the Milanese on the design and construction of their new cathedral. The case of the Parler family is symptomatic both of the dramatic increase in the number of recorded names of artists and architects during the Gothic period, and of the international character of Gothic art and architecture, despite sometimes pronounced regional variations.

# GOTHIC EUROPE

## FRANCE

▌ The birthplace of Gothic art and architecture was Saint-Denis, where Abbot Suger used rib vaults with pointed arches to rebuild the Carolingian royal church and filled the windows of the ambulatory with stained glass. On the west facade, Suger introduced sculpted figures on the portal jambs, a feature that appeared shortly later on the Royal Portal of Chartres Cathedral. Saint-Denis, the west facade of Chartres, and Laon Cathedral are the key monuments of Early Gothic (1140–1194) architecture.

▌ After a fire in 1194, Chartres Cathedral was rebuilt with flying buttresses, four-part nave vaults, and a three-story elevation of nave arcade, triforium, and clerestory. These features set the pattern for High Gothic (1194–1300) cathedrals. French architects sought to construct naves of soaring height. The vaults of Amiens Cathedral are 144 feet high.

▌ Flying buttresses made possible huge stained-glass windows. High Gothic windows employed delicate lead cames and bar tracery. The colored glass converted natural sunlight into divine light (*lux nova*), dramatically transforming the character of church interiors.

▌ High Gothic jamb statues broke out of the architectural straitjacket of their Early Gothic predecessors. At Chartres, Reims, and elsewhere, the sculpted figures move freely and sometimes converse with their neighbors.

▌ The High Gothic Rayonnant court style of Louis IX gave way in the Late Gothic (1300–1500) period to the Flamboyant style, in which flamelike tracery formed brittle decorative webs, as at Saint-Maclou in Rouen.

▌ The prosperity of the era also led to a boom in secular architecture. Important examples are the fortified circuit wall of Carcassonne, the hall of the cloth guild in Bruges, and the house of the financier Jacques Coeur in Bourges.

▌ In the 13th century, Paris was the intellectual capital of Europe and home to numerous workshops of professional lay artists specializing in the production of luxurious illuminated manuscripts. These urban for-profit ancestors of modern publishing houses usurped the role of monastic scriptoria.

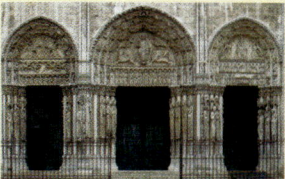

Royal Portal, Chartres Cathedral, ca. 1145–1155

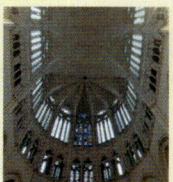

Amiens Cathedral, begun 1220

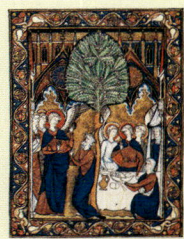

*Psalter of Saint Louis,* 1253–1270

## ENGLAND

▌ The Parisian Gothic style spread rapidly throughout Europe during the 13th century, but many regional styles developed, as in the Romanesque period. English Gothic churches, such as Salisbury Cathedral, differ from their French counterparts in their wider and shorter facades, flat east ends, double transepts, and sparing use of flying buttresses.

▌ Especially characteristic of English Gothic architecture is the elaboration of architectural patterns, which often disguise the underlying structure of the buildings. For example, the fan vaults of the chapel of Henry VII at Westminster Abbey in London transform the logical rib vaults of French buildings into decorative fancy in the Late Gothic Perpendicular style.

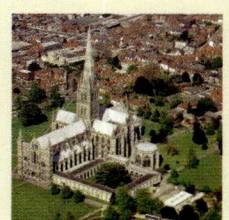

Salisbury Cathedral, Salisbury, 1220–1258

## HOLY ROMAN EMPIRE

▌ Nicholas of Verdun was the leading artist of the Meuse River valley, an area renowned for enamel- and metalwork. Nicholas's altars and shrines provide an idea of the sumptuous nature of the furnishings of Gothic churches. His innovative figural style influenced the development of Gothic sculpture.

▌ German architects eagerly embraced the French Gothic architectural style at Cologne Cathedral and elsewhere. German originality manifested itself most clearly in the Gothic period in sculpture, which often featured emotionally charged figures in dramatic poses and also revived the art of portraiture. Statues of secular historical figures are key elements of the sculptural programs of Naumburg and Bamberg cathedrals.

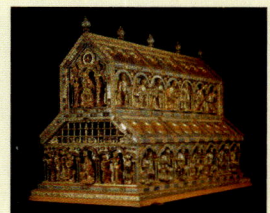

Nicholas of Verdun, *Shrine of the Three Kings,* ca. 1190

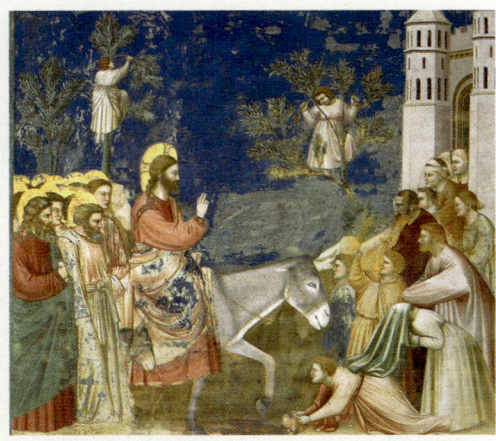

Giotto's cycle of biblical frescoes in the Arena Chapel includes 38 framed panels depicting the lives of the Virgin, her parents, and Jesus. The passion cycle opens with *Entry into Jerusalem.*

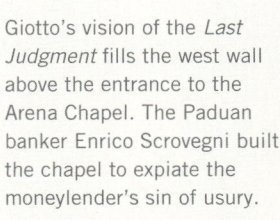

Giotto's vision of the *Last Judgment* fills the west wall above the entrance to the Arena Chapel. The Paduan banker Enrico Scrovegni built the chapel to expiate the moneylender's sin of usury.

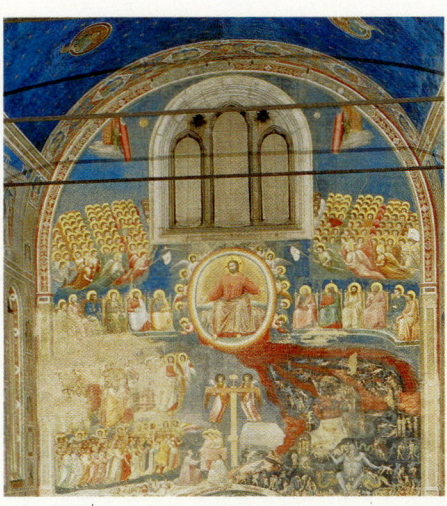

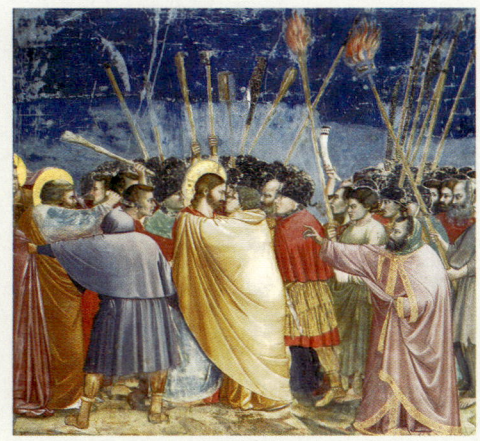

Giotto was a pioneer in pursuing a naturalistic approach to representation based on observation. In *Betrayal of Jesus,* he revived the classical tradition of depicting some figures from the rear.

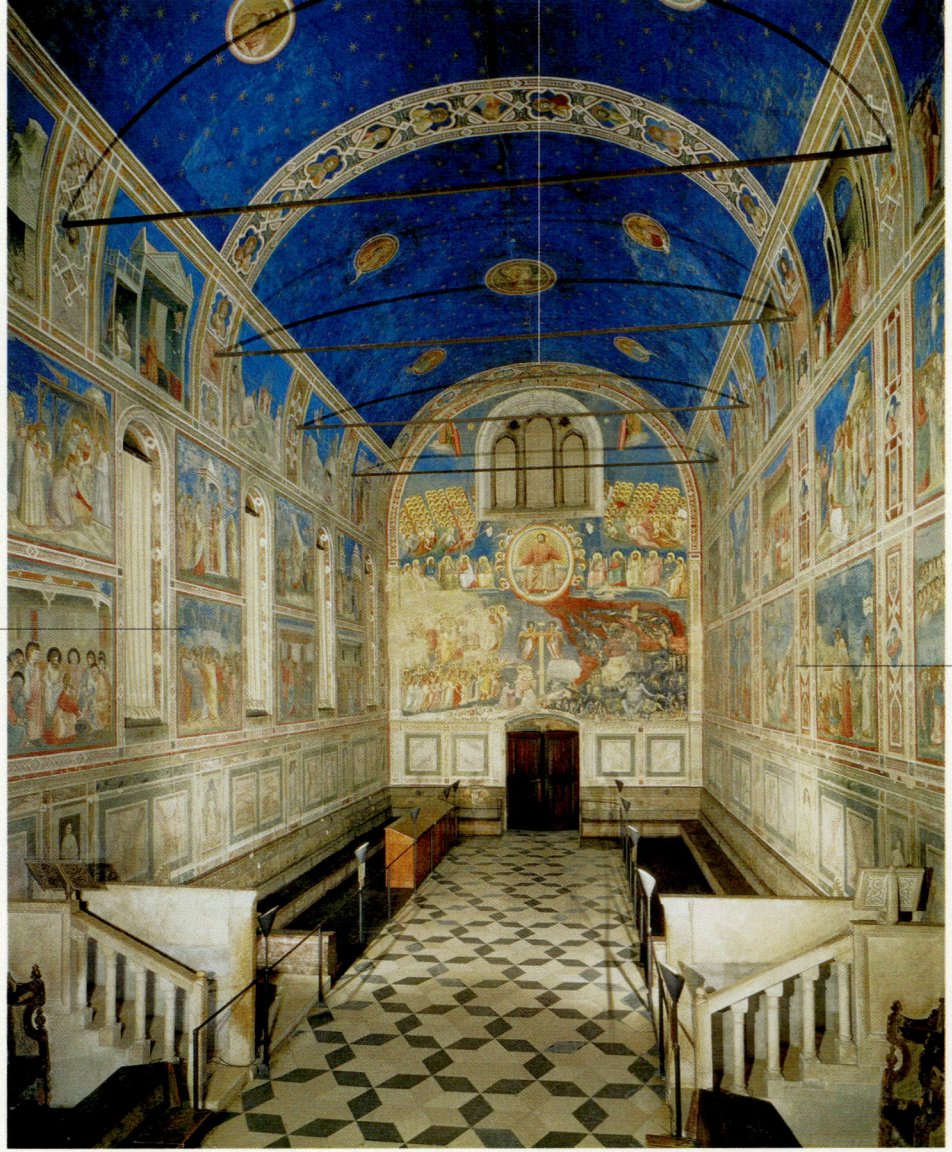

14-1 GIOTTO DI BONDONE, interior of the Arena Chapel (Cappella Scrovegni; looking west), Padua, Italy, 1305–1306.

# LATE MEDIEVAL ITALY

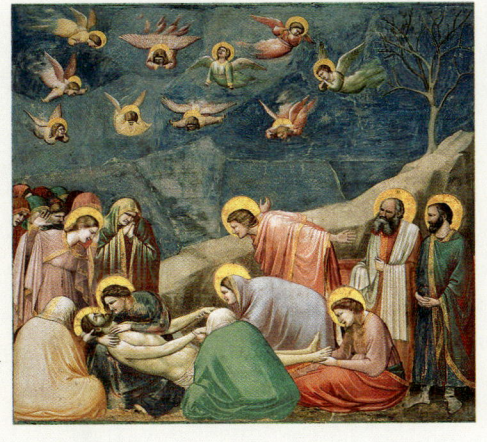

Giotto was also a master of composition. In *Lamentation*, the rocky slope behind the figures leads the viewer's eye toward the heads of Mary and the dead Jesus at the lower left.

## LATE MEDIEVAL OR PROTO-RENAISSANCE?

**A**rt historians debate whether the art of Italy between 1200 and 1400 is the last phase of medieval art or the beginning of the rebirth, or *Renaissance*, of Greco-Roman *naturalism*. All agree, however, the pivotal figure of this age was the Florentine painter GIOTTO DI BONDONE (ca. 1266–1337), whose masterwork was the fresco cycle of the Arena Chapel (FIG. **14-1**) in Padua. A banker, Enrico Scrovegni, built the chapel on a site adjacent to his palace in the hope it would expiate the moneylender's sin of usury. Consecrated in 1305, the chapel takes its name from an ancient Roman arena (*amphitheater*) nearby.

Some scholars have suggested Giotto himself may have been the chapel's architect, because its design so perfectly suits its interior decoration. The rectangular hall has only six windows, all in the south wall, leaving the other walls as almost unbroken and well-illuminated surfaces for painting. In 38 framed panels, Giotto presented the most poignant incidents from the lives of the Virgin and her parents, Joachim and Anna, in the top level, and, in the middle and lower levels, the life and mission (middle), and the passion and resurrection (bottom) of Jesus. The climactic event of the cycle of human salvation, *Last Judgment*, covers most of the west wall above the chapel's entrance.

The *Entry into Jerusalem, Betrayal of Jesus,* and *Lamentation* panels reveal the essentials of Giotto's style. In contrast to the common practice of his day, Giotto based his method of pictorial expression on observation of the natural world—the approach championed by the ancient Greeks and Romans but largely abandoned in the Middle Ages. Subtly scaled to the chapel's space, Giotto's stately and slow-moving half-life-size figures act out the religious dramas convincingly and with great restraint. The biblical actors are sculpturesque, simple, and weighty, often *foreshortened* (seen from an angle) and modeled with light and shading in the classical manner. They convey individual emotions through their postures and gestures. Giotto's naturalism displaced the Byzantine style in Italy (see Chapter 9), inaugurating an age some scholars call "early scientific." By stressing the preeminence of sight for gaining knowledge of the world, Giotto and his successors contributed to the foundation of empirical science. They recognized that the visual world must be observed before it can be analyzed and understood. Praised in his own and later times for his fidelity to nature, Giotto was more than a mere imitator of it. He showed his generation a new way of seeing. With Giotto, Western painters turned away from the spiritual world—the focus of medieval European artists—and once again moved resolutely toward the visible world as the inspiration for their art.

# 13TH CENTURY

When the Italian humanists of the 16th century condemned the art of the late Middle Ages in northern Europe as *"Gothic"* (see Chapter 13), they did so by comparing it with the contemporaneous art of Italy, which consciously revived *classical** art. Italian artists and scholars regarded medieval artworks as distortions of the noble art of the Greeks and Romans. Interest in the art of classical antiquity was not entirely absent during the medieval period, however, even in France, the center of the Gothic style. For example, on the west front of Reims Cathedral, the 13th-century statues of Christian *saints* and angels (FIG. 13-24) reveal the unmistakable influence of ancient Roman art on French sculptors. However, the classical revival that took root in Italy during the 13th and 14th centuries was much more pervasive and longer-lasting.

## Sculpture

Italian admiration for classical art surfaced early on at the court of Frederick II, king of Sicily (r. 1197–1250) and Holy Roman emperor (r. 1220–1250). Frederick's nostalgia for Rome's past grandeur fostered a revival of classical sculpture in Sicily and southern Italy not unlike the classical *renovatio* (renewal) Charlemagne encouraged in Germany and France four centuries earlier (see Chapter 11).

**NICOLA PISANO** The sculptor Nicola d'Apulia (Nicholas of Apulia), better known as NICOLA PISANO (active ca. 1258–1278) after his adopted city (see "Italian Artists' Names," page 405, and MAP 14-1), received his early training in southern Italy under Frederick's rule. In 1250, Nicola traveled northward and eventually settled in Pisa. Then at the height of its political and economic power, the maritime city was a magnet for artists seeking lucrative commissions. Nicola specialized in carving marble reliefs and ornamentation for large *pulpits* (raised platforms from which priests led church services), completing the first (FIG. 14-2) in 1260 for Pisa's century-old baptistery (FIG. 12-26, *left*). Some elements of the pulpit's design carried on medieval traditions—for example, the *trefoil* (triple-curved) *arches* and the lions supporting some of the *columns*—but Nicola also incorporated classical elements. The large *capitals* with two rows of thick overlapping leaves crowning the columns are a Gothic variation of the *Corinthian capital* (see page 151 and FIG. 5-73, or page xxii–xxiii in Volume II and Book D). The arches are round, as in Roman architecture, rather than pointed (*ogival*), as in Gothic buildings. Also, each of the large rectangular relief panels resembles the sculptured front of a Roman *sarcophagus* (coffin; for example, FIG. 7-70).

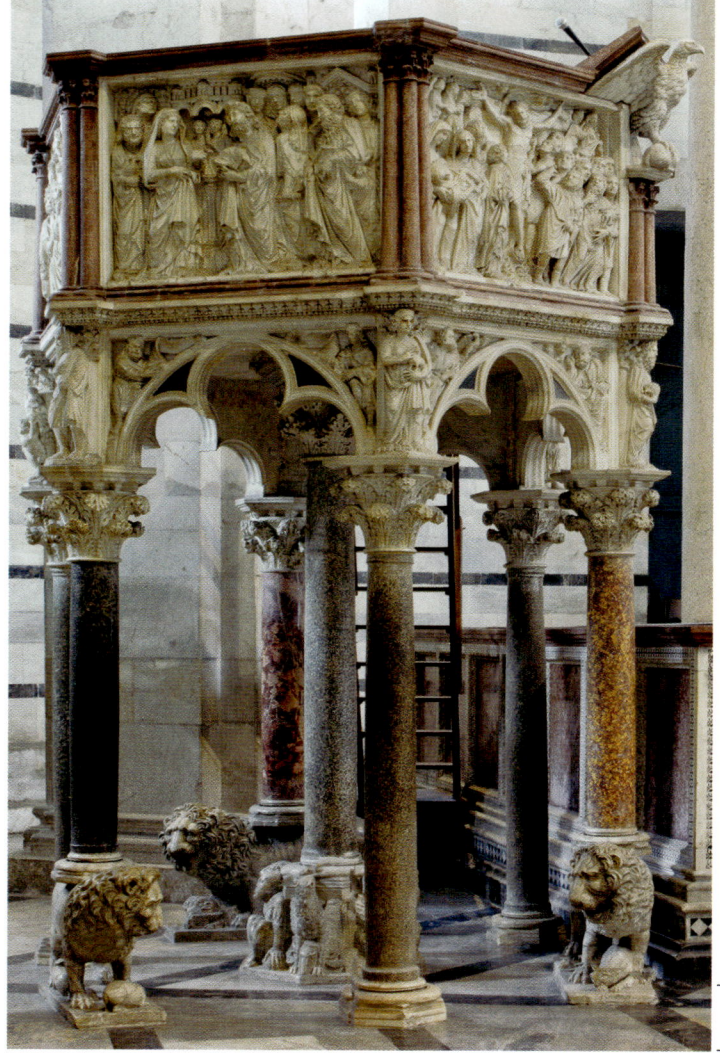

**14-2** NICOLA PISANO, **pulpit of the baptistery, Pisa, Italy, 1259–1260. Marble, 15′ high.** ◼

Nicola Pisano's Pisa baptistery pulpit retains many medieval features, for example, the trefoil arches and the lions supporting columns, but the figures derive from ancient Roman sarcophagus reliefs.

*In *Art through the Ages* the adjective "Classical," with uppercase *C,* refers specifically to the Classical period of ancient Greece, 480–323 BCE. Lowercase "classical" refers to Greco-Roman antiquity in general, that is, the period treated in Chapters 5, 6, and 7.

---

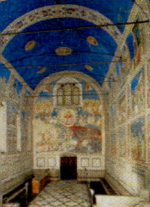

# LATE MEDIEVAL ITALY

| 13th Century | 14th Century |
|---|---|
| ▍ Bonaventura Berlinghieri and Cimabue are the leading painters working in the Italo-Byzantine style, or *maniera greca* | ▍ In Florence, Giotto, considered the first Renaissance artist, pioneers a naturalistic approach to painting based on observation |
| ▍ Nicola and Giovanni Pisano, father and son, represent two contrasting sculptural styles, the classical and the Gothic respectively | ▍ In Siena, Duccio softens the maniera greca and humanizes religious subject matter |
| ▍ Fresco cycles in Rome and Assisi foreshadow the revolutionary art of Giotto | ▍ Secular themes emerge as important subjects in civic commissions, as in the frescoes of Siena's Palazzo Pubblico |
| | ▍ Florence, Siena, and Orvieto build new cathedrals that are stylistically closer to Early Christian basilicas than to French Gothic cathedrals |

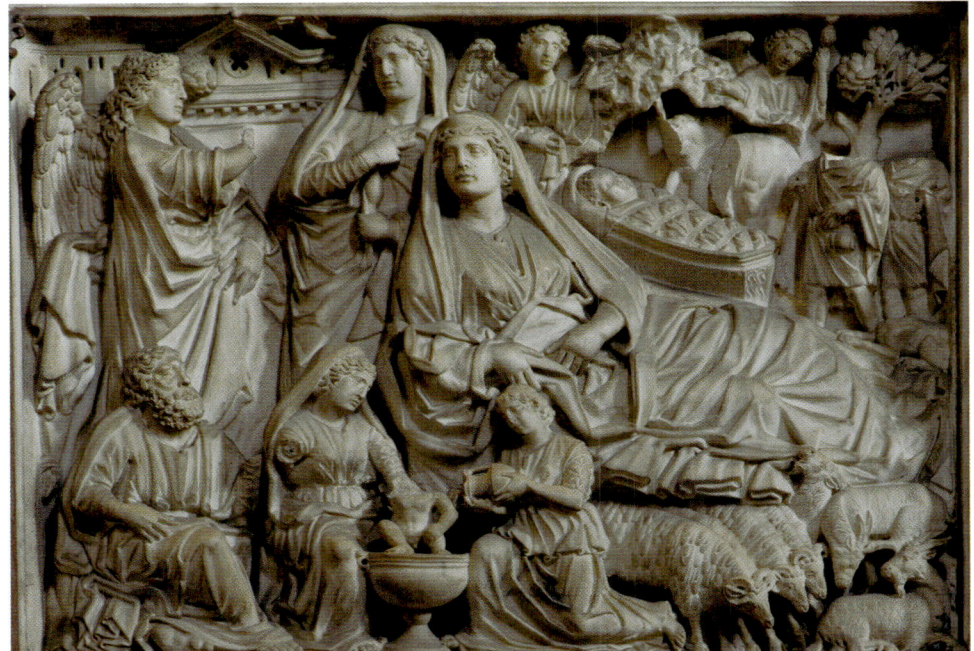

14-3 NICOLA PISANO, *Annunciation, Nativity,* and *Adoration of the Shepherds,* relief panel on the baptistery pulpit, Pisa, Italy, 1259–1260. Marble, 2′ 10″ × 3′ 9″.

Classical sculpture inspired the faces, beards, coiffures, and draperies, as well as the bulk and weight of Nicola's figures. The *Nativity* Madonna resembles lid figures on Roman sarcophagi.

1 ft.

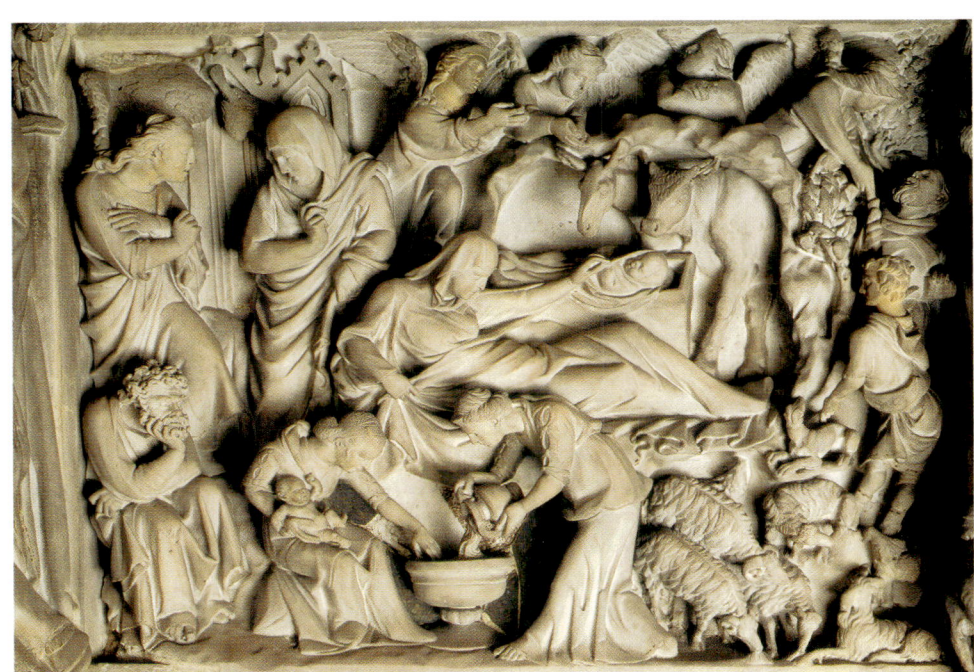

14-4 GIOVANNI PISANO, *Annunciation, Nativity,* and *Adoration of the Shepherds,* relief panel on the pulpit of Sant'Andrea, Pistoia, Italy, 1297–1301. Marble, 2′ 10″ × 3′ 4″.

The French Gothic style had a greater influence on Giovanni Pisano, Nicola's son. Giovanni arranged his figures loosely and dynamically. They display a nervous agitation, as if moved by spiritual passion.

1 ft.

The densely packed large-scale figures of the individual panels also seem to derive from the compositions found on Roman sarcophagi. One of these panels (FIG. 14-3) depicts scenes from the infancy cycle of Christ (see "The Life of Jesus in Art," Chapter 8, pages 240–241, or pages xxx–xxxi, in Volume II and Book D), including *Annunciation* (*top left*), *Nativity* (*center* and *lower half*), and *Adoration of the Shepherds* (*top right*). Mary appears twice, and her size varies. The focus of the composition is the reclining Virgin of *Nativity,* whose posture and drapery are reminiscent of those of the lid figures on Etruscan (FIGS. 6-5 and 6-15) and Roman (FIG. 7-61) sarcophagi. The face types, beards, and coiffures, as well as the bulk and weight of Nicola's figures, also reveal the influence of classical relief sculpture. Art historians have even been able to pinpoint the models of some of the pulpit figures on Roman sarcophagi in Pisa.

**GIOVANNI PISANO** Nicola's son, GIOVANNI PISANO (ca. 1250–1320), likewise became a sought-after sculptor of church pulpits. Giovanni's pulpit in Sant'Andrea at Pistoia also has a panel (FIG. 14-4) featuring *Nativity* and related scenes. The son's version of the subject offers a striking contrast to his father's thick carving and placid, almost stolid presentation of the religious narrative. Giovanni arranged the figures loosely and dynamically. They twist and bend in excited animation, and the deep spaces between them suggest their motion. In *Annunciation* (*top left*), the Virgin shrinks from the angel's sudden appearance in a posture of alarm touched with humility. The same spasm of apprehension contracts her supple body as she reclines in *Nativity* (*center*). The drama's principals share in a peculiar nervous agitation, as if spiritual passion suddenly moves all of them. Only the shepherds and the sheep (*right*)

# The Great Schism, Mendicant Orders, and Confraternities

In 1305, the College of Cardinals (the collective body of all cardinals) elected a French pope, Clement V (r. 1305–1314), who settled in Avignon. Subsequent French popes remained in Avignon, despite their announced intentions to return to Rome. Understandably, the Italians, who saw Rome as the rightful capital of the universal Church, resented the Avignon papacy. The conflict between the French and Italians resulted in the election in 1378 of two popes—Clement VII, who resided in Avignon (and who does not appear in the Catholic Church's official list of popes), and Urban VI (r. 1378–1389), who remained in Rome. Thus began what became known as the Great Schism. After 40 years, Holy Roman Emperor Sigismund (r. 1410–1437) convened a council that resolved this crisis by electing a new Roman pope, Martin V (r. 1417–1431), who was acceptable to all.

The pope's absence from Italy during much of the 14th century contributed to an increase in prominence of *monastic orders*. The Augustinians, Carmelites, and Servites became very active, ensuring a constant religious presence in the daily life of Italians, but the largest and most influential monastic orders were the *mendicants* (begging friars)—the Franciscans, founded by Francis of Assisi (FIG. 14-5), and the Dominicans, founded by the Spaniard Dominic de Guzman (ca. 1170–1221). These mendicants renounced all worldly goods and committed themselves to spreading God's word, performing good deeds, and ministering to the sick and dying. The Dominicans, in particular, contributed significantly to establishing urban educational institutions. The Franciscans and Dominicans became very popular in Italy because of their devotion to their faith and the more personal relationship with God they encouraged. Although both mendicant orders worked for the glory of God, a degree of rivalry nevertheless existed between the two. For example, in Florence they established their churches on opposite sides of the city—Santa Croce (FIG. I-4), the Franciscan church, on the eastern side, and the Dominicans' Santa Maria Novella (FIG. 14-6A) on the western (MAP 21-1).

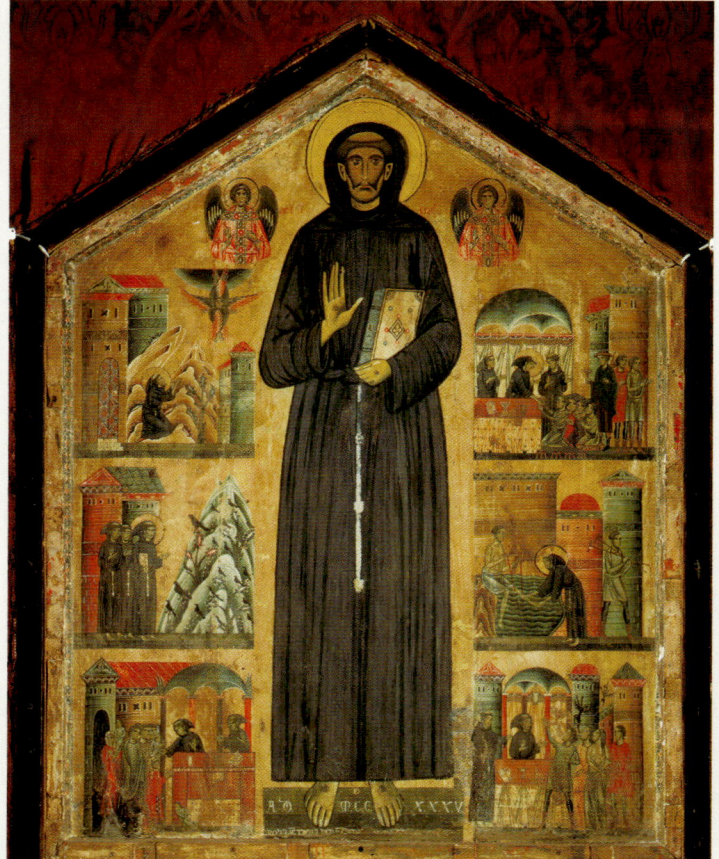

**14-5** BONAVENTURA BERLINGHIERI, *Saint Francis Altarpiece,* San Francesco, Pescia, Italy, 1235. Tempera on wood, 5′ × 3′ × 6′. 🎥

Berlinghieri painted this altarpiece in the Italo-Byzantine style, or maniera greca, for the mendicant (begging) order of Franciscans. It is the earliest known representation of Saint Francis of Assisi.

1 ft.

*Confraternities,* organizations consisting of laypersons who dedicated themselves to strict religious observance, also grew in popularity during the 14th and 15th centuries. The mission of confraternities included tending the sick, burying the dead, singing hymns, and performing other good works. The confraternities as well as the mendicant orders continued to play an important role in Italian religious life through the 16th century. The numerous artworks and monastic churches they commissioned have ensured their enduring legacy.

---

do not yet share in the miraculous event. The swiftly turning, sinuous draperies, the slender figures they enfold, and the general emotionalism of the scene are features not found in Nicola Pisano's interpretation. The father worked in the classical tradition, the son in a style derived from French Gothic. These styles were two of the three most important ingredients in the formation of the distinctive and original art of 14th-century Italy.

## Painting and Architecture

The third major stylistic element in late medieval Italian art was the Byzantine tradition (see Chapter 9). Throughout the Middle Ages, the Byzantine style dominated Italian painting, but its influence

was especially strong after the fall of Constantinople in 1204, which precipitated a migration of Byzantine artists to Italy.

**BONAVENTURA BERLINGHIERI** One of the leading painters working in the Italo-Byzantine style, or *maniera greca* (Greek style), was BONAVENTURA BERLINGHIERI (active ca. 1235–1244) of Lucca. His most famous work is the *Saint Francis Altarpiece* (FIG. 14-5) in the church of San Francesco (Saint Francis) in Pescia. Painted in 1235 using *tempera* on wood panel (see "Tempera and Oil Painting," Chapter 20, page 539), the *altarpiece* honors Saint Francis of Assisi (ca. 1181–1226), whose most important shrine (FIG. 14-5A), at Assisi itself, boasts the most extensive cycle of

## Italian Artists' Names

In contemporary societies, people have become accustomed to a standardized method of identifying individuals, in part because of the proliferation of official documents such as driver's licenses, passports, and student identification cards. Modern names consist of given names (names selected by the parents) and family names, although the order of the two (or more) names varies from country to country. In China, for example, the family name precedes the given name (see Chapters 16 and 33).

This kind of regularity in names was not, however, the norm in premodern Italy. Many individuals were known by their place of birth or adopted hometown. Nicola Pisano (FIGS. 14-2 and 14-3) was "Nicholas the Pisan," Giulio Romano was "Julius the Roman," and Domenico Veneziano was "the Venetian." Leonardo da Vinci ("Leonard from Vinci") hailed from the small town of Vinci, near Florence (MAP 14-1). Art historians therefore refer to these artists by their given names, not the names of their towns. (The title of Dan Brown's best-selling novel should have been *The Leonardo Code*, not *The Da Vinci Code*.)

Nicknames were also common. Giorgione was "Big George." People usually referred to Tommaso di Cristoforo Fini as Masolino ("Little Thomas") to distinguish him from his more famous pupil, Masaccio ("Brutish Thomas"). Guido di Pietro was called Fra Angelico (the Angelic Friar). Cenni di Pepo is remembered as Cimabue (FIG. 14-6), which means "bull's head."

Names were also impermanent and could be changed at will. This flexibility has resulted in significant challenges for historians, who often must deal with archival documents and records referring to the same artist by different names.

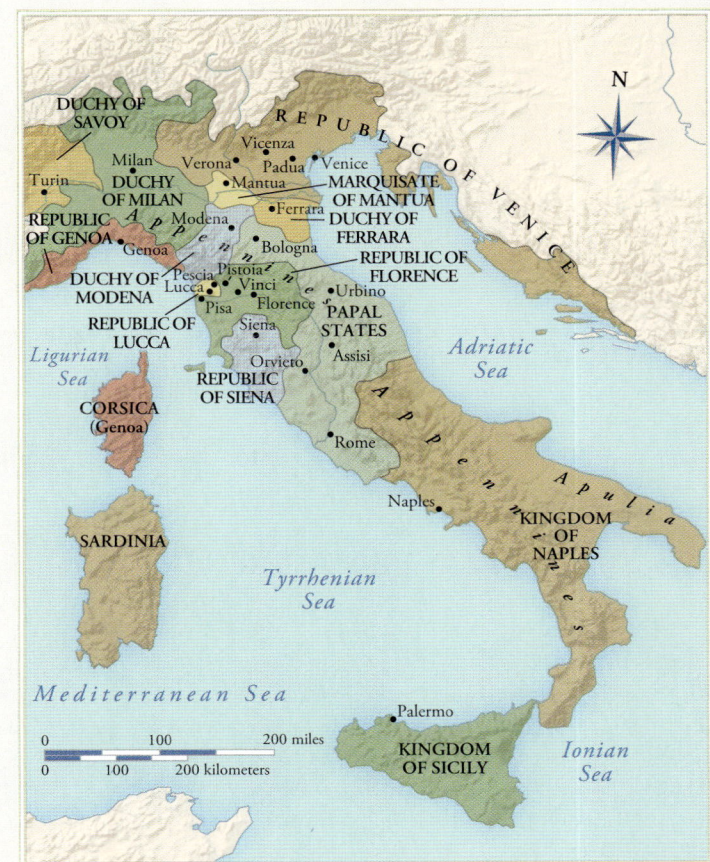

MAP 14-1 Italy around 1400.

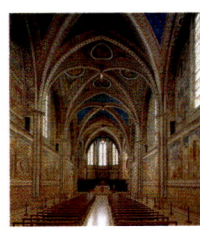

14-5A San Francesco, Assisi, 1228–1253.

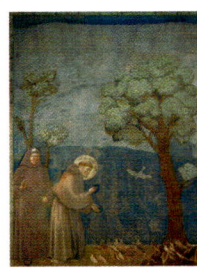

14-5B ST. FRANCIS MASTER, *Preaching to the Birds*, ca. 1290–1300.

frescoes from 13th-century Italy. Berlinghieri depicted Francis wearing the costume later adopted by all Franciscan monks: a coarse clerical robe tied at the waist with a rope. The saint displays the *stigmata*—marks resembling Christ's wounds—that miraculously appeared on his hands and feet. Flanking Francis are two angels, whose frontal poses, prominent halos, and lack of modeling reveal the Byzantine roots of Berlinghieri's style. So, too, does the use of *gold leaf* (gold beaten into tissue-paper-thin sheets, then applied to surfaces), which emphasizes the image's flatness and spiritual nature. The narrative scenes along the sides of the panel provide an active contrast to the stiff formality of the large central image of Francis. At the upper left, taking pride of place at the saint's right, Francis receives the stigmata. Directly below, the saint preaches to the birds, a subject that also figures prominently in the fresco program (FIG. 14-5B) of San Francesco at Assisi, the work of a painter art historians call the SAINT FRANCIS MASTER. These and the scenes depicting Francis's

miracle cures strongly suggest Berlinghieri's source was one or more Byzantine *illuminated manuscripts* (compare FIG. 9-17) with biblical narrative scenes.

Berlinghieri's *Saint Francis Altarpiece* also highlights the increasingly prominent role of religious orders in late medieval Italy (see "The Great Schism, Mendicant Orders, and Confraternities," page 404). Saint Francis's Franciscan order worked diligently to impress on the public the saint's valuable example and to demonstrate the order's commitment to teaching and to alleviating suffering. Berlinghieri's Pescia altarpiece, painted only nine years after Francis's death, is the earliest known signed and dated representation of the saint. Appropriately, Berlinghieri's panel focuses on the aspects of the saint's life the Franciscans wanted to promote, thereby making visible (and thus more credible) the legendary life of this holy man. Saint Francis believed he could get closer to God by rejecting worldly goods, and to achieve this he stripped himself bare in a public square and committed himself to a strict life of fasting, prayer, and meditation. His followers considered the appearance of stigmata on Francis's hands and feet (clearly visible in the saint's frontal image, which resembles a Byzantine *icon*) as God's blessing, and viewed Francis as a second Christ. Fittingly, four of the six narrative scenes on the altarpiece depict miraculous healings, connecting Saint Francis even more emphatically to Christ.

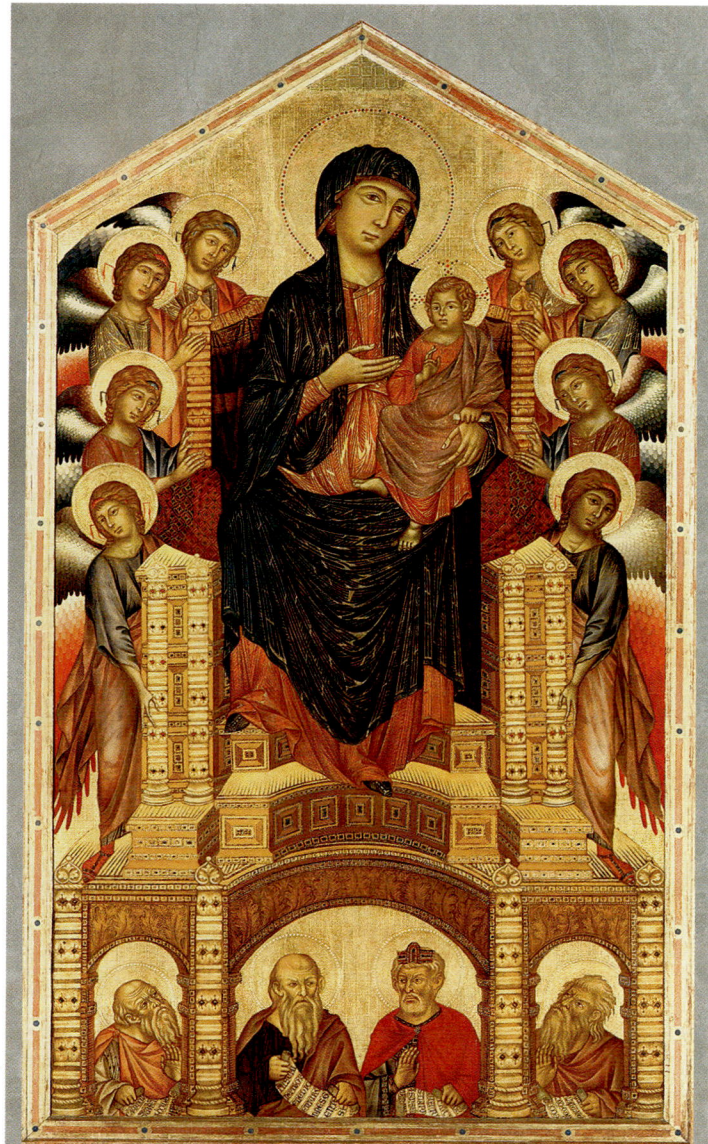

**14-6** CIMABUE, *Madonna Enthroned with Angels and Prophets,* from Santa Trinità, Florence, ca. 1280–1290. Tempera and gold leaf on wood, 12′ 7″ × 7′ 4″. Galleria degli Uffizi, Florence. ◼◀

Cimabue was one of the first artists to break away from the maniera greca. Although he relied on Byzantine models, Cimabue depicted the Madonna's massive throne as receding into space.

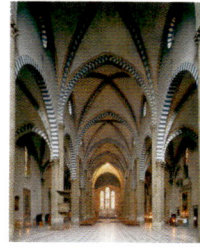

**14-6A** Santa Maria Novella, Florence, begun ca. 1246. ◼◀

**CIMABUE** One of the first artists to break from the Italo-Byzantine style that dominated 13th-century Italian painting was Cenni di Pepo, better known as CIMABUE (ca. 1240–1302). Cimabue challenged some of the major conventions of late medieval art in pursuit of a new naturalism, the close observation of the natural world—the core of the classical tradition. He painted *Madonna Enthroned with Angels and Prophets* (FIG. 14-6) for Santa Trinità (Holy Trinity) in Florence, the Benedictine church near the Arno River built between 1258 and 1280, roughly contemporaneous with the Dominican church of Santa Maria Novella (FIG. 14-6A). The composition and the gold background reveal the painter's reliance on Byzantine models (compare FIG. 9-18).

Cimabue also used the gold embellishments common to Byzantine art for the folds of the Madonna's robe, but they are no longer merely decorative patterns. In his panel they enhance the three-dimensionality of the drapery. Furthermore, Cimabue constructed a deeper space for the Madonna and the surrounding figures to inhabit than was common in Byzantine art. The Virgin's throne, for example, is a massive structure and Cimabue convincingly depicted it as receding into space. The overlapping bodies of the angels on each side of the throne and the half-length prophets who look outward or upward from beneath it reinforce the sense of depth.

# 14TH CENTURY

In the 14th century, Italy consisted of numerous independent *city-states,* each corresponding to a geographic region centered on a major city (MAP 14-1). Most of the city-states, such as Venice, Florence, Lucca, and Siena, were republics—constitutional oligarchies governed by executive bodies, advisory councils, and special commissions. Other powerful 14th-century states included the Papal States, the Kingdom of Naples, and the Duchies of Milan, Modena, Ferrara, and Savoy. As their names indicate, these states were politically distinct from the republics, but all the states shared in the prosperity of the period. The sources of wealth varied from state to state. Italy's port cities expanded maritime trade, whereas the economies of other cities depended on banking or the manufacture of arms or textiles.

The outbreak of the Black Death (bubonic plague) in the late 1340s threatened this prosperity, however. Originating in China, the Black Death swept across Europe. The most devastating natural disaster in European history, the plague eliminated between 25 and 50 percent of the Continent's population in about five years. The Black Death devastated Italy's inhabitants. In large Italian cities, where people lived in relatively close proximity, the death tolls climbed as high as 50 to 60 percent of the population. The bubonic plague had a significant effect on art. It stimulated religious bequests and encouraged the commissioning of devotional images. The focus on sickness and death also led to a burgeoning in hospital construction.

Another significant development in 14th-century Italy was the blossoming of a vernacular (commonly spoken) literature, which dramatically affected Italy's intellectual and cultural life. Latin remained the official language of Church liturgy and state documents. However, the creation of an Italian vernacular literature (based on the Tuscan dialect common in Florence) expanded the audience for philosophical and intellectual concepts because of its greater accessibility. Dante Alighieri (1265–1321, author of *The Divine Comedy*), the poet and scholar Francesco Petrarch (1304–1374), and Giovanni Boccaccio (1313–1375, author of *Decameron*) were most responsible for establishing this vernacular literature.

**RENAISSANCE HUMANISM** The development of a vernacular literature was one important sign that the essentially religious view of the world dominating medieval Europe was about to change dramatically in what historians call the *Renaissance.* Although religion continued to occupy a primary position in the lives of Europeans, a growing concern with the natural world, the individual, and humanity's worldly existence characterized the Renaissance period—the 14th through the 16th centuries. The word *renaissance* in French and English (*rinascità* in Italian) refers to a "rebirth" of art and culture. A revived interest in classical cultures—indeed, the veneration of classical antiquity as a model—was central to this rebirth. The notion of the Renaissance representing the restoration of the glorious past of Greece and Rome gave rise to the concept of the "Middle Ages" as the era falling between antiquity and the Renaissance. The transition from the medieval to the Renaissance, though dramatic, did not come about abruptly, however. In fact, much that is medieval persisted in the Renaissance and in later periods.

Fundamental to the development of the Italian Renaissance was *humanism,* which emerged during the 14th century and became a central component of Italian art and culture in the 15th and 16th centuries. Humanism was more a code of civil conduct, a theory of education, and a scholarly discipline than a philosophical system. As their name suggests, Italian humanists were concerned chiefly with human values and interests as distinct from—but not opposed to—religion's otherworldly values. Humanists pointed to classical cultures as particularly praiseworthy. This enthusiasm for antiquity, represented by the elegant Latin of Cicero (106–43 BCE) and the Augustan age, involved study of Latin literature and a conscious emulation of what proponents believed were the Roman civic virtues. These included self-sacrificing service to the state, participation in government, defense of state institutions (especially the administration of justice), and stoic indifference to personal misfortune in the performance of duty. With the help of a new interest in and knowledge of Greek, the humanists of the late 14th and 15th centuries recovered a large part of Greek as well as Roman literature and philosophy that had been lost, left unnoticed, or cast aside in the Middle Ages. Indeed, classical cultures provided humanists with a model for living in this world, a model primarily of human focus derived not from an authoritative and traditional religious dogma but from reason.

Ideally, humanists sought no material reward for services rendered. The sole reward for heroes of civic virtue was fame, just as the reward for leaders of the holy life was sainthood. For the educated, the lives of heroes and heroines of the past became as edifying as the lives of the saints. Petrarch wrote a book on illustrious men, and his colleague Boccaccio complemented it with 106 biographies of famous women—from Eve to Joanna, queen of Naples (r. 1343–1382). Both Petrarch and Boccaccio were famous in their own day as poets, scholars, and men of letters—their achievements equivalent in honor to those of the heroes of civic virtue. In 1341 in Rome, Petrarch received the laurel wreath crown, the ancient symbol of victory and merit. The humanist cult of fame emphasized the importance of creative individuals and their role in contributing to the renown of the city-state and of all Italy.

## Giotto

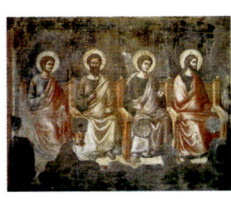

14-6B CAVALLINI, *Last Judgment,* ca. 1290–1295.

Critics from Giorgio Vasari† to the present day have regarded Giotto di Bondone (FIG. 14-1) as the first Renaissance painter. A pioneer in pursuing a naturalistic approach to representation based on observation, he made a much more radical break with the past than did Cimabue, whom Vasari identified as Giotto's teacher. Scholars still debate the sources of Giotto's style, however. One formative influence must have been Cimabue's work,

although Vasari lauded Giotto as having eclipsed his master by abandoning the "crude maniera greca." The 13th-century *murals* of San Francesco at Assisi (FIGS. 14-5A and 14-5B) and those of PIETRO CAVALLINI (ca. 1240–ca. 1340) in Rome (FIG. 14-6B) may also have influenced the young Giotto. French Gothic sculpture (which Giotto may have seen but which was certainly familiar to him from the work of Giovanni Pisano, who had spent time in Paris) and ancient Roman art probably also contributed to Giotto's artistic education. Yet no mere synthesis of these varied influences could have produced the significant shift in artistic approach that has led some scholars to describe Giotto as the father of Western pictorial art. Renowned in his own day, his reputation has never faltered. Regardless of the other influences on his artistic style, his true teacher was nature—the world of visible things.

*MADONNA ENTHRONED* On nearly the same great scale as Cimabue's enthroned Madonna (FIG. 14-6) is Giotto's panel (FIG. 14-7) depicting the same subject, painted for the high altar

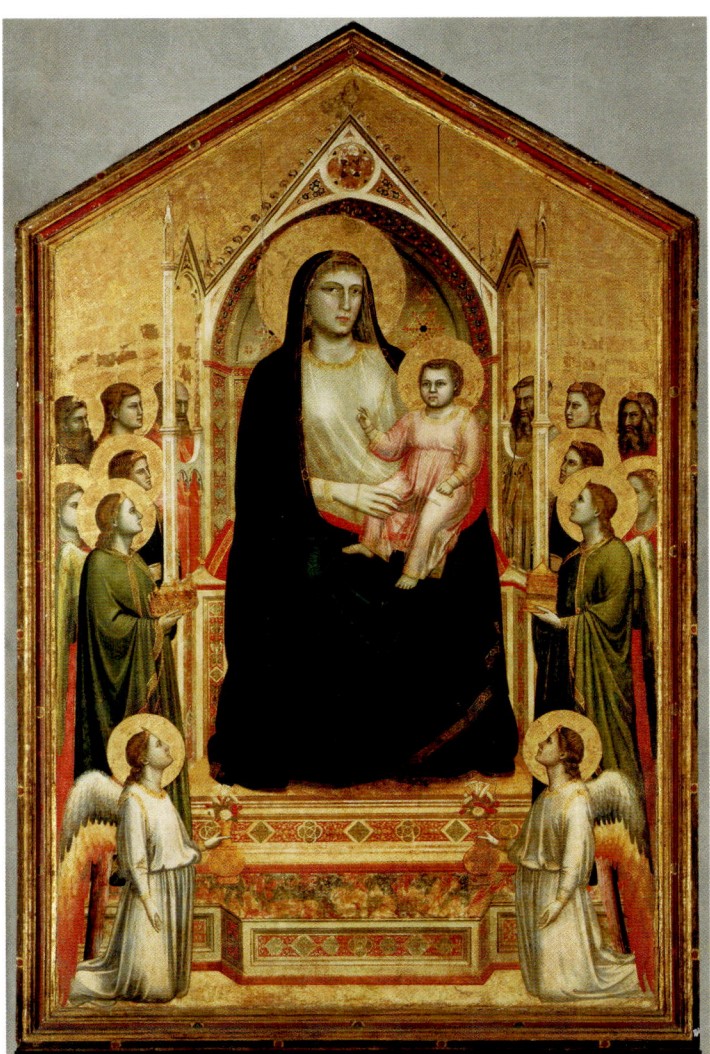

1 ft.

**14-7 GIOTTO DI BONDONE,** *Madonna Enthroned,* **from the Church of Ognissanti, Florence, ca. 1310. Tempera and gold leaf on wood, 10′ 8″ × 6′ 8″. Galleria degli Uffizi, Florence.**

Giotto displaced the Byzantine style in Italian painting and revived classical naturalism. His figures have substance, dimensionality, and bulk, and give the illusion they could throw shadows.

†Giorgio Vasari (1511–1574) was both a painter and an architect. Today, however, people associate him primarily with his landmark book, *Lives of the Most Eminent Painters, Sculptors, and Architects,* first published in 1550. Despite inaccuracies, Vasari's *Lives* is an invaluable research tool. It is the major contemporary source of information about Italian Renaissance art and artists.

# Fresco Painting

Fresco painting has a long history, particularly in the Mediterranean region, where the Minoans (FIGS. 4-7 to 4-9B) used it as early as the 17th century BCE. *Fresco* (Italian for "fresh") is a mural-painting technique involving the application of permanent limeproof pigments, diluted in water, on freshly laid lime plaster. Because the surface of the wall absorbs the pigments as the plaster dries, fresco is one of the most durable painting techniques. The stable condition of the ancient Minoan frescoes, as well as those found at Pompeii and other Roman sites (FIGS. 7-17 to 7-26), in San Francesco (FIGS. 14-5A and 14-5B) at Assisi, and in the Arena Chapel (FIGS. 14-1 and 14-8 to 14-8B) at Padua, testify to the longevity of this painting method. The colors have remained vivid (although dirt and soot have necessitated cleaning—most famously in the Vatican's Sistine Chapel; FIG. 22-18B) because of the chemically inert pigments the artists used. In addition to this *buon fresco* (good, that is, true fresco) technique, artists used *fresco secco* (dry fresco). Fresco secco involves painting on dried lime plaster, the method the ancient Egyptians favored (FIGS. 3-28 and 3-29). Although the finished product visually approximates buon fresco, the plaster wall does not absorb the pigments, which simply adhere to the surface, so fresco secco is not as permanent as buon fresco.

The buon fresco process is time-consuming and demanding and requires several layers of plaster. Although buon fresco methods vary, generally the artist prepares the wall with a rough layer of lime plaster called the *arriccio* (brown coat). The artist then transfers the composition to the wall, usually by drawing directly on the arriccio with a burnt-orange pigment called *sinopia* (most popular during the 14th century), or by transferring a *cartoon* (a full-size preparatory drawing). Cartoons increased in usage in the 15th and 16th centuries, largely replacing sinopia underdrawings. Finally, the painter lays the *intonaco* (painting coat) smoothly over the drawing in sections (called *giornate*—Italian for "days") only as large as the artist expects to complete in that session. (In Giotto's *Lamentation*

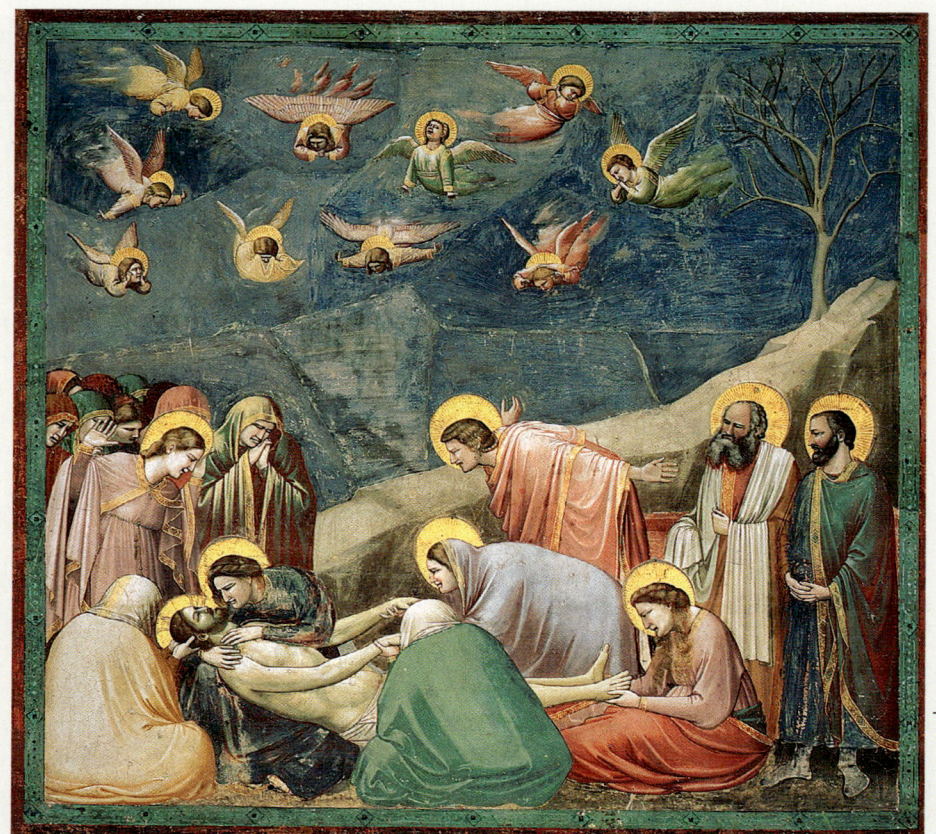

**14-8** GIOTTO DI BONDONE, *Lamentation,* Arena Chapel (Cappella Scrovegni), Padua, Italy, ca. 1305. Fresco, 6' 6¾" × 6' ¾". ◼◂

Giotto painted *Lamentation* in several sections, each corresponding to one painting session. Artists employing the buon fresco technique must complete each section before the plaster dries.

[FIG. 14-8], the giornate are easy to distinguish.) The buon fresco painter must apply the colors quickly, because once the plaster is dry, it will no longer absorb the pigment. Any unpainted areas of the intonaco after a session must be cut away so that fresh plaster can be applied for the next giornata.

In areas of high humidity, such as Venice, fresco was less appropriate because moisture is an obstacle to the drying process. Over the centuries, fresco became less popular, although it did experience a revival in the 1930s with the Mexican muralists (FIGS. 29-73 and 29-74).

of Florence's Church of the Ognissanti (All Saints). Although still portrayed against the traditional gold background, Giotto's Madonna rests within her Gothic throne with the unshakable stability of an ancient marble goddess (compare FIG. 7-30). Giotto replaced Cimabue's slender Virgin, fragile beneath the thin ripplings of her drapery, with a weighty, queenly mother. In Giotto's painting, the Madonna's body is not lost—indeed, it is asserted. Giotto even showed Mary's breasts pressing through the thin fabric of her white undergarment. Gold highlights have disappeared from her heavy robe. Giotto aimed instead to construct a figure with substance, dimensionality, and bulk—qualities suppressed in favor of a spiritual immateriality in Byzantine and Italo-Byzantine art. Works painted in the new style portray statuesque figures projecting into the light and giving the illusion they could throw shadows. Giotto's *Madonna Enthroned* marks the end of medieval painting in Italy and the beginning of a new naturalistic approach to art.

**ARENA CHAPEL** Projecting on a flat surface the illusion of solid bodies moving through space presents a double challenge. Constructing the illusion of a weighty, three-dimensional body also requires constructing the illusion of a space sufficiently ample to contain that body. In his *fresco* cycles (see "Fresco Painting," page 408), Giotto constantly strove to reconcile these two aspects of illusionistic painting. His murals in Enrico Scrovegni's Arena Chapel (FIG. 14-1) at Padua show his art at its finest. In 38 framed scenes (FIGS. **14-8, 14-8A,** and **14-8B**), Giotto presented one of the most impressive and complete Christian pictorial cycles ever rendered. The narrative unfolds on the north and south walls in three zones, reading from top to bottom. Below, imitation marble veneer—reminiscent of ancient Roman decoration (FIG. 7-51), which Giotto may have seen—alternates with personified Virtues and Vices painted in *grisaille* (monochrome grays, often used for modeling in paintings) to resemble sculpture. On the west wall above the chapel's entrance is Giotto's dramatic *Last Judgment,* the culminating scene also of Pietro Cavallini's late-13th-century fresco cycle (FIG. 14-6B) in Santa Cecilia in Trastevere in Rome. The chapel's vaulted ceiling is blue, an azure sky dotted with golden stars symbolic of Heaven. Medallions bearing images of Christ, Mary, and various prophets also appear on the vault. Giotto painted the same blue in the backgrounds of the narrative panels on the walls below. The color thereby functions as a unifying agent for the entire decorative scheme.

The panel in the lowest zone of the north wall, *Lamentation* (FIG. 14-8), illustrates particularly well the revolutionary nature of Giotto's style. In the presence of boldly foreshortened angels, seen head-on with their bodies receding into the background and darting about in hysterical grief, a congregation mourns over the dead Savior just before his entombment. Mary cradles her son's body, while Mary Magdalene looks solemnly at the wounds in Christ's feet and Saint John the Evangelist throws his arms back dramatically. Giotto arranged a shallow stage for the figures, bounded by a thick diagonal rock incline defining a horizontal ledge in the foreground. Though narrow, the ledge provides firm visual support for the figures. The rocky setting recalls the landscape of a 12th-century Byzantine mural (FIG. 9-29) at Nerezi in Macedonia. Here, the steep slope leads the viewer's eye toward the picture's dramatic focal point at the lower left. The postures and gestures of Giotto's figures convey a broad spectrum of grief. They range from Mary's almost fierce despair to the passionate outbursts of Mary Magdalene and John to the philosophical resignation of the two disciples at the right and the mute sorrow of the two hooded mourners in the foreground. In *Lamentation,* a single event provokes a host of individual responses in figures that are convincing presences both physically and psychologically. Painters before Giotto rarely attempted, let alone achieved, this combination of naturalistic representation, compositional complexity, and emotional resonance.

The formal design of the *Lamentation* fresco—the way Giotto grouped the figures within the constructed space—is worth close study. Each group has its own definition, and each contributes to the rhythmic order of the composition. The strong diagonal of the rocky ledge, with its single dead tree (the tree of knowledge of good and evil, which withered after Adam and Eve's original sin), concentrates the viewer's attention on the heads of Christ and his mother, which Giotto positioned dynamically off center. The massive bulk of the seated mourner in the painting's left corner arrests and contains all movement beyond Mary and her dead son. The seated mourner to the right establishes a relation with the center figures, who, by gazes and gestures, draw the viewer's attention back to Christ's head. Figures seen from the back, which are frequent in Giotto's compositions (compare FIG. 14-8B), represent an innovation in the development away from the formal Italo-Byzantine style. These figures emphasize the foreground, aiding the visual placement of the intermediate figures farther back in space. This device, the very contradiction of Byzantine frontality, in effect puts viewers behind the "observer figures," who, facing the action as spectators, reinforce the sense of stagecraft as a model for painting.

Giotto's new devices for depicting spatial depth and body mass could not, of course, have been possible without his management of light and shade. He shaded his figures to indicate both the direction of the light illuminating their bodies and the shadows (the diminished light), thereby giving the figures volume. In *Lamentation,* light falls upon the upper surfaces of the figures (especially the two central bending figures) and passes down to dark in their garments, separating the volumes one from the other and pushing one to the fore, the other to the rear. The graded continuum of light and shade, directed by an even, neutral light from a single steady source—not shown in the picture—was the first step toward the development of *chiaroscuro* (the use of contrasts of dark and light to produce modeling) in later Renaissance painting (see Chapter 21).

The stagelike settings made possible by Giotto's innovations in *perspective* (the depiction of three-dimensional objects in space on a two-dimensional surface) and lighting suited perfectly the dramatic narrative the Franciscans emphasized then as a principal method for educating the faithful in their religion. In this new age of humanism, the old stylized presentations of the holy mysteries had evolved into *mystery plays.* Actors extended the drama of the Mass into one- and two-act tableaus and scenes and then into simple narratives offered at church portals and in city squares. (Eventually, confraternities also presented more elaborate religious dramas called *sacre rappresentazioni*—holy representations.) The great increase in popular sermons to huge city audiences prompted a public taste for narrative, recited as dramatically as possible. The arts of illusionistic painting, of drama, and of sermon rhetoric with all their theatrical flourishes developed simultaneously and were mutually influential. Giotto's art masterfully synthesized dramatic narrative, holy lesson, and truth to human experience in a visual idiom of his own invention, accessible to all. Not surprisingly, Giotto's frescoes served as textbooks for generations of Renaissance painters.

## Siena

Among 14th-century Italian city-states, the Republics of Siena and Florence were the most powerful. Both were urban centers of bankers and merchants with widespread international contacts and large sums available for the commissioning of artworks (see "Artists' Guilds, Artistic Commissions, and Artists' Contracts," page 410).

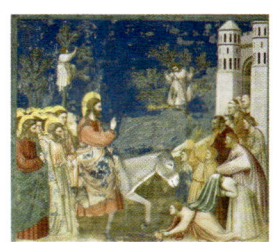

14-8A GIOTTO, *Entry into Jerusalem,* ca. 1305.

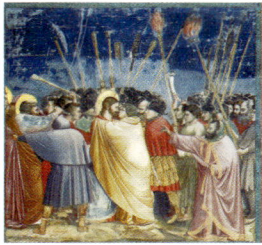

14-8B GIOTTO, *Betrayal of Jesus,* ca. 1305.

# Artists' Guilds, Artistic Commissions, and Artists' Contracts

The structured organization of economic activity during the 14th century, when Italy had established a thriving international trade and held a commanding position in the Mediterranean world, extended to many trades and professions. *Guilds* (associations of master craftspeople, apprentices, and tradespeople), which had emerged during the 12th century, became prominent. These associations not only protected members' common economic interests against external pressures, such as taxation, but also provided them with the means to regulate their internal operations (for example, work quality and membership training).

Because of today's international open art market, the notion of an "artists' union" may seem strange. The general public tends to think of art as the creative expression of an individual artist. However, artists did not always enjoy this degree of freedom. Historically, they rarely undertook major artworks without receiving a specific commission. The patron contracting for the artist's services could be a civic group, religious entity, private individual, or even the artists' guild itself. Guilds, although primarily business organizations, contributed to their city's religious and artistic life by subsidizing the building and decoration of numerous churches and hospitals. For example, the wool manufacturers' guild oversaw the start of Florence Cathedral (FIGS. 14-18 and 14-18A) in 1296, and the wool merchants' guild supervised the completion of its dome (FIG. 21-30A). The guild of silk manufacturers and goldsmiths provided the funds to build Florence's foundling hospital, the Ospedale degli Innocenti (FIG. 21-31).

Monastic orders, confraternities, and the popes were also major art patrons. In addition, wealthy families and individuals—for example, the Paduan banker Enrico Scrovegni (FIG. 14-1)—commissioned artworks for a wide variety of reasons. Besides the aesthetic pleasure these patrons derived from art, the images often also served as testaments to the patron's piety, wealth, and stature. Because artworks during this period were the product of service contracts, a patron's needs or wishes played a crucial role in the final form of any painting, sculpture, or building. Some early contracts between patrons and artists still exist. Patrons normally asked artists to submit drawings or models for approval, and they expected the artists they hired to adhere closely to the approved designs. The contracts usually stipulated certain conditions, such as the insistence on the artist's own hand in the production of the work, the quality of pigment and amount of gold or other precious items to be used, completion date, payment terms, and penalties for failure to meet the contract's terms.

A few extant 13th- and 14th-century painting contracts are especially illuminating. Although they may specify the subject to be represented, these binding legal documents always focus on the financial aspects of the commission and the responsibilities of the painter to the patron (and vice versa). In a contract dated November 1, 1301, between Cimabue (FIG. 14-6) and another artist and the Hospital of Santa Chiara in Pisa, the artists agree to supply an altarpiece

> with colonnettes, tabernacles, and predella, painted with histories of the divine majesty of the Blessed Virgin Mary, of the apostles,

of the angels, and with other figures and pictures, as shall be seen fit and shall please the said master of or other legitimate persons for the hospital.*

Other terms of the Santa Chiara contract specify the size of the panel and require the artists to use gold and silver gilding for parts of the altarpiece.

The contract for the construction of an altarpiece was usually a separate document, because it necessitated employing the services of a master carpenter. For example, on April 15, 1285, the leading painter of Siena, Duccio di Buoninsegna (FIGS. 14-9 to 14-11), signed a contract with the rectors of the Confraternity of the Laudesi, the lay group associated with the Dominican church of Santa Maria Novella (FIG. 14-6A) in Florence. The contract specified only that Duccio was to provide the painting, not its frame—and it imposed conditions the painter had to meet if he was to be paid.

> [The rectors] promise . . . to pay the same Duccio . . . as the payment and price of the painting of the said panel that is to be painted and done by him in the way described below . . . 150 lire of the small florins. . . . [Duccio, in turn, promises] to paint and embellish the panel with the image of the blessed Virgin Mary and of her omnipotent Son and other figures, according to the wishes and pleasure of the lessors, and to gild [the panel] and do everything that will enhance the beauty of the panel, his being all the expenses and the costs. . . . If the said panel is not beautifully painted and it is not embellished according to the wishes and desires of the same lessors, they are in no way bound to pay him the price or any part of it.†

Sometimes patrons furnished the materials and paid artists by the day instead of a fixed amount. That was the arrangement Duccio made on October 9, 1308, when he agreed to paint the *Maestà* (FIG. 14-9) for the high altar of Siena Cathedral.

> Duccio has promised to paint and make the said panel as well as he can and knows how, and he further agreed not to accept or receive any other work until the said panel is done and completed. . . . [The church officials promise] to pay the said Duccio sixteen solidi of the Sienese denari as his salary for the said work and labor for each day that the said Duccio works with his own hands on the said panel . . . [and] to provide and give everything that will be necessary for working on the said panel so that the said Duccio need contribute nothing to the work save his person and his effort.‡

In all cases, the artists worked for their patrons and could count on being compensated for their talents and efforts only if the work they delivered met the standards of those who ordered it.

*Translated by John White, *Duccio: Tuscan Art and the Medieval Workshop* (London: Thames & Hudson, 1979), 34.
†Translated by James H. Stubblebine, *Duccio di Buoninsegna and His School* (Princeton, N.J.: Princeton University Press, 1979), 1: 192.
‡Stubblebine, *Duccio*, 1: 201.

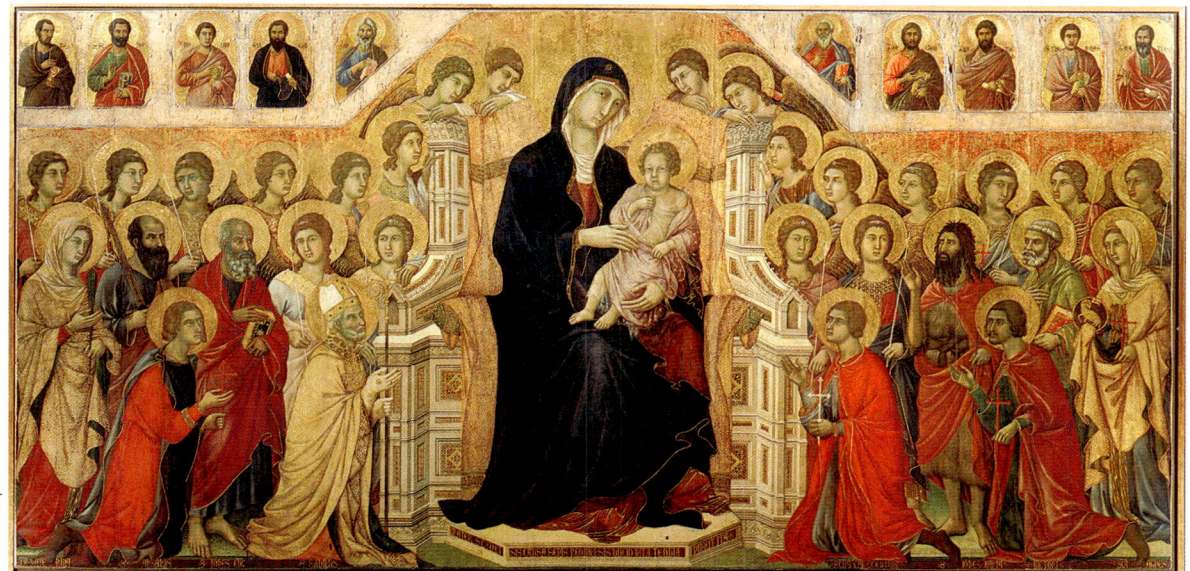

**14-9** DUCCIO DI BUONINSEGNA, *Virgin and Child Enthroned with Saints,* principal panel of the *Maestà* altarpiece, from Siena Cathedral, Siena, Italy, 1308–1311. Tempera and gold leaf on wood, 7′ × 13′. Museo dell'Opera del Duomo, Siena. ◼

Duccio derived the formality and symmetry of his composition from Byzantine painting, but relaxed the rigidity and frontality of the figures, softened the drapery, and individualized the faces.

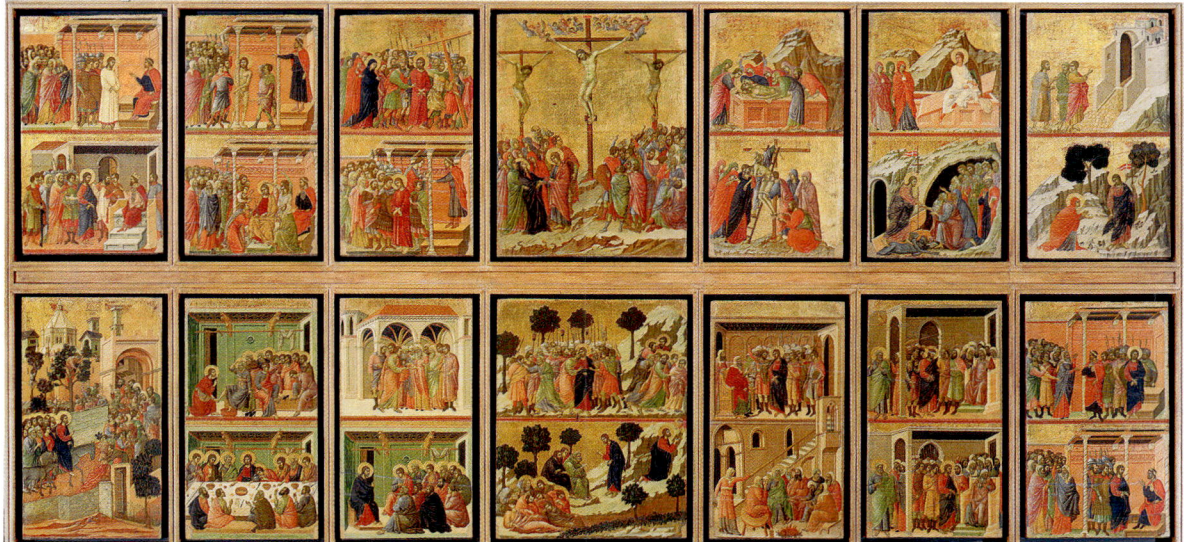

**14-10** DUCCIO DI BUONINSEGNA, *Life of Jesus,* 14 panels from the back of the *Maestà* altarpiece, from Siena Cathedral, Siena, Italy, 1308–1311. Tempera and gold leaf on wood, 7′ × 13′. Museo dell'Opera del Duomo, Siena.

On the back of the *Maestà* altarpiece, Duccio painted Jesus' passion in 24 scenes on 14 panels, beginning with *Entry into Jerusalem* (FIG. 14-10A), at the lower left, through *Noli me tangere,* at top right.

**DUCCIO** The works of DUCCIO DI BUONINSEGNA (active ca. 1278–1318) represent Sienese art at its most supreme. His most famous painting, the immense altarpiece called *Maestà* (*Virgin Enthroned in Majesty;* FIG. 14-9), replaced a much smaller painting of the Virgin Mary on the high altar of Siena Cathedral (FIG. 14-12A). The Sienese believed the Virgin had brought them victory over the Florentines at the battle of Monteperti in 1260, and she was the focus of the religious life of the republic. Duccio and his assistants began work on the prestigious commission in 1308 and completed *Maestà* in 1311, causing the entire city to celebrate. Shops closed and the bishop led a great procession of priests, civic officials, and the populace at large in carrying the altarpiece from Duccio's studio outside the city gate through the Campo (FIG. 14-15) up to its home on Siena's highest hill. So great was Duccio's stature that church officials permitted him to include his name in the dedicatory inscription on the front of the altarpiece on the Virgin's footstool: "Holy Mother of God, be the cause of peace for Siena and of life for Duccio, because he painted you thus."

As originally executed, Duccio's *Maestà* consisted of the seven-foot-high central panel (FIG. 14-9) with the dedicatory inscription,

surmounted by seven *pinnacles* above, and a *predella,* or raised shelf, of panels at the base, altogether some 13 feet high. Painted in tempera front and back (FIG. 14-10), the work unfortunately can no longer be seen in its entirety, because of its dismantling in subsequent centuries. Many of Duccio's panels are on display today as single masterpieces, scattered among the world's museums.

The main panel on the front of the altarpiece represents the Virgin enthroned as queen of Heaven amid choruses of angels and saints. Duccio derived the composition's formality and symmetry, along with the figures and facial types of the principal angels and saints, from Byzantine tradition. But the artist relaxed the strict frontality and rigidity of the figures. They turn to each other in quiet conversation. Further, Duccio individualized the faces of the four saints kneeling in the foreground, who perform their ceremonial gestures without stiffness. Similarly, he softened the usual Byzantine hard body outlines and drapery patterning. The folds of the garments, particularly those of the female saints at both ends of the panel, fall and curve loosely. This is a feature familiar in French Gothic works (FIG. 13-37) and is a mark of the artistic dialogue between Italy and northern Europe in the 14th century.

Despite these changes revealing Duccio's interest in the new naturalism, he respected the age-old requirement that as an altarpiece, *Maestà* would be the focus of worship in Siena's largest and most important church, its *cathedral,* the seat of the bishop of Siena. As such, Duccio knew *Maestà* should be an object holy in itself—a work of splendor to the eyes, precious in its message and its materials. Duccio thus recognized how the function of the altarpiece naturally limited experimentation in depicting narrative action and producing illusionistic effects (such as Giotto's) by modeling forms and adjusting their placement in pictorial space.

Instead, the queen of Heaven panel is a miracle of color composition and texture manipulation, unfortunately not fully revealed in photographs. Close inspection of the original reveals what the Sienese artist learned from other sources. In the 13th and 14th centuries, Italy was the distribution center for the great silk trade from China and the Middle East (see "The Silk Road," Chapter 16, page 458). After processing the silk in city-states such as Lucca and Florence, the Italians exported the precious fabric throughout Europe to satisfy an immense market for sumptuous dress. (Dante, Petrarch, and many other humanists decried the appetite for luxury in costume, which to them represented a decline in civic and moral virtue.) People throughout Europe (Duccio and other artists among them) prized fabrics from China, Persia, Byzantium, and the Islamic world. In *Maestà,* Duccio created the glistening and shimmering effects of textiles, adapting the motifs and design patterns of exotic materials. Complementing the luxurious fabrics and the (lost) gilded wood frame are the halos of the holy figures, which feature tooled decorative designs in gold leaf (*punchwork*). But Duccio, like Giotto (FIG. 14-7), eliminated almost all the gold patterning of the figures' garments in favor of creating three-dimensional volume. Traces remain only in the Virgin's red dress.

In contrast to the main panel, the predella and the back (FIG. 14-10) of *Maestà* present an extensive series of narrative panels of different sizes and shapes, beginning with *Annunciation* and culminating with Christ's *Resurrection* and other episodes following his *Crucifixion* (see "The Life of Jesus in Art," Chapter 11, pages

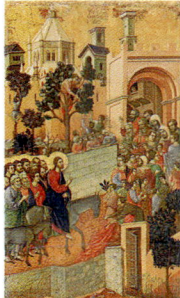

240–241, or pages xxx–xxxi in Volume II and Book D). The section reproduced here, consisting of 24 scenes in 14 panels, relates Christ's passion. Duccio drew the details of his scenes from the accounts in all four Gospels. The viewer reads the pictorial story in zig-zag fashion, beginning with *Entry into Jerusalem* (FIG. **14-10A**) at the lower left. *Crucifixion* is at the top cen-

**14-10A** DUCCIO, *Entry into Jerusalem,* 1308–1311.

**14-11** DUCCIO DI BUONINSEGNA, *Betrayal of Jesus,* panel on the back of the *Maestà* altarpiece, from Siena Cathedral, Siena, Italy, 1309–1311. Tempera and gold leaf on wood, 1′ 10$\frac{1}{2}$″ × 3′ 4″. Museo dell'Opera del Duomo, Siena.

In this dramatic depiction of Judas's betrayal of Jesus, the actors display a variety of individual emotions. Duccio here took a decisive step toward the humanization of religious subject matter.

ter. The narrative ends with Christ's appearance to Mary Magdalene (*Noli me tangere*) at the top right. Duccio consistently dressed Jesus in blue robes in most of the panels, but beginning with *Transfiguration,* he gilded the Savior's garment.

On the front panel, Duccio showed himself as the great master of the formal altarpiece. However, he allowed himself greater latitude for experimentation in the small accompanying panels, front and back. (Worshipers could always view both sides of the altarpiece because the high altar stood at the center of the sanctuary.) *Maestà*'s biblical scenes reveal Duccio's powers as a narrative painter. In *Betrayal of Jesus* (FIG. **14-11;** compare FIG. 14-8B), for example, the artist represented several episodes of the event—the betrayal of Jesus by Judas's false kiss, the disciples fleeing in terror, and Peter cutting off the ear of the high priest's servant. Although the background, with its golden sky and rock formations, remains traditional, the style of the figures before it has changed radically. The bodies are not the flat frontal shapes of Italo-Byzantine art. Duccio imbued them with mass, modeled them with a range of tonalities from light to dark, and arranged their draperies around them convincingly. Even more novel and striking is the way the figures seem to react to the central event. Through posture, gesture, and even facial expression, they display a variety of emotions. Duccio carefully differentiated among the anger of Peter, the malice of Judas (echoed in the faces of the throng about Jesus), and the apprehension and timidity of the fleeing disciples. These figures are actors in a religious drama the artist interpreted in terms of thoroughly human actions and reactions. In this and the other narrative panels, for example, Jesus' *Entry into Jerusalem* (FIG. 14-10A), a theme treated also by Giotto in the Arena Chapel (FIG. 14-8A), Duccio took a decisive step toward the humanization of religious subject matter.

**ORVIETO CATHEDRAL** While Duccio was working on *Maestà* for Siena's most important church, a Sienese architect, LORENZO MAITANI, received the commission to design Orvieto's Cathedral (FIG. **14-12**). The Orvieto *facade,* like the earlier facade of Siena Cathedral (FIG. **14-12A**), begun by Giovanni Pisano (FIG. 14-4), demonstrates the appeal of the decorative vocabulary of French Gothic architecture in Italy at the end of the 13th and beginning of the 14th century. Characteristically French are the pointed gables over Orvieto Cathedral's three doorways, the *rose window* and

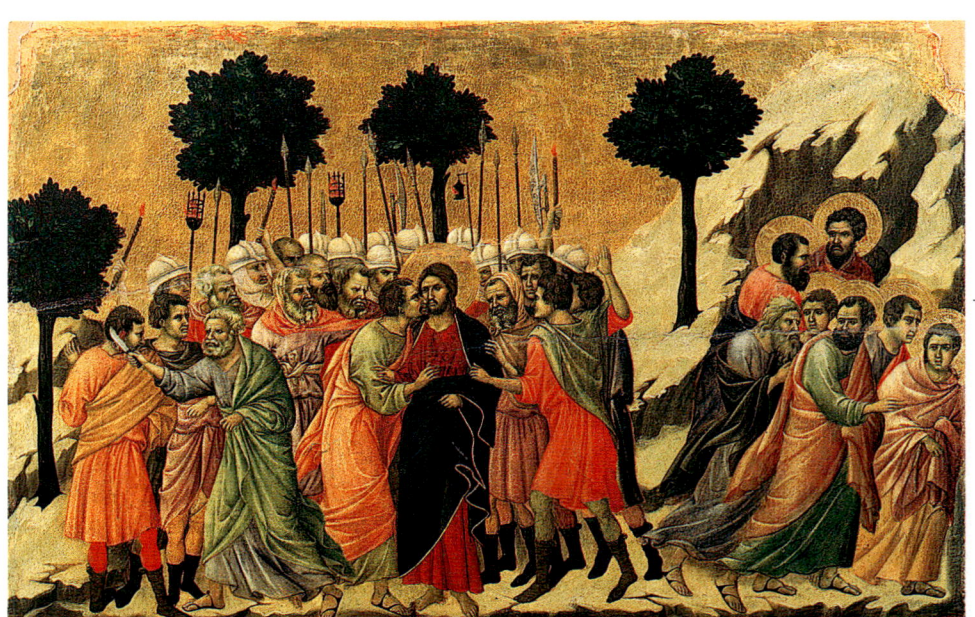

1 ft.

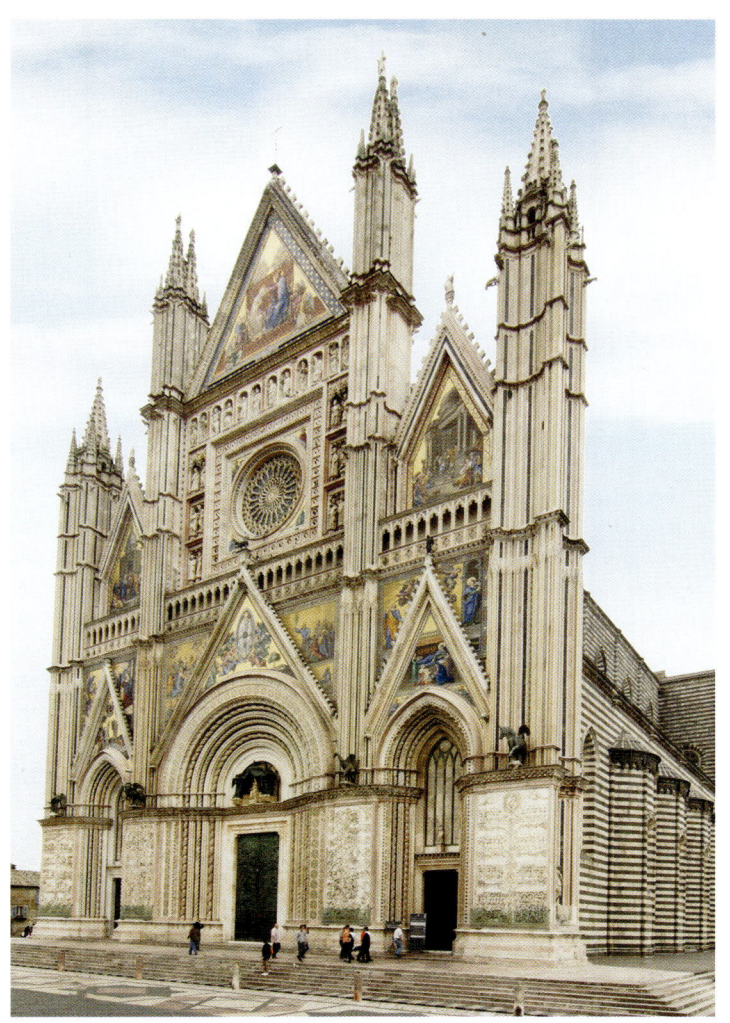

14-12 LORENZO MAITANI, Orvieto Cathedral (looking northeast), Orvieto, Italy, begun 1310. ◼️🎥

The pointed gables over the doorways, the rose window, and the large pinnacles derive from French Gothic architecture, but the facade of Orvieto Cathedral masks a traditional timber-roofed basilica.

statues in niches in the upper zone, and the four large *pinnacles* dividing the facade into three *bays* (see "The Gothic Cathedral," Chapter 13, page 373, or page xxvi in Volume II and Book D). The outer pinnacles serve as miniature substitutes for the tall northern European west-front towers. Maitani's facade, however, is a Gothic overlay masking a marble-revetted *basilican* structure in the Tuscan *Romanesque* tradition, as the three-quarter view of the cathedral in FIG. 14-12 reveals. Few Italian architects fully embraced the Gothic style. The Orvieto facade resembles a great altar screen, its single plane covered with carefully placed carved and painted decoration. In principle, Orvieto belongs with Pisa Cathedral (FIG. 12-26) and other earlier Italian buildings, rather than with the French cathedrals at Amiens (FIG. 13-19) and Reims (FIG. 13-23). Inside, Orvieto Cathedral has a timber-roofed *nave* with a two-story *elevation* (columnar *arcade* and *clerestory*) in the Early Christian manner. Both the *chancel arch* framing the *apse* and the nave arcade's arches are round as opposed to pointed.

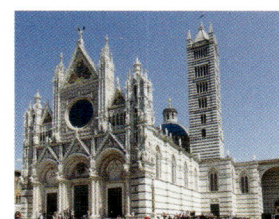

14-12A Siena Cathedral, begun ca. 1226. ◼️🎥

**SIMONE MARTINI** Duccio's successors in the Sienese school also produced innovative works. SIMONE MARTINI (ca. 1285–1344) was a pupil of Duccio's and may have assisted him in painting *Maestà*. Martini was a close friend of Petrarch's, and the poet praised him highly for his portrait of "Laura" (the woman to whom Petrarch dedicated his sonnets). Martini worked for the French kings in Naples and Sicily and, in his last years, produced paintings for the papal court at Avignon, where he came in contact with French painters. By adapting the insubstantial but luxuriant patterns of the Gothic style to Sienese art and, in turn, by acquainting painters north of the Alps with the Sienese style, Martini was instrumental in creating the so-called *International style*. This new style swept Europe during the late 14th and early 15th centuries because it appealed to the aristocratic taste for brilliant colors, lavish costumes, intricate ornamentation, and themes involving splendid processions.

The *Annunciation* altarpiece (FIG. **14-13**) Martini created for Siena Cathedral features elegant shapes and radiant color, fluttering line, and weightless figures in a spaceless setting—all hallmarks of the artist's style.

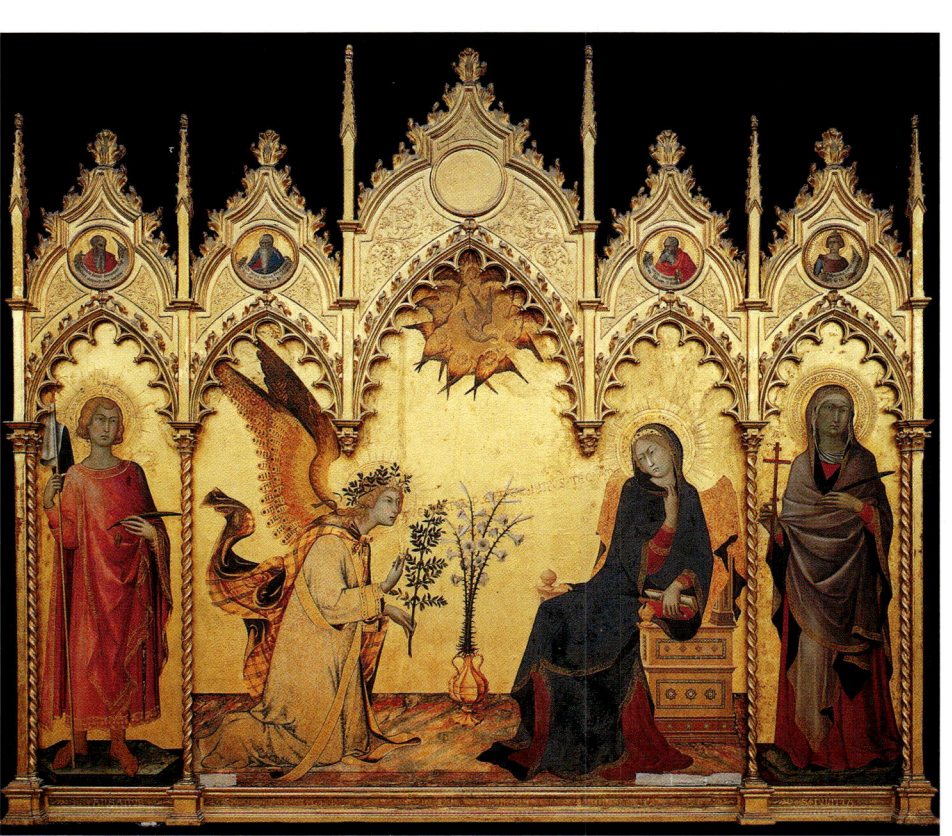

1 ft.

14-13 SIMONE MARTINI and LIPPO MEMMI, *Annunciation* altarpiece, from Siena Cathedral, 1333 (frame reconstructed in the 19th century). Tempera and gold leaf on wood, center panel 10′ 1″ × 8′ 8¾″. Galleria degli Uffizi, Florence.

A pupil of Duccio's, Martini was instrumental in the creation of the International style. Its hallmarks are elegant shapes, radiant color, flowing line, and weightless figures in golden, spaceless settings.

# Artistic Training in Renaissance Italy

In Italy during the 14th through 16th centuries, training to become a professional artist capable of earning membership in the appropriate guild (see "Artists' Guilds," page 410) was a laborious and lengthy process. Aspiring artists started their training at an early age, anywhere from age 7 to 15. Their fathers would negotiate an arrangement with a master artist whereby each youth lived with that master for a specified number of years, usually five or six. During that time, the boys served as apprentices to the master of the workshop, learning the trade. (This living arrangement served as a major obstacle for female artists, because it was inappropriate for young girls to live in a male master's household.) The guilds supervised this rigorous training. They wanted not only to ensure their professional reputations by admitting only the most talented members but also to control the number of artists (and thereby limit competition). Toward this end, they frequently tried to regulate the number of apprentices working under a single master.

The skills apprentices learned varied with the type of studio they joined. Those apprenticed to painters learned to grind pigments, draw, prepare wood panels for painting, gild, and lay plaster for fresco. Sculptors in training learned to manipulate different materials—wood, stone, *terracotta* (baked clay), wax, bronze, or stucco—although many sculpture workshops specialized in only one or two of these materials. For stone carving, apprentices learned their craft by blocking out the master's designs for statues. As their skills developed, apprentices took on increasingly difficult tasks.

Cennino Cennini (ca. 1370–1440) explained the value of this apprenticeship system, and in particular, the advantages for young artists in studying and copying the works of older masters, in an influential book he published in 1400, *Il Libro dell'Arte* (*The Handbook of Art*):

> Having first practiced drawing for a while, . . . take pains and pleasure in constantly copying the best things which you can find done by the hand of great masters. And if you are in a place where many good masters have been, so much the better for you. But I give you this advice: take care to select the best one every time, and the one who has the greatest reputation. And, as you go on from day to day, it will be against nature if you do not get some grasp of his style and of his spirit. For if you undertake to copy after one master today and after another one tomorrow, you will not acquire the style of either one or the other, and you will inevitably, through

enthusiasm, become capricious, because each style will be distracting your mind. You will try to work in this man's way today, and in the other's tomorrow, and so you will not get either of them right. If you follow the course of one man through constant practice, your intelligence would have to be crude indeed for you not to get some nourishment from it. Then you will find, if nature has granted you any imagination at all, that you will eventually acquire a style individual to yourself, and it cannot help being good; because your hand and your mind, being always accustomed to gather flowers, would ill know how to pluck thorns.*

After completing their apprenticeships, artists entered the appropriate guilds. For example, painters, who ground pigments, joined the guild of apothecaries. Sculptors were members of the guild of stoneworkers, and goldsmiths entered the silk guild, because metalworkers often stretched gold into threads wound around silk for weaving. Guild membership served as certification of the artists' competence, but did not mean they were ready to open their own studios. New guild-certified artists usually served as assistants to master artists, because until they established their reputations, they could not expect to receive many commissions, and the cost of establishing their own workshops was high. In any case, this arrangement was not permanent, and workshops were not necessarily static enterprises. Although well-established and respected studios existed, workshops could be organized around individual masters (with no set studio locations) or organized for a specific project, especially an extensive decoration program.

Generally, assistants to painters were responsible for gilding frames and backgrounds, completing decorative work, and, occasionally, rendering architectural settings. Artists regarded figures, especially those central to the represented subject, as the most important and difficult parts of a painting, and the master reserved these for himself. Sometimes assistants painted secondary or marginal figures but only under the master's close supervision. That was probably the case with Simone Martini's *Annunciation* altarpiece (FIG. 14-13), in which the master painted the Virgin and angel, and the flanking saints are probably the work of his assistant, Lippo Memmi.

*Translated by Daniel V. Thompson Jr., *Cennino Cennini, The Craftsman's Handbook* (*Il Libro dell'Arte*) (New York: Dover Publications, 1960; reprint of 1933 ed.), 14–15.

---

The complex etiquette of the European chivalric courts probably dictated the presentation. The angel Gabriel has just alighted, the breeze of his passage lifting his mantle, his iridescent wings still beating. The gold of his sumptuous gown signals he has descended from Heaven to deliver his message. The Virgin, putting down her book of devotions, shrinks demurely from Gabriel's reverent genuflection—an appropriate act in the presence of royalty. Mary draws about her the deep blue, golden-hemmed mantle, colors befitting the queen of Heaven. Between the two figures is a vase of white lilies, symbolic of the Virgin's purity. Despite Mary's modesty and diffidence and the tremendous import of the angel's message, the scene subordinates drama to court ritual, and structural experimentation to surface splendor. The intricate *tracery* of the richly

tooled (reconstructed) French Gothic–inspired frame and the elaborate punchwork halos (by then a characteristic feature of Sienese panel painting) enhance the tactile magnificence of *Annunciation*.

Simone Martini and his student and assistant, LIPPO MEMMI (active ca. 1317–1350), signed the altarpiece and dated it (1333). The latter's contribution to *Annunciation* is still a matter of debate, but most art historians believe he painted the two lateral saints. These figures, which are reminiscent of the jamb statues of Gothic church portals, have greater solidity and lack the linear elegance of Martini's central pair. Given the nature of medieval and Renaissance workshop practices, it is often difficult to distinguish the master's hand from those of assistants, especially if the master corrected or redid part of the pupil's work (see "Artistic Training in Renaissance Italy," page 414).

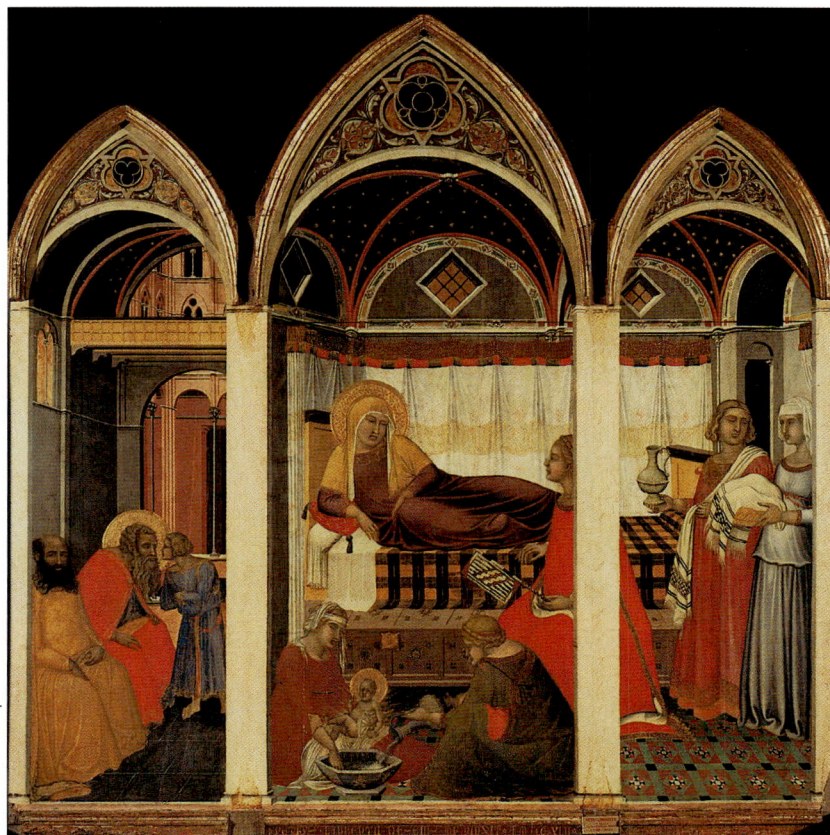

1 ft.

**14-14** Pietro Lorenzetti, *Birth of the Virgin,* from the altar of Saint Savinus, Siena Cathedral, Siena, Italy, 1342. Tempera on wood, 6′ 1″ × 5′ 11″. Museo dell'Opera del Duomo, Siena.

In this triptych, Pietro Lorenzetti revived the pictorial illusionism of ancient Roman murals and painted the architectural members dividing the panel as if they extended back into the painted space.

**PIETRO LORENZETTI** Another of Duccio's students, Pietro Lorenzetti (active 1320–1348), contributed significantly to the general experiments in pictorial realism taking place in 14th-century Italy. Surpassing even his renowned master, Lorenzetti achieved a remarkable degree of spatial illusionism in his *Birth of the Virgin* (FIG. **14-14**), a large *triptych* (three-part panel painting) created for the altar of Saint Savinus in Siena Cathedral. Lorenzetti painted the wooden architectural members dividing the altarpiece into three sections as though they extended back into the painted space. Viewers seem to look through the wooden frame (added later) into a boxlike stage, where the event takes place. That one of the vertical members cuts across a figure, blocking part of it from view, strengthens the illusion. In subsequent centuries, artists exploited this use of architectural elements to enhance the illusion of painted figures acting out a drama a mere few feet away. This kind of pictorial illusionism characterized ancient Roman mural painting (FIGS. 7-18 and 7-19, *right*) but had not been practiced in Italy for a thousand years.

Lorenzetti's setting for his holy subject also represented a marked step in the advance of worldly realism. Saint Anne—who, like Nicola Pisano's Virgin in *Nativity* (FIG. 14-3), resembles a reclining figure on the lid of a Roman sarcophagus (FIG. 7-61)—props herself up wearily as the midwives wash the child and the women bring gifts. She is the center of an episode occurring in an upper-class Italian house of the period. A number of carefully observed domestic details and the scene at the left, where Joachim eagerly awaits news of the delivery, create the illusion that the viewer has opened the walls of Saint Anne's house and peered inside. Lorenzetti's altarpiece is noteworthy both for the painter's innovations in spatial illusionism and for his careful inspection and recording of details of the everyday world.

**PALAZZO PUBBLICO** Not all Sienese painting of the early 14th century was religious in character. One of the most important fresco cycles of the period (FIGS. 14-16 and 14-17) was a civic commission for Siena's Palazzo Pubblico ("public palace" or city hall). Siena was a proud commercial and political rival of Florence. The secular center of the community, the civic meeting hall in the main square (the Campo, or Field), was almost as great an object of civic pride as the city's cathedral (FIG. 14-12A). The Palazzo Pubblico (FIG. **14-15**) has a slightly concave

**14-15** Palazzo Pubblico (looking east), Siena, Italy, 1288–1309. ◀

Siena's Palazzo Pubblico has a concave facade and a gigantic tower visible for miles around. The tower served as both a defensive lookout over the countryside and a symbol of the city-state's power.

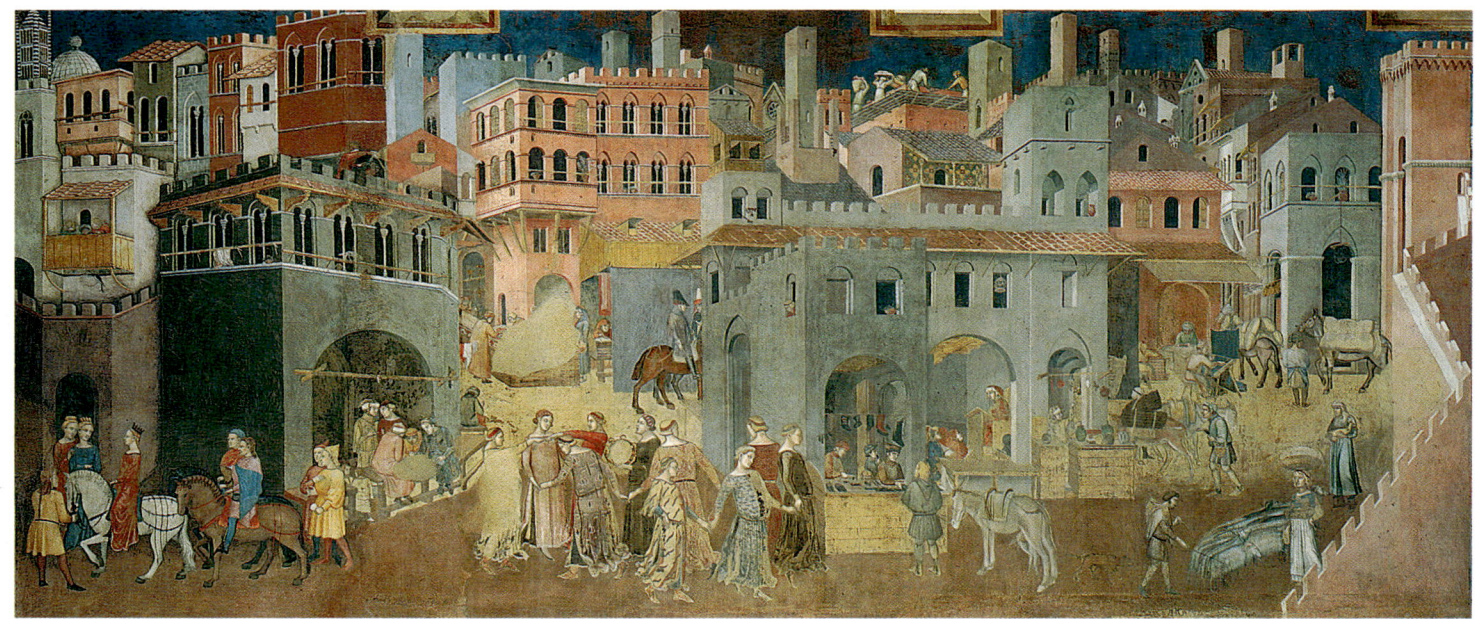

**14-16** Ambrogio Lorenzetti, *Peaceful City,* detail from *Effects of Good Government in the City and in the Country,* east wall, Sala della Pace, Palazzo Pubblico, Siena, Italy, 1338–1339. Fresco. ■◄

In the Hall of Peace (FIG. 14-16A) of Siena's city hall (FIG. 14-15), Ambrogio Lorenzetti painted an illusionistic panorama of the bustling city. The fresco served as an allegory of good government in the Sienese republic.

facade (to conform to the irregular shape of the Campo) and a gigantic tower visible from miles around (compare FIGS. 13-29 and 14-18B). The imposing building and tower must have earned the admiration of Siena's citizens as well as of visitors to the city, inspiring in them respect for the republic's power and success. The tower served as a lookout over the city and the countryside around it and as a bell tower (*campanile*) for ringing signals of all kinds to the populace. Siena, as other Italian city-states, had to defend itself against neighboring cities and often against kings and emperors. In addition, it had to secure itself against internal upheavals common in the history of the Italian city-republics. Class struggle, feuds among rich and powerful families, and even uprisings of the whole populace against the city governors were constant threats in medieval Italy. The heavy walls and *battlements* (fortified *parapets*) of the Sienese town hall eloquently express how frequently the city governors needed to defend themselves against their own citizens. The Palazzo Pubblico tower, out of reach of most missiles, incorporates *machicolated galleries* (galleries with holes in their floors to enable defenders to dump stones or hot liquids on attackers below) built out on *corbels* (projecting supporting architectural members) for defense of the tower's base.

**AMBROGIO LORENZETTI** The painter entrusted with the major fresco program in the Palazzo Pubblico was Pietro Loren-

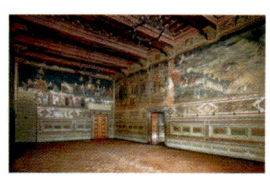

**14-16A** Sala della Pace, Siena, 1338–1339.

zetti's brother AMBROGIO LORENZETTI (active 1319–1348). In the frescoes Ambrogio produced for the Sala della Pace (Hall of Peace; FIG. 14-16A), he elaborated his brother's advances in illusionistic representation in spectacular fashion while giving visual form to Sienese civic concerns. The subjects of Ambrogio's murals are *Allegory of Good Government, Bad Government and the Effects of Bad Government in the City,* and *Effects of Good Government in the City and in the Country.* The turbulent politics of the Italian cities—the violent party struggles, the overthrow and reinstatement of governments—called for solemn reminders of fair and just administration, and the city hall was just the place to display these allegorical paintings. Indeed, the leaders of the Sienese government who commissioned this fresco series had undertaken the "ordering and reformation of the whole city and countryside of Siena."

In *Effects of Good Government in the City and in the Country,* Ambrogio depicted the urban and rural effects of good government. *Peaceful City* (FIG. 14-16) is a panoramic view of Siena, with its clustering palaces, markets, towers, churches, streets, and walls, reminiscent of the townscapes of ancient Roman murals (FIG. 7-19, *left*). The city's traffic moves peacefully, guild members ply their trades and crafts, and radiant maidens, clustered hand in hand, perform a graceful circling dance. Dancers were regular features of festive springtime rituals. Here, their presence also serves as a metaphor for a peaceful commonwealth. The artist fondly observed the life of his city, and its architecture gave him an opportunity to apply Sienese artists' rapidly growing knowledge of perspective.

As the viewer's eye passes through the city gate to the countryside beyond its walls, Ambrogio's *Peaceful Country* (FIG. 14-17) presents a bird's-eye view of the undulating Tuscan terrain with its villas, castles, plowed farmlands, and peasants going about their occupations at different seasons of the year. Although it is an allegory, not a mimetic picture of the Sienese countryside on a specific day, Lorenzetti particularized the view of Tuscany—as well as the city view—by careful observation and endowed the painting with the character of a portrait of a specific place and environment. *Peaceful Country* represents one of the first appearances of *landscape* in Western art since antiquity (FIG. 7-20).

An allegorical figure of Security hovers above the hills and fields, unfurling a scroll promising safety to all who live under the rule of law. But Siena could not protect its citizens from the plague sweeping through Europe in the mid-14th century. The Black Death (see page 406) killed thousands of Sienese and may have ended the careers of both Lorenzettis. They disappear from historical records in 1348.

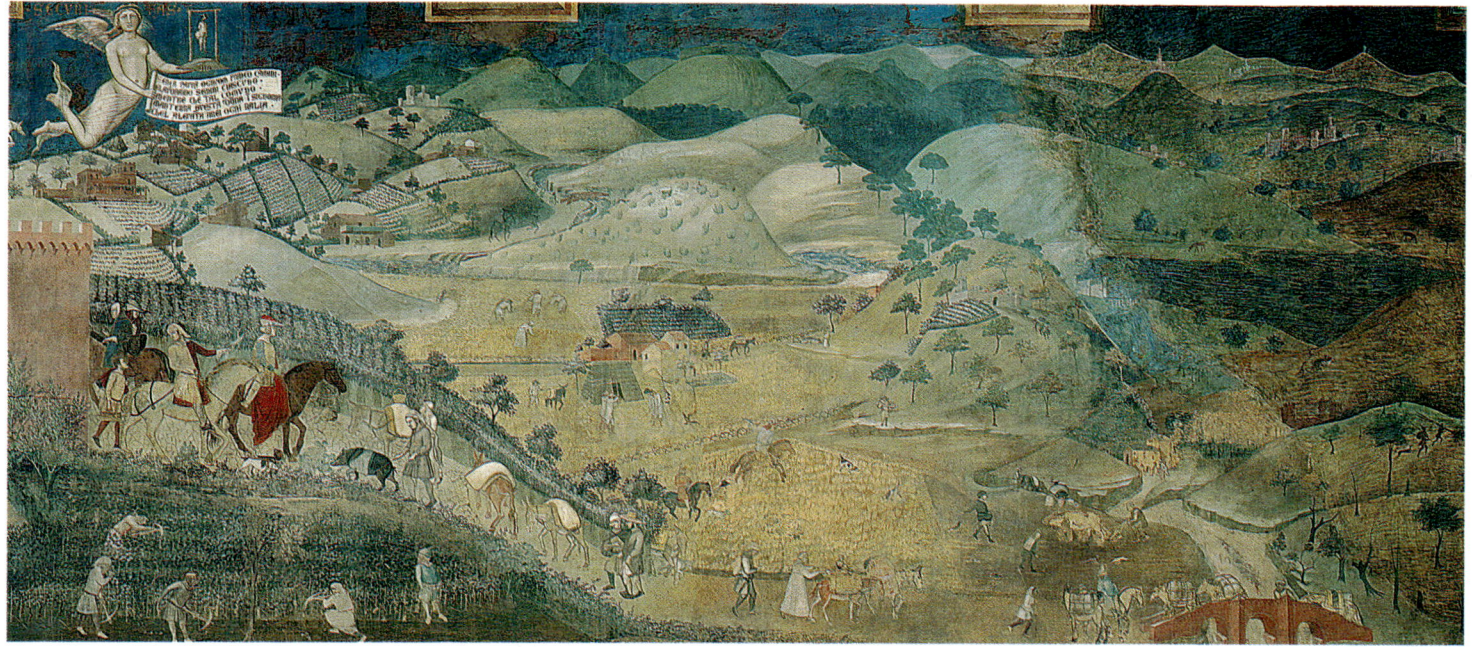

**14-17** Ambrogio Lorenzetti, *Peaceful Country,* detail from *Effects of Good Government in the City and in the Country,* east wall, Sala della Pace (FIG. 14-16A), Palazzo Pubblico (FIG. 14-15), Siena, Italy, 1338–1339. Fresco. ◼◀

This sweeping view of the countryside is one of the first instances of landscape painting in Western art since antiquity. The winged figure of Security promises safety to all who live under Sienese law.

## Florence

Like Siena, the Republic of Florence was a dominant city-state during the 14th century. The historian Giovanni Villani (ca. 1270–1348), for example, described Florence as "the daughter and the creature of Rome," suggesting a preeminence inherited from the Roman Empire. Florentines were fiercely proud of what they perceived as their economic and cultural superiority. Florence controlled the textile industry in Italy, and the republic's gold *florin* was the standard coin of exchange everywhere in Europe.

**FLORENCE CATHEDRAL** Florentines translated their pride in their predominance into such landmark buildings as Santa Maria del Fiore (FIGS. **14-18** and **14-18A**), Florence's cathedral, the center for the most important religious observances in the city. Arnolfo di Cambio (ca. 1245–1302) began work on the cathedral (*Duomo* in Italian) in 1296, three years before he received the commission to build the city's town hall, the Palazzo della Signoria (FIG. **14-18B**). Intended as the "most beautiful and honorable church in Tuscany," the cathedral reveals the competitiveness Florentines felt with cities such as Siena (FIG. 14-12A) and Pisa (FIG. 12-26). Church authorities planned for the

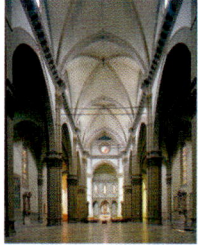

**14-18A** Nave, Florence Cathedral, begun 1296.

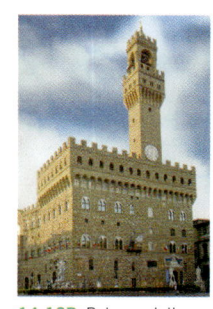

**14-18B** Palazzo della Signoria, Florence, 1299–1310.

**14-18** Arnolfo di Cambio and others, aerial view of Santa Maria del Fiore (and the Baptistery of San Giovanni; looking northeast), Florence, Italy, begun 1296. Campanile designed by Giotto di Bondone, 1334. ◼◀

The Florentine Duomo's marble revetment carries on the Tuscan Romanesque architectural tradition, linking this basilican church more closely to Early Christian Italy than to Gothic France.

Duomo to hold the city's entire population, and although its capacity is only about 30,000 (Florence's population at the time was slightly less than 100,000), the building seemed so large even the noted architect Leon Battista Alberti (see Chapter 21) commented it seemed to cover "all of Tuscany with its shade." The builders ornamented the cathedral's surfaces, in the old Tuscan fashion, with marble-encrusted geometric designs, matching the *revetment* (decorative wall paneling) to that of the facing 11th-century Romanesque baptistery of San Giovanni (FIGS. 12-27 and 14-18, *left*).

The vast gulf separating Santa Maria del Fiore from its northern European counterparts becomes evident in a comparison between the Florentine church and the High Gothic cathedrals of Amiens (FIG. 13-19), Reims (FIG. 13-23), and Cologne (FIG. 13-52). Gothic architects' emphatic stress on the vertical produced an awe-inspiring upward rush of unmatched vigor and intensity. The French and German buildings express organic growth shooting heavenward, as the pierced, translucent stone tracery of the spires merges with the atmosphere. Florence Cathedral, in contrast, clings to the ground and has no aspirations to flight. All emphasis is on the horizontal elements of the design, and the building rests firmly and massively on the ground. The clearly defined simple geometric volumes of the cathedral show no tendency to merge either into each other or into the sky.

Giotto di Bondone designed the Duomo's campanile in 1334. In keeping with Italian tradition (FIGS. 12-21 and 12-26), it stands apart from the church. In fact, it is essentially self-sufficient and could stand anywhere else in the city without looking out of place. The same cannot be said of the towers of Amiens, Reims, and Cologne cathedrals. They are essential elements of the structures behind them, and it would be unthinkable to detach one of them and place it somewhere else. No individual element of Gothic churches seems capable of an independent existence. One form merges into the next in a series of rising movements pulling the eye upward and never permitting it to rest until it reaches the sky. The Florentine campanile is entirely different. Neatly subdivided into cubic sections, Giotto's tower is the sum of its component parts. Not only could this tower be removed from the building without adverse effects, but also each of the parts—cleanly separated from each other by continuous moldings—seems capable of existing independently as an object of considerable aesthetic appeal. This compartmentalization is reminiscent of the Romanesque style, but it also forecasts the ideals of Renaissance architecture. Artists hoped to express structure in the clear, logical relationships of the component parts and to produce self-sufficient works that could exist in complete independence. Compared with northern European towers, Giotto's campanile has a cool and rational quality more appealing to the intellect than to the emotions.

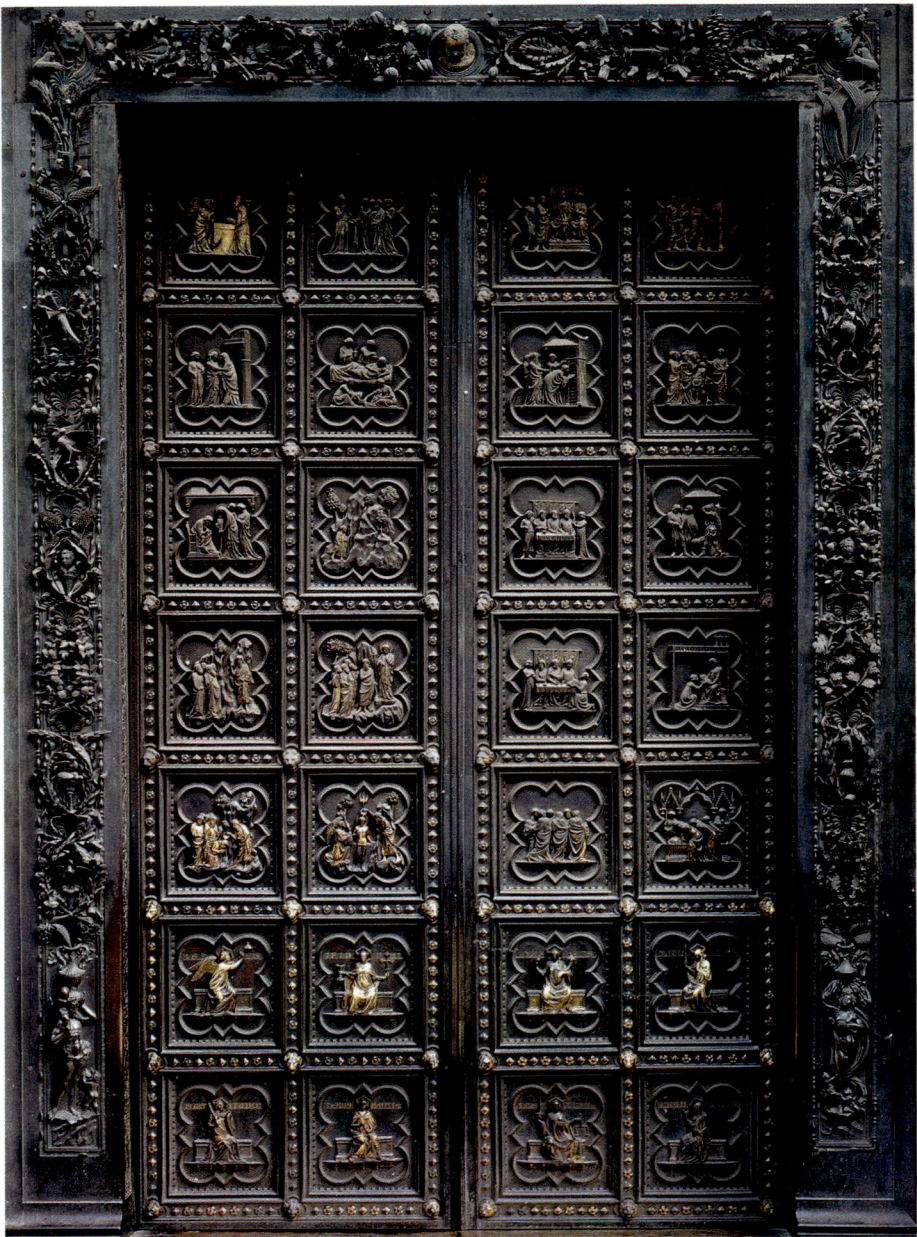

**14-19** ANDREA PISANO, south doors of the Baptistery of San Giovanni (FIG. 12-27), Florence, Italy, 1330–1336. Gilded bronze, doors 16′ × 9′ 2″; individual panels 1′ 7¼″ × 1′ 5″. (The door frames date to the mid-15th century.)

Andrea Pisano's bronze doors have 28 panels with figural reliefs in French Gothic quatrefoil frames. The lower eight depict Christian virtues. The rest represent the life of Saint John the Baptist.

1 ft.

The facade of Florence Cathedral was not completed until the 19th century, and then in a form much altered from its original design. In fact, until the 17th century, Italian builders exhibited little concern for the facades of their churches, and dozens remain unfinished to this day. One reason for this may be that Italian architects did not conceive the facades as integral parts of the structures but rather, as in the case of Orvieto Cathedral (FIG. 14-12), as screens that could be added to the church exterior at any time.

A generation after work began on Florence's church, the citizens decided also to beautify their 11th-century baptistery (FIGS. 12-27 and 14-18, *left*) with a set of bronze doors (FIG. **14-19**) for the south entrance to the building. The sponsors were the members of

Florence's guild of wool importers, who competed for business and prestige with the wool manufacturers' association, an important sponsor of the cathedral building campaign. The wool-importers' guild hired ANDREA PISANO (ca. 1290–1348), a native of Pontedera in the territory of Pisa—unrelated to Nicola and Giovanni Pisano (see "Italian Artists' Names," page 405)—to create the doors. Andrea designed 28 bronze panels for the doors, each cast separately, of which 20 depict episodes from the life of Saint John the Baptist, to whom the Florentines dedicated their baptistery. Eight panels (at the bottom) represent personified Christian virtues. The *quatrefoil* (four-lobed, cloverlike) frames are of the type used earlier for reliefs flanking the doorways of Amiens Cathedral (FIG. 13-19), suggesting French Gothic sculpture was one source of Andrea's style. The gilded figures stand on projecting ledges in each quatrefoil. Their proportions and flowing robes also reveal a debt to French sculpture, but the compositions, both in general conception (small groups of figures in stagelike settings) and in some details, owe a great deal to Giotto, for whom Andrea had earlier executed reliefs for the cathedral's campanile, perhaps according to Giotto's designs.

The wool importers' patronage of the baptistery did not end with this project. In the following century, the guild paid for the even more prestigious east doors (FIGS. 21-9 and 21-10), directly across from the cathedral's west facade, and also for a statue of Saint John the Baptist on the facade of Or San Michele, a multipurpose building housing a 14th-century tabernacle (FIG. 14-19A) by ANDREA ORCAGNA (active ca. 1343–1368) featuring the painting *Madonna and Child Enthroned with Saints* by BERNARDO DADDI (active ca. 1312–1348).

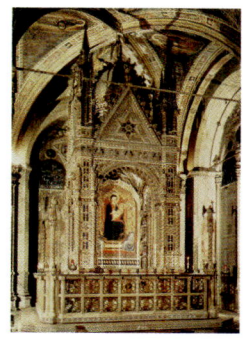

14-19A ORCAGNA, Or San Michele tabernacle, 1355–1359.

## Pisa

Siena and Florence were inland centers of commerce. Pisa was one of Italy's port cities, which, with Genoa and Venice (MAP 14-1), controlled the rapidly growing maritime avenues connecting western Europe with the lands of Islam, with Byzantium and Russia, and with China. As prosperous as Pisa was as a major shipping power, however, it was not immune from the disruption the Black Death wreaked across all of Italy and Europe in the late 1340s. Concern with death, a significant theme in art even before the onset of the plague, became more prominent in the years after midcentury.

**CAMPOSANTO** *Triumph of Death* is a tour de force of death imagery (FIG. 14-20). The creator of this large-scale (over 18 by 49 feet) fresco remains disputed. Some art historians attribute the work to FRANCESCO TRAINI (active ca. 1321–1363), while others argue for BUONAMICO BUFFALMACCO (active 1320–1336). Painted on the wall of the Camposanto (Holy Field), the enclosed burial ground adjacent to Pisa's cathedral (FIG. 12-26), the fresco captures the horrors of death and forces viewers to confront their mortality. The painter rendered each scene with naturalism and emotive power. In the left foreground (FIG. 14-20, *top*), young aristocrats, mounted in a stylish cavalcade, encounter three coffin-encased corpses in differing stages of decomposition. As the horror of the confrontation with death strikes them, the ladies turn away with delicate disgust, while a gentleman holds his nose. (The animals, horses and dogs, sniff excitedly.) At the far left, the hermit Saint Macarius unrolls a scroll bearing an inscription commenting on the folly of pleasure and

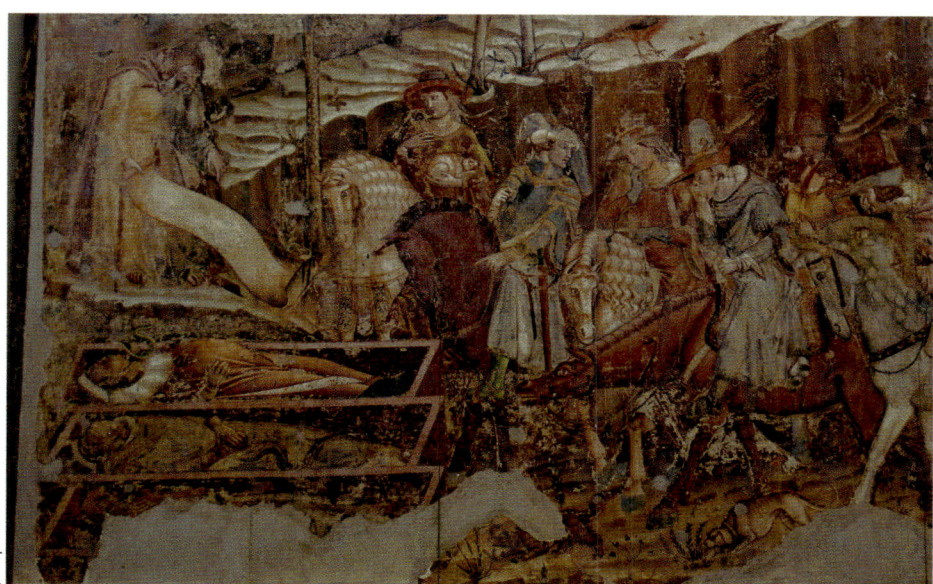

1 ft.

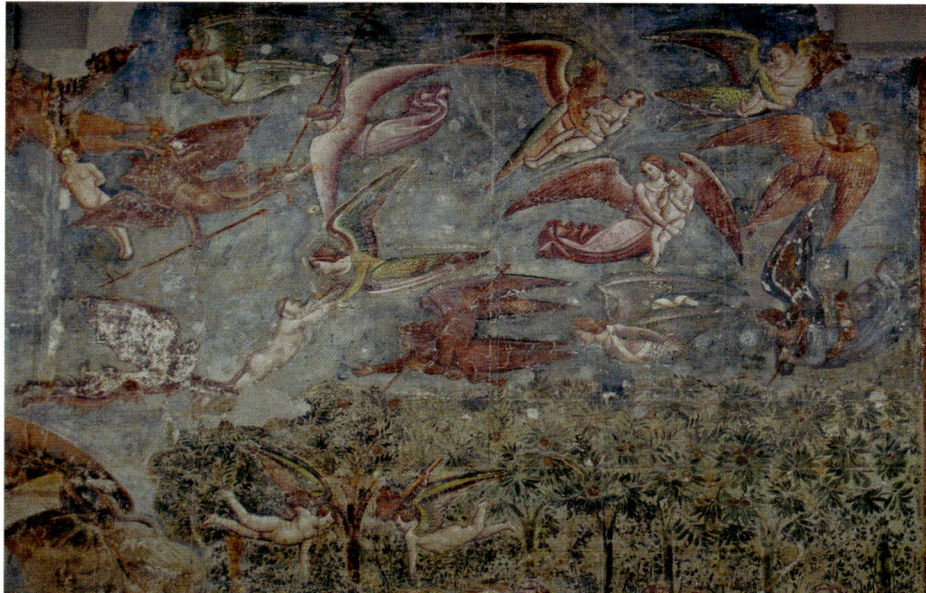

1 ft.

**14-20** FRANCESCO TRAINI or BUONAMICO BUFFALMACCO, two details of *Triumph of Death*, 1330s. Full fresco, 18′ 6″ × 49′ 2″. Camposanto, Pisa. ◼◀

Befitting its location on a wall in Pisa's Camposanto, the enclosed burial ground adjacent to the cathedral, this fresco captures the horrors of death and forces viewers to confront their mortality.

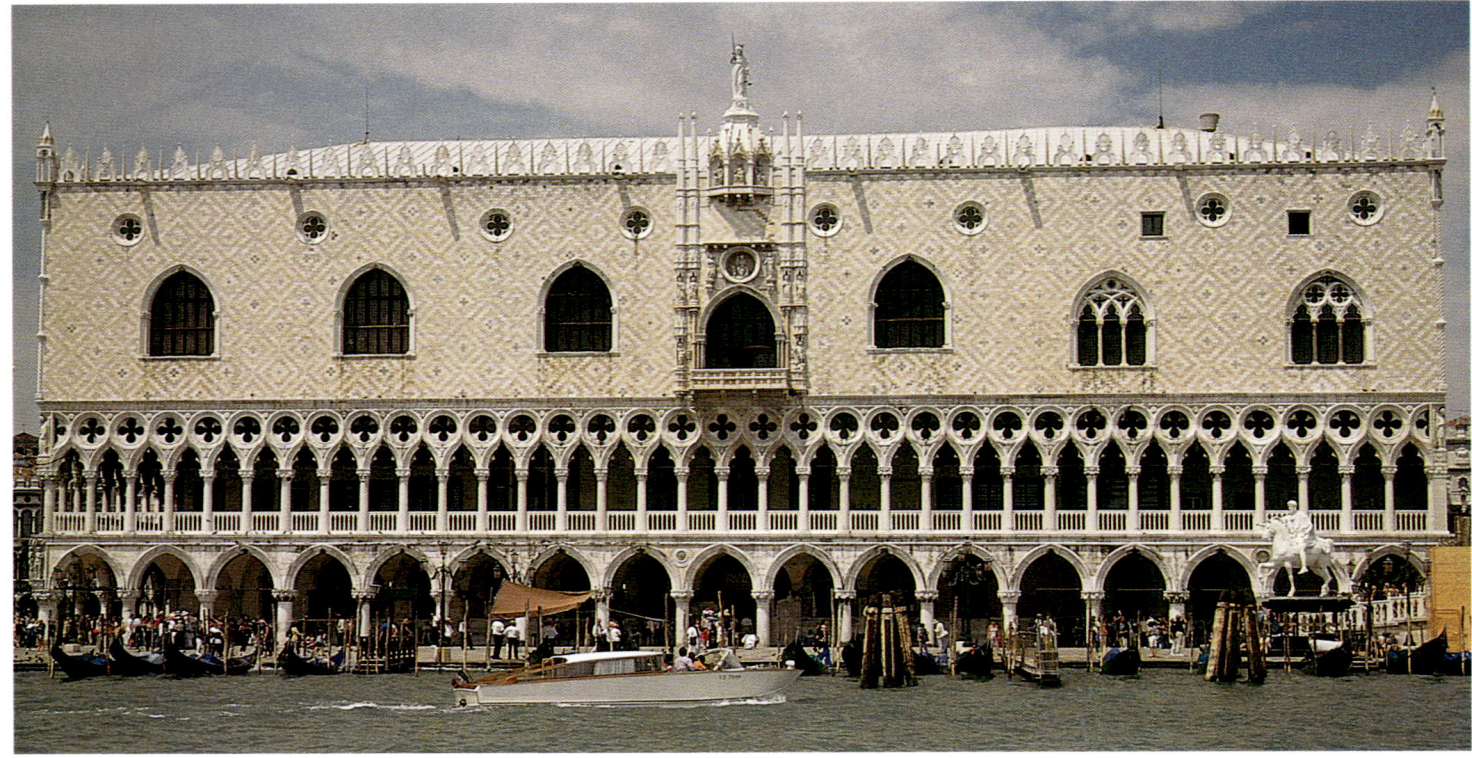

**14-21** Doge's Palace, Venice, Italy, begun ca. 1340–1345; expanded and remodeled, 1424–1438.

The delicate patterning in cream- and rose-colored marbles, the pointed and ogee arches, and the quatrefoil medallions of the Doge's Palace constitute a Venetian variation of northern Gothic architecture.

the inevitability of death. On the far right, ladies and gentlemen ignore dreadful realities, occupying themselves in an orange grove with music and amusements while above them (FIG. 14-20, *bottom*) angels and demons struggle for the souls of the corpses heaped in the foreground.

In addition to these direct and straightforward scenes, the mural contains details conveying more subtle messages. For example, the painter depicted those who appear unprepared for death—and thus unlikely to achieve salvation—as wealthy and reveling in luxury. Given that the Dominicans—an order committed to a life of poverty (see "Mendicant Orders," page 404)—participated in the design for this fresco program, this imagery surely was a warning against greed and lust.

## Venice

One of the wealthiest cities of late medieval Italy—and of Europe—was Venice, renowned for its streets of water. Situated on a lagoon on the northeastern coast of Italy, Venice was secure from land attack and could rely on a powerful navy for protection against invasion from the sea. Internally, Venice was a tight corporation of ruling families that, for centuries, provided stable rule and fostered economic growth.

**DOGE'S PALACE** The Venetian republic's seat of government was the Doge's (Duke's) Palace (FIG. **14-21**). Begun around 1340 to 1345 and significantly remodeled after 1424, it was the most ornate public building in medieval Italy. In a stately march, the first level's short and heavy columns support rather severe *pointed arches* that look strong enough to carry the weight of the upper structure. Their rhythm doubles in the upper arcades, where more slender columns carry *ogee arches* (made up of double-curving lines), which terminate in flamelike tips between medallions pierced with quatrefoils. Each story is taller than the one beneath it, the topmost as high as the two lower arcades combined. Yet the building does not look top-heavy. This is due in part to the complete absence of articulation in the top story and in part to the walls' delicate patterning, in cream- and rose-colored marbles, which makes them appear paper-thin. The Doge's Palace represents a delightful and charming variant of Late Gothic architecture. Colorful, decorative, light and airy in appearance, the Venetian palace is ideally suited to this unique Italian city that floats between water and sky.

# LATE MEDIEVAL ITALY

## 13TH CENTURY

❚ Diversity of style characterizes the art of 13th-century Italy, with some artists working in the *maniera greca,* or Italo-Byzantine style, some in the mode of Gothic France, and others in the newly revived classical tradition.

❚ The leading painters working in the Italo-Byzantine style were Bonaventura Berlinghieri and Cimabue. Both drew inspiration from Byzantine icons and illuminated manuscripts. Berlinghieri's *Saint Francis Altarpiece* is the earliest dated portrayal of Saint Francis of Assisi, who died in 1226.

❚ Trained in southern Italy in the court style of Frederick II (r. 1197–1250), Nicola Pisano was a master sculptor who settled in Pisa and carved pulpits incorporating marble panels that, both stylistically and in individual motifs, derive from ancient Roman sarcophagi. Nicola's son, Giovanni Pisano, also was a sculptor of church pulpits, but his work more closely reflects the Gothic sculpture of France.

❚ At the end of the century, in Rome and Assisi, Pietro Cavallini and other fresco painters created mural programs foreshadowing the revolutionary art of Giotto.

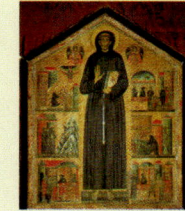

Bonaventura Berlinghieri,
*Saint Francis Altarpiece,* 1235

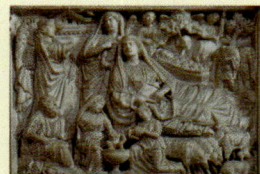

Nicola Pisano, Pisa Baptistery
pulpit, 1259–1260

## 14TH CENTURY

❚ During the 14th century, Italy suffered the most devastating natural disaster in European history—the Black Death—but it was also the time when Renaissance humanism took root. Although religion continued to occupy a primary position in Italian life, scholars and artists became increasingly concerned with the natural world.

❚ Art historians regard Giotto di Bondone of Florence as the first Renaissance painter. An architect as well, Giotto designed the bell tower of Florence's Cathedral. His masterpiece is the fresco program of the Arena Chapel in Padua, where he established himself as a pioneer in pursuing a naturalistic approach to representation based on observation, which was at the core of the classical tradition in art. The Renaissance marked the rebirth of classical values in art and society.

❚ The greatest master of the Sienese school of painting was Duccio di Buoninsegna, whose *Maestà* still incorporates many elements of the *maniera greca.* He relaxed the frontality and rigidity of his figures, however, and in the narrative scenes on the back of the gigantic altarpiece in Siena Cathedral took a decisive step toward humanizing religious subject matter by depicting actors displaying individual emotions.

❚ Secular themes also came to the fore in 14th-century Italy, most notably in Ambrogio Lorenzetti's frescoes for Siena's Palazzo Pubblico. His depictions of the city and its surrounding countryside are among the first landscapes in Western art since antiquity.

❚ The prosperity of the 14th century led to many major building campaigns, including new cathedrals in Florence, Siena, and Orvieto, and new administrative palaces in Florence, Siena, and Venice. Florence's 11th-century baptistery also received new bronze doors by Andrea Pisano.

❚ The 14th-century architecture of Italy underscores the regional character of late medieval art. Orvieto Cathedral's facade, for example, incorporates some elements of the French Gothic vocabulary, but it is a screen masking a timber-roofed structure with round arches in the nave arcade in the Early Christian tradition.

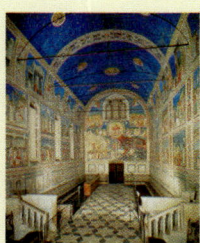

Giotto, Arena Chapel,
Padua, ca. 1305

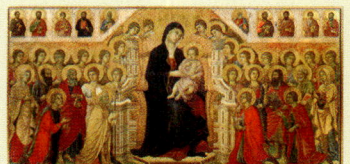

Duccio, *Maestà,* Siena Cathedral,
1308–1311

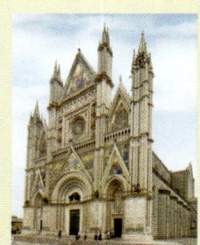

Orvieto Cathedral,
begun 1310

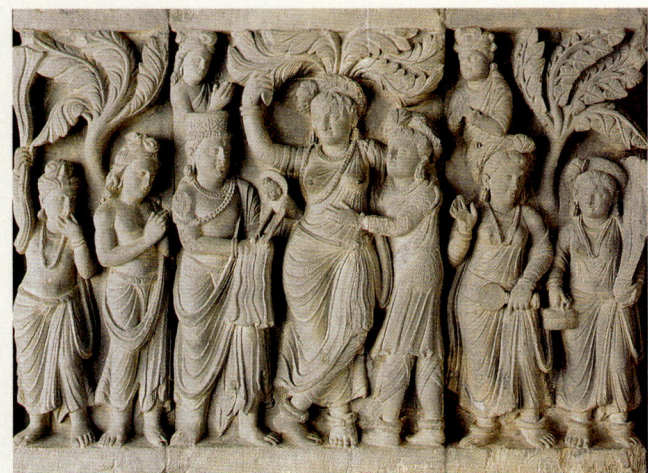

This frieze is one of the earliest pictorial narratives of the Buddha's life. At the left, Queen Maya gives birth to Prince Siddhartha, the future Buddha, who emerges from her right hip.

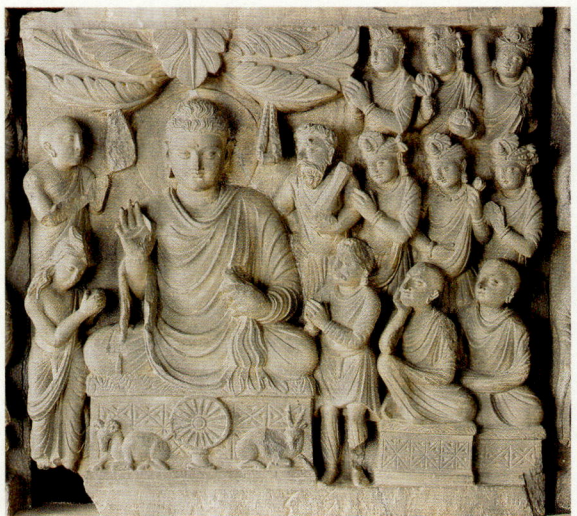

Here, the Buddha, seated in the Deer Park at Sarnath with his right hand raised in a gesture of blessing, preaches his first sermon in which he reveals the Eightfold Path to nirvana.

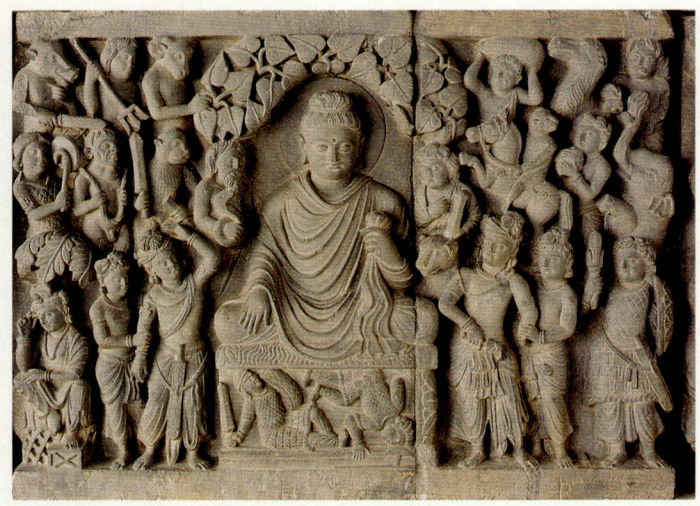

In the next scene, the Buddha sits beneath the Bodhi tree while the soldiers and demons of the evil Mara attempt to distract him from his quest for knowledge, but they are not successful.

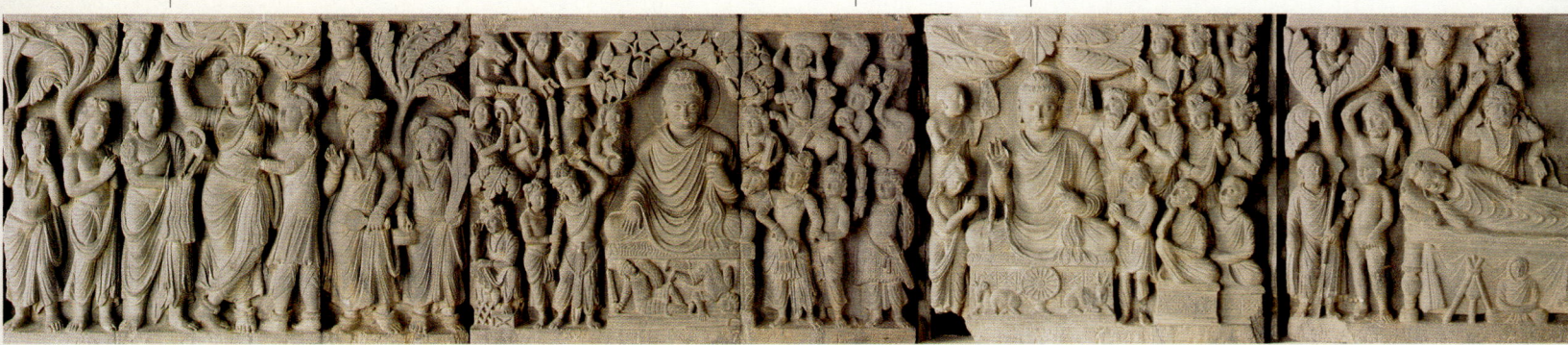

**15-1** The life and death of the Buddha, frieze from Gandhara, Pakistan, second century CE. Schist, 2′ 2⅜″ × 9′ 6⅛″. Freer Gallery of Art, Washington, D.C.

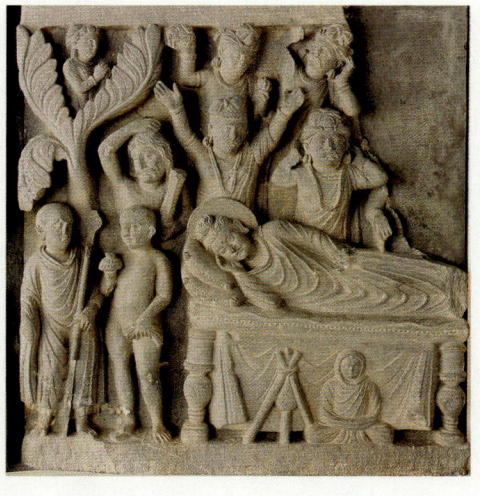

In the final scene, the Buddha lies dying among his devotees, who wail in grief, save for one meditating monk who realizes the Buddha has achieved nirvana and release from suffering.

# SOUTH AND SOUTHEAST ASIA BEFORE 1200

## THE LIFE OF THE BUDDHA

The Buddha (Enlightened One) was born around 563 BCE as Prince Siddhartha Gautama, the eldest son of the king of the Shakya clan. A prophecy foretold he would grow up to be either a world conqueror or a great religious leader. His father preferred the secular role for young Siddhartha and groomed him for kingship by shielding the boy from the hardships of the world. When he was 29, however, the prince rode out of the palace, abandoned his wife and family, and encountered for himself the pain of old age, sickness, and death. Siddhartha responded to the suffering he witnessed by renouncing his opulent life and becoming a wandering ascetic searching for knowledge through meditation. Six years later, he achieved complete enlightenment, or buddhahood, while meditating beneath a pipal tree (the Bodhi tree) at Bodh Gaya ("place of enlightenment") in eastern India. Known from that day on as Shakyamuni ("wise man of the Shakya clan"), the Buddha preached his first sermon in the Deer Park at Sarnath. There he set in motion the Wheel (*chakra*) of the Law (*dharma*) and expounded the Four Noble Truths, the core insights of Buddhism: (1) life is suffering; (2) the cause of suffering is desire; (3) one can overcome and extinguish desire; (4) the way to conquer desire and end suffering is to follow the Buddha's Eightfold Path of right understanding, right thought, right speech, right action, right livelihood, right effort, right mindfulness, and right concentration. The Buddha's path leads to *nirvana,* the cessation of the endless cycle of painful life, death, and rebirth. The Buddha continued to preach until his death at age 80.

One of the earliest pictorial narrative cycles of the Buddha's life is a stone frieze (FIG. **15-1**) from Gandhara, a region largely in Pakistan today, close to the Afghanistan border. Depicted, in chronological order from left to right, are the Buddha's birth at Lumbini, the enlightenment at Bodh Gaya, the first sermon at Sarnath, and the Buddha's death at Kushinagara. At the left, Queen Maya gives birth to Prince Siddhartha, who emerges from her right hip. Receiving him is the god Indra. Elegantly dressed ladies, one with a fan of peacock feathers, suggest the opulent court life the Buddha left behind. In the next scene, the Buddha sits beneath the Bodhi tree while the soldiers and demons of the evil Mara attempt to distract him from his quest for knowledge. They are unsuccessful, and the Buddha then preaches the Eightfold Path to nirvana in the Deer Park at Sarnath. The sculptor set the scene by placing two deer and the Wheel of the Law beneath the figure of the Buddha. In the final section of the frieze, the parinirvana, the Buddha lies dying among his devotees, some of whom wail in grief, while one monk, who realizes the Buddha has been permanently released from suffering, remains tranquil in meditation.

# SOUTH ASIA

In the third millennium BCE, a great civilization arose over a wide geographic area along the Indus River in Pakistan and extended into India as far south as Gujarat and east beyond Delhi (MAP 15-1). Thus, when Alexander the Great and his army reached India in 326 BCE, they encountered a civilization already more than 2,000 years old. In fact, the remains of the first cities in the Indus Valley predate the palaces of Homer's Trojan War heroes (FIGS. 4-15 and 4-19) by a millennium. Archaeologists have dubbed this early South Asian culture the Indus Civilization.

# Indus Civilization

The Indus Civilization flourished from about 2600 to 1500 BCE. The most important excavated Indus sites are Mohenjo-daro and Harappa in present-day Pakistan. Both were fully developed cities featuring streets oriented to compass points and multistoried houses built of carefully formed and precisely laid kiln-baked bricks. Their inhabitants engaged in trade with cities as far away as modern Iraq, but in sharp contrast to the contemporaneous civilizations of Mesopotamia and Egypt (see Chapters 2 and 3), no surviving Indus building has yet been identified as a temple or a palace.

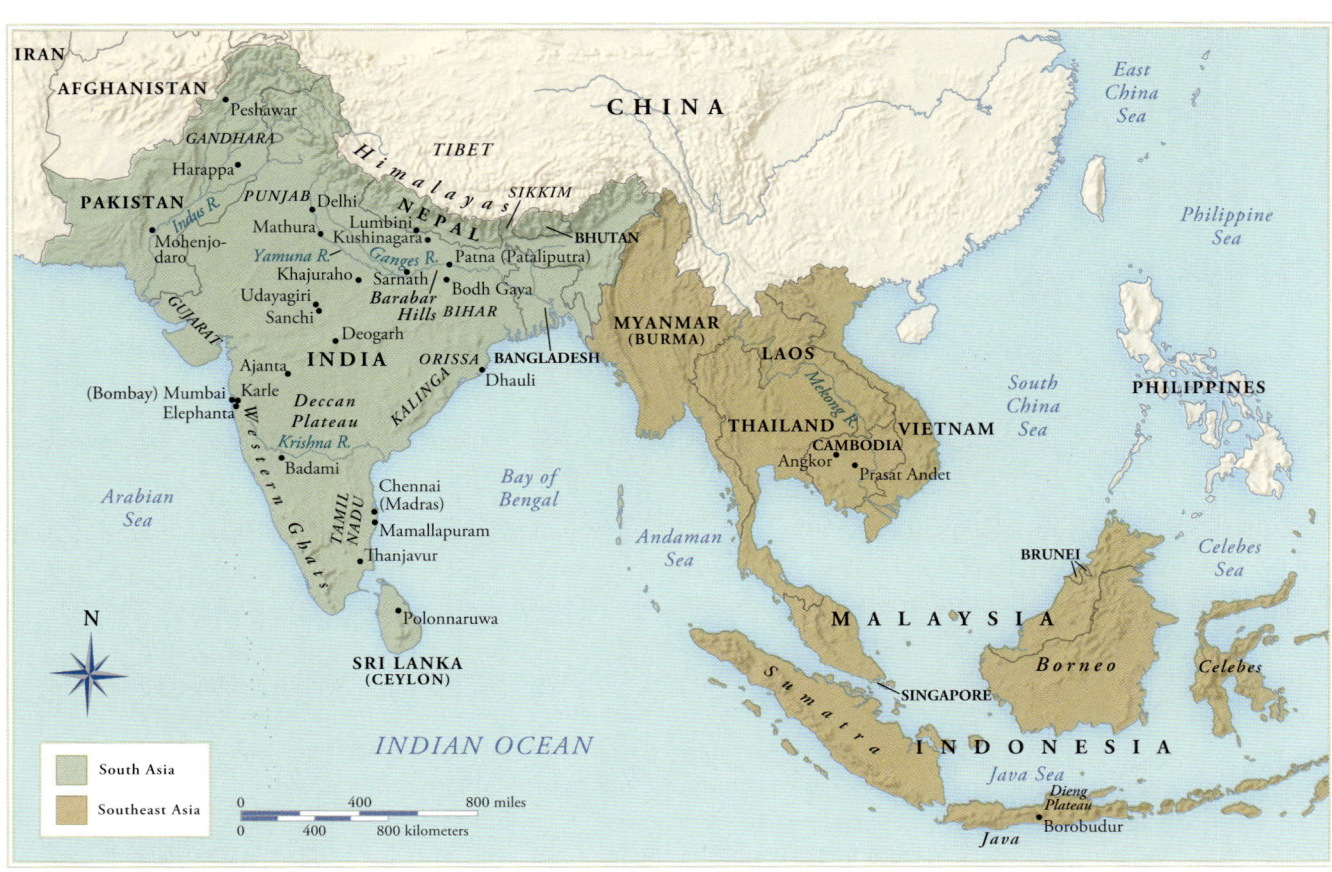

MAP 15-1 South and Southeast Asian sites before 1200.

## SOUTH AND SOUTHEAST ASIA BEFORE 1200

| | BCE | | CE | | |
|---|---|---|---|---|---|
| 2600 **Indus** 1500 | 323 **Maurya** 185 | **Shunga, Andhra, Kushan** 320 | **Gupta and Post-Gupta** 647 | **Medieval** 1200 |

| | | | | |
|---|---|---|---|---|
| ▌First South Asian cities in the Indus Valley have rational plans and sophisticated water-supply and sewage systems ▌Indus art is small-scale and has stylistic parallels in the art of Mesopotamia | ▌Ashoka (r. 272–231 BCE) converts to Buddhism and builds the original Great Stupa at Sanchi. He also sets up pillars with animal capitals throughout his kingdom—the oldest preserved monumental stone artworks in India | ▌Construction of stupas and rock-cut chaitya halls in Buddhist monasteries ▌First representations of the Buddha in human form based on prototypes in Greco-Roman art | ▌Gupta sculptors establish the canonical image of the Buddha ▌Earliest mural paintings in the Buddhist caves of Ajanta ▌Oldest preserved Hindu monumental stone temples and sculptures | ▌Emergence of distinct regional styles in South Asian Hindu temple architecture ▌Regional variations on Indian architectural and sculptural prototypes appear throughout Southeast Asia |

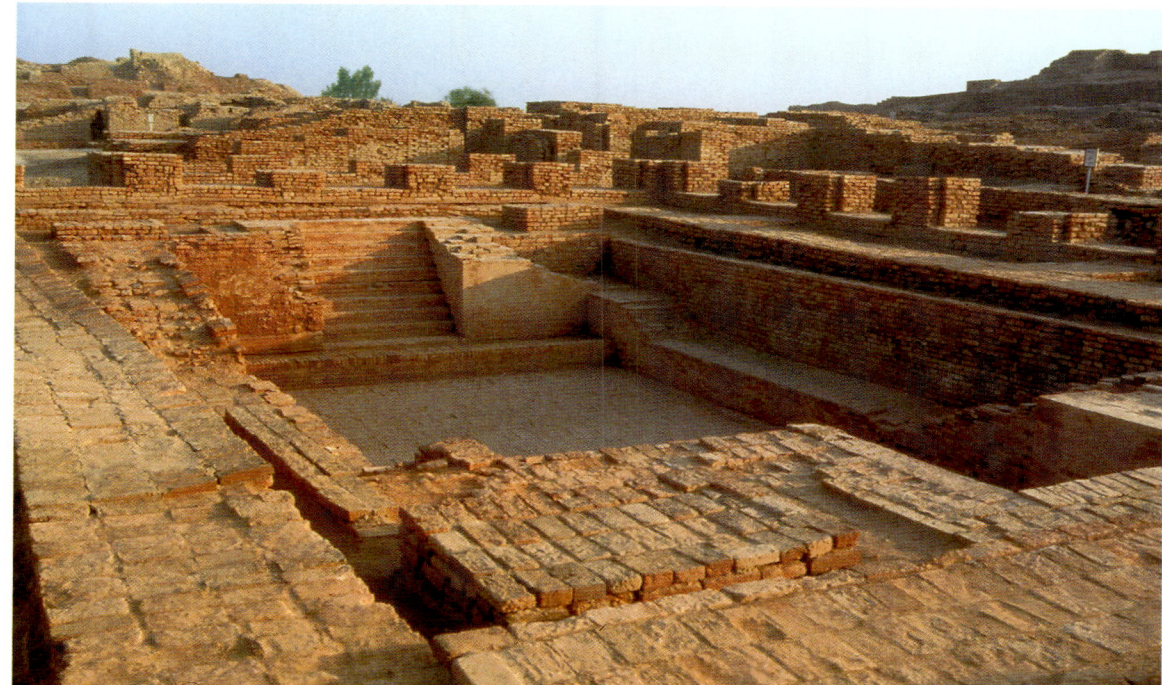

The Indus cities of the third millennium BCE had sophisticated water-supply and sewage systems, which made possible this brick complex used for ritual bathing of a kind still practiced in South Asia today.

**MOHENJO-DARO** The Indus cities also boasted one of the world's first sophisticated systems of water supply and sewage. Throughout Mohenjo-daro, hundreds of wells provided fresh water to homes incorporating some of the oldest recorded private bathing areas and toilet facilities, with drainage into public sewers. In the heart of the city stood the so-called Great Bath, a complex of rooms centered on a sunken brick pool (FIG. **15-2**) 39 feet long, 23 feet wide, and 8 feet deep. The Indus builders made the pool watertight by sealing the joints between the bricks with bitumen, an asphaltlike material also used in Mesopotamia. The bath was probably not a purely recreational facility but rather a place for ritual bathing of the kind still practiced in South Asia today.

Surprisingly, excavators have discovered little art from the long-lived Indus Civilization, and all of the objects found are small. Perhaps the most impressive preserved sculpture represents a robed male figure (FIG. **15-3**) with half-closed eyes, a low forehead, and a closely trimmed beard with shaved upper lip. He wears a headband with a central circular emblem, matched by a similar armband. Holes on each side of his neck suggest he also wore a necklace of precious metal. *Trefoils* (cloverlike designs with three stylized leaves) decorate his elegant robe. They, as well as the circles of the head- and armbands, originally held red paste and shell inlays, as did the eyes. Scholars often compare the Mohenjo-daro statuette with Sumerian sculptures, where the trefoil motif appears in sacred contexts, and refer to the person portrayed as a "priest-king," the ambiguous term used for some Sumerian leaders. The identity and rank of the Mohenjo-daro figure are uncertain, however. Nonetheless, the elaborate costume and precious materials make clear he was an elite individual.

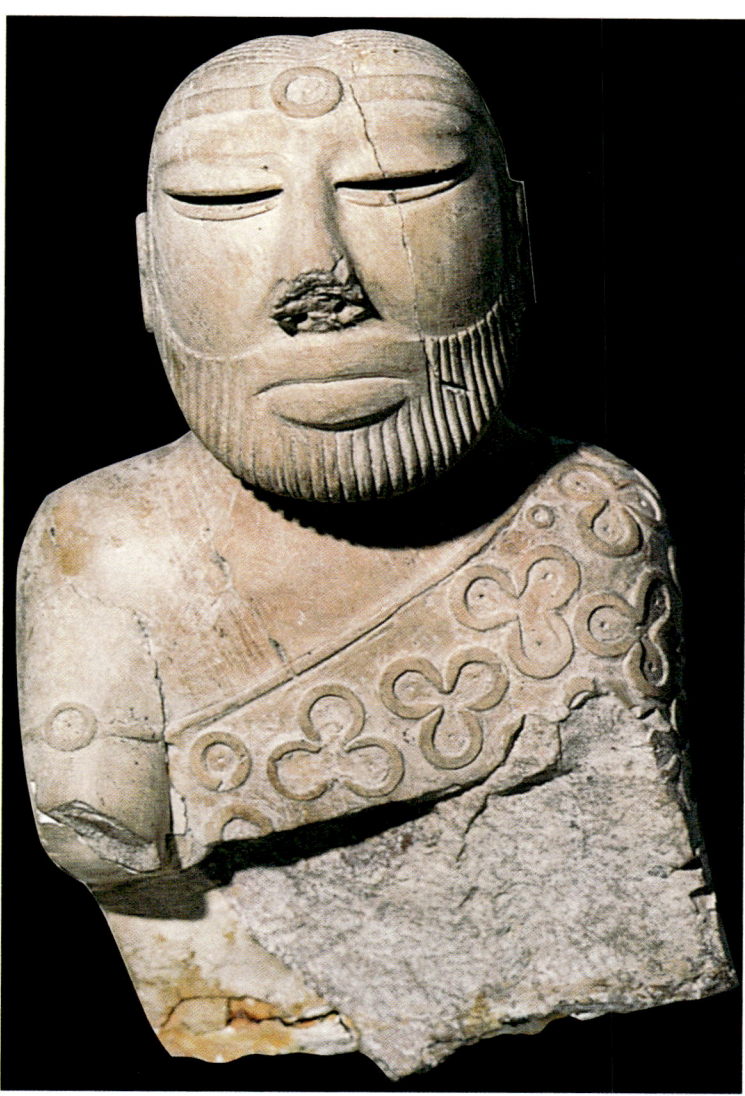

1 in.

**15-3** Robed male figure, from Mohenjo-daro, Pakistan, ca. 2000–1900 BCE. Steatite, $6\frac{7}{8}''$ high. National Museum of Pakistan, Karachi.

Little art survives from the Indus Civilization, and all of it is of small scale. This bearded figure, which scholars think represents a priest-king, has iconographic similarities to some Sumerian sculptures.

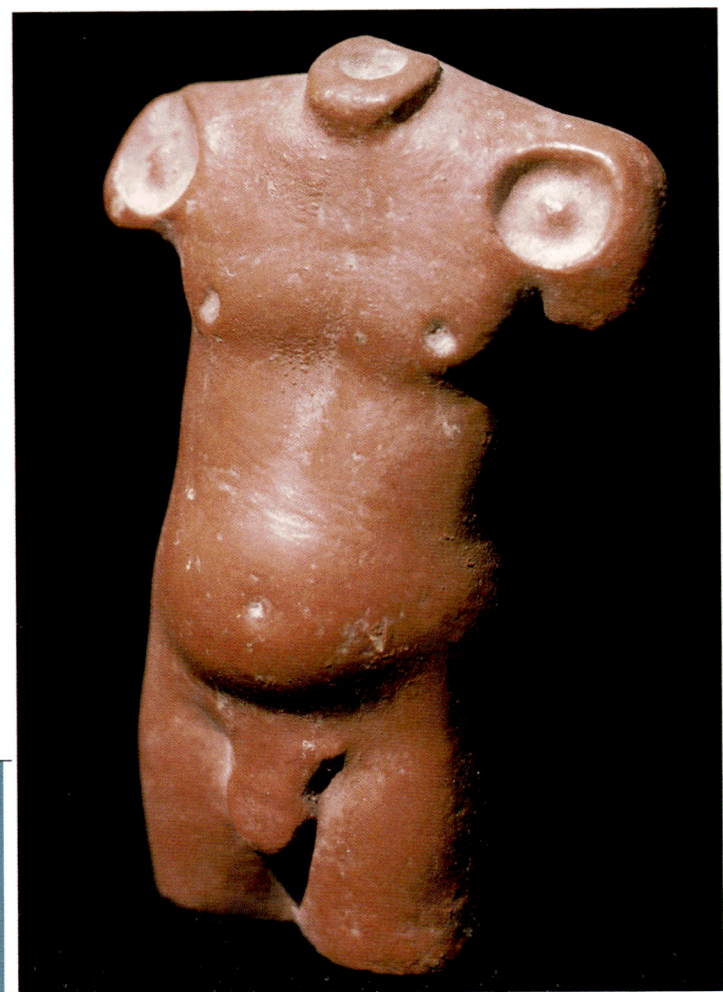

1 in.

**15-4** Nude male torso, from Harappa, Pakistan, ca. 2000–1900 BCE. Red sandstone, $3\frac{3}{4}''$ high. National Museum, New Delhi.

This miniature figure, with its emphasis on sensuous polished surfaces and swelling curves, already displays many of the stylistic traits common to South Asian sculpture for thousands of years.

**HARAPPA** Quite different in style is the fragmentary miniature red sandstone male figure (FIG. **15-4**) found at Harappa. Scholars usually compare this nude figure, which is less than 4 inches in height, with Greek statues of much later date, but the treatment of anatomy separates it sharply from the classical tradition. The highly polished surface of the stone and the swelling curves of the abdomen reveal the Indus artist's interest in the fluid movement of a living body, not in the logical anatomical structure of Greek sculpture. This sense of pulsating vigor and the emphasis on sensuous surfaces would continue to be chief characteristics of South Asian sculpture for thousands of years.

**INDUS SEALS** The most common Indus art objects are steatite seals with incised designs. They are similar in many ways to the stamp seals found at contemporaneous sites in Mesopotamia (see "Mesopotamian Seals," Chapter 2, page 39). Most of the Indus examples have an animal or tiny narrative carved on the face, along with an as-yet-untranslated script. On the back, a *boss* (circular knob) with a hole permitted insertion of a string so that the owner could wear the seal or hang it on a wall. As in the ancient Near East, the Indus peoples sometimes used the seals to make impressions on clay, apparently for securing trade goods wrapped in textiles. The animals most frequently represented include the humped bull,

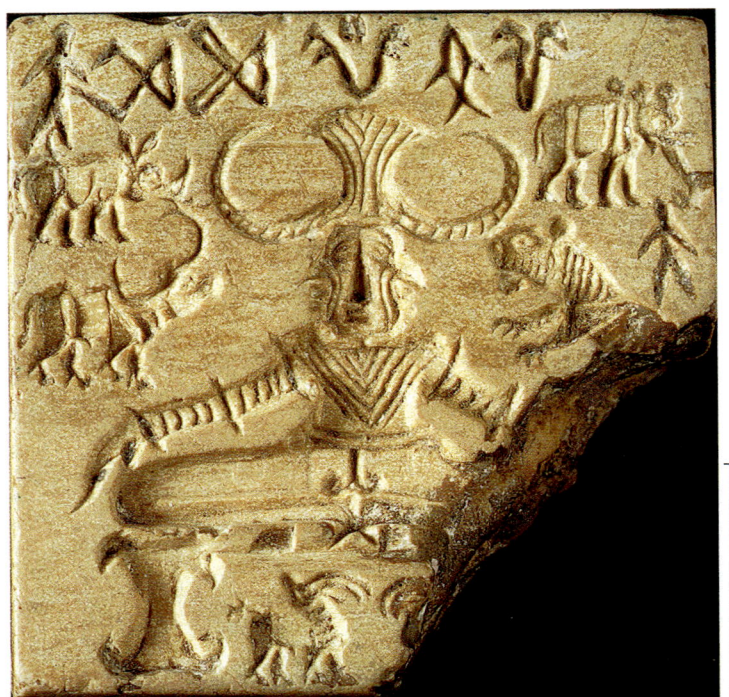

$\frac{1}{2}$ in.

**15-5** Seal with seated figure in yogic posture, from Mohenjo-daro, Pakistan, ca. 2300–1750 BCE. Steatite coated with alkali and baked, $1\frac{3}{8}'' \times 1\frac{3}{8}''$. National Museum, New Delhi.

This seal depicting a (three-faced?) figure wearing a horned headdress and seated in a yogic posture indicates this important Indian meditative practice began as early as the Indus Civilization.

elephant, rhinoceros, and tiger. The seal carvers portrayed all the animals in strict profile, as did the painters and relief sculptors of all other early cultures. Some of the narrative seals indicate the Indus peoples considered trees sacred, as both Buddhists and Hindus did later. Many scholars have suggested religious and ritual continuities between the Indus Civilization and later Indian culture.

One of the most elaborate seals (FIG. **15-5**) depicts a male figure with a horned headdress and, perhaps, three faces, seated (with erect penis) among the profile animals that regularly appear alone on other seals. The figure's position—folded legs with heels pressed together and arms resting on the knees—suggests a yogic posture (compare FIG. 15-12). *Yoga* is a method for controlling the body and relaxing the mind used in later Indian religions to yoke, or unite, the practitioner to the divine. Although most scholars reject the identification of this figure as a prototype of the multiheaded Hindu god Shiva (FIG. 15-18) as Lord of Beasts, the yogic posture proves this important Indian meditative practice began as early as the Indus Civilization.

## Vedic and Upanishadic Period

By 1700 BCE, the urban phase of the Indus Civilization had ended in most areas. The production of sculptures, seals, and script gradually ceased, and village life replaced urban culture. Very little art survives from the next thousand years, but the religious foundations laid during this period helped define most later South and Southeast Asian art.

**VEDAS** The basis for the new religious ideas were the oral hymns of the Aryans, a mobile herding people from Central Asia who occupied the Punjab, an area of northwestern India, in the second

# Buddhism and Buddhist Iconography

The earliest form of Buddhism is Theravada (Path of the Elders) Buddhism. Practiced by the historical Buddha's disciples at the monasteries they founded after his death, Theravada Buddhism seeks to aid individuals wishing to follow Shakyamuni Buddha's path to enlightenment and nirvana. The new religion developed and changed over time, however, as the Buddha's teachings spread from India throughout Asia. The second major school of Buddhist thought, Mahayana (Great Path) Buddhism, emerged around the beginning of the Common Era (CE). Mahayana Buddhists refer to Theravada Buddhism as Hinayana (Lesser Path) Buddhism and believe in a larger goal than nirvana for an individual—namely, buddhahood for all. Mahayana Buddhists also revere *bodhisattvas* (Buddhas-to-be), exemplars of compassion who restrain themselves at the threshold of nirvana to aid others in earning merit and achieving buddhahood. Theravada Buddhism became the dominant sect in southern India, Sri Lanka, and mainland Southeast Asia, whereas Mahayana Buddhism took root in northern India and spread to China, Korea, Japan, and Nepal.

A third important Buddhist sect, especially popular in East Asia, venerates the Amitabha Buddha (Amida in Japanese), the Buddha of Infinite Light and Life. The devotees of this Buddha hope to be reborn in the Pure Land Paradise of the West, where the Amitabha resides and can grant them salvation. In Pure Land teachings, people have no possibility of attaining enlightenment on their own but can achieve paradise by faith alone.

The earliest (first century CE) depictions of the Buddha in human form show him as a robed monk. Artists distinguished the Enlightened One from monks and bodhisattvas by *lakshanas,* body attributes indicating the Buddha's suprahuman nature. These distinguishing marks include an *urna,* or curl of hair between the eyebrows, shown as a dot; an *ushnisha,* a cranial bump shown as hair on the earliest images (FIGS. 15-1, 15-11, 15-11A, and 15-12) but later as part of the head (FIG. 15-13); and, less frequently, palms and soles imprinted with a wheel (FIG. 15-12). Artists also often depicted the Buddha with elongated ears, the result of wearing heavy royal jewelry in his youth, but the enlightened Shakyamuni is rarely bejeweled, though many bodhisattvas are (FIG. 15-14). Sometimes the Buddha appears with a halo, or sun disk, behind his head (FIGS. 15-11, 15-11A, 15-12, and 15-13).

Representations of the Buddha also feature a repertory of *mudras,* or hand gestures, conveying fixed meanings. These include the *dhyana* (meditation) mudra, with the right hand over the left, palms upward (FIG. 15-11); the *bhumisparsha* (earth-touching) mudra, right hand down reaching to the ground, calling the earth to witness the Buddha's enlightenment (FIG. 15-1); the *dharmachakra* (Wheel of the Law, or teaching) mudra, a two-handed gesture with right thumb and index finger forming a circle (FIG. 15-13); and the *abhaya* (do not fear) mudra, right hand up, palm outward, a gesture of protection or blessing (FIGS. 15-1, 15-11A, and 15-12).

Episodes from the Buddha's life are among the most popular subjects in all Buddhist artistic traditions. No single text provides the complete or authoritative narrative of the Buddha's life and death. Thus, numerous versions and variations exist, allowing for a rich artistic repertory. Four of the most important events (see "The Life of the Buddha," page 423) are his birth at Lumbini from the side of his mother, Queen Maya (FIG. 15-1); the achievement of buddhahood while meditating beneath the Bodhi tree at Bodh Gaya (FIG. 15-1); the Buddha's first sermon at Sarnath (FIGS. 15-1 and 15-13); and his attainment of nirvana (*parinirvana*) when he died at Kushinagara (FIGS. 15-1 and 15-28). Buddhists established monasteries and monuments at the four sites where these key events occurred, although the Buddha himself disapproved of all luxury, including lavish religious shrines featuring costly figural art.

---

millennium BCE. The Aryans ("Noble Ones") spoke Sanskrit, the earliest language yet identified in South Asia. Around 1500 BCE, they composed the first of four *Vedas*. These Sanskrit compilations of religious learning (*Veda* means "knowledge") included hymns intended for priests (called Brahmins) to chant or sing. The Brahmins headed a social hierarchy, or caste system, perhaps of pre-Aryan origin, that still forms the basis of Indian society today. Below the priests were the warriors, traders, and manual laborers (including artists and architects), respectively. The Aryan religion centered on sacrifice, the ritual enactment of often highly intricate and lengthy ceremonies in which the priests placed materials, such as milk and soma (an intoxicating drink), into a fire that carried the sacrifices to the gods in the heavens. If the Brahmins performed these rituals accurately, the gods would fulfill the prayers of those who sponsored the sacrifices. These gods, primarily male, included Indra, Varuna, Surya, and Agni, gods associated, respectively, with rain, the ocean, the sun, and fire. The Aryans apparently did not create images of these deities.

**UPANISHADS** The next phase of South Asian urban civilization developed east of the Indus heartland, in the Ganges River valley. Here, from 800 to 500 BCE, religious thinkers composed a variety of texts called the *Upanishads*. Among the innovative ideas in the Upanishads were *samsara, karma,* and *moksha* (or *nirvana*). *Samsara* is the belief that individuals are born again after death in an almost endless round of rebirths. The type of rebirth can vary. One can be reborn as a human being, an animal, or even a god. An individual's past actions (*karma*), either good or bad, determine the nature of future rebirths. The ultimate goal of a person's religious life is to escape—*moksha* (liberation) or *nirvana* (cessation)—from the cycle of birth and death by merging the individual self into the vital force of the universe.

**HINDUISM AND BUDDHISM** Hinduism and Buddhism, the two major modern religions originating in Asia, developed in the late centuries BCE and the early centuries CE. Hinduism, the dominant religion in India today, discussed in more detail later, has its origins in Aryan religion. The founder of Buddhism was the Buddha (see "The Life of the Buddha," page 423), who advocated the path of *asceticism,* or self-discipline and self-denial, as the means to free oneself from attachments to people and possessions, thus ending rebirth (see "Buddhism and Buddhist Iconography," above). Buddhists call the escape from the cycle of birth, death, and rebirth "nirvana" (cessation). Hindus call it "moksha" (liberation). Unlike

# Ashoka's Conversion to Buddhism

The reign of the Maurya king Ashoka marks both the beginning of monumental stone art and architecture (FIGS. 15-6, 15-6A, and 15-6B) in India and the first official sponsorship of Buddhism. The effect of Ashoka's conversion to Buddhism on the later history of art and religion in Asia cannot be overstated. An edict carved into a rock at Dhauli in the ancient region of Kalinga (roughly equivalent to the modern state of Orissa on the Bay of Bengal) records Ashoka's embrace of nonviolence and of the Buddha's teachings after an especially bloody conquest that claimed more than 100,000 lives. The inscription also captures Ashoka's missionary zeal, which spread Buddhism far beyond the boundaries of his kingdom.

> The Beloved of the Gods [Ashoka], conqueror of the Kalingas, is moved to remorse now. For he has felt profound sorrow and regret because the conquest of a people previously unconquered involves slaughter, death, and deportation. . . . [King Ashoka] now thinks that even a person who wrongs him must be forgiven . . . [and he] considers moral conquest [conquest by dharma] the most important conquest. He has achieved this moral conquest repeatedly both here and among the peoples living beyond the borders of his kingdom. . . . Even in countries which [King Ashoka's] envoys have not reached, people have heard about dharma and about [the king's] ordinances and instructions in dharma. . . . This edict on dharma has been inscribed so that my sons and great-grandsons who may come after me should not think new conquests worth achieving. . . . Let them consider moral conquest the only true conquest.*

The story of Ashoka's renunciation of violent aggression at Kalinga still resonates today. It inspired one of the most important 20th-century Indian sculptors to take up the theme and imbue it with contemporary meaning (FIG. 32-11).

*Rock Edict XIII. Translated by N. A. Nikam and Richard McKeon, *The Edicts of Asoka* (Chicago: University of Chicago Press, 1959), 27–30.

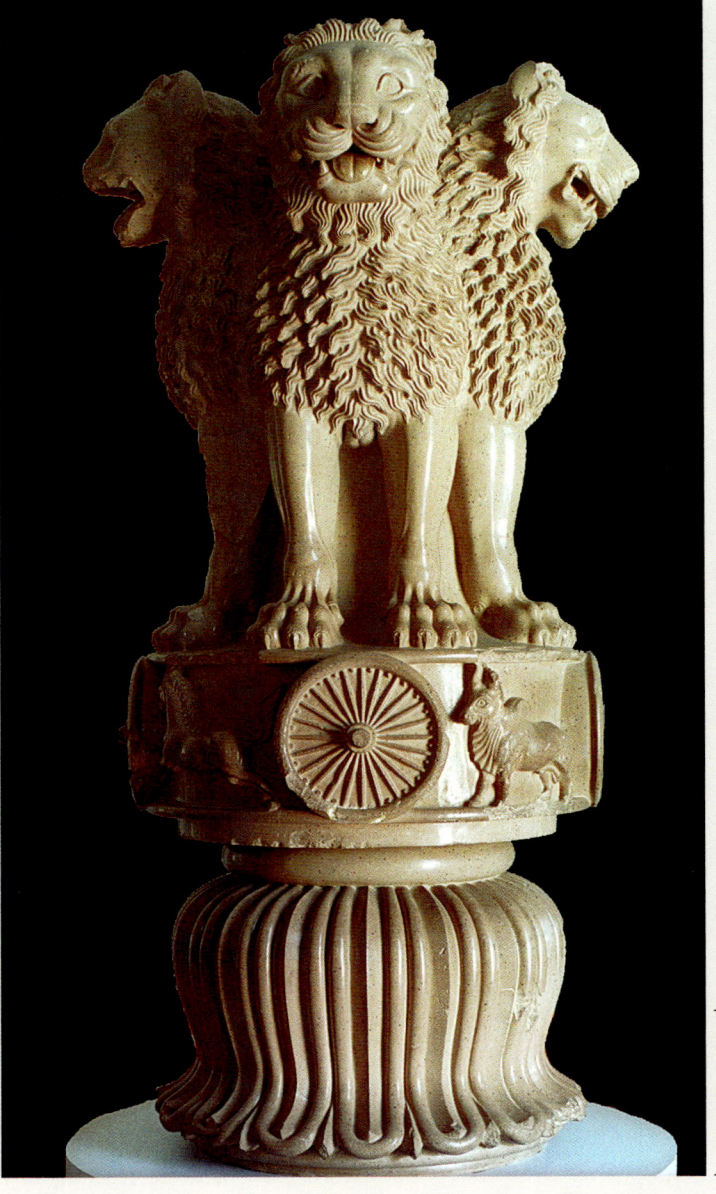

**15-6** Lion capital of the column set up by Ashoka at Sarnath, India, ca. 250 BCE. Polished sandstone, 7′ high. Archaeological Museum, Sarnath.

Ashoka formulated a legal code based on the Buddha's teachings and inscribed those laws on columns he set up throughout his kingdom. The lions on this capital supported the Wheel of the Law.

1 ft.

---

their predecessors in South Asia, both Hindus and Buddhists use images of gods and holy persons in religious rituals. To judge from surviving works, Buddhism has the older artistic tradition. The earliest Buddhist monuments date to the Maurya period.

## Maurya Dynasty

In 326 BCE, after conquering the Persian Empire (see Chapter 5), Alexander the Great reached the Indus River, but his troops refused to go forward. Reluctantly, Alexander abandoned his dream of conquering India and headed home. After Alexander's death three years later, his generals divided his empire among themselves. One of them, Seleucus Nicator, reinvaded India, but Chandragupta Maurya (r. 323–298 BCE), founder of the Maurya dynasty, defeated

him in 305 BCE and eventually consolidated almost all of present-day India under his domain. Chandragupta's capital was Pataliputra (modern Patna) in northeastern India, far from the center of the Indus Civilization (MAP 15-1). Megasthenes, Seleucus's ambassador to the Maurya court, described Pataliputra in his book on India as a large and wealthy city enclosed within mighty wooden walls so extensive the circuit had 64 gates and 570 towers.

**ASHOKA** The greatest Maurya ruler was Ashoka (r. 272–231 BCE), who left his imprint on history by converting to Buddhism and spreading the Buddha's teaching throughout and beyond India (see "Ashoka's Conversion to Buddhism," above). Ashoka formulated a legal code based on the Buddha's dharma and inscribed his laws on enormous *monolithic* (one-piece stone) columns set up through-

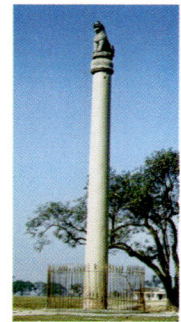

15-6A Lion pillar, Lauriya Nandangarh, ca. 245 BCE.

out his kingdom. Ashoka's pillars, one of which (FIG. 15-6A) still stands at Lauriya Nandangarh, reached 30 to 40 feet high and were the first monumental stone artworks in India. The pillars penetrated deep into the ground, connecting earth and sky, forming an "axis of the universe," a pre-Buddhist concept that became an important motif in Buddhist architecture. The columns stood along pilgrimage routes to sites associated with the Buddha and on the roads leading to Pataliputra.

Capping Ashoka's pillars were elaborate *capitals,* also carved from a single block of stone. The finest (FIG. 15-6) comes from Sarnath, where the Buddha gave his first sermon and set the Wheel of the Law into motion. At 7 feet high, it and a contemporaneous statue representing a fertility goddess (FIG. 15-6B) found near the Mauryan capital are among the earliest works of monumental sculpture in South Asia. Stylistically, the Sarnath lion capital owes much to ancient Mesopotamia and Persia, especially the Achaemenid art

of Persepolis (FIG. 2-26), but its iconography is Buddhist. Two pairs of back-to-back lions (texts often refer to the Buddha as "the lion") stand on a round *abacus* decorated with four wheels and four animals symbolizing the four quarters of the world. The lions once carried a large stone wheel on their backs. The wheel (*chakra*) is a reference to the Wheel of the Law but also indicated Ashoka's stature as a *chakravartin* ("holder of the wheel"), a universal king imbued with divine authority. The open mouths of the four lions facing the four quarters of the world may signify the worldwide announcement of the Buddha's message.

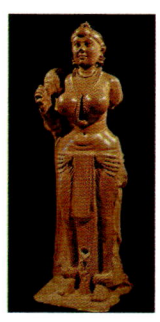

15-6B Yakshi with fly whisk, Didarganj, mid-third century BCE.

## Shunga, Andhra, and Kushan Dynasties

The Maurya dynasty came to an abrupt end when its last ruler was assassinated by one of his generals, who founded a new dynasty in his own name. The Shungas, however, never ruled an empire as extensive as the Maurya kingdom. The Shunga realm comprised only central India, and the Andhras, who controlled the Deccan plateau to the south, usurped their power in the early first century BCE. By the middle of that century, an even greater empire, the Kushan, rose in northern India. Its most celebrated king was Kanishka, who came to power during the late first or early second century CE and who set up capitals at Peshawar and other sites in Gandhara. The Kushans grew rich on trade between China and the west along one of the main caravan routes bringing the luxuries of the Orient to the Roman Empire (see "The Silk Road," Chapter 16, page 458). Kanishka even struck coins modeled on the imperial coinage of Rome, some featuring Greco-Roman deities, but Kanishka's coins also carried portraits of himself and images of the Buddha and various Hindu deities.

SANCHI The unifying characteristic of this age of regional dynasties in South Asia was the patronage of Buddhism. One important Buddhist monastery, founded during Ashoka's reign and in use for more than a thousand years, is at Sanchi in central India. It consists of many buildings constructed over the centuries, including *viharas* (celled structures where monks live), large *stupas* (see "The Stupa," page 430), *chaitya halls* (halls with rounded, or *apsidal,* ends for housing smaller stupas), and temples for sheltering images.

The Great Stupa at Sanchi dates originally to Ashoka's reign, but its present form (FIG. 15-7), with its tall stone fence and four gates, dates from about 50 BCE to 50 CE. The solid earth-and-rubble dome stands 50 feet high. Worshipers enter through one of

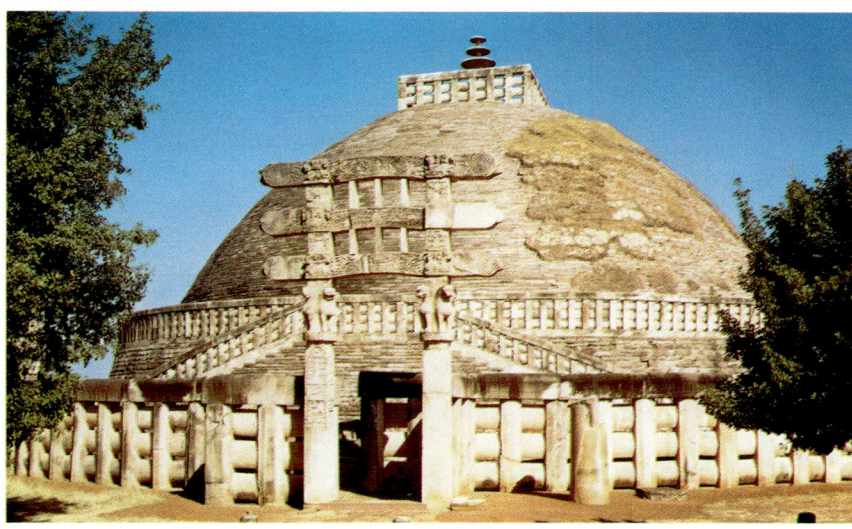

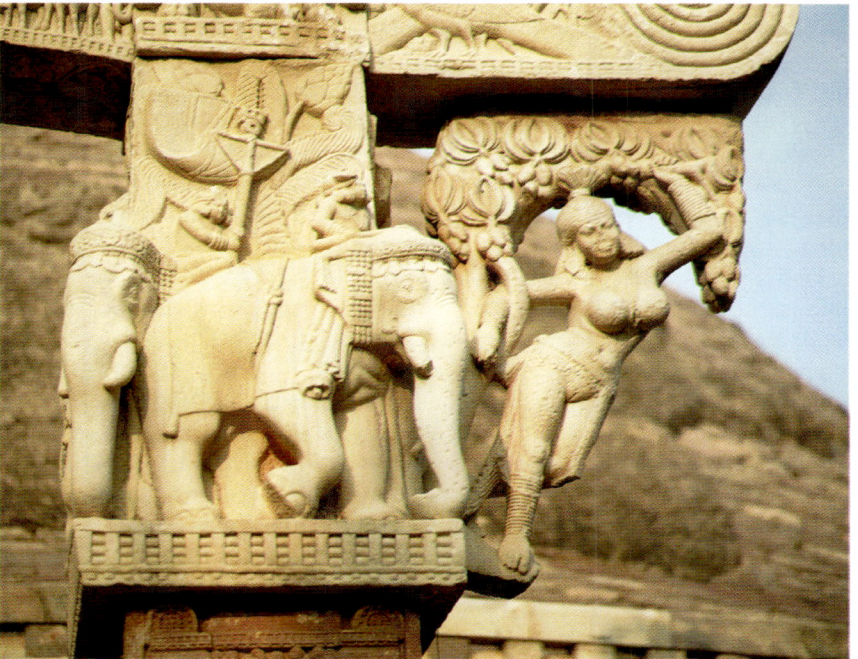

1 ft.

15-7 *Top: Great Stupa (looking north), Sanchi, India, third century BCE to first century CE. Bottom:* Elephants and yakshi, detail of the east torana, mid-first century BCE to early first century CE. Sandstone, 5′ high.

The Sanchi stupa is an earthen mound containing relics of the Buddha. Buddhists walk around stupas in a clockwise direction. They believe the circular movement brings devotees into harmony with the cosmos.

# The Stupa

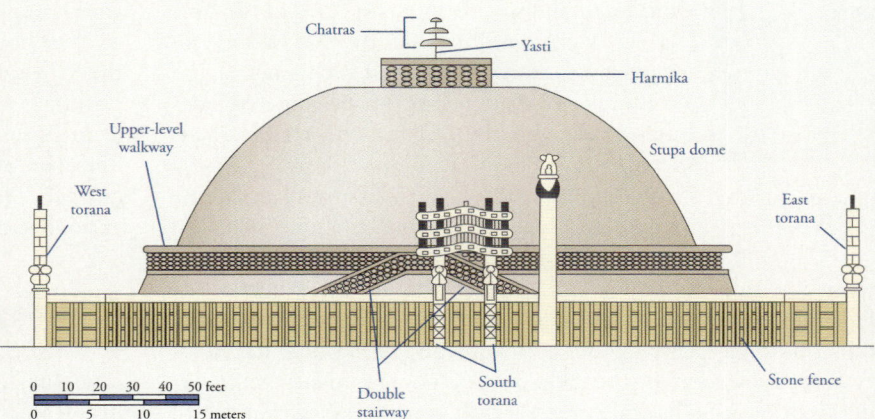

An essential element of Buddhist sanctuaries is the *stupa,* a large circular mound modeled on earlier South Asian burial mounds of a type familiar in many other ancient cultures (FIGS. 4-20 and 6-6). The stupa was not a tomb, however, but a monument housing relics of the Buddha. When the Buddha died, his followers placed his cremated remains in eight *reliquaries,* or containers, similar in function to the later reliquaries housed in medieval churches at pilgrimage sites throughout the Christian world (see "The Veneration of Relics," Chapter 12, page 336). But unlike their Western equivalents, which were put on display, the Buddha's relics were buried in solid earthen mounds (stupas) that could not be entered. In the mid-third century BCE, Ashoka opened the original eight stupas and spread the Buddha's relics among thousands of stupas in all corners of his realm. Buddhists venerated the Buddha's remains by *circumambulation,* walking around the stupa in a clockwise direction. The circular movement, echoing the movement of the earth and the sun, brought the devotee into harmony with the cosmos. Stupas come in many sizes, from tiny handheld objects to huge structures, such as the Great Stupa at Sanchi (FIG. 15-7), constructed originally by Ashoka and later enlarged.

The monumental stupas are three-dimensional *mandalas,* or sacred diagrams of the universe. The domed stupa itself represents the world mountain, with the cardinal points marked by *toranas,* or gateways (FIGS. 15-8 and 15-8A). The *harmika,* positioned atop the stupa dome, is a stone fence or railing that encloses a square

**15-8** Diagram of the Great Stupa, Sanchi, India, third century BCE to first century CE.

Stupas are three-dimensional mandalas (sacred diagrams of the universe). The domed stupa represents the world mountain with a yasti at the top corresponding to the axis of the universe. Toranas mark the cardinal points.

area symbolizing the sacred domain of the gods. At the harmika's center, a *yasti,* or pole, corresponds to the axis of the universe, a motif already present in Ashoka's pillars (FIG. 15-6A). Three *chatras,* or stone disks, assigned various meanings, crown the yasti. The yasti rises from the mountain-dome and passes through the harmika, thus uniting this world with the heavenly paradise. A stone fence often encloses the entire structure, clearly separating the sacred space containing the Buddha's relics from the profane world outside.

the gateways, walk on the lower circumambulation path, then climb the stairs on the south side to circumambulate at the second level (FIG. **15-8**). Carved onto different parts of the Great Stupa are more than 600 brief inscriptions of donors to the project. Hundreds of individuals (more than a third of them women) made the monument's construction possible. Veneration of the Buddha was open to all, not just the monks, and common laypeople, who hoped to accrue merit for future rebirths with their gifts, made most of the dedications.

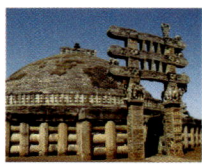

**15-8A** East torana, Great Stupa, Sanchi, ca. 50 BCE–50 CE.

The reliefs on the four toranas (FIG. **15-8A**) at Sanchi depict the story of the Buddha's life and those of his past lives (*jatakas*). In Buddhist belief, everyone has had innumerable past lives, including Siddhartha. During Siddhartha's former lives, as recorded in the jatakas, he accumulated sufficient merit to achieve enlightenment and become the Buddha. In the life stories recounted in the Sanchi torana reliefs, however, the Buddha never appears in human form. Instead, the artists used symbols, for example, footprints, a parasol, or an empty seat, to indicate the Buddha's presence. Some scholars regard these symbols as markers of where the Buddha once was so that others can follow in his footsteps.

Also carved on the east torana is a scantily clad, sensuous woman called a *yakshi* (FIG. 15-7, *bottom*). These goddesses, worshiped throughout India, personify fertility and vegetation and were long-established statuary types (FIG. 15-6B) in the repertoire of South Asian sculptors. The Sanchi yakshi reaches up to hold a mango tree branch while pressing her left foot against the trunk, which causes the tree to flower. Buddhist artists later adopted this pose, with its rich associations of procreation and abundance, for representing the Buddha's mother, Maya, giving birth (FIG. 15-1). Thus, South Asian artists adopted pan-Indian symbolism, such as the woman under the tree, when formulating Buddhist iconography.

**KARLE** The chaitya hall (FIGS. **15-9** and **15-10**) carved out of the living rock at Karle in imitation of earlier wooden structures is the best early example of a Buddhist stupa hall. Datable around 50 to 100 CE, the Karle hall has a pillared *ambulatory* (walking path), enabling worshipers to circumambulate the stupa placed at the back of the sacred cave. The hall also has excellent acoustics for devotional chanting. At nearly 45 feet high and 125 feet long, it surpasses in size even the rock-cut chamber (FIG. 3-23) of the temple of the Egyptian pharaoh Ramses II. Elaborate capitals atop the rock-cut pillars depict men and women riding on elephants (compare FIG. 15-8). Outside,

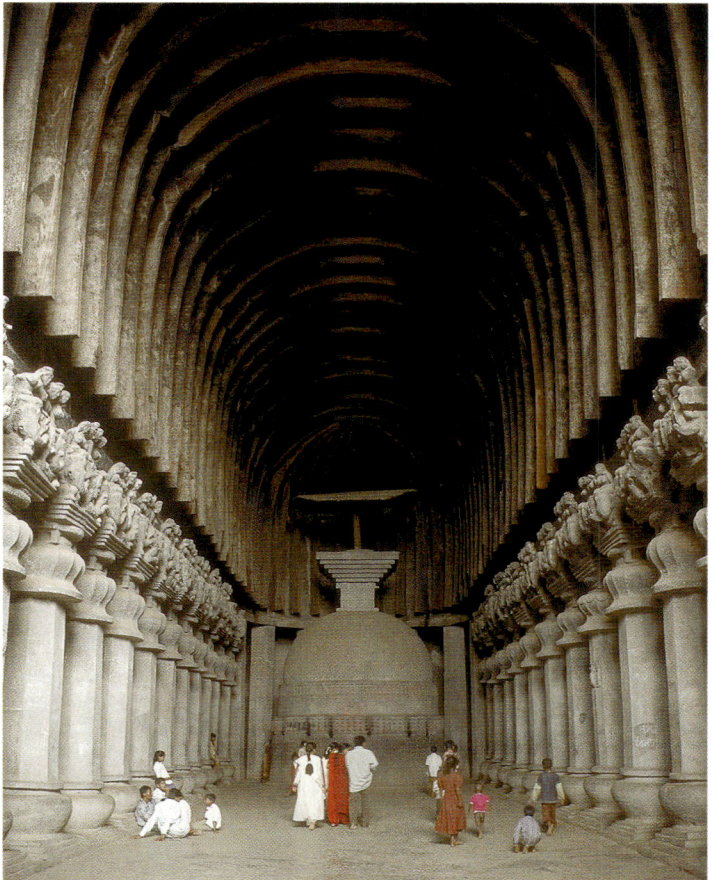

**15-9** Interior of the chaitya hall, Karle, India, ca. 50–100 CE.

Chaitya halls in Buddhist monasteries house stupas. The rock-cut cave at Karle imitates earlier wooden halls. The massive interior (45 feet tall, 125 feet long) has excellent acoustics for devotional chanting.

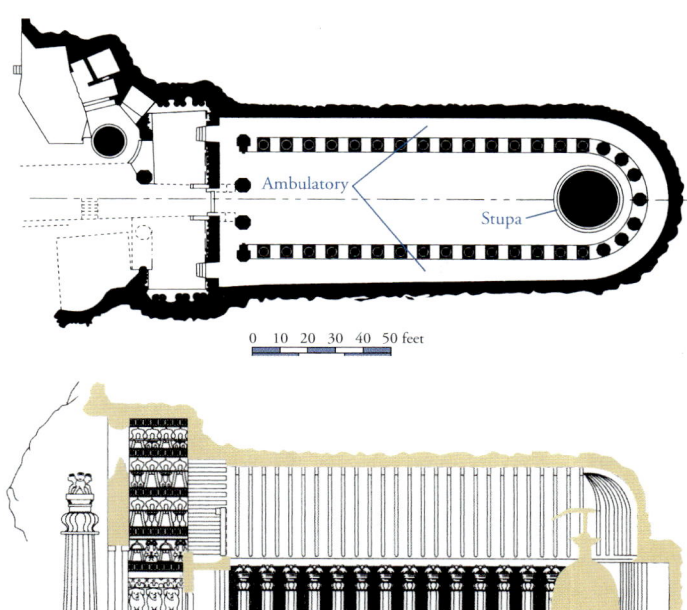

**15-10** Plan (*top*) and section (*bottom*) of the chaitya hall, Karle, India, ca. 50–100 CE.

An early example of Buddhist architecture, the chaitya hall at Karle is carved out of the rock. It has a pillared ambulatory enabling worshipers to circumambulate the stupa in the apse of the cave.

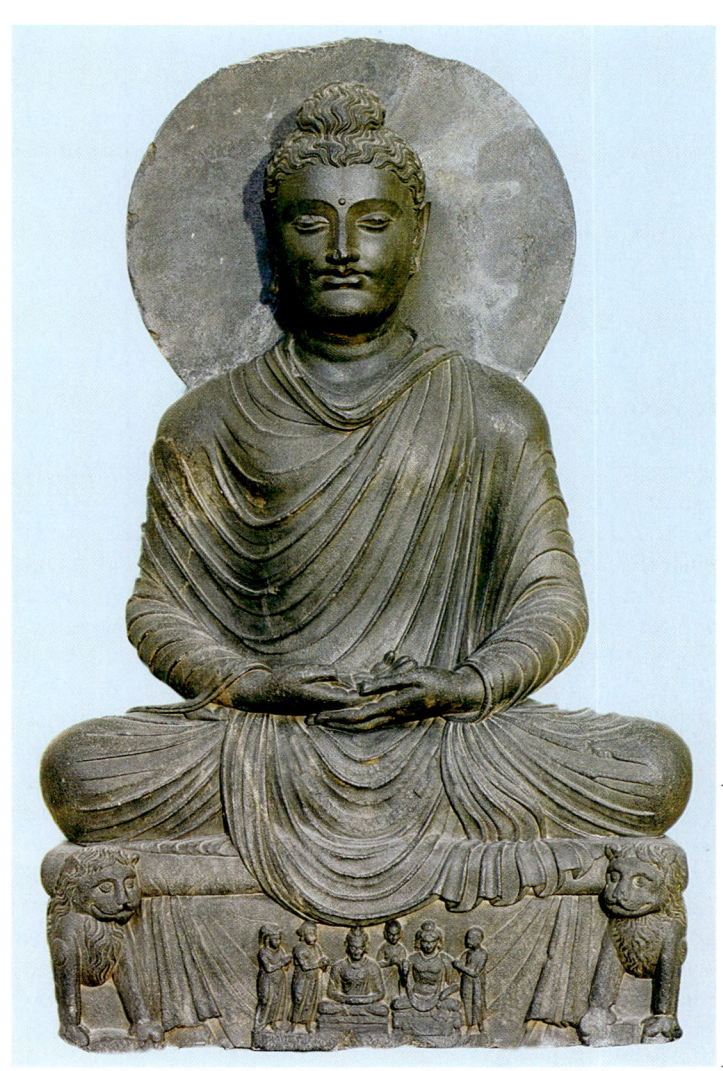

**15-11** Meditating Buddha, from Gandhara, Pakistan, second century CE. Gray schist, 3′ 7½″ high. National Museums of Scotland, Edinburgh. ■◀

Many early portrayals of the Buddha in human form come from Gandhara and depict the Enlightened One as a robed monk. The style of this Gandharan Buddha owes much to Greco-Roman art.

amorous couples (*mithunas*) flank the entrance. As do the yakshis at Sanchi, these auspicious figures symbolize the creative life force.

**GANDHARA** The first anthropomorphic representations of the Buddha probably appeared in the first century CE. Scholars still debate what brought about this momentous shift in Buddhist iconography, but one factor may have been the changing perception of the Buddha himself. Originally revered as an enlightened mortal, the Buddha increasingly became regarded as a divinity. Consequently, the Buddha's followers desired images of him to worship.

Many early portrayals of the Buddha in human form come from the Gandhara region. A second-century CE statue (FIG. **15-11**) carved in gray schist, the local stone, shows the Buddha, with halo, ushnisha, and urna, dressed in a monk's robe, seated in a cross-legged yogic posture similar to that of the male figure with horned headdress on the Indus seal (FIG. 15-5). The Buddha's hands overlap, palms upward, in the dhyana mudra, the gesture of meditation see "Buddhism," page 427). This statue and similar

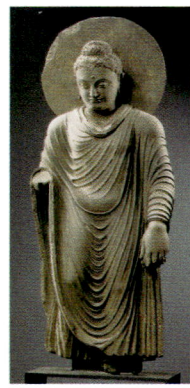

15-11A Standing Buddha, Gandhara, second to third century CE.

Gandharan representations of the Buddha, standing (FIG. 15-11A) as well as seated, owe a great deal to Greco-Roman art, both in the treatment of body forms, such as the sharp, arching brows and continuous profile of forehead and nose (FIG. 5-41), and in the draping of the togalike garment (FIG. 7-71).

One of the earliest pictorial narratives in which the Buddha appears in human form also comes from Gandhara: the frieze (FIG. 15-1) in the Freer Gallery depicting the Buddha's birth at Lumbini, the enlightenment at Bodh Gaya, the first sermon at Sarnath, and the Buddha's death at Kushinagara. Although the iconography of the frieze is Buddhist with roots in earlier South Asian art—the representation of Queen Maya giving birth to Prince Siddhartha derives from depictions of yakshis (FIG. 15-7, *bottom*)—Roman reliefs must have served as stylistic models for the sculptors. For example, the distribution of standing and equestrian figures over the relief ground, with those behind the first row seemingly suspended in the air, is familiar in Roman art of the second and third centuries CE (FIGS. 7-65 and 7-70). The figure of the Buddha on his deathbed has parallels in the reclining figures on the lids of Roman sarcophagi (FIG. 7-61). The type of hierarchical composition in which a large central figure sits between balanced tiers of smaller onlookers is also common in Roman imperial art (FIG. 7-76).

**MATHURA** Contemporaneous with but stylistically distinct from the Gandharan sculptures are the Buddha images from Mathura, a city about 90 miles south of Delhi that was also part of the Kushan Empire. The Mathura statues (for example, FIG. 15-12) have closer links to the Indian portrayals of *yakshas,* the male equivalents of the yakshis. Indian artists represented yakshas as robust, powerful males with broad shoulders and open, staring eyes. Mathura Buddhas, carved from red sandstone, as was the Harappa nude man (FIG. 15-4), retain these characteristics but wear a monk's robe (with right shoulder bare) and lack the yakshas' jewelry and other signs of wealth. The robe appears almost transparent, revealing the full, fleshy body beneath. In FIG. 15-12, the Buddha sits in a yogic posture on a lion throne under the Bodhi tree, attended by fly-whisk bearers. He raises his right hand palm-out in the abhaya

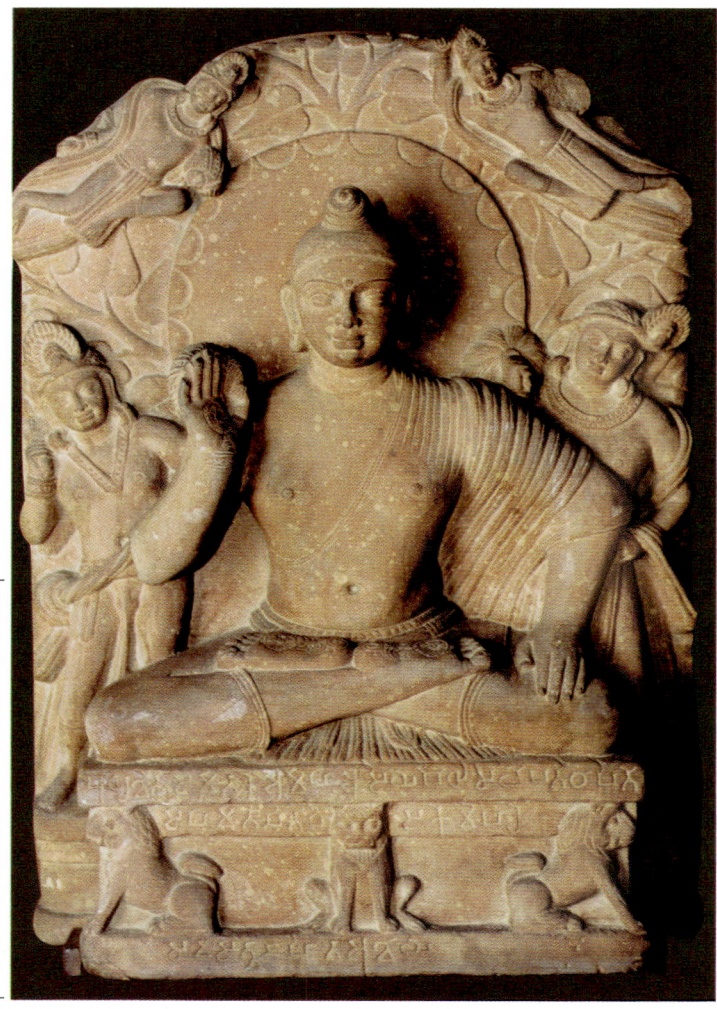

1 ft.

**15-12** Buddha seated on lion throne, from Mathura, India, second century CE. Red sandstone, 2′ 3½″ high. Archaeological Museum, Muttra.

Stylistically distinct from the Gandharan Buddhas are those of Mathura. In this statue depicting the Buddha under the Bodhi tree, the Buddha has the body type of a yaksha but wears a monk's robe.

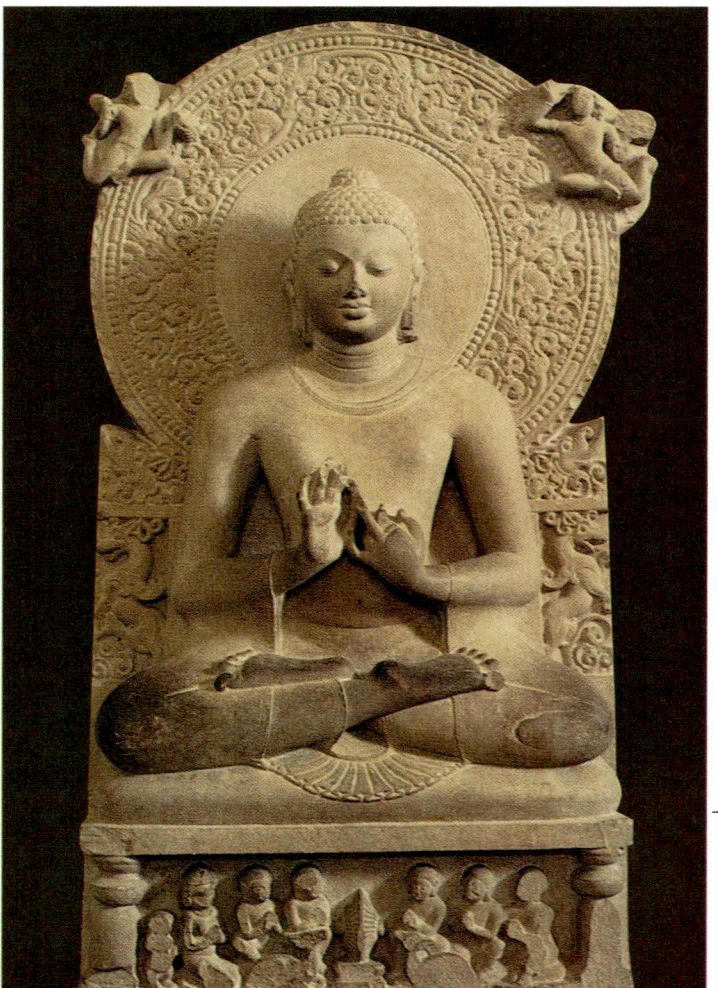

1 ft.

**15-13** Seated Buddha preaching first sermon, from Sarnath, India, second half of fifth century. Tan sandstone, 5′ 3″ high. Archaeological Museum, Sarnath.

Gupta artists formulated the canonical sculpted image of the Buddha, combining the Gandharan monastic-robe type with the Mathuran soft, full-bodied figure attired in clinging garments.

## The Painted Caves of Ajanta

Art historians assume India had a rich painting tradition in ancient times, but because early Indian artists often used perishable materials, such as palm leaf and wood, and because of the tropical climate in much of India, nearly all early Indian painting has disappeared. At Ajanta in the Deccan region, however, paintings cover the walls, pillars, and ceilings of several caves datable to the second half of the fifth century.

The detail reproduced here (FIG. 15-14) comes from one of the restored murals in cave 1 at Ajanta. The bodhisattva Padmapani sits among a crowd of devotees, both princes and commoners. With long, dark hair hanging down below a jeweled crown, he stands holding his attribute, a blue lotus flower, in his right hand. The painter rendered with finesse the sensuous form of the richly attired bodhisattva, gently modeling the figure with gradations of color and delicate highlights and shading, especially evident in the face and neck. The artist also carefully considered the placement of the painting in the cave, putting it on the left wall of the entrance to the antechamber of the main shrine. From that location the bodhisattva gazes downward at worshipers entering the antechamber on their way to the rock-cut Buddha image in a cell at the back of the cave.

To create the Ajanta murals, the painters—professional lay artists rather than monks—first applied two layers of clay mixed with straw and other materials to the walls. They then added a third layer of fine white lime plaster. Unlike true fresco painting (see "Fresco Painting," Chapter 14, page 408), in which painters apply colors to wet plaster, the Indian painters waited for the lime to dry. This method produces less durable results, and the Ajanta murals have suffered water damage over the centuries. The artists next outlined the figures in dark red and painted in the details of faces,

**15-14** Bodhisattva Padmapani, detail of a wall painting in the antechamber of cave 1, Ajanta, India, second half of fifth century.

In this early example of Indian painting in an Ajanta cave, the artist rendered the sensuous form of the richly attired bodhisattva with gentle gradations of color and delicate highlights and shadows.

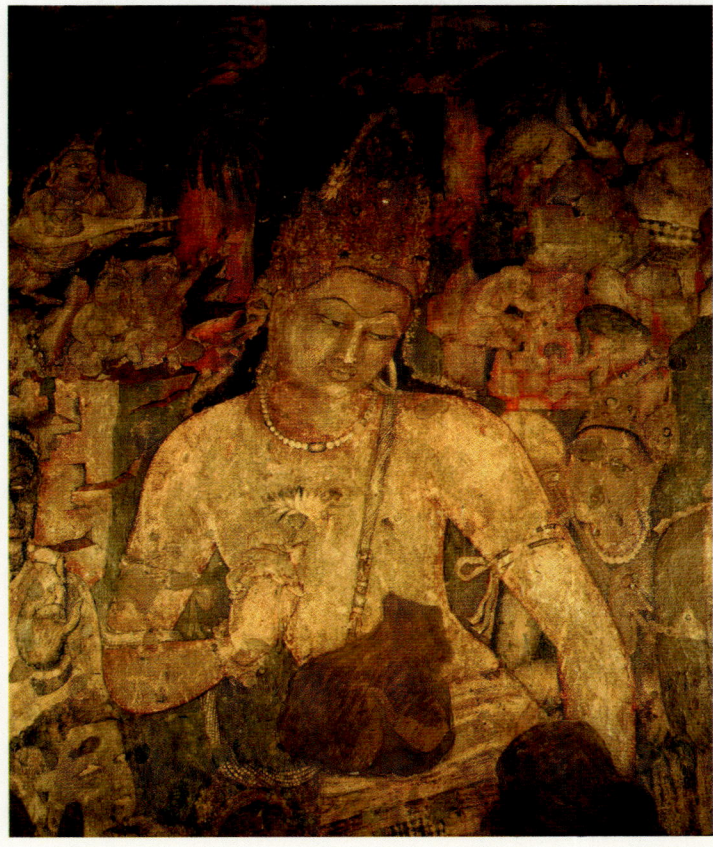

costumes, and jewelry. The Ajanta palette consisted of six basic water-soluble colors, produced mostly from local minerals: white, from lime; black, from soot; red and yellow, from ocher; and green, from glauconite. Blue, used sparingly, came from costly lapis lazuli imported from Afghanistan. The last step was to polish the painted surface with a smooth stone.

---

gesture, indicating to worshipers they need have no fear. His hands and feet bear the mark of the Wheel of the Law. The inscription reveals a Buddhist nun named Amoha-asi dedicated the sculpture "to the welfare and happiness of all sentient beings."

## The Gupta and Post-Gupta Periods

Around 320* a new empire arose in north-central India. The Gupta emperors chose Pataliputra as their capital, deliberately associating themselves with the prestige of the former Maurya Empire. The heyday of this dynasty was under Chandragupta II (r. 375–415), whose very name recalled the first Maurya emperor. The Guptas were great patrons of art and literature.

**SARNATH** Under the Guptas, artists formulated what became the canonical image of the Buddha, combining the Gandharan monastic robe covering both shoulders (FIGS. 15-1, 15-11, and 15-11A)

* From this point on, all dates in this chapter are CE unless otherwise stated.

with the soft, full-bodied Buddha figures with clinging garments of Mathuran sculpture (FIG. 15-12). These disparate styles beautifully merge in a fifth-century statue (FIG. **15-13**) of the Buddha from Sarnath. The statue's smooth, unadorned surfaces conform to the Indian notion of perfect body form and emphasize the figure's spirituality. The Buddha's eyes are downcast in meditation, and he holds his hands in front of his body in the Wheel-turning gesture, preaching his first sermon. Below the Buddha is a scene with the Wheel of the Law at the center between two (now partially broken) deer symbolizing the Deer Park at Sarnath. Buddha images such as this one became so popular that temples housing Buddha statues seem largely to have superseded the stupa as the norm in Buddhist sacred architecture.

**BUDDHIST AJANTA** The new popularity of Buddha imagery is evident in the mural and ceiling paintings of cave 1 (FIG. **15-14**) and the many other caves carved into the mountainside at Ajanta, northeast of Bombay (see "The Painted Caves of Ajanta," above). Ajanta owes its fame today to those paintings, but the site had been

added more than 20 new caves to the site. Another Ajanta Buddhist monument is cave 19, which boasts a chaitya hall (FIG. **15-15**) contemporaneous with the murals in cave 1. The typological similarity of the fifth-century Ajanta chaitya hall to the earlier example at Karle (FIG. 15-9) is immediately clear and is consistent with the conservative nature of religious architecture in all cultures. At Ajanta, however, sculptors carved on the front of the stupa an image of the Buddha standing between columns.

**HINDU AJANTA** At Ajanta, as at many other sites in India, Buddhists and Hindus (and adherents of other faiths) practiced their religions side by side. For example, at the same time painters were at work on the Buddhist murals in cave 1, the Hindu Vakataka king Harishena (r. 462–481) and members of his court were the sponsors of new Hindu caves at the monastery. Buddhism and Hinduism are not monotheistic religions, such as Judaism, Christianity, and Islam. Instead, Buddhists and Hindus approach the spiritual through many gods and varying paths, which permits mutually tolerated differences. In fact, in Hinduism, the Buddha was one of the 10 incarnations of Vishnu, one of the three principal Hindu deities (see "Hinduism and Hindu Iconography," page 435).

**UDAYAGIRI** More early Buddhist than Hindu art has survived in India because the Buddhists constructed their monasteries with durable materials such as stone and brick. But in the Gupta period, Hindu stone sculpture and architecture began to rival the great Buddhist monuments of South Asia. The oldest Hindu cave temples are at Udayagiri, near Sanchi. They date to the early fifth century, some 600 years after the first Buddhist examples. Although the Udayagiri temples are architecturally simple and small, the site boasts monumental relief sculptures showing an already fully developed religious iconography. One of these reliefs (FIG. **15-16**), carved in a shallow niche of rock, shows a 13-foot-tall Vishnu in his incarnation as the boar Varaha. The avatar has a human body and a boar's head. Vishnu assumed this form when he rescued the earth—personified as the goddess Bhudevi clinging to the boar's tusk—from being carried off to the bottom of the ocean. Vishnu stands with one foot resting on the coils of a snake king (note the

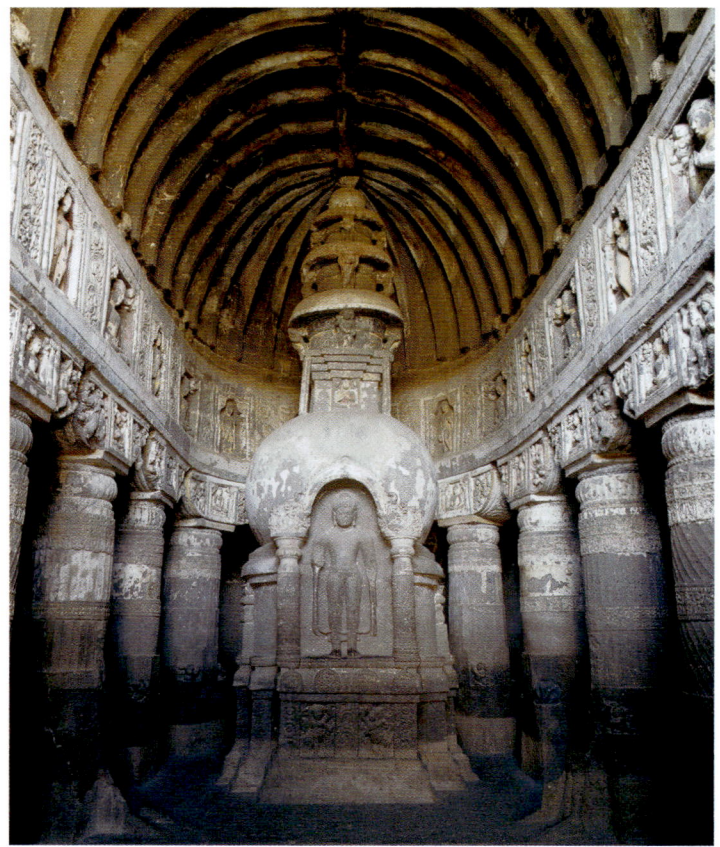

**15-15** Interior of cave 19, Ajanta, India, second half of fifth century.

The popularity of Gupta Buddha statues led to a transformation in Indian religious architecture. Cave 19 at Ajanta is a chaitya hall with an image of the Buddha carved on the front of its stupa.

home to a small Buddhist monastery for centuries. During the second half of the fifth century, that is, about the same time a Gupta sculptor created the classic seated Buddha of Sarnath, royal patrons of the local Vakataka dynasty, allied to the Guptas by marriage,

**15-16** *Boar Avatar of Vishnu Rescues the Earth,* cave 5, Udayagiri, India, early fifth century. Relief 22′ × 13′; Vishnu 12′ 8″ high.

The oldest Hindu cave temples are at Udayagiri, a site that also boasts some of the earliest Hindu stone sculptures, such as this huge relief of Vishnu as the boar Varaha rescuing the earth.

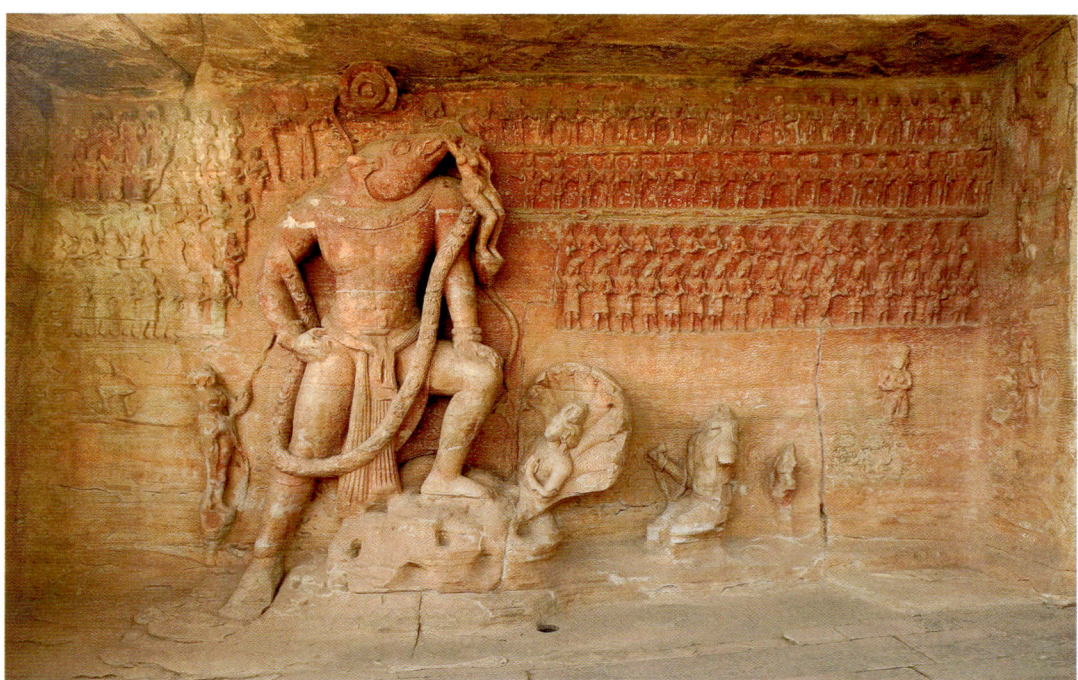

1 ft.

# Hinduism and Hindu Iconography

Unlike Buddhism (and Christianity, Islam, and other religions), Hinduism recognizes no founder or great prophet. Hinduism also has no descriptive definition but means "the religion of the Indians." Both "India" and "Hindu" have a common root in the name of the Indus River. The practices and beliefs of Hindus vary tremendously, but the literary origins of Hinduism date to the Vedic period, and some aspects of Hindu practice apparently were already present in the Indus Civilization of the third millennium BCE. Ritual sacrifice by Brahmin priests is central to Hinduism, as it was to the Aryans. The goal of sacrifice is to please a deity in order to achieve release (*moksha*, liberation) from the endless cycle of birth, death, and rebirth (*samsara*) and become one with the universal spirit.

Not only is Hinduism a religion of many gods, but the Hindu deities have various natures and take many forms. This multiplicity suggests the all-pervasive nature of the Hindu gods. The three most important deities are the gods Shiva and Vishnu and the goddess Devi. Each of the three major sects of Hinduism today considers one of these three to be supreme—Shiva in Shaivism, Vishnu in Vaishnavism, and Devi in Shaktism. (*Shakti* is the female creative force.)

**Shiva** is the Destroyer, but, consistent with the multiplicity of Hindu belief, he is also a regenerative force. In the latter role, Shiva can be represented in the form of a *linga* (a phallus or cosmic pillar). When Shiva appears in human form in Hindu art, he frequently has multiple limbs and heads (FIGS. 15-17, 15-18, and 15-27), signs of his suprahuman nature, and matted locks piled atop his head, crowned by a crescent moon. Sometimes he wears a serpent scarf and has a third eye on his forehead (the emblem of his all-seeing nature). Shiva rides the bull **Nandi** (FIG. 15-17) and often carries a *trident,* a three-pronged pitchfork.

**Vishnu** is the Preserver of the Universe. Artists frequently portray him with four arms (FIGS. 15-20 and 15-31) holding various attributes, including a conch-shell trumpet and discus. He sometimes reclines on a serpent floating on the waters of the cosmic sea (FIGS. 15-20 and 15-31). When the evil forces of the universe become too strong, he descends to earth to restore balance and assumes different forms (*avatars,* or incarnations), including a boar (FIG. 15-16), fish, and tortoise, as well as **Krishna,** the divine lover (FIG. 32-7), and even the Buddha himself.

**Devi** is the Great Goddess who takes many forms and has many names. Hindus worship her alone or as a consort of male gods (**Parvati** or **Uma,** wife of Shiva; **Lakshmi,** wife of Vishnu), as

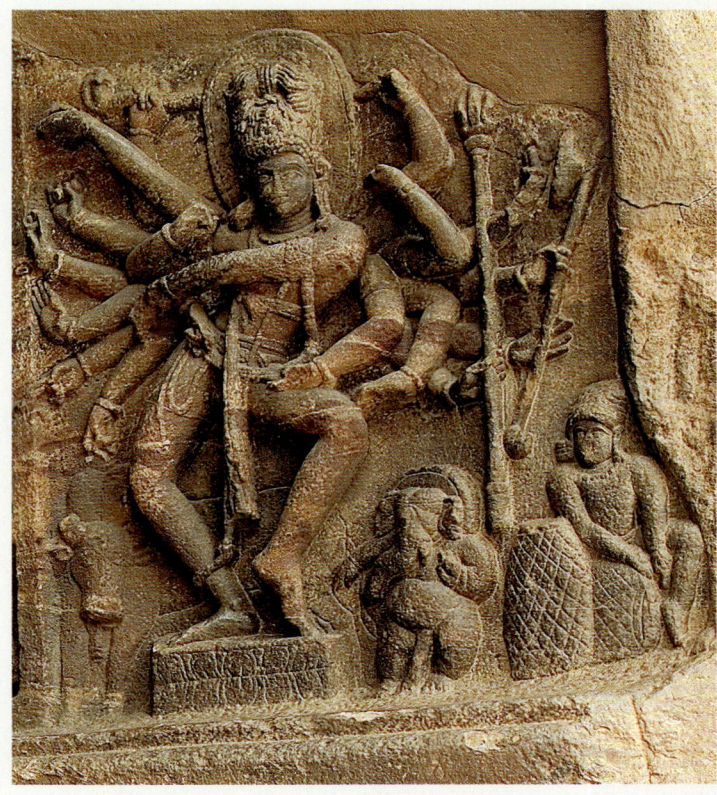

**15-17** Dancing Shiva, rock-cut relief, cave 1, Badami, India, late sixth century.

Shiva here dances the cosmic dance and has 18 arms, some holding objects, others forming mudras. Hindu gods often have multiple limbs to indicate their suprahuman nature and divine powers.

well as **Radha,** lover of Krishna (FIG. 32-7). She has both benign and horrific forms; she both creates and destroys. In one manifestation, she is **Durga,** a multiarmed goddess who often rides a lion (FIG. 15-22). Her son is the elephant-headed **Ganesha** (FIG. 15-17).

The stationary images of deities in Hindu temples are often made of stone. Hindus periodically remove portable images of their gods, often of bronze (FIG. 15-27), from the temple, particularly during festivals to enable many worshipers to take *darshan* (seeing the deity and being seen by the deity) at one time. In temples dedicated to Shiva, the stationary form is the linga.

---

multiple hoods behind his human head), who represents the conquered demon that attempted to abduct the earth. Rows of gods and sages form lines to witness the event.

The relief served a political as well as a religious purpose. The patron of the relief was a local king who honored the great Gupta king Chandragupta II in a nearby inscription dated to the year 401. Many scholars believe the local king wanted viewers to see Chandragupta (who had visited the site) as saving his kingdom by ridding it of its enemies in much the same way Varaha saved the earth.

**BADAMI** During the sixth century, the Huns brought down the Gupta Empire, and various regional dynasties rose to power. In the Deccan plateau of central India, the Chalukya kings ruled from their capital at Badami. There, Chalukya sculptors carved a series of reliefs in the walls of halls cut into the cliff above the city. One relief (FIG. 15-17), datable to the late sixth century, shows Shiva dancing the cosmic dance, his 18 arms swinging rhythmically in an arc. Some of the hands hold objects, and others form prescribed mudras. At the lower right, the elephant-headed Ganesha tentatively

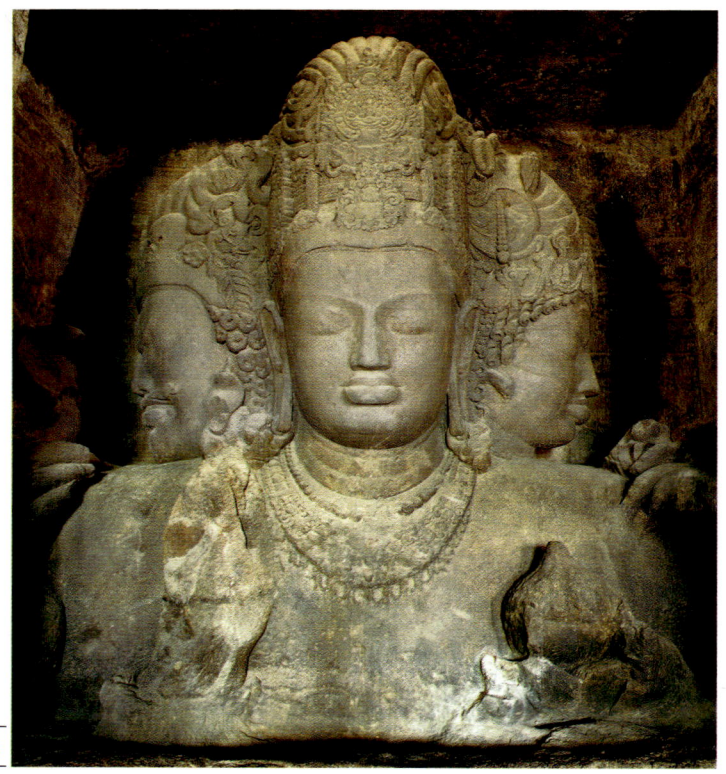

**15-18** Shiva as Mahadeva, cave 1, Elephanta, India, ca. 550–575. Basalt, Shiva 17′ 10″ high.

This immense rock-cut image of Shiva as Mahadeva ("Great God") emerges out of the depths of the Elephanta cave as worshipers' eyes adjust to the darkness. Shiva has both male and female faces.

sents Shiva's destructive side. Shiva holds these two opposing forces in check, and the central face expresses their balance. The cyclic destruction and creation of the universe, which the side faces also symbolize, are part of Indian notions of time, matched by the cyclic pattern of death and rebirth (samsara).

**DEOGARH** The excavated cave shrines just considered are characteristic of early Hindu religious architecture, but temples constructed using quarried stone became more important as Hinduism evolved over the centuries. As they did with the cave temples, the Hindus initially built rather small and simple temples but decorated them with narrative reliefs displaying a fully developed iconography. The Vishnu Temple (FIG. **15-19**) at Deogarh in north-central India, datable to the early sixth century, is among the first Hindu temples constructed with stone blocks. A simple square structure, it has an elaborately decorated doorway at the front and a relief in a niche on each of the other three sides. Sculpted guardians and mithunas protect the doorway at Deogarh, because it is the transition point between the dangerous outside and the sacred. The temple culminates in a tall tower, originally at least 40 feet high.

The reliefs in the three niches of the Deogarh temple depict important episodes in the saga of Vishnu. On the south (FIG. **15-20**), Vishnu sleeps on the coils of the giant serpent Ananta, whose multiple heads form a kind of umbrella around the god's face. While Lakshmi massages her husband's legs (he has cramps as he gives birth), the four-armed Vishnu dreams the universe into reality. A lotus plant (said to have grown out of Vishnu's navel) supports the four-headed Hindu god of creation, Brahma. Flanking him are other important Hindu divinities, including Shiva on his bull. Below are six figures. The four at the right are personifications of Vishnu's various powers. They will defeat the two armed demons at the left. The

mimics Shiva. Nandi, Shiva's bull mount, stands at the left. Artists often represented Hindu deities as part human and part animal (FIG. 15-16) or, as in the Badami relief, as figures with multiple body parts. Such composite and multilimbed forms indicate the subjects are not human but suprahuman gods with supernatural powers.

**ELEPHANTA** Another portrayal of Shiva as a suprahuman being is in a third Hindu cave site, on Elephanta, an island in Bombay's harbor that early Portuguese colonizers named after a life-size stone elephant sculpture there. A king of the Kalachuri dynasty took control of Elephanta in the sixth century, and he may have commissioned the largest of the island's cave temples. Just inside the west entrance to the cave is a shrine housing Shiva's linga, the god's emblem. Deep within the temple, in a niche once closed off with wooden doors, is a nearly 18-foot-high rock-cut image (FIG. **15-18**) of Shiva as Mahadeva, the "Great God" or Lord of Lords. Mahadeva appears to emerge out of the depths of the cave as worshipers' eyes become accustomed to the darkness. This image of Shiva has three faces, each showing a different aspect of the deity. (A fourth, unseen at the back, is implied—the god has not emerged fully from the rock.) The central face expresses Shiva's quiet, balanced demeanor. The clean planes of the face contrast with the richness of the piled hair encrusted with jewels. The two side faces differ significantly. The one on the right is female, with framing hair curls. The left face is a grimacing male with a curling mustache who wears a cobra as an earring. The female (Uma) indicates the creative aspect of Shiva. The fierce male (Bhairava) repre-

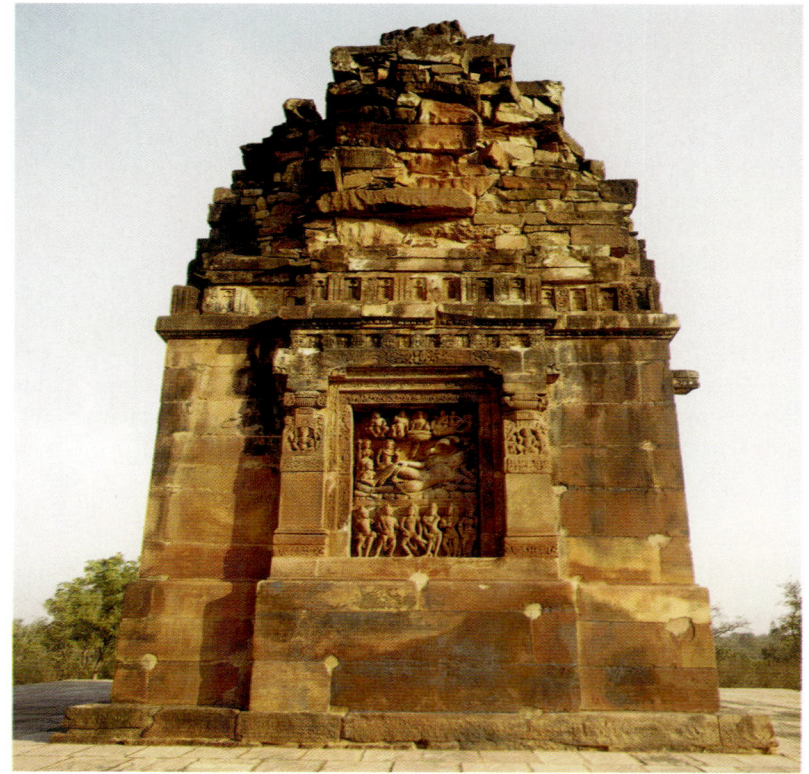

**15-19** Vishnu Temple (looking north), Deogarh, India, early sixth century.

One of the first masonry Hindu temples, the Vishnu Temple at Deogarh is a simple square building with a tower. Sculpted guardians protect its entrance. Narrative reliefs adorn the three other sides.

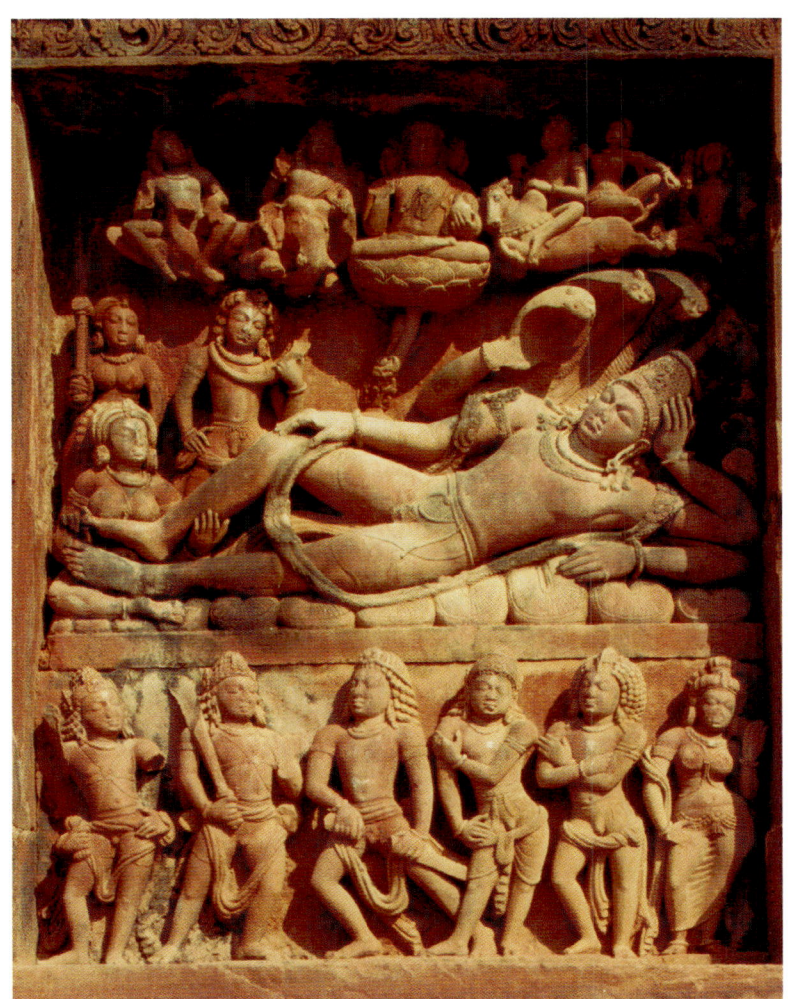

**15-20** *Vishnu Asleep on the Serpent Ananta,* relief panel on the south facade of the Vishnu Temple, Deogarh, India, early sixth century.

Sculptors carved the reliefs of the Vishnu Temple at Deogarh in classic Gupta style. In the south panel, the four-armed Vishnu sleeps on the serpent Ananta as he dreams the universe into reality.

sculptor carved all the figures in the classic Gupta style, with smooth bodies and clinging garments (compare FIG. 15-13).

# Early Medieval Period

During the several centuries corresponding to the early medieval period in Europe (see Chapter 11), the early Islamic period in Mesopotamia and Persia (see Chapter 10), the Tang and Song dynasties in China (see Chapter 16), and the Hakuho, Nara, and Heian periods in Japan (see Chapter 17), regional dynasties ruled parts of India. Among the most important of these kingdoms were the Palas and Chandellas in northern India and the Pallavas and Cholas in the south. Whereas Buddhism spread rapidly throughout eastern Asia, in medieval India it gradually declined, and the various local kings vied with one another to build glorious shrines to the Hindu gods.

**MAMALLAPURAM** In addition to cave temples and masonry temples, Indian architects created a third type of monument: freestanding temples carved out of rocky outcroppings. Sculpted monolithic temples are rare. Some of the earliest and most impressive are at Mamallapuram, south of Madras on the Bay of Bengal, where they are called *rathas,* or "chariots" (that is, vehicles of the gods). In the late seventh century, the Pallava dynasty ordered five rathas (FIG. **15-21**) carved out of a

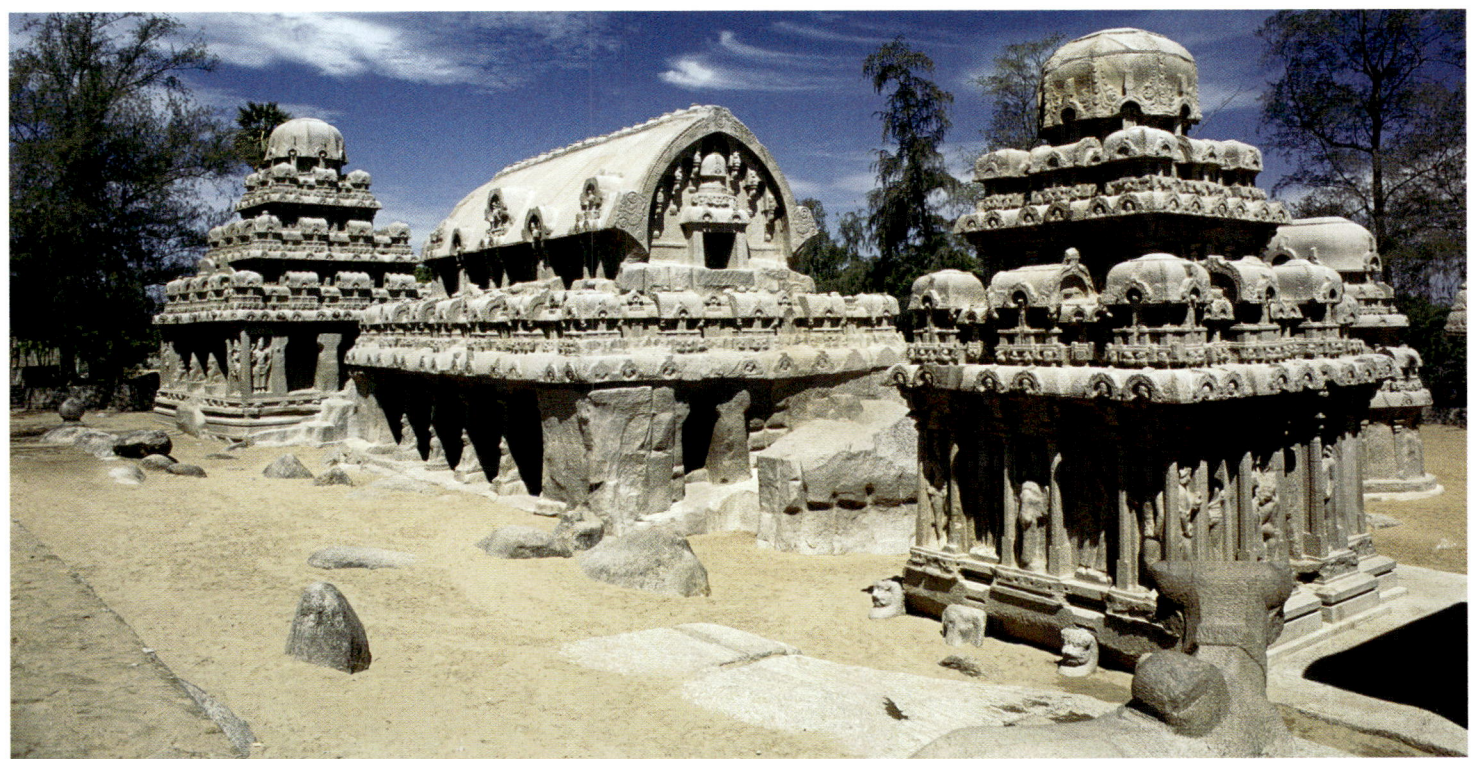

**15-21** Rock-cut rathas (looking southwest), Mamallapuram, India, second half of seventh century. From *left* to *right:* Dharmaraja, Bhima, and Arjuna rathas.

Indian architects also created temples by sculpting them from the living rock. The seventh-century rathas ("chariots" of the gods) at Mamallapuram were all carved from a single huge granite outcropping.

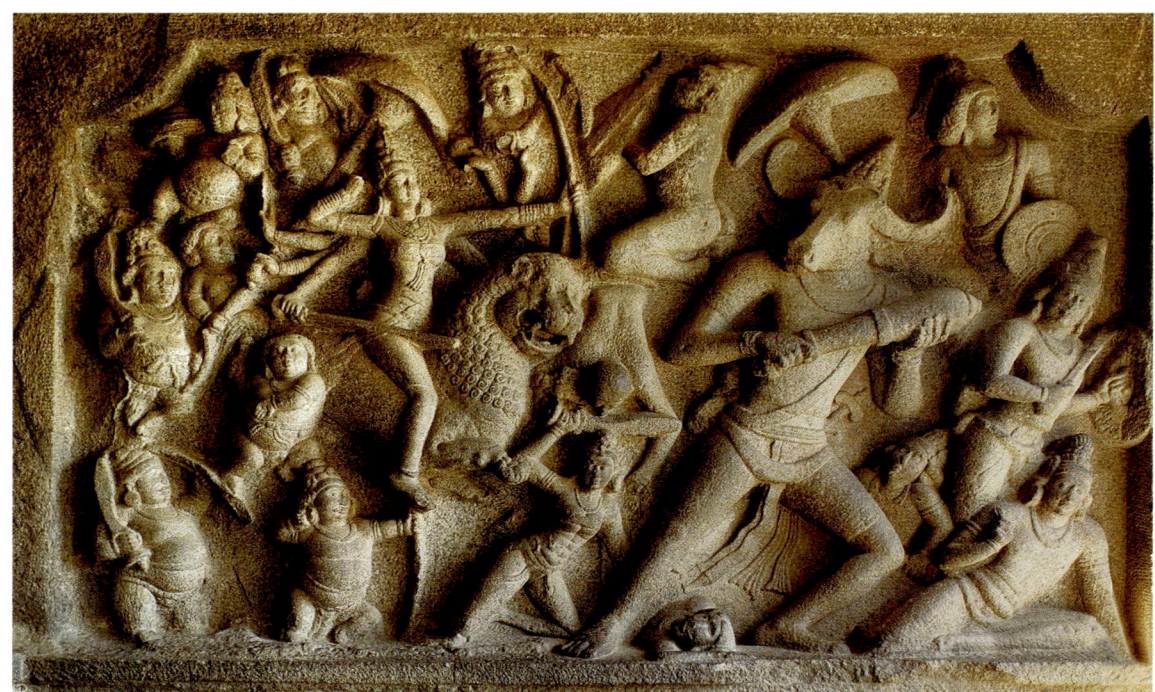

**15-22** *Durga Slaying the Buffalo Demon Manisha,* rock-cut relief in the Mahishasuramardini cave temple, Mamallapuram, India, seventh century CE. Granite, 9′ high.

The supreme Hindu goddess Devi here takes the form of Durga riding a lion. Wielding weapons in her eight hands, Durga defeats the demon Manisha, symbolizing the triumph of good over evil.

single huge granite boulder jutting out from the sand. The group is of special interest because it illustrates the variety of temple forms at this period, based on earlier wooden structures, before a standard masonry type of temple became the norm in southern India.

The largest Mamallapuram ratha, the Dharmaraja (FIG. 15-21, *left*), dedicated to Shiva, is an early example of the typical southern-style temple with stepped-pyramid *vimana* (see "Hindu Temples," page 439). The tower ascends in pronounced tiers of cornices decorated with miniature shrines. The lower walls include carved columns and figures of deities inside niches. The Bhima ratha to the right, dedicated to Vishnu, has a rectangular plan and a rounded roof. The next ratha, the Arjuna, is a smaller example of the southern Indian type. At the end of the row (not visible in FIG. 15-21) sits the very small Draupadi ratha, modeled on a thatched hut and dedicated to Durga, a form of the supreme Hindu goddess Devi. The two largest temples were never finished.

**DURGA AND MANISHA** The Hindu warrior goddess who defends civilization against the evil forces at work in the world is Durga ("She who is difficult to oppose"). On one wall of the Mahishasuramardini cave temple at Mamallapuram, Durga rides into battle on the back of a lion, leading an army of chubby dwarfs against the buffalo-headed, human-bodied demon Manisha (FIG. 15-22), as recounted in one of the most important early works of Hindu literature, the *Devi Mahatmya.* The combat symbolizes for Hindus the struggle between good and evil, order and disorder.

In the Mamallapuram cave relief, the buffalo demon is a giant, far larger than the slender and elegantly dressed eight-armed goddess who stretches her bow to launch an arrow against her foe. Her other arms wield additional weapons given to her by the male Hindu deities when they beseeched her to do battle on their behalf against the terrible Manisha. Durga is therefore a fearsome force despite her delicate appearance. The club-bearing demon recoils from her onslaught. He and his allies have begun their retreat, although he turns his head to look back at Durga. The victory of the goddess over the physically more powerful demon eloquently conveys the message that for the Hindu faithful, good will triumph over evil.

The horizontal format of the relief, the piling up of figures over the surface, and the dramatic and effective way the sculptor has communicated the chaos of hand-to-hand combat all recall Late Antique Roman sarcophagi, such as the *Ludovisi Battle Sarcophagus* (FIG. 7-70). The relief is one of several major works of narrative relief sculpture at Mamallapuram. By far the largest—featuring life-size figures—probably represents the *Descent of the Ganges River* (FIG. **15-22A**).

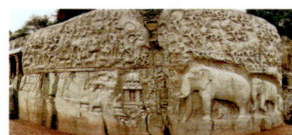

**15-22A** *Descent of the Ganges,* Mamallapuram, ca. 600–650.

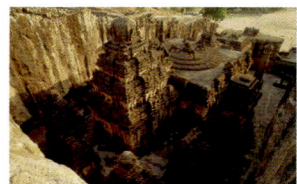

**15-22B** Kailasanatha Temple, Ellora, second half of eighth century.

**THANJAVUR** More ambitious than the rathas of Mamallapuram is the eighth-century rock-cut Kailasanatha Temple (FIG. **15-22B**) at Ellora, a forerunner of the largest known freestanding Hindu temples in the southern Indian tradition (see "Hindu Temples," page 439). Under the Cholas, whose territories extended into part of Sri Lanka and even Java, architects constructed southern-type temples of unprecedented size. The Rajarajeshvara Temple (FIG. **15-23**) at Thanjavur, dedicated in 1010 to Shiva as the Lord of Rajaraja, was the largest and tallest temple (210 feet high) in India at the time. The temple stands inside a walled precinct. It consists of a stairway leading to two flat-roofed mandapas, the larger one having 36 pillars, and to the garbha griha in the base of the enormous pyramidal vimana, which is as much an emblem of the Cholas' secular power as of their devotion to Shiva. On the exterior walls of the lower stories are numerous reliefs in niches depicting the god in his various forms.

**KHAJURAHO** At the same time the Cholas were building the Rajarajeshvara Temple at Thanjavur in the south, the Chandella dynasty was constructing northern-style temples at Khajuraho. The Vishvanatha Temple (FIG. **15-24**) is one of more than 20 large, elaborate temples at that site. Vishvanatha ("Lord of the World") is

# Hindu Temples

The Hindu temple is the home of the gods on earth and the place where they make themselves visible to humans. At the core of all Hindu temples is the *garbha griha* ("womb chamber"), which houses images or symbols of the deity—for example, Shiva's linga (see "Hinduism," page 435). Only Brahmin priests may enter this inner sanctuary and make offerings to the gods. Worshipers, however, may stand at the threshold and behold the deity as manifest by its image. In the elaborate multiroomed temples of later Hindu architecture, the worshipers and priests progress through a series of ever more sacred spaces, usually on an east-west axis. Hindu priests and architects attached great importance to each temple's plan and sought to make it conform to the sacred geometric diagram (*mandala*) of the universe.

Architectural historians, following ancient Indian texts, divide Hindu temples into two major typological groups tied to geography. The most important distinguishing feature of the **northern** style of temple (FIG. 15-24) is its beehivelike tower or *shikhara* ("mountain peak"), capped by an *amalaka,* a ribbed cushionlike form, derived from the shape of the amala fruit (believed to have medicinal powers). Amalakas appear on the corners of the lower levels of the shikhara too. Northern temples also have smaller towerlike roofs over the halls (*mandapas*) leading to the garbha griha.

**Southern** temples (FIG. 15-23) can easily be recognized by the flat roofs of their pillared mandapas and by their shorter towered shrines, called *vimanas,* which lack the curved profile of their northern counterparts and resemble multilevel pyramids.

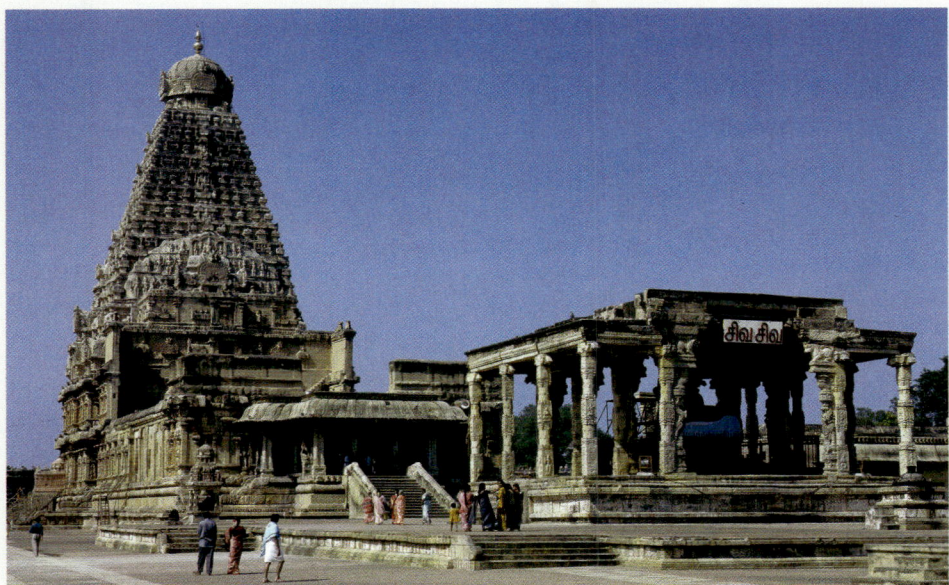

**15-23** Rajarajeshvara Temple (looking southeast), Thanjavur, India, ca. 1010.

The Rajarajeshvara Temple at Thanjavur is an example of the southern type of Hindu temple. Two flat-roofed mandapas lead to the garbha griha in the base of its 210-foot-tall pyramidal vimana.

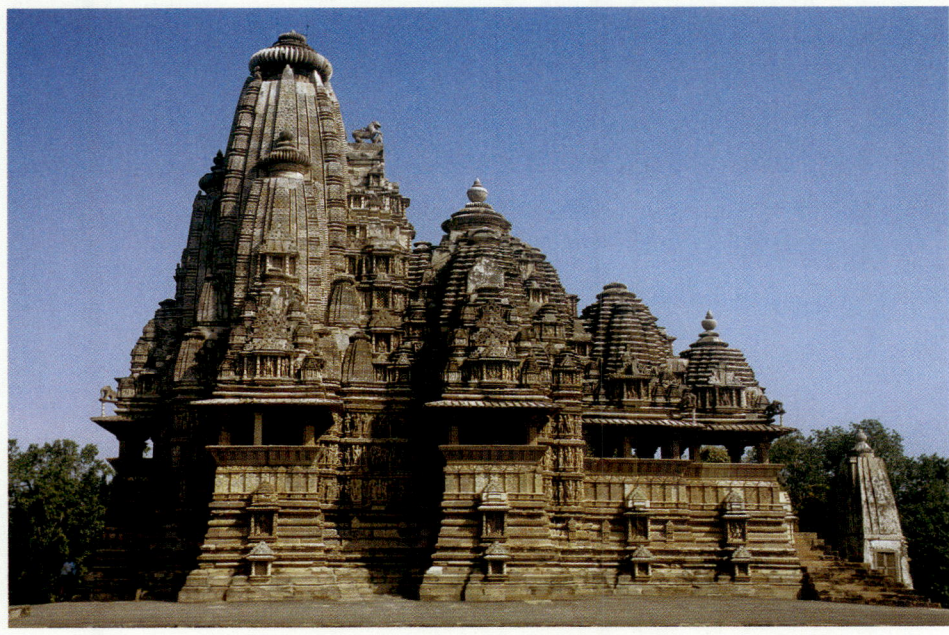

**15-24** Vishvanatha Temple (looking north), Khajuraho, India, ca. 1000.

The Vishvanatha Temple is a northern Hindu temple type. It has four towers, each taller than the preceding one, symbolizing Shiva's mountain home. The largest tower is the beehive-shaped shikhara.

another of the many names for Shiva. Dedicated in 1002, the structure has three towers over the mandapas, each rising higher than the preceding one, leading to the tallest tower at the rear, in much the same way the foothills of the Himalayas, Shiva's home, rise to meet their highest peak. The mountain symbolism applies to the interior plan (FIG. **15-25**) of the Vishvanatha Temple as well. Under the tallest tower, the shikhara, is the garbha griha, the small and dark inner sanctuary chamber, like a cave, which houses the image of the deity. Thus, temples such as the Vishvanatha symbolize constructed mountains with caves, comparable to the cave temples at Elephanta and other Indian sites. In all cases, the deity manifests himself or herself within the cave and takes various forms in sculptures. The temple-mountains, however, are not intended to appear natural but rather are perfect mountains designed using ideal mathematical proportions.

The reliefs of Thanjavur's Rajarajeshvara Temple are typical of southern temple decoration, which is generally limited to images of deities. The exterior walls of Khajuraho's Vishvanatha Temple are equally typical of northern temples in the profusion of sculptures (FIG. **15-26**) depicting mortals as well as gods, especially pairs of men and women (mithunas) embracing or engaged in sexual intercourse in an extraordinary range of positions. The use of seminude yakshis and amorous couples as motifs on religious buildings in India has a very long history, going back to the earliest architectural traditions, both Hindu and Buddhist (Sanchi, FIG. 15-8, and Karle). As in the earlier examples, the erotic sculptures of Khajuraho suggest fertility and the propagation of life and serve as auspicious protectors of the sacred precinct.

**SHIVA AS NATARAJA** Portable objects also play an important role in Hinduism. The statuette (FIG. **15-27**) of Shiva from Tamil Nadu, cast in solid bronze around 1000, recalls the sixth-century

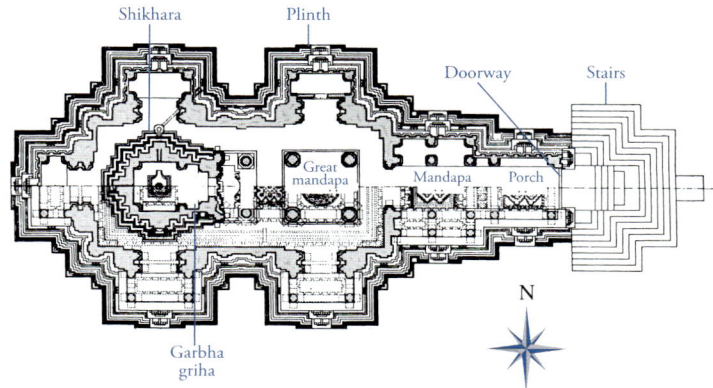

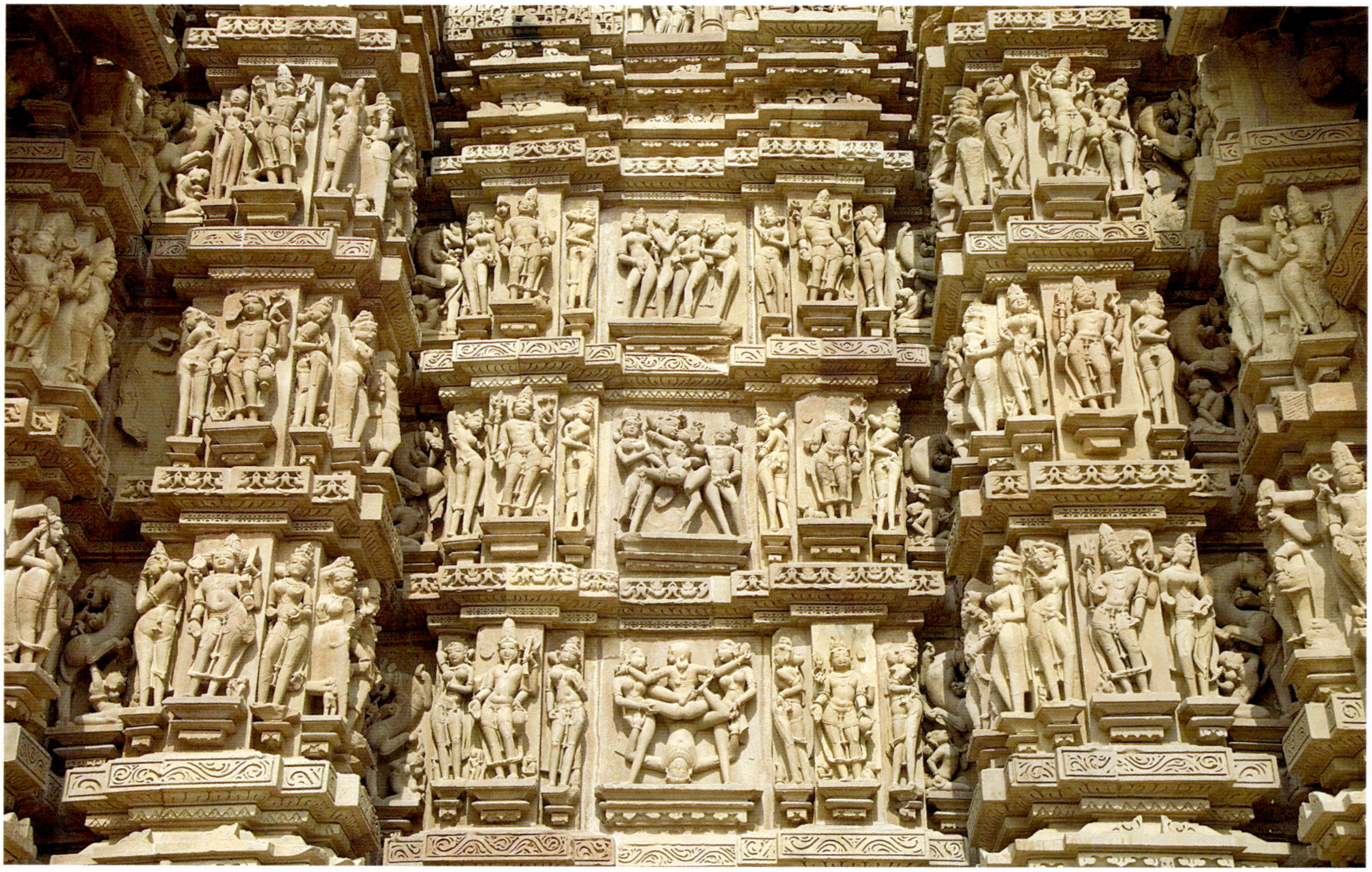

**15-25** Plan of the Vishvanatha Temple, Khajuraho, India, ca. 1000.

Under the shikhara of the Vishvanatha Temple is the garbha griha, the dark inner sanctuary chamber resembling a cave, which houses the image of the deity. Only priests can enter the garbha griha.

**15-26** Mithuna reliefs, detail of the north side of the Vishvanatha Temple, Khajuraho, India, ca. 1000.

Northern Hindu temples usually feature reliefs depicting deities and amorous couples (mithunas). The erotic sculptures suggest the propagation of life and serve as protectors of the sacred precinct.

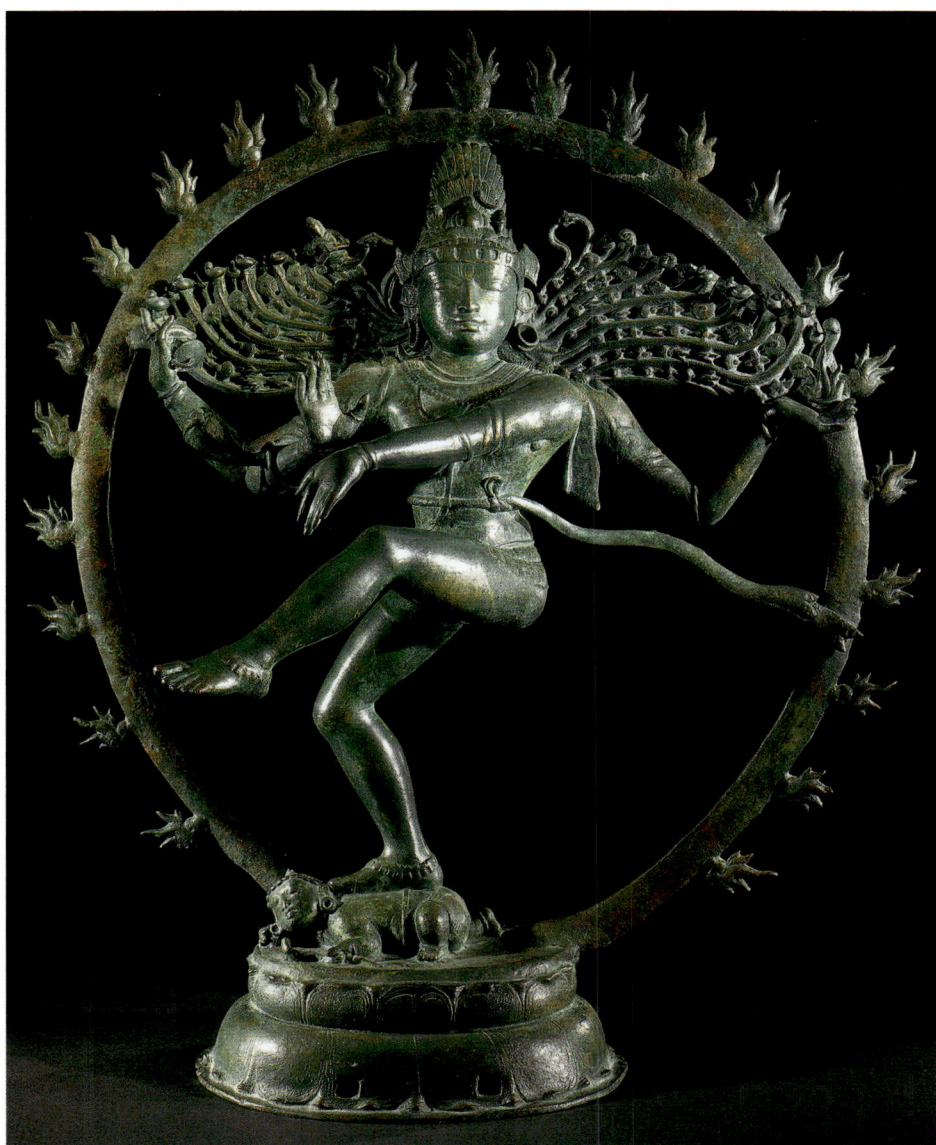

15-27 Shiva as Nataraja, from Tamil Nadu, India, ca. 1000. Bronze. British Museum, London.

One of many portable images of the gods used in Hindu worship, this solid-bronze statuette of Shiva as Lord of the Dance depicts the god balancing on one leg atop a dwarf representing ignorance.

of the god but the god itself. All must treat the image as a living being. Worship of the deity involves caring for him as if he were an honored person. Bathed, clothed, given foods to eat, and taken for outings, the image also receives gifts—songs, lights (lit oil lamps), good smells (incense), and flowers, things the god can enjoy through the senses. The food given to the god is particularly important, as he eats the "essence," leaving the remainder for the worshiper. The food is then *prasada* ("grace"), sacred because it came in contact with the divine. In an especially religious household, the deity resides as an image and receives the food for each meal before the family eats. When the god resides in a temple, it is the duty of the priests to feed, clothe, and take care of him.

The Chola dynasty ended in the 13th century, a time of political, religious, and cultural change in South Asia. At this point, Buddhism survived in only some areas of India. It soon died out completely there, although the late form of northern Indian Buddhism continued in Tibet and Nepal. At the same time, Islam, which had arrived in India as early as the eighth century, became a potent political force with the establishment of the Delhi sultanate in 1206. Hindu and Islamic art assumed preeminent roles in India in the 13th century (see Chapter 32).

# SOUTHEAST ASIA

Art historians once considered the art of Southeast Asia an extension of Indian civilization. Because of the Indian character of many Southeast Asian monuments, scholars hypothesized that Indian artists had constructed and decorated them and that Indians had colonized Southeast Asia. Today, researchers have concluded no Indian colonization occurred. The expansion of Indian culture to Southeast Asia during the first millennium CE was peaceful and nonimperialistic, a by-product of trade. In the early centuries CE, ships bringing trade goods from India and China to Rome passed through Southeast Asia on the monsoon winds. The local tribal chieftains quickly saw an opportunity to participate, mainly with their own forest products, such as aromatic woods, bird feathers, and spices. Accompanying the trade goods from India were Sanskrit, Buddhism, and Hinduism—and Buddhist and Hindu art. But the Southeast Asian peoples soon modified Indian art to make it their own. Art historians now recognize Southeast Asian art and architecture as a distinctive and multifaceted tradition.

relief (FIG. 15-17) in the Badami cave, but it is one of many examples of moveable images of deities created under the Chola kings and still used in Hindu rituals today. Here, Shiva dances as Nataraja ("Lord of the Dance") by balancing on one leg atop Apasmara, the dwarf of ignorance, which the god stamps out as he dances. Shiva extends all four arms, two of them touching the flaming *nimbus* ("light of glory") encircling him. These two upper hands also hold a small drum (right hand) and a flame (left hand). Shiva creates the universe to the drumbeat's rhythm. The small fire represents destruction. Shiva's lower left hand points to his upraised foot, indicating the foot as the place where devotees can find refuge and enlightenment. The god's lower right hand, raised in the abhaya mudra, tells worshipers to come forward without fear. As Shiva spins, his matted hair comes loose and spreads like a fan on both sides of his head.

At times, worshipers insert poles into the holes on the base of the Tamil Nadu Shiva to carry it, but even when stationary, the statuette would not appear as it does in FIG. 15-27. Rather, when Hindus worship the Shiva Nataraja, they dress the image, cover it with jewels, and garland it with flowers. The only bronze part visible is the face, marked with colored powders and scented pastes. Considered the embodiment of the deity, the image is not a symbol

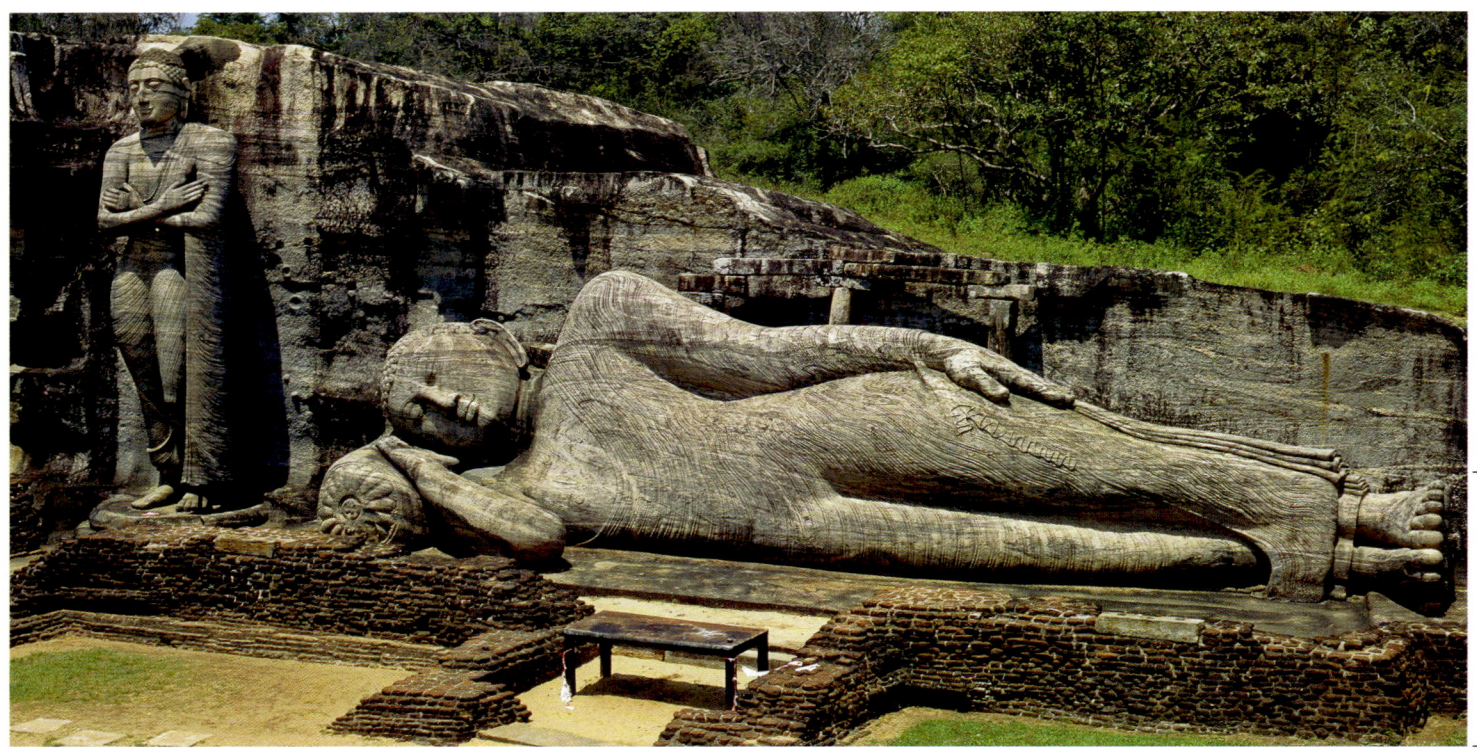

**15-28** *Death of the Buddha (Parinirvana)*, Gal Vihara, near Polonnaruwa, Sri Lanka, 11th to 12th century. Granulite, Buddha 10′ × 46′.

The sculptor of this colossal recumbent Sri Lankan Buddha emulated the classic Gupta style of a half millennium earlier in the figure's clinging robe, rounded face, and coiffure.

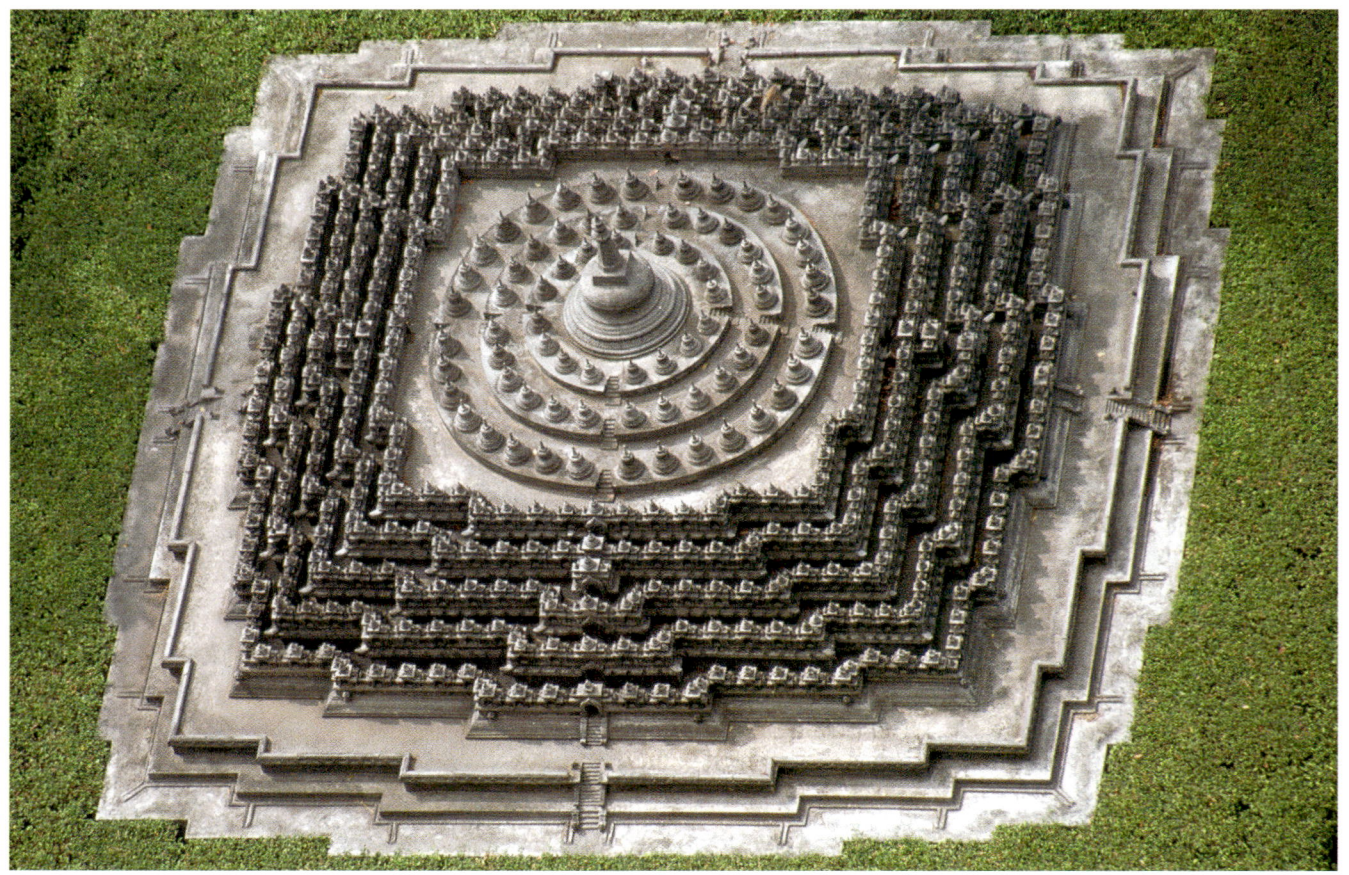

**15-29** Aerial view of Borobudur, Java, Indonesia, ca. 800.

Borobudur is a gigantic, unique Buddhist monument. Built on nine terraces with more than 1,500 stupas and 1,500 statues and reliefs, it takes the form of a cosmic mountain, which worshipers circumambulate.

## Sri Lanka

Sri Lanka (formerly Ceylon) is an island located at the very tip of the Indian subcontinent. Theravada Buddhism, the oldest form of Buddhism, stressing worship of the historical Buddha (Shakyamuni Buddha), arrived in Sri Lanka as early as the third century BCE. From there it spread to other parts of Southeast Asia. With the demise of Buddhism in India in about the 13th century, Sri Lanka now has the longest-lived Buddhist tradition in the world.

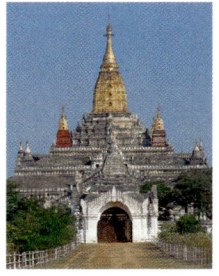

**GAL VIHARA** One of the largest sculptures in Southeast Asia is the 46-foot-long recumbent Buddha (FIG. **15-28**) carved out of a rocky outcropping at Gal Vihara in the 11th or 12th century. To the left of the Buddha, much smaller in scale, stands his cousin and chief disciple, Ananda, arms crossed, mourning Shakyamuni's death. (At about the same time, the Burmese built a temple [FIG. **15-28A**] in honor of Ananda at Bagan.) Although more than a half millennium later

15-28A Ananda Temple, Bagan, begun 1091.

in date, the Sri Lankan representation of the Buddha's parinirvana reveals its sculptor's debt to the classic Gupta sculptures of India, with their clinging garments, rounded faces, and distinctive renditions of hair (compare FIG. 15-13). Other Southeast Asian monuments, in contrast, exhibit a marked independence from Indian models.

## Java

On the island of Java, part of the modern nation of Indonesia, the period from the 8th to the 10th centuries brought construction of both Hindu and Buddhist monuments.

**BOROBUDUR** Unique in both form and meaning, Borobudur (FIG. **15-29**) is a Buddhist monument of colossal size, measuring about 400 feet per side at the base and about 98 feet tall. Built over a small hill on nine terraces accessed by four stairways aligned with the cardinal points, the structure contains literally millions of blocks of volcanic stone. Visitors ascending the massive monument on their way to the summit encounter more than 500 life-size Buddha images, at least 1,000 relief panels, and some 1,500 stupas of various sizes.

Scholars debate the intended meaning of Borobudur. Most think it is a constructed cosmic mountain, a three-dimensional mandala where worshipers pass through various realms on their way to ultimate enlightenment. As they circumambulate the structure, pilgrims first see reliefs illustrating the karmic effects of different kinds of human behavior, then reliefs depicting jatakas of the Buddha's earlier lives, and, farther up, events from the life of Shakyamuni. On the circular terraces near the summit, each stupa is hollow and houses

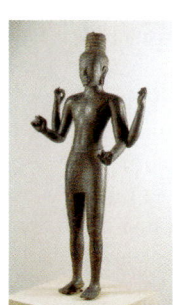

a statue of the seated Buddha, who has achieved spiritual enlightenment and preaches using the Wheel-turning mudra. At the very top is the largest, sealed stupa. It may once have contained another Buddha image, but it may also have been left empty to symbolize the formlessness of true enlightenment. Although scholars have interpreted the iconographic program in different ways, all agree on two essential points: that Borobudur is dependent on Indian art, literature, and religion, and that nothing comparable exists in India itself. Borobudur's sophistication, complexity, and originality underline how completely the

15-29A Bodhisattva Maitreya, Prakhon Chai, eighth to ninth century.

Javanese, and Southeast Asians in general, had absorbed, rethought, and reformulated Indian religion and art by 800. (In Thailand, for example, sculptors created a unique iconography for bodhisattvas [FIG. **15-29A**] combining Buddhist and Hindu elements.)

## Cambodia

In 802, at about the same time the Javanese built Borobudur, the Khmer king Jayavarman II (r. 802–850) founded the Angkor dynasty, which ruled Cambodia for the next 400 years and sponsored the construction of hundreds of monuments, including gigantic Buddhist monasteries (*wats*). For at least two centuries before the founding of Angkor, the Khmer (the predominant ethnic group in Cambodia) produced Indian-related sculpture of exceptional quality. Images of Vishnu were particularly important during the pre-Angkorian period.

**HARIHARA** A statue of Vishnu (FIG. **15-30**) from Prasat Andet shows the Hindu god in his manifestation as Harihara (Shiva-Vishnu). To represent Harihara, the sculptor divided the statue

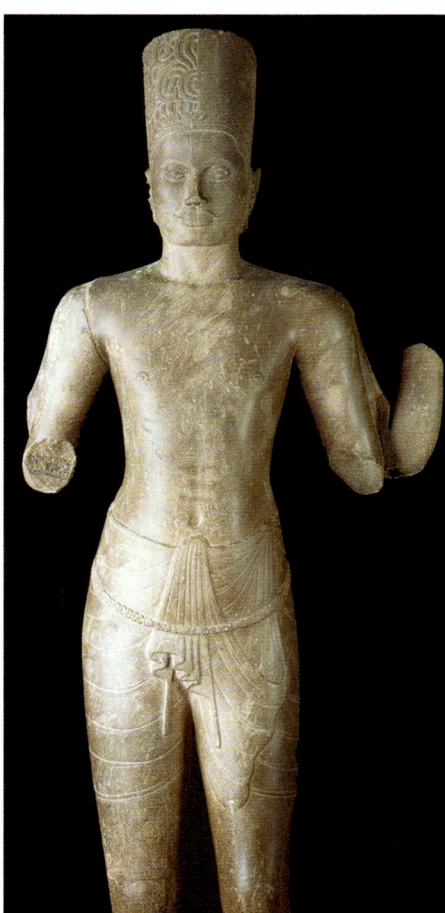

**15-30** Harihara, from Prasat Andet, Cambodia, early seventh century. Stone, 6′ 3″ high. National Museum, Phnom Penh.

Harihara is a composite of Shiva (the god's right side) and Vishnu (on the left). Stylistically indebted to Gupta sculpture, the Khmer statue is freestanding so that it could be viewed from all sides.

1 ft.

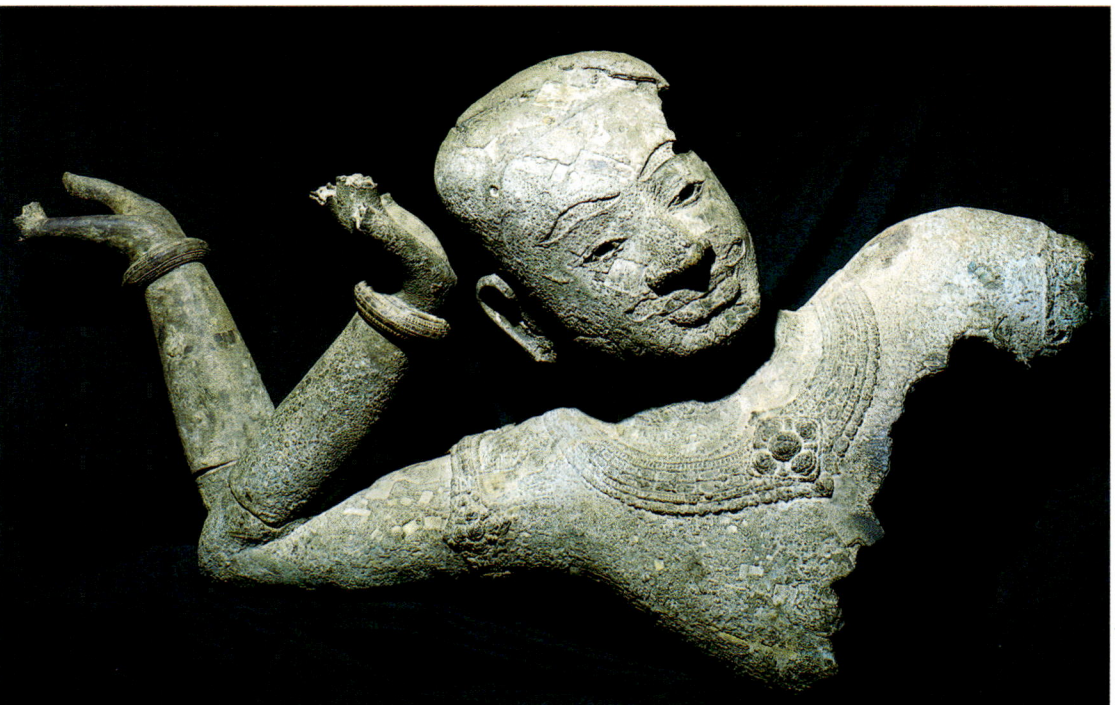

**15-31** *Vishnu Lying on the Cosmic Ocean,* from the Mebon Temple on an island in the western baray, Angkor, Cambodia, 11th century. Bronze, fragment 8′ long.

This fragmentary hollow-cast bronze statue was originally more than 20 feet long and inlaid with gold, silver, and jewels. It portrays Vishnu asleep on the cosmic ocean at the moment of the universe's creation.

1 ft.

vertically, with Shiva on the god's right side, Vishnu on his left. The tall headgear reflects the division most clearly. The Shiva half, embellished with the winding locks of an ascetic, contrasts with the kingly Vishnu's plain miter. Attributes (now lost) held in the four hands also helped differentiate the two sides. Stylistically, the Cambodian statue, like the Sri Lankan parinirvana group (FIG. 15-28), derives from Indian sculptures (FIG. 15-13) of Gupta style. But unlike almost all stone sculpture in India, carved in relief on slabs or stelae, this Khmer image is in the round. The Harihara's broken arms and ankles vividly attest to the vulnerability of this format. The Khmer sculptors, however, wanted their statues to be seen from all sides in the center of the garbha grihas of brick temples.

**VISHNU ON THE COSMIC OCEAN** The Khmer kings were exceedingly powerful and possessed enormous wealth. A now-fragmentary statue (FIG. **15-31**) portraying Vishnu lying on the cosmic ocean testifies to both the luxurious nature of much Khmer art and to the mastery of Khmer bronze-casters. The surviving portion is about 8 feet long. In complete form, at well over 20 feet long, the Vishnu statue was among the largest bronzes of the ancient and medieval worlds, surpassed only by such lost wonders as the statue of Athena (FIG. 5-46) in the Parthenon and the 120-foot-tall colossus of the Roman emperor Nero (see "The Golden House of Nero," Chapter 7, page 202). Originally, gold and silver inlays and jewels embellished the Vishnu image, and the god wore a separate miter on his head. The subject of the gigantic statue is the same as that carved in relief (FIG. 15-20) on the Deogarh Vishnu Temple. Vishnu lies asleep on the cosmic ocean at the moment of the creation of the universe. In the myth, a lotus stem grows from Vishnu's navel, its flower supporting Brahma, the creator god. In this statue, Vishnu probably had a waterspout emerging from his navel, indicating his ability to create the waters as well as to create Brahma and protect the earth. The statue occupied an island temple in the western *baray* (reservoir) of Angkor.

**ANGKOR WAT** For more than four centuries, successive kings worked on construction of the Angkor site. Founded by Indravarman (r. 877–889), Angkor is an engineering marvel, a vast complex of temples and palaces within a rectangular grid of canals and reservoirs fed by local rivers. Each of the Khmer kings built a temple mountain at Angkor and installed his personal god—Shiva, Vishnu, or the Buddha—on top and gave the god part of his own royal name, implying the king was a manifestation of the deity. When the king died, the Khmer believed the god reabsorbed him, because he had been the earthly portion of the deity during his lifetime, so they worshiped the king's image as the god. This concept of kingship approaches deification of the ruler, familiar in many other societies, such as pharaonic Egypt (see Chapter 3).

Of all the Khmer kings' monuments, Angkor Wat (FIG. **15-32**) is the most spectacular. Built by Suryavarman II (r. 1113–1150), it is the largest of the many Khmer temple complexes. Angkor Wat rises from a huge rectangle of land delineated by a moat measuring about 5,000 by 4,000 feet. Like the other Khmer temples, its purpose was to associate the king with his personal god, in this case Vishnu. The centerpiece of the complex is a tall stepped tower surrounded by four smaller towers connected by covered galleries. The five towers symbolize the five peaks of Mount Meru, the sacred mountain at the center of the universe. Two more circuit walls with galleries, towers, and gates enclose the central block. Thus, as one progresses inward through the complex, the towers rise ever higher, paralleling the towers of Khajuraho's Vishvanatha Temple (FIG. 15-24) but in a more complex sequence and on a much grander scale.

Throughout Angkor Wat, stone reliefs glorify both Vishnu in his various avatars and Suryavarman II. A relief (FIG. **15-33**) on the inner wall of the lowest gallery shows the king holding court. Suryavarman II sits on an elaborate wooden throne, its bronze legs rising as cobra heads. Kneeling retainers, smaller than the king because they are lesser figures in the Khmer hierarchy, hold a forest of umbrellas and fans, emblems of Suryavarman's exalted rank. In the reliefs of Angkor Wat, religion and politics are united.

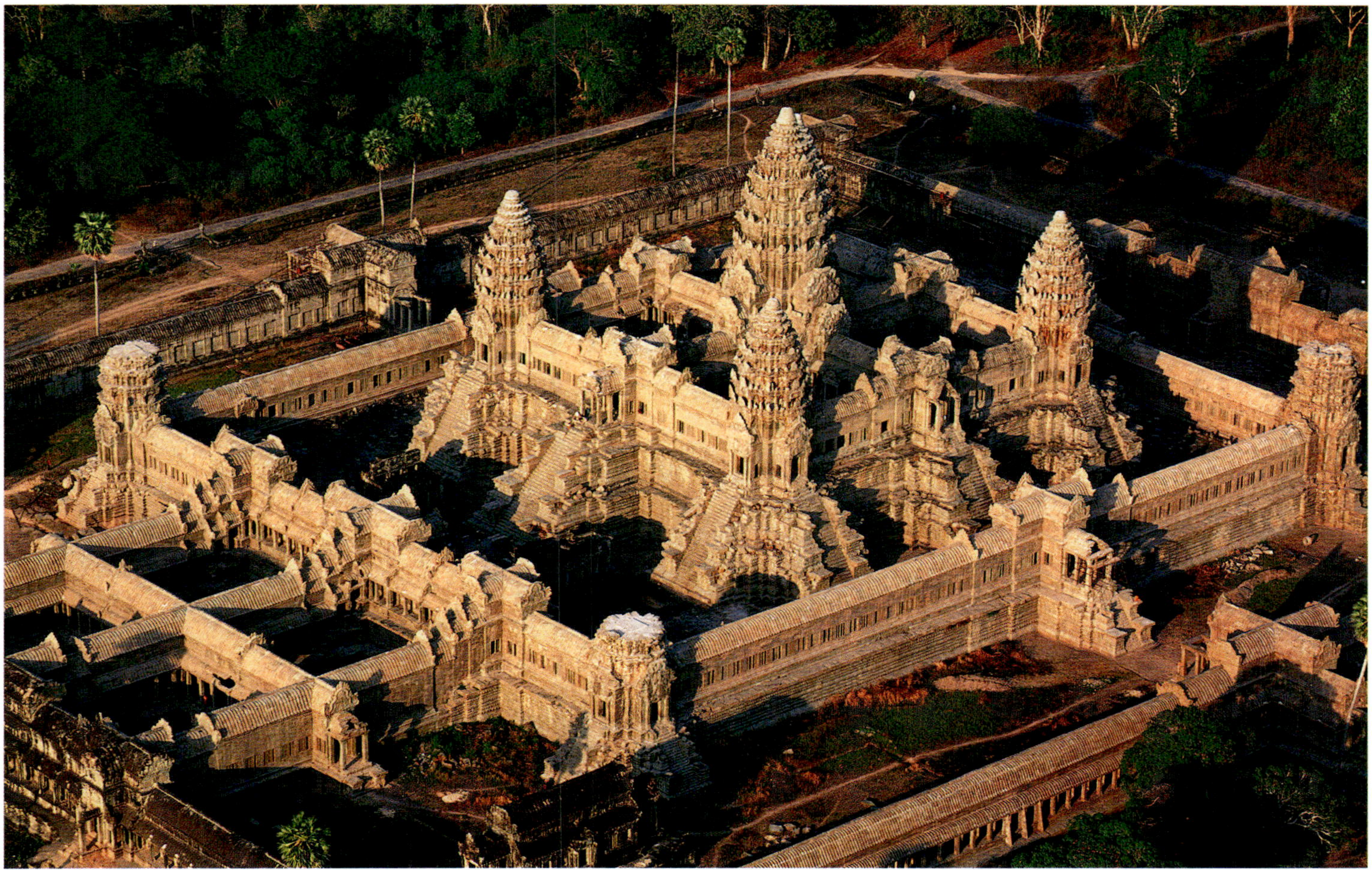

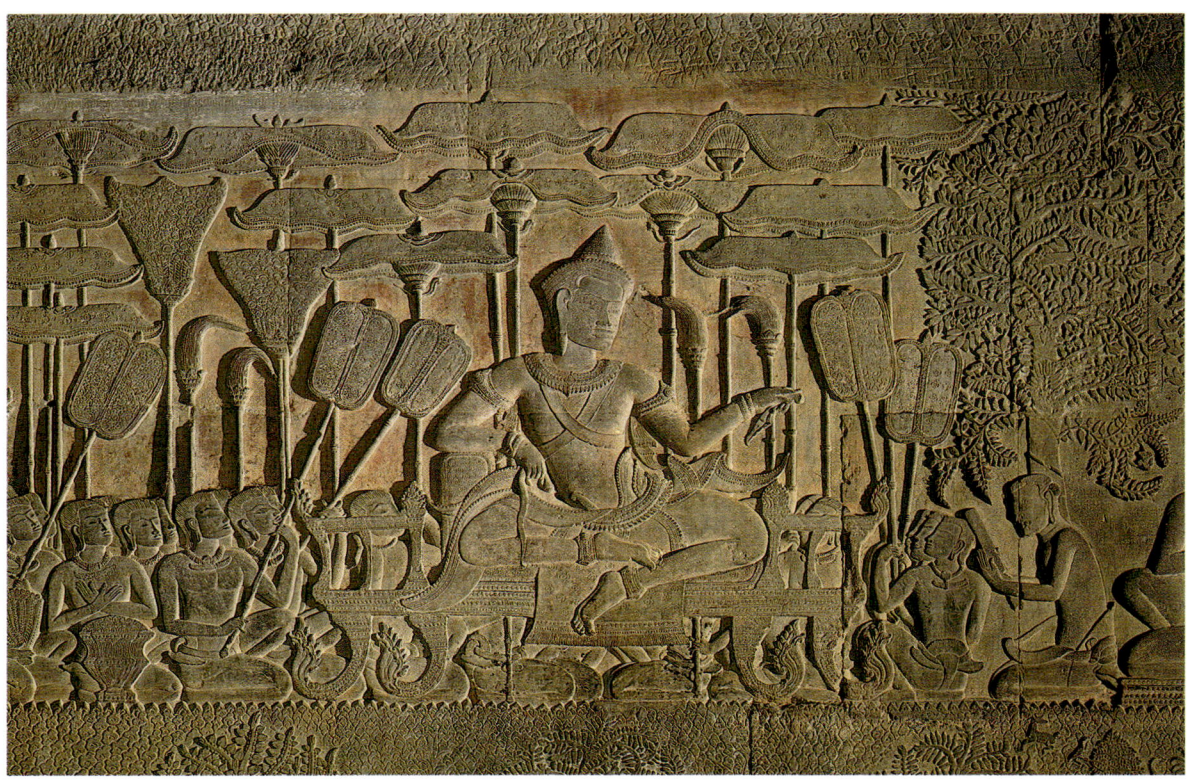

**15-32** Aerial view of Angkor Wat (looking northeast), Angkor, Cambodia, first half of 12th century.

Angkor Wat, built by Suryavarman II to associate the Khmer king with the god Vishnu, has five towers symbolizing the five peaks of Mount Meru, the sacred mountain at the center of the universe.

**15-33** King Suryavarman II holding court, detail of a stone relief, lowest gallery, south side, Angkor Wat, Angkor, Cambodia, first half of 12th century.

The reliefs of Angkor Wat glorify Vishnu in his various incarnations and Suryavarman II, whom the sculptor depicted holding court and surrounded by his attendants, all of smaller scale than the king.

**15-34** Towers of the Bayon, Angkor Thom, Cambodia, ca. 1200.

Jayavarman VII embraced Buddhism instead of Hinduism. His most important temple, the Bayon, has towers carved with giant faces probably depicting either the bodhisattva Lokeshvara or the king himself.

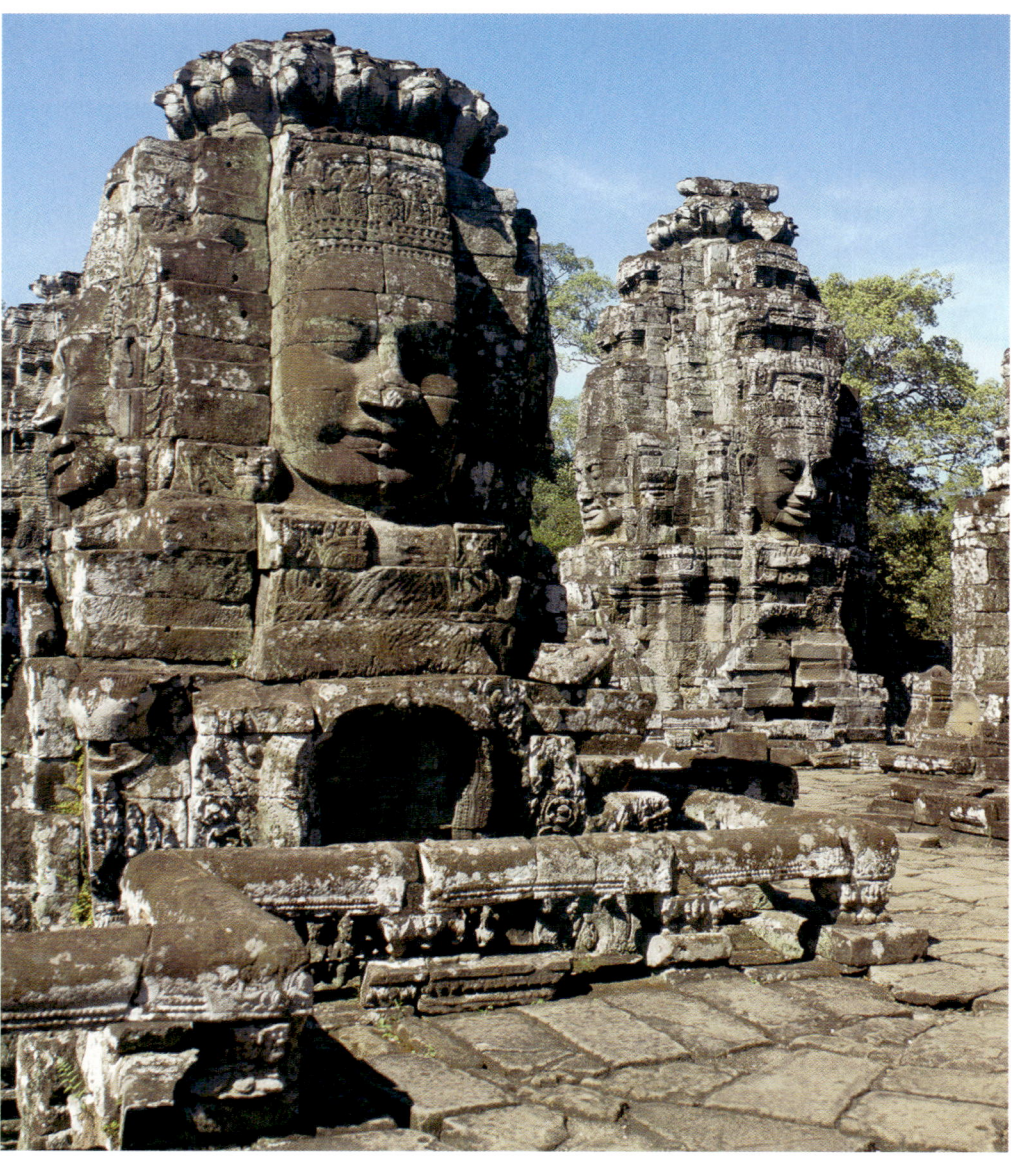

**BAYON** Jayavarman VII (r. 1181–1219), Suryavarman II's son, ruled over much of mainland Southeast Asia and built more during his reign than all the Khmer kings preceding him combined. His most important temple, the Bayon (FIG. **15-34**), is a complicated monument constructed with unique circular terraces surmounted by towers carved with giant faces. Jayavarman turned to Buddhism from the Hinduism the earlier Khmer rulers embraced, but he adapted his new creed to make the Buddha and the bodhisattva Lokeshvara ("Lord of the World") into divine prototypes of the king, in the Khmer tradition. The faces on the Bayon towers perhaps portray Lokeshvara, intended to indicate the watchful compassion emanating in all directions from the capital. Other researchers have proposed that the faces depict Jayavarman himself. The king's great experiment in religion and art was short-lived, but it also marked the point of change in Southeast Asia when Theravada Buddhism began to dominate most of the mainland. Chapter 32 chronicles this important development.

During the first to fourth centuries, Buddhism also spread to other parts of Asia—to China, Korea, and Japan. Although the artistic traditions in these countries differ greatly from one another, they share, along with Southeast Asia, a tradition of Buddhist art and an ultimate tie with India. Chapters 16 and 17 trace the changes Buddhist art underwent in East Asia, along with the region's other rich artistic traditions.

# SOUTH AND SOUTHEAST ASIA BEFORE 1200

## INDUS CIVILIZATION ca. 2600–1500 BCE

▎ One of the world's earliest civilizations arose in the Indus Valley in the third millennium BCE. Indus cities, such as Mohenjo-daro and Harappa, had streets oriented to the compass points and sophisticated water-supply and sewage systems.

▎ Little Indus art survives, mainly seals with incised designs and small-scale sculptures such as the statue of a priest-king from Mohenjo-daro. Indus sculptures have stylistic parallels with the art of Mesopotamia, with which the South Asian cities engaged in trade.

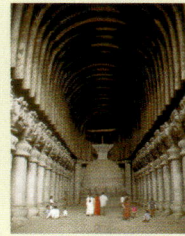

Robed male figure,
Mohenjo-daro, ca. 2600–1900 BCE

## MAURYA DYNASTY 323–185 BCE

▎ Chandragupta Maurya (r. 323–298 BCE), founder of the dynasty bearing his name, established his capital at Pataliputra in northeastern India and repelled the Greeks from South Asia in 305 BCE.

▎ The greatest Maurya ruler was Ashoka (r. 272–231 BCE), who converted to Buddhism and spread the Buddha's teaching throughout South Asia. Ashoka was the builder of the original Great Stupa at Sanchi and set up 30- to 40-foot-tall pillars with animal capitals throughout his kingdom. These columns, the first monumental stone artworks in India, owe a stylistic debt to Achaemenid Persian sculpture, but the iconography is Buddhist.

Lion capital of Ashoka,
Sarnath, ca. 250 BCE

## SHUNGA, ANDHRA, AND KUSHAN DYNASTIES ca. 185 BCE–320 CE

▎ The unifying characteristic of this age of regional dynasties in South Asia was the patronage of Buddhism. In addition to the stupa, the chief early type of Buddhist sacred architecture was the pillared rock-cut chaitya hall.

▎ The first representations of the Buddha in human form probably date to the first century CE. Gandharan Buddha statues owe a strong stylistic debt to Greco-Roman art.

▎ By the second century CE, the iconography of the life of the Buddha from his birth at Lumbini to his death at Kushinagara was well established.

Chaitya hall, Karle,
ca. 50 CE

## GUPTA AND POST-GUPTA PERIODS ca. 320–647

▎ Gupta sculptors formulated the canonical Buddha image in the fifth century, combining Gandharan iconography with a soft, full-bodied figure in clinging garments.

▎ The Gupta-period Buddhist caves of Ajanta are the best surviving examples of early mural painting in India.

▎ The oldest Hindu monumental stone temples and sculptures date to the fifth and sixth centuries, including the rock-cut reliefs of Udayagiri, Badami, and Elephanta, and the Vishnu Temple at Deogarh.

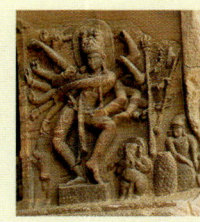

Dancing Shiva, Badami,
late sixth century

## MEDIEVAL PERIOD 7th to 12th Centuries

▎ Several distinctive South Asian regional styles emerged in Hindu religious architecture during the medieval period. Northern temples, such as the Vishvanatha Temple at Khajuraho, feature a series of small towers leading to a tall beehive-shaped tower, or shikhara, over the garbha griha. Southern temples, such as the Rajarajeshvara Temple at Thanjavur, have flat-roofed pillared halls (mandapas) leading to a pyramidal tower (vimana).

▎ In Southeast Asia, medieval art and architecture reflect Indian prototypes, but many local styles developed. The most distinctive monuments of the period are Borobudur on Java and the temples of the Khmer kings at Angkor in Cambodia.

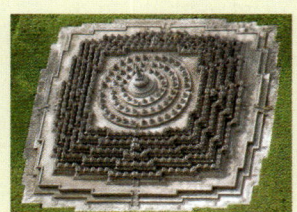

Borobudur, Java, ca. 800

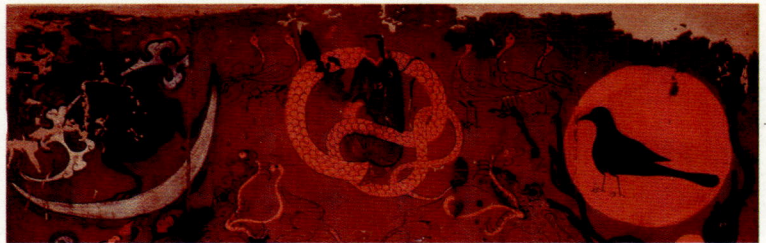

The tomb of the marquise of Dai contained many treasures, most notably a T-shaped painted silk banner draped over her coffin. The upper part represents Heaven, with the silvery moon and red sun.

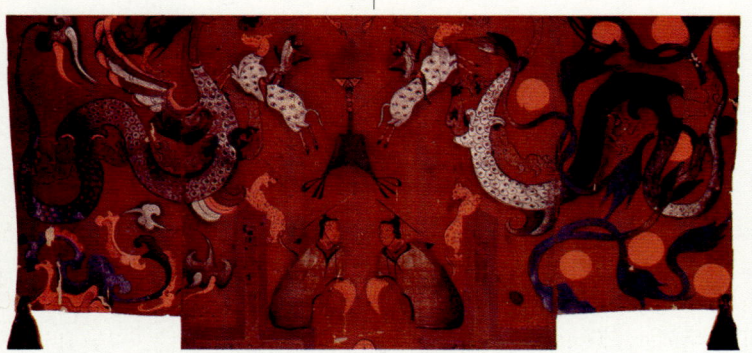

In the celestial realm at the top of the T, between and below the two heavenly orbs—the moon and its symbol, the toad, and the sun and its symbol, the raven—are dragons and immortal beings.

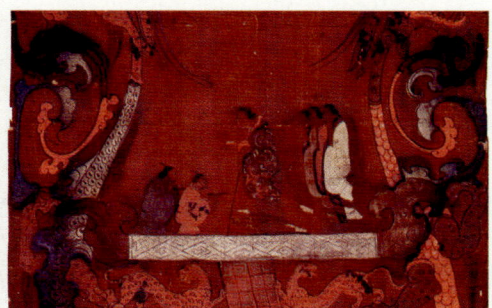

At the center of the vertical section of the banner, the standing figure on the first white platform is probably the marquise of Dai, awaiting her ascent to Heaven, where she can gain immortality.

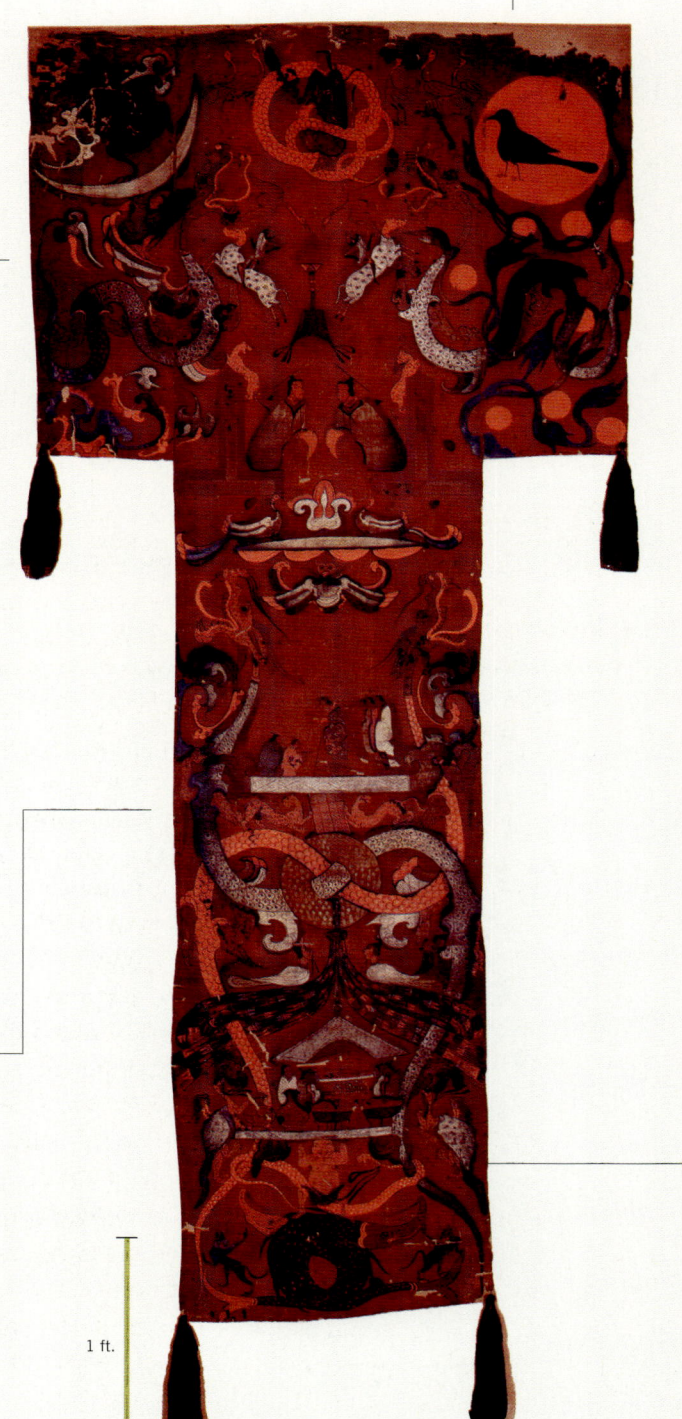

1 ft.

**16-1** Funeral banner, from tomb 1 (tomb of the marquise of Dai), Mawangdui, China, Han dynasty, ca. 168 BCE. Painted silk, 6′ 8¾″ × 3′ ¼″. Hunan Provincial Museum, Changsha.

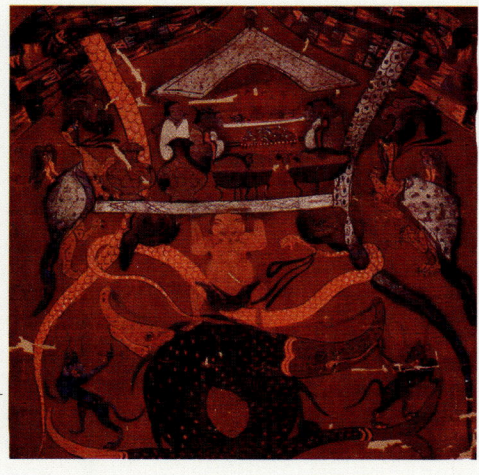

The lowest portion of the banner found in the marquise's tomb depicts the noblewoman's funeral. The two representations of her are among the earliest portraits in Chinese art.

# CHINA AND KOREA TO 1279

## CHINESE SILK FOR THE AFTERLIFE

In 1972, archaeologists excavated the tomb of the marquise of Dai at Mawangdui. The tomb contained a rich array of goods for use during burial ceremonies and to accompany the noblewoman into the afterlife. Among the finds were decorated lacquer utensils, rich textiles, and an astonishingly well-preserved corpse in the innermost of four nested *sarcophagi*. Most remarkable, however, was the discovery of a painted T-shaped silk banner (FIG. **16-1**) draped over the marquise's coffin.

Silk is the finest natural fabric ever produced. It comes from the cocoons of caterpillars called silkworms. The manufacture of silk was a well-established industry in China by the second millennium BCE. Silk farmers raise silkworms from eggs, which they place in trays. The farmers also must grow mulberry trees or purchase mulberry leaves, the silkworms' only food source. The silkworms form cocoons out of very fine filaments they extrude as liquid from their bodies. The filaments soon solidify with exposure to air. Before the transformed caterpillars emerge as moths and badly damage the silk, the farmers kill them with steam or high heat. They soften the cocoons in hot water and unwind the filaments onto a reel. The filaments are so fine that workers generally unwind the threads from five to ten cocoons together to bond into a single strand while the filaments are still soft and sticky. Later, the silk workers twist several strands together to form a thicker yarn and then weave the yarn on a loom to produce silk cloth. Both the yarn and the cloth can be dyed, and the silk fabric can be decorated by weaving threads of different colors together in special patterns (*brocades*) or by stitching in threads of different colors (*embroidery*). Greatly admired, Chinese silk and the secrets of its production gradually spread across the ancient world along what came to be called the Silk Road (see "The Silk Road," page 458).

The marquise's funerary banner is an early masterpiece of painting on silk. Scholars generally agree the area within the cross at the top of the T represents Heaven. Most of the vertical section below is the human realm. At the very bottom is the Underworld. In the heavenly realm, dragons and immortal beings appear between and below two orbs—the red sun and its symbol, the raven, on the right, and the silvery moon and its symbol, the toad, on the left. Below, the standing figure on the first white platform near the center of the vertical section is probably the marquise of Dai herself—one of the first portraits in Chinese art. The woman awaits her ascent to Heaven, where she can attain immortality. Nearer the bottom, the artist depicted her funeral. Between these two sections are two intertwining dragons. Their tails reach down to the Underworld and their heads point to Heaven, unifying the entire composition.

# CHINA

East Asia is a vast area, varied both topographically and climatically. Dominated by the huge land mass of China, the region also encompasses the peninsula of Korea and the islands of Japan (MAP 16-1). China's landscape includes sandy plains, mighty rivers, towering mountains, and fertile farmlands. Its political and cultural boundaries have varied over the millennia, and at times it has grown geographically to about twice the area of the United States, encompassing Tibet, Chinese Turkestan (Xinjiang), Mongolia, Manchuria, and parts of Korea. China boasts the world's largest population and is ethnically diverse. The spoken language varies so much that speakers of different dialects do not understand one another. The written language, however, which employs *characters* (signs recording spoken words, even if those words are spoken differently in the various dialects), has made possible a shared Chinese literary, philosophic, and religious tradition.

## Neolithic Age

Discoveries in recent decades have expanded the already rich Chinese archaeological record enormously and have provided evidence of settled village life as far back as the seventh or early sixth millennium BCE. Excavators have uncovered Neolithic sites with large multifamily houses constructed of wood, bamboo, wattle, daub, and mud plaster and equipped with hearths. These early villages

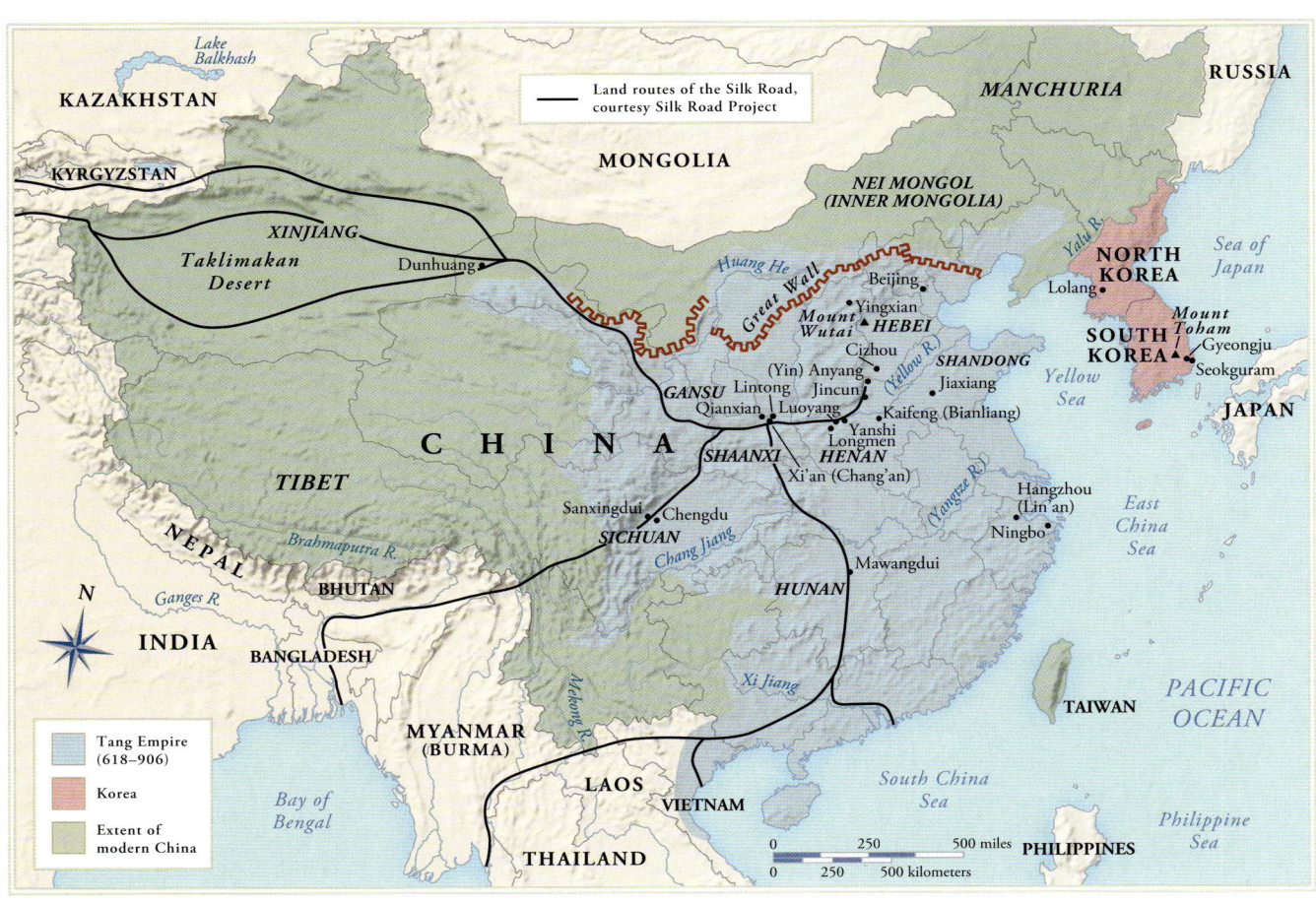

**MAP 16-1** China during the Tang dynasty.

# CHINA AND KOREA TO 1279

| | Neolithic to Shang | | Zhou and Qin | | Han and Period of Disunity | | | Tang | | Song and Liao | |
|---|---|---|---|---|---|---|---|---|---|---|---|
| 7000 | | 1500 | 1050 | | 206 | 581 | 618 | | 907 | | 1279 |

BCE | CE

- Chinese ceramists produce sophisticated pottery before the invention of the potter's wheel
- Shang artists perfect the piece-mold technique of bronze-casting

- Zhou artists excel in fashioning luxurious objects in bronze, lacquer, and jade
- The First Emperor of Qin builds an immense burial mound guarded by 6,000 terracotta soldiers

- Han buildings feature interlocking clusters of wooden brackets
- Earliest Chinese image of the Buddha, 338 CE
- Xie He formulates "Six Canons" of Chinese painting, early sixth century

- Chang'an, the Tang capital, is the most magnificent city in the world
- Golden age of Chinese painting on silk scrolls
- Major sculpted and painted Buddhist temples

- China becomes the world's most technologically advanced society
- Apogee of landscape painting under the Song emperors
- Liao dynasty builds the world's tallest wooden building

## Chinese Earthenwares and Stonewares

China has no rival in the combined length and richness of its ceramic history. Beginning with the makers of the earliest pots in prehistoric villages (FIG. 16-2), ancient Chinese potters showed a flair for shaping carefully prepared and kneaded clay into diverse, often dramatic and elegant vessel forms. Until Chinese potters developed true *porcelains* (extremely fine, hard white ceramics; see "Chinese Porcelain," Chapter 33, page 997) around 1300, they produced only two types of clay vessels or objects—earthenwares and stonewares. For both types, potters used clays colored by mineral impurities, especially iron compounds ranging from yellow to brownish-black.

The clay bodies of *earthenwares* (FIG. 16-2), fired at low temperatures in open pits or simple kilns, remain soft and porous, thus allowing liquids to seep through. Chinese artists also used the low-fire technique to produce terracotta sculptures, even life-size figures of humans and animals (FIG. 16-6). Over time, Chinese potters developed kilns enabling them to fire their clay vessels at much higher temperatures—more than 2,000 degrees Fahrenheit. These elevated temperatures produce *stonewares,* named for their stone-like hardness and density.

Potters in China excelled at the various techniques commonly used to decorate earthenwares and stonewares. Most of these decorative methods depend on changes occurring in the kiln to chemical compounds found in clay as natural impurities. When fired, many compounds change color dramatically, depending on the conditions in the kiln. For example, if little oxygen remains in a hot kiln, iron oxide (rust) turns either gray or brownish-black, whereas an abundance of oxygen produces a reddish hue (see "Greek Vase Painting," Chapter 5, page 110).

Chinese potters also decorated vessels simply by painting their surfaces. In one of the oldest decorative techniques, the potters applied *slip* (a mixture of clay and water like a fine, thin mud)—by painting, pouring, or dipping—to a clay body not yet fully dry. The natural varieties of clay produced a broad, if not bright, range of colors, as seen in Neolithic vessels (FIG. 16-2). But Chinese potters often added compounds such as iron oxide to the slip to change or intensify the colors. After the vessels had partially dried, the potters could incise lines through the slip down to the clay body to produce designs such as those seen in later Chinese stonewares (FIG. 16-21). Chinese artists also inlaid designs, carving them into plain vessel surfaces and then filling them with slip or soft clay of a contrasting color. These techniques spread throughout East Asia (FIG. 16-29).

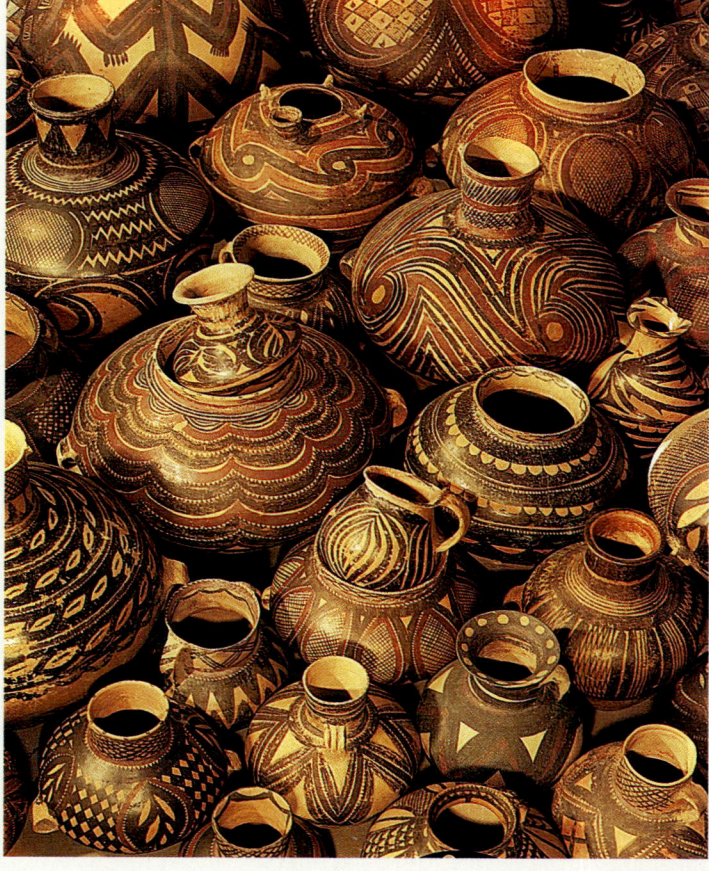

**16-2** Yangshao Culture vases, from Gansu Province, China, mid-third millennium BCE.

Chinese artists produced vessels of many different shapes even before the invention of the potter's wheel and decorated them with abstract motifs in red and brownish-black on a cream-colored ground.

To produce a hard, glassy surface after firing, potters coated plain or decorated vessels with a *glaze,* a finely ground mixture of minerals. They often used clear or highly translucent glazes, but opaque, richly colored glazes also became common. Sometimes painters allowed the thick glazes to run down the side of a vase or a figurine (FIG. 16-18) to produce dramatic effects.

also had pens for domesticated animals, kilns for pottery production, pits for storage and refuse, and cemeteries for the dead. Chinese Neolithic artisans produced impressive artworks, especially from jade and clay.

**YANGSHAO POTTERY** Mastery of the art of pottery occurred at a very early date in China. The potters of the Yangshao Culture, which arose along the Yellow River in northeastern China, produced fine decorated *earthenware* bowls (see "Chinese Earthenwares and Stonewares," above) even before the invention of the potter's wheel in the fourth millennium BCE. In the third millennium, the Yangshao potters of Gansu Province formed by hand and then painted vessels (FIG. 16-2) of astonishing sophistication. The multiplicity of shapes suggests the vessels served a wide variety of functions in daily life, but most of the finds come from graves. Decoration is in red and brownish-black on a cream-colored ground. Some pots and bowls include stylized animal motifs, but most feature abstract designs. The painters reveal a highly refined aesthetic sensibility, effectively integrating a variety of angular and curvilinear geometric motifs, including stripes, zigzags, lozenges, circles, spirals, and waves.

## Shang Bronze-Casting

A mong the finest bronzes of the second millennium BCE are those that Shang artists created using piece molds. The Shang bronze-workers began the process by producing a solid clay model of the desired object. When the model dried to durable hardness, they pressed damp clay around it to form a mold that hardened but remained somewhat flexible. At that point, they carefully cut the mold in pieces, removed the pieces from the model, and baked the pieces in a kiln to form hard earthenware sections. Sculptors then carved the intricate details of the relief decoration into the inner surfaces of the piece molds. Next, the artists shaved the model to reduce its size to form a core for the piece mold. They next reassembled the mold around the model using bronze spacers to preserve a void between the model and the mold—a space equivalent to the layer of wax used in the lost-wax method (see "Hollow-Casting Life-Size Bronze Statues," Chapter 5, page 130). The Shang bronze-casters then added a final clay layer on the outside to hold everything together, leaving open ducts for pouring molten bronze into the space between the model and the mold and for venting gases. Once the mold cooled, they broke it apart, removed the new bronze vessel, and cleaned and polished it.

Shang bronzes show mastery in casting rivaling that of any other ancient civilization. The great numbers of cast-bronze vessels strongly suggest well-organized workshops. Shang bronzes held wine, water, grain, or meat for sacrificial rites. Each vessel's shape matched its intended purpose. All feature surfaces densely covered with abstract and animal motifs. On the guang illustrated here (FIG. 16-3), the multiple designs and their fields of background spirals integrate so closely with the form of the libation-pouring vessel that they are not merely an external embellishment but an

**16-3** Guang, probably from Anyang, China, Shang dynasty, 12th or 11th century BCE. Bronze, 6½″ high. Asian Art Museum of San Francisco (Avery Brundage Collection).

Shang artists perfected casting elaborate bronze vessels covered with animal motifs. The animal forms, real and imaginary, on this libation guang are probably connected with the world of spirits.

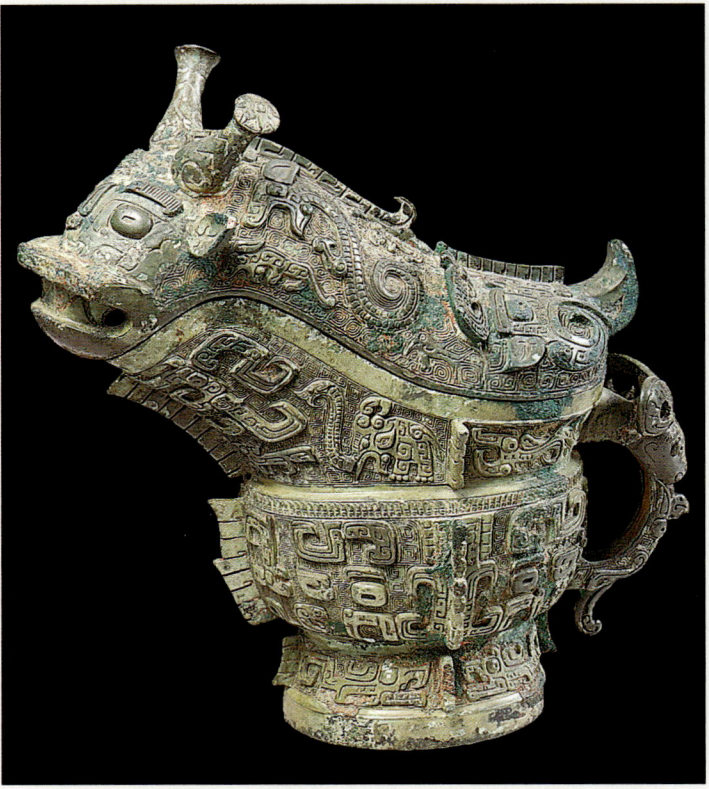

1 in.

integral part of the sculptural whole. Some motifs on the guang's side may represent the eyes of a tiger and the horns of a ram. A horned animal forms the front of the lid, and at the rear is a horned head with a bird's beak. Another horned head appears on the handle. Fish, birds, elephants, rabbits, and more abstract composite creatures swarm over the surface against a background of spirals. The fabulous animal forms, real and imaginary, on Shang bronzes are unlikely to have been purely decorative. They probably inhabit the world of spirits addressed in the rituals.

## Shang Dynasty and Sanxingdui

During the past century, archaeologists have begun to confirm the existence of China's earliest royal dynasties, long thought to have been mythical. In 1959, for example, at Yanshi in Henan Province, excavators found what they believe to be traces of the Xia (ca. 2000–1600 BCE), China's oldest dynasty. Much better documented, however, is the Shang dynasty (ca. 1600–1050 BCE), the first great Chinese dynasty of the Bronze Age. The Shang kings ruled from a series of royal capitals in the Yellow River valley and vied for power and territory with the rulers of neighboring states. In 1928, excavations at Anyang (ancient Yin) brought to light the last Shang capital. There, archaeologists found a large number of objects—turtle shells, animal bones, and bronze containers—inscribed in the earliest form of the Chinese language. These fragmentary records and the other finds at Anyang provide important information about the

Shang kings and their affairs. They reveal a warlike, highly stratified society. Walls of pounded earth protected Shang cities. Servants, captives, and even teams of charioteers with chariots and horses accompanied Shang kings to their tombs, a practice also documented in Mesopotamia at the Royal Cemetery at Ur (see Chapter 2).

The excavated tomb furnishings include weapons and a great wealth of objects in jade, ivory, lacquer, and bronze. Not only the kings received lavish burials. The tomb of Fu Hao, the wife of Wu Ding (r. ca. 1215–1190 BCE), contained an ivory beaker inlaid with turquoise and more than a thousand jade and bronze objects. The Chinese used many of the vessels found in Shang tombs, for example, the guang (FIG. 16-3), shaped like a covered gravy boat, in sacrifices to ancestors and in funerary ceremonies. In some cases families set up shrines for ancestor worship above the burial sites. Shang artists cast their elaborate bronze vessels in piece molds (see "Shang Bronze-Casting," above).

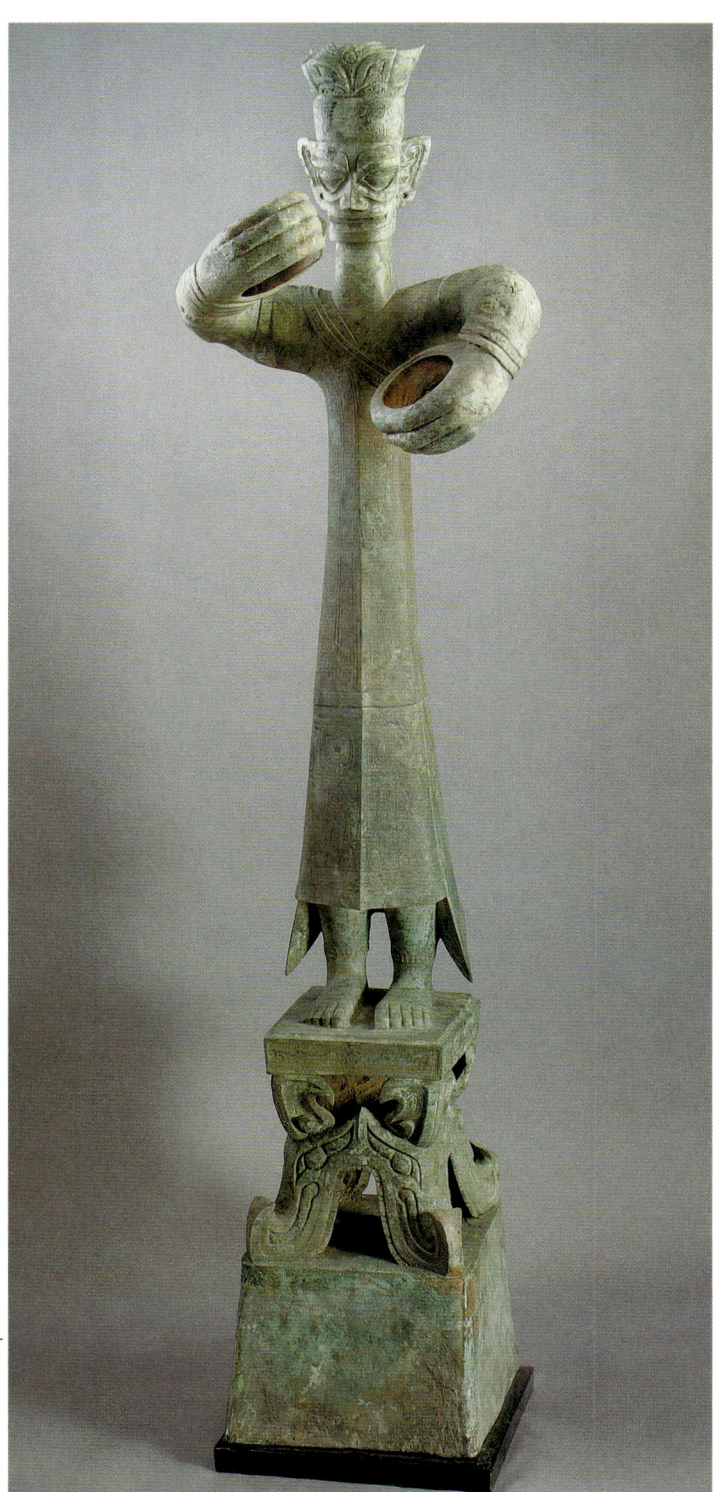

1 ft.

**16-4** Standing male figure, from pit 2, Sanxingdui, China, ca. 1200–1050 BCE. Bronze, 8′ 5″ high, including base. Museum, Sanxingdui.

Excavations at Sanxingdui have revealed a civilization contemporaneous with the Shang but with a different artistic aesthetic. This over-life-size statue has elongated proportions and large, staring eyes.

**SANXINGDUI** Recent excavations in other regions of China have greatly augmented historical understanding of the Bronze Age. They suggest that at the same time Anyang flourished under its Shang rulers in northern China, so did other major cen-

ters with distinct aesthetic traditions. In 1986, pits at Sanxingdui, near Chengdu in southwestern China, yielded a treasure of elephant tusks and objects in gold, bronze, jade, and clay of types never before discovered. They attest to an independent kingdom of enormous wealth contemporaneous with the better-known Shang dynasty.

The most dramatic find at Sanxingdui was a bronze statue (FIG. **16-4**) more than 8 feet tall. Chinese representations of the human figure on this scale are otherwise unknown at this early date. The Sanxingdui statue matches anything from Anyang in masterful casting technique. Very different in subject and style from the Shang bronzes, the over-life-size bronze figure initially shocked art historians who had formed their ideas about Bronze Age Chinese aesthetics based solely on Shang material. The figure—of unknown identity—is highly stylized, with elongated proportions and large, staring eyes. It stands on a base composed of four legs formed of fantastic animal heads with horns and trunklike snouts. The statue tapers gently as it rises, and the figure gradually becomes rounder. Just below the neck, great arms branch dramatically outward, ending in oversized hands that once held an object, most likely one of the many elephant tusks buried in pit 2 with the bronze statue. Surface decorations of squared spirals and hook-pointed curves are all that link this monumental statue with the small-scale and intricate Shang piece-mold bronze vessels (FIG. 16-3). Systematic excavations and chance finds will probably produce more surprises in the future and cause art historians to revise once again their picture of Chinese art in the second half of the second millennium BCE.

## Zhou Dynasty

Around 1050 BCE, the Zhou, former vassals of the Shang, captured Anyang and overthrew their Shang overlords. The Zhou dynasty proved to be the longest lasting in China's history—so long historians divide the Zhou era into two periods: Western Zhou (ca. 1050–771 BCE) and Eastern Zhou (770–256 BCE). The dividing event is the transfer of the Zhou capital from Chang'an (modern Xi'an) in the west to Luoyang in the east. The closing centuries of Zhou rule include a long period of warfare among competing states (Warring States Period, ca. 475–221 BCE). The Zhou fell to one of these states, the Qin, in 256 BCE.

**ZHOU JADE** Under the Zhou, the development of markets and the introduction of bronze coinage brought heightened prosperity and a taste for lavish products, such as bronzes inlaid with gold and silver. Late Zhou bronzes feature scenes of hunting, religious rites, and magic practices. These may relate to the subjects and compositions of lost paintings mentioned in Zhou literature. Other materials favored in the late Zhou period were *lacquer,* a varnish-like substance made from the sap of the Asiatic sumac, used to decorate wood furniture and other objects (see "Lacquered Wood," Chapter 33, page 995, and FIG. 33-8), and jade (see "Chinese Jade," page 454).

The manufacture of jade objects for burial with the dead, beginning in Neolithic times, reached a peak of technical perfection during the Zhou dynasty. Among the most common finds in tombs of the period are *bi* disks (FIG. **16-5**)—thin, flat circular pieces of jade with a hole in the center, which may have symbolized the circle of Heaven. Bi disks were status symbols in life as well as treasured items the dead took with them to the afterlife. After a battle, for example, the victors forced their defeated foes to relinquish their bi disks as symbols of their submission. The disks also had high monetary value.

## Chinese Jade

The Chinese first used jade—or more precisely, nephrite—for artworks and ritual objects in the Neolithic period. Nephrite polishes to a more lustrous, slightly buttery finish than jadeite (the stone Chinese sculptors preferred from the 18th century on), which is quite glassy. Both stones are beautiful, come in colors other than the well-known green, and are tough, hard, and heavy. In China, those qualities became metaphors for the fortitude and moral perfection of superior persons. The Chinese also believed jade possessed magical qualities that could protect the dead. In one Han dynasty tomb, for example, archaeologists discovered the bodies of a prince and princess dressed in suits composed of more than 2,000 jade pieces sewn together with gold wire.

Because of its extreme hardness, jade could not be carved with the Neolithic sculptor's stone tools. Researchers have speculated on how these early artists were able to cut, shape, and incise the nephrite objects found at many Neolithic Chinese sites. The sculptors probably used cords embedded with sand to incise lines into the surfaces. Sand placed in a bamboo tube drill could perforate the hard stone, but the process would have been long and arduous, requiring great patience as well as superior skill.

Even after the invention of bronze tools, Chinese sculptors still had to rely on grinding and abrasion rather than simple drilling and chiseling to produce their intricately shaped, pierced, and engraved works. An example is the *bi* (FIG. 16-5) shown here, said to have come from a royal Eastern Zhou tomb at Jincun. Rows of raised spirals, created by laborious grinding and polishing, decorate the disk itself. Within the inner circle and around the outer edge of the bi are elegant dragons. The Chinese thought dragons inhabited the water and flew between Heaven and Earth, bringing rain, so these animals long have been symbols of good fortune in East Asia. They also symbolized the rulers' power to mediate between Heaven and Earth. To sculpt the dragons on the bi from Jincun required long hours of work to pierce through the hard jade. The bi testifies to the Zhou sculptor's mastery of this difficult material.

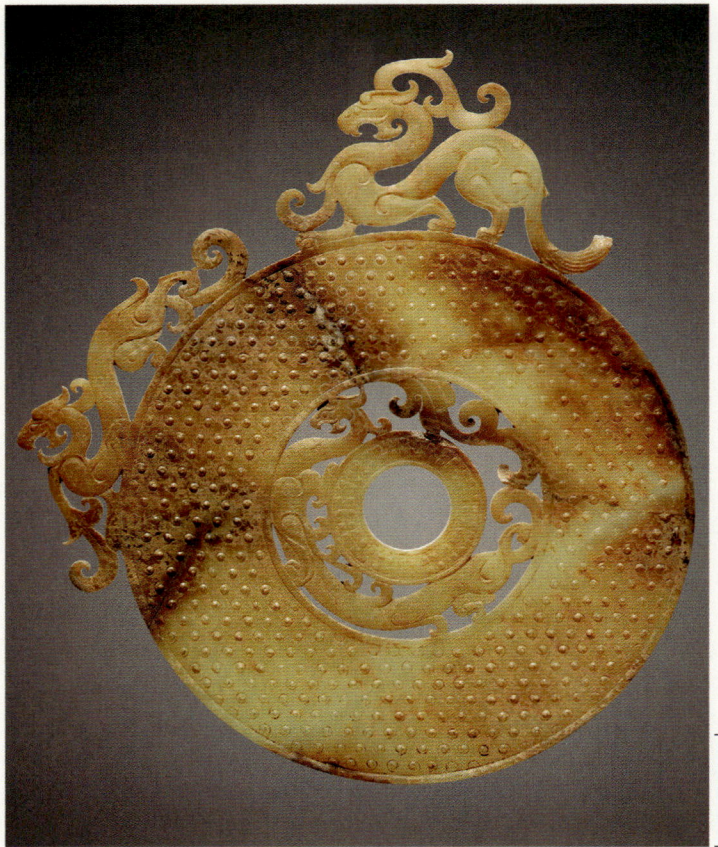

1 in.

**16-5** Bi disk with dragons, from Jincun(?), near Luoyang, China, Eastern Zhou dynasty, fourth to third century BCE. Nephrite, 6½″ in diameter. Nelson-Atkins Museum of Art, Kansas City.

This intricately shaped jade bi required hours of grinding, piercing, engraving, and polishing to produce. Dragons were Chinese symbols of good fortune and flew between Heaven and Earth.

## Qin Dynasty

During the Warring States Period, China endured more than two centuries of political and social turmoil. This was also a time of intellectual and artistic upheaval, when conflicting schools of philosophy, including Legalism, Daoism, and Confucianism, emerged. Order was finally restored when the powerful armies of the ruler of the state of Qin (from which the modern name "China" derives) conquered all rival states. Known to history by his title, Qin Shi Huangdi (First Emperor of Qin), between 221 and 210 BCE he controlled an area equal to about half of modern China, much larger than the territories of any of the earlier Chinese dynasties. During his reign, Shi Huangdi ordered the linkage of active fortifications along the northern border of his realm to form the famous Great Wall. The wall defended China against the fierce nomadic peoples of the north, especially the Huns, who eventually made their way to eastern Europe. By sometimes brutal methods, the First Emperor

consolidated rule through a centralized bureaucracy and adopted standardized written language, weights and measures, and coinage. He also repressed all schools of thought other than Legalism, which espoused absolute obedience to the state's authority and advocated strict laws and punishments. Chinese historians have harshly condemned the First Emperor, but the bureaucratic system he put in place long outlasted his reign. Its success was due in large part to Shi Huangdi's decision to replace the feudal lords with talented salaried administrators and to reward merit rather than to favor high birth.

**TERRACOTTA ARMY, LINTONG** In 1974, excavations started at the site of the immense burial mound of the First Emperor of Qin at Lintong. For its construction, the ruler conscripted more than 700,000 laborers, and the project continued after his death. The mound itself remains unexcavated, but archae-

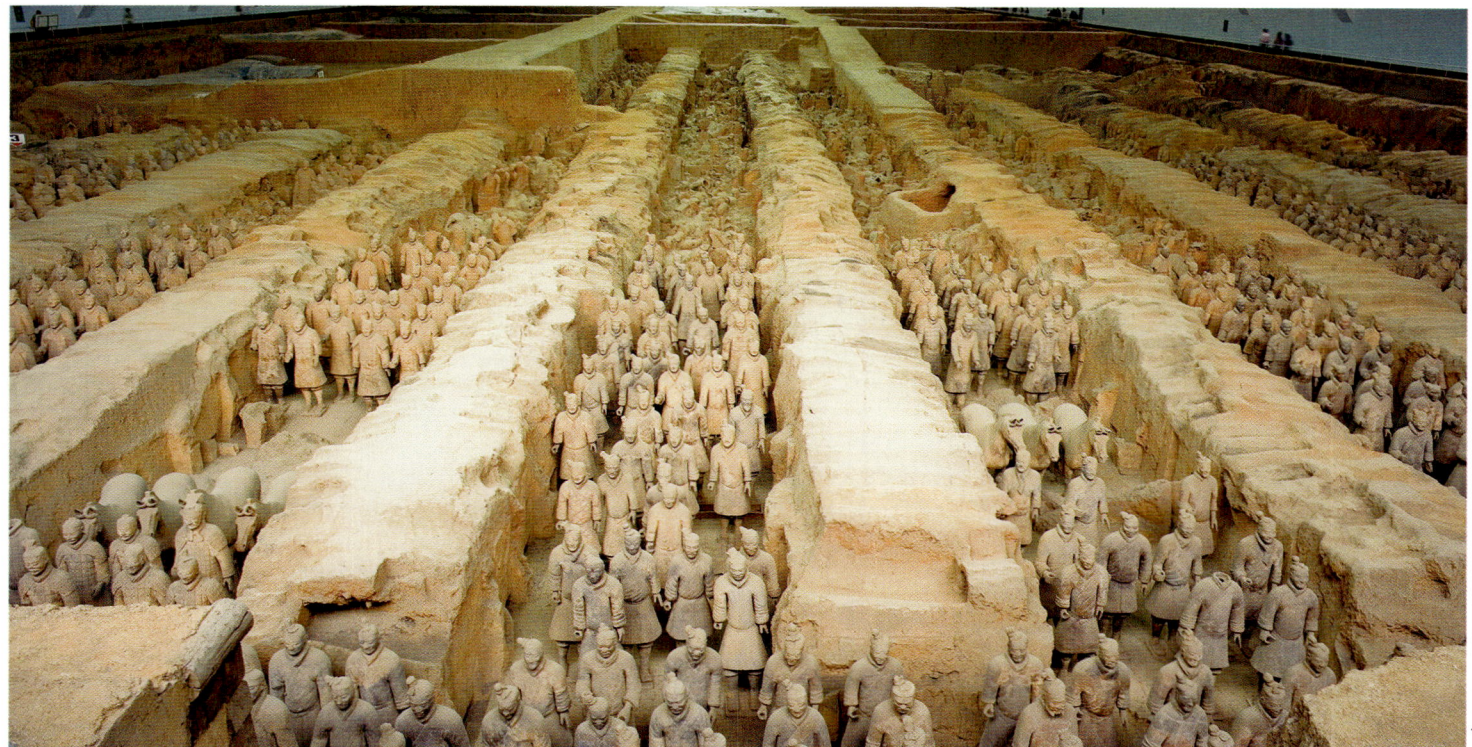

**16-6** Army of the First Emperor of Qin in pits next to his burial mound, Lintong, China, Qin dynasty, ca. 210 BCE. Painted terracotta, average figure 5′ 10⅞″ high. ◼◀

The First Emperor was buried beneath an immense mound guarded by more than 6,000 life-size terracotta soldiers. Although produced from common molds, every figure has an individualized appearance.

ologists believe it contains a vast treasure-filled underground funerary palace designed to match the fabulous palace the emperor occupied in life. The historian Sima Qian (136–85 BCE) described both palaces, but scholars did not take his account seriously until the discovery of pits around the tomb containing more than 6,000 life-size painted terracotta figures (FIG. **16-6**) of soldiers and horses, as well as bronze horses and chariots. The terracotta army served as the First Emperor's bodyguard deployed in perpetuity outside his tomb.

The Lintong army, consisting of statues of cavalry, chariots, archers, lancers, and hand-to-hand fighters, was one of the 20th century's greatest archaeological discoveries. Lesser versions of Shi Huangdi's army have since been uncovered at other Chinese sites, suggesting the First Emperor's tomb became the model for many others. The huge assemblage at Lintong testifies to a high degree of organization in the Qin imperial workshop. Manufacturing this army of statues required a veritable army of sculptors and painters as well as a large number of huge kilns. The First Emperor's artisans could have opted to use the same molds over and over again to produce thousands of identical soldiers standing in strict formation. In fact, they did employ the same molds repeatedly for different parts of the statues but assembled the parts in many different combinations. Consequently, the stances, arm positions, garment folds, equipment, coiffures, and facial features vary, sometimes slightly, sometimes markedly, from statue to statue. Additional hand modeling of the cast body parts before firing enabled the sculptors to differentiate the figures even more. The Qin painters undoubtedly added further variations to the appearance of the terracotta army. The result of these efforts was a brilliant balance of uniformity and individuality.

## Han Dynasty

Soon after the First Emperor's death, the people who had suffered under his reign revolted, assassinated his corrupt and incompetent son, and founded the Han dynasty in 206 BCE. The Han ruled China for four centuries, integrating many of the Qin reforms in a more liberal governing policy. They also extended China's southern and western boundaries, penetrating far into Central Asia (present-day Xinjiang). Han merchants even traded indirectly with distant Rome via the so-called Silk Road (see "The Silk Road," page 458).

**WU FAMILY SHRINES** Excavations of Han dynasty tombs have uncovered some of the finest examples of Chinese painting, such as the silk funerary banner of the marquise of Dai (FIG. 16-1), and of bronze-casting, for example, the *boshan* (incense burner) of Prince Liu Sheng (FIG. **16-6A**). The most important stone sculptures of this period are the pictorial narratives on the walls of the Wu family shrines in a cemetery at Jiaxiang in Shandong Province. The shrines, which date between 147 and 168 CE, document the emergence under the Han dynasty of private, nonaristocratic families as patrons of reli-

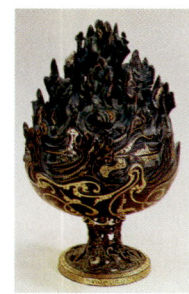

**16-6A** Incense burner of Prince Liu Sheng, ca. 113 BCE.

gious and mythological art having political overtones. Dedicated to deceased male family members, the Wu shrines are simple in form, consisting of three low walls and a pitched roof. On the interior surfaces, sculptors carved flat polished images that stand out against an equally flat, though roughly textured, ground. The historical scenes include a representation of the third-century BCE hero Jing Ke's attempt to assassinate the tyrannical First Emperor of Qin.

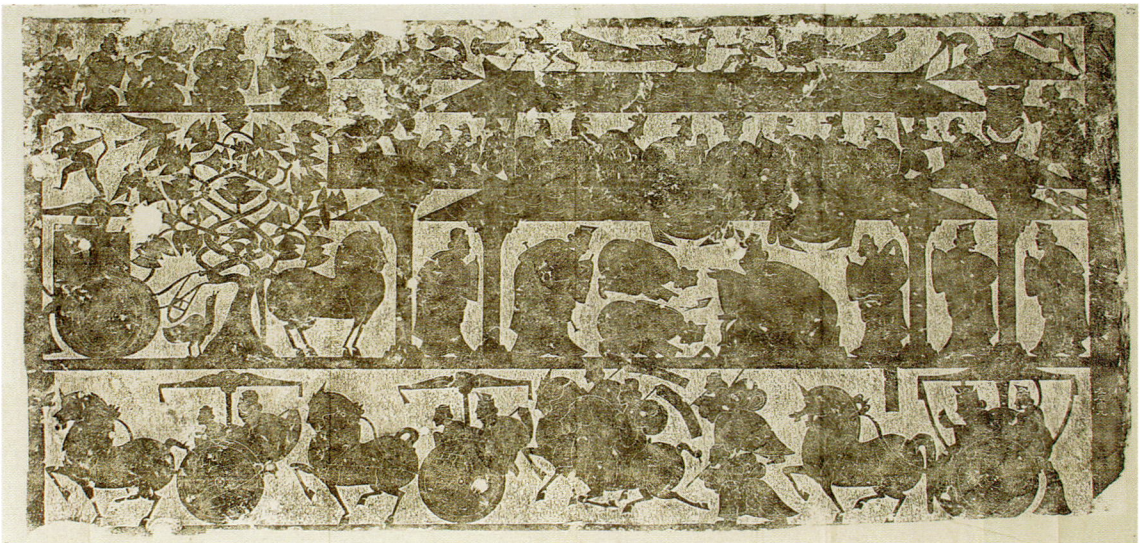

**16-7** The archer Yi(?) and a reception in a mansion, Wu family shrine, Jiaxiang, China, Han dynasty, 147–168 CE. Rubbing of a stone relief, 3′ × 5′.

The Wu family shrines depict legendary, historical, and contemporaneous subjects. Here, the hero Yi shoots down suns to save Earth from scorching. To the right is a ceremonial scene in a Han mansion.

1 ft.

On the slab shown in FIG. **16-7**, a *rubbing* (an impression made by placing dampened paper over the surface and rubbing ink onto the portions adhering to the relief carving) taken from the shrine wall depicts an archer at the upper left who is probably the hero Yi. He saves Earth from scorching by shooting down the nine extra suns, represented as crows in the Fusang tree. (The small orbs below the sun on the marquise of Dai's banner [FIG. 16-1] probably allude to the same story.) The lowest zone shows a procession of umbrella-carriages moving to the left. Above, underneath the overhanging eaves of a two-story mansion, robed men bearing gifts pay homage to a central figure of uncertain identity, represented as larger and therefore more important. Two men kneel before the larger figure. Women occupy the upper story. Again, one figure, at the center and facing forward, is singled out as the most important. The identities of the individual figures are unknown. Interpretations vary widely, and in the past decade, scholars have discovered some of the Wu reliefs have recarved inscriptions, leading them to question even the traditional date of the slab. Nonetheless, these scenes of homage and loyalty are consistent with the Confucian ideals of Han society (see "Daoism and Confucianism," page 463).

**WUWEI FLYING HORSE** Han sculptors also excelled in bronze-casting. Of the many surviving bronze figurines of this period, those discovered in 1969 at Wuwei in Gansu Province in the brick tomb of Governor-General Zhang are of special interest. The tomb contained almost 100 cast-bronze sculptures of horses, chariots, and soldiers—a miniature version of the life-size army (FIG. 16-6) guarding the tomb of the First Emperor of Qin. The figurine illustrated here (FIG. **16-8**) represents a distinctive breed of horse from Turkestan. It differs from all the others in Zheng's tomb because it is not prancing or standing still but galloping, or, more accurately, flying, because one hoof rests on a swallow with spread wings. The sculptor posed the horse with its head tilted to one side but presented the animal's body in a pure profile. (Compare the horses pulling carts in the reliefs [FIG. 16-7] of the Wu family shrine.) The Wuwei horse has an even more elegant silhouette, with its legs spread widely and its tail lifted behind it like a fifth leg, balancing the curved neck and the rear left leg. Zhang's airborne horse suggests the journey from his tomb will take him heavenward to an immortal afterlife.

**HAN HOUSES AND PALACES** No remains of Han domestic buildings survive, but ceramic models of houses deposited in Han tombs, together with representations such as those in the Wu family shrines, provide information about Chinese residential architecture and construction techniques during the early centuries CE. An unusually large painted earthenware model (FIG. **16-9**) reproduces a Han house with sharply projecting tiled roofs resting on a framework of timber posts, lintels, and brackets. This construction method (FIG. **16-10**) typifies much Chinese architecture even today (see "Chinese Wooden Construction," page 457). Descriptions of Han palaces suggest they were grandiose versions of the type of house reproduced in this model but with more luxurious decoration, including mural paintings and walls of lacquered wood.

1 in.

**16-8** Flying horse, from the tomb of Governor-General Zhang, Wuwei, China, Han dynasty, late second century CE. Bronze, 1′ 1½″ high. Gansu Provincial Museum, Lanzhou.

Found in a late Han dynasty tomb, this cast-bronze galloping, flying horse has one hoof on a swallow with spread wings, suggesting the deceased's heavenward journey to the afterlife.

# Chinese Wooden Construction

Although the basic unit of Chinese architecture, the rectangular hall with columns supporting a roof, was common in many ancient civilizations, Chinese buildings have two major distinguishing features: the curving silhouettes of their roofs and their method of construction. The Chinese, like other ancient peoples, used wood to construct their earliest buildings. Although those structures do not survive, scholars believe many of the features giving East Asian architecture its distinctive character may date to the Zhou dynasty. Even the simple buildings reproduced on Han stone carvings (FIG. 16-7) and in clay models (FIG. 16-9) reveal a style and a method of construction long basic to China.

The typical Chinese hall has a pitched roof with projecting eaves. Wooden columns, lintels, and brackets provide the support. The walls have no weight-bearing function but serve only as screens separating inside from outside and room from room. The colors of Chinese buildings, predominantly red, black, yellow, and white, are also distinctive. Chinese timber architecture is customarily multicolored throughout, save for certain parts left in natural color, such

as railings made of white marble. The builders usually painted the screen walls and the columns red. Chinese designers often chose dazzling combinations of colors and elaborate patterns for the beams, brackets, eaves, rafters, and ceilings. Artists painted or lacquered the surfaces to protect the timber from rot and wood parasites, as well as to produce an arresting aesthetic effect.

The drawing reproduced here (FIG. 16-10) shows the basic construction method of Chinese architecture, with the major components of a Chinese building labeled. The builders laid *beams* between columns, decreasing the length of the beams as the structure rose. The beams supported vertical *struts,* which in turn supported higher beams and eventually the *purlins* running the length of the building and carrying the roof's sloping *rafters.* Unlike the rigid elements of the triangular trussed timber roof common in the West, which produce flat sloping rooflines, the varying lengths of the Chinese cross beams and the variously placed purlins can create curved profiles. Early Chinese roofs have flat profiles (FIGS. 16-7 and 16-9), but curving rafters (FIGS. 16-10 and 16-22) later became the norm, not only in China but throughout East Asia. The interlocking clusters of brackets were capable of supporting roofs with broad overhanging *eaves,* another typical feature of Chinese architecture. Multiplication of the *bays* (spaces between the columns) could extend the building's length to any dimension desired, although each bay could be no wider or longer than the length of a single tree trunk. The proportions of the structural elements could be fixed into *modules* (basic units), allowing for standardization of parts and thus rapid construction. The Chinese wooden construction system was so sophisticated that highly skilled workers could fit the parts together without using any adhesive substance, such as mortar or glue, and still build very large, stable structures capable of standing for centuries.

1 ft.

**16-9** Model of a house, Han dynasty, first century CE. Painted earthenware, 4′ 4″ high. Nelson-Atkins Museum of Art, Kansas City.

This Han house model provides invaluable information about the form, coloration, and construction methods of Chinese architecture. The flat profile of the rooflines is typical of earlier Chinese buildings.

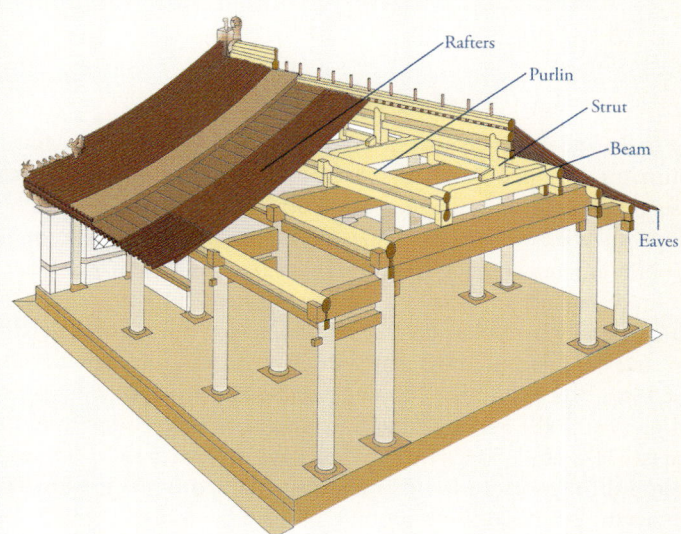

**16-10** Chinese raised beam construction (after L. Liu).

Chinese walls have no weight-bearing function. They serve only as screens separating inside from outside and room from room. Tang dynasty and later buildings usually have curved rafters and eaves.

## The Silk Road

The Chinese began to produce silk (see "Chinese Silk for the Afterlife," page 449) as early as the second millennium BCE, and people soon coveted the luxury fabric throughout Asia and beyond. Romans knew of silk as early as the second century BCE and treasured it for garments and hangings. Silk came to Rome along the ancient fabled Silk Road—a network of caravan routes across Central Asia linking China and the Mediterranean world (MAP 16-1). The western part, between the Mediterranean region and India, developed first, due largely to the difficult geographic conditions in northeastern India. In Central Asia, the caravans had to skirt the Taklimakan Desert, one of the most inhospitable environments on earth, as well as climb high, dangerous mountain passes. Very few traders traveled the entire distance. Along the way, goods usually passed through the hands of people from many lands, who often only dimly understood the ultimate origins and destinations of what they traded. The Roman passion for silk ultimately led to the modern name for these caravan routes, but silk was far from the only product traded along the way. Gold, ivory, gems, glass, lacquer, incense, furs, spices, cotton, linens, exotic animals, and other merchandise precious enough to warrant the risks passed along the Silk Road.

Ideas moved along the Silk Road as well. Most important perhaps, the caravans brought Buddhism to China from India in the first century CE, opening a significant new chapter in both the history of religion and the history of art in China.

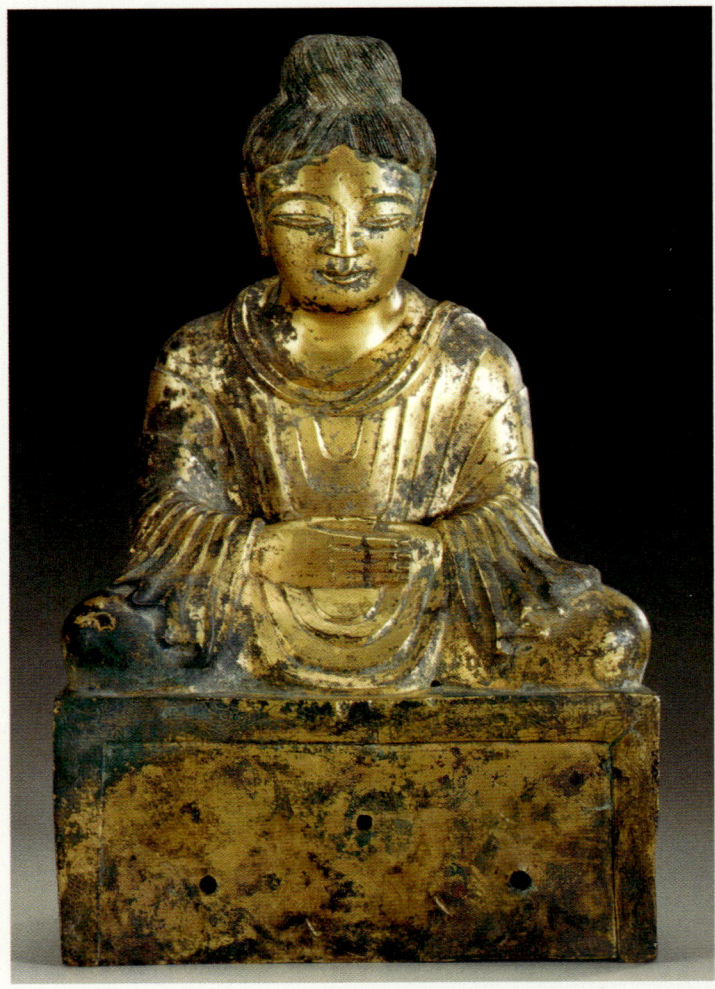

**16-11** Shakyamuni Buddha, from Hebei Province, Later Zhao dynasty, Period of Disunity, 338. Gilded bronze, 1′ 3½″ high. Asian Art Museum of San Francisco, San Francisco (Avery Brundage Collection).

The Silk Road brought not only trade goods to China but also Buddhism. This earliest datable Chinese Buddha image is stylistically indebted to Gandharan prototypes (FIG. 15-11).

1 in.

## Period of Disunity

For three and a half centuries, from 220 to 581,* civil strife divided China into competing states. Scholars variously refer to this era as the Period of Disunity or the period of the Six Dynasties or of the Northern and Southern Dynasties. In the history of this extremely complex era, one development deserves special mention—the occupation of northern China by peoples who were not ethnically Han Chinese and who spoke non-Chinese languages. It was in the northern states, connected to India by the desert caravan routes of the Silk Road (see "The Silk Road," above), that Buddhism first took root in China during the Han dynasty. Certain practices shared with Daoism (see "Daoism and Confucianism," page 463), such as withdrawal from ordinary society, helped Buddhism gain an initial foothold in the north. But Buddhism's promise of hope beyond the troubles of this world earned it an ever broader audience during the upheavals of the Period of Disunity. In addition, the fully developed Buddhist system of thought attracted intellectuals. Buddhism never fully displaced Confucianism and Daoism, but it did prosper throughout China for centuries and had a profound influence on the further development of the religious forms of those two native traditions.

**ZHAO BUDDHA** A gilded bronze statuette (FIG. **16-11**) in San Francisco representing Shakyamuni, the historical Buddha, bears an inscription giving its date as 338. Although some scholars have argued that the inscription is a later addition, many art historians accept the statuette as the earliest precisely datable Chinese image of the Buddha, created during the Later Zhao dynasty (319–351). The oldest Chinese Buddhist texts describe the Buddha as golden and radiating light. This no doubt accounts for the choice of gilded bronze as the sculptor's medium. In both style and iconography, this early Buddha resembles the prototype conceived and developed at Gandhara (FIGS. 15-1, 15-11, and 15-11A). The Chinese figure recalls its presumed South Asian models in the flat, relief-like handling of the robe's heavy concentric folds, the ushnisha (cranial bump) on the head, and the cross-legged position. So new were the icon and its meaning, however, that the Chinese sculptor misrepresented the canonical dhyana mudra, or meditation gesture (see "Buddhism and Buddhist Iconography," Chapter 15, page 427).

*From this point on, all dates in this chapter are CE unless otherwise stated.

# Chinese Painting Materials and Formats

Mural paintings in caves (FIG. 16-15) were popular in China, as they were in South Asia (FIG. 15-14), but Chinese artists also employed several other materials and formats for their works. The basic requirements for paintings not on walls were the same as for writing—a round tapered brush, soot-based ink, and either silk or paper. The Chinese were masters of the brush. Sometimes they used modulated lines for contours and interior details that elastically thicken and thin to convey depth and mass. In other works, they used *iron-wire lines* (thin, unmodulated lines with a suggestion of tensile strength) to define each figure in their paintings. Chinese painters also used richly colored minerals as pigments, finely ground and suspended in a gluey medium, and watery washes of mineral and vegetable dyes. The formats of Chinese paintings on silk or paper tend to be personal and intimate, and they are usually best viewed by only one or two people at a time. The most common types are listed here.

*Hanging scrolls* (FIGS. 16-14A, 16-19, 16-24, and 16-25). Chinese painters often mounted pictures on, or painted directly on, unrolled vertical scrolls for display on walls.

*Handscrolls* (FIGS. 16-12, 16-16, 16-20, and 16-23A). Artists also frequently attached paintings to, or painted directly on, long, narrow scrolls the viewer unrolled horizontally, section by section from right to left.

*Album leaves* (FIGS. 16-23 and 33-15). Many Chinese artists painted small panels on paper leaves, which collectors placed in albums.

*Fans* (FIG. 33-14). Stiff round or arched folding fans were also popular painting formats.

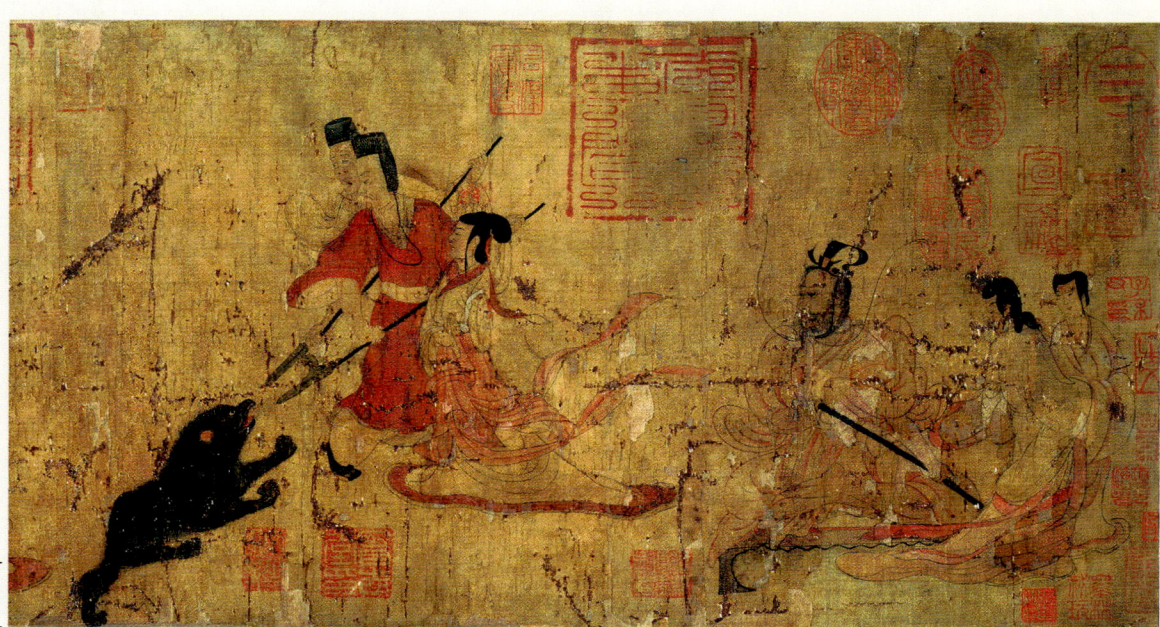

1 in.

**16-12** Attributed to GU KAIZHI, *Lady Feng and the Bear,* detail of *Admonitions of the Instructress to the Court Ladies,* Period of Disunity, late fourth century. Handscroll, ink and colors on silk, $9\frac{3}{4}''\times 11'\ 4\frac{1}{2}''$. British Museum, London.

Chinese handscrolls are unrolled and read from right to left. This section of an early scroll depicts Lady Feng's act of heroism to save the life of her emperor, a perfect model of Confucian behavior.

Here, the Buddha clasps his hands across his stomach. In South Asian art, the Buddha turns his palms upward, with thumbs barely touching in front of his torso.

**LADY FENG'S HEROISM** Secular arts also flourished in the Period of Disunity, as rulers sought calligraphers and painters to lend prestige to their courts. The most famous early Chinese painter with whom extant works can be associated was GU KAIZHI (ca. 344–406). Gu was a friend of important members of the Eastern Jin dynasty (317–420) and won renown as a calligrapher, a painter of court portraits, and a pioneer of landscape painting. A *handscroll* (see "Chinese Painting Materials and Formats," above) attributed to Gu Kaizhi in the 11th century is not by his hand, but it exemplifies the key elements of his art. Called *Admonitions of the Instructress to the Court Ladies,* the horizontal scroll contains painted scenes and accompanying explanatory text. Like all Chinese handscrolls, this one was unrolled and read from right to left, with only a small section exposed for viewing at one time.

The section illustrated here (FIG. **16-12**) records a well-known act of heroism—Lady Feng saving her emperor's life by placing herself between him and an attacking bear, a perfect model of Confucian behavior. As in many early Chinese paintings, the artist set the figures against a blank background with only a minimal setting for the scene, although in other works Gu provided landscape settings for his narratives. The figures' poses and fluttering drapery ribbons, in concert with individualized facial expressions, convey a clear quality of animation. This style accords well with painting ideals expressed in texts of the time, when representing inner vitality and spirit took precedence over reproducing surface appearances (see "Xie He's Six Canons," page 460).

## Xie He's Six Canons

China has a long and rich history of scholarship on painting, preserved today in copies of texts from as far back as the fourth century and in citations to even earlier sources. Few of the first texts on painting survive, but later authors often quoted them, preserving parts of some important works for posterity. Thus, educated Chinese painters and their clients could steep themselves in a rich art historical tradition. Perhaps the most famous subject of later commentary is a set of six "canons" (laws) of painting Xie He formulated in the early sixth century. The canons, as translated by James Cahill, are as follows:

1. Engender a sense of movement through spirit consonance.
2. Use the brush with the bone method.
3. Responding to things, depict their forms.
4. According to kind, describe appearances [with color].
5. Dividing and planning, positioning and arranging.
6. Transmitting and conveying earlier models through copying and transcribing.*

Xie employed only four characters for each of these succinct and cryptic laws. Several variant translations have been proposed, and scholars actively debate the precise meaning of each canon. Interpreting the canons in connection with extant paintings is often difficult but nonetheless offers valuable insights into what the Chinese of Xie's day and later valued in painting.

The simplest canons to understand are the third, fourth, and fifth, because they show Chinese painters' concern for accuracy in rendering forms and colors and for care in composition, artistic concerns common in many cultures. However, separating form and color into different laws gives written expression to a distinctive feature of early Chinese painting. Painters such as Gu Kaizhi (FIG. 16-12) and Yan Liben (FIG. 16-16) used an outline-and-color technique. Their brushed-ink outline drawings employ flat applications of color. To suggest volume, they used ink shading along edges, such as drapery folds.

Also noteworthy is the order of the laws, suggesting Chinese painters' primary concern: to convey the vital spirit of their subjects and their own sensitivity to that spirit. Next in importance was the handling of the brush and the careful placement of strokes, especially of ink. The sixth canon also speaks to a standard Chinese painting practice: copying. Chinese painters, like painters in other cultures throughout history, trained by copying the works of their teachers and other artists (see "Artistic Training in Renaissance Italy," Chapter 14, page 414). In addition, Chinese artists often copied famous paintings as sources of forms and ideas for their own works and to preserve great works created using fragile materials. In China, as elsewhere, change and individual development occurred in constant reference to the past, the artists always preserving some elements of it.

*James Cahill, "The Six Laws and How to Read Them," *Ars Orientalis* 4 (1961), 372–381.

---

**MEETING OF TWO BUDDHAS** A gilded bronze statuette (FIG. **16-13**) shows how the sculptors of the Northern Wei dynasty (386–534) transformed the Gandhara-derived style of earlier Buddhist art in China (FIG. 16-11). Dated 518, the piece was probably a private devotional object in a domestic setting or a votive offering in a temple. It represents the meeting of Shakyamuni Buddha (at the viewer's right) and Prabhutaratna, the Buddha who had achieved nirvana in the remote past, as recounted in the *Lotus Sutra,* an encyclopedic collection of Buddhist thought and poetry. When Shakyamuni was preaching on Vulture Peak, Prabhutaratna's stupa miraculously appeared in the sky. Shakyamuni opened it and revealed Prabhutaratna himself, who had promised to be present whenever the Lotus Sutra was preached. Shakyamuni sat beside him and continued to expound the Lotus Sutra's teachings. The meeting of the two Buddhas symbolized the continuity of Buddhist thought across the ages.

Behind each Buddha is a *mandorla* (flamelike almond-shaped nimbus). Both figures sit in the *lalitasana* pose—one leg folded and the other hanging down. This standard pose, which indicates

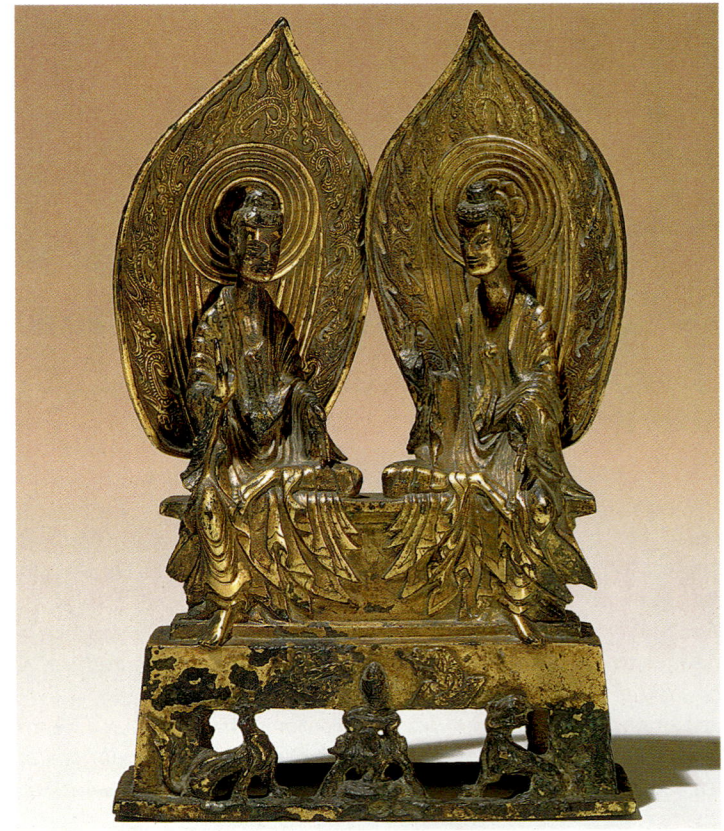

**16-13** Shakyamuni and Prabhutaratna, from Hebei Province, Northern Wei dynasty, 518. Gilded bronze, 10¼" high. Musée Guimet, Paris.

The sculptor of this statuette transformed the Gandhara-derived style of earlier Chinese Buddhist art (FIG. 16-11). The bodies have elongated proportions, and the garment folds form sharp ridges.

1 in.

relaxation, underscores the ease of communication between the two Buddhas. Their bodies have elongated proportions, and their smiling faces have sharp noses and almond eyes. The folds of the garments drop like a waterfall from their shoulders to their knees and spill over onto the pedestal, where they form sharp ridges resembling the teeth of a saw. The rhythmic sweep and linear elegance of the folds recall the brushwork of contemporaneous Chinese painting.

**BUDDHIST CAVES** The Northern Wei dynasty was also responsible for beginning work at the great Longmen Cave complex near Luoyang, further developed under the Tang dynasty (FIG. 16-14). Modeled on the cave temples of India (see Chapter 15), the Longmen and other Chinese complexes feature rock-cut shrines decorated with sculptures and paintings. The Longmen site alone eventually grew to encompass 2,345 shrines and more

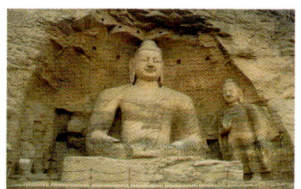

16-13A Seated Buddha, cave 20, Yungang, ca. 460–470.

than 100,000 statues and 2,800 inscriptions, attesting to the importance of Buddhism in China at this time. The Northern Wei emperors also sponslored Buddhist caves at the Yungang Grottoes near Datong, notably cave 20 with its colossal rock-cut image of the seated Buddha (FIG. 16-13A).

## Sui and Tang Dynasties

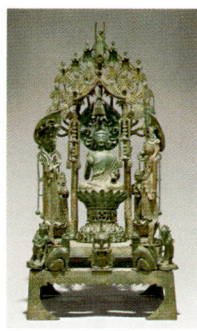

16-13B Sui altarpiece with Amitabha and attendants, 593.

The emperors of the short-lived Sui dynasty (r. 581–618) succeeded in reuniting China and prepared the way for the brilliant Tang dynasty, but few high-quality works survive from the 37-year Sui reign. One Sui masterpiece is a small altarpiece (FIG. 16-13B) now in Boston, dated by inscription to 593.

Under the Tang emperors (r. 618–907), China entered a period of unequaled magnificence (MAP 16-1). Chinese armies marched across Central Asia, prompting an influx of foreign peoples, wealth, and ideas into China. Traders, missionaries, and other travelers journeyed to the cosmopolitan Tang capital at Chang'an, and the Chinese, in turn, ventured westward. Chang'an, laid out on a grid scheme, occupied more than 30 square miles. It was the greatest city in the world during the seventh and eighth centuries.

**VAIROCANA BUDDHA** In its first century, the new dynasty continued to support Buddhism and to sponsor great monuments for Buddhist worshipers. One of the most spectacular Tang Buddhist sculptures is carved into the face of a cliff in the Longmen Cave complex. The colossal relief (FIG. 16-14), which dominates the entire site, features a central figure of the Buddha 44 feet tall—seated. An inscription records that the project was completed in 676 when Gaozong (r. 649–683) was the Tang emperor and that in 672 the empress Wu Zetian underwrote a substantial portion of the considerable cost with her private funds. Wu Zetian was an exceptional woman by any standard, and when Gaozong died in 683, she declared herself emperor and ruled until 705, when she was forced to abdicate at age 82.

Wu Zetian's Buddha is the Vairocana Buddha, not the historical Buddha of FIGS. 16-11, 16-13, and 16-13A, but the Mahayana Cosmic Buddha, the Buddha of Boundless Space and Time (see "Buddhism," Chapter 15, page 427). Flanking him are two of his monks, attendant bodhisattvas, and guardian figures—all smaller than the Buddha but still of colossal size. The sculptors represented the Buddha in serene majesty. An almost geometric regularity of contour and smoothness of planes emphasize the volume of the massive figure. The folds of his robes fall in a few concentric arcs. The artists suppressed surface detail in the interest of monumental simplicity and dignity.

**DUNHUANG GROTTOES** The westward expansion of the Tang Empire increased the importance of Dunhuang, the westernmost gateway to China on the Silk Road. Dunhuang long had been a wealthy, cosmopolitan trade center, a Buddhist pilgrimage destination, and home to thriving communities of Buddhist monks and nuns of varied ethnicity, as well as to adherents of other religions. In the course of several centuries beginning in the Period of Disunity, the Chinese cut hundreds of sanctuaries with painted murals into the soft rock of the cliffs near Dunhuang. Known today as the Mogao Grottoes and in antiquity as the Caves of a Thousand

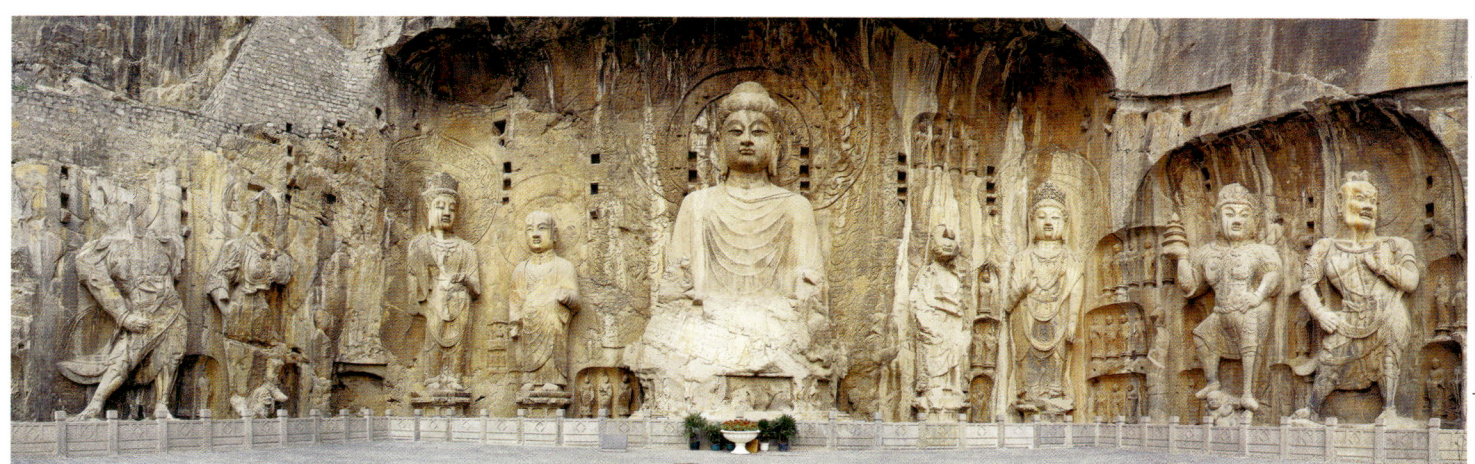

10 ft.

16-14 Vairocana Buddha, disciples, and bodhisattvas, Fengxian Temple, Longmen Caves, Luoyang, China, Tang dynasty, completed 676. Limestone, Buddha, 44′ high. ◼◀

Empress Wu Zetian sponsored these colossal rock-cut sculptures. The Tang artists represented the Mahayana Cosmic Buddha in serene majesty, suppressing surface detail in favor of monumental simplicity.

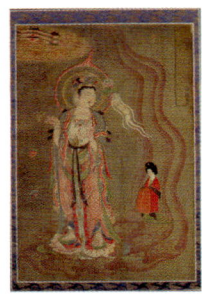

16-14A Bodhisattva
Guanyin, Dunhuang,
late 9th or early 10th
century.

Buddhas, the Dunhuang cave temples also contain sculptured images of painted unfired clay and stucco and painted silk scrolls (FIG. 16-14A). The earliest recorded dedication of a cave at Dunhuang was in 366, but the oldest extant caves date to the early fifth century. The Dunhuang Grottoes are especially important because in 845 the emperor Wuzong instituted a major persecution, destroying 4,600 Buddhist temples and 40,000 shrines and forcing the return of 260,500 monks and nuns to lay life. Wuzong's policies did not affect Dunhuang, then under Tibetan rule, so the site preserves much of the type of art lost elsewhere.

*Paradise of Amitabha* (FIG. 16-15) in Dunhuang cave 172 shows how the splendor of the Tang era and religious teachings could come together in a powerful image. Buddhist Pure Land sects, especially those centered on Amitabha, Buddha of the West, had captured the popular imagination in the Period of Disunity under the Six Dynasties and continued to flourish during the Tang dynasty. Pure Land teachings asserted that individuals had no hope of attaining enlightenment through their own power because of the waning of the Buddha's law. Instead, they could obtain rebirth in a realm free from spiritual corruption simply through faith in Amitabha's promise of salvation. Richly detailed, brilliantly colored pictures steeped in the opulence of the Tang dynasty, such as this one, greatly aided worshipers in gaining

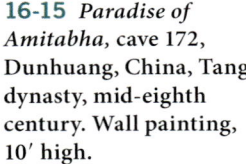

16-15A Foguang Si, Mount Wutai, ca. 857.

faith by visualizing the wonders of the Pure Land Paradise. Amitabha sits in the center of a raised platform against a backdrop of ornate buildings characteristic of the Tang era (compare the Foguang Si [Buddha Radiance Temple] at Mount Wutai [FIG. 16-15A]).

The Buddha's principal bodhisattvas and lesser divine attendants surround him. Before them a celestial dance takes place. Bodhisattvas had strong appeal in East Asia as compassionate beings ready to achieve buddhahood but dedicated to humanity's salvation. Some received direct worship and became the main subjects of sculpture and painting.

**YAN LIBEN** Although few examples of Tang painting exist today, many art historians regard the early Tang dynasty as the golden age of Chinese figure painting. In perfect accord with contemporaneous and later Chinese poets' and critics' glowing descriptions of Tang painting style are the unrestored portions of *The Thirteen Emperors* (FIG. 16-16), a masterpiece of line drawing and colored washes long attributed to YAN LIBEN (d. 673). Born into an aristocratic family and the son of a famous artist, Yan was prime minister under the emperor Gaozong as well as a celebrated painter. This handscroll depicts 13 Chinese rulers from the Han to the Sui dynasties. Its purpose was to portray these historical figures as exemplars of moral and political virtue, in keeping with the Confucian ideal of learning from the past (see "Daoism and Confucianism," page 463). Each emperor stands or sits in an undefined space. The emperor's greater size relative to his attendants immediately establishes his superior stature. Simple shading in the faces and the robes gives the figures an added semblance of volume and presence.

The detail in FIG. 16-16 represents Emperor Xuan of the Chen dynasty (557–589) seated among his attendants, two of whom carry the ceremonial fans that signify his rank and focus the viewer's attention on him. Xuan stands out from the others also because of his dark robes. His majestic serenity contrasts with his attendants' animated poses, which vary sharply from figure to figure, lending vitality to the composition.

**TOMB OF YONGTAI** Wall paintings in the tomb of the Tang princess Yongtai (684–701) at Qianxian, near Chang'an, permit an analysis of court painting styles unobscured by problems of

16-15 *Paradise of Amitabha,* cave 172, Dunhuang, China, Tang dynasty, mid-eighth century. Wall painting, 10′ high.

This richly detailed, brilliantly colored mural aided worshipers at Dunhuang to visualize the wonders of the Pure Land Paradise promised to those who had faith in Amitabha, the Buddha of the West.

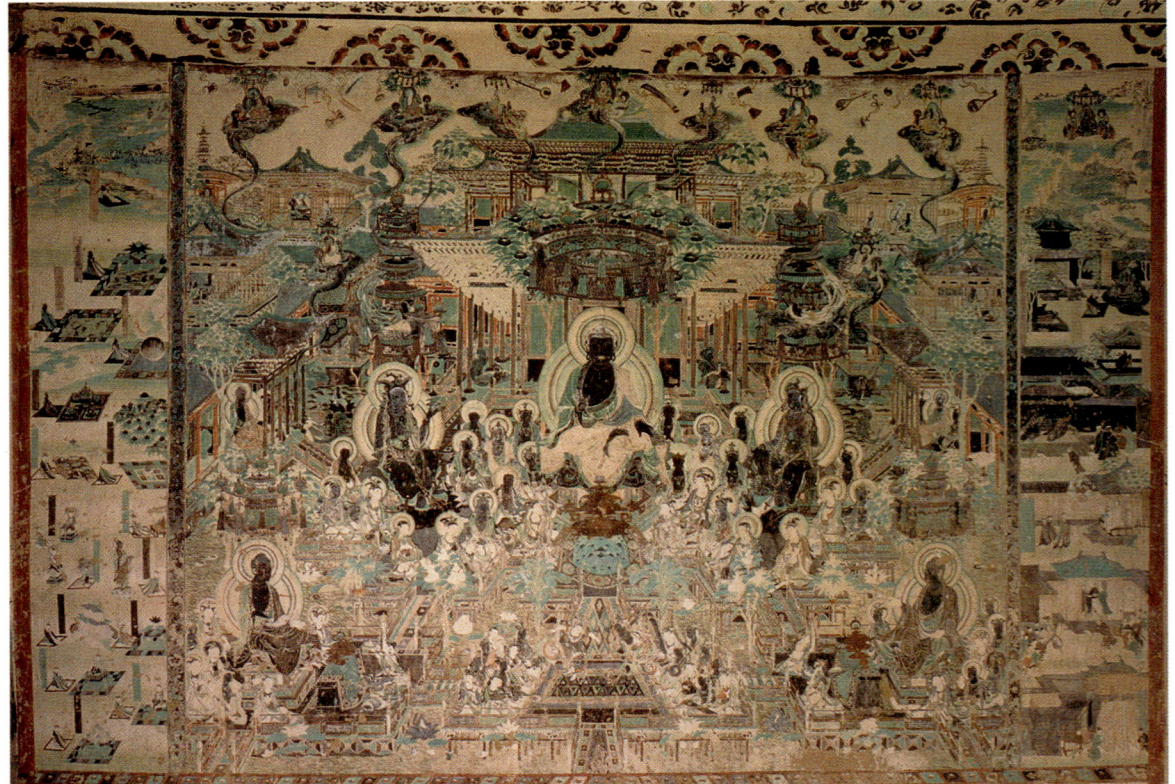

1 ft.

## Daoism and Confucianism

Daoism and Confucianism are both philosophies and religions native to China. Both schools of thought attracted wide followings during the Warring States Period (ca. 475–221 BCE) when political turbulence led to social unrest.

Daoism emerged out of the metaphysical teachings attributed to Laozi (604?–531? BCE) and Zhuangzi (370?–301? BCE). It takes its name from Laozi's treatise *Daodejing* (*The Way and Its Power*). Daoist philosophy stresses an intuitive awareness, nurtured by harmonious contact with nature, and shuns everything artificial. Daoists seek to follow the universal path, or principle, called the Dao, whose features cannot be described but only suggested through analogies. For example, the Dao is said to be like water, always yielding but eventually wearing away the hard stone that does not yield. For Daoists, strength comes from flexibility and inaction. Historically, Daoist principles encouraged retreat from society in favor of personal cultivation in nature and the achievement of a perfect balance between *yang*, active masculine energy, and *yin*, passive feminine energy.

Confucius (Kong Fuzi, or Master Kong, 551–479 BCE) was born in the state of Lu (roughly modern Shandong Province) to an aristocratic family that had fallen on hard times. From an early age, he showed a strong interest in the rites and ceremonies that helped unite people into an orderly society. As he grew older, he developed a deep concern for the suffering the civil conflict of his day caused. Thus, he adopted a philosophy he hoped would lead to order and stability. The *junzi* ("superior person" or "gentleman") who possesses *ren* ("human-heartedness") personified the ideal social order Confucius sought. Although the term *junzi* originally assumed noble birth, in Confucian thought anyone can become a junzi by cultivating the virtues Confucius espoused, especially empathy for suffering, pursuit of morality and justice, respect for ancient ceremonies, and adherence to traditional social relationships, such as those between parent and child, elder and younger sibling, husband and wife, and ruler and subject.

Confucius's disciple Mencius (or Mengzi, 371?–289? BCE) developed his master's ideas further, stressing that the deference to age and rank at the heart of the Confucian social order brings a reciprocal responsibility. For example, a king's legitimacy depends on the goodwill of his people. A ruler should share his joys with his subjects and will know his laws are unjust if they bring suffering to the people.

Confucius spent much of his adult life trying to find rulers willing to apply his teachings, but he died in disappointment. However, he and Mencius profoundly influenced Chinese thought and social practice. Chinese traditions of venerating deceased ancestors and outstanding leaders encouraged the development of Confucianism as a religion as well as a philosophic tradition. Eventually, Emperor Wu (r. 140–87 BCE) of the Han dynasty established Confucianism as the state's official doctrine. Thereafter, it became the primary subject of the civil service exams required for admission into and advancement within government service.

*Confucian* and *Daoist* are broad, imprecise terms scholars often use to distinguish aspects of Chinese culture stressing social responsibility and order (Confucian, for example, FIGS. 16-12 and 16-16) from those emphasizing cultivation of individuals, often in reclusion (Daoist, for example, FIGS. 16-19 and 16-23). But both philosophies share the idea that anyone can cultivate wisdom or ability, regardless of birth.

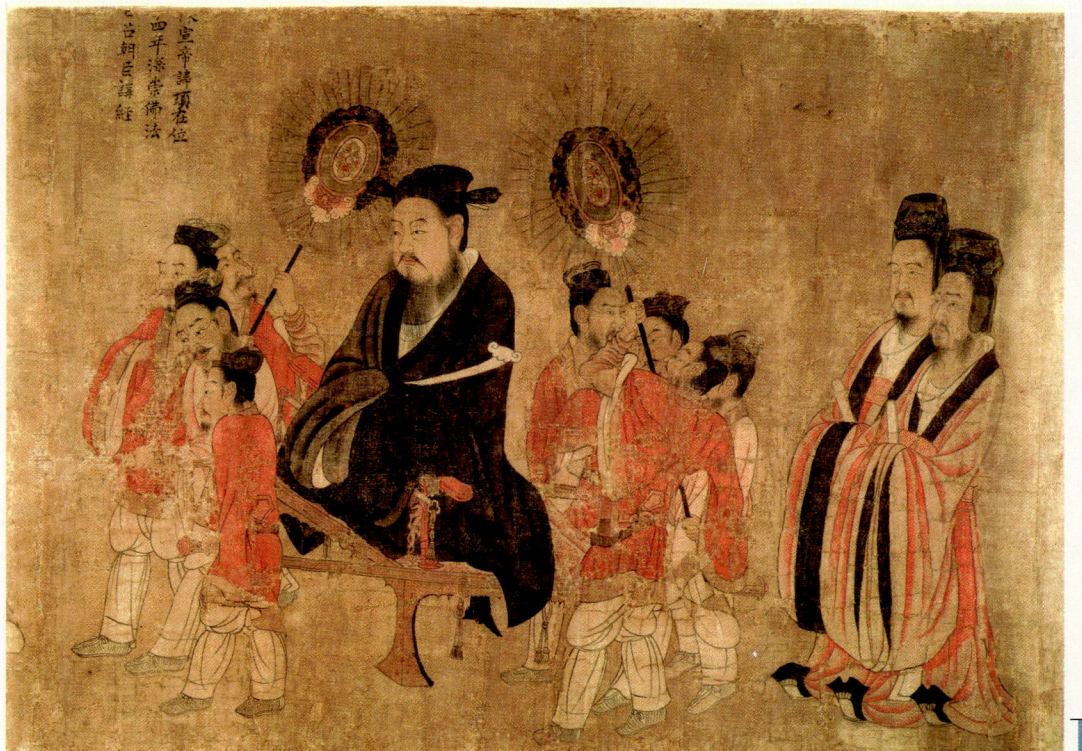

**16-16** Attributed to YAN LIBEN, *Emperor Xuan and Attendants*, detail of *The Thirteen Emperors*, Tang dynasty, ca. 650. Handscroll, ink and colors on silk, detail 1′ 8¼″ × 1′ 5½″; full scroll 17′ 5″ long. Museum of Fine Arts, Boston.

This handscroll portrays 13 Chinese rulers as Confucian exemplars of moral and political virtue. Yan Liben, a celebrated Tang painter, was a master of line drawing and colored washes.

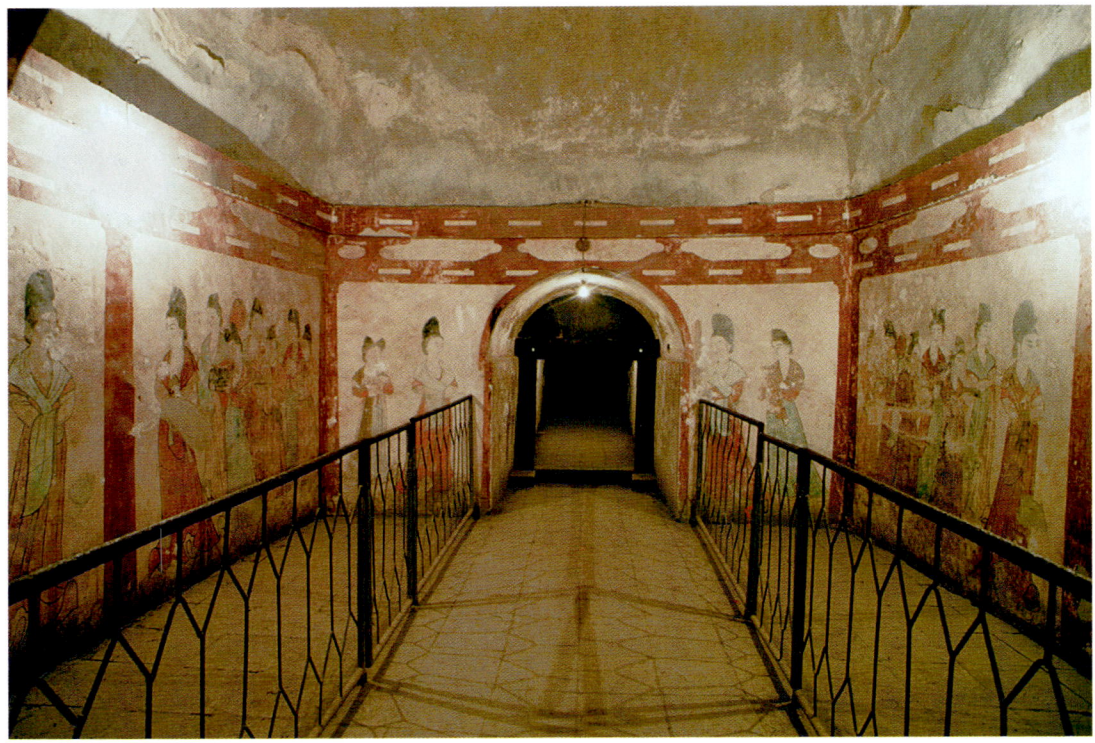

1 ft.

authenticity and reconstruction. When she was 17 years old, Yongtai was either murdered or forced to commit suicide by Wu Zetian, sponsor of the colossal rock-cut image of the Vairocana Buddha (FIG. 16-14) at Luoyang. Yongtai's underground tomb dates to 706, however, because her formal burial had to await Wu Zetian's death. The murals illustrated here (FIG. **16-17**) depict palace ladies and their attendants, images of pleasant court life to accompany the princess into her afterlife. The figures appear as if on a shallow stage, but the artist did not provide any indications of background or setting. The women, arranged in two rows, assume a variety of poses, some seen full-face, others in three-quarter views, both from the front and the back. The device of paired figures facing into and out of the picture space appears often in paintings of this period and effectively conveys depth. Thick, even contour lines describe full-volumed faces and suggest solid forms beneath the drapery, all with the utmost economy. This simplicity of form and line, along with the measured cadence of the poses, results in an air of monumental dignity.

**TANG CERAMIC SCULPTURE** Tang ceramists also achieved renown and produced thousands of earthenware figures of people, domesticated animals, and fantastic creatures for burial in tombs. These statuettes attest to a demand for ceramic sculpture by a much wider group of patrons than ever before, but terracotta funerary sculpture has a long history in China. The most spectacular example is the ceramic army (FIG. 16-6) of the First Emperor of Qin. The subjects of the Tang figurines are also much more diverse than in earlier periods. The depiction of a broad range of foreigners, including Semitic traders and Central Asian musicians on camels, accurately reflects the cosmopolitanism of Tang China.

The artists painted some figurines with colored slips and decorated others, such as the spirited, handsomely adorned neighing horse in FIG. **16-18,** with colorful lead glazes that ran in dramatic streams down the objects' sides when fired (see "Chinese Earthenwares and Stonewares," page 451). The popularity of the horse as a

subject of Chinese art (compare FIG. 16-8) reflects the importance the emperors placed on the quality of their stables. The breed represented here is powerful in build. Its beautifully arched neck terminates in a small, elegant head. Richly harnessed and saddled, the horse testifies to its rider's nobility.

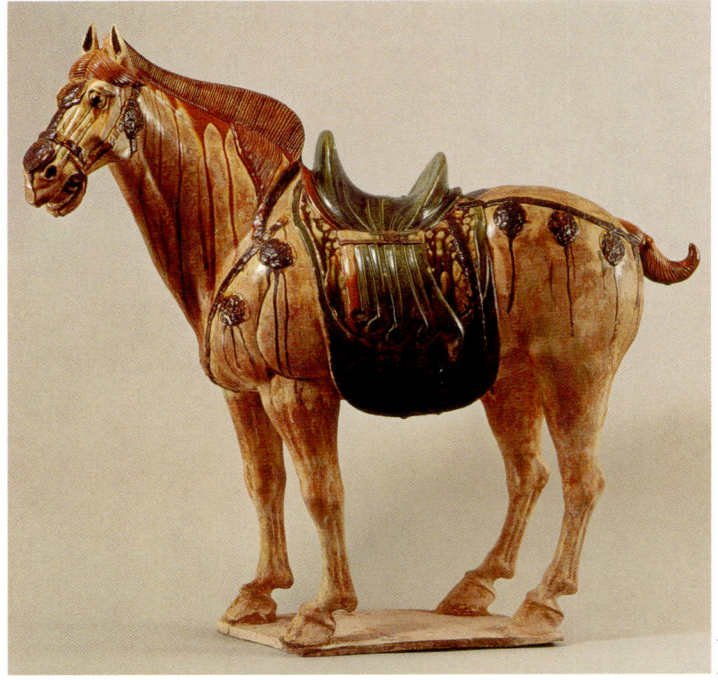

1 in.

**16-18** Neighing horse, Tang dynasty, eighth to ninth century. Glazed earthenware, 1′ 8″ high. Victoria & Albert Museum, London.

Tang ceramists achieved renown for their earthenware figurines decorated with colorful lead glazes that ran in dramatic streams down the sides when a piece was fired, as in this statuette.

## Song and Liao Dynasties

The last century of Tang rule brought many popular uprisings and the empire's gradual disintegration. After an interim of internal strife known as the Five Dynasties period (907–960), General Zhao Kuangyin succeeded in consolidating the country once again. He established himself as the first emperor (r. 960–976) of the Song dynasty (960–1279), which ruled China from a capital in the north at Bianliang (modern Kaifeng) during the Northern Song period (960–1127). The Song emperors curtailed many of the hereditary privileges of the elite class. They also made political appointments on the basis of scores on civil service examinations, and education became a more important prerequisite for Song officials than high birth.

The three centuries of Song rule, including the Southern Song period (1127–1279) when the capital was at Lin'an (modern Hangzhou) in southern China, were also a time of extraordinary technological innovation. Under the Song dynasty, the Chinese invented the magnetic compass for sea navigation, printing with moveable clay type, paper money, and gunpowder. Song China was the most technologically advanced society in the world in the early second millennium.

**FAN KUAN** For many art historians, the Song dynasty also marks the apogee of Chinese landscape painting, which first emerged as a major subject during the Period of Disunity. Although many of the great Northern Song masters worked for the imperial court, FAN KUAN (ca. 960–1030) was a Daoist recluse (see "Daoism and Confucianism," page 463) who shunned the cosmopolitan life of Bianliang. He believed nature was a better teacher than were other artists, and he spent long days in the mountains studying configurations of rocks and trees and the effect of sunlight and moonlight on natural forms. Just as centuries later, Giorgio Vasari (1511–1574) would credit Italian Renaissance artists with the exploration and perfection of naturalistic painting (see Chapter 21), so did Song critics laud Fan and other leading Chinese painters of the day as the first masters of the recording of light, shade, distance, and texture—several centuries earlier than in Europe. Yet, the comparison with 15th- and 16th-century Italy is misleading. Chinese landscape painters did not aim to produce portraits of specific places seen from a fixed viewpoint. They did not seek to imitate or to reproduce nature. Rather, they sought to capture the essence of nature and of its individual elements using brush and ink on silk. Their paintings are tributes to nature, not representations of unique rock or tree formations.

In *Travelers among Mountains and Streams* (FIG. **16-19**), Fan painted a vertical landscape of massive mountains rising from the distance. The overwhelming natural forms dwarf the few human and animal figures (for example, the mule train in the lower right corner), which the artist reduced to minute proportions. The nearly seven-foot-long silk hanging scroll cannot contain nature's grandeur, and the landscape continues in all directions beyond its borders. Fan showed some elements from level ground (for example, the great boulder in the foreground), and others obliquely from the top (the shrubbery on the highest cliff). The shifting perspectives lead the viewer's eye on a journey through the mountains. To appreciate the painted landscape fully, an observer must focus not only on the larger composition but also on intricate details and on the character of each brushstroke. Numerous "texture strokes" help model massive forms and convey a sense of tactile surfaces. For the face of the mountain, for example, Fan employed small, pale brush marks, the kind of texture stroke the Chinese call "raindrop strokes."

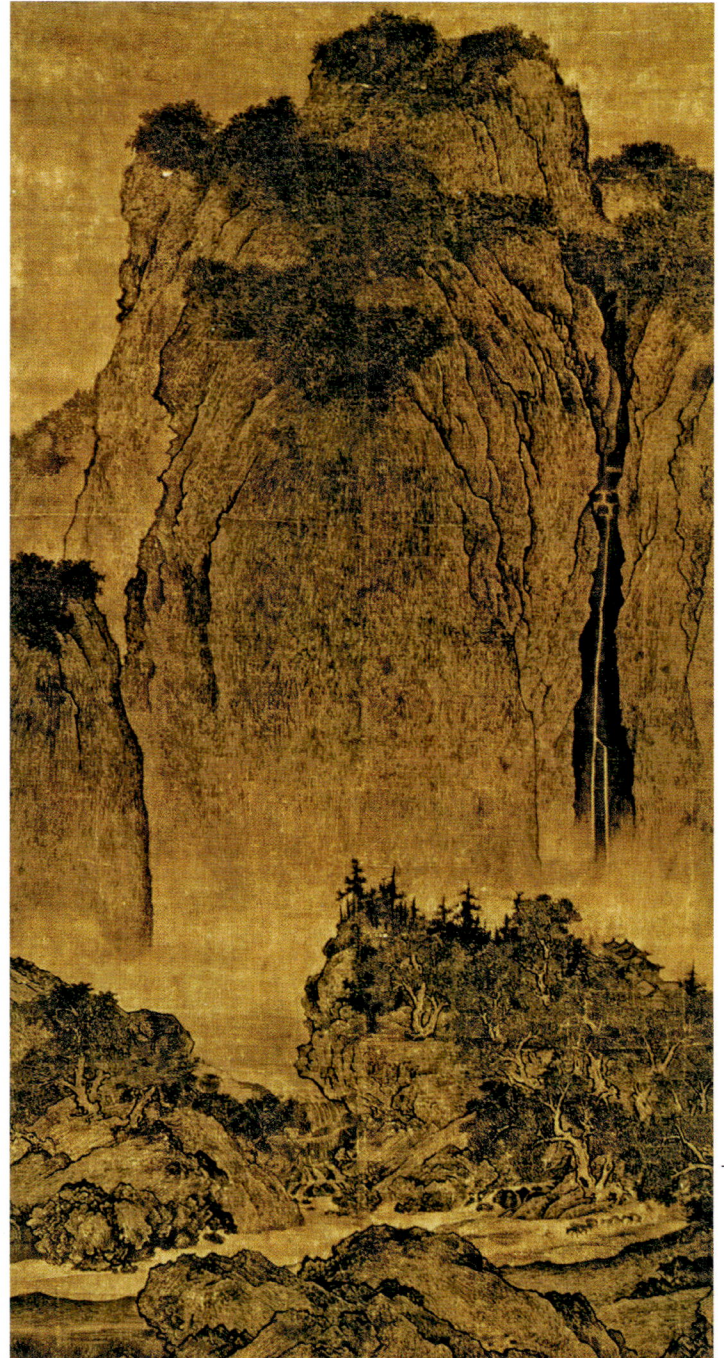

1 ft.

**16-19** FAN KUAN, *Travelers among Mountains and Streams*, **Northern Song period, early 11th century. Hanging scroll, ink and colors on silk, 6′ 7$\frac{1}{4}$″ × 3′ 4$\frac{1}{4}$″. National Palace Museum, Taibei.**

Fan Kuan, a Daoist recluse, spent long days in the mountains studying the effects of light on rock formations and trees. He was one of the first masters at recording light, shade, distance, and texture.

**HUIZONG** A century after Fan Kuan painted in the mountains of Shanxi, HUIZONG (1082–1135; r. 1101–1126) assumed the Song throne at Bianliang. Less interested in governing than in the arts, the new emperor brought the country to near bankruptcy and lost much of China's territory to the armies of the Tartar Jin dynasty (1115–1234), who captured the Song capital in 1126 and took Huizong as a prisoner. He died in their hands nine years later. An

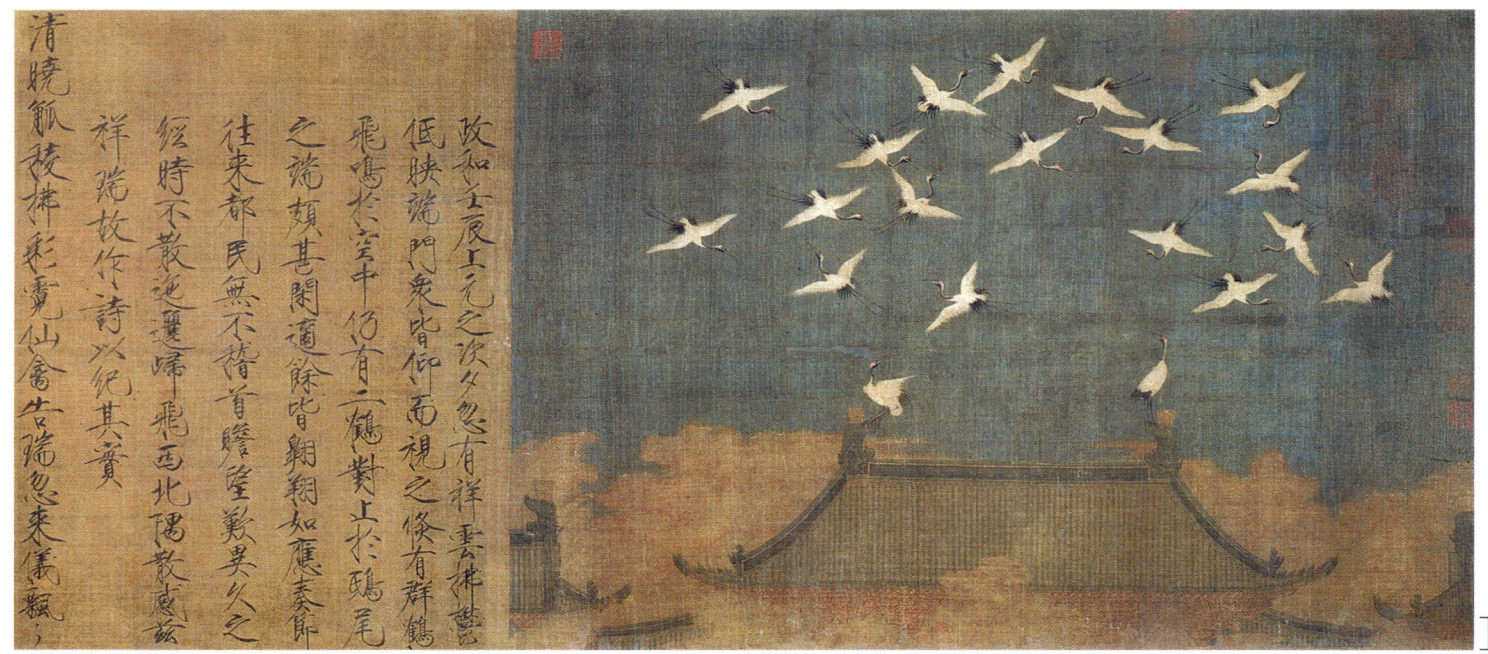

**16-20** Attributed to HUIZONG, *Auspicious Cranes,* Northern Song period, 1112. Section of a handscroll, ink and colors on silk, 1′ 8⅛″ × 4′ 6⅜″. Liaoning Provincial Museum, Shenyang.

The Chinese regarded the white cranes that appeared at Huizong's palace as an auspicious sign. This painting of the event is a masterful combination of elegant composition and realistic observation.

accomplished poet, calligrapher, and painter, Huizong reorganized the imperial painting academy and required the study of poetry and calligraphy as part of the official training of court painters. *Calligraphy,* or the art of writing, was highly esteemed in China throughout its history, and prominent inscriptions are frequent elements of Chinese paintings (see "Calligraphy and Inscriptions on Chinese Paintings," Chapter 33, page 997). Huizong also promoted the careful study both of nature and of the classical art of earlier periods, and was an avid art collector as well as the sponsor of a comprehensive catalogue of the vast imperial art holdings.

A short handscroll (FIG. **16-20**) usually attributed to Huizong is more likely the work of court painters under his direction, but it displays the emperor's style as both calligrapher and painter. Huizong's characters represent one of many styles of Chinese calligraphy. They consist of thin strokes, and each character is meticulously aligned with its neighbors to form neat vertical rows. The painting depicts cranes flying over the roofs of Bianliang. It is a masterful combination of elegant composition and realistic observation. The painter carefully recorded the black and red feathers of the white cranes and depicted the birds from a variety of viewpoints to suggest they were circling around the roof. Huizong did not, however, choose this subject because of his interest in the anatomy and flight patterns of birds. The painting was a propaganda piece commemorating the appearance of 20 white cranes at the palace gates during a festival in 1112. The Chinese interpreted the

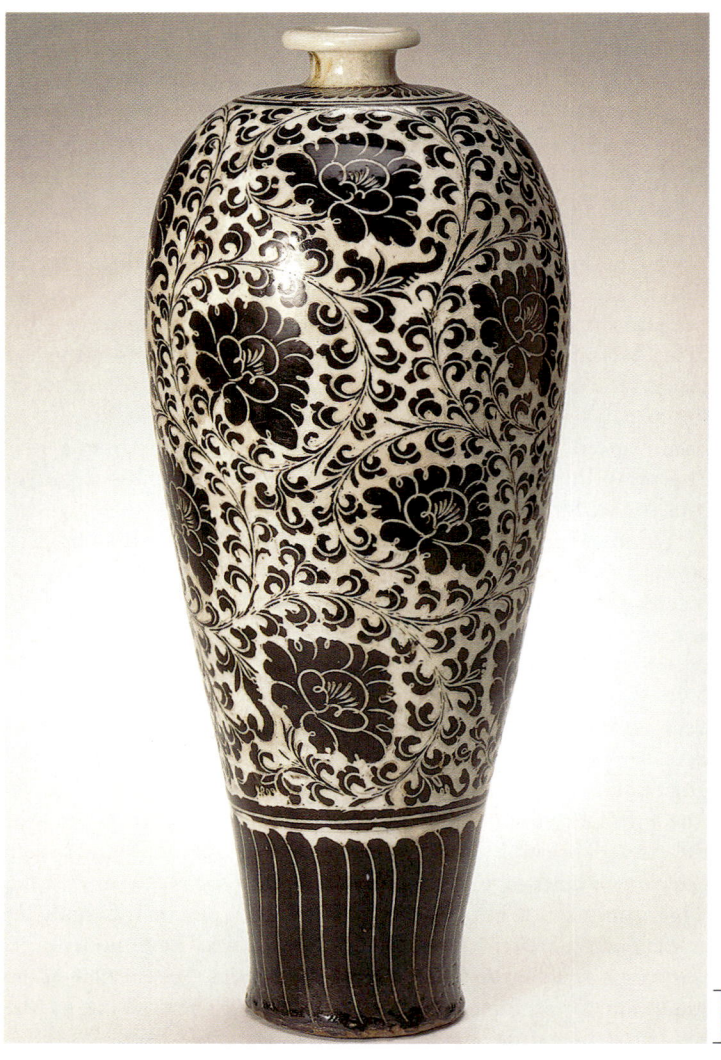

**16-21** Meiping vase, from Xiuwi, China, Northern Song period, 12th century. Stoneware, Cizhou type, with sgraffito decoration, 1′ 7½″ high. Asian Art Museum of San Francisco, San Francisco (Avery Brundage Collection).

Chinese potters developed the sgraffito technique (incising through a colored slip) during the Northern Song period. This vase features vines and flowers created by cutting through a black slip.

appearance of the cranes as an auspicious sign, proof Heaven had blessed Huizong's rule. Although few would ever have viewed the handscroll, painted banners featuring the cranes were displayed on special occasions, where they could be seen by a larger public.

**CIZHOU POTTERY** Song artists also produced superb ceramics. Some reflect their patrons' interests in antiquities and imitate the powerful forms of the Shang and Zhou bronzes. However, Song ceramics more commonly had elegant shapes with fluid silhouettes. Many featured monochrome glazes, such as the famous celadon wares, also produced in Korea (FIG. 16-29), but a quite different kind of pottery emerged in northern China, loosely classed as Cizhou (after the city in Hebei Province that was the center of production). The example shown here (FIG. 16-21) is a vase of the high-shouldered shape known as *meiping*. Chinese potters developed the subtle techniques of *sgraffitto* (incising the design through a colored slip) during the Northern Song period. They achieved the intricate black-and-white design on this meiping by cutting through a black slip (see "Chinese Earthenwares and Stonewares," page 451). The vase's tightly twining vine and flower-petal motifs closely embrace the vessel in a perfect accommodation of surface design to vase shape.

**FOGUANG SI PAGODA** For two centuries during the Northern Song period, the Liao dynasty (907–1125) ruled part of northern China. The Liao emperors were important patrons of architecture, painting, and sculpture (for example, the statue of Bodhi-

sattva Guanyin, FIG. **16-21A**). In 1056, the Liao dynasty built the Foguang Si Pagoda (FIG. **16-22**), the tallest wooden building ever constructed, at Yingxian in Shanxi Province. The *pagoda,* or tower—the building type most often associated with Buddhism in China and other parts of East Asia—is the most eye-catching feature of a Buddhist temple complex. It somewhat resembles the tall towers of Indian temples (see "Hindu Temples," Chapter 15, page 439) and their distant ancestor, the Buddhist stupa (see "The Stupa," Chapter 15, page 430). As did stupas, many early pagodas housed relics and provided a focus for devotion to the Buddha. Later pagodas served other functions, such as housing sacred images and texts. The Chinese and Koreans built both stone and brick pagodas, but wooden pagodas were also common and became the standard in Japan (FIG. 17-9).

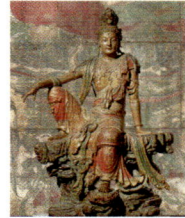

16-21A Bodhisattva Guanyin seated on Potalaka, 11th or early 12th century.

The nine-story octagonal pagoda at Yingxian is 216 feet tall and made entirely of wood (see "Chinese Wooden Construction," page 457). Sixty giant, four-tiered bracket clusters carry the floor beams and projecting eaves of the five main stories. They rest on two concentric rings of columns at each level. Alternating main stories and windowless mezzanines with cantilevered balconies, set back farther on each story as the tower rises, form a combined elevation of nine stories. Along with the open veranda on the ground level and the soaring pinnacle, the balconies visually lighten the building's mass.

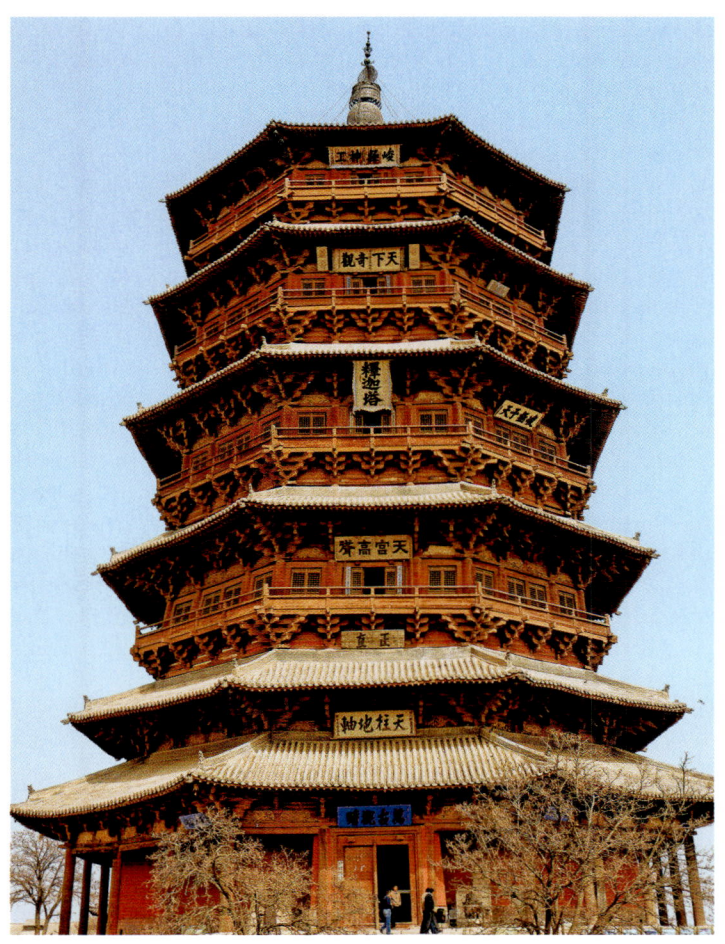

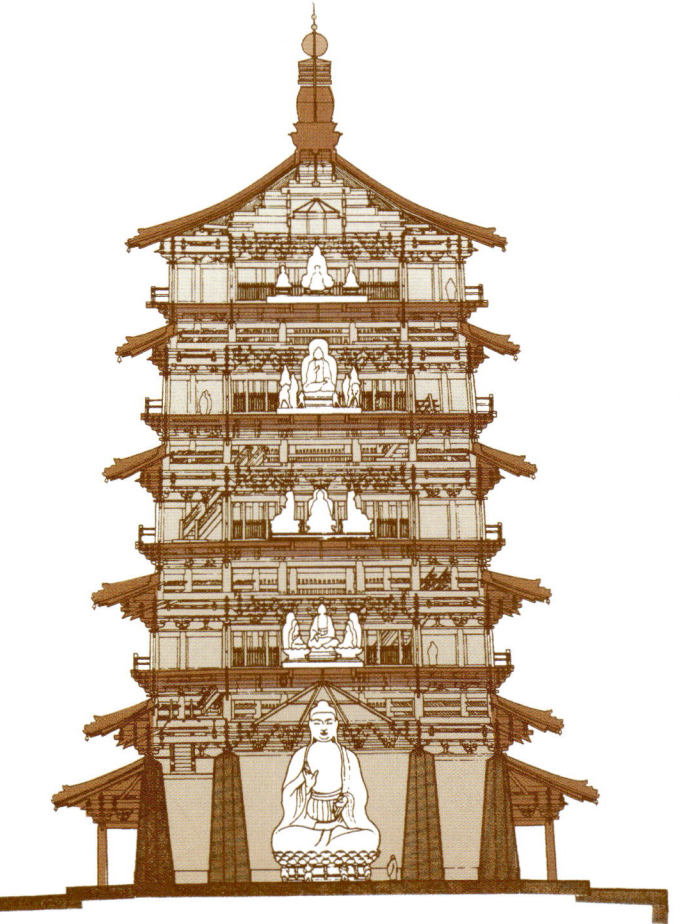

**16-22** View (*left*) and cross-section (*right;* after L. Liu) of Foguang Si Pagoda, Yingxian, China, Liao dynasty, 1056.

The tallest wooden building in the world is this Buddhist pagoda at Yingxian. The nine-story tower shows the Chinese wooden beam-and-bracket construction system at its most ingenious.

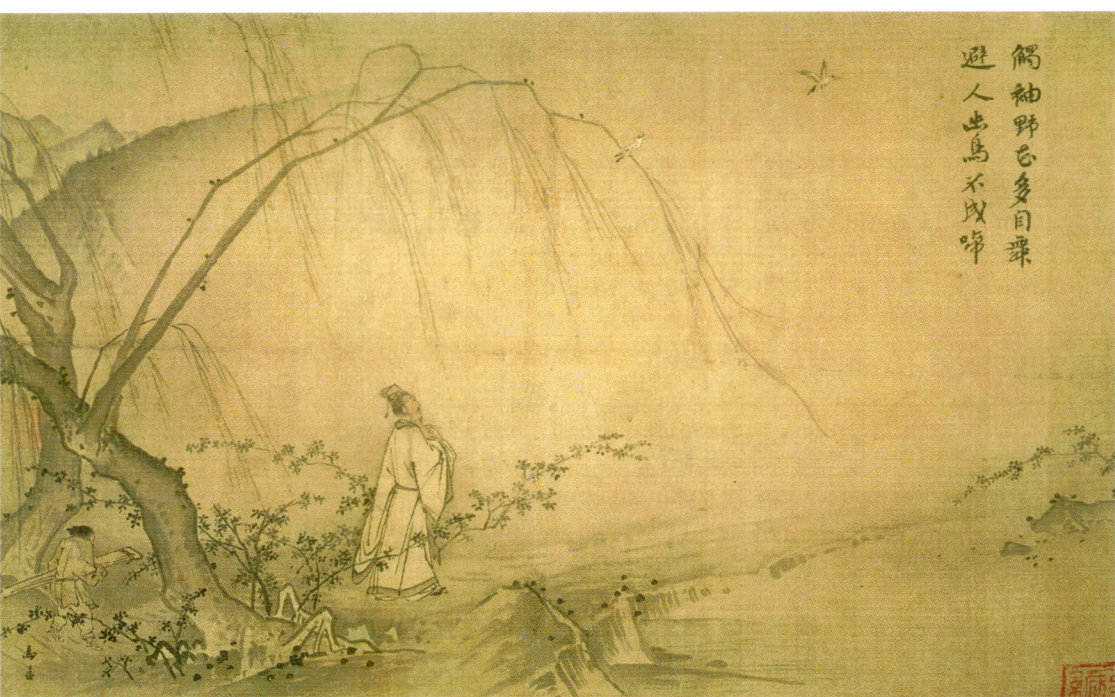

**16-23** MA YUAN, *On a Mountain Path in Spring,* Southern Song period, early 13th century. Album leaf, ink and colors on silk, 10¾″ × 17″. National Palace Museum, Taibei.

In contrast to Fan (FIG. 16-19), Ma reduced the landscape on this album leaf to a few elements and confined them to one part of the page. A large, solitary figure gazes into the infinite distance.

The cross-section (FIG. 16-22, *right*) shows the symmetrical placement of statues of the Buddha inside, the colossal scale of the ground-floor statue, and the intricacy of the beam-and-bracket system at its most ingenious.

## SOUTHERN SONG PERIOD

When the Jin captured Bianliang and the emperor Huizong in 1126 and took control of northern China, Gaozong (r. 1127–1162), Huizong's sixth son, escaped and eventually established a new Song capital in the south at Lin'an (present-day Hangzhou). From there, he and his successors during the Southern Song period ruled their reduced empire until 1279.

Court sponsorship of painting continued in the new capital, and, as in the Northern Song period, some emperors took a direct interest in the painters of the imperial painting academy. During the reign of Ningzong (r. 1194–1224), members of the court, including Ningzong himself and Empress Yang, frequently added brief poems to the paintings created under their direction. Some painters belonged to families that had worked for the Song emperors for several generations.

## MA YUAN

The most famous Song painters came from the Ma family, which began working for the Song dynasty during the Northern Song period. MA YUAN (ca. 1160–1225) painted *On a Mountain Path in Spring* (FIG. **16-23**), a silk album leaf, for Ningzong in the early 13th century. In his composition, as in those of his contemporary,

**16-23A** XIA GUI, *Twelve Views from a Thatched Hut,* ca. 1200–1225.

XIA GUI (active ca. 1195–1230; FIG. **16-23A**), in striking contrast to Fan Kuan's much larger *Travelers among Mountains and Streams* (FIG. 16-19), Ma reduced the landscape to a few elements and confined the natural setting to the foreground and left side of the page. A large, solitary figure gazes out into the infinite distance. Framing him are the carefully placed diagonals of willow branches. Near the upper right corner, a bird flies toward the couplet Ningzong added in ink, demonstrating his mastery of both poetry and calligraphy:

> *Brushed by his sleeves, wild flowers dance in the wind;*
> *Fleeing from him, hidden birds cut short their songs.*

Some scholars have suggested the author of the two-line poem was Empress Yang, but the inscription is in Ningzong's hand. In any case, landscape paintings such as this one are perfect embodiments of the Chinese ideals of peace and unity with nature.

## ZHOU JICHANG

Other Southern Song painters focused on religious themes. Although Neo-Confucianism, a blend of traditional Chinese thought and selected Buddhist concepts, became the leading philosophy, traditional Buddhist themes remained popular subjects for paintings. ZHOU JICHANG (ca. 1130–1190) painted *Lohans Giving Alms to Beggars* (FIG. **16-24**) around 1178 as part of a series of 100 scrolls produced at the southern coastal city of Ningbo for an abbot who invited individual donors to pay for the paintings as offerings in the nearby Buddhist temple. *Lohans* are enlightened disciples of the Buddha who have achieved freedom from rebirth (nirvana) by suppression of all desire for earthly things. Their charge was to protect Buddhist law until the arrival of the Buddha of the Future. In his Ningbo scroll, Zhou arranged the foreground, middle ground, and background vertically to clarify the lohans' positions relative to one another and to the beggars. The lohans move with slow dignity in a plane above the ragged wretches who scramble miserably for the alms their serene benefactors throw down. The extreme difference in deportment between the two groups distinguishes their status, as do their contrasting features. The lohans' vividly colored attire, flowing draperies, and quiet gestures set them off from the dirt-colored and jagged shapes of the people physically and spiritually beneath them. In this painting, consistent with Xie's principles (see "Xie He's Six Canons," page 460), Zhou used color for symbolic and decorative purposes, not to imitate nature or depict the appearance of individual forms. The composition of the landscape—the cloudy platform and lofty peaks of the lohans and the desertlike setting of the beggars—also distinguishes the two spheres of being.

## LIANG KAI

A new school of Buddhist thought, Chan Buddhism (see "Chan Buddhism," page 470), which stressed the quest for personal enlightenment through meditation, also flourished under the Song dynasty. LIANG KAI (active early 13th century) was a master of an abbreviated, expressive style of ink painting that found great favor among Chan monks in China, Korea, and Japan. He served in the painting academy of the imperial court in Hangzhou, and his early works include poetic landscapes typical of the Southern Song. Later in life, he left the court and concentrated on figure painting, including Chan subjects.

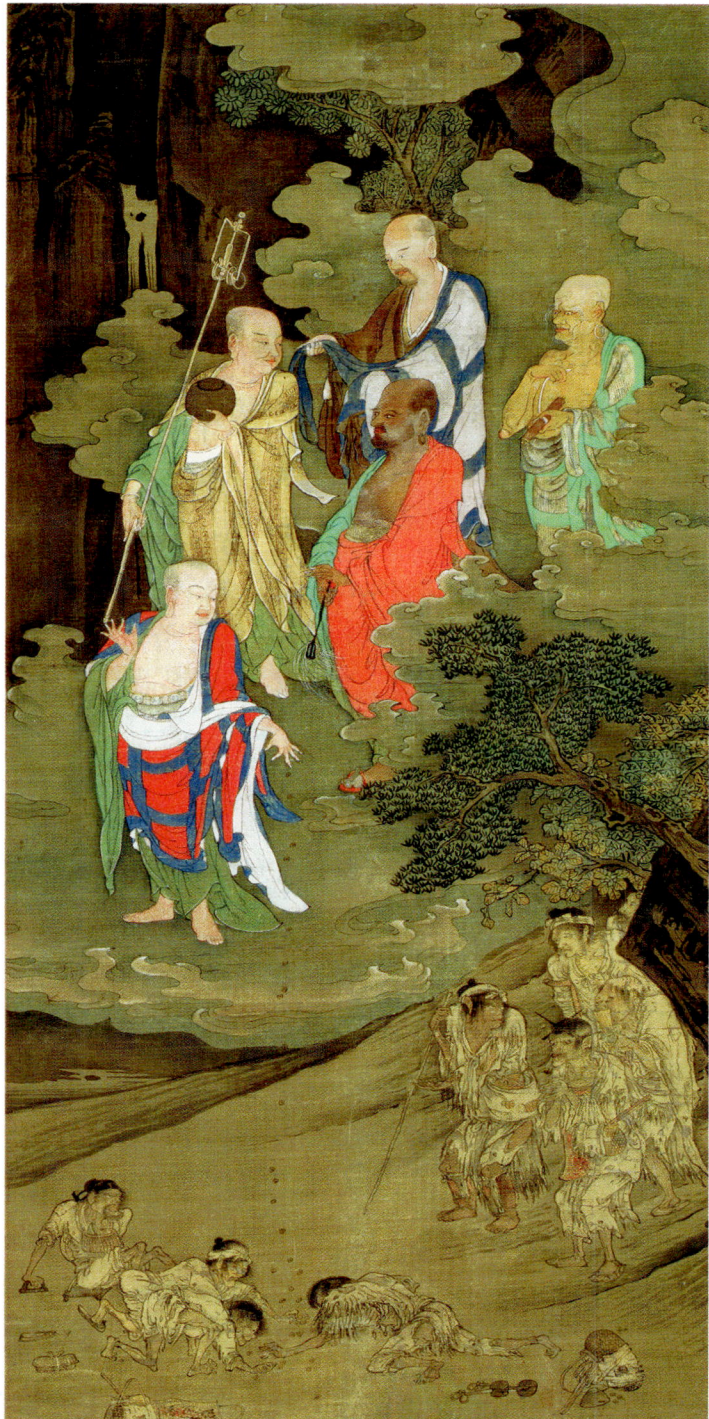

1 in.

**16-24** Zhou Jichang, *Lohans Giving Alms to Beggars,* Southern Song period, ca. 1178. Hanging scroll, ink and colors on silk, 3′ 7⅞″ × 1′ 8⅞″. Museum of Fine Arts, Boston.

Zhou chose a vertical arrangement of the figures in the fore-, middle-, and background in order to elevate the enlightened lohans in their bright attire above the ragged, dirt-colored beggars.

Surviving works attributed to Liang include an ink painting (FIG. **16-25**) of the Sixth Chan Patriarch, Huineng, crouching as he chops bamboo. In Chan thought, the performance of even mundane tasks such as chopping bamboo had the potential to become a spiritual exercise. In fact, this scene specifically depicts the patriarch's "Chan moment," when the sound of the blade striking the bamboo resonated within his spiritually attuned mind to propel him through the final doorway to enlightenment. The scruffy,

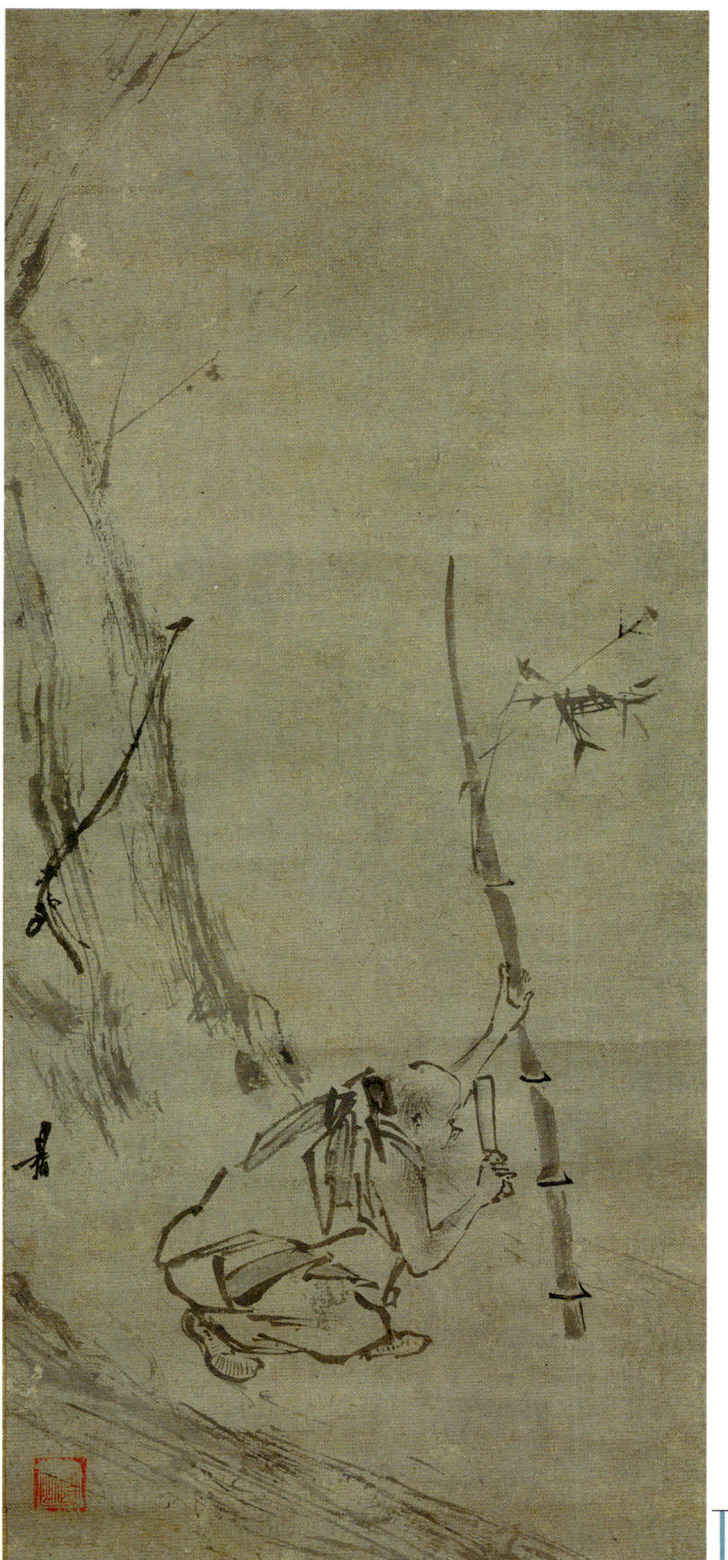

1 in.

**16-25** Liang Kai, *Sixth Chan Patriarch Chopping Bamboo,* Southern Song period, early 13th century. Hanging scroll, ink on paper, 2′ 5¼″ high. Tokyo National Museum, Tokyo.

On this hanging scroll, Liang, a renowned master of ink painting, depicted the Sixth Chan Patriarch's "Chan moment," when the chopping sound of his blade propelled the patriarch to enlightenment.

caricature-like representation of the revered figure suggests that worldly matters, such as physical appearance or signs of social status, do not burden Huineng's mind.

## Chan Buddhism

Under the Song emperors (960–1279), the new school of *Chan* Buddhism gradually gained importance, until it was second only to Neo-Confucianism. The Chan school traced its origins through a series of patriarchs (the founder and early leaders, joined in a master–pupil lineage). The First Chan Patriarch was Bodhidharma, a semilegendary sixth-century Indian missionary. By the time of the Sixth Chan Patriarch, Huineng (638–713; FIG. 16-25), in the early Tang period, the religious forms and practices of the school were already well established.

Although Chan monks adapted many of the rituals and ceremonies of other schools over the course of time, they focused on the cultivation of the mind or spirit of the individual in order to break through the illusions of ordinary reality, especially by means of meditation. In Chan thought, the means of enlightenment lie within the individual, and direct personal experience with some ultimate reality is the necessary step to its achievement. Meditation

is a critical practice. In fact, the word *Chan* is a translation of the Sanskrit word for "meditation." Bodhidharma is said to have meditated so long in a cave his arms and legs withered away.

Chan Buddhism has two major schools of thought. The Northern school holds that enlightenment comes only gradually after long meditation, but the Southern school believes the breakthrough to enlightenment can be sudden and spontaneous. Huineng, for example, achieved his "Chan moment" when he heard the sharp sound of a cutting blade strike a bamboo stick—the subject of an early-13th-century hanging scroll (FIG. 16-25) by the Southern Song painter Liang Kai.

Chan Buddhist beliefs influenced art and aesthetics as they developed in China and spread to Korea and Japan. In Japan, Chan (Japanese *Zen*) had an especially extensive, long-term influence on the arts and remains an important school of Buddhism there today (see "Zen Buddhism," Chapter 34, page 1007).

Liang used a variety of brushstrokes in the execution of this deceptively simple picture. Most are pale and wet, ranging from the fine lines of Huineng's beard to the broad texture strokes of the tree. A few darker strokes, which define the vine growing around the tree and the patriarch's clothing, offer visual accents in the painting. This kind of quick and seemingly casual execution of paintings has traditionally been interpreted as a sign of a painter's ability to produce compelling pictures spontaneously as a result of superior training and character, or, in the Chan setting, progress toward enlightenment.

# KOREA

Korea is a northeast Asian peninsula that shares borders with China and Russia and faces the islands of Japan (MAPS 16-1 and 17-1). Korea's pivotal location is a key factor in understanding the relationship of its art to that of China and the influence of Korea's art on that of Japan. Ethnically, the Koreans are related to the peoples of eastern Siberia and Mongolia as well as to the Japanese. At first, the Koreans used Chinese characters to write Korean words, but later they invented their own phonetic alphabet. Korean art, although frequently based on Chinese models, is not merely derivative but has, like Korean civilization, a distinct identity.

## Three Kingdoms Period

Pottery-producing cultures appeared on the Korean peninsula in the Neolithic period no later than 6000 BCE, and the Korean Bronze Age dates from about 1000 BCE. Bronze technology came to Korea from the area that is today northeastern China (formerly known as Manchuria). About 100 BCE, during the Han dynasty, the Chinese established outposts in Korea. The most important was Lolang, which became a prosperous commercial center. By the middle of the century, however, three native kingdoms—Goguryeo, Baekje, and Silla—controlled most of the Korean peninsula and reigned for more than seven centuries until Silla completed its conquest of its neighbors in 668. During this era, known as the Three Kingdoms period (ca. 57 BCE–688 CE), Korea remained in continuous contact with both China and Japan. Buddhism came to Korea from China

in the fourth century CE, first in Goguryeo and Baekje and then in the Silla kingdom. The Koreans in turn transmitted it from the peninsula to Japan in the sixth century.

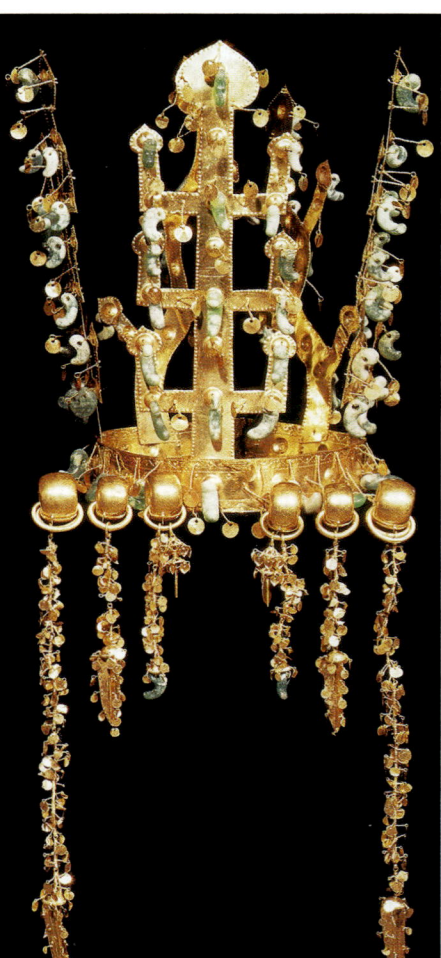

**16-26** Crown, from the north mound of the Cheonmachong tomb (tomb 98), Hwangnam-dong, near Gyeongju, Korea, Three Kingdoms Period, fifth to sixth century. Gold and jade, $10\frac{3}{4}$" high. Gyeongju National Museum, Gyeongju.

This gold-and-jade crown from a Silla tomb attests to the wealth of that kingdom and the skill of its artists. The uprights may be stylized tree and antler forms symbolizing life and supernatural power.

1 in.

**SILLA CROWN** Tombs of the Silla kingdom have yielded spectacular artifacts representative of the wealth and power of its rulers. Finds in the region of Gyeongju, the Silla capital, justify the city's ancient name—Kumsong (City of Gold). The gold-and-jade crown (FIG. 16-26) from the Cheonmachong (Heavenly Horse) tomb at Hwangnam-dong, near Gyeongju, dated to the fifth or sixth century, also attests to the high quality of artisanship among Silla artists. The crown's major elements, the band and the uprights, as well as the myriad spangles adorning them, were cut from sheet gold and embossed along the edges. Gold rivets and wires secure the whole, as do the comma-shaped pieces of jade further embellishing the crown. Archaeologists interpret the uprights as stylized tree and antler forms believed to symbolize life and supernatural power. The Cheonmachong crown has no Chinese counterpart, although the technique of working sheet gold may have come to Korea from northeast China.

**BODHISATTVA MAITREYA** The introduction of Buddhism to Korea in the fourth century created a demand for images of the Buddha and of bodhisattvas. The style and iconography of early Korean Buddhist art usually depended on Chinese models, but later examples depart from Chinese prototypes and mark the maturation of a distinct regional artistic tradition. A three-foot-tall gilt cast-bronze statue (FIG. 16-27), made either in the Baekje or Silla kingdom in the early seventh century CE, represents Bodhisattva Maitreya seated in meditation. Maitreya, the future Buddha who will succeed Shakyamuni, the historical Buddha, wears only a simple necklace, in contrast to the rich jewelry of most Chinese bodhisattvas, and his trilobed crown is also a characteristic Korean feature. The bodhisattva's chest is bare, but he wears a long skirt over his lower body, the folds of which cascade over his seat and onto the ground. Maitreya has crossed his right leg and placed his

right foot on his left thigh. He leans his chin on his right hand, a posture connoting contemplation. His right elbow in turn rests on his right thigh. The slender proportions of the figure have parallels in Chinese bronzes of the Northern Wei dynasty, for example, the group of Shakyamuni and Prabhutaratna (FIG. 16-13) from Hebei Province, but the treatment of the drapery folds differs sharply.

## Unified Silla Kingdom

Aided by China's emperor, the Silla kingdom conquered the Goguryeo and Baekje kingdoms and unified Korea in 668. The era of the Unified Silla Kingdom (688–935) is roughly contemporaneous with the Tang dynasty's brilliant culture in China, and many consider the era Korea's golden age.

**SEOKGURAM** The Silla rulers embraced Buddhism both as a source of religious enlightenment and as a protective force. They considered the magnificent Buddhist temples they constructed in and around their capital of Gyeongju to be supernatural defenses against external threats as well as places of worship. Unfortunately, none of these temples survived Korea's turbulent history. However, there remains at Seokguram, near the summit of Mount Toham, northeast of the city, a splendid granite Buddhist monument (FIG. 16-28). Scant surviving records suggest it was built under the supervision of Kim Tae-song, a member of the royal family who

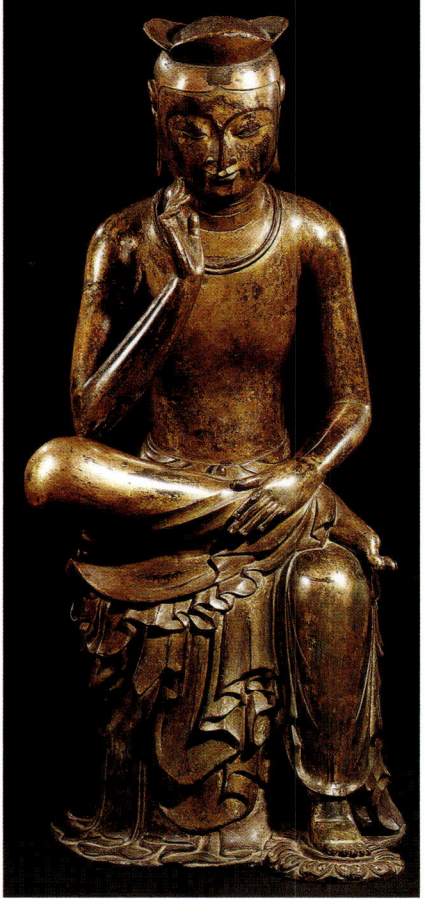

**16-27** Meditating Bodhisattva Maitreya, Three Kingdoms period, early seventh century CE. Gilt bronze, 2′ 11⅞″ high. National Museum of Korea, Seoul.

The introduction of Buddhism to Korea created a demand for Buddhist images. An early masterpiece of Korean Buddhist sculpture is this gilt-bronze statue of Maitreya, the Buddha of the Future.

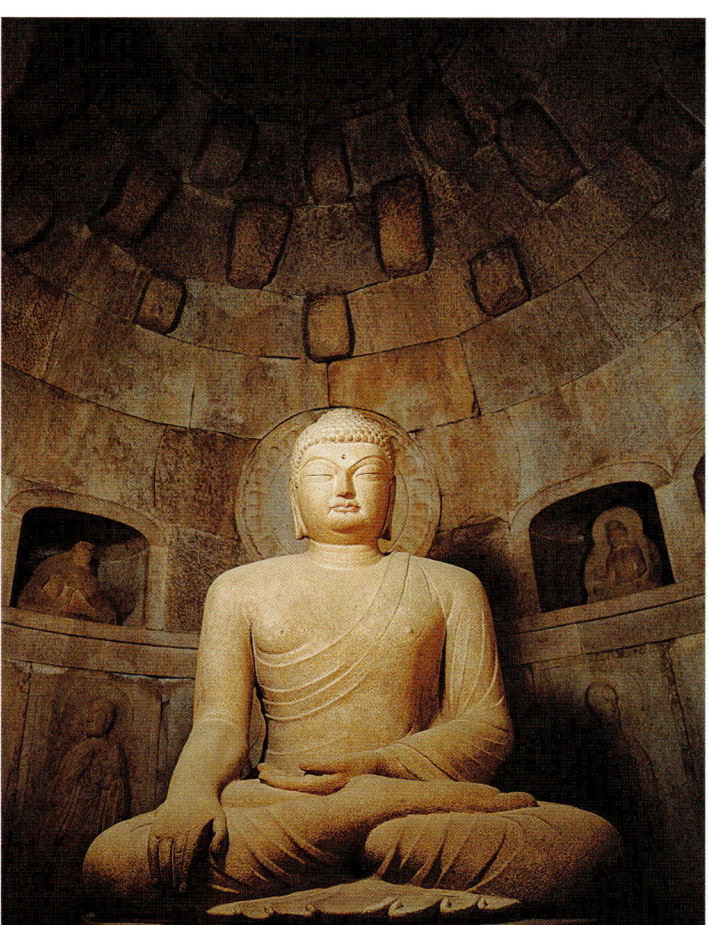

**16-28** Shakyamuni Buddha, in the rotunda of the cave temple, Seokguram, Korea, Unified Silla Kingdom, 751–774. Granite, 11′ high.

Unlike rock-cut Chinese Buddhist shrines, this Korean cave temple was constructed of granite blocks. Dominating the rotunda is a huge statue depicting the Buddha at the moment of enlightenment.

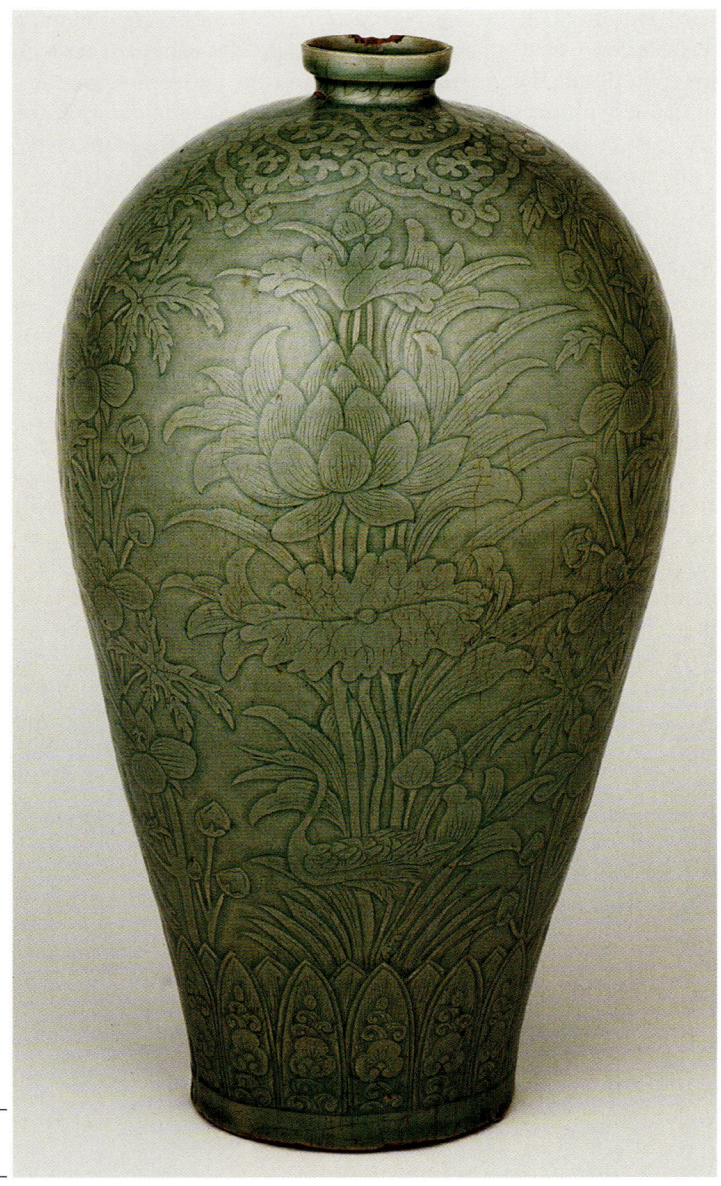

1 in.

**16-29** Maebyeong vase, Goryeo dynasty, 12th century. Porcellaneous stoneware with incised decoration under celadon glaze, 1′ 4″ tall. Philadelphia Museum of Art, Philadelphia (purchased with the Fiske Kimball Fund and the Marie Kimball Fund, 1974).

Celadon wares feature highly translucent iron-pigmented glazes with incised designs. This green maebyeong vase has herons interspersed among mallow and lotus blossoms.

served as prime minister. He initiated construction in 742 to honor his parents in his previous life. Certainly, the intimate scale of Seokguram and the quality of its reliefs and freestanding figures support the idea it was a private chapel for royalty.

The main *rotunda* (circular area under a dome) measures about 21 feet in diameter. Despite its modest size, the Seokguram project required substantial resources. Unlike the Chinese Buddhist caves at Yungang (FIG. 16-13A), Longmen (FIG. 16-14), and Dunhuang (FIG. 16-15), the interior wall surfaces and sculpture were not cut from the rock in the process of excavation. Instead, workers assembled hundreds of granite pieces of various shapes and sizes, attaching them with stone rivets instead of mortar.

Sculpted images of bodhisattvas, lohans, and guardians line the lower zone of the wall. Above, 10 niches contain miniature statues of seated bodhisattvas and believers. All these figures face inward toward the 11-foot-tall statue of Shakyamuni, which dominates the chamber and faces the entrance. Carved from a single block of granite, the image represents the Buddha as he touched the earth to call it to witness the realization of his enlightenment at Bodh Gaya (FIG. 15-1). Although remote in time and place from the Sarnath Buddha in India (FIG. 15-13), this majestic image remains faithful to its iconographic prototype. More immediately, the Korean statue draws on the robust, round-faced figures of Tang China (FIG. 16-14), and its drapery is a more schematic version of the fluid type found in Tang sculpture. However, no close precedents exist for the figure's distinctly broad-shouldered dignity combined with harmonious proportions. Art historians consider this Korean statue one of the finest images of the Buddha in East Asia.

## Goryeo Dynasty

Although Buddhism was the established religion of Korea, Confucianism, introduced from China during the Silla era, increasingly shaped social and political conventions. In the ninth century, the three old kingdoms began to reemerge as distinct political entities, and although the Unified Silla and Goryeo kingdoms overlapped (between about 918 and 935), by 935 the Goryeo (from Goguryeo) had taken control, and they dominated for the next three centuries. In 1231 the Mongols, who had invaded China, pushed into Korea, beginning a war lasting 30 years. In the end, the Goryeo had to submit to forming an alliance with the Mongols, who eventually conquered all of China (see Chapter 33).

**CELADON WARE** Goryeo potters in the 12th century produced the famous Korean *celadon* wares, admired worldwide. The finest celadon wares feature ornate engraved and inlaid designs over which the ceramists applied highly translucent iron-pigmented glazes, fired in an oxygen-deprived kiln to become gray, pale blue, pale green, or brownish-olive. A masterful example of celadon ware is the plum-shaped (*maebyeong* in Korean, *meiping* in Chinese, FIG. 16-21) vase (FIG. **16-29**) that once belonged to the American financier and art collector J. P. Morgan. Dating to the later Goryeo period, it is the largest maebyeong vase known and was decorated using the inlay technique for which Goryeo potters were famous. The artist incised delicate motifs of herons interspersed among mallow and lotus blossoms into the clay's surface and then filled the grooves with white and colored slip. Then the potter scraped the surface of the vessel and finally covered the entire maebyeong with the celadon blue-green glaze. The incised motifs are broader at the top than at the bottom, reflecting the potter's sure sense of the dynamic relationship between ornamentation and ceramic volume.

**CHINA, KOREA, AND JAPAN** China's achievements in virtually every field spread beyond even the boundaries of the vast empires it sometimes controlled. Although Buddhism was born in India, the Chinese adaptations and transformations of its teachings, religious practices, and artistic forms were those that spread farther east. China's neighbors owe China an immense cultural debt, but Korea was the crucial artistic, cultural, and religious link between the mainland and the islands of Japan, the subject of Chapter 17.

# CHINA AND KOREA BEFORE 1280

### NEOLITHIC TO SHANG DYNASTY ca. 7000–1050 BCE

▌ The history of Chinese art begins with the production of Neolithic earthenware pottery in the fourth millennium BCE.

▌ The Shang dynasty (r. ca. 1600–1050 BCE), which ruled the Yellow River valley, was the first great Chinese dynasty of the Bronze Age. Shang bronze-workers were among the best in the ancient world and created a wide variety of elaborately decorated vessels using a sophisticated piece-mold casting process.

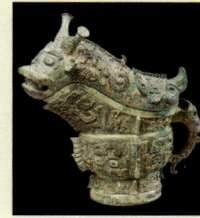

Guang, Anyang,
12th or 11th century BCE

### ZHOU AND QIN DYNASTIES 1050–206 BCE

▌ The Zhou dynasty was the longest in China's history. The Western Zhou kings (r. ca. 1050–771 BCE) ruled from Chang'an and the Eastern Zhou kings (r. 770–256 BCE) from Luoyang. During the last centuries of Zhou rule, Daoism and Confucianism gained wide followings in China. Zhou artists produced lavish works in bronze, lacquer, and especially jade.

▌ China's First Emperor founded the short-lived Qin dynasty (r. 221–206 BCE) after defeating the Zhou and all other rival states. A terracotta army of more than 6,000 soldiers guarded the First Emperor's burial mound at Lintong. The tomb itself remains unexcavated.

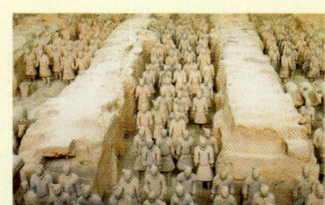

Army of the First Emperor of Qin,
Lintong, ca. 210 BCE

### HAN DYNASTY AND PERIOD OF DISUNITY 206 BCE–581 CE

▌ The Han dynasty (r. 206 BCE–220 CE) extended China's boundaries to the south and west and even traded indirectly with Rome via the fabled Silk Road. Han tombs have yielded rich finds, including painted silks, bronze figurines, jade burial suits, and earthenware models of wooden buildings.

▌ Civil strife divided China into competing states from 220 to 581 CE. The earliest Chinese images of the Buddha date to this so-called Period of Disunity, during which Xie He (early sixth century) formulated his six canons of Chinese painting.

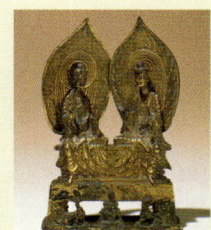

Shakyamuni and
Prabhutaratna, 518

### TANG DYNASTY AND UNIFIED SILLA KINGDOM 618–935

▌ China enjoyed unequaled prosperity and power under the Tang emperors (r. 618–907), whose capital at Chang'an became the greatest and most cosmopolitan city in the world.

▌ The Tang dynasty was the golden age of Chinese figure painting. The few surviving works include *The Thirteen Emperors* handscroll by Yan Liben illustrating historical figures as exemplars of Confucian ideals. The Dunhuang caves provide evidence of the magnificence of Tang Buddhist art, especially mural painting.

▌ Korea also enjoyed an artistic golden age at this time under the Unified Silla Kingdom (r. 688–935).

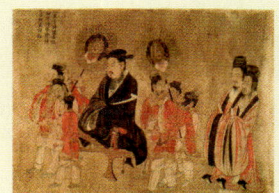

Yan Liben,
*The Thirteen Emperors*, ca. 650

### SONG AND LIAO DYNASTIES 960–1279

▌ Song China (Northern Song, r. 960–1127, capital at Bianliang; Southern Song, r. 1127–1279, capital at Lin'an) was the most technologically advanced society in the world in the early second millennium. The Song era also marked the apogee of Chinese landscape painting. Among the leading artists were Fan Kuan and Ma Yuan.

▌ For part of this period, the Liao dynasty (r. 907–1125) controlled northern China and erected the tallest wooden building in the world, the Foguang Si Pagoda.

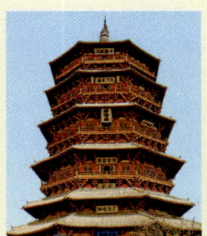

Foguang Si Pagoda,
Yingxian, 1056

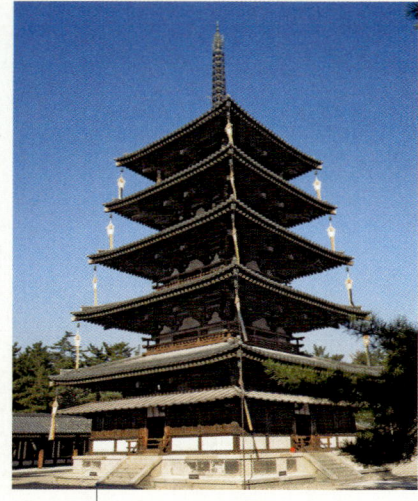

The pagoda of a Japanese Buddhist temple complex housed relics of the Buddha. The Horyuji pagoda is 122 feet tall. The towering height connoted the soaring spirit of Buddhist faith.

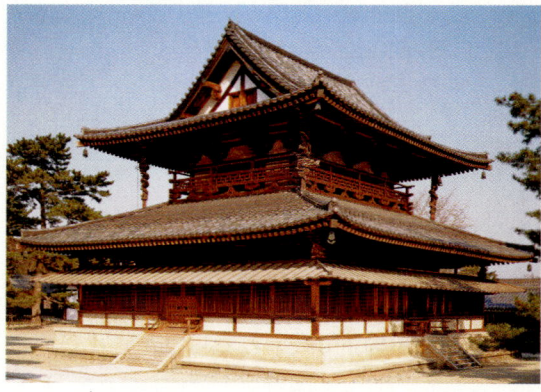

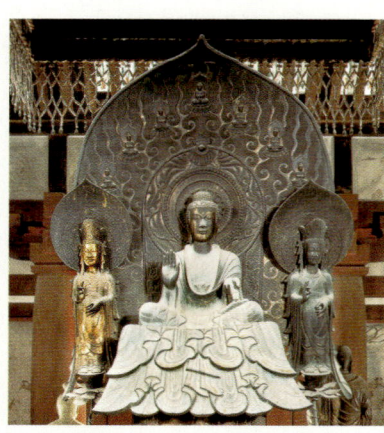

The Horyuji kondo was a replacement for an earlier hall destroyed by fire. Priests rescued its Buddha triad, carved by the master sculptor Tori Busshi, and reinstalled the group in the later structure.

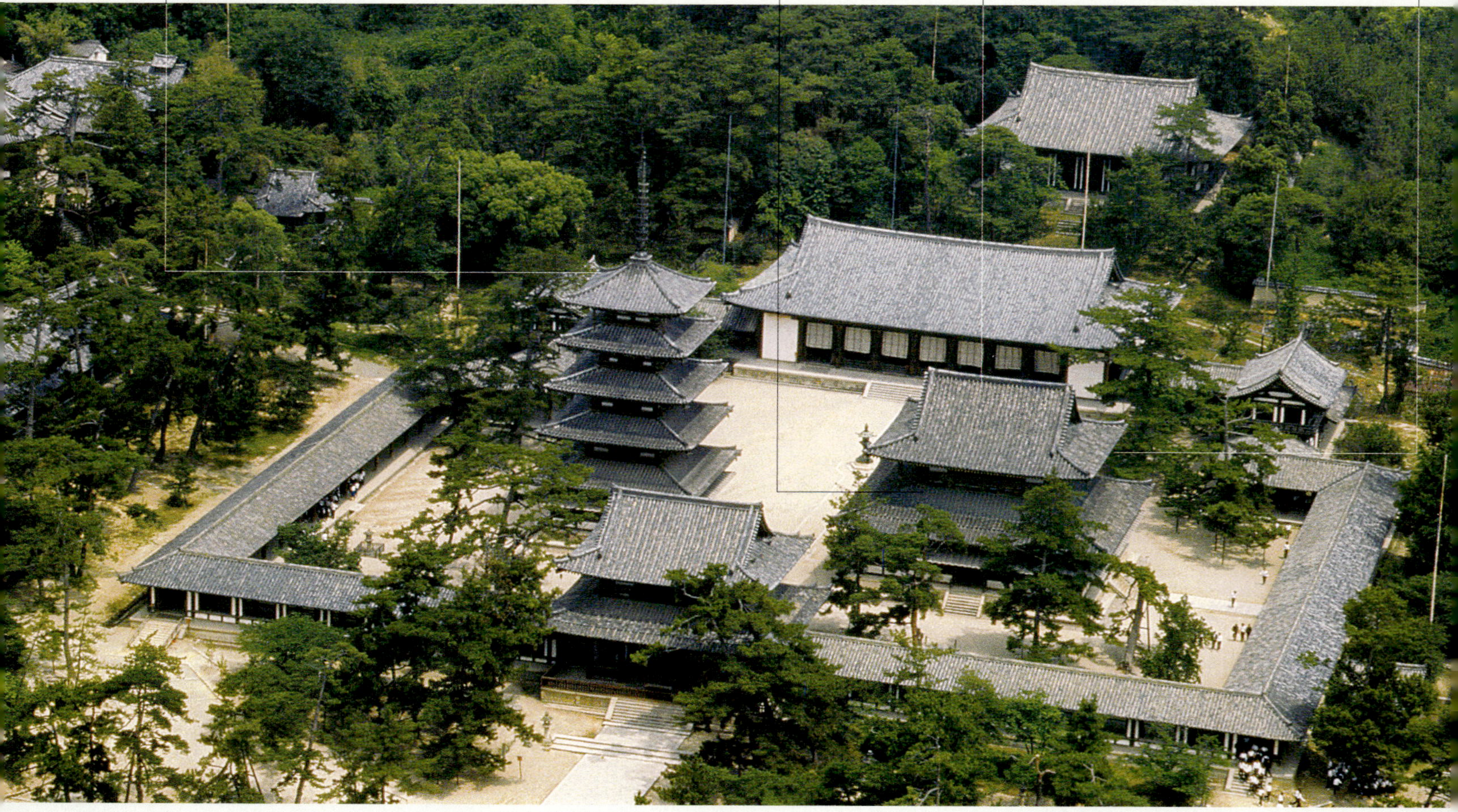

The kondo, or Golden Hall, of a Buddhist temple complex housed statues of the Buddha and bodhisattvas. The Horyuji kondo follows Chinese models in its construction method and curved roofline.

**17-1** Aerial view of the Horyuji temple complex (looking northwest), Nara Prefecture, Japan, Nara period, ca. 680.

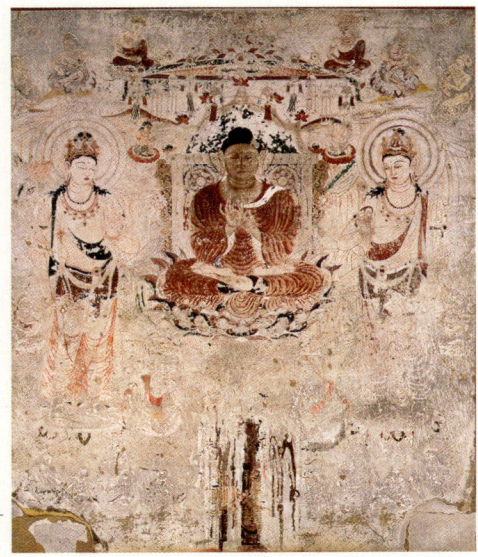

Adorning the Horyuji Golden Hall were mural paintings of the Buddhas of the Four Directions, including Amida, the Buddha of Immeasurable Light and Infinite Life, seated in his Western Pure Land.

# JAPAN BEFORE 1333

## BUDDHISM SPREADS TO JAPAN

The Japanese archipelago (MAP 17-1) consists of four main islands—Hokkaido, Honshu, Shikoku, and Kyushu—and hundreds of smaller ones, a surprising number of them inhabited. Japanese culture, however, does not share the isolation of some island civilizations, but rather has long demonstrated responsiveness to imported ideas—Buddhism among them.

Buddhism arrived in Japan in 552 CE in the form of a gift of Buddhist scriptures and a Buddha statue from a Korean king to the Japanese emperor. The most important early Japanese Buddhist temple complex is at Horyuji (FIG. 17-1), seven miles south of present-day Nara. Fire destroyed the first (sixth-century) temple on the site, which housed a bronze *Buddha triad* (Buddha flanked by two bodhisattvas) dated 632. Shaka—the Japanese name for the historical Buddha (Shakyamuni in Sanskrit)—sits in front of a flaming mandorla (a lotus-petal-shaped nimbus). The sculptor was TORI BUSSHI (*busshi* means "maker of Buddhist images").

Temple officials later installed Tori's group in the rebuilt seventh-century *kondo* of the Nara complex. The kondo, or Golden Hall, was the main hall for worship and contained statues of the Buddha and the bodhisattvas the temple honored. Other key buildings in the Horyuji and similar Japanese Buddhist temple complexes include the *kodo,* or lecture hall, for both monks and laypersons to listen to the reading of sacred texts, and a pagoda, which housed relics of the Buddha. The Horyuji pagoda is five stories and 122 feet tall. The towering height—accentuated by the decreasing size of the roofs from bottom to top—connotes the soaring spirit of Buddhist faith. Both the Horyuji kondo and pagoda underscore Japan's openness to other East Asian artistic traditions. Following Chinese models, the Japanese builders used ceramic tiles as roofing material and adopted the distinctive curved roofline of Tang (FIG. 16-15A) and later Chinese architecture.

In addition to Tori's Buddha triad, the Horyuji kondo boasted some of the finest examples of Buddhist wall painting in East Asia. The pictorial program celebrated the Buddhas of the Four Directions, including Amida (Amitabha in Sanskrit), the Buddha of Immeasurable Light and Infinite Life, who was ruler of the Western Pure Land Paradise. Some scholars believe the painters who executed the Horyuji murals were not Japanese but Chinese or Korean—further evidence of the fruitful artistic and cultural exchanges between the Japanese islands and the mainland. The introduction of Buddhism to Japan in 552 CE so profoundly changed the character of Japanese art and architecture that scholars traditionally divide the early history of art in Japan into pre-Buddhist and Buddhist eras.

# JAPAN BEFORE BUDDHISM

Japan's earliest distinct culture antedated the birth of the Buddha (see "The Life of the Buddha," Chapter 15, page 423) by roughly 10,000 years and lasted for several millennia, far longer than the entire later history of art in Japan.

## Jomon

Art historians call the earliest art-producing culture of Japan the Jomon (ca. 10,500–300 BCE). The term *jomon* ("cord markings") refers to the technique Japanese potters of this era used to decorate earthenware vessels. The Jomon people were hunter-gatherers, but unlike most such societies, which were nomadic, the Jomon enjoyed surprisingly settled lives. Their villages consisted of pit dwellings—shallow round excavations with raised earthen rims and thatched roofs. Their settled existence permitted the Jomon people to develop distinctive ceramic technology, even before their development of agriculture. In fact, archaeologists have dated some ceramic *sherds* (pottery fragments) found in Japan to before 10,000 BCE—older than sherds from any other area of the world.

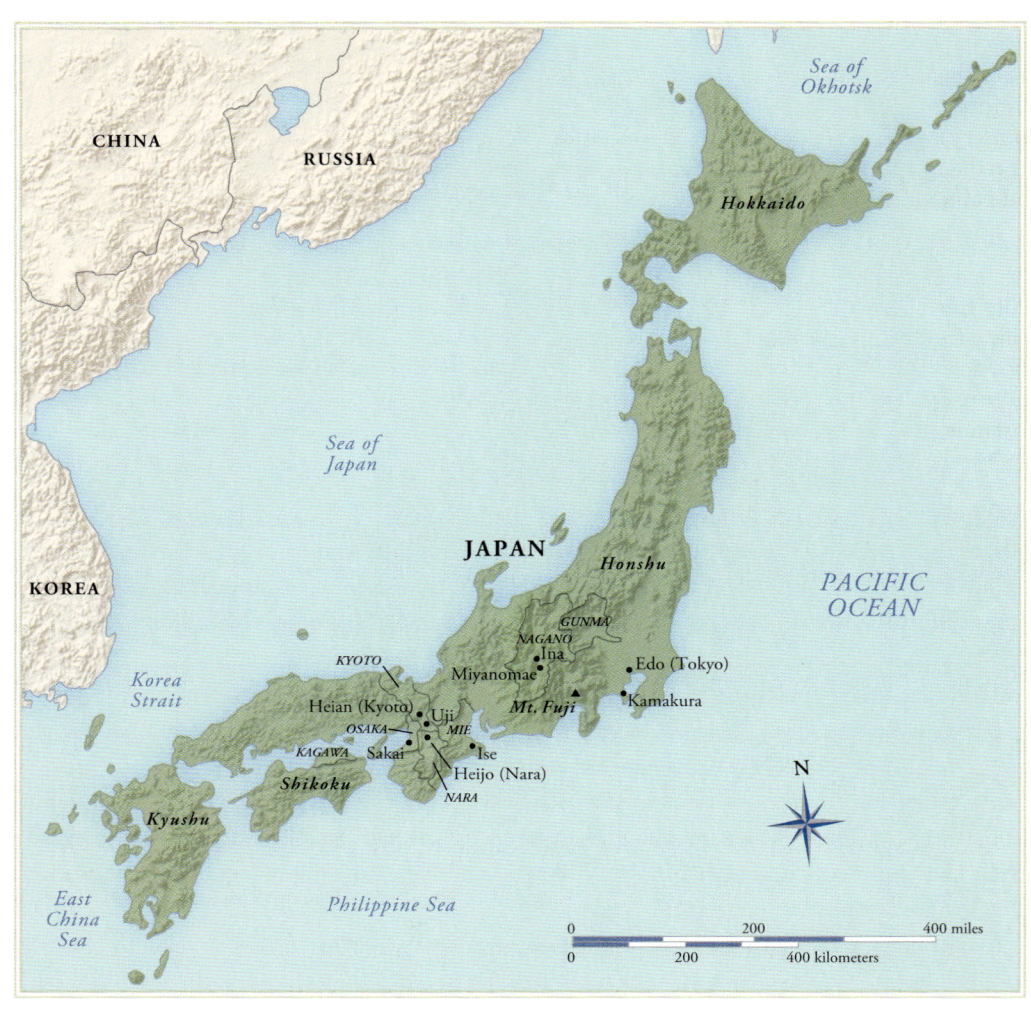

**MAP 17-1** Japan before 1333.

# JAPAN BEFORE 1333

| BCE | CE | | | | | |
|---|---|---|---|---|---|---|
| Jomon and Yayoi | Kofun | Asuka and Nara | | Heian | Kamakura | |
| 10,500 — 300 | 300 — 552 | 552 — 784 | 794 | 794 — 1185 | 1185 — 1332 | |

- ❙ Neolithic Jomon ceramists produce distinctive pottery having cordlike decoration
- ❙ Yayoi metalworkers cast bronze bells modeled on Han Chinese prototypes

- ❙ Japanese elite patrons construct monumental keyhole-shaped burial mounds and place cylindrical clay figures (haniwa) around and on top of them

- ❙ Buddhism arrives in Japan from Korea in 552, initiating the Asuka period
- ❙ The imperial government establishes its capital at Nara in 710 and builds Buddhist temple complexes following Chinese models

- ❙ The imperial capital moves to Heiankyo (Kyoto) in 794, and Esoteric Buddhism takes hold in Japan
- ❙ Narrative scroll painting becomes a major art form

- ❙ Power shifts from the Japanese emperor to the shoguns of Kamakura
- ❙ Sculptors create realistic portraits in wood with rock-crystal eyes

**MIDDLE JOMON POTTERY** In addition to rope markings, incised lines and applied coils of clay adorned Jomon pottery surfaces. The most impressive examples come from the Middle Jomon period (2500–1500 BCE). Much of the population then lived in the mountainous inland region, where local variations in ceramic form and surface treatment abounded. However, all Jomon potters shared a highly developed feeling for modeled, rather than painted, ceramic ornamentation. Jomon pottery displays such a wealth of applied clay coils, striped incisions, and sometimes quasi-figural motifs that the sculptural treatment in certain instances even jeopardizes the basic functionality of the vessel. Jomon vessels served a wide variety of purposes, from storage to cooking to bone burial. Some of the most elaborate pots may have been used in communal rituals. A dramatic example (FIG. **17-2**) from Miyanomae characteristically shows an intricately modeled surface and a partially sculpted rim. Jomon pottery contrasts strikingly with China's most celebrated Neolithic earthenwares (FIG. 16-2), which emphasize basic ceramic form and painted decoration.

## Yayoi

Jomon culture gradually gave way to Yayoi (ca. 300 BCE–300 CE). The period takes its name from the Yayoi district of Tokyo, where archaeologists initially discovered evidence of this first post-Jomon civilization, but the culture emerged in Kyushu, the southernmost of the main Japanese islands, and spread northward. Increased interaction with both China and Korea and immigration from Korea brought dramatic social and technological transformations during the Yayoi period. The Japanese continued to live in pit dwellings, but their villages grew in size, and they developed fortifications, indicating a perceived need for defense. In the third century CE, Chinese visitors noted Japan had walled towns, many small kingdoms, and a highly stratified social structure. Wet-rice agriculture provided the social and economic foundations for this development. The Yayoi period was a time of tremendous change in Japanese material culture as well. Yayoi ceramists produced vessels that were less sculptural than Jomon pottery and sometimes polychrome, and they developed bronze-casting and loom weaving.

**DOTAKU** Among the most intriguing objects Yayoi artisans fashioned were *dotaku,* or bells. They resemble Han Chinese bell forms, but the Yayoi did not use dotaku as musical instruments. The bronze bells, which are oval in section and range in height from 5 inches to more than 4 feet, were treasured ceremonial objects, and the Japanese often deposited them in graves. Cast in clay molds, these bronzes generally featured raised geometric decoration presented in bands or blocks. On some of the hundreds of surviving dotaku, including the medium-size example illustrated here (FIG. **17-3**), the ornamentation consists of simple line drawings of people, animals, and boats, often in scenes of hunting and fishing or agricultural activities. The dotaku engravings are the earliest extant examples of pictorial art in Japan.

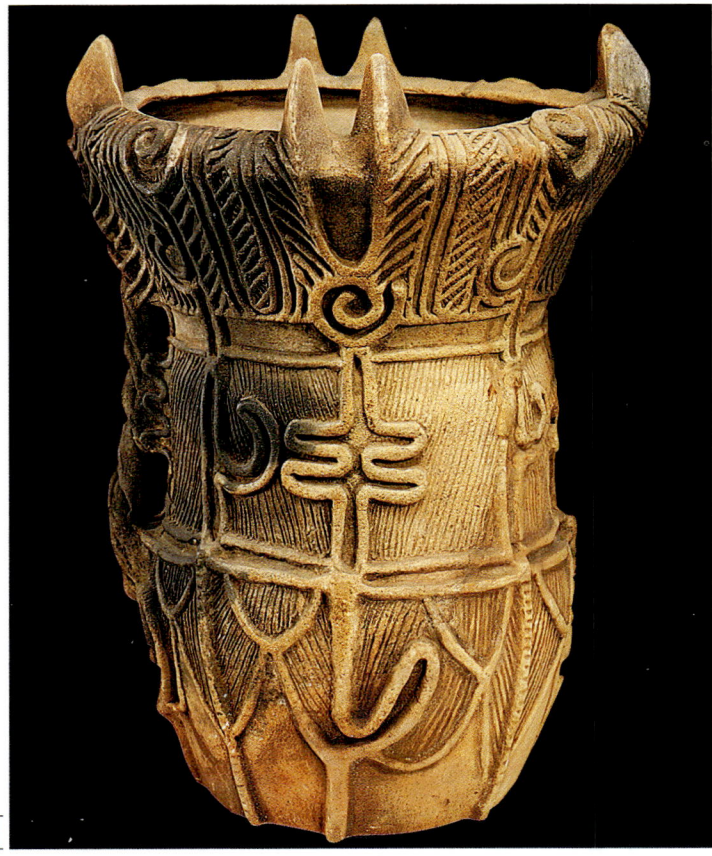

**17-2** Vessel, from Miyanomae, Nagano Prefecture, Japan, Middle Jomon period, ca. 2500–1500 BCE. Earthenware, 1′ 11⅔″ high. Tokyo National Museum, Tokyo.

Jomon pottery is the earliest art form of Japan. Characteristic features are the applied clay coils, striped incisions, and quasi-figural motifs that sometimes jeopardize the functionality of the vessel.

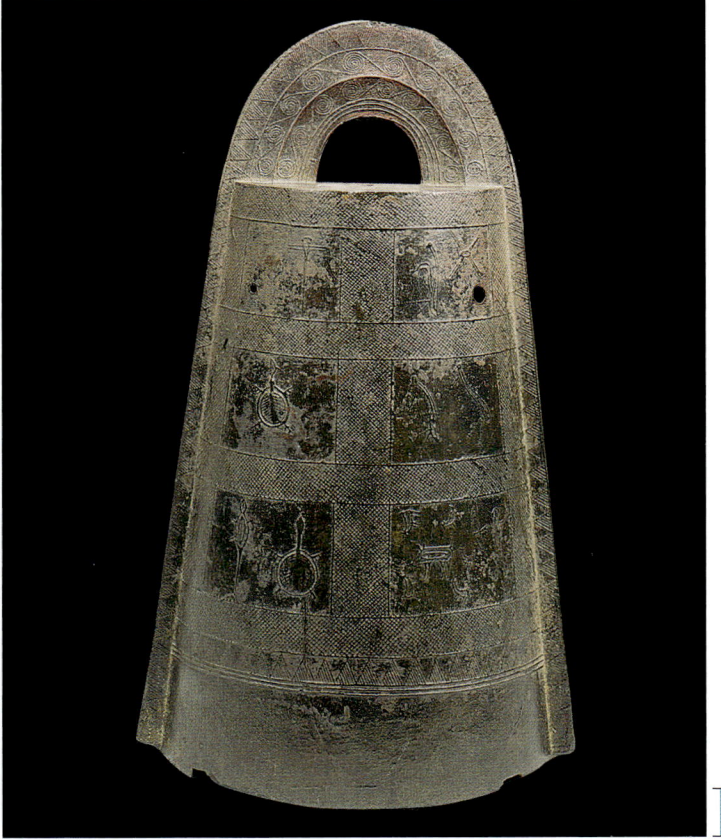

**17-3** Dotaku with incised figural motifs, from Kagawa Prefecture, Japan, late Yayoi period, ca. 100–300 CE. Bronze, 1′ 4⅞″ high. Tokyo National Museum, Tokyo.

Yayoi dotaku were based on Han Chinese bells, but they were not musical instruments. Dotaku feature geometric decoration and the earliest Japanese images of humans and animals.

# Kofun

Historians named the succeeding Kofun period (ca. 300–552)* after the enormous earthen burial mounds, or *tumuli*, that had begun to appear in the third century. (*Ko* means "old"; *fun* means "tomb.") The tumuli grew dramatically in number and scale in the fourth century and, as in Greece (FIG. 4-20) and Italy (FIG. 6-6) many centuries earlier, served to proclaim the power and wealth of those buried in them.

**TOMB OF NINTOKU** The largest tumulus (FIG. **17-4**) in Japan is at Sakai. Most scholars identify it as the tomb of Emperor Nintoku, although others think the tumulus postdates his death in 399. The central mound, which takes the "keyhole" form that was standard for tumuli during the Kofun period, is 1,574 feet long and rises to a height of 114 feet. Surrounded by three moats, the entire site covers 458 acres. The best-preserved Kofun tumuli have a stone-walled burial chamber near the summit of the mound. Inside were the deceased's coffin and numerous objects to take into the afterlife. The objects buried with exalted individuals such as Emperor Nintoku included imperial regalia, swords, comma-shaped jewels, and bronze mirrors. The mirrors, which the Japanese believed offered magical protection, came from China, but the form of the Kofun keyhole tombs and many of the other burial goods suggest even closer connections with Korea. For example, the comma-shaped jewels closely resemble those found on Korean Silla crowns (FIG. 16-26), but the Japanese counterparts are simpler and fashioned of gilt bronze.

**HANIWA** The Japanese also placed unglazed ceramic sculptures called *haniwa* on and around Kofun tumuli. These sculptures, usually several feet in height, as is the warrior shown here (FIG. **17-5**), are distinctly Japanese. Compared with the Chinese terracotta soldiers and horses (FIG. 16-6) buried with the First Emperor of Qin, these statues appear deceptively whimsical as variations on a cylindrical theme (*hani* means "clay," *wa* means "circle"). Yet haniwa sculptors skillfully adapted the basic clay cylinder into a host of forms, from abstract shapes to objects, animals (for example, deer, bears, horses, and monkeys), and human figures, such as warriors and female shamans. These artists altered the shapes of the cylinders, emblazoned them with applied ornaments, excised or built up forms, and then painted the haniwa. The variety of figure types suggests the haniwa did not function as military guards but perhaps rather represented the realm the deceased ruled during his life. The Japanese set the statues both in curving rows around the tumulus and in groups around a haniwa house placed directly over the deceased's

*From this point on, all dates in this chapter are CE unless otherwise stated.

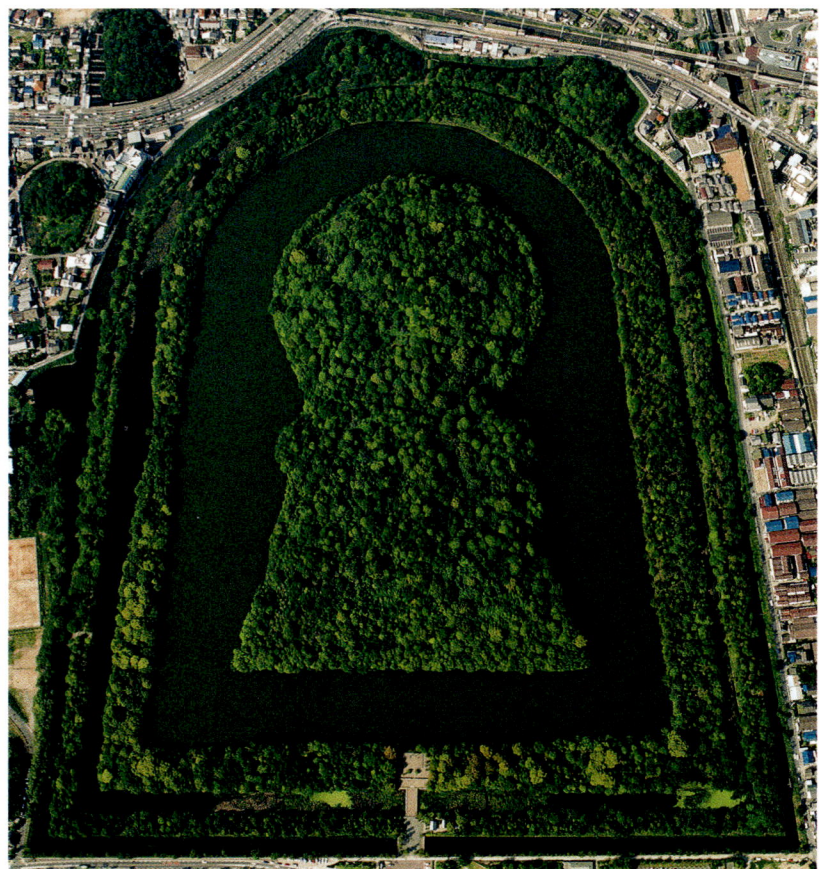

**17-4** Tomb of Emperor Nintoku (looking northeast), Sakai, Osaka Prefecture, Japan, Kofun period, late fourth to early fifth century.

The largest Kofun tumulus, attributed to Emperor Nintoku, has a keyhole shape and three surrounding moats. About 20,000 clay haniwa originally stood on the gigantic earthen mound.

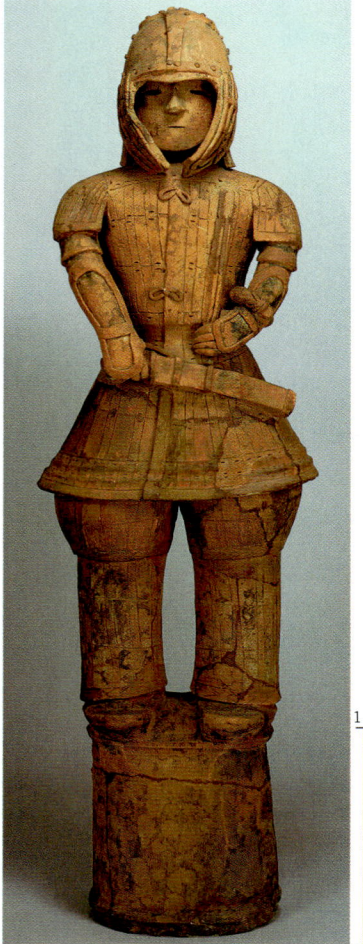

burial chamber. Presumably, the number of sculptures reflected the stature of the dead person. The arrangement may mimic a funeral procession in honor of the dead. Emperor Nintoku's tumulus had about 20,000 haniwa statues placed around the mound.

**SHINTO** The religious system the Japanese embraced during the Yayoi and Kofun eras is Shinto (see "Shinto," page 479). The Japanese imperial clan traces its origins to the Shinto sun goddess Amaterasu. Her shrine (FIG. **17-6**) at Ise in a forest near the Isuzu River is the most important Shinto religious center. The location, use, and ritual reconstruction of the Ise Jingu (Ise Shrine) every 20 years reflect the primary characteristics of Shinto—sacred space, ritual renewal, and purification.

**17-5** Haniwa warrior, from Gunma Prefecture, Japan, Kofun period, fifth to mid-sixth century. Low-fired clay, 4′ 3¼″ high. Tokyo National Museum, Tokyo. ◼◂

During the Kofun period, the Japanese set up cylindrical clay statues (haniwa) of humans, animals, and objects on burial tumuli. They may represent the realm the deceased ruled during his life.

## Shinto

The early beliefs and practices of pre-Buddhist Japan, which form a part of the belief system later called Shinto ("Way of the Gods"), did not derive from the teachings of any individual founding figure or distinct leader. Nor do formal scriptures, in the strict sense, exist for these beliefs and practices. Shinto developed in Japan in conjunction with the advent of agriculture during the Yayoi period. Japanese religious practices thus originally focused on the needs of this agrarian society and included agricultural rites surrounding planting and harvesting. Villagers venerated and prayed to a multitude of local deities or spirits called *kami*. The early Japanese believed kami existed in mountains, waterfalls, trees, and other features of nature, as well as in charismatic people, and they venerated not only the kami themselves but also the places the kami occupied, which the ancient Japanese considered sacred.

Each clan (a local group claiming a common ancestor, and the basic societal unit during the Kofun period) had its own protector kami, to whom members offered prayers in the spring for successful planting and in the fall for good harvests. Clan members built shrines consisting of several buildings for the veneration of kami. Priests made offerings of grains and fruits at these shrines and prayed on behalf of the clans. Rituals of divination, water purifica-

tion, and ceremonial cleansing at the shrines proliferated. Visitors to the shrine area had to wash before entering in a ritual of spiritual and physical purification.

Purity was such a critical aspect of Japanese religious beliefs that people would abandon buildings and even settlements if negative events, such as poor harvests, suggested spiritual defilement. Even the early imperial court moved several times to newly built towns to escape impurity and its consequences. Such purification concepts are also the basis for the cyclical rebuilding of the sanctuaries at grand shrines. The buildings of the inner shrine (FIG. 17-6) at Ise, for example, have been rebuilt every 20 years for more than a millennium with few interruptions. Rebuilding rids the sacred site of physical and spiritual impurities that otherwise might accumulate. During reconstruction, the old shrine remains standing until carpenters build an exact duplicate next to it. In this way, the Japanese have preserved ancient forms with great precision.

When Buddhism arrived in Japan from the mainland in the sixth century, Shinto practices changed. For example, until the introduction of Buddhism, painted or carved images of Shinto deities did not exist. Yet despite the eventual predominance of Buddhism in Japan, Shinto remains a vital religion for many Japanese.

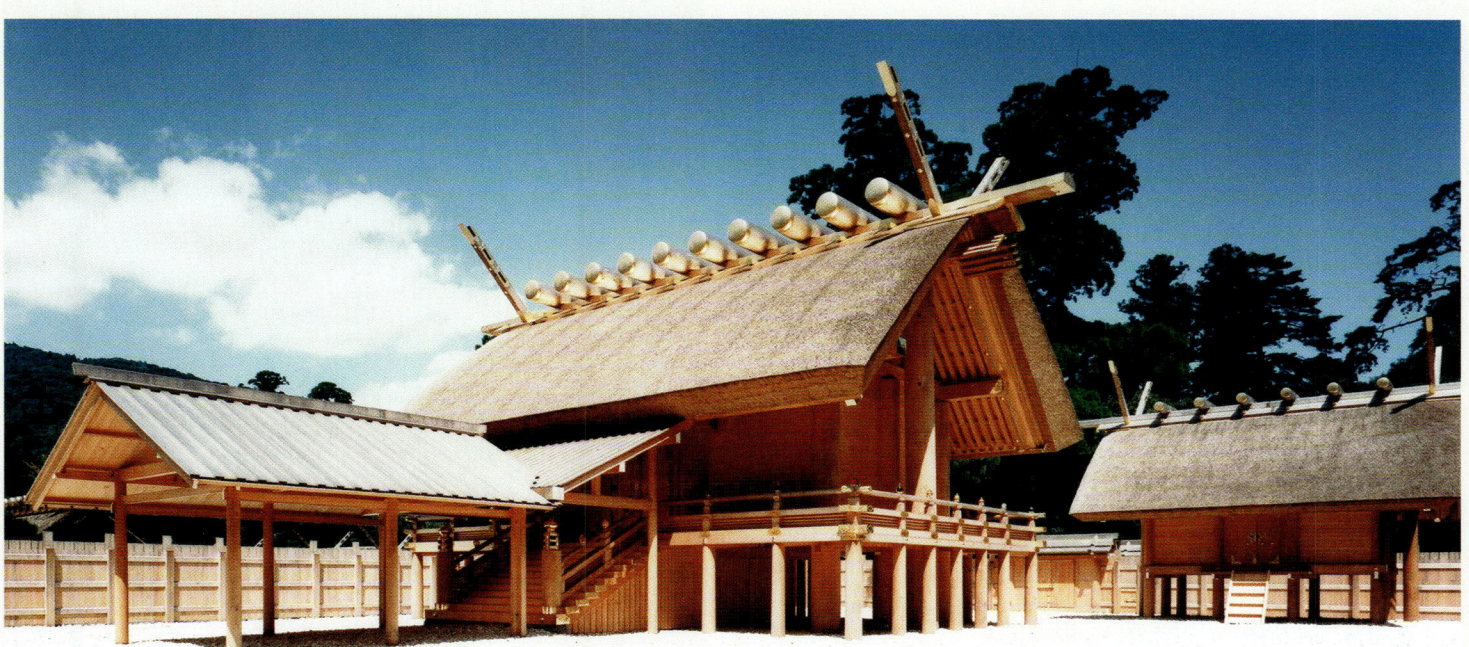

**17-6** **Main hall (looking northwest) of the Ise Jingu, Ise, Mie Prefecture, Japan, Kofun period or later; rebuilt in 1993.**

The most important Shinto shrine in Japan honors the sun goddess Amaterasu. Constructed of wood with a thatch roof and rebuilt every 20 years, the shrine reflects the form of early Japanese granaries.

Traditionally attributed to the Kofun period, the shrine is probably of later date, but it still serves as a representative example of sacred architecture in ancient Japan. Although Japanese shrine architecture varies tremendously, scholars believe the Ise Shrine preserves some of the earliest design elements. Yet the shrine is unique because of its connection to the Japanese imperial family. No other shrines may

be constructed with the identical design. The original source for the form of the Ise complex's main hall appears to be Japanese granaries, which were among the most important buildings in Japan's early agrarian society. Not every aspect of the Ise Shrine is equally ancient. The three main structures of the inner shrine nonetheless convey some sense of Japanese architecture before the introduction of

Buddhism and before the development of more elaborately constructed and adorned buildings.

Aside from the thatched roofs and some metallic decorations, the sole construction material at Ise is wood, fitted together in a *mortise-and-tenon* system, in which the builders slip the wallboards into slots in the pillars. Two massive freestanding posts (once great cypress trunks), one at the center of each end of the main sanctuary, support most of the weight of the *ridgepole,* the beam at the crest of the roof. The golden-hued cypress columns and planks contrast in color and texture with the white gravel covering the sacred grounds. The roof was thatch, which the Japanese smoked, sewed into bundles, and then laid in layers. The smooth shearing of the entire surface produced a gently changing contour. Today, cypress bark covers the roof. Decorative elements (originally having a structural function) enhance the roofline, and include *chigi,* extensions of the rafters at each end of the roof, and *katsuogi,* wooden logs placed at right angles across the ridgepole to hold the thatch of the roof in place. The Ise Shrine highlights the connection, central to Shinto, between nature and spirit. Not only are the construction materials derived from the natural world, but the shrine also stands at a specific location where the builders believed a kami had taken up residence.

# BUDDHIST JAPAN

In 552, according to traditional interpretation, King Syong Myong, ruler of Baekje, one of Korea's Three Kingdoms (see Chapter 16), sent Emperor Kimmei (r. 539–571) of Japan a gilded-bronze statue of the Buddha along with *sutras* (Buddhist scriptures) translated into Chinese, at the time the written language of East Asia. The Korean king urged the Japanese emperor to convert to Buddhism. Resistance to the new religion was initially fierce and led to civil strife and armed conflict between opposing Japanese factions. Syong Myong's gift nonetheless marked the beginning of the Asuka period (552–645), during which the ruling elite embraced major elements of continental culture that had been gradually filtering into Japan. These cultural components, which ultimately became firmly established in Japan, included Chinese writing, Confucianism (see "Daoism and Confucianism," Chapter 16, page 463), and Buddhism (see "Buddhism and Buddhist Iconography," Chapter 15, page 427). Older beliefs and practices (those that came to be known as Shinto) continued to have significance (and do to the present day), especially as agricultural rituals and imperial court rites. As time passed, Shinto deities even gained new identities as local manifestations of Buddhist deities.

In 645, a series of reforms led to the establishment of a centralized government in place of the individual clans that controlled Japan's different regions. This shift marked the beginning of the Nara period (645–784), when the Japanese court, ruling from a series of capitals south of modern Kyoto, increasingly adopted the forms and rites of the Chinese court. In 710, the Japanese finally established what they intended as a permanent capital at Heijo (present-day Nara). City planners laid out the new capital on a symmetrical grid closely modeled on the plan of the Chinese capital of Chang'an.

## Asuka and Nara

In the arts associated with Buddhist practices, Japan followed Korean and Chinese prototypes very closely, especially during the Asuka and Nara periods. In fact, early Buddhist architecture in Japan adhered so closely to mainland standards (although generally with a considerable time lag) that surviving Japanese temples have helped greatly in the reconstruction of what has been almost completely lost on the Asian continent.

**TORI BUSSHI** Among the earliest extant examples of Japanese Buddhist sculpture is the bronze Buddha triad (FIG. 17-7) by Tori Busshi at Horyuji (FIG. 17-1), dated 632. According to the inscription on the Buddha's halo, Empress Suiko (r. 593–628) commissioned the work as a votive offering when her nephew, Prince Shotuku Taishi, the leading champion of Buddhism and Confucian principles of governance in Asuka Japan, fell ill in 621. When Shotuku died, the empress dedicated the triad to the prince's well-being in his next life and to his hoped-for rebirth in Paradise. The central figure in the triad is Shaka, seated with his right hand raised in the abhaya mudra ("fear-not gesture"; see "Buddhism and Buddhist Iconography," Chapter 15, page 427). The flaming mandorla that forms a backdrop to the historical Buddha incorporates small figures of other Buddhas. The sculptor was a descendant of a Chinese immigrant, and the Horyuji Buddha triad reflects the style of the early to mid-sixth century in China and Korea, a style that featured elongated heads and elegant drapery folds forming gravity-defying swirls. The vibrant patterns of the Buddha's garment contrast with the serenity of his pose and expression.

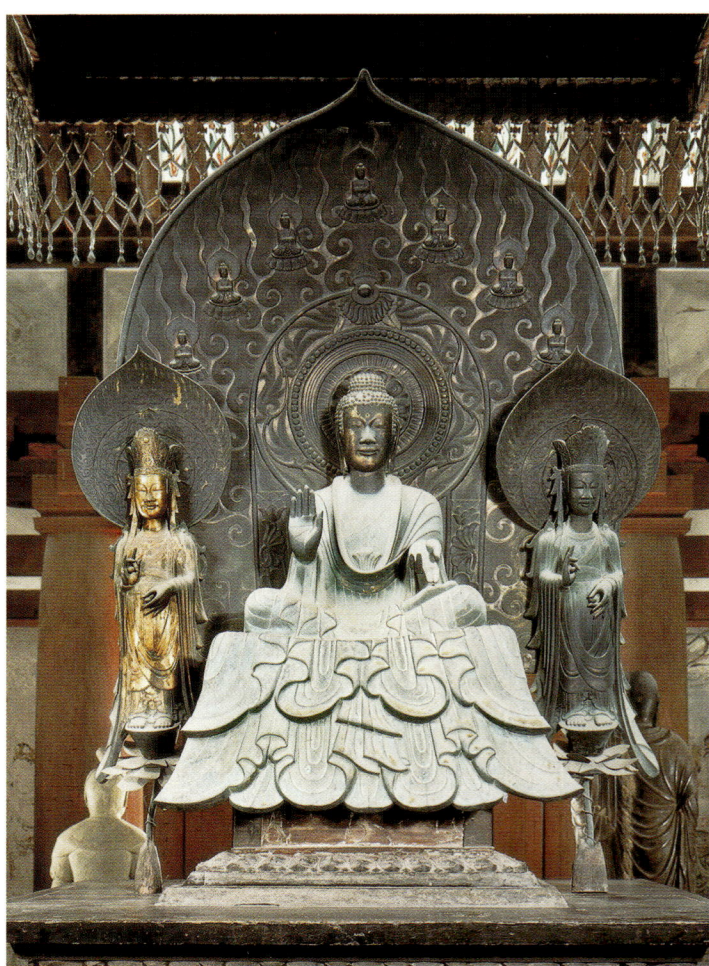

**17-7** TORI BUSSHI, Shaka triad, kondo, Horyuji, Nara Prefecture, Japan, Asuka period, 623. Bronze, central figure 2′ 10″ high. ◼◀

Tori's Shaka triad (the historical Buddha and two bodhisattvas) is among the earliest Japanese Buddhist sculptures. The elongated heads and elegant swirling drapery reflect Chinese models.

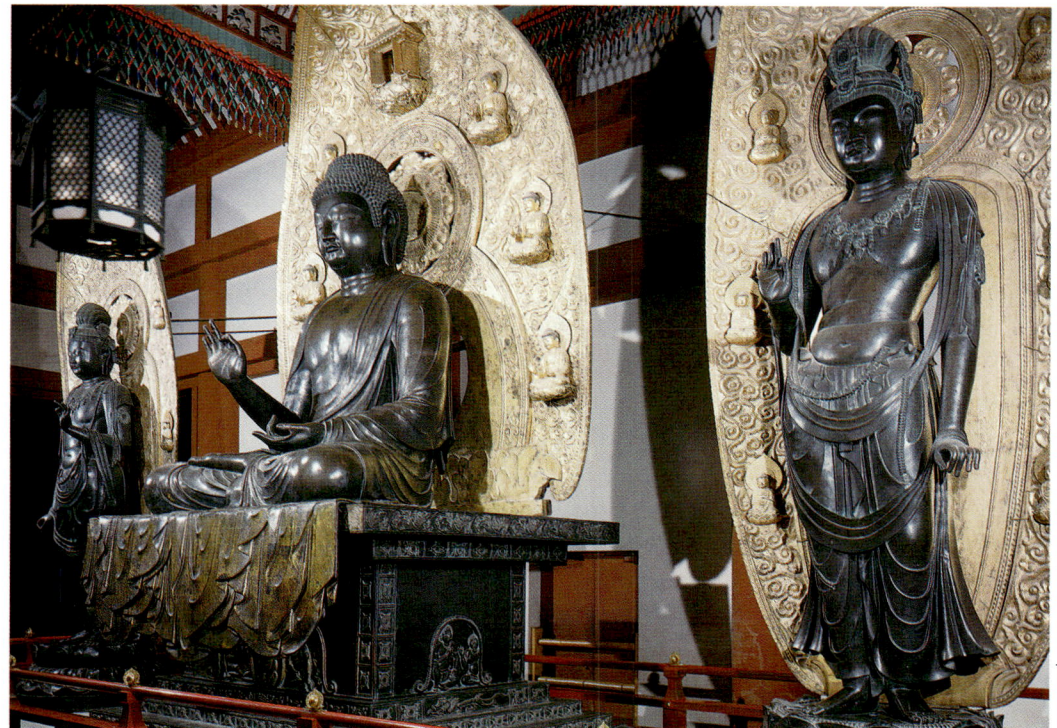

**17-8** Yakushi triad, kondo, Yakushiji, Nara Prefecture, Japan, Nara period, late seventh or early eighth century. Bronze, central figure 8′ 4″ high, including base and mandorla. ◼◂

The sculptor of this Buddha triad favored greater anatomical definition and shape-revealing drapery than did Asuka artist Tori Busshi. The Nara statues display the sensuality of Indian sculpture.

1 ft.

**YAKUSHI TRIAD** In the early Nara period, Japanese sculptors began to move beyond the Asuka style in favor of new ideas and forms coming out of Tang China and Korea. More direct relations with China also narrowed the time lag between developments there and their transfer to Japan. In the bronze (originally gilded) triad of Yakushi (the Indian Bhaisajyaguru, the Buddha of Healing who presides over the Eastern Pure Land; FIG. **17-8**) in the kondo of the late-seventh-century Yakushiji temple complex in Nara, the sculptor favored greater anatomical definition and shape-revealing drapery over the dramatic stylizations of Tori's triad. The statues of

the attendant Bodhisattvas Nikko and Gakko, especially, reveal the long stylistic trail back through China (FIG. 16-14) to the sensuous fleshiness and outthrust-hip poses of Indian sculpture (FIGS. 15-7, *bottom,* and 15-13).

**HORYUJI KONDO** Tori Busshi created his Shaka triad for an Asuka Buddhist temple complex at Horyuji (FIG. 17-1), founded by Prince Shotuku near his own estate outside Nara. Fire destroyed the Asuka temple, but the priests rescued Tori's statue and reinstalled it around 680 in the kondo (FIG. **17-9**) of the successor Nara-era

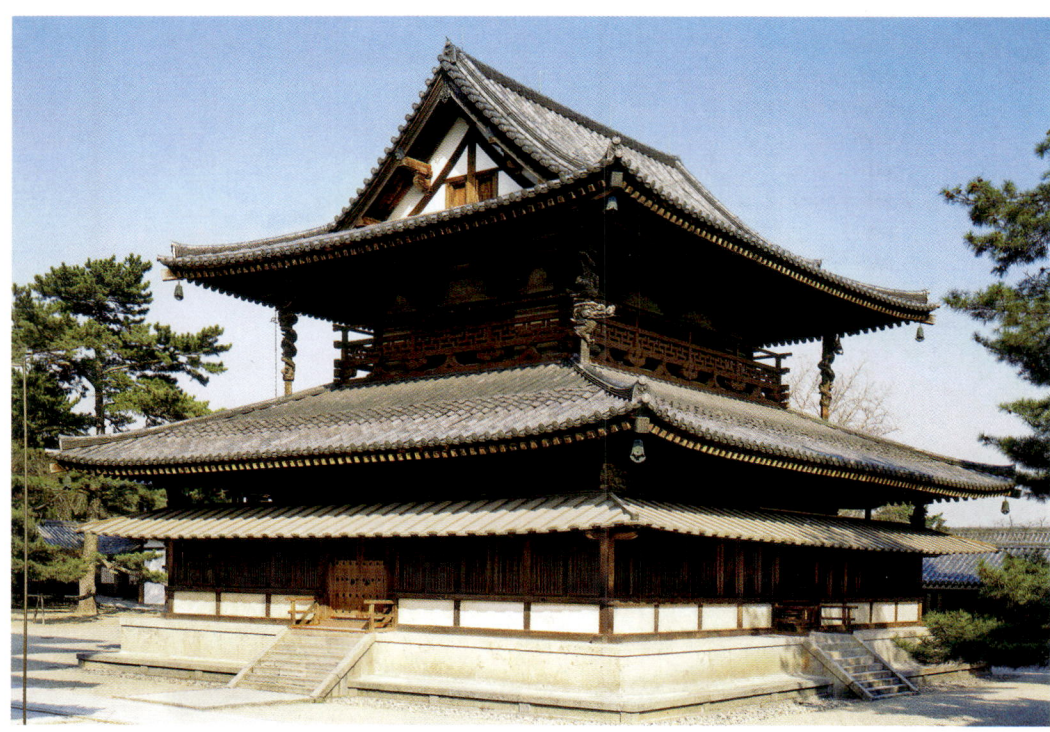

**17-9** Kondo (looking southeast), Horyuji, Nara Prefecture, Japan, Nara period, ca. 680.

The kondo, or Golden Hall, of a Buddhist temple complex housed statues of the Buddha and bodhisattvas. The Horyuji kondo follows Chinese models in its construction method and curved roofline.

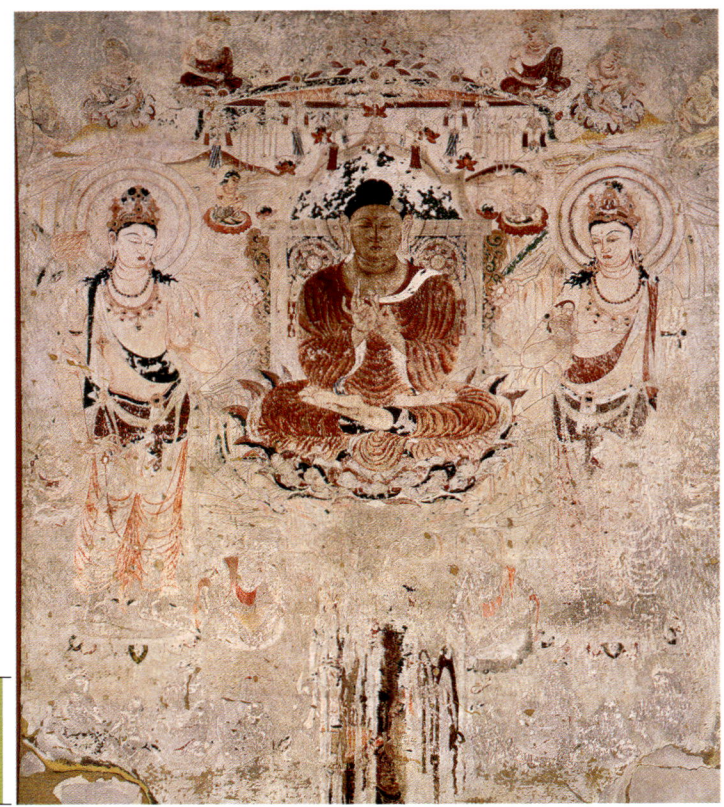

1 ft.

**17-10** Amida triad, photograph before fire damage of the mural formerly in the kondo, Horyuji, Nara Prefecture, Japan, Nara period, ca. 710. Ink and colors, 10′ 3″ × 8′ 6″. Original mural now in the Horyuji Treasure House, Nara.

The murals of the Horyuji kondo represented the Buddhas of the Four Directions. Amida, the Buddha of the Western Pure Land, has red iron-wire lines and reflects Chinese Tang painting style.

complex. Although periodically repaired and somewhat altered (the covered porch is an eighth-century addition; the upper railing dates to the 17th century), the structure retains its graceful but sturdy forms beneath the modifications. The main pillars (not visible in FIG. 17-9 due to the porch addition) decrease in diameter from bottom to top. The tapering provides an effective transition between the more delicate brackets above and the columns' stout forms. Also somewhat masked by the added porch is the harmonious reduction in scale from the first to the second story.

Until a disastrous fire in 1949, visitors to the Horyuji complex could view important early examples of Japanese Buddhist mural painting. Executed around 710, when Nara became the Japanese capital, these

**17-11** Daibutsuden (looking north), odaiji, Nara, Japan, Nara period, 743; rebuilt ca. 1700.

The Daibutsuden of the Todaiji temple complex is the largest wooden building in the world. Commissioned by Emperor Shomu in 743, the Great Buddha Hall originally had 11 bays instead of the current 7.

paintings are poorly preserved today and best studied in old color photographs. The most important paintings depicted the Buddhas of the Four Directions. As do the other three, Amida (FIG. **17-10**), the Buddha of the Western Pure Land, sits enthroned in his fabled paradise, attended by bodhisattvas. The exclusive worship of Amida later became a major trend in Japanese Buddhism, and much grander depictions of his paradise appeared, resembling those at Dunhuang (FIG. 16-15) in China. Here, however, the representation is simple and iconic.

Although executed on a dry wall, the Japanese painting process involved techniques similar to fresco, such as transferring designs from paper to wall by piercing holes in the paper and pushing colored powder through the perforations (*pouncing*). As in the Buddha triad (FIG. 17-8) at Yakushiji, the mature Tang style, with its echoes of Indian sensuality, surfaces in this work. The smooth brush lines, thoroughly East Asian, give the figures their substance and life. These lines, often seen in Buddhist painting, are called *iron-wire lines* because they are thin and of unvarying width with a suggestion of tensile strength. As in many other Buddhist paintings, the lines are red instead of black. The identity of the painters of these pictures is unknown, but they may have been Chinese or Korean rather than Japanese.

**DAIBUTSUDEN, TODAIJI** At the Todaiji temple complex at Nara, the kondo is known as the Daibutsuden (FIG. **17-11**), or Great Buddha Hall. Originally constructed in the eighth century, the current Daibutsuden dates to the early 18th century. The Nara-period temple housed a 53-foot-tall bronze image of the Cosmic Buddha, Roshana (Sanskrit, Vairocana), inspired by Chinese colossal stone statues (FIG. 16-14) of this type. The commissioning of Todaiji and its Great Buddha (Daibutsu) by Emperor Shomu (r. 724–749) in 743 was historically important as part of an imperial attempt to unify and strengthen the country by enlisting religious authority to reinforce imperial power. The temple served as the administrative center of a network of branch temples built in every province. Thus, the consolidation of imperial authority and thorough penetration of Buddhism throughout the country went hand in hand. The dissemination of a common religion contributed to the eventual disruption of the clan system and the unification of disparate

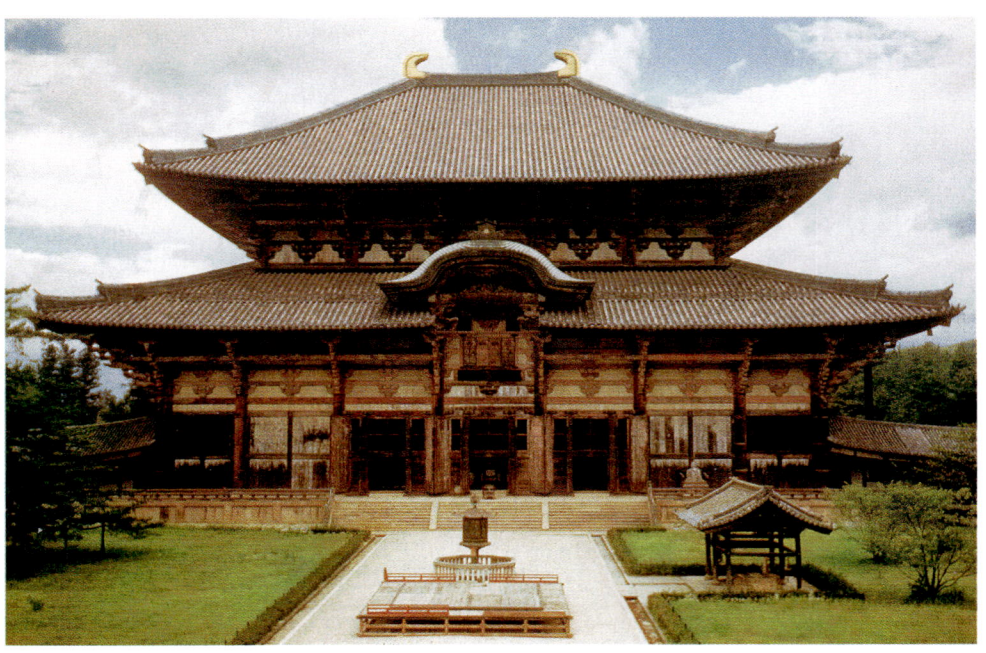

political groups. The building and the Daibutsu within were so important that court and government officials as well as Buddhist dignitaries from China and India attended the opening ceremonies on April 9, 752. Chinese Buddhist monks also arrived in Japan in large numbers and were instrumental in spreading Buddhist teachings throughout Japan. Sadly, the current building is significantly smaller than the original. Today, the Daibutsuden has 7 bays, the original had 11. Yet even in its diminished size, the Todaiji Great Buddha Hall is the largest wooden building in the world.

## Heian

In 784, possibly to escape the power of the Buddhist priests in Nara, the imperial house moved its capital north, eventually relocating in 794 in what became its home until modern times. Originally called Heiankyo ("capital of peace and tranquility"), its name today is Kyoto. The Heian period (794–1185) of Japanese art takes its name from the new capital. Early in the period, Japan maintained fairly close ties with China, but from the middle of the ninth century on, relations between Japan and China deteriorated so rapidly that by the end of that century, court-sponsored contacts had ceased. Japanese culture became much more self-directed than it had been in the preceding few centuries.

**ESOTERIC BUDDHISM** Among the major developments during the early Heian period was the introduction of Esoteric Buddhism to Japan from China. The name reflects the secret transmission of its teachings. Two Esoteric sects made their appearance: Tendai in 805 and Shingon in 806. The teachings of Tendai were based on the *Lotus Sutra,* one of the Buddhist scriptural narratives, and *Shingon* (True Word) teachings on two other sutras. Both Tendai and Shingon Buddhists believe all individuals possess buddha nature and can achieve enlightenment through meditation rituals and careful living. To aid focus during meditation, Shingon disciples use special hand gestures (mudras) and recite particular words or syllables (*mantras* in Sanskrit, *shingon* in Japanese). Shingon became the primary form of Buddhism in Japan through the mid-10th century.

**TAIZOKAI MANDARA** Because of the emphasis on ritual and meditation in Shingon, the arts flourished during the early Heian period. Both paintings and sculptures provided followers with visualizations of specific Buddhist deities and allowed them to contemplate the transcendental concepts central to the religion. Of particular importance in Shingon meditation was the *mandara* (*mandala* in Sanskrit), a diagram of the cosmic universe. The most famous Japanese mandaras are the Womb World (Taizokai) and the Diamond World (Kongokai). Together they formed a complementary pair on the wall of a Shingon kondo. The central motif in the Womb World is the lotus of compassion. In the Diamond World it is the diamond scepter of wisdom. The Womb World is composed of 12 zones, each representing one of the various dimensions of buddha nature (for example, universal knowledge, wisdom, achievement, and purity). The Taizokai mandara illustrated here (FIG. **17-12**) is among the oldest and best preserved in Japan. It is on display today with a corresponding Kongokai mandara at Kyoogokokuji (Toji), the Shingon teaching center established at Kyoto in 823. Many of the figures hold lightning bolts, symbolizing the power of the mind to destroy human passion. Both the Toji Womb World mandara and its Diamond World counterpart reflect Chinese models.

**PHOENIX HALL, UJI** During the middle and later Heian period, belief in the vow of Amida, the Buddha of the Western Pure Land, to save believers through rebirth in his realm gained great prominence among the Japanese aristocracy. Eventually, the simple message of Pure Land (Jodo, in Japanese) Buddhism—universal salvation—facilitated the spread of Buddhism to all classes of Japanese society. The most important surviving monument in Japan related to Pure Land beliefs is the

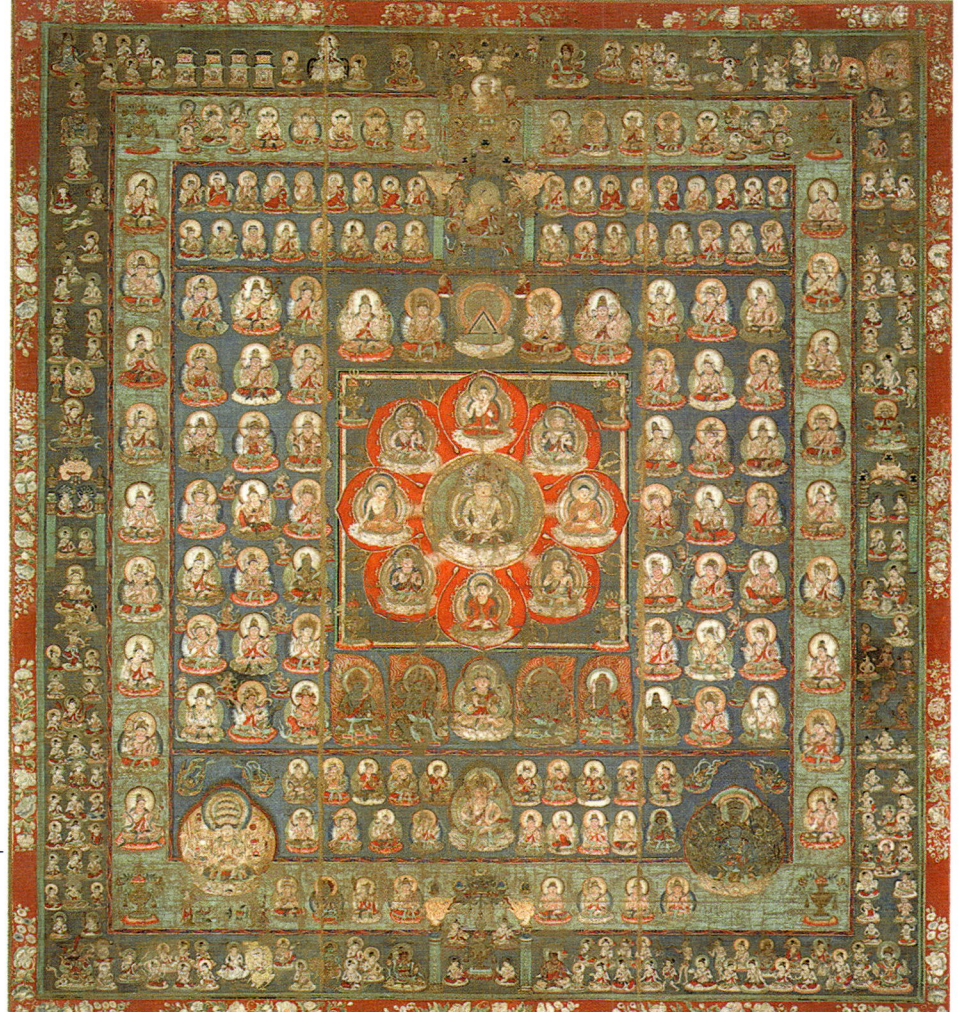

1 ft.

**17-12** Taizokai (Womb World) mandara, Kyoogokokuji (Toji), Kyoto, Japan, Heian period, second half of ninth century. Hanging scroll, color on silk, $6' \times 5'\frac{5}{8}''$.

The Womb World mandara is a diagram of the cosmic universe composed of 12 zones representing the dimensions of Buddha nature. Mandaras played a central role in Esoteric Buddhist meditation.

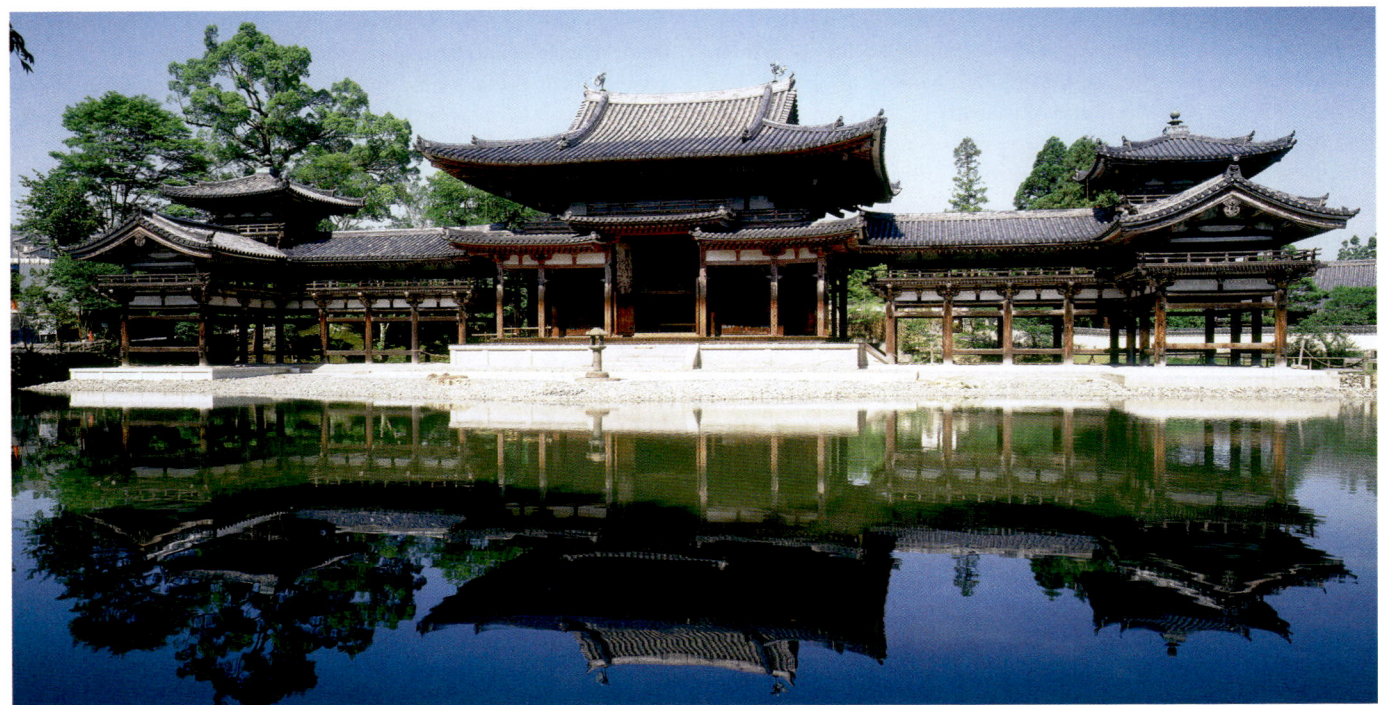

**17-13** Phoenix Hall (looking west), Byodoin, Uji, Kyoto Prefecture, Japan, Heian period, 1053.

The Phoenix Hall's elaborate winged form evokes images of Amida's palace in the Western Pure Land. Situated on a pond, the temple suggests the floating weightlessness of celestial architecture.

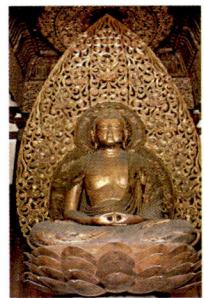

17-13A JOCHO, Seated Amida, Phoenix Hall, Uji, 1053.

Phoenix Hall (FIG. **17-13**) of the Byodoin, a Heian Buddhist temple complex at Uji, south of Kyoto. Fujiwara Yorimichi (990–1074), the powerful regent for three emperors between 1016 and 1068, built the temple in memory of his father, Fujiwara no Michinaga (966–1027), on the grounds of Michinaga's summer villa at Uji. Dedicated in 1053, the Phoenix Hall houses a gilded and lacquered wood statue (FIG. **17-13A**) of Amida by the master sculptor JOCHO (d. 1057). The building's elaborate winged form evokes images of the Buddha's palace in his Pure Land, as depicted in East Asian paintings (FIG. 16-15) in which the architecture reflects the design of Chinese palaces. By placing only light pillars on the exterior, elevating the wings, and situating the whole on a reflective pond, the Phoenix Hall builders suggested the floating weightlessness of celestial architecture. The building's name derives from its overall birdlike shape and from two bronze phoenixes decorating the ridgepole ends. In eastern Asia, people believed these birds alighted on lands properly ruled. Here, they represent imperial might, sometimes associated especially with the empress. The authority of the Fujiwara family derived primarily from the marriage of daughters to the imperial line.

**TALE OF GENJI** Japan's most admired literary classic is *Tale of Genji*, written around 1000 by Murasaki Shikubu (usually referred to as Lady Murasaki; ca. 978–ca. 1025), a lady-in-waiting at the court. Recounting the lives and loves of Prince Genji and his descendants, *Tale of Genji* provides readers with a view of Heian court culture (see "Heian Court Culture," page 485). The oldest extant examples of illustrated copies are fragments from

a deluxe set of early-12th-century handscrolls (see "Chinese Painting Materials and Formats," Chapter 16, page 459). From textual and physical evidence, scholars have suggested the set originally consisted of about 10 handscrolls produced by 5 teams of artisans. Each team consisted of a nobleman talented in calligraphy, a chief painter who drew the compositions in ink, and assistants who added the color. The script is primarily *hiragana,* a sound-based writing

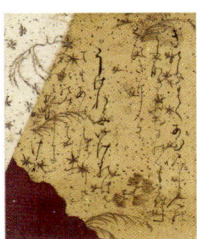

17-13B FUJIWARA NO SADANOBU, *Ishiyama-gire,* early 12th century.

system developed in Japan from Chinese characters. Whereas Japanese scribes employed Chinese characters for Chinese poetry, hiragana became the primary script for Japanese court poetry. One Heian master of hiragana calligraphy was FUJIWARA NO SADANOBU (1088–ca. 1156; FIG. **17-13B**). In *the Genji* handscrolls, pictures alternate with text, as in Gu Kaizhi's *Admonitions* scrolls (FIG. 16-12). However, the Japanese work focuses on emotionally charged moments in personal relationships, rather than on lessons in exemplary behavior.

In the scene illustrated here (FIG. **17-14**), Genji meets with his greatest love near the time of her death. The bush-clover in the garden identifies the season as autumn, a time associated with the fading of life and love. A radically upturned ground plane and strong diagonal lines suggest three-dimensional space. The painter omitted roofs and ceilings to provide a privileged view of the interior spaces where the action takes place. The unusual angles were also metaphors for the emotions of the characters depicted. Flat fields of unshaded color emphasize the painting's two-dimensional character. Rich patterns in the textiles and architectural ornamentation produce a feeling of sumptuousness. The human figures appear constructed of stiff layers of contrasting fabrics, and the artist

# Heian Court Culture

During the Nara and especially the Heian periods, the Japanese imperial court developed as the center of an elite culture. In a time of peace and prosperity, the aristocracy had the leisure to play musical instruments and write poetry. Exchanging poems became a common social practice and a frequent preoccupation of lovers. Both men and women produced poems as well as paintings and calligraphy that critics generally consider "classical" today. Heian court members, especially those from the great Fujiwara clan that dominated the court for a century and a half and built the Phoenix Hall (FIG. 17-13) at Uji, compiled the first great anthologies of Japanese poetry and wrote Japan's most influential secular prose.

A lady-in-waiting to an empress of the early 11th century wrote the best-known work of literature in Japan, *Tale of Genji.*

Known as Lady Murasaki, the author is one of many women who were important writers, especially of diaries and poems. Generally considered the world's first lengthy novel (the English translation is almost a thousand pages), *Tale of Genji* tells of the life and loves of Prince Genji and, after his death, of his heirs. The novel and much of Japanese literature consistently display sensitivity to the sadness inherent in the transience of love and life. These human sentiments are often intertwined with the seasonality of nature. For example, the full moon, flying geese, crying deer, and certain plants symbolize autumn, which in turn evokes somber emotions, fading love, and dying. These concrete but evocative images frequently appear in paintings, such as the illustrated scrolls of *Tale of Genji* (FIG. 17-14).

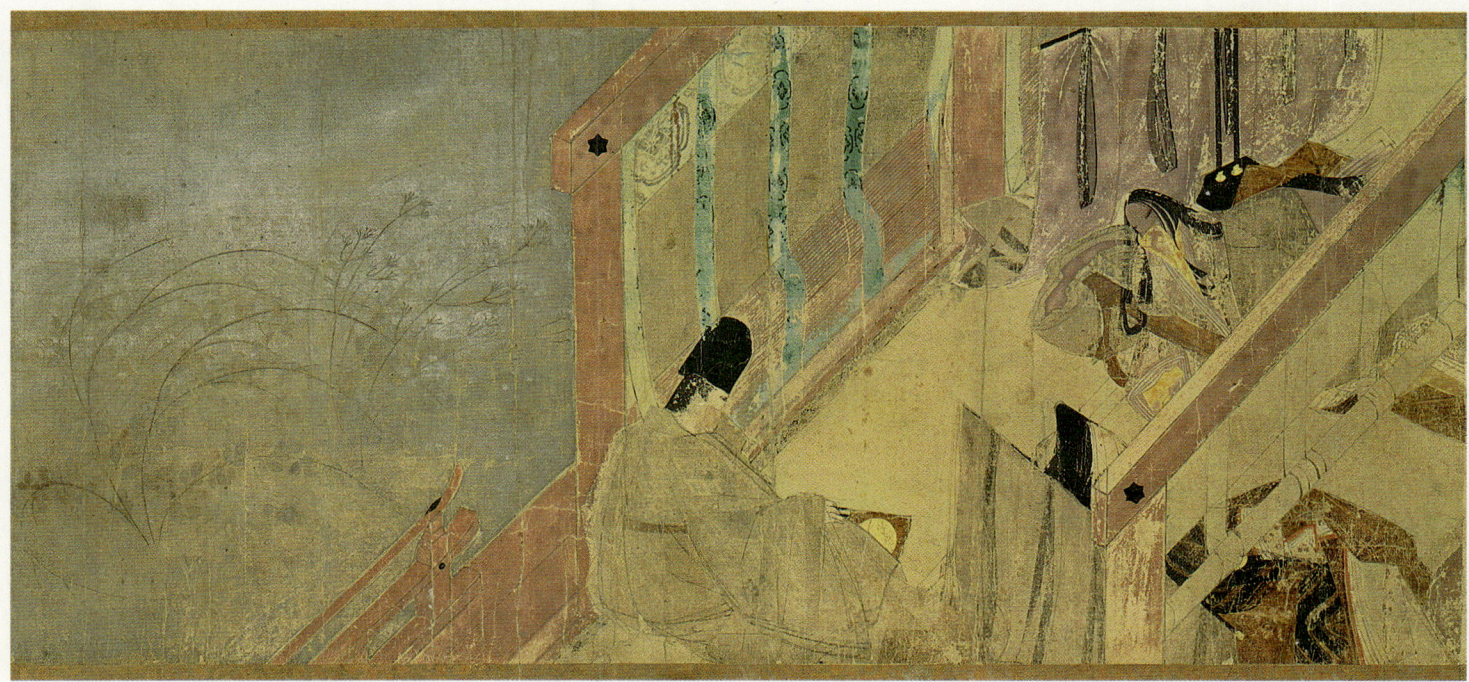

1 in.

**17-14** *Genji Visits Murasaki,* from the Minori chapter, *Tale of Genji,* Heian period, first half of 12th century. Handscroll, ink and color on paper, 8⅝″ high. Goto Art Museum, Tokyo. ◼◀

In this handscroll of Lady Murasaki's *Tale of Genji,* the upturned ground and diagonal lines suggest three-dimensional space. Flat color fields emphasize the painting's two-dimensionality.

simplified and generalized the aristocratic faces, using a horizontal line for each eye and a hook for the nose. This lack of individualization may reflect societal restrictions on looking directly at exalted persons. Later Japanese critics considered several formal features of the *Genji* illustrations—native subjects, bright mineral pigments, lack of emphasis on strong brushwork, and general flatness—typical of *yamato-e,* or "native-style painting." (*Yamato* means "Japan" and the term describes anything characteristically Japanese.)

### *LEGENDS OF MOUNT SHIGI* Heian painting was diverse in both style and subject matter. *Legends of Mount Shigi,* painted

during the late 12th century, represents a different facet of Heian narrative handscroll painting. The stories belong to a genre of pious Buddhist tales devoted to miraculous events involving virtuous individuals. Unlike the *Genji* scrolls, short segments of text and pictures do not alternate. Instead, the painters took advantage of the scroll format to present several scenes in a long, unbroken stretch. For example, the first scroll shows the same travelers at several stages of their journey through a continuous landscape.

The *Mount Shigi* scrolls illustrate three miracles associated with a Buddhist monk named Myoren who resided in a hut close to a small temple on the slopes of Mount Shigi near Nara. The

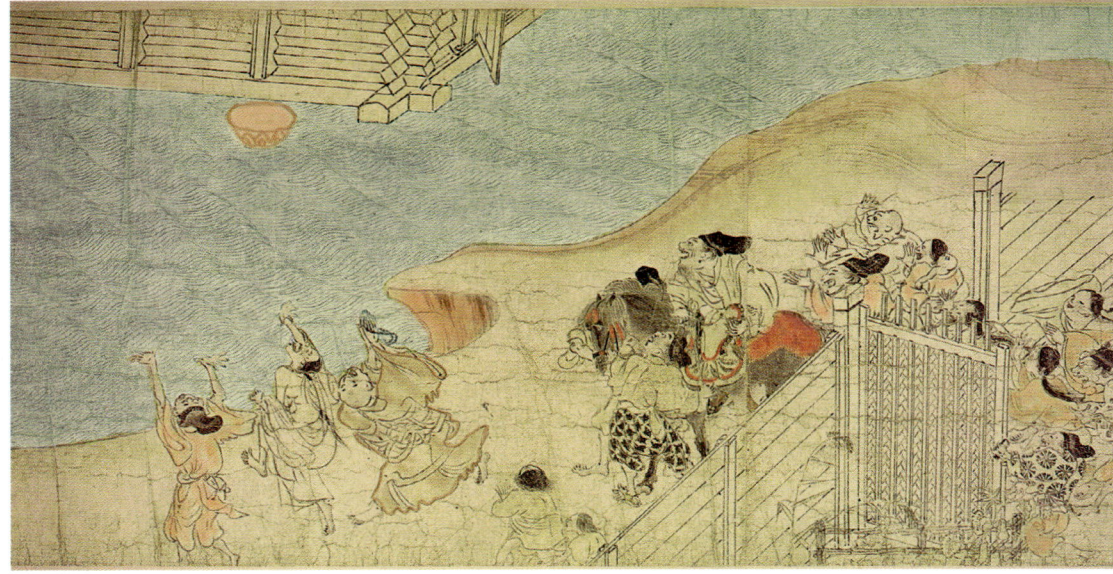

**17-15** *The Flying Storehouse,* from *Legends of Mount Shigi,* Heian period, late 12th century. Handscroll, ink and colors on paper, 1' ½" high. Chogosonshiji, Nara.

This Heian handscroll illustrating a Buddhist miracle differs from the *Genji* scroll (FIG. 17-14) in both subject and style. The artist exaggerated each feature of the gesticulating and scurrying figures.

1 in.

first relates the story of the flying storehouse (FIG. **17-15**) and depicts Myoren's *begging bowl* (the bowl Buddhist monks use to collect alms, either money or food) lifting the rice-filled granary of a greedy farmer and, through the power of the monk's faith, carrying it off to Myoren's mountaintop hut. The painter used a multitude of rapid brushstrokes and pale colors to depict the astonished landowner, his attendants, and several onlookers in various attitudes and poses. Some grimace, others gesticulate wildly and scurry about in frantic amazement. As in the *Genji* scroll, the *Shigi* painter represented the architecture from above, but in striking contrast to the generic faces of the *Genji* illustrations, the artist exaggerated each figure's features.

## Kamakura

In the late 12th century, a series of civil wars between rival warrior families led to the end of the Japanese imperial court as a major political and social force. The victors, headed by the Minamoto family, established their *shogunate* (military government) at Kamakura in eastern Japan. The imperial court remained in Kyoto as the theoretical source of political authority, but real power resided with the *shoguns*. The first shogun was Minamoto Yoritomo (1147–1199), on whom the emperor officially bestowed the title in 1185. The ensuing period of Japanese art is called the Kamakura period (1185–1332), named for the shogunate's headquarters. Under the Kamakura shoguns, more frequent and positive contact with China brought with it an appreciation for recent cultural developments there, ranging from new architectural styles to Zen Buddhism.

**SHUNJOBO CHOGEN** Rebuilding in Nara after the destruction the civil wars inflicted presented an early opportunity for architectural experimentation. A leading figure in planning and directing the reconstruction efforts was the priest Shunjobo Chogen (1120–1206), who sources say made three trips to China between 1166 and 1176. After learning about contemporary Chinese architecture, he oversaw the rebuilding of Todaiji (FIG. 17-11), among other projects, with generous donations from Minamoto Yoritomo. Chogen's portrait statue (FIG. 17-16), probably carved shortly after his death at age 86, is one of the most striking examples of the high level of naturalism prevalent in the early Kamakura period. It features finely painted details and a powerful rendering of the signs of aging, including sunken cheeks and eye sockets, lined face and neck, and

slumping posture. Details such as the nervous handling of prayer beads capture the personality as well as the appearance of the priest. The statue displays fine Heian carving techniques combined with an increased concern for natural volume and detail learned from studying, among other sources, surviving Nara-period works and sculptures imported from Song China. Enhancing the natural quality of this and other Kamakura portrait statues is the use of inlaid rock crystal for the eyes, a technique unique to Japan.

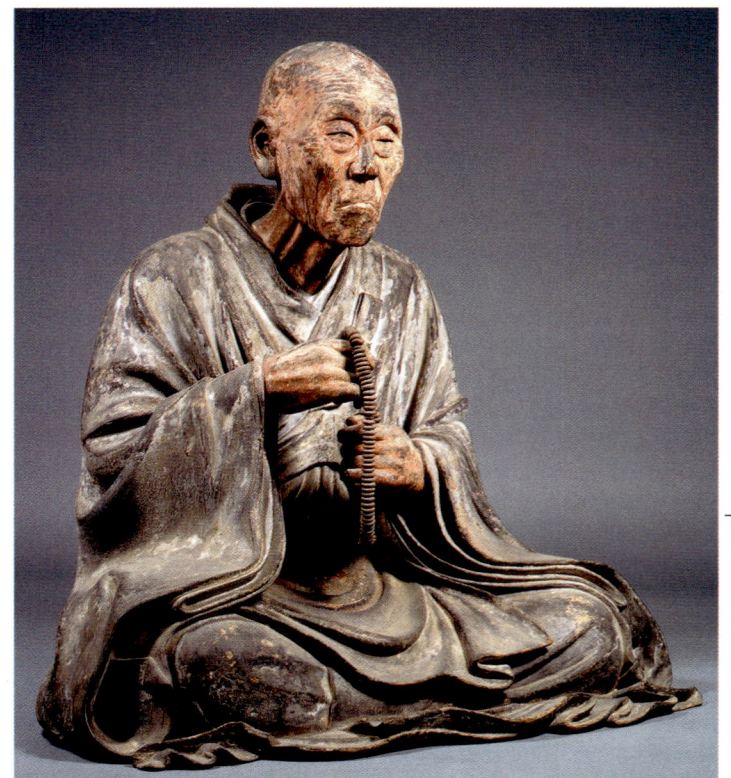

1 ft.

**17-16** Portrait statue of the priest Shunjobo Chogen, Todaiji, Nara, Japan, Kamakura period, ca. 1206. Painted cypress wood, 2' 8⅜" high.

Kamakura artists' interest in naturalism is evident in this moving portrait of a seated priest. The statue is noteworthy for its finely painted details and powerful rendering of personality and old age.

## Heian and Kamakura Artistic Workshops

Until the late Heian period, major artistic commissions came almost exclusively from the imperial court or the great temples. As shogun warrior families gained wealth and power, they too became great art patrons—in many cases closely following established preferences in subject and style.

Artists, for the most part, did not work independently but rather were affiliated with workshops. Indeed, until recently, hierarchically organized male workshops produced most Japanese art. Membership in these workshops was often based on familial relationships. Dominating each workshop was a master, and many of his main assistants and apprentices were relatives. Outsiders of considerable skill sometimes joined workshops, often through marriage or adoption. The eldest son usually inherited the master's position, after rigorous training in the necessary skills from a very young age. Therefore, one meaning of the term *art school* in Japan is a network of workshops tracing their origins to the same master, a kind of artistic clan. Inside the workshops, the master and senior assistants handled the most important production stages, but artists of lower rank helped with the more routine work. The Kamakura portrait statue (FIG. 17-17) of the priest Kuya preaching, for example, was the work of Kosho, whose family workshop traced its artistic roots to a sculptor who lived 150 years before Kosho learned his craft.

Artistic cooperation also surfaced in court bureaus, an alternative to family workshops. These official bureaus, housed at the imperial palace, had emerged by the Heian period. The imperial painting bureau accrued particular fame. Teams of court painters, led by the bureau director, produced pictures such as the scenes in the *Tale of Genji* handscrolls (FIG. 17-14). This system remained vital into the Kamakura period and well beyond. Under the direction of a patron or the patron's representative, the master painter laid out the composition by brushing in the initial outlines and contours. Under his supervision, junior painters applied the colors. The master then completed the work by brushing in fresh contours and details such as facial features. Very junior assistants and apprentices assisted in the process by preparing paper, ink, and pigments. Unlike mastership in hereditarily run workshops, competition among several families determined control of the court painting bureau during the Heian and Kamakura periods.

**17-17** KOSHO, Portrait statue of the priest Kuya preaching, Kamakura period, early 13th century. Painted wood with inlaid eyes, 3′ 10¼″ high. Rokuharamitsuji, Kyoto.

Kosho, a leading Kamakura sculptor, depicted Kuya as a frail priest roaming the countryside chanting the six syllables of the prayer to Amida, shown as six tiny Buddhas emerging from his mouth.

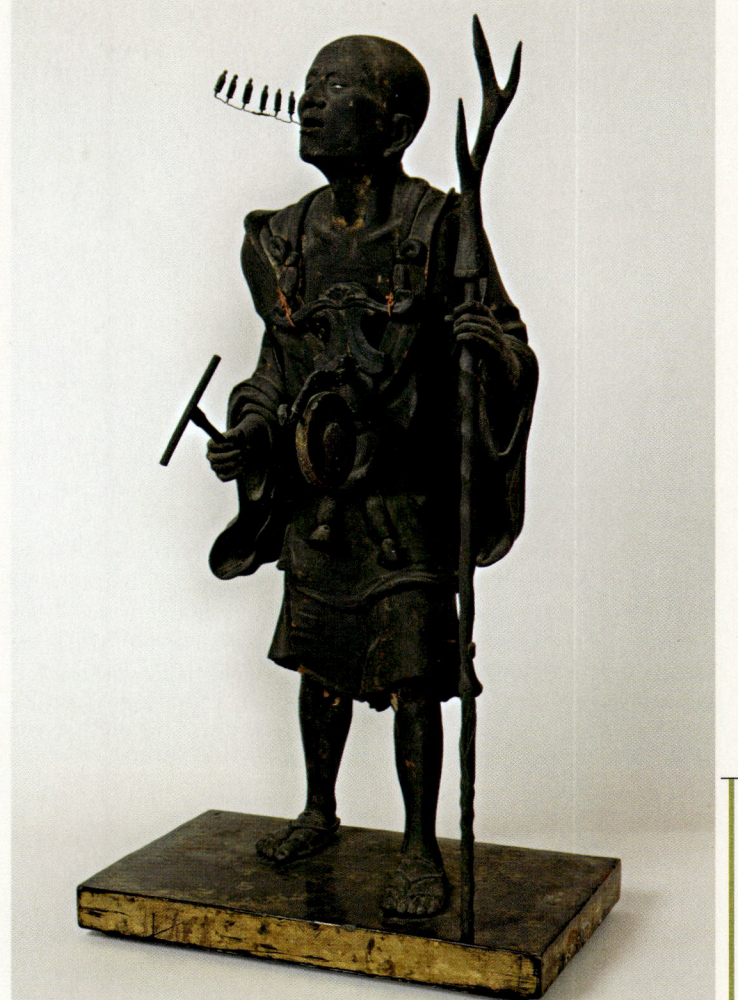

1 ft.

The bureaus and family workshops did not control all art production, however. Priest-artists trained in temple workshops to make Buddhist art objects for public viewing as well as images for private priestly meditation. Amateur painting was common among aristocrats of all ranks. As they did for poetry composition and calligraphy, aristocrats frequently sponsored painting competitions, in which both women and men participated. In fact, court ladies probably played a significant role in developing the painting style seen in the *Genji* scrolls, and a few participated in public projects.

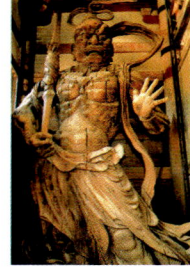

**KOSHO** The name of the sculptor of Shunjobo Chogen's portrait is not known, but a contemporaneous portrait (FIG. **17-17**) of the highest quality survives by KOSHO (d. 1237), one of the great Kamakura masters of realistic sculpture. Kosho was the fourth of six sons of the sculptor UNKEI (d. 1223; FIG. **17-17A**), who was in turn the son of a sculptor of the impor-

**17-17A** UNKEI, *Agyo*, Todaiji, 1203.

tant Kei School (see "Heian and Kamakura Artistic Workshops," above), which traced its lineage to the mid-11th-century master Jocho (FIG. 17-13A). Art historians generally regard the portrait statue of the priest Kuya (903–972) to be Kosho's best work. Kuya converted to Amidism, an early form of Pure Land Buddhism (see "Buddhism," Chapter 15, page 427), after killing a deer. Horrified at what he had done, he devoted the rest of his life to roaming the countryside preaching faith in Amida. Kuya always dressed in ragged clothes and held a walking staff topped by the antlers of the

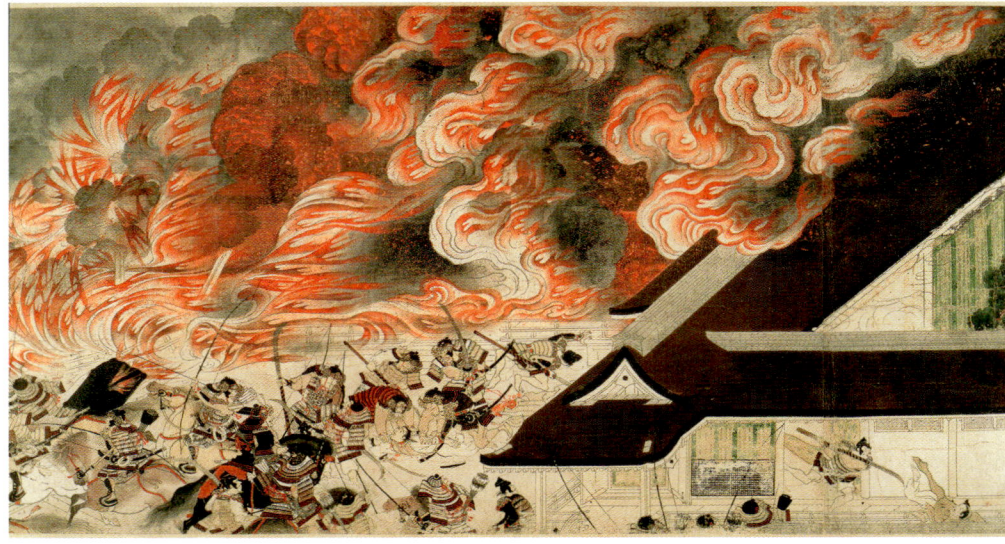

17-18 *Night Attack on the Sanjo Palace,* from *Events of the Heiji Period,* Kamakura period, 13th century. Handscroll, ink and colors on paper, 1′ 4¼″ high; complete scroll, 22′ 10″ long. Museum of Fine Arts, Boston (Fenollosa-Weld Collection).

The *Heiji* scroll is an example of historical narrative painting. Staccato brushwork and vivid flashes of color beautifully capture the drama of the night attack and burning of Goshirakawa's palace.

1 in.

deer whose life he took. Everywhere he went he chanted the six-syllable *nembutsu* prayer professing total faith in the compassion of Amida Buddha (*Namu Amida Butsu*) while beating a gong.

Kosho's wooden statue is an imaginary portrait, but it is so convincing in its naturalistic depiction of a frail old man of faith it seems as if Kuya posed for the portrait, even though he had been dead for more than two centuries when Kosho carved this statue for the Rokuharamitsuji temple in Kyoto. Kuya walks with his left foot advanced and his antler-topped staff in his left hand. His gong

hangs from a yoke over his shoulders, and he holds his striker in his right hand. Most remarkable is the way Kosho represented Kuya chanting. He placed six miniature Buddhas on a wire emerging from Kuya's mouth, one for each syllable of his chant.

*ATTACK ON SANJO PALACE* All the painting types flourishing in the Heian period continued to prosper in the Kamakura period. A striking example of handscroll painting is *Events of the Heiji Period,* which dates to the 13th century and illustrates another facet of Japanese painting—historical narrative. The scroll depicts some civil-war battles at the end of the Heian period. The section reproduced here (FIG. **17-18**) represents the nighttime attack on the Sanjo palace during which the retired emperor Goshirakawa (r. 1155–1158) was taken prisoner and his palace burned. Swirling flames and billowing clouds of smoke dominate the composition. Below, soldiers on horseback and on foot do battle. As in other Heian and Kamakura scrolls, the artist represented the buildings from above at a sharp angle. Noteworthy here are the painter's staccato brushwork and the vivid flashes of color that beautifully capture the drama of the event.

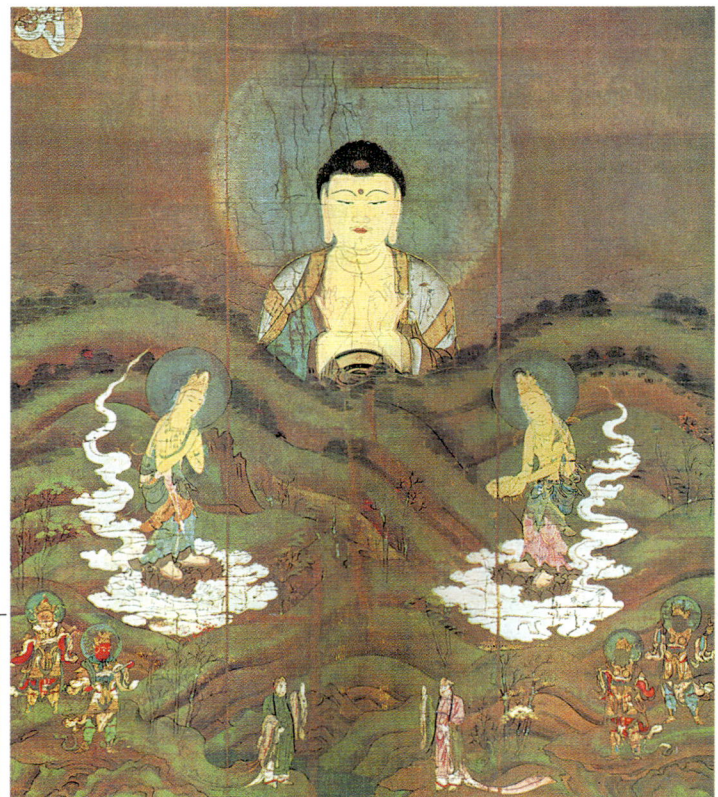

17-19 *Amida Descending over the Mountains,* Zenrinji, Kyoto, Japan, Kamakura period, 13th century. Hanging scroll, ink and colors on silk, 4′ 3⅛″ × 3′ 10½″.

Scrolls depicting Amida descending to convey the dead to the Pure Land Paradise were often hung in the room of a dying person. Here, the rendering of Amida has an iconic character.

1 ft.

*AMIDA DESCENDING* Buddhism and Buddhist painting also remained vital in the Kamakura period, and elite patrons continued to commission major Pure Land artworks. Pure Land Buddhism in Japan stressed the saving power of Amida, who, if called on, hastened to believers at the moment of death and conveyed them to his Pure Land. Pictures of this scene were often hung in the presence of a dying person, who recited Amida's name to ensure salvation. In *Amida Descending over the Mountains* (FIG. **17-19**), a gigantic Amida rises from behind the mountains against the backdrop of a dark sky. His two main attendant bodhisattvas, Kannon and Seishi, have already descended. The painter depicted them as if they were addressing the deceased directly. Below, two boys point to the approaching divinities. In contrast to these gesticulating figures, Amida is still and frontal, which gives his image an iconic quality. Particularly striking is the way in which Amida's halo (nimbus) resembles a rising moon, an image long admired in Japan for its spiritual beauty.

The Kamakura period ended the way it began—with civil war. After several years of conflict beginning in 1332, one shogun emerged supreme and governed Japan from his headquarters in the Muramachi district of Kyoto. The art and architecture of Japan from 1336 to 1980 are the subject of Chapter 34.

# JAPAN BEFORE 1333

## JOMON AND YAYOI PERIODS ca. 10,500 BCE–300 CE

▌ The Jomon (ca. 10,500–300 BCE) is Japan's earliest distinct culture. It takes its name from the applied clay cordlike coil decoration of Jomon pottery.

▌ Archaeologists unearthed the first evidence for the Yayoi culture (ca. 300 BCE–300 CE) in the Yayoi district of Tokyo, but the culture emerged in Kyushu and spread northward. Increasing contact with the East Asian mainland is evident in the form of Yayoi dotaku, which were modeled on Han Chinese bells but were not musical instruments.

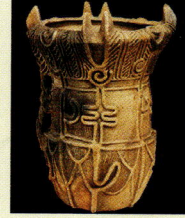

Middle Jomon vessel, ca. 2,500–1,500 BCE

## KOFUN PERIOD ca. 300–552

▌ Kofun means "old tomb," and great earthen keyhole-shaped burial mounds are the primary characteristic of the last pre-Buddhist period of Japanese art. The largest tumulus in Japan, attributed to Emperor Nintoku, who died in 399, is at Sakai.

▌ About 20,000 clay cylindrical figures (haniwa) stood around and atop the Sakai tumulus. Haniwa sculptures depict inanimate objects and animals as well as human figures, including warriors. The haniwa may represent the realm the deceased ruled during life.

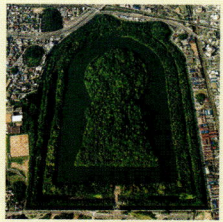

Tomb of Emperor Nintoku, Sakai, late 4th to early 5th century

## ASUKA AND NARA PERIODS 552–784

▌ Buddhism came to Japan from Korea in 552, and the first Japanese Buddhist artworks, such as Tori Busshi's Shaka triad at Horyuji, date to the Asuka period (552–645).

▌ During the Nara period (645–784), a centralized imperial government was established, with its capital at Nara from 710 to 784. Nara architecture, for example, the Horyuji kondo, followed Tang Chinese models in the use of ceramic roof tiles and the adoption of a curved roofline. The Daibutsuden constructed at Todaiji in 743 is the largest wooden building in the world.

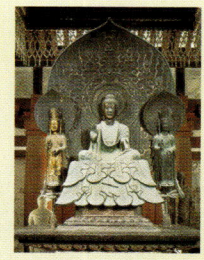

Tori Busshi, Shaka triad, 623

## HEIAN PERIOD 794–1185

▌ In 794 the imperial family moved the capital to Heiankyo (Kyoto). Shortly thereafter, Esoteric Buddhism arrived in Japan and created demand for painted mandaras of the Womb World and the Diamond World in order to facilitate meditation.

▌ A masterpiece of Heian Buddhist architecture is the Phoenix Hall of the Byodoin at Uji, which evokes images of the celestial architecture of the Buddha's Pure Land of the West.

▌ Narrative scroll painting was a major Heian art form. Illustrated scrolls of Lady Murasaki's *Tale of Genji* feature the distinctive combination of elevated viewpoints that suggest three-dimensional space and flat colors that emphasize the painting's two-dimensional character.

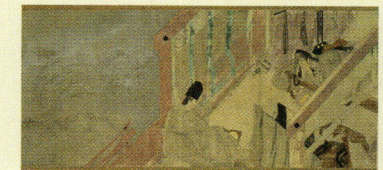

*Tale of Genji*, first half of 12th century

## KAMAKURA PERIOD 1185–1332

▌ In 1185, power shifted from the Japanese emperor to the first shogun of Kamakura. The shoguns became great patrons of art and architecture.

▌ Kamakura painting is diverse in both subject and style and includes historical narratives, such as *Events of the Heiji Period,* and Buddhist hanging scrolls.

▌ Kamakura wood portraits—for example, the seated statue of the priest Shunjobo Chogen—are noteworthy for their realism and the use of rock crystal for the eyes.

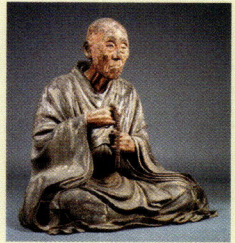

Shunjobo Chogen, ca. 1206

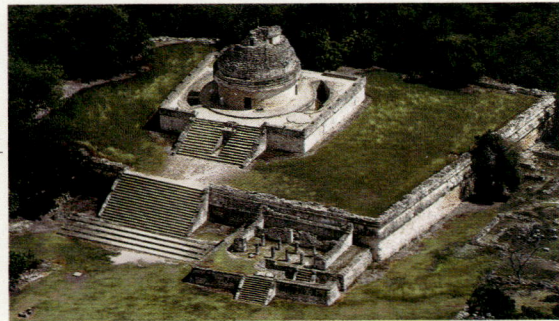

One of the most unusual Maya buildings is the Caracol ("snail shell") at Chichén Itzá. It encloses a spiral staircase and was probably both a temple to Kulkulcán and an astronomical observatory.

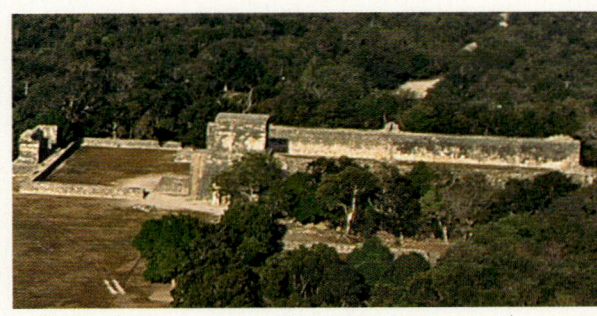

Chichén Itzá boasts the largest ball court in Mesoamerica. The rules of the ball game remain obscure, but the games were important rituals that often ended in the death of captured enemies.

The characteristic Maya temple was a stepped pyramidal platform with a shrine on the top. Chichén Itzá's, which has 365 steps on four sides, was a temple to Kulkulcán, the feathered-serpent god.

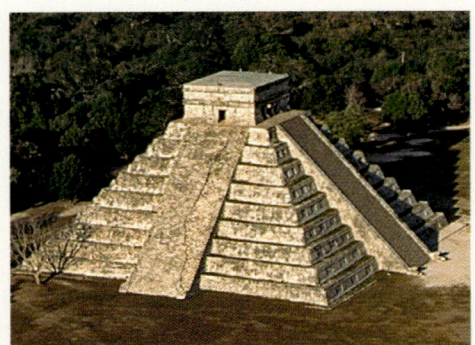

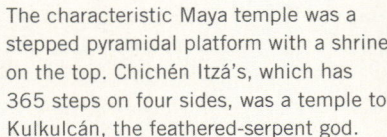

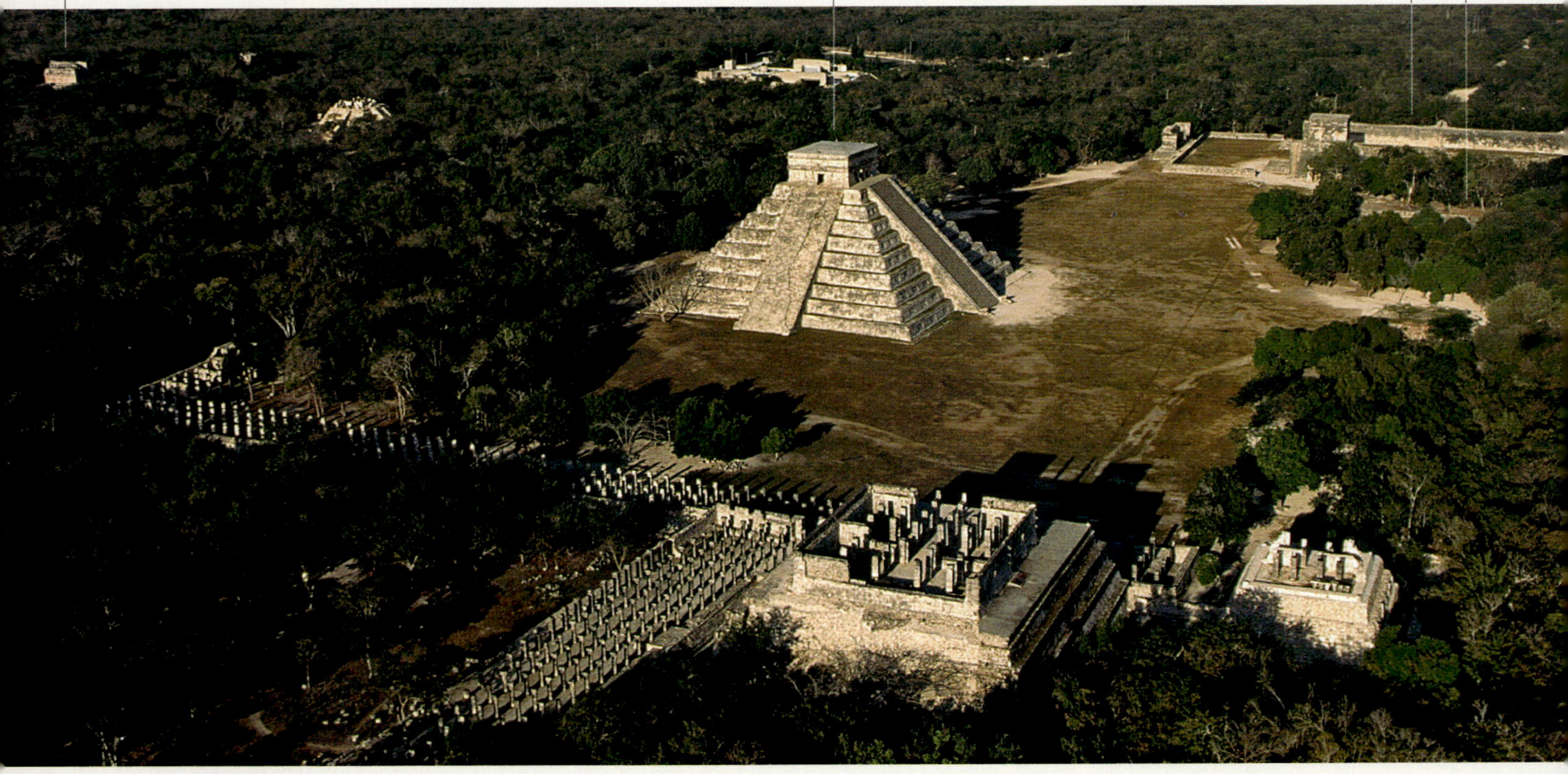

**18-1** Aerial view (looking southwest) of the Maya city of Chichén Itzá, Mexico, centered on the Castillo, ca. 800–900 CE. ◼◀

# NATIVE ARTS OF THE AMERICAS BEFORE 1300

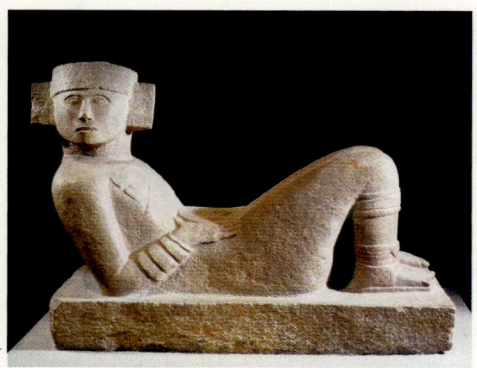

Inside the Kulkulcán temple was a *chacmool* statue similar to this one from the nearby Platform of the Eagles. Chacmools are fallen warriors with receptacles on their chests to receive sacrificial offerings.

## ANCIENT CITIES IN A NEW WORLD

During the millennium and a half before Europeans discovered what for them was a "New World," the native peoples of the Western Hemisphere constructed some of the world's largest cities. Teotihuacán, for example, near present-day Mexico City, was a great metropolis covering nine square miles. The city, which had a population of nearly 200,000 at its peak in the sixth century CE, was widely influential throughout Mesoamerica.

The most famous of the many civilizations that flourished in the Americas before 1300 was the Maya. Renowned for their great urban centers and imposing temple-pyramids carved out of the dense rain and scrub forests of Mexico, Guatemala, Honduras, and Belize, the Maya were also skilled in mathematics and astronomy, developed a complex written language, and kept detailed historical records.

One of the best preserved Maya sites—and most frequently visited because of its proximity to the popular vacation destination of Cancún in the Yucatán Peninsula—is Chichén Itzá (FIG. **18-1**). The city dates to the period archaeologists have dubbed the Postclassic, that is, the late period, beginning around 900 CE. Some of its major buildings are typical, however, of earlier Classic sites, such as Copán in Honduras and Tikal in Guatemala.

Dominating Chichén Itzá's main northern plaza is a gigantic pyramidal stepped platform crowned by a temple to Kukulcán, the feathered-serpent god. Oriented to the four cardinal points, the pyramid has nine levels and 365 steps collectively on its four sides. Solar connections abound in Maya architecture, and during the winter and summer equinoxes, the sun's rays create the illusion of the serpent-god on the pyramid's steps.

Chichén Itzá also boasts the largest ball court in Mesoamerica, almost 500 feet long. There, skilled athletes competed in ball games that are poorly understood today, but that often resulted in the sacrifice of captives forced to play—and always lose. Archaeologists have found sculptures representing fallen warriors (*chacmools*) at several locations around the main plaza, including the pyramid-temple of Kukulcán. The chacmools probably figured in the sacrificial rites connected with the ritual ball games. More unusual is the round and domed temple nicknamed the Caracol ("snail-shell") by the Spanish conquerors because of its internal spiral staircase. It probably doubled as an astronomical observatory. Eventually, Chichén Itzá, as so many other abandoned Maya cities, became absorbed into the thick vegetation that still hems in the site—to be rediscovered and explored centuries later by modern archaeologists.

# THE ANCIENT AMERICAS

The origins of the indigenous peoples of the Americas are still uncertain. Sometime no later than 30,000 to 10,000 BCE, these first Americans probably crossed the now-submerged land bridge called Beringia, which connected the shores of the Bering Strait between Asia and North America. Some migrants may have reached the Western Hemisphere via boats traveling along the Pacific coast of North America. These Stone Age nomads were hunter-gatherers. They made tools only of bone, pressure-flaked stone, and wood. They had no knowledge of agriculture but possibly some of basketry. They could control fire and probably built simple shelters. For many centuries, they spread out until they occupied the two American continents. But they were always few in number. When the first Europeans arrived at the end of the 15th century (see Chapter 35), the total population of the Western Hemisphere may not have exceeded 40 million.

Between 8000 and 2000 BCE, some of the migrants learned to fish, farm cotton, and domesticate plants such as squash and maize (corn). The nomads settled in villages and learned to make ceramic utensils and figurines. Metal technology developed only in the Andean region of South America (eventually spreading north into present-day Mexico) and, although extremely refined, generally met only the need for ornamentation, not for tools. With these skills as a base, many cultures rose and fell over long periods.

Several of the peoples of North, Central, and South America had already reached a high level of social complexity and technological achievement by the early centuries CE. Although most relied on stone tools, did not use the wheel (except for toys), and had no pack animals but the llama (in South America), the early Americans developed complex agricultural techniques and excelled in the engineering arts associated with the planning and construction of cities, civic and domestic buildings, roads and bridges, and irrigation and drainage systems. They carved monumental stone statues and reliefs, painted extensive murals, and mastered the arts of weaving, pottery, and metalwork. In Mesoamerica, the Maya and other cultural groups even had a highly developed writing system and knowledge of mathematical calculation that enabled them to keep precise records and create a sophisticated calendar and a highly accurate astronomy.

These advanced civilizations went into rapid decline, however, in the 16th century when the Europeans introduced new diseases to the Western Hemisphere, and Hernán Cortés (1485–1547), Francisco Pizarro (1471–1541), and their armies conquered the Aztec and Inka empires. Some native elites survived and adapted to the Spanish presence, but the conquerors destroyed most of the once-glorious American cities in their zeal to obliterate all traces of non-Christian worship. The forces of nature—erosion and the encroachment of tropical forests—caused the abandonment of other sites. But despite the ruined state of the pre-Hispanic cities of the Americas today, archaeologists and art historians have been able to reconstruct much of the art and architectural history of the Western Hemisphere before its inhabitants made contact with Europeans. This chapter examines in turn the artistic achievements of the native peoples of Mesoamerica, South America, and North America before 1300. Chapter 35 treats the art and architecture of the Americas from 1300 to the present.

# MESOAMERICA

The term *Mesoamerica* describes the region comprising part of present-day Mexico, Guatemala, Belize, Honduras, and the Pacific coast of El Salvador (MAP **18-1**). Mesoamerica was the homeland of several of the great *pre-Columbian* civilizations—those that flourished before the arrival of Christopher Columbus (1451–1506) and the subsequent European invasion.

The principal regions of pre-Columbian Mesoamerica are the Gulf Coast region (Olmec and Classic Veracruz cultures); the states of Jalisco, Colima, and Nayarit (collectively known as West Mexico); Chiapas, Yucatán, Quintana Roo, and Campeche states in Mexico, the Petén area of Guatemala, Belize, and Honduras (Maya culture); southwestern Mexico and the state of Oaxaca (Zapotec and Mixtec cultures); and the central plateau surrounding modern Mexico City (Teotihuacán, Toltec, and Aztec cultures). These civilizations were often influential over extensive areas.

The Mexican highlands are a volcanic and seismic region. In highland Mexico, great reaches of arid plateau land, fertile for maize and other crops wherever water is available, lie between heavily forested mountain slopes, which at some places rise to a perpetual snow level. The moist tropical rain forests of the coastal plains yield

## NATIVE ARTS OF THE AMERICAS BEFORE 1300

| BCE | CE | | | |
|---|---|---|---|---|
| 1200 | 400 | 300 | 900 | 1300 |
| ▪ Colossal ruler portraits of the Olmec (ca. 900–400 BCE), the "mother culture" of Mesoamerica<br>▪ Temple complexes and relief stelae set up at Chavín de Huántar (ca. 800–200 BCE) in Andean South America | ▪ Construction of the Avenue of the Dead and the pyramids of Teotihuacán in Preclassic (ca. 400 BCE–300 CE) Mesoamerica<br>▪ The Paracas (ca. 400 BCE–200 CE) culture in Peru produces extraordinary textiles<br>▪ Adena (ca. 500–1 BCE) build the first great mounds in North America | ▪ The Maya construct vast complexes of temple-pyramids, palaces, plazas, and ball courts in Classic (ca. 300–900) Mesoamerica<br>▪ The Nasca (ca. 200 BCE–600 CE) create 800 miles of earth drawings around 500 CE<br>▪ The Tiwanaku (ca. 100–1000) and Wari (ca. 500–800) cultures flourish in northern Bolivia and southern Peru | ▪ Construction of a huge pyramid-temple and the largest ball court in Mesoamerica at the Postclassic (ca. 900–1521) Maya site of Chichén Itzá<br>▪ Cahokia, Illinois, with 120 mounds is the largest city in North America during the Mississippian culture (ca. 800–1500)<br>▪ In the American Southwest, the Mimbres (ca. 1000–1250) produce black-and-white painted bowls, and the Ancestral Puebloans build a complex with 800 rooms at Chaco Canyon (ca. 850–1050) | |

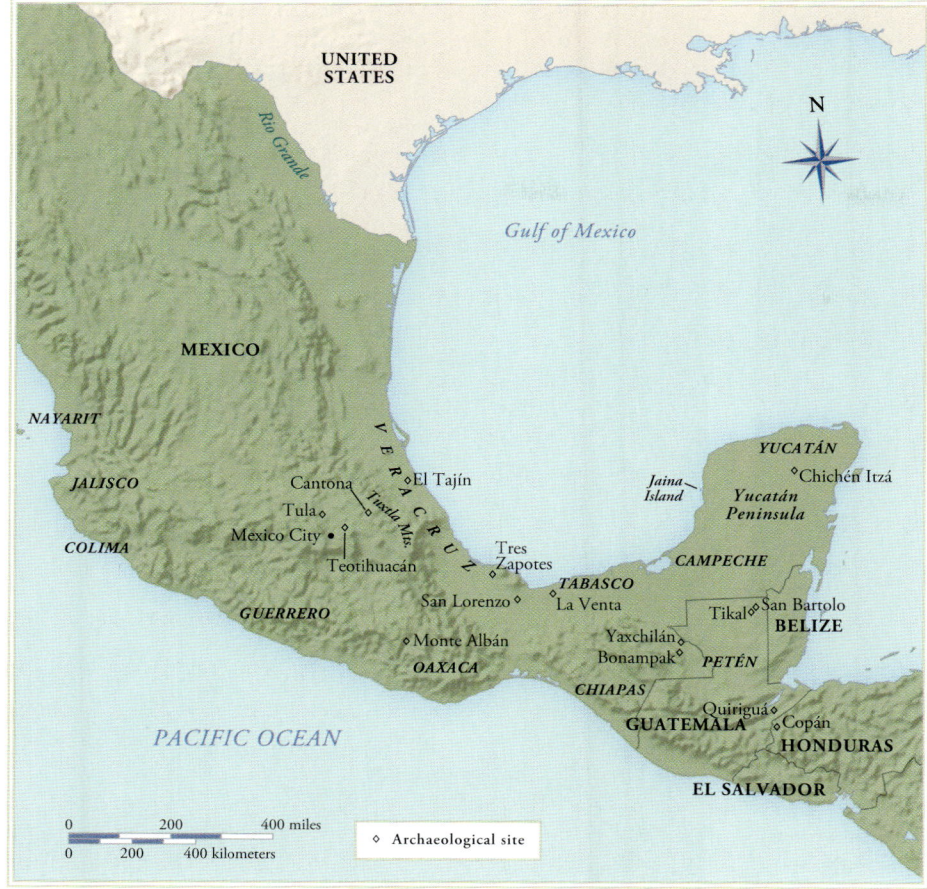

**MAP 18-1** Early sites in Mesoamerica.

Scholars can now list many Maya rulers by name and fix the dates of their reigns with precision. Other writing systems, such as that of the Zapotec, who began to record dates at a very early time, are less well understood, but researchers are making rapid progress in their interpretation. Historians have now established a widely accepted Mesoamerican chronology divided into three epochs, with some overlapping of subperiods. The Preclassic (Formative), which marks the rise of elites and the first major works of art and architecture, extends from 2000 BCE to about 300 CE. The Classic period runs from about 300 to 900. The Postclassic begins about 900 and ends with the Spanish conquest in 1521.

## Olmec and Preclassic West Mexico

Archaeologists often refer to the Olmec culture of the present-day states of Veracruz and Tabasco as the "mother culture" of Mesoamerica, because many distinctive Mesoamerican religious, social, and artistic traditions can be traced to it. Recent excavations, however, have revealed other important centers during the Preclassic period. The notion of a linear evolution of all Mesoamerican art and architecture from the Olmec is giving way to a more complex, multicenter picture of early Mesoamerica.

rich crops, when the land can be cleared. In Yucatán, a subsoil of limestone furnishes abundant material for both building and carving. This limestone tableland merges with the vast Petén region of Guatemala, which separates Mexico from Honduras. Yucatán and the Petén, where dense rain forest alternates with broad stretches of grassland, boast some of the most spectacular Maya ruins, including the site of Chichén Itzá (FIG. 18-1). The great mountain chains of Mexico and Guatemala extend into Honduras and slope sharply down to tropical coasts. Highlands and mountain valleys, with their chill and temperate climates, alternate dramatically with the humid climate of tropical rain forest and coastlines.

The variegated landscape of Mesoamerica may have much to do with the diversity of languages its native populations speak. Researchers have documented no fewer than 14 linguistic families. Many of the languages spoken in the pre–Spanish conquest period survive to this day. Various Mayan languages linger in Guatemala and southern Mexico. The Náhuatl of the Aztecs endures in the Mexican highlands. The Zapotec and Mixtec languages persist in Oaxaca and its environs. Diverse as the languages of these peoples were, their cultures otherwise had much in common. The Mesoamerican peoples shared maize cultivation, religious beliefs and rites, myths, social structures, customs, and arts.

Archaeologists, with ever-increasing refinement of technique, have been uncovering, describing, and classifying Mesoamerican monuments for more than a century. In the 1950s, linguists made important breakthroughs in deciphering the Maya *hieroglyphic* script, and epigraphers have made further progress in recent decades.

Settling in the tropical lowlands of the Gulf of Mexico, the Olmec peoples cultivated a terrain of rain forest and alluvial lowland washed by numerous rivers flowing into the gulf. Here, between approximately 1500 and 400 BCE, social organization assumed the form later Mesoamerican cultures adapted and developed. The mass of the population—food-producing farmers scattered in hinterland villages—provided the sustenance and labor that maintained a hereditary caste of rulers, hierarchies of priests, functionaries, and artisans. The nonfarming population presumably lived, arranged by rank, within precincts that served ceremonial, administrative, and residential functions and perhaps also were marketplaces. At regular intervals, the whole community convened for ritual observances at the religious-civic centers of towns such as San Lorenzo and La Venta. These centers were the formative architectural expressions of the structure and ideals of Olmec society.

**OLMEC RULER PORTRAITS** At La Venta, low clay-and-earthen platforms and stone fences enclosed two great courtyards. At one end of the larger area was a mound almost 100 feet high. Although now very eroded, this early pyramid, built of earth and adorned with colored clays, may have been intended to mimic a mountain, held sacred by Mesoamerican peoples as both a life-giving source of water and a feared destructive force. (Volcanic eruptions and earthquakes still wreak havoc in this region.) The La Venta layout is an early form of the temple-pyramid-plaza complex aligned on a north-south axis that characterized later Mesoamerican ceremonial center design.

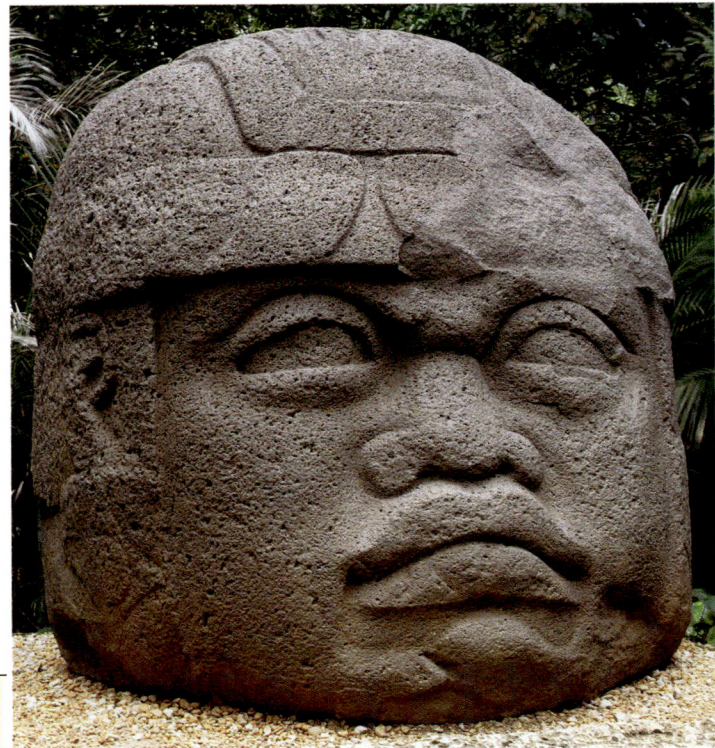

1 ft.

**18-2** Colossal head, La Venta, Mexico, Olmec, ca. 900–400 BCE. Basalt, 9′ 4″ high. Museo-Parque La Venta, Villahermosa.

The identities of the Olmec colossi are uncertain, but their individualized features and distinctive headgear as well as later Maya practice suggest these heads portray rulers rather than deities.

Four colossal basalt heads (FIG. **18-2**), weighing about 10 tons each and standing between 6 and 10 feet high, face out from the plaza. Archaeologists have discovered more than a dozen similar heads at San Lorenzo and Tres Zapotes. Almost as much of an achievement as the carving of these huge stones with stone tools was their transportation across the 60 miles of swampland from the nearest known basalt source, the Tuxtla Mountains. Although the identities of these colossi are uncertain, their individualized features and distinctive headgear and ear ornaments, as well as the later Maya practice of carving monumental ruler portraits, suggest the Olmec heads portray rulers rather than gods. The sheer size of the heads and their intensity of expression evoke great power, whether mortal or divine.

**JADE CELTS** The Olmec also made paintings in caves, fashioned ceramic figurines, and carved sculptures in jade, a prized, extremely hard, dark green stone they acquired from unknown sources far from their homeland. Sometimes the Olmec carved jade into ax-shaped polished forms art historians call *celts,* which they then buried under their ceremonial courtyards or platforms, perhaps in connection with rites associated with maize agriculture. The celt shape could be modified into a figural form, combining relief carving with incising. Olmec sculptors used stone-tipped drills and abrasive materials, such as sand, to carve jade. The subjects represented include figures combining human and animal features and postures, such as the *were-jaguar* illustrated here (FIG. **18-3**), which may be a maize deity. The Olmec human-animal representations may also refer to the belief that religious practitioners underwent dangerous transformations to wrest power from supernatural forces and harness it for the good of the community.

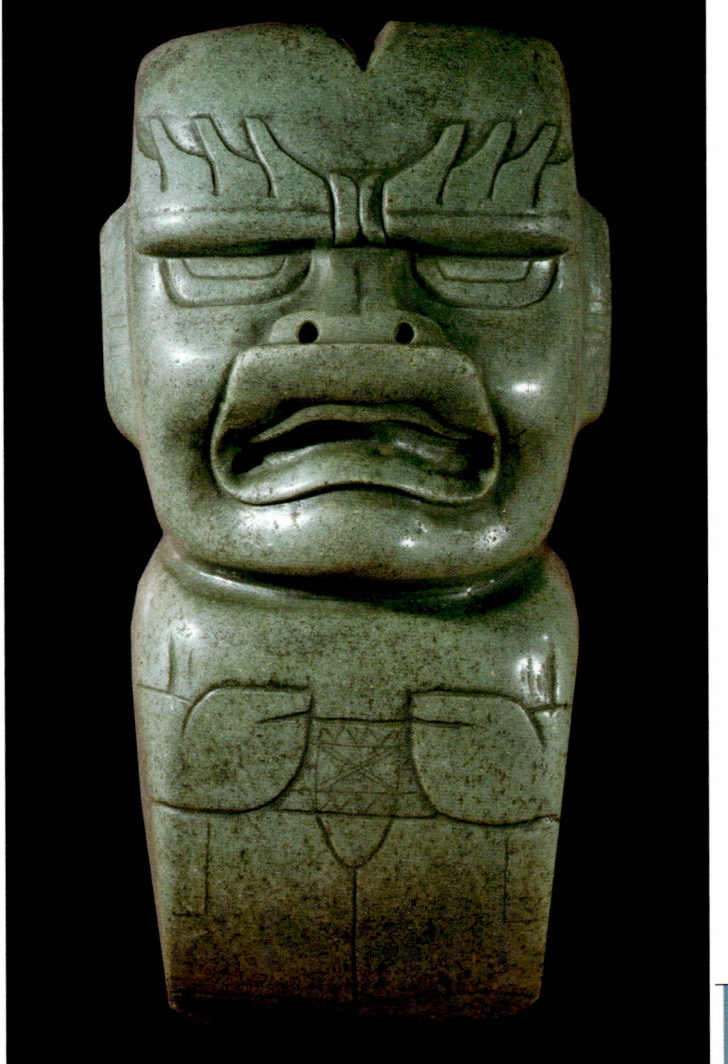

1 in.

**18-3** Ceremonial ax in the form of a were-jaguar, from La Venta, Mexico, Olmec, ca. 900–400 BCE. Jadeite, 11½″ high. British Museum, London.

Olmec celts often represent composite human-animal figures. They may reflect the Mesoamerican belief that religious practitioners underwent dangerous transformations on behalf of the community.

**WEST MEXICO** Far to the west of the tropical heartland of the Olmec are the Preclassic sites along Mexico's Pacific coast. Historians have long thought the ancient peoples of the modern West Mexican states of Nayarit, Jalisco, and Colima existed at Mesoamerica's geographic and cultural fringes. Recent archaeological discoveries, however, have revealed that although the West Mexicans did not produce large-scale stone sculpture, they did build permanent structures. These included tiered platforms and ball courts (see "The Mesoamerican Ball Game," page 501), architectural features found in nearly all Mesoamerican cultures and as far north as the North American Southwest. Yet West Mexico is best known for its rich tradition of clay sculpture. The sculptures come from tombs consisting of shafts as deep as 50 feet with chambers at their base. Because scientific excavations began only recently, much of what is known about West Mexican tomb contents derives primarily from the artifacts grave robbers found and sold. Researchers believe, however, the West Mexicans built most of these tombs and filled them with elaborate offerings during the late Preclassic period, the half millennium before 300 CE.

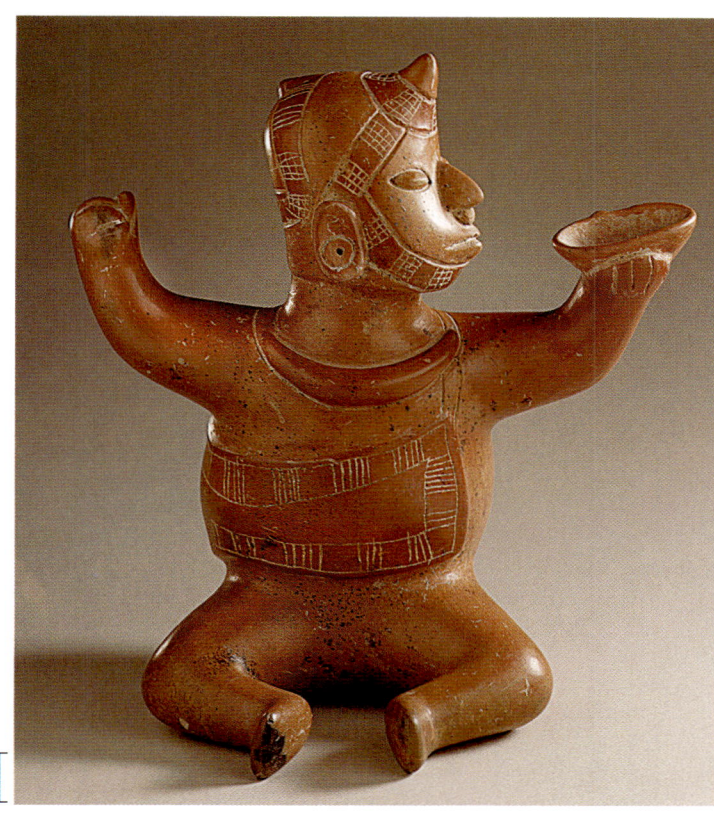

**18-4** Seated figure with drinking cup, from Colima, Mexico, ca. 200 BCE–500 CE. Clay with orange and red slip, 1′ 1″ high. Los Angeles County Museum of Art (Proctor Stafford Collection, purchased with funds provided by Mr. and Mrs. Allan C. Balch).

Preclassic West Mexico is famous for its ceramic sculptures. This one may depict a religious practitioner with a horn on his forehead or a political leader wearing a shell ornament—or someone serving both roles.

1 in.

The large ceramic figures found in the Colima tombs are consistently a highly burnished red orange, in contrast to the distinctive polychrome surfaces of the majority of other West Mexican ceramics. The area also is noted for small-scale clay narrative scenes that include modeled houses and temples and numerous solid figurines shown in a variety of lively activities. These sculptures, which almost exclusively depict elite ritual activities, are not found in any other ancient Mesoamerican culture, and their meaning is often uncertain. For example, scholars are unsure whether the figure illustrated here (FIG. **18-4**) is a religious practitioner with a horn on his forehead (a common indigenous symbol of special powers) or a political leader wearing a shell ornament (often a Mesoamerican emblem of rulership)—or a person serving both roles.

## Teotihuacán

At Olmec sites, the characteristic later Mesoamerican temple-pyramid-plaza layout appeared in embryonic form. At Teotihuacán (FIG. **18-5**), northeast of modern Mexico City, the Preclassic scheme

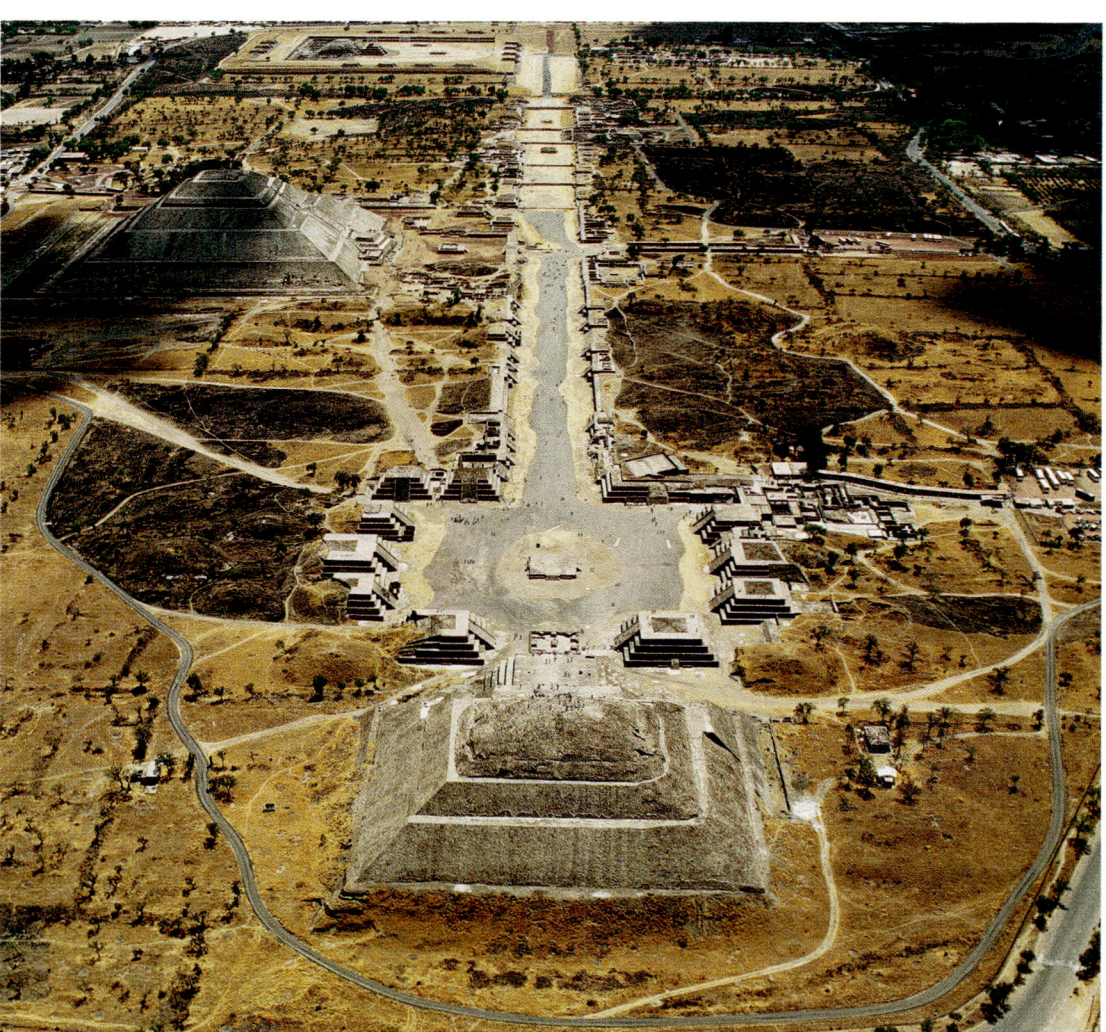

**18-5** Aerial view of Teotihuacán (looking south), Mexico. Pyramid of the Moon (*foreground*), Pyramid of the Sun (*top left*), and the Citadel (*background*), all connected by the Avenue of the Dead; main structures ca. 50–250 CE. ◼◀

At its peak around 600 CE, Teotihuacán was the world's sixth-largest city. It featured a grid plan, a two-mile-long main avenue, and monumental pyramids echoing the shapes of nearby mountains.

underwent a massive expansion into a genuine city. Teotihuacán was a large, densely populated metropolis that fulfilled a central civic, economic, and religious role for the region and indeed for much of Mesoamerica. Built up between about 100 BCE and 600 CE, when fire ravaged the city, the site's major monuments date to the late Preclassic period between 50 and 250 CE. Teotihuacán covers nine square miles, laid out in a grid pattern with the axes oriented by sophisticated surveying. The city's orientation and the placement of some of its key monuments apparently relate to astronomical phenomena.

At its peak, around 600 CE, Teotihuacán may have had as many as 125,000 to 200,000 residents, which would have made it then the sixth-largest city in the world. Divided into numerous wardlike sectors, this metropolis must have had a uniquely cosmopolitan character, with Zapotec peoples located in the city's western wards, and merchants from Veracruz living in the eastern wards, importing their own pottery and building their houses and tombs in the style of their homelands. The city's urbanization did nothing to detract from its sacred nature. In fact, it vastly augmented Teotihuacán's importance as a religious center. The Aztecs, who visited Teotihuacán regularly and reverently long after it had been abandoned, gave it its current name, which means "the place of the gods." Because the city's inhabitants left only a handful of undeciphered hieroglyphs, linguists do not yet even know what language they spoke. The names of many major features of the site are unknown. The Avenue of the Dead and the Pyramids of the Sun and Moon are later Aztec designations that do not necessarily relate to the original names of these streets and buildings.

North-south and east-west axes, each four miles in length, divide the grid plan into quarters. The scheme recalls Hellenistic and Roman urban planning (compare FIGS. 5-76 and 7-43) and is very unusual in Mesoamerica before the Aztecs. The main north-south axis, the Avenue of the Dead (FIG. 18-5), is 130 feet wide and connects the Pyramid of the Moon complex with the Citadel and its Temple of Quetzalcoatl. This two-mile stretch is not a continuously flat street but is broken by sets of stairs, giving pedestrians a constantly changing view of the surrounding buildings and landscape.

**PYRAMIDS** The largest structures at Teotihuacán are the stepped temple platforms popularly called pyramids, as in Egypt (see Chapter 3), but there is no connection between these two ancient cultures. The Preclassic Pyramid of the Sun (FIG. 18-5, *top left*), facing west on the east side of the Avenue of the Dead, dates to the first century CE. The city's centerpiece, it rises to a height of more than 200 feet in its restored state, which may not accurately reflect the pyramid's original appearance. The Pyramid of the Moon (FIG. 18-5, *foreground*) is a century or more later, around 150 to 250 CE. The shapes of the monumental structures at Teotihuacán echo the surrounding mountains. Their imposing mass and scale surpass those of all other Mesoamerican sites. Rubble-filled and faced with the local volcanic stone, the pyramids consist of stacked squared platforms diminishing in perimeter from the base to the top. Unlike the Stepped Pyramid of Djoser (FIG. 3-4) in Egyptian Saqqara, the Teotihuacán pyramids have ramped stairways that once led to crowning temples constructed of perishable materials such as wood and thatch. A distinctive feature of Teotihuacán construction is the alternation of sloping (*talud*) and vertical (*tablero*) rubble layers. The employment of *talud-tablero construction* at other sites is a sure sign of Teotihuacán influence.

The Teotihuacanos built the Pyramid of the Sun over a cave, which they reshaped and filled with ceramic offerings. The pyramid

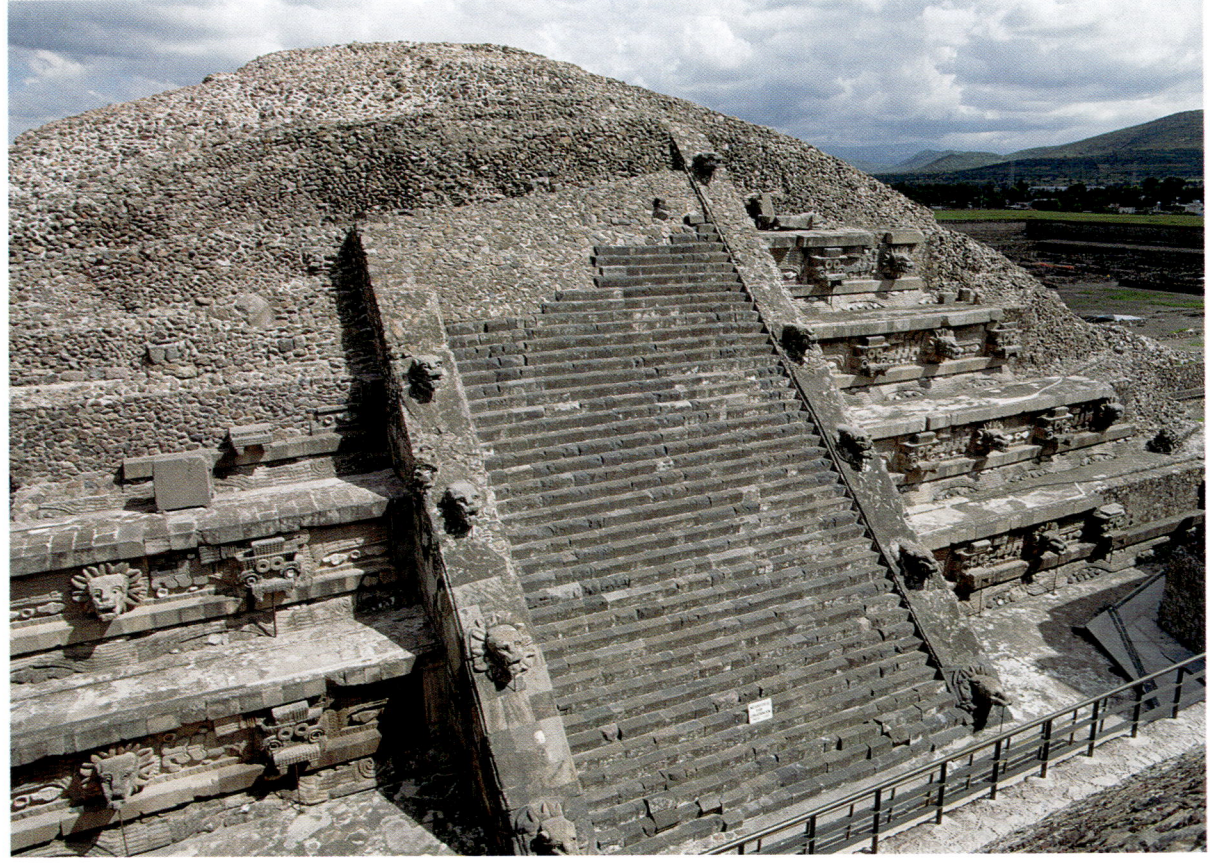

**18-6** Temple of Quetzalcoatl (looking southeast), the Citadel, Teotihuacán, Mexico, third century CE. ◧◧

The stone heads of Quetzalcoatl decorating this temple are the earliest Mesoamerican representations of the feathered-serpent god. Excavators found sacrificial victims beneath and around the pyramid.

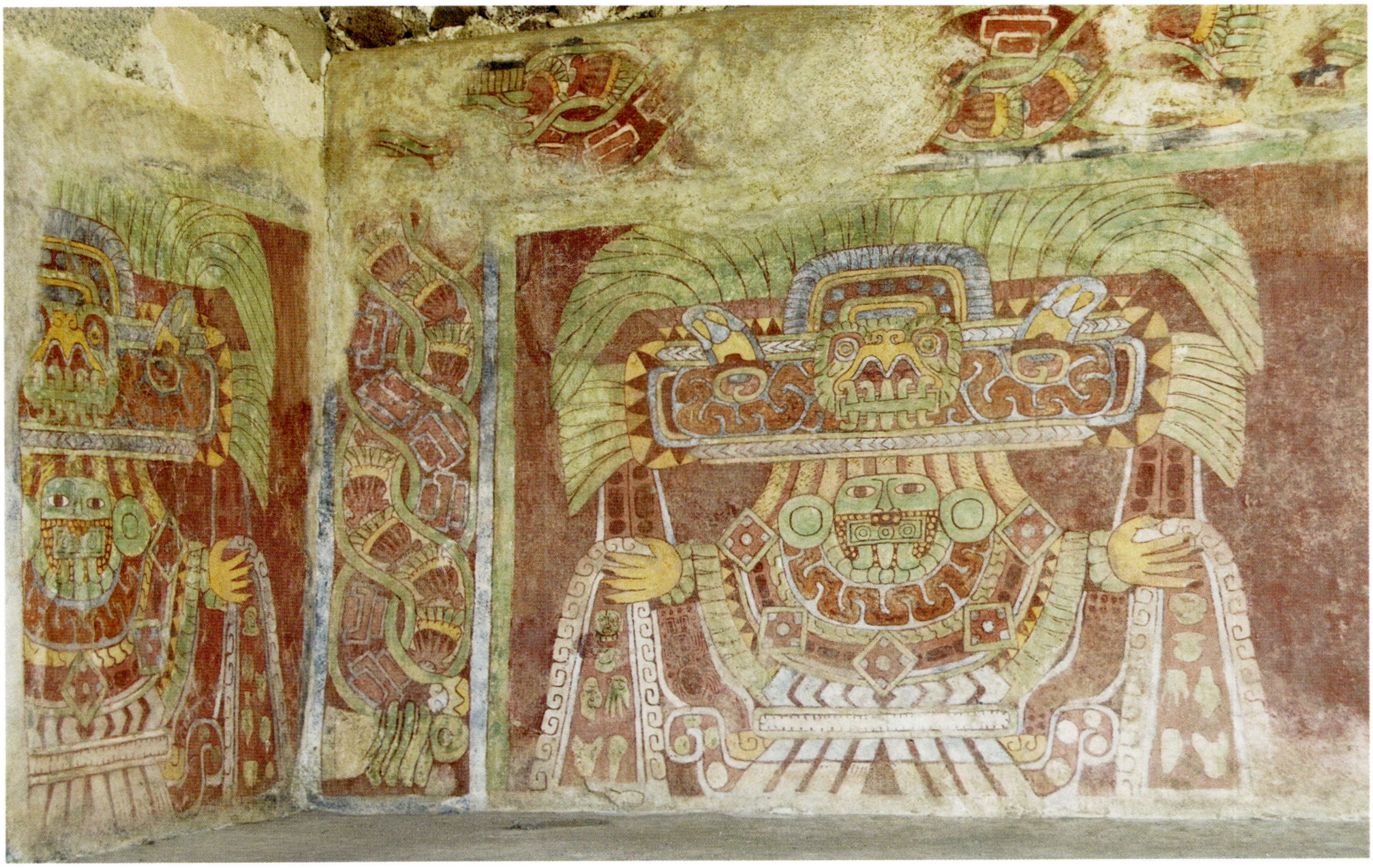

**18-7** Goddess, wall painting from the Tetitla apartment complex at Teotihuacán, Mexico, 650–750 CE. Pigments over clay and plaster.

Elaborate mural paintings adorned Teotihuacán's elite residential compound. This example may depict the city's principal deity, a goddess wearing a jade mask and a large feathered headdress.

may have marked a sacred spring within the now-dry cave. Excavators found children buried at the four corners of each of the pyramid's tiers. The Aztec sacrificed children to bring rainfall, and Teotihuacán art abounds with references to water, so the Teotihuacanos may have shared the Aztec preoccupation with rain and agricultural fertility. The city's inhabitants rebuilt the Pyramid of the Moon (currently being excavated) at least five times in Teotihuacán's early history. It may have been positioned to mimic the shape of Cerro Gordo, the volcanic mountain behind it, undoubtedly an important source of life-sustaining streams.

**QUETZALCOATL** At the south end of the Avenue of the Dead is the great quadrangle of the Citadel (FIG. 18-5, *background*). It encloses a smaller pyramidal shrine datable to the third century CE, the Temple of Quetzalcoatl (FIG. **18-6**). Quetzalcoatl, the "feathered serpent," was a major god in the Mesoamerican pantheon at the time of the Spanish conquest, hundreds of years after the fall of Teotihuacán. The Aztecs associated him with wind, rain clouds, and life. Beneath the temple, archaeologists found a tomb looted in antiquity, perhaps belonging to a Teotihuacano ruler. The discovery has led them to speculate the Teotihuacanos buried their elite in or under pyramids, as did the Maya. Surrounding the tomb both beneath and around the pyramid were the remains of at least a hundred sacrificial victims. Some wore necklaces made of strings of human jaws, both real and sculpted from shell. As did most other Mesoamerican groups, the Teotihuacanos invoked and

appeased their gods through human sacrifice. The presence of such a large number of victims also may reflect Teotihuacán's militaristic expansion. Throughout Mesoamerica, the victors often sacrificed captured warriors.

The temple's sculptured panels, which feature projecting stone heads of Quetzalcoatl alternating with heads of a long-snouted scaly creature with rings on its forehead, decorate each of the temple's six terraces. This is the first unambiguous representation of the feathered serpent in Mesoamerica. The scaly creature's identity is unclear. Linking these alternating heads are low-relief carvings of feathered-serpent bodies and seashells. The latter both reflect Teotihuacán contact with the peoples of the Mexican coasts and symbolize water, an essential ingredient for the sustenance of an agricultural economy.

**MURAL PAINTING** As in most ancient Mesoamerican cities, brightly painted stucco once covered Teotihuacán's buildings and streets. Elaborate murals also decorated the walls of the rooms of its elite residential compounds. The paintings (FIGS. **18-7** and **18-7A**) chiefly depict deities, ritual

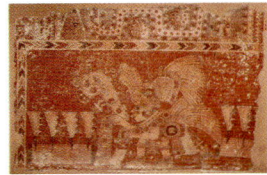

**18-7A** Bloodletting mural, Teotihuacán, ca. 600–700 CE.

activities, and processions of priests, warriors, and even animals. Experimenting with a variety of surfaces, materials, and techniques over the centuries, Teotihuacán muralists finally settled on applying pigments to a smooth lime-plaster surface coated with clay. They then polished the surface to a high sheen. Although some Teotihuacán paintings have a restricted palette of varying tones of red (largely derived from the mineral hematite), creating subtle contrasts between figure and ground, most employ vivid hues arranged in flat, carefully outlined patterns.

The mural illustrated here (FIG. 18-7) depicts an earth or nature goddess. Some scholars think she was the city's principal deity. Always shown frontally with her face covered by a jade mask, she is dwarfed by her large feathered headdress and reduced to a bust placed upon a stylized pyramid. She stretches her hands out to provide liquid streams filled with bounty—a motif common in many cultures, including ancient Mesopotamia (FIGS. 2-17 and 2-18A). The stylized human hearts flanking the frontal bird mask in the Teotihuacano goddess's headdress reflect the ancient Mesoamerican belief that human sacrifice is essential to agricultural renewal.

The influence of Teotihuacán was all-pervasive in Mesoamerica. The Teotihuacanos established colonies as far away as the southern borders of Maya civilization, in the highlands of Guatemala, some 800 miles from Teotihuacán.

## Classic Maya

The Olmec and Teotihuacán civilizations made a strong contribution to the development of Classic Maya culture. As was true of Teotihuacán, the foundations of Maya civilization date to the Preclassic period, perhaps 600 BCE or even earlier. At that time, the Maya, who occupied the moist lowland areas of Belize, southern Mexico, Guatemala, and Honduras, seem to have abandoned their early, somewhat egalitarian pattern of village life and adopted a hierarchical autocratic society. This system evolved into the typical Maya city-state governed by hereditary rulers and ranked nobility. How and why this happened are still unknown, but the Classic Maya culture endured for 600 years.

Although the causes of the beginning and end of Classic Maya civilization are obscure, researchers are gradually revealing its history, religion, ceremonies, conventions, and patterns of daily life through scientific excavation and progress made in decoding Mayan script. Two important breakthroughs have radically altered the understanding of both Mayan writing and the Maya worldview. The first was the realization that the Maya depicted their rulers (rather than gods or anonymous priests) in their art and noted their rulers' achievements in their texts. The second was that Mayan writing is largely phonetic—that is, the hieroglyphs consist of signs representing sounds in the Mayan language. Fortunately, the Spaniards recorded the various Mayan languages in colonial texts and dictionaries. Descendants of the Maya still speak most of the ancient languages today, facilitating the translation of many ancient Mayan hieroglyphs.

The Maya possessed a highly developed knowledge of arithmetic calculation and the ability to observe and record the movements of the sun, the moon, and numerous planets. They contrived an intricate but astonishingly accurate calendar with a fixed-zero date, and although their structuring of time was radically different in form from the Western calendar used today, it was just as precise and efficient. With their calendar, the Maya established the genealogical lines of their rulers, which certified their claim to rule, and created the only true written history in ancient America. Although other ancient Mesoamerican societies, even in the Preclassic period, also possessed calendars, only the Maya calendar can be translated directly into today's system of measuring time.

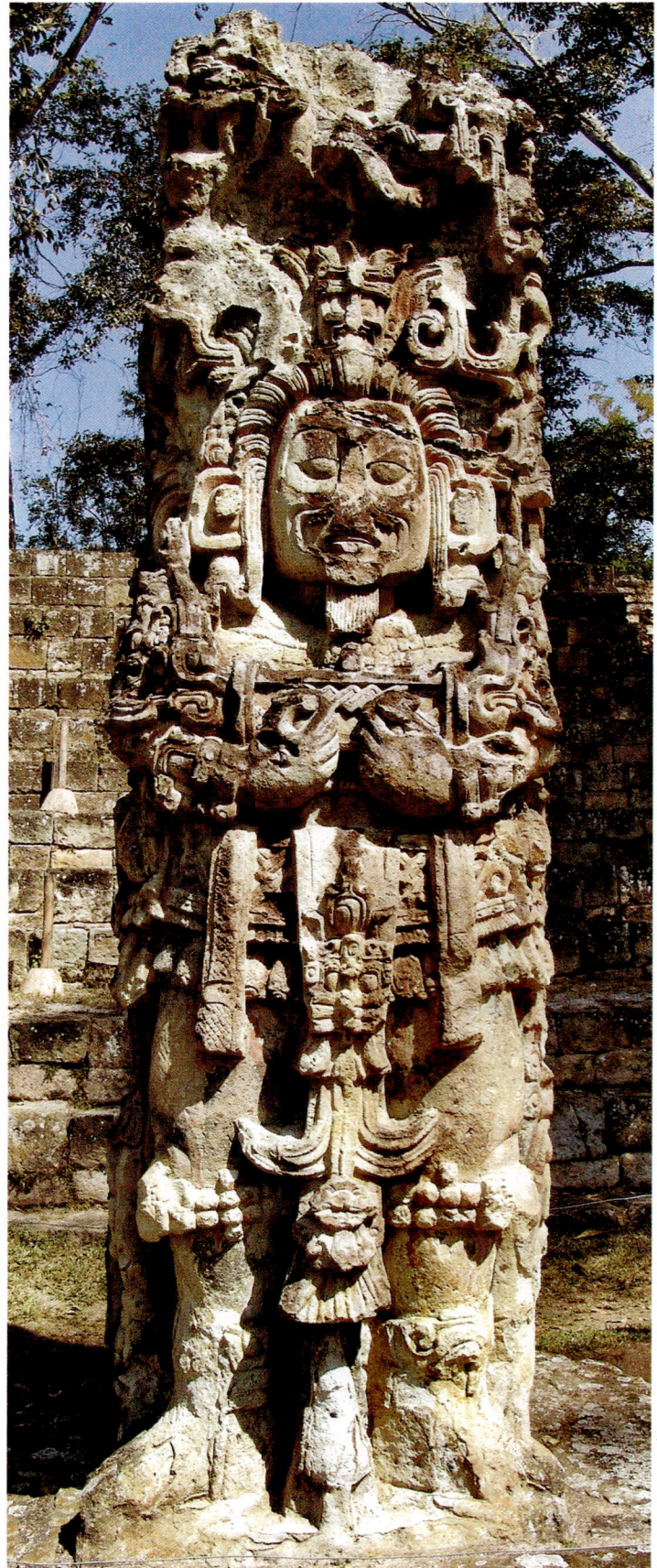

1 ft.

**18-8** Stele D portraying Ruler 13 (Waxaklajuun-Ub'aah-K'awiil), Great Plaza, Copán, Honduras, Maya, 736 CE. Stone, 11′ 9″ high.

This 12-foot stele portrays one of Copán's most important rulers as an over-life-size figure wearing an elaborate headdress and holding a double-headed serpent bar, symbol of his sacred authority.

**ARCHITECTURE AND RITUAL** Vast complexes of terraced temple-pyramids, palaces, plazas, ball courts (see "The Mesoamerican Ball Game," page 501), and residences of the governing elite dotted the Maya area. Unlike Teotihuacán, no single Maya site ever achieved complete dominance as the center of power. The new architecture, and the art embellishing it, advertised the power of the rulers, who appropriated cosmic symbolism and stressed their descent from gods to reinforce their claims to legitimate rule.

The Maya erected their most sacred and majestic buildings in enclosed, centrally located precincts within their cities. Archaeologists call these areas the "site core"—the religious and administrative nucleus for a population of dispersed farmers settled throughout a suburban area of many square miles. There, the Maya rulers staged dramatic rituals within spacious sculpture-filled plazas. In both life and art, the ruling families and troops of priests, nobles, and retainers wore extravagant, vividly colorful cotton textiles, feathers, jaguar skins, and jade, all emblematic of rank and wealth. On the different levels of the painted and polished temple platforms, the ruling classes performed the rites in clouds of incense to the music of maracas, flutes, and drums. The Maya thus transformed the architectural complex at each city's center into a theater of religion and statecraft.

**COPÁN** Because Copán, on the western border of Honduras, has more hieroglyphic inscriptions and well-preserved carved monuments than any other site in the Americas, it was one of the first Maya sites excavated. It also has proved one of the richest in the trove of architecture, sculpture, and artifacts recovered. Conspicuous plazas dominated the heart of the city. In Copán's Great Plaza, the Maya set up tall, sculpted stone *stelae*. Carved with the portraits of the rulers who erected them, these stelae also recorded their names, dates of reign, and notable achievements in glyphs on the front, sides, or back.

Stele D (FIG. **18-8**), set up in 736 CE, represents one of the city's foremost rulers, Waxaklajuun-Ub'aah-K'awiil (r. 695–738), whose name means "18 are the apparitions of the god K'awiil." Scholars often call him Ruler 13 in the Copán dynastic sequence of 16 rulers. During his long reign, the city may have reached its greatest physical extent and range of political influence. On Stele D, Ruler 13 wears an elaborate headdress and ornamented kilt and sandals. He holds across his chest a double-headed serpent bar, symbol of his sacred authority. His features are distinctly Maya, although highly idealized. The Maya elite usually required sculptors and painters to depict them as eternally youthful. The dense, deeply carved ornamental details framing the face and figure in florid profusion stand almost clear of the block and wrap around the sides of the stele. The high relief, originally painted, gives the impression of an over-life-size freestanding statue, although an incised hieroglyphic text is on the flat back side of the stele. A powerful ruler who erected many stelae and buildings at Copán, including one of Mesoamerica's best-preserved (and carefully restored) ball courts (FIG. **18-9;** see "The Mesoamerican Ball Game," page 501), Ruler 13 eventually suffered a humiliating end. In 738, the king of neighboring Quiriguá captured and beheaded him.

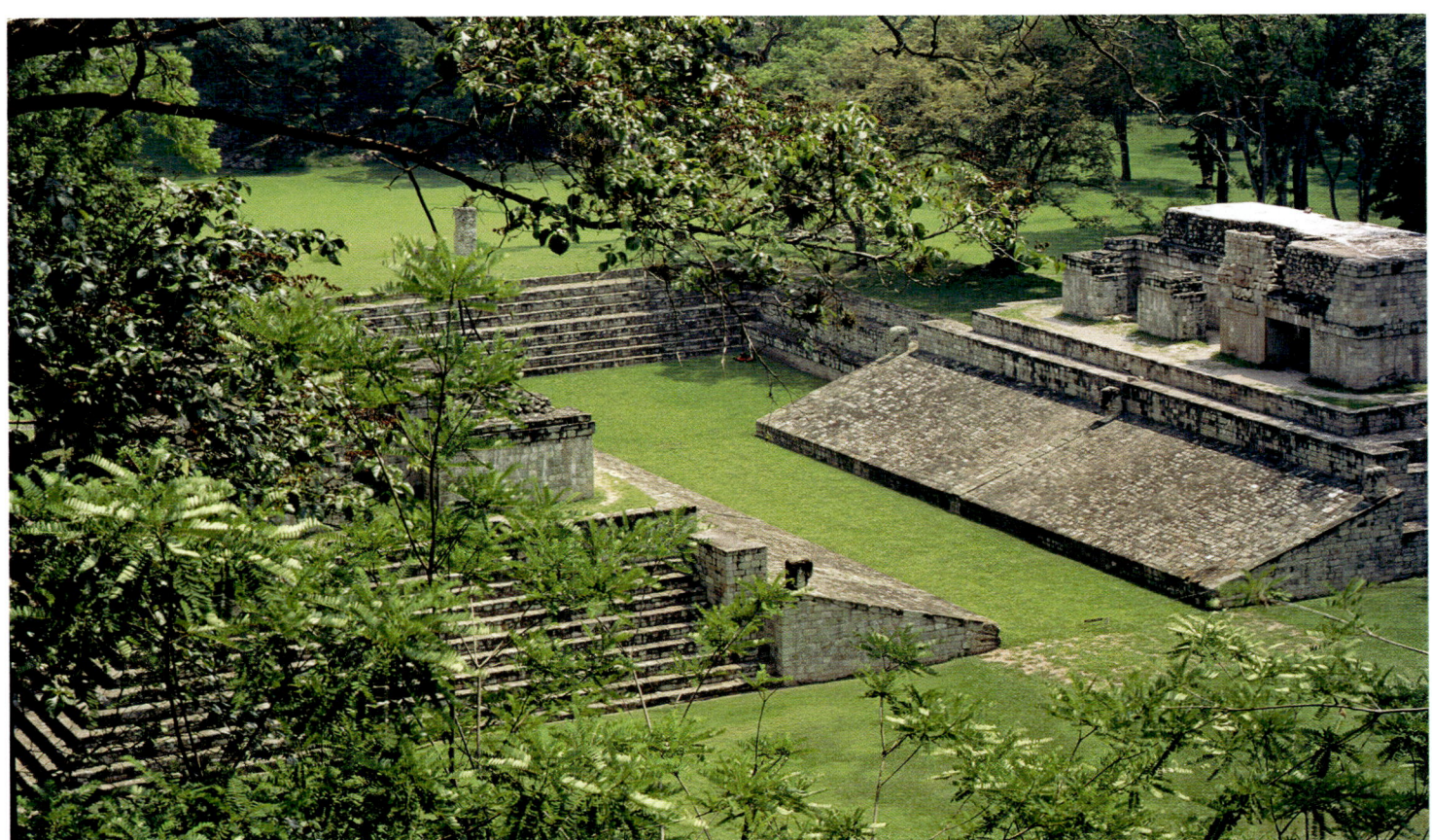

**18-9** Ball court (looking northeast), Middle Plaza, Copán, Honduras, Maya, 738 CE.

Ball courts were common in Mesoamerican cities. Copán's is 93 feet long. The rules of the ball game itself are unknown, but games sometimes ended in human sacrifice of captives taken in battle.

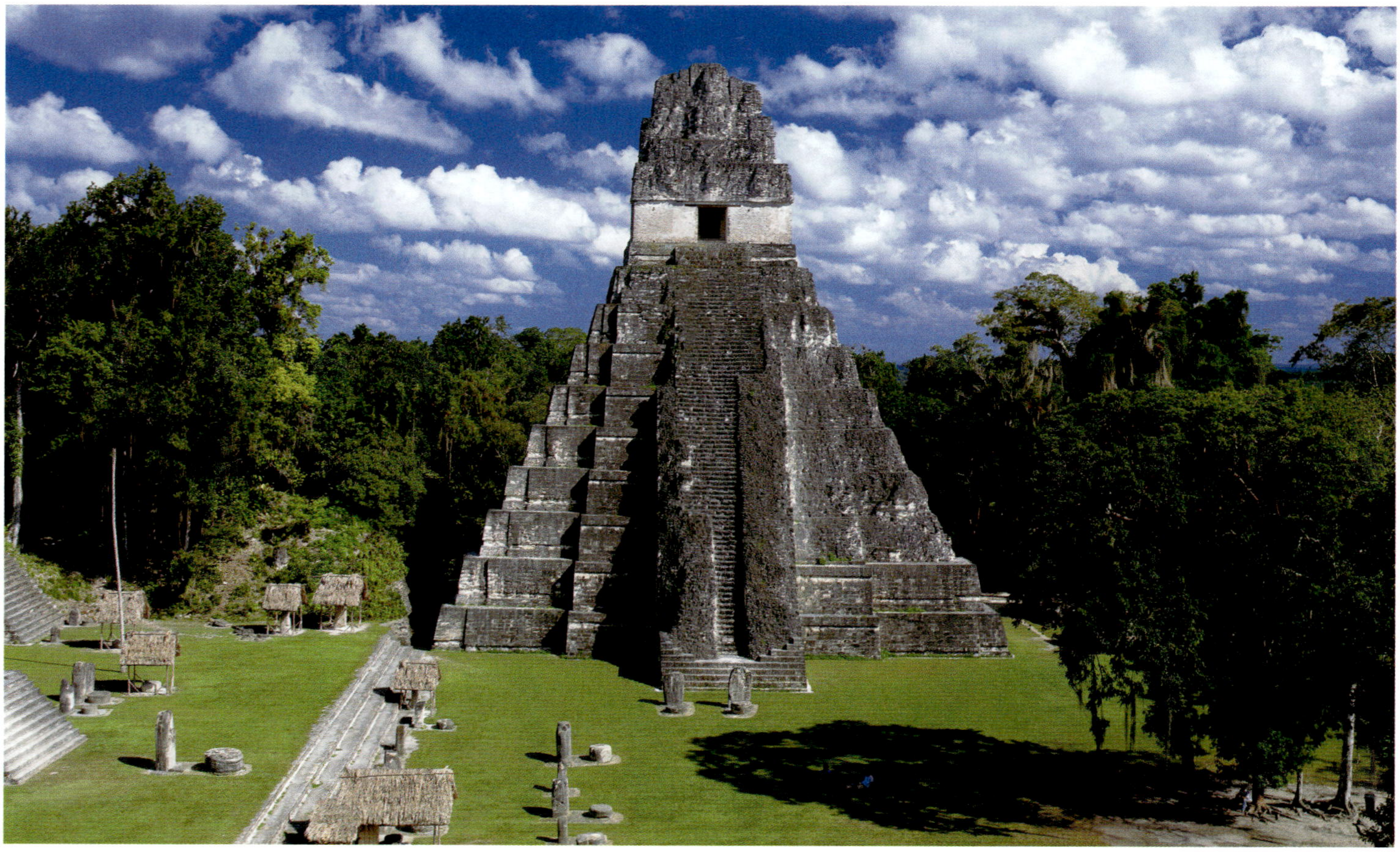

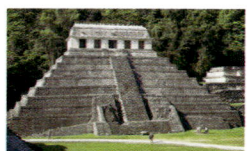

**18-10** Temple I (Temple of the Giant Jaguar), Tikal, Guatemala, Maya, ca. 732 CE.

Temple I at Tikal is a 145-foot-tall pyramid that was the temple-mausoleum of Hasaw Chan K'awiil, who died in 732 CE. The nine tiers of the pyramid probably refer to the nine levels of the Underworld.

**18-10A** Temple of the Inscriptions, Palenque, ca. 675–690 CE.

**TIKAL** Another great Maya site of the Classic period is Tikal in Guatemala, some 150 miles north of Copán. Tikal is one of the oldest and largest Maya cities. Together with its suburbs, Tikal originally covered some 75 square miles and served as the ceremonial center of a population of perhaps 75,000. The Maya did not lay out central Tikal on a grid plan as did the designers of contemporaneous Teotihuacán. Instead, causeways connected irregular groupings. Modern surveys have uncovered the remains of as many as 3,000 separate structures in an area of about six square miles. The site's nucleus is the Great Plaza, an open area studded with stelae and bordered by large stone structures. The Maya engineers graded the plaza and other areas of the city to conduct rainwater into the city's reservoirs. Dominating the Great Plaza are two soaring pyramids, taller than the surrounding rain forest, which face each other across the open square. The larger pyramid (FIG. **18-10**), Temple I (also called the Temple of the Giant Jaguar after a motif on one of its carved wooden lintels), reaches a height of about 145 feet, about twice the height of the late-seventh-century Temple of the Inscriptions (FIG. **18-10A**) at Palenque in Mexico, but more than 50 feet shorter and much narrower than the Preclassic Pyramid of the Sun (FIG. 18-5, *top left*) at Teotihuacán. Considerable evidence indicates the builders of Palenque and Tikal and other Maya sites painted the exteriors of their temples red or red, white, and other bright colors.

The Temple of the Giant Jaguar at Tikal is the temple-mausoleum of one of the city's greatest rulers, Hasaw Chan K'awiil, who died in 732 CE. The Maya buried him in a vaulted chamber under the pyramid's base. The towering structure consists of nine sharply inclining platforms, probably a reference to the nine levels of the Underworld, and a three-chambered temple reached by a narrow stairway. Surmounting the temple is an elaborately sculpted *roof comb,* a vertical architectural projection that once bore the ruler's gigantic portrait modeled in stucco.

**JAINA** As did their West Mexican predecessors (FIG. 18-4), the Maya excelled at modeling small-scale figures in clay. The extant examples are remarkably lifelike and display an almost unlimited variety of postures and gestures, made possible by the malleable nature of the medium. The figures, often cast in molds, also represent a wider range of human types and activities than is commonly depicted on Maya stelae. Ball players (FIG. **18-11**), women weaving, older men, dwarfs, supernatural beings, and amorous couples, as well as elaborately attired rulers and warriors, are the most common subjects. Many of the hollow figurines are also whistles. All are products of ceramic workshops on the mainland, but burials on the island cemetery of Jaina, off the western coast of Yucatán, have yielded hundreds of clay statuettes, including the ball player illustrated here. Traces of blue remain on the man's belt, remnants of the vivid pigments that once covered many of these figurines. The Maya used "Maya blue," a combination of a particular kind of clay and indigo, a vegetable dye, to paint both ceramics and murals.

# The Mesoamerican Ball Game

After witnessing the native ball game of Mexico soon after their arrival, the 16th-century Spanish conquerors took Aztec ball players back to Europe to demonstrate the novel sport. Their chronicles remark on the athletes' great skill, the heavy wagering that accompanied the competition, and the ball itself, made of rubber, a substance the Spaniards had never seen before.

Native Americans played the game throughout Mesoamerica and into the southwestern United States, beginning at least 3,400 years ago, the date of the earliest known ball court. The Olmec were apparently avid players. Their very name—a modern invention in Náhuatl, the Aztec language—means "rubber people," after the latex-growing region they inhabited. Not only do ball players appear in Olmec art, but archaeologists also have found remnants of sunken earthen ball courts and even rubber balls at Olmec sites.

The Olmec earthen playing field evolved in other Mesoamerican cultures into a plastered masonry surface, I- or T-shaped in plan, flanked by two parallel sloping or straight walls. Sometimes the walls were wide enough to support small structures on top, as at Copán (FIG. 18-9). At other sites, temples stood at either end of the ball court. These structures were common features of Mesoamerican cities. At Cantona in the Mexican state of Puebla, for example, archaeologists have uncovered 22 ball courts even though only a small portion of the site has been excavated. Teotihuacán (FIG. 18-5) is an exception. Excavators have not yet found a ball court there, but mural paintings at the site illustrate people playing the game with portable markers and sticks. Most ball courts were adjacent to the important civic structures of Mesoamerican cities, such as palaces and temple-pyramids, as at Copán.

Historians know surprisingly little about the rules of the ball game itself, not even how many players were on the field or how they scored goals. Unlike a modern soccer field with its standard dimensions, Mesoamerican ball courts vary widely in size. The largest known—at Chichén Itzá (FIG. 18-1)—is nearly 500 feet long. Copán's is about 93 feet long. Some have stone rings set high up on their walls at right angles to the ground, but many courts lack this feature, so it is uncertain whether the players aimed to get the ball through a ring in order to score a point. Alternatively, players may have scored goals by bouncing the ball against the walls and into the end zones. As in soccer, players could not touch the ball with their hands but used their heads, elbows, hips, and legs. They wore thick leather belts, and sometimes even helmets, and padded their knees and arms against the blows of the fast-moving, solid rubber ball. Typically, the Maya portrayed ball players wearing heavy protective clothing and kneeling, poised to deflect the ball (FIG. 18-11).

Although widely enjoyed as a competitive spectator sport, the ball game did not serve solely for entertainment. The ball, for example, may have represented a celestial body such as the sun, its move-

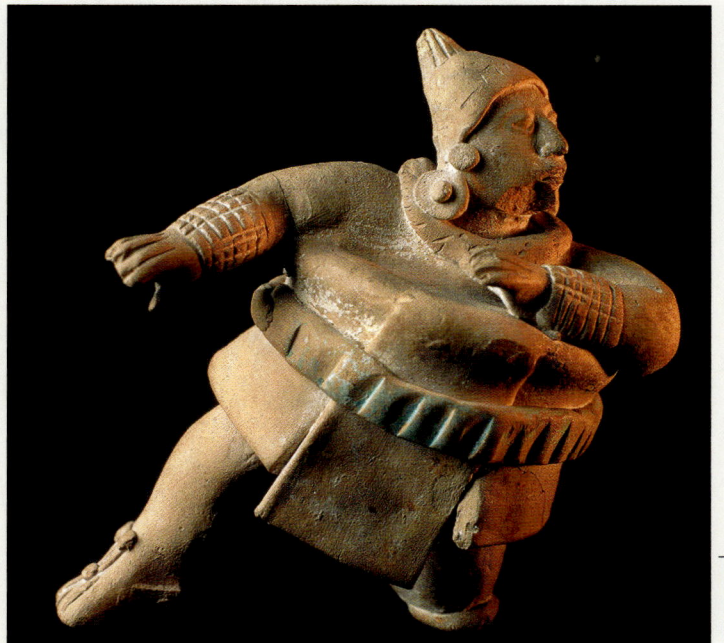

1 in.

**18-11** Ball player, from Jaina Island, Mexico, Maya, 700–900 CE. Painted clay, 6¼″ high. Museo Nacional de Antropología, Mexico City.

Maya ceramic figurines represent a wide range of human types and activities. This kneeling ball player wears a thick leather belt and arm- and kneepads to protect him from the hard rubber ball.

ments over the court imitating the sun's daily passage through the sky. Reliefs on the walls of ball courts at certain sites make clear the game sometimes culminated in human sacrifice, probably of captives taken in battle and then forced to participate in a game they were predestined to lose.

Accounts of ball games also appear in Mesoamerican mythology. In the Maya epic known as the *Popol Vuh* (*Council Book*), first written down in Spanish in the colonial period, the evil lords of the Underworld force a legendary pair of twins to play ball. The brothers lose, and the victors sacrifice them. The sons of one twin eventually travel to the Underworld and, after a series of trials including a ball game, outwit the lords and kill them. They revive their father, buried in the ball court after his earlier defeat at the hands of the Underworld gods. The younger twins rise to the heavens to become the sun and the moon, and the father becomes the god of maize, principal sustenance of all Mesoamerican peoples. The ball game and its aftermath, then, were a metaphor for the cycle of life, death, and regeneration that permeated Mesoamerican religion.

This pigment has proved virtually indestructible, unlike other colors the Maya used, which have mostly disappeared over time. Like the larger terracotta figures of West Mexico, these figurines accompanied the dead on their inevitable voyage to the Underworld.

The excavations at Jaina, however, have revealed nothing more that might clarify the meaning and function of the figures. Male figurines do not come exclusively from burials of male individuals, for example.

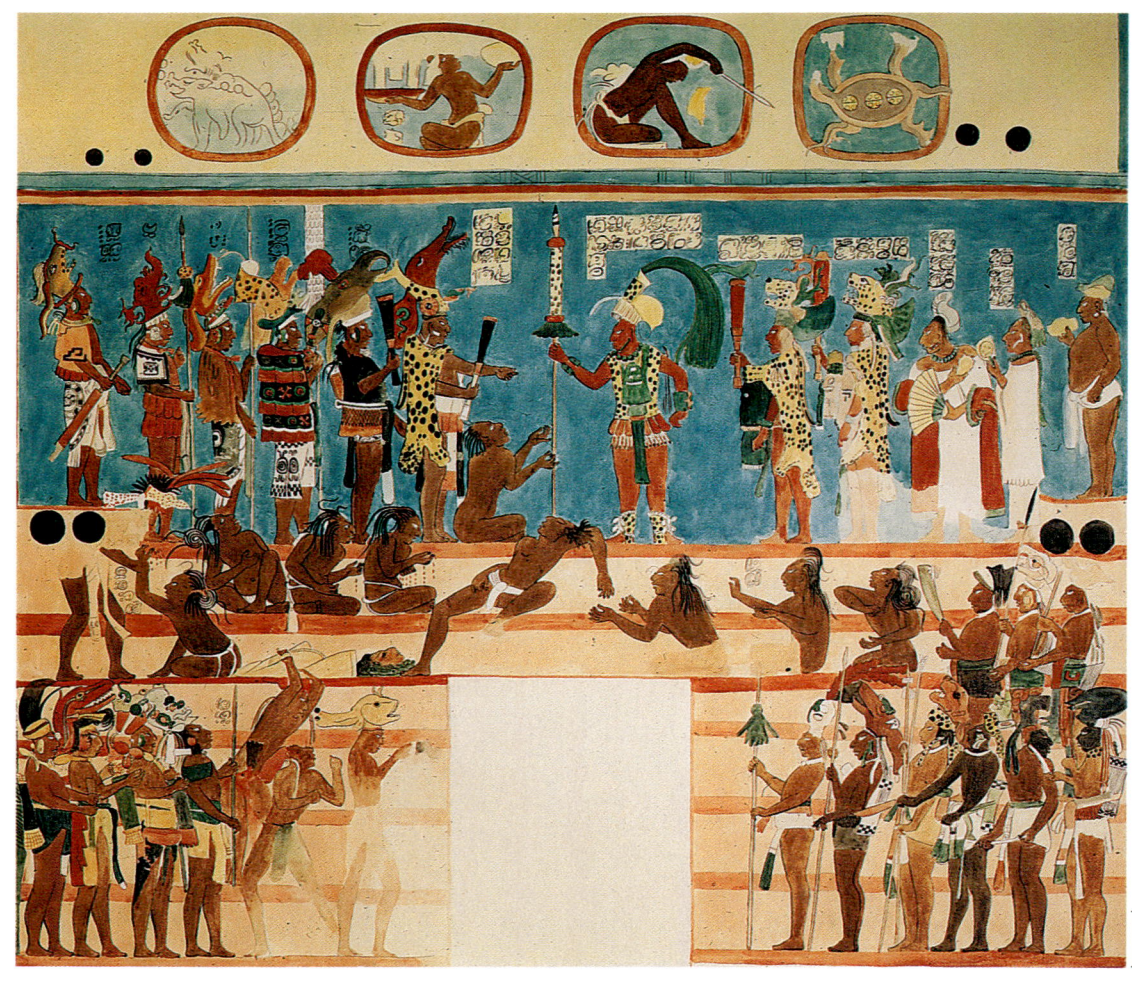

**18-12** Presentation of captives to Lord Chan Muwan, room 2 of structure 1, Bonampak, Mexico, Maya, ca. 790 CE. Mural, 17′ × 15′; watercolor copy by Antonio Tejeda. Peabody Museum, Harvard University, Cambridge.

The figures in this mural— a cross between fresco and tempera—may be standing on a pyramid's steps. At the top, the richly attired Chan Muwan reviews naked captives, with mutilated hands, awaiting death.

1 ft.

**BONAMPAK** The vivacity of the Jaina figurines and their variety of pose, costume, and occupation have parallels in the mural paintings of Bonampak (Mayan for "painted walls") in southeastern Mexico. Three chambers in one Bonampak structure contain murals recording important aspects of Maya court life. The illustrated example (FIG. **18-12**) shows warriors surrounding captives on a terraced platform. The figures have naturalistic proportions and overlap, twist, turn, and gesture. The artists used fluid lines to outline the figures, working with color to indicate both texture and volume. The Bonampak painters combined their pigments—both mineral and organic—with a mixture of water, crushed limestone, and vegetable gums and applied them to their stucco walls in a technique best described as a cross between *fresco* and *tempera*.

Circumstantial details abound in the Bonampak murals. The information revealed is comprehensive, explicit, and presented with the fidelity of an eyewitness report. Royal personages are identifiable by both their physical features and their costumes, and accompanying inscriptions provide the precise day, month, and year for the events recorded. All the scenes at Bonampak relate the events and ceremonies welcoming a new royal heir (shown as a toddler in some scenes). They include presentations, preparations for a royal fete, dancing, battle, and the taking and sacrificing of prisoners. On all occasions of state, public bloodletting was an integral part of Maya ritual. The ruler, his consort, and certain members of the nobility drew blood from their bodies and sought union with the supernatural world. The slaughter of captives taken in war regularly accompanied this ceremony. Indeed, Mesoamerican cultures undertook warfare largely to provide victims for sacrifice. The torture and eventual execution of prisoners served both to nourish the gods and to strike fear into enemies and the general populace.

The scene (FIG. 18-12) in room 2 of structure 1 depicts the presentation of prisoners to Lord Chan Muwan. The painter arranged the figures in registers that may represent a pyramid's steps. On the uppermost step, against a blue background, is a file of gorgeously appareled nobles wearing animal headgear. Conspicuous among them on the right are retainers clad in jaguar pelts and jaguar headdresses. Also present is Chan Muwan's wife (third from right). The ruler himself, in jaguar jerkin and high-backed sandals, stands at the center, facing a crouching victim who appears to beg for mercy. Naked captives, anticipating death, crowd the middle level. One of them, already dead, sprawls at the ruler's feet. Others dumbly contemplate the blood dripping from their mutilated hands. The lower zone, cut through by a doorway into the structure housing the murals, shows clusters of attendants who are doubtless of inferior rank to the lords of the upper zone. The stiff formality of the victors contrasts graphically with the supple imploring attitudes and gestures of the hapless victims. The Bonampak victory was short-lived, however. The artists never finished the murals, and soon after the dates written on the walls, the Maya apparently abandoned the site.

The Bonampak murals are the most famous Maya wall paintings, but they are not unique. In 2001 at San Bartolo in northeastern Guatemala, American archaeologists discovered the earliest examples yet found. They date to around 100 BCE, almost a millennium before the Bonampak murals.

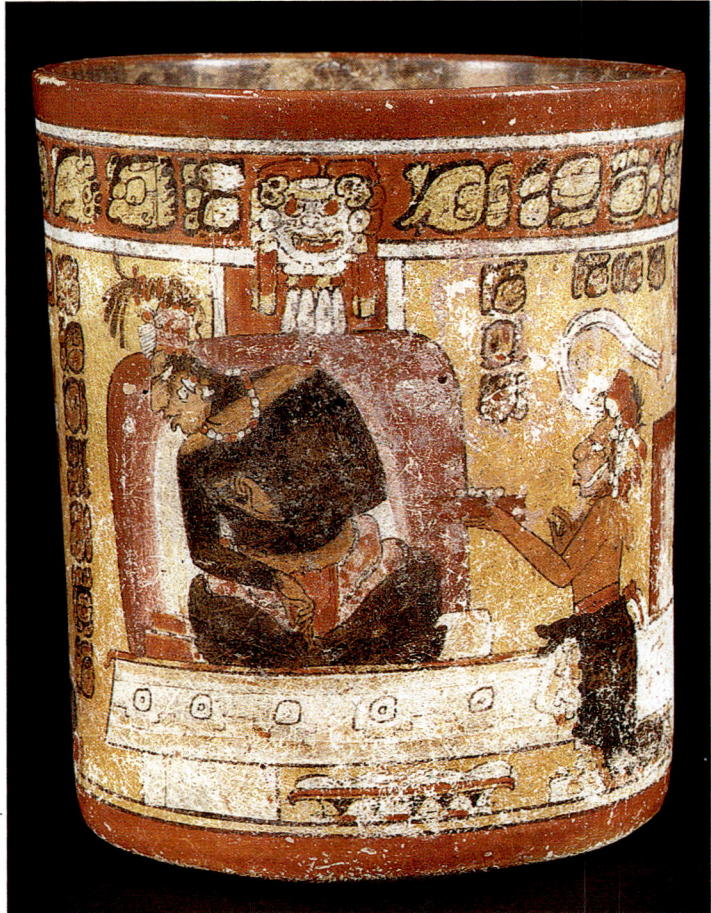

18-13 Enthroned Maya lord and attendants, cylinder vase, probably from Altamira, Mexico, Maya, ca. 672–830 CE. Polychrome ceramic, 8″ high. Dumbarton Oaks Research Library and Collections, Washington, D.C.

Maya polychrome ceramics depict a variety of subjects ranging from mythology to daily life. This cylinder vase shows an enthroned Maya lord at a ritual involving drinking and dancing.

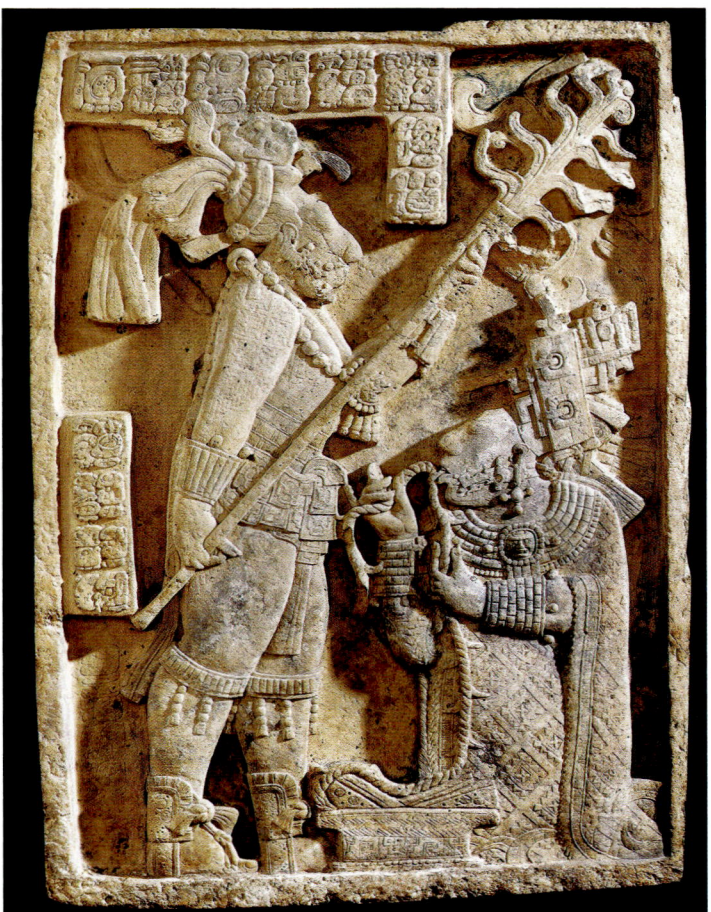

18-14 Shield Jaguar and Lady Xoc, lintel 24 of temple 23, Yaxchilán, Mexico, Maya, ca. 725 CE. Limestone, 3′ 7″ × 2′ 6½″. British Museum, London.

The carved lintels of this eighth-century temple document the central role elite women played in Maya society. Lady Xoc pierces her tongue in a bloodletting ritual intended to induce a visionary state.

**CYLINDER VASES** Frescoes such as those at Bonampak and San Bartolo once liberally adorned the walls of Maya civic and religious buildings, but surviving examples are rare. Fortunately, as in ancient Greece (see Chapter 5), painted ceramics have been found in large numbers at Maya sites. But Maya painted pottery, in contrast to most Greek vase paintings, is polychrome. Produced using colored slips fired at low temperatures in open pits to achieve a lustrous surface, Maya vases approximate the appearance of mural painting much more closely than do the black-and-red compositions on Greek vases. Hieroglyphic labels are common and identify many of the figures and events depicted and also record individual artist's names. Sometimes the texts describe the contents of the vessels. Cylinder vases often contained cacao, a much-prized chocolate drink, but others were gifts to the dead and never used in daily life.

The scene on the cylinder vase illustrated here (FIG. **18-13**), like those on similar vessels, wraps around the entire exterior surface. At the center is an enthroned, bare-chested Maya lord wearing a feathered headdress. He engages in animated conversation with two seated noblemen to his right. A lidded cylinder vase is at his side. A kneeling attendant at his left offers him a bowl. The drawing style is typical of Maya ceramics. Black contour lines are prominent, and

the artist filled in the outlines with flat colors—mostly red, orange, and brown—on a creamy slip background. The painted hieroglyphs describe this as a ritual scene involving drinking and dancing. The inscriptions also name the participants and the artist.

**YAXCHILÁN** Elite women played an important role in Maya society, and some surviving artworks document their high status. The painted reliefs on the lintels of temple 23 at Yaxchilán represent an elite woman as a central figure in Maya ritual. Lintel 24 (FIG. **18-14**) depicts the ruler Itzamna B'ahlam II (r. 681–742 CE), known as Shield Jaguar, and his principal wife, Lady Xoc. She is magnificently outfitted in an elaborate woven garment, headdress, and jewels. With a barbed cord she pierces her tongue in a bloodletting ceremony (compare FIG. 18-7A) that, according to accompanying inscriptions, celebrated the birth of a son to one of the ruler's other wives as well as an alignment between the planets Saturn and Jupiter. The celebration must have taken place in a dark chamber or at night because Shield Jaguar provides illumination with a blazing torch. These ceremonies induced an altered state of consciousness in order to connect the bloodletter with the supernatural world. (Lintel 25 depicts Lady Xoc and her vision of an ancestor emerging from the mouth of a serpent.)

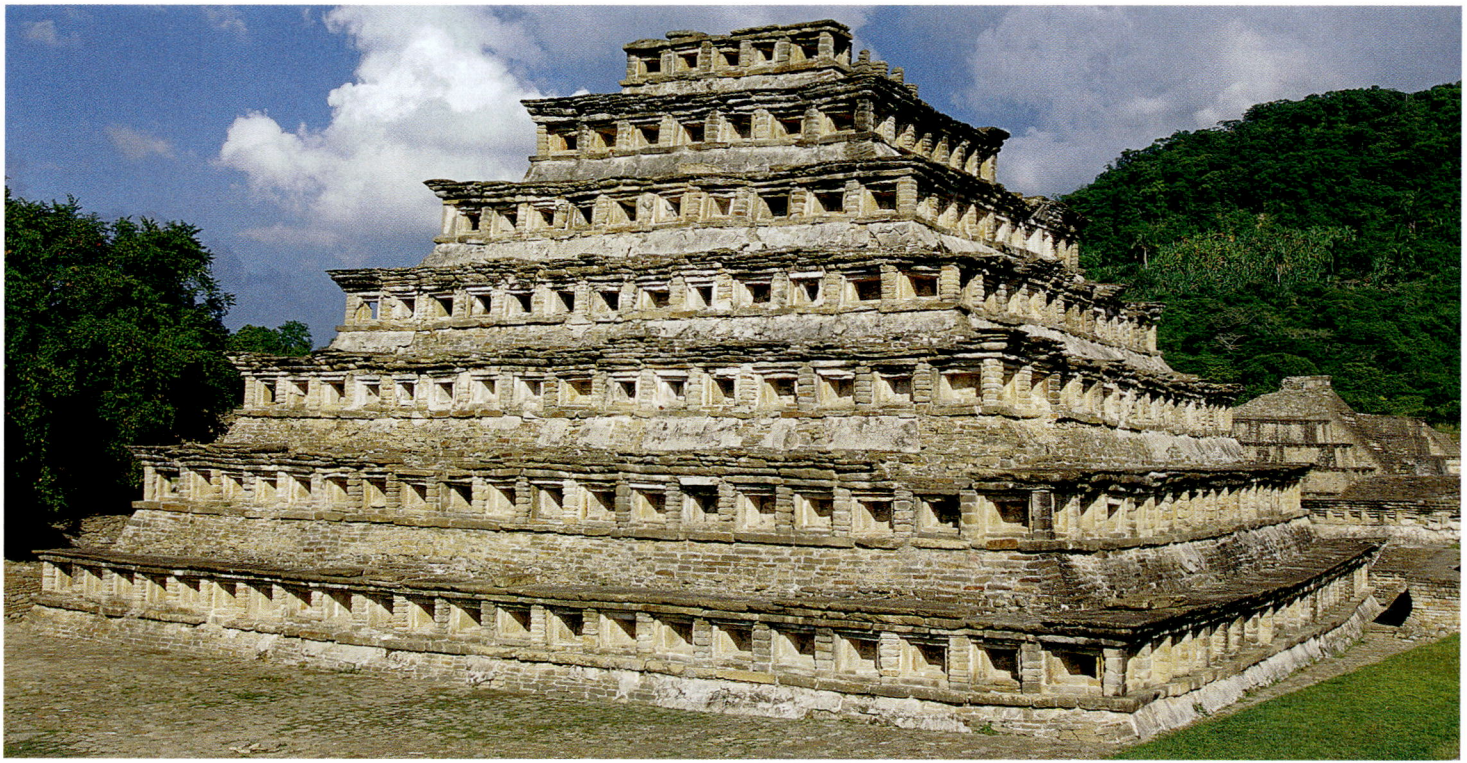

**18-15** Pyramid of the Niches (looking northeast), El Tajín, Mexico, Classic Veracruz, sixth century CE.

The Pyramid of the Niches, although only 66 feet tall, has 365 niches, one for each day of the solar year. It is one of many Mesoamerican monuments connected with astronomy and the calendar.

## Classic Veracruz

The Maya is the most famous Classic Mesoamerican culture today, and its remains are the most abundant. Still, other cultures also flourished, and some of their surviving monuments rival those of the Maya in size and sophistication. In the Veracruz plain, for example, the heir to the Olmec culture was a civilization archaeologists call Classic Veracruz. The name of the people who occupied the area at the time is unknown.

**EL TAJÍN** The major Classic Veracruz site is El Tajín, which explorers discovered in the dense rain forest of the Gulf of Mexico coast in 1785. At its peak, El Tajín was a thriving city of hundreds of acres and tens of thousands of inhabitants. The excavated portion of the city has already revealed 17 ball courts. The building that dominates the ceremonial center of El Tajín is the so-called Pyramid of the Niches (FIG. **18-15**), a sixth-century CE structure of unusual form. In spite of its small size (only 66 feet tall), the Pyramid of the Niches encases an earlier smaller pyramid. The later structure has a steep staircase on its east side and six stories, each one incorporating a row of niches on each of the four sides, 365 in all. The number of niches, which corresponds to the number of days in a solar year, is unlikely to be coincidental. The Pyramid of the Niches is one of many examples of the close connection between the form of Mesoamerican monuments and astronomical observations and the measurement of time.

## Postclassic Mexico

Throughout Mesoamerica, the Classic period ended at different times with the disintegration of the great civilizations. Teotihuacán's political and cultural empire, for example, began to wane around 600, when fire destroyed the city center. Archaeologists have not yet determined the cause, but within a century, the Teotihuacanos had deserted the formerly great metropolis. Around 900, the Maya abandoned many of their sites to the jungle, leaving a few northern Maya cities to flourish for another century or two before they, too, became depopulated. The Classic culture of the Zapotecs, centered at Monte Albán in the state of Oaxaca, came to an end around 700, and the neighboring Mixtec peoples assumed supremacy in this area during the Postclassic period. Classic El Tajín survived the general crisis afflicting the others but burned sometime in the 12th century. War and confusion followed the collapse of the Classic civilizations and facilitated the breakup of the great states into small, local political entities isolated in fortified sites. The disintegration encouraged even more warlike regimes and chronic aggression. The militant city-state of Chichén Itzá (FIG. 18-1) dominated Yucatán, while in central Mexico the Toltec and the later Aztec peoples, both ambitious migrants from the north, forged empires by force of arms.

**CHICHÉN ITZÁ** Yucatán, a flat, low limestone peninsula covered with scrub vegetation, lies north of the rolling and densely forested region of the Guatemalan Petén. During the Classic period, Mayan-speaking peoples sparsely inhabited this northern region. For reasons still the subject of debate, when the southern Maya abandoned their Classic sites after 900, the northern Maya continued to build many new temples in this area. They also experimented with construction techniques and materials to a much greater extent than their counterparts farther south. Piers and columns appeared in doorways, and stone mosaics enlivened facades. The northern groups also invented a new type of construction, a solid core of coarse rubble faced on both sides with a veneer of square limestone plates.

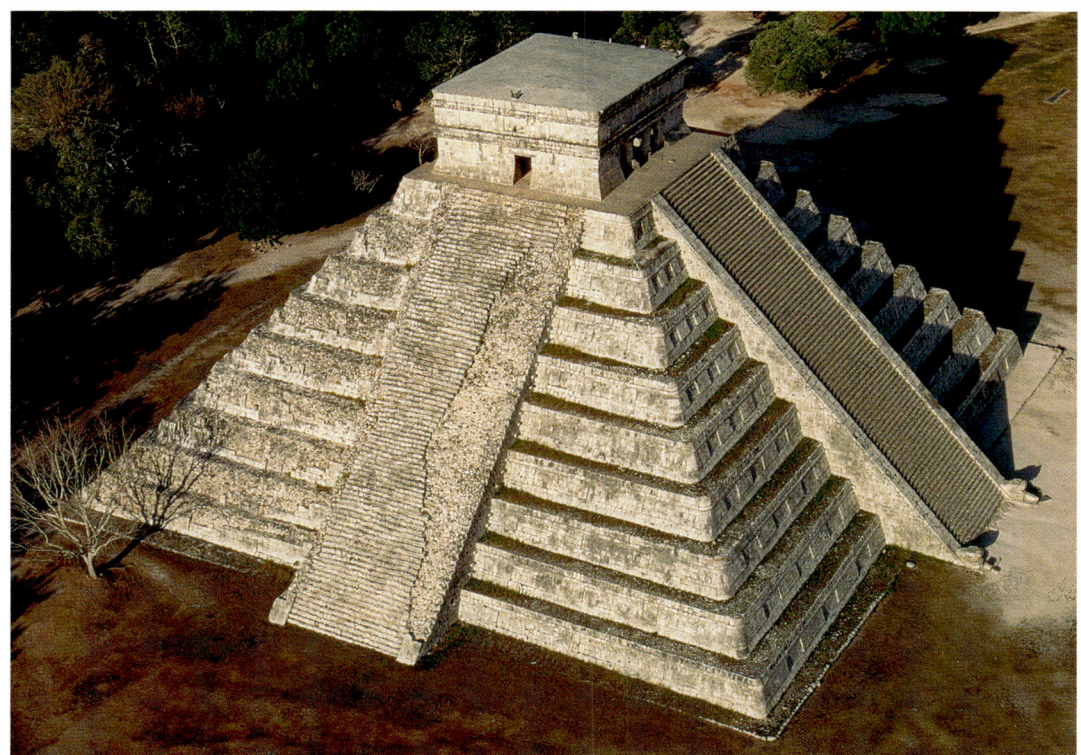

**18-16** Aerial view of the Castillo (looking southwest), Chichén Itzá, Mexico, Maya, ca. 800–900 CE. ◼◀

A temple to Kulkulcán sits atop this pyramid featuring a total of 365 stairs on its four sides. At the winter and summer equinoxes, the sun casts a shadow in the shape of a serpent along the northern staircase.

Dominating the main northern plaza (FIG. 18-1) of Chichén Itzá today is the 98-foot-high pyramid (FIG. **18-16**) the Spaniards nicknamed the Castillo (Castle). Like Temple I at Tikal (FIG. 18-10), this pyramid has nine levels. Atop the structure is a temple dedicated to Kukulcán, the Maya equivalent of Quetzalcoatl, and, as at El Tajín (FIG. 18-15), the design of the Castillo is tied to the solar year. The north side has 92 steps and the other three sides 91 steps each for a total of 365. At the winter and summer equinoxes, the sun casts a shadow along the northern staircase of the pyramid.

Because of the pyramid's silhouette and the angle of the sun, the shadow takes the shape of a serpent that slithers along the pyramid's face as the sun moves across the sky.

Excavations inside the Castillo in 1937 revealed an earlier nine-level pyramid within the later and larger structure. Inside was a chamber with a throne in the form of a red jaguar and a stone figure of the chacmool type depicting a fallen warrior. Chacmools (for example, FIG. **18-17**, found on the so-called Platform of the Eagles near the Castillo) recline on their backs and have receptacles on

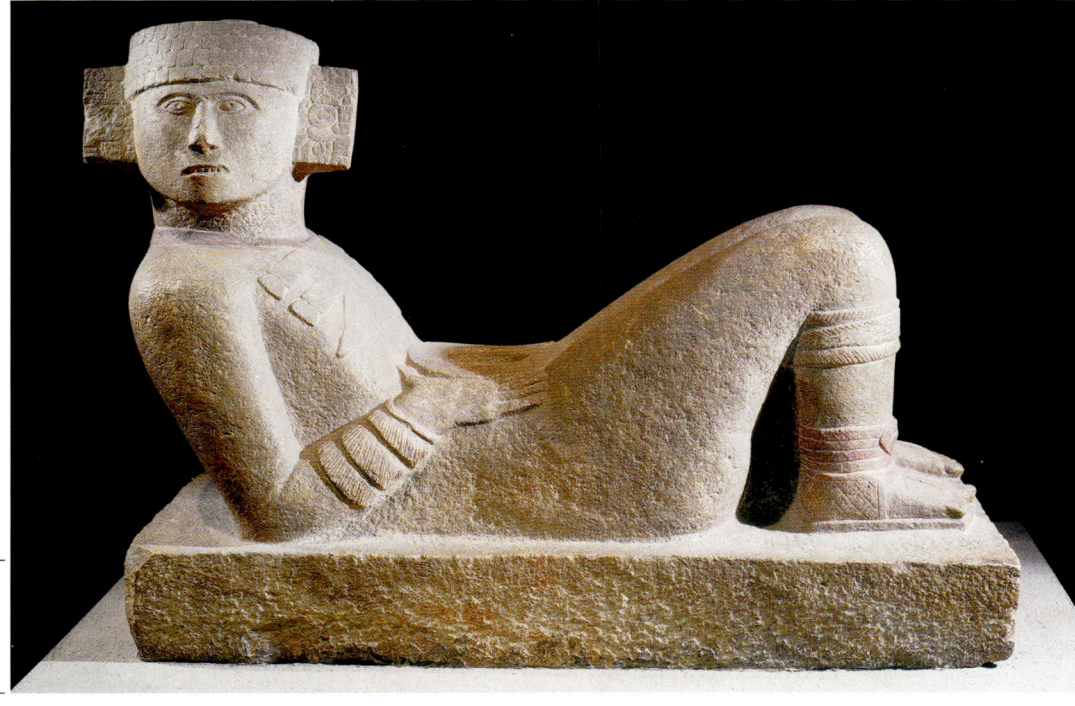

**18-17** Chacmool, from the Platform of the Eagles, Chichén Itzá, Mexico, Maya, ca. 800–900 CE. Stone, 4′ 10½″ high. Museo Nacional de Antropología, Mexico City. ◼◀

Chacmools represent fallen warriors reclining on their backs with receptacles on their chests to receive sacrificial offerings. Excavators discovered one in the throne chamber inside an earlier pyramid within the Castillo (FIG. 18-16).

1 ft.

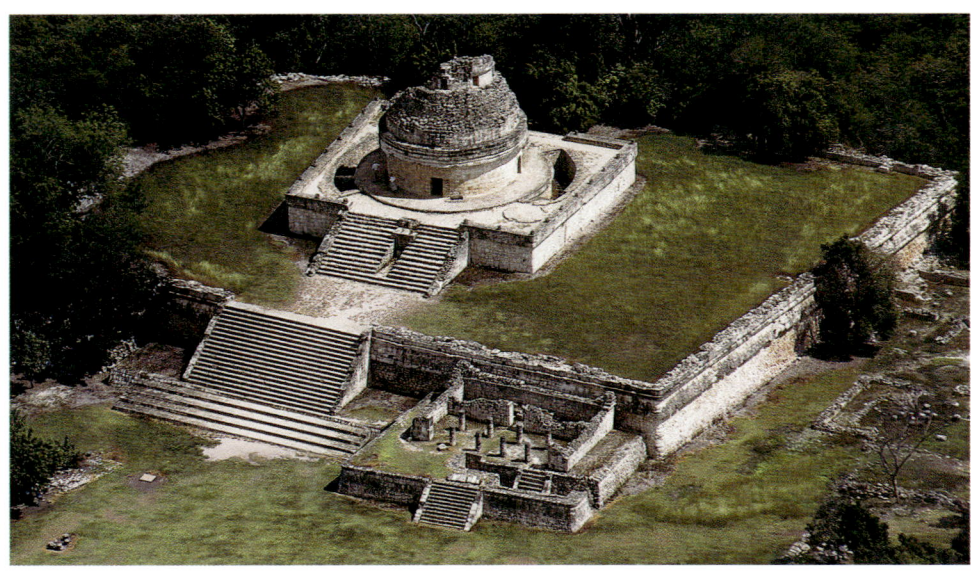

their chests to receive ritual offerings, probably of sacrificial victims. The name, coined by Augustus Le Plongeon (1826–1908), an early explorer of Maya (and Peruvian) sites, means "red jaguar paw" in Mayan. The distinctive forms of Mesoamerican chacmools made a deep impression upon some 20th-century sculptors.

The Caracol (FIG. **18-18**) at Chichén Itzá, with its snail-shaped interior stairway, establishes that the northern Maya were as inventive with architectural form as they were experimental with construction and materials. A cylindrical tower rests on a broad terrace that is in turn supported by a larger rectangular platform measuring 169 by 232 feet. The tower, composed of two concentric walls, encloses a circular staircase that leads to a small chamber near the top of the structure. In plan, the building recalls the cross-section of a conch shell (hence the building's Spanish nickname), which was an attribute of the feathered serpent, and round temples were dedicated to him in central Mexico. This building may therefore also have been a temple to Kukulcán. Windows along the Caracol's staircase and an opening at the summit probably were used for astronomical observation.

**TULA** The rulers of the Aztec Empire, the most powerful in Mesoamerican history (see Chapter 35), claimed descent from the Toltecs, whose name means "makers of things." Little is known about the Toltecs, and scholars are rethinking the traditional view that they were invaders from the north whose arrival in central Mexico contributed to the fall of the Classic civilizations. In any case, the Toltecs occupied Tula, north of Mexico City, from about 900 to 1200. Feared warriors as well as master artisans and farmers, they also constructed imposing temples and set up stone statues. Most impressive are the four colossal *atlantids* (male statue-columns; FIG. **18-19**) built up of four stone drums each that stand atop Pyramid B at Tula. Whether the atlan-

tids portray rulers in military dress or anonymous armed warriors is uncertain, but their function is clear. These images of brutal authority stand eternally at attention, warding off all hostile forces. They wear feathered headdresses and, as breastplates, stylized butterflies, heraldic symbols of the Toltecs. In one hand they clutch a bundle of darts and in the other an *atlatl* (spear-thrower), typical weapons of highland Mexico. The figures originally supported a temple roof, now missing. Their architectural function dictated the rigidity of pose, compactness, and strict simplicity of contour of the figures.

By 1180, the last Toltec ruler abandoned Tula, and most of his people followed. Some years later, the city was catastrophically destroyed, its ceremonial buildings burned to their foundations, its walls torn down, and the straggling remainder of its population scattered. The exact reasons for the Toltecs' departure and for their city's destruction are unknown, but they left a power vacuum in Mexico that the Aztecs eventually filled three centuries later.

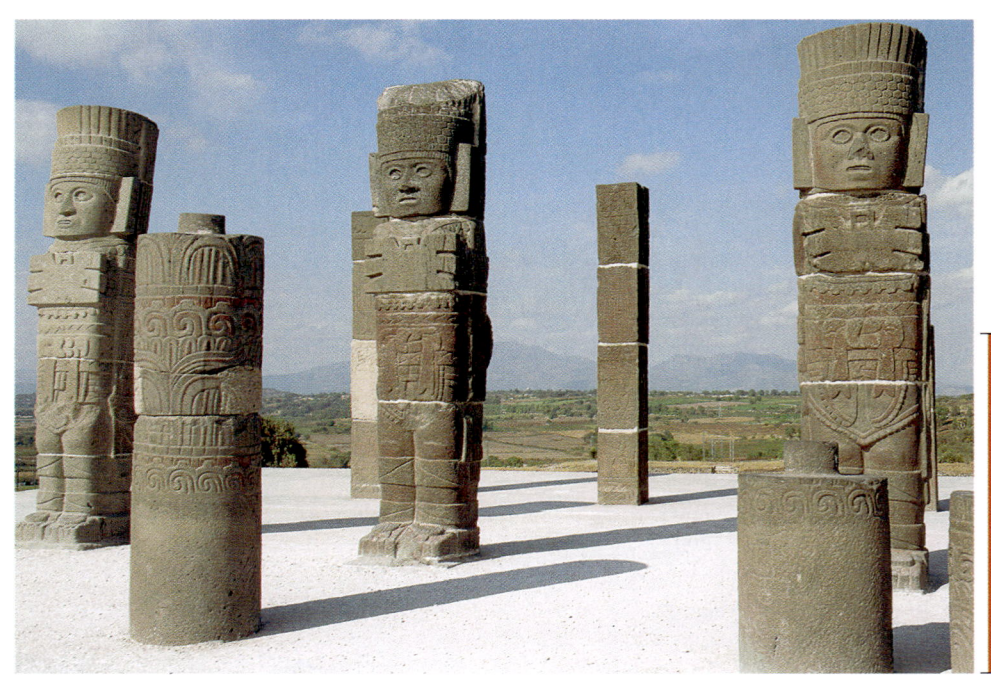

10 ft.

# INTERMEDIATE AREA

Between the highly developed civilizations of Mesoamerica and the South American Andes lies a region archaeologists have dubbed the "Intermediate Area." Comprising parts of El Salvador, Honduras, Ecuador, and Venezuela, and all of Panama, Costa Rica, Nicaragua, and Colombia, at the time of the European invasion it was by no means a unified political territory but rather was divided among many small rival chiefdoms. Although the people of the Intermediate Area did not produce monumental architecture on the scale of their neighbors to the north and south and, unlike the Mesoamericans, left no written records, they too were consummate artists. Potters in the Intermediate Area made some of the earliest ceramics of the Americas, and they continued to create an astonishing variety of terracotta vessels and figures until the time of the Spanish conquest. Among the other arts practiced in the Intermediate Area were stone sculpture, jade carving, and especially the highly prized art of goldworking. The first Europeans to make contact here were astonished to see the natives appearing in public nearly naked but covered in gold jewelry. The legend of El Dorado, a Colombian chief who coated himself in gold as part of his accession rites, was largely responsible for the Spanish invaders' ruthless plunder of the region.

**TAIRONA** In northern Colombia (MAP 18-2), the Sierra Nevada de Santa Marta rises above the Caribbean. The topography of lofty mountains and river valleys provided considerable isolation and the independent development of various groups. The inhabitants of this region after about 1000 CE included a group known as the Tairona, whose goldsmiths were among the finest in the Western Hemisphere. They produced technologically advanced and aesthetically sophisticated work in gold mostly by cutting and hammering thin gold sheets. The Tairona smiths, however, who had to obtain gold by trade, used the *lost-wax process* in part to preserve the scarce amount of the precious metal available to them. Tairona pendants were not simply rich accessories for costumes but amulets or talismans representing powerful beings who gave the wearer protection and status. The pendant shown here (FIG. **18-20**), cast in a gold-and-copper alloy called tumbaga, represents a bat-faced man—perhaps a masked man rather than a composite being, or a man in the process of spiritual transformation. In local mythology, the first animal created was the bat. This bat-man wears an immense headdress composed of two birds in the round, two great beaked heads, and a series of spirals crowned by two overarching stalks. The harmony of repeated curvilinear motifs, the rhythmic play of their contours, and the precise delineation of minute detail attest to the artist's technical control and aesthetic sensitivity.

# SOUTH AMERICA

As in Mesoamerica, until their defeat at the hands of the Spanish conquistadors, the indigenous peoples of Andean South America (MAP **18-2**) erected towering monuments and produced sophisticated paintings, sculptures, ceramics, and textiles. Although less well studied than the ancient Mesoamerican cultures, the South American civilizations are older, and in some ways they surpassed the accomplishments of their northern counterparts. Andean peoples, for example, mastered metalworking much earlier, and their monumental architecture predates that of the earliest Mesoamerican culture, the Olmec, by more than a millennium. The peoples of northern Chile even began to mummify their dead at least 500 years before the Egyptians.

The Central Andean region of South America lies between Ecuador and northern Chile, its western border the Pacific Ocean.

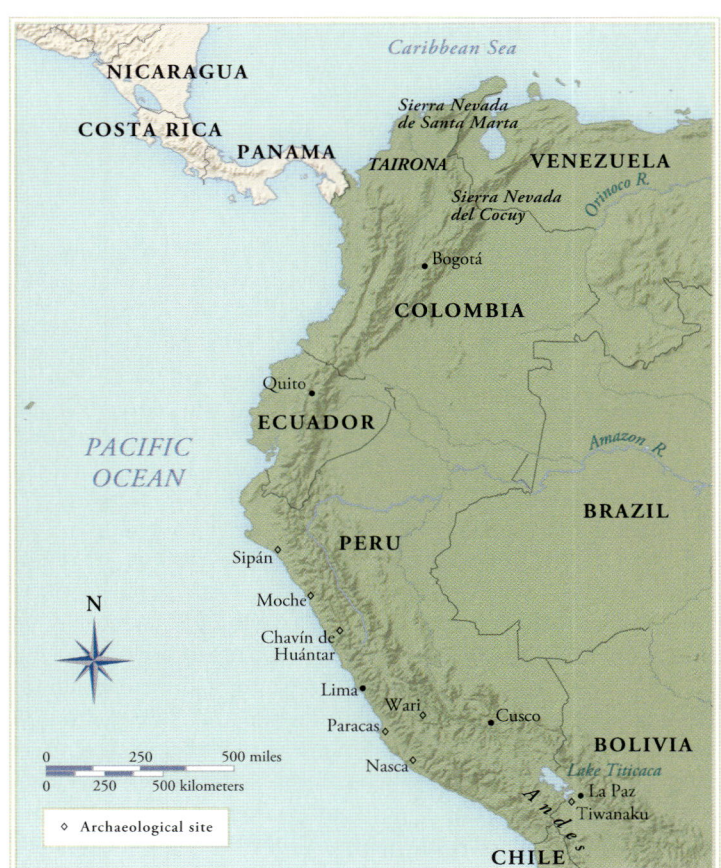

1 in.

**18-20** Pendant in the form of a bat-faced man, from northeastern Colombia, Tairona, after 1000 CE. Tumbaga, $5\frac{1}{4}''$ high. Metropolitan Museum of Art, New York (Jan Mitchell and Sons Collection).

The peoples of the Intermediate Area between Mesoamerica and Andean South America were expert goldsmiths. This pendant depicting a bat-faced man with a large headdress served as an amulet.

**MAP 18-2** Early sites in Andean South America.

It consists of three well-defined geographic zones, running north and south and roughly parallel to one another. The narrow western coastal plain is a desert crossed by rivers, creating habitable fertile valleys. Next, the high peaks of the great Cordillera of the Andes hem in plateaus of a temperate climate. The region's inland border, the eastern slopes of the Andes, is a hot and humid jungle.

Andean civilizations flourished both in the highlands and on the coast. Highland cave dwellers fashioned the first rudimentary art objects by 8800 BCE. Weavers began to fashion sophisticated textiles as early as 2500 BCE, and the firing of clay began in Peru before 1800 BCE. Beginning about 800 BCE, Andean chronology alternates between periods historians call "horizons," when a single culture appears to have dominated a broad geographic area for a relatively long period, and "intermediate periods" characterized by more independent regional development. The Chavín culture (ca. 800–200 BCE) represents the first period, Early Horizon; the Tiwanaku and Wari cultures (ca. 600–1000 CE) the Middle Horizon; and the Inka Empire (discussed in Chapter 35) the Late Horizon. Among the many regional styles that flourished between these horizons, the most important are the Early Intermediate period (ca. 200 BCE–700 CE) Paracas and Nasca cultures of the south coast of Peru, and the Moche in the north.

The discovery of complex ancient communities documented by radiocarbon dating is changing the picture of early South American cultures. Planned communities boasting organized labor systems and monumental architecture dot the narrow river valleys that drop from the Andes to the Pacific Ocean. In the Central Andes, these early sites began to develop around 3000 BCE, about a millennium before the invention of pottery there. Carved gourds and some fragmentary cotton textiles survive from this early period. They depict composite creatures, such as crabs turning into snakes, as well as doubled and then reversed images, both hallmarks of later Andean art.

The architecture of the early coastal sites typically consists of large U-shaped flat-topped platforms—some as high as a 10-story building—around sunken courtyards. Many had numerous small chambers on top. Construction materials included both uncut fieldstones and handmade *adobes* (sun-dried mud bricks) in the shape of cones, laid point to point in coarse mud plaster to form walls and platforms. These complexes almost always faced toward the Andes, source of the life-giving rivers on which these communities depended for survival. Mountain worship, which continues in the Andean region to this day, was probably the focus of early religious practices as well. In the highlands, archaeologists also have discovered large ceremonial complexes. In place of the numerous interconnecting rooms found atop many coastal mounds, the highland examples have a single small chamber at the top, often with a stone-lined firepit in the center. These pits probably played a role in ancient fire rituals. Excavators have found burnt offerings in the pits, often of exotic objects such as marine shells and tropical bird feathers.

## Chavín

Named after the ceremonial center of Chavín de Huántar, located in the northern highlands of Peru, the Chavín culture of the Early Horizon period developed and spread throughout much of the coastal region and the highlands during the first millennium BCE. Once thought to be the "mother culture" of the Andean region, archaeologists now view the Chavín culture as the culmination of developments that began elsewhere some 2,000 years earlier.

The Old Temple of Chavín de Huántar was an important pilgrimage site. Dated to the first millennium BCE, it resembles some of the sacred complexes of the earliest Andean cultures but is much larger. It is a U-shaped, stone-faced structure with wings up to

83 yards long facing east between two rivers. Although at first glance its three stories appear to be a solid stepped platform, in fact narrow passageways, small chambers, and stairways penetrate the temple in a labyrinthine pattern. No windows, however, light the interior spaces. The few members of Chavín society with access to these rooms must have witnessed secret and sacred torch-lit ceremonies. Fronting the temple are sunken courts, an arrangement also adopted from earlier coastal sites.

The temple complex at Chavín de Huántar is famous for its extensive stone carvings. The most common subjects are composite creatures combining feline, avian, reptilian, and human features. Consisting largely of low relief on panels, cornices, and columns, and some rarer instances of freestanding sculpture, Chavín carving is essentially shallow, linear incision. An immense oracular cult image stood in the center of the temple's oldest part. Other examples of sculpture in the round include heads of mythological creatures pegged into the exterior walls.

***RAIMONDI STELE*** Found in the main temple at Chavín de Huántar and named after its discoverer, the *Raimondi Stele* (FIG. **18-21**) represents a figure called the "staff god." He appears in various versions from Colombia to northern Bolivia but always holds staffs. Seldom, however, do the representations have the

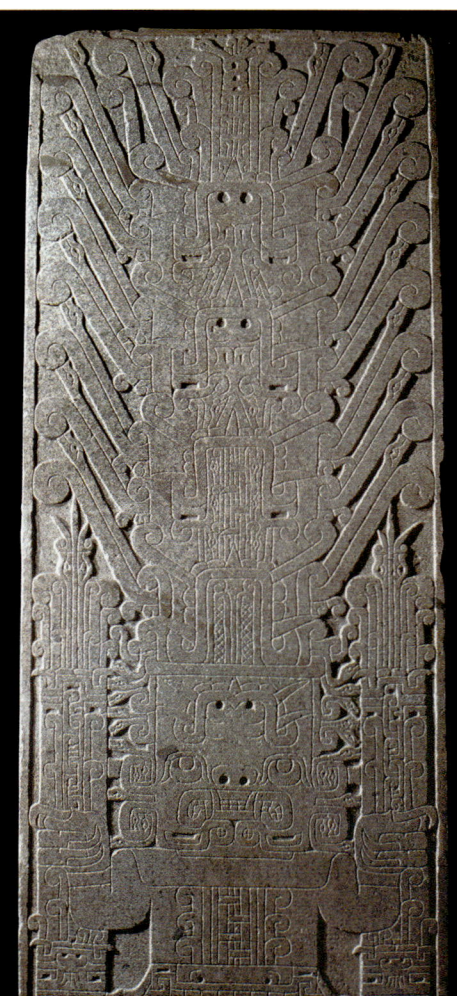

**18-21** *Raimondi Stele,* from the main temple, Chavín de Huántar, Peru, ca. 800–200 BCE. Green diorite, 6′ high. Instituto Nacional de Cultura, Lima.

The *Raimondi Stele* staff god wears a headdress of faces and snakes. Seen upside down, the god's face becomes two faces. The ability of gods to transform themselves is a core aspect of Andean religion.

1 ft.

degree of elaboration found at Chavín. The Chavín staff god gazes upward, frowns, and bares his teeth. His elaborate headdress dominates the upper two-thirds of the slab. Inverting the image reveals that the headdress consists of a series of fanged jawless faces, each emerging from the mouth of the one above it. Snakes abound. They extend from the deity's belt, make up part of the staffs, serve as whiskers and hair for the deity and the headdress creatures, and form a braid at the apex of the composition. The *Raimondi Stele* clearly illustrates the Andean artistic tendency toward both multiplicity and dual readings. Upside down, the god's face turns into two faces. The ability of gods to transform before viewers' eyes is a core aspect of Andean religion.

Chavín iconography spread widely throughout the Andean region via portable media such as goldwork, textiles, and ceramics. For example, more than 300 miles from Chavín on the south coast of Peru, archaeologists have discovered cotton textiles with imagery recalling Chavín sculpture. Painted staff-bearing female deities, apparently local manifestations or consorts of the highland staff god, decorate these large cloths, which may have served as wall hangings in temples. Ceramic vessels found on the north coast of Peru also carry motifs similar to those found on Chavín stone carvings.

## Paracas, Nasca, and Moche

Several coastal traditions developed during the millennium from about 400 BCE to 700 CE. The most prominent were the Paracas (ca. 400 BCE–200 CE), Nasca (ca. 200 BCE–600 CE), and Moche (ca. 1–700 CE). Together they exemplify the great variations within Peruvian art styles.

**PARACAS** The Paracas culture occupied a desert peninsula and a nearby river valley on the south coast of Peru. Outstanding among the Paracas arts are the funerary textiles used to wrap the bodies of the dead in multiple layers. These textiles, buried in shaft tombs beneath the sands and preserved because of the dry desert climate, are among the enduring masterpieces of Andean art (see "Andean Weaving," page 510). Most are of woven cotton with designs embroidered onto the fabric in alpaca or vicuña wool imported from the highlands. The weavers, probably exclusively women, used more than 150 vivid colors, the majority derived from plants. Feline, bird, and serpent motifs appear on many of the textiles, but the human figure, real or mythological, predominates. Humans dressed up as or changing into animals are common motifs on the grave mantles—consistent with the Andean transformation theme noted on the *Raimondi Stele* (FIG. 18-21). On one well-preserved mantle (FIG. **18-22**), a figure with prominent eyes appears scores of times over the surface. The flowing hair and the slow kicking motion of the legs suggest the figure is flying or floating while carrying batons and fans, or according to some scholars, knives and hallucinogenic mushrooms. On other mantles, the figures carry the skulls or severed heads of enemies. Art historians have interpreted the flying figures either as Paracas religious practitioners dancing or flying during an ecstatic trance or as images of the deceased. Despite endless repetitions of the figure, variations of detail occur throughout each textile, notably in the figures' positions and in subtle color changes.

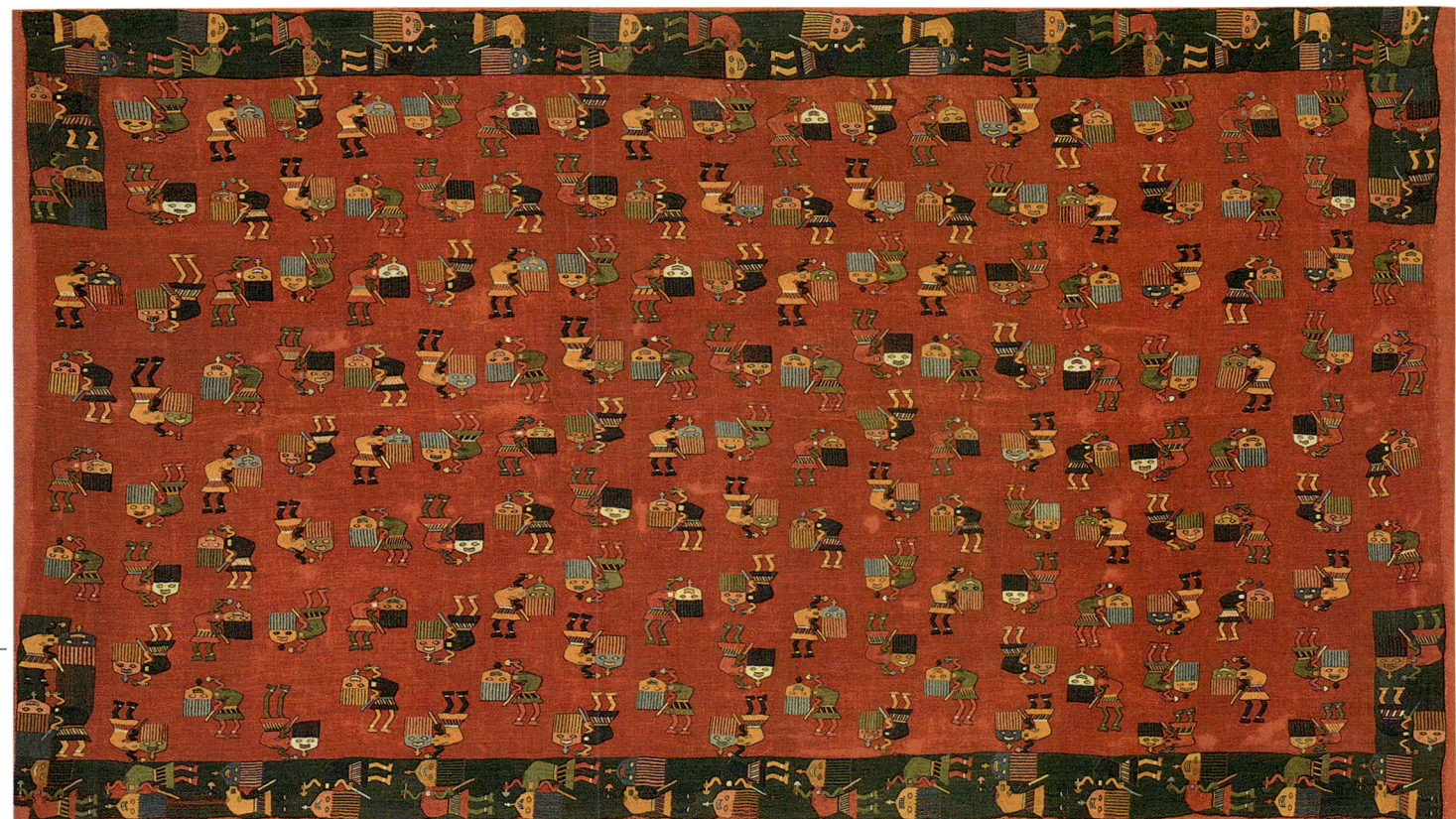

1 ft.

**18-22** Embroidered funerary mantle, from the southern coast of Peru, Paracas, first century CE. Plain-weave camelid fiber with stem-stitch embroidery of camelid wool, 4′ 7⅞″ × 7′ 10⅞″. Museum of Fine Arts, Boston (William A. Paine Fund).

Paracas weavers created elaborate mantles to wrap around the bodies of the dead. The flying or floating figure repeated endlessly on this mantle is probably the deceased or a religious practitioner.

# Andean Weaving

When the Inka first encountered the Spanish conquistadors, they found the Europeans' fixation on gold and silver puzzling. The Inka valued finely woven cloth just as highly as precious metal. Textiles and clothing dominated every aspect of their existence. Storing textiles in great warehouses, their leaders demanded cloth as tribute, gave it as gifts, exchanged it during diplomatic negotiations, and even burned it as a sacrificial offering. Although both men and women participated in cloth production, the Inka rulers selected the best women weavers from around the empire and sequestered them for life to produce textiles exclusively for the elite.

Andean weavers manufactured their textiles by spinning into yarn the cotton grown in five different shades on the warm coast and the fur sheared from highland llamas, alpacas, vicuñas, or guanacos, and then weaving the yarn into cloth. Rare tropical bird feathers and small plaques of gold and silver were sometimes sewn onto cloth destined for the nobility. Andean weavers mastered nearly every textile technique known today, many executed with a simple device known as a *backstrap loom*. Similar looms are still in use in the Andes. The weavers stretch the long *warp* (vertical) threads between two wooden bars. The top bar is tied to an upright. A belt or backstrap, attached to the bottom bar, encircles the waist of the seated weaver, who maintains the tension of the warp threads by leaning back. The weaver passes the *weft* (horizontal) threads over and under the warps and pushes them tightly against each other to produce the finished cloth. In ancient textiles, the sturdy cotton often formed the warp, and the wool, which can be dyed brighter colors, served to create complex designs in the weft.

*Embroidery,* the sewing of threads onto a finished ground cloth to form contrasting designs, was the specialty of the Paracas culture (FIG. 18-22).

The dry deserts of coastal Peru have preserved not only numerous textiles from different periods but also hundreds of finely worked baskets containing spinning and weaving implements. These tools are invaluable sources of information about Andean textile production processes. The baskets found in documented contexts came from women's graves, attesting to the close identity between weaving and women, the reverence for the cloth-making process, and the Andean belief that textiles were necessary in the afterlife.

A special problem all weavers confront is they must visualize the entire design in advance and cannot easily change it during the weaving process. No records exist of how Andean weavers learned, retained, and passed on the elaborate patterns they wove into cloth, but some painted ceramics depict weavers at work, apparently copying designs from finished models. However, the inventiveness of individual weavers is evident in the endless variety of colors and patterns in surviving Andean textiles. This creativity often led Andean artists to design textiles that are highly abstract and geometric. Paracas embroideries (FIG. 18-22), for example, may depict humans, down to the patterns on the tunics they wear, yet the weavers reduced the figures to their essentials in order to focus on their otherworldly role. The Wari compositions (FIG. 18-28) are the culmination of this tendency toward abstraction in which figural motifs become stunning blocks of color that overwhelm the subject matter itself.

---

**NASCA** The Nasca culture takes its name from the Nasca River valley south of Paracas. The early centuries of the Nasca civilization ran concurrently with the closing centuries of the Paracas culture, and Nasca style emulated Paracas style. The Nasca won renown for their pottery, and thousands of their ceramic vessels survive. These usually have round bottoms, double spouts connected by bridges, and smoothly burnished polychrome surfaces. The subjects of their painted decoration vary greatly, but plants, animals, and composite mythological creatures, part human and part animal, are most common. Nasca painters often represented ritual impersonators, some of whom, like the Paracas flying figures (FIG. 18-22), hold trophy heads and weapons. On the vessel illustrated here (FIG. **18-23**) are two costumed flying figures. The painter reduced their bodies and limbs to abstract appendages and focused on the heads. The figures wear a multicolored necklace, a whiskered gold mouthpiece, circular disks hanging from the ears, and a rayed crown on the forehead. Masks or heads with streaming hair,

**18-23** Bridge-spouted vessel with flying figures, from the Nasca River valley, Peru, Nasca, ca. 50–200 CE. Painted ceramic, $5\frac{1}{2}''$ high. Art Institute of Chicago, Chicago (Kate S. Buckingham Endowment).

The Nasca were masters of pottery painting. The painter of this bridge-spouted vessel depicted two crowned and bejeweled flying figures, probably ritual impersonators with trophy heads.

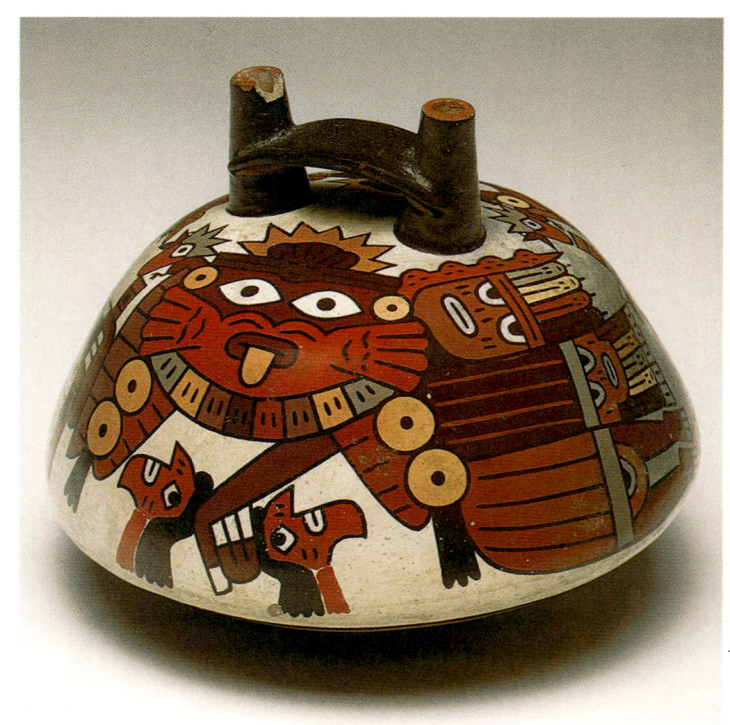

1 in.

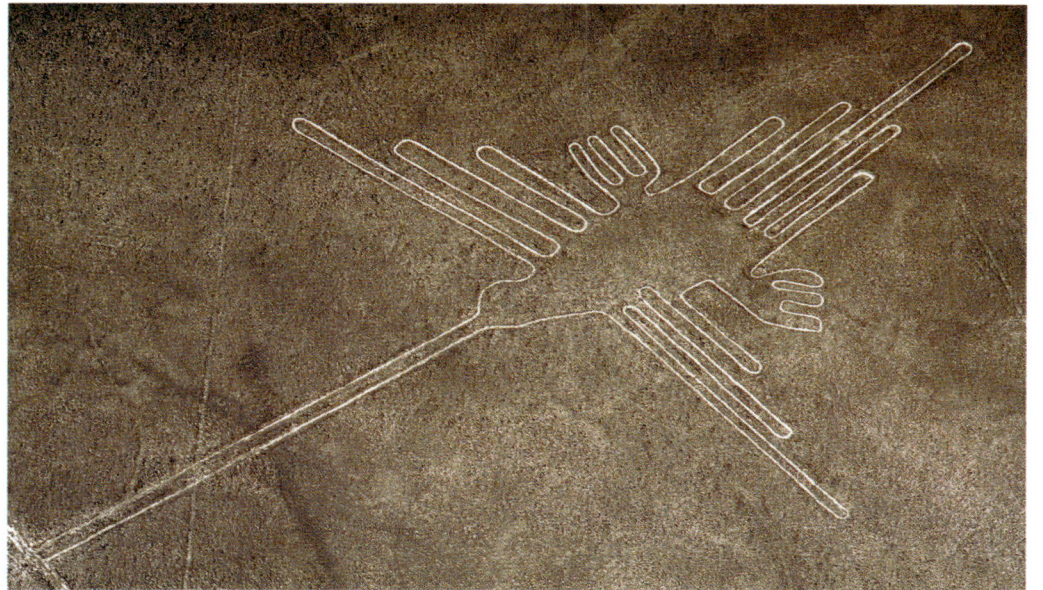

possibly more trophy heads, flow over the impersonators' backs, increasing the sense of motion.

Nasca artists also depicted figures on a gigantic scale. Some 800 miles of lines drawn in complex networks on the dry surface of the Nasca Plain have long attracted world attention because of their colossal size, which defies human perception from the ground. Preserved today are about three dozen images of birds, fish, and plants, including a hummingbird (FIG. **18-24**) several hundred feet long. The Nasca artists also drew geometric forms, such as trapezoids, spirals, and straight lines running for miles. Artists produced the Nasca Lines, as art historians have dubbed these immense earth drawings, by selectively removing the dark top layer of stones to expose the light clay and calcite below. The Nasca created the lines quite easily from available materials and using rudimentary geometry. Small groups of workers have made modern reproductions of them with relative ease. The lines seem to be paths laid out using simple stone-and-string methods. Some lead in traceable directions across the deserts of the Nasca River drainage. Others have many shrinelike nodes punctuating the lines, like the knots on a cord. Some lines converge at central places usually situated close to water sources and seem to be associated with water supply and irrigation. They may have marked pilgrimage routes for those who journeyed to local or regional shrines on foot. Altogether, the vast arrangement of the Nasca Lines is a system—not a meaningless maze but a traversable map that plotted the whole terrain of Nasca material and spiritual concerns. Remarkably, until quite recently, the peoples of highland Bolivia made and used similar ritual pathways in association with shrines, demonstrating the tenacity of the Andean indigenous belief systems.

**MOCHE** Among the most famous art objects the ancient Peruvians produced are the painted clay vessels of the Moche, who occupied a series of river valleys on the north coast of Peru around the same time the Nasca flourished to the south. Among ancient civilizations, only the Greeks and the Maya (FIG. 18-13) surpassed the Moche in the information recorded on their ceramics. Moche pots illustrate architecture, metallurgy, weaving, the brewing of chicha (fermented maize beer), human deformities and diseases, and even sexual acts. Moche vessels are predominantly flat-bottomed stirrup-spouted jars derived from Chavín prototypes. The potters generally decorated them with a *bichrome* (two-color) slip. Although the Moche made early vessels by hand without the aid of a potter's wheel, they fashioned later ones in two-piece molds. Thus, numerous near-duplicates survive. Moche potters continued to refine the stirrup spout, making it an elegant slender tube, much narrower than the Chavín examples. The portrait vessel illustrated here (FIG. **18-25**) is an elaborate example of a common Moche type. It may depict the face of a warrior, a ruler, or even a royal retainer whose image may have been buried with many other pots to accompany his dead master. The realistic rendering of the physiognomy is particularly striking.

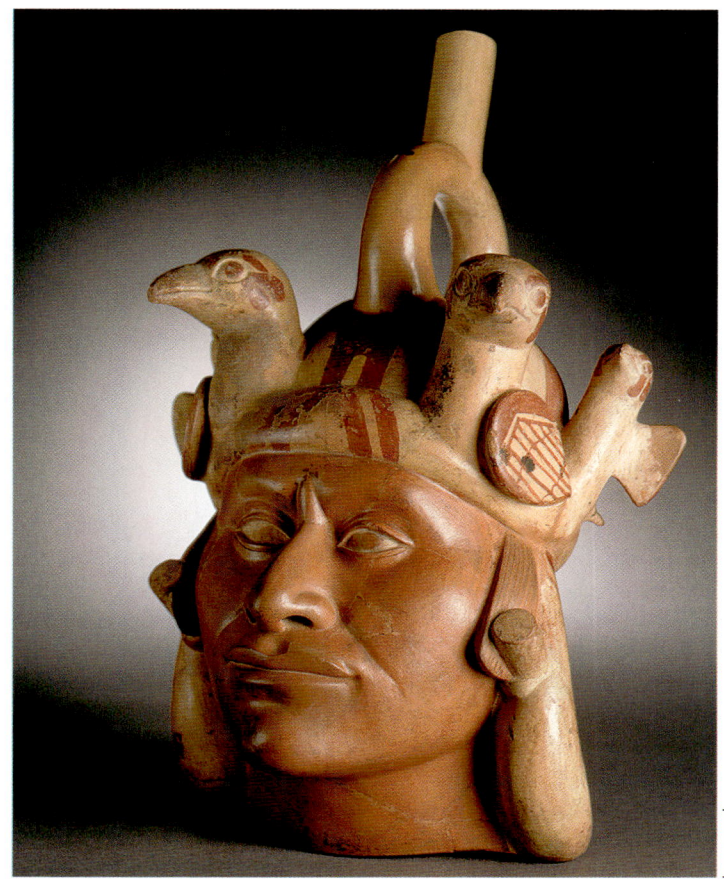

**18-25** Vessel in the shape of a portrait head, from the northern coast of Peru, Moche, fifth to sixth century CE. Painted clay, 1' $\frac{1}{2}$" high. Museo Arqueológico Rafael Larco Herrera, Lima.

1 in.

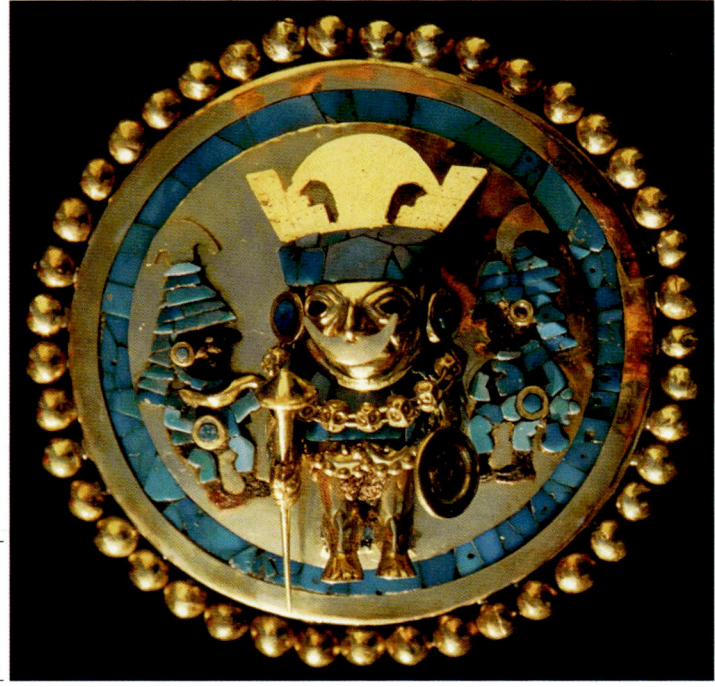

1 in.

**18-26** Ear ornament, from Sipán, Peru, Moche, ca. 300 CE. Gold and turquoise, 4⅘″ diameter. Bruning Archaeological Museum, Lambayeque.

This ear ornament from a Sipán tomb depicts a warrior priest and two retainers. The priest carries a war club and shield and wears an owl-head-bead necklace. The costume corresponds to archaeological finds.

**SIPÁN** Elite men, along with retinues of sacrificial victims, appear to be the occupants of several rich Moche tombs excavated near the village of Sipán on the arid northwest coast of Peru. The Sipán burials have yielded a treasure of golden artifacts and more than a thousand ceramic vessels. The discovery of the tombs in the late 1980s created a great stir in the archaeological world, contributing significantly to the knowledge of Moche culture. Beneath a large adobe platform adjacent to two high but greatly eroded pyramids, excavators found the most impressive of several lavish graves, the tomb of a man known today as the Lord of Sipán or the Warrior Priest. The splendor of the trappings adorning his corpse, the quantity and quality of the sumptuous accessories, and the bodies of the retainers buried with him indicate he was a personage of the highest rank. Indeed, the Lord of Sipán may have been one of the warrior priests so often depicted on Moche ceramic wares and murals (and on a golden pyramid-shaped rattle in this very tomb) assaulting his enemies and participating in sacrificial ceremonies.

**18-27** Gateway of the Sun, Bolivia, Tiwanaku, ca. 375–700 CE. Stone, 9′ 10″ high.

The Gateway of the Sun probably led into a sacred area. The central figure is a version of the Chavín staff god (FIG. 18-21). Originally painted, the relief was also inlaid with turquoise and covered with gold.

An ear ornament (FIG. **18-26**) of turquoise and gold found in one Sipán tomb shows a warrior priest clad much like the Lord of Sipán. Two retainers appear in profile to the left and right of the central figure. Represented frontally, he carries a war club and shield and wears a necklace of owl-head beads. The figure's bladelike, crescent-shaped helmet is a replica of the large golden one buried with the Sipán lord. The war club and shield also match finds in the Warrior Priest's tomb. The figure wears an ear ornament that is a simplified version of the ornament it decorates. Other details also correspond to excavated objects—for example, the removable nose ring hanging down over the mouth. The value of the Sipán find is incalculable for what it reveals about elite Moche culture and for its confirmation of the accuracy of the iconography of Moche artworks.

## Tiwanaku and Wari

The bleak highland country of southeastern Peru and southwestern Bolivia contrasts markedly with the warm valleys of the coast. In the Bolivian mountains, the Tiwanaku culture (ca. 100–1000 CE) developed beginning in the second century CE. North of the Paracas society in Peru, the Wari culture (ca. 500–800 CE) dominated parts of the dry coast.

**TIWANAKU** Named after its principal archaeological site on the southern shore of Lake Titicaca, the Tiwanaku culture flourished for nearly a millennium, spreading to the adjacent coastal area as well as to other highland regions, eventually extending from southern Peru to northern Chile. Tiwanaku was an important ceremonial center. Its inhabitants constructed grand buildings using the region's fine sandstone, andesite, and diorite.

Tiwanaku's imposing Gateway of the Sun (FIG. **18-27**) is a huge monolithic block of andesite pierced by a single doorway. Moved in ancient times from its original location within the site, the gateway now forms part of an enormous walled platform. Relief sculpture crowns the gate. The central figure is a Tiwanaku version of the Chavín staff god (FIG. 18-21). Larger than all the other figures and presented frontally, he dominates the composition and

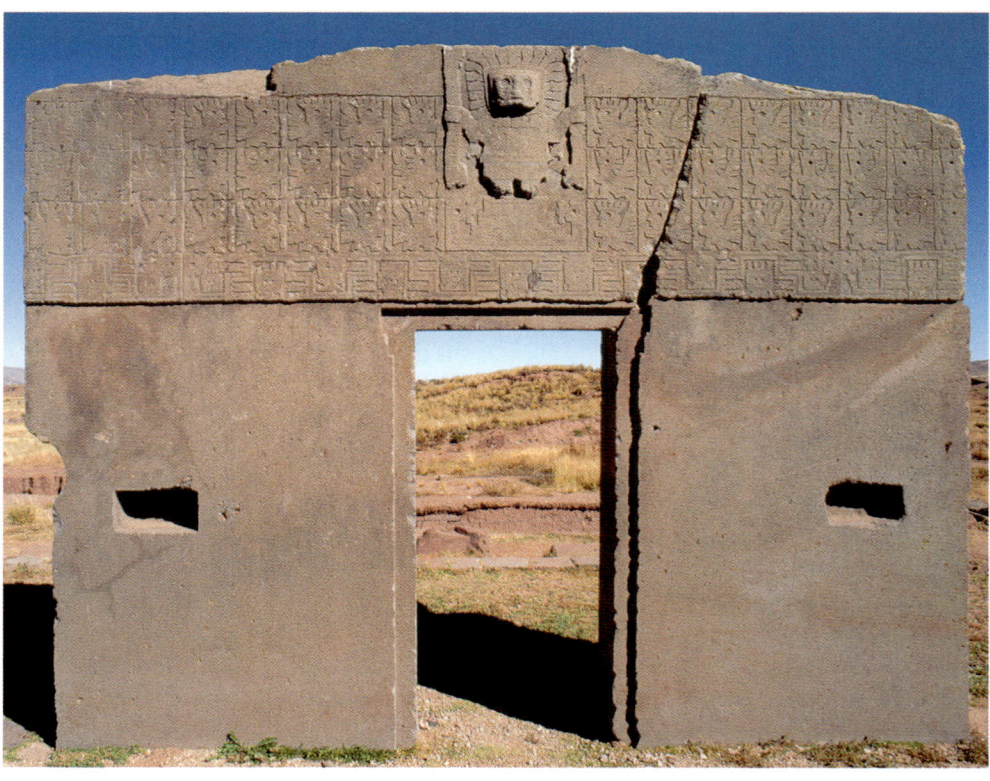

presides over the passageway. Rays project from his head. Many terminate in puma heads, representing the power of the highlands' fiercest predator. The staff god—possibly a sky and weather deity rather than the sun deity the rayed head suggests—appears in art throughout the Tiwanaku horizon, associated with smaller attendant figures. Those of the Gateway of the Sun are winged and have human or condor heads. Like the puma, the condor is an impressive carnivore, the largest raptor in the world. Sky and earth beings thus converge on the gate, which probably served as the doorway to a sacred area, a place of transformation. The reliefs were once colorfully painted. The figures' eyes apparently also had turquoise inlays, and gold covered the surfaces. The effect undoubtedly was dazzling.

**WARI** The flat, abstract, and repetitive figures surrounding the central figure on the Gateway of the Sun recall woven textile designs. Indeed, the people of the Tiwanaku culture, like those of the Paracas, were consummate weavers, although many fewer textiles survive from the damp highlands. Many examples of weaving, especially tunics, survive from the contemporaneous Wari culture in Peru, however.

Although Wari weavers fashioned cloth from both wool and cotton fibers, as did their Paracas predecessors (FIG. 18-22), the resemblance between the two textile styles ends there. Whereas Paracas weavers embroidered motifs onto the plain woven surface, their Wari counterparts wove the designs directly into the fabric, the weft threads packed densely over the warp threads in a technique known as *tapestry* (see "Embroidery and Tapestry," Chapter 12, page 362). Some particularly fine pieces have more than 200 weft threads per inch. Furthermore, unlike the relatively naturalistic individual figures depicted on Paracas mantles, those appearing on Wari textiles are so closely connected and so abstract as to be nearly unrecognizable. In the tunic shown here, known as the *Lima Tapestry* (FIG. 18-28), the Wari designer expanded or compressed each figure in a different way and placed them in vertical rows pressed between narrow red bands of plain cloth. Elegant tunics such as this one must have been prestige garments made for the elite. A close connection existed between clothing and status in many ancient American societies, especially in the Inka Empire that eventually dominated Andean South America (see Chapter 35).

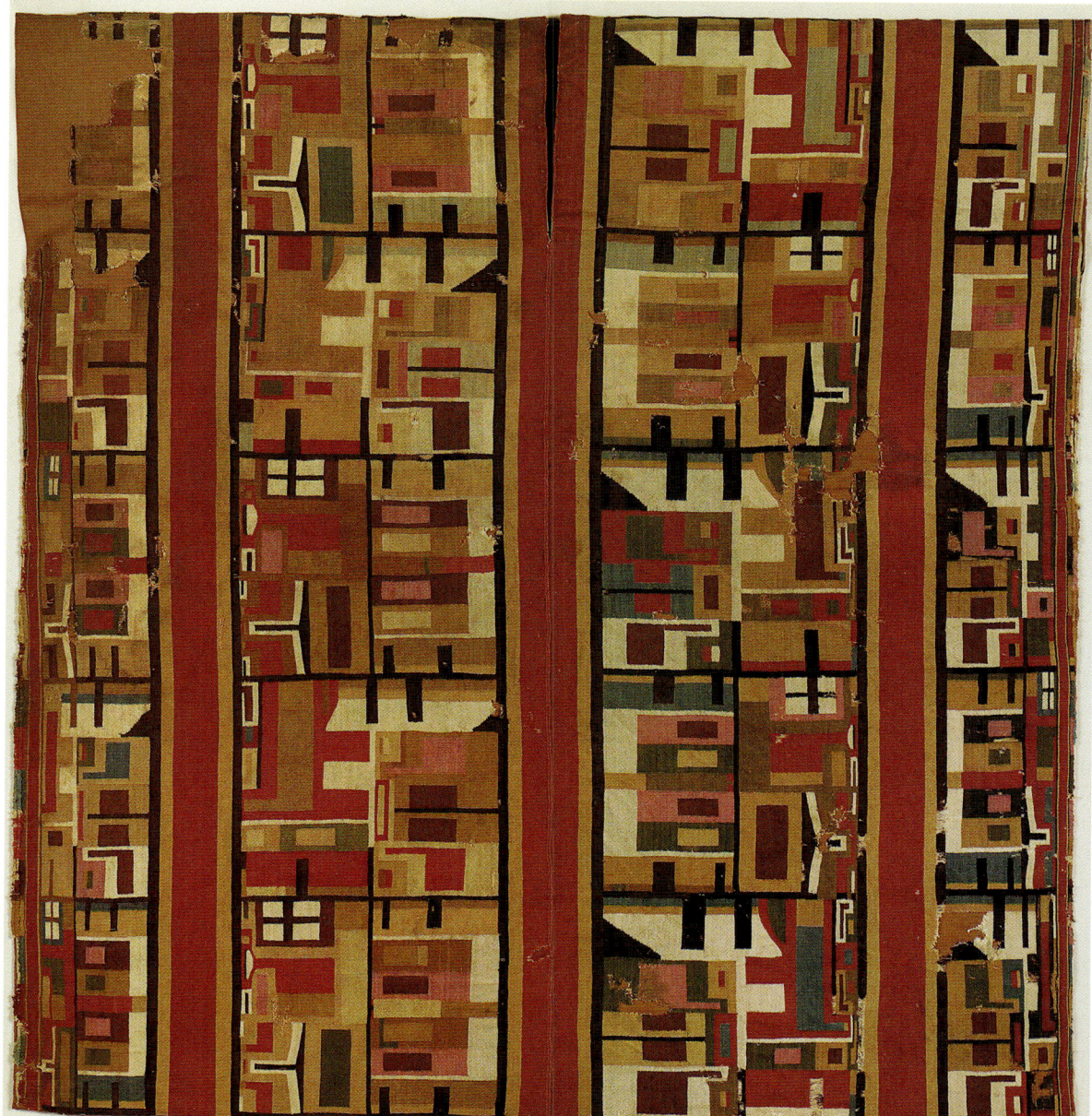

**18-28** *Lima Tapestry,* **tunic, from Peru, Wari, ca. 500–800 CE.** $3' 3\frac{3}{8}'' \times 2' 11\frac{3}{8}''$**. Museo Nacional de Antropología Arqueología e Historia del Perú, Lima.**

Whereas Paracas mantles (FIG. 18-22) are embroideries, Wari textiles are tapestries with the motifs woven directly into the fabric. The figures on this tunic are so abstract as to be nearly unrecognizable.

1 ft.

# NORTH AMERICA

In many parts of the United States and Canada, archaeologists have identified indigenous cultures dating as far back as 12,000 years ago. Most of the surviving art objects, however, come from the last 2,000 years. Scholars divide the vast and varied territory of North America (MAP 18-3) into cultural regions based on the geography and relative homogeneity of language and social and artistic patterns. Native lifestyles varied widely over the continent, ranging from small bands of migratory hunters to settled—at times even urban—agriculturalists. Among the art-producing peoples who inhabited the continent before the arrival of Europeans are the Eskimos of Alaska and the Inuit of Canada, who hunted and fished across the Arctic from Greenland to Siberia, and the maize farmers of the American Southwest, who wrested water from their arid environment and built effective irrigation systems as well as roads and spectacular cliff dwellings. Farmers also settled in the vast, temperate Eastern Woodlands—ranging from eastern Canada to Florida and from the Atlantic to the Great Plains west of the Mississippi. Some of them left behind great earthen mounds that once functioned as their elite residences or burial places.

## Eskimo

The Eskimoan peoples originally migrated to North America across the Bering Strait. During the early first millennium CE, a community of Eskimo sea-mammal hunters and tool makers occupied parts of Alaska during the Norton, or Old Bering Sea, culture that began around 500 BCE.

**IPIUTAK MASK** Archaeologists have uncovered major works of Eskimo art at the Ipiutak site at Point Hope. The finds include a variety of burial goods as well as tools. A burial mask (FIG. 18-29) datable to around 100 CE is of special interest. The artist fashioned the mask out of walrus ivory, the material used for most Arctic artworks because of the scarcity of wood in the region. The mask consists of nine carefully shaped parts, interrelated to produce several faces, both human and animal, echoing the transformation theme noted in other ancient American cultures. The confident, subtle composition in shallow relief is a tribute to the artist's imaginative control over the material. The mask's abstract circles and curved lines are common motifs on the decorated tools discovered at Point Hope. For centuries, the Eskimo also carved human and animal figures, always at small scale, reflecting a nomadic lifestyle requiring the creation of portable objects.

## Woodlands

Early Native American artists also excelled in working stone into a variety of utilitarian and ceremonial objects. Some early cultures, such as those of the Woodlands east of the Mississippi River, also

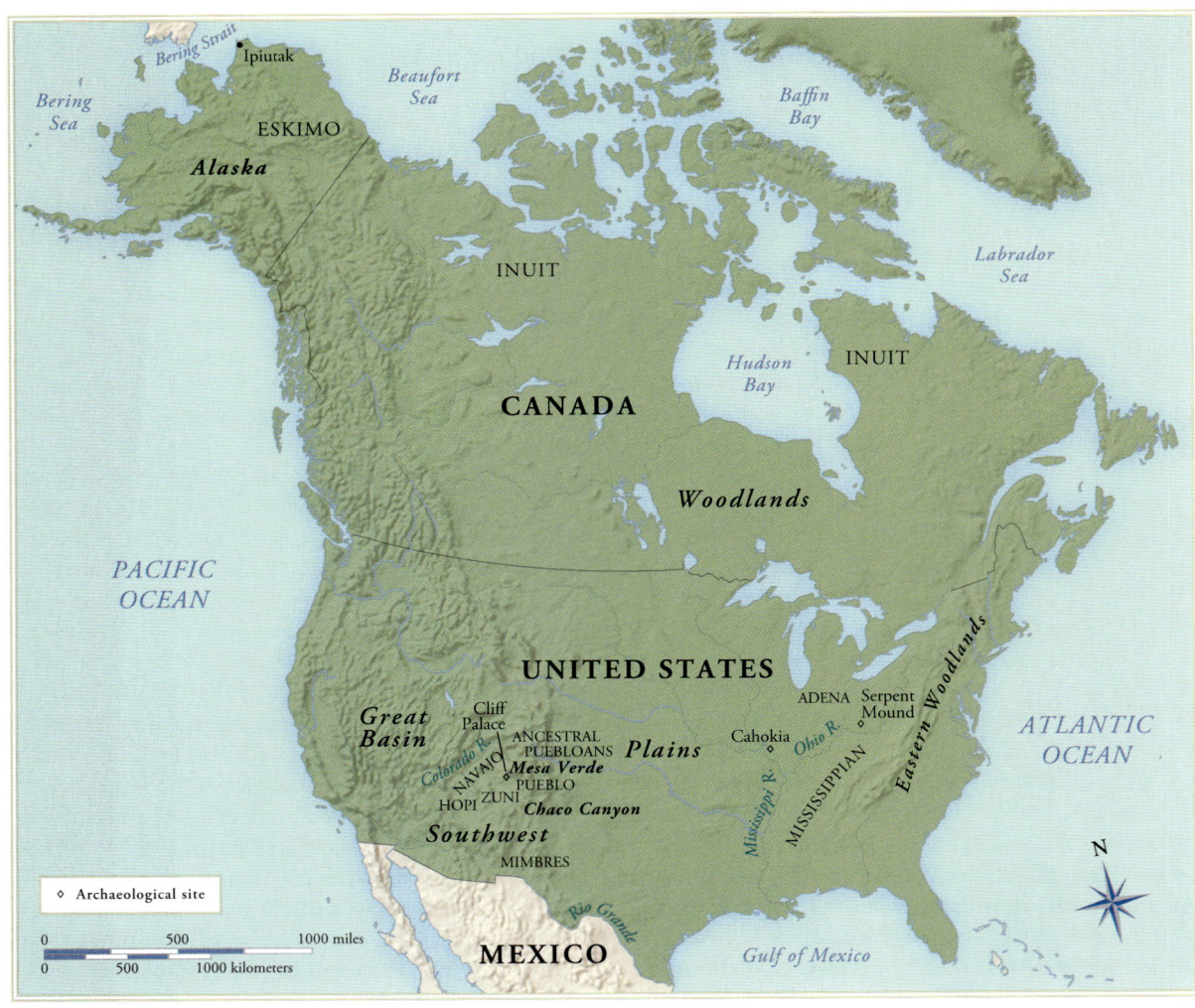

**MAP 18-3** Early Native American sites in North America. ◼️▶

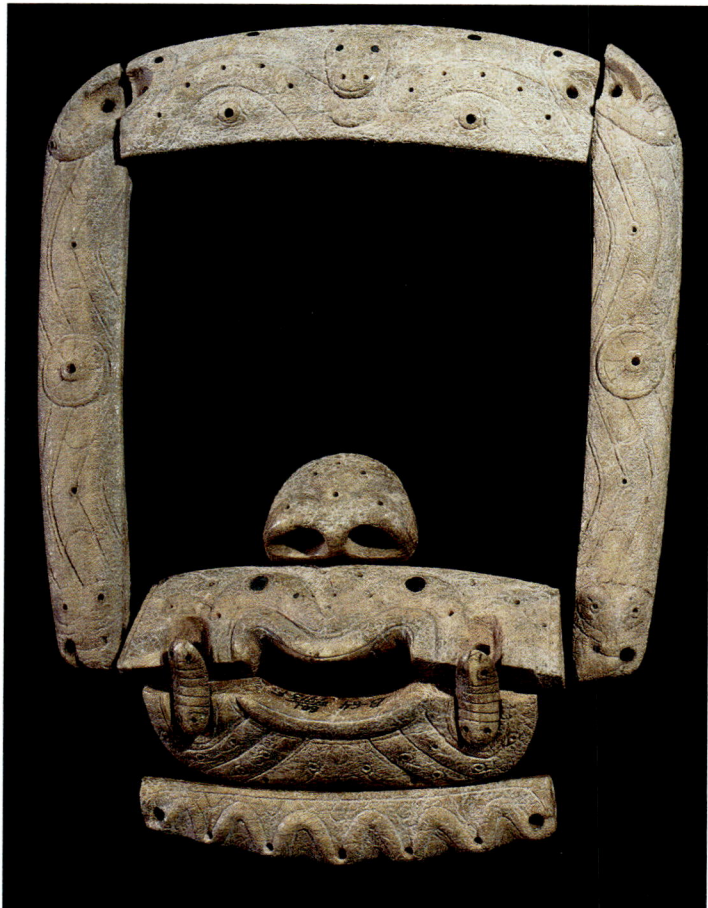

1 in.

**18-29** Burial mask, from Point Hope, Alaska, Ipiutak, ca. 100 CE. Ivory, greatest width 9½″. American Museum of Natural History, New York.

Carved out of walrus ivory, this mask consists of nine parts that can be combined to produce several faces, both human and animal, echoing the transformation theme common in ancient American art.

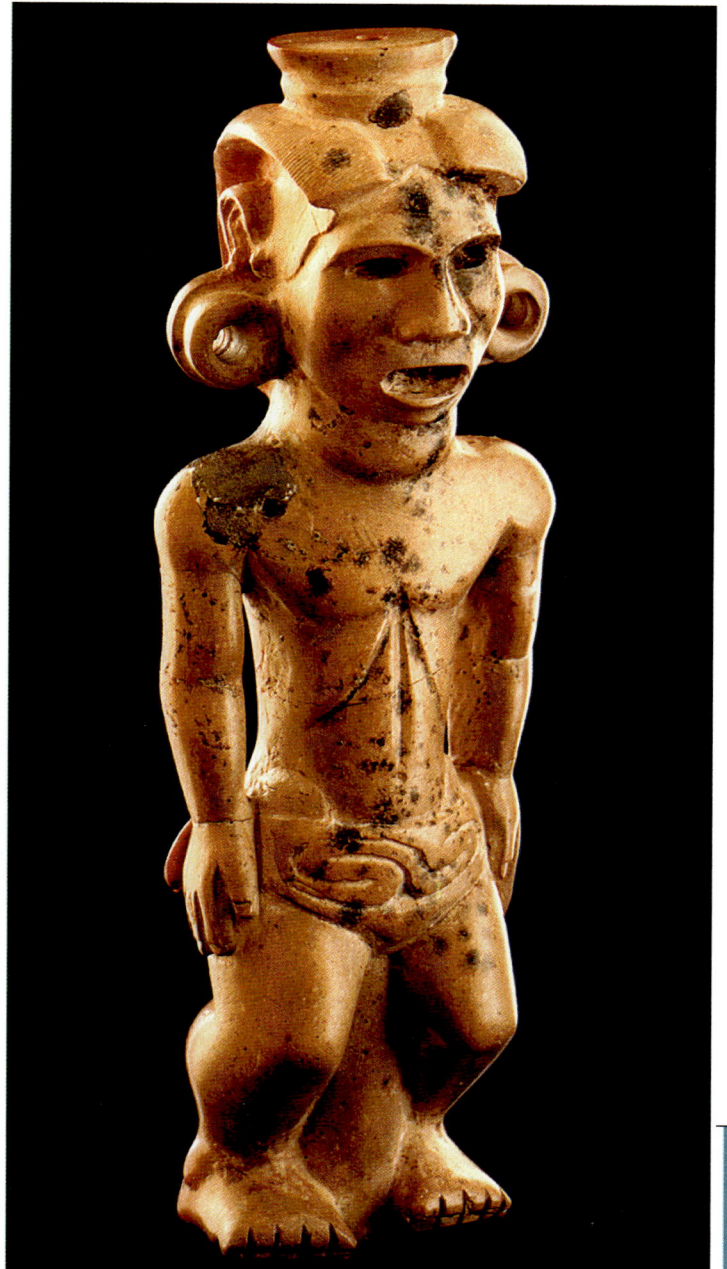

1 in.

**18-30** Pipe, from a mound in Ohio, Adena, ca. 500–1 BCE. Stone, 8″ high. Ohio Historical Society, Columbus.

Smoking was an important ritual in ancient North America, and the Adena often buried pipes with men for use in the afterlife. This example resembles some Mesoamerican sculptures in form and costume.

established great urban centers with populations sometimes exceeding 20,000.

**ADENA** Archaeologists have found remains of the Adena culture of Ohio at about 500 sites in the Central Woodlands. The Adena buried their elite in great earthen mounds and often placed ceremonial pipes in the graves. Smoking was an important social and religious ritual in many Native American cultures, and pipes were treasured status symbols men wanted to take with them into the afterlife. The Adena pipe shown here (FIG. **18-30**), carved between 500 BCE and the end of the millennium, takes the shape of a standing man. The figure has naturalistic joint articulations and musculature, a lively flexed-leg pose, and an alert facial expression—all combining to suggest movement. In form and costume (note the prominent ear spools), the figure resembles some Mesoamerican sculptures.

**MISSISSIPPIAN** The Adena were the first great mound builders of North America, but the Mississippian culture, which emerged around 800 CE and eventually encompassed much of the eastern United States, surpassed all earlier Woodlands groups in the size and complexity of their communities. One Mississippian mound site, Cahokia in southern Illinois, was the largest city in North America in the early second millennium CE, with a population of at least 20,000 and an area of more than six square miles. There were approximately 120 mounds at Cahokia. The grandest, 100 feet tall and built in stages between about 900 and 1200 CE, was Monk's Mound (FIG. **18-30A**). It aligns with the position of the sun at the equinoxes and may have served as an astronomical observatory as well as the site of agricultural ceremonies. Topping each stage were wooden structures the Mississippians eventually destroyed in preparation for the building of a new layer.

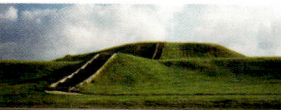

**18-30A** Monk's Mound, Cahokia, ca. 1050–1200 CE.

# Serpent Mound

Serpent Mound (FIG. 18-31) is one of the largest and best known of the Woodlands effigy mounds, but it is the subject of considerable controversy. First excavated in the 1880s, Serpent Mound represents one of the first efforts at preserving a Native American site from destruction at the hands of pot hunters and farmers. For a long time after its exploration, archaeologists attributed construction of the mound to the Adena culture, which flourished in the Ohio area during the last several centuries BCE. Radiocarbon dates taken from the mound, however, indicate the people known as Mississippians built it much later. Unlike most other ancient mounds, for example, Monk's Mound (FIG. 18-30A) in Cahokia, Illinois, Serpent Mound contained no evidence of burials or temples. Serpents, however, were important in Mississippian iconography, appearing, for instance, etched on shell gorgets similar to the one reproduced in FIG. 18-32. The Mississippians strongly associated snakes with the earth and the fertility of crops. A stone figurine found at one Mississippian site depicts a woman digging her hoe into the back of a large serpentine creature whose tail turns into a vine of gourds.

Some researchers have proposed another possible meaning for the construction of Serpent Mound. The date suggested for it is 1070, not long after the brightest appearance in recorded history of Halley's Comet in 1066, an astronomical event recorded on the 11th-century *Bayeux Tapestry* (FIGS. 12-37 and 12-38) as an important omen. Could Serpent Mound have been built in response to the same comet lighting up the North American heavens? Scholars have even suggested the serpentine form of the mound replicates Halley's Comet streaking across the night sky. Whatever its meaning, an earthwork as large and elaborate as Serpent Mound could only have been built by a large labor force under the firm direction of a powerful elite eager to leave its mark on the landscape forever.

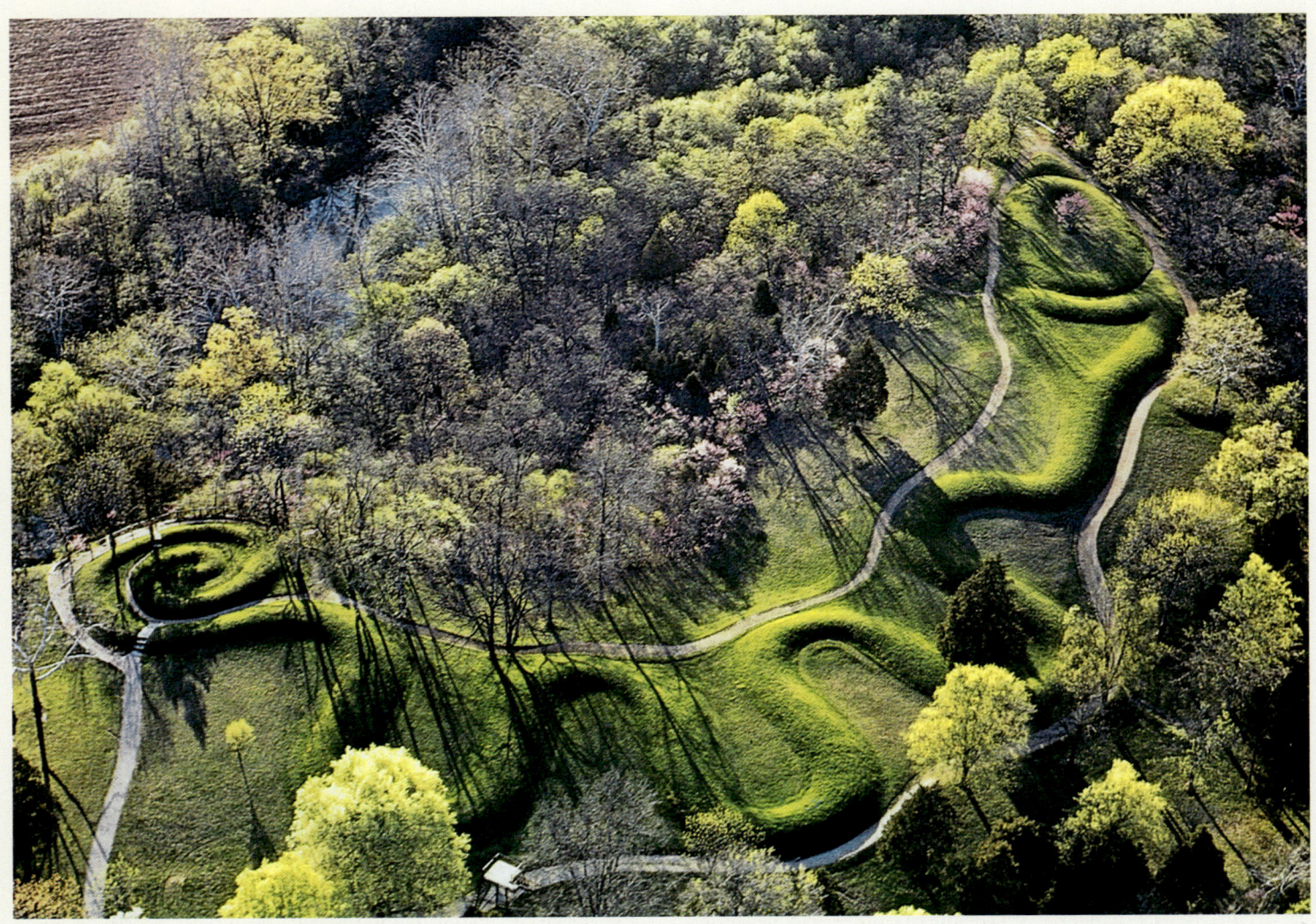

**18-31** Serpent Mound, Ohio, Mississippian, ca. 1070 CE. 1200' long, 20' wide, 5' high.

The Mississippians constructed effigy mounds in the form of animals and birds. This mound seems to depict a serpent. Some scholars, however, think it replicates the path of Halley's Comet in 1066.

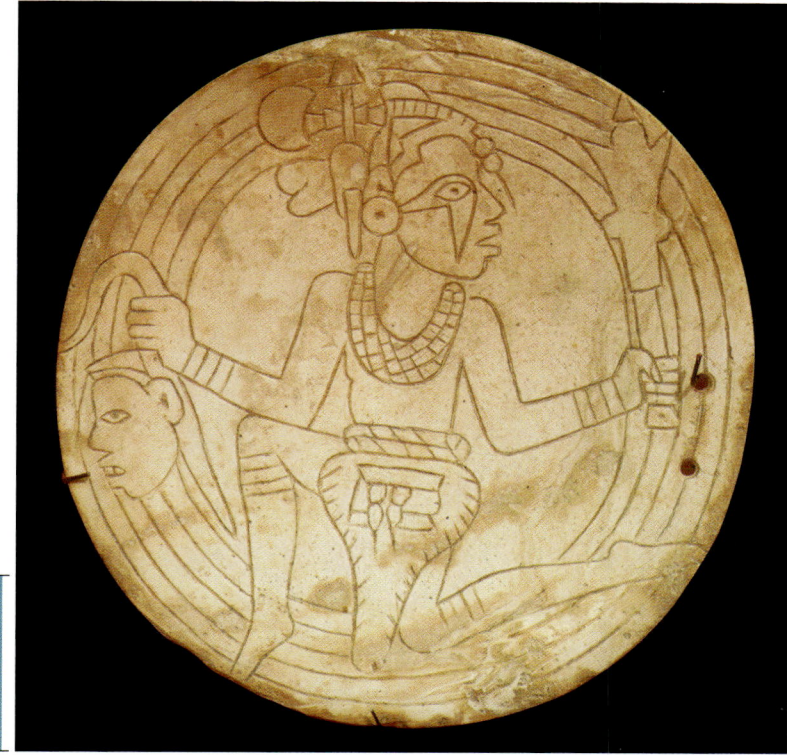

1 in.

**18-32** Incised gorget with running warrior, from Sumner County, Tennessee, Mississippian, ca. 1250–1300 CE. Shell, 4″ wide. National Museum of the American Indian, Washington, D.C.

This neck pendant was probably a gift to the dead to ensure safe passage to the afterlife. It represents a running Mississippian warrior holding a mace in one hand and a severed human head in the other.

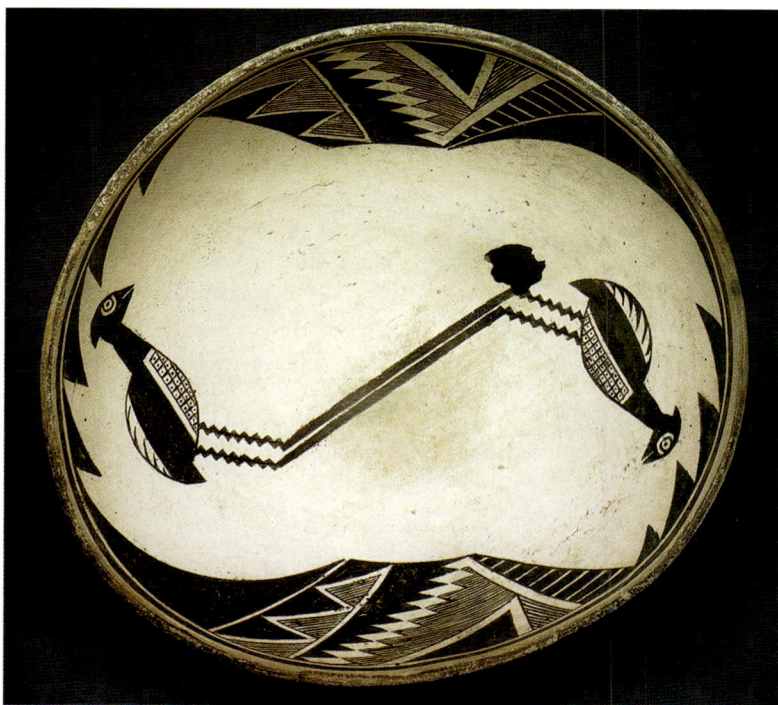

1 in.

**18-33** Bowl with two cranes and geometric forms, from New Mexico, Mimbres, ca. 1250 CE. Painted ceramic, diameter 1′ $\frac{1}{2}$″. Art Institute of Chicago, Chicago (Hugh L. and Mary T. Adams Fund).

Native Americans have been producing pottery for more than 2,000 years, long before the introduction of the potter's wheel. Mimbres bowls feature black-and-white animals and abstract patterns.

The Mississippians also constructed *effigy mounds* (mounds built in the form of animals or birds). One of the best preserved is Serpent Mound (FIG. **18-31**), a twisting earthwork on a bluff overlooking a creek in Ohio. It measures nearly a quarter mile from its open jaw (FIG. 18-31, *top right*), which seems to clasp an oval-shaped mound in its mouth, to its tightly coiled tail (*far left*). Both its date and meaning are controversial (see "Serpent Mound," page 516).

The Mississippian peoples, like their predecessors in North America, also manufactured small portable art objects. The shell *gorget*, or neck pendant, was a favorite item. One example (FIG. **18-32**), found at a site in Tennessee, dates from around 1250 to 1300 CE and depicts a running warrior, shown in the same kind of composite profile and frontal view with bent arms and legs used to suggest motion in other ancient cultures (compare, for instance, FIG. 5-16). The Tennessee warrior wears an elaborate headdress incorporating an arrow. He carries a mace in his left hand and a severed human head in his right. On his face is the painted forked eye of a falcon. Most Mississippian gorgets come from burial and temple mounds, and archaeologists believe they were gifts to the dead to ensure their safe arrival and prosperity in the land of the spirits. Other art objects found in similar contexts include fine mica cutouts and embossed copper cutouts of hands, bodies, snakes, birds, and other presumably symbolic forms.

## Southwest

In the Southwest, Native Americans have been producing pottery since the late first millennium BCE, but the most impressive examples of decorated pottery date to after 1000 CE.

**MIMBRES** The Mimbres culture of southwestern New Mexico, which flourished between approximately 1000 and 1250 CE, is renowned for its black-on-white painted bowls. Mimbres bowls have been found in burials under house floors, inverted over the head of the deceased and ritually "killed" by puncturing a small hole at the base, perhaps to allow the spirits of the deceased to join their ancestors in the sky (which contemporary Southwestern peoples view as a dome). The bowl illustrated here (FIG. **18-33**) dates to around 1250 and features an animated graphic rendering of two black cranes on a white ground. The contrast between the bowl's abstract border designs and the birds creates a dynamic tension. Thousands of different compositions appear on Mimbres pottery. They range from lively and complex geometric patterns to abstract renditions of humans, animals, and composite mythological beings. Almost all are imaginative creations by artists who seem to have been determined not to repeat themselves. Their designs emphasize linear rhythms balanced and controlled within a clearly defined border. Because the potter's wheel was unknown in the Americas, the artists constructed their pots out of coils of clay, creating countless sophisticated shapes of varied size, always characterized by technical excellence. Although historians have no direct knowledge about the potters' identities, the fact that pottery making was usually women's work in the Southwest during the historical period (see "Gender Roles in Native American Art," Chapter 35, page 1030) suggests the Mimbres potters also may have been women.

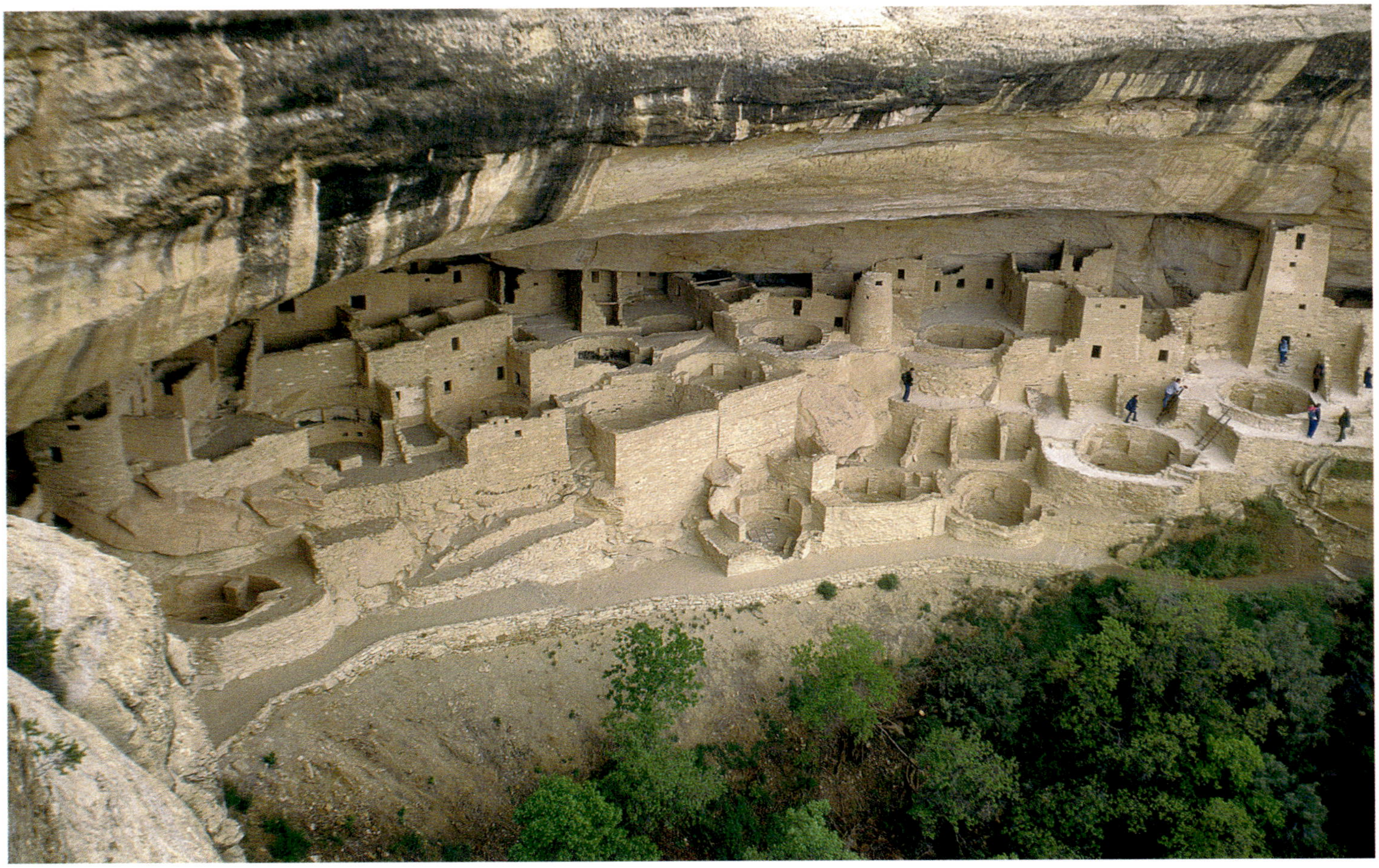

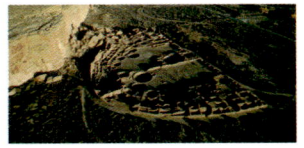

**18-34** Cliff Palace (looking northeast), Mesa Verde National Park, Colorado, Ancestral Puebloan, ca. 1150–1300 CE.

Cliff Palace, wedged into a sheltered ledge to heat the pueblo in winter and shade it during the hot summer months, contains about 200 stone-and-timber rooms plastered inside and out with adobe.

**18-33A** Pueblo Bonito, Chaco Canyon, ca. 850–1050 CE.

## ANCESTRAL PUEBLOANS

The Ancestral Puebloans, formerly known as the Anasazi, were northern neighbors of the Mimbres. (Anasazi means "enemy ancestors" in Navajo, a term the descendants of these early Native Americans have understandably rejected.) The Ancestral Puebloans emerged as an identifiable culture around 200 CE, but their art did not reach its peak until about 1000. The many ruined *pueblos* (urban settlements) scattered throughout the Southwest reveal the Ancestral Puebloans' masterful building skills. In Chaco Canyon (FIG. **18-33A**), New Mexico, for example, they built a great semicircle of 800 rooms reaching to five stepped-back stories, the largest of several similar sites in and around the canyon. Chaco Canyon was the center of a wide trade network extending as far as Mexico.

Sometime in the late 12th century, a drought occurred, and the Ancestral Puebloans largely abandoned their open canyon-floor dwelling sites to move farther north to the steep-sided canyons and lusher environment of Mesa Verde in southwestern Colorado. Cliff Palace (FIG. **18-34**) is wedged into a sheltered ledge above a valley floor. It contains about 200 rectangular rooms (mostly communal dwellings) of carefully laid stone and timber, once plastered inside and out with adobe. The location for Cliff Palace was not accidental. The Ancestral Puebloans designed it to take advantage of the sun to heat the pueblo in winter and the sheltering ledge to shade it during the hot summer months. Scattered in the foreground of FIG. 18-34 are two dozen large circular roofed semisubterranean structures called *kivas*. The Ancestral Puebloans entered the kivas using a ladder extending through a hole in the flat roof. These rooms were the spiritual centers of native Southwest life, male council houses where the elders stored ritual regalia and where private rituals and preparations for public ceremonies took place—and still do.

The Ancestral Puebloans did not disappear but gradually evolved into the various Pueblo peoples who still live in Arizona, New Mexico, Colorado, and Utah. They continue to speak their native languages, practice deeply rooted rituals, and make pottery in the traditional manner. Their art is discussed in Chapter 35.

# NATIVE ARTS OF THE AMERICAS BEFORE 1300

## MESOAMERICA

▮ The Olmec (ca. 1200–400 BCE) is often called the "mother culture" of Mesoamerica. At La Venta and elsewhere, the Olmec built pyramids and ball courts and carved colossal basalt portraits of their rulers during the Preclassic period.

▮ In contrast to the embryonic civic centers of the Olmec, Teotihuacán in the Valley of Mexico was a huge metropolis laid out on a strict grid plan. Its major pyramids and plazas date to the late Preclassic period (ca. 50–250 CE).

▮ The Maya occupied parts of Mexico, Belize, Guatemala, and Honduras. During the Classic period (ca. 300–900 CE), at Copán, Tikal, and other sites, they built vast complexes of temple-pyramids, palaces, plazas, and ball courts and decorated them with monumental sculptures and mural paintings glorifying their rulers and gods. The Maya also left extensive written records and possessed a sophisticated knowledge of astronomy and arithmetic calculation.

▮ The most famous Postclassic (ca. 900–1521) Maya site is Chichén Itzá in the Yucatán Peninsula, which boasts a huge pyramid-temple to Kulkulcán and the largest ball court in Mesoamerica.

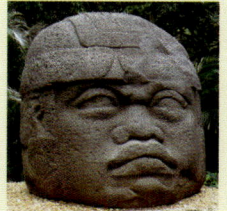

Colossal head, La Venta, Olmec, ca. 900–400 BCE

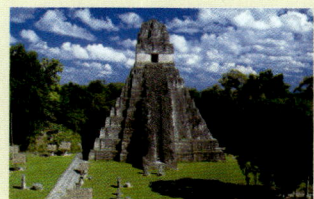

Temple I, Tikal, Maya, ca. 732 CE

## SOUTH AMERICA

▮ The ancient civilizations of South America are even older than those of Mesoamerica. The earliest Andean sites began to develop around 3000 BCE.

▮ At Chavín de Huántar in Peru, archaeologists have excavated U-shaped temple complexes and monumental statues and reliefs dating between about 800 and 200 BCE, during the Early Horizon period.

▮ The Paracas (ca. 400 BCE–200 CE), Nasca (ca. 200 BCE–600 CE), and Moche (ca. 1–700 CE) cultures of the Early Intermediate period in Peru produced extraordinary textiles, distinctive painted ceramics, and turquoise-inlaid goldwork. The subjects range from composite human-animals to ruler portraits. Most monumental are the Nasca Lines, which may have marked pilgrimage routes.

▮ The Tiwanaku (ca. 100–1000 CE) and Wari (ca. 500–800 CE) cultures of northern Bolivia and southern Peru flourished during the Middle Horizon period. Tiwanaku is noteworthy for its monumental stone architecture. The Wari produced magnificent tapestries.

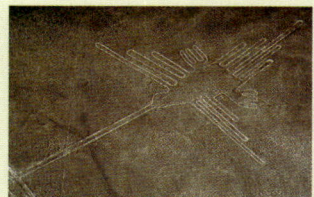

Hummingbird, Nasca, ca. 500 CE

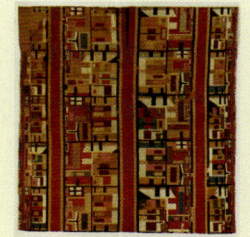

*Lima Tapestry*, Wari, ca. 500–800 CE

## NORTH AMERICA

▮ The indigenous cultures of the United States and Canada date as far back as 10,000 BCE, but most of the surviving art objects date from the last 2,000 years. The Eskimo, for example, produced small-scale artworks in ivory beginning in the early first millennium CE, reflecting a nomadic lifestyle requiring portable objects.

▮ The peoples of the Mississippian culture (ca. 800–1500 CE) were great mound builders. Cahokia in Illinois encompassed about 120 mounds and was the largest city in North America during the early second millennium CE.

▮ In the Southwest, Native Americans have been producing pottery for more than 2,000 years. The black-and-white painted bowls of the Mimbres (ca. 1000–1250 CE) are among the finest. The Ancestral Puebloans were master builders of pueblos, urban settlements of stone and wood, often plastered with adobe. The pueblo at Chaco Canyon, New Mexico, had about 800 rooms. Cliff Palace, Colorado, is noteworthy for its sophisticated design, wedged into a sheltered ledge to take advantage of the winter sun and the summer shade.

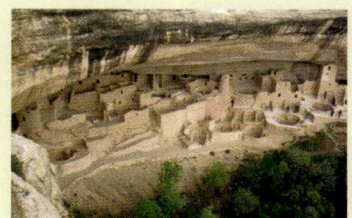

Cliff Palace, Colorado, Ancestral Puebloan, ca. 1150–1300 CE

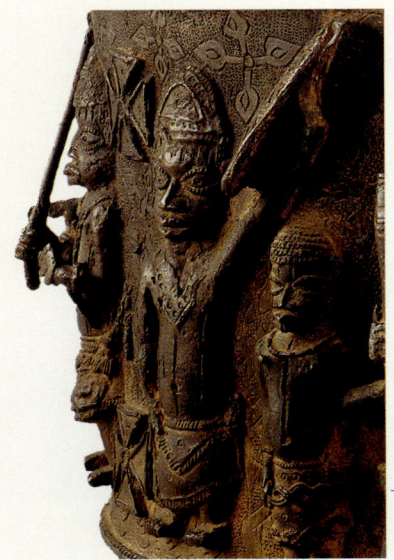

The unknown artist who cast this *ikegobo* drew attention to the king by placing attendant figures to his left and right who each raise one arm to point to his head.

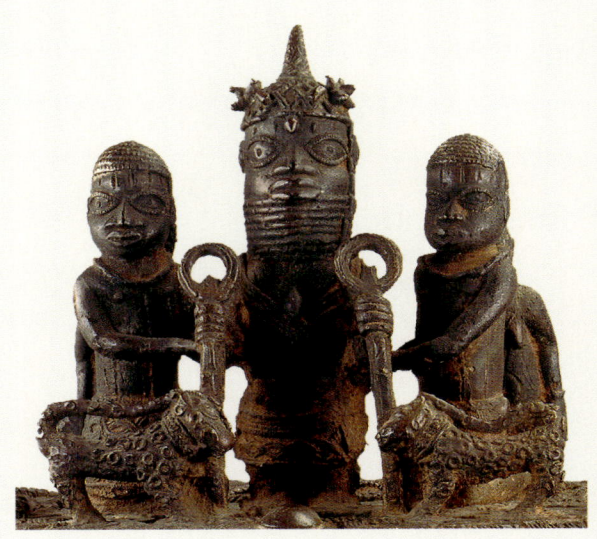

One of the Benin king's praise names is "great head," and on this cast-bronze royal altar, the artist represented him larger than all other figures and with a disproportionately large head.

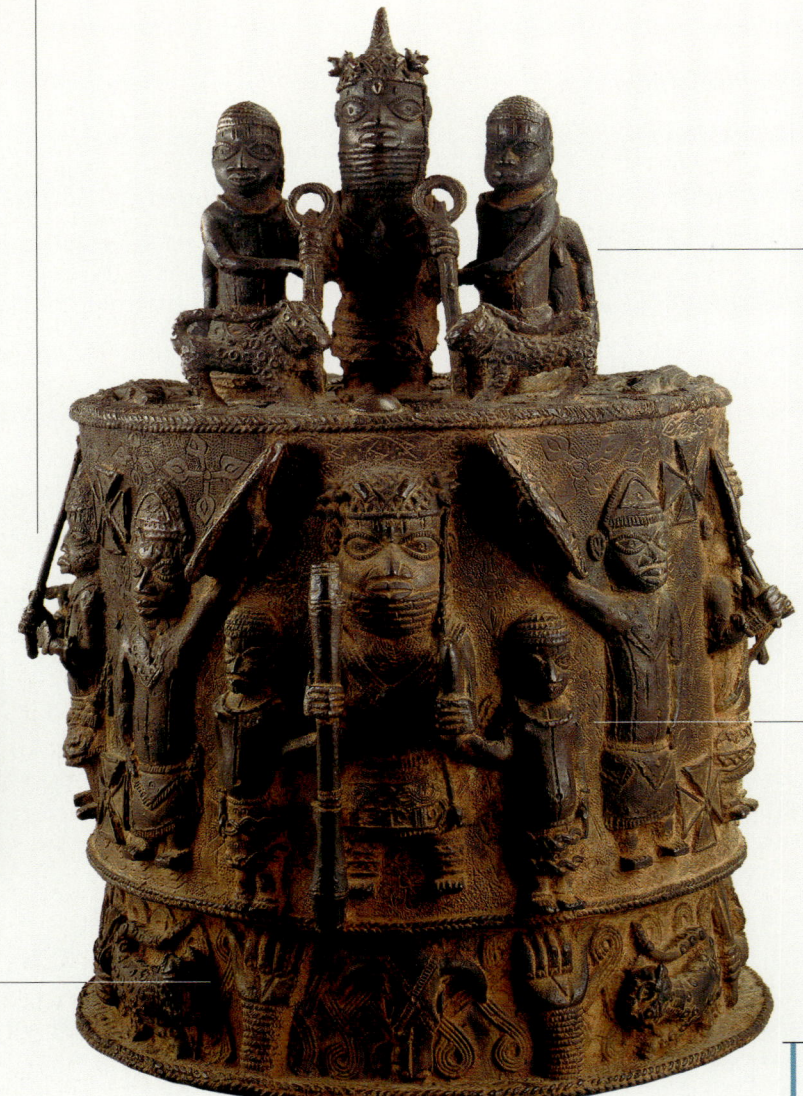

An *ikegobo* is an altar to the hand, the symbol of personal achievement in Benin society. The band at the bottom of this altar features hands alternating with other emblems of royal power.

**19-1** Altar to the Hand (ikegobo), from Benin, Nigeria, ca. 1735–1750. Brass, 1′ 5½″ high. British Museum, London (gift of Sir William Ingram). ◼◀

1 in.

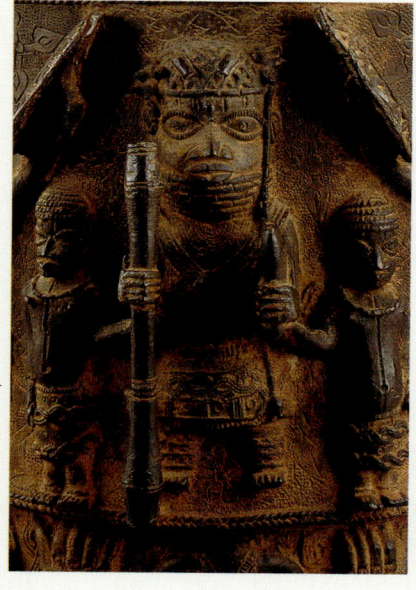

The sacred king, or *oba*, depicted twice on this portable altar is probably Eresonyen, who ruled Benin about 1735–1750. He wears a multistrand coral necklace emblematic of his high office.

## SACRED KINGSHIP IN BENIN

Some of the oldest paintings yet discovered, for example those from the Apollo 11 Cave in Namibia (FIG. 1-3), come from Africa, and African art is as diverse as the continent is vast. Most African artworks created before 1800 are difficult to date and interpret. The art of the Benin kingdom, just west of the lower reaches of the Niger River in what is today Nigeria (not to be confused with the modern Republic of Benin), is exceptional. The kingdom, most likely established in the 13th century, reached the apex of its wealth and power in the 16th century. Benin kingship was hereditary and considered sacred, and the purpose of the finest preserved Benin artworks was to honor the ruling *oba,* his family, and his ancestors. The names and dates of many of the Benin kings are known, and numerous extant artworks can even be confidently attributed to specific rulers.

The 18th-century cast-brass royal shrine illustrated here (FIG. 19-1), on which the oba appears twice, underscores the centrality of the sacred king in Benin culture. Called an *ikegobo* and about a foot and a half tall, it is a portable altar to the hand, which symbolized personal achievement in Benin society, both on the battlefield and in peacetime. The altar features symmetrical hierarchical compositions centered on the dominant king, probably Eresonyen, who ruled Benin around 1735 to 1750, and who appears on the altar wearing the multistrand coral necklace emblematic of his high office. He is the central figure on the top of the altar, flanked by smaller (and therefore lesser) members of his court, usually identified as priests. In front of the king and his attendant priests is a pair of leopards, animals the sacred king sacrificed and symbolic of his power over all creatures. Similar compositions are common in Benin arts, as exemplified by the royal plaque (FIG. I-1) discussed in the Introduction. On the ikegobo, as was the norm throughout Africa, the artist distorted the king's proportions to emphasize his head, the seat of his will and power. Benin men celebrate a festival of the head called Igue, and one of the king's praise names is "great head."

King Eresonyen appears again as the largest figure on the cylindrical body of the altar. As in the freestanding group at the top, the size of the figures in relief varies with their importance at the Benin court. The sculptor drew attention to the sacred oba by placing him at the center, where two attendant figures raise their arms to point to his head. Around the base are more leopards, ram and elephant heads, and crocodiles (not all visible in FIG. 19-1), and the all-important hands symbolizing royal power and accomplishment. The oba and other high-ranking officials offered sacrifices at the ikegobo to ensure the king's continued strength and achievement.

# AFRICAN PEOPLES AND ART FORMS

Africa (MAP 19-1, page 524) is a vast continent of 52 nations comprising more than one-fifth of the world's land mass and many distinct topographical and ecological zones. Parched deserts occupy northern and southern regions, high mountains rise in the east, and three great rivers—the Niger, the Congo, and the Nile—and their lush valleys support agriculture and large settled populations. More than 2,000 distinct ethnic, cultural, and linguistic groups, often but inaccurately called "tribes," long have inhabited the African continent. These population groups historically have ranged in size from a few hundred, in hunting and gathering bands, to 20 million or more. Councils of elders often governed smaller groups, whereas larger populations sometimes formed a centralized state under a king, as in Benin (FIG. 19-1).

Despite this great variety, African peoples share many core beliefs and practices. These include honoring ancestors, worshiping nature deities, and elevating rulers to sacred status. Most Africans also consult diviners or fortune tellers. These beliefs have given rise to many richly expressive art traditions. Some have close equivalents in Western cultures, for example, figural sculpture, sacred and secular architecture, and rock engraving and painting. But other art forms, poorly documented until recent times because of their perishable nature and because they did not conform to Western notions of "artworks," also played key roles in African life. These include the art of body decoration and modification, costumes, and masks.

Given the size of the African continent and the diversity of ethnic groups, it is not surprising that African art varies enormously in subject, materials, and function. Nomadic and seminomadic peoples excel in the arts of personal adornment and also produce rock engravings and paintings depicting animals and rituals. Farmers, in contrast, often create figural sculpture in terracotta, wood, and metal for display in shrines to legendary ancestors or nature deities held responsible for the health of crops and the well-being of the people. The regalia, art, and architecture of kings and their courts, as elsewhere in the world, celebrate the wealth and power of the rulers themselves. Nearly all African peoples lavish artistic energy on the decoration of their bodies to express their identity and status, and many communities mount richly layered festivals, including masquerades, to celebrate harvests and the New Year and to commemorate the deaths of leaders.

This chapter surveys the early, and often difficult to date, art and architecture of sub-Saharan Africa from prehistoric times through the 18th century (see "Dating African Art and Identifying African Artists," page 523). The discussion includes the effects on Africans and African art of the first contacts with Europeans, which began along the seacoasts in the late 15th century, but excludes the art and architecture of Egypt and of Roman and Islamic North Africa, already treated in Chapters 3, 7, and 10 respectively. Chapter 37 treats African art of the past two centuries, from the beginning of European colonization to 1980. Contemporary African art is considered in its global context in Chapter 31.

# PREHISTORY AND EARLY CULTURES

Thousands of rock engravings and paintings found at hundreds of sites across the continent constitute the earliest known African art. Some painted animals (FIG. 1-3) from the Apollo 11 Cave in southwestern Africa date to perhaps as long ago as 25,000 years, earlier than all but the oldest *Paleolithic* (Old Stone Age) art of Europe (see Chapter 1). Because humankind apparently originated in Africa, archaeologists may yet discover the world's earliest art there as well.

## Rock Art

The greatest concentrations of rock art are in the Sahara to the north, the Horn of Africa in the east, and the Kalahari Desert to the south, as well as in caves and on rock outcroppings in southern Africa. Accurately naturalistic renderings as well as stylized images on rock surfaces show animals and humans in many different positions and activities, singly or in groups, stationary or in motion. Most of these works date to within the past 4,000 to 6,000 years, but some may have been created as early as 8000 BCE. They provide a rich record of the environment, human activities, and animal species in prehistoric times.

TASSILI N'AJJER  A 7,000-year-old painting (FIG. 19-2) from Tassili n'Ajjer in southeastern Algeria in the central Sahara (at that time a verdant savannah) is one of the earliest and finest surviving examples of rock art. The painter depicted a running woman with convincing animation and significant detail. The dotted marks on her shoulders, legs, and torso probably indicate she is wearing body paint applied for a ritual. Her face, however, is featureless, a common

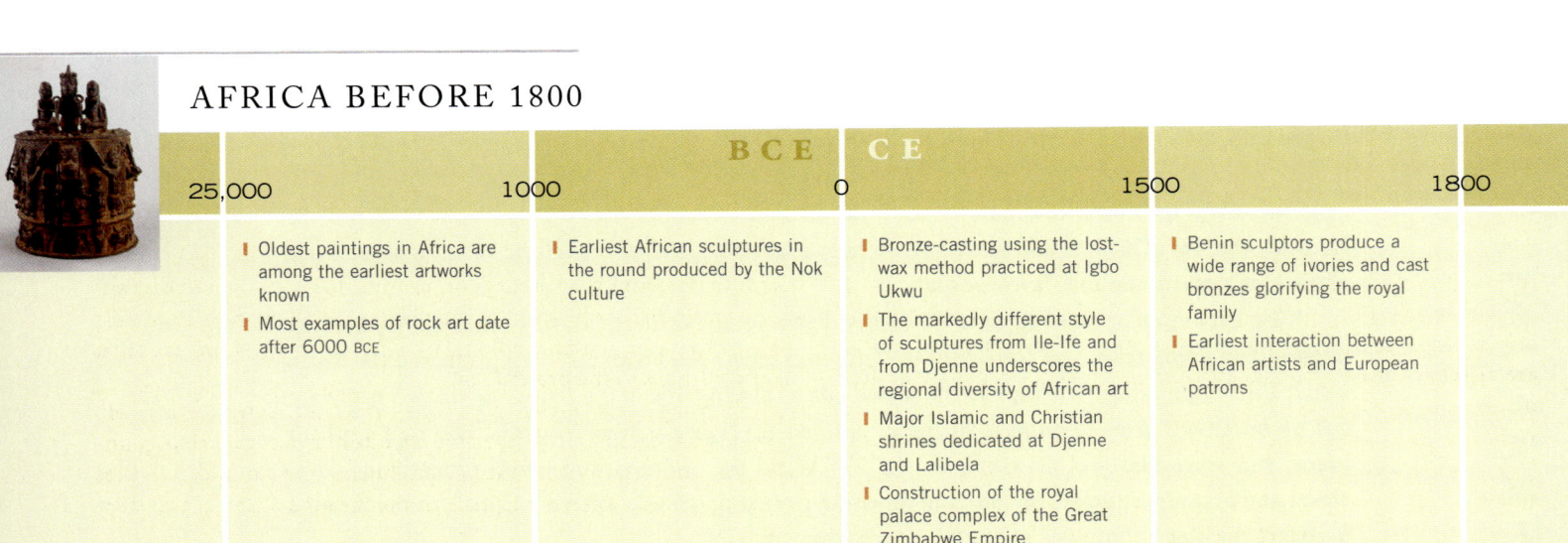

## AFRICA BEFORE 1800

| | 25,000 | 1000 | BCE / CE 0 | 1500 | 1800 |
|---|---|---|---|---|---|
| | ▮ Oldest paintings in Africa are among the earliest artworks known <br> ▮ Most examples of rock art date after 6000 BCE | ▮ Earliest African sculptures in the round produced by the Nok culture | ▮ Bronze-casting using the lost-wax method practiced at Igbo Ukwu <br> ▮ The markedly different style of sculptures from Ile-Ife and from Djenne underscores the regional diversity of African art <br> ▮ Major Islamic and Christian shrines dedicated at Djenne and Lalibela <br> ▮ Construction of the royal palace complex of the Great Zimbabwe Empire | ▮ Benin sculptors produce a wide range of ivories and cast bronzes glorifying the royal family <br> ▮ Earliest interaction between African artists and European patrons | |

# Dating African Art and Identifying African Artists

**M**ost African objects bear neither labels nor signatures, and consequently it is nearly impossible to date them precisely or to identify their makers definitively. As in the West, this is especially true for the oldest surviving artworks (FIGS. I-1 and 19-2), but in Africa the absence of documentary information persisted until quite recently. Early collectors did not even bother to ask the names of living artists or when they made their works. Although a firm chronology for the full range of African arts is currently beyond reach, broad historical trends are reasonably clear. Still, until archaeologists conduct more extensive fieldwork in sub-Saharan Africa, many artworks will remain difficult to date even within a century, and whole cultures will continue to be poorly documented. Some African peoples, however, have left written documents that help date their artworks, even when their methods of measuring time differ from those used today. Other cultures, such as the Benin kingdom (FIGS. I-1, 19-1, and 19-13), preserve detailed oral records of past events. Historians can check these against the accounts of European travelers and traders.

When artists are members of craft or occupational guilds—such as blacksmiths and brass-casters in Western Sudan—commissions go to the group chief, and the specific artist who worked on the commission may never be known. Nevertheless, art historians can identify individual hands if an artist's work is distinctive. Documentation now exists for several hundred artists, even if most of their names are lost. For some sculptors who worked in the late 19th or early 20th centuries, however, scholars have been able to compile fairly detailed biographies (see "African Artists," Chapter 37, page 1071).

Where documentation on authorship or dating is fragmentary or unavailable, art historians sometimes try to establish chronology from an object's style, although, as discussed in the Introduction, stylistic analysis is a subjective tool. Scientific techniques such as *radiocarbon dating* (measuring the decay rate of carbon isotopes in organic matter to provide dates for wood, fiber, and ivory) and *thermoluminescence* (dating the amounts of radiation found in fired clay objects) have also proved useful but cannot provide precise dates. Nonetheless, art historians are slowly writing the history of African art, even if large gaps remain to be filled.

One major problem impeding compilation of an accurate history of art in Africa is illegal and uncontrolled excavation. By removing artworks from the ground, treasure hunters disturb or ruin the objects' original contexts and reduce or eliminate the possibility of establishing accurate chronologies. This phenomenon is not unique to Africa, however (see "Archaeology, Art History, and the Art Market," Chapter 4, page 88). Archaeologists on all continents

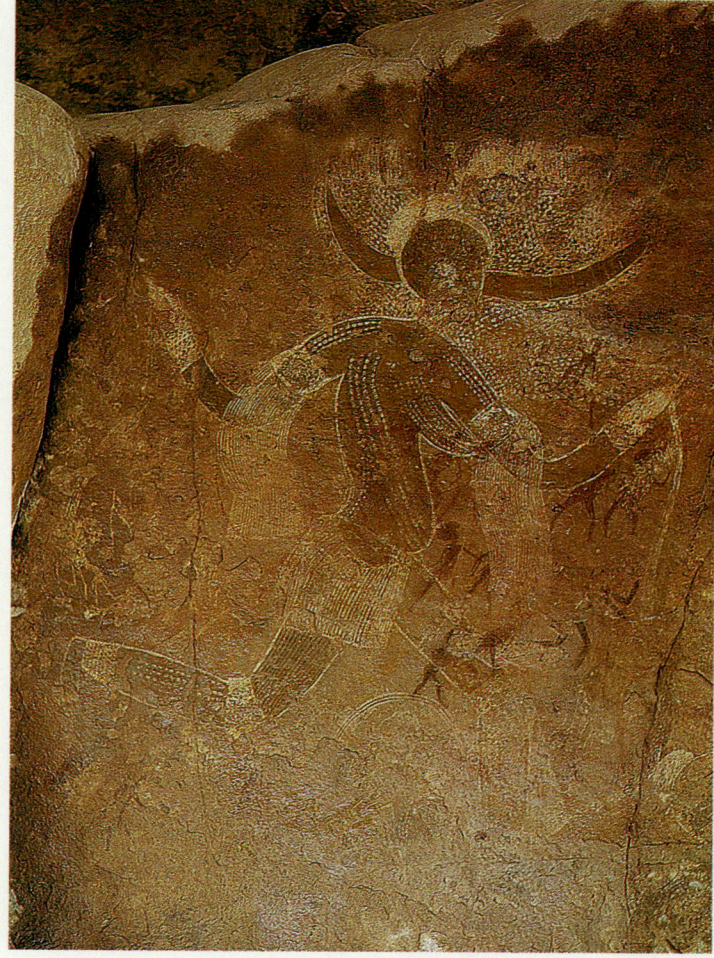

**19-2** Running woman, rock painting, from Tassili n'Ajjer, Algeria, ca. 6000–4000 BCE.

Prehistoric rock paintings are difficult to date and interpret. This Algerian example represents a running woman wearing body paint, raffia skirt, and horned headgear, apparently in a ritual context.

confront the problem of looting and the consequent loss of knowledge about the provenance and original function of objects collectors wish to acquire. That is the unfortunate result of the worldwide appreciation of African art that began in the early 20th century, when many European artists looked to "primitive art" for inspiration (see "Primitivism and Colonialism," Chapter 29, page 846).

trait in the earliest art of Europe as well as Africa (see Chapter 1). The white parallel patterns attached to her arms and waist probably represent flowing raffia decorations and a raffia skirt. Horns are also part of her ceremonial attire—shown, as typically in prehistoric art (see Chapter 1), in the *twisted perspective,* or *composite view,* that is, seen from the front even though on a profile head. Notably, the artist painted this detailed image over a field of much smaller painted human beings, an example of why it is often so dif-

ficult to date and interpret art on rock surfaces, as subsequent superimpositions are frequent. Nonetheless, scholars have been able to establish a rough chronology for African rock art, an art form that continues to the present day.

Although the precise meaning of most African rock art also remains uncertain, a considerable literature exists describing, analyzing, and interpreting the varied human and animal activities shown, as well as the evidently symbolic, more abstract patterns.

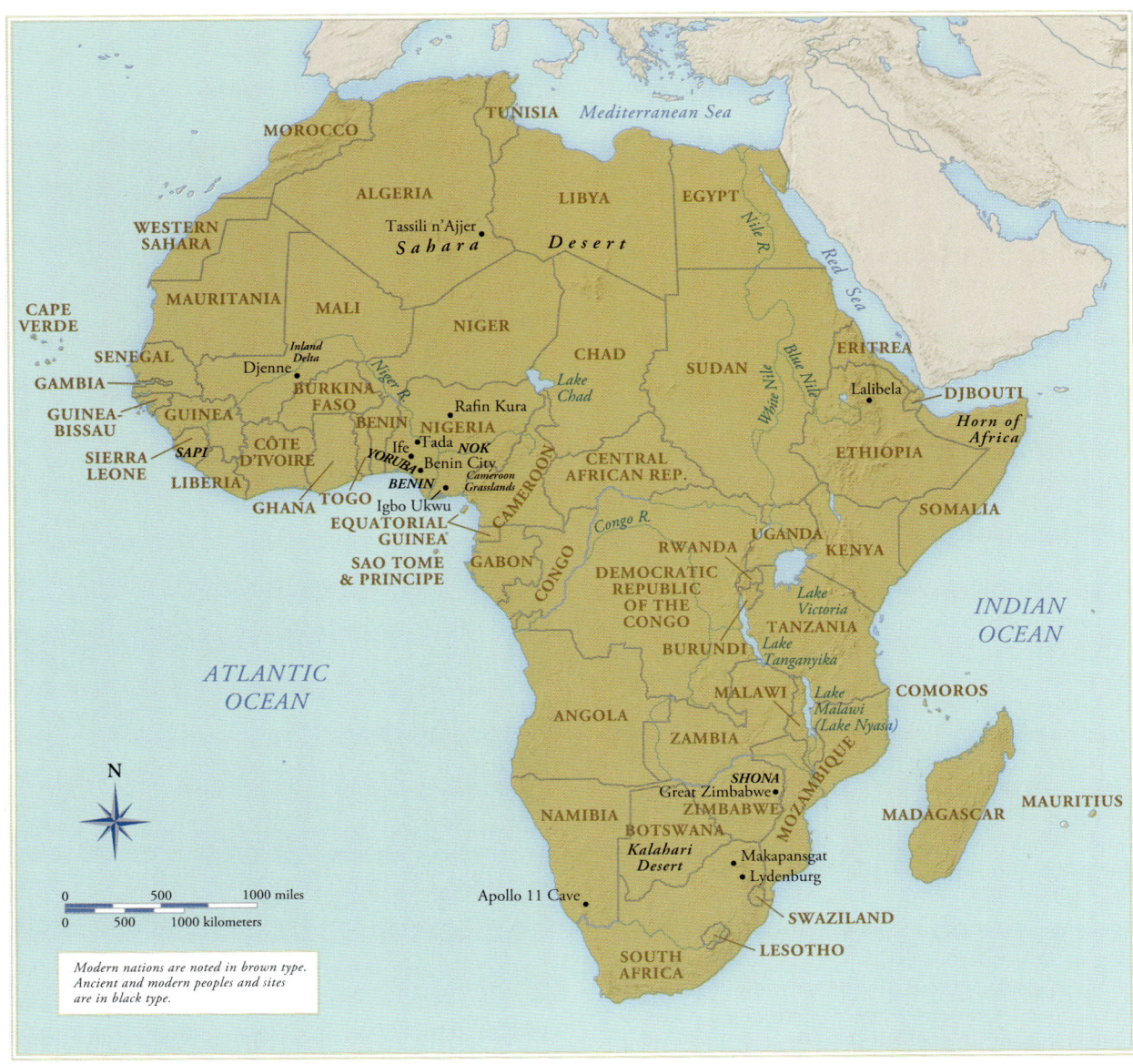

**MAP 19-1** Precolonial African peoples and sites.

The human and humanlike figures may include representations of supernatural beings as well as mortals. Some scholars have, in fact, interpreted the woman from Tassili n'Ajjer as a horned deity instead of a human wearing ceremonial headgear.

## Nok and Lydenburg

Outside Egypt and neighboring Nubia (see Chapter 3), the earliest African sculptures in the round have been found at several sites in central Nigeria archaeologists collectively call the Nok culture. Scholars disagree on whether the Nok sites were unified politically or socially. Named after the site where these sculptures were first discovered in 1928, Nok art dates between 500 BCE and 200 CE. Hundreds of Nok-style human and animal heads, body parts, and figures have been found accidentally during tin-mining operations, but unfortunately not in their original context.

**NOK** A representative Nok terracotta head (FIG. **19-3**), found at Rafin Kura, is a fragment of what was originally a full figure. Preserved

fragments of other statues indicate the Nok sculptors fashioned a variety of types, including standing, seated, and kneeling figures. The heads are disproportionately large compared with the bodies. The head shown here has an expressive face with large alert eyes, flaring nostrils, and parted lips. The pierced eyes, mouth, and ear holes are characteristic of Nok sculpture and probably helped to equalize the heating of the hollow clay head during the firing process. The coiffure with incised grooves, the raised eyebrows, the perforated triangular eyes, and the sharp jaw line suggest the sculptor carved some details of the head while modeling the rest. The function of the Nok terracottas is unclear, but the broken tube around the neck of the Rafin Kura figure may be a bead necklace, an indication the person portrayed held an elevated position in Nok society. The gender of the Nok artists is also unknown, but because the primary ceramists and clay sculptors across the continent have traditionally been women, Nok women may have sculpted these heads as well (see "Gender Roles in African Art Production," Chapter 37, page 1070).

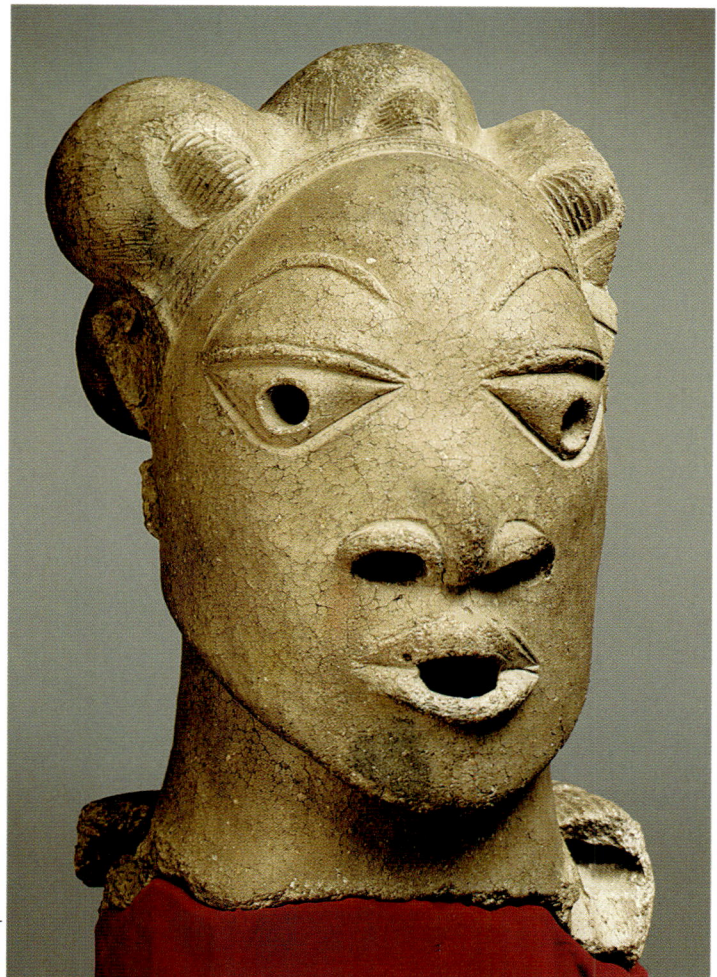

**19-3** Nok head, from Rafin Kura, Nigeria, ca. 500 BCE–200 CE. Terracotta, 1′ 2 3/16″ high. National Museum, Lagos.

The earliest African sculptures in the round come from Nigeria. The Nok culture produced expressive terracotta heads with large eyes, mouths, and ears. Piercing equalized the heat during the firing process.

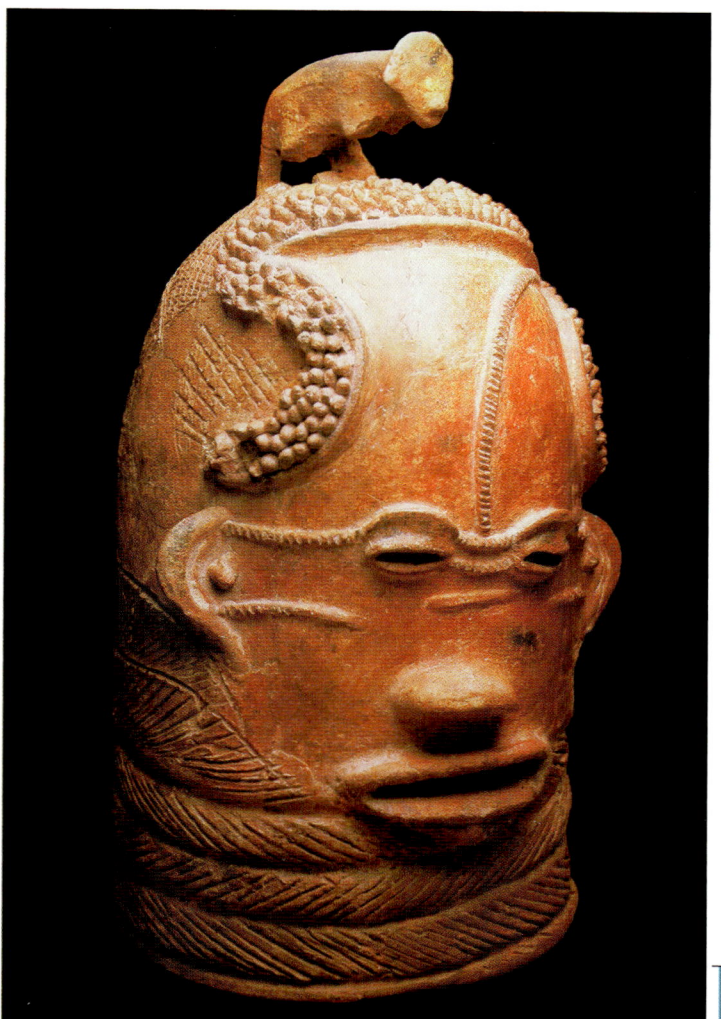

**19-4** Head, from Lydenburg, South Africa, ca. 500 CE. Terracotta, 1′ 2 15/16″ high. IZIKO Museums of Cape Town, Cape Town.

This Lydenburg head resembles an inverted terracotta pot and may have been a helmet mask. The sculptor depicted the features by applying thin clay fillets. The scarification marks are signs of beauty.

**LYDENBURG** Later than the Nok examples are the seven life-size terracotta heads discovered carefully buried in a pit outside the town of Lydenburg in present-day South Africa. Radiocarbon evidence indicates the heads date to about 500 CE. The Lydenburg head illustrated here (FIG. **19-4**), reconstructed from fragments, has a humanlike form, although its inverted pot shape differs markedly from the more naturalistic Nok heads. The artist formed the eyes, ears, nose, and mouth, as well as the hairline, by applying thin clay fillets onto the head. The same method produced what are probably *scarification* marks (scars intentionally created to form patterns on the flesh) on the forehead, temples, and between the eyes. Incised linear patterns also adorn the back of the head. (This head is among the earliest artworks documenting the ancient African practice of beautifying the body through the creation of scars, a custom different from, but comparable to, the Polynesian tradition of tattooing bodies; see "Tattoo in Polynesia," Chapter 36, page 1055). The horizontal neck bands, with their incised surfaces, resemble the ringed or banded necks Africans still consider signs of beauty in many parts of the continent. In Africa, it is not uncommon for the human body itself to become a work of art. A small, unidentifiable animal sits atop the Lydenburg head (compare FIG. 4-12). In the absence of contemporaneous written documents, scholars can only guess at

the use and meaning of a head such as this one, but it is noteworthy that animals appear only on those Lydenburg heads large enough to have served as helmet masks. The head, therefore, probably had a ceremonial function.

## Igbo Ukwu

By the 9th or 10th century, a West African bronze-casting tradition of great sophistication had developed in the lower Niger area, just east of that great river. Dozens of objects in an intricate refined style have been unearthed at Igbo Ukwu. The ceramic, copper, bronze, and iron artifacts include basins (FIG. **19-4A**), bowls, altar stands, staffs, swords, scabbards, knives, and pendants. In one grave, archaeologists discovered numerous prestige objects—copper anklets, armlets, spiral ornaments, a fan handle, and more than 100,000 beads, which may have been used as a form of currency. The tomb also contained three elephant tusks, a beaded arm-

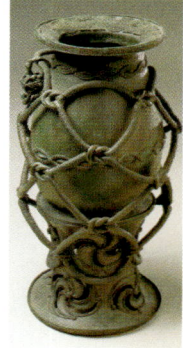

**19-4A** Roped water basin, Igbo Ukwu, 9th to 10th centuries CE.

## Art and Leadership in Africa

The relationships between leaders and art forms are strong, complex, and universal in Africa. Political, spiritual, and social leaders—kings, chiefs, titled people, and religious specialists—have the power and wealth to obtain the services of the best artists and acquire the most sumptuous materials to adorn themselves (FIG. 37-23), furnish their homes and palaces (FIGS. 37-6, 37-16, and 37-16A), and make visible the cultural and religious organizations they lead (FIGS. 19-1 and 37-13). Leaders also possess the power to dispense art or the prerogative to use it.

A number of formal or structural principles or trends characterize leaders' arts and thus set them off from the popular arts of ordinary Africans. Leaders' arts—for example, the lavish layered regalia of chiefs and kings (FIG. 19-6)—tend to be durable and fashioned of costly materials, such as ivory (FIG. 19-13), beads, copper alloys, and other metals. Some of the objects made specifically for African leaders, such as stools or chairs (FIG. 37-6), ornate clothing (FIG. 37-23), and special weaponry, draw attention to their superior status. Handheld objects, for example, staffs (FIG. 19-1), spears, knives, scepters, pipes, and fly whisks (FIG. 19-5), extend a leader's reach and magnify his or her gestures. Other objects associated with leaders, such as fans (FIG. I-1), shields, and umbrellas, protect the leaders both physically and spiritually. Sometimes the regalia and implements of an important person are so heavy they render the leader virtually immobile (FIG. 37-23), suggesting the temporary holder of an office is less significant than the eternal office itself. In African art, leaders not only appear wearing and holding the trappings of their high offices. Artists commonly portrayed them as larger-than-life figures flanked by diminutive attendants (FIGS. I-1 and 19-1) or mounted on undersized horses (FIGS. I-1 and 19-5). Often the leaders, both male and female, have facial scars (FIGS. 19-5, 19-6A, and 19-13) denoting their elevated status in society.

Although leaders' arts are easy to recognize in centralized, hierarchical societies, such as the Benin kingdom (FIGS. I-1, 19-1, 19-13, and 37-13), leaders among less centralized peoples have been no less conversant with the power of art to move people and effect change. For example, African leaders often oversee religious rituals in which they may be less visible than the forms they commission and manipulate: shrines, altars, festivals, and rites of passage such as funerals, the last being especially elaborate and festive in many parts of Africa. The arts that leaders control thus help create pageantry, mystery, and spectacle, enriching and changing the lives of the people.

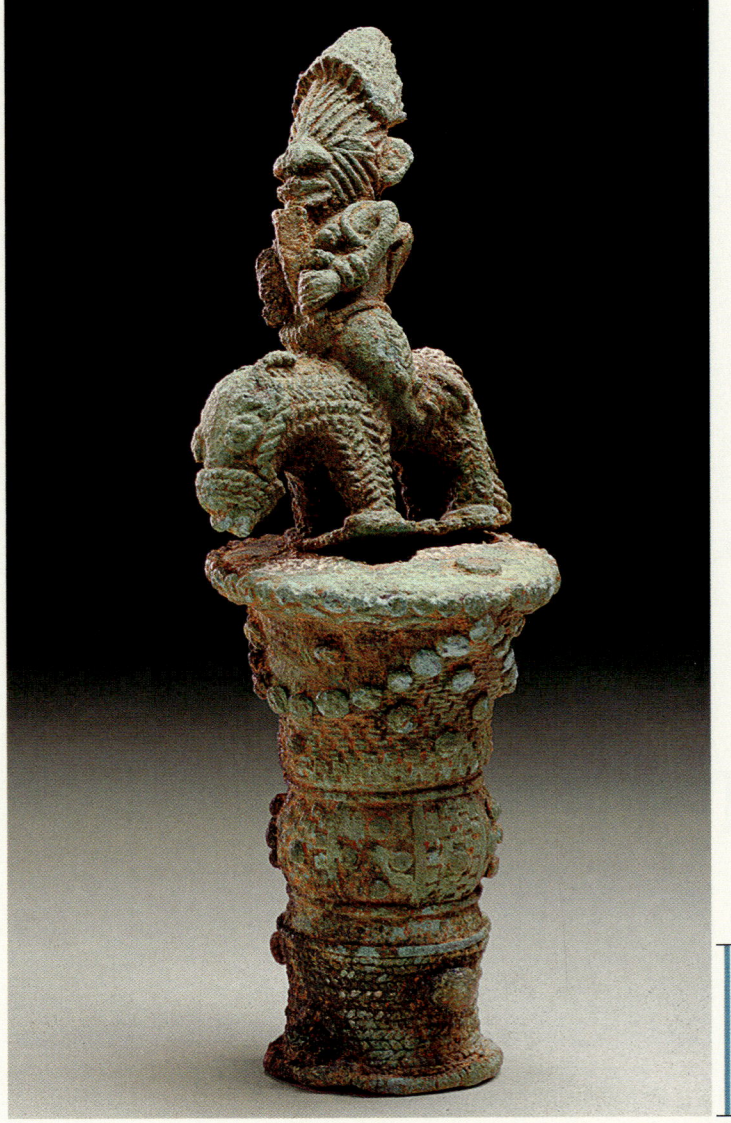

1 in.

**19-5** Equestrian figure on fly-whisk hilt, from Igbo Ukwu, Nigeria, 9th to 10th centuries CE. Copper-alloy bronze, figure 6 3/16″ high. National Museum, Lagos. ◼️📹

The oldest preserved African lost-wax cast bronze is this fly-whisk hilt, which a leader used to extend his reach and magnify his gestures. The artist exaggerated the size of the ruler compared with his steed.

---

let, a crown, and a bronze leopard's skull. These items, doubtless the regalia of a leader (see "Art and Leadership in Africa," above), whether secular or religious, are the earliest cast-metal objects known from regions south of the Sahara.

**EQUESTRIAN FLY WHISK** A lost-wax cast-bronze sculpture (FIG. 19-5), the earliest yet found in Africa, came from the same grave at Igbo Ukwu. It depicts an equestrian figure on a fly-whisk handle. The African artist made the handle using a casting method similar to that documented much earlier in Mesopotamia (FIG. 2-12)

and the Mediterranean (see "Hollow-Casting," Chapter 5, page 130). The sculpture's upper section comprises a figure seated on a horse, a symbol of power in many parts of West Africa, and the lower part is an elaborately embellished handle with beaded and threadlike patterns. As is common in African art, the sculptor intentionally represented the rider as much larger than his steed and also exaggerated the size of the man's head. The prominent facial stripes are another instance of scarification. Here the scars probably are marks of titled status. Similar examples of facial modification can still be found among Igbo-speaking peoples today.

## Ruler Portraiture at Ile-Ife

Just after the turn of the 19th century, the German anthropologist Leo Frobenius (1873–1938) "discovered" the sculpture of Ile-Ife in the Lower Niger River region. Because of the refinement and naturalism of the statues and heads he saw, Frobenius, who, like most Europeans, had preconceived notions about the "primitive" nature of African art, could not believe these sculptures were the work of local artists. Rather, he ascribed authorship to ancient Greece, where he knew many instances of similarly lifelike statuary. Other scholars traced the Ile-Ife works to ancient Egypt, along with patterns of sacred kingship they also believed originated several thousand miles away in the Nile Valley. But excavations in and around Ile-Ife, especially near the king's palace, have conclusively established that ancient Nigerian sculptors were indeed the artists who made the extraordinary sculptures in stone, terracotta, and copper alloys found at Ile-Ife. Radiocarbon dating places these works as early as the 11th or 12th century. Most of the finds date to what archaeologists have dubbed the "Pavement Era" of the 12th to 14th centuries, when the Yoruba paved several rectangular areas of their capital at Ile-Ife with bricklike ceramic sherds. These paved precincts were probably ritual centers where the Yoruba displayed the images of their deceased rulers on altars. The sculptures served the kings in ceremonies of installation, in funerals, and in annual festivals reaffirming the sacred power of the ruler and the allegiance of his people.

As is the case with the full-length portrait of the king illustrated here (FIG. 19-6) and the head (FIG. 19-6A) from the royal palace complex, the Ife sculptors usually modeled both heads and bodies in a strikingly naturalistic manner, apart from blemishes or signs of age, which they intentionally omitted. Thus, Ife style is lifelike but at the same time idealized. The artists portrayed most people as young adults in the prime of life and without any disfiguring warts or wrinkles. Some life-size heads, although still idealized, take naturalism so far as to give the impression of being individual portraits. This is especially true of a group of 19 heads cast in copper alloys that scholars are quite certain record the features of specific persons, although nearly all their names are lost. Several of the Ife heads have small holes above the forehead (FIG. 19-6A) and around the lips and jaw, and were found with black beads. The perforations and beads suggest the heads once had beaded crowns with veils, such as those known among Yoruba kings today, and perhaps human hair as well. Elaborate beadwork, a Yoruba royal prerogative, is also a salient feature of the Ife king's image in FIG. 19-6.

The hundreds of terracotta and copper-alloy heads, body parts and fragments, animals, and ritual vessels from Ile-Ife attest to a

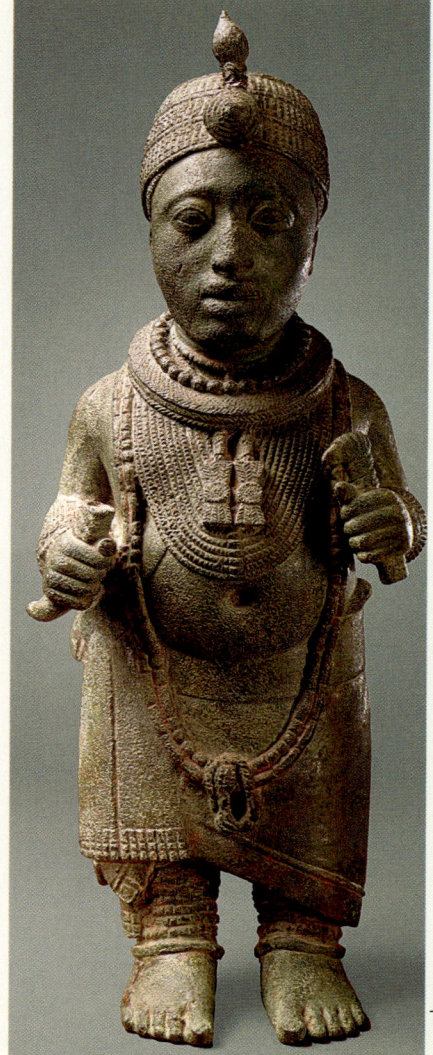

19-6 King, from Ita Yemoo (Ife), Nigeria, 11th to 12th centuries. Zinc-brass, 1′ 6½″ high. Museum of Ife Antiquities, Ife. ◼◀

Unlike most African sculptures, this royal figure has a naturalistically modeled torso and facial features approaching portraiture. The head, however, the locus of wisdom, is disproportionately large.

1 in.

remarkable period of African art during which sensitive, meticulously rendered idealized naturalism prevailed. To this day, works in this style stand in vivid contrast to the vast majority of African objects, which show the human figure in many different, quite strongly conventionalized styles. Diversity of style in the art of a continent as vast and ancient as Africa should surprise no one, however.

# 11TH TO 18TH CENTURIES

Although kings ruled some African population groups from an early date, the best evidence for royal arts in Africa comes from the several centuries between about 1000 and the beginning of European colonization in the 19th century.* During this period, Africans also constructed major houses of worship for the religions of Christianity and Islam, both of which originated in the Middle East but quickly gained adherents south of the Sahara.

*From this point on, all dates in this chapter are CE unless otherwise stated.

## Ile-Ife

Africans have long considered Ile-Ife, about 200 miles west of Igbo Ukwu in southwestern Nigeria, the cradle of Yoruba civilization, the place where the gods Oduduwa and Obatala created the earth and its peoples. Tradition also names Oduduwa the first *oni* (ruler) of Ile-Ife and the ancestor of all Yoruba kings.

**ILE-IFE KING** Ife artists often portrayed their sacred kings in sculpture. One of the most impressive examples is a statuette (FIG. **19-6**) of an Ife *oni* (king), cast in a zinc-brass alloy, datable to the 11th or 12th century. This and many similar representations

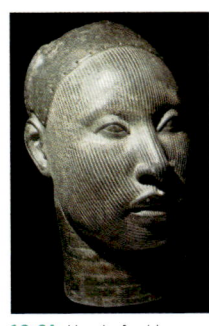

**19-6A** Head of a king, Ile-Ife, 12th to 13th centuries. ◼️◄

of Ife rulers—for example, a 12th- or 13th-century head (FIG. **19-6A**) found in the Wunmonije palace complex—are exceptional in Africa because of the artists' naturalism in recording facial features and fleshy anatomy (see "Ruler Portraiture at Ile-Ife," page 527). The naturalism does not extend to body proportions, however. The heads of the Ife rulers, for example, are disproportionately large compared with their bodies. For modern Yoruba, the head is the locus of wisdom, destiny, and the essence of being, and these ideas probably developed at least 800 years ago, accounting for the emphasis on the head in Ife statuary. In the statuette illustrated here, the artist also took great care to indicate the man's status as a sacred ruler by precisely reproducing the details of the king's heavily beaded costume, crown, and jewelry.

**TADA SEATED MAN** Usually thought to be the work of a sculptor from Ile-Ife but perhaps attesting to an independent artistic center is a statuette (FIG. **19-7**) of a seated figure found about 120 miles from the Yoruba capital on the banks of the Niger River near the village of Tada. Although the naturalistic rendition of the head and body of the Tada figure is typical of sculptures (FIGS. 19-6 and 19-6A) found at or near Ile-Ife, the relaxed seated posture is unique. The Tada figure also wears only a simple cap and a patterned fabric wrapped around the hips, and it is unlikely the sculpture portrays a king. The seated posture, however, suggests the figure, cast in several pieces, may have been placed on a throne. It is possible the Yoruba dressed the statue in royal regalia, now lost. Also distinguishing this sculpture from those of Ile-Ife is the more naturalistic proportional relationship between the head and body. The material—almost pure copper—also separates the Tada figure from contemporaneous Ile-Ife sculptures.

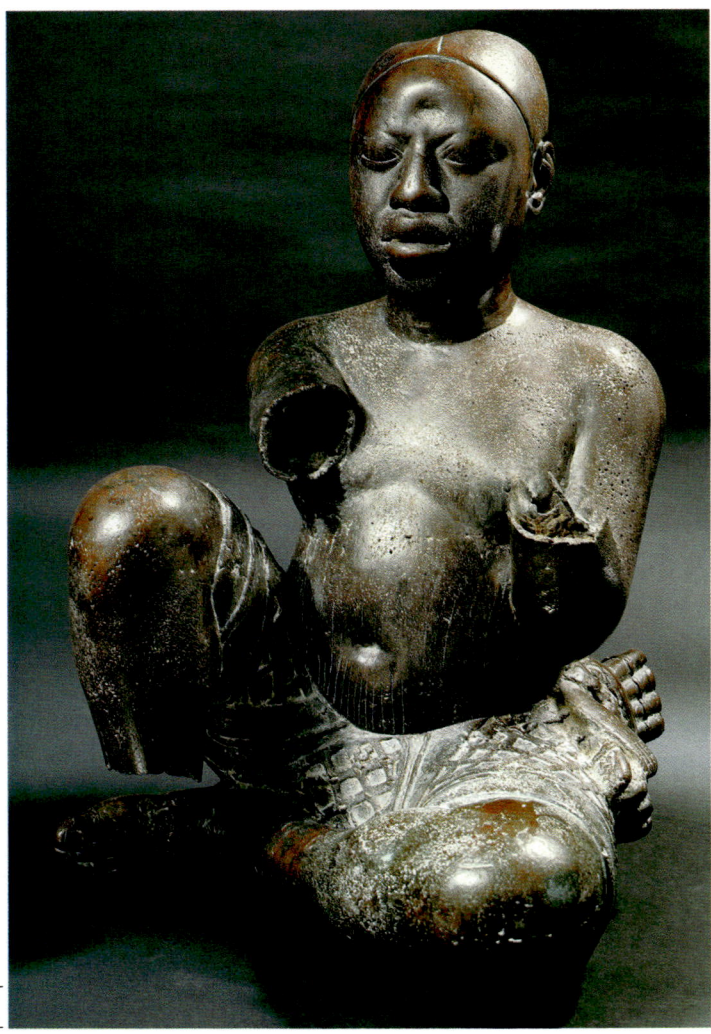

1 in.

**19-7** Seated man, from Tada, Nigeria, 13th to 14th centuries. Copper, 1′ 9⅛″ high. National Museum, Lagos.

Although stylistically related to the naturalistic zinc-brass sculptures of Ile-Ife, this unique copper seated figure found 120 miles away may be the product of a distinct regional workshop.

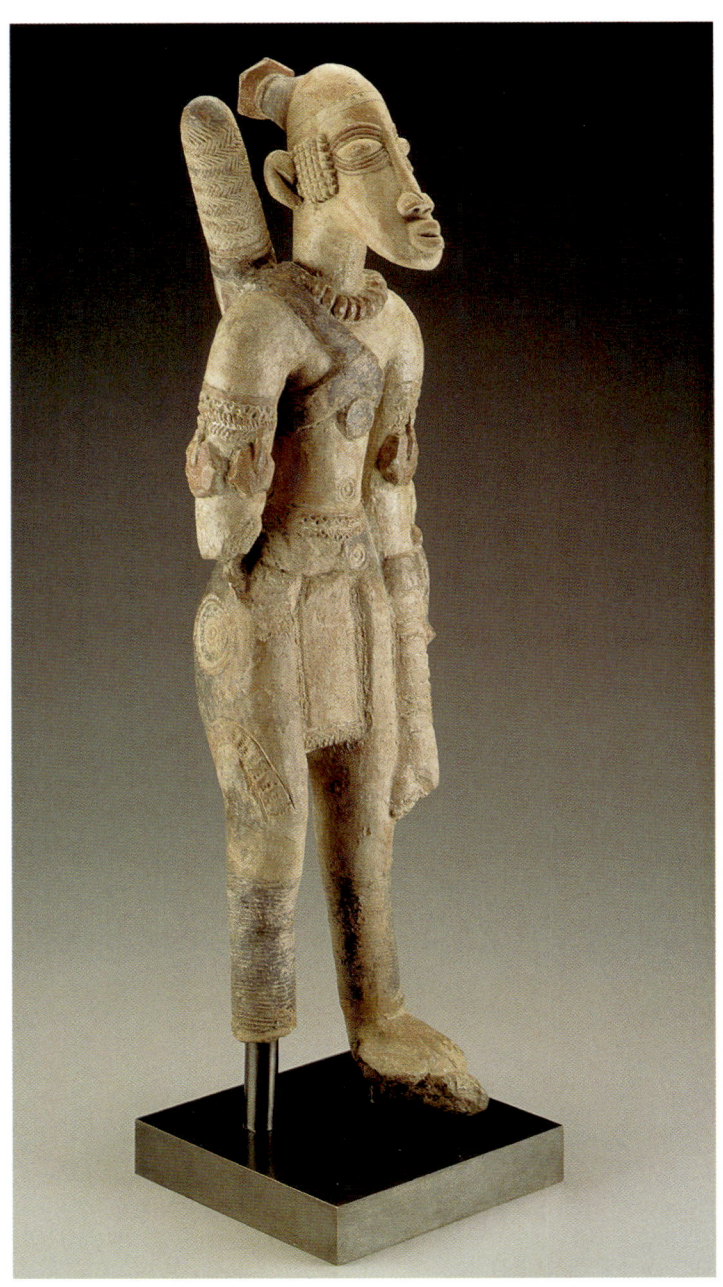

1 in.

**19-8** Archer, from Djenne, Mali, 13th to 15th centuries. Terracotta, 2′ ⅜″ high. National Museum of African Art, Washington, D.C.

Djenne terracottas present a striking contrast to statues from Ile-Ife. This archer is thin with tubular limbs and an elongated head featuring a prominent chin, bulging eyes, and large nose.

Discoveries such as this one are reminders of how incomplete is the record of early African art. Additional finds may one day establish whether Ile-Ife was a unique center for the production of naturalistic statuary during the first half of the second millennium or rather one of several stylistically related regional workshops.

## Djenne and Lalibela

The inland floodplain of the Niger River was for the African continent a kind of "fertile crescent" analogous to ancient Mesopotamia (see Chapter 2). By about 800, a walled town, Djenne in present-day Mali, had been built on high ground left dry during the flooding season. At this site, archaeologists have uncovered evidence of many specialist workshops of blacksmiths, sculptors, potters, and other artisans.

**DJENNE TERRACOTTAS** Hundreds of sensitively modeled terracotta sculptures, most dating to between 1100 and 1500, have been found at numerous sites in the Djenne region. Production tapered off sharply, however, with the arrival of Islam, whose adherents shunned figural art in religious contexts (see Chapter 10). Unfortunately, as is true of the Nok terracottas, the vast majority of the surviving Djenne sculptures came from illegal excavations, and all contextual information about them has been destroyed. The subject matter includes male and female couples, people with what some scholars interpret as lesions and swellings, and snake-entwined figures. The Djenne sculptors depicted the human figures in a variety of postures—seated, reclining, kneeling, standing, and on horseback. Some are warriors. Others wear elaborate jewelry, but many are without adornment or attributes. The range of subjects and postures is extraordinary at this date.

The terracotta figure illustrated here (FIG. **19-8**) dates to the 13th to 15th centuries and represents a Djenne warrior with a quiver of arrows on his back and knives strapped to his left arm. The proportions of the figure present a striking contrast to those from Ile-Ife and Tada (FIGS. 19-6 and 19-7)—thin and tall with tubular limbs and an elongated head with a prominent chin, bulging eyes, and large nose, characteristic features of the distinctive Djenne style.

**GREAT MOSQUE, DJENNE** One of the most ambitious examples of *adobe* (sun-dried mud-brick) architecture in the world is at Djenne's Great Mosque (FIG. **19-9**), first built in the 13th century and reconstructed in 1906–1907 after a fire destroyed the earlier building in 1830. The mosque has a large courtyard in front of a roofed prayer hall, emulating the plan of many of the oldest mosques known (see "The Mosque," Chapter 10, page 288), and the *qibla* wall faces Mecca, as in all mosques. The facade, however, is unlike any in the Middle East and features soaring adobe towers and vertical buttresses resembling engaged columns that produce a majestic rhythm. The many rows of protruding wooden beams further enliven the walls but also serve a practical function as perches for workers undertaking the essential recoating of sacred clay on the exterior that occurs during an annual festival.

**BETA GIORGHIS, LALIBELA** Many early African cultures maintained trade networks that sometimes extended well beyond the continent. The exchange of goods also brought an exchange of artistic ideas and forms. One striking example is Lalibela in the rugged highlands of present-day Ethiopia, where land travel is difficult. Christianity arrived in Ethiopia in the early fourth

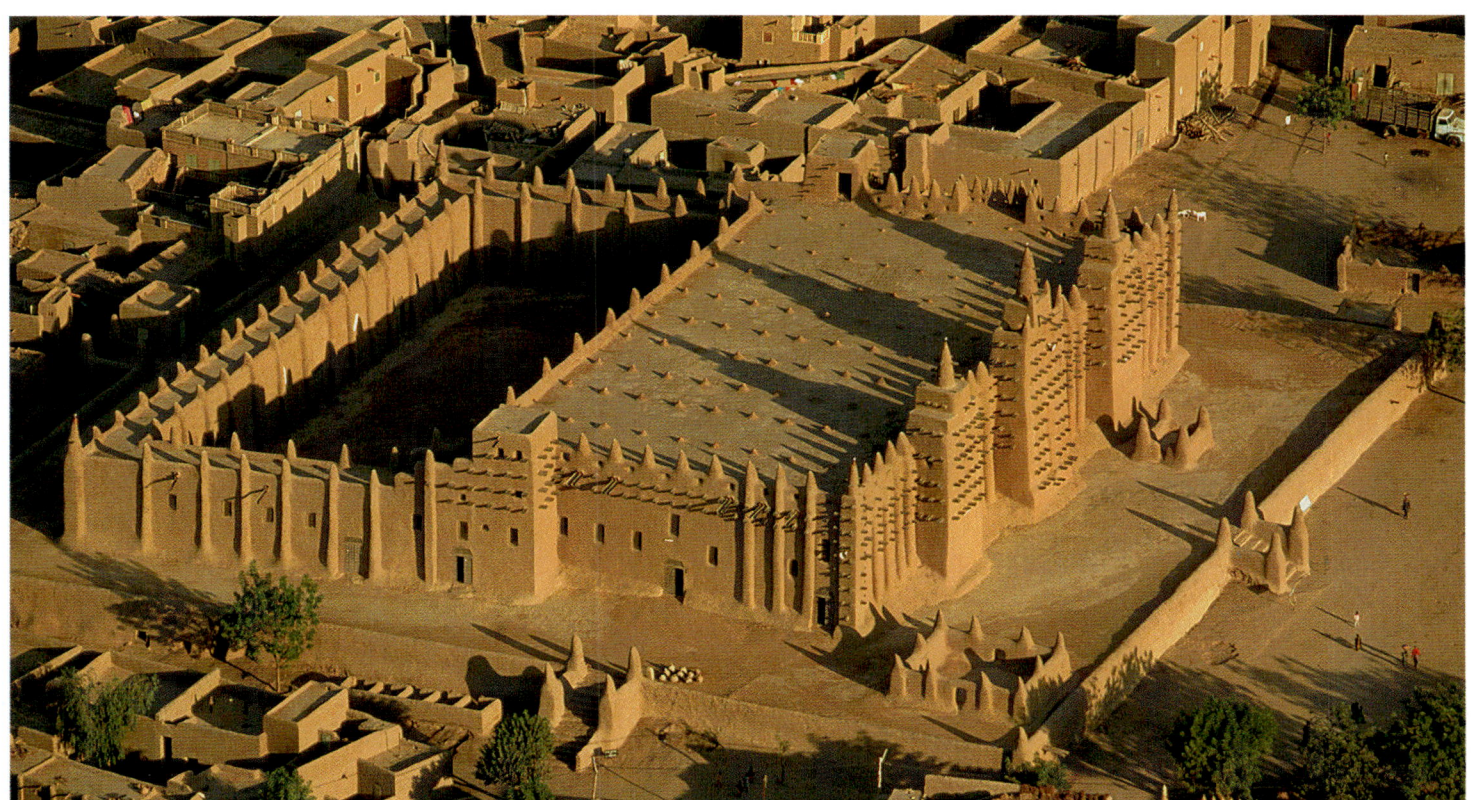

**19-9** Aerial view of the Great Mosque (looking northwest), Djenne, Mali, begun 13th century, rebuilt 1906–1907.

The Great Mosque at Djenne resembles Middle Eastern mosques in plan (large courtyard in front of a roofed prayer hall), but the construction materials—adobe and wood—are distinctly African.

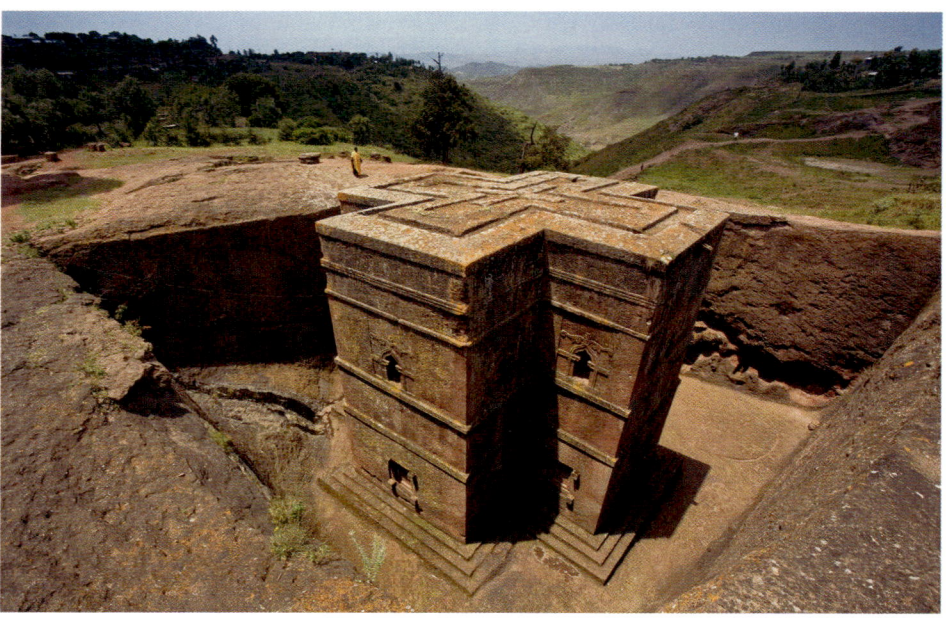

**19-10** Beta Giorghis (Church of Saint George), Lalibela, Ethiopia, ca. 1220.

The Christian king Lalibela sought to build a New Jerusalem in Ethiopia. The rock-cut church of Saint George emulates Byzantine models and has a Greek-cross plan and internal dome.

century, when the region was part of the indigenous Aksum Empire. In the early 13th century, King Lalibela (r. 1181–1211) of the Zagwe dynasty commissioned 11 churches to be cut from the bedrock at his capital of Roha (renamed Lalibela in his honor after his death). The king wished to transform his city into a "New Jerusalem," a pilgrimage site for Ethiopian Christians, which it still is today. Pilgrims can visit all 11 churches because they are linked by tunnels and walkways below ground level.

Not the largest but probably the latest and in many ways the most interesting of these rock-cut churches is Beta Giorghis (FIG. **19-10**), the Church of Saint George, which Lalibela's stonemasons cut out of the red tufa in the form of a Greek cross, revealing a familiarity with contemporaneous Byzantine architecture (see Chapter 9). About 43 feet tall, the roof of the structure has a 40-by-40-foot Greek cross sculpted in relief, underscoring the sacred shape of the church. Inside is a hollowed-out dome beneath the cruciform roof. Rock-cut buildings are rare but well documented in Egypt, Jordan, and India (see Chapters 3, 7, and 15). Some of the most complex designs are at Lalibela. Carving from the bedrock a complex building such as Beta Giorghis, with all its details, required careful planning and highly skilled labor. The volcanic bedrock is soft and easily worked, but the designer had to visualize all aspects of the complete structure before the work began because there was no possibility of revision or correction.

## Great Zimbabwe

Many of the earliest artworks found in Africa come from the southern part of the continent (for example, FIG. 1-3). The most famous southern African site is a complex of stone ruins at the large southeastern political center called Great Zimbabwe. First occupied in the 11th century, the site features walled enclosures and towers dating from about the late 13th to the middle of the 15th centuries. At that time, the Great Zimbabwe Empire had a wide trade network. Finds of beads and pottery from the Near East and China, along with copper and gold objects, underscore that

Great Zimbabwe was a prosperous trade center long before Europeans began their coastal voyaging in the late 15th century.

**GREAT ENCLOSURE** Most scholars agree Great Zimbabwe was a royal residence with special areas for the ruler, his wives, and nobles, including an open court for ceremonial gatherings (the royal hill complex). At the zenith of the empire's power, as many as 18,000 people may have lived in the surrounding area, with most of the commoners residing outside the enclosed complex reserved for royalty. Although the habitations themselves have not survived, the enclosures remain. They are unusual for their size and the excellence of their stonework. Some perimeter walls are 30 feet tall. One of these, known as the Great Enclosure (FIG. **19-11**), houses one large and several small conical, towerlike stone structures, which archaeologists have interpreted symbolically as masculine (large) and feminine (small) forms, but their precise significance is unknown. The form of the large tower suggests a granary. Grain bins were symbols of royal power and generosity, as the ruler received tribute in grain and dispensed it to the people in times of need.

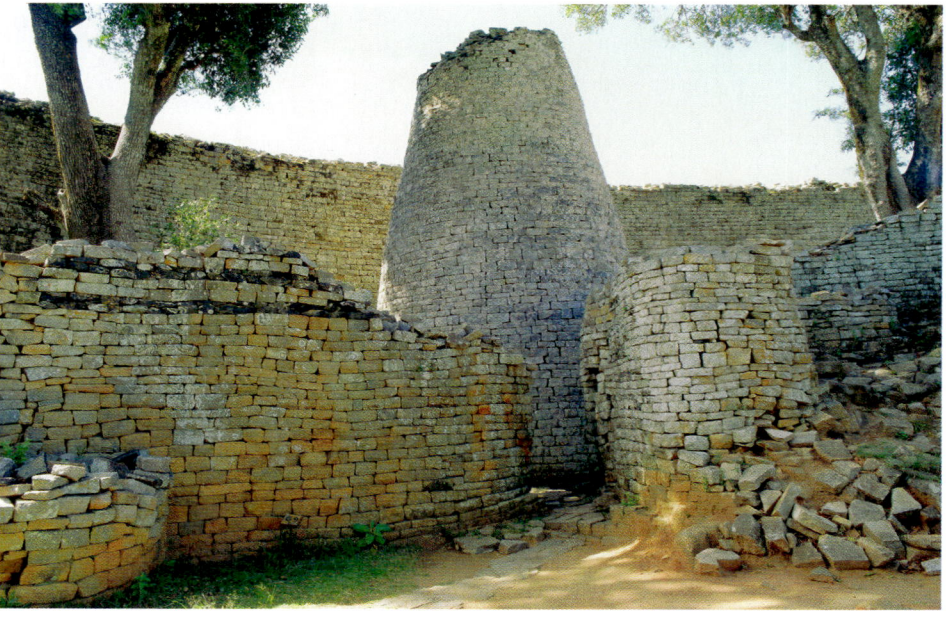

**19-11** Walls and tower, Great Enclosure, Great Zimbabwe, Zimbabwe, 14th century.

The Great Zimbabwe Empire in southern Africa had a trade network that extended to Mesopotamia and China. Thirty-foot-high stone walls and conical towers surrounded the royal residence.

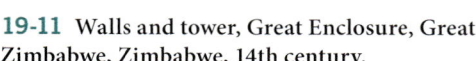

**SOAPSTONE MONOLITHS** Explorations at Great Zimbabwe have yielded eight soapstone *monoliths* (sculptures carved from a single block of stone). Seven came from the royal hill complex and probably stood in shrines to ancestors. The eighth monolith (FIG. 19-12), found in an area now considered the ancestral shrine of the ruler's first wife, stands several feet tall. Some have interpreted the bird at the top as symbolizing the king or his ancestors. (Ancestral spirits among the present-day Shona-speaking peoples of the area take the form of birds, especially eagles, believed to communicate between the sky and the earth.) The crocodile on the front of the monolith may represent the wife's elder male ancestors. The circles beneath the bird are called "eyes of the crocodile" in Shona and may symbolically represent elder female ancestors. The double- and single-chevron motifs may stand for young male and young female ancestors, respectively. The bird seems to be a bird of prey, such as an eagle, but this and other bird sculptures from the site have feet with five humanlike toes, rather than an eagle's three-toed talons. The Great Zimbabwe birds are of no known species, and some scholars have speculated the five-toed bird and the crocodile symbolize previous rulers who would have acted as messengers between the living and the dead, as well as between the sky and the earth.

# Benin

According to oral tradition, the first Benin king in the 13th century was the grandson of a Yoruba king of Ile-Ife. Benin reached its greatest power and geographical extent in the 16th century. The kingdom's vicissitudes and slow decline thereafter culminated in 1897, when the British burned and sacked the Benin palace and city. Benin City thrives today, however, and the palace, where the Benin king continues to live, has been partially rebuilt. In addition to expertly cast copper-alloy sculptures (FIGS. I-1 and 19-1), Benin artists have produced sophisticated artworks in ivory, wood, ceramic, and wrought iron. The hereditary oba and his court still use and dispense art objects as royal favors to title holders and other chiefs (see "Art and Leadership," page 526).

**QUEEN MOTHER IVORY** Among the masterworks of Benin art are the cast-brass altar (FIG. 19-1) honoring Oba Eresonyen, already discussed, and an extraordinary ivory head of a woman, now in the Metropolitan Museum of Art (FIG. **19-13**), which a Benin king almost certainly wore at his waist. A nearly identical pendant, fashioned from the same piece of ivory, is in the British Museum. Oba Esigie (r. ca. 1504–1550), under whom the Benin kingdom flourished and expanded with Portuguese aid, probably commissioned the pair.

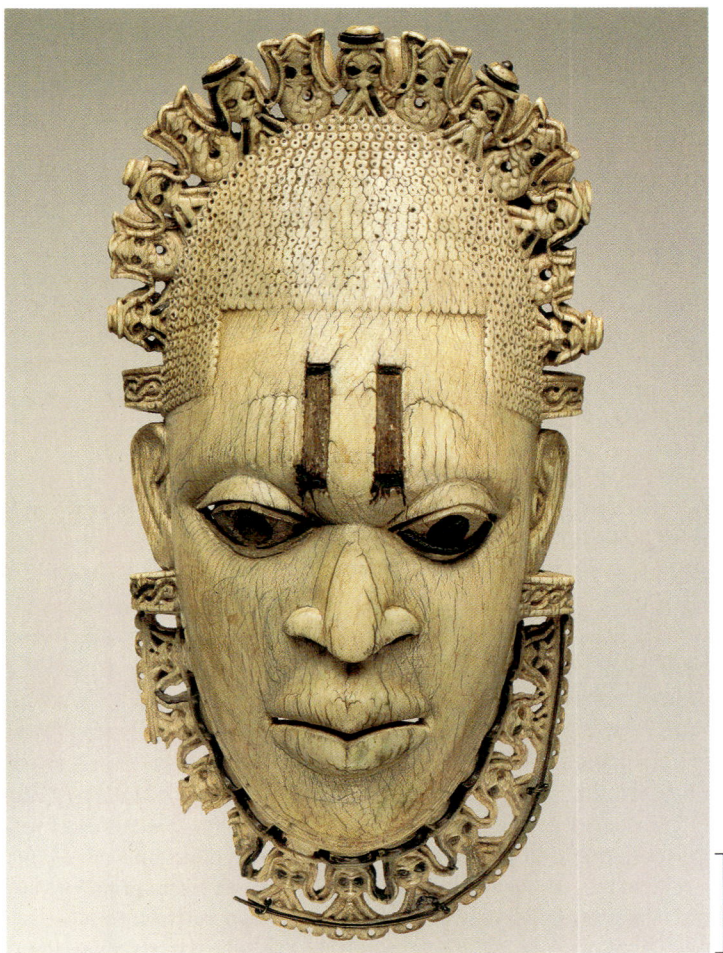

**19-12** Monolith with bird and crocodile, from Great Zimbabwe, Zimbabwe, 15th century. Soapstone, bird 1′ 2½″ high. Great Zimbabwe Site Museum, Great Zimbabwe.

This soapstone monolith stood in the ancestral shrine of a Great Zimbabwe ruler's wife. The bird and crocodile may symbolize previous rulers who act as messengers between the living and dead.

**19-13** Waist pendant of a queen mother, from Benin, Nigeria, ca. 1520. Ivory and iron, 9⅜″ high. Metropolitan Museum of Art, New York (Michael C. Rockefeller Memorial Collection, gift of Nelson A. Rockefeller, 1972).

This head probably portrays Idia, mother of Oba Esigie, who wore it on his waist. Above Idia's head are Portuguese heads and mudfish, symbols of trade and of the sea god Olokun.

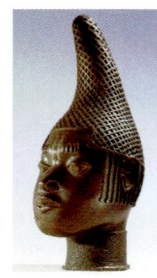

19-13A Head of a queen mother, Benin, ca. 1520–1550.

Esigie's mother, Idia, helped him in warfare, and in return he created for her the title of Queen Mother, *iy'oba,* and built her a separate palace and court. He and his successors also set up altars to their mothers on which they displayed bronze portraits (for example, FIG. 19-13A) of them.

The ivory pendant illustrated here (FIG. 19-13) most likely represents Idia and is remarkable for its sensitive naturalism. On its crown are alternating bearded Portuguese heads and mudfish, symbolic references respectively to Benin's trade and diplomatic relationships with the Portuguese and to Olokun, god of the sea, wealth, and creativity. The mudfish, equally at home on land and in the sea, also symbolized the dual human/divine aspect of the ruler. Another series of Portuguese heads adorns the lower part of the carving. In the late 15th and 16th centuries, the Benin people probably associated the Portuguese, with their large ships from across the sea, their powerful weapons, and their wealth in metals, cloth, and other goods, with Olokun, the deity they deemed responsible for abundance and prosperity.

## Sapi

Between 1490 and 1540, some peoples on the Atlantic coast of Africa in present-day Sierra Leone, whom the Portuguese collectively called the Sapi, created art not only for themselves but also for Portuguese explorers and traders, who brought the objects back to Europe.

**SAPI SALTCELLARS** The Portuguese commissions included delicate spoons, forks, and elaborate containers usually referred to as saltcellars, as well as boxes, hunting horns, and knife handles. Salt was a valuable commodity, used both as a flavoring and as a food preservative. Costly saltcellars were prestige items that graced the tables of the European elite (compare FIG. 22-52). Sapi sculptors meticulously carved the saltcellars from elephant tusk ivory, which was plentiful in those early days and was one of the coveted exports in early West and Central African trade with Europe. The ivories the Sapi produced for export are a fascinating hybrid art form. Characterized by refined detail and careful finish, they are the earliest examples of African tourist art.

Art historians have attributed the saltcellar shown here (FIG. **19-14**), almost 17 inches high, to the MASTER OF THE SYMBOLIC EXECUTION, one of the three major Sapi ivory carvers during the period. This saltcellar, which depicts an execution scene, is one of the artist's best pieces and the source of the assigned name. A kneeling figure with a shield in one hand holds an ax (restored) in the other hand over another seated figure about to lose his head. On the ground before the executioner, six severed heads grimly testify to the executioner's power. A double zigzag line separates the lid of the globular container from the rest of the vessel. This vessel rests in turn on a circular platform held up by slender rods adorned with crocodile images. Two male and two female figures sit between these rods, grasping them. The men wear European-style pants and have long, straight hair. The women wear skirts, and the elaborate raised patterns on their upper chests surely represent decorative scars.

The European components of this saltcellar are the overall design of a spherical container on a pedestal and some of the geometric patterning on the base and the sphere, as well as certain elements of dress, such as the shirts and hats. Distinctly African are the style of the human heads and figures and their proportions, the latter skewed here to emphasize the head, as so often seen in African art. Identical large noses with flaring nostrils, as well as the conventions for rendering eyes and lips, characterize Sapi stone figures

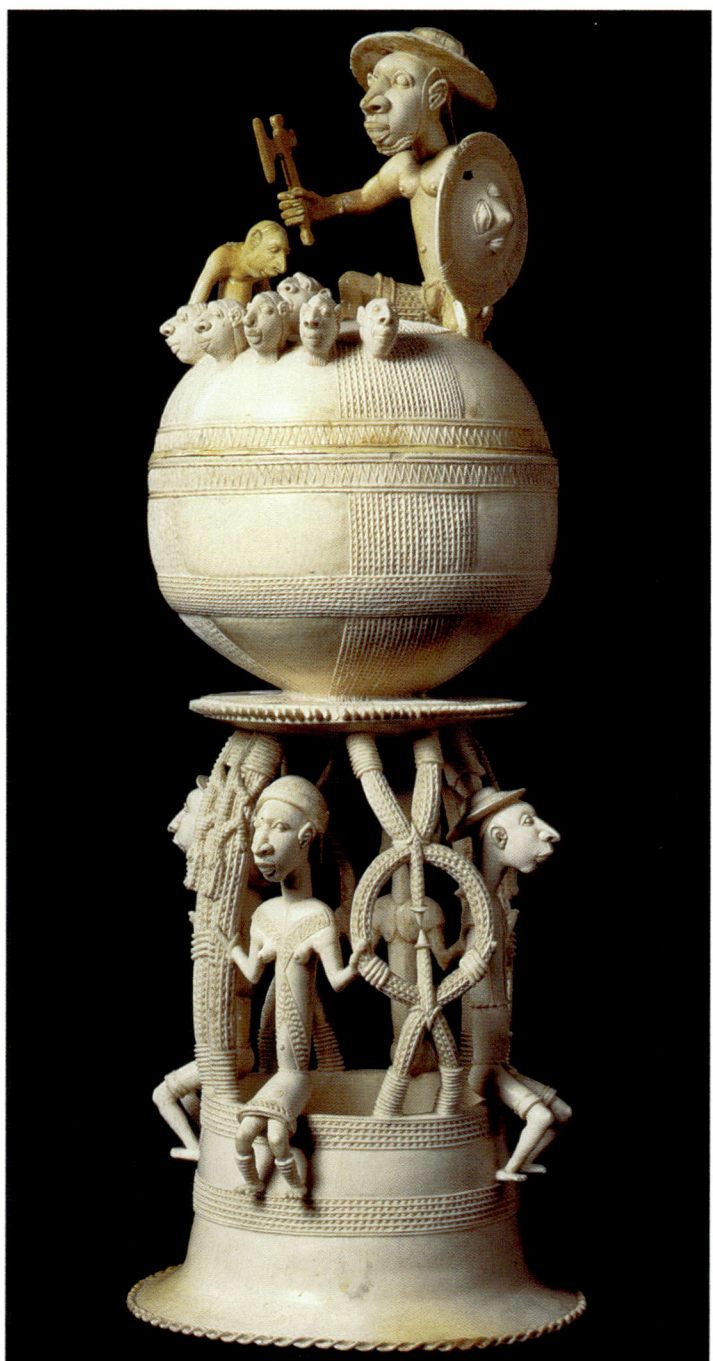

1 in.

19-14 MASTER OF THE SYMBOLIC EXECUTION, saltcellar, Sapi-Portuguese, from Sierra Leone, ca. 1490–1540. Ivory, 1′ 4⅞″ high. Museo Nazionale Preistorico e Etnografico Luigi Pigorini, Rome.

The Sapi exported saltcellars combining African and Portuguese traits. This one represents an execution scene with an African-featured man wearing European pants seated among severed heads.

from the same region and period. Scholars do not know whether it was the African carver or the European patron who specified the subject matter and the configurations of various parts, but the Sapi works testify to a fruitful artistic interaction between Africans and Europeans during the early 16th century.

The impact of European art became much more pronounced in the late 19th and especially the 20th centuries. These developments and the continuing vitality of the native arts in Africa are examined in Chapter 37.

# AFRICA BEFORE 1800

## PREHISTORY, CA. 25,000–1000 BCE

❚ Humankind apparently originated in Africa, and some of the oldest known artworks come from the Apollo 11 Cave (FIG. 1-3) in southwestern Africa. Most African rock art, however, is no earlier than 6000 BCE. Some of the oldest examples are at Tassili n'Ajjer in northwestern Africa.

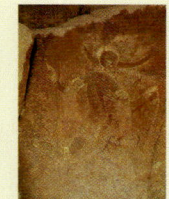

Running woman, Tassili n'Ajjer, ca. 6000–4000 BCE

## EARLY CULTURES, CA. 1000 BCE–1000 CE

❚ The Nok culture of central Nigeria produced the oldest African examples of sculpture in the round between 500 BCE and 200 CE. The pierced eyes, noses, and mouths helped equalize the heat during the firing process.

❚ The earliest examples of African bronze-casting using the lost-wax method are the 9th- or 10th-century CE sculptures found at Igbo Ukwu (Nigeria).

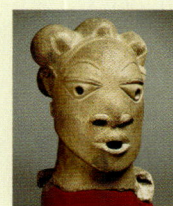

Nok terracotta head, ca. 500 BCE–200 CE

## 11TH TO 15TH CENTURIES

❚ The sculptors of Ile-Ife (Nigeria) fashioned images of their kings in an unusually naturalistic style during the 11th and 12th centuries, but the heads of the figures are disproportionately large, as in most African artworks.

❚ The terracotta sculptures of Djenne (Mali), datable about 1100–1500, encompass an extraordinary variety of subjects, including warriors and equestrian figures. They display a distinctive style featuring tubular limbs and elongated heads.

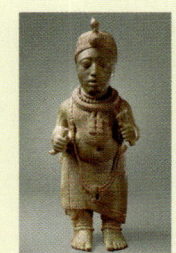

Ife king, 11th to 12th centuries

❚ In northern Africa, converts to Islam and Christianity constructed major religious shrines that emulated foreign models but employed different building materials and methods, for example, the adobe Great Mosque at Djenne and the rock-cut church of Beta Giorghis (Saint George) at Lalibela (Ethiopia).

❚ In southern Africa, the Great Zimbabwe Empire conducted prosperous trade with Mesopotamia and China long before the first contact with Europeans. Impressive stone walls and towers enclosed the royal palace complex.

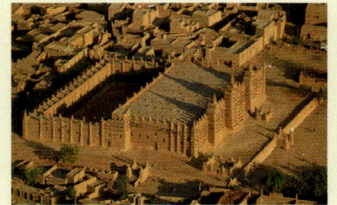

Great Mosque, Djenne, 13th century

## 16TH TO 18TH CENTURIES

❚ The Benin kingdom in the Lower Niger region, probably founded in the 13th century, reached its zenith in the 16th century. Benin sculptors excelled in ivory carving and bronze-casting, producing artworks that glorified the royal family.

❚ An early example of the interaction between African artists and European patrons is the series of Sapi ivory saltcellars from Sierra Leone datable between 1490 and 1540.

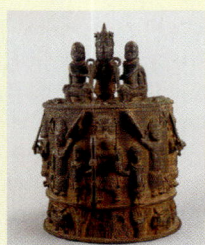

Benin altar to the hand, ca. 1735–1750

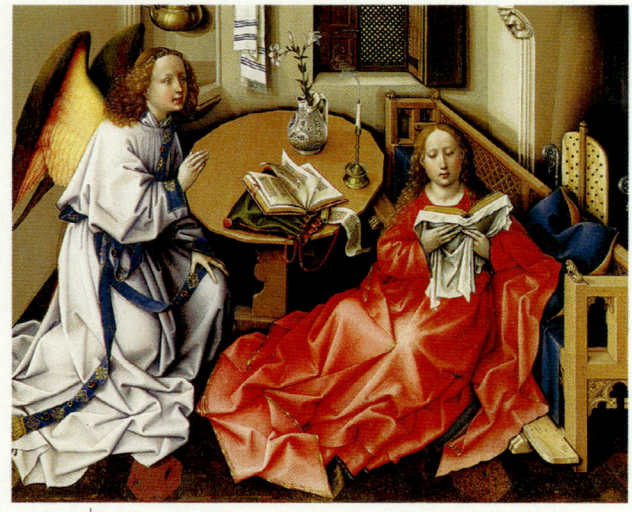

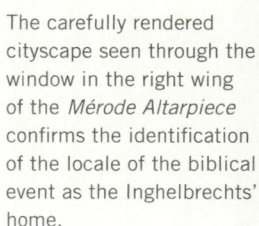

The carefully rendered cityscape seen through the window in the right wing of the *Mérode Altarpiece* confirms the identification of the locale of the biblical event as the Inghelbrechts' home.

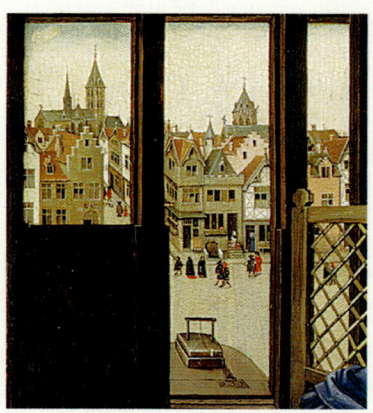

Campin was the leading painter of Tournai. In the *Mérode Altarpiece*, he set *Annunciation* in a Flemish merchant's home in which the objects represented have symbolic significance.

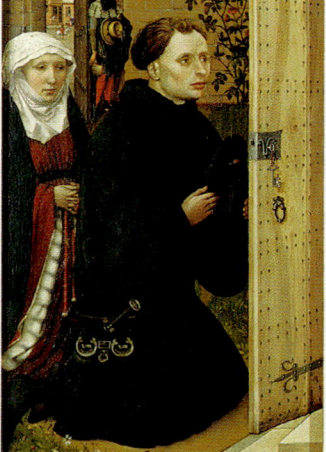

In the altarpiece's left wing, Campin depicted his patrons, Peter Inghelbrecht and Margarete Scrynmakers, as kneeling witnesses to the announcement of the Virgin's miraculous pregnancy.

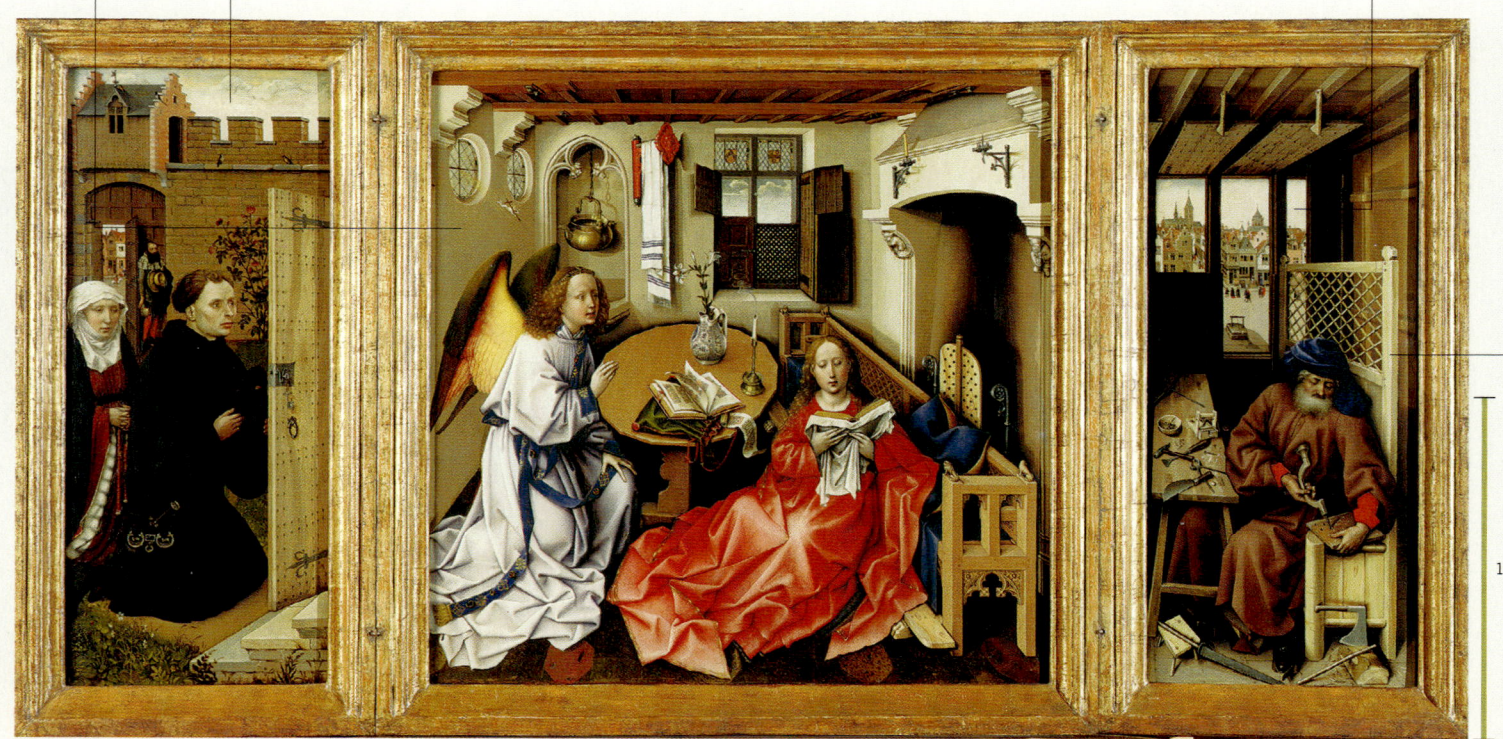

1 ft.

**20-1** ROBERT CAMPIN (MASTER OF FLÉMALLE), *Mérode Altarpiece* (open), ca. 1425–1428. Oil on wood, center panel 2′ 1$\frac{3}{8}$″ × 2′ $\frac{7}{8}$″, each wing 2′ 1$\frac{3}{8}$″ × 10$\frac{7}{8}$″. Metropolitan Museum of Art, New York (The Cloisters Collection, 1956). ◼◀

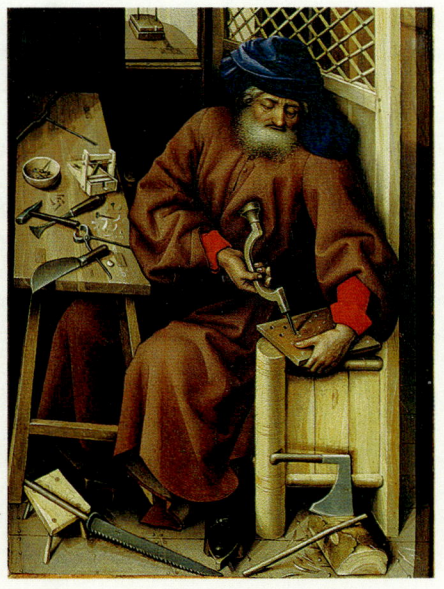

Joseph, in his workshop and unaware of the angel's arrival, has constructed two mousetraps, symbols of the theological concept that Christ is bait set in the trap of the world to catch the Devil.

# LATE MEDIEVAL AND EARLY RENAISSANCE NORTHERN EUROPE

## THE VIRGIN IN A FLEMISH HOME

In 15th-century Flanders—a region corresponding to what is today Belgium, the Netherlands, Luxembourg, and part of northern France—lay patrons far outnumbered the clergy in the commissioning of religious artworks. Especially popular were small altarpieces for household prayer, such as the *Mérode Altarpiece* (FIG. **20-1**), the most famous work by the "MASTER OF FLÉMALLE," whom many scholars identify as ROBERT CAMPIN (ca. 1378–1444), the leading painter of Tournai. Perhaps the most striking feature of these private devotional images is the integration of religious and secular concerns. For example, artists often presented biblical scenes as taking place in a Flemish home. Religion was such an integral part of Flemish life that separating the sacred from the secular was almost impossible—and undesirable. Moreover, the presentation in religious art of familiar settings and objects no doubt strengthened the direct bond the patron or viewer felt with biblical figures.

The *Annunciation* theme, as prophesied in Isaiah 7:14, occupies the Mérode triptych's central panel. The archangel Gabriel approaches Mary, who sits reading inside a well-kept home. The view through the window in the right wing and the depicted accessories, furniture, and utensils confirm the locale as Flanders. However, the objects represented are not merely decorative. They also function as symbols. The book, extinguished candle, and lilies on the table, the copper basin in the corner niche, the towels, fire screen, and bench all symbolize the Virgin's purity and her divine mission.

In the right panel, Joseph, apparently unaware of the angel's arrival, has constructed two mousetraps, symbolic of the theological concept that Christ is bait set in the trap of the world to catch the Devil. The ax, saw, and rod Campin painted in the foreground of Joseph's workshop not only are tools of the carpenter's trade but also are mentioned in Isaiah 10:15. In the left panel, the closed garden is symbolic of Mary's purity, and the flowers Campin included relate to Mary's virtues, especially humility.

The altarpiece's donor, Peter Inghelbrecht, a wealthy merchant, and his wife, Margarete Scrynmakers, kneel in the garden and witness the momentous event through an open door. *Donor portraits*—portraits of the individual(s) who commissioned (or "donated") the work—became very popular in the 15th century. In this instance, in addition to asking to be represented in their altarpiece, the Inghelbrechts probably specified the subject. Inghelbrecht means "angel bringer," a reference to the *Annunciation* theme of the central panel. Scrynmakers means "cabinet- or shrine-makers," referring to the workshop scene in the right panel.

# NORTHERN EUROPE IN THE 15TH CENTURY

As the 15th century opened, Rome and Avignon were still the official seats of two competing popes (see "The Great Schism," Chapter 14, page 404), and the Hundred Years' War (1337–1453) between France and England still raged. The general European movement toward centralized royal governments, begun in the 12th century, continued apace, but the corresponding waning of *feudalism* brought social turmoil. Nonetheless, despite widespread conflict and unrest, a new economic system emerged—the early stage of European capitalism. In response to the financial requirements of trade, new credit and exchange systems created an economic network of enterprising European cities. Trade in money accompanied trade in commodities, and the former financed industry. Both were in the hands of international trading companies, such as those of Jacques Coeur in Bourges (see Chapter 13) and the Medici in Florence (see Chapter 21). In 1460, Flemish entrepreneurs established the first international commercial stock exchange in Antwerp. In fact, the French word for stock market (*bourse*) comes from the name of the van der Beurse family of Bruges, the wealthiest city in 15th-century Flanders.

Art also thrived in northern Europe during this time under royal, ducal, church, and private patronage. Two developments in particular were of special significance: the adoption of oil-based pigment as the leading medium for painting, and the blossoming of printmaking as a major art form, which followed the invention of moveable type. These new media had a dramatic influence on artistic production worldwide.

## BURGUNDY AND FLANDERS

In the 15th century, Flanders (MAP **20-1**) was not an independent state but a region under the control of the duke of Burgundy, the ruler of the fertile east-central region of France still famous for its

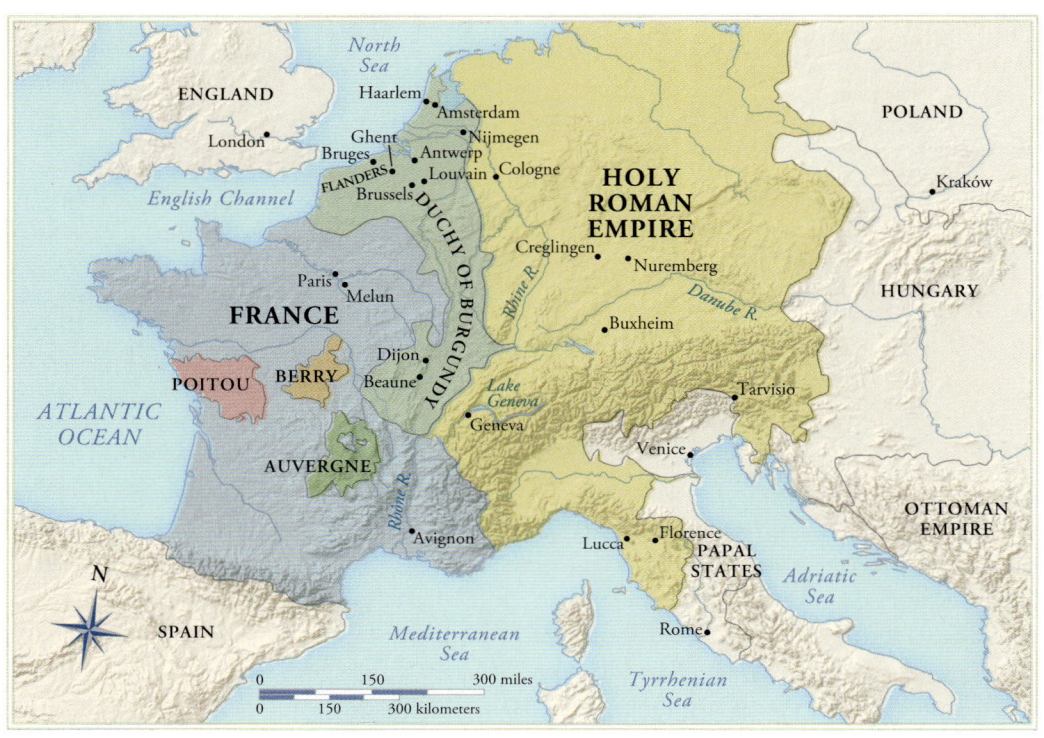

MAP 20-1  France, the duchy of Burgundy, and the Holy Roman Empire in 1477.

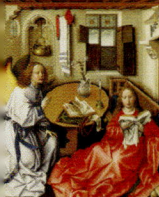

# LATE MEDIEVAL AND EARLY RENAISSANCE NORTHERN EUROPE

| 1385 | 1425 | 1450 | 1475 | 1500 |
|---|---|---|---|---|
| ▪ Claus Sluter carves life-size statues of biblical figures with portraitlike features for Philip the Bold, duke of Burgundy<br><br>▪ The Limbourg brothers expand the illusionistic capabilities of manuscript illumination for Jean, duke of Berry | ▪ Robert Campin, Jan van Eyck, and Rogier van der Weyden popularize the use of oil paints in Flanders to record the exact surface appearance of objects, fabrics, faces, and landscapes<br><br>▪ Flemish painters establish portraiture as a major art form<br><br>▪ German graphic artists pioneer woodcut printing, making art affordable to the masses | ▪ The second generation of Flemish master painters—Petrus Christus, Dirk Bouts, and Hugo van der Goes—continue to use oil paints for altarpieces featuring naturalistic representations of religious themes<br><br>▪ In Germany, Johannes Gutenberg invents moveable type and prints the first Bibles on a letterpress | ▪ In Flanders, Hans Memling specializes in portraiture and paintings of the Madonna and Child<br><br>▪ The Late Gothic style lingers in Germany in the large wooden altarpieces carved by Veit Stoss and Tilman Riemenschneider<br><br>▪ Martin Schongauer becomes the first northern European master of metal engraving | |

wines. Duke Philip the Bold (r. 1363–1404) was one of four sons of King John II (r. 1350–1364) of France. In 1369, Philip married Margaret de Mâle, the daughter of the count of Flanders, and acquired territory in the Netherlands. Thereafter, the major source of Burgundian wealth was Bruges, the city that made Burgundy a dangerous rival of France, which then, as in the Gothic age (see Chapter 13), was a smaller kingdom geographically than the modern nation-state. Bruges initially derived its wealth from the wool trade but soon expanded into banking, becoming the financial clearinghouse for all of northern Europe. Indeed, Bruges so dominated Flanders that the duke of Burgundy eventually chose to make the city his capital and moved his court there from Dijon. Due to the expanded territory and the prosperity of the duchy of Burgundy, Philip the Bold and his successors were probably the most powerful northern European rulers during the first three quarters of the 15th century. Although members of the French royal family, they usually supported England (on which they relied for the raw materials used in their wool industry) during the Hundred Years' War and, at times, controlled much of northern France, including Paris, the seat of the French monarchy. At the height of Burgundian power, the reigning duke's lands stretched from the Rhône River to the North Sea.

## Chartreuse de Champmol

The dukes of Burgundy were great patrons of the arts. They fully appreciated that artworks could support their dynastic and political goals as well as adorn their castles and townhouses. Philip the Bold's grandest artistic enterprise was the building of the Chartreuse de Champmol, near Dijon. A *chartreuse* ("charter house" in English) is a Carthusian *monastery*. The Carthusian order, founded by Saint Bruno in the late 11th century at Chartreuse, near Grenoble in southeastern France, consisted of monks who devoted their lives to solitary living and prayer. Unlike monastic orders that earned income from farming and other work, the Carthusians generated no revenues. Philip's generous endowment at Champmol was therefore the sole funding for an ambitious artistic program inspired by Saint-Denis, the royal abbey of France and burial site of the French kings (FIGS. 13-2 to 13-3A). The architect the duke chose was DROUET DE DAMMARTIN, who had worked for Philip's brother, King Charles V (r. 1364–1380), on the Louvre (FIG. 20-16), the French royal palace in Paris. Philip intended the Dijon chartreuse to become a ducal *mausoleum* and serve both as a means of securing salvation in perpetuity for the Burgundian dukes (the monks prayed continuously for the souls of the ducal family) and as a dynastic symbol of Burgundian power.

**CLAUS SLUTER** In 1389, Philip the Bold placed the Haarlem (Netherlands) sculptor CLAUS SLUTER (active ca. 1380–1406) in charge of the sculptural program (FIGS. 20-2 and 20-2A) for the Chartreuse de Champmol. For the portal (FIG. 20-2A) of the monastery's chapel, Sluter's workshop produced statues of the duke and his wife kneeling before the Virgin and Child. For the cloister, Sluter designed a large sculptural fountain located in a well (FIG. 20-2). The well served as a water source for the monastery, but water

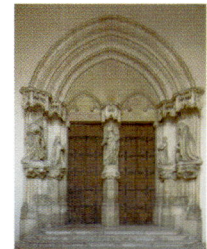

20-2A SLUTER, Chartreuse de Champmol portal, 1385–1393. ◼️

probably did not spout from the fountain because the Carthusian commitment to silence and prayer would have precluded anything that produced sound.

Sluter's *Well of Moses* features statues of Moses and five other prophets (David, Daniel, Isaiah, Jeremiah, and Zachariah) surrounding a base that once supported a 25-foot-tall group of Christ on the cross, the Virgin Mary, John the Evangelist, and Mary Magdalene. The Carthusians called the

20-2 CLAUS SLUTER, *Well of Moses,* Chartreuse de Champmol, Dijon, France, 1395–1406. Limestone, painted and gilded by JEAN MALOUEL, Moses 6′ high. ◼️

The *Well of Moses,* a symbolic fountain of life made for the duke of Burgundy, originally supported a *Crucifixion* group. Sluter's figures recall French Gothic jamb statues but are far more realistic.

1 ft.

*Well of Moses* a *fons vitae,* a fountain of everlasting life. The blood of the crucified Christ symbolically flowed down over the grieving angels and Old Testament prophets, spilling into the well below, washing over Christ's prophetic predecessors and redeeming anyone who would drink water from the well. Whereas the models for the Dijon chapel statues were the sculptured portals of French Gothic cathedrals, the inspiration for the *Well of Moses* may have come in part from contemporaneous *mystery plays* in which actors portraying prophets frequently delivered commentaries on events in Christ's life.

The six figures are much more realistically rendered than Gothic jamb statues (FIGS. 13-18 and 13-18A), and the prophets have almost portraitlike features and distinct individual personalities and costumes. David is an elegantly garbed Gothic king, Moses an elderly horned prophet (compare FIG. 12-35) with a waist-length beard. Sluter's intense observation of natural appearance provided him with the information necessary to sculpt the prophets in minute detail. Heavy draperies with voluminous folds swathe the life-size figures. The artist succeeded in making their difficult, complex surfaces seem remarkably naturalistic. He enhanced this effect by skillfully differentiating textures, from coarse drapery to smooth flesh and silky hair. Originally, paint, much of which has flaked off, further augmented the naturalism of the figures. (The painter was JEAN MALOUEL [ca. 1365–1415], another Netherlandish master.) This fascination with the specific and tangible in the visible world became one of the chief characteristics of 15th-century Flemish art.

**MELCHIOR BROEDERLAM** Philip the Bold also commissioned a major altarpiece for the main altar in the chapel of the Chartreuse. A collaborative project between two Flemish artists, this altarpiece consisted of a large sculptured shrine by Jacques de Baerze (active ca. 1384–1399) and a pair of painted exterior panels (FIG. **20-3**) by MELCHIOR BROEDERLAM (active ca. 1387–1409).

Altarpieces were a major art form north of the Alps in the late 14th and 15th centuries. From their position behind the altar, they served as backdrops for the Mass. The Mass represents a ritual celebration of the Holy *Eucharist.* At the Last Supper, Christ commanded his apostles to repeat in memory of him the communion credo that he is tendering them his body to eat and his blood to drink, as reenacted in the Eucharist (see "The Life of Jesus in Art," Chapter 8, pages 240–241, or xxx–xxxi in Volume II and Book D). This act serves as the nucleus of the Mass, which involves this reenactment as well as prayer and contemplation of the Word of God. Because the Mass involves not only a memorial rite but complex Christian doctrinal tenets as well, art has traditionally played an important role in giving visual form to these often complex theological concepts for the Christian faithful. Like sculpted medieval church *tympana,* these altarpieces had a didactic role, especially for the illiterate. They also reinforced Church doctrines for viewers and stimulated devotion.

Given their function as backdrops to the Mass, it is not surprising many altarpieces depict scenes directly related to Christ's sacrifice. The Champmol altarpiece, or *retable,* for example, features sculpted passion scenes on the interior. These public altarpieces most often took the form of *polyptychs*—hinged multipaneled paintings or multiple carved relief panels. The hinges enabled the clergy to close the polyptych's side wings over the central panel(s). Artists decorated both the exterior and interior of the altarpieces. This multi-image format provided the opportunity to construct narratives through a sequence of images, somewhat as in manuscript illustration. Although concrete information is lacking about

when the clergy opened and closed these altarpieces, the wings probably remained closed on regular days and open on Sundays and feast days. On this schedule, viewers could have seen both the interior and exterior—diverse imagery at various times according to the liturgical calendar.

The painted wings (FIG. 20-3) of the *Retable de Champmol* depict *Annunciation* and *Visitation* on the left panel and *Presentation into the Temple* and *Flight into Egypt* on the right panel. Dealing with Christ's birth and infancy, Broederlam's painted images on the altarpiece's exterior set the stage for de Baerze's interior sculpted passion scenes (not illustrated). The exterior panels are an unusual amalgam of different styles, locales, and religious symbolism. The two paintings include both landscape and interior scenes. Broederlam depicted the buildings in both Romanesque and Gothic styles (see Chapters 12 and 13). Scholars have suggested the juxtaposition of different architectural styles in the left panel is symbolic. The *rotunda* (round building, usually with a dome) refers to the Old Testament, whereas the Gothic porch relates to the New Testament. In the right panel, a statue of a Greco-Roman god falls from the top of a column as the holy family approaches. These and other details symbolically announce the coming of the new order under Christ. Stylistically, Broederlam's panels are a mixture of three-dimensional rendition of the landscape and buildings with a solid gold background and flat golden halos for the holy figures, regardless of the positions of their heads. Despite these lingering medieval pictorial conventions, the altarpiece is an early example of many of the artistic developments that preoccupied European artists throughout the 15th century, especially the illusionistic depiction of three-dimensional objects and the naturalistic representation of landscape.

## Jan van Eyck

The *Retable de Champmol* also foreshadowed another significant development in 15th-century art—the widespread adoption of *oil paints* (see "Tempera and Oil Painting," page 539). Oil paints facilitated the exactitude in rendering details so characteristic of northern European painting. Although the Italian biographer Giorgio Vasari (1511–1574) and other 16th-century commentators credited Jan van Eyck (FIGS. 20-4 to 20-7) with the invention of oil painting, recent evidence has revealed oil paints had been known for some time, well before Melchior Broederlam used oils for Philip the Bold's Dijon altarpiece and Robert Campin painted the *Mérode Altarpiece* (FIG. 20-1) for Peter Inghelbrecht. Flemish painters built up their pictures by superimposing translucent paint layers on a layer of underpainting, which in turn had been built up from a carefully planned drawing made on a panel prepared with a white ground. With the oil medium, artists could create richer colors than previously possible, giving their paintings an intense tonality, the illusion of glowing light, and enamel-like surfaces. These traits differed significantly from the high-keyed color, sharp light, and rather *matte* (dull) surface of *tempera.* The brilliant and versatile oil medium suited perfectly the formal intentions of the generation of Flemish painters after Broederlam, including Campin (FIG. 20-1) and van Eyck, who aimed for sharply focused clarity of detail in their representation of objects ranging in scale from large to almost invisible.

***GHENT ALTARPIECE*** The first Netherlandish painter to achieve international fame was JAN VAN EYCK (ca. 1390–1441), who in 1425 became the court painter of Philip the Good, duke of Burgundy (r. 1419–1467). In 1432, he moved his studio to Bruges, where the duke maintained his official residence. That same

## Tempera and Oil Painting

The generic words *paint* and *pigment* encompass a wide range of substances artists have used through the ages. Fresco aside (see "Fresco Painting," Chapter 14, page 408), during the 14th century, egg *tempera* was the material of choice for most painters, both in Italy and northern Europe. Tempera consists of egg combined with a wet paste of ground pigment. In his influential guidebook *Il libro dell'arte* (*The Artist's Handbook,* 1437), Cennino Cennini (ca. 1370–ca. 1440) noted that artists mixed only the egg yolk with the ground pigment, but analyses of paintings from this period have revealed some artists chose to use the entire egg. Images painted with tempera have a velvety sheen. Artists usually applied tempera to the painting surface with a light touch because thick application of the pigment mixture results in premature cracking and flaking.

Some artists used oil paints as far back as the eighth century, but not until the early 1400s did oil painting become widespread. Melchior Broederlam (FIG. 20-3) and other Flemish artists were among the first to employ oils extensively (often mixing them with tempera), and Italian painters quickly followed suit. The discovery of better drying components in the early 15th century enhanced the setting capabilities of oils. Rather than apply these oils in the light, flecked brushstrokes tempera encouraged, artists laid down the oils in transparent layers, or *glazes,* over opaque or semiopaque underlayers. In this manner, painters could build up deep tones through repeated glazing. Unlike works in tempera, whose surface dries quickly due to water evaporation, oils dry more uniformly and slowly, giving the artist time to rework areas. This flexibility must have been particularly appealing to artists who worked very deliberately, such as the Flemish masters discussed in this chapter, as well as the Italian Leonardo da Vinci (see Chapter 22). Leonardo also preferred oil paint because its gradual drying process and consistency enabled him to blend the pigments, thereby creating the impressive *sfumato* (smoky) effect that contributed to his fame.

Both tempera and oils can be applied to various surfaces. Through the early 16th century, wood panels served as the foundation for most paintings. Italians painted on poplar. Northern European artists used oak, lime, beech, chestnut, cherry, pine, and silver fir. Availability of these timbers determined the choice of wood. Linen canvas became increasingly popular in the late 16th century. Although evidence suggests artists did not intend permanency for their early images on canvas, the material proved particularly useful in areas such as Venice where high humidity warped wood panels and made fresco unfeasible. Further, until artists began to use wooden bars to stretch the canvas to form a taut surface, canvas paintings were more portable than wood panels.

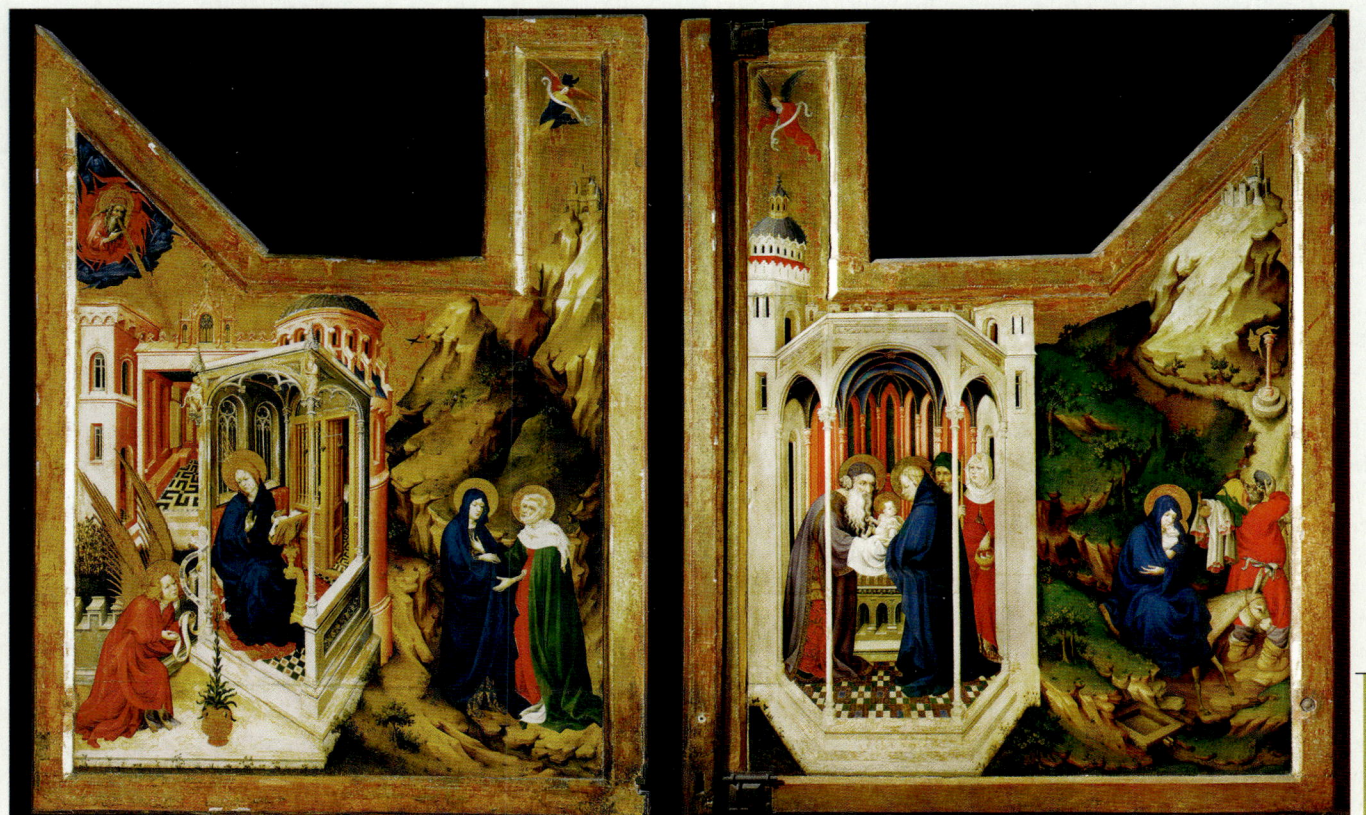

1 ft.

**20-3** MELCHIOR BROEDERLAM, *Retable de Champmol,* from the chapel of the Chartreuse de Champmol, Dijon, France, installed 1399. Oil on wood, each wing 5′ 5¾″ × 4′ 1¼″. Musée des Beaux-Arts, Dijon.

This early example of oil painting attempts to represent the three-dimensional world on a two-dimensional surface, but the gold background and flat halos recall medieval pictorial conventions.

year, he completed the *Ghent Altarpiece* (FIGS. 20-4 and 20-5), which, according to an inscription, his older brother HUBERT VAN EYCK (ca. 1366–1426) had begun. This retable is one of the largest (nearly 12 feet tall) of the 15th century. Jodocus Vyd, diplomat-retainer of Philip the Good, and his wife, Isabel Borluut, commissioned this polyptych as the centerpiece of the chapel Vyd built in the church originally dedicated to Saint John the Baptist (since 1540, Saint Bavo Cathedral). Vyd's largesse and the political and social connections the *Ghent Altarpiece* revealed to its audience contributed to Vyd's appointment as burgomeister (chief magistrate) of Ghent shortly after the unveiling of the work. Two of the exterior panels (FIG. 20-4) depict the donors. The husband and wife, painted in illusionistically rendered niches, kneel with their hands clasped in prayer. They gaze piously at illusionistic stone sculptures of Ghent's patron saints, Saint John the Baptist and Saint John the Evangelist (who was probably also Vyd's patron saint). The *Annunciation* appears on the upper register, with a careful representation of a Flemish town outside the painted window of the center panel. In the uppermost arched panels, van Eyck depicted the Old Testament prophets Zachariah and Micah, along with *sibyls*, Greco-Roman mythological female prophets whose writings the Christian Church interpreted as prophecies of Christ.

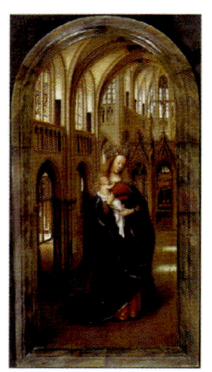

20-5A VAN EYCK, *Madonna in a Church,* ca. 1425–1430.

When opened (FIG. 20-5), the altarpiece reveals a sumptuous, superbly colored painting of humanity's redemption through Christ. In the upper register, God the Father—wearing the pope's triple tiara, with a worldly crown at his feet, and resplendent in a deep-scarlet mantle—presides in majesty. To God's right is the Virgin, represented, as in the Gothic age and in an earlier van Eyck *diptych* (two-paneled painting; FIG. 20-5A), as the queen of Heaven, with a crown of 12 stars upon her head. Saint John the Baptist sits to God's left. To either side is a choir of angels, with an angel playing an organ on the right. Adam and Eve appear in the far panels. The inscriptions in the arches above Mary and Saint John extol the Virgin's virtue and purity and Saint John's greatness as the forerunner of Christ. The inscription above the Lord's head translates as "This is God, all-powerful in his divine majesty; of all the best, by the gentleness of his goodness; the most liberal giver, because of his infinite generosity." The step behind the crown at the Lord's feet bears the inscription, "On his head, life without death. On his brow, youth without age. On his right, joy without sadness. On his left, security without fear." The entire altarpiece amplifies the central theme of salvation. Even though humans, symbolized by Adam and Eve, are sinful, they will be saved because God, in his infinite love, will sacrifice his own son for this purpose.

The panels of the lower register extend the symbolism of the upper. In the central panel, the community of saints comes from the four corners of the earth through an opulent, flower-spangled landscape. They proceed toward the altar of the lamb and the octagonal fountain of life (compare FIG. 20-2). The book of Revelation passage recounting the *Adoration of the Lamb* is the main reading on All Saints' Day (November 1). The lamb symbolizes the sacrificed son of God, whose heart bleeds into a chalice, while into the fountain spills the "pure river of water of life, clear as crystal, pro-

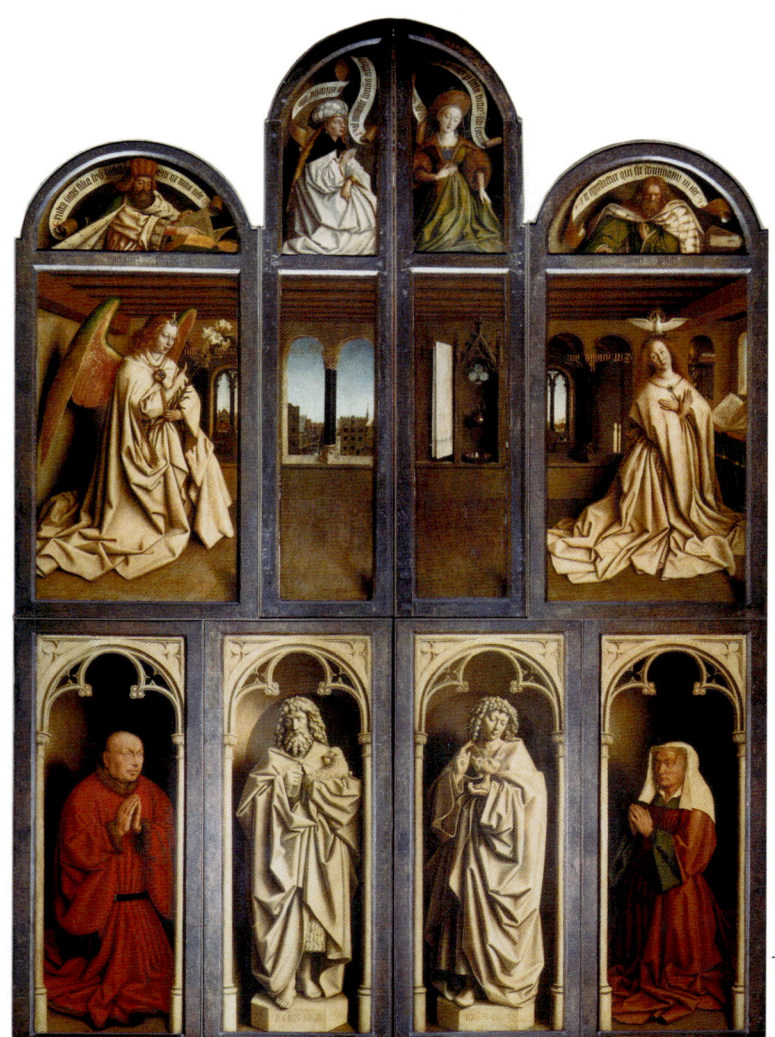

20-4 HUBERT and JAN VAN EYCK, *Ghent Altarpiece* (closed), Saint Bavo Cathedral, Ghent, Belgium, completed 1432. Oil on wood, 11′ 5″ × 7′ 6″. ◼◀

Monumental painted altarpieces were popular in Flemish churches. Artists decorated both the interiors and exteriors of these polyptychs, which often, as here, included donor portraits.

1 ft.

ceeding out of the throne of God and of the Lamb" (Rev. 22:1). On the right, the 12 apostles and a group of martyrs in red robes advance. On the left appear prophets. In the right background come the virgin martyrs, and in the left background the holy confessors approach. On the lower wings, hermits, pilgrims, knights, and judges approach from left and right. They symbolize the four cardinal virtues: Temperance, Prudence, Fortitude, and Justice, respectively. The altarpiece celebrates the whole Christian cycle from the fall of man to the redemption, presenting the Church triumphant in heavenly Jerusalem.

Van Eyck used oil paints to render the entire altarpiece in a shimmering splendor of color that defies reproduction. No small detail escaped the painter. With pristine specificity, he revealed the beauty of the most insignificant object as if it were a work of piety as much as a work of art. He depicted the soft texture of hair, the glitter of gold in the heavy brocades, the luster of pearls, and the flashing of gems, all with loving fidelity to appearance. This kind of meticulous attention to recording the exact surface appearance of humans, animals, objects, and landscapes, already evident in

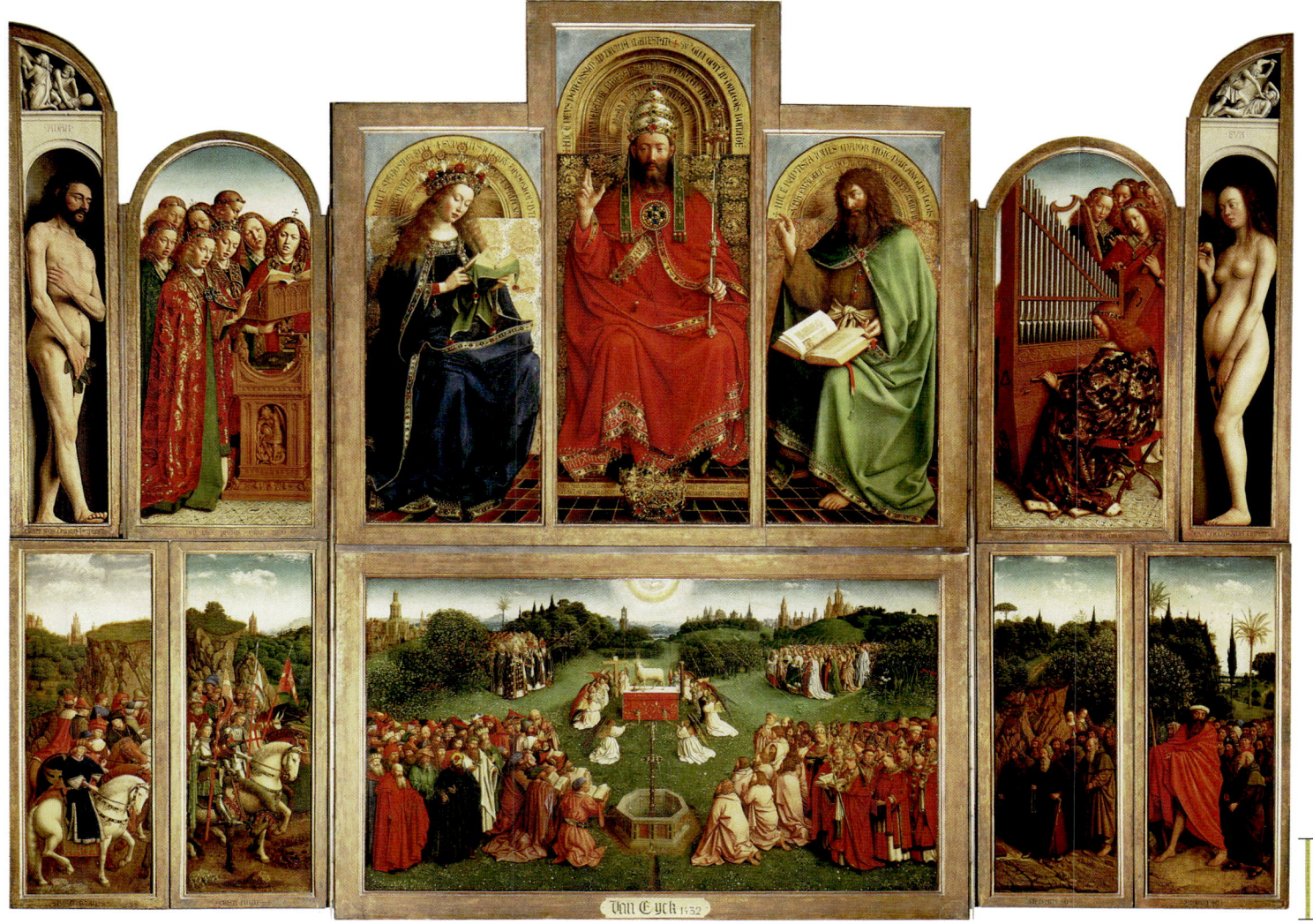

**20-5** HUBERT and JAN VAN EYCK, *Ghent Altarpiece* (open), Saint Bavo Cathedral, Ghent, Belgium, completed 1432. Oil on wood, 11′ 5″ × 15′ 1″. ◼◀

In this sumptuous painting of salvation from the original sin of Adam and Eve, God the Father presides in majesty. Van Eyck used oil paints to render every detail with loving fidelity to appearance.

the *Mérode Altarpiece* (FIG. 20-1), became the hallmark of Flemish panel painting in the 15th century.

**GIOVANNI ARNOLFINI** Emerging capitalism led to an urban prosperity that fueled the growing bourgeois market for art objects, particularly in Bruges, Antwerp, and, later, Amsterdam. This prosperity contributed to a growing interest in secular art in addition to religious artworks. Both the *Mérode Altarpiece* and the *Ghent Altarpiece* include painted portraits of their donors. These paintings marked a significant revival of portraiture, a genre that had languished since antiquity.

A purely secular portrait, but one with religious overtones, is Jan van Eyck's oil painting of *Giovanni Arnolfini and His Wife* (FIG. 20-6). Van Eyck depicted the Lucca financier (who had established himself in Bruges as an agent of the Medici family) in his home, a setting that is simultaneously mundane yet charged with the spiritual. Arnolfini holds the hand of his second wife, whose name is not known. According to the traditional interpretation of the painting, van Eyck recorded the couple taking their marriage

vows. As in the *Mérode Altarpiece* (FIG. 20-1), almost every object portrayed carries meaning. The cast-aside clogs indicate this event is taking place on holy ground. The little dog symbolizes fidelity (the common canine name *Fido* originated from the Latin *fido,* "to trust"). Behind the pair, the curtains of the marriage bed have been opened. The bedpost's *finial* (crowning ornament) is a tiny statue of Saint Margaret, patron saint of childbirth. (The bride is not yet pregnant, although the fashionable costume she wears makes her appear so.) From the finial hangs a whisk broom, symbolic of domestic care. The oranges on the chest below the window may refer to fertility. The single candle burning in the left rear holder of the ornate chandelier and the mirror, in which the viewer sees the entire room reflected, symbolize the all-seeing eye of God. The small medallions set into the mirror frame show tiny scenes from the passion of Christ and represent God's promise of salvation for the figures reflected on the mirror's convex surface. Viewers of the period would have been familiar with many of the objects included in the painting because of traditional Flemish customs. Husbands customarily presented brides with clogs, and the solitary lit candle

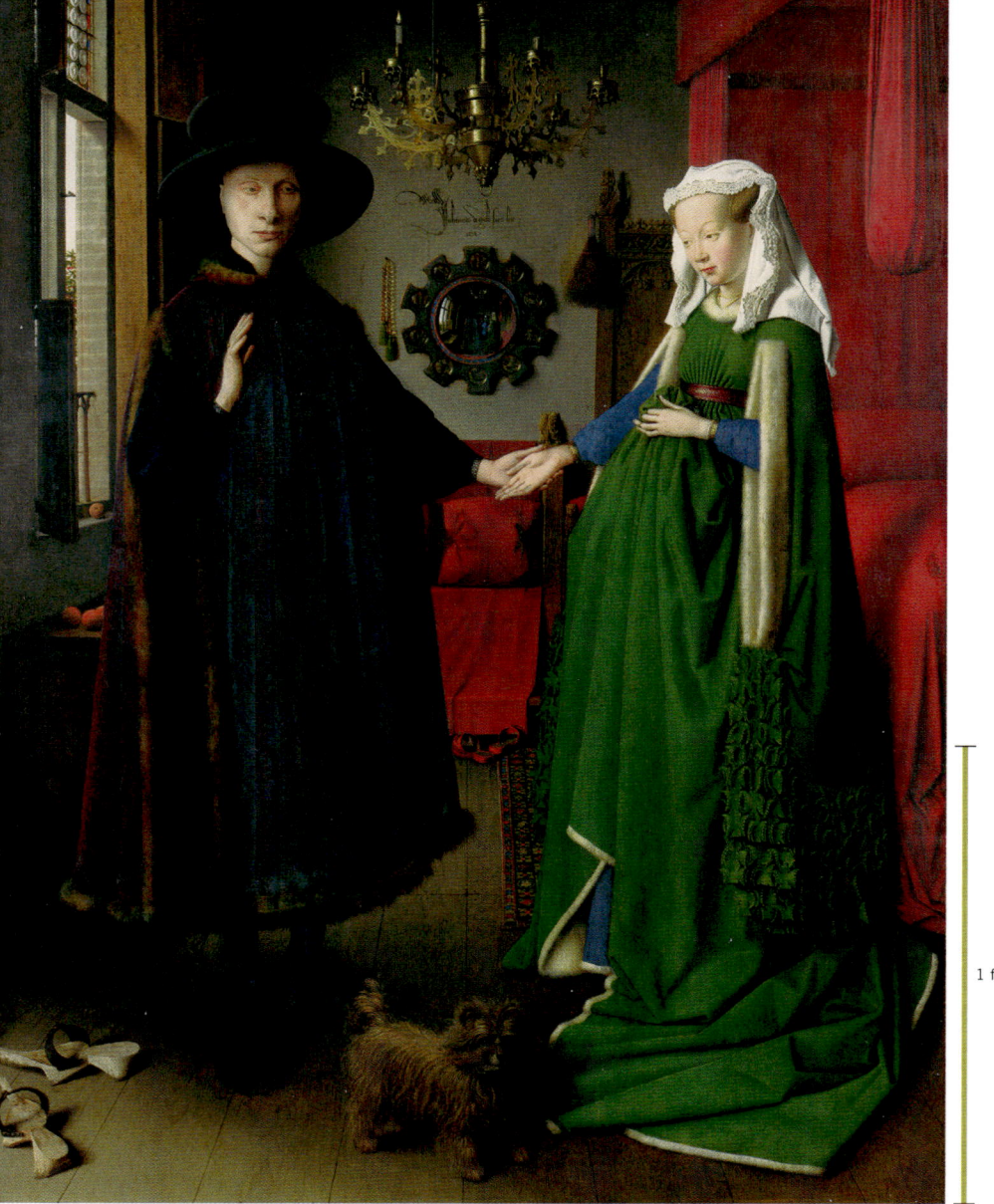

1 ft.

in the chandelier was part of Flemish marriage practices. Van Eyck's placement of the two figures suggests conventional gender roles—the woman stands near the bed and well into the room, whereas the man stands near the open window, symbolic of the outside world.

Van Eyck enhanced the documentary nature of this scene by exquisitely painting each object. He carefully distinguished textures and depicted the light from the window on the left reflecting off various surfaces. He also augmented the scene's credibility by including the convex mirror (complete with its spatial distortion, brilliantly recorded), because viewers can see not only the principals, Arnolfini and his wife, but also two persons who look into the room through the door. (Arnolfini's raised right hand may be a gesture of greeting to the two men.) One of these must be the artist himself, as the florid inscription above the mirror, *Johannes de Eyck fuit hic* ("Jan van Eyck was here"), announces he was present. The picture's purpose, then, would have been to record and sanctify this marriage.

Most scholars now reject this traditional reading of the painting, however. The room is a public reception area, not a bedchamber, and it has been suggested that Arnolfini is conferring legal privileges on his wife to conduct business in his absence. In either case, the artist functions as a witness. The self-portrait of van Eyck in the mirror also underscores the painter's self-consciousness as a professional artist whose role deserves to be recorded and remembered. (Compare the 12th-century monk Eadwine's self-portrait as "prince of scribes" [FIG. 12-36], a very early instance of an artist engaging in "self-promotion.")

*MAN IN A RED TURBAN* In 15th-century Flanders, artists also painted secular portraits without the layer of religious inter-

pretation present in the Arnolfini double portrait. These private commissions began to multiply as both artists and patrons became interested in the reality (both physical and psychological) portraits could reveal. For various reasons, great patrons embraced the opportunity to have their likenesses painted. They wanted to memorialize themselves in their dynastic lines and to establish their identities, ranks, and stations with images far more concrete than heraldic coats of arms. Portraits also served to represent state officials at events they could not attend. Sometimes, royalty, nobility, and the very rich would send artists to paint the likeness of a prospective bride or groom. For example, when young King Charles VI of France sought a bride, he dispatched a painter to three different royal courts to make portraits of the candidates.

In *Man in a Red Turban* (FIG. 20-7), the man van Eyck portrayed looks directly at the viewer. This is the first known Western painted portrait in a thousand years where the sitter does so. The

## Framed Paintings

Until the 20th century, when painters began simply to affix canvas to wooden *stretcher bars* to provide a taut painting surface devoid of ornamentation, artists considered the frame an integral part of the painting. Frames served a number of functions, some visual, others conceptual. For paintings such as large-scale altarpieces that were part of a larger environment, frames often served to integrate the painting with its surroundings. Frames could also be used to reinforce the illusionistic nature of the painted image. For example, the Italian painter Giovanni Bellini, in his *San Zaccaria Altarpiece* (FIG. 22-32), duplicated the carved pilasters of the architectural frame in the painting itself, thereby enhancing the illusion of space and giving the painted figures an enhanced physical presence. In the *Ghent Altarpiece,* the frame seems to cast shadows on the floor between the angel and Mary in the *Annunciation* (FIG. 20-4, *top.*) More commonly, artists used frames specifically to distance the viewer from the (often otherworldly) scene by calling attention to the separation of the image from the viewer's space.

Most 15th- and 16th-century paintings included elaborate frames the artists themselves helped design and construct. Extant contracts reveal the frame could account for as much as half of the cost of an altarpiece. Frequently, the commissions called for painted or gilded frames, adding to the expense. For small works, artists sometimes affixed the frames to the panels before painting, creating an insistent visual presence as they worked. Occasionally, a single piece of wood served as both panel and frame, and the artist carved the painting surface from the wood, leaving the edges as a frame. Larger images with elaborate frames, such as altarpieces, required the services of a woodcarver or stonemason. The painter worked closely with the individual constructing the frame to ensure its appropriateness for the image(s) produced.

Unfortunately, over time, many frames have been removed from their paintings. For instance, in 1566 church officials dismantled the *Ghent Altarpiece* and detached its elaborately carved frame in order to protect the sacred work from Protestant *iconoclasts* (see Chapter 23). As ill luck would have it, when the panels were reinstalled in 1587, no one could find the frame. Sadly, the absence of many of the original frames of old paintings deprives viewers today of the painter's complete artistic vision. Conversely, when the original frames exist, they sometimes provide essential information, such as the subject, name of the painter, and date. For

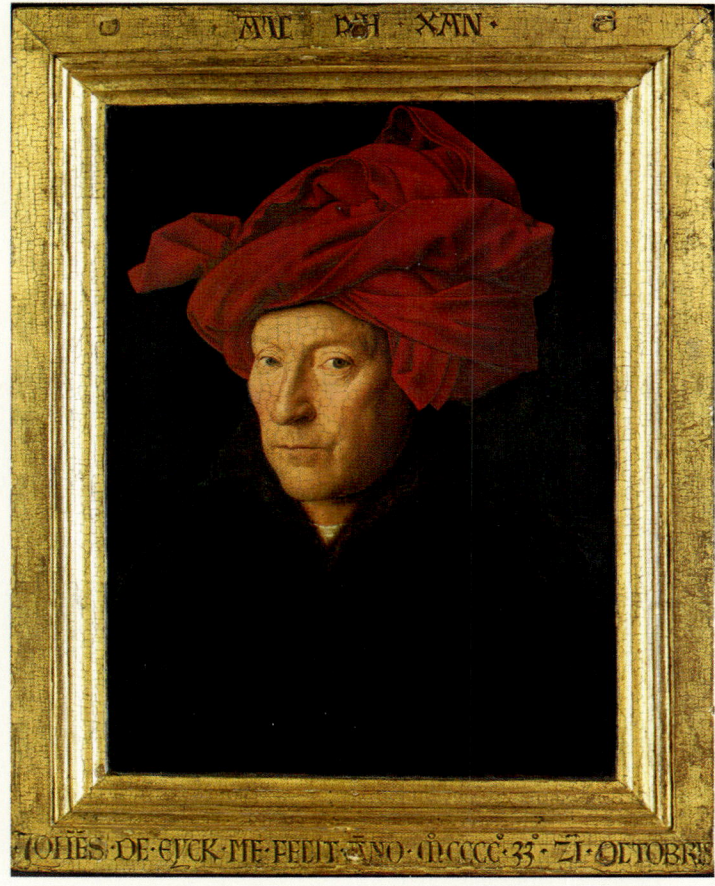

1 in.

**20-7** JAN VAN EYCK, *Man in a Red Turban,* 1433. Oil on wood, 1′ 1⅛″ × 10¼″. National Gallery, London.

*Man in a Red Turban* is the first known Western painted portrait in a thousand years in which the sitter looks directly at the viewer. The inscribed frame suggests it is a self-portrait.

example, the inscriptions on the frame of Jan van Eyck's *Man in a Red Turban* (FIG. 20-7) state he painted it on October 21, 1433, and the inclusion of "As I can" and omission of the sitter's name suggest the painting is a self-portrait.

level, composed gaze, directed from a true three-quarter head pose, must have impressed observers deeply. The painter created the illusion that from whatever angle a viewer observes the face, the eyes return that gaze. Van Eyck, with his considerable observational skill and controlled painting style, injected a heightened sense of specificity into this portrait by including beard stubble, veins in the bloodshot left eye, and weathered, aged skin. Although a definitive identification of the sitter has yet to be made, most scholars consider *Man in a Red Turban* a self-portrait, which van Eyck painted by looking at his image in a mirror (as he depicted himself

in the mirror in the Arnolfinis' home). The inscriptions on the frame (see "Framed Paintings," above) reinforce this identification. Across the top, van Eyck wrote "As I can" in Flemish using Greek letters. (One suggestion is this portrait was a demonstration piece intended for prospective clients, who could compare the painting with the painter and judge what he "could do" in terms of recording a faithful likeness. Across the bottom appears the statement (in Latin) "Jan van Eyck made me" and the date. The use of both Greek and Latin suggests the artist's view of himself as a successor to the fabled painters of antiquity.

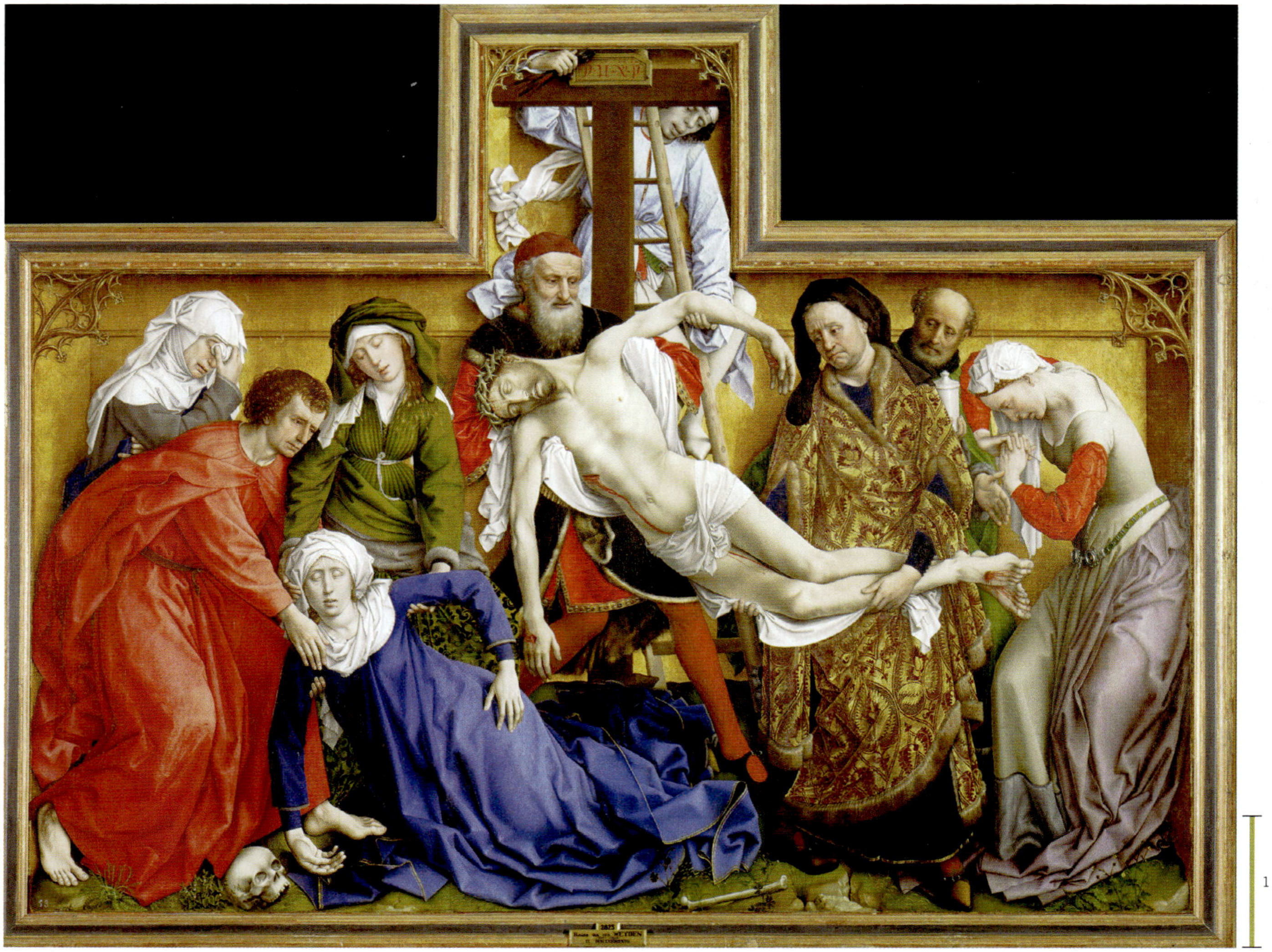

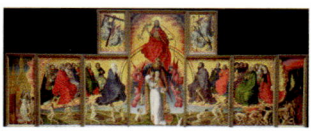

**20-8** ROGIER VAN DER WEYDEN, *Deposition*, center panel of a triptych from Notre-Dame hors-les-murs, Louvain, Belgium, ca. 1435. Oil on wood, 7′ 2⅝″ × 8′ 7⅛″. Museo del Prado, Madrid. ◼◀

*Deposition* resembles a relief carving in which the biblical figures act out a drama of passionate sorrow as if on a shallow theatrical stage. The painting makes an unforgettable emotional impression.

## Rogier van der Weyden

When Jan van Eyck received the commission for the *Ghent Altarpiece,* ROGIER VAN DER WEYDEN (ca. 1400–1464) was an assistant in the workshop of Robert Campin (FIG. 20-1), but the younger painter's fame eventually rivaled van Eyck's. Rogier quickly became renowned for his dynamic compositions stressing human action and drama. He concentrated on Christian themes such as *Deposition* (FIG. **20-8**) and other episodes in the life of Jesus that elicited powerful emotions, for example, *Crucifixion* and *Pietà* (the Virgin Mary cradling the dead body of her son), moving observers deeply by vividly portraying the sufferings of Christ. He also painted a dramatic vision of *Last Judgment* (FIG. **20-8A**).

**20-8A** VAN DER WEYDEN, *Last Judgment Altarpiece,* ca. 1444–1448. ◼◀

**DEPOSITION** One of Rogier's early masterworks is his 1435 *Deposition* (FIG. 20-8), the center panel of a triptych commissioned by the archers' guild of Louvain for the church of Notre-Dame hors-les-murs (Notre-Dame "outside the [town] walls"). Rogier acknowledged the patrons of this large painting by incorporating the crossbow (the guild's symbol) into the decorative tracery in the corners. Instead of creating a deep landscape setting, as van Eyck might have, Rogier compressed the figures and action onto a shallow stage with a golden back wall, imitating the large sculptured shrines so popular in the 15th century, especially in the Holy Roman Empire (FIGS. 20-19 and 20-20). The device admirably served his purpose of expressing maximum action within a limited space. The painting, with the artist's crisp drawing and precise modeling of forms, resembles a stratified relief carving. A series of lateral undulating movements gives the group a compositional unity, a formal cohesion Rogier strengthened by depicting the desolating anguish many of the figures share. Present are the Virgin and several of her half-sisters, Joseph of Arimathea, Nicodemus, Saint John the Evangelist, and Mary Magdalene. The similar poses of Christ and his mother further unify the composition and reflect the belief that Mary suffered the same pain at the crucifixion as her son. Their echoing postures also resemble the shape of a crossbow.

Few painters have equaled Rogier van der Weyden in rendering passionate sorrow as it vibrates through a figure or distorts a tearstained face. His depiction of the agony of loss in *Deposition* is

## The Artist's Profession in Flanders

As in Italy (see "Artistic Training," Chapter 14, page 414), guilds controlled artistic production in Flanders. To pursue a craft, individuals had to belong to the guild controlling that craft. Painters, for example, sought admission to the Guild of Saint Luke, the patron saint of painters because Luke made a portrait of the Virgin Mary (FIG. 20-9). The path to eventual membership in the guild began, for men, at an early age, when the father apprenticed his son in boyhood to a master, with whom the young aspiring painter lived. The master taught the fundamentals of his craft—how to make implements, prepare panels with *gesso* (plaster mixed with a binding material), and mix colors, oils, and varnishes. Once the youth mastered these procedures and learned to work in the master's traditional manner, he usually spent several years working as a journeyman in various cities, observing and absorbing ideas from other masters. He then was eligible to become a master and could apply for admission to the guild. Fees could be very high, especially if an artist was not a citizen of the same city. Sometimes, an artist seeking admission to a guild would marry the widow of a member. A woman could inherit her husband's workshop but not run it. Guild membership was essential for establishing an artist's reputation and for obtaining commissions. The guild inspected paintings to evaluate workmanship and ensure its members used quality materials. It also secured adequate payment for its artists' labor.

Women had many fewer opportunities than men to train as artists, in large part because of social and moral constraints that forbade women to reside as apprentices in the homes of male masters. Moreover, from the 16th century, when academic training courses supplemented and then replaced guild training, until the 20th century, women would not as a rule expect or be permitted instruction in figure painting, because it involved dissection of cadavers and study of the nude male model. Flemish women interested in pursuing art as a career, for example, Caterina van Hemessen (FIG. 23-18), most often received tutoring from fathers and husbands who were professionals and whom the women assisted in all the technical procedures of the craft. Despite these obstacles, membership records of the art guilds of Bruges and other cities reveal a substantial number of Flemish

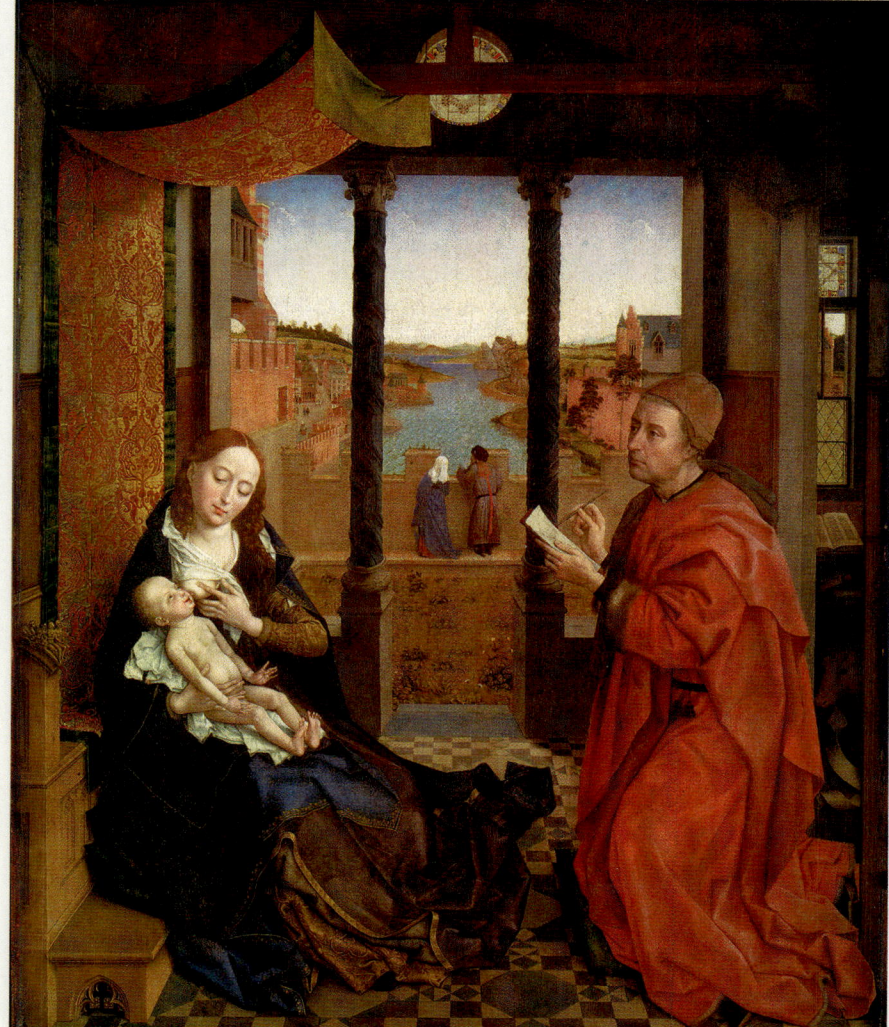

**20-9** ROGIER VAN DER WEYDEN, *Saint Luke Drawing the Virgin*, ca. 1435–1440. Oil and tempera on wood, 4′ 6$\frac{1}{8}$″ × 3′ 7$\frac{5}{8}$″. Museum of Fine Arts, Boston (gift of Mr. and Mrs. Henry Lee Higginson).

Probably commissioned by the painters' guild in Brussels, this painting honors the first Christian artist and the profession of painting. Saint Luke may be a self-portrait of Rogier van der Weyden.

1 ft.

women were able to establish themselves as artists during the 15th century. That they succeeded in negotiating the difficult path to acceptance as professionals is a testament to both their tenacity and their artistic skill.

among the most authentic in religious art and creates an immediate and unforgettable emotional effect on the viewer. It was probably Rogier whom Michelangelo had in mind when, according to the Portuguese painter Francisco de Hollanda (1517–1584), the Italian master observed, "Flemish painting [will] please the devout better than any painting of Italy, which will never cause him to shed a tear, whereas that of Flanders will cause him to shed many."[1]

*SAINT LUKE* Slightly later in date is Rogier's *Saint Luke Drawing the Virgin* (FIG. 20-9), probably painted for the Guild of Saint Luke, the artists' guild in Brussels. The panel depicts the patron saint of painters drawing the Virgin Mary using a *silverpoint* (a sharp *stylus* that creates a fine line). The theme paid tribute to the profession of painting in Flanders (see "The Artist's Profession in Flanders," above) by drawing attention to the venerable history

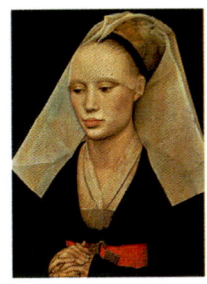

20-9A VAN DER WEYDEN, *Portrait of a Lady*, ca. 1460.

of the painter's craft and documenting the preparatory work required before the artist could begin painting the figures and setting. Portrait painting was a major source of income for Flemish artists, and Rogier was one of the best (FIG. 20-9A). In fact, many scholars believe Rogier's Saint Luke is a self-portrait, identifying the Flemish painter with the first Christian artist and underscoring the holy nature of painting. Rogier shared with Campin and van Eyck the aim of recording every detail of a scene with loving fidelity to optical appearance, seen here in the rich fabrics, the floor pattern, and the landscape visible through the window. Also, as his older colleagues did, Rogier imbued much of the representation with symbolic significance. At the right, the ox identifies the figure recording the Virgin's features as Saint Luke (see "The Four Evangelists," Chapter 11, page 314). The carved armrest of the Virgin's bench depicts Adam, Eve, and the serpent, reminding the viewer that Mary is the new Eve and Christ the new Adam who will redeem humanity from original sin.

## Later Flemish Painters

Robert Campin, Jan van Eyck, and Rogier van der Weyden were the leading figures of the first generation of "Northern Renaissance" painters. (Art historians usually transfer to northern Europe, with less validity than in its original usage, the term *Renaissance*, coined to describe the conscious revival of classical art in Italy. They also use the uppercase designation *Northern European* as a stylistic term parallel to Italian, as opposed to the geographic designation *northern European*.) The second generation of Flemish masters, active during the latter half of the 15th century, had much in common with their illustrious predecessors, especially a preference for using oil paints to create naturalistic representations, often, although not always, of traditional Christian subjects for installation in churches.

**PETRUS CHRISTUS** One work of uncertain Christian content is *A Goldsmith in His Shop* (FIG. 20-10) by PETRUS CHRISTUS (ca. 1410–1472), who settled in Bruges in 1444. According to the traditional interpretation, *A Goldsmith in His Shop* portrays Saint Eligius (who was initially a master goldsmith before committing his life to God) sitting in his stall, showing an elegantly attired couple a selection of rings. The bride's betrothal girdle lies on the table as a symbol of chastity, and the woman reaches for the ring the goldsmith weighs. The artist's inclusion of a crystal container for Eucharistic wafers (on the lower shelf to the right of Saint Eligius) and the scales (a reference to the last judgment) supports a religious interpretation of this painting and continues the Flemish tradition of imbuing everyday objects with symbolic significance. A halo once encircled the goldsmith's head, seemingly confirming the religious nature of this scene. Scientists have determined, however, that the halo was a later addition by another artist, and restorers have removed it.

Most scholars now think the painting, although not devoid of religious content, should be seen as a vocational painting of the type often produced for installation in Flemish guild chapels. Although the couple's presence suggests a marriage portrait, the patrons were probably not the couple portrayed but rather the goldsmiths' guild in Bruges. Saint Eligius was the patron saint of gold- and silversmiths, blacksmiths, and metalworkers, all of whom shared a chapel

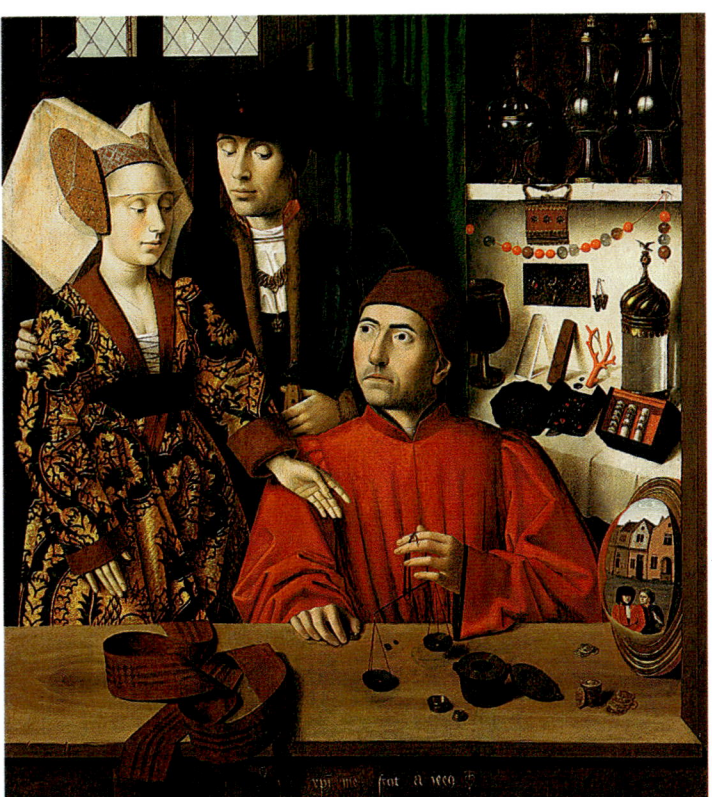

20-10 PETRUS CHRISTUS, *A Goldsmith in His Shop*, 1449. Oil on wood, 3′ 3″ × 2′ 10″. Metropolitan Museum of Art, New York (Robert Lehman Collection, 1975).

Once thought to depict Eligius, the patron saint of goldsmiths, Christus's painting, made for the Bruges goldsmiths guild, is more likely a generic scene of a couple shopping for a wedding ring.

in a building adjacent to their meetinghouse. The reconsecration of this chapel took place in 1449, the same date as the Christus painting. Therefore, it seems probable the artist painted *A Goldsmith in His Shop*, which illustrates an economic transaction and focuses on the goldsmith's profession, specifically for the guild chapel.

Christus went to great lengths to produce a historically credible image. For example, the variety of objects depicted in the painting serves as advertisement for the goldsmiths' guild. Included are the goldsmiths' raw materials (precious stones, beads, crystal, coral, and seed pearls) scattered among finished products (rings, buckles, and brooches). The pewter vessels on the upper shelves are donation pitchers, which town leaders gave to distinguished guests. All these meticulously painted objects not only attest to the centrality and importance of goldsmiths to both the secular and sacred communities but also enhance the naturalism of the painting. The convex mirror in the foreground showing another couple and a street with houses serves to extend the painting's space into the viewer's space, further creating the illusion of reality, as in van Eyck's Arnolfini portrait (FIG. 20-6).

**DIRK BOUTS** In *Last Supper* (FIG. 20-11), DIRK BOUTS (ca. 1415–1475) of Haarlem chose a different means of suggesting spatial recession. The painting is the central panel of the *Altarpiece of the Holy Sacrament*, which the Confraternity of the Holy Sacrament in Louvain commissioned

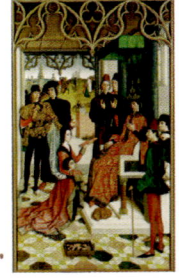

20-11A BOUTS, *Justice of Otto III*, ca. 1470–1475. ◼

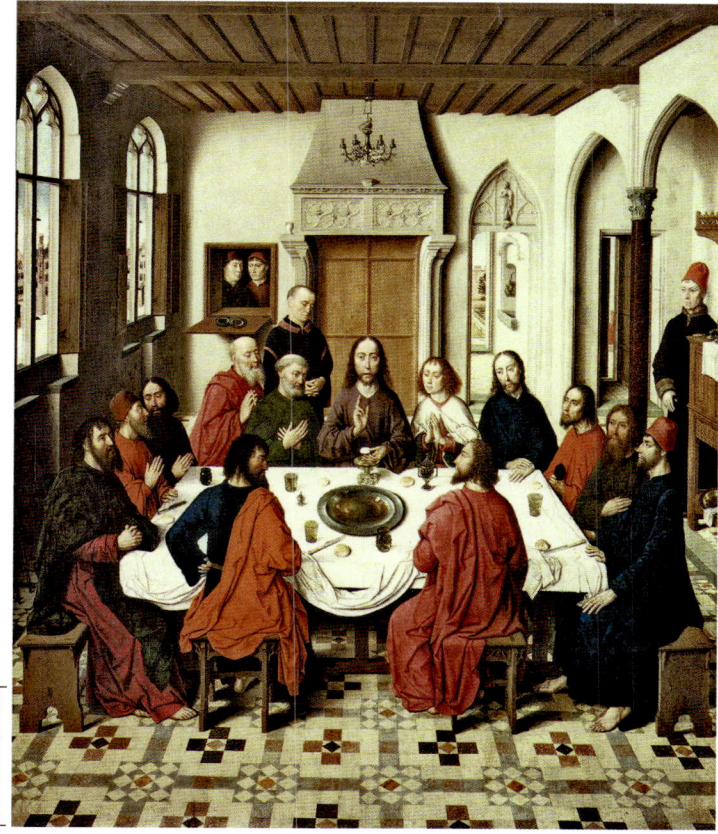

1 ft.

20-11 DIRK BOUTS, *Last Supper,* center panel of the *Altarpiece of the Holy Sacrament,* Saint Peter's, Louvain, Belgium, 1464–1468. Oil on wood, 6′ × 5′. ◼◀

One of the earliest Northern European paintings to employ Renaissance linear perspective, this *Last Supper* includes four servants in Flemish attire—portraits of the altarpiece's patrons.

perpendicular to the picture plane) lead to the vanishing point in the center of the mantelpiece above Christ's head. The small side room, however, has its own vanishing point, and neither it nor the vanishing point of the main room falls on the horizon of the landscape seen through the windows, as in Italian Renaissance paintings.

In *Last Supper,* Bouts did not focus on the biblical narrative itself but instead presented Christ in the role of a priest performing a ritual from the liturgy of the Christian Church—the consecration of the Eucharistic wafer. This contrasts strongly with other depictions of the same subject, which often focused on Judas's betrayal or on Christ's comforting of John. The Confraternity of the Holy Sacrament dedicated itself to the worship of the Eucharist, and the smaller panels on the altarpiece's wings depict Old Testament *prefigurations* of the Eucharist. Bouts also added four servants (two in the window and two standing) not mentioned in the biblical account, all dressed in Flemish attire. These are portraits of the four members of the confraternity who contracted Bouts to paint the altarpiece, continuing the Flemish tradition of inserting into representations of biblical events portraits of the painting's patrons, first noted in the *Mérode Altarpiece* (FIG. 20-1).

## HUGO VAN DER GOES

By the mid-15th century, Flemish art had achieved renown throughout Europe. The *Portinari Altarpiece* (FIG. 20-12), for example, is a large-scale Flemish work in a family chapel in Florence, Italy. The artist who received the commission was HUGO VAN DER GOES (ca. 1440–1482), the dean of the painters' guild of Ghent from 1468 to 1475. Hugo painted the triptych for Tommaso Portinari, an Italian shipowner and agent for the powerful Medici family of Florence. Portinari appears on the wings

in 1464, four years before Bouts became the city's official painter and produced a series of panels—*Justice of Otto III* (FIG. **20-11A**)—for Louvain's town hall. Bouts's *Last Supper* is one of the earliest Northern Renaissance paintings to demonstrate the use of a *vanishing point* (see "Linear and Atmospheric Perspective," Chapter 21, page 567) for creating *perspective.* All of the central room's *orthogonals* (converging diagonal lines imagined to be behind and

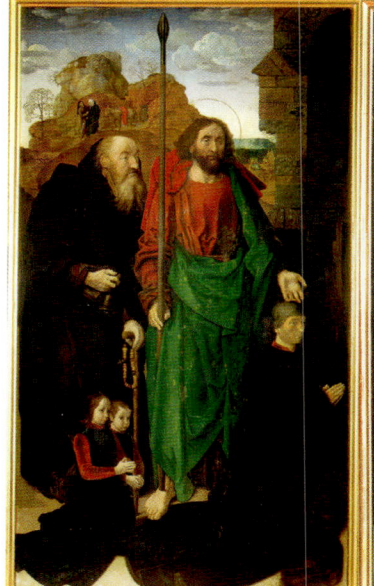
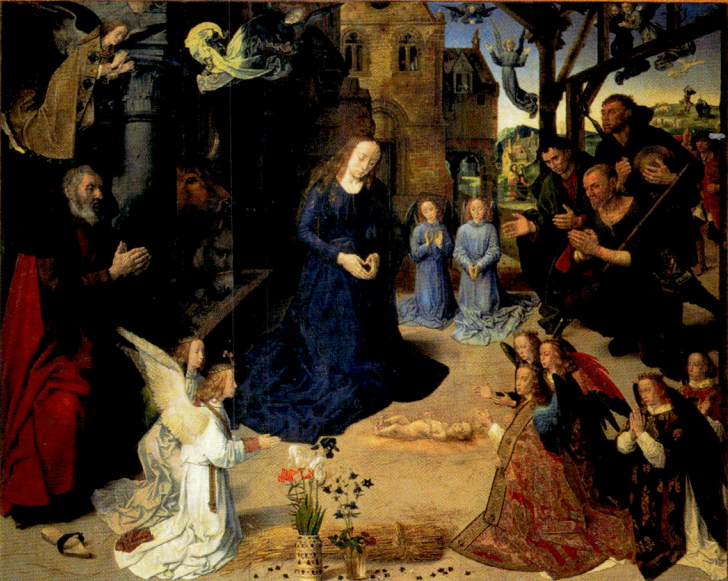
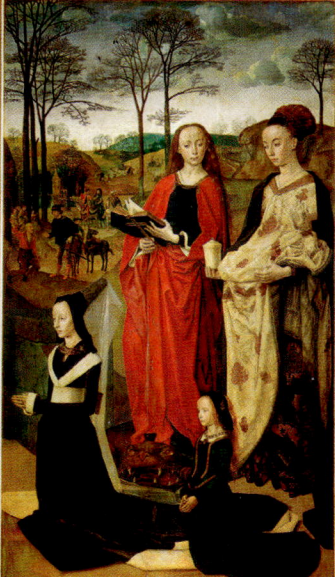

1 ft.

20-12 HUGO VAN DER GOES, *Portinari Altarpiece* (open), from Sant'Egidio, Florence, Italy, ca. 1476. Tempera and oil on wood, center panel 8′ 3½″ × 10′, each wing 8′ 3½″ × 4′ 7½″. Galleria degli Uffizi, Florence.

This altarpiece is a rare instance of the awarding of a major commission in Italy to a Flemish painter. The Florentines admired Hugo's realistic details and brilliant portrayal of human character.

of the altarpiece with his family and their patron saints. The subject of the central panel is *Adoration of the Shepherds*. On this large surface, Hugo displayed a scene of solemn grandeur, muting the high drama of the joyous occasion. The Virgin, Joseph, and the angels seem to brood on the suffering to come rather than to meditate on the miracle of Jesus' birth. Mary kneels, somber and monumental, on a tilted ground, a device the painter used to situate the main actors at the center of the panel. (The compositional device may derive from the tilted stage floors of 15th-century mystery plays.) Three shepherds enter from the right rear. Hugo represented them in attitudes of wonder, piety, and gaping curiosity. Their lined faces, work-worn hands, and uncouth dress and manner seem immediately familiar.

The architecture and a continuous wintry northern European landscape unify the three panels. Symbols surface throughout the altarpiece. Iris and columbine flowers are emblems of the sorrows of the Virgin. The angels represent the 15 joys of Mary. A sheaf of wheat stands for Bethlehem (the "house of bread" in Hebrew), a reference to the Eucharist. The harp of David, emblazoned over the building's portal in the middle distance (just to the right of the Virgin's head), signifies the ancestry of Christ. To stress the meaning and significance of the illustrated event, Hugo revived medieval pictorial devices. Small scenes shown in the background of the altarpiece represent (from left to right) the flight into Egypt, the annunciation to the shepherds, and the arrival of the magi. Hugo's variation in the scale of his figures to differentiate them by their importance to the central event also reflects older traditions. Still,

he put a vigorous, penetrating realism to work in a new direction, characterizing human beings according to their social level while showing their common humanity.

After Portinari placed the altarpiece in his family's chapel in the Florentine church of Sant'Egidio, it created a considerable stir among Italian artists. Although the painting may have seemed unstructured to them, Hugo's masterful technique and what the Florentines deemed incredible realism in representing drapery, flowers, animals, and, above all, human character and emotion made a deep impression on them. At least one Florentine artist, Domenico Ghirlandaio (FIGS. 21-26 and 21-27), paid tribute to the Flemish master by using Hugo's most striking motif, the adoring shepherds, in one of his own *Nativity* paintings.

**HANS MEMLING** Hugo's contemporary, HANS MEMLING (ca. 1430–1494), became a citizen of Bruges in 1465 and received numerous commissions from the city's wealthy merchants, Flemish and foreign alike. He specialized in portraits of his patrons (one of whom was Tommaso Portinari) and images of the Madonna. Memling's many paintings of the Virgin portray young, slight, pretty princesses, each holding a doll-like infant Christ. The center panel of the *Saint John Altarpiece* depicts the *Virgin with Saints and Angels* (FIG. **20-13**). The patrons of this altarpiece—two brothers and two sisters of the order of the Hospital of Saint John in Bruges—appear on the exterior side panels (not illustrated). In the central panel, two angels, one playing a musical instrument and the other holding a book, flank the Virgin. To the sides of Mary's throne

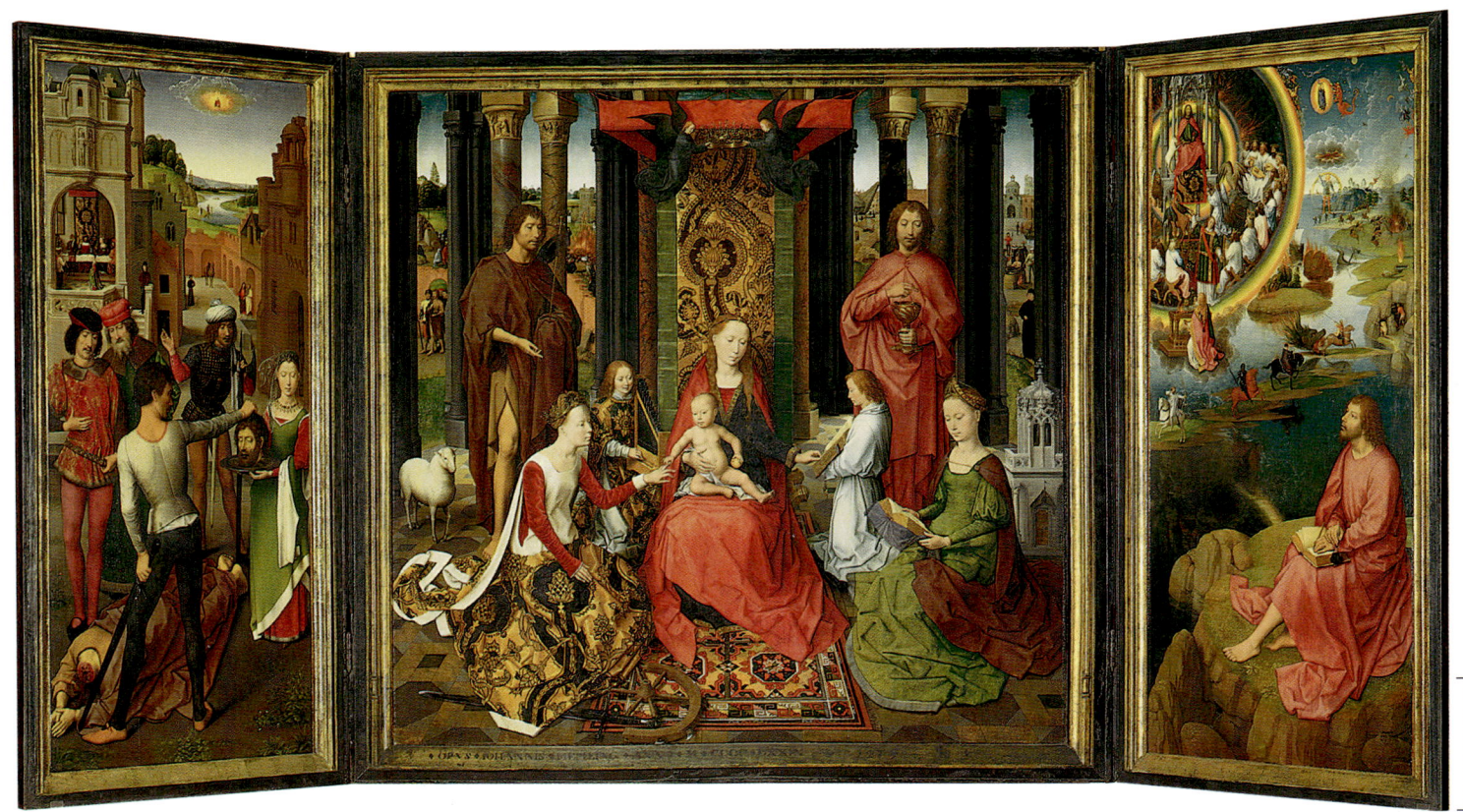

1 ft.

**20-13** HANS MEMLING, *Virgin with Saints and Angels,* center panel of the *Saint John Altarpiece,* Hospitaal Sint Jan, Bruges, Belgium, 1479. Oil on wood, center panel 5′ 7¾″ × 5′ 7¾″, each wing 5′ 7¾″ × 2′ 7⅛″.

Memling specialized in images of the Madonna. His *Saint John Altarpiece* exudes an opulence that results from the sparkling and luminous colors and the realistic depiction of rich tapestries and brocades.

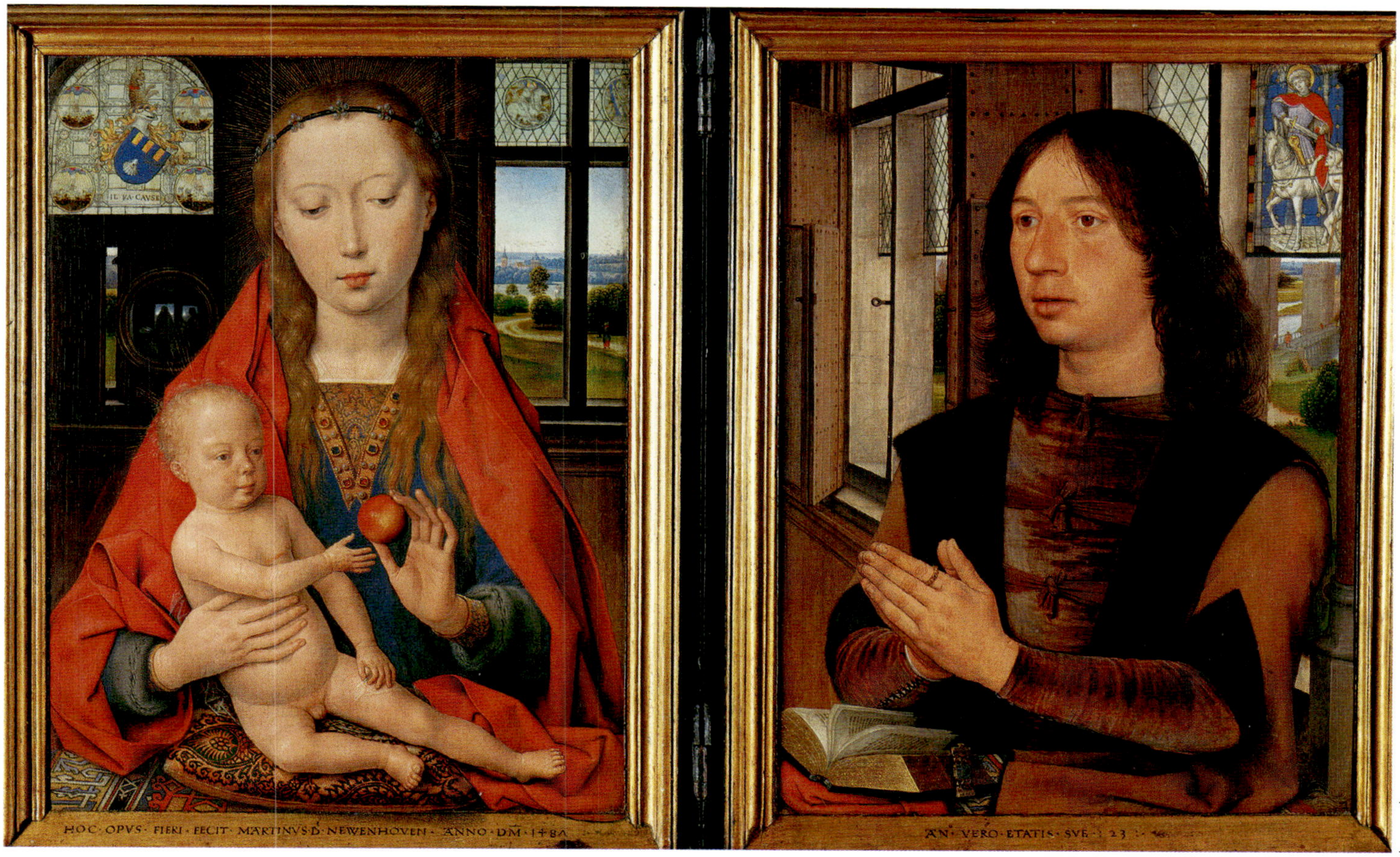

**20-14** HANS MEMLING, *Diptych of Martin van Nieuwenhove*, 1487. Oil on wood, each panel 1′ 5¾″ × 1′ 1″. Memlingmuseum, Bruges.

In this diptych the Virgin and Child pay a visit to the home of 23-year-old Martin van Nieuwenhove. A round convex mirror reflects the three figures and unites the two halves of the diptych spatially.

stand Saint John the Baptist on the left and Saint John the Evangelist on the right, and seated in the foreground are Saints Catherine and Barbara. This gathering celebrates the *mystic marriage* of Saint Catherine of Alexandria, one of many virgin saints believed to have entered into a spiritual marriage with Christ. As one of the most revered virgins of Christ, Saint Catherine provided a model of devotion that resonated with women viewers (especially nuns). The altarpiece exudes an opulence that results from the rich colors, meticulously depicted tapestries and brocades, and the serenity of the figures. The composition is balanced and serene, the color sparkling and luminous, and the execution of the highest technical quality.

Memling combined portraiture and Madonna imagery again in a much less ambitious—and more typical—work (FIG. **20-14**) commissioned by Martin van Nieuwenhove, the scion of an important Bruges family that held various posts in the civic government. Martin himself served as burgomeister (mayor) of Bruges in 1497. The painting takes the form of a diptych, with the patron portrayed on the right wing and praying to the Madonna and Child on the left wing. According to inscriptions on the frames, van Nieuwenhove commissioned the work in 1487 when he was 23 years old (he died in 1500).

The format of the van Nieuwenhove diptych follows the pattern Memling used earlier for his wedding triptych of *Tommaso Portinari and Maria Baroncelli* (FIG. **20-14A**) but with only a single (male) portrait. The left panel representing the Madonna

and Child is probably similar to the lost central section of the Portinari triptych. Memling's portrayals of the Virgin and Child differ little in his smaller, private devotional works and his larger altarpieces (FIG. 20-13) and consistently feature a tender characterization of the young Virgin and her nude in-

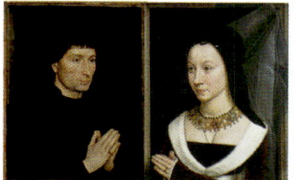

**20-14A** MEMLING, *Tommaso Portinari and Maria Baroncelli*, ca. 1470.

fant son. Here, however, Memling set both the Madonna and her patron in the interior of a well-appointed Flemish home featuring stained-glass windows. The window to the left of the Virgin's head bears van Nieuwenhove's coat of arms. The window behind the donor depicts his patron saint, Martin of Tours. These precisely recorded details identify the home as van Nieuwenhove's (the Minnewater Bridge in Bruges is visible through the open window), and the Madonna and Child have honored him by coming to his private residence. The conceit is a familiar one in Flemish painting. An early example is the *Annunciation* taking place in the home of Peter Inghelbrecht in Robert Campin's *Mérode Altarpiece* (FIG. 20-1). In the Memling portrait diptych, the Christ Child sits on the same ledge as the donor's open prayer book. Also uniting the two wings of the diptych is the round convex mirror behind the Virgin's right shoulder in which the viewer sees the reflection of the Virgin and van Nieuwenhove as well as the rest of the room (compare FIGS. 20-6 and 20-10).

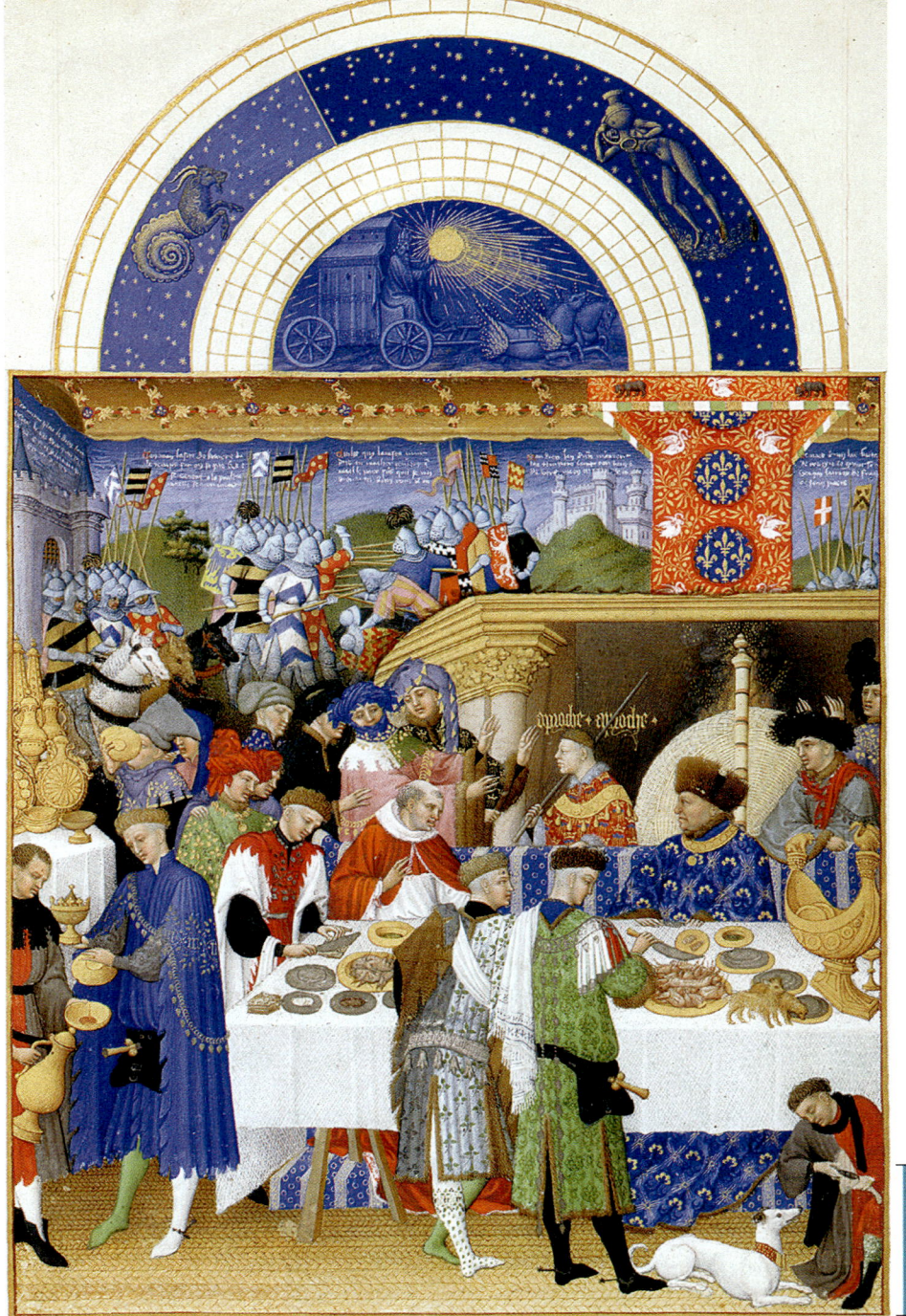

# FRANCE

In contrast to the prosperity and peace Flanders enjoyed during the 15th century, in France the Hundred Years' War crippled economic enterprise and prevented political stability. The anarchy of war and the weakness of the kings gave rise to a group of duchies, each with significant power and the resources to commission major artworks. The strongest and wealthiest of these has already been examined—the duchy of Burgundy, which controlled Flanders. But the dukes of Berry, Bourbon, and Nemours as well as members of the French royal court were also important art patrons.

## Manuscript Painting

During the 15th century, French artists built on the achievements of Gothic painters (see Chapter 13) and produced exquisitely refined illuminated manuscripts. Among the most significant developments in French manuscript painting was a new conception and presentation of space. Paintings in manuscripts took on more pronounced characteristics as illusionistic scenes. Increased contact with Italy, where Renaissance artists had revived the pictorial principles of classical antiquity, may have influenced French painters' interest in illusionism.

**LIMBOURG BROTHERS** The most innovative early-15th-century manuscript illuminators were the three LIMBOURG BROTHERS—POL, HERMAN, and JEAN—from Nijmegen in the Netherlands. They were nephews of Jean Malouel, the court artist of Philip the Bold. Following in the footsteps of earlier illustrators such as Jean Pucelle (FIGS. 13-36 and 13-36A), the Limbourg brothers expanded the illusionistic capabilities of illumination. Trained in the Netherlands, the brothers moved to Paris no later than 1402, and between 1405 and their death in 1416, probably from the plague, they worked in Paris and Bourges for Jean, duke of Berry (r. 1360–1416) and brother of King Charles V (r. 1364–1380) of France and of Philip the Bold of Burgundy.

The duke ruled the western French regions of Berry, Poitou, and Auvergne (MAP 20-1). He was an avid art patron and focused on collecting manuscripts, jewels, and rare artifacts. Among the more than 300 manuscripts the duke owned were Pucelle's *Belleville Breviary* (FIG. 13-36) and the *Hours of Jeanne d'Évreux* (FIG. 13-36A) as well as *Les Très Riches Heures du Duc de Berry* (*The Very Sumptuous Hours of*

the Duke of Berry; FIGS. **20-15** and **20-16**), which he commissioned the Limbourg brothers to produce. A Book of Hours, like a *breviary,* was a book used for reciting prayers (see "Medieval Books," Chapter 11, page 312). As prayer books, they replaced the traditional *psalters* (books of psalms), which were the only liturgical books in private hands until the mid-13th century. The centerpiece of a Book of Hours was the "Office [prayer] of the Blessed Virgin," which contained liturgical passages to be read privately at set times during the day, from *matins* (dawn prayers) to *compline* (the last of the prayers recited daily). An illustrated calendar containing local religious feast days usually preceded the Office of the Blessed Virgin. Penitential psalms, devotional prayers, litanies to the saints, and other prayers, including those of the dead and of the Holy Cross, followed the center-

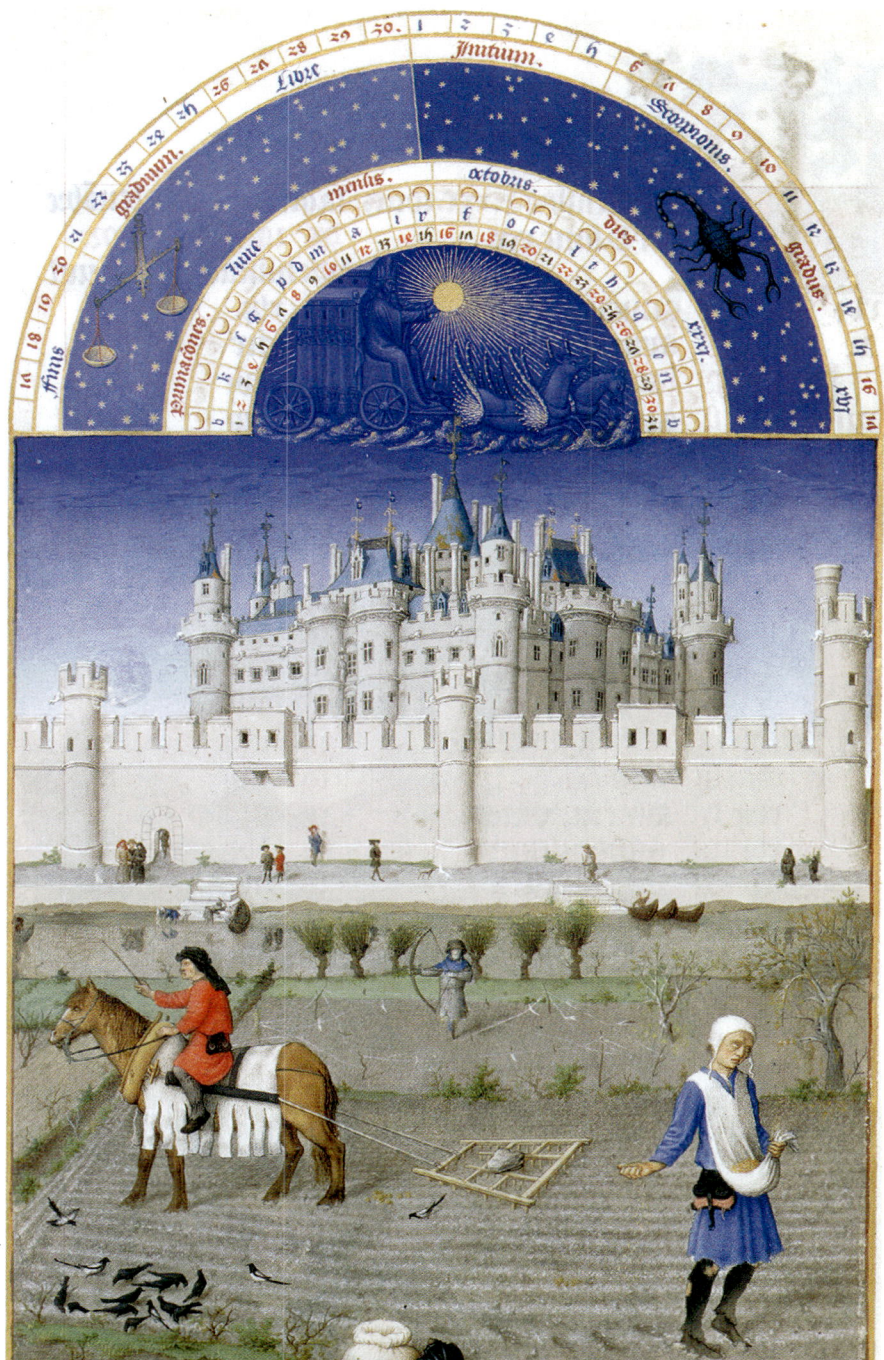

**20-16** LIMBOURG BROTHERS (POL, HERMAN, JEAN), *October,* from *Les Très Riches Heures du Duc de Berry,* 1413–1416. Colors and ink on vellum, $8\frac{7}{8}'' \times 5\frac{3}{8}''$. Musée Condé, Chantilly. ■◄

The Limbourg brothers expanded the illusionistic capabilities of manuscript painting with their care in rendering architectural details and convincing depiction of cast shadows.

The full-page calendar pictures of *Les Très Riches Heures* are the most famous in the history of manuscript illumination. They represent the 12 months in terms of the associated seasonal tasks, alternating scenes of nobility and peasantry. Above each picture is a *lunette* in which the Limbourgs depicted the zodiac signs and the chariot of the sun as it makes its yearly cycle through the heavens. Beyond its function as a religious book, *Les Très Riches Heures* also visually captures the power of the duke and his relationship to the peasants. For example, the colorful calendar picture for January (FIG. 20-15) portrays a New Year's reception at court. The duke appears as magnanimous host, his head circled by the fire screen, almost halolike, behind him. His chamberlain stands next to him, urging the guests forward with the words "*aproche, aproche.*" The lavish spread of food on the table and the large tapestry on the back wall augment the richness and extravagance of the setting and the occasion.

In contrast, the illustration for October (FIG. 20-16) focuses on the peasantry. Here, the Limbourg brothers depicted a sower, a harrower on horseback, and washerwomen, along with city dwellers, who promenade in front of the Louvre (the French king's residence at the time, now one of the world's great art museums). The peasants do not appear discontented as they go about their assigned tasks. Surely this imagery flattered the duke's sense of himself as a compassionate master. The growing artistic interest in naturalism is evident here in the careful way the painter recorded the architectural details of the Louvre and in the convincing shadows of the people and objects (such as the archer scarecrow and the horse) in the scene.

1 in.

piece. Books of Hours became favorite possessions of the northern European aristocracy during the 14th and 15th centuries. (Mary, the last duchess of Burgundy, commissioned a Book of Hours in which she was portrayed praying; FIG. **20-16A**. It is the masterpiece of the illuminator known as the MASTER OF MARY OF BURGUNDY, possi-

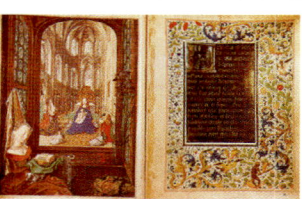

**20-16A** *Hours of Mary of Burgundy,* ca. 1480.

bly ALEXANDER BENING [ca. 1444–1519].) These sumptuous books eventually became available to affluent burghers and contributed to the decentralization of religious practice that was one factor in the Protestant Reformation in the early 16th century (see Chapter 23).

horse) in the scene.

As a whole, *Les Très Riches Heures* reinforced the image of the duke of Berry as a devout man, cultured bibliophile, sophisticated art patron, and powerful and magnanimous leader. Further, the expanded range of subject matter, especially the prominence of *genre* subjects in a religious book, reflected the increasing integration of religious and secular concerns in both art and life at the time. Although all three Limbourg brothers worked on *Les Très Riches Heures,* art historians have never been able to ascertain definitively which brother painted which images. Given the common practice of collaboration on artistic projects at this time, however, the determination of specific authorship is not very important.

## Panel Painting

Images for private devotional use were popular in France, as in Flanders, and the preferred medium was oil paint on wood panels.

**JEAN FOUQUET** Among the French artists whose paintings were in demand was JEAN FOUQUET (ca. 1420–1481), who worked for King Charles VII (r. 1422–1461, the patron and client of Jacques Coeur; FIG. 13-30) and for the duke of Nemours. Fouquet painted a diptych (FIG. **20-17**) for Étienne Chevalier, who, despite his lowly origins, became Charles VII's treasurer in 1452. In the left panel of the *Melun Diptych* (named for its original location in Melun Cathedral), Chevalier appears with his patron saint, Saint Stephen (Étienne in French). Appropriately, Fouquet's donor portrait of Chevalier depicts his prominent patron as devout—kneeling, with hands clasped in prayer. The representation of the pious donor with his standing saint recalls Flemish art, as do the three-quarter stances and the realism of Chevalier's portrait. The artist portrayed Saint Stephen, whose head also has a portraitlike quality, holding the stone of his martyrdom (death by stoning) atop a volume of the holy scriptures, thereby ensuring that viewers properly identify the saint. Fouquet rendered the entire image in meticulous detail and included a highly ornamented architectural setting.

In its original diptych form (the two panels are now in different museums), the viewer would follow the gaze of Chevalier and Saint Stephen over to the right panel, which depicts the Virgin Mary and Christ Child in a most unusual way—with marblelike flesh, surrounded by red and blue *cherubs* (chubby winged child angels). The juxtaposition of these two images enabled the patron to bear witness to the sacred. The integration of sacred and secular (especially the political or personal), prevalent in other northern European artworks, also emerges here, which complicates the reading of this diptych. Agnès Sorel (1421–1450), the mistress of King Charles VII, was Fouquet's model for the Virgin Mary, whose left breast is exposed and who does not look at the viewer. Chevalier commissioned this painting after Sorel's death, probably by poisoning while pregnant with the king's child. Thus, in addition to the religious interpretation of this diptych, there is surely a personal and political narrative here as well.

# HOLY ROMAN EMPIRE

Because the Holy Roman Empire (whose core was Germany) did not participate in the drawn-out saga of the Hundred Years' War, its economy remained stable and prosperous. Without a dominant court to commission artworks, wealthy merchants and clergy became the primary German patrons during the 15th century.

## Panel Painting

The art of the early Northern Renaissance in the Holy Roman Empire displays a pronounced stylistic diversity. Some artists followed developments in Flemish painting, and large-scale altarpieces featuring naturalistically painted biblical themes were familiar sights in the Holy Roman Empire.

**KONRAD WITZ** Among the most notable 15th-century German altarpieces is the *Altarpiece of Saint Peter*, painted in 1444 for the chapel of Notre-Dame des Maccabées in the Cathedral of Saint Peter in Geneva, Switzerland. KONRAD WITZ (ca. 1400–1446), whose studio was in Basel, painted one exterior wing of this triptych with a

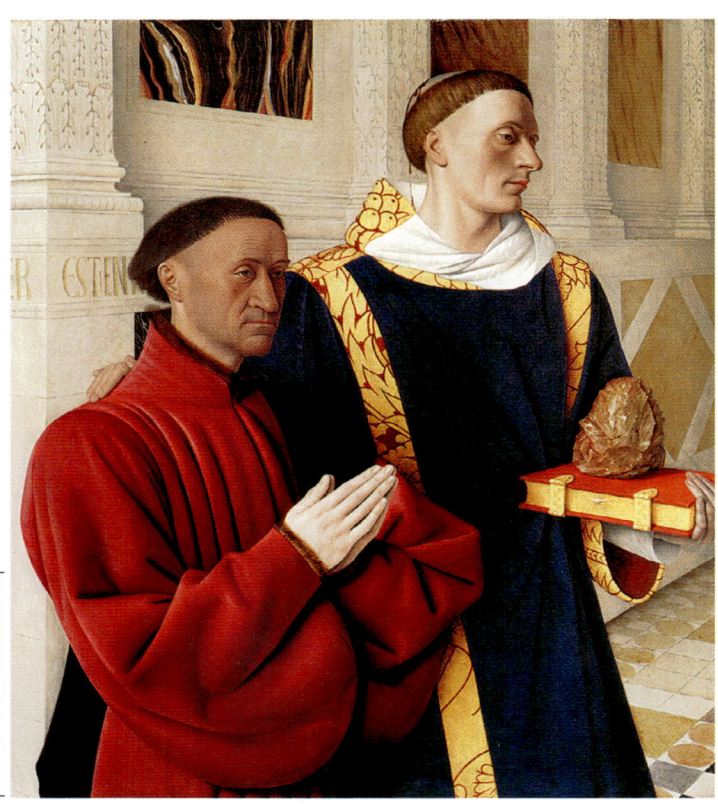
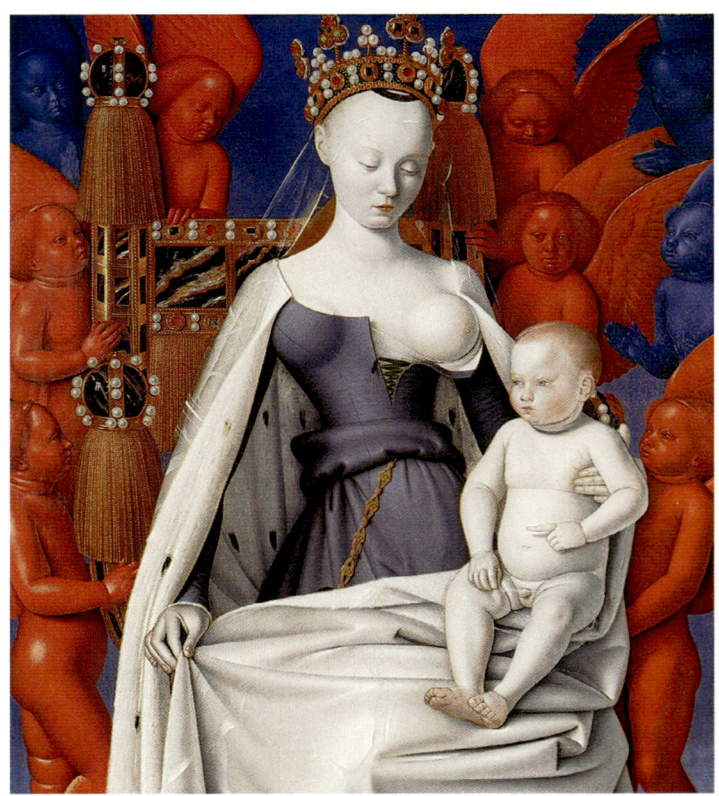

**20-17** JEAN FOUQUET, *Melun Diptych.* Left wing: *Étienne Chevalier and Saint Stephen,* ca. 1450. Oil on wood, 3′ $\frac{1}{2}$″ × 2′ 9$\frac{1}{2}$″. Gemäldegalerie, Staatliche Museen zu Berlin, Berlin. Right wing: *Virgin and Child,* ca. 1451. Oil on wood, 3′ 1$\frac{1}{4}$″ × 2′ 9$\frac{1}{2}$″. Koninklijk Museum voor Schone Kunsten, Antwerp.

Fouquet's meticulous representation of a pious kneeling donor with a standing patron saint recalls Flemish painting, as do the three-quarter stances and the realism of the portraits.

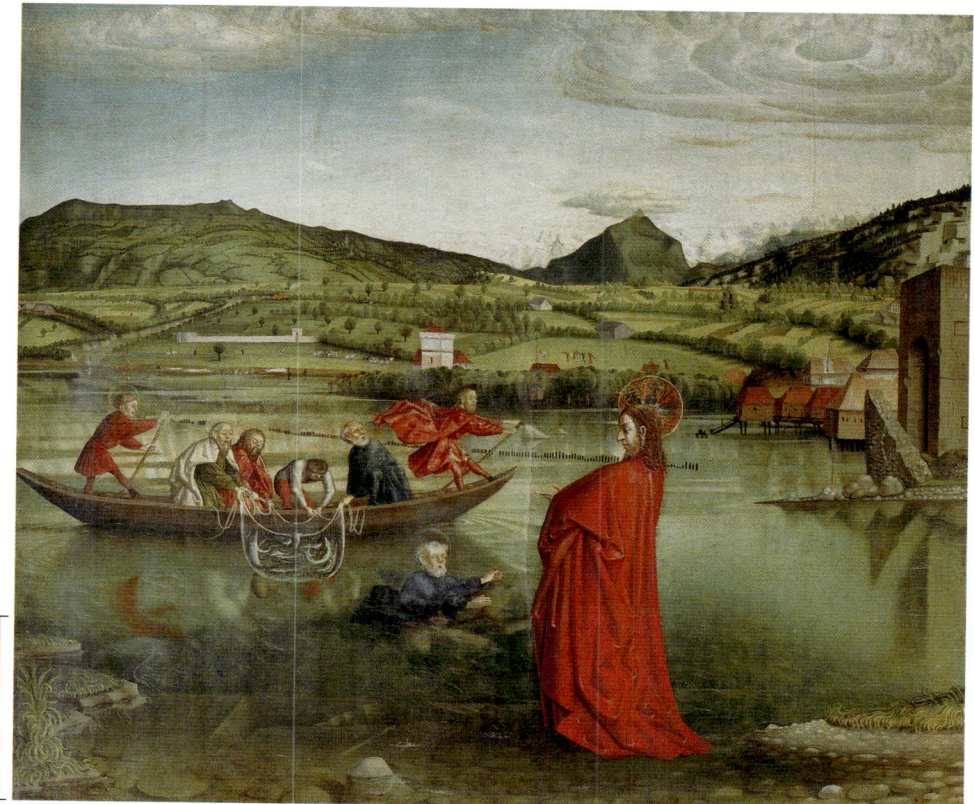

**20-18** KONRAD WITZ, *Miraculous Draught of Fish,* exterior wing of *Altarpiece of Saint Peter,* from the Chapel of Notre-Dame des Maccabées, Cathedral of Saint Peter, Geneva, Switzerland, 1444. Oil on wood, 4' 3" × 5' 1". Musée d'Art et d'Histoire, Geneva.

Konrad Witz set this biblical story on Lake Geneva. The painting is one of the first 15th-century works depicting a specific locale and is noteworthy for the painter's skill in rendering water effects.

representation of *Miraculous Draught of Fish* (FIG. **20-18**). The other exterior wing (not illustrated) depicts the release of Saint Peter from prison. The central panel is lost. On the interior wings, Witz painted scenes of *Adoration of the Magi* and of Saint Peter's presentation of the donor (Bishop François de Mies) to the Virgin and Child. *Miraculous Draught of Fish* shows Peter, the first pope, unsuccessfully trying to emulate Christ walking on water. Some scholars think the choice of subject is a commentary on the part of Witz's patron, the Swiss cardinal, on the limited power of the pope in Rome.

The painting is particularly significant because of the landscape's prominence. Witz showed precocious skill in the study of water ef-

fects—the sky glaze on the slowly moving lake surface, the mirrored reflections of the figures in the boat, and the transparency of the shallow water in the foreground. He observed and represented the landscape so carefully that art historians have been able to determine the exact location shown. Witz presented a view of the shores of Lake Geneva, with the town of Geneva on the right and Le Môle Mountain in the distance behind Christ's head. This painting is one of the first 15th-century works depicting a specific, identifiable site.

The work of other leading German painters of the mid-15th century, for example, STEFAN LOCHNER (ca. 1400–1451), retained medieval features to a much greater degree, as is immediately evident in a comparison between Witz's landscape and Lochner's *Madonna in the Rose Garden* (FIG. **20-18A**).

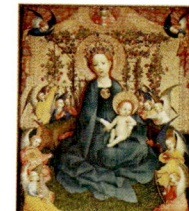

**20-18A** LOCHNER, *Madonna in the Rose Garden,* ca. 1440.

## Sculpture

In contrast to Flanders, where painted altarpieces were the norm, in the Holy Roman Empire many of the leading 15th-century artists specialized in carving large wooden retables. These grandiose sculpted altarpieces reveal the power of the lingering Late Gothic style.

**VEIT STOSS** The sculptor VEIT STOSS (1447–1533) trained in the Upper Rhine region but settled in Kraków (in present-day Poland) in 1477. In that year, he began work on a monumental altarpiece (FIG. **20-19**) for the church of Saint Mary in Kraków. In the central boxlike shrine, huge carved and painted figures, some nine feet high,

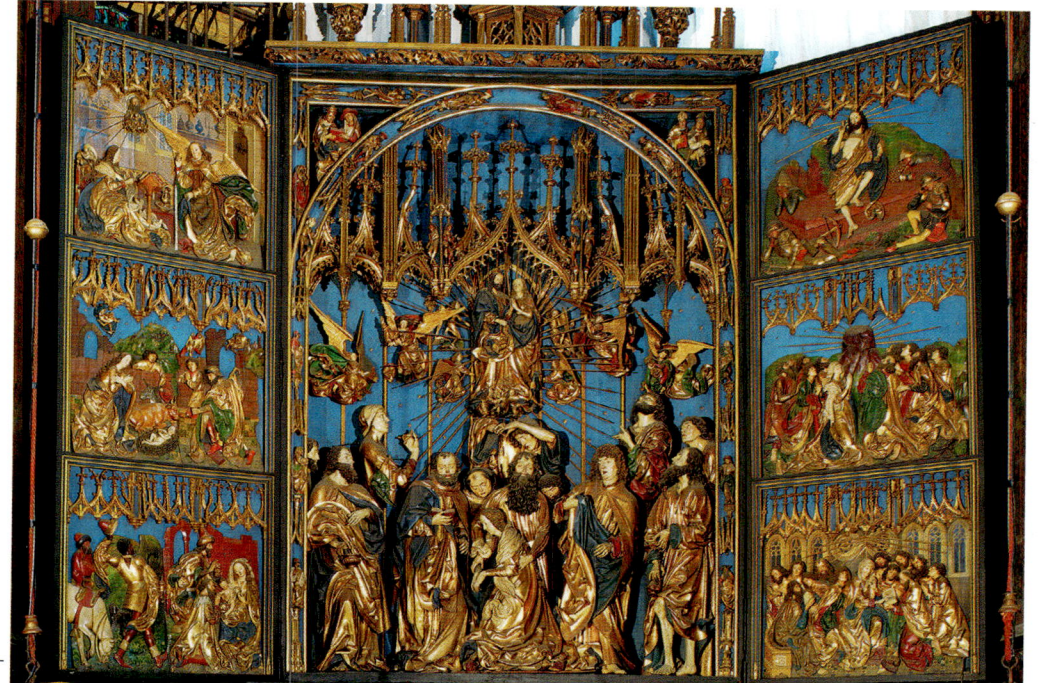

**20-19** VEIT STOSS, *Death and Assumption of the Virgin* (wings open), altar of the Virgin Mary, church of Saint Mary, Kraków, Poland, 1477–1489. Painted and gilded wood, center panel 23' 9" high.

In this huge sculptured and painted altarpiece, Stoss used every figural and ornamental element from the vocabulary of Gothic art to heighten the emotion and to glorify the sacred event.

Holy Roman Empire **553**

represent Death and Assumption of the Virgin. On the wings, Stoss portrayed scenes from the lives of Christ and Mary. The altar forcefully expresses the intense piety of Gothic culture in its late phase, when artists used every figural and ornamental motif in the repertoire of Gothic art to heighten the emotion and to glorify sacred events. In the Kraków altarpiece, Christ's disciples congregate around the Virgin, who collapses, dying. One of them supports her, while another wrings his hands in grief. Stoss posed others in attitudes of woe and psychic shock, striving for realism in every minute detail. He engulfed the figures in restless, twisting, and curving swaths of drapery whose broken and writhing lines unite the whole tableau in a vision of agitated emotion. The artist's massing of sharp, broken, and pierced forms that dart flamelike through the composition—at once unifying and animating it—recalls the design principles of Late Gothic architecture (FIG. 13-27). Indeed, in the Kraków altarpiece, Stoss merged sculpture and architecture, enhancing their union with paint and gilding.

**TILMAN RIEMENSCHNEIDER** *Assumption of the Virgin* is also the subject of the center panel (FIG. **20-20**) of the *Creglingen Altarpiece,* created by TILMAN RIEMENSCHNEIDER (ca. 1460–1531) of Würzburg for a parish church in Creglingen, Germany. He incorporated intricate Gothic forms, especially in the altarpiece's elaborate canopy, but unlike Stoss, he did not paint the figures or the background. By employing an endless and restless line running through the garments of the figures, Riemenschneider succeeded in setting the whole design into fluid motion, and no individual element functions without the rest. The draperies float and flow around bodies lost within them, serving not as descriptions but as design elements that tie the figures to one another and to the framework. A look of psychic strain, a facial expression common in Riemenschneider's work, heightens the spirituality of the figures, immaterial and weightless as they appear.

## Graphic Arts

A new age blossomed in the 15th century with a sudden technological advance that had widespread effects—the invention by Johannes Gutenberg (ca. 1400–1468) of moveable type around 1450 and the development of the printing press. Printing had been known in China centuries before but had never fostered, as it did in 15th-century Europe, a revolution in written communication and in the generation and management of information. Printing provided new and challenging media for artists, and the earliest form was the *woodcut* (see "Woodcuts, Engravings, and Etchings," page 556). Artists produced inexpensive woodcuts such as the *Buxheim Saint Christopher* (FIG. **20-20A**) before the development of moveable-type printing. But when a rise in literacy and the improved economy necessitated production of illustrated books on a grand scale, artists met the challenge of bringing the woodcut picture onto the same page as the letterpress.

**MICHAEL WOLGEMUT** The so-called *Nuremberg Chronicle,* a history of the world produced in Nuremberg by ANTON KOBERGER (ca. 1445–1513) with more than 650 illustrations by the workshop of MICHAEL WOLGEMUT (1434–1519), documents this achievement. The hand-colored illustration (FIG. **20-21**) spread across two facing pages represents *Radeburga* (modern Radeberg, near Dresden). The blunt, simple lines of the woodcut technique give a detailed perspective of the city, its harbor and

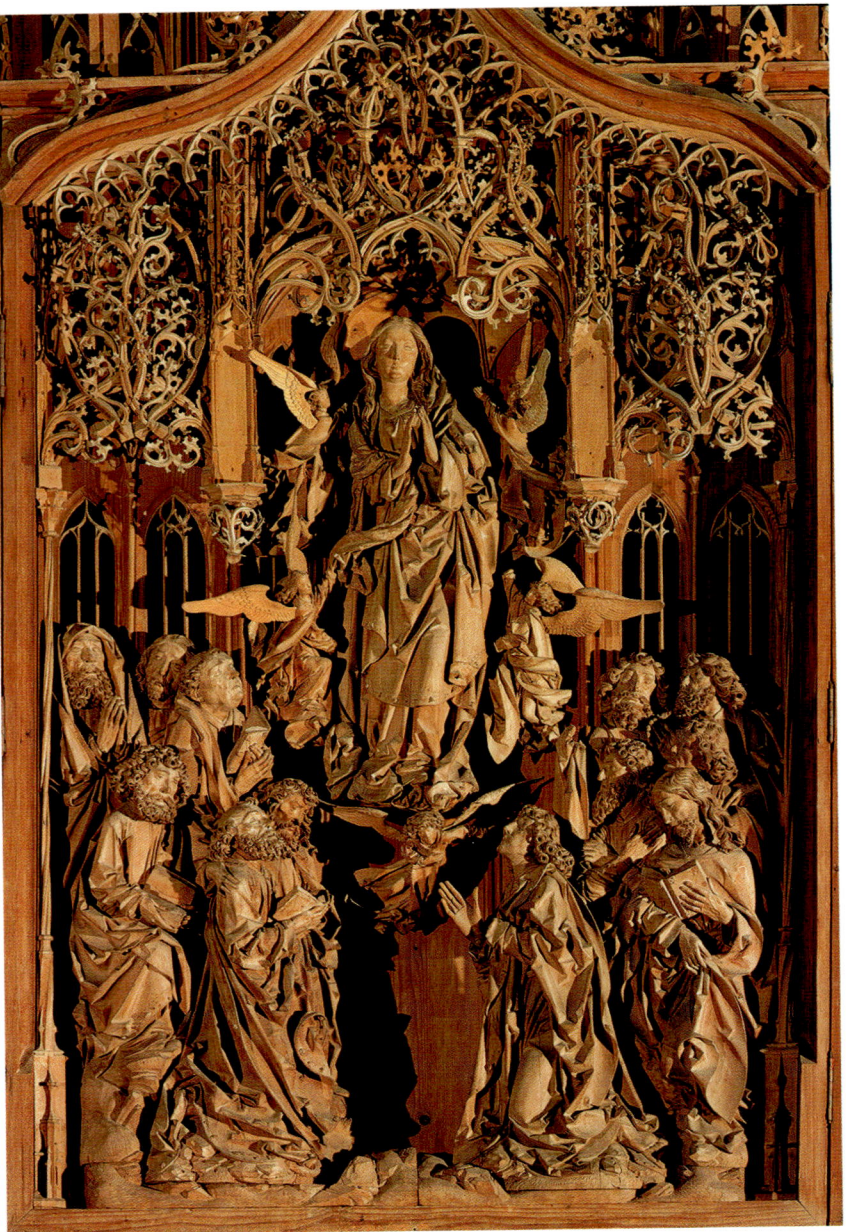

**20-20** TILMAN RIEMENSCHNEIDER, *Assumption of the Virgin,* **center panel of** *Creglingen Altarpiece,* **parish church, Creglingen, Germany, ca. 1495–1499. Lindenwood, 6′ 1″ wide.**

Riemenschneider specialized in carving large wood retables. His works feature intricate Gothic tracery and religious figures whose bodies are almost lost within their swirling garments.

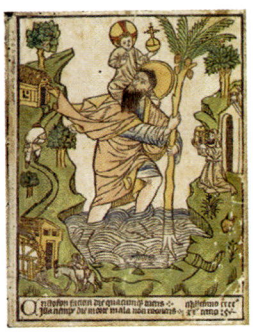

**20-20A** *Buxheim Saint Christopher,* 1423.

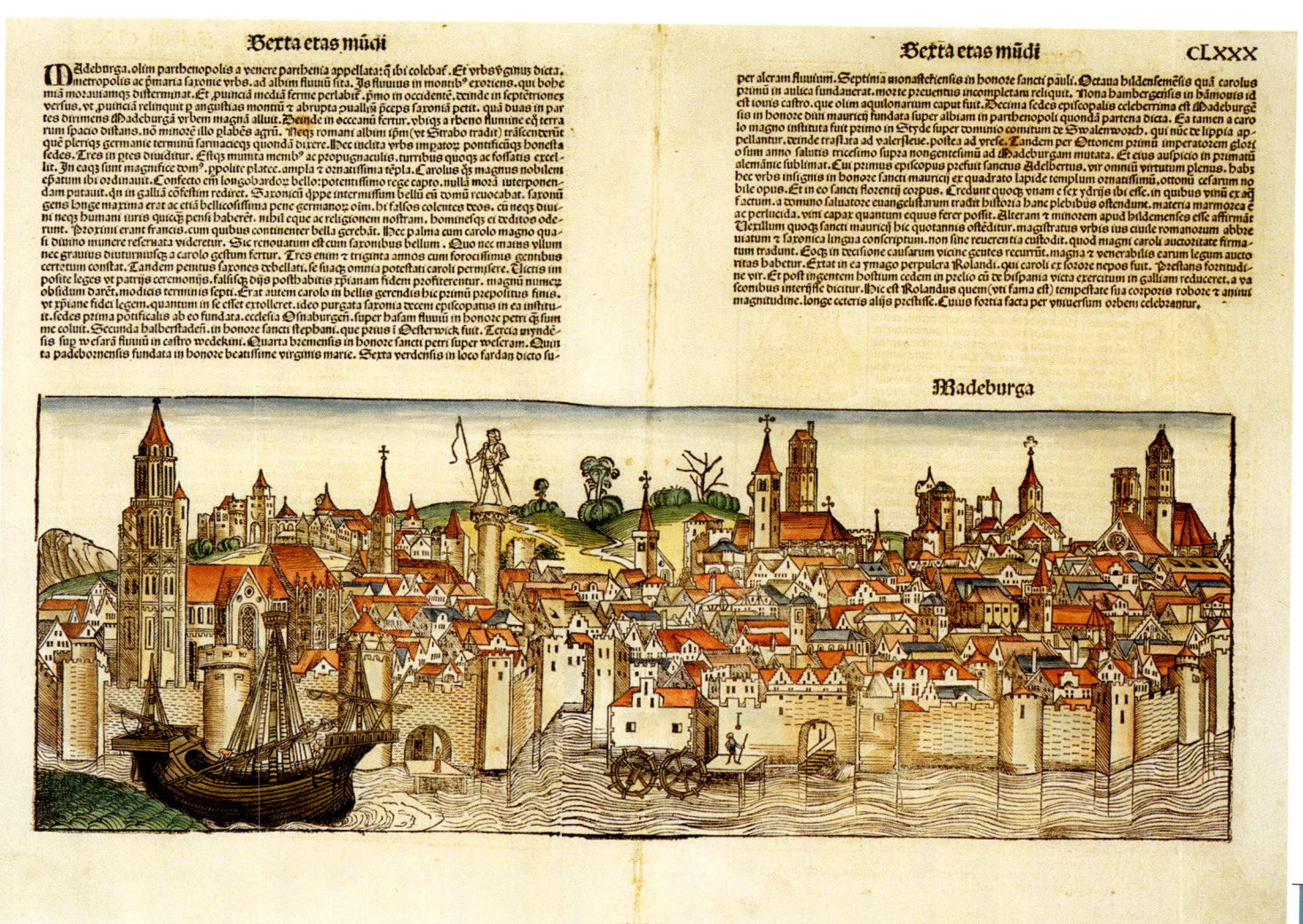

Berta etas mūdi

Madeburga.olim parthenopolis a venere parthenia appellata:q̄ ibi colebaƒ.Et vrbs v̄gınus dicta. metropolis ac pmaria saxonie vrbs.ad albim fluuiū sita. Is fluuius in montib⁹ exoriens.qui bohe miā moraunamq̄s distermmat.Et.puincia medıā ferme perlabıƒ.pmo in occidente.deınde in septemones versus,vt.puinciā relinquıt p̄ angustias montiū ⁊ abrupta puallıꝗ ꝑ̄eps saxoniā petit.quā duas in par tes dimmens Madeburgā vrbem magnā alluit.Deınde in occeanū fertur.vbiꝗ a rheno flumine eꝗ terra rum spacio distans.nō mınoze illo plabes agrū. Neꝗ romani albim ıp̄m(vt Strabo tradit) trāscenuerūt q̄ plerıꝗ germanie terminū farmaciecꝗ quondā dicere.Hec mclita vrbs impatoꝛ pontıficıꝗ bonesta sedes.Tres in p̄tes dıuıdıtur.Estꝗ munıta memb⁹ ac pꝛopugnaculıs.turribus quoꝗ ac fossatıs excel lit.In eaꝗ sunt magnifice tem⁹.polıte place.ampla ⁊ oꝛnatıssıma tep̄la.Carolus ꝗs magnus nobılent eꝑ̄atum ıbı oꝛdınauıt.Confecto cm̄ longobardo bello:potentıssımo rege capto,nulla moza ıuterponen dam putauıt.qñ in gallıā cōfestū redıret.Saxonıcı ꝑ̄pe intermıssum bellū cū tomū reuocabat.saxonıı gens longe maxima erat ac etıā bellicosıssıma pene germanoꝛ oım.bı falsos colentes tros.cū neꝗ dıuı nı neꝗ humanı ıurıs quıcꝗ pensı haberet.nıhıl eque ac relıgıonem nostram.homınesꝗ eı exdıtos ode runt.ꝓxımı erant francıs.cum quıbus contınenter bella gerebāt.Hec palma eum carolo magno qua sı dıuıno munere reservata vıderetur.Sıc renouatum est cum saxonıbus bellum.Quo nec maıus vllum nec grauıus dıuturnıusꝗ a carolo gestum fertur.Tres enım ⁊ trıgınta annos cum feroçıssımıs gentıbus certetuım constat.Tandem penıtus saxones tebellatı.se suaꝗ omnıa potestatı carolı permısere.Dıctıs ım posıte leges vt patrıꝗs ceremonıꝗs.falsısꝗ dꝰs posth abıtıs xp̄ıanam fidem profiterentur.magnū numeꝛ obsıdum darēt.modıcıa termınıs septı.Erat autem carolo in bellıs gerendıs hıc pꝛımı ꝓepositus finıs. vt xp̄ıane fidei legem.quantum in se esset extolleret.ıdeo purgata saxonıa tecem episcopatus in ea ınstıtu ıt.sedes pꝛıma pontıficalıs ab eo fundata.ecclesıa Osnaburgen.super basam fluuıı in bonoze petrı ꝗs fun me colıt.Secunda halberstadeñ.ın bonoze sancti stephanı.que pꝛıus ı Oesterwıck fuıt.Tercıa myndeñ sıs sup̄ w̄esarā fluuıū ın castro wedekını.Quarta bremeñsıs ın bonoze sancti petrı super w̄eseram.Quın ta padebozneñsıs fundata ın bonoze beatıssıme vırgınıs marıe. Sexta verdeñsıs ın loco fardan dıcto su

Berta etas mūdi            CLXXX

per aleram fluuıım.Septınıa monasterıeñsıs ın bonoze sancti paulı.Octaua hıldenseñesıs quā carolus pꝛımū ın aulıca fundauerat.moꝛte pꝛeuentus ıncompletam relıquıt.Nona bambergeñsıs ın bāmouıs ıd est ıouıs castro.que olım aquılonarıum caput fuıt.Decıma sedes episcopalıs celeberrıma est Madeburgē sıs ın bonoze dñı maurıcı fundata super albıam ın parthenopolı quondā partena dicta.Ea tamen a caro lo magno ınstıtuta fuıt pꝛımo ın Stryde super tomınıo comıtum te Swalenwoꝛch.quı nūc̄ te lıppıa ap pellantur.deınde trasflata ad valerfleue.postea ad wrele.Tandem per Ottonem pꝛımı ımperatozem glozı o sum anno salutıs trıcesımo supꝛa nongentesımū ad Madeburgam mutata.Et sub auspıcıo ın pꝛımatū alemanıe sublımat.Cuı pꝛımus episcopus pꝛefuıt sanctus Adelbertus.vır omnıū vırtutum plenus.habꝓ hec vrbs ınsıgnıs ın bonoze sancti maurıcı et quadrato lapıde templum oꝛnatıssımū.ottonıs cesarum no bıle opus.Et ın eo sancti flozentıı cozpus.Credunt quoꝗ vnam et ser ydrıꝗs ıbı esse.ın quıbus vınū et aꝗ factum.a tomıno saluatoze euangelıstarum tradıt hıstozıa hanc plebıbus ostendunt.materıa marmozea e ac perlucıda.vını capax quantum equus ferre possıt.Alteram ⁊ mınotem apud hıldemeñses esse affırmāt Uexıllum quoꝗ sancti maurıcı hıc quotannıs ostēdıtur.magıstratus vrbıs ıus cıuıle romanozum abbꝛe uıatum ⁊ saxonıca lıngua conscrıptum.non sıne reuerentıa custodıt.quod magnı carolı auctozıtate fırma tum tradunt.Eoꝗs ın tecısıone causarum vıcıne gentes recurrunt.magna ⁊ venerabılıs earum legum aucto rıtas habetur.Erat ın ea ymago pꝛepulcra Rolandı.quı carolı et sozoze nepos fuıt.Pꝛestans foꝛtıtudı ne vır.Et post ıngentem hostıum cedem ın pꝛelıo cū a̅ bıspanıa vıcta exercıtum ın gallıam reduceret.a va sconıbus ıntersıffe dıcıtur.Hıc est Rolandus quem(vtı fama est)tempestate sua cozpozıs robote ⁊ anımı magnıtudıne.longe ceterıs alıꝗs pꝛestıffe.Cuıus foꝛtıa facta per vnıuersum oꝛbem celebꝛantur.

Madeburga

1 in.

**20-21** MICHAEL WOLGEMUT and shop, *Radeburga* page from the *Nuremberg Chronicle,* 1493. Woodcut. Printed by ANTON KOBERGER.

The *Nuremberg Chronicle* is an early example of woodcut illustrations in printed books. The more than 650 pictures include detailed views of towns, but they are generic rather than specific portrayals.

shipping, its walls and towers, its churches and municipal buildings, and the baronial castle on the hill. Despite the numerous architectural structures, historians cannot determine whether this illustration represents the artist's accurate depiction of the city or is the product of a fanciful imagination. Artists often reprinted the same image as illustrations of different cities, and this depiction of Radeburga is very likely a generic view. Regardless, the work is a monument to a new craft, which expanded in concert with the art of the printed book.

**MARTIN SCHONGAUER** The woodcut medium hardly had matured when the technique of *engraving* (see "Woodcuts, Engravings, and Etchings," page 556), begun in the 1430s and well developed by 1450, proved much more flexible. Predictably, in the second half of the century, engraving began to replace the woodcut process, for making both book illustrations and widely popular single prints.

MARTIN SCHONGAUER (ca. 1430–1491) was the most skilled and subtle 15th-century Northern Renaissance master of metal engraving. His *Saint Anthony Tormented by Demons* (FIG. **20-22**) shows both the versatility of the medium and the artist's mastery

of it. The stoic saint is caught in a revolving thornbush of spiky demons, who claw and tear at him furiously. With unsurpassed skill and subtlety, Schongauer incised lines of varying thickness and density into a metal plate and created marvelous distinctions of tonal values and textures—from smooth skin to rough cloth, from the furry and feathery to the hairy and scaly. The use of *cross-hatching* (sets of engraved lines at right angles) to describe forms, which Schongauer probably developed, became standard among German graphic artists. The Italians preferred *parallel hatching* (FIG. 21-30) and rarely adopted cross-hatching, which, in keeping with the general Northern European approach to art, tends to describe the surfaces of things rather than their underlying structures.

Schongauer probably engraved *Saint Anthony* between 1480 and 1490. By then, the political geography of Europe had changed dramatically. Charles the Bold, who had assumed the title of duke of Burgundy in 1467, died in 1477, bringing to an end the Burgundian dream of forming a strong middle kingdom between France and the Holy Roman Empire. After Charles's death at the battle of Nancy, the French monarchy reabsorbed the southern Burgundian lands, and the Netherlands passed to the Holy Roman Empire

*Holy Roman Empire* **555**

# Woodcuts, Engravings, and Etchings

With the invention of moveable type in the 15th century and the new widespread availability of paper from commercial mills, the art of printmaking developed rapidly in Europe. A *print* is an artwork on paper, usually produced in multiple impressions. The set of prints an artist creates from a single print surface is called an *edition*. As with books manufactured on a press, the printmaking process involves the transfer of ink from a printing surface to paper. This can be accomplished in several ways. During the 15th and 16th centuries, artists most commonly used the *relief* and *intaglio* methods of printmaking.

Artists produce relief prints, the oldest and simplest of the printing methods, by carving into a surface, usually wood. Relief printing requires artists to conceptualize their images negatively—that is, they remove the surface areas around the images using a gouging instrument. Thus, when the printmaker inks the ridges that carry the design, the hollow areas remain dry, and a positive image results when the artist presses the printing block against paper. Because artists produce *woodcuts* through a subtractive process (removing parts of the material), it is difficult to create very thin, fluid, and closely spaced lines. As a result, woodcut prints (for example, FIGS. 20-21 and 20-21A) tend to exhibit stark contrasts and sharp edges.

In contrast to the production of relief prints, the intaglio method involves a positive process. The artist *incises* (cuts) an image on a metal plate, often copper. The image can be created on the plate manually (*engraving* or *drypoint*; for example, FIG. 20-22) using a tool (a *burin* or *stylus*) or chemically (*etching*; for example, FIG. 25-16). In the etching process, an acid bath eats into the exposed parts of the plate where the artist has drawn through an acid-resistant coating. When the artist inks the surface of the intaglio plate and wipes it clean, the ink is forced into the incisions. Then the artist runs the plate and paper through a roller press, and the paper absorbs the remaining ink, creating the print. Because the artist "draws" the image onto the plate, intaglio prints differ in character from relief prints. Engravings, drypoints, and etchings generally present a wider variety of linear effects, as is immediately evident in a comparison of the roughly contemporaneous woodcut of *Tarvisium* (FIG. 20-21) by Michael Wolgemut and Martin Schongauer's engraving of *Saint Anthony Tormented by Demons* (FIG. 20-22). Intaglio prints also often reveal to a greater extent evidence of the artist's touch, the result of the hand's changing pressure and shifting directions.

The paper and inks artists use also affect the finished look of the printed image. During the 15th and 16th centuries, European printmakers used papers produced from cotton and linen rags that papermakers mashed with water into a pulp. The papermakers then applied a thin layer of this pulp to a wire screen and allowed it to dry to create the paper. As contact with Asia increased, printmakers made greater use of what was called Japan paper (of mulberry fibers) and China paper. Artists, then as now, could select from a

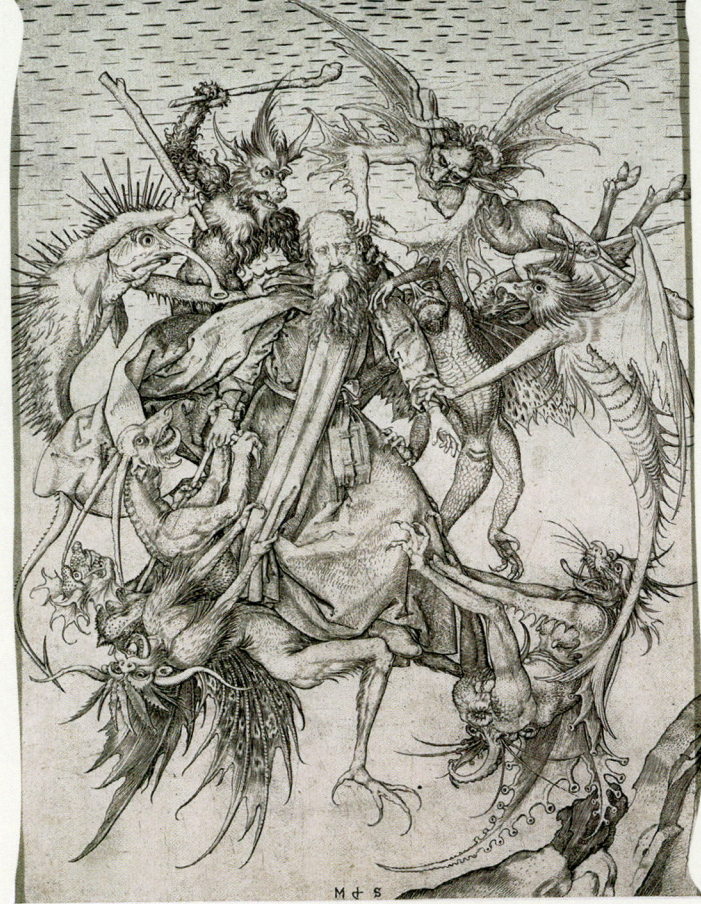

**20-22** MARTIN SCHONGAUER, *Saint Anthony Tormented by Demons*, ca. 1480–1490. Engraving, $1' \frac{1}{4}'' \times 9''$. Fondazione Magnani Rocca, Corte di Mamiano.

Schongauer was the most skilled of the early masters of metal engraving. By using a burin to incise lines in a copper plate, he was able to create a marvelous variety of tonal values and textures.

wide variety of inks. The type and proportion of the ink ingredients affect the consistency, color, and oiliness of inks, which various papers absorb differently.

Paper is lightweight, and the portability of prints has appealed to artists over the years. The opportunity to produce numerous impressions from the same print surface also made printmaking attractive to 15th- and 16th-century artists. In addition, prints can be sold at lower prices than paintings or sculptures. Consequently, prints reached a much wider audience than did one-of-a-kind artworks. The number and quality of existing 15th- and 16th-century European prints attest to the importance of the new print medium.

by virtue of the dynastic marriage of Charles's daughter, Mary of Burgundy (FIG. 20-16A), to Maximilian of Habsburg, inaugurating a new political and artistic era in northern Europe (see Chapter 23). The next two chapters, however, explore Italian developments in painting, sculpture, and architecture during the 15th and 16th centuries.

# LATE MEDIEVAL AND EARLY RENAISSANCE NORTHERN EUROPE

## BURGUNDY AND FLANDERS

❚ The most powerful rulers north of the Alps during the first three-quarters of the 15th century were the dukes of Burgundy. They controlled Flanders, which derived its wealth from wool and banking, and were great art patrons.

❚ Duke Philip the Bold (r. 1363–1404) endowed the Carthusian monastery at Champmol, near Dijon, which became a ducal mausoleum. He employed Claus Sluter, whose *Well of Moses* features innovative statues of prophets with portraitlike features and realistic costumes.

❚ Flemish painters popularized the use of oil paints on wood panels. By superimposing translucent glazes, they created richer colors than possible using tempera or fresco. One of the earliest examples of oil painting is Melchior Broederlam's *Retable de Champmol* (1339).

❚ A major art form in churches and private homes alike was the altarpiece with folding wings. In Robert Campin's *Mérode Altarpiece,* the *Annunciation* takes place in a Flemish home. The work's donors, depicted on the left wing, are anachronistically present as witnesses to the sacred event. Typical of "Northern Renaissance" painting, the everyday objects depicted often have symbolic significance.

❚ Jan van Eyck, Rogier van der Weyden, and others established portraiture as an important art form in 15th-century Flanders. Their subjects were successful businessmen, both Flemish and foreign, for example, the Italian financier Giovanni Arnolfini. Rogier's *Saint Luke Drawing the Virgin,* a celebration of the painter's craft, is probably a self-portrait.

❚ Among the other major Flemish painters were Petrus Christus and Hans Memling of Bruges, Dirk Bouts of Louvain, and Hugo van der Goes of Ghent, all of whom produced both altarpieces for churches and portraits for the homes of wealthy merchants. Hugo achieved such renown that he won a commission to paint an altarpiece for a church in Florence. The Italians marveled at the Flemish painter's masterful technique and extraordinary realism.

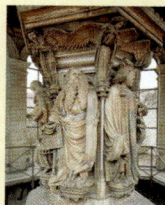

Sluter, *Well of Moses,*
1395-1406

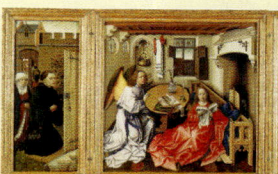

Campin, *Mérode Altarpiece,*
ca. 1425–1428

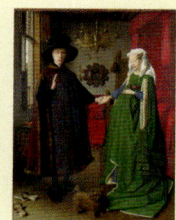

Van Eyck, *Giovanni Arnolfini
and His Wife,* 1434

## FRANCE

❚ During the 15th century, the Hundred Years' War crippled the French economy, but dukes and members of the royal court still commissioned some notable artworks.

❚ The Limbourg brothers expanded the illusionistic capabilities of manuscript illumination in the Book of Hours they produced for Jean, duke of Berry (r. 1360–1416) and brother of King Charles V (r. 1364–1380). Their full-page calendar pictures alternately represent the nobility and the peasantry, always in seasonal, naturalistic settings with realistically painted figures.

❚ French court art—for example, Jean Fouquet's *Melun Diptych*—owes a large debt to Flemish painting in style and technique as well as in the integration of sacred and secular themes.

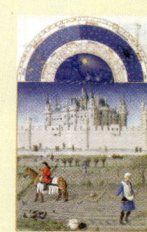

Limbourg brothers, *Les Très Riches
Heures du Duc de Berry,* 1413–1416

## HOLY ROMAN EMPIRE

❚ The Late Gothic style remained popular in 15th-century Germany for large carved wooden retables featuring highly emotive figures amid Gothic tracery.

❚ The major German innovation of the 15th century was the development of the printing press, which publishers soon used to produce books with woodcut illustrations. Woodcuts are relief prints in which the artist carves out the areas around the lines to be printed.

❚ German artists were also the earliest masters of engraving. The intaglio technique allows for a wider variety of linear effects because the artist incises the image directly onto a metal plate.

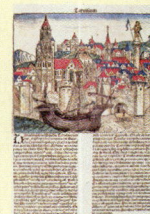

Wolgemut, *Nuremberg
Chronicle,* 1493

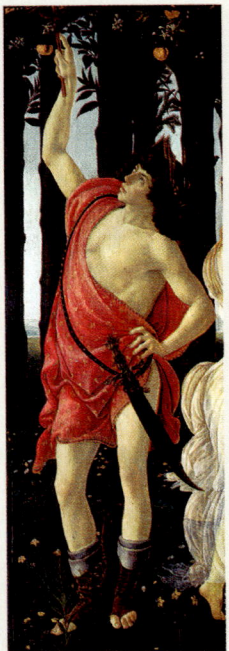

Mercury is the most enigmatic figure in Botticelli's lyrical painting celebrating love in springtime, probably a commemoration of the May 1482 wedding of Lorenzo di Pierfrancesco de' Medici.

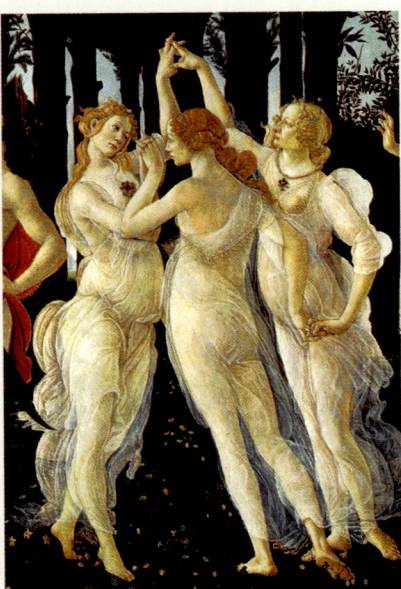

The dancing Three Graces closely resemble ancient prototypes Botticelli must have studied, but in 15th-century Florence, the Graces are clothed, albeit in thin, transparent garments.

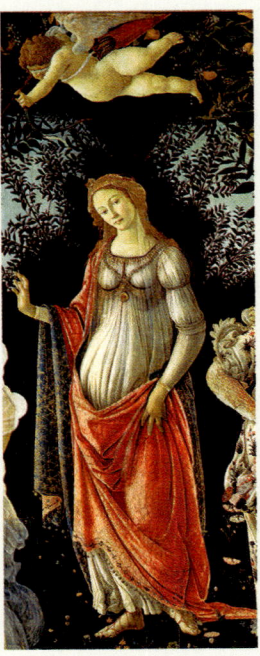

Cupid hovers over Venus, the central figure in this mythological allegory. The sky seen through the opening in the landscape behind Venus forms a kind of halo around the goddess of love's head.

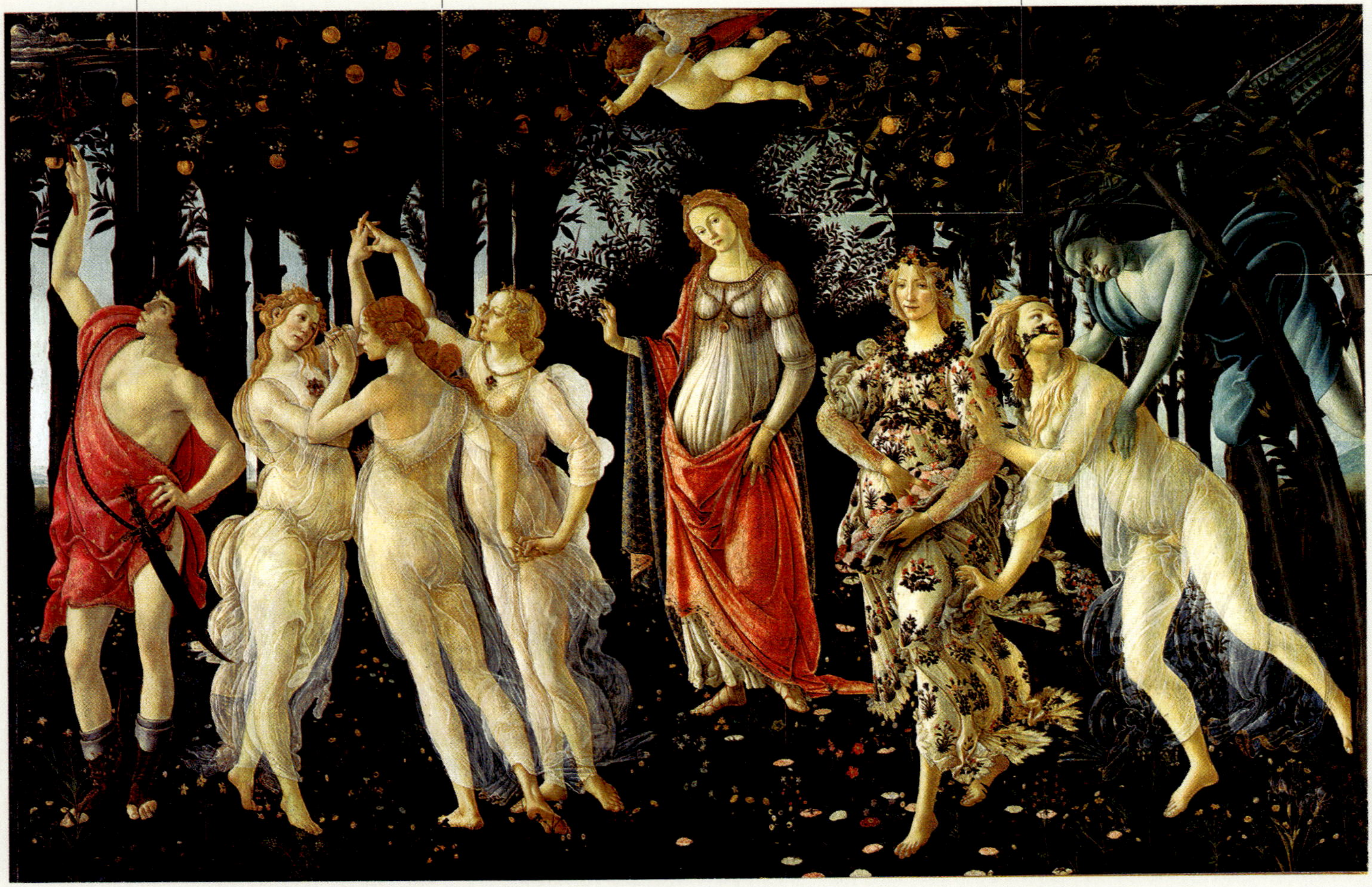

**21-1** SANDRO BOTTICELLI, *Primavera*, ca. 1482. Tempera on wood, 6′ 8″ × 10′ 4″. Galleria degli Uffizi, Florence. ◼️

1 ft.

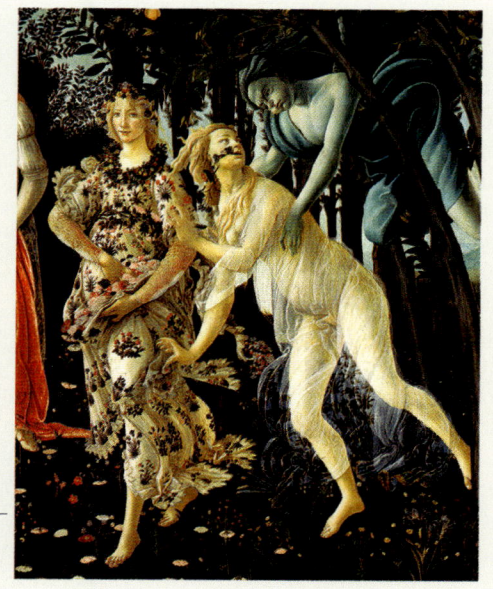

The blue ice-cold Zephyrus, the west wind, carries off and marries the nymph Chloris, whom he transforms into Flora, goddess of spring, appropriately shown wearing a rich floral gown.

21

# THE RENAISSANCE IN QUATTROCENTO ITALY

FRAMING THE ERA

## MEDICI PATRONAGE AND CLASSICAL LEARNING

The Medici family of Florence has become synonymous with the extraordinary cultural phenomenon called the Italian Renaissance. By early in the 15th century (the '400s, or *Quattrocento* in Italian), the banker Giovanni di Bicci de' Medici (ca. 1360–1429) had established the family fortune. His son Cosimo (1389–1464) became a great patron of art and of learning in the broadest sense. For example, Cosimo provided the equivalent of $20 million to establish the first public library since the ancient world. Cosimo's grandson Lorenzo (1449–1492), called "the Magnificent," was a member of the Platonic Academy of Philosophy and gathered about him a galaxy of artists and gifted men in all fields. He spent lavishly on buildings, paintings, and sculptures. Indeed, scarcely a single great Quattrocento architect, painter, sculptor, philosopher, or humanist scholar failed to enjoy Medici patronage.

Of all the Florentine masters the Medici employed, perhaps the most famous today is SANDRO BOTTICELLI (1444–1510). His work is a testament to the intense interest that the Medici and Quattrocento humanist scholars and artists had in the art, literature, and mythology of the Greco-Roman world—often interpreted by writers, painters, and sculptors alike in terms of Christianity according to the philosophical tenets of Neo-Platonism.

Botticelli painted *Primavera* (*Spring*; FIG. **21-1**) for Lorenzo di Pierfrancesco de' Medici (1463–1503), one of Lorenzo the Magnificent's cousins. Venus stands just to the right of center with her son Cupid hovering above her head. Botticelli drew attention to Venus by opening the landscape behind her to reveal a portion of sky that forms a kind of halo around the goddess of love's head. To her right, seemingly the target of Cupid's arrow, are the dancing Three Graces, based closely on ancient prototypes but clothed, albeit in thin, transparent garments. At the right, the blue ice-cold Zephyrus, the west wind, is about to carry off and marry the nymph Chloris, whom he transforms into Flora, goddess of spring, appropriately shown wearing a rich floral gown. At the far left, the enigmatic figure of Mercury turns away from all the others and reaches up with his distinctive staff, the *caduceus,* perhaps to dispel storm clouds. The sensuality of the representation, the appearance of Venus in springtime, and the abduction and marriage of Chloris all suggest the occasion for the painting was young Lorenzo's wedding in May 1482. But the painting also sums up the Neo-Platonists' view that earthly love is compatible with Christian theology. In their reinterpretation of classical mythology, Venus as the source of love provokes desire through Cupid. Desire can lead either to lust and violence (Zephyr) or, through reason and faith (Mercury), to the love of God. *Primavera,* read from right to left, served to urge the newlyweds to seek God through love.

# RENAISSANCE HUMANISM

The humanism Petrarch and Boccaccio promoted during the 14th century (see Chapter 14) fully blossomed in the 15th century. Increasingly, Italians in elite circles embraced the tenets underlying humanism—an emphasis on education and on expanding knowledge (especially of classical antiquity), the exploration of individual potential and a desire to excel, and a commitment to civic responsibility and moral duty. Quattrocento Italy also enjoyed an abundance of artistic talent. The fortunate congruence of artistic genius, the spread of humanism, and economic prosperity nourished the Renaissance, forever changing the direction and perception of art in the Western world.

For the Italian humanists, the quest for knowledge began with the legacy of the Greeks and Romans—the writings of Socrates, Plato, Aristotle, Ovid, and others. The development of a literature based on the commonly spoken Tuscan dialect expanded the audience for humanist writings. Further, the invention of moveable metal type in Germany around 1445 (see Chapter 20) facilitated the printing and wide distribution of books. Italians enthusiastically embraced this new printing process. By 1464, Subiaco (near Rome) boasted a press, and by 1469, Venice had established one as well. Among the first books printed in Italy using these new presses was Dante's *Divine Comedy,* his vernacular epic about Heaven, Purgatory, and Hell. The production of editions in Foligno (1472), Mantua (1472), Venice (1472), Naples (1477 and 1478–1479), and Milan (1478) testifies to the widespread popularity of Dante's work.

The humanists also avidly acquired information in a wide range of fields, including botany, geology, geography, optics, medicine, and engineering. Leonardo da Vinci's phenomenal expertise in many fields—from art and architecture to geology, aerodynamics, hydraulics, botany, and military science, among many others—still defines the modern notion of the "Renaissance man." Humanism also fostered a belief in individual potential and encouraged individual achievement, as well as civic responsibility. Whereas people in medieval society accorded great power to divine will in determining the events that affected lives, those in Renaissance Italy adopted a more secular stance. Humanists not only encouraged individual improvement but also rewarded excellence with fame and honor. Achieving and excelling through hard work became moral imperatives.

Quattrocento Italy witnessed constant fluctuations in its political and economic spheres, including shifting power relations among the numerous city-states and the rise of princely courts (see "Italian Princely Courts," page 591). *Condottieri* (military leaders) with large numbers of mercenary troops at their disposal played a major role in the ongoing struggle for power. Princely courts, such as those in Urbino and Mantua, emerged as cultural and artistic centers alongside the great art centers of the 14th century, especially the Republic of Florence. The association of humanism with education and culture appealed to accomplished individuals of high status, and humanism had its greatest impact among the elite and powerful, whether in the republics or the princely courts. These individuals were in the best position to commission art. As a result, humanist ideas came to permeate Italian Renaissance art. The intersection of art with humanist doctrines during the Renaissance is evident in the popularity of subjects selected from classical history or mythology (for example, FIG. 21-1); in the increased concern with developing perspective systems and depicting anatomy accurately; in the revival of portraiture and other self-aggrandizing forms of patronage; and in citizens' extensive participation in civic and religious art commissions.

# FLORENCE

Because high-level patronage required significant accumulated wealth, those individuals, whether princes or merchants, who had managed to prosper came to the fore in artistic circles. The best-known Italian Renaissance art patrons were the Medici of the Republic of Florence (see "Medici Patronage and Classical Learning," page 559), yet the earliest important artistic commission in 15th-century Florence (MAP 21-1) was not a Medici project but rather a competition held by the Cathedral of Santa Maria del Fiore and sponsored by the city's guild of wool merchants.

## Sculpture

In 1401, the cathedral's art directors held a competition to make bronze doors for the east portal of the Baptistery of San Giovanni (FIG. 12-27). Artists and public alike considered this commission particularly prestigious because the east entrance to the baptistery faced the cathedral (FIG. 14-18). The competition is historically

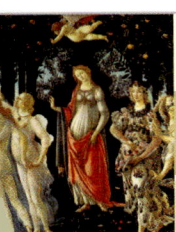

# THE RENAISSANCE IN QUATTROCENTO ITALY

| 1400 | 1425 | 1450 | 1475 | 1500 |
|---|---|---|---|---|
| ▮ Ghiberti wins the competition to design new doors for Florence's baptistery<br>▮ Nanni di Banco, Donatello, and others create statues for Or San Michele<br>▮ Masaccio carries Giotto's naturalism further in the Brancacci chapel<br>▮ Brunelleschi develops linear perspective and designs the Ospedale degli Innocenti, the first Renaissance building | ▮ Ghiberti installs the *Gates of Paradise* facing Florence Cathedral<br>▮ Donatello revives freestanding nude male statuary<br>▮ Michelozzo builds the new Medici palace in Florence<br>▮ Alberti publishes his treatise on painting | ▮ Federico da Montefeltro brings Piero della Francesca to the Urbino court<br>▮ Alberti designs palaces and churches in Florence and Mantua<br>▮ Mantegna creates illusionistic paintings for the Camera Picta in Mantua | ▮ Botticelli paints Neo-Platonic mythological allegories for the Medici<br>▮ Alberti publishes his treatise on architecture<br>▮ Pope Sixtus IV employs leading painters to decorate the Sistine Chapel<br>▮ Savonarola condemns humanism and the Medici flee Florence | |

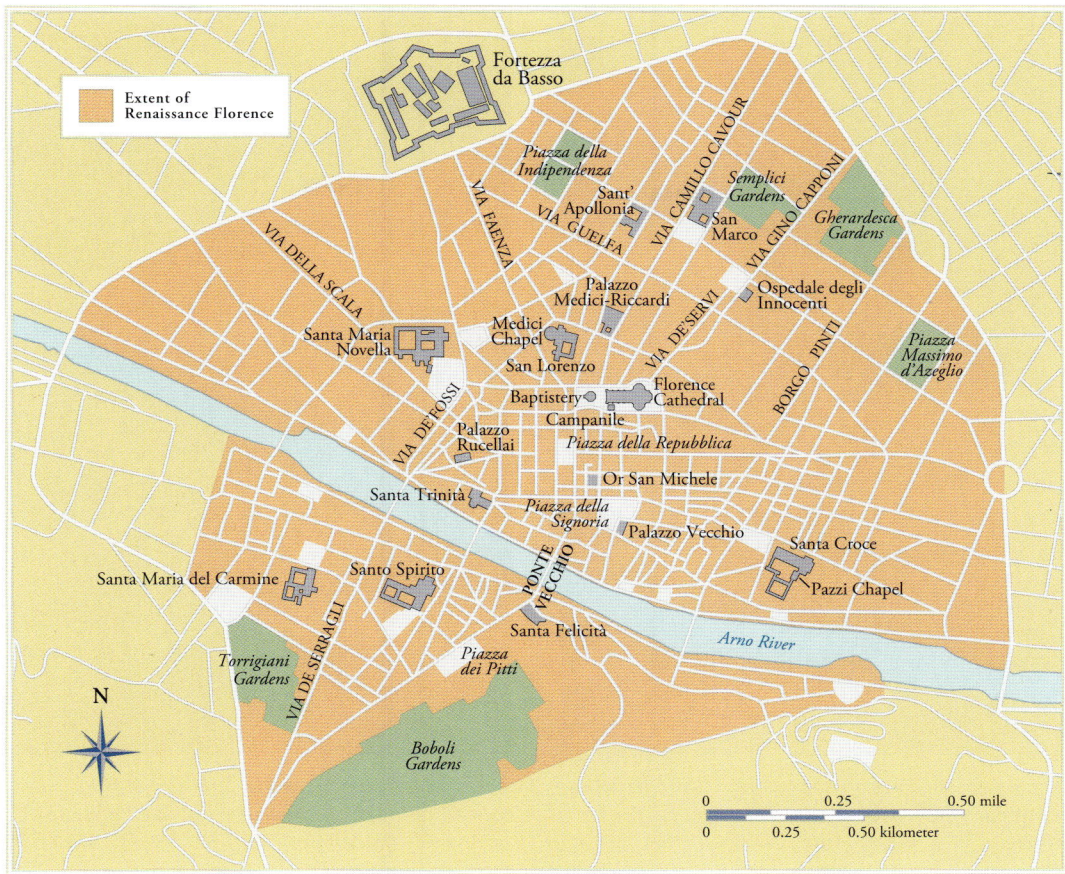

**MAP 21-1** Renaissance Florence.

important not only for the quality of the work submitted by those seeking the commission but also because it already showcased several key elements associated with mature Renaissance art: personal or, in this case, guild patronage as both a civic imperative and a form of self-promotion; the esteem accorded to individual artists; and the development of a new pictorial illusionism.

***SACRIFICE OF ISAAC*** Between 1330 and 1335, Andrea Pisano had designed the south doors (FIG. 14-19) of the baptistery. The jurors of the 1401 competition for the second set of doors required each entrant to submit a relief panel depicting the sacrifice of Isaac in a similar French Gothic quatrefoil frame. This episode from the book of Genesis centers on God's order to Abraham to sacrifice his son Isaac as a demonstration of Abraham's devotion (see "Jewish Subjects in Christian Art," Chapter 8, page 238). As Abraham was about to comply, an angel intervened and stopped him from plunging the knife into his son's throat. Because of the parallel between Abraham's willingness to sacrifice Isaac and God's sacrifice of his son Jesus to redeem humankind, Christians viewed the sacrifice of Isaac as a *prefiguration* (prophetic forerunner) of Jesus' crucifixion. Both refer to *covenants* (binding agreements between God and humans), and given that the sacrament of baptism initiates the newborn or the convert into these covenants, Isaac's sacrifice was an appropriate choice for baptistery doors.

Contemporary developments, however, may also have been an important factor in the selection of this theme. In the late 1390s, Giangaleazzo Visconti, the first duke of Milan (r. 1378–1395), began a military campaign to take over the Italian peninsula. By 1401, when the cathedral's art directors initiated the baptistery doors competition, Visconti's troops had surrounded Florence, and its in-

dependence was in serious jeopardy. Despite dwindling water and food supplies, Florentine officials exhorted the public to defend the city's freedom. For example, the humanist chancellor Coluccio Salutati (1331–1406) urged his fellow citizens to adopt the republican ideal of civil and political liberty associated with ancient Rome and to identify themselves with its spirit. To be a citizen of the Florentine Republic was to be Roman. Freedom was the distinguishing virtue of both societies. The story of Abraham and Isaac, with its theme of sacrifice, paralleled the message Florentine officials had conveyed to rally the public's support. The wool merchants, asserting both their preeminence among Florentine guilds and their civic duty, may have selected the biblical subject with this in mind. The Florentines' reward for their faith and sacrifice came in 1402, when Visconti died suddenly, ending the invasion threat.

**BRUNELLESCHI AND GHIBERTI** The jury selected seven semifinalists from among the many artists who entered the widely advertised competition. Only the panels of the two finalists, FILIPPO BRUNELLESCHI (1377–1446) and LORENZO GHIBERTI (1378–1455), have survived. As instructed, both artists used the same French-style frames Andrea Pisano had used for the south doors (FIG. 14-19) and depicted the same moment of the narrative—the angel's interruption of the action. Brunelleschi's entry (FIG. **21-2**) is a vigorous interpretation of the theme and recalls the emotional agitation of Giovanni Pisano's relief sculptures (FIG. 14-4). Abraham seems suddenly to have summoned the dreadful courage needed to murder his son at God's command. He lunges forward, robes flying, and exposes Isaac's throat to the knife. Matching Abraham's energy, the saving angel flies in from the left, grabbing Abraham's arm to stop the killing. Brunelleschi's figures demonstrate his

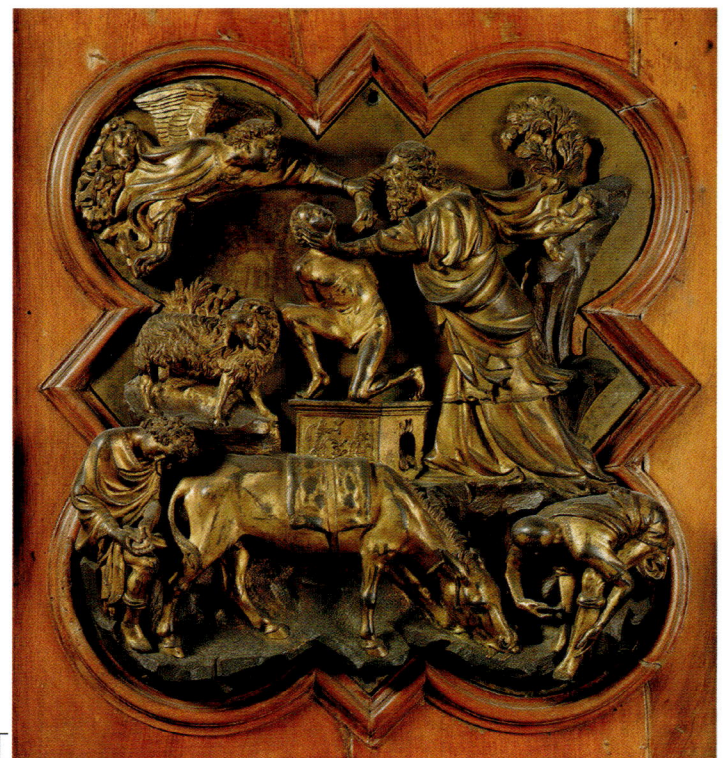

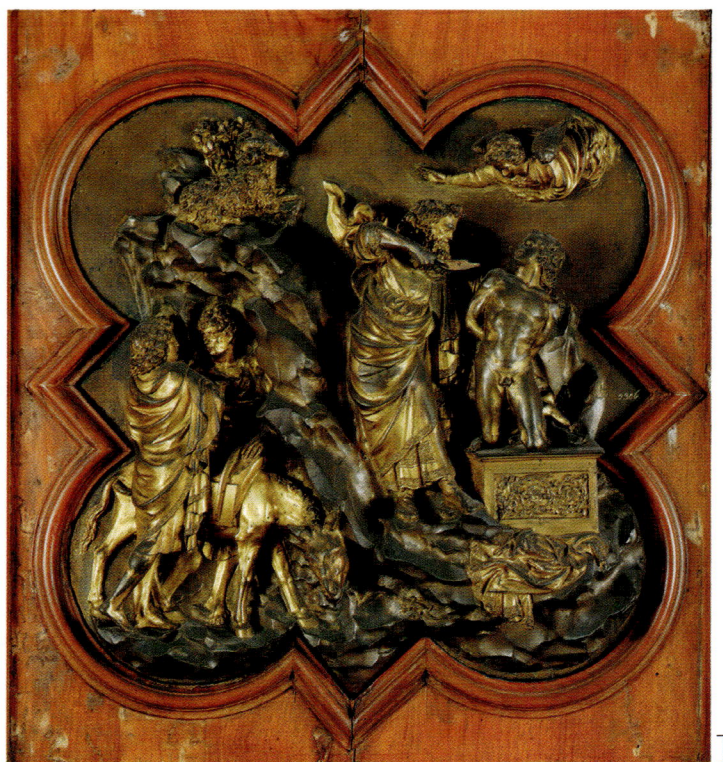

1 in.

1 in.

**21-2** FILIPPO BRUNELLESCHI, *Sacrifice of Isaac,* competition panel for east doors of the Baptistery of San Giovanni, Florence, Italy, 1401–1402. Gilded bronze, 1′ 9″ × 1′ 5½″. Museo Nazionale del Bargello, Florence.

Brunelleschi's entry in the competition to create new bronze doors for the Florentine baptistery shows a frantic angel about to halt an emotional, lunging Abraham clothed in swirling Gothic robes.

**21-3** LORENZO GHIBERTI, *Sacrifice of Isaac,* competition panel for east doors of the Baptistery of San Giovanni, Florence, Italy, 1401–1402. Gilded bronze, 1′ 9″ × 1′ 5½″. Museo Nazionale del Bargello, Florence.

In contrast to Brunelleschi's panel (FIG. 21-2), Ghiberti's entry in the baptistery competition features gracefully posed figures that recall classical statuary. Isaac's altar has a Roman acanthus frieze.

ability to represent faithfully and dramatically all the elements in the biblical narrative.

Whereas Brunelleschi imbued his image with violent movement and high emotion, Ghiberti, the youngest artist in the competition, emphasized grace and smoothness. In Ghiberti's panel (FIG. **21-3**), Abraham appears in a typically Gothic pose with outthrust hip (compare FIG. 13-26) and seems to contemplate the act he is about to perform, even as he draws back his arm to strike. The figure of Isaac, beautifully posed and rendered, recalls Greco-Roman statuary and could be regarded as the first classical nude since antiquity. (Compare, for example, the torsion of Isaac's body and the dramatic turn of his head with the posture of the Hellenistic statue of a Gaul plunging a sword into his own chest, FIG. 5-80). Unlike his medieval predecessors, Ghiberti revealed a genuine appreciation of the nude male form and a deep interest in how the muscular system and skeletal structure move the human body. Even the altar on which Isaac kneels displays Ghiberti's emulation of antique models. Decorating it are acanthus scrolls of a type that commonly adorned Roman temple friezes in Italy and throughout the former Roman Empire (for example, FIG. 7-32). These classical references reflect the influence of humanism in Quattrocento Italy. Ghiberti's entry in the baptistery competition is also noteworthy for the artist's interest in spatial illusion. The rocky landscape seems to emerge from the blank panel toward the viewer, as does the strongly foreshortened angel. Brunelleschi's image, in contrast, emphasizes the planar orientation of the surface.

Ghiberti's training included both painting and metalwork. His careful treatment of the gilded bronze surfaces, with their sharply and accurately incised detail, proves his skill as a goldsmith. That Ghiberti cast his panel in only two pieces (thereby reducing the amount of bronze needed) no doubt also impressed the selection committee. Brunelleschi's panel consists of several cast pieces. Thus, not only would Ghiberti's doors, as proposed, be lighter and more impervious to the elements, but they also represented a significant cost savings. The younger artist's submission clearly had much to recommend it, both stylistically and technically, and the judges awarded the commission to him. Ghiberti's pride in winning the competition is evident in his description of the award, which also reveals the fame and glory increasingly accorded to individual achievement in 15th-century Italy:

> To me was conceded the palm of the victory by all the experts and by all who had competed with me. To me the honor was conceded universally and with no exception. To all it seemed that I had at that time surpassed the others without exception, as was recognized by a great council and an investigation of learned men.... There were thirty-four judges from the city and the other surrounding countries. The testimonial of the victory was given in my favor by all.[1]

**OR SAN MICHELE** A second major Florentine sculptural project of the early 1400s was the sculptural decoration of the exterior of Or San Michele, an early-14th-century building prominently located on the main street connecting the Palazzo della Signoria

(FIG. 14-18B; seat of the *Signoria,* Florence's governing body) and the cathedral (MAP 21-1). At various times, Or San Michele housed a church, a granary, and the headquarters of Florence's guilds. City officials had assigned niches on the building's four sides to specific guilds, instructing each guild to place a statue of its patron saint in its niche. Nearly a century after completion of Or San Michele, however, the guilds had filled only 5 of the 14 niches. In 1406, the Signoria issued a dictum requiring the guilds to comply with the original plan to embellish their assigned niches. A few years later, Florence was once again under siege, this time by King Ladislaus (r. 1399–1414) of Naples. Ladislaus had marched north, occupied Rome and the Papal States (MAP 14-1) by 1409, and threatened to overrun Florence. As they had done when Visconti was at the republic's doorstep, Florentine officials urged citizens to stand firm and defend their city-state from tyranny. Once again, Florence escaped unscathed. Ladislaus, on the verge of military success in 1414, fortuitously died. The guilds may well have viewed this new threat as an opportunity to perform their civic duty by rallying their fellow Florentines while also promoting their own importance and position in Florentine society. By 1423, statues by Ghiberti and other leading Florentine artists were on display in the nine remaining niches of Or San Michele.

**NANNI DI BANCO** Among the niches filled during the Neapolitan king's siege was the one assigned to the Florentine guild of stone- and woodworkers. They chose a guild member, the sculptor NANNI DI BANCO (ca. 1380–1421), to create four life-size marble statues of the guild's martyred patron saints. These four Christian sculptors had defied an order from Emperor Diocletian (r. 284–305) to carve a statue of a Roman deity. In response, the emperor ordered them put to death. Because they placed their faith above all else, these saints were perfect role models for the 15th-century Florentines whom city leaders exhorted to stand fast in the face of Ladislaus's armies.

Nanni's sculptural group, *Four Crowned Saints* (FIG. **21-4**), is an early Renaissance attempt to solve the problem of integrating figures and space on a monumental scale. The artist's positioning of the figures, which stand in a niche that is *in* but confers some separation *from* the architecture, furthered the gradual emergence of sculpture from its architectural setting. This process began with works such as the 13th-century statues (FIG. 13-24) on the jambs of the west facade portals of Reims Cathedral. At Or San Michele, the niche's spatial recess presented Nanni di Banco with a dramatic new possibility for the interrelationship of the figures. By placing them in a semicircle within their deep niche and relating them to one another by their postures and gestures, as well as by the arrangement of robes, the Quattrocento sculptor arrived at a unified spatial composition. A remarkable psychological unity also connects these unyielding figures, whose bearing expresses the discipline and integrity necessary to face adversity. As the figure on the right speaks, pointing to his right, the two men opposite listen and the one next to him looks out into space, pondering the meaning of the words and reinforcing the formal cohesion of the figural group with psychological cross-references.

In *Four Crowned Saints,* Nanni also displayed a deep respect for and close study of Roman portrait statues. The emotional intensity of the faces of the two inner saints owes much to the extraordinarily moving portrayals in stone of third-century Roman emperors (FIGS. 7-68 and 7-68A), and the bearded heads of the outer saints reveal a familiarity with second-century imperial portraiture (FIGS. 7-59 and 7-59A). Often, when Renaissance artists sought to

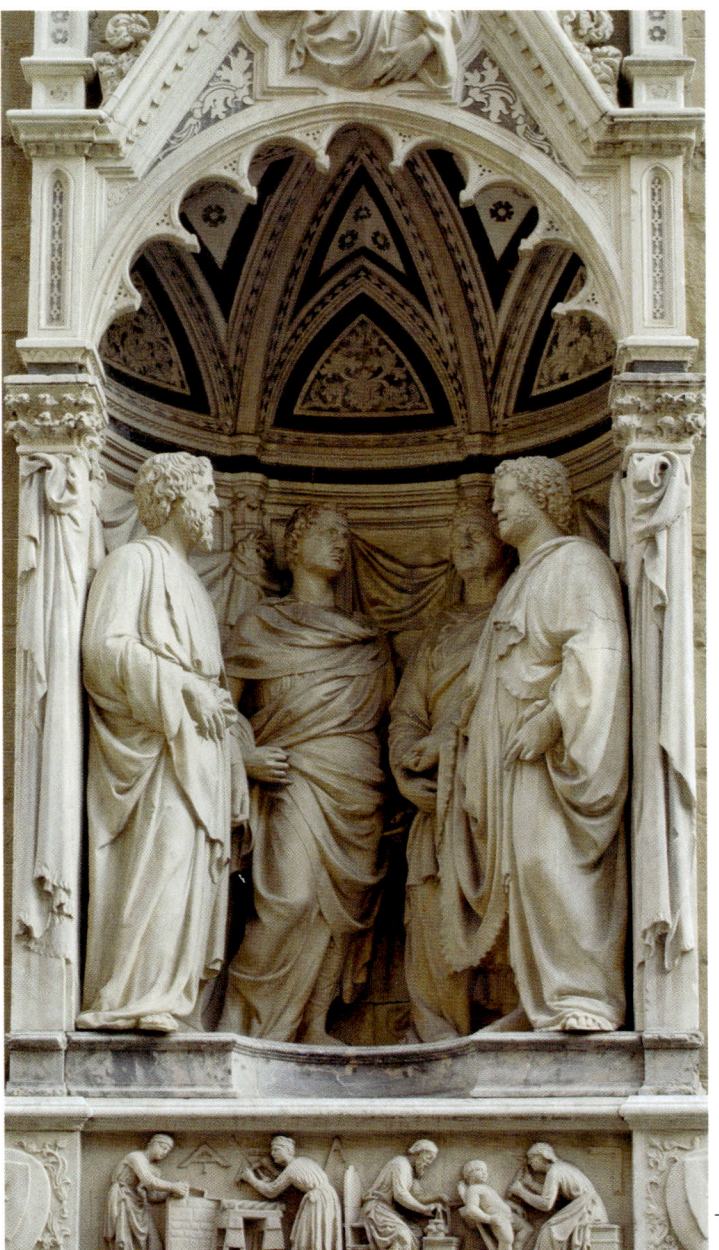

1 ft.

**21-4** NANNI DI BANCO, *Four Crowned Saints,* Or San Michele, Florence, Italy, ca. 1410–1416. Marble, figures 6′ high. Modern copy in exterior niche. Original sculpture in museum on second floor of Or San Michele, Florence. ◼◀

Nanni's group representing the four martyred patron saints of Florence's sculptors guild is an early example of Renaissance artists' attempt to liberate statuary from its architectural setting.

portray individual personalities, they turned to ancient Roman models for inspiration, but they did not simply copy them. Rather, they strove to interpret or offer commentary on their classical models in the manner of humanist scholars dealing with classical texts.

**DONATELLO** Another sculptor who carved statues for Or San Michele's niches was Donato di Niccolo Bardi, called DONATELLO (ca. 1386–1466), who incorporated Greco-Roman sculptural principles in his *Saint Mark* (FIG. **21-5**), executed for the guild of

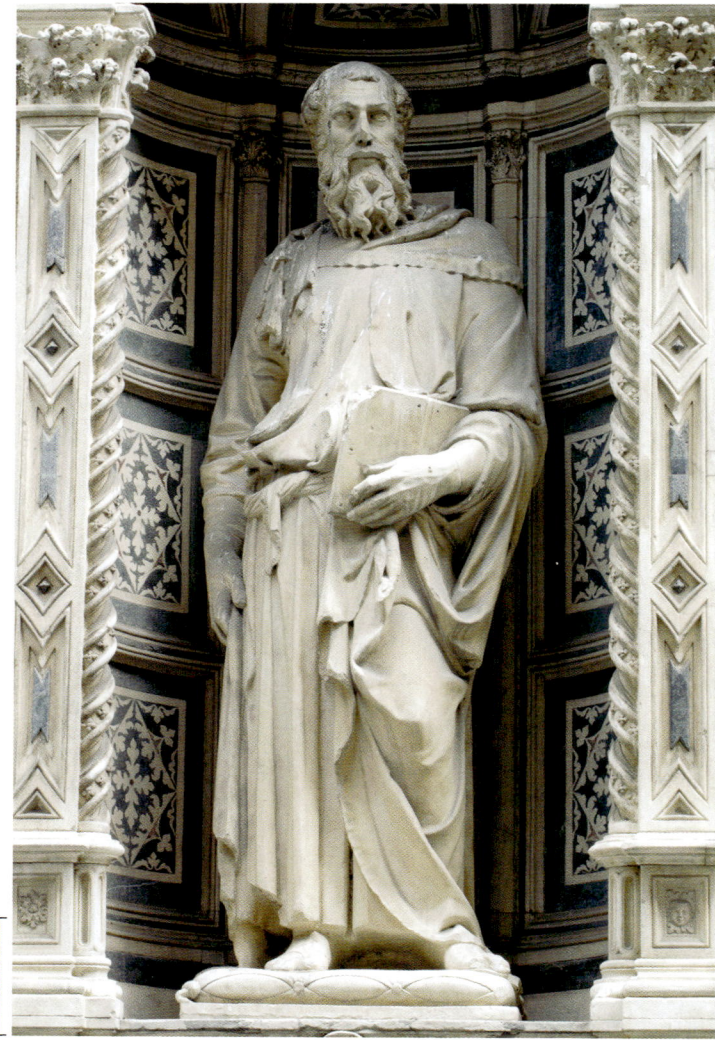

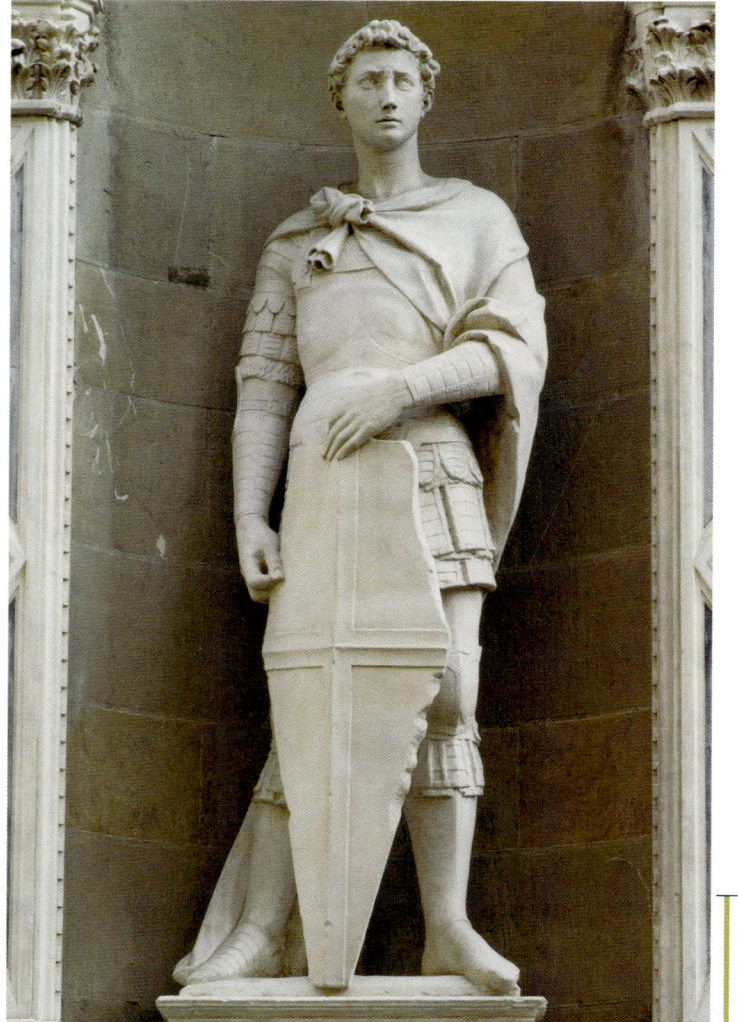

**21-5** Donatello, *Saint Mark,* Or San Michele, Florence, Italy, ca. 1411–1413. Marble, figure 7′ 9″ high. Modern copy in exterior niche. Original sculpture in museum on second floor of Or San Michele, Florence. ◼◂

In this statue carved for the guild of linen makers and tailors, Donatello introduced classical contrapposto into Quattrocento sculpture. The drapery falls naturally and moves with the body.

**21-6** Donatello, *Saint George,* Or San Michele, Florence, Italy, ca. 1410–1415. Marble, figure 6′ 10″ high. Modern copy in exterior niche. Original statue in Museo Nazionale del Bargello, Florence. ◼◂

Donatello's statue for the armorers guild once had a bronze sword and helmet. The warrior saint stands defiantly, ready to spring from his niche to defend Florence, his sword pointed at the spectator.

linen makers and tailors. In this sculpture, Donatello took a fundamental step toward depicting motion in the human figure by recognizing the principle of weight shift, or *contrapposto.* Greek sculptors of the fifth century BCE were the first to grasp that the act of standing requires balancing the position and weight of the different parts of the human body, as they demonstrated in works such as *Kritios Boy* (FIG. 5-34) and *Doryphoros* (FIG. 5-40). In contrast to earlier sculptors, Greek artists recognized the human body is not a rigid mass but a flexible structure that moves by continuously shifting its weight from one supporting leg to the other, its constituent parts moving in consonance. Donatello reintroduced this concept into Renaissance statuary. As the saint's body "moves," his garment "moves" with it, hanging and folding naturally from and around different body parts so that the viewer senses the figure as a nude human wearing clothing, not as a stone statue with arbitrarily incised drapery. Donatello's *Saint Mark* is the first Renaissance statue whose voluminous robe (the pride of the Florentine guild that paid for the statue) does not conceal but

accentuates the movement of the arms, legs, shoulders, and hips. This development further contributed to the sculpted figure's independence from its architectural setting. Saint Mark's stirring limbs, shifting weight, and mobile drapery suggest impending movement out of the niche.

**SAINT GEORGE** For the Or San Michele niche of the guild of armorers and swordmakers, Donatello made a statue of *Saint George* (FIG. **21-6**). The saintly knight stands proudly with his shield in front of him. He once held a bronze sword in his right hand and wore a bronze helmet on his head, both fashioned by the sponsoring guild. The statue continues the Gothic tradition of depicting warrior saints on church facades, as seen in the statue of Saint Theodore (FIG. 13-18) on the westernmost jamb of the south *transept* portal of Chartres Cathedral, but here it has a civic role to play. Saint George stands in a defiant manner—ready to spring from his niche to defend Florence against attack from another Visconti or Ladislaus, his sword jutting out threateningly at all

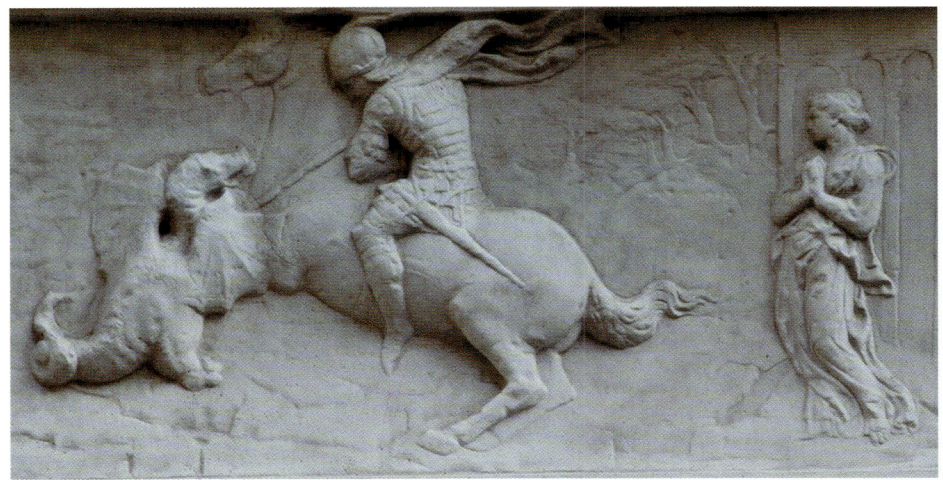

21-7 DONATELLO, *Saint George and the Dragon*, relief below the statue of Saint George (FIG. 21-6), Or San Michele, Florence, Italy, ca. 1417. Marble, 1′ 3¼″ × 3′ 11¼″. Modern copy on exterior of Or San Michele. Original relief in Museo Nazionale del Bargello, Florence. ◼◀

Donatello's relief marks a turning point in Renaissance sculpture. He took a painterly approach, creating an atmospheric effect by using incised lines. The depth of the background cannot be measured.

1 in.

passersby. The saint's body is taut, and Donatello gave him a face filled with nervous energy.

Directly below the statue's base is Donatello's marble relief representing *Saint George and the Dragon* (FIG. 21-7). Commissioned about two years after the sculptor installed his statue in the niche, the relief marks a turning point in Renaissance sculpture. Even the landscapes in the baptistery competition reliefs (FIGS. 21-2 and 21-3) are modeled forms seen against a blank background. In *Saint George and the Dragon,* Donatello created an atmospheric effect by using incised lines. It is impossible to talk about a background plane in this work. The landscape recedes into distant space, and the depth of that space cannot be measured. The sculptor conceived the relief as a window onto an infinite vista.

**FEAST OF HEROD** Donatello's mastery of relief sculpture is also evident in *Feast of Herod* (FIG. 21-8), a bronze relief on the baptismal font in Siena Cathedral. Some of the figures, especially the dancing Salome (to the right), derive from classical reliefs, but nothing in Greco-Roman art can match the illusionism of Donatello's rendition of this biblical scene. In Donatello's relief, Salome has already delivered the severed head of John the Baptist, which the kneeling executioner offers to King Herod. The other figures recoil in horror in two groups. At the right, one man covers his face with his hand. At the left, Herod and two terrified children shrink back in dismay. The psychic explosion drives the human elements apart, leaving a gap across which the emotional electricity crackles. This masterful stagecraft obscures another drama Donatello was playing out on the stage itself. His *Feast of Herod* marks the introduction of rationalized perspective in Renaissance art. As in *Saint George and the Dragon* (FIG. 21-7), Donatello opened the space of the action well into the distance. But here he employed the new mathematically based science of linear perspective to depict two arched courtyards and the groups of attendants in the background.

**RENAISSANCE PERSPECTIVE** In the 14th century, Italian artists, such as Giotto, Duccio, and the Lorenzetti brothers, had used several devices to indicate distance, but with the development of *linear perspective,* Quattrocento artists acquired a way to make the illusion of distance certain and consistent (see "Linear and Atmospheric Perspective," page 567). In effect, they conceived the picture plane as a transparent window through which the observer looks to see the constructed pictorial world. This discovery was enormously important, for it made possible what has

been called the "rationalization of sight." It brought all random and infinitely various visual sensations under a simple rule that could be expressed mathematically. Indeed, Renaissance artists' interest in linear perspective reflects the emergence at this time of modern science itself. Of course, 15th-century artists were not primarily scientists. They simply found perspective an effective way to order and clarify their compositions. Nonetheless, there can be little doubt that linear perspective, with its new mathematical certitude, conferred a kind of aesthetic legitimacy on painting by making the picture measurable and exact. The projection of measurable objects on flat surfaces not only influenced the character of Renaissance paintings but also made possible scale drawings, maps, charts, graphs, and diagrams—means of exact representation that laid the foundation for modern science and technology.

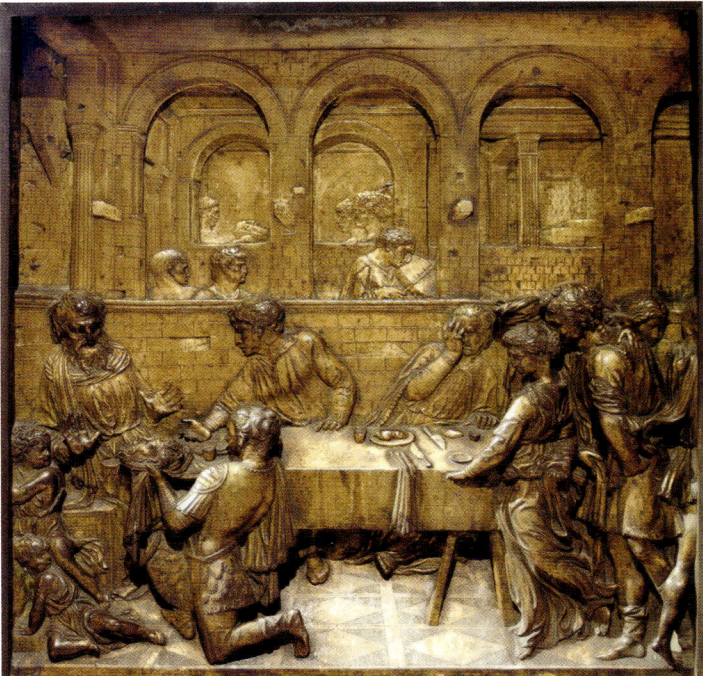

1 in.

21-8 DONATELLO, *Feast of Herod,* panel on the baptismal font of Siena Cathedral, Siena, Italy, 1423–1427. Gilded bronze, 1′ 11½″ × 1′ 11½″. ◼◀

Donatello's *Feast of Herod* marked the introduction of rationalized perspective space in Renaissance relief sculpture. Two arched courtyards of diminishing size open the space of the action into the distance.

In Ghiberti's later doors for the Florentine baptistery, the sculptor abandoned the Gothic quatrefoil frames for the biblical scenes (compare FIG. 21-3) and employed painterly illusionistic devices.

The inventor (or rediscoverer) of linear perspective was Filippo Brunelleschi. In his biography of the Florentine artist, written around 1480, Antonio Manetti (1423–1497) emphasized the importance of the scientific basis of Brunelleschi's system:

> [Filippo Brunelleschi] propounded and realized what painters today call perspective, since it forms part of that science which, in effect, consists of setting down properly and rationally the reductions and enlargements of near and distant objects as perceived by the eye of man: buildings, plains, mountains, places of every sort and location, with figures and objects in correct proportion to the distance in which they are shown. He originated the rule that is essential to whatever has been accomplished since his time in that area. We do not know whether centuries ago the ancient painters . . . knew about perspective or employed it rationally. If indeed they employed it by rule (I did not previously call it a science without reason) as he did later, . . . [no] records about it have been discovered. . . . Through industry and intelligence [Brunelleschi] either rediscovered or invented it.[2]

**GATES OF PARADISE** Lorenzo Ghiberti, Brunelleschi's chief rival in the baptistery competition, was, with Donatello, among the first artists to embrace Brunelleschi's unified system for representing space. Ghiberti's enthusiasm for perspective illusion is on display in the new east doors (FIG. **21-9**) for Florence's baptistery (FIG. 12-27), which the cathedral officials commissioned him to make in 1425. Ghiberti's patrons moved his first pair of doors to the north entrance to make room for the new ones they commissioned him to make for the prestigious east side. Michelangelo later declared Ghiberti's second doors as "so beautiful that they would do well for the gates of Paradise."[3] In the *Gates of Paradise,* as the doors have been called since then, Ghiberti abandoned the quatrefoil frames of Andrea Pisano's south doors (FIG. 14-19) and his own earlier doors and reduced the number of panels from 28 to 10. Each panel contains a relief set in plain molding and depicts an episode from the Old Testament. The complete gilding of the reliefs creates an effect of great splendor and elegance.

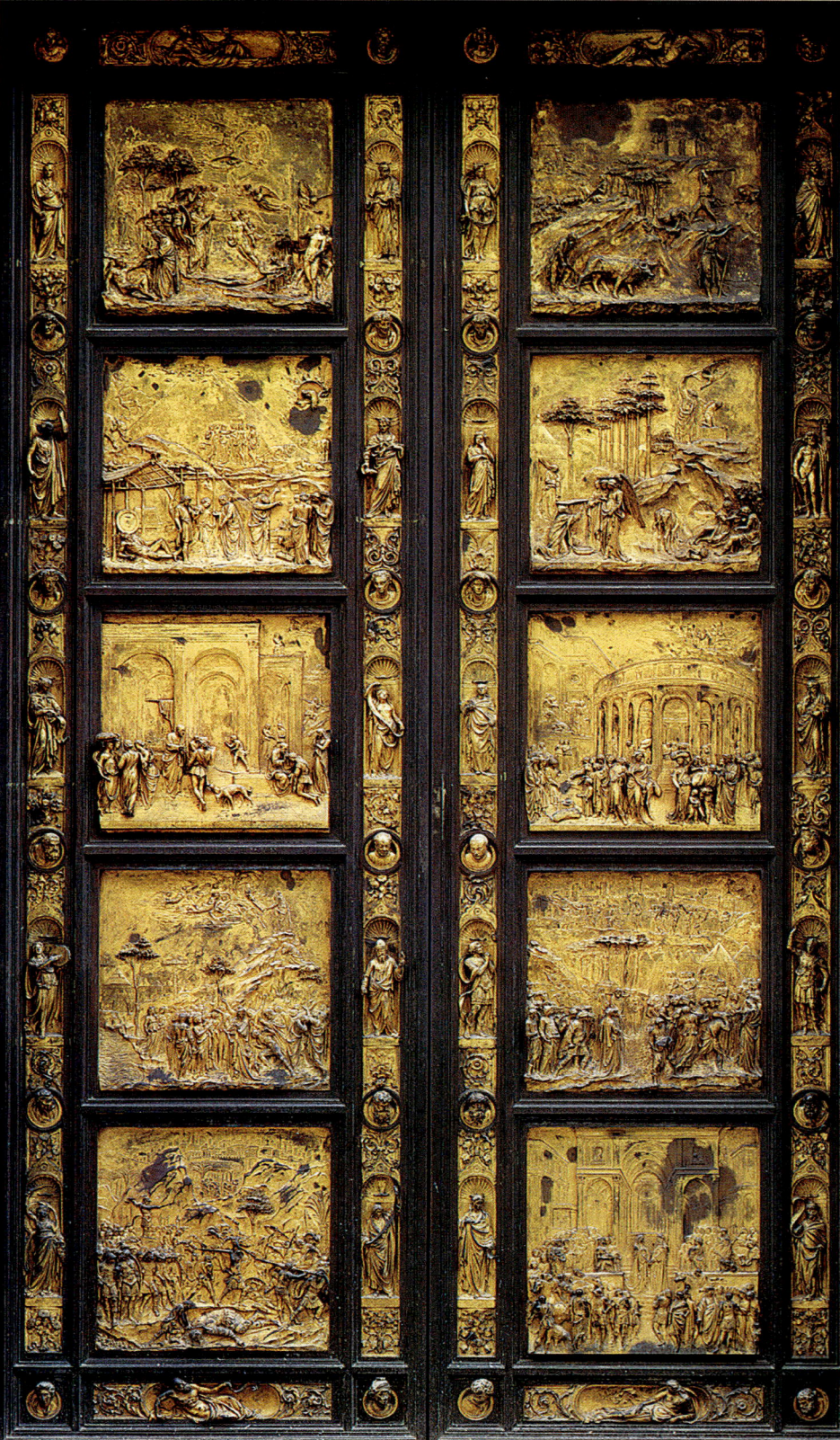

1 ft.

The individual panels, such as *Isaac and His Sons* (FIG. **21-10**), clearly recall painting techniques in their depiction of space as well as in their treatment of the narrative. Some exemplify more fully than painting many of the principles the architect and theorist Leon Battista Alberti formulated in his 1435 treatise, *On Painting.* In his relief, Ghiberti created the illusion of space partly through the use of linear perspective and partly by sculptural means. He

# Linear and Atmospheric Perspective

Scholars long have noted the Renaissance fascination with perspective. In essence, portraying perspective involves constructing a convincing illusion of space in two-dimensional imagery while unifying all objects within a single spatial system. Renaissance artists were not the first to focus on depicting illusionistic space. Both the Greeks and the Romans were well versed in perspective rendering. Many frescoes of buildings and colonnades (for example, FIG. 7-19, *right*) using a Renaissance-like system of converging lines adorn the walls of Roman houses. However, the Renaissance rediscovery of and interest in perspective contrasted sharply with the portrayal of space during the Middle Ages, when spiritual concerns superseded the desire to depict objects illusionistically.

Renaissance knowledge of perspective included both *linear perspective* and *atmospheric perspective*.

▌ **Linear perspective.** Developed by Filippo Brunelleschi, linear perspective enables artists to determine mathematically the relative size of rendered objects to correlate them with the visual recession into space. The artist first must identify a horizontal line that marks, in the image, the horizon in the distance (hence the

term *horizon line*). The artist then selects a *vanishing point* on that horizon line (often located at the exact center of the line). By drawing *orthogonals* (diagonal lines) from the edges of the picture to the vanishing point, the artist creates a structural grid that organizes the image and determines the size of objects within the image's illusionistic space. Among the works that provide clear examples of linear perspective are Ghiberti's *Isaac and His Sons* (FIGS. 21-10 and 21-11), Masaccio's *Holy Trinity* (FIG. 21-21), and Perugino's *Christ Delivering the Keys of the Kingdom to Saint Peter* (FIG. 21-41).

▌ **Atmospheric perspective.** Unlike linear perspective, which relies on a structured mathematical system, atmospheric perspective involves optical phenomena. Artists using atmospheric perspective (sometimes called *aerial perspective*) exploit the principle that the farther back the object is in space, the blurrier, less detailed, and bluer it appears. Further, color saturation and value contrast diminish as the image recedes into the distance. Leonardo da Vinci used atmospheric perspective to great effect in works such as *Madonna of the Rocks* (FIG. 22-2) and *Mona Lisa* (FIG. 22-5).

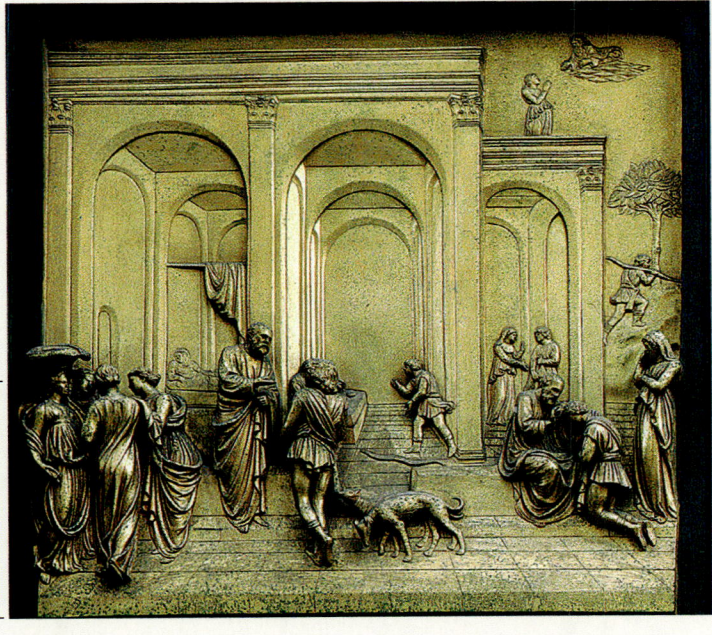

1 ft.

**21-10** LORENZO GHIBERTI, *Isaac and His Sons* (detail of FIG. 21-9), east doors (*Gates of Paradise*), Baptistery of San Giovanni, Florence, Italy, 1425–1452. Gilded bronze, 2′ 7½″ × 2′ 7½″. Museo dell'Opera del Duomo, Florence. ◼◀

In this relief, Ghiberti employed linear perspective to create the illusion of distance, but he also used sculptural aerial perspective, with forms appearing less distinct the deeper they are in space.

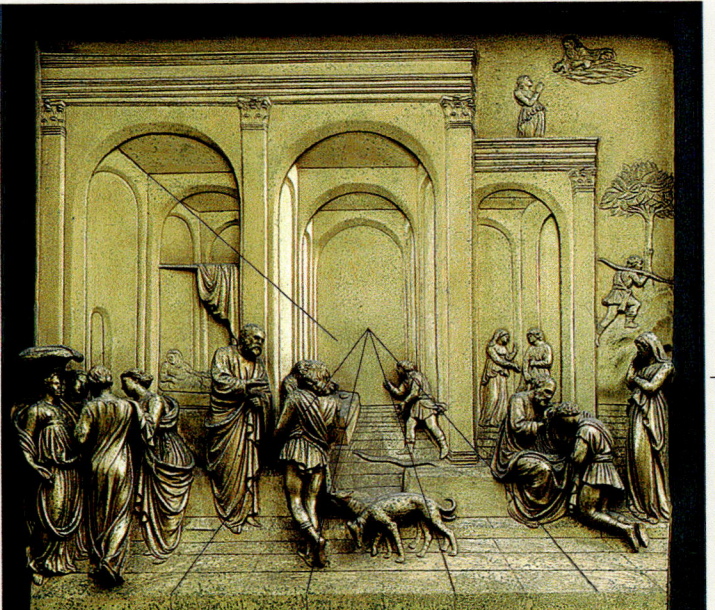

1 ft.

**21-11** Perspective diagram of FIG. 21-10. ◼◀

All of the orthogonals of the floor tiles in this early example of linear perspective converge on a vanishing point on the central axis of the composition, but the orthogonals of the architecture do not.

represented the pavement on which the figures stand according to a painter's vanishing-point perspective construction (see "Linear and Atmospheric Perspective," above, and FIG. 21-11), but the figures themselves appear almost fully in the round. In fact, some of their heads stand completely free. As the eye progresses upward,

the relief increasingly flattens, concluding with the architecture in the background, which Ghiberti depicted using barely raised lines. In this manner, the artist created a sort of sculptor's atmospheric perspective, with forms appearing less distinct the deeper they are in space. Regardless of the height of the reliefs, however, the size of each figure decreases in exact correspondence to its distance from the foreground, just as do the dimensions of the floor tiles, as specified in Alberti's treatise.

Ghiberti described the baptistery's east doors as follows:

> I strove to imitate nature as closely as I could, and with all the perspective I could produce [to have] excellent compositions rich with many figures. In some scenes I placed about a hundred figures, in some less, and in some more. . . . There were ten stories, all [sunk] in frames because the eye from a distance measures and interprets the scenes in such a way that they appear round. The scenes are in the lowest relief and the figures are seen in the planes; those that are near appear large, those in the distance small, as they do in reality. I executed this entire work with these principles.[4]

In the reliefs of the *Gates of Paradise,* Ghiberti achieved a greater sense of depth than had previously seemed possible in sculpture. His principal figures do not occupy the architectural space he created for them. Rather, the artist arranged them along a parallel plane in front of the grandiose architecture. (According to Leon Battista Alberti, in his *On the Art of Building,* the grandeur of the architecture reflects the dignity of the events shown in the foreground.) Ghiberti's figure style mixes a Gothic patterning of rhythmic line, classical poses and motifs, and a new realism in characterization, movement, and surface detail. Ghiberti retained the medieval narrative method of presenting several episodes within a single frame. In *Isaac and His Sons,* the women in the left foreground attend the birth of Esau and Jacob in the left background. In the central foreground, Isaac sends Esau and his dogs to hunt game. In the right foreground, Isaac blesses the kneeling Jacob as Rebecca looks on. Yet viewers experience little confusion because of Ghiberti's careful and subtle placement of each scene. The figures, in varying degrees of projection, gracefully twist and turn, appearing to occupy and move through a convincing stage space, which Ghiberti deepened by showing some figures from behind. The classicism derives from the artist's close study of ancient art. Ghiberti admired and collected classical sculpture, bronzes, and coins. Their influence appears throughout the panel, particularly in the figure of Rebecca, which Ghiberti based on a popular Greco-Roman statuary type. The emerging practice of collecting classical art in the 15th century had much to do with the incorporation of classical motifs and the emulation of classical style in Renaissance art.

**DONATELLO,** *DAVID* The use of perspective systems in relief sculpture and painting represents only one aspect of the Renaissance revival of classical principles and values in the arts. Another was the revival of the freestanding nude statue. The first Renaissance sculptor to portray the nude male figure in statuary was Donatello. He probably cast his bronze *David* (FIG. **21-12**) sometime between 1440 and 1460 for display in the courtyard (FIG. 21-38) of the Medici palace in Florence. In the Middle Ages, the clergy regarded nude statues as both indecent and idolatrous, and nudity in general appeared only rarely in art—and then only in biblical or moralizing contexts, such as the story of Adam and Eve or depictions of sinners in Hell. With *David,* Donatello reinvented the classical nude. His subject, however, was not a Greco-Roman god, hero, or athlete but the youthful biblical slayer of Goliath who had become the symbol of the Florentine Republic—and therefore an ideal choice of subject for the residence of the most powerful family in Florence. The Medici were aware of Donatello's earlier *David* in Florence's town hall (FIG. 14-18B), which the artist had produced during the threat of invasion by King Ladislaus. Their selection

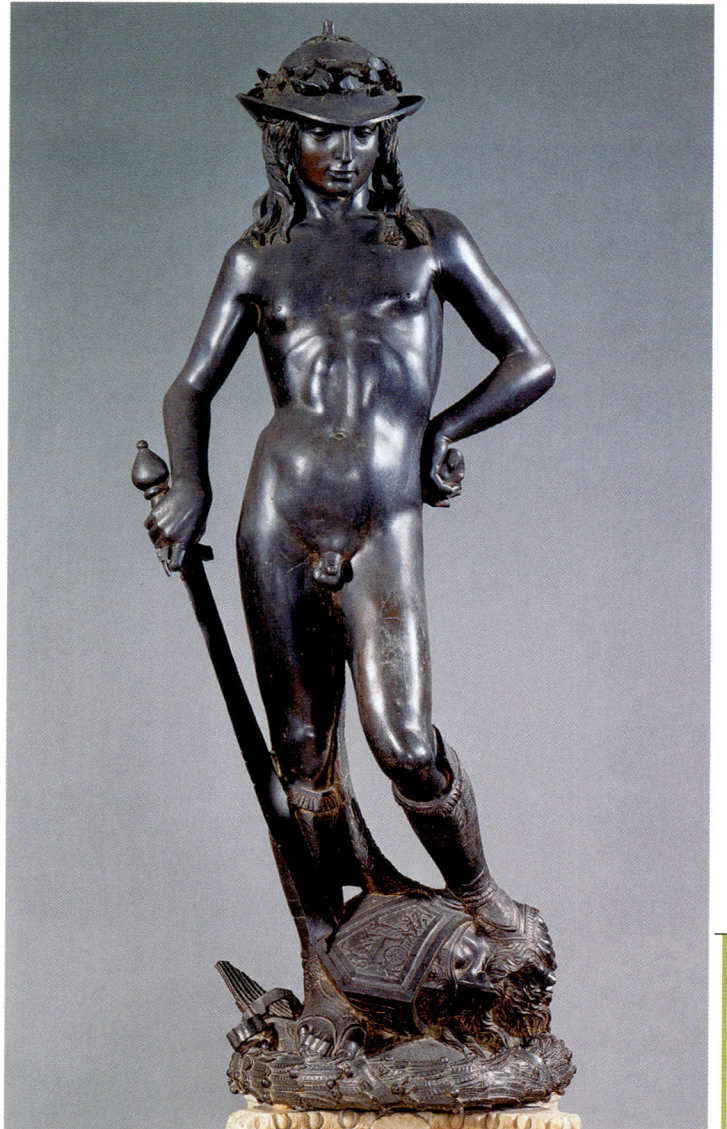

**21-12** DONATELLO, *David,* ca. 1440–1460. Bronze, 5′ 2¼″ high. Museo Nazionale del Bargello, Florence. ◼◀

Donatello's *David* possesses both the relaxed contrapposto and the sensuous beauty of nude Greek gods (FIG. 5-63). The revival of classical statuary style appealed to the sculptor's patrons, the Medici.

of the same subject suggests the Medici identified themselves with Florence or, at the very least, saw themselves as responsible for Florence's prosperity and freedom. The invoking of classical poses and formats also appealed to the Medici as humanists. Donatello's *David* possesses both the relaxed classical contrapposto stance and the proportions and sensuous beauty of the gods (FIG. 5-63) of Praxiteles, a famous Greek sculptor. These qualities were, not surprisingly, absent from medieval figures—and they are also lacking, for different

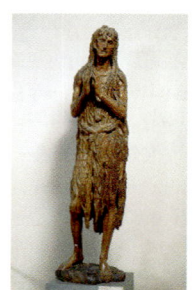

**21-12A** DONATELLO, *Penitent Mary Magdalene,* ca. 1455.

reasons, in Donatello's depiction of the aged Mary Magdalene. The contrast between the sculptor's *David* and his *Penitent Mary Magdalene* (FIG. **21-12A**) demonstrates the extraordinary versatility of this Florentine master.

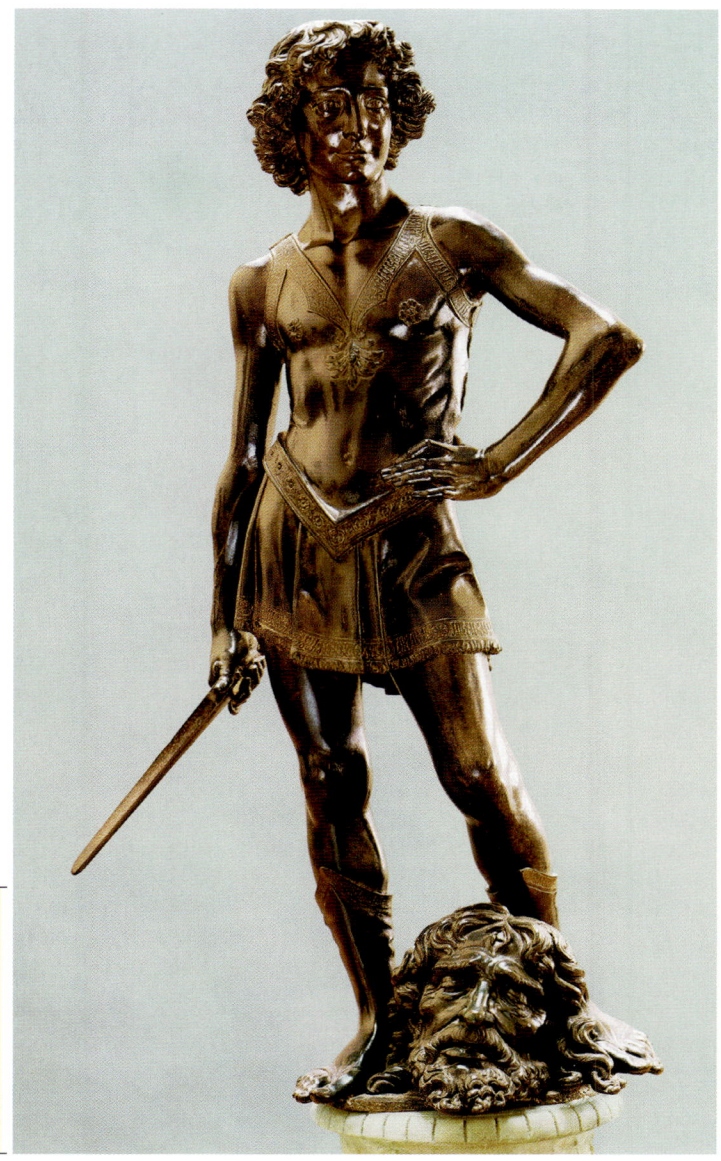

1 ft.

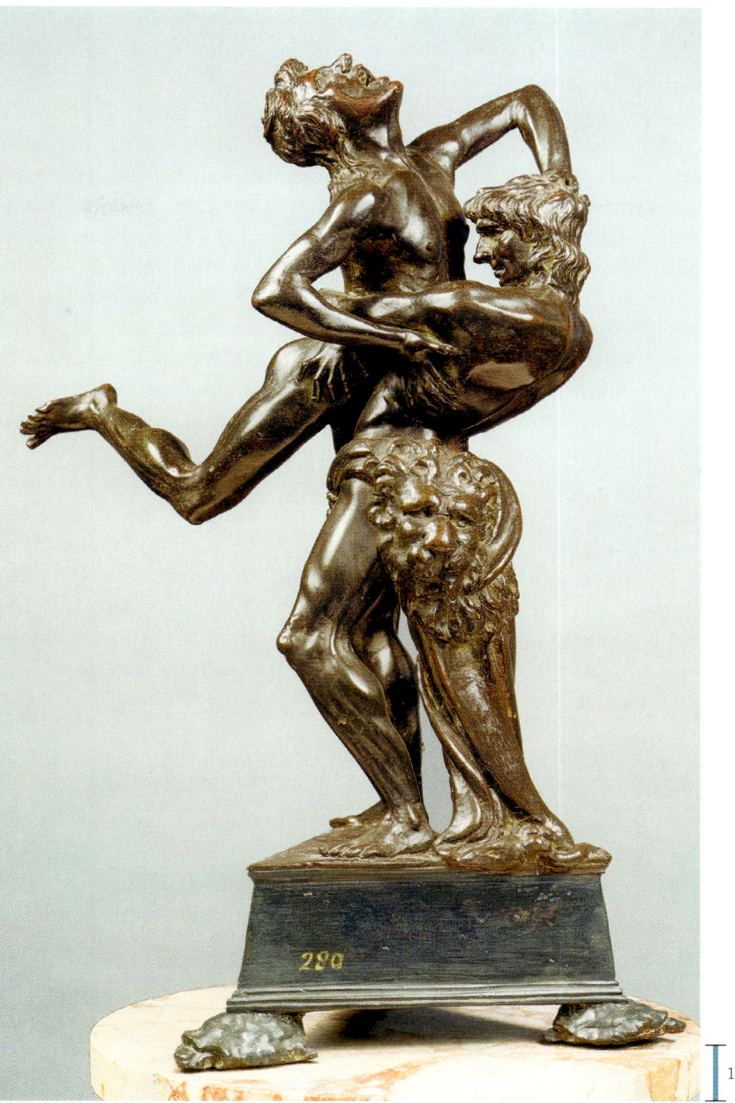

1 in.

**VERROCCHIO** Another *David* (FIG. **21-13**), by ANDREA DEL VERROCCHIO (1435–1488), one of the most important sculptors during the second half of the 15th century, reaffirms the Medici family's identification with the heroic biblical king and with Florence. A painter as well as a sculptor, Verrocchio directed a flourishing *bottega* (studio-shop) in Florence that attracted many students, among them Leonardo da Vinci. Verrocchio's *David* contrasts strongly in its narrative realism with the quiet classicism of Donatello's *David.* Verrocchio's hero is a sturdy, wiry young apprentice clad in a leather doublet who stands with a jaunty pride. As in Donatello's version, Goliath's head lies at David's feet. He poses like a hunter with his kill. The easy balance of the weight and the lithe, still thinly adolescent musculature, with prominent veins, show how closely Verrocchio read the biblical text and how clearly he knew the psychology of brash young men. The Medici eventually sold Verrocchio's bronze *David* to the Florentine government for placement in the Palazzo della Signoria. After the expulsion of the Medici from Florence, civic officials appropriated Donatello's *David* for civic use and moved it to the city hall as well.

**POLLAIUOLO** As noted in the discussion of Botticelli's *Primavera* (FIG. 21-1), the Renaissance interest in classical culture naturally also led to the revival of Greco-Roman mythological themes in art. The Medici were Florence's leading patrons in this sphere as well. Around 1470, ANTONIO DEL POLLAIUOLO (ca. 1431–1498), who was also an important painter and engraver (FIG. 21-30), received a Medici commission to produce a small-scale sculpture, *Hercules and Antaeus* (FIG. **21-14**). The subject matter, derived from Greek mythology, and the emphasis on human anatomy reflect the Medici preference for humanist imagery. Even more specifically, the Florentine seal had featured Hercules since the end of the 13th century. As commissions such as the two *David* sculptures demonstrate, the Medici clearly embraced every opportunity to associate themselves with the glory of the Florentine Republic and claimed much of the credit for its preeminence.

In contrast to the placid presentation of Donatello's *David* (FIG. 21-12), Pollaiuolo's *Hercules and Antaeus* exhibits the stress and strain of the human figure in violent action. This sculpture departs dramatically from the convention of frontality that had dominated statuary during the Middle Ages and the Early Renaissance. Not quite 18 inches high, *Hercules and Antaeus* embodies the ferocity and vitality of elemental physical conflict. The group illustrates the wrestling match between Antaeus (Antaios), a giant and son of the goddess Earth, and Hercules (Herakles), a theme the Greek painter Euphronios had represented on an ancient Greek vase (FIG. 5-23) 2,000 years before. According to the Greek myth, each time Hercules threw him down, Antaeus sprang up again, his strength renewed by contact with the earth. Finally, Hercules held him aloft—so Antaeus could not touch the ground—and strangled him around the waist. Pollaiuolo strove to convey the final excruciating moments of the struggle—the strained sinews of the combatants, the clenched teeth of Hercules, and the kicking and screaming of Antaeus. The figures intertwine and interlock as they fight, and the flickering reflections of light on the dark gouged bronze surface contribute to a fluid play of planes and the effect of agitated movement.

**TOMB OF LEONARDO BRUNI** Given the increased emphasis on individual achievement and recognition that humanism fostered, it is not surprising portraiture enjoyed a revival in the 15th century. In addition to likenesses of elite individuals made during their lifetime, commemorative portraits of the deceased were common in Quattrocento Italy, as in ancient Rome. Leonardo Bruni (1369–1444) of Arezzo was one of the leading Early Renaissance humanist scholars. Around 1403 he wrote a *laudatio* (essay of praise) in honor of Florence, celebrating the city as the heir of the ancient Roman Republic. His most ambitious work, published in 1429 when he served as Florence's chancellor (1427–1444), was a history of the Florentine Republic. When Bruni died on March 9, 1444, the Signoria ordered a state funeral "according to ancient custom," during which the eminent humanist Giannozzo Manetti (1396–1459) delivered the eulogy and placed a laurel wreath on the head of Bruni's toga-clad corpse. The Florentine government also commissioned BERNARDO ROSSELLINO (1409–1464) to carve a monumental tomb (FIG. **21-15**) for the right wall of the nave of Santa Croce (FIG. I-4) honoring the late chancellor. Rossellino was the most prominent member of a family of stonecutters from Settignano, a town near Florence noted for its quarries.

Rossellino's monument in honor of Leonardo Bruni established the wall tomb as a major genre of Italian Renaissance sculpture. (Later examples include Michelangelo's tombs of the Medici [FIG. 22-16] in Florence and of Pope Julius II [FIGS. 22-14 and 22-15] in Rome.) The tomb is rich in color—white, black, and red marbles with selective gilding. Rossellino based his effigy of Bruni on ancient Roman sarcophagi (FIG. 7-61). The chancellor lies on a funerary bier supported by Roman eagles atop a sarcophagus resting on the foreparts of lions. Bruni, dressed in a toga and crowned with a laurel wreath, as during his state funeral, holds one of his books, probably his history of Florence. The realism of Bruni's head has led many scholars to postulate that Rossellino based his portrait on a wax death mask following ancient Roman practice (see "Roman Ancestor Portraits," Chapter 7, page 185). Two winged Victories hold aloft a plaque with a Latin inscription stating that History mourns the death of Leonardus, Eloquence is now si-

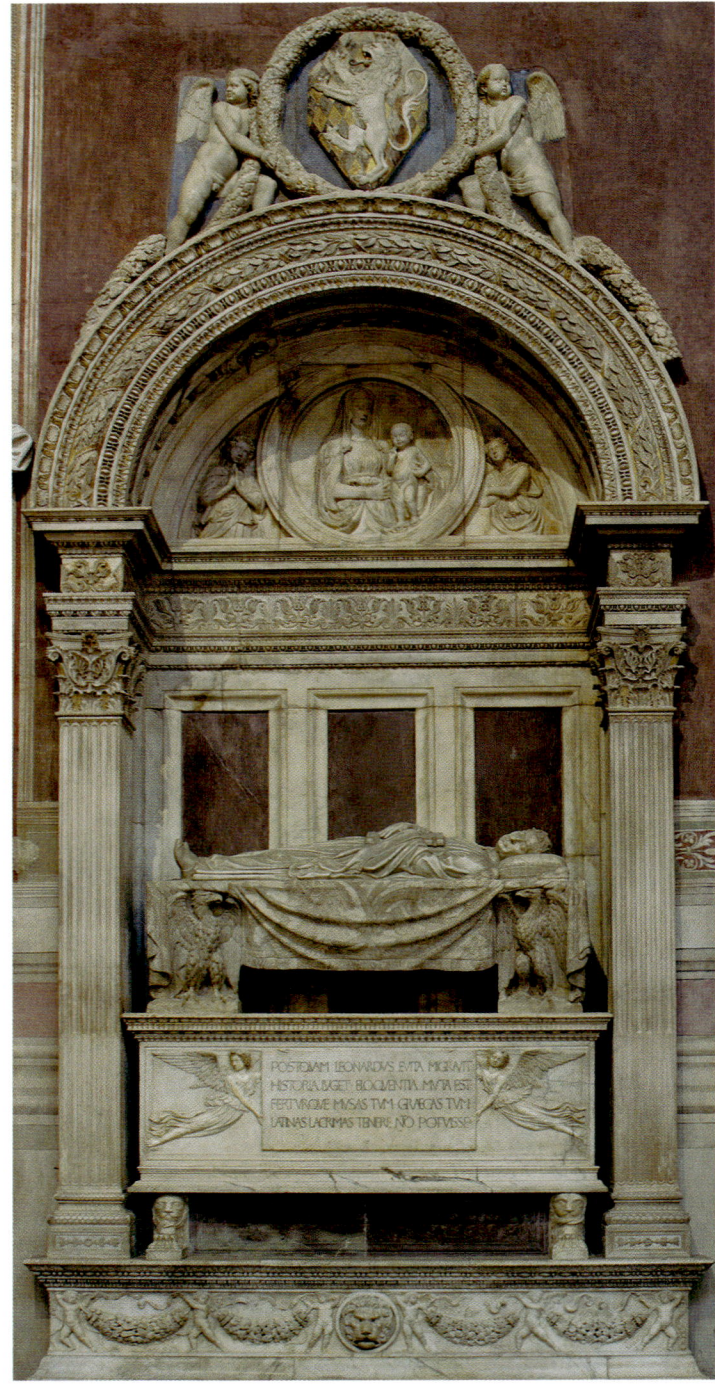

1 ft.

**21-15** BERNARDO ROSSELLINO, tomb of Leonardo Bruni, Santa Croce, Florence, Italy, ca. 1444–1450. Marble, 23′ 3½″ high. ◼

Rossellino's tomb in honor of the humanist scholar and Florentine chancellor Leonardo Bruni combines ancient Roman and Christian motifs. It established the pattern for Renaissance wall tombs.

lenced, and the Greek and Latin muses cannot hold back their tears. Framing the effigy is a round-arched niche with Corinthian pilasters. The base of the tomb is a frieze of *putti* (cupids) carrying garlands, a standard motif on Roman sarcophagi, which also commonly have lions as supports (FIG. 7-70). The classically inspired tomb stands in sharp contrast to the Gothic tomb (FIG. 13-42A) of King Edward II in Gloucester Cathedral. But the Renaissance tomb is a creative variation of classical models, not a copy, and the motifs are a mix of classical and Christian themes. In the lunette beneath

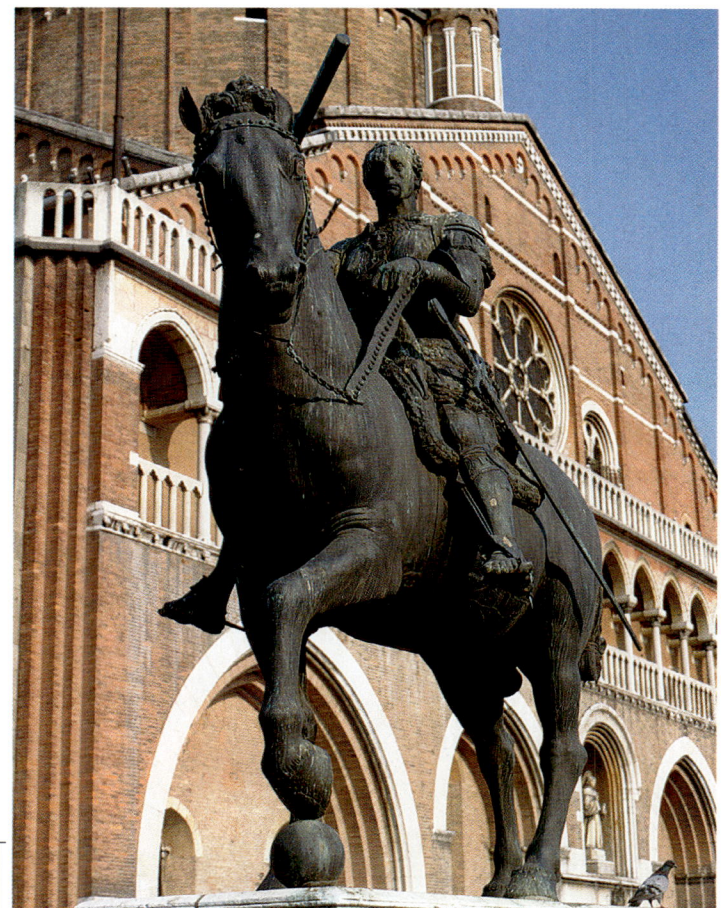

1 ft.

**21-16** Donatello, *Gattamelata* (equestrian statue of Erasmo da Narni), Piazza del Santo, Padua, Italy, ca. 1445–1453. Bronze, 12′ 2″ high.

Donatello based his gigantic portrait of a Venetian general on equestrian statues of ancient Roman emperors (FIG. 7-59). Together, man and horse convey an overwhelming image of irresistible strength.

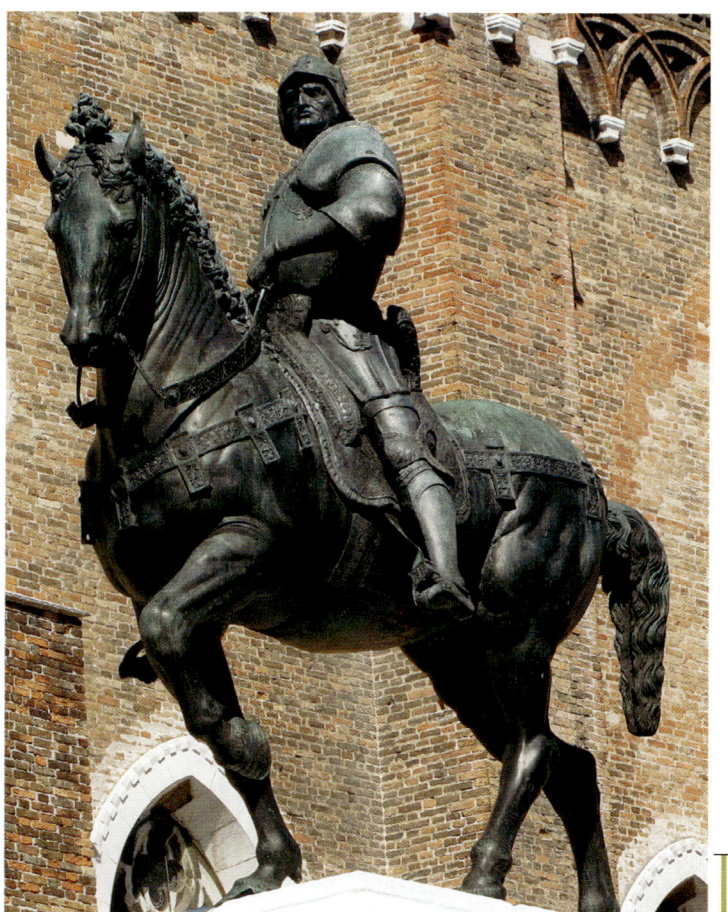

1 ft.

**21-17** Andrea del Verrocchio, *Bartolommeo Colleoni* (equestrian statue), Campo dei Santi Giovanni e Paolo, Venice, Italy, ca. 1481–1496. Bronze, 13′ high.

Eager to compete with Donatello's *Gattamelata* (FIG. 21-16), Colleoni provided the funds for his own equestrian statue in his will. The statue stands on a pedestal even taller than Gattamelata's.

the arch is a tondo of the Madonna and Child between praying angels. Above the arch, two putti hold up a wreath circling the lion of the Florentine Republic. A lion's head is also the central motif in the putto-and-garland frieze below the deceased's coffin.

*GATTAMELATA* The grandest and most costly Quattrocento portraits in the Roman tradition were over-life-size bronze equestrian statues. The supremely versatile Donatello also excelled in this genre. In 1443, he left Florence for northern Italy to accept a rewarding commission from the Republic of Venice to create a commemorative monument in honor of the recently deceased Venetian condottiere Erasmo da Narni, nicknamed Gattamelata ("honeyed cat," a wordplay on his mother's name, Melania Gattelli). Although Gattamelata's family paid for the general's portrait (FIG. **21-16**), the Venetian senate formally authorized its placement in the square in front of the church of Sant'Antonio in Padua, the condottiere's birthplace. Equestrian statues occasionally had been set up in Italy in the late Middle Ages, but Donatello's *Gattamelata* was the first since antiquity to rival the grandeur of Roman imperial mounted portraits, such as that of Marcus Aurelius (FIG. 7-59), which the artist must have seen in Rome. Donatello's contemporaries, one of whom described Gattamelata as sitting on his horse "with great magnificence like a triumphant Caesar,"[5] recognized this reference to antiquity. The statue stands on a lofty base, set

apart from its surroundings, celebrating the Renaissance liberation of sculpture from architecture. Massive and majestic, the great horse bears the armored general easily, for, unlike the sculptor of the Marcus Aurelius statue, Donatello did not represent the Venetian commander as superhuman and disproportionately larger than his horse. Gattamelata dominates his mighty steed by force of character rather than sheer size. The Italian rider, his face set in a mask of dauntless resolution and unshakable will, is the very portrait of the Renaissance individualist. Such a man—intelligent, courageous, ambitious, and frequently of humble origin— could, by his own resourcefulness and on his own merits, rise to a commanding position in the world. Together, man and horse convey an overwhelming image of irresistible strength and unlimited power—an impression Donatello reinforced visually by placing the left forefoot of the horse on an orb, reviving a venerable ancient symbol for hegemony over the earth (compare FIG. 11-12). The imperial imagery is all the more remarkable because Erasmo da Narni was not a head of state.

*BARTOLOMMEO COLLEONI* Verrocchio also received a commission to fashion an equestrian statue of another condottiere who fought for the Venetians, Bartolommeo Colleoni (1400–1475). His portrait (FIG. **21-17**) provides a counterpoint to Donatello's statue. Eager to garner the same fame the *Gattamelata* portrait

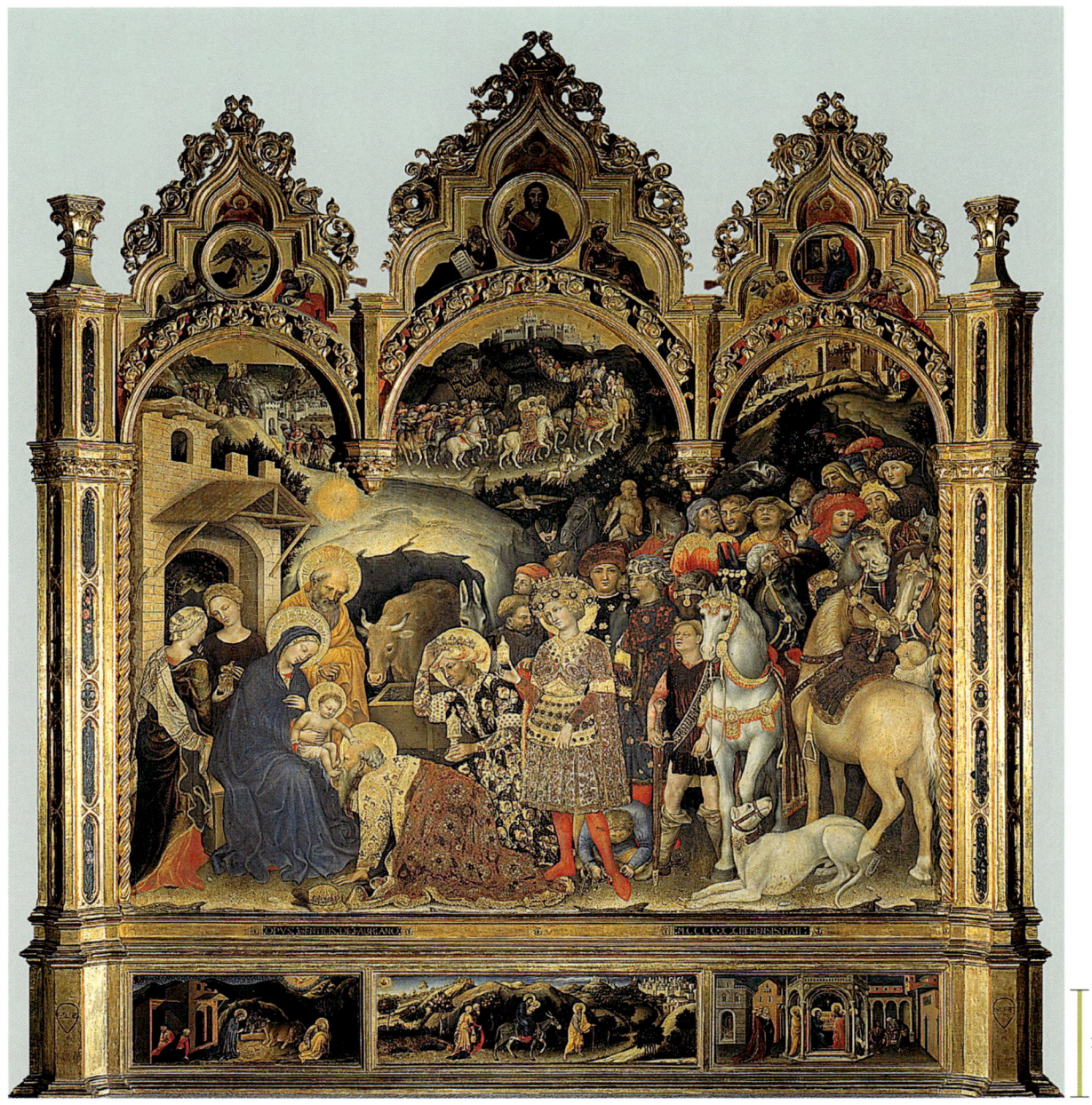

**21-18** Gentile da Fabriano, *Adoration of the Magi,* altarpiece from the Strozzi chapel, Santa Trinità, Florence, Italy, 1423. Tempera on wood, 9′ 11″ × 9′ 3″. Galleria degli Uffizi, Florence.

Gentile was the leading Florentine painter working in the International style. He successfully blended naturalistic details with Late Gothic splendor in color, costume, and framing ornamentation.

achieved, Colleoni provided funds in his will for his own statue. Because both Donatello and Verrocchio executed their statues after the deaths of their subjects, neither artist knew personally the individual he portrayed. The result is a fascinating difference of interpretation (like that between their two *Davids*) as to the demeanor of a professional captain of armies. Verrocchio placed the statue of the bold equestrian general on a pedestal even taller than the one Donatello used for *Gattamelata,* elevating it so viewers could see the dominating, aggressive figure from all approaches to the piazza (the Campo dei Santi Giovanni e Paolo). In contrast with the near repose of *Gattamelata,* the *Colleoni* horse moves in a prancing stride, arching and curving its powerful neck, while the commander seems suddenly to shift his whole weight to the stirrups and rise from the saddle with a violent twist of his body. The artist depicted both horse and rider with an exaggerated tautness—the animal's bulging muscles and the man's fiercely erect and rigid body together convey brute strength. In *Gattamelata,* Donatello created a portrait of grim sagacity. Verrocchio's *Bartolommeo Colleoni* is a portrait of merciless might.

## Painting

In Quattrocento Italy, humanism and the celebration of classical artistic values also largely determined the character of panel and mural painting. The new Renaissance style did not, however, immediately displace all vestiges of the Late Gothic style. In particular, the International style, the dominant mode in painting around 1400 (see Chapter 14), persisted well into the 15th century.

## Cennino Cennini on Imitation and Emulation in Renaissance Art

Although many of the values championed by Renaissance humanists endure to the present day, the premium that modern Western society places on artistic originality is a fairly recent phenomenon. In contrast, imitation and emulation were among the concepts Renaissance artists most valued. Many 15th- and 16th-century artists, of course, developed unique, recognizable styles, but convention, in terms of both subject matter and representational practices, predominated. In Italian Renaissance art, certain themes, motifs, and compositions appear with great regularity, fostered by training practices that emphasized the importance of tradition for aspiring Renaissance artists.

**Imitation** The starting point in a young artist's training (see "Artistic Training in Renaissance Italy," Chapter 14, page 414) was imitation. Italian Renaissance artists believed the best way to learn was to copy the works of masters. Accordingly, much of an apprentice's training consisted of copying exemplary artworks. Leonardo da Vinci filled his sketchbooks with drawings of well-known sculptures and frescoes, and Michelangelo spent days sketching artworks in churches around Florence and Rome.

**Emulation** The next step was emulation, which involved modeling one's art after that of another artist. Although imitation still provided the foundation for this practice, an artist used features of another's art only as a springboard for improvements or innovations. Thus, developing artists went beyond previous artists and attempted to prove their own competence and skill by improving on established and recognized masters. Comparison and a degree of competition were integral to emulation. To evaluate the "improved" artwork, viewers had to be familiar with the original "model."

Renaissance artists believed developing artists would ultimately arrive at their own unique style through this process of imitation and emulation. Cennino Cennini (ca. 1370–1440) explained the value of this training procedure in a book he published around 1400, *Il Libro dell'Arte* (*The Artist's Handbook*), which served as a practical guide to artistic production:

> Having first practiced drawing for a while, . . . take pains and pleasure in constantly copying the best things which you can find done by the hand of great masters. And if you are in a place where many good masters have been, so much the better for you. But I give you this advice: take care to select the best one every time, and the one who has the greatest reputation. And, as you go on from day to day, it will be against nature if you do not get some grasp of his style and of his spirit. For if you undertake to copy after one master today and after another one tomorrow, you will not acquire the style of either one or the other, and you will inevitably, through enthusiasm, become capricious, because each style will be distracting your mind. You will try to work in this man's way today, and in the other's tomorrow, and so you will not get either of them right. If you follow the course of one man through constant practice, your intelligence would have to be crude indeed for you not to get some nourishment from it. Then you will find, if nature has granted you any imagination at all, that you will eventually acquire a style individual to yourself, and it cannot help being good; because your hand and your mind, being always accustomed to gather flowers, would ill know how to pluck thorns.*

*Translated by Daniel V. Thompson Jr., *Cennino Cennini, The Craftsman's Handbook* (*Il Libro dell'Arte*), (New York: Dover Publications, 1960; reprint of 1933 ed.), 14–15.

**GENTILE DA FABRIANO** The leading Quattrocento master of the International Style was GENTILE DA FABRIANO (ca. 1370–1427), who in 1423 painted *Adoration of the Magi* (FIG. **21-18**) as the altarpiece for the family chapel of Palla Strozzi (1372–1462) in the church of Santa Trinità in Florence. At the beginning of the 15th century, the Strozzi family was the wealthiest in the city. The altarpiece, with its elaborate gilded Gothic frame, is testimony to the patron's lavish tastes. So too is the painting itself, with its gorgeous surface and sumptuously costumed kings, courtiers, captains, and retainers accompanied by a menagerie of exotic animals. Gentile portrayed all these elements in a rainbow of color with extensive use of gold. The painting presents all the pomp and ceremony of chivalric etiquette in a religious scene centered on the Madonna and Child. Although the style is fundamentally International Gothic, Gentile inserted striking naturalistic details. For example, the artist depicted animals from a variety of angles and foreshortened the forms convincingly, most notably the horse at the far right seen in a three-quarter rear view. Gentile did the same with human figures, such as the kneeling man removing the spurs from the standing *magus* in the center foreground. In the left panel of the predella, Gentile painted what may have been the first nighttime *Nativity* scene with the central light source—the radiant Christ Child—introduced

into the picture itself. Although predominantly conservative, Gentile demonstrated he was not oblivious to Quattrocento experimental trends and could blend naturalistic and inventive elements skillfully and subtly into a traditional composition without sacrificing Late Gothic splendor in color, costume, and framing ornamentation.

**MASACCIO** The artist who epitomizes the innovative spirit of early-15th-century Florentine painting was Tommaso di ser Giovanni di Mone Cassai, known as MASACCIO (1401–1428). Although his presumed teacher, Masolino da Panicale (see "Italian Artists' Names," Chapter 14, page 405), had worked in the International Style, Masaccio broke sharply from the normal practice of imitating his master's style (see "Cennino Cennini on Imitation and Emulation in Renaissance Art," above). He moved suddenly, within the short span of six years, into unexplored territory. Most art historians recognize no other painter in history to have contributed so much to the development of a new style in so short a time as Masaccio, whose untimely death at age 27 cut short his brilliant career. Masaccio was the artistic descendant of Giotto (see Chapter 14), whose calm, monumental style he carried further by introducing a whole new repertoire of representational devices that generations of Renaissance painters later studied and developed.

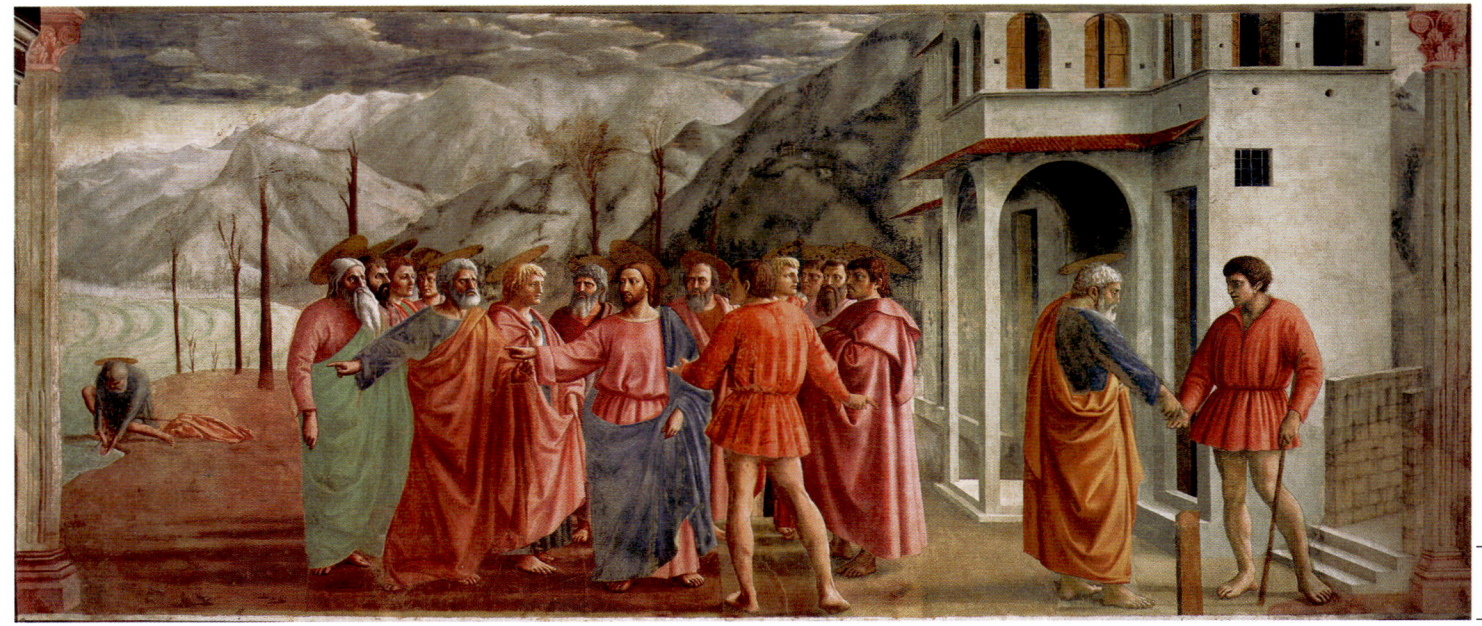

**21-19** Masaccio, *Tribute Money*, Brancacci chapel, Santa Maria del Carmine, Florence, Italy, ca. 1424–1427. Fresco, 8′ 4⅛″ × 19′ 7⅛″. ◼◤

Masaccio's figures recall Giotto's in their simple grandeur, but they convey a greater psychological and physical credibility. He modeled his figures with light coming from a source outside the picture.

**BRANCACCI CHAPEL**  The frescoes Masaccio painted in the family chapel that Felice Brancacci (1382–1447) sponsored in Santa Maria del Carmine in Florence provide excellent examples of his innovations. In *Tribute Money* (FIG. **21-19**), painted shortly before his death, Masaccio depicted an episode from the Gospel of Matthew (17:24–27). As the tax collector confronts Jesus at the entrance to the Roman town of Capernaum, Jesus directs Saint Peter to the shore of Lake Galilee. There, as Jesus foresaw, Peter finds the tribute coin in the mouth of a fish and returns to pay the tax. Masaccio divided the story into three parts within the fresco. In the center, Jesus, surrounded by his disciples, tells Peter to retrieve the coin from the fish, while the tax collector stands in the foreground, his back to spectators and hand extended, awaiting payment. At the left, in the middle distance, Peter extracts the coin from the fish's mouth, and, at the right, he thrusts the coin into the tax collector's hand.

Masaccio's figures recall Giotto's in their simple grandeur, but they convey a greater psychological and physical credibility. Masaccio created the figures' bulk through modeling not with a flat, neutral light lacking an identifiable source but with a light coming from a specific source outside the picture. The light comes from the right and strikes the figures at an angle, illuminating the parts of the solids obstructing its path and leaving the rest in shadow, producing the illusion of deep sculptural relief. Between the extremes of light and dark, the light appears as a constantly active but fluctuating force highlighting the scene in varying degrees. Giotto used light only to model the masses. In Masaccio's works, light has its own nature, and the masses are visible only because of its direction and intensity. The viewer can imagine the light as playing over forms—revealing some and concealing others, as the artist directs it. The figures in *Tribute Money* are solemn and weighty, but they also move freely and reveal body structure, as do Donatello's statues. Masaccio's representations adeptly suggest bones, muscles, and the pressures and tensions of joints. Each figure conveys a maximum of contained energy. *Tribute Money* helps the viewer understand Giorgio Vasari's comment: "[T]he works made before his

[Masaccio's] day can be said to be painted, while his are living, real, and natural."[6]

Masaccio's arrangement of the figures is equally inventive. They do not stand in a line in the foreground. Instead, the artist grouped them in circular depth around Jesus, and he placed the whole group in a spacious landscape, rather than in the confined stage space of earlier frescoes. The group itself generates the foreground space and the architecture on the right amplifies it. Masaccio depicted the building in perspective, locating the vanishing point, where all the orthogonals converge, at Jesus' head. He also diminished the brightness of the colors as the distance increases, an aspect of atmospheric perspective. Although ancient Roman painters used aerial perspective (FIG. 7-20), medieval artists had abandoned it. Thus, it virtually disappeared from art until Masaccio and his contemporaries rediscovered it. They came to realize that the light and air interposed between viewers and what they see are two parts of the visual experience called "distance."

In an awkwardly narrow space at the entrance to the Brancacci chapel, to the left of *Tribute Money*, Masaccio painted *Expulsion of Adam and Eve from Eden* (FIG. **21-20**), another fresco displaying the representational innovations of *Tribute Money*. For example, the sharply slanted light from an outside source creates deep relief, with lights placed alongside darks, and acts as a strong unifying agent. Masaccio also presented the figures with convincing structural accuracy, thereby suggesting substantial body weight. Further, the hazy background specifies no locale but suggests a space around and beyond the figures. Adam's feet, clearly in contact with the ground, mark the human presence on earth, and the cry issuing from Eve's mouth voices her anguish. The angel does not force them physically from Eden. Rather, they stumble on blindly, the angel's will and their own despair driving them. The composition is starkly simple, its message incomparably eloquent.

**HOLY TRINITY**  Masaccio's *Holy Trinity* fresco (FIG. **21-21**) in Santa Maria Novella is another of the young artist's masterworks and

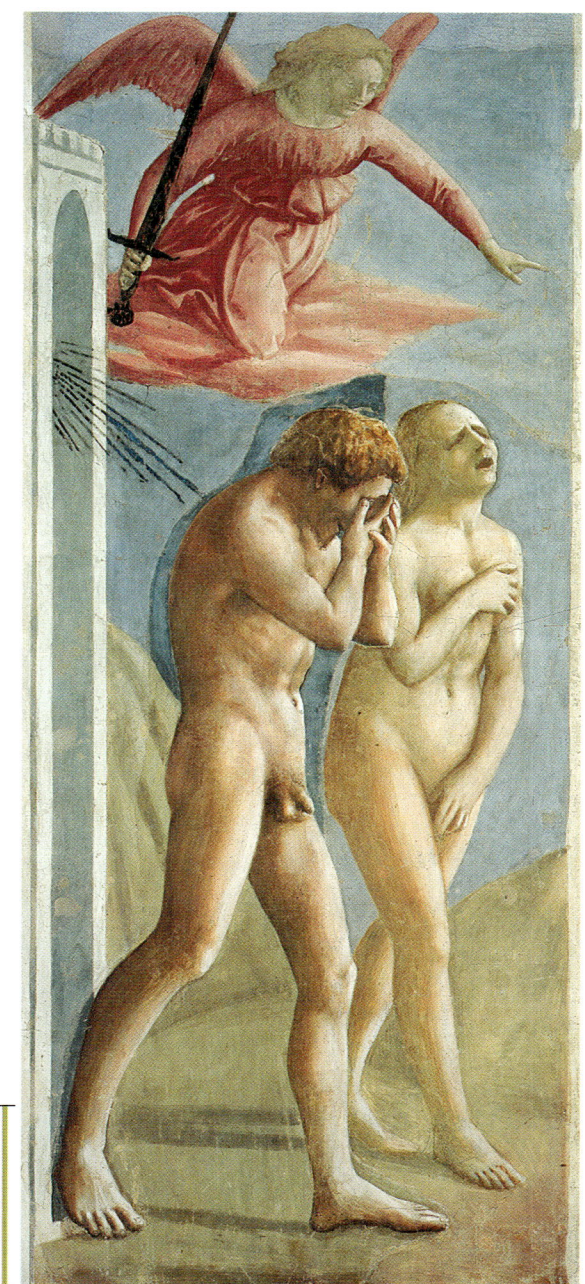

**21-20** MASACCIO, *Expulsion of Adam and Eve from Eden,* Brancacci chapel, Santa Maria del Carmine, Florence, Italy, ca. 1424–1427. Fresco, 7′ × 2′ 11″. ◼️◣

Adam and Eve, expelled from Eden, stumble on blindly, driven by the angel's will and their own despair. The hazy background specifies no locale but suggests a space around and beyond the figures.

1 ft.

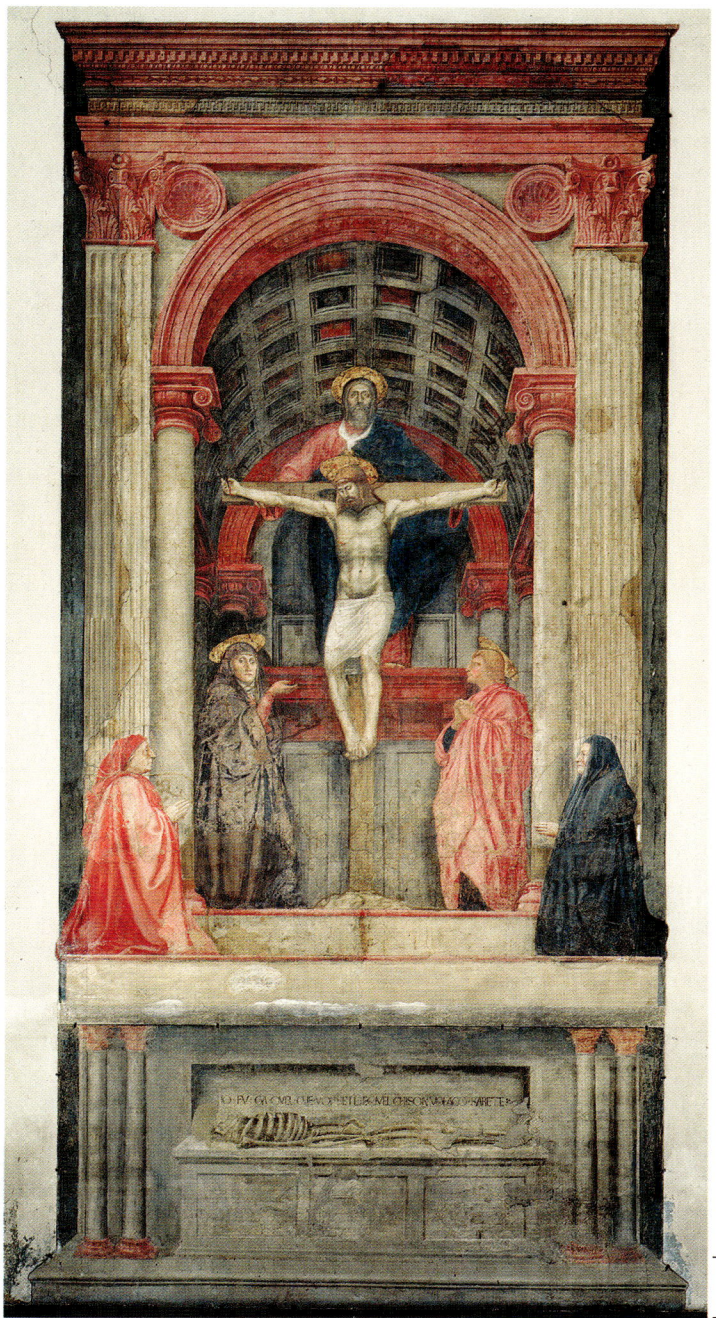

**21-21** MASACCIO, *Holy Trinity,* Santa Maria Novella, Florence, Italy, ca. 1424–1427. Fresco, 21′ 10⅝″ × 10′ 4¾″.

Masaccio's pioneering *Holy Trinity* is the premier early-15th-century example of the application of mathematics to the depiction of space according to Brunelleschi's system of perspective.

1 ft.

the premier early-15th-century example of the application of mathematics to the depiction of space. Masaccio painted the composition on two levels of unequal height. Above, in a barrel-vaulted chapel reminiscent of a Roman *triumphal arch* (FIGS. 7-40 and 7-44B; compare FIG. 21-49A), the Virgin Mary and Saint John appear on either side of the crucified Christ. God the Father emerges from behind Christ, supporting the arms of the cross and presenting his son to the worshiper as a devotional object. The dove of the Holy Spirit hovers between God's head and Christ's head. Masaccio also included portraits of the donors of the painting, Lorenzo Lenzi and his wife, who kneel just in front of the *pilasters* framing the chapel's

entrance. Below, the artist painted a tomb containing a skeleton. An inscription in Italian above the skeleton reminds the spectator, "I was once what you are, and what I am you will become."

The illusionism of *Holy Trinity* is breathtaking. In this fresco, Masaccio brilliantly demonstrated the principles and potential of Brunelleschi's new science of perspective. Indeed, some art historians have suggested Brunelleschi may have collaborated with Masaccio. The vanishing point of the composition is at the foot of the cross. With this point at eye level, spectators look up at the Trinity and down at the tomb. About 5 feet above the floor level, the vanishing point pulls the two views together, creating the illusion of a real structure transecting the wall's vertical plane. Whereas the tomb appears to project forward into the church, the chapel recedes visually behind the wall and appears as an extension of the spectator's space. This adjustment of the picture's space to the viewer's position was an important innovation in illusionistic painting that other artists of the Renaissance and the later Baroque period would develop further. Masaccio was so exact in his metrical proportions it is possible to calculate the dimensions of the chapel (for example, the span of the painted vault is 7 feet and the depth of the chapel is 9 feet). Thus, he achieved not only a successful illusion but also a rational measured coherence that is responsible for the unity and harmony of the fresco. *Holy Trinity* is, however, much more than a demonstration of Brunelleschi's perspective or of the painter's ability to represent fully modeled figures bathed in light. In this painting, Masaccio also powerfully conveyed one of the central tenets of Christian faith. The ascending pyramid of figures leads viewers from the despair of death to the hope of resurrection and eternal life through Christ's crucifixion.

**FRA ANGELICO** As Masaccio's *Holy Trinity* clearly demonstrates, humanism and religion were not mutually exclusive. In fact, for many Quattrocento Italian artists, humanist concerns were not a primary consideration. The art of FRA ANGELICO (ca. 1400–1455) focused on serving the Roman Catholic Church. In the late 1430s, the abbot of the Dominican monastery of San Marco (Saint Mark) in Florence asked Fra Angelico to produce a series of frescoes for the monastery. The Dominicans (see "Mendicant Orders," Chapter 14, page 404) of San Marco had dedicated themselves to lives of prayer and work, and the religious compound was mostly spare and austere to encourage the monks to immerse themselves in their devotional lives. Fra Angelico's *Annunciation* (FIG. **21-22**) appears at the top of the stairs leading to the friars' cells. Appropriately, Fra

Angelico presented the scene of the Virgin Mary and the Archangel Gabriel with simplicity and serenity. The two figures appear in a plain *loggia* resembling the *portico* of San Marco's *cloister,* and the artist painted all the fresco elements with a pristine clarity. As an admonition to heed the devotional function of the images, Fra Angelico included a small inscription at the base of the image: "As you venerate, while passing before it, this figure of the intact Virgin, beware lest you omit to say a Hail Mary." Like most of Fra Angelico's paintings, *Annunciation,* with its simplicity and directness, still has an almost universal appeal and fully reflects the artist's simple, humble character.

**ANDREA DEL CASTAGNO** Fra Angelico's younger contemporary ANDREA DEL CASTAGNO (ca. 1421–1457) also accepted a commission to produce a series of frescoes for a religious establishment. Castagno's *Last Supper* (FIG. **21-23**) in the *refectory* (dining hall) of Sant'Apollonia in Florence, a convent for Benedictine nuns, manifests both a commitment to the biblical narrative and an interest in perspective. The lavishly painted room Jesus and his 12 disciples occupy suggests the artist's absorption with creating the illusion of three-dimensional space. However, closer scrutiny reveals inconsistencies, such as how Renaissance perspective systems make it impossible to see both the ceiling from inside and the roof from outside, as Castagno depicted. The two side walls also do not appear parallel. Castagno chose a conventional compositional format, with the figures seated at a horizontally placed table. He derived the apparent self-absorption of most of the disciples and the malevolent features of Judas (who sits alone on the outside of the table) from the Gospel of Saint John, rather than the more familiar version of the last supper recounted in the Gospel of Saint Luke. Castagno's dramatic and spatially convincing depiction of the event no doubt was a powerful presence for the nuns during their daily meals.

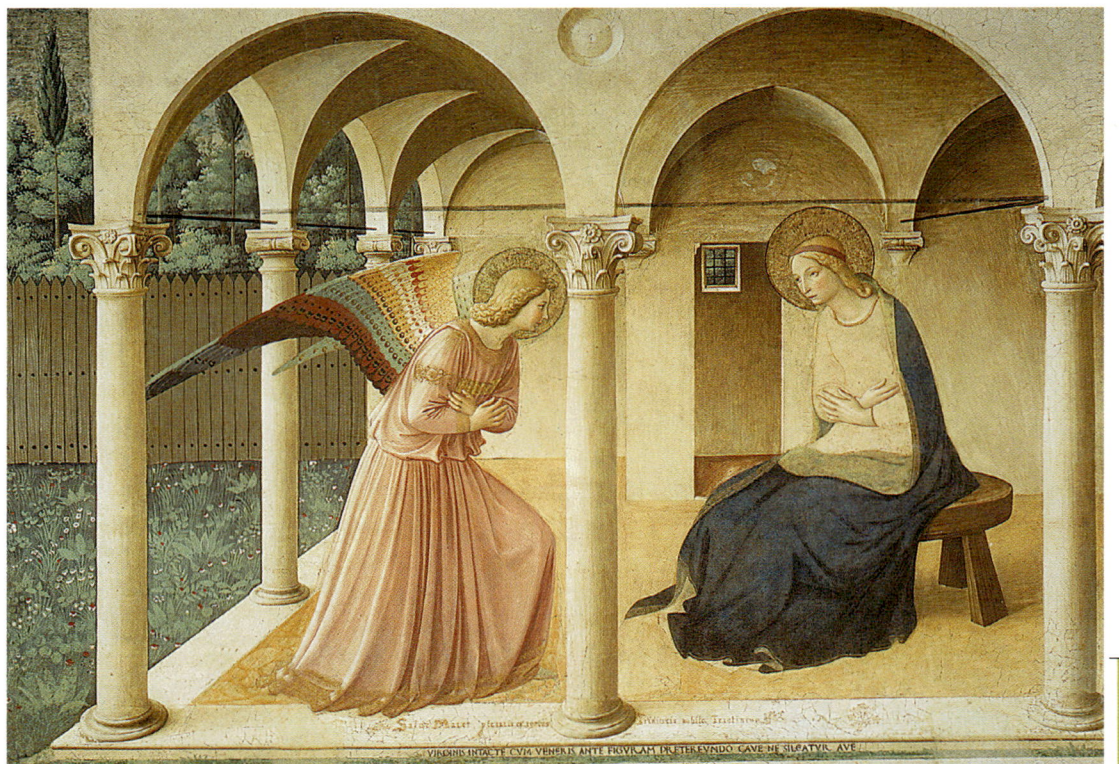

**21-22** FRA ANGELICO, *Annunciation,* San Marco, Florence, Italy, ca. 1438–1447. Fresco, 7′ 1″ × 10′ 6″.

Painted for the Dominican monks of San Marco, Fra Angelico's fresco is simple and direct. Its figures and architecture have a pristine clarity befitting the fresco's function as a devotional image.

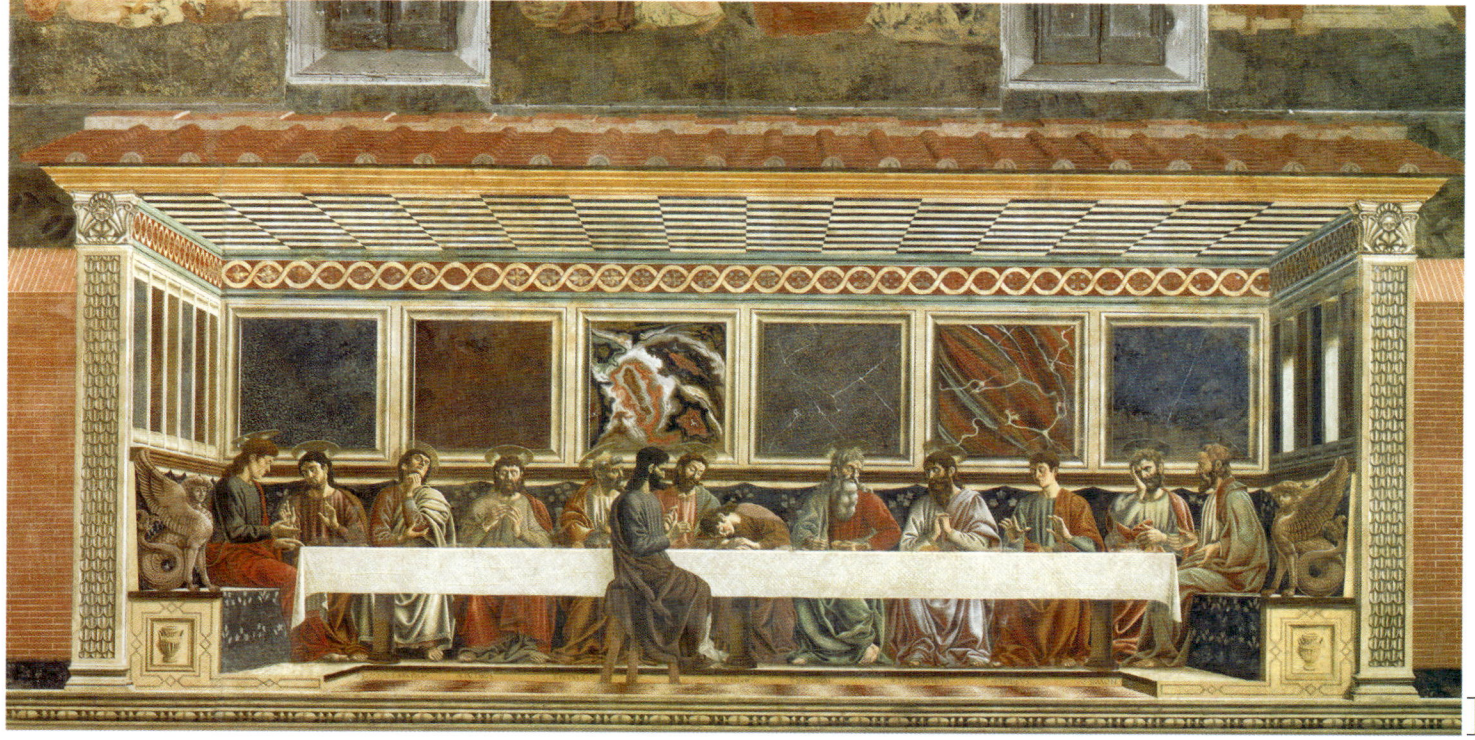

**21-23** ANDREA DEL CASTAGNO, *Last Supper,* refectory of the monastery of Sant'Apollonia, Florence, Italy, 1447. Fresco, 15′ 5″ × 32′. ◀

Judas sits isolated in this *Last Supper* based on the Gospel of Saint John. The figures are small compared with the setting, reflecting Castagno's preoccupation with the new science of perspective.

**FRA FILIPPO LIPPI** Another younger contemporary of Fra Angelico, FRA FILIPPO LIPPI (ca. 1406–1469), was also a friar—but there all resemblance ends. Fra Filippo was unsuited for monastic life. He indulged in misdemeanors ranging from forgery and embezzlement to the abduction of a pretty nun, Lucretia, who became his mistress and the mother of his son, the painter Filippino Lippi (1457–1504). Only the intervention of the Medici on his behalf at the papal court preserved Fra Filippo from severe punishment and total disgrace. An orphan, Fra Filippo spent his youth in a monastery adjacent to the church of Santa Maria del Carmine, and when he was still in his teens, he must have met Masaccio there and witnessed the decoration of the Brancacci chapel. Fra Filippo's early work survives only in fragments, but these show he tried to work with Masaccio's massive forms. Later, probably under the influence of Ghiberti's and Donatello's relief sculptures, he developed a linear style that emphasized the contours of his figures and enabled him to suggest movement through flying and swirling draperies.

In a painting from Fra Filippo's later years, *Madonna and Child with Angels* (FIG. **21-24**), the Virgin sits in prayer at a slight angle to the viewer. Her body casts a shadow on the window frame behind her. But the painter's primary interest was not in space but in line, which unifies the composition and contributes to the precise and smooth delineation of forms. The Carmelite brother interpreted his subject in a surprisingly worldly manner. The Madonna

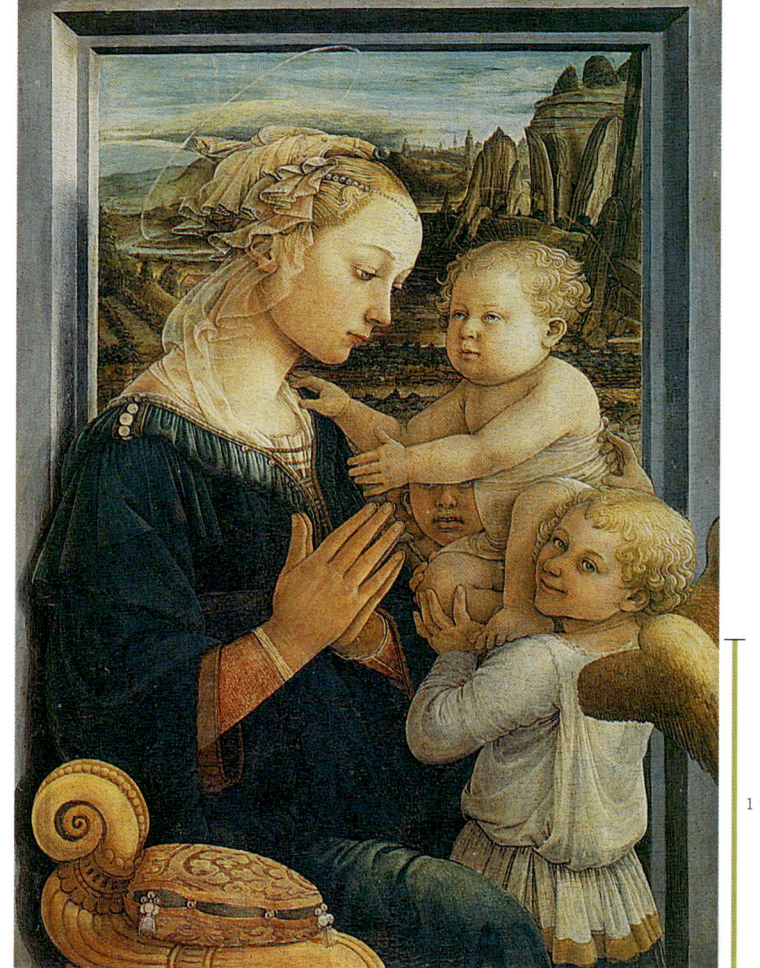

**21-24** FRA FILIPPO LIPPI, *Madonna and Child with Angels,* ca. 1460–1465. Tempera on wood, 2′ 11½″ × 2′ 1″. Galleria degli Uffizi, Florence.

Fra Filippo, a monk guilty of many misdemeanors, represented the Virgin and Christ Child in a distinctly worldly manner, carrying the humanization of the holy family further than any artist before him.

Florence **577**

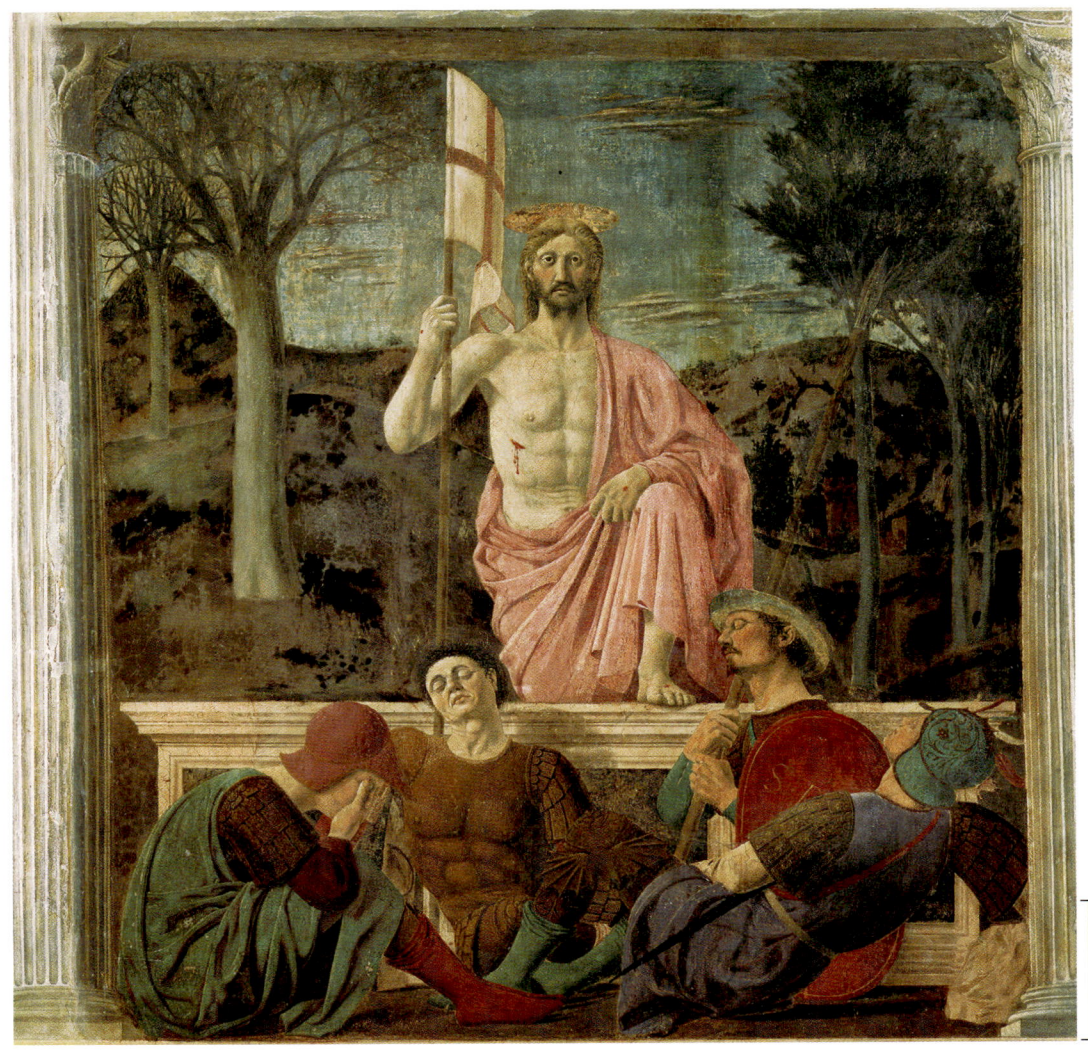

1 ft.

is a beautiful young mother, albeit with a transparent halo, in an elegantly furnished Florentine home, and neither she nor the Christ Child, whom two angels hold up, has a solemn expression. One of the angels, in fact, sports the mischievous, puckish grin of a boy refusing to behave for the pious occasion. Significantly, all figures reflect the use of live models (perhaps Lucretia for the Madonna). Fra Filippo plainly relished the charm of youth and beauty as he found it in this world. He preferred the real in landscape also. The background, seen through the window, incorporates recognizable features of the Arno valley. Compared with the earlier Madonnas by Giotto (FIG. 14-7) and Duccio (FIG. 14-9), this work shows how far artists had carried the humanization of the religious theme. Whatever the ideals of spiritual perfection may have meant to artists in past centuries, Renaissance artists realized those ideals in terms of the sensuous beauty of this world.

**PIERO DELLA FRANCESCA** One of the most renowned painters in 15th-century Italy was PIERO DELLA FRANCESCA (ca. 1420–1492), a native of Borgo San Sepolcro in southeastern Tuscany, who worked for diverse patrons, including the Medici in Florence and Federico de Montefeltro in Urbino (FIG. 21-43). In Tuscany, his commissions included frescoes of Christ's *Resurrection* (FIG. **21-25**) for the town hall of his birthplace and *Legend of the True Cross* (FIG. **21-25A**) for the church of San Francesco at Arezzo. He painted *Resurrection* at the request of the Borgo San Sepolcro civic council on the wall

facing the entrance to its newly remodeled Palazzo Comunale. Normally, the subjects chosen for city halls were scenes of battles, townscapes, or allegories of enlightened governance, as in Siena's Palazzo Pubblico (FIGS. 14-16, 14-16A, and 14-17). But the San Sepolcro council chose instead a religious subject. The town's name—Holy Sepulcher—derived from the legend that two 10th-century saints, Arcanus and Egidius, brought a fragment of Christ's tomb to the town from the Holy Land. Christ's *Resurrection* was also the subject of the central panel of the altarpiece painted between 1346 and 1348 by the Sienese painter Niccolò di Segna for the cathedral of San Sepolcro.

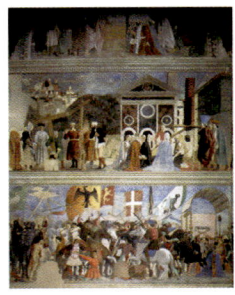

**21-25A** PIERO DELLA FRANCESCA, *Legend of the True Cross,* ca. 1450–1455.

In Piero's *Resurrection,* the viewer witnesses the miracle of the risen Christ through the Corinthian columns of a classical portico (preserved only in part because the painting was trimmed during its installation in a new location). Piero chose a viewpoint corresponding to the viewer's position and depicted the architectural frame at a sharp angle from below. The Roman soldiers who have fallen asleep when they should be guarding the tomb are also seen from below in a variety of foreshortened poses. (The bareheaded guard second from the left with his head resting on Christ's sarcophagus may be a self-portrait of the artist.) The soldiers form the

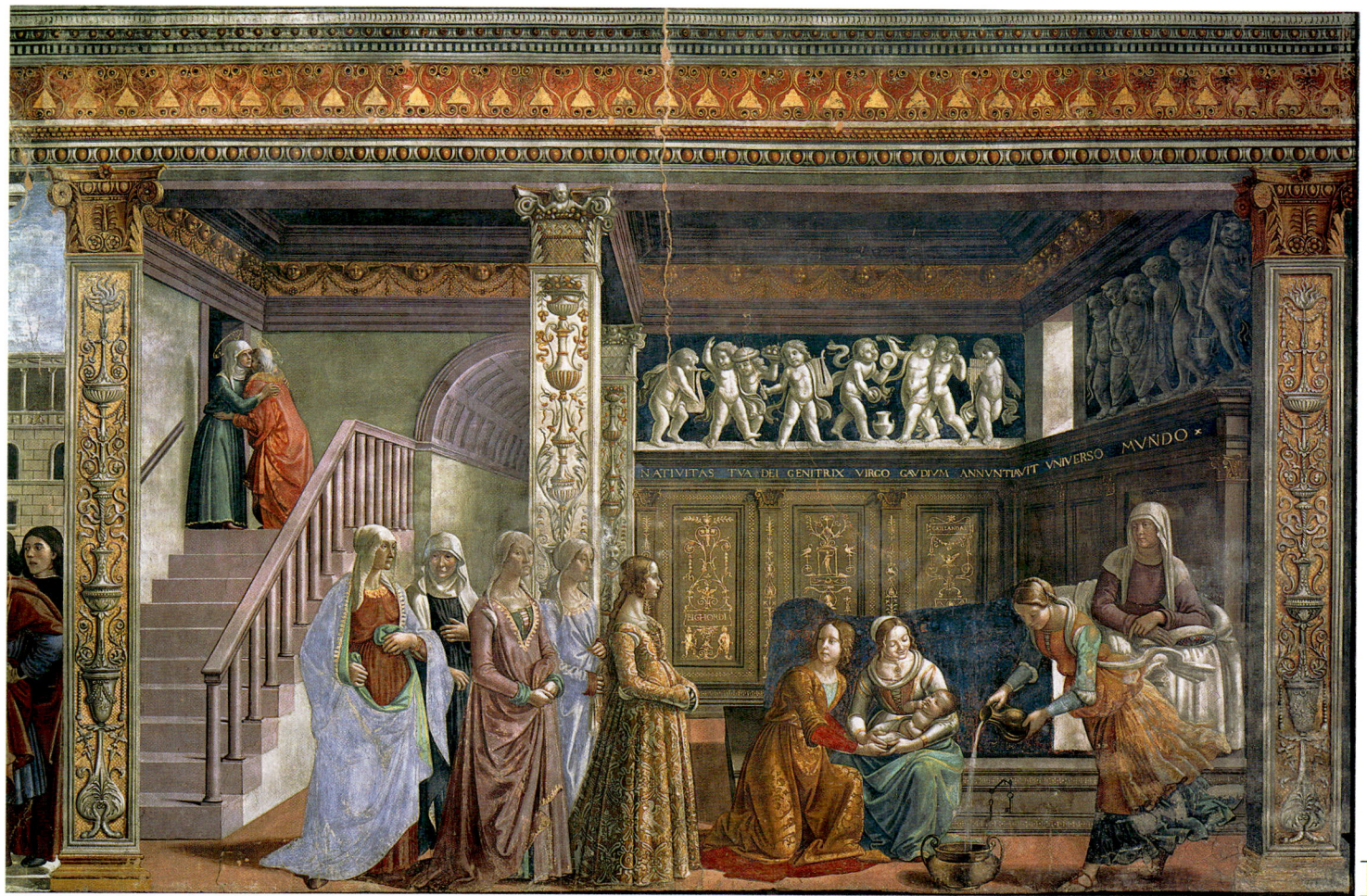

**21-26** Domenico Ghirlandaio, *Birth of the Virgin,* Cappella Maggiore, Santa Maria Novella, Florence, Italy, ca. 1485–1490. Fresco, 24′ 4″ × 14′ 9″. ◼◂

Ludovica Tornabuoni holds as prominent a place in Ghirlandaio's fresco as she must have held in Florentine society—evidence of the secularization of sacred themes in 15th-century Italian painting.

base of a compositional triangle culminating at Christ's head. For Christ, Piero violated the perspective of the rest of the fresco and used a head-on view of the resurrected savior, imbuing the figure with an iconic quality. Christ's muscular body has the proportions of Greco-Roman nude statues. His pastel cloak stands out prominently from the darker colors of the soldiers' costumes. Christ holds the banner of his victory over death and displays his wounds. His face has portraitlike features. The tired eyes and somber expression are the only indications of his suffering on the cross.

**DOMENICO GHIRLANDAIO** Although projects undertaken with church, civic, and Medici patronage were significant sources of income for Florentine artists, other wealthy families also offered attractive commissions. Toward the end of the 15th century, DOMENICO GHIRLANDAIO (1449–1494) received the contract for an important project for Giovanni Tornabuoni, one of the wealthiest Florentines of his day. Tornabuoni asked Ghirlandaio to paint a cycle of frescoes depicting scenes from the lives of the Virgin and Saint John the Baptist for the choir of Santa Maria Novella (FIG. 14-6A), the Dominican church where Masaccio had earlier painted his revolutionary *Holy Trinity* (FIG. 21-21). In *Birth of the Virgin* (FIG. **21-26**), Mary's mother, Saint Anne, reclines in a palatial Renaissance room embellished with fine wood inlay and sculpture, while midwives

prepare the infant's bath. From the left comes a solemn procession of women led by a young Tornabuoni family member, probably Ludovica, Giovanni's only daughter. Ghirlandaio's composition epitomizes the achievements of Quattrocento Florentine painting: clear spatial representation, statuesque figures, and rational order and logical relations among all figures and objects. If any remnant of earlier traits remains here, it is the arrangement of the figures, which still cling somewhat rigidly to layers parallel to the picture plane. New, however, and in striking contrast to the dignity and austerity of Fra Angelico's frescoes (FIG. 21-22) for the Dominican monastery of San Marco, is the dominating presence of the donor's family in the religious tableau. Ludovica holds as prominent a place in the composition (close to the central axis) as she must have held in Florentine society. Her appearance in the painting (a different female member of the house appears in each fresco) is conspicuous evidence of the secularization of sacred themes. Artists depicted living persons of high rank not only as present at biblical dramas (as Masaccio did in *Holy Trinity*) but also even stealing the show from the saints—as here, where the Tornabuoni women upstage the Virgin and Child. The display of patrician elegance tempers the biblical narrative and subordinates the fresco's devotional nature.

Ghirlandaio also painted individual portraits of wealthy Florentines. His 1488 panel painting of an aristocratic young woman is

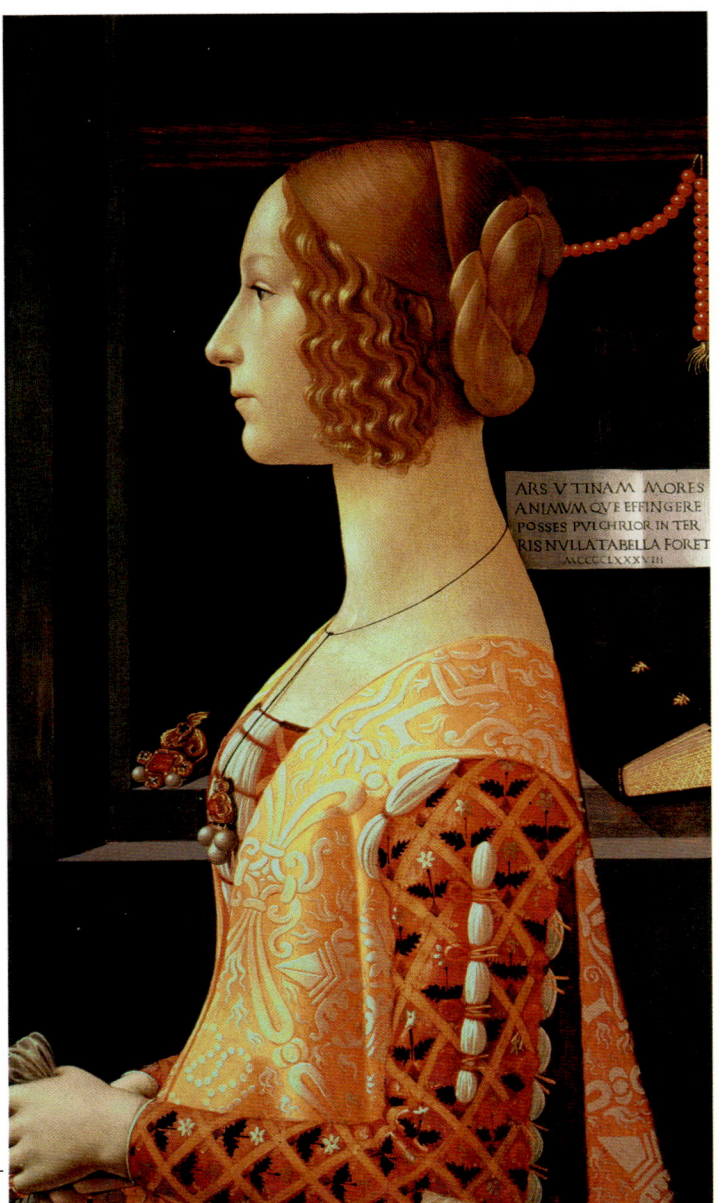

**21-27** DOMENICO GHIRLANDAIO, *Giovanna Tornabuoni*(?), 1488. Oil and tempera on wood, 2′ 6″ × 1′ 8″. Museo Thyssen-Bornemisza, Madrid.

Renaissance artists revived the ancient art of portraiture. This portrait reveals the wealth, courtly manners, and humanistic interest in classical literature that lie behind much 15th-century Florentine art.

probably a portrait of Giovanna Tornabuoni (FIG. **21-27**), a member of the powerful Albizzi family and wife of Lorenzo Tornabuoni, one of Lorenzo Medici's cousins. Although artists at this time were beginning to employ three-quarter and full-face views for portraits (FIG. 21-29A) in place of the more traditional profile pose, Ghirlandaio used the older format. This did not prevent him from conveying a character reading of the sitter. His portrait reveals the proud bearing of a sensitive and beautiful young woman. It also tells viewers much about the advanced state of culture in Florence, the value and careful cultivation of beauty in life and art, the breeding of courtly manners, and the great wealth behind it all. In addition, the painting shows the powerful attraction classical literature held for Italian humanists. In the background, an epitaph (Giovanna Tornabuoni died in childbirth in 1488 at age 20) quotes the ancient Roman poet Martial:

> If art could depict character and soul,
> No painting on earth would be more beautiful.[7]

**PAOLO UCCELLO** A masterpiece of this secular side of Quattrocento art is *Battle of San Romano* (FIG. **21-28**) by PAOLO UCCELLO (1397–1475), a Florentine painter trained in the International Style. The large panel painting is one of three Lorenzo de' Medici acquired for his bedchamber in the palatial Medici residence (FIGS. 21-37 and 21-38) in Florence. There is some controversy about the date of the painting because documents have been discovered suggesting Lorenzo may have purchased at least two of the paintings from a previous owner instead of commissioning the full series himself. The scenes commemorate the Florentine victory over the Sienese in 1432 and must have been painted no earlier than the mid-1430s if not around 1455, the traditional date assigned to the commission. In the panel illustrated, Niccolò da Tolentino (ca. 1350–1435), a friend and supporter of Cosimo de' Medici, leads the charge against the Sienese. Although the painting focuses on Tolentino's military exploits, it also acknowledges the Medici, albeit in symbolic form. The bright orange fruit behind the raised lances on the left are *mela medica* (Italian, "medicinal apples"). Because the name *Medici* means

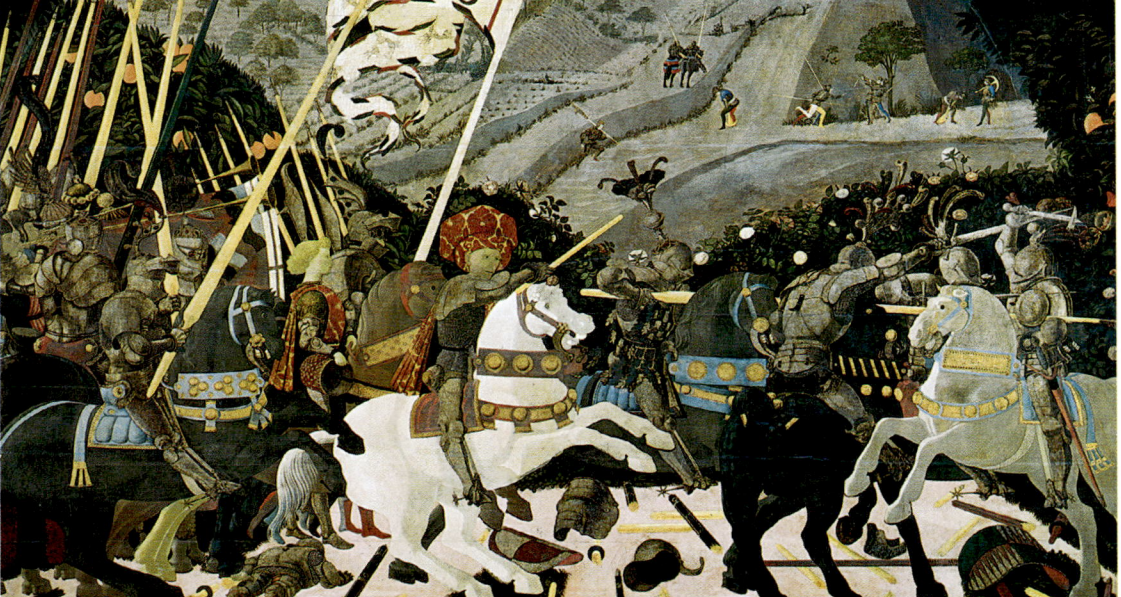

**21-28** PAOLO UCCELLO, *Battle of San Romano,* ca. 1435 or ca. 1455. Tempera on wood, 6′ × 10′ 5″. National Gallery, London.

In this panel once in Lorenzo de' Medici's bedchamber, Niccolò da Tolentino leads the charge against the Sienese. The foreshortened spears and figures reveal Uccello's fascination with perspective.

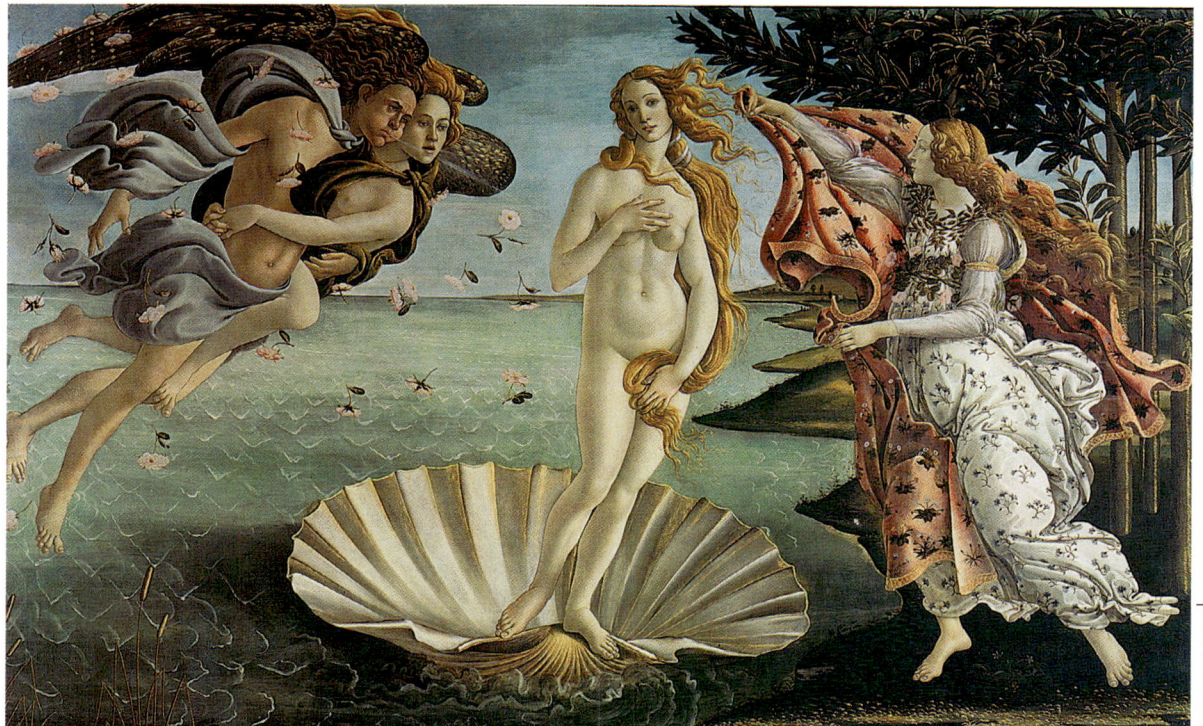

21-29 SANDRO BOTTICELLI, *Birth of Venus*, ca. 1484–1486. Tempera on canvas, 5′ 9″ × 9′ 2″. Galleria degli Uffizi, Florence. ◼◀

Inspired by an Angelo Poliziano poem and classical Aphrodite statues (FIG. 5-62), Botticelli revived the theme of the female nude in this elegant and romantic representation of Venus born of sea foam.

1 ft.

"doctors," this fruit was a fitting symbol of the family. Orange apples also appear in Botticelli's *Primavera* (FIG. 21-1). Their inclusion here suggests that at least this panel was a Medici commission, if all three were not.

In *Battle of San Romano*, Uccello created a composition that recalls the International style processional splendor of Gentile da Fabriano's *Adoration of the Magi* (FIG. 21-18) yet also reflects Uccello's obsession with perspective. In contrast with Gentile, who emphasized surface decoration, Uccello painted life-size, classically inspired figures arranged in the foreground and, in the background, a receding landscape resembling the low cultivated hillsides between Florence and Lucca. He foreshortened broken spears, lances, and a fallen soldier and carefully placed them along the converging orthogonals of the perspective system to create a base plane akin to a checkerboard, on which he then placed the larger volumes in measured intervals. The rendering of three-dimensional form, used by other painters for representational or expressive purposes, became for Uccello a preoccupation. For him, it had a magic of its own, which he exploited to satisfy his inventive and original imagination.

## BOTTICELLI, *BIRTH OF VENUS*

Also painted for the Medici and rivaling *Primavera* (FIG. 21-1) in fame is Sandro Botticelli's *Birth of Venus* (FIG. **21-29**). The theme was the subject of a poem by Angelo Poliziano (1454–1494), a leading humanist of the day. In Botticelli's lyrical painting of Poliziano's retelling of the Greek myth, Zephyrus, carrying Chloris, blows Venus, born of the sea foam and carried on a cockle shell, to her sacred island, Cyprus. There, the nymph Pomona runs to meet her with a brocaded mantle. The lightness and bodilessness of the winds move all the figures without effort. Draperies undulate easily in the gentle gusts, perfumed by rose petals that fall on the whitecaps. In this painting, unlike in *Primavera*, Botticelli depicted Venus as nude. As noted earlier, the nude, especially the female nude, was exceedingly rare during the Middle Ages. The artist's use (especially on such a large scale—roughly life-size) of an ancient Venus statue (a Hellenistic variant of Praxiteles' famous *Aphrodite of Knidos*, FIG. 5-62) as a

model could have drawn harsh criticism. But in the more accommodating Renaissance culture and under the protection of the powerful Medici, the depiction went unchallenged, in part because *Birth of Venus*, which has several mythological figures in common with *Primavera*, is susceptible to a Neo-Platonic reading. Marsilio Ficino (1433–1499), for example, made the case in his treatise *On Love* (1469) that those who embrace the contemplative life of reason—including, of course, the humanists in the Medici circle—will immediately contemplate spiritual and divine beauty whenever they behold physical beauty.

Botticelli's style is clearly distinct from the earnest search many other artists pursued to comprehend humanity and the natural world through a rational, empirical order. Indeed, Botticelli's elegant and beautiful linear style (he was a pupil of Fra Filippo Lippi, FIG. 21-24) seems removed from all the scientific knowledge 15th-century artists had gained in the areas of perspective and anatomy. For example, the seascape in *Birth of Venus* is a flat backdrop devoid of atmospheric perspective. Botticelli's style paralleled the Florentine allegorical pageants that were chivalric tournaments structured around allusions to classical mythology. The same trend is evident in the poetry of the 1470s and 1480s. Artists and poets at this time did not directly imitate classical antiquity but used the myths, with delicate perception of their charm, in a way still tinged with medieval romance. Ultimately, Botticelli created a style of visual poetry parallel to the love poetry of Lorenzo de' Medici. His paintings possess a lyricism and courtliness that appealed to cultured Florentine patrons, whether the Medici themselves or associates of the family (FIG. **21-29A**).

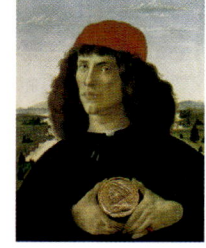

21-29A BOTTICELLI, *Young Man Holding a Medal*, ca. 1474–1475. ◼◀

## ENGRAVING

Although the most prestigious commissions in 15th-century Florence were for large-scale panel paintings and frescoes and for monumental statues and reliefs, some artists also produced important small-scale works, such as Pollaiuolo's

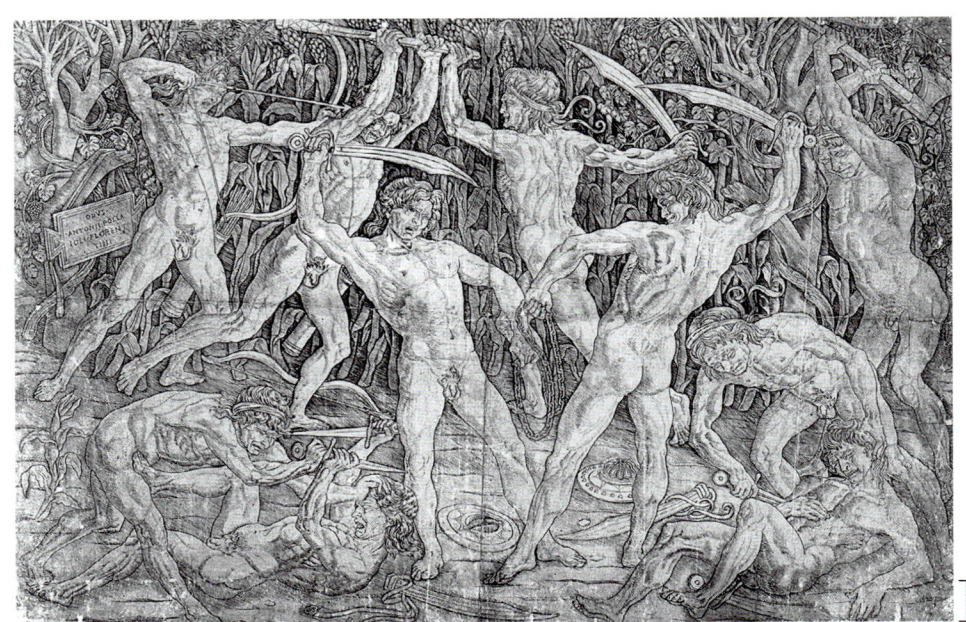

**21-30** Antonio del Pollaiuolo, *Battle of Ten Nudes,* ca. 1465. Engraving, 1′ 3⅛″ × 1′ 11¼″. Metropolitan Museum of Art, New York (bequest of Joseph Pulitzer, 1917).

Pollaiuolo was fascinated by how muscles and sinews activate the human skeleton. He delighted in showing nude figures in violent action and from numerous foreshortened viewpoints.

1 in.

*Hercules and Antaeus* (FIG. 21-14). Pollaiuolo also experimented with the new medium of engraving, which northern European artists had pioneered around the middle of the century. But whereas German graphic artists, such as Martin Schongauer (FIG. 20-22), described their forms with hatching that followed the forms, Italian engravers, such as Pollaiuolo, preferred parallel hatching. The former method was in keeping with the general northern European approach to art, which tended to describe surfaces of forms rather than their underlying structures, whereas the latter better suited the anatomical studies that preoccupied Pollaiuolo and his Italian contemporaries.

*Battle of Ten Nudes* (FIG. **21-30**), like Pollaiuolo's *Hercules and Antaeus* (FIG. 21-14), reveals the artist's interest in the realistic presentation of human figures in action. Earlier artists, such as Donatello (FIG. 21-12) and Masaccio (FIG. 21-20), had dealt effectively with the problem of rendering human anatomy, but they usually depicted their figures at rest or in restrained motion. As is evident in his engraving as well as in his sculpture, Pollaiuolo took delight in showing violent action. He conceived the body as a powerful machine and liked to display its mechanisms, such as knotted muscles and taut sinews that activate the skeleton as ropes pull levers. To show this to best effect, Pollaiuolo developed a figure so lean and muscular it appears *écorché* (as if without skin), with strongly accentuated delineations at the wrists, elbows, shoulders, and knees. *Battle of Ten Nudes* shows this figure type in a variety of poses and from numerous viewpoints, enabling Pollaiuolo to demonstrate his prowess in rendering the nude male figure. In this, he was a kindred spirit of late-sixth-century Greek vase painters, such as Euthymides (FIG. 5-23), who had experimented with foreshortening for the first time in history. Even though the figures in *Ten Nudes* hack and slash at one another without mercy, they nevertheless seem somewhat stiff and frozen because Pollaiuolo depicted *all* the muscle groups at maximum tension. Not until several decades later did an even greater anatomist, Leonardo da Vinci, observe that only some of the body's muscle groups participate in any one action, while the others remain relaxed.

## Architecture

Filippo Brunelleschi's ability to codify a system of linear perspective derived in part from his skill as an architect. Although according to his biographer, Antonio Manetti, Brunelleschi turned to architecture out of disappointment over the loss to Lorenzo Ghiberti of the commission for the baptistery doors (FIGS. 21-2 and 21-3), he continued to work as a sculptor for several years and received commissions for sculpture as late as 1416. It is true, however, that as the 15th century progressed, Brunelleschi's interest turned increasingly toward architecture. Several trips to Rome (the first in 1402,

probably with his friend Donatello), where the ruins of ancient Rome captivated him, heightened his fascination with architecture. His close study of Roman monuments and his effort to make an accurate record of what he saw may have been the catalyst that led Brunelleschi to develop his revolutionary system of geometric linear perspective.

### OSPEDALE DEGLI INNOCENTI

At the end of the second decade of the 15th century, Brunelleschi received two important architectural commissions in Florence—to construct a dome (FIG. **21-30A**) for the city's late medieval cathedral (FIG. 14-18), and to design the Ospedale degli Innocenti (Hospital of the Innocents, FIG. 21-31), a home for Florentine orphans and foundlings. The latter commission came from Florence's guild of silk manufacturers and goldsmiths, of which Brunelleschi, a goldsmith, was a member. The

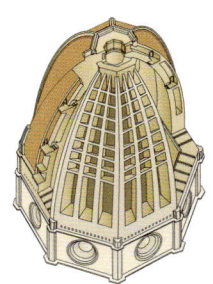

**21-30A** Brunelleschi, Florence Cathedral dome, 1420–1436. ◼

site chosen for the orphanage, adjacent to the church of the Santissima Annunziata (Most Holy Annunciation), was appropriate. The church housed a miracle-working image of the Annunciation that attracted large numbers of pilgrims. With the construction of the new foundling hospital, the Madonna would now watch over infants as well, assisted by the guild, which supported the orphanage with additional charitable donations.

Most scholars regard Brunelleschi's Ospedale degli Innocenti as the first building to embody the new Renaissance architectural style. As in earlier similar buildings, the facade of the Florentine orphanage is a loggia opening onto the street, a sheltered portico where, in this case, parents could anonymously deliver unwanted children to the care of the foundling hospital. Brunelleschi's arcade consists of a series of round arches on slender Corinthian columns. Each bay is a domed compartment with a *pediment*-capped window above. Both plan and elevation conform to a *module* that embodies the rationality of classical architecture. Each column is 10 *braccia* (approximately 20 feet; 1 braccia, or arm, equals 23 inches) tall. The distance between the columns of the facade and the distance between the columns and the wall are also 10 braccia. Thus, each of the bays is a cubical unit 10 braccia wide, deep, and high. The

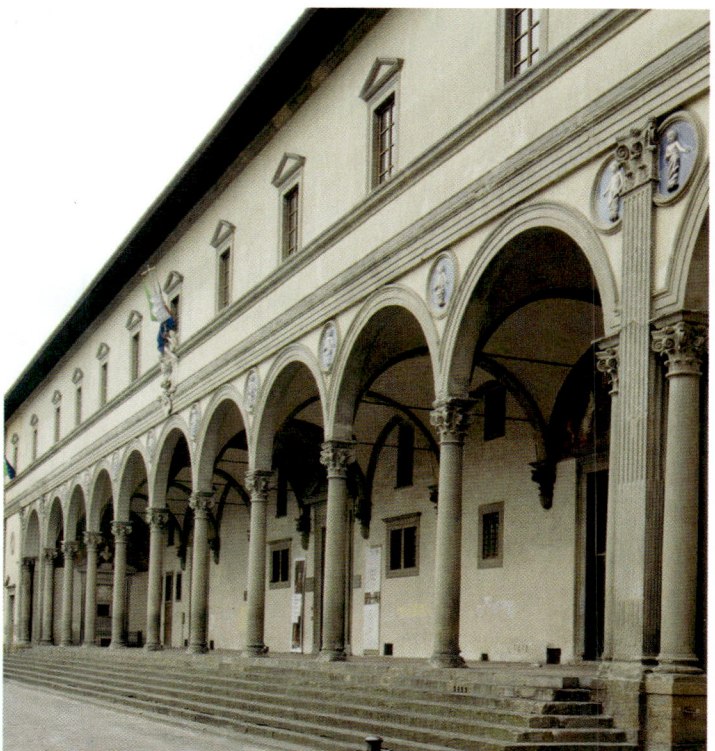

**21-31** Filippo Brunelleschi, **Loggia of the Ospedale degli Innocenti (Foundling Hospital; looking northeast), Florence, Italy, begun 1419.** ◼◀

Often called the first Renaissance building, the loggia of the orphanage sponsored by Florence's silk and goldsmith guild features a classically austere design based on a module of 10 braccia.

height of the columns also equals the diameter of the arches (except in the two outermost bays, which are slightly wider and serve as framing elements in the overall design). The color scheme, which would become a Brunelleschi hallmark, is austere: white stucco walls with gray *pietra serena* ("serene stone") columns and moldings. In 1487, Andrea della Robbia (1435–1525), nephew of Luca della Robbia (FIG. 21-36A) and his successor as head of the family workshop, added more color to the loggia in the form of a series of *glazed terracotta roundels,* one above each column, depicting a baby in swaddling clothes (no two are identical)—the only indication on the building's facade of its charitable function.

**SANTO SPIRITO** Begun around 1436 and completed, with some changes, after Brunelleschi's death, Santo Spirito (FIG. **21-32**) is one of two *basilican* churches the architect built in Florence. (The other is San Lorenzo; FIG. **21-32A**.) Santo Spirito showcases the clarity and classically inspired rationality that characterize Brunelleschi's mature designs. Brunelleschi laid out this *cruciform* building in either multiples or segments of the dome-covered *crossing square.* The aisles, subdivided into small squares

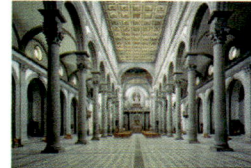

**21-32A** Brunelleschi, San Lorenzo, ca. 1421–1469. ◼◀

covered by shallow, saucer-shaped vaults, run all the way around the flat-roofed central space. They have the visual effect of compressing the longitudinal design into one more comparable to a *central plan,* because the various aspects of the interior resemble one another, no matter where an observer stands. Originally, this centralization effect would have been even stronger. Brunelleschi had planned to extend the aisles across the front of the nave as well, as shown on the plan (FIG. **21-33**, *left*). However, adherence to that design would have de-

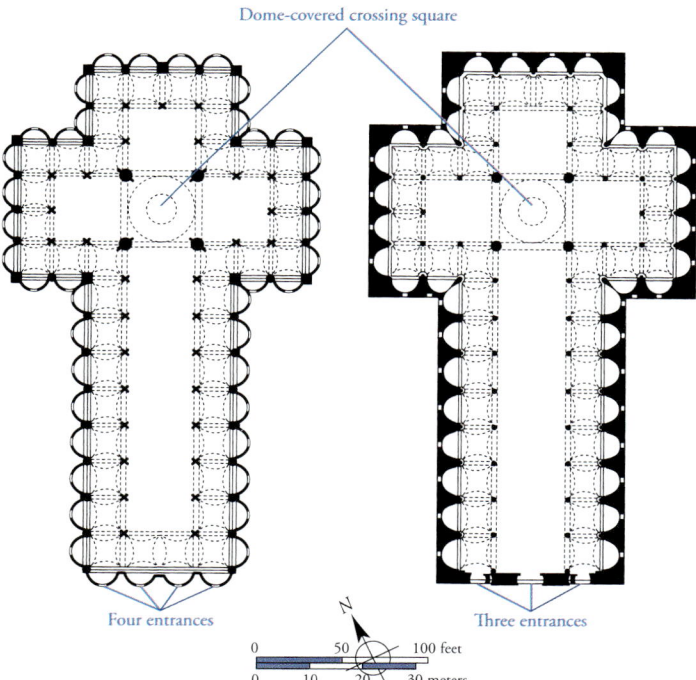

**21-33** Filippo Brunelleschi, **early plan (*left*) and plan as constructed (*right*) of Santo Spirito, Florence, Italy, designed 1434–1436; begun 1446.**

Santo Spirito displays the classically inspired rationality of Brunelleschi's mature style in its all-encompassing modular scheme based on the dimensions of the dome-covered crossing square.

**21-32** Filippo Brunelleschi, **interior of Santo Spirito (looking northeast), Florence, Italy, designed 1434–1436; begun 1446.** ◼◀

The austerity of the decor and the mathematical clarity of the interior of Santo Spirito contrast sharply with the soaring drama and spirituality of the nave arcades and vaults of Gothic churches.

## Italian Renaissance Family Chapel Endowments

During the 14th through 16th centuries in Italy, wealthy families regularly endowed chapels in or adjacent to major churches. These family chapels were usually on either side of the choir near the altar at the church's east end. Particularly wealthy families sponsored chapels in the form of separate buildings constructed adjacent to churches. For example, the Medici Chapel (Old Sacristy) abuts San Lorenzo in Florence. Other powerful banking families—the Baroncelli, Bardi, and Peruzzi—each sponsored chapels in the Florentine church of Santa Croce. The Pazzi family commissioned a chapel (FIGS. 21-34 to 21-36) adjacent to Santa Croce, and the Brancacci family sponsored the decorative program (FIGS. 21-19 and 21-20) of their chapel in Santa Maria del Carmine.

These families endowed chapels to ensure the well-being of the souls of individual family members and ancestors. The chapels served as burial sites and as spaces for liturgical celebrations and commemorative services. Chapel owners sponsored Masses for the dead, praying to the Virgin Mary and the saints for intercession on behalf of their deceased loved ones.

Changes in Christian doctrine prompted these concerted efforts to enhance donors' chances for eternal salvation. Until the 13th century, most Christians believed that after death, souls went either to Heaven or to Hell. In the late 1100s and early 1200s, the concept of Purgatory—a way station between Heaven and Hell where souls could atone for sins before judgment day—increasingly won favor. Pope Innocent III (1198–1216) officially recognized the existence of such a place in 1215. Because Purgatory represented a chance for the faithful to improve the likelihood of eventually gaining admission to Heaven, Christians eagerly embraced this opportunity.

When the Church extended this idea for believers to improve their prospects while alive, charitable work, good deeds, and devotional practices proliferated. Family chapels provided the space

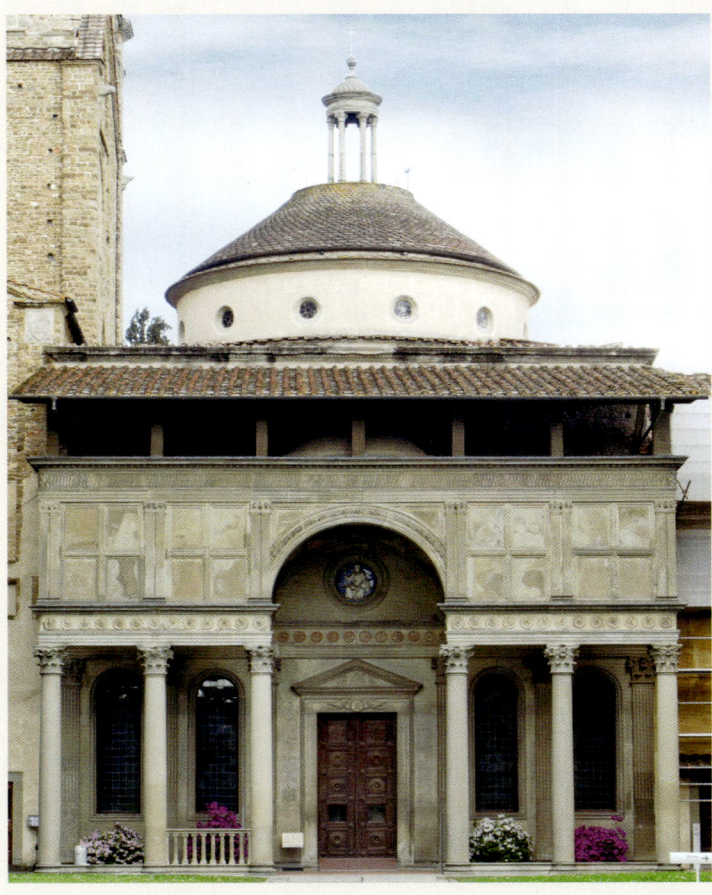

**21-34** FILIPPO BRUNELLESCHI, facade of the Pazzi Chapel, Santa Croce, Florence, Italy, begun 1433. ◼◀

The Pazzi family erected this chapel as a gift to the Franciscan church of Santa Croce. It served as the monks' chapter house and is one of the first independent Renaissance central-plan buildings.

necessary for the performance of devotional rituals. Most chapels included altars, as well as chalices, vestments, candlesticks, and other objects used in the Mass. Most patrons also commissioned decorations, such as painted altarpieces, frescoes on the walls, and sculptural objects. The chapels were therefore not only expressions of piety and devotion but also opportunities for donors to enhance their stature in the larger community.

manded four entrances in the facade, instead of the traditional and symbolic three, a feature hotly debated during Brunelleschi's lifetime and changed after his death. Successor builders also modified the appearance of the exterior walls (FIG. 21-33, *right*) by filling in the recesses between the projecting semicircular chapels to convert the original highly sculpted wall surface into a flat one.

The major features of Santo Spirito's interior (FIG. 21-32), however, are much as Brunelleschi designed them. In this modular scheme, as in the loggia of the Ospedale degli Innocenti (FIG. 21-31), a mathematical unit served to determine the dimensions of every aspect of the church. This unit—the crossing bay measuring 20 by 20 braccia—subdivided throughout the plan creates a rhythmic harmony. Fixed ratios also determined the elevation. For example, the nave is twice as high as it is wide, and the arcade and clerestory are of equal height, which means the height of the arcade equals

the nave's width. Astute observers can read the proportional relationships among the interior's parts as a series of mathematical equations. The austerity of the decor enhances the rationality of the design and produces a restful and tranquil atmosphere. Brunelleschi left no space for expansive wall frescoes that would only detract from the clarity of his architectural scheme. The calculated logic of the design echoes that of ancient Roman buildings, such as the Pantheon (FIG. 7-50, *right*). The rationality of Santo Spirito contrasts sharply, however, with the soaring drama and spirituality of the nave arcades and vaults of Gothic churches (for example, FIGS. 13-19 and 13-20). It even deviates from the design of Florence Cathedral's nave (FIG. 14-18A), whose verticality is restrained in comparison to its northern European counterparts. Santo Spirito fully expresses the new Renaissance spirit that placed its faith in reason rather than in the emotions.

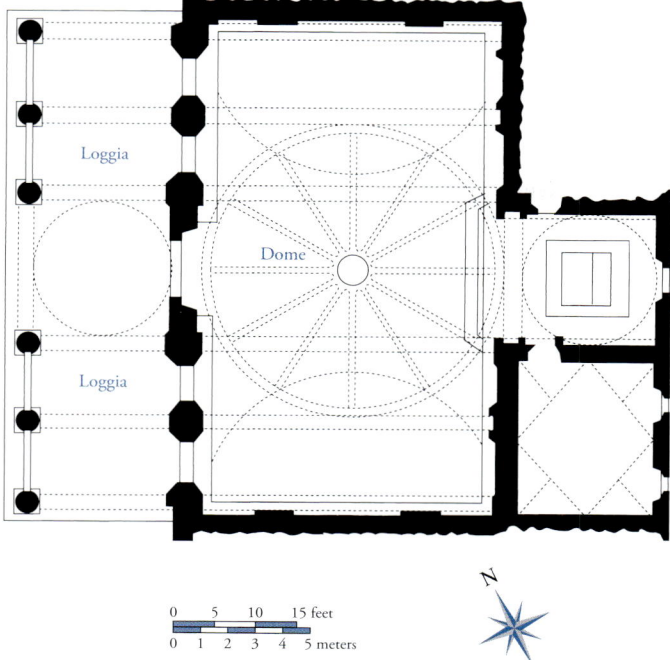

**21-35** FILIPPO BRUNELLESCHI, plan of the Pazzi Chapel, Santa Croce, Florence, Italy, begun 1433.

Although the Pazzi Chapel is rectangular, rather than square or round, Brunelleschi created a central plan by placing all emphasis on the dome-covered space at the heart of the building.

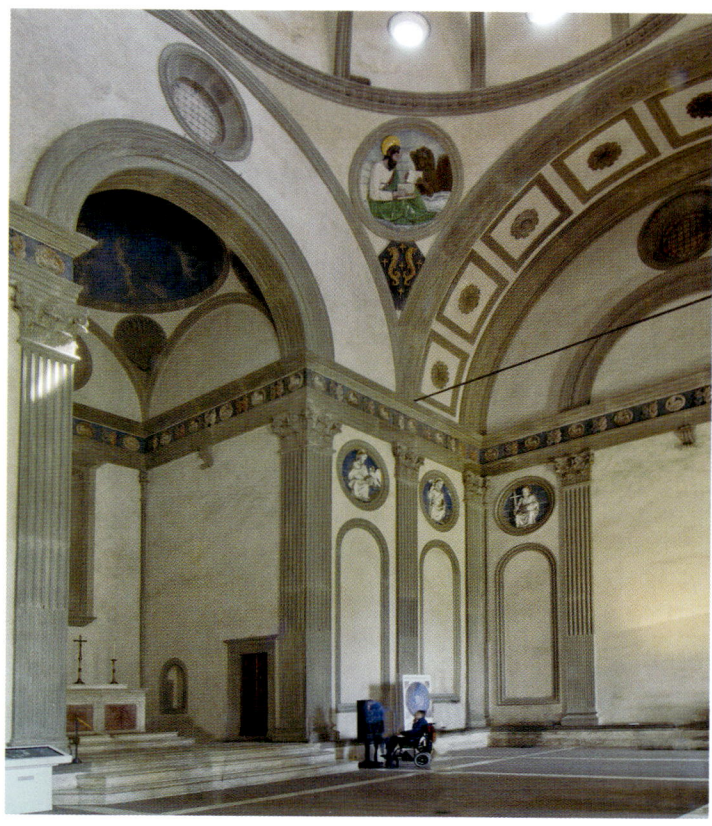

**21-36** FILIPPO BRUNELLESCHI, interior of the Pazzi Chapel (looking northeast), Santa Croce, Florence, Italy, begun 1433. ◼◂

The interior trim of the Pazzi Chapel is gray pietra serena, which stands out against the white stuccoed walls and crisply defines the modular relationships of Brunelleschi's plan and elevation.

**PAZZI CHAPEL** Brunelleschi's apparent effort to impart a centralized effect to the interior of Santo Spirito suggests that he found intriguing the compact and self-contained qualities of central-plan buildings—for example, the Pantheon (FIGS. 7-49 to 7-51) and the Florentine Baptistery of San Giovanni (FIG. 12-27). He had already explored this interest in his design for the chapel (FIG. 21-34) the Pazzi family donated to the Franciscan church of Santa Croce in Florence (see "Italian Renaissance Family Chapel Endowments," page 584). Brunelleschi began to work on the project around 1423, but construction continued until the 1460s, long after his death. The exterior probably does not reflect Brunelleschi's original design. The loggia, admirable as it is, likely was added as an afterthought, perhaps by the sculptor-architect Giuliano da Maiano (1432–1490). The Pazzi Chapel served as the *chapter house* (meeting hall) of the local chapter of Franciscan monks. Historians have suggested the monks needed the expansion to accommodate more of their brethren.

Behind the loggia stands one of the first independent Renaissance buildings conceived basically as a central-plan structure. Although the Pazzi Chapel's plan (FIG. 21-35) is rectangular, rather than square or round, Brunelleschi placed all emphasis on the central dome-covered space. The short barrel-*vault* sections bracing the dome on two sides appear to be incidental appendages. The interior trim (FIG. 21-36) is Brunelleschi's favorite gray pietra serena, which stands out against the white stuccoed walls and crisply defines the modular relationships of plan and elevation. As he did in his design for the Ospedale degli Innocenti (FIG. 21-31) and later for Santo Spirito (FIG. 21-32), Brunelleschi used a basic unit that enabled him to construct a balanced, harmonious, and regularly proportioned space.

Circular medallions, or *tondi,* in the dome's *pendentives* (see "Pendentives and Squinches," Chapter 9, page 262) consist of glazed terracotta reliefs representing the four evangelists. The technique for manufacturing these baked clay reliefs was of recent invention. Around 1430, LUCA DELLA ROBBIA (1400–1482) perfected the application of vitrified (heat-fused) colored potters' glazes to sculpture (FIG. 21-36A). Inexpensive, durable, and decorative, they became extremely popular and provided the basis for a flourishing family business. Luca's nephew Andrea della Robbia produced roundels for Brunelleschi's loggia of the Ospedale degli Innocenti (FIG. 21-31) in 1487, and Andrea's sons, Giovanni della Robbia (1469–1529) and Girolamo della Robbia (1488–1566), carried on this tradition well into the 16th century. Most of the tondi in the Pazzi Chapel are the work of Luca della Robbia himself. Together with the images of the 12 apostles on the pilaster-framed wall panels, they add striking color accents to the tranquil interior.

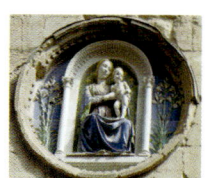

**21-36A** LUCA DELLA ROBBIA, *Madonna and Child,* ca. 1455–1460. ◼◂

**PALAZZO MEDICI** It seems curious that Brunelleschi, the most renowned architect of his time, did not participate in the upsurge of palace building Florence experienced in the 1430s and 1440s. This proliferation of palazzi testified to the stability of the Florentine economy and to the affluence and confidence of the city's leading citizens. Brunelleschi, however, confined his efforts in this field to work on the Palazzo di Parte Guelfa (headquarters of Florence's then-ruling "party") and to a rejected model for a new palace that Cosimo de' Medici intended to build.

When the Medici returned to Florence in 1434 after a brief exile imposed upon them by other elite families who resented the Medicis' consolidation of power, Cosimo, aware of the importance of public perception, attempted to maintain a lower profile and to wield his power from behind the scenes. In all probability, this attitude accounted for his rejection of Brunelleschi's design for the Medici residence, which he evidently found too imposing and ostentatious to be politically wise. Cosimo eventually awarded the commission to MICHELOZZO DI BARTOLOMMEO (1396–1472), a young architect who had been Donatello's collaborator in several sculptural enterprises. Although Cosimo passed over Brunelleschi, his architectural style nevertheless deeply influenced Michelozzo. To a limited extent, the Palazzo Medici (FIG. 21-37) reflects Brunelleschian principles.

Later bought by the Riccardi family (hence the name Palazzo Medici-Riccardi), who almost doubled the facade's length in the 18th century, the palace, both in its original and extended form, is a simple, massive structure. Heavy *rustication* (rough, unfinished masonry) on the ground floor accentuates its strength. Michelozzo divided the building block into stories of decreasing height by using long, unbroken *stringcourses* (horizontal bands), which give it coherence. *Dressed* (smooth, finished) masonry on the second level and an even smoother surface on the top story modify the severity of the ground floor and make the building appear progressively lighter as the eye moves upward. The extremely heavy *cornice,* which Michelozzo related not to the top story but to the building as a whole, dramatically reverses this effect. Like the ancient Roman cornices that served as Michelozzo's models (compare FIGS. 7-32, 7-40, and 7-44B), the Palazzo Medici-Riccardi cornice is a very effective lid for the structure, clearly and emphatically defining its proportions. Michelozzo perhaps also was inspired by the many extant examples of Roman rusticated masonry, and Roman precedents even exist for the juxtaposition of rusticated and dressed stone masonry on the same facade (FIG. 7-34). However, nothing in the ancient world precisely compares with Michelozzo's design. The Palazzo Medici exemplifies the simultaneous respect for and independence from the antique—features that characterize the Early Renaissance in Italy. The classicism and fortresslike appearance of the palace stand in vivid contrast to the Late Gothic delicacy of the facade (FIG. 21-37A) of the so-called Ca d'Oro ("House of Gold"), the roughly contemporaneous palace of the wealthy Venetian merchant Marino Contarini. The comparison underscores the marked regional differences between the art and architecture of Florence and Venice (see Chapter 22).

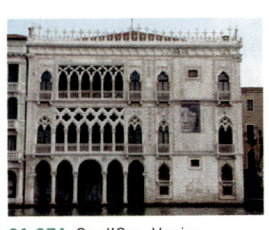

21-37A Ca d'Oro, Venice, 1421–1437. ◼◀

The heart of the Palazzo Medici is an open colonnaded court (FIG. 21-38) that clearly shows Michelozzo's debt to Brunelleschi. The round-arched colonnade, although more massive in its proportions, closely resembles Brunelleschi's foundling-hospital loggia (FIG. 21-31) and the nave colonnades of Santo Spirito (FIG. 21-32) and San Lorenzo (FIG. 21-32A). The Palazzo Medici's internal court surrounded by an arcade was the first of its kind and influenced a long line of descendants in Renaissance domestic architecture.

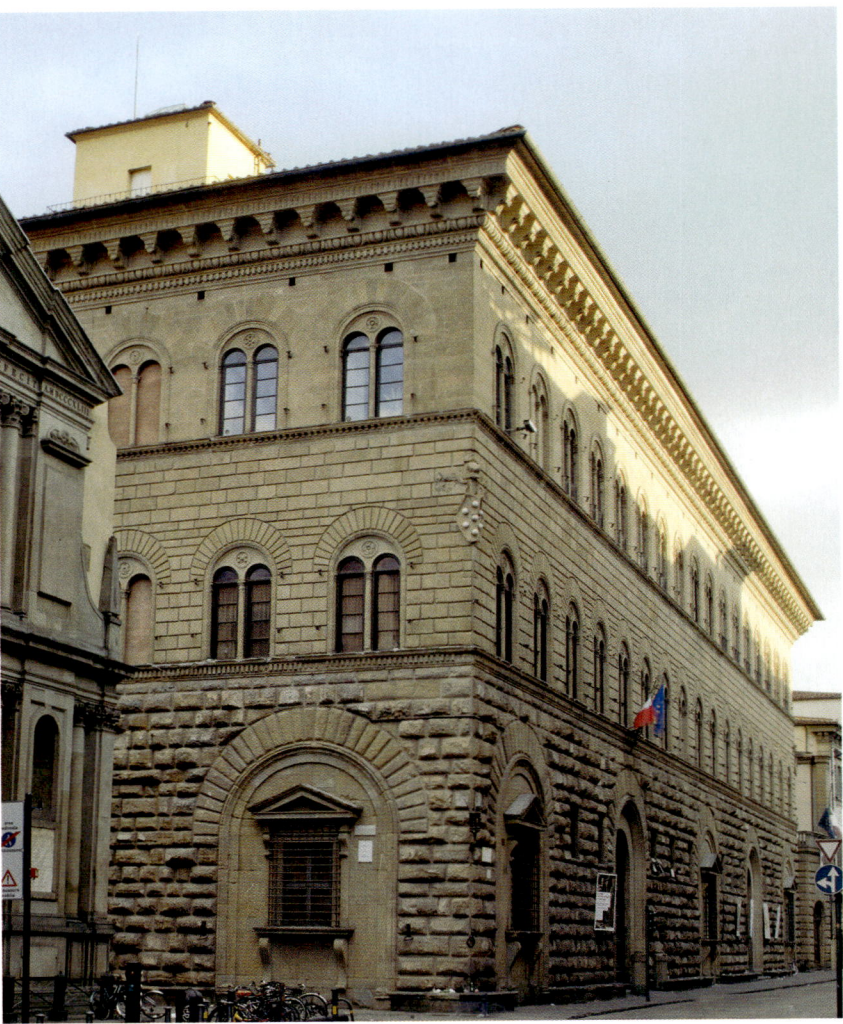

21-37 MICHELOZZO DI BARTOLOMMEO, east facade of the Palazzo Medici-Riccardi (looking southwest) Florence, Italy, begun 1445. ◼◀

The Medici palace, with its combination of dressed and rusticated masonry and classical moldings, draws heavily on ancient Roman architecture, but Michelozzo creatively reinterpreted his models.

**LEON BATTISTA ALBERTI** Although he entered the profession of architecture rather late in life, LEON BATTISTA ALBERTI (1404–1472) nevertheless made a remarkable contribution to architectural design. He was the first to study seriously the ancient Roman architectural treatise of Vitruvius (see page 167), and his knowledge of it, combined with his own archaeological investigations, made him the first Renaissance architect to understand classical architecture in depth. Alberti's most influential theoretical work, *On the Art of Building* (written about 1450, published in 1486), although inspired by Vitruvius, contains much original material. Alberti advocated a system of ideal proportions and believed the central plan was the ideal form for churches. He also considered incongruous the combination of column and arch, which had persisted since Roman times and throughout the Middle Ages. For Alberti, the arch was a wall opening that should be supported only by a section of wall (a pier), not by an independent sculptural element (a column), as in Brunelleschi and Michelozzo's buildings.

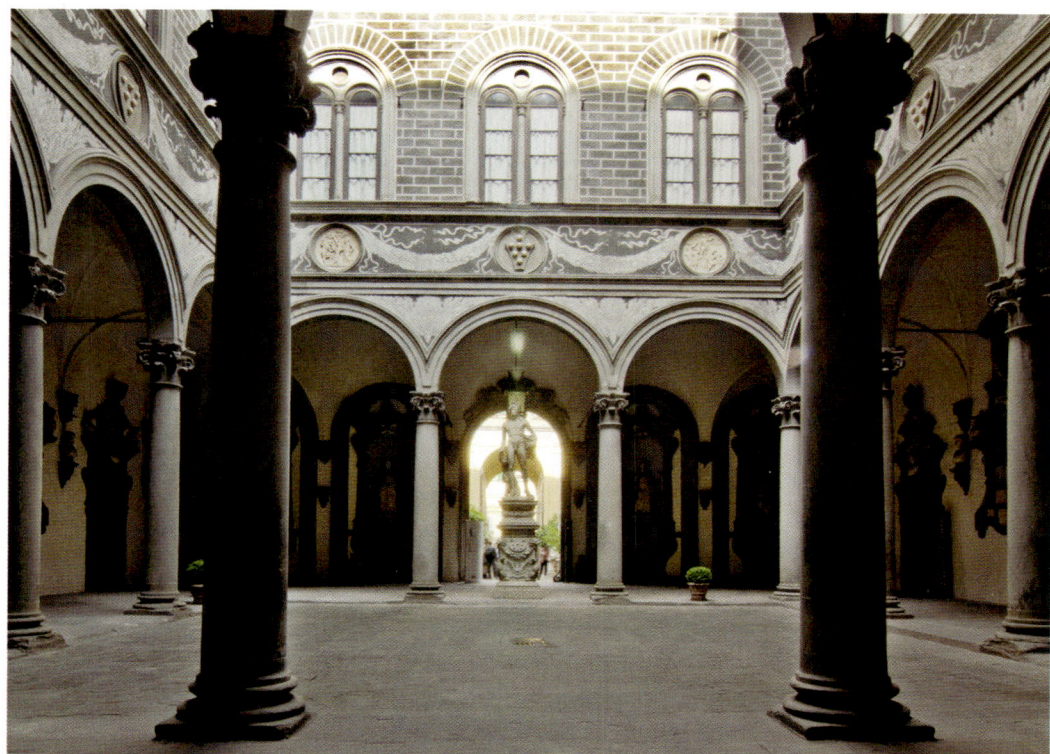

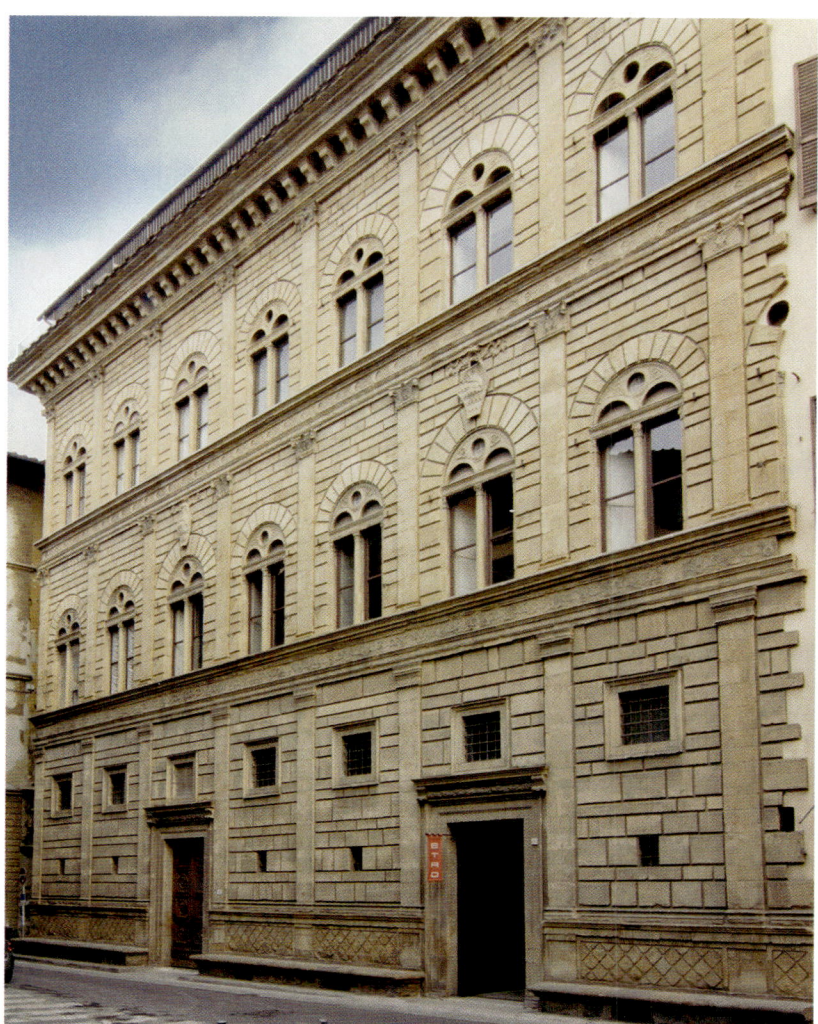

**PALAZZO RUCELLAI** Alberti's architectural style represents a scholarly application of classical elements to contemporaneous buildings. He designed the Palazzo Rucellai (FIG. **21-39**) in Florence, although his pupil and collaborator, Bernardo Rossellino (FIG. 21-15), constructed the building using Alberti's plans and sketches. The facade of the palace is much more severe than that of the Palazzo Medici-Riccardi (FIG. 21-37). Pilasters define each story, and a classical cornice crowns the whole. Between the smooth pilasters are subdued and uniform wall surfaces. Alberti created the sense that the structure becomes lighter in weight toward its top by adapting the ancient Roman manner of using different capitals for each story. He chose *Tuscan* (the Etruscan variant of the Greek *Doric order;* FIG. 5-13, *left,* or page xxii in Volume II and Book D) for the ground floor, *Composite* (the Roman combination of *Ionic volutes* with the acanthus leaves of the *Corinthian;* FIG. 5-73 or page xxiii in Volume II and Book D) for the second story,

**21-39** LEON BATTISTA ALBERTI and BERNARDO ROSSELLINO, Palazzo Rucellai (looking northwest), Florence, Italy, ca. 1452–1470. ◼◀

Alberti was an ardent student of classical architecture. By adapting the Roman use of different orders for each story, he created the illusion that the Palazzo Rucellai becomes lighter toward its top.

and Corinthian for the third floor. Alberti modeled his facade on the most imposing Roman ruin of all, the Colosseum (FIG. 7-37), but he was no slavish copyist. On the Colosseum's facade, the capitals employed are, from the bottom up, Tuscan, Ionic, and Corinthian. Moreover, Alberti adapted the Colosseum's varied surface to a flat facade, which does not allow the deep penetration of the building's mass that is so effective in the Roman structure. By converting his ancient model's *engaged columns* (half-round columns attached to a wall) into shallow pilasters that barely project from the wall, Alberti created a large-meshed linear net. Stretched tightly across the front of his building, it not only unifies the three levels but also emphasizes the wall's flat, two-dimensional qualities.

**SANTA MARIA NOVELLA** The Rucellai family also commissioned Alberti to design the facade (FIG. **21-40**) of the 13th-century Gothic church of Santa Maria Novella in Florence. Here, Alberti took his cue from a *Romanesque* design—that of the Florentine church of San Miniato al Monte. Following his medieval model, he designed a small, pseudoclassical, pediment-capped temple front for the facade's upper part and supported it with a pilaster-framed arcade incorporating the six tombs and three doorways of the Gothic building. But in the organization of these elements, Alberti applied Renaissance principles. The height of Santa Maria Novella (to the pediment tip) equals its width. Consequently, the entire facade can be inscribed in a square. Throughout the facade, Alberti defined areas and related them to one another in terms of proportions that can be expressed in simple numerical ratios. For example, the upper structure can be encased in a square one-fourth the size of the main square. The cornice separating the two levels divides the major square in half so that the lower portion of the building is a rectangle twice as wide as it is high. In his treatise, Alberti wrote at length about the necessity of employing harmonic proportions to achieve beautiful buildings. Alberti shared this conviction with Brunelleschi, and this fundamental dependence on classically derived mathematics distinguished their architectural work from that of their medieval predecessors. They believed in the eternal and universal validity of numerical ratios as the source of beauty. In this respect, Alberti and Brunelleschi revived the true spirit of the High Classical age of ancient Greece, as epitomized by the architect Iktinos and the sculptor Polykleitos, who produced canons of proportions for the perfect temple and the perfect statue (see "The Perfect Temple," and "Polykleitos's Prescription for the Perfect Statue," Chapter 5, pages 105 and 132). Still, it was not only a desire to emulate Vitruvius and the Greek masters that motivated Alberti to turn to mathematics in his quest for beauty. His contemporary, the Florentine humanist Giannozzo Manetti (1396–1459), had argued that Christianity itself possessed the order and logic of mathematics. In his 1452 treatise, *On the Dignity and Excellence of Man,* Manetti insisted Christian religious truths were as self-evident as mathematical axioms.

The Santa Maria Novella facade was an ingenious solution to a difficult design problem. On one hand, it adequately expressed the organization of the structure attached to it. On the other hand, it subjected preexisting and quintessentially medieval features, such as the large round window on the second level, to a rigid geometrical order that instilled a quality of classical calm and reason. This facade also introduced a feature of great historical consequence—the scrolls that simultaneously unite the broad lower and narrow upper levels and screen the sloping roofs over the aisles. With variations, similar spirals appeared in literally hundreds of church facades throughout the Renaissance and Baroque periods.

**GIROLAMO SAVONAROLA** In the 1490s, Florence underwent a political, cultural, and religious upheaval. Florentine artists and their fellow citizens responded then not only to humanist ideas but also to the incursion of French armies and especially to the preaching of the Dominican monk Girolamo Savonarola (1452–1498), the reformist priest-dictator who denounced the humanistic secularism of the Medici and their artists, philosophers, and poets. Savonarola exhorted the people of Florence to repent their sins, and when Lorenzo de' Medici died in 1492, the priest prophesied the downfall of the city and of Italy and assumed absolute control of the state. As did a large number of citizens, Savonarola believed the Medici family's political, social, and religious power had corrupted Florence and invited the scourge of foreign invasion. Savonarola encouraged citizens to burn their classical texts, scientific treatises, and philosophical publications. The Medici fled in 1494. Scholars still debate the significance of Savonarola's brief span of power. Apologists for the undoubtedly sincere monk deny his actions played a role in the decline of Florentine culture at the end of the 15th century. But the puritanical spirit that moved Savonarola must have dampened considerably the enthusiasm for classical antiquity of the Florentine Early Renaissance. Certainly, Savonarola's condemnation of humanism as heretical nonsense, and his banishing of the Medici, Tornabuoni, and other wealthy families from Florence, deprived local artists of some of their major patrons, at least in the short term. There were, however, commissions aplenty for artists elsewhere in Italy.

**21-40** Leon Battista Alberti, west facade of Santa Maria Novella, Florence, Italy, 1456–1470. ◼◀

Alberti's design for the facade of this Gothic church features a pediment-capped temple front and pilaster-framed arcades. Numerical ratios are the basis of the proportions of all parts of the facade.

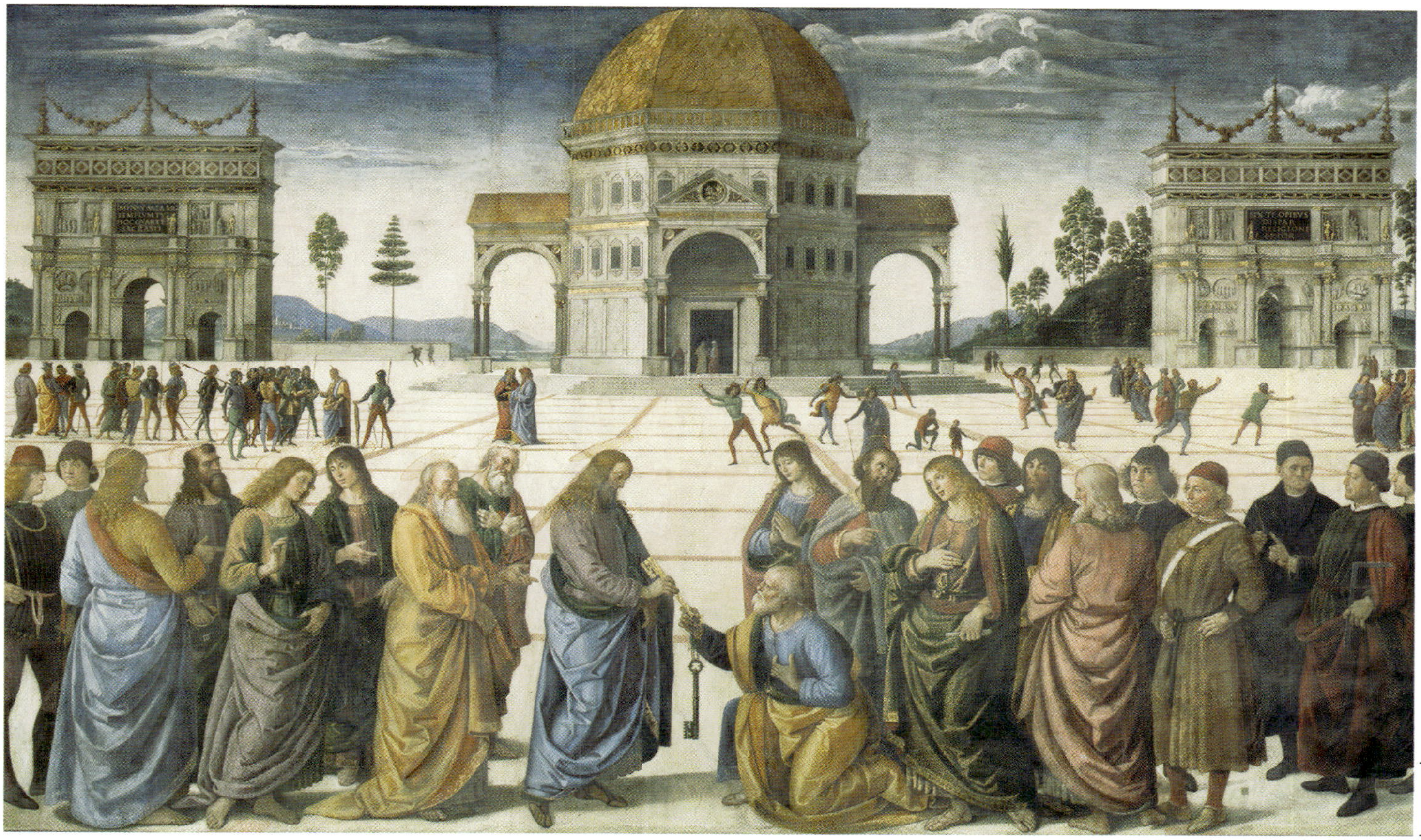

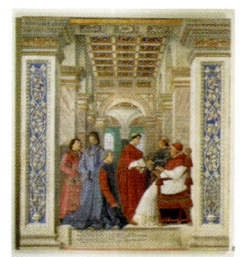

21-41 PERUGINO, *Christ Delivering the Keys of the Kingdom to Saint Peter*, Sistine Chapel, Vatican, Rome, Italy, 1481–1483. Fresco, 11′ 5½″ × 18′ 8½″.

Painted for the Vatican, this fresco depicts the event on which the papacy bases its authority. The converging lines of the pavement connect the action in the foreground with the background.

# THE PRINCELY COURTS

Although Florentine artists led the way in creating the Renaissance in art and architecture, the arts flourished throughout Italy in the 15th century. The princely courts in Rome, Urbino, Mantua, and elsewhere also deserve credit for nurturing Renaissance art (see "Italian Princely Courts and Artistic Patronage," page 591). Whether the "prince" was a duke, condottiere, or pope, the considerable wealth the heads of these courts possessed, coupled with their desire for recognition, fame, and power, resulted in major art commissions.

## Rome and the Papal States

Although not a secular ruler, the pope in Rome was the head of a court with enormous wealth at his disposal. In the 16th and 17th centuries, the popes became the major patrons of art and architecture in Italy (see Chapters 22 and 24), but even during the Quattrocento, the papacy was the source of some significant artistic commissions.

**PERUGINO** Between 1481 and 1483, Pope Sixtus IV (r. 1471–1484) summoned a group of artists to Rome to decorate the walls of the newly completed Sistine Chapel (MAP 22-1 and FIG. 22-1). Among the artists the pope employed were Botticelli, Ghirlandaio, and Pietro Vannucci, known as PERUGINO (ca. 1450–1523) because his birthplace was Perugia in Umbria. The project followed immediately the completion of the new Vatican library, which the pope also or-

dered decorated with frescoes by MELOZZO DA FORLÌ (1438–1494; FIG. 21-41A) and others. Perugino's contribution to the Sistine Chapel fresco cycle was *Christ Delivering the Keys of the Kingdom to Saint Peter* (FIG. 21-41). The papacy had, from the beginning, based its claim to infallible and total authority over the Roman Catholic Church on this biblical event, and therefore the subject was one of obvious appeal to Sixtus IV. In Perugino's fresco, Christ

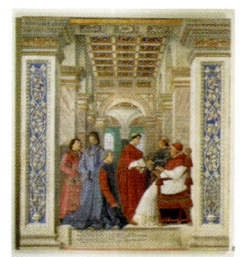

21-41A MELOZZO DA FORLÌ, *Sixtus IV Confirming Platina*, ca. 1477–1481.

hands the keys to Saint Peter, who stands amid an imaginary gathering of the 12 apostles and Renaissance contemporaries. These figures occupy the apron of a great stage space that extends into the distance to a point of convergence in the doorway of a central-plan temple. (Perugino used parallel and converging lines in the pavement to mark off the intervening space; compare FIGS. 21-10 and 21-11.) Figures in the middle distance complement the near group, emphasizing its density and order by their scattered arrangement. At the corners of the great piazza, duplicate triumphal arches serve as the base angles of a distant compositional triangle whose apex is in the central building. Perugino modeled the arches closely on the Arch of Constantine (FIG. 7-75) in Rome. Although an anachronism in a painting depicting a scene from Christ's life, the arches served to underscore the close ties between Saint Peter and Constantine, the first Christian emperor of Rome and builder of the great basilica (FIG. 8-9)

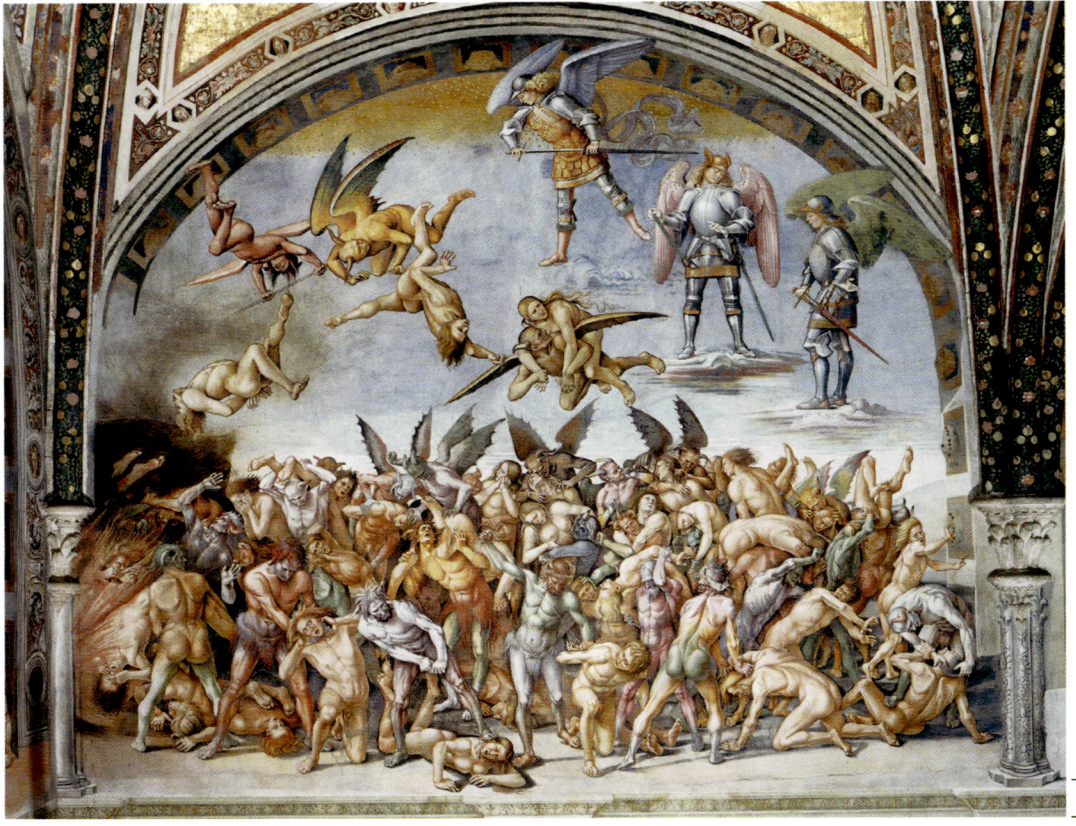

**21-42** Luca Signorelli, *The Damned Cast into Hell,* San Brizio chapel, Orvieto Cathedral, Orvieto, Italy, 1499–1504. Fresco, 23′ wide. ◼◀

Few figure compositions of the 15th century have the same psychic impact as Signorelli's fresco of writhing, foreshortened muscular bodies tortured by demons in Hell.

1 ft.

over Saint Peter's tomb. Christ and Peter flank the triangle's central axis, which runs through the temple's doorway, the vanishing point of Perugino's perspective scheme. Brunelleschi's new spatial science allowed the Umbrian artist to organize the action systematically. The composition interlocks both two-dimensional and three-dimensional space, and the placement of central actors emphasizes the axial center.

**LUCA SIGNORELLI** Another Umbrian painter Sixtus IV employed for the decoration of the Sistine Chapel was LUCA SIGNORELLI (ca. 1445–1523), in whose work the fiery passion of Savonarola's sermons found its pictorial equal. Signorelli further developed Pollaiuolo's interest in the depiction of muscular bodies in violent action in a wide variety of poses and foreshortenings. In the San Brizio chapel in the cathedral of the papal city of Orvieto (MAP 14-1), Signorelli painted for Pope Alexander VI (r. 1492–1503) scenes depicting the end of the world, including *The Damned Cast into Hell* (FIG. **21-42**). Few Quattrocento figure compositions equal Signorelli's in psychic impact. Saint Michael and the hosts of Heaven hurl the damned into Hell, where, in a dense, writhing mass, they are vigorously tortured by demons, some winged. The horrible consequences of a sinful life had not been so graphically depicted since Gislebertus carved his vision of *Last Judgment* (FIG. 12-1) in the west *tympanum* of Saint-Lazare at Autun around 1130. The figures—nude, lean, and muscular—assume every conceivable posture of anguish. Signorelli was a master both of foreshortening the human figure and depicting bodies in violent movement. Although each figure is clearly a study from a model, Signorelli incorporated the individual studies into a convincing and coherent narrative composition. Terror and rage pass like storms through the wrenched and twisted bodies. The fiends, their hair flaming and their bodies the color of putrefying flesh, lunge at their victims in ferocious frenzy.

## Urbino

Under the patronage of Federico da Montefeltro (1422–1482), Urbino, southeast of Florence across the Appenines (MAP 14-1), became an important center of Renaissance art and culture. In fact, the humanist writer Paolo Cortese (1465–1540) described Federico as one of the two greatest artistic patrons of the 15th century (the other was Cosimo de' Medici). Federico was a condottiere so renowned for his military expertise that he was in demand by popes and kings, and soldiers came from across Europe to study under his direction.

**PIERO DELLA FRANCESCA** One of the artists who received several commissions from Federico was Piero della Francesca, who had already established a major reputation in his native Tuscany. At the Urbino court, Piero produced both official portraits and religious works for Federico, among them a double portrait (FIG. **21-43**) of the count and his second wife, Battista Sforza (1446–1472), and the *Brera Altarpiece* (FIG. **21-43A**), in which Federico kneels before the enthroned Madonna and saints.

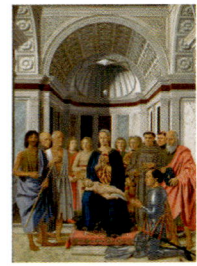

**21-43A** PIERO DELLA FRANCESCA, *Brera Altarpiece,* ca. 1472–1474.

Federico de Montefeltro married Battista Sforza in 1460 when she was 14 years old. The daughter of Alessandro Sforza (1409–1473), lord of Pesaro and brother of the duke of Milan, Battista was a well-educated humanist who proved to be an excellent administrator of Federico's territories during his frequent military campaigns. She gave birth to eight daughters in 11 years and finally, on January 25, 1472, to the male heir for which the couple had prayed. When the countess died of pneumonia five months later at age 26, Federico went into mourning for virtually the rest of his life. He never remarried.

# Italian Princely Courts and Artistic Patronage

During the Renaissance, the absence of a single sovereign ruling all of Italy and the fragmented nature of the independent city-states (MAP 14-1) provided a fertile breeding ground for the ambitions of power-hungry elites. In the 15th century, princely courts proliferated throughout the peninsula. A prince was in essence the lord of a territory, and, despite this generic title, he could have been a duke, marquis, count, cardinal, pope, or condottiere. At this time, major princely courts emerged in papal Rome (FIGS. 21-41, 21-41A, and 21-42), Milan, Naples, Ferrara, Savoy, Urbino (FIGS. 21-43, 21-43A, and 21-44), and Mantua (FIGS. 21-45 to 21-50). Rather than denoting a specific organizational structure or physical entity, the term *princely court* refers to a power relationship between the prince and the territory's inhabitants based on imperial models. Each prince worked tirelessly to preserve and extend his control and authority, seeking to establish a societal framework of people who looked to him for employment, favors, protection, prestige, and leadership. The importance of these princely courts derived from their role as centers of power and culture.

The efficient functioning of a princely court required a sophisticated administrative structure. Each prince employed an extensive household staff, ranging from counts, nobles, cooks, waiters, stewards, footmen, stable hands, and ladies-in-waiting to dog handlers, leopard keepers, pages, and runners. The duke of Milan had more than 40 chamberlains to attend to his personal needs alone. Each prince also needed an elaborate bureaucracy to oversee political, economic, and military operations and to ensure his continued control. These officials included secretaries, lawyers, captains, ambassadors, and condottieri. Burgeoning international diplomacy and trade made each prince the center of an active and privileged sphere. Their domains extended to the realm of culture, for they saw themselves as more than political, military, and economic leaders. As the wealthiest individuals in their regions, princes possessed the means to commission numerous artworks and buildings. Art functioned in several capacities in the princely courts—as evidence of princely sophistication and culture, as a form of prestige or commemoration, as propaganda, as a demonstration of wealth—in addition to being a source of visual pleasure.

Princes often researched in advance the reputations and styles of the artists and architects they commissioned. Such assurances of excellence were necessary, because the quality of the work reflected not solely on the artist but on the patron as well. Yet despite the importance of individual style, princes sought artists who also were willing, at times, to subordinate their personal styles to work collaboratively on large-scale projects.

Princes bestowed on selected individuals the title of "court artist." Serving as a court artist had its benefits, among them a guaranteed salary (not always forthcoming), living quarters in the palace, liberation from guild restrictions, and, on occasion, status as a member of the prince's inner circle, perhaps even a knighthood. For artists struggling to elevate their profession from the ranks of craftspeople, working for a prince presented a marvelous opportunity. Until the 16th century, artists had limited status, and people considered them in the same class as small shopkeepers and petty merchants. Indeed, at court dinners, artists most often sat with the other members of the salaried household: tailors, cobblers, barbers, and upholsterers. Thus, the possibility of advancement was a powerful and constant incentive.

Princes demanded a great deal from court artists. Artists not only created the frescoes, portraits, and sculptures that have become their legacies but also designed tapestries, seat covers, costumes, masks, and decorations for various court festivities. Because princes constantly received ambassadors and dignitaries and needed to maintain a high profile to reinforce their authority, lavish social functions were the norm. Artists often created gifts for visiting nobles and potentates. Recipients judged these gifts on the quality of both the work and the materials. By using expensive materials—gold leaf, silver leaf, lapis lazuli (a rich azure-blue stone imported from Afghanistan), silk, and velvet brocade—and employing the best artists, princes could impress others with their wealth and good taste.

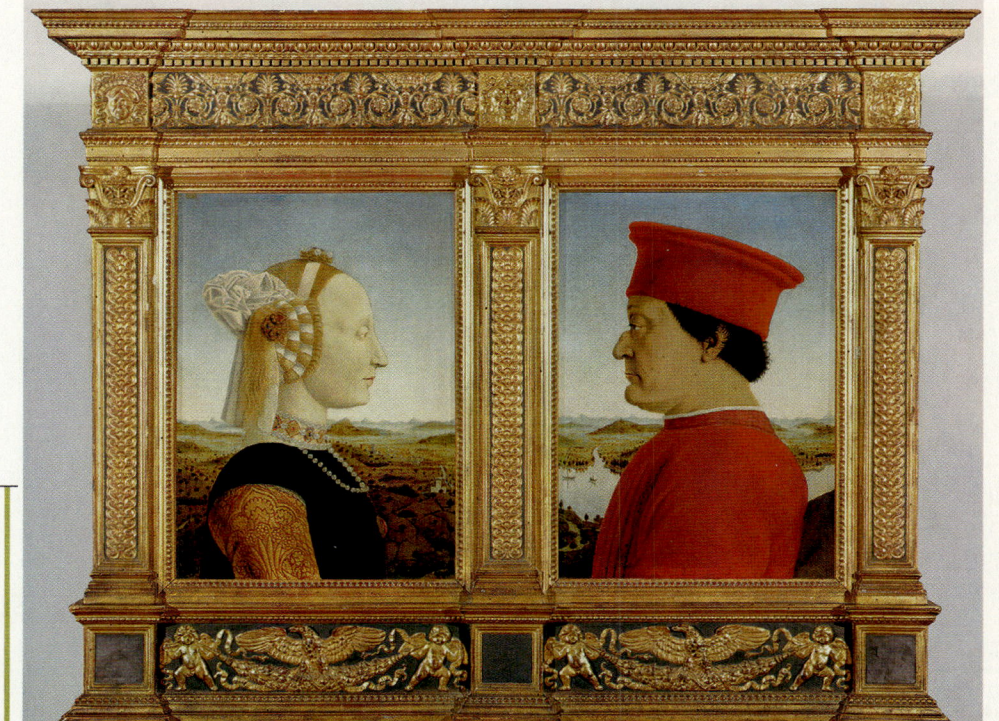

1 ft.

**21-43** PIERO DELLA FRANCESCA, *Battista Sforza and Federico da Montefeltro*, ca. 1472–1474. Oil and tempera on wood in modern frame, each panel 1′ 6½″ × 1′ 1″. Galleria degli Uffizi, Florence. ◼◀

Piero's portraits of Federico da Montefeltro and his recently deceased wife combine the profile views on Roman coins with the landscape backgrounds of Flemish portraiture (FIG. 20-14).

Federico commissioned Piero della Francesca to paint their double portrait shortly after Battista's death to pay tribute to her and to have a memento of their marriage. The present frame is a 19th-century addition. Originally, the two portraits formed a hinged diptych. The format—two bust-length portraits with a landscape background—follows Flemish models, such as the portraits by Hans Memling (FIGS. 20-14 and 20-14A), as does Piero's use of oil-based pigment (see "Tempera and Oil Painting," Chapter 20, page 539). Piero would have been familiar with northern European developments because Federico employed Flemish painters at his court. But Piero depicted the Urbino count and countess in profile, in part to emulate the profile portraits of Roman rulers on coins (FIG. 7-81, *left*) that Renaissance humanists avidly collected, and in part to conceal the disfigured right side of Federico's face. (He lost his right eye and part of the bridge of his nose in a tournament in 1450.) That injury also explains why Federico is on the right in left profile (compare FIG. 21-43A). Roman coins normally show the emperor in right profile, and Renaissance marriage portraits almost always place the husband at the viewer's left.

Piero probably based Battista's portrait on her death mask, and the pallor of her skin may be a reference to her death. Latin inscriptions on the reverse of the two portraits refer to Federico in the present tense and to Battista in the past tense, confirming the posthumous date of her portrait. The backs of the panels also bear paintings. They represent Federico and Battista in triumphal chariots accompanied by personifications of their respective virtues, including Justice, Prudence, and Fortitude (Federico) and Faith, Charity, and Chastity (Battista). The placement of scenes of triumph on the reverse of profile portraits also emulates ancient Roman coinage.

***FLAGELLATION*** Piero may also have painted his most enigmatic work, *Flagellation* (FIG. **21-44**), for Federico da Montefeltro. The setting for the passion drama is the portico of Pontius Pilate's palace in Jerusalem. Curiously, the focus of the composition is not Jesus but the group of three large figures in the foreground, whose identity scholars still debate. Some have described the bearded figure as a Turk and interpreted the painting as a commentary on the capture in 1453 of Christian Constantinople by the Muslims (see Chapter 9). Other scholars, however, identify the three men as biblical figures, including King David, one of whose psalms Christian theologians believed predicted the conspiracy against Jesus. In any case, the three men appear to discuss the event in the background. As Pilate, the seated judge, watches, Jesus, bound to a column topped

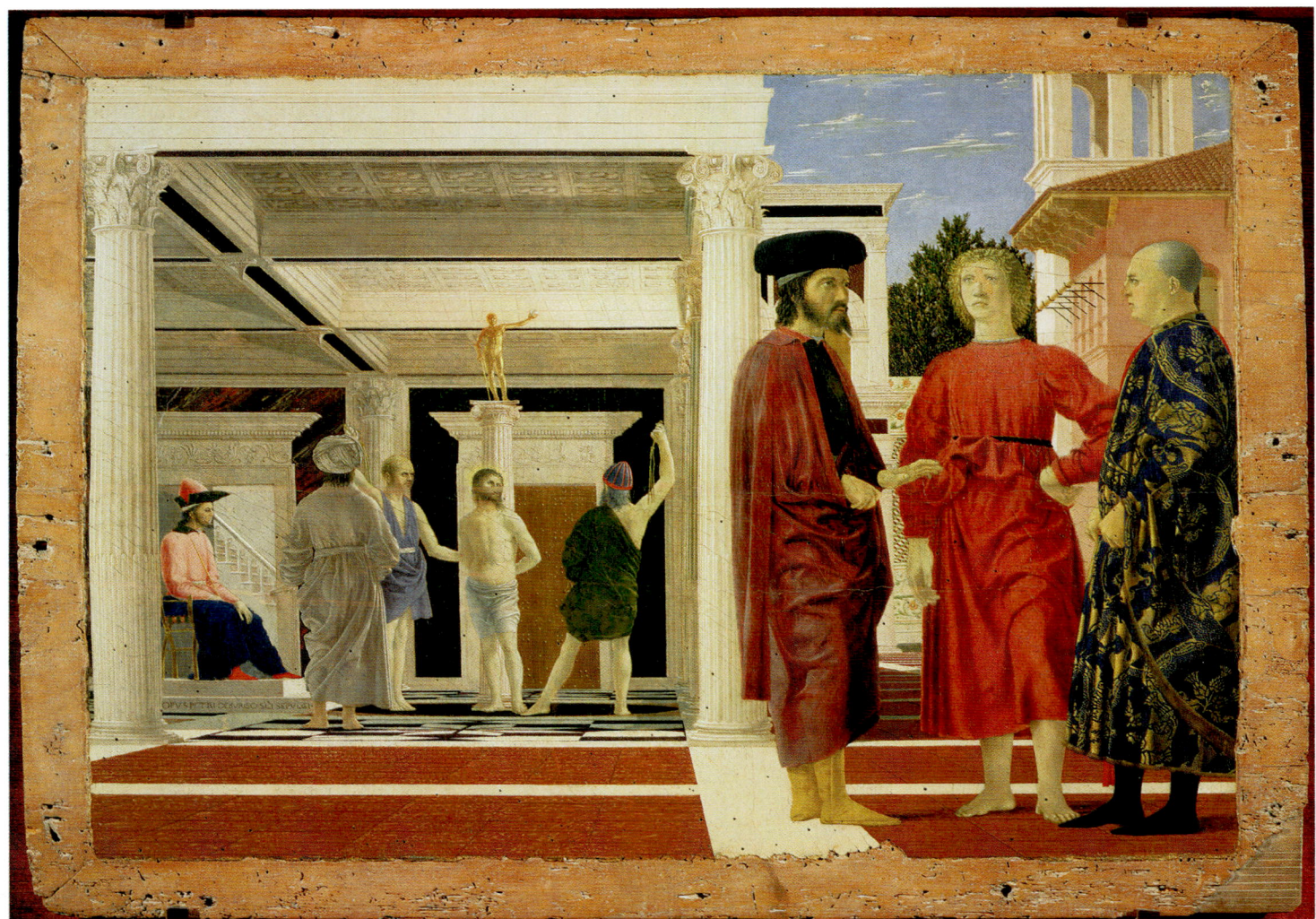

**21-44** PIERO DELLA FRANCESCA, *Flagellation*, ca. 1455–1465. Oil and tempera on wood, 1′ 11$\frac{1}{8}$″ × 2′ 8$\frac{1}{4}$″. Galleria Nazionale delle Marche, Urbino.

In this enigmatic painting, the three unidentified foreground figures appear to be discussing the biblical tragedy taking place in Pilate's palace, which Piero rendered in perfect perspective.

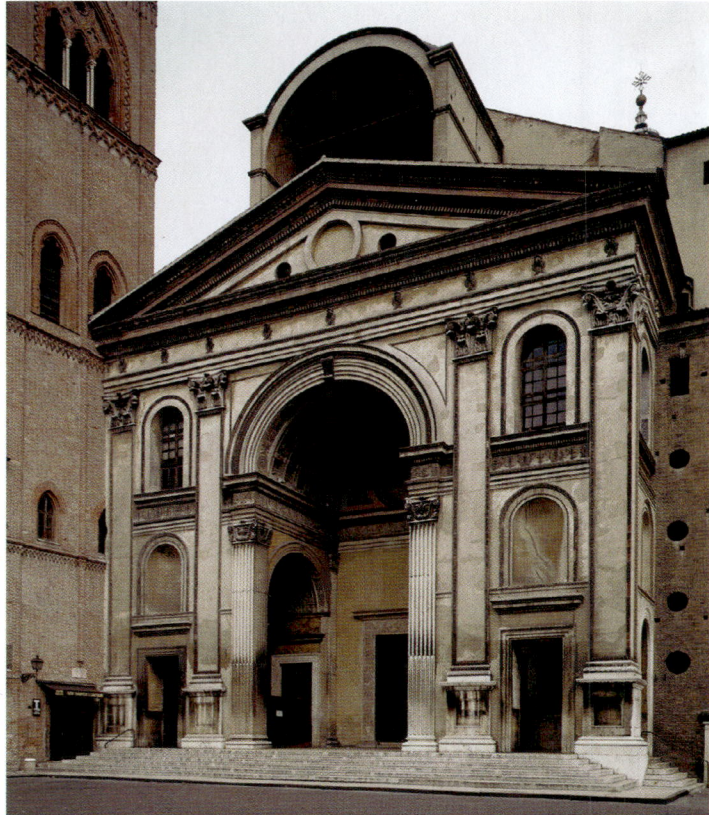

**21-45** LEON BATTISTA ALBERTI, west façade of Sant'Andrea, Mantua, Italy, designed 1470, begun 1472.

Alberti's design for Sant'Andrea reflects his study of ancient Roman architecture. Employing a colossal order, the architect combined a triumphal arch and a Roman temple front with pediment.

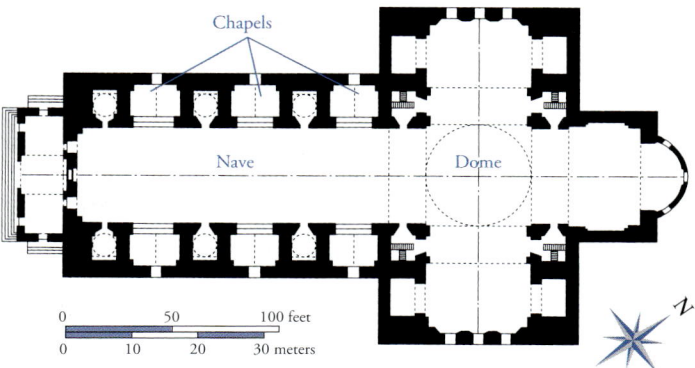

**21-46** LEON BATTISTA ALBERTI, plan of Sant'Andrea, Mantua, Italy, designed 1470, begun 1472.

In his architectural treatise, Alberti criticized the traditional basilican plan as impractical. He designed Sant'Andrea as a single huge hall with independent chapels branching off at right angles.

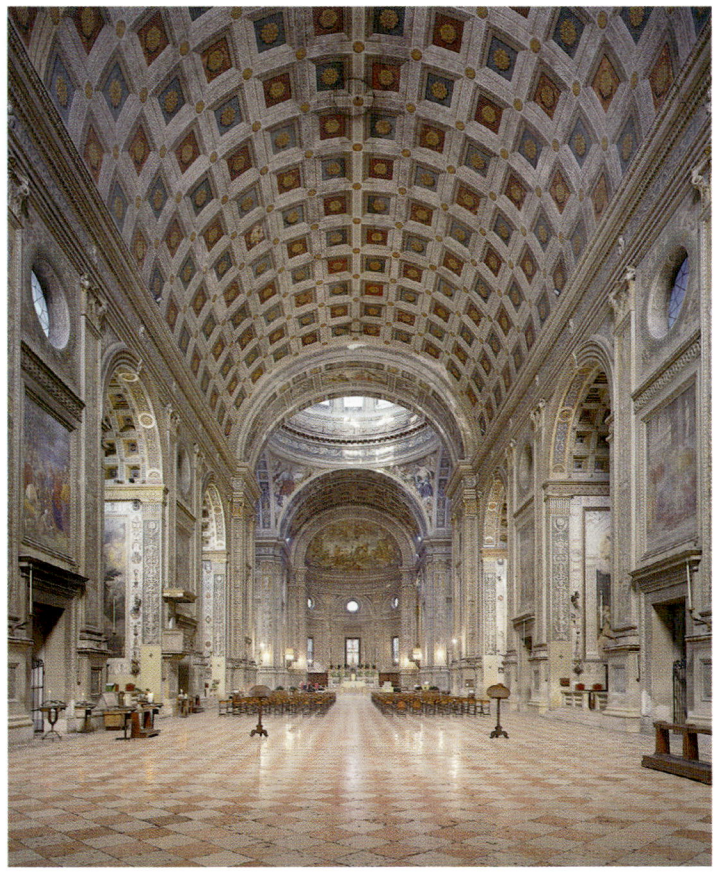

**21-47** LEON BATTISTA ALBERTI, interior of Sant'Andrea (looking east), Mantua, Italy, designed 1470, begun 1472.

For the nave of Sant'Andrea, Alberti abandoned the medieval columnar arcade. The tremendous vaults suggest that Constantine's Basilica Nova (FIG. 7-78) in Rome may have served as a prototype.

by a classical statue, is about to be whipped. Piero's perspective is so meticulous the floor pattern can be reconstructed perfectly as a central porphyry (purple marble) circle with surrounding squares composed of various geometric shapes. Whatever the solution to the iconographical puzzle of Piero's *Flagellation,* the small wood panel reveals a mind cultivated by mathematics. The careful delineation of architecture suggests an architect's vision, certainly that of a man entirely familiar with compass and ruler. Piero planned his compositions almost entirely by his sense of the exact and lucid structures defined by mathematics. He believed the highest beauty resides in forms that have the clarity and purity of geometric figures. Toward the end of his long career, Piero, a skilled geometrician, wrote the first theoretical treatise on systematic perspective, after having practiced the art with supreme mastery for almost a lifetime. His association with the architect Leon Battista Alberti at Ferrara and at Rimini (FIGS. 21-46 and 21-47) around 1450–1451 probably turned his attention fully to perspective (a science in which Alberti was an influential pioneer; see page 566) and helped determine his later, characteristically architectonic compositions. This approach appealed to Federico, a patron fascinated by architectural space and its depiction.

## Mantua

Marquis Ludovico Gonzaga (1412–1478) ruled the court of Mantua in northeastern Italy (MAP 14-1) during the mid-15th century. A famed condottiere like Federico de Montefeltro, Gonzaga established his reputation as a fierce military leader while general of the

Milanese armies. The visit of Pope Pius II (r. 1458–1464) to Mantua in 1459 stimulated the marquis's determination to transform his city into one all Italy would envy.

**SANT'ANDREA** One of the major projects Gonzaga instituted was the redesign and replacement of the 11th-century church of Sant'Andrea (FIGS. 21-45 to 21-47). Gonzaga turned to the renowned architect Leon Battista Alberti (FIGS. 21-39 and 21-40) for

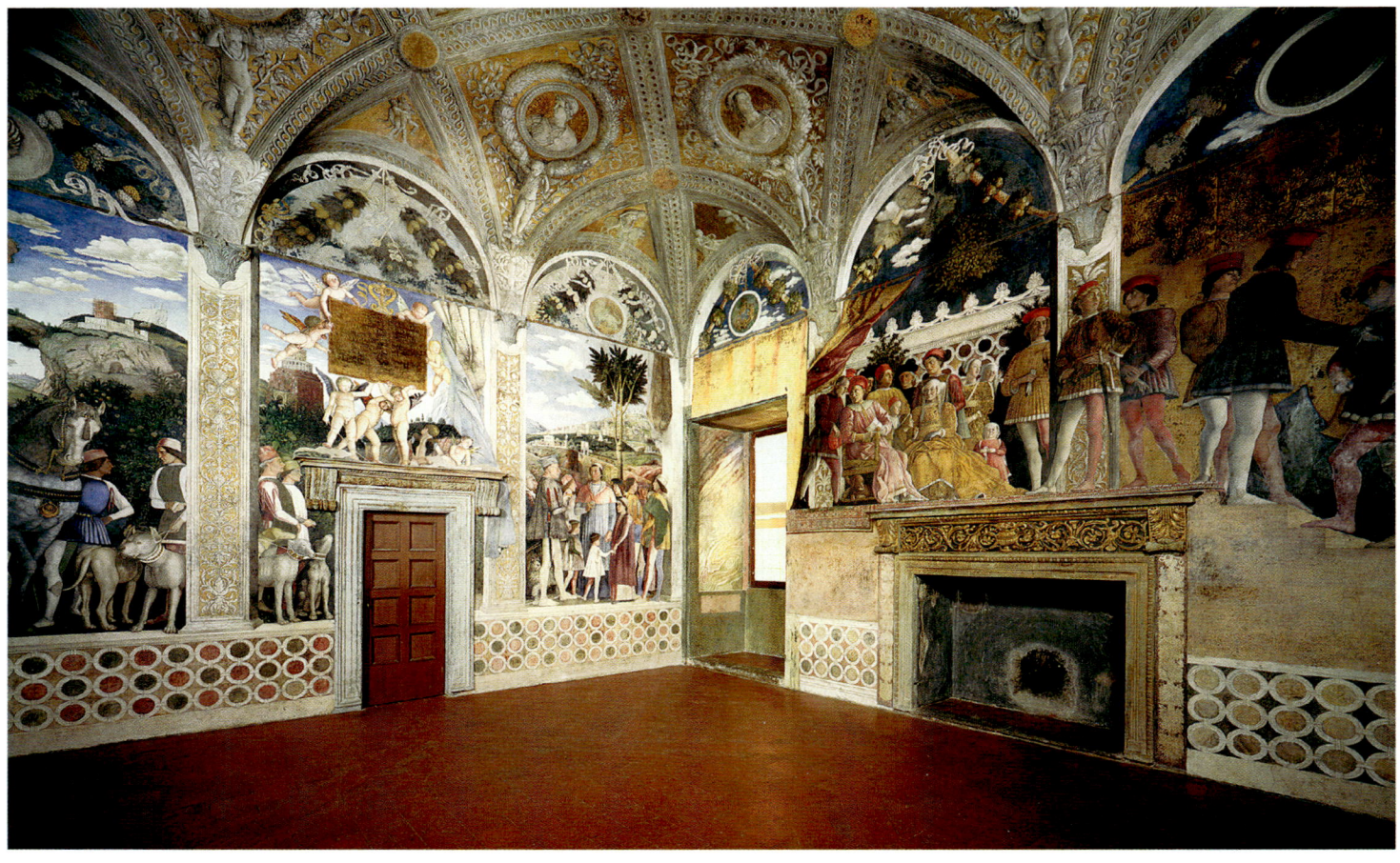

21-48 ANDREA MANTEGNA, interior of the Camera Picta (Painted Chamber), Palazzo Ducale, Mantua, Italy, 1465–1474. Fresco.

Working for Ludovico Gonzaga, who established Mantua as a great art city, Mantegna produced for the duke's palace the first completely consistent, illusionistic decoration of an entire room.

this important commission. The facade (FIG. 21-45) Alberti designed incorporated two major ancient Roman architectural motifs—the temple front and the triumphal arch. The combination was already a familiar feature of Roman buildings still standing in Italy. For example, many triumphal arches, including an Augustan (late first century BCE) arch at Rimini on Italy's northeast coast, feature a pediment over the arcuated passageway and engaged columns, but there is no close parallel in antiquity for Alberti's eclectic and ingenious design. The Renaissance architect's concern for proportion led him to equalize the vertical and horizontal dimensions of the facade, which left it considerably shorter than the church behind it. Because of the primary importance of visual appeal, many Renaissance architects made this concession not only to the demands of a purely visual proportionality in the facade but also to the facade's relation to the small square in front of it, even at the expense of continuity with the body of the building. Yet structural correspondences to the building do exist in Sant'Andrea's facade. The pilasters are the same height as those on the nave's interior walls, and the large barrel vault over the central portal, with smaller barrel vaults branching off at right angles, introduces on a smaller scale the arrangement of the church's nave and chapels (FIGS. 21-46 and 21-47). The facade pilasters, as part of the wall, run uninterrupted through three stories in an early application of the *colossal* or *giant order* that became a favorite motif of Michelangelo (see Chapter 22).

The tremendous vaults in the interior of Sant'Andrea suggest Alberti's model may have been Constantine's Basilica Nova (FIG. 7-78) in Rome—erroneously thought in the Middle Ages and Renaissance to be a Roman temple. Consistent with his belief that arches should not be used with freestanding columns, Alberti abandoned the medieval columnar arcade Brunelleschi still used in Santo Spirito (FIG. 21-32) and San Lorenzo (FIG. 21-32A). Thick walls alternating with vaulted chapels, interrupted by a massive dome over the *crossing,* support the huge coffered barrel vault. Because FILIPPO JUVARA (1678–1736) added the present dome in the 18th century, the effect may be somewhat different from what Alberti planned. Regardless, the vault calls to mind the vast interior spaces and dense enclosing masses of Roman architecture. In his treatise, Alberti criticized the traditional basilican plan (with continuous aisles flanking the central nave) as impractical because the colonnades conceal the ceremonies from the faithful in the aisles. For this reason, he designed a single huge hall (FIG. 21-47) with independent chapels branching off at right angles (FIG. 21-46). This break with a Christian building tradition that had endured for a thousand years was extremely influential in later Renaissance and Baroque church planning.

**ANDREA MANTEGNA** Like other princes, Ludovico Gonzaga believed an impressive palace was an important visual expression of his authority. One of the most spectacular rooms in the

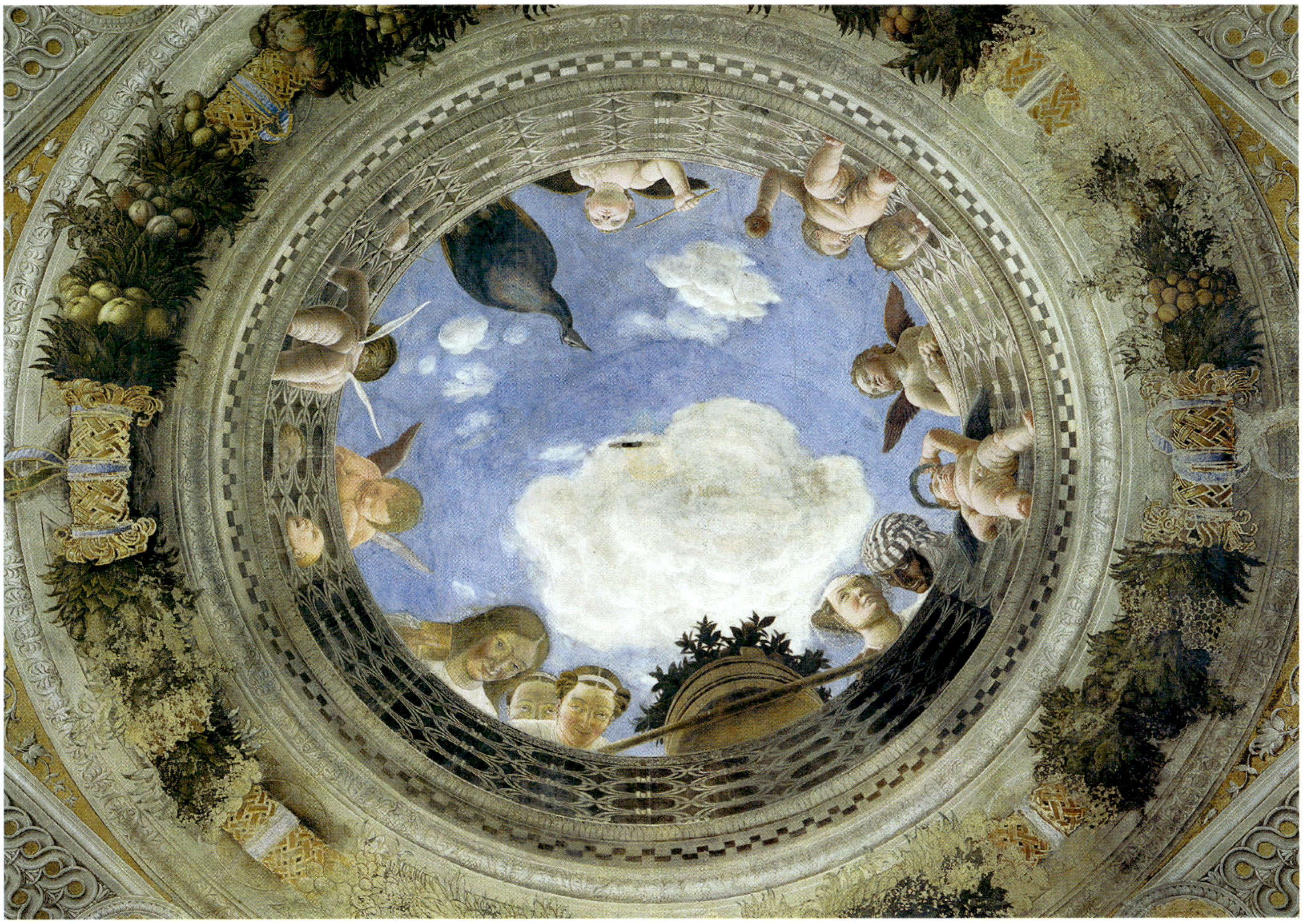

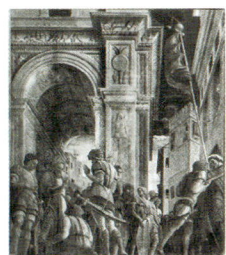

**21-49** ANDREA MANTEGNA, ceiling of the Camera Picta (Painted Chamber), Palazzo Ducale, Mantua, Italy, 1465–1474. Fresco, 8′ 9″ in diameter. ◼◀

Inside the Camera Picta, the viewer becomes the viewed as figures gaze into the room from a painted oculus opening onto a blue sky. This is the first perspective view of a ceiling from below.

Palazzo Ducale (ducal palace) is the duke's bedchamber and audience hall, the so-called Camera degli Sposi ("Room of the Newlyweds"), originally the Camera Picta ("Painted Room"; FIGS. **21-48** and **21-49**). ANDREA MANTEGNA (ca. 1431–1506) of Padua took almost nine years to complete the extensive fresco program in which he sought to aggrandize Ludovico Gonzaga and his family. The particulars of each scene are still a matter of scholarly debate, but any viewer standing in the Camera Picta surrounded by the spectacle and majesty of courtly life cannot help but be thoroughly impressed by both the commanding presence and elevated status of the patron and the dazzling artistic skills of Mantegna.

In the Camera Picta, Mantegna performed a triumphant feat by producing the first completely consistent illusionistic decoration of an entire room. By integrating real and painted architectural elements, Mantegna illusionistically dissolved the room's walls in a manner foretelling 17th-century Baroque decoration (see Chapter 24). The Camera Picta recalls the efforts of Italian painters more than 15 centuries earlier at Pompeii and elsewhere to merge mural painting and architecture in frescoes of the so-called Second Style of Roman painting (FIGS. 7-18 and 7-19). Mantegna's *trompe l'oeil* (French, "deceives the eye") design, however, went far beyond anything preserved from ancient Italy. The Renaissance painter's daring experimentalism led him to complete the room's decoration with the first perspective of a ceiling (FIG. 21-49) seen from below (called, in Italian, *di sotto in sù,* "from below upward"). Baroque ceiling decorators later broadly developed this technique. Inside the Camera Picta, the viewer becomes the viewed as figures look down into the room from the painted *oculus* ("eye"). Seen against the convincing illusion of a cloud-filled blue sky, several putti, strongly foreshortened, set the amorous mood of the Room of the Newlyweds, as the painted spectators (who are not identified) smile down on the scene. The prominent peacock, perched precariously as if ready to swoop down into the room, is an attribute of Juno, Jupiter's bride, who oversees lawful marriages. This brilliant feat of illusionism is the climax of decades of experimentation with perspective representation by numerous Quattrocento artists as well as by Mantegna himself—for example, in his frescoes (FIG. **21-49A**) in the Church of the Eremitani in Padua.

**21-49A** MANTEGNA, *Saint James Led to Martyrdom,* 1454–1457.

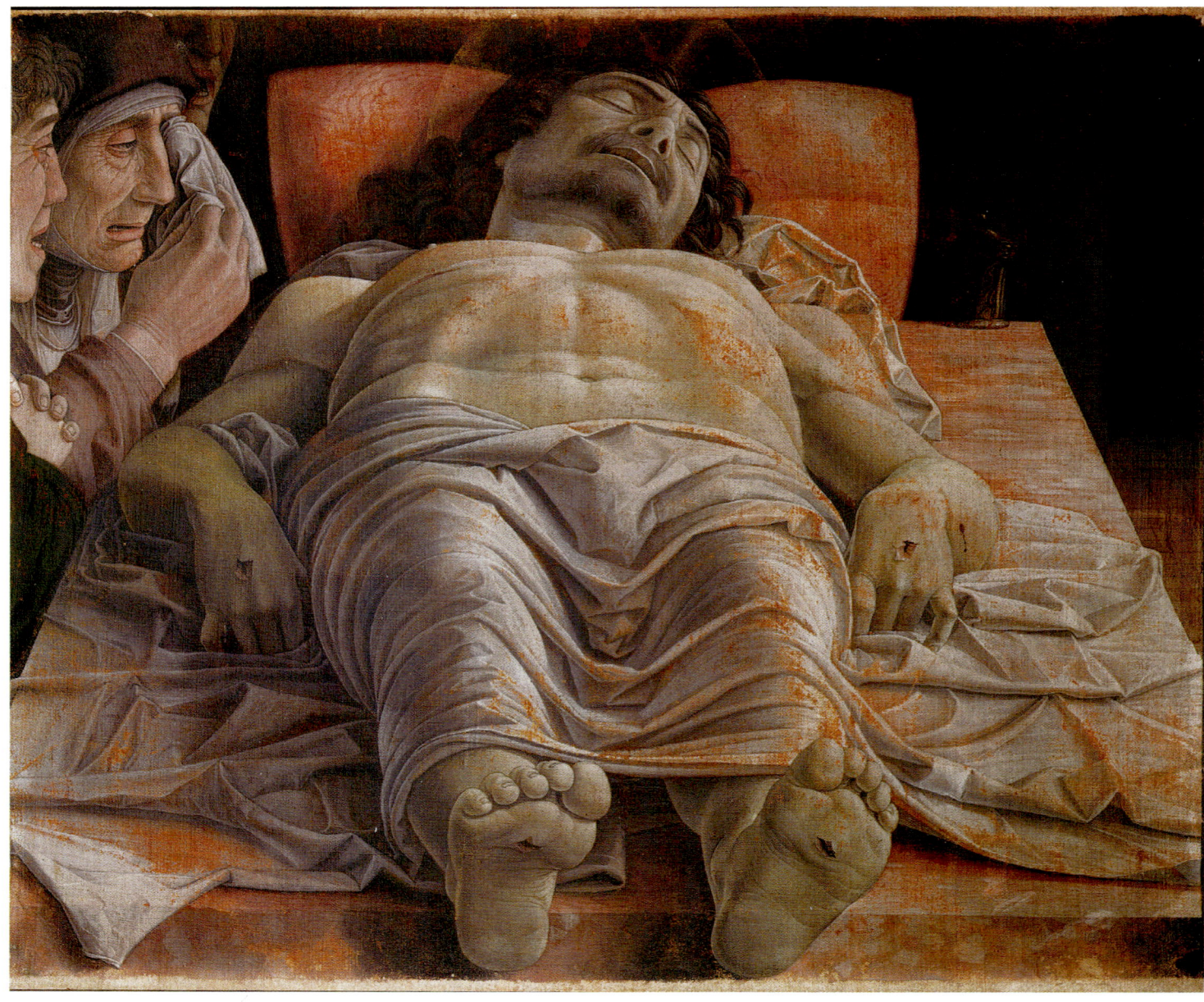

**21-50** ANDREA MANTEGNA, *Foreshortened Christ* (*Lamentation over the Dead Christ*), ca. 1500. Tempera on canvas, 2′ 2¾″ × 2′ 7⅞″. Pinacoteca di Brera, Milan. ■◀

In this work of overwhelming emotional power, Mantegna presented both a harrowing study of a strongly foreshortened cadaver and an intensely poignant depiction of a biblical tragedy.

**FORESHORTENED CHRIST** One of Mantegna's later paintings (FIG. 21-50) is another example of the artist's mastery of perspective. In fact, Mantegna seems to have set up for himself difficult problems in perspective simply for the joy he took in solving them. The painting often called *Lamentation over the Dead Christ,* but recorded under the name *Foreshortened Christ* at the time of Mantegna's death, is a work of overwhelming power. At first glance, as its 16th-century title implies, this painting seems to be a strikingly realistic study in foreshortening. Careful scrutiny, however, reveals Mantegna reduced the size of Christ's feet, which, as he clearly knew, would cover much of the body if properly represented according to the rules of perspective, in which the closest objects, people, or body parts are the largest. Thus, tempering naturalism with artistic license, Mantegna presented both a harrowing study of a strongly foreshortened cadaver and an intensely poignant depiction of a biblical tragedy. The painter's harsh, sharp line seems to cut the surface as if it were metal and conveys, by its grinding edge, the theme's corrosive emotion. Remarkably, in the supremely gifted hands of Mantegna, all of Quattrocento science here serves the purpose of devotion.

# THE RENAISSANCE IN QUATTROCENTO ITALY

## FLORENCE

▌ The fortunate congruence of artistic genius, the spread of humanism, and economic prosperity nourished the flowering of the new artistic culture historians call the Renaissance—the rebirth of classical values in art and life. The greatest center of Renaissance art in the 15th century was Florence, home of the powerful Medici, who were among the most ambitious art patrons in history.

▌ Some of the earliest examples of the new Renaissance style in sculpture are the statues Nanni di Banco and Donatello made for Or San Michele. Donatello's *Saint Mark* reintroduced the classical concept of contrapposto into Renaissance statuary. His later *David* was the first nude male statue since antiquity. Donatello was also a pioneer in relief sculpture, the first to incorporate the principles of linear and atmospheric perspective, devices also employed brilliantly by Lorenzo Ghiberti in his *Gates of Paradise* for the Florentine baptistery.

▌ The Renaissance interest in classical culture naturally also led to the revival of Greco-Roman mythological themes in art, for example, Antonio del Pollaiuolo's *Hercules and Antaeus,* and to the revival of equestrian portraits, such as Donatello's *Gattamelata* and Andrea del Verrocchio's *Bartolommeo Colleoni.*

▌ Although some painters continued to work in the Late Gothic International Style, others broke fresh ground by exploring new modes of representation. Masaccio's figures recall Giotto's, but have a greater psychological and physical credibility, and the light shining on Masaccio's figures comes from a source outside the picture. His *Holy Trinity* epitomizes Early Renaissance painting in its convincing illusionism, achieved through Filippo Brunelleschi's new science of linear perspective, yet it remains effective as a devotional painting in a church setting.

▌ The secular side of Quattrocento Italian painting is on display in historical works, such as Paolo Uccello's *Battle of San Romano* and Domenico Ghirlandaio's portrait *Giovanna Tornabuoni.* The humanist love of classical themes comes to the fore in the works of Sandro Botticelli, whose lyrical *Primavera* and *Birth of Venus* were inspired by poetry and Neo-Platonic philosophy.

▌ Italian architects also revived the classical style. Brunelleschi's Ospedale degli Innocenti showcases the clarity and Roman-inspired rationality of 15th-century Florentine architecture. The model for Leon Battista Alberti's influential 1450 treatise *On the Art of Building* was a similar work by the ancient Roman architect Vitruvius.

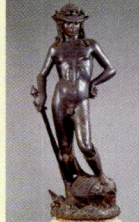

Donatello, *David,* ca. 1440–1460

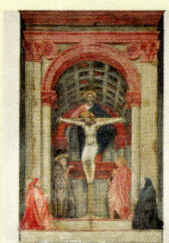

Masaccio, *Holy Trinity,* ca. 1424–1427

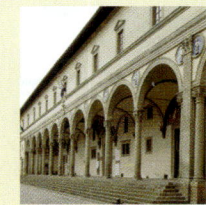

Brunelleschi, Ospedale degli Innocenti, begun 1419

## THE PRINCELY COURTS

▌ Although Florentine artists led the way in creating the Renaissance in art and architecture, the papacy in Rome and the princely courts in Urbino, Mantua, and elsewhere also were major art patrons.

▌ Among the important papal commissions of the Quattrocento was the decoration of the walls of the Sistine Chapel with frescoes, including Perugino's *Christ Delivering the Keys of the Kingdom to Saint Peter,* a prime example of linear perspective.

▌ Under the patronage of Federico da Montefeltro, Urbino became a major center of Renaissance art and culture. The leading painter in Federico's employ was Piero della Francesca, a master of color and light and the author of the first theoretical treatise on perspective.

▌ Mantua became an important art center under Marquis Ludovico Gonzaga, who commissioned Alberti to rebuild the church of Sant'Andrea. Alberti applied the principles he developed in his architectural treatise to the project and freely adapted forms from Roman religious and civic architecture.

▌ Gonzaga hired Andrea Mantegna to decorate the Camera Picta of the ducal palace, in which the painter produced the first completely consistent illusionistic decoration of an entire room.

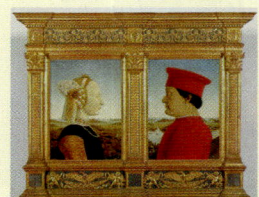

Piero della Francesca, *Battista Sforza and Federico da Montefeltro,* 1472–1474

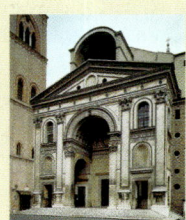

Alberti, Sant'Andrea, Mantua, 1470

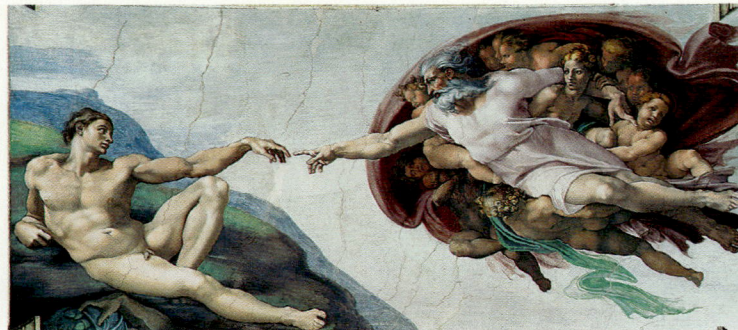

Michelangelo, the Renaissance genius who was primarily a sculptor, reluctantly spent almost four years painting the ceiling of the Sistine Chapel under commission from Pope Julius II.

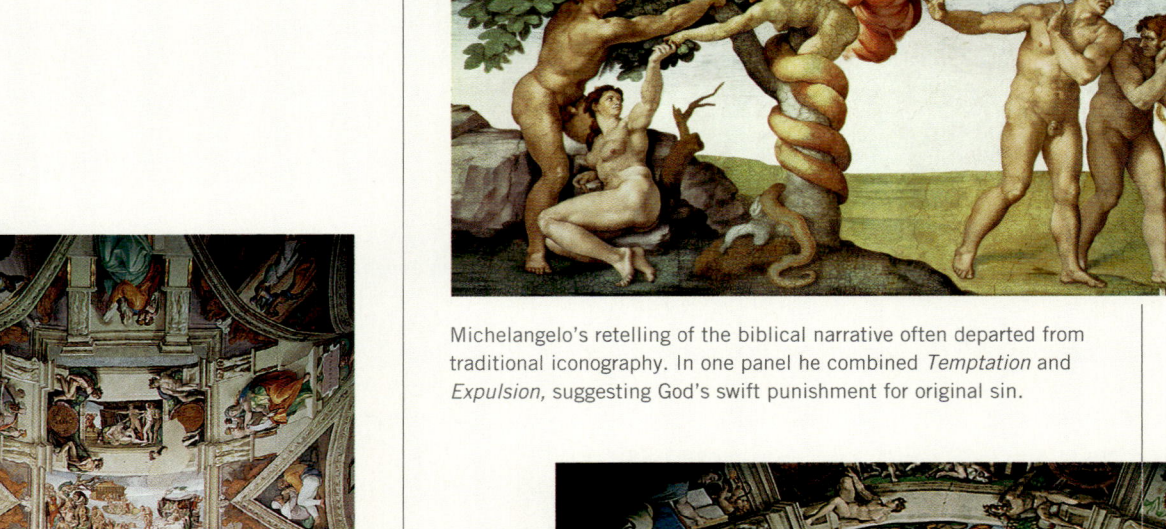

Michelangelo's retelling of the biblical narrative often departed from traditional iconography. In one panel he combined *Temptation* and *Expulsion*, suggesting God's swift punishment for original sin.

The fresco cycle illustrates the creation and fall of humankind as related in Genesis. Michelangelo always painted with a sculptor's eye. His heroic figures resemble painted statues.

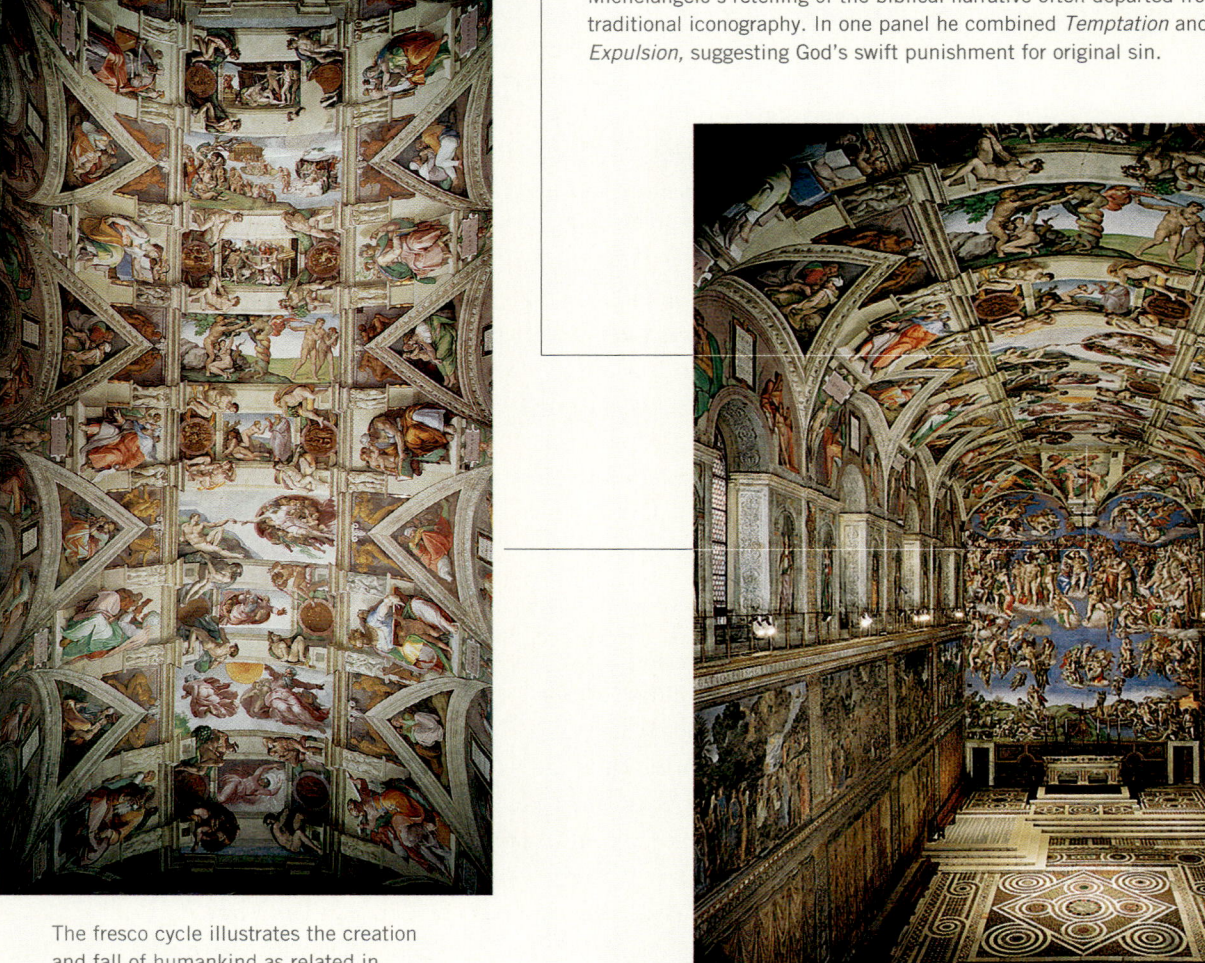

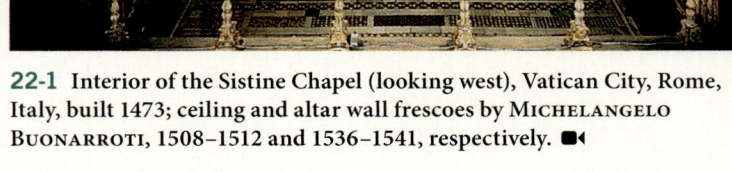

**22-1** Interior of the Sistine Chapel (looking west), Vatican City, Rome, Italy, built 1473; ceiling and altar wall frescoes by MICHELANGELO BUONARROTI, 1508–1512 and 1536–1541, respectively. ◼◀

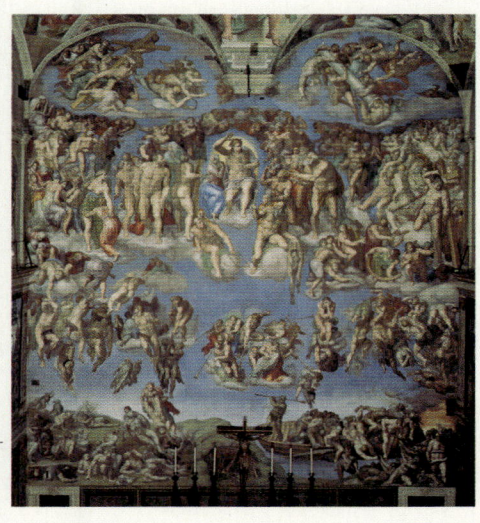

Michelangelo completed his fresco cycle in the Sistine Chapel for another pope—Paul III—with this terrifying vision of the fate awaiting sinners at the *Last Judgment.* It includes his self-portrait.

# RENAISSANCE AND MANNERISM IN CINQUECENTO ITALY

FRAMING THE ERA

## MICHELANGELO IN THE SERVICE OF JULIUS II

Michelangelo Buonarroti (1475–1564) was the first artist in history whose prodigious talent and brooding personality matched today's image of the temperamental artistic genius. His self-imposed isolation, creative furies, proud independence, and daring innovations led Italians of his era to speak of the charismatic personality of the man and the expressive character of his works in one word—*terribilità,* the sublime shadowed by the awesome and the fearful. Yet, unlike most modern artists, who create works in their studios and offer them for sale later, Michelangelo and his contemporaries produced most of their paintings and sculptures under contract for wealthy patrons who dictated the content—and sometimes the form—of their artworks.

In Italy in the 1500s—the *Cinquecento*—the greatest art patron was the Catholic Church headed by the pope in Rome. Michelangelo's most famous work today—the ceiling of the Sistine Chapel (FIG. **22-1**) in the Vatican palace (MAPS **22-1** and 24-1)—was, in fact, a commission he did not want. His patron was Julius II (r. 1503–1513), an immensely ambitious man who sought to extend his spiritual authority into the temporal realm, as other medieval and Renaissance popes had done. Julius selected his name to associate himself with Julius Caesar and found inspiration in ancient Rome. His enthusiasm for engaging in battle earned Julius the designation "warrior-pope," but his ten-year papacy was most notable for his patronage of the arts. He understood well the propagandistic value of visual imagery and upon his election immediately commissioned artworks that would present an authoritative image of his rule and reinforce the primacy of the Catholic Church.

When Julius asked Michelangelo to take on the challenge of providing frescoes for the ceiling of the Sistine Chapel, the artist insisted painting was not his profession (a protest that rings hollow after the fact, but Michelangelo's major works until then had been in sculpture). The artist had no choice, however, but to accept the pope's assignment.

In the Sistine Chapel frescoes, as in his sculpture, Michelangelo relentlessly concentrated his expressive purpose on the human figure. To him, the body was beautiful not only in its natural form but also in its spiritual and philosophical significance. The body was the manifestation of the character of the soul. In the *Creation of Adam, Temptation and Expulsion,* and *Last Judgment* frescoes, Michelangelo represented the body in its most elemental aspect—in the nude or simply draped, with no background and no ornamental embellishment. He always painted with a sculptor's eye for how light and shadow reveal volume and surface. It is no coincidence that many of the figures in the Sistine Chapel seem to be painted statues.

# HIGH AND LATE RENAISSANCE

The art and architecture of 16th-century Italy built on the foundation of the Early Renaissance of the 15th century, but no single artistic style characterized Italian 16th-century art, and regional differences abounded, especially between central Italy (Florence and Rome) and Venice. The period opened with the brief era art historians call the High Renaissance—the quarter century between 1495 and the deaths of Leonardo da Vinci in 1519 and Raphael in 1520. The Renaissance style and the interest in classical culture, perspective, proportion, and human anatomy dominated the remainder of the 16th century (the Late Renaissance), but a new style, called Mannerism, challenged Renaissance naturalism almost as soon as Raphael had

been laid to rest (inside the ancient Roman Pantheon, FIG. 7-51). The one constant in Cinquecento Italy is the astounding quality, both technical and aesthetic, of the art and architecture produced.

Indeed, the modern notion of the "fine arts" and the exaltation of the artist-genius originated in Renaissance Italy. Humanist scholars and art patrons alike eagerly adopted the ancient Greek philosopher Plato's view of the nature of poetry and of artistic creation in general: "All good poets . . . compose their beautiful poems not by art, but because they are inspired and possessed. . . . For not by art does the poet sing, but by power divine."[1] In Cinquecento Italy, the pictorial arts achieved the high status formerly held only by poetry. During the High Renaissance, artists first became international celebrities, none more so than Leonardo da Vinci, Raphael, and Michelangelo.

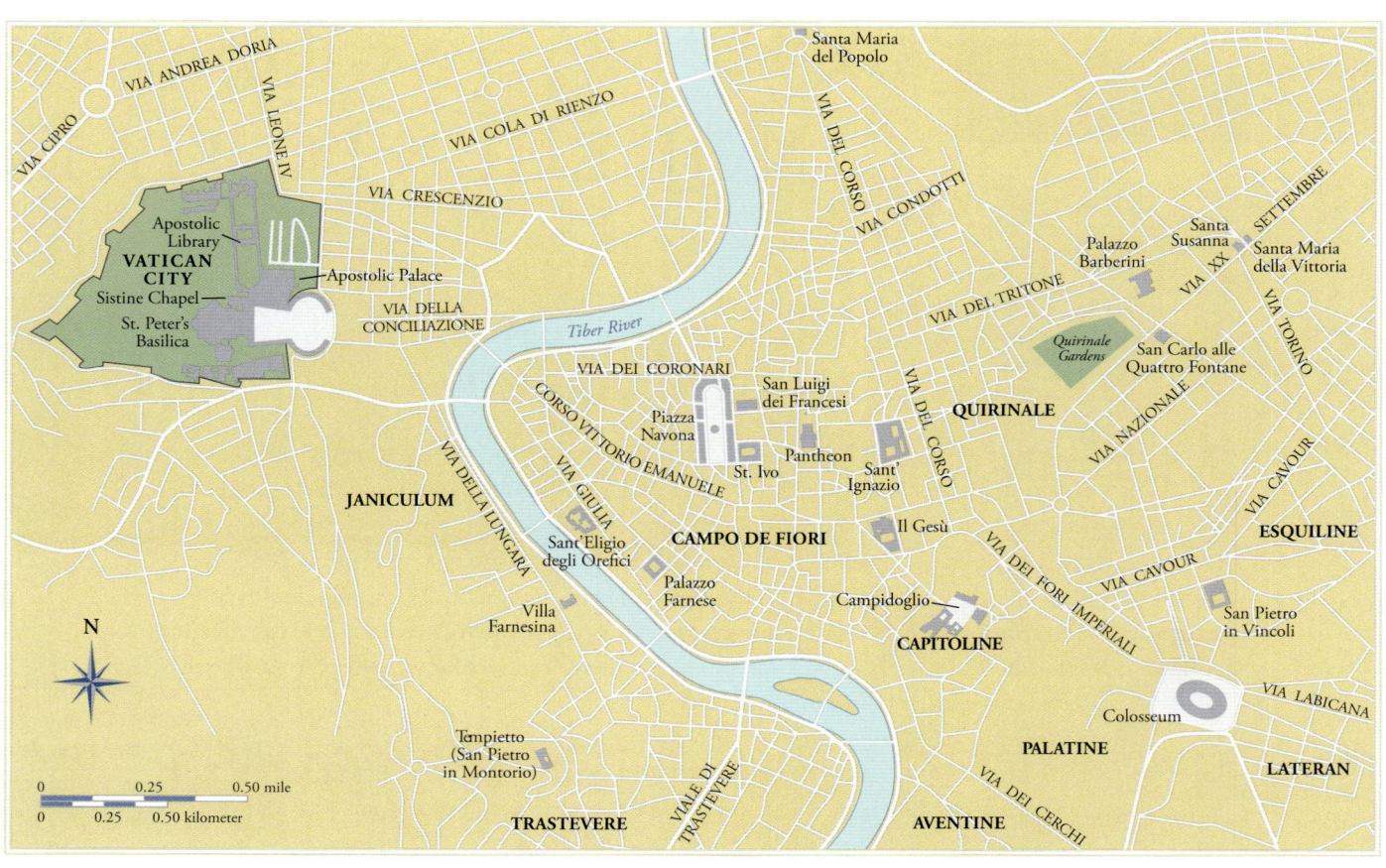

**MAP 22-1** Rome with Renaissance and Baroque monuments.

## RENAISSANCE AND MANNERISM IN CINQUECENTO ITALY

| 1495 | 1520 | 1550 | 1575 | 1600 |
|---|---|---|---|---|
| ▌ Leonardo da Vinci paints *Last Supper* in Milan and *Mona Lisa* in Florence<br><br>▌ High Renaissance art emerges in Rome under Pope Julius II<br><br>▌ Raphael paints *School of Athens* for the papal apartments<br><br>▌ Michelangelo carves *David* for the Palazzo della Signoria in Florence and paints the ceiling of the Sistine Chapel in Rome | ▌ Paul III launches the Counter-Reformation<br><br>▌ Michelangelo paints *Last Judgment* in the Sistine Chapel<br><br>▌ In Venice, Titian uses rich colors and establishes oil on canvas as the preferred medium of Western painting<br><br>▌ Mannerism emerges as an alternative to High Renaissance style in the work of Pontormo, Parmigianino, Bronzino, and Giulio Romano | ▌ Council of Trent defends religious art<br><br>▌ Andrea Palladio becomes chief architect of the Venetian Republic<br><br>▌ Giorgio Vasari publishes *Lives of the Most Eminent Painters, Sculptors, and Architects* | ▌ Tintoretto is the leading Venetian Mannerist painter<br><br>▌ Veronese creates a huge illusionistic ceiling painting for the Doge's Palace<br><br>▌ Giovanni da Bologna uses spiral compositions for Mannerist statuary groups<br><br>▌ Construction of Il Gesù in Rome | |

# Leonardo da Vinci

Born in the small town of Vinci, near Florence, LEONARDO DA VINCI (1452–1519) trained in the studio of Andrea del Verrocchio (FIGS. 21-13 and 21-17). The quintessential "Renaissance man," Leonardo possessed unequaled talent and an unbridled imagination. Art was but one of his innumerable interests, the scope and depth of which were without precedent. His unquenchable curiosity is evident in the voluminous notes he interspersed with sketches in his notebooks dealing with botany, geology, geography, cartography, zoology, military engineering, animal lore, anatomy, and aspects of physical science, including hydraulics and mechanics. Leonardo stated repeatedly that his scientific investigations made him a better painter. That is undoubtedly the case. For example, Leonardo's in-depth exploration of optics provided him with a thorough understanding of perspective, light, and color. Leonardo was a true artist-scientist. Indeed, his scientific drawings (FIG. 22-6) are themselves artworks.

Leonardo's great ambition in his painting, as well as in his scientific endeavors, was to discover the laws underlying the processes and flux of nature. With this end in mind, he also studied the human body and contributed immeasurably to the fields of physiology and psychology. Leonardo believed reality in an absolute sense is inaccessible and humans can know it only through its changing images. He considered the eyes the most vital organs and sight the most essential function. Better to be deaf than blind, he argued, because through the eyes, individuals can grasp reality most directly and profoundly.

**LEONARDO IN MILAN** Around 1481, Leonardo left Florence after offering his services to Ludovico Sforza (1451–1508), the son and heir apparent of the ruler of Milan. The political situation in Florence was uncertain, and Leonardo may have felt his particular skills would be in greater demand in Milan, providing him with the opportunity for increased financial security. He devoted most of a letter to Ludovico to advertising his competence and his qualifications as a military engineer, mentioning only at the end his abilities as a painter and sculptor. The letter illustrates the relationship between Renaissance artists and their patrons (see "Michelangelo in the Service of Julius II," page 599) as well as Leonardo's breadth of competence. That he should select expertise in military engineering as his primary attraction for the Sforzas is an index of the period's instability.

> And in short, according to the variety of cases, I can contrive various and endless means of offence and defence. . . . In time of peace I believe I can give perfect satisfaction and to the equal of any other in architecture and the composition of buildings, public and private; and in guiding water from one place to another. . . . I can carry out sculpture in marble, bronze, or clay, and also I can do in painting whatever may be done, as well as any other, be he whom he may.[2]

Ludovico accepted Leonardo's offer, and the Florentine artist remained in Milan for almost 20 years.

***MADONNA OF THE ROCKS*** Shortly after settling in Milan, Leonardo painted *Madonna of the Rocks* (FIG. **22-2**) as the central panel of an altarpiece for the chapel of the Confraternity of the Immaculate Conception in San Francesco Grande. The painting builds on Masaccio's understanding and usage of chiaroscuro, the subtle play of light and dark. Modeling with light and shadow and expressing emotional states were, for Leonardo, the heart of painting:

> A good painter has two chief objects to paint—man and the intention of his soul. The former is easy, the latter hard, for it must be

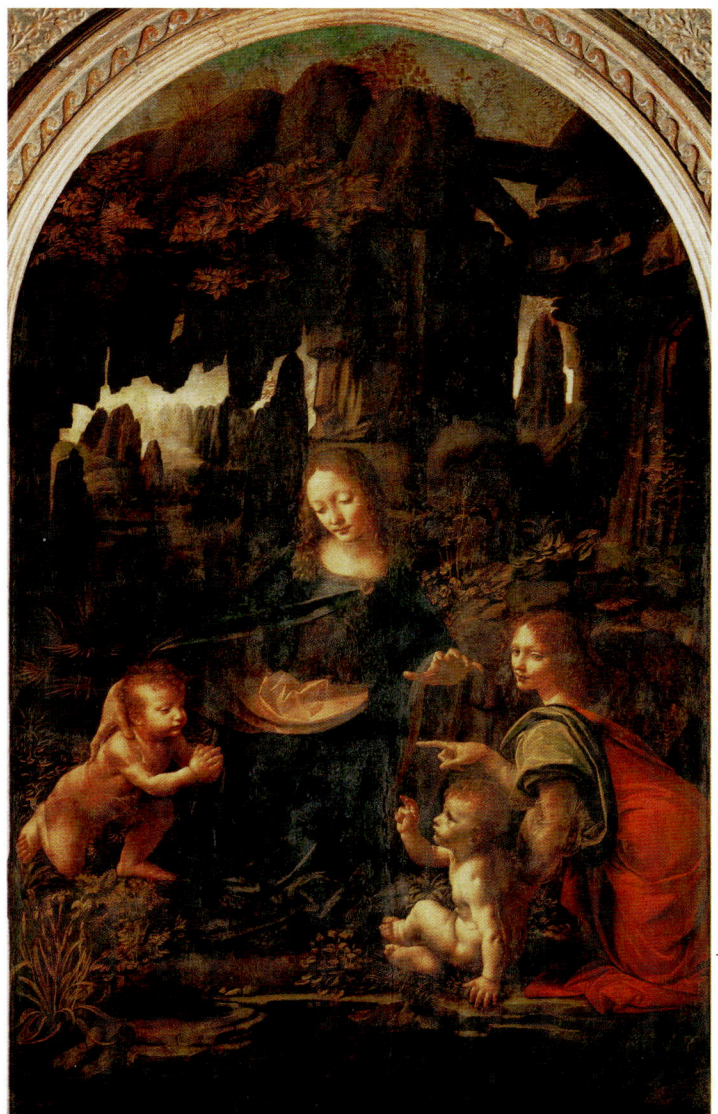

**22-2** LEONARDO DA VINCI, *Madonna of the Rocks,* from San Francesco Grande, Milan, Italy, begun 1483. Oil on wood (transferred to canvas), 6′ 6½″ × 4′. Musée du Louvre, Paris. ◼◂

Leonardo used gestures and a pyramidal composition to unite the Virgin, John the Baptist, the Christ Child, and an angel in this work, in which the figures share the same light-infused environment.

expressed by gestures and the movement of the limbs. . . . A painting will only be wonderful for the beholder by making that which is not so appear raised and detached from the wall.[3]

Leonardo presented the figures in *Madonna of the Rocks* in a pyramidal grouping and, more notably, as sharing the same environment. This groundbreaking achievement—the unified representation of objects in an atmospheric setting—was a manifestation of his scientific curiosity about the invisible substance surrounding things. The Madonna, Christ Child, infant John the Baptist, and angel emerge through nuances of light and shade from the half-light of the cavernous visionary landscape. Light simultaneously veils and reveals the forms, immersing them in a layer of atmosphere. Leonardo's effective use of atmospheric perspective is the result in large part of his mastery of the relatively new medium of oil painting, which had previously been used mostly by northern European painters (see "Tempera and Oil Painting," Chapter 20, page 539). The four figures pray, point, and bless, and these acts and

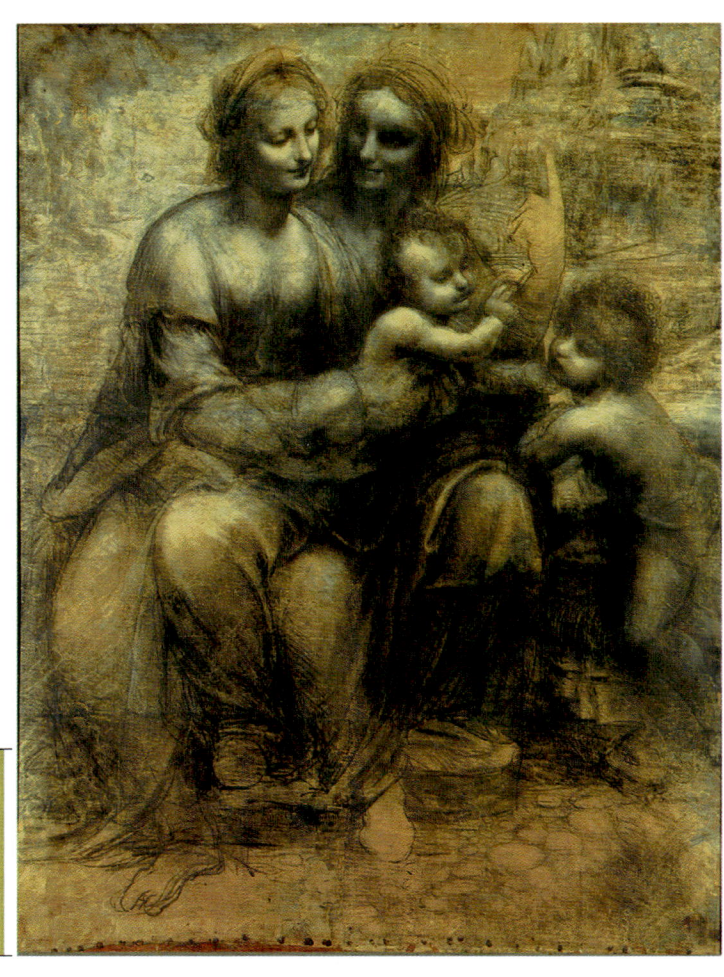

**22-3** Leonardo da Vinci, cartoon for *Madonna and Child with Saint Anne and the Infant Saint John,* ca. 1505–1507. Charcoal heightened with white on brown paper, 4′ 6″ × 3′ 3″. National Gallery, London. ◼◀

In this cartoon for a painting of the Madonna and Child and two saints, Leonardo drew a scene of tranquil grandeur filled with monumental figures reminiscent of classical statues.

1 ft.

gestures, although their meanings are uncertain, visually unite the individuals portrayed. The angel points to the infant John and, through his outward glance, involves the viewer in the tableau. John prays to the Christ Child, who blesses him in return. The Virgin herself completes the series of interlocking gestures, her left hand reaching toward the Christ Child and her right hand resting protectively on John's shoulder. The melting mood of tenderness, which the caressing light enhances, suffuses the entire composition. By creating an emotionally compelling, visually unified, and spatially convincing image, Leonardo succeeded in expressing "the intention of [man's] soul."

**MADONNA AND CHILD CARTOON** Leonardo's style fully emerges in *Madonna and Child with Saint Anne and the Infant Saint John* (FIG. **22-3**), a preliminary drawing (*cartoon*) for a painting (see "Renaissance Drawings," page 604) he made in 1505 or shortly thereafter. Here, the glowing light falls gently on the majestic forms in a scene of tranquil grandeur and balance. Leonardo ordered every part of his cartoon with an intellectual pictorial logic that results in an appealing visual unity. The figures are robust and monumental, the stately grace of their movements reminiscent of the Greek statues of goddesses (FIG. 5-49) in the pediments of the

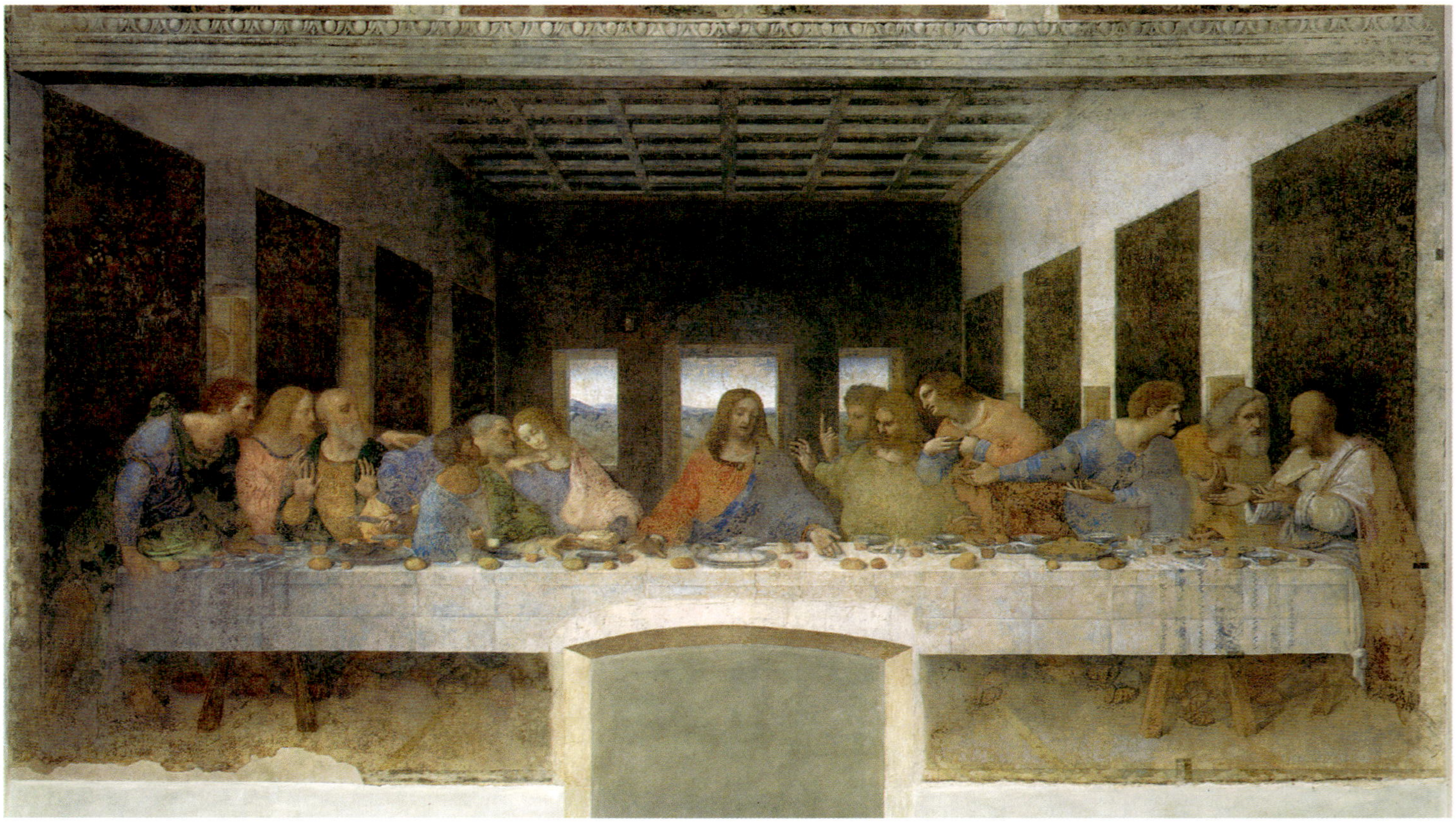

1 ft.

**22-4** Leonardo da Vinci, *Last Supper,* ca. 1495–1498. Oil and tempera on plaster, 13′ 9″ × 29′ 10″. Refectory, Santa Maria delle Grazie, Milan. ◼◀

Christ has just announced that one of his disciples will betray him, and each one reacts. Christ is both the psychological focus of Leonardo's fresco and the focal point of all the converging perspective lines.

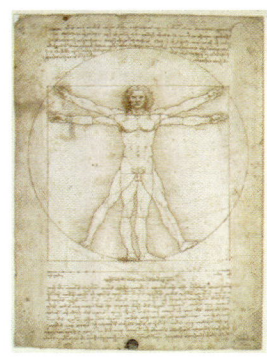

**22-3A** LEONARDO, *Vitruvian Man,* ca. 1485–1490.

Parthenon. Leonardo's infusion of the principles of classical art into his designs, however, cannot be attributed to specific knowledge of Greek monuments. He and his contemporaries never visited Greece. Their acquaintance with classical art extended only to Etruscan and Roman monuments, Roman copies of Greek statues in Italy, and ancient texts describing Greek and Roman works of art and architecture, especially Vitruvius's treatise *On Architecture* (FIG. **22-3A**).

**LAST SUPPER** For the refectory of the church of Santa Maria delle Grazie in Milan, Leonardo painted *Last Supper* (FIG. **22-4**), which both formally and emotionally is Leonardo's most impressive work. Jesus and his 12 disciples sit at a long table placed parallel to the picture plane in a simple, spacious room. The austere setting amplifies the painting's highly dramatic action. Jesus, with outstretched hands, has just said, "One of you is about to betray me" (Matt. 26:21). A wave of intense excitement passes through the group as each disciple asks himself and, in some cases, his neighbor, "Is it I?" (Matt. 26:22). Leonardo visualized a sophisticated conjunction of the dramatic "One of you is about to betray me" with the initiation of the ancient liturgical ceremony of the Eucharist, when Jesus, blessing bread and wine, said, "This is my body, which is given for you. Do this for a commemoration of me. . . . This is the chalice, the new testament in my blood, which shall be shed for you" (Luke 22:19–20).

In the center, Jesus appears isolated from the disciples and in perfect repose, the calm eye of the swirling emotion around him. The central window at the back, whose curved pediment arches above his head, frames his figure. The pediment is the only curve in the architectural framework, and it serves here, along with the diffused light, as a halo. Jesus' head is the focal point of all converging perspective lines in the composition. Thus, the still, psychological focus and cause of the action is also the perspective focus, as well as the center of the two-dimensional surface. The two-dimensional, the three-dimensional, and the psychodimensional focuses are the same.

Leonardo presented the agitated disciples in four groups of three, united among and within themselves by the figures' gestures and postures. The artist sacrificed traditional iconography to pictorial and dramatic consistency by placing Judas on the same side of the table as Jesus and the other disciples (compare FIG. 21-23). Judas's face is in shadow (the light source in the painting corresponds to the windows in the Milanese refectory). He clutches a money bag in his right hand as he reaches his left forward to fulfill Jesus' declaration: "But yet behold, the hand of him that betrayeth me is with me on the table" (Luke 22:21). The two disciples at the table ends are quieter than the others, as if to bracket the energy of the composition, which is more intense closer to Jesus, whose serenity both halts and intensifies it. The disciples register a broad range of emotional responses, including fear, doubt, protestation, rage, and love. Leonardo's numerous preparatory studies—using live models—suggest he thought of each figure as carrying a particular charge and type of emotion. Like a stage director, he read the Gospel story carefully, and scrupulously cast his actors as the Bible described their roles. In this work, as in his other religious paintings, Leonardo revealed his extraordinary ability to apply his voluminous knowledge about the observable world to the pictorial representation of a religious scene, resulting in a psychologically complex and compelling painting.

Leonardo's *Last Supper* is unfortunately in poor condition today, even after the completion in 1999 of a cleaning and restoration project lasting more than two decades. In a bold experiment, Leonardo had mixed oil and tempera, applying much of it *a secco* (to dried, rather than wet, plaster) in order to create a mural that more closely approximated oil painting on canvas or wood instead of fresco. But because the wall did not absorb the pigment as in the *buon fresco* technique, the paint quickly began to flake (see "Fresco Painting," Chapter 14, page 408). The humidity of Milan further accelerated the deterioration. The restoration involved extensive scholarly, chemical, and computer analysis. Like similar projects elsewhere, however, most notably in the Sistine Chapel (FIGS. 22-1 and 22-18B), this one was not without controversy. One scholar has claimed 80 percent of what is visible today is the work of the modern restorers, not Leonardo.

**MONA LISA** Leonardo's *Mona Lisa* (FIG. **22-5**) is probably the world's most famous portrait. The sitter's identity is still the subject of scholarly debate, but in his biography of Leonardo, Giorgio Vasari asserted she was Lisa di Antonio Maria Gherardini, the wife of Francesco del Giocondo, a wealthy Florentine—hence, "Mona

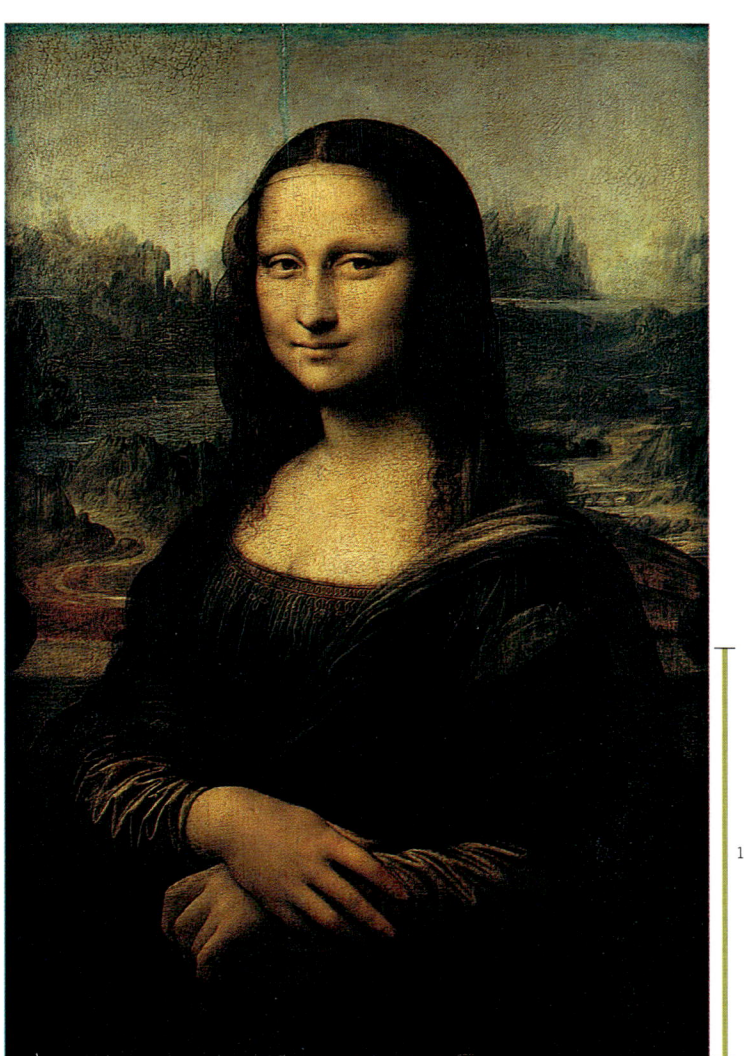

1 ft.

**22-5** LEONARDO DA VINCI, *Mona Lisa,* ca. 1503–1505. Oil on wood, 2′ 6¼″ × 1′ 9″. Musée du Louvre, Paris.

Leonardo's skill with chiaroscuro and atmospheric perspective is on display in this new kind of portrait depicting the sitter as an individual personality who engages the viewer psychologically.

# Renaissance Drawings

In Cinquecento Italy, drawing (or *disegno*) assumed a position of greater artistic prominence than ever before. Until the late 15th century, the expense of drawing surfaces and their lack of availability limited the production of preparatory sketches. Most artists drew on *parchment* (prepared from the skins of calves, sheep, and goats) or on *vellum* (made from the skins of young animals; FIG. 13-31). Because of the high cost of these materials, drawings in the 14th and 15th centuries tended to be extremely detailed and meticulously executed. Artists often drew using a silverpoint stylus (FIG. 20-9) because of the fine line it produced and the sharp point it maintained. The introduction in the late 15th century of less expensive paper made of fibrous pulp produced for the developing printing industry (see "Woodcuts, Engravings, and Etchings," Chapter 20, page 556) enabled artists to experiment more and to draw with greater freedom. As a result, sketches proliferated. Artists executed these drawings in pen and ink (FIG. 22-6), chalk, charcoal (FIG. 22-3), brush, and graphite or lead.

During the Renaissance, the importance of drawing transcended the mechanical or technical possibilities it afforded artists, however. The term *disegno* referred also to design, an integral component of good art. Design was the foundation of art, and drawing was the fundamental element of design. In his 1607 treatise *L'idea de' pittori, scultori ed architteti,* Federico Zuccari (1542–1609), director of the Accademia di San Luca (Academy of Saint Luke), the Roman painting academy, summed up this philosophy when he stated that drawing is the external physical manifestation (*disegno esterno*) of an internal intellectual idea or design (*disegno interno*).

The design dimension of art production became increasingly important as artists cultivated their own styles. The early stages of artistic training largely focused on imitation and emulation (see "Cennino Cennini on Imitation and Emulation," Chapter 21, page 573), but to achieve widespread recognition, artists had to develop their own styles. Although the artistic community and public

**22-6** LEONARDO DA VINCI, *The Fetus and Lining of the Uterus,* ca. 1511–1513. Pen and ink with wash over red chalk and traces of black chalk on paper, $1' \times 8\frac{5}{8}''$. Royal Library, Windsor Castle. ◼◂

The introduction of less expensive paper in the late 15th century enabled artists to draw more frequently. Leonardo's analytical anatomical studies epitomize the scientific spirit of the Renaissance.

1 in.

at large acknowledged technical skill, the conceptualization of the artwork—its theoretical and formal development—was paramount. Disegno, or design in this case, represented an artist's conceptualization and intention. In the literature of the period, the terms often invoked to praise esteemed artists included *invenzione* (invention), *ingegno* (innate talent), *fantasia* (imagination), and *capriccio* (originality).

---

(an Italian contraction of *ma donna,* "my lady") Lisa." Despite the uncertainty of this identification, Leonardo's portrait is a convincing representation of an individual. Unlike earlier portraits, it does not serve solely as an icon of status. Indeed, Mona Lisa wears no jewelry and holds no attribute associated with wealth. She sits quietly, her hands folded, her mouth forming a gentle smile, and her gaze directed at the viewer. Renaissance etiquette dictated a woman should not look directly into a man's eyes. Leonardo's portrayal of this self-assured young woman without the trappings of power but engaging the audience psychologically is thus quite remarkable.

The enduring appeal of *Mona Lisa* derives in large part from Leonardo's decision to set his subject against the backdrop of a mysterious uninhabited landscape. This setting, with roads and

bridges seemingly leading nowhere, recalls that of his *Madonna of the Rocks* (FIG. 22-2). The composition also resembles Fra Filippo Lippi's *Madonna and Child with Angels* (FIG. 21-24) with figures seated in front of a window through which the viewer glimpses a distant landscape. Originally, the artist represented Mona Lisa in a loggia. A later owner trimmed the painting, eliminating the columns, but partial column bases remain to the left and right of Mona Lisa's shoulders.

The painting is darker today than 500 years ago and the colors are less vivid, but *Mona Lisa* still reveals Leonardo's fascination and skill with chiaroscuro and atmospheric perspective. The portrait is a prime example of the artist's famous smoky *sfumato* (misty haziness)—his subtle adjustment of light and blurring of precise planes.

**ANATOMICAL STUDIES** *Mona Lisa* is also exceptional because Leonardo completed very few paintings. His perfectionism, relentless experimentation, and far-ranging curiosity diffused his efforts. However, the drawings (see "Renaissance Drawings," page 604) in his notebooks preserve an extensive record of his ideas. His interests focused increasingly on science in his later years, and he embraced knowledge of all facets of the natural world. His investigations in anatomy yielded drawings of great precision and beauty of execution. *The Fetus and Lining of the Uterus* (FIG. 22-6), although it does not meet 21st-century standards for accuracy (for example, Leonardo regularized the uterus's shape to a sphere, and his characterization of the lining is incorrect), was an astounding achievement in its day. Leonardo's analytical anatomical studies epitomize the scientific spirit of the Renaissance, establishing that era as a prelude to the modern world and setting it in sharp contrast to the preceding Middle Ages. Although Leonardo may not have been the first scientist of the modern world (at least not in today's sense of the term), he did originate the modern method of scientific illustration incorporating *cutaway* views. Scholars have long recognized the importance of his drawings for the development of anatomy as a science, especially in an age predating photographic methods such as X-rays.

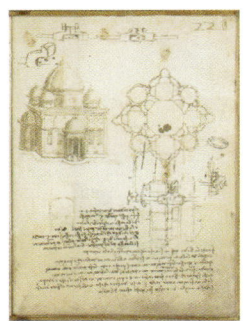

22-6A LEONARDO, central-plan church, ca. 1487–1490.

Leonardo also won renown in his time as both architect and sculptor, although no extant buildings or sculptures can be definitively attributed to him. From his many drawings of central-plan structures (FIG. 22-6A), it is evident he shared the interest of other Renaissance architects in this building type. As for Leonardo's sculptures, numerous drawings of monumental equestrian statues survive, and he made a full-scale model for a monument to Francesco Sforza (1401–1466), Ludovico's father. The French used the statue as a target and shot it to pieces when they occupied Milan in 1499.

Leonardo left Milan at that time and served for a while as a military engineer for Cesare Borgia (1476–1507), who, with the support of his father, Pope Alexander VI (r. 1492–1503), tried to conquer the cities of the Romagna region in north-central Italy and create a Borgia duchy. Leonardo eventually returned to Milan in the service of the French. At the invitation of King Francis I (FIG. 23-12), he then went to France, where he died at the château of Cloux in 1519.

## Raphael

Alexander VI's successor was Julius II (see page 599). Among the many projects the ambitious new pope sponsored were a design for a modern Saint Peter's (FIGS. 22-22 and 22-23) to replace the timber-roofed fourth-century basilica (FIG. 8-9), the decoration of the papal apartments (FIG. 22-9), and the construction of his tomb (FIGS. 22-14 and 22-15), in addition to commissioning Michelangelo to paint the Sistine Chapel ceiling (FIGS. 22-1 and 22-17).

In 1508, Julius II called Raffaello Santi (or Sanzio), known as RAPHAEL (1483–1520) in English, to the papal court in Rome (see "Italian Princely Courts," Chapter 21, page 591). Born in a small town in Umbria near Urbino, Raphael probably learned the rudiments of his art from his father, Giovanni Santi (d. 1494), a painter connected with the ducal court of Federico da Montefeltro (FIG. 21-43), before entering the studio of Perugino (FIG. 21-41) in Perugia. Although strongly influenced by Perugino, Leonardo, and others, Raphael developed an individual style exemplifying the ideals of High Renaissance art.

***MARRIAGE OF THE VIRGIN*** Among Raphael's early works is *Marriage of the Virgin* (FIG. 22-7), which he painted for the chapel of Saint Joseph in the church of San Francesco in Città di Castello, southeast of Florence. The subject was a fitting one for Saint Joseph. According to the *Golden Legend* (a 13th-century collection of stories about the lives of the saints), Joseph competed with other suitors for Mary's hand. The high priest was to give the Virgin to whichever suitor presented to him a rod that had miraculously bloomed. Raphael depicted Joseph with his flowering rod in his left hand. In his right hand, Joseph holds the wedding ring he is about to place on Mary's finger. Other virgins congregate at the left, and the unsuccessful suitors stand on the right. One of them breaks his rod in half over his knee in frustration, giving Raphael an opportunity to demonstrate his mastery of foreshortening. The perspective system he used is the one he learned from Perugino (compare FIG. 21-41). The temple in the background is Raphael's version of a centrally planned building, featuring Brunelleschian arcades (FIG. 21-31).

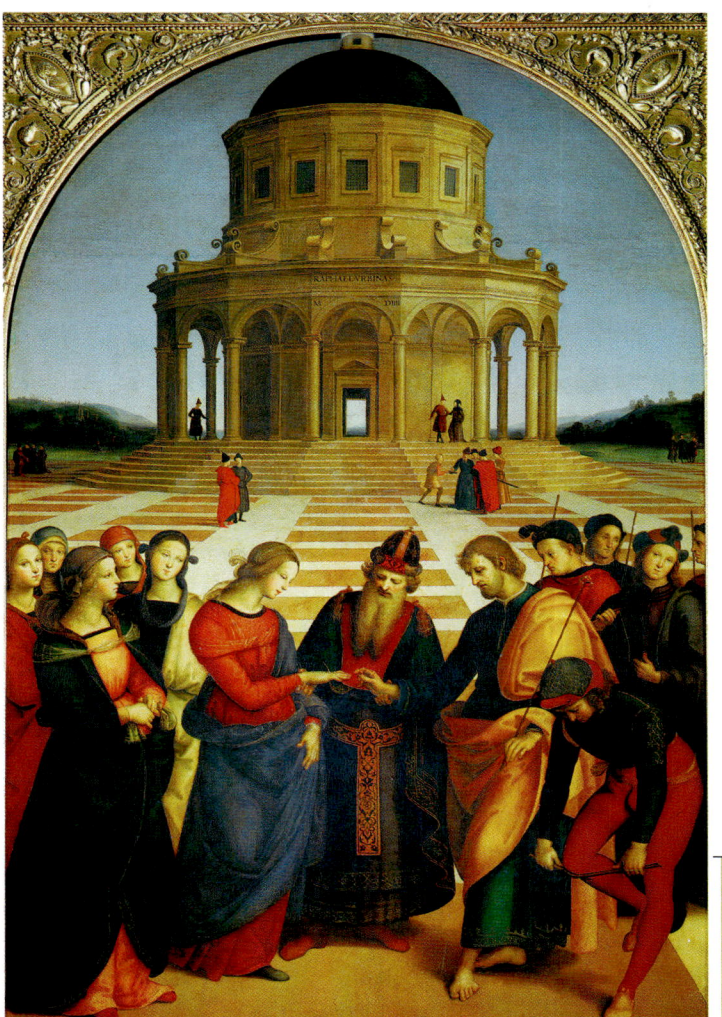

22-7 RAPHAEL, *Marriage of the Virgin,* from the Chapel of Saint Joseph, San Francesco, Città di Castello, Italy, 1504. Oil on wood, 5′ 7″ × 3′ 10½″. Pinacoteca di Brera, Milan.

In this early work depicting the marriage of the Virgin to Saint Joseph, Raphael demonstrated his mastery of foreshortening and of the perspective system he learned from Perugino (FIG. 21-41).

Emulating Leonardo's pyramidal composition (FIG. 22-2) but rejecting his dusky modeling and mystery, Raphael set his Madonna in a well-lit landscape and imbued her with grace, dignity, and beauty.

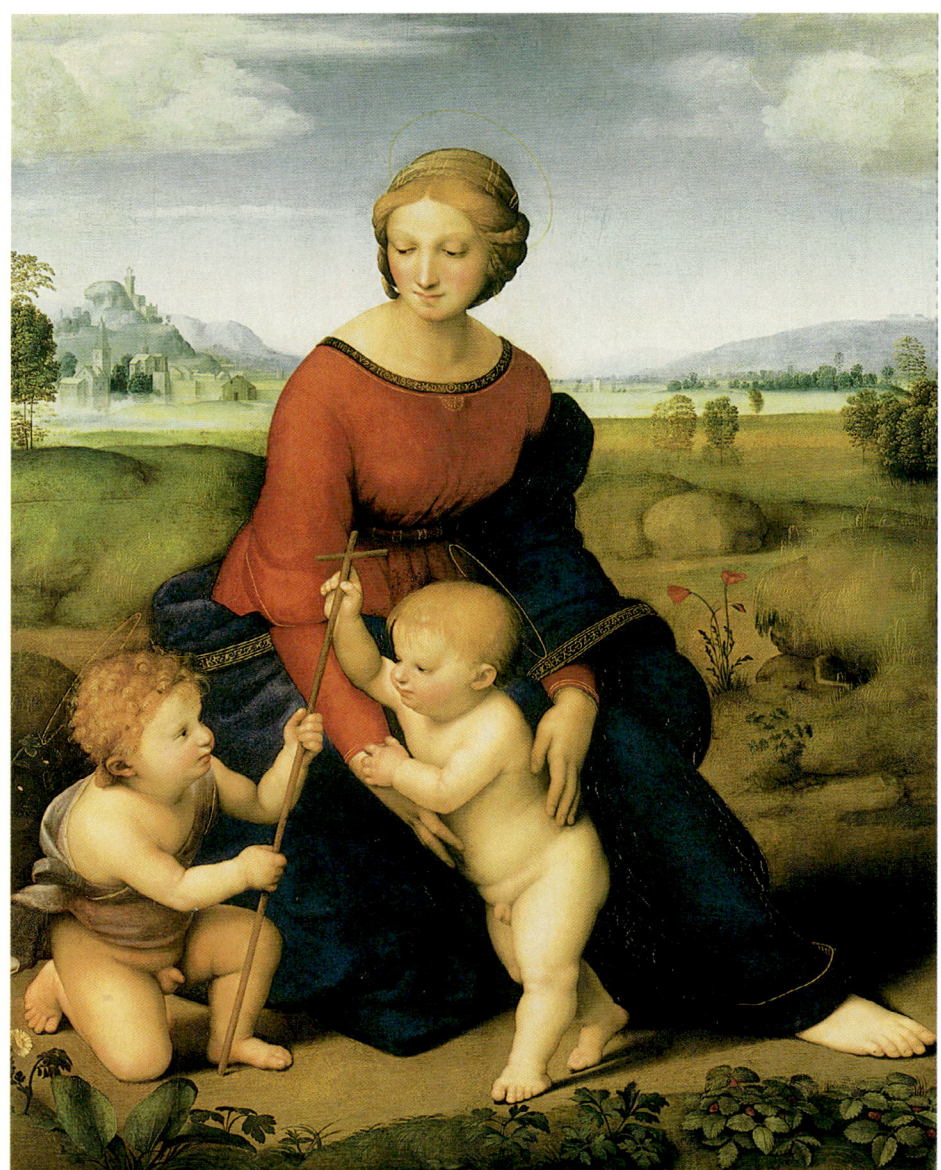

*MADONNA IN THE MEADOW* Raphael spent the four years from 1504 to 1508 in Florence. There, still in his early 20s, he discovered that the painting style he had learned so painstakingly from Perugino was already outmoded (as was Brunelleschi's Early Renaissance architectural style). Florentine crowds flocked to the church of Santissima Annunziata to see Leonardo's recently unveiled cartoon of the Virgin, Christ Child, Saint Anne, and Saint John (probably an earlier version of FIG. 22-3). Under Leonardo's influence, Raphael began to modify the Madonna compositions he had employed in Umbria. In *Madonna in the Meadow* (FIG. **22-8**) of 1505–1506, Raphael adopted Leonardo's pyramidal composition and modeling of faces and figures in subtle chiaroscuro. Yet the Umbrian artist placed the large, substantial figures in a Peruginesque landscape, with his former master's typical feathery trees in the middle ground. Although Raphael experimented with Leonardo's dusky modeling, he tended to return to Perugino's lighter tonalities and blue skies. Raphael preferred clarity to obscurity, not fascinated, as Leonardo was, with mystery. Raphael quickly achieved fame for his Madonnas. His work, as well as Leonardo's, deeply influenced Raphael's slightly younger contemporary, ANDREA DEL SARTO (1486–1530), whose most famous painting is *Madonna of the Harpies* (FIG. **22-8A**).

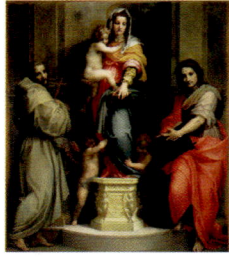

**22-8A** ANDREA DEL SARTO, *Madonna of the Harpies,* 1517.

*SCHOOL OF ATHENS* Three years after completing *Madonna in the Meadow,* Raphael received one of the most important painting commissions Julius II awarded—the decoration of the papal apartments in the Apostolic Palace of the Vatican (MAP 24-1). Of the suite's several rooms (*stanze*), Raphael painted the Stanza della Segnatura (Room of the Signature—the papal library, where Julius II signed official documents) and the Stanza d'Eliodoro (Room of Heliodorus—the pope's private audience room, named for one of the paintings there). His pupils completed the others, following his sketches. On the four walls of the Stanza della Segnatura, Raphael presented images symbolizing the four branches of human knowledge and wisdom under the headings *Theology,*

*Law* (*Justice*), *Poetry,* and *Philosophy*—the learning required of a Renaissance pope. Given Julius II's desire for recognition as both a spiritual and temporal leader, it is appropriate the *Theology* and *Philosophy* frescoes face each other. The two images present a balanced picture of the pope—as a cultured, knowledgeable individual and as a wise, divinely ordained religious authority.

In Raphael's *Philosophy* mural (commonly called *School of Athens,* FIG. **22-9**), the setting is not a "school" but a congregation of the great philosophers and scientists of the ancient world. Raphael depicted these luminaries, revered by Renaissance humanists, conversing and explaining their various theories and ideas. The setting is a vast hall covered by massive vaults that recall ancient Roman architecture, especially the much-admired coffered barrel vaults of the Basilica Nova (FIG. 7-78). Colossal statues of Apollo and Athena, patron deities of the arts and of wisdom, oversee the interactions. Plato and Aristotle are the central figures around whom Raphael carefully arranged the others. Plato holds his book *Timaeus* and points to Heaven, the source of his inspiration, while Aristotle carries his book *Nichomachean Ethics* and gestures toward the earth, from which his observations of reality sprang. Appropriately,

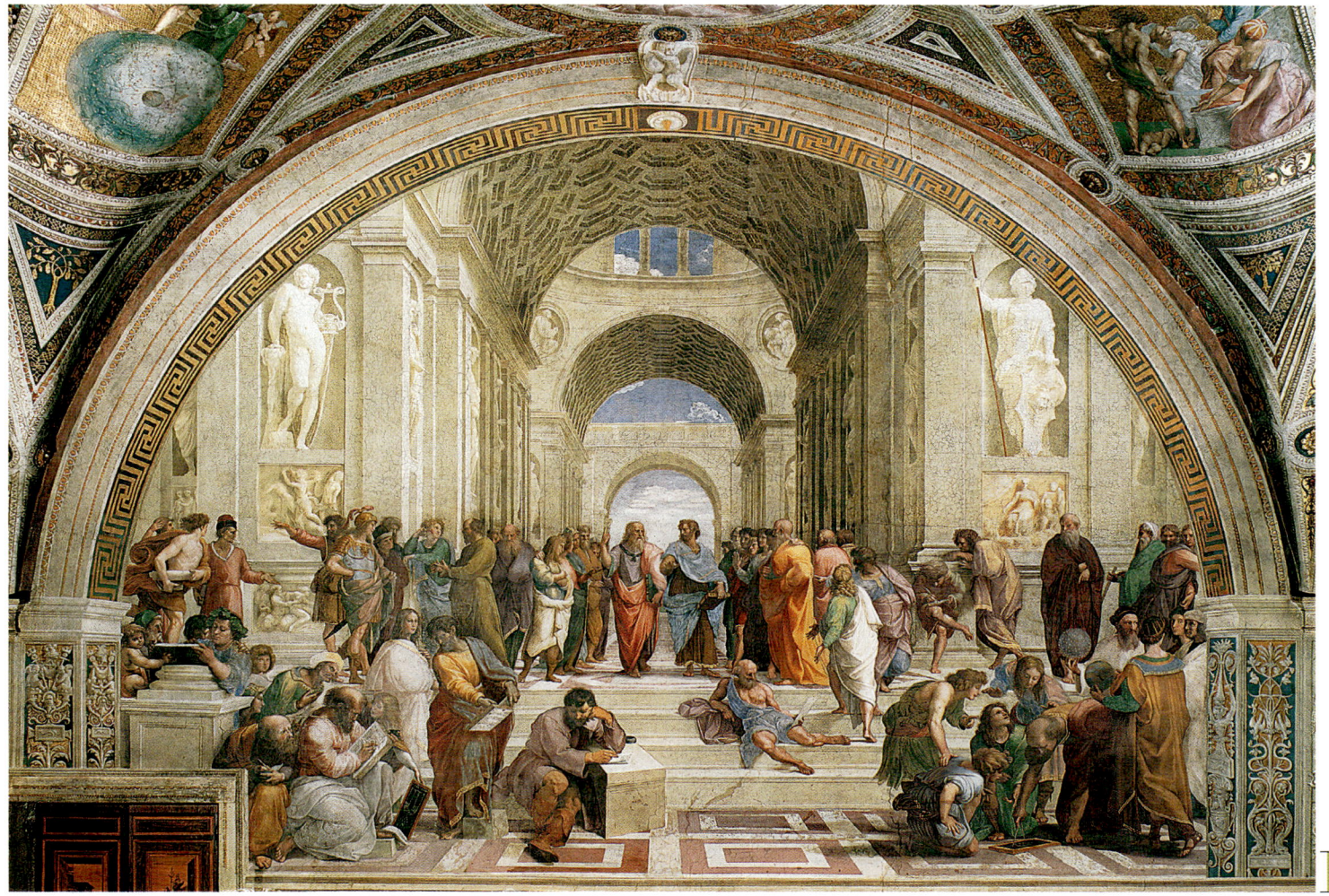

**22-9** RAPHAEL, *Philosophy* (*School of Athens*), Stanza della Segnatura, Vatican Palace, Rome, Italy, 1509–1511. Fresco, 19′ × 27′. ◼◀

Raphael included himself in this gathering of great philosophers and scientists whose self-assurance conveys calm reason. The setting recalls the massive vaults of the Basilica Nova (FIG. 7-78).

ancient philosophers, men concerned with the ultimate mysteries that transcend this world, stand on Plato's side. On Aristotle's side are the philosophers and scientists concerned with nature and human affairs. At the lower left, Pythagoras writes as a servant holds up the harmonic scale. In the foreground, Heraclitus (probably a portrait of Michelangelo) broods alone. Diogenes sprawls on the steps. At the right, students surround Euclid, who demonstrates a theorem. Euclid may be a portrait of the architect Bramante, whom Julius II had recently commissioned to design the new church (FIGS. 22-22 and 22-23) to replace Constantine's 1,200-year-old Saint Peter's (FIG. 8-9). (The architectural setting of *School of Athens* approximates Bramante's design for the interior of Saint Peter's; compare FIG. 24-5.) At the extreme right, just to the right of the astronomers Zoroaster and Ptolemy, both holding globes, Raphael included his self-portrait.

The groups appear to move easily and clearly, with eloquent poses and gestures that symbolize their doctrines and present an engaging variety of figural positions. The self-assurance and natural dignity of the figures convey calm reason, balance, and measure—those qualities Renaissance thinkers admired as the heart of philosophy. Significantly, Raphael placed himself among the mathematicians and scientists in *School of Athens*. Certainly, the evolution of pictorial science approached perfection in this fresco

in which Raphael convincingly depicted a vast space on a two-dimensional surface.

The artist's psychological insight matured along with his mastery of the problems of perspective representation. All the characters in Raphael's *School of Athens,* like those in Leonardo's *Last Supper* (FIG. 22-4), communicate moods that reflect their beliefs, and the artist's placement of each figure tied these moods together. From the center, where Plato and Aristotle stand, Raphael arranged the groups of figures in an ellipse with a wide opening in the foreground. Moving along the floor's perspective pattern, the viewer's eye penetrates the assembly of philosophers and continues, by way of the reclining Diogenes, up to the here-reconciled leaders of the two great opposing camps of Renaissance philosophy. The vanishing point falls on Plato's left hand, drawing attention to *Timaeus*. In the Stanza della Segnatura, Raphael reconciled and harmonized not only the Platonists and Aristotelians but also classical humanism and Christianity, surely a major factor in the fresco's appeal to Julius II.

***LEO X*** Succeeding Julius II as Raphael's patron was Pope Leo X (r. 1513–1521). By this time, Raphael had achieved renown throughout Italy and moved in the highest circles of the papal court. The new pope entrusted the Umbrian artist with so many projects in

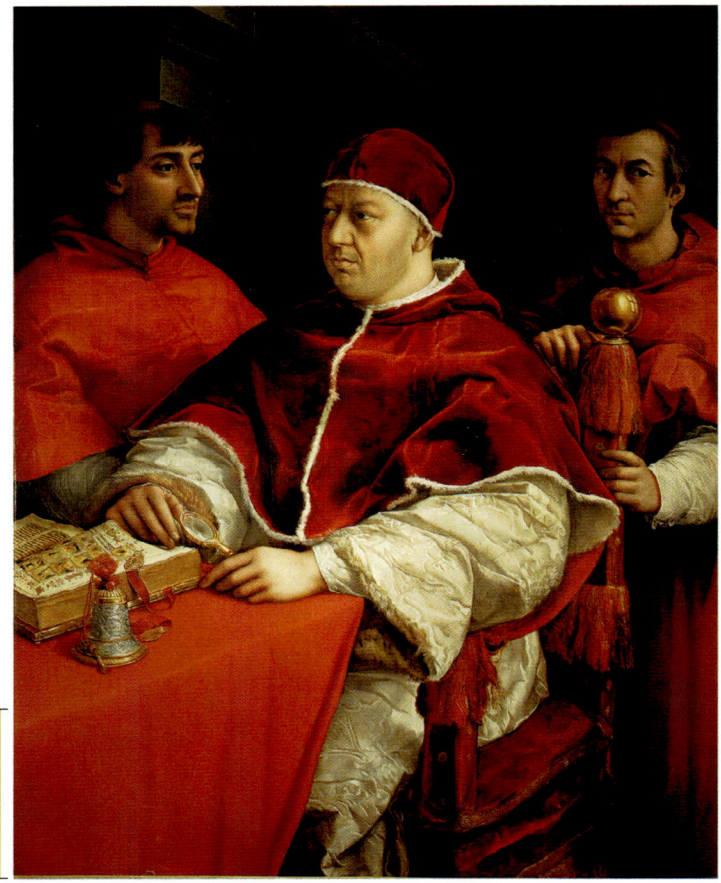

**22-10** RAPHAEL, *Pope Leo X with Cardinals Giulio de' Medici and Luigi de' Rossi*, ca. 1517. Oil on wood, 5′ $\frac{5}{8}$″ × 3′ 10$\frac{7}{8}$″. Galleria degli Uffizi, Florence.

In this dynastic portrait of the Medici pope and two Medici cardinals, Raphael depicted Leo X as an art collector and man of learning. The meticulous details reveal a debt to Netherlandish painting.

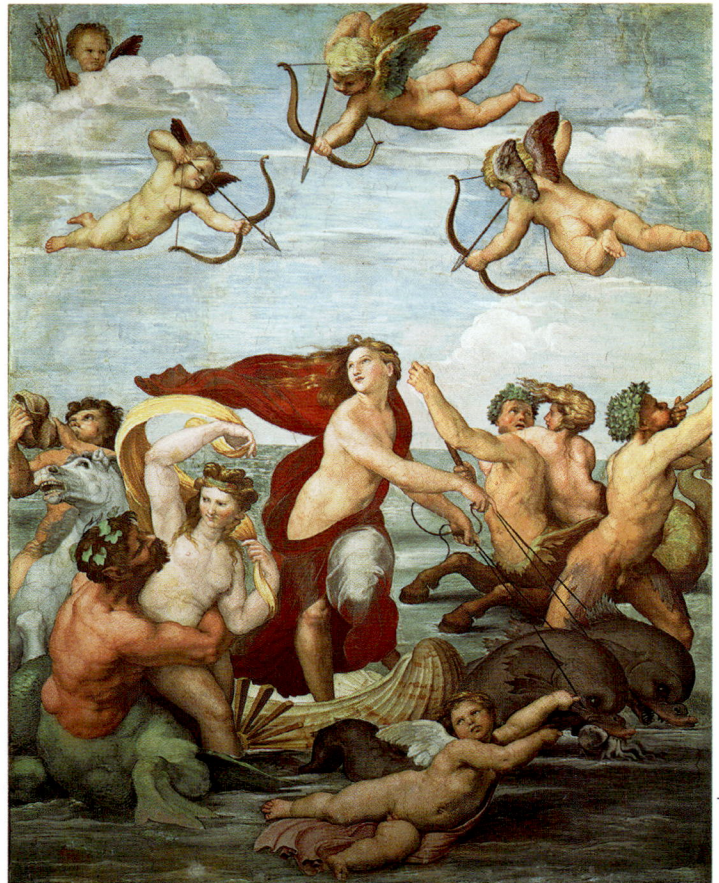

**22-11** RAPHAEL, *Galatea*, Sala di Galatea, Villa Farnesina, Rome, Italy, ca. 1513. Fresco, 9′ 8″ × 7′ 5″.

Based on a poem by Poliziano, Raphael's fresco depicts Galatea fleeing from Polyphemus. The painting, made for the banker Agostino Chigi's private palace, celebrates human beauty and zestful love.

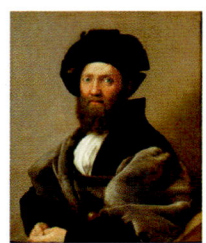

**22-10A** RAPHAEL, *Baldassare Castiglione*, ca. 1514.

Rome, including overseeing construction of Saint Peter's, that Raphael became a wealthy man at a young age. Leo himself (Giovanni de' Medici) was a scion of Italy's most famous family. The second son of Lorenzo the Magnificent, he received a princely humanistic education. His election as pope came only a year after the return of the Medici to Florence following nearly two decades of exile (see Chapter 21), and Leo used his position to advance the family's interests. The portrait (FIG. 22-10) he commissioned Raphael to paint in 1517—a few years after the artist portrayed the famed courtier Baldassare Castiglione (FIG. 22-10A)—is, in essence, a dynastic portrait. Appropriately, the pope dominates the canvas, seated in his study before a table with an illuminated 14th-century manuscript, the magnifying glass he required because of his myopia, and a bell engraved with classical decorative motifs. Raphael portrayed Leo as he doubtless wished to be represented—as a man of learning and a collector of beautiful objects rather than as a head of state. To the pope's right is his cousin Cardinal Giulio de' Medici, who became Pope Clement VII (r. 1523–1534). Behind Leo's chair is Luigi de' Rossi (1474–1519), his cousin on his mother's side, whom the pope appointed cardinal.

The three men look neither at one another nor at the painter or spectator, but are absorbed in their own thoughts.

Raphael's mastery of the oil technique is evident in every detail. His depiction of the rich satin, wool, velvet, and fur garments the three men wear skillfully conveys their varied textures. His reproduction of the book on the pope's desk is so meticulous that scholars have been able to identify it as the *Hamilton Bible* in the Berlin Staatsbibliothek, open to folio 400 verso, the beginning of the Gospel of Saint John with illustrations of Christ's passion. The light illuminating the scene comes from the right—from a window reflected in the spherical brass finial of the pope's chair, in which the viewer can also see the indistinct form of the painter. In details such as these, Raphael revealed his knowledge and admiration of earlier Netherlandish painting, especially the work of Jan van Eyck (see Chapter 20).

***GALATEA*** As a star at the papal court, Raphael also enjoyed the patronage of other prominent figures in Rome. Agostino Chigi (1465–1520), an immensely wealthy banker who managed the Vatican's financial affairs, commissioned Raphael to decorate his palace on the Tiber River with scenes from classical mythology. Outstanding among the frescoes Raphael painted in the small but splendid Villa Farnesina is *Galatea* (FIG. 22-11), which he based on

## Leonardo and Michelangelo on Painting versus Sculpture

Both Leonardo da Vinci and Michelangelo produced work in a variety of artistic media, earning enviable reputations not just as painters and sculptors but as architects and draftsmen as well. The two disagreed, however, on the relative merits of the different media. In particular, Leonardo, with his intellectual and analytical mind, preferred painting to sculpture, which he denigrated as manual labor. In contrast, Michelangelo, who worked in a more intuitive manner, saw himself primarily as a sculptor. Two excerpts from their writings reveal their positions on the relationship between the two media.

Leonardo da Vinci wrote the following in his so-called *Treatise on Painting*:

> Painting is a matter of greater mental analysis, of greater skill, and more marvelous than sculpture, since necessity compels the mind of the painter to transform itself into the very mind of nature, to become an interpreter between nature and art. Painting justifies by reference to nature the reasons of the pictures which follow its laws: in what ways the images of objects before the eye come together in the pupil of the eye; which, among objects equal in size, looks larger to the eye; which, among equal colors will look more or less dark or more or less bright; which, among things at the same depth, looks more or less low; which, among those objects placed at equal height, will look more or less high, and why, among objects placed at various distances, one will appear less clear than the other.
>
> This art comprises and includes within itself all visible things such as colors and their diminution, which the poverty of sculpture cannot include. Painting represents transparent objects but the sculptor will show you the shapes of natural objects without artifice. The painter will show you things at different distances with variation of color due to the air lying between the objects and the eye; he shows you mists through which visual images penetrate with difficulty; he shows you rain which discloses within it clouds with mountains and valleys; he shows the dust which discloses within it and beyond it the combatants who stirred it up; he shows streams of greater or lesser density; he shows fish playing between the surface of the water and its bottom; he shows the polished pebbles of various colors lying on the washed sand at the bottom of rivers, surrounded by green plants; he shows the stars at various heights above us, and thus he achieves innumerable effects which sculpture cannot attain.*

As if in response, although decades later, Michelangelo wrote these excerpts in a letter to Benedetto Varchi (1502–1565), a Florentine poet best known for his 16-volume history of Florence:

> I believe that painting is considered excellent in proportion as it approaches the effect of relief, while relief is considered bad in proportion as it approaches the effect of painting.
>
> I used to consider that sculpture was the lantern of painting and that between the two things there was the same difference as that between the sun and the moon. But . . . I now consider that painting and sculpture are one and the same thing.
>
> Suffice that, since one and the other (that is to say, both painting and sculpture) proceed from the same faculty, it would be an easy matter to establish harmony between them and to let such disputes alone, for they occupy more time than the execution of the figures themselves. As to that man [Leonardo] who wrote saying that painting was more noble than sculpture, if he had known as much about the other subjects on which he has written, why, my serving-maid would have written better!†

*Leonardo da Vinci, *Treatise on Painting*, 51. In Robert Klein and Henri Zerner, *Italian Art 1500–1600: Sources and Documents* (Evanston, Ill.: Northwestern University Press, 1966), 7–8.
†Michelangelo to Benedetto Varchi, Rome, 1549. In Klein and Zerner, *Italian Art 1500–1600*, 13–14.

*Stanzas for the Joust of Giuliano de' Medici* by Angelo Poliziano, whose poetry had earlier inspired Botticelli to paint *Birth of Venus* (FIG. 21-29). In Raphael's fresco, Galatea flees on a shell drawn by leaping dolphins to escape her uncouth lover, the cyclops Polyphemus (painted on another wall by a different artist). Sea creatures and playful cupids surround her. The painting is an exultant song in praise of human beauty and zestful love. Compositionally, Raphael enhanced the liveliness of the image by placing the sturdy figures around Galatea in bounding and dashing movements that always return to her as the energetic center. The cupids, skillfully foreshortened, repeat the circling motion. Raphael conceived his figures sculpturally, and Galatea's body—supple, strong, and vigorously in motion—contrasts with Botticelli's delicate, hovering, almost dematerialized Venus while suggesting the spiraling compositions of Hellenistic statuary (FIG. 5-80). In *Galatea*, classical myth presented in monumental form, in vivacious movement, and in a spirit of passionate delight resurrects the naturalistic art and poetry of the Greco-Roman world.

## Michelangelo

Although Michelangelo is most famous today as the painter of the Sistine Chapel frescoes (FIG. 22-1), he was also an architect, poet, engineer, and, first and foremost, a sculptor. Michelangelo considered sculpture superior to painting because the sculptor shares in the divine power to "make man" (see "Leonardo and Michelangelo on Painting versus Sculpture," above). Drawing a conceptual parallel to Plato's ideas, Michelangelo believed the image the artist's hand produces must come from the idea in the artist's mind. The idea, then, is the reality the artist's genius has to bring forth. But artists are not the creators of the ideas they conceive. Rather, they find their ideas in the natural world, reflecting the absolute idea, which, for the artist, is beauty. One of Michelangelo's best-known observations about sculpture is that the artist must proceed by finding the idea—the image locked in the stone. By removing the excess stone, the sculptor extricates the idea from the block (FIG. I-16), bringing forth the living form. The artist, Michelangelo felt, works for many

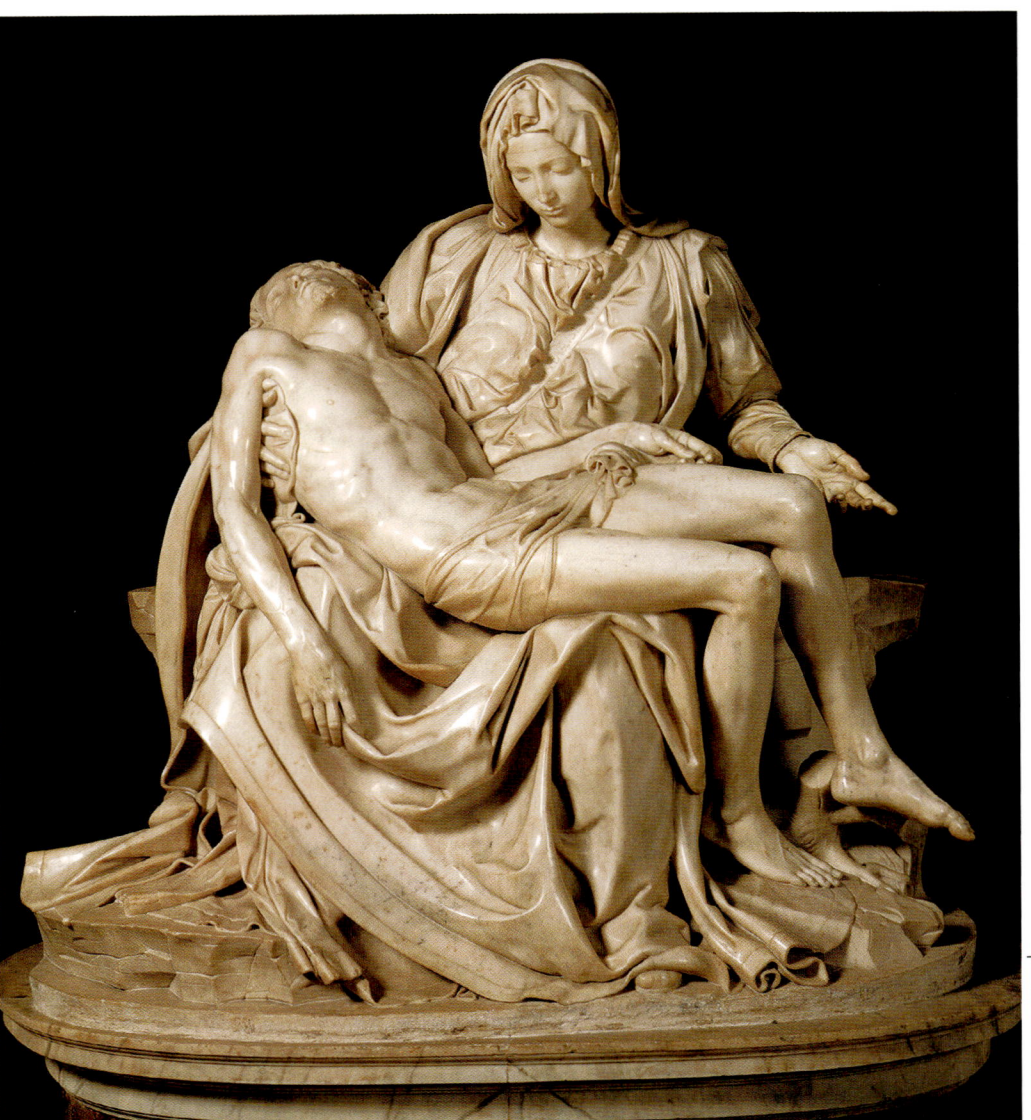

Michelangelo's representation of Mary
cradling Christ's corpse captures the
sadness and beauty of the young Virgin
but was controversial because the Madonna
seems younger than her son.

1 ft.

years to discover this unceasing process of revelation and "arrives late at
novel and lofty things."⁴

Michelangelo did indeed arrive "at novel and lofty things," for
he broke sharply from the lessons of
his predecessors and contemporaries
in one important respect. He mis-
trusted the application of mathematical methods as guarantees of beauty
in proportion. Measure and proportion, he believed, should be "kept in
the eyes." Vasari quoted Michelangelo
as declaring "it was necessary to have
the compasses in the eyes and not
in the hand, because the hands work
and the eye judges."⁵ Thus, Michelangelo set aside Vitruvius, Alberti, Leonardo, and others who tirelessly sought
the perfect measure, and insisted the
artist's inspired judgment could identify other pleasing proportions. In addition, Michelangelo argued the artist must not be bound, except by the
demands made by realizing the idea.
This assertion of the artist's authority was typical of Michelangelo and
anticipated the modern concept of the
right to a self-expression of talent lim-
ited only by the artist's own judgment. The artistic license to aspire
far beyond the "rules" was, in part, a manifestation of the pursuit
of fame and success that humanism fostered. In this context, Michelangelo created works in architecture, sculpture, and painting
that departed from High Renaissance regularity. He put in its stead
a style of vast, expressive strength conveyed through complex, eccentric, and often titanic forms looming before the viewer in tragic
grandeur.

As a youth, Michelangelo was an apprentice in the studio of
the painter Domenico Ghirlandaio (FIGS. 21-26 and 21-27), but he
left before completing his training. Although Michelangelo later
claimed he owed nothing artistically to anyone, he made detailed
drawings based on the work of the great Florentines Giotto and
Masaccio. Early on, he came to the attention of Lorenzo the Magnificent and studied sculpture under one of Lorenzo's favorite artists, Bertoldo di Giovanni (ca. 1420–1491), a former collaborator of
Donatello's. When the Medici fell in 1494, Michelangelo fled Florence for Bologna, where the sculptures of the Sienese artist Jacopo
della Quercia (1367–1438) impressed him.

***PIETÀ*** Michelangelo made his first trip to Rome in the summer
of 1496, and two years later, still in his early 20s, he produced his
first masterpiece there: a *Pietà* (FIG. **22-12**) for the French cardinal Jean de Bilhères Lagraulas (1439–1499). The cardinal commissioned the statue to be placed in the rotunda attached to the south
transept of Old Saint Peter's (FIG. 8-9) in which he was to be buried
beside other French churchmen. (The work is now on view in the
new church [FIG. 24-4] that replaced the fourth-century basilica.)
The theme—Mary cradling the dead body of Christ in her lap—was
a staple in the repertoire of French and German artists (FIG. 13-50),
and Michelangelo's French patron doubtless chose the subject. The
Italian, however, rendered the northern European theme in an unforgettable manner. Michelangelo transformed marble into flesh,
hair, and fabric with a sensitivity for texture almost without parallel. The polish and luminosity of the exquisite marble surface can be
fully appreciated only in the presence of the original. Breathtaking,
too, is the tender sadness of the beautiful and youthful Mary as she
mourns the death of her son. In fact, her age—seemingly less than
that of Christ—was a subject of controversy from the moment the
statue was unveiled. Michelangelo explained Mary's ageless beauty
as an integral part of her purity and virginity. Beautiful, too, is the
son whom she holds. Christ seems less to have died a martyr's crucifixion than to have drifted off into peaceful sleep in Mary's maternal arms. His wounds are barely visible.

***DAVID*** Michelangelo returned to Florence in 1501. In 1495, during the Medici exile, the Florentine Republic had ordered the transfer of Donatello's *David* (FIG. 21-12) from the Medici residence to the Palazzo della Signoria to join Verrocchio's *David* (FIG. 21-13) there. The importance of David as a civic symbol led the Florence Cathedral building committee to invite Michelangelo to work a great block of marble left over from an earlier aborted commission into still another *David* statue for the Signoria. The colossal statue (FIG. **22-13**)—Florentines referred to it as "the Giant"—Michelangelo created from that block forever assured his reputation as an extraordinary talent. Vasari, for example, extolled the work, claiming

> without any doubt [Michelangelo's *David*] has put in the shade every other statue, ancient or modern, Greek or Roman . . . [The statue] was intended as a symbol of liberty [in front of Florence's city hall], signifying that just as David had protected his people and governed them justly, so whoever ruled Florence should vigorously defend the city and govern it with justice.[6]

Despite the traditional association of David with heroic triumph over a fearsome adversary, Michelangelo chose to represent the young biblical warrior not after his victory, with Goliath's head at his feet (as Donatello and Verrocchio had done), but before the encounter, with David sternly watching his approaching foe. *David* exhibits the characteristic representation of energy in reserve that imbues Michelangelo's later figures with the tension of a coiled spring. The anatomy of David's body plays an important part in this prelude to action. His rugged torso, sturdy limbs, and large hands and feet alert viewers to the triumph to come. Each swelling vein and tightening sinew amplifies the psychological energy of David's pose.

Michelangelo doubtless had the classical nude in mind when he conceived his *David*. Like many of his colleagues, he greatly admired Greco-Roman statues, in particular the skillful and precise rendering of heroic physique. Without strictly imitating the antique style, the Renaissance sculptor captured in his portrayal of the biblical hero the tension of Lysippan athletes (FIG. 5-65) and the psychological insight and emotionalism of Hellenistic statuary (FIGS. 5-80, 5-81, and 5-89). His *David* differs from Donatello's and Verrocchio's creations in much the same way later Hellenistic statues departed from their Classical predecessors (see Chapter 5). Michelangelo abandoned the self-contained compositions of the 15th-century *David* statues by abruptly turning the hero's head toward his gigantic adversary. This *David* is compositionally and emotionally connected to an unseen presence beyond the statue, a feature also of Hellenistic sculpture (FIG. 5-86). As early as 1501, then, Michelangelo invested his efforts in presenting towering, pent-up emotion rather than calm, ideal beauty. He transferred his own doubts, frustrations, and passions into the great figures he created or planned.

**TOMB OF JULIUS II** The formal references to classical antiquity in Michelangelo's *David* surely appealed to Julius II, who associated himself with the humanists and with Roman emperors. Thus, this sculpture and the fame that accrued to Michelangelo on its completion called the artist to the pope's attention, leading shortly thereafter to major papal commissions. The first project Julius II commissioned from Michelangelo was the pontiff's tomb, to be placed in Old Saint Peter's. The sculptor's original 1505 design called for a freestanding, two-story structure with some 28 statues. The proposed monument, of unprecedented size (compare FIG. 21-15), would have given Michelangelo the latitude to sculpt

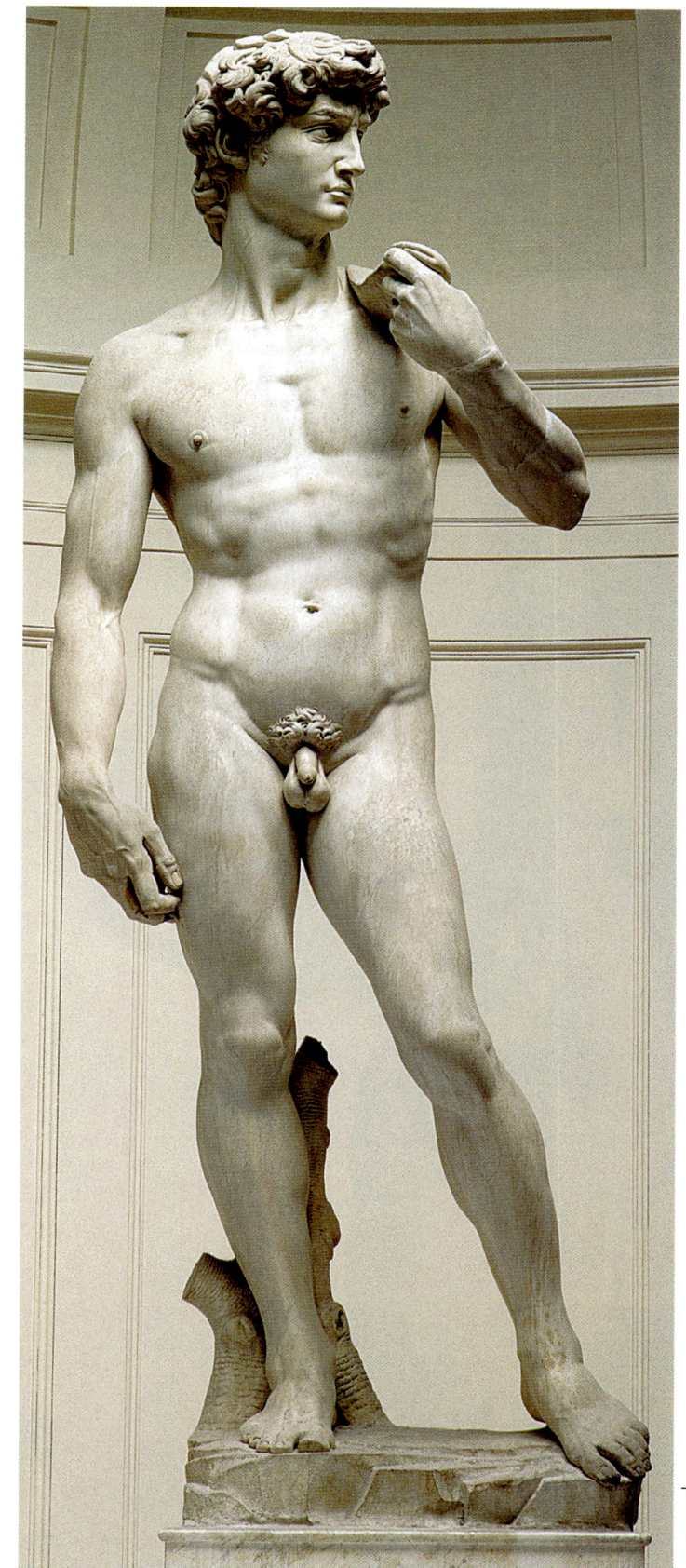

**22-13** MICHELANGELO BUONARROTI, *David*, from Piazza della Signoria, Florence, Italy, 1501–1504. Marble, 17′ high. Galleria dell'Accademia, Florence. ◼◀

In this colossal statue, Michelangelo represented David in heroic classical nudity, capturing the tension of Lysippan athletes (FIG. 5-65) and the emotionalism of Hellenistic statuary (FIGS. 5-80 and 5-81).

numerous human figures while providing Julius II with a grandiose memorial that would associate the Cinquecento pope with the first pope, Peter himself. Shortly after Michelangelo began work on this project, the pope interrupted the commission, possibly because funds had to be diverted to the rebuilding of Saint Peter's. After Julius II's death in 1513, Michelangelo reluctantly reduced the scale of the project step-by-step until, in 1542, a final contract specified a simple wall tomb with fewer than one-third of the originally planned figures. Michelangelo completed the tomb in 1545 and saw it placed in San Pietro in Vincoli (MAP 22-1), where Julius II had served as a cardinal before his accession to the papacy. Given Julius's ambitions, it is safe to say that had he seen the final design of his tomb, or known where it would eventually be located, he would have been bitterly disappointed.

The spirit of the tomb may be summed up in *Moses* (FIG. **22-14**), which Michelangelo carved between 1513 and 1515 during one of his sporadic resumptions of work on the project. Meant to be seen from below and to be balanced with seven other massive forms related to it in spirit, *Moses* in its final comparatively paltry setting does not convey the impact originally intended. Michelangelo depicted the Old Testament prophet seated, the Tablets of the Law under one arm and his hands gathering his voluminous beard. The horns on Moses's head were a convention in Christian art (based on a mistranslation of the Hebrew word for "rays") and helped Renaissance viewers identify the prophet (compare FIGS. 12-35 and 20-2). Here, as in his *David*, Michelangelo used the device of the turned head, in this case to concentrate the expression of awful wrath stirring in the prophet's mighty frame and eyes. Moses' muscles

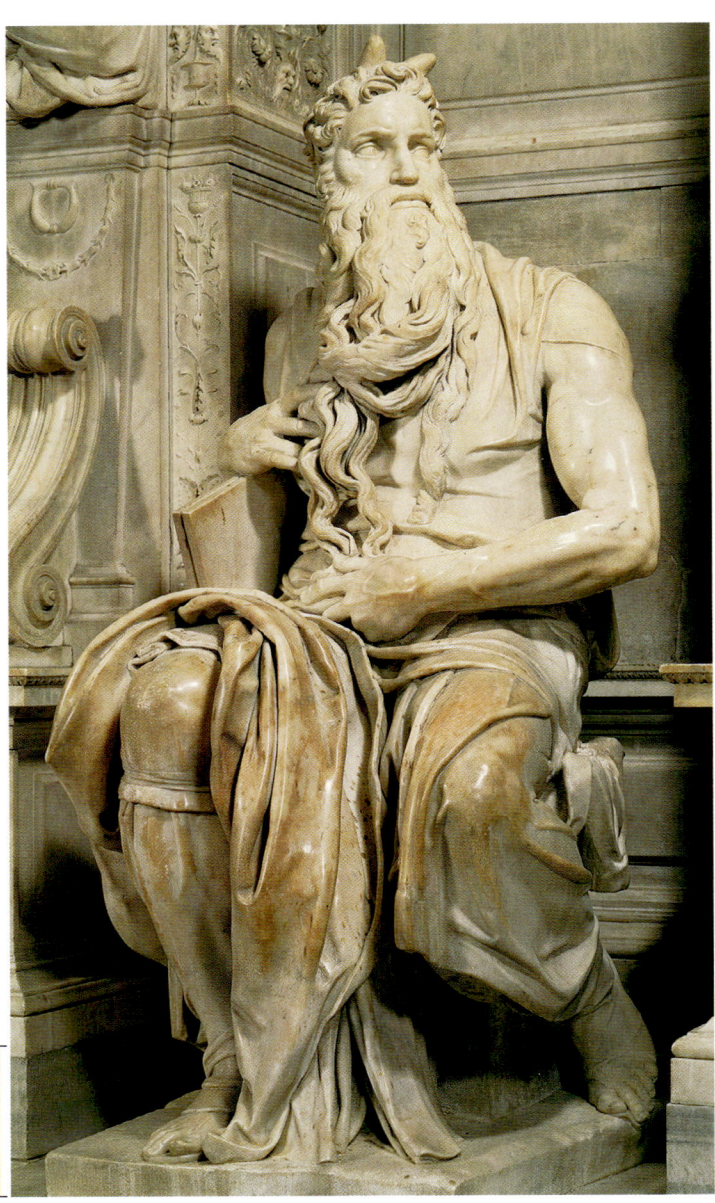

1 ft.

**22-14** MICHELANGELO BUONARROTI, *Moses*, from the tomb of Pope Julius II, Rome, Italy, ca. 1513–1515. Marble, 7′ 8½″ high. San Pietro in Vincoli, Rome. ◼◀

Not since Hellenistic times had a sculptor captured as much pent-up energy, both emotional and physical, in a seated statue as Michelangelo did in the over-life-size *Moses* he carved for Julius II's tomb.

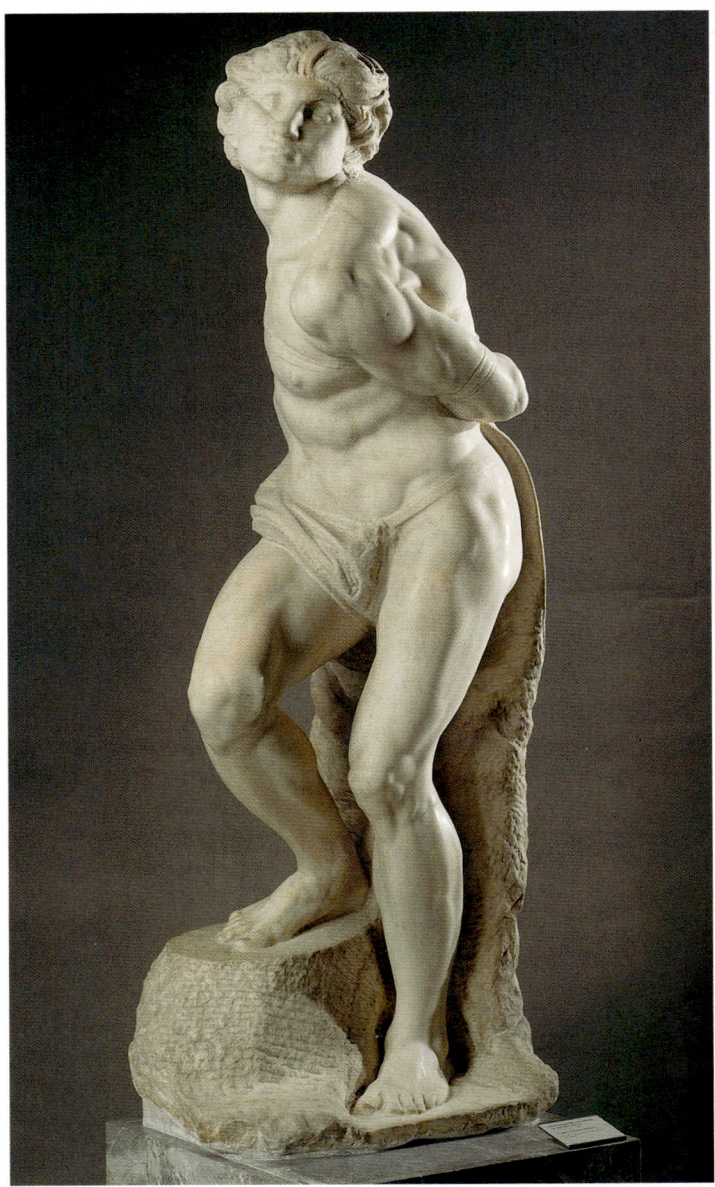

1 ft.

**22-15** MICHELANGELO BUONARROTI, *Bound Slave* (*Rebellious Slave*), from the tomb of Pope Julius II, Rome, Italy, ca. 1513–1516. Marble, 7′ 5⁄8″ high. Musée du Louvre, Paris.

For Pope Julius II's grandiose tomb, Michelangelo planned a series of statues of captives or slaves in various attitudes of revolt and exhaustion. This defiant figure exhibits a violent contrapposto.

bulge, his veins swell, and his great legs seem to begin slowly to move. Not since Hellenistic times had a sculptor captured so much pent-up energy—both emotional and physical—in a seated statue (FIGS. 5-86 and 5-89).

Michelangelo also intended to incorporate in the pope's tomb some 20 statues of captives, popularly known as slaves, in various attitudes of revolt and exhaustion. Art historians have traditionally believed *Bound Slave,* or *Rebellious Captive* (FIG. **22-15**), and the unfinished statue shown in FIG. I-16 to be two of those destined for Julius's tomb. Some scholars now doubt this attribution, and some even reject the identification of the statues as "slaves" or "captives." Whatever their identity, these statues, like Michelangelo's *David* and *Moses,* testify to the sculptor's ability to create figures embodying powerful emotional states. In *Bound Slave,* the defiant figure's

violent contrapposto is the image of frantic but impotent struggle. Michelangelo based his whole art on his conviction that whatever can be said greatly through sculpture and painting must be said through the human figure.

**TOMB OF GIULIANO DE' MEDICI** Following the death of Julius II, Michelangelo, like Raphael, went into the service of Leo X and his successor, Clement VII. These Medici popes chose not to perpetuate a predecessor's fame by permitting Michelangelo to complete Julius's tomb. Instead, they (Pope Leo X and the then-cardinal Giulio de' Medici; FIG. 22-10) commissioned him in 1519 to build a funerary chapel, the New Sacristy, attached to Brunelleschi's San Lorenzo (FIG. 21-32A) in Florence. At opposite sides of the New Sacristy stand Michelangelo's sculpted tombs of Giuliano (1478–1516), duke of Nemours (south of Paris), and Lorenzo (1492–1519), duke of Urbino, son and grandson of Lorenzo the Magnificent. Giuliano's tomb (FIG. **22-16**) is compositionally the twin of Lorenzo's. Michelangelo finished neither tomb. Scholars believe he intended to place pairs of recumbent river gods at the bottom of the sarcophagi, balancing the pairs of figures resting on the sloping sides, but Michelangelo's grand design for the tombs remains a puzzle.

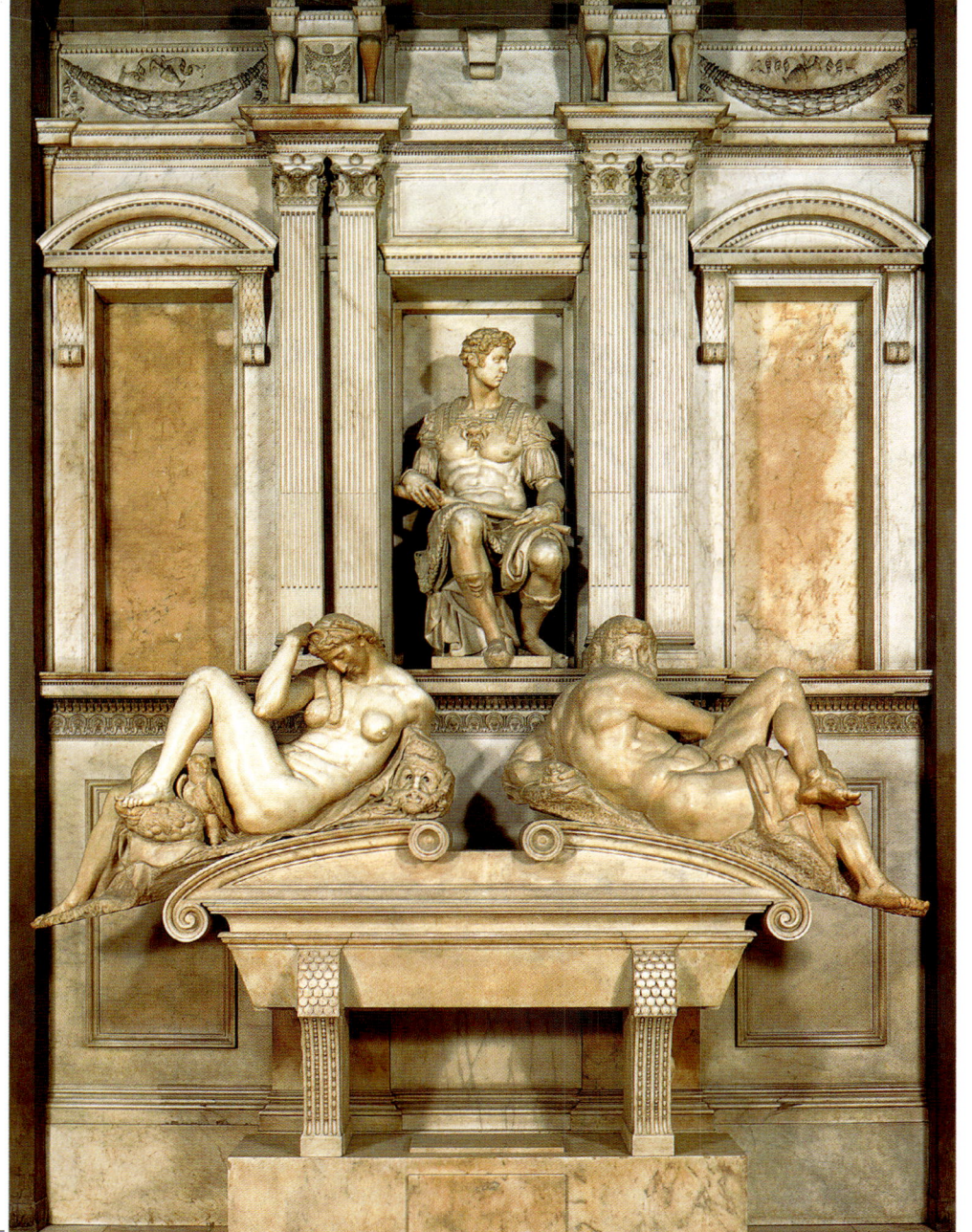

According to the traditional interpretation, the arrangement Michelangelo planned, but never completed, mirrors the soul's ascent through the levels of the Neo-Platonic universe. Neo-Platonism, the school of thought based on Plato's idealistic, spiritualistic philosophy, experienced a renewed popularity in the 16th-century humanist community. The lowest level of the tomb, which the river gods represent, would have signified the Underworld of brute matter, the source of evil. The two statues on the sarcophagi would symbolize the realm of time—the specifically human world of the cycles of dawn, day, evening, and night. Humanity's state in this world of time was one of pain and anxiety, of frustration and exhaustion. At left, the muscular female Night—Michelangelo used male models even for his female figures—and, at right, the male Day appear to be chained into

**22-16** MICHELANGELO BUONARROTI, tomb of Giuliano de' Medici, New Sacristy (Medici Chapel), San Lorenzo, Florence, Italy, 1519–1534. Marble, central figure 5' 11" high.

Michelangelo's portrait of Giuliano de' Medici in Roman armor depicts the deceased as the model of the active and decisive man. Below are the anguished, twisting figures of Night and Day.

1 ft.

never-relaxing tensions. Both exhibit the anguished twisting of the body's masses in contrary directions seen also in Michelangelo's *Bound Slave* (FIG. 22-15; compare FIG. I-16) and in his Sistine Chapel paintings (FIGS. 22-18 and 22-18A). This contortion is a staple of Michelangelo's figural art. Day, with a body the thickness of a great tree and the anatomy of Hercules (or of a reclining Greco-Roman river god that may have inspired Michelangelo's statue), strains his huge limbs against each other, his unfinished visage rising menacingly above his shoulder. Night, the symbol of rest, twists as if in troubled sleep, her posture wrenched and feverish. The artist surrounded her with an owl, poppies, and a hideous mask symbolic of nightmares. Some scholars argue, however, that the Night and Day personifications allude not to humanity's pain but to the life cycle and the passage of time leading ultimately to death.

On their respective tombs, sculptures of Lorenzo and Giuliano appear in niches at the apex of the structures. Transcending worldly existence, they represent the two ideal human types—the contemplative man (Lorenzo) and the active man (Giuliano). Giuliano (FIG. 22-16) sits clad in the armor of a Roman emperor and holds a commander's baton, his head turned alertly as if in council (he looks toward the statue of the Virgin at one end of the chapel). Across the room, Lorenzo appears wrapped in thought, his face in deep shadow. Together, they symbolize the two ways human beings might achieve union with God—through meditation or through the active life fashioned after that of Christ. In this sense, they are not individual portraits. Indeed, Michelangelo declined to sculpt likenesses of Lorenzo and Giuliano. Who, he asked, would care what they looked like in a thousand years? This attitude is consistent with Michelangelo's interests. Throughout his career he demonstrated less concern for facial features and expressions than for the overall human form. The rather generic visages of the two Medici captains of the Church attest to this view. For the artist, the contemplation of what lies beyond the corrosion of time counted more.

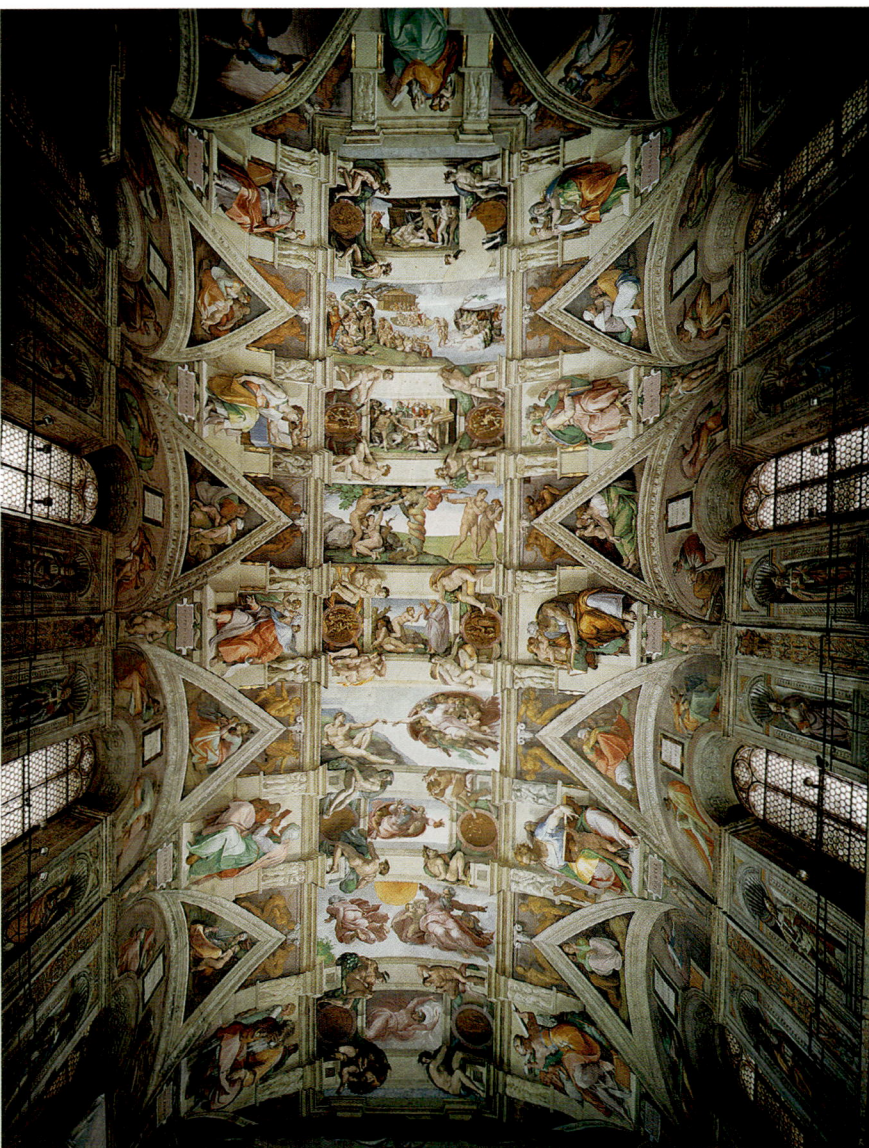

**22-17** MICHELANGELO BUONARROTI, ceiling of the Sistine Chapel, Vatican City, Rome, Italy, 1508–1512. Fresco, 128′ × 45′. ◼◄

Michelangelo labored almost four years for Pope Julius II on the frescoes for the ceiling of the Sistine Chapel. He painted more than 300 figures illustrating the creation and fall of humankind.

**SISTINE CHAPEL CEILING** When Julius II suspended work on his tomb, the pope offered the bitter Michelangelo the commission to paint the ceiling (FIG. 22-17) of the Sistine Chapel (FIG. 22-1) in 1508. The artist reluctantly assented in the hope the tomb project could be revived. Michelangelo faced enormous difficulties in painting the Sistine ceiling: its dimensions (some 5,800 square feet), its height above the pavement (almost 70 feet), and the complicated perspective problems the vault's height and curve presented, as well as his inexperience in the fresco technique. (Michelangelo had to redo the first section he completed because of faulty preparation of the intonaco; see "Fresco Painting," Chapter 14, page 408.) Yet, in less than four years, Michelangelo produced an extraordinary series of monumental frescoes incorporating his patron's agenda, Church doctrine, and his own interests. In depicting the most august and solemn themes of all, the creation, fall, and redemption of humanity—subjects most likely selected by Julius II with input from Michelangelo and Cardinal Marco Vigerio della Rovere (1446–1516)—Michelangelo spread a colossal compositional scheme across the vast surface. He succeeded in weaving together more than 300 figures in an ultimate grand drama of the human race.

A long sequence of narrative panels describing the creation, as recorded in Genesis, runs along the crown of the vault, from *God's Separation of Light and Darkness* (above the altar) to *Drunkenness of Noah* (nearest the entrance to the chapel). Thus, as viewers enter the chapel, look up, and walk toward the altar, they review, in reverse order, the history of the fall of humankind. The Hebrew prophets and ancient sibyls who foretold the coming of Christ appear seated in large thrones on both sides of the central row of scenes from Genesis, where the vault curves down. In the four corner *pendentives*, Michelangelo placed four Old Testament scenes with David, Judith, Haman, and Moses and the Brazen Serpent. Scores of lesser figures also appear. The ancestors of Christ (FIG. 22-18B) fill the triangular compartments above the windows, nude youths punctuate the corners of the central panels, and small pairs of putti in *grisaille* (monochrome painting using shades of gray to imitate sculpture)

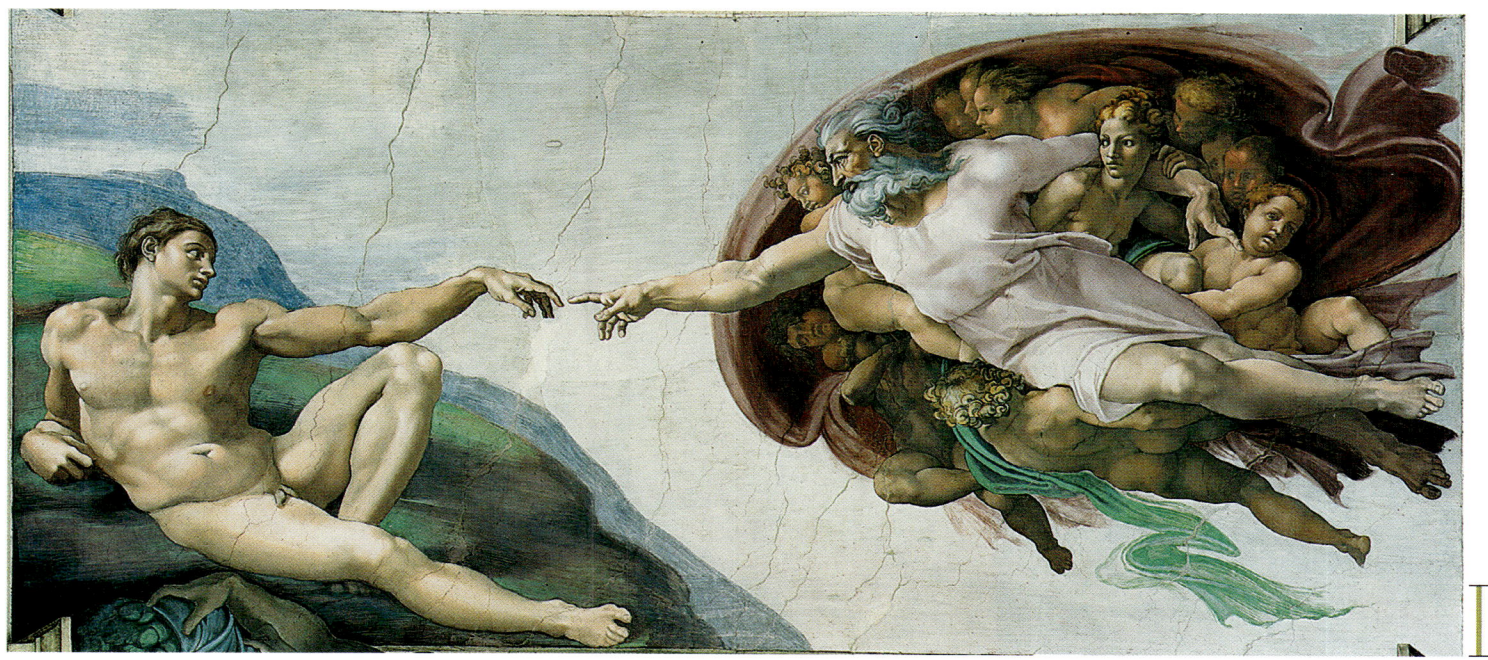

**22-18** MICHELANGELO BUONARROTI, *Creation of Adam,* detail of the ceiling of the Sistine Chapel (FIG. 22-17), Vatican City, Rome, Italy, 1511–1512. Fresco, 9′ 2″ ×18′ 8″. ◼◀

Life leaps to Adam like a spark from the extended hand of God in this fresco, which recalls the communication between gods and heroes in the classical myths Renaissance humanists admired so much.

support the painted cornice surrounding the entire central corridor. The overall conceptualization of the ceiling's design and narrative structure not only presents a sweeping chronology of Christianity but also is in keeping with Renaissance ideas about Christian history. These ideas included interest in the conflict between good and evil and between the energy of youth and the wisdom of age. The conception of the entire ceiling was astounding in itself, and the articulation of it in its thousands of details was a superhuman achievement.

Unlike Andrea Mantegna's decoration of the ceiling of the Camera Picta (FIGS. 21-48 and 21-49) in Mantua, the strongly marked unifying architectural framework in the Sistine Chapel does not construct "picture windows" framing illusions within them. Rather, the viewer focuses on figure after figure, each sharply outlined against the neutral tone of the architectural setting or the plain background of the panels.

***CREATION OF ADAM*** The two central panels of Michelangelo's ceiling represent *Creation of Adam* (FIG. **22-18**) and *Fall of*

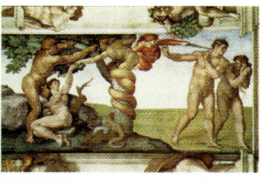

**22-18A** MICHELANGELO, *Fall of Man,* ca. 1510.

*Man* (FIG. **22-18A**). In both cases, Michelangelo rejected traditional iconographical convention in favor of bold new interpretations of the momentous events. In *Creation of Adam,* God and Adam confront each other in a primordial unformed landscape of which Adam is still a material part, heavy as earth. The Lord transcends the earth, wrapped in a billowing cloud of drapery and borne up by his powers. Life leaps to Adam like a spark from the extended and mighty hand of God. The communication between gods and heroes, so familiar in classical myth, is here concrete. This blunt depiction of the Lord as ruler of Heaven in the classical, Olympian sense indicates how easily High Renaissance thought joined classical and Christian traditions. Yet the classical trappings do not obscure the essential Christian message.

Beneath the Lord's sheltering left arm is a woman, apprehensively curious but as yet uncreated. Scholars traditionally believed she represented Eve, but many now think she is the Virgin Mary (with the Christ Child at her knee). If the second identification is correct, it suggests Michelangelo incorporated into his fresco one of the essential tenets of Christian faith—the belief that Adam's original sin eventually led to the sacrifice of Christ, which in turn made possible the redemption of all humankind (see "Jewish Subjects in Christian Art," Chapter 8, page 238).

As God reaches out to Adam, the viewer's eye follows the motion from right to left, but Adam's extended left arm leads the eye back to the right, along the Lord's right arm, shoulders, and left arm to his left forefinger, which points to the Christ Child's face. The focal point of this right-to-left-to-right movement—the fingertips of Adam and the Lord—is dramatically off-center. Michelangelo replaced the straight architectural axes found in Leonardo's compositions with curves and diagonals. For example, the bodies of the two great figures are complementary—the concave body of Adam fitting the convex body and billowing "cloak" of God. Thus, motion directs not only the figures but also the whole composition. The reclining positions of the figures, the heavy musculature, and the twisting poses are all intrinsic parts of Michelangelo's style.

The photographs of the Sistine Chapel reproduced here record the appearance of Michelangelo's frescoes after the completion of a 12-year cleaning project (1977–1989). The painstaking restoration (FIG. **22-18B**) elicited considerable controversy because it revealed vivid colors that initially shocked art historians, producing accusations the restorers were destroying Michelangelo's masterpieces. That reaction, however, was largely attributable to

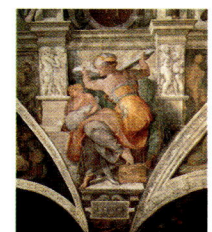

**22-18B** Sistine Chapel restoration, 1977–1989.

the fact that for centuries no one had ever seen Michelangelo's frescoes except covered with soot and grime.

High and Late Renaissance **615**

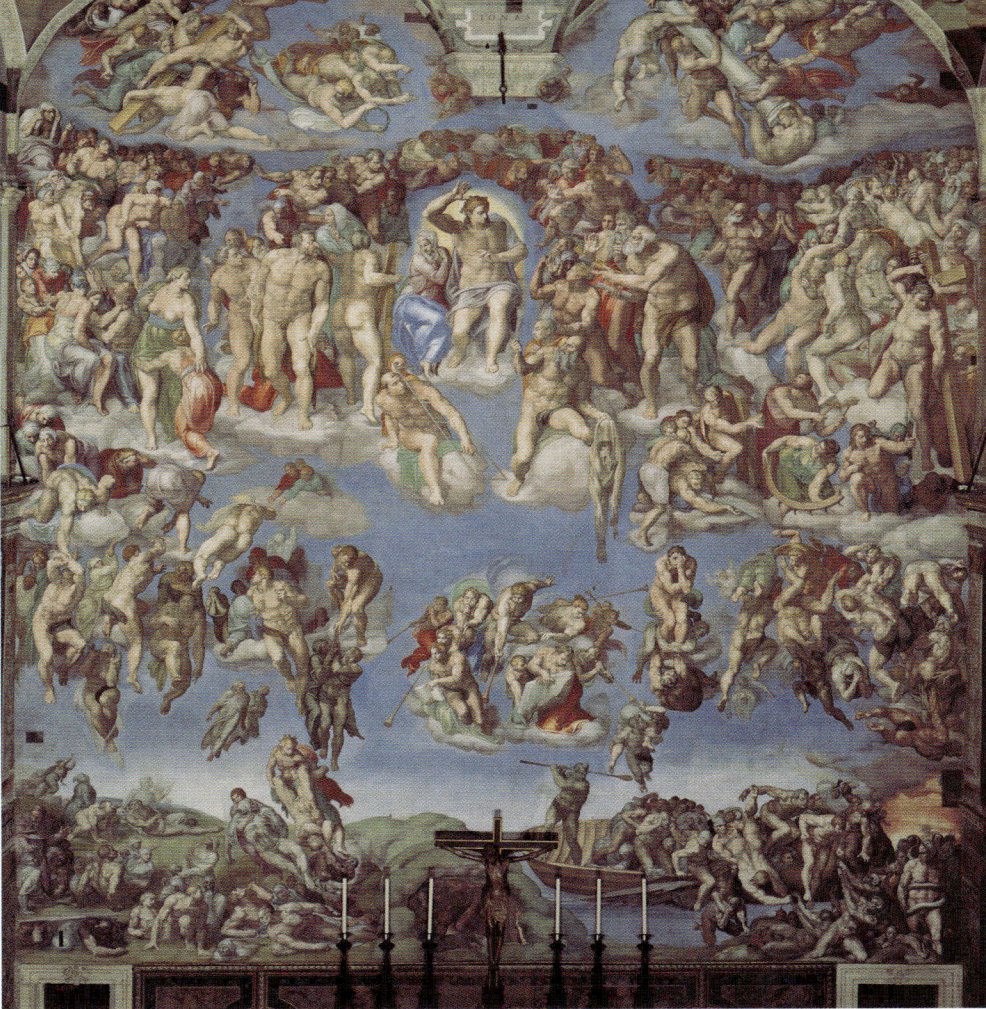

**22-19** MICHELANGELO BUONARROTI, *Last Judgment,* altar wall of the Sistine Chapel, Vatican City, Rome, Italy, 1536–1541. Fresco, 48′ × 44′. ◼◀

Michelangelo completed his fresco cycle in the Sistine Chapel with this terrifying vision of the fate awaiting sinners. Near the center, he placed his own portrait on the flayed skin Saint Bartholomew holds.

10 ft.

## THE COUNTER-REFORMATION

Paul III (r. 1534–1549) succeeded Clement VII as pope in 1534 at a time of widespread dissatisfaction with the leadership and policies of the Roman Catholic Church. Led by clerics such as Martin Luther and John Calvin in the Holy Roman Empire (see Chapter 23), early-16th-century reformers directly challenged papal authority, especially regarding secular issues. Disgruntled Catholics voiced concerns about the sale of *indulgences* (pardons for sins, reducing the time a soul spent in purgatory), nepotism (the appointment of relatives to important positions), and high Church officials pursuing personal wealth. This Reformation movement resulted in the establishment of Protestantism, with sects such as Lutheranism and Calvinism. Central to Protestantism was a belief in personal faith rather than adherence to decreed Church practices and doctrines. Because the Protestants believed the only true religious relationship was the personal relationship between an individual and God, they were, in essence, eliminating the need for Church intercession, which is central to Catholicism.

The Catholic Church, in response, mounted a full-fledged campaign to counteract the defection of its members to Protestantism. Led by Paul III, this response, the Counter-Reformation, consisted of numerous initiatives. The Council of Trent, which met intermittently from 1545 through 1563, was a major component of this effort. Composed of cardinals, archbishops, bishops, abbots, and theologians, the Council of Trent dealt with issues of Church doctrine, including many the Protestants contested. Many papal commissions during this period can be viewed as an integral part of the Counter-Reformation effort. Popes long had been aware of the power of visual imagery to construct and reinforce ideological claims, and 16th-century popes exploited this capability (see "Religious Art in Counter-Reformation Italy," page 617).

*LAST JUDGMENT* Among Paul III's first papal commissions was an enormous (48 feet tall) fresco for the Sistine Chapel. Michelangelo agreed to paint *Last Judgment* (FIG. **22-19**) on the chapel's altar (west) wall. Here, the artist depicted Christ as the stern judge of the world—a giant who raises his mighty right arm in a gesture of damnation so broad and universal as to suggest he will destroy all creation. The choirs of Heaven surrounding him pulse with anxiety and awe. Crowded into the space below are trumpeting angels, the ascending figures of the just, and the downward-hurtling figures of the damned. On the left, the dead awake and assume flesh. On the right, demons, whose gargoyle masks and burning eyes revive the demons of Romanesque tympana (FIG. 12-1), torment the damned.

Michelangelo's terrifying vision of the fate awaiting sinners goes far beyond even Signorelli's gruesome images (FIG. 21-42). Martyrs who suffered especially agonizing deaths crouch below the judge. One of them, Saint Bartholomew, who was skinned alive, holds the flaying knife and the skin, its face a grotesque self-portrait of Michelangelo. The figures are huge and violently twisted, with small heads and contorted features. Yet while this immense fresco impresses on viewers Christ's wrath on judgment day, it also holds out hope. A group of saved souls—the elect—crowd around Christ, and on the far right appears a figure with a cross, most likely the Good Thief (crucified with Christ) or a saint martyred by crucifixion, such as Saint Andrew.

# Religious Art in Counter-Reformation Italy

Both Catholics and Protestants took seriously the role of devotional imagery in religious life. However, their views differed dramatically. Catholics deemed art valuable for cultivating piety. Protestants believed religious imagery encouraged idolatry and distracted the faithful from the goal of developing a personal relationship with God (see Chapter 23). As part of the Counter-Reformation effort, Pope Paul III convened the Council of Trent in 1545 to review controversial Church doctrines. At its conclusion in 1563, the Council issued the following edict:

> The holy council commands all bishops and others who hold the office of teaching and have charge of the *cura animarum* [literally, "cure of souls"—the responsibility of laboring for the salvation of souls], that in accordance with the usage of the Catholic and Apostolic Church, received from the primitive times of the Christian religion, and with the unanimous teaching of the holy Fathers and the decrees of sacred councils, they above all instruct the faithful diligently in matters relating to intercession and invocation of the saints, the veneration of relics, and the legitimate use of images. . . . Moreover, that the images of Christ, of the Virgin Mother of God, and of the other saints are to be placed and retained especially in the churches, and that due honor and veneration is to be given them; . . . because the honor which is shown them is referred to the prototypes which they represent, so that by means of the images which we kiss and before which we uncover the head and prostrate

ourselves, we adore Christ and venerate the saints whose likeness they bear. That is what was defined by the decrees of the councils, especially of the Second Council of Nicaea, against the opponents of images.

Moreover, let the bishops diligently teach that by means of the stories of the mysteries of our redemption portrayed in paintings and other representations the people are instructed and confirmed in the articles of faith, which ought to be borne in mind and constantly reflected upon; also that great profit is derived from all holy images, not only because the people are thereby reminded of the benefits and gifts bestowed on them by Christ, but also because through the saints the miracles of God and salutary examples are set before the eyes of the faithful, so that they may give God thanks for those things, may fashion their own life and conduct in imitation of the saints and be moved to adore and love God and cultivate piety. . . . That these things may be the more faithfully observed, the holy council decrees that no one is permitted to erect or cause to be erected in any place or church, howsoever exempt, any unusual image unless it has been approved by the bishop.*

*Canons and Decrees of the Council of Trent,* December 3–4, 1563. Quoted in Robert Klein and Henri Zerner, *Italian Art 1500–1600: Sources and Documents* (Evanston, Ill.: Northwestern University Press, 1966), 120–121.

---

**UNFINISHED *PIETÀ*** Six years after completing the *Last Judgment* fresco and nearly 50 years after carving the *Pietà* (FIG. 22-12) for the burial chapel of Cardinal Jean de Bilhères Lagraulas, Michelangelo, already in his 70s, began work on another *Pietà* (FIG. **22-20**), this one destined for his own tomb in Santa Maria Maggiore in Rome. For this group, the aged master set for himself an unprecedented technical challenge—to surpass the sculptors of the ancient *Laocoön* (FIG. 5-89) and carve four life-size figures from a single marble block. He did not succeed. Christ's now-missing left leg became detached, perhaps because of a flaw in the marble, and in 1555 Michelangelo abandoned the project and began to smash the statue. His assistants intervened, and he eventually permitted one of them, Tiberio Calcagni (1532–1565), to repair some of the damage and finish the work in part.

In composition and tone, this later *Pietà*—actually a *Deposition* group (see "The Life of Jesus in Art," Chapter 8, pages 240–241, or pages xxx–xxxi in Volume II)—stands in stark contrast to the work of Michelangelo's youth. The composition is vertical with three figures—the Virgin, Mary Magdalene, and Nicodemus—supporting the lifeless body of Christ, the slumping form of which may have been inspired by a famous Roman copy of Myron's *Discus*

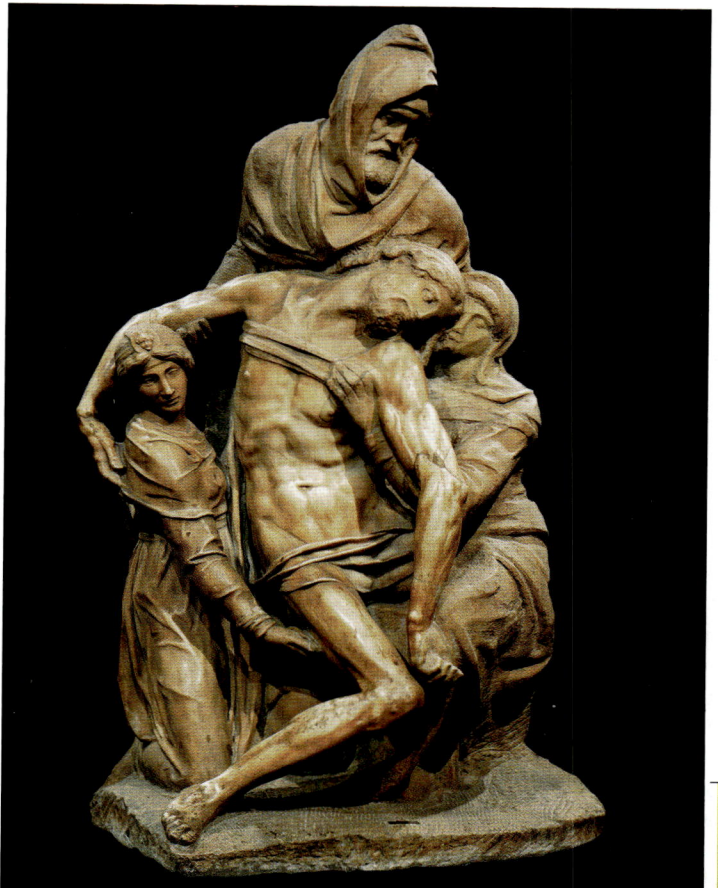

**22-20** MICHELANGELO BUONARROTI, *Pietà,* ca. 1547–1555. Marble, 7′ 8″ high. Museo dell'Opera del Duomo, Florence.

Left unfinished, this *Pietà,* begun when Michelangelo was in his 70s and intended for his own tomb, includes a self-portrait of the sculptor as Nicodemus supporting the lifeless body of the Savior.

1 ft.

*Thrower* (FIG. 5-39). The Virgin is now a subsidiary figure, half hidden by her son, whose left leg originally rested on her left thigh, a position suggesting sexual union, which elicited harsh criticism— a possible reason Michelangelo smashed the statue. The undersized Mary Magdalene is in a kneeling position, and her hand does not make contact with Christ's flesh, underscoring the sacred nature of the Savior's body. Forming the apex of the composition is the hooded Nicodemus, a self-portrait of Michelangelo. This late work is therefore very personal in nature. The sculptor placed himself in direct contact with Christ, without the intercession of priests or saints, a heretical concept during the Counter-Reformation and another possible explanation why Michelangelo never completed the statue.

## Architecture

Michelangelo was an accomplished architect as well as a sculptor and painter, and his Vatican commissions included designing a new church to replace the basilica Constantine erected over the site of Saint Peter's burial place (Old Saint Peter's, FIG. 8-9). By the 15th century, it was obvious the ancient timber-roofed church was insufficient for the needs and aspirations of the Renaissance papacy. Rebuilding the fourth-century basilica would occupy some of the leading architects of Italy for more than a century.

**BRAMANTE** The first in the distinguished line of architects of the new Saint Peter's was DONATO D'ANGELO BRAMANTE (1444–1514). Born in Urbino and trained as a painter (perhaps by Piero della Francesca), Bramante went to Milan in 1481 and, as Leonardo did, stayed there until the French arrived in 1499. In Milan, he abandoned painting to become his generation's most renowned architect. Under the influence of Filippo Brunelleschi, Leon Battista Alberti, and perhaps Leonardo, all of whom strongly favored the art and architecture of classical antiquity, Bramante developed the High Renaissance form of the central-plan church.

**TEMPIETTO** The architectural style Bramante championed was, consistent with the humanistic values of the day, based on ancient Roman models. Bramante's first major work in the classical mode was the small architectural gem known as the Tempietto (FIG. **22-21**) on the Janiculum hill overlooking the Vatican. The building received its name because, to contemporaries, it had the look of a small ancient temple. "Little Temple" is, in fact, a perfect nickname for the structure, because the round temples of Roman Italy (FIG. 7-4) directly inspired Bramante's design. King Ferdinand (r. 1479–1516) and Queen Isabella of Spain commissioned the Tempietto to mark the presumed location of Saint Peter's crucifixion. Bramante undertook the project in 1502, but construction may not have begun until the end of the decade. Today the Tempietto stands inside the rectangular cloister of the church of San Pietro in Montorio, but Bramante planned, although never executed, a circular colonnaded courtyard to frame the "temple." His intent was to coordinate the Tempietto and its surrounding portico by aligning the columns of the two structures.

The Tempietto's design is severely rational with its sober circular *stylobate* (stepped temple platform) and the austere *Tuscan* style of the colonnade. Bramante achieved a wonderful balance and harmony in the relationship of the parts (dome, drum, and base) to one another and to the whole. Conceived as a tall domed cylinder projecting from the lower, wider cylinder of its colonnade, this small building incorporates all the qualities of a sculptured monument. Bramante's sculptural eye is most evident in the rhythmical play of light and shadow around the columns and balustrade and across the deep-set rectangular windows alternating with shallow shell-capped niches in the *cella* (central room of a temple), walls, and drum. Although the Tempietto, superficially at least, may resemble a Greek *tholos* (a circular shrine; FIG. 5-72), and although antique models provided the inspiration for all its details, the combination of parts and details was new and original. (Classical tholoi, for instance, had neither drum nor balustrade.)

**22-21** DONATO D'ANGELO BRAMANTE, Tempietto, San Pietro in Montorio, Rome, Italy, begun 1502.

Contemporaries celebrated Bramante as the first architect to revive the classical style. Roman temples (FIG. 7-4) inspired his "little temple," but Bramante combined the classical parts in new ways.

One of the main differences between the Early and High Renaissance styles of architecture is the former's emphasis on detailing flat wall surfaces versus the latter's sculptural handling of architectural masses. Bramante's Tempietto initiated the High Renaissance era in architecture. Andrea Palladio, a brilliant theorist as well as a major later 16th-century architect (FIGS. 22-28 to 22-31), included the Tempietto in his survey of ancient temples because Bramante was "the first to bring back to light the good and beautiful architecture that from antiquity to that time had been hidden."[7] Round in plan and elevated on a base that isolates it from its surroundings, the Tempietto conforms to Alberti's and Palladio's strictest demands for an ideal church.

## NEW SAINT PETER'S

As noted, Bramante was the architect Julius II selected to design a replacement for the Constantinian basilican church of Old Saint Peter's (FIG. 8-9). The earlier building had fallen into considerable disrepair and, in any event, did not suit this ambitious pope's taste for the colossal. Julius wanted to gain control over all Italy and to make the Rome of the popes the equal of (if not more splendid than) the Rome of the caesars. He intended the new building to serve, as did Constantine's church, as a *martyrium* to mark the apostle's grave, but the pope also hoped to install his own tomb (FIGS. 22-14 and 22-15) in the new Saint Peter's.

Bramante's ambitious design (FIG. 22-22) for the new church consisted of a cross with arms of equal length, each terminating in an apse. A large dome would have covered the crossing, and smaller domes over subsidiary chapels would have capped the diagonal axes of the roughly square plan. Bramante's design also called for a boldly sculptural treatment of the walls and piers under the dome. The organization of the interior space was complex in the extreme:

nine interlocking crosses, five of them supporting domes. The scale of Bramante's Saint Peter's was titanic. The architect boasted he would place the dome of the Pantheon (FIGS. 7-49 to 7-51) over the Basilica Nova (Basilica of Constantine; FIG. 7-78).

A commemorative medal (FIG. 22-23) by CRISTOFORO FOPPA CARADOSSO (ca. 1452–1526) shows how Bramante planned to accomplish that feat. As in the Pantheon, Saint Peter's dome would be hemispherical, but Bramante broke up the massive unity of the ancient temple by adding two towers and a medley of domes and porticos. In light of Julius II's interest in the Roman Empire, using the Pantheon as a model was entirely appropriate. That Bramante's design for the new Saint Peter's appeared on a commemorative medal is in itself significant. Such medals proliferated in the 15th century, reviving the ancient Roman practice of placing images of important imperial building projects on the reverse side of coins. Roman coins also bore on the fronts portraits of the emperors who commissioned the buildings. Julius II appears on the front of the Caradosso medal.

## MICHELANGELO, SAINT PETER'S

During Bramante's lifetime, construction of Saint Peter's did not advance beyond the erection of the crossing piers and the lower choir walls. After his death, the work passed from one architect to another and, in 1546, to Michelangelo. With the Church facing challenges to its supremacy, Pope Paul III surely felt a sense of urgency about the completion of this project. Michelangelo's work on Saint Peter's became a long-term show of dedication, thankless and without pay. Among Michelangelo's difficulties was his struggle to preserve and carry through Bramante's original plan (FIG. 22-22), which he praised and chose to retain as the basis for his own

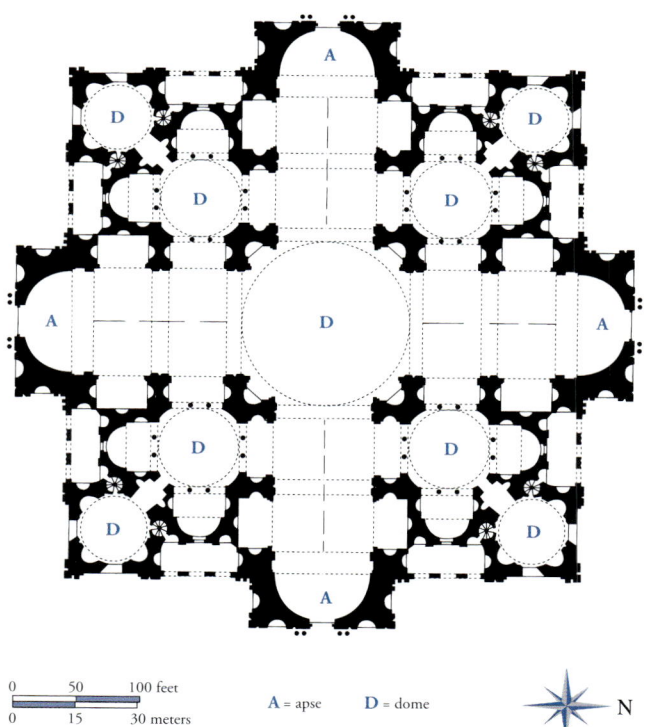

**22-22** DONATO D'ANGELO BRAMANTE, plan for Saint Peter's, Vatican City, Rome, Italy, 1505.

Bramante proposed to replace the Constantinian basilica of Saint Peter's (FIG. 8-9) with a central-plan church featuring a cross with arms of equal length, each of which terminated in an apse.

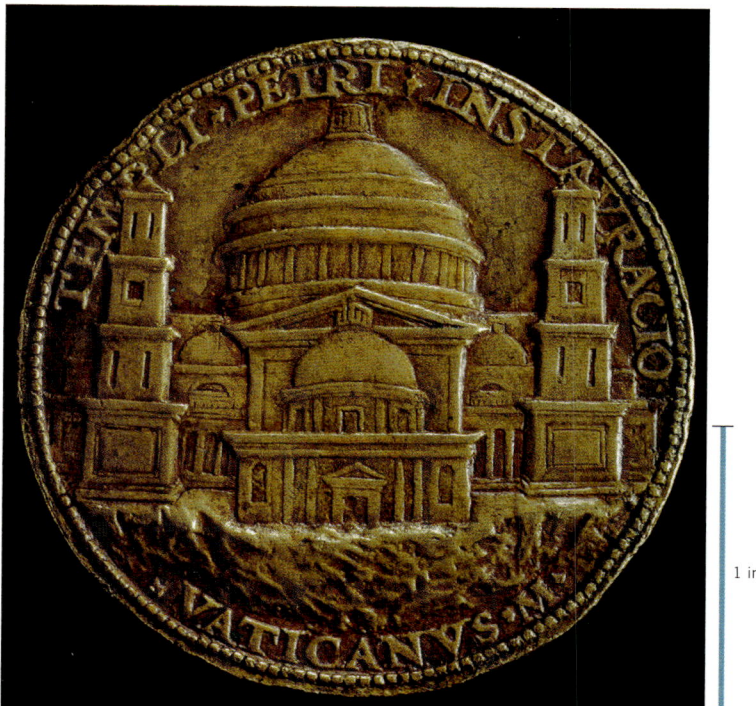

1 in.

**22-23** CRISTOFORO FOPPA CARADOSSO, reverse side of a medal showing Bramante's design for Saint Peter's, 1506. Bronze, $2\frac{1}{4}''$ diameter. British Museum, London.

Bramante's unexecuted 1506 design for Saint Peter's called for a large dome over the crossing, smaller domes over the subsidiary chapels, and a boldly sculptural treatment of the walls and piers.

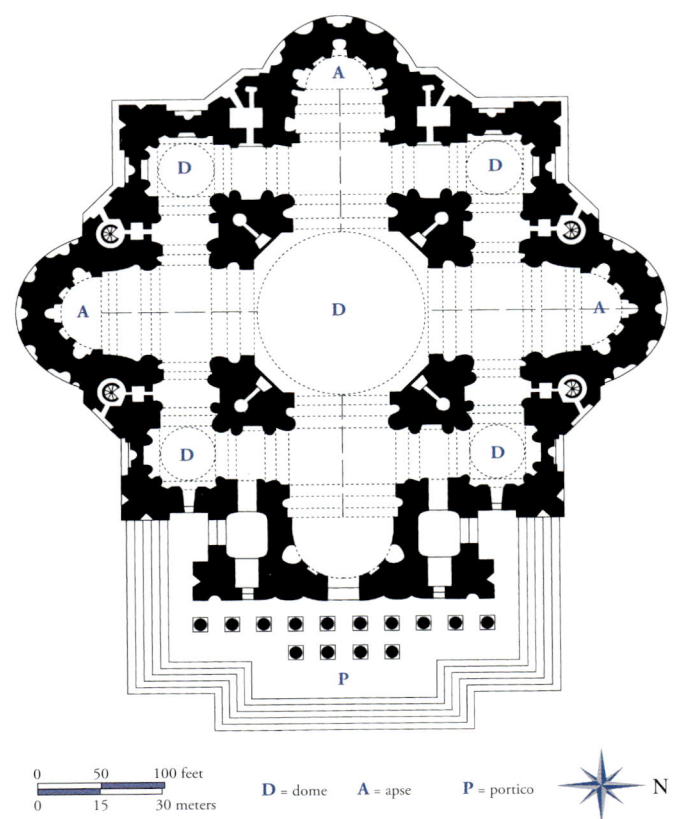

**22-24** MICHELANGELO BUONARROTI, plan for Saint Peter's, Vatican City, Rome, Italy, 1546.

In his modification of Bramante's plan (FIG. 22-22), Michelangelo reduced the central component from a number of interlocking crosses to a compact domed Greek cross inscribed in a square.

0  50  100 feet
0  15  30 meters
**D** = dome  **A** = apse  **P** = portico  **N**

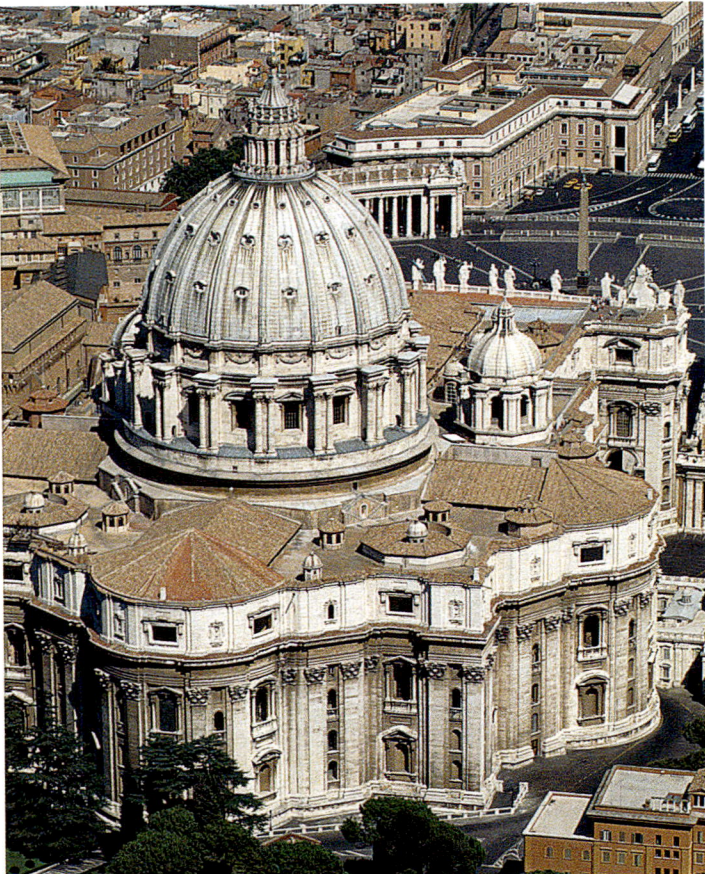

**22-25** MICHELANGELO BUONARROTI, Saint Peter's (looking northeast), Vatican City, Rome, Italy, 1546–1564. Dome completed by GIACOMO DELLA PORTA, 1590.

The west end of Saint Peter's offers the best view of Michelangelo's intentions. The giant pilasters of his colossal order march around the undulating wall surfaces of the central-plan building.

design (FIG. **22-24**). Michelangelo shared Bramante's conviction that a central plan was the ideal form for a church. Always a sculptor at heart, Michelangelo carried his obsession with human form over to architecture and reasoned that buildings should follow the form of the human body. This meant organizing their units symmetrically around a central axis, as the arms relate to the body or the eyes to the nose. "For it is an established fact," he wrote, "that the members of architecture resemble the members of man. Whoever neither has been nor is a master at figures, and especially at anatomy, cannot really understand architecture."[8]

In his modification of Bramante's plan, Michelangelo reduced the central component from a number of interlocking crosses to a compact domed *Greek cross* inscribed in a square and fronted with a double-columned portico. Without destroying the centralizing features of Bramante's plan, Michelangelo, with a few strokes of the pen, converted its crystalline complexity into massive, cohesive unity. His treatment of the building's exterior further reveals his interest in creating a unified and cohesive design. Because of later changes to the front of the church, the west (apse) end (FIG. **22-25**) offers the best view of Michelangelo's style and intention. His design incorporated the colossal order, the two-story pilasters first seen in more reserved fashion in Alberti's Mantuan church of Sant'Andrea (FIG. 21-45). The giant pilasters seem to march around the undulating wall surfaces, confining the movement without interrupting it. The architectural sculpturing here extends up from the ground through the attic stories and into the drum and dome, unifying the whole building from base to summit.

The domed west end—as majestic as it is today and as influential as it has been on architecture throughout the centuries—is not quite as Michelangelo intended it. Originally, he had planned a dome with an ogival section, like the one Brunelleschi designed for Florence Cathedral (FIGS. 14-18 and 21-30A). But in his final version, he decided on a hemispherical dome to temper the verticality of the design of the lower stories and to establish a balance between dynamic and static elements. However, when Giacomo della Porta executed the dome (FIGS. 22-25 and 24-4) after Michelangelo's death, he restored the earlier high design, ignoring Michelangelo's later version. Giacomo's reasons were probably the same ones that had impelled Brunelleschi to use an ogival section for the Florentine dome—greater stability and ease of construction. The result is the dome seems to rise from its base, rather than rest firmly on it— an effect Michelangelo might not have approved.

**PALAZZO FARNESE** Another architectural project Michelangelo took over at the request of Paul III was the construction of the lavish private palace the pope had commissioned when he was still Cardinal Alessandro Farnese. The future pope had selected ANTONIO DA SANGALLO THE YOUNGER (1483–1546) to design the Palazzo Farnese (FIG. **22-26**) in Rome. (At Antonio's death in 1546, Michelangelo assumed control of the building's completion, while also overseeing the reorganization of the Capitoline Hill

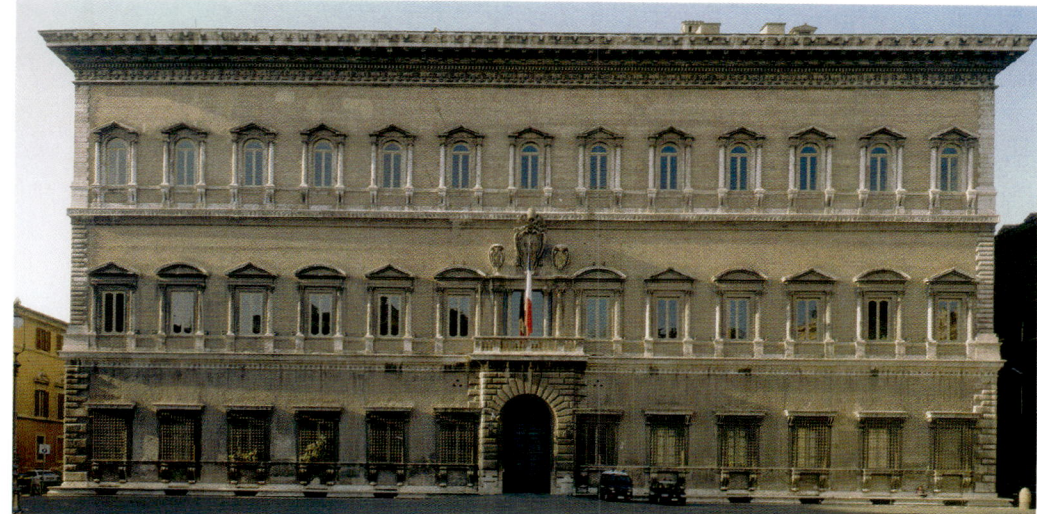

**22-26** Antonio da Sangallo the Younger, Palazzo Farnese (looking southeast), Rome, Italy, 1517–1546; completed by Michelangelo Buonarroti, 1546–1550.

Paul III's construction of a lavish private palace in Rome reflects his ambitions for his papacy. The facade features a rusticated central doorway and alternating triangular and segmental pediments.

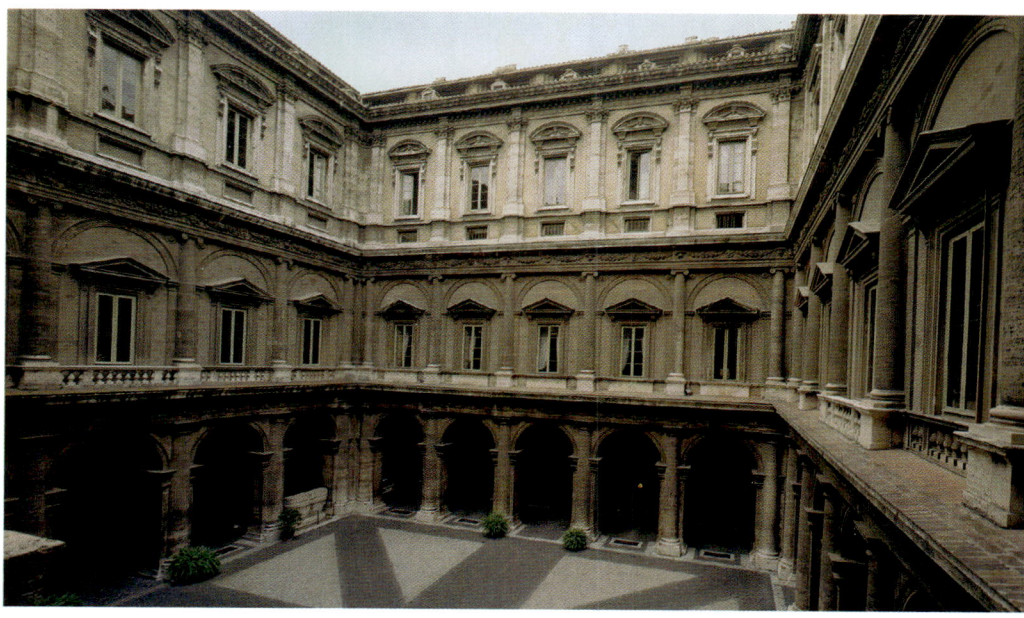

**22-27** Antonio da Sangallo the Younger, courtyard of the Palazzo Farnese, Rome, Italy, ca. 1517–1546. Third story and attic by Michelangelo Buonarroti, 1546–1550.

The interior courtyard of the Palazzo Farnese set the standard for later Italian palaces. It fully expresses the order, regularity, simplicity, and dignity of the High Renaissance style in architecture.

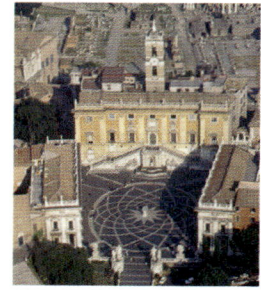

**22-26A** Michelangelo, Campidoglio, Rome, 1538–1564.

[FIG. **22-26A**] for the pope.) Antonio, the youngest of a family of architects, went to Rome around 1503 and became Bramante's draftsman and assistant. He is the perfect example of the professional architect. Indeed, his family constituted an architectural firm, often planning and drafting for other architects.

The broad, majestic front of the Palazzo Farnese asserts to the public the exalted station of a great family. It is significant that Paul chose to enlarge greatly the original rather modest palace to its present form after his accession to the papacy in 1534, reflecting his ambitions both for his family and for the papacy. Facing a spacious paved square, the facade is the very essence of princely dignity in architecture. The *quoins* (rusticated building corners) and cornice firmly anchor the rectangle of the smooth front, and lines of windows (the central row with alternating triangular and *segmental* [curved] pediments, in Bramante's fashion) mark a majestic march across it. The window frames are not flush with the wall, as in the Palazzo Medici-Riccardi (FIG. 21-37), but project from its surface, so instead of being a flat, thin plane, the facade is a spatially active three-dimensional mass. The rusticated doorway and second-story balcony, surmounted by the Farnese coat of arms, emphasize the central axis and bring the design's horizontal and vertical forces into harmony. This centralizing feature, absent from the palaces of Michelozzo (FIG. 21-37) and Alberti (FIG. 21-39), is the external opening of a central corridor axis running through the entire building and continuing in the garden beyond. Around this axis, Sangallo arranged the rooms with strict regularity.

The interior courtyard (FIG. **22-27**) displays stately column-framed arches on the first two levels, as in the Colosseum (FIG. 7-37). On the third level, Michelangelo incorporated his sophisticated variation on that theme (based in part on the Colosseum's fourth-story Corinthian pilasters), with overlapping pilasters replacing the weighty columns of Sangallo's design. The Palazzo Farnese set the standard for Italian Renaissance palaces and fully expresses the classical order, regularity, simplicity, and dignity of the High Renaissance.

High and Late Renaissance    **621**

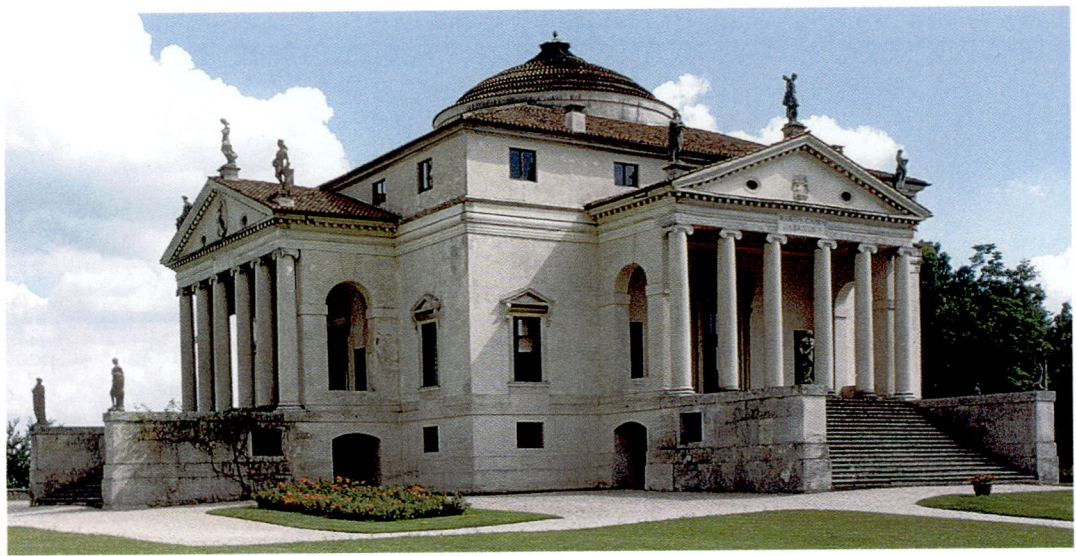

22-28 ANDREA PALLADIO, Villa Rotonda (formerly Villa Capra; looking south), near Vicenza, Italy, ca. 1550–1570.

The Villa Rotonda has four identical facades, each one resembling a Roman temple with a columnar porch. In the center is a great dome-covered rotunda modeled on the Pantheon (FIG. 7-49).

**VENICE** For centuries a major Mediterranean port, Venice served as the gateway to the Orient. After reaching the height of its commercial and political power during the 15th century, the city saw its fortunes decline in the 16th century. Even so, Venice and the Papal States were the only Italian sovereignties to retain their independence during the century of strife. Either France or Spain dominated all others. Although the discoveries in the New World and the economic shift from Italy to areas such as the Netherlands were largely responsible for the decline of Venice, even more immediate and pressing events drained its wealth and power. After their conquest of Constantinople (see Chapters 9 and 10), the Turks began to vie with the Venetians for control of the eastern Mediterranean. The Ottoman Empire evolved into a constant threat to Venice. Early in the century, the European powers of the League of Cambrai also attacked the Italian port city. Formed and led by Pope Julius II, who coveted Venetian holdings on Italy's mainland, the league included Spain, France, and the Holy Roman Empire, in addition to the Papal States. Despite these challenges, Venice developed a flourishing, independent, and influential school of artists.

**ANDREA PALLADIO** The chief architect of the Venetian Republic from 1570 until his death a decade later was Andrea di Pietro of Padua, known as ANDREA PALLADIO (1508–1580). (The surname derives from Pallas Athena, Greek goddess of wisdom, an appropriate reference for an architect schooled in the classical tradition of Alberti and Bramante.) Palladio began his career as a stonemason and decorative sculptor in Vicenza. At age 30, however, he turned to architecture, the ancient literature on architecture, engineering, topography, and military science. In order to study the ancient buildings firsthand, Palladio made several trips to Rome. In 1556, he illustrated Daniele Barbaro's edition of Vitruvius's *De architectura* and later wrote his own treatise on architecture, *I quattro libri dell'architettura* (*The Four Books of Architecture*), originally published in 1570. That work had wide-ranging influence on succeeding generations of architects throughout Europe. Palladio's influence outside Italy, most significantly in England and in colonial America (see Chapter 26), was stronger and more lasting than any other architect's.

Palladio accrued his significant reputation from his many designs for villas, built on the Venetian mainland. Nineteen still stand, and they especially influenced later architects. The same spirit that prompted the ancient Romans to build villas in the countryside

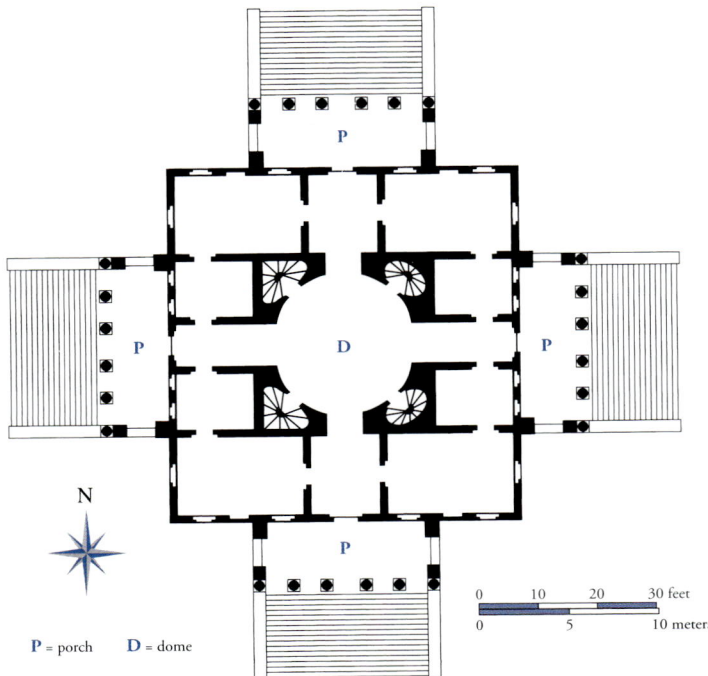

22-29 ANDREA PALLADIO, plan of the Villa Rotonda (formerly Villa Capra), near Vicenza, Italy, ca. 1550–1570.

Andrea Palladio published an influential treatise on architecture in 1570. Consistent with his design theories, all parts of the Villa Rotonda relate to one another in terms of mathematical ratios.

motivated a similar villa-building boom in 16th-century Venice, which, with its very limited space, was highly congested. But a longing for the countryside was not the only motive. Declining fortunes prompted the Venetians to develop their mainland possessions with new land investment and reclamation projects. Citizens who could afford to do so set themselves up as aristocratic farmers and developed swamps into productive agricultural land. The villas were thus aristocratic farms surrounded by service outbuildings (like the much later American plantations, which emulated many aspects of Palladio's architectural style). Palladio generally arranged the outbuildings in long, low wings branching out from the main building and enclosing a large rectangular court area.

**VILLA ROTONDA** Palladio's most famous villa, Villa Rotonda (FIG. 22-28), near Vicenza, is exceptional because the architect did not build it for an aspiring gentleman farmer but for a retired monsignor who wanted a villa for social events. Palladio planned and designed Villa Rotonda, located on a hilltop, as a kind of *belvedere* (literally "beautiful view"; in architecture, a structure with a view of the countryside or the sea), without the usual wings of secondary buildings. It has a central plan (FIG. 22-29) featuring four identical facades with projecting porches, each of which resembles a Roman Ionic temple. In placing a traditional temple porch in front of a dome-covered unit, Palladio doubtless had the Pantheon (FIG. 7-49) in mind. But, as Bramante did in his Tempietto (FIG. 22-21), Palladio transformed his model into a new design without parallel in antiquity. Each of the villa's four porches is a platform for enjoying a different view of the surrounding landscape. In this design, the central dome-covered rotunda logically functions as a circular reception area from which visitors may turn in any direction for the preferred view. The result is a building with functional parts systematically related to one another in terms of calculated mathematical relationships. Villa Rotonda embodies all the qualities of self-sufficiency and formal completeness most Renaissance architects sought.

**SAN GIORGIO MAGGIORE** One of the most dramatically placed buildings in Venice is San Giorgio Maggiore (FIG. 22-30), directly across the Grand Canal from Piazza San Marco. Palladio began work on the church a few years before he succeeded JACOPO SANSOVINO (1486–1570; FIG. 22-30A) as Venice's official architect. Dissatisfied with earlier solutions to the problem of integrating a high central nave and lower aisles into a unified facade design, Palladio solved it by superimposing a tall and narrow classical porch on a low broad one. This solution reflects the building's interior arrangement (FIG. 22-31) and in that sense is strictly logical, but the

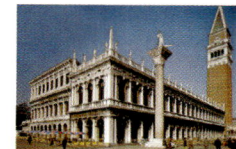

**22-30A** SANSOVINO, Mint and Library, Venice, begun 1536.

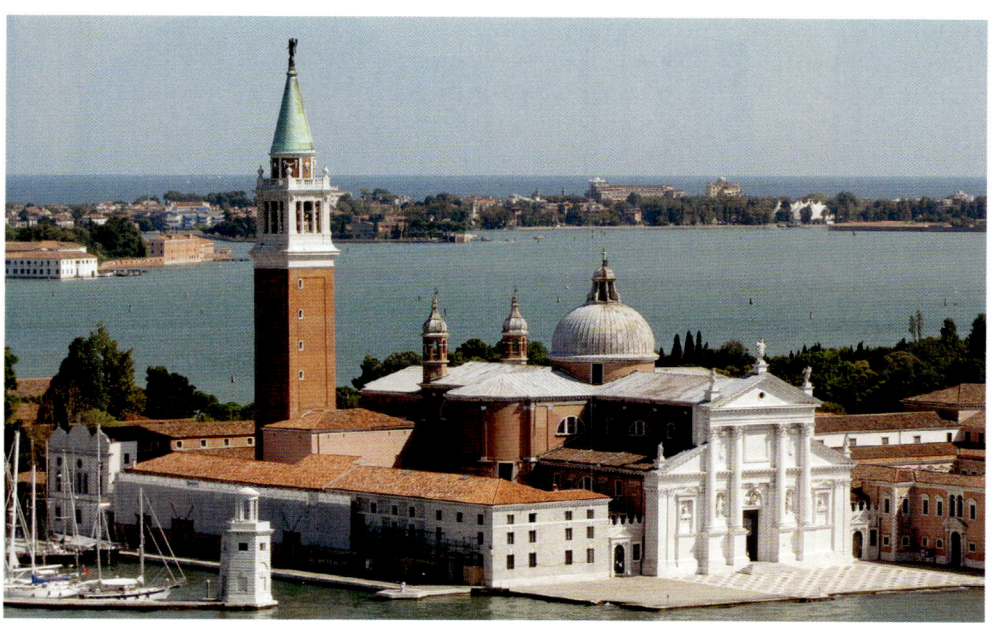

**22-30** ANDREA PALLADIO, San Giorgio Maggiore (looking southeast), Venice, Italy, begun 1566.

Dissatisfied with earlier solutions to the problem of integrating a high central nave and lower aisles into a unified facade, Palladio superimposed a tall and narrow classical porch on a low broad one.

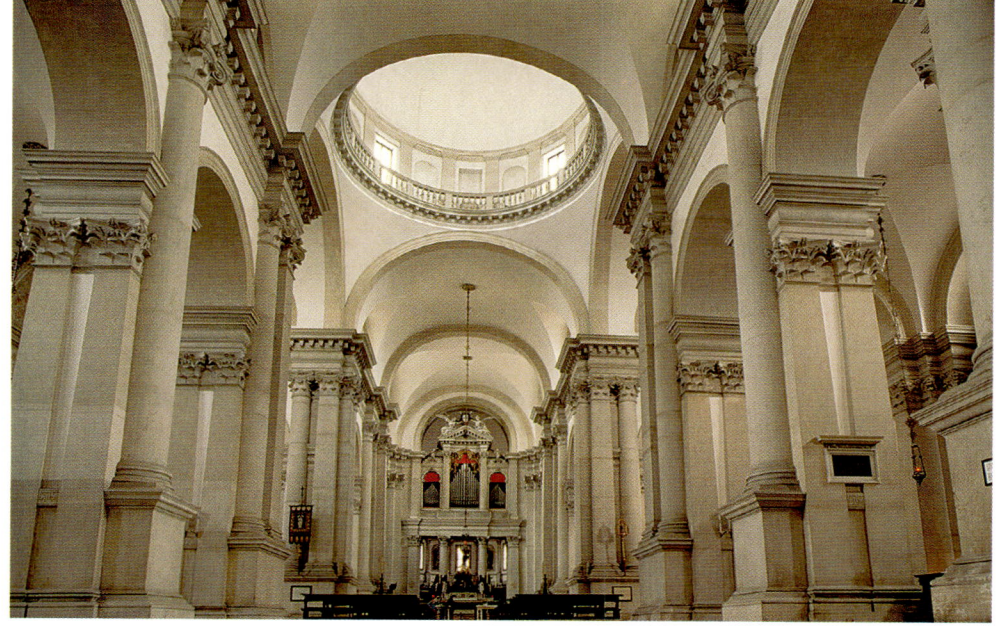

**22-31** ANDREA PALLADIO, interior of San Giorgio Maggiore (looking east), Venice, Italy, begun 1566.

In contrast to the somewhat irrational intersection of two temple facades on the exterior of San Giorgio Maggiore, Palladio's interior is strictly logical, consistent with classical architectural theory.

intersection of two temple facades is irrational and ambiguous, consistent with contemporaneous developments in Mannerist architecture (see page 632). Palladio's design also created the illusion of three-dimensional depth, an effect intensified by the strong projection of the central columns and the shadows they cast. The play of shadow across the building's surfaces, its reflection in the water, and its gleaming white against sea and sky create a remarkably colorful effect. The interior of the church lacks the ambiguity of the facade and exhibits strong roots in High Renaissance architectural style. Light floods the interior and crisply defines the contours of the rich wall decorations, all beautifully and "correctly" profiled—the exemplar of what classical architectural theory meant by "rational" organization.

## Venetian Painting

In the 16th century, the Venetians developed a painting style distinct from that of Rome and Florence. Artists in the maritime republic showed a special interest in recording the effect of Venice's soft-colored light on figures and landscapes. The leading Venetian master at the turn of the century was Giovanni Bellini, who contributed significantly to creating the High Renaissance painting style in Venice.

**GIOVANNI BELLINI** Trained in the International Style by his father, Jacopo, a student of Gentile da Fabriano (FIG. 21-18), GIOVANNI BELLINI (ca. 1430–1516) worked in the family shop and did not develop his own style until after his father's death in 1470. His early independent works show the dominant influence of his brother-in-law Andrea Mantegna (FIGS. 21-48 to 21-50). But in the late 1470s, he came into contact with the work of the Sicilian-born painter Antonello da Messina (ca. 1430–1479). Antonello received his early training in Naples, where he must have encountered Flemish painting and mastered using mixed oil (see "Tempera and Oil Painting," Chapter 20, page 539). This more flexible medium is wider in coloristic range than either tempera or fresco. Antonello arrived in Venice in 1475 and during his two-year stay introduced his Venetian colleagues to the possibilities the new oil technique offered. In Saint Fran-

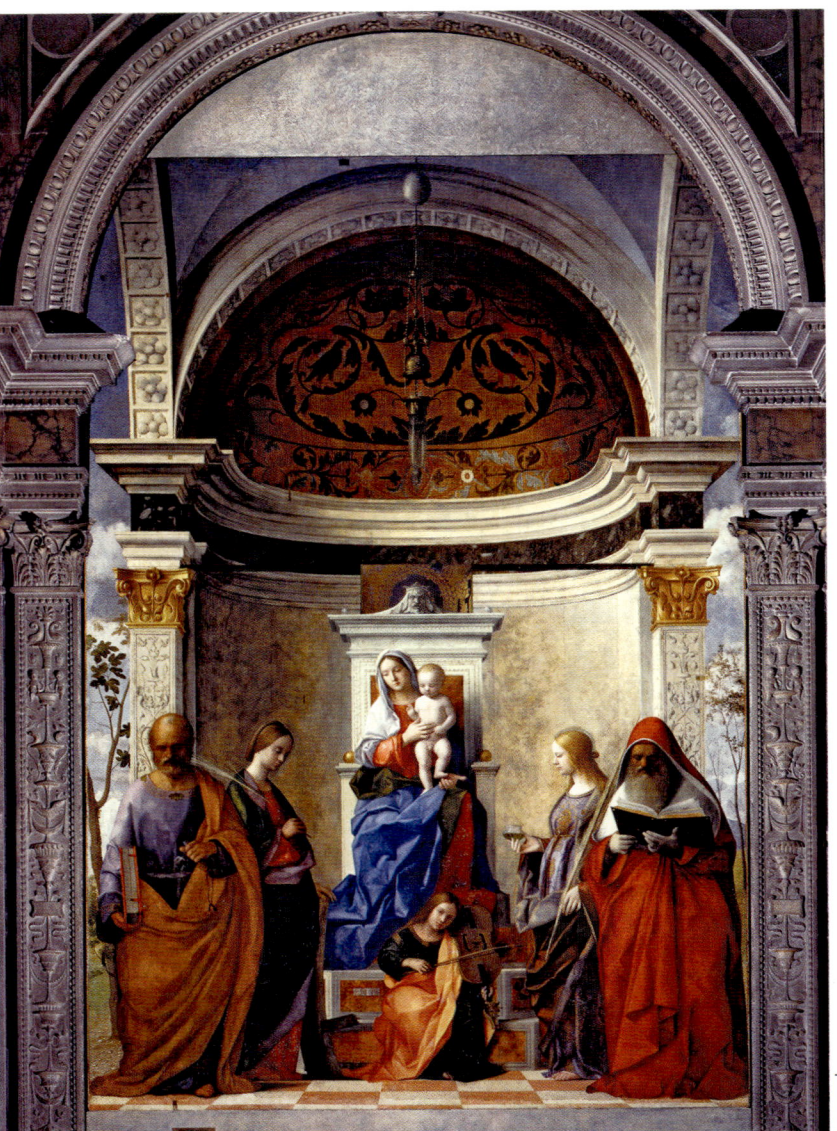

**22-32** GIOVANNI BELLINI, *Madonna and Child with Saints* (*San Zaccaria Altarpiece*), 1505. Oil on wood transferred to canvas, 16′ 5$\frac{1}{2}$″ × 7′ 9″. San Zaccaria, Venice.

In this *sacra conversazione* uniting saints from different eras, Bellini created a feeling of serenity and spiritual calm through the harmonious and balanced presentation of color and light.

cis in the Desert (FIG. **22-31A**), his most famous work of this period, Bellini used a mixture of oil and tempera. As a direct result of Bellini's contact with Antonello, Bellini abandoned Mantegna's harsh linear style and developed a sensuous coloristic manner destined to characterize Venetian painting for a century.

**22-31A** BELLINI, *Saint Francis in the Desert,* ca. 1470–1480.

**SAN ZACCARIA ALTARPIECE** Bellini earned great recognition for his many Madonnas, which he painted both in half-length (with or without accompanying saints) on small devotional panels and in full-length on large, monumental altarpieces of the sacra conversazione (holy conversation) type. In the sacra conversazione, which became a popular theme for religious paintings from the middle of the 15th century on, saints from different epochs occupy the same space and seem to converse either with one another or

with the audience. (Raphael employed much the same conceit in his School of Athens, FIG. 22-9, where he gathered Greek philosophers of different eras.) Bellini carried on the tradition in one of his earliest major commissions, the San Zaccaria Altarpiece (FIG. **22-32**). The Virgin Mary sits enthroned, holding the Christ Child, with saints flanking her. Bellini placed the group in a carefully painted shrine. Attributes aid the identification of all the saints: Saint Lucy holding a tray with her plucked-out eyes displayed on it; Peter with his key and book; Catherine with the palm of martyrdom and the broken wheel; and Jerome with a book (representing his translation of the Bible into Latin). At the foot of the throne sits an angel playing a viol. The painting radiates a feeling of serenity and spiritual calm. Viewers derive this sense less from the figures (no interaction occurs among them) than from Bellini's harmonious and balanced presentation of color and light. Line is not the chief agent of form, as it generally is in paintings produced in Rome and Florence.

Indeed, outlines dissolve in light and shadow. Glowing color produces a soft radiance that envelops the forms with an atmospheric haze and enhances their majestic serenity.

**FEAST OF THE GODS** Painted a quarter century later, *Feast of the Gods* (FIG. **22-33**) was a collaboration between Bellini and his greatest student, Titian (FIGS. 22-35 to 22-41). Bellini also drew from the work of another pupil, Giorgione (FIG. 22-34), who developed his master's landscape backgrounds into poetic Arcadian reveries. Derived from Arcadia, a region in southern Greece, the term *Arcadian* referred, by the time of the Renaissance, to an idyllic place of rustic peace and simplicity. After Giorgione's premature death, Bellini embraced his student's interests and, in *Feast of the Gods,* developed a new kind of mythological painting. The duke of Ferrara, Alfonso d'Este (r. 1505–1534), commissioned this work for the Camerino d'Alabastro (Alabaster Room), a private apartment in the Palazzo Ducale complex. Alfonso hired four painters—Bellini, Titian, Raphael, and Fra Bartolommeo (1472–1517) of Florence—to provide four paintings of related mythological subjects for the room, carefully selected for the duke by the humanist scholar Mario Equicola (1470–1515). Both Raphael and Fra Bartolommeo died before fulfilling the commission. Although for his painting Bellini drew some of the figures from the standard repertoire of Greco-Roman art—most notably, the nymph carrying a vase on her head and the sleeping nymph in the lower right corner—the Olympian gods appear as peasants enjoying a picnic in a shady glade. The ancient literary source was the Roman poet Ovid's *Fasti* (1:391–440; 6:319–348), which describes the gods banqueting. Satyrs attend the gods, nymphs bring jugs of wine, and couples engage in love play. At the far right, Priapus lifts the dress of the sleeping nymph with exposed breast. (All four paintings in the Camerino centered on Venus or Bacchus, the Roman gods of love and wine.) The mellow light of a long afternoon glows softly around the gathering, caressing the surfaces of colorful fabrics, smooth flesh, and polished metal. Here, Bellini communicated the delight the Venetian school took in the beauty of texture revealed by the full resources of gently and subtly harmonized color. Behind the warm, lush tones of the figures, a background of cool green tree-filled glades extends into the distance. At the right, a screen of trees creates a verdant shelter. The atmosphere is idyllic, a lush countryside providing a setting for the never-ending pleasure of the immortal gods.

With Bellini, Venetian art became the great complement of the schools of Florence and Rome. The Venetians' instrument was color, that of the Florentines and Romans sculpturesque form. Scholars often distill the contrast between these two approaches down to *colorito* (colored or painted) versus *disegno* (drawing and design). Whereas most central Italian artists emphasized careful design preparation based on preliminary drawing (see "Renaissance Drawings," page 604), Venetian artists focused on color and the process of paint application. In addition, the general thematic focus of their work differed. Venetian artists painted the poetry of the senses and delighted in nature's beauty and the pleasures of humanity. Artists in Florence and Rome gravitated toward more intellectual themes—the epic of humanity, the masculine virtues, the grandeur of the ideal, and the lofty conceptions of religion involving the heroic and sublime. Much of the later history of Western art involves a dialogue between these two traditions.

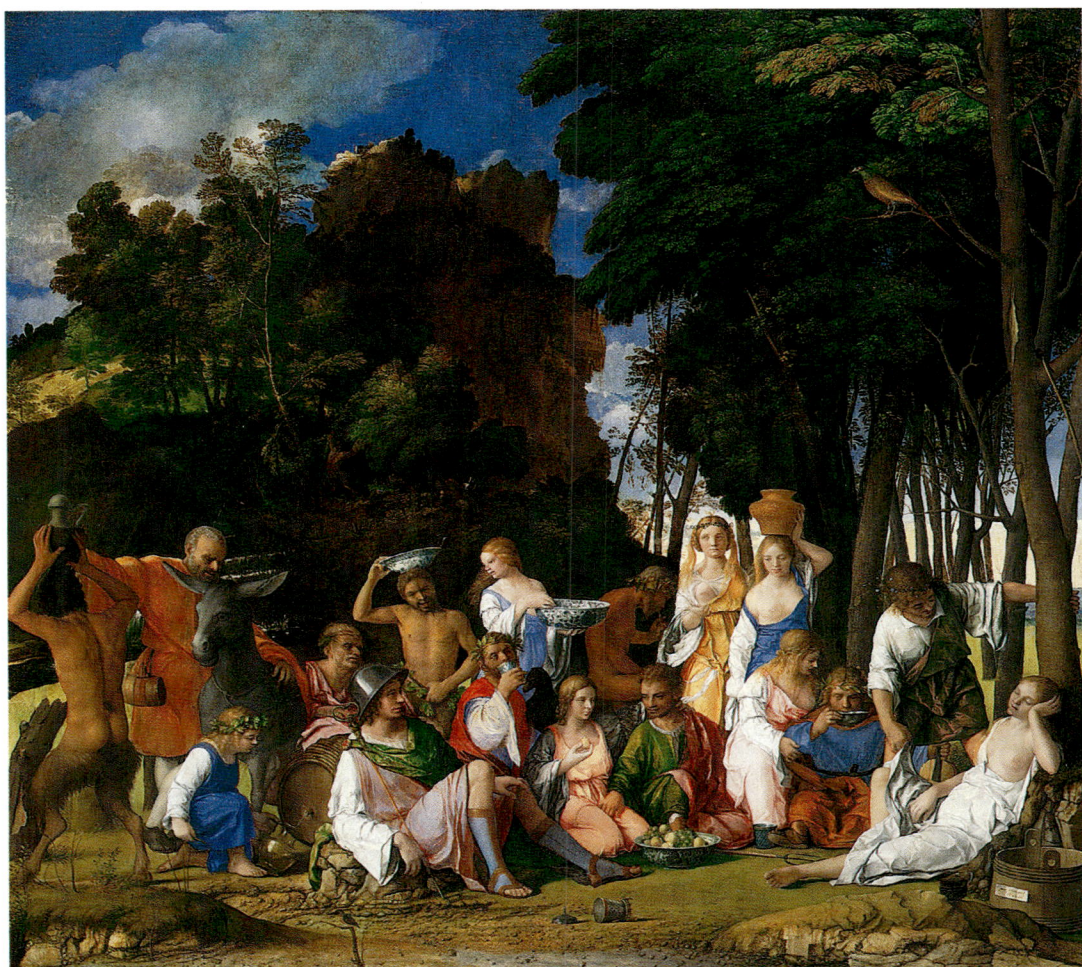

**22-33** GIOVANNI BELLINI and TITIAN, *Feast of the Gods,* from the Camerino d'Alabastro, Palazzo Ducale, Ferrara, Italy, 1529. Oil on canvas, 5′ 7″ × 6′ 2″. National Gallery of Art, Washington (Widener Collection).

In *Feast of the Gods,* based on Ovid's *Fasti,* Bellini developed a new kind of mythological painting in which the Olympian deities appear as peasants enjoying a picnic in the soft afternoon light.

1 ft.

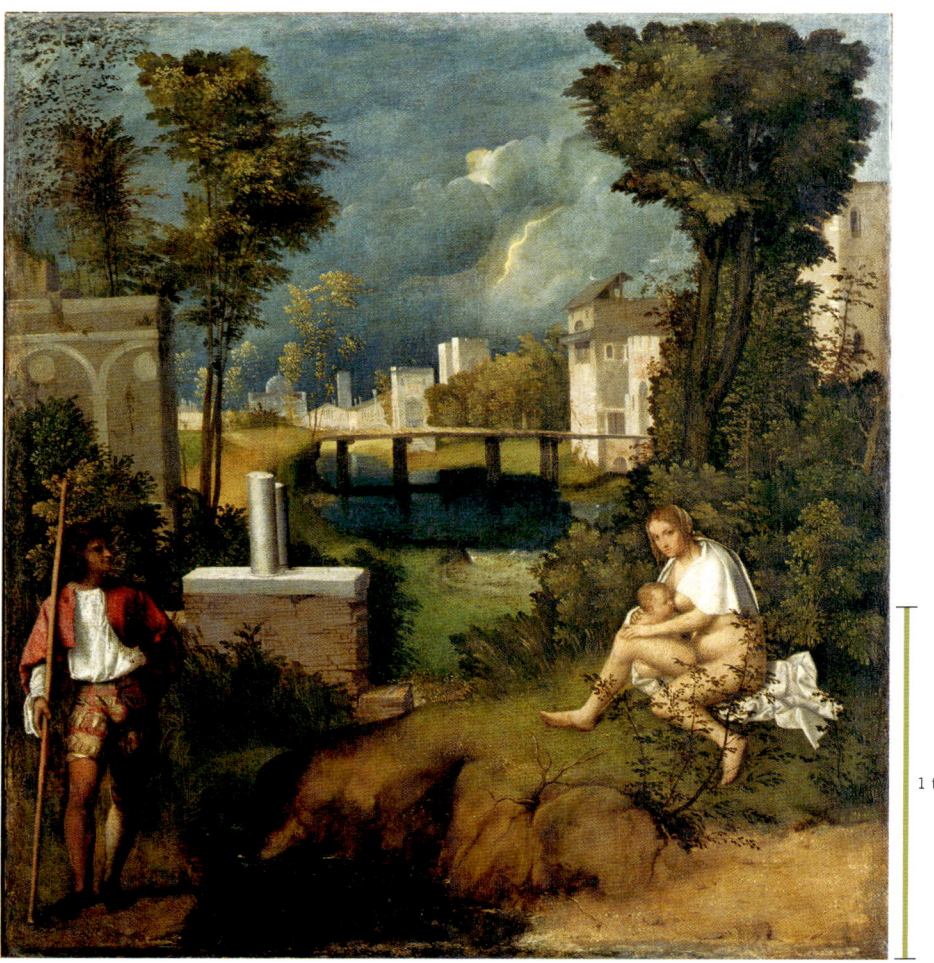

**22-34** Giorgione da Castelfranco, *The Tempest*, ca. 1510. Oil on canvas, 2′ 8¼″ × 2′ 4¾″. Galleria dell'Accademia, Venice.

The subject of this painting set in a lush landscape beneath a stormy sky is uncertain, contributing, perhaps intentionally, to the painting's enigmatic quality and intriguing air.

**GIORGIONE** Describing Venetian art as "poetic" is particularly appropriate, given the development of *poesia,* or painting meant to operate in a manner similar to poetry. Both classical and Renaissance poetry inspired Venetian artists, and their paintings focused on the lyrical and sensual. Thus, in many Venetian artworks, discerning concrete narratives or subjects is virtually impossible. That is certainly the case with *The Tempest* (FIG. **22-34**), a painting that continues to defy interpretation. It is the greatest work attributed to the short-lived GIORGIONE DA CASTELFRANCO (ca. 1477–1510), the Venetian artist who deserves much of the credit for developing the poetic manner of painting. To an even greater extent than in Bellini's later *Feast of the Gods* (for which Giorgione's work served as inspiration for his teacher, Bellini), a lush landscape fills most of Giorgione's *Tempest*. Stormy skies and lightning in the middle background threaten the tranquility of the pastoral setting, however. Pushed off to both sides are the few human figures depicted—a young woman nursing a baby in the right foreground and a man

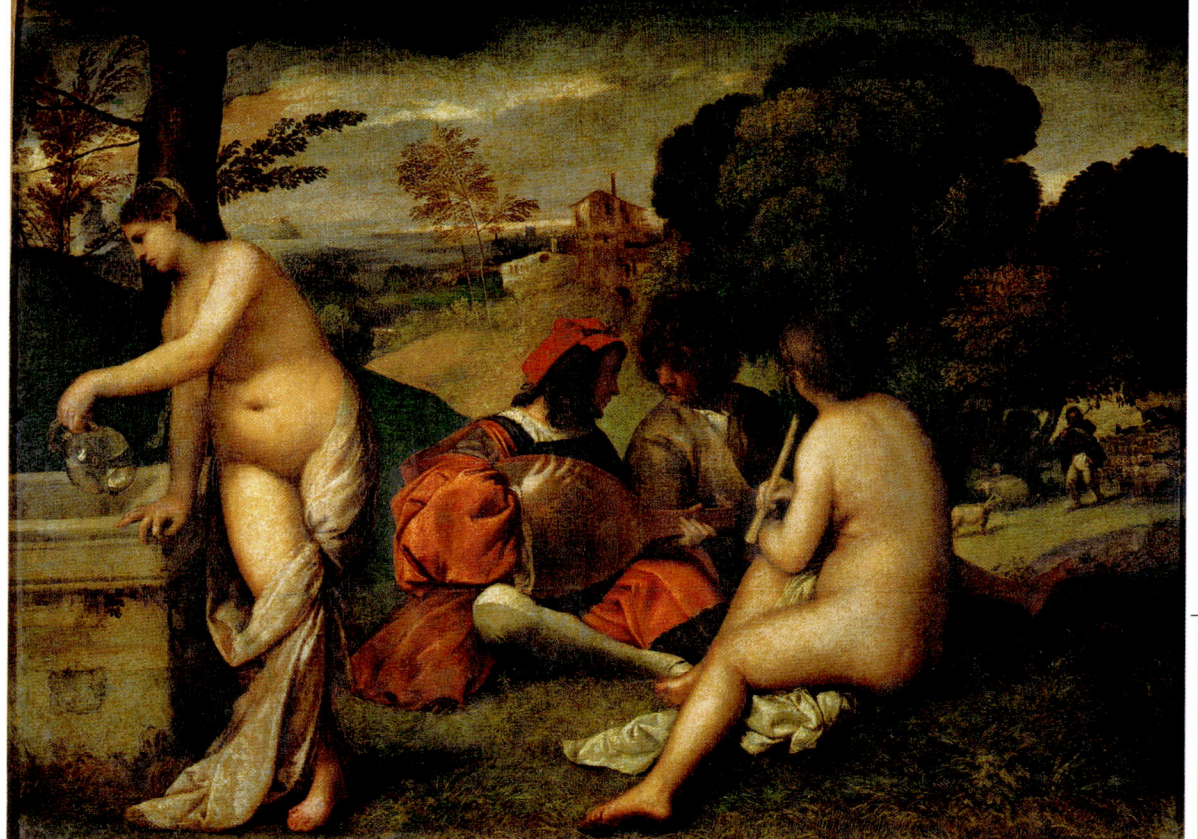

**22-35** Titian, *Pastoral Symphony,* ca. 1508–1511. Oil on canvas, 3′ 7¼″ × 4′ 6¼″. Musée du Louvre, Paris.

Venetian art conjures poetry. In this painting, Titian so eloquently evoked the pastoral mood that the uncertainty about the picture's meaning is not distressing. The mood and rich color are enough.

carrying a *halberd* (a combination spear and battle-ax—but he is not a soldier) on the left. Much scholarly debate has centered on the painting's subject, fueled by X-rays of the canvas that revealed Giorgione altered many of the details as work progressed. Most notably, a seated nude woman originally occupied the position where Giorgione subsequently placed the standing man. The changes the painter made have led many art historians to believe Giorgione did not intend the painting to have a definitive narrative, which is appropriate for a Venetian poetic rendering. Other scholars have suggested various mythological and biblical narratives. The uncertainty about the subject contributes to the painting's intriguing air.

**TITIAN** Giorgione's masterful handling of light and color and his interest in landscape, poetry, and music—Vasari reported he was an accomplished lutenist and singer—influenced not only his much older yet constantly inquisitive master, Bellini, but also his younger contemporary, Tiziano Vecelli, called TITIAN (ca. 1490–1576) in English. Indeed, a masterpiece long attributed to Giorgione—*Pastoral Symphony* (FIG. **22-35**)—is now widely believed to be an early work of Titian. Out of dense shadow emerge the soft forms of figures and landscape. Titian, a supreme colorist and master of the oil medium, cast a mood of tranquil reverie and dreaminess over the entire scene, evoking the landscape of a lost but never forgotten paradise. As in Giorgione's *Tempest,* the theme is as enigmatic as the lighting. Two nude women, accompanied by two clothed young men, occupy the bountiful landscape through which a shepherd passes. In the distance, a villa crowns a hill. The artist so eloquently evoked the pastoral mood that the viewer does not find the uncertainty about the picture's precise meaning distressing. The mood is enough. The shepherd symbolizes the poet. The pipes and lute symbolize his poetry. The two women accompanying the young men may be thought of as their invisible inspiration, their muses. One turns to lift water from the sacred well of poetic inspiration. The voluptuous bodies of the women, softly modulated by the smoky shadow, became the standard in Venetian art. The fullness of their figures contributes to their effect as poetic personifications of nature's abundance.

***ASSUMPTION OF THE VIRGIN*** On Bellini's death in 1516, the Republic of Venice appointed Titian as its official painter. Shortly thereafter, the prior of the Franciscan basilica of Santa Maria Gloriosa dei Frari commissioned Titian to paint a monumental altarpiece (nearly 23 feet high) for the high altar of the church. In *Assumption of the Virgin* (FIG. **22-36**), a fitting theme for the shrine of the "glorious Saint Mary," Titian's remarkable coloristic sense and his ability to convey light through color are again on display. The subject is the ascent of the Virgin to Heaven on a great white cloud borne aloft by putti. Above, golden clouds, so luminous they seem to glow and radiate light into the church, envelop the Virgin, whose head is on the vertical axis of the composition. God the Father appears above, slightly off-center, awaiting Mary with open arms. Below, closest to the viewer, over-life-size apostles gesticulate wildly as they witness the glorious event. Through his mastery of the oil medium—fresco was not a good choice for Venetian churches because of the dampness and salinity of this city with saltwater streets—Titian used vibrant color to infuse the image with intensity and amplify the drama.

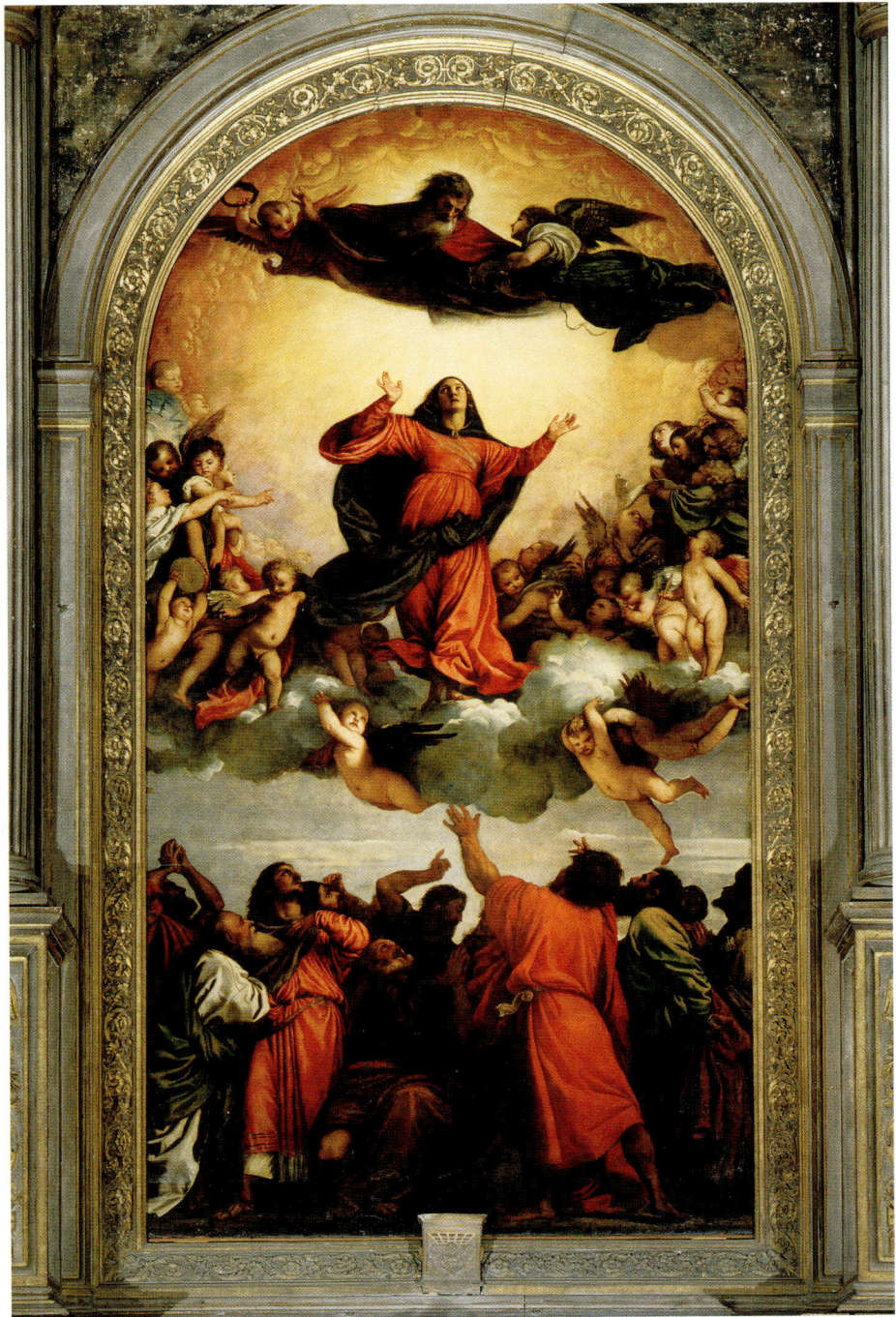

**22-36** TITIAN, *Assumption of the Virgin*, 1515–1518. Oil on wood, 22′ 7½″ × 11′ 10″. Santa Maria Gloriosa dei Frari, Venice.

Titian won renown for his ability to convey light through color. In this dramatic depiction of the Virgin Mary's ascent to Heaven, the golden clouds seem to glow and radiate light into the church.

1 ft.

**22-37** TITIAN, *Madonna of the Pesaro Family*, 1519–1526. Oil on canvas, 15′ 11″ × 8′ 10″. Pesaro Chapel, Santa Maria Gloriosa dei Frari, Venice.

In this dynamic composition presaging a new kind of pictorial design, Titian placed the figures on a steep diagonal, positioning the Madonna, the focus of the composition, well off the central axis.

1 ft.

**PESARO MADONNA** A year after installing *Assumption of the Virgin* in the main altar of the Venetian church of the Frari, Titian received a commission to paint *Madonna of the Pesaro Family* (FIG. **22-37**) for the same church. Jacopo Pesaro (d. 1547), bishop of Paphos in Cyprus and commander of the papal fleet, had led a successful expedition in 1502 against the Turks during the Venetian-Turkish war. He dedicated a family chapel in Santa Maria Gloriosa and donated Titian's altarpiece in gratitude. In a stately sunlit setting in what may be the Madonna's palace in Heaven, Mary receives the commander, who kneels dutifully at the foot of her throne. A soldier (Saint George?) behind the commander carries a banner with the *escutcheons* (shields with coats of arms) of the Borgia pope, Alexander VI, and of Pesaro. Behind him is a turbaned Turk, a prisoner of war of the Christian forces. Saint Peter appears on the steps of the throne, and Saint Francis introduces other Pesaro family members (all male—Italian depictions of donors in this era typically excluded women and children), who kneel solemnly in the right foreground. Thus, Titian entwined the human and the heavenly, depicting the Madonna and saints honoring the achievements of a specific man. A quite worldly transaction takes place (albeit beneath a heavenly cloud bearing angels) between a queen and her court and loyal servants, consistent with Renaissance protocol and courtly splendor.

A prime characteristic of High Renaissance painting is the massing of monumental figures, singly and in groups, within a weighty and majestic architecture. But here Titian did not compose a horizontal and symmetrical arrangement, as did Leonardo in *Last Supper* (FIG. 22-4) and Raphael in *School of Athens* (FIG. 22-9). Rather, he placed the figures on a steep diagonal, positioning the Madonna, the focus of the composition, well off the central axis. Titian drew attention to her with the perspective lines, the inclination of the figures, and the directional lines of gaze and gesture. The banner inclining toward the left beautifully brings the design into equilibrium, balancing the rightward and upward tendencies of its main direction. This kind of composition is more dynamic than most High Renaissance examples and presaged a new kind of pictorial design—one built on movement rather than rest.

**BACCHUS AND ARIADNE** After the deaths of Raphael and Fra Bartolommeo, Titian took over their commissions to paint bacchanalian scenes for Alfonso d'Este's Camerino d'Alabastro in addition to his own assignment. Titian also contributed the landscape background to Bellini's *Feast of the Gods* (FIG. 22-33). Completed in 1523, *Meeting of Bacchus and Ariadne* (FIG. **22-38**), based on an ancient Latin poem by Catullus, is a roughly six-feet-square canvas in which Bacchus, accompanied by a boisterous group, arrives on the island of Naxos in a leopard-drawn chariot to save Ariadne, whom Theseus had abandoned there. Consistent with the mythological subject, Titian looked to classical art for models and derived one of the figures, the snake-entwined satyr, from the recently unearthed

*Laocoön* (FIG. 5-89), a marble statue that also made an indelible impression on Michelangelo and many others. Titian's rich and luminous colors add greatly to the sensuous appeal of the painting, making it perfect for what Alfonso called his "pleasure chamber."

**VENUS OF URBINO** In 1538, at the height of his powers, Titian painted the so-called *Venus of Urbino* (FIG. **22-39**) for Guidobaldo II, who became the duke of Urbino the following year (r. 1539–1574). The title (given to the painting later) elevates to the status of classical mythology what is probably a representation of a sensual Italian woman in her bedchamber. Whether the subject is divine or mortal, Titian based his version on an earlier (and pioneering) painting of Venus (not illustrated) by Giorgione. Here, Titian established the compositional elements and the standard for paintings of the reclining female nude, regardless of the many ensuing variations. This "Venus" reclines on the gentle slope of her luxurious pillowed couch. Her softly rounded body contrasts with the sharp vertical edge of the curtain behind her, which serves to direct the viewer's attention to her left hand and pelvis as well as to divide the foreground from the background. At the woman's feet is a slumbering lapdog—where Cupid would be if this were Venus. In the right background, near the window opening onto a landscape, two servants bend over a chest, apparently searching for garments (Renaissance households stored clothing in carved wooden chests

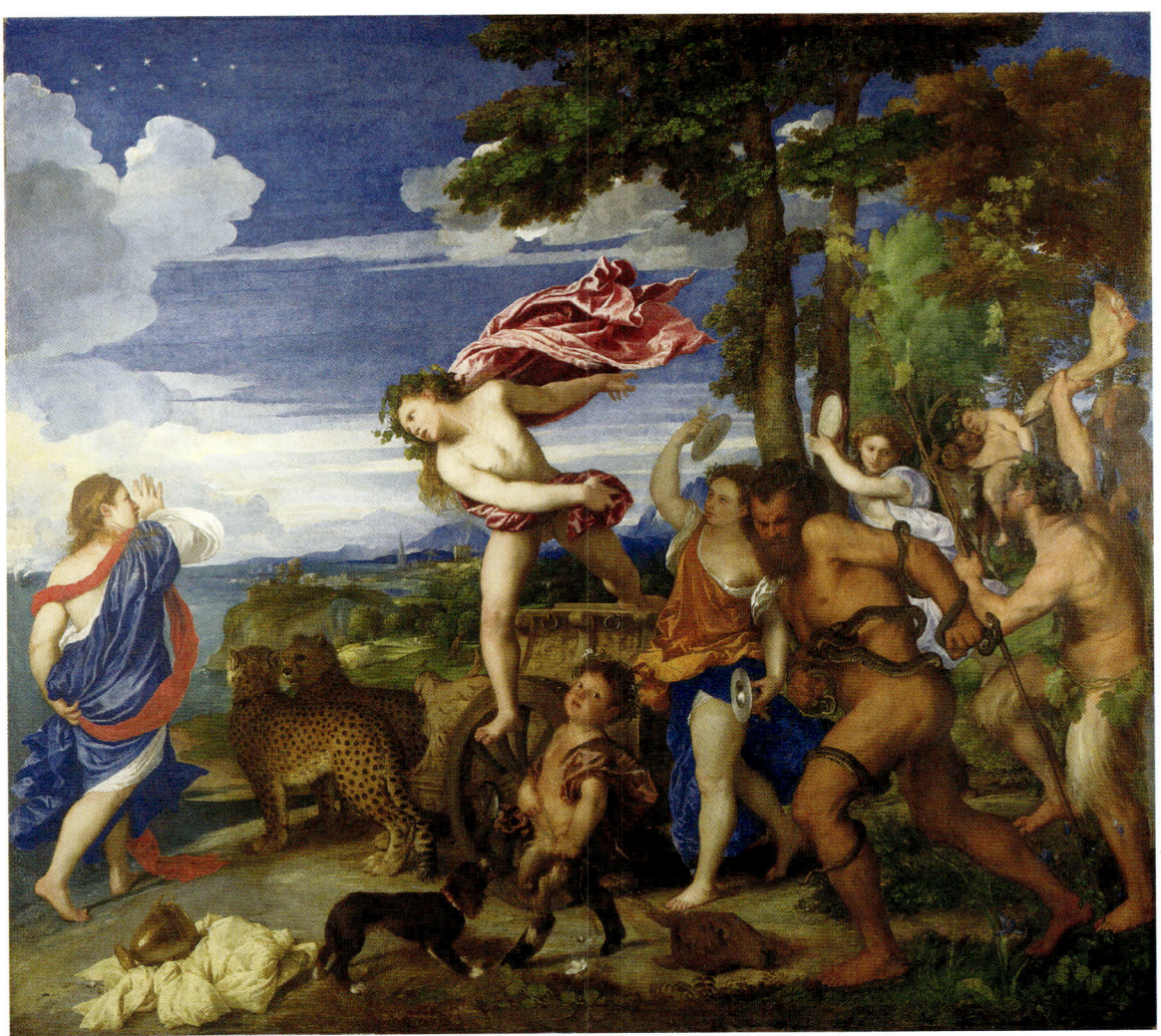

**22-38** TITIAN, *Meeting of Bacchus and Ariadne*, from the Camerino d'Alabastro, Palazzo Ducale, Ferrara, Italy, 1522–1523. Oil on canvas, 5′ 9″ × 6′ 3″. National Gallery, London.

Titian's rich and luminous colors add greatly to the sensuous appeal of this mythological painting in which he based one of the figures on the recently unearthed *Laocoön* (FIG. 5-89).

1 ft.

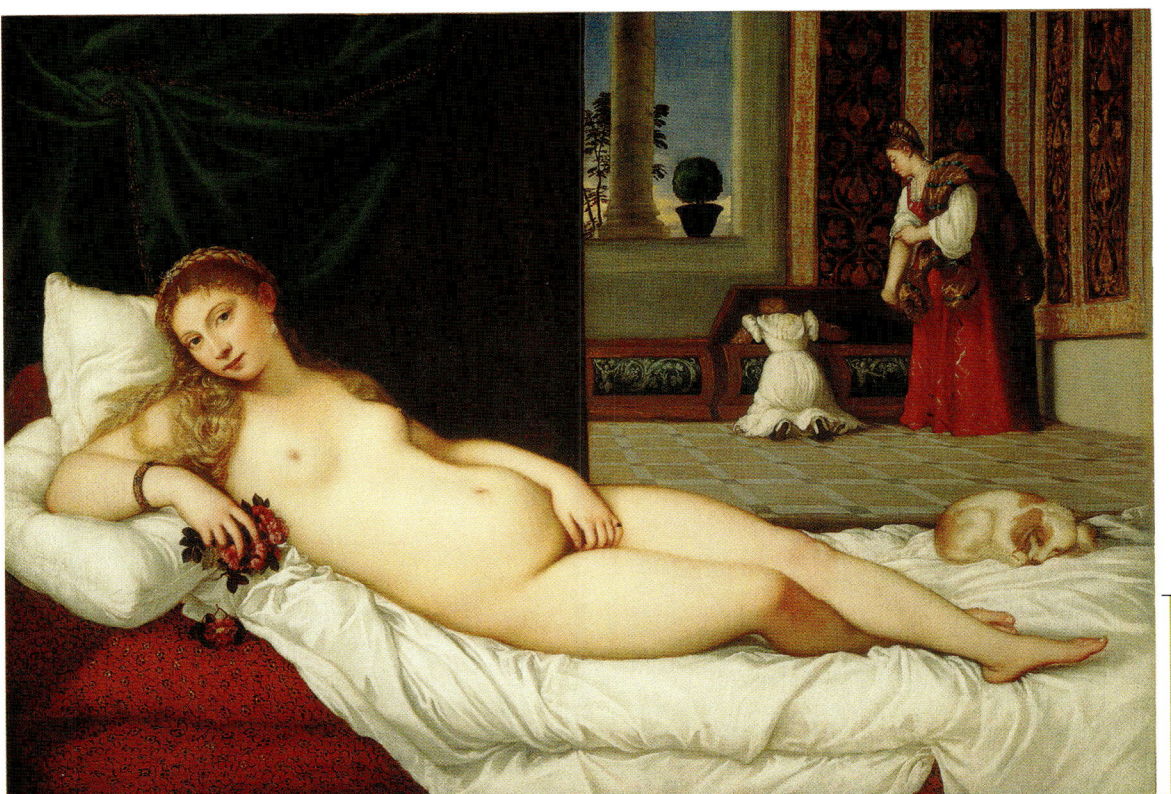

**22-39** TITIAN, *Venus of Urbino*, 1536–1538. Oil on canvas, 3′ 11″ × 5′ 5″. Galleria degli Uffizi, Florence. ◼

Titian established oil color on canvas as the preferred painting medium in Western art. Here, he also set the standard for representations of the reclining female nude, whether divine or mortal.

1 ft.

High and Late Renaissance　**629**

# Women in the Renaissance Art World

The Renaissance art world was decidedly male-dominated. Few women could become professional artists because of the many obstacles they faced. In particular, for centuries, training practices mandating residence in a master's house (see "Artists' Guilds," Chapter 14, page 410) precluded women from acquiring the necessary experience. In addition, social proscriptions, such as those preventing women from drawing from nude models, hampered an aspiring woman artist's advancement through the accepted avenues of artistic training.

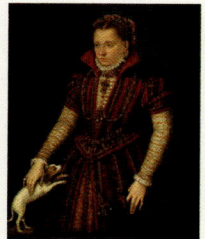

22-40A FONTANA, *Portrait of a Noblewoman*, ca. 1580.

Still, some determined Renaissance women surmounted these barriers and produced not only considerable bodies of work but earned enviable reputations as well. One was Sofonisba Anguissola (FIG. 22-47), who was so accomplished she can be considered the first Italian woman to have ascended to the level of international art celebrity. LAVINIA FONTANA (1552–1614; FIG. 22-40A) also achieved notable success, and her paintings constitute the largest surviving body of work by any woman artist before 1700. Fontana learned her craft from her father, Prospero Fontana (1512–1597), a leading Bolognese painter. (Paternal training was the norm for aspiring women artists.) She was in demand as a portraitist and received commissions from important patrons, including members of the ruling Habsburg family. She even spent time as an official painter to the papal court in Rome.

Perhaps more challenging for women than the road to becoming a professional painter was the mastery of sculpture, made more difficult by the physical demands of the medium. Yet Properzia de' Rossi (ca. 1490–1530) established herself as a professional sculptor and was the only woman artist Giorgio Vasari included in his comprehensive publication, *Lives of the Most Eminent Painters, Sculptors, and Architects*. Active in the early 16th century, she died of the plague in 1530, bringing her promising career to an early end.

Beyond the realm of art production, Renaissance women exerted significant influence as art patrons. Scholars only recently have begun to explore systematically the role of women in commissioning works of art. As a result, current knowledge is sketchy at best but suggests women played a much more extensive role than previously acknowledged. Among the problems researchers face in their quest to clarify women's activities as patrons is that women often wielded their influence and decision-making power behind the scenes. Many of them acquired their positions through marriage. Their power was thus indirect and provisional, based on their husbands' wealth and status. Thus, documentation of the networks within which women patrons operated and of the processes they used to exert power in a society dominated by men is less substantive than for male patrons.

One of the most important Renaissance patrons, male or female, was Isabella d'Este (1474–1539), the marquess of Mantua. The daughter of Ercole d'Este, duke of Ferrara (r. 1471–1505), and brought up in the cultured princely court there, Isabella married Francesco Gonzaga, marquis of Mantua (1466–1519), in 1490. The marriage gave Isabella access to the position and wealth necessary to pursue her interest in becoming a major art patron. An avid collector, she enlisted the aid of agents who scoured Italy for appealing artworks. Isabella

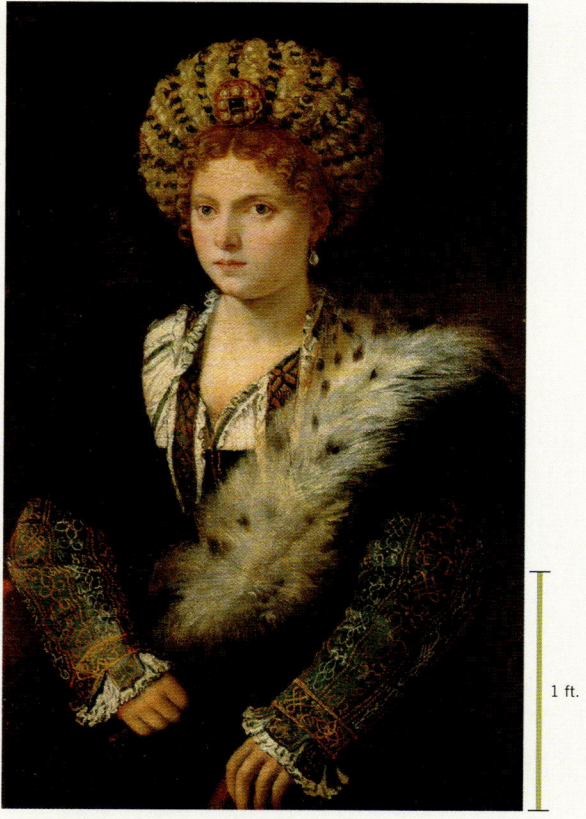

**22-40** TITIAN, *Isabella d'Este*, 1534–1536. Oil on canvas, $3' 4\frac{1}{8}'' \times 2' 1\frac{3}{16}''$. Kunsthistorisches Museum, Vienna.

Isabella d'Este was one of the most powerful women of the Renaissance era. When, at age 60, she commissioned Titian to paint her portrait, she insisted the artist depict her in her 20s.

did not limit her collection to painting and sculpture but included ceramics, glassware, gems, cameos, medals, classical texts, musical manuscripts, and musical instruments.

Undoubtedly, Isabella was a proud and ambitious woman well aware of how art could boost her fame and reputation. Accordingly, she commissioned several portraits of herself from the most esteemed artists of her day—Leonardo da Vinci, Andrea Mantegna, and Titian (FIG. 22-40). The detail and complexity of many of her contracts with artists reveal her insistence on control over the artworks.

Other Renaissance women positioned themselves as serious art patrons. One was Caterina Sforza (1462–1509), daughter of Galeazzo Maria Sforza (heir to the duchy of Milan), who married Girolamo Riario (1443–1488) in 1484. The death of her husband, lord of Imola and count of Forlì, gave Sforza, who survived him by two decades, access to power denied most women. Another female art patron was Lucrezia Tornabuoni (1425–1482), who married Piero di Cosimo de' Medici (1416–1469), one of many Medici, both men and women, who earned reputations as unparalleled art patrons. Further archival investigation of women's roles in Renaissance Italy undoubtedly will produce more evidence of how women established themselves as patrons and artists and the extent to which they contributed to the flourishing of Renaissance art.

## Palma il Giovane on Titian

An important change occurring in Titian's time was the almost universal adoption of canvas, with its rough-textured surface, in place of wood panels for paintings. Titian's works established oil-based pigment on canvas as the typical medium of the Western pictorial tradition thereafter. Palma il Giovane, one of Titian's students, who completed the *Pietà* (FIG. 22-41) Titian intended for his tomb in Santa Maria Gloriosa dei Frari in Venice, wrote a valuable account of his teacher's working methods and of how Titian used the new medium to great advantage:

Titian [employed] a great mass of colors, which served . . . as a base for the compositions. . . . I too have seen some of these, formed with bold strokes made with brushes laden with colors, sometimes of a pure red earth, which he used, so to speak, for a middle tone, and at other times of white lead; and with the same brush tinted with red, black and yellow he formed a highlight; and observing these principles he made the promise of an exceptional figure appear in four brushstrokes. . . . Having constructed these precious foundations he used to turn his pictures to the wall and leave them there without looking at them, sometimes for several months. When he wanted to apply his brush again he would examine them with the utmost rigor . . . to see if he could find any faults. . . . In this way, working on the figures and revising them, he brought them to the most perfect symmetry that the beauty of art and nature can reveal. . . . [T]hus he gradually covered those quintessential forms with living flesh, bringing them

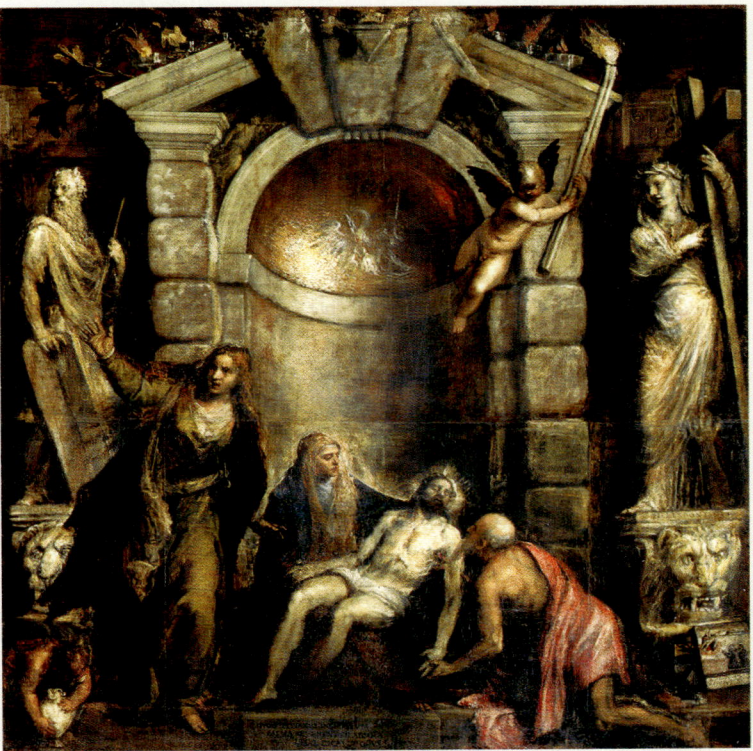

**22-41** TITIAN and PALMA IL GIOVANE, *Pietà*, ca. 1570–1576. Oil on canvas, 11′ 6″ × 12′ 9″. Galleria dell'Accademia, Venice.

In this late work characterized by broad brushstrokes and a thick impasto, Titian portrayed himself as the penitent Saint Jerome kneeling before the dead Christ. Titian intended the work for his own tomb.

1 ft.

by many stages to a state in which they lacked only the breath of life. He never painted a figure all at once and . . . in the last stages he painted more with his fingers than his brushes.*

*Quoted in Francesco Valcanover, "An Introduction to Titian," in Valcanover, *Titian: Prince of Painters* (Venice: Marsilio Editori, 1990), 23–24.

---

called *cassoni*) to clothe their reclining nude mistress. Beyond them, a smaller vista opens into a landscape. Titian masterfully constructed the view backward into the room and the division of the space into progressively smaller units.

As in other Venetian paintings, color plays a prominent role in *Venus of Urbino*. The red tones of the matron's skirt and the muted reds of the tapestries against the neutral whites of the matron's sleeves and the kneeling girl's gown echo the deep Venetian reds set off against the pale neutral whites of the linen and the warm ivory gold of the flesh. The viewer must study the picture carefully to realize the subtlety of color planning. For instance, the two deep reds (in the foreground cushions and in the background skirt) play a critical role in the composition as a gauge of distance and as indicators of an implied diagonal opposed to the real one of the reclining figure. Here, Titian used color not simply to record surface appearance but also to organize his placement of forms.

***ISABELLA D'ESTE*** Titian was a highly esteemed portraitist as well and in great demand. More than 50 portraits by his hand survive. One of the best is *Isabella d'Este* (FIG. **22-40**), Titian's portrait of one of the most prominent women of the Renaissance (see "Women in the Renaissance Art World," page 630). Isabella was the sister of Alfonso d'Este, for whom Titian painted three mythological scenes

for the Ferrara ducal palace. At 16, she married Francesco Gonzaga, marquis of Mantua, and through her patronage of art and music was instrumental in developing the Mantuan court into an important cultural center. Portraits by Titian generally emphasize his psychological reading of the subject's head and hands. Thus, Titian sharply highlighted Isabella's face, whereas her black dress fades into the undefined darkness of the background. The unseen light source also illuminates Isabella's hands, and Titian painted her sleeves with incredible detail to further draw viewers' attention to her hands. This portrait reveals not only Titian's skill but the patron's wish too. Painted when Isabella was 60 years old, the portrait depicts her in her 20s—at her specific request. Titian used an earlier likeness of her as his guide, but his portrait is no copy. Rather, it is a distinctive portrayal of his poised and self-assured patron that owes little to its model.

***PIETÀ*** As Michelangelo had done late in his life, Titian began to contemplate death and salvation and around 1570 decided to create a memorial for his tomb. He, too, chose *Pietà* (FIG. **22-41**) as the theme, albeit for a painting, not a statuary group, as in Michelangelo's case (FIG. 22-20). Intended for the altar of his burial chapel in the right aisle of Santa Maria Gloriosa dei Frari in Venice, which housed two of his earlier altarpieces (FIGS. 22-36 and 22-37),

Titian's *Pietà* remained unfinished when he died of the plague in 1576. His assistant, Jacopo Negretti, known as PALMA IL GIOVANE (1548–1628)—Palma the Younger—piously completed the painting.

Titian set the scene of grief over Christ's death in a rusticated niche reminiscent of the bays of Sansovino's Mint (FIG. 22-30A, *left*) on the Canale San Marco. The Virgin cradles her son's body, while Mary Magdalene runs forward with her right arm raised in a gesture of extreme distress. (Echoing her form, but in reverse, is the torch-carrying angel added by Palma.) The other penitent mourner is Saint Jerome, seen from behind kneeling at Christ's side. His head has the features of the aged, balding Titian—another parallel with Michelangelo's *Pietà.* Both artists apparently wanted to portray themselves touching Jesus' body, hoping for their salvation.

For this huge (roughly 12 feet square) canvas, Titian employed one of his favorite compositional devices (compare FIG. 22-37), creating a bold diagonal movement beginning at Jerome's feet and leading through Christ, the Virgin, and Mary Magdalene to the statue of Moses with the Ten Commandments at the left. (The other statue represents the Hellespontine Sibyl. The votive painting leaning against its pedestal depicts Titian and his son Orazio, who also died of the plague in 1576, praying before another *Pietà.*) But unlike Titian's early and mature works, in which he used smooth and transparent oil glazes, this *Pietà,* as his other late paintings, features broken brushstrokes and rough, uneven patches of pigment built up like paste (*impasto*) that catch the light. Many Baroque painters, especially Peter Paul Rubens and Rembrandt van Rijn (see Chapter 25), subsequently adopted Titian's innovative and highly expressive manner of applying thick paint to canvas (see "Palma il Giovane on Titian," page 631).

# MANNERISM

The Renaissance styles of Rome, Florence, and Venice dominated Italian painting, sculpture, and architecture for most of the 16th century, but already in the 1520s another style—Mannerism—had emerged in reaction to it. *Mannerism* is a term derived from the Italian word *maniera,* meaning "style" or "manner." In the field of art history, the term *style* usually refers to a characteristic or representative mode, especially of an artist or period (for example, Titian's style or Gothic style). *Style* can also refer to an absolute quality of fashion (for example, someone has "style"). Mannerism's style (or representative mode) is characterized by style (being stylish, cultured, elegant).

## Painting

Among the features most closely associated with Mannerism is artifice. Of course, all art involves artifice, in the sense that art is not "natural"—it is something humans fashion. But many artists, including High Renaissance painters such as Leonardo and Raphael, chose to conceal that artifice by using devices such as perspective and shading to make their representations of the world look natural. In contrast, Mannerist painters consciously revealed the constructed nature of their art. In other words, Renaissance artists generally strove to create art that appeared natural, whereas Mannerist artists were less inclined to disguise the contrived nature of art production. This is why artifice is a central feature of discussions about Mannerism, and why Mannerist works can seem, appropriately, "mannered." The conscious display of artifice in Mannerism often reveals itself in imbalanced compositions and unusual complexities, both visual and conceptual. Ambiguous space, departures from expected conventions, and unusual presentations of traditional themes also surface frequently in Mannerist art.

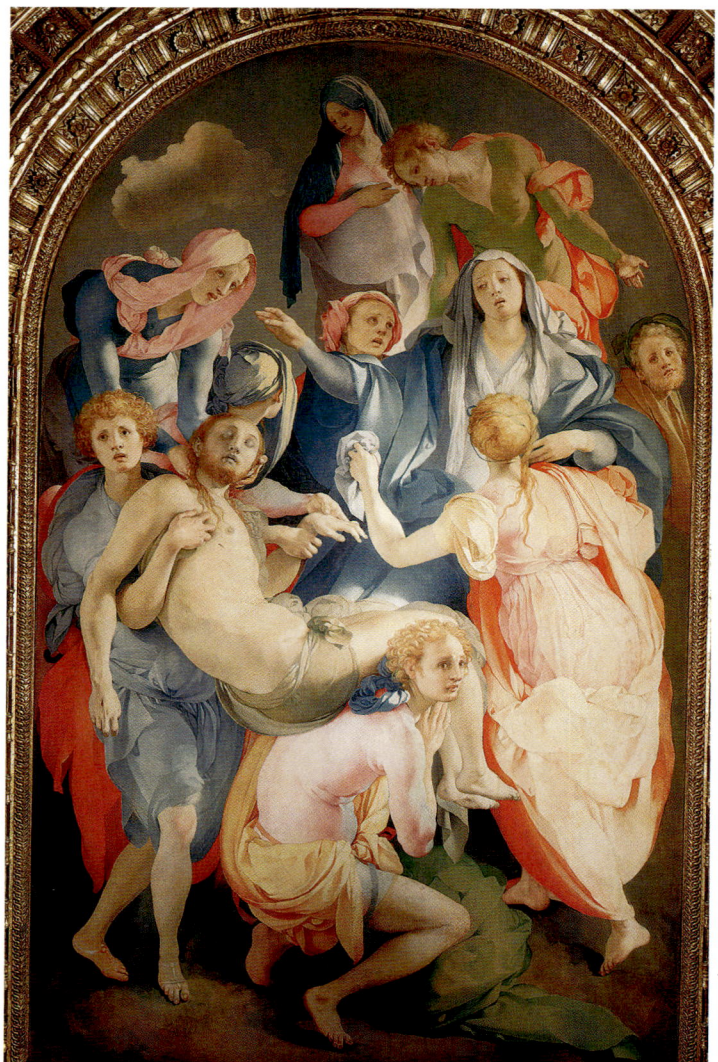

1 ft.

**22-42** JACOPO DA PONTORMO, *Entombment of Christ,* Capponi chapel, Santa Felicità, Florence, Italy, 1525–1528. Oil on wood, 10′ 3″ × 6′ 4″. ◼◂

Mannerist paintings such as this one represent a departure from the compositions of the earlier Renaissance. Instead of concentrating masses in the center of the painting, Pontormo left a void.

**PONTORMO** *Entombment of Christ* (FIG. **22-42**) by the Florentine painter Jacopo Carucci, known as JACOPO DA PONTORMO (1494–1557) after his birthplace, exhibits almost all the stylistic features characteristic of Mannerism's early phase in painting—as does *Fall of the Rebel Angels* (FIG. **22-42A**) by Pontormo's older contemporary DOMENICO BECCAFUMI (1481–1551). Christ's descent from the cross and subsequent entombment had frequently been depicted in art (see "The Life of Jesus in Art," Chapter 8, pages 240–241, or on pages xxs–xxsi in Volume II and Book D),

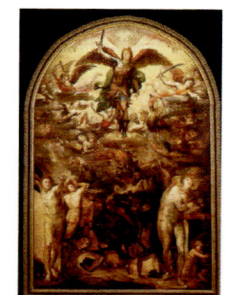

**22-42A** BECCAFUMI, *Fall of the Rebel Angels,* ca. 1524.

and Pontormo exploited the familiarity 16th-century viewers would have had by playing off their expectations. For example, he omitted from the painting both the cross and Christ's tomb, and consequently scholars debate whether he meant to represent *Descent from the Cross* or *Entombment.* Also, instead of presenting the action as taking place across the perpendicular picture plane, as artists such as Raphael and Rogier van der Weyden (FIG. 20-8) had done in their paintings of these episodes from Christ's passion, Pontormo rotated the conventional figural groups along a vertical axis. As a result, the Virgin Mary falls back (away from the viewer) as she releases her dead son's hand. Unlike High Renaissance artists, who had concentrated their masses in the center of the painting, Pontormo left a void. This emptiness accentuates the grouping of hands filling that hole, calling attention to the void—symbolic of loss and grief. The artist enhanced the painting's ambiguity with the curiously anxious glances the figures cast in all directions. (The bearded young man at the upper right who gazes at the viewer is probably a self-portrait of Pontormo.) Athletic bending and twisting characterize many of the figures, with distortions (for example, the torso of the foreground figure bends in an anatomically impossible way), elastic elongation of the limbs, and heads rendered as uniformly small and oval. The contrasting colors, primarily light blues and pinks, add to the dynamism and complexity of the work. The painting represents a departure from the balanced, harmoniously structured compositions of the High Renaissance.

**PARMIGIANINO** Girolamo Francesco Maria Mazzola of Parma, known as PARMIGIANINO (1503–1540), achieved a reputation as a gifted painter while still in his teens. When he was 21, a visit to a barber's shop, where he saw his reflection in a convex mirror, inspired him to paint a self-portrait (FIG. 22-43) of unique format with the intention of presenting it to Pope Clement VII as a demonstration of his virtuosity. According to Vasari, the pope proclaimed the work a "marvel," and Parmigianino, who possessed charm and good looks as well as artistic talent, quickly became the favorite painter of the elite in Rome, the successor to Raphael, who had died just four years before Parmigianino's arrival at the papal court.

To imitate the appearance of a convex mirror, Parmigianino had a carpenter prepare a section of a wooden sphere of the same size and shape as a barber's mirror (about 10 inches in diameter) and used oil glazes to produce a surface luster that heightens the illusion of the viewer looking into a mirror and not at a painting. The viewer in this case is also the painter, whose handsome countenance Vasari described as an angel's, not a man's. The pope remarked that Parmigianino's portrait of himself in his studio was "astonishing" in its success in creating the appearance of someone gazing at his reflection. As in a real convex mirror, the artist's face—at the center of the reflective surface and some distance from it—is free of distortion, but his hand and sleeve are of exaggerated size. The emphasis on the hand no doubt is also a statement on Parmigianino's part about the supreme importance of the painter's hand in fashioning an artwork. That emphasis on artifice as the essence of painting is the core principle of Mannerism.

***MADONNA WITH THE LONG NECK*** Parmigianino's best-known work, however, is *Madonna with the Long Neck* (FIG. 22-44), which exemplifies the elegant stylishness that was a principal aim

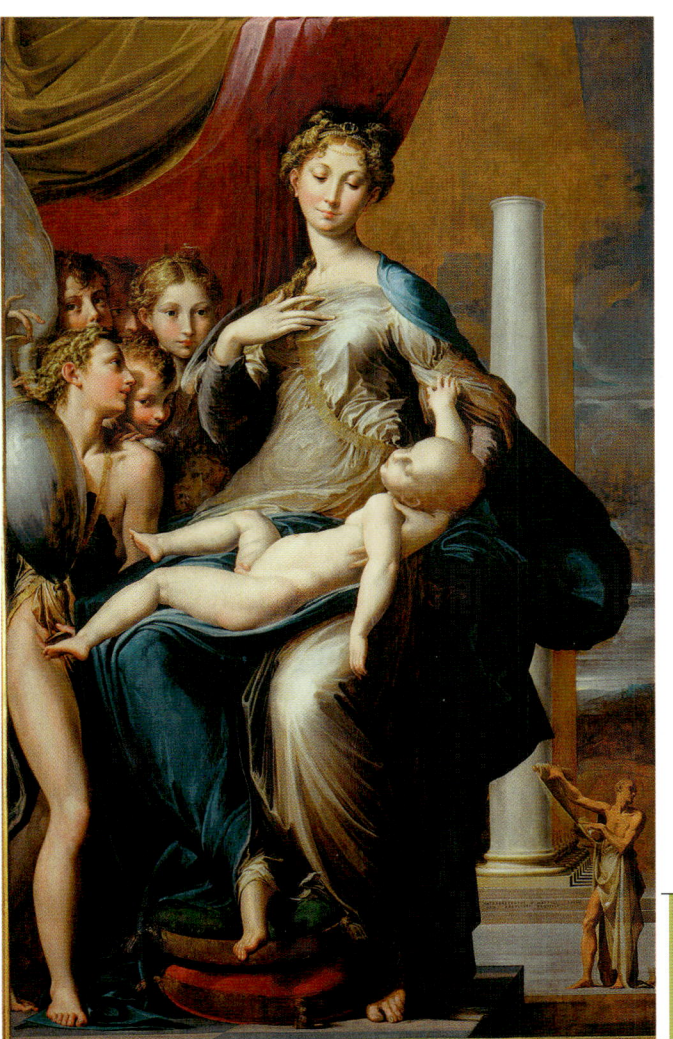

**22-44** PARMIGIANINO, *Madonna with the Long Neck,* from the Baiardi chapel, Santa Maria dei Servi, Parma, Italy, 1534–1540. Oil on wood, 7′ 1″ × 4′ 4″. Galleria degli Uffizi, Florence. ◼️

Parmigianino's Madonna displays the stylish elegance that was a principal aim of Mannerism. Mary has a small oval head, a long slender neck, attenuated hands, and a sinuous body.

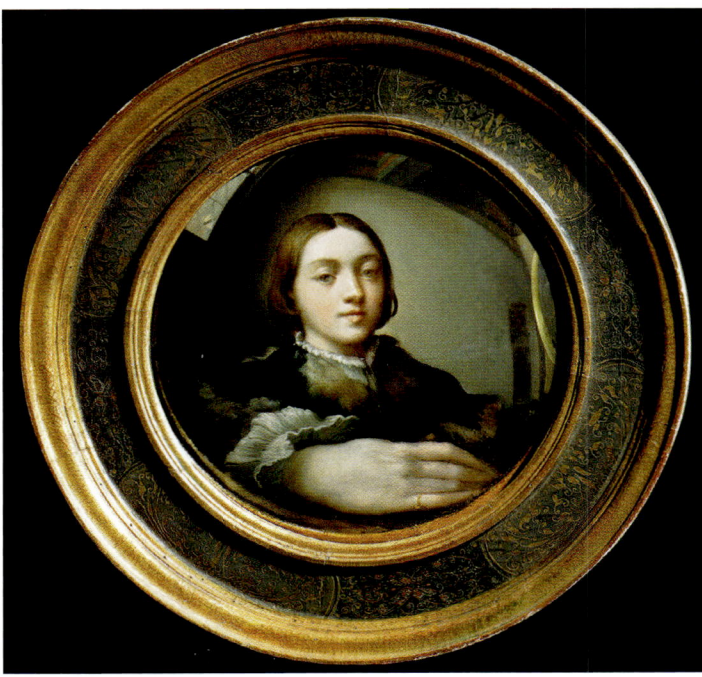

1 in.

**22-43** PARMIGIANINO, *Self-Portrait in a Convex Mirror,* 1524. Oil on wood, 9⅝″ diameter. Kunsthistorisches Museum, Vienna.

Painted to impress Pope Clement VII with his virtuosity, Parmigianino's self-portrait brilliantly reproduces the young Mannerist's distorted appearance as seen in a barber's convex mirror.

1 ft.

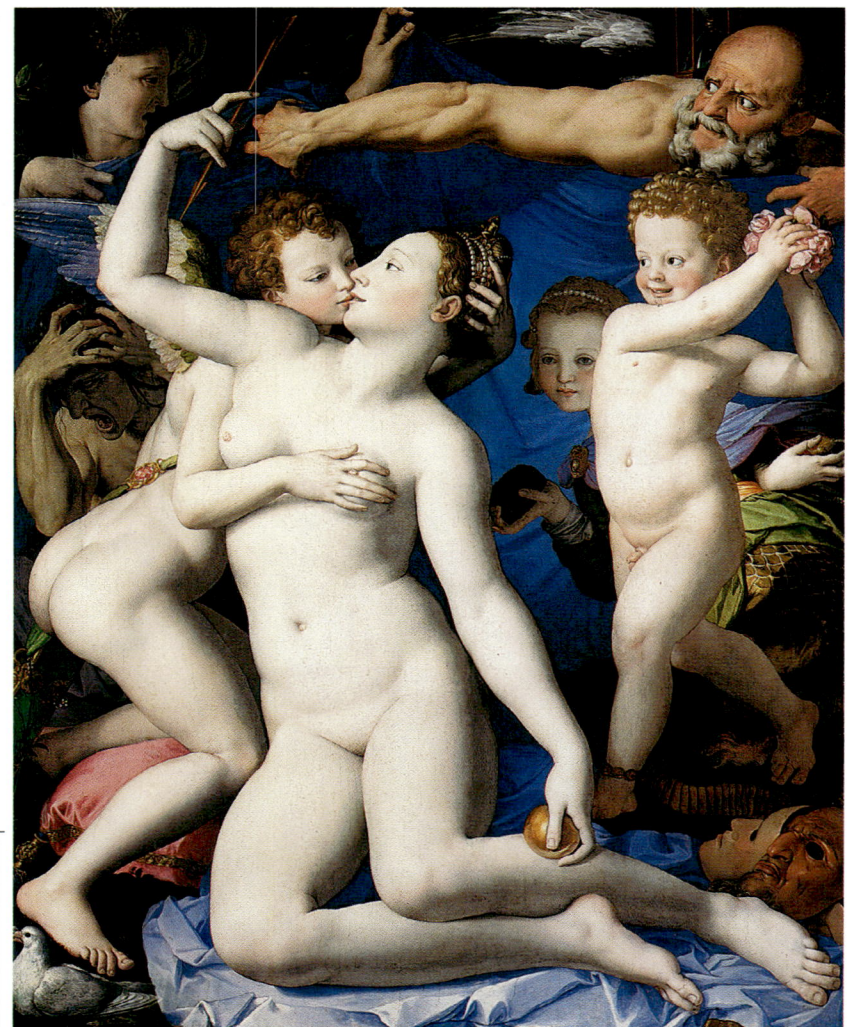

1 ft.

**22-45** BRONZINO, *Venus, Cupid, Folly, and Time,* ca. 1546. Oil on wood, 4′ 9½″ × 3′ 9¾″. National Gallery, London.

In this painting of Cupid fondling his mother Venus, Bronzino demonstrated a fondness for learned allegories with lascivious undertones. As in many Mannerist works, the meaning is ambiguous.

**BRONZINO** *Venus, Cupid, Folly, and Time* (FIG. **22-45**), by Agnolo di Cosimo, called BRONZINO (1503–1572), also displays all the chief features of Mannerist painting. A pupil of Pontormo, Bronzino was a Florentine and painter to the first grand duke of Tuscany, Cosimo I de' Medici (r. 1537–1574). In this painting, which Cosimo commissioned as a gift for King Francis I of France (FIG. 23-12), Bronzino demonstrated the Mannerists' fondness for learned allegories that often had lascivious undertones, a shift from the simple and monumental statements and forms of the High Renaissance. Bronzino depicted Cupid—here an adolescent who has reached puberty, not an infant—fondling his mother, Venus, while Folly prepares to shower them with rose petals. Time, who appears in the upper right corner, draws back the curtain to reveal the playful incest in progress. Other figures in the painting represent other human qualities and emotions, including Envy. The masks, a favorite device of the Mannerists, symbolize deceit. The picture seems to suggest that love—accompanied by envy and plagued by inconstancy—is foolish and that lovers will discover its folly in time. But as in many Mannerist paintings, the meaning here is ambiguous, and interpretations of the painting vary. Compositionally, Bronzino placed the figures around the front plane, and they almost entirely block the space. The contours are strong and sculptural, the surfaces of enamel smoothness. Of special interest are the heads, hands, and feet, for the Mannerists considered the extremities the carriers of grace, and the clever depiction of them as evidence of artistic skill.

***ELEANORA OF TOLEDO*** In 1540, Cosimo I de' Medici married Eleanora of Toledo (1519–1562), daughter of Charles V's viceroy in Naples, and thereby cemented an important alliance with the Spanish court. Several years later Cosimo asked Bronzino to paint Eleanora and their second son, Giovanni (FIG. **22-46**), who then was about three years old. Bronzino painted dozens of portraits of members of the Medici family, but never portrayed Eleanora with any of her daughters (she and Cosimo had three daughters as well as eight sons). This painting therefore should be seen as a formal dynastic portrait intended to present the duke's wife as the mother of one of his heirs.

As in other Bronzino portraits (FIG. **22-46A**), the subjects appear aloof and emotionless. Bronzino idealized both Eleanora and Giovanni, giving both of them perfect features and blemishless skin that glows like alabaster. Eleanora's figure takes up most of the panel's surface, and Bronzino further underscored her primacy by lightening the blue background around her head, creating a halolike frame for her face and perhaps associating the mother and son with the Madonna and Christ Child. Seated with one arm around Giovanni and the other resting on her lap, Eleanora looks out at the viewer with cool detachment. She is richly attired in a brocaded gown and wears a costly pearl necklace and a tiara. The painter reproduced the various textures of fabric, jewels, hair, and flesh with supreme skill. The boy stands stiffly, staring forward, suppressing all playful thoughts in

**22-46A** BRONZINO, *Portrait of a Young Man,* ca. 1530–1545. ◼◂

of Mannerism. In Parmigianino's hands, this traditional, usually sedate, religious subject became a picture of exquisite grace and precious sweetness. The Madonna's small oval head, her long and slender neck, the otherworldly attenuation and delicacy of her hand, and the sinuous, swaying elongation of her frame—all are marks of the aristocratic, sumptuous courtly taste of Mannerist artists and patrons alike. Parmigianino amplified this elegance by expanding the Madonna's form as viewed from head to toe. On the left stands a bevy of angelic creatures, melting with emotions as soft and smooth as their limbs. On the right, the artist included a line of columns without capitals and an enigmatic figure with a scroll, whose distance from the foreground is immeasurable and ambiguous—the antithesis of rational Renaissance perspective diminution of size with distance.

Although the elegance and sophisticated beauty of the painting are due in large part to the Madonna's attenuated limbs, that exaggeration is not solely decorative in purpose. *Madonna with the Long Neck* takes its subject from a simile in medieval hymns comparing the Virgin's neck with a great ivory tower or column, such as the one Parmigianino depicted to the right of the Madonna.

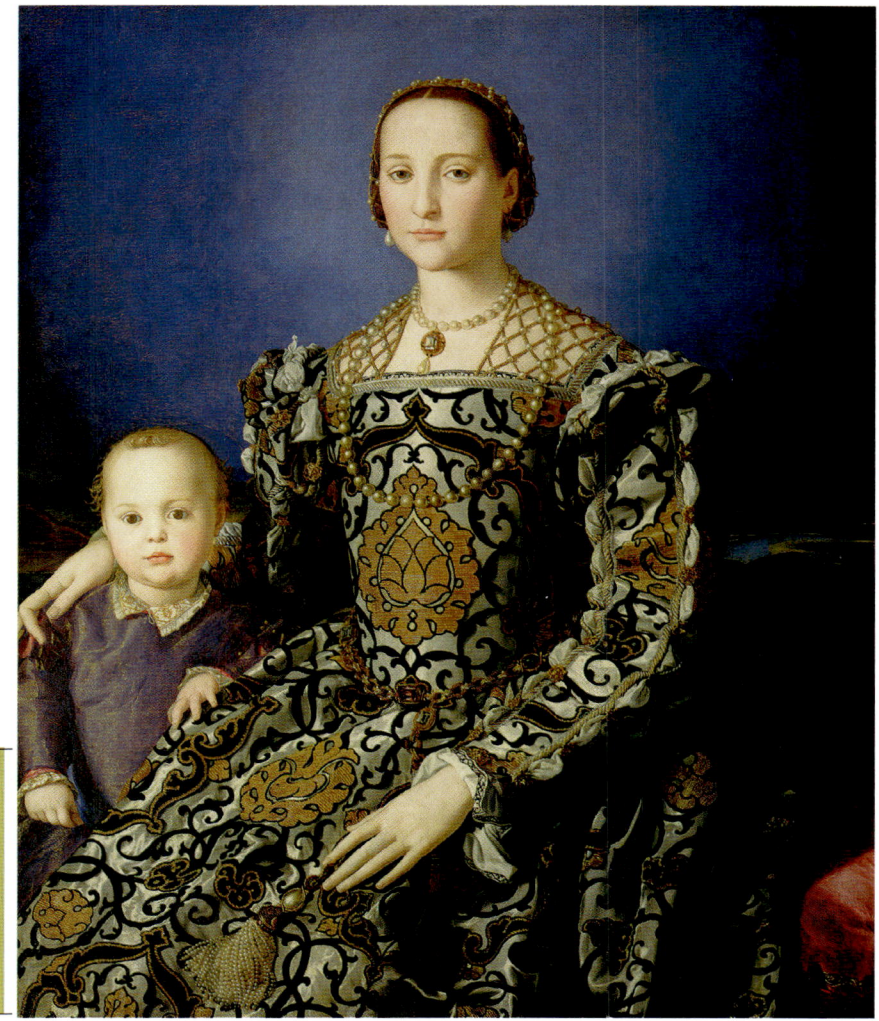

**22-46** BRONZINO, *Eleanora of Toledo and Giovanni de' Medici,* ca. 1546. Oil on wood, 3′ 9¼″ × 3′ 1¾″. Galleria degli Uffizi, Florence. ◼◀

Bronzino was the official portraitist of Grand Duke Cosimo de' Medici. His portrayal of Cosimo's Spanish wife and their second son features rich costumes and coolly detached personalities.

order to behave as expected on this formal occasion. Bronzino's portrayal of Eleanora and Giovanni is in some ways less a portrait of a mother and child than of a royal audience.

**SOFONISBA ANGUISSOLA** The aloof formality of Bronzino's dynastic portrait is much relaxed in the portraiture of SOFONISBA ANGUISSOLA (ca. 1532–1625) of Cremona in northern Italy. Anguissola introduced a new kind of group portrait of irresistible charm, characterized by an informal intimacy and subjects that are often moving, conversing, or engaged in activities. Like many of the other works she produced before emigrating to Spain in 1559, the portrait illustrated here (FIG. **22-47**) represents members of her family. Against a neutral ground, Anguissola placed her two sisters and brother in an affectionate pose meant not for official display but for private showing. The sisters, wearing matching striped gowns, flank their brother, who caresses a lapdog. The older sister (at the left) summons the dignity required for the occasion, while the boy looks quizzically at the portraitist with an expression of naive curiosity, and the other girl diverts her attention toward something or someone to the painter's left.

Anguissola's use of relaxed poses and expressions, her sympathetic personal presentation, and her graceful treatment of the forms brought her international acclaim (see "Women in the Renaissance Art World," page 630). She received praise from the aged Michelangelo, was court painter to Phillip II (r. 1556–1598) of Spain, and, at the end of her life, gave advice on art to a young admirer of her work, Anthony Van Dyck (FIG. 25-5), the great Flemish master.

**22-47** SOFONISBA ANGUISSOLA, *Portrait of the Artist's Sisters and Brother,* ca. 1555. Oil on wood, 2′ 5¼″ × 3′ 1½″. Methuen Collection, Corsham Court, Wiltshire.

Anguissola was the leading woman artist of her time. Her contemporaries admired her use of relaxed poses and expressions in intimate and informal group portraits such as this one of her family.

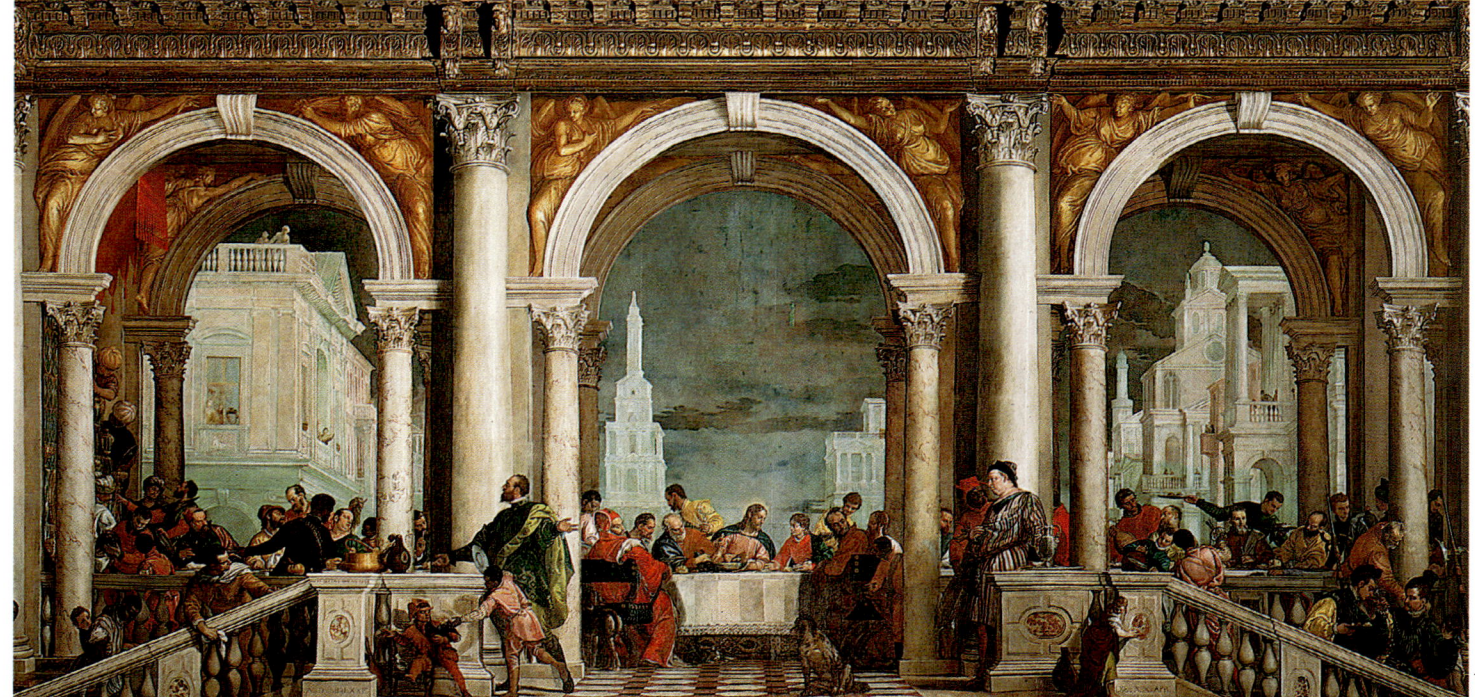

1 ft.

**TINTORETTO** Venetian painting of the later 16th century built on established High Renaissance Venetian ideas, but incorporated many elements of the Mannerist style. Jacopo Robusti, known as TINTORETTO (1518–1594), claimed to be a student of Titian and aspired to combine Titian's color with Michelangelo's drawing, but art historians consider Tintoretto the outstanding Venetian representative of Mannerism. He adopted many Mannerist pictorial devices, which he employed to produce works imbued with dramatic power, depth of spiritual vision, and glowing Venetian color schemes.

Toward the end of Tintoretto's life, his art became spiritual, even visionary, as solid forms melted away into swirling clouds of dark shot through with fitful light. In Tintoretto's *Last Supper* (FIG. **22-48**), painted for the right wall next to the high altar in Andrea Palladio's church of San Giorgio Maggiore (FIG. 22-31), the figures appear in a dark interior illuminated by a single light in the upper left of the image. The shimmering halos establish the biblical nature of the scene. The ability of this dramatic scene to engage viewers was fully in keeping with Counter-Reformation ideals

**22-49** PAOLO VERONESE, *Christ in the House of Levi,* from the refectory of Santi Giovanni e Paolo, Venice, Italy, 1573. Oil on canvas, 18′ 3″ × 42′. Galleria dell'Accademia, Venice.

Veronese's paintings feature superb color and majestic classical settings. The Catholic Church accused him of impiety for including dogs and dwarfs near Christ in this work originally titled *Last Supper*.

(see "Religious Art in Counter-Reformation Italy," page 617) and the Catholic Church's belief in the didactic nature of religious art.

Tintoretto's *Last Supper* incorporates many Mannerist devices, including an imbalanced composition and visual complexity. In terms of design, the contrast with Leonardo's *Last Supper* (FIG. 22-4) is both extreme and instructive. Leonardo's composition, balanced and symmetrical, parallels the picture plane in a geometrically organized and closed space. The figure of Christ is the tranquil center of the drama and the perspective focus. In Tintoretto's painting, Christ is above and beyond the converging perspective lines racing diagonally away from the picture surface, creating disturbing effects of limitless depth and motion. The viewer locates Tintoretto's Christ via the light flaring, beaconlike, out of darkness. The contrast of the two pictures reflects the direction Renaissance painting took in the 16th century, as it moved away from architectonic clarity of space and neutral lighting toward the dynamic perspectives and dramatic chiaroscuro of the coming Baroque.

**VERONESE** Among the great Venetian masters was Paolo Caliari of Verona, called PAOLO VERONESE (1528–1588). Whereas Tintoretto gloried in monumental drama and deep perspectives, Veronese specialized in splendid pageantry painted in superb color and set within majestic classical architecture. Like Tintoretto, Veronese painted on a huge scale, with canvases often as large as 20 by 30 feet or more. His usual subjects, painted for the refectories of wealthy monasteries, afforded him an opportunity to display magnificent companies at table.

Veronese painted *Christ in the House of Levi* (FIG. 22-49), originally called *Last Supper*, for the dining hall of Santi Giovanni e Paolo in Venice. In a great open loggia framed by three monumental arches, Christ sits at the center of the splendidly garbed elite of Venice. In the foreground, with a courtly gesture, the very image of gracious grandeur, the chief steward welcomes guests. Robed lords, their colorful retainers, dogs, and dwarfs crowd into the spacious loggia. Painted during the Counter-Reformation, this depiction prompted criticism from the Catholic Church. The Holy Office of the Inquisition accused Veronese of impiety for painting lowly creatures so close to the Lord, and it ordered him to make changes at his own expense. Reluctant to do so, he simply changed the painting's title, converting the subject to a less solemn one. As Palladio looked to the example of classically inspired High Renaissance architecture, so Veronese returned to High Renaissance composition, its symmetrical balance, and its ordered architectonics. His shimmering colors span the whole spectrum, although he avoided solid colors in favor of half shades (light blues, sea greens, lemon yellows, roses, and violets), creating veritable flowerbeds of tone.

10 ft.

**22-50** PAOLO VERONESE, *Triumph of Venice*, ca. 1585. Oil on canvas, 29′ 8″ × 19′. Hall of the Grand Council, Doge's Palace, Venice.

Veronese's immense oval ceiling painting presents a tableau of Venice crowned by Fame amid columns, clouds, and personifications. Baroque painters adopted this 45-degree view from the ground.

The Venetian Republic employed both Tintoretto and Veronese to decorate the grand chambers and council rooms of the Doge's Palace (FIG. 14-21). A great and popular decorator, Veronese revealed himself a master of imposing illusionistic ceiling compositions, such as *Triumph of Venice* (FIG. 22-50). Here, within an oval frame, he presented Venice, crowned by Fame, enthroned between two great twisted columns in a balustraded loggia, garlanded with clouds, and attended by figures symbolic of its glories. Unlike Mantegna's *di sotto in sù* (FIG. 21-49) perspective, Veronese's is not a projection directly up from below, but at a 45-degree angle to spectators, a technique used by many later Baroque decorators (see Chapter 24).

**22-51** CORREGGIO, *Assumption of the Virgin*, 1526–1530. Fresco, 35′ 10″ × 37′ 11″. Parma Cathedral, Parma.

Working long before Veronese, Correggio, the teacher of Parmigianino, won little fame in his day, but his illusionistic ceiling designs, such as this one in Parma Cathedral, inspired many Baroque painters.

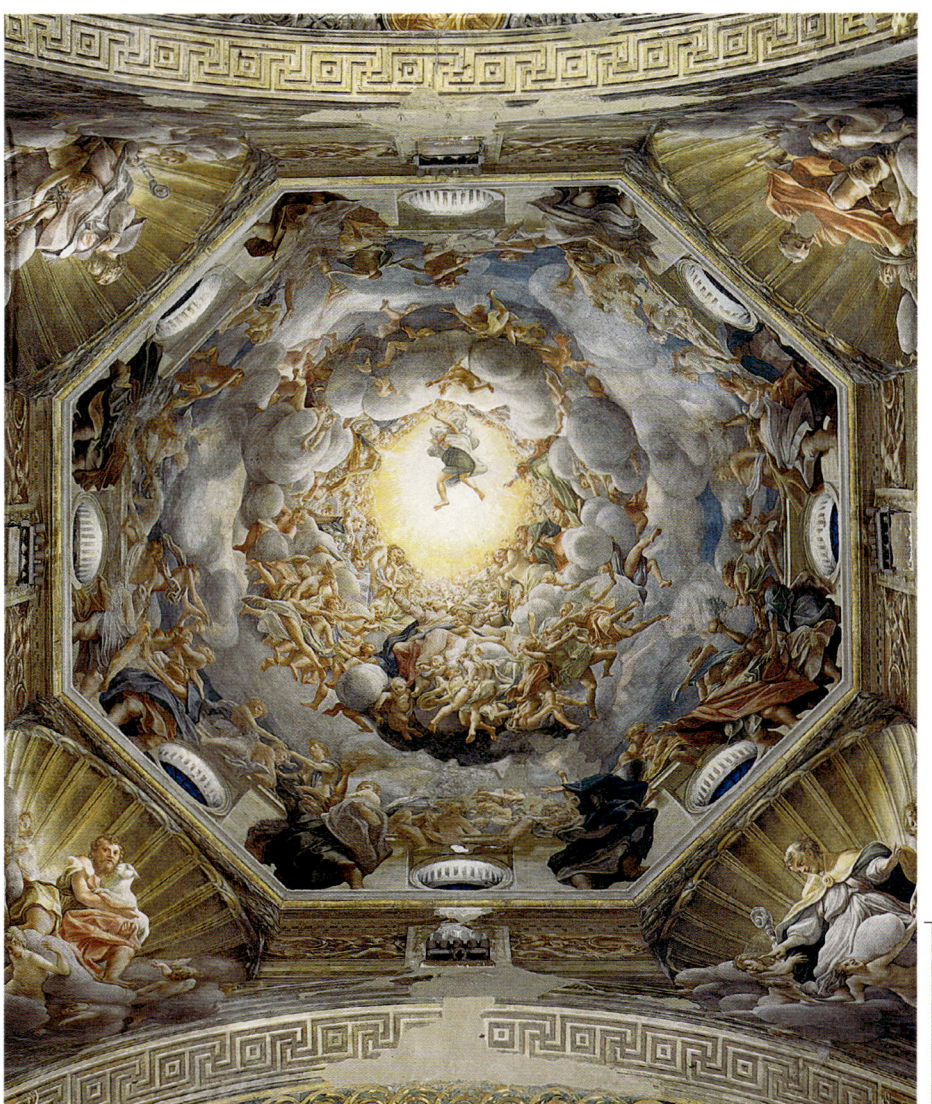

10 ft.

**CORREGGIO** One painter who developed a unique personal style almost impossible to classify was Antonio Allegri, known as CORREGGIO (ca. 1489–1534) from his birthplace, near Parma. The teacher of Parmigianino, Correggio pulled together many stylistic trends, including those of Leonardo, Raphael, and the Venetians. Working more than a half century before Veronese, Correggio's most enduring contribution was his development of illusionistic ceiling perspectives. In Parma Cathedral, he painted away the entire dome with his *Assumption of the Virgin* (FIG. **22-51**). Opening up the *cupola,* the artist showed worshipers a view of the sky, with concentric rings of clouds where hundreds of soaring figures perform a wildly pirouetting dance in celebration of the Assumption. Versions of these angelic creatures became permanent tenants of numerous Baroque churches in later centuries. Correggio was also an influential painter of religious panels, anticipating in them many other Baroque compositional devices. Correggio's *Assumption of the Virgin* predates Veronese's *Triumph of Venice* by more than a half century, but contemporaries expressed little appreciation for his achievement. Later, during the 17th century, Baroque painters recognized him as a kindred spirit.

## Sculpture

Mannerism extended beyond painting. Artists translated its principles into sculpture and architecture as well.

**BENVENUTO CELLINI** Among those who made their mark as Mannerist sculptors was BENVENUTO CELLINI (1500–1571), the author of a fascinating autobiography. It is difficult to imagine a medieval artist composing an autobiography. Only in the Renaissance, with the birth of the notion of individual artistic genius, could a work such as Cellini's (or Vasari's *Lives*)

**22-52** BENVENUTO CELLINI, *Saltcellar of Francis I,* 1540–1543. Gold, enamel, and ebony, 10¼″ × 1′ 1⅛″. Stolen in 2003 from the Kunsthistorisches Museum, Vienna.

Famed as a master goldsmith, Cellini fashioned this costly saltcellar for the table of Francis I of France. The elongated proportions of the figures clearly reveal Cellini's Mannerist approach to form.

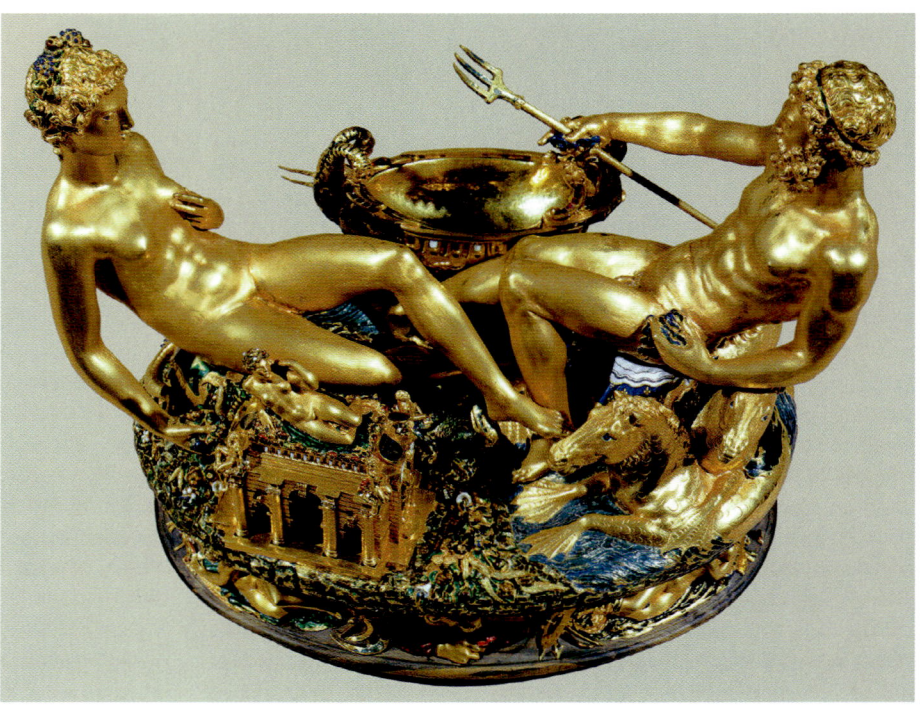

1 in.

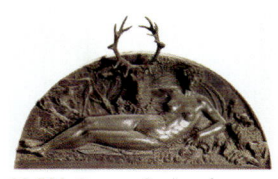

have been conceived and written. Cellini's literary self-portrait presents him not only as a highly accomplished artist but also as a statesman, soldier, and lover, among many other roles. He was, first of all, a goldsmith, but only one of his major works in that medium survives, the saltcellar (FIG. 22-52) he made for the royal table of Francis I (FIG. 23-12). The king had hired Cellini with a retainer of an annual salary, supplemented by fees for the works he produced, for example, his *Genius of Fontainebleau* (FIG. 22-52A) for the royal hunting lodge outside Paris. The price Francis paid Cellini for the luxurious gold-and-*enamel* saltcellar illustrated here was almost 50 percent greater than the artist's salary for the year. Neptune and Tellus (or, as Cellini named them, Sea—the source of salt—and Land) recline atop an ebony base decorated with relief figures of Dawn, Day, Twilight, Night, and the four winds—some based on Michelangelo's statues in the Medici Chapel (FIG. 22-16) in San Lorenzo. The boat next to Neptune's right leg contained the salt, and the triumphal arch (compare FIG. 7-75) next to the right leg of the earth goddess held the pepper. The elongated proportions of the figures, especially the slim, small-breasted figure of Tellus, whom ancient artists always represented as a matronly woman (FIG. 7-30), reveal Cellini's Mannerist approach to form.

**GIOVANNI DA BOLOGNA** The lure of Italy drew a brilliant young Flemish sculptor, Jean de Boulogne, to Italy, where he practiced his art under the equivalent Italian name of GIOVANNI DA BOLOGNA (1529–1608). Giovanni's *Abduction of the Sabine Women* (FIG. 22-53) exemplifies Mannerist principles of figure composition. Drawn from the legendary history of early Rome, the group of figures received its current title—relating how the Romans abducted wives for themselves from the neighboring Sabines—only after its exhibition. Earlier, it was *Paris Abducting Helen,* among other mythological titles. In fact, Giovanni did not intend to depict any particular subject. He created the group as a demonstration piece. His goal was to achieve a dynamic spiral figural composition involving an old man, a young man, and a woman, all nude in the tradition of ancient statues portraying deities and mythological figures. Although Giovanni would have known Antonio Pollaiuolo's *Hercules and Antaeus* (FIG. 21-14), whose Greek hero lifts his opponent off the ground, he turned directly to ancient sculpture for inspiration, especially to *Laocoön* (FIG. 5-89). *Abduction of the Sabine Women* includes references to that universally admired statue in the crouching old man and in the woman's up-flung arm. The three bodies interlock on a vertical axis, creating an ascending spiral movement.

To appreciate the sculpture fully, the viewer must walk around it, because the work changes radically according to the viewing point. One factor contributing to the shifting imagery is the prominence of open spaces passing through the masses (for example, the space between an arm and a body), which have as great an effect as the solids. This sculpture was the first large-scale group since classical antiquity designed to be seen from multiple viewpoints, in striking contrast to Pollaiuolo's group, which the artist fashioned to be seen from the angle shown in FIG. 21-14. Giovanni's figures do not break out of this spiral vortex but remain as if contained within a cylinder. Nonetheless, they display athletic flexibility and Michelangelesque potential for action.

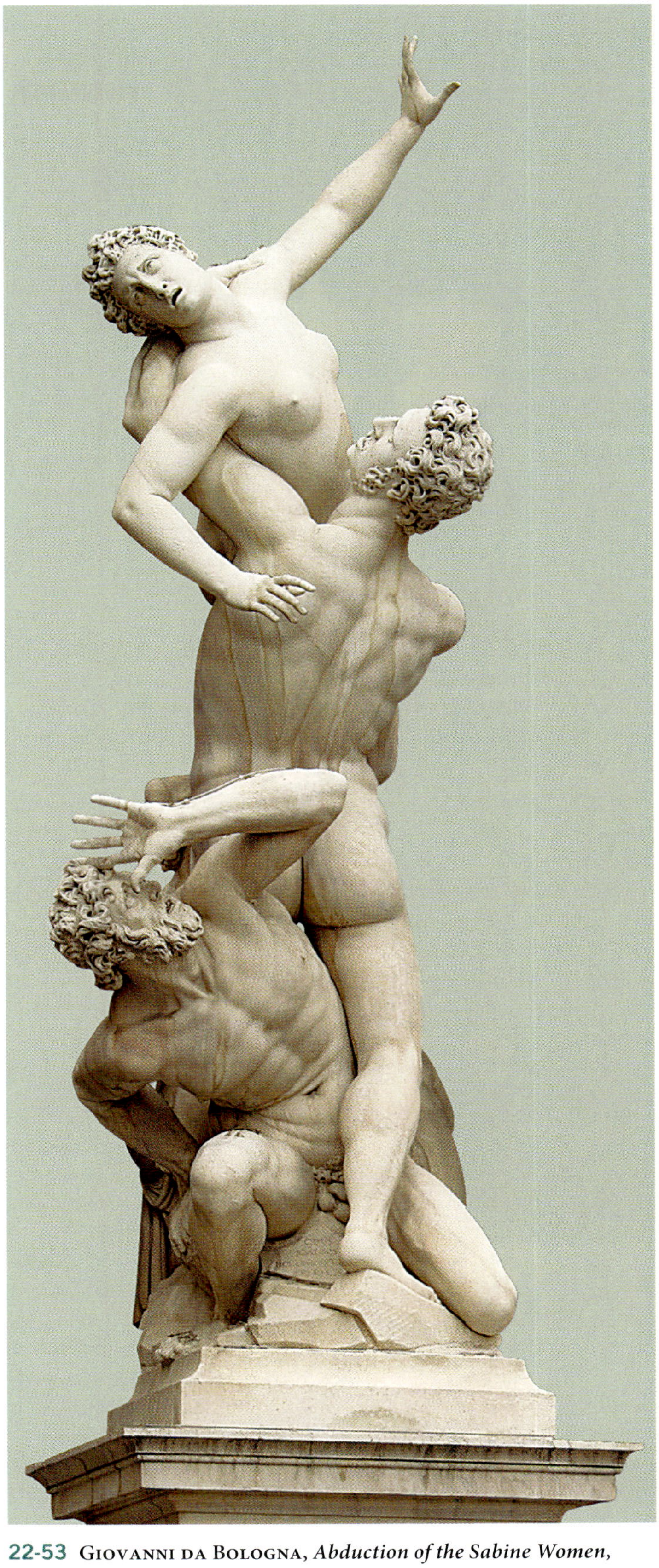

1 ft.

**22-53** GIOVANNI DA BOLOGNA, *Abduction of the Sabine Women,* Loggia dei Lanzi, Piazza della Signoria, Florence, Italy, 1579–1583. Marble, 13′ 5½″ high. ◼◀

This sculpture was the first large-scale group since classical antiquity designed to be seen from multiple viewpoints. The three bodies interlock to create a vertical spiral movement.

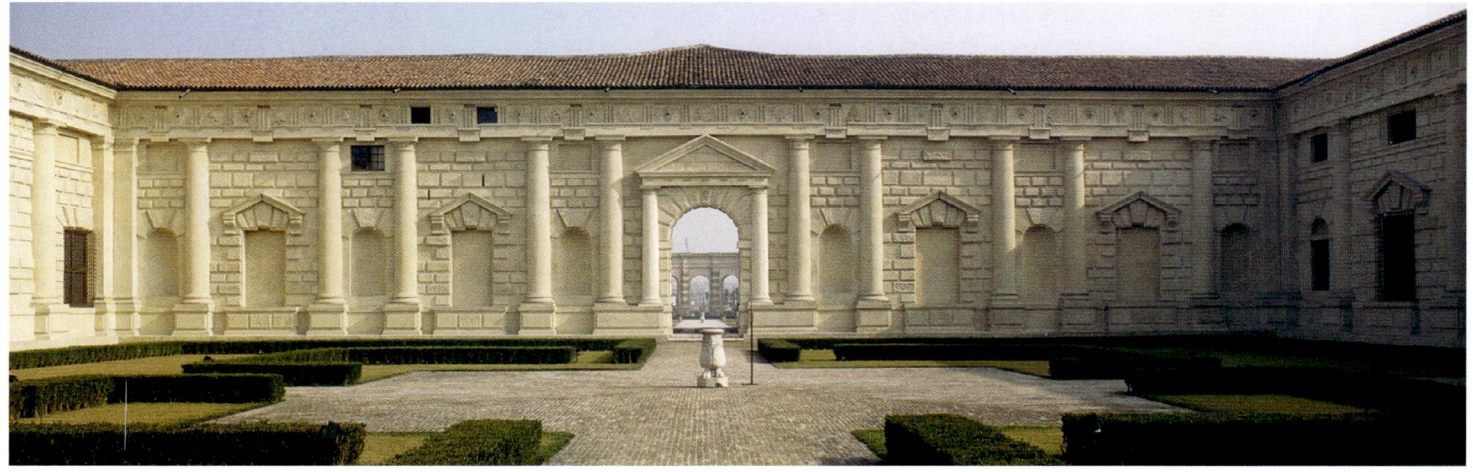

**22-54** GIULIO ROMANO, courtyard of the Palazzo del Tè (looking southeast), Mantua, Italy, 1525–1535.

The Mannerist divergences from architectural convention, for example, the slipping triglyphs, are so pronounced in the Palazzo del Tè that they constitute a parody of Bramante's classical style.

# Architecture

Mannerist architects used classical architectural elements in a highly personal and unorthodox manner, rejecting the balance, order, and stability that were the hallmarks of the High Renaissance style, and aiming instead to reveal the contrived nature of architectural design.

**GIULIO ROMANO** Applying that anticlassical principle was the goal of GIULIO ROMANO (ca. 1499–1546) when he designed the Palazzo del Tè (FIG. **22-54**) in Mantua and, with it, formulated almost the entire architectural vocabulary of Mannerism. Early in his career, Giulio was Raphael's chief assistant in decorating the Vatican stanze. After Raphael's premature death in 1520, Giulio became his master's artistic executor, completing Raphael's unfinished frescoes and panel paintings. In 1524, Giulio went to Mantua, where he found a patron in Duke Federigo Gonzaga (r. 1530–1540), for whom he built and decorated (FIG. **22-54A**) the Palazzo del Tè between 1525 and 1535. Gonzaga intended the palace to serve as both suburban summer residence and stud farm for his famous stables. Originally planned as a relatively modest country villa, Giulio's building so pleased his patron that Gonzaga soon commissioned the architect to enlarge the structure. In a second building campaign, Giulio expanded the villa to a palatial scale by adding three wings, which he placed around a square central court. This once-paved court, which functions both as a passage and as the focal point of the design, has a nearly urban character. Its surrounding buildings form a self-enclosed unit with a large garden, flanked by a stable, attached to it on the east side.

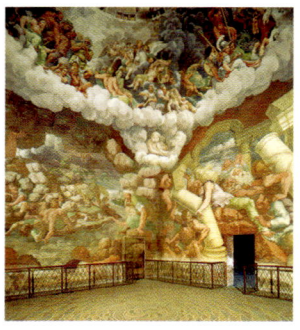

**22-54A** GIULIO ROMANO, *Fall of the Giants*, 1530–1532.

Giulio's Mannerist style is on display in the facades facing the palace's courtyard (FIG. 22-54), where the divergences from architectural convention are pronounced. Indeed, the Palazzo del Tè constitutes an enormous parody of Bramante's classical style, a veritable Mannerist manifesto announcing the artifice of architectural design. In a building laden with structural surprises and contradictions, the courtyard is the most unconventional of all. The *keystones* (central *voussoirs*), for example, either have not fully settled or seem to be slipping from the arches—and, more eccentric still, Giulio even placed voussoirs in the pediments over the rectangular niches, where no arches exist. The massive Tuscan columns flanking these niches carry incongruously narrow *architraves*. That these architraves break midway between the columns stresses their apparent structural insufficiency, and they seem unable to support the weight of the *triglyphs* of the *Doric frieze* above (see "Doric and Ionic Orders," Chapter 5, page 116, or on page xxii in Volume II and Book D), which threaten to crash down on the head of anyone foolish enough to stand beneath them. To be sure, only a highly sophisticated observer can appreciate Giulio's witticism. Recognizing some quite subtle departures from the norm presupposes a thorough familiarity with the established rules of classical architecture. That the duke delighted in Giulio's mannered architectural inventiveness speaks to his cultivated taste.

**LAURENTIAN LIBRARY** Although he personifies the High Renaissance artist, Michelangelo, like Giulio Romano, also experimented with architectural designs that flouted most of the classical rules of order and stability. The restless nature of Michelangelo's genius is evident in the vestibule (FIG. **22-55**) he designed for the Medici library adjoining the Florentine church of San Lorenzo. The Laurentian Library had two contrasting spaces Michelangelo had to unite: the long horizontal of the library proper and the vertical of the vestibule. The need to place the vestibule windows up high (at the level of the reading room) determined the narrow verticality of the vestibule's elevation and proportions. Much taller than it is wide, the vestibule gives the impression of a vertically compressed, shaftlike space. Anyone schooled exclusively in the classical architecture of Bramante and the High Renaissance would have been appalled by Michelangelo's indifference here to classical norms in proportion and in the application of the rules of the classical orders. For example, he used columns in pairs and sank them into the walls, where they perform no supporting function. Michelangelo also split columns in halves around corners. Elsewhere, he placed scroll *corbels* on the walls beneath columns. They seem to

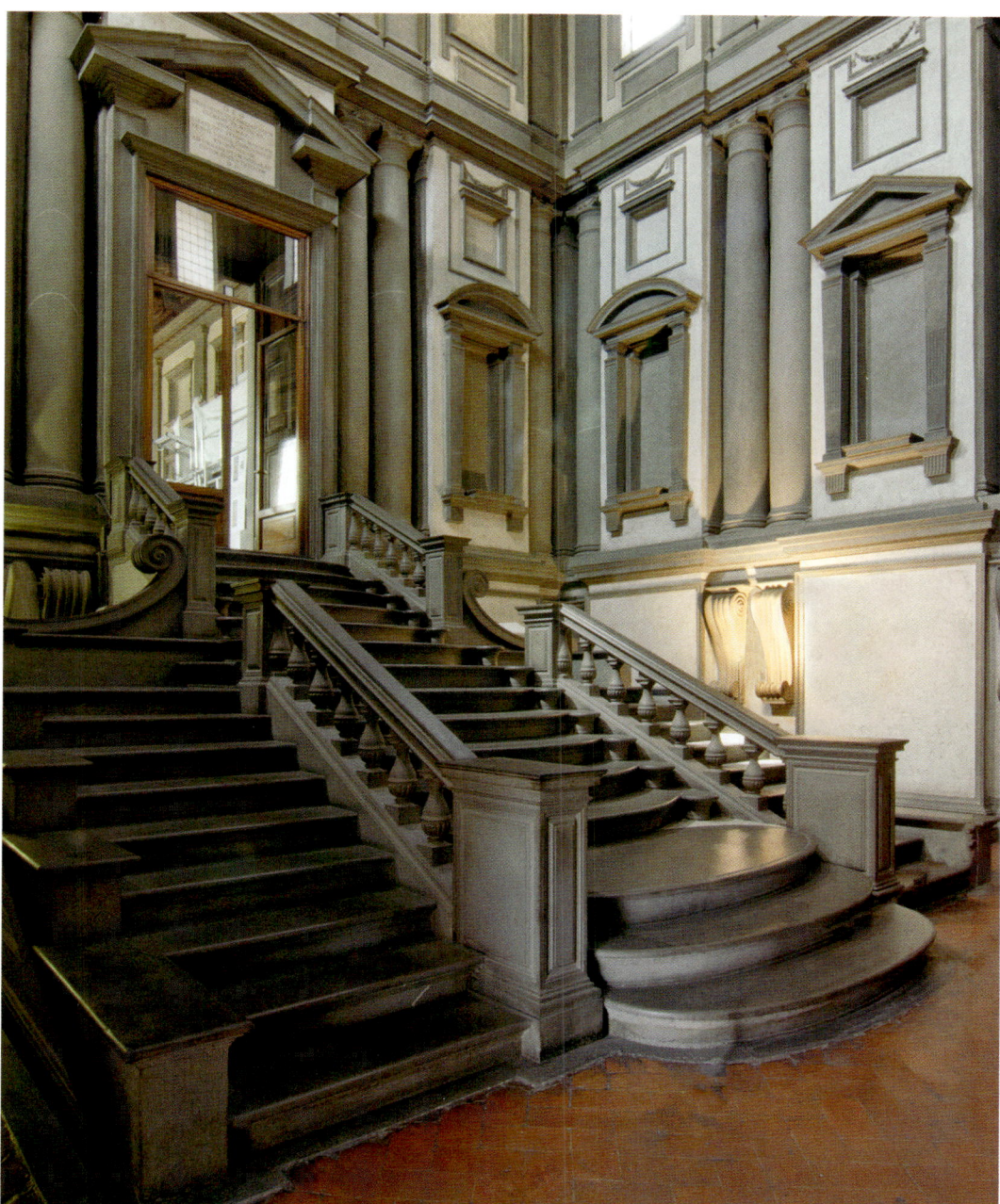

**22-55** Michelangelo
Buonarroti, vestibule of the
Laurentian Library, Florence, Italy,
1524–1534; staircase, 1558–1559. ◼◀

With his customary independence
of spirit, Michelangelo, working in a
Mannerist mode in the Laurentian
Library vestibule, disposed willfully
of almost all the rules of classical
architecture.

hang from the moldings, holding up nothing. He arbitrarily broke through pediments as well as through cornices and stringcourses. He sculpted pilasters that taper downward instead of upward. In short, the High Renaissance master, working in a Mannerist mode, disposed willfully and abruptly of classical architecture. Moreover, in the vast, flowing stairway (the latest element of the vestibule) that protrudes tonguelike into the room from the "mouth" of the doorway to the library, Michelangelo foreshadowed the dramatic movement of Baroque architecture (see Chapter 24). With his customary trailblazing independence of spirit, Michelangelo created an interior space that conveyed all the strains and tensions found in his statuary and in his painted figures. Michelangelo's art began in the style of the Quattrocento, developed into the epitome of High Renaissance art, and, at the end, moved toward Mannerism. He was 89 when he died in 1564, still hard at work on Saint Peter's and other projects. Few artists, then or since, could escape his influence.

**IL GESÙ** Probably the most influential building of the later Cinquecento was the mother church of the Jesuit order. The activity of the Society of Jesus, known as the Jesuits, was an important component of the Counter-Reformation. Ignatius of Loyola (1491–1556), a Spanish nobleman who dedicated his life to the service of God, founded the Jesuit order. He attracted a group of followers, and in 1540 Pope Paul III formally recognized his group as a religious order. The Jesuits were the papacy's invaluable allies in its quest to reassert the supremacy of the Catholic Church. Particularly successful in the field of education, the order established numerous schools. In addition, its members were effective missionaries and carried the message of Catholicism to the Americas, Asia, and Africa.

As a major participant in the Counter-Reformation, the Jesuit order needed a church appropriate to its new prominence. Because Michelangelo was late in providing the designs for their church,

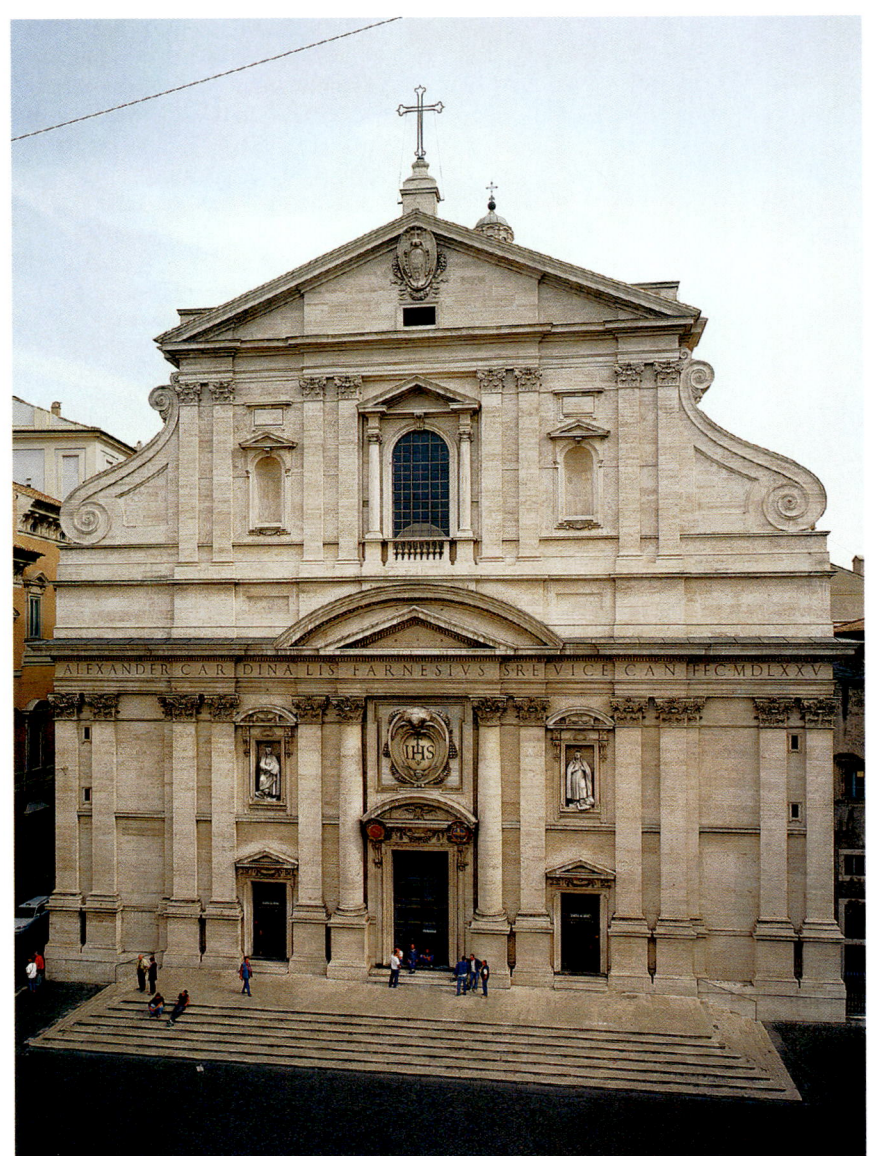

**22-56** GIACOMO DELLA PORTA, west facade of Il Gesù, Rome, Italy, ca. 1575–1584.

In Giacomo della Porta's innovative design, the march of pilasters and columns builds to a climax at the central bay. Many Roman Baroque church facades are architectural variations of Il Gesù.

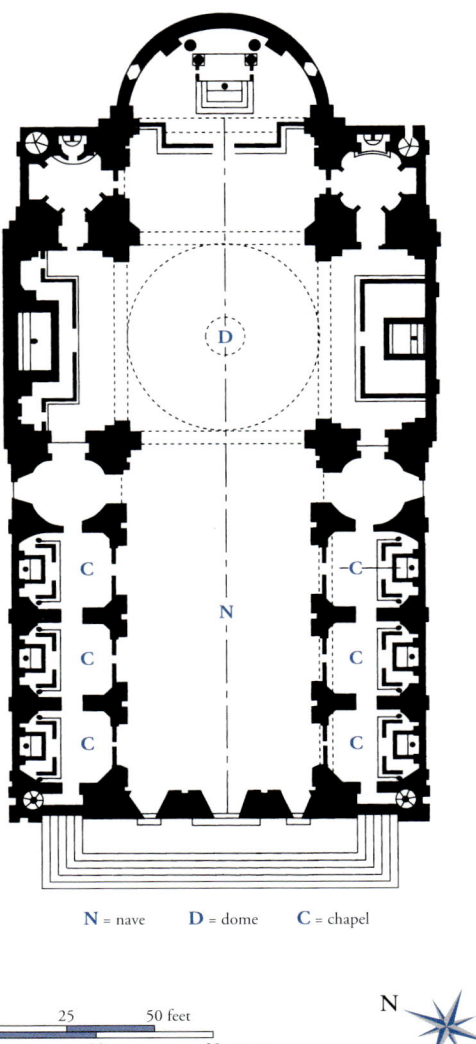

**N** = nave    **D** = dome    **C** = chapel

**22-57** GIACOMO DA VIGNOLA, plan of Il Gesù, Rome, Italy, 1568.

Giacomo da Vignola's plan for Il Gesù, with its exceptionally wide nave with side chapels instead of aisles—ideal for grand processions—won wide acceptance in the Catholic world.

called Il Gesù, or Church of Jesus, in 1568 the Jesuits turned to GIACOMO DELLA PORTA (ca. 1533–1602), who was responsible for the facade (FIG. **22-56**)—and who later designed the dome of Saint Peter's (FIG. 22-25)—and GIACOMO DA VIGNOLA (1507–1573), who designed the ground plan (FIG. **22-57**).

The plan of Il Gesù reveals a monumental expansion of Alberti's scheme for Sant'Andrea (FIGS. 21-46 and 21-47) in Mantua. Here, the nave takes over the main volume of space, making the structure a great hall with side chapels. A dome emphasizes the approach to the altar. The wide acceptance of the Gesù plan in the Catholic world, even in modern times, speaks to its ritual efficacy. The opening of the church building into a single great hall provides an almost theatrical setting for large promenades and processions (which combined social with priestly functions). Above all, the ample space could accommodate the great crowds that gathered to hear the eloquent preaching of the Jesuits.

The facade of Il Gesù was also not entirely original, but it too had an enormous influence on later church design. The union of the lower and upper stories, achieved by scroll buttresses, harks back to Alberti's Santa Maria Novella (FIG. 21-40). Its classical pediment is familiar in Alberti's work (FIG. 21-45), as well as in that of Palladio (FIGS. 22-28 and 22-30). The paired pilasters appear in Michelangelo's design for Saint Peter's (FIG. 22-25). Giacomo della Porta skillfully synthesized these existing motifs and unified the two stories. The horizontal march of the pilasters and columns builds to a dramatic climax at the central bay, and the bays of the facade snugly fit the nave-chapel system behind them. Many Roman church facades of the 17th century are architectural variations on della Porta's design. Chronologically and stylistically, Il Gesù belongs to the Late Renaissance, but its enormous influence on later churches marks it as one of the significant monuments for the development of Italian Baroque church architecture, discussed in Chapter 24.

# RENAISSANCE AND MANNERISM IN CINQUECENTO ITALY

## HIGH AND LATE RENAISSANCE 1495–1600

❚ During the High (1495–1520) and Late (1520–1600) Renaissance periods in Italy, artists, often in the employ of the papacy, further developed the interest in classical cultures, perspective, proportion, and human anatomy that had characterized Quattrocento Italian art.

❚ The major regional artistic centers were Florence and Rome in central Italy and Venice in the north. Whereas most Florentine and Roman artists emphasized careful design preparation based on preliminary drawing (*disegno*), Venetian artists focused on color and the process of paint application (*colorito*).

❚ Leonardo da Vinci, the quintessential "Renaissance man," won renown as a painter for his *sfumato* (misty haziness) and for his psychological insight in depicting biblical narrative (*Last Supper*) and contemporary personalities (*Mona Lisa*).

❚ Raphael favored lighter tonalities than Leonardo and clarity over obscurity. His sculpturesque figures appear in landscapes under blue skies (*Madonna of the Meadows*) or in grandiose architectural settings rendered in perfect perspective (*School of Athens*).

❚ Michelangelo was a pioneer in several media, including architecture, but his first love was sculpture. He carved (*David, Moses*) and painted (Sistine Chapel ceiling) emotionally charged figures with heroic physiques, preferring pent-up energy to Raphael's calm, ideal beauty.

❚ The leading architect of the early 16th century was Bramante, who championed the classical style of the ancients. He based his design for the Tempietto—the first High Renaissance building—on antique models, but the combination of parts was new and original.

❚ Andrea Palladio, an important theorist as well as architect, carried on Bramante's classical style during the Late Renaissance. Renowned for his villa designs, he had a lasting influence upon later European and American architecture.

❚ The greatest master of the Venetian painting school was Titian, famed for his rich surface textures and dazzling display of color in all its nuances. In paintings such as *Meeting of Bacchus and Ariadne,* he established oil color on canvas as the standard medium of the Western pictorial tradition.

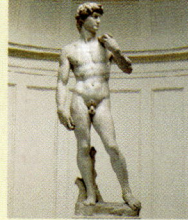

Michelangelo, *David,*
1501–1504

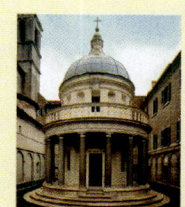

Bramante, Tempietto, Rome,
begun 1502

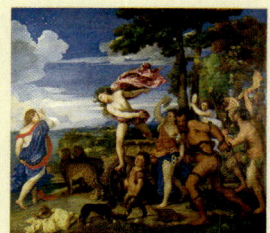

Titian, *Meeting of Bacchus
and Ariadne,* 1522–1523

## MANNERISM 1520–1600

❚ Mannerism emerged in the 1520s in reaction to the High Renaissance style of Leonardo and Raphael. A prime feature of Mannerist art is artifice. Renaissance painters generally strove to create art that appeared natural, whereas Mannerist artists were less inclined to disguise the contrived nature of art production. Ambiguous space, departures from expected conventions, and unusual presentations of traditional themes are hallmarks of Mannerist painting.

❚ Parmigianino's *Madonna with the Long Neck* epitomizes the elegant stylishness of Mannerist painting. The elongated proportions of the figures, the enigmatic line of columns without capitals, and the ambiguous position of the figure with a scroll are the antithesis of High Renaissance classical proportions, clarity of meaning, and rational perspective.

❚ Mannerism was also a sculptural style. Benvenuto Cellini created a costly saltcellar for the table of the French king Francis I. The figures, based on antique statuary, have the slim waists and long limbs that appealed to Mannerist taste.

❚ The leading Mannerist architect was Giulio Romano, who rejected the balance, order, and stability of the High Renaissance style. In the Palazzo del Tè in Mantua, which he also decorated with frescoes, the divergences from architectural convention parody Bramante's classical style and include triglyphs that slip out of the Doric frieze.

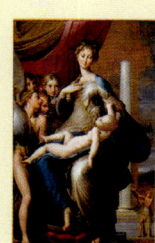

Parmigianino, *Madonna with
the Long Neck,* 1534–1540

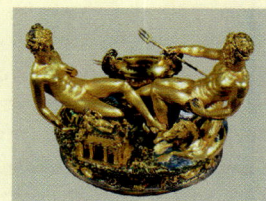

Cellini, *Saltcellar of Francis I,*
1540–1543

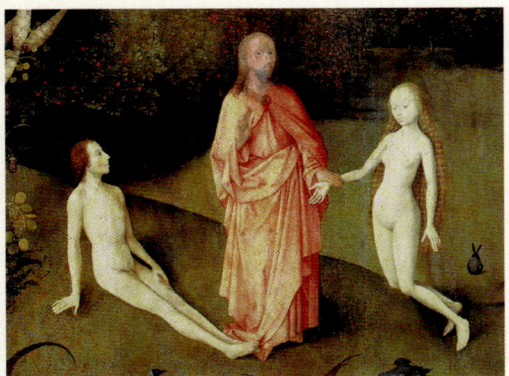

*Garden of Earthly Delights* is Bosch's most enigmatic painting, but scholars agree it depicts Paradise in the left and central panels and Hell in the right wing. At the left, God as Christ presents Eve to Adam.

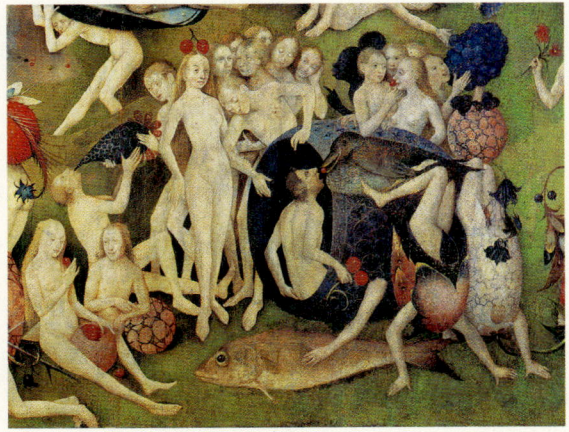

In the fantastic sunlit landscape that is Bosch's Paradise, scores of nude people in the prime of life blithely cavort. The oversize fruits are fertility symbols, and the scene celebrates procreation.

In the inky darkness of Bosch's Hell are unidentifiable objects that are imaginative variations on chemical apparatus of the day. Alchemy is a prominent theme of the work.

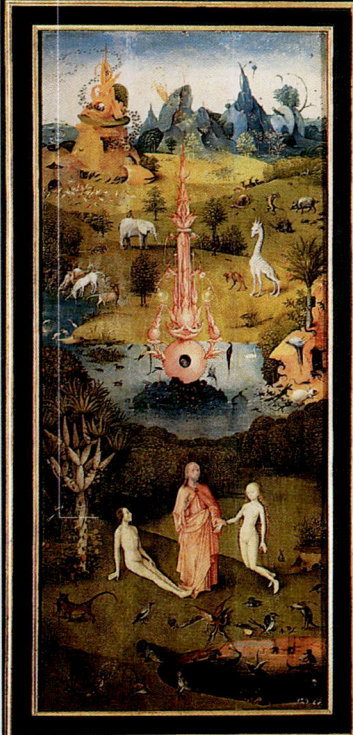 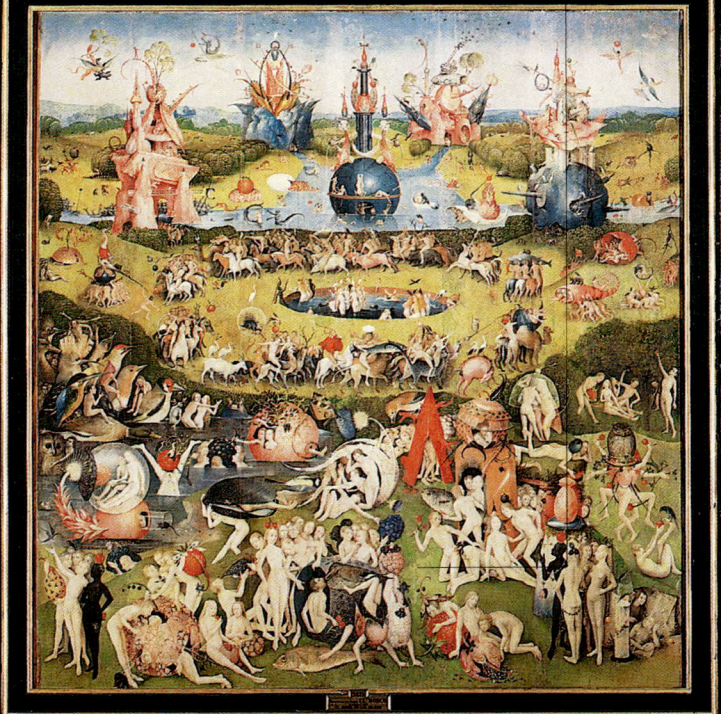

1 ft.

**23-1** Hieronymus Bosch, *Garden of Earthly Delights*, 1505–1510. Oil on wood, center panel 7′ 2⅝″ × 6′ 4¾″, each wing 7′ 2⅝″ × 3′ 2¼″. Museo del Prado, Madrid. ◼

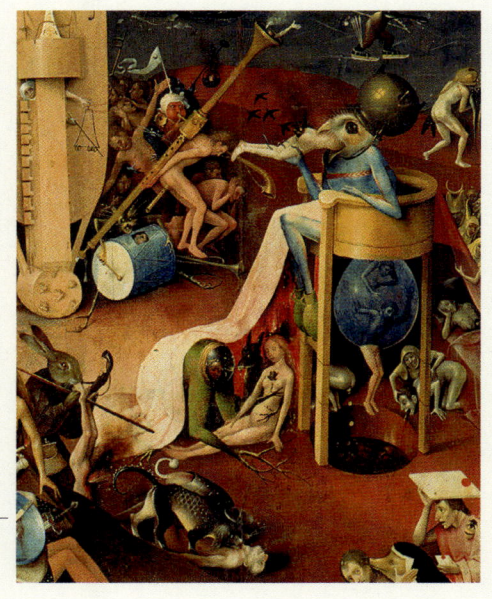

The horrors of Hell include beastly creatures devouring people, and sinners enduring tortures tailored to their conduct while alive. A glutton vomits eternally. A miser defecates gold coins.

# HIGH RENAISSANCE AND MANNERISM IN NORTHERN EUROPE AND SPAIN

## EARTHLY DELIGHTS IN THE NETHERLANDS

The leading Netherlandish painter of the early 16th century was HIERONYMUS BOSCH (ca. 1450–1516), one of the most fascinating and puzzling artists in history. Bosch's most famous painting, the *Garden of Earthly Delights* (FIG. 23-1), is also his most enigmatic, and no interpretation has ever won universal acceptance. Although the work is a monumental triptych, which would suggest a religious function as an altarpiece, *Garden of Earthly Delights* was on display in the palace of Henry III of Nassau, regent of the Netherlands, no later than seven years after its completion. This suggests the triptych was a secular commission, and some scholars have proposed that given the work's central themes of sex and procreation, the painting may commemorate a wedding. Marriage was a familiar theme in Netherlandish painting (FIGS. 20-6 and 20-10). Any similarity to earlier paintings ends there, however. Whereas Jan van Eyck and Petrus Christus grounded their depictions of betrothed couples in 15th-century life and custom, Bosch's image portrays a visionary world of fantasy and intrigue—a painted world without close parallel until the advent of Surrealism more than 400 years later (see Chapter 29).

In the left panel, God (in the form of Christ) presents Eve to Adam in a landscape, presumably the Garden of Eden. Bosch's wildly imaginative setting includes an odd pink fountainlike structure in a body of water and an array of fanciful and unusual animals, including a giraffe, an elephant, and winged fish.

The central panel is a continuation of Paradise, a sunlit landscape filled with nude people, all in the prime of youth, blithely cavorting amid bizarre creatures and unidentifiable objects. The youths play with abandon. Some stand on their hands or turn somersaults. The numerous fruits and birds (fertility symbols) in the scene suggest procreation, and, indeed, many of the figures pair off as couples.

In contrast to the orgiastic overtones of the central panel is the terrifying image of Hell in the right wing, where viewers must search through the inky darkness to find all of the fascinating though repulsive details Bosch recorded. Beastly creatures devour people, while other condemned souls endure tortures tailored to their conduct while alive. A glutton must vomit eternally. A miser defecates gold coins. A spidery monster fondles a promiscuous woman. Scholars have traditionally interpreted Bosch's triptych as a warning of the fate awaiting the sinful, decadent, and immoral, but as a secular work, *Garden of Earthly Delights* may have been intended for a learned audience fascinated by *alchemy*—the study of seemingly magical chemical changes. Details throughout the triptych are based on chemical apparatus of the day, which Bosch knew well because his in-laws were pharmacists.

# NORTHERN EUROPE IN THE 16TH CENTURY

The dissolution of the Burgundian Netherlands in 1477 led in the early 16th century to a realignment in the European geopolitical landscape (MAP 23-1). France and the Holy Roman Empire absorbed the former Burgundian territories and increased their power. But by the end of the century, through calculated marriages, military exploits, and ambitious territorial expansion, Spain was the dominant European state. Throughout the Continent, monarchs increasingly used art and architecture to glorify their reigns and to promote a stronger sense of cultural and political unity among their subjects, thereby laying the foundation for today's European nations. Wealthy merchants also cultivated art as a status symbol, as the commissioning and collecting of artworks became less and less the exclusive province of the aristocracy. Some artists, most notably Albrecht Dürer (FIGS. 23-4 to 23-7), became successful businessmen themselves by selling their works to the public.

These important societal changes occurred against the backdrop of a momentous religious crisis. Concerted attempts to reform Western Christendom led to the Reformation and the establishment of Protestantism (as distinct from Catholicism), which in turn prompted the Catholic Church's response, the Counter-Reformation (see Chapter 22). Ultimately, the Reformation split the Western Church in half and produced a hundred years of civil war between Protestants and Catholics. But the tumultuous religious conflict engulfing 16th-century Europe did not prevent—and may, in fact, have accelerated—the exchange of intellectual and artistic ideas, because artists frequently moved from one area to another in search of religious freedom and lucrative commissions. Catholic Italy and the (mostly) Protestant Holy Roman Empire shared in a lively commerce—economic and cultural—and 16th-century art throughout

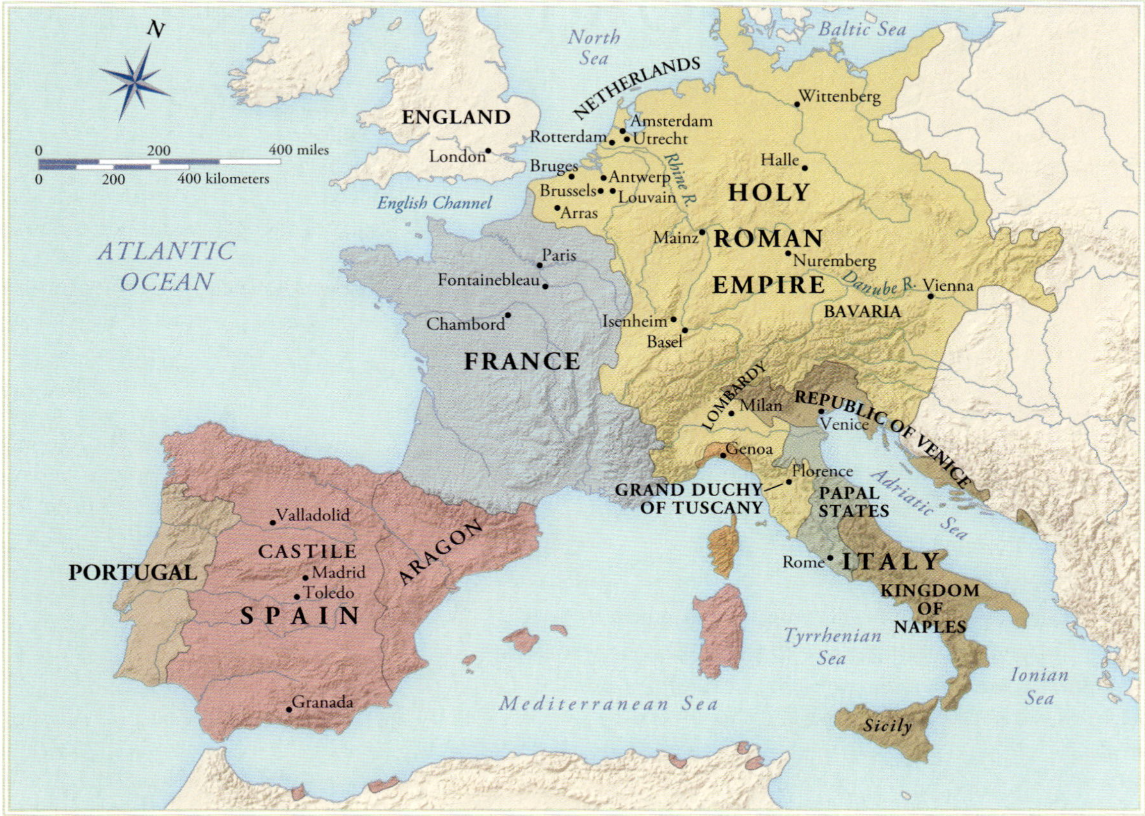

MAP 23-1 Europe in the early 16th century.

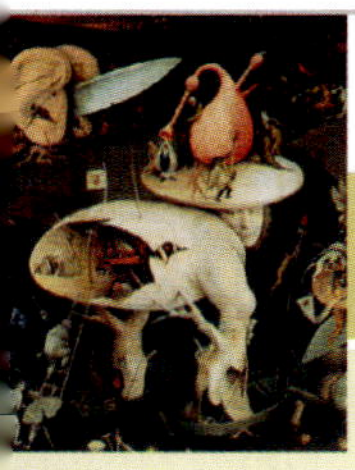

## HIGH RENAISSANCE AND MANNERISM IN NORTHERN EUROPE AND SPAIN

| 1500 | 1530 | 1560 | 1600 |
|---|---|---|---|

**1500**

▌ In Catholic countries, commissions for religious works, such as the *Isenheim Altarpiece*, continue, but, consistent with Reformation values, Protestant patrons prefer secular themes, including portraiture, classical mythology, and the macabre

▌ Albrecht Dürer, master printmaker, becomes the first international art celebrity outside Italy

**1530**

▌ In France under Henry II (r. 1547–1559), architectural designs are a mix of Italian and Northern Renaissance elements

▌ Netherlandish painters inject moralizing religious messages into seemingly secular genre paintings

▌ Hans Holbein, Caterina van Hemessen, and Levina Teerlinc achieve renown as portrait painters

**1560**

▌ Pieter Bruegel the Elder, the greatest Netherlandish artist of the mid-16th century, produces masterful landscapes that nonetheless focus on human activities

▌ Greek-born El Greco settles in Toledo and creates paintings that are a uniquely personal mix of Byzantine and Italian Mannerist elements. His hybrid style captured the fervor of Spanish Catholicism

**1600**

Europe was a major beneficiary of that exchange. Humanism filtered up from Italy and spread throughout northern Europe. Northern humanists, like their southern counterparts, cultivated knowledge of classical cultures and literature, but they focused more on reconciling humanism with Christianity.

Among the most influential of these "Christian humanists" were the Dutch-born Desiderius Erasmus (1466–1536) and the Englishman Thomas More (1478–1535). Erasmus demonstrated his interest in both Italian humanism and religion with his "philosophy of Christ," emphasizing education and scriptural knowledge. Both an ordained priest and avid scholar, Erasmus published his most famous essay, *In Praise of Folly*, in 1509. In this widely read work, he satirized not just the Church but various social classes as well. His ideas were to play an important role in the development of the Reformation, but he consistently declined to join any of the Reformation sects. Equally erudite was Thomas More, who served King Henry VIII (r. 1509–1547). Henry eventually ordered More's execution because of his opposition to England's break with the Catholic Church. In France, François Rabelais (ca. 1494–1553), a former monk who advocated rejecting stagnant religious dogmatism, disseminated the humanist spirit.

The turmoil emerging during the 16th century lasted well into the 17th century and permanently affected the face of Europe. The concerted challenges to established authority and the persistent philosophical inquiry eventually led to the rise of new political systems (for example, the nation-state) and new economic systems (such as capitalism).

# HOLY ROMAN EMPIRE

Although at the opening of the 16th century, many in the Holy Roman Empire (MAP 23-1) expressed dissatisfaction with the Church in Rome, Martin Luther had not yet posted the *Ninety-five Theses* that launched the Protestant Reformation. The Catholic clergy in Germany still offered artists important commissions to adorn churches and other religious institutions.

**MATTHIAS GRÜNEWALD** Matthias Neithardt, known conventionally as MATTHIAS GRÜNEWALD (ca. 1480–1528), worked for the archbishops of Mainz in several capacities, from court painter and decorator to architect, hydraulic engineer, and superintendent of works. Grünewald eventually moved to northern Germany, where he settled at Halle in Saxony. Around 1510, he began work on the *Isenheim Altarpiece* (FIG. **23-2**), a complex and fascinating monument reflecting Catholic beliefs and incorporating several references to Catholic doctrines, such as the lamb (symbol of the son of God), whose wound spurts blood into a chalice in the *Crucifixion* scene (FIG. 23-2, *top*) on the exterior of the altarpiece.

Created for the monastic hospital order of Saint Anthony of Isenheim, the *Isenheim Altarpiece* takes the form of a wooden shrine (carved around 1505 by NIKOLAUS HAGENAUER, active 1493–1538) featuring large gilded and polychromed statues of Saints Anthony Abbot, Augustine, and Jerome in the main zone and smaller statues of Christ and the 12 apostles in the predella (FIG. 23-2, *bottom*). To Hagenauer's centerpiece, Grünewald added two pairs of painted moveable wings that open at the center. Hinged at the sides, one pair stands directly behind the other. Grünewald painted the exterior panels of the first pair (visible when the altarpiece is closed,

FIG. 23-2, *top*) between 1510 and 1515: *Crucifixion* in the center, *Saint Sebastian* on the left, *Saint Anthony Abbot* on the right, and *Lamentation* in the predella. When these exterior wings are open, four additional scenes (not illustrated)—*Annunciation, Angelic Concert, Madonna and Child,* and *Resurrection*—appear. Opening this second pair of wings exposes Hagenauer's interior shrine, flanked by Grünewald's panels depicting *Meeting of Saints Anthony and Paul* and *Temptation of Saint Anthony* (FIG. 23-2, *bottom*).

The placement of this altarpiece in the choir of a church adjacent to the monastery's hospital dictated much of the imagery. Saints associated with the plague and other diseases and with miraculous cures, such as Saints Anthony and Sebastian, appear prominently in the *Isenheim Altarpiece*. Grünewald's panels specifically address the themes of dire illness and miraculous healing and accordingly emphasize the suffering of the order's patron saint, Anthony. The painted images served as warnings, encouraging increased devotion from monks and hospital patients. They also functioned therapeutically by offering some hope to the afflicted. Indeed, Saint Anthony's legend emphasized his dual role as vengeful dispenser of justice (by inflicting disease) and benevolent healer.

One of the most memorable scenes is *Temptation of Saint Anthony* (FIG. 23-2, *bottom right*). It is a terrifying image of the five temptations, depicted as an assortment of ghoulish and bestial creatures in a dark landscape, attacking the saint. In the foreground Grünewald painted a grotesque image of a man, whose oozing boils, withered arm, and distended stomach all suggest a horrible disease. Medical experts have connected these symptoms with ergotism (a disease caused by ergot, a fungus that grows especially on rye). Although doctors did not discover the cause of this disease until about 1600, people lived in fear of its recognizable symptoms (convulsions and gangrene). The public referred to this illness as "Saint Anthony's Fire," and it was one of the major diseases treated at the Isenheim hospital. The gangrene often compelled amputation, and scholars have noted that the two moveable halves of the altarpiece's predella (FIG. 23-2, *top*), if slid apart, make it appear as if Christ's legs have been amputated. The same observation applies to the two main exterior panels. Due to the off-center placement of the cross, opening the left panel "severs" one arm from the crucified figure.

Thus, Grünewald carefully selected and presented his altarpiece's iconography to be particularly meaningful for viewers at this hospital. In the interior shrine, the artist balanced the horrors of the disease and the punishments awaiting those who did not repent with scenes such as *Meeting of Saints Anthony and Paul,* depicting the two saints, healthy and aged, conversing peacefully. Even the exterior panels (the closed altarpiece; FIG. 23-2, *top*) convey these same concerns. *Crucifixion* emphasizes Christ's pain and suffering, but the knowledge that this act redeemed humanity tempers the misery. In addition, Saint Anthony appears in the right wing as a devout follower of Christ who, like Christ and for Christ, endured intense suffering for his faith. Saint Anthony's appearance on the exterior thus reinforces the themes Grünewald intertwined throughout this entire work—themes of pain, illness, and death, as well as those of hope, comfort, and salvation. Grünewald also brilliantly used color to enhance the effect of the painted scenes of the altarpiece. He intensified the contrast of horror and hope by playing subtle tones and soft harmonies against shocking dissonances of color.

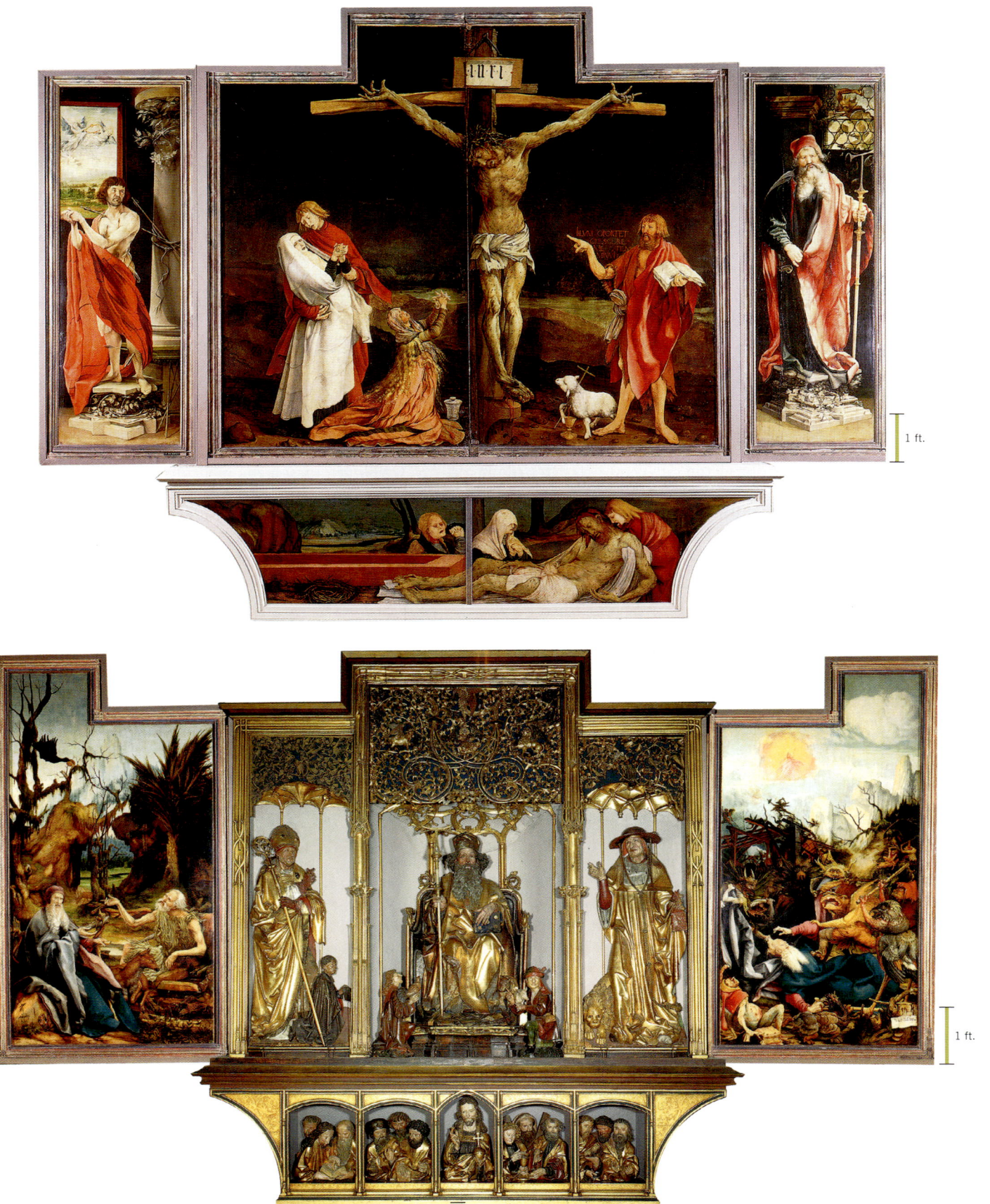

**23-2** MATTHIAS GRÜNEWALD, *Isenheim Altarpiece* (closed, *top;* open, *bottom*), from the chapel of the Hospital of Saint Anthony, Isenheim, Germany, ca. 1510–1515. Oil on wood, center panel 9′ 9½″ × 10′ 9″, each wing 8′ 2½″ × 3′ ½″, predella 2′ 5½″ × 11′ 2″. Shrine carved by NIKOLAUS HAGENAUER, ca. 1505. Painted and gilt limewood, 9′ 9½″ × 10′ 9″. Musée d'Unterlinden, Colmar.

Befitting its setting in a monastic hospital, Matthias Grünewald's *Isenheim Altarpiece* includes painted panels depicting suffering and disease but also miraculous healing, hope, and salvation.

**HANS BALDUNG GRIEN** The son of a prosperous attorney and the brother of a university professor, HANS BALDUNG GRIEN (ca. 1484–1545) chose to pursue painting and printmaking as a profession rather than the law or letters. He settled in Strasbourg, a center of humanistic learning, where he enjoyed a long and successful career. Baldung produced some religious works, although none on the scale of the *Isenheim Altarpiece.* His reputation rested primarily on his exploration of nontraditional subjects, such as witchcraft.

*Witches' Sabbath* (FIG. **23-3**) is a *chiaroscuro woodcut,* a recent German innovation. The technique requires the use of two blocks of wood instead of one. The printmaker carves and inks one block in the usual way in order to produce a traditional black-and-white print (see "Woodcuts, Engravings, and Etchings," Chapter 20, page 556). Then the artist cuts a second block consisting of broad highlights to be inked in grays or colors and printed over the first block's impression. Chiaroscuro woodcuts therefore incorporate some of the qualities of painting and feature tonal subtleties absent in traditional woodcuts.

Witchcraft was a counter-religion in the 15th and 16th centuries involving magical rituals, secret potions, and devil worship. Witches prepared brews they inhaled or rubbed into their skin, sending them into hallucinogenic trances in which they allegedly flew through the night sky on broomsticks or goats. The popes condemned all witches, and Church inquisitors vigorously pursued these demonic heretics and subjected them to torture to wrest confessions from them. Witchcraft fascinated Baldung, and he turned to the subject repeatedly. For him and his contemporaries, witches were evil forces in the world, threats to man—as was Eve herself, whom Baldung also frequently depicted as a temptress responsible for original sin.

In *Witches' Sabbath,* Baldung depicted a night scene in a forest featuring a coven of naked witches. Female nudity and macabre scenes were persistent elements in Baldung's art (compare FIG. **23-3A**). These themes were popular with the public, who avidly purchased his relatively inexpensive prints. The coven in

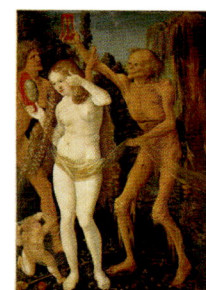

**23-3A** BALDUNG GRIEN, *Death and the Maiden,* 1509–1511.

this woodcut includes both young seductresses and old hags. They gather around a covered jar from which a fuming concoction escapes into the air. One young witch rides through the night sky on a goat. She sits backward—Baldung's way of suggesting witchcraft is the inversion of the true religion, Christianity.

**ALBRECHT DÜRER** The dominant artist of the early 16th century in the Holy Roman Empire was ALBRECHT DÜRER (1471–1528) of Nuremberg. Dürer was the first artist outside Italy to become an international celebrity. He traveled extensively, visiting and studying in Colmar, Basel, Strasbourg, Venice, Antwerp, and Brussels, among other locales. As a result of these travels, Dürer met many of the leading humanists and artists of his time, including Erasmus of Rotterdam and the Venetian master Giovanni Bellini (FIGS. 22-31A, 22-32, and 22-33). A man of exceptional talents and tremendous energy, Dürer achieved widespread fame in his own time and has enjoyed a lofty reputation ever since.

Fascinated with the classical ideas of the Italian Renaissance, Dürer was among the first Northern Renaissance artists to travel to Italy expressly to study Italian art and its underlying theories at their source. After his first journey in 1494–1495 (the second was in 1505–1506), he incorporated many Italian developments into his art. Art historians have acclaimed Dürer as the first artist north of the Alps to understand fully the basic aims of the Renaissance in Italy. Like Leonardo da Vinci, Dürer wrote theoretical treatises on a variety of subjects, such as perspective, fortification, and the ideal in human proportions. Unlike Leonardo, he both finished and published his writings. Dürer also was the first northern European artist to leave a record of his life and career through his correspondence, a detailed and eminently readable diary, and a series of self-portraits.

**SELF-PORTRAITS** Dürer's earliest preserved self-portrait—a silverpoint drawing now in the Albertina in Vienna—dates to 1484, when he was only 13, two years before he began his formal education as an apprentice in the workshop of Michel Wolgemut (FIG. 20-21). In 1498, a few years after his first visit to Italy, he painted a likeness of himself in the

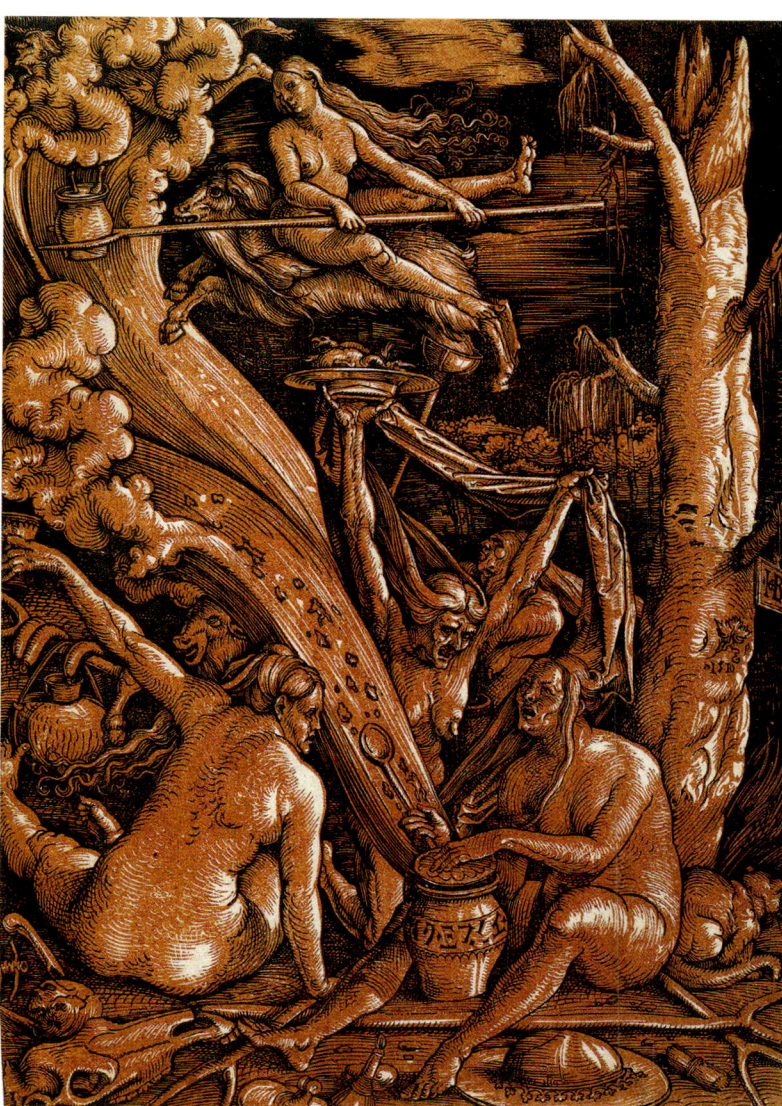

**23-3** HANS BALDUNG GRIEN, *Witches' Sabbath,* 1510. Chiaroscuro woodcut, 1′ 2$\frac{7}{8}$″ × 10$\frac{1}{4}$″. British Museum, London.

Baldung's woodcut depicts witches gathered around a cauldron containing a secret potion. One witch flies mounted backward on a goat, suggesting witchcraft is the inversion of Christianity.

1 in.

**FALL OF MAN** Dürer's fame in his own day, as today, rested more on his achievements as a printmaker than as a painter. Trained as a goldsmith by his father before he took up painting and printmaking, he developed an extraordinary proficiency in handling the burin, the engraving tool. This technical ability, combined with a feeling for the form-creating possibilities of line, enabled him to produce a body of graphic work few artists have rivaled for quality and number. Dürer created numerous book illustrations. He also circulated and sold prints in single sheets, which people of ordinary means could buy, expanding his audience considerably. Aggressively marketing his prints with the aid of an agent, Dürer became a wealthy man from the sale of these works. His wife, who served as his manager, and his mother also sold his prints at markets. Through his graphic works, he exerted strong influence throughout northern Europe and also in Italy. The lawsuit Dürer brought in 1506 against an Italian artist for copying his prints reveals his business acumen. Scholars generally regard this lawsuit as the first in history over artistic copyright.

One of Dürer's early masterpieces, *Fall of Man* (*Adam and Eve*; FIG. **23-5**), represents the first distillation of his studies of the Vitruvian theory of human proportions (compare FIG. 22-3A), a theory based on arithmetic ratios. Clearly outlined against the dark

**23-4** ALBRECHT DÜRER, *Self-Portrait*, 1500. Oil on wood, 2′ 2¼″ × 1′ 7¼″. Alte Pinakothek, Munich.

Dürer here presents himself as a frontal Christlike figure reminiscent of medieval icons. It is an image of the artist as a divinely inspired genius, a concept inconceivable before the Renaissance.

**23-4A** DÜRER, *Great Piece of Turf*, 1503.

Italian mode—a seated half-length portrait in three-quarter view in front of a window through which the viewer sees a landscape. The *Self-Portrait* reproduced here (FIG. **23-4**), painted just two years later, is markedly different in character. Inscribed with his monogram and the date (*left*) and four lines (*right*) stating the painting depicts him at age 28, the panel portrays the artist in a fur-trimmed coat in a rigid frontal posture against a dark background. Dürer has a short beard and shoulder-length hair, and the portrait intentionally evokes medieval devotional images of Christ. The position of Dürer's right hand resembles but does not duplicate (which would have been blasphemous) Christ's standard gesture of blessing in Byzantine icons (FIG. 9-33). The focus on the hand is also a reference to the artist's hand as a creative instrument. Doubtless deeply affected by the new humanistic view that had emerged in Renaissance Italy of the artist as a divinely inspired genius, Dürer responded by painting himself as a Christlike figure. He also embraced Italian artists' interest in science, as is evident in his botanically accurate 1503 watercolor study *Great Piece of Turf* (FIG. **23-4A**).

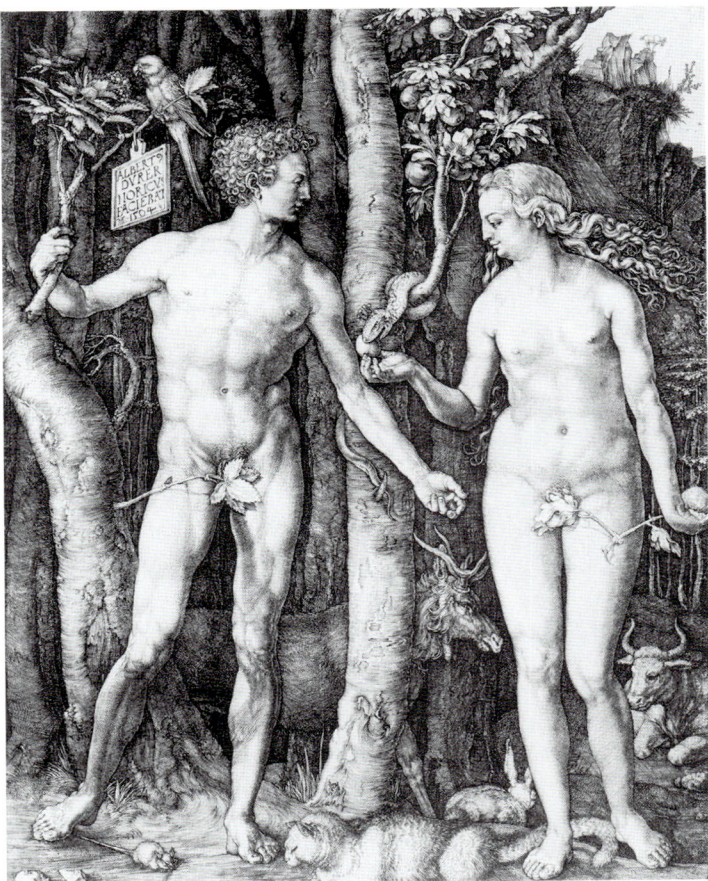

**23-5** ALBRECHT DÜRER, *Fall of Man* (*Adam and Eve*), 1504. Engraving, 9⅞″ × 7⅝″. Museum of Fine Arts, Boston (centennial gift of Landon T. Clay).

Dürer was the first Northern Renaissance artist to achieve international celebrity. *Fall of Man,* with two figures based on ancient statues, reflects his studies of the Vitruvian theory of human proportions.

background of a northern European forest, the two idealized figures of Adam and Eve stand in poses reminiscent of specific classical statues probably known to Dürer through graphic representations. Preceded by numerous geometric drawings in which the artist attempted to systematize sets of ideal human proportions in balanced contrapposto poses, the final print presents Dürer's concept of the "perfect" male and female figures. Yet he tempered this idealization with naturalism, demonstrating his well-honed observational skills in his rendering of the background foliage and animals (compare FIGS. 23-4A and 23-5A). The gnarled bark of the trees and the feathery leaves authenticate the scene, as do the various creatures skulking underfoot. The animals populating the print are symbolic. The choleric cat, the melancholic elk, the sanguine rabbit, and the phlegmatic ox represent humanity's temperaments based on the "four humors," body fluids that were the basis of theories developed by the ancient Greek physician Hippocrates

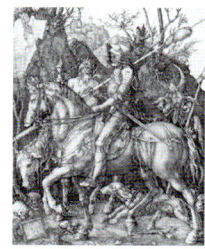

23-5A DÜRER, *Knight, Death, and the Devil,* 1513.

and practiced in medieval physiology. The tension between cat and mouse in the foreground symbolizes the relation between Adam and Eve at the crucial moment in *Fall of Man.*

*MELENCOLIA I* Dürer took up the theme of the four humors, specifically melancholy, in one of his most famous engravings, *Melencolia I* (FIG. 23-6), which many scholars regard as a kind of self-portrait of Dürer's artistic psyche as well as a masterful example of the artist's ability to produce a wide range of tonal values and textures. (Erasmus praised Dürer as "the Apelles [the most renowned ancient Greek painter] of black lines,"[1] and the German artist's mastery of all aspects of printmaking is evident also in his woodcuts, for example, FIG. I-9.)

The Italian humanist Marsilio Ficino (1433–1499) had written an influential treatise (*De vita triplici,* 1482–1489) in which he asserted that artists were distinct from the population at large because they were born under the sign of the planet Saturn, named for the ancient Roman god. They shared that deity's melancholic temperament because they had an excess of black bile, one of the four body humors, in their systems. Artists therefore were "saturnine"—eccentric and capable both of inspired artistic frenzy and melancholic depression. Raphael had depicted Michelangelo in the guise of the brooding Heraclitus in his *School of Athens* (FIG. 22-9), and Dürer used a similarly posed female figure for his winged personification of Melancholy in *Melencolia I.* (In 1510, in *De occulta philosophia,* Heinrich Cornelius Agrippa of Nettesheim [1486–1535] identified three levels of melancholy. The first was artistic melancholy, which explains the Roman numeral on the banner carried by the bat—a creature of the dark—in Dürer's engraving.) All around the brooding figure of Melancholy are the tools of the artist and builder (compare FIG. 13-32)—compass, hammer, nails, and saw among them—but they are useless to the frustrated artist while he is suffering from melancholy. Melancholy's face is obscured by shadow, underscoring her state of mind, but Dürer also included a burst of light on the far horizon behind the bat, an optimistic note suggesting artists can overcome their depression and produce works of genius—such as this engraving.

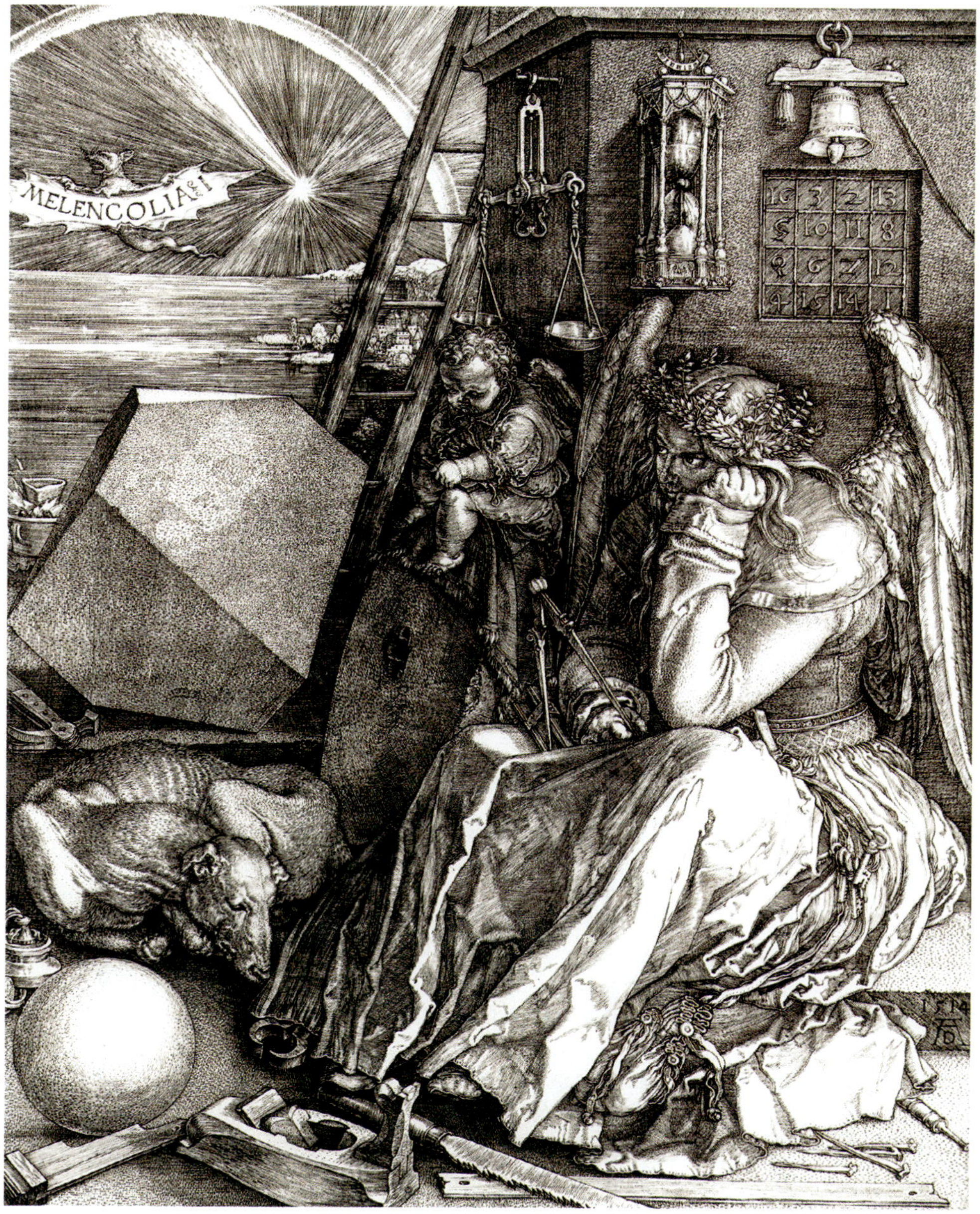

23-6 ALBRECHT DÜRER, *Melencolia I,* 1514. Engraving, $9\frac{3}{8}'' \times 7\frac{1}{2}''$. Victoria & Albert Museum, London.

In this "self-portrait" of his artistic personality, Dürer portrayed Melancholy as a brooding winged woman surrounded by the tools of the artist and builder but incapable of using them.

1 in.

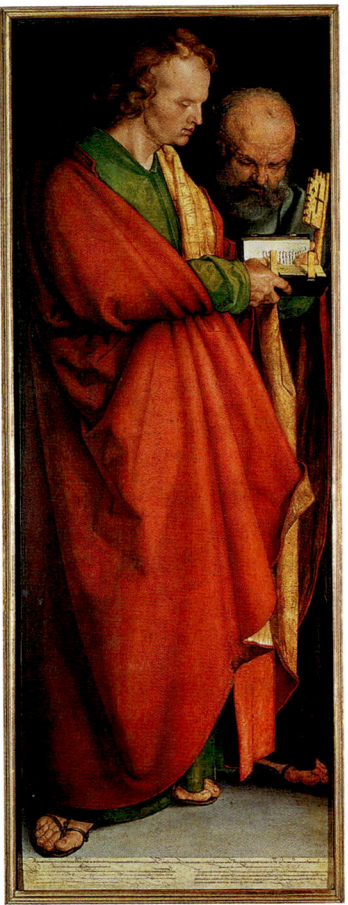

1 ft.

**23-7** ALBRECHT DÜRER, *Four Apostles*, 1526. Oil on wood, each panel 7′ 1″ × 2′ 6″. Alte Pinakothek, Munich. ◼◀

Dürer's support for Lutheranism surfaces in his portraitlike depictions of four saints on two painted panels. Peter, representative of the pope in Rome, plays a secondary role behind John the Evangelist.

**FOUR APOSTLES** Dürer's major work in the oil medium is *Four Apostles* (FIG. **23-7**), a two-panel oil painting he produced without commission and presented to the city fathers of Nuremberg in 1526 to be hung in the city hall. Saints John and Peter appear on the left panel, Mark and Paul on the right. In addition to showcasing Dürer's mastery of the oil technique, of his brilliant use of color and light and shade, and of his ability to imbue the four saints with individual personalities and portraitlike features, *Four Apostles* documents Dürer's support for the German theologian Martin Luther (1483–1546), who sparked the Protestant Reformation. Dürer conveyed his Lutheran sympathies by his positioning of the figures. He relegated Saint Peter (as representative of the pope in Rome) to a secondary role by placing him behind John the Evangelist. John assumed particular prominence for Luther because of the evangelist's focus on Christ's person in his Gospel. In addition, Peter and John both read from the Bible, the single authoritative source of religious truth, according to Luther. Dürer emphasized the Bible's centrality by depicting it open to the passage "In the beginning was the Word, and the Word was with God, and the Word was God" (John 1:1). At the bottom of the panels, Dürer included quotations from the four apostles' books, using Luther's German translation of the New Testament. The excerpts warn against the coming of perilous times and the preaching of false prophets who will distort God's word.

**LUTHER AND THE REFORMATION** The Protestant Reformation, which came to fruition in the early 16th century, had its roots in long-term, growing dissatisfaction with Catholic Church leadership. The deteriorating relationship between the faithful and the Church of Rome's hierarchy stood as an obstacle for the millions who sought a meaningful religious experience. Particularly damaging was the perception that the Roman popes concerned themselves more with temporal power and material wealth than with the salvation of Church members. The fact that many 15th-century popes and cardinals came from wealthy families, such as the Medici (FIG. 22-10), intensified this perception. It was not only those at the highest levels who seemed to ignore their spiritual duties. Archbishops, bishops, and abbots began to accumulate numerous offices, thereby increasing their revenues but making it more difficult for them to fulfill all of their responsibilities. By 1517, dissatisfaction with the Church had grown so widespread that Luther felt free to challenge papal authority openly by posting in Wittenberg his *Ninety-five Theses*, in which he enumerated his objections to Church practices, especially the sale of indulgences. *Indulgences* were Church-sanctioned remittances (or reductions) of time Catholics had to spend in Purgatory for confessed sins. The increasing frequency of their sale suggested that those who could afford to purchase indulgences were buying their way into Heaven.

Luther's goal was significant reform and clarification of major spiritual issues, but his ideas ultimately led to the splitting of Christendom. According to Luther, the Catholic Church's extensive ecclesiastical structure needed casting out, for it had no basis in scripture. The Bible and nothing else could serve as the foundation for Christianity. Luther declared the pope the Antichrist (for which the pope excommunicated him), called the Church the "whore of Babylon," and denounced ordained priests. He also rejected most of Catholicism's sacraments other than baptism and communion, decrying them as obstacles to salvation (see "Catholic and Protestant Views of Salvation," page 653, and FIG. **23-8**). Luther maintained that for Christianity to be restored to its original purity, the Church needed cleansing of all the doctrinal impurities that had collected through the ages. Luther advocated the Bible as the source of all religious truth. The Bible—the sole scriptural authority—was the word of God, which did not exist in the Church's councils, law, and rituals. Luther facilitated the lay public's access to biblical truths by producing the first translation of the Bible in a vernacular language.

**ART AND THE REFORMATION** In addition to doctrinal differences, Catholics and Protestants took divergent stances on the role of visual imagery in religion. Catholics embraced church decoration as an aid to communicating with God (see "Religious Art in Counter-Reformation Italy," Chapter 22, page 617). In contrast, Protestants believed images of Christ, the Virgin, and saints could lead to idolatry and distracted viewers from focusing on the real reason for their presence in church—to communicate directly with God. Because of this belief, Protestant churches were relatively bare, and the extensive church pictorial programs found especially in Italy but also in northern Europe (FIGS. 20-19, 20-20, and 23-2) were not as prominent in Protestant churches.

The Protestant concern over the role of religious imagery at times escalated to outright *iconoclasm*—the objection to and destruction of religious imagery. In encouraging a more personal relationship with God, Protestant leaders spoke out against much of the religious art being produced. In his 1525 tract *Against the*

## Catholic and Protestant Views of Salvation

A central concern of the Protestant reformers was the question of how Christians achieve salvation. Rather than perceive salvation as something for which weak and sinful humans must constantly strive through good deeds performed under the watchful eye of a punitive God, Martin Luther argued that faithful individuals attained redemption solely by God's bestowal of his grace. Therefore, people cannot earn salvation. Further, no ecclesiastical machinery with all its miraculous rites and indulgent forgivenesses could save sinners face-to-face with God. Only absolute faith in Christ could redeem sinners and ensure salvation. Redemption by faith alone, with the guidance of scripture, was the fundamental doctrine of Protestantism.

In *Law and Gospel* (FIG. 23-8), a woodcut dated about a dozen years after Luther set the Reformation in motion with his *Ninety-five Theses*, Lucas Cranach the Elder gave visual expression to the doctrinal differences between Protestantism and Catholicism. Cranach contrasted Catholicism (based on Old Testament law, according

to Luther) and Protestantism (based on the Gospel belief in God's grace) in two images separated by a centrally placed tree. On the left half, judgment day has arrived, as represented by Christ's appearance at the top of the scene, hovering amid a cloud halo and accompanied by angels and saints. Christ raises his left hand in the traditional gesture of damnation, and, below, a skeleton drives off a terrified person to burn for eternity in Hell. This person tried to live a good and honorable life, but despite his efforts, he fell short. Moses stands to the side, holding the tablets of the law—the Ten Commandments Catholics follow in their attempt to attain salvation. In contrast to this Catholic reliance on good works and clean living, Protestants emphasized God's grace as the source of redemption. Accordingly, God showers the sinner in the right half of the print with grace, as streams of blood flow from the crucified Christ. At the far left are Adam and Eve, whose original sin necessitated Christ's sacrifice. In the lower right corner of the woodcut, Christ emerges from the tomb and promises salvation to all who believe in him.

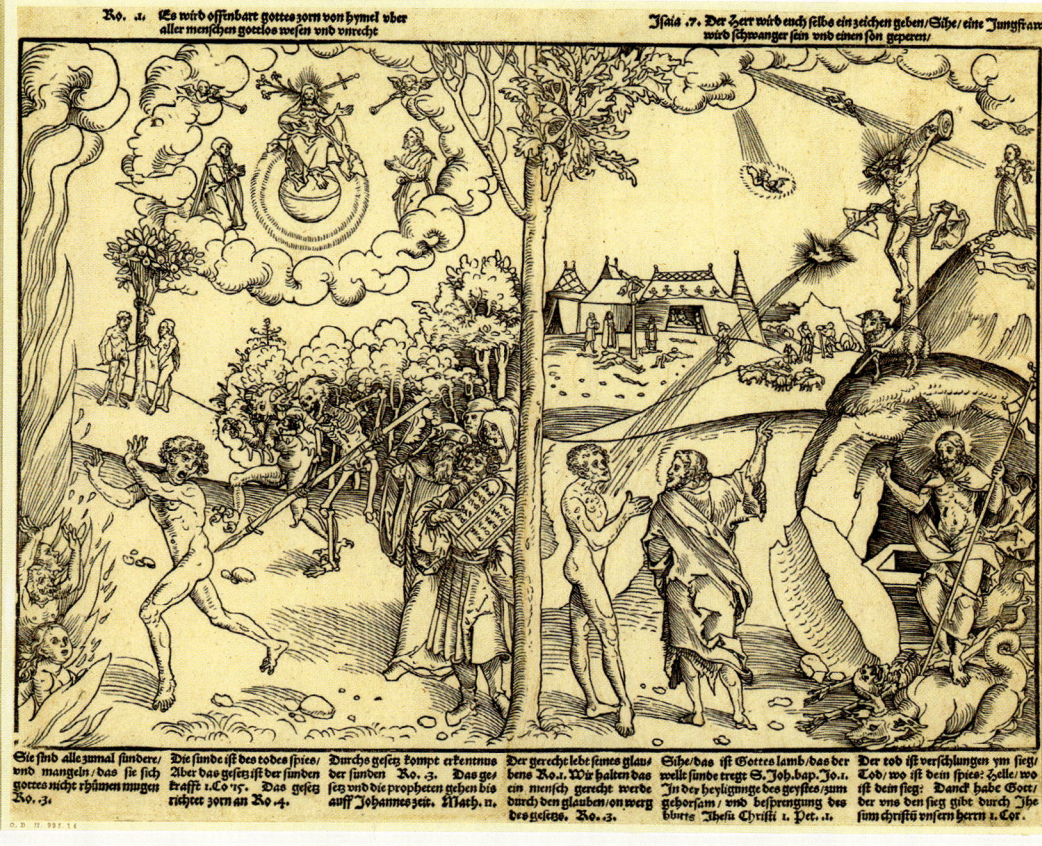

**23-8** LUCAS CRANACH THE ELDER, *Law and Gospel*, ca. 1530. Woodcut, $10\frac{5}{8}'' \times 1' \frac{3}{4}''$. **British Museum, London.**

Lucas Cranach was a close friend of Martin Luther, whose *Ninety-five Theses* launched the Reformation in 1517. This woodcut contrasts Catholic and Protestant views of how to achieve salvation.

1 in.

*Heavenly Prophets in the Matter of Images and Sacraments,* Martin Luther explained his attitude toward religious imagery:

> I approached the task of destroying images by first tearing them out of the heart through God's Word and making them worthless and despised. . . . For when they are no longer in the heart, they can do no harm when seen with the eyes. . . . I have allowed and

not forbidden the outward removal of images. . . . And I say at the outset that according to the law of Moses no other images are forbidden than an image of God which one worships. A crucifix, on the other hand, or any other holy image is not forbidden.[2]

Two influential Protestant theologians based in Switzerland—Ulrich Zwingli (1484–1531) and French-born John Calvin (Jean

Cauvin, 1509–1564)—were more vociferous in cautioning their followers about the potentially dangerous nature of religious imagery. Zwingli and Calvin's condemnation of religious imagery often led to eruptions of iconoclasm. Particularly violent waves of iconoclastic fervor swept Basel, Zurich, Strasbourg, and Wittenberg in the 1520s. In an episode known as the Great Iconoclasm, bands of Calvinists visited Catholic churches in the Netherlands in 1566, shattering stained-glass windows, smashing statues, and destroying paintings and other artworks they perceived as idolatrous. These strong reactions to art not only reflect the religious fervor of the time but also serve as dramatic demonstrations of the power of art—and of how much art mattered.

**LUCAS CRANACH THE ELDER** The artist most closely associated with the Protestant Reformation and with Martin Luther in particular was LUCAS CRANACH THE ELDER (1472–1553). Cranach and Luther were godfathers to each other's children, and many scholars have dubbed Cranach "the painter of the Reformation." Cranach was also an accomplished graphic artist who used the new, inexpensive medium of prints on paper to promote Lutheran ideology (FIG. 23-8). Cranach's work encompasses a wide range of themes, however. For example, for aristocratic Saxon patrons he produced a large number of paintings of classical myths featuring female nudes in suggestive poses. One classical theme he depicted several times was *Judgment of Paris,* of which the small panel (FIG. **23-9**) now in Karlsruhe is the best example. Homer records the story, but Cranach's source was probably the second-century CE Roman author Lucian's elaboration of the tale. Mercury chose a handsome young shepherd named Paris to be the judge of a beauty contest among three goddesses—Juno, wife of Jupiter; Minerva, Jupiter's virgin daughter and goddess of wisdom and war; and Venus, the goddess of love (see "The Gods and Goddesses of Mount Olympus," Chapter 5, page 107, or on page xxix in Volume II and Book D). According to Lucian, each goddess attempted to bribe Paris with rich rewards if he chose her. Venus won by offering Paris the most beautiful woman in the world, Helen of Troy, and thus set in motion the epic war between the Greeks and Trojans recounted in Homer's *Iliad.*

Cranach's painting could never be confused with an ancient depiction of the myth. The setting is a German landscape with a Saxon castle in the background, and the seated shepherd is a knight in full armor wearing a fashionable hat. Mercury, an aged man (as he never is in ancient art), also wearing armor, bends over to draw Paris's attention to the three goddesses. They are nude save for their transparent veils, their fine jewelry, and, in the case of Juno, an elegant hat. Loosely based on classical representations of the Three Graces (compare FIG. 21-1)—ancient artists did not depict Juno or Minerva undressed—Cranach's goddesses do not have the proportions (or modesty) of Praxiteles' *Aphro-*

*dite of Knidos* (FIG. 5-62). Slender, with small heads and breasts and long legs, they pose seductively before the judge. Venus performs a dance for Paris, but he seems indifferent to all three goddesses. Only the rearing horse appears to be excited by the spectacle—a touch of humor characteristic of Cranach.

**ALBRECHT ALTDORFER** As elsewhere in 16th-century Europe, some artists in the Holy Roman Empire worked in the employ of rulers, and their work promoted the political agendas of their patrons. In 1529, for example, the duke of Bavaria, Wilhelm IV (r. 1508–1550), commissioned ALBRECHT ALTDORFER (ca. 1480–1538) to paint *Battle of Issus* (FIG. **23-10**) at the commencement of his military campaign against the invading Turks. The panel depicts Alexander the Great's defeat of King Darius III of Persia in 333 BCE at a town called Issus on the Pinarus River. Altdorfer announced the subject—which the Greek painter Philoxenos of Eretria (FIG. 5-70) had represented two millennia before—in the Latin inscription suspended in the sky. The parallels between the historical and contemporary conflicts were no doubt significant

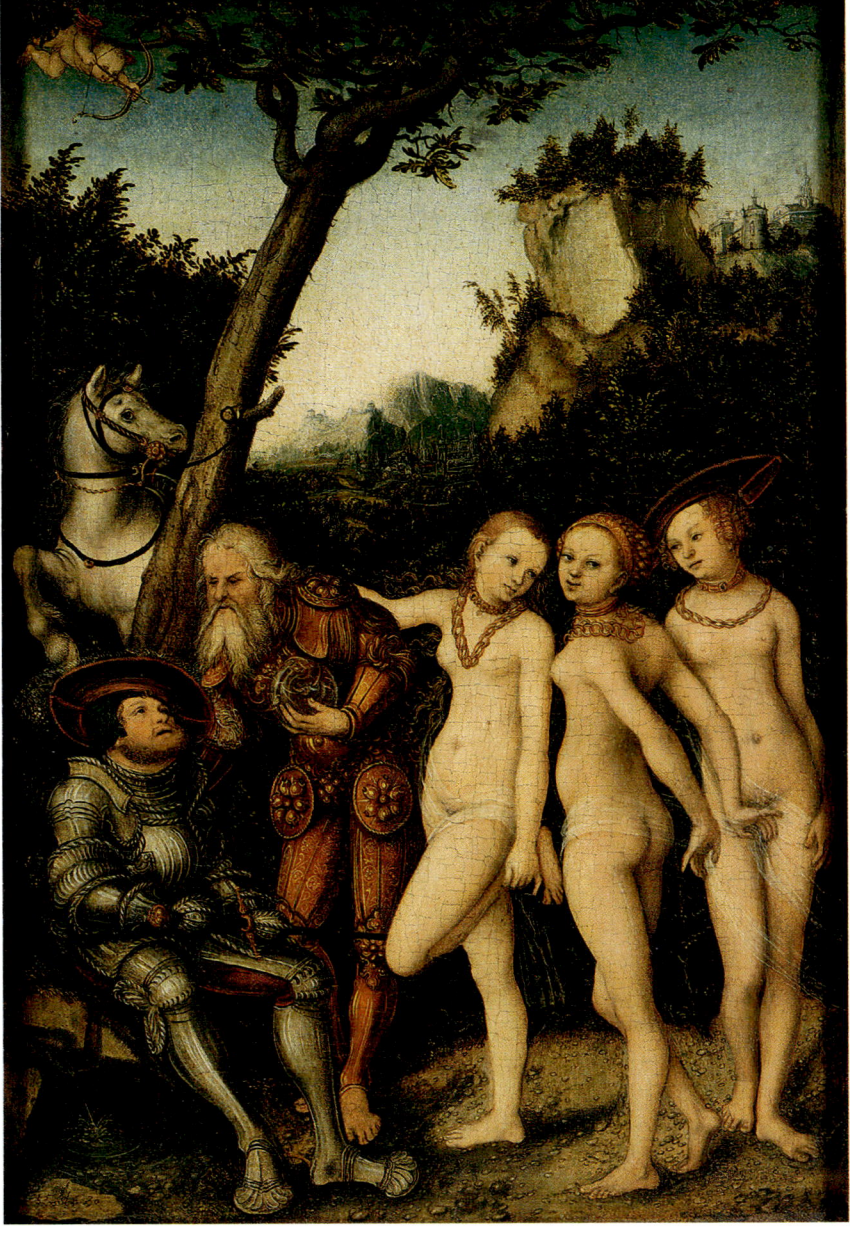

**23-9** LUCAS CRANACH THE ELDER, *Judgment of Paris,* 1530. Oil on wood, 1′ 1½″ × 9½″. Staatliche Kunsthalle, Karlsruhe.

For aristocratic German patrons, Cranach painted many classical myths featuring seductive female nudes. In his *Judgment of Paris,* the Greek shepherd is a knight in armor in a Saxon landscape.

1 in.

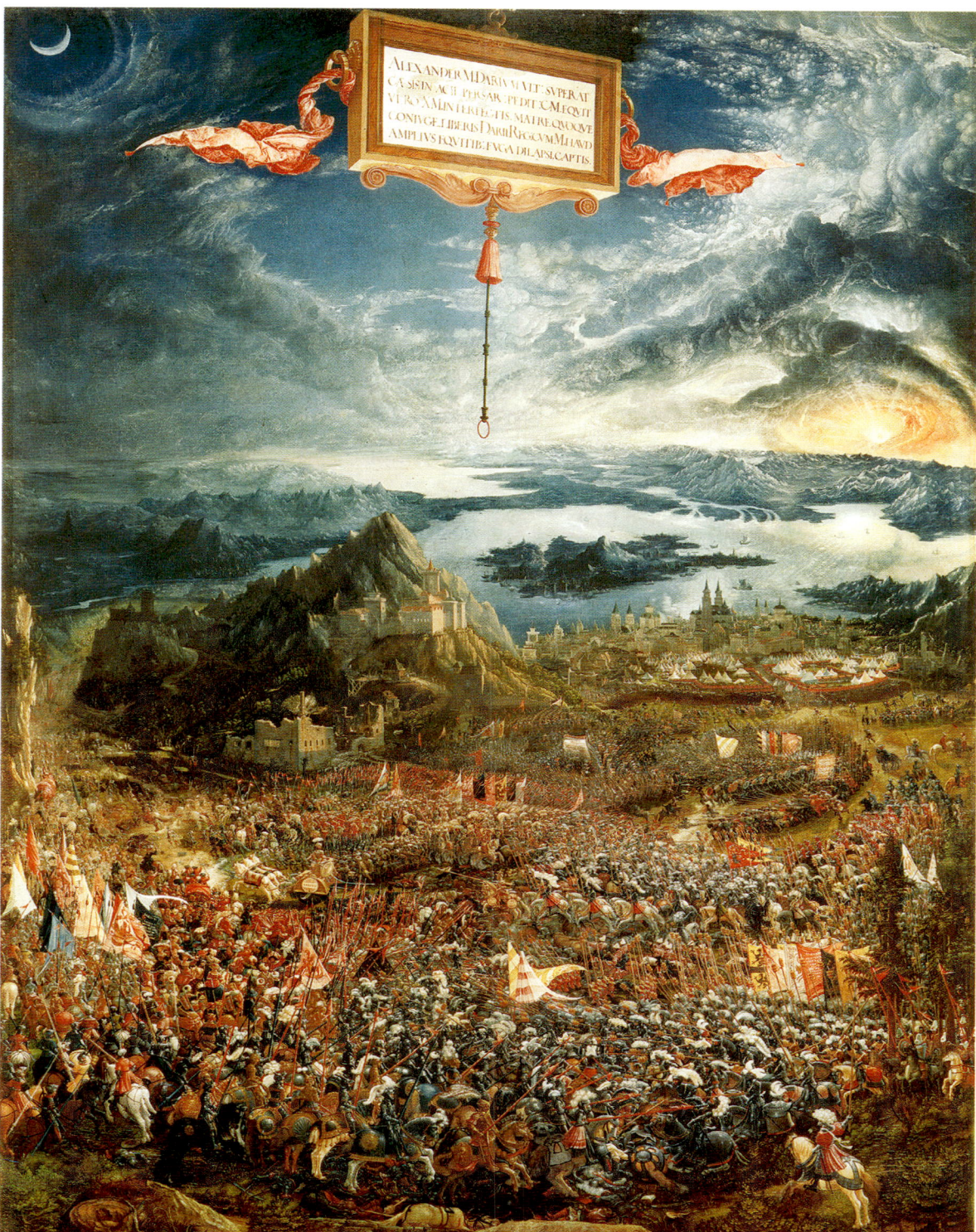

Interweaving history and 16th-century politics, Albrecht Altdorfer painted Alexander the Great's defeat of the Persians for a patron who had just embarked on a military campaign against the Turks.

1 ft.

to the duke. Both involved Western societies engaged in battles against Eastern foes with different values—the Persians in antiquity and the Turks in 1528. Altdorfer reinforced this connection by attiring the figures in 16th-century armor and depicting them engaged in contemporary military alignments.

*Battle of Issus* also reveals Altdorfer's love of landscape. The battle takes place in an almost cosmological setting. From a bird's-eye view, the clashing armies swarm in the foreground. In the distance, craggy mountain peaks rise next to still bodies of water. Amid swirling clouds, a blazing sun descends. Although the spectacular topography may appear invented, Altdorfer derived his depiction of the landscape from maps. Specifically, he set the scene in the eastern Mediterranean with a view from Greece to the Nile in Egypt. In addition, Altdorfer may have acquired his information about this battle from the German scholar Johannes Aventinus (1477–1534), whose account of Alexander's victory describes the bloody daylong battle. Appropriately, given Alexander's designation as the "sun god," the sun sets over the victorious Greeks on the right, while a small crescent moon (a symbol of ancient Persia) hovers in the upper left corner over the retreating enemy forces.

Holy Roman Empire     **655**

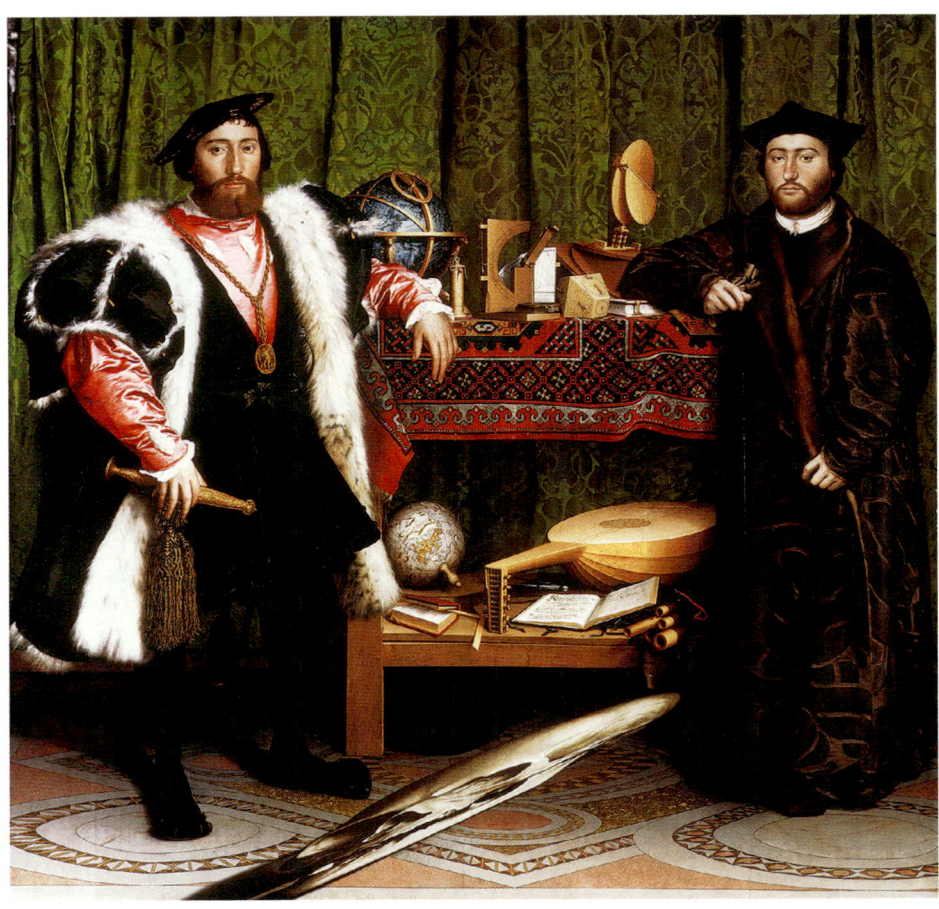

**23-11** Hans Holbein the Younger, *The French Ambassadors*, 1533. Oil and tempera on wood, 6′ 8″ × 6′ 9½″. National Gallery, London. ◼◄

In this double portrait, Holbein depicted two humanists with a collection of objects reflective of their worldliness and learning, but he also included an anamorphic skull, a reminder of death.

**HANS HOLBEIN** Also in the employ of the rich and powerful for much of his career was Hans Holbein the Younger (ca. 1497–1543), who excelled as a portraitist. Trained by his father, Holbein produced portraits consistent with the northern European tradition of close realism that had emerged in 15th-century Flemish art (see Chapter 20). The surfaces of Holbein's paintings are as lustrous as enamel, and the details are exact and exquisitely drawn. Yet he also incorporated Italian ideas about monumental composition and sculpturesque form.

Holbein began his artistic career in Basel, where he knew Erasmus of Rotterdam. Because of the immediate threat of a religious civil war in Basel, Erasmus suggested Holbein leave for England and gave him a recommendation to Thomas More, chancellor of England under Henry VIII. Holbein quickly obtained important commissions, for example, to paint a double portrait of the French ambassadors to England, Jean de

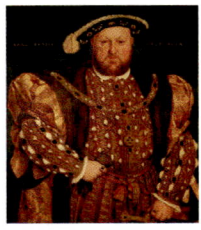

**23-11A** Holbein the Younger, *Henry VIII*, 1540.

Dinteville and Georges de Selve (FIG. **23-11**), and within a few years of his arrival, he became the official painter to the English court, producing numerous portraits of Henry VIII (FIG. **23-11A**).

*The French Ambassadors* (FIG. 23-11) exhibits Holbein's considerable talents—his strong sense of composition, his subtle linear patterning, his gift for portraiture, his marvelous sensitivity to color, and his faultless technique. The two men, both ardent humanists, stand at opposite ends of a side table covered with an oriental rug and a collection of objects reflective of their worldliness and their interest in learning and the arts. These include mathematical and astronomical models and implements, a lute with a broken string, compasses, a sundial, flutes, globes, and an open hymnbook with Luther's translation of *Veni, Creator Spiritus* and of the Ten Commandments.

Of particular interest is the long gray shape that slashes diagonally across the picture plane and interrupts the stable, balanced, and serene composition. This form is an *anamorphic image,* a distorted image recognizable only when viewed with a special device, such as a cylindrical mirror, or by looking at the painting at an acute angle. In this case, if the viewer stands off to the right, the gray slash becomes a skull. Although scholars disagree on the skull's precise meaning, it certainly refers to death. Artists commonly incorporated skulls into paintings as reminders of mortality. Indeed, Holbein depicted a skull on the metal medallion on Jean de Dinteville's hat. Holbein may have intended the skulls, in conjunction with the crucifix that appears half hidden behind the curtain in the upper left corner, to encourage viewers to ponder death and resurrection.

This painting may also allude to the growing tension between secular and religious authorities. Jean de Dinteville was a titled landowner, Georges de Selve a bishop. The inclusion of Luther's translations next to the lute with the broken string (a symbol of discord) may subtly refer to this religious strife. In any case, *The French Ambassadors* is a painting of supreme artistic achievement. Holbein rendered the still-life objects with the same meticulous care as he did the men themselves, the woven design of the deep emerald curtain behind them, and the floor tiles, drawn in perfect perspective.

# FRANCE

As *The French Ambassadors* illustrates, France in the early 16th century continued its efforts to secure widespread recognition as a political power and cultural force. The French kings were major patrons of art and architecture.

**FRANCIS I** Under the rule of Francis I (r. 1515–1547), the French established a firm foothold in Milan and its environs. Francis waged a campaign (known as the Habsburg-Valois Wars) against Charles V (the Spanish king and Holy Roman emperor; r. 1516–1558), which occupied him from 1521 to 1544. These wars involved disputed territories—southern France, the Netherlands, the Rhineland, northern Spain, and Italy—and reflect France's central role in the shifting geopolitical landscape.

The French king also took a strong position in the religious controversies of his day. By the mid-16th century, the split between Catholics and Protestants had become so pronounced that subjects often felt compelled either to accept the religion of their sovereign or emigrate to a territory where the sovereign's religion corresponded with their own. France was predominantly Catholic, and in 1534, Francis declared Protestantism illegal. The state persecuted its Protestants, the Huguenots, a Calvinist sect, and drove them underground. (Calvin fled from France to Switzerland two years later.) The Huguenots' commitment to Protestant Calvinism eventually led to one of the bloodiest religious massacres in European history when the Huguenots and Catholics clashed in Paris in August 1572. The violence quickly spread throughout France with the support of many nobles, which presented a serious threat to the king's authority.

In art as well as politics and religion, Francis I was a dominant figure. To elevate his country's cultural profile, he invited several esteemed Italian artists to his court, Leonardo da Vinci among them (see Chapter 22). Under Francis, the Church, the primary patron of art and architecture in medieval France, yielded that position to the French monarchy.

**JEAN CLOUET** As the rulers of antiquity had done, Francis commissioned portraits of himself to assert his authority. The finest is the portrait (FIG. **23-12**) JEAN CLOUET (ca. 1485–1541) painted about a decade after Francis became king. It portrays the French monarch as a worldly ruler magnificently bedecked in silks and brocades, wearing a gold chain with a medallion of the Order of Saint Michael, a French order Louis XI founded in 1469. Legend has it that Francis (known as the "merry monarch") was a great lover and the hero of hundreds of "gallant" deeds. Appropriately, he appears suave and confident, with his hand resting on the pommel of a dagger. Despite the careful detail, the portrait also exhibits an elegantly formalized quality, the result of Clouet's suppression of modeling, which flattens features, seen particularly in Francis's neck. The disproportion between the king's small head and his broad body, swathed in heavy layers of fabric, adds to the formalized nature.

Francis and his court favored art that was at once elegant, erotic, and unorthodox. Appropriately, Mannerism appealed to them most, and Francis thus brought Benvenuto Cellini (FIGS. 22-52 and 22-52A) to France with the promise of a lucrative retainer. He put two prominent Florentine Mannerists—Rosso Fiorentino and Francesco Primaticcio—in charge of decorating the new royal palace at Fontainebleau.

**CHÂTEAU DE CHAMBORD** Francis I also indulged his passion for building by commissioning several large *châteaux,* among them the Château de Chambord (FIG. **23-13**). Reflecting more peaceful times, these châteaux, developed from medieval castles, served as country houses for royalty, who usually built them near forests for use as hunting lodges. Many, including Chambord, still featured protective surrounding moats, however. Construction of the Château de Chambord began in 1519, but Francis I never saw its

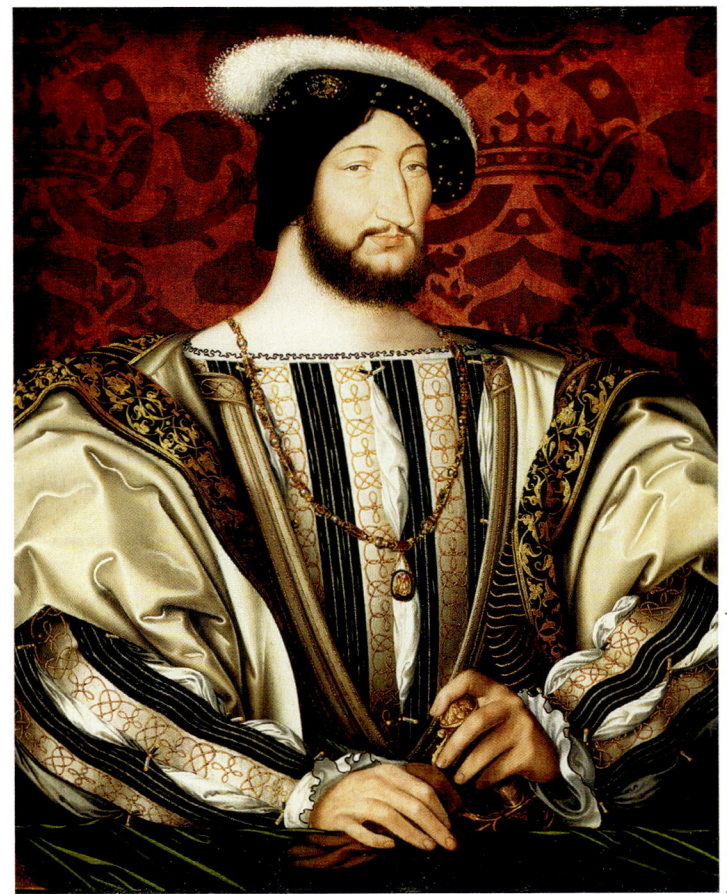

23-12 JEAN CLOUET, *Francis I,* ca. 1525–1530. Tempera and oil on wood, 3′ 2″ × 2′ 5″. Musée du Louvre, Paris.

Clouet's portrait of Francis I in elegant garb reveals the artist's attention to detail but also the flattening of features and disproportion between head and body, giving the painting a formalized quality.

1 ft.

completion. Chambord's plan, originally drawn by a pupil of Giuliano da Sangallo (FIGS. 22-26 and 22-27), includes a central square block with four corridors, in the shape of a cross, and a broad central staircase that gives access to groups of rooms—ancestors of the modern suite of rooms or apartments. At each of the four corners, a

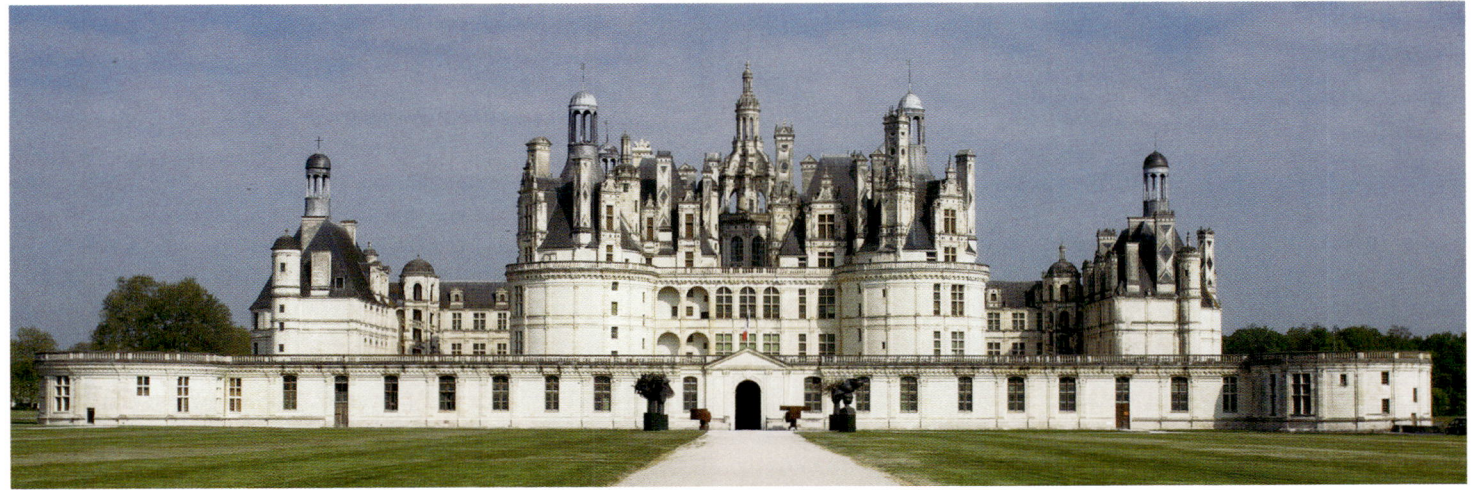

23-13 Château de Chambord (looking northwest), Chambord, France, begun 1519. ◼◀

French Renaissance châteaux, which developed from medieval castles, served as country houses for royalty. King Francis I's Château de Chambord reflects Italian palazzo design, but it has a Gothic roof.

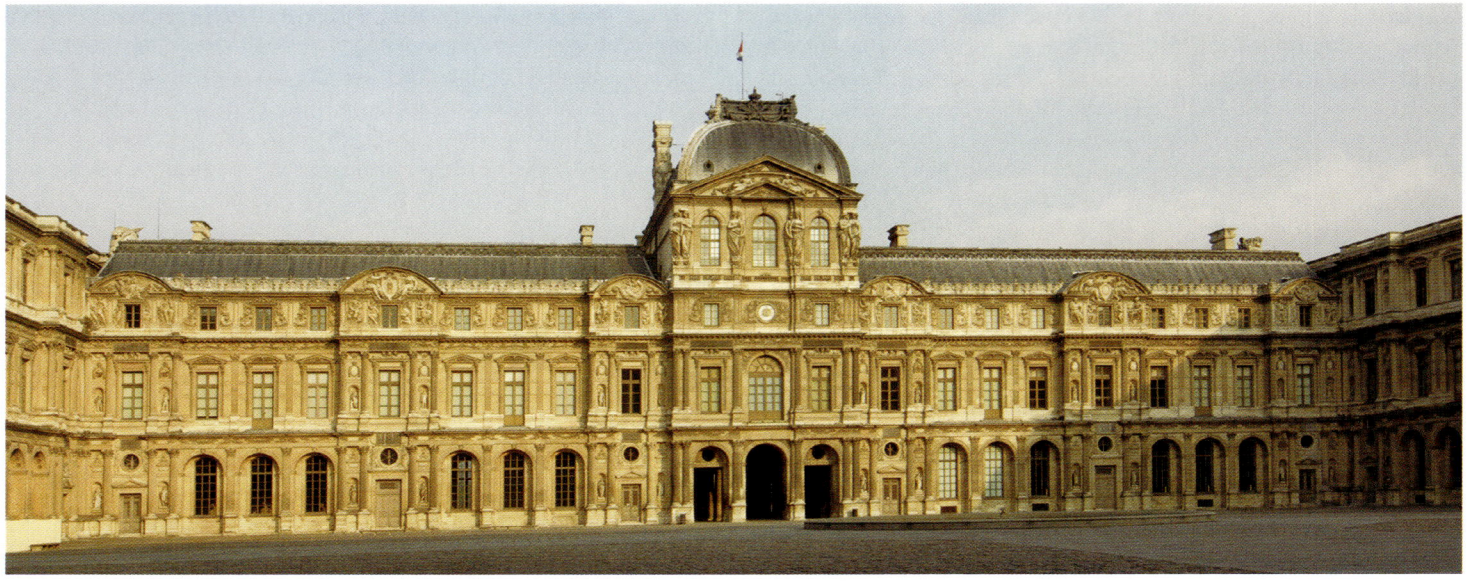

**23-14** PIERRE LESCOT, west wing of the Cour Carré (Square Court, looking west) of the Louvre, Paris, France, begun 1546. ◼◤

Lescot's design for the Louvre palace reflects the Italian Renaissance classicism of Bramante, but the decreasing height of the stories, large windows, and steep roof are northern European features.

round tower punctuates the square plan. From the exterior, Chambord presents a carefully contrived horizontal accent on three levels, with continuous moldings separating its floors. Windows align precisely, one exactly over another. The Italian Renaissance palazzo served as the model for this matching of horizontal and vertical features, but above the third level the structure's lines break chaotically into a jumble of high dormers, chimneys, and lanterns that recall soaring, ragged Gothic silhouettes on the skyline.

**LOUVRE, PARIS** Chambord, despite its Italian elements, is essentially a French building. During the reign of Francis's successor, Henry II (r. 1547–1559), however, translations of Italian architectural treatises appeared, and Italian architects themselves came to work in France. Moreover, the French turned to Italy for study and travel. These exchanges caused a more extensive revolution in style than had transpired earlier, although certain French elements derived from the Gothic tradition persisted. This incorporation of Italian architectural ideas characterizes the redesigned Louvre in Paris, originally a medieval palace and fortress (FIG. 20-16). Since Charles V's renovation of the Louvre in the mid-14th century, the castle had fallen into a state of disrepair. Francis I initiated the project to update and expand the royal palace, but died before the work was well under way. His architect, PIERRE LESCOT (1510–1578), continued under Henry II and produced the classical style most closely associated with 16th-century French architecture.

Lescot and his associates were familiar with the architectural style of Bramante and his school. In the west wing of the Cour Carré (Square Court; FIG. **23-14**) of the Louvre, each of the stories forms a complete order, and the cornices project enough to furnish a strong horizontal accent. The arcading on the ground story reflects the ancient Roman use of arches and produces more shadow than in the upper stories due to its recessed placement, thereby strengthening the design's visual base. On the second story, the pilasters rising from bases and the alternating curved and angular pediments supported by consoles have direct antecedents in several High Renaissance palaces (for example, FIG. 22-26). Yet the decreasing height of the stories, the scale of the windows (proportionately much larger

than in Italian Renaissance buildings), and the steep roof are northern European elements. Especially French are the pavilions jutting from the wall. A motif the French long favored—double columns framing a niche—punctuates the pavilions. The richly articulated wall surfaces feature relief sculptures by JEAN GOUJON (ca. 1510–1565), who had previously collaborated with Lescot on the Fountain of the Innocents (FIG. **23-14A**) in Paris. Other northern European countries imitated this French classical manner—its double-columned pavilions, tall and wide windows, profuse statuary, and steep roofs—although with local variations. The modified classicism the French produced became the model for building projects north of the Alps through most of the 16th century.

**23-14A** GOUJON, Fountain of the Innocents, 1547–1549.

# THE NETHERLANDS

With the demise of the duchy of Burgundy in 1477 and the division of that territory between France and the Holy Roman Empire, the Netherlands at the beginning of the 16th century consisted of 17 provinces (corresponding to modern Holland, Belgium, and Luxembourg). The Netherlands was among the most commercially advanced and prosperous European countries. Its extensive network of rivers and easy access to the Atlantic Ocean provided a setting conducive to overseas trade, and shipbuilding was one of the most profitable enterprises. The region's commercial center shifted toward the end of the 15th century, partly because of the buildup of silt in the Bruges estuary. Traffic relocated to Antwerp, which became the hub of economic activity in the Netherlands after 1510. As many as 500 ships a day passed through Antwerp's harbor, and large trading companies from England, the Holy Roman Empire, Italy, Portugal, and Spain established themselves in the city.

During the second half of the 16th century, Philip II of Spain (r. 1556–1598) controlled the Netherlands. Philip had inherited the region from his father Charles V, and he sought to force the

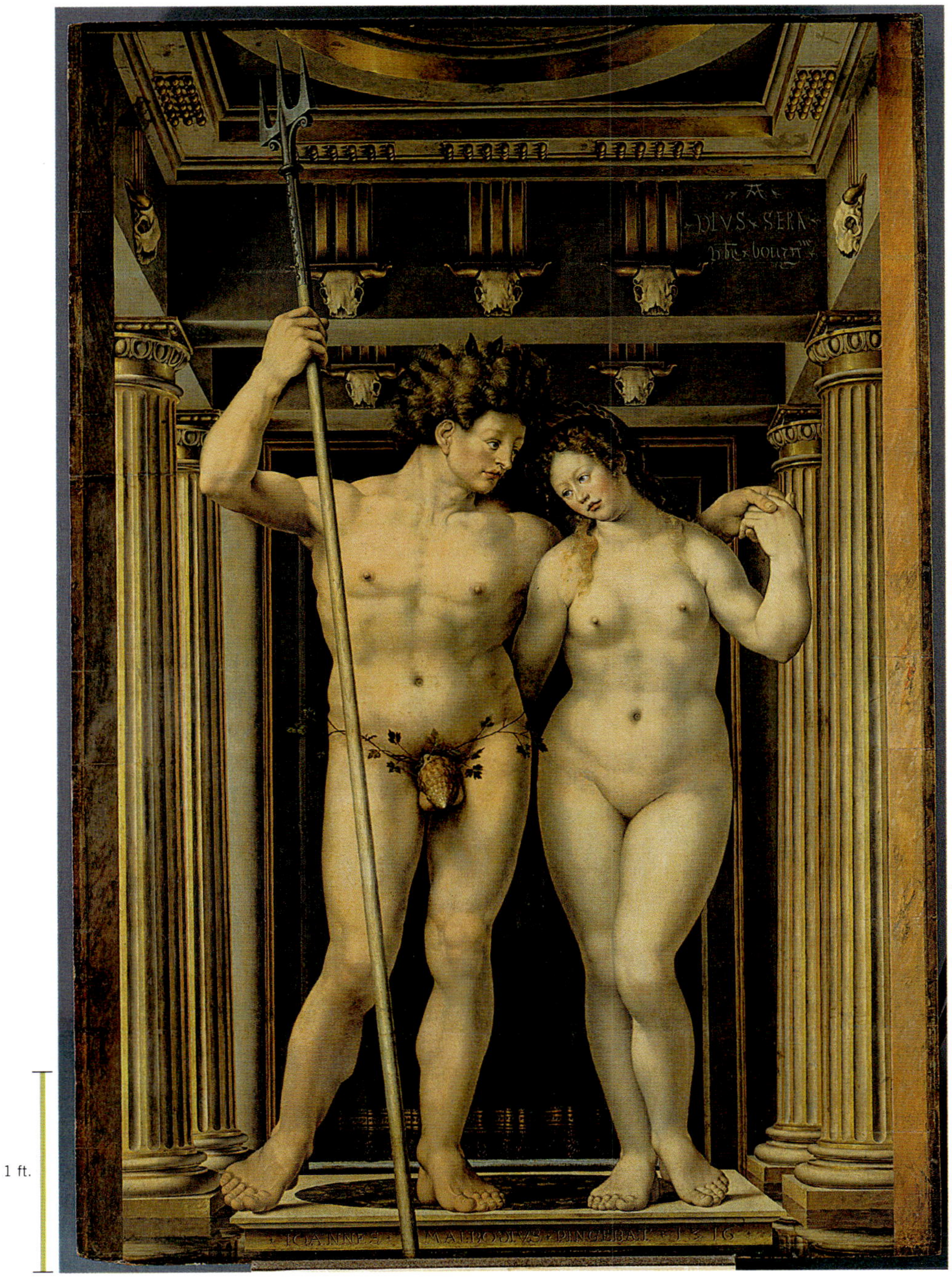

Dürer's *Fall of Man* (FIG. 23-5) inspired the poses of Gossaert's classical deities, but the architectural setting is probably based on sketches of ancient buildings Gossaert made during his trip to Rome.

who traveled to Italy and became fascinated with classical antiquity and mythology (FIG. **23-15**), although he also painted traditional Christian themes (FIG. **23-15A**). Giorgio Vasari, the Italian artist and biographer and Gossaert's contemporary, wrote that "Jean Gossart [*sic*] of Mabuse

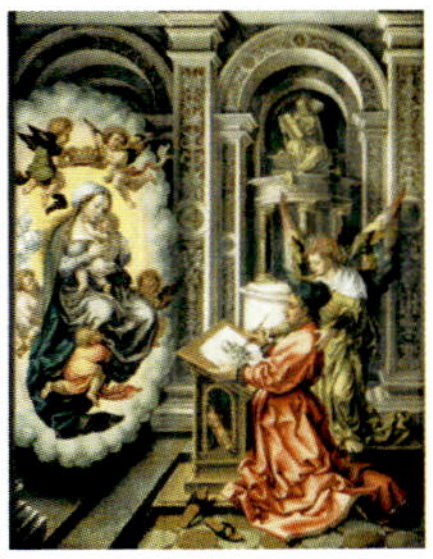

23-15A GOSSAERT, *Saint Luke Drawing the Virgin*, ca. 1520–1525.

was almost the first who took from Italy into Flanders the true method of making scenes full of nude figures and poetical inventions,"[3] although Gossaert derived much of his classicism from Albrecht Dürer.

Indeed, Dürer's *Fall of Man* (FIG. 23-5) inspired the composition and poses in Gossaert's *Neptune and Amphitrite* (FIG. 23-15). However, in contrast to Dürer's exquisitely small engraving, Gossaert's painting is more than six feet tall and four feet wide. The artist executed the painting with characteristic Netherlandish polish, skillfully drawing and carefully modeling the figures. Gossaert depicted the sea god with his traditional attribute, the trident, and wearing a laurel wreath and an ornate conch shell in place of Dürer's fig leaf. Amphitrite is fleshy and, like Neptune, stands in a contrapposto stance. The architectural frame, which resembles the cella of a classical temple (FIG. 5-46), is an unusual mix of Doric and Ionic elements and *bucrania* (ox skull decorations), a common motif in ancient architectural ornamentation.

entire population to become Catholic. His heavy-handed tactics and repressive measures led in 1579 to revolt and the formation of two federations: the Union of Arras, a Catholic union of southern Netherlandish provinces, which remained under Spanish dominion, and the Union of Utrecht, a Protestant union of northern provinces, which became the Dutch Republic (MAP 25-1).

Large-scale altarpieces and other religious works continued to be commissioned for Catholic churches, but with the rise of Protestantism in the Netherlands, artists increasingly favored secular subjects. Netherlandish art of this period provides a wonderful glimpse into the lives of various strata of society, from nobility to peasantry, capturing their activities, environment, and values.

**JAN GOSSAERT** As in the Holy Roman Empire and France, developments in Italian Renaissance art interested many Netherlandish artists. JAN GOSSAERT (ca. 1478–1535) was one of those

Gossaert likely based the classical setting on sketches he had made of ancient buildings while in Rome. He had traveled to Italy with Philip, bastard of Burgundy, this painting's patron. A Burgundian admiral (hence the Neptune reference), Philip became a bishop and kept this work in the innermost room of his castle.

**QUINTEN MASSYS** Antwerp's growth and prosperity, along with its wealthy merchants' propensity for collecting and purchasing art, attracted artists to the city. Among them was QUINTEN MASSYS (ca. 1466–1530), who became Antwerp's leading master after 1510. The son of a Louvain blacksmith, Massys demonstrated a willingness to explore the styles and modes of a variety of models, from Jan van Eyck and Rogier van der Weyden to Albrecht Dürer, Hieronymus Bosch, and Leonardo da Vinci. Yet his eclecticism was subtle and discriminating, enriched by an inventiveness that gave a personal stamp to his paintings.

Massys's depiction of a secular financial transaction is also a commentary on Netherlandish values. The banker's wife shows more interest in the money-weighing than in her prayer book.

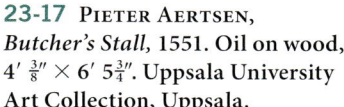

In *Money-Changer and His Wife* (FIG. 23-16), Massys presented a professional man transacting business. He holds scales, checking the weight of coins on the table. The artist's detailed rendering of the figures, setting, and objects suggests a fidelity to observable fact, and provides insight into developing commercial practices. But *Money-Changer and His Wife* is also a commentary on Netherlandish values and mores. The painting highlights the financial transactions that were an increasingly prominent part of 16th-century secular life in the Netherlands and that distracted Christians from their religious duties. The banker's wife, for example, shows more interest in watching her husband weigh money than in reading her prayer book. Massys incorporated into his painting numerous references to the importance of a moral, righteous, and spiritual life, including a carafe with water and a candlestick, traditional religious symbols. The couple ignores them, focusing solely on money. On the right, through a window, an old man talks with another man, a reference to idleness and gossip. The reflected image in the convex mirror on the counter offsets this image of sloth and foolish chatter. There, a man reads what is most likely a Bible or prayer book. Behind him is a church steeple. An inscription on the original frame (now lost) read, "Let the balance be just and the weights equal" (Lev. 19:36), an admonition that applies both to the money-changer's professional conduct and the eventual last judgment. Nonetheless, the couple in this painting has tipped the balance in favor of the pursuit of wealth.

**PIETER AERTSEN** This tendency to inject reminders about spiritual well-being into paintings of everyday life emerges again in *Butcher's Stall* (FIG. 23-17) by PIETER AERTSEN (ca. 1507–1575), who worked in Antwerp for more than three decades. At first glance, this painting appears to be a descriptive *genre* scene (one from daily

23-17 PIETER AERTSEN, *Butcher's Stall*, 1551. Oil on wood, 4′ ⅜″ × 6′ 5¾″. Uppsala University Art Collection, Uppsala.

*Butcher's Stall* appears to be a genre painting, but in the background, Joseph leads a donkey carrying Mary and the Christ Child. Aertsen balanced images of gluttony with allusions to salvation.

life). On display is an array of meat products—a side of a hog, chickens, sausages, a stuffed intestine, pig's feet, meat pies, a cow's head, a hog's head, and hanging entrails. Also visible are fish, pretzels, cheese, and butter. As did Massys, Aertsen embedded strategically placed religious images in his painting. In the background, Joseph leads a donkey carrying Mary and the Christ Child. The holy family stops to offer alms to a beggar and his son, while the people behind the holy family wend their way toward a church. Furthermore, the crossed fishes on the platter and the pretzels and wine in the rafters on the upper left all refer to "spiritual food" (pretzels were often served as bread during Lent). Aertsen accentuated these allusions to salvation through Christ by contrasting them to their opposite— a life of gluttony, lust, and sloth. He represented this degeneracy with the oyster and mussel shells (which Netherlanders believed possessed aphrodisiacal properties) scattered on the ground on the painting's right side, along with the people seen eating and carousing nearby under the roof. Underscoring the general theme is the placard at the right advertising land for sale—Aertsen's moralistic reference to a recent scandal involving the transfer of land from an Antwerp charitable institution to a land speculator. The sign appears directly above the vignette of the Virgin giving alms to the beggar.

**CATERINA VAN HEMESSEN** With the accumulation of wealth in the Netherlands, portraits increased in popularity. The self-portrait (FIG. 23-18) by CATERINA VAN HEMESSEN (1528–1587)

is the first known northern European self-portrait by a woman. Here, she confidently presented herself as an artist who interrupts her work to gaze at the viewer. She holds brushes, a palette, and a *maulstick* (a stick used to steady the hand while painting) in her left hand, and delicately applies pigment to the canvas with her right hand. The artist ensured proper identification (and credit) through the inscription in the painting: "Caterina van Hemessen painted me / 1548 / her age 20." Professional women artists remained unusual in the 16th century in large part because of the difficulty in obtaining formal training (see "The Artist's Profession in Flanders," Chapter 20, page 545). Caterina was typical in having been trained by her father, Jan Sanders van Hemessen (ca. 1500–1556), a well-known painter.

**LEVINA TEERLINC** Another Netherlandish woman who achieved a successful career as an artist was LEVINA TEERLINC (1515–1576) of Bruges. She established such a high reputation that Henry VIII and his successors invited her to England to paint miniatures for them. There, she was a formidable rival of some of her male contemporaries at the court, such as Holbein (FIG. 23-11A), and received greater compensation for her work than they did for theirs. Teerlinc's considerable skill is evident in a life-size portrait (FIG. 23-19) attributed to her, which depicts Elizabeth I as a composed, youthful princess. Daughter of Henry VIII and Anne

**23-18** CATERINA VAN HEMESSEN, *Self-Portrait,* 1548. Oil on wood, 1′ ¾″ × 9⅞″. Kunstmuseum Basel, Basel. ◼️

In this first known northern European self-portrait by a woman, Caterina van Hemessen represented herself as a confident artist momentarily interrupting her work to look out at the viewer.

**23-19** Attributed to LEVINA TEERLINC, *Elizabeth I as a Princess,* ca. 1559. Oil on wood, 3′ 6¾″ × 2′ 8¼″. Royal Collection, Windsor Castle, Windsor. ◼️

Teerlinc received greater compensation for her work for the British court than did her male contemporaries. Her considerable skill is evident in this life-size portrait of Elizabeth I as a young princess.

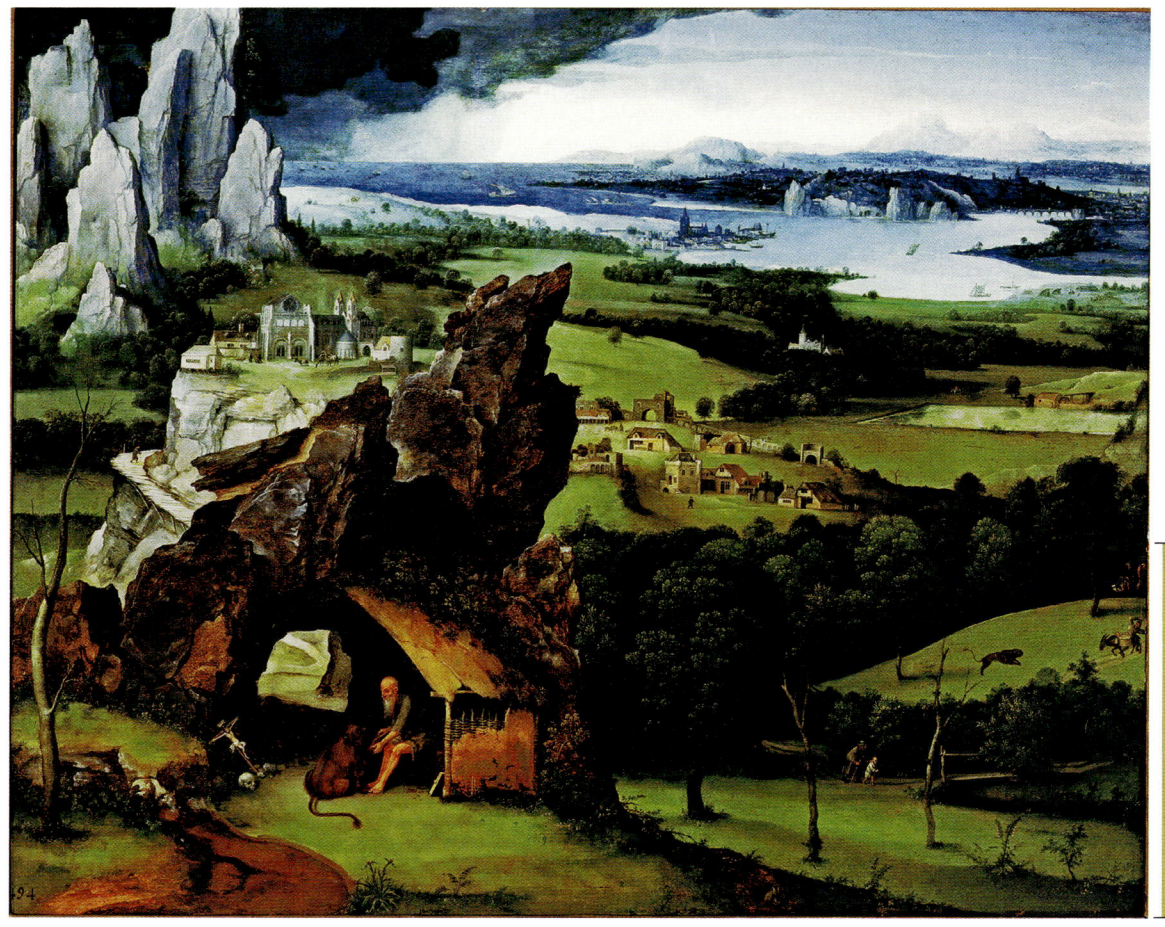

1 ft.

Boleyn, Elizabeth was probably in her late 20s when she posed for this portrait. Appropriate to her station in life, Elizabeth wears an elegant brocaded gown, extravagant jewelry, and a headdress based on a style her mother popularized.

That van Hemessen and Teerlinc enjoyed such success is a testament to their determination and skill, given the difficulties women faced in a profession dominated by men. Women also played an important role as patrons in 16th-century northern Europe. Politically powerful women such as Margaret of Austria (regent of the Netherlands during the early 16th century; 1480–1530) and Mary of Hungary (queen consort of Hungary; 1505–1558) were avid collectors and patrons, and contributed significantly to the thriving state of the arts. As did other art patrons, these women collected and commissioned art not only for the aesthetic pleasure it provided but also for the status it bestowed on them and the cultural sophistication it represented.

**JOACHIM PATINIR** In addition to portrait and genre painting, landscape painting flourished in the Netherlands. Particularly well known for his landscapes was JOACHIM PATINIR (d. 1524). In fact, the word *Landschaft* (landscape) first emerged in German literature as a characterization of an artistic category when Dürer described Patinir as a "good landscape painter." In *Landscape with Saint Jerome* (FIG. **23-20**), Patinir subordinated the saint, who removes a thorn from a lion's paw in the foreground, to the exotic and detailed landscape. Craggy rock formations, verdant rolling fields, villages with church steeples, expansive bodies of water, and a dramatic sky fill most of the panel. Patinir amplified the sense of distance by masterfully using color to enhance the visual effect of recession and advance.

**PIETER BRUEGEL THE ELDER** The greatest Netherlandish painter of the mid-16th century was PIETER BRUEGEL THE ELDER (ca. 1528–1569). Influenced by Patinir, Bruegel was also a landscape painter, but in his paintings, no matter how huge a slice of the world he depicted, human activities remain the dominant theme. As did many of his contemporaries, Bruegel traveled to Italy, where he probably spent almost two years, going as far south as Sicily. Unlike other artists, however, Bruegel chose not to incorporate classical elements into his paintings.

Bruegel's *Netherlandish Proverbs* (FIG. **23-21**) depicts a Netherlandish village populated by a wide range of people (nobility, peasants, and clerics). From a bird's-eye view, the spectator encounters a mesmerizing array of activities reminiscent of the topsy-turvy scenes of Bosch (FIG. **23-1**), but the purpose and meaning of Bruegel's anecdotal details are clear. By illustrating more than a hundred proverbs in this one painting, the artist indulged his Netherlandish audience's obsession with proverbs and passion for detailed and clever imagery. As the viewer scrutinizes the myriad vignettes within the painting, Bruegel's close observation and deep understanding of human nature become apparent. The proverbs depicted include, on the far left, a man in blue gnawing on a pillar ("He bites the column"—an image of hypocrisy). To his right, a man "beats his head against a wall" (an ambitious idiot). On the roof a man "shoots one arrow after the other, but hits nothing" (a shortsighted fool). In the far distance, the "blind lead the blind"—a subject to which Bruegel returned several years later in one of his most famous paintings (not illustrated).

In contrast to Patinir's Saint Jerome, lost in the landscape, the myriad, raucous cast of characters of Bruegel's *Netherlandish Proverbs* fills the panel, so much so the artist almost shut out the sky. *Hunters in the Snow* (FIG. **23-22**) and *Fall of Icarus*

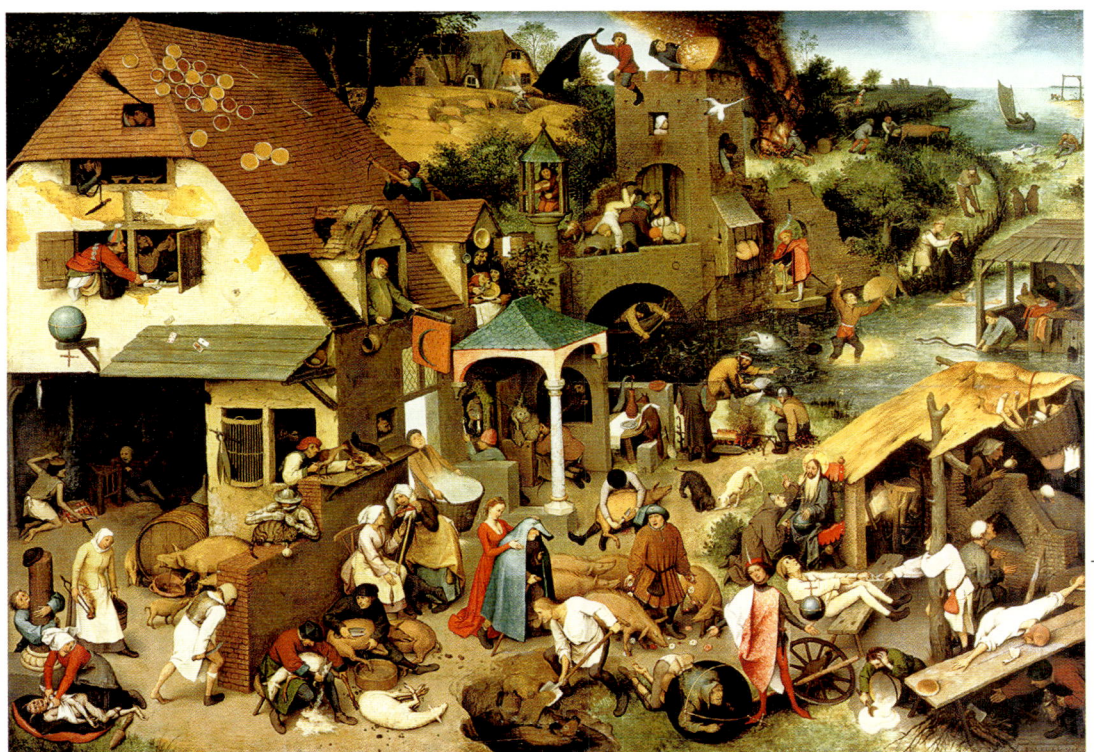

**23-21** PIETER BRUEGEL THE ELDER, *Netherlandish Proverbs*, 1559. Oil on wood, 3′ 10″ × 5′ 4⅛″. Gemäldegalerie, Staatliche Museen zu Berlin, Berlin. ◼◀

In this painting of a Netherlandish village, Bruegel indulged his audience's obsession with proverbs and passion for clever imagery, and demonstrated his deep understanding of human nature.

1 ft.

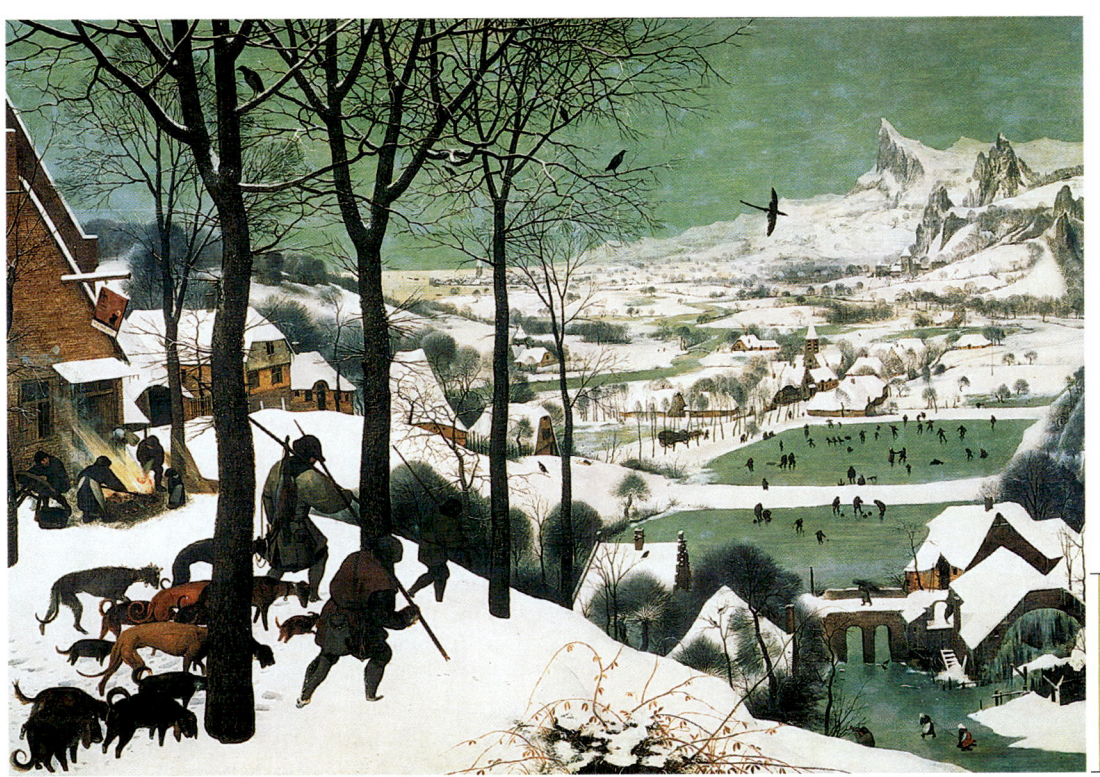

**23-22** PIETER BRUEGEL THE ELDER, *Hunters in the Snow*, 1565. Oil on wood, 3′ 10⅛″ × 5′ 3¾″. Kunsthistorisches Museum, Vienna.

In *Hunters in the Snow,* one of a series of paintings illustrating different seasons, Bruegel draws the viewer diagonally deep into the landscape by his mastery of line, shape, and composition.

1 ft.

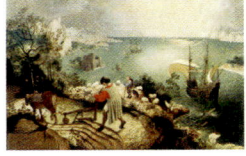

**23-22A** BRUEGEL THE ELDER, *Fall of Icarus*, ca. 1555–1556.

(FIG. **23-22A**) are very different in character and illustrate the dynamic variety of Bruegel's work. *Hunters* is one of a series of six paintings (some scholars think there were originally twelve) illustrating seasonal changes. The series grew out of the tradition of depicting seasons and peasants in Books of Hours (FIGS. 20-15 and 20-16). The painting shows human figures and landscape locked in winter cold, reflect-

ing the particularly severe winter of 1565, when Bruegel produced the work. The weary hunters return with their hounds, women build fires, skaters skim the frozen pond, and the town and its church huddle in their mantle of snow. Bruegel rendered the landscape in an optically accurate manner. It develops smoothly from foreground to background and draws the viewer diagonally into its depths. The painter's consummate skill in using line and shape and his subtlety in tonal harmony make this one of the great landscape paintings in Western art.

# SPAIN

Spain's ascent to power in Europe began in the mid-15th century with the marriage of Isabella of Castile (1451–1504) and Ferdinand of Aragon (1452–1516) in 1469. By the end of the 16th century, Spain had emerged as the dominant European power. Under the Habsburg rulers Charles V and Philip II, the Spanish Empire controlled a territory greater in extent than any ever known—a large part of Europe, the western Mediterranean, a strip of North Africa, and vast expanses in the New World. Spain acquired many of its New World colonies through aggressive overseas exploration. Among the most notable conquistadors sailing under the Spanish flag were Christopher Columbus (1451–1506), Vasco Nuñez de Balboa (ca. 1475–1517), Ferdinand Magellan (1480–1521), Hernán Cortés (1485–1547), and Francisco Pizarro (ca. 1470–1541). The Habsburg Empire, enriched by New World plunder, supported the most powerful military force in Europe. Spain defended and then promoted the interests of the Catholic Church in its battle against the inroads of the Protestant Reformation. Indeed, Philip II earned the title "Most Catholic King." Spain's crusading spirit, nourished by centuries of war with Islam, engaged body and soul in forming the most Catholic civilization of Europe and the Americas. In the 16th century, for good or for ill, Spain left the mark of its power, religion, language, and culture on two hemispheres.

**COLEGIO DE SAN GREGORIO** During the 15th century and well into the 16th, a Late Gothic style of architecture, the Plateresque, prevailed in Spain. *Plateresque* derives from the Spanish word *platero* (silversmith), and delicately executed ornamentation resembling metalwork is the defining characteristic of the Plateresque style. The Colegio de San Gregorio (Seminary of Saint Gregory; FIG. **23-23**) in the Castilian city of Valladolid handsomely exemplifies the Plateresque manner, which Spanish expansion into the Western Hemisphere also brought to "New Spain" (FIG. **23-23A**). Great carved retables, like the German altarpieces that influenced them (FIGS. 20-19, 20-20, and 23-2, *bottom*), appealed to church patrons and architects in Spain, and the portals of Plateresque facades often resemble elegantly carved retables set into an otherwise blank wall. The Plateresque entrance of San Gregorio is a lofty sculptured stone screen bearing no functional relation to the architecture behind it. On the entrance level, lacelike tracery reminiscent of Moorish design hems the flamboyant ogival arches. (Spanish hatred of the Moors did not prevent Spanish architects from adapting Moorish motifs.) A great screen, paneled into sculptured compartments, rises above the tracery. In the center, the branches of a huge pomegranate tree (symbolizing Granada, the Moorish capital of Spain the Habsburgs captured in 1492; see Chapter 10) wreathe the coat of arms of King Ferdinand and Queen Isabella. Cupids play among the tree branches, and, flanking the central panel, niches frame armed pages of the court, heraldic wild men symbolizing aggression, and armored soldiers, attesting to Spain's proud new militancy. In typical Plateresque and Late Gothic fashion, the activity of a thousand intertwined motifs unifies the whole design, which, in sum, creates an exquisitely carved panel greatly expanded in scale from the retables that inspired it.

**23-23A** Casa de Montejo, Mérida, 1549.

**EL ESCORIAL** Under Philip II, the Plateresque style gave way to an Italian-derived classicism that also characterized

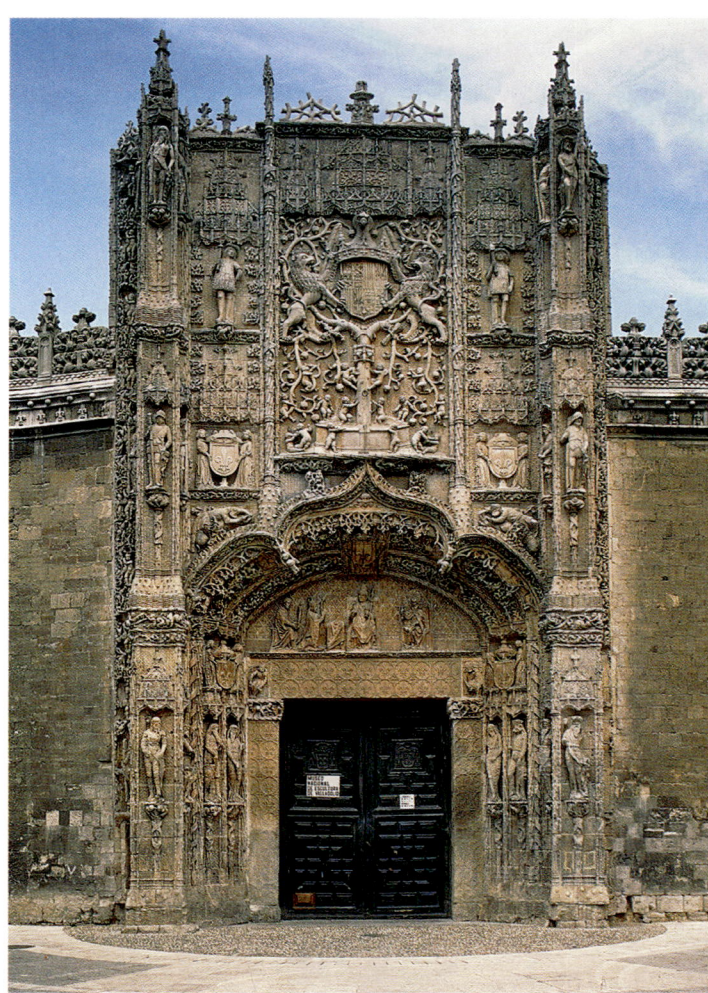

**23-23** Portal, Colegio de San Gregorio, Valladolid, Spain, ca. 1498.

The Plateresque architectural style takes its name from *platero* (Spanish, "silversmith"). At the center of this portal's Late Gothic tracery is the coat of arms of King Ferdinand and Queen Isabella.

16th-century French architecture (FIG. 23-13). The Italian style is on display in the expansive complex called El Escorial (FIG. **23-24**), which JUAN BAUTISTA DE TOLEDO (d. 1567) and JUAN DE HERRERA (ca. 1530–1597), principally the latter, constructed for Philip II. In his will, Charles V stipulated that a "dynastic pantheon" be built to house the remains of past and future monarchs of Spain. Philip II, obedient to his father's wishes, chose a site some 30 miles northwest of Madrid in rugged terrain with barren mountains. Here, he built El Escorial, not only a royal mausoleum but also a church, a monastery, and a palace. Legend has it that the gridlike plan for the enormous complex, 625 feet wide and 520 feet deep, symbolized the gridiron on which Saint Lawrence, El Escorial's patron saint, suffered his martyrdom.

The vast structure is in keeping with Philip's austere character, his passionate Catholic religiosity, his proud reverence for his dynasty, and his stern determination to impose his will worldwide. He insisted that in designing El Escorial, the architects focus on simplicity of form, severity in the whole, nobility without arrogance, and majesty without ostentation. The result is a classicism of Doric severity, ultimately derived from Italian architecture and with the grandeur of Saint Peter's (FIGS. 24-3 and 24-4) implicit in the scheme, but unique in European architecture.

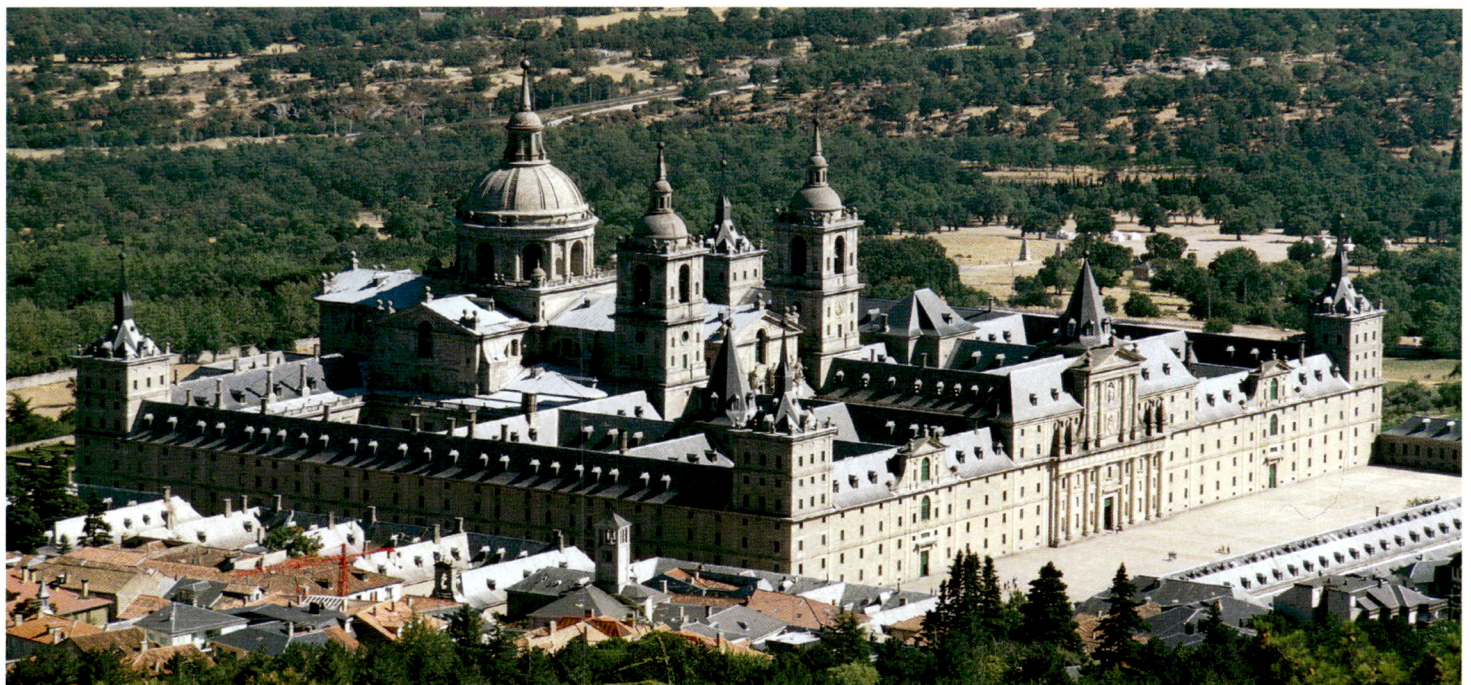

**23-24** Juan de Herrera and Juan Bautista de Toledo, aerial view (looking southeast) of El Escorial, near Madrid, Spain, 1563–1584.

Conceived by Charles V and built by Philip II, El Escorial is a royal mausoleum, church, monastery, and palace in one. The complex is classical in style with severely plain walls and massive towers.

Only the three entrances, with the dominant central portal framed by superimposed orders and topped by a pediment in the Italian fashion, break the long sweep of the structure's severely plain walls. Massive square towers punctuate the four corners. The stress on the central axis, with its subdued echoes in the two flanking portals, anticipates the three-part organization of later Baroque facades (see Chapter 24). The construction material for the entire complex (including the church)—granite, a difficult stone to work—conveys a feeling of starkness and gravity. The church's massive facade and the austere geometry of the interior complex, with its blocky walls and ponderous arches, produce an effect of overwhelming strength and weight. The entire complex is a monument to the collaboration of a great king and remarkably understanding architects. El Escorial stands as the overpowering architectural expression of Spain's spirit in its heroic epoch and of the character of Philip II, the extraordinary ruler who directed it.

**EL GRECO**   Reflecting the increasingly international character of European art as well as the mobility of artists, the greatest Spanish painter of the era was not a Spaniard. Born on Crete, Domenikos Theotokopoulos, called EL GRECO (ca. 1547–1614), emigrated to Italy as a young man. In his youth, he absorbed the traditions of Late Byzantine frescoes and mosaics. While still young, El Greco went to Venice, where he worked in Titian's studio, although Tintoretto's paintings seem to have made a stronger impression on him (see Chapter 22). A brief trip to Rome explains the influences of Roman and Florentine Mannerism on his work. By 1577, he had left for Spain to spend the rest of his life in Toledo.

El Greco's art is a strong personal blending of Byzantine and Mannerist elements. The intense emotionalism of his paintings, which naturally appealed to Spanish piety, and a great reliance on and mastery of color bound him to 16th-century Venetian art and to Mannerism. El Greco's art was not strictly Spanish (although it

appealed to certain sectors of that society), for it had no Spanish antecedents and little effect on later Spanish painters. Nevertheless, El Greco's hybrid style captured the fervor of Spanish Catholicism.

*Burial of Count Orgaz* (FIG. **23-25**), painted in 1586 for the church of Santo Tomé in El Greco's adoptive home, Toledo, vividly expressed that fervor. El Greco based the painting on the legend that the count of Orgaz, who had died some three centuries before and who had been a great benefactor of Santo Tomé, was buried in the church by Saints Stephen and Augustine, who miraculously descended from Heaven to lower the count's body into its sepulcher. In the painting, El Greco carefully distinguished the terrestrial and celestial spheres. The brilliant Heaven that opens above irradiates the earthly scene. The painter represented the terrestrial realm with a firm realism, whereas he depicted the celestial, in his quite personal manner, with elongated undulating figures, fluttering draperies, and a visionary swirling cloud. Below, the two saints lovingly lower the count's armor-clad body, the armor and heavy draperies painted with all the rich sensuousness of the Venetian school. A solemn chorus of personages dressed in black fills the background. In the carefully individualized features of these figures (who include El Greco himself in a self-portrait, and his young son, Jorge Manuel, as well as the priest who commissioned the painting and the Spanish king Philip II), El Greco demonstrated he was also a great portraitist.

The upward glances of some of the figures below and the flight of an angel above link the painting's lower and upper spheres. The action of the angel, who carries the count's soul in his arms as Saint John and the Virgin intercede for it before the throne of Christ, reinforces this connection. El Greco's deliberate change in style to distinguish between the two levels of reality gives the viewer an opportunity to see the artist's early and late manners in the same work, one below the other. His relatively sumptuous and realistic presentation of the earthly sphere is still strongly rooted in Venetian art,

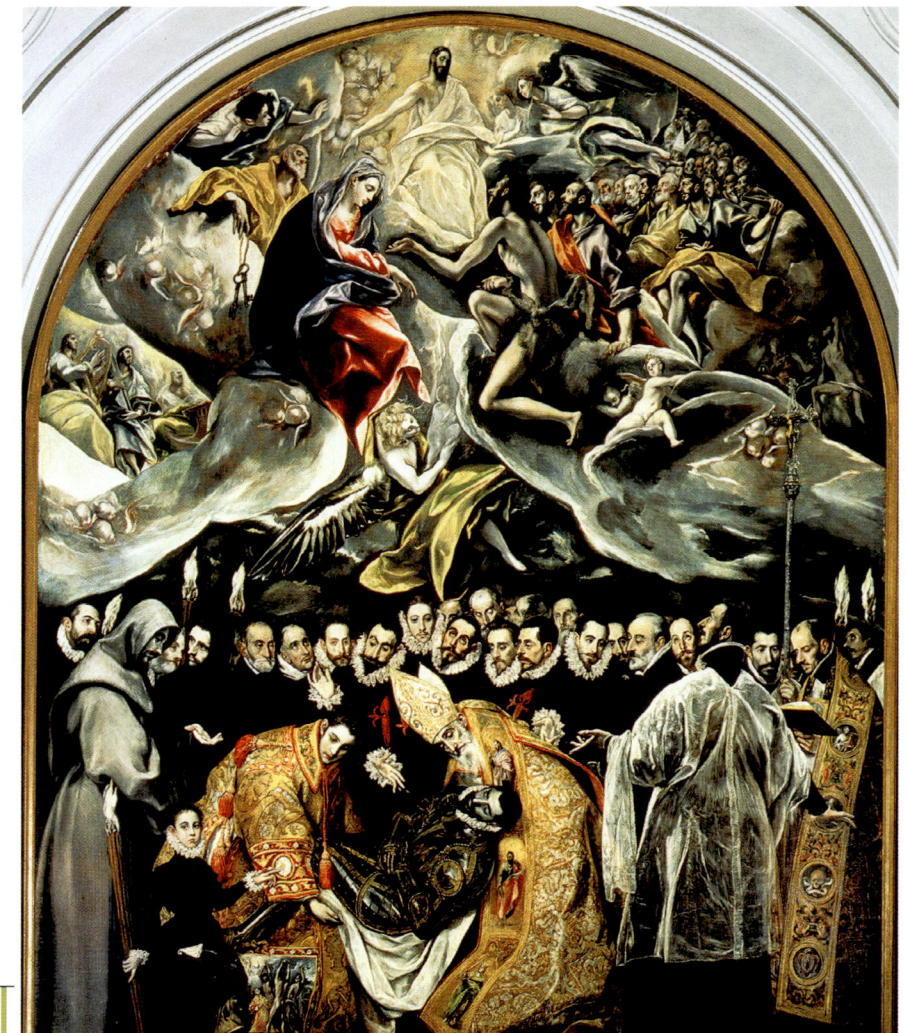

**23-25** EL GRECO, *Burial of Count Orgaz*, 1586. Oil on canvas, 16′ × 12′. Santo Tomé, Toledo.

El Greco's art is a blend of Byzantine and Italian Mannerist elements. His intense emotional content captured the fervor of Spanish Catholicism, and his dramatic use of light foreshadowed the Baroque style.

but the abstractions and distortions El Greco used to show the immaterial nature of the heavenly realm characterize his later style. His elongated figures existing in undefined spaces, bathed in a cool light of uncertain origin, explain El Greco's usual classification as a Mannerist, but it is difficult to apply that label to him without reservation. Although he used Mannerist formal devices, El Greco's primary concerns were emotion and conveying his religious fervor or arousing that of others. The forcefulness of his paintings is the result of his unique, highly developed expressive style.

***VIEW OF TOLEDO*** El Greco's singular vision is equally evident in one of his latest works, *View of Toledo* (FIG. **23-26**), the only pure landscape he ever painted. As does so much of El Greco's work, this painting breaks sharply with tradition. The Greek-born artist depicted the Spanish city from a nearby hilltop and drew attention to the great spire of Toledo's cathedral by leading the viewer's eye along the diagonal line of the bridge crossing the Tajo and continuing with the city's walls. El Greco knew Toledo intimately, and every building is recognizable, although he rearranged some of their positions, moving, for example, the Alcazar palace to the right of the cathedral. Yet he rendered no structure in meticulous detail, as most Renaissance painters would have done, and the color palette is not true to nature but limited to greens and grays. The atmosphere is eerie. Dramatic bursts of light in the stormy sky cast a ghostly pall over the city. The artist applied oil pigment to canvas in broad brushstrokes typical of his late, increasingly abstract painting style, with the result that the buildings and trees do not have sharp contours and almost seem to shake.

Art historians have compared *View of Toledo* to Giorgione da Castelfranco's *Tempest* (FIG. 22-34) and the dramatic lighting to works by Tintoretto (FIG. 22-48), and indeed, El Greco's Venetian training is evident. Still, the closest parallels lie not in the past but in the future—in paintings such as Vincent van Gogh's *Starry Night* (FIG. 28-18) and in 20th-century Expressionism and Surrealism (see Chapter 29). El Greco's art is impossible to classify using conventional labels. Although he had ties to Mannerism and foreshadowed developments of the Baroque era in Spain and Italy—examined in the next chapter—he was a singular artist with a unique vision.

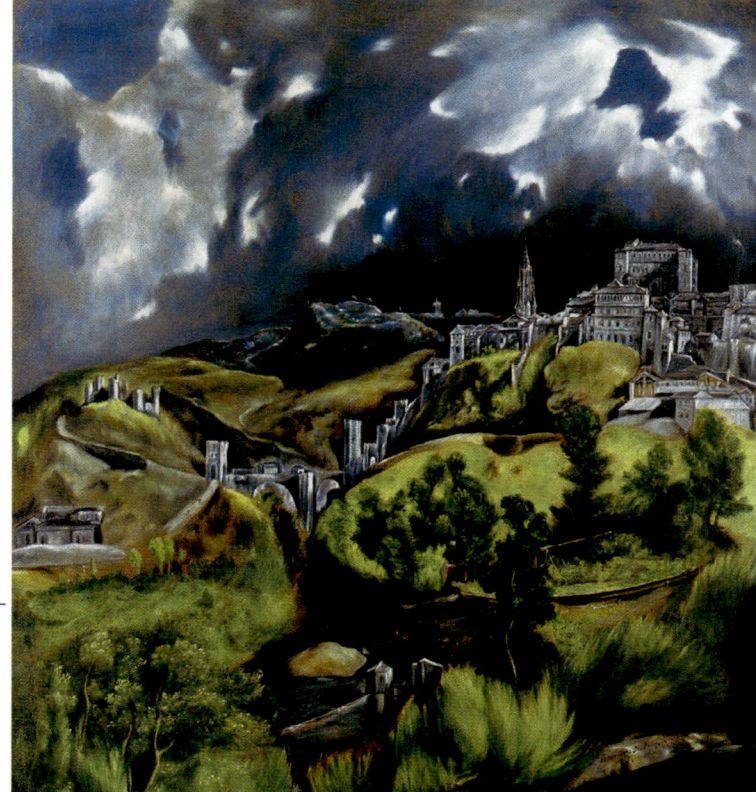

**23-26** EL GRECO, *View of Toledo*, ca. 1610. Oil on canvas, 3′ 11¾″ × 3′ 6¾″. Metropolitan Museum of Art, New York (H. O. Havemeyer Collection. Bequest of Mrs. H. O. Havemeyer, 1929).

*View of Toledo* is the only pure landscape El Greco ever produced. The dark, stormy sky casts a ghostly pall over the city. The painting exemplifies the artist's late, increasingly abstract style.

1 ft.

1 ft.

# HIGH RENAISSANCE AND MANNERISM IN NORTHERN EUROPE AND SPAIN

## HOLY ROMAN EMPIRE

▌ Widespread dissatisfaction with the Church in Rome led to the Protestant Reformation, splitting Christendom in half. Protestants objected to the sale of indulgences and rejected most of the sacraments of the Catholic Church. They also condemned ostentatious church decoration as a form of idolatry that distracted the faithful from communication with God.

▌ As a result, Protestant churches were relatively bare, but art, especially prints, still played a role in Protestantism. Lucas Cranach the Elder, for example, effectively used visual imagery to contrast Catholic and Protestant views of salvation in his woodcut *Law and Gospel.*

▌ The greatest printmaker of the Holy Roman Empire was Albrecht Dürer, who was also a painter. Dürer was the first artist outside Italy to become an international celebrity. His work ranged from biblical subjects to botanical studies. *Fall of Man* reflects Dürer's studies of the Vitruvian theory of human proportions and of classical statuary. Dürer's engravings rival painting in tonal quality.

▌ Other German artists, such as Albrecht Altdorfer, achieved fame as landscape painters. Hans Holbein was a renowned portraitist who became court painter in England. His *French Ambassadors* portrays two worldly humanists and includes a masterfully rendered anamorphic skull.

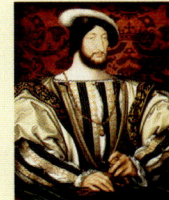

Dürer, *Fall of Man*, 1504

Holbein, *The French Ambassadors,* 1533

## FRANCE

▌ King Francis I fought against Holy Roman Emperor Charles V and declared Protestantism illegal in France. An admirer of Italian art, he invited several prominent Italian painters and sculptors to work at his court and decorate his palace at Fontainebleau.

▌ French architecture of the 16th century mixes Italian and Northern Renaissance elements, as in Pierre Lescot's design of the renovated Louvre palace and Francis's château at Chambord, which combines classical motifs derived from Italian palazzi with a Gothic roof silhouette.

Clouet, *Francis I,* ca. 1525–1530

## THE NETHERLANDS

▌ The Netherlands was one of the most commercially advanced and prosperous countries in 16th-century Europe. Much of Netherlandish art of this period provides a picture of contemporary life and values.

▌ Pieter Aertsen of Antwerp, for example, painted *Butcher's Stall,* which seems to be a straightforward genre scene but includes the holy family offering alms to a beggar in the background, providing a stark contrast between gluttony and religious piety.

▌ Landscapes were the specialty of Joachim Patinir. Pieter Bruegel's repertory also included landscape painting. His *Hunters in the Snow* is one of a series of paintings depicting seasonal changes and the activities associated with them, as in traditional Books of Hours.

▌ Women artists of the period include Caterina van Hemessen, who painted the earliest northern European self-portrait of a woman, and Levina Teerlinc, who produced portraits for the English court.

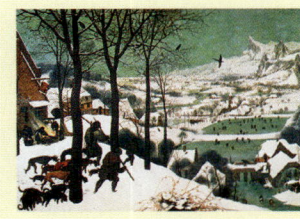

Bruegel, *Hunters in the Snow,* 1565

## SPAIN

▌ At the end of the 16th century, Spain was the dominant power in Europe with an empire greater in extent than any ever known, including vast territories in the New World.

▌ The Spanish Plateresque style of architecture takes its name from *platero* (silversmith) and features delicate ornamentation resembling metalwork.

▌ Under Philip II the Plateresque style gave way to an Italian-derived classicism, seen at its best in El Escorial, a royal mausoleum, monastery, and palace complex near Madrid.

▌ The leading painter of 16th-century Spain was the Greek-born El Greco, who combined Byzantine style, Italian Mannerism, and the religious fervor of Catholic Spain in works such as *Burial of Count Orgaz.*

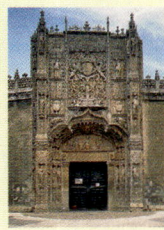

Colegio de San Gregorio, Valladolid, ca. 1498

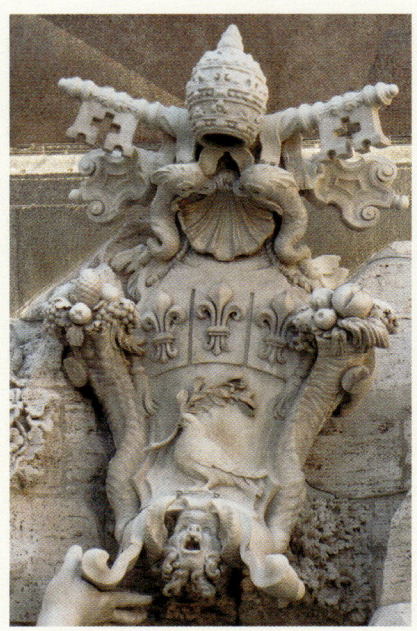

As water flows from a travertine grotto supporting an ancient Egyptian obelisk, Bernini's marble personifications of major rivers of four continents twist and gesticulate emphatically.

Crowning the grotto is Pope Innocent X's coat of arms and atop the obelisk is the Pamphili family's dove symbolizing the Holy Spirit and Christianity's triumph in all parts of the then-known world.

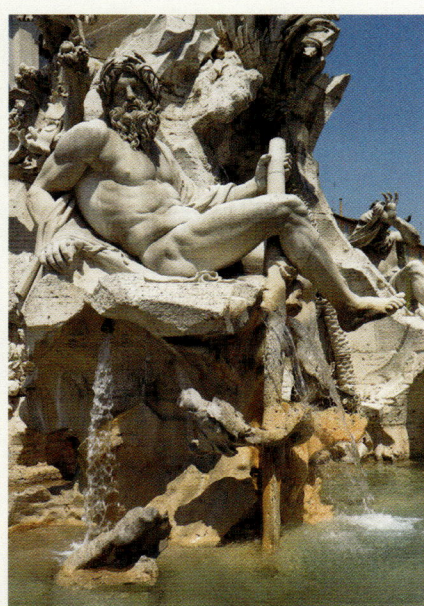

Each of the four rivers has an identifying attribute. The Ganges (Asia), easily navigable, holds an oar. The Plata (Americas) has a hoard of coins, signifying the wealth of the New World.

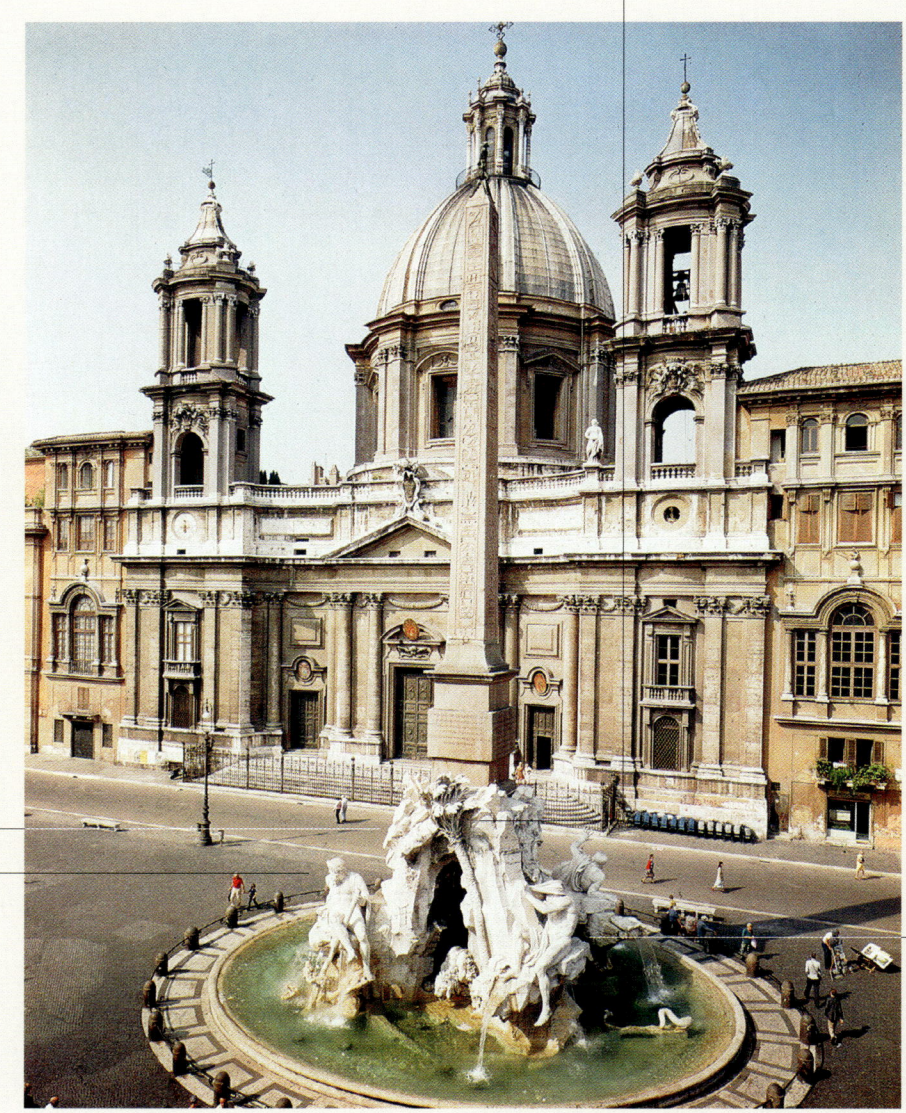

24-1 Gianlorenzo Bernini, Fountain of the Four Rivers (looking southwest with Sant'Agnese in Agone in the background), Piazza Navona, Rome, Italy, 1648–1651. ◀◣

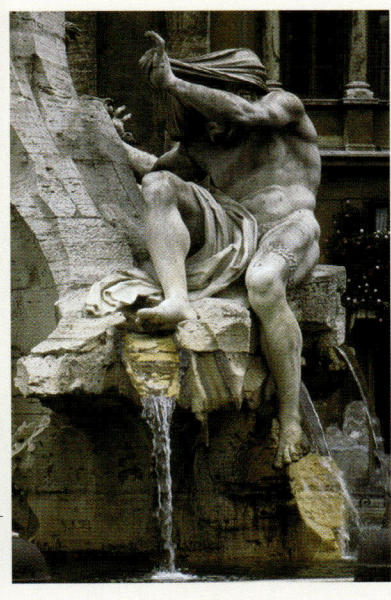

The Danube (Europe) gazes awestruck at the papal arms, and the Nile (Africa) covers his face—Bernini's acknowledgment that the Nile's source was unknown to Europeans at the time.

# THE BAROQUE IN ITALY AND SPAIN

## BAROQUE ART AND SPECTACLE

**O**ne of the most popular tourist attractions in Rome is the Fountain of the Four Rivers (FIG. 24-1) in Piazza Navona by GIANLORENZO BERNINI (1598–1680). Architect, painter, sculptor, playwright, and stage designer, Bernini was one of the most important and imaginative artists of the Baroque era in Italy and its most characteristic and sustaining spirit. Nonetheless, the fountain's patron, Pope Innocent X (r. 1644–1655), did not want Bernini to win this commission. Bernini had been the favorite sculptor of the Pamphili pope's predecessor, Urban VIII (r. 1623–1644), who spent so extravagantly on art and himself and his family that he nearly bankrupted the Vatican treasury. Innocent emphatically opposed the excesses of the Barberini pope and shunned Bernini, awarding new papal commissions to other sculptors and architects. Bernini was also in disgrace at the time because of his failed attempt to erect bell towers for the new facade (FIG. 24-3) of Saint Peter's. When Innocent announced a competition for a fountain in Piazza Navona (MAP 22-1), site of the Pamphili family's palace and parish church, Sant'Agnese in Agone (FIG. 24-1, *rear*), he pointedly did not invite Bernini to submit a design. However, the renowned sculptor succeeded in having a model of his proposed fountain placed where the pope would see it. When Innocent examined it, he was so captivated he declared the only way anyone could avoid employing Bernini was not to look at his work.

Bernini's bold design, executed in large part by his assistants, called for a sculptured travertine grotto supporting an ancient obelisk Innocent had transferred to Piazza Navona from the circus of the Roman emperor Maxentius (r. 305–312) on the Via Appia. The piazza was once the site of the stadium of Domitian (r. 81–96), a long and narrow arena for athletic contests, which explains the piazza's unusual shape and the church's name (*agone* means "foot race" in Italian). Water rushes from the artificial grotto into a basin filled with marble statues personifying major rivers of four continents—the Danube (Europe), Nile (Africa), Ganges (Asia), and Plata (Americas). The reclining figures twist and gesticulate, consistent with Baroque taste for movement and drama. The Nile covers his face—Bernini's way of acknowledging the Nile's source was unknown at the time. The Rio de la Plata has a hoard of coins, signifying the wealth of the New World. The Ganges, easily navigable, holds an oar. The Danube, awestruck, reaches up to the papal coat of arms. A second reference to Innocent X is the Pamphili dove at the apex of the obelisk, which also symbolizes the Holy Spirit and the triumph of Christianity in all parts of the then-known world. The scenic effect of the cascading water would have been heightened whenever Piazza Navona was flooded for festival pageants. Bernini's fountain epitomizes the Baroque era's love for uniting art and spectacle.

# "BAROQUE" ART AND ARCHITECTURE

Art historians traditionally describe 17th-century European art as *Baroque,* but the term is problematic because the period encompasses a broad range of styles and genres. Although its origin is unclear, "Baroque" may have come from the Portuguese word *barroco,* meaning an irregularly shaped pearl. Use of the term can be traced to the late 18th century, when critics disparaged the Baroque period's artistic production, in large part because of perceived deficiencies in comparison with the art of the Italian Renaissance. Over time, this negative connotation faded, but the term stuck. "Baroque" remains useful to describe the distinctive new style that emerged during the early 1600s—a style of complexity and drama seen especially in Italian art of this period. Whereas Renaissance artists reveled in the precise, orderly rationality of classical models, Baroque artists embraced dynamism, theatricality, and elaborate ornamentation, all used to spectacular effect, often on a grandiose scale, as in Bernini's Four Rivers Fountain (FIG. 24-1).

## ITALY

Although in the 16th century the Roman Catholic Church launched the Counter-Reformation in response to—and as a challenge to—the Protestant Reformation, the considerable appeal of Protestantism continued to preoccupy the popes throughout the 17th century. The Treaty of Westphalia (see Chapter 25) in 1648 had formally recognized the principle of religious freedom, serving to validate Protestantism (predominantly in the German states). With the Catholic Church as the leading art patron in 17th-century Italy, the aim of much of Italian Baroque art was to restore Roman Catholicism's predominance and centrality. The Council of Trent, one 16th-century Counter-Reformation initiative, firmly resisted Protestant objections to using images in religious worship, insisting on their necessity for teaching the laity (see "Religious Art in Counter-Reformation Italy," Chapter 22, page 617). Baroque art in Italy was therefore often overtly didactic.

### Architecture and Sculpture

Italian 17th-century art and architecture, especially in Rome, embodied the renewed energy of the Counter-Reformation and communicated it to the populace. At the end of the 16th century, Pope Sixtus V (r. 1585–1590) had played a key role in the Catholic Church's lengthy campaign to reestablish its preeminence. He

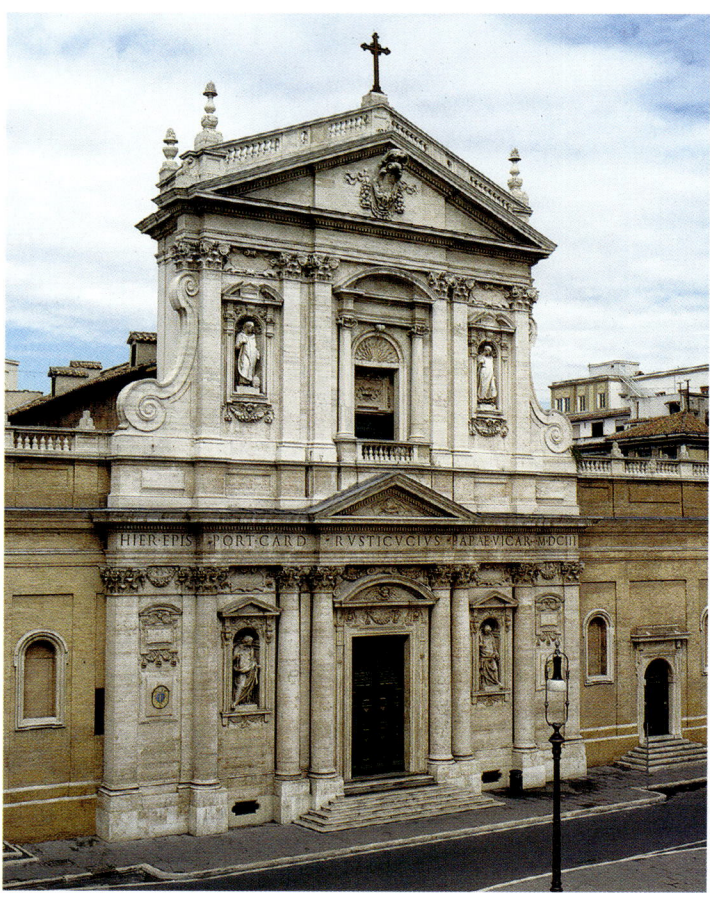

**24-2** CARLO MADERNO, facade of Santa Susanna (looking north), Rome, Italy, 1597–1603.

Santa Susanna's facade is one of the earliest manifestations of the Baroque spirit. The rhythm of the columns and pilasters mounts dramatically toward the emphatically stressed vertical axis.

augmented the papal treasury and intended to rebuild Rome as an even more magnificent showcase of Church power. Between 1606 and 1667, several strong and ambitious popes—Paul V, Urban VIII, Innocent X, and Alexander VII—made many of Sixtus V's dreams a reality. Rome still bears the marks of their patronage everywhere.

**SANTA SUSANNA** The facade (FIG. 24-2) CARLO MADERNO (1556–1629) designed at the turn of the century for the Roman church of Santa Susanna stands as one of the earliest manifestations of the

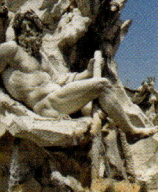

# THE BAROQUE IN ITALY AND SPAIN

| 1600 | 1625 | 1650 | 1675 | 1700 |
|---|---|---|---|---|
| ▌ Paul V commissions Maderno to complete Saint Peter's<br><br>▌ Carracci introduces quadro riportato fresco painting in the Palazzo Farnese<br><br>▌ Caravaggio pioneers tenebrism in Baroque painting<br><br>▌ Bernini creates *David* and *Apollo and Daphne* for Cardinal Scipione Borghese | ▌ Borromini designs San Carlo alle Quattro Fontane and the Chapel of Saint Ivo in Rome<br><br>▌ Gentileschi, the leading woman artist of the 17th century, achieves international renown<br><br>▌ Ribera and Zurburán paint scenes of martyrdom in Catholic Spain<br><br>▌ Philip IV of Spain appoints Velázquez court painter | ▌ Bernini designs the colonnaded oval piazza in front of Saint Peter's<br><br>▌ Murillo creates the canonical image of the *Virgin of the Immaculate Conception*<br><br>▌ Velázquez paints *Las Meninas* | ▌ Gaulli and Pozzo paint illusionistic ceiling frescoes in Il Gesù and Sant'Ignazio<br><br>▌ Guarini brings the Baroque architectural style of Rome to Turin | |

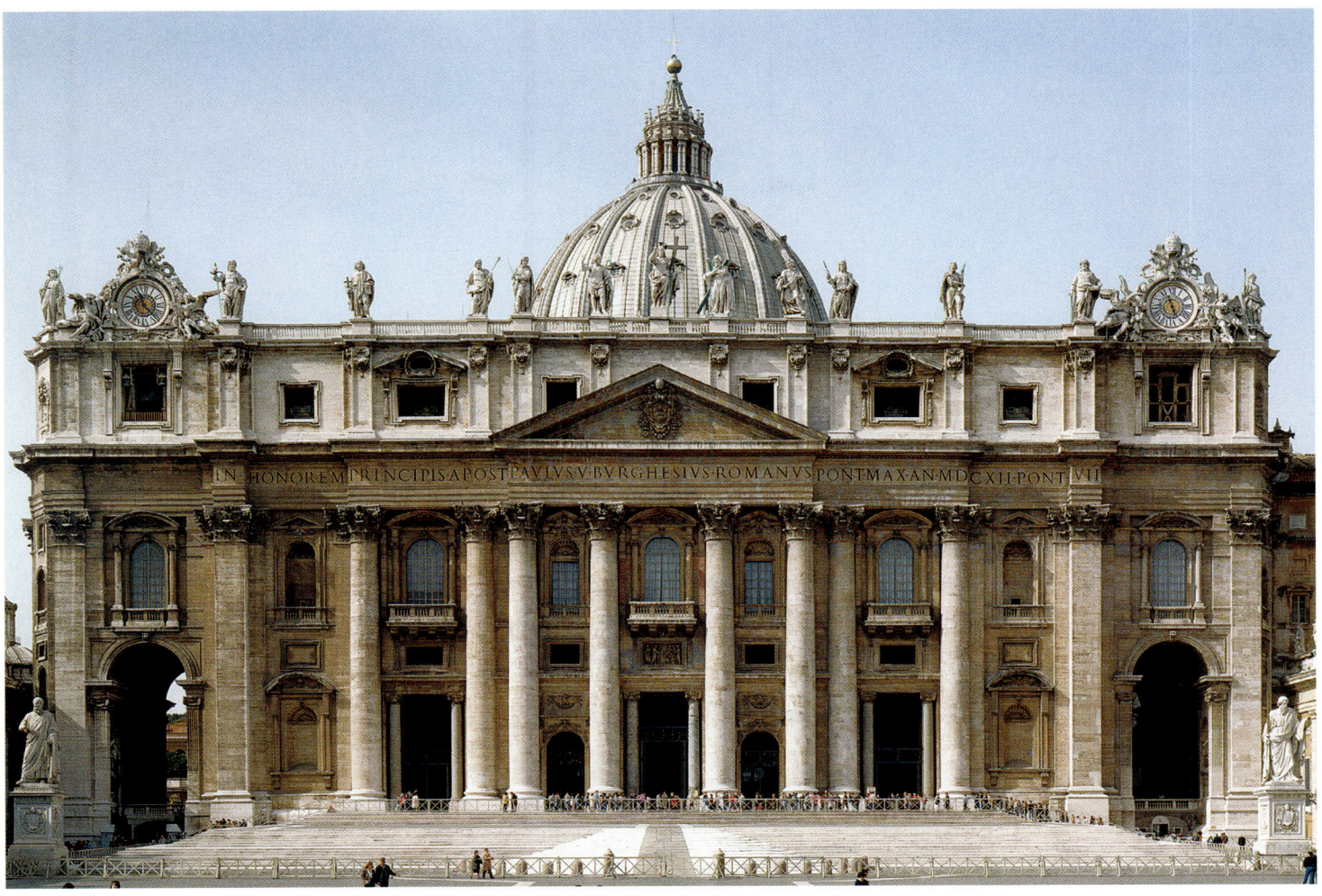

**24-3** CARLO MADERNO, east facade of Saint Peter's, Vatican City, Rome, Italy, 1606–1612.

For the facade of Saint Peter's, Maderno elaborated on his design for Santa Susanna (FIG. 24-2), but the two outer bays with bell towers were not part of his plan and detract from the verticality he sought.

Baroque artistic spirit. In its general appearance, Maderno's facade resembles Giacomo della Porta's immensely influential design for Il Gesù (FIG. 22-56), the church of the Jesuits in Rome. But the later facade has a greater verticality that concentrates and dramatizes the major features of its model. The tall central section projects forward from the horizontal lower story, and the scroll buttresses connecting the two levels are narrower and set at a sharper angle. The elimination of an arch framing the pediment over the doorway further enhances the design's vertical thrust. The rhythm of Santa Susanna's vigorously projecting columns and pilasters mounts dramatically toward the emphatically stressed central axis. The recessed niches, which contain statues and create pockets of shadow, heighten the sculptural effect.

**MADERNO AND SAINT PETER'S** The drama inherent in Santa Susanna's facade appealed to Pope Paul V (r. 1605–1621), who commissioned Maderno in 1606 to complete Saint Peter's in Rome. As the symbolic seat of the papacy, the church Constantine originally built over the first pope's tomb (see Chapter 8) was the very emblem of Western Christendom. In light of Counter-Reformation concerns, the Baroque popes wanted to conclude

the already century-long rebuilding project and reap the prestige embodied in the mammoth new church. In many ways Maderno's facade (FIG. 24-3) is a gigantic expansion of the elements of Santa Susanna's first level. But the compactness and verticality of the smaller church's facade are not as prominent because Saint Peter's enormous breadth counterbalances them. Mitigating circumstances must be taken into consideration when assessing this design, however. Because Maderno had to match the preexisting core of an incomplete building, he did not have the luxury of formulating a totally new concept for Saint Peter's. Moreover, the facade's two outer bays with bell towers were not part of Maderno's original design. Hence, had the facade been constructed according to the architect's initial concept, it would have exhibited greater verticality and visual coherence.

Maderno's plan (MAP 24-1) also departed from the Renaissance central plans for Saint Peter's designed by Bramante (FIG. 22-22) and, later, by Michelangelo (FIG. 22-24). Paul V asked Maderno to add three nave bays to the earlier nucleus because Church officials had decided the central plan was too closely associated with ancient temples, such as the Pantheon (FIG. 7-49). Further, the spatial organization of the longitudinal basilican plan of the original

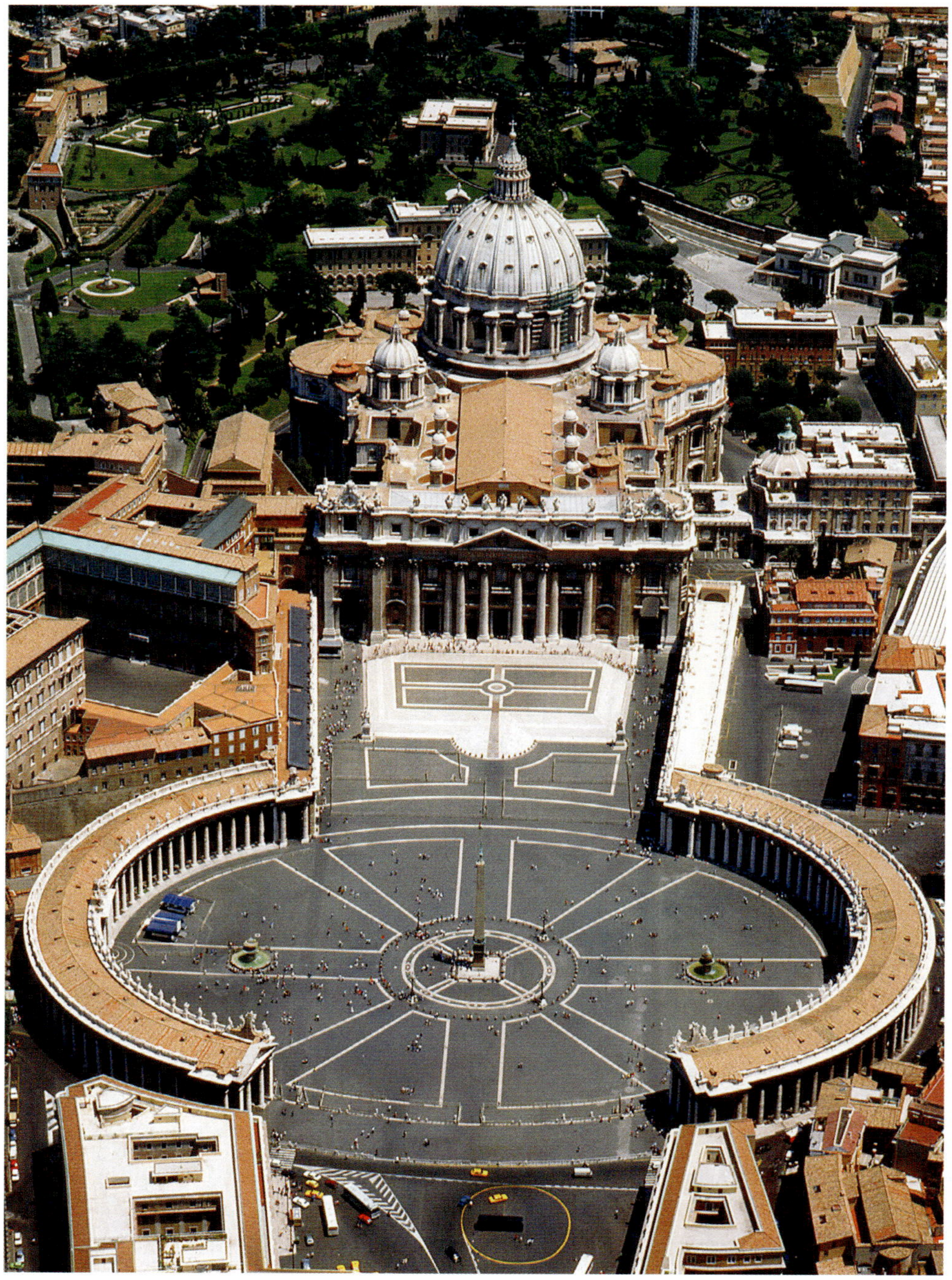

24-4 Aerial view of Saint Peter's (looking west), Vatican City, Rome, Italy. Piazza designed by GIANLORENZO BERNINI, 1656–1667.

The dramatic gesture of embrace Bernini's colonnade makes as worshipers enter Saint Peter's piazza symbolizes the welcome the Catholic Church wished to extend during the Counter-Reformation.

fourth-century church (FIG. 8-9) reinforced the symbolic distinction between clergy and laity and also was much better suited for religious processions. Lengthening the nave, however, pushed the dome farther back from the facade, and all but destroyed the effect Michelangelo had planned—a structure pulled together and dominated by its dome. When viewed at close range, the dome barely emerges above the facade's soaring frontal plane. Seen from farther back (FIG. 24-3), it appears to have no drum. Visitors must move back quite a distance from the front (or fly over the church, FIG. 24-4) to see the dome and drum together. Today, visitors to the Vatican can appreciate the effect Michelangelo intended only by viewing Saint Peter's from the back (FIG. 22-25).

## BERNINI AND SAINT PETER'S

Old Saint Peter's had a large forecourt, or *atrium* (FIG. 8-9, *right*), in front of the church proper, and in the mid-17th century, Gianlorenzo Bernini, who had long before established his reputation as a supremely gifted architect and sculptor (see page 669), received the prestigious commission to construct a monumental colonnade-framed *piazza* (plaza; FIG. **24-4**) in front of Maderno's facade. Bernini's design had to incorporate two preexisting structures on the site—an obelisk the ancient Romans had brought from Egypt (which Pope Sixtus V had moved to its present location in 1585 as part of his vision of Christian triumph in Rome) and a fountain Maderno constructed in front of the church. Bernini coopted these features to define the long axis of a vast oval embraced by two colonnades joined to Maderno's facade. Four rows of huge Tuscan columns make up the two colonnades, which terminate in classical temple fronts. The colonnades extend a dramatic gesture of embrace to all who enter the piazza, symbolizing the welcome the Roman Catholic Church gave its members during the Counter-Reformation. Bernini himself referred to his colonnades as the welcoming arms of Saint Peter's.

Beyond their symbolic resonance, the colonnades served visually to counteract the natural perspective and bring the facade closer to the viewer. (Bernini's mastery of perspective in architecture is even more evident in his contemporaneous design for the Scala Regia [FIG. **24-4A**] of the Vatican palace, a project he undertook at the request of Pope Alexander VII [r. 1655–1667].) Emphasizing the facade's height in this manner, Bernini subtly and effectively compensated for its extensive width. Thus, a Baroque transformation expanded the compact central designs of Bramante and Michelangelo into a dynamic complex of axially ordered elements that reach out and enclose spaces of vast dimension. By its sheer scale and theatricality, the completed Saint Peter's fulfilled the desire of the Counter–Reformation Church to present an awe-inspiring and authoritative vision of itself.

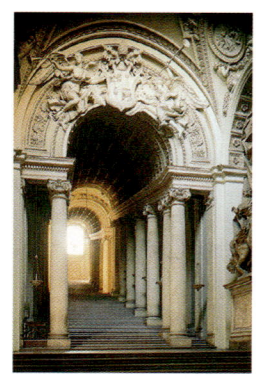

24-4A BERNINI, Scala Regia, Vatican, 1663–1666.

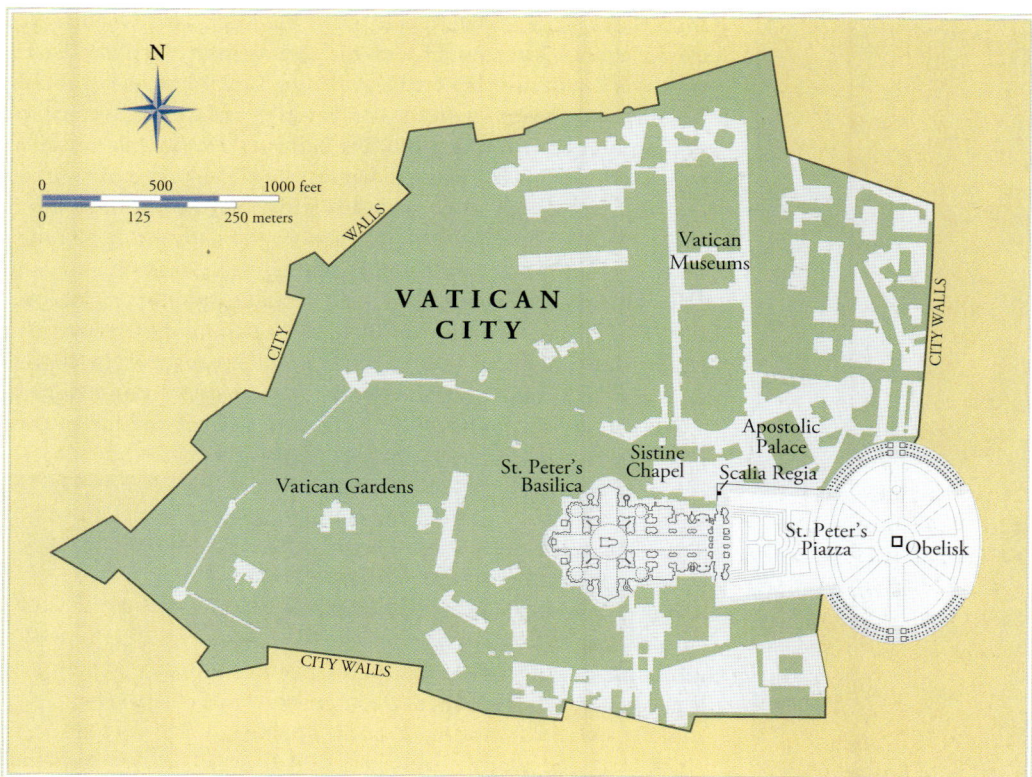

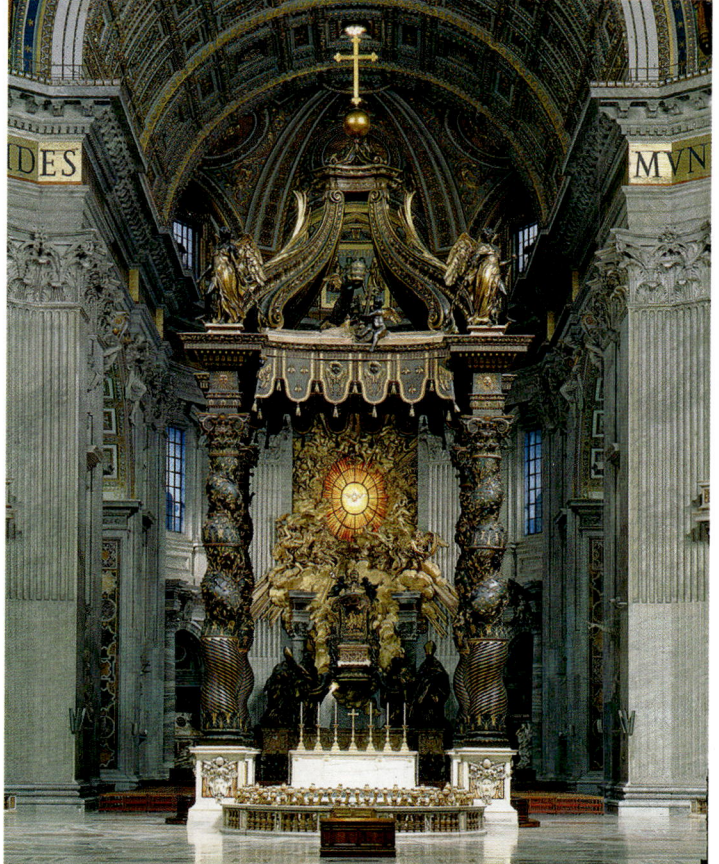

**24-5** GIANLORENZO BERNINI, baldacchino (looking west), Saint Peter's, Vatican City, Rome, Italy, 1624–1633.

Bernini's baldacchino serves both functional and symbolic purposes. It marks Saint Peter's tomb and the high altar, and it visually bridges human scale to the lofty vaults and dome above.

**BALDACCHINO** Prior to being invited to design the piazza in front of Saint Peter's, Bernini had won the commission to erect a gigantic bronze *baldacchino* (FIG. **24-5**) under Giacomo della Porta's dome (FIG. 22-25). Completed between 1624 and 1633, the canopylike structure (*baldacco* is Italian for "silk from Baghdad," such as for a cloth canopy) stands almost 100 feet high (the height of an average eight-story building) and serves both functional and symbolic purposes. It marks the high altar and the tomb of Saint Peter, and it visually bridges human scale to the lofty vaults and dome above. Further, for worshipers entering the nave of the huge church, it provides a dramatic, compelling presence at the crossing. Its columns also create a visual frame for the elaborate sculpture representing the throne of Saint Peter (the Cathedra Petri) at the far end of Saint Peter's (FIG. 24-5, *rear*). On a symbolic level, the structure's decorative elements speak to the power of the Catholic Church and of Pope Urban VIII. Partially fluted and wreathed with vines, the baldacchino's four spiral columns are Baroque versions of the comparable columns of the ancient baldacchino over the same spot in Old Saint Peter's, thereby invoking the past to reinforce the primacy of the Roman Catholic Church in the 17th century. At the top of the vine-entwined columns, four colossal angels stand guard at the upper corners of the canopy. Forming the canopy's apex are four serpentine brackets that elevate the orb and the cross. Since the time of Constantine (FIG. 7-81, *right*; compare FIG. 9-2), the orb and the cross had served as symbols of the Church's triumph. The baldacchino also features numerous bees, symbols of Urban VIII's family, the Barberini. The structure effectively gives visual form to the triumph of Christianity and the papal claim to doctrinal supremacy.

The construction of the baldacchino was itself a remarkable feat. Each of the bronze columns consists of five sections cast from wood models using the *lost-wax process* (see "Hollow-Casting Life-Size Bronze Statues," Chapter 5, page 130). Although Bernini did some of the work himself, including cleaning and repairing the wax molds and doing the final cleaning and *chasing* (engraving and embossing) of the bronze casts, he contracted out much of the project to experienced bronze-casters and sculptors. The superstructure is predominantly cast bronze, although some of the sculptural elements are brass or wood. The enormous scale of the baldacchino required a considerable amount of bronze. On Urban VIII's orders, workmen dismantled the portico of the Pantheon (FIG. 7-49) to acquire the bronze for the baldacchino—ideologically appropriate, given the Church's rejection of polytheism.

The concepts of triumph and grandeur permeate every aspect of the 17th-century design of Saint Peter's. Suggesting a great and solemn procession, the main axis of the complex traverses the piazza (marked by the central obelisk) and enters Maderno's nave. It comes to a temporary halt at the altar beneath Bernini's baldacchino, but it continues on toward its climactic destination at another great altar in the apse.

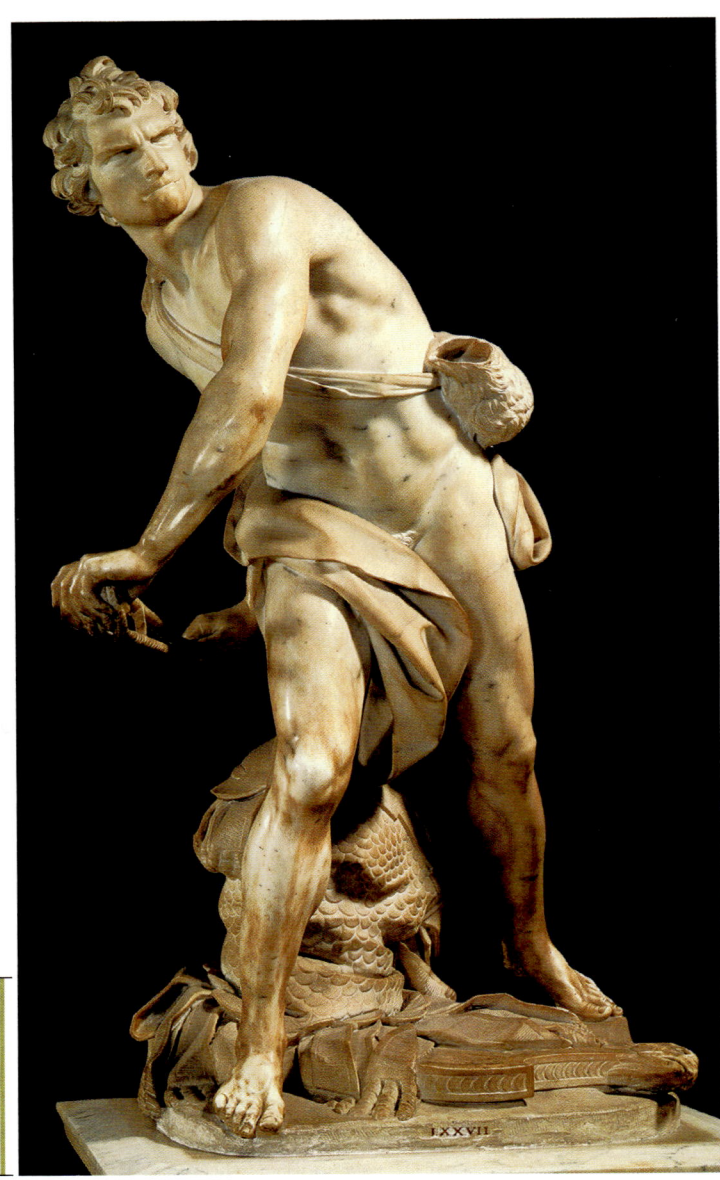

from those earlier masterpieces, however. Michelangelo portrayed David before his encounter with his gigantic adversary, and Donatello and Verrocchio depicted David after his triumph over Goliath. Bernini chose to represent the combat itself and aimed to catch the split-second of maximum action. Bernini's *David,* his muscular legs widely and firmly planted, begins the violent, pivoting motion that will launch the stone from his sling. (A bag full of stones is at David's left hip, suggesting he thought the fight would be tough and long.) Unlike Myron, the fifth-century BCE Greek sculptor who froze his *Discus Thrower* (FIG. 5-39) at a fleeting moment of inaction, Bernini selected the most dramatic of an implied sequence of poses, requiring the viewer to think simultaneously of the continuum and of this tiny fraction of it. The suggested continuum imparts a dynamic quality to the statue. In Bernini's *David,* the energy confined in Michelangelo's figures (FIGS. 22-14 and 22-15) bursts forth. The Baroque statue seems to be moving through time and through space. This kind of sculpture cannot be inscribed in a cylinder or confined in a niche. Its unrestrained action demands space around it. Nor is it self-sufficient in the Renaissance sense, as its pose and attitude direct attention beyond it to the unseen Goliath. Bernini's *David* moves out into the space surrounding it, as do Apollo and Daphne in the marble group (FIG. **24-6A**) he carved for the same patron, Cardinal Scipione Borghese (1576–1633). Further, the expression

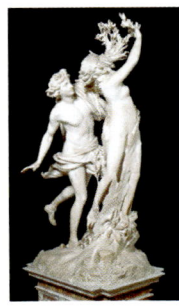

**24-6A** BERNINI, *Apollo and Daphne,* 1623–1624.

**24-6** GIANLORENZO BERNINI, *David,* 1623. Marble, 5′ 7″ high. Galleria Borghese, Rome. ◼◀

Bernini's sculptures are expansive and theatrical, and the element of time plays an important role in them. His emotion-packed *David* seems to be moving through both time and space.

**DAVID** Bernini's baldacchino is, like his Four Rivers Fountain (FIG. 24-1), a masterpiece of the sculptor's craft even more than the architect's. In fact, although Bernini achieved an international reputation as an architect, his fame rests primarily on his sculpture. The biographer Filippo Baldinucci (1625–1696) observed: "[T]here was perhaps never anyone who manipulated marble with more facility and boldness. He gave his works a marvelous softness . . . making the marble, so to say, flexible."[1] Bernini's sculpture is expansive and theatrical, and the element of time usually plays an important role in it, as in the pronounced movement of the personified rivers—and the cascading water—in his Piazza Navona fountain.

A sculpture that predates both the Four Rivers Fountain and Saint Peter's baldacchino is Bernini's *David* (FIG. **24-6**). The Baroque master surely knew the Renaissance statues of the biblical hero fashioned by Donatello (FIG. 21-12), Verrocchio (FIG. 21-13), and Michelangelo (FIG. 22-13). Bernini's *David* differs fundamentally

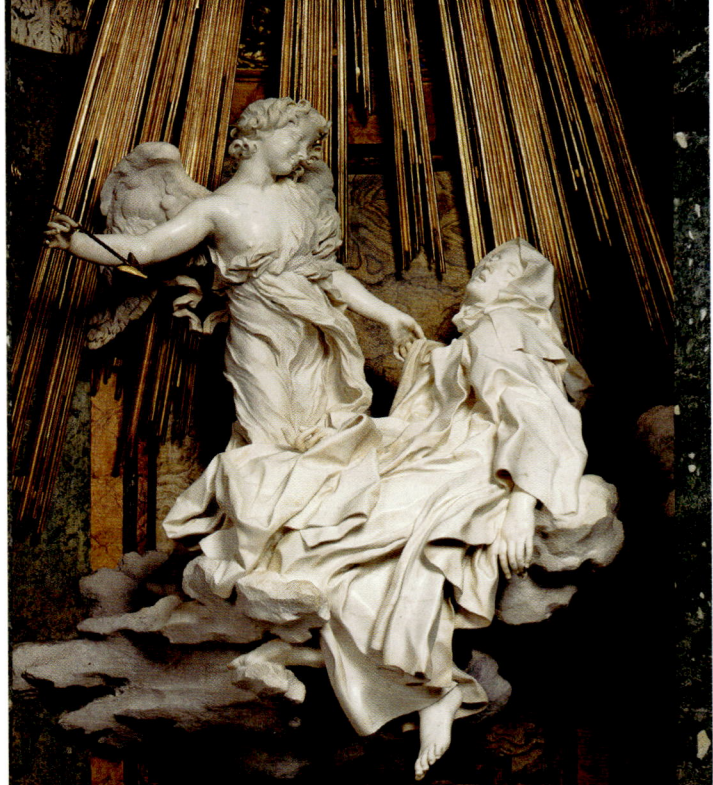

**24-7** GIANLORENZO BERNINI, *Ecstasy of Saint Teresa,* Cornaro chapel, Santa Maria della Vittoria, Rome, Italy, 1645–1652. Marble, height of group 11′ 6″. ◼◀

The passionate drama of Bernini's depiction of Saint Teresa correlated with the ideas of Ignatius Loyola, who argued that the re-creation of spiritual experience would encourage devotion and piety.

In the Cornaro chapel, Bernini, the quintessential Baroque artist, marshaled the full capabilities of architecture, sculpture, and painting to create an intensely emotional experience for worshipers.

conversion occurred after the death of her father, when she fell into a series of trances, saw visions, and heard voices. Feeling a persistent pain, she attributed it to the fire-tipped arrow of divine love an angel had thrust repeatedly into her heart. In her writings, Saint Teresa described this experience as making her swoon in delightful anguish.

In Bernini's hands, the entire Cornaro chapel became a theater for the production of this mystical drama. The niche in which it takes place appears as a shallow *proscenium* (the part of the stage in front of the curtain) crowned with a broken Baroque pediment and ornamented with polychrome marble. On either side of the chapel, sculpted portraits of members of the family of Cardinal Federico Cornaro (1579–1673) watch the heavenly drama unfold from choice balcony seats. Bernini depicted the saint in ecstasy, unmistakably a mingling of spiritual and physical passion, swooning back on a cloud, while the smiling angel aims his arrow. The

of intense concentration on David's face contrasts vividly with the classically placid visages of Donatello's and Verrocchio's versions and is more emotionally charged even than Michelangelo's. The tension in David's face augments the dramatic impact of Bernini's sculpture.

***ECSTASY OF SAINT TERESA*** Another work displaying the motion and emotion that are hallmarks of Italian Baroque art is Bernini's *Ecstasy of Saint Teresa* (FIG. 24-7) in the Cornaro chapel (FIG. 24-8) of the Roman church of Santa Maria della Vittoria. The work exemplifies the Baroque master's refusal to limit his statues to firmly defined spatial settings. For this commission, Bernini marshaled the full capabilities of architecture, sculpture, and painting to charge the entire chapel with palpable tension. In the Cornaro chapel, Bernini drew on the considerable knowledge of the theater he derived from writing plays and producing stage designs. The marble sculpture that serves as the chapel's focus depicts Saint Teresa of Avila (1515–1582), a nun of the Carmelite order and one of the great mystical saints of the Spanish Counter-Reformation. Her

sculptor's supreme technical virtuosity is evident in the visual differentiation in texture among the clouds, rough nun's cloth, gauzy material, smooth flesh, and feathery wings—all carved from the same white marble. Light from a hidden window of yellow glass pours down on golden rays suggesting the radiance of Heaven, whose painted representation covers the vault.

The passionate drama of Bernini's *Ecstasy of Saint Teresa* correlated with the ideas disseminated earlier by Ignatius Loyola (1491–1556), who founded the Jesuit order in 1534 and whom the Catholic Church canonized as Saint Ignatius in 1622. In his book *Spiritual Exercises,* Ignatius argued that the re-creation of spiritual experiences in artworks would do much to increase devotion and piety. Thus, theatricality and sensory impact were useful vehicles for achieving Counter-Reformation goals (see "Religious Art in Counter-Reformation Italy," Chapter 22, page 617). Bernini was a devout Catholic, which undoubtedly contributed to his understanding of those goals. His inventiveness, technical skill, sensitivity to his patrons' needs, and energy made him the quintessential Italian Baroque artist.

24-9 FRANCESCO BORROMINI, facade of San Carlo alle Quattro Fontane (looking south), Rome, Italy, 1638–1641.

Borromini rejected the notion that a church should have a flat frontispiece. He set San Carlo's facade in undulating motion, creating a dynamic counterpoint of concave and convex elements.

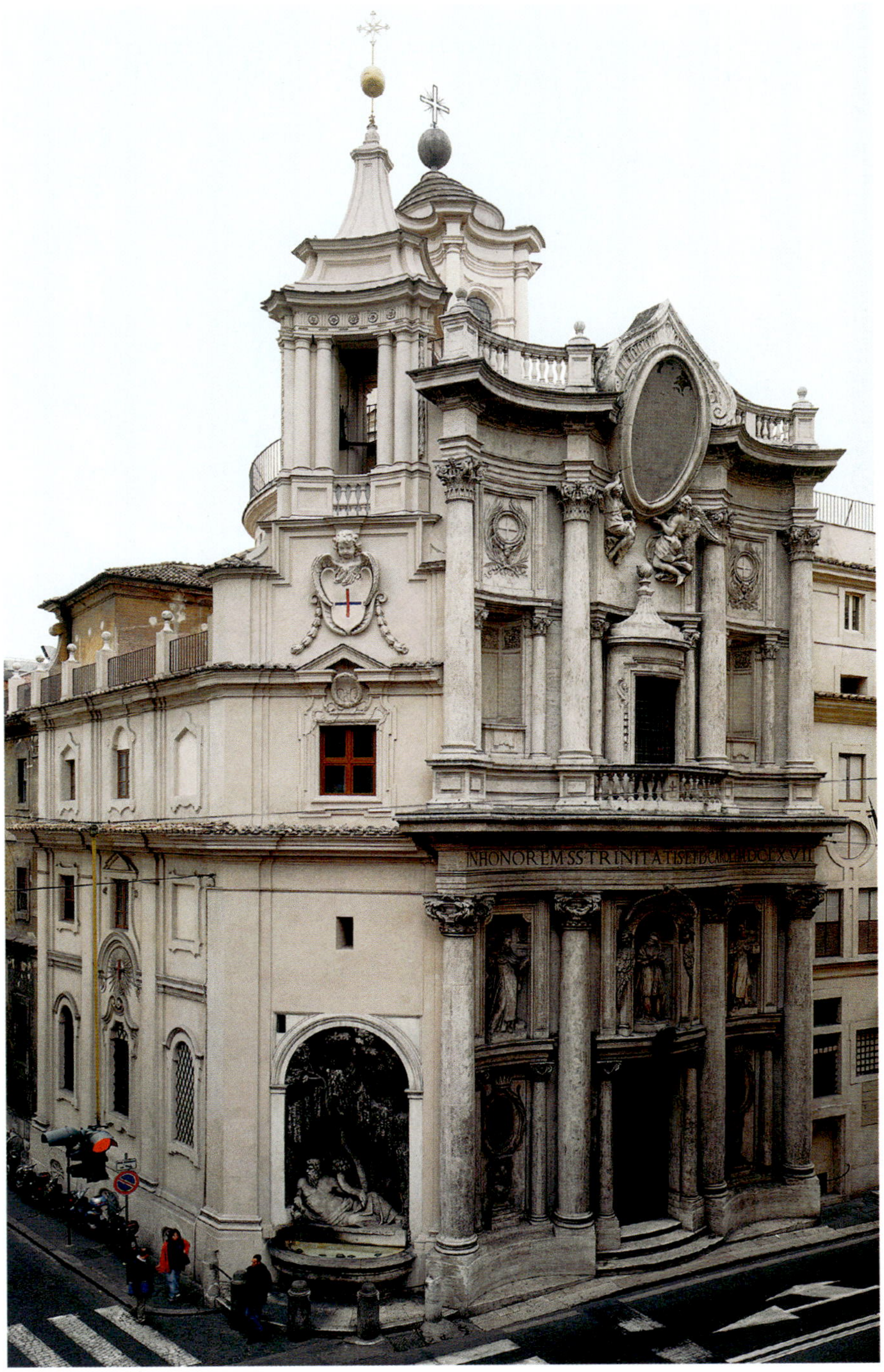

## SAN CARLO ALLE QUATTRO FONTANE

As gifted as Bernini was as an architect, FRANCESCO BORROMINI (1599–1667) took Italian Baroque architecture to even greater dramatic heights. In the little church of San Carlo alle Quattro Fontane (Saint Charles at the Four Fountains; FIG. 24-9), Borromini went much further than any of his predecessors or contemporaries in emphasizing a building's sculptural qualities. Although Maderno incorporated sculptural elements in his designs for the facades of Santa Susanna (FIG. 24-2) and Saint Peter's (FIG. 24-3), those church fronts still develop along relatively lateral planes. Borromini set his facade in undulating motion, creating a dynamic counterpoint of concave and convex elements on two levels (for example, the sway of the cornices). He enhanced the three-dimensional effect with deeply recessed niches. This facade is not the traditional flat frontispiece that defines a building's outer limits. It is a pulsating, engaging screen inserted between interior and exterior space, designed not to separate but to provide a fluid transition between the two. In fact, San Carlo has not one but two facades, underscoring the functional interrelation of the building and its environment. The second facade, a narrow bay crowned with its own small tower, turns away from the main facade and, following the curve of the street, faces an intersec-

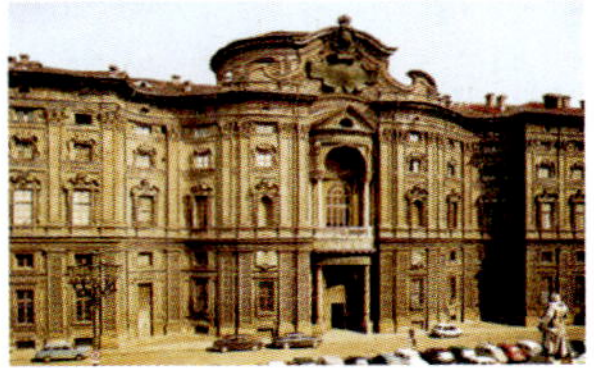

24-9A GUARINI, Palazzo Carignano, Turin, 1679–1692.

tion. Borromini's innovative style had an enormous influence on later Baroque architects throughout Italy. The Palazzo Carignano (FIG. 24-9A) in Turin, for example, designed by GUARINO GUARINI (1624–1683), depends heavily on Borromini's work in Rome.

The interior of San Carlo alle Quattro Fontane is not only Borromini's ingenious response to an awkward site but also a provocative variation on the theme of the centrally planned church. In plan (FIG. 24-10), San Carlo is a hybrid of a *Greek cross* (a cross with four arms of equal length) and an oval, with a long axis between entrance and apse. The side walls move in an undulating flow that reverses the facade's motion. Vigorously projecting columns define the space into which they protrude just as much as they accent the walls to which they are attached. Capping this molded interior space is a deeply coffered oval dome (FIG. 24-11) that seems to float on the light entering through windows hidden in its base. Rich variations on the basic theme of the oval—dynamic curves relative to the static circle—create an interior that flows from entrance to altar, unimpeded by the segmentation so characteristic of Renaissance buildings.

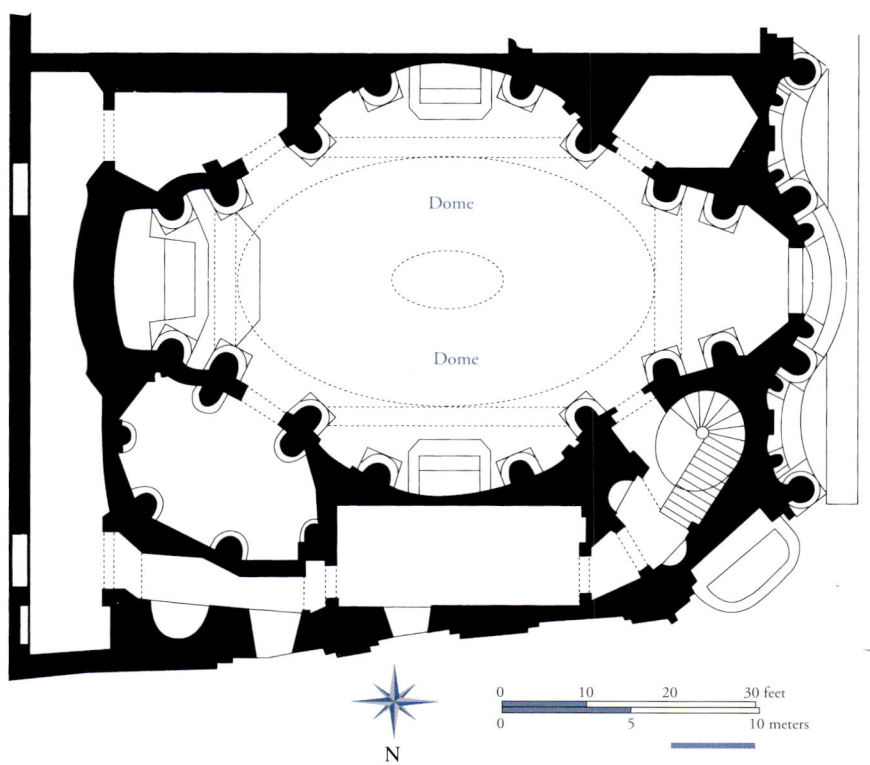

**24-10** FRANCESCO BORROMINI, plan of San Carlo alle Quattro Fontane, Rome, Italy, 1638–1641.

The plan of San Carlo is a hybrid of a Greek cross and an oval. The walls pulsate in a way that reverses the facade's movement. The molded, dramatically lit space flows from entrance to altar.

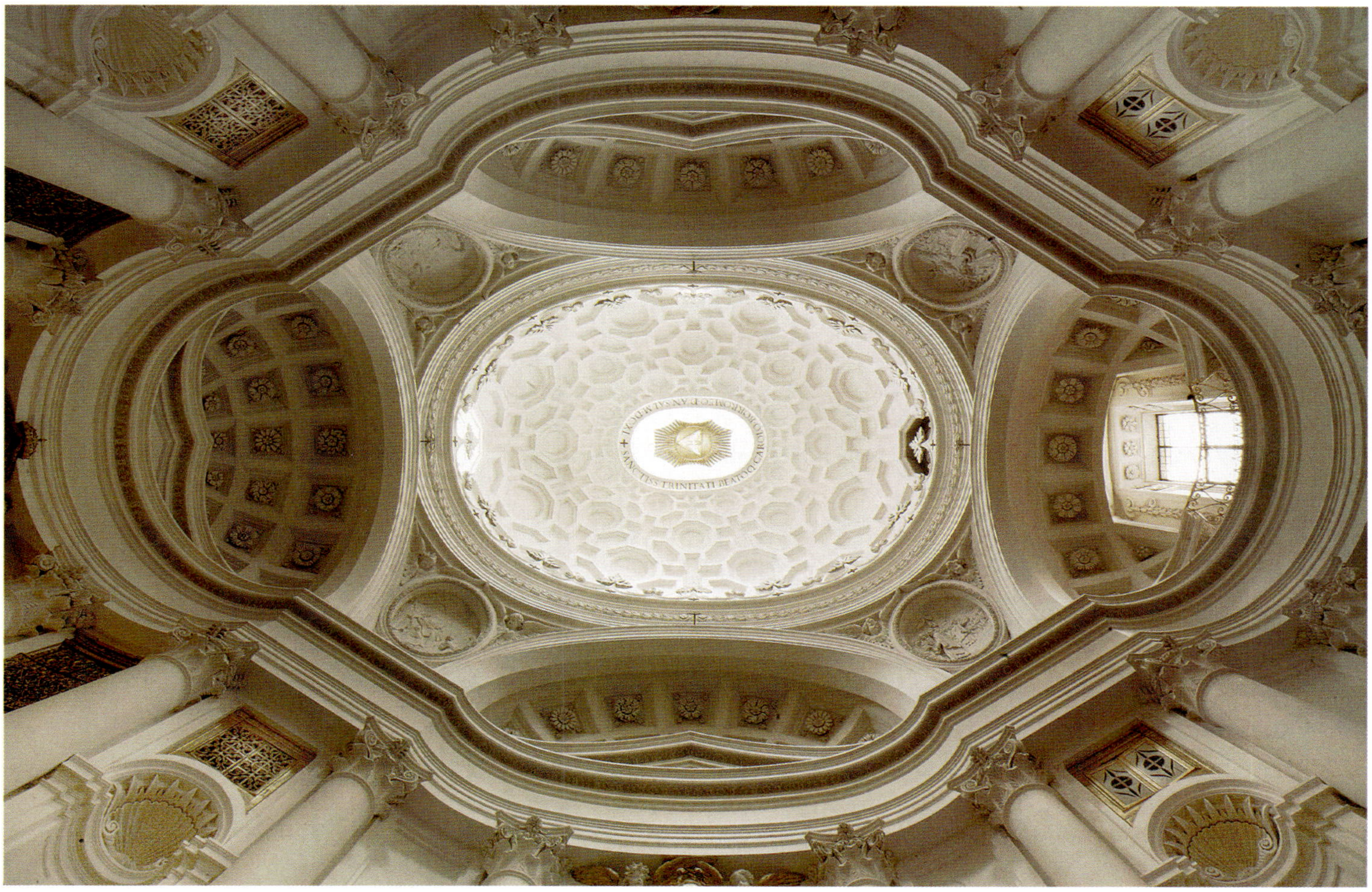

Dome

Dome

| 0 | 10 | 20 | 30 feet |
| 0 | | 5 | 10 meters |

N

**24-11** FRANCESCO BORROMINI, San Carlo alle Quattro Fontane (view into dome), Rome, Italy, 1638–1641.

In place of a traditional round dome, Borromini capped the interior of San Carlo with a deeply coffered oval dome that seems to float on the light entering through windows hidden in its base.

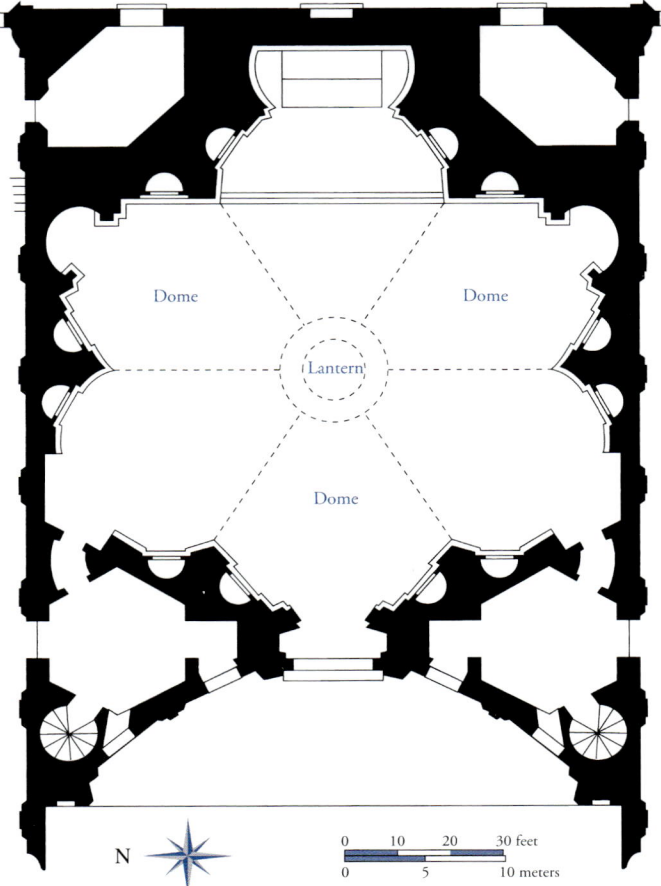

**24-12** Francesco Borromini, *Chapel of Saint Ivo (looking east), College of the Sapienza, Rome, Italy, begun 1642.*

In characteristic fashion, Borromini played concave against convex forms on the upper level of the Chapel of Saint Ivo. Pilasters restrain the forces that seem to push the bulging forms outward.

**24-13** Francesco Borromini, plan of the Chapel of Saint Ivo, College of the Sapienza, Rome, Italy, begun 1642.

The interior elevation of Borromini's Saint Ivo chapel fully reflects all the elements of its highly complex plan, which is star-shaped with rounded points and apses on all sides.

**CHAPEL OF SAINT IVO** Borromini carried the unification of interior space even further in the Chapel of Saint Ivo (FIG. **24-12**) at the east end of the courtyard of the College of the Sapienza (Wisdom) in Rome. In his characteristic manner, Borromini played concave against convex forms on the upper level of the chapel's exterior. The arcaded courtyard, which frames the lower levels of the chapel's facade, had already been constructed when Borromini began work, and he adjusted his design to achieve a harmonious merging of the new and older parts of the college. Above the inward-curving lower two stories of the Saint Ivo chapel rises a convex drumlike structure that supports the dome's lower parts. Clusters of pilasters restrain the forces that seem to push the bulging forms outward. Buttresses above the pilasters curve upward to brace a tall, ornate lantern topped by a spiral that, screwlike, seems to fasten the structure to the sky.

The centralized plan (FIG. **24-13**) of the interior of the Saint Ivo chapel is that of a star with rounded points and apses on all sides. Indentations and projections along the angled curving walls create a highly complex plan, with all the elements fully reflected in the interior elevation. From floor to lantern, the wall panels rise in a continuously tapering sweep halted only momentarily by a single horizontal cornice (FIG. **24-14**). Thus, the dome is not a separate unit placed on a supporting block, as in Renaissance buildings. It is an organic part that evolves out of and shares the qualities of the supporting walls, and it cannot be separated from them. This carefully designed progression up through the lantern creates a dynamic and cohesive shell that encloses and energetically molds a scalloped fragment of space. Few architects have matched Borromini's ability to translate extremely complicated designs into masterfully unified structures, but some later architects, including Guarini, an accomplished mathematician as well as architect, designed even more complex domes (FIG. **24-14A**).

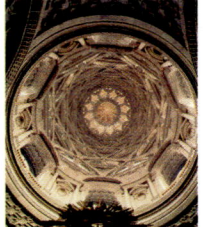

**24-14A** Guarini, Chapel of the Holy Shroud, Turin, 1667–1694.

## Painting

Although architecture and sculpture provided the most obvious vehicles for manipulating space and creating theatrical effects, painting continued to be an important art form in 17th-century Italy. Among the most noted Italian Baroque painters were Annibale Carracci and Caravaggio, whose styles, although different, were both thoroughly in accord with the period.

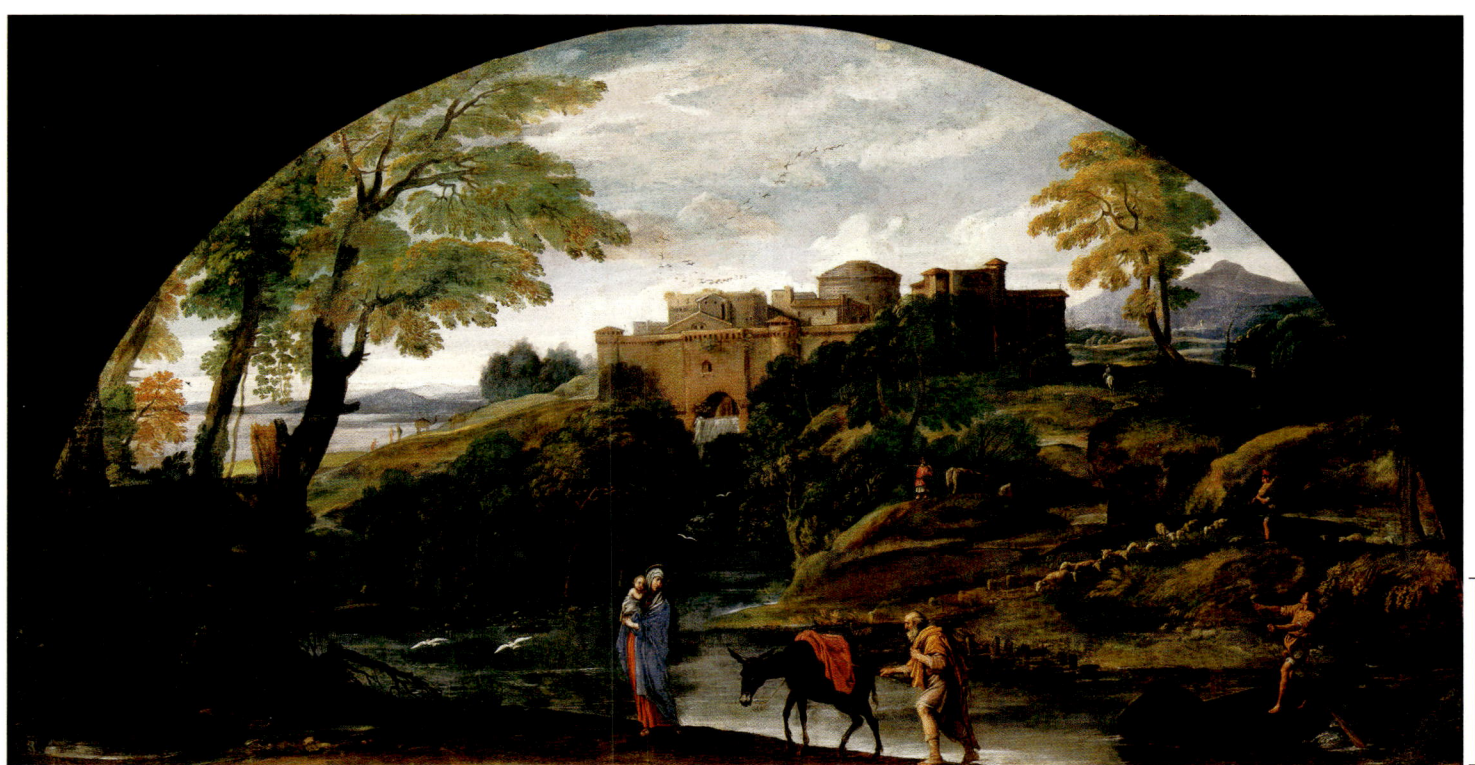

24-14 FRANCESCO BORROMINI, Chapel of Saint Ivo (view into dome), College of the Sapienza, Rome, Italy, begun 1642.

Unlike Renaissance domes, Borromini's Baroque dome is an organic part that evolves out of and shares the qualities of the supporting walls, and it cannot be separated from them.

cant institution of its kind in the history of Western art. The Carracci established it on the premises that art can be taught—the basis of any academic philosophy of art—and that art instruction must include the classical and Renaissance traditions in addition to the study of anatomy and life drawing.

In *Flight into Egypt* (FIG. **24-15**), based on the biblical narrative from Matthew 2:13–14, Annibale Carracci created the "ideal" or "classical" landscape, in which nature appears ordered by divine law and human reason. Tranquil hills and fields, quietly gliding streams, serene skies, unruffled foliage, shepherds with their flocks—all the props of the pastoral scene and mood familiar in Venetian Renaissance paintings

**ANNIBALE CARRACCI** A native of Bologna, ANNIBALE CARRACCI (1560–1609) received much of his training at an art academy founded there by several members of his family, among them his cousin Ludovico Carracci (1555–1619) and brother Agostino Carracci (1557–1602). The Bolognese academy was the first signifi-

(FIG. 22-35)—expand to fill the picture space in *Flight into Egypt* and similar paintings. Carracci regularly included screens of trees in the foreground, dark against the sky's even light. In contrast to many Renaissance artists, he did not create the sense of deep space through linear perspective but rather by varying light and shadow

1 ft.

24-15 ANNIBALE CARRACCI, *Flight into Egypt*, 1603–1604. Oil on canvas, 4′ × 7′ 6″. Galleria Doria Pamphili, Rome.

Carracci's landscapes idealize antiquity and the idyllic life. Here, the pastoral setting takes precedence over the narrative of Mary, the Christ Child, and Saint Joseph wending their way slowly to Egypt.

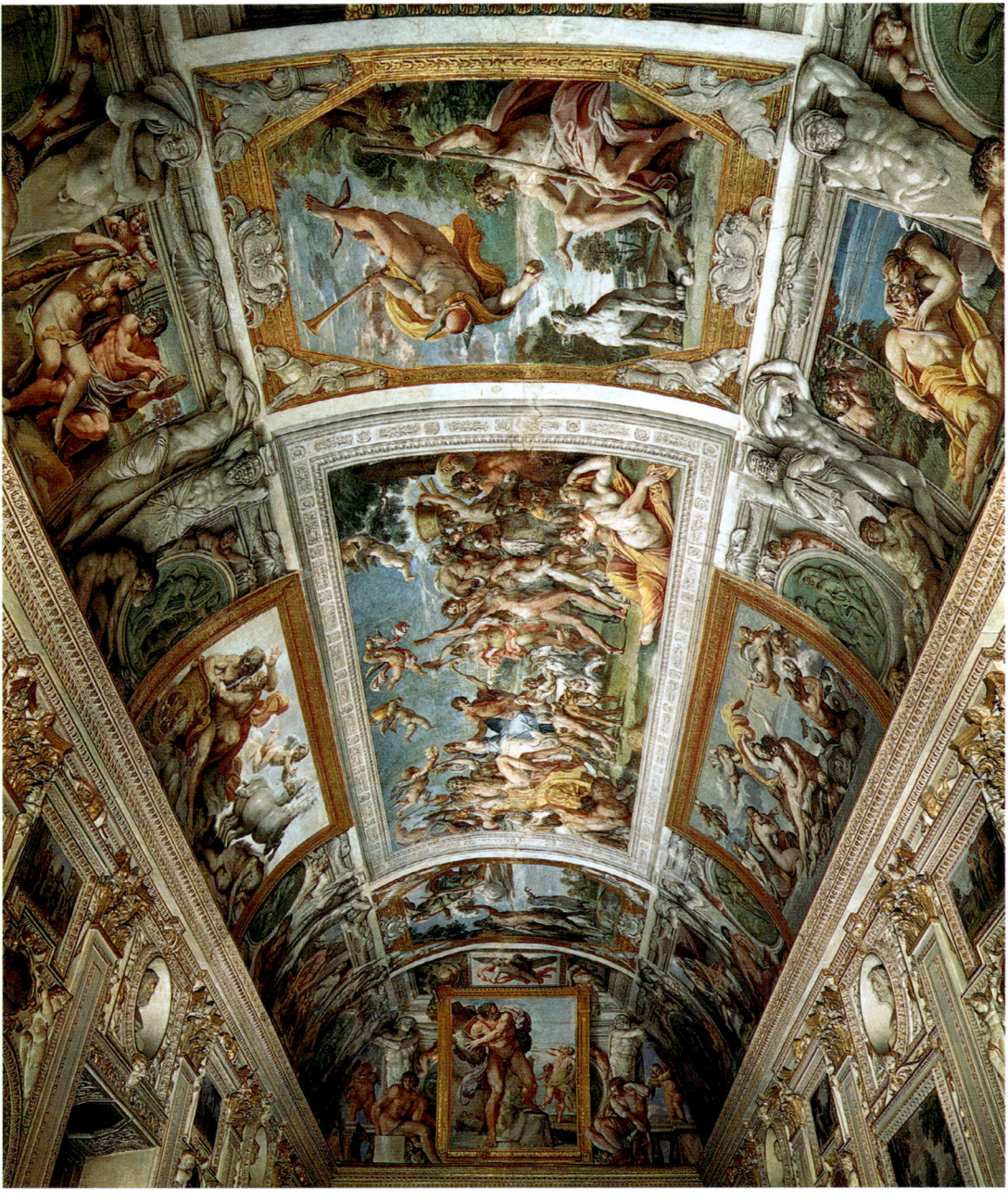

**24-16** Annibale Carracci, *Loves of the Gods,* ceiling frescoes in the gallery, Palazzo Farnese (FIG. 22-26), Rome, Italy, 1597–1601. ◼◀

On the shallow curved vault of this gallery in the Palazzo Farnese, Carracci arranged the mythological scenes in a quadro riportato format resembling easel paintings on a wall.

to suggest expansive atmosphere. In *Flight into Egypt,* streams or terraces, carefully placed one above the other and narrowed, zigzag through the terrain, leading the viewer's eyes back to the middle ground. There, many Venetian Renaissance landscape artists depicted walled towns or citadels, towers, temples, monumental tombs, and villas (as Carracci did in *Flight into Egypt*). These constructed environments captured idealized antiquity and the idyllic life. Although the artists often took the subjects for these classically rendered scenes from religious or heroic stories, they favored pastoral landscapes over narratives. Here, Annibale greatly diminished the size of Mary, the Christ Child, and Saint Joseph, who simply become part of the landscape as they wend their way slowly to Egypt after having been ferried across a stream.

***LOVES OF THE GODS*** Carracci's most notable works are his frescoes (FIG. **24-16**) in the Palazzo Farnese in Rome. Cardinal Odoardo Farnese (1573–1626), a wealthy descendant of Pope Paul III,

who built the palace (FIG. 22-26) in the 16th century, commissioned Annibale to decorate the ceiling of the palace's gallery to celebrate the wedding of the cardinal's brother. Appropriately, the title of the fresco's iconographic program is *Loves of the Gods*—interpretations of the varieties of earthly and divine love in classical mythology.

Carracci arranged the scenes in a format resembling framed easel paintings on a wall, but in the Farnese gallery the paintings cover a shallow curved vault. The term for this type of simulation of easel painting for ceiling design is *quadro riportato* (transferred framed painting). By adapting the northern European and Venetian tradition of easel painting to the Florentine and Roman fresco tradition, Carracci reoriented the direction of painting in central Italy. He made quadro riportato fashionable for more than a century.

Flanking the framed pictures are polychrome seated nude youths, who turn their heads to gaze at the scenes around them, and

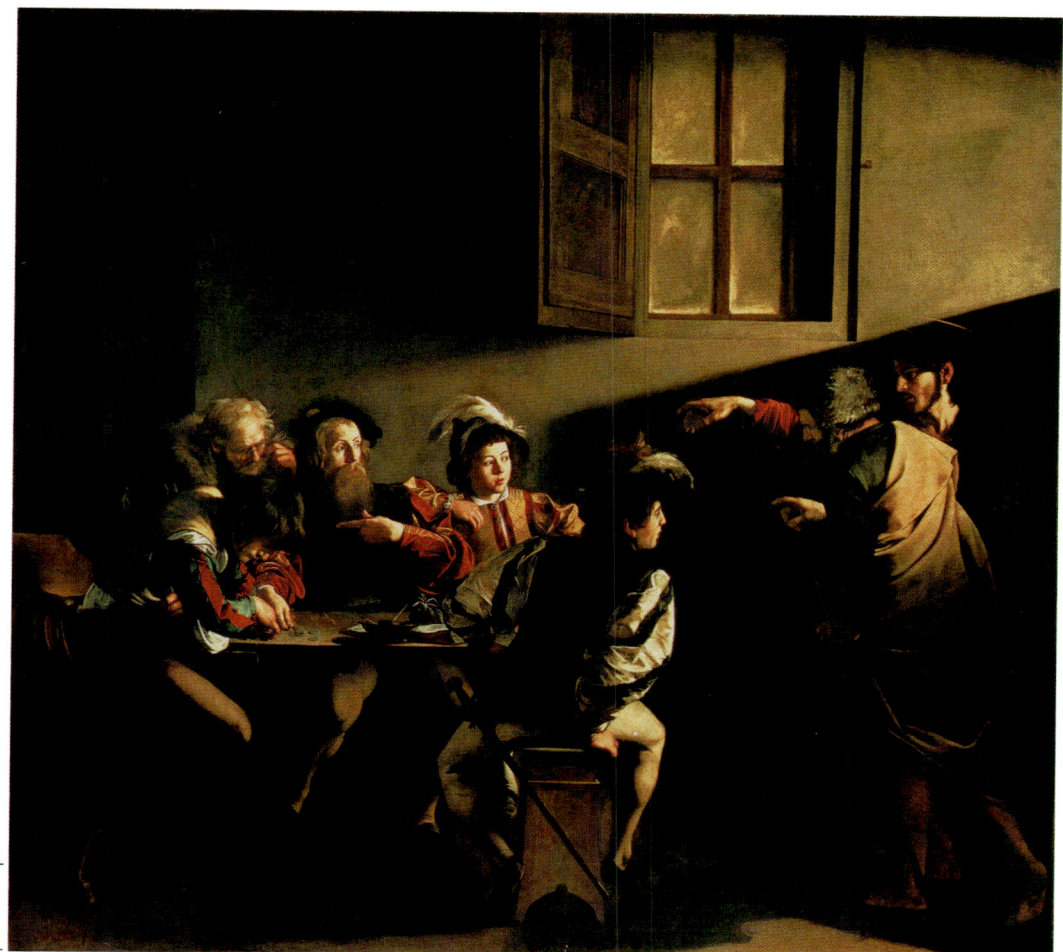

**24-17** CARAVAGGIO, *Calling of Saint Matthew*, ca. 1597–1601. Oil on canvas, 11′ 1″ × 11′ 5″. Contarelli chapel, San Luigi dei Francesi, Rome. ◼◀

The stark contrast of light and dark was a key feature of Caravaggio's style. Here, Christ, cloaked in mysterious shadow, summons Levi the tax collector (Saint Matthew) to a higher calling.

are an important source of information about the artist), Caravaggio received many commissions, both public and private, and numerous painters paid him the supreme compliment of borrowing from his innovations. His influence on later artists, as much outside Italy as within, was immense. In his art, Caravaggio injected naturalism into both religion and the classics, reducing them to human dramas played out in the harsh and dingy settings of his time and place. The unidealized figures he selected from the fields and the streets of Italy, however, were effective precisely because of their familiarity.

standing Atlas figures painted to resemble marble statues. Carracci derived these motifs from the Sistine Chapel ceiling (FIG. 22-17), but he did not copy Michelangelo's figures. Notably, the chiaroscuro of the Farnese gallery frescoes differs for the pictures and the figures surrounding them. Carracci modeled the figures inside the panels in an even light. In contrast, light from beneath illuminates the outside figures, as if they were tangible three-dimensional beings or statues lit by torches in the gallery below. This interest in illusion, already manifest in the Renaissance, continued in the grand ceiling compositions (FIGS. 24-21 to 24-24) of the mature Baroque. In the crown of the vault, the long panel, *Triumph of Bacchus,* is an ingenious mixture of Raphael's drawing style and lighting and Titian's more sensuous and animated figures. Carracci succeeded in adjusting their authoritative styles to create something of his own—no easy achievement.

**CARAVAGGIO** Michelangelo Merisi, known as CARAVAGGIO (1573–1610) after his northern Italian birthplace, developed a unique style that had tremendous influence throughout Europe. His outspoken disdain for the classical masters (probably more rhetorical than real) drew bitter criticism from many painters, one of whom denounced him as the "anti-Christ of painting." Giovanni Pietro Bellori (1613–1696), the most influential critic of the age and an admirer of Annibale Carracci, believed Caravaggio's refusal to emulate the models of his distinguished predecessors threatened the whole classical tradition of Italian painting that had reached its zenith in Raphael's work (see "Giovanni Pietro Bellori on Annibale Carracci and Caravaggio," page 682). Yet despite this criticism and the problems in Caravaggio's troubled life (police records

*CALLING OF SAINT MATTHEW* An early Caravaggio masterpiece, *Calling of Saint Matthew* (FIG. 24-17), is one of two large canvases honoring Saint Matthew the artist created for the Contarelli chapel in San Luigi dei Francesi (Saint Louis of the French) in Rome. Caravaggio received the commission for the San Luigi paintings upon the recommendation of Cardinal Del Monte, for whom the artist had recently painted *Musicians* (FIG. **24-17A**). The commonplace setting of the painting—a tavern with unadorned walls—is typical of Caravaggio. Into this mundane environment, cloaked in mysterious shadow and almost unseen, Christ, identifiable

**24-17A** CARAVAGGIO, *Musicians,* ca. 1595.

initially only by his indistinct halo, enters from the right. With a commanding gesture, he summons Levi, the Roman tax collector, to a higher calling. The astonished Levi—his face highlighted for the viewer by the beam of light emanating from an unspecified source above Christ's head and outside the picture—points to himself in disbelief. Although Christ's extended arm is reminiscent of the Lord's in Michelangelo's *Creation of Adam* (FIG. 22-18), the position of his hand and wrist is similar to Adam's. This reference was highly appropriate, because the Church considered Christ to be the second Adam. Whereas Adam was responsible for the fall of humankind, Christ is the vehicle of its redemption. The conversion of Levi (who became Matthew) brought his salvation.

## Giovanni Pietro Bellori on Annibale Carracci and Caravaggio

The written sources to which art historians turn as aids in understanding the art of the past are invaluable, but they reflect the personal preferences and prejudices of the writers. Pliny the Elder, for example, claimed in the first century CE that "art ceased" after the death of Alexander the Great—a remark usually interpreted as expressing his disapproval of Hellenistic art in contrast to Classical art (see Chapter 5).* Giorgio Vasari, the biographer and champion of Italian Renaissance artists, condemned Gothic art as "monstrous and barbarous," and considered medieval art in general a distortion of the noble art of the Greeks and Romans (see Chapter 13).† Giovanni Pietro Bellori, the leading biographer of Baroque artists, similarly recorded his admiration for Renaissance classicism as well as his distaste for Mannerism and realism in his opposing evaluations of Annibale Carracci and Caravaggio.

In the opening lines of his *Vita* (Life) of Carracci, Bellori praised "the divine Raphael . . . [whose art] raised its beauty to the summit, restoring it to the ancient majesty of . . . the Greeks and the Romans" and lamented that soon after, "artists, abandoning the study of nature, corrupted art with the *maniera*, that is to say, with the fantastic idea based on practice and not on imitation." But fortunately, Bellori observed, just "when painting was drawing to its end," Annibale Carracci rescued "the declining and extinguished art."‡

Bellori especially lauded Carracci's Palazzo Farnese frescoes (FIG. 24-16):

> No one could imagine seeing anywhere else a more noble and magnificent style of ornamentation, obtaining supreme excellence in the compartmentalization and in the figures and executed with the grandest manner in the design with the just proportion and the great strength of chiaroscuro. . . . Among modern works they have no comparison.§

In contrast, Bellori characterized Caravaggio as talented and widely imitated but misguided in his rejection of classicism in favor of realism.

[Caravaggio] began to paint according to his own inclinations; not only ignoring but even despising the superb statuary of antiquity and the famous paintings of Raphael, he considered nature to be the only subject fit for his brush. As a result, when he was shown the most famous statues of [the ancient sculptors] Phidias [FIG. 5-46] and Glykon [FIG. 5-66] in order that he might use them as models, his only answer was to point toward a crowd of people, saying that nature had given him an abundance of masters. . . . [W]hen he came upon someone in town who pleased him he made no attempt to improve on the creations of nature.**

[Caravaggio] claimed that he imitated his models so closely that he never made a single brushstroke that he called his own, but said rather that it was nature's. Repudiating all other rules, he considered the highest achievement not to be bound to art. For this innovation he was greatly acclaimed, and many talented and educated artists seemed compelled to follow him . . . Nevertheless he lacked *invenzione*, decorum, *disegno*, or any knowledge of the science of painting. The moment the model was taken from him, his hand and his mind became empty. . . . Thus, as Caravaggio suppressed the dignity of art, everybody did as he pleased, and what followed was contempt for beautiful things, the authority of antiquity and Raphael destroyed. . . . Now began the imitation of common and vulgar things, seeking out filth and deformity.††

*Pliny, *Natural History*, 25.52.
† Giorgio Vasari, *Introduzione alle tre arti del disegno* (1550), ch. 3.
‡Giovanni Pietro Bellori, *Le vite de' pittori, scultori e architetti moderni* (Rome, 1672). Translated by Catherine Enggass, *The Lives of Annibale and Agostino Carracci by Giovanni Pietro Bellori* (University Park: Pennsylvania University Press, 1968), 5–6.
§Ibid., 33.
**Translated by Howard Hibbard, *Caravaggio* (New York: Harper & Row, 1983), 362.
††Ibid., 371–372.

---

**CONVERSION OF SAINT PAUL** A piercing ray of light illuminating a world of darkness and bearing a spiritual message is also a central feature of *Conversion of Saint Paul* (FIG. 24-18), which Caravaggio painted for the Cerasi chapel in Santa Maria del Popolo. He depicted the saint-to-be at the moment of his conversion, flat on his back with his arms thrown up. In the background, an old groom seems preoccupied with caring for the horse. At first inspection, little here suggests the momentous significance of the unfolding spiritual event. The viewer could be witnessing a mere stable accident, not a man overcome by a great miracle. Although many of his contemporaries criticized Caravaggio for departing from traditional depictions of religious scenes, the eloquence and humanity with which he imbued his paintings impressed many others.

To compel worshipers' interest and involvement in Paul's conversion, Caravaggio employed a variety of ingenious formal devices. Here, as in the slightly later *Entombment* (FIG. 24-18A), he used a perspective and a chiaroscuro intended to bring viewers as close as possible to the scene's space and action, almost as if they

were participants. The low horizon line augments the sense of inclusion. Further, Caravaggio designed *Conversion of Saint Paul* for its specific location on the chapel wall, positioned at the line of sight of an average-height person standing at the chapel entrance. The sharply lit figures emerge from the dark background as if illuminated by the light from the chapel's windows. The lighting resembles that of a stage production and is analogous to the rays in Bernini's *Ecstasy of Saint Teresa* (FIGS. 24-7 and 24-8).

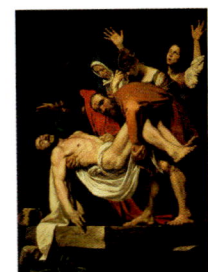

**24-18A** CARAVAGGIO, *Entombment*, ca. 1603.

Caravaggio's figures are still heroic with powerful bodies and clearly delineated contours in the Renaissance tradition, but the stark and dramatic contrast of light and dark, which at first shocked and then fascinated his contemporaries, obscures the more traditional aspects of his style. Art historians call Caravaggio's use of dark settings enveloping their occupants—which profoundly

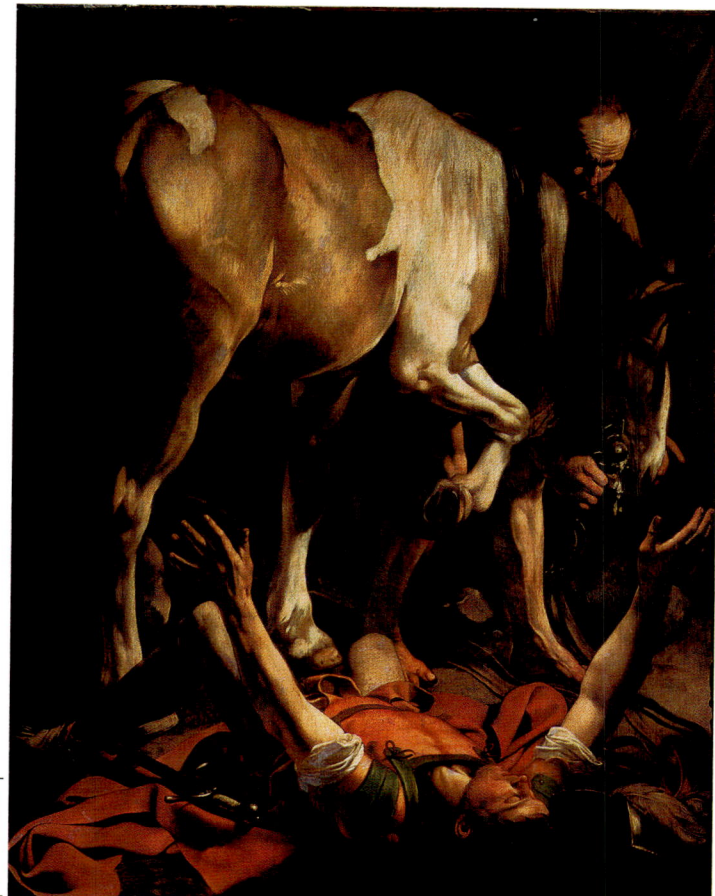

**24-18** CARAVAGGIO, *Conversion of Saint Paul*, ca. 1601. Oil on canvas, 7′ 6″ × 5′ 9″. Cerasi chapel, Santa Maria del Popolo, Rome.

Caravaggio used perspective, chiaroscuro, and dramatic lighting to bring viewers into this painting's space and action, almost as if they were participants in Saint Paul's conversion to Christianity.

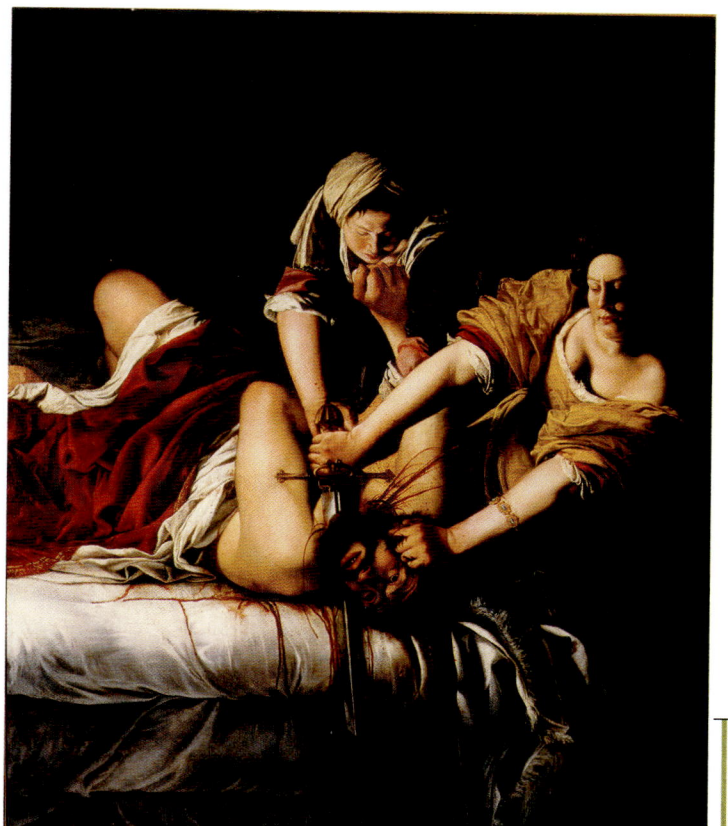

**24-19** ARTEMISIA GENTILESCHI, *Judith Slaying Holofernes,* ca. 1614–1620. Oil on canvas, 6′ 6⅓″ × 5′ 4″. Galleria degli Uffizi, Florence. ◼◀

Narratives involving heroic women were a favorite theme of Gentileschi. In *Judith Slaying Holofernes,* the dramatic lighting of the action in the foreground emulates Caravaggio's tenebrism.

influenced European art, especially in Spain and the Netherlands— *tenebrism,* from the Italian word *tenebroso,* or "shadowy" manner. In Caravaggio's work, tenebrism also contributed greatly to the essential meaning of his pictures. In *Conversion of Saint Paul,* the dramatic spotlight shining down upon the fallen Paul is the light of divine revelation converting him to Christianity.

**ARTEMISIA GENTILESCHI** Caravaggio's combination of naturalism and drama appealed both to patrons and artists, and he had many followers. Among them was the most celebrated woman artist of the era, ARTEMISIA GENTILESCHI (ca. 1593–1653), whose father Orazio (1563–1639), her teacher, was himself strongly influenced by Caravaggio. The daughter's successful career, pursued in Florence, Venice, Naples, and Rome, helped disseminate Caravaggio's style throughout the peninsula.

In *Judith Slaying Holofernes* (FIG. **24-19**), Gentileschi adopted the tenebrism and what might be called the "dark" subject matter Caravaggio favored. Significantly, she chose a narrative involving a heroic woman, a favorite theme of hers. The story, from the book of Judith, relates the delivery of Israel from the Assyrians. Having succumbed to Judith's charms, the Assyrian general Holofernes invited her to his tent for the night. When he fell asleep, Judith cut off his head. In this version of the scene (Gentileschi produced more than one painting of the subject), Judith and her maidservant behead Holofernes. Blood spurts everywhere as the two women

summon all their strength to wield the heavy sword. The tension and strain are palpable. The controlled highlights on the action in the foreground recall Caravaggio's work and heighten the drama here as well.

*LA PITTURA* During the brief period Orazio Gentileschi was the official painter of the English king Charles I (r. 1625–1649), Artemisia painted perhaps her most unusual work, an allegory of Painting (*La Pittura*; FIG. **24-20**). Most art historians believe the painting, which was in the collection of the king at the time of his execution in 1649, is a self-portrait.

Gentileschi's personified image of Painting as a woman closely follows the prescription for representing *La Pittura* in a widely circulated handbook by Cesare Ripa (d. 1622) called *Iconologia,* published in 1593. Until the 16th century, only Poetry and Music had a fixed iconography. The inclusion of Painting in Ripa's handbook reflects the newly elevated status painters held during the Renaissance. He describes *La Pittura* as a beautiful woman with disheveled hair painting with her brush in one hand and holding her palette in the other. She wears a gold chain with a pendant in the form of a mask, because masks imitate faces and painting is the art of imitation. The chain symbolizes the continuous linkage of master to pupil from generation to generation. Gentileschi incorporated all of these traits into her painting, but instead of representing *La Pittura* as a frontal, emblematic figure, she portrayed her as actively

# The Letters of Artemisia Gentileschi

Artemisia Gentileschi (FIG. 24-20) was the most renowned woman painter in Europe during the first half of the 17th century and the first woman ever admitted to membership in Florence's Accademia del Disegno (Academy of Design). As did other women who could not become apprentices in all-male studios (see "The Artist's Profession," Chapter 20, page 545), she learned her craft from her father. Never forgotten in subsequent centuries, Artemisia's modern fame stems from the seminal 1976 exhibition *Women Artists: 1550–1950*,* which opened a new chapter in feminist art history.

In addition to scores of paintings created for wealthy patrons, among them the king of England and the grand duke of Tuscany, Gentileschi left behind 28 letters, some of which reveal she believed patrons treated her differently because of her gender. Three 1649 letters written in Naples to Don Antonio Ruffo (1610–1678) in Messina make her feelings explicit.

> I fear that before you saw the painting you must have thought me arrogant and presumptuous. . . . [I]f it were not for Your Most Illustrious Lordship . . . I would not have been induced to give it for one hundred and sixty, because everywhere else I have been I was paid one hundred *scudi* per figure. . . . You think me pitiful, because a woman's name raises doubts until her work is seen.[†]

> I was mortified to hear that you want to deduct one third from the already very low price that I had asked. . . . It must be that in your heart Your Most Illustrious Lordship finds little merit in me.[‡]

> As for my doing a drawing and sending it, [tell the gentleman who wishes to know the price for a painting that] I have made a solemn vow never to send my drawings because people have cheated me. In particular, just today I found myself [in the situation] that, having done a drawing of souls in Purgatory for the Bishop of St. Gata, he, in order to spend less, commissioned another painter to do the painting using my work. If I were a man, I can't imagine it would have turned out this way, because when the concept has been real-

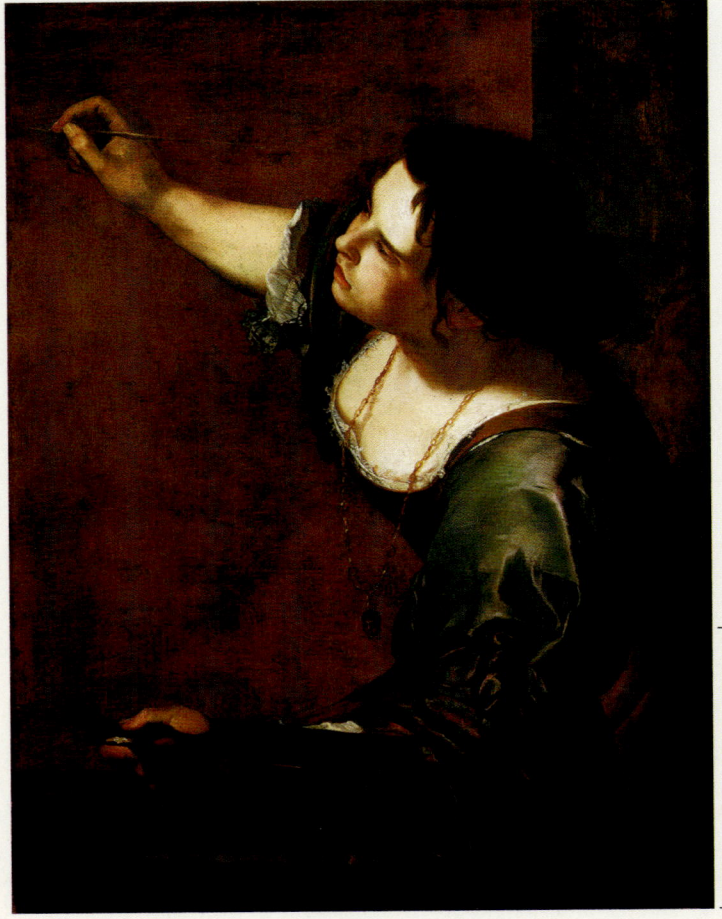

**24-20** ARTEMISIA GENTILESCHI, *Self-Portrait as the Allegory of Painting*, ca. 1638–1639. Oil on canvas, 3′ 2$\frac{7}{8}$″ × 2′ 5$\frac{5}{8}$″. Royal Collection, Kensington Palace, London. ◼️

Gentileschi here portrayed herself in the guise of *La Pittura* (Painting) with brush and palette. To paint a self-portrait from the side, Gentileschi had to set up a pair of mirrors to record her features.

1 ft.

ized and defined with lights and darks, and established by means of planes, the rest is a trifle.[§]

*Ann Sutherland Harris and Linda Nochlin, *Women Artists: 1550–1950* (Los Angeles: Los Angeles County Museum of Art, 1976), 118–124.
[†]Letter dated Janary 30, 1649. Translated by Mary D. Garrard, *Artemisia Gentileschi: The Image of the Female Hero in Italian Baroque Art* (Princeton, N.J.: Princeton University Press, 1989), 390.
[‡]Letter dated October 23, 1649. Ibid., 395–396.
[§]Letter dated November 13, 1649. Ibid., 397–398.

engaged in her craft, seen from her left side. The viewer's eye follows the line of her left arm through the curve of her shoulders and right arm to her right hand, the instrument of artistic genius. It is noteworthy that the canvas in this painting is blank. This is not a self-portrait of the artist at work on a specific painting (compare FIGS. 23-18, 25-11, 26-15, and 26-16) but a portrait of Gentileschi as Painting herself.

In almost all Renaissance and Baroque self-portraits, the artist gazes at the viewer. The frontal view not only provides the fullest view of the artist's features, but it is also the easiest to paint because the artist needs only to look in a mirror in order to record his or her features (FIG. 22-43). To create this self-portrait, however, Gentileschi had to set up two mirrors in order to paint her likeness from

an angle, a highly original break from tradition and an assertion of her supreme skill in a field dominated by men (see "The Letters of Artemisia Gentileschi," above).

**GUIDO RENI** Caravaggio was not the only early-17th-century painter to win a devoted following. GUIDO RENI (1575–1642), known to his many admirers as "the divine Guido," trained in the Bolognese art academy founded by the Carracci family. The influence of Annibale Carracci and Raphael is evident in *Aurora* (FIG. 24-21), a ceiling fresco in the Casino Rospigliosi in Rome. Aurora (Dawn) leads Apollo's chariot, while the Hours dance about it. Guido conceived *Aurora* as a quadro riportato, following the format of the paintings in Annibale's *Loves of the Gods* (FIG. 24-16), and

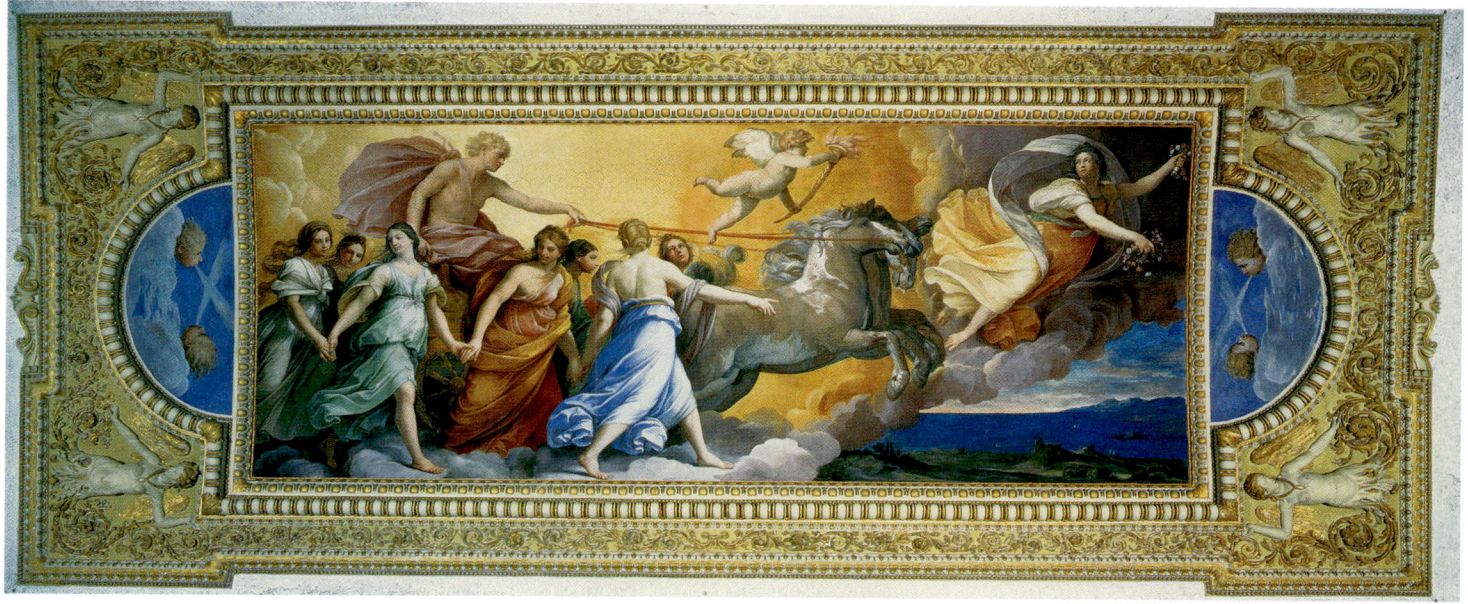

**24-21** GUIDO RENI, *Aurora*, ceiling fresco in the Casino Rospigliosi, Rome, Italy, 1613–1614.

The "divine Guido" conceived *Aurora* as a quadro riportato, reflecting his training in the Bolognese art academy. The scene of Dawn leading Apollo's chariot derives from ancient Roman reliefs.

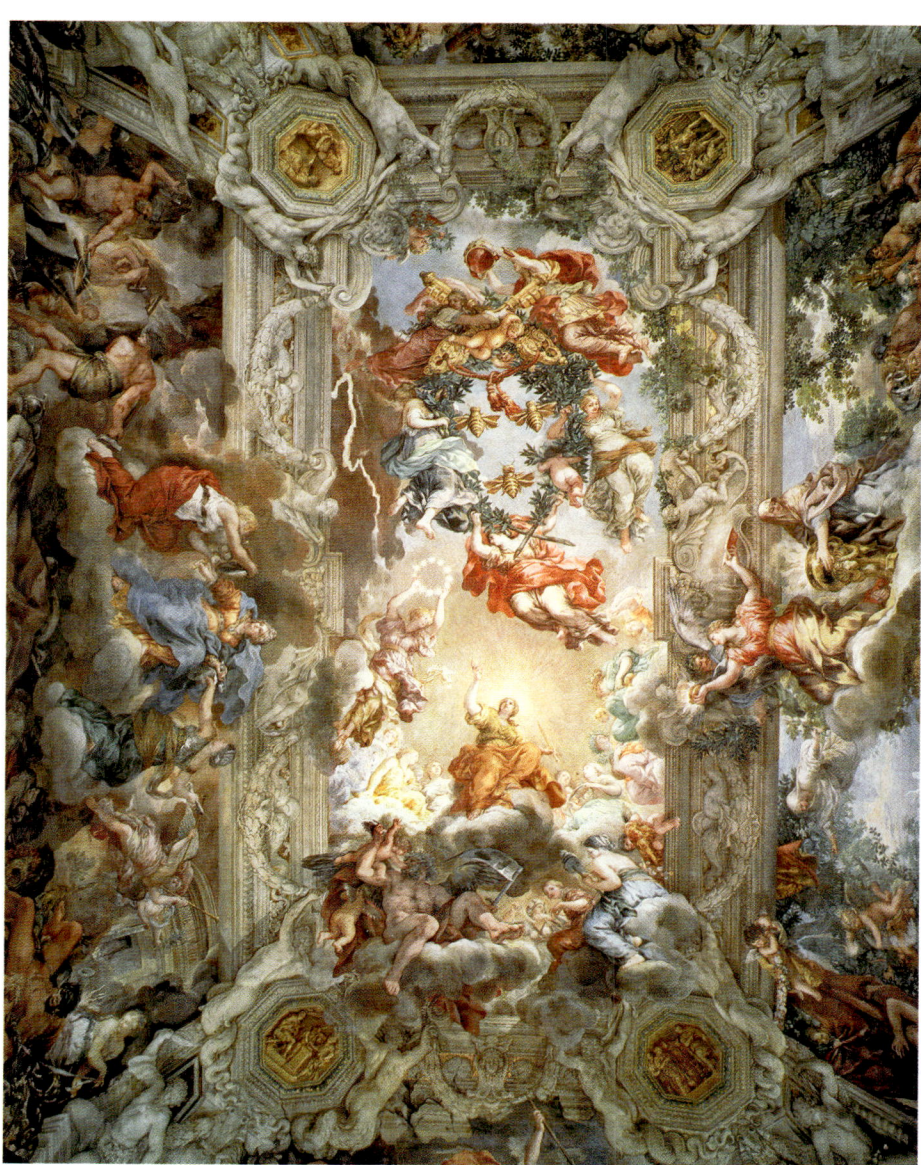

**24-22** PIETRO DA CORTONA, *Triumph of the Barberini,* ceiling fresco in the Gran Salone, Palazzo Barberini, Rome, Italy, 1633–1639.

In this dramatic ceiling fresco, Divine Providence appears in a halo of radiant light directing Immortality, holding a crown of stars, to bestow eternal life on the family of Pope Urban VIII.

provided the quadro with a complex and convincing illusionistic frame. The fresco exhibits a fluid motion, soft modeling, and sure composition, although without Raphael's sculpturesque strength. It is an intelligent interpretation of the Renaissance master's style. Consistent with the precepts of the Bolognese academy, the painter also looked to antiquity for models. The ultimate sources for the *Aurora* composition were Roman reliefs (FIG. 7-42) and coins depicting emperors in triumphal chariots accompanied by flying Victories and other personifications.

**PIETRO DA CORTONA** The experience of looking up at a painting is different from viewing a painting hanging on a wall. The considerable height and the expansive scale of most ceiling frescoes induce a feeling of awe. Patrons who wanted to burnish their public image or control their legacy found monumental ceiling frescoes to be perfect vehicles. In 1633, Pope Urban VIII commissioned a ceiling fresco for the Gran Salone (the main reception hall) of the Palazzo Barberini in Rome. The most important decorative commission of the 1630s, the lucrative assignment went to PIETRO DA CORTONA (1596–1669), a Tuscan architect and painter who had moved to Rome two decades before. The grandiose and spectacular *Triumph of the Barberini* (FIG. **24-22**) overwhelms spectators with

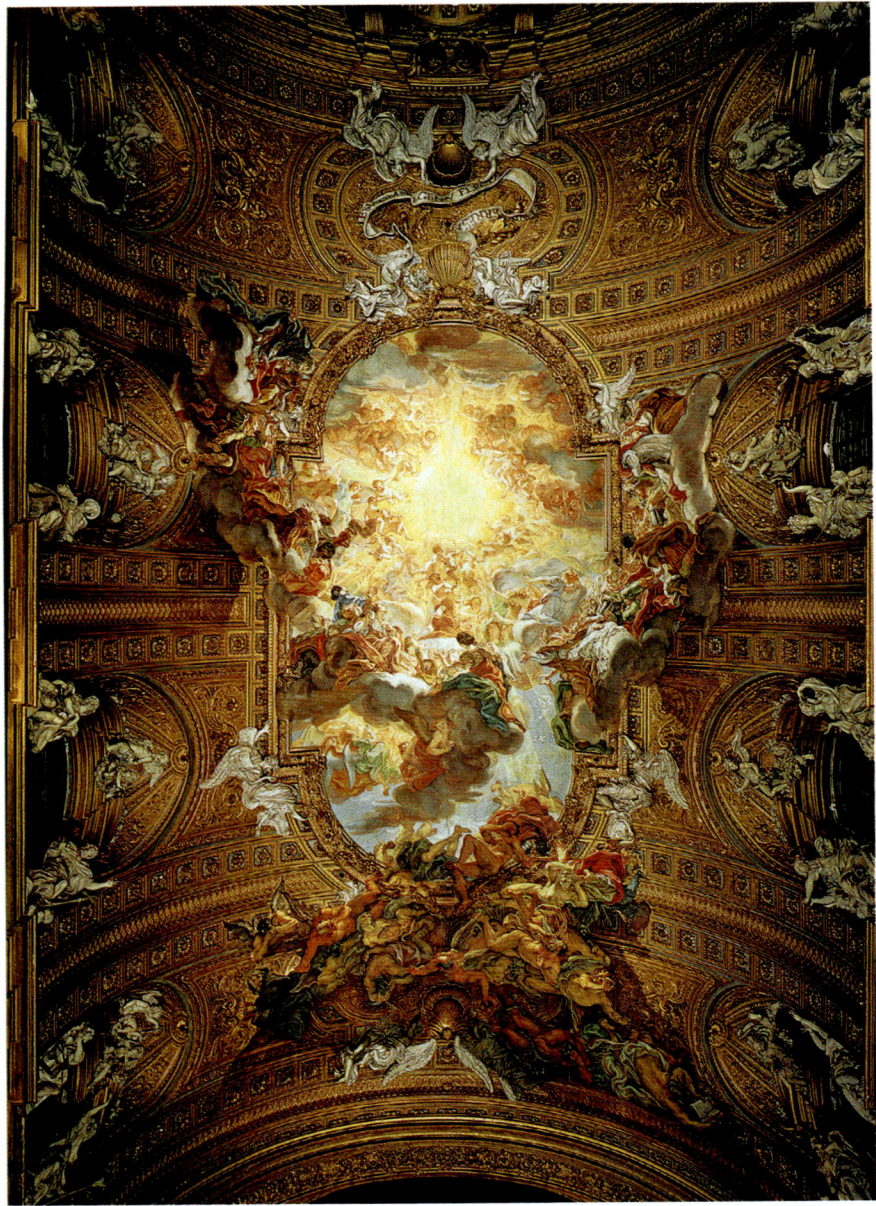

In the nave of Il Gesù, gilded architecture opens up to offer the faithful a glimpse of Heaven. To heighten the illusion, Gaulli painted figures on stucco extensions that project outside the painting's frame.

the glory of the Barberini family (and Urban VIII in particular). The iconographic program for this fresco, designed by the poet Francesco Bracciolini (1566–1645), centered on the accomplishments of the Barberini. Divine Providence appears in a halo of radiant light directing Immortality, holding a crown of stars, to bestow eternal life on the family. The virtues Faith, Hope, and Charity hold aloft a gigantic laurel wreath (also a symbol of immortality), which frames three bees (the Barberini family's symbols, which also appeared in Bernini's baldacchino, FIG. 24-5). Also present are the papal tiara and keys announcing the personal triumphs of Urban VIII.

**GIOVANNI BATTISTA GAULLI** The dazzling spectacle of ceiling frescoes also proved very effective for commissions illustrating religious themes. Church authorities realized paintings high above the ground offered perfect opportunities to impress on worshipers the glory and power of the Catholic Church. In conjunction with the theatricality of Italian Baroque architecture and sculpture, monumental frescoes on church ceilings contributed to creating transcendent spiritual environments well suited to the needs of the Catholic Church in Counter-Reformation Rome.

*Triumph of the Name of Jesus* (FIG. **24-23**) in the nave of Il Gesù (FIGS. 22-56 and 22-57) vividly demonstrates the dramatic impact Baroque ceiling frescoes could have. As the mother church of the Jesuit order, Il Gesù played a prominent role in Counter-Reformation efforts. In this immense fresco by GIOVANNI BATTISTA GAULLI (1639–1709), gilded architecture opens up in the center of the ceiling to offer the faithful a stunning glimpse of Heaven. Gaulli represented Jesus as a barely visible monogram (IHS) in a blinding radiant light floating heavenward. In contrast, sinners experience a violent descent back to Earth. The painter glazed the gilded architecture to suggest shadows, thereby enhancing the scene's illusionistic quality. To further heighten the illusion, Gaulli painted many of the sinners on three-dimensional stucco extensions projecting outside the painting's frame.

**FRA ANDREA POZZO** Another master of ceiling decoration was FRA ANDREA POZZO (1642–1709), a lay brother of the Jesuit order and a master of perspective, on which he wrote an influential treatise. Pozzo designed and executed the vast ceiling fresco *Glorification of Saint Ignatius* (FIG. **24-24**) for the church of Sant'Ignazio in Rome. Like Il Gesù, Sant'Ignazio was a prominent Counter-Reformation church because of its dedication to the founder of the Jesuit order. The Jesuits played a major role in Catholic education and sent legions of missionaries to the New World and Asia. As

Gaulli did in Il Gesù, Pozzo created the illusion of Heaven opening up above the congregation. To accomplish this, the artist painted an extension of the church's architecture into the vault so the roof seems to be lifted off. As Heaven and Earth commingle, Christ receives Saint Ignatius in the presence of figures personifying the four corners of the world. A disk in the nave floor marks the spot where the viewer should stand to gain the whole perspective illusion. For worshipers looking up from this point, the vision is complete. They find themselves in the presence of the heavenly and spiritual.

The effectiveness of Italian Baroque religious art depended on the drama and theatricality of individual images, as well as on the interaction and fusion of architecture, sculpture, and painting. Sound enhanced this experience. Architects designed churches with acoustical effects in mind, and in an Italian Baroque church filled with music, the power of both image and sound must have been immensely moving. Through simultaneous stimulation of both the senses of sight and hearing, the faithful might well have been transported into a trancelike state that would, indeed, as the great English poet John Milton (1608–1674) eloquently stated in *Il Penseroso* (1631), "bring all Heaven before [their] eyes."[2]

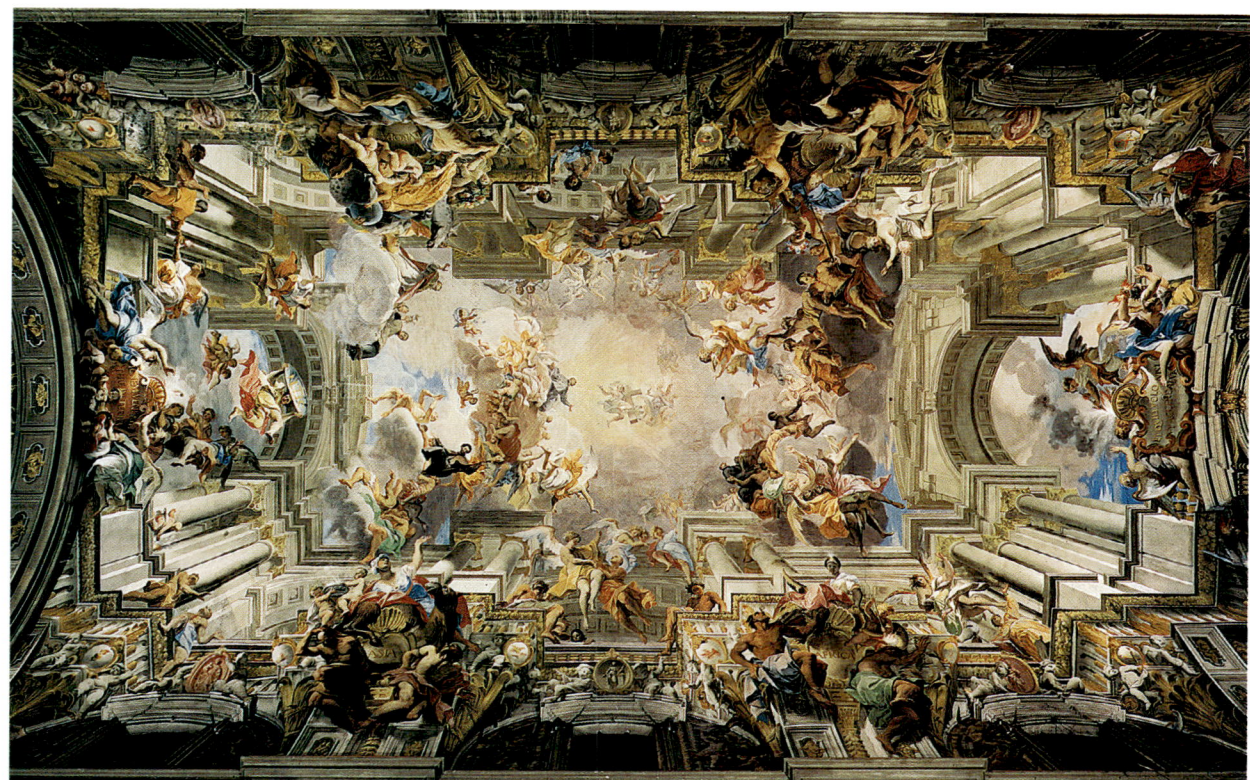

By merging real and painted architecture, Pozzo created the illusion the vaulted ceiling of Sant'Ignazio has been lifted off and the nave opens to Heaven above the worshipers' heads.

# SPAIN

During the 16th century, Spain had established itself as an international power. The Habsburg kings had built a dynastic state encompassing Portugal, part of Italy, the Netherlands, and extensive areas of the New World (see Chapters 23 and 35). By the beginning of the 17th century, however, the Habsburg Empire was struggling, and although Spain mounted an aggressive effort during the Thirty Years' War (see Chapter 25), by 1660 the imperial age of the Spanish Habsburgs was over. In part, the demise of the Habsburg Empire was due to economic woes. The military campaigns Philip III (r. 1598–1621) and his son Philip IV (r. 1621–1665) waged during the Thirty Years' War were costly and led to higher taxes. The increasing tax burden placed on Spanish subjects in turn incited revolts and civil war in Catalonia and Portugal in the 1640s, further straining an already fragile economy.

## Painting

Although the dawn of the Baroque period found the Spanish kings struggling to maintain control of their dwindling empire, both Philip III and Philip IV realized the prestige great artworks brought and the value of visual imagery in communicating to a wide audience. Thus, both of them continued to spend lavishly on art.

**JUAN SÁNCHEZ COTÁN** One painter who made a major contribution to the development of Spanish art, although he did not receive any royal commissions, was JUAN SÁNCHEZ COTÁN (1560–1627). Born in Orgaz, outside Toledo, Sánchez Cotán moved to Granada and became a Carthusian monk in 1603. Although he painted religious subjects, his greatest works are the *still lifes* (paintings of artfully arranged inanimate objects) he produced before entering monastic life (and never thereafter). Few in number, they nonetheless established still-life painting as an important genre in 17th-century Spain.

*Still Life with Game Fowl* (FIG. **24-25**) is one of Sánchez Cotán's most ambitious compositions, but it conforms to the pattern he adopted for all of his still lifes. A niche or a window—the artist clearly wished the setting to be indeterminate—fills the entire surface of the canvas. At the bottom, fruits and vegetables, including a melon—cut open with a slice removed—rest on a ledge. Above, suspended on strings from a nail or hook outside the frame, are a quince and four game fowl. All are meticulously rendered and

1 ft.

**24-25** JUAN SÁNCHEZ COTÁN, *Still Life with Game Fowl*, ca. 1600–1603. Oil on canvas, 2' 2¾" × 2' 10⅞". Art Institute of Chicago, Chicago (gift of Mr. and Mrs. Leigh B. Block).

Sánchez Cotán established still life as an important genre in Spain. His compositions feature brightly illuminated fruits, vegetables, and birds, hanging or on a ledge, against a dark background.

brightly illuminated, enhancing the viewer's sense of each texture, color, and shape, yet the background is impenetrable shadow. The sharp and unnatural contrast between light and dark imbues the still life with a sense of mystery absent, for example, in Dutch still-life paintings (FIGS. 23-17, 25-1, 25-22, and 25-23). There may, in fact, be a spiritual reference. Sánchez Cotán once described his 11 paintings of fruits, vegetables, and birds as "offerings to the Virgin"—probably a reference to the Virgin as the *fenestra coeli* ("window to Heaven") and the source of spiritual food for the faithful.

**BARTOLOMÉ ESTEBAN MURILLO** In the 17th century, Spain maintained its passionate commitment to Catholic orthodoxy, and as in Counter-Reformation Italy, Spanish Ba-

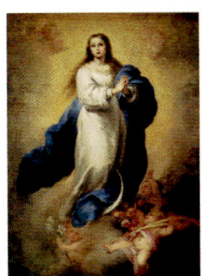

24-25A MURILLO, *Immaculate Conception,* ca. 1661–1670.

roque artists sought ways to move viewers and to encourage greater devotion and piety. BARTOLOMÉ ESTEBAN MURILLO (1617–1682), for example, formulated the canonical image of the *Virgin of the Immaculate Conception* (FIG. **24-25A**), in which Mary is a beautiful young woman ascending to Heaven. But scenes of death and martyrdom also had great appeal in Spain. They provided artists with opportunities both to depict extreme emotion and to elicit passionate feelings in viewers. Spain prided itself on its saints—Saint Teresa of Avila (FIG. 24-8) and Saint Ignatius Loyola (FIG. 24-24) were both Spanish-born—and martyrdom scenes surfaced frequently in Spanish Baroque art.

**JOSÉ DE RIBERA** As a young man, JOSÉ (JUSEPE) DE RIBERA (ca. 1588–1652) emigrated to Naples and fell under the spell of Caravaggio, whose innovative style he introduced to Spain. Emulating Caravaggio, Ribera made naturalism and compelling drama primary ingredients of his paintings, which often embraced brutal themes, reflecting the harsh times of the Counter-Reformation and the Spanish taste for stories showcasing courage and devotion. Ribera's *Martyrdom of Saint Philip* (FIG. **24-26**) is grim and dark in subject and form. Scorning idealization of any kind, Ribera represented Philip's executioners hoisting him into position after tying him to a cross, the instrument of Christ's own martyrdom. The saint's rough, heavy body and swarthy, plebeian features express a kinship between him and his tormentors, who are similar to the types of figures found in Caravaggio's paintings. The patron of this painting is unknown, but it is possible Philip IV commissioned the work, because Saint Philip was the king's patron saint.

**FRANCISCO DE ZURBARÁN** Another prominent Spanish painter of dramatic works was FRANCISCO DE ZURBARÁN (1598–1664), whose primary patrons throughout his career were rich Spanish monastic orders. Many of his paintings are quiet and contemplative, appropriate for prayer and devotional purposes. Zurbarán painted *Saint Serapion* (FIG. **24-27**) as a devotional image for the funerary chapel of the monastic Order of Mercy in Seville. The saint, who participated in the Third Crusade of 1196, suffered martyrdom while preaching the Gospel to Muslims. According to one account, the monk's captors tied him to a tree and then tortured and decapitated him. The Order of Mercy dedicated itself

**24-26** JOSÉ DE RIBERA, *Martyrdom of Saint Philip,* ca. 1639. Oil on canvas, 7′ 8″ × 7′ 8″. Museo del Prado, Madrid.

Martyrdom scenes were popular in Counter-Reformation Spain. Scorning idealization of any kind, Ribera represented Philip's executioners hoisting him into position to die on a cross.

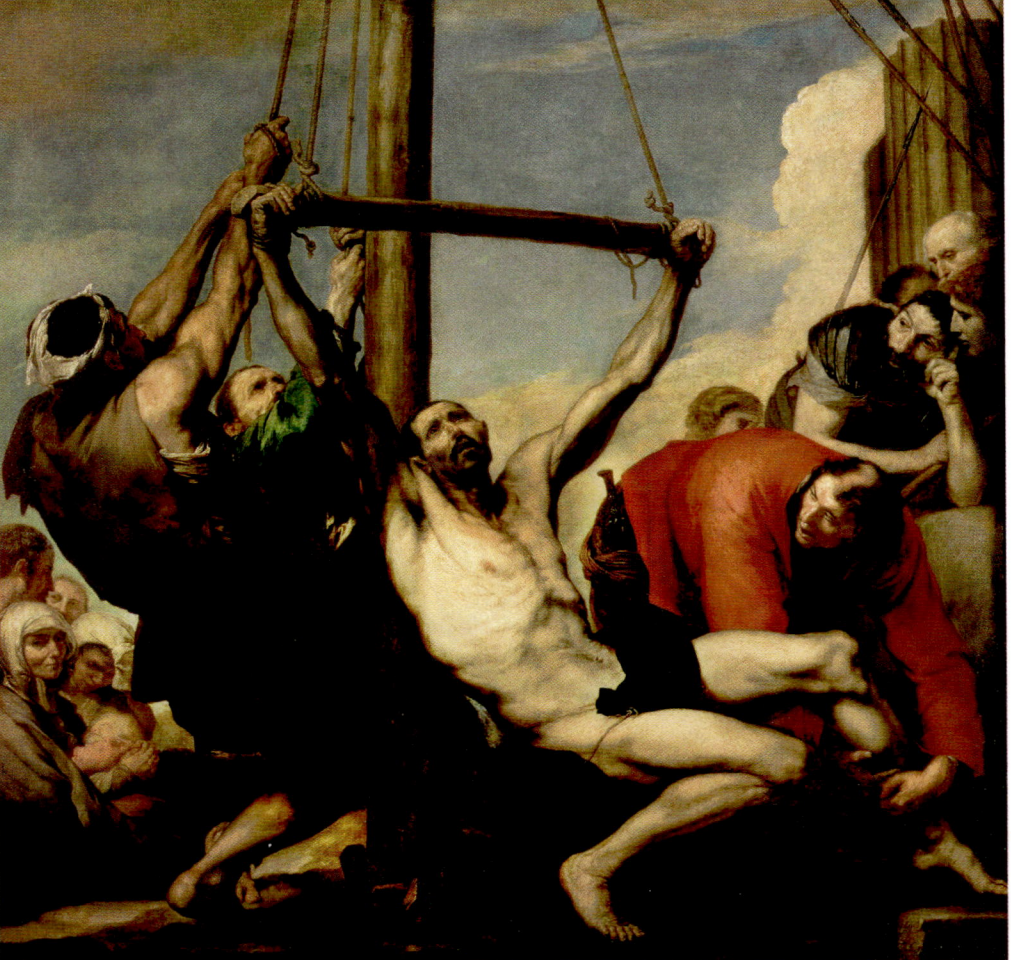

1 ft.

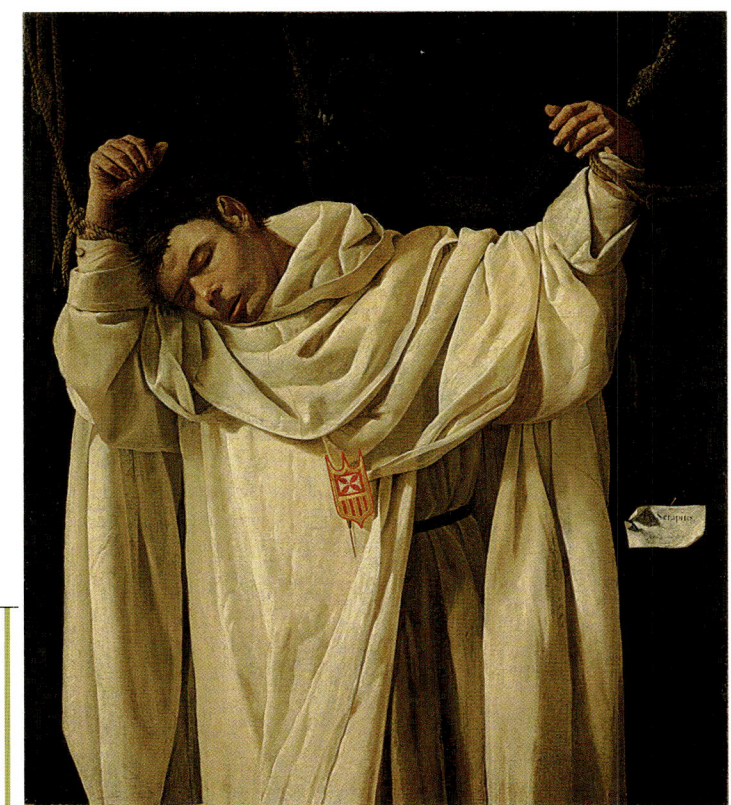

**24-27** Francisco de Zurbarán, *Saint Serapion,* 1628. Oil on canvas, 3′ 11½″ × 3′ 4¾″. Wadsworth Atheneum Museum of Art, Hartford (The Ella Gallup Sumner and Mary Catlin Sumner Collection Fund).

The light shining on Serapion calls attention to his tragic death and increases the painting's dramatic impact. The monk's coarse features label him as common, evoking empathy from a wide audience.

1 ft.

to self-sacrifice, and Serapion's membership in this order amplified the resonance of Zurbarán's painting. In *Saint Serapion,* the monk emerges from a dark background and fills the foreground. The bright light shining on him calls attention to the saint's tragic death and increases the dramatic impact of the image. In the background are two barely visible tree branches. A small note next to the saint identifies him for viewers. The coarse features of the Spanish monk label him as common, no doubt evoking empathy from a wide audience.

**DIEGO VELÁZQUEZ** The foremost Spanish painter of the Baroque age—and the greatest beneficiary of royal patronage—was Diego Velázquez (1599–1660). An early work, *Water Carrier of Seville* (FIG. **24-28**), painted when Velázquez was only about 20 years old, already reveals his impressive command of the painter's craft. In this genre scene that seems to convey a deeper significance, Velázquez rendered the figures with clarity and dignity, and his careful and convincing depiction of the water jugs in the foreground, complete with droplets of water, adds to the scene's credibility. The plebeian nature of the figures and the contrast of darks and lights again reveal the influence of Caravaggio, whose work Velázquez had studied.

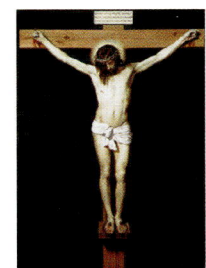

**24-28A** Velázquez, *Christ on the Cross,* ca. 1631–1632.

As did many other Spanish artists, Velázquez produced religious pictures, for example, *Christ on the Cross* (FIG. **24-28A**), as well as genre scenes, but his renown in his day rested primarily on the works he painted for King Philip IV (see "Velázquez and Philip IV," page 690). After the king appointed Velázquez court painter, the artist largely abandoned both religious and genre subjects in favor of royal portraits (FIG. **24-28B**) and canvases recording historical events.

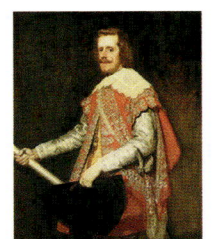

**24-28B** Velázquez, *Philip IV,* 1644.

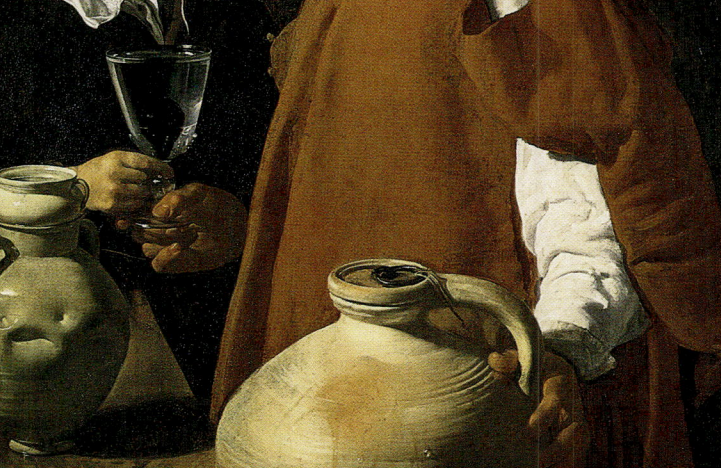

1 ft.

**24-28** Diego Velázquez, *Water Carrier of Seville,* ca. 1619. Oil on canvas, 3′ 5½″ × 2′ 7½″. Victoria & Albert Museum, London.

In this early work—a genre scene that seems to convey a deeper significance—the contrast of darks and lights, and the plebian nature of the figures, reveal Velázquez's debt to Caravaggio.

Spain **689**

# Velázquez and Philip IV

Trained in Seville, Diego Velázquez was quite young when he came to the attention of Philip IV. The painter's immense talent impressed the king, and Philip named him chief court artist and palace chamberlain, a position that also involved overseeing the rapidly growing royal art collection and advising the king on acquisitions and display. Among the works in Philip IV's possession were paintings by Titian, Annibale Carracci, Guido Reni, Albrecht Dürer, and Velázquez's famous Flemish contemporary, Peter Paul Rubens (see Chapter 25).

With the exception of two extended trips to Italy and a few excursions, Velázquez remained in Madrid for the rest of his life. His close relationship with Philip IV and his high office as chamberlain gave him prestige and a rare opportunity to fulfill the promise of his genius. One sign of Velázquez's fertile imagination as well as mastery of the brush is that he was able to create timeless artworks out of routine assignments to commemorate the achievements of his patron, as he did in his record of the Spanish victory over the Dutch in 1625 (*Surrender of Breda*, FIG. 24-29). Velázquez also painted dozens of portraits of Philip IV (FIG. 24-28B) and his family and retinue, including *Las Meninas* (FIG. 24-30), one of the greatest paintings in the history of Western art, a work Philip admired so much he displayed it in his personal office.

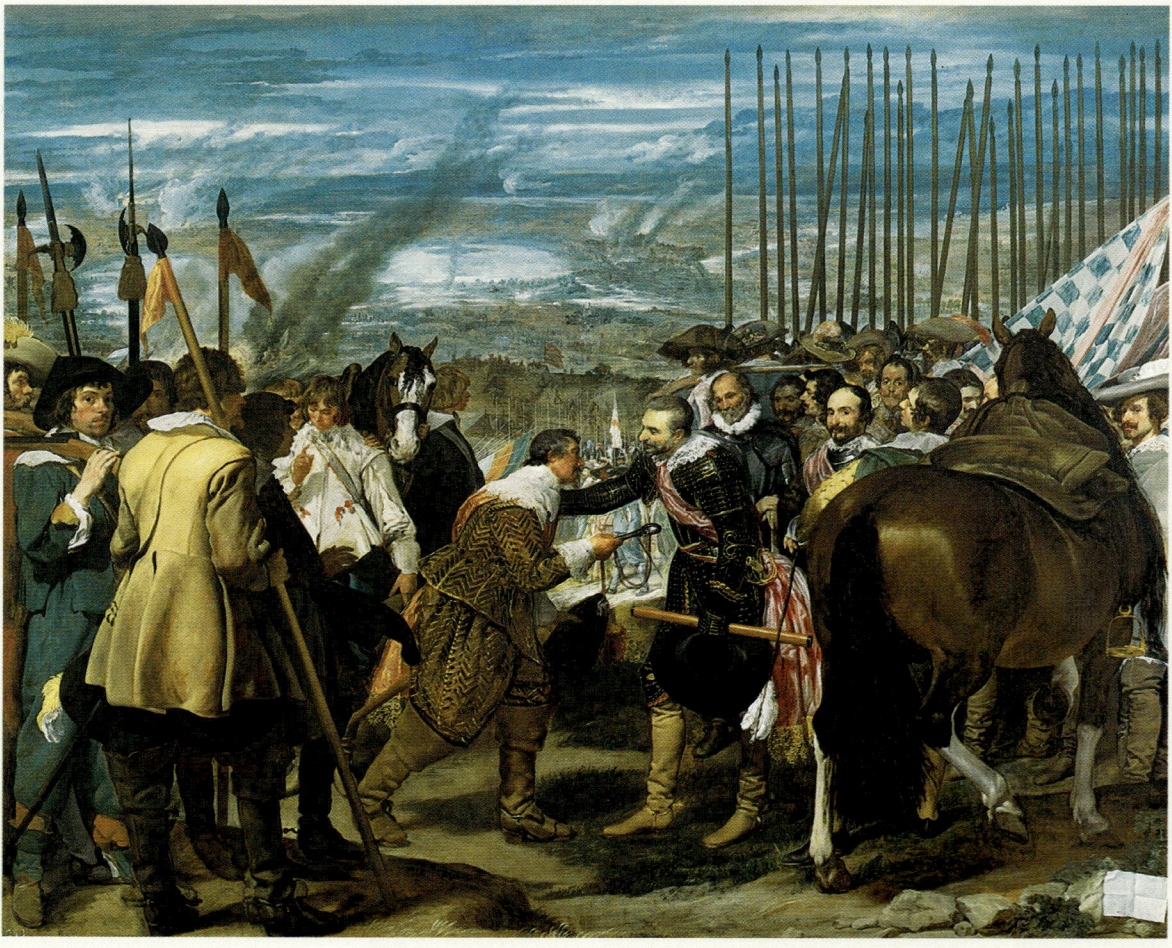

**24-29** Diego Velázquez, *Surrender of Breda*, 1634–1635. Oil on canvas, 10′ 1″ × 12′ 1⁄2″. Museo del Prado, Madrid.

As Philip IV's court artist, Velázquez produced many history paintings, including fictional representations such as this one depicting the Dutch mayor of Breda surrendering to the Spanish general.

1 ft.

**SURRENDER OF BREDA** In 1635, Velázquez painted *Surrender of Breda* (FIG. 24-29) as part of an extensive program of decoration for the Hall of Realms in Philip IV's new secondary pleasure palace in Madrid, the Palacio del Buen Retiro. The huge canvas (more than 12 feet long and almost as tall) was one of 10 paintings celebrating recent Spanish military successes around the globe. It commemorates the Spanish victory over the Dutch at Breda in 1625. Among the most troublesome situations for Spain was the conflict in the Netherlands. Determined to escape Spanish control, the northern Netherlands broke from the Habsburg Empire in the late 16th century. Skirmishes continued to flare up along the border between the northern (Dutch) and southern (Spanish) Netherlands, and in 1625 Philip IV sent General Ambrogio di Spínola to Breda to reclaim the town for Spain.

Velázquez depicted the victorious Spanish troops, organized and well armed, on the right side of the painting. In sharp contrast, the defeated Dutch on the left appear bedraggled and disorganized. In the center foreground, the mayor of Breda, Justinus of Nassau, hands the city's keys to the Spanish general—although no encounter of this kind ever occurred. Velázquez's fictional record of the event glorifies not only the strength of the Spanish military but the benevolence of Spínola as well. Velázquez did not portray the Spanish general astride his horse, lording over the vanquished Dutch mayor, but rather painted him standing and magnanimously stopping Justinus from kneeling. Indeed, the terms of surrender were notably lenient, and Spínola allowed the Dutch to retain their arms—which they used to recapture the city in 1637.

**LAS MENINAS**  After an extended visit to Rome from 1648 to 1651, Velázquez returned to Spain. In 1656, he painted his greatest work, *Las Meninas* (*The Maids of Honor;* FIG. **24-30**). The setting is the artist's studio in the palace of the Alcázar, the official royal residence in Madrid. After the death of Prince Baltasar Carlos in 1646, Philip IV ordered part of the prince's chambers converted into a studio for Velázquez. The painter represented himself stand-

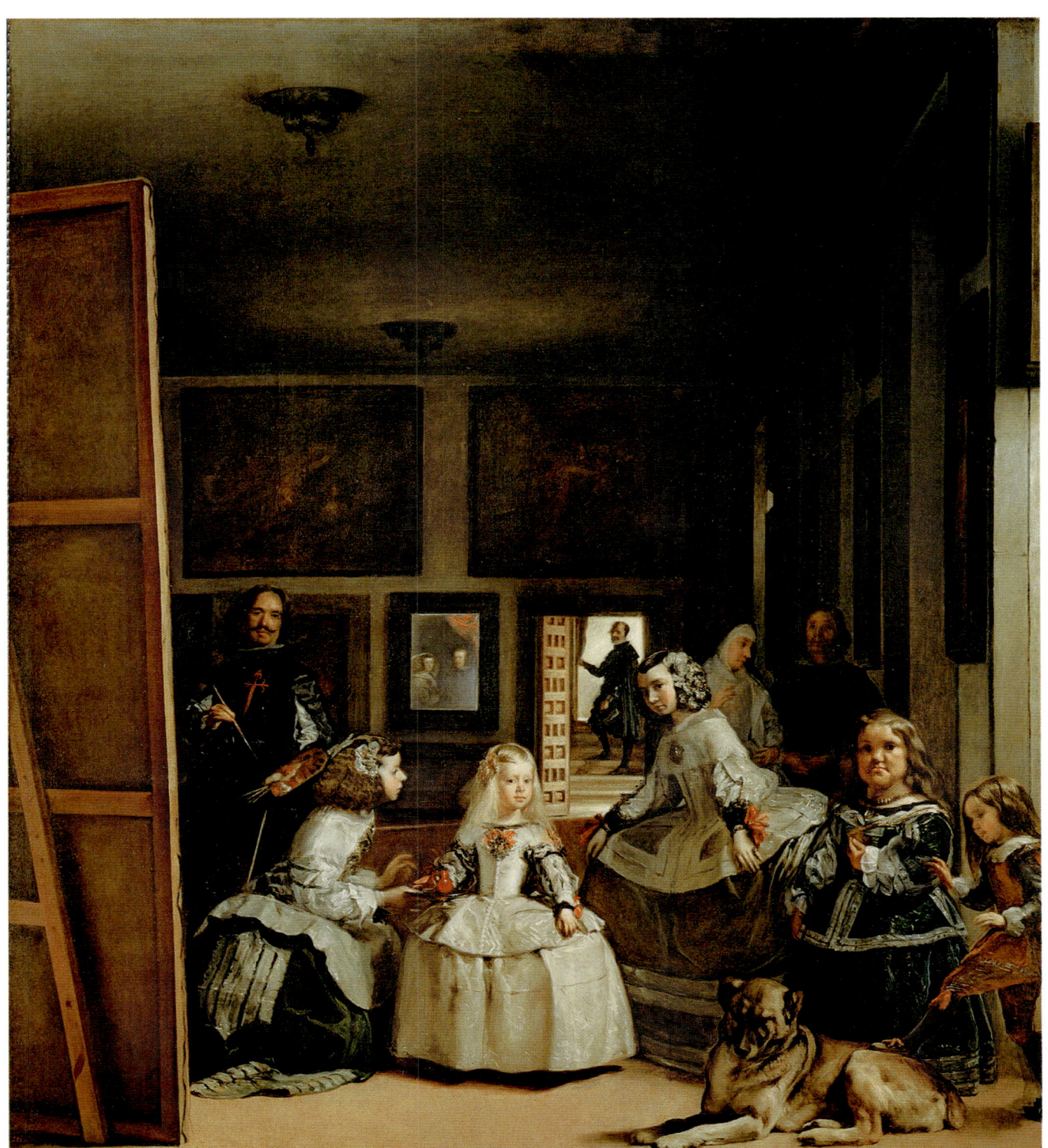

1 ft.

**24-30**  DIEGO VELÁZQUEZ, *Las Meninas* (*The Maids of Honor*), 1656. Oil on canvas, 10′ 5″ × 9′. Museo del Prado, Madrid. ◼◖

Velázquez intended this huge and complex work, with its cunning contrasts of real, mirrored, and picture spaces, to elevate both himself and the profession of painting in the eyes of Philip IV.

ing before a large canvas. The young Infanta (Princess) Margarita appears in the foreground with her two maids-in-waiting, her favorite dwarfs, and a large dog. In the middle ground are a woman in widow's attire and a male escort. In the background, a chamberlain stands in a brightly lit open doorway. Scholars have been able to identify everyone in the room, including the two meninas and the dwarfs.

*Las Meninas* is noteworthy for its visual and narrative complexity. Indeed, art historians have yet to agree on any particular reading or interpretation. A central issue preoccupying scholars has been what, exactly, is taking place in *Las Meninas*. What is Velázquez depicting on the huge canvas in front of him? He may be painting this very picture—an informal image of the infanta and her entourage. Alternately, Velázquez may be painting a portrait of King Philip IV and Queen Mariana, whose reflections appear in the mirror on the far wall. If so, that would suggest the presence of the king and queen in the viewer's space, outside the confines of the picture. Other scholars have proposed that the mirror image is not a reflection of the royal couple standing in Velázquez's studio but a reflection of the portrait the artist is in the process of painting on the canvas before him. This question will probably never be definitively resolved.

More generally, *Las Meninas* is Velázquez's attempt to elevate both himself and his profession. As first painter to the king and as chamberlain of the palace, Velázquez was conscious not only of the importance of his court office but also of the honor and dignity belonging to his profession as a painter. Throughout his career, Velázquez hoped to be ennobled by royal appointment to membership in the ancient and illustrious Order of Santiago (Saint James). Because he lacked a sufficiently noble lineage, he gained entrance only with difficulty at the very end of his life, and then only through the pope's dispensation. In the painting, Velázquez wears the order's red cross on his doublet, painted there, legend says, by Philip IV. In all likelihood, Velázquez painted it. In the artist's mind, *Las Meninas* might have embodied the idea of the great king visiting his studio, as Alexander the Great visited the studio of the painter Apelles in ancient times. The figures in the painting all appear to acknowledge the royal presence. Placed among them in equal dignity is Velázquez, face-to-face with his sovereign.

The location of the completed painting reinforced this act of looking—of seeing and being seen. *Las Meninas* hung in Philip IV's personal office in another part of the palace. Thus, although occasional visitors admitted to the king's private quarters may have seen this painting, Philip was the primary audience. Each time he stood before the canvas, he again participated in the work as the probable subject of Velázquez's painting within the painting and as the object of the figures' gazes. In *Las Meninas,* Velázquez elevated the

art of painting, in the person of the painter, to the highest status. The king's presence enhanced this status—either in person as the viewer of *Las Meninas* or as a reflected image in the painting itself. The paintings that appear in *Las Meninas* further reinforced this celebration of the painter's craft. On the wall above the doorway and the mirror, two faintly recognizable pictures are copies made by Velázquez's son-in-law, Juan del Mazo (ca. 1612–1667), of paintings by Peter Paul Rubens. The paintings depict the immortal gods as the source of art. Ultimately, Velázquez sought ennoblement not for himself alone but for his art as well.

*Las Meninas* is extraordinarily complex visually. Velázquez's optical report of the event, authentic in every detail, pictorially summarizes the various kinds of images in their different levels and degrees of reality. He portrayed the realities of image on canvas, of mirror image, of optical image, and of the two painted images. This work—with its cunning contrasts of real spaces, mirrored spaces, picture spaces, and pictures within pictures—itself appears to have been taken from a large mirror reflecting the entire scene. This would mean the artist did not paint the princess and her suite as the main subjects of *Las Meninas* but himself in the process of painting them. *Las Meninas* is a pictorial summary and a commentary on the essential mystery of the visual world, as well as on the ambiguity that results when different states or levels interact or are juxtaposed.

Velázquez employed several devices in order to achieve this visual complexity. For example, the extension of the composition's pictorial depth in both directions is noteworthy. The open doorway and its ascending staircase lead the eye beyond the artist's studio, and the mirror and the outward glances of several of the figures incorporate the viewer's space into the picture as well. (Compare how the mirror in Jan van Eyck's *Giovanni Arnolfini and His Wife* [FIG. 20-6] similarly incorporates the area in front of the canvas into the picture, although less obviously and without a comparable extension of space beyond the rear wall of the room.) Velázquez also masterfully observed and represented form and shadow. Instead of putting lights abruptly beside darks, following Caravaggio, Velázquez allowed a great number of intermediate values of gray to come between the two extremes. His matching of tonal gradations approached effects later discovered in the age of photography.

The inclusion of the copies of two Rubens paintings hanging on the wall in Velázquez's studio is the Spanish master's tribute to the great Flemish painter, one of the towering figures who made the 17th century one of the most important in the history of art in northern Europe. The works of Rubens, Rembrandt, and the other leading Baroque painters, sculptors, and architects of Flanders, the Dutch Republic, France, and England are the subject of Chapter 25.

# THE BAROQUE IN ITALY AND SPAIN

## ITALY

▌ Art historians call the art of 17th-century Italy and Spain *Baroque,* a term that probably derives from the Portuguese word for an irregularly shaped pearl. Baroque art is dynamic and theatrical in vivid contrast to the precision and orderly rationality of Renaissance classicism.

▌ Baroque architects emphatically rejected the classical style. Gianlorenzo Bernini's colonnade framing the piazza in front of Saint Peter's is not a traditional rectangular atrium but two curving arms welcoming worshipers.

▌ Francesco Borromini emphasized the sculptural qualities of buildings. The facades of his churches—for example, San Carlo alle Quattro Fontane—are not flat frontispieces but undulating surfaces that provide a fluid transition from exterior to interior space. The interiors of his buildings pulsate with energy and feature complex domes that grow organically from curving walls.

▌ Guarino Guarini brought Borromini's innovative Baroque architectural style to Turin and designed even more complex domes than those the Roman master created.

▌ Bernini achieved even greater renown as a sculptor. His *David* represents the biblical hero in action, hurling stones at Goliath. In *Ecstasy of Saint Teresa,* Bernini marshaled the full capabilities of architecture, sculpture, and painting to create an intensely emotional experience for worshipers, consistent with the Counter-Reformation principle of using artworks to inspire devotion and piety.

▌ In painting, Caravaggio broke new ground by employing stark and dramatic contrasts of light and dark (tenebrism) and by setting religious scenes in everyday locales filled with rough-looking common people. An early masterpiece, *Calling of Saint Matthew,* for example, takes place in an ordinary tavern.

▌ Caravaggio's combination of drama and realism attracted both admiring followers, including Artemisia Gentileschi, the leading woman painter of the 17th century, and harsh critics. The biographer Giovanni Pietro Bellori, for example, deplored Caravaggio's abandonment of the noble style of Raphael and the ancients and his "suppression of the dignity of art." He preferred the more classical style of Annibale Carracci and the Bolognese art academy.

▌ Illusionistic ceiling paintings were very popular in Baroque Italy. The major ceiling painters were Pietro da Cortona, Giovanni Battista Gaulli, and Fra Andrea Pozzo. In Sant'Ignazio in Rome, Pozzo created the illusion that Heaven is opening up above worshipers' heads by merging the church's architecture with the painted nave vault.

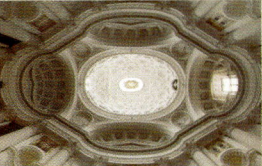

Borromini, San Carlo alle Quattro Fontane, Rome, 1638–1641

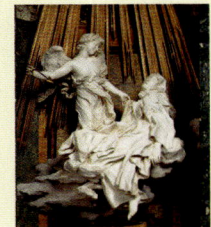

Bernini, *Ecstasy of Saint Teresa,* 1645–1652

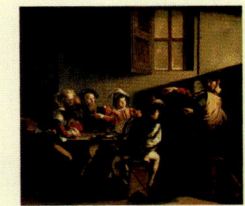

Caravaggio, *Calling of Saint Matthew,* ca. 1597–1601

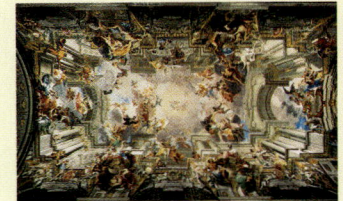

Pozzo, *Glorification of Saint Ignatius,* 1691–1694

## SPAIN

▌ Although the power of the Habsburg kings declined during the 17th century, the royal family, which was devoutly Catholic, continued to spend lavishly on art. Spanish artists eagerly embraced the drama and emotionalism of Italian Baroque art. Scenes of death and martyrdom were popular in Counter-Reformation Spain. Painters such as José de Ribera and Francisco de Zurbarán adopted Caravaggio's lighting and realism to produce moving images of martyred saints.

▌ The greatest Spanish Baroque painter was Diego Velázquez, court painter to Philip IV. Velázquez painted themes ranging from genre and religious subjects to royal portraits and historical events. His masterwork, *Las Meninas,* is extraordinarily complex and mixes real spaces, mirrored spaces, picture spaces, and pictures within pictures. It is a celebration of the art of painting itself.

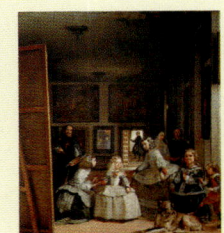

Velázquez, *Las Meninas,* 1656

In the 17th century, an important new class of patrons emerged in the Dutch Republic—successful merchants who took pride in their material possessions, the fruit of worldwide trade.

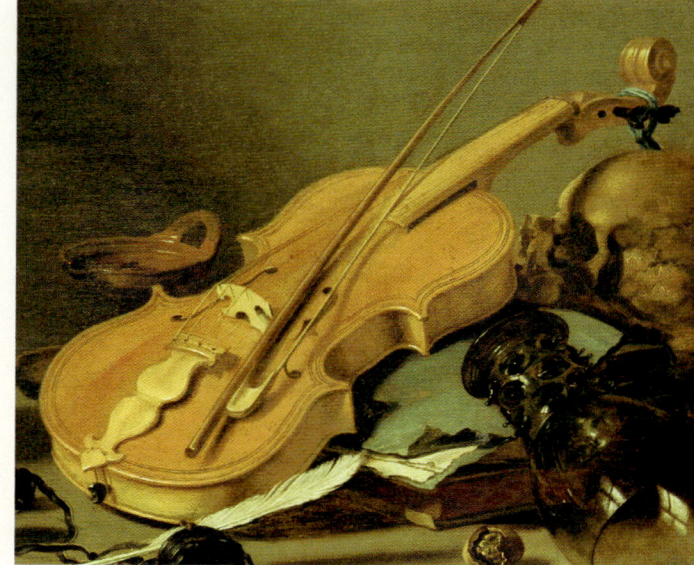

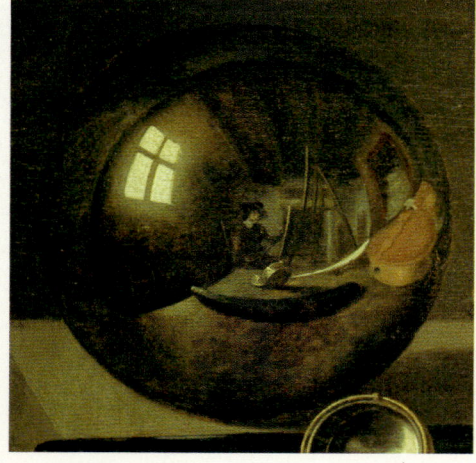

Claesz's mastery of the oil medium is evident in details such as the glass ball on the left side of the table, in which the viewer sees the reflected image of the artist painting this still life.

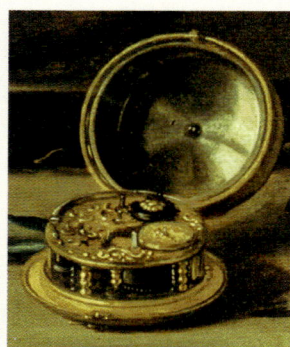

Dutch Baroque still-life paintings are meticulously crafted images that are both scientific in their accurate portrayal of devices such as this timepiece and poetic in their beauty and lyricism.

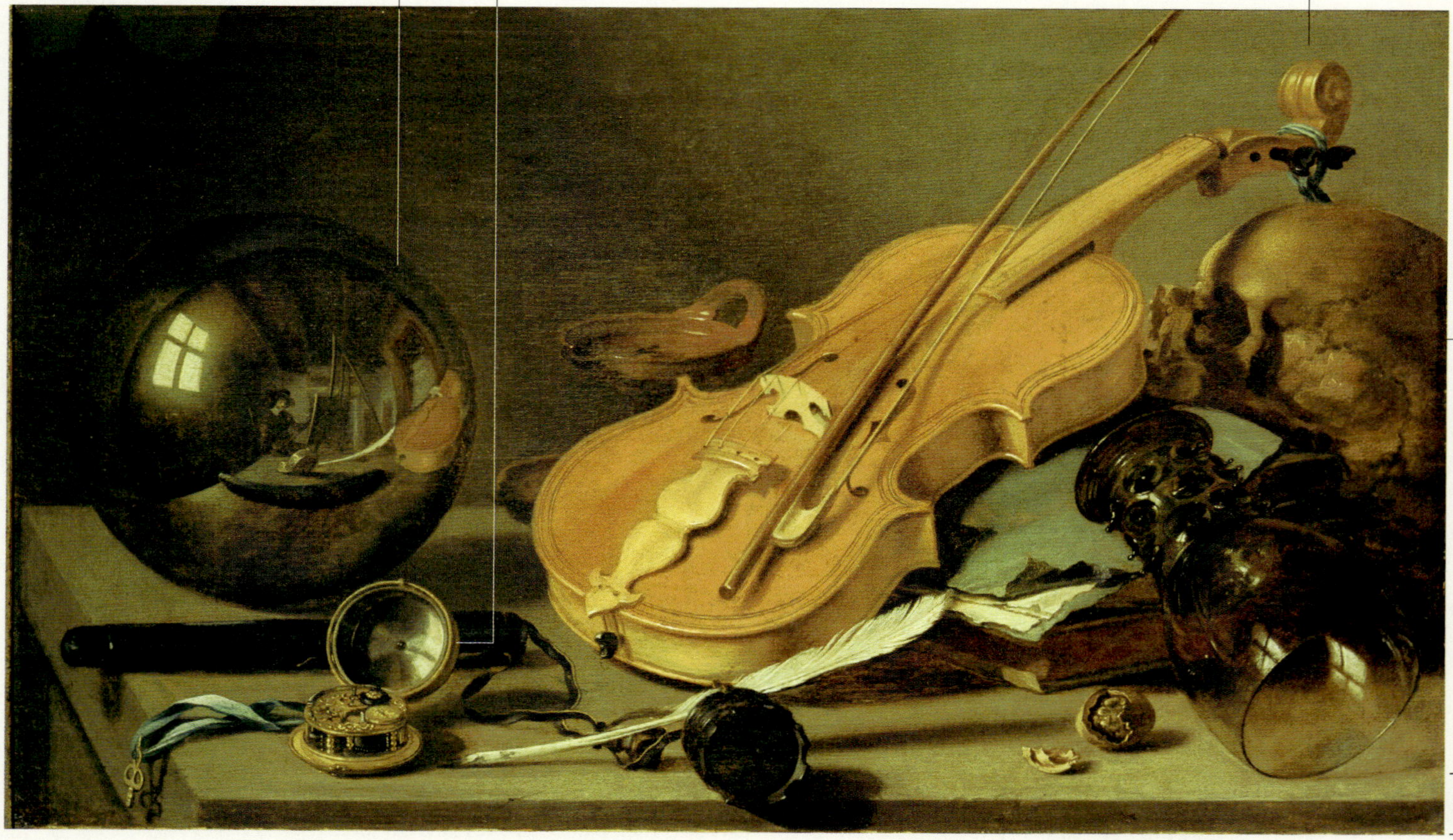

1 in.

**25-1** PIETER CLAESZ, *Vanitas Still Life*, 1630s. Oil on panel, 1′ 2″ × 1′ 11½″. Germanisches Nationalmuseum, Nuremberg.

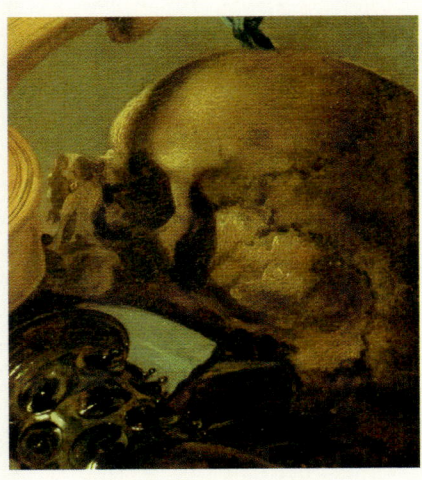

# THE BAROQUE IN NORTHERN EUROPE

Calvinist morality tempered Dutch citizens' delight in accumulated wealth. In this vanitas still life, the skull and timepiece are *mementi mori*, reminders of life's transience.

## STILL-LIFE PAINTING IN THE DUTCH REPUBLIC

In 1648, after decades of continuous border skirmishes with the Spaniards, the northern Netherlands achieved official recognition as the United Provinces of the Netherlands (the Dutch Republic; MAP **25-1**). The new independent republic owed its ascendance largely to its success in international trade. Dutch ships laden with goods roamed the world, sailing as far as North and South America, western Africa, China, Japan, and the Pacific islands.

Peter Mundy, a widely traveled Englishman, commented in 1640 on the irony that the Dutch Republic produced almost nothing on its own land yet enjoyed great wealth and could afford rare commodities from around the world:

> For although the land (and that with much labour) is brought only to pasture . . . yet by means of their shipping they are plentifully supplied with what the earth affords for the use of man . . . from any part of the world . . . Europe, Asia, Africa or America . . . with the most precious and rich commodities of those parts.[1]

The prosperous Dutch were justifiably proud of their accomplishments, and the popularity of still-life paintings—particularly images of accumulated goods—reflected this pride. These paintings of worldly possessions marked the emergence of an important new class of art patrons—wealthy merchants—who had tastes distinctly different from those of the leading patrons elsewhere in Baroque Europe, namely royalty and the Catholic Church. Dutch still lifes, which were well suited to the Protestant ethic rejecting most religious art, are among the finest ever painted. They are meticulously crafted images both scientific in their optical accuracy and poetic in their beauty and lyricism.

One of the best Dutch paintings of this genre is *Vanitas Still Life* (FIG. **25-1**) by PIETER CLAESZ (1597–1660), in which the painter presented the material possessions of a prosperous household strewn across a tabletop or dresser. The ever-present morality and humility central to the Calvinist faith tempered Dutch pride in worldly goods, however. Thus, although Claesz fostered the appreciation and enjoyment of the beauty and value of the objects he depicted, he also reminded the viewer of life's transience by incorporating references to death. Art historians call works of this type *vanitas* (vanity) paintings, and each feature a *memento mori* (reminder of death). In *Vanitas Still Life*, references to mortality include the skull, timepiece, tipped glass, and cracked walnut. All suggest the passage of time or something or someone that was here but now is gone. Claesz emphasized this element of time (and demonstrated his technical virtuosity) by including a self-portrait reflected in the glass ball on the left side of the table. He appears to be painting this still life. But in an apparent challenge to the message of inevitable mortality that vanitas paintings convey, the portrait serves to immortalize the artist.

# WAR AND TRADE
# IN NORTHERN EUROPE

During the 17th and early 18th centuries, numerous geopolitical shifts occurred in Europe as the fortunes of individual countries waxed and waned. Pronounced political and religious friction resulted in widespread unrest and warfare. Indeed, between 1562 and 1721, all of Europe was at peace for a mere four years. The major conflict of this period was the Thirty Years' War (1618–1648), which ensnared Spain, France, Sweden, Denmark, the Netherlands, Germany, Austria, Poland, the Ottoman Empire, and the Holy Roman Empire. Although the outbreak of the war had its roots in the conflict between militant Catholics and militant Protestants, the driving force quickly shifted to secular, dynastic, and nationalistic concerns. Among the major political entities vying for expanded power and authority in Europe were the Bourbon dynasty of France and the Habsburg dynasties of Spain and the Holy Roman Empire. The war, which concluded with the Treaty of Westphalia in 1648, was largely responsible for the political restructuring of Europe (MAP 25-1). As a result, the United Provinces of the Netherlands (the Dutch Republic), Sweden, and France expanded their authority. Spanish and Danish power diminished. In addition

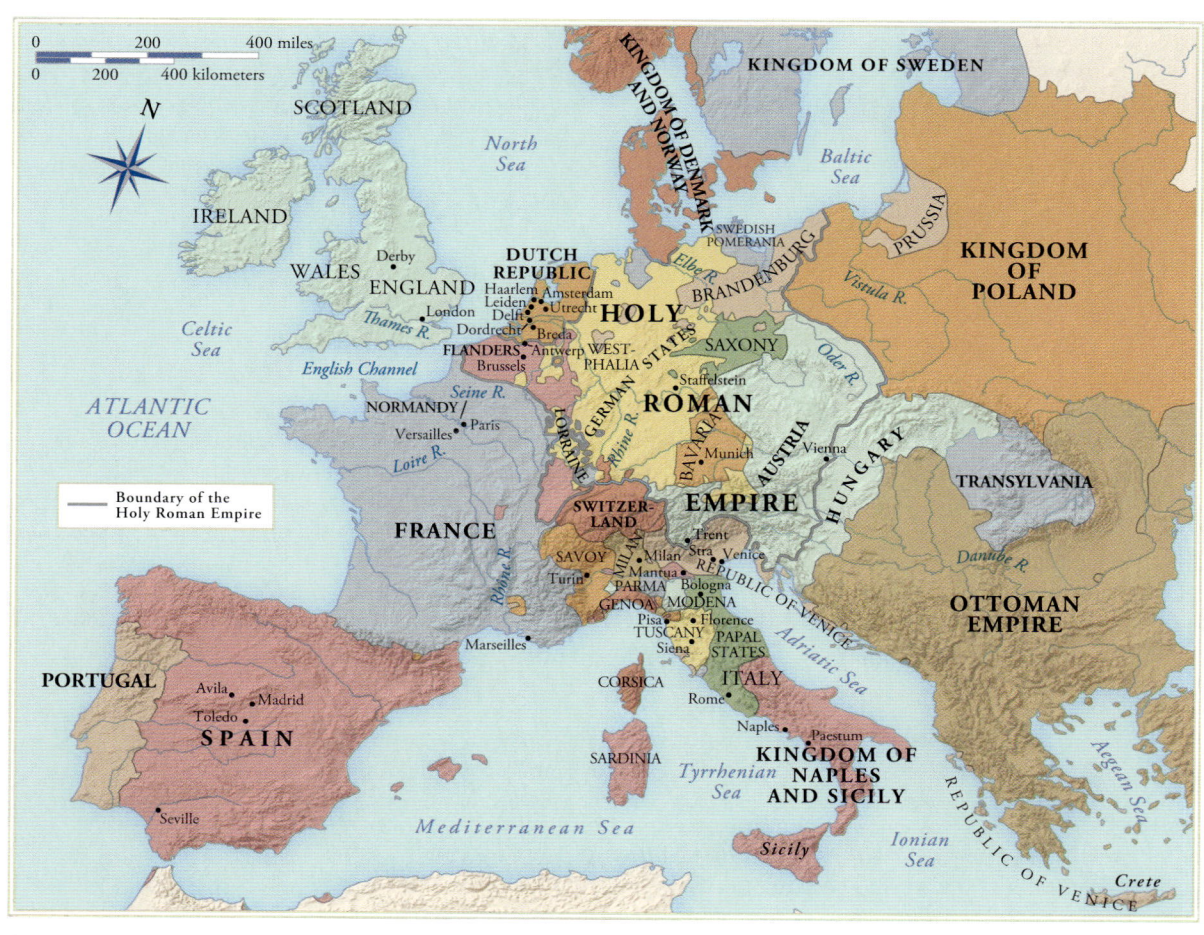

**MAP 25-1** Europe in 1648 after the Treaty of Westphalia.

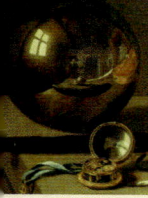

# THE BAROQUE IN NORTHERN EUROPE

| 1600 | 1625 | 1650 | 1675 | 1700 |
|---|---|---|---|---|
| I Peter Paul Rubens is the leading painter in Catholic Flanders<br><br>I The founding of the Bank of Amsterdam in 1609 initiates an era of Dutch preeminence in international trade<br><br>I In the northern Netherlands, Calvinist patrons favor genre scenes, portraits, and still lifes | I Frans Hals achieves renown for his group portraits of Dutch burghers<br><br>I Rembrandt, the foremost Dutch Baroque painter, is also a master of etching<br><br>I The Treaty of Westphalia concludes the Thirty Years' War in 1648 | I Jacob van Ruisdael and other Dutch artists specialize in landscape painting<br><br>I Jan Vermeer uses a camera obscura as an aid in painting domestic interiors<br><br>I Nicholas Poussin champions classical "grand manner" painting in Rome | I Louis XIV, the Sun King, builds the palace at Versailles<br><br>I Sir Christopher Wren designs Saint Paul's Cathedral in London | |

to reconfiguring territorial boundaries, the Treaty of Westphalia in essence granted freedom of religious choice throughout Europe. This treaty thus marked the abandonment of the idea of a united Christian Europe, and accepted the practical realities of secular political systems. The building of today's nation-states was emphatically under way.

The 17th century also brought heightened economic competition to Europe. Much of the foundation for worldwide mercantilism—extensive voyaging and geographic exploration, improved cartography, and advances in shipbuilding—had been laid in the previous century. In the 17th century, however, changes in financial systems, lifestyles, and trading patterns, along with expanding colonialism, fueled the creation of a worldwide marketplace. The Dutch founded the Bank of Amsterdam in 1609, which eventually became the center of European transfer banking. By establishing a system in which merchant firms held money on account, the bank relieved traders of having to transport precious metals as payment. Trading practices became more complex. Rather than simple reciprocal trading, triangular trade (trade among three parties) allowed for a larger pool of desirable goods. Exposure to an ever-growing array of goods affected European diets and lifestyles. Coffee (from island colonies) and tea (from China) became popular beverages during the early 17th century. Equally explosive was the growth of sugar use. Sugar, tobacco, and rice were slave crops, and the slave trade expanded to meet the demand for these goods. Traders captured and enslaved Africans and shipped them to European colonies and the Americas to provide the requisite labor force for producing these commodities.

The resulting worldwide mercantile system permanently changed the face of Europe. The prosperity international trade generated affected social and political relationships, necessitating new rules of etiquette and careful diplomacy. With increased disposable income, more of the newly wealthy spent money on art, significantly expanding the market for artworks, especially small-scale paintings for private homes.

# FLANDERS

In the 16th century, the Netherlands had come under the crown of Habsburg Spain when Emperor Charles V retired, leaving the Spanish kingdoms, their Italian and American possessions, and the Netherlandish provinces to his only legitimate son, Philip II (r. 1556–1598). (Charles bestowed his imperial title and German lands on his brother.) Philip's repressive measures against the Protestants led the northern provinces to break from Spain and set up the Dutch Republic. The southern provinces remained under Spanish control and retained Catholicism as their official religion. The political distinction between modern Holland and Belgium more or less reflects this original separation, which in the 17th century signaled not only religious but also artistic differences.

## Painting

The leading art of 17th-century Flanders (the Spanish Netherlands) was painting. Flemish Baroque painters retained close connections to the Baroque art of Catholic Europe. The Dutch schools of painting developed their own subjects and styles, consistent with their reformed religion and the new political, social, and economic structure of the Dutch Republic.

**PETER PAUL RUBENS** The greatest 17th-century Flemish painter was PETER PAUL RUBENS (1577–1640), a towering figure in the history of Western art. Rubens built on the innovations of the Italian Renaissance and Baroque masters to formulate the first truly pan-European painting style. Rubens's art is an original and powerful synthesis of the manners of many masters, especially Michelangelo, Titian, Carracci, and Caravaggio. His style had wide appeal, and his influence was international. Among the most learned individuals of his time, Rubens possessed an aristocratic education and a courtier's manner, diplomacy, and tact, which, with his facility for language, made him the associate of princes and scholars. He became court painter to the dukes of Mantua (descended from Mantegna's patrons), friend of King Philip IV (r. 1621–1665) of Spain and his adviser on collecting art, painter to Charles I (r. 1625–1649) of England and Marie de' Medici (1573–1642) of France, and permanent court painter to the Spanish governors of Flanders. Rubens also won the confidence of his royal patrons in matters of state, and they often entrusted him with diplomatic missions of the highest importance. Rubens employed scores of associates and apprentices to produce a steady stream of paintings for an international clientele. In addition, he functioned as an art dealer, buying and selling contemporary artworks and classical antiquities for royal and aristocratic clients throughout Europe, who competed with one another in amassing vast collections of paintings and sculptures, one of which

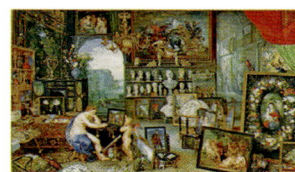
25-1A BRUEGHEL and RUBENS, *Allegory of Sight*, ca. 1617–1618.

became the subject of a painting (FIG. **25-1A**) by Rubens and JAN BRUEGEL THE ELDER (1568–1625). Rubens's many enterprises made him a rich man, able to afford a magnificent townhouse in Antwerp and a castle in the countryside. Rubens, like Raphael, was a successful and renowned artist, a consort of kings, a shrewd man of the world, and a learned philosopher.

***ELEVATION OF THE CROSS*** Rubens departed Flanders for Italy in 1600 and remained there until 1608. During these years, he studied the works of Italian Renaissance and Baroque masters and laid the foundations of his mature style. Shortly after returning home, he painted *Elevation of the Cross* (FIG. **25-2**) for the church of Saint Walburga in Antwerp. Later moved to the city's cathedral, the altarpiece is one of numerous commissions for religious works Rubens received at this time. By investing in sacred art, Flemish churches sought to affirm their allegiance to Catholicism and Spanish Habsburg rule after a period of Protestant iconoclastic fervor in the region.

Rubens's interest in Italian art, especially the works of Michelangelo and Caravaggio, is evident in the Saint Walburga triptych. The choice of this episode from the passion cycle provided Rubens with the opportunity to depict heavily muscled men in unusual poses straining to lift the heavy cross with Christ's body nailed to it. Here, as in his *Lion Hunt* (FIG. I-14), Rubens, deeply impressed by Michelangelo's twisting sculpted and painted figures, showed his prowess in representing foreshortened anatomy and the contortions of violent action. Rubens placed the body of Christ on the cross as a diagonal that cuts dynamically across the picture while inclining back into it. The whole composition seethes with a power that comes from strenuous exertion, from elastic human sinew taut with effort. The tension is emotional as well as physical, as reflected

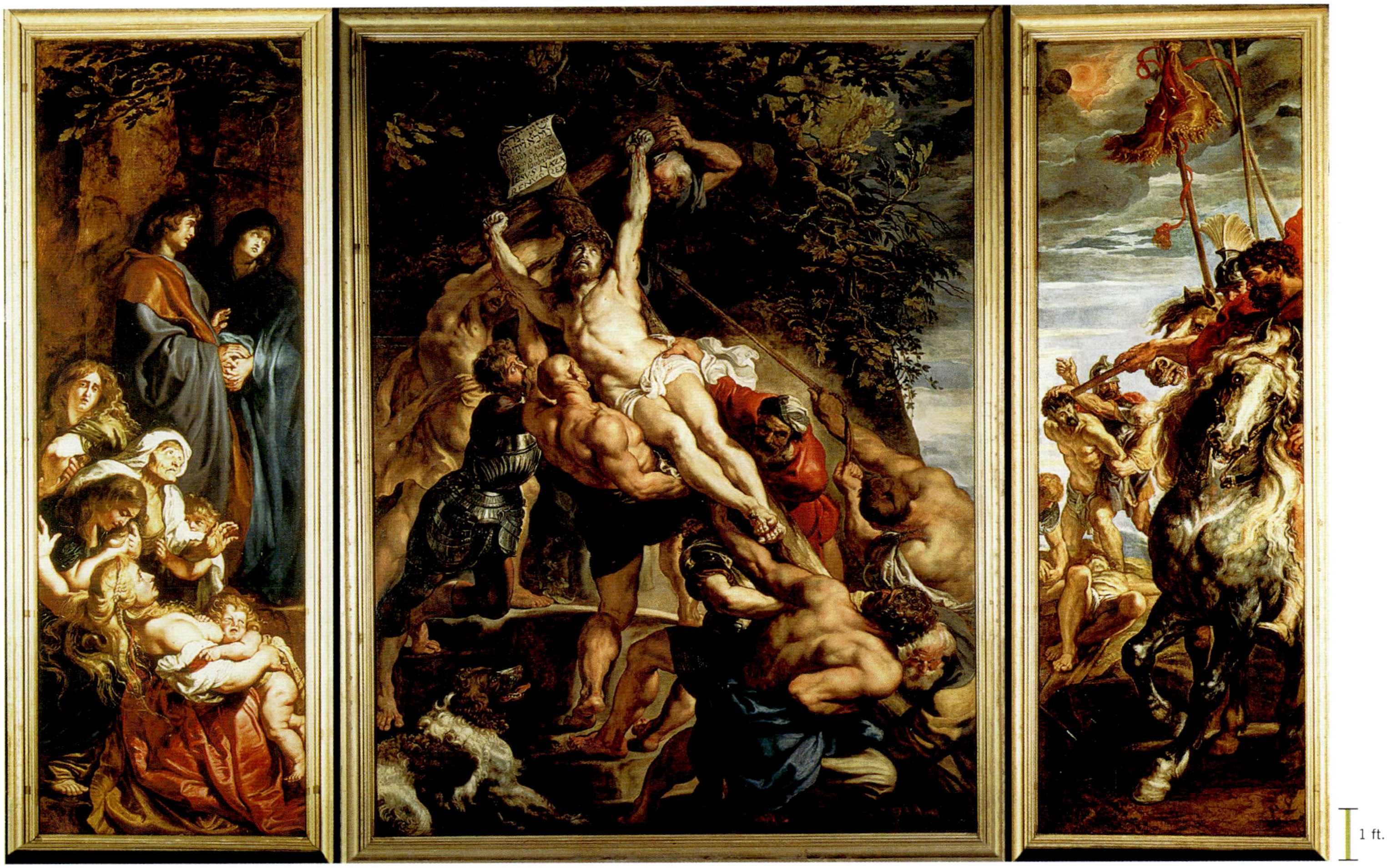

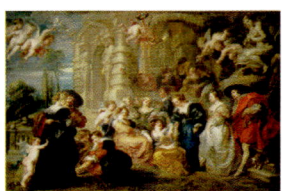

**25-2** PETER PAUL RUBENS, *Elevation of the Cross,* from Saint Walburga, Antwerp, 1610. Oil on wood, center panel 15′ 1⅞″ × 11′ 1½″, each wing 15′ 1⅞″ × 4′ 11″. Antwerp Cathedral, Antwerp.

In this triptych, Rubens explored foreshortened anatomy and violent action. The whole composition seethes with a power that comes from heroic exertion. The tension is emotional as well as physical.

not only in Christ's face but also in the features of his followers. Bright highlights and areas of deep shadow inspired by Caravaggio's tenebrism, hallmarks of Rubens's work at this stage of his career, enhance the drama.

Although Rubens later developed a much subtler coloristic style in paintings such as *Garden of Love* (FIG. **25-2A**), the human body in action, draped or undraped, male or female, remained the focus of his art. This interest, combined with his voracious intellect, led Rubens to copy the works of classical antiquity and of the Italian masters.

**25-2A** RUBENS, *Garden of Love,* 1630–1632.

During his last two years in Rome (1606 to 1608), Rubens made many black-chalk drawings of great artworks, including figures in Michelangelo's Sistine Chapel frescoes (FIG. 22-17) and the ancient marble group (FIG. 5-89) of Laocoön and his two sons. In a Latin treatise he wrote titled *De imitatione statuarum* (*On the Imitation of Statues*), Rubens stated: "I am convinced that in order to achieve the highest perfection one needs a full understanding of the [ancient] statues, indeed a complete absorption in them; but one must make judicious use of them and before all avoid the effect of stone."[2]

***MARIE DE' MEDICI*** Rubens's interaction with royalty and aristocracy provided him with an understanding of the ostentation and spectacle of Baroque (particularly Italian) art that appealed to the wealthy and privileged. Rubens, the born courtier, reveled in the pomp and majesty of royalty. Likewise, those in power embraced the lavish spectacle that served the Catholic Church so well in Italy. The magnificence and splendor of Baroque imagery reinforced the authority and right to rule of the highborn. Among Rubens's royal patrons was Marie de' Medici, a member of the famous Florentine house and widow of Henry IV (r. 1589–1610), the first Bourbon king of France. She commissioned Rubens to paint a series of huge canvases memorializing and glorifying her career. Between 1622 and 1626, Rubens, working with amazing creative energy, produced with the aid of his many assistants 21 historical-allegorical pictures designed to hang in the queen's new palace, the Luxembourg, in Paris.

In *Arrival of Marie de' Medici at Marseilles* (FIG. **25-3**), a 13-foot-tall tableau, Marie disembarks at that southern French port after her sea voyage from Italy. An allegorical personification of France, draped in a cloak decorated with the *fleur-de-lis* (the floral symbol of French royalty; compare FIG. 25-24), welcomes her. The sea and sky rejoice at the queen's safe arrival. Neptune

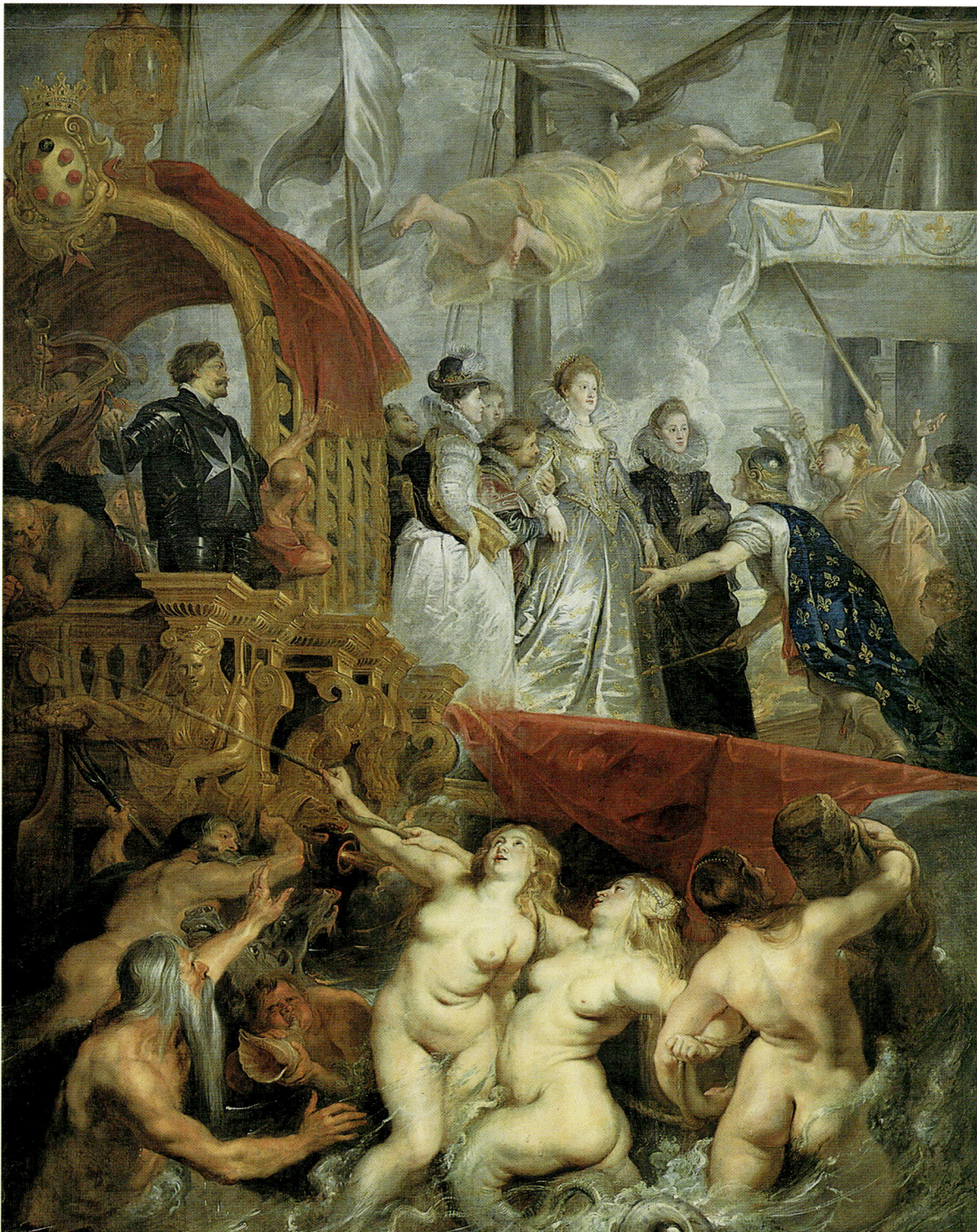

25-3 PETER PAUL
RUBENS, *Arrival of
Marie de' Medici at
Marseilles,* 1622–1625.
Oil on canvas,
12′ 11½″ × 9′ 7″. Musée
du Louvre, Paris.

Rubens painted 21 large
canvases glorifying Marie
de' Medici's career. In
this historical-allegorical
picture of robust figures
in an opulent setting,
the sea and sky rejoice
at the queen's arrival in
France.

1 ft.

and the Nereids (daughters of the sea god Nereus) salute her, and the winged and trumpeting personified Fame swoops overhead. Conspicuous in the galley's opulently carved stern-castle, under the Medici coat of arms, stands the imperious commander of the vessel, the only immobile figure in the composition. In black and silver, this figure makes a sharp accent amid the swirling tonality of ivory, gold, and red. Rubens enriched the surfaces with a decorative splendor that pulls the whole composition together. The audacious vigor that customarily enlivens the painter's figures, beginning with the monumental, twisting sea creatures, vibrates through the entire design.

**CONSEQUENCES OF WAR** Rubens's diplomatic missions gave him great insight into European politics, and he never ceased

# Rubens on *Consequences of War*

In the ancient and medieval worlds, artists rarely wrote commentaries on the works they produced. (The Greek sculptor Polykleitos is a notable exception; see "Polykleitos's Prescription for the Perfect Statue," Chapter 5, page 132.) Beginning with the Renaissance, however, the increased celebrity artists enjoyed and the ready availability of paper encouraged artists to record their intentions in letters to friends and patrons.

In March 1638, Peter Paul Rubens wrote a letter to Justus Sustermans (1597–1681), court painter of Grand Duke Ferdinando II de' Medici of Tuscany, explaining his *Consequences of War* (FIG. 25-4) and his attitude toward the European military conflicts of his day.

> The principal figure is Mars, who has left the open temple of Janus (which in time of peace, according to Roman custom, remained closed) and rushes forth with shield and blood-stained sword, threatening the people with great disaster. He pays little heed to Venus, his mistress, who, accompanied by Amors and Cupids, strives with caresses and embraces to hold him. From the other side, Mars is dragged forward by the Fury Alekto, with a torch in her hand. Near by are monsters personifying Pestilence and Famine, those inseparable partners of War. On the ground, turning her back, lies a woman with a broken lute, representing Harmony, which is incompatible with the discord of War. There is also a mother with her child in her arms, indicating that fecundity, procreation and charity are thwarted by War, which corrupts and destroys everything. In addition, one sees an architect thrown on his back, with his instruments in his hand, to show that which in time of peace is constructed for the use and ornamentation of the City, is hurled to the ground by the force of arms and falls to ruin. I believe, if I remember rightly, that you will find on the ground, under the feet of Mars a book and a drawing on paper, to imply that he treads underfoot all the arts and letters. There ought also to be a bundle of darts or arrows, with the band which held them together undone; these when bound form the symbol of Concord. Beside them is the caduceus and an olive branch, attribute of Peace; these are also cast aside. That grief-stricken woman clothed in black, with torn veil, robbed of all her jewels and other ornaments, is the unfortunate Europe who, for so many years now, has suffered plunder, outrage, and misery, which are so injurious to everyone that it is unnecessary to go into detail. Europe's attribute is the globe, borne by a small angel or genius, and surmounted by the cross, to symbolize the Christian world.*

*Translated by Kristin Lohse Belkin, *Rubens* (London: Phaidon, 1998), 288–289.

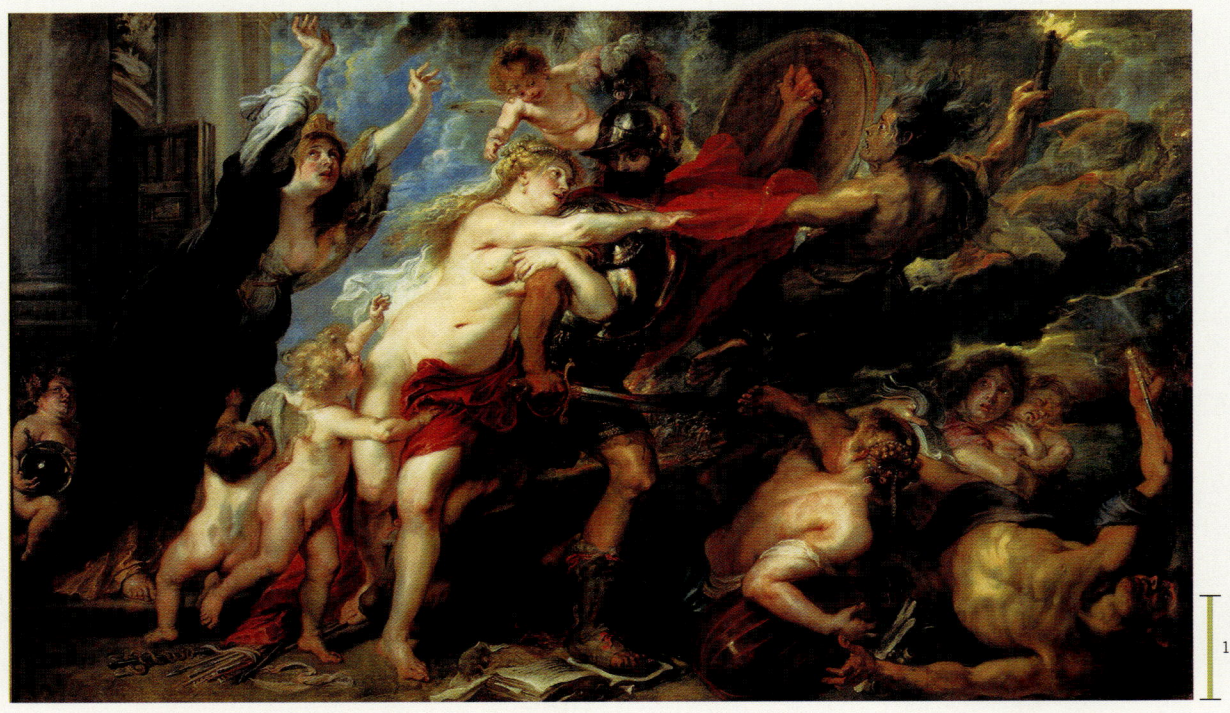

**25-4** **PETER PAUL RUBENS**, *Consequences of War*, 1638–1639. Oil on canvas, 6′ 9″ × 11′ 3⅞″. Palazzo Pitti, Florence.

Since the Renaissance, artists have left behind many letters shedding light on their lives and work. In a 1638 letter, Rubens explained the meaning of each figure in this allegorical painting.

to promote peace. Throughout most of his career, however, war was constant. When commissioned in 1638 to produce a painting (FIG. 25-4) for Ferdinando II de' Medici, the grand duke of Tuscany (r. 1621–1670), Rubens took the opportunity to express his attitude toward the Thirty Years' War (see "Rubens on *Consequences of War*," above). The fluid articulation of human forms in this work and the energy emanating from the chaotic scene are hallmarks of Rubens's mature style.

**ANTHONY VAN DYCK** Most of the leading painters of the next generation in Flanders were at one time Rubens's assistants. The master's most famous pupil was ANTHONY VAN DYCK (1599–1641). Early on, the younger man, unwilling to be overshadowed by Rubens's undisputed stature, left his native Antwerp for Genoa and then London, where he became court portraitist to Charles I. Although Van Dyck created dramatic compositions of high quality, his specialty became the portrait. He developed a courtly manner of great elegance that influenced many artists throughout Europe and resounded in English portrait painting well into the 19th century.

In one of his finest works, *Charles I Dismounted* (FIG. 25-5), the ill-fated English king stands in a landscape with the Thames River in the background. An equerry and a page attend him. The portrait is a stylish image of relaxed authority, as if the king is out for a casual ride in his park, but no one can mistake the regal poise and the air of absolute authority that Charles's Parliament resented and was soon to rise against. Here, the king turns his back on his attendants as he surveys his domain. Van Dyck's placement of the monarch is exceedingly artful. He stands off center but balances the composition with a single keen glance at the viewer. Van Dyck even managed to portray Charles I, who was of short stature, in a position to look down on the observer.

**CLARA PEETERS** Some Flemish 17th-century artists specialized in still-life painting, as did Sánchez Cotán (FIG. 24-25) in Spain. A pioneer of this genre was CLARA PEETERS (1594–ca. 1657), a native of Antwerp who spent time in Holland and laid the groundwork for Pieter Claesz (FIG. 25-1) and other Dutch masters of still-life painting, including Willem Kalf (FIG. 25-22) and Rachel Ruysch (FIG. 25-23). Peeters won renown for her depictions

of food and flowers together, and for still lifes featuring bread and fruit, known as *breakfast pieces*. In *Still Life with Flowers, Goblet, Dried Fruit, and Pretzels* (FIG. 25-6), Peeters's considerable skills are on full display. One of a series of four paintings, each of which depicts a typical early-17th-century meal, this breakfast piece reveals Peeters's virtuosity in depicting a wide variety of objects convincingly, from the smooth, reflective surfaces of the glass and silver goblets to the soft petals of the blooms in the vase. Peeters often painted the objects in her still lifes against a dark background, thereby negating any sense of deep space (compare FIG. 24-25). In this breakfast piece, she enhanced the sense of depth in the foreground by placing the leaves of the flower on the stone ledge as though they were encroaching into the viewer's space.

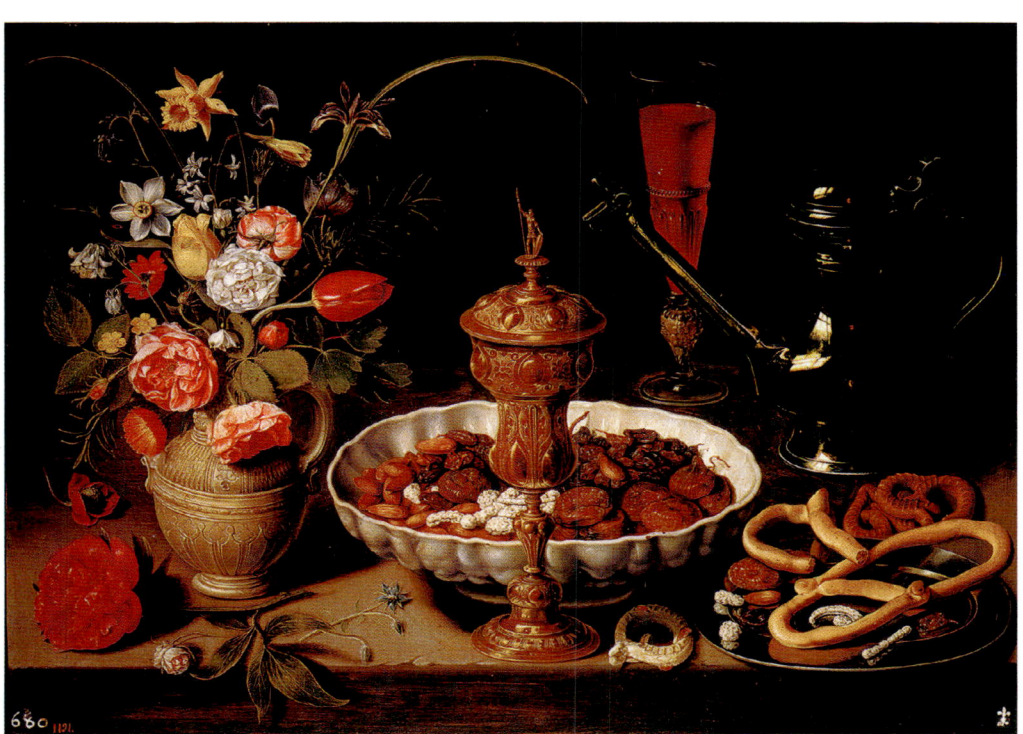

# DUTCH REPUBLIC

With the founding of the Bank of Amsterdam in 1609, Amsterdam emerged as the financial center of the Continent. In the 17th century, the city had the highest per capita income in Europe. The Dutch economy also benefited enormously from the country's expertise on the open seas, which facilitated establishing far-flung colonies. By 1650, Dutch trade routes extended to North America, South America, the west coast of Africa, China, Japan, Southeast Asia, and much of the Pacific. Due to this prosperity and in the absence of an absolute ruler, political power increasingly passed into the hands of an urban patrician class of merchants and manufacturers, especially in cities such as Amsterdam, Haarlem, and Delft. All of these bustling cities were located in Holland (the largest of the seven United Provinces), which explains why historians informally use the name "Holland" to refer to the entire country.

## Ter Brugghen, van Honthorst, Hals, Leyster

Religious differences were a major consideration during the northern Netherlands' insistent quest for independence during the 16th and early 17th centuries. Whereas Spain and the southern Netherlands were Catholic, the people of the northern Netherlands were predominantly Protestant. The prevailing Calvinism demanded a puritanical rejection of art in churches, and thus artists produced relatively little religious art in the Dutch Republic at this time (especially compared with the volume of commissions created in the wake of the Counter-Reformation in areas dominated by Catholicism; see Chapter 24).

**HENDRICK TER BRUGGHEN** Some artists in the Dutch Republic did produce religious art, however. HENDRICK TER BRUGGHEN (1588–1629) of Utrecht, for example, painted *Calling of Saint Matthew* (FIG. **25-7**) in 1621 after returning from a trip to Italy, selecting as his subject a theme Caravaggio had painted (FIG. 24-17) for the church of San Luigi dei Francesi in Rome. The moment of the narrative chosen and the naturalistic depiction of the figures echo Caravaggio's work. But although ter Brugghen was an admirer of the Italian master, he dispensed with Caravaggio's stark contrasts of dark and light and instead presented the viewer with a more colorful palette of soft tints. Further, the Dutch painter compressed the figures into a small but well-lit space, creating an intimate effect compared with Caravaggio's more spacious setting.

**MERCANTILIST PATRONAGE** Given the absence of an authoritative ruler and the Calvinist concern for the potential misuse of religious art, commissions from royalty or the Catholic Church, prominent in the art of other countries, were uncommon in the United Provinces. With the new prosperity, however, an expanding class of merchants with different tastes emerged as art patrons. In contrast to Italian, Spanish, and Flemish Baroque art, 17th-century Dutch art centered on genre scenes, landscapes, portraits of middle-class men and women, and still lifes, all of which appealed to the newly prosperous Dutch merchants (see "Still-Life Painting in the Dutch Republic," page 695, and "Middle-Class Patronage and the Art Market in the Dutch Republic," page 703).

**GERRIT VAN HONTHORST** Typical of 17th-century Dutch genre scenes is *Supper Party* (FIG. **25-8**) by GERRIT VAN HONTHORST (1590–1656). In this painting, van Honthorst presented an informal gathering of unidealized figures. While a musician serenades the group, his companions delight in watching a young woman feeding a piece of chicken to a man whose hands are both occupied—one holds a jug and the other a glass. Van Honthorst spent several years in Italy, and while there he carefully studied Caravaggio's work, as did fellow Utrecht painter Hendrick ter Brugghen. The Italian artist's influence surfaces in the mundane tavern setting and the nocturnal lighting of *Supper Party*. Fascinated by nighttime effects, van Honthorst frequently placed a hidden light source in his pictures and used it as a pretext to work with dramatic and starkly contrasting dark and light effects. Seemingly lighthearted genre scenes were popular in Baroque Holland, but Dutch viewers could also interpret them moralistically. For example, *Supper Party* can be read as a warning against the sins of gluttony (represented by the man on the right) and lust (the woman feeding the glutton is, in all likelihood, a prostitute with her aged procuress at her side). Or perhaps the painting represents the loose companions of the Prodigal Son (Luke 15:13)—panderers and prostitutes drinking, singing, strumming, and laughing. Strict Dutch Calvinists no doubt approved of such interpretations. Others simply took delight in the immediacy of the scenes and skill of artists such as van Honthorst.

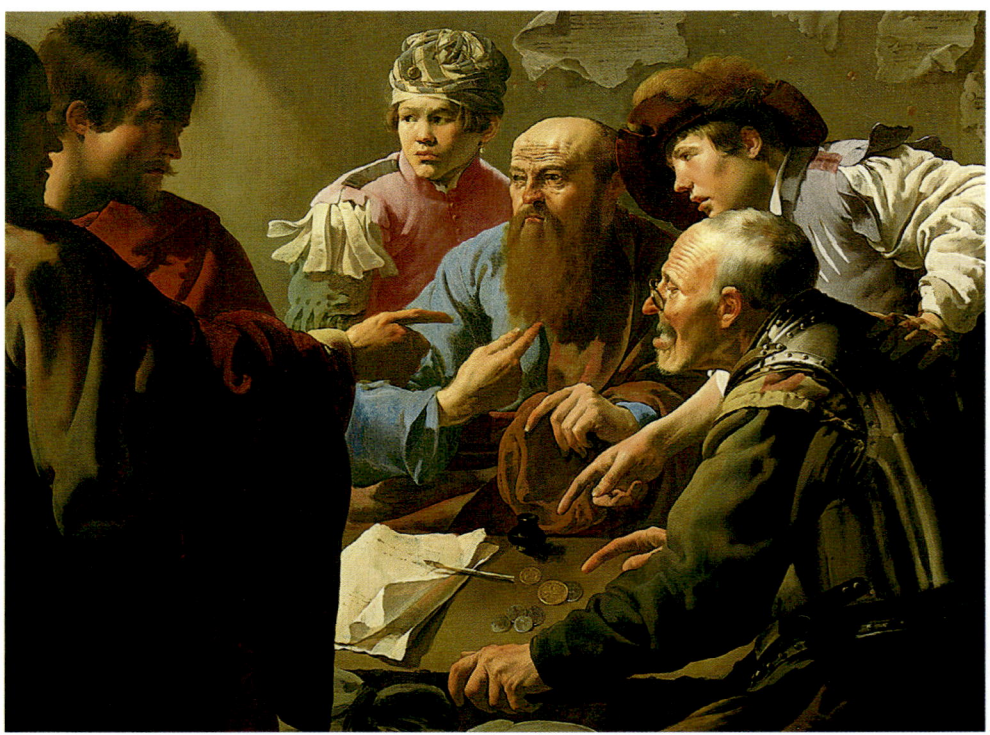

**25-7** HENDRICK TER BRUGGHEN, *Calling of Saint Matthew*, 1621. Oil on canvas, 3′ 4″ × 4′ 6″. Centraal Museum, Utrecht.

Although middle-class patrons in the Protestant Dutch Republic preferred genre scenes, still lifes, and portraits, some artists, including Hendrick ter Brugghen, also painted religious scenes.

1 ft.

# Middle-Class Patronage and the Art Market in the Dutch Republic

Throughout history, the wealthy have been the most avid art collectors. Indeed, the money necessary to commission major artworks from leading artists can be considerable. During the 17th century in the Dutch Republic, however, the prosperity a large proportion of the population enjoyed significantly expanded the range of art patrons. As a result, one distinguishing hallmark of Dutch art production during the Baroque period was how it catered to the tastes of a middle-class audience, broadly defined. An aristocracy and an upper class of ship owners, rich businesspeople, high-ranking officers, and directors of large companies still existed, and these groups continued to be major patrons of the arts. But with the expansion of the Dutch economy, traders, craftspeople, bureaucrats, and soldiers also commissioned and collected art.

Although steeped in the morality and propriety central to the Calvinist ethic, members of the Dutch middle class sought ways to announce their success and newly acquired status. House furnishings, paintings, tapestries, and porcelain were among the items they collected and displayed in their homes. The Calvinist disdain for excessive ostentation, however, led Dutch collectors to favor small, low-key works—portraits of bourgeois men and women (FIGS. 25-9, 25-10, 25-12, and 25-13), still lifes (FIGS. 25-1, 25-22, and 25-23), genre scenes (FIGS. 25-8, 25-19, and 25-21), and landscapes (FIGS. 25-17, 25-18, 25-18A, and 25-18B). This focus contrasted with the Italian Baroque penchant for large-scale, dazzling ceiling frescoes and opulent room decoration (see Chapter 24). Indeed, the stylistic, as opposed to the chronological, designation "Baroque" is ill suited to these 17th-century northern European artworks.

It is risky to generalize about the spending and collecting habits of the Dutch middle class, but probate records, contracts, and archived inventories reveal some interesting facts. These records suggest an individual earning between 1,500 and 3,000 guilders a year could live quite comfortably. A house could be purchased for 1,000 guilders. Another 1,000 guilders could buy all the necessary furnishings for a middle-class home, including a significant amount of art, particularly paintings. Although there was, of course, considerable variation in prices, many artworks were very affordable. Prints, for example, were extremely cheap because of the high number of copies artists produced of each picture. Paintings of interior and genre scenes were relatively inexpensive in 17th-century Holland, perhaps costing one or two guilders each. Small landscapes fetched between three and four guilders. Commissioned portraits were the most costly. The size of the work and quality of the frame, as well as the reputation of the artist, were other factors in determining the price of a painting, regardless of the subject.

With the exception of portraits, Dutch artists produced most of their paintings for an anonymous market, hoping to appeal to a wide audience. To ensure success, artists in the United Provinces adapted to the changed conditions of art production and sales. They marketed their paintings in many ways, selling their works directly to buyers who visited their studios and through art dealers, exhibitions, fairs, auctions, and even lotteries. Because of the uncertainty of these sales mechanisms (as opposed to the certainty of an ironclad contract for a commission from a church or king), artists became more responsive to market demands. Specialization became common among Dutch artists. For example, painters might limit their practice to portraits, still lifes, or landscapes—the most popular genres among middle-class patrons.

Artists did not always sell their paintings. Frequently they used their work to pay off loans or debts. Tavern debts, in particular, could be settled with paintings, which may explain why many art dealers (such as Jan Vermeer and his father before him) were also innkeepers. This connection between art dealing and other businesses eventually solidified, and innkeepers, for example, often would have art exhibitions in their taverns hoping to make a sale. The institutions of today's open art market—dealers, galleries, auctions, and estate sales—owe their establishment to the emergence in the 17th century of a prosperous middle class in the Dutch Republic.

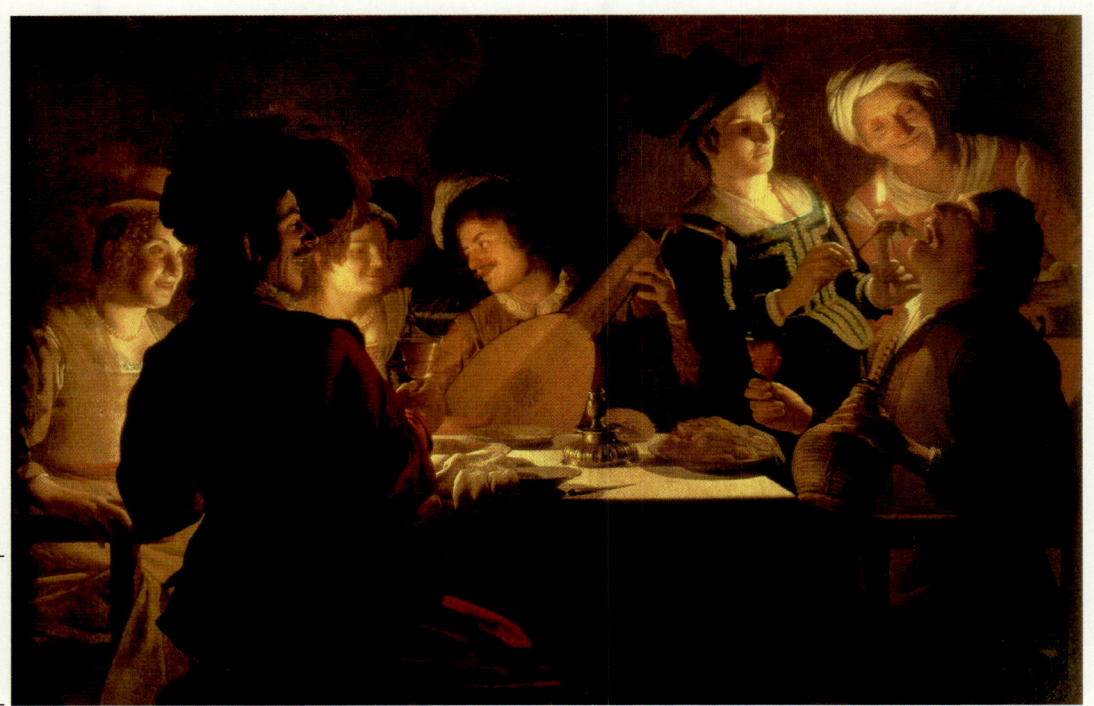

1 ft.

**25-8** GERRIT VAN HONTHORST, *Supper Party,* 1620. Oil on canvas, 4′ 8″ × 7′. Galleria degli Uffizi, Florence.

Genre scenes were popular subjects among middle-class Dutch patrons. Gerrit van Honthorst's *Supper Party* may also have served as a Calvinist warning against the sins of gluttony and lust.

**FRANS HALS** Many Dutch artists excelled in portraiture in response to popular demand. FRANS HALS (ca. 1581–1666), the leading painter in Haarlem, was one of those who made portraits his specialty. Portrait artists traditionally relied heavily on convention—for example, specific poses, settings, attire, and furnishings—to convey a sense of the sitter. Because the subject was usually someone of status or note, such as a pope, king, duchess, or wealthy banker, the artist's goal was to produce an image appropriate to the subject's station in life. With the increasing number of Dutch middle-class patrons, portrait painting became more challenging. The Calvinists shunned ostentation, instead wearing subdued and dark clothing with little variation or decoration, and the traditional conventions became inappropriate and thus unusable. Despite these difficulties, or perhaps because of them, Hals produced lively portraits that seem far more relaxed than traditional formulaic portraiture. He injected an engaging spontaneity into his images and conveyed the individuality of his sitters as well. His manner of execution intensified the casualness, immediacy, and intimacy in his paintings. Because the touch of Hals's brush was as light and fleeting as the moment he captured the pose, the figure, the highlights on clothing, and the facial expression all seem instantaneously created.

**ARCHERS OF SAINT HADRIAN** Hals's most ambitious portraits reflect the widespread popularity in the Dutch Republic of vast canvases commemorating the participation of Dutch burghers in civic organizations. These commissions presented greater difficulties to the painter than requests to depict a single sitter. Hals rose to the challenge and achieved great success with this new portrait genre. His *Archers of Saint Hadrian* (FIG. **25-9**) is typical in that the subject is one of the many Dutch civic militia groups that claimed credit for liberating the Dutch Republic from Spain. As other companies did, the Archers met on their saint's feast day in dress uniform for a grand banquet. The celebrations sometimes lasted an entire week, prompting an ordinance limiting them to three or four days. These events often included sitting for a group portrait.

In *Archers of Saint Hadrian,* Hals attacked the problem of how to represent each militia member satisfactorily yet retain action and variety in the composition. Whereas earlier group portraits in the Netherlands were rather ordered and regimented images, Hals sought to enliven the depictions. In his portrait of the Saint Hadrian militiamen, each member is both part of the troop and an individual with a distinct physiognomy. The sitters' movements and moods vary markedly. Some engage the viewer directly. Others look away or at a companion. Some are stern, others animated. Each archer is equally visible and clearly recognizable. The uniformity of attire—black military dress, white ruffs, and sashes—did not deter Hals from injecting spontaneity into the work. Indeed, he used those elements to create a lively rhythm extending throughout the composition and energizing the portrait. The impromptu effect— the preservation of every detail and fleeting facial expression—is, of course, the result of careful planning. Yet Hals's vivacious brush appears to have moved instinctively, directed by a plan in his mind but not traceable in any preparatory scheme on the canvas.

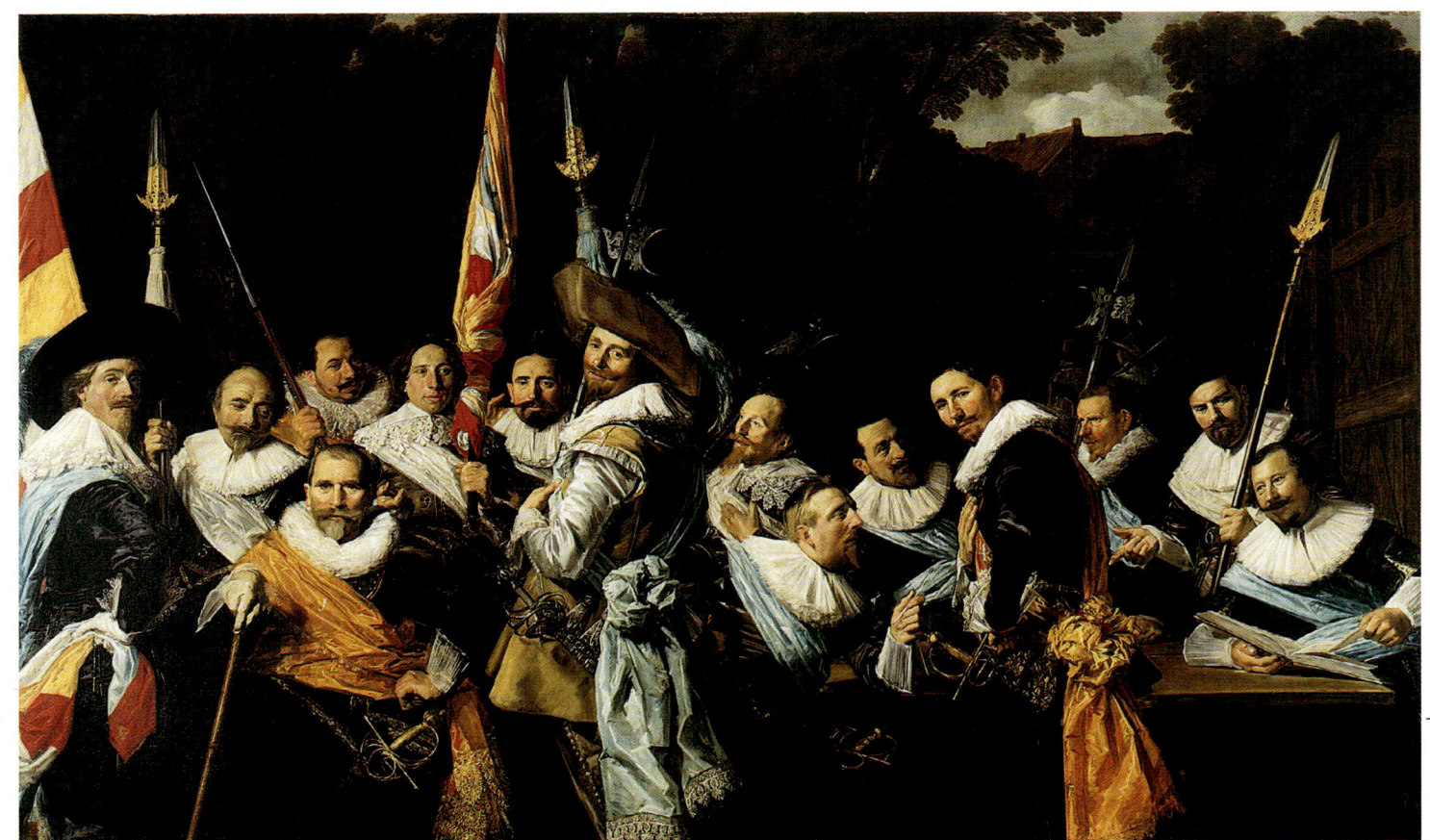

1 ft.

**25-9** FRANS HALS, *Archers of Saint Hadrian,* ca. 1633. Oil on canvas, 6′ 9″ × 11′. Frans Halsmuseum, Haarlem. ◼️

In this brilliant composition, Hals succeeded in solving the problem of portraying each individual in a group portrait while retaining action and variety in the painting as a whole.

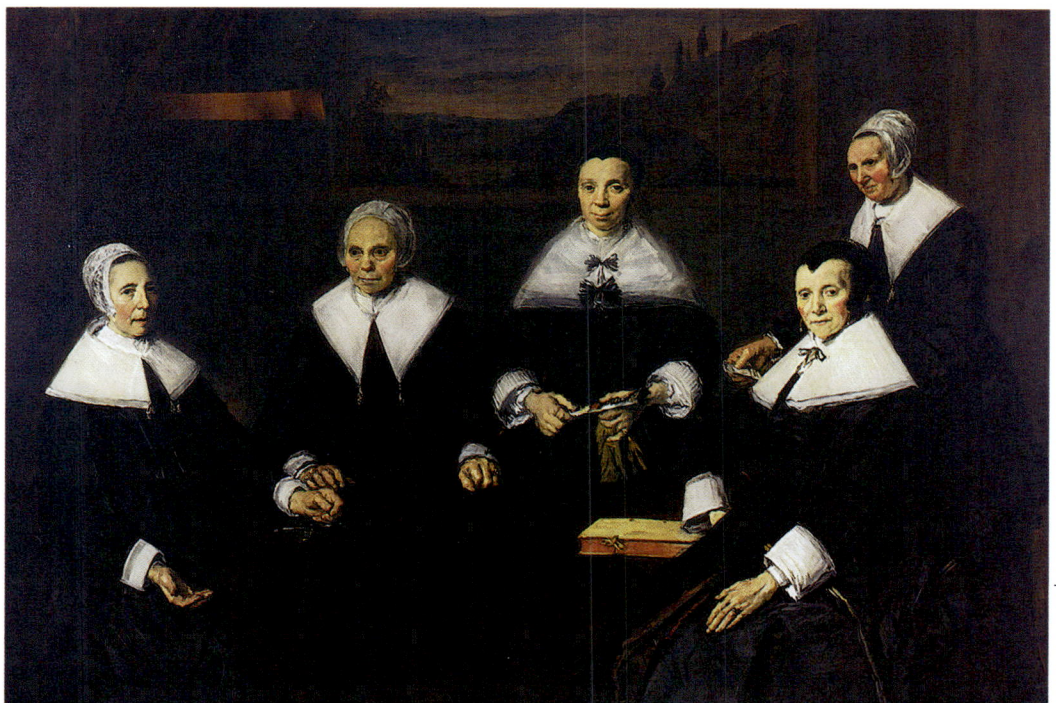

**25-10** FRANS HALS, *The Women Regents of the Old Men's Home at Haarlem*, 1664. Oil on canvas, 5′ 7″ × 8′ 2″. Frans Halsmuseum, Haarlem. ◼◀

Dutch women played a major role in public life as regents of charitable institutions. A stern puritanical sensibility suffuses Hals's group portrait of the regents of Haarlem's old men's home.

1 ft.

**WOMEN REGENTS OF HAARLEM** Hals also produced group portraits of Calvinist women engaged in charitable work. The finest is *The Women Regents of the Old Men's Home at Haarlem* (FIG. **25-10**). Although Dutch women had primary responsibility for the welfare of the family and the orderly operation of the home, they also populated the labor force in the cities. Among the more prominent roles educated Dutch women played in public life were as regents of orphanages, hospitals, old age homes, and prisons. In Hals's portrait, the Haarlem regents sit quietly in a manner becoming of devout Calvinists. Unlike the more relaxed, seemingly informal character of his other group portraits, a stern, puritanical, and composed sensibility suffuses Hals's portrayal of these regents. The women—all carefully distinguished as individuals—gaze out from the painting with expressions ranging from dour disinterest to kindly concern. The somber and virtually *monochromatic* (one-color) palette, punctuated only by the white accents of the clothing, contributes to the painting's restraint. Both the coloration and the mood of Hals's portrait are appropriate for this commission. Portraying the Haarlem regents called for a very different kind of portrait from those Hals made of men at festive militia banquets.

**JUDITH LEYSTER** Some of Hals's students developed thriving careers of their own as portraitists. One was JUDITH LEYSTER (1609–1660), whose *Self-Portrait* (FIG. **25-11**) reveals the strong training she received. It is detailed, precise, and accurate but also imbued with the spontaneity found in her master's works. In her portrait, Leyster succeeded at communicating a great deal about herself. She depicted herself as an artist, seated in front of a painting on an easel. The palette in her left hand and brush in her right announce the painting as her creation. She thus invites the viewer to evaluate her skill, which both the fiddler on the canvas and the image of herself demonstrate as considerable. Although she produced a wide range of paintings, including still lifes and floral pieces, her specialty was genre scenes such as the comic image seen on the easel. Leyster's quick smile and relaxed pose as she stops her work to meet the viewer's gaze reveal her self-assurance. Although presenting herself as an artist, Leyster did not paint herself wearing the traditional artist's smock, as her more famous contemporary Rembrandt did in his 1659–1660 self-portrait (FIG. 25-15). Her elegant attire distinguishes her socially as a member of a well-to-do family, another important aspect of Leyster's identity.

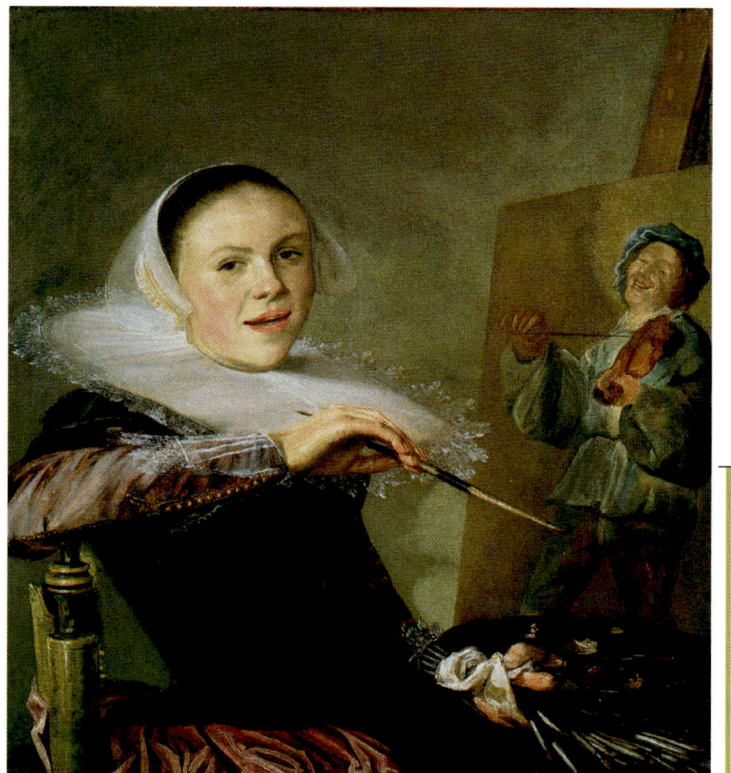

**25-11** JUDITH LEYSTER, *Self-Portrait*, ca. 1630. Oil on canvas, 2′ 5¾″ × 2′ 1⅝″. National Gallery of Art, Washington, D.C. (gift of Mr. and Mrs. Robert Woods Bliss). ◼◀

Although presenting herself as an artist specializing in genre scenes, Leyster wears elegant attire instead of a painter's smock, placing her socially as a member of a well-to-do family.

1 ft.

# Rembrandt

REMBRANDT VAN RIJN (1606–1669), Hals's younger contemporary and the leading Dutch painter of his time, was an undisputed genius—an artist of great versatility, a master of light and shadow, and a unique interpreter of the Protestant conception of scripture. Born in Leiden, he moved to Amsterdam around 1631, where he could attract a more extensive clientele than possible in his native city. Rembrandt had trained as a history painter in Leiden, but in Amsterdam he immediately entered the lucrative market for portraiture and soon became renowned for that genre.

***ANATOMY LESSON OF DR. TULP*** In a painting he completed shortly after he arrived in Amsterdam, *Anatomy Lesson of Dr. Tulp* (FIG. **25-12**), Rembrandt deviated even further from the traditional staid group portrait than had Hals. Despite Hals's determination to enliven his portraits, he still evenly spread his subjects across the canvas. In contrast, Rembrandt chose to portray the members of the surgeons' guild (who commissioned this group portrait) clustered on the painting's left side. In the foreground appears the corpse Dr. Tulp, a noted physician, is in the act of dissecting. Rembrandt diagonally placed and foreshortened the corpse, activating the space by disrupting the strict horizontal, planar orientation typical of traditional portraiture. He depicted each of the "students" specifically, and although they wear virtually identical attire, their poses and facial expressions suggest the varying degrees of intensity with which they watch Dr. Tulp's demonstration—or ignore it. One, at the apex of Rembrandt's triangular composition of bodies, gazes at the viewer instead of at the operating table. Another directs his attention to the open book (an anatomy manual) at the cadaver's feet. Rembrandt produced this painting when he was 26 and just beginning his career. His innovative approach to group portraiture is therefore all the more remarkable.

***NIGHT WATCH*** Rembrandt amplified the complexity and energy of the group portrait in *The Company of Captain Frans Banning Cocq* (FIG. **25-13**), better known as *Night Watch*. This more commonly used title is a misnomer, however. The painting is not of a nocturnal scene. Rembrandt used light in a masterful way, and dramatic lighting certainly enhances the image. Still, the painting's darkness (which explains the commonly used title) is the result of the varnish the artist used, which darkened considerably over time. It was not the painter's intention to portray his subjects moving about at night.

This painting was one of many civic-guard group portraits Dutch artists produced during this period.

From the limited information available about the commission, it appears the two officers, Captain Frans Banning Cocq and Lieutenant Willem van Ruytenburch, along with 16 members of their militia, contributed to Rembrandt's fee. (Despite the prominence of the girl just to the left of center, scholars have yet to ascertain her identity.) *Night Watch* was one of six paintings by different artists commissioned by various groups around 1640 for the assembly and banquet hall of Amsterdam's new Musketeers Hall, the largest and most prestigious interior space in the city. Unfortunately, in 1715, when city officials moved Rembrandt's painting to Amsterdam's town hall, they trimmed it on all sides, leaving an incomplete record of the artist's resolution of the challenge of portraying this group.

Even in its truncated form, *The Company of Captain Frans Banning Cocq* succeeds in capturing the excitement and frenetic activity of men preparing for a parade. Comparing this militia group portrait with Hals's *Archers of Saint Hadrian* (FIG. 25-9) reveals Rembrandt's inventiveness in enlivening what was, by then, becoming a conventional format for Dutch group portraits. Rather than present assembled men posed in orderly fashion, the younger artist chose to portray the company members rushing about in the act of organizing themselves, thereby animating the image considerably. At the same time, he managed to record the three most important stages of using a musket—loading, firing, and readying the weapon for reloading—details that must have pleased his patrons.

***RETURN OF THE PRODIGAL SON*** The Calvinist injunction against religious art did not prevent Rembrandt from making a series of religious paintings and prints. In the Dutch Republic, paintings depicting biblical themes were not objects of devotion, but they still brought great prestige, and Rembrandt and other artists vied to demonstrate their ability to narrate holy scripture in dramatic new ways. One of Rembrandt's earliest biblical paintings, *Blinding of Samson* (FIG. **24-13A**), reveals the young artist's debt to Rubens and Caravaggio. His mature works, however, differ markedly from the

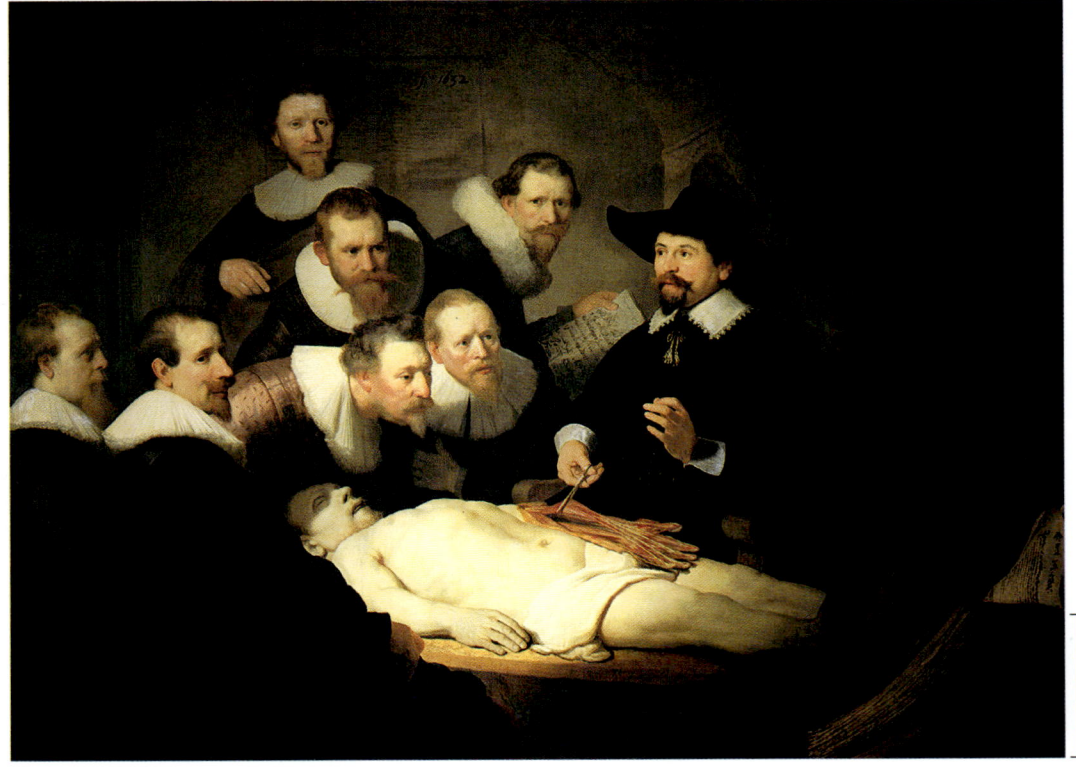

**25-12** REMBRANDT VAN RIJN, *Anatomy Lesson of Dr. Tulp*, 1632. Oil on canvas, 5′ 3¾″ × 7′ 1¼″. Mauritshuis, The Hague. ◼◀

In this early work, Rembrandt used an unusual composition, arranging members of Amsterdam's surgeons' guild clustered on one side of the painting as they watch Dr. Tulp dissect a corpse.

1 ft.

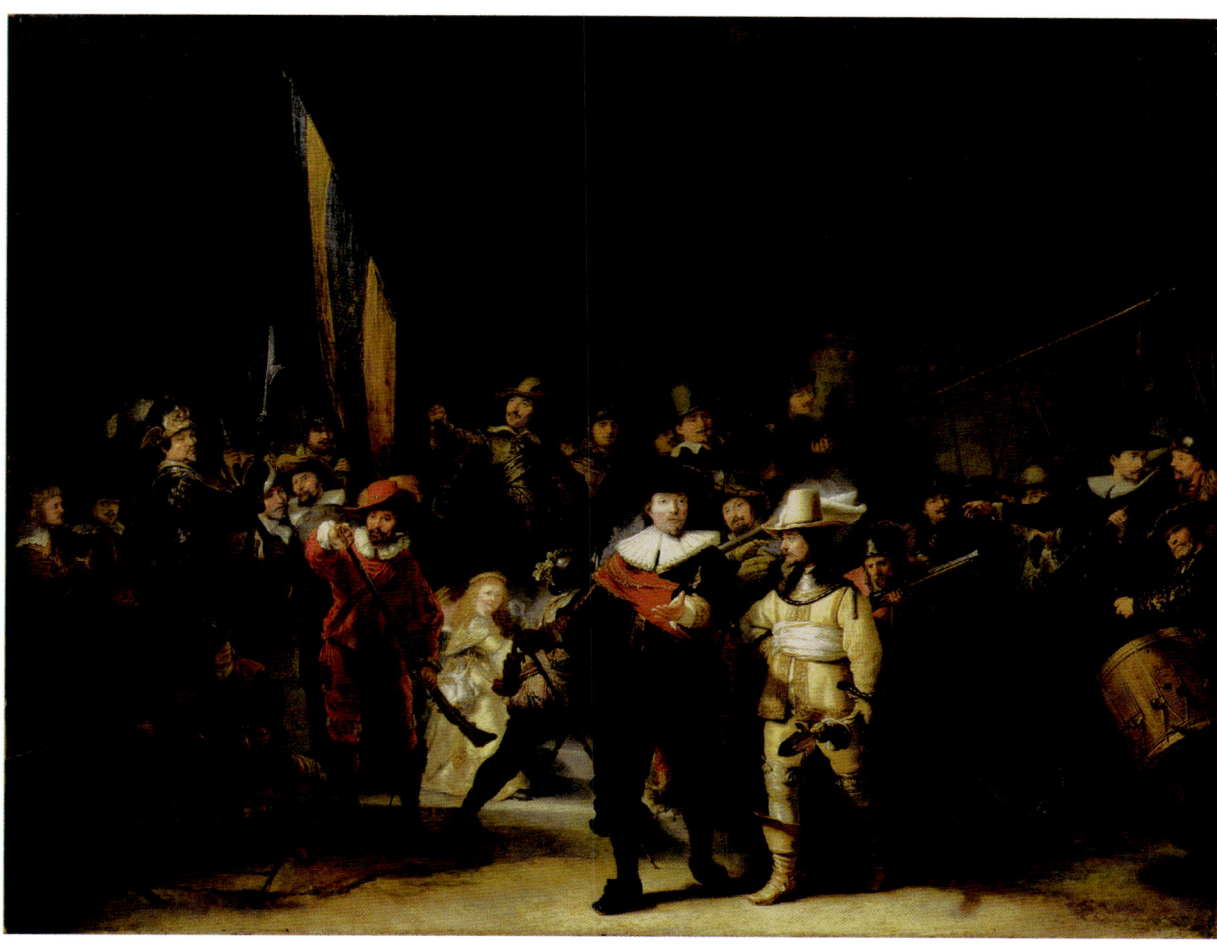

25-13 REMBRANDT VAN RIJN, *The Company of Captain Frans Banning Cocq* (*Night Watch*), 1642. Oil on canvas, 11′ 11″ × 14′ 4″ (trimmed from original size). Rijksmuseum, Amsterdam.

Rembrandt's dramatic use of light contributes to the animation of this militia group portrait in which the artist showed the company members rushing to organize themselves for a parade.

1 ft.

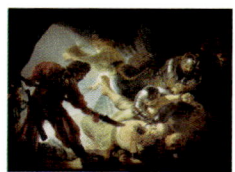

25-13A REMBRANDT, *Blinding of Samson*, 1636.

religious art of Baroque Italy and Flanders. Rembrandt had a special interest in probing the states of the human soul. The spiritual stillness of his later religious paintings is that of inward-turning contemplation, far from the choirs and trumpets and the heavenly tumult of Bernini (FIG. 24-7) or Pozzo (FIG. 24-24).

The Dutch artist's psychological insight and his profound sympathy for human affliction produced, at the end of his life, one of the most moving pictures in all religious art, *Return of the Prodigal Son* (FIG. 25-14). In this biblical parable, the younger of two sons leaves his home and squanders his wealth on a life of sin. When he becomes poor and hungry and sees the error of his ways, he returns home. In Rembrandt's painting, the forgiving father tenderly embraces his lost son, who crouches before him in weeping contrition, while three figures, immersed to varying degrees in the soft shadows, note the lesson of mercy. The light, everywhere mingled with shadow, directs the viewer's attention by illuminating the father and son and largely veiling the witnesses. Its focus is the beautiful, spiritual face of the old man. Secondarily, the light touches the contrasting stern face of the foremost witness. The painting demonstrates the degree to which Rembrandt developed a personal style completely in tune with the simple eloquence of the biblical passage.

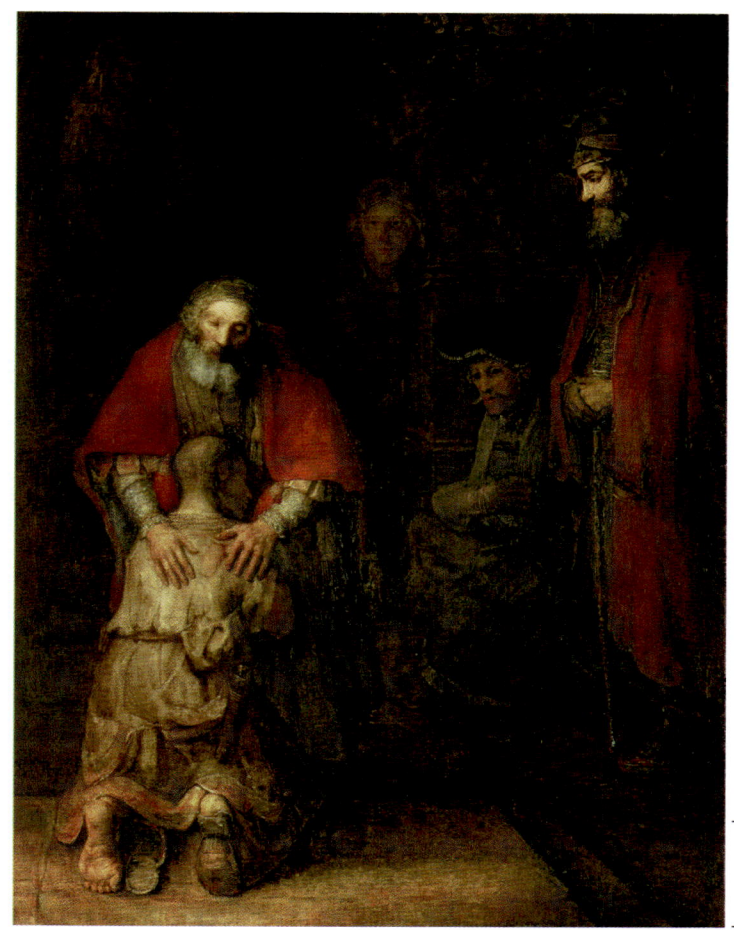

25-14 REMBRANDT VAN RIJN, *Return of the Prodigal Son*, ca. 1665. Oil on canvas, 8′ 8″ × 6′ 9″. Hermitage Museum, Saint Petersburg.

The spiritual stillness of Rembrandt's religious paintings is that of inward-turning contemplation, in vivid contrast to the heavenly tumult of Italian Baroque Counter-Reformation works.

1 ft.

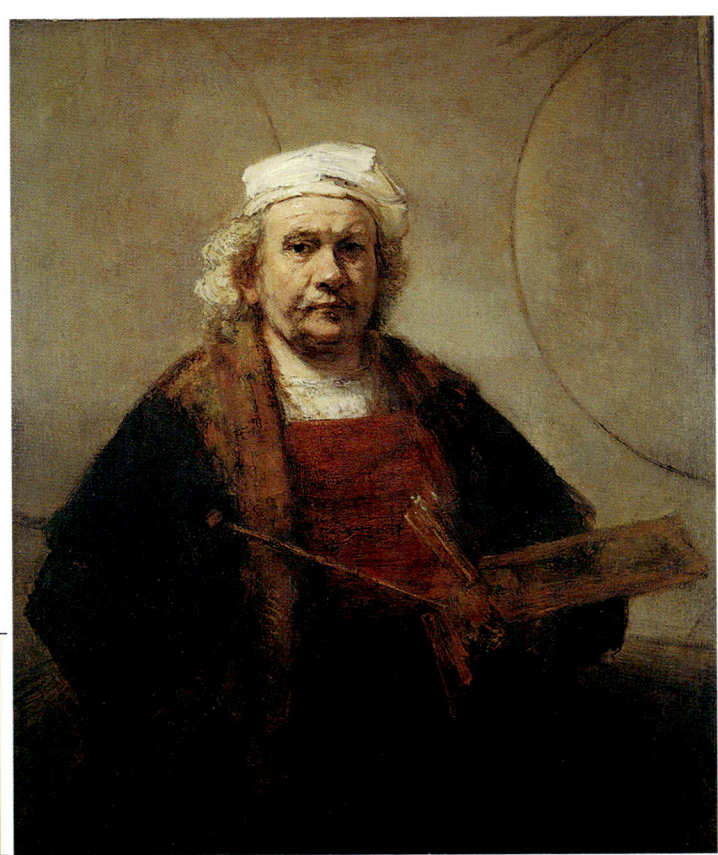

**25-15** REMBRANDT VAN RIJN, *Self-Portrait,* ca. 1659–1660. Oil on canvas, 3′ 8¾″ × 3′ 1″. Kenwood House, London (Iveagh Bequest). ◼◀

In this late self-portrait, Rembrandt's interest in revealing the soul is evident in the attention given to his expressive face. The controlled use of light and the nonspecific setting contribute to this focus.

**GRADATIONS OF LIGHT** From the few paintings by Rembrandt discussed thus far, it should be clear the artist's use of light is among the hallmarks of his style. Rembrandt's pictorial method involved refining light and shade into finer and finer nuances until they blended with one another. Earlier painters' use of abrupt lights and darks gave way, in the work of artists such as Rembrandt and Velázquez (FIGS. 24-28 to 24-30), to gradation. Although these later artists sacrificed some of the dramatic effects of sharp chiaroscuro, a greater fidelity to appearances more than offsets those sacrifices. In fact, the recording of light in small gradations is closer to reality because the eye perceives light and dark not as static but as always subtly changing.

In general, Renaissance artists represented forms and faces in a flat, neutral modeling light (even Leonardo's shading is of a standard kind). They represented the *idea* of light, rather than showed how humans perceive light. Artists such as Rembrandt discovered gradations of light and dark as well as degrees of differences in pose, in the movements of facial features, and in psychic states. They arrived at these differences optically, not conceptually or in terms of some ideal. Rembrandt found that by manipulating the direction, intensity, and distance of light and shadow, and by varying the surface texture with tactile brushstrokes, he could render subtle nuances of character and mood, both in individuals and whole scenes. He discovered for the modern world that variation of light and shade, subtly modulated, can be read as emotional differences. In the visible world, light, dark, and the wide spectrum of values

between the two are charged with meanings and feelings that sometimes are independent of the shapes and figures they modify. The theater and the photographic arts have used these discoveries to great dramatic effect.

**SELF-PORTRAITS** Rembrandt carried over the spiritual quality of his religious works into his later portraits (FIGS. **25-15** and **25-15A**) by the same means—what could be called the "psychology of light." Light and dark are not in conflict in his portraits. They are reconciled, merging softly and subtly to produce the visual equivalent of quietness. Their prevailing mood is one of tranquil meditation, of philosophical resignation, of musing recollection—indeed, a whole cluster of emotional tones heard only in silence.

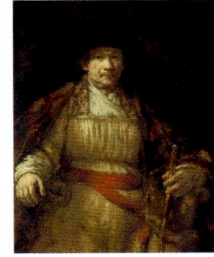

**25-15A** REMBRANDT, *Self-Portrait,* 1658.

In his self-portrait now in Kenwood House (FIG. 25-15), the light source outside the upper left of the painting bathes the painter's face in soft highlights, leaving the lower part of his body in shadow. The artist depicted himself as possessing dignity and strength, and the portrait serves as a summary of the many stylistic and professional concerns that occupied him throughout his career. Rembrandt's distinctive use of light is evident, as is the assertive brushwork suggesting his confidence and self-assurance. He presented himself as a working artist holding his brushes, palette, and maulstick (compare FIG. 23-18) and wearing his studio garb—a smock and painter's turban. The circles on the wall behind him (the subject of much scholarly debate) may allude to a legendary sign of artistic virtuosity—the ability to draw a perfect circle freehand. Rembrandt's abiding interest in revealing the human soul emerges here in his careful focus on his expressive visage. His controlled use of light and the nonspecific setting contribute to this focus. Further, X-rays of the painting have revealed that Rembrandt originally depicted himself in the act of painting. His final resolution, with the viewer's attention drawn to his face, produced a portrait not just of the artist but of the man as well. Indeed, Rembrandt's nearly 70 self-portraits in various media have no parallel in sheer quantity. They reflect the artist's deeply personal connection to his craft.

**ETCHINGS** Rembrandt's virtuosity also extended to the graphic media, especially etching (see "Woodcuts, Engravings, and Etchings," Chapter 20, page 556). Many printmakers adopted etching after its perfection early in the 17th century, because the technique afforded greater freedom than engraving in drawing the design. The etcher covers a copper plate with a layer of wax or varnish, and then incises the design into this surface with a pointed tool, exposing the metal below but not cutting into its surface. Next, the artist immerses the plate in acid, which etches, or eats away, the exposed parts of the metal, acting in the same way the burin does in engraving. The medium's softness gives etchers greater carving freedom than woodcutters and engravers have working directly in more resistant wood and metal. If Rembrandt had never painted, he still would be renowned, as he principally was in his lifetime, for his prints. Prints were a major source of income for Rembrandt, as they were for Albrecht Dürer (see Chapter 23), and he often reworked the plates so they could be used to produce a new issue or edition. This constant reworking was unusual within the context of 17th-century printmaking practices.

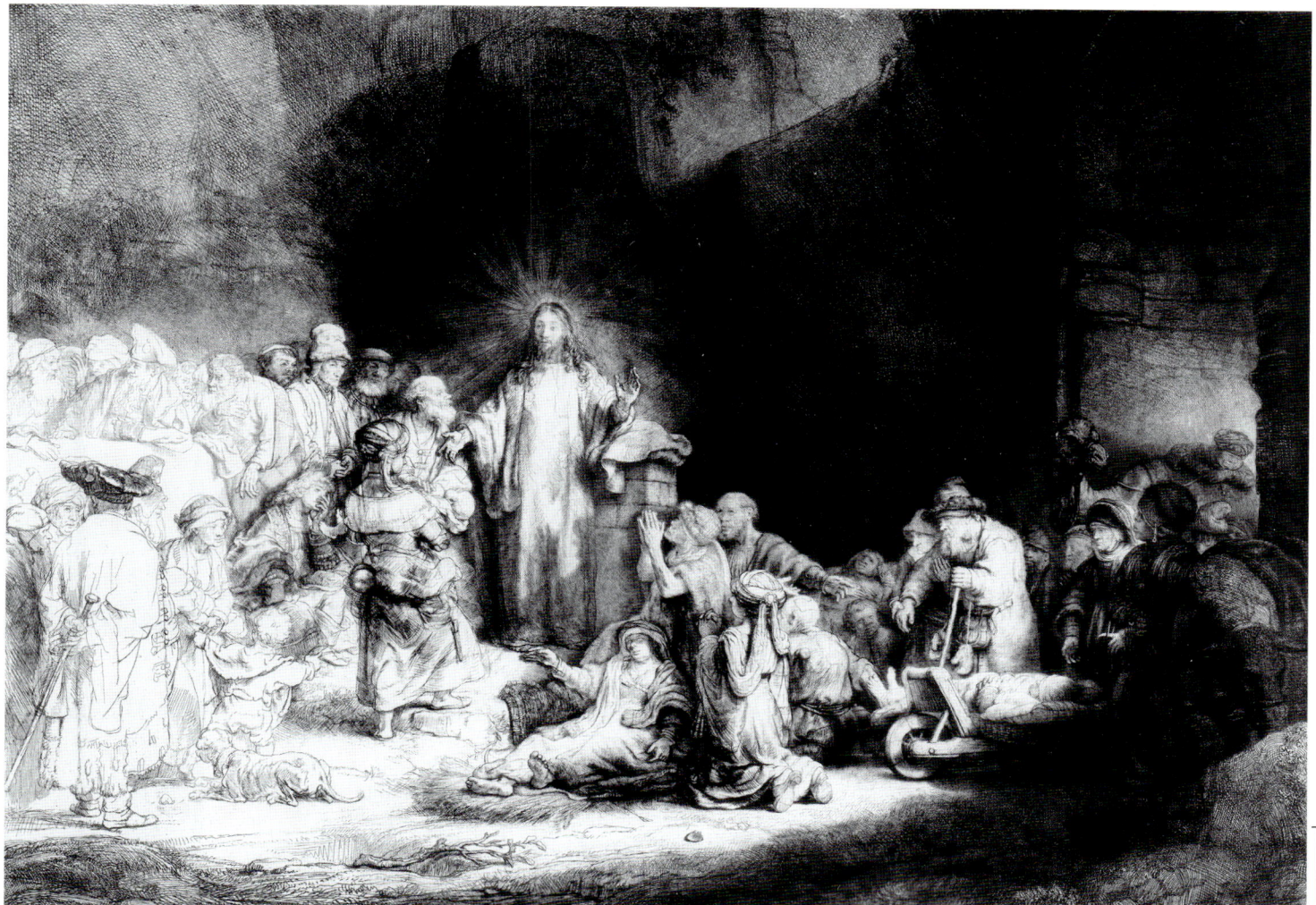

**25-16** REMBRANDT VAN RIJN, *Christ with the Sick around Him, Receiving the Children* (*Hundred-Guilder Print*), ca. 1649. Etching, 11″ × 1′ 3¼″. Pierpont Morgan Library, New York.

Rembrandt's mastery of the newly perfected medium of etching is evident in his expert use of light and dark to draw attention to Christ as he preaches compassionately to the blind and lame.

*HUNDRED-GUILDER PRINT* One of Rembrandt's most celebrated etchings is *Christ with the Sick around Him, Receiving the Children* (FIG. **25-16**). Indeed, the title by which this work has been known since the early 18th century, *Hundred-Guilder Print,* refers to the high sale price it brought during Rembrandt's lifetime. (As noted, a comfortable house could be purchased for 1,000 guilders.) *Christ with the Sick* demonstrates the artist's mastery of all aspects of the printmaker's craft, for Rembrandt used both engraving and etching to depict the figures and the setting. As in his other religious works, Rembrandt suffused this print with a deep and abiding piety, presenting the viewer not the celestial triumph of the Catholic Church but the humanity and humility of Jesus. Christ appears in the center preaching compassionately to, and simultaneously blessing, the blind, the lame, and the young, who are spread throughout the composition in a dazzling array of standing, kneeling, and lying positions. Also present is a young man in elegant garments with his head in his hand, lamenting Christ's insistence that the wealthy need to give their possessions to the poor in order to gain entrance to Heaven. The tonal range of the print is remarkable. At the right, the figures near the city gate are in deep shadow. At the left, the figures, some rendered almost exclusively in outline, are in bright light—not the light of day but the illumination radiating from Christ himself. A second, unseen source of light comes from the right and casts the shadow of the praying man's arms and head onto Christ's tunic. Technically and in terms of its humanity, *Hundred-Guilder Print* is Rembrandt's supreme achievement as a printmaker.

## Cuyp and Ruisdael

Due to topography and politics, the Dutch had a unique relationship to the land, one that differed from attitudes of people living in other European countries. After gaining independence from Spain, the Dutch undertook an extensive reclamation project lasting almost a century. Dikes and drainage systems cropped up across the countryside. Because of the effort expended on these endeavors, the Dutch developed a distinctly direct relationship to the land. The reclamation also affected Dutch social and economic life. The marshy and swampy nature of much of the terrain made it less desirable for large-scale exploitation, so the extensive feudal landowning system elsewhere in Europe never developed in the United Provinces. Most Dutch families owned and worked their own farms, cultivating a feeling of closeness to the land. Consequently, landscape scenes abound in 17th-century Dutch art.

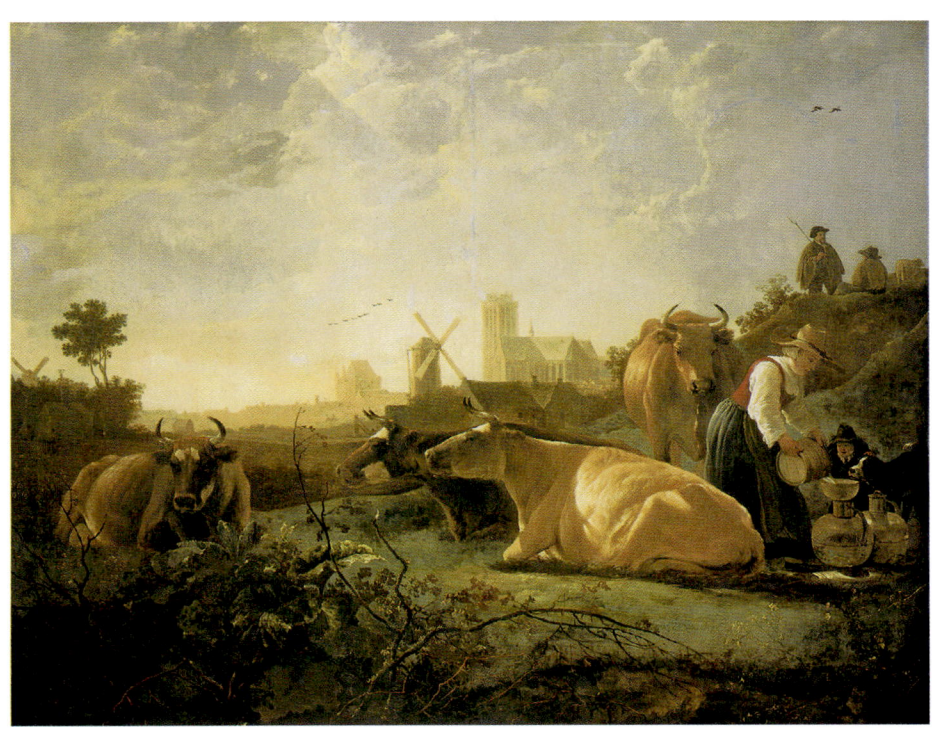

**25-17** Aelbert Cuyp, *Distant View of Dordrecht, with a Milkmaid and Four Cows, and Other Figures (The "Large Dort")*, late 1640s. Oil on canvas, 5′ 1″ × 6′ 4⅞″. National Gallery, London.

Unlike idealized Italian Renaissance landscapes, Cuyp's painting portrays a particular locale. The cows, shepherds, and milkmaid refer to the Dutch Republic's important dairy industry.

**AELBERT CUYP** One Dutch artist who established his reputation as a specialist in landscape painting was AELBERT CUYP (ca. 1620–1691). His works were the products of careful observation and a deep respect for and understanding of Dutch topography. *Distant View of Dordrecht, with a Milkmaid and Four Cows, and Other Figures* (FIG. **25-17**) reveals Cuyp's substantial skills. Unlike the idealized classical landscapes in many Italian Renaissance paintings, this landscape is particularized. The church in the background, for example, is a faithful representation of the Grote Kerk in Dordrecht. The dairy cows, shepherds, and milkmaid in the foreground refer to a cornerstone of Dutch agriculture—the demand for dairy products such as butter and cheese, which increased with the development of urban centers. The credibility of this and similar paintings rests on Cuyp's pristine rendering of each detail.

**JACOB VAN RUISDAEL** Depicting the Dutch landscape with precision and sensitivity was also a specialty of JACOB VAN RUISDAEL (ca. 1628–1682). In *View of Haarlem from the Dunes at Overveen* (FIG. **25-18**), Ruisdael provided an overarching view of this major Dutch city. The specificity of the artist's image—the Saint Bavo church in the background, the numerous windmills that refer to the land reclamation efforts, and the figures in the foreground stretching linen to be bleached (a major industry in Haarlem)—reflects the pride Dutch painters took in recording their homeland and the activities of their fellow citizens. Nonetheless, in this painting the inhabitants and dwellings are so minuscule they blend into the land itself, unlike the figures in Cuyp's view of Dordrecht. Moreover, the horizon line is low, so the sky fills almost three-quarters of the picture space, and the sun illuminates the landscape only in patches, where

it has broken through the clouds above. In *View of Haarlem*, Ruisdael not only captured the appearance of a specific locale but also succeeded in imbuing the work with a quiet serenity that is almost spiritual. Less typical of his work, but also one of the great landscape paintings of the 17th century, is Ruisdael's allegorical *Jewish Cemetery* (FIG. **25-18A**).

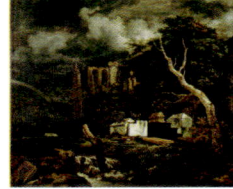

**25-18A** RUISDAEL, *Jewish Cemetery*, ca. 1655–1660.

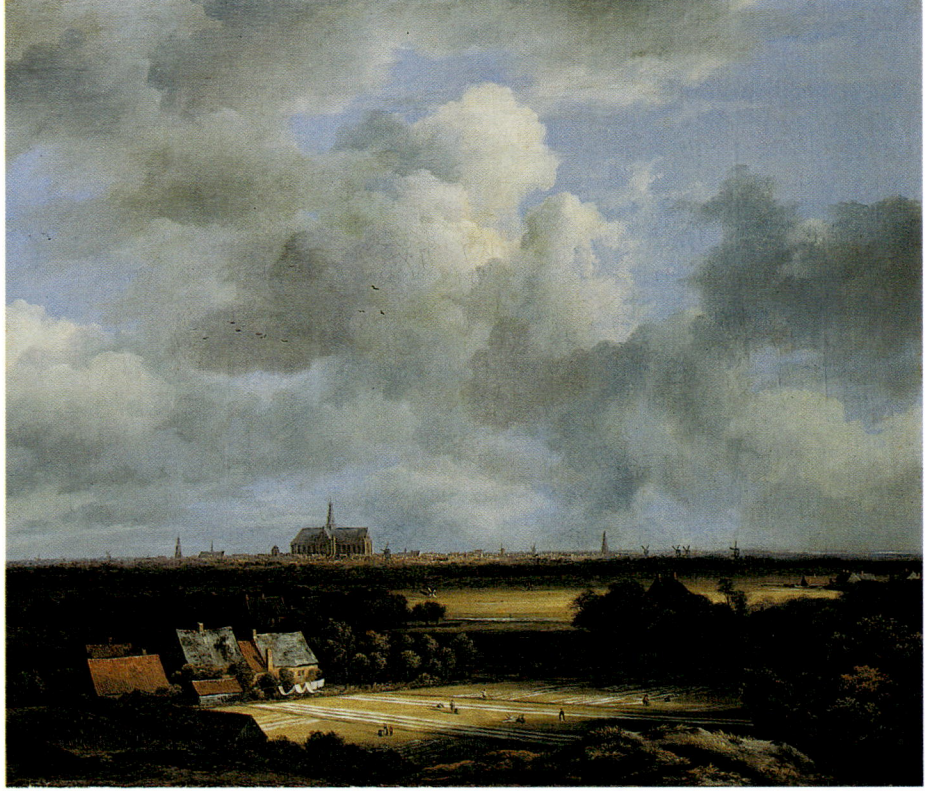

**25-18** Jacob van Ruisdael, *View of Haarlem from the Dunes at Overveen*, ca. 1670. Oil on canvas, 1′ 10″ × 2′ 1″. Mauritshuis, The Hague.

In this painting, Ruisdael succeeded in capturing a specific, realistic view of Haarlem, its windmills, and Saint Bavo church, but he also imbued the landscape with a quiet serenity approaching the spiritual.

## Vermeer

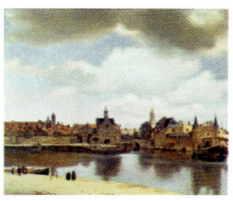

**25-18B** Vermeer, *View of Delft,* ca. 1661.

Although he also painted landscapes, such as *View of Delft* (FIG. **25-18B**), JAN VERMEER (1632–1675) made his reputation as a painter of interior scenes, another popular subject among middle-class patrons. These paintings offer the viewer glimpses into the private lives of prosperous, responsible, and cultured citizens of the United Provinces. Despite his fame as a painter today, Vermeer derived much of his income from his work as an innkeeper and art dealer in Delft (see "Middle-Class Patronage and the Art Market," page 703), and he completed no more than 35 paintings that can be definitively attributed to him. He began his career as a painter of biblical and historical themes but soon abandoned those traditional subjects in favor of domestic scenes. Flemish artists of the 15th century also had painted domestic interiors, but sacred personages often occupied those scenes (for example, FIG. 20-1). In contrast, Vermeer and his contemporaries composed neat, quietly opulent interiors of Dutch middle-class dwellings with men, women, and children engaging in household tasks or at leisure. Women are the primary occupants of Vermeer's homes, and his paintings are highly idealized depictions of the social values of Dutch burghers.

**WOMAN HOLDING A BALANCE** In one of Vermeer's finest canvases, *Woman Holding a Balance* (FIG. **25-19**), a beautiful young woman wearing a veil and a fur-trimmed jacket stands in a room in her home. Light coming from a window illuminates the scene, as in many of the artist's paintings. The woman stands before a table on which are spread her most precious possessions—pearl necklaces, gold chains, and gold coins, which reflect the sunlight that also shines on the woman's face and the fingers of her right hand. In fact, the perspective orthogonals direct the viewer's attention neither to the woman's head nor to her treasures but to the hand in which she holds a balance for weighing gold. The scales, however, are empty—in perfect balance, the way Ignatius of Loyola advised Catholics (Vermeer was a Catholic convert in the Protestant Dutch Republic) to lead a temperate, self-aware life and to balance one's sins with virtuous behavior. The mirror on the wall may refer to self-knowledge, but it may also symbolize, as do the pearls and gold, the sin of vanity. Bolstering that interpretation is the large framed *Last Judgment* painting on the back wall in which Christ, weigher of souls, appears in a golden aureole directly above the young woman's head. Therefore, this serene domestic scene is pregnant with hidden meaning. The woman holds the scales in balance and contemplates the kind of life (one free from the temptations of worldly riches) she must lead in order to be judged favorably on judgment day.

Vermeer, like Rembrandt, was a master of pictorial light and used it with immense virtuosity. He could render space so convincingly through his depiction of light that in his works the picture surface functions as an invisible glass pane through which the viewer looks into the constructed illusion. Art historians believe Vermeer used as tools both mirrors and the *camera obscura,* an ancestor of the modern camera based on passing light through a tiny pinhole or lens to project an image on a screen or the wall of a room. (In later versions, artists projected the image on a ground-glass wall of a box whose opposite wall contained the pinhole or lens.) Vermeer did not simply copy the camera's image, however. Instead, the camera obscura and the mirrors helped him obtain results he reworked compositionally, placing his figures and the furniture of a room in a beautiful stability of quadrilateral shapes. Vermeer's compositions evoke a matchless classical serenity. Enhancing this quality are colors so true to the optical facts and so subtly modulated they suggest Vermeer was far ahead of his time in color science. For example, Vermeer realized shadows are not colorless and dark, adjoining colors affect each other, and light is composed of colors. Thus, he painted reflections off of surfaces in colors modified by others nearby. Some scholars have suggested Vermeer also perceived the phenomenon modern photographers call "circles of confusion," which appear on out-of-focus negatives. Vermeer could have seen them in images projected by the camera obscura's primitive lenses. He approximated these effects with light dabs that, in close view, give the impression of an image slightly "out of focus." When the observer draws back a step, however, as if adjusting the lens, the color spots cohere, giving an astonishingly accurate illusion of the third dimension.

**25-19** JAN VERMEER, *Woman Holding a Balance,* ca. 1664. Oil on canvas, 1' 3$\frac{5}{8}$" × 1' 2". National Gallery of Art, Washington, D.C. (Widener Collection).

Vermeer's woman holding empty scales in perfect balance, ignoring pearls and gold on the table, is probably an allegory of the temperate life. On the wall behind her is a *Last Judgment* painting.

1 in.

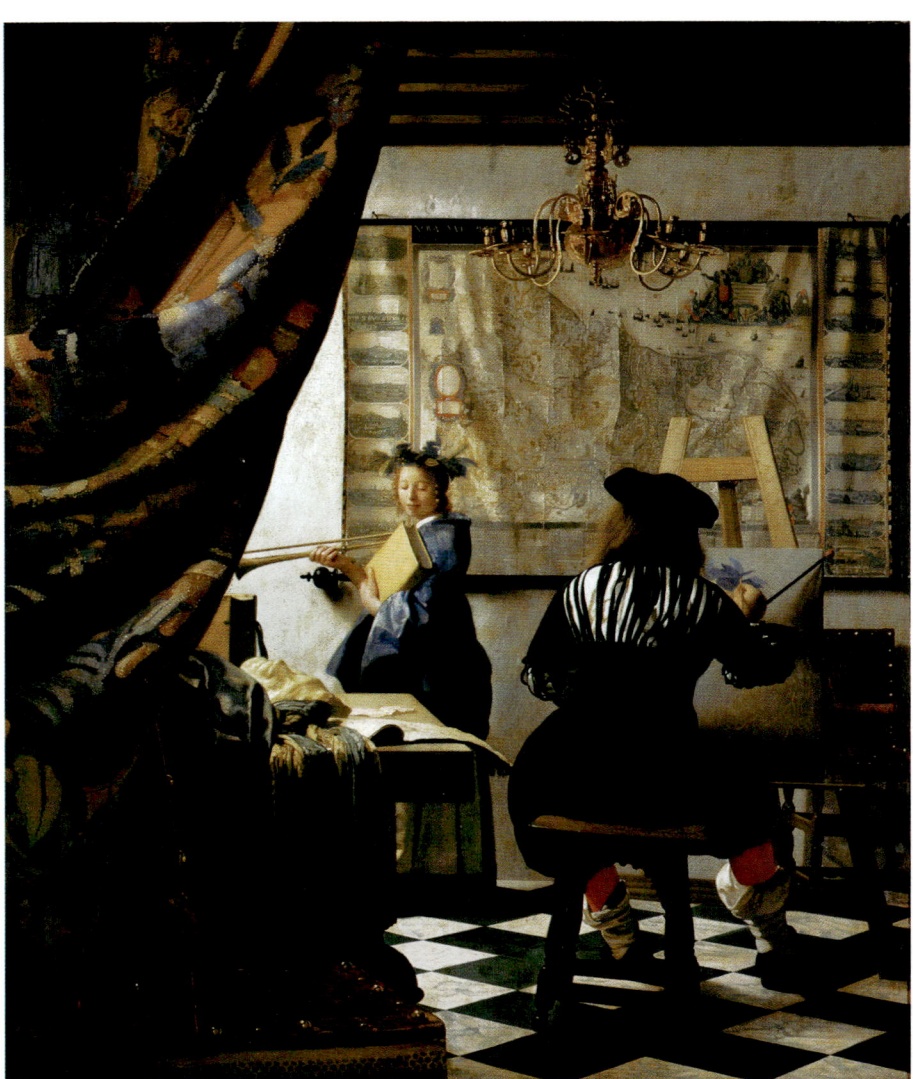

**THE ART OF PAINTING** Vermeer's stylistic precision and commitment to his profession are evident in *Allegory of the Art of Painting* (FIG. **25-20**). The artist himself appears in the painting, with his back to the viewer and dressed in "historical" clothing (reminiscent of Burgundian attire). He is hard at work on a painting of the model standing before him wearing a laurel wreath and holding a trumpet and book, traditional attributes of Clio, the muse of history. The map of the provinces (an increasingly common wall adornment in Dutch homes) on the back wall serves as yet another reference to history. As

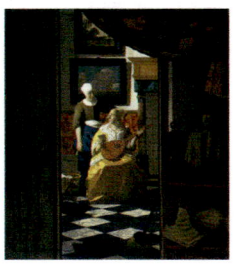

in *Woman Holding a Balance* and *The Letter* (FIG. **25-20A**), another of Vermeer's domestic scenes, the viewer is outside the space of the action, looking in through the drawn curtain, which also separates the artist in his studio from the rest of the house. Some

**25-20A** VERMEER, *The Letter*, 1666.

art historians have suggested the light radiating from an unseen window on the left, illuminating both the model and the canvas being painted, alludes to the light of artistic inspiration. Accordingly, many scholars have interpreted this painting as an allegory—a reference to painting inspired by history. Vermeer's mother-in-law confirmed this allegorical reading in 1677 while seeking to retain the painting after the artist's death, when 26 of his works were scheduled to be sold to pay his widow's debts. She listed the painting in her written claim as "the piece . . . wherein the Art of Painting is portrayed."[3]

## Steen

Whereas Vermeer's paintings reveal the charm and beauty of Dutch domesticity, the works of JAN STEEN (ca. 1625–1679) provide a counterpoint. In *Feast of Saint Nicholas* (FIG. **25-21**), instead of depicting a tidy, calm Dutch household, Steen opted for a scene of chaos and disruption. Saint Nicholas has just visited this residence, and the children are in an uproar as they search their shoes for the

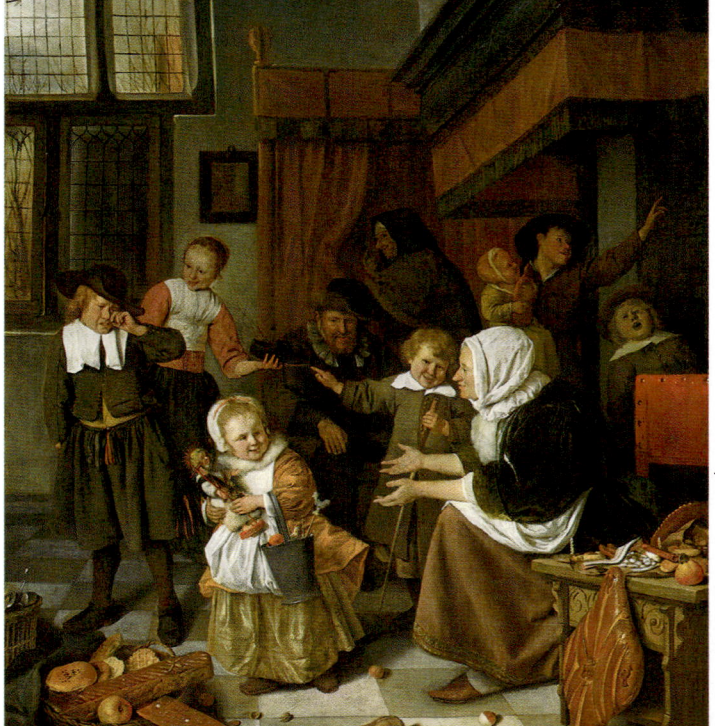

Christmas gifts he has left. Some children are delighted. The little girl in the center clutches her gifts, clearly unwilling to share with the other children despite her mother's pleas. Others are disappointed. The boy on the left is in tears because he received only a birch rod. An appropriately festive atmosphere reigns, which contrasts sharply with the decorum prevailing in Vermeer's works. As do the paintings of other Dutch artists, Steen's lively scenes often take on an allegorical dimension and moralistic tone. Steen frequently used children's activities as satirical comments on foolish adult behavior. *Feast of Saint Nicholas* is not his only allusion to selfishness, pettiness, and jealousy.

## Kalf and Ruysch

As already discussed (see "Still-Life Painting in the Dutch Republic," page 695), Dutch patrons had a keen interest in still lifes. In addition to Peter Claesz (FIG. 25-1), the leading Dutch still-life painters included Willem Kalf and Rachel Ruysch.

**WILLEM KALF** As Dutch prosperity increased, precious objects and luxury items made their way into still-life paintings. *Still Life with a Late Ming Ginger Jar* (FIG. **25-22**) by WILLEM KALF (1619–1693) reflects the wealth Dutch citizens had accrued and the painter's exquisite skills, both technical and aesthetic. Kalf highlighted the breadth of Dutch maritime trade through his depiction of the Indian floral carpet and the Chinese jar used to store ginger (a luxury item). He delighted in recording the lustrous sheen of fabric and the light glinting off reflective surfaces. As is evident in this image, Kalf's works present an array of ornamental objects, such as the Venetian and Dutch glassware and the silver dish. The inclusion of the watch, Mediterranean peach, and peeled lemon suggests this work, like Claesz's *Vanitas Still Life* (FIG. 25-1), is also a vanitas painting, consistent with Calvinist values.

**RACHEL RUYSCH** As living objects that soon die, flowers, particularly cut blossoms, appeared frequently in vanitas paintings. However, floral painting as a distinct genre also flourished in the Dutch Republic. One of the leading practitioners of this art was RACHEL RUYSCH (1663–1750), who from 1708 to 1716 served as court painter to the elector Palatine (the ruler of the Palatinate, a former division of Bavaria) in Düsseldorf, Germany. Ruysch's father was a professor of botany and anatomy, which may account for her interest in and knowledge of plants and insects. She acquired an international reputation for her lush paintings, such as *Flower Still Life* (FIG. **25-23**). In this canvas, the lavish floral arrangement is so full, many of the blossoms seem to be spilling out of the vase. Ruysch's careful arrangement of the painting's elements is evident in her composing the flowers to create a diagonal running from the lower left to the upper right corner of the canvas, offsetting the opposing diagonal of the table edge.

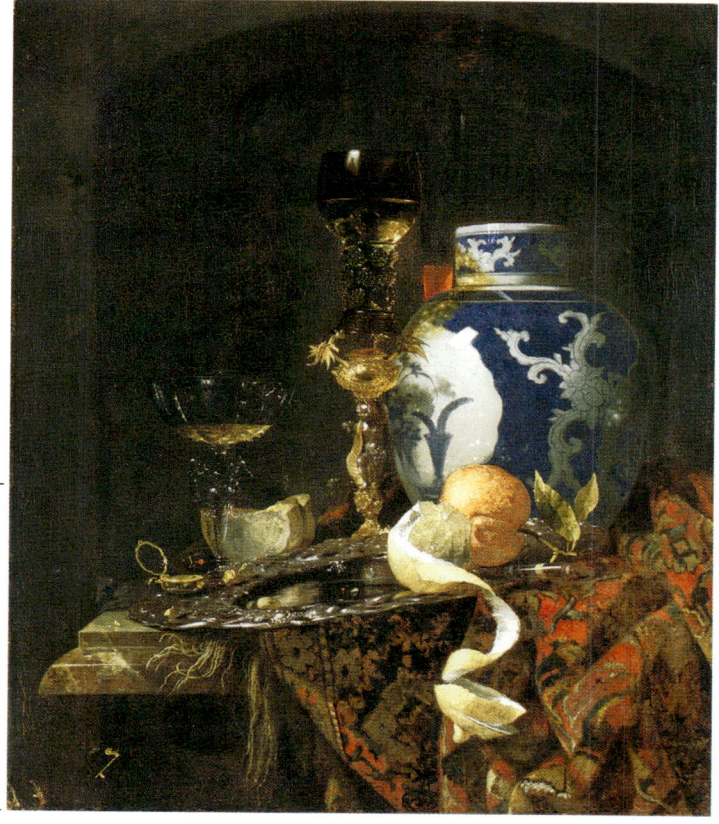

**25-22** WILLEM KALF, *Still Life with a Late Ming Ginger Jar,* 1669. Oil on canvas, 2′ 6″ × 2′ 1¾″. Indianapolis Museum of Art, Indianapolis (gift in commemoration of the 60th anniversary of the Art Association of Indianapolis, in memory of Daniel W. and Elizabeth C. Marmon).

The opulent objects, especially the Indian carpet and Chinese jar, attest to the prosperous Dutch maritime trade. Kalf's inclusion of a watch suggests this painting may be a vanitas still life.

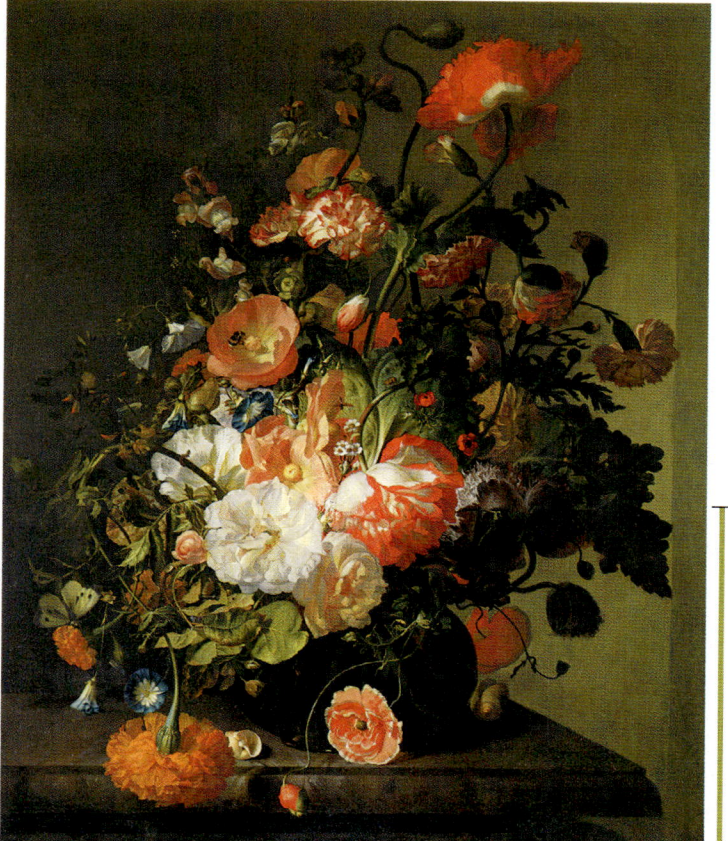

**25-23** RACHEL RUYSCH, *Flower Still Life,* after 1700. Oil on canvas, 2′ 5¾″ × 1′ 11⅞″. Toledo Museum of Art, Toledo (purchased with funds from the Libbey Endowment, gift of Edward Drummond Libbey). ◼◂

Flower paintings were very popular in the Dutch Republic. Ruysch achieved international renown for her lush paintings of floral arrangements, noted also for their careful compositions.

# FRANCE

In France, monarchical authority had been increasing for centuries, culminating in the reign of Louis XIV (r. 1661–1715), who sought to determine the direction of French society and culture. Although its economy was not as expansive as the Dutch Republic's, France became Europe's largest and most powerful nation in the 17th century. Against this backdrop, the arts flourished.

## Louis XIV

The preeminent French art patron of the 17th century was King Louis XIV himself. Determined to consolidate and expand his power, Louis was a master of political strategy and propaganda. He established a carefully crafted and nuanced relationship with the nobility, granting them sufficient benefits to keep them pacified but simultaneously maintaining rigorous control to avoid insurrection or rebellion. He also ensured subservience by anchoring his rule in *divine right* (belief in a king's absolute power as God's will), rendering Louis's authority incontestable. So convinced was Louis of his importance and centrality to the French kingdom that he eagerly adopted the title "le Roi Soleil" ("the Sun King"). Like the sun, Louis XIV was the center of the universe.

The Sun King's desire for control extended to all realms of French life, including art. Louis and his principal adviser, Jean-Baptiste Colbert (1619–1683), strove to organize art and architecture in the service of the state. They understood well the power of art as propaganda and the value of visual imagery for cultivating a public persona, and they spared no pains to raise great symbols and monuments to the king's absolute power. Louis and Colbert sought to regularize taste and establish the classical style as the preferred French manner. The founding of the Royal Academy of Painting and Sculpture in 1648 served to advance this goal.

**PORTRAITURE** Louis XIV maintained a workshop of artists, each with a specialization—for example, faces, fabric, architecture, landscapes, armor, or fur. Thus, many of the king's portraits were a group effort, but the finest is the work of one artist. *Louis XIV*

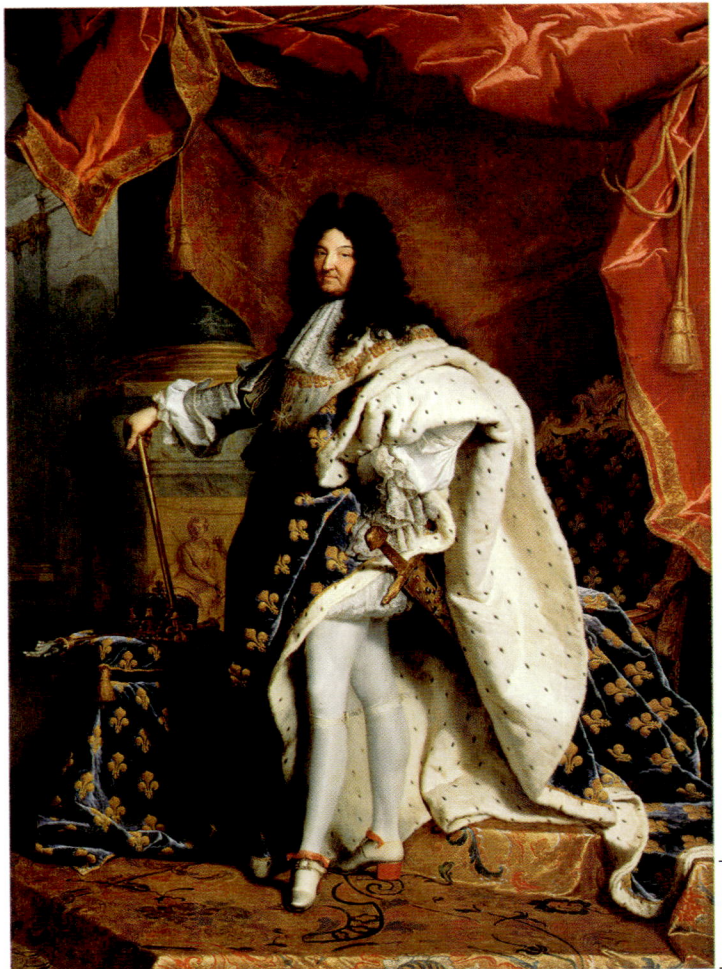

**25-24** HYACINTHE RIGAUD, *Louis XIV*, 1701. Oil on canvas, 9′ 2″ × 6′ 3″. Musée du Louvre, Paris. ◼️

In this portrait set against a stately backdrop, Rigaud portrayed the 5′ 4″ Sun King wearing red high-heeled shoes and with his ermine-lined coronation robes thrown over his left shoulder.

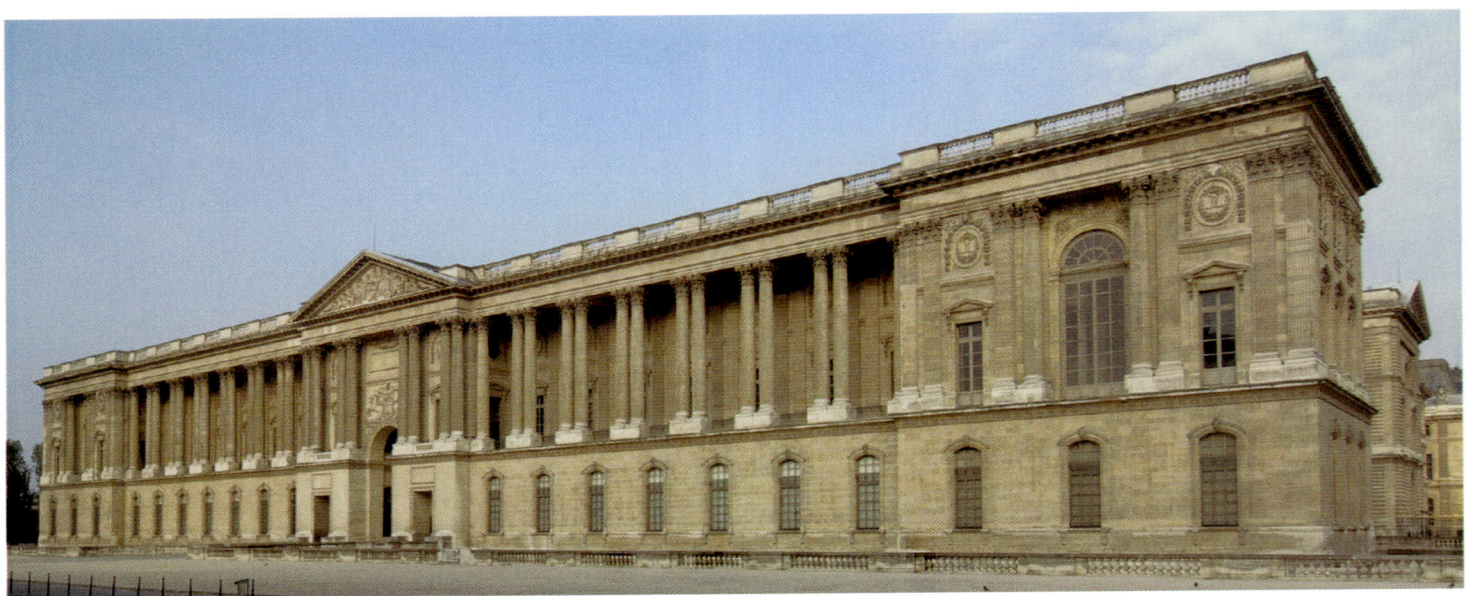

**25-25** CLAUDE PERRAULT, LOUIS LE VAU, and CHARLES LE BRUN, east facade of the Louvre (looking southwest), Paris, France, 1667–1670. ◼️

The design of the Louvre's east facade is a brilliant synthesis of French and Italian classical elements, including a central pavilion resembling an ancient temple front with a pediment.

(FIG. 25-24) by HYACINTHE RIGAUD (1659–1743) successfully conveys the image of an absolute monarch. The king, age 63 when Rigaud painted this work, stands with his left hand on his hip and gazes directly at the viewer. His elegant ermine-lined fleur-de-lis coronation robes (compare FIG. 25-3) hang loosely from his left shoulder, suggesting an air of haughtiness. Louis also draws his garment back to expose his legs. (The king was a ballet dancer in his youth and was proud of his well-toned legs.) The portrait's majesty derives in large part from the composition. The Sun King is the unmistakable focal point of the image, and Rigaud placed him so he seems to look down on the viewer. (Louis XIV was only five feet four inches tall—a fact that drove him to invent the red-heeled shoes he wears in the portrait.) The carefully detailed environment in which the king stands also contributes to the painting's stateliness and grandiosity. Indeed, when the king was not present, Rigaud's portrait, which hung over the throne, served in his place, and courtiers knew never to turn their backs on the painting.

**THE LOUVRE** The first great architectural project Louis XIV and his adviser Colbert undertook was the closing of the east side of the Louvre's Cour Carré (FIG. 23-14), left incomplete by Pierre Lescot in the 16th century. The king summoned Gianlorenzo Bernini (see Chapter 24) from Rome to submit plans, but Bernini envisioned an Italian palace on a monumental scale, which would have involved the demolition of all previous work. His plan rejected, Bernini indignantly returned to Rome. Louis then turned to three

French architects—CLAUDE PERRAULT (1613–1688), LOUIS LE VAU (1612–1670), and CHARLES LE BRUN (1619–1690)—for the Louvre's east facade (FIG. 25-25). The design is a brilliant synthesis of French and Italian classical elements, culminating in a new and definitive formula. The facade has a central and two corner projecting columnar pavilions resting on a stately podium. The central pavilion is in the form of a classical temple front. To either side is a giant colonnade of paired columns, resembling the columned flanks of a temple folded out like wings. The designers favored an even roofline, balustraded and broken only by the central pediment, over the traditional French pyramidal roof of the Louvre's west wing (FIG. 23-14). The emphatically horizontal sweep of the 17th-century facade brushed aside all memory of Gothic verticality. The stately proportions and monumentality of the Baroque design were both an expression of the new official French taste and a symbol of centrally organized authority.

**VERSAILLES PALACE** Work on the Louvre barely had begun when Louis XIV decided to convert a royal hunting lodge at Versailles, south of Paris, into a great palace. He assembled a veritable army of architects, decorators, sculptors, painters, and landscape designers under the general management of Charles Le Brun. In their hands, the conversion of a simple lodge into the palace of Versailles (FIG. 25-26) became the greatest architectural project of the age—a defining statement of French Baroque style and an undeniable symbol of Louis XIV's power and ambition.

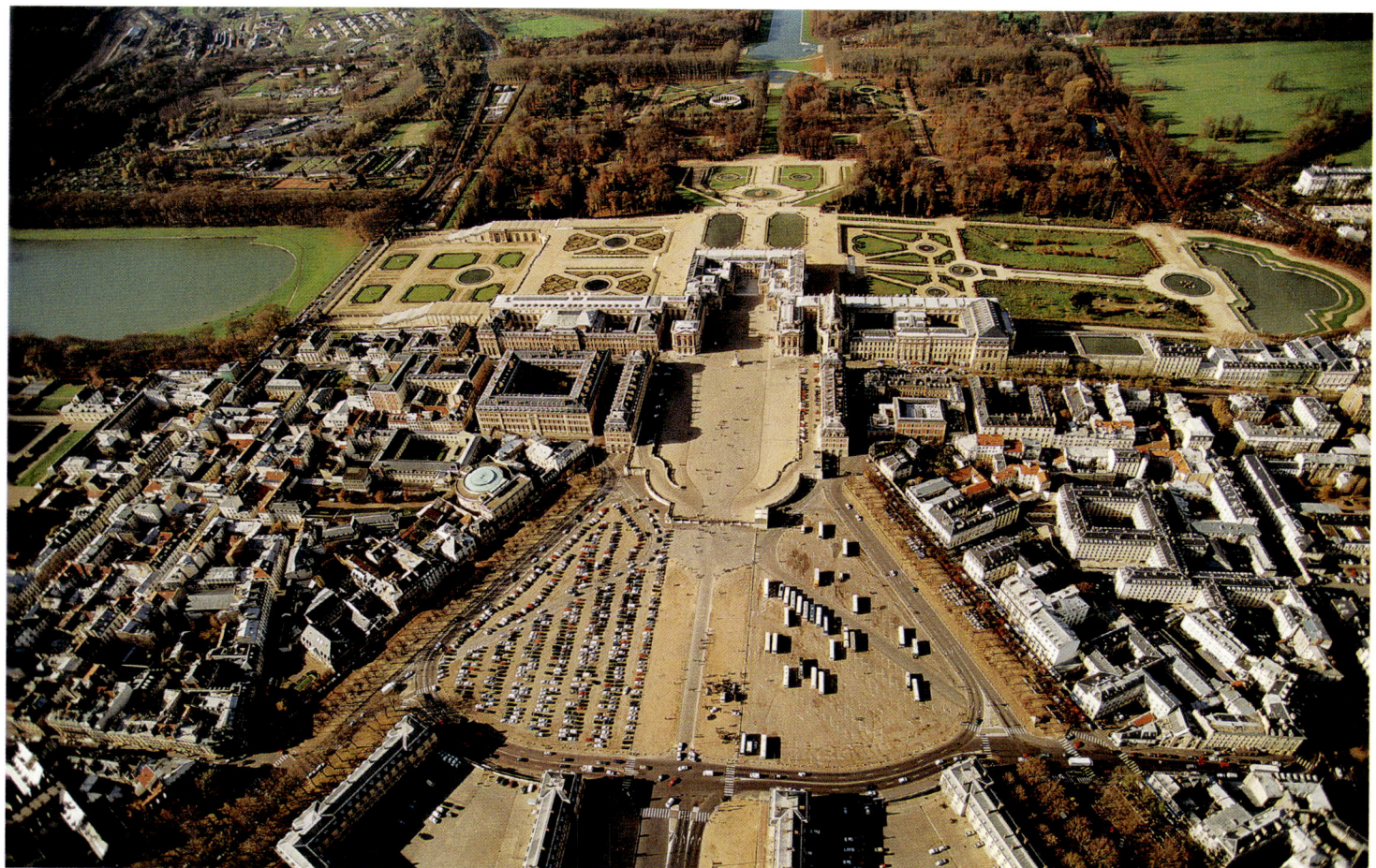

**25-26** JULES HARDOUIN-MANSART, CHARLES LE BRUN, and ANDRÉ LE NÔTRE, aerial view of the palace and gardens (looking northwest), Versailles, France, begun 1669.

Louis XIV ordered his architects to convert a royal hunting lodge at Versailles into a gigantic palace and park with a satellite city whose three radial avenues intersect in the king's bedroom.

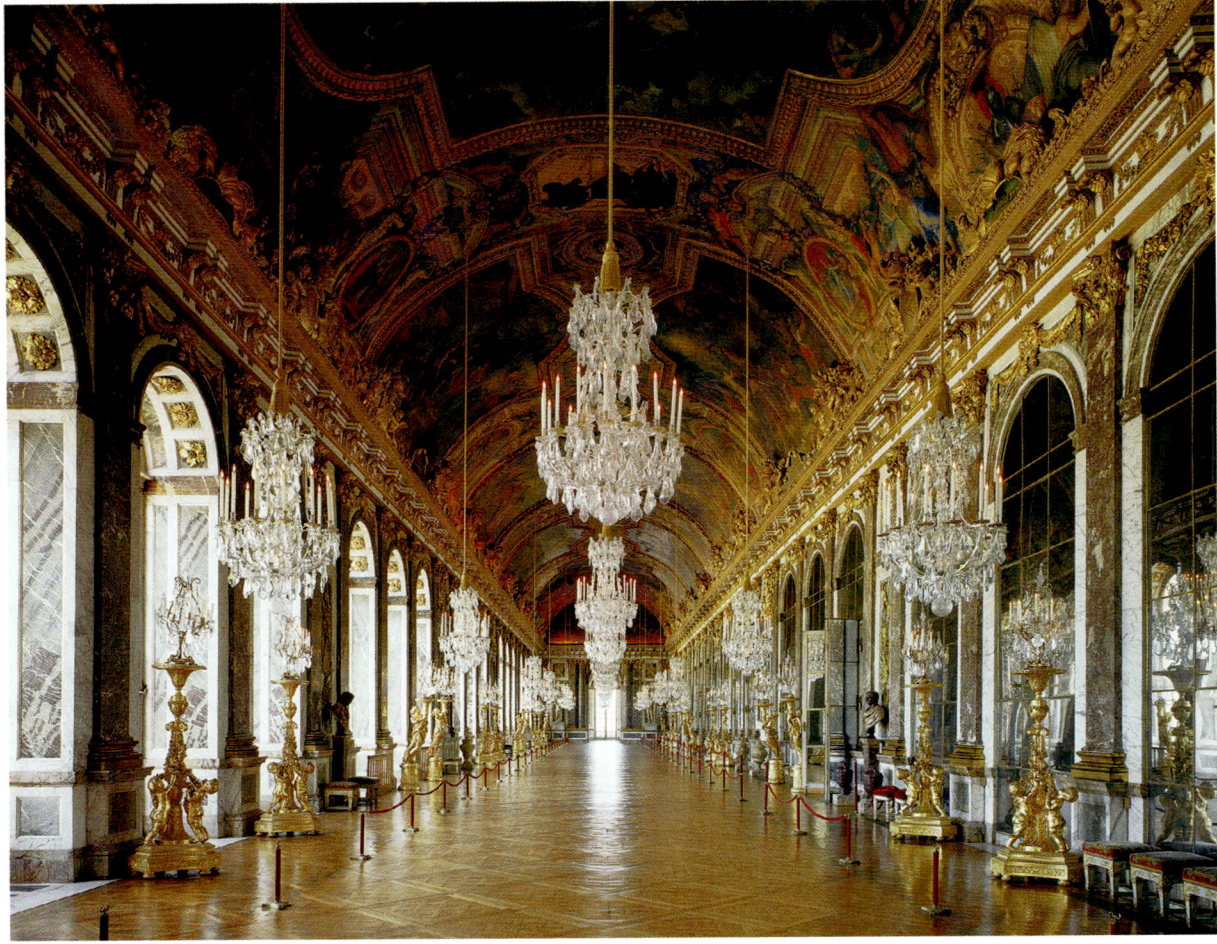

**25-27** Jules Hardouin-Mansart and Charles Le Brun, Galerie des Glaces (Hall of Mirrors), palace of Versailles, Versailles, France, ca. 1680.

This hall overlooks the Versailles park from the second floor of Louis XIV's palace. Hundreds of mirrors illusionistically extend the room's width and once reflected gilded and jeweled furnishings.

Planned on a gigantic scale, the project called not only for a large palace flanking a vast park but also for the construction of a satellite city to house court and government officials, military and guard detachments, courtiers, and servants (undoubtedly to keep them all under the king's close supervision). Le Brun laid out this town to the east of the palace along three radial avenues that converge on the palace. Their axes, in a symbolic assertion of the ruler's absolute power over his domains, intersected in the king's spacious bedroom, which served as an official audience chamber. The palace itself, more than a quarter mile long, is perpendicular to the dominant east-west axis running through the associated city and park.

Every detail of the extremely rich decoration of the palace's interior received careful attention. The architects and decorators designed everything from wall paintings to doorknobs in order to reinforce the splendor of Versailles and to exhibit the very finest sense of artisanship. Of the literally hundreds of rooms within the palace, the most famous is the Galerie des Glaces, or Hall of Mirrors (FIG. **25-27**), designed by Jules Hardouin-Mansart (1646–1708) and Le Brun. This hall overlooks the park from the second floor and extends along most of the width of the central block. Although deprived of its original sumptuous furniture, which included gold and silver chairs and bejeweled trees, the Galerie des Glaces retains much of its splendor today. Hundreds of mirrors, set into the wall opposite the windows, alleviate the hall's tunnel-like quality and illusionistically extend the width of the room. The mirror, that ultimate source of illusion, was a favorite element of Baroque interior design. Here, it also enhanced the dazzling extravagance of the great festivals Louis XIV was so fond of hosting.

**VERSAILLES PARK** The enormous palace might appear unbearably ostentatious were it not for its extraordinary setting in a vast park, which makes the palace seem almost an adjunct. From the Galerie des Glaces, the king and his guests could enjoy a sweeping vista down the park's tree-lined central axis and across terraces, lawns, pools, and lakes toward the horizon. The park of Versailles, designed by André Le Nôtre (1613–1700), must rank among the world's greatest artworks in both size and concept. Here, the French architect transformed an entire forest into a park. Although its geometric plan may appear stiff and formal, the park in fact offers an almost unlimited assortment of vistas, as Le Nôtre used not only the multiplicity of natural forms but also the terrain's slightly rolling contours with stunning effectiveness.

The formal gardens near the palace provide a rational transition from the frozen architectural forms to the natural living ones. Here, the elegant shapes of trimmed shrubs and hedges define the tightly designed geometric units. Each unit is different from its neighbor and has a focal point in the form of a sculptured group, a pavilion, a reflecting pool, or perhaps a fountain. Farther away from the palace, the design loosens as trees, in shadowy masses, screen or frame views of open countryside. Le Nôtre carefully composed all vistas for maximum effect. Light and shadow, formal and informal, dense growth and open meadows—all play against one another in unending combinations and variations. No photograph or series of photographs can reveal the design's full richness. The park unfolds itself only to those walking through it. In this respect, it is a temporal artwork. Its aspects change with the time of day, the seasons, and the relative position of the observer.

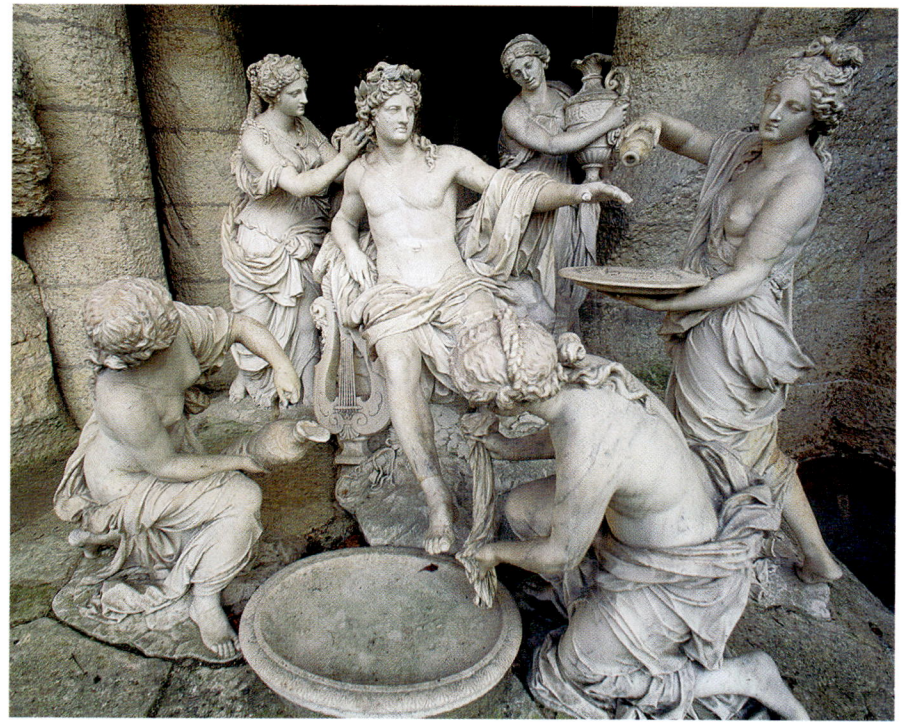

**25-28** FRANÇOIS GIRARDON and THOMAS REGNAUDIN, *Apollo Attended by the Nymphs,* Grotto of Thetis, Park of Versailles, Versailles, France, ca. 1666–1672. Marble, life-size.

Girardon's study of ancient sculpture and Poussin's figure compositions influenced the design of this mythological group in a grotto above a dramatic waterfall in the gardens of Versailles.

**GROTTO OF THETIS** For the Grotto of Thetis above a dramatic waterfall in the gardens of Versailles, FRANÇOIS GIRARDON (1628–1715) designed *Apollo Attended by the Nymphs* (FIG. **25-28**). Both stately and graceful, the nymphs have a compelling charm as they minister to the god Apollo at the end of the day. (The three nymphs in the background are the work of THOMAS REGNAUDIN [1622–1706].) Girardon's close study of Greco-Roman sculpture heavily influenced his design of the figures, and the figure compositions of the most renowned French painter of the era, Nicholas Poussin (FIG. 25-31), inspired their arrangement. Since Apollo was often equated with the sun god (see "The Gods and Goddesses of Mount Olympus," Chapter 5, page 107, or page xxix in Volume II and Book D), the group refers obliquely to Louis XIV as the Roi Soleil. This doubtless helped to assure the work's success at court. Girardon's classical style and mythological symbolism well suited France's glorification of royal majesty.

**ROYAL CHAPEL** In 1698, Hardouin-Mansart received the commission to add a Royal Chapel to the Versailles palace complex. The chapel's interior (FIG. **25-29**) is essentially rectangular, but because its apse is as high as the nave, the fluid central space takes on a curved Baroque quality. However, the light entering through the large clerestory windows lacks the directed dramatic effect of the Italian Baroque, instead illuminating the interior's precisely chiseled details brightly and evenly. Pier-supported arcades carry a majestic row of Corinthian columns defining the royal gallery. The royal pew is at the rear, accessible directly from the king's apartments. Amid the restrained decoration, only the illusionistic ceiling paintings, added in 1708 and 1709 by ANTOINE COYPEL (1661–1722), suggest the drama and complexity of Italian Baroque art.

As a symbol of absolute power, Versailles has no equal. It also expresses, in the most monumental terms of its age, the rationalistic creed—based on scientific advances, such as the physics of Sir Isaac

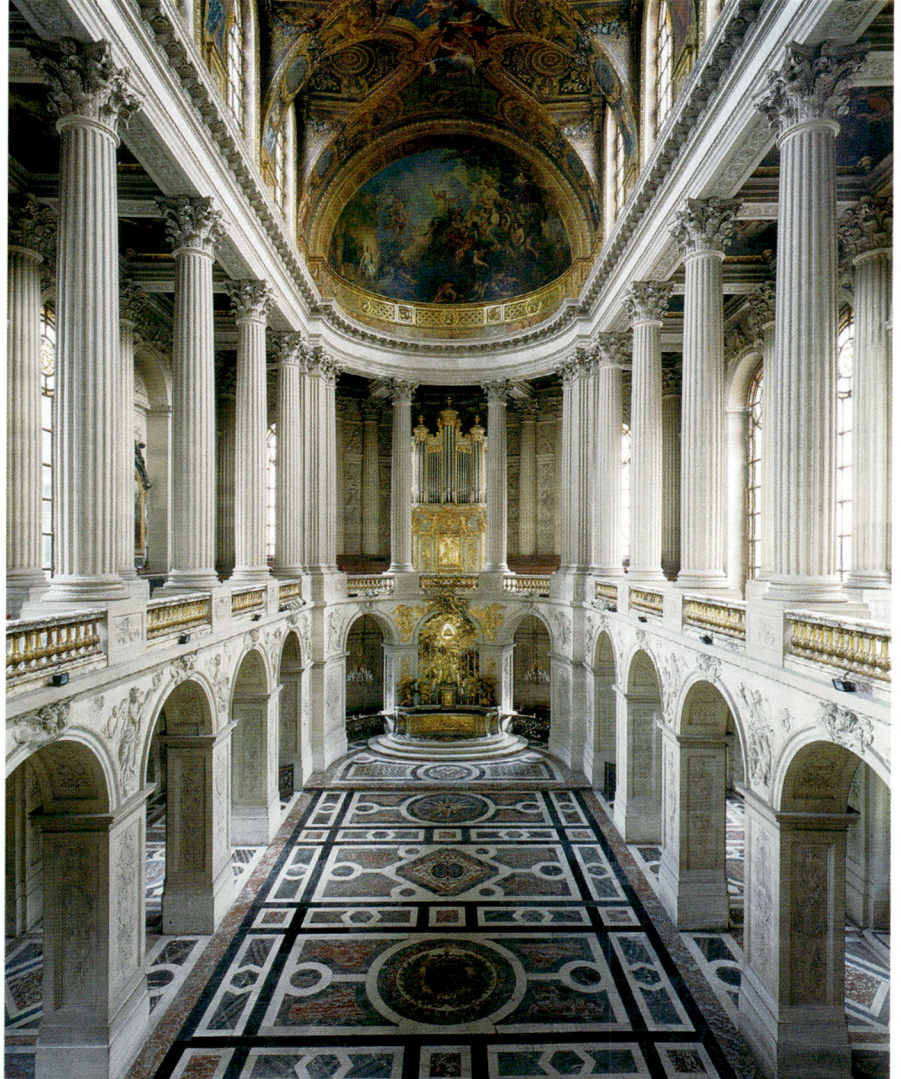

**25-29** JULES HARDOUIN-MANSART, interior of the Royal Chapel, with ceiling decorations by ANTOINE COYPEL, palace of Versailles, Versailles, France, 1698–1710.

Because the apse is as high as the nave, the central space of the Royal Chapel at Versailles has a curved Baroque quality. Louis XIV could reach the royal pew directly from his apartments.

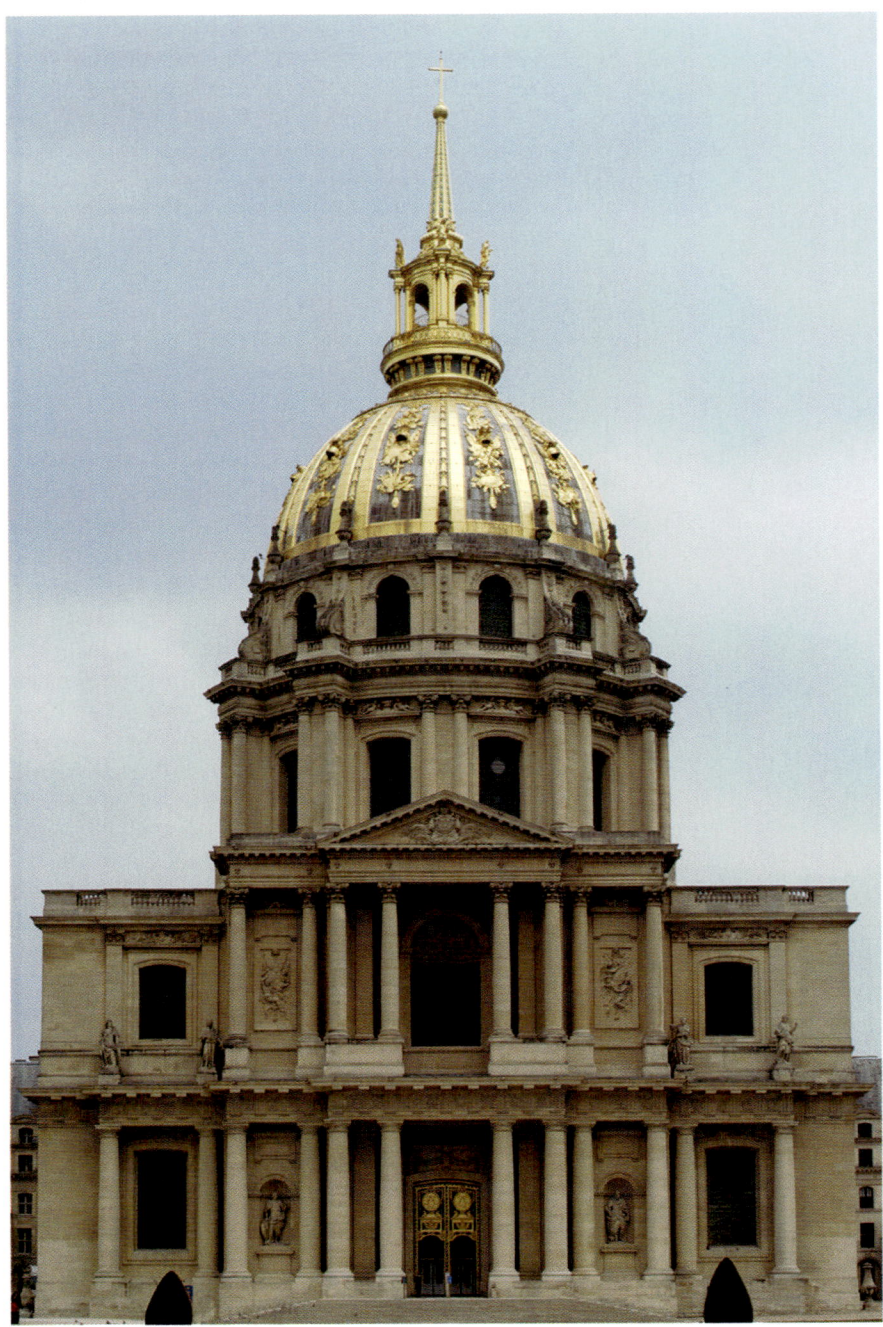

**25-30** JULES HARDOUIN-MANSART, Église du Dôme (looking north), Church of the Invalides, Paris, France, 1676–1706. ◼️

Hardouin-Mansart's church marries the Italian and French architectural styles. The grouping of the orders is similar to the Italian Baroque manner but without the dramatic play of curved surfaces.

established for the disabled soldiers of his many wars. Two firmly separated levels, the upper one capped by a pediment, compose the frontispiece. The grouping of the orders and of the bays they frame is not unlike that in Italian Baroque architecture but without the dramatic play of curved surfaces characteristic of many 17th-century Italian churches, for example, Borromini's San Carlo (FIG. 24-9) in Rome. The compact facade is low and narrow in relation to the vast drum and dome, seeming to serve simply as a base for them. The overpowering dome, conspicuous on the Parisian skyline, is itself expressive of the Baroque love for dramatic magnitude, as is the way its designer aimed for theatrical effects of light and space. The dome consists of three shells, the lowest cut off so a visitor to the interior looks up through it to the one above, which is filled with light from hidden windows in the third, outermost dome. CHARLES DE LA FOSSE (1636–1716) painted the second dome in 1705 with an Italian-inspired representation of the heavens opening up to receive Saint Louis, patron of France (see "Louis IX, the Saintly King," Chapter 13, page 385).

## Poussin

Louis XIV's embrace of classicism enticed many French artists to study Rome's ancient and Renaissance monuments. But even before the Sun King ascended to the throne in 1661, NICOLAS POUSSIN (1594–1665) of Normandy had spent most of his life in Rome, where he produced grandly severe paintings modeled on those of Titian and Raphael. He also carefully formulated a theoretical explanation of his method and was ultimately responsible for establishing classical painting as an important ingredient of 17th-century French art (see "Poussin's Notes for a Treatise on Painting," page 719). His classical style presents a striking contrast to the contemporaneous Baroque style of his Italian counterparts in Rome (see Chapter 24), underscoring the multifaceted character of the art of 17th-century Europe.

*ET IN ARCADIA EGO* Poussin's *Et in Arcadia Ego* (*Even in Arcadia, I* [am present]; FIG. **25-31**) exemplifies the "grand manner" of painting the artist advocated. It features a lofty subject rooted in the classical world and figures based on antique statuary. Rather than depicting dynamic movement and intense emotions, as his Italian contemporaries in Rome did, Poussin emulated the rational order and stability of Raphael's paintings. Dominating the foreground are three shepherds living in the idyllic land of Arcadia. They study an inscription on a tomb as a statuesque female figure quietly places her hand on the shoulder of one of them. She may be the spirit of death, reminding these mortals, as does the inscription, that death is found even in Arcadia, supposedly a spot of paradisiacal bliss. The countless draped female statues surviving in Italy from Roman times supplied the models for this figure, and the posture of the youth with one foot resting on a boulder derives from Greco-Roman statues of Neptune, the sea god, leaning on his trident. The classically compact and balanced grouping of the figures, the even light, and the thoughtful and reserved mood complement Poussin's classical figure types.

Newton (1642–1727) and the mathematical philosophy of René Descartes (1596–1650)—that all knowledge must be systematic and all science must be the consequence of the intellect imposed on matter. The majestic and rational design of Versailles proudly proclaims the mastery of human intelligence (and the mastery of Louis XIV) over the disorderliness of nature.

**ÉGLISE DU DÔME, PARIS** Another of Hardouin-Mansart's masterworks, the Église du Dôme (FIG. **25-30**), or Church of the Invalides, in Paris, also marries the Italian Baroque and French classical architectural styles. An intricately composed domed square of great scale, the church adjoins the veterans hospital Louis XIV

# Poussin's Notes for a Treatise on Painting

As the leading proponent of classical painting in 17th-century Rome, Nicolas Poussin outlined the principles of classicism in notes for an intended treatise on painting, left incomplete at his death. In those notes, Poussin described the essential ingredients necessary to produce a beautiful painting in "the grand manner":

> The grand manner consists of four things: subject-matter or theme, thought, structure, and style. The first thing that, as the foundation of all others, is required, is that the subject-matter shall be grand, as are battles, heroic actions, and divine things. But assuming that the subject on which the painter is laboring is grand, his next consideration is to keep away from minutiae . . . [and paint only] things magnificent and grand . . . Those who elect mean subjects take refuge in them because of the weakness of their talents.*

> The idea of beauty does not descend into matter unless this is prepared as carefully as possible. This preparation consists of three things: arrangement, measure, and aspect or form. Arrangement means the relative position of the parts; measure refers to their size; and form consists of lines and colors. Arrangement and relative position of the parts and making every limb of the body hold its natural place are not sufficient unless measure is added, which gives to each limb its correct size, proportionate to that of the whole body [compare "Polykleitos's Prescription for the Perfect Statue," Chapter 5, page 132], and unless form joins in, so that the lines will be drawn with grace and with a harmonious juxtaposition of light and shadow.†

Poussin applied these principles in paintings such as *Et in Arcadia Ego* (FIG. 25-31), a work peopled with perfectly proportioned statuesque figures attired in antique garb.

*Translated by Robert Goldwater and Marco Treves, eds., *Artists on Art*, 3d ed. (New York: Pantheon Books, 1958), 155.
†Ibid., 156.

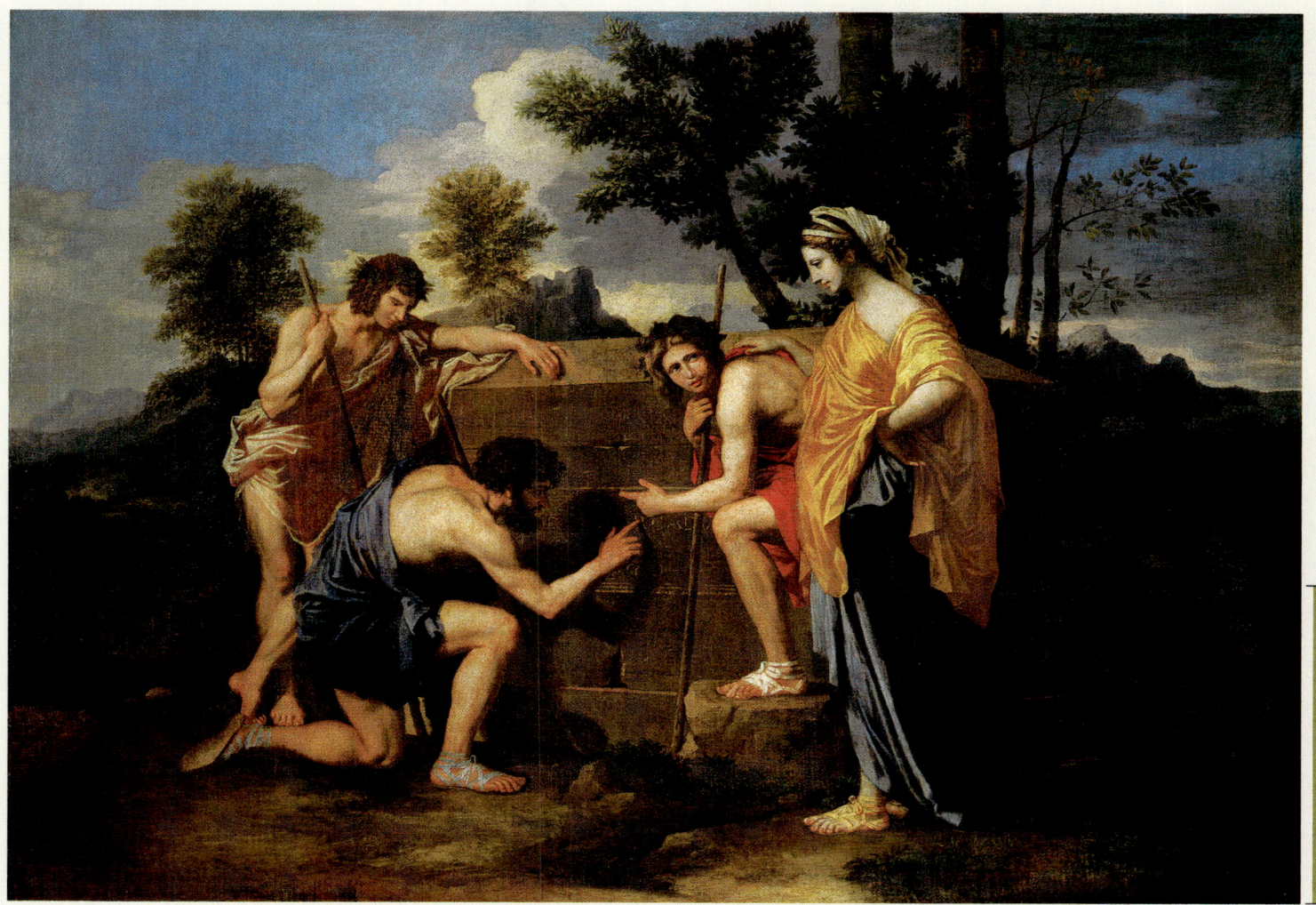

1 ft.

**25-31** NICOLAS POUSSIN, *Et in Arcadia Ego,* ca. 1655. Oil on canvas, 2′ 10″ × 4′. Musée du Louvre, Paris.

Poussin was the leading proponent of classicism in 17th-century Rome. His "grand manner" paintings are models of "arrangement and measure" and incorporate figures inspired by ancient statuary.

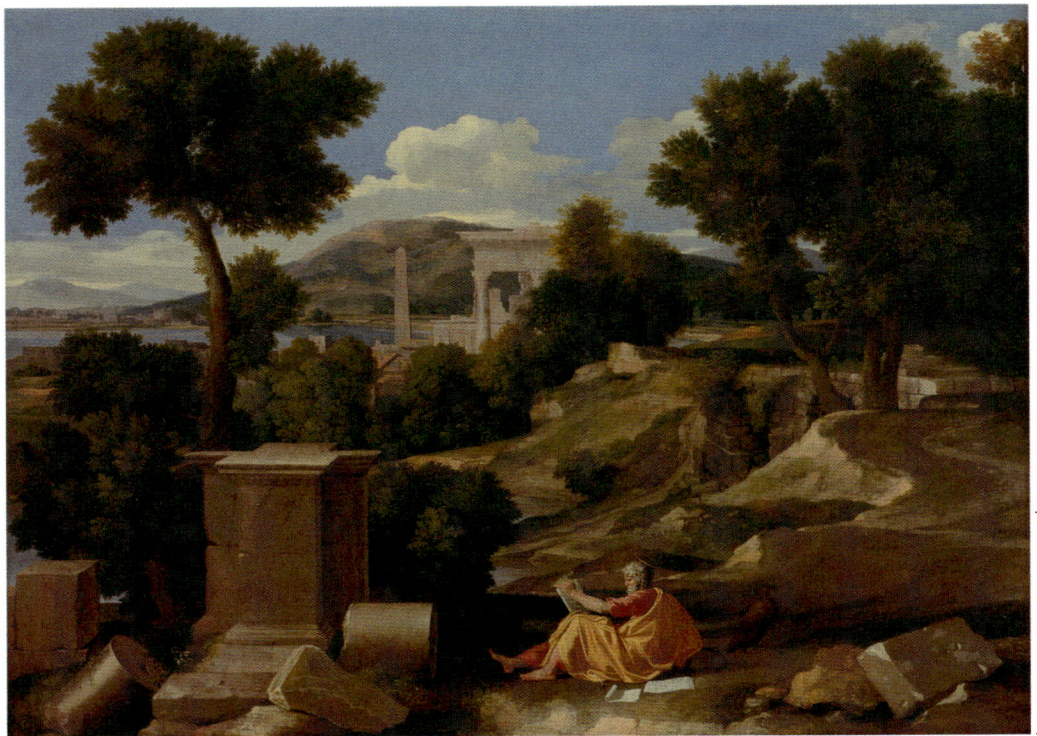

25-32 NICOLAS POUSSIN, *Landscape with Saint John on Patmos*, 1640. Oil on canvas, 3' 3½" × 4' 5⅝". Art Institute of Chicago, Chicago (A. A. Munger Collection). ◼◄

Poussin placed Saint John in a classical landscape amid broken columns, an obelisk, and a ruined temple, suggesting the decay of great civilizations and the coming of the new Christian era.

1 ft.

*SAINT JOHN ON PATMOS* In *Et in Arcadia Ego*, monumental figures dominate the landscape setting, but the natural world looms large in many of Poussin's paintings. *Landscape with Saint John on Patmos* (FIG. 25-32) is one of a pair of canvases Poussin painted for Gian Maria Roscioli (d. 1644), secretary to Pope Urban VIII. The second landscape represents Saint Matthew, reclining in right profile, who faced Saint John when the two canvases, now in different museums on different continents, hung side by side in Rome. An eagle stands behind John, just as an angel, Matthew's attribute, stands beside him. John, near the end of his life on the Greek island of Patmos, composed the book of Revelation, his account of the end of the world and the second coming of Christ, a prophetic vision of violent destruction and the last judgment. Poussin's setting, however, is a serene classical landscape beneath a sunny sky. (He created a similar setting in *Burial of Phocion* [FIG. 25-32A], which he painted later in the decade.) Saint John reclines in the foreground, posed like a Greco-Roman river god, amid shattered columns and a pedestal for a statue that disappeared long ago. In the middle ground, two oak trees frame the ruins of a classical temple and an Egyptian obelisk, many of which the Romans brought to their capital from the Nile and the popes reused in their building projects, for example, in the piazza in front of Saint Peter's (FIG. 24-4) and in Bernini's Fountain of the Four Rivers (FIG. 24-1). The decaying buildings suggest the decline of great empires—to be replaced by Christianity in a new era. In the distance are hills, sky, and clouds, all of which Poussin represented with pristine clarity, ignoring the rules of atmospheric perspective. His landscapes are not portraits of specific places, as are the Dutch landscapes of Ruisdael (FIG. 25-18) and Vermeer (FIG. 25-18B). Rather, they are imaginary settings constructed according to classical rules of design. Poussin's clouds, for example, echo the contours of his hills.

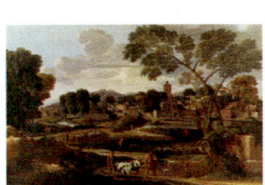

25-32A POUSSIN, *Burial of Phocion*, 1648.

## Claude Lorrain

Claude Gellée, called CLAUDE LORRAIN (1600–1682) after his birthplace in the duchy of Lorraine, rivaled Poussin in fame. Claude modulated in a softer style Poussin's disciplined rational art, with its sophisticated revelation of the geometry of landscape. Unlike the figures in Poussin's pictures, those in Claude's landscapes tell no dramatic story, point out no moral, praise no hero, and celebrate no saint. Indeed, the figures in Claude's paintings often appear to be added as mere excuses for the radiant landscape itself. For the French artist, painting involved essentially one theme—the beauty of a broad sky suffused with the golden light of dawn or sunset glowing through a hazy atmosphere and reflecting brilliantly off rippling water.

In *Landscape with Cattle and Peasants* (FIG. 25-33), the figures in the right foreground chat in animated fashion. In the left foreground, cattle relax contentedly. In the middle ground, cattle amble slowly away. The well-defined foreground, distinct middle ground, and dim background recede in serene orderliness, until all form dissolves in a luminous mist. Atmospheric and linear perspective reinforce each other to turn a vista into a typical Claudian vision, an ideal classical world bathed in sunlight in infinite space (compare FIG. I-12).

Claude's formalizing of nature with balanced groups of architectural masses, screens of trees, and sheets of water followed the great tradition of classical landscape. It began with the backgrounds of Venetian paintings (FIGS. 22-33 to 22-35) and continued in the art of Annibale Carracci (FIG. 24-15) and Poussin (FIGS. 25-32 and 25-32A). Yet Claude, like the Dutch painters, studied the light and the atmospheric nuances of nature, making a unique contribution. He recorded carefully in hundreds of sketches the look of the Roman countryside, its gentle terrain accented by stone-pines, cypresses, and poplars and by the ever-present ruins of ancient aqueducts, tombs, and towers. He made these the fundamental elements of his compositions. Travelers could understand the picturesque beauties of the outskirts of Rome in Claude's landscapes.

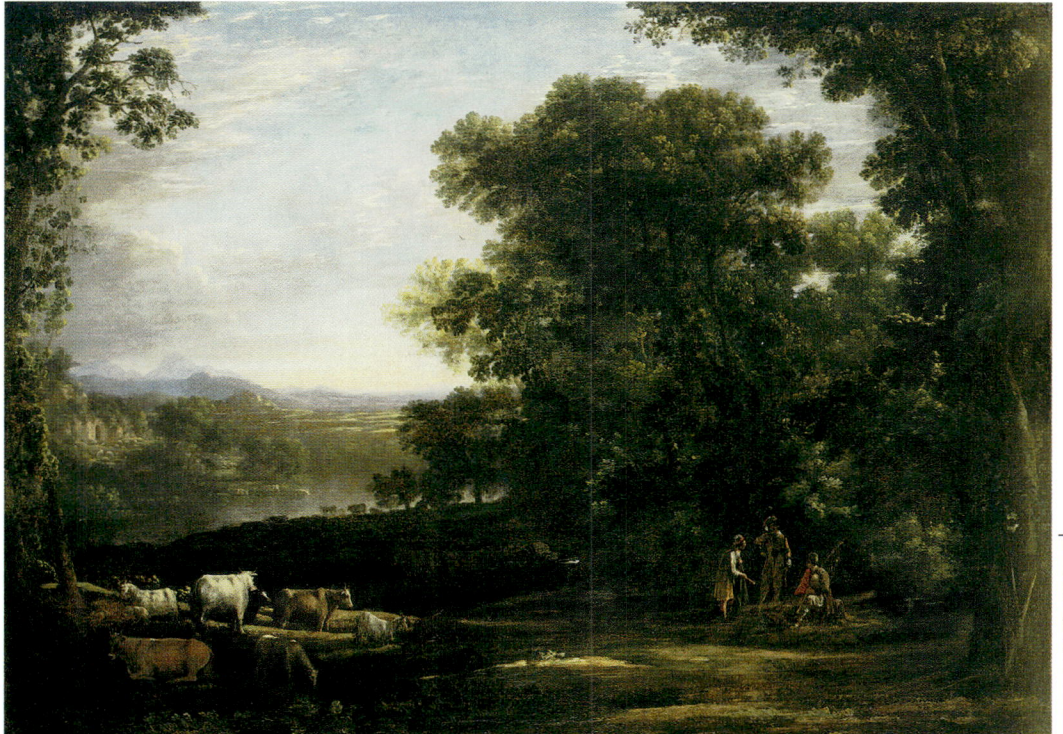

1 ft.

Claude achieved his marvelous effects of light by painstakingly placing tiny value gradations, which imitated, though on a very small scale, the range of values of outdoor light and shade. Avoiding the problem of high-noon sunlight overhead, Claude preferred, and convincingly represented, the sun's rays as they gradually illuminated the morning sky or, with their dying glow, set the pensive mood of evening. Thus, he matched the moods of nature with those of human subjects. Claude's infusion of nature with human feeling and his recomposition of nature in a calm equilibrium greatly appealed to many landscape painters of the 18th and early 19th centuries.

## Le Nain, Callot, La Tour

Although classicism was an important element of French art during the 17th and early 18th centuries, not all artists embraced the "grand manner."

**LOUIS LE NAIN** The works of LOUIS LE NAIN (ca. 1593–1648) have more in common with contemporaneous Dutch art than Renaissance or ancient art. Nevertheless, subjects that in Dutch painting were opportunities for boisterous good humor (FIG. 25-21), Le Nain treated with somber stillness. *Family of Country People* (FIG. **25-34**) reflects the thinking of 17th-century French social theorists who celebrated the natural virtue of peasants who worked the soil. Le Nain's painting expresses the grave dignity of one peasant family made stoic and resigned by hardship. These drab country folk surely had little reason for merriment. The peasant's lot, never easy, was miserable during the Thirty Years' War.

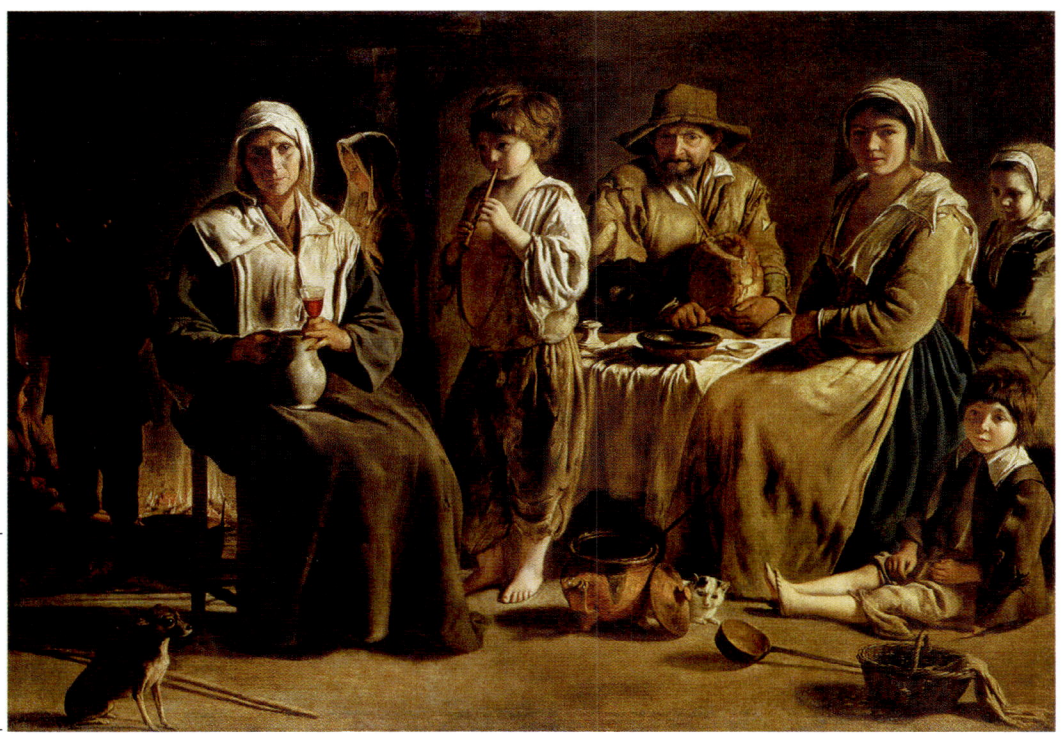

1 ft.

France    721

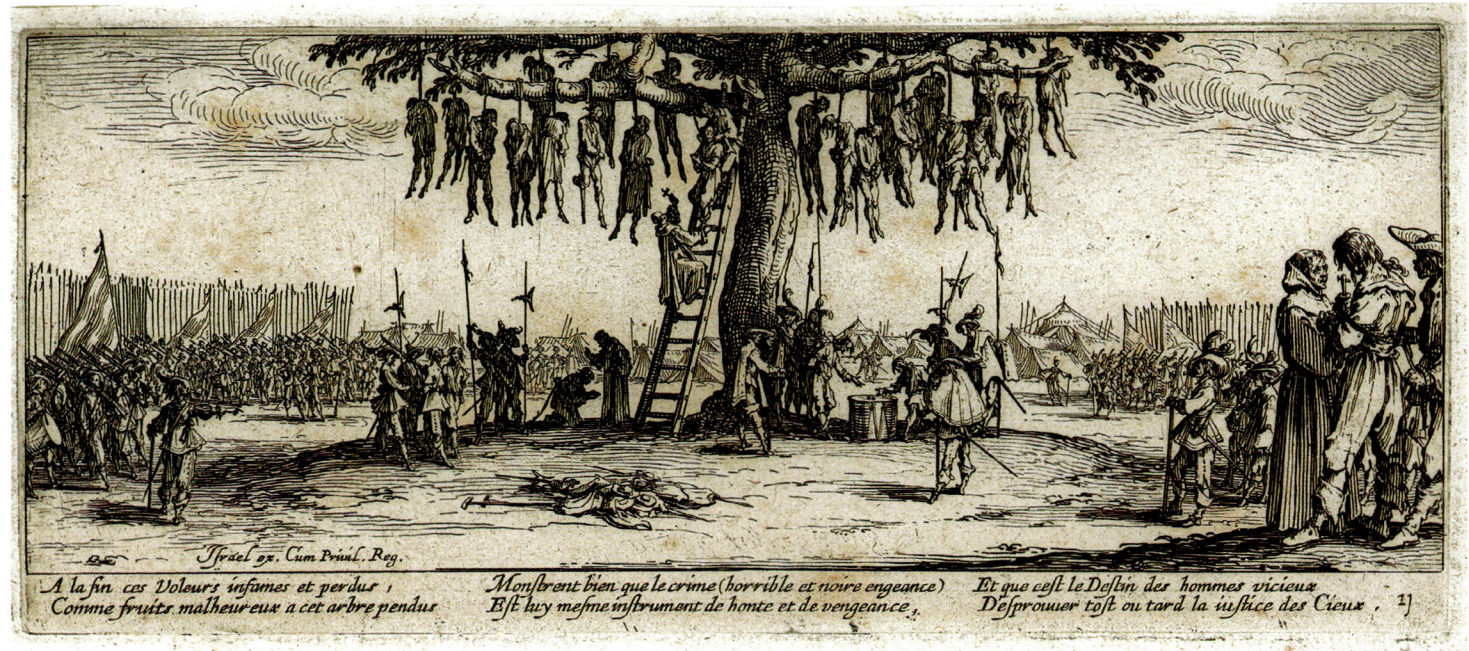

A la fin ces Voleurs infames et perdus ,    Monstrent bien que le crime (horrible et noire engeance)    Et que cest Le Destin des hommes vicieux
Comme fruits malheureux a cet arbre pendus    Est luy mesme instrument de honte et de vengeance ,    Desprouuer tost ou tard la iustice des Cieux .    21

**25-35** JACQUES CALLOT, *Hanging Tree,* from the *Miseries of War* series, 1629–1633. Etching, 3¾″ × 7¼″. Bibliothèque Nationale, Paris.

Callot's *Miseries of War* etchings were among the first realistic pictorial records of the human disaster of military conflict. *Hanging Tree* depicts a mass execution of thieves in the presence of an army.

The anguish and frustration of the peasantry, suffering from the cruel depredations of unruly armies living off the countryside, often erupted in violent revolts that the same armies savagely suppressed. This family, however, is pious, docile, and calm. Because Le Nain depicted peasants with dignity and quiet resignation, despite their harsh living conditions, some scholars have suggested he intended his paintings to please wealthy urban patrons.

**JACQUES CALLOT** Two other prominent artists from Lorraine were Jacques Callot and Georges de La Tour. JACQUES CALLOT (ca. 1592–1635) conveyed a sense of military life during these troubled times in a series of prints called *Miseries of War.* Callot confined himself almost exclusively to the art of etching and was widely influential—Rembrandt was among those who knew and learned from his work. Callot perfected the medium of etching, developing a very hard surface for the copper plate to enable fine and precise delineation with the needle. His quick, vivid touch and faultless drawing produced panoramas sparkling with sharp details of life—and death—despite their small size (roughly 4 by 7 inches). In the *Miseries of War* series, he observed these details coolly, presenting without comment images based on events he must have witnessed in the wars in Lorraine.

In *Hanging Tree* (FIG. **25-35**), Callot depicted a mass execution of thieves (identified in the text at the bottom of the etching). The event takes place in the presence of a disciplined army, drawn up on parade with banners, muskets, and lances, their tents in the background. Hanged men sway in clusters from the branches of a huge cross-shaped tree. A monk climbs a ladder, holding up a crucifix to a man while the executioner adjusts the noose around the man's neck. At the foot of the ladder, another victim kneels to receive absolution. Under the crucifix tree, men roll dice on a drumhead, hoping to win the belongings of the executed. (This is probably an allusion to the soldiers who cast lots for the gar-

ments of the crucified Christ.) In the right foreground, a hooded priest consoles a bound man. Callot's *Miseries of War* etchings are among the first realistic pictorial records of the human disaster of armed conflict.

**GEORGES DE LA TOUR** France, unlike the Dutch Republic, was a Catholic country, and religious themes, although not as common as in Italian and Spanish Baroque art (see Chapter 24), occupied some 17th-century French painters. Among the French artists who painted biblical subjects was GEORGES DE LA TOUR (1593–1652). His work, particularly his use of light, suggests a familiarity with Caravaggio's art, which he may have learned about from painters in Utrecht, such as ter Brugghen and van Honthorst (FIGS. 25-7 and 25-8). Although La Tour used the devices of Caravaggio's Dutch followers, his effects are strikingly different from theirs. His *Adoration of the Shepherds* (FIG. **25-36**) makes use of the night setting favored by the Utrecht school, much as van Honthorst portrayed it. But here, the light, its source shaded by an old man's hand, falls upon a very different company in a very different mood. A group of humble men and women, coarsely clad, gather in prayerful vigil around a luminous baby Jesus. Without the aid of the title, this work might be construed as a genre piece, a narrative of some event from peasant life. Nothing in the environment, placement, poses, dress, or attributes of the figures distinguishes them as the Virgin Mary, Joseph, Christ Child, or shepherds. The artist did not even paint halos. The light is not spiritual but material: it comes from a candle. La Tour's scientific scrutiny of the effects of light, as it throws precise shadows on surfaces intercepting it, nevertheless had religious intention and consequence. The light illuminates a group of ordinary people held in a mystic trance induced by their witnessing the miracle of the incarnation. In this timeless tableau of simple people, La Tour eliminated the dogmatic significance and traditional iconography of the incarnation. Still, these people

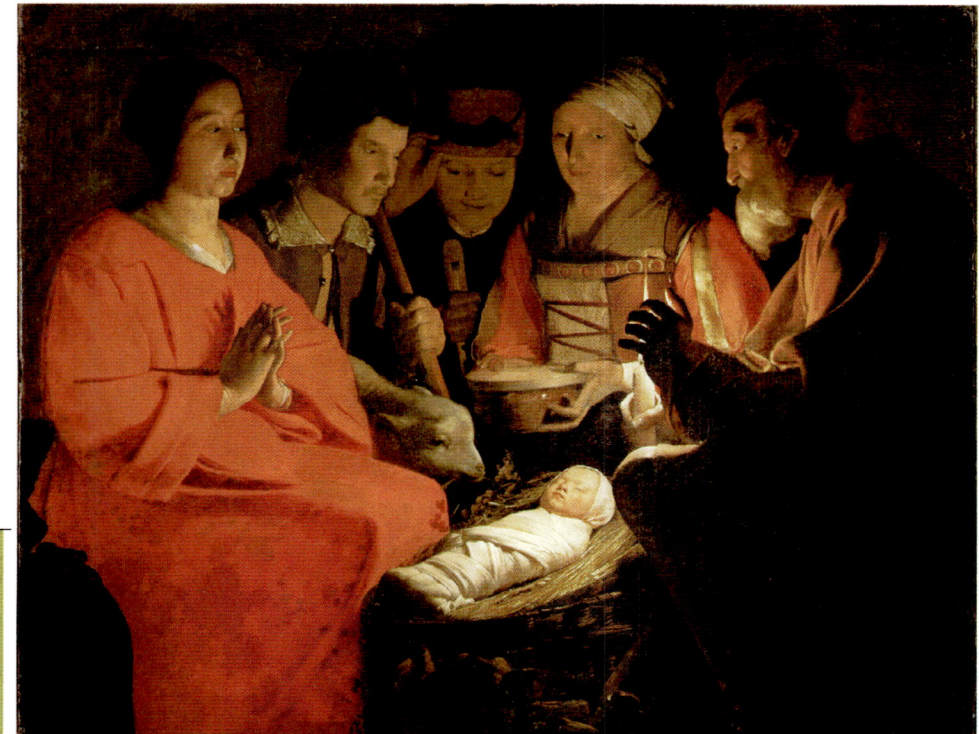

25-36 GEORGES DE LA TOUR, *Adoration of the Shepherds,* 1645–1650. Oil on canvas, 3′ 6″ × 4′ 6″. Musée du Louvre, Paris.

Without the aid of the title, this candlelit nighttime scene could be a genre piece instead of a biblical narrative. La Tour did not even paint halos around the heads of the holy figures.

1 ft.

## ENGLAND

In England, in sharp distinction to France, the common law and the Parliament kept royal power in check. England also differed from France (and Europe in general) in other significant ways. Although an important part of English life, religion was not the contentious issue it was on the Continent. The religious affiliations of the English included Catholicism, Anglicanism, Protestantism, and Puritanism (the English version of Calvinism). In the economic realm, England was the one country (other than the Dutch Republic) to take advantage of the opportunities overseas trade offered. As an island, Britain (which after 1603 consisted of England, Wales, and Scotland), like the Dutch Republic, possessed a large and powerful navy, as well as excellent maritime capabilities.

reverently contemplate something they regard as holy. The devout of any religious persuasion can read this painting, regardless of their familiarity with the biblical account.

The supernatural calm pervading *Adoration of the Shepherds* is characteristic of the mood of Georges de La Tour's art. He achieved this by eliminating motion and emotive gesture (only the light is dramatic), by suppressing surface detail, and by simplifying body volumes. These stylistic traits are among those associated with classical and Renaissance art. Thus, several apparently contradictory elements meet in the work of La Tour: classical composure, fervent spirituality, and genre realism.

### Jones and Wren

In the realm of art, the most significant English achievements were in the field of architecture, much of it, as in France, incorporating classical elements.

**INIGO JONES** The most important English architect of the first half of the 17th century was INIGO JONES (1573–1652), architect to Kings James I (r. 1603–1625) and Charles I (FIG. 25-5). Jones spent considerable time in Italy. He greatly admired the classical authority and restraint of Andrea Palladio's structures and studied with great care his treatise on architecture (see Chapter 22). Jones took many motifs from Palladio's villas and palaces, and he adopted Palladio's basic design principles for his own architecture. The nature of his achievement is evident in the buildings he designed for his royal patrons, among them the Banqueting House (FIG. **25-37**) at Whitehall in London. For this structure, a symmetrical block of great clarity and dignity,

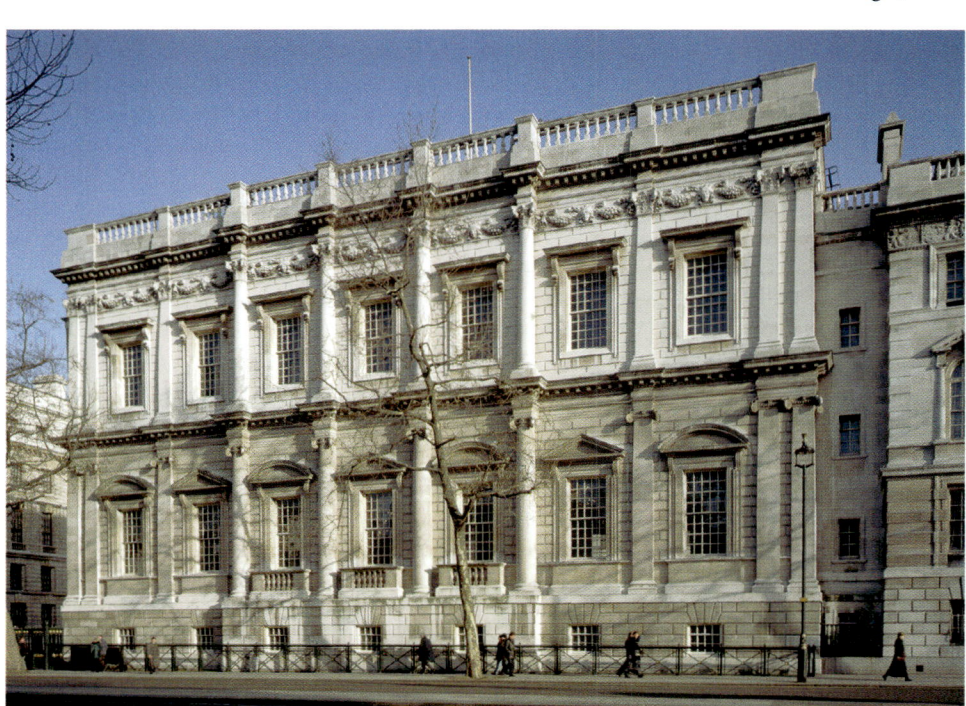

25-37 INIGO JONES, **Banqueting House (looking northeast), Whitehall, London, England, 1619–1622.**

Jones was a great admirer of the classical architecture of Palladio, and he adopted motifs from the Italian architect's villas and palaces for the buildings he designed for his royal patrons.

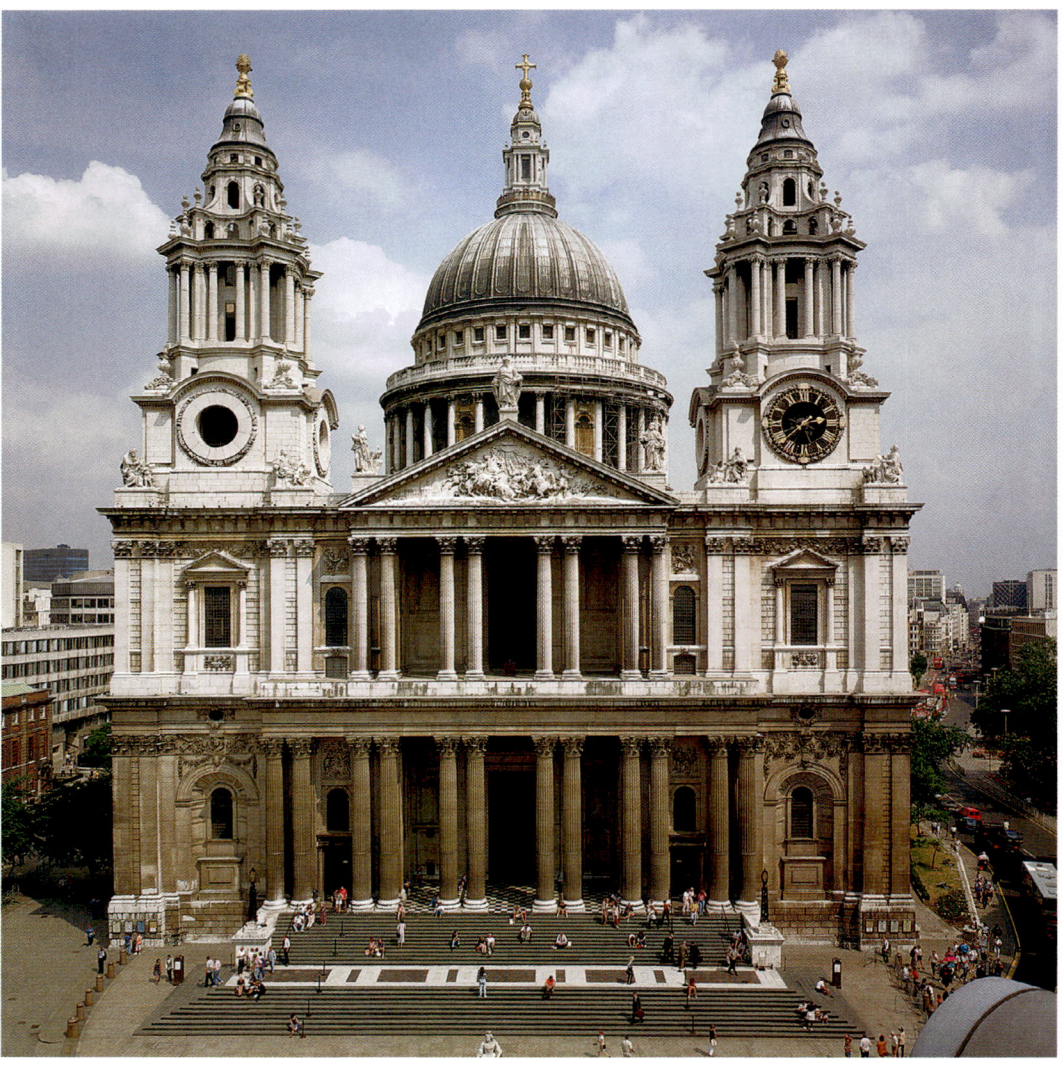

Jones superimposed two orders, using columns in the center and pilasters near the ends. The balustraded roofline, uninterrupted in its horizontal sweep, antedates the Louvre's east facade (FIG. 25-25) by more than 40 years. Palladio would have recognized and approved all of the design elements, but the building as a whole is not a copy of his work. Although relying on the revered Italian's architectural vocabulary and syntax, Jones retained his independence as a designer. For two centuries his influence in English architecture was almost as authoritative as Palladio's.

**CHRISTOPHER WREN** London's majestic Saint Paul's Cathedral (FIG. **25-38**) is the work of England's most renowned architect, CHRISTOPHER WREN (1632–1723). A mathematical genius and skilled engineer whose work won Isaac Newton's praise, Wren became professor of astronomy in London at age 25. Mathematics led to architecture, and Charles II (r. 1649–1685) asked Wren to prepare a plan for restoring the old Gothic church of Saint Paul. Wren proposed to remodel the building based on Roman structures. Within a few months, the Great Fire of London, which destroyed the old structure and many churches in the city in 1666, gave Wren his opportunity. Although Jones's work strongly influenced him, Wren also traveled in France, where the splendid palaces and state buildings being created in and around Paris at the time of the com-

petition for the Louvre design must have impressed him. Wren also closely studied prints illustrating Baroque architecture in Italy. In Saint Paul's, he harmonized Palladian, French, and Italian Baroque features.

In view of its size, the cathedral was built with remarkable speed—in little more than 30 years—and Wren lived to see it completed. The building's form underwent constant refinement during construction, and Wren did not determine the final appearance of the towers until after 1700. In the splendid skyline composition, two foreground towers act effectively as foils to the great dome. Wren must have known similar schemes Italian architects had devised for Saint Peter's (FIG. 24-4) in Rome to solve the problem of the relationship between the facade and dome. Certainly, the influence of Borromini (FIG. 24-12) is evident in the upper levels and lanterns of the towers. The lower levels owe a debt to Palladio (FIG. 22-30), and the superposed paired columnar porticos recall the Louvre's east facade (FIG. 25-25). Wren's skillful eclecticism brought all these foreign features into a monumental unity.

Wren designed many other London churches after the Great Fire. Even today, Wren's towers and domes punctuate the skyline of London. Saint Paul's dome is the tallest of all. Wren's legacy was significant and long-lasting, both in England and in colonial America (see Chapter 26).

# THE BAROQUE IN NORTHERN EUROPE

## FLANDERS

▌ In the 17th century, Flanders remained Catholic and under Spanish control. Flemish Baroque art is more closely tied to the Baroque art of Italy than is the art of much of the rest of northern Europe.

▌ The leading Flemish painter of this era was Peter Paul Rubens, whose work and influence were international in scope. A diplomat as well as an artist, he counted kings and queens among his patrons and friends. His paintings exhibit Baroque splendor in color and ornament, and feature robust and foreshortened figures in swirling motion.

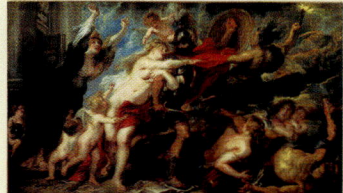

Rubens, *Consequences of War,*
1638–1639

## DUTCH REPUBLIC

▌ The Dutch Republic received official recognition of its independence from Spain in the Treaty of Westphalia of 1648. Worldwide trade and banking brought prosperity to its predominantly Protestant citizenry, which largely rejected church art in favor of private commissions of portraits, genre scenes, landscapes, and still lifes.

▌ Frans Hals produced innovative portraits of middle-class patrons in which a lively informality replaced the formulaic patterns of traditional portraiture. Aelbert Cuyp and Jacob van Ruisdael specialized in landscapes depicting specific places, not idealized Renaissance settings. Peter Claesz, Willem Kalf, and others painted vanitas still lifes featuring meticulous depictions of worldly goods amid reminders of death.

▌ Rembrandt van Rijn, the greatest Dutch artist of the age, treated a broad range of subjects, including religious themes and portraits. His oil paintings are notable for their dramatic impact and subtle gradations of light and shade as well as the artist's ability to convey human emotions. Rembrandt was also a master printmaker renowned for his etchings.

▌ Jan Vermeer specialized in painting the occupants of serene, comfortable Dutch homes. His convincing representation of interior spaces depended in part on his employment of the camera obscura. Vermeer was also a master of light and color and understood shadows are not colorless.

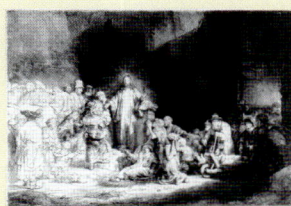

Rembrandt, *Hundred-Guilder Print,*
ca. 1649

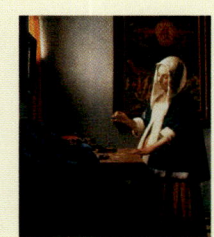

Vermeer, *Woman Holding
a Balance,* ca. 1664

## FRANCE AND ENGLAND

▌ The major art patron in 17th-century France was the Sun King, the absolutist monarch Louis XIV, who expanded the Louvre and built a gigantic palace-and-garden complex at Versailles featuring sumptuous furnishings and sweeping vistas. Among the architects Louis employed were Charles Le Brun and Jules Hardouin-Mansart, who succeeded in marrying Italian Baroque and French classical styles.

▌ The leading French proponent of classical painting was Nicolas Poussin, who spent most of his life in Rome and championed the "grand manner" of painting. This style called for heroic or divine subjects and classical compositions with figures often modeled on ancient statues.

▌ Claude Lorraine, whose fame rivaled Poussin's, specialized in classical landscapes rendered in linear and atmospheric perspective. His compositions often incorporated ancient ruins.

▌ In 17th-century England, architecture was the most important art form. Two architects who achieved international fame were Inigo Jones and Christopher Wren, who harmonized the architectural principles of Andrea Palladio with the Italian Baroque and French classical styles.

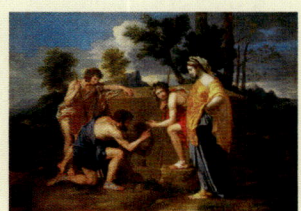

Poussin, *Et in Arcadia Ego,*
ca. 1655

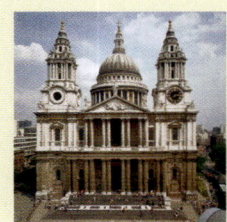

Wren, Saint Paul's, London,
1675–1710

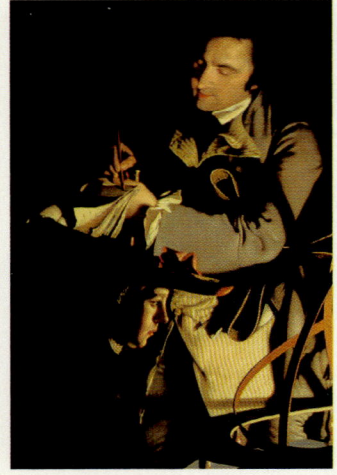

Joseph Wright of Derby specialized in dramatically lit paintings celebrating the scientific advances of the Enlightenment era. Here, a man listening to a learned lecture takes careful notes.

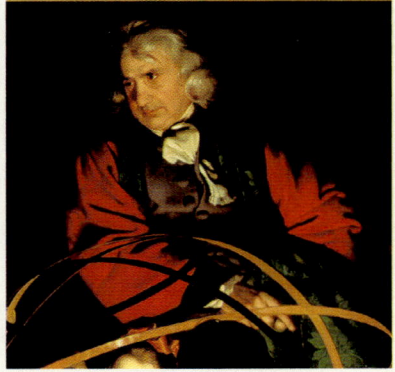

At the center of Wright's canvas, a scholar demonstrates an orrery, a mechanical model of the solar system in which each planet revolves around the sun at the correct relative velocity.

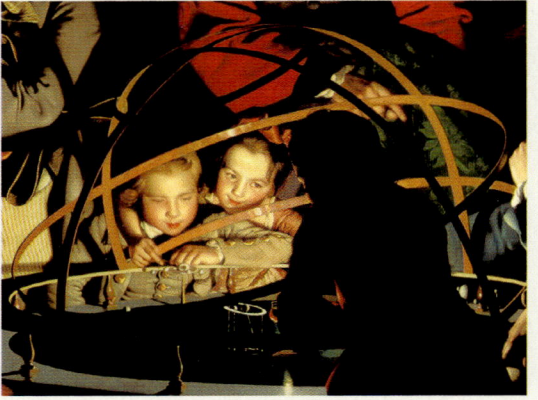

Awestruck children crowd close to the orbs representing the planets within the arcing bands symbolizing their orbits. Light from a lamp creates shadows, heightening the drama of the scene.

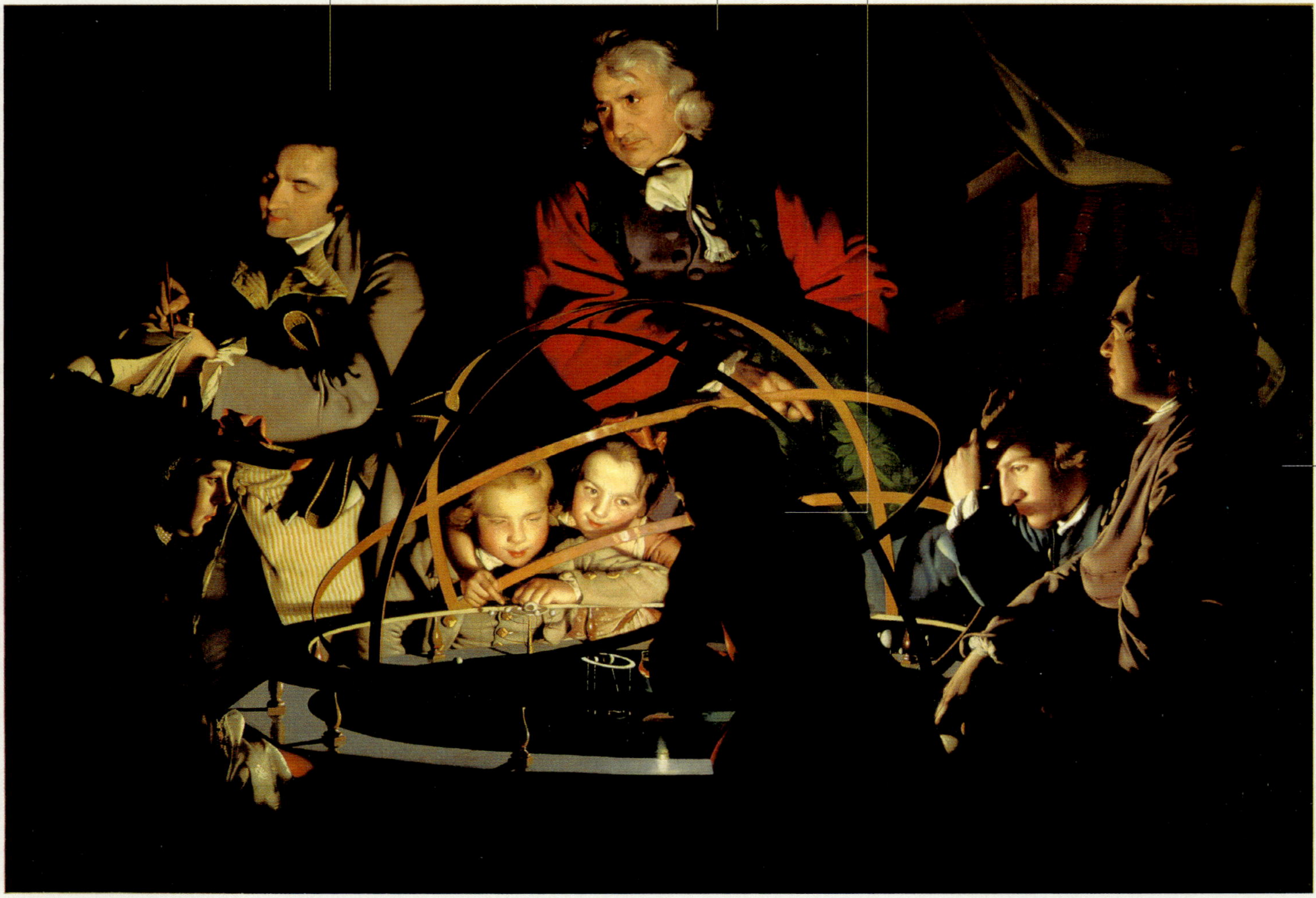

1 ft.

**26-1**  JOSEPH WRIGHT OF DERBY, *A Philosopher Giving a Lecture at the Orrery,* ca. 1763–1765. Oil on canvas, 4′ 10″ × 6′ 8″. Derby Museums and Art Gallery, Derby.

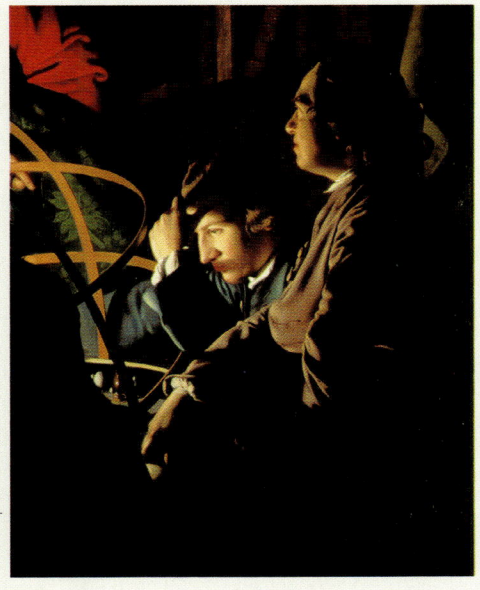

The wonders of scientific knowledge mesmerize everyone in Wright's painting, adults as well as children. At the right, two gentlemen pay rapt attention to the demonstration.

# 26

# ROCOCO TO NEOCLASSICISM: THE 18TH CENTURY IN EUROPE AND AMERICA

FRAMING THE ERA

## ART AND SCIENCE IN THE ERA OF ENLIGHTENMENT

The dawn of the *Enlightenment* in the 18th century brought a new way of thinking critically about the world and about humankind, independently of religion, myth, or tradition. Enlightenment thinkers rejected unfounded beliefs in favor of empirical evidence and promoted the questioning of all assertions. Thus, the Enlightenment encouraged and stimulated the habit and application of mind known as the "scientific method" and fostered technological invention. The scientific advances of the Enlightenment era affected the lives of everyone, and most people enthusiastically responded to wonders of the Industrial Revolution such as the steam engine, which gave birth to the modern manufacturing economy and the prospect of a seemingly limitless supply of goods and services.

The fascination science had for ordinary people as well as for the learned is the subject of *A Philosopher Giving a Lecture at the Orrery* (FIG. **26-1**) by the English painter JOSEPH WRIGHT OF DERBY (1734–1797). Wright studied painting near Birmingham (MAP 27-2), the center of the Industrial Revolution, and specialized in dramatically lit scenes showcasing modern scientific instruments and experiments. In this painting, a scholar demonstrates a mechanical model of the solar system called an *orrery,* in which each planet (represented by a metal orb) revolves around the sun (a lamp) at the correct relative velocity. Light from the lamp pours forth from in front of the boy silhouetted in the foreground to create shadows that heighten the drama of the scene. Awestruck children crowd close to the tiny orbs representing the planets within the arcing bands symbolizing their orbits. An earnest listener makes notes, while the lone woman seated at the left and the two gentlemen at the right pay rapt attention. Scientific knowledge mesmerizes everyone in Wright's painting. The artist visually reinforced the fascination with the orrery by composing his image in a circular fashion, echoing the device's orbital design. The postures and gazes of all the participants and observers focus attention on the cosmic model. Wright scrupulously and accurately rendered every detail of the figures, the mechanisms of the orrery, and even the books and curtain in the shadowy background.

Wright's choice of subjects and realism in depicting them appealed to the great industrialists of his day, including Josiah Wedgwood (1730–1795), who pioneered many techniques of mass-produced pottery, and Sir Richard Arkwright (1732–1792), whose spinning frame revolutionized the textile industry. Both men often purchased paintings by Wright featuring scientific advances. To them, the Derby artist's elevation of the theories and inventions of the Industrial Revolution to the plane of history painting was exciting and appropriately in tune with the new era of Enlightenment.

# A CENTURY OF REVOLUTIONS

In 1700, Louis XIV still ruled France as the Sun King (see Chapter 25), presiding over his realm and French culture from his palatial residence at Versailles (FIG. 25-26). The French king's palace inspired the construction of many other

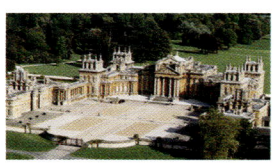

26-1A VANBRUGH and HAWKSMOOR, Blenheim Palace, 1705–1725.

grandiose homes on the Continent and across the English Channel during the early 18th century, including Blenheim Palace (FIG. 26-1A), which SIR JOHN VANBRUGH (1664–1726) and NICHOLAS HAWKSMOOR (1661–1736) designed for the duke of Marlborough. By 1800, however, revolutions had overthrown the monarchy in France and achieved independence for the British colonies in America (MAP 26-1). The 18th century also gave birth to a revolution of a different kind—the Industrial Revolution, which began in England and soon transformed the economies of continental Europe and North America and eventually the world.

Against this backdrop of revolutionary change, social as well as political, economic, and technological, came major transformations in the arts. Compare, for example, Antoine Watteau's *Pilgrimage to Cythera* (FIG. 26-7), painted 1717–1719, which unfolds in a lush landscape and celebrates the romantic dalliances of the moneyed elite, with Jacques-Louis David's 1784 *Oath of the Horatii* (FIG. 26-25), set in an austere Doric hall and glorifying the civic virtue and heroism of an ancient Roman family. The two works have little in common other than both are French oil paintings. In the 18th century, shifts in style and subject matter were both rapid and significant.

# ROCOCO

The death of Louis XIV in 1715 brought many changes in French high society. The elite quickly abandoned the court of Versailles for the pleasures of town life. Although French citizens still owed allegiance to a monarch, the early 18th century brought a resurgence of aristocratic social, political, and economic power. Members of the nobility not only exercised their traditional privileges (for example, exemption from certain taxes and from forced labor on public works) but also sought to expand their power. In the cultural realm, aristocrats reestablished their predominance as art patrons.

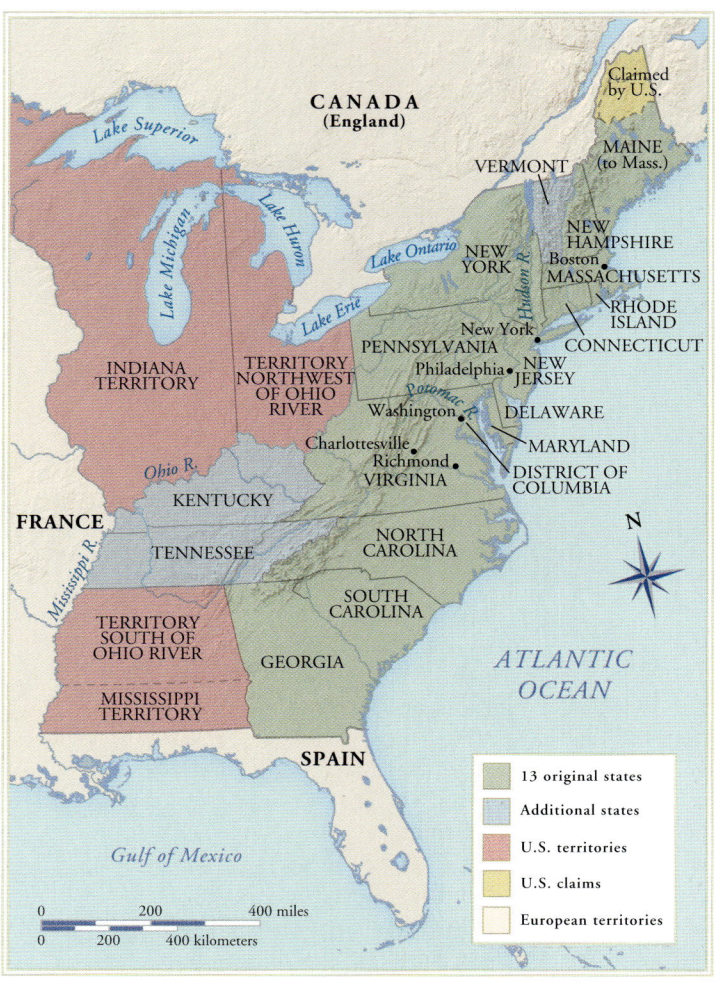

MAP 26-1   The United States in 1800.

The *hôtels* (townhouses) of Paris soon became the centers of a new, softer style called *Rococo*. Associated with the regency (1715–1723) following the death of Louis XIV and with the reign of Louis XV (r. 1723–1774), the Rococo style in art and architecture was the perfect expression of the lighthearted elegance the wealthy cultivated in their opulent homes (see "Femmes Savants and Salon Culture," page 729).

---

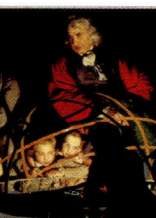

# ROCOCO TO NEOCLASSICISM:
## THE 18TH CENTURY IN EUROPE AND AMERICA

| 1700 | 1725 | 1750 | 1775 | 1800 |
|---|---|---|---|---|
| ▌ The Rococo style becomes the rage in the opulent townhouses of Paris<br><br>▌ Watteau creates a new painting genre—the *fête galante* | ▌ Neumann adapts the intimate Rococo domestic style to ecclesiastical architecture<br><br>▌ Chardin rejects the frivolity of Rococo painting in favor of "natural" art<br><br>▌ Canaletto paints views of Venice as souvenirs of the Grand Tour of Italy | ▌ The Enlightenment admiration for Greece and Rome prompts a Neoclassical revival in architecture<br><br>▌ During the Industrial Revolution, Wright celebrates scientific advances in dramatically lit paintings<br><br>▌ First use of iron in bridge construction at Coalbrookdale, England | ▌ Reynolds achieves renown for Grand Manner portraits<br><br>▌ Vigée-Lebrun and Labille-Guiard gain admission to the French Royal Academy of Painting and Sculpture<br><br>▌ David becomes the painter-ideologist of the French Revolution<br><br>▌ Jefferson promotes Neoclassicism as the official architectural style of the new American republic | |

## Femmes Savants and Salon Culture

The feminine look of the Rococo style suggests the taste and social initiative of women, and to a large extent, women dominated the cultural sphere during the Rococo age. In the 18th century, aristocratic women—including Madame de Pompadour (1721–1764), mistress of Louis XV of France; Maria Theresa (1717–1780), archduchess of Austria and queen of Hungary and Bohemia; and Empresses Elizabeth (r. 1741–1762) and Catherine the Great (r. 1762–1796) of Russia—held some of the most influential positions in Europe. Female taste also was a defining factor in numerous smaller courts as well as in the private sphere.

In the early 1700s, Paris was the social capital of Europe, and the Rococo salon (FIG. 26-2) was the center of Parisian society. Wealthy, ambitious, and clever society hostesses competed to attract the most famous and accomplished people to their salons. The medium of social intercourse was conversation spiced with wit, repartee as quick and deft as a fencing match. Artifice reigned supreme, and participants considered enthusiasm or sincerity in bad taste.

The women who hosted these salons, whether in Paris or elsewhere in Europe (FIG. 26-3), referred to themselves as *femmes savants*—learned women. Chief among them was Julie de Lespinasse (1732–1776), one of the most articulate, urbane, and intelligent French women of the time. She held daily salons from five o'clock until nine in the evening. The memoirs of Jean François Marmontel (1723–1799), published in 1827, documented the liveliness of these gatherings and the remarkable nature of this hostess.

> The circle was formed of persons who were not bound together. She [Julie de Lespinasse] had taken them here and there in society, but so well assorted were they that once [in her salon] they fell into harmony like the strings of an instrument touched by an able hand. Following out that comparison, I may say that she played the instrument with an art that came of genius; she seemed to know what tone each string would yield before she touched it; I mean to say that our minds and our natures were so well known to her that in order to bring them into play she had but to say a word. Nowhere was conversation more lively, more brilliant, or better regulated than at her house. It was a rare phenomenon indeed, the

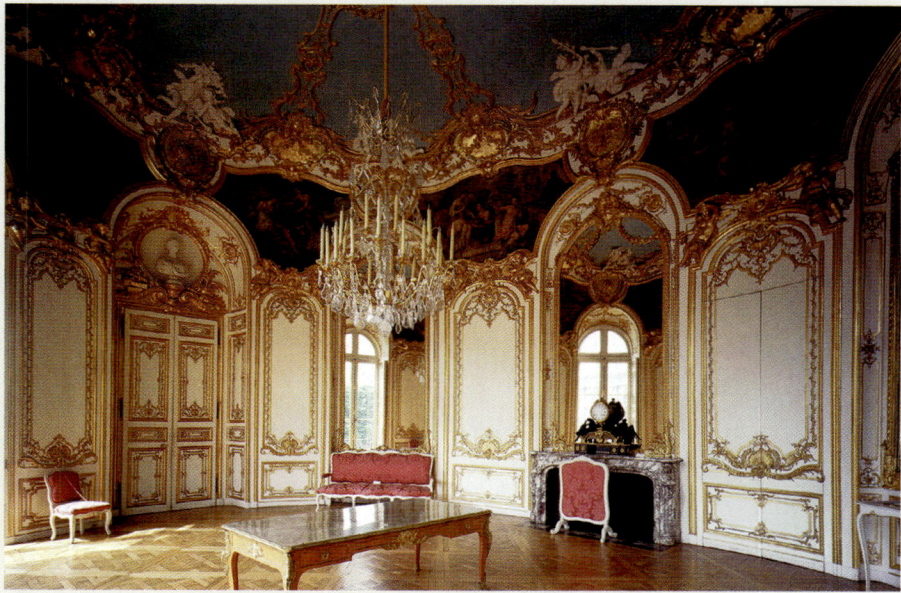

**26-2** GERMAIN BOFFRAND, Salon de la Princesse, with paintings by CHARLES-JOSEPH NATOIRE and sculptures by JEAN-BAPTISTE LEMOYNE, Hôtel de Soubise, Paris, France, 1737–1740.

Rococo rooms such as this one, featuring sinuous curves, gilded moldings and mirrors, small sculptures and paintings, and floral ornamentation, were the center of Parisian social and intellectual life.

> degree of tempered, equable heat which she knew so well how to maintain, sometimes by moderating it, sometimes by quickening it. The continual activity of her soul was communicated to our souls, but measurably; her imagination was the mainspring, her reason the regulator. Remark that the brains she stirred at will were neither feeble nor frivolous. . . . Her talent for casting out a thought and giving it for discussion to men of that class, her own talent in discussing it with precision, sometimes with eloquence, her talent for bringing forward new ideas and varying the topic—always with the facility and ease of a fairy . . . these talents, I say, were not those of an ordinary woman. It was not with the follies of fashion and vanity that daily, during four hours of conversation, without languor and without vacuum, she knew how to make herself interesting to a wide circle of strong minds.*

*Jean François Marmontel, *Memoirs of Marmontel* (1827), translated by Brigit Patmore (London: Routledge, 1930), 270.

## Architecture

Rococo appeared in France in about 1700, primarily as a style of interior design. The French Rococo exterior was most often simple, or even plain, but Rococo exuberance took over the interior. The term derived from the French word *rocaille* (pebble), but it referred especially to the small stones and shells used to decorate grotto interiors. Shells or forms resembling shells were the principal motifs in Rococo ornamentation.

**SALON DE LA PRINCESSE** A typical French Rococo room is the Salon de la Princesse (FIG. **26-2**) in the Hôtel de Soubise in Paris, designed by GERMAIN BOFFRAND (1667–1754) in collaboration with the painter JOSEPH NATOIRE (1700–1777) and the sculptor JEAN-BAPTISTE LEMOYNE (1704–1778). Parisian salons such as this one were the center of Rococo social life. They usurped the role Louis XIV's Versailles palace (FIG. 25-26) played in the 17th century, when the Sun King set the tone for French culture. In the

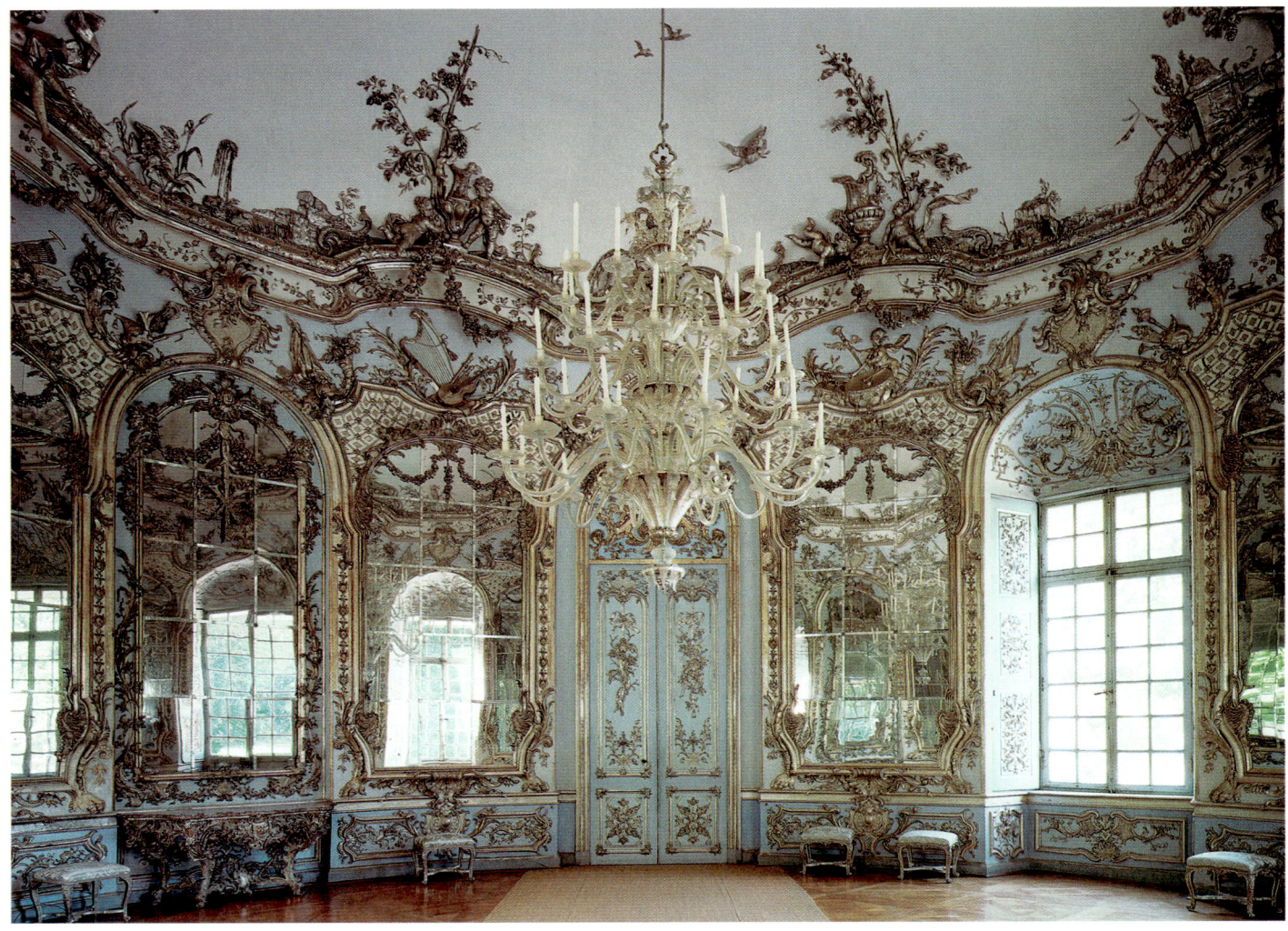

**26-3** FRANÇOIS DE CUVILLIÉS, Hall of Mirrors, the Amalienburg, Nymphenburg Palace park, Munich, Germany, early 18th century.

Designed by a French architect, this circular hall in a German lodge displays the Rococo architectural style at its zenith, dazzling the eye with the organic interplay of mirrors, crystal, and stucco relief.

early 18th century, the centralized and grandiose palace-based culture of Baroque France gave way to a much more intimate and decentralized culture based in private homes. The new architectural style mirrored this social and cultural shift. A comparison between the Salon de la Princesse and the Galerie des Glaces (FIG. 25-27) at Versailles reveals how Boffrand softened the strong architectural lines and panels of the earlier style into flexible, sinuous curves luxuriantly multiplied in mirror reflections. The walls melt into the vault. Irregular painted shapes, surmounted by sculpture and separated by the ubiquitous rocaille shells, replace the hall's cornices. Painting, architecture, and sculpture combine to form a single ensemble. The profusion of curving tendrils and sprays of foliage blend with the shell forms to give an effect of freely growing nature, suggesting the designer permanently bedecked the Rococo room for a festival.

French Rococo interiors were lively total works of art. Exquisitely wrought furniture, enchanting small sculptures, ornamented mirror frames, delightful ceramics and silver, small paintings, and decorative *tapestries* complemented the architecture, relief sculptures, and mural paintings. Unfortunately, the Salon de la Princesse has lost most of the moveable furnishings that once contributed so much to its total ambience. Visitors can imagine, however,

how this and similar Rococo rooms—with their alternating gilded moldings, vivacious relief sculptures, and daintily colored ornamentation of flowers and garlands—must have harmonized with the chamber music played in them, with the elaborate costumes of satin and brocade, and with the equally elegant etiquette and sparkling wit of the people who graced them.

**AMALIENBURG** The French Rococo style quickly spread beyond Paris. The Amalienburg, a small lodge the French architect FRANÇOIS DE CUVILLIÉS (1695–1768) built in the park of the Nymphenburg Palace in Munich, is a prime example of Germany's adoption of the Parisian style. The most spectacular room in the lodge is the circular Hall of Mirrors (FIG. **26-3**), a silver-and-blue ensemble of architecture, stucco relief, silvered bronze mirrors, and crystal. The hall dazzles the eye with myriad scintillating motifs, forms, and figurations and showcases the full ornamental repertoire of the Rococo style at its zenith. Silvery light, reflected and amplified by windows and mirrors, bathes the room and creates shapes and contours that weave rhythmically around the upper walls and the ceiling coves. Everything seems organic, growing, and in motion, an ultimate refinement of illusion the architect, artists, and artisans created with virtuoso flourishes.

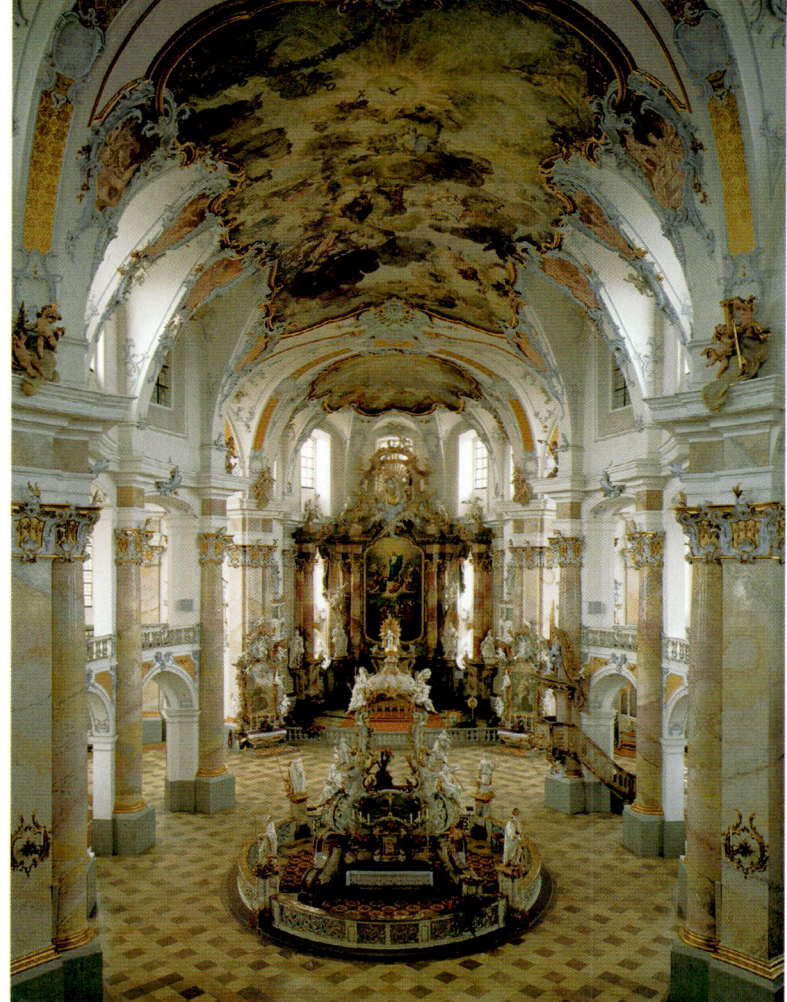

**26-4** Balthasar Neumann, interior of the pilgrimage church of Vierzehnheiligen (looking east), near Staffelstein, Germany, 1743–1772.

Neumann adapted the intimate Rococo style to ecclesiastical architecture. Vierzehnheiligen's interior is light and delicate in contrast to the dynamic energy of Italian Baroque church designs.

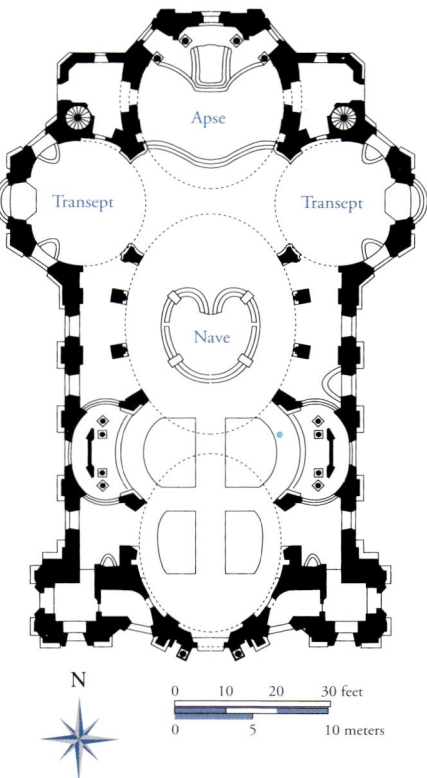

**26-5** Balthasar Neumann, plan of the pilgrimage church of Vierzehnheiligen, near Staffelstein, Germany, 1743–1772.

Vierzehnheiligen's plan features undulating lines and a dynamic composition of tangent ovals and circles. It is even more complex than Borromini's influential church plans (FIGS. 24-10 and 24-13).

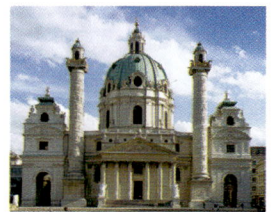

**26-3A** Fischer von Erlach, Karlskirche, Vienna, 1716–1737.

**VIERZEHNHEILIGEN** Rococo style was not exclusively a domestic phenomenon, however. Although in the early 18th century, some architects, such as Johann Bernhard Fischer von Erlach (1656–1723), continued to design churches incorporating Baroque and classical elements—for example, Karlskirche (FIG. **26-3A**) in Vienna—others eagerly adopted the Rococo style for ecclesiastical architecture. One of the most splendid examples is the pilgrimage church of Vierzehnheiligen (Fourteen Saints; FIGS. **26-4** and **26-5**) near Staffelstein (MAP 25-1), which the German architect Balthasar Neumann (1687–1753) began as construction was about to be concluded on the grandiose palace (FIG. **26-5A**) he had designed in 1719 for the prince-bishops of Würzburg. The interior (FIG. 26-4) of Neumann's church exhibits a vivacious play of architectural fantasy that retains the dynamic energy of Italian Baroque architecture (see Chapter 24) but not its drama. Numerous large windows in the richly decorated walls of Vierzehnheiligen flood the interior with an even, bright, and cheerful light. The feeling is one of lightness and delicacy.

Vierzehnheiligen's plan (FIG. 26-5) reveals the influence of Francesco Borromini (FIGS. 24-10 and 24-13), as does the contemporaneous Wieskirche (Church of the Meadow; FIG. **26-5B**) by Dominikus Zimmermann (1685–1766). The Staffelstein plan, however, is even more complex than the plans for Borromini's churches in Rome. Neumann, perhaps deliberately, banished all straight lines. The composition, made up of tangent ovals and circles, achieves a quite different interior effect within the essential outlines of a traditional rectilinear basilican church with a nave, transept, and apse. Undulating space is in continuous motion, creating unlimited vistas bewildering in their variety and surprise effects. The structure's features pulse, flow, and commingle as if they were ceaselessly in the process of being molded. The design's fluidity of line, the floating and hovering surfaces, the interwoven spaces, and the dematerialized masses combine to suggest a "frozen" counterpart to the intricacy of voices in a Baroque fugue by Johann Sebastian Bach (1685–1750). The church is a brilliant ensemble of architecture, painting, sculpture, and music that dissolves the boundaries among the arts.

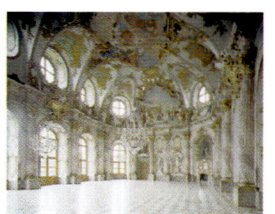

**26-5A** Neumann, Kaisersaal, Würzburg, 1719–1744.

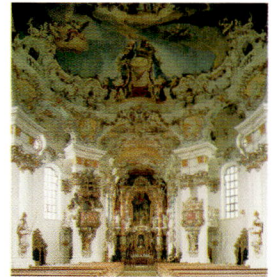

**26-5B** Zimmermann, Wieskirche, Füssen, 1745–1754.

## Painting and Sculpture

The unification of diverse artistic media that characterizes the Rococo style did not preclude the rise to prominence of painters of independent works. Chief among them were Antoine Watteau, François Boucher, and Jean-Honoré Fragonard in France.

**ANTOINE WATTEAU** The painter whom scholars most closely associate with French Rococo is ANTOINE WATTEAU (1684–1721). The sharp differences between the Rococo and Baroque ages in France quickly become evident by contrasting Watteau's *L'Indifférent* (*The Indifferent One*; FIG. **26-6**) with Rigaud's portrait of Louis XIV (FIG. 25-24). Rigaud portrayed pompous majesty in supreme glory, as if the French monarch were reviewing throngs of bowing courtiers at Versailles. Watteau's painting is more delicate and lighter in both color and tone. The artist presented a languid, gliding dancer whose stilted minuet might constitute a parody of the monarch's solemnity if the paintings were hung together. (The contrast in scale would be equally stark: The portrait of Louis XIV is almost 10 feet tall. Watteau's dancer is 10 inches tall.) In Rigaud's portrait, stout architecture, bannerlike curtains, flowing ermine, and fleur-de-lis exalt the king. In Watteau's painting, the dancer moves in a rainbow shimmer of color, emerging onto the stage of the intimate comic opera to the silken sounds of strings. As in architecture, this contrast of paintings also highlights the shift in artistic patronage from one era to the next.

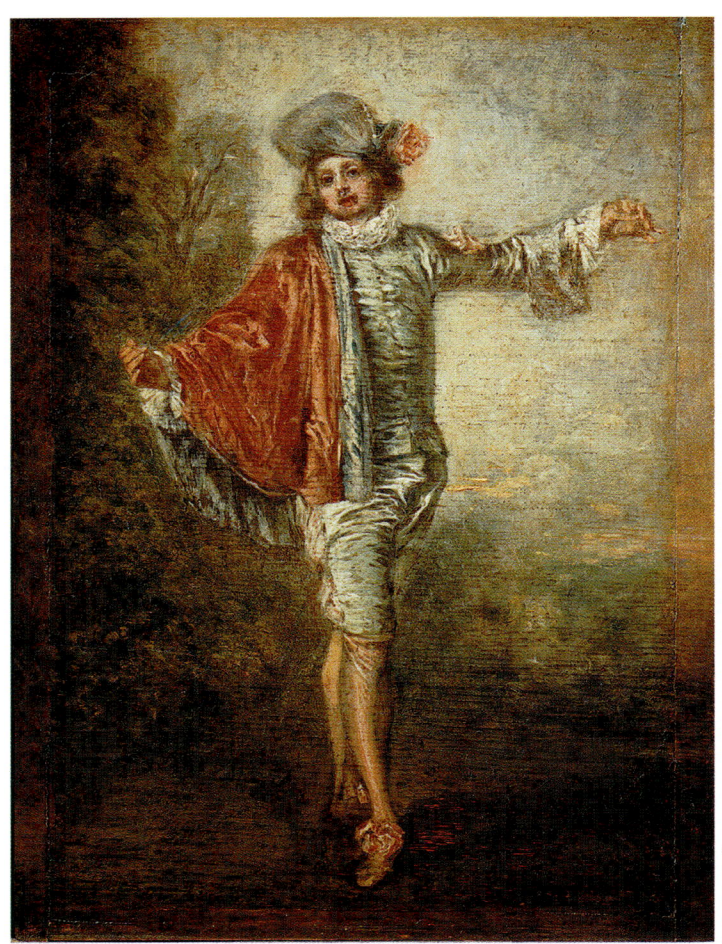

**26-6** ANTOINE WATTEAU, *L'Indifférent*, ca. 1716. Oil on canvas, 10″ × 7″. Musée du Louvre, Paris. ◼◀

This small Rococo painting of a dancer exhibits lightness and delicacy in both color and tone. It differs significantly from Rigaud's majestic portrait (FIG. 25-24) of the pompous Louis XIV.

1 in.

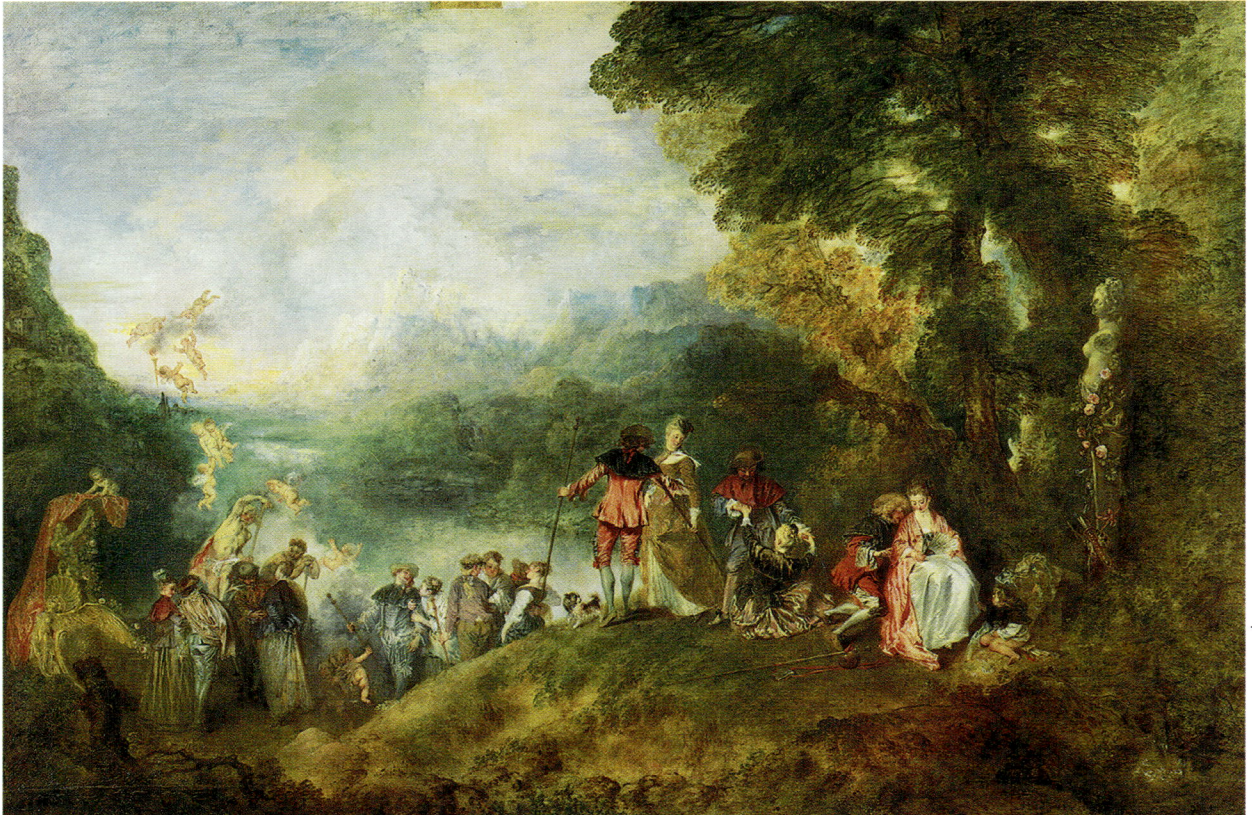

**26-7** ANTOINE WATTEAU, *Pilgrimage to Cythera*, 1717. Oil on canvas, 4′ 3″ × 6′ 4½″. Musée du Louvre, Paris. ◼◀

Watteau's *fête galante* paintings depict the outdoor amusements of French upper-class society. The haze of color, subtly modeled shapes, gliding motion, and air of suave gentility match Rococo taste.

1 ft.

Whereas royal patronage, particularly on the part of Louis XIV, dominated the French Baroque period, Rococo was the culture of a wider aristocracy in which private patrons dictated taste.

***PILGRIMAGE TO CYTHERA*** Watteau was largely responsible for creating a specific type of Rococo painting, called a *fête galante* (amorous festival) painting. These paintings depicted the outdoor entertainment or amusements of French high society. The premier example of a fête galante painting is Watteau's masterpiece (painted in two versions), *Pilgrimage to Cythera* (FIG. 26-7). The painting was the artist's entry for admission to the French Royal Academy of Painting and Sculpture (see "Academic Salons," Chapter 28, page 802). In 1717 the fête galante was not an acceptable category for submission, but rather than reject Watteau's candidacy, the academy created a new category to accommodate his entry. At the turn of the 18th century, two competing doctrines sharply divided the membership of the French academy. Many members followed Nicolas Poussin in teaching that form was the most important element in painting, whereas "colors in painting are as allurements for persuading the eyes."[1] Colors were additions for effect and not really essential. The other group took Rubens as its model and proclaimed the natural supremacy of color and the coloristic style as the artist's proper guide. Depending on which doctrine they supported, academy members were either *Poussinistes* or *Rubénistes*. Watteau was Flemish and Rubens's coloristic style heavily influenced his work. With Watteau in their ranks, the Rubénistes carried the day, establishing Rococo painting as the preferred style of the early 18th century.

Watteau's *Pilgrimage to Cythera* (FIG. 26-7) presents luxuriously costumed lovers who have made a "pilgrimage" to Cythera, the island of eternal youth and love, sacred to Aphrodite. (Some art historians think the lovers are returning from Cythera rather than having just arrived. Watteau provided few clues to settle the question definitively.) The elegant figures move gracefully from the protective shade of a woodland park, filled with amorous cupids and voluptuous statuary. Watteau's figural poses blend elegance and sweetness. He composed his generally quite small paintings from albums of drawings in which he sought to capture slow movement from difficult and unusual angles, searching for the smoothest, most poised, and most refined attitudes. As he experimented with nuances of posture and movement, Watteau also strove for the most exquisite shades of color difference, defining in a single stroke the shimmer of silk at a bent knee or the iridescence that touches a glossy surface as it emerges from shadow. The haze of color, the subtly modeled shapes, the gliding motion, and the air of suave gentility appealed greatly to Watteau's wealthy patrons, whom, as he was dying from tuberculosis, he still depicted as carefree and at leisure in his most unusual painting, *Signboard of Gersaint* (FIG. **26-7A**).

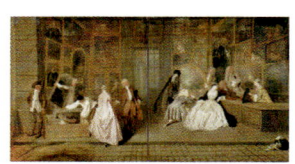

26-7A WATTEAU, *Signboard of Gersaint*, 1721.

**FRANÇOIS BOUCHER** After Watteau's death at age 36 brought his brilliant career to a premature end, FRANÇOIS BOUCHER (1703–1770) rose to the dominant position in French painting, in large part because he was Madame de Pompadour's favorite artist. Although Boucher was an excellent portraitist, his success rested primarily on his graceful canvases depicting Arcadian shepherds, nymphs, and goddesses cavorting in shady glens engulfed in pink and sky-blue light. *Cupid a Captive* (FIG. 26-8) presents a rosy pyramid of infant and female flesh set off against a cool, leafy background, with fluttering draperies both hiding and revealing the nudity of the figures. Boucher used the full range of Italian

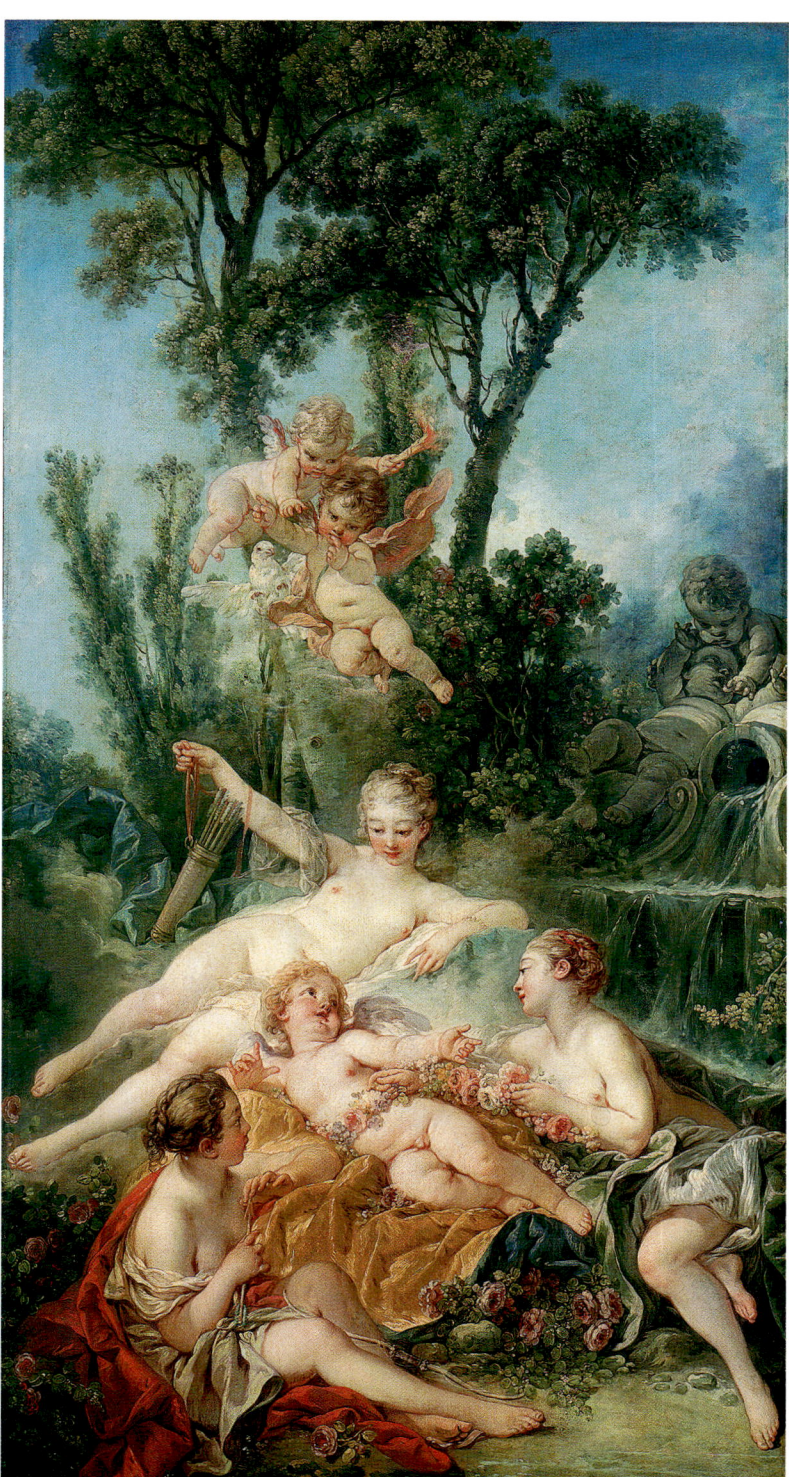

1 ft.

**26-8** FRANÇOIS BOUCHER, *Cupid a Captive*, 1754. Oil on canvas, 5′ 6″ × 2′ 10″. **Wallace Collection, London.** ◼◀

Boucher was Madame de Pompadour's favorite artist. In this Rococo tableau, he painted a pyramid of rosy infant and female flesh and fluttering draperies set off against a cool, leafy background.

and French Baroque devices—the dynamic play of crisscrossing diagonals, curvilinear forms, and slanting recessions—to create his masterly composition. But he dissected powerful Baroque curves into a multiplicity of decorative flourishes, dissipating Baroque drama into sensual playfulness. Lively and lighthearted, Boucher's artful Rococo fantasies became mirrors for his affluent French patrons to behold the ornamental reflections of their cherished pastimes.

**JEAN-HONORÉ FRAGONARD**  Boucher's greatest student, JEAN-HONORÉ FRAGONARD (1732–1806), was a first-rate colorist whose decorative skill almost surpassed his master's. An example of his manner can stand as characteristic not only of his work but also of the later Rococo in general. In *The Swing* (FIG. **26-9**), a young gentleman has convinced an unsuspecting old bishop to swing the young man's pretty sweetheart higher and higher, while her lover (and the work's patron), in the lower left corner, stretches out to admire her ardently from a strategic position on the ground. The young lady flirtatiously and boldly kicks off her shoe toward the little statue of Cupid. The infant love god holds his finger to his lips. The landscape emulates Watteau's—a luxuriant perfumed bower in

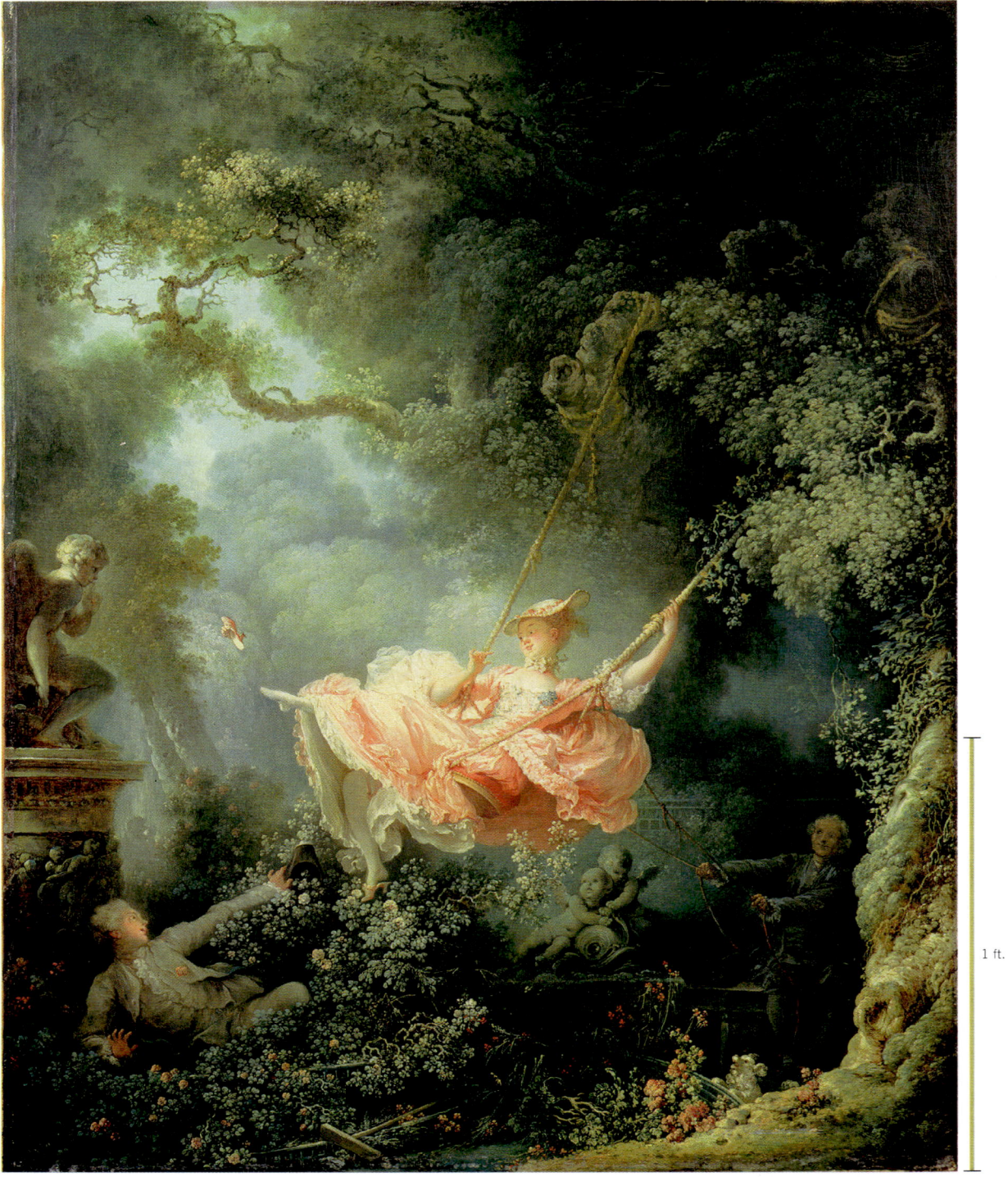

1 ft.

**26-9**  JEAN-HONORÉ FRAGONARD, *The Swing,* 1766. Oil on canvas, 2′ 8⅝″ × 2′ 2″. Wallace Collection, London. ◼◀

Fragonard's *Swing* epitomizes Rococo style. Pastel colors and soft light complement a scene in which a young lady flirtatiously kicks off her shoe at a statue of Cupid while her lover watches.

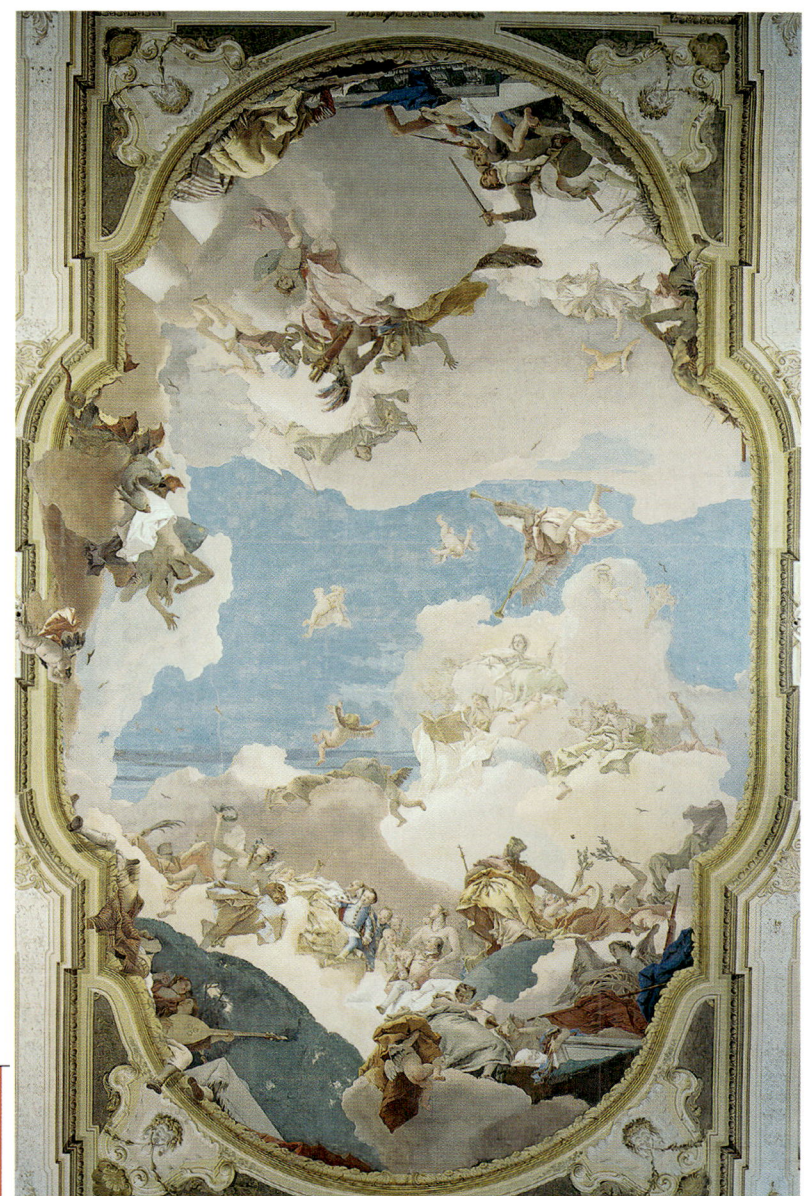

10 ft.

**26-10** GIAMBATTISTA TIEPOLO, *Apotheosis of the Pisani Family,* ceiling painting in the Villa Pisani, Stra, Italy, 1761–1762. Fresco, 77′ 1″ × 44′ 3″.

A master of illusionistic ceiling painting in the Baroque tradition, Tiepolo adopted the bright and cheerful colors and weightless figures of Rococo easel paintings for huge frescoes.

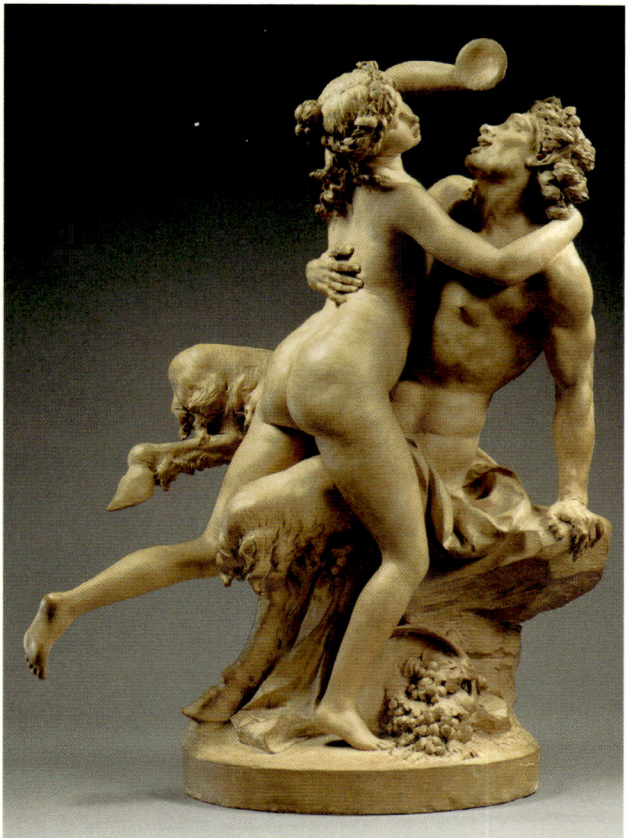

1 in.

**26-11** CLODION, *Nymph and Satyr Carousing,* ca. 1780–1790. Terracotta, 1′ 11¼″ high. Metropolitan Museum of Art, New York (bequest of Benjamin Altman, 1913).

The erotic playfulness of Boucher and Fragonard is evident in Clodion's tabletop terracotta sculptures representing sensuous fantasies often involving satyrs and nymphs, the followers of Bacchus.

a park that very much resembles a stage scene for comic opera. The glowing pastel colors and soft light convey, almost by themselves, the theme's sensuality.

**GIAMBATTISTA TIEPOLO** *The Swing* is less than 3 feet in height and Watteau's *L'Indifférent* (FIG. 26-6), as already noted, barely 10 inches tall. But the intimate Rococo style could also be adapted for paintings of huge size, as the work of GIAMBATTISTA TIEPOLO (1696–1770) demonstrates. A Venetian, Tiepolo worked for patrons in Austria, Germany, and Spain, as well as in Italy. He was a master of illusionistic ceiling decoration in the Baroque tradition, but favored the bright, cheerful colors and relaxed compositions of Rococo easel paintings. In *Apotheosis of the Pisani Family* (FIG. **26-10**), a ceiling fresco in the Villa Pisani at Stra in northern Italy (MAP 25-1), Tiepolo depicted seemingly weightless figures fluttering through vast sunlit skies and fleecy clouds, their forms casting dark accents

against the brilliant light of high noon. The painter elevated Pisani family members to the rank of gods in a heavenly scene recalling the ceiling paintings of Pozzo (FIG. 24-24). But while retaining 17th-century illusionism in his works, Tiepolo softened the rhetoric and created pictorial schemes of great elegance and grace, unsurpassed for their sheer effectiveness as decor.

**CLODION** Rococo was nontheless a style best suited for small-scale works projecting a mood of sensual intimacy. Claude Michel, called CLODION (1738–1814), specialized in small, lively sculptures representing sensuous Rococo fantasies. Clodion lived and worked in Rome for several years after winning a cherished Prix de Rome (Rome Prize) from the French royal academy to study art and paint or sculpt in the eternal city. Clodion's work incorporates echoes of Italian Mannerist sculpture. His small group, *Nymph and Satyr Carousing* (FIG. **26-11**), depicts two followers of Bacchus, the Roman god of wine. The sensuous nymph who rushes to pour wine from a cup into the open mouth of a semihuman goat-legged satyr is reminiscent of the nude female figures of Benvenuto Cellini (FIGS. 22-52 and 22-52A), who worked at Fontainebleau for Francis I, and of Giovanni da Bologna (FIG. 22-53), a French Mannerist sculptor who moved to Italy. The erotic playfulness of Boucher and Fragonard is also evident in Clodion's 2-foot-tall terracotta group destined for display on a marble tabletop in an elegant Rococo salon.

# THE ENLIGHTENMENT

The aristocratic culture celebrated in Rococo art did not go unchallenged during the 18th century. Indeed, the feudal system that served as the foundation of social and economic life in Europe dissolved, and the rigid social hierarchies that provided the basis for Rococo art and patronage relaxed. By the end of the 18th century, revolutions had erupted in France and America. A major factor in these political, social, and economic changes was the Enlightenment.

## Philosophy and Science

Enlightenment thinkers championed an approach to the acquisition of knowledge based on empirical observation and scientific experimentation (see "Art and Science in the Era of Enlightenment," page 727). Enlightenment-era science had roots in the work of René Descartes (1596–1650), Blaise Pascal (1623–1662), Isaac Newton (1642–1727), and Gottfried Wilhelm von Leibnitz (1646–1716) in the 17th century. England and France were the principal centers of the Enlightenment, though its dictums influenced the thinking of intellectuals throughout Europe and in the American colonies. Benjamin Franklin (1706–1790), Thomas Jefferson (1743–1826), and other American notables embraced its principles.

**NEWTON AND LOCKE** Of particular importance for Enlightenment thought was the work of Isaac Newton and John Locke (1632–1704) in England. In his scientific studies, Newton insisted on empirical proof of his theories and encouraged others to avoid metaphysics and the supernatural—realms that extended beyond the natural physical world. This emphasis on both tangible data and concrete experience became a cornerstone of Enlightenment thought. In addition, Newton's experiments revealed rationality in the physical world, and Enlightenment thinkers transferred that concept to the sociopolitical world by promoting a rationally organized society. Locke, whose works acquired the status of Enlightenment gospel, developed these ideas further. According to Locke's "doctrine of empiricism," knowledge comes through sensory perception of the material world. From these perceptions alone people form ideas. Locke asserted human beings are born good, not cursed by original sin. The laws of nature grant them the natural rights of life, liberty, and property as well as the right to freedom of conscience. Government is by contract, and its purpose is to protect these rights. If and when government abuses these rights, the citizenry has the further natural right of revolution. Locke's ideas empowered people to take control of their own destinies.

**PHILOSOPHES** The work of Newton and Locke also inspired many French intellectuals, or *philosophes.* These thinkers conceived of individuals and societies at large as parts of physical nature. They shared the conviction the ills of humanity could be remedied by applying reason and common sense to human problems. They criticized the powers of church and state as irrational limits placed on political and intellectual freedom. They believed by accumulating and propagating knowledge, humanity could advance by degrees to a happier state than it had ever known. This conviction matured into the "doctrine of progress" and its corollary doctrine, the "perfectibility of humankind." Previous societies, for the most part, perceived the future as inevitable—the cycle of life and death. They believed religious beliefs determined fate. The notion of progress—the systematic and planned improvement of society—first developed during the 18th century and continues to influence 21st-century thought.

**DIDEROT** Animated by their belief in human progress and perfectibility, the philosophes took on the task of gathering knowledge and making it accessible to all who could read. Their program was, in effect, the democratization of knowledge. Denis Diderot (1713–1784) greatly influenced the Enlightenment's rationalistic and materialistic thinking. He became editor of the pioneering *Encyclopédie,* a compilation of articles written by more than a hundred contributors, including all the leading philosophes. The *Encyclopédie* was truly comprehensive (its formal title was *Systematic Dictionary of the Sciences, Arts, and Crafts*) and included all available knowledge—historical, scientific, and technical as well as religious and moral—and political theory. The first volume appeared in 1751 and the last of the 35 volumes of text and illustrations in 1780. Other Enlightenment authors produced different compilations of knowledge. Diderot's contemporary, Georges-Louis Leclerc (1707–1788), Comte de Buffon, undertook a kind of encyclopedia of the natural sciences. His *Natural History,* a monumental work of 44 volumes, was especially valuable for its zoological study. Buffon's contemporary, the Swedish botanist Carolus Linnaeus (1707–1778), established a system of plant classification.

The political, economic, and social consequences of this increase in knowledge and the doctrine of progress were explosive. It is no coincidence the French Revolution, the American Revolution, and the Industrial Revolution in England all occurred during this period. These upheavals precipitated yet other major changes, including the growth of cities and of an urban working class, and the expansion of colonialism as the demand for cheap labor and raw materials increased. This enthusiasm for growth gave birth to the doctrine of Manifest Destiny—the ideological justification for continued territorial expansion. Thus, the Age of Enlightenment ushered in a new way of thinking and affected historical developments worldwide.

**VOLTAIRE** François Marie Arouet, better known as Voltaire (1694–1778), was the most representative figure—almost the personification—of the Enlightenment spirit. Voltaire was instrumental in introducing Newton and Locke to the French intelligentsia. He hated, and attacked through his writings, the arbitrary despotic rule of kings, the selfish privileges of the nobility and the church, religious intolerance, and, above all, the injustice of the French *ancien regime* (the "old order"). In his numerous books and pamphlets, which the authorities regularly condemned and burned, he protested against government persecution of the freedoms of thought and religion. Voltaire believed humankind could never be happy until an enlightened society removed the traditional obstructions to the progress of the human mind. His personal and public involvement in the struggle against established political and religious authority gave authenticity to his ideas. Voltaire persuaded a whole generation that fundamental changes were necessary, paving the way for a revolution in France he never intended and probably would never have approved. Voltaire did not believe "all men are created equal," the credo of Jean-Jacques Rousseau, Thomas Jefferson, and the American Declaration of Independence.

**INDUSTRIAL REVOLUTION** The Enlightenment emphasis on scientific investigation and technological invention opened up new possibilities for human understanding of the world and for control of its material forces. Research into the phenomena of electricity and combustion, along with the discovery of oxygen and the power of steam, had enormous consequences. Steam power as an adjunct to, or replacement for, human labor initiated a new era in world history, beginning with the Industrial Revolution in England. These and other technological advances—admiringly

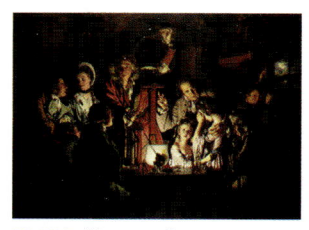

recorded in the paintings of Joseph Wright of Derby (FIGS. 26-1 and **26-11A**)—epitomized the Enlightenment notion of progress and gave birth to the Industrial Revolution. Most scholars mark the dawn of that technological revolution in the 1740s with the invention of steam engines in England for industrial production. By 1850, England could boast the world's first manufacturing economy. Within a century, the harnessed power of steam, coal, oil, iron, steel, and electricity working in concert transformed Europe. These scientific and technological advances also affected the arts, particularly through the invention of photography (see Chapter 27) and the use of new materials for constructing buildings.

**COALBROOKDALE BRIDGE**    The first use of iron in bridge design was in the cast-iron bridge (FIG. **26-12**) built over the Severn River, near Coalbrookdale in England (MAP 30-1), where ABRAHAM DARBY III (1750–1789), one of the bridge's two designers, ran his family's cast-iron business. The Darby family had spearheaded the evolution of the iron industry in England, and they vigorously supported the investigation of new uses for the material. The fabrication of cast-iron rails and bridge elements inspired Darby to work with architect THOMAS F. PRITCHARD (1723–1777) in designing the Coalbrookdale Bridge. The cast-iron armature supporting the roadbed springs from stone pier to stone pier until it leaps the final 100 feet across the Severn River gorge. The style of the graceful center arc echoes the grand arches of Roman aqueducts (FIG. 7-33). At the same time, the exposed structure of the bridge's cast-iron parts prefigured the skeletal use of iron and steel in the 19th century, when exposed structural armatures became expressive factors in the design of buildings such as the Crystal Palace (FIG. 27-47) in England and the Eiffel Tower (FIG. 28-38) in France.

**ROUSSEAU**    The second key figure of the French Enlightenment, who was also instrumental in preparing the way ideologically for the French Revolution, was Jean-Jacques Rousseau (1712–1778). Voltaire believed the salvation of humanity lay in the advancement of science and the rational improvement of society. In contrast, Rousseau argued the arts, sciences, society, and civilization in general had corrupted "natural man"—people in their primitive state. He was convinced humanity's only salvation lay in a return to something like "the ignorance, innocence and happiness" of its original condition. According to Rousseau, human capacity for feeling, sensibility, and emotions came before reason: "To exist is to feel; our feeling is undoubtedly earlier than our intelligence, and we had feelings before we had ideas." Nature alone must be the guide: "All our natural inclinations are right." Fundamental to Rousseau's thinking was the notion "Man by nature is good . . . he is depraved and perverted by society." He rejected the idea of progress, insisting "Our minds have been corrupted in proportion as the arts and sciences have improved."[2] Rousseau's elevation of feelings above reason as the most primitive—and hence the most "natural"—of human expressions led him to exalt as the ideal the peasant's simple life, with its honest and unsullied emotions.

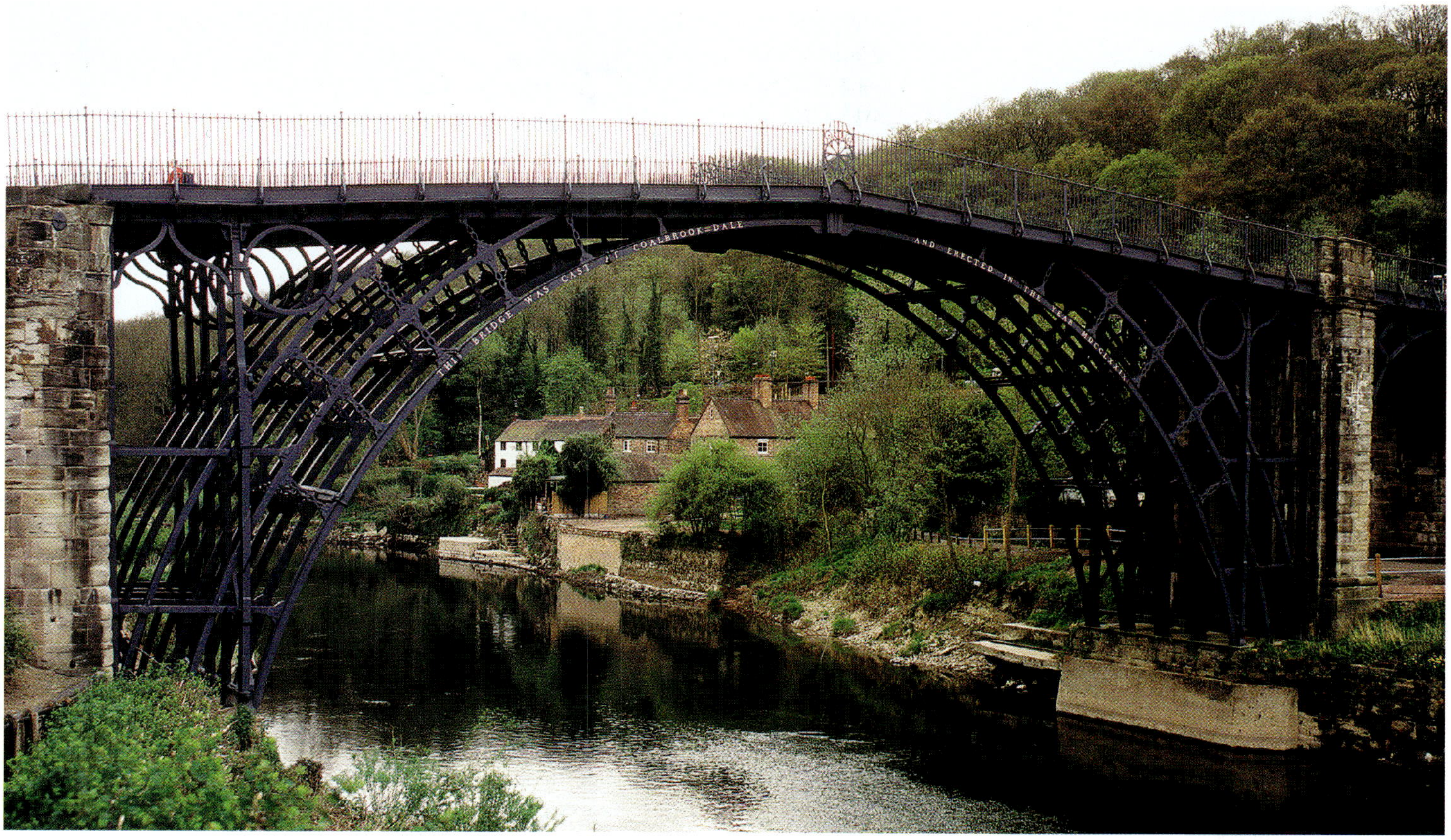

**26-12**    ABRAHAM DARBY III and THOMAS F. PRITCHARD, iron bridge (looking northwest), Coalbrookdale, England, 1776–1779.

The first use of iron in bridge design was in this bridge over the Severn River. The Industrial Revolution brought engineering advances and new materials that revolutionized architectural construction.

## Diderot on Chardin and Boucher

Denis Diderot was a pioneer in the field of art criticism as well as in the encyclopedic compilation of human knowledge. Between 1759 and 1781, he contributed reviews of the biennial Salon of the French Royal Academy of Painting and Sculpture (see "Academic Salons," Chapter 28, page 802) to the Parisian journal *Correspondence littéraire*. In his review of the 1763 Salon, Diderot had the following praise for Chardin's still lifes and for naturalism in painting.

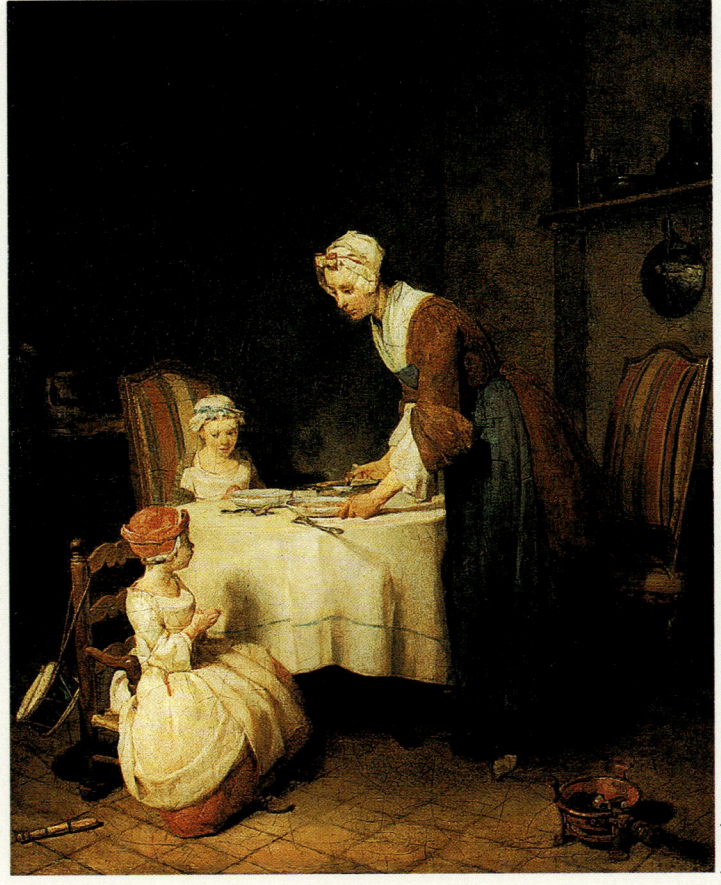

**26-13** Jean-Baptiste-Siméon Chardin, *Saying Grace*, 1740. Oil on canvas, 1′ 7″ × 1′ 3″. Musée du Louvre, Paris.

Chardin embraced naturalism and celebrated the simple goodness of ordinary people, especially mothers and children, who lived in a world far from the frivolous Rococo salons of Paris.

1 in.

There are many small pictures by Chardin at the Salon, almost all of them depicting fruit with the accoutrements for a meal. This is nature itself. The objects stand out from the canvas and they are so real that my eyes are fooled by them. . . . In order to look at other people's paintings, I feel as though I need different eyes; but to look at Chardin's, I need only keep the ones nature gave me and use them properly. If I had painting in mind as a career for my child, I'd buy this one [and have him copy it]. . . . Yet nature itself may be no more difficult to copy. . . . O Chardin, it's not white, red or black pigment that you grind on your palette but rather the very substance of objects; it's real air and light that you take onto the tip of your brush and transfer onto the canvas. . . . It's magic, one can't understand how it's done: thick layers of colour, applied one on top of the other, each one filtering through from underneath to create the effect. . . . Close up, everything blurs, goes flat and disappears. From a distance, everything comes back to life and reappears.*

Diderot could write scathing reviews as well as lavish praise on the leading artists of his day. He admired Chardin (FIG. 26-13) because his work was the antithesis of the Rococo manner in painting, which Diderot deplored. Here, for example, is what Diderot had to say about François Boucher (FIG. 26-8), who also exhibited in the Salon of 1763, and his younger protégés emulating his Rococo style:

What a misuse of talent! How much time gone to waste! You could have had twice the effect for half the effort. . . . When one writes, does one have to write everything? And when one paints, does one have to paint everything? . . . This man is the ruination of all young apprentice painters. Barely able to handle a brush and hold a palette, they torture themselves stringing together infantile garlands, painting chubby crimson bottoms, and hurl themselves headlong into all kinds of follies which cannot be redeemed by originality, fire, tenderness nor by any magic in their models. For they lack all of these.†

*Translated by Kate Tunstall, in Charles Harrison, Paul Wood, and Jason Gaiger, eds., *Art in Theory 1648–1815: An Anthology of Changing Ideas* (Oxford: Blackwell, 2000), 604.
†Ibid., 603–604.

## "NATURAL" ART

Rousseau's views, popular and widely read, were largely responsible for the turning away from the Rococo sensibility in the arts and the formation of a taste for the "natural," as opposed to the artificial and frivolous.

**CHARDIN** Reflecting Rousseau's values, Jean-Baptiste-Siméon Chardin (1699–1779) painted quiet scenes of domestic life, which offered the opportunity to praise the simple goodness of ordinary people, especially mothers and young children, who in spirit, occupation, and environment lived far from corrupt society. In *Saying Grace* (FIG. 26-13), Chardin ushers the viewer into a modest room where a mother and her two daughters are about to dine. The mood of quiet attention is at one with the hushed lighting and mellow color and with the closely studied still-life accessories whose worn surfaces tell their own humble domestic history. The viewer witnesses a moment of social instruction, when mother and older sister supervise the younger sister in the simple, pious ritual of giving thanks to God before a meal. The simplicity of the composition reinforces the subdued charm of this scene, with the three figures highlighted against the dark background. Chardin was the poet of the commonplace and the master of its nuances. A gentle sentiment

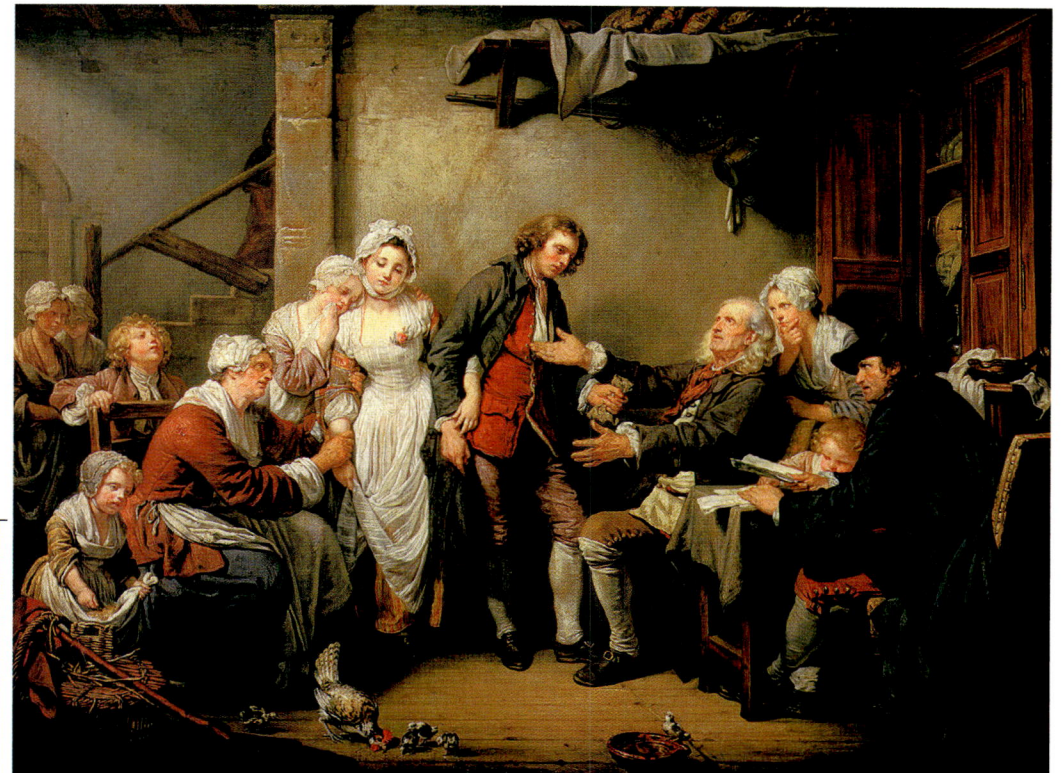

26-14 JEAN-BAPTISTE GREUZE, *Village Bride*, 1761. Oil on canvas, 3′ × 3′ 10½″. Musée du Louvre, Paris.

Greuze was a master of sentimental narrative, which appealed to a new audience that admired "natural" virtue. Here, in an unadorned room, a father blesses his daughter and her husband-to-be.

prevails in all his pictures, an emotion not contrived and artificial but born of the painter's honesty, insight, and sympathy. Chardin's paintings had wide appeal, even in unexpected places. Louis XV, the royal personification of the Rococo in his life and tastes, once owned *Saying Grace*. The painter was also a favorite of Diderot, the leading art critic of the day as well as the editor of the *Encylopédie* (see "Diderot on Chardin and Boucher," page 738).

**JEAN-BAPTISTE GREUZE** The sentimental narrative in art became the specialty of French artist JEAN-BAPTISTE GREUZE (1725–1805), whose most popular work, *Village Bride* (FIG. **26-14**), sums up the characteristics of the genre. The setting is an unadorned room in a rustic dwelling. In a notary's presence, the elderly father has passed his daughter's dowry to her youthful husband-to-be and blesses the pair, who gently take each other's arms. The old mother tearfully gives her daughter's arm a farewell caress, while the youngest sister melts in tears on the shoulder of the demure bride. An envious older sister broods behind her father's chair. Rosy-faced, healthy children play around the scene. The picture's story is simple—the happy climax of a rural romance. The picture's moral is just as clear—happiness is the reward of "natural" virtue.

Greuze produced this work at a time when the audience for art was expanding. The strict social hierarchy that provided the foundation for Rococo art and patronage gave way to a bourgeois economic and social system. The newly important bourgeois class embraced art, and paintings such as *Village Bride* particularly appealed to ordinary hard-working people. They carefully analyzed each gesture and each nuance of sentiment and reacted with tumultuous enthusiasm. At the 1761 Salon of the Royal Academy, Greuze's picture received enormous attention. Diderot, who reviewed the exhibition for *Correspondence littéraire,* reported it was difficult to get near the canvas because of the throngs of admirers.

**ÉLISABETH-LOUISE VIGÉE-LEBRUN** Another manifestation of the "naturalistic" impulse in 18th-century French art was the emergence of a new mode of portraiture exemplified by *Self-Portrait* (FIG. **26-15**) by ÉLISABETH-LOUISE VIGÉE-LEBRUN (1755–1842). The painter looks directly at viewers and pauses in her work to return their gaze. Although her mood is lighthearted and her costume's details echo the serpentine curve Rococo artists and wealthy patrons loved, nothing about Vigée-Lebrun's pose or her mood speaks of Rococo frivolity. Hers is the self-confident stance of a woman whose art has won her an independent role in society. She

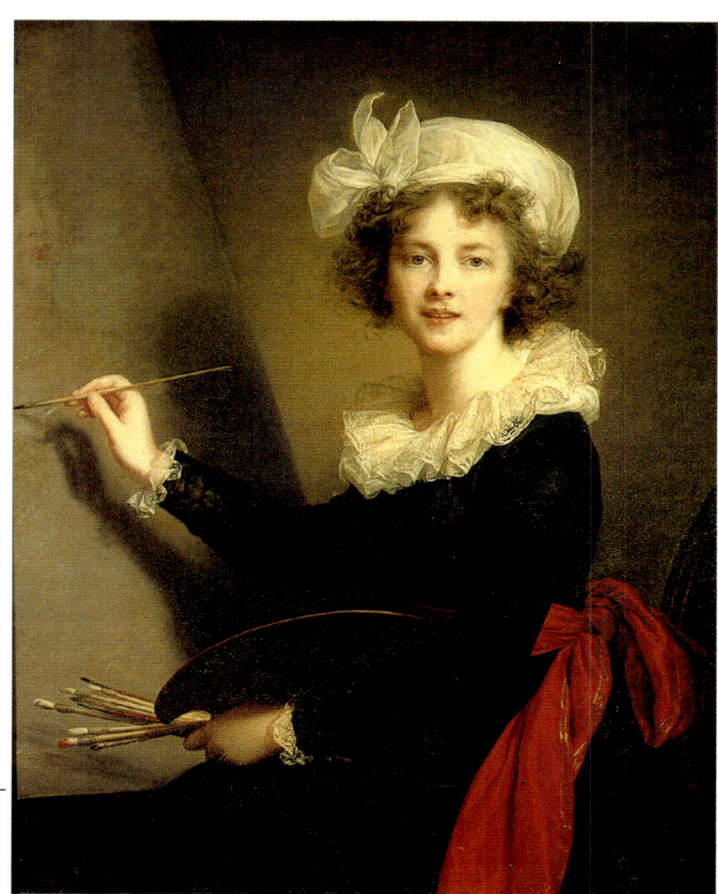

26-15 ÉLISABETH-LOUISE VIGÉE-LEBRUN, *Self-Portrait*, 1790. Oil on canvas, 8′ 4″ × 6′ 9″. Galleria degli Uffizi, Florence.

Vigée-Lebrun was one of the few women admitted to the Royal Academy of Painting and Sculpture. In this self-portrait, she depicted herself confidently painting the likeness of Queen Marie Antoinette.

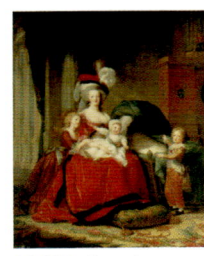

portrayed herself in a close-up, intimate view at work on one of the many portraits (for example, FIG. **26-15A**) she painted of her most important patron, Queen Marie Antoinette (1755–1793). Like many of her contemporaries, Vigée-Lebrun lived a life of extraordinary personal and economic independence, working for the nobility throughout Europe. She was famous for the force and grace of her portraits, especially those of highborn ladies and royalty. She was successful during the age of the late monarchy in France and was one of the few women admitted to the Royal Academy of Painting and Sculpture. After the French Revolution, however, the academy rescinded her membership, because women were no longer welcome, but she enjoyed continued success owing to her talent, wit, and ability to forge connections with those in power in the postrevolutionary period.

**ADÉLAÏDE LABILLE-GUIARD** Six years older than Vigée-Lebrun, ADÉLAÏDE LABILLE-GUIARD (1749–1803) was the second-most important woman painter in Paris at the end of the 18th century, but she never achieved the renown enjoyed by her younger rival. She trained with François-Élie Vincent (1708–1790) and later with his son François-André Vincent (1746–1816), whom she married after her divorce from her first husband, Louis-Nicolas Guiard, a clerk. Like Vigée-Lebrun, Labille-Guiard boasted royal patronage but not of the same order. She became the official painter of the "mesdames"—the aunts of King Louis XVI—in 1787, four years after she was admitted to the royal painting academy on the same day as Vigée-Lebrun. The two painters captured the remaining two of four memberships reserved for women, a quota Labille-Guiard worked hard to lift after gaining admission. The two artists took opposite sides during the French Revolution, and Labille-Guiard painted portraits of some of the uprising's leaders, including one of the few known portraits of Maximilien Robespierre (1758–1794), the most prominent figure calling for the death of King Louis XVI.

A comparison between Labille-Guiard's *Self-Portrait with Two Pupils* (FIG. **26-16**) and Vigée-Lebrun's *Self-Portrait* (FIG. 26-15) underscores the two women's different self-images. The younger painter presented herself at work on a portrait of her most important patron, Marie Antoinette. The subject of the canvas Labille-Guiard is painting is unknown. Her self-portrait focuses instead on her role as a teacher. She had as many as nine women in her studio at one time. Here, two apprentices—dressed more simply than their elegantly clad instructor—cluster behind her, one intently studying the painting in progress, the other, as Labille-Guiard, gazing at the viewer. The three figures form a classical pyramidal composition, echoed by the easel. In the V formed by the two triangles is a portrait bust of the artist's father. Appropriately for this early feminist, her muse is a man, a reversal of the traditional gender roles.

**WILLIAM HOGARTH** Across the Channel, a truly English style of painting emerged with WILLIAM HOGARTH (1697–1764), who satirized the lifestyle of the newly prosperous middle class with comic zest. Traditionally, the British imported painters from the Continent—Holbein, Rubens, and Van Dyck among them. Hogarth waged a lively campaign throughout his career against the English feeling of dependence on, and inferiority to, these artists. Although Hogarth would have been the last to admit it, his own painting owed much to the work of his contemporaries in France, the Rococo

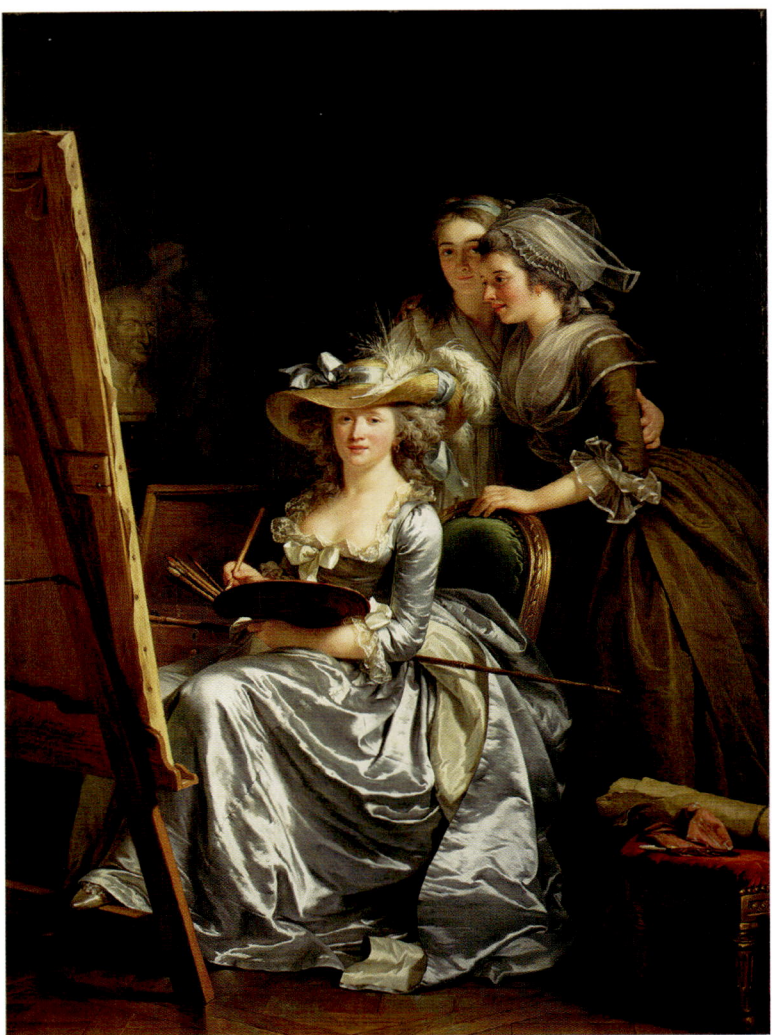

1 ft.

**26-16** ADÉLAÏDE LABILLE-GUIARD, *Self-Portrait with Two Pupils*, 1785. Oil on canvas, 6′ 11″ × 4′ 11½″. Metropolitan Museum of Art, New York (gift of Julia A. Berwind, 1953).

In contrast to Vigée-Lebrun (FIG. 26-15), Labille-Guiard, her older contemporary, depicted herself as a teacher. Her father's bust portrait serves as her muse in a reversal of traditional gender roles.

artists. Yet his subject matter, frequently moral in tone, was distinctively English. This was the great age of English satirical writing, and Hogarth—who admired that literary genre and included Henry Fielding (1701–1754), the author of *Tom Jones,* among his closest friends—clearly saw himself as translating satire into the visual arts.

Hogarth's favorite device was to make a series of narrative paintings and prints, in a sequence similar to chapters in a book or scenes in a play, following a character or group of characters in their encounters with some social evil. *Breakfast Scene* (FIG. **26-17**), from *Marriage à la Mode,* is one in a sequence of six paintings satirizing the marital immoralities of the moneyed classes in England. In it, the marriage of a young viscount is just beginning to founder. The husband and wife are tired after a long night spent in separate pursuits. While the wife stayed at home for an evening of cards and music-making, her young husband had been away from the house for a night of suspicious business. He thrusts his hands deep into the empty money-pockets of his breeches, while his wife's small dog sniffs inquiringly at a woman's lacy cap protruding from his coat pocket. A steward, his hands full of unpaid bills, raises his eyes in despair at the actions of his noble master and mistress. The house is palatial, but Hogarth filled it with witty clues to the dubious taste of

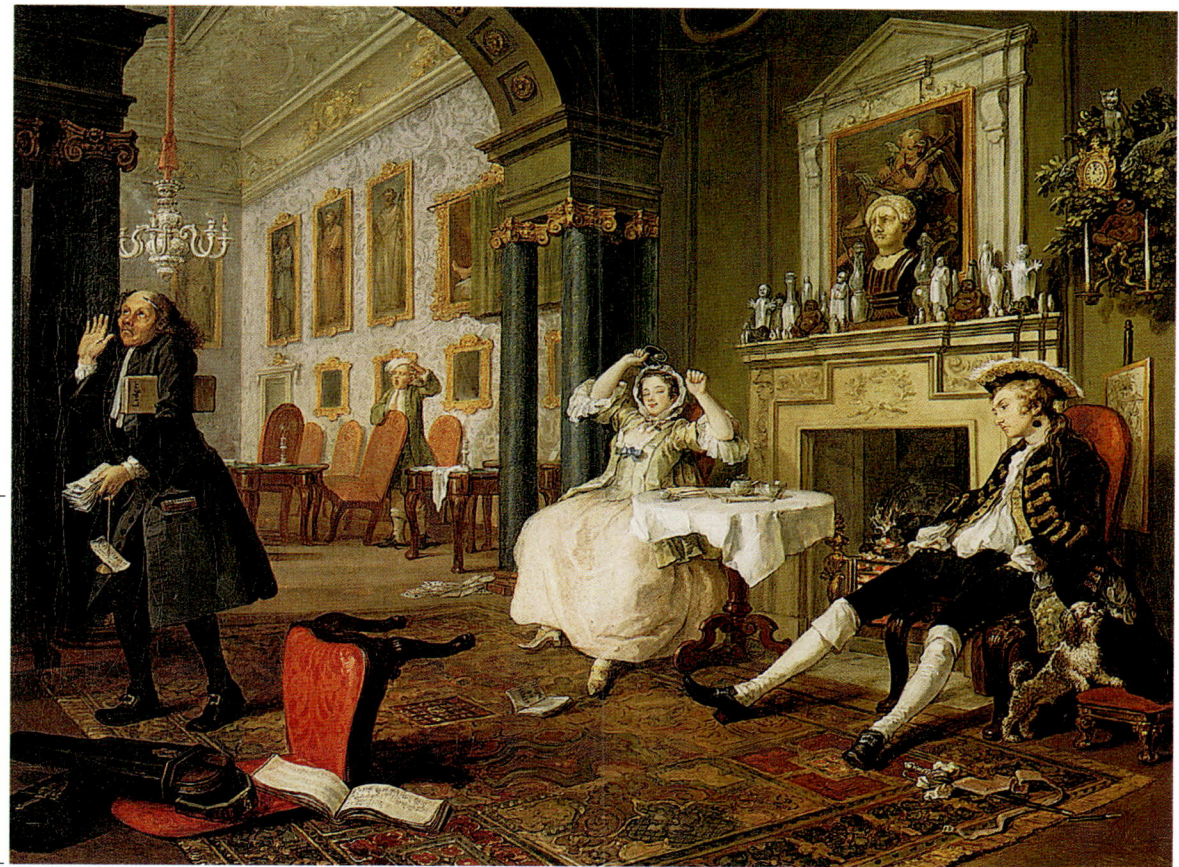

26-17 WILLIAM
HOGARTH, *Breakfast
Scene,* from *Marriage
à la Mode,* ca. 1745.
Oil on canvas,
2′ 4″ × 3′. National
Gallery, London.

Hogarth won fame for
his paintings and prints
satirizing English life with
comic zest. This is one of
a series of six paintings in
which he chronicled the
marital immoralities of
the moneyed class.

1 ft.

its occupants. For example, the row of pious religious paintings on
the upper wall of the distant room concludes with a curtained canvas
undoubtedly depicting an erotic subject. According to the custom of
the day, ladies could not view this discretely hidden painting, but at
the pull of a cord, the master and his male guests could enjoy a tableau of cavorting figures. In *Breakfast Scene,* as in all his work, Hogarth proceeded as a novelist might, elaborating on his subject with
carefully chosen detail, the discovery of which heightens the comedy.

Hogarth designed the marriage series to be published as a set
of engravings. The prints of this and his other moral narratives
were so popular that unscrupulous entrepreneurs produced unauthorized versions almost as fast as the artist created his originals.
The popularity of these prints speaks not only to the appeal of their
subjects but also to the democratization of knowledge and culture
the Enlightenment fostered and to the exploitation of new printing
technologies that opened the way for a more affordable and widely
disseminated visual culture.

## THOMAS GAINSBOROUGH

A contrasting blend of "naturalistic"
representation and Rococo setting is
found in *Mrs. Richard Brinsley Sheridan* (FIG. **26-18**), a characteristic
portrait by British painter THOMAS
GAINSBOROUGH (1727–1788). Gainsborough presented Mrs. Sheridan as
a lovely, informally dressed woman
seated in a rustic landscape faintly
reminiscent of Watteau (FIG. 26-7)
in its soft-hued light and feathery
brushwork. Gainsborough's goal
was to match the natural, unspoiled

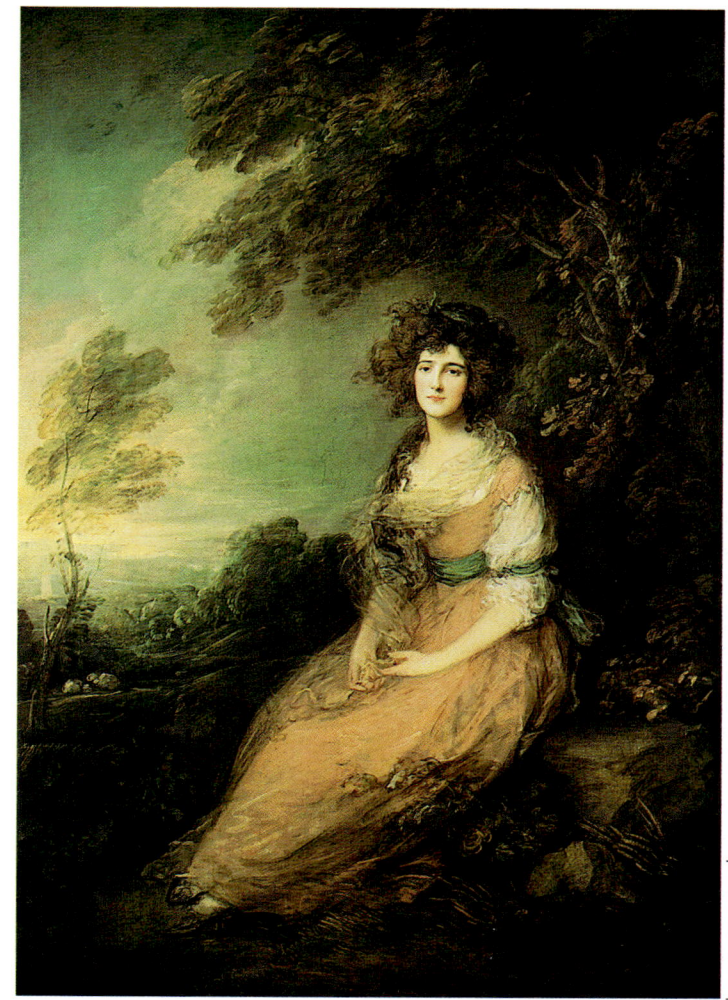

26-18 THOMAS
GAINSBOROUGH, *Mrs.
Richard Brinsley Sheridan,*
1787. Oil on canvas,
7′ 2⅝″ × 5′ ⅝″. National
Gallery of Art, Washington,
D.C. (Andrew W. Mellon
Collection).

In this life-size portrait,
Gainsborough sought to match
Mrs. Sheridan's natural beauty
with that of the landscape.
The rustic setting, soft-hued
light, and feathery brushwork
recall Rococo painting.

1 ft.

beauty of the landscape with that of his sitter. Mrs. Sheridan's dark brown hair blows freely in the slight wind, and her clear "English complexion" and air of ingenuous sweetness contrast sharply with the pert sophistication of the subjects of Continental Rococo portraits. Gainsborough planned to give the picture a more pastoral air by adding several sheep, but he did not live long enough to complete the canvas. Even without the sheep, the painting clearly expresses Gainsborough's deep interest in the landscape setting. Although he won greater fame in his time for his portraits, he had begun as a landscape painter and always preferred painting scenes of nature to depicting individual likenesses.

**JOSHUA REYNOLDS** Morality of a more heroic tone than found in the work of Greuze, yet in harmony with "naturalness," included the virtues of honor, valor, and love of country. The Enlightenment concept of "nobility," especially in the view of Rousseau, referred to character, not to aristocratic birth. As the century progressed and people felt the tremors of coming revolutions, the virtues of courage and resolution, patriotism, and self-sacrifice assumed greater importance. Having risen from humble origins, the modern military hero, not the decadent aristocrat, brought the excitement of war into the company of the "natural" emotions.

SIR JOSHUA REYNOLDS (1723–1792) specialized in what became known as *Grand Manner portraiture* and often painted likenesses of key participants in the great events of the latter part of the 18th century. Although clearly depicting specific individuals, Grand Manner portraits elevated the sitters by conveying refinement and elegance. Painters communicated a person's grace and class through certain standardized conventions, such as the large scale of the figure relative to the canvas, the controlled pose, the landscape setting, and the low horizon line.

Reynolds painted *Lord Heathfield* (FIG. **26-19**) in 1787. The sitter was a perfect subject for a Grand Manner portrait—a burly, ruddy English officer, the commandant of the fortress at Gibraltar. Heathfield had doggedly defended the British stronghold against the Spanish and French, and later received the honorary title Baron Heathfield of Gibraltar. Here, he holds the huge key to the fortress, the symbol of his victory. He stands in front of a curtain of dark smoke rising from the battleground, flanked by one cannon pointing ineffectively downward and another whose tilted barrel indicates it lies uselessly on its back. Reynolds portrayed the features of the general's heavy, honest face and his uniform with unidealized realism. But Lord Heathfield's posture and the setting dramatically suggest the heroic themes of battle, courage, and patriotism.

**BENJAMIN WEST** Some American artists also became well known in England. BENJAMIN WEST (1738–1820), born in Pennsylvania on what was then the colonial frontier (MAP 26-1), traveled to Europe early in life to study art and then went to England, where he met with almost immediate success. A cofounder of the Royal Academy of Arts, West succeeded Reynolds as its president. He became official painter to George III (r. 1760–1801) and retained that position even during the strained period of the American Revolution.

In *Death of General Wolfe* (FIG. **26-20**), West depicted the mortally wounded young English commander just after his defeat of the French in the decisive battle of Quebec in 1759, which gave Canada to Great Britain. Because his subject was a recent event, West clothed his characters in contemporary costumes (although the military uniforms are not completely accurate in all details). However, West blended this realism of detail with the grand tradition of history painting by arranging his figures in a complex and

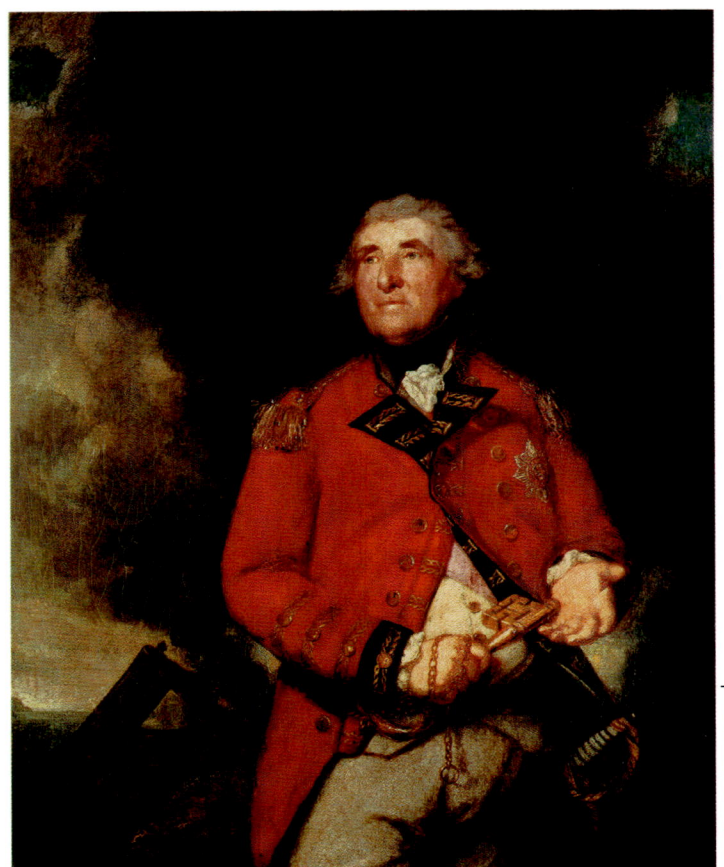

**26-19** SIR JOSHUA REYNOLDS, *Lord Heathfield,* 1787. Oil on canvas, 4′ 8″ × 3′ 9″. National Gallery, London.

In this Grand Manner portrait, Reynolds depicted the English commander who defended Gibraltar. As is typical for this genre, Heathfield stands in a dramatic pose and his figure takes up most of the canvas.

theatrically ordered composition. His modern hero dies among grieving officers on the field of victorious battle in a way that suggests the death of a saint. (The composition, in fact, derives from paintings of the lamentation over the dead Christ.) West wanted to present this hero's death in the service of the state as a martyrdom charged with religious emotions. His innovative and highly effective combination of the conventions of traditional heroic painting with a look of modern realism influenced history painting well into the 19th century.

**JOHN SINGLETON COPLEY** American artist JOHN SINGLETON COPLEY (1738–1815) matured as a painter in the Massachusetts Bay Colony. Like West, Copley later emigrated to England, where he absorbed the fashionable English portrait style. But unlike Grand Manner portraiture, Copley's *Paul Revere* (FIG. **26-21**), painted before the artist left Boston, conveys a sense of directness and faithfulness to visual fact that marked the taste for honesty and plainness noted by many late-18th- and 19th-century visitors to America. When Copley painted his portrait, Revere was not yet the familiar hero of the American Revolution. In the picture, he is working at his profession of silversmithing. The setting is plain, the lighting clear and revealing. Revere sits in his shirtsleeves, bent over a teapot in progress. He pauses and turns his head to look the observer straight in the eyes. The painter treated the reflections in the polished wood of the tabletop with as much care as he did Revere's

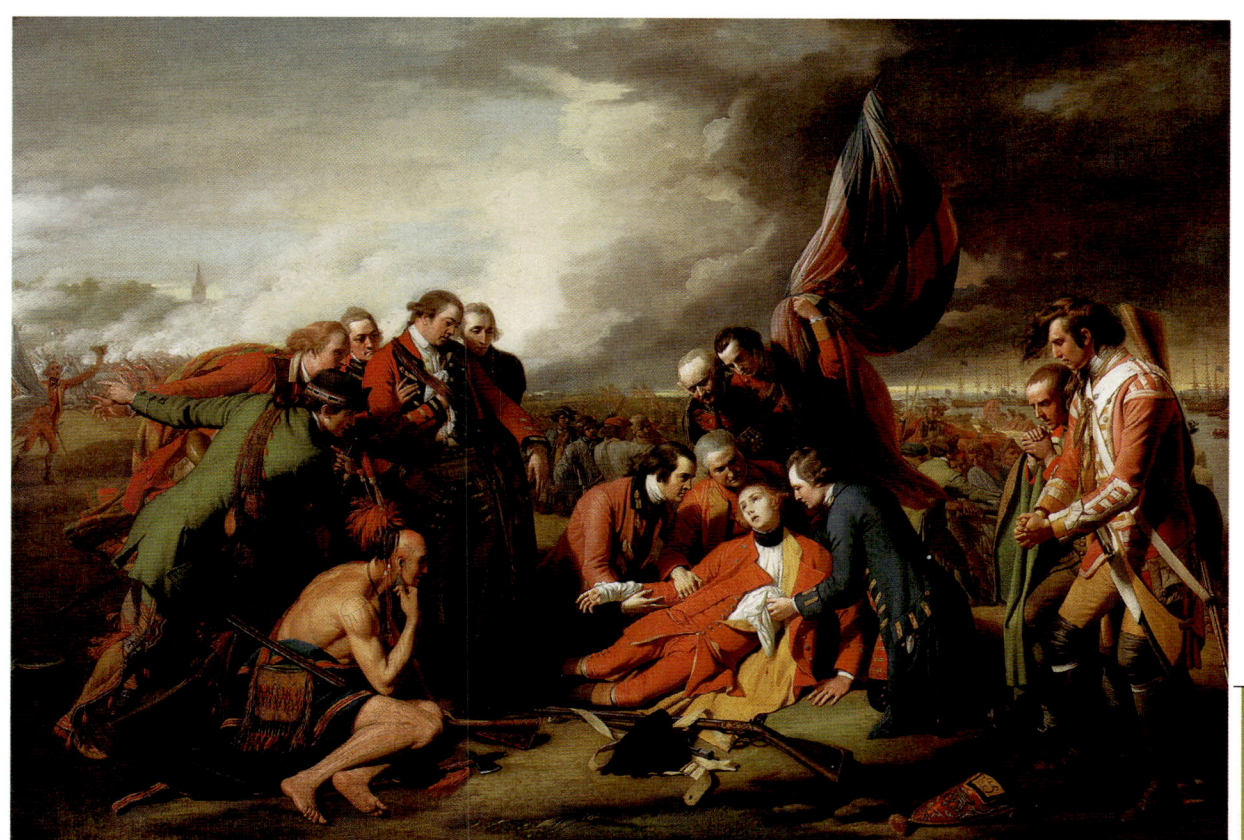

**26-20** BENJAMIN WEST, *Death of General Wolfe,* 1771. Oil on canvas, 4′ 11½″ × 7′. National Gallery of Canada, Ottawa (gift of the Duke of Westminster, 1918).

West's great innovation was to blend contemporary subject matter and costumes with the grand tradition of history painting. Here, the painter likened General Wolfe's death to that of a martyred saint.

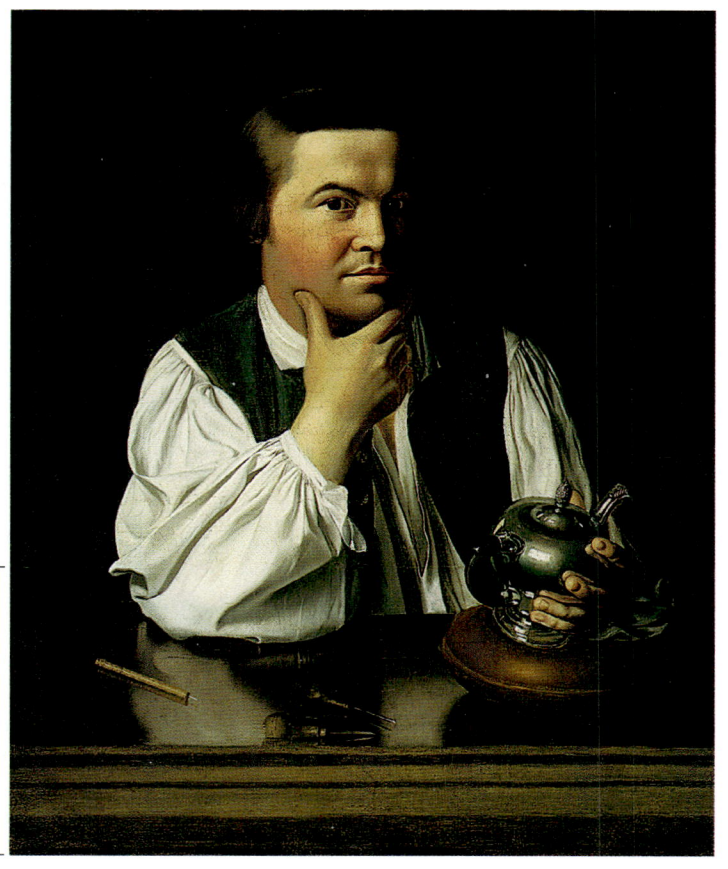

figure, his tools, and the teapot resting on its leather graver's pillow. Copley gave special prominence to Revere's eyes by reflecting intense reddish light onto the darkened side of his face and hands. The informality and the sense of the moment link this painting to contemporaneous English and Continental portraits. But the spare style and the emphasis on the sitter's down-to-earth character differentiate this American work from its European counterparts.

**THE GRAND TOUR** The 18th-century public also sought "naturalness" in artists' depictions of landscapes. Documentation of specific places became popular, in part due to growing travel opportunities and expanding colonialism. These depictions of geographic settings also served the needs of the many scientific expeditions mounted during the century and satisfied the desires of genteel tourists for mementos of their journeys. By this time, a Grand Tour of the major sites of Europe was an essential part of every well-bred person's education (see "The Grand Tour and Veduta Painting," page 744). Those who embarked on a tour of the Continent wished to return with souvenirs to help them remember their experiences and impress those at home with the wonders

**26-21** JOHN SINGLETON COPLEY, *Paul Revere,* ca. 1768–1770. Oil on canvas, 2′ 11⅛″ × 2′ 4″. Museum of Fine Arts, Boston (gift of Joseph W., William B., and Edward H. R. Revere).

In contrast to Grand Manner portraiture, Copley's *Paul Revere* emphasizes his subject's down-to-earth character, differentiating this American work from its European counterparts.

# The Grand Tour and Veduta Painting

Although travel throughout Europe was commonplace in the 18th century, Italy became an especially popular destination. This "pilgrimage" of aristocrats, the wealthy, politicians, and diplomats from France, England, Germany, Flanders, Sweden, the United States, Russia, Poland, and Hungary came to be known as the Grand Tour. Italy's allure fueled the revival of classicism, and the popularity of Neoclassical art drove the fascination with Italy. One British observer noted: "All our religion, all our arts, almost all that sets us above savages, has come from the shores of the Mediterranean."*

The Grand Tour was not simply leisure travel. The education available in Italy to the inquisitive mind made such a tour an indispensable experience for anyone who wished to make a mark in society. The Enlightenment had made knowledge of ancient Rome and Greece imperative, and a steady stream of Europeans and Americans traveled to Italy in the late 18th and early 19th centuries. These tourists aimed to increase their knowledge of literature, the visual arts, architecture, theater, music, history, customs, and folklore. Given this extensive agenda, it is not surprising a Grand Tour could take a number of years to complete. Most travelers moved from location to location, following an established itinerary.

The British were the most avid travelers, and they conceived the initial "tour code," including required itineraries to important destinations. Although they designated Rome early on as the primary destination in Italy, visitors traveled as far north as Venice and as far south as Naples. Eventually, Paestum, Sicily, Florence, Siena, Pisa, Genoa, Milan, Bologna, and Parma (MAP 25-1) all appeared in guidebooks and in paintings. Joseph Wright of Derby (FIGS. 26-1 and 26-11A) and Joseph Mallord William Turner (FIG. 27-22) were among the many British artists to undertake a Grand Tour.

Many visitors to Italy returned home from their Grand Tour with a painting by Antonio Canaletto, the leading painter of scenic views (vedute) of Venice. It must have been very cheering on a gray winter afternoon in England to look up and see a sunny, panoramic view such as that in Canaletto's Riva degli Schiavoni, Venice (FIG. 26-22), with its cloud-studded sky, picturesque water traffic, and well-known Venetian landmarks painted in scrupulous perspective and minute detail. (The Doge's Palace [FIG. 14-21] is at the left in Riva degli Schiavoni.) Canaletto usually made drawings "on

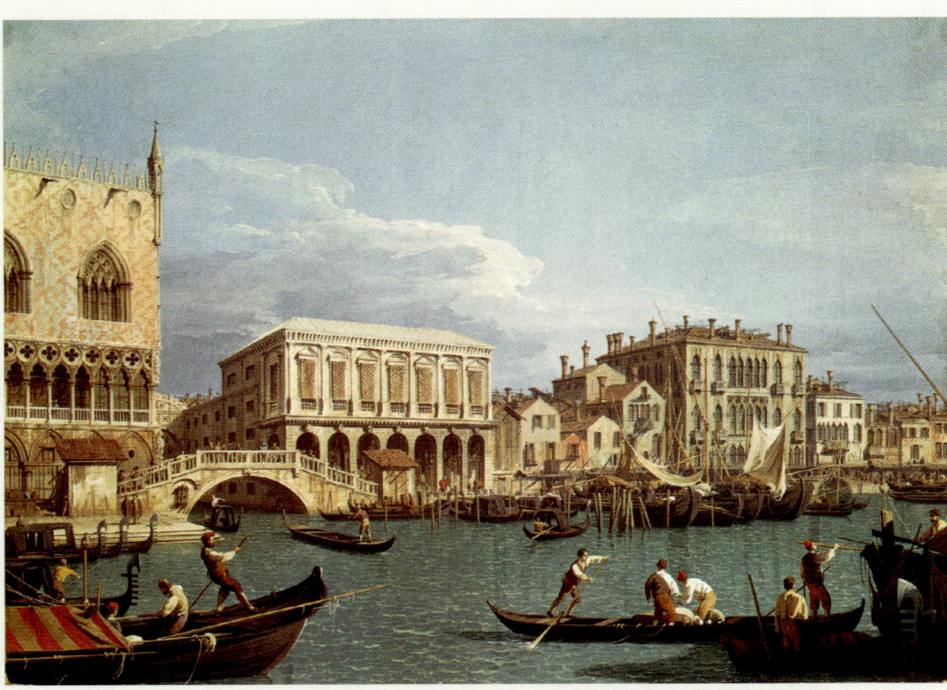

**26-22** ANTONIO CANALETTO, *Riva degli Schiavoni, Venice*, ca. 1735–1740. Oil on canvas, 1′ 6½″ × 2′ ⅞″. Toledo Museum of Art, Toledo.

Canaletto was the leading painter of Venetian *vedute,* which were treasured souvenirs for 18th-century travelers visiting Italy on a Grand Tour. He used a camera obscura for his on-site drawings.

location" to take back to his studio and use as sources for paintings. To help make the on-site drawings true to life, he often used a camera obscura, as Vermeer (FIGS. 25-19 to 25-20A) did before him. These instruments were darkened chambers (some of them virtually portable closets) with optical lenses fitted into a hole in one wall through which light entered to project an inverted image of the subject onto the chamber's opposite wall. The artist could trace the main details from this image for later reworking and refinement. The camera obscura enabled artists to create convincing representations incorporating the variable focus of objects at different distances. Canaletto's paintings give the impression of capturing every detail, with no "editing." In fact, he presented each site according to Renaissance perspective conventions and exercised great selectivity about which details to include and which to omit to make a coherent and engagingly attractive veduta.

*Cesare de Seta, "Grand Tour: The Lure of Italy in the Eighteenth Century," in Andrew Wilton and Ilaria Bignamini, eds., *Grand Tour: The Lure of Italy in the Eighteenth Century* (London: Tate Gallery, 1996), 13.

they had seen. The English were especially eager collectors of travel pictures. Venetian artists in particular found it profitable to produce paintings of the most characteristic *vedute* (scenic views) of their city to sell to British visitors. Chief among those artists was

ANTONIO CANALETTO (1697–1768), whose works, for example *Riva degli Schiavoni, Venice* (*Bank of the Slaves, Venice*; FIG. **26-22**), English tourists avidly acquired as evidence of their visit to Italy's magical city of water.

## The Excavations of Herculaneum and Pompeii

Among the developments stimulating the European fascination with classical antiquity was the initiation of systematic excavations at two ancient Roman cities on the Bay of Naples—Herculaneum and Pompeii—in 1738 and 1748, respectively. The violent eruption of Mount Vesuvius in August 79 CE had buried both cities under volcanic ash and lava (see "An Eyewitness Account of the Eruption of Mount Vesuvius," Chapter 7, page 188), protecting the sites for hundreds of years from looters and the ravages of nature. Consequently, the 18th-century excavations yielded an unprecedented number of well-preserved paintings, sculptures, vases, and other household objects, and provided rich evidence for reconstructing Roman art and life. As a result, European ideas about and interest in ancient Rome expanded tremendously, and collectors eagerly acquired as many of the newly discovered antiquities as they could. One of the most avid collectors was Sir William Hamilton (1731–1803), British consul in Naples from 1764 to 1800, who purchased numerous painted vases and other ancient objects and then sold them to the British Museum in 1772. The finds at Pompeii and Herculaneum, therefore, quickly became available to a wide public.

"Pompeian" style soon became all the rage in England, as is evident, for example, in Robert Adam's Etruscan Room (FIG. 26-23) at Osterley Park House, which was inspired by the frescoes of the Third and early Fourth Styles of Roman mural painting (FIGS. 7-21 and 7-22). Adam took decorative motifs (medallions, urns, vine scrolls, sphinxes, and tripods) from Roman art and arranged them sparsely within broad, neutral spaces and slender margins, as in his elegant, linear ancient models. This new Neoclassical style almost entirely displaced the curvilinear Rococo (FIGS. 26-2 and 26-3) in the homes of the wealthy after midcentury. Adam was also an archaeologist, and he had explored and written accounts of the ruins of Diocletian's palace (FIG. 7-74) at Split. Kedleston House in Derbyshire, Adelphi Terrace in London, and a great many other structures he designed show how the Split palace influenced his work.

The archaeological finds from Herculaneum and Pompeii also affected garden and landscape design, fashion, and tableware.

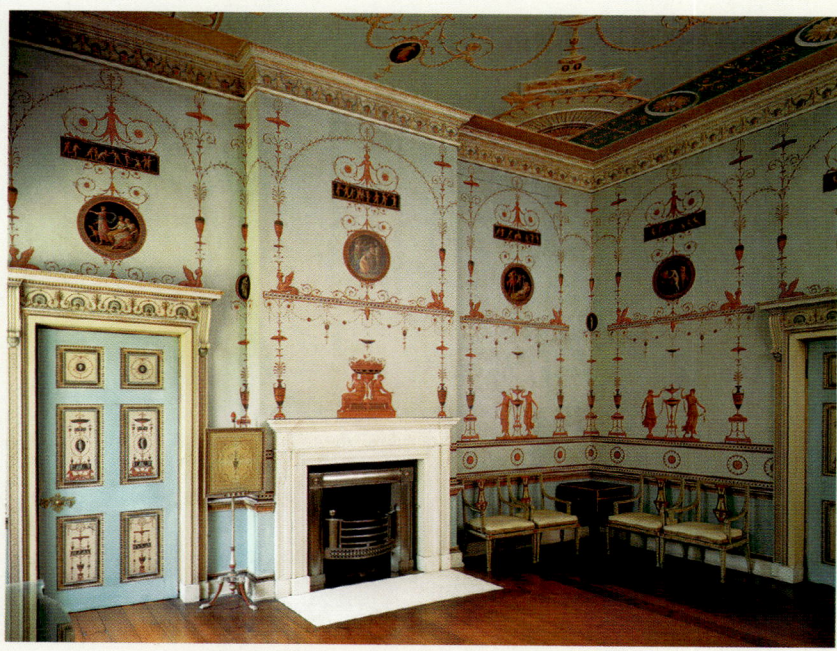

**26-23** ROBERT ADAM, Etruscan Room, Osterley Park House, Middlesex, England, begun 1761. Reconstructed in the Victoria & Albert Museum, London.

Inspired by archaeological discoveries at Herculaneum and Pompeii in the mid-18th century, Adam incorporated decorative motifs from Roman mural painting into his Etruscan Room at Osterley Park.

Clothing based on classical garb became popular, and Emma, Lady Hamilton (1761–1815), Sir William's wife, often gave lavish parties dressed in delicate Greek-style drapery. Neoclassical taste also determined the pottery designs of John Flaxman (1755–1826) and Josiah Wedgwood. Wedgwood established his reputation in the 1760s with his creamware inspired by ancient art. He eventually produced vases based on what were then thought to be Etruscan designs (they were, in fact, imported Greek vases deposited in Etruscan tombs) and expanded his business by producing small busts of classical figures as well as cameos and medallions adorned with copies of antique reliefs and statues.

# NEOCLASSICISM

One of the defining characteristics of the late 18th century was a renewed admiration for classical antiquity, which the Grand Tour was instrumental in fueling. This interest gave rise to the artistic movement known as *Neoclassicism,* which incorporated the subjects and styles of ancient art. Painting, sculpture, and architecture, however, were only the most prominent manifestations of Neoclassicism. Fascination with Greek and Roman culture was widespread and extended to the public culture of fashion and home decor. The Enlightenment's emphasis on rationality in part explains this classical focus, because the geometric harmony of classical art and architecture embodied Enlightenment ideals. In addition, classical cultures represented the pinnacle of civilized society. Greece and

Rome served as models of enlightened political organization. With their traditions of liberty, civic virtue, morality, and sacrifice, these cultures were ideal models during a period of great political upheaval. Given these traditional associations, it is not coincidental that Neoclassicism was particularly appealing during the French and American revolutions.

Further whetting the public appetite for classicism were the excavations near Naples of Herculaneum and Pompeii, which the volcanic eruption of Mount Vesuvius had buried (see "The Excavations of Herculaneum and Pompeii," above). Soon, murals based on the paintings unearthed in the excavations began to appear in European townhouses, such as the Etruscan Room (FIG. **26-23**) by ROBERT ADAM (1728–1792) in Osterley Park House in Middlesex, begun in 1761.

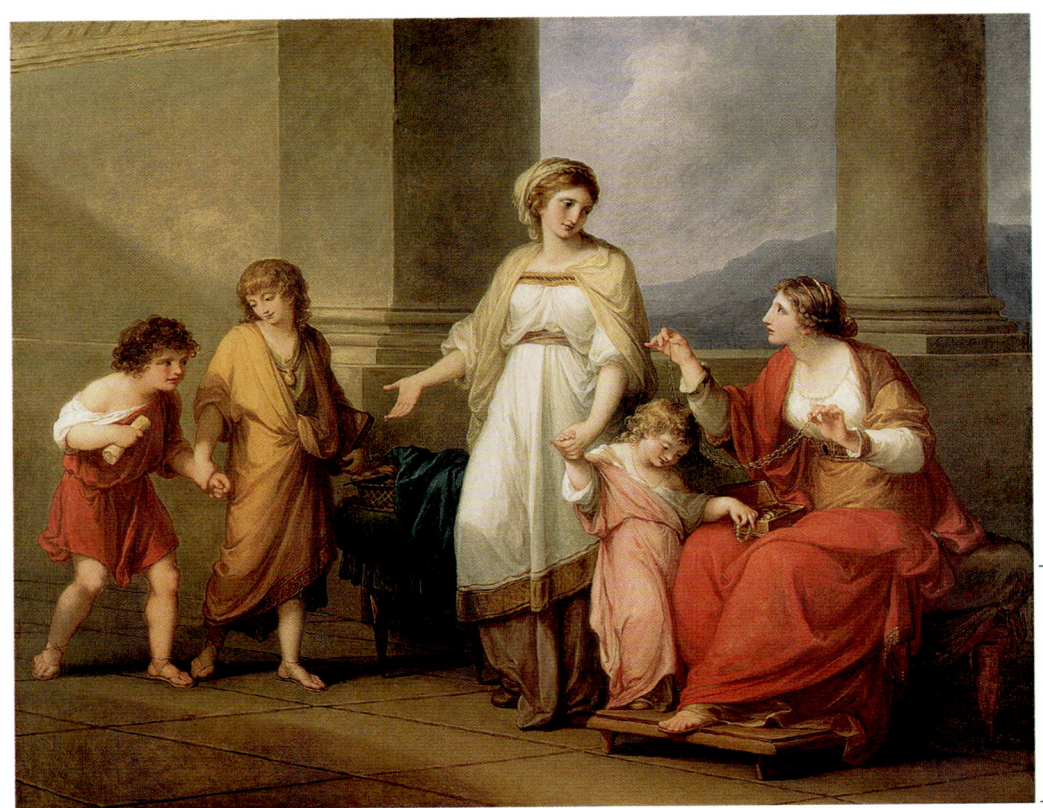

**26-24** Angelica Kauffmann, *Cornelia Presenting Her Children as Her Treasures,* or *Mother of the Gracchi,* ca. 1785. Oil on canvas, 3′ 4″ × 4′ 2″. Virginia Museum of Fine Arts, Richmond (Adolph D. and Wilkins C. Williams Fund).

Kauffmann's painting of a virtuous Roman mother who presented her children to a visitor as her jewels exemplifies the Enlightenment fascination with classical antiquity and with classical art.

1 ft.

**WINCKELMANN** The enthusiasm for classical antiquity also permeated much of the scholarship of the time. In the late 18th century, the ancient world increasingly became the focus of academic research. A visit to Rome inspired Edward Gibbon (1737–1794) to begin his monumental *Decline and Fall of the Roman Empire,* which appeared between 1776 and 1788. Earlier, in 1755, Johann Joachim Winckelmann (1717–1768), widely recognized as the first modern art historian, published *Reflections on the Imitation of Greek Works in Painting and Sculpture,* in which the German scholar unequivocally designated Greek art as the most perfect to come from human hands. For Winckelmann, classical art was far superior to the "natural" art of his day.

> Good taste, which is becoming more prevalent throughout the world, had its origins under the skies of Greece.... The only way for us to become great ... is to imitate the ancients.... In the masterpieces of Greek art, connoisseurs and imitators find not only nature at its most beautiful but also something beyond nature, namely certain ideal forms of its beauty.... A person enlightened enough to penetrate the innermost secrets of art will find beauties hitherto seldom revealed when he compares the total structure of Greek figures with most modern ones, especially those modelled more on nature than on Greek taste.[3]

In his later *History of Ancient Art* (1764), Winckelmann carefully described major works of classical art and positioned each one within a huge inventory organized by subject matter, style, and period. Before Winckelmann, art historians had focused on biography, as did Giorgio Vasari and Giovanni Pietro Bellori in the 16th and 17th centuries (see "Giovanni Pietro Bellori on Annibale Carracci and Caravaggio," Chapter 24, page 682). Winckelmann thus initiated one modern art historical method thoroughly in accord with Enlightenment ideas of ordering knowledge—a system of description and classification that provided a pioneering model for the understanding of stylistic evolution. Winckelmann's familiarity with classical art derived predominantly (as was the norm) from Roman works and Roman copies of Greek art in Italy. Yet Winckelmann was instrumental in bringing to scholarly attention the differences between Greek and Roman art. Thus, he paved the way for more thorough study of the distinct characteristics of the art and architecture of these two cultures.

## Painting

Winckelmann's influence extended beyond the world of scholarship. He also was instrumental in promoting Neoclassicism as a major stylistic movement in late-18th-century painting. He was, for example, the scholar who advised his countryman Anton Raphael Mengs (1728–1779) on classical iconography when Mengs painted *Parnassus* (FIG. **26-23A**), the fresco many art historians regard as the first Neoclassical painting.

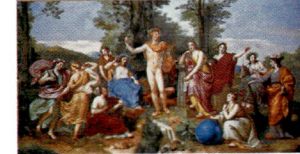

**26-23A** Mengs, *Parnassus,* 1761.

**ANGELICA KAUFFMANN** Another pioneer of Neoclassical painting was Angelica Kauffmann (1741–1807). Born in Switzerland and trained in Italy, Kauffmann spent many of her productive years in England. A student of Reynolds (FIG. 26-19), she was a founding member of the British Royal Academy of Arts and enjoyed an enviable reputation. Her *Cornelia Presenting Her Children as Her Treasures,* or *Mother of the Gracchi* (FIG. **26-24**), is an *exemplum virtutis* (example or model of virtue) drawn from Greek and Roman history and literature. The moralizing pictures of Greuze (FIG. 26-14) and Hogarth (FIG. 26-17) already had marked a change in taste, but Kauffmann replaced the modern setting and character of their works. She clothed her actors in ancient Roman garb and posed them in statuesque attitudes within Roman interiors. The theme of *Mother of the Gracchi* is the virtue of Cornelia, mother of the future political leaders Tiberius and Gaius Gracchus, who, in the second century BCE, attempted to reform the Roman Republic. Cornelia reveals her character in this scene, which takes place after a visitor had shown off her fine jewelry and then haughtily insisted Cornelia show hers. Instead of taking out her own precious adornments, Cornelia brought her sons forward, presenting them as her jewels. The architectural setting is severely Roman, with no

# David on Greek Style and Public Art

Jacques-Louis David was the leading Neoclassical painter in France at the end of the 18th century. He championed a return to Greek style and the painting of inspiring heroic and patriotic subjects. In 1796 he made the following statement to his pupils:

> I want to work in a pure Greek style. I feed my eyes on antique statues, I even have the intention of imitating some of them. The Greeks had no scruples about copying a composition, a gesture, a type that had already been accepted and used. They put all their attention and all their art on perfecting an idea that had been already conceived. They thought, and they were right, that in the arts the way in which an idea is rendered, and the manner in which it is expressed, is much more important than the idea itself. To give a body and a perfect form to one's thought, this—and only this—is to be an artist.*

David also strongly believed paintings depicting noble events in ancient history, such as his *Oath of the Horatii* (FIG. 26-25), would serve to instill patriotism and civic virtue in the public at large in postrevolutionary France. In November 1793 he wrote:

> [The arts] should help to spread the progress of the human spirit, and to propagate and transmit to posterity the striking examples of the efforts of a tremendous people who, guided by reason and philosophy, are bringing back to earth the reign of liberty, equality, and law. The arts must therefore contribute forcefully to the education of the public. . . . The arts are the imitation of nature in her most beautiful and perfect form. . . .

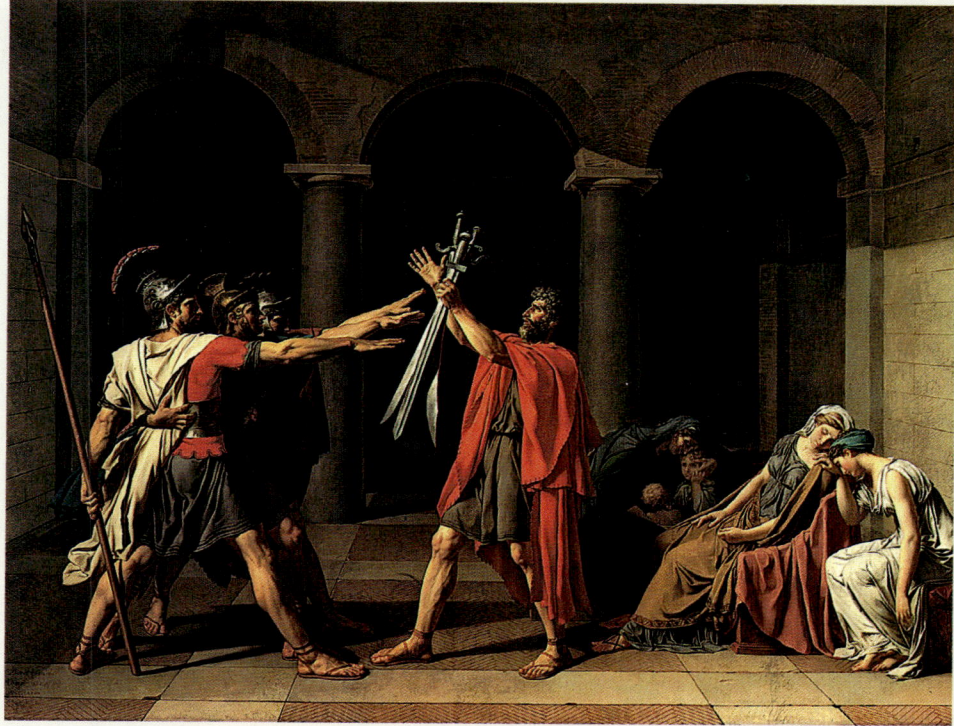

**26-25** JACQUES-LOUIS DAVID, *Oath of the Horatii*, 1784. Oil on canvas, 10′ 10″ × 13′ 11″. Musée du Louvre, Paris. ◼◀

David was the Neoclassical painter-ideologist of the French Revolution. This huge canvas celebrating ancient Roman patriotism and sacrifice features statuesque figures and classical architecture.

> [T]hose marks of heroism and civic virtue offered the eyes of the people [will] electrify the soul, and plant the seeds of glory and devotion to the fatherland.†

*Translated by Robert Goldwater and Marco Treves, eds., *Artists on Art*, 3d ed. (New York: Pantheon Books, 1958), 206.
†Ibid., 205.

---

Rococo motif in evidence, and the composition and drawing have the simplicity and firmness of low-relief carving, qualities shared with Mengs's *Parnassus* (FIG. 26-23A).

**JACQUES-LOUIS DAVID** The Enlightenment idea of a participatory and knowledgeable citizenry lay behind the revolt against the French monarchy in 1789, but the immediate causes of the French Revolution were France's economic crisis and the clash between the Third Estate (bourgeoisie, peasantry, and urban and rural workers) and the First and Second Estates (the clergy and nobility, respectively). They fought over the issue of representation in the legislative body, the Estates-General, which had been convened to discuss taxation as a possible solution to the economic problem. However, the ensuing revolution revealed the instability of the monarchy and of French society's traditional structure and resulted in a succession of republics and empires as France struggled to find a way to adjust to these fundamental changes.

JACQUES-LOUIS DAVID (1748–1825) became the Neoclassical painter-ideologist of the French Revolution. A distant relative of François Boucher (FIG. 26-8), he followed the Rococo painter's style until a period of study in Rome won the younger man over to the classical art tradition. David favored academic teachings about using the art of the ancients and of the great Renaissance masters as models. He, as Winckelmann, rebelled against Rococo style as an "artificial taste" and exalted the "perfect form" of Greek art (see "David on Greek Style and Public Art," above).

**OATH OF THE HORATII** David concurred with the Enlightenment belief that the subject of an artwork should have a moral. Paintings representing noble deeds in the past could inspire virtue in the present. A milestone painting in the Neoclassical master's career, *Oath of the Horatii* (FIG. 26-25), depicts a story from pre-Republican Rome, the heroic phase of Roman history. The topic was not too obscure for David's audience. Pierre Corneille (1606–1684) had retold this story of conflict between love and patriotism, first recounted by the ancient Roman historian Livy, in a play performed in Paris several years earlier. According to the story, the leaders of the warring cities of Rome and Alba decided to resolve their conflicts in a series of encounters waged by three representatives from each side. The Romans chose as their champions the three Horatius brothers, who had to face the three sons of the Curatius family from Alba. A sister of the Horatii, Camilla, was the bride-to-be of one of the Curatius sons, and the wife of the youngest Horatius was the sister of the Curatii. David's painting shows the Horatii as they swear on their swords, held high by their father, to win or die for Rome, oblivious to the anguish and sorrow of the Horatii women.

*Oath of the Horatii* is a paragon of the Neoclassical style. Not only does the subject matter deal with a narrative of patriotism and sacrifice excerpted from Roman history, but the painter also employed formal devices to present the image with force and clarity. The action unfolds in a shallow space much like a stage setting, defined by a severely simple architectural framework. David deployed his statuesque and carefully modeled figures across the space, close to the foreground, in a manner reminiscent of ancient relief sculpture. The rigid, angular, and virile forms of the men on the left effectively contrast with the soft curvilinear shapes of the distraught women on the right. This juxtaposition visually pits virtues the Enlightenment leaders ascribed to men (such as courage, patriotism, and unwavering loyalty to a cause) against the emotions of love, sorrow, and despair the women in the painting express. The French viewing audience perceived such emotionalism as characteristic of the female nature. The message was clear and of a type readily identifiable to the prerevolutionary French public. The picture created a sensation at its first exhibition in Paris in 1785. Although David had painted it under royal patronage and did not intend the painting as a revolutionary statement, *Oath of the Horatii* aroused his audience to patriotic zeal. The Neoclassical style soon became the semiofficial voice of the French Revolution.

***DEATH OF MARAT*** When the revolution broke out in 1789, David threw in his lot with the Jacobins, the radical and militant revolutionary faction. He accepted the role of de facto minister of propaganda, organizing political pageants and ceremonies requiring floats, costumes, and sculptural props. David believed art could play an important role in educating the public and that dramatic paintings emphasizing patriotism and civic virtue would prove effective as rallying calls. However, rather than continuing to create artworks focused on scenes from antiquity, David began to portray scenes from the French Revolution itself.

In 1793, David painted *Death of Marat* (FIG. **26-26**), which he wanted not only to serve as a record of an important event in the struggle to overthrow the monarchy but also to provide inspiration and encouragement to the revolutionary forces. The painting commemorates the assassination that year of Jean-Paul Marat (1743–1793), an influential writer who was David's friend. The artist depicted the martyred revolutionary in his bathtub after Charlotte Corday (1768–1793), a member of a rival political faction, stabbed him to death. (Marat suffered from a painful skin disease and required frequent medicinal baths.) David presented the scene with directness and clarity. The cold neutral space above Marat's figure slumped in the tub produces a chilling oppressiveness. The painter vividly placed all narrative details in the foreground—the knife, the wound, the blood, the letter with which Corday gained entrance—to sharpen the sense of pain and outrage. David masterfully composed the painting to present Marat as a tragic martyr who died

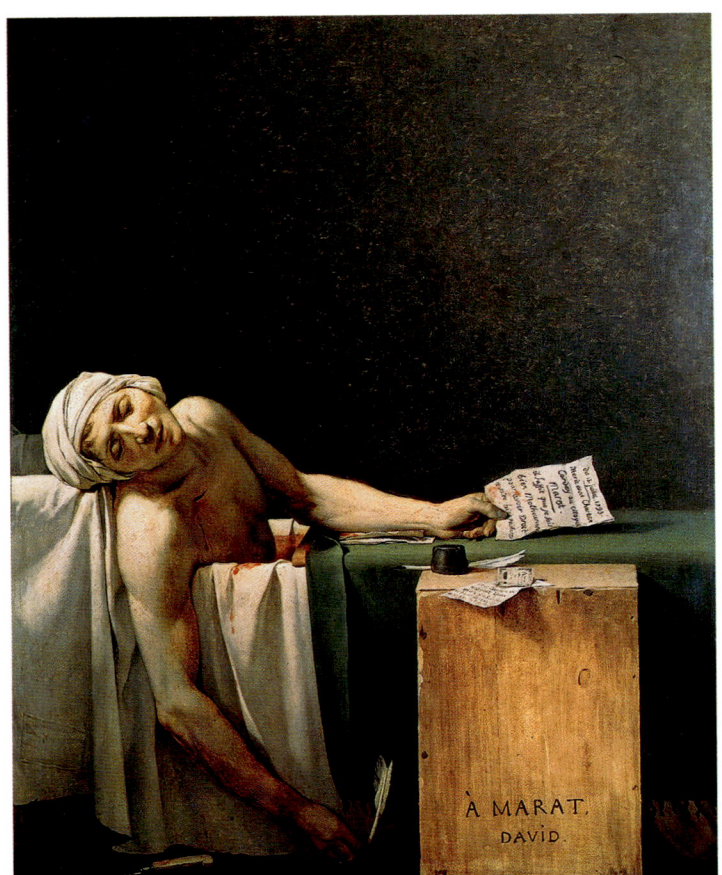

**26-26** JACQUES-LOUIS DAVID, *Death of Marat*, 1793. Oil on canvas, 5′ 5″ × 4′ 2½″. Musées Royaux des Beaux-Arts de Belgique, Brussels. ◼◀

David depicted the revolutionary Marat as a tragic martyr, stabbed to death in his bath. Although the painting displays severe Neoclassical spareness, its convincing realism conveys pain and outrage.

in the service of the revolution. He based Marat's figure on Christ in Michelangelo's *Pietà* (FIG. 22-12) in Saint Peter's in Rome. The reference to Christ's martyrdom made the painting a kind of "altarpiece" for the new civic "religion," inspiring the French people with the saintly dedication of their slain leader.

## Architecture and Sculpture

Architects in the Enlightenment era also formed a deep admiration for the Greco-Roman past. Fairly early in the 18th century, they began to turn away from the theatricality and ostentation of Baroque design, still evident in grandiose structures such as Blenheim Palace (FIG. 26-1A) in England and Karlskirche (FIG. 26-3A) in Austria, as well as from the delicate flourishes of Rococo salons (FIGS. 26-2 and 26-3), palaces (FIG. 26-5A), and churches (FIGS. 26-4 and 26-5B). The style they instead embraced offered a more streamlined antique look.

**PANTHÉON** The Parisian church of Sainte-Geneviève, now the Panthéon (FIG. **26-27**), by JACQUES-GERMAIN SOUFFLOT (1713–1780) stands as testament to the revived interest in classical architecture. The Roman ruins at Baalbek in Lebanon, especially the titanic colonnade of the temple of Jupiter, provided much of the inspiration for Soufflot's design. The columns, reproduced with studied archaeological precision, stand out from walls that are severely blank, except for a repeated garland motif near the top. The colonnaded dome, a Neoclassical version of the domes of Saint

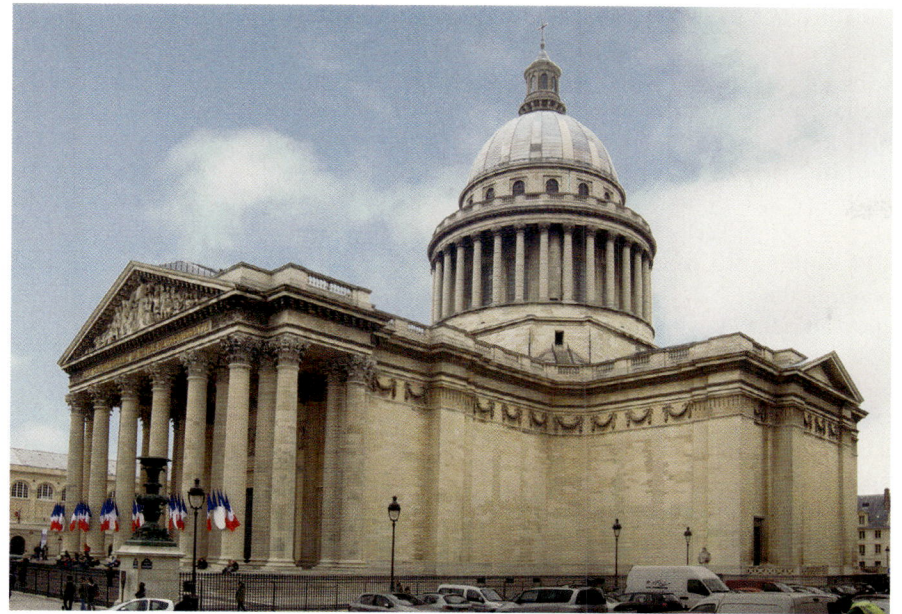

**26-27** Jacques-Germain Soufflot, Panthéon (Sainte-Geneviève; looking northeast), Paris, France, 1755–1792.

Soufflot's Panthéon is a testament to the Enlightenment admiration for Greece and Rome. It combines a portico based on an ancient Roman temple with a colonnaded dome and a Greek-cross plan.

cal systems ranging from Athenian democracy to Roman imperial rule. Thus, parliamentary England joined revolutionary France in embracing Neoclassicism. In England, Neoclassicism's appeal also was due to its clarity and simplicity. These characteristics provided a stark contrast to the complexity and opulence of Baroque art, then associated with the flamboyant rule of absolute monarchy. In English architecture, the preference for a simple and rational style derived indirectly from the authority of the ancient Roman architect Vitruvius through Andrea Palladio (FIGS. 22-28 to 22-31) in the 16th century and Inigo Jones (FIG. 25-37) in the 17th.

Richard Boyle (1695–1753), earl of Burlington, strongly restated Jones's Palladian doctrine in the new Neoclassical idiom in Chiswick House (FIG. **26-28**), which he built on London's outskirts with the help of William Kent (ca. 1686–1748). Paving the way for this shift in style was, among other things, the publication of Colin Campbell's *Vitruvius Britannicus* (1715), three volumes of engravings of ancient buildings, prefaced by a denunciation of Italian Baroque and high praise for Palladio and Jones. Chiswick House is a free variation on the theme of Palladio's Villa Rotonda (FIG. 22-28). The exterior design provided a clear alternative to the colorful splendor of Versailles (FIG. 25-26). In its simple symmetry, unadorned planes, right angles, and precise proportions, Chiswick looks very classical and rational. But the Palladian-style villa's setting within informal gardens, where a charming irregularity of layout and freely growing uncropped foliage dominate the scene, mitigates the classical severity and rationality. Just as the owners of English villas cultivated irregularity in the landscaping surrounding their homes, they sometimes preferred interiors ornamented in a style more closely related to Rococo decoration. At Chiswick, the interior design creates a luxurious Baroque foil to the stern symmetry of the exterior and the plan.

Palladian classicism prevailed in English architecture until about 1760, when it began to evolve into Neoclassicism. Playing a pivotal role in the shift from a dependence on Renaissance examples to ancient models was the publication in 1762 of the first volume of *Antiquities of Athens*

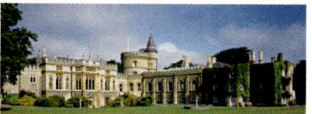

**26-27A** Walpole, Strawberry Hill, Twickenham, 1749–1777.

Peter's (FIG. 22-25) in Rome, the Église du Dôme (FIG. 25-30) in Paris, and Saint Paul's (FIG. 25-38) in London, rises above a Greek-cross plan. Both the dome and the vaults rest on an interior grid of splendid freestanding Corinthian columns, as if the portico's colonnade continued within. Although the whole effect, inside and out, is Roman, the structural principles employed were essentially Gothic. Soufflot was one of the first 18th-century builders to apply the logical engineering of Gothic cathedrals (see "The Gothic Cathedral," Chapter 13, page 373) to modern buildings. With few exceptions, however, such as Strawberry Hill (FIG. **26-27A**), owned and largely designed by Horace Walpole (1717–1797), the revival of interest in the Gothic architectural style did not take hold until the following century (see Chapter 27 and FIGS. 27-43 and 27-43A).

**CHISWICK HOUSE** The appeal of classical architecture extended well beyond French borders. The popularity of Greek and Roman cultures was due not only to their association with morality, rationality, and integrity but also to their connection to politi-

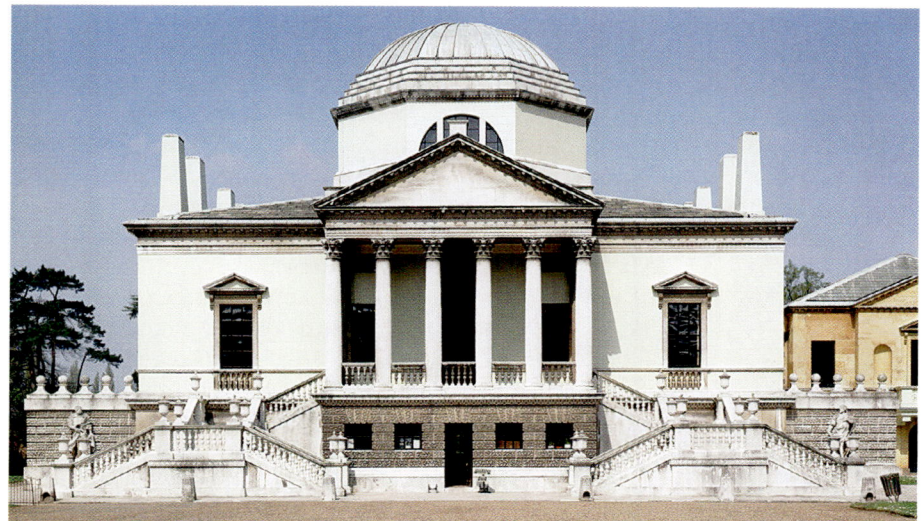

**26-28** Richard Boyle and William Kent, Chiswick House (looking northwest), near London, England, begun 1725.

For this English villa, Boyle and Kent emulated the simple symmetry and unadorned planes of the Palladian architectural style. Chiswick House is a free variation on the Villa Rotonda (FIG. 22-28).

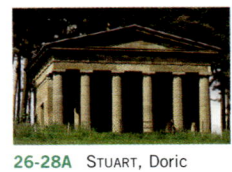

by two British painters and architects, JAMES STUART (1713–1788) and Nicholas Revett (1720–1804). Indeed, the purest expression of Greek-inspired architecture in 18th-century England was Stuart's design for the Doric portico (FIG. 26-28A) at Hagley Park.

**STOURHEAD PARK** English architects also made a significant contribution to the history of architecture by developing the *picturesque garden* in the 18th century, a garden designed in accord with the Enlightenment taste for the "natural." This approach to landscape architecture was in strong opposition to the formality and symmetry of Continental gardens such as those of the palace at Versailles (FIG. 25-26), which epitomized the imposition of rational order on untamed nature. Despite their "unordered" appearance, English gardens were carefully planned and often made allusions to classical antiquity, satisfying the demands of their patrons to surround themselves with mementos of the Grand Tour (see "The Grand Tour," page 744) they undertook in their youth.

An early masterpiece of this genre is the park at Stourhead (FIG. 26-29), designed by HENRY FLITCROFT (1697–1769) in collaboration with the property's owner, HENRY HOARE (1705–1785), the son of a wealthy banker. Hoare's country estate in Wiltshire overlooked a lush valley in which Flitcroft created an irregularly shaped artificial lake by damming up the Stour River. Around it, he placed a winding path leading to and from a grotto adorned with statues of a river god and a nymph. The twisting road and the grotto conjured for Hoare the voyage of Aeneas and the entrance to the Underworld in Virgil's *Aeneid,* required reading (in the original Latin) for any properly educated British gentleman. Flitcroft also placed around Hoare's version of Lake Avernus a bridge with five arches modeled on Andrea Palladio's bridge at Vicenza and pavilions that are free variations on famous classical buildings, including the Temple of Venus (FIG. 7-72) at Baalbek and the Pantheon (FIG. 7-49) in Rome.

Flitcroft sited all the structures strategically to create vistas resembling those in the paintings of Claude Lorrain (FIG. 25-33), beloved by those who had completed a Grand Tour. In fact, the view reproduced here of Flitcroft's Pantheon beyond the Palladian bridge on the far side of the lake at Stourhead specifically emulates Claude's 1672 *Landscape with Aeneas at Delos* in the National Gallery in London, in turn inspired by the *Aeneid.* Still, consistent with the eclectic tastes of 18th-century patrons, Hoare's park also contains Chinese bridges, a Turkish tent, and a Gothic tower.

**THOMAS JEFFERSON** Because the appeal of Neoclassicism was due in part to the values with which it was associated— morality, idealism, patriotism, and civic virtue—it is not surprising that in the new American republic (MAP 26-1), THOMAS JEFFERSON (1743–1826) spearheaded a movement to adopt Neoclassicism as the national architectural style. Jefferson—economist, educational theorist, gifted amateur architect, as well as stateman—admired Palladio immensely and read carefully the Italian architect's *Four Books of Architecture.* Later, while minister to France, he studied 18th-century French classical architecture and city planning and visited the Maison Carrée (FIG. 7-32), an ancient Roman temple at Nîmes. After his European sojourn, Jefferson completely remodeled Monticello (FIG. 26-30), his home near Charlottesville, Virginia, which he originally had designed in a different style. The final version of Monticello is somewhat reminiscent of Palladio's Villa Rotonda (FIG. 22-28) and of Chiswick House (FIG. 26-28), but its materials are the local wood and brick used in Virginia.

**UNIVERSITY OF VIRGINIA** Jefferson's Neoclassicism was an extension of the Enlightenment belief in the perfectibility of human beings and in the power of art to help achieve that perfection. When he became president, he selected Benjamin Latrobe (1764–1820) to build the U.S. Capitol in Washington, D.C., specifying that Latrobe use a Roman style. Jefferson's choice in part reflected his admiration for the beauty of the Roman buildings he had seen in Europe and in part his association of those buildings

**26-29** HENRY FLITCROFT and HENRY HOARE, the park at Stourhead, England, 1743–1765.

Flitcroft's design for Hoare's Wiltshire estate included a replica of the Pantheon overlooking an artificial lake and a grotto alluding to Aeneas's journey to the Underworld from Lake Avernus.

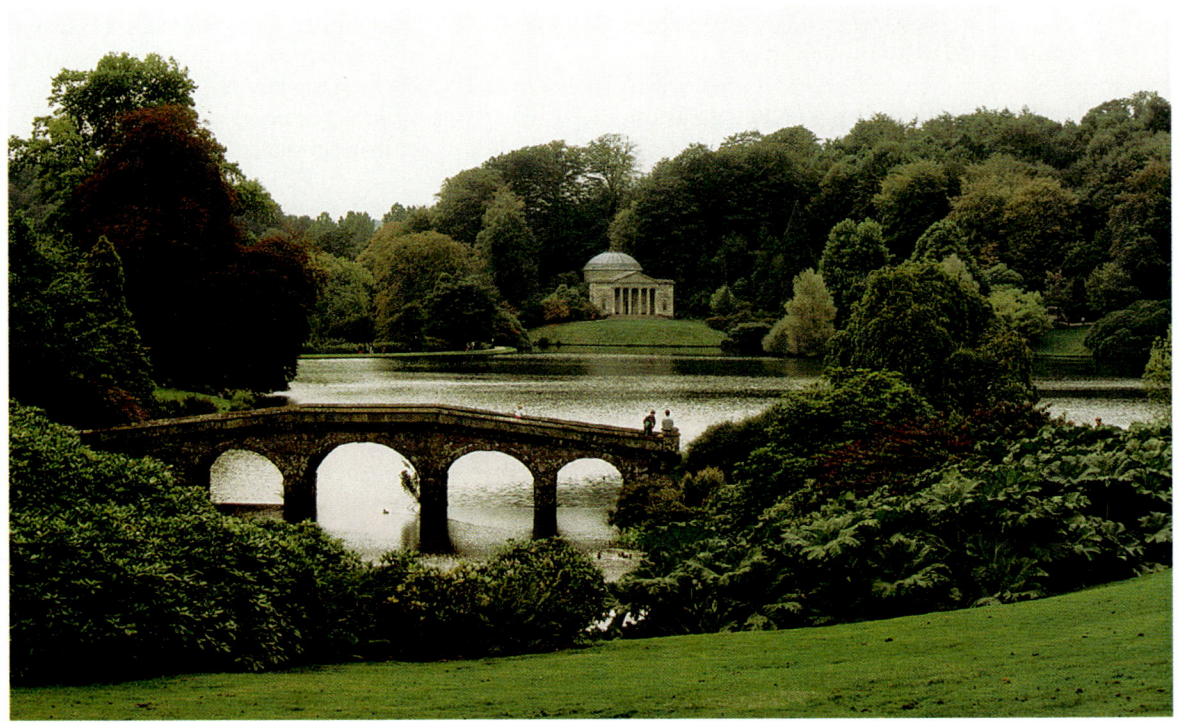

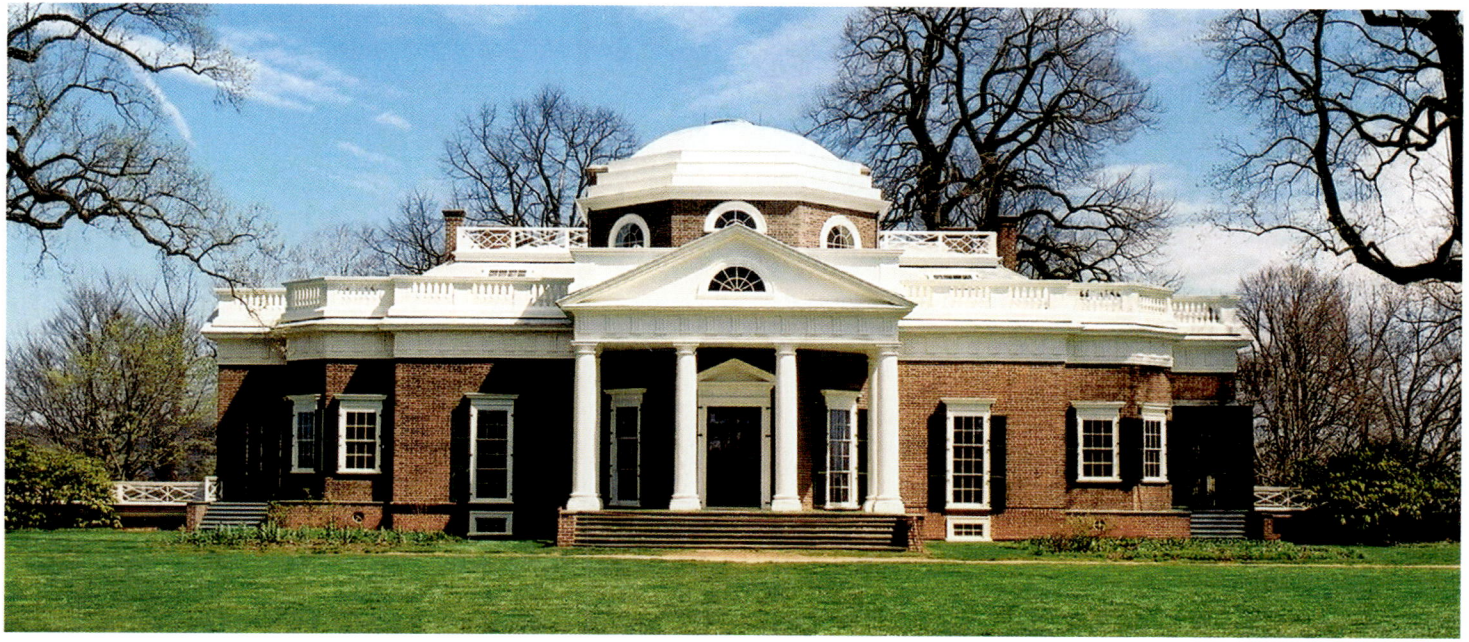

**26-30** THOMAS JEFFERSON, Monticello, Charlottesville, Virginia, 1770–1806. ■◀

Jefferson led the movement to adopt Neoclassicism as the architectural style of the United States. Although built of local materials, his Palladian Virginia home recalls Chiswick House (FIG. 26-28).

with an idealized Roman republican government and, through that, with the democracy of ancient Greece.

In his own designs for public buildings, Jefferson also looked to Rome for models. He modeled the State Capitol in Richmond, Virginia, on the Maison Carrée (FIG. 7-32). For the University of Virginia, which he founded, Jefferson turned to the Pantheon (FIG. 7-49). The Rotunda (FIG. **26-31**) is the centerpiece of Jefferson's "academical village" in Charlottesville. It sits on an elevated platform at one end of a grassy quadrangle ("the Lawn"), framed by Neoclassical pavilions and colonnades—just as temples in Roman forums (FIGS. 7-12 and 7-44) stood at one short end of a colonnaded square. Each of the ten pavilions (five on each side) resembles a small classical temple. No two are exactly alike. Jefferson ex-

perimented with variations of all the different classical orders in his pavilions. He had thoroughly absorbed the principles of classical architecture and clearly delighted in borrowing motifs from major buildings. Jefferson was no mere copyist, however. His designs were highly original—and, in turn, frequently emulated.

**JEAN-ANTOINE HOUDON** Neoclassicism also became the preferred style for public sculpture in the new American republic. When members of the Virginia legislature wanted to erect a life-size marble statue of Virginia-born George Washington (1732–1799), they awarded the commission to the leading French Neoclassical sculptor of the late 18th century, JEAN-ANTOINE HOUDON (1741–1828). Houdon had already carved a bust portrait of Benjamin Franklin

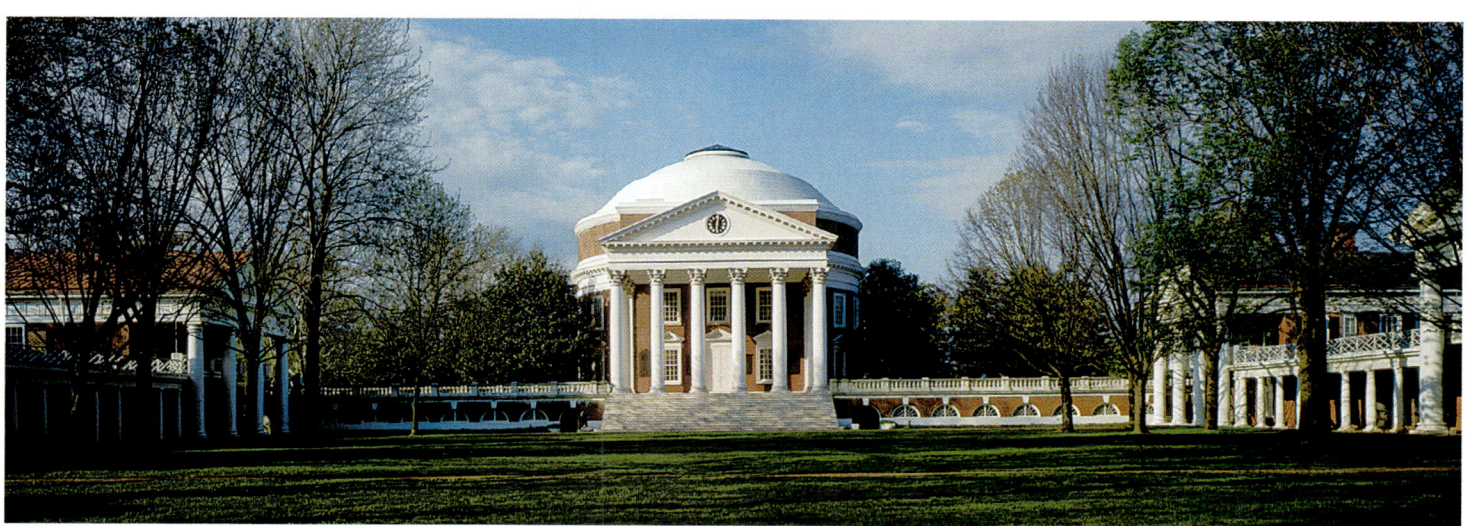

**26-31** THOMAS JEFFERSON, Rotunda and Lawn (looking north), University of Virginia, Charlottesville, Virginia, 1819–1826.

Modeled on the Pantheon (FIG. 7-49), Jefferson's Rotunda sits like a temple in a Roman forum on an elevated platform overlooking the colonnaded Lawn of the University of Virginia.

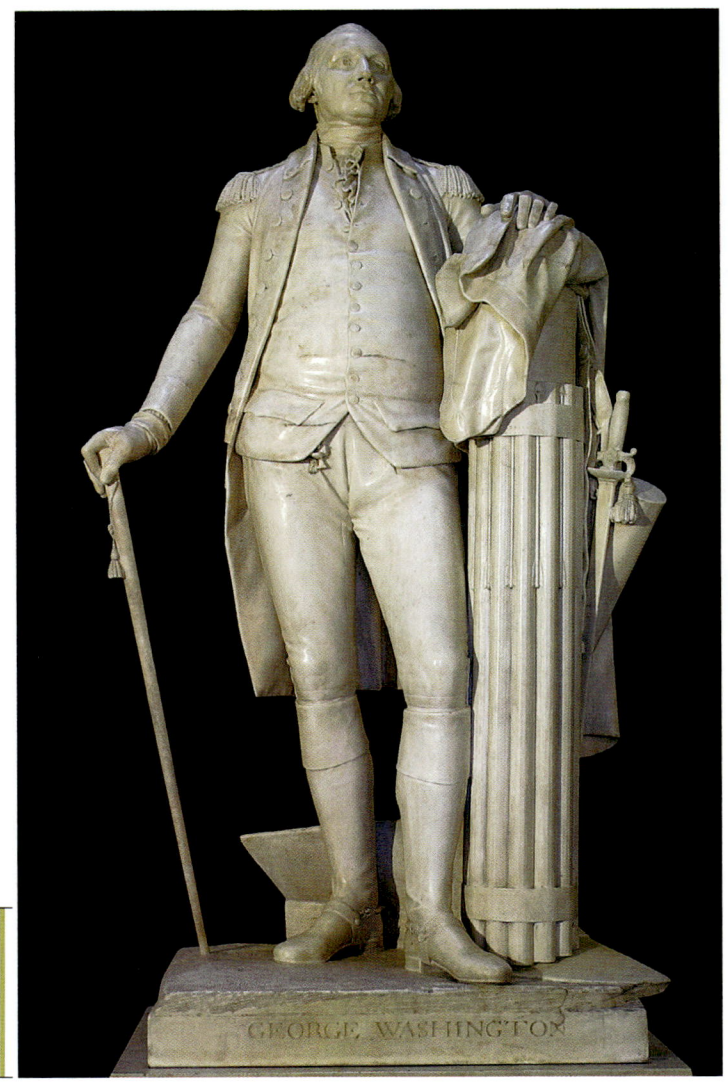

**26-32** JEAN-ANTOINE HOUDON, *George Washington*, 1788–1792. Marble, 6′ 2″ high. State Capitol, Richmond.

Houdon portrayed Washington in contemporary garb, but he incorporated the Roman *fasces* and Cincinnatus's plow in the statue, because Washington similarly had returned to his farm after his war service.

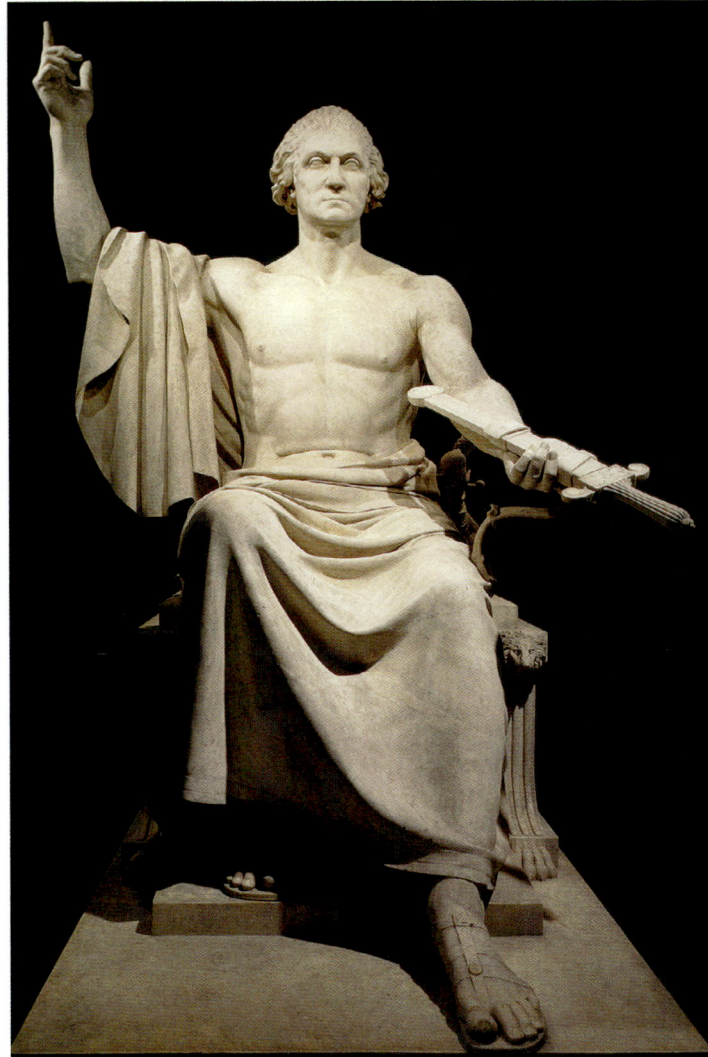

**26-33** HORATIO GREENOUGH, *George Washington*, 1840. Marble, 11′ 4″ high. Smithsonian American Art Museum, Washington, D.C.

In this posthumous portrait, Greenough likened Washington to a god by depicting him seminude and enthroned in the manner of Phidias's Olympian statue of Zeus, king of the Greek gods.

(1706–1790) when he was America's ambassador to France. His portrait of Washington (FIG. **26-32**) is the sculptural equivalent of a painted Grand Manner portrait (FIG. 26-19). But although Washington wears 18th-century garb, the statue makes overt reference to the Roman Republic. The "column" on which Washington leans is a bundle of rods with an ax attached—the ancient Roman *fasces,* an emblem of authority (used much later as the emblem of Mussolini's Fascist—the term derives from "fasces"—government in 20th-century Italy). The 13 rods symbolize the 13 original states. The plow behind Washington alludes to Cincinnatus, a patrician of the early Roman Republic who was elected dictator during a time of war and resigned his position as soon as victory had been achieved in order to return to his farm. Washington wears the badge of the Society of the Cincinnati (visible beneath the bottom of his waistcoat), an association founded in 1783 for officers in the revolutionary army who had resumed their peacetime roles. Tellingly, Washington no longer holds his sword in Houdon's statue.

**HORATIO GREENOUGH** After his death, Washington gradually took on almost godlike stature as the "father of his country." In 1840 the U.S. Congress commissioned American sculptor HORATIO GREENOUGH (1805–1852) to create a statue (FIG. **26-33**) of the country's first president for the Capitol. Greenough used Houdon's portrait as his model for the head, but he portrayed Washington as seminude and enthroned, as Phidias depicted Zeus in the famous lost statue he made for the god's temple at Olympia in ancient Greece. The colossal statue—Washington is more than 11 feet tall, seated—epitomizes the Neoclassical style, but it did not win favor with either the Congress that commissioned it or the public. Although no one ever threw Greenough's statue into the Potomac River, as one congressman suggested, the legislators never placed it in its intended site beneath the Capitol dome. In fact, by 1840 the Neoclassical style itself was no longer in vogue. The leading artists of Europe and America had embraced a new style, Romanticism, examined in the next chapter.

# ROCOCO TO NEOCLASSICISM: THE 18TH CENTURY IN EUROPE AND AMERICA

## ROCOCO

❚ In the early 18th century, the centralized and grandiose palace-based culture of Baroque France gave way to the much more intimate Rococo culture based in the townhouses of Paris. There, aristocrats and intellectuals gathered for witty conversation in salons featuring delicate colors, sinuous lines, gilded mirrors, elegant furniture, and small paintings and sculptures.

❚ The leading Rococo painter was Antoine Watteau, whose usually small canvases feature light colors and elegant figures in ornate costumes moving gracefully through lush landscapes. His *fête galante* paintings depict the outdoor amusements of French high society.

❚ Watteau's successors included François Boucher and Jean-Honoré Fragonard, who carried on the Rococo style late into the 18th century. In Italy, Giambattista Tiepolo adapted the Rococo manner to huge ceiling frescoes in the Baroque tradition.

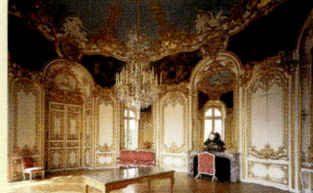

Boffrand, Salon de la Princesse, Paris 1737–1740

## THE ENLIGHTENMENT

❚ By the end of the 18th century, revolutions had overthrown the monarchy in France and achieved independence for the British colonies in America. A major factor was the Enlightenment, a new way of thinking critically about the world independently of religion and tradition.

❚ The Enlightenment promoted scientific questioning of all assertions and embraced the doctrine of progress, epitomized by the Industrial Revolution, which began in England in the 1740s. The paintings of Joseph Wright of Derby celebrated the scientific inventions of the Enlightenment era.

❚ The Enlightenment also made knowledge of ancient Rome imperative for the cultured elite, and Europeans and Americans in large numbers undertook a Grand Tour of Italy. Among the most popular souvenirs of the Grand Tour were Antonio Canaletto's *vedute* of Venice rendered in precise Renaissance perspective with the aid of a camera obscura.

❚ Rejecting the idea of progress, Rousseau, one of the leading French *philosophes,* argued for a return to natural values and exalted the simple, honest life of peasants. His ideas had a profound impact on artists such as Jean-Baptiste-Siméon Chardin and Jean-Baptiste Greuze, who painted sentimental narratives about rural families.

❚ The taste for naturalism also led to the popularity of portrait paintings with landscape backgrounds, a specialty of Thomas Gainsborough, and to a reawakening of interest in realism. Benjamin West represented the protagonists in his history paintings wearing contemporary costumes.

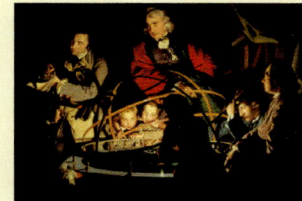

Wright, *A Lecture at the Orrery,* ca. 1763–1765

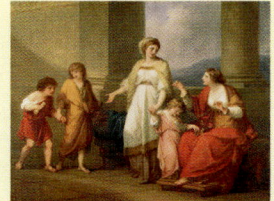

Canaletto, *Riva degli Schiavoni, Venice,* ca. 1735–1740

## NEOCLASSICISM

❚ The Enlightenment revival of interest in Greece and Rome, which spurred systematic excavations at Herculaneum and Pompeii, also gave rise in the late 18th century to the artistic movement known as Neoclassicism, which incorporated the subjects and styles of ancient art.

❚ One pioneer of the new style was Angelica Kauffmann, who often chose subjects drawn from Roman history for her paintings. Jacques-Louis David, who exalted classical art as "the imitation of nature in her most beautiful and perfect form," also favored ancient Roman themes. Painted on the eve of the French Revolution, *Oath of the Horatii,* set in a severe classical hall, served as an example of patriotism and sacrifice.

❚ Architects also eagerly embraced the Neoclassical style. Ancient Roman and Italian Renaissance structures inspired Jacques-Germain Soufflot's Panthéon in Paris and Richard Boyle's Chiswick House near London. A Greek temple in Athens was the model for James Stuart's Doric portico in Worcestershire.

❚ In the United States, Thomas Jefferson adopted the Neoclassical style in his designs for Monticello and the University of Virginia. He championed Neoclassicism as the official architectural style of the new American republic because it represented for him idealism, patriotism, and civic virtue.

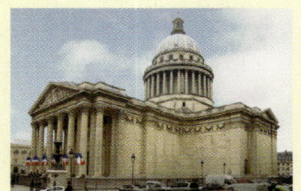

Kauffmann, *Mother of the Gracchi,* ca. 1785

Soufflot, Panthéon, Paris, 1755–1792

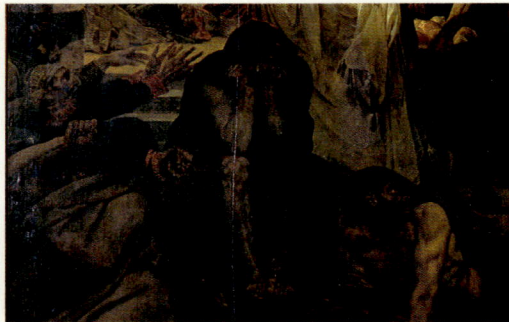

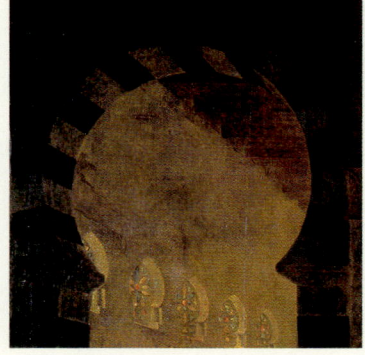

In the shadows of the left side of the huge canvas are dying and dead Arabs, including a seated man in despair. Gros based the figure on one of the damned in Michelangelo's *Last Judgment* (FIG. 22-19).

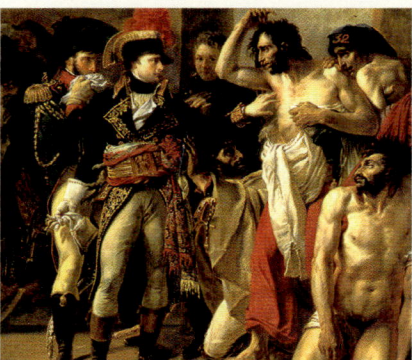

Napoleon, fearless among the plague-stricken, reaches out to touch one man's sores. Gros portrayed the French general as Christlike, implying he possessed miraculous power to heal the sick.

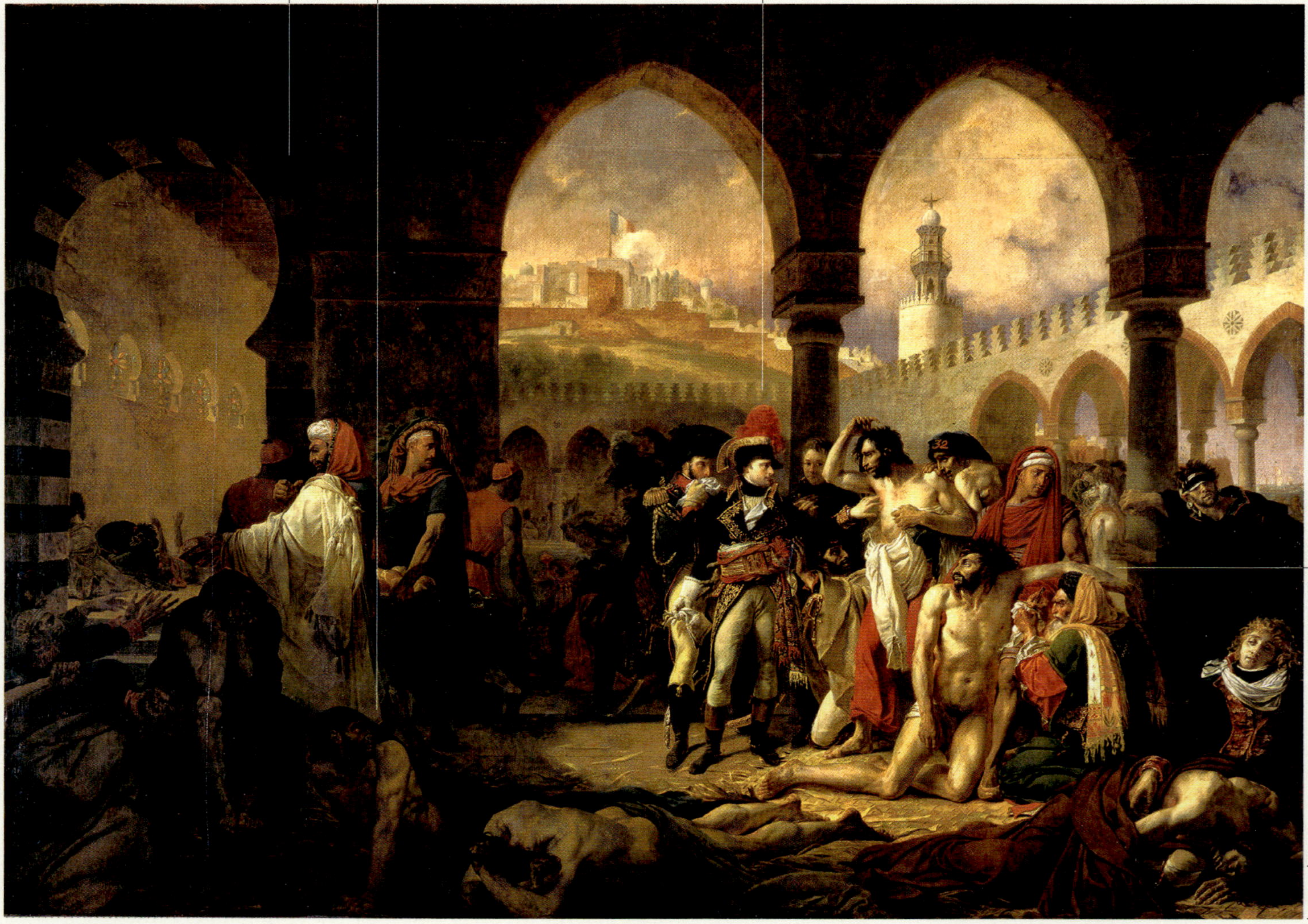

Foreshadowing Romanticism, Gros carefully recorded the exotic people, costumes, and architecture of Jaffa, including the distinctive Islamic striped horseshoe arches of the mosque-hospital.

1 ft.

1 ft.

**27-1** ANTOINE-JEAN GROS, *Napoleon at the Plague House at Jaffa,* 1804. Oil on canvas, 17′ 5″ × 23′ 7″. Musée du Louvre, Paris.

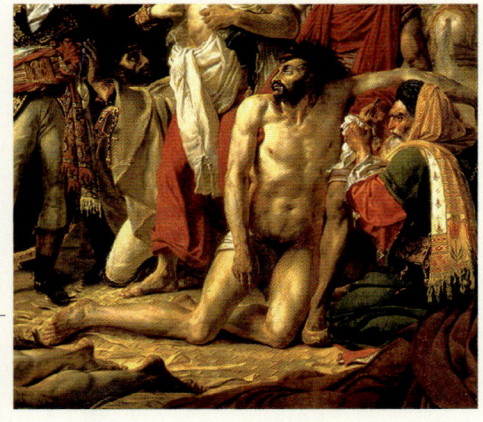

Among the dying whom Napoleon has come to comfort is a kneeling nude man with left arm extended. His posture recalls that of the dead Christ in Michelangelo's emotional *Pietà* (FIG. 22-20).

# ROMANTICISM, REALISM, PHOTOGRAPHY: EUROPE AND AMERICA, 1800 TO 1870

**FRAMING THE ERA**

## NAPOLEON AT JAFFA

In the opening decade of the 19th century, many of the leading French artists produced major artworks glorifying the most powerful man in Europe at the time—Napoleon Bonaparte (1769–1821), since 1799 First Consul of the French Republic and from 1804 to 1815, Emperor of the French. One of those artists was ANTOINE-JEAN GROS (1771–1835), a pupil of Jacques-Louis David (FIGS. 26-25 and 26-26), Napoleon's favorite painter. Gros, like David, produced several paintings that contributed to Napoleon's growing mythic status. In *Napoleon at the Plague House at Jaffa* (FIG. **27-1**), the artist, at Napoleon's request, recorded an incident during an outbreak of the bubonic plague in the course of the general's Syrian campaign of 1799. This fearsome disease struck Muslim and French forces alike, and to quell the growing panic and hysteria, on March 11, 1799, Napoleon himself visited the mosque at Jaffa that had been converted into a hospital for those who had contracted the dreaded disease. Gros depicted Napoleon's staff officers covering their noses against the stench of the place, whereas Napoleon, amid the dead and dying, is fearless and in control. He comforts those still alive, who are clearly awed by his presence and authority. Indeed, by depicting the French leader having removed his glove to touch the sores of a plague victim, Gros implied Napoleon possessed the miraculous power to heal. The composition recalls scenes of the doubting Thomas touching Christ's wound. Here, however, Napoleon is not Saint Thomas but a Christlike figure tending to the sick, as in Rembrandt's *Hundred-Guilder Print* (FIG. 25-16), which Gros certainly knew. The French painter also based the despairing seated figure at the lower left on the comparable figure (one of the damned) in Michelangelo's *Last Judgment* (FIG. 22-19). The kneeling nude man with extended arm at the right recalls the dead Christ in Michelangelo's late *Pietà* (FIG. 22-20).

The action in *Napoleon at the Plague House in Jaffa* unfolds against the exotic backdrop of the horseshoe arches and Moorish arcades of the mosque-hospital's courtyard (compare FIG. 10-9). On the left are Muslim doctors distributing bread and ministering to plague-stricken Arabs in the shadows. On the right, in radiant light, are Napoleon and his soldiers in their splendid tailored uniforms. David had used this polarized compositional scheme and an arcaded backdrop to great effect in his *Oath of the Horatii* (FIG. 26-25), and Gros emulated these features in this painting. However, the younger artist's fascination with the exoticism of the Muslim world, as is evident in his attention to the details of architecture and costume, represented a departure from Neoclassicism. This, along with Gros's emphasis on death, suffering, and an emotional rendering of the scene, presaged core elements of the artistic movement that would soon displace Neoclassicism—Romanticism.

# ART UNDER NAPOLEON

The revolution of 1789 initiated a new era in France, but the overthrow of the monarchy also opened the door for Napoleon Bonaparte to exploit the resulting disarray and establish a different kind of monarchy with himself at its head. In 1799, after serving in various French army commands and leading major campaigns in Italy and Egypt, Napoleon became First Consul of the French Republic, a title with clear and intentional links to the ancient Roman Republic (see Chapter 7). During the next 15 years, the ambitious general gained control of almost all of continental Europe in name or through alliances (MAP 27-1). In May 1804, for example, he became king of Italy. Later that year, the pope journeyed to Paris for Napoleon's coronation as Emperor of the French (FIG. 27-2). In 1812, however, Napoleon launched a disastrous invasion of Russia that ended in retreat, and in 1815 he suffered a devastating defeat at the hands of the British at Waterloo in present-day Belgium. Forced to abdicate the imperial throne, Napoleon went into exile on the island of Saint Helena in the South Atlantic, where he died six years later.

After Napoleon's death, the political geography of Europe changed dramatically (MAP 27-2, page 758), but in many ways the more significant changes during the first half of the 19th century

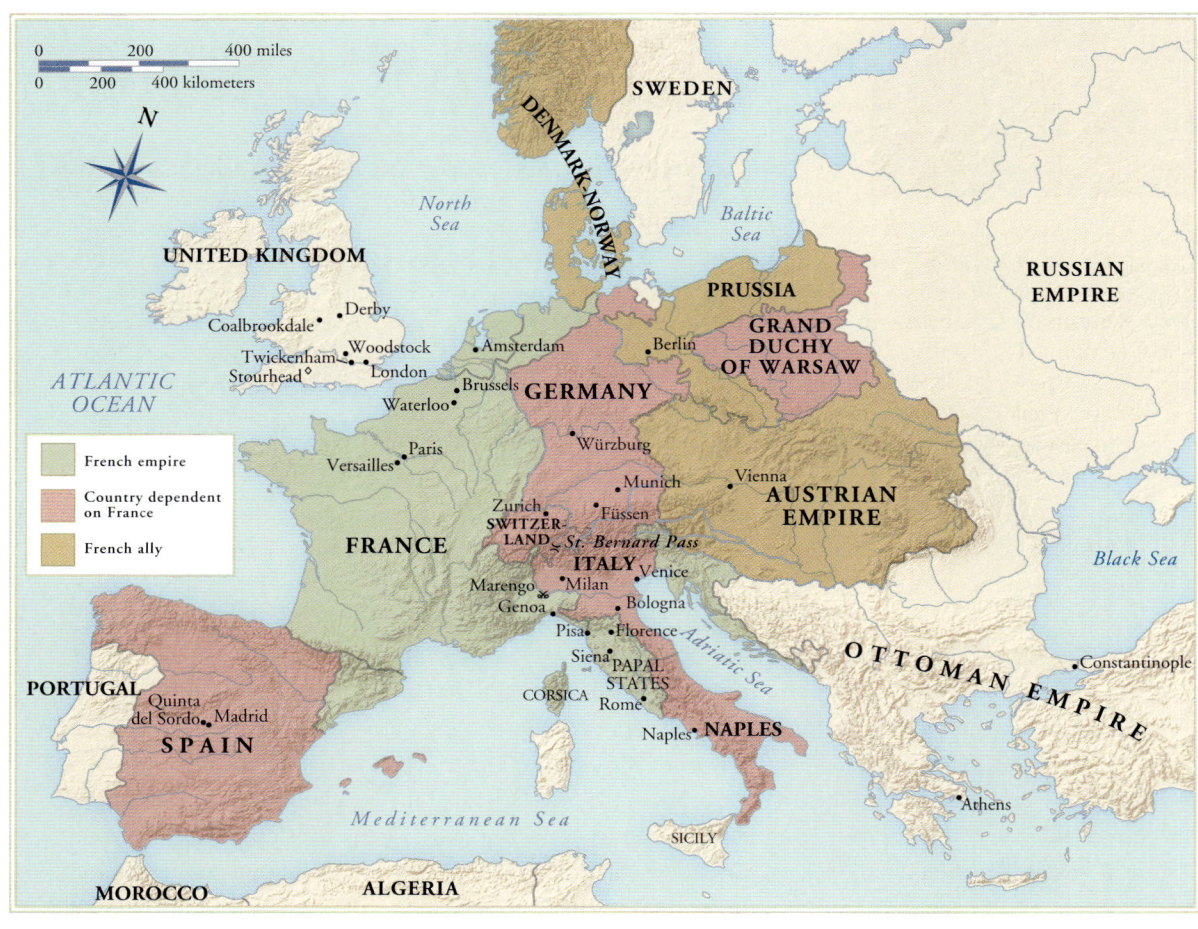

**MAP 27-1** The Napoleonic Empire in 1815.

Map legend:
- French empire
- Country dependent on France
- French ally

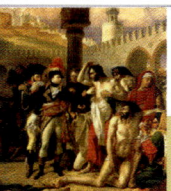

## ROMANTICISM, REALISM, PHOTOGRAPHY: EUROPE AND AMERICA, 1800 TO 1870

| 1800 | 1815 | 1840 | 1870 |
|------|------|------|------|

- Napoleon appoints David as First Painter of the Empire and brings Canova from Rome to Paris
- Vignon designs La Madeleine, Napoleon's Neoclassical "temple of glory"
- Gros, Girodet, and Ingres form a bridge between Neoclassicism and Romanticism

- Romanticism is the leading art movement in Europe. Delacroix and other painters favor exotic and fantastic subjects featuring unleashed emotion, vibrant color, and bold brushstrokes
- Friedrich, Turner, Cole, and other Romantic artists specialize in painting transcendental landscapes
- Gothic style enjoys a revival in architecture
- Daguerre and Talbot invent photography

- Courbet exhibits his work in the Pavilion of Realism. He and other Realist painters in Europe and America insist people and events of their own time are the only valid subjects for art
- Manet's paintings get a hostile reception because of their shocking subject matter and nonillusionistic style
- Paxton pioneers prefabricated glass-and-iron construction in the Crystal Palace
- Technological advances enable artists to make on-the-spot photographs of the Civil War

were technological and economic. The Industrial Revolution caused a population boom in European cities, and railroads spread to many parts of the Continent, facilitating the transportation of both goods and people. Transformation also occurred in the art world. The century opened with Neoclassicism still supreme, but by 1870 Romanticism and Realism in turn had captured the imagination of artists and public alike. New construction techniques had a major impact on architectural design, and the invention of photography revolutionized picturemaking of all kinds.

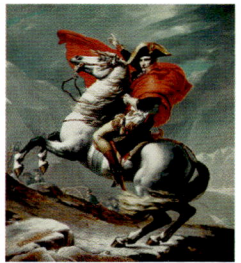

27-1A DAVID, *Napoleon Crossing Saint-Bernard,* 1800–1801.

**DAVID AND NAPOLEON** At the fall of the French revolutionary Maximilien Robespierre and his party in 1794, Jacques-Louis David, who had aligned himself personally and through his work with the revolutionary forces, barely escaped with his life. He stood trial and went to prison. After his release in 1795, he worked hard to resurrect his career. When Napoleon approached David in 1804 and offered him the position of First Painter of the Empire, David seized the opportunity. The artist, who had earlier painted a series of portraits of the emperor on horseback crossing the Alps (FIG. 27-1A), exemplified Neoclassicism, the artistic style Napoleon favored because he aspired to rule an empire that might one day rival ancient Rome's. The French emperor consequently embraced all links with the classical past as symbolic sources of authority.

**CORONATION OF NAPOLEON** The new emperor was well aware of the power of art for constructing a public image and of David's ability to produce inspiring patriotic images. The most grandiose work First Painter David produced for his new imperial patron was *Coronation of Napoleon* (FIG. 27-2), an immense (20 by 32 feet) canvas documenting the pomp and pageantry of the crowning ceremony of December 1804. To a large extent, David adhered to historical fact in depicting Napoleon's coronation, duly recording, for example, the appearance of the interior of Paris's Notre Dame Cathedral as the emperor's architects Charles Percier (1764–1838) and Pierre-François-Léonard Fontaine (1762–1853) had decorated it for the occasion. David also faithfully portrayed those in attendance: Napoleon; his wife Josephine (1763–1814), who kneels to receive her crown; Pope Pius VII (r. 1800–1823), seated behind Napoleon; Joseph (1768–1814) and Louis (1778–1846) Bonaparte; Napoleon's ministers; the retinues of the emperor and empress; a representative group of the clergy; and David himself, seated among the rows of spectators in the balconies. Preliminary studies and drawings reveal, however, that, at Napoleon's request, David made changes to his initially accurate record of the event. For example, the emperor insisted the painter depict the pope with his hand raised in blessing. Further, Napoleon's mother, who had refused to attend the coronation, appears prominently in the center background.

Given the number of figures and details David had to incorporate in his painting, it is remarkable he was able to impose upon the lavish pageant the structured composition central to the Neoclassical style. As in his *Oath of the Horatii* (FIG. 26-25), David presented

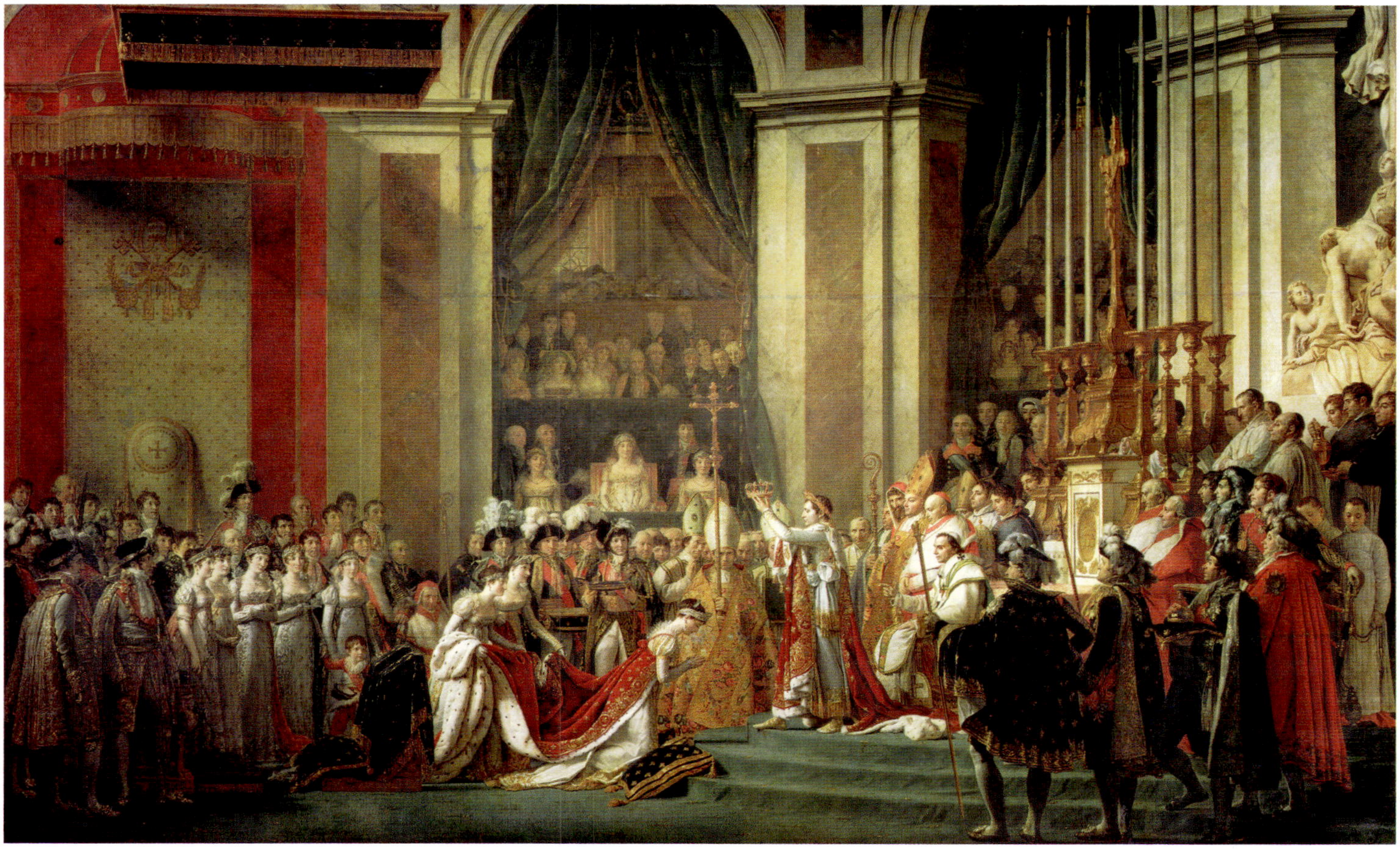

27-2 JACQUES-LOUIS DAVID, *Coronation of Napoleon,* 1805–1808. Oil on canvas, 20′ 4½″ × 32′ 1¾″. Musée du Louvre, Paris.

As First Painter of the Empire, David recorded Napoleon at his December 1804 coronation crowning his wife with the pope as witness, thus underscoring the authority of the state over the church.

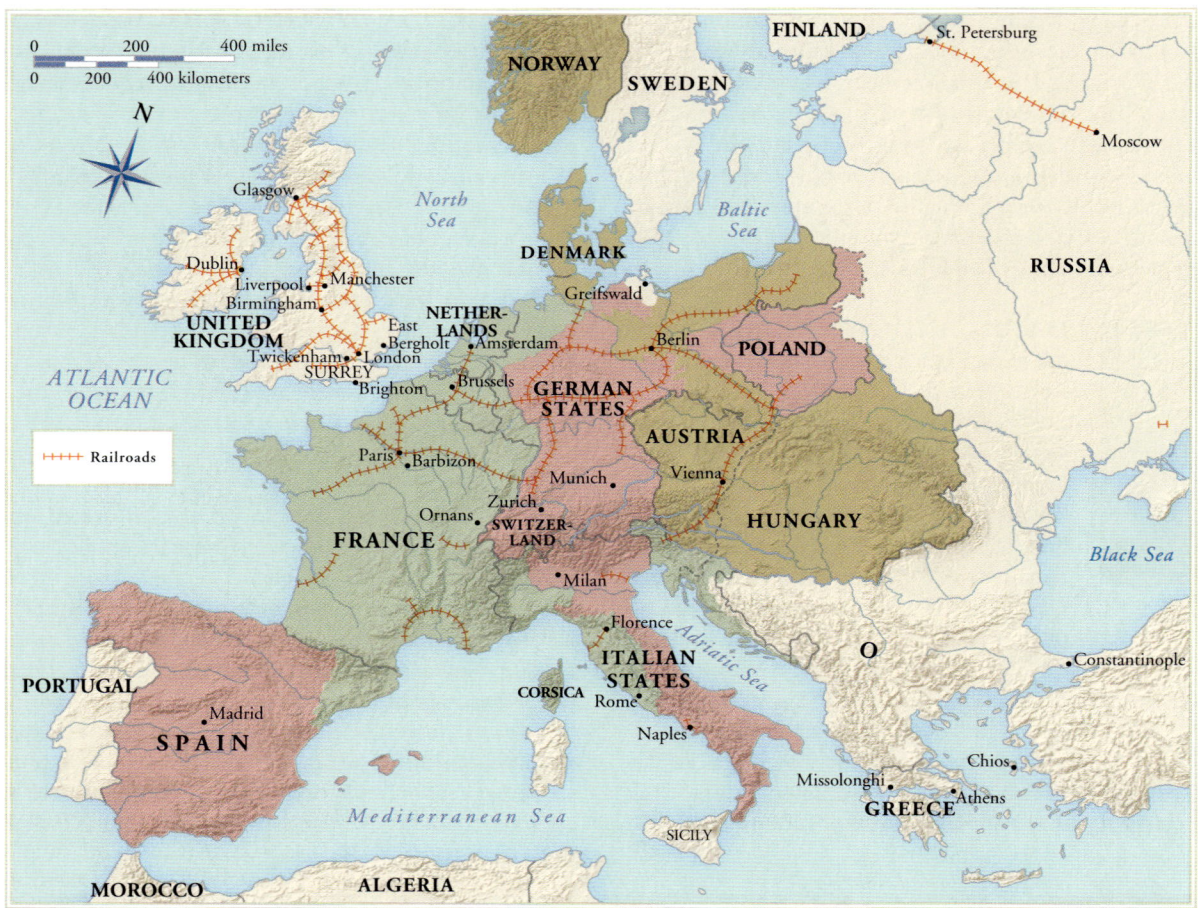

MAP 27-2 Europe around 1850.

the action as if on a theater stage—which in this instance was literally the case, even if the stage Percier and Fontaine constructed was inside a church. In addition, as he did in his arrangement of the men and women in *Oath of the Horatii,* David conceptually divided the painting to highlight polarities. The pope, prelates, and priests representing the Catholic Church appear on the right. The members of Napoleon's imperial court are on the left. The relationship between church and state was one of this period's most contentious issues. Napoleon's decision to crown himself, rather than to allow the pope to perform the coronation, as was traditional, reflected Napoleon's concern about the church-state power relationship. For the painting commemorating the occasion, the emperor insisted David depict the moment when, having already crowned himself,

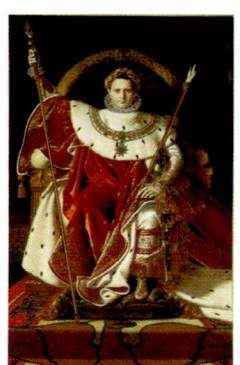

27-2A INGRES, *Napoleon on His Imperial Throne,* 1806.

Napoleon placed a crown on his wife's head, further underscoring his authority. Thus, although this painting appears at first to be a detailed, objective record of a historical event, it is, in fact, a carefully crafted tableau designed to present Napoleon in the way he wished to be seen. In that respect, as well as stylistically, David was emulating the artists in the employ of the ancient Roman emperors (see Chapter 7), as did his pupil, JEAN-AUGUSTE-DOMINIQUE INGRES (1780–1867) in a contemporaneous portrait (FIG. 27-2A) of Napoleon enthroned.

**LA MADELEINE** Napoleon also embraced Neoclassical architecture as an ideal vehicle for expressing his imperial authority. For example, the emperor resumed construction of the church of La Madeleine (FIG. 27-3) in Paris, which had been interrupted in 1790. However, he converted the building into a "temple of glory" for France's imperial armies. (The structure reverted again to a church after Napoleon's defeat and long before its completion in 1842.) Designed by PIERRE VIGNON (1763–1828), the grandiose Napoleonic temple includes a high podium and broad flight of stairs leading to a deep porch in the front. These architectural features, coupled with the Corinthian columns, recall Roman temples in France, such as the Maison Carrée (FIG. 7-32) at Nîmes, making La Madeleine a symbolic link between the Napoleonic and Roman empires. Curiously, the building's classical shell surrounds an interior covered by a sequence of three domes, a feature found in Byzantine and Romanesque churches. Vignon in essence clothed a traditional church in the costume of imperial Rome.

**ANTONIO CANOVA** Neoclassical sculpture also was in vogue under Napoleon. His favorite sculptor was ANTONIO CANOVA (1757–1822), who somewhat reluctantly left a successful career in Italy to settle in Paris and serve the emperor. Once in France, Canova became Napoleon's admirer and made numerous portraits, all in the Neoclassical style, of the emperor and his family. The most remarkable is the marble portrait (FIG. 27-4) of Napoleon's sister, Pauline Borghese (1780–1825), as Venus. Initially, Canova, who had gained renown for his sculptures of classical gods and heroes—for

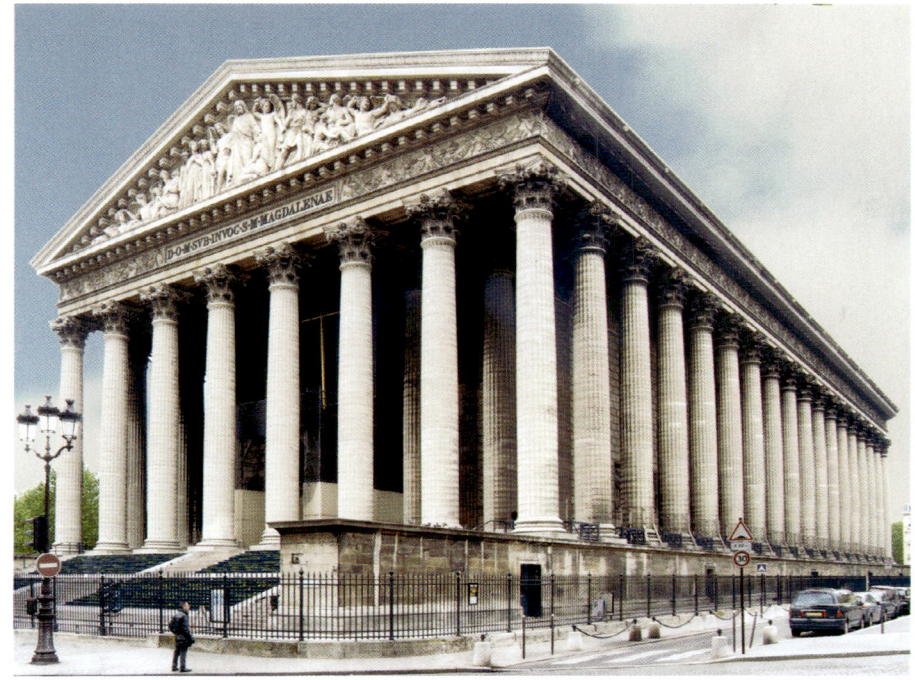

The French public never got to admire Canova's portrait, however. Napoleon had arranged the marriage of his sister to an heir of the noble Roman Borghese family. Once Pauline was in Rome, her behavior was less than dignified, and the public gossiped extensively about her affairs. Pauline's insistence on being represented as the goddess of love reflected her self-perception. Because of his wife's questionable reputation, Prince Camillo Borghese (1775–1832), the work's official patron, kept the sculpture sequestered in the Villa Borghese in Rome (where it still is). Borghese allowed relatively few people to see the portrait. Still, knowledge of the existence of the sculpture was widespread and increased the notoriety of both artist and subject.

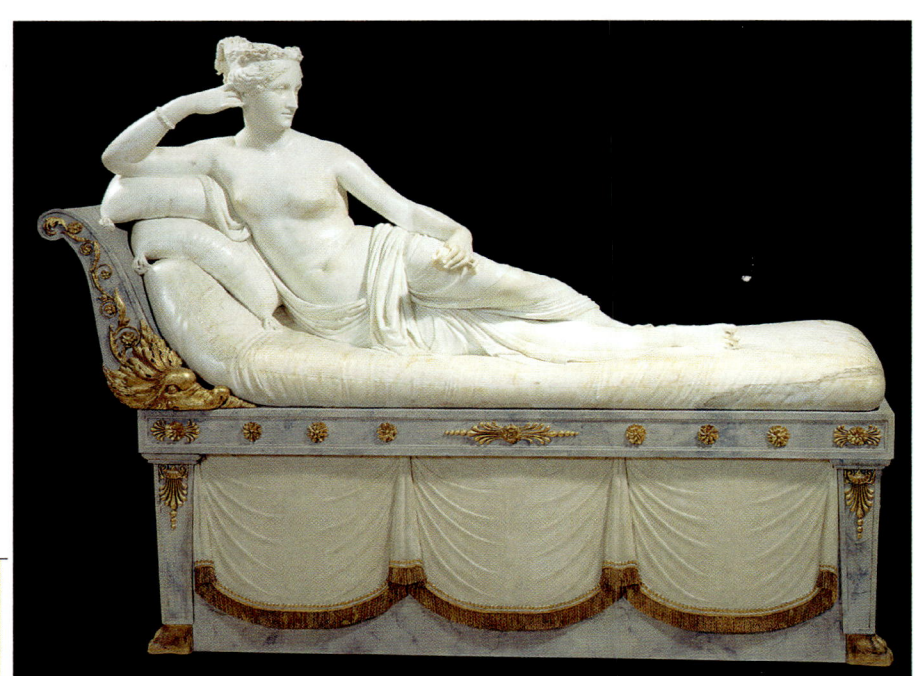

27-4A CANOVA, Cupid and Psyche, 1787–1793.

example, *Cupid and Psyche* (FIG. 27-4A)—had suggested depicting Borghese as Diana, goddess of the hunt. Pauline, however, demanded she be portrayed as Venus, the goddess of love. Thus she appears, reclining on a divan and gracefully holding the golden apple, the symbol of the goddess's triumph in the judgment of Paris. Canova clearly based his work on Greek statuary—the sensuous pose and seminude body recall Hellenistic works such as *Venus de Milo* (FIG. 5-83)—and the reclining figure has parallels on Roman sarcophagus lids (FIG. 7-61; compare FIG. 6-5).

**DAVID'S STUDENTS** Given David's stature as an artist in Napoleonic France, along with the popularity of Neoclassicism, it is not surprising the First Painter attracted numerous students and developed an active and flourishing teaching studio (see "David on Greek Style," Chapter 26, page 747). He gave practical instruction to and deeply influenced many important artists of the period. So strong was David's commitment to classicism that he encouraged all his students to learn Latin, the better to immerse themselves in and understand classical culture. David even initially demanded his pupils select their subjects from Plutarch, the ancient author of *Lives of the Noble Greeks and Romans* and a principal source of Neoclassical subject matter. Due to this thorough classical foundation, David's students all produced work that at its core retains Neoclassical elements. Yet David was far from authoritarian in his teaching, and he encouraged his students to find their own artistic identities. The work of his three most famous students—Gros (FIG. 27-1), Ingres (FIGS. 27-2A, 27-6, and 27-7), and Girodet-Trioson (FIGS. 27-5 and 27-5A)—represents a departure from the structured confines of Neoclassicism. David's pupils laid the foundation for the Romantic movement (see page 762) by exploring the realm of the exotic and the erotic, and often by turning to fictional narratives for the subjects of their paintings, as the Romantic artists would also do.

27-4 ANTONIO CANOVA, *Pauline Borghese as Venus*, 1808. Marble, 6' 7″ long. Galleria Borghese, Rome.

1 ft.

Girodet's depiction of Native American lovers in the Louisiana wilderness appealed to the French public's fascination with what it perceived as the passion and primitivism of the New World.

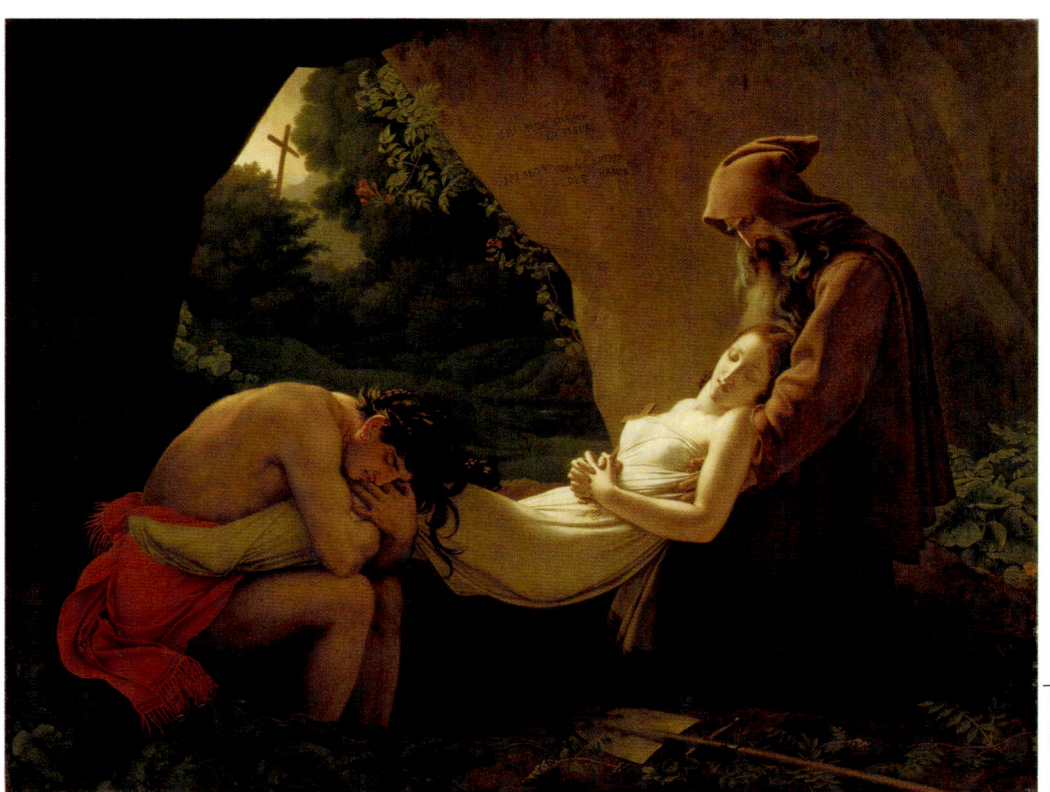

**GIRODET-TRIOSON** *Burial of Atala* (FIG. **27-5**) by ANNE-LOUIS GIRODET-TRIOSON (1767–1824) is an important bridge between Neoclassicism and Romanticism. Girodet based the painting on *The Genius of Christianity,* a novel by François René de Chateaubriand (1768–1848). The section of the novel dealing with Atala appeared as an excerpt a year before the publication of the entire book in 1802. Both the excerpt and the novel were enormously successful, and as a result, Atala became almost a cult figure. The exoticism and eroticism integral to the narrative accounted in large part for the public's interest in *The Genius of Christianity.* Set in Louisiana, Chateaubriand's work focuses on two young Native Americans, Atala and Chactas. The two, from different tribes, fall in love and run away together through the wilderness. Erotic passion permeates the story, and Atala, sworn to lifelong virginity, finally commits suicide rather than break her oath. Girodet's painting depicts this tragedy. Atala's grief-stricken lover, Chactas, buries the heroine in the shadow of a cross. Assisting in the burial is a cloaked priest, whose presence is appropriate given Chateaubriand's emphasis on the revival of Christianity (and the Christianization of the New World) in his novel. Like Gros's depiction of the exotic Muslim world of Jaffa (FIG. 27-1), Girodet's representation of American Indian lovers in the Louisiana wilderness appealed to the public's fascination (whetted by the Louisiana Purchase in 1803) with what it perceived as the passion and primitivism of Native American life in the New World. *Burial of*

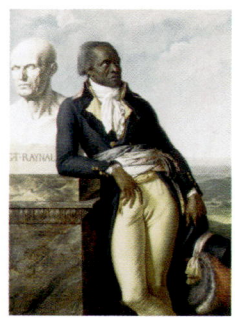

27-5A GIRODET-TRIOSON, *Jean-Baptiste Belley,* 1797.

*Atala* speaks here to emotions, rather than inviting philosophical meditation or revealing some grand order of nature and form. Unlike David's appeal in *Oath of the Horatii* (FIG. 26-25) to feelings that inspire public action, the appeal here is to the viewer's private world of fantasy and emotion. But Girodet-Trioson also occasionally addressed contemporary themes in his work, as he did in his portrait (FIG. **27-5A**) of Jean-Baptiste Belley, a French legislator and former slave.

**INGRES** David's greatest pupil, J.-A.-D. Ingres (FIG. 27-2A), arrived at David's studio in the late 1790s after Girodet-Trioson had left to establish an independent career. Ingres's study there was to be short-lived, however, as he soon broke with David on matters of style. Ingres adopted what he believed to be a truer and purer Greek style than David's Neoclassical manner. The younger artist employed flat, linear forms approximating those found in Greek vase painting (see Chapter 5), and often placed the main figures in the foreground of his composition, emulating classical low-relief sculpture.

***APOTHEOSIS OF HOMER*** Ingres exhibited his huge composition *Apotheosis of Homer* (FIG. **27-6**) at the Salon of 1827 (see "Academic Salons," Chapter 28, page 802). The painting presented in a single statement the doctrines of ideal form and of Neoclassical taste, and generations of academic painters remained loyal to that style. Winged Victory (or Fame) crowns the epic poet Homer, who sits like a god on a throne before an Ionic temple. At Homer's feet are two statuesque women, personifications of the *Iliad* and the *Odyssey,* the offspring of his imagination. Symmetrically grouped about him is a company of the "sovereign geniuses"—as Ingres called them—who expressed humanity's highest ideals in philosophy, poetry, music, and art. To Homer's left are the Greek poet Anacreon with his lyre, Phidias with his sculptor's hammer, the philosophers Plato and Socrates, and other ancient worthies of different eras. They gather together in the painter's world of suspended time as Raphael united them in *School of Athens* (FIG. 22-9), which was the inspiration for *Apotheosis of Homer.* To the far right in Ingres's assembly of literary and artistic giants are the Roman poets Horace and Vergil, and two Italians: Dante, and, conspicuously, Raphael. Among the forward group on the painting's left side are Poussin (pointing) and Shakespeare (half concealed). At the right are French writers Jean Baptiste Racine, Molière, Voltaire, and François de Salignac de la Mothe Fénelon. Ingres had planned a much larger and more inclusive group, but he never completed the project.

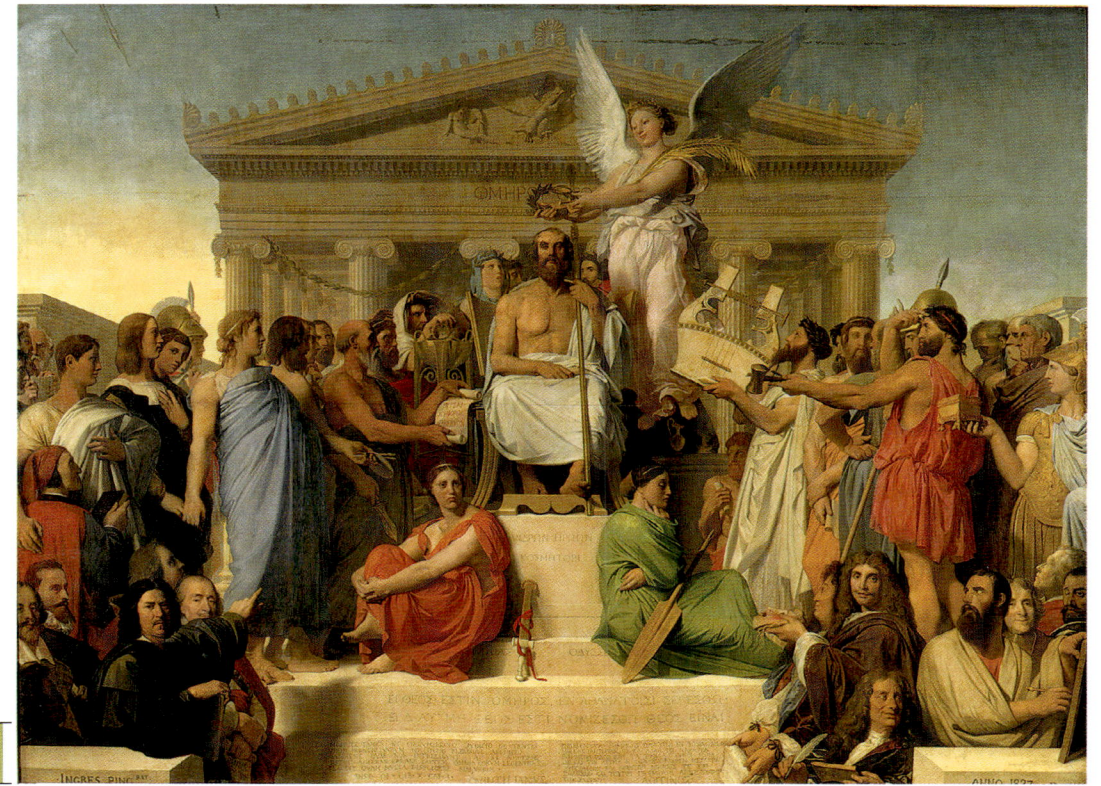

1 ft.

languid pose, small head and elongated limbs, and the generally cool color scheme reveal the painter's debt to Parmigianino (FIG. 22-44) and the Italian Mannerists. However, by converting the figure to an *odalisque* (woman in a Turkish harem), Ingres, unlike Canova, made a strong concession to the burgeoning Romantic taste for the exotic.

This rather strange mixture of artistic allegiances—the combination of precise classical form and Romantic themes—prompted

**GRANDE ODALISQUE** Despite his commitment to ideal form and careful compositional structure, Ingres also produced works that, like those of Gros and Girodet, his contemporaries saw as departures from Neoclassicism. The most famous is *Grande Odalisque* (FIG. **27-7**). The subject—the reclining nude female figure—followed the grand tradition of antiquity and the Renaissance (FIGS. 22-16 and 22-39) in sculpture as well as painting, as did Canova's *Pauline Borghese as Venus* (FIG. 27-4). *Grande Odalisque* again shows Ingres's admiration for Raphael in his borrowing of that master's type of female head (FIGS. 22-7 and 22-8). The figure's

confusion, and when Ingres first exhibited *Grande Odalisque* in 1814, the painting drew acid criticism. Critics initially saw Ingres as a rebel in terms of both the form and content of his works. They did not cease their attacks until the mid-1820s, when a greater enemy of David's Neoclassical style, Eugène Delacroix, appeared on the scene. Then critics suddenly perceived that Ingres's art, despite its innovations and deviations, still contained crucial elements adhering to the Neoclassical taste for the ideal. In fact, Ingres soon became the leader of the academic forces in their battle against the "barbarism" of Delacroix, Théodore Géricault, and the Romantic movement.

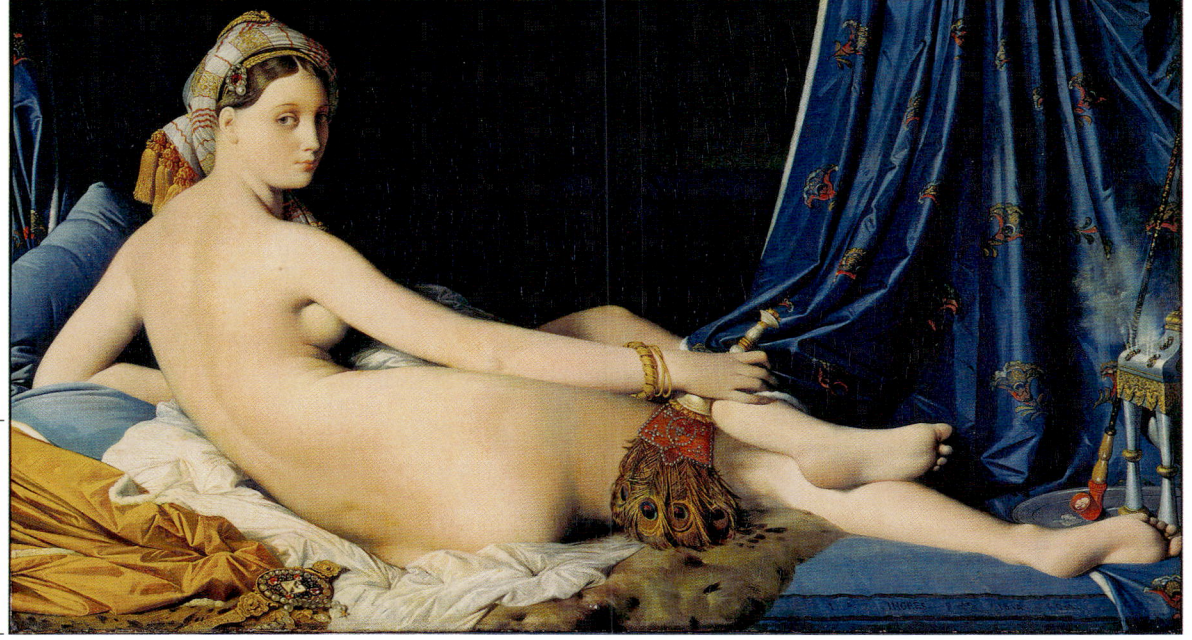

1 ft.

# ROMANTICISM

Whereas Neoclassicism's rationality reinforced Enlightenment thought (see Chapter 26), particularly Voltaire's views, Rousseau's ideas contributed to the rise of *Romanticism*. Rousseau's exclamation "Man is born free, but is everywhere in chains!"—the opening line of his *Social Contract* (1762)—summarizes a fundamental Romantic premise. Romanticism emerged from a desire for freedom—not only political freedom but also freedom of thought, of feeling, of action, of worship, of speech, and of taste. Romantics asserted freedom was the right and property of all. They believed the path to freedom was through imagination rather than reason and functioned through feeling rather than through thinking.

The allure of the Romantic spirit grew dramatically during the late 18th century, when the term originated among German literary critics. Their aim was to distinguish peculiarly "modern" traits from the Neoclassical traits that already had displaced Baroque and Rococo design elements. Consequently, some scholars refer to Romanticism as a phenomenon that began around 1750 and ended about 1850, but most use the term more narrowly to denote a movement that flourished from about 1800 to 1840, between Neoclassicism and Realism.

## Roots of Romanticism

The transition from Neoclassicism to Romanticism represented a shift in emphasis from reason to feeling, from calculation to intuition, and from objective nature to subjective emotion. Among Romanticism's manifestations were the interests in the medieval period and in the sublime. For people living in the 18th century, the Middle Ages were the "dark ages," a time of barbarism, superstition, dark mystery, and miracle. The Romantic imagination stretched its perception of the Middle Ages into all the worlds of fantasy open to it, including the ghoulish, the infernal, the terrible, the nightmarish, the grotesque, the sadistic, and all the imagery that comes from the chamber of horrors when reason sleeps. Related to the imaginative sensibility was the period's notion of the sublime. Among the individuals most involved in studying the sublime was the British politician and philosopher Edmund Burke (1729–1797). In *A Philosophical Enquiry into the Origins of Our Ideas of the Sublime and Beautiful* (1757), Burke articulated his definition of the sublime—feelings of awe mixed with terror. Burke observed that pain or fear evoked the most intense human emotions and that these emotions could also be thrilling. Thus, raging rivers and great storms at sea could be sublime to their viewers.

Accompanying this taste for the sublime was the taste for the fantastic, the occult, and the macabre—for the adventures of the soul voyaging into the dangerous reaches of the imagination.

**HENRY FUSELI** The concept of the nightmare is the subject of a 1781 painting (FIG. **27-8**) by HENRY FUSELI (1741–1825). Swiss by birth, Fuseli settled in England and eventually became a member of the Royal Academy and an instructor there. Largely self-taught, he contrived a distinctive manner to express the fantasies of his vivid imagination. Fuseli specialized in night moods of horror and in dark fantasies—in the demonic, in the macabre, and often in the sadistic. In *The Nightmare,* a beautiful young woman lies asleep, draped across the bed with her limp arm dangling over the side. An *incubus,* a demon believed in medieval times to prey, often sexually, on sleeping women, squats ominously on her body. In the background, a ghostly horse with flaming eyes bursts into the scene from beyond the curtain. Despite the temptation to see the painting's title as a pun because of this horse, the word *nightmare* in fact derives from "night" and "Mara." Mara was a spirit in Scandinavian mythology who tormented and suffocated sleepers. Fuseli was among the first to attempt to depict the dark terrain of the human subconscious that became fertile ground for later artists to harvest.

**WILLIAM BLAKE** In their images of the sublime and the terrible, Romantic artists often combined something of Baroque dynamism with naturalistic details in their quest for grippingly moving visions. These elements became the mainstay of Romantic art and contrasted with the more intellectual, rational Neoclassical themes and compositions. The two were not mutually exclusive, however. Gros, Girodet-Trioson, and Ingres effectively integrated elements of Neoclassicism with Romanticism. So, too, did the visionary English poet, painter, and engraver WILLIAM BLAKE (1757–1827). Blake greatly admired ancient Greek art because it exemplified for him the mathematical and thus the eternal, and his work often incorporated classical references. Yet Blake did not align himself with prominent Enlightenment figures. Like many other Romantic

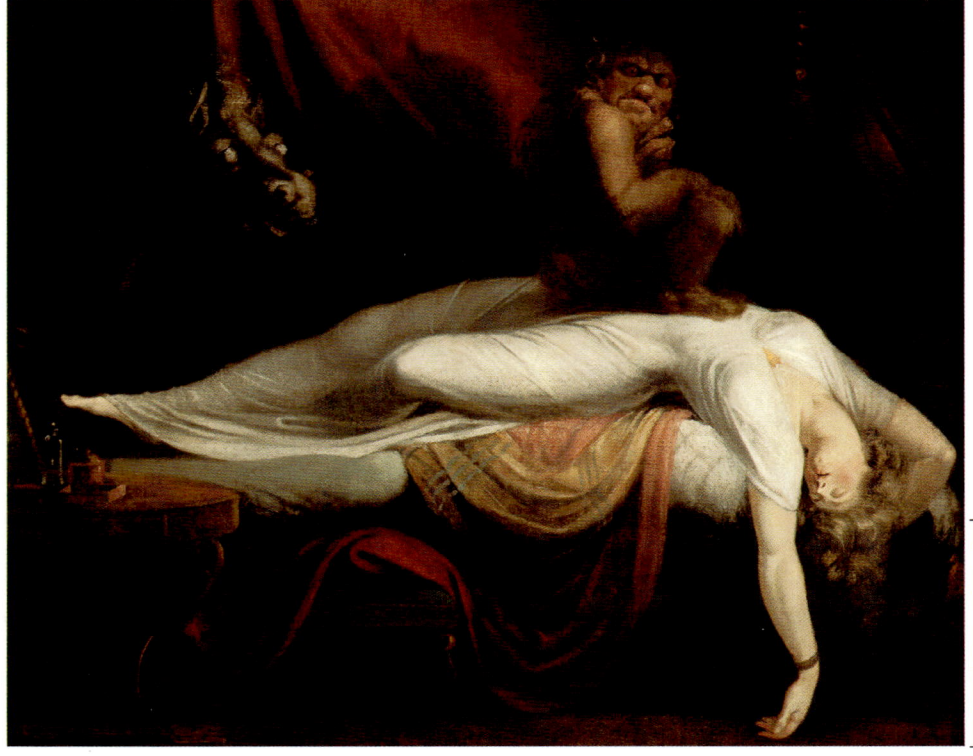

**27-8** HENRY FUSELI, *The Nightmare,* 1781. Oil on canvas, 3′ 3¾″ × 4′ 1½″. Detroit Institute of the Arts (Founders Society purchase with funds from Mr. and Mrs. Bert L. Smokler and Mr. and Mrs. Lawrence A. Fleishman).

The transition from Neoclassicism to Romanticism marked a shift in emphasis from reason to feeling. Fuseli was among the first painters to depict the dark terrain of the human subconscious.

1 ft.

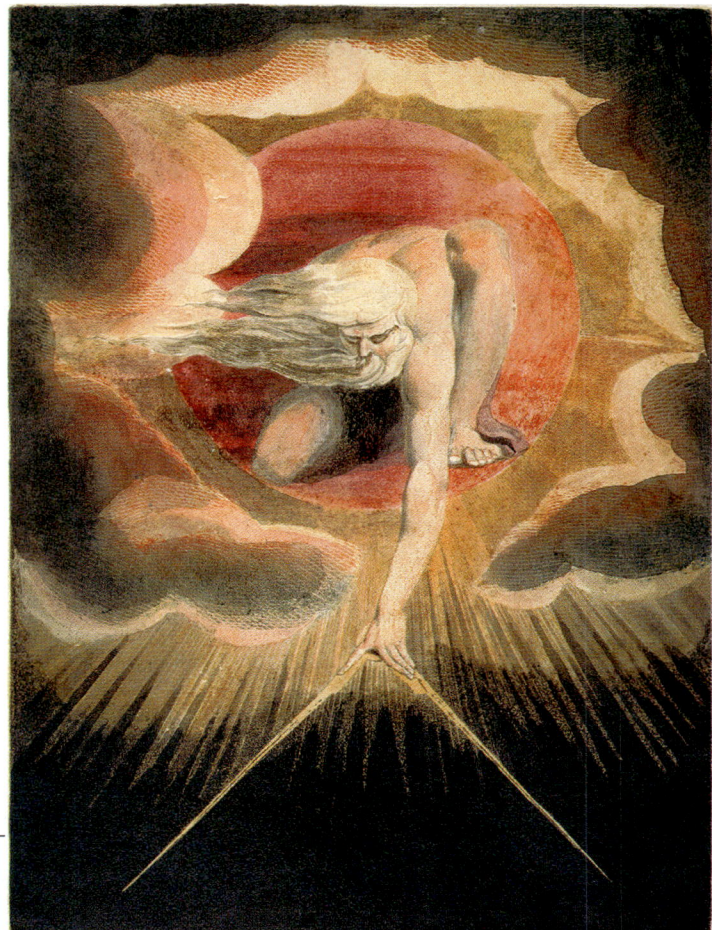

**27-9** WILLIAM BLAKE, *Ancient of Days,* frontispiece of *Europe: A Prophecy,* 1794. Metal relief etching, hand colored, $9\frac{1}{2}'' \times 6\frac{3}{4}''$. Pierpont Morgan Library, New York.

Although art historians classify Blake as a Romantic artist, he incorporated classical references in his works. Here, ideal classical anatomy merges with the inner dark dreams of Romanticism.

artists, he also found the art of the Middle Ages appealing. Blake derived the inspiration for many of his paintings and poems from his dreams. The importance he attached to these nocturnal experiences led him to believe the rationalist search for material explanations of the world stifled the spiritual side of human nature. He also believed the stringent rules of behavior that orthodox religions imposed killed the individual creative impulse.

Blake's vision of the Almighty in *Ancient of Days* (FIG. **27-9**) combines his ideas and interests in a highly individual way. For Blake, this figure united the concept of the Creator with that of wisdom as a part of God. He chose *Ancient of Days* as the frontispiece for his book *Europe: A Prophecy,* and juxtaposed it with a quotation ("When he set a compass upon the face of the deep") from Proverbs 8:27. The speaker is Wisdom, who tells the reader how she was with the Lord through all the time of the creation (Prov. 8:22–23, 27–30). Energy fills Blake's composition. The Almighty leans forward from a fiery orb, peering toward earth and unleashing power through his outstretched left arm into twin rays of light. These emerge between his spread fingers like an architect's measuring instrument—a conception of creation with precedents in Gothic manuscript painting (FIG. 13-32). Here, however, a mighty wind surges through the Creator's thick hair and beard. Only the strength

of his Michelangelesque physique keeps him firmly planted on his heavenly perch. In this image Blake merged ideal classical anatomy with the inner dark dreams of Romanticism.

## Spain and France

From its roots in the work of Fuseli, Blake, and other late-18th-century artists, Romanticism gradually displaced Neoclassicism as the dominant painting style of the first half of the 19th century. Romantic artists, including Francisco Goya in Spain and Théodore Géricault and Eugène Delacroix in France, reveled in exploring the exotic, erotic, and fantastic.

**FRANCISCO GOYA** Although FRANCISCO JOSÉ DE GOYA Y LUCIENTES (1746–1828) was David's contemporary, their work has little in common. Goya, however, did not arrive at his general dismissal of Neoclassicism without considerable thought about the Enlightenment and the Neoclassical penchant for rationality and order. In *The Sleep of Reason Produces Monsters* (FIG. **27-10**), an

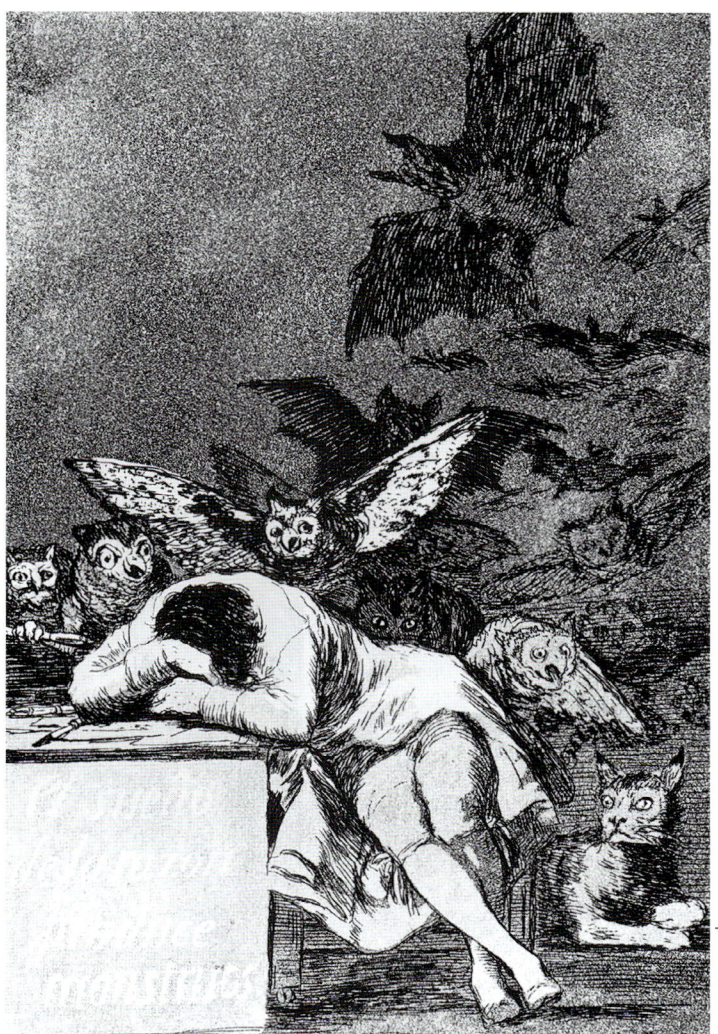

**27-10** FRANCISCO GOYA, *The Sleep of Reason Produces Monsters,* from *Los Caprichos,* ca. 1798. Etching and aquatint, $8\frac{1}{2}'' \times 5\frac{7}{8}''$. Metropolitan Museum of Art, New York (gift of M. Knoedler & Co., 1918).

In this print, Goya depicted himself asleep while threatening creatures converge on him, revealing his commitment to the Romantic spirit—the unleashing of imagination, emotions, and nightmares.

etching from a series titled *Los Caprichos* (*The Caprices*), Goya depicted himself asleep, slumped onto a desk, while threatening creatures converge on him. Seemingly poised to attack the artist are owls (symbols of folly) and bats (symbols of ignorance). The viewer might read this as a portrayal of what emerges when reason is suppressed and, therefore, as advocating Enlightenment ideals. However, the print also can be interpreted as Goya's commitment to the creative process and the Romantic spirit—the unleashing of imagination, emotions, and even nightmares.

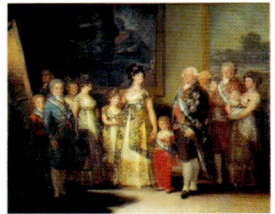

27-10A GOYA, *Family of Charles IV*, 1800.

**THIRD OF MAY, 1808** Much of Goya's multifaceted work deals not with Romantic fantasies but with contemporary events. In 1786, he became an official artist in the court of Charles IV (r. 1788–1808) and produced portraits of the king and his family (FIG. **27-10A**). Dissatisfaction with the king's rule increased dramatically during Goya's tenure at the court, and the Spanish people eventually threw their support behind the king's son, Ferdinand VII, in the hope he would initiate reform. To overthrow his father and mother, Queen Maria Luisa (1751–1819), Ferdinand enlisted the aid of Napoleon Bonaparte, who possessed uncontested authority and military expertise at that time. Napoleon had designs on the Spanish throne and thus readily agreed to send French troops to Spain. Not surprisingly, as soon as he ousted Charles IV, Napoleon revealed his plan to rule Spain himself by installing his brother Joseph Bonaparte (r. 1808–1813) on the Spanish throne.

The Spanish people, finally recognizing the French as invaders, sought a way to expel the foreign troops. On May 2, 1808, Spaniards attacked Napoleon's soldiers in a chaotic and violent clash. In retaliation and as a show of force, the French responded the next day by rounding up and executing Spanish citizens. This tragic event is the subject of Goya's most famous painting, *Third of*

*May, 1808* (FIG. **27-11**), commissioned in 1814 by Ferdinand VII (r. 1813–1833), who had reclaimed the throne after the ouster of the French. In emotional fashion, Goya depicted the anonymous murderous wall of Napoleonic soldiers ruthlessly executing the unarmed and terrified Spanish peasants. The artist encouraged empathy for the Spaniards by portraying horrified expressions and anguish on their faces, endowing them with a humanity lacking in the French firing squad. Moreover, the peasant about to be shot throws his arms out in a cruciform gesture reminiscent of Christ's position on the cross. Goya enhanced the emotional drama of the massacre by using stark darks and lights and by extending the time frame depicted. Although Goya captured the specific moment when one man is about to be executed, he also recorded the bloody bodies of others lying dead on the ground. Still others have been herded together to be shot in a few moments.

**SATURN** Over time, Goya became increasingly disillusioned and pessimistic, and his declining health further contributed to this state of mind. Among Goya's later works are the "Black Paintings," frescoes he painted on the walls of his farmhouse in Quinta del Sordo, outside Madrid. Because Goya created these works solely on his terms and for his private viewing, they provide great insight into the artist's outlook, which is terrifying and disturbing. *Saturn Devouring One of His Children* (FIG. **27-12**) depicts the raw carnage and violence of Saturn (the Greek god Kronos; see "The Gods and Goddesses of Mount Olympus," Chapter 5, page 107, or page xxix in Volume II and Book D), wild-eyed and monstrous, as he consumes one of his offspring. Because of the similarity of Kronos and *khronos* (the Greek word for "time"), Saturn has come to be associated with time. This has led some to interpret Goya's painting as an expression of the artist's despair over the passage of time. Despite the simplicity of the image, it conveys a wildness, boldness, and brutality that evokes an elemental response from all viewers. Goya's work, rooted both in personal and national history, presents darkly emotional images well in keeping with Romanticism.

**27-11** FRANCISCO GOYA, *Third of May, 1808,* 1814–1815. Oil on canvas, 8′ 9″ × 13′ 4″. Museo del Prado, Madrid. ◼◀

Goya encouraged empathy for the massacred Spanish peasants by portraying horrified expressions on their faces, endowing them with a humanity lacking in the French firing squad.

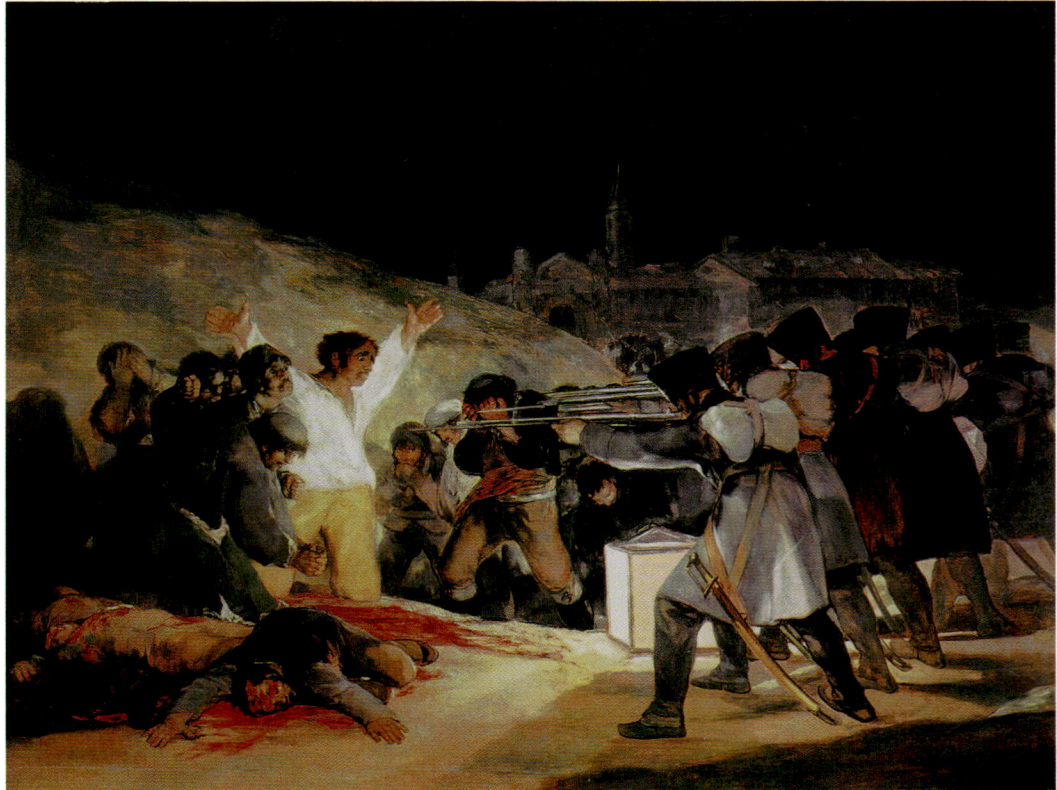

1 ft.

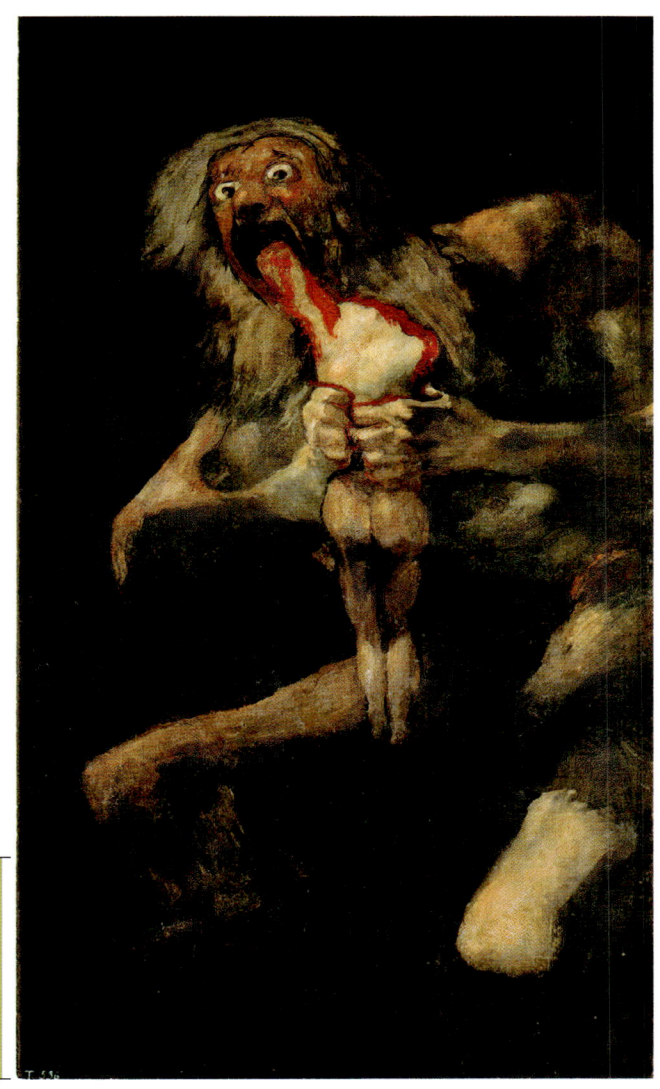

1 ft.

**27-12** Francisco Goya, *Saturn Devouring One of His Children,* 1819–1823. Fresco, later detached and mounted on canvas, 4′ 9⅛″ × 2′ 8⅝″. Museo del Prado, Madrid.

This disturbing fresco in Goya's farmhouse uses a mythological tale to express the aging artist's despair over the passage of time. Saturn's Greek name *Kronos* is similar to the Greek word for "time."

**THÉODORE GÉRICAULT** In France, one of the artists most closely associated with the Romantic movement was Théodore Géricault (1791–1824), who studied with an admirer of David, Pierre-Narcisse Guérin (1774–1833). Although Géricault retained an interest in the heroic and the epic and completed rigorous training in classical drawing, he chafed at the rigidity of the Neoclassical style, instead producing works that captivate viewers with their drama, visual complexity, and emotional force.

***RAFT OF THE MEDUSA*** Géricault's most ambitious project was a gigantic canvas (approximately 16 by 23 feet) titled *Raft of the Medusa* (FIG. **27-13**), exhibited in the Salon of 1819, seven years after he burst onto the Parisian art scene with *Charging Chasseur* (FIG. **27-13A**). In both works, Géricault abandoned the idealism of Neoclassicism and embraced the theatricality of Romanticism. The subject of *Raft of the Medusa* is the 1816 shipwreck off the African coast of the French frigate *Medusa*, which ran aground on a reef due to the incompetence of the captain, a political appointee. In an attempt to sur-

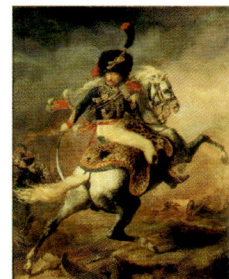

**27-13A** Géricault, *Charging Chasseur,* 1812.

vive, 150 passengers built a makeshift raft from pieces of the disintegrating ship. The raft drifted for 12 days, and the number still alive dwindled to 15. Finally, a ship spotted the raft and rescued the emaciated survivors. This horrendous event was political dynamite once it became public knowledge.

In *Raft of the Medusa,* which took Géricault eight months to complete, the artist sought to capture the horror, chaos, and emotion of the tragedy yet invoke the grandeur and impact of Neoclassical history painting.

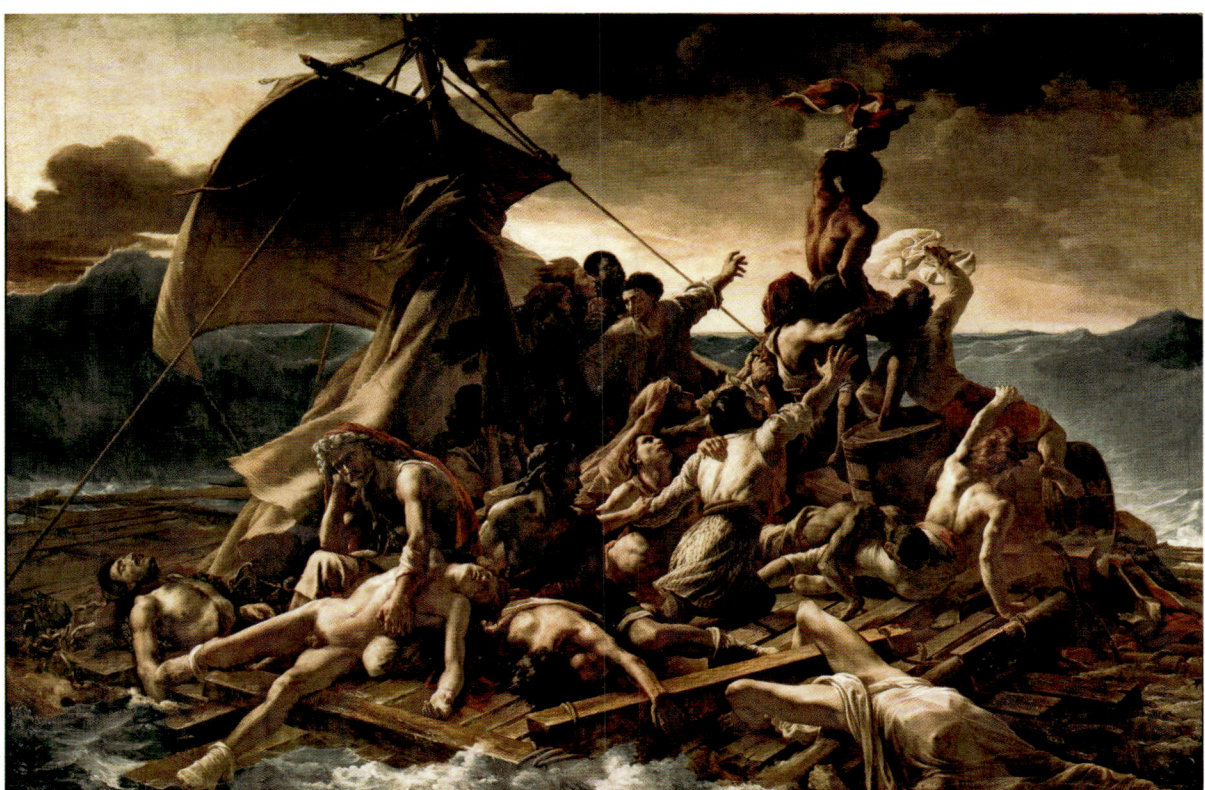

1 ft.

**27-13** Théodore Géricault, *Raft of the Medusa,* 1818–1819. Oil on canvas, 16′ 1″ × 23′ 6″. Musée du Louvre, Paris. ◼◀

In this gigantic history painting, Géricault rejected Neoclassical compositional principles and, in the Romantic spirit, presented a jumble of writhing bodies in every attitude of suffering, despair, and death.

Romanticism   **765**

Géricault went to great lengths to ensure the accuracy of his representation. He visited hospitals and morgues to examine corpses, interviewed the survivors, and had a model of the raft constructed in his studio. In the painting, the few despairing survivors summon what little strength they have left to flag down the passing ship far on the horizon. The subdued palette and prominent shadows lend an ominous pall to the scene. Géricault departed from the straightforward organization of Neoclassical compositions and instead presented a jumble of writhing bodies. He arranged the survivors and several corpses in a powerful X-shaped composition, and piled one body on another in every attitude of suffering, despair, and death (recalling the plague-stricken figures in Gros's *Napoleon at the Plague House at Jaffa,* FIG. 27-1). One light-filled diagonal axis stretches from bodies at the lower left up to the black man raised on his comrades' shoulders and waving a piece of cloth toward the horizon. The cross axis descends from the dark, billowing sail at the upper left to the shadowed upper torso of the body trailing in the open sea. Géricault's decision to place the raft at a diagonal so that a corner juts outward further draws viewers into the tragic scene. Indeed, it seems as though some of the corpses are sliding off the raft into the viewing space.

*Raft of the Medusa* is also the artist's commentary on the practice of slavery. Géricault was a member of an abolitionist group that sought ways to end the slave trade in the colonies, the cause promoted in the French legislature by Jean-Baptiste Belley (FIG. 27-5A). Given Géricault's antipathy to slavery, it is appropriate he placed Jean Charles, a black soldier who was one of the few survivors, at the top of the pyramidal heap of bodies.

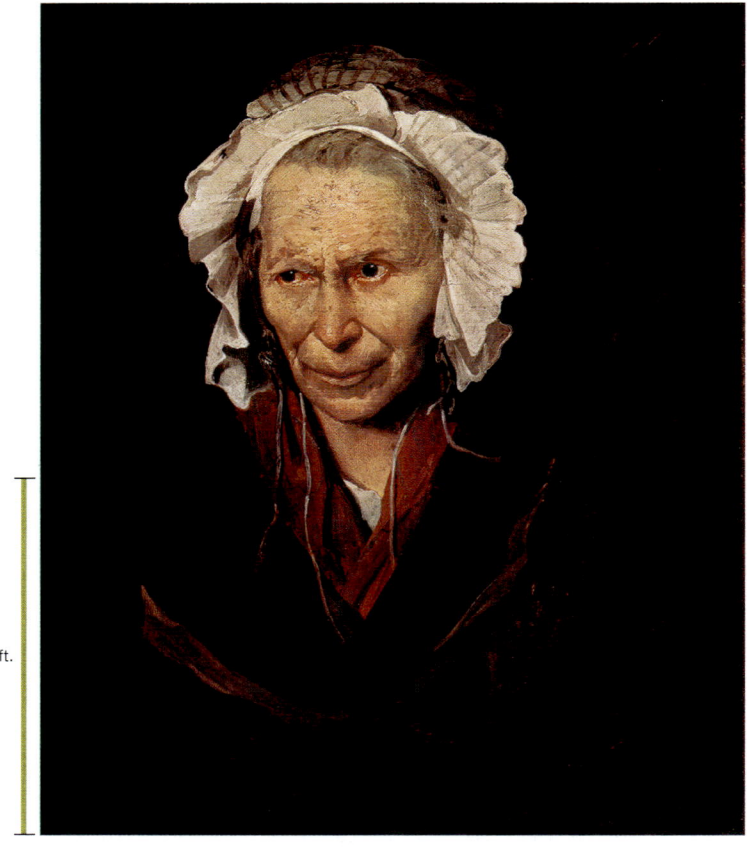

1 ft.

**27-14** THÉODORE GÉRICAULT, *Insane Woman,* 1822–1823. Oil on canvas, 2′ 4″ × 1′ 9″. Musée des Beaux-Arts, Lyons.

The insane and the influence of aberrant states of mind on the appearance of the human face fascinated Géricault and other Romantic artists, who rebelled against Enlightenment rationality.

**INSANE WOMAN** Mental aberration and irrational states of mind could not fail to interest the rebels against Enlightenment rationality. Géricault, like Goya, examined the influence of mental states on the human face and believed, as many of his contemporaries did, that a face accurately revealed character, especially at the moment of death (FIG. 27-11) and in madness (FIG. 27-12). Géricault made many studies of the inmates of hospitals and institutions for the criminally insane, and he studied the severed heads of guillotine victims. Scientific and artistic curiosity often accompanied the morbidity of the Romantic interest in derangement and death.

*Insane Woman* (FIG. **27-14**) is one of several of Géricault's portraits of the insane possessing a peculiar hypnotic power. The woman looks away from the viewer, her mouth tense and her eyes red-rimmed with suffering. The portrait presents the psychic facts with astonishing authenticity and breaks sharply with traditional portraiture in which the sitter's visage is idealized, the expression placid, and the setting designed to communicate the elevated stature of the person portrayed.

**EUGÈNE DELACROIX** Art historians often present the history of painting during the first half of the 19th century as a contest between two major artists—Ingres, the Neoclassical draftsman, and EUGÈNE DELACROIX (1798–1863; FIG. 27-50), the Romantic colorist. Their dialogue recalls the quarrel between the Poussinistes and the Rubénistes at the end of the 17th century and the beginning of the 18th (see Chapter 26). The Poussinistes were conservative defenders of academism who insisted that drawing was superior to color, whereas the Rubénistes proclaimed the importance of color over line (line quality being more intellectual and thus more restrictive than color). Delacroix's works were products of his view that the artist's powers of imagination would in turn capture and inflame the viewer's imagination. Literature of imaginative power served Delacroix (and many of his contemporaries) as a useful source of subject matter (see "The Romantic Spirit in Art, Music, and Literature," page 767). Théophile Gautier (1811–1872), the prominent Romantic critic and novelist, recalled:

> In those days painting and poetry fraternized. The artists read the poets, and the poets visited the artists. We found Shakespeare, Dante, Goethe, Lord Byron and Walter Scott in the studio as well as in the study. There were as many splashes of color as there were blots of ink in the margins of those beautiful books which we endlessly perused. Imagination, already excited, was further fired by reading those foreign works, so rich in color, so free and powerful in fantasy.[1]

**DEATH OF SARDANAPALUS** Delacroix's 1827 *Death of Sardanapalus* (FIG. **27-15**) is perhaps the grandest Romantic pictorial drama ever painted. Although inspired by the 1821 narrative poem *Sardanapalus* by Lord Byron (1788–1824), the painting does not illustrate that text faithfully. Delacroix depicted the last hour of the Assyrian king Ashurbanipal (r. 668–627 BCE; FIG. 2-23), whom the Greeks called Sardanapalus. The king has just received news of his armies' defeat and the enemies' entry into his city. The setting Delacroix painted is much more tempestuous and crowded than Byron described, and orgiastic destruction has replaced the sacrificial suicide of the poem. Sardanapulus reclines on his funeral pyre, soon to be set alight, and gloomily watches the destruction of all of his most precious possessions—his women, slaves, horses, and treasure. The king's favorite concubine throws herself on the bed, determined to go up in flames with her master. The Assyrian ruler presides like a genius of evil over the tragic scene. Most conspicuous

# The Romantic Spirit in Art, Music, and Literature

The appeal of Romanticism, with its emphasis on freedom and feeling, extended well beyond the realm of the visual arts. The imagination and vision that characterized Romantic paintings and sculptures were equally moving and riveting in musical or written form. In European music, literature, and poetry, the Romantic spirit was a dominant presence during the late 18th and early 19th centuries. Composers and authors alike rejected classicism's structured order in favor of the emotive and expressive. In music, the compositions of Franz Schubert (1797–1828), Franz Liszt (1811–1886), Frédéric Chopin (1810–1849), and Johannes Brahms (1833–1897) emphasized the melodic or lyrical. For these composers, music had the power to express the unspeakable and to communicate the subtlest and most powerful human emotions.

In literature, Romantic poets such as John Keats (1795–1821), William Wordsworth (1770–1850), and Samuel Taylor Coleridge (1772–1834) published volumes of poetry manifesting the Romantic interest in lyrical drama. *Ozymandias,* by Percy Bysshe Shelley (1792–1822), transported readers to faraway, exotic locales. The setting of Lord Byron's *Sardanapalus* is the ancient Assyrian Empire (see Chapter 2). Byron's poem conjures images of eroticism and fury unleashed—images Eugène Delacroix made concrete in his painting *Death of Sardanapalus* (FIG. 27-15). One of the best examples of the Romantic spirit is the engrossing novel *Frankenstein,* written in 1818 by Shelley's wife, Mary Wollstonecraft Shelley (1797–1851). This fantastic tale of a monstrous creature run amok remains popular to the present day. As was true of many Romantic artworks, the novel not only embraced emotionalism but also rejected the rationalism underlying Enlightenment thought. Dr. Frankenstein's monster was a product of science, and the novel is an indictment of the tenacious belief in science that Voltaire and other Enlightenment thinkers promoted. *Frankenstein* served as a cautionary tale of the havoc that could result from unrestrained scientific experimentation and from the arrogance of scientists.

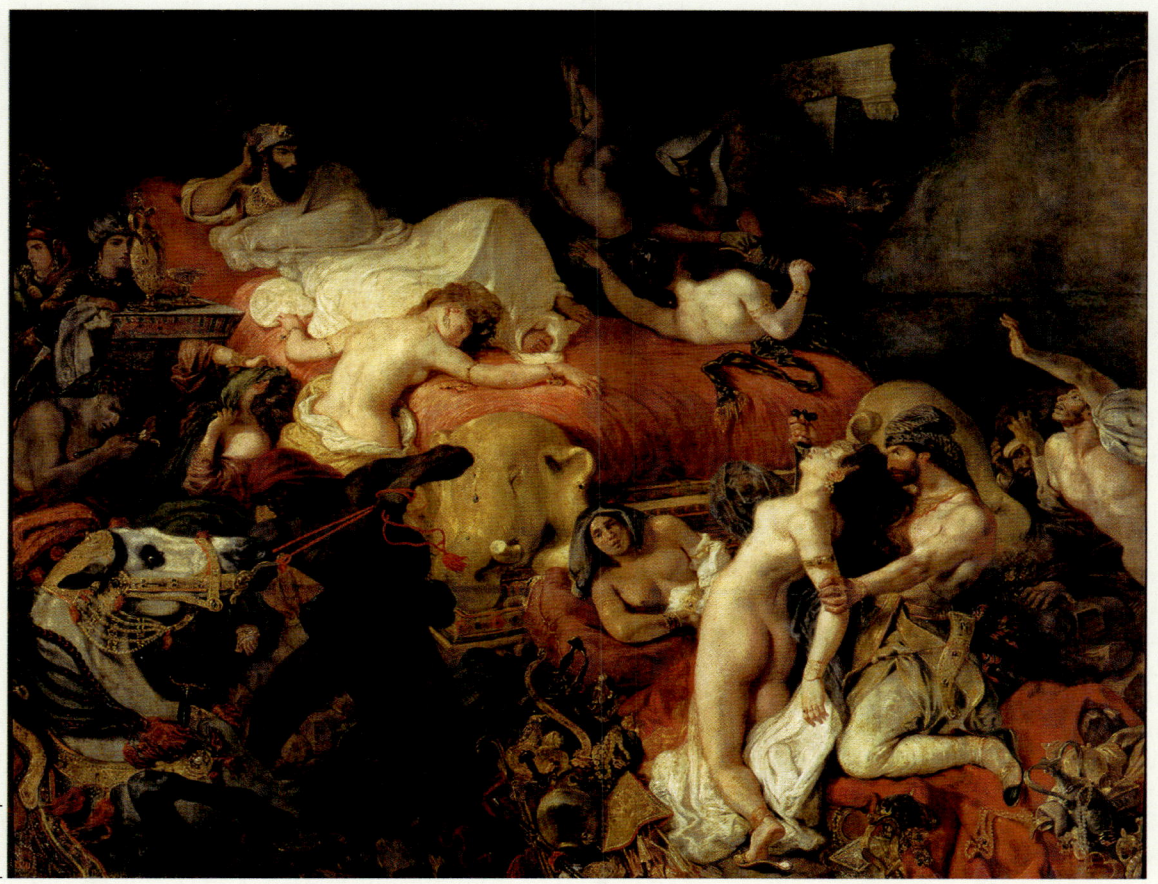

1 ft.

**27-15** EUGÈNE DELACROIX, *Death of Sardanapalus,* 1827. Oil on canvas, 12′ 1½″ × 16′ 2⅞″. Musée du Louvre, Paris. ◼◀

Inspired by Byron's 1821 poem, Delacroix painted the Romantic spectacle of an Assyrian king on his funeral pyre. The richly colored and emotionally charged canvas is filled with exotic figures.

are the tortured and dying bodies of the harem women. In the foreground, a muscular slave plunges his knife into the neck of one woman. Delacroix filled this awful spectacle of suffering and death with the most daringly difficult and tortuous poses, and chose the richest intensities of hue. With its exotic and erotic overtones, *Death of Sardanapalus* tapped into the Romantic fantasies of 19th-century viewers.

Although *Death of Sardanapalus* is a seventh-century BCE drama, Delacroix, as Géricault, also turned to current events, particularly tragic or sensational ones, for his subject matter. For ex-

ample, he produced several images based on the Greek War for Independence (1821–1829), including a huge canvas painted while the war was in progress recording the Turkish massacre of the Greeks of Chios (FIG. **27-15A**). The French perception of the Greeks locked in a brutal struggle for freedom from the cruel and exotic Ottoman Turks generated great interest in Romantic circles.

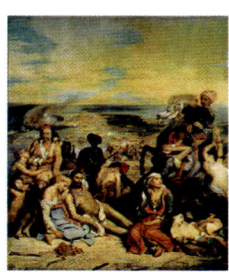

**27-15A** DELACROIX, *Massacre at Chios,* 1822–1824.

**27-16** EUGÈNE DELACROIX, *Liberty Leading the People,* 1830. Oil on canvas, 8′ 6″ × 10′ 8″. Musée du Louvre, Paris. 🎥◀

In a balanced mix of history and poetic allegory, Delacroix captured the passion and energy of the 1830 revolution in this painting of Liberty leading the Parisian uprising against Charles X.

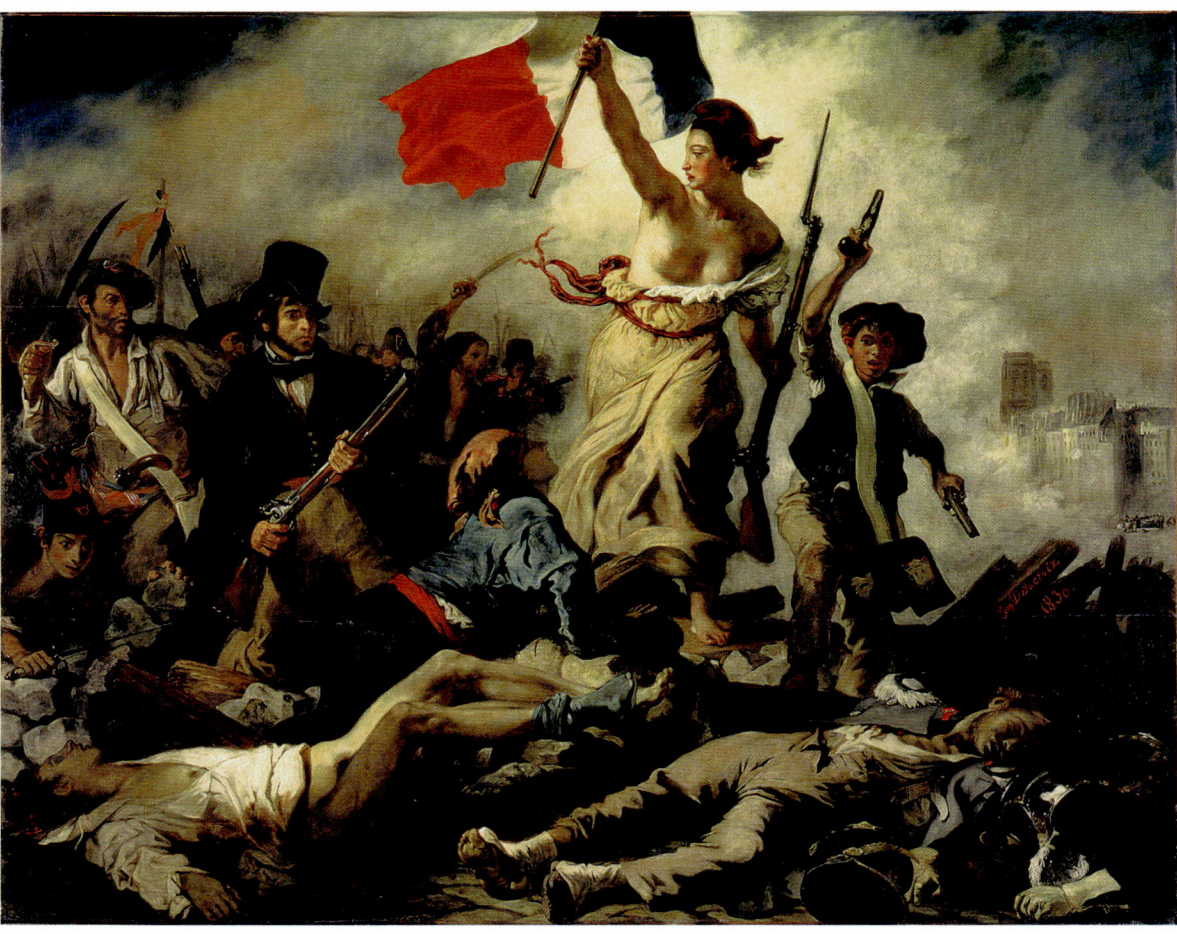

1 ft.

***LIBERTY LEADING THE PEOPLE*** Closer to home, Delacroix captured the passion and energy of the 1830 revolution in *Liberty Leading the People* (FIG. **27-16**). Based on the Parisian uprising against Charles X (r. 1824–1830) at the end of July 1830, it depicts the allegorical personification of Liberty defiantly thrusting forth the republic's tricolor banner as she urges the masses to fight on. The scarlet Phrygian cap (the symbol of a freed slave in antiquity) she wears reinforces the urgency of this struggle. Arrayed around Liberty are bold Parisian types—the street boy brandishing his pistols, the menacing worker with a cutlass, and the intellectual dandy in a top hat brandishing a musket. As in Géricault's *Raft of the Medusa* (FIG. 27-13), dead bodies are all around. In the background, the towers of Notre-Dame (FIG. 13-11) rise through the smoke and haze. The painter's inclusion of this recognizable Parisian landmark announces the specificity of locale and event, balancing contemporary historical fact with poetic allegory.

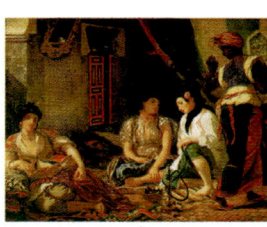

**27-17A** DELACROIX, *Women of Algiers,* 1834.

***TIGER HUNT*** An enormously influential event in Delacroix's life that affected his art in both subject and form was his visit to North Africa in 1832 (see "Delacroix in Morocco," page 769). Things he saw there shocked his imagination with fresh impressions that lasted throughout his life and resulted in paintings such as *Tiger Hunt* (FIG. **27-17**), which he completed more than two decades after his trip. Among the canvases he painted immediately upon his return is *Women of Algiers* (FIG. **27-17A**), which captivated the public

when exhibited in the 1834 Salon. Delacroix's African experience further heightened his already considerable awareness of the expressive power of color and light. What Delacroix knew about color he passed on to later painters of the 19th century, particularly the Impressionists (see Chapter 28). He observed that pure colors are as rare in nature as lines and that color appears only in an infinitely varied scale of different tones, shadings, and reflections, which he tried to re-create in his paintings. He recorded his observations in his journal, which became for later painters and scholars a veritable handbook of pre-Impressionist color theory. Although Delacroix anticipated the later development of Impressionist color science, that art-science had to await the discoveries by Michel Eugène Chevreul (1786–1889) and Hermann von Helmholtz (1821–1894) of the laws of light decomposition and the properties of complementary colors. Only then could the problems of color perception and juxtaposition in painting be properly formulated (see "19th-Century Color Theory," Chapter 28, page 813). Nevertheless, Delacroix's observations were significant, and he advised other artists not to fuse their brushstrokes, as those strokes would appear to fuse naturally from a distance.

No other painter of the time explored the domain of Romantic subject and mood as thoroughly and definitively as Delacroix. His technique was impetuous, improvisational, and instinctive, rather than deliberate, studious, and cold. It epitomized Romantic colorist painting, catching the impression quickly and developing it in the execution process. His contemporaries commented on how furiously Delacroix worked once he had an idea, keeping the whole painting progressing at once. The fury of his attack matched the fury of his imagination and his subjects.

# Delacroix in Morocco

Romantic painters often depicted exotic faraway places they had never seen, but Eugène Delacroix journeyed to Morocco in 1832 and discovered in the sun-drenched landscape—and in the hardy and colorful Moroccans dressed in robes reminiscent of the Roman toga—new insights into a culture built on proud virtues. He found in North Africa a culture more classical than anything European Neoclassicism could conceive. In a letter to his friend Fréderic Villot dated February 29, 1832, he wrote:

> This place is made for painters. . . . [B]eauty abounds here; not the over-praised beauty of fashionable paintings. The heroes of David and Co. with their rose-pink limbs would cut a sorry figure beside these children of the sun, who moreover wear the dress of classical antiquity with a nobler air, I dare assert.*

In a second letter, written June 4, 1832, he reported to Auguste Jal:

> You have seen Algiers and you can imagine what the natives of these regions are like. Here there is something even simpler and more primitive; there is less of the Turkish alloy; I have Romans and Greeks on my doorstep: it makes me laugh heartily at David's Greeks, apart, of course, from his sublime skill as a painter. I know now what they were really like; . . . If painting schools persist in [depicting classical subjects], I am convinced, and you will agree

with me, that they would gain far more from being shipped off as cabin boys on the first boat bound for the Barbary coast than from spending any more time wearing out the classical soil of Rome. Rome is no longer to be found in Rome.†

The gallantry, valor, and fierce love of liberty of the Moroccans made them, in Delacroix's eyes, unspoiled heroes uncontaminated by European decadence. The Moroccan voyage reinforced Delacroix's Romantic conviction that beauty exists in the fierceness of nature, natural processes, and natural beings, especially animals. After he experienced Morocco, more and more of Delacroix's subjects involved combats between beasts or between beasts and men. He painted snarling tangles of lions and tigers, battles between horses, and clashes of Muslims with great cats in swirling hunting scenes using compositions reminiscent of those of Rubens (FIG. I-14), as in his 1854 painting *Tiger Hunt* (FIG. 27-17), which clearly speaks to the Romantic interest in faraway lands and exotic cultures.

*Translated by Jean Stewart, in Charles Harrison, Paul Wood, and Jason Gaiger, eds., *Art in Theory 1815–1900: An Anthology of Changing Ideas* (Oxford: Blackwell, 1998), 87.
†Ibid., 88.

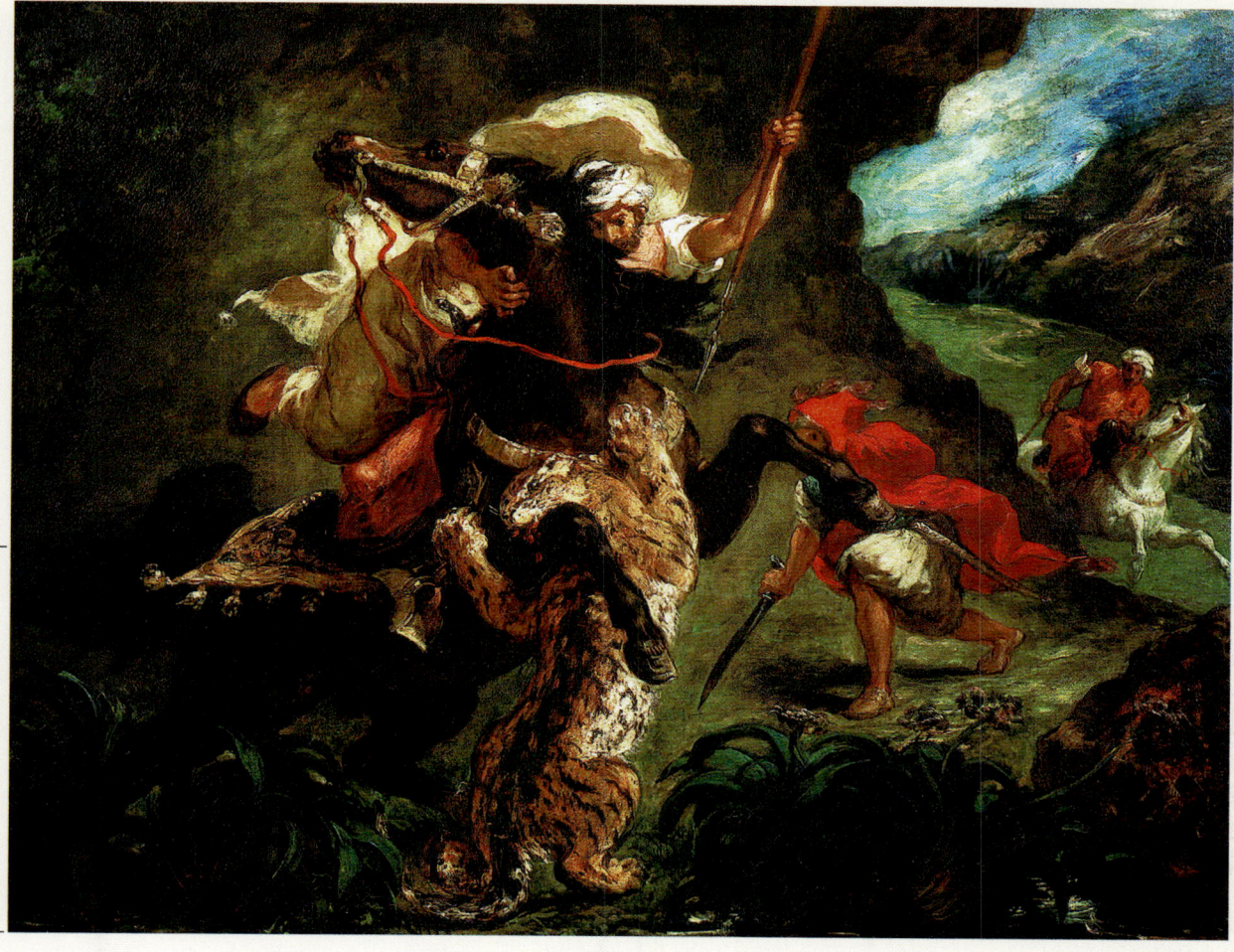

1 ft.

**27-17** EUGÈNE DELACROIX, *Tiger Hunt,* 1854. Oil on canvas, 2′ 5″ × 3′. Musée d'Orsay, Paris.

Delacroix's 1832 trip to Morocco inspired *Tiger Hunt* and had a lasting impact on his art. His paintings of men battling ferocious beasts are consistent with the Romantic interest in exotic places.

**FRANÇOIS RUDE** The Romantic spirit pervaded all media during the early 19th century. As did the painters of the period, many sculptors produced work incorporating both Neoclassical and Romantic elements. The colossal limestone group *Departure of the Volunteers of 1792* (FIG. **27-18**), also called *La Marseillaise,* is one example. The relief, the work of FRANÇOIS RUDE (1784–1855), decorates one of the gigantic piers of the Arc de Triomphe in Paris. This French landmark was an 1806 Napoleonic commission designed by Jean François Thérèse Chalgrin (1739–1811) on the model of the triumphal arches of ancient Rome (FIGS. 7-40, 7-44B, and 7-75). Work on the arch stopped after Napoleon's defeat but resumed in 1833. Three years later, workmen inserted Rude's group (and three similar ones by other sculptors) into the completed arch. The sculpture depicts the volunteers of 1792 departing to defend France's borders against the foreign enemies of the revolution. The Roman goddess of war, Bellona (who here personifies liberty as well as the "Marseillaise," the revolutionary hymn that is now France's national anthem), soars above patriots of all ages, exhorting them forward with her thundering battle cry. The figures recall David's classically armored (FIG. 26-25) or nude heroes, as do the rhetorical gestures of the wide-flung arms and the striding poses. Yet the violence of motion, the jagged contours, and the densely packed, overlapping

masses relate more closely to the compositional method of dramatic Romanticism, as found in the canvases of Géricault (FIG. 27-13) and Delacroix (FIG. 27-16). Indeed, the allegorical figure in *La Marseillaise* is the spiritual sister of Delacroix's Liberty. Rude's stone figure shares the same Phrygian cap, the badge of liberty, with Delacroix's earlier painted figure, but Rude's soldiers wear classical costumes or are heroically nude, whereas those in Delacroix's painting appear in modern Parisian dress. Both works are allegorical, but one looks to the past and the other to the present.

## Landscape Painting

Landscape painting came into its own in the 19th century as a fully independent and respected genre. Briefly eclipsed at the century's beginning by the taste for ideal form, which favored figural composition and history, landscape painting flourished as leading painters adopted the genre as their specialty. Increasing tourism, which came courtesy of improved and expanded railway systems both in Europe (MAP 27-2) and America, contributed to the popularity of landscape painting.

The notion of the picturesque became particularly resonant in the Romantic era. Already in the 18th century, artists had regarded the pleasurable, aesthetic mood that natural landscape inspired as making the landscape itself "picturesque"—that is, worthy of being painted. Rather than simply describe nature, Romantic poets and artists often used nature as allegory. In this manner, artists commented on spiritual, moral, historical, or philosophical issues. Landscape painting was a particularly effective vehicle for such commentary.

In the early 19th century, most northern European (especially German) landscape painting to some degree expressed the Romantic view (first extolled by Rousseau) of nature as a "being" that included the totality of existence in organic unity and harmony. In nature—"the living garment of God," as German poet and dramatist Johann Wolfgang von Goethe (1749–1832) called it—artists found an ideal subject to express the Romantic theme of the soul unified with the natural world. As all nature was mysteriously permeated by "being," landscape artists had the task of interpreting the signs, symbols, and emblems of universal spirit disguised within visible material things. Artists no longer merely beheld a landscape but participated in its spirit, becoming translators of nature's transcendent meanings.

**CASPAR DAVID FRIEDRICH** Among the first northern European artists to depict the Romantic transcendental landscape was CASPAR DAVID FRIEDRICH (1774–1840). For Friedrich, landscapes were temples, and his paintings were altarpieces. The reverential mood of his works demands from the viewer the silence appropriate to sacred places filled with a divine presence. *Abbey in the Oak Forest* (FIG. **27-19**) serves as a solemn requiem. Under a winter sky, through the leafless oaks of a snow-covered cemetery, a funeral procession bears a coffin into the ruins of a Gothic church Friedrich based on the remains of Eldana Abbey in Greifswald. The emblems of death are everywhere—the season's desolation, the leaning crosses and tombstones, the black of mourning the grieving wear, the skeletal trees, and the destruction time has wrought on the church. The painting is a kind of meditation on human mortality. As Friedrich himself remarked: "Why, it has often occurred to me to ask myself, do I so frequently choose death, transience, and the grave as subjects for my paintings? One must submit oneself many times to death in order some day to attain life everlasting."[2] The artist's sharp-focused rendering of details demonstrates his keen perception of everything in the physical environment relevant to his message. Friedrich's work

10 ft.

**27-18** FRANÇOIS RUDE, *Departure of the Volunteers of 1792* (*La Marseillaise*), Arc de Triomphe, Paris, France, 1833–1836. Limestone, 41′ 8″ high. ◼◄

This historical-allegorical sculpture features the Roman war goddess Bellona, but the violent motion, jagged contours, and densely packed masses typify Romantic painting compositions.

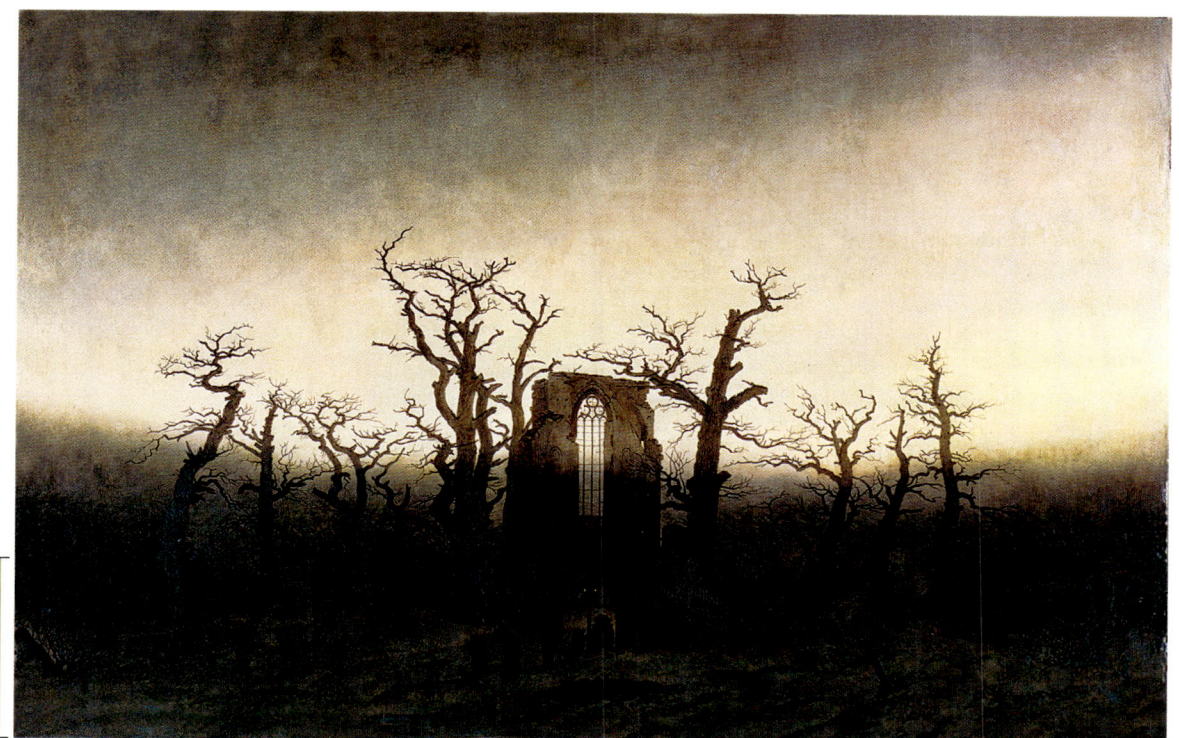

**27-19** CASPAR DAVID FRIEDRICH, *Abbey in the Oak Forest*, 1810. Oil on canvas, $4' \times 5'\, 8\frac{1}{2}''$. Nationalgalerie, Staatliche Museen zu Berlin, Berlin. ◼️◀

Friedrich was a master of the Romantic transcendental landscape. The reverential mood of this winter scene with a ruined Gothic church and cemetery demands the silence appropriate to sacred places.

balances inner and outer experience. "The artist," he wrote, "should not only paint what he sees before him, but also what he sees within him. If he does not see anything within him, he should give up painting what he sees before him."[3] Although Friedrich's works may not have the theatrical energy of the paintings of Géricault or Delacroix, a resonant and deep emotion pervades them.

***WANDERER ABOVE A SEA OF MIST*** In *Abbey in the Oak Forest* and many of Friedrich's landscapes, the human figure plays an insignificant role. Indeed, in many instances the human actors are difficult even to discern. But in other paintings, one or more figures seen from behind gazing at the natural vista dominate the canvas. In *Wanderer above a Sea of Mist* (FIG. **27-20**), probably Friedrich's most famous painting, a solitary man dressed in German attire suggestive of a bygone era stands on a rocky promontory and leans on his cane. He surveys a vast panorama of clouds, mountains, and thick mist. Because Friedrich chose a point of view on the level of the man's head, the viewer has the sensation of hovering in space behind him—an impossible position that enhances the aura of mystery the scene conveys. Scholars dispute whether Friedrich intended the viewer to identify with the man seen from behind or if he wanted the viewer to contemplate the man gazing at the misty landscape. In either case, the painter communicated an almost religious awe at the beauty and vastness of the natural world. *Wanderer above a Sea of Mist* perfectly expresses the Romantic notion of the sublime in nature.

**JOHN CONSTABLE** In England, one of the most momentous developments in Western history—the Industrial Revolution—had a profound impact on the evolution of Romantic landscape painting. Although discussion of the Industrial Revolution invariably focuses on technological advances, factory development, and growth of urban centers (see Chapter 26), industrialization had no less pronounced an effect on the countryside and the land itself. The detrimental economic effect the Industrial Revolution had

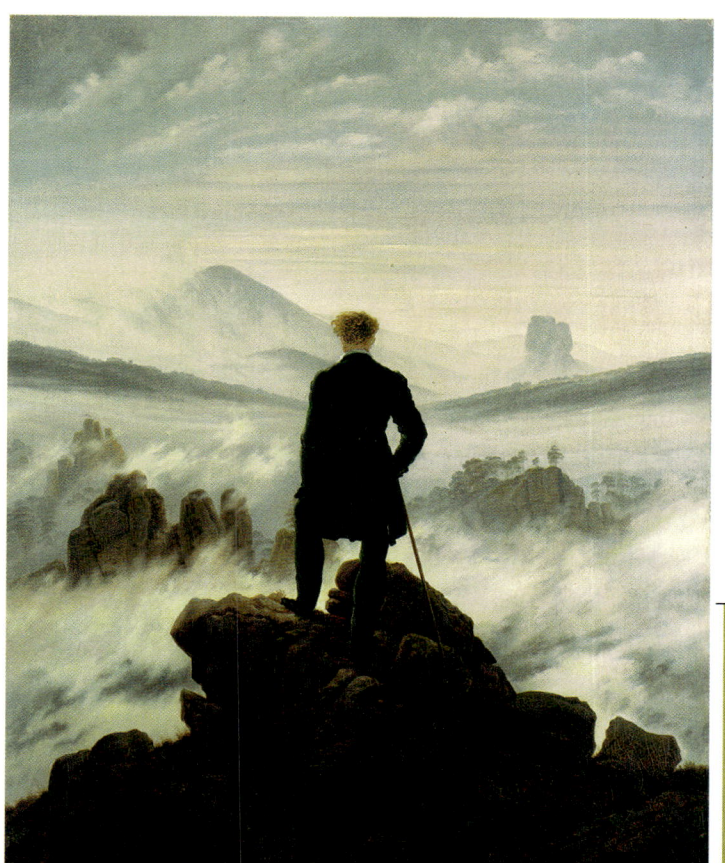

**27-20** CASPAR DAVID FRIEDRICH, *Wanderer above a Sea of Mist*, 1817–1818. Oil on canvas, $3'\, 1\frac{3}{4}'' \times 2'\, 5\frac{3}{8}''$. Hamburger Kunsthalle, Hamburg.

Friedrich's painting of a solitary man on a rocky promontory gazing at a vast panorama of clouds, mountains, and thick mist perfectly expresses the Romantic notion of the sublime in nature.

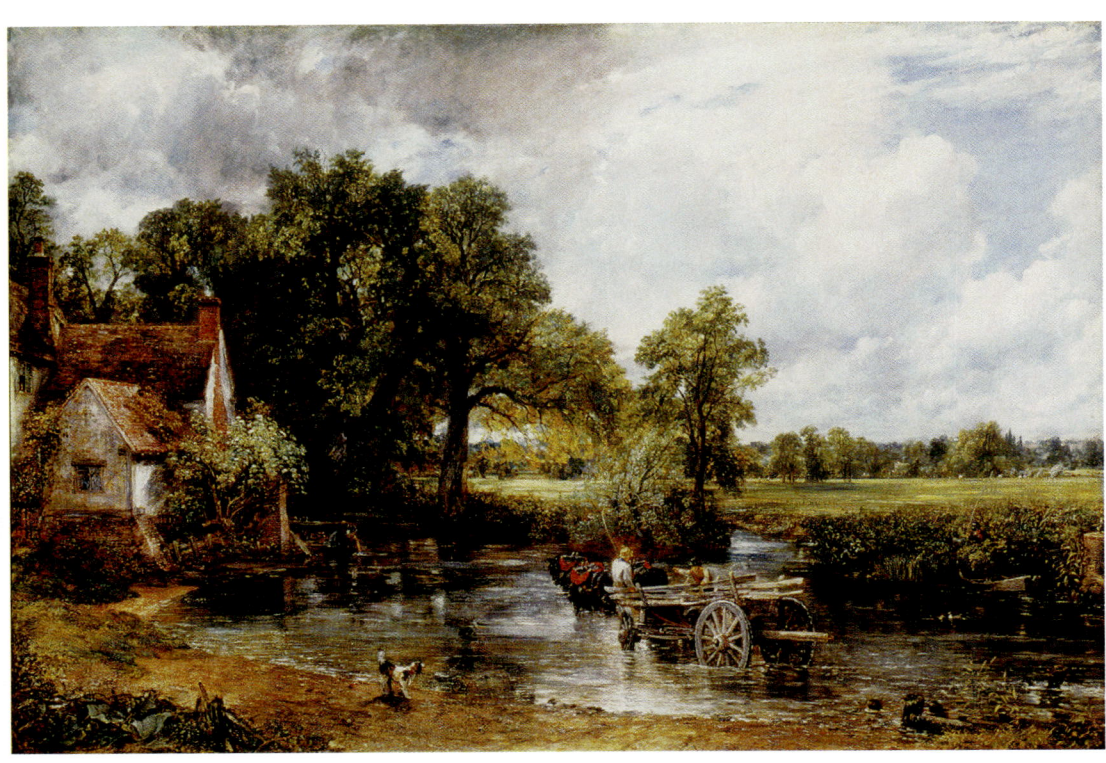

**27-21** John Constable, *The Haywain,* 1821. Oil on canvas, 4' 3¼" × 6' 1". National Gallery, London.

*The Haywain* is a nostalgic view of the disappearing English countryside during the Industrial Revolution. Constable had a special gift for capturing the texture that climate and weather give to landscape.

1 ft.

on prices for agrarian products produced significant unrest in the English countryside. In particular, increasing numbers of displaced farmers could no longer afford to farm their small land plots.

John Constable (1776–1837) addressed this agrarian crisis in his landscape paintings. He made countless studies from nature for each of his canvases, which helped him produce in his paintings the convincing sense of reality that won so much praise from his contemporaries. In his quest for the authentic landscape, Constable studied it as a meteorologist (which he was by avocation). His special gift was for capturing the texture that climate and weather, which delicately veil what is seen, give to landscape. Constable's use of tiny dabs of local color, stippled with white, created a sparkling shimmer of light and hue across the canvas surface—the vibration itself suggestive of movement and process.

*The Haywain* (FIG. **27-21**) is representative of Constable's art and reveals much about his outlook. A small cottage sits on the left of this placid, picturesque scene of the countryside, and in the center foreground, a man leads a horse and wagon across the stream. Billowy clouds float lazily across the sky. The muted greens and golds and the delicacy of Constable's brushstrokes complement the scene's tranquility. The artist portrayed the oneness with nature the Romantic poets sought. The relaxed figures are not observers but participants in the landscape's "being."

In terms of content, *The Haywain* is significant for precisely what it does not show—the civil unrest of the agrarian working class and the resulting outbreaks of violence and arson. The people populating Constable's landscapes blend into the scenes and are at one with nature. Rarely does the viewer see workers engaged in tedious labor. Indeed, this painting has a nostalgic, wistful air to it, and reflects Constable's memories of a disappearing rural pastoralism. The artist's father was a rural landowner of considerable wealth, and many of the scenes Constable painted (*The Haywain* included) depict his family's property near East Bergholt in Suffolk, East Anglia. This nostalgia, presented in such naturalistic terms, renders Constable's works Romantic in tone. That the painter felt a kindred spirit with the Romantic artists is revealed by his comment, "Painting is but another word for feeling."[4]

**J.M.W. TURNER** Constable's contemporary in the English school of landscape painting, Joseph Mallord William Turner (1775–1851), produced work that also responded to encroaching industrialization. However, whereas Constable's paintings are serene and precisely painted, Turner's feature turbulent swirls of frothy pigment. The passion and energy of Turner's works reveal the Romantic sensibility that was the foundation for his art and also clearly illustrate Edmund Burke's concept of the sublime—awe mixed with terror.

Among Turner's most notable works is *The Slave Ship* (FIG. **27-22**). Its subject is a 1783 incident reported in a widely read book titled *The History of the Abolition of the Slave Trade,* by Thomas Clarkson. Because the book had just been reprinted in 1839, Clarkson's account probably prompted Turner's choice of subject for this 1840 painting. The incident involved the captain of a slave ship who, on realizing his insurance company would reimburse him only for slaves lost at sea but not for those who died en route, ordered the sick and dying slaves thrown overboard. Appropriately, the painting's full title is *The Slave Ship* (*Slavers Throwing Overboard the Dead and Dying, Typhoon Coming On*). Turner's frenzied emotional depiction of this act matches its barbaric nature. The artist transformed the sun into an incandescent comet amid flying scarlet clouds. The slave ship moves into the distance, leaving in its wake a turbulent sea choked with the bodies of slaves sinking to their deaths. The relative scale of the minuscule human forms compared with the vast sea and overarching sky reinforces the sense of the sublime, especially the immense power of nature over humans. Almost lost in the boiling colors are the event's particulars, but on close inspection, the viewer can discern the iron shackles and manacles around the wrists and ankles of the drowning slaves, cruelly denying them any chance of saving themselves.

A key ingredient of Turner's highly personal style is the emotive power of pure color. The haziness of the painter's forms and the indistinctness of his compositions intensify the colors and energetic brushstrokes. Turner's innovation in works such as *The Slave Ship* was to release color from any defining outlines so as to express both the forces of nature and the painter's emotional response to them. In his paintings, the reality of color is at one with the reality of feeling. Turner's methods had an incalculable effect on the later

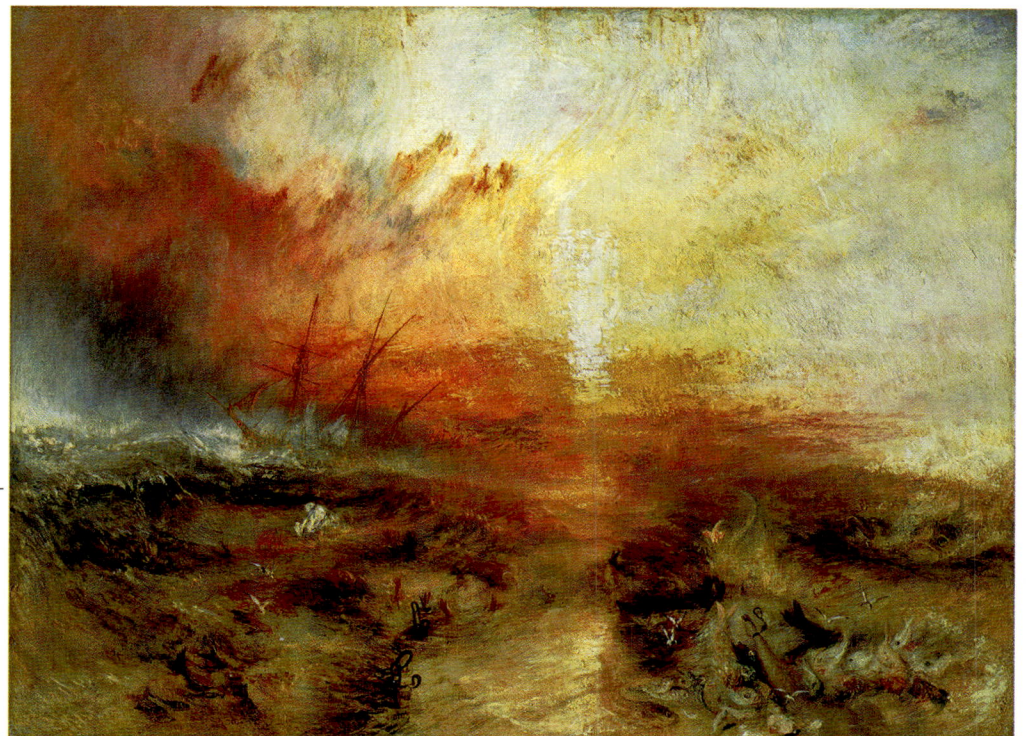

**27-22** JOSEPH MALLORD WILLIAM TURNER, *The Slave Ship* (*Slavers Throwing Overboard the Dead and Dying, Typhoon Coming On*), 1840. Oil on canvas, 2' 11¼" × 4'. Museum of Fine Arts, Boston (Henry Lillie Pierce Fund).

The essence of Turner's innovative style is the emotive power of color. He released color from any defining outlines to express both the forces of nature and the painter's emotional response to them.

1 ft.

development of painting. His discovery of the aesthetic and emotive power of pure color and his pushing of the medium's fluidity to a point where the paint itself is almost the subject were important steps toward 20th-century abstract art, which dispensed with shape and form altogether (see Chapter 30).

**THOMAS COLE** In America, landscape painting was the specialty of a group of artists known as the Hudson River School, so named because its members drew their subjects primarily from the uncultivated regions of New York's Hudson River Valley, although many of these painters depicted scenes from across the country. As did the early-19th-century landscape painters in Germany and England, the artists of the Hudson River School not only presented Romantic panoramic landscape views but also participated in the

ongoing exploration of the individual's and the country's relationship to the land. American landscape painters frequently focused on identifying qualities that made America unique. One American painter of English birth, THOMAS COLE (1801–1848), often referred to as the leader of the Hudson River School, articulated this idea:

Whether he [an American] beholds the Hudson mingling waters with the Atlantic—explores the central wilds of this vast continent, or stands on the margin of the distant Oregon, he is still in the midst of American scenery—it is his own land; its beauty, its magnificence, its sublimity—all are his; and how undeserving of such a birthright, if he can turn towards it an unobserving eye, an unaffected heart![5]

Another issue that surfaced frequently in Hudson River School paintings was the moral question of America's direction as a civilization. Cole addressed this question in *The Oxbow* (*View from Mount Holyoke, Northampton, Massachusetts, after a Thunderstorm*; FIG. **27-23**). A splendid scene opens before the viewer, dominated by the lazy oxbow-shaped turning of the Connecticut River. Cole divided the composition in two, with the dark, stormy wilderness on the left and the more developed civilization on the right. The minuscule artist in the bottom center of the painting (wearing a top hat), dwarfed by the landscape's scale, turns to the viewer as if to ask for input in deciding the country's future course. Cole's depictions of expansive wilderness incorporated reflections and moods romantically appealing to the public.

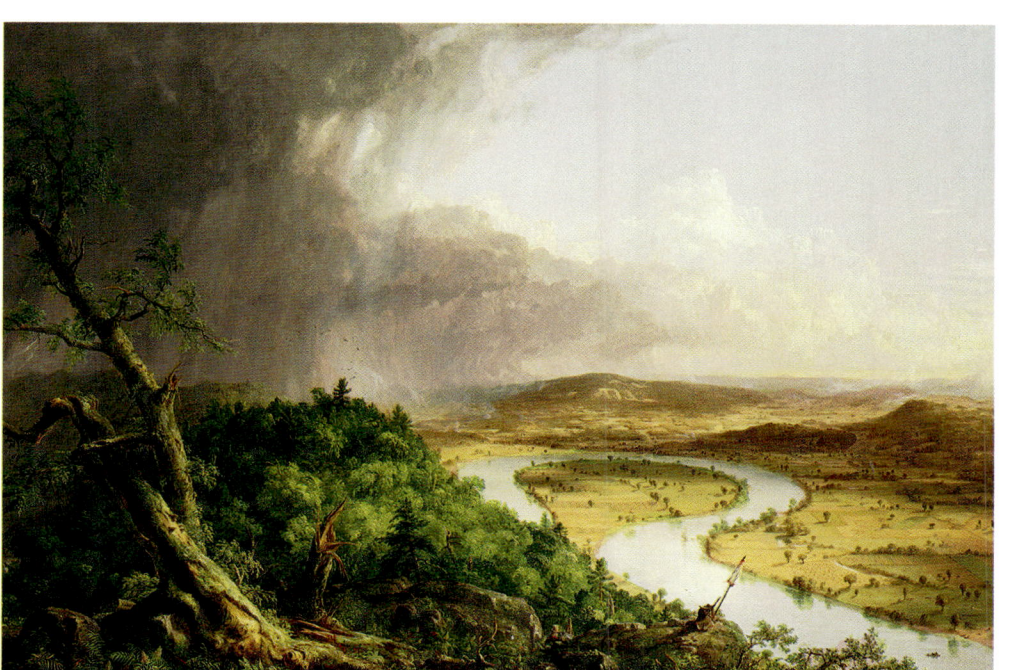

**27-23** THOMAS COLE, *The Oxbow* (*View from Mount Holyoke, Northampton, Massachusetts, after a Thunderstorm*), 1836. Oil on canvas, 4' 3½" × 6' 4". Metropolitan Museum of Art, New York (gift of Mrs. Russell Sage, 1908). ◼◄

Cole divided his canvas into dark wilderness on the left and sunlit civilization on the right. The minuscule painter at the bottom center seems to be asking for advice about America's future course.

1 ft.

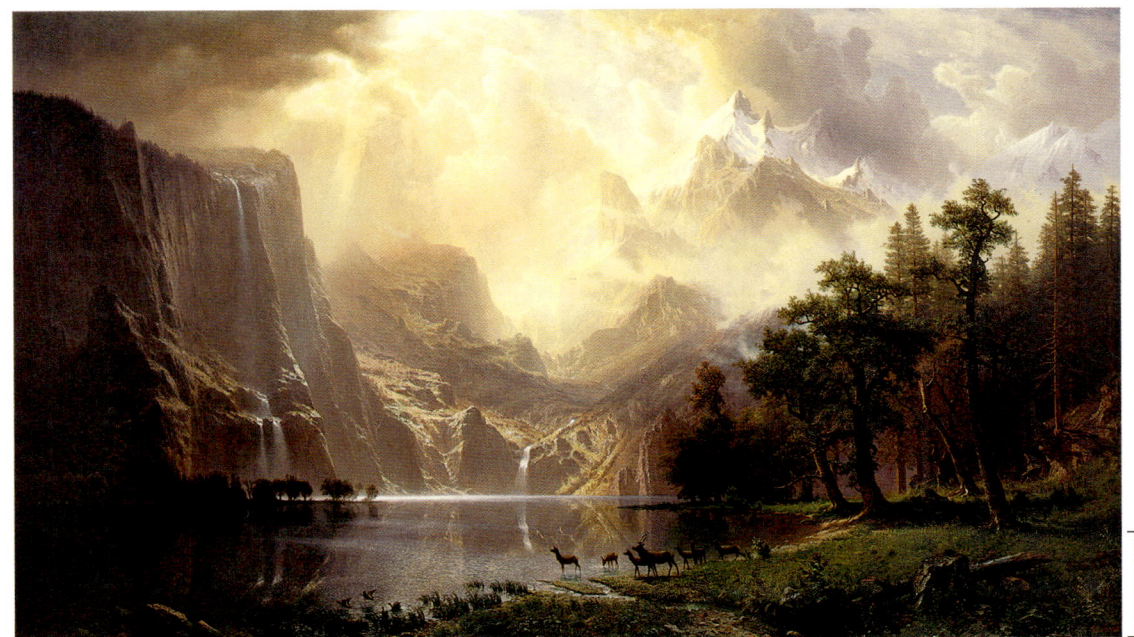

**27-24** ALBERT BIERSTADT, *Among the Sierra Nevada Mountains, California*, 1868. Oil on canvas, 6′ × 10′. National Museum of American Art, Smithsonian Institution, Washington, D.C.

Bierstadt's panoramic landscape presents the breathtaking natural beauty of the American West, reinforcing the 19th-century doctrine of Manifest Destiny, which justified America's western expansion.

1 ft.

**ALBERT BIERSTADT** Other Hudson River artists used the landscape genre as an allegorical vehicle to address moral and spiritual concerns. ALBERT BIERSTADT (1830–1902) traveled west in 1858 and produced many paintings depicting the Rocky Mountains, Yosemite Valley, and other dramatic locales. These works, such as *Among the Sierra Nevada Mountains, California* (FIG. **27-24**), present breathtaking scenery and natural beauty. This panoramic view (the painting is 10 feet wide) is awe-inspiring. Deer and waterfowl appear at the edge of a placid lake, and steep and rugged mountains soar skyward on the left and in the distance. A stand of trees, uncultivated and wild, frames the lake on the right. To underscore the almost transcendental nature of this scene, Bierstadt depicted the sun's rays breaking through the clouds overhead, which suggests a heavenly consecration of the land. That Bierstadt's focus was the American West is not insignificant. By

calling national attention to the splendor and uniqueness of the regions beyond the Rocky Mountains, Bierstadt's paintings reinforced the idea of Manifest Destiny. This popular 19th-century doctrine held that westward expansion across the continent was the logical destiny of the United States. As John L. O'Sullivan (1813–1895) expounded in the earliest known use of the term in 1845, "Our manifest destiny [is] to overspread the continent allotted by Providence for the free development of our yearly multiplying millions."[6] Paintings of the scenic splendor of the West helped to mute growing concerns over the realities of conquest, the displacement of Native Americans, and the exploitation of the environment. It should come as no surprise that among those most eager to purchase Bierstadt's work were mail-service magnates and railroad builders—entrepreneurs and financiers involved in westward expansion.

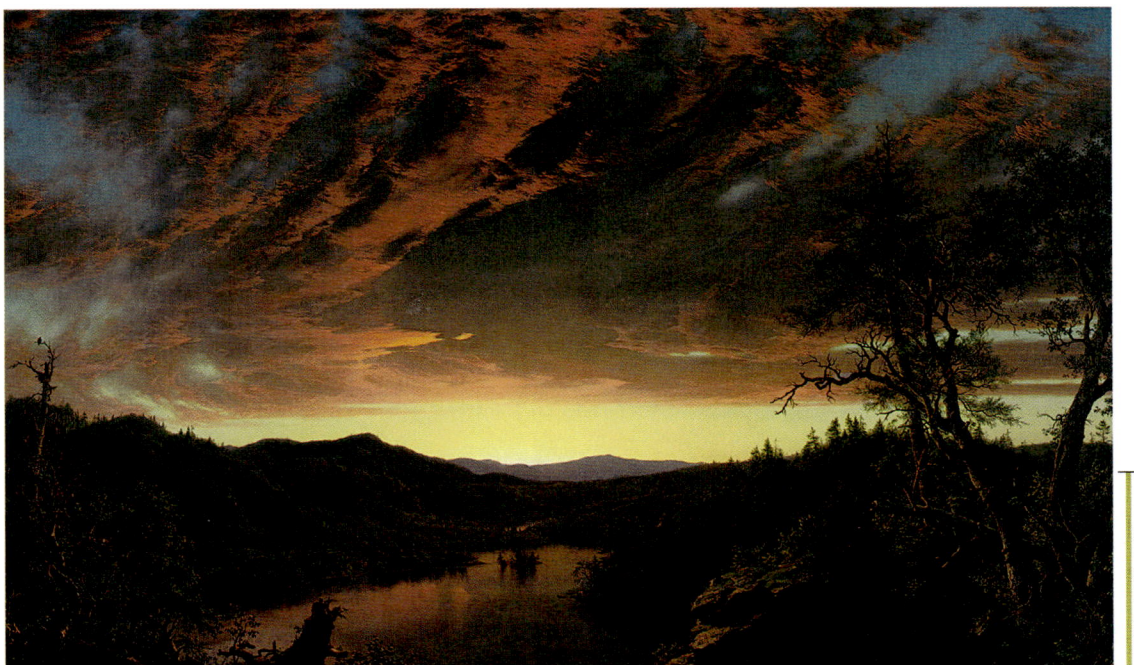

**27-25** FREDERIC EDWIN CHURCH, *Twilight in the Wilderness*, 1860s. Oil on canvas, 3′ 4″ × 5′ 4″. Cleveland Museum of Art, Cleveland (Mr. and Mrs. William H. Marlatt Fund).

Church's paintings eloquently express the Romantic notion of the sublime. Painted during the Civil War, this wilderness landscape presents an idealistic view of America free of conflict.

1 ft.

**FREDERIC CHURCH** Another painter usually associated with the Hudson River School was FREDERIC EDWIN CHURCH (1826–1900), but his interest in landscape scenes extended beyond America. He traveled widely—to South America, Mexico, Europe, the Middle East, Newfoundland, and Labrador. Church's paintings are firmly in the idiom of the Romantic sublime, yet they also reveal contradictions and conflicts in the constructed mythology of American providence and character. *Twilight in the Wilderness* (FIG. 27-25) presents a panoramic view of the sun setting over the majestic landscape. Beyond Church's precise depiction of the magnificent spectacle of nature, the painting, like Constable's *Haywain* (FIG. 27-21), is remarkable for what it does not depict. As did Constable, Church and the other Hudson River School painters worked in a time of great upheaval. *Twilight in the Wilderness* dates to the 1860s, when the Civil War was tearing apart the no-longer-united states. Yet this painting does not display evidence of turbulence or discord. Indeed, it does not include even a single figure. By constructing such an idealistic and comforting view, Church contributed to the national mythology of righteousness and divine providence—a mythology that had become increasingly difficult to maintain in the face of conflict.

Landscape painting was immensely popular in the late 18th and early 19th centuries, in large part because it provided viewers with breathtaking and sublime spectacles of nature. Artists also could allegorize nature, and it was rare for a landscape painting not to touch on spiritual, moral, historical, or philosophical issues. Landscape painting became the perfect vehicle for artists (and the viewing public) to "naturalize" conditions, rendering debate about contentious issues moot and eliminating any hint of conflict.

# REALISM

Advances in industrial technology during the early 19th century reinforced Enlightenment faith in the connection between science and progress. Both intellectuals and the general public increasingly embraced *empiricism* and *positivism*. To empiricists, the basis of knowledge is observation and direct experience. Positivists

ascribed to the philosophical model developed by Auguste Comte (1798–1857), who believed scientific laws governed the environment and human activity and could be revealed through careful recording and analysis of observable data. Comte's followers promoted science as the mind's highest achievement and advocated a purely empirical approach to nature and society.

## France

*Realism* was a movement that developed in France around mid-century against this backdrop of an increasing emphasis on science. Consistent with the philosophical tenets of the empiricists and positivists, Realist artists argued that only the contemporary world—what people can see—was "real." Accordingly, Realists focused their attention on the people and events of their own time and disapproved of historical and fictional subjects on the grounds they were neither visible nor present and therefore were not real.

**GUSTAVE COURBET** The leading figure of the Realist movement in 19th-century art was GUSTAVE COURBET (1819–1877). In fact, even though he shunned labels, Courbet used the term *Realism* when exhibiting his own works (see "Courbet on Realism," page 776). The Realists' sincerity about scrutinizing their environment led them to paint subjects artists had traditionally deemed unworthy of depiction—the mundane and trivial, working-class laborers and peasants, and so forth. Moreover, by depicting these subjects on a scale and with an earnestness and seriousness previously reserved for historical, mythological, and religious painting, Realist artists sought to establish parity between contemporary subject matter and the traditional themes of "high art."

**THE STONE BREAKERS** An early work that exemplifies Courbet's championing of everyday life as the only valid subject for the modern artist is *The Stone Breakers* (FIG. 27-26), in which the Realist painter presented a glimpse into the life of rural menial laborers. Courbet represented in a straightforward manner two men—one about 70, the other quite young—in the act of breaking stones, traditionally the lot of the lowest members of French society. By juxtaposing youth and age, Courbet suggested those born

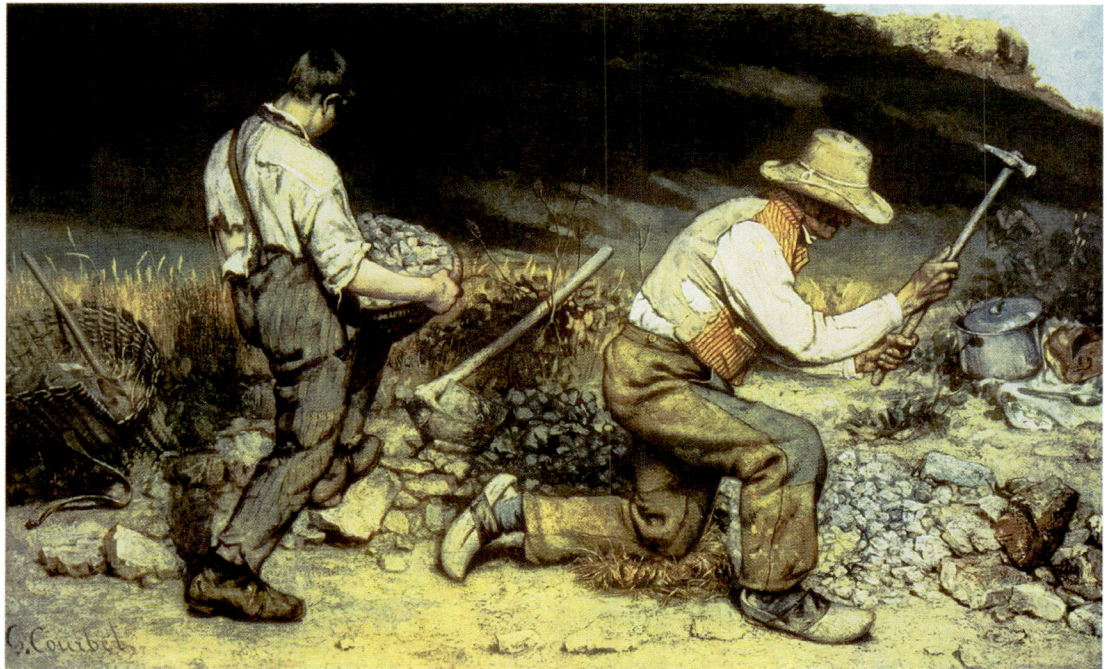

**27-26** GUSTAVE COURBET, *The Stone Breakers*, 1849. Oil on canvas, 5′ 3″ × 8′ 6″. Formerly Gemäldegalerie, Dresden (destroyed in 1945).

Courbet was the leading figure in the Realist movement. Using a palette of dirty browns and grays, he conveyed the dreary and dismal nature of menial labor in mid-19th-century France.

1 ft.

## Courbet on Realism

The academic jury selecting work for the 1855 Salon (part of the Exposition Universelle in Paris that year) rejected two of Courbet's paintings, declaring his subjects and figures were too coarse (so much so as to be plainly "socialistic") and too large. Typical of Courbet's work are *The Stone Breakers* (FIG. 27-26), which depicts menial laborers, and *Burial at Ornans* (FIG. 27-27), which represents the funeral of an ordinary man and is nearly 22 feet long. In response to the jury's decision, Courbet withdrew all of his works, including those that had been accepted, and set up his own exhibition outside the grounds, calling it the Pavilion of Realism. This was in itself a bold action. Courbet was the first artist ever known to have staged a private exhibition of his own work. His pavilion and the statement he issued to explain the paintings shown there amounted to the Realist movement's manifesto. Although Courbet maintained he founded no school and was of no school, he did, as the name of his pavilion suggests, accept the term *Realism* as descriptive of his art.

The statement Courbet distributed at his pavilion reads in part:

> The title of "realist" has been imposed upon me . . . Titles have never given a just idea of things; were it otherwise, the work would be superfluous. . . . I have studied the art of the moderns, avoiding any preconceived system and without prejudice. I have no more wanted to imitate the former than to copy the latter; nor have I thought of achieving the idle aim of "art for art's sake." No! I have simply wanted to draw from a thorough knowledge of tradition the reasoned and free sense of my own individuality. . . . To be able to translate the customs, ideas, and appearances of my time as I see them—in a word, to create a living art—this has been my aim.*

Six years later, on Christmas Day, 1861, Courbet wrote an open letter, published a few days later in the *Courier du dimanche,* addressed to prospective students. In the letter, the painter reflected on the nature of his art.

> [An artist must apply] his personal faculties to the ideas and the events of the times in which he lives. . . . [A]rt in painting should consist only of the representation of things that are visible and tangible to the artist. Every age should be represented only by its own artists, that is to say, by the artists who have lived in it. I also maintain that painting is an essentially concrete art form and can consist only of the representation of both real and existing things. . . . An abstract object, not visible, nonexistent, is not within the domain of painting.†

Courbet's most famous statement, however, is his blunt dismissal of academic painting, in which he concisely summed up the core principle of Realist painting:

> I have never seen an angel. Show me an angel, and I'll paint one.‡

*Translated by Robert Goldwater and Marco Treves, eds., *Artists on Art from the XIV to the XX Century* (New York: Pantheon), 295.
†Translated by Petra ten-Doesschate Chu, *Letters of Gustave Courbet* (Chicago: University of Chicago Press, 1992), 203–204.
‡Quoted by Vincent van Gogh in a July 1885 letter to his brother Theo, in Ronald de Leeuw, *The Letters of Vincent van Gogh* (New York: Penguin, 1996), 302.

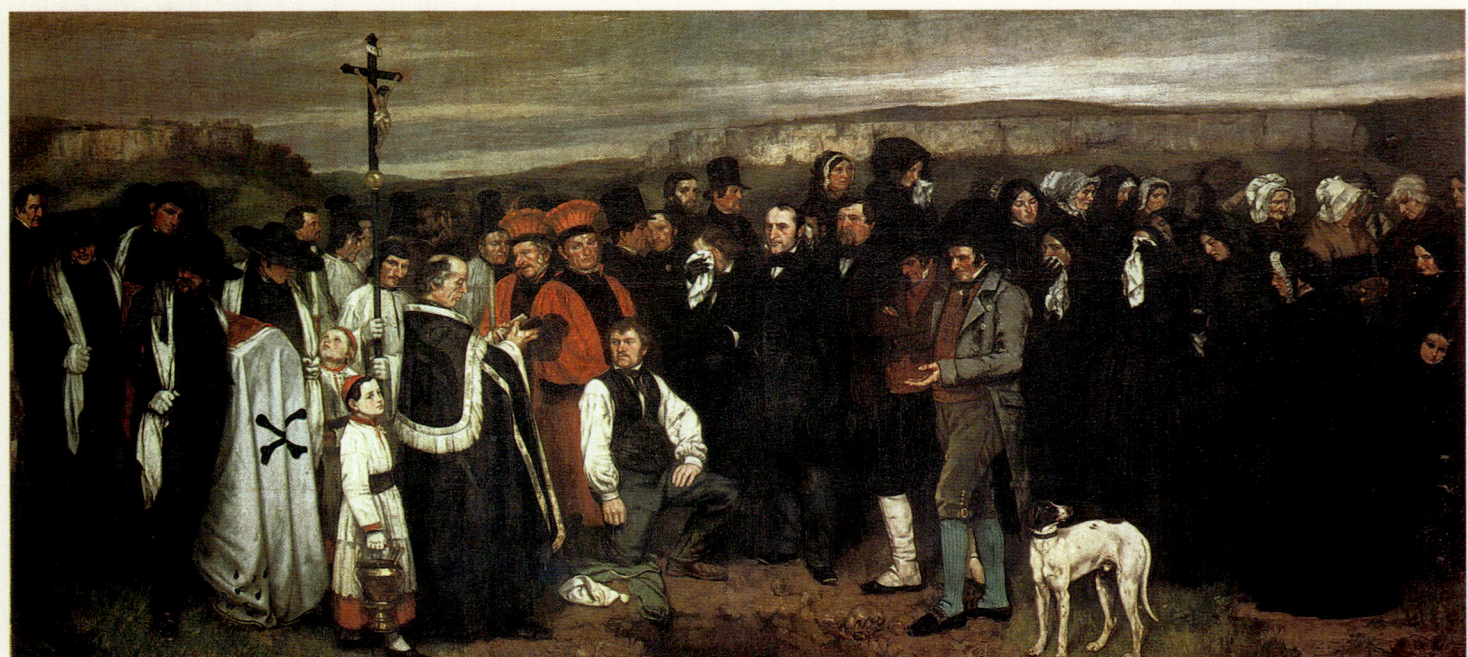

1 ft.

**27-27** GUSTAVE COURBET, *Burial at Ornans,* 1849. Oil on canvas, 10′ 3½″ × 21′ 9½″. Musée d'Orsay, Paris.

Although as monumental in scale as a traditional history painting, *Burial at Ornans* horrified critics because of the ordinary nature of the subject and Courbet's starkly antiheroic composition.

to poverty remain poor their entire lives. The artist neither romanticized nor idealized the men's work but depicted their thankless toil with directness and accuracy. Courbet's palette of dirty browns and grays further conveys the dreary and dismal nature of the task, and the angular positioning of the older stone breaker's limbs suggests a mechanical monotony.

Courbet's interest in the working poor as subject matter had a special resonance for his mid-19th-century French audience. In 1848, laborers rebelled against the bourgeois leaders of the newly formed Second Republic and against the rest of the nation, demanding better working conditions and a redistribution of property. The army quelled the uprising in three days, but not without long-lasting trauma and significant loss of life. The 1848 revolution raised the issue of labor as a national concern. Courbet's depiction of stone breakers in 1849 was thus timely and populist.

***BURIAL AT ORNANS*** Many art historians regard Courbet's *Burial at Ornans* (FIG. 27-27) as his masterpiece. The huge (10 by 22 feet) canvas depicts a funeral set in a bleak provincial landscape outside the artist's home town. Attending the funeral are the types of ordinary people Honoré de Balzac (1799–1850) and Gustave Flaubert (1821–1880) presented in their novels. While an officious clergyman reads the Office of the Dead, those attending cluster around the excavated gravesite, their faces registering all degrees of response to the ceremony. Although the painting has the monumental scale of a traditional history painting, the subject's ordinariness and the starkly antiheroic composition horrified critics. Arranged in a wavering line extending across the enormous breadth of the canvas are three groups—the somberly clad women at the back right, a semicircle of similarly clad men by the open grave, and assorted churchmen at the left. This wall of figures blocks any view into deep space. The faces are portraits. Some of the models were Courbet's sisters (three of the women in the front row, toward the right) and friends. Behind and above the figures are bands of overcast sky and barren cliffs. The dark pit of the grave opens into the viewer's space in the center foreground. Despite the unposed

look of the figures, Courbet controlled the composition in a masterful way by his sparing use of bright color. In place of the heroic, the sublime, and the dramatic, Courbet aggressively presented the viewer with the mundane realities of daily life and death. In 1857, Jules-François-Félix Husson Champfleury (1821–1889), one of the first critics to recognize and appreciate Courbet's work, wrote of *Burial at Ornans,* "[I]t represents a small-town funeral and yet reproduces the funerals of *all* small towns."[7] Unlike the theatricality of Romanticism, Realism captured the ordinary rhythms of daily life.

Of great importance for the later history of art, Realism also involved a reconsideration of the painter's primary goals and departed from the established emphasis on illusionism. Accordingly, Realists called attention to painting as a pictorial construction by the ways they applied pigment or manipulated composition. Courbet's intentionally simple and direct methods of expression in composition and technique seemed unbearably crude to many of his more traditional contemporaries, who called him a primitive. Although his bold, somber palette was essentially traditional, Courbet often used the *palette knife* for quickly placing and unifying large daubs of paint, producing a roughly wrought surface. His example inspired the young artists who worked for him (and later Impressionists such as Claude Monet and Auguste Renoir; see Chapter 28), but the public accused him of carelessness and critics wrote of his "brutalities."

***JEAN-FRANÇOIS MILLET*** As did Courbet, Jean-François Millet (1814–1878) found his subjects in the people and occupations of the everyday world. Millet was one of a group of French painters of country life who, to be close to their rural subjects, settled near the village of Barbizon in the forest of Fontainebleau. This Barbizon School specialized in detailed pictures of forest and countryside. Millet, their most prominent member, was of peasant stock and identified with the hard lot of the country poor. In *The Gleaners* (FIG. 27-28), he depicted three impoverished women— members of the lowest level of peasant society—performing the backbreaking task of gleaning. Landowning nobles traditionally permitted peasants to glean, or collect, the wheat scraps left in the field after the harvest. Millet characteristically placed his monumental figures in the foreground, against a broad sky. Although the field stretches back to a rim of haystacks, cottages, trees, distant workers, and a flat horizon, the gleaners quietly doing their tedious and time-consuming work dominate the canvas.

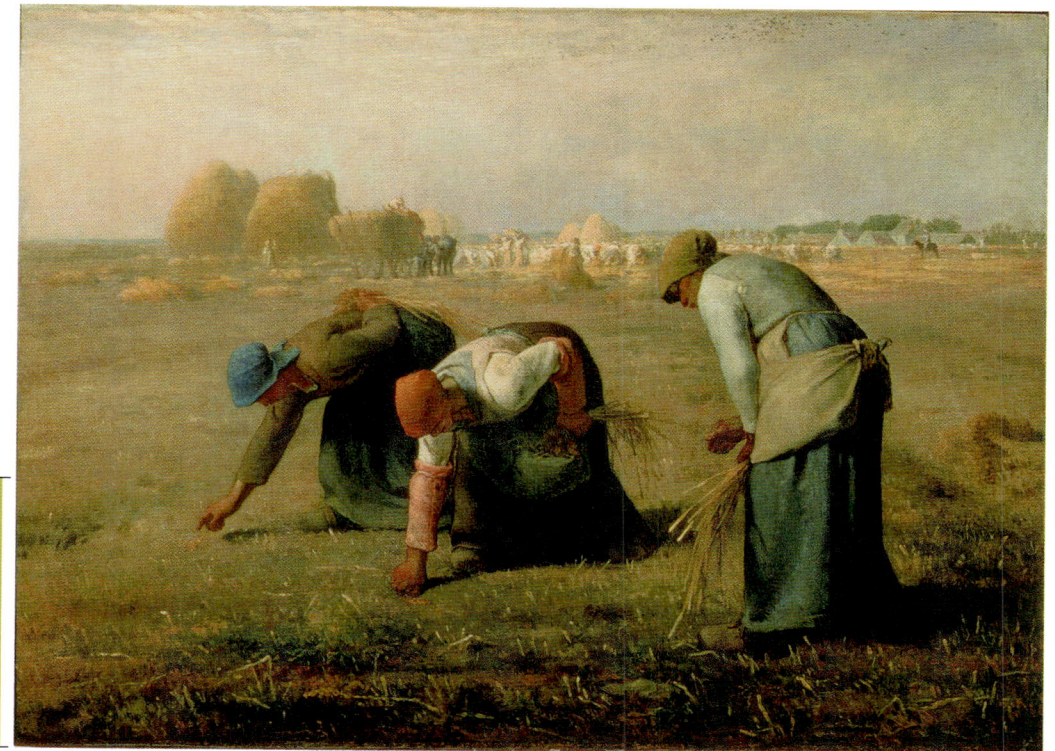

1 ft.

**27-28** Jean-François Millet, *The Gleaners,* 1857. Oil on canvas, 2′ 9″ × 3′ 8″. Musée d'Orsay, Paris.

Millet and the Barbizon School painters specialized in depictions of French country life. Here, Millet portrayed three impoverished women gathering the scraps left in the field after a harvest.

## Lithography

In 1798, the German printmaker Alois Senefelder (1771–1834) created the first prints using stone instead of metal plates or wooden blocks. In contrast to earlier printing techniques (see "Woodcuts, Engravings, and Etchings," Chapter 20, page 556), in which the artist applied ink either to a raised or incised surface, in *lithography* (Greek, "stone writing") the printing and nonprinting areas of the plate are on the same plane.

The chemical phenomenon fundamental to lithography is the repellence of oil and water. The lithographer uses a greasy, oil-based crayon to draw directly on a stone plate and then wipes water onto the stone, which clings only to the areas the drawing does not cover.

Next, the artist rolls oil-based ink onto the stone, which adheres to the drawing but is repelled by the water. When the artist presses the stone against paper, only the inked areas—the drawing—transfer to the paper. Color lithography requires multiple plates, one for each color, and the printmaker must take special care to make sure each impression lines up perfectly with the previous one so that each color prints in its proper place.

One of the earliest masters of this new printmaking process was Honoré Daumier, whose politically biting lithographs (FIG. 27-29) published in a widely read French journal reached an audience of unprecedented size.

**27-29** HONORÉ DAUMIER, *Rue Transnonain*, 1834. Lithograph, $1' \times 1' 5\frac{1}{2}''$. Philadelphia Museum of Art, Philadelphia (bequest of Fiske and Marie Kimball).

Daumier used the recent invention of lithography to reach a wide audience for his social criticism and political protest. This print records the horrific 1834 massacre in a workers' housing block.

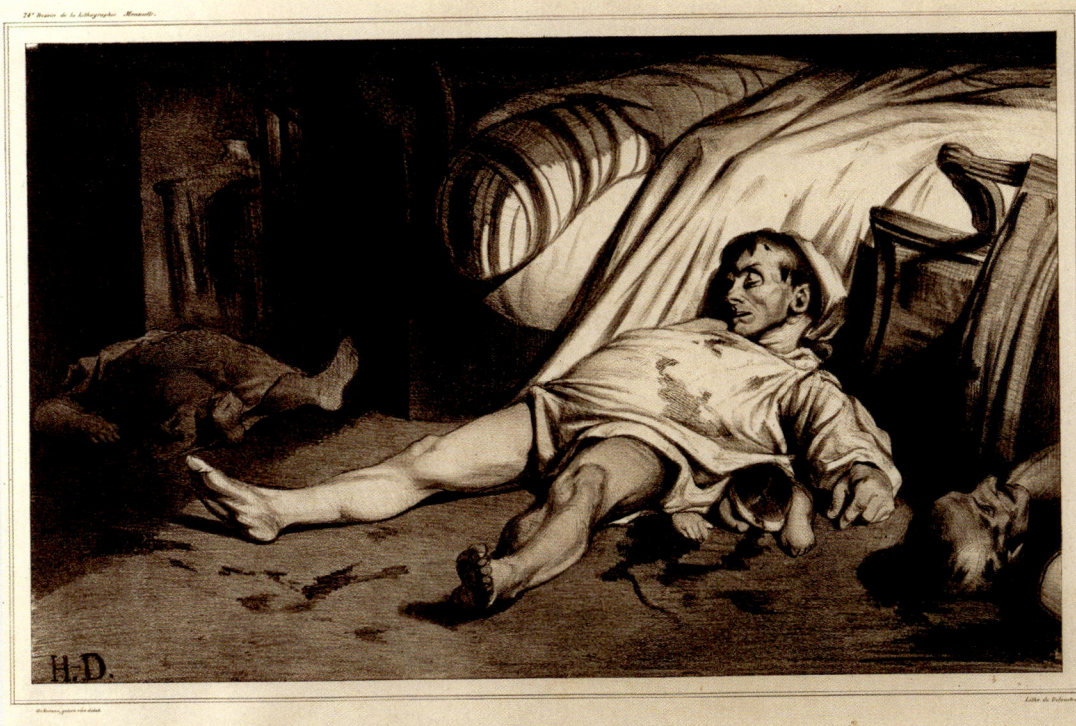

RUE TRANSNONAIN, LE 15 AVRIL, 1834

1 in.

Although Millet's paintings evoke a sentimentality absent from Courbet's, the French public still reacted to his work with disdain and suspicion. In the aftermath of the 1848 revolution, Millet's investiture of the poor with solemn grandeur did not meet with approval from the prosperous classes. In particular, middle-class landowners resisted granting gleaning rights, and thus Millet's relatively dignified depiction of gleaning antagonized them. The middle class also linked the poor with the dangerous, newly defined working class, which was finding outspoken champions in men such as Karl Marx (1818–1883), Friedrich Engels (1820–1895), and the novelists Émile Zola (1840–1902) and Charles Dickens (1812–1870). Socialism was a growing movement, and both its views on property and its call for social justice, even economic equality, threatened and frightened the bourgeoisie. Millet's sympathetic portrayal of the poor seemed to much of the public to be a political manifesto.

**HONORÉ DAUMIER** Because people widely recognized the power of art to serve political ends, the political and social agitation accompanying the violent revolutions in France and the rest of Europe in the later 18th and early 19th centuries prompted the French people to suspect artists of subversive intention. A person could be jailed for too bold a statement in the press, in literature, in art—even in music and drama. Realist artist HONORÉ DAUMIER (1808–1879) was a defender of the urban working classes, and in his art he boldly confronted authority with social criticism and political protest. In response, the authorities imprisoned the artist. A painter, sculptor, and, like Dürer, Rembrandt, and Goya, one of history's great printmakers, Daumier produced *lithographs* (see "Lithography," above) that enabled him to create an unprecedented number of prints, thereby reaching an exceptionally large and broad audience. In addition to producing individual prints for sale,

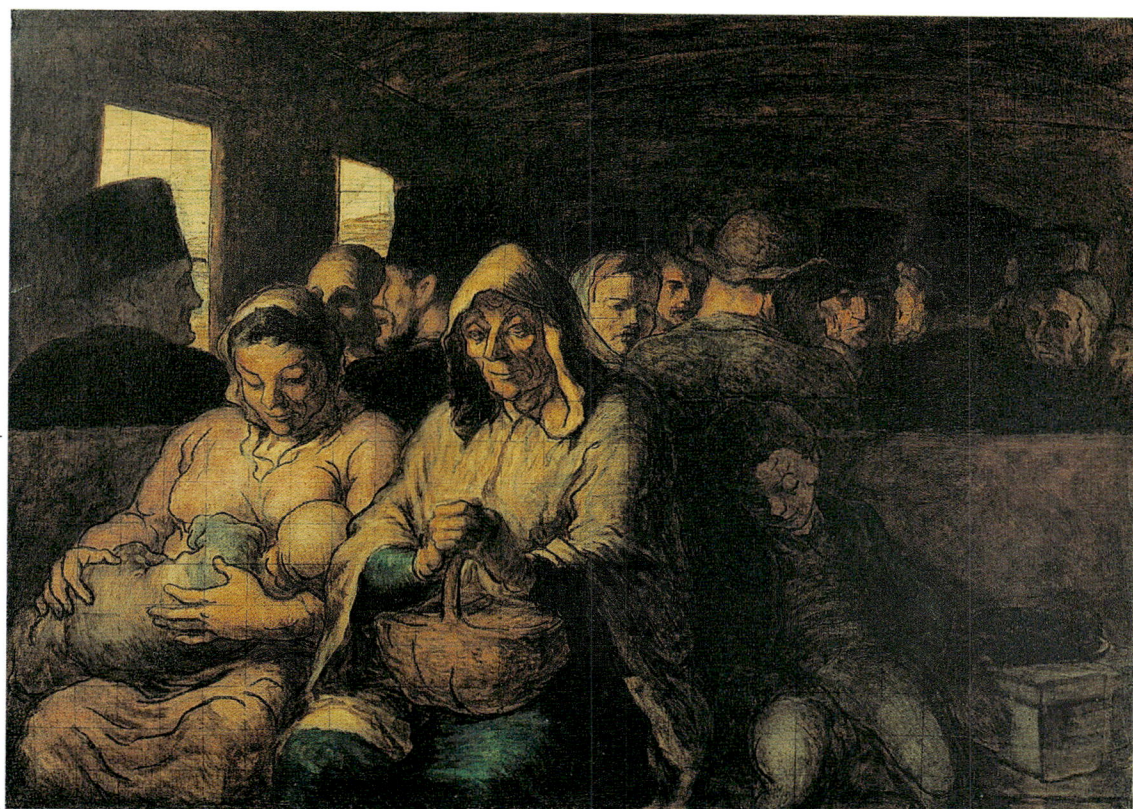

27-30 HONORÉ DAUMIER, *Third-Class Carriage,* ca. 1862. Oil on canvas, 2′ 1¾″ × 2′ 11½″. Metropolitan Museum of Art, New York (H. O. Havemeyer Collection, bequest of Mrs. H. O. Havemeyer, 1929).

Daumier frequently depicted the plight of the disinherited masses of 19th-century industrialization. Here, he portrayed the anonymous poor cramped together in a grimy third-class railway carriage.

1 ft.

Daumier also contributed satirical lithographs to the widely read, liberal French Republican journal *Caricature,* further increasing the number of people exposed to his work. In *Caricature,* Daumier mercilessly lampooned the foibles and misbehavior of politicians, lawyers, doctors, and the rich bourgeoisie in general.

*RUE TRANSNONAIN* Daumier's lithograph *Rue Transnonain* (FIG. 27-29) depicts an atrocity having the same shocking impact as Goya's *Third of May, 1808* (FIG. 27-11). The title refers to a street in Paris where an unknown sniper killed a civil guard, part of a government force trying to repress a worker demonstration. Because the fatal shot had come from a workers' housing block, the remaining guards immediately stormed the building and massacred all of its inhabitants. With Goya's power, Daumier created a view of the slaughter from a sharp angle of vision. But unlike Goya, he depicted not the dramatic moment of execution but the terrible, quiet aftermath. The limp bodies of the workers—and of a child crushed beneath his father's corpse—lie amid violent disorder. The print's power lies in its factualness. Daumier's pictorial manner is rough and spontaneous, and that approach to representation, which is a central characteristic of Realist art, accounts in large measure for its remarkable force.

*THIRD-CLASS CARRIAGE* For his paintings, Daumier chose the same kind of subjects and representational manner as in his graphic work, especially after the 1848 revolution. His unfinished *Third-Class Carriage* (FIG. 27-30) provides a glimpse into the cramped and grimy railway cars of the 1860s. The riders are poor and can afford only third-class tickets. First- and second-class carriages had closed compartments, but third-class passengers had to cram together on hard benches stretching from one end of their carriage to the other. The disinherited masses of 19th-century industrialization were Daumier's indignant concern. He depicted

them in the unposed attitudes and unplanned arrangements of the millions thronging the modern cities—anonymous, insignificant, dumbly patient with a lot they could not change. Daumier saw people as they ordinarily appeared, their faces vague, impersonal, and blank—unprepared for any observers. He tried to achieve the real by isolating a random collection of the unrehearsed details of human existence from the continuum of ordinary life. Daumier's vision anticipated the spontaneity and candor of scenes captured with the camera by the end of the century.

**ROSA BONHEUR** The most celebrated woman artist of the 19th century was MARIE-ROSALIE (ROSA) BONHEUR (1822–1899). The winner of the gold medal at the Salon of 1848, Bonheur became in 1894 the first woman officer in the French Legion of Honor. As was typical for women since the Renaissance (see "The Artist's Profession," Chapter 20, page 545), Bonheur received her artistic training from her father, Oscar-Raymond Bonheur (1796–1849), who was a proponent of *Saint-Simonianism,* an early-19th-century utopian socialist movement that championed the education and enfranchisement of women. As a result of her father's influence, Bonheur launched her career believing that as a woman and an artist, she had a special role to play in creating a new and perfect society. A Realist passion for accuracy in painting drove Bonheur, but she resisted depicting the problematic social and political themes seen in the work of Courbet, Millet, Daumier, and other Realists. Rather, she turned to the animal world—not, however, to the exotic wild animals that so fascinated Delacroix (FIG. 27-17), but to animals common in the French countryside, especially horses, but also rabbits, cows, and sheep. She went to great lengths to observe the anatomy of living horses at the great Parisian horse fair and spent long hours studying the anatomy of carcasses in the Paris slaughterhouses.

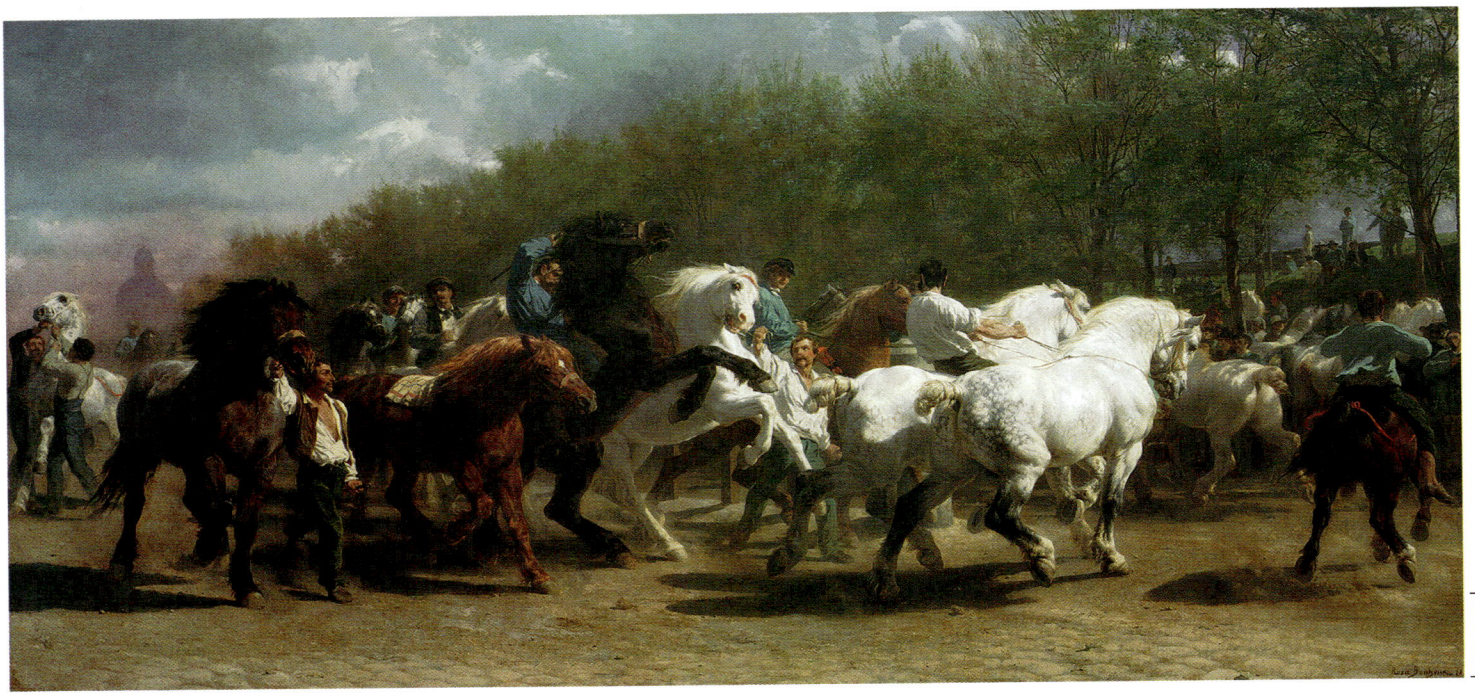

**27-31** ROSA BONHEUR, *The Horse Fair*, 1853–1855. Oil on canvas, 8′ $\frac{1}{4}$″ × 16′ 7$\frac{1}{2}$″. Metropolitan Museum of Art, New York (gift of Cornelius Vanderbilt, 1887).

Bonheur was the most celebrated woman artist of the 19th century. A Realist, she went to great lengths to record accurately the anatomy of living horses, even studying carcasses in slaughterhouses.

For *The Horse Fair* (FIG. 27-31), Bonheur's best-known work, the artist chose a panoramic composition similar to that in Courbet's *Burial at Ornans* (FIG. 27-27). She filled her broad canvas with the sturdy farm Percherons and their grooms seen on parade at the annual Parisian horse sale. Some horses, not quite broken, rear up. Others plod or trot, guided on foot or ridden by their keepers. Bonheur recorded the Percherons' uneven line of march, their thunderous pounding, and their seemingly overwhelming power based on her close observation of living animals, even though she acknowledged some inspiration from the Parthenon frieze (FIG. 5-50, *top*). The dramatic lighting, loose brushwork, and rolling sky also reveal her admiration of Géricault's style (FIGS. 27-13 and 27-13A). The equine drama in *The Horse Fair* captivated viewers, who eagerly bought engraved reproductions of Bonheur's painting, making it one of the most popular artworks of the century.

**ÉDOUARD MANET** As pivotal a figure in 19th-century European art as Gustave Courbet was the painter ÉDOUARD MANET (1832–1883). Like Courbet, Manet was influential in articulating Realist principles, but the younger artist also played an important role in the development of Impressionism in the 1870s (see Chapter 28). Manet's *Le Déjeuner sur l'Herbe* (*Luncheon on the Grass;* FIG. 27-32), widely recognized only later as a seminal work in the history of art, depicts two clothed men and one nude and one clothed woman at a picnic. Consistent with Realist principles, Manet based all four figures on real people. The seated nude is Victorine Meurend (Manet's favorite model at the time), and the gentlemen are his brother Eugène (with cane) and probably the sculptor Ferdinand Leenhof, although scholars have suggested other identifications. The two men wear fashionable Parisian attire of the 1860s. The nude woman is a distressingly unidealized figure who also seems disturbingly unabashed and at ease, gazing directly at the viewer without shame or flirtatiousness.

This audacious painting outraged the French public. Rather than a traditional pastoral scene, for example, Titian's *Pastoral Symphony* (FIG. 22-35), populated by anonymous idealized figures in an idyllic setting, *Le Déjeuner* featured ordinary men and promiscuous women in a Parisian park. One hostile critic, no doubt voicing public opinion, said: "A commonplace woman of the demimonde, as naked as can be, shamelessly lolls between two dandies dressed to the teeth. These latter look like schoolboys on a holiday, perpetrating an outrage to play the man. . . . This is a young man's practical joke—a shameful, open sore."[8] Manet surely anticipated criticism of his painting, but shocking the public was not his primary aim. His goal was more complex and far more ambitious. With *Le Déjeuner,* he sought to reassess the nature of painting. The work contains sophisticated references and allusions to many artistic genres—history painting, portraiture, pastoral scenes, nudes, and even religious scenes. *Le Déjeuner* is Manet's impressive synthesis and critique of the entire history of painting.

The negative response to Manet's painting on the part of public and critics alike extended beyond subject matter. The painter's manner of presenting his figures also elicited severe criticism. He rendered the men and women in soft focus and broadly painted the landscape, including the pool in which the second woman bathes. The loose manner of painting contrasts with the clear forms of the harshly lit foreground trio and of the pile of discarded female clothes and picnic foods at the lower left. The lighting creates strong contrasts between dark and highlighted areas. In the main figures, many values are summed up in one or two lights or darks. The effect is both to flatten the forms and set them off sharply from the setting. Form, rather than a matter of line, is only a function of paint and light. Manet aimed to move away from illusionism toward an open acknowledgment of painting's properties, such as the flatness of the painting surface, which would become a core principle of many later 19th-century painters as well as their successors

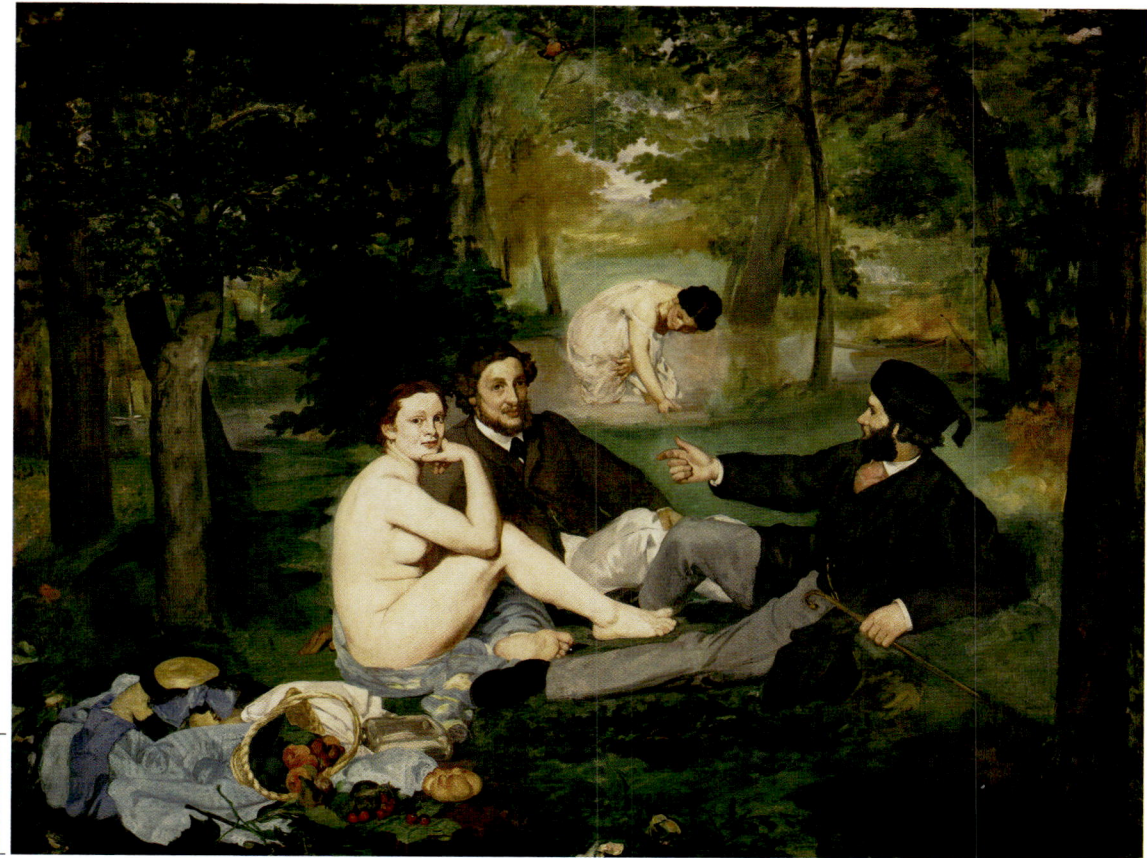

Manet shocked his contemporaries with both his subject matter and manner of painting. Moving away from illusionism, he used colors to flatten form and to draw attention to the painting surface.

to the present day. The mid-19th-century French public, however, saw only a crude sketch lacking the customary finish of paintings exhibited in the Paris Salon. The style of the painting, coupled with the unorthodox subject matter, made *Le Déjeuner sur l'Herbe* one of the most controversial artworks ever created.

**OLYMPIA** Even more scandalous to the French viewing public, however, was Manet's *Olympia* (FIG. **27-33**), painted the same year. Manet's subject was a young white prostitute (Olympia was a common "professional" name for prostitutes in 19th-century France). She reclines on a bed that extends across the full width of

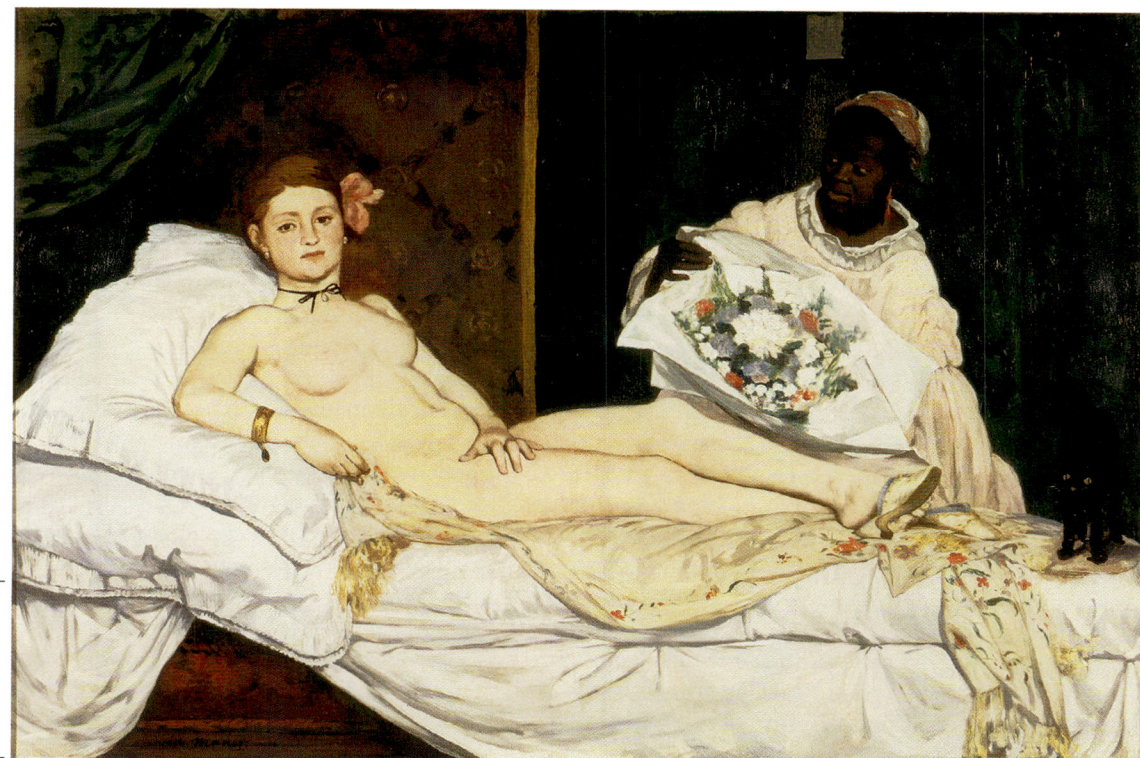

**27-33** Édouard Manet, *Olympia*, 1863. Oil on canvas, 4′ 3″ × 6′ 2¼″. Musée d'Orsay, Paris. ■◀

Manet's painting of a nude prostitute and her black maid carrying a bouquet from a client scandalized the public. Critics also faulted his rough brushstrokes and abruptly shifting tonalities.

Realism **781**

the painting (and beyond) and is nude except for a thin black ribbon tied around her neck, a bracelet on her arm, an orchid in her hair, and fashionable slippers on her feet. Like the seated nude in *Le Déjeuner,* Olympia meets the viewer's eye with a look of cool indifference. The only other figure in the painting is a black maid, who presents Olympia a bouquet of flowers from a client.

*Olympia* horrified public and critics alike. Although images of prostitutes were not unheard of during this period, the shamelessness of Olympia and her look verging on defiance shocked viewers. The depiction of a black woman was also not new to painting, but the French public perceived Manet's inclusion of both a black maid and a nude prostitute as evoking moral depravity, inferiority, and animalistic sexuality. The contrast of the black servant with the fair-skinned courtesan also conjured racial divisions. One critic described Olympia as "a courtesan with dirty hands and wrinkled feet . . . her body has the livid tint of a cadaver displayed in the morgue; her outlines are drawn in charcoal and her greenish, bloodshot eyes appear to be provoking the public, protected all the while by a hideous Negress."[9] From this statement, it is clear viewers were responding not solely to the subject matter but to Manet's artistic style as well. The painter's brushstrokes are much rougher and the shifts in tonality are far more abrupt than those found in traditional academic painting. This departure from accepted practice exacerbated the audacity of the subject matter. *Olympia*—indeed, all of Manet's work—represented a radical departure from the academic style then in favor, as exemplified by the work of Adolphe-William Bouguereau (1825–1905; FIG. 27-33A), an artist largely forgotten today, although he was a towering figure in the French art world during the second half of the 19th century.

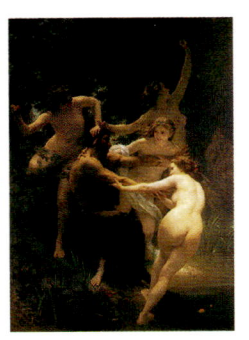

27-33A BOUGUEREAU, *Nymphs and a Satyr,* 1873.

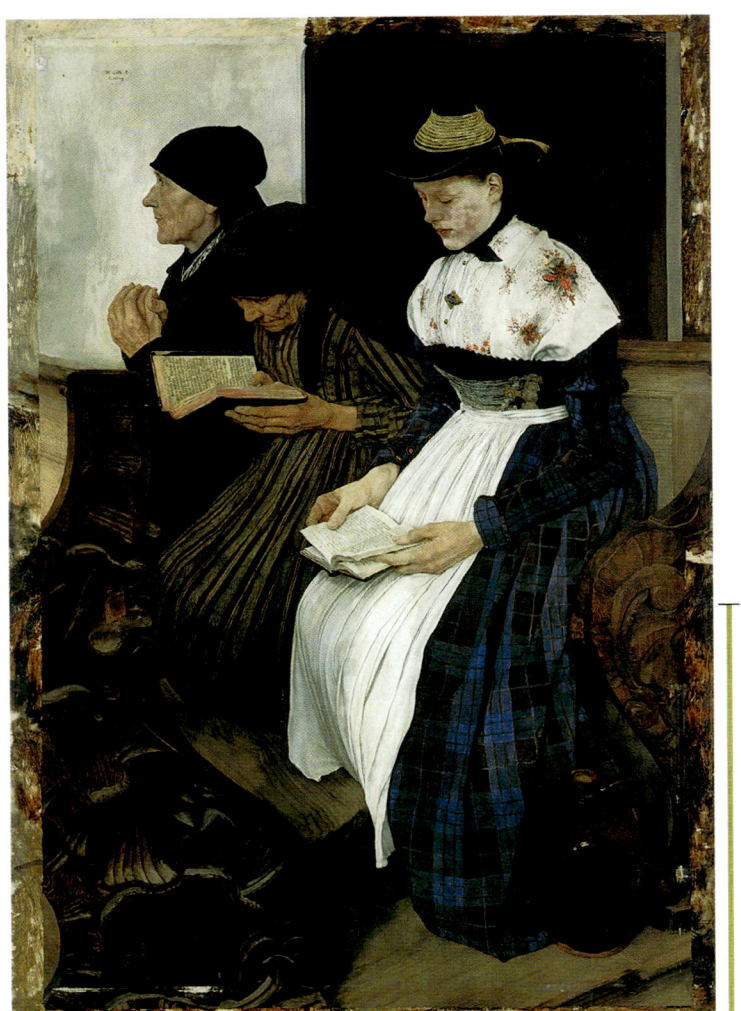

27-34 WILHELM LEIBL, *Three Women in a Village Church,* 1878–1882. Oil on canvas, 2′ 5″ × 2′ 1″. Hamburger, Kunsthalle, Hamburg.

French Realism spread quickly to Germany, where Leibl painted this moving depiction of simple peasant women of different generations holding their prayer books in hands roughened by work.

## Germany and the United States

Although French artists took the lead in promoting the depiction of the realities of modern life as the only valid goal for artists, the Realist movement was neither exclusively French nor confined to Europe.

**WILHELM LEIBL** In Germany, WILHELM LEIBL (1844–1900) shared French Realists' commitment to representing the contemporary world and real people in his paintings. *Three Women in a Village Church* (FIG. 27-34) is typical of Leibl's work, which focused on country life. The painting records a sacred moment—the moment of prayer—in the life of three women of different generations. Dressed in rustic costume, their Sunday-church best, they quietly pursue their devotions, their prayer books held in large hands roughened by work. Their manners and their dress reflect their unaffected nature, untouched by the refinements of urban life. Leibl highlighted their natural virtues: simplicity, honesty, steadfastness, patience. He spent three years working on this image of peasants in their village church, often under impossible conditions of lighting and temperature. Despite the meticulous application of paint and sharpness of focus, the picture is a moving expression of the artist's compassionate view of his subjects, a reading of character without sentimentality.

**WINSLOW HOMER** Realism received an especially warm welcome in the United States. One of the leading American Realist painters was WINSLOW HOMER (1836–1910) of Boston. Homer experienced at first hand the most momentous event of his era—the Civil War. In 1860, he joined the Union campaign as an artist-reporter for *Harper's Weekly.* At the end of the war, he painted *Veteran in a New Field* (FIG. 27-35). Although it is relatively simple and direct, Homer's painting is a significant commentary on the effects and aftermath of America's catastrophic national conflict. At the center of the canvas is a man with his back to the viewer, harvesting wheat. Homer identified him as a veteran by including his uniform and canteen carelessly thrown on the ground in the lower right corner. The man's current occupation, however, is as a farmer, and he has cast aside his former role as a soldier. The veteran's involvement in meaningful and productive work implies a smooth transition from war to peace. This postwar transition to work and the fate of disbanded soldiers were national concerns. Echoing the sentiments behind Houdon's portrayal of George Washington as the new Cincinnatus (FIG. 26-32), the *New York Weekly Tribune* commented: "Rome took her great man from the plow, and made him a dictator—we must now take our soldiers from the camp and make them farmers."[10] America's ability to effect a smooth transition was seen as evidence of its national strength. "The peaceful and harmonious

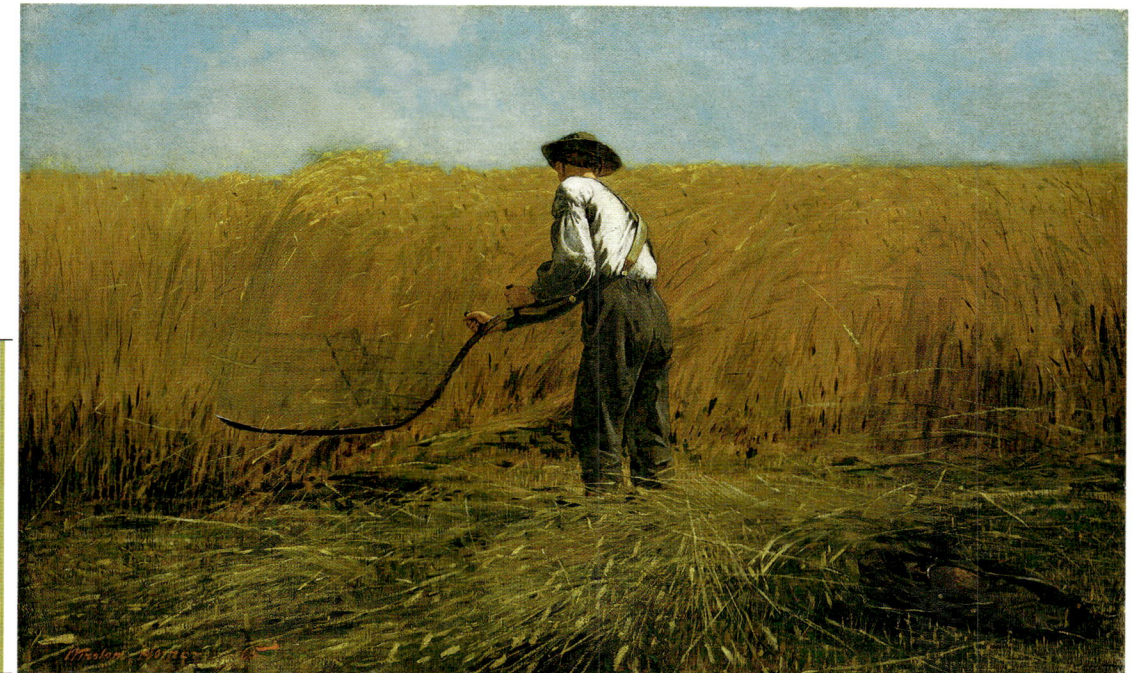

27-35 WINSLOW HOMER, *Veteran in a New Field*, 1865. Oil on canvas, 2′ $\frac{1}{8}$″ × 3′ 2$\frac{1}{8}$″. Metropolitan Museum of Art, New York (bequest of Miss Adelaide Milton de Groot, 1967).

This veteran's productive work implies a smooth transition to peace after the Civil War, but Homer placed a single-bladed scythe—the Grim Reaper's tool—in his hands, symbolizing the deaths of soldiers.

1 ft.

disbanding of the armies in the summer of 1865," poet Walt Whitman (1819–1892) wrote, was one of the "immortal proofs of democracy, unequall'd in all the history of the past."[11] Homer's painting thus reinforced the perception of the country's greatness.

*Veteran in a New Field* also comments symbolically about death. By the 1860s, farmers used cradled scythes to harvest wheat. For this detail, however, Homer rejected realism in favor of symbolism. The former soldier's tool is a single-bladed scythe. The artist thus transformed the man who lived through the Civil War into a symbol of Death—the Grim Reaper himself. In addition to being a tribute to the successful transition to peace, *Veteran in a New Field* is an elegy to the thousands of soldiers who did not return from the war. It may also be a lamentation on the recent assassination of President Abraham Lincoln.

**THOMAS EAKINS** Even more resolutely a Realist than Homer was Philadelphia-born THOMAS EAKINS (1844–1916), whose work reflects his keen appetite for recording the realities of the human experience. Eakins studied both painting and medical anatomy in Philadelphia before undertaking further study under French artist Jean-Léon Gérôme (1824–1904). Eakins aimed to paint things as he saw them rather than as the public might wish them portrayed. This attitude was very much in tune with 19th-century American taste, combining an admiration for accurate depiction with a hunger for truth.

The too-brutal Realism of Eakins's early masterpiece, *The Gross Clinic* (FIG. **27-36**), prompted the art jury to reject it for the Philadelphia exhibition celebrating the American independence centennial in 1876. The painting portrays the renowned surgeon Dr. Samuel Gross in the operating amphitheater of the Jefferson Medical College in Philadelphia, where the painting hung for 130 years until its sale in 2006 to raise funds for the college. Eakins's decision to depict

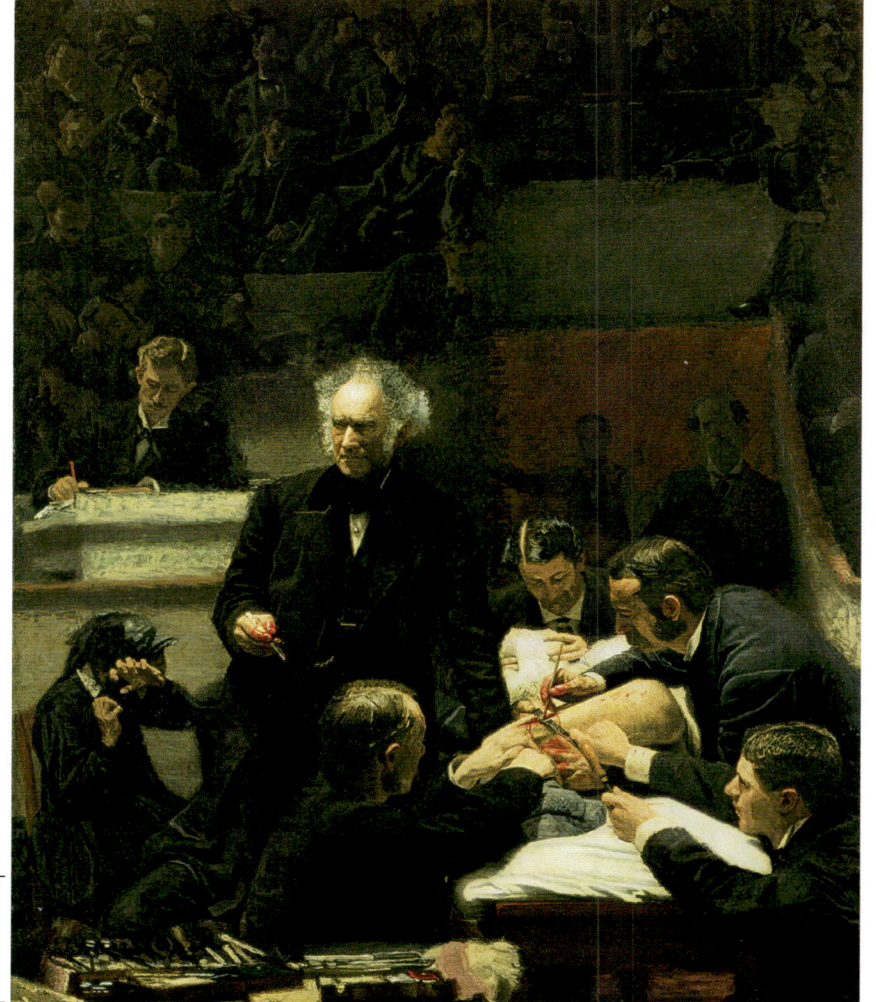

1 ft.

27-36 THOMAS EAKINS, *The Gross Clinic*, 1875. Oil on canvas, 8′ × 6′ 6″. Philadelphia Museum of Art, Philadelphia. ◼◀

The too-brutal realism of Eakins's depiction of a medical college operating amphitheater caused this painting's rejection from the Philadelphia exhibition celebrating America's centennial.

an operation in progress reflects the public's increasing faith that scientific and medical advances could enhance—and preserve—lives. Dr. Gross, with bloody fingers and scalpel, lectures about his surgery on a young man's leg. The patient suffered from osteomyelitis, a bone infection. Watching the surgeon, acclaimed for his skill in this particular operation, are several colleagues—all of whom historians have identified—and the patient's mother, who covers her face. Also present is an anesthetist, who holds a cloth over the patient's face. Anesthetics had been introduced in 1846, and their development eliminated a major obstacle to extensive surgery. The painting is an unsparing description of an unfolding event, with a good deal more reality than many viewers could endure. "It is a picture," one critic said, "that even strong men find difficult to look at long, if they can look at it at all."[12]

Consistent with the dominance of empiricism in the latter half of the 19th century, Eakins believed careful observation—and, where relevant, scientific knowledge—were prerequisites for his art, and he created his paintings in a deliberate, methodical way based on firsthand study of his subject. For example, Eakins's focus on anatomical correctness led him to investigate the human form and humans in motion, both with regular photographic apparatuses and with a special camera devised by the French kinesiologist (a person who studies the physiology of body movement) Étienne-Jules Marey (1830–1904). Eakins later collaborated with Eadweard Muybridge (FIG. 27-54) in the photographic study of animal and human action of all types, anticipating the 20th-century invention of the motion picture.

**JOHN SINGER SARGENT** The expatriate American artist JOHN SINGER SARGENT (1856–1925), born in Florence, Italy, was a younger contemporary of Eakins. Sargent developed a looser, more dashing Realist portrait style, in contrast to Eakins's carefully rendered details. Sargent studied art in Paris before settling in London, where he won renown both as a cultivated and cosmopolitan gentleman and as an accomplished portrait painter. He learned his adept application of paint in thin layers and his effortless achievement of quick and lively illusion from his study of Velázquez, whose masterpiece, *Las Meninas* (FIG. 24-30), may have influenced Sargent's family portrait *The Daughters of Edward Darley Boit* (FIG. 27-37). The four girls (the children of one of Sargent's close friends) appear in a hall and small drawing room in their Paris home. The informal, eccentric arrangement of their slight figures suggests how much at ease they are within this familiar space and with objects such as the monumental Japanese vases, the red screen, and the fringed rug, whose scale subtly emphasizes the children's diminutive stature. Sargent must have known the Boit daughters well. Relaxed and trustful, they gave the artist an opportunity to record a gradation of young innocence. He sensitively captured the naive, wondering openness of the little girl in the foreground, the grave artlessness of the 10-year-old child, and the slightly self-conscious poise of the adolescents. Sargent's casual positioning of the figures and seemingly random choice of the setting communicate a sense of spontaneity. The children seem to be attending momentarily to an adult who has asked them to interrupt their activity. The painting embodies the Realist belief that the artist's business is to record modern people in modern contexts.

**HENRY OSSAWA TANNER**
Typical of the Realist painter's desire to depict the lives of ordinary people engaged in everyday activities is the early work of African American artist HENRY OSSAWA TANNER (1859–1937). Tanner studied art with Eakins before moving to Paris. There he combined Eakins's belief in careful study from nature with a desire to portray with dignity the life of the working people he had been raised among as a minister's son in Pennsylvania. The mood in *The Thankful Poor* (FIG. 27-38) is one of quiet devotion not far removed from the Realism of Millet (FIG. 27-28) and

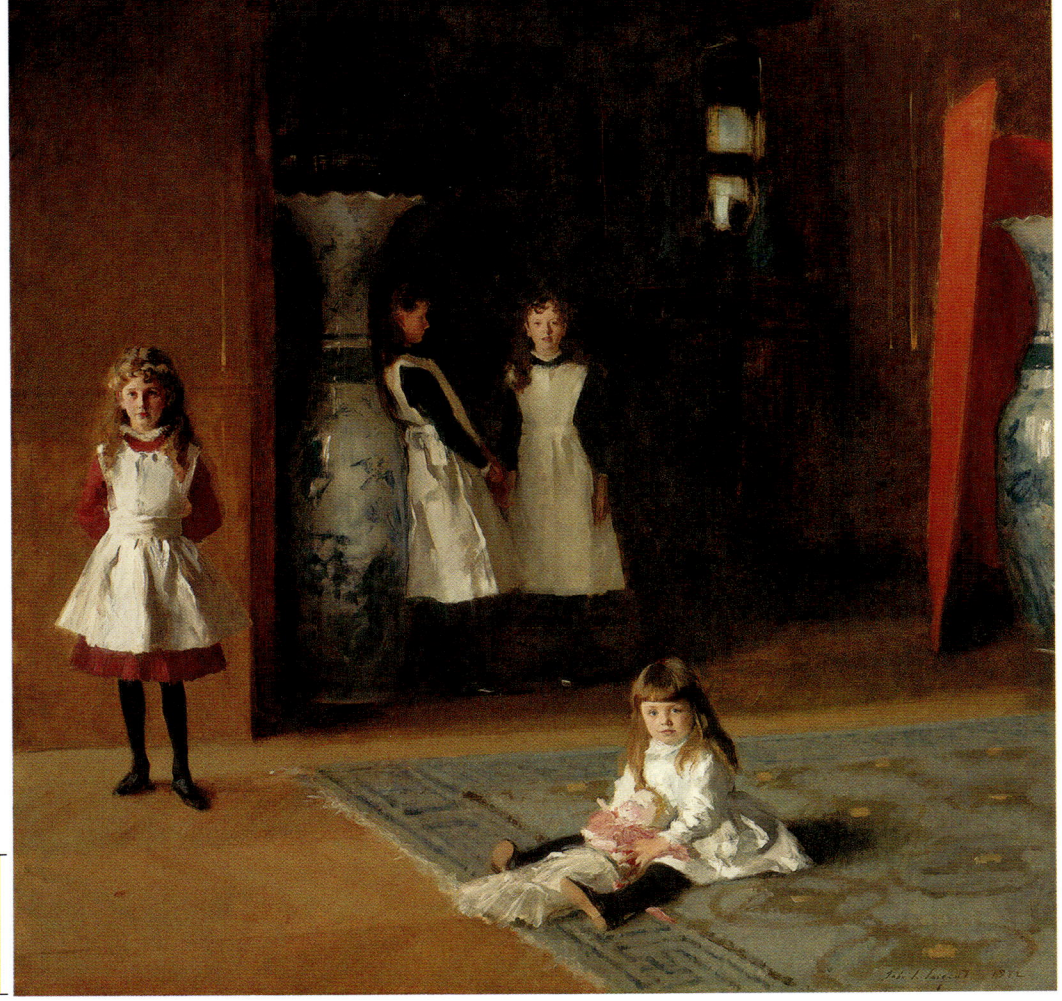

**27-37** JOHN SINGER SARGENT, *The Daughters of Edward Darley Boit*, 1882. Oil on canvas, 7′ 3 3/8″ × 7′ 3 5/8″. Museum of Fine Arts, Boston (gift of Mary Louisa Boit, Florence D. Boit, Jane Hubbard Boit, and Julia Overing Boit, in memory of their father, Edward Darley Boit).

Sargent's casual positioning of the Boit sisters creates a sense of the momentary and spontaneous, consistent with Realist painters' interest in recording modern people in modern contexts.

1 ft.

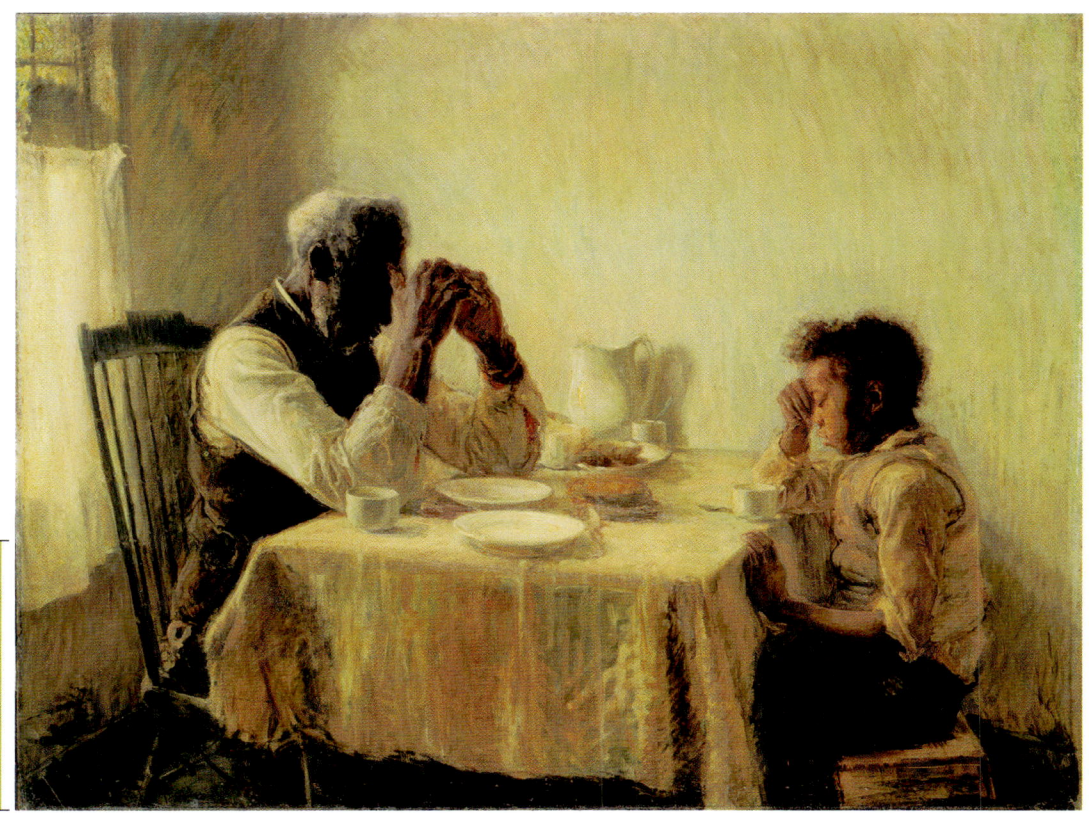

**27-38** HENRY OSSAWA TANNER, *The Thankful Poor,* 1894. Oil on canvas, 2′ 11½″ × 3′ 8¼″. Collection of William H. and Camille Cosby.

Tanner combined the Realists' belief in careful study from nature with a desire to portray with dignity the life of African American families. Expressive lighting reinforces the painting's reverent spirit.

1 ft.

Leibl (FIG. 27-34). Tanner painted the grandfather, grandchild, and main objects in the room in great detail, whereas everything else dissolves into loose strokes of color and light. Expressive lighting reinforces the painting's reverent spirit, with deep shadows intensifying the man's devout concentration and golden light pouring in the window to illuminate the quiet expression of thanksgiving on the younger face. The deep sense of sanctity expressed here in terms of everyday experience became increasingly important for Tanner. Within a few years of completing *The Thankful Poor,* he began painting biblical subjects grounded in direct study from nature and in the love of Rembrandt that had inspired him from his days as a Philadelphia art student.

**EDMONIA LEWIS** About 15 years older than Tanner, the sculptor EDMONIA LEWIS (ca. 1845–after 1909), the daughter of a Chippewa mother and African American father, produced work stylistically indebted to Neoclassicism but depicting contemporary Realist themes. *Forever Free* (FIG. **27-39**) is a marble sculpture Lewis carved while living in Rome, surrounded by examples of both classical and Renaissance art. It represents two freed African American slaves. The man stands heroically in a contrapposto stance reminiscent of classical statues. His right hand rests on the shoulder of the kneeling woman, and his left hand holds aloft a broken manacle and chain as literal and symbolic references to his former servitude. Produced four years after President Lincoln's issuance of the Emancipation Proclamation, *Forever Free* (originally titled *The Morning*

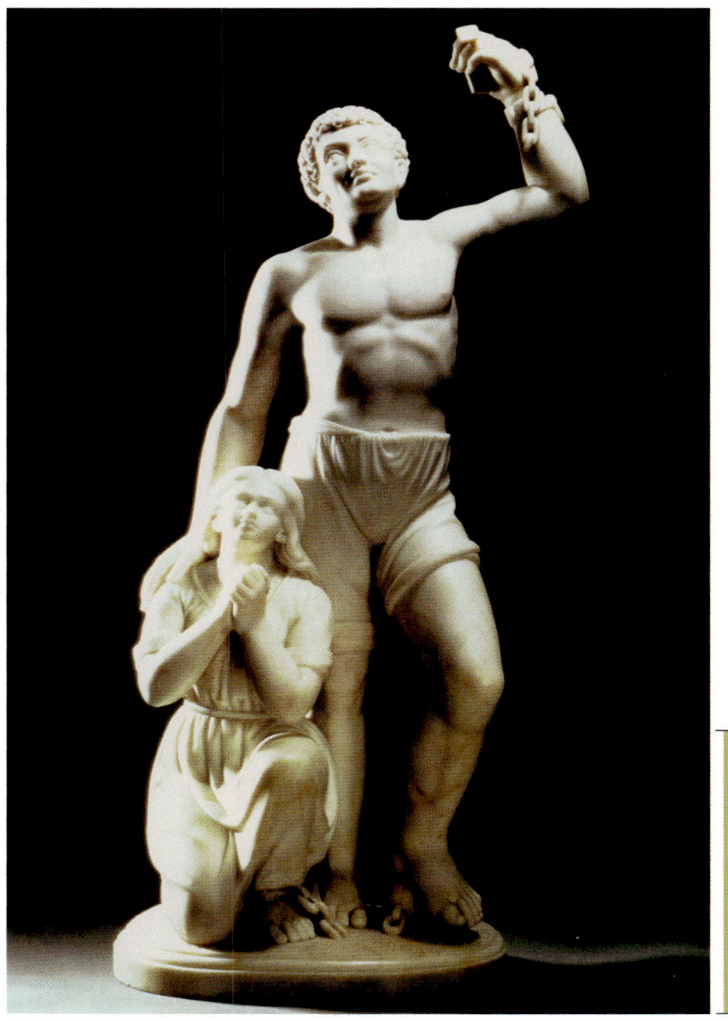

**27-39** EDMONIA LEWIS, *Forever Free,* 1867. Marble, 3′ 5¼″ high. James A. Porter Gallery of Afro-American Art, Howard University, Washington, D.C.

Lewis was a sculptor whose work owes a stylistic debt to Neoclassicism but depicts contemporary Realist themes. She carved *Forever Free* four years after Lincoln's Emancipation Proclamation.

1 ft.

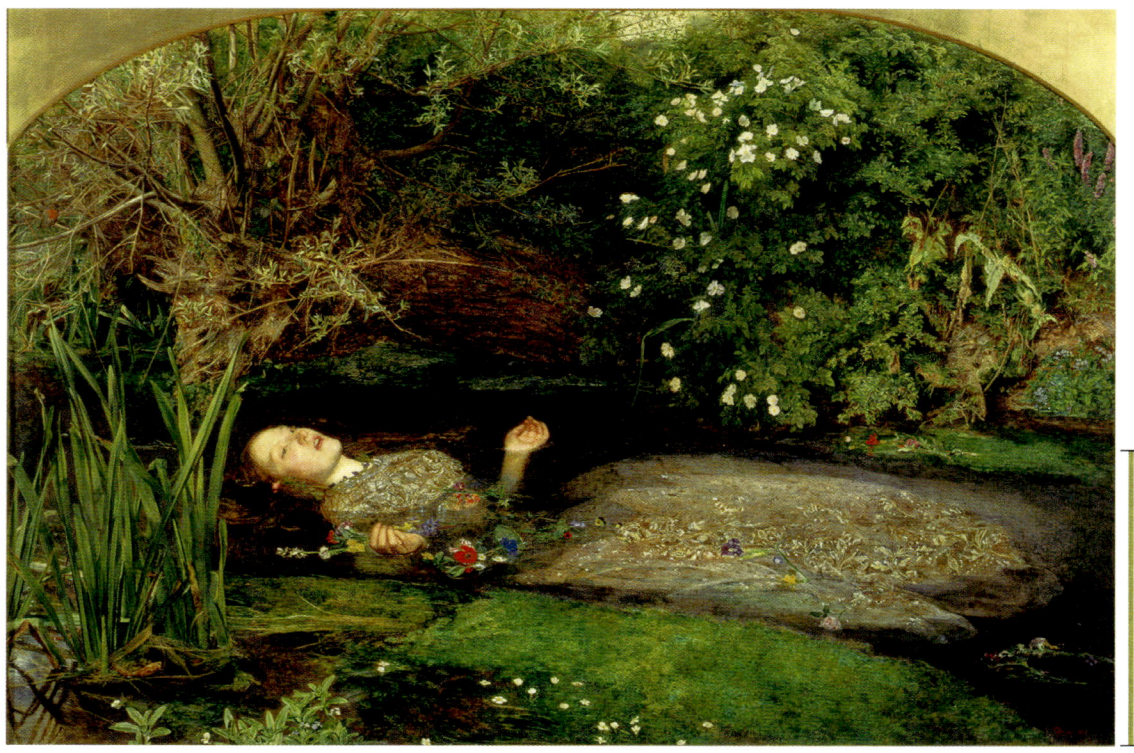

**27-40** JOHN EVERETT MILLAIS, *Ophelia,* 1852. Oil on canvas, 2′ 6″ × 3′ 8″. Tate Gallery, London. ◼◀

Millet was a founder of the Pre-Raphaelite Brotherhood, whose members refused to be limited to the contemporary scenes that strict Realists portrayed. The drowning of Ophelia is a Shakespearean subject.

1 ft.

*of Liberty*) was widely perceived as an abolitionist statement. However, other factors caution against an overly simplistic reading. For example, scholars have debated the degree to which the sculptor attempted to inject a statement about gender relationships into this statue and whether the kneeling position of the woman is a reference to female subordination in the African American community.

Lewis's accomplishments as a sculptor speak to the increasing access to training available to women in the 19th century. Educated at Oberlin College (the first American college to grant degrees to women), Lewis financed her trip to Rome with the sale of medallions and marble busts. Her success in a field dominated by white male artists is a testament to both her skill and her determination.

## Pre-Raphaelite Brotherhood

Realism did not appeal to all artists, of course. In England, a group of painters who called themselves the *Pre-Raphaelite Brotherhood* refused to be limited to the contemporary scenes strict Realists portrayed. These artists chose instead to represent fictional, historical, and fanciful subjects, albeit with a significant degree of convincing illusion.

**JOHN EVERETT MILLAIS** One of the founders of the Pre-Raphaelite Brotherhood was JOHN EVERETT MILLAIS (1829–1896). So painstakingly careful was Millais in his study of visual facts closely observed from nature that Charles Baudelaire (1821–1867) called him "the poet of meticulous detail." The Pre-Raphaelite Brotherhood, organized in 1848, wished to create fresh and sincere art, free from what its members considered the tired and artificial manner propagated in the academies by the successors of Raphael. Influenced by the critic, artist, and writer John Ruskin (1819–1900), the Pre-Raphaelites shared his distaste for the materialism and ugliness of the contemporary industrializing world. They also expressed appreciation for the spirituality and idealism (as well as the art and artisanship) of past times, especially the Middle Ages and the Early Renaissance.

Millais's *Ophelia* (FIG. **27-40**) garnered enthusiastic praise when the painter exhibited it in the Exposition Universelle in Paris in 1855—the exhibition at which Courbet set up his Pavilion of Realism. The subject, from Shakespeare's *Hamlet* (4.7.176–179), is the drowning of Ophelia, who, in her madness, is unaware of her plight:

> *Her clothes spread wide,*
> *And mermaidlike awhile they bore her up—*
> *Which time she chanted snatches of old tunes,*
> *As one incapable of her own distress.*

To make the pathos of the scene visible, Millais became a faithful and feeling witness of its every detail, reconstructing it with a lyricism worthy of the original poetry. Although the scene is fictitious and therefore one Realist painters would have rejected, Millais worked diligently to present it with unswerving fidelity to visual fact. He painted the background on site at a spot along the Hogsmill River in Surrey. For the figure of Ophelia, Millais had a friend lie in a heated bathtub full of water for hours at a time.

**DANTE GABRIEL ROSSETTI** Another founder of the Pre-Raphaelite Brotherhood was DANTE GABRIEL ROSSETTI (1828–1882), who established an enviable reputation as both a painter and poet. Like other members of the group, Rossetti focused on literary and biblical themes in his art. He also produced numerous portraits of women that projected an image of ethereal beauty and melded apparent opposites—for example, a Victorian prettiness with sensual allure. His *Beata Beatrix* (FIG. **27-41**) is ostensibly a portrait of a literary figure—Beatrice, from Dante's *Vita Nuova*—as she overlooks Florence in a trance after being mystically transported to Heaven. Yet the portrait also had personal resonance for Rossetti. It served as a memorial to his wife, Elizabeth Siddal (the model for Millais's *Ophelia*). Siddal had died shortly before Rossetti began this painting in 1862. In the image, the woman (Siddal-Beatrice) sits in a trancelike state, while a red dove (a messenger of both love

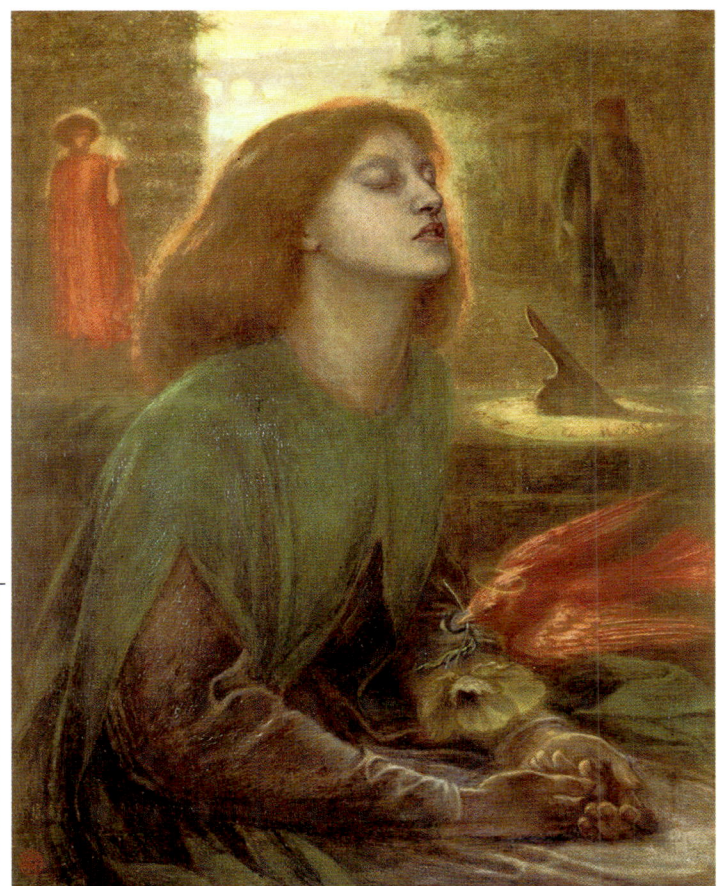

1 ft.

**27-41** Dante Gabriel Rossetti, *Beata Beatrix,* ca. 1863. Oil on canvas, 2′ 10″ × 2′ 2″. Tate Gallery, London.

This painting of a beautiful and sensuous woman is ostensibly a literary portrait of Dante's Beatrice, but the work also served as a memorial to Rossetti's wife, who died of an opium overdose.

and death) deposits a poppy (symbolic of sleep and death) in her hands. Because Siddal died of an opium overdose, the presence of the poppy assumes greater significance.

# ARCHITECTURE

At the opening of the 19th century, Napoleon had co-opted the classical style as the official architectural expression of his empire. Neoclassicism was in vogue elsewhere in Europe and in the new American republic too, but other historical styles also enjoyed revivals at the same time architects were exploring the expressive possibilities that new construction technologies had fostered. The buildings constructed during the 19th century are consequently among the most stylistically diverse in history.

**ALTES MUSEUM, BERLIN** After the fall of Napoleon, who had occupied the Prussian capital of Berlin from 1806 to 1808, a fervent nationalistic spirit emerged in Germany. One manifestation of Prussian nationalism was the decision to build Europe's first public art museum to house the extensive and growing royal collection. The commission went to Karl Friedrich Schinkel (1781–1841), who worked in many revival styles during his career, including Romanesque, Gothic, and Italian Renaissance, but who chose the Neoclassical style for what he and Crown Prince Friedrich Wilhelm III (1755–1861) conceived as a "temple of culture."

The Altes (Old) Museum (FIG. 27-42), constructed on an island in the Spree River across from the royal palace in Berlin, is not truly templelike, however. Rather, with its broad facade of 18 Ionic columns on a high podium, it more closely resembles a Greek stoa (FIG. 5-77) than a pediment-capped classical temple. Noteworthy for its perfect proportions, Schinkel's austere design expresses nobility, tradition, and elite culture, now made accessible to the public in a building whose style Europeans associated with the democratic values of ancient Greece and Rome.

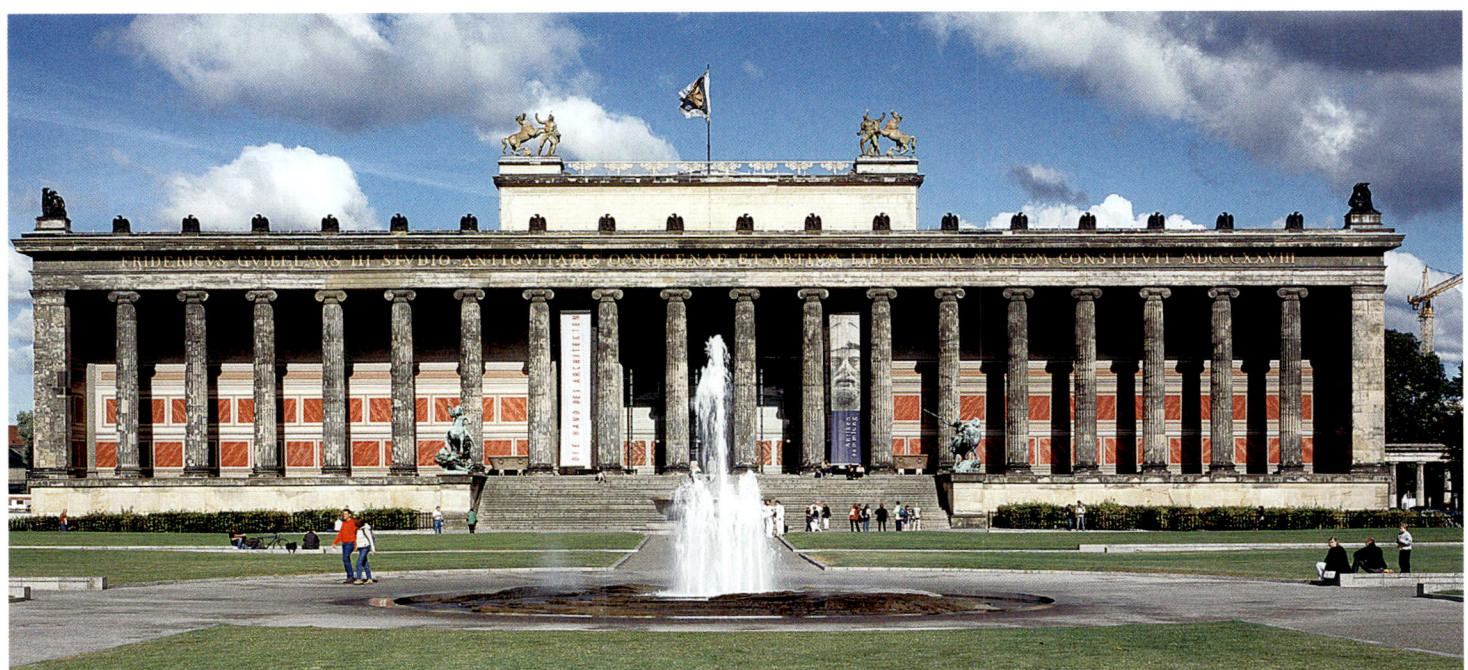

**27-42** Karl Friedrich Schinkel, Altes Museum, Berlin, Germany, 1822–1830.

Schinkel conceived the first public art museum in Europe as a Neoclassical "temple of culture." The Altes Museum's facade of 18 Ionic columns resembles an ancient Greek stoa (FIG. 5-77).

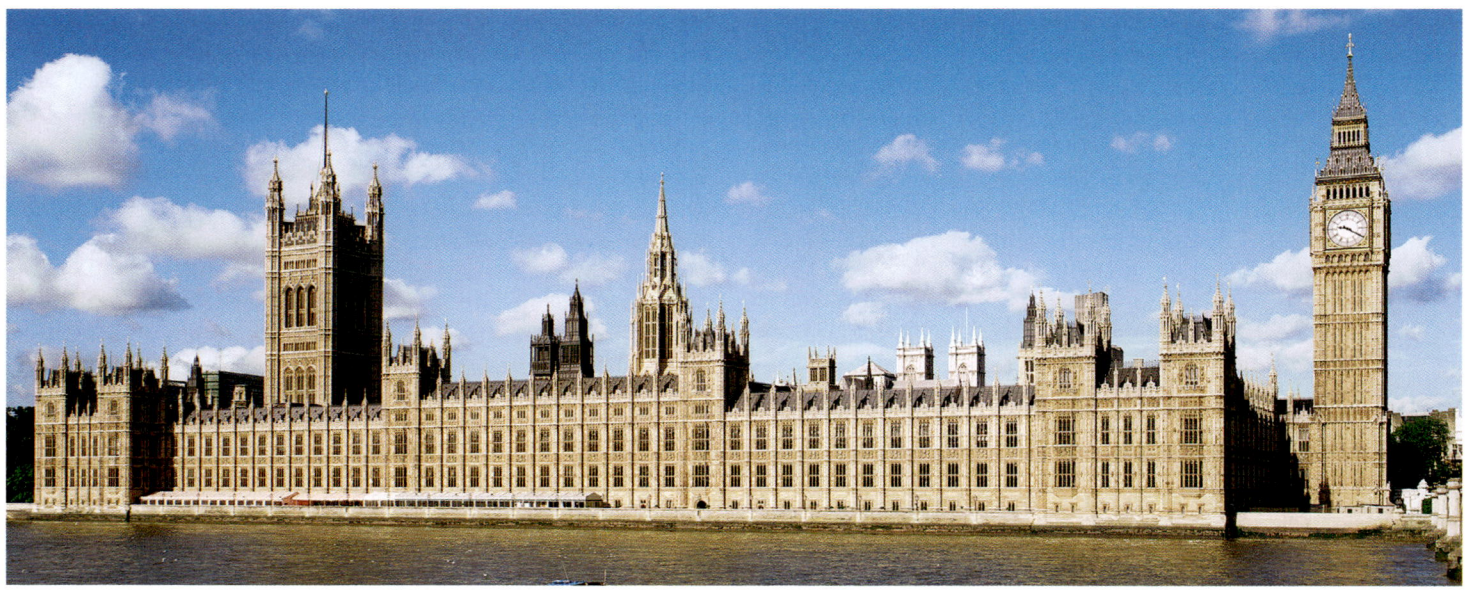

**27-43** CHARLES BARRY and AUGUSTUS WELBY NORTHMORE PUGIN, Houses of Parliament, London, England, designed 1835. ◼◀

During the 19th century, architects revived many historical styles, often reflecting nationalistic pride. The Houses of Parliament have an exterior veneer and towers that recall English Late Gothic style.

The Neoclassical facade masks a very practical plan that has no model in classical temples or stoas. A broad central staircase leads into a foyer and then a cubical central block, which projects above the facade's colonnade. The central block houses a sculpture-filled domed rotunda loosely based on the Pantheon (FIGS. 7-50 and 7-51) in Rome. To either side is a courtyard whose windows provide light to the painting galleries all around. Large windows on the side and rear walls of the Altes Museum also illuminate the galleries. The museum was revolutionary in organizing the artworks it contained in chronological order, emphasizing the history of art, as opposed to simply displaying aesthetic treasures (compare FIG. 25-1A).

**GOTHIC REVIVAL** As 19th-century scholars gathered the documentary materials of European history in encyclopedic enterprises, each nation came to value its past as evidence of the validity of its ambitions and claims to greatness. Intellectuals appreciated the art of the remote past as a product of cultural and national genius. Italy, of course, had its Roman ruins, which had long inspired later architects. A reawakening of interest in Gothic architecture also surfaced at this time, even in France under Napoleon. In 1802, Chateaubriand published his influential *Genius of Christianity*—the source for Girodet-Trioson's *Burial of Atala* (FIG. 27-5)—which defended religion on the grounds of its beauty and mystery rather than on the grounds of truth. Gothic cathedrals, according to Chateaubriand, were translations of the sacred groves of the ancient Gauls into stone and should be cherished as manifestations of France's holy history. One result of this new nationalistic respect for the Gothic style was that Eugène Emmanuel Viollet-le-Duc (1814–1879) received a commission in 1845 to restore the interior of Paris's Notre Dame to its Gothic splendor after removing the Baroque and Napoleonic (FIG. 27-2) alterations.

**HOUSES OF PARLIAMENT** England also celebrated its medieval heritage with *Neo-Gothic* buildings. In London, when the old Houses of Parliament burned in 1834, the Parliamentary Commission decreed that designs for the new building be either Gothic or Elizabethan. CHARLES BARRY (1795–1860), with the assistance of AUGUSTUS WELBY NORTHMORE PUGIN (1812–1852), submitted the winning design (FIG. 27-43) in 1835. By this time, architectural style had become a matter of selection from the historical past. Barry had traveled widely in Europe, Greece, Turkey, Egypt, and Palestine, studying the architecture of each place. He preferred the classical Renaissance styles, but he had designed some earlier Neo-Gothic buildings, and Pugin successfully influenced him in the direction of English Late Gothic. Pugin was one of a group of English artists and critics who saw moral purity and spiritual authenticity in the religious architecture of the Middle Ages and revered the careful medieval artisans who built the great cathedrals. The Industrial Revolution was flooding the market with cheaply made and ill-designed commodities. Machine work was replacing handicraft. Many, Pugin included, believed in the necessity of restoring the old artisanship, which they felt embodied honesty as well as quality. Pugin was also the author of the influential *True Principles of Pointed or Christian Architecture* (1841), which RICHARD UPJOHN (1802–1878) consulted for his Neo-Gothic Trinity Church (FIG. 27-43A) in New York City. The design of the Houses of Parliament, however, is not genuinely Gothic, despite its picturesque tower groupings (the Clock Tower, housing Big Ben, at one end, and the Victoria Tower at the other). The building has a formal axial plan and a kind of Palladian regularity beneath its Neo-Gothic detail. Pugin himself said of it, "All Grecian, Sir. Tudor [English Late Gothic] details on a classical body."[13]

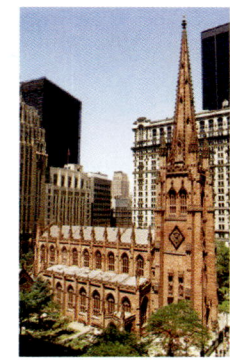

**27-43A** UPJOHN, Trinity Church, New York, 1841–1852.

**ROYAL PAVILION** Although the Neoclassical and Neo-Gothic styles dominated early-19th-century architecture, exotic new approaches of all manner soon began to appear, due in part to European imperialism and in part to the Romantic spirit permeating all the arts. Great Britain's forays throughout the world, particularly India, had exposed English culture to a broad range of non-Western artistic styles. The Royal Pavilion (FIG. 27-44), designed

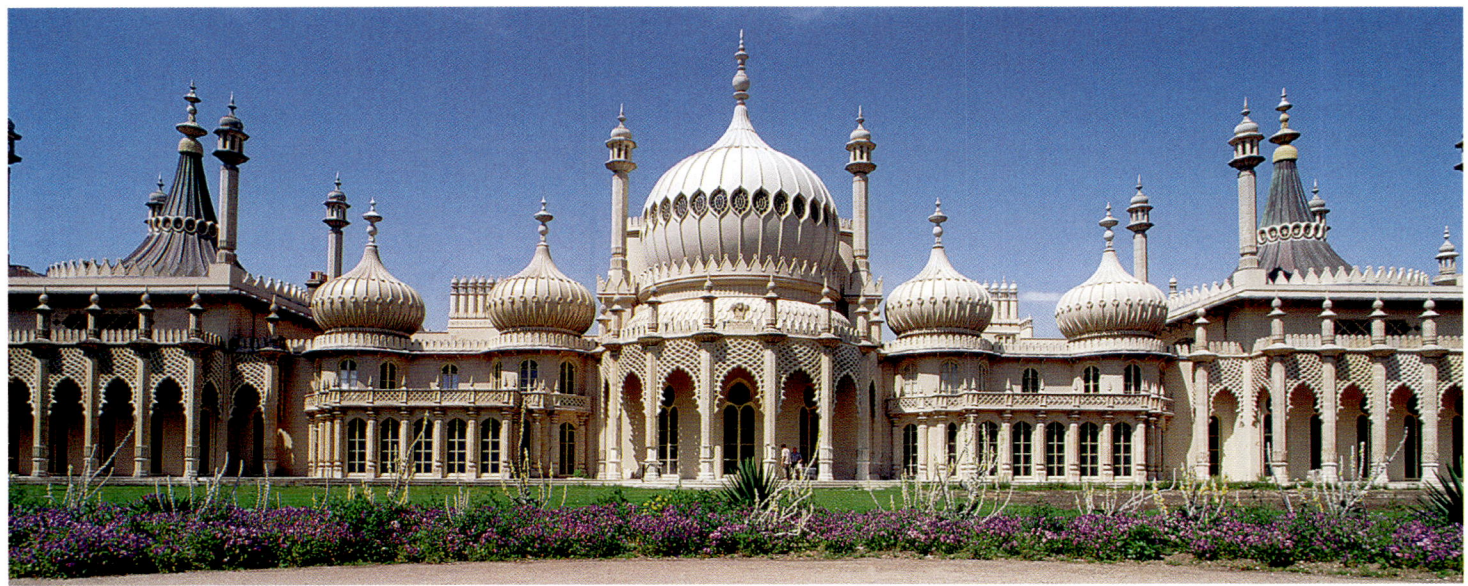

**27-44** JOHN NASH, Royal Pavilion, Brighton, England, 1815–1818.

British territorial expansion brought a familiarity with many exotic styles. This palatial "Indian Gothic" seaside pavilion is a conglomeration of Islamic domes, minarets, and screens.

by JOHN NASH (1752–1835), exhibits a wide variety of these styles. Nash was an established architect, known for Neoclassical buildings in London, when the prince regent (later King George IV) asked him to design a royal pleasure palace in the seaside resort of Brighton. The architecture of Greece, Egypt, and China influenced the interior décor of the Royal Pavilion, but the fantastic exterior is a conglomeration of Islamic domes, minarets, and screens architectural historians describe as "Indian Gothic." Underlying the exotic facade is a cast-iron skeleton, an early (if hidden) use of this material in noncommercial construction. Nash also put this metal to fanciful use, creating life-size palm-tree columns in cast iron to support the Royal Pavilion's kitchen ceiling. The building, an appropriate enough backdrop for gala throngs pursuing pleasure by the seaside, has served as a prototype for countless playful architectural exaggerations still found in European and American resorts.

**PARIS OPÉRA** Another style that found favor in 19th-century architecture was the Baroque, because it was well suited to convey-ing a grandeur worthy of the riches the European elite acquired during this age of expansion. The Paris Opéra (FIG. **27-45**), designed by CHARLES GARNIER (1825–1898), mirrored the opulent lives of these privileged few. The opera house has a festive and spectacularly theatrical Neo-Baroque front and two wings resembling Baroque domed central-plan churches. Inside, intricate arrangements of corridors, vestibules, stairways, balconies, alcoves, entrances, and exits facilitate easy passage throughout the building and provide space for entertainment and socializing at intermissions.

The Baroque grandeur of the layout and of the building's ornamental appointments are characteristic of an architectural style called *Beaux-Arts,* which flourished in the late 19th and early 20th centuries in France. Based on ideas taught at the dominant École des Beaux-Arts (School of Fine Arts) in Paris, the Beaux-Arts style incorporated classical principles (such as symmetry in design, including interior spaces extending radially from a central core or axis) and featured extensive exterior ornamentation. As an example of a Beaux-Arts building, Garnier's Opéra proclaims, through its majesty and lavishness, its function as a gathering place for fashionable audiences in an era of conspicuous wealth. The style was so attractive to the moneyed classes who supported the arts that theaters and opera houses continued to reflect the Paris Opéra's design until World War I transformed society (see Chapter 29).

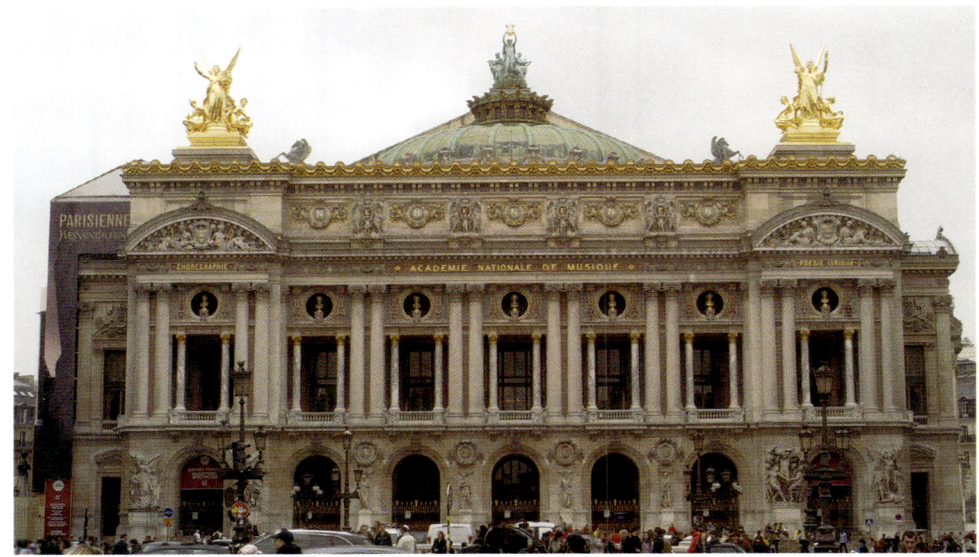

**27-45** CHARLES GARNIER, Opéra (looking north), Paris, France, 1861–1874. ■◀

For Paris's opera house, Garnier chose a festive and spectacularly theatrical Neo-Baroque facade well suited to a gathering place for fashionable audiences in an age of conspicuous wealth.

**27-46** HENRI LABROUSTE, reading room of the Bibliothèque Sainte-Geneviève, Paris, France, 1843–1850.

The exterior of this Parisian library looks like a Renaissance palazzo, but the interior has an exposed cast-iron skeleton, which still incorporates classical Corinthian capitals and Renaissance scrolls.

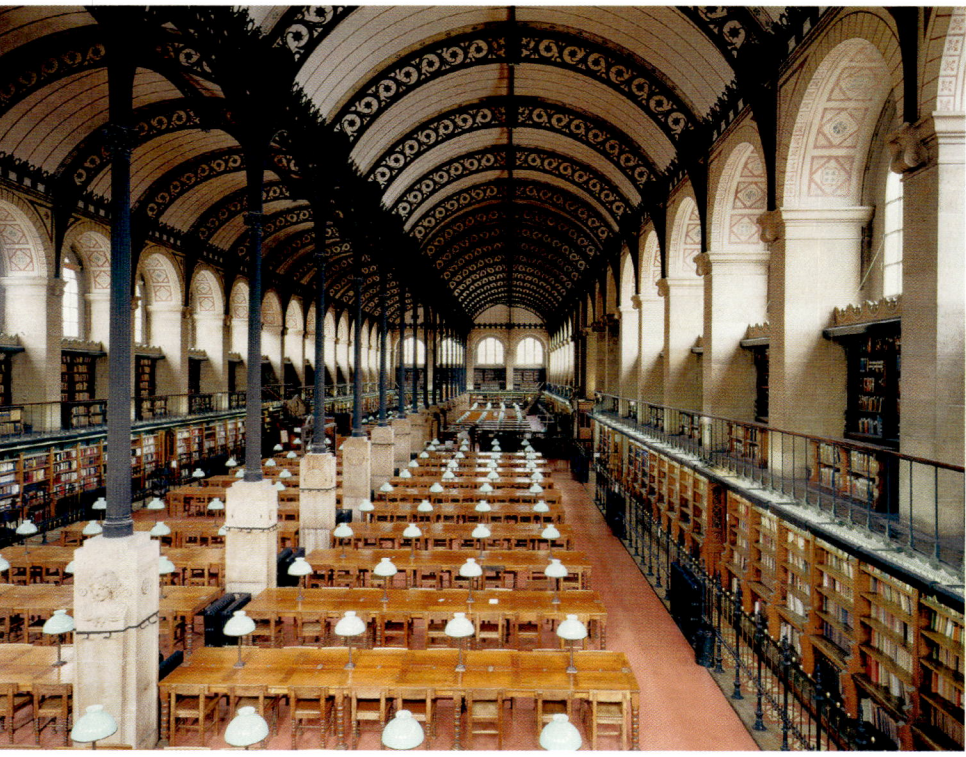

## SAINTE-GENEVIÈVE LIBRARY

Work on Garnier's opera house began in 1861, but by the middle of the 19th century, many architects had already abandoned sentimental and Romantic designs from the past. Since the 18th century, bridges had been constructed of cast iron (FIG. 26-12) because of its tensile strength and resistance to fire, and steel became available after 1860 as a building material that enabled architects to create new designs involving vast enclosed spaces, as in the great train sheds of railroad stations (FIG. 28-4) and in exposition halls. Most other utilitarian architecture—factories, warehouses, dockyard structures, mills, and the like—long had been built simply and without historical ornamentation.

The Bibliothèque Sainte-Geneviève, built by HENRI LABROUSTE (1801–1875), is an interesting mix of Renaissance revival style and modern cast-iron construction. The library's two-story facade with arched windows recalls Renaissance palazzo designs, but Labrouste exposed the structure's metal skeleton on the interior. The lower story of the building housed the book stacks. The upper floor featured a spacious reading room (FIG. 27-46) consisting essentially of two barrel-vaulted halls, roofed in terracotta and separated by a row of slender cast-iron columns on concrete pedestals. The columns, recognizably Corinthian, support the iron roof arches pierced with intricate vine-scroll ornamentation derived from the Renaissance

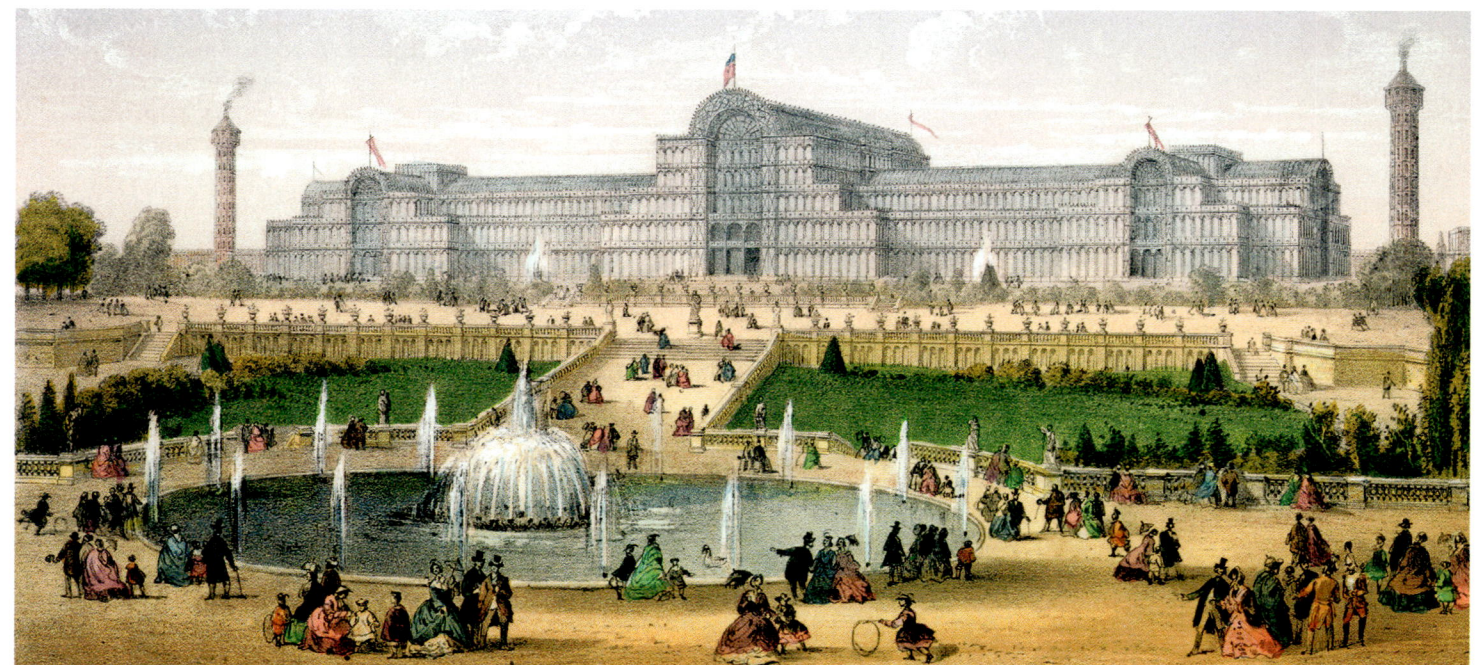

**27-47** JOSEPH PAXTON, Crystal Palace, London, England, 1850–1851; enlarged and relocated at Sydenham, England, 1852–1854. Detail of a color lithograph by ACHILLE-LOUIS MARTINET, ca. 1862. Private collection.

The tensile strength of iron enabled Paxton to experiment with a new system of glass-and-metal roof construction. Constructed of prefabricated parts, the vast Crystal Palace required only six months to build.

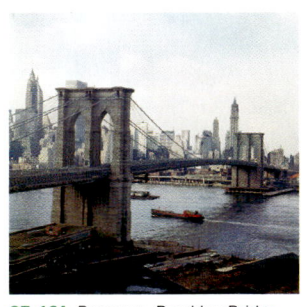

27-46A ROEBLING, Brooklyn Bridge, 1867–1883.

architectural repertoire. Labrouste's design highlights how the peculiar properties of the new structural material aesthetically transformed the shapes of traditional masonry architecture. But it is also clear how reluctant some 19th-century architects were to surrender traditional forms, even when fully aware of new possibilities for design and construction. Architects scoffed at "engineers' architecture" for many years and continued to clothe their steel-and-concrete structures in the Romantic "drapery" of a historical style. For example, the designer of the Brooklyn Bridge (FIG. 27-46A), JOHN AUGUSTUS ROEBLING (1806–1869), combined the latest steel technology with motifs from Gothic and Egyptian architecture.

**CRYSTAL PALACE** Completely "undraped" construction first became popular in the conservatories (greenhouses) of English country estates. JOSEPH PAXTON (1801–1865) built several of these structures for his patron, the duke of Devonshire. In the largest—300 feet long—he used an experimental system of glass-and-metal roof construction. Encouraged by the success of this system, Paxton submitted a winning glass-and-iron building design in the competition for the hall to house the Great Exhibition of 1851 in London, organized to present "works of industry of all nations." Paxton constructed the exhibition building, the Crystal Palace (FIG. 27-47), with prefabricated parts. This enabled workers to build the vast structure in the then-unheard-of time of six months and to dismantle it quickly at the exhibition's closing to avoid permanent obstruction of the park. The plan borrowed much from Roman and Christian basilicas, with a central flat-roofed "nave" and a barrel-vaulted crossing "transept." The design provided ample interior space to contain displays of huge machines as well as to accommodate decorative touches in the form of large working fountains and giant trees. The public admired the Crystal Palace so much that the workers who dismantled it put up an enlarged version of the glass-and-steel exhibition hall at a new location on the outskirts of London at Sydenham, where it remained until fire destroyed it in 1936. Fortunately, a few old black-and-white photographs and several color lithographs (FIG. 27-47) preserve a record of the Crystal Palace's appearance.

# PHOTOGRAPHY

A technological device of immense consequence for the modern experience was invented shortly before the mid-19th century: the camera, with its attendant art of photography. From the time Frenchman LOUIS-JACQUES-MANDÉ DAGUERRE (1789–1851) and Briton WILLIAM HENRY FOX TALBOT (1800–1877) announced the first practical photographic processes in 1839, people have celebrated photography's ability to make convincing pictures of people, places, and things. The relative ease of the process, even in its earliest and most primitive form, seemed a dream come true for scientists and artists, who for centuries had grappled with less satisfying methods of capturing accurate images of their subjects. Photography also perfectly suited an age that saw the emergence of Realism as an art movement and a pronounced shift of artistic patronage away from the elite few toward a broader base of support. The growing and increasingly powerful middle class

embraced both the comprehensible images of the new artistic medium and their lower cost.

For the traditional artist, photography suggested new answers to the great debate about what is real and how to represent the real in art. Because photography easily and accurately enabled the reproduction of three-dimensional objects on a two-dimensional surface, the new medium also challenged the place of traditional modes of pictorial representation originating in the Renaissance. Artists as diverse as Delacroix, Ingres, Courbet, and the Impressionist Edgar Degas (see Chapter 28) welcomed photography as a helpful auxiliary to painting. Other artists, however, feared the camera was a mechanism that would displace the painstaking work of skilled painters. From the moment of its invention, photography threatened to expropriate the realistic image, until then the exclusive property of painting. But just as some painters looked to the new medium of photography for answers on how best to render an image in paint, so some photographers looked to painting for suggestions about ways to imbue the photographic image with qualities beyond simple reproduction. Indeed, the first subjects photographers chose to record were traditional painting themes, for example, still lifes and portraits—in part to establish photography as a legitimate artistic medium on a par with painting. A debate immediately began over whether the photograph was an art form or if the camera was merely a scientific instrument. An 1862 court case provided the answer: Photography was an art, and photographs were entitled to copyright protection.

Artists themselves were instrumental in the development of the new photographic technology. The camera obscura was familiar to 18th-century artists. In 1807, the invention of the *camera lucida* (lighted room) replaced the enclosed chamber of the camera obscura. Now the photographer aimed a small prism lens, hung on a stand, downward at an object. The lens projected the image of the object onto a sheet of paper. Artists using either of these devices found the process long and arduous, no matter how accurate the resulting work. All yearned for a more direct way to capture a subject's image. Two very different scientific inventions that accomplished this—the *daguerreotype* and the *calotype* (see "Daguerreotypes, Calotypes, and Wet-Plate Photography," page 792)—appeared almost simultaneously in France and England in 1839.

**DAGUERREOTYPES** The French government presented the new daguerreotype process at the Academy of Science in Paris on January 7, 1839, with the understanding that its details would be made available to all interested parties without charge (although the inventor received a large annuity in appreciation). Soon, people worldwide began making pictures with the daguerreotype "camera" (a name shortened from camera obscura) in a process almost immediately christened "photography," from the Greek *photos* (light) and *graphos* (writing). From the start, the possibilities of the process as a new art medium intrigued painters. Paul Delaroche (1797–1856), a leading academic painter of the day, wrote in an official report to the French government that anticipated the 1862 legal ruling:

> Daguerre's process completely satisfies all the demands of art, carrying certain essential principles of art to such perfection that it must become a subject of observation and study even to the most accomplished painters. The pictures obtained by this method are as remarkable for the perfection of the details as for the richness and harmony of the general effect. Nature is reproduced in them not only with truth, but also with art.[14]

# Daguerreotypes, Calotypes, and Wet-Plate Photography

The earliest photographic processes were the *daguerreotype* (FIGS. 27-48 and 27-49), named after L.J.M. Daguerre, and the *calotype* (FIG. 27-54). Daguerre was an architect and theatrical set painter and designer. This background led Daguerre and a partner to open a popular entertainment called the Diorama. Audiences witnessed performances of "living paintings" created by changing the lighting effects on a "sandwich" composed of a painted backdrop and several layers of painted translucent front curtains. Daguerre used a camera obscura for the Diorama, but he wanted to find a more efficient and effective procedure. Through a mutual acquaintance, he met Joseph Nicéphore Niépce (1765–1833), who in 1826 had successfully made a permanent picture of the cityscape outside his upper-story window by exposing, in a camera obscura, a metal plate covered with a light-sensitive coating. Niépce's process, however, had the significant drawback that it required an eight-hour exposure time. After Niépce died in 1833, Daguerre continued his work, making two important discoveries. Latent development—that is, bringing out the image through treatment in chemical solutions—considerably shortened the length of time needed for exposure. Daguerre also discovered a better way to "fix" the image by chemically stopping the action of light on the photographic plate, which otherwise would continue to darken until the image turned solid black.

The daguerreotype reigned supreme in photography until the 1850s, but the second major photographic invention, the ancestor of the modern negative-print system, eventually replaced it. On January 31, 1839, less than three weeks after Daguerre unveiled his method in Paris, William Henry Fox Talbot presented a paper on his "photogenic drawings" to the Royal Institution in London. As early as 1835, Talbot made "negative" images by placing objects on sensitized paper and exposing the arrangement to light. This created a design of light-colored silhouettes recording the places where opaque or translucent objects had blocked light from darkening the paper's emulsion. In his experiments, Talbot next exposed sensitized papers inside simple cameras and, with a second sheet, created "positive" images. He further improved the process with more light-sensitive chemicals and a chemical development of the negative image. This technique enabled multiple prints. However, in Talbot's process, which he named the calotype (from the Greek word *kalos,* "beautiful"), the photographic images incorporated the texture of the paper. This produced a slightly blurred, grainy effect very different from the crisp detail and wide tonal range available with the daguerreotype. Also discouraging widespread adoption of the calotype were the stiff licensing and equipment fees charged for many years after Talbot patented his new process in 1841.

One of the earliest masters of an improved kind of calotype photography was the multitalented Frenchman known as Nadar (FIGS. 27-50 and 27-51). He used glass negatives and albumen (prepared with egg white) printing paper (FIGS. 27-52 and 27-53), which could record finer detail and a wider range of light and shadow than Talbot's calotype process. The new *wet-plate* technology (so named because the photographic plate was exposed, developed, and fixed while wet) almost at once became the universal way of making negatives until 1880. However, wet-plate photography had drawbacks. The plates had to be prepared and processed on the spot. Working outdoors meant taking along a portable darkroom—a wagon, tent, or box with light-tight sleeves for the photographer's arms.

Refinements of these early processes served photographers well for a century and a half but have been largely supplanted today by digital photography (see Chapter 31).

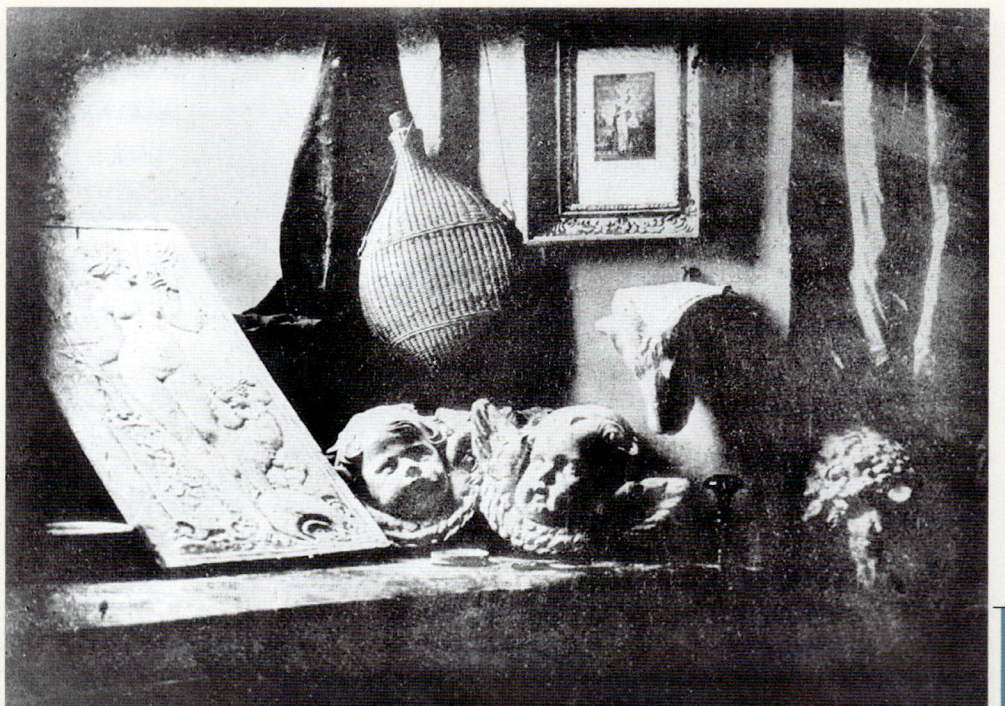

**27-48** LOUIS-JACQUES-MANDÉ DAGUERRE, *Still Life in Studio,* 1837. Daguerreotype, $6\frac{1}{4}'' \times 8\frac{1}{4}''$. Société Française de Photographie, Paris. ◼◀

One of the first plates Daguerre produced after perfecting his new photographic process was this still life, in which he was able to capture amazing detail and finely graduated tones of light and shadow.

1 in.

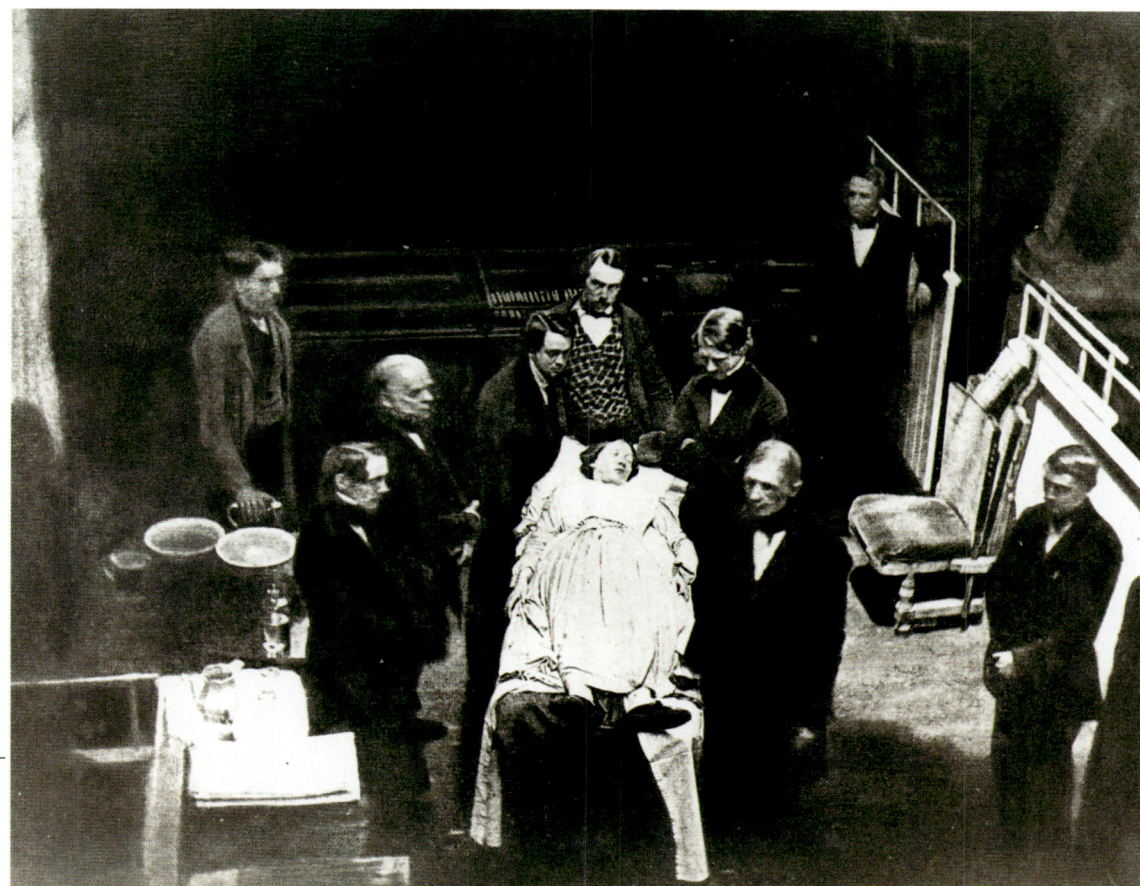

27-49 JOSIAH JOHNSON HAWES and ALBERT SANDS SOUTHWORTH, *Early Operation under Ether, Massachusetts General Hospital*, ca. 1847. Daguerreotype, $6\frac{1}{2}'' \times 8\frac{1}{2}''$. Massachusetts General Hospital Archives and Special Collections, Boston. ◾◄

In this early daguerreotype, which predates Eakins's *The Gross Clinic* (FIG. 27-36) by almost 30 years, Hawes and Southworth demonstrated the documentary power of the new medium of photography.

1 in.

Unlike photographs people make today, whether printed from traditional film negatives or from computerized digital images, each daguerreotype is a unique work. *Still Life in Studio* (FIG. **27-48**) is one of the first successful plates Daguerre produced after perfecting his method. The process captured every detail—the subtle forms, the varied textures, the finely graduated tones of light and shadow—in Daguerre's carefully constructed tableau. The three-dimensional forms of the sculptures, the basket, and the bits of cloth spring into high relief. The inspiration for the composition came from 17th-century Dutch vanitas still lifes, such as those of Pieter Claesz (FIG. 25-1). As did Claesz, Daguerre arranged his objects to reveal their textures and shapes clearly. Unlike a painter, Daguerre could not alter anything within his arrangement to create a stronger image. However, he could suggest a symbolic meaning through his choice of objects. Like the skull and timepiece in Claesz's painting, Daguerre's sculptural and architectural fragments and the framed print of an embrace suggest even art is vanitas and will not endure forever.

**HAWES AND SOUTHWORTH** In the United States, photographers began to make daguerreotypes within two months of Daguerre's presentation in Paris. Two particularly avid and resourceful advocates of the new medium were JOSIAH JOHNSON HAWES (1808–1901), a painter, and ALBERT SANDS SOUTHWORTH (1811–1894), a pharmacist and teacher. Together, they ran a daguerreotype studio in Boston specializing in portraiture, then popular due to the shortened exposure time required for the process (although it was still long enough to require head braces to help subjects remain motionless while photographers recorded their images).

The partners also took their equipment outside the studio to record places and events of particular interest to them. One resultant image is *Early Operation under Ether, Massachusetts General Hospital* (FIG. **27-49**). This daguerreotype, taken from the vantage point of the gallery of a hospital operating room, put the viewer in the position of medical students looking down on a lecture-demonstration typical throughout the 19th century. An image of historical record, this early daguerreotype predates Eakins's *Gross Clinic* (FIG. 27-36) by almost three decades. The focus of attention in *Early Operation* is the white-draped patient surrounded by a circle of darkly clad doctors. The details of the figures and the room's furnishings are in sharp focus, but the slight blurring of several of the figures betrays motion during the exposure. The elevated viewpoint flattens the spatial perspective and emphasizes the relationships of the figures in ways the Impressionists, especially Degas, found intriguing.

**NADAR** Portraiture was one of the first photography genres to use a technology that improved the calotype. Making portraits was an important economic opportunity for most photographers, as Southworth and Hawes proved, but the greatest of the early portrait photographers was undoubtedly Gaspar-Félix Tournachon. Known simply as NADAR (1820–1910), Tournachon was a French novelist, journalist, enthusiastic balloonist, and caricaturist, who became an early champion of photography. Photographic studies for his caricatures led Nadar to open a portrait studio. So talented was he at capturing the essence of his subjects that the most important people in France, including Delacroix, Daumier, Courbet, and Manet, flocked to his studio to have their portraits made. Nadar said he sought in his work "that instant of understanding that puts you in touch with the model—helps you sum him up,

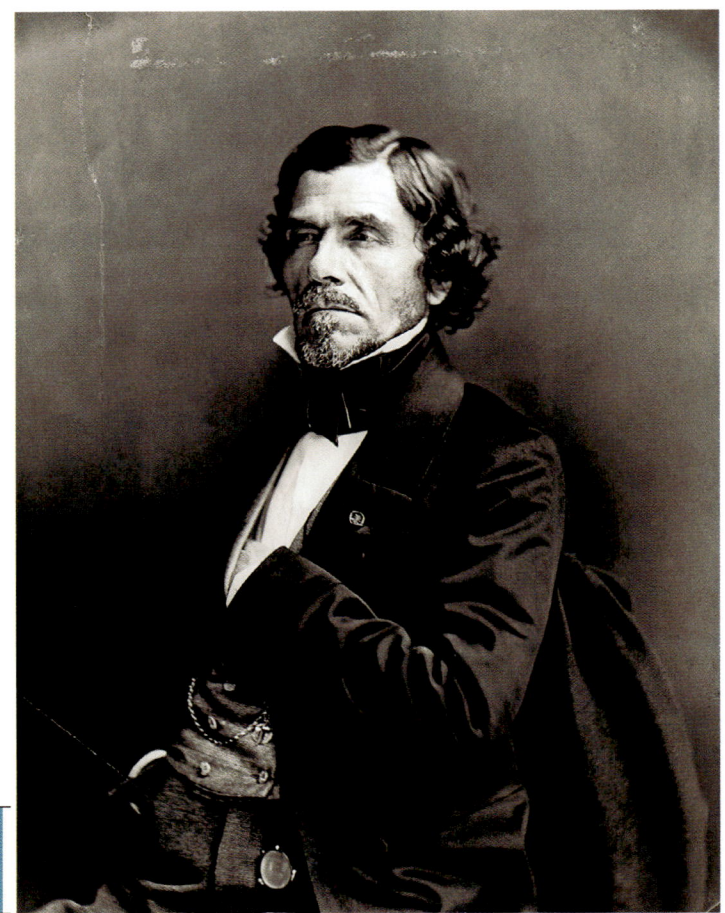

**27-50** Nadar, *Eugène Delacroix*, ca. 1855. Modern print, $8\frac{1}{2}'' \times 6\frac{2}{3}''$, from the original negative. Bibliothèque Nationale, Paris.

Nadar was one of the earliest portrait photographers. His prints of the leading artists of the day, such as this one of Delacroix, reveal the sitters' personalities as well as record their features.

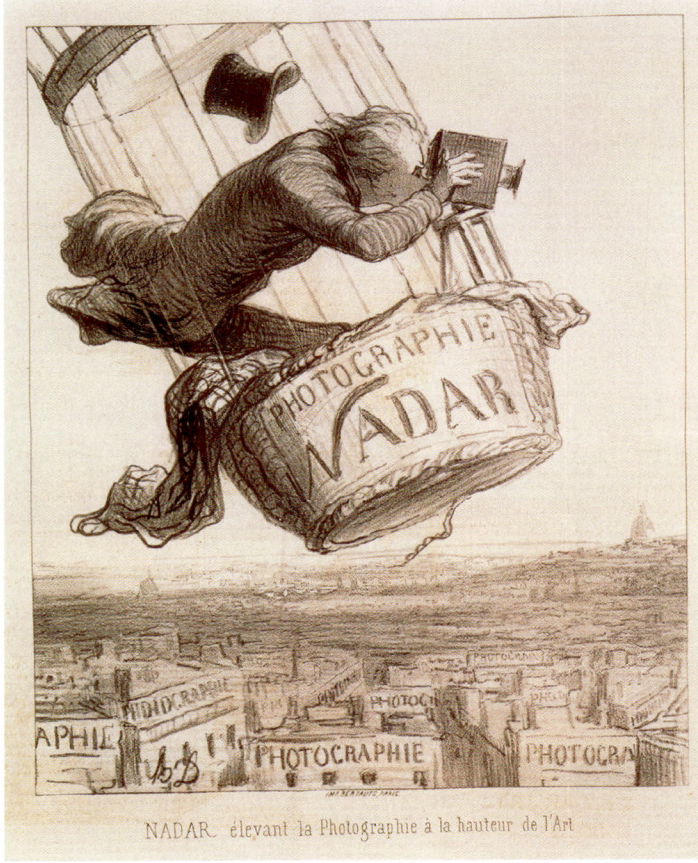

NADAR élevant la Photographie à la hauteur de l'Art

**27-51** Honoré Daumier, *Nadar Raising Photography to the Height of Art*, 1862. Lithograph, $10\frac{3}{4}'' \times 8\frac{3}{4}''$. Museum of Fine Arts, Boston.

Daumier's lithograph of Nadar (FIG. 27-50) in a balloon "elevating the art of photography" commemorates a court decision acknowledging photographs as artworks protected by copyright.

guides you to his habits, his ideas, and character and enables you to produce . . . a really convincing and sympathetic likeness, an intimate portrait."[15]

Nadar's *Eugène Delacroix* (FIG. **27-50**) shows the painter at the height of his career. In this photograph, the artist appears with remarkable presence. Even in half-length, his gesture and expression create a mood that seems to reveal much about him. Perhaps Delacroix responded to Nadar's famous gift for putting his clients at ease by assuming the pose that best expressed his personality. The new photographic materials made possible the rich range of tones in Nadar's images.

Nadar achieved so much fame for his wet-plate photographic portraits (see "Daguerreotypes, Calotypes, and Wet-Plate Photography," page 792) that he became the subject of a Daumier lithograph (FIG. **27-51**) that provides incisive and amusing commentary about the struggle of photography to be recognized as a fine art. Daumier made his print in response to the 1862 court decision acknowledging photographs were indeed artworks. In the lithograph, Nadar energetically takes pictures with his camera as his balloon rises over Parisian rooftops—Daumier's literal representation of the elevation of photography's status the French judge reaffirmed. The image also refers to the fact that Nadar was a staunch advocate of balloon transportation and aerial reconnaissance. He produced the first aerial photographs of Paris in 1858 from his balloon *Le Géant* (The Giant).

**JULIA MARGARET CAMERON** Among the most famous portrait photographers in 19th-century England was Julia Margaret Cameron (1815–1879), who did not take up photography seriously until the age of 48. Although she produced images of many well-known men of the period, including Charles Darwin, Alfred Tennyson, and Thomas Carlyle, she photographed more women than men, as was true of many women photographers. *Ophelia, Study No. 2* (FIG. **27-52**) typifies her portrait style. Cameron often depicted her female subjects as characters in literary or biblical narratives. The slightly blurred focus also became a distinctive feature of her work—the byproduct of photographing with a lens with a short focal length, which allowed only a small area of sharp focus. The blurriness adds an ethereal, dreamlike tone to the photographs, appropriate for Cameron's fictional "characters." Her photograph of Ophelia has a mysterious, fragile quality reminiscent of Pre-Raphaelite paintings (FIG. 27-41) of literary heroines.

**TIMOTHY O'SULLIVAN** Photographers were quick to realize the documentary power of their new medium. Thus began the story of photography's influence on modern life and of the immense changes it brought to communication and information management. Historical events could be recorded in permanent form on the spot for the first time. The photographs taken of the Crimean War (1856) by Roger Fenton (1819–1869) and of the American Civil War by Mathew B. Brady (1823–1896), Alexander Gardner (1821–1882),

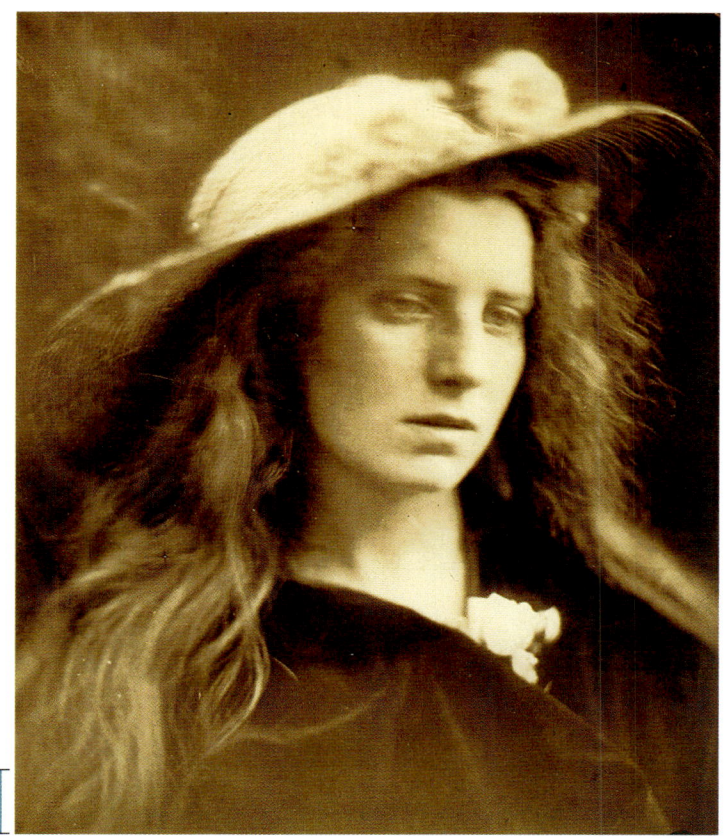

**27-52** JULIA MARGARET CAMERON, *Ophelia, Study No. 2*, 1867. Albumen print, 1′ 1″ × 10⅔″. George Eastman House, Rochester (gift of Eastman Kodak Company; formerly Gabriel Cromer Collection).

Cameron was a prominent 19th-century photographer who often depicted her female subjects as characters in literary or biblical narratives. The slightly blurred focus is a distinctive feature of her work.

and TIMOTHY O'SULLIVAN (1840–1882) remain unsurpassed as incisive accounts of military life, unsparing in their truth to detail and poignant as expressions of human experience.

Of the Civil War photographs, the most moving are the inhumanly objective records of combat deaths. Perhaps the most reproduced of these Civil War photographs is Gardner's print of O'Sullivan's *A Harvest of Death, Gettysburg, Pennsylvania* (FIG. **27-53**). Although viewers could regard this image as simple reportage, it also functions to impress on people the high price of war. Corpses litter the battlefield as far as the eye can see. O'Sullivan presented a scene stretching far to the horizon. As the photograph modulates from the precise clarity of the bodies of Union soldiers in the foreground, boots stolen and pockets picked, to the indistinct corpses in the distance, the suggestion of innumerable other dead soldiers is unavoidable. This "harvest" is far more sobering and depressing than that in Winslow Homer's Civil War painting, *Veteran in a New Field* (FIG. 27-35). Though it was years before photolithography could reproduce photographs such as this in newspapers, photographers exhibited them publicly. They made an impression newsprint engravings never could.

**27-53** TIMOTHY O'SULLIVAN, *A Harvest of Death, Gettysburg, Pennsylvania*, 1863. Negative by Timothy O'Sullivan. Albumen print by ALEXANDER GARDNER, 6¾″ × 8¾″. New York Public Library (Astor, Lenox and Tilden Foundations, Rare Books and Manuscript Division), New York. 🎥

Wet-plate technology enabled photographers to record historical events on the spot— and to comment on the high price of war, as in this photograph of dead Union soldiers at Gettysburg in 1863.

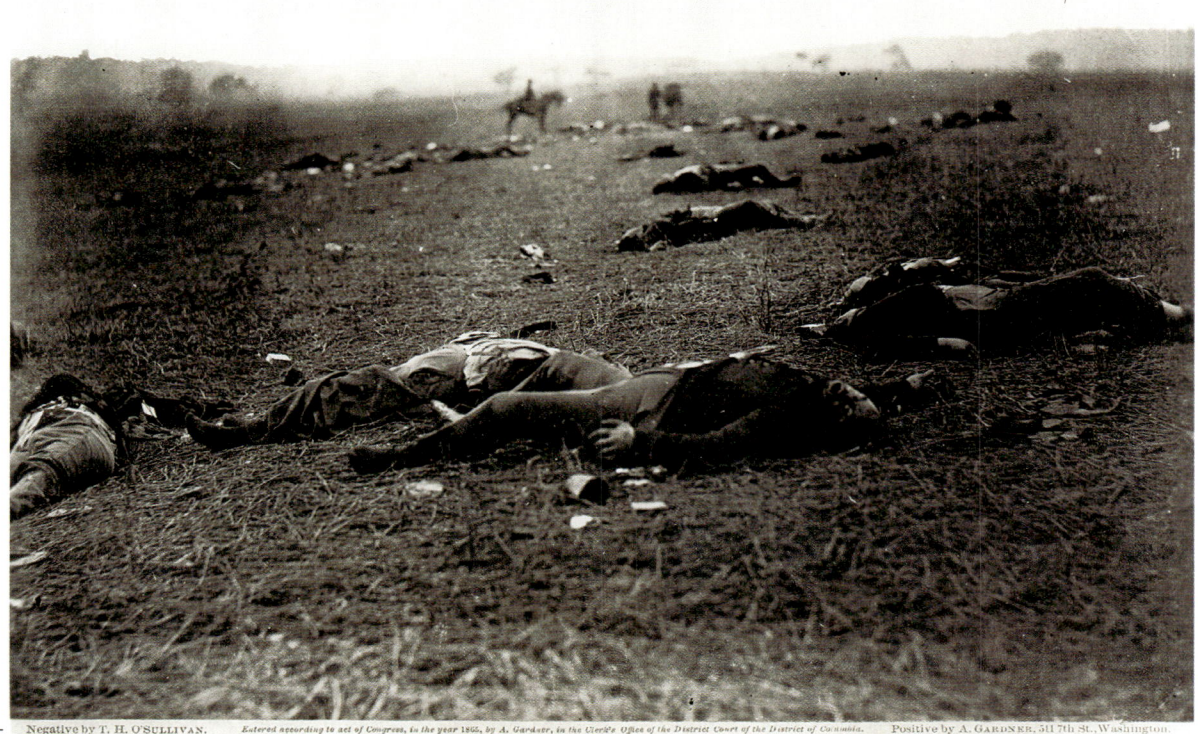

Negative by T. H. O'SULLIVAN.    Entered according to act of Congress, in the year 1865, by A. Gardner, in the Clerk's Office of the District Court of the District of Columbia.    Positive by A. GARDNER, 511 7th St., Washington.

A HARVEST OF DEATH, GETTYSBURG, PENNSYLVANIA.

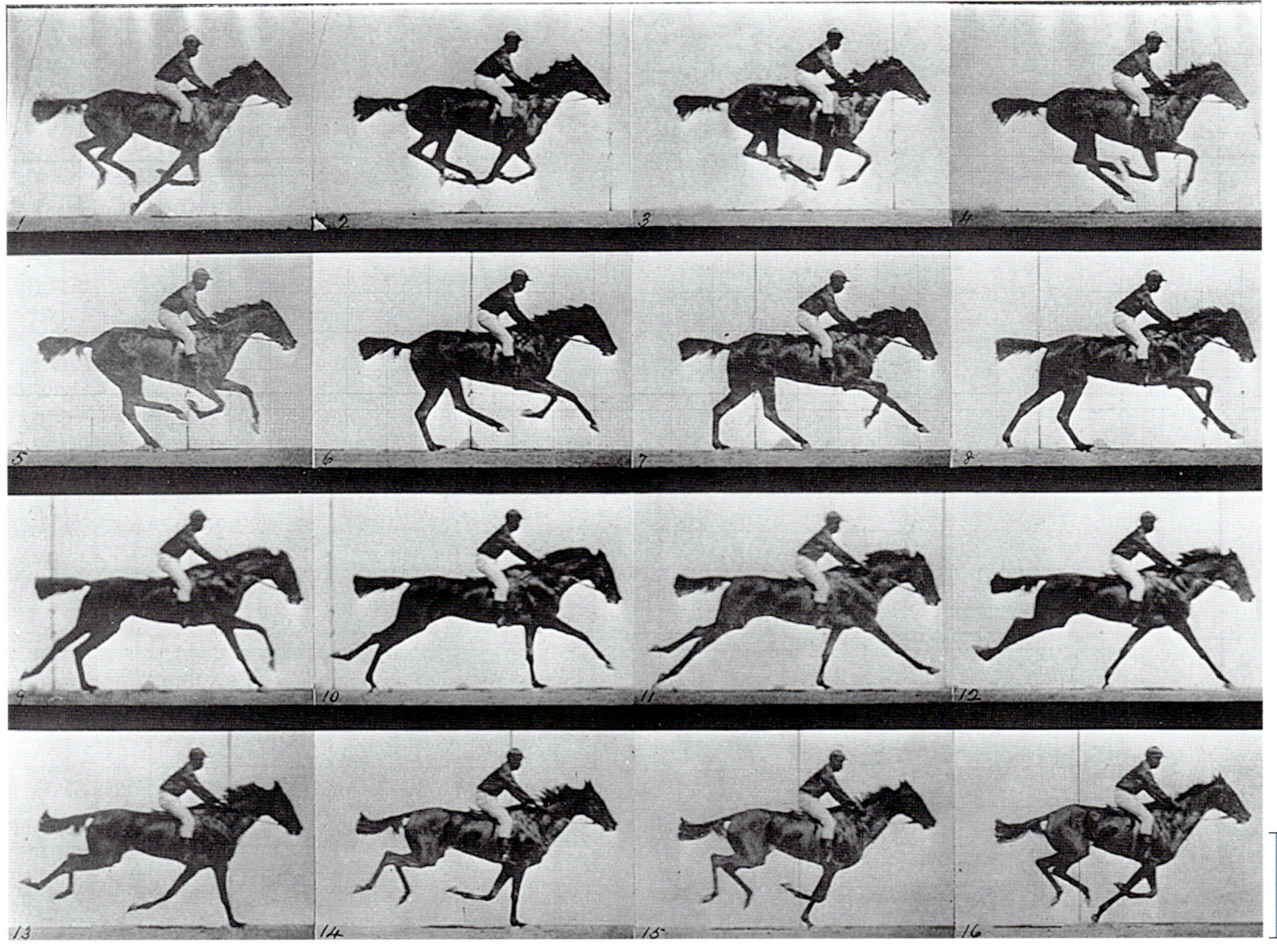

1 in.

**27-54** EADWEARD MUYBRIDGE, *Horse Galloping,* 1878. Calotype print, 9″ × 12″. George Eastman House, Rochester. ◼◀

Muybridge specialized in photographic studies of the successive stages in human and animal motion—details too quick for the human eye to capture. Modern cinema owes a great deal to his work.

**EADWEARD MUYBRIDGE** The Realist photographer and scientist EADWEARD MUYBRIDGE (1830–1904) came to the United States from England in the 1850s and settled in San Francisco, where he established a prominent international reputation for his photographs of the western United States. In 1872, the governor of California, Leland Stanford (1824–1893), sought Muybridge's assistance in settling a bet about whether, at any point in a stride, all four feet of a horse galloping at top speed are off the ground. Through his sequential photography, as seen in *Horse Galloping* (FIG. **27-54**), Muybridge proved they were. This experience was the beginning of Muybridge's photographic studies of the successive stages in human and animal motion—details too quick for the human eye to capture. These investigations culminated in 1885 at the University of Pennsylvania with a series of multiple-camera motion studies that recorded separate photographs of progressive moments in a single action. Muybridge's discoveries received extensive publicity through the book *Animal Locomotion* (1887), and his motion photographs earned him a place in the history of science, as well

as art. These sequential motion studies, along with those of Eakins and Marey, influenced many other artists, including their contemporary, the painter and sculptor Edgar Degas (FIG. 28-10), and 20th-century artists such as Marcel Duchamp (FIG. 29-35).

Muybridge presented his work to scientists and general audiences with a device called the *zoopraxiscope,* which he invented to project his sequences of images (mounted on special glass plates) onto a screen. The result was so lifelike one viewer said it "threw upon the screen apparently the living, moving animals. Nothing was wanting but the clatter of hoofs upon the turf."[16] The illusion of motion in Muybridge's photographic exhibits was the result of a physical fact of human eyesight called "persistence of vision." Stated simply, it means the brain retains whatever the eye sees for a fraction of a second after the eye stops seeing it. Thus, viewers saw a rapid succession of different images merging one into the next, producing the illusion of continuous change. This illusion lies at the heart of the motion-picture industry that debuted in the 20th century. Thus, with Muybridge's innovations in photography, yet another new art form was born—the cinema.

# ROMANTICISM, REALISM, PHOTOGRAPHY: EUROPE AND AMERICA, 1800 TO 1870

## ART UNDER NAPOLEON

- As Emperor of the French from 1804 to 1815, Napoleon embraced the Neoclassical style in order to associate his regime with the empire of ancient Rome. Roman temples were the models for La Madeleine in Paris, which Pierre Vignon built as a temple of glory for France's imperial armies.

- Napoleon chose Jacques-Louis David as First Painter of the Empire. His favorite sculptor was Antonio Canova, who carved marble Neoclassical portraits of the imperial family, including a reclining image of Napoleon's sister, Pauline Borghese, in the guise of Venus.

- The beginning of a break from Neoclassicism can already be seen in the work of some of David's students, including Gros, Girodet-Trioson, and Ingres, all of whom painted some exotic subjects reflecting Romantic taste.

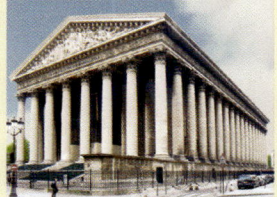

Vignon, La Madeleine, Paris, 1807–1842

## ROMANTICISM

- The roots of Romanticism are in the 18th century, but usually the term more narrowly denotes the artistic movement that flourished from 1800 to 1840, between Neoclassicism and Realism. Romantic artists gave precedence to feeling and imagination over Enlightenment reason. Romantic painters explored the exotic, erotic, and fantastic in their art.

- In Spain, Francisco Goya's *Los Caprichos* series celebrated the unleashing of imagination, emotions, and even nightmares. In France, Eugène Delacroix led the way in depicting Romantic narratives set in faraway places and distant times. Ancient Assyria, for example, is the subject of his colorful *Death of Sardanapalus*.

- Romantic painters often chose landscapes as an ideal subject to express the theme of the soul unified with the natural world. Masters of the transcendental landscape include Friedrich in Germany, Constable and Turner in England, and Cole, Bierstadt, and Church in the United States.

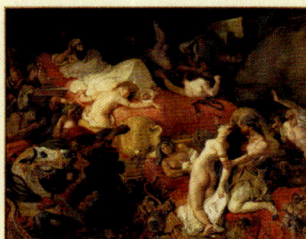

Delacroix, *Death of Sardanapalus*, 1827

## REALISM

- Realism developed as an artistic movement in mid-19th-century France. Its leading proponent was Gustave Courbet, whose paintings of menial laborers and ordinary people exemplify his belief that painters should depict only their own time and place. Honoré Daumier boldly confronted authority with his satirical lithographs commenting on the plight of the urban working classes. Édouard Manet shocked the public with his paintings featuring promiscuous women, and his rough brushstrokes, which emphasized the flatness of the painting surface, paved the way for modern abstract art.

- Among the leading American Realists were Winslow Homer, Thomas Eakins, and John Singer Sargent. Eakins's painting of surgery in progress was too brutally realistic for the Philadelphia art jury that rejected it.

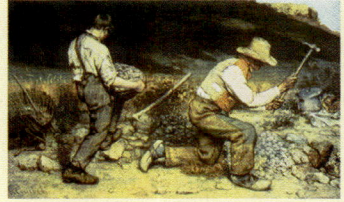

Courbet, *The Stone Breakers*, 1849

## ARCHITECTURE

- Territorial expansion, the Romantic interest in exotic locales and earlier eras, and nationalistic pride led to the revival in the 19th century of older architectural styles, especially the Gothic, exemplified by London's Houses of Parliament.

- By the middle of the century, many architects had already abandoned sentimental and Romantic designs from the past in favor of exploring the possibilities of cast-iron construction, as in Henri Labrouste's Saint-Geneviève Library in Paris and Joseph Paxton's Crystal Palace in London.

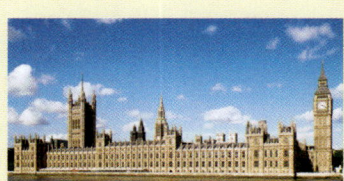

Barry and Pugin, Houses of Parliament, London, 1835

## PHOTOGRAPHY

- In 1839, Daguerre in Paris and Talbot in London invented the first practical photographic processes. In 1862, a French court formally recognized photography as an art form subject to copyright protection. Many of the earliest photographers, including Nadar and Cameron, specialized in portrait photography, but others, including Hawes, Southworth, and O'Sullivan in the United States quickly realized the documentary power of the new medium. Muybridge's sequential photos of human and animal motion were the forerunners of the modern cinema.

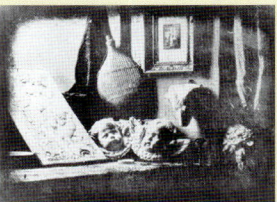

Daguerre, *Still Life in Studio*, 1837

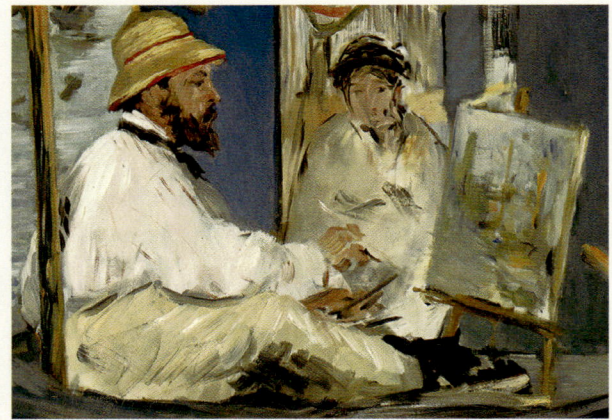

In summer 1874, Manet recorded Monet painting—*en plein air* directly on canvas without any preliminary sketchpreliminar— in his floating studio on the Seine at Argenteuil, 22 minutes from Paris by train.

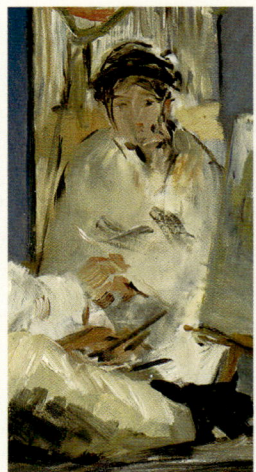

With Monet is his wife, Camille Doncieux. Monet, underappreciated as an artist, had recently sold some paintings, enabling the couple to purchase the small boat he equipped with a cabin and easel.

In this painting, Manet adopted not only Monet's Impressionist subject matter but also the younger artist's short brushstrokes and fascination with the reflection of sunlight on water.

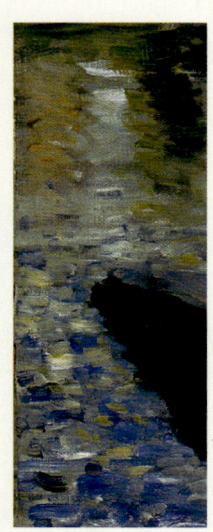

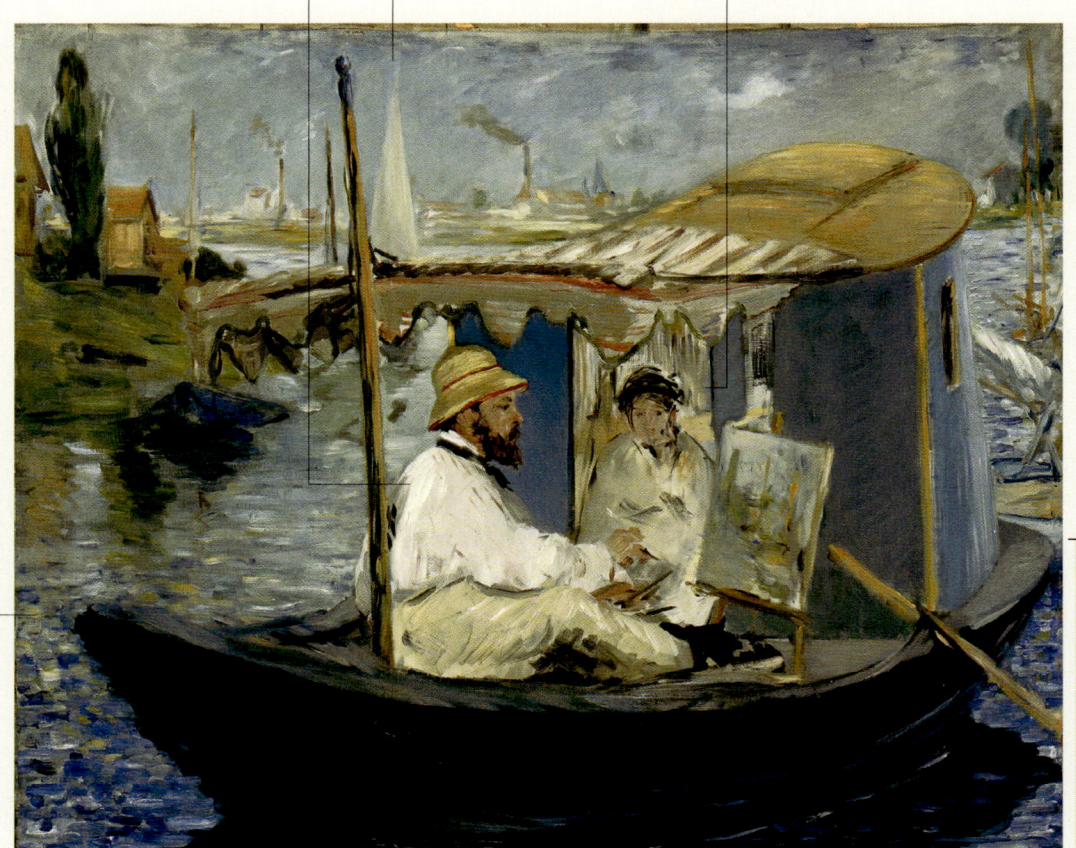

**28-1** Édouard Manet, *Claude Monet in His Studio Boat,* 1874. Oil on canvas, 2′ 8″ × 3′ 3¼″. Neue Pinakothek, Munich. ◼◀

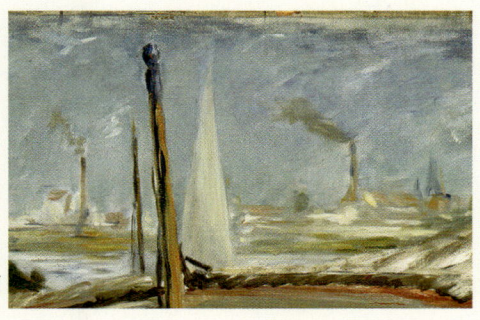

In the distance are the factories and smokestacks of Argenteuil. Manet thus recorded the two poles of modern life—the leisure activities of the bourgeosie and the industrialization along the Seine.

# IMPRESSIONISM, POST-IMPRESSIONISM, SYMBOLISM: EUROPE AND AMERICA, 1870 TO 1900

## IMPRESSIONS OF MODERN LIFE

*Impressionism* was an art movement born in late-19th-century industrialized, urbanized Paris as a reaction to the sometimes brutal and chaotic transformation of French life, which made the world seem unstable and insubstantial. As the poet and critic Charles Baudelaire (1821–1867) observed in his 1860 essay *The Painter of Modern Life*: "[M]odernity is the transitory, the fugitive, the contingent."[1] Accordingly, Impressionist painters built upon the innovations of the Realists in turning away from traditional mythological and religious themes in favor of daily life, but they sought to convey the elusiveness and impermanence of the subjects they portrayed.

In 1872, the painter CLAUDE MONET (1840–1926), a leading Impressionist, moved to Argenteuil, a prosperous industrial town on the Seine (MAP **28-1**) that was also a favorite leisure destination of the city dwellers of Paris—only 22 minutes by train from the Saint-Lazare train station (FIG. 28-4). Situated at a point where the river widened into a deep basin, Argenteuil was an ideal spot for boating of all kinds, from casual rowing to formal regattas. In 1873, after accumulating enough money from recent sales of his paintings, the underappreciated and financially strapped Monet was able to purchase a small boat, which he equipped with a tiny wooden cabin and a striped awning and used as his floating studio.

During the summer of 1874, Édouard Manet (FIGS. 27-32 and 27-33) joined Monet at Argenteuil and painted side-by-side with the younger artist. One day, Manet recorded Monet in his studio boat (FIG. **28-1**) at work on *Sailboats on the Seine, Argenteuil,* a painting now in the Fine Arts Museum of San Francisco. Monet, wearing a straw hat, sits at the front of the boat with his easel before him. Camille Doncieux, Monet's wife (compare FIG. 28-2A), is at once the painter's admirer and his muse. In the distance are the factories and smokestacks that represent the opposite pole of life at Argenteuil. In capturing both the leisure activities of the bourgeoisie and the industrialization along the Seine in the 1870s on the same canvas, Manet, like Monet, was fulfilling Baudelaire's definition of "the painter of modern life."

*Claude Monet in His Studio Boat* is noteworthy as a document of Monet's preference for painting outdoors (*en plein air*)—a radical practice at the time—in order to record his "impression" of the Seine by placing colors directly on a white canvas without any preliminary sketch—also a sharp break from traditional studio techniques. The painting further attests to Monet's influence on his older friend Manet, who here adopted the younger painter's subject matter, short brushstrokes, and fascination with the reflection of light on water.

FRAMING THE ERA

# MARXISM, DARWINISM, MODERNISM

The momentous developments of the early 19th century in Europe—industrialization, urbanization, and increased economic and political interaction worldwide—matured during the latter half of the century. The Industrial Revolution born in England spread so rapidly to the Continent and the United States that historians often refer to the third quarter of the 19th century as the second Industrial Revolution. Whereas the first Industrial Revolution centered on textiles, steam, and iron, the second focused on steel, electricity, chemicals, and oil. The discoveries in these fields provided the foundation for developments in plastics, machinery, building construction, and automobile manufacturing and paved the way for the invention of the radio, electric light, telephone, and electric streetcar.

A significant consequence of industrialization was urbanization. The number and size of Western cities grew dramatically during the latter part of the 19th century, largely due to migration from the countryside. Farmers in large numbers relocated to urban centers because expanded agricultural enterprises squeezed smaller property owners from their land. The widely available work opportunities in the cities, especially in the factories, were also a major factor in this population shift. Improving health and living conditions in the cities further contributed to their explosive growth.

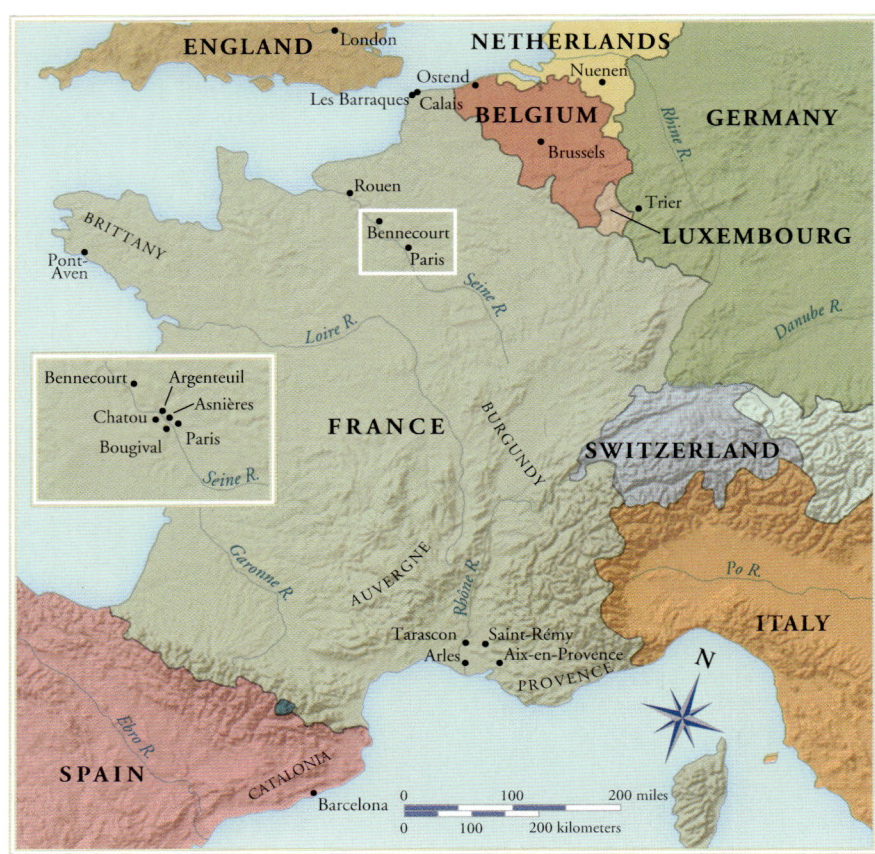

**MAP 28-1** France around 1870.

**MARXISM AND DARWINISM** The rise of the urban working class was fundamental to the ideas of Karl Marx (1818–1883), one of the era's dominant figures. Born in Trier, Germany, Marx received a doctorate in philosophy from the University of Berlin. After moving to Paris, he met fellow German Friedrich Engels (1820–1895), who became his lifelong collaborator. Together they wrote *The Communist Manifesto* (1848), which called for the working class to overthrow the capitalist system. As did other 19th-century empiricists, Marx believed scientific, rational law governed nature and, indeed, all human history. For Marx, economic forces based on class struggle induced historical change. Throughout history, insisted Marx, those who controlled the means of production conflicted with those whose labor they exploited for their own enrichment—a dynamic he called "dialectical materialism." Marx advocated the creation of a socialist state in which the working class seized power and destroyed capitalism. This new political, social, and economic system—Marxism—held great appeal for the oppressed as well as for many intellectuals.

Equally influential was the English naturalist Charles Darwin (1809–1882), whose theory of natural selection did much to increase interest in science. Darwin and his compatriot Alfred Russel Wallace (1823–1913), working independently, proposed a model for the process of evolution based on mechanistic laws, rather than attributing evolution to random chance or God's plan. They postulated a competitive system in which only the fittest survived. Darwin's controversial ideas, as presented in *On the Origin of Species by Means of Natural Selection* (1859), contradicted the biblical narrative of creation. By challenging traditional religious beliefs, Darwinism contributed to growing secularism.

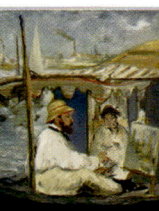

## IMPRESSIONISM, POST-IMPRESSIONISM, SYMBOLISM: EUROPE AND AMERICA, 1870 TO 1900

| 1870 | 1880 | 1890 | 1900 |
|------|------|------|------|
| ▌ Claude Monet and the Impressionists mount their first independent exhibition in Paris<br>▌ Monet, Pierre-Auguste Renoir, Berthe Morisot, and other Impressionists paint landscapes and bourgeois life outdoors<br>▌ European artists begin to collect Japanese prints<br>▌ Gustave Moreau explores eroticism and fantasy in Symbolist paintings | ▌ Georges Seurat develops pointillism<br>▌ Vincent van Gogh moves to France and explores the expressive power of color<br>▌ Auguste Rodin receives the commission for *Gates of Hell*<br>▌ Alexandre-Gustave Eiffel builds the Eiffel Tower in Paris | ▌ Paul Cézanne seeks "to do Poussin over entirely from nature"<br>▌ The Art Nouveau movement emerges in architecture and the decorative arts<br>▌ Gustav Klimt's paintings epitomize fin-de-siècle culture in Austria<br>▌ Louis Sullivan builds steel, glass, and stone skyscrapers in America | |

Other theorists and social thinkers, most notably British philosopher Herbert Spencer (1820–1903), applied Darwin's principles to the rapidly changing socioeconomic realm. As in the biological world, they asserted, industrialization's intense competition led to the survival of the most economically fit companies, enterprises, and countries. The social Darwinists provided Western nations with justification for the colonization of peoples and cultures they deemed less advanced. By 1900, the major economic and political powers had divided up much of the world. The French had colonized most of North Africa and Indochina, while the British occupied India, Australia, and large areas of Africa, including Nigeria, Egypt, Sudan, Rhodesia, and the Union of South Africa. The Dutch were a major presence in the Pacific, and the Germans, Portuguese, Spanish, and Italians all established themselves in various areas of Africa.

**MODERNISM** The combination of extensive technological changes and increased exposure to other cultures, coupled with the rapidity of these changes, led to an acute sense in Western cultures of the world's impermanence. Darwin's ideas of evolution and Marx's emphasis on a continuing sequence of conflicts reinforced this awareness of a constantly shifting reality. These societal changes in turn fostered a new and multifaceted artistic approach that art historians call *modernism*. Modernist artists seek to capture the images and sensibilities of their age, but modernism transcends the simple depiction of the contemporary world—the goal of Realism (see Chapter 27). Modernist artists also critically examine the premises of art itself, as Manet did in his seminal 1863 painting *Le Déjeuner sur l'Herbe* (FIG. 27-32). Modernism thus implies certain concerns about art and aesthetics internal to art production, regardless of whether the artist is portraying modern life. Clement Greenberg (1909–1994), an influential American art critic who wrote about the revolutionary art movements of the decades following World War II (see Chapter 30), explained:

> The essence of Modernism lies . . . in the use of the characteristic methods of a discipline to criticize the discipline itself—not in order to subvert it, but to entrench it more firmly in its area of competence. . . . Realistic, illusionist art had dissembled the medium, using art to conceal art. Modernism used art to call attention to art. The limitations that constitute the medium of painting—the flat surface, the shape of the support, the properties of pigment—were treated by the Old Masters as negative factors that could be acknowledged only implicitly or indirectly. Modernist painting has come to regard these same limitations as positive factors that are to be acknowledged openly.[2]

Although the work of Gustave Courbet and the Realists already expressed this modernist viewpoint, modernism emerged even more forcefully in the late-19th-century movements that art historians call Impressionism, Post-Impressionism, and Symbolism.

# IMPRESSIONISM

A hostile critic applied the term *Impressionism* in response to Claude Monet's *Impression: Sunrise* (FIG. 28-2), exhibited in the first Impressionist show in 1874 (see "Academic Salons and Independent Art Exhibitions," page 802). Although the critic intended the label to be derogatory, by the third Impressionist show in 1878, the artists had embraced it and were calling themselves Impressionists.

**CLAUDE MONET** Artists and critics had used the term *Impressionism* before, but only in relation to sketches. Impression-ist paintings do incorporate the qualities of sketches—abbreviation, speed, and spontaneity. This is apparent in *Impression: Sunrise* (FIG. 28-2), in which Monet made no attempt to disguise the brushstrokes or blend the pigment to create smooth tonal gradations and an optically accurate scene. This concern with acknowledging the paint and the canvas surface continued the modernist exploration the Realists began. Beyond this connection to the sketch, Impressionism operated at the intersection of what the artists saw and what they felt. In other words, the "impressions" these artists recorded in their paintings were neither purely objective descriptions of the exterior world nor solely subjective responses, but the interaction between the two. They were sensations—the Impressionists' subjective and personal responses to nature.

In sharp contrast to traditional studio artists, Monet painted outdoors, often on the banks of the Seine (FIG. 28-2A) northwest of Paris or in a boat on the river (FIG. 28-1). Painting *en plein air* sharpened Monet's focus on the roles light and color play in capturing an instantaneous representation of atmosphere and climate. Monet carried the

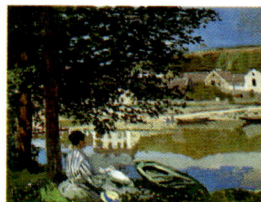

28-2A MONET, *Bank of the Seine, Bennecourt*, 1868.

systematic investigation of light and color further than any other Impressionist, but all of them recognized the importance of carefully observing and understanding how light and color operate. Such thorough study enabled the Impressionists to present images that truly conveyed a sense of the momentary and transitory. Lila Cabot Perry (1848–1933), a student of Monet's late in his career, gave this description of Monet's approach:

> I remember his once saying to me: "When you go out to paint, try to forget what objects you have before you—a tree, a house, a field, or whatever. Merely think, here is a little square of blue, here an oblong of pink, here a streak of yellow, and paint it just as it looks to you, the exact color and shape, until it gives your own naïve impression of the scene before you."[3]

Scientific studies of light and the invention of chemically synthesized pigments increased artists' sensitivity to the multiplicity of colors in nature and gave them new colors for their work. After scrutinizing the effects of light and color on forms, the Impressionists concluded that *local color*—an object's color in white light—becomes modified by the quality of the light shining on it, by reflections from other objects, and by the effects juxtaposed colors produce. Shadows do not appear gray or black, as many earlier painters thought, but seem to be composed of colors modified by reflections or other conditions. If artists use complementary colors (see "19th-Century Color Theory," page 813) side by side over large enough areas, the colors intensify each other, unlike the effect of small quantities of adjoining mixed pigments, which blend into neutral tones. Furthermore, the "mixing" of colors by juxtaposing them on a canvas produces a more intense hue than the same colors mixed on the palette. It is not strictly true the Impressionists used only primary hues, placing them side by side to create secondary colors (blue and yellow, for example, to create green). But they did achieve remarkably brilliant effects with their characteristically short, choppy brushstrokes, which so accurately caught the vibrating quality of light. The fact their canvas surfaces look unintelligible at close range and their forms and objects appear only when the eye fuses the strokes at a certain distance accounts for much of the early adverse criticism leveled at their work. Some critics even accused the Impressionists of firing their paint at the canvas with pistols.

## Academic Salons and Independent Art Exhibitions

For both artists and art historians, modernist art stands in marked contrast—indeed in forceful opposition—to academic art, that is, to the art promoted by the established art schools such as the Royal Academy of Painting and Sculpture in France (founded in 1648) and the Royal Academy of Arts in Britain (founded in 1768). These academies provided instruction for art students and sponsored exhibitions, exerting tight control over the art scene. The annual exhibitions, called "Salons" in France, were highly competitive, as was membership in these academies. Subsidized by the government, the French Royal Academy supported a limited range of artistic expression, focusing on traditional subjects and highly polished technique. Because of the challenges modernist art presented to established artistic conventions, the juries for the Salons and other exhibitions often rejected the works more adventurous artists wished to display, thereby preventing the public from viewing any art other than the officially sanctioned forms of expression. When, however, the 1855 jury rejected some of Gustave Courbet's paintings, the artist reacted by setting up his own Pavilion of Realism (see "Courbet on Realism," Chapter 27, page 776). Years later, he wrote:

> [I]t is high time that someone have the courage to be an honest man and that he say that the Academy is a harmful, all-consuming institution, incapable of fulfilling the goal of its so-called mission.*

Growing dissatisfaction with the decisions of the French Academy's jurors prompted Napoleon III (r. 1852–1870) in 1863 to establish the Salon des Refusés (Salon of the Rejected) to show all of the works not accepted for exhibition in the regular Salon. Édouard Manet's *Le Déjeuner sur l'Herbe* (FIG. 27-32) was among them. The public greeted it and the entire exhibition with derision. One reviewer of the rejected works summed up the prevailing attitude:

> This exhibition, at once sad and grotesque, . . . offers abundant proof . . . that the jury always displays an unbelievable leniency. Save for one or two questionable exceptions there is not a painting which deserves the honor of the official galleries . . . There is even something cruel about this exhibition; people laugh as they do at a farce.†

In 1867, after further rejections, Manet, following Courbet, mounted a private exhibition of 50 of his paintings outside the Paris World's Fair. Six years later, Claude Monet (FIG. 28-2) and the other Impressionists formed their own society and began mounting shows of their works in Paris. This action provided the Impressionists much freedom, for they did not have to contend with the Royal Academy's authoritative and confining viewpoint. The Impressionist exhibitions took place at one- or two-year intervals from 1874 until 1886.

Another group of artists unhappy with the official Salon's conservative nature adopted the same renegade idea. In 1884, these artists formed the Société des Artistes Indépendants (Society of Independent Artists) and held annual Salons des Indépendants. Georges Seurat's *A Sunday on La Grande Jatte* (FIG. 28-16) was one of the paintings in the Independents' 1886 salon.

As the art market expanded, venues for the exhibition of art increased. Art circles and societies sponsored private shows in which both amateurs and professionals participated. Dealers became more aggressive in promoting the artists they represented by mounting exhibitions in a variety of spaces, some fairly intimate and small, others large and grandiose. All of these proliferating opportunities for exhibition gave French artists alternatives to the traditional constraints of the Salon and provided fertile breeding ground for the development of radically new art forms and styles.

*Letter to Jules-Antoine Castagnary, October 17, 1868. Translated by Petra ten-Doesschate Chu, *Letters of Gustave Courbet* (Chicago: University of Chicago Press, 1992), 346.
†Maxime du Camp, in *Revue des deux mondes,* 1863, quoted in George Heard Hamilton, *Manet and His Critics* (New Haven: Yale University Press, New Haven, Conn., 1986), 42–43.

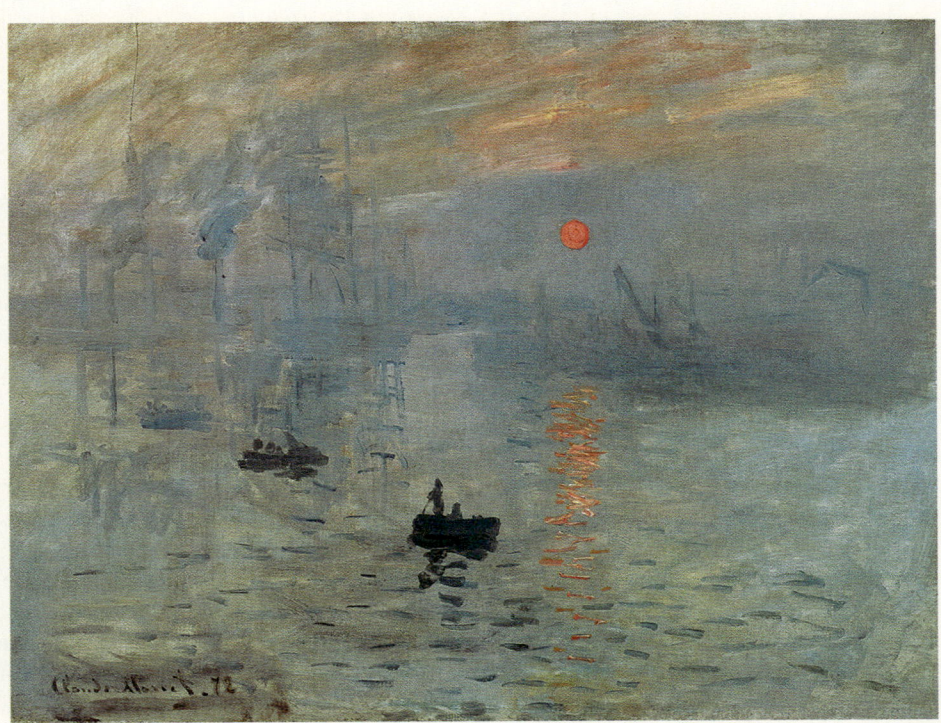

**28-2** CLAUDE MONET, *Impression: Sunrise*, 1872. Oil on canvas, 1' 7½″ × 2' 1½″. Musée Marmottan, Paris.

A hostile critic applied the derogatory term *Impressionism* to this painting because of its sketchy quality and undisguised brushstrokes. Monet and his circle embraced the label for their movement.

1 in.

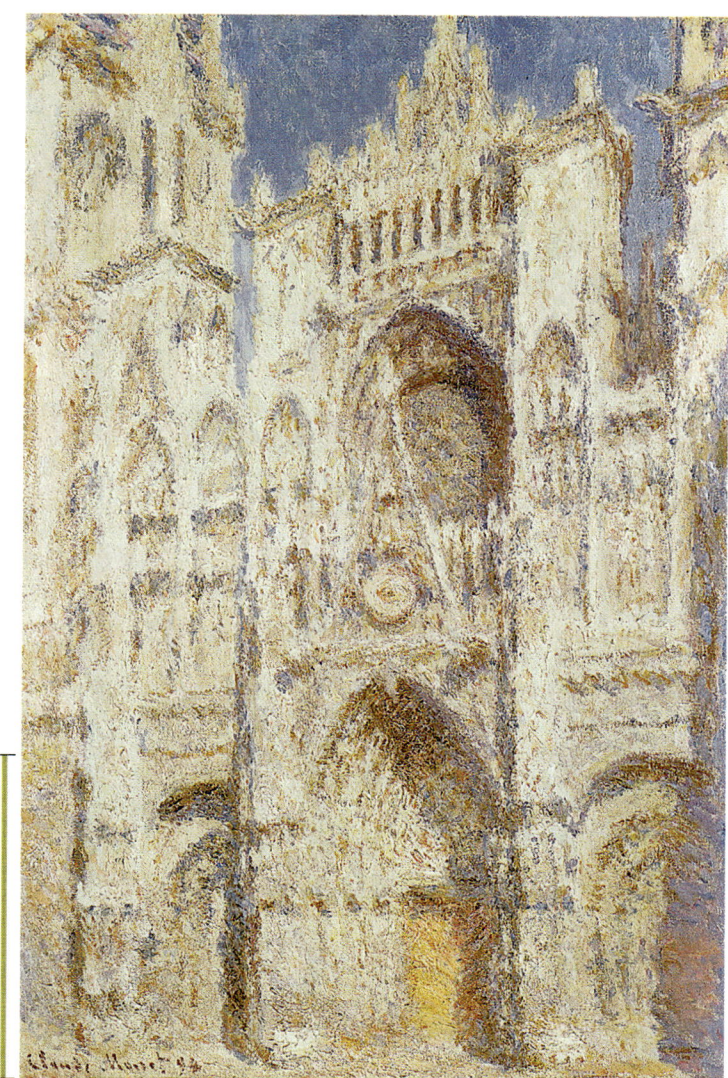

28-3 CLAUDE MONET, *Rouen Cathedral: The Portal (in Sun)*, 1894. Oil on canvas, 3′ 3¼″ × 2′ 1⅞″. Metropolitan Museum of Art, New York (Theodore M. Davis Collection, bequest of Theodore M. Davis, 1915).

Monet painted a series of views of Rouen Cathedral at different times of day and under various climatic conditions. The real subject of this painting is not the building but the sunlight shining on it.

**ROUEN CATHEDRAL** Monet's intensive study of the phenomena of light and color is especially evident in several series of paintings he made of the same subject. In one series, he painted more than three dozen views of Rouen Cathedral, northwest of Paris. For each canvas in the series, Monet observed the cathedral from nearly the same viewpoint but at different times of the day or under various climatic conditions. In the painting illustrated here (FIG. 28-3), Monet depicted the church bathed in bright light. With scientific precision, he carefully recorded the passing of time as seen in the movement of light over identical forms. In fact, the real subject of Monet's painting—as the title *Rouen Cathedral: The Portal (in Sun)* implies—is not the cathedral, which he showed only in part, but the sunlight on the building's main portal. Later critics accused Monet and his companions of destroying form and order for fleeting atmospheric effects, but Monet focused on light and color precisely to reach a greater understanding of the appearance of form.

**SAINT-LAZARE** Most of the Impressionists painted scenes in and around Paris, the heart of modern life in France. Monet's *Saint-Lazare Train Station* (FIG. 28-4) depicts a dominant aspect of the contemporary urban scene. The expanding railway network had made travel more convenient, bringing throngs of people into Paris and enabling city dwellers to reach rural areas quickly. In this painting, Monet captured the energy and vitality of Paris's modern transportation hub. The train, emerging from the steam and smoke it emits, rumbles into the station. In the background haze are the tall buildings that were becoming a major component of the Parisian landscape. Monet's agitated paint application contributes to the sense of energy and conveys the atmosphere of urban life.

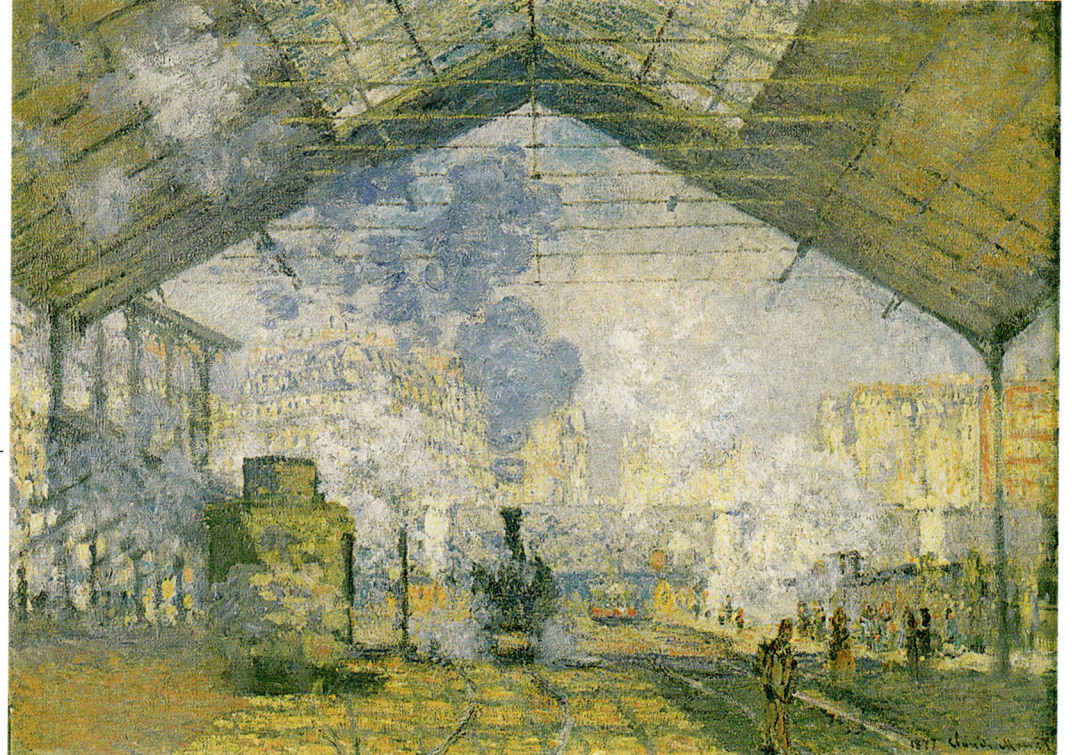

28-4 CLAUDE MONET, *Saint-Lazare Train Station*, 1877. Oil on canvas, 2′ 5¾″ × 3′ 5″. Musée d'Orsay, Paris.

Impressionist paintings are unintelligible at close range, but the eye fuses the brushstrokes at a distance. The agitated application of paint contributes to the sense of energy in this urban scene.

Georges Rivière (1855–1943), a critic and friend of some of the Impressionists, saw this painting in the third Impressionist exhibition and recorded the essence of what Monet had tried to achieve:

> Like a fiery steed, stimulated rather than exhausted by the long trek that it has only just finished, [the locomotive] tosses its mane of smoke, which lashes the glass roof of the main hall. . . . We see the vast and manic movements at the station where the ground shakes with every turn of the wheel. The platforms are sticky with soot, and the air is full of that bitter scent exuded by burning coal. As we look at this magnificent picture, we are overcome by the same feelings as if we were really there, and these feelings are perhaps even more powerful, because in the picture the artist has conveyed his own feelings as well.[4]

**GUSTAVE CAILLEBOTTE** Other Impressionists also represented facets of city life, although not always using Monet's impressionistic brushstrokes. The setting of *Paris: A Rainy Day* (FIG. **28-5**) by GUSTAVE CAILLEBOTTE (1849–1893) is a junction of spacious boulevards resulting from the redesigning of Paris begun in 1852. The city's population had reached close to 1.5 million by midcentury. To accommodate this congregation of humanity—and to facilitate the movement of troops in the event of another revolution—Napoleon III ordered Paris rebuilt. The emperor named Baron Georges Haussmann (1809–1891), a city superintendent, to oversee the entire project. In addition to new water and sewer systems, street lighting, and new residential and commercial buildings, a major component of the new Paris was the creation of the wide, open boulevards seen in Caillebotte's painting. These great avenues, whose construction caused the demolition of thousands of old buildings and streets, transformed medieval Paris into the present-day city, with its superb vistas and wide uninterrupted arteries for the flow of vehicular and pedestrian traffic. Caillebotte chose to focus on these markers of the city's rapid urbanization.

Although Caillebotte did not dissolve his image into the broken color and brushwork characteristic of Impressionism, he did use an informal and asymmetrical composition. The figures seem randomly placed, with the frame cropping them arbitrarily, suggesting the transitory nature of the street scene. Well-dressed Parisians of the leisure class share the viewer's space. Despite the sharp focus of *Paris: A Rainy Day,* the picture captures the artist's "impression" of urban life.

**CAMILLE PISSARRO** Other Impressionists also found Paris's spacious boulevards and avenues—the product of "Haussmannization"—attractive subjects for paintings. *La Place du Théâtre Français* (FIG. **28-6**) is one of many panoramic scenes of the city CAMILLE PISSARRO (1830–1903) painted. The artist recorded the blurred dark accents against a light ground that constituted his visual sensations of a crowded Parisian square viewed from several stories above street level. The moment Pissarro captured on his canvas is not so much of fugitive light effects as it is of the street life, achieved through a deliberate casualness in the arrangement of figures. To accomplish this sense of spontaneity, Pissarro sometimes used photography to record the places he wished to paint, as did many of his fellow Impressionists. Indeed, the visual parallels between Impressionist paintings and photographs are striking. In *La Place du Théâtre Français,* these parallels include the arbitrary cutting off of figures at the edges of the painting and the curious flattening spatial effect produced by the high viewpoint.

**BERTHE MORISOT** Many Impressionist paintings depict scenes from resort areas on the seashore or along the Seine River, such as Argenteuil (FIG. 28-1), Bennencourt (FIG. 28-2A), Bougival, and Chatou (MAP 28-1). The railway line running to and from Saint-Lazare station connected Argenteuil to Paris, so transportation was not an obstacle. Parisians often would take the train out to these resort areas for a day of sailing, picnicking, and strolling

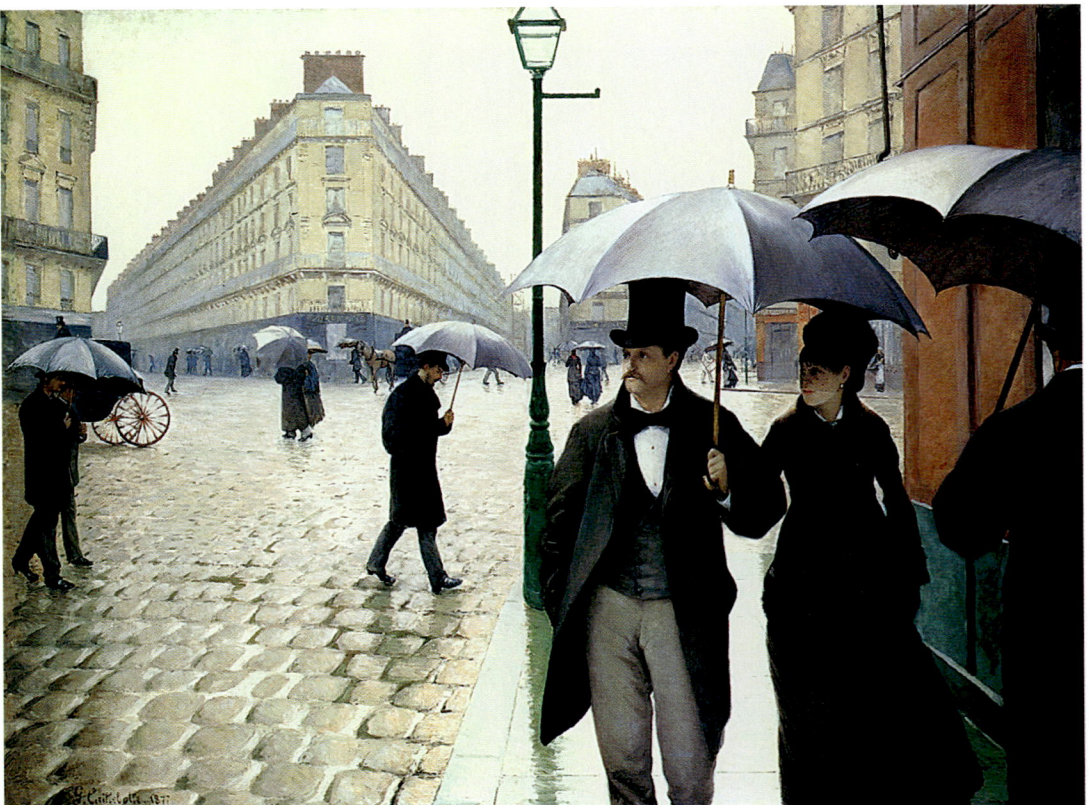

**28-5** GUSTAVE CAILLEBOTTE, *Paris: A Rainy Day,* 1877. Oil on canvas, 6′ 9″ × 9′ 9″. Art Institute of Chicago, Chicago (Worcester Fund).

Although Caillebotte did not use Impressionistic broken brushstrokes, the seemingly randomly placed figures and the arbitrary cropping of the vista suggest the transitory nature of modern life.

1 ft.

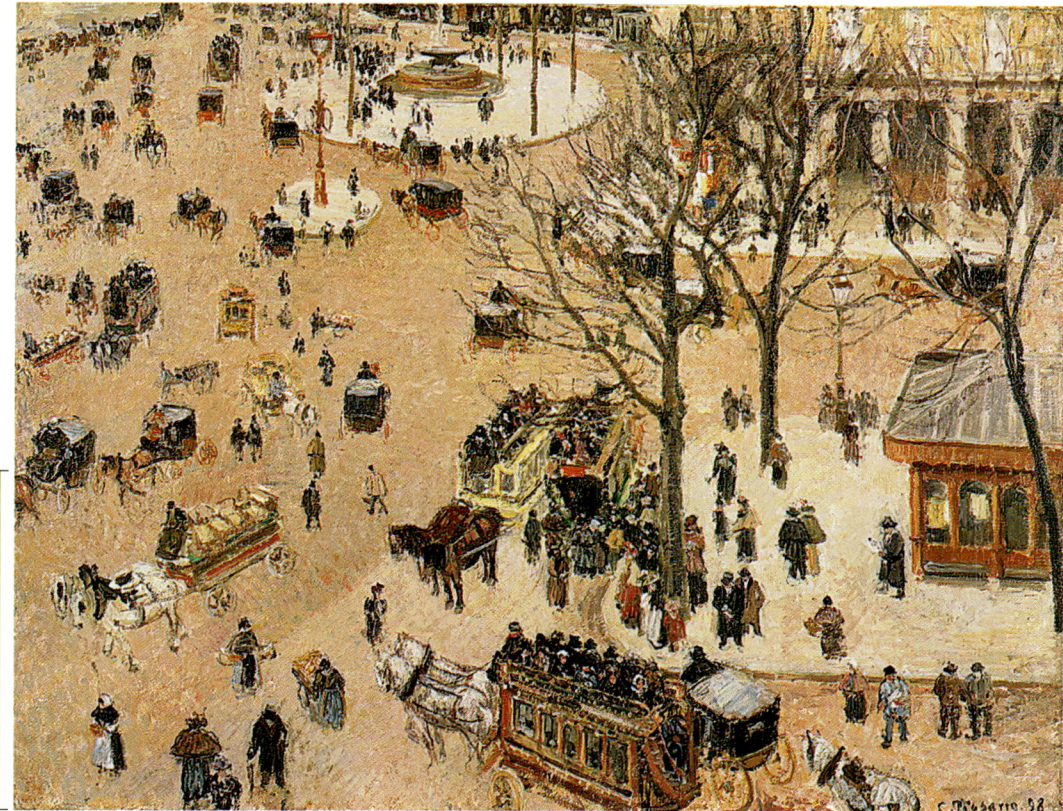

1 ft.

along the Seine. BERTHE MORISOT (1841–1895), Édouard Manet's sister-in-law, regularly exhibited with the Impressionists. Most of her paintings focus on domestic subjects, the one realm of Parisian life where society allowed an upper-class woman such as Morisot free access, but she also produced many outdoor scenes, including *Villa at the Seaside* (FIG. 28-7), painted in 1874, and *Summer's Day* (FIG. 28-7A), in 1879. The subject and style of both works correlate well with Impressionist concerns.

The setting of *Villa at the Seaside* is the shaded veranda of a summer hotel at a fashionable seashore resort. A woman elegantly but not ostentatiously dressed sits gazing out across the railing to a sun-lit beach. Her child, its discarded toy boat a splash of red, gazes at the passing sails on the placid sea. The mood is of relaxed leisure. Morisot used the

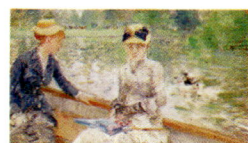

28-7A MORISOT, *Summer's Day,* 1879. ◼◀

open brushwork and the *plein air* lighting characteristic of Impressionism. Sketchy brushstrokes record her quick perceptions. Nowhere did Morisot linger on contours or enclosed details. She presented the scene in a slightly filmy, soft focus conveying a feeling of airiness. The composition also recalls the work of other Impressionists. The figures fall informally into place, as someone who shared their intimate space would perceive them. Morisot was both immensely ambitious and talented, as her ability to catch the pictorial moment demonstrates. She escaped the hostile criticism directed at most of the other Impressionists. People praised her work for its sensibility, grace, and delicacy.

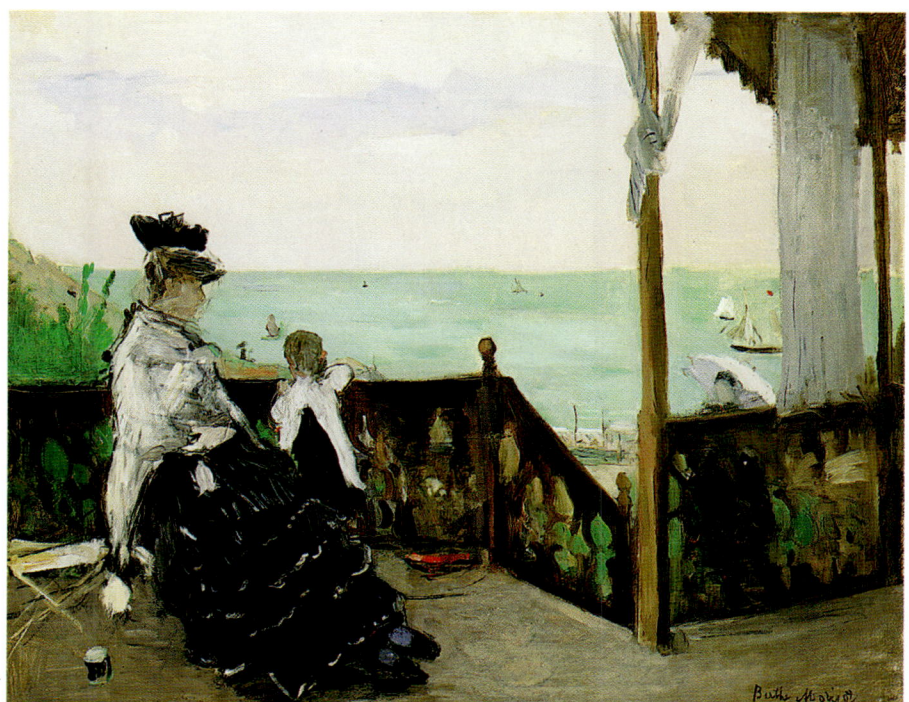

1 in.

28-7 BERTHE MORISOT, *Villa at the Seaside,* 1874. Oil on canvas, 1' 7¾" × 2' ⅛". Norton Simon Art Foundation, Los Angeles. ◼◀

In this informal view of a woman and child enjoying their leisure time at a fashionable seashore resort, Morisot used swift, sketchy strokes of light colors to convey a feeling of airiness.

# Renoir on the Art of Painting

Many 19th-century artists were concerned with the theoretical basis of picturemaking. One of the most cogent statements on this subject is Pierre-Auguste Renoir's concise summary of how he, as an Impressionist, painted pictures and what he hoped to achieve as an artist.

> I arrange my subject as I want it, then I go ahead and paint it, like a child. I want a red to be sonorous, to sound like a bell; if it doesn't turn out that way, I add more reds and other colors until I get it. I am no cleverer than that. I have no rules and no methods; . . . I have no secrets. I look at a nude; there are myriads of tiny tints. I must find the ones that will make the flesh on my canvas live and quiver. . . . [I]f they could explain a picture, it wouldn't be art. Shall I tell you what I think are the two qualities of art? It must be indescribable and it must be inimitable. . . . The work of art must seize upon you, wrap you up in itself, carry you away. It is the means by which the artist conveys his passions. . . . I want people to feel that neither the setting nor the figures are dull and lifeless.*

There is certainly nothing dull or lifeless about *Le Moulin de la Galette* (FIG. 28-8), in which Renoir depicted throngs of people gathered in a popular Parisian dance hall. Some crowd the tables and chatter, while others dance energetically. So lively is the atmosphere the viewer can virtually hear the sounds of music, laughter, and tinkling glasses. The painter dappled the whole scene with sunlight and shade, artfully blurred into the figures to produce precisely the effect of floating and fleeting light the Impressionists so cultivated. Renoir's casual unposed placement of the figures and the suggested continuity of space, spreading in all directions and only accidentally limited by the frame, position the viewer as a participant rather than as an outsider. Whereas classical art sought to express universal and timeless qualities, Impressionism attempted to depict just the opposite—the incidental, momentary, and passing aspects of reality.

*Quoted in Eric Protter, ed., *Painters on Painting* (New York: Grosset & Dunlap, 1971), 145.

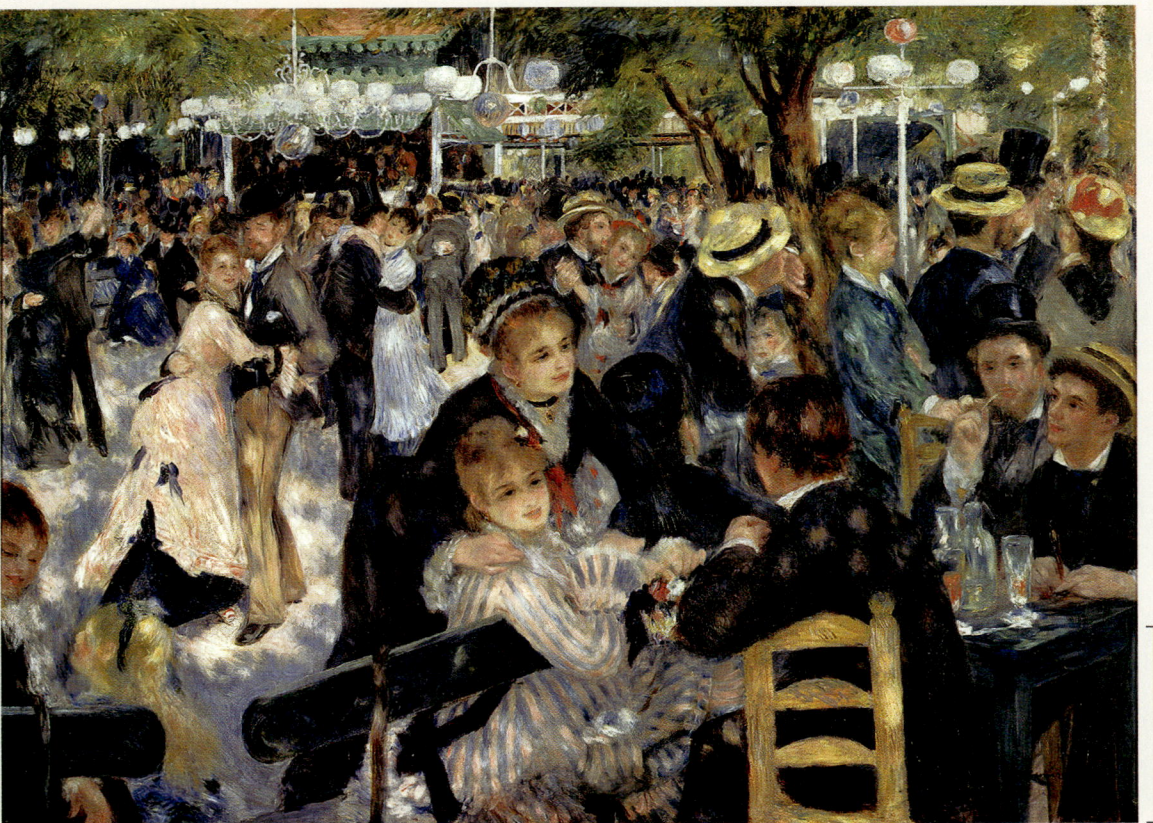

**28-8** PIERRE-AUGUSTE RENOIR, *Le Moulin de la Galette*, 1876. Oil on canvas, 4′ 3″ × 5′ 8″. Musée d'Orsay, Paris. ◼️

Renoir's painting of this popular Parisian dance hall is dappled by sunlight and shade, artfully blurred into the figures to produce the effect of floating and fleeting light the Impressionists cultivated.

1 ft.

**PIERRE-AUGUSTE RENOIR** Ample time for leisure activities was another facet of the new, industrialized Paris, and scenes of dining and dancing, café-concerts, opera, ballet, and other forms of urban recreation became mainstays of Impressionism. Although seemingly unrelated, industrialization facilitated these pursuits. With the advent of set working hours, people's schedules became more regimented, enabling them to plan their favorite pastimes. One Impressionist who turned repeatedly to Parisian nightlife for the subjects of his canvases was PIERRE-AUGUSTE RENOIR (1841–1919), who in 1874 painted *en plein air* alongside Monet and Manet at Argenteuil (FIG. 28-1) and was also one of the most eloquent writers on the aims of Impressionism (see "Renoir on the Art of Painting," above). His *Le Moulin de la Galette* (FIG. 28-8) of 1876 is a superb example of this Impressionist genre.

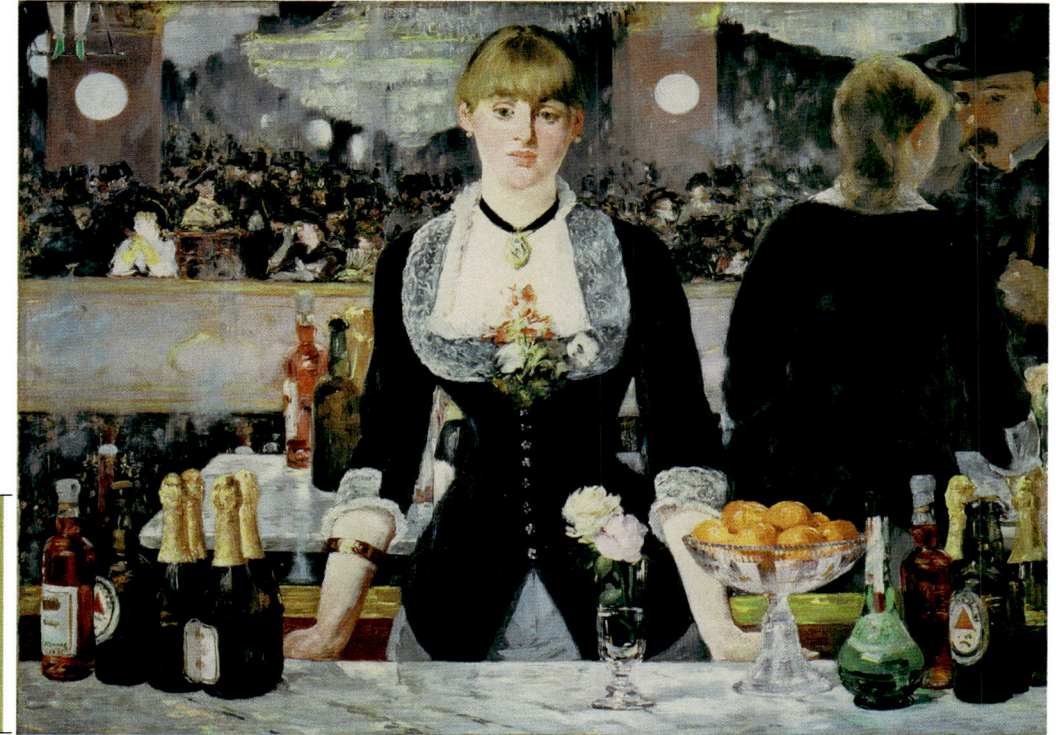

28-9 ÉDOUARD MANET, *A Bar at the Folies-Bergère,* 1882. Oil on canvas, 3′ 1″ × 4′ 3″. Courtauld Institute of Art Gallery, London. ◼◀

In this painting set in a Parisian café, Manet called attention to the canvas surface by creating spatial inconsistencies, such as the relationship between the barmaid and her apparent reflection in a mirror.

of modeling and perspective are minimal. This painting method further calls attention to the surface by forcing the viewer to scrutinize the work to make sense of the scene. But it is difficult to do so, because visual discrepancies immediately emerge. For example, what initially seems easily recognizable as a mirror behind the barmaid creates confusion throughout the rest of the painting. Is the woman on the right the barmaid's reflection? If both figures are the same person, it is impossible to reconcile the spatial relationship between the barmaid, the mirror, the bar's frontal horizontality, and the barmaid's seemingly displaced reflection. These visual contradictions reveal Manet's insistence on calling attention to the pictorial structure of his painting, in keeping with his modernist interest in examining the basic premises of the medium.

**ÉDOUARD MANET** The immensely versatile Manet, whose career bridged Realism (FIGS. 27-32 and 27-33) and Impressionism (FIG. 28-1), also depicted Parisian nightlife. One of his later works in the Impressionist mode is *A Bar at the Folies-Bergère* (FIG. 28-9), painted in 1882. The Folies-Bergère was a popular café with music-hall performances, one of the fashionable gathering places for Parisian revelers that many Impressionists frequented. In Manet's painting, a barmaid, centrally placed, looks out from the canvas but seems disinterested or lost in thought, divorced from her patrons as well as from the viewer. Manet blurred and roughly applied the brushstrokes, particularly those in the background, and the effects

**EDGAR DEGAS** Impressionists also depicted more-formal leisure activities. The fascination EDGAR DEGAS (1834–1917) had with patterns of motion brought him to the Paris Opéra (FIG. 27-45) and its ballet school. There, his keen observational power took in the formalized movements of classical ballet, one of his favorite subjects. In *The Rehearsal* (FIG. 28-10), Degas used several devices to bring the observer into the pictorial space. The frame cuts off the spiral stair, the windows in the background, and the group of figures in the right foreground. The figures are not at the center of a

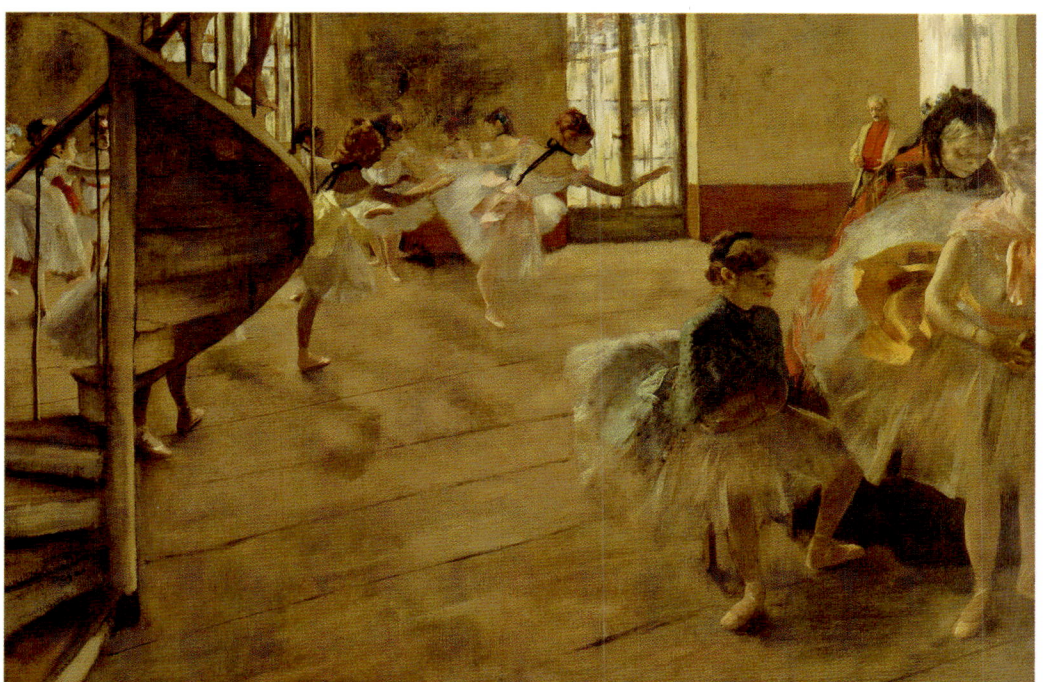

28-10 EDGAR DEGAS, *The Rehearsal,* 1874. Oil on canvas, 1′ 11″ × 2′ 9″. Glasgow Art Galleries and Museum, Glasgow (Burrell Collection). ◼◀

The arbitrarily cut-off figures of dancers, the patterns of light splotches, and the blurry images reveal Degas's interest in reproducing fleeting moments, as well as his fascination with photography.

# Japonisme

Despite Europe's and America's extensive colonization during the 19th century, Japan avoided Western intrusion until 1853–1854, when Commodore Matthew Perry (1794–1858) and American naval forces exacted trading and diplomatic privileges from Japan. From the increased contact, Westerners became familiar with Japanese culture. So intrigued were the French with Japanese art and culture that they coined a specific term—*Japonisme*—to describe the Japanese aesthetic, which, because of both its beauty and exoticism, greatly appealed to the fashionable segment of Parisian society. In 1867 at the Exposition Universelle in Paris, the Japanese pavilion garnered more attention than any other. Soon, Japanese kimonos, fans, lacquer cabinets, tea caddies, folding screens, tea services, and jewelry flooded Paris. Japanese-themed novels and travel books were immensely popular as well. As demand for Japanese merchandise grew in the West, the Japanese began to develop import-export businesses, and the foreign currency flowing into Japan helped to finance much of its industrialization.

Artists in particular were great admirers of Japanese art. Among those the Japanese aesthetic influenced were the Impressionists and Post-Impressionists, especially Édouard Manet, Edgar Degas, Mary Cassatt, James Abbott McNeill Whistler, Henri de Toulouse-Lautrec, Paul Gauguin, and Vincent van Gogh. Indeed, van Gogh collected and copied Japanese prints (FIG. 28-16B; compare FIG. 34-1). For the most part, the Japanese presentation of space in woodblock prints (see "Japanese Woodblock Prints," Chapter 34, page 1016), which were more readily available in the West than any other Asian art form, intrigued these artists. Because of the simplicity of the woodblock printing process, the Japanese prints feature broad areas of flat color with a limited amount of modulation or gradation. This flatness interested modernist painters, who sought ways to call attention to the picture surface. The right side of Degas's *The Tub* (FIG. 28-11), for example, has this two-dimensional quality. Degas, in fact, owned a print by Japanese artist Torii Kiyonaga depicting eight women at a bath in various poses and states of undress. That print inspired Degas's painting. A comparison between Degas's bather and a detail (FIG. 28-12) of a bather from another of Kiyonaga's prints is striking, although Degas did not closely copy any of the Japanese artist's figures. Instead, he absorbed the essence of Japanese compositional style and the distinctive angles employed in representing human figures, and he translated them into the Impressionist mode.

The decorative quality of Japanese images also appealed to the artists associated with the Arts and Crafts movement in England. Artists such as William Morris (FIG. 28-34) and Charles Rennie Mackinstosh (FIG. 28-35) found Japanese prints attractive because those artworks intersected nicely with two fundamental Arts and Crafts principles: art should be available to the masses, and functional objects should be artistically designed.

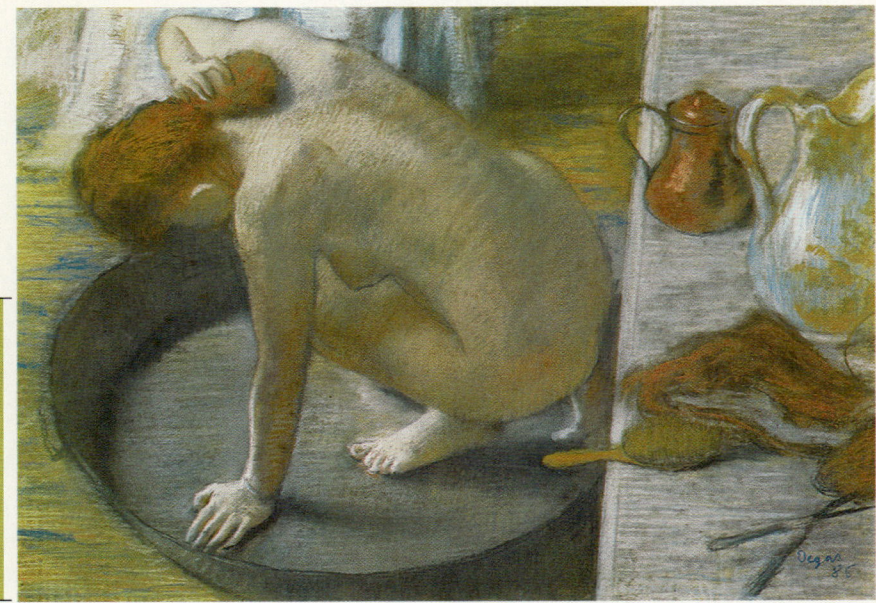

1 in.

28-11 EDGAR DEGAS, *The Tub*, 1886. Pastel, 1′ 11½″ × 2′ 8⅜″. Musée d'Orsay, Paris. ◼▸

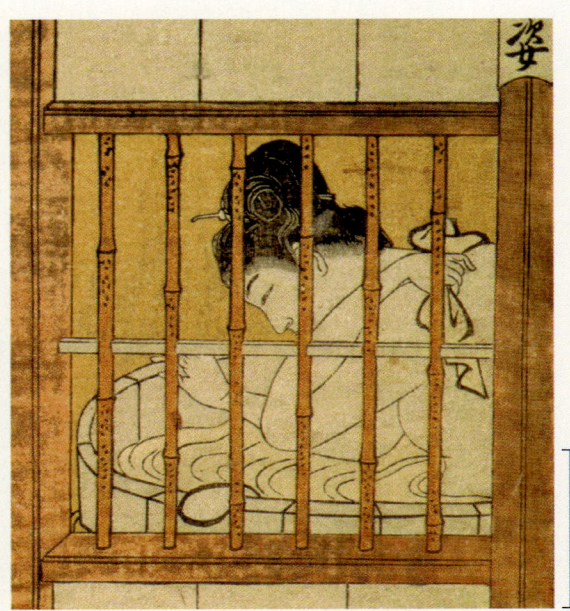

1 in.

28-12 TORII KIYONAGA, detail of *Two Women at the Bath*, ca. 1780. Color woodblock, full print 10½″ × 7½″, detail 3¾″ × 3½″. Musée Guimet, Paris.

*The Tub* reveals the influence of Japanese prints, especially the sharp angles that artists such as Kiyonaga used in representing figures. Degas translated his Japanese model into the Impressionist mode.

classically balanced composition. Instead, Degas arranged them in a seemingly random manner. The prominent diagonals of the wall bases and floorboards lead the viewer's eye into and along the directional lines of the dancers. Finally, as is customary in Degas's ballet pictures, a large, off-center, empty space creates the illusion of a continuous floor connecting the observer with the pictured figures.

The often arbitrarily cut-off figures, the patterns of light splotches, and the blurriness of the images in this and other Degas works indicate the artist's interest in reproducing single moments. They also reveal his fascination with photography. Degas not only studied the photographs of others but regularly used a camera to make preliminary studies for his works, particularly photographing figures in interiors. Japanese woodblock prints (see "Japonisme," page 808) were another inspirational source for paintings such as *The Rehearsal*. The cunning spatial projections in Degas's paintings probably derived in part from Japanese prints, such as those by Suzuki Harunobu (FIG. 34-12). Japanese artists used diverging lines not only to organize the flat shapes of figures but also to direct the viewer's attention into the picture space. The Impressionists, acquainted with these woodblocks as early as the 1860s, greatly admired the spatial organization, familiar and intimate themes, and flat unmodeled color areas of the Japanese prints, and avidly incorporated these features into their own paintings.

**THE TUB** Although color and light were major components of the Impressionists' quest to capture fleeting sensations, these artists considered other formal elements as well. Degas, for example, became a master of line, so much so his works often differ significantly from those of Monet and Renoir. Degas specialized in studies of figures in rapid and informal action, recording the quick impression of arrested motion, as is evident in *The Rehearsal* (FIG. 28-10). He often employed lines to convey this sense of movement. In *The Tub* (FIG. **28-11**), inspired by a Japanese print similar to the one illustrated here (FIG. **28-12**) by TORII KIYONAGA (1752–1815), a young woman crouches in a washing tub. Degas outlined the major objects in the painting—the woman, tub, and pitchers—and covered all surfaces with linear hatch marks. He was able to achieve this leaner quality by using *pastels,* his favorite medium. With these dry sticks of powdered pigment, Degas drew directly on the paper, as one would with a piece of chalk, thus accounting for the linear basis of his work. Although the applied pastel is subject to smudging, the colors tend to retain their autonomy, so they appear fresh and bright.

*The Tub* also reveals how Degas's work, like that of the other Impressionists, continued the modernist exploration of the premises of painting by acknowledging the artwork's surface. Although the viewer clearly perceives the woman as a depiction of a three-dimensional form in space, the tabletop or shelf on the right of the image appears severely tilted, so much so it seems to parallel the picture plane. The two pitchers on the table complicate this visual conflict between the table's flatness and the illusion of the bathing woman's three-dimensional volume. The limited foreshortening of the pitchers and their shared edge, in conjunction with the rest of the image, create a visual perplexity for the viewer.

**MARY CASSATT** In the Salon of 1874, Degas admired a painting by a young American artist, MARY CASSATT (1844–1926), the daughter of a Philadelphia banker. Degas befriended and influ-

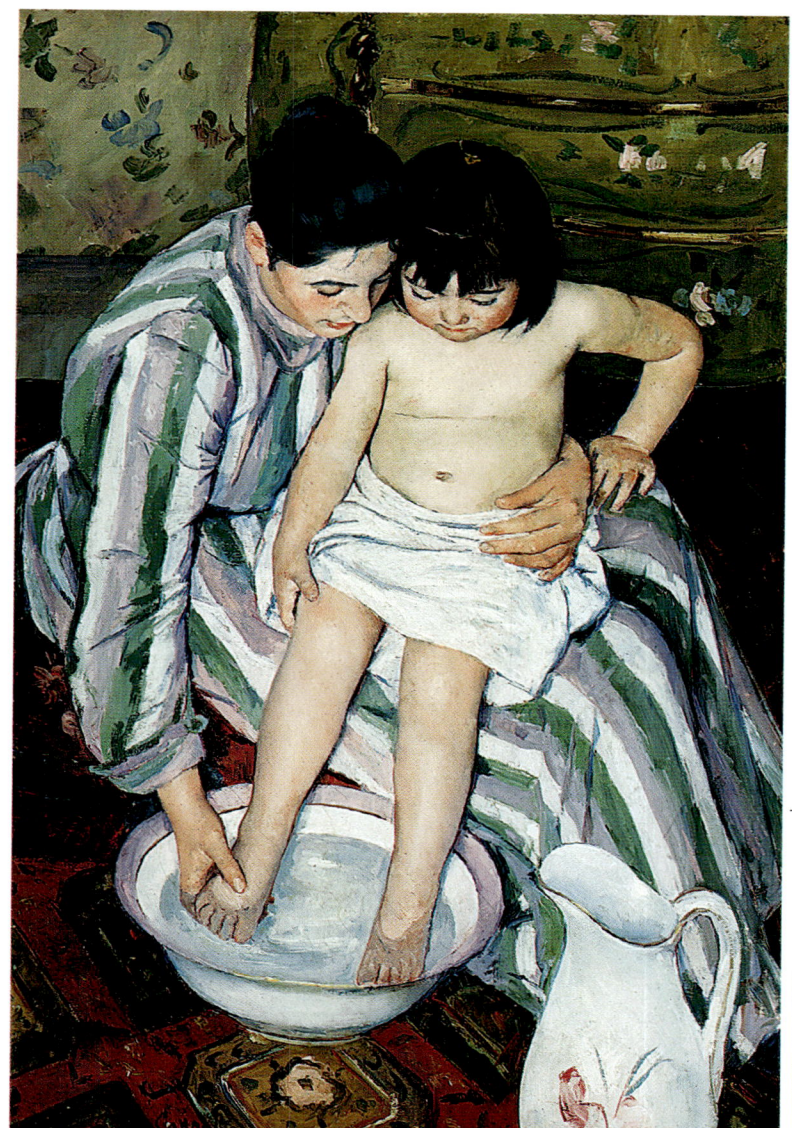

1 ft.

**28-13** MARY CASSATT, *The Bath*, ca. 1892. Oil on canvas, 3′ 3″ × 2′ 2″. Art Institute of Chicago, Chicago (Robert A. Walker Fund). ◼◀

Cassatt's compositions owe much to Degas and Japanese prints, but her subjects differ from those of most Impressionist painters, in part because, as a woman, she could not frequent cafés.

enced Cassatt, who exhibited regularly with the Impressionists. She had trained as a painter before moving to Europe to study masterworks in France and Italy. As a woman, she could not easily frequent the cafés with her male artist friends, and she had the responsibility of caring for her aging parents, who had moved to Paris to join her. Because of these restrictions, Cassatt's subjects, like Morisot's (FIG. 28-7), were principally women and children, whom she presented with a combination of objectivity and genuine sentiment. Works such as *The Bath* (FIG. **28-13**) show the tender relationship between a mother and child. As in Degas's *The Tub,* the visual solidity of the mother and child contrasts with the flattened patterning of the wallpaper and rug. Cassatt's style in this work owed much to the compositional devices of Degas and of Japanese prints, but the painting's design has an originality and strength all its own.

## Whistler on "Artistic Arrangements"

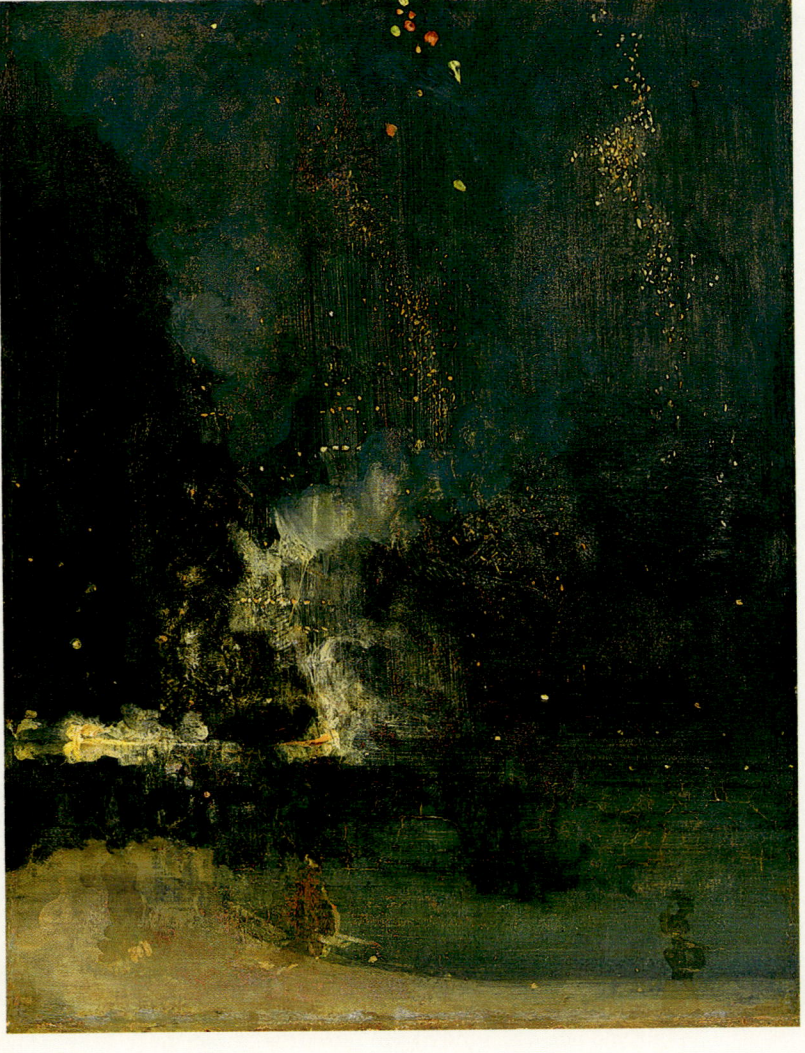

**28-14** JAMES ABBOTT McNEILL WHISTLER, *Nocturne in Black and Gold* (*The Falling Rocket*), ca. 1875. Oil on panel, 1′ 11⅝″ × 1′ 6½″. Detroit Institute of Arts, Detroit (gift of Dexter M. Ferry Jr.).

In this painting, Whistler displayed an Impressionist's interest in conveying the atmospheric effects of fireworks at night, but he also emphasized the abstract arrangement of shapes and colors.

Underscoring the insistence by late-19th-century artists, both in Europe and America, that paintings are independent two-dimensional artworks and not windows opening onto the three-dimensional world, American-born James Abbott Mc-Neill Whistler, who produced his most famous works in London, called his paintings "arrangements" or "nocturnes." *Nocturne in Black and Gold* (FIG. 28-14) is a daring painting with gold flecks and splatters representing an exploded firework punctuating the darkness of the night sky. More interested in conveying the atmospheric effects than in providing details of the scene, Whistler emphasized creating a harmonious arrangement of shapes and colors on the rectangle of his canvas, an approach many 20th-century artists adopted. Whistler's works angered many 19th-century viewers, however. The British critic John Ruskin (1819–1900) responded to this painting by writing a scathing review accusing Whistler of "flinging a pot of paint in the public's face" with his style. In reply, Whistler sued Ruskin for libel. During the trial, Ruskin's attorney asked Whistler about the subject of *Nocturne*:

"What is your definition of a Nocturne?"

"It is an arrangement of line, form, and colour first; . . . Among my works are some night pieces; and I have chosen the word Nocturne because it generalizes and amplifies the whole set of them. . . . The nocturne in black and gold is a night piece and represents the fireworks at Cremorne [Gardens in London]."

"Not a view of Cremorne?"

"If it were a view of Cremorne, it would certainly bring about nothing but disappointment on the part of the beholders. It is an artistic arrangement."*

The court transcript notes the spectators in the courtroom laughed at that response, but Whistler won the case. However, his victory had sadly ironic consequences for him. The judge in the case, showing where his—and the public's—sympathies lay, awarded the artist only one farthing (less than a penny) in damages and required him to pay all of the court costs, which ruined him financially.

*Quoted in Charles Harrison, Paul Wood, and Jason Gaiger, *Art in Theory, 1815–1900* (Oxford: Blackwell, 1998), 835–836.

**JAMES WHISTLER** Another American expatriate artist in Europe was JAMES ABBOTT McNEILL WHISTLER (1834–1903), who spent time in Paris before settling finally in London. He met many of the French Impressionists, and his art, for example, *Nocturne in Black and Gold,* or *The Falling Rocket* (FIG. **28-14**), is a unique combination of some of their concerns and his own (see "Whistler on 'Artistic Arrangements,'" above). Whistler shared the Impressionists' interests in the subject of contemporary life and the sensations color produces on the eye. To these influences he added his own desire to create harmonies paralleling those achieved in music.

Nature contains the elements, in color and form, of all pictures, as the keyboard contains the notes of all music. But the artist is born to pick, and choose, and group with science, these elements, that the result may be beautiful—as the musician gathers his notes, and forms his chords, until he brings forth from chaos glorious harmony.[5]

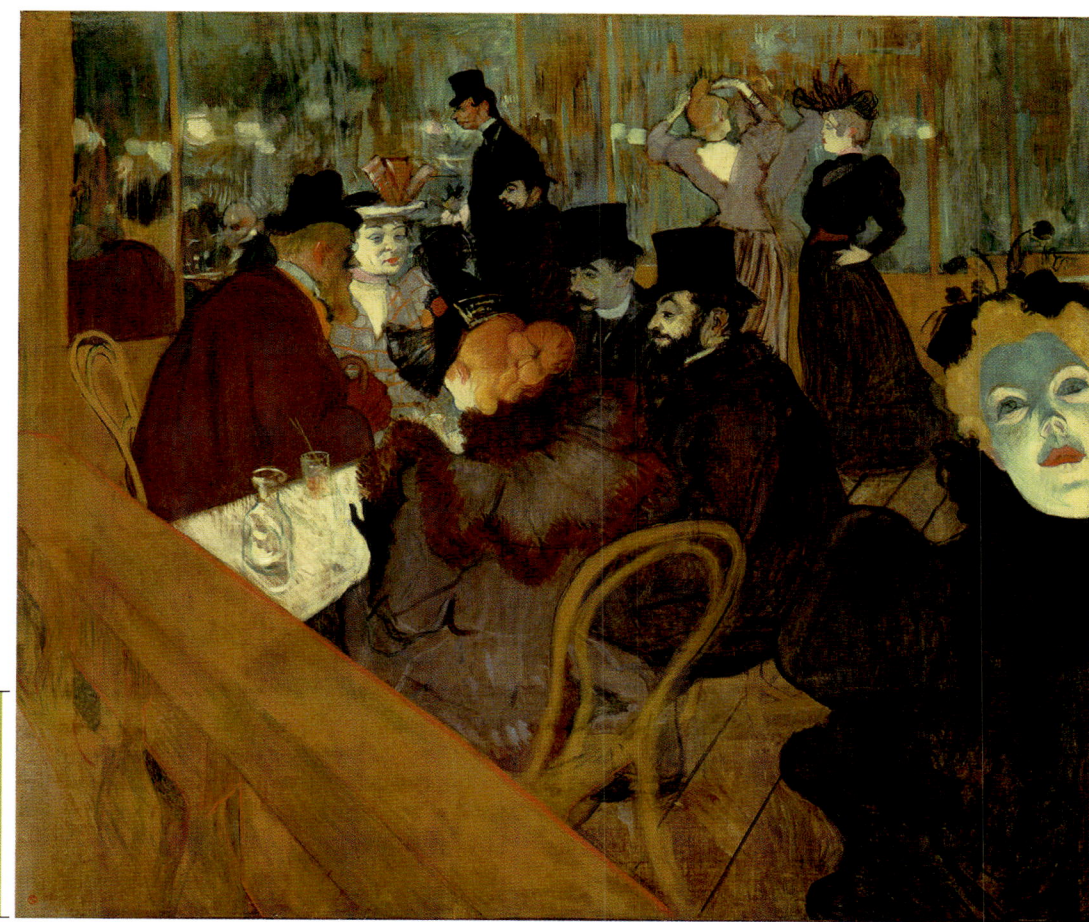

28-15 HENRI DE TOULOUSE-
LAUTREC, *At the Moulin Rouge*,
1892–1895. Oil on canvas,
4′ × 4′ 7″. Art Institute of
Chicago, Chicago (Helen Birch
Bartlett Memorial Collection).

Degas, Japanese prints, and
photography influenced this
painting's oblique composition,
but the glaring lighting, masklike
faces, and dissonant colors are
distinctly Toulouse-Lautrec's.

1 ft.

# POST-IMPRESSIONISM

By 1886 most critics and a large segment of the public accepted the Impressionists as serious artists. Just when their images of contemporary life no longer seemed crude and unfinished, however, some of these painters and a group of younger followers came to feel the Impressionists were neglecting too many of the traditional elements of picturemaking in their attempts to capture momentary sensations of light and color on canvas. In a conversation with the influential art dealer Ambroise Vollard (1866–1939) in about 1883, Renoir commented: "I had wrung impressionism dry, and I finally came to the conclusion that I knew neither how to paint nor how to draw. In a word, impressionism was a blind alley, as far as I was concerned."[6] By the 1880s, some artists were more systematically examining the properties and the expressive qualities of line, pattern, form, and color. Among them were Dutch-born Vincent van Gogh and the French painter Paul Gauguin, who focused their artistic efforts on exploring the expressive capabilities of formal elements, and Georges Seurat and Paul Cézanne, also from France, who were more analytical in orientation. Because their art had its roots in Impressionist precepts and methods, but was not stylistically homogeneous, these artists and others, including Henri de Toulouse-Lautrec, became known as the *Post-Impressionists.*

**HENRI DE TOULOUSE-LAUTREC** Closest to the Impressionists in many ways was the French artist HENRI DE TOULOUSE-LAUTREC (1864–1901), who deeply admired Degas and shared the Impressionists' interest in capturing the sensibility of modern life. His work, however, has an added satirical edge to it and often borders on caricature. Genetic defects stunted his growth and partially crippled him, leading to his self-exile from the high society his ancient aristocratic name entitled him to enter. He became a denizen of the night world of Paris, consorting with a tawdry population of entertainers, prostitutes, and other social outcasts. He reveled in the energy of the city's music halls, such as the Moulin Rouge (FIG. 28-15) and the Jardin de Paris (FIG. 28-15A), cafés, and bordellos. *At the Moulin Rouge* reveals the influences of Degas, of Japanese prints, and of photography in the oblique and asymmetrical composition, the spatial diagonals, and the strong line patterns with added dissonant colors. But although Toulouse-Lautrec based everything he painted on firsthand observation and the scenes he captured were already familiar to viewers in the work of the Impressionists, he so emphasized or exaggerated each element that the tone is new. Compare, for instance, the mood of *At the Moulin Rouge* with the relaxed and casual atmosphere of Renoir's *Le Moulin de la Galette* (FIG. 28-8). Toulouse-Lautrec's scene is nightlife, with its glaring artificial light, brassy music, and assortment of corrupt, cruel, and masklike faces. (He included himself in the background—the diminutive man wearing a derby hat accompanying the very tall man, his cousin.) Such distortions by simplification of the figures and faces anticipated Expressionism (see Chapter 29), when artists' use of formal elements—for example, brighter colors and bolder lines than ever before—increased the effect of the images on observers.

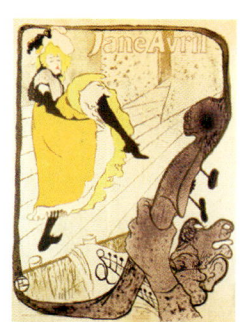

28-15A TOULOUSE-LAUTREC,
*Jane Avril,* 1893.

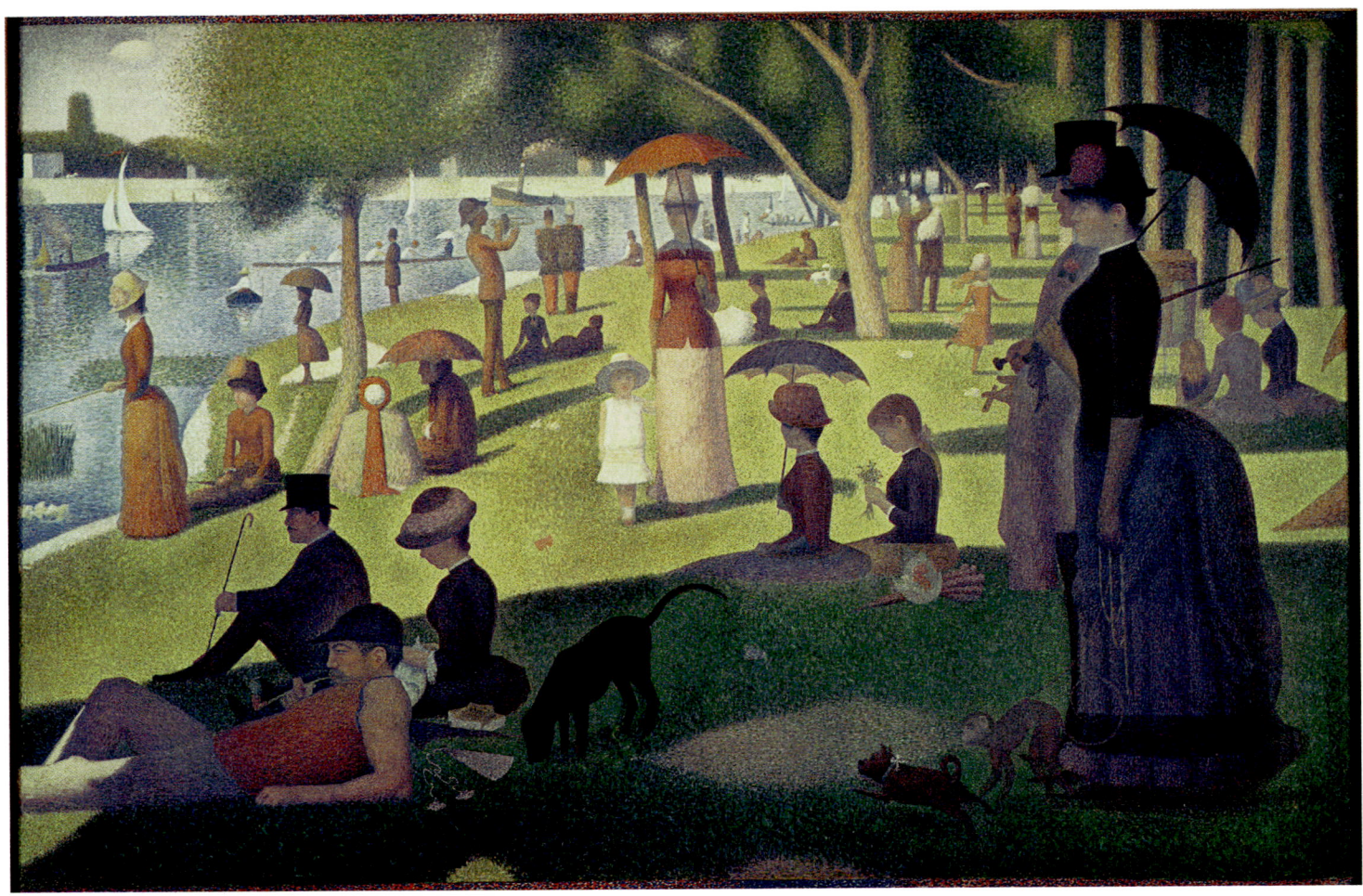

1 ft.

**28-16** GEORGES SEURAT, *A Sunday on La Grande Jatte,* 1884–1886. Oil on canvas, 6′ 9″ × 10′. Art Institute of Chicago, Chicago (Helen Birch Bartlett Memorial Collection, 1926). ◼◂

Seurat's color system—pointillism—involved dividing colors into their component parts and applying those colors to the canvas in tiny dots. The forms become comprehensible only from a distance.

**GEORGES SEURAT** The themes GEORGES SEURAT (1859–1891) addressed in his paintings were also Impressionist subjects, but he depicted them in a resolutely intellectual way. He devised a disciplined and painstaking system of painting focused on color analysis. Seurat was less concerned with the recording of immediate color sensations than he was with their careful and systematic organization into a new kind of pictorial order. He disciplined the free and fluent play of color characterizing Impressionism into a calculated arrangement based on scientific color theory. Seurat's system, known as *pointillism* or *divisionism,* involved carefully observing color and separating it into its component parts (see "Pointillism and 19th-Century Color Theory," page 813). The artist then applies these pure component colors to the canvas in tiny dots (points) or daubs. Thus, the shapes, figures, and spaces in the image become comprehensible only from a distance, when the viewer's eyes blend the many pigment dots.

Seurat introduced pointillism to the French public at the eighth and last Impressionist exhibition in 1886, where he displayed *A Sunday on La Grande Jatte* (FIG. **28-16**). The subject of the painting is consistent with Impressionist recreational themes, and Seurat also shared the Impressionists' interest in analyzing light and color. But Seurat's rendition of Parisians at leisure is rigid and remote, unlike the spontaneous representations of Impressionism. Seurat's pointillism instead produced a carefully composed and painted image. By using meticulously calculated values, the painter carved out a deep rectangular space. He played on repeated motifs both to create flat patterns and to suggest spatial depth. Reiterating the profile of the female form, the parasol, and the cylindrical forms of the figures, Seurat placed each in space to set up a rhythmic movement in depth as well as from side to side. Sunshine fills the picture, but the painter did not break the light into transient patches of color. Light, air, people, and landscape are formal elements in an abstract design in which line, color, value, and shape cohere in a precise and tightly controlled organization. Seurat's orchestration of the many forms across the monumental (almost 7 by 10 feet) canvas created a rhythmic cadence harmonizing the entire composition.

Seurat once stated: "They see poetry in what I have done. No, I apply my method, and that is all there is to it."[7] Despite this claim, Seurat's art is much more than a scientifically based system. *La Grande Jatte* reveals the painter's recognition of the tenuous and shifting social and class relationships at the time. La Grande Jatte (The Big Bowl) is an island in the Seine River near Asnières, one of late-19th-century Paris's rapidly growing industrial suburbs. Seurat's painting captures public life on a Sunday—a congregation of people from various classes, from the sleeveless worker lounging in the left foreground, to the middle-class man and woman seated next to him. Most of the people wear their Sunday best, making class distinctions less obvious.

**VINCENT VAN GOGH** In marked contrast to Seurat, VINCENT VAN GOGH (1853–1890) explored the capabilities of colors

# Pointillism and 19th-Century Color Theory

In the 19th century, advances in the sciences contributed to changing theories about color and how people perceive it. Many physicists and chemists immersed themselves in studying optical reception and the behavior of the human eye in response to light of differing wavelengths. They also investigated the psychological dimension of color. These new ideas about color and its perception provided a framework within which artists such as Georges Seurat (FIG. 28-16) worked. Although historians do not know which publications on color Seurat himself read, he no doubt relied on aspects of these evolving theories to develop pointillism.

Discussions of color often focus on *hue* (for example, red, yellow, and blue), but it is important to consider the other facets of color—*saturation* (the hue's brightness or dullness) and *value* (the hue's lightness or darkness). Most artists during the 19th century understood the concepts of *primary colors* (red, yellow, and blue), *secondary colors* (orange, purple, and green), and *complementary colors* (red and green, yellow and purple, blue and orange; see Introduction, page 7).

Chemist Michel-Eugène Chevreul (1786–1889) extended artists' understanding of color dynamics by formulating the law of *simultaneous contrasts* of colors. Chevreul asserted juxtaposed colors affect the eye's reception of each, making the two colors as dissimilar as possible, both in hue and value. For example, placing light green next to dark green has the effect of making the light green look even lighter and the dark green darker. Chevreul further provided an explanation of *successive contrasts*—the phenomenon of colored afterimages. When a person looks intently at a color (green, for example) and then shifts to a white area, the fatigued eye momentarily perceives the complementary color (red).

Charles Blanc (1813–1882), who coined the term *optical mixture* to describe the visual effect of juxtaposed complementary colors, asserted the smaller the areas of adjoining complementary colors, the greater the tendency for the eye to "mix" the colors, so that the viewer perceives a grayish or neutral tint. Seurat used this principle frequently in his paintings.

Also influential for Seurat was the work of physicist Ogden Rood (1831–1902), who published his ideas in *Modern Chromatics, with Applications to Art and Industry* in 1879. Expanding on the ideas of Chevreul and Blanc, Rood constructed an accurate and understandable diagram of contrasting colors. Further (and particularly significant to Seurat), Rood explored representing color gradation. He suggested artists could achieve gradation by placing small

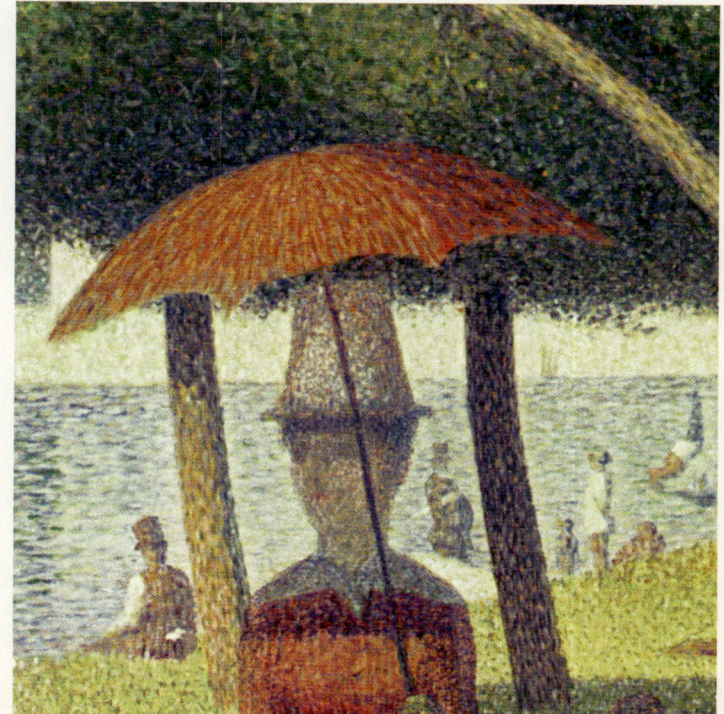

Detail of *A Sunday on La Grande Jatte* (FIG. 28-16).

dots or lines of color side by side, which he observed blended in the eye of the beholder when viewed from a distance.

The color experiments of Seurat and other late-19th-century artists were also part of a larger discourse about human vision and how people see and understand the world. The theories of physicist Ernst Mach (1838–1916) focused on the psychological experience of sensation. He believed humans perceive their environments in isolated units of sensation the brain then recomposes into a comprehensible world. Another scientist, Charles Henry (1859–1926), also pursued research into the psychological dimension of color—how colors affect people, and under what conditions. He went even further to explore the physiological effects of perception. Seurat's work, though characterized by a systematic and scientifically minded approach, also incorporated his concerns about the emotional tone of the images.

and distorted forms to express his emotions as he confronted nature. The son of a Dutch Protestant pastor, van Gogh believed he had a religious calling and did missionary work in the coal-mining area of Belgium. Repeated professional and personal failures brought him close to despair. Only after he turned to painting did he find a way to communicate his experiences. He completed his first major work, *The Potato Eaters* (FIG. **28-16A**), when he was 32 years old. Five years later, considering himself a failure as an artist and an outcast not only from artistic circles but also from society at large, van Gogh fatally shot himself. He sold only one painting during his lifetime. Since his death, however, van Gogh's reputation and the

appreciation of his art have grown dramatically. Subsequent painters, especially the Fauves and German Expressionists (see Chapter 29), built on van Gogh's use of color and the expressiveness of his art. This kind of influence is an important factor in determining artistic significance, and it is no exaggeration to state that today van Gogh is one of the most revered artists in history.

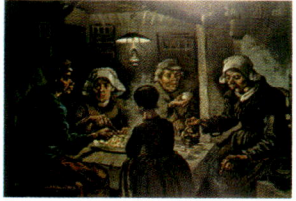

28-16A VAN GOGH, *The Potato Eaters*, 1885.

# The Letters of Vincent van Gogh

Throughout his life, Vincent van Gogh wrote letters to his brother Theo van Gogh (1857–1891), a Parisian art dealer, on matters both mundane and philosophical. The letters are precious documents of the vicissitudes of the painter's life and reveal his emotional anguish. In many of the letters, van Gogh also forcefully stated his views about art, including his admiration for Japanese prints (FIG. 28-16B). In one letter, he told Theo: "In both my life and in my painting, I can very well do without God but I cannot, ill as I am, do without something which is greater than I, . . . the power to create."* For van Gogh, the power to create involved the expressive use of color. "Instead of trying to reproduce exactly what I have before my eyes, I use color more arbitrarily so as to express myself forcibly."[†] Color in painting, he argued, is "not locally true from the point of view of the delusive realist, but color suggesting some emotion of an ardent temperament."[‡]

Some of van Gogh's letters contain vivid descriptions of his paintings, which are invaluable to art historians in gauging his intentions and judging his success. For example, about *Night Café* (FIG. 28-17), he wrote:

> I have tried to express the terrible passions of humanity by means of red and green. The room is blood red and dark yellow with a green billiard table in the middle; there are four citron-yellow lamps with a glow of orange and green. Everywhere there is a clash and contrast of the most disparate reds and greens in the figures

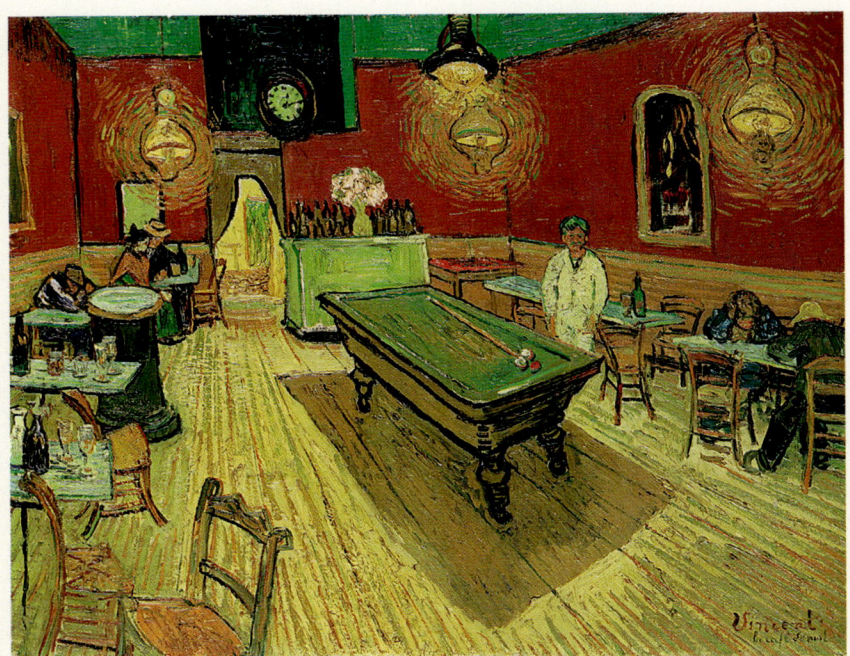

**28-17** VINCENT VAN GOGH, *Night Café*, 1888. Oil on canvas, 2′ 4½″ × 3′. Yale University Art Gallery, New Haven (bequest of Stephen Carlton Clark).

In *Night Café*, van Gogh explored ways colors and distorted forms can express emotions. The thickness, shape, and direction of the brushstrokes create a tactile counterpart to the intense colors.

1 ft.

of little sleeping hooligans, in the empty, dreary room, in violet and blue. The blood-red and the yellow-green of the billiard table, for instance, contrast with the soft, tender Louis XV green of the counter, on which there is a pink nosegay. The white coat of the landlord, awake in a corner of that furnace, turns citron-yellow, or pale luminous green.[§]

*Vincent van Gogh to Theo van Gogh, September 3, 1888, in W. H. Auden, ed., *Van Gogh: A Self-Portrait. Letters Revealing His Life as a Painter* (New York: Dutton, 1963), 319.
[†]August 11, 1888. Ibid., 313.
[‡]September 8, 1888. Ibid., 321.
[§]September 8, 1888. Ibid., 320.

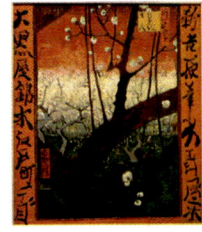

**28-16B** VAN GOGH, *Flowering Plum Tree*, 1887.

**NIGHT CAFÉ** Van Gogh moved to Paris in 1886, where he began to collect—and copy (FIG. 28-16B)—Japanese prints. In 1888, he relocated to Arles in southern France, where he painted *Night Café* (FIG. 28-17), one of his most important and innovative canvases. Although the subject is apparently benign, van Gogh invested it with a charged energy. As he stated in a letter to his brother Theo (see "The Letters of Vincent van Gogh," above), he wanted the painting to convey an oppressive atmosphere—" a place where one can ruin oneself, go mad, or commit a crime."[8] The proprietor rises like a specter from the edge of the billiard table, which the painter depicted in such a steeply tilted perspective that it threatens to slide out of the painting into the viewer's space. Van Gogh communicated the "madness" of the place by selecting vivid hues whose juxtaposition augmented their intensity. His insistence on the expressive values of color led him to develop a corresponding expressiveness in his paint application. The thickness, shape, and direction of his brushstrokes created a tactile counterpart to his intense color schemes. He moved the brush vehemently back and forth or at right angles, giving a textilelike effect, or squeezed dots or streaks onto his canvas from his paint tube. This bold, almost slapdash attack enhanced the intensity of his colors.

**STARRY NIGHT** Similarly illustrative of van Gogh's "expressionist" method is *Starry Night* (FIG. 28-18), which the artist painted in 1889, the year before his death. At this time, van Gogh was living at the asylum of Saint-Paul-de-Mausole in Saint-Rémy, near Arles, where he had committed himself. In *Starry Night,* the artist did not represent the sky's appearance. Rather, he communicated his feelings about the electrifying vastness of the universe, filled with whirling and exploding stars, with the earth and humanity huddling beneath it. The church nestled in the center of the village is, perhaps, van

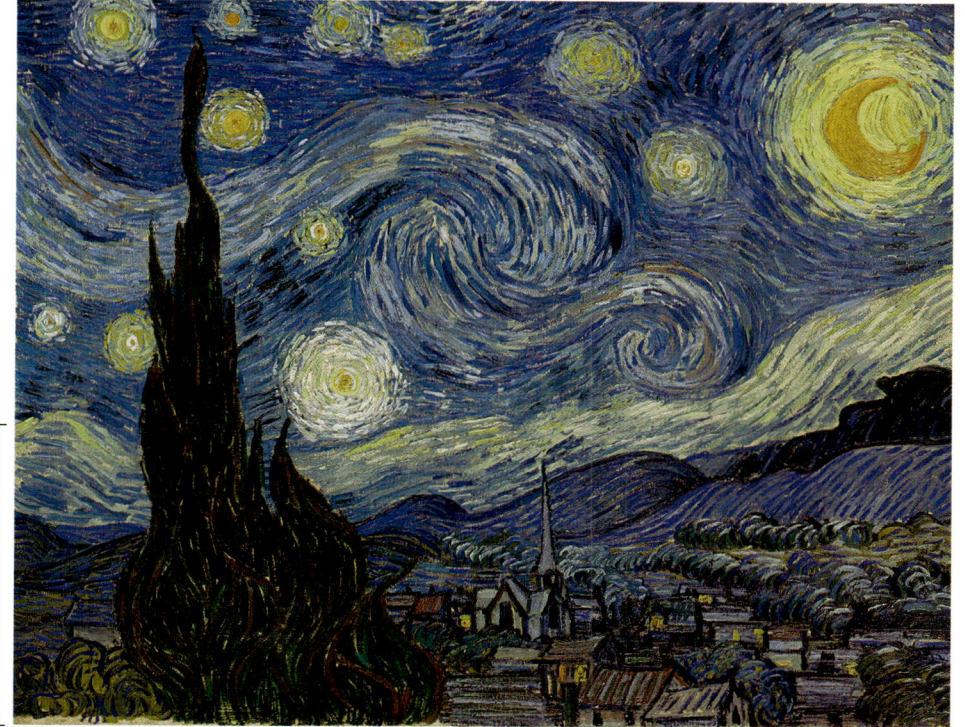

28-18 VINCENT VAN GOGH, *Starry Night,* 1889. Oil on canvas, 2′ 5″ × 3′ ¼″. Museum of Modern Art, New York (acquired through the Lillie P. Bliss Bequest). ◼◀

In this late work, van Gogh painted the vast night sky filled with whirling and exploding stars, the earth huddled beneath it. The painting is an almost abstract pattern of expressive line, shape, and color.

1 ft.

lent brushstrokes, the color suggests a quiet but pervasive depression. A letter van Gogh wrote to his brother on July 16, 1888, reveals his contemplative state of mind:

Perhaps death is not the hardest thing in a painter's life. . . . [L]ooking at the stars always makes me dream, as simply as I dream over the black dots representing towns and villages on a map. Why, I ask myself, shouldn't the shining dots of the sky be as accessible as the black dots on the map of France? Just as we take the train to get to Tarascon or Rouen, we take death to reach a star.[9]

**PAUL GAUGUIN** After painting as an amateur, PAUL GAUGUIN (1848–1903) took lessons with Camille Pissarro and then resigned

Gogh's attempt to express or reconcile his conflicted views about religion. Although the style of *Starry Night* suggests a very personal vision, this work does correspond in many ways to the view available to the painter from the window of his room in Saint-Paul-de-Mausole. The existence of cypress trees and the placement of the constellations have been confirmed as matching the view visible to van Gogh during his stay in the asylum. Still, the artist translated everything he saw into his unique vision. Given van Gogh's determination to "use color . . . to express [him]self forcibly," the dark, deep blue suffusing the entire painting cannot be overlooked. Together with the turbu-

from his prosperous brokerage business in 1883 to devote his time entirely to painting. As van Gogh did, Gauguin rejected objective representation in favor of subjective expression. He also broke with the Impressionists' studies of minutely contrasted hues because he believed color above all must be expressive. For Gauguin, the artist's power to determine the colors in a painting was a central element of creativity. However, whereas van Gogh's heavy, thick brushstrokes were an important component of his expressive style, Gauguin's color areas appear flatter, often visually dissolving into abstract patches or patterns.

In 1886, attracted by Brittany's unspoiled culture, its ancient Celtic folkways, and the still-medieval Catholic piety of its people, Gauguin moved to Pont-Aven. Although in the 1870s and 1880s, Brittany had been transformed into a profitable market economy, Gauguin still viewed the Bretons as "natural" men and women, perfectly at ease in their unspoiled peasant environment. At Pont-Aven, he painted *Vision after the Sermon* (FIG. **28-19**), also known as *Jacob Wrestling with the Angel,* a work in which he decisively rejected both Realism and Impressionism. The painting shows Breton women, wearing their starched white Sunday caps and black dresses, visualizing the

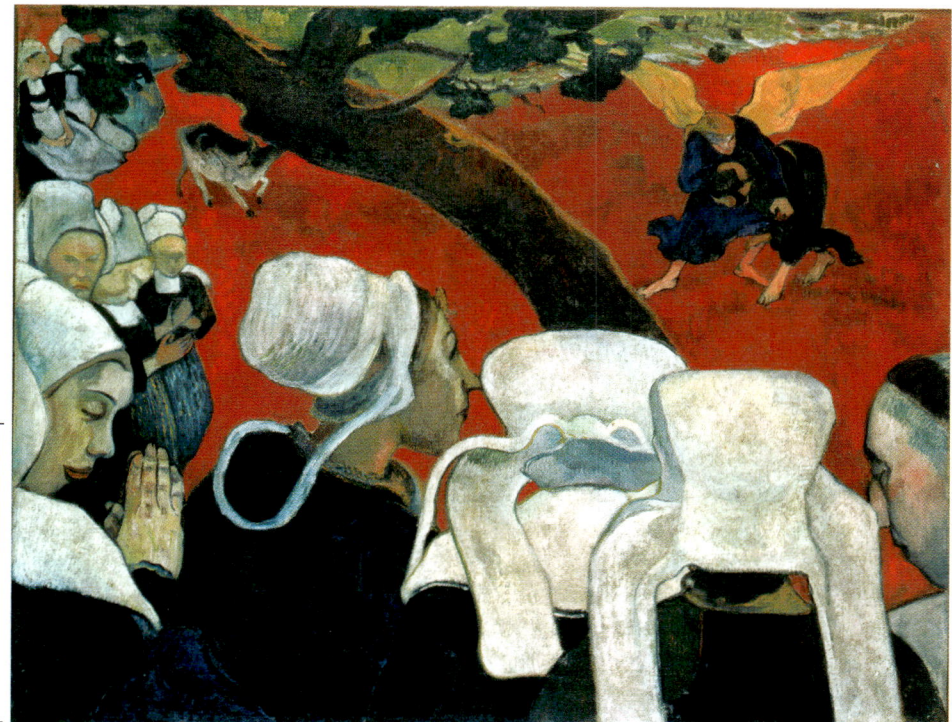

1 ft.

28-19 PAUL GAUGUIN, *Vision after the Sermon* (*Jacob Wrestling with the Angel*), 1888. Oil on canvas, 2′ 4¾″ × 3′ ½″. National Gallery of Scotland, Edinburgh. ◼◀

Gauguin admired Japanese prints, stained glass, and cloisonné enamels. Their influences are evident in this painting of Breton women, in which firm outlines enclose large areas of unmodulated color.

# Gauguin on *Where Do We Come From?*

Paul Gauguin's *Where Do We Come From? What Are We? Where Are We Going?* (FIG. 28-20), painted in Tahiti in 1897, was, in the artist's judgment, his most important work. It can be read as a summary of his artistic methods and of his views on life. The scene is a tropical landscape, populated with native women and children. Despite the setting, most of the canvas surface, other than the figures, consists of broad areas of flat color, which convey a lushness and intensity.

Two of Gauguin's letters to friends contain lengthy discussions of this work and shed important light on the artist's intentions and on the painting's meaning.

> Where are we going? Near to death an old woman. . . . What are we? Day to day existence. . . . Where do we come from? Source. Child. Life begins. . . . Behind a tree two sinister figures, cloaked in garments of sombre colour, introduce, near the tree of knowledge, their note of anguish caused by that very knowledge in contrast to some simple beings in a virgin nature, which might be paradise as conceived by humanity, who give themselves up to the happiness of living.*

> I wanted to kill myself. I went to hide in the mountains, where my corpse would have been eaten up by ants. I didn't have a revolver but I did have arsenic . . . Was the dose too large, or was it the fact of vomiting, which overcame the effects of the poison by getting

rid of it? I know not. . . . . Before I died I wanted to paint a large canvas that I had worked out in my head, and all month long I worked day and night at fever pitch. I can assure you it's nothing like a canvas by Puvis de Chavannes [FIG. 28-23], with studies from nature, then a preparatory cartoon, etc. No, it's all done without a model, feeling my way with the tip of the brush on a piece of sackcloth that is full of knots and rough patches; so it looks terribly unpolished. [Contrary to this assertion, Gauguin did make a detailed preliminary drawing, now in the Louvre, for *Where Do We Come From?* He is here altering the facts in order to establish a persona for himself as an inspired genius who created great works without recourse to traditional studio methods.] People will say it is slipshod, unfinished . . . [but] I do believe that not only is this painting worth more than all the previous ones but also that I will never do a better one or another like it. I put all my energy into it before dying, such painful passion amid terrible circumstances . . . and life burst from it.†

*Where Do We Come From?* is, therefore, a sobering, pessimistic image of the life cycle's inevitability.

*Letter to Charles Morice, March 1898. Translated by Belinda Thompson, *Gauguin by Himself* (Boston: Little, Brown, 1993), 270–271.
†Letter to Daniel de Monfreid, February 1898. Translated by Thompson, ibid., 257–258.

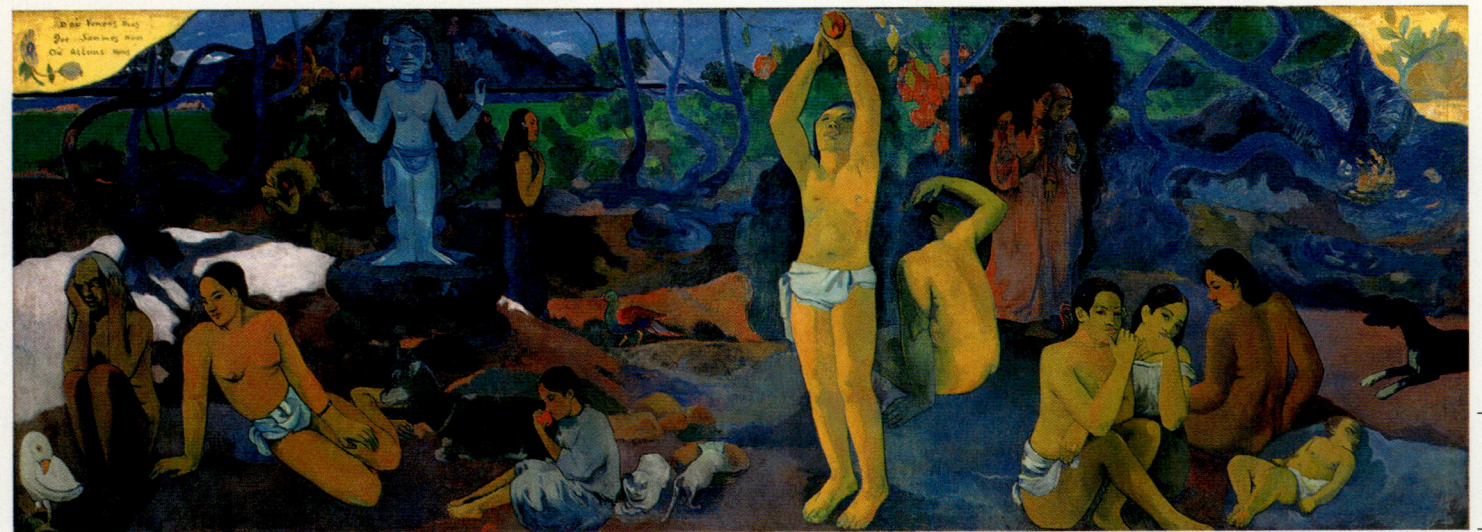

**28-20** PAUL GAUGUIN, *Where Do We Come From? What Are We? Where Are We Going?* 1897. Oil on canvas, 4′ 6¾″ × 12′ 3″. Museum of Fine Arts, Boston (Tompkins Collection).

In search of a place far removed from European materialism, Gauguin moved to Tahiti, where he used native women and tropical colors to present a pessimistic view of the inevitability of the life cycle.

sermon they have just heard in church on Jacob's encounter with the Holy Spirit (Gen. 32:24–30). The women pray devoutly before the apparition, as they would have before the roadside crucifix shrines that were characteristic features of the Breton countryside. Gauguin departed from optical realism and composed the picture elements to focus the viewer's attention on the idea and intensify its message.

The images are not what the Impressionist eye would have seen and replicated but what memory would have recalled and imagination would have modified. Thus the artist twisted the perspective and allotted the space to emphasize the innocent faith of the unquestioning women, and he shrank Jacob and the angel, wrestling in a ring enclosed by a Breton stone fence, to the size of fighting cocks.

Wrestling matches were regular features at the entertainment held after high mass, so Gauguin's women are spectators at a contest that was, for them, a familiar part of their culture.

Gauguin did not unify the picture with a horizon perspective, light and shade, or naturalistic use of color. Instead, he abstracted the scene into a pattern. Pure unmodulated color fills flat planes and shapes bounded by firm line: white caps, black dresses, and the red field of combat. The shapes are angular, even harsh. The caps, the sharp fingers and profiles, and the hard contours suggest the austerity of peasant life and ritual. Gauguin admired Japanese prints, stained glass, and *cloisonné* metalwork (FIGS. 11-2 and 11-3). These art forms contributed to his daring experiment to transform traditional painting and Impressionism into abstract, expressive patterns of line, shape, and pure color. His revolutionary method found its first authoritative expression in *Vision after the Sermon*.

**WHERE DO WE COME FROM?** After a brief period of association with van Gogh in Arles in 1888, Gauguin, in his restless search for provocative subjects and for an economical place to live, settled in Tahiti (MAP 36-1). The South Pacific island attracted Gauguin because he believed it offered him a life far removed from materialistic Europe and an opportunity to reconnect with nature. Upon his arrival, he discovered that Tahiti, under French control since 1842, had been extensively colonized. Disappointed, Gauguin tried to maintain his vision of an untamed paradise by moving to the Tahitian countryside, where he expressed his fascination with primitive life in a series of canvases in which he often based the design, although indirectly, on native motifs. The tropical flora of the island inspired the colors he chose for these paintings—unusual harmonies of lilac, pink, and lemon.

Despite the allure of the South Pacific, Gauguin continued to struggle with life. His health suffered, and his art had a hostile reception. In 1897, worn down by these obstacles, Gauguin decided to take his own life, but not before painting a large canvas titled *Where Do We Come From? What Are We? Where Are We Going?* (FIG. 28-20), which he wrote about in letters to his friends (see "Gauguin on *Where Do We Come From?*" page 816). His attempt to commit suicide in Tahiti was unsuccessful, but Gauguin died a few years later, in 1903, in the Marquesas Islands, his artistic genius still unrecognized.

**PAUL CÉZANNE** Although a lifelong admirer of Delacroix, PAUL CÉZANNE (1839–1906) allied himself early in his career with the Impressionists, especially Pissarro (FIG. 28-6). He at first accepted their color theories and their faith in subjects chosen from everyday life, but his own studies of the Old Masters in the Louvre persuaded him Impressionism lacked form and structure. Cézanne declared he wanted to "make of Impressionism something solid and durable like the art of the museums."[10]

The basis of Cézanne's art was his unique way of studying nature in works such as *Mont Sainte-Victoire* (FIG. 28-21), one of many views he painted of this mountain near his home in Aix-en-Provence. His aim was not truth in appearance, especially not photographic truth, nor was it the "truth" of Impressionism. Rather, he sought a lasting structure behind the formless and fleeting visual information the eyes absorb. Instead of employing the Impressionists' random approach when he was face-to-face with nature, Cézanne developed a more analytical style. His goal was to order the lines, planes, and colors comprising nature. He constantly and painstakingly checked his painting against the part of the scene—he called it the "motif"—he was studying at the moment. In a March 1904 letter, Cézanne stated his goal as a painter: "[to do] Poussin over entirely from nature . . . in the open air, with color and light, instead of one of those works imagined in a studio, where

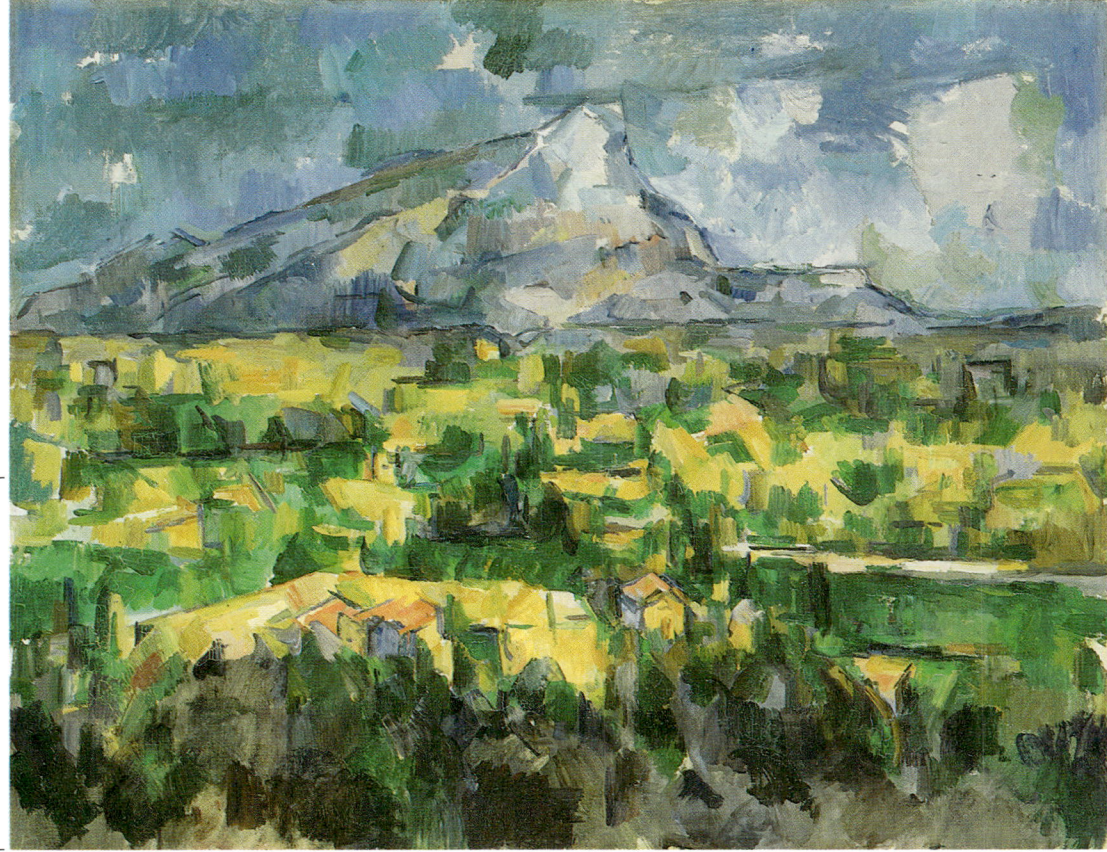

**28-21** PAUL CÉZANNE, *Mont Sainte-Victoire*, 1902–1904. Oil on canvas, 2′ 3½″ × 2′ 11¼″. Philadelphia Museum of Art, Philadelphia (George W. Elkins Collection). ◼◀

In his landscapes, Cézanne replaced the transitory visual effects of changing atmospheric conditions—the Impressionists' focus—with careful analysis of the lines, planes, and colors of nature.

1 ft.

everything has the brown coloring of feeble daylight without reflections from the sky and sun."[11] He sought to achieve Poussin's effects of distance, depth, structure, and solidity not by using traditional perspective and chiaroscuro but by recording the color patterns he deduced from an optical analysis of nature.

With special care, Cézanne explored the properties of line, plane, and color and their interrelationships. He studied the effect of every kind of linear direction, the capacity of planes to create the sensation of depth, the intrinsic qualities of color, and the power of colors to modify the direction and depth of lines and planes. To create the illusion of three-dimensional form and space, Cézanne focused on carefully selecting colors. He understood the visual properties—hue, saturation, and value—of different colors vary (see "Color Theory," page 813). Cool colors tend to recede, whereas warm ones advance. By applying to the canvas small patches of juxtaposed colors, some advancing and some receding, Cézanne created volume and depth in his works. On occasion, the artist depicted objects chiefly in one hue and achieved convincing solidity by modulating the intensity (or saturation). At other times, he juxtaposed contrasting colors—for example, green, yellow, and red—of similar saturation (usually in the middle range rather than the highest intensity) to compose specific objects, such as fruit or bowls.

In *Mont Sainte-Victoire,* Cézanne replaced the transitory visual effects of changing atmospheric conditions, effects that preoccupied Monet, with a more concentrated, lengthier analysis of the colors in large lighted spaces. The main space stretches out behind and beyond the canvas plane and includes numerous small elements, such as roads, fields, houses, and the viaduct at the far right, each seen from a slightly different viewpoint. Above this shifting, receding perspective rises the largest mass of all, the mountain, with an effect—achieved by equally stressing background and foreground contours—of being simultaneously near and far away. This portrayal approximates the experience a person has when viewing the landscape forms piecemeal. The relative proportions of objects vary rather than being fixed by strict perspective, such as that normally found in a photograph. Cézanne immobilized the shifting colors of Impressionism into an array of clearly defined planes composing the objects and spaces in his scene. Describing his method in a letter to a fellow painter, he wrote:

> [T]reat nature by the cylinder, the sphere, the cone, everything in proper perspective so that each side of an object or a plane is directed towards a central point. Lines parallel to the horizon give breadth . . . Lines perpendicular to this horizon give depth. But nature for us men is more depth than surface, whence the need of introducing into our light vibrations, represented by reds and yellows, a sufficient amount of blue to give the impression of air.[12]

**BASKET OF APPLES** Still life was another good vehicle for Cézanne's experiments, as he could arrange a limited number of selected objects to provide a well-ordered point of departure. So analytical was Cézanne in preparing, observing, and painting still lifes (in contrast to the Impressionist emphasis on spontaneity) that he had to abandon using real fruit and flowers because they tended to rot. In *Basket of Apples* (FIG. **28-22**), the objects have lost something of their individual character as bottles and fruit and have almost become cylinders and spheres. Cézanne captured the solidity of each object by juxtaposing color patches. His interest in the study of volume and solidity is evident from the disjunctures in the painting—the table edges are discontinuous, and various objects seem to be depicted from different vantage points. In his zeal to understand three-dimensionality and to convey the placement of forms relative to the space around them, Cézanne explored his still-life arrangements from different viewpoints. This resulted in paintings that, though conceptually coherent, do not appear optically realistic. Cézanne created what might be called, paradoxically, an architecture of color.

In keeping with the modernist concern with the integrity of the painting surface, Cézanne's methods never allow the viewer to disregard the actual two-dimensionality of the picture plane.

**28-22** PAUL CÉZANNE, *Basket of Apples,* ca. 1895. Oil on canvas, 2′ ⅜″ × 2′ 7″. Art Institute of Chicago, Chicago (Helen Birch Bartlett Memorial Collection, 1926). ◼◀

Cézanne's still lifes reveal his analytical approach to painting. He captured the solidity of bottles and fruit by juxtaposing color patches, but the resulting abstract shapes are not optically realistic.

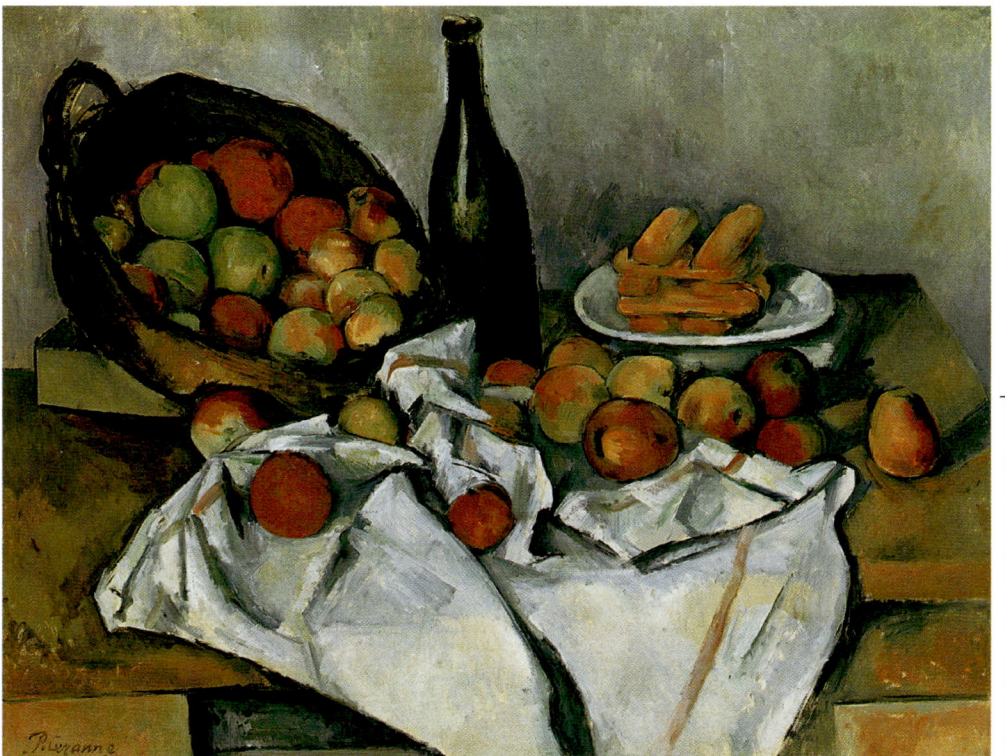

1 ft.

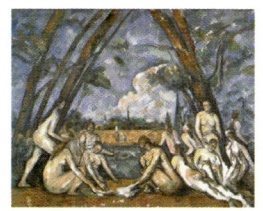

In this manner, Cézanne achieved a remarkable feat—presenting the viewer with two-dimensional and three-dimensional images simultaneously. His late works, such as his unfinished *The Large Bathers* (FIG. **28-22A**), profoundly influenced the development of Cubism in the early 20th century (see Chapter 29).

# SYMBOLISM

The Impressionists and Post-Impressionists believed their emotions and sensations were important elements for interpreting nature, but the depiction of nature remained a primary focus of their efforts. By the end of the 19th century, the representation of nature became completely subjective. Artists no longer sought to imitate nature but created free interpretations of it, concerned solely with expressing their individual spirit. They rejected the optical world as observed in favor of a fantasy world, of forms they conjured in their free imagination, with or without reference to things conventionally seen. Color, line, and shape, divorced from conformity to the optical image, became symbols of personal emotions in response to the world. Deliberately choosing to stand outside of convention and tradition, artists spoke in signs and symbols, as if they were prophets.

Many of the artists following this path adopted an approach to subject and form that associated them with a general European movement called *Symbolism*. Symbolists, whether painters or writers, disdained Realism as trivial. The task of Symbolist artists, both visual and verbal, was not to see things but to see through them to a significance and reality far deeper than what superficial appearance revealed. In this function, as the poet Arthur Rimbaud (1854–1891) insisted, artists became beings of extraordinary insight. (One group of Symbolist painters called itself the *Nabis,* the Hebrew word for

"prophet.") Rimbaud, whose poems had great influence on the artistic community, went so far as to say, in his *Letter from a Seer* (1871), that to achieve the seer's insight, artists must become deranged. In effect, they must systematically unhinge and confuse the everyday faculties of sense and reason, which served only to blur artistic vision. The artists' mystical vision must convert the objects of the commonsense world into symbols of a reality beyond that world and, ultimately, a reality from within the individual. Elements of Symbolism appeared in the works of van Gogh and Gauguin, but their art differed from mainstream Symbolism in their insistence on showing unseen powers as linked to a physical reality, instead of attempting to depict an alternate, wholly interior life.

The extreme subjectivism of the Symbolists led them to cultivate all the resources of fantasy and imagination, no matter how deeply buried or obscure. Moreover, they urged artists to stand against the vulgar materialism and conventional mores of industrial and middle-class society. Above all, the Symbolists wished to purge literature and art of anything utilitarian, to cultivate an exquisite aesthetic sensitivity. The subjects of the Symbolists, conditioned by this reverent attitude toward art and exaggerated aesthetic sensation, became increasingly esoteric and exotic, mysterious, visionary, dreamlike, and fantastic. Perhaps not coincidentally, contemporary with the Symbolists, Sigmund Freud (1856–1939), the founder of psychoanalysis, began the age of psychiatry with his *Interpretation of Dreams* (1900), an introduction to the concept and the world of unconscious experience.

**PIERRE PUVIS DE CHAVANNES** Although he never formally identified himself with the Symbolists, the French painter PIERRE PUVIS DE CHAVANNES (1824–1898) became the "prophet" of those artists. Puvis rejected Realism and Impressionism and went his own way in the 19th century, serenely unaffected by these movements. He produced an ornamental and reflective art—a dramatic rejection of Realism's noisy everyday world. In *Sacred Grove* (FIG. **28-23**), which may have influenced Seurat's *Grande Jatte*

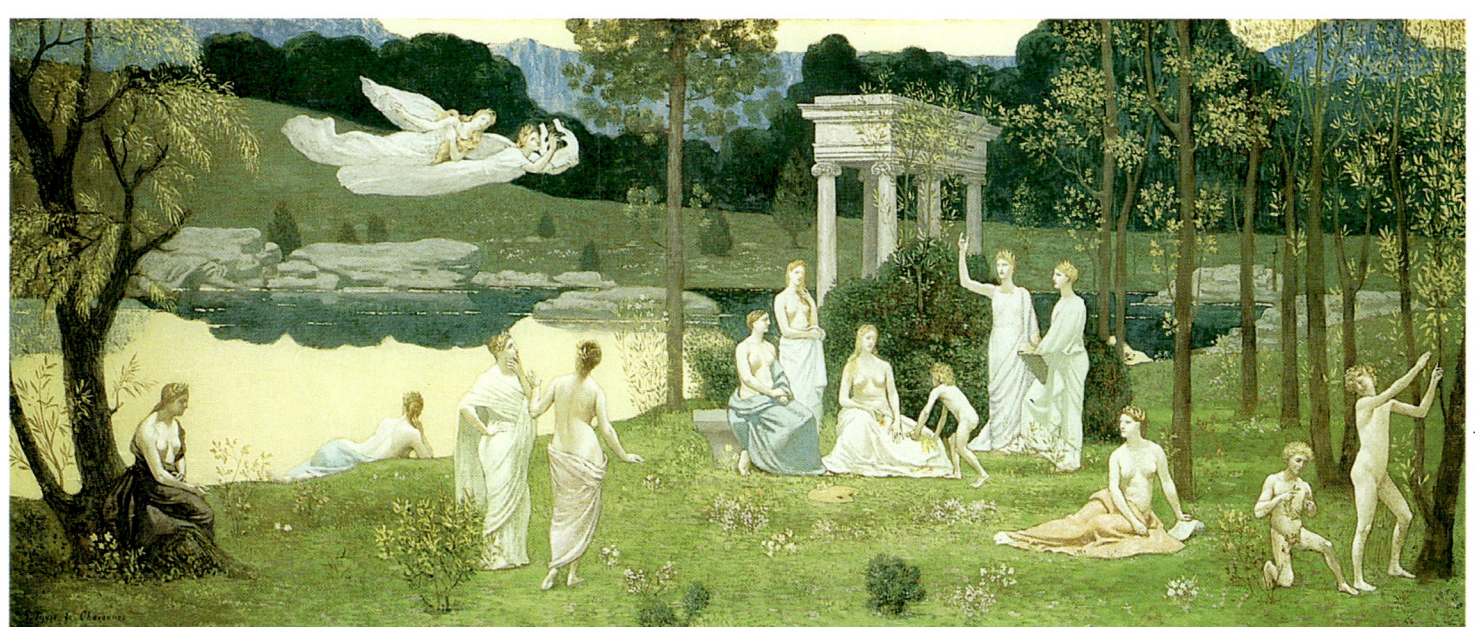

**28-23** PIERRE PUVIS DE CHAVANNES, *Sacred Grove,* 1884. Oil on canvas, 2′ 11½″ × 6′ 10″. Art Institute of Chicago, Chicago (Potter Palmer Collection).

The Symbolists revered Puvis de Chavannes for his rejection of Realism. His statuesque figures in timeless poses inhabit a tranquil landscape, their gestures suggesting a symbolic ritual significance.

(FIG. 28-16), he deployed statuesque figures in a tranquil landscape with a classical shrine. Suspended in timeless poses, the figures' contours are simple and sharp, and their modeling is as shallow as *bas-relief*. The calm and still atmosphere suggests some consecrated place where all movements and gestures have a permanent ritual significance. The stillness and simplicity of the forms, the linear patterns their rhythmic contours create, and the suggestion of their symbolic weight constitute a type of anti-Realism. Puvis garnered support from a wide range of artists. The conservative French Academy and the government applauded his classicism. The Symbolists revered Puvis for his vindication of imagination and his independence from the capitalist world of materialism and the machine.

**GUSTAVE MOREAU**  In keeping with Symbolist tenets, GUSTAVE MOREAU (1826–1898) gravitated toward subjects inspired by dreaming, which was as remote as possible from the everyday world. Moreau presented these subjects sumptuously, and his natural love of sensuous design led him to incorporate gorgeous color, intricate line, and richly detailed shape in all his paintings.

*The Apparition* (FIG. **28-24**), one of two versions of the same subject Moreau submitted to the Salon of 1876, treats a theme that fascinated him and many of his contemporaries—the *femme fatale* (fatal woman), the destructive temptress of men. The seductive heroine here is the biblical Salome (Mark 6:211–28), who danced enticingly before her stepfather, King Herod, and demanded in return the head of Saint John the Baptist (compare FIG. 21-8). In Moreau's representation of the story, Herod sits in the background, enthroned not in a Middle Eastern palace but in a classical columnar hall resembling a Roman triumphal arch. Salome is in the foreground, scantily clad in a gold- and gem-encrusted costume. She points to an apparition hovering in the air at the level of Herod's head. In a radiant circle of light is the halo-framed head of John the Baptist that Salome

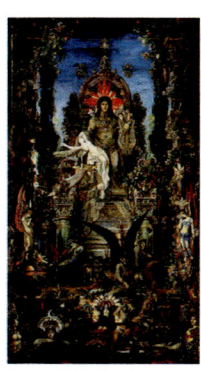

28-24A MOREAU, *Jupiter and Semele*, ca. 1875.

desired, dripping with blood but with eyes wide open. The combination of hallucinatory imagery, eroticism, precise drawing, rich color, and opulent setting is the hallmark of Moreau's highly original style (compare FIG. **28-24A**). His paintings foreshadow the work of the Surrealists in the next century (see Chapter 29).

**ODILON REDON**  Like Moreau, fellow French Symbolist ODILON REDON (1840–1916) was a visionary. He had been aware of an intense inner world since childhood and later wrote of "imaginary things" haunting him. Redon adapted the Impressionist palette and stippling brushstroke for a very different purpose. In *The Cyclops* (FIG. **28-25**), Redon projected a figment of the imagination as if it were visible, coloring it whimsically with a rich profusion of fresh saturated hues that harmonized with the mood he felt fit the subject. The fetal head of the shy, simpering Polyphemus, with its single huge loving eye, rises balloonlike above the sleeping Galatea. The image born of the dreaming world and the color

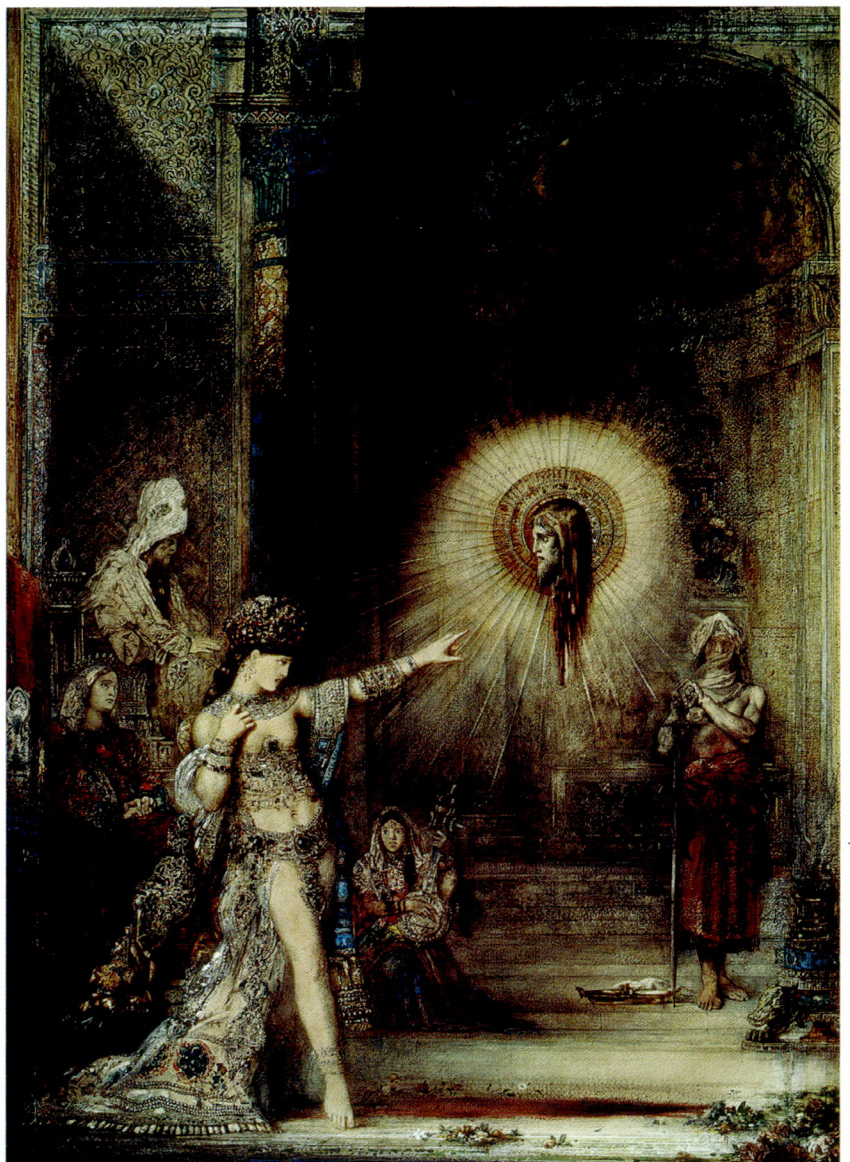

**28-24** GUSTAVE MOREAU, *The Apparition*, 1874–1876. Watercolor on paper, 3′ 5¾″ × 2′ 4⅜″. Musée du Louvre, Paris.

Moreau's painting of Salome, a biblical femme fatale, combines hallucinatory imagery, eroticism, precise drawing, rich color, and an opulent setting—hallmarks of Moreau's Symbolist style.

1 ft.

analyzed and disassociated from the waking world come together here at the artist's will. The contrast with Raphael's representation of the same subject (FIG. 22-11) could hardly be more striking. As Redon himself observed: "All my originality consists . . . in making unreal creatures live humanly by putting, as much as possible, the logic of the visible at the service of the invisible."[13]

**HENRI ROUSSEAU**  The imagination of HENRI ROUSSEAU (1844–1910) engaged a different but equally powerful world of personal fantasy. Gauguin had journeyed to the South Seas in search of primitive innocence. Rousseau was a "primitive" without leaving Paris—a self-taught amateur who turned to painting full-time only after his retirement from service in the French government. Nicknamed "Le Douanier" (The Customs Inspector), he first exhibited in the Salon of 1885 when he was 41. Derided by the critics, Rousseau turned to the Salon des Indépendants in 1886 and thereafter

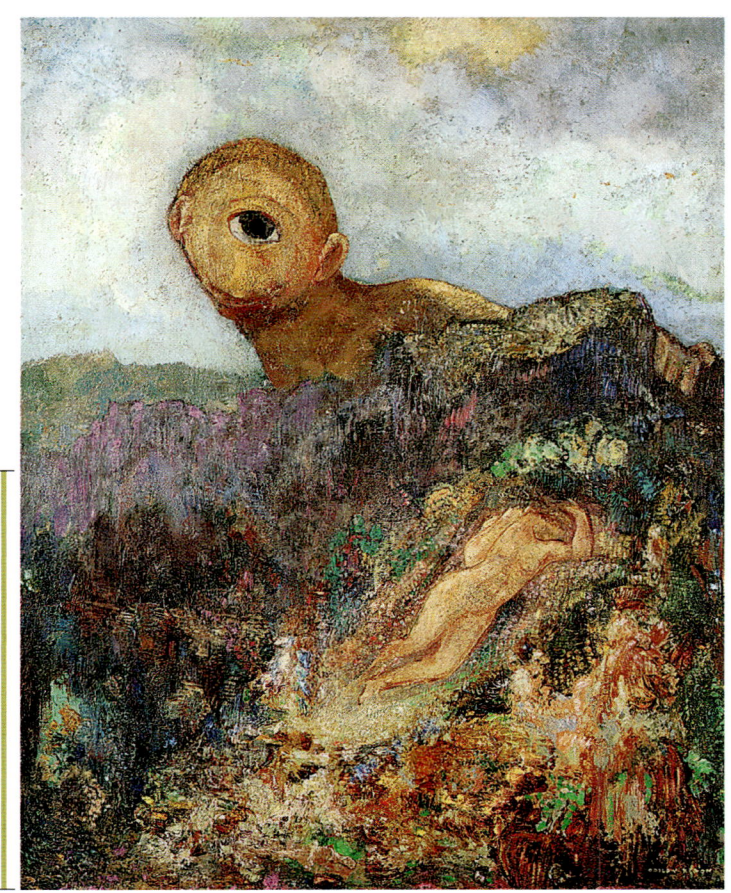

**28-25** ODILON REDON, *The Cyclops,* 1898. Oil on canvas, 2′ 1″ × 1′ 8″. Kröller-Müller Foundation, Otterlo.

In *The Cyclops,* the Symbolist painter Odilon Redon projected a figment of the imagination as if it were visible, coloring it whimsically with a rich profusion of hues adapted from the Impressionist palette.

exhibited his works there almost every year until his death. Even in that more liberal venue, Rousseau still received almost universally unfavorable reviews because of his lack of formal training, imperfect perspective, doll-like figures, and settings resembling constructed theater sets more than natural landscapes. Rousseau compensated for his apparent visual, conceptual, and technical naïveté with a natural talent for design and an imagination teeming with exotic images of mysterious tropical landscapes, which are the setting for two of his most famous works, *Sleeping Gypsy* (FIG. **28-26**) of 1897 and *The Dream* (FIG. **28-26A**), painted 13 years later. In the earlier painting, the recumbent figure occupies a desert

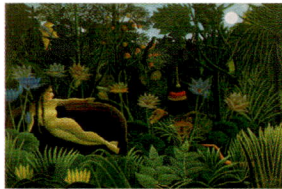

**28-26A** ROUSSEAU, *The Dream,* 1910.

world, silent and secret, and dreams beneath a pale, perfectly round moon. In the foreground, a lion resembling a stuffed, but somehow menacing, animal doll sniffs at the gypsy. A critical encounter impends—an encounter of the type that recalls the uneasiness of a person's vulnerable subconscious self during sleep—a subject of central importance to Rousseau's contemporary, Sigmund Freud. Rousseau's art of drama and fantasy has its own sophistication and, after the artist's death, influenced the development of Surrealism (see Chapter 29).

**JAMES ENSOR** Not all Symbolist artists were French. The leading Belgian painter of the late 19th century was JAMES ENSOR (1860–1949), the son of an expatriate Englishman and a Flemish mother, who spent most of his life in the seaside resort village of Ostend, far from the artistic centers of Europe. In 1883 he cofounded Les Vingts (The Twenty), a group of Belgian artists who staged unjuried exhibitions in Brussels modeled on the independent salons of Paris. A fervent nationalist, he left the group when it began to exhibit the work of foreign artists. In fact, Ensor's most monumental

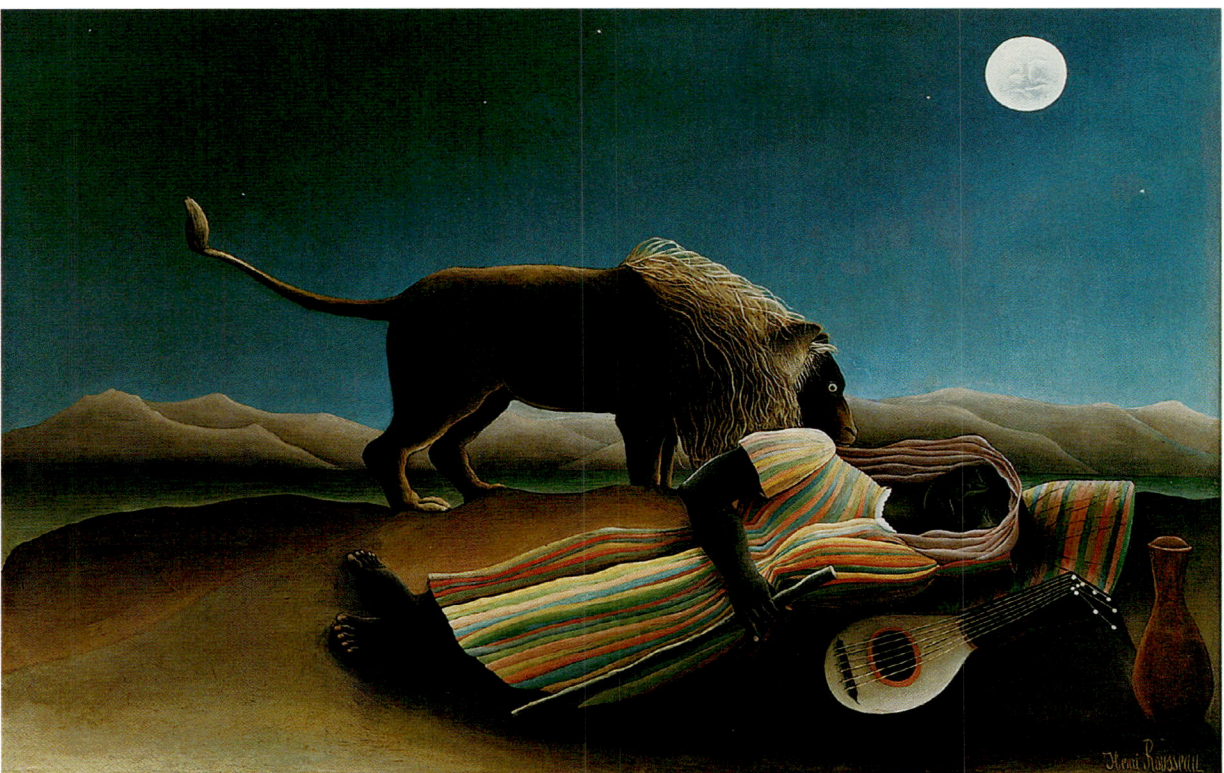

**28-26** HENRI ROUSSEAU, *Sleeping Gypsy,* 1897. Oil on canvas, 4′ 3″ × 6′ 7″. Museum of Modern Art, New York (gift of Mrs. Simon Guggenheim).

In *Sleeping Gypsy,* Rousseau depicted a doll-like but menacing lion sniffing at a recumbent dreaming figure in a mysterious landscape. The painting suggests the vulnerable subconscious during sleep.

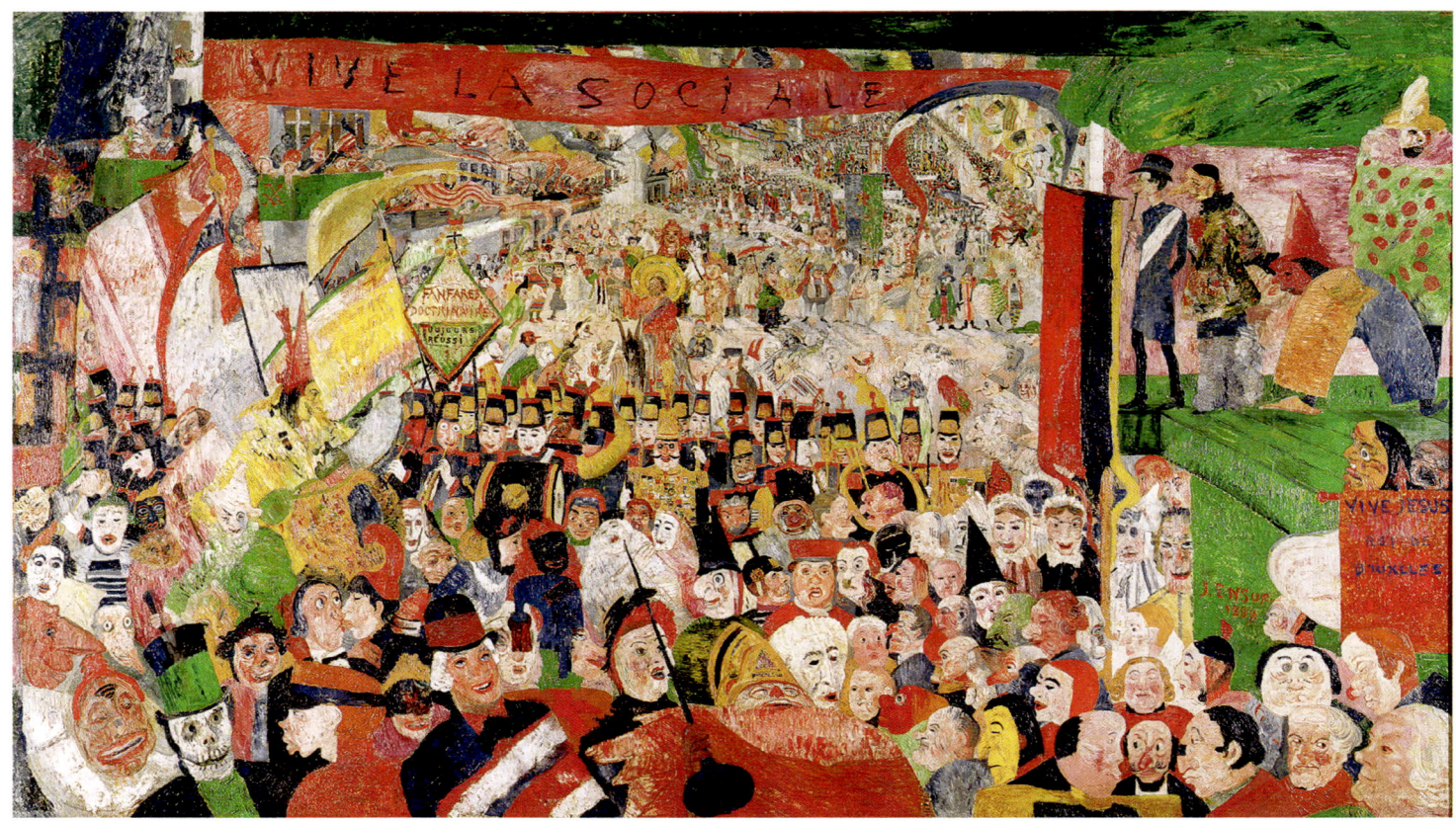

**28-27** JAMES ENSOR, *Christ's Entry into Brussels in 1889*, 1888. Oil on canvas, 8′ 3½″ × 14′ 1½″. J. Paul Getty Museum, Los Angeles.

Ensor's gigantic canvas is an indictment of corrupt modern values. Christ enters Brussels on a donkey in 1889, ignored by the dense crowd of soldiers and citizens wearing grotesque, grimacing masks.

work, *Christ's Entry into Brussels in 1889* (FIG. **28-27**), is very likely a critical response to Georges Seurat's *La Grande Jatte* (FIG. 28-16), exhibited by Les Vingt in 1887.

Whereas Seurat's canvas celebrates the leisure activities of contented bourgeois Parisians, Ensor's even larger (14 feet long) painting is a socialist commentary on the decadence and alienation of urban life at the end of the 19th century. The giant canvas is the artist's pessimistic vision of how Christ would be greeted if he entered the Belgian capital in 1889. Christ is a small and insignificant figure on a donkey in the background of the painting, ignored by the dense crowd of soldiers and citizens wearing grotesque masks inspired by the papier-mâché carnival masks Ensor's family sold in their curio shop in Ostend. Some of the people carry banners and signs. One reads "Long Live Jesus, King of Brussels," another "Long Live Socialism." Complementing the ugly, grimacing masked faces of the anonymous crowd, which eloquently express Ensor's condemnation of the corrupt values of modern society, are the discordant combination of reds, blues, and greens and the coarse texture of the thickly applied oil pigment. As an indictment of the immorality of modern life, Ensor's canvas has few equals.

**EDVARD MUNCH** Also linked in spirit to the Symbolists were the English artist AUBREY BEARDSLEY (1872–1898; FIG. **28-27A**) and the Norwegian EDVARD MUNCH (1863–1944). Munch felt deeply the pain of human life. He believed humans were powerless before the great natural forces of death and love. The emotions associated with them—jealousy, loneliness, fear, desire, despair—became the theme of most of his art. Because Munch's goal was

to describe the conditions of "modern psychic life," as he put it, Realist and Impressionist techniques were inappropriate, focusing as they did on the tangible world. In the spirit of Symbolism, Munch used color, line, and figural distortion for expressive ends. Influenced by Gauguin, Munch produced both paintings and prints whose high emotional charge was a major source of inspiration for the German Expressionists in the early 20th century (see Chapter 29).

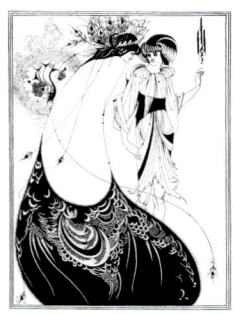

**28-27A** BEARDSLEY, *The Peacock Skirt*, 1894.

Munch's *The Scream* (FIG. **28-28**) exemplifies his style. The image—a man standing on a bridge or jetty in a landscape—comes from the real world, but Munch's treatment of the image departs significantly from visual reality. *The Scream* evokes a visceral, emotional response from the viewer because of the painter's dramatic presentation. The man in the foreground, simplified to almost skeletal form, emits a primal scream. The landscape's sweeping curvilinear lines reiterate the shapes of the man's mouth and head, almost like an echo, as the cry seems to reverberate through the setting. The fiery red and yellow stripes that give the sky an eerie glow also contribute to this work's resonance. Munch wrote a revealing epigraph to accompany the painting: "I stopped and leaned against the balustrade, almost dead with fatigue. Above the blue-black fjord hung the clouds, red as blood and tongues of fire. My friends had left me, and alone, trembling with anguish, I became aware of the vast, infinite cry of nature."[14] Appropriately, the original title of this work was *Despair*.

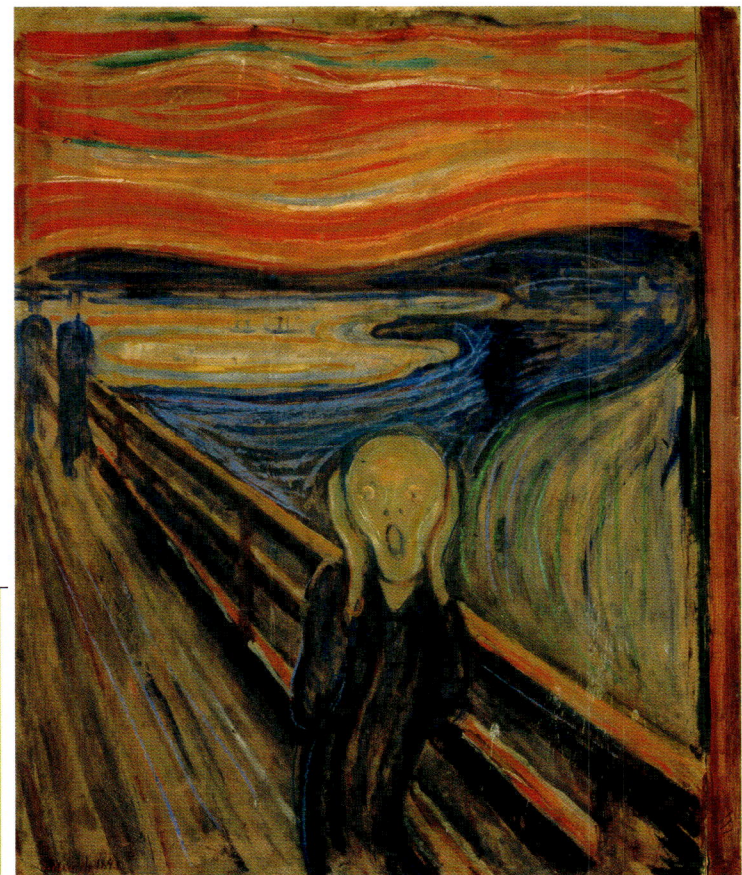

**28-28** Edvard Munch, *The Scream,* 1893. Tempera and pastels on cardboard, 2′ 11¾″ × 2′ 5″. National Gallery, Oslo.

Although grounded in the real world, *The Scream* departs significantly from visual reality. Munch used color, line, and figural distortion to evoke a strong emotional response from the viewer.

**FIN-DE-SIÈCLE** Historians have adopted the term *fin-de-siècle,* which literally means "end of the century," to describe the spirit of dissolution and anxiety that characterized European, and especially Austrian, culture of the late 1800s. This designation is not merely chronological but also refers to a certain sensibility. The increasingly large and prosperous middle classes aspired to the advantages the aristocracy traditionally enjoyed. They too strove to live "the good life," which evolved into a culture of decadence and indulgence. Characteristic of the fin-de-siècle period was an intense preoccupation with sexual drives, powers, and perversions. People at the end of the century also immersed themselves in an exploration of the unconscious. This culture was unrestrained and freewheeling, but the determination to enjoy life masked an anxiety prompted by significant political upheaval and an uncertain future. The country most closely associated with fin-de-siècle culture was Austria.

**GUSTAV KLIMT** The Viennese artist Gustav Klimt (1863–1918) captured this period's flamboyance in his work but tempered it with unsettling undertones. In *The Kiss* (FIG. **28-29**), his best-known work, Klimt depicted a couple locked in an embrace. The setting is ambiguous, an indeterminate place apart from time and space. Moreover, all the viewer sees of the embracing couple is a small segment of each body—and virtually nothing of the man's face. The rest of the canvas dissolves into shimmering, extravagant flat patterning. This patterning has clear ties to Art Nouveau and to the Arts and Crafts movement (discussed later) and also evokes the conflict between two- and three-dimensionality intrinsic to the work of Degas and other modernists. In *The Kiss,* however, those patterns also signify gender contrasts—rectangles for the man's garment, circles for the woman's. Yet the patterning also unites the two lovers into a single formal entity, underscoring their erotic union.

**GERTRUDE KÄSEBIER** Photography, which during the 19th century most people regarded as the ultimate form of Realism, could also be manipulated by artists to produce effects more akin to painting than to factual records of contemporary life. After the first great breakthroughs (see Chapter 27), which bluntly showed what was before the eye, some photographers began to pursue

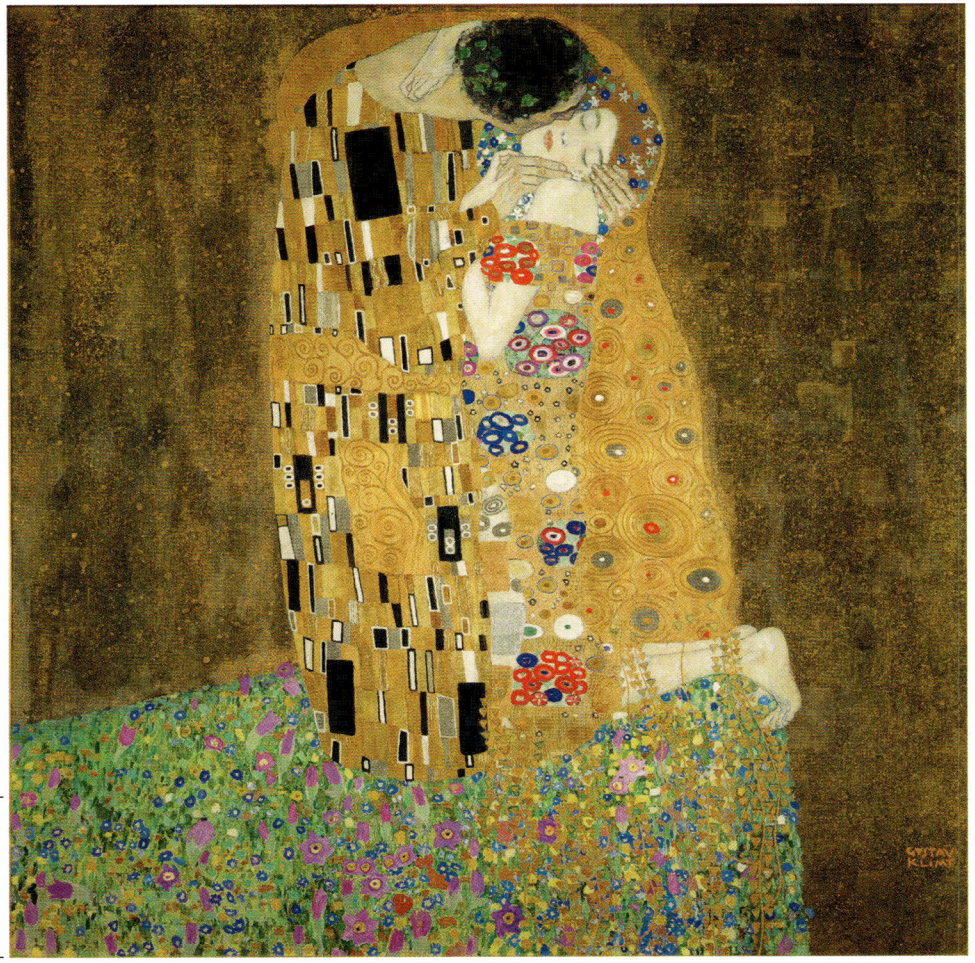

**28-29** Gustav Klimt, *The Kiss,* 1907–1908. Oil on canvas, 5′ 10¾″ × 5′ 10¾″. Österreichische Galerie Belvedere, Vienna. ◼◀

In this opulent Viennese fin-de-siècle painting, Klimt revealed only a small segment of each lover's body. The rest of his painting dissolves into shimmering, extravagant flat patterning.

entire image slightly. In *Blessed Art Thou among Women,* the soft focus invests the whole scene with an aura of otherworldly peace. The photograph showcases Käsebier's ability to inject a sense of the spiritual and the divine into scenes from everyday life.

## SCULPTURE

The three-dimensional art of sculpture could not capture the optical sensations many painters favored in the later 19th century. Its very nature—its tangibility and solidity—suggests permanence. Consequently, the sculptors of this period pursued artistic goals markedly different from those of contemporaneous painters and photographers.

**JEAN-BAPTISTE CARPEAUX** In France, JEAN-BAPTISTE CARPEAUX (1827–1875) combined an interest in Realism with a love of ancient, Renaissance, and Baroque sculpture. He based his group *Ugolino and His Children* (FIG. **28-31**) on a passage in Dante's *Inferno* (33.58–75) in which Count Ugolino and his four sons starve to death while shut up in a tower. In Hell, Ugolino relates to Dante how, in a moment of extreme despair, he bit both his hands in grief. His children, thinking he did it because of his hunger, offered him

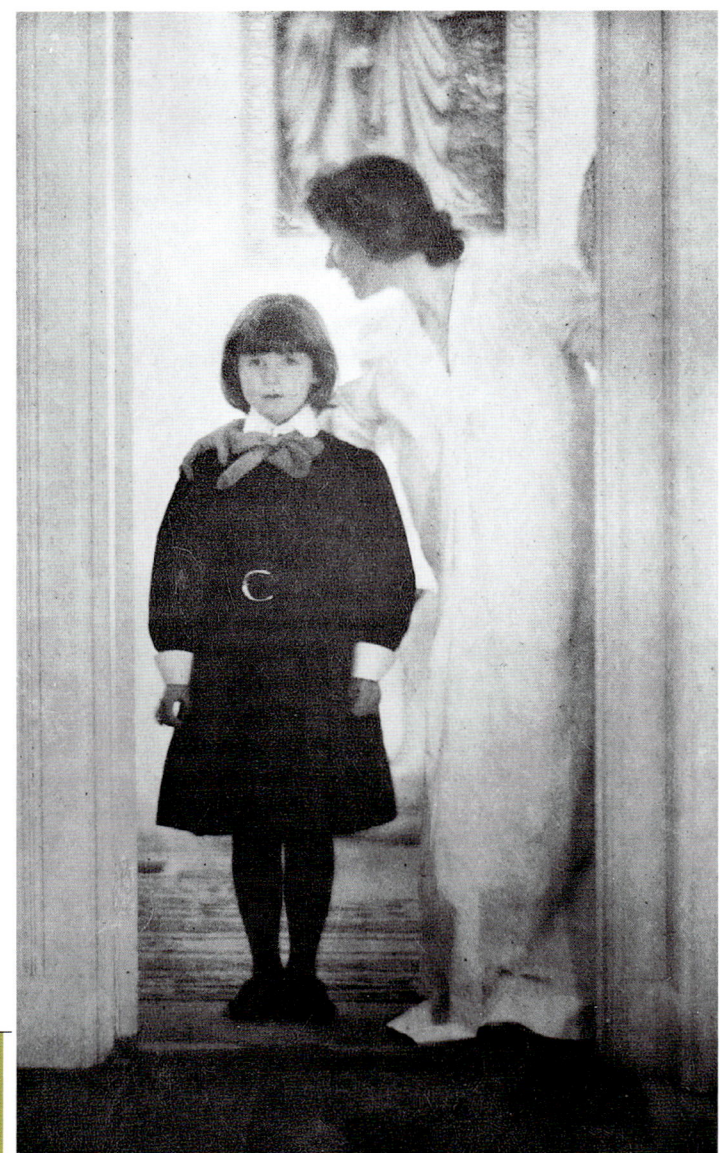

1 ft.

**28-30** GERTRUDE KÄSEBIER, *Blessed Art Thou among Women,* 1899. Platinum print on Japanese tissue, $9\frac{3}{8}'' \times 5\frac{1}{2}''$. Museum of Modern Art, New York (gift of Mrs. Hermine M. Turner).

Symbolist Käsebier injected a sense of the spiritual and the divine into scenes from everyday life. The deliberately soft focus of this photograph invests the scene with an aura of otherworldly peace.

new ways of using the medium as a vehicle of artistic expression. A leading practitioner of what might be called the pictorial style in photography was the American GERTRUDE KÄSEBIER (1852–1934), who took up the camera in 1897 after raising a family and working as a portrait painter. She soon became famous for photographs with Symbolist themes, such as *Blessed Art Thou among Women* (FIG. **28-30**). The title repeats the phrase the angel Gabriel used to announce to the Virgin Mary that she will be the mother of Jesus. In the context of Käsebier's photography, the words suggest a parallel between the biblical Mother of God and the modern mother in the image, who both protects and sends forth her daughter. The white setting and the mother's pale gown shimmer in soft focus behind the serious girl, who wears darker tones and whom the photographer captured with sharper focus. Käsebier deliberately combined an out-of-focus background with a sharp or almost-sharp foreground in order to achieve an expressive effect by blurring the

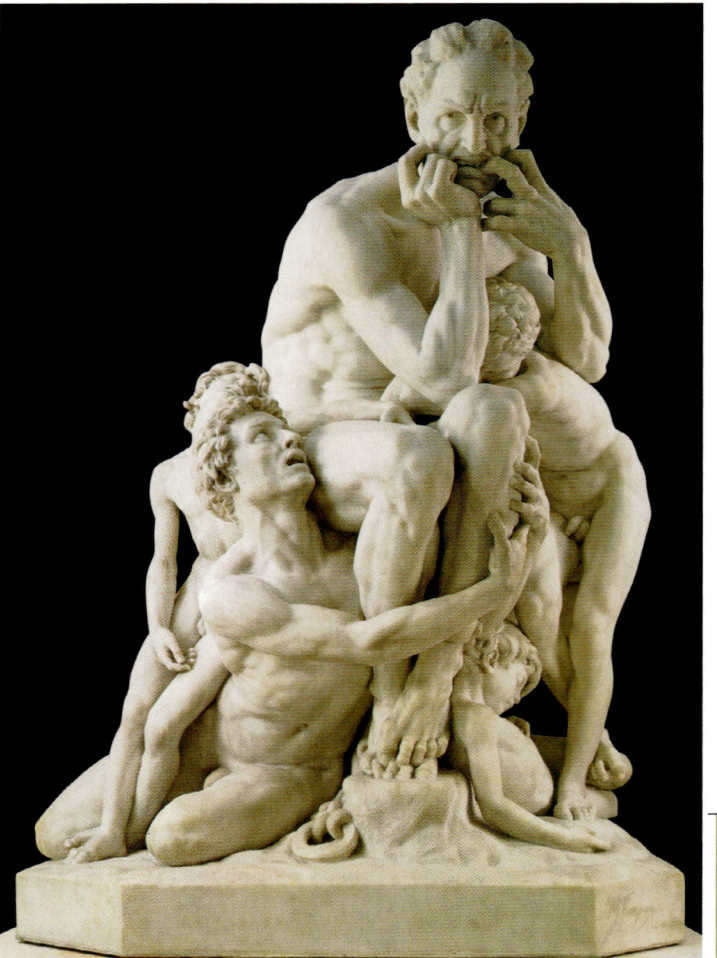

1 ft.

**28-31** JEAN-BAPTISTE CARPEAUX, *Ugolino and His Children,* 1865–1867. Marble, 6′ 5″ high. Metropolitan Museum of Art, New York (Josephine Bay Paul and C. Michael Paul Foundation, Inc., and the Charles Ulrich and Josephine Bay Foundation, Inc., gifts, 1967).

As in Dante's *Inferno,* Carpeaux represented Ugolino biting his hands in despair as he and his sons await death by starvation. The twisted forms suggest the self-devouring torment of frustration.

## Rodin on Movement in Art and Photography

Photography had a profound effect on 19th-century art, and many artists used photographs as an aid in capturing "reality" on canvas or in stone. Eadweard Muybridge's photographs of a galloping horse (FIG. 27-54), for example, definitively established that at certain times all four hooves of the animal are in the air. But not all artists believed photography was "true to life." The sculptor Auguste Rodin (FIGS. 28-32, 28-32A, and 28-33) was one of the doubters.

I have always sought to give some indication of movement [in my statues]. I have very rarely represented complete repose. I have always endeavoured to express the inner feelings by the mobility of the muscles. . . . The illusion of life is obtained in our art by good modelling and by movement. . . . [M]ovement is the transition from one attitude to another. . . . Have you ever attentively examined instantaneous photographs of walking figures? . . . [Photographs] present the odd appearance of a man suddenly stricken with paralysis and petrified in his pose. . . . If, in fact, in instantaneous photographs, the figures, though taken while moving, seem suddenly fixed in mid-air, it is because, all parts of the body being reproduced exactly at the same twentieth or fortieth of a second, there is no progressive development of movement as there is in art. . . . [I]t is the artist who is truthful and it is photography which lies, for in reality time does not stop.*

* Translated by Robin Fedden, in Elizabeth Gilmore Holt, ed., *From the Classicists to the Impressionists: Art and Architecture in the 19th Century* (New Haven, Conn.: Yale University Press, 1966; reprint 1986), 406–409.

**28-32** AUGUSTE RODIN, *Walking Man*, 1905. Bronze, 6′ 11¾″ high. Musée d'Orsay, Paris.

In this study for a statue of Saint John the Baptist, Rodin depicted a headless and armless figure in midstride. *Walking Man* demonstrates Rodin's mastery of anatomy and ability to capture transitory motion.

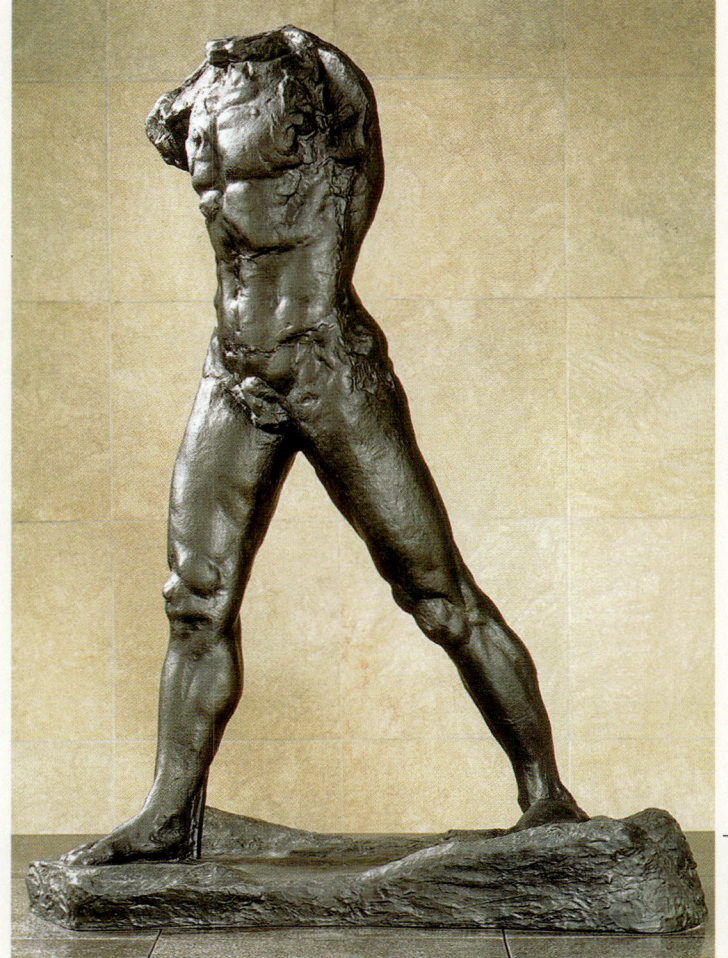

1 ft.

---

their own flesh as food. In Carpeaux's statuary group, the powerful forms—twisted, intertwined, and densely concentrated—suggest the self-devouring torment of frustration and despair wracking the unfortunate Ugolino. A careful student of Michelangelo's male figures, Carpeaux also said he had the Laocoön group (FIG. 5-89) in mind. Certainly, the storm and stress of *Ugolino and His Children* recall similar characteristics of that ancient work. Regardless of these influences, the sense of vivid reality in the anatomy of Carpeaux's figures shows the artist's interest in study from life. The French public did not share that interest, however, and preferred the idealized bodies of classical sculptures—one of the reasons Carpeaux was forced to remove *The Dance* (FIG. **28-31A**) from the facade of the Paris opera house (FIG. 27-45).

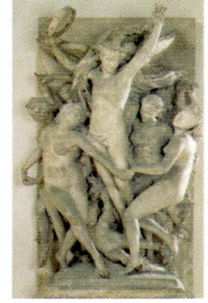

**28-31A** CARPEAUX, *The Dance*, 1867–1869.

**AUGUSTE RODIN** The leading French sculptor of the later 19th century was AUGUSTE RODIN (1840–1917), who conceived and executed his sculptures with a Realist sensibility. The human body in

motion (see "Rodin on Movement in Art and Photography," above) fascinated Rodin, as it did Eakins and Muybridge (FIG. 27-54) before him. Rodin was also well aware of the Impressionists' innovations. Although color was not a significant factor in Rodin's work, the influence of Impressionism is evident in the artist's abiding concern for the effect of light on sculpted surfaces. When focusing on the human form, he joined his profound knowledge of anatomy and movement with special attention to the body's exterior, saying, "The sculptor must learn to reproduce the surface, which means all that vibrates on the surface, soul, love, passion, life. . . . Sculpture is thus the art of hollows and mounds, not of smoothness, or even polished planes."[15] Primarily a modeler of pliable material rather than a carver of hard wood or stone, Rodin worked his surfaces with fingers sensitive to the subtlest variations of surface, catching the fugitive play of constantly shifting light on the body. In his studio, he often would have a model move around in front of him while he created preliminary versions of his sculptures with coils of clay.

In *Walking Man* (FIG. **28-32**), a preliminary study for the sculptor's *Saint John the Baptist Preaching*, Rodin succeeded in representing a fleeting moment in cast bronze. He portrayed a headless and armless figure in midstride at the moment when weight is transferred across the pelvis from the back leg to the front. In addition to capturing the sense of the transitory, Rodin demonstrated his mastery of realistic detail in his meticulous rendition of muscle, bone, and tendon.

***GATES OF HELL*** Rodin also made many nude and draped studies for each of the figures in two of his most ambitious works—the life-size group *Burghers of Calais* (FIG. 28-32A) and the *Gates of Hell* (FIG. 28-33), which occupied the sculptor for two decades. After he failed to gain admission to the École des Beaux-Arts, Rodin enrolled in the École Impériale Spéciale de Dessin et Mathématiques, the French school of decorative arts, known as the "Petit École" (Little School) because it was a lesser version of the more prestigious Beaux-Arts academy. Nonetheless, Rodin gained attention for the outstanding realism of some of his early sculptures, and on August 16, 1880, he received a major governmental commission to design a pair of doors for a planned Museum of Decorative Arts in Paris. Rodin worked on the project for 20 years, but the museum was never built (the Musée d'Orsay now occupies the intended site). It was not until after the sculptor's death that others cast his still-unfinished doors in bronze.

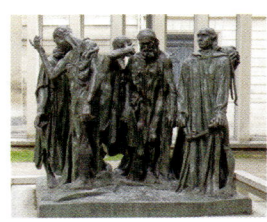

28-32A RODIN, *Burghers of Calais*, 1884–1889.

The commission permitted Rodin to choose his own subject. He selected *The Gates of Hell,* based on Dante's *Inferno* and Baudelaire's *Flowers of Evil.* Originally inspired by Lorenzo Ghiberti's *Gates of Paradise* (FIG. 21-9), which he had seen in Florence, Rodin quickly abandoned the idea of a series of framed narrative panels and decided instead to cover each of the doors with a continuous writhing mass of tormented men and women, sinners condemned to Dante's second circle of Hell for their lust. Because of the varying height of the relief and the variegated surfaces, the figures seem to be in flux, moving in and out of an undefined space in a reflection of their psychic turmoil. The dreamlike (or rather, the nightmarish) vision connects Rodin with the Symbolists, and the pessimistic mood exemplifies the fin-de-siècle spirit. The swirling composition and emotionalism recall Eugène Delacroix's *Death of Sardanapalus* (FIG. 27-15) and Michelangelo's *Last Judgment* (FIG. 22-19). But Rodin's work defies easy stylistic classification.

The nearly 200 figures of *The Gates of Hell* spill over onto the jambs and the lintel. Rodin also included freestanding figures, which, cast separately in multiple versions, are among his most famous works. Above the doors, *The Three Shades* is a trio of twisted nude male figures, essentially the same figure with elongated arms in three different positions. The group evokes Jean Baptiste Carpeaux's *Ugolino and His Children* (FIG. 28-31). *The Thinker,* Rodin's famous seated nude man with a powerful body who rests his chin

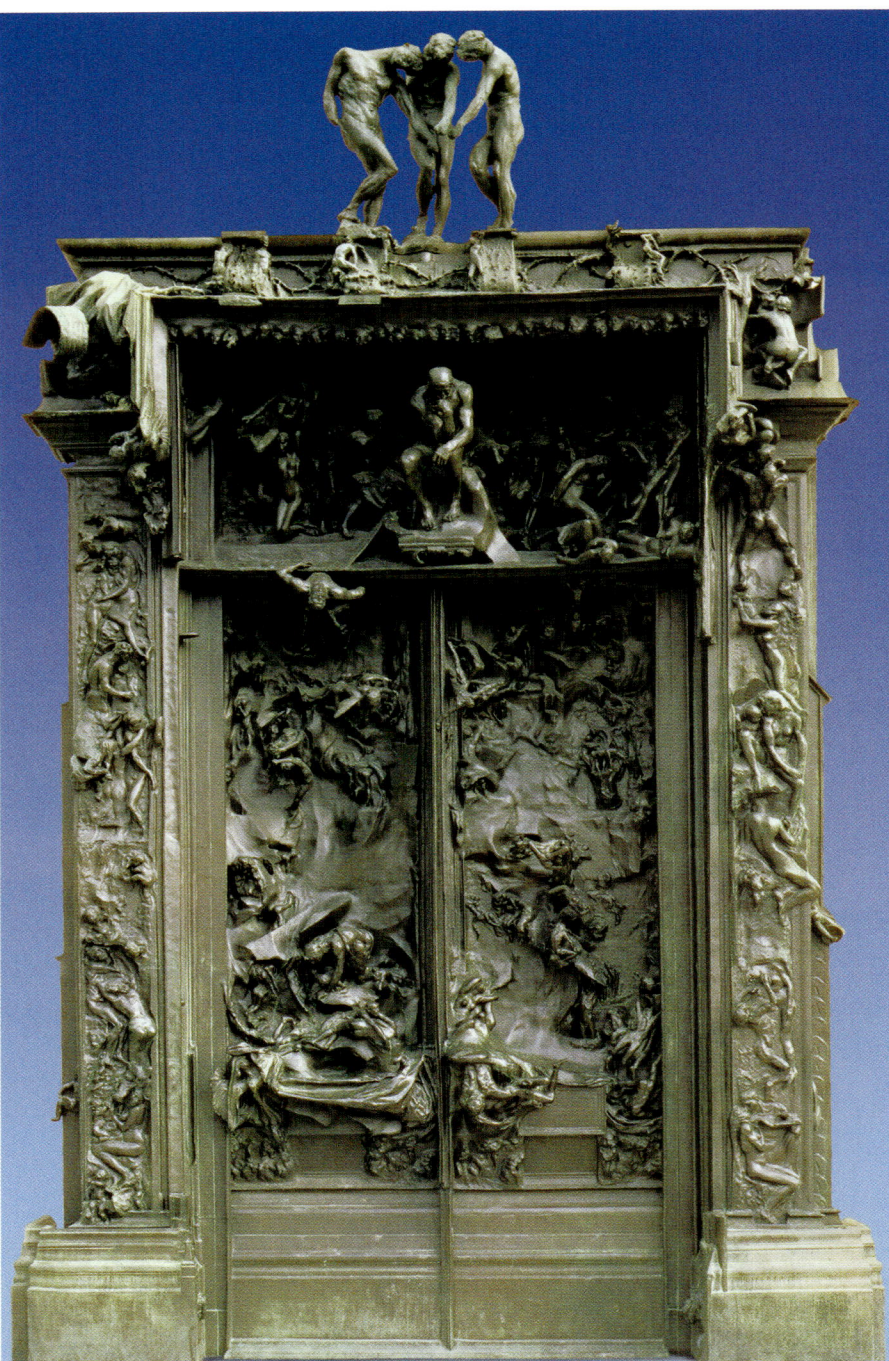

1 ft.

28-33 AUGUSTE RODIN, *The Gates of Hell*, 1880–1900 (cast in 1917). Bronze, 20′ 10″ × 13′ 1″. Musée Rodin, Paris.

Rodin's most ambitious work, inspired by Dante's *Inferno* and Ghiberti's *Gates of Paradise* (FIG. 21-9), presents nearly 200 tormented sinners in relief below *The Three Shades* and *The Thinker.*

on his clenched right hand, ponders the fate of the tormented souls on the doors below. *The Gates of Hell,* more than 20 feet tall, was Rodin's most ambitious project. It greatly influenced the painters and sculptors of the Expressionist movements of the early 20th century (see Chapter 29).

Rodin's ability to capture the quality of the transitory through his highly textured surfaces while revealing larger themes and deeper, lasting sensibilities is one of the reasons he had a strong influence on 20th-century artists. Because many of his works, such as

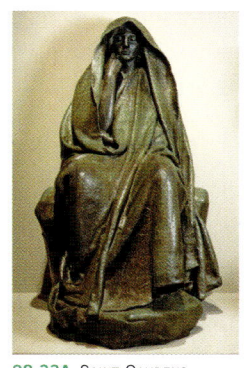

28-33A SAINT-GAUDENS, *Adams Memorial*, 1886–1891.

*Walking Man,* were deliberate fragments, he was also instrumental in creating a taste for the incomplete, an aesthetic many later sculptors embraced enthusiastically.

## AUGUSTUS SAINT-GAUDENS

Other leading sculptors of the late 19th century pursued more traditional goals, however. In America, for example, AUGUSTUS SAINT-GAUDENS (1848–1907) produced monumental statues expressing the majestic calm of ancient Greek and Roman sculpture, as in his *Adams Memorial* (FIG. **28-33A**) in Washington, D.C.

# ARCHITECTURE AND DECORATIVE ARTS

The decisive effects of industrialization were impossible to ignore, and although many artists embraced this manifestation of "modern life" or at least explored its effects, other artists, especially those associated with the Arts and Crafts movement in England, decried the impact of rampant industrialism. This movement, which developed during the last decades of the 19th century, was shaped by the ideas of John Ruskin, the critic who skewered Whistler's "arrangements" (see "Whistler," page 810), and the artist William Morris. Both men shared a distrust of machines and industrial capitalism, which they believed alienated workers from their own nature. Accordingly, they advocated an art "made by the people for the people

as a joy for the maker and the user."[16] This condemnation of capitalism and support for manual laborers were consistent with the tenets of socialism, and many artists in the Arts and Crafts movement, especially in England, considered themselves socialists and participated in the labor movement.

This democratic, or at least populist, attitude carried over to the art they produced as well. Members of the Arts and Crafts movement dedicated themselves to making functional objects with high aesthetic value for a wide public. They advocated a style based on natural, rather than artificial, forms, which often consisted of repeated designs of floral or geometric patterns. For Ruskin, Morris, and others in the Arts and Crafts movement, high-quality artisanship and honest labor were crucial ingredients of superior works of decorative art.

**WILLIAM MORRIS** To promote these ideals, WILLIAM MORRIS (1834–1896) formed a decorating firm dedicated to Arts and Crafts principles: Morris, Marshall, Faulkner, and Company, Fine Arts Workmen in Painting, Carving, Furniture, and Metals. His company did a flourishing business producing wallpaper, textiles, furniture, books, rugs, stained glass, tiles, and pottery. In 1867, Morris received the commission to decorate the Green Dining Room (FIG. **28-34**) at London's South Kensington Museum (now the Victoria & Albert Museum), the center of public art education and home of decorative art collections. The range of room features—windows, lights, and *wainscoting* (paneling on the lower part of interior walls)—Morris created for this unified, beautiful, and functional environment was all-encompassing. Nothing escaped his eye. Morris's design for this room also reveals the penchant of Arts and Crafts designers for intricate patterning.

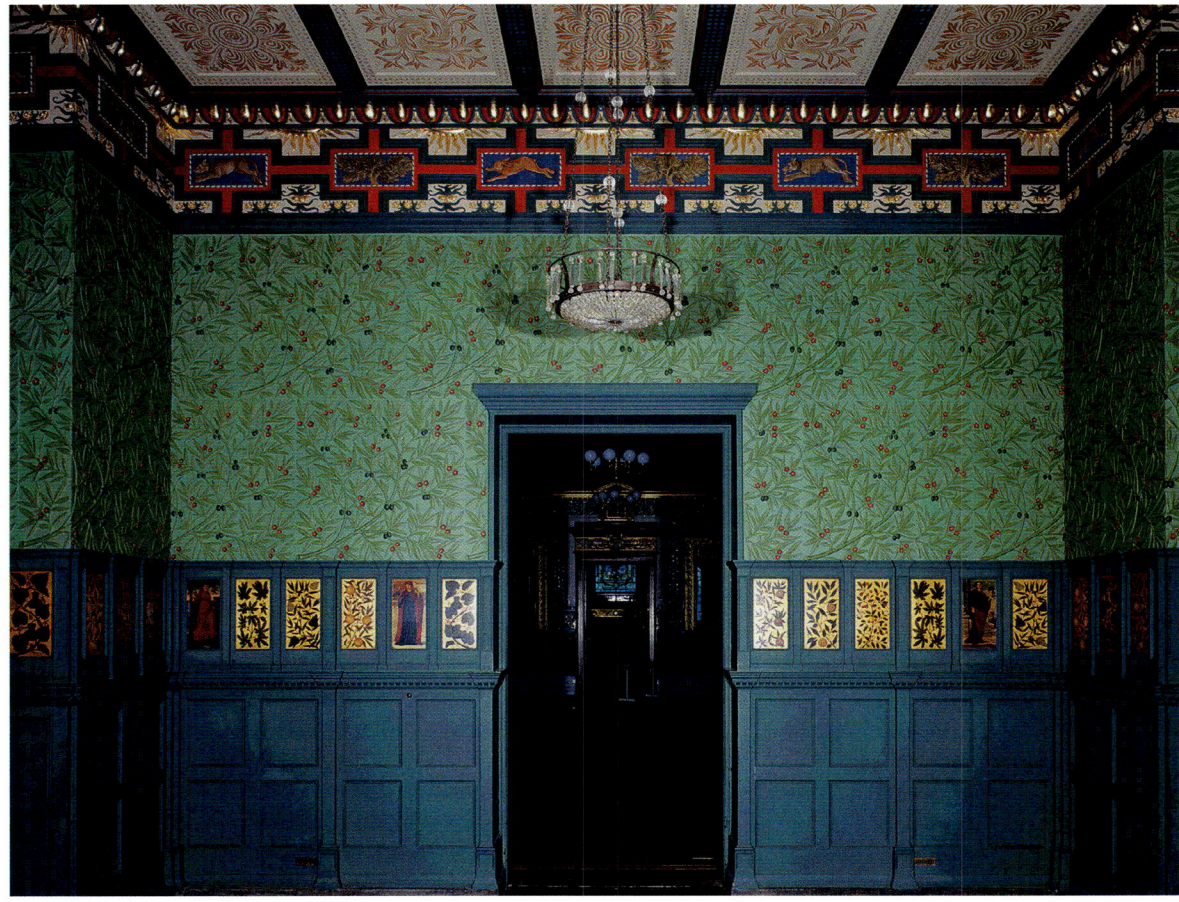

**28-34** WILLIAM MORRIS, Green Dining Room, South Kensington Museum (now Victoria & Albert Museum), London, England, 1867.

William Morris was a founder of the Arts and Crafts movement. His Green Dining Room exemplifies the group's dedication to creating intricately patterned yet unified and functional environments.

28-35 CHARLES RENNIE MACKINTOSH and MARGARET MACDONALD MACKINTOSH, Ladies' Luncheon Room, Ingram Street Tea Room, Glasgow, Scotland, 1900–1912. Reconstructed (1992–1995) in the Glasgow Art Galleries and Museum, Glasgow.

The Mackintoshes' Ladies' Luncheon Room in Glasgow features functional and exquisitely designed Arts and Crafts decor, including stained-glass windows and pristinely geometric furnishings.

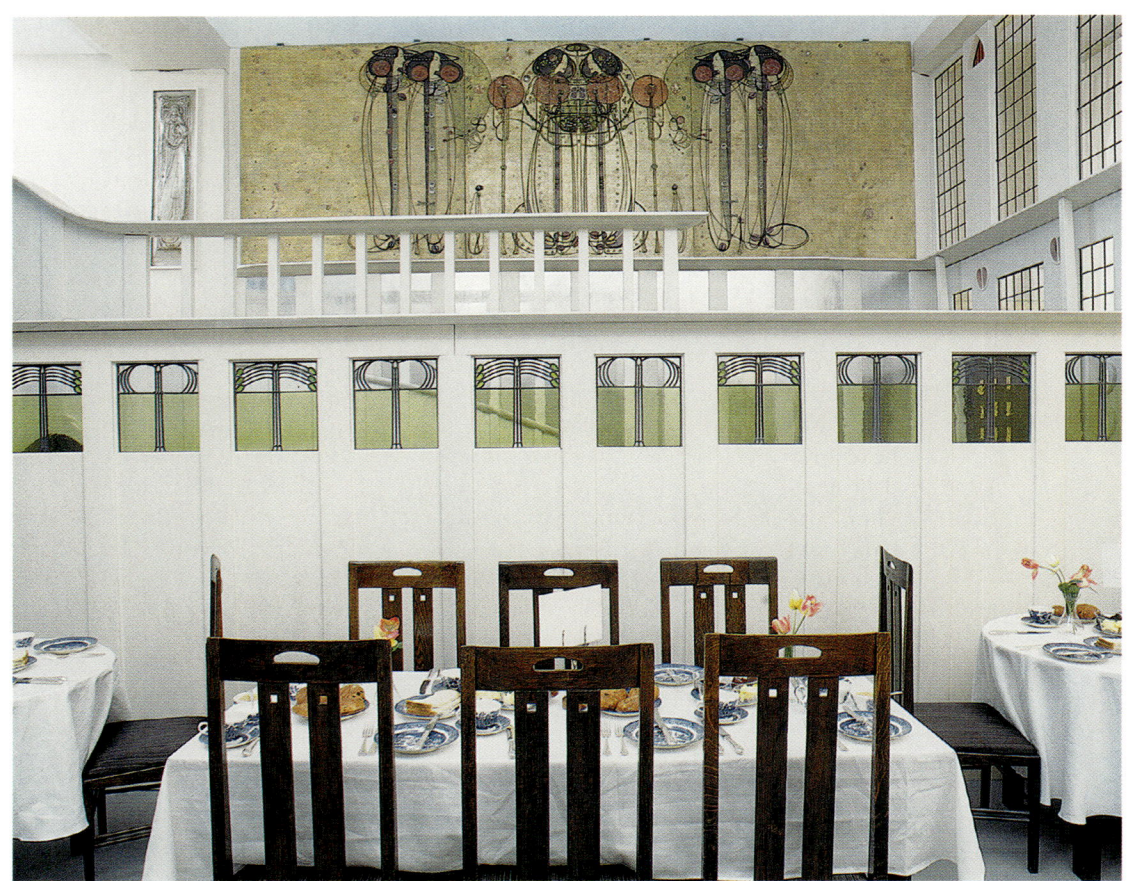

**CHARLES RENNIE MACKINTOSH** Numerous Arts and Crafts societies in America, England, and Germany carried on this ideal of artisanship. In Scotland, CHARLES RENNIE MACKINTOSH (1868–1929) designed a number of tea rooms, including the Ladies' Luncheon Room (FIG. 28-35) located in the Ingram Street Tea Room in Glasgow. The room decor is consistent with Morris's vision of a functional, exquisitely designed art. The chairs, stained-glass windows, and large panels of colored gesso with twine, glass beads, thread, mother-of-pearl, and tin leaf—made by MARGARET MACDONALD MACKINTOSH (1864–1933), an artist-designer and Mackintosh's wife, who collaborated with him on many projects—are all pristinely geometric and rhythmical in design.

**ART NOUVEAU** An important international architectural and design movement that developed out of the ideas the Arts and Crafts movement promoted was *Art Nouveau* (New Art), which took its name from a shop in Paris called L'Art Nouveau. Known by that name in France, Belgium, Holland, England, and the United States, the style had other names in other places: *Jugendstil* in Austria and Germany (after the magazine *Jugend,* "youth"), *Modernismo* in Spain, and *Floreale* in Italy. Proponents of this movement tried to synthesize all the arts in a determined attempt to create art based on natural forms that could be mass-produced for a large audience. The Art Nouveau style adapted the twining plant form to the needs of architecture, painting, sculpture, and all of the decorative arts.

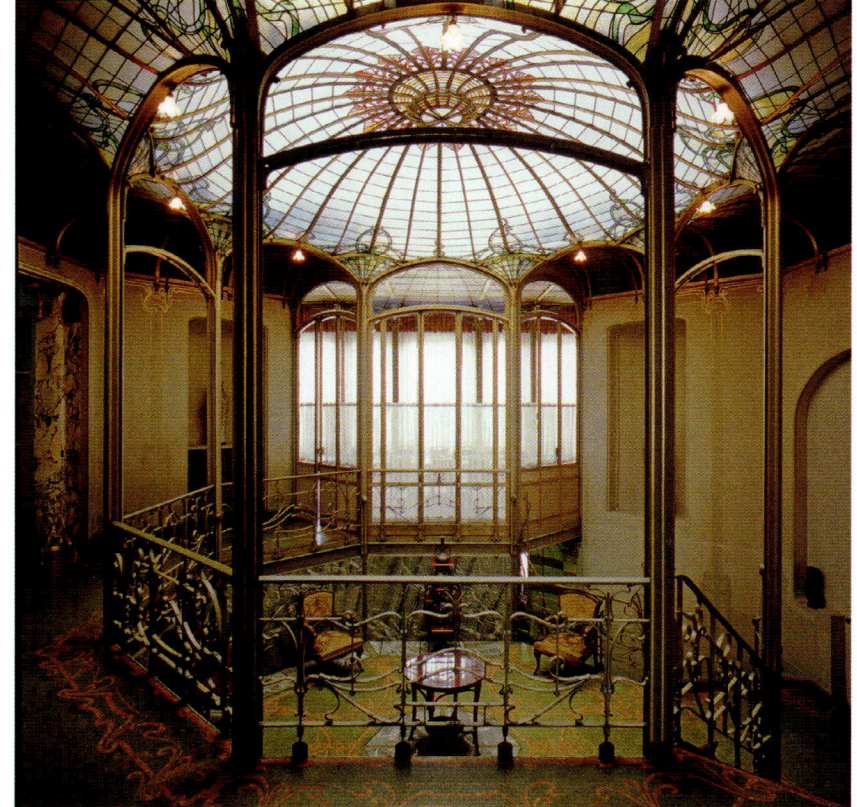

28-36 VICTOR HORTA, staircase in the Van Eetvelde House, Brussels, 1895.

The Art Nouveau movement was an attempt to create art and architecture based on natural forms. Here, every detail conforms to the theme of the twining plant and functions as part of a living whole.

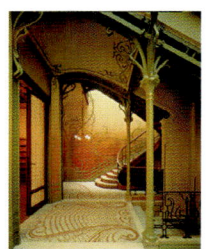

**28-36A** HORTA, Tassel House, Brussels, 1892–1893.

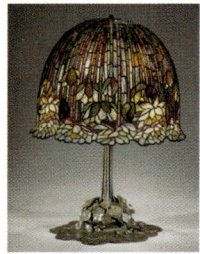

**28-36B** TIFFANY, water lily lamp, 1904–1915.

**VICTOR HORTA** The mature Art Nouveau style of the 1890s is on display in the houses the Belgian architect VICTOR HORTA (1861–1947) designed. A characteristic example is the staircase (FIG. **28-36**) in the Van Eetvelde House, which Horta built in Brussels in 1895, three years after designing the Tassel House (FIG. **28-36A**), his first major commission. Every detail of the Van Eetvelde interior functions as part of a living whole. Furniture, drapery folds, veining in the lavish stone paneling, and the patterning of the door moldings join with real plants to provide graceful counterpoints for the twining-plant theme. Metallic tendrils curl around the railings and posts, delicate metal tracery fills the glass dome, and floral and leaf motifs spread across the fabric panels of the screen. Flower and plant motifs also figure prominently in the immensely popular stained-glass lamps (FIG. **28-36B**) of LOUIS COMFORT TIFFANY (1848–1933).

The Art Nouveau style reflects several influences. In addition to the rich, foliated two-dimensional ornamentation of Arts and Crafts design and that movement's respect for materials, the sinuous whiplash curve of Japanese print designs (FIG. 34-13) inspired Art Nouveau artists. Art Nouveau also borrowed from the expressively patterned styles of van Gogh (FIGS. 28-17 and 28-18), Gauguin (FIGS. 28-19 and 28-20), and their Post-Impressionist and Symbolist contemporaries.

**ANTONIO GAUDI** Art Nouveau achieved its most personal expression in the work of the Spanish architect ANTONIO GAUDI (1852–1926). Before becoming an architect, Gaudi had trained as an ironworker. As many young artists of his time, he longed to create a style both modern and appropriate to his country. Taking inspiration from Moorish architecture and from the simple architecture of his native Catalonia, Gaudi developed a personal aesthetic. He conceived a building as a whole and molded it almost as a sculptor might shape a figure from clay. Although work on his designs proceeded slowly under the guidance of his intuition and imagination, Gaudi was a master who invented many new structural techniques that facilitated construction of his visions. His Barcelona apartment house, Casa Milá (FIG. **28-37**), is a wondrously free-form mass wrapped around a street corner. Lacy iron railings enliven the swelling curves of the cut-stone facade. Dormer windows peep from the undulating tiled roof, from which fantastically writhing chimneys poke energetically into the air above. The rough surfaces of the stone walls suggest naturally worn rock. The entrance portals look like eroded sea caves, but their design also may reflect the excitement that swept Spain following the 1879 discovery of Paleolithic cave paintings at Altamira (FIG. 1-9). Gaudi felt each of his buildings was symbolically a living thing, and the passionate naturalism of his Casa Milá is the spiritual kin of early-20th-century Expressionist painting and sculpture (see Chapter 29).

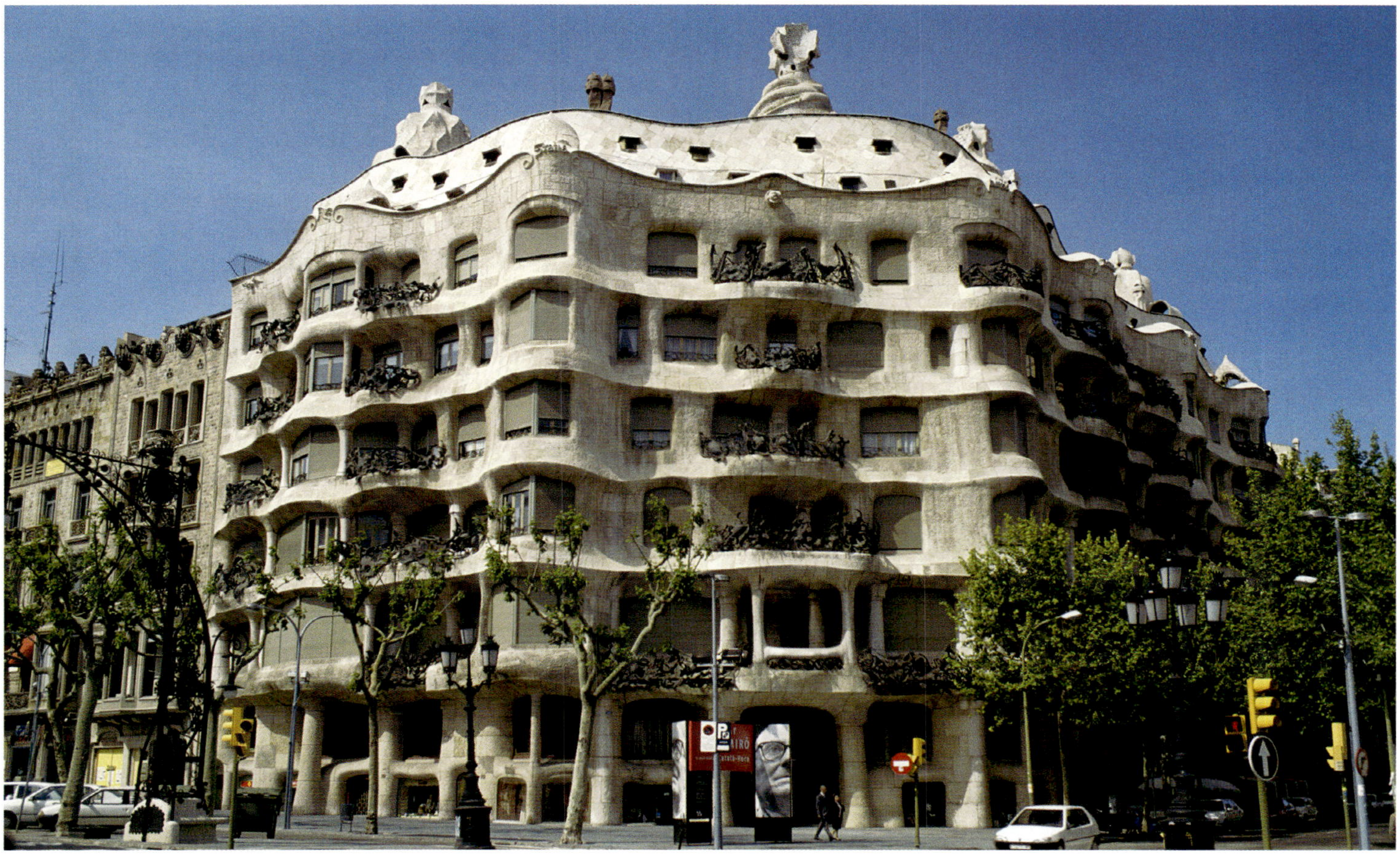

**28-37** ANTONIO GAUDI, Casa Milá (looking north), Barcelona, Spain, 1907.

Spanish Art Nouveau architect Gaudi conceived this apartment house as if it were a gigantic sculpture to be molded from clay. Twisting chimneys cap the undulating roof and walls.

Architecture and Decorative Arts **829**

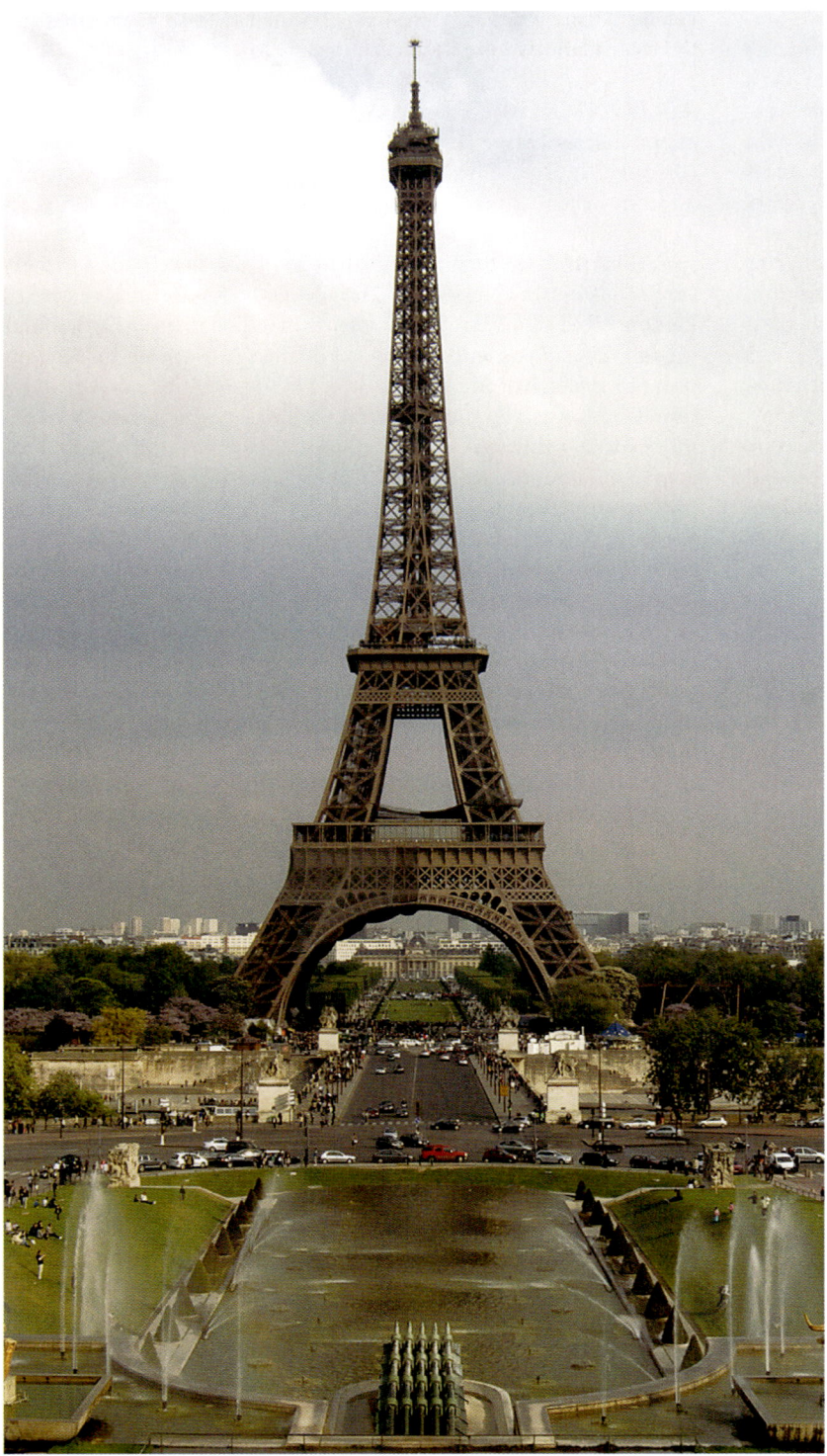

**28-38** ALEXANDRE-GUSTAVE EIFFEL, Eiffel Tower (looking southeast), Paris, France, 1889. ◧◀

New materials and technologies and the modernist aesthetic fueled radically new architectural designs in the late 19th century. Eiffel jolted the world with the exposed iron skeleton of his tower.

**ALEXANDRE-GUSTAVE EIFFEL** In the later 19th century, new technologies and the changing needs of urbanized, industrialized society affected architecture throughout the Western world. Since the 18th century, bridges had been built of cast iron (FIG. 26-12), which enabled engineering advancements in the construction of larger, stronger, and more fire-resistant structures. Steel, available after 1860, made it possible for architects to enclose ever larger spaces, such as those found in railroad stations (FIG. 28-4) and exposition halls. The Realist impulse also encouraged architectural designs that honestly expressed a building's purpose, rather than elaborately disguising its function. The elegant metal-skeleton structures of the French engineer-architect ALEXANDRE-GUSTAVE EIFFEL (1832–1923) were responses to this idea, and they constituted an important contribution to the development of the 20th-century skyscraper. A native of Burgundy, Eiffel trained in Paris before beginning a distinguished career designing exhibition halls, bridges, and the interior armature for France's anniversary gift to the United States—the *Statue of Liberty* by Frédéric Auguste Bartholdi (1834–1904).

Eiffel designed his best-known work, the Eiffel Tower (FIG. **28-38**), for an exhibition in Paris in 1889. Originally seen as a symbol of modern Paris and still considered a symbol of 19th-century civilization, the elegant iron tower thrusts its needle shaft 984 feet above the city, making it at the time of its construction (and for some time thereafter) the world's tallest structure. The tower rests on four giant supports connected by gracefully arching open-frame skirts that provide a pleasing mask for the heavy horizontal girders needed to strengthen the legs. Visitors can take two successive elevators to the top, or they can use the internal staircase. Either way, the view of Paris and the Seine from the tower is incomparable, as is the design of the tower itself. The transparency of Eiffel's structure blurs the distinction between interior and exterior to an extent never before achieved or even attempted. This interpenetration of inner and outer space became a hallmark of 20th-century art and architecture. Eiffel's tower and the earlier iron skeletal frames designed by Labrouste (FIG. 27-46) and Paxton (FIG. 27-47) jolted the architectural profession into a realization that modern materials and processes could germinate a completely new style and a radically innovative approach to architectural design.

**AMERICAN SKYSCRAPERS** The desire for greater speed and economy in building, as well as for a reduction in fire hazards, prompted the use of cast and wrought iron for many building programs, especially commercial ones. Designers in both England and the United States enthusiastically developed cast-iron architecture until a series of disastrous fires in the early 1870s in New York, Boston, and Chicago demonstrated that cast iron by itself was far from impervious to fire. This discovery led to encasing the metal in masonry, combining the first material's strength with the second's fire resistance.

In cities, convenience required closely grouped buildings, and increased property values forced architects literally to raise the roof. Even an attic could command high rentals if the builders installed one of the new elevators, used for the first time in the Equitable Building in New York (1868–1871). Metal, which could support these towering structures, gave birth to the American skyscraper.

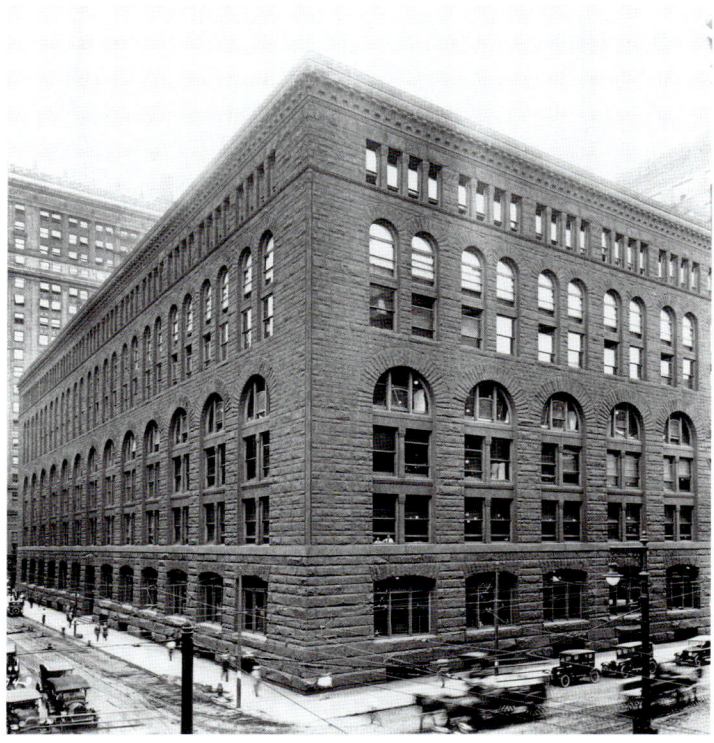

**28-39** Henry Hobson Richardson, Marshall Field wholesale store, Chicago, 1885–1887 (demolished 1930).

Richardson was a pioneer in designing commercial structures using a cast-iron skeleton encased in fire-resistant masonry. This construction technique enabled the insertion of large windows in the walls.

**HENRY HOBSON RICHARDSON** One of the pioneers in designing these modern commercial structures was Henry Hobson Richardson (1838–1886), but he also had a profound respect for earlier architectural styles. Because Richardson had a special fondness for the Romanesque architecture of the Auvergne area in France, he frequently used heavy round arches and massive masonry walls. Architectural historians sometimes consider his work to constitute a Romanesque revival related to the Neo-Gothic style (FIGS. 27-43 and 27-43A). This designation does not do credit to the originality and quality of most of the buildings Richardson designed during his brief 18-year practice. Trinity Church in Boston and his smaller public libraries, residences, railroad stations, and courthouses in New England and elsewhere best demonstrate his vivid imagination and the solidity (the sense of enclosure and permanence) so characteristic of his style. However, his most important and influential building was the Marshall Field wholesale store (FIG. **28-39**) in Chicago, begun in 1885 and demolished in 1930. This vast building occupied an entire city block. Designed for the most practical of purposes, it nonetheless recalled historical styles without imitating them. The tripartite elevation of a Renaissance palace (FIG. 21-37) or of the Roman aqueduct (FIG. 7-33) near Nîmes, France, may have been close to Richardson's mind. But he used no classical ornamentation, made much of the massive courses of masonry, and, in the strong horizontality of the window-sills and the interrupted courses defining the levels, stressed the long sweep of the building's lines, as well as the edifice's ponderous weight. Although the structural frame still lay behind and in conjunction with the masonry screen, the great glazed arcades opened up the walls of the monumental store. They pointed the way to the modern total penetration of walls and the transformation of them into mere screens or curtains that serve both to echo the underlying structural grid and to protect it from the weather.

**LOUIS HENRY SULLIVAN** As skyscrapers proliferated, architects refined the visual vocabulary of these buildings. Louis Henry Sullivan (1856–1924), whom many architectural historians call the first truly modern architect, arrived at a synthesis of industrial structure and ornamentation that perfectly expressed the spirit of late-19th-century commerce. To achieve this, he used the latest technological developments to create light-filled, well-ventilated office buildings and adorned both exteriors and interiors with ornate embellishments. Such decoration served to connect commerce and culture, and imbued these white-collar workspaces with a sense of refinement and taste. These characteristics are evident in the Guaranty (Prudential) Building (FIG. **28-40**) in Buffalo, built

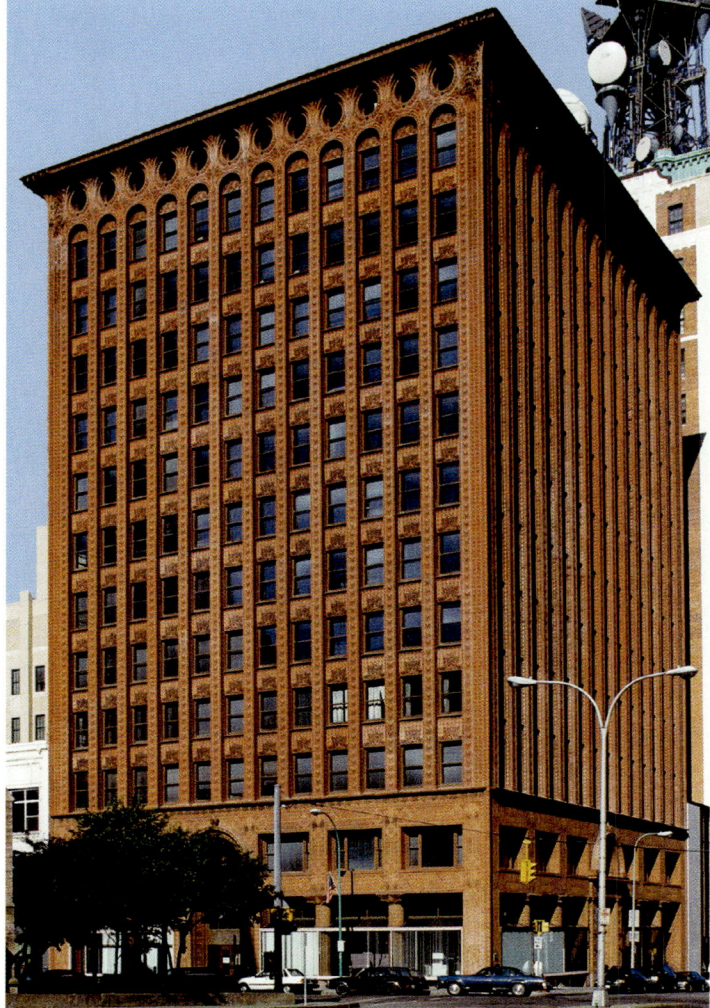

**28-40** Louis Henry Sullivan, Guaranty (Prudential) Building (looking southwest), Buffalo, New York, 1894–1896.

Sullivan drew on the latest technologies to create this light-filled, well-ventilated Buffalo office building. He added ornate surface embellishments to impart a sense of refinement and taste.

Architecture and Decorative Arts    **831**

**28-41** LOUIS HENRY SULLIVAN, Carson, Pirie, Scott Building (looking southeast), Chicago, 1899–1904.

Sullivan's slogan was "form follows function." He tailored the design of this steel, glass, and stone Chicago department store to meet the needs of its employees and customers.

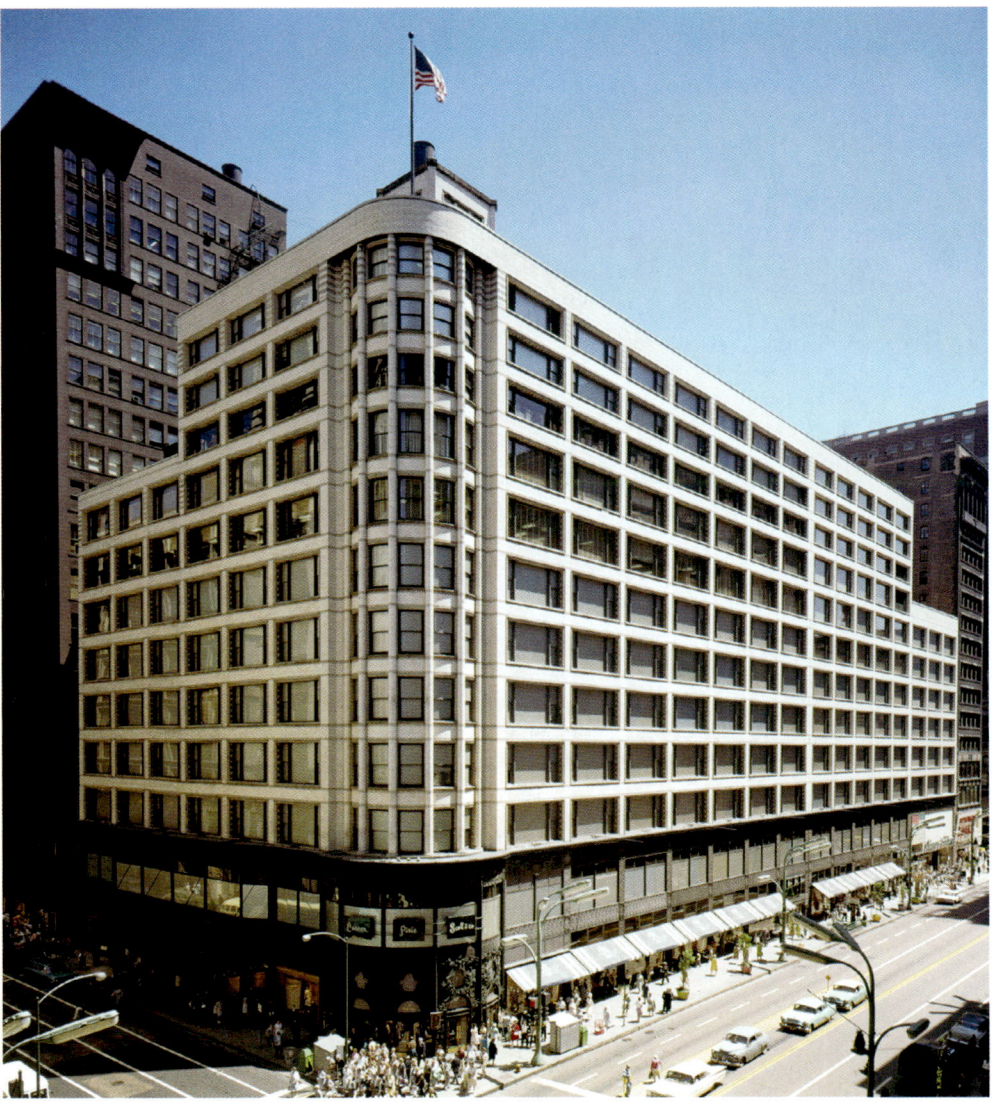

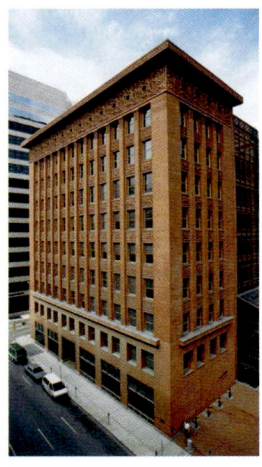

**28-40A** SULLIVAN, Wainwright Building, St. Louis, 1890–1891.

between 1894 and 1896, and in his earlier Wainwright Building (FIG. **28-40A**) in St. Louis. The Buffalo skyscraper is steel, sheathed with terracotta. The imposing scale of the building and the regularity of the window placements served as an expression of the large-scale, refined, and orderly office work taking place within. Sullivan tempered the severity of the structure with lively ornamentation, both on the piers and cornice on the exterior of the building and on the stairway balustrades, elevator cages, and ceiling in the interior. The Guaranty Building illustrates Sullivan's famous dictum "form follows function," which became the slogan of many early-20th-century architects. Still, Sullivan did not advocate a rigid and doctrinaire correspondence between exterior and interior design. Rather, he espoused a free and flexible relationship—one his pupil

Frank Lloyd Wright (see Chapter 29) later described as similar to that between the hand's bones and tissue.

Sullivan also designed the Carson, Pirie, Scott Building (FIG. **28-41**) in Chicago. Built between 1899 and 1904, this department store required broad, open, well-illuminated display spaces. Sullivan again used a minimal structural steel skeleton to achieve this goal. The architect gave over the lowest two levels of the building to an ornament in cast iron (of his invention) made of wildly fantastic motifs. He regarded the display windows as pictures, which merited elaborate frames. As in the Guaranty Building, Sullivan revealed his profound understanding of the maturing consumer economy and tailored the Carson, Pirie, Scott Building to meet the functional and symbolic needs of its users.

Thus, in architecture as well as in the pictorial arts, the late 19th century was a period during which artists challenged traditional modes of expression, often emphatically rejecting the past. Architects and painters as different as Sullivan, Monet, van Gogh, and Cézanne, each in his own way, contributed significantly to the entrenchment of modernism as the new cultural orthodoxy of the early 20th century (see Chapter 29).

# IMPRESSIONISM, POST-IMPRESSIONISM, SYMBOLISM: EUROPE AND AMERICA, 1870 TO 1900

## IMPRESSIONISM

▌ A hostile critic applied the term *Impressionism* to the paintings of Claude Monet because of their sketchy quality. The Impressionists—Monet, Pierre-Auguste Renoir, Edgar Degas, and others—strove to capture fleeting moments and transient effects of light and climate on canvas. They also focused on recording the contemporary urban scene in Paris, frequently painting bars, dance halls, the ballet, wide boulevards, and railroad stations.

▌ Complementing the Impressionists' sketchy, seemingly spontaneous brushstrokes are the compositions of their paintings. Reflecting the influence of Japanese prints and photography, Impressionist works often have arbitrarily cut-off figures and settings seen at sharply oblique angles.

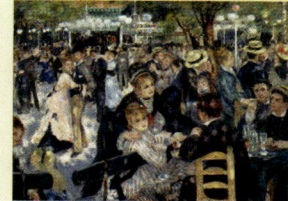

Renoir, *Le Moulin de la Galette*, 1876

## POST-IMPRESSIONISM AND SYMBOLISM

▌ Post-Impressionism is not a unified style. The term refers to the group of late-19th-century artists, including Georges Seurat, Vincent van Gogh, Paul Gauguin, and Paul Cézanne, who followed the Impressionists and took painting in new directions. Seurat refined the Impressionist approach to color and light into pointillism—the disciplined application of pure color in tiny daubs. Van Gogh explored the capabilities of colors and distorted forms to express emotions. Gauguin, an admirer of Japanese prints, moved away from Impressionism in favor of large areas of flat color bounded by firm lines. Cézanne replaced the transitory visual effects of the Impressionists with a rigorous analysis of the lines, planes, and colors that make up landscapes and still lifes.

▌ Gustave Moreau, Odilon Redon, and Henri Rousseau were the leading French Symbolists. They disdained Realism as trivial and sought to depict a reality beyond that of the everyday world, rejecting materialism and celebrating fantasy and imagination. Their subjects were often mysterious, exotic, and sensuous.

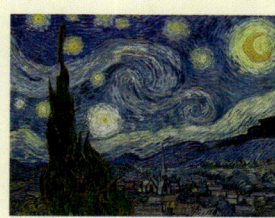

van Gogh, *Starry Night*, 1889

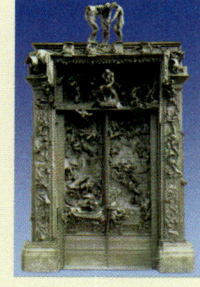

Rousseau, *Sleeping Gypsy*, 1897

## SCULPTURE

▌ Sculpture cannot capture transitory optical effects or explore the properties of color and line, and late-19th-century sculptors pursued goals different from those of contemporaneous painters.

▌ The leading figure of the era was Auguste Rodin, who explored Realist themes and the representation of movement. His vision of tormented, writhing figures in Hell connects his work with the Symbolists. Rodin also made statues that were deliberate fragments, creating a taste for the incomplete that appealed to many later sculptors.

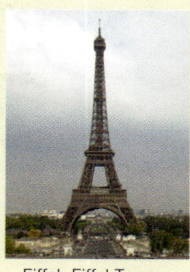

Rodin, *Gates of Hell*, 1880–1900

## ARCHITECTURE AND DECORATIVE ARTS

▌ Not all artists embraced the industrialization transforming daily life during the 19th century. The Arts and Crafts movement in England and the international Art Nouveau style formed in opposition to modern mass production. Both schools advocated natural forms and high-quality craftsmanship.

▌ New technologies and the changing needs of urbanized, industrialized society transformed architecture in the late 19th century. The exposed iron skeleton of the Eiffel Tower jolted architects into realizing how modern materials and processes could revolutionize architectural design. Henry Hobson Richardson and Louis Sullivan were pioneers in designing the first metal, stone, and glass skyscrapers.

Eiffel, Eiffel Tower, Paris, 1889

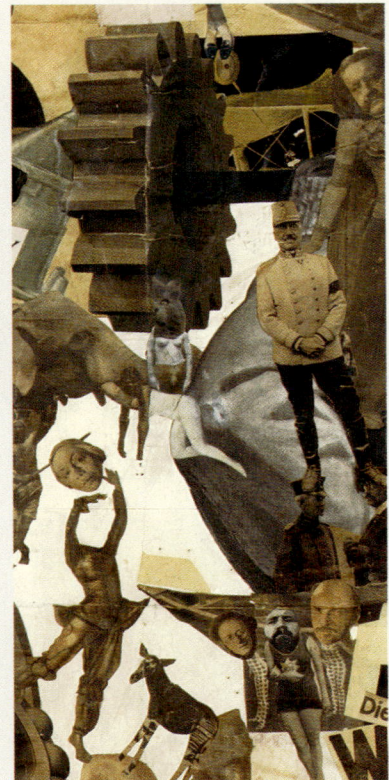

The cut-out photos in Höch's photomontage appear to be randomly selected, but they are carefully arranged. The leading figures of the Weimar Republic (the "anti-Dadaists") are at the top right.

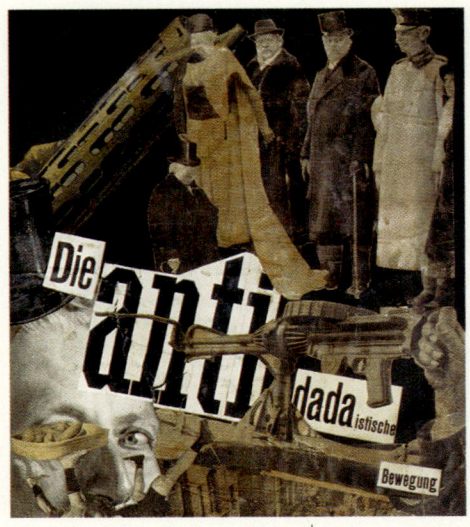

The many photos pasted together in *Cut with a Kitchen Knife* include mass-produced machine parts. In the lower left of this detail, the artist Käthe Kollwitz's head floats above a dancer's body.

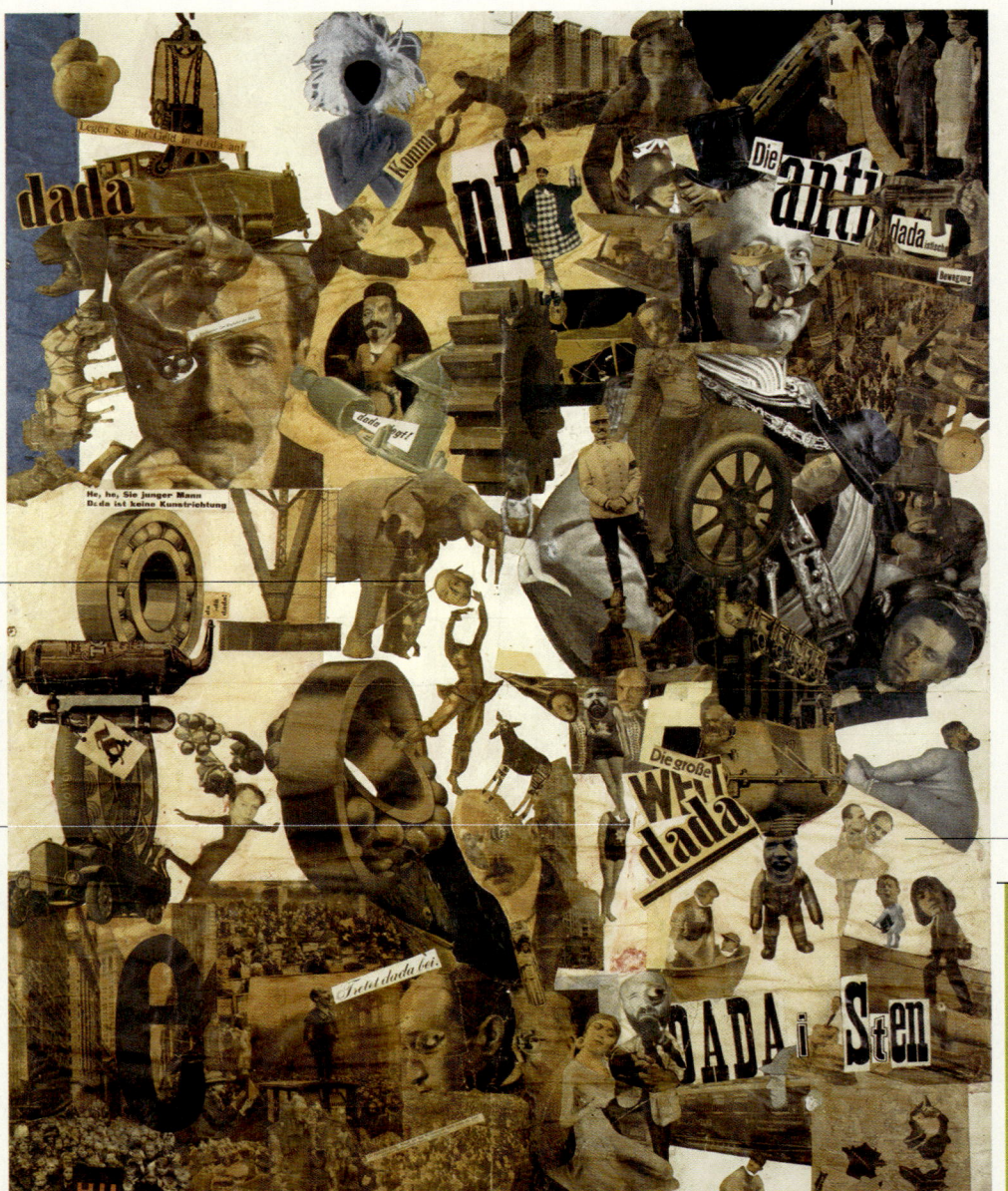

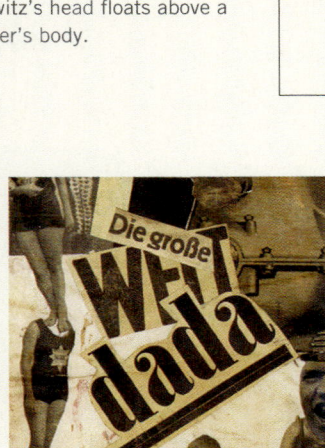

The letters cut from various publications are of different typefaces and font sizes, contributing to the sense of dislocation throughout. Near the center are the words "The great Dada world."

**29-1** HANNAH HÖCH, *Cut with the Kitchen Knife Dada through the Last Weimar Beer Belly Cultural Epoch of Germany*, 1919–1920. Photomontage, 3′ 9″ × 2′ 11½″. Neue Nationalgalerie, Staatliche Museen zu Berlin, Berlin. ◼◖

1 ft.

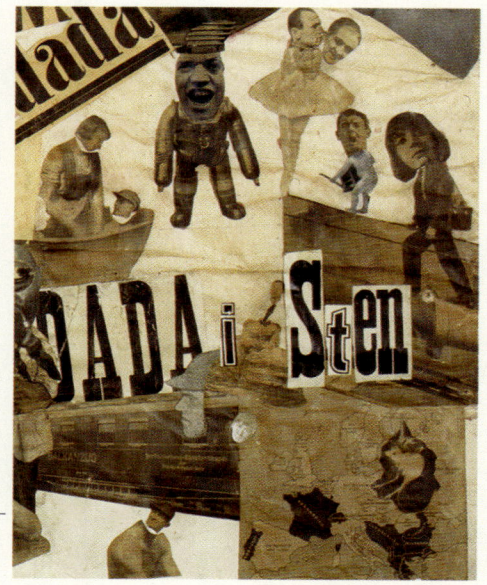

# MODERNISM IN EUROPE AND AMERICA, 1900 TO 1945

**FRAMING THE ERA**

## GLOBAL WAR, ANARCHY, AND DADA

World War I—the "Great War"—broke out in 1914, unleashing slaughter and devastation on a scale unprecedented in history. More than nine million soldiers died in four years. Britain alone lost 60,000 men on the opening day of the battle of the Somme. The negotiated formal end of hostilities in 1919 redrew the political map of Europe (MAP **29-1**). Peace, however, could not erase the scars of a global conflict that had altered the worldview of millions. One major consequence of the Great War was the emergence of an artistic movement known as *Dada*. The Dadaists believed reason and logic had been responsible for the insane spectacle of collective homicide that was World War I, and they concluded the only route to salvation was through political anarchy, the irrational, and the intuitive.

In Berlin, Dada took on an activist political edge. The Berlin Dadaists pioneered a variation of the technique called *collage* in French (FIG. 29-17)—creating artistic compositions from cut pieces of paper. The Berliners christened their version *photomontage*, because their assemblages consisted almost entirely of pieces of magazine photographs, usually combined into deliberately antilogical compositions. Collage lent itself well to the Dada desire to exploit chance in the creation of art—and anti-art.

One of the Berlin Dadaists who perfected the photomontage technique was HANNAH HÖCH (1889–1978). Höch's photomontages advanced the absurd illogic of Dada by presenting viewers with chaotic, contradictory, and satiric compositions. They also provided scathing and insightful commentary on two of the most dramatic developments during the Weimar Republic (1918–1933) in Germany—the redefinition of women's social roles and the explosive growth of mass print media. Höch incorporated both themes in *Cut with the Kitchen Knife Dada through the Last Weimar Beer Belly Cultural Epoch of Germany* (FIG. **29-1**), in which she arranged in seemingly haphazard fashion—often with a touch of typically wicked Dada humor—an eclectic mixture of cutout photos. Closer inspection, however, reveals the artist's careful selection and placement of the photographs. For example, the key figures in the Weimar Republic are together at the upper right (identified as the "anti-Dada movement"). Some of Höch's fellow Dadaists appear among images of Karl Marx and Vladimir Lenin, aligning Dada with other revolutionary forces in what she prominently labeled with cutout lettering "Die grosse Welt dada" (the great Dada world). Höch also positioned herself in the topsy-turvy Dada world she created. A photograph of her head appears in the lower right corner, juxtaposed with a map of Europe showing which countries had granted women the right to vote—a commentary on the power both women and Dada had to destabilize society.

# GLOBAL UPHEAVAL
# AND ARTISTIC REVOLUTION

The first half of the 20th century was a period of significant upheaval worldwide. Between 1900 and 1945, the major industrial powers fought two global wars, witnessed the rise of Communism, Fascism, and Nazism, and suffered the Great Depression. These decades were also a time of radical change in the arts when painters and sculptors challenged some of the most basic assumptions about the purpose of art and what form an artwork should take. Throughout history, artistic revolution has often accompanied political, social, and economic upheaval, but never before had the new directions artists explored been as pronounced or as long-lasting as those born during the first half of the last century.

**AVANT-GARDE** As did other members of society, artists felt deeply the effects of the political and economic disruptions of the early 20th century. As the old social orders collapsed and new ones, from communism to corporate capitalism, took their places, artists searched for new definitions of and uses for art in a changed world. Already in the 19th century, each successive modernist movement had challenged artistic conventions with ever-greater intensity. This relentless questioning of the status quo gave rise to the notion of an artistic *avant-garde*. The term, which means "front guard," derives from 19th-century French military usage. The avant-garde were the troops sent ahead of the army's main body to reconnoiter and make occasional raids on the enemy. Politicians who deemed themselves visionary and forward-thinking subsequently adopted the term. It then migrated to the art world in the 1880s, when artists and critics used it to refer to the Realists, Impressionists, and Post-Impressionists—artists who were ahead of their time and who transgressed the limits of established art forms.

These trailblazing rebels rejected the classical, academic, and traditional, and zealously explored the premises and formal qualities of painting, sculpture, and other media. Although the general public found avant-garde art incomprehensible, the principles underlying 19th-century modernism appealed to increasing numbers of artists as the 20th century dawned.

# EUROPE, 1900 TO 1920

Avant-garde artists in all their diversity became a major force during the opening decades of the 20th century, beginning with the artistic movement known as *Fauvism*.

## Fauvism

In 1905, at the third Salon d'Automne (Autumn Salon) in Paris, a group of young painters exhibited canvases so simplified in design and so shockingly bright in color that a startled critic, Louis Vauxcelles (1870–1943), described the artists as *fauves* (wild beasts). The Fauves were totally independent of the French Academy and the "official" Salon (see "Academic Salons and Independent Art Exhibitions," Chapter 28, page 802). Driving the Fauve movement was a desire to develop an art having the directness of Impressionism but employing intense color juxtapositions for expressive ends.

Building on the legacy of artists such as Vincent van Gogh and Paul Gauguin (see Chapter 28), the Fauves went even further in liberating color from its descriptive function and exploring the effects different colors have on emotions. The Fauves produced portraits, landscapes, still lifes, and nudes of spontaneity and verve, with rich surface textures, lively linear patterns, and, above all, bold colors. They employed startling contrasts of vermilion and emerald green and of cerulean blue and vivid orange held together by sweeping brushstrokes and bold patterns in an effort to release internal feelings.

The Fauve painters never officially organized, and the looseness of both personal connections and stylistic affinities caused the Fauve movement to begin to disintegrate almost as soon as it emerged. Within five years, most of the artists had departed from a strict adherence to Fauve principles and developed their own more

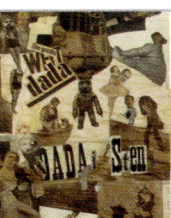

# MODERNISM IN EUROPE AND AMERICA, 1900 TO 1945

| 1900 | 1910 | 1920 | 1930 | 1945 |
|---|---|---|---|---|
| ▌European artists build on the innovations of the Impressionists and Post-Impressionists and explore new avenues of artistic expression<br><br>▌Henri Matisse and the Fauves free color from its descriptive function<br><br>▌German Expressionist groups—Die Brücke and Der Blaue Reiter—produce paintings featuring bold colors and distorted forms<br><br>▌In America, Frank Lloyd Wright promotes "natural architecture" in his expansive "prairie houses" | ▌Pablo Picasso and Georges Braque radically challenge the traditional Western way of making pictures with their Cubist dissection of forms<br><br>▌The Italian Futurists celebrate dynamic motion and modern technology in paintings and statues<br><br>▌Vassily Kandinsky pursues complete abstraction in painting<br><br>▌The Dadaists explore the role of chance in often irreverent artworks<br><br>▌The Armory Show introduces American artists and the public to avant-garde developments in Europe | ▌In the wake of World War I, German Neue Sachlichkeit painters depict the horrors of global conflict<br><br>▌The Surrealists seek ways to visualize the world of the unconscious and investigate automatism as a means of creating art<br><br>▌De Stijl artists create "pure plastic art" using geometric forms and primary colors<br><br>▌Constantine Brancusi and Barbara Hepworth promote abstraction in sculpture<br><br>▌The Bauhaus advocates the integration of all the arts in its vision of "total architecture"<br><br>▌Photography emerges as an important art form in the work of Alfred Stieglitz and Edward Weston | ▌Aaron Douglas and Jacob Lawrence explore African American history in the Harlem Renaissance<br><br>▌Alexander Calder creates abstract sculptures with moving parts<br><br>▌Grant Wood and the Regionalists celebrate life in rural America in paintings rejecting European abstraction<br><br>▌José Orozco and Diego Rivera paint vast mural cycles recording Mexican history<br><br>▌Dorothea Lange and Margaret Bourke-White achieve renown for their documentary photography | |

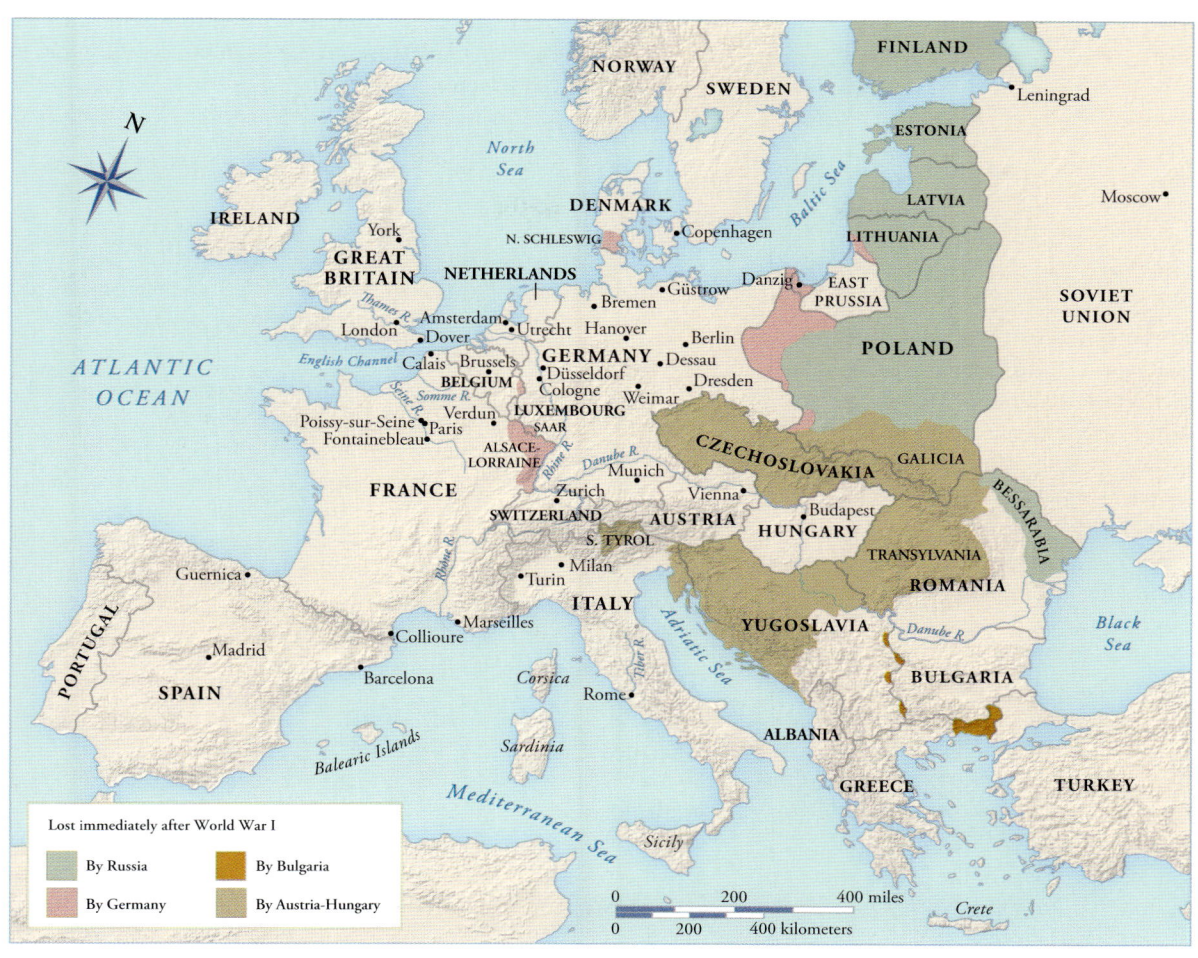

MAP 29-1 Europe at the end of World War I

Lost immediately after World War I

| | |
|---|---|
| By Russia | By Bulgaria |
| By Germany | By Austria-Hungary |

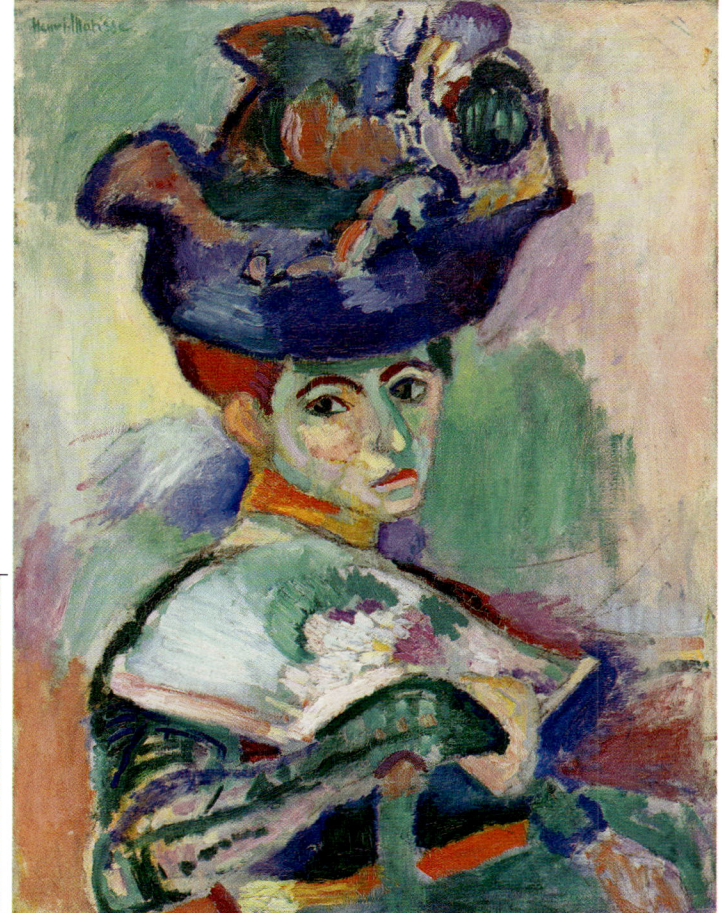

1 ft.

personal styles. During its brief existence, however, Fauvism made a remarkable contribution to the direction of art by demonstrating color's structural, expressive, and aesthetic capabilities.

**HENRI MATISSE** The dominant figure of the Fauve group was HENRI MATISSE (1869–1954), who believed color could play a primary role in conveying meaning and focused his efforts on developing this notion. In an early painting, *Woman with the Hat* (FIG. **29-2**), Matisse depicted his wife, Amélie, in a rather

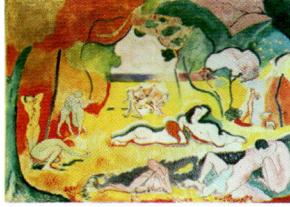

29-2A MATISSE, *Le Bonheur de Vivre,* 1905–1906.

conventional manner compositionally, but the seemingly arbitrary colors immediately startle the viewer, as does the sketchiness of the forms. The entire image—the woman's face, clothes, hat, and background—consists of patches and splotches of color juxtaposed in ways that sometimes produce jarring contrasts. Matisse explained his approach: "What characterized fauvism was that we rejected imitative colors, and that with pure colors we obtained stronger reactions."[1] For Matisse and the Fauves, therefore, color became the formal element most responsible for pictorial coherence and the primary conveyor of meaning (see "Matisse on Color," page 838, and FIG. **29-2A**).

**29-2** HENRI MATISSE, *Woman with the Hat,* 1905. Oil on canvas, 2′ 7¾″ × 1′ 11½″. San Francisco Museum of Modern Art, San Francisco (bequest of Elise S. Haas).

Matisse's portrayal of his wife, Amélie, features patches and splotches of seemingly arbitrary colors. He and the other Fauve painters used color not to imitate nature but to produce a reaction in the viewer.

# Matisse on Color

In an essay entitled "Notes of a Painter," published in the Parisian journal *La Grande Revue* on Christmas Day, 1908, Henri Matisse responded to his critics and set forth his principles and goals as a painter. The following excerpts help explain what Matisse was trying to achieve in paintings such as *Harmony in Red* (FIG. 29-3).

What I am after, above all, is expression. . . . Expression, for me, does not reside in passions glowing in a human face or manifested by violent movement. The entire arrangement of my picture is expressive: the place occupied by the figures, the empty spaces around them, the proportions, everything has its share. Composition is the art of arranging in a decorative manner the diverse elements at the painter's command to express his feelings. . . .

Both harmonies and dissonances of colour can produce agreeable effects. . . . Suppose I have to paint an interior: I have before me a cupboard; it gives me a sensation of vivid red, and I put down a red which satisfies me. A relation is established between this red and the white of the canvas. Let me put a green near the red, and make the floor yellow; and again there will be relationships between the green or yellow and the white of the canvas which will satisfy me. . . . A new combination of colours will succeed the first and render the totality of my representation. I am forced to transpose

until finally my picture may seem completely changed when, after successive modifications, the red has succeeded the green as the dominant colour. I cannot copy nature in a servile way; I am forced to interpret nature and submit it to the spirit of the picture. From the relationship I have found in all the tones there must result a living harmony of colours, a harmony analogous to that of a musical composition. . . .

The chief function of colour should be to serve expression as well as possible. . . . My choice of colours does not rest on any scientific theory; it is based on observation, on sensitivity, on felt experiences. . . . I simply try to put down colours which render my sensation. There is an impelling proportion of tones that may lead me to change the shape of a figure or to transform my composition. Until I have achieved this proportion in all parts of the composition I strive towards it and keep on working. Then a moment comes when all the parts have found their definite relationships, and from then on it would be impossible for me to add a stroke to my picture without having to repaint it entirely.*

*Translated by Jack D. Flam, *Matisse on Art* (London: Phaidon, 1973), 32–40.

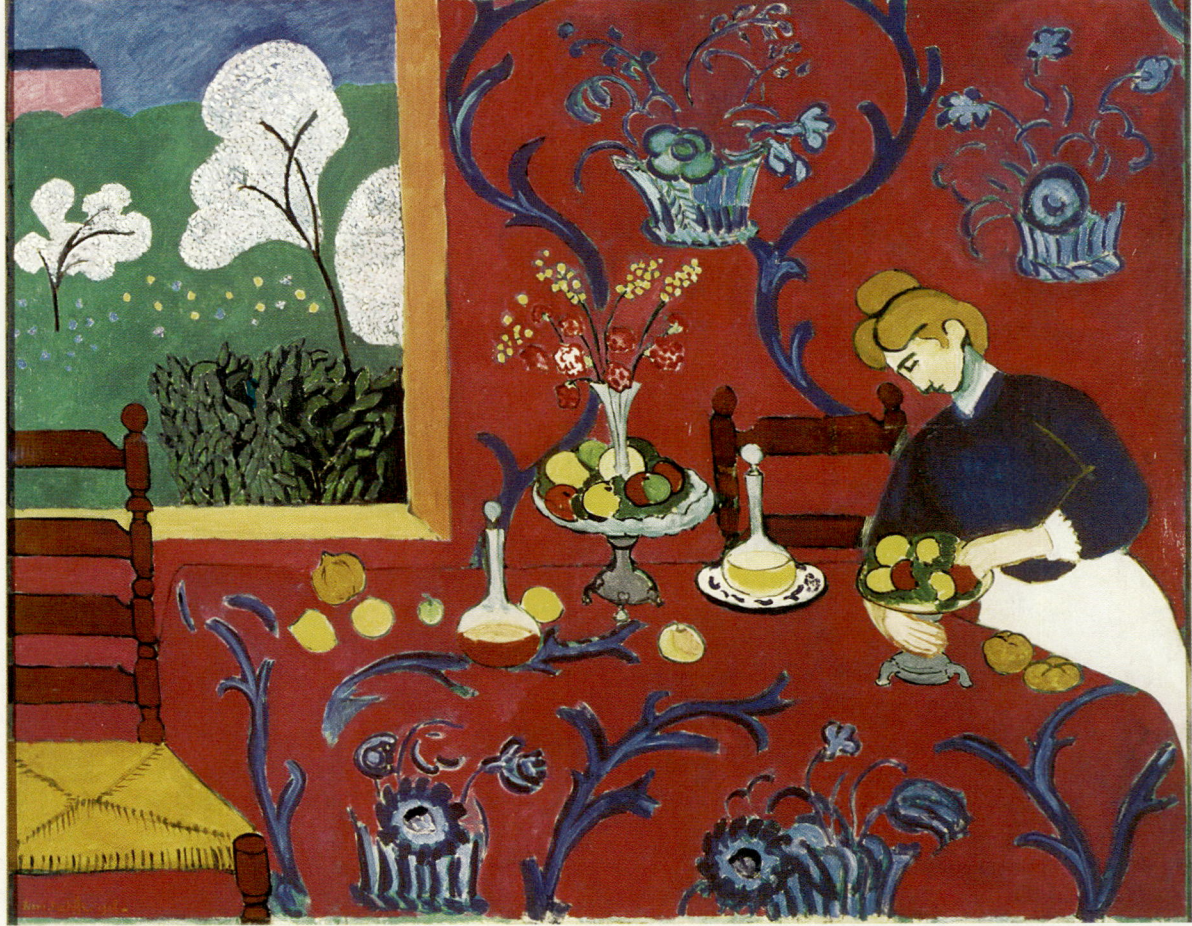

**29-3** HENRI MATISSE, *Red Room* (*Harmony in Red*), 1908–1909. Oil on canvas, 5′ 11″ × 8′ 1″. State Hermitage Museum, Saint Petersburg. ◼

Matisse believed painters should choose compositions and colors that express their feelings. Here, the table and wall seem to merge because they are the same color and have identical patterning.

1 ft.

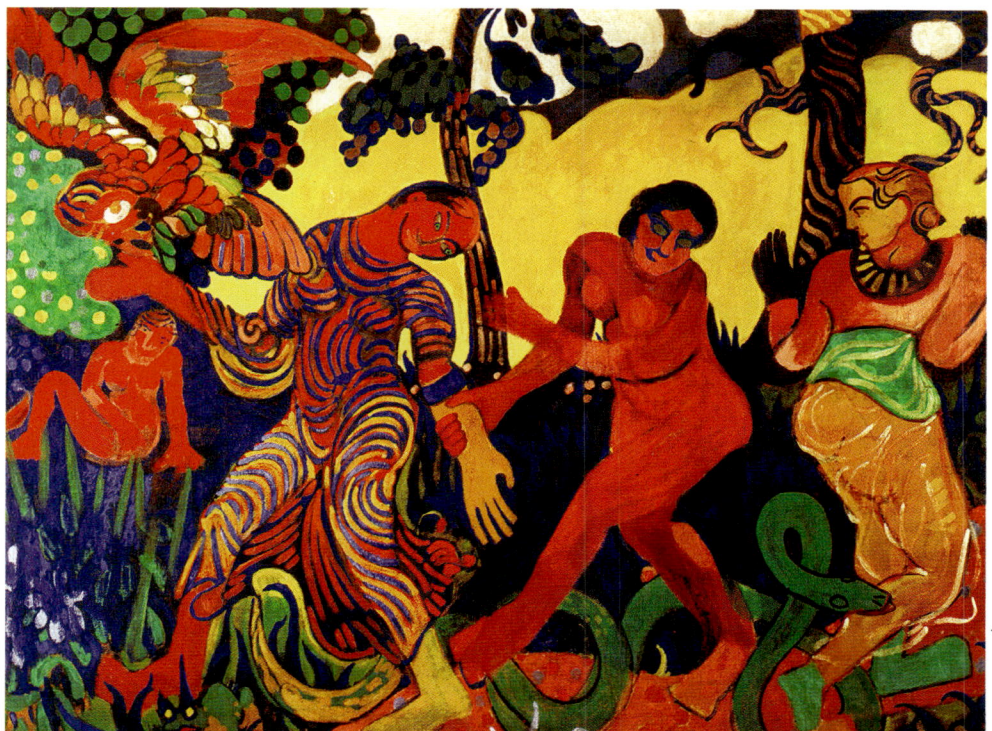

Derain worked closely with Matisse, but the tropical setting and the bold colors of *The Dance* also reflect Derain's study of Gauguin's paintings (FIGS. 28-19 and 28-20), as does the flattened perspective.

1 ft.

*HARMONY IN RED* These color discoveries reached maturity in Matisse's *Red Room* (*Harmony in Red*; FIG. 29-3). The subject is the interior of a comfortable, prosperous household with a maid placing fruit and wine on the table, but Matisse's canvas is radically different from traditional paintings of domestic interiors (for example, FIGS. 25-19 and 25-20A). The Fauve painter depicted objects in simplified and schematized fashion and flattened out the forms. For example, Matisse eliminated the front edge of the table, rendering the table, with its identical patterning, as flat as the wall behind it. The window at the upper left could also be a painting on the wall, further flattening the space. Everywhere, the colors contrast richly and intensely. Matisse's process of overpainting reveals the importance of color for striking the right chord in the viewer. Initially, this work was predominantly green. Then Matisse repainted it blue, but blue also did not seem appropriate. Not until he repainted the canvas red did Matisse feel he had found the right color for the "harmony" he wished to compose.

**ANDRÉ DERAIN** Another leading Fauve painter was ANDRÉ DERAIN (1880–1954). As did Matisse, with whom he worked closely, Derain sought to employ color for aesthetic and compositional coherence and to elicit emotional responses. *The Dance* (FIG. 29-4), in which several figures, some nude, others clothed, frolic in a lush landscape (compare FIG. 29-4A), is

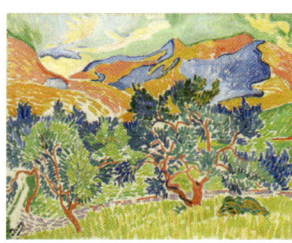

one of Derain's best paintings. The tropical setting and the bold colors reflect in part Derain's study of Gauguin's canvases (FIGS. 28-19 and 28-20), as does the flattened perspective. Derain used color to delineate space, and he indicated light and shadow not by differences in value but by contrasts of hue. For the

**29-4A** DERAIN, *Mountains at Collioure,* 1905.

Fauves, as for Gauguin and van Gogh, color does not describe the local tones of objects but expresses the picture's content.

## German Expressionism

The immediacy and boldness of the Fauve images appealed to many artists, including the German *Expressionists*. However, although color plays a prominent role in German painting of the early 20th century, the "expressiveness" of the German images is due as much to the Expressionists' wrenching distortions of form, ragged outlines, and agitated brushstrokes.

**ERNST LUDWIG KIRCHNER** The first group of German Expressionists—*Die Brücke* (The Bridge)—gathered in Dresden in 1905 under the leadership of ERNST LUDWIG KIRCHNER (1880–1938). The group members thought of themselves as paving the way for a more perfect age by bridging the old age and the new, hence their name. Kirchner's early studies in architecture, painting, and the graphic arts had instilled in him a deep admiration for German medieval art. As did the British artists associated with the Arts and Crafts movement, such as William Morris (FIG. 28-34), Die Brücke artists modeled themselves on medieval craft guilds whose members lived together and practiced all the arts equally. Kirchner described their lofty goals in a ringing 1913 statement published in the form of a woodcut titled *Chronik der Brücke:*

> With faith in progress and in a new generation of creators and spectators we call together all youth. As youth, we carry the future and want to create for ourselves freedom of life and of movement against the long-established older forces. Everyone who reproduces that which drives him to creation with directness and authenticity belongs to us.[2]

Die Brücke artists protested the hypocrisy and materialistic decadence of those in power. Kirchner, in particular, focused much of his attention on the detrimental effects of industrialization, such as the alienation of individuals in cities, which he felt fostered a mechanized and impersonal society. The tensions leading to World War I further exacerbated the discomfort and anxiety of the German Expressionists.

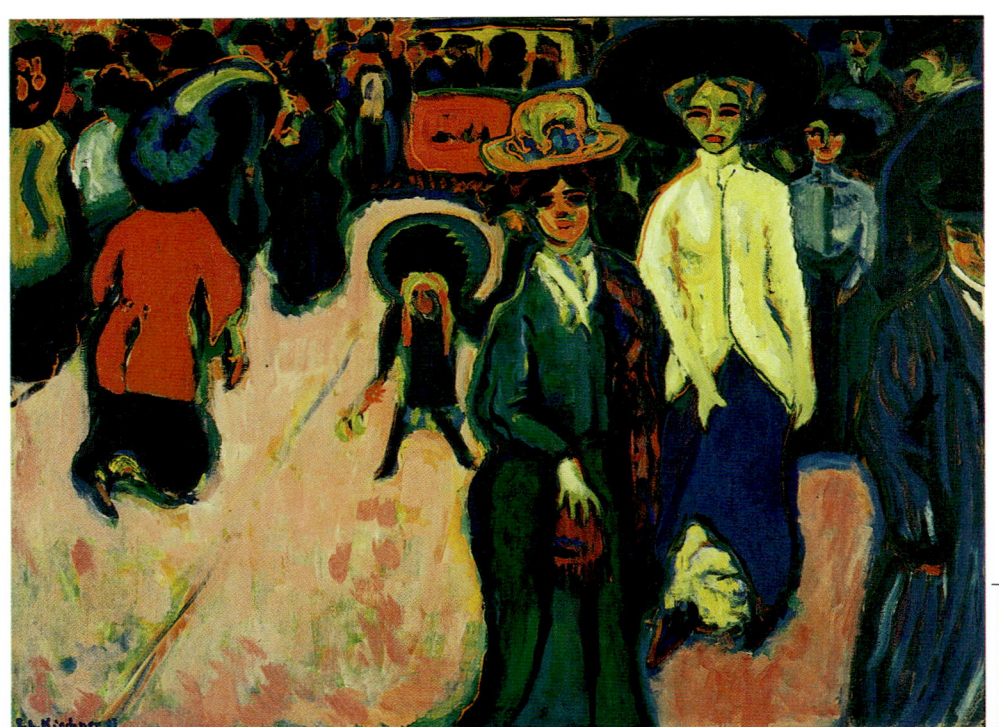

29-5 ERNST LUDWIG KIRCHNER, *Street, Dresden*, 1908 (dated 1907). Oil on canvas, 4' 11¼" × 6' 6⅞". Museum of Modern Art, New York. ◼◂

Kirchner's perspective distortions, disquieting figures, and color choices reflect the influence of the Fauves and of Edvard Munch (FIG. 28-28), who made similar expressive use of formal elements.

Kirchner's *Street, Dresden* (FIG. 29-5) provides a glimpse into the frenzied urban activity of a bustling German city before World War I. Rather than offering the distant, panoramic urban view of the Impressionists (FIG. 28-5), Kirchner's street scene is jarring and dissonant in both composition and color. The women in the foreground loom large, approaching somewhat menacingly. The steep perspective of the street, which threatens to push the women directly into the viewer's space, increases their confrontational nature. Harshly rendered, the women's features make them appear ghoulish, and the garish, clashing colors—juxtapositions of bright orange, emerald green, chartreuse, and pink—add to the expressive impact of the image. Kirchner's perspective distortions, disquieting figures, and color choices reflect the influence of the work of Edvard Munch, who made similar expressive use of formal elements in *The Scream* (FIG. 28-28).

**EMIL NOLDE** Much older than most Die Brücke artists was Emil Hansen, who changed his name in 1902 to EMIL NOLDE (1867–1956) after his birthplace in northern Germany. The younger artists invited him to join their group in 1906, but Nolde, an introvert who preferred to work alone, left Die Brücke the next year. By 1913, the group had dissolved, but a commonality of interests and painterly style continued to link Nolde and the other Die Brücke artists throughout their careers. The content of Nolde's work centered, for the most part, on religious imagery. In contrast to the quiet spirituality and restraint of traditional religious images, however, Nolde's paintings, for example, *Saint Mary of Egypt among Sinners* (FIG. 29-6), are visceral and forceful. Mary, before her conversion, entertains lechers whose lust magnifies their brutal ugliness. The distortions of form and color (especially the jarring juxtaposition of blue and orange) and the rawness of the brushstrokes amplify the harshness of the leering faces.

Borrowing ideas from van Gogh, Munch, the Fauves, and African and Oceanic art (see "Primi-

tivism and Colonialism," page 846, and FIG. 29-6A), Nolde and the other Die Brücke artists created images that derive much of their power from a dissonance and seeming lack of finesse. The harsh colors, aggressively brushed paint, and distorted forms expressed the painters' feelings about the injustices of society and their belief in a healthful union of human beings and nature.

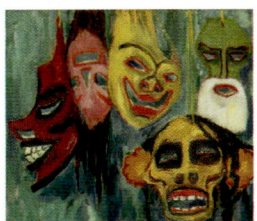

29-6A NOLDE, *Masks*, 1911.

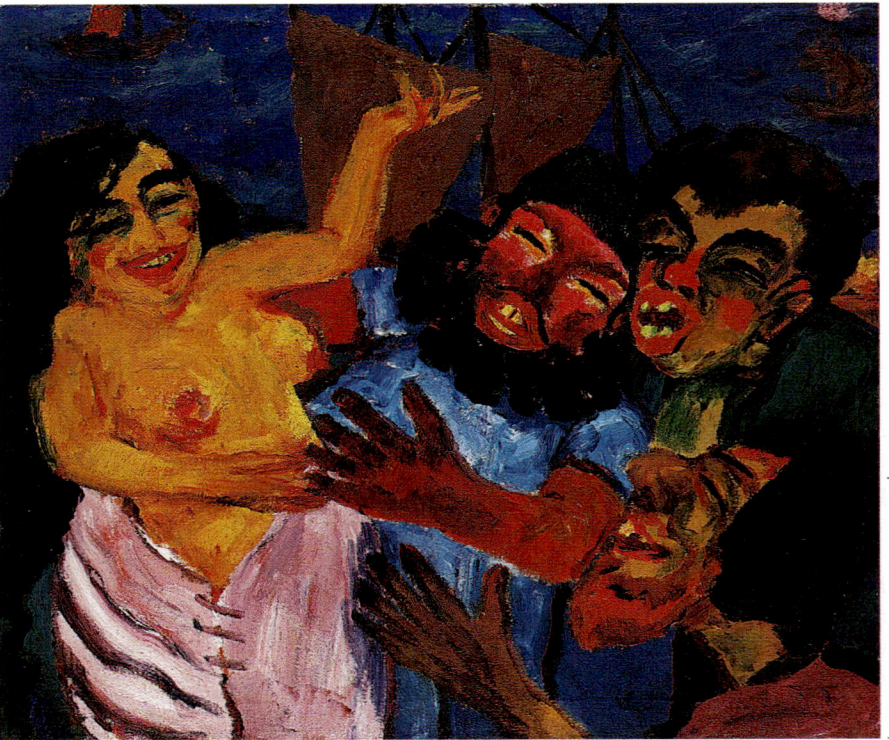

29-6 EMIL NOLDE, *Saint Mary of Egypt among Sinners*, 1912. Left panel of a triptych, oil on canvas, 2' 10" × 3' 3". Hamburger Kunsthalle, Hamburg.

In contrast to the quiet spirituality of traditional religious images, Nolde's paintings produce visceral emotions and feature distorted forms, jarring color juxtapositions, and raw brushstrokes.

# Science and Art in the Early 20th Century

In the early 20th century, radical new ways of thinking emerged in both science and art, forcing people to revise how they understood the world. In particular, the values and ideals that were the legacy of the Enlightenment (see Chapter 26) began to yield to new perspectives. Intellectuals countered 18th- and 19th-century assumptions about progress and reason with ideas challenging traditional notions about the physical universe, the structure of society, and human nature. Modernist artists fully participated in this reassessment and formulated innovative theoretical bases for their work. Accordingly, much early-20th-century Western art is a rejection of traditional limitations and definitions both of art and of the universe.

Fundamental to the Enlightenment was faith in science. Because of its basis in empirical, or observable, fact, science provided a mechanistic conception of the universe, which reassured a populace that was finding traditional religions less certain. As promoted in the classic physics of Isaac Newton (1642–1727), the universe was a huge machine consisting of time, space, and matter. In the early 20th century, many scientists challenged this model of the universe in what amounted to a second scientific and technological revolution. Particularly noteworthy was the work of physicists Max Planck (1858–1947), Albert Einstein (1879–1955), Ernest Rutherford (1871–1937), and Niels Bohr (1885–1962). With their discoveries, each of these scientists shattered the existing faith in the objective reality of matter and, in so doing, paved the way for a new model of the universe. Planck's quantum theory (1900) raised questions about the emission of atomic energy. In his 1905 paper "The Electrodynamics of Moving Bodies," Einstein carried Planck's work further by introducing his theory of relativity. He argued that space and time are not absolute, as postulated in Newtonian physics. Rather, Einstein explained, time and space are relative to the observer and linked in

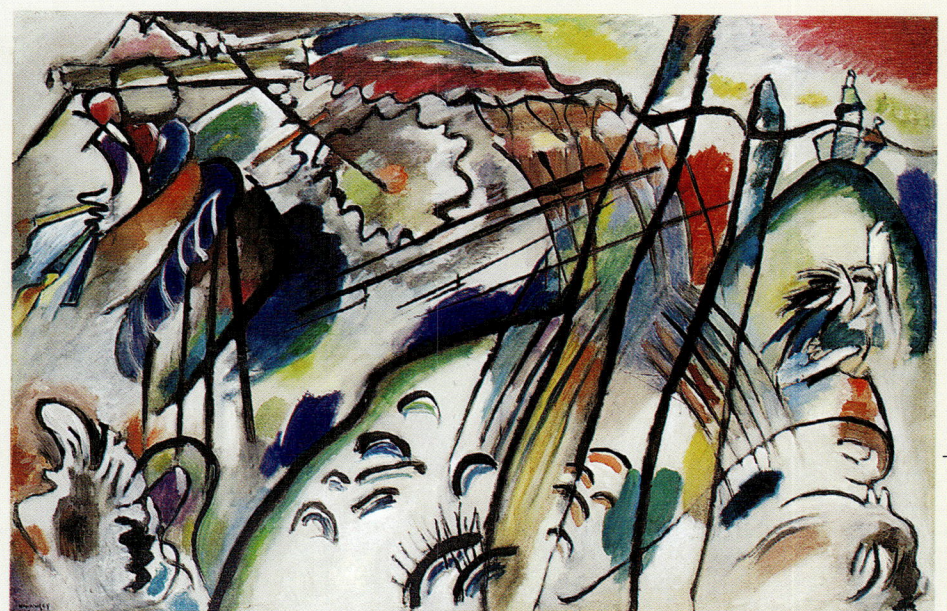

29-7 VASSILY KANDINSKY, *Improvisation 28* (second version), 1912. Oil on canvas, 3′ 7⅞″ × 5′ 3⅞″. Solomon R. Guggenheim Museum, New York (gift of Solomon R. Guggenheim, 1937).

The theories of Einstein and Rutherford convinced Kandinsky that material objects had no real substance. He was one of the first painters to explore complete abstraction in his canvases.

what he called a four-dimensional space-time continuum. He also concluded that matter, rather than a solid, tangible reality, was another form of energy. Einstein's famous equation, $E = mc^2$, where $E$ stands for energy, $m$ for mass, and $c$ for the speed of light, provided a formula for understanding atomic energy. Rutherford's and Bohr's exploration of atomic structure between 1906 and 1913 contributed to this new perception of matter and energy. Together, all these scientific discoveries constituted a changed view of physical nature and contributed to the growing interest in abstraction, as opposed to the mimetic representation of the world, among early-20th-century artists such as Vassily Kandinsky (FIG. 29-7).

---

**VASSILY KANDINSKY** A second major German Expressionist group, *Der Blaue Reiter* (The Blue Rider), formed in Munich in 1911. The two founding members, Vassily Kandinsky and Franz Marc, whimsically selected this name because of their mutual interest in the color blue and horses. As did Die Brücke, this group produced paintings that captured their feelings in visual form while also eliciting intense visceral responses from viewers.

Born in Russia, VASSILY KANDINSKY (1866–1944) moved to Munich in 1896 and soon developed a spontaneous and aggressively avant-garde expressive style. Indeed, Kandinsky was one of the first artists to explore complete abstraction, as in *Improvisation 28* (FIG. 29-7), painted in 1912. Kandinsky fueled his elimination of representational elements with his interest in theosophy (a religious and philosophical belief system incorporating a wide range of tenets from, among other sources, Buddhism and mysticism) and the occult, as well as with advances in the sciences. A true intellectual, widely read in philosophy, religion, history, and the other arts, especially music, Kandinsky was also one of the few early modernists to read with some comprehension the new scientific theories of the era (see "Science and Art in the Early 20th Century," above). Scientists' exploration of atomic structure, for example, convinced Kandinsky that material objects had no real substance, thereby shattering his faith in a world of tangible things. He articulated his ideas in an influential treatise, *Concerning the Spiritual in Art*, published in 1912. Artists, Kandinsky believed, must express their innermost feelings by orchestrating color, form, line, and space. *Improvisation 28* is one of numerous works Kandinsky produced that convey feelings with color juxtapositions, intersecting

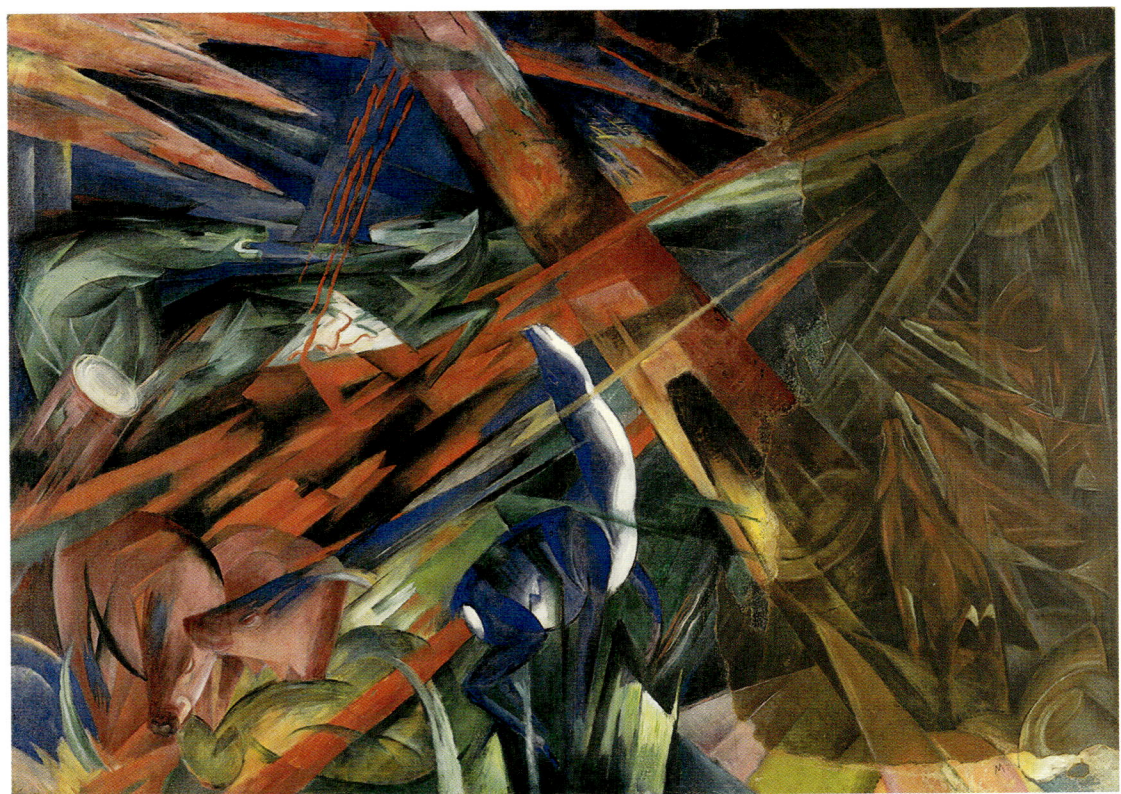

**29-8** Franz Marc, *Fate of the Animals*, 1913. Oil on canvas, 6′ 4¾″ × 8′ 9½″. Kunstmuseum Basel, Basel.

Marc developed a system of correspondences between specific colors and feelings or ideas. In this apocalyptic scene of animals trapped in a forest, the colors of severity and brutality dominate.

1 ft.

linear elements, and implied spatial relationships. Ultimately, Kandinsky saw these abstractions as evolving blueprints for a more enlightened and liberated society emphasizing spirituality.

**FRANZ MARC** As did many of the other German Expressionists, Franz Marc (1880–1916), the cofounder of Der Blaue Reiter, grew increasingly pessimistic about the state of humanity, especially as World War I loomed on the horizon. His perception of human beings as deeply flawed led him to turn to the animal world for his subjects. Animals, he believed, were more pure than humanity and thus more appropriate vehicles to express an inner truth. In his quest to imbue his paintings with greater emotional intensity, Marc focused on color and developed a system of correspondences between specific colors and feelings or ideas. In a letter to a fellow Blaue Reiter, Marc explained: "Blue is the *male* principle, severe and spiritual. Yellow is the *female* principle, gentle, happy and sensual. Red is *matter,* brutal and heavy."[3]

*Fate of the Animals* (FIG. **29-8**) represents the culmination of Marc's efforts to create, in a sense, an iconography of color. Painted in 1913, when the tension of impending cataclysm had pervaded society, the animals appear trapped in a forest amid falling trees, some apocalyptic event destroying both the forest and the animals inhabiting it. The painter distorted the entire scene and shattered it into fragments. Significantly, the lighter and brighter colors—the passive, gentle, and cheerful ones—are absent, and the colors of severity and brutality dominate the work. On the back of the canvas Marc wrote: "All being is flaming suffering." The artist discovered just how well his painting portended war's anguish and tragedy when he ended up at the front the following year. His experiences in battle prompted him to tell his wife in a letter: "[*Fate of the Animals*] is like a premonition of this war—horrible and shattering. I can hardly conceive that I painted it."[4] Marc's contempt for people's inhumanity and his attempt to express that through his art ended, with tragic irony, in his death in action in 1916.

**KÄTHE KOLLWITZ** The emotional range of German Expressionism extends from passionate protest and satirical bitterness to the poignantly expressed pity for the poor in the prints of Käthe Kollwitz (1867–1945), for example, *Woman with Dead Child* (FIG. **29-9**). Kollwitz and her younger contemporary Paula Modersohn-Becker (1876–1907; FIG. **29-9A**) studied at the Union of Berlin Women Artists and had no formal association with any Expressionist group. Working in a variety of printmaking techniques, including woodcut, lithography, and etching, Kollwitz explored a range of issues from the overtly political to the deeply personal.

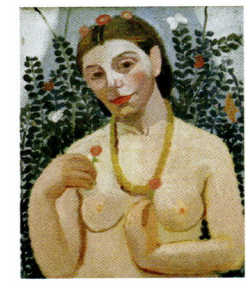

**29-9A** Modersohn-Becker, *Self-Portrait,* 1906.

One image Kollwitz explored in depth, producing a number of print variations, was a mother with her dead child. Although she initially derived the theme from the Christian *Pietà,* Kollwitz transformed it into a universal statement of maternal loss and grief. In the etching and lithograph illustrated here (FIG. 29-9), she replaced the reverence and grace pervading most depictions of Mary holding the dead Christ (FIG. 22-12) with an animalistic passion. The grieving mother ferociously grips the body of her dead child. The primal nature of the undeniably powerful image is in keeping with the aims of the Expressionists. Not since the Gothic age in Germany (FIG. 13-50) had any artist produced a mother-and-son group with a comparable emotional impact. Because Kollwitz used her son Peter as the model for the dead child, the image was no doubt all the more personal to her. The print stands as a poignant premonition. Peter died fighting in World War I at age 21.

**EGON SCHIELE** Also related in spirit to but not associated with any German Expressionist group was the Austrian artist Egon Schiele (1890–1918), who during his tragically brief but

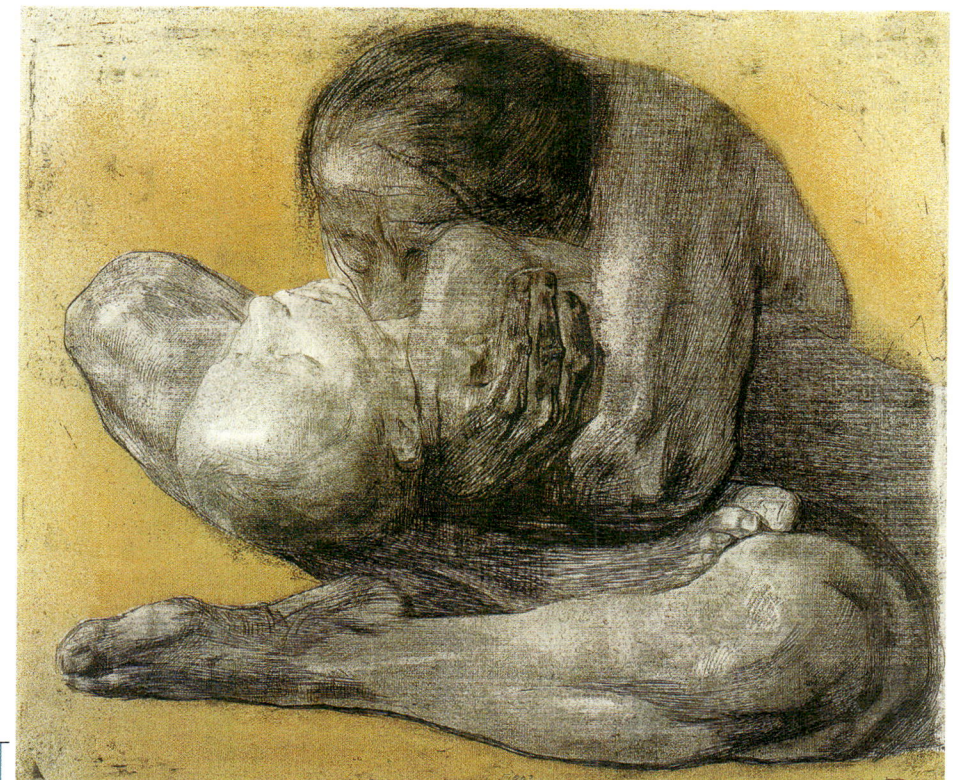

**29-9** Käthe Kollwitz, *Woman with Dead Child*, 1903. Etching and soft-ground etching, overprinted lithographically with a gold tone plate, 1′ 4⅝″ × 1′ 7⅛″. British Museum, London.

The theme of a mother mourning over her dead child comes from images of the *Pietà* in Christian art, but Kollwitz transformed it into a powerful universal statement of maternal loss and grief.

prolific career produced more than 3,000 paintings and drawings. The bulk of them are nude figure studies of men and women in *gouache* and watercolor on paper, including approximately a hundred self-portraits (FIG. **29-10**) exemplifying early-20th-century Expressionist painters' intense interest in emotional states. As a teenager, Schiele watched the slow, painful deterioration of his father, who contracted syphilis and died when Egon was 15. The experience had a profound impact on the artist, who ever after associated sex with physical and emotional pain and death.

Schiele began formal art training the year after his father died. He enrolled in Vienna's Academy of Fine Art in 1906, where he became a protégé of Gustav Klimt (FIG. 28-29), who invited Schiele to exhibit some of his works with his own and those of, among others, Vincent van Gogh and Edvard Munch. The emotional content of their work made a deep impression upon Schiele, who nonetheless far surpassed van Gogh, Munch, and all of his contemporaries, including the sculptor WILHELM LEHMBRUCK (1881–1919; FIG. **29-10A**), in the portrayal of emaciated bodies and tormented psyches. Indeed, Schiele once spent 24 days in prison for producing what a judge ruled was pornographic art.

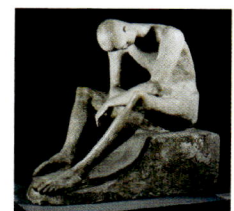

29-10A LEHMBRUCK, *Seated Youth*, 1917.

Schiele's 1910 nude portrait of himself grimacing (FIG. 29-10) is a characteristic example of his mature work. He stands frontally, staring at himself in the large mirror he kept in his studio. There is no background. The edges of the paper sever his lower legs and right elbow. In some portraits Schiele portrayed himself with amputated limbs, and his body is always that of a malnourished man whose muscles show through transparent flesh. The pose is awkward, twisted, and pained. The elongated fingers of the hands seem useless, incapable of holding anything. It is hard to imagine a nude body breaking more sharply with the classical tradition of heroic male nudity. Schiele's self-portrait is that of a martyr who has suffered both physically and psychologically. (He portrayed himself in several paintings as Saint Sebastian pierced by arrows.) Schiele's unhappy life ended when he contracted the Spanish flu in 1918. He was only 28 years old.

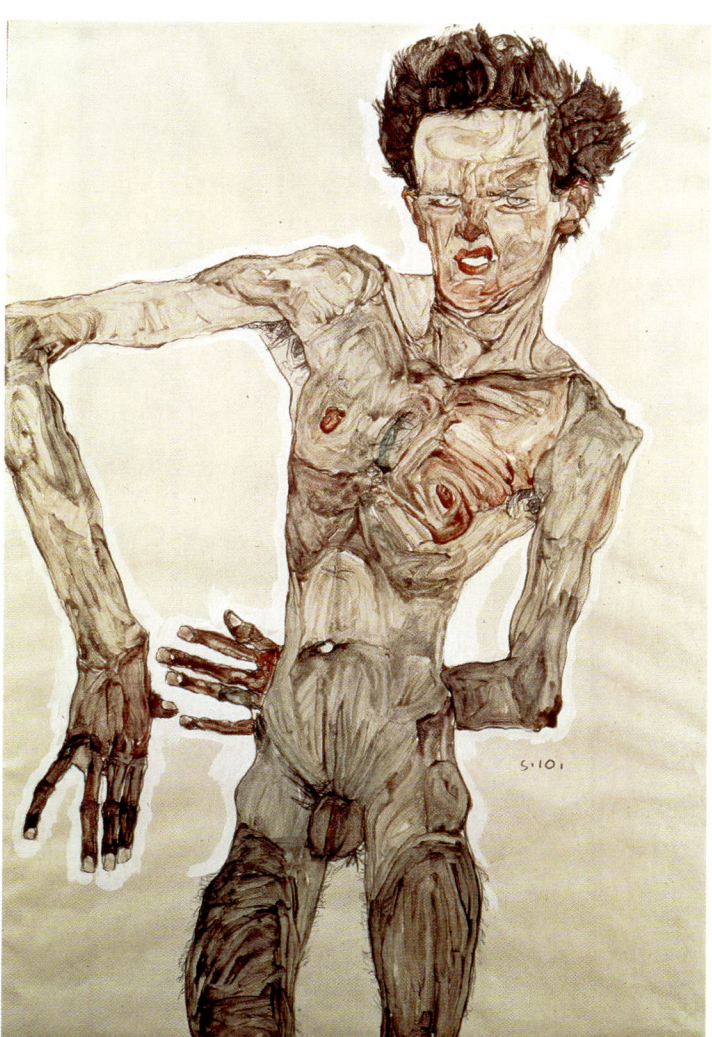

**29-10** Egon Schiele, *Nude Self-Portrait, Grimacing*, 1910. Gouache, watercolor, and pencil on paper, 1′ 10″ × 1′ 2⅜″. Albertina, Vienna.

Breaking sharply with the academic tradition of heroic male nudity, Schiele, a Viennese Expressionist, often portrayed himself with an emaciated body, twisted limbs, and a grimacing expression.

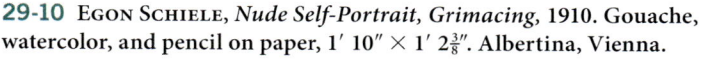

## Gertrude and Leo Stein and the Avant-Garde

One of the many unexpected developments in the history of art is that two Americans—Gertrude (1874–1946) and Leo (1872–1947) Stein—played pivotal roles in the history of the European avant-garde. The Steins provided a hospitable environment in their Paris home for artists, writers, musicians, collectors, and critics to socialize and discuss progressive art and ideas. Born in Pennsylvania, the Stein siblings moved to 27 rue de Fleurus in Paris in 1903. Gertrude's experimental writing stimulated her interest in the latest developments in the arts. Conversely, the avant-garde ideas discussed in her home influenced Gertrude's unique poetry, plays, and other works. She is perhaps best known for *The Autobiography of Alice B. Toklas* (1933), a unique memoir written in the persona of her longtime lesbian companion.

The Steins' interest in the exciting and invigorating debates taking place in avant-garde circles led them to welcome visitors to their Saturday salons, which included lectures, thoughtful discussions, and spirited arguments. Often, these gatherings lasted until dawn and included not only their French friends but also visiting Americans, Britons, Swedes, Germans, Hungarians, Spaniards, Poles, and Russians. Among the hundreds who visited the Steins were artists Henri Matisse, Pablo Picasso, Georges Braque, Mary Cassatt, Marcel Duchamp, Alfred Stieglitz, and Arthur B. Davies; writers Ernest Hemingway, F. Scott Fitzgerald, John dos Passos, Jean Cocteau, and Guillaume Apollinaire; art dealers Daniel Kahnweiler and Ambroise Vollard; critics Roger Fry and Clive Bell; and collectors Sergei Shchukin and Ivan Morozov.

The Steins were avid art collectors, and the works they hung in their home attracted many visitors. One of the first paintings Leo purchased was Matisse's notorious *Woman with the Hat* (FIG. 29-2), and he subsequently bought many more by Matisse—including *Le Bonheur de Vivre* (FIG. 29-2A)—along with works by Gauguin, Cézanne, Renoir, Picasso, and Braque. Picasso, who developed a close friendship with Gertrude, painted her portrait (FIG. 29-11) in 1907. Gertrude loved the painting so much she kept it by her all her life and bequeathed it to the Metropolitan Museum of Art only upon her death in 1946.

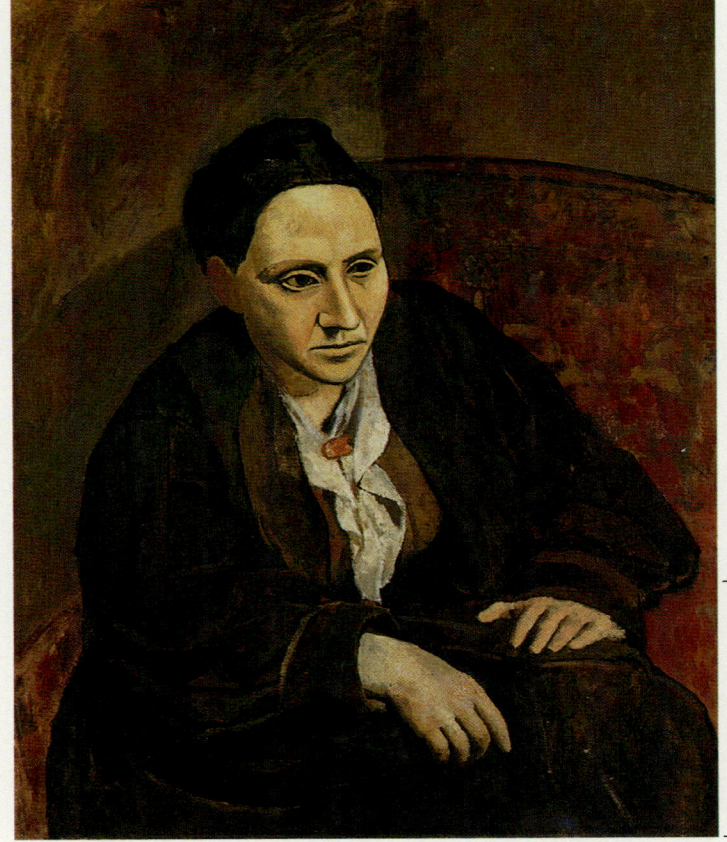

1 ft.

**29-11** PABLO PICASSO, *Gertrude Stein*, 1906–1907. Oil on canvas, 3′ 3⅜″ × 2′ 8″. Metropolitan Museum of Art, New York (bequest of Gertrude Stein, 1947). ◼◀

Picasso had left this portrait of his friend and patron unfinished until he decided to incorporate the planar simplicity of ancient Iberian stone sculptures into his depiction of her face.

## Primitivism and Cubism

The Expressionist departure from any strict adherence to illusionism in art was a path other artists followed. Among those who most radically challenged prevailing artistic conventions and moved most aggressively into the realm of abstraction was Pablo Picasso.

**PABLO PICASSO** Born in Spain four years after Gustave Courbet's death, PABLO PICASSO (1881–1973) mastered all aspects of late-19th-century Realist technique by the time he entered the Barcelona Academy of Fine Art in the late 1890s. His prodigious talent led him to experiment with a wide range of visual expression, first in Spain and then in Paris, where he settled in 1904. An artist whose importance to the history of art is uncontested, Picasso made staggering contributions to new ways of representing the surrounding world. Perhaps the most prolific artist in history, he explored virtually every artistic medium during his lengthy career, but remained a traditional artist in making careful preparatory studies for each major work. Nonetheless, Picasso epitomized

modernism in his enduring quest for innovation, which resulted in sudden shifts from one style to another. By the time he settled permanently in Paris, Picasso's work had evolved from Spanish painting's sober Realism through an Impressionistic phase to the so-called Blue Period (1901–1904), when, in a melancholy state of mind, he used primarily blue colors to depict worn, pathetic, and alienated figures. In 1904, Picasso's palette changed to lighter and brighter colors during his Rose (or Pink) Period (1904–1906), but some of the canvases he painted during those years, such as *Family of Saltimbanques* (FIG. 29-11A), retain the pessimistic overtones of the Blue Period.

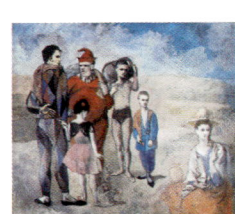

**29-11A** PICASSO, *Family of Saltimbanques*, 1905.

***GERTRUDE STEIN*** By 1906, Picasso was searching restlessly for new ways to depict form. He found clues in the ancient Iberian sculpture of his homeland and other "primitive" cultures.

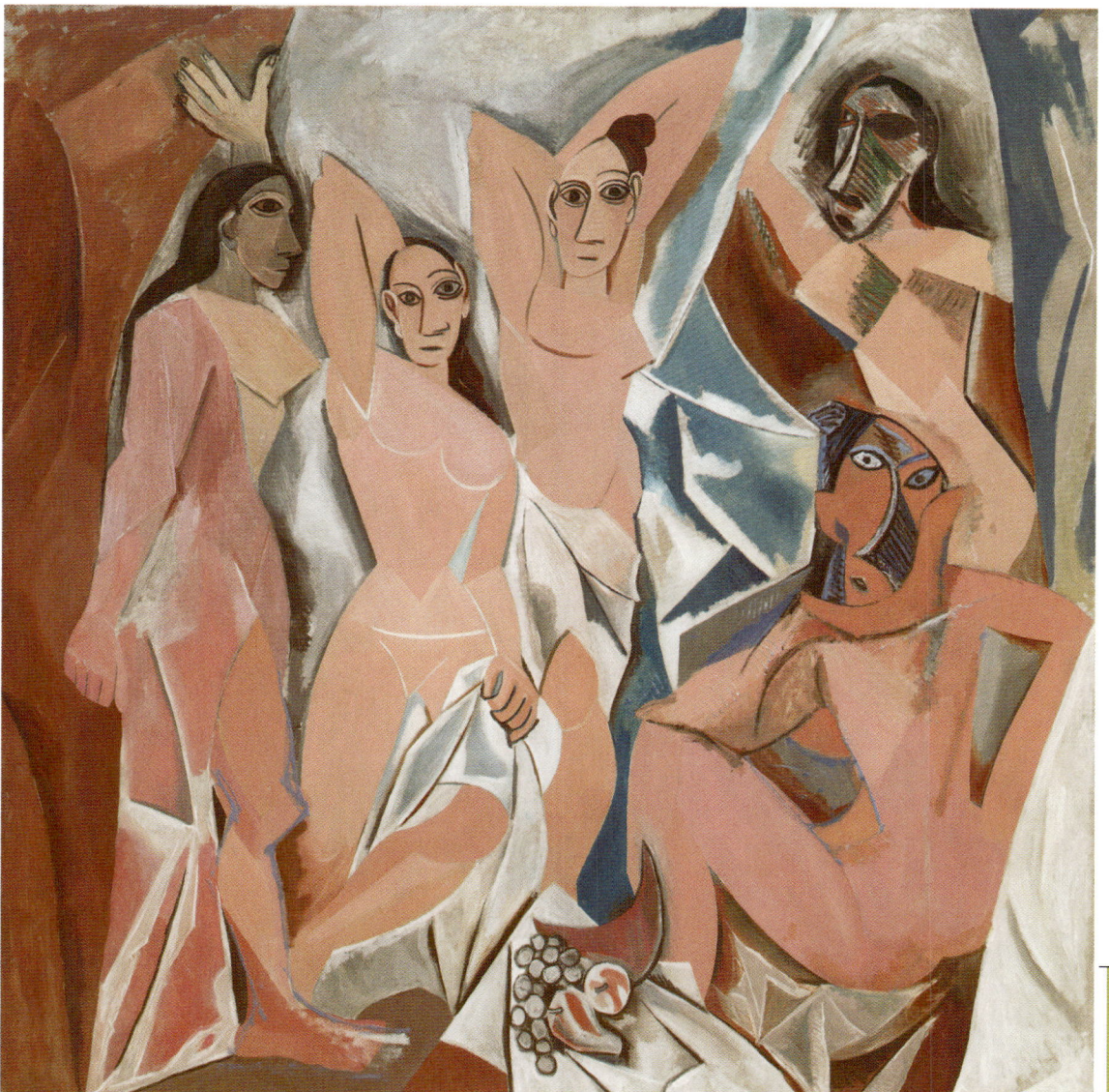

29-12 PABLO PICASSO, *Les Demoiselles d'Avignon*, 1907. Oil on canvas, 8′ × 7′ 8″. Museum of Modern Art, New York (acquired through the Lillie P. Bliss Bequest).
■◀

African and ancient Iberian sculpture and Cézanne's late paintings influenced this pivotal work, with which Picasso opened the door to a radically new method of representing forms in space.

1 ft.

Inspired by these sources, Picasso returned to a portrait of *Gertrude Stein* (FIG. **29-11**), his friend and patron (see "Gertrude and Leo Stein and the Avant-Garde," page 844). Picasso had left the portrait unfinished after Stein posed for more than 80 sittings earlier in the year. On resuming work, Picasso painted Stein's head as a simplified planar form, incorporating aspects derived from Iberian stone heads. Although the disparity between the style of the face and the rest of the figure is striking, together they provide an insightful portrait of a forceful, vivacious woman. More important, Picasso had discovered a new approach to the representation of the human form.

**DEMOISELLES D'AVIGNON** The influence of "primitive" art also surfaces in *Les Demoiselles d'Avignon* (*The Young Ladies of Avignon*; FIG. **29-12**), which opened the door to a radically new method of representing form in space. Picasso began the work as a symbolic picture to be titled *Philosophical Bordello*, portraying two male clients (who, based on surviving drawings, had features resembling Picasso's) intermingling with women in the reception room of a brothel on Avignon Street in Barcelona. One was a sailor. The other carried a skull, an obvious reference to death. By the time the artist finished, he had eliminated the male figures and simpli-

fied the room's details to a suggestion of drapery and a schematic foreground still life. Picasso had become wholly absorbed in the problem of finding a new way to represent the five female figures in their interior space. Instead of depicting the figures as continuous volumes, he fractured their shapes and interwove them with the equally jagged planes representing drapery and empty space. Indeed, the space, so entwined with the bodies, is virtually illegible. Here Picasso pushed Cézanne's treatment of form and space (FIGS. 28-21 to 28-22A) to a new level. The tension between Picasso's representation of three-dimensional space and his conviction a painting is a two-dimensional design on the surface of a stretched canvas is a tension between representation and abstraction.

The artist extended the radical nature of *Les Demoiselles d'Avignon* even further by depicting the figures inconsistently. Ancient Iberian sculptures inspired the calm, ideal features of the three young women at the left, as they had the head of Gertrude Stein (FIG. 29-11). The energetic, violently striated features of the two heads to the right emerged late in Picasso's production of the work and grew directly from his increasing fascination with the power of African sculpture (see "'Primitivism' and Colonialism," page 846), which the artist studied in Paris's Trocadéro ethnography museum

## Primitivism and Colonialism

The art of Africa, Oceania, and the native peoples of the Americas was a major source of inspiration for many early-20th-century modernist artists. Art historians refer to the incorporation of stylistic elements from these "non-Western" cultures as *primitivism*. Both terms imply the superiority of Western civilization and Western art, but many modernist artists admired these artworks precisely because they embodied different stylistic preferences and standards. Some artists, for example Henri Matisse and Pablo Picasso (FIG. 29-13), became enthusiastic collectors of "primitive art," but all of them could view non-Western objects in the many European and American anthropological and ethnographic museums that had begun to proliferate during the second half of the 19th century.

In 1882, the Musée d'Ethnographie du Trocadéro (now the Musée du quai Branly) in Paris opened its doors to the public. The Musée Permanent des Colonies (now the Musée National des Arts d'Afrique et d'Océanie) in Paris also provided the public with a wide array of objects—weapons, tools, basketwork, headdresses—from colonial territories, as did the Musée Africain in Marseilles. In Berlin, the Museum für Völkerkunde housed almost 10,000 African objects by 1886, when it opened for public viewing. Even the Expositions Universelles—regularly scheduled exhibitions in France designed to celebrate industrial progress—included products from Oceania and Africa after 1851. By the beginning of the 20th century, significant non-Western collections were on view in museums in Liverpool, Glasgow, Edinburgh, London, Hamburg, Stuttgart, Vienna, Berlin, Munich, Leiden, Copenhagen, and Chicago.

The formation of these collections was a by-product of the frenzied imperialist expansion central to the geopolitical dynamics of the 19th century and much of the 20th century. Most of the Western powers maintained colonies as raw-material sources, as manufacturing markets, and as territorial acquisitions. For example, the United States, France, and Holland all kept a colonial presence in the Pacific. Britain, France, Germany, Belgium, Holland, Spain, and Portugal divided up the African continent. People often perceived these colonial cultures as "primitive" and referred to many of the non-Western artifacts displayed in museums as "artificial curiosities" or "fetish objects." Indeed, the exhibition of these objects collected during expeditions to the colonies served to reinforce the "need" for a colonial presence in these countries. Colonialism often had a missionary dimension. These objects, which often depicted strange gods or creatures, reinforced the perception these peoples were "barbarians" who needed to be "civilized" or "saved," and this perception justified colonialism and its missionary aspects worldwide.

Whether avant-garde artists were aware of the imperialistic implications of their appropriation of non-Western culture is unclear. Certainly, however, many artists reveled in the energy and freshness of non-Western images and forms. These different cultural products provided Western artists with new ways of looking at their own art. Matisse always maintained he saw African sculptures as simply "good sculptures . . . like any other."* Picasso, in contrast, believed "the masks weren't just like any other pieces of

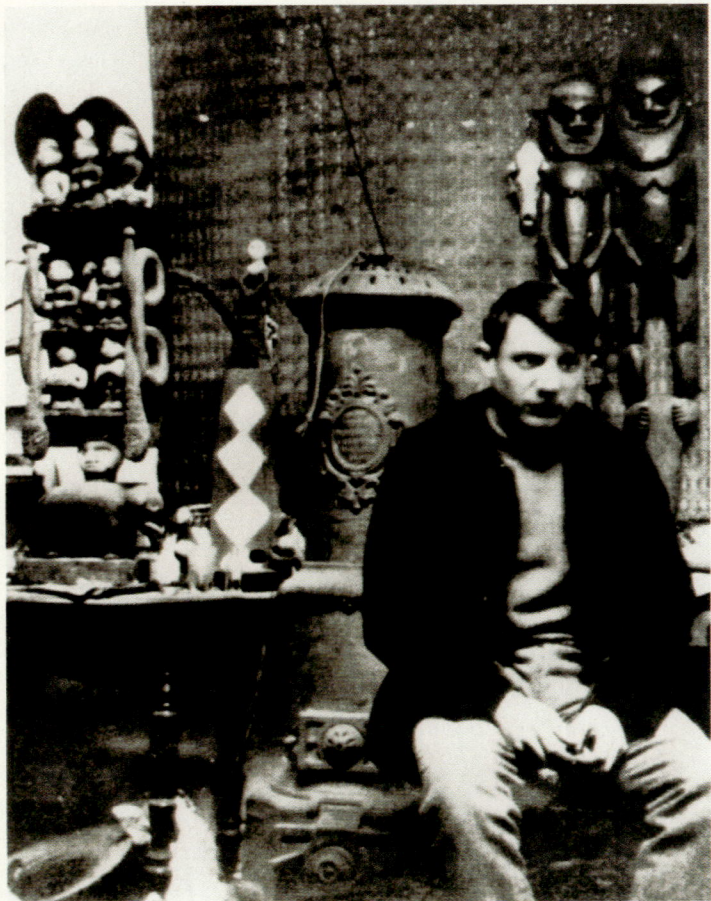

29-13 FRANK GELETT BURGESS, photograph of Pablo Picasso in his studio in the rue Ravignan, Paris, France, 1908. Musée Picasso, Paris. ◼️

Picasso was familiar with ancient Iberian art from his homeland and studied African and other "primitive" art in Paris's Trocadéro museum. He kept his own collection of primitive art in his studio.

sculpture. Not at all. They were magic things. . . . mediators" between humans and the forces of evil, and he sought to capture their power as well as their forms in his paintings. "[In the Trocadéro] I understood why I was a painter. . . . All alone in that awful museum, with masks, dolls . . . *Les Demoiselles d'Avignon* [FIG. 29-12] must have come to me that day."† "Primitive art" seemed to embody a directness, closeness to nature, and honesty that appealed to modernist artists determined to reject conventional models. Non-Western art served as an important revitalizing and energizing force in Western art.

*Jean-Louis Paudrat, "From Africa," in William Rubin, ed., *"Primitivism" in 20th Century Art: Affinity of the Tribal and the Modern* (New York: Museum of Modern Art, 1984), 1:141.
†Ibid.

and collected and kept in his Paris studio (FIG. 29-13). Perhaps responding to the energy of these two new heads, Picasso also revised their bodies. He broke them into more ambiguous planes suggesting a combination of views, as if the observer sees the figures from more than one place in space at once. The woman seated at the lower right shows these multiple angles most clearly, seeming to present the viewer simultaneously with a three-quarter back view from the left, another from the right, and a front view of the head that suggests seeing the figure frontally as well. Gone is the traditional concept of an orderly, constructed, and unified pictorial space mirroring the world. In its place are the rudimentary beginnings of a new representation of the world as a dynamic interplay of time and space. Clearly, *Les Demoiselles d'Avignon* represents a dramatic departure from the careful presentation of a visual reality. Explained Picasso: "I paint forms as I think them, not as I see them."[5]

**GEORGES BRAQUE AND CUBISM**  For many years, Picasso showed *Les Demoiselles* only to other painters. One of the first to see it was GEORGES BRAQUE (1882–1963), a Fauve painter who found it so challenging he began to rethink his own painting style. Using the painting's revolutionary elements as a point of departure, together Braque and Picasso formulated *Cubism* around 1908 in the belief the art of painting had to move far beyond the description of visual reality. Cubism represented a radical turning point in the history of art, nothing less than a dismissal of the pictorial illusionism that had dominated Western art since the Renaissance. The Cubists rejected naturalistic depictions, preferring compositions of shapes and forms abstracted from the conventionally perceived world. They pursued the analysis of form central to Cézanne's artistic explorations by dissecting everything around them into their many constituent features, which they then recomposed, by a new logic of design, into a coherent, independent aesthetic picture. The Cubists' rejection of accepted artistic practice illustrates both the period's aggressive avant-garde critique of pictorial convention and the public's dwindling faith in a safe, concrete Newtonian world in the face of the physics of Einstein and others (see "Science and Art," page 841).

The new style received its name after Matisse described some of Braque's work to the critic Louis Vauxcelles as having been painted "with little cubes." In his review, Vauxcelles described the new paintings as "cubic oddities."[6] The French writer and theorist Guillaume Apollinaire (1880–1918) summarized well the central concepts of Cubism in 1913:

> Authentic cubism [is] the art of depicting new wholes with formal elements borrowed not from the reality of vision, but from that of conception. This tendency leads to a poetic kind of painting which stands outside the world of observation; for, even in a simple cubism, the geometrical surfaces of an object must be opened out in order to give a complete representation of it. . . . Everyone must agree that a chair, from whichever side it is viewed, never ceases to have four legs, a seat and a back, and that, if it is robbed of one of these elements, it is robbed of an important part.[7]

Most art historians refer to the first phase of Cubism, developed jointly by Picasso and Braque, as *Analytic Cubism,* because in essence it is a painterly analysis of the structure of form. Because Cubists could not achieve the kind of total view Apollinaire described by the traditional method of drawing or painting models from one position, they began to dissect the forms of their subjects and to present their analysis of form across the canvas surface.

*THE PORTUGUESE*  Georges Braque's painting *The Portuguese* (FIG. 29-14) exemplifies Analytic Cubism. The subject is a Portuguese musician the artist recalled seeing years earlier in a bar in Marseilles. Braque dissected the man and his instrument and placed the resulting forms in dynamic interaction with the space around them. Unlike the Fauves and German Expressionists, who used vibrant colors, the Cubists chose subdued hues—here solely brown tones—in order to focus attention on form. In *The Portuguese,* Braque carried his analysis so far viewers must work diligently to discover clues to the subject. The construction of large intersecting planes suggests the forms of a man and a guitar. Smaller shapes interpenetrate and hover in the large planes. The way Braque treated light and shadow reveals his departure from conventional artistic practice. Light and dark passages suggest both chiaroscuro modeling and transparent planes that enable viewers to see through one level to another. Solid forms emerge only to be canceled almost immediately by a different reading of the subject.

The stenciled letters and numbers Braque included add to the painting's complexity. Letters and numbers are flat shapes, but as elements of a Cubist painting such as *The Portuguese,* they enable the

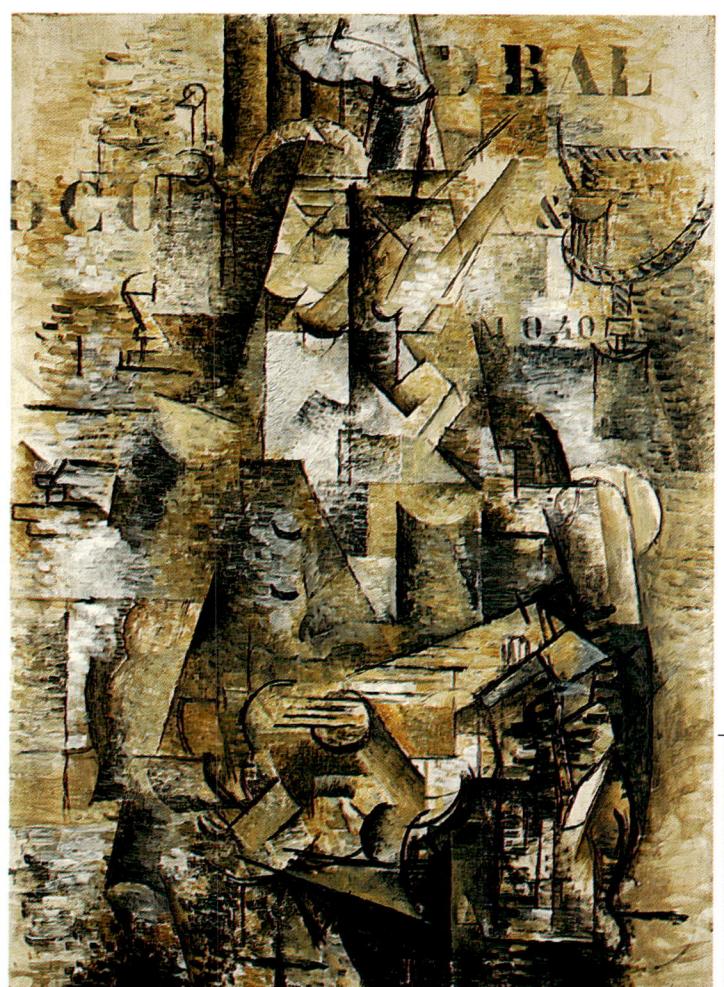

1 ft.

**29-14**  GEORGES BRAQUE, *The Portuguese,* 1911. Oil on canvas, 3′ 10⅛″ × 2′ 8″. Kunstmuseum Basel, Basel (gift of Raoul La Roche, 1952). ◼◀

The Cubists rejected the pictorial illusionism that had dominated Western art for centuries. Here, Braque concentrated on dissecting form and placing it in dynamic interaction with space.

painter to play with viewers' perception of two- and three-dimensional space. The letters and numbers lie flat on the painted canvas surface, yet the shading and shapes of other forms seem to flow behind and underneath them, pushing the letters and numbers forward into the viewing space. Occasionally, they seem attached to the surface of some object within the painting. Ultimately, the constantly shifting imagery makes it impossible to arrive at any definitive or final reading of the image. Examining this kind of painting is a disconcerting excursion into ambiguity and doubt, especially since the letters and numbers seem to anchor the painting in the world of representation, thereby exacerbating the tension between representation and abstraction. Analytical Cubist paintings radically disrupt expectations about the representation of space and time.

**ROBERT DELAUNAY** Art historians generally regard the suppression of color as crucial to Cubism's success, but ROBERT DELAUNAY (1885–1941), Picasso's and Braque's contemporary, worked toward a kind of color Cubism. Apollinaire gave the name *Orphism* to Delaunay's version of Cubism, after Orpheus, the Greek god of music. Apollinaire believed art, like music, was distinct from the representation of the visible world. But Delaunay's own name for his art was *Simultané-isme*. "Simultaneity" for Delaunay meant the application of 19th-century theories about the perception and psychology of color (see "19th-Century Color Theory," Chapter 28, page 813) to create spatial effects and kaleidoscopic movement solely through color contrasts. He insisted color in painting was both form and subject, and as early as 1912 he began to paint purely abstract compositions with titles such as *Simultaneous Disks, Simultaneous Windows,* and *Simultaneous Contrasts.* Delaunay developed his ideas about color use in dialogue with his Russian-born wife, Sonia (1885–1974), also an important modernist artist. She created paintings, quilts, and other textile arts, and book covers that exploited the expressive capabilities of color. As a result of their artistic explorations, both Delaunays became convinced the rhythms of modern life could best be expressed through color harmonies and dissonances.

A salient feature of modern life for Delaunay was technological innovation, and the engineering marvels of the late 19th and early 20th centuries figure prominently in his paintings. In 1914 he immortalized the engineer, inventor, and aviator Louis Blériot (1872–1936) in one of his boldest Orphic canvases. *Homage to Blériot* (FIG. **29-15**) is an almost purely abstract composition that celebrates Blériot's great achievement of being the first person to fly across the English Channel, which he accomplished in a monoplane of his own design. The 22-mile flight from Les Barraques, near Calais, France, to Dover, England, on July 25, 1909, lasted 37 minutes and made Blériot an instant international celebrity. It also brought him a prize of 1,000 British pounds, which a London newspaper had offered as a challenge to all aviators. At the time Delaunay commemorated the event, Blériot was manufacturing warplanes for use by French pilots and their allies during World War I. Blériot's monoplane appears at the upper right of Delaunay's painting, above another triumph of French engineering, the Eiffel

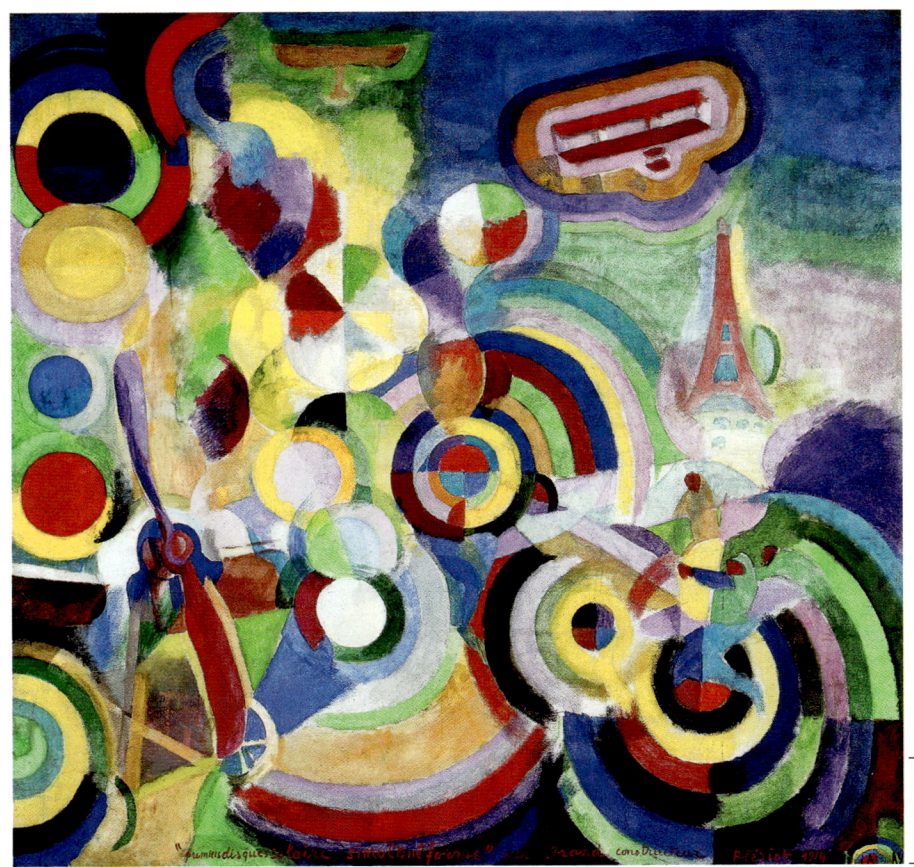

**29-15** ROBERT DELAUNAY, *Homage to Blériot,* 1914. Oil on canvas, 8′ 2½″ × 8′ 3″. Kunstmuseum Basel, Basel (Emanuel Hoffman Foundation).

In this Orphic Cubist composition, Delaunay paid tribute to Louis Blériot, the first person to fly across the English Channel. Blériot's monoplane is at the upper right, above the Eiffel Tower.

Tower (FIG. 28-38), one of Delaunay's favorite subjects (FIG. **29-15A**). Filling the rest of the canvas are a propeller (at the lower left) and mostly circular abstract shapes suggestive of whirling propellers and blazing suns.

**SYNTHETIC CUBISM** In 1912, Cubism entered a new phase that art historians have dubbed *Synthetic Cubism*. In this later Cubist style, instead of dissecting forms, artists constructed paintings and

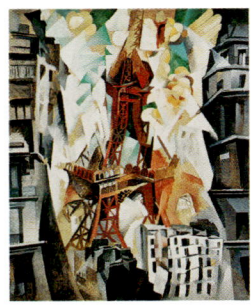

**29-15A** DELAUNAY, *Champs de Mars,* 1911.

drawings from objects and shapes cut from paper or other materials. The work marking the point of departure for this new style was Picasso's *Still Life with Chair-Caning* (FIG. **29-16**), a mixed-media painting in which Picasso imprinted a photolithographed pattern of a cane chair seat on the canvas and then pasted a piece of oilcloth on it. Framed with rope, this work challenges viewers' understanding of reality. The photographically replicated chair caning seems so "real" one expects the holes to break any brushstrokes laid upon it. But the chair caning, although optically suggestive of the real, is only an illusion or representation of an object. In contrast, the painted abstract areas do not refer to tangible objects in the real world. Yet the fact they do not imitate anything makes them more "real" than the chair caning. No pretense exists. Picasso extended the visual play by making the letter *U* escape from the space of the accompanying *J* and *O*

# Picasso on Cubism

In 1923, almost a decade after Picasso and Braque launched an artistic revolution with their Analytic (FIG. 29-14) and Synthetic (FIG. 29-16) Cubist paintings, Picasso granted an interview to the painter and critic Marius de Zayas (1880–1961). Born in Mexico, de Zayas had settled in New York City in 1907, and in 1911 had been instrumental in mounting the first exhibition in the United States of Picasso's works. In their conversation, the approved English translation of which appeared in the journal *The Arts* under the title "Picasso Speaks," the artist set forth his views about Cubism and the nature of art in general.

> We all know that Art is not truth. Art is a lie that makes us realize truth, at least the truth that is given us to understand. The artist must know the manner whereby to convince others of the truthfulness of his lies. . . . They speak of naturalism in opposition to modern painting. I would like to know if anyone has ever seen a natural work of art. Nature and art, being two different things, cannot be the same thing. Through art we express our conception of what nature is not. . . .

> Cubism is no different from any other school of painting. The same principles and the same elements are common to all. . . . Many think that Cubism is an art of

transition, an experiment which is to bring ulterior results. Those who think that way have not understood it. Cubism is not either a seed or a foetus, but an art dealing primarily with forms, and when a form is realized it is there to live its own life. . . . Mathematics, trigonometry, chemistry, psychoanalysis, music, and whatnot, have been related to Cubism to give it an easier interpretation. All this has been pure literature, not to say nonsense, . . . Cubism has kept itself within the limits and limitations of painting, never pretending to go beyond it. Drawing, design, and color are understood and practiced in Cubism in the spirit and manner that they are

understood and practiced in all other schools. Our subjects might be different, as we have introduced into painting objects and forms that were formerly ignored. . . . [I]n our subjects, we keep the joy of discovery, the pleasure of the unexpected; our subject itself must be a source of interest.*

*Marius de Zayas, "Picasso Speaks," *The Arts* (May 1923), 315–326. Reprinted in Herschel B. Chipp, *Theories of Modern Art: A Source Book by Artists and Critics* (Berkeley and Los Angeles: University of California Press, 1968), 263–266.

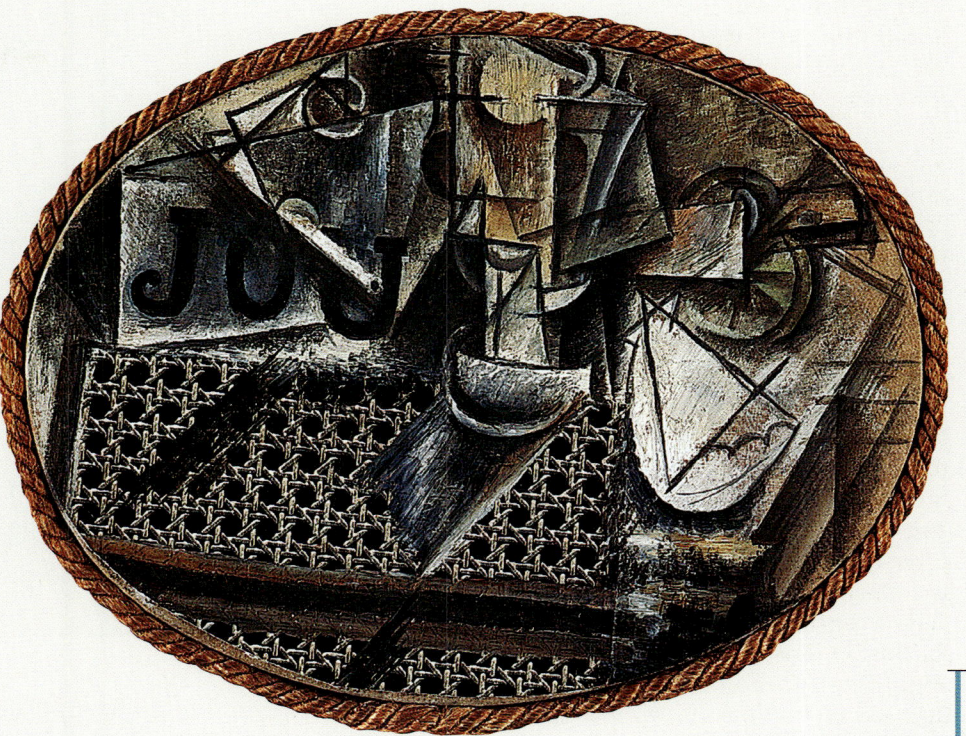

**29-16** PABLO PICASSO, *Still Life with Chair-Caning,* 1912. Oil, oilcloth, and rope on canvas, $10\frac{5}{8}'' \times 1' \ 1\frac{3}{4}''$. Musée Picasso, Paris. ◼◀

This painting includes a piece of oilcloth imprinted with the photolithographed pattern of a cane chair seat. Framed with a piece of rope, the still life challenges the viewer's understanding of reality.

1 in.

and partially covering it with a cylindrical shape that pushes across its left side. The letters *JOU,* which appear in many Cubist paintings, formed part of the masthead of the daily French newspapers (*journaux*) often found among the objects represented. Picasso and Braque especially delighted in the punning references to *jouer* and *jouir*—the French verbs meaning "to play" and "to enjoy."

Although most discussions of Cubism focus on the formal innovations of Picasso, Braque, and Delaunay, it is important to note that the public also viewed the revolutionary nature of Cubism in sociopolitical terms. Many people considered Cubism's challenge

to artistic convention and tradition a subversive attack on 20th-century society. In fact, many modernist artists and writers of the period allied themselves with various anarchist groups whose social critiques and utopian visions appealed to progressive thinkers. It was, therefore, not difficult to see radical art, such as Cubism, as having political ramifications. Many critics in the French press consistently equated Cubism's disdain for tradition with anarchism and revolution. Picasso himself, however, never viewed Cubism as a protest movement or even different in kind from traditional painting (see "Picasso on Cubism," above).

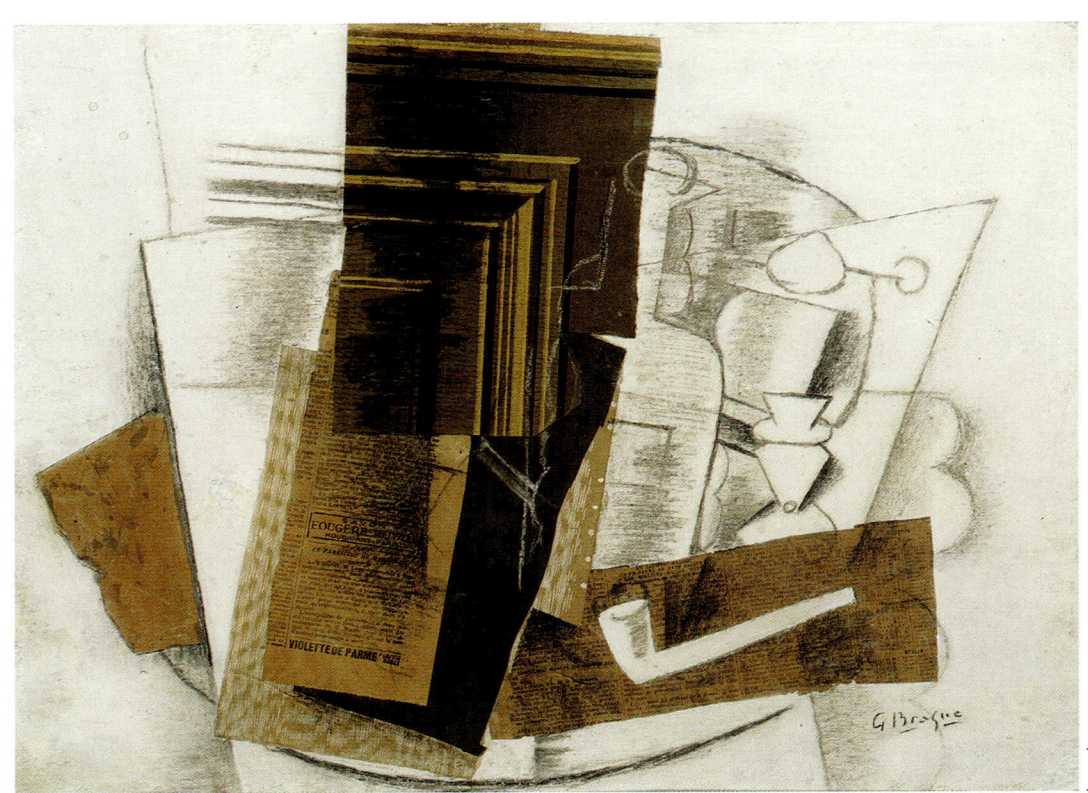

**29-17** GEORGES BRAQUE, *Bottle, Newspaper, Pipe, and Glass,* 1913. Charcoal and various papers pasted on paper, 1′ 6⅞″ × 2′ 1¼″. Private collection, New York. ◼◀

This Cubist collage of glued paper is a visual game to be deciphered. The pipe in the foreground, for example, seems to lie on the newspaper, but it is a cutout revealing the canvas surface.

**COLLAGE** After *Still Life with Chair-Caning,* both Picasso and Braque continued to explore the medium of *collage* introduced into the realm of "high art" (as opposed to unselfconscious "folk art") in that work. From the French word *coller,* meaning "to stick," a collage is a composition of bits of objects, such as newspaper or cloth, glued to a surface. Braque's *Bottle, Newspaper, Pipe, and Glass* (FIG. **29-17**) is a type of collage called *papier collé* ("stuck paper") in which the artist glues assorted paper shapes to a drawing or painting. In Braque's papier collé, charcoal lines and shadows provide clues to the Cubist multiple views of various surfaces and objects. Roughly rectangular strips of printed and colored paper dominate the composition. The paper imprinted with wood grain and moldings provides an illusion whose concreteness contrasts with the lightly rendered objects on the right. Five pieces of paper overlap one another in the center of the composition to create a layering of flat planes that both echo the space the lines suggest and establish the flatness of the work's surface. All shapes in the image seem to oscillate, pushing forward and dropping back in space. Shading seems to carve space into flat planes in some places and to turn planes into transparent surfaces in others. The pipe in the foreground illustrates this complex visual interplay especially well. Although it appears to lie on the newspaper, it is in fact a form cut through the printed paper to reveal the canvas surface, which Braque lightly modeled with charcoal. The artist thus kept his audience aware that *Bottle, Newspaper, Pipe, and Glass* is an artwork, a visual game to be deciphered, and not an attempt to reproduce nature.

Picasso explained the goals of Cubist collage in this way:

> Not only did we try to displace reality; reality was no longer in the object. . . . [In] the *papier collé* . . . [w]e didn't any longer want to fool the eye; we wanted to fool the mind. . . . If a piece of newspaper can be a bottle, that gives us something to think about in connection with both newspapers and bottles, too.[8]

Like all collage, the papier collé technique was modern in its medium—mass-produced materials never before found in high art—and modern in the way the artist embedded the art's "message" in the imagery and in the nature of these everyday materials.

*GUERNICA* Picasso continued to experiment with different artistic styles and media right up until his death in 1973. Celebrated primarily for his brilliant formal innovations, he was nonetheless acutely aware of politics throughout his life. As Picasso watched his homeland descend into civil war in the late 1930s, his involvement in political issues grew even stronger. He declared: "[P]ainting is not made to decorate apartments. It is an instrument for offensive and defensive war against the enemy."[9] Picasso got the opportunity to use art as a weapon in January 1937 when the Spanish Republican government-in-exile in Paris asked Picasso to produce a major work for the Spanish Pavilion at the Paris International Exposition that summer. He did not formally accept the invitation, however, until he received word that Guernica, the capital of the Basque region (an area in southern France and northern Spain populated by Basque speakers), had been almost totally destroyed in an air raid on April 26, 1937. Nazi pilots acting on behalf of the rebel general Francisco Franco (1892–1975) bombed the city at the busiest hour of a market day, killing or wounding many of Guernica's 7,000 citizens as well as leveling buildings. The event jolted Picasso into action. By the end of June, he had completed *Guernica* (FIG. **29-18**), a mural-sized canvas of immense power.

Despite the painting's title, Picasso made no specific reference to the event in *Guernica.* The imagery includes no bombs and no German planes. It is a universal visceral outcry of human grief. In the center, along the lower edge of the painting, lies a slain warrior clutching a broken and useless sword. A gored horse tramples him and rears back in fright as it dies. On the left, a shrieking, anguished woman cradles her dead child. On the far right, a woman on fire runs screaming from a burning building, while another woman flees mindlessly. In the upper right corner, a woman, represented by only a head, emerges from the burning building, thrusting forth a light to illuminate the horror. Overlooking the destruction is a bull, which, according to the artist, represents "brutality and darkness."[10]

In *Guernica,* Picasso brilliantly used aspects of his earlier Cubist discoveries to expressive effect, particularly the fragmentation of objects and the dislocation of anatomical features. This Cubist

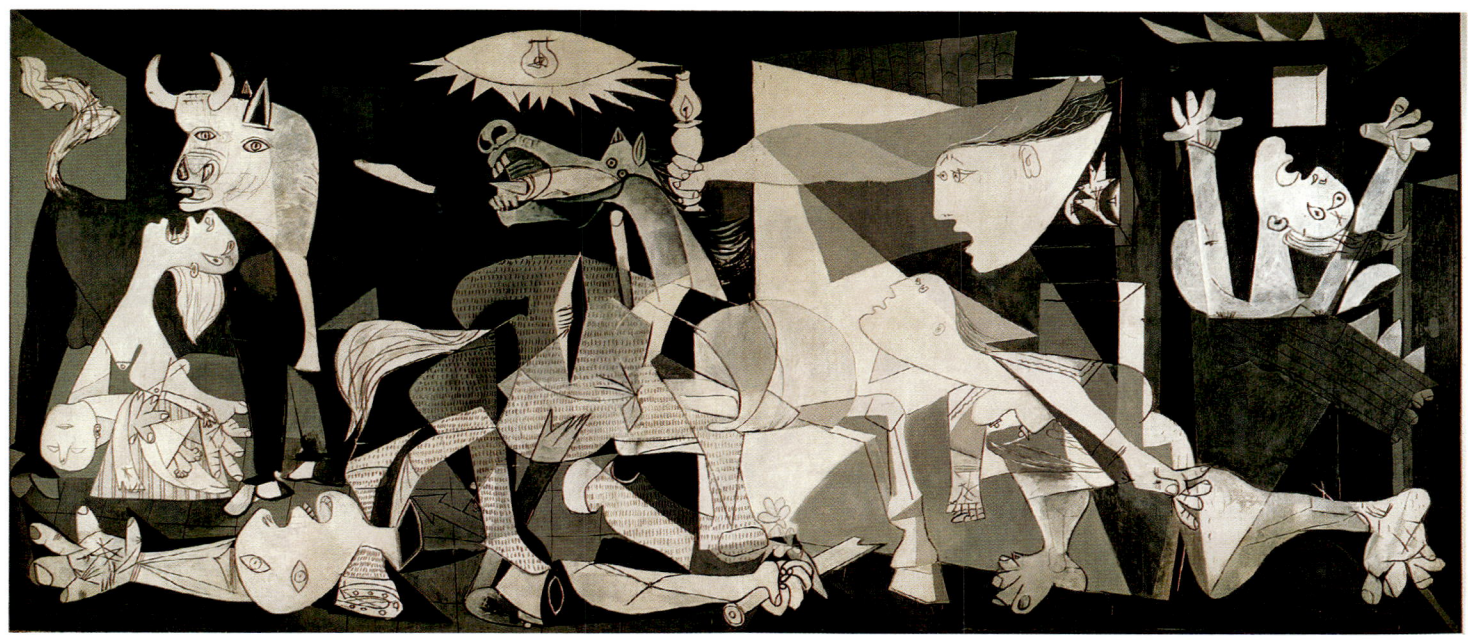

1 ft.

**29-18** PABLO PICASSO, *Guernica,* 1937. Oil on canvas, 11′ 5½″ × 25′ 5¾″. Museo Nacional Centro de Arte Reina Sofía, Madrid. ◼◂

Picasso used Cubist techniques, especially the fragmentation of objects and dislocation of anatomical features, to expressive effect in this condemnation of the Nazi bombing of the Basque capital.

fragmentation gave visual form to the horror of the aerial bombardment of the Basque people. What happened to these figures in the artist's act of painting—the dissections and contortions of the human form—paralleled what happened to them in real life. To emphasize the scene's severity and starkness, Picasso reduced his palette to black, white, and shades of gray, suppressing color once again, as he had in his Analytic Cubist works.

*GUITAR* Cubism not only opened new avenues for representing form on two-dimensional surfaces. It also inspired new approaches to sculpture. Picasso created *Guitar* (FIG. **29-19**) in 1912. As in his Cubist paintings, this sculpture operates at the intersection of two- and three-dimensionality. Picasso took the form of a guitar—an image that surfaces in many of his paintings as well, in-

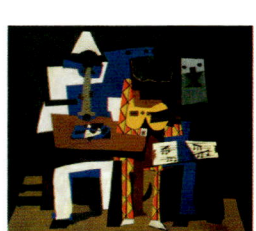

**29-19A** PICASSO, *Three Musicians,* 1921.

cluding *Three Musicians* (FIG. **29-19A**)—and explored its volume via flat planar cardboard surfaces. (FIG. 29-19 reproduces the *maquette,* or model. The finished sculpture was to be made of sheet metal.) By presenting what is essentially a cutaway view of a guitar, Picasso allowed viewers to examine both surface and interior space, both mass and void. This, of course, was completely in keeping with the Cubist program. Some scholars have suggested Picasso derived the cylindrical form that serves as the sound hole on the guitar from the eyes on masks from the Ivory Coast of Africa. African masks were a continuing and persistent source of inspiration for the artist (see "Primitivism," page 846). Here, however, Picasso seems to have transformed the anatomical features of African masks into a part of a musical instrument—dramatic evidence of his unique, innovative artistic vision. Ironically—and intentionally—the sound hole, the central void in a real guitar, is, in Picasso's *Guitar,* the only solid form.

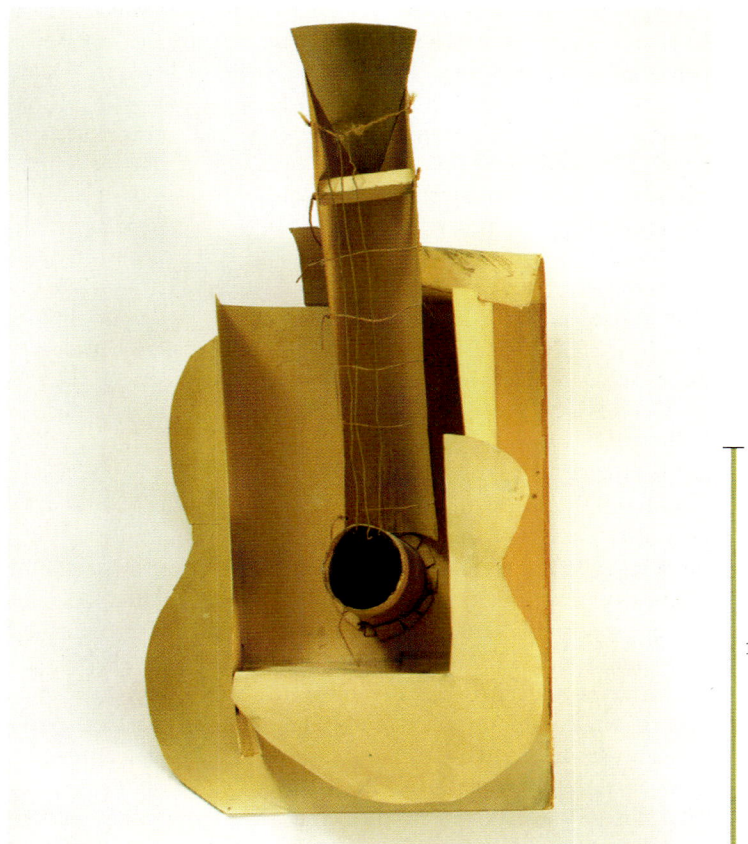

1 ft.

**29-19** PABLO PICASSO, maquette for *Guitar,* 1912. Cardboard, string, and wire (restored), 2′ 1¼″ × 1′ 1″ × 7½″. Museum of Modern Art, New York.

In this model for a sculpture of sheet metal, Picasso presented what is essentially a cutaway view of a guitar, allowing the viewer to examine both surface and interior space, both mass and void.

Europe, 1900 to 1920 **851**

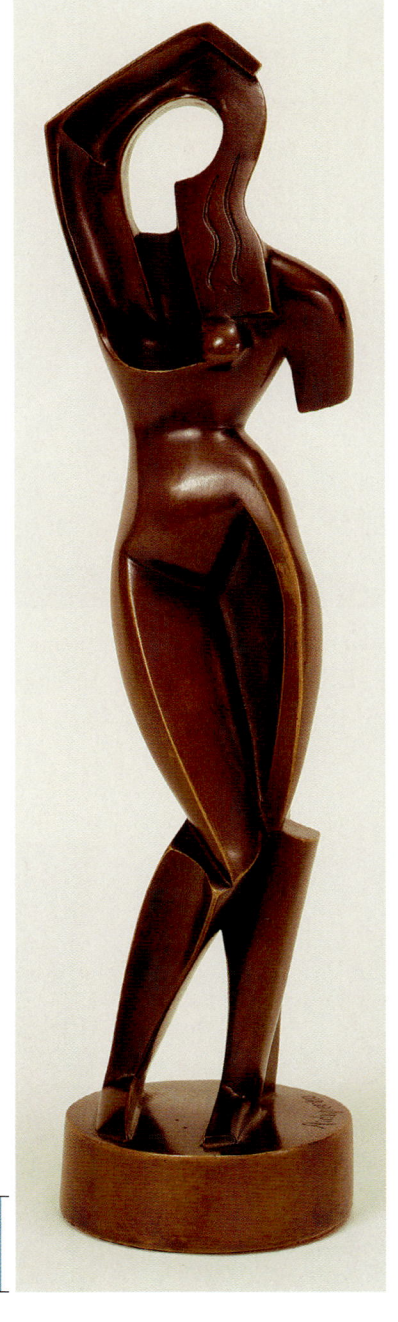

**29-20** ALEKSANDR ARCHIPENKO, *Woman Combing Her Hair*, 1915. Bronze, 1′ 1¾″ × 3¼″ × 3⅛″. Museum of Modern Art, New York (acquired through the Lillie P. Bliss Bequest).

In this statuette, Archipenko introduced, in place of the head, a void with a shape of its own that figures importantly in the whole design. The void is not simply the negative counterpart of the volume.

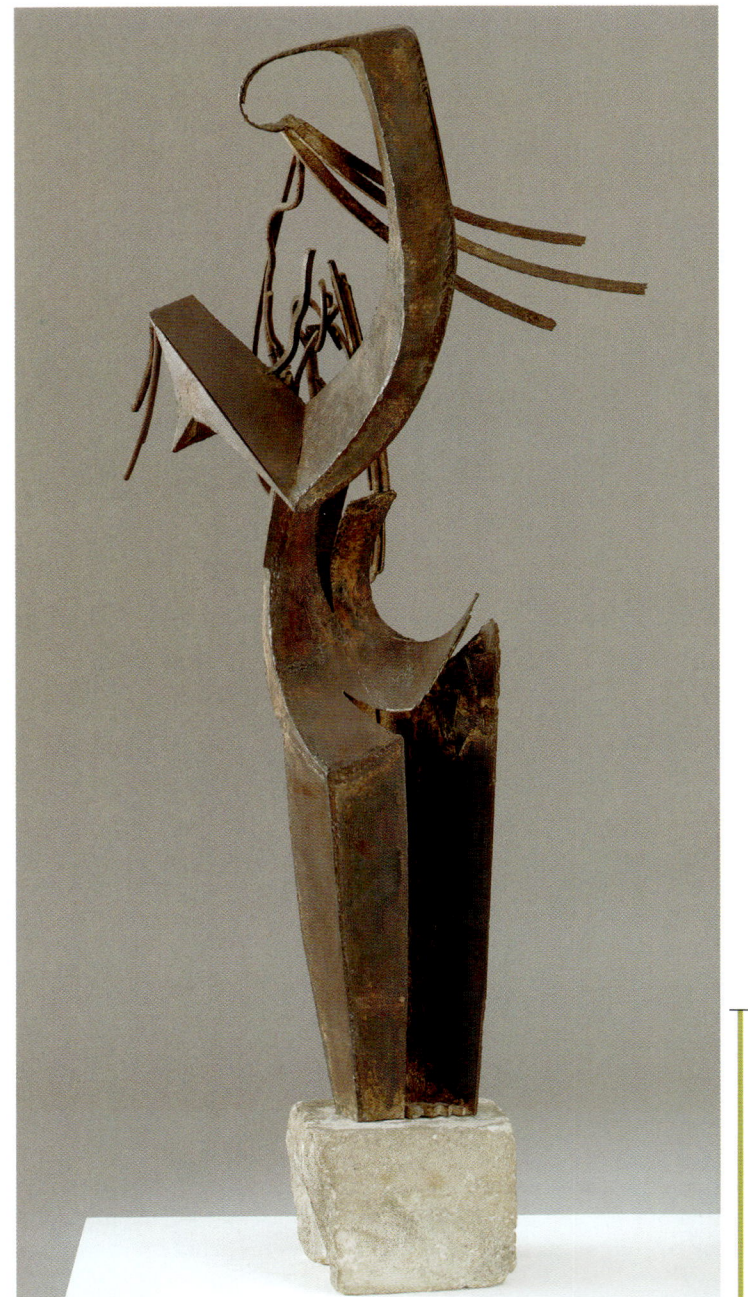

**29-21** JULIO GONZÁLEZ, *Woman Combing Her Hair,* 1936. Iron, 4′ 4″ × 1′ 11½″ × 2′ ⅝″. Museum of Modern Art, New York (Mrs. Simon Guggenheim Fund).

Using prefabricated metal pieces, González reduced his figure to an interplay of curves, lines, and planes—virtually a complete abstraction without any vestiges of traditional representational art.

**ALEKSANDR ARCHIPENKO** The Russian sculptor ALEKSANDR ARCHIPENKO (1887–1964) similarly explored the Cubist notion of spatial ambiguity and the relationship between solid forms and space. In *Woman Combing Her Hair* (FIG. **29-20**), Archipenko introduced, in place of the head, a void with a shape of its own that figures importantly in the whole design. Enclosed spaces have always existed in figurative sculpture—for example, the space between the arm and the body when the hand rests on the hip (FIG. 21-13). But in Archipenko's statuette the space penetrates the figure's continuous mass and is a defined form equal in importance to the mass of the bronze. It is not simply the negative counterpart to the volume as it is in traditional statues. Archipenko's *Woman* shows the same fluid intersecting planes seen in Cubist painting, and the relation of the planes to each other is equally complex. Thus, both in painting and sculpture, the Cubists broke through traditional limits and transformed these media.

**JULIO GONZÁLEZ** Among the other notable sculptors of the early 20th century were JULIO GONZÁLEZ (1876–1942; FIG. **29-21**) and JACQUES LIPCHITZ (1891–1973). Lipchitz's works, such as *Bather* (FIG. **29-21A**), are three-dimensional equivalents of the Analytical Cubist canvases of Picasso and Braque (FIG. 29-14). González was a friend of Picasso who shared his interest in the artistic possibilities of new materials and new methods borrowed from both industrial technology and

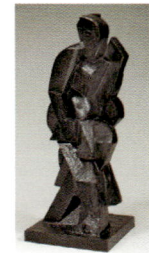

**29-21A** LIPCHITZ, *Bather*, 1917.

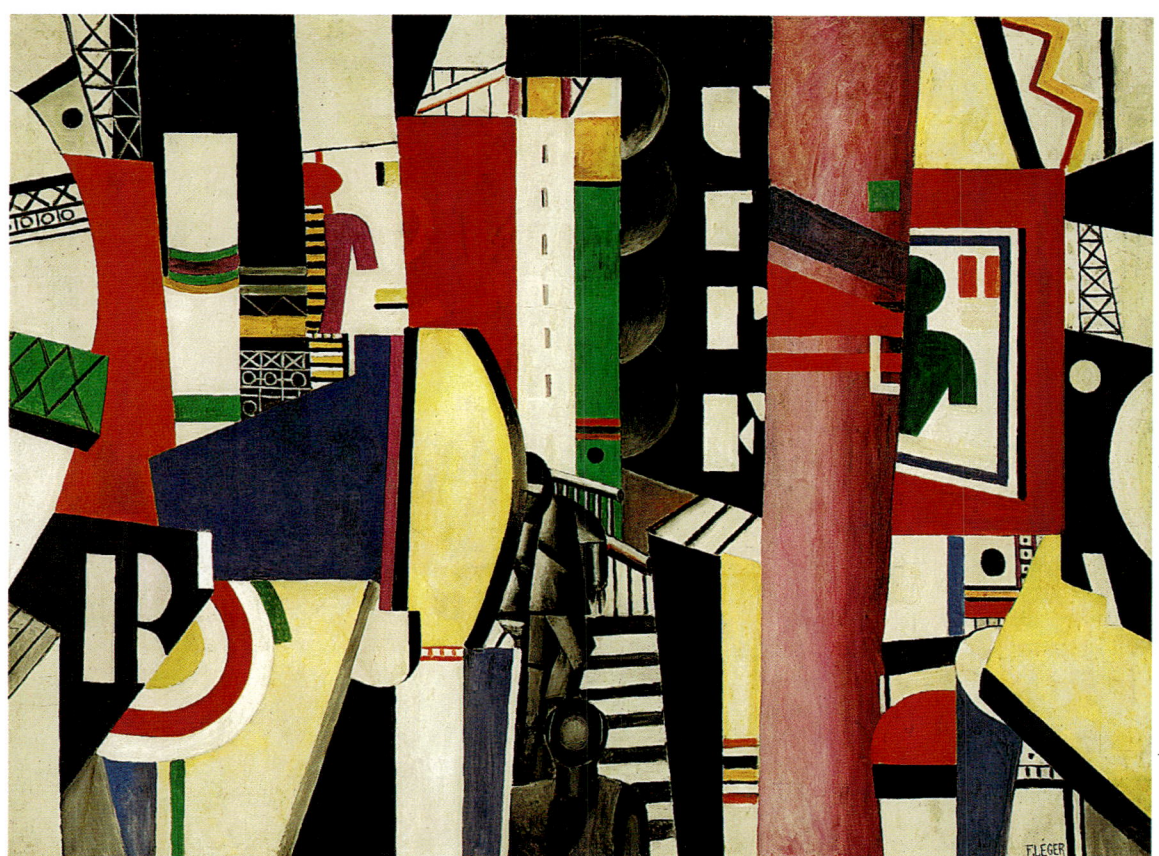

29-22 FERNAND LÉGER, *The City,* 1919. Oil on canvas, 7′ 7″ × 9′ 9½″. Philadelphia Museum of Art, Philadelphia (A. E. Gallatin Collection).

Léger championed the "machine aesthetic." In *The City,* he captured the mechanical commotion of urban life, incorporating the effects of billboard ads, flashing lights, and noisy traffic.

1 ft.

traditional metalworking. Born into a family of metalworkers in Barcelona, González helped Picasso construct a number of welded sculptures. This contact with Picasso in turn enabled González to refine his own sculptural vocabulary. Using prefabricated bars, sheets, or rods of welded or wrought iron and bronze, González created dynamic sculptures with both linear elements and volumetric forms. A comparison between his *Woman Combing Her Hair* (FIG. 29-21) and Archipenko's version of the same subject (FIG. 29-20) is instructive. Archipenko's figure still incorporates the basic shapes of a woman's body. González reduced his figure to an interplay of curves, lines, and planes—virtually a complete abstraction without any vestiges of traditional representational art. Although González's sculpture received only limited exposure during his lifetime, his work greatly influenced later abstract artists working in welded metal (FIG. 30-16).

**FERNAND LÉGER AND PURISM** Best known today as one of the most important modernist architects, Le Corbusier (FIG. 29-68) was also a painter. In 1918 he founded a movement called *Purism,* which opposed Synthetic Cubism on the grounds it was becoming merely an esoteric, decorative art out of touch with the machine age. Purists maintained machinery's clean functional lines and the pure forms of its parts should direct artists' experiments in design, whether in painting, architecture, or industrially produced objects. This "machine aesthetic" inspired FERNAND LÉGER (1881–1955), a French artist who had painted with the Cubists. He devised an effective compromise of tastes, bringing together meticulous Cubist analysis of form with Purism's broad simplification and machinelike finish of the design components. He retained from his Cubist practice a preference for cylindrical and tube-shaped motifs, suggestive of machined parts such as pistons and cylinders.

Léger's works have the sharp precision of the machine, whose beauty and quality he was one of the first artists to appreciate. For example, in his film *Ballet Mécanique* (1924), Léger contrasted inanimate objects such as functioning machines with humans in dancelike variations. Preeminently the painter of modern urban life, Léger incorporated into works such as *The City* (FIG. **29-22**) the massive effects of modern posters and billboard advertisements, the harsh flashing of electric lights, and the noise of traffic. The monumental scale of *The City,* an early work incorporating the aesthetic of Synthetic Cubism, suggests Léger, had he been given the opportunity, would have been one of the great mural painters of his age. In a definitive way, he depicted the mechanical commotion of urban life, including the robotic movements of mechanized people (FIG. **29-22A**).

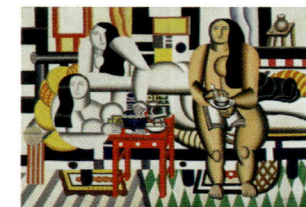

29-22A LÉGER, *Three Women,* 1921.

## Futurism

Artists associated with another early-20th-century movement, *Futurism,* pursued many of the ideas the Cubists explored. Equally important to the Futurists, however, was their well-defined sociopolitical agenda. Inaugurated and given its name by the charismatic Italian poet and playwright Filippo Tommaso Marinetti (1876–1944) in 1909, Futurism began as a literary movement but soon encompassed the visual arts, cinema, theater, music, and architecture. Indignant over the political and cultural decline of Italy, the Futurists published numerous manifestos in which they aggressively

## Futurist Manifestos

On April 11, 1910, a group of young Italian artists published *Futurist Painting: Technical Manifesto* in Milan in an attempt to apply the writer Filippo Tommaso Marinetti's views on literature to the visual arts. Signed jointly by Umberto Boccioni, Carlo Carrà, Luigi Russolo, Giacomo Balla, and Gino Severini, the manifesto also appeared in an English translation supervised by Marinetti himself. It states in part:

> On account of the persistency of an image on the retina, moving objects constantly multiply themselves [and] their form changes . . . Thus a running horse has not four legs, but twenty. . . .
>
> What was true for the painters of yesterday is but a falsehood today. . . . To paint a human figure you must not paint it; you must render the whole of its surrounding atmosphere. . . . [T]he vivifying current of science [must] soon deliver painting from academic tradition. . . . The shadows which we shall paint shall be more luminous than the highlights of our predecessors, and our pictures, next to those of the museums, will shine like blinding daylight compared with deepest night. . . .
>
> We declare . . . that all forms of imitation must be despised, all forms of originality glorified . . . that all subjects previously used must be swept aside in order to express our whirling life of steel, of pride, of fever and of speed . . . that movement and light destroy the materiality of bodies.*

Two years later, Boccioni published a *Technical Manifesto of Futurist Sculpture,* in which he argued traditional sculpture was "a monstrous anachronism" and modern sculpture should be

> a translation, in plaster, bronze, glass, wood or any other material, of those atmospheric planes which bind and intersect things. . . . Let's . . . proclaim the absolute and complete abolition of finite lines and the contained statue. Let's split open our figures and place the environment inside them. We declare that the environment must form part of the plastic whole.†

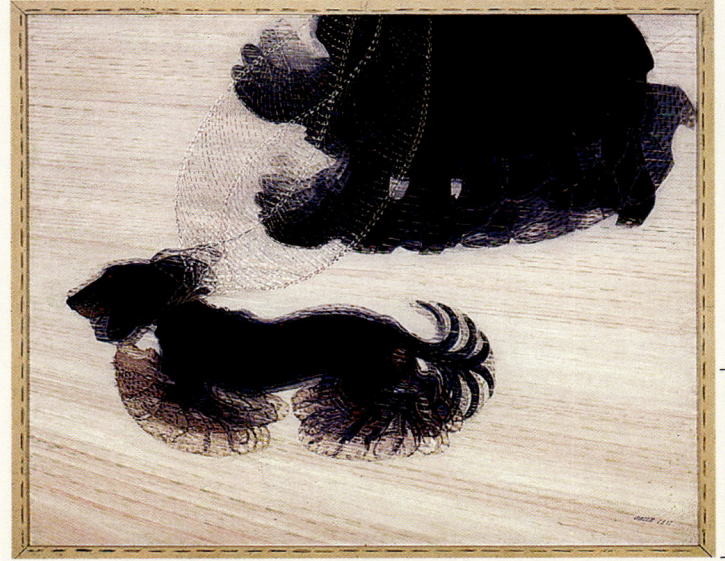

**29-23** GIACOMO BALLA, *Dynamism of a Dog on a Leash,* 1912. Oil on canvas, 2′ 11¾″ × 3′ 7¼″. Albright-Knox Art Gallery, Buffalo (bequest of A. Conger Goodyear, gift of George F. Goodyear, 1964). ◼◀

The Futurists' interest in motion and in the Cubist dissection of form is evident in Balla's painting of a passing dog and its owner. Simultaneity of views was central to the Futurist program.

The sculptures of Boccioni (FIG. 29-24) and the paintings of Balla (FIG. 29-23) and Severini (FIG. 29-25) are the perfect expressions of these Futurist principles and goals.

*Futurist Painting: Technical Manifesto* (*Poesia,* April 11, 1910). Translated by Filippo Tommaso Marinetti, in Umbro Apollonio, ed., *Futurist Manifestos* (Boston: Museum of Fine Arts, 1970), 27–31.
†Translated by Robert Brain, in Apollonio, *Futurist Manifestos,* 51–65.

advocated revolution, both in society and in art. As did Die Brücke, the Futurists aimed at ushering in a new, more enlightened era.

In their quest to launch Italian society toward a glorious future, the Futurists championed war as a means of washing away the stagnant past. Indeed, they saw war as a cleansing agent. Marinetti declared: "We will glorify war—the only true hygiene of the world."[11] The Futurists agitated for the destruction of museums, libraries, and similar repositories of accumulated culture, which they described as mausoleums. They also called for radical innovation in the arts. Of particular interest to the Futurists were the speed and dynamism of modern technology, an interest shared by Delaunay (FIGS. 29-15 and 29-15A) and Léger (FIGS. 29-22 and 29-22A). Marinetti insisted a racing "automobile adorned with great pipes like serpents with explosive breath . . . is more beautiful than the *Victory of Samothrace*"[12]—a reference to the Greek statue (FIG. 5-82) in the Musée du Louvre that for early-20th-century artists represented classicism and the glories of past civilizations.

Appropriately, Futurist art often focused on motion in time and space, incorporating the Cubist discoveries derived from the analysis of form.

**GIACOMO BALLA** The Futurists' interest in motion and in the Cubist dissection of form is evident in *Dynamism of a Dog on a Leash* (FIG. **29-23**), in which GIACOMO BALLA (1871–1958) represented a passing dog and its owner, whose skirts are just within visual range. Balla achieved the effect of motion by repeating shapes, for example, the dog's legs and tail and the swinging line of the leash. Simultaneity of views, as in Cubism, was central to the Futurist program (see "Futurist Manifestos," above).

**UMBERTO BOCCIONI** One of the cosigners of the Futurist manifesto was UMBERTO BOCCIONI (1882–1916), who produced what is perhaps the definitive work of Futurist sculpture, *Unique Forms of Continuity in Space* (FIG. **29-24**). This piece highlights the formal and spatial effects of motion rather than their source,

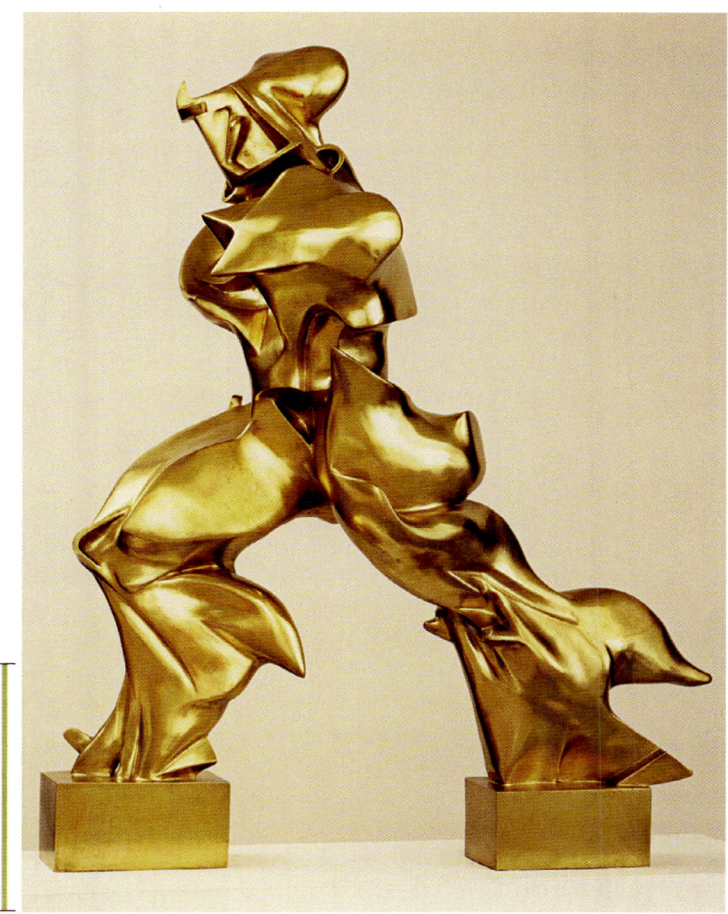

**29-24** UMBERTO BOCCIONI, *Unique Forms of Continuity in Space,* 1913 (cast 1931). Bronze, 3′ 7⅞″ × 2′ 10⅞″ × 1′ 3¾″. Museum of Modern Art, New York (acquired through the Lillie P. Bliss Bequest). ◼◀

Boccioni's Futurist manifesto for sculpture advocated abolishing the enclosed statue. This running figure's body is so expanded it almost disappears behind the blur of its movement.

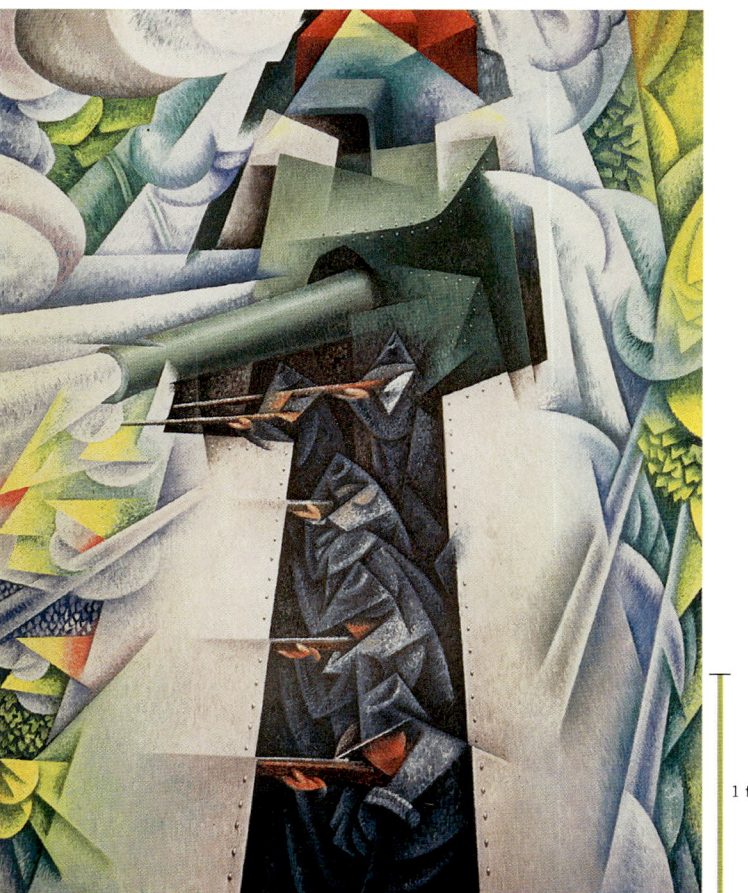

**29-25** GINO SEVERINI, *Armored Train,* 1915. Oil on canvas, 3′ 10″ × 2′ 10⅛″. Collection of Richard S. Zeisler, New York. ◼◀

Severini's glistening armored train with protruding cannon reflects the Futurist faith in the cleansing action of war. The painting captures the dynamism and motion central to the Futurist manifesto.

the striding human figure. The figure is so expanded, interrupted, and broken in plane and contour it almost disappears behind the blur of its movement—just as people, buildings, and stationary objects become blurred when seen from an automobile traveling at great speed on a highway. Boccioni's search for sculptural means for expressing dynamic movement reached a monumental expression in *Unique Forms.* In its power and sense of vital activity, this sculpture surpasses similar efforts in Futurist painting to create images symbolic of the dynamic quality of modern life. Although Boccioni's figure bears a curious resemblance to the *Nike of Samothrace* (FIG. 5-82), the ancient sculptor suggested motion only through posture and agitated drapery, not through distortion and fragmentation of the human body.

This Futurist representation of motion in sculpture has its limitations, however. The eventual development of the motion picture, based on the rapid sequential projection of fixed images, produced more convincing illusions of movement. And several decades later in sculpture, Alexander Calder (FIG. 29-78) pioneered the development of kinetic sculpture—sculptures with parts that really move. But in the early 20th century, Boccioni was unsurpassed for his ability to capture the sensation of motion in statuary.

**GINO SEVERINI** The painting *Armored Train* (FIG. **29-25**) by GINO SEVERINI (1883–1966) also encapsulates the Futurist program—politically as well as artistically. Severini depicted a high-tech armored train with its rivets glistening and a huge booming cannon protruding from the top. Submerged in the bowels of the train, soldiers in a row point guns at an unseen target. In Cubist fashion, Severini depicted all of the elements of the painting, from the soldiers to the smoke emanating from the cannon, broken into facets and planes, suggesting action and movement. *Armored Train* reflects the Futurists' passion for speed and the "whirling life of steel," and their faith in the cleansing action of war. Not only are the colors predominantly light and bright, but death and destruction—the tragic consequences of war—are absent from Severini's painting. This sanitized depiction of armed conflict contrasts sharply with Francisco Goya's *The Third of May, 1808* (FIG. 27-11), which also depicts a uniform row of anonymous soldiers in the act of shooting. Goya, however, graphically presented the dead and those about to be shot, and the dark tones he used cast a dramatic and sobering pall.

Once World War I broke out, the Futurist group began to disintegrate, largely because so many of them felt compelled (given the Futurist support for the war) to join the Italian Army. Some of them, including Umberto Boccioni, died in the war.

# Dada

Although the Futurists celebrated World War I and the changes they hoped it would effect, the mass destruction and chaos that conflict unleashed horrified other artists. Humanity had never before witnessed such wholesale slaughter on so grand a scale over such an extended period. Millions died or sustained grievous wounds in great battles. For example, in 1916, the battle of Verdun (lasting five months) produced a half million casualties. The new technology of armaments, bred from the age of steel, made the Great War a "war of the guns." In the face of massed artillery hurling millions of tons of high explosives and gas shells and in the sheets of fire from thousands of machine guns in armored vehicles of the kind celebrated in Futurist canvases (FIG. 29-25), attack was suicidal. Battle movement congealed into the stalemate of trench warfare, stretching from the English Channel almost to Switzerland. The mud, filth, and blood of the trenches, the pounding and shattering of incessant shell fire, and the terrible deaths and mutilations were a devastating psychological, as well as physical, experience for a generation brought up with the doctrine of progress and a belief in the fundamental values of civilization. The introduction of poison gas in 1915 added to the horror of humankind's inhumanity.

With the war as a backdrop, many artists contributed to the artistic and literary movement that became known as *Dada* (see page 835). This movement emerged, in large part, in reaction to what many of these artists saw as nothing more than an insane spectacle of collective homicide. Although Dada began independently in New York and Zurich, it also emerged in Paris, Berlin, and Cologne, among other cities. Dada was more a mindset or attitude than a single identifiable style. As André Breton (1896–1966), founder of the slightly later Surrealist movement, explained: "Cubism was a school of painting, futurism a political movement: DADA is a state of mind."[13] The Dadaists believed Enlightenment reasoning had produced global devastation, and consequently they turned away from logic in favor of the irrational. Thus, an element of absurdity is a cornerstone of Dada—reflected in the movement's very name. Many explanations exist for the choice of "Dada," but according to an oft-repeated anecdote, the Dadaists chose the word at random by sticking a knife into a French-German dictionary (hence the title Hannah Höch chose for her Dada photomontage (FIG. 29-1). *Dada* is French for "a child's hobby horse." The word satisfied the Dadaists' desire for something nonsensical.

The Dadaists' pessimism and disgust surfaced in their disdain for convention and tradition. These artists made a concerted and sustained attempt to undermine cherished notions and assumptions about art. Because of this destructive dimension, art historians often describe Dada as a nihilistic enterprise. Dada's nihilism and its derisive iconoclasm can be read at random from the Dadaists' numerous manifestos and declarations of intent:

> Dada knows everything. Dada spits on everything. Dada says "knowthing," Dada has no fixed ideas. Dada does not catch flies. Dada is bitterness laughing at everything that has been accomplished, sanctified. . . . Dada is never right. . . . No more painters, no more writers, no more religions, no more royalists, no more anarchists, no more socialists, no more police, no more airplanes, no more urinary passages. . . . Like everything in life, Dada is useless, everything happens in a completely idiotic way. . . . We are incapable of treating seriously any subject whatsoever, let alone this subject: ourselves.[14]

Although cynicism and pessimism inspired the Dadaists, what they developed was phenomenally influential and powerful. By attacking convention and logic, the Dada artists unlocked new avenues for creative invention, thereby fostering a more serious examination of the basic premises of art than had prior movements. But the Dadaists could also be lighthearted in their subversiveness. Although horror and disgust about the war initially prompted Dada, an undercurrent of humor and whimsy—sometimes sardonic or irreverent—runs through much of the art. For example, Marcel Duchamp painted a moustache and goatee on a reproduction of Leonardo's *Mona Lisa* (FIG. 29-27A). The French painter Francis Picabia (1879–1953), Duchamp's collaborator in setting up Dada in New York, nailed a toy monkey to a board and labeled it *Portrait of Cézanne.*

In its emphasis on the spontaneous and intuitive, Dada paralleled the views of Sigmund Freud (1856–1939) and Carl Jung (1875–1961). Freud was a Viennese doctor who developed the fundamental principles for what became known as psychoanalysis. In his book *The Interpretation of Dreams* (1900), Freud argued unconscious and inner drives (of which people are largely unaware) control human behavior. Jung, a Swiss psychiatrist who developed Freud's theories further, believed the unconscious is composed of two facets, a personal unconscious and a collective unconscious. The collective unconscious comprises memories and associations all humans share, such as archetypes and mental constructions. According to Jung, the collective unconscious accounts for the development of myths, religions, and philosophies.

Particularly interested in the exploration of the unconscious that Freud advocated, the Dada artists believed art was a powerfully practical means of self-revelation and catharsis, and the images arising out of the subconscious mind had a truth of their own, independent of conventional vision. A Dada filmmaker, Hans Richter (1888–1976), summarized the attitude of the Dadaists:

> Possessed, as we were, of the ability to entrust ourselves to "chance," to our conscious as well as our unconscious minds, we became a sort of public secret society. . . . We laughed at everything. . . . But laughter was only the expression of our new discoveries, not their essence and not their purpose. Pandemonium, destruction, anarchy, anti-everything of the World War? How could Dada have been anything but destructive, aggressive, insolent, on principle and with gusto?[15]

**JEAN ARP** One prominent Dada artist whose works illustrate Richter's element of chance was Zurich-based JEAN (HANS) ARP (1887–1966). Arp pioneered the use of chance in composing his images. Tiring of the look of some Cubist-related collages he was making, he took some sheets of paper, tore them into roughly shaped squares, haphazardly dropped them onto a sheet of paper on the floor, and glued them into the resulting arrangement. The rectilinearity of the shapes guaranteed a somewhat regular design (which Arp no doubt enhanced by adjusting the random arrangement into a quasi-grid), but chance had introduced an imbalance that seemed to Arp to restore to his work a special mysterious vitality he wanted to preserve. *Collage Arranged According to the Laws of Chance* (FIG. **29-26**) is one of the works he created by this method. The operations of chance were for Dadaists a crucial part of this kind of improvisation. As Richter stated: "For us chance was the 'unconscious mind' that Freud had discovered in 1900. . . . Adoption of chance had another purpose, a secret one. This was to restore to the work of art its primeval magic power and to find a way back to the immediacy it had lost through contact with . . . classicism."[16] Arp's

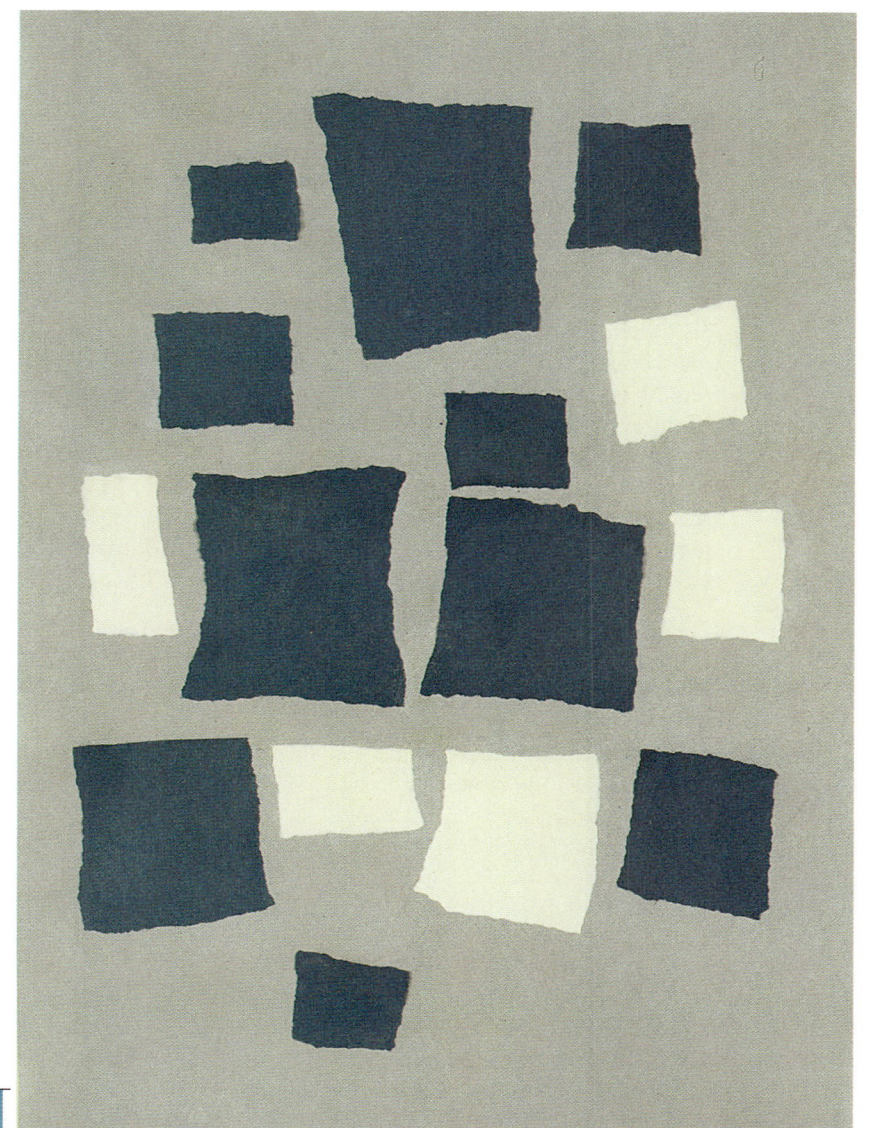

**29-26** Jean (Hans) Arp, *Collage Arranged According to the Laws of Chance*, 1916–1917. Torn and pasted paper, 1′ 7$\frac{1}{8}$″ × 1′ 1$\frac{5}{8}$″. Museum of Modern Art, New York. ■◀

In this collage, Arp dropped torn paper squares onto a sheet of paper and then glued them where they fell. His reliance on chance in composing images reinforced the anarchy inherent in Dada.

renunciation of artistic control and reliance on chance when creating his compositions reinforced the anarchy and subversiveness inherent in Dada.

**MARCEL DUCHAMP** Perhaps the most influential Dadaist was MARCEL DUCHAMP (1887–1968), a Frenchman who became the central artist of New York Dada but was also active in Paris. In 1913, he exhibited his first "readymade" sculptures, which were mass-produced common objects—"found objects" the artist selected and sometimes "rectified" by modifying their substance or combining them with another object. The creation of readymades, he insisted, was free from any consideration of either good or bad taste, qualities shaped by a society he and other Dada artists found aesthetically bankrupt. Perhaps his most outrageous readymade was *Fountain* (FIG. **29-27**), a porcelain urinal presented on its back, signed "R. Mutt," and dated (1917). The "artist's signature" was, in fact, a witty pseudonym derived from the Mott plumbing company's name and that of the shorter man of the then-popular Mutt and Jeff comic-strip duo. As with Duchamp's other readymades and "assisted readymades" such as *L.H.O.O.Q.* (FIG. **29-27A**), he did not select the urinal for exhibition because of its aesthetic qualities. The "art" of this "artwork" lay in the artist's choice of object, which had the effect of conferring the status of art on it and forcing viewers to see the object in a new light. As Duchamp wrote in a "defense" published in 1917, after an exhibition committee rejected *Fountain* for display: "Whether Mr. Mutt with his own hands made the fountain or not has no importance. He CHOSE it. He took an ordinary article of life, placed it so that its useful significance disappeared under the new title and point of view—created a new thought for that object."[17] It is hard to imagine a more aggressive challenge to artistic conventions than Dada works such as *Fountain*.

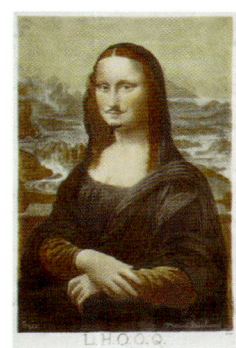

**29-27A** DUCHAMP, *L.H.O.O.Q.*, 1919.

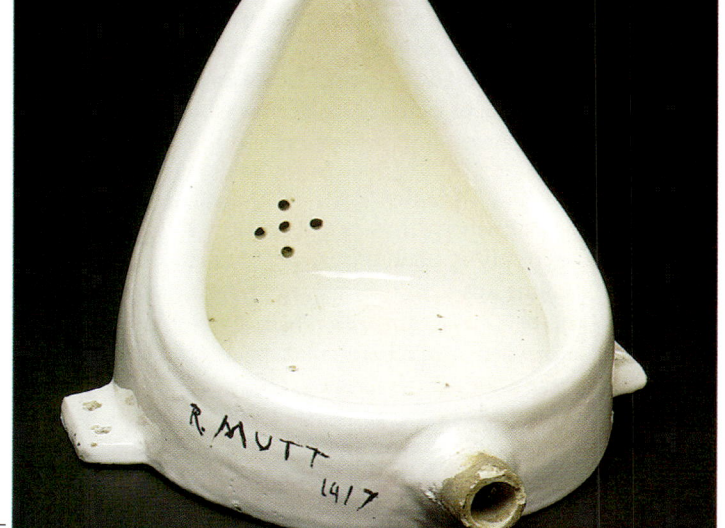

**29-27** MARCEL DUCHAMP, *Fountain* (second version), 1950 (original version produced 1917). Glazed sanitary china with black paint, 1′ high. Philadelphia Museum of Art, Philadelphia.

Duchamp's "readymade" sculptures were mass-produced objects the Dada artist modified. In *Fountain*, he conferred the status of art on a urinal and forced people to see the object in a new light.

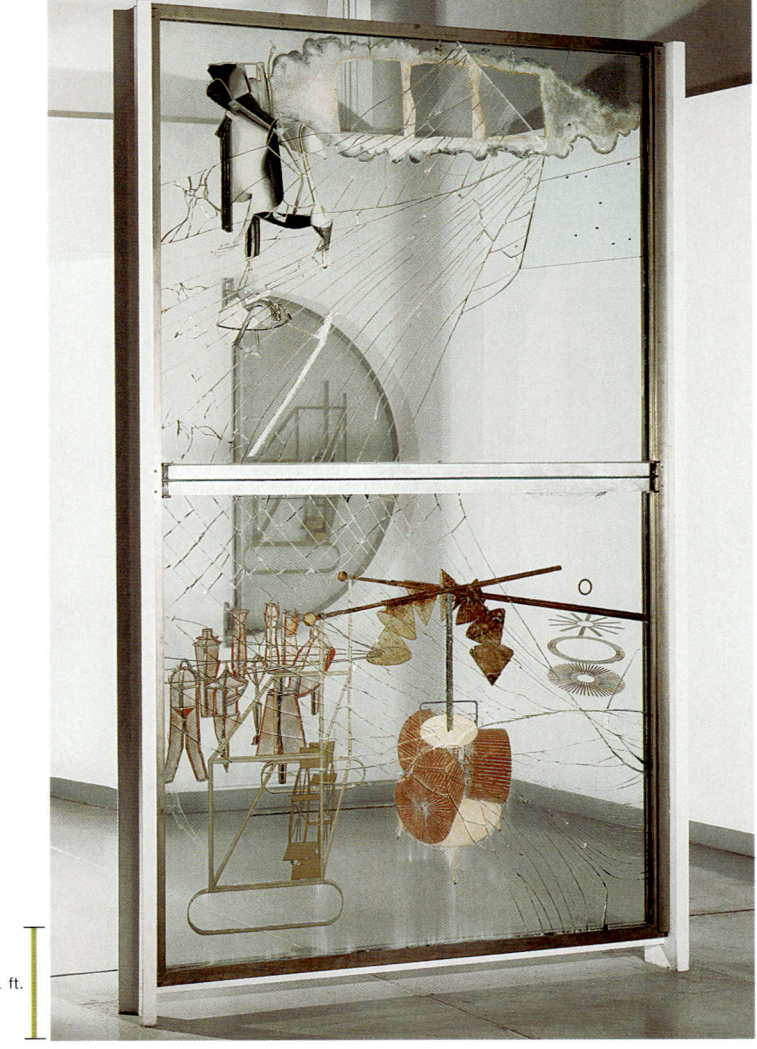

1 ft.

**29-28** Marcel Duchamp, *The Bride Stripped Bare by Her Bachelors, Even (The Large Glass)*, 1915–1923. Oil, lead, wire, foil, dust, and varnish on glass, 9′ 1½″ × 5′ 9⅛″. Philadelphia Museum of Art, Philadelphia (Katherine S. Dreier Bequest).

*The Large Glass* is a simultaneously playful and serious examination of humans as machines. The bride is a motor fueled by "love gasoline," and the male figures in the lower half also move mechanically.

**THE LARGE GLASS** Among the most visually and conceptually challenging of Duchamp's works is *The Bride Stripped Bare by Her Bachelors, Even* (FIG. **29-28**), often called *The Large Glass*. Begun in 1915 and abandoned by Duchamp as unfinished in 1923, *The Large Glass* is a simultaneously playful and serious examination of humans as machines. Consisting of oil paint, wire, and lead foil sandwiched in between two large glass panels, the artwork presents an array of images, some apparently mechanical, others diagrammatic, and yet others seemingly abstract in nature. Duchamp provided some clues to the intriguing imagery in a series of notes accompanying the work. The top half of *The Large Glass* represents "the bride," whom Duchamp has depicted as "basically a motor" fueled by "love gasoline." In contrast, the bachelors appear as uniformed male figures in the lower half of the composition. They too move mechanically. The chocolate grinder in the center of the lower glass pane represents masturbation ("the bachelor grinds his own chocolate"). In *The Large Glass,* Duchamp provided his own whimsical but insightful ruminations into the ever-confounding realm of desire and sexuality. In true

Dadaist fashion, chance completed the work. During the transportation of *The Large Glass* from an exhibition in 1927, the glass panes shattered. Rather than replace the broken glass, Duchamp painstakingly pieced together the glass fragments. After encasing the reconstructed work, broken panes and all, between two heavier panes of glass, Duchamp declared the work completed "by chance."

Duchamp (and the generations of artists after him profoundly influenced by his art and especially his attitude) considered life and art matters of chance and choice freed from the conventions of society and tradition. In Duchamp's approach to art and life, each act was individual and unique. Every person's choice of found objects would be different, for example, and each person's throw of the dice would be at a different instant and probably would yield a different number. This philosophy of utter freedom for artists was fundamental to the history of art in the 20th century—in America as well as Europe. Duchamp spent much of World War I in New York, where he painted *Nude Descending a Staircase* (FIG. 29-35) and inspired a group of American artists and collectors with his radical rethinking of the role of artists and of the nature of art.

**KURT SCHWITTERS** Early on, Dada spread to Germany. In Berlin, Hannah Höch produced photomontages (FIG. 29-1) featuring sharp political commentary. In Hanover, KURT SCHWITTERS (1887–1948) followed a gentler muse. Inspired by Cubist collage but working nonobjectively, Schwitters found visual poetry in the cast-off junk of modern society and scavenged in trash bins for materials, which he pasted and nailed together into designs such as *Merz 19* (FIG. **29-29**). The term *Merz,* which Schwitters used as a generic title for a whole series of collages, derived nonsensically from the German word *Kommerzbank* (commerce bank) and appeared as a word fragment in one of his compositions. Although nonobjective, his collages still resonate with the meaning of the fragmented found objects they contain. The recycled elements of Schwitters's collages, like Duchamp's readymades, acquire new meanings through their new uses and locations. Elevating objects that are essentially trash to the status of high art certainly fits within the parameters of the Dada program and parallels the absurdist dimension of much of Dada art. Contradiction, paradox, irony, and even blasphemy were Dada's bequest to later artists.

## Suprematism and Constructivism

Dada was a movement born of pessimism and cynicism. Not all early-20th-century artists, however, reacted to the profound turmoil of the times by retreating from society. Some artists promoted utopian ideals, believing staunchly in art's ability to contribute to improving society and all humankind. These efforts often surfaced in the face of significant political upheaval, as was the case with Suprematism and Constructivism in Russia.

**KAZIMIR MALEVICH** Despite Russia's distance from Paris, the center of the international art world in the early 20th century, Russians had a long history of cultural contact and interaction with western Europe. Wealthy Russians, such as Ivan Morozov (1871–1921) and Sergei Shchukin (1854–1936), amassed extensive collections of Impressionist, Post-Impressionist, and avant-garde paintings. Shchukin, who participated in the salons at the Steins' home in Paris (see "Gertrude and Leo Stein," page 844), became particularly enamored with the work of both Picasso and Matisse. By the mid-1910s, he had acquired 37 paintings by Matisse and 51 by Picasso. Because of their access to collections such as these, Russian artists were familiar with the latest artistic developments, especially Fauvism, Cubism, and Futurism.

One Russian artist who pursued the revolutionary direction Cubism introduced was KAZIMIR MALEVICH (1878–1935). Malevich

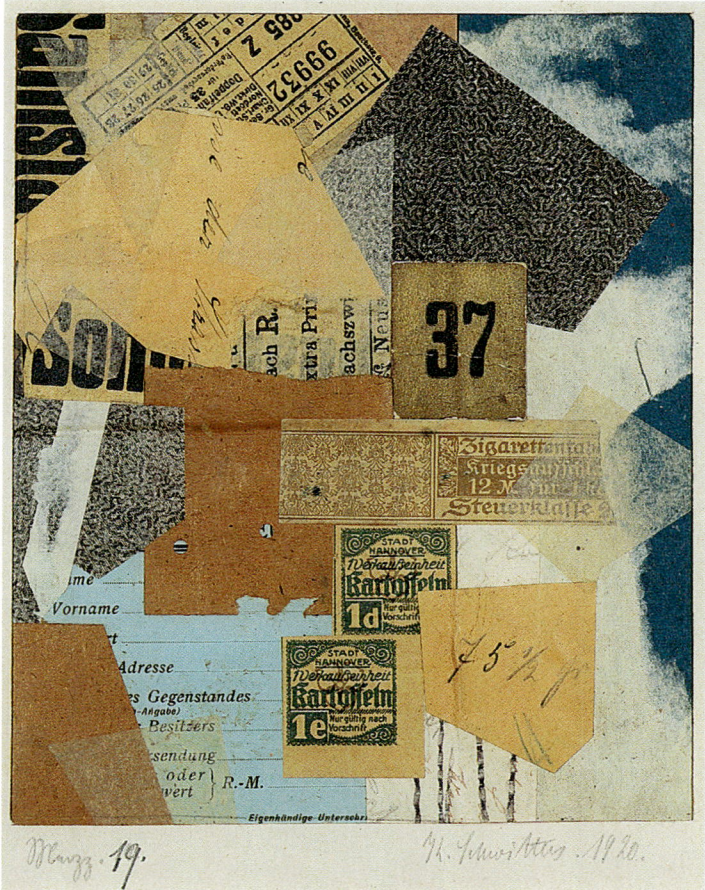

**29-29** KURT SCHWITTERS, *Merz 19*, 1920. Paper collage, $7\frac{1}{4}'' \times 5\frac{7}{8}''$. Yale University Art Gallery, New Haven (gift of Collection Société Anonyme).

Inspired by Cubist collage but working nonobjectively, Schwitters found visual poetry in the cast-off junk of modern society, which he pasted and nailed together into striking Dada compositions.

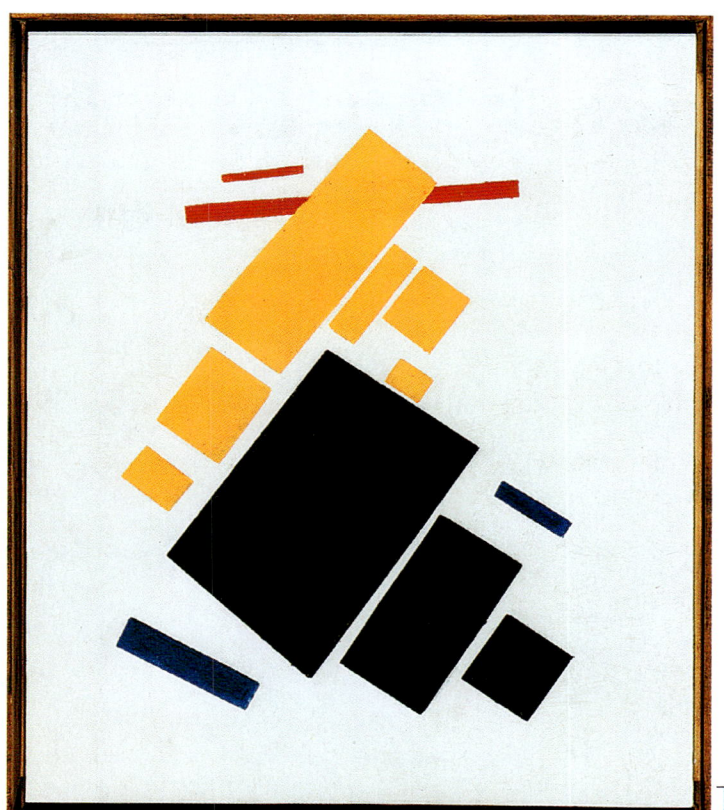

**29-30** KAZIMIR MALEVICH, *Suprematist Composition: Airplane Flying*, 1915 (dated 1914). Oil on canvas, $1'\ 10\frac{7}{8}'' \times 1'\ 7''$. Museum of Modern Art, New York. ◼◀

Malevich developed an abstract style he called Suprematism to convey that the supreme reality in the world is pure feeling. Here, the brightly colored rectilinear shapes float against white space.

developed an abstract style to convey his belief that the supreme reality in the world is "pure feeling," which attaches to no object. Thus, this belief called for new, nonobjective forms in art—shapes not related to objects in the visible world. Malevich had studied painting, sculpture, and architecture and had worked his way through most of the avant-garde styles of his youth before deciding none could express pure feeling. He christened his new artistic approach *Suprematism,* explaining: "Under Suprematism I understand the supremacy of pure feeling in creative art. To the Suprematist, the visual phenomena of the objective world are, in themselves, meaningless; the significant thing is feeling, as such, quite apart from the environment in which it is called forth."[18]

The basic form of Malevich's new Suprematist nonobjective art was the square. Combined with its relatives, the straight line and the rectangle, the square soon filled his paintings, such as *Suprematist Composition: Airplane Flying* (FIG. **29-30**). In this work, the brightly colored shapes float against and within a white space, and the artist placed them in dynamic relationship to one another. Malevich believed all peoples would easily understand his new art because of the universality of its symbols. It used the pure language of shape and color, to which everyone could respond intuitively.

Having formulated his artistic approach, Malevich welcomed the Russian Revolution, which broke out in 1917 as a result of widespread dissatisfaction with the regime of Tsar Nicholas II (r. 1894–1917). Russian workers staged a general strike in protest, and the tsar abdicated in March. In late 1917, the Bolsheviks, a faction of Russian Social Democrats that promoted violent revolution, wrested control of the country from the ruling provisional government. Once in power, their leader, Vladimir Lenin (1870–1924), nationalized the land and turned it over to the local rural soviets (councils of workers' and soldiers' deputies). After extensive civil war, the Communists, as they now called themselves, succeeded in retaining control of Russia and taking over an assortment of satellite countries in eastern Europe. This new state adopted the official name Union of Soviet Socialist Republics (USSR, or Soviet Union) in 1923.

Malevich viewed the revolution as an opportunity to wipe out past traditions and begin a new culture. He believed his art could play a major role in that effort because of its universal accessibility. But, after a short period when the new regime heralded avant-garde art, the political leaders of the Soviet Union decided their new communist society needed a more "practical" art. Soviet authorities promoted a "realistic," illusionistic art that they thought a wide public could understand and that they hoped would teach citizens about their new government. This horrified Malevich. To him, true art could never have a practical connection with life:

Every social idea, however great and important it may be, stems from the sensation of hunger; every art work, regardless of how small and insignificant it may seem, originates in pictorial or plastic feeling. It is high time for us to realize that the problems of art lie far apart from those of the stomach or the intellect.[19]

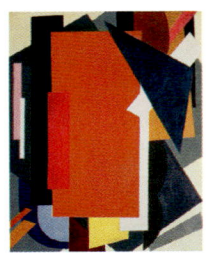

**29-30A** POPOVA, *Architectonic Painting,* 1916–1917.

Disappointed and unappreciated by the public, Malevich eventually gravitated toward other disciplines, such as mathematical theory and geometry, logical fields given his interest in pure abstraction, but his work and his theories made a profound impression on other artists, especially in Russia. These included LYUBOV POPOVA (1889–1924), who joined Malevich's Suprematist movement in 1916. Popova's most notable works are the series of canvases she named *Architectonic Paintings* (FIG. **29-30A**).

**NAUM GABO** The Russian-born sculptor NAUM GABO (1890–1977) also wanted to create an innovative art to express a new reality, and like Malevich, he believed art should spring from sources separate from the everyday world. For Gabo, the new reality was the space-time world described by early-20th-century scientists (see "Science and Art," page 841). As he wrote in *The Realistic Manifesto,* published with his brother Anton Pevsner (1886–1962) in 1920:

> Space and time are the only forms on which life is built and hence art must be constructed. . . . The realization of our perceptions of the world in the forms of space and time is the only aim of our pictorial and plastic art. . . . We renounce the thousand-year-old delusion in art that held the static rhythms as the only elements of the plastic and pictorial arts. We affirm in these arts a new element, the kinetic rhythms, as the basic forms of our perception of real time.[20]

Gabo was one of the Russian sculptors known as Constructivists. The name *Constructivism* may have come originally from the title *Construction,* which the Russian artist Vladimir Tatlin (FIG. 29-32) used for some relief sculptures he made in 1913 and 1914. Gabo explained he called himself a Constructivist partly because he built up his sculptures piece by piece in space, instead of carving or modeling them in the traditional way. Although Gabo experimented briefly with real motion in his work, most of his sculptures relied on the relationship of mass and space to suggest the nature of space-time. To indicate the volumes of mass and space more clearly in his sculpture, Gabo used some of the new synthetic plastic materials, including celluloid, nylon, and Lucite, to create constructions whose space seems to flow through as well as around the transparent materials. In works such as *Column* (FIG. **29-31**), Gabo opened up the column's circular mass so viewers could experience the volume of space it occupies. Two transparent planes extend through its diameter, crossing at right angles at the center of the implied cylindrical column shape. The opaque colored planes at the base and the inclined open ring set up counter-rhythms to the crossed upright planes. They establish the sense of dynamic kinetic movement Gabo always sought to express as an essential part of reality.

## Architecture

A third art movement that emerged in the Soviet Union in the years immediately following the Russian Revolution was *Productivism,* which was an offshoot of the Constructivist movement. The Productivists sought to design a better environment for human beings.

**VLADIMIR TATLIN** One of the most gifted leaders of the Productivism movement was VLADIMIR TATLIN (1885–1953). The Russian Revolution was the signal to Tatlin, as it had been to Malevich, that the hated old order was about to end. In utopian fashion, he and the other Productivists aspired to play a significant role in creating

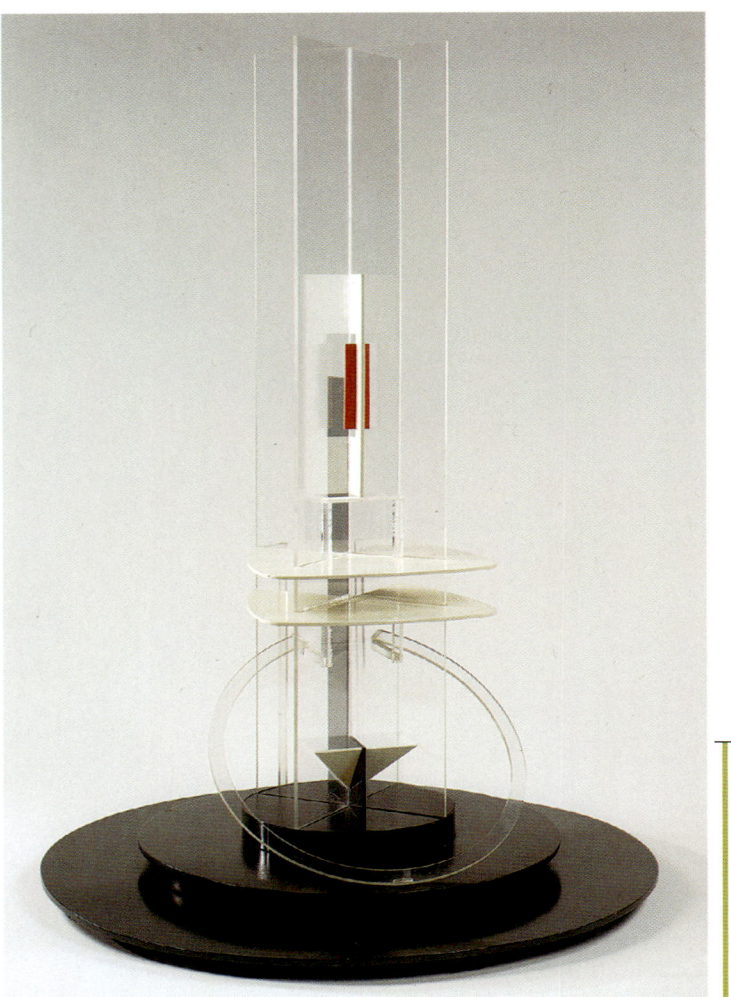

1 ft.

**29-31** NAUM GABO, *Column,* ca. 1923 (reconstructed 1937). Perspex, wood, metal, glass, 3′ 5″ × 2′ 5″ × 2′ 5″. Solomon R. Guggenheim Museum, New York.

Gabo's Constructivist sculptures rely on the relationship of mass and space to suggest the nature of space-time. Space seems to flow through as well as around the transparent materials he used.

a new world, one that would fully use the power of industrialization to benefit all people. Initially, like Malevich and Gabo, Tatlin believed nonobjective art was ideal for the new society, free as such art was from any past symbolism. But after the 1917 revolution, Tatlin enthusiastically abandoned abstract art for "functional art" and designed products such as an efficient stove and workers' clothing.

Tatlin's most famous work is *Monument to the Third International* (FIG. **29-32**), which, in its reductive geometry, connects Productivism to the artistic programs of the Suprematists and Constructivists. Tatlin received the commission from the Department of Artistic Work of the People's Commissariat for Enlightenment in early 1919 to honor the Russian Revolution. He envisioned a huge glass-and-iron building that—at 1,300 feet—would have been one-third taller than the Eiffel Tower (FIG. 28-38). Widely influential, "Tatlin's Tower," as it became known, served as a model for those seeking to encourage socially committed and functional art. On its proposed site in the center of Moscow, it would have functioned as a propaganda and news center for the Soviet people. Within a dynamically tilted spiral cage, three geometrically shaped chambers were to rotate around a central axis, each chamber housing

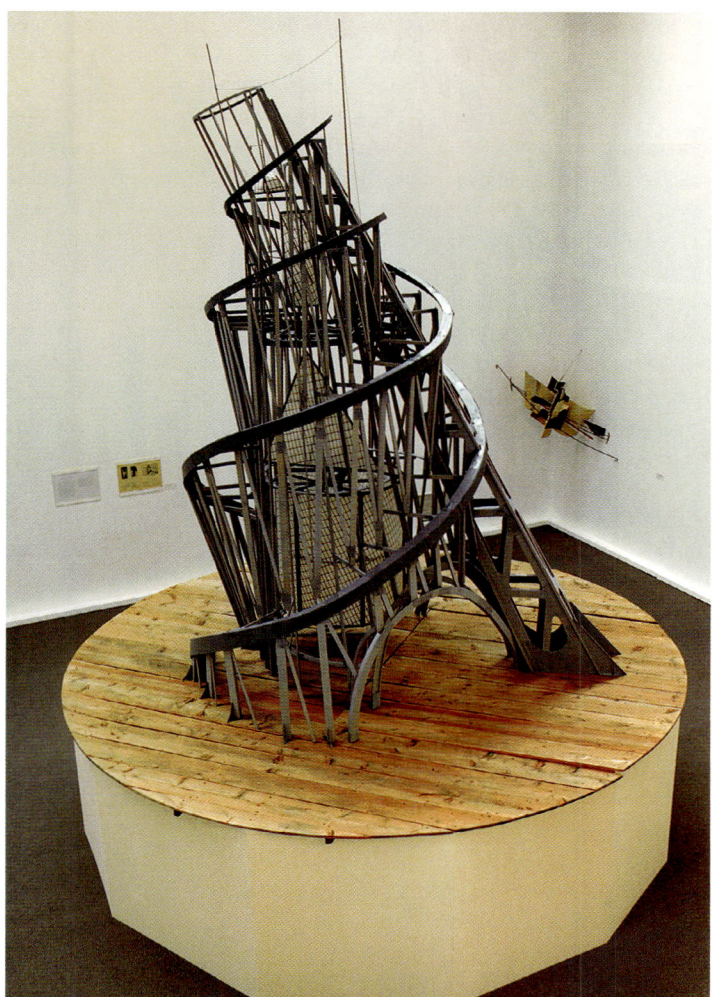

**29-32** VLADIMIR TATLIN, *Monument to the Third International,* 1919–1920. Reconstruction of the lost model, 1992-1993. Kunsthalle, Düsseldorf.

"Tatlin's Tower" was an ambitious avant-garde design for a Soviet governmental building with three geometrically shaped chambers rotating at different speeds within a dynamically tilted spiral cage.

**ADOLF LOOS** In Germany, ADOLF LOOS (1870–1933) was the most influential architectural theorist during the opening decades of the 20th century. Loos trained as an architect at the Dresden College of Technology and then traveled to the United States to attend the 1893 Columbia Exposition in Chicago. Although he apparently found no work as an architect in Chicago, he remained there three years. During that time he became familiar with the buildings (FIGS. 28-40, 28-40A, and 28-41) and theories of Louis Sullivan, whose 1892 essay *Ornament in Architecture* affected Loos profoundly. In that treatise, Sullivan suggested architects consider banishing all ornamentation from their buildings for a period of years "in order that our thought might concentrate acutely upon the production of buildings well formed and comely in the nude."

Loos carried Sullivan's ideas even further in a series of essays in which he railed against the excesses of the Art Nouveau style (FIGS. 28-40 and 28-40A), which was the rage in Europe at the turn of the century. He published his major statement on the subject in 1908 under the title *Ornament and Crime*. Loos equated architectural ornamentation with the "amoral" tattoos of Papua New Guinea (see "Tattoo in Polynesia," Chapter 36, page 1055, and FIGS. I-19 and 36-16) and asserted that modern men who tattooed themselves were either criminals or degenerates. Ornamentation in architecture was also a crime, both on aesthetic grounds and because it wasted labor and materials.

Loos put his ideas to work in his 1910 design for the Viennese home of the painter Lilly Steiner (1884–1962). Cubical in form with a garden facade in the shape of a shallow U, the Steiner House (FIG. **29-33**) has a reinforced-concrete skeleton and a severe white stucco shell devoid of ornamentation of any kind, even moldings separating the floors. The windows are simple unframed sheets of plate glass, symmetrically arranged. Walter Gropius would later build upon Loos's ideas about pure, functional architectural design at the Bauhaus (see "Walter Gropius and the Bauhaus," page 885, and FIG. 29-66), where he promoted "avoiding all romantic embellishment and whimsy."

facilities for a different type of governmental activity and rotating at a different speed. The one at the bottom, a huge cylindrical glass structure for lectures and meetings, was to revolve once a year. Higher up was a cone-shaped chamber that would rotate monthly and serve administrative functions. At the top, a cubic information center would have revolved daily, issuing news bulletins and proclamations via the most modern means of communication. These included an open-air news screen (illuminated at night) and a special instrument designed to project words on the clouds on any overcast day. The proposed decreasing size of the chambers as visitors ascended the monument paralleled the decision-making hierarchy in the political system, with the most authoritative, smallest groups near the building's apex. The design thus served as a visual reinforcement of a social and political reality. Unfortunately, due to Russia's desperate economic situation in the 1920s, Tatlin's Tower was never built. But Tatlin worked out his ambitious design in now-lost metal and wood models exhibited on various official occasions. The only records of these models are a few drawings and photographs, but they have permitted faithful reconstructions of the design, such as the one reproduced in FIG. 29-32.

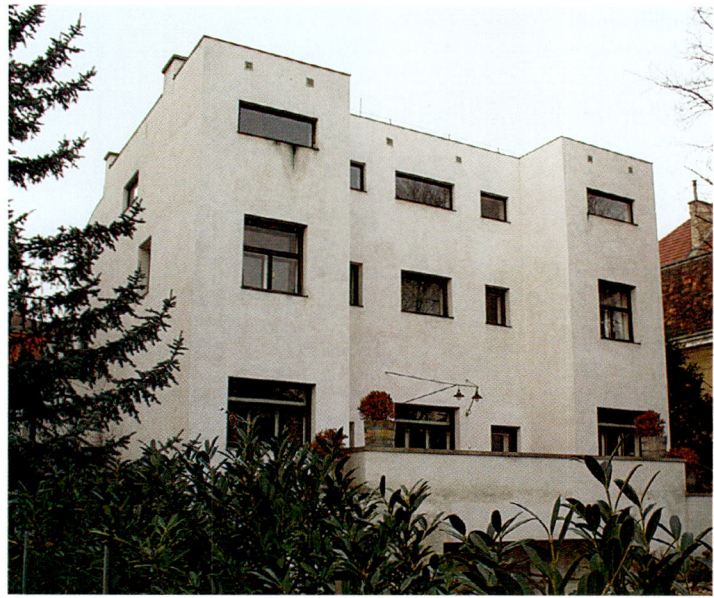

**29-33** ADOLF LOOS, garden facade of the Steiner House (looking northwest), Vienna, Austria, 1910.

For Loos, decoration was a "criminal" waste of labor and materials. His Steiner House is a cubical mass with a white stucco shell devoid of ornamentation and without even moldings separating floors.

# UNITED STATES, 1900 TO 1930

Avant-garde experiments in the arts were not limited to Europe. Increasingly common transatlantic travel during the later 19th and early 20th centuries resulted in a lively exchange of artistic ideas among European and American artists. For example, John Singer Sargent (FIG. 27-37), Mary Cassatt (FIG. 28-13), and James Abbott McNeill Whistler (FIG. 28-14) spent much of their productive careers in Europe, whereas many European artists ended their careers in the United States, especially in anticipation of and, later, in the wake of World War I. American artists wishing to pursue modernist ideas at home received encouragement from a number of wealthy and visionary patrons, mostly women (see "Art 'Matronage' in the United States," page 865).

## Painting and Sculpture

In the opening decade of the 20th century, when most American artists knew little about the revolutionary work of their European counterparts, the goal of many of the leading painters was to present a realistic, unvarnished look at American life. In this regard, their work paralleled that of the French Realists in the mid-19th century (see Chapter 27).

**JOHN SLOAN AND THE EIGHT** The most important group of American Realist artists was The Eight—eight painters who gravitated into the circle of the influential and evangelical artist and teacher Robert Henri (1865–1929). Henri urged his followers to make "pictures from life,"[21] and accordingly, these artists pursued with zeal the production of images depicting the rapidly changing urban landscape of New York City. Because these vignettes often captured the bleak and seedy aspects of city life, The Eight eventually became known as the Ash Can School. Some critics referred to them as "the apostles of ugliness."

A prominent member of The Eight was JOHN SLOAN (1871–1951). A self-described "incorrigible window watcher,"[22] Sloan constantly wandered the streets of New York, observing human drama. He focused much of his attention on the working class, which he perceived as embodying the realities of life. So sympathetic was Sloan to the plight of workers that he joined the Socialist Party in 1909 and eventually ran for public office on the Socialist ticket. In paintings such as *Sixth Avenue and 30th Street* (FIG. **29-34**), Sloan revealed his ability to capture both the visual and social realities of American urban life. When he painted this image in 1907, Sloan lived on West 23rd Street, on the outskirts of the Tenderloin District, an area cluttered with brothels, dance halls, saloons, gambling dens, and cheap hotels. *Sixth Avenue* depicts a bustling intersection. Bracketing the throngs of people filling the intersection are elevated train tracks on the left and a row of storefronts and apartment buildings on the right. These two defining elements of city life converge in the far center background of the painting. Sloan's portrayals of New York also feature a cross-section of the population of the city at the opening of the 20th century. In the foreground of *Sixth Avenue,* Sloan prominently placed three women. One, in a shabby white dress, is a drunkard, stumbling along with her pail of beer. Two streetwalkers stare at her. In turn, two well-dressed men gaze at the prostitutes. Sloan's depiction of the women allied him with reformers of the time, who saw streetwalkers not as immoral but as victims of an unfair social and economic system. At a time when traditional art centered on genteel and proper society, Sloan's forthright depiction of prostitutes was categorically "Realist."

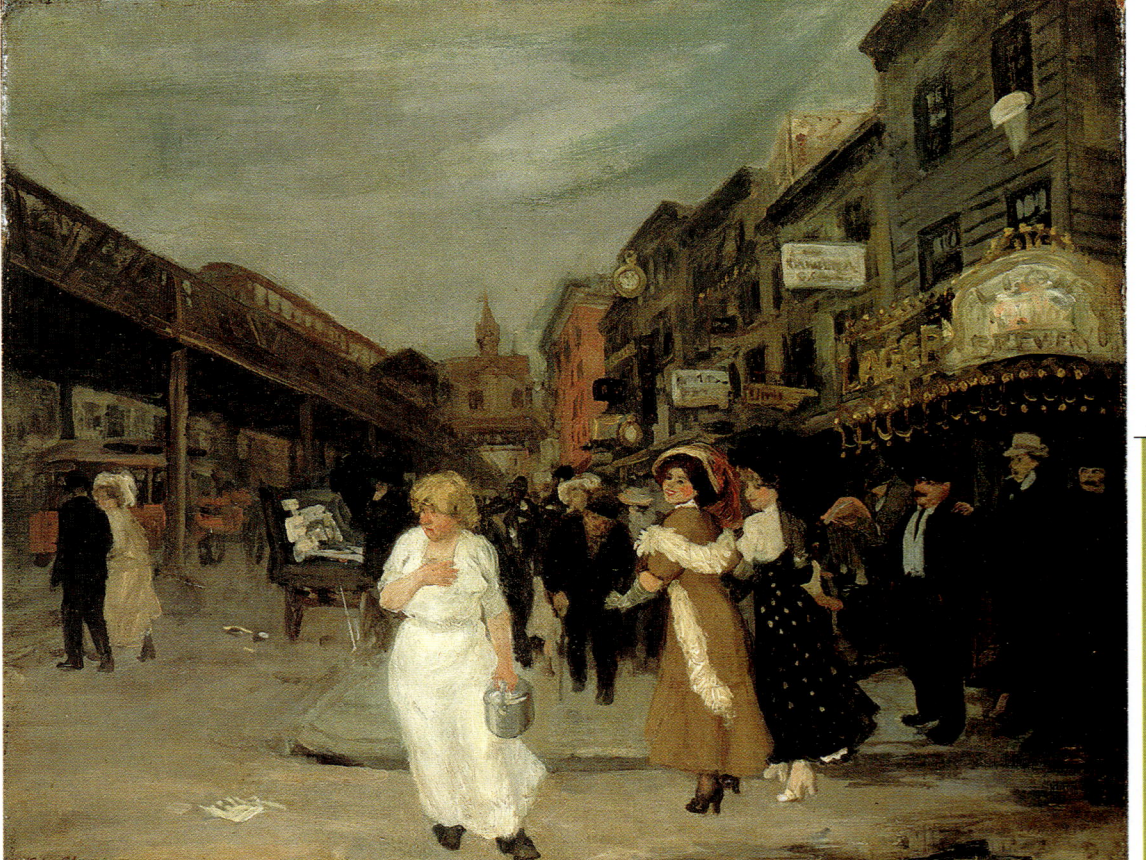

**29-34** JOHN SLOAN, *Sixth Avenue and Thirtieth Street, New York City,* 1907. Oil on canvas, 2′ ¼″ × 2′ 8″. Philadelphia Museum of Art, Philadelphia (gift of Meyer P. Potamkin and Vivian O. Potamkin, 2000).

A prominent member of the American Realist group called The Eight, Sloan captured in his paintings the bleak and seedy aspects of the rapidly changing urban landscape of New York City.

1 ft.

# The Armory Show

From February 17 to March 15, 1913, the American public flocked in large numbers to view the International Exhibition of Modern Art at the 69th Regiment Armory in New York City. The "Armory Show," as it came universally to be called, was an ambitious endeavor organized primarily by two artists, Walt Kuhn (1877–1949) and Arthur B. Davies (1862–1928). The show included more than 1,600 artworks by American and European artists. Among the European artists represented were Matisse, Derain, Picasso, Braque, Duchamp (FIG. 29-35), Kandinsky, Kirchner, Lehmbruck, and Brancusi. In addition to exposing Americans to the latest European artistic developments, the Armory Show also provided American artists with a prime showcase for their work. The foreword to the exhibition catalog spelled out the goals of the organizers:

> The American artists exhibiting here consider the exhibition of equal importance for themselves as for the public. The less they find their work showing signs of the developments indicated in the Europeans, the more reason they will have to consider whether or not painters or sculptors here have fallen behind . . . the forces that have manifested themselves on the other side of the Atlantic.*

On its opening, this provocative exhibition served as a lightning rod for commentary, immediately attracting heated controversy. The *New York Times* described the show as "pathological" and called the modernist artists "cousins to the anarchists," while the magazine *Art and Progress* compared them to "bomb throwers, lunatics, depravers."† Other critics demanded the exhibition be closed as a menace to public morality. The *New York Herald,* for example, asserted: "The United States is invaded by aliens, thousands of whom constitute so many perils to the health of the body politic. Modernism is of precisely the same heterogeneous alien origin and is imperiling the republic of art in the same way."‡

Nonetheless, the exhibition was an important milestone in the history of art in the United States. The Armory Show traveled to Chicago and Boston after it closed in New York and was a significant catalyst for the reevaluation of the nature and purpose of American art.

*Quoted in Herschel B. Chipp, *Theories of Modern Art: A Source Book by Artists and Critics* (Berkeley and Los Angeles: University of California Press, 1968), 503.
†Quoted in Sam Hunter, John Jacobus, and Daniel Wheeler, *Modern Art,* rev. 3d. ed. (Upper Saddle River, N.J.: Prentice Hall, 2005), 250.
‡Quoted in Francis K. Pohl, *Framing America: A Social History of American Art,* 2d ed. (New York: Thames & Hudson, 2002), 341.

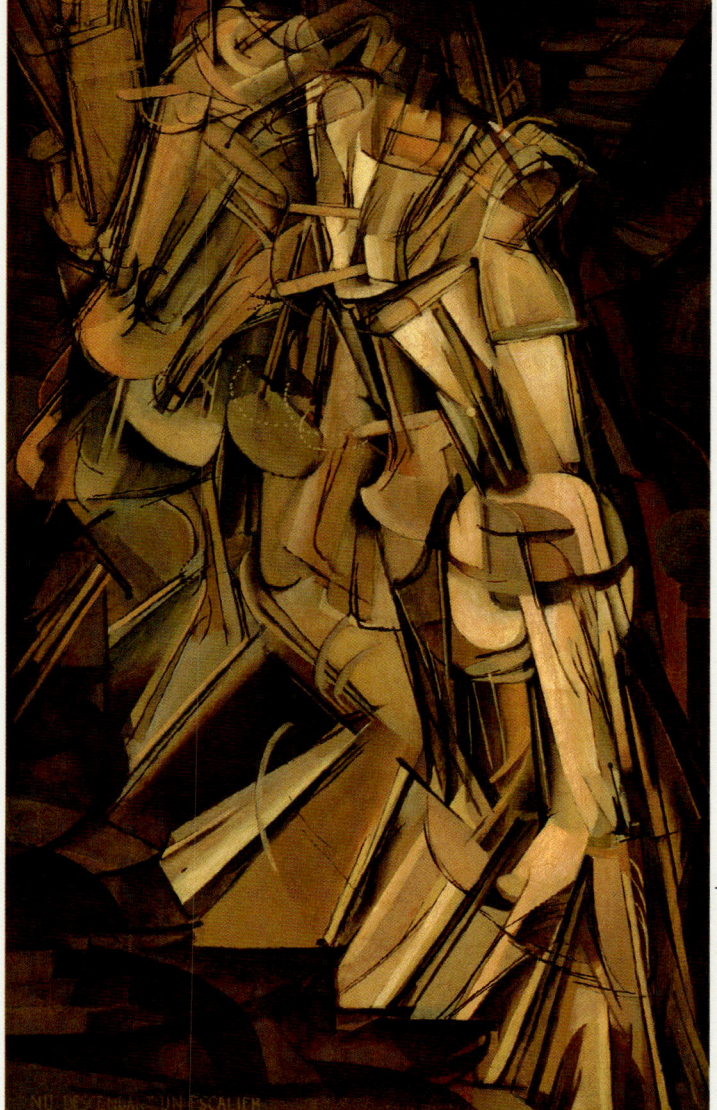

1 ft.

**29-35** MARCEL DUCHAMP, *Nude Descending a Staircase, No. 2,* 1912. Oil on canvas, 4′ 10″ × 2′ 11″. Philadelphia Museum of Art, Philadelphia (Louise and Walter Arensberg Collection).

The Armory Show introduced European modernism to America. Duchamp's figure moving in a time continuum owes a debt to Cubism and Futurism. The press gave it a hostile reception.

**ARMORY SHOW** The relative isolation of American artists from developments across the Atlantic came to an abrupt end in early 1913 when the Armory Show opened in New York City (see "The Armory Show," above). Although later recognized as the seminal event in the development of American modernist art, the exhibition received a hostile response from the press. The work the journalists and critics most maligned was Marcel Duchamp's *Nude Descending a Staircase, No. 2* (FIG. 29-35). The painting represents a single figure in motion down a staircase in a time continuum and suggests the effect of a sequence of overlaid film stills. Unlike the Dada works by Duchamp (FIGS. 29-27, 29-27A, and 29-28), *Nude Descending a Staircase* shares many characteristics with the work of the Cubists and the Futurists. The monochromatic palette is reminiscent of Analytic Cubism, as is Duchamp's faceted presentation of the human form. The artist's interest in depicting the figure in motion reveals an affinity for the Futurists' ideas. One critic described this work as "an explosion in a shingle factory,"[23] and newspaper cartoonists delighted in lampooning the painting.

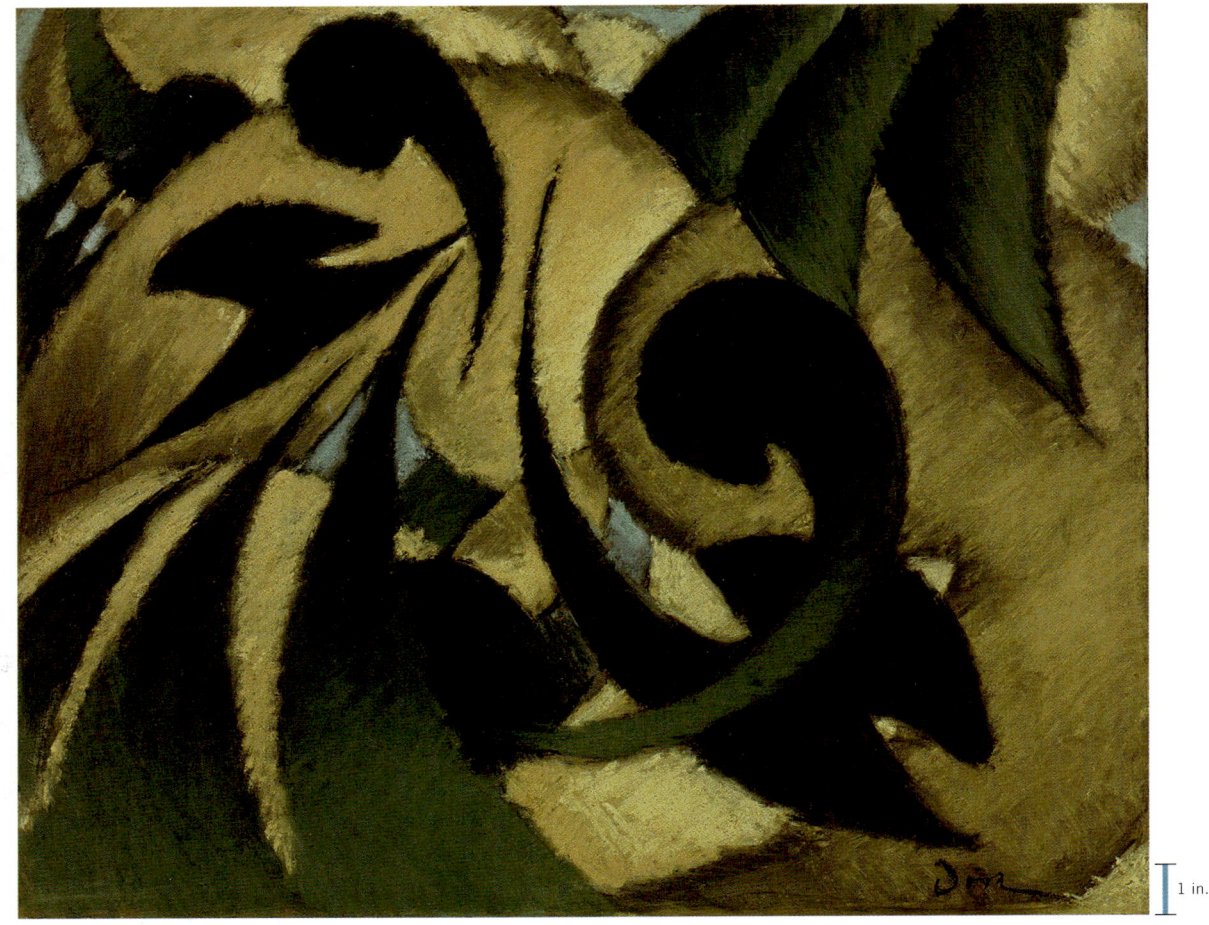

1 in.

**29-36** ARTHUR DOVE, *Nature Symbolized No. 2,* ca. 1911. Pastel on paper, 1′ 6″ × 1′ 9⅝″. Art Institute of Chicago, Chicago (Alfred Stieglitz Collection).

Dove was one of the first painters to produce completely nonobjective canvases. Using only abstract shapes and color, he sought to capture the essence of nature and of pulsating organic growth.

**ARTHUR DOVE** Among the American modernists who exhibited their work in the Armory Show was ARTHUR DOVE (1880–1946). After graduating from Cornell University, Dove worked briefly as a commercial artist in New York and then in 1907 left for Paris, where he encountered the paintings of Henri Matisse (FIGS. 29-2, 29-2A, and 29-3) and André Derain (FIGS. 29-4 and 29-4A). Dove returned to New York in 1910. He occupies a special place in the evolution of modernist art in the United States because he began painting completely nonobjective paintings at about the same time as Vassily Kandinsky but apparently without any knowledge of Kandinsky's *Improvisation* series (FIG. 29-7).

Dove spent most of his life on farms in rural New York and Connecticut and loved the textures and colors of the American landscape. He sought to capture in his paintings the essence of nature, especially its pulsating energy, but without representing nature directly. A characteristic and aptly named example of his abstract renditions of fields, vegetation, and sky is *Nature Symbolized No. 2* (FIG. 29-36), which he probably painted in 1911. Incorporating some of the principles and forms of Cubism but without representing any identifiable objects or landscape elements, Dove used swirling and jagged lines and a palette of mostly green, black, and sandy yellow to capture the essence of vegetation sprouting gloriously from fertile soil beneath patches of blue sky. He once described his goal as the creation of "rhythmic paintings" expressing nature's "spirit" through shape and color.

**MAN RAY** Another American artist who incorporated the latest European trends in his work was Emmanuel Radnitzky, who assumed the name MAN RAY (1890–1976). Ray was a close associate of Duchamp's in the 1920s. During that decade, Ray produced art having a decidedly Dada spirit, and he often incorporated found objects in his paintings, sculptures, movies, and photographs.

Trained as an architectural draftsman and engineer, Ray earned his living as a graphic designer and portrait photographer, and developed an innovative photographic technique relying on chance. In contrast to traditional photographs, Ray produced his images without using a camera. He placed objects directly on photographic paper and then exposed the paper to light. Ray dubbed these photographs, which in effect created themselves, *Rayographs.*

As did many other artists of this period, Ray had a keen interest in mass-produced objects and technology, as well as a dedication to exploring the psychological realm of human perception of the exterior world. Like Schwitters, he used the dislocation of ordinary things from their everyday settings to surprise his viewers into new awareness. His displacement of found objects was particularly effective in works such as *Cadeau* (*Gift;* FIG. 29-37). For this sculpture, with characteristic Dada humor, he equipped a laundry iron with a row of wicked-looking tacks, subverting its proper function. Ray's "gift" would rip to shreds any garment the recipient tried to press with it.

## Art "Matronage" in the United States

Until the 20th century, a leading reason for the dearth of women artists was that professional institutions restricted women's access to artistic training. For example, the proscription against women participating in life-drawing classes, a staple of academic artistic training, in effect denied women the opportunity to become professional artists. Another explanation for the absence of women from the traditional art historical canon is that art historians have not considered as "high art" many of the art objects women have traditionally produced (for example, quilts or basketry).

By the early 20th century, however, many of the impediments to a woman's becoming a recognized artist had been removed. Today, women are a major presence in the art world. One of the developments in the early 20th century that laid the groundwork for this change was the prominent role American women played as art patrons. These "art matrons" provided financial, moral, and political support to cultivate the advancement of the arts in America. Chief among them were Gertrude Vanderbilt Whitney, Lillie P. Bliss, Mary Quinn Sullivan, Abby Aldrich Rockefeller, Isabella Stewart Gardner, Peggy Guggenheim, and Jane Stanford.*

Gertrude Vanderbilt Whitney (1875–1942) was a practicing sculptor and enthusiastic collector. To assist young American artists such as Robert Henri and John Sloan (FIG. 29-34) in exhibiting their work, she opened the Whitney Studio in 1914. By 1929, dissatisfied with the recognition accorded young, progressive American artists, she offered her entire collection of 500 works to the Metropolitan Museum of Art in New York City. Her offer rejected, she founded her own museum in New York, the Whitney Museum of American Art. She chose as the first director a visionary and energetic woman, Juliana Force (1876–1948), who inaugurated a pioneering series of monographs on living American artists and organized lecture series by influential art historians and critics. Through the efforts of these two women, the Whitney Museum became a major force in American art.

A trip to Paris in 1920 whetted the interest of Peggy Guggenheim (1898–1979) in avant-garde art. As did Whitney, Guggenheim collected art and eventually opened a gallery in England to exhibit the work of innovative artists. She continued her support for modernist art after her return to the United States. Guggenheim's New York gallery, called Art of This Century, was instrumental in advancing the careers of many artists, including her husband, Max Ernst (FIG. 29-53). She eventually moved her art collection to a lavish Venetian palace, where the public can still view the important artworks she acquired.

Other women who contributed significantly to the arts were Lillie P. Bliss (1864–1931), Mary Quinn Sullivan (1877–1939), and Abby Aldrich Rockefeller (1874–1948). Philanthropists, art collectors, and educators, these influential and far-sighted women saw the need for a museum to collect and exhibit modernist art. Together they established the Museum of Modern Art in New York City in 1929, which became (and continues to be) the most influential museum of modern art in the world (see "The Museum of Modern Art," page 895), and collects American as well as European modernist art, for example, Man Ray's *Cadeau* (FIG. 29-37).

Isabella Stewart Gardner (1840–1924) and Jane Stanford (1828–1905) also undertook the ambitious project of founding museums. The Isabella Stewart Gardner Museum in Boston, established in 1903,

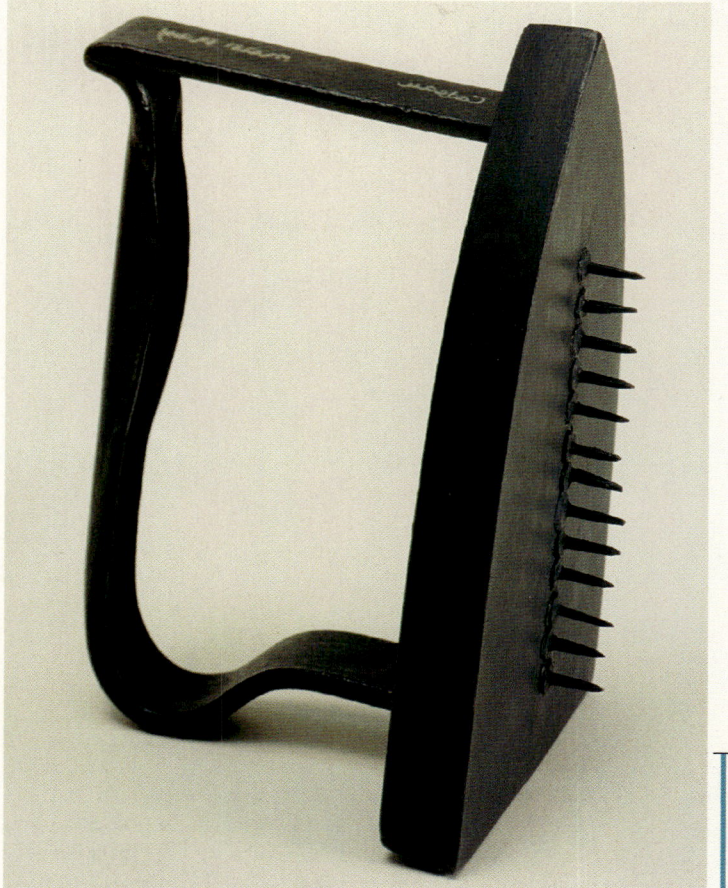

1 in.

**29-37** MAN RAY, *Cadeau* (*Gift*), ca. 1958 (replica of 1921 original). Painted flatiron with row of 13 tacks with heads glued to the bottom, $6\frac{1}{8}'' \times 3\frac{5}{8}'' \times 4\frac{1}{2}''$. Museum of Modern Art, New York (James Thrall Soby Fund).

With characteristic Dada humor, the American artist Man Ray equipped a laundry iron with a row of wicked-looking spikes, subverting its proper function of smoothing and pressing.

houses a well-chosen and comprehensive collection of art of many periods. The Stanford Museum, the first American museum west of the Mississippi, got its start in 1905 on the grounds of Stanford University, which Leland Stanford Sr. and Jane Stanford founded after the tragic death of their son. The Stanford Museum houses a wide range of objects, including archaeological and ethnographic artifacts. These two driven women committed much of their time, energy, and financial resources to ensure the success of their museums, and were intimately involved in their institutions' day-to-day operations.

The museums these women established flourish today, attesting to the extraordinary vision of these "art matrons" and the remarkable contributions they made to the advancement of art in the United States.

*Art historian Wanda Corn coined the term *art matronage* in the catalog *Cultural Leadership in America: Art Matronage and Patronage* (Boston: Isabella Stewart Gardner Museum, 1997).

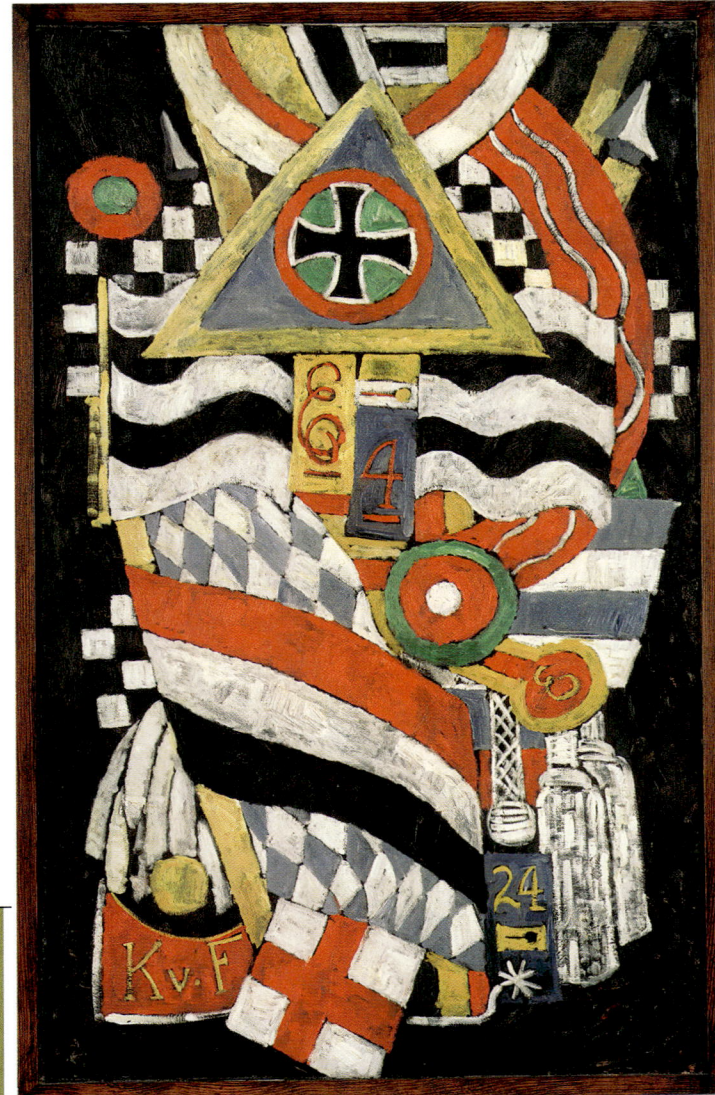

**29-38** MARSDEN HARTLEY, *Portrait of a German Officer*, 1914. Oil on canvas, 5′ 8¼″ × 3′ 5⅜″. Metropolitan Museum of Art, New York (Alfred Stieglitz Collection).

In this elegy to a lover killed in battle, Hartley arranged military-related images against a somber black background. The flattened, planar presentation reveals the influence of Synthetic Cubism.

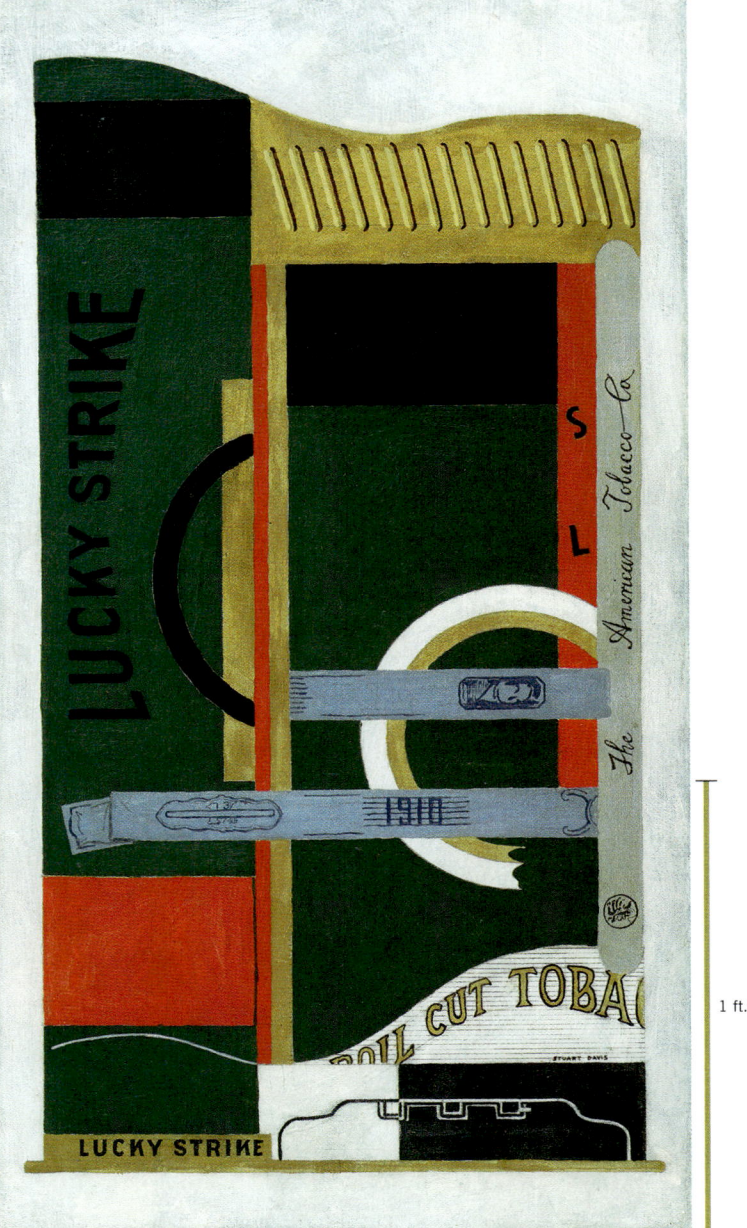

**29-39** STUART DAVIS, *Lucky Strike*, 1921. Oil on canvas, 2′ 9¼″ × 1′ 6″. Museum of Modern Art, New York (gift of the American Tobacco Company, Inc.). © Estate of Stuart Davis/Licensed by VAGA, New York.

Tobacco products fascinated Davis, a heavy smoker. In *Lucky Strike,* he depicted a cigarette package in fragmented form, recalling Cubism, and imbued his painting with an American jazz rhythm.

**MARSDEN HARTLEY** One American artist who developed a personal style influenced by Cubism and German Expressionism was MARSDEN HARTLEY (1877–1943). In 1912, Hartley traveled to Europe, visiting Paris, where he became acquainted with the work of the Cubists, and Munich, where he gravitated to the Blaue Reiter circle. Kandinsky's work particularly impressed Hartley, and he developed a style he called "Cosmic Cubism." In 1913, he moved to Berlin. With the heightened militarism in Germany and the eventual outbreak of World War I, Hartley immersed himself in military imagery.

*Portrait of a German Officer* (FIG. **29-38**) is one of Hartley's best paintings of this period. It depicts an array of military-related images: German imperial flags, regimental insignia, badges, and emblems such as the Iron Cross. Although this image resonates in the general context of wartime militarism, important elements in the painting had personal significance for Hartley. In particular,

the painting includes references to his lover, Lieutenant Karl von Freyberg, who lost his life in battle a few months before Hartley painted this "portrait." Von Freyberg's initials appear in the lower left corner. His age when he died (24) appears in the lower right corner, and his regiment number (4) appears in the center of the painting. Also incorporated is the letter E for von Freyberg's regiment, the Bavarian Eisenbahn. The influence of Synthetic Cubism is evident in the flattened, planar presentation of the elements, which almost appear as abstract patterns. The somber black background against which the artist placed the colorful stripes, patches, and shapes casts an elegiac pall over the painting.

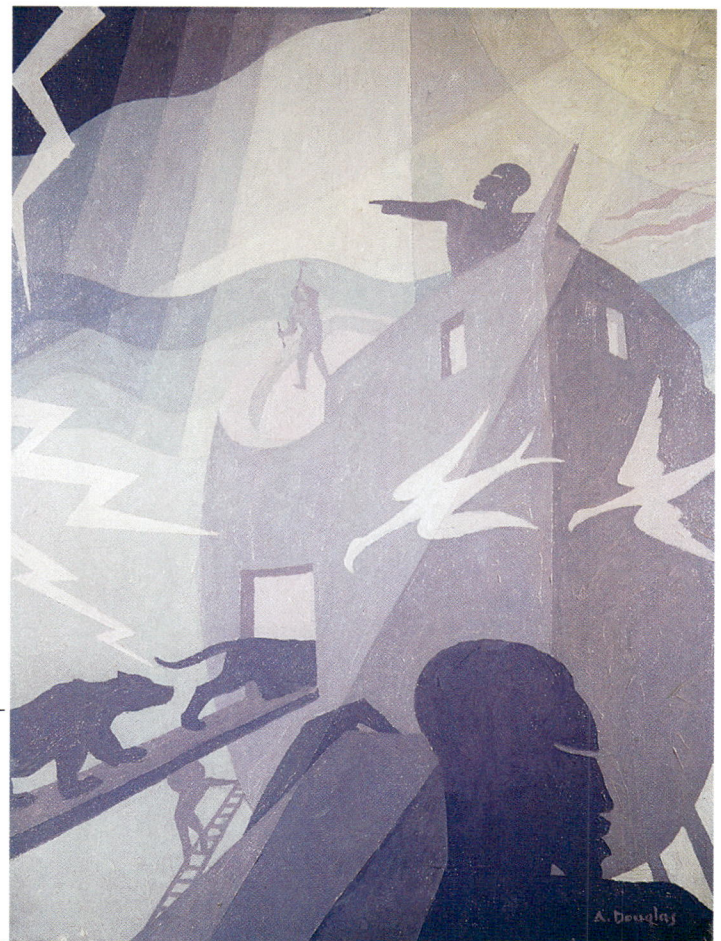

**29-40** AARON DOUGLAS, *Noah's Ark,* ca. 1927. Oil on Masonite, 4′ × 3′. Fisk University Galleries, University of Tennessee, Nashville.

In *Noah's Ark* and other paintings of the cultural history of African Americans, Douglas incorporated motifs from African sculpture and the transparent angular planes characteristic of Synthetic Cubism.

**STUART DAVIS** Philadelphia-born STUART DAVIS (1894–1964) created what he believed was a modern American art style by combining the flat shapes of Synthetic Cubism with his sense of jazz tempos and his perception of the energy of fast-paced American culture. *Lucky Strike* (FIG. **29-39**) is one of several tobacco still lifes Davis began in 1921. Davis was a heavy smoker, and tobacco products and their packaging fascinated him. He insisted the introduction of packaging in the late 19th century was evidence of high civilization and therefore, he concluded, of the progressiveness of American culture. Davis depicted the Lucky Strike package in fragmented form, reminiscent of Synthetic Cubist collages. However, although the work does incorporate flat printed elements, these are illusionistically painted, rather than glued onto the canvas. The discontinuities and the interlocking planes imbue *Lucky Strike* with a dynamism and rhythm not unlike American jazz or the pace of life in a lively American metropolis. *Lucky Strike* is resolutely both American and modern.

**AARON DOUGLAS** Also deriving his personal style from Synthetic Cubism was African American artist AARON DOUGLAS (1898–1979), who used the style to represent symbolically the historical and cultural memories of his people. Born in Kansas,

Douglas studied in Nebraska and Paris before settling in New York City, where he became part of the flowering of art and literature in the 1920s known as the Harlem Renaissance. Spearheaded by writers and editors Alain Locke (1886–1953) and Charles Spurgeon Johnson (1883–1956), the Harlem Renaissance was a manifestation of the desire of African Americans to promote their cultural accomplishments. They also aimed to cultivate pride among fellow African Americans and to foster racial tolerance across the United States. Expansive and diverse, the fruits of the Harlem Renaissance included the writings of authors such as Langston Hughes, Countee Cullen, and Zora Neale Hurston; the jazz and blues of Duke Ellington, Bessie Smith, Eubie Blake, Fats Waller, and Louis Armstrong; the photographs of James Van Der Zee and Prentice H. Polk; and the paintings and sculptures of Meta Warrick Fuller and Augusta Savage.

Douglas arrived in New York City in 1924 and became one of the most sought-after graphic artists in the African American community. Encouraged to create art that would express the cultural history of his race, Douglas incorporated motifs from African sculpture into compositions painted in a version of Synthetic Cubism stressing transparent angular planes. *Noah's Ark* (FIG. **29-40**) was one of seven paintings based on a book of poems by James Weldon Johnson (1871–1938) called *God's Trombones: Seven Negro Sermons in Verse.* Douglas used flat planes to evoke a sense of mystical space and miraculous happenings. In *Noah's Ark*, lightning strikes and rays of light crisscross the pairs of animals entering the ark, while men load supplies in preparation for departure. The artist suggested deep space by differentiating the size of the large human head and shoulders of the worker at the bottom and the small person at work on the far deck of the ship. Yet the composition's unmodulated color shapes create a pattern on the Masonite surface that cancels any illusion of three-dimensional depth. Here, Douglas used Cubism's formal language to express a powerful religious vision. Seven years later, employed by the U.S. government to create murals for the Harlem branch of the New York Public Library, he addressed a contemporary rather than a biblical subject: the history of Africans in America (FIG. **29-40A**).

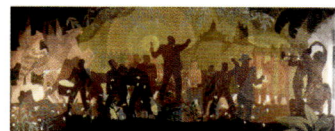

**29-40A** DOUGLAS, *Slavery through Reconstruction,* 1934.

**PRECISIONISM** Another distinctly American art movement in the post–Armory Show period was *Precisionism.* Although not an organized group, the Precisionists shared a fascination with the machine's "precision" and its importance in modern life. Although new technologies captured the imaginations of many European artists, especially the Futurists, Americans generally seemed more enamored by the prospects of a mechanized society than did Europeans. Even the Frenchman Francis Picabia, Duchamp's collaborator, noted: "Since machinery is the soul of the modern world, and since the genius of machinery attains its highest expression in America, why is it not reasonable to believe that in America the art of the future will flower most brilliantly?"[24] Precisionism, however, expanded beyond the exploration of machine imagery. Many artists associated with this group gravitated toward Synthetic Cubism's flat, sharply delineated planes as an appropriate visual idiom for their imagery, adding to the clarity and precision of their work. Eventually, Precisionism came to be characterized by a merging of a familiar native style in American architecture and artifacts with a modernist vocabulary derived largely from Synthetic Cubism.

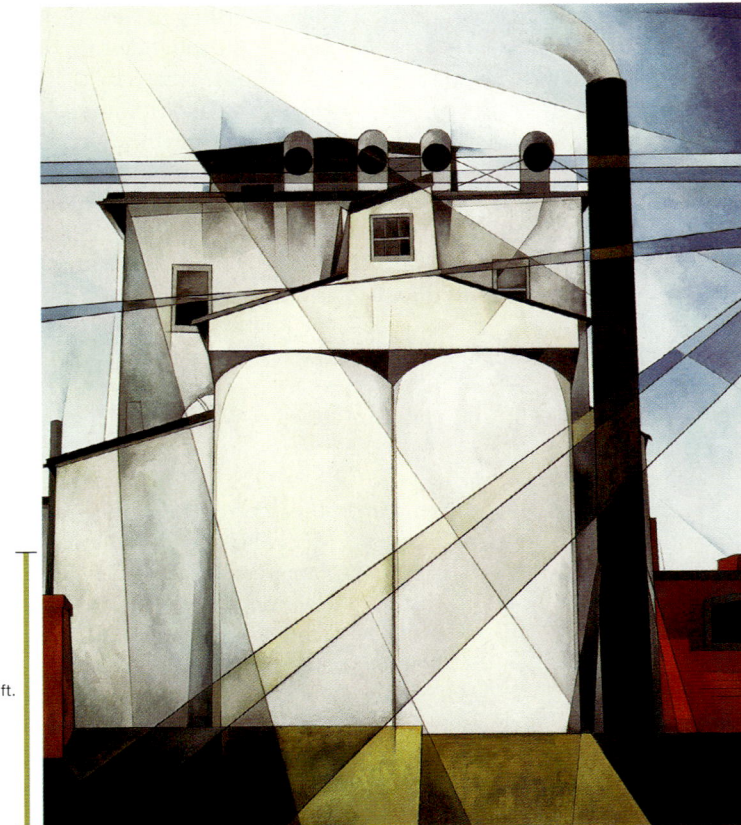

**29-41** CHARLES DEMUTH, *My Egypt,* 1927. Oil on composition board, 2′ 11¾″ × 2′ 6″. Whitney Museum of American Art, New York (purchased with funds from Gertrude Vanderbilt Whitney).

Demuth was one of the leading Precisionists—American artists who extolled the machine age. This painting depicts grain elevators reduced to geometric forms amid Cubist transparent diagonal planes.

**CHARLES DEMUTH** Two of the leading Precisionists hailed from Pennsylvania—Charles Sheeler (1883–1965) and CHARLES DEMUTH (1883–1935). Sheeler traveled to Italy and France in 1909, and Demuth spent the years 1912–1914 in Paris, but both artists rejected pure abstraction and favored American subjects, especially industrial landscapes. Demuth's *My Egypt* (FIG. **29-41**) incorporates the spatial discontinuities characteristic of Cubism into a typically Precisionist depiction of an industrial site near Lancaster, the painter's birthplace. Demuth reduced the John W. Eshelman and Sons grain elevators to simple geometric forms. The grain elevators remain recognizable and solid, but the "beams" of transparent planes and the diagonal force lines threaten to destabilize the image and recall Cubist fragmentation of space. The degree to which Demuth intended to extol the American industrial scene is unclear. The title, *My Egypt,* is sufficiently ambiguous in tone to accommodate differing readings. On the one hand, Demuth could have been suggesting a favorable comparison between the Egyptian pyramids and American grain elevators as cultural icons. On the other hand, the title could be read cynically, as a negative comment on the limitations of American culture.

**GEORGIA O'KEEFFE** The work of Wisconsin-born GEORGIA O'KEEFFE (1887–1986) changed stylistically throughout her career. During the 1920s, O'Keeffe was a Precisionist. She had moved from the tiny town of Canyon, Texas, to New York City in 1918, and although she had visited the city before, what she found there excited her. "You have to live in today," she told a friend. "Today the

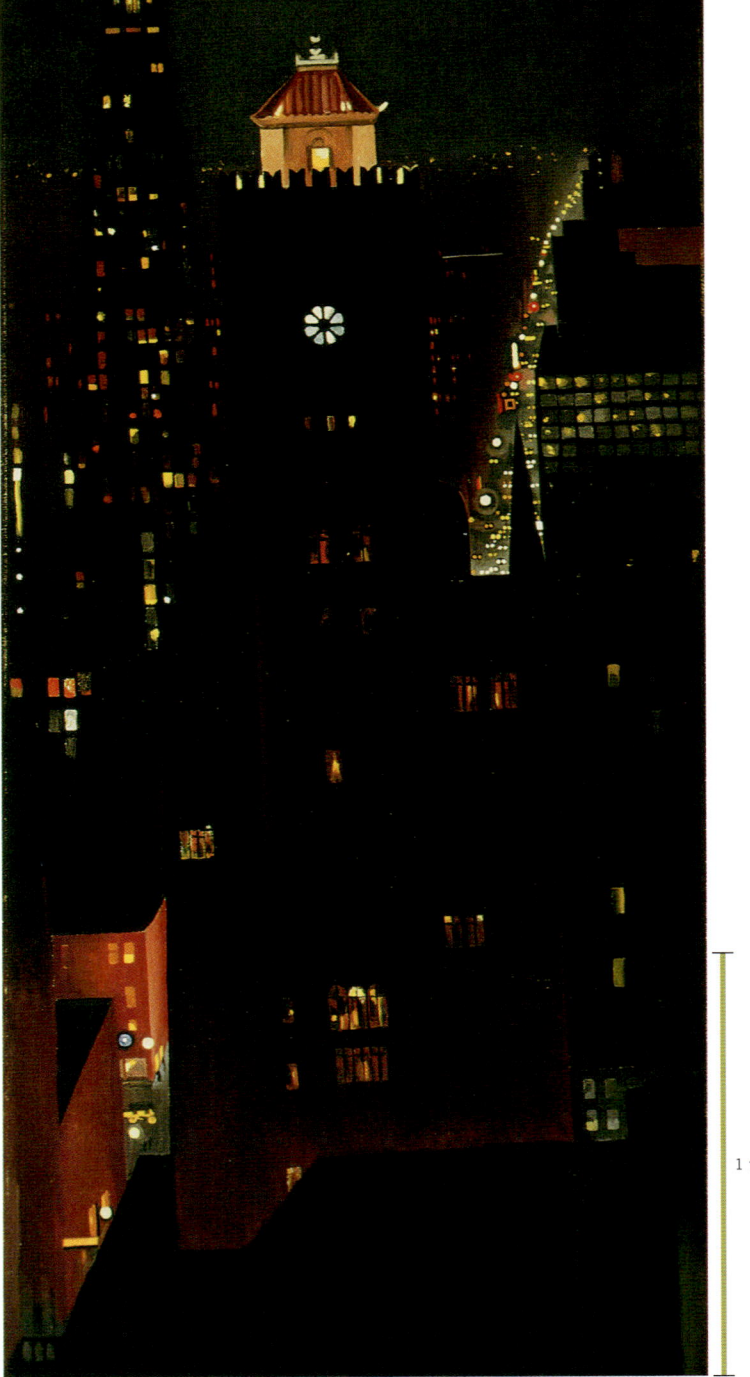

**29-42** GEORGIA O'KEEFFE, *New York, Night,* 1929. Oil on canvas, 3′ 4⅛″ × 1′ 7⅛″. Sheldon Memorial Art Gallery, Lincoln (Nebraska Art Association, Thomas C. Woods Memorial Collection).

O'Keeffe's Precisionist representation of New York's soaring skyscrapers reduces the buildings to large, simple, dark planes punctuated by small windows that add rhythm and energy to the image.

city is something bigger, more complex than ever before in history. And nothing can be gained from running away. I couldn't even if I could."[25] While in New York, O'Keeffe met Alfred Stieglitz (FIGS. 29-43 and 29-43A), who played a major role in promoting the avant-garde in the United States. Stieglitz had established an art gallery at 291 Fifth Avenue in New York. In "291," as the gallery came to be called, he exhibited the latest in both European and

American art. Thus, 291, like the Armory Show, played an important role in the history of early-20th-century art in America. Stieglitz had seen and exhibited some of O'Keeffe's earlier work, and he drew her into his avant-garde circle of painters and photographers. He became one of O'Keeffe's staunchest supporters and, eventually, her husband. The interest of Stieglitz and his circle in capturing the sensibility of the machine age intersected with O'Keeffe's fascination with the fast pace of city life, and she produced paintings during this period, such as *New York, Night* (FIG. **29-42**), featuring the soaring skyscrapers dominating the city. As did other Precisionists, O'Keeffe reduced her images to simple planes, here punctuated by small rectangular windows that add rhythm and energy to the image, countering the monolithic darkness of the looming buildings.

Despite O'Keeffe's affiliation with the Precisionist movement and New York, she is best known for her paintings of cow skulls and of flowers. For example, in *Jack in the Pulpit No. 4* (FIG. I-5), she reveals her interest in stripping subjects to their purest forms and colors to heighten their expressive power. In this work, O'Keeffe reduced the incredible details of a flower to a symphony of basic colors, shapes, textures, and vital rhythms. Exhibiting the natural flow of curved planes and contour, O'Keeffe simplified the form almost to the point of complete abstraction. The fluid planes unfold like undulant petals from a subtly placed axis—the white jetlike streak—in a vision of the slow, controlled motion of growing life. O'Keeffe's painting, in its graceful, quiet poetry, reveals the organic reality of the object by strengthening its characteristic features.

## Photography

Among the most significant artistic developments during the decades between the two world wars was the emergence of photography as a respected branch of the fine arts. The person most responsible for elevating the stature of photography was Alfred Stieglitz.

**ALFRED STIEGLITZ** Taking his camera everywhere he went, ALFRED STIEGLITZ (1864–1946) photographed whatever he saw around him, from the bustling streets of New York City to cloudscapes in upstate New York and the faces of friends and relatives. He believed in making only "straight, unmanipulated" photographs. Thus, he exposed and printed them using basic photographic processes, without resorting to techniques such as double-exposure or double-printing that would add information absent in the subject when he released the shutter. Stieglitz said he wanted the photographs he made with this direct technique "to hold a moment, to record something so completely that those who see it would relive an equivalent of what has been expressed."[26]

Stieglitz began a lifelong campaign to win a place for photography among the fine arts while he was a student of photochemistry in Germany. Returning to New York, he founded the Photo-Secession group, which mounted traveling exhibitions in the United States and sent loan collections abroad, and he published an influential journal titled *Camera Work*. In his own works, Stieglitz specialized in photographs of his environment and saw these subjects in terms of arrangements of forms and of the "colors" of his black-and-white materials. His aesthetic approach crystallized during the making of *The Steerage* (FIG. **29-43**), taken during a voyage to Europe with his first wife and daughter in 1907. Traveling first class, Stieglitz rapidly grew bored with the company of the prosperous passengers in his section of the ship. He walked as far forward on the first-class level as he could, when the rail around the opening onto the lower deck brought him up short. This level was for the steerage passengers the U.S. government sent back to Europe after refusing them entrance into the country. Later, Stieglitz described what happened next:

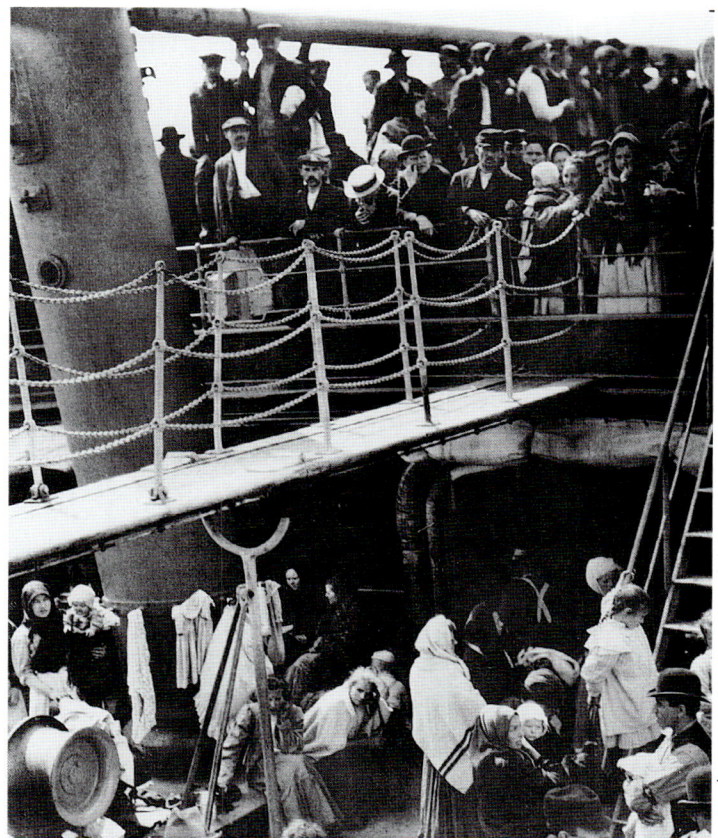

**29-43** ALFRED STIEGLITZ, *The Steerage*, 1907 (print 1915). Photogravure (on tissue), $1' \frac{3}{8}'' \times 10\frac{1}{8}''$. Amon Carter Museum, Fort Worth. ◼◀

Stieglitz waged a lifelong campaign to win a place for photography among the fine arts. This 1907 image is a haunting mixture of found patterns of forms and human activity. It stirs deep emotions.

The scene fascinated me: A round hat; the funnel leaning left, the stairway leaning right; the white drawbridge, its railing made of chain; white suspenders crossed on the back of a man below; circular iron machinery; a mast that cut into the sky, completing a triangle. I stood spellbound. I saw shapes related to one another—a picture of shapes, and underlying it, a new vision that held me: simple people; the feeling of ship, ocean, sky; a sense of release that I was away from the mob called rich. Rembrandt came into my mind and I wondered would he have felt as I did. . . . I had only one plate holder with one unexposed plate. Could I catch what I saw and felt? I released the shutter. If I had captured what I wanted, the photograph would go far beyond any of my previous prints. It would be a picture based on related shapes and deepest human feeling—a step in my own evolution, a spontaneous discovery.[27]

This description reveals Stieglitz's abiding interest in the formal elements of the photograph—an insistently modernist focus that emerges in even more extreme form in his *Equivalent* series (FIG. **29-43A**) of the 1920s. The finished print fulfilled Stieglitz's vision so well that it shaped his future photographic work, and its haunting mixture of found patterns and human activity has continued to stir viewers' emotions to this day.

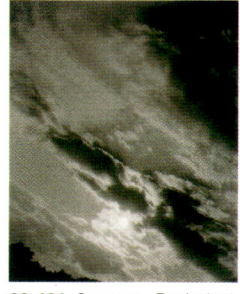

**29-43A** STIEGLITZ, *Equivalent*, 1923. ◼◀

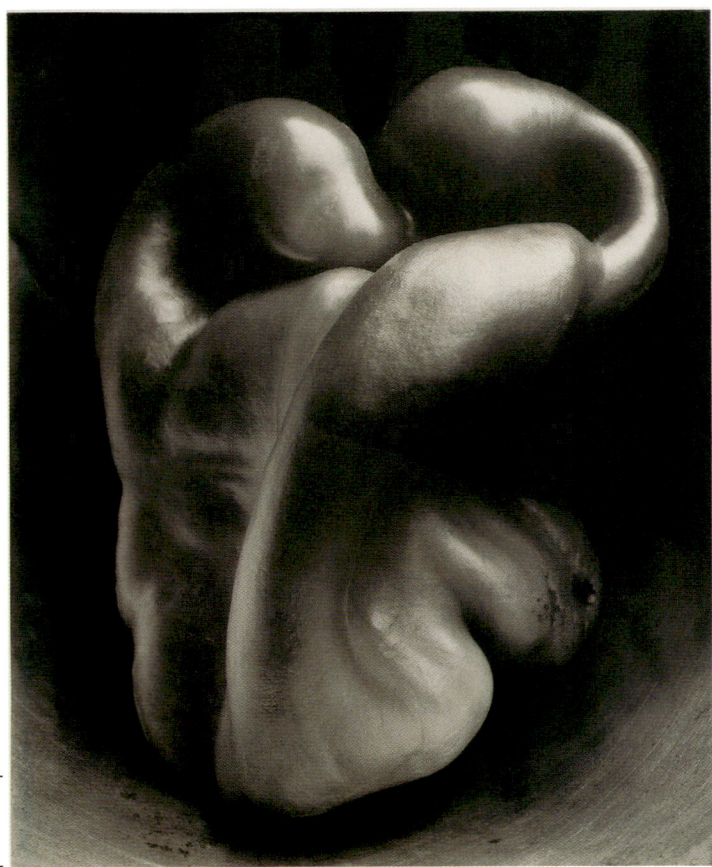

29-44 EDWARD WESTON, *Pepper No. 30*, 1930. Gelatin silver print, $9\frac{1}{2}'' \times 7\frac{1}{2}''$. Center for Creative Photography, University of Arizona, Tucson.

Weston "previsualized" his still lifes, choosing the exact angle, lighting, and framing he desired. His vegetables often resemble human bodies, in this case a seated nude seen from behind.

**EDWARD WESTON** Like Alfred Stieglitz, in whose 291 Gallery he exhibited his work, EDWARD WESTON (1886–1958) played a major role in establishing photography as an important artistic medium. But unlike Stieglitz, who worked outdoors and sought to capture transitory moments in his photographs, Weston meticulously composed and carefully lit his subjects in a controlled studio setting, whether he was doing still lifes of peppers, shells, and other natural forms of irregular shape, or figure studies. The 1930 photograph of a pepper illustrated here (FIG. 29-44) is the 30th in a large series and an outstanding example of this genre. In contrast to Weston's photographs of sections of nude human bodies (FIG. 29-44A), his still-life photographs show the entire object, albeit tightly framed. (Compare Geor-

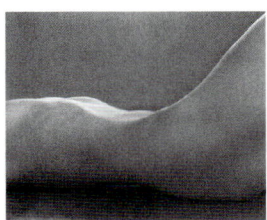

29-44A WESTON, *Nude*, 1925.

gia O'Keeffe's *Jack-in-the-Pulpit No. 4* [FIG. I-5] painted the same year.) The artificial lighting accentuates the undulating surfaces and crevices of the vegetable. Weston left nothing to chance, choosing the exact angle and play of light over the object, "previsualizing" the final photographic print before snapping the camera's shutter.

In a kind of reversal of his approach to photographing nudes, which he often transformed into landscapes, Weston frequently chose peppers whose shapes reminded him of human bodies. *Pepper No. 30* looks like a seated nude figure seen from behind with raised arms emerging from broad shoulders. Viewers can read the vertical crease down the center of the vegetable as the spinal column leading to the buttocks. Although highly successful as a purely abstract composition of shapes and of light and dark, Weston's still life also conveys mystery and sensuality through its dramatic lighting and rich texture.

## Architecture

As did other artists, many early-20th-century architects in the United States looked to Europe for inspiration, but distinctive American styles also emerged that in turn had a major influence on architectural design worldwide.

**FRANK LLOYD WRIGHT** One of the most striking personalities in the development of modern architecture on either side of the Atlantic was FRANK LLOYD WRIGHT (1867–1959). Born in Wisconsin, Wright moved to Chicago, where he eventually joined the firm headed by Louis Sullivan (FIGS. 28-40, 28-40A, and 28-41). Wright set out to create an American "architecture of democracy."[28] Always a believer in "natural" and "organic" buildings, Wright saw architecture as serving free individuals who have the right to move within a "free" space, envisioned as a nonsymmetrical design interacting spatially with its natural surroundings. He sought to develop an organic unity of planning, structure, materials, and site. Wright identified the principle of continuity as fundamental to understanding his view of organic unity:

> Classic architecture was all fixation. . . . Now why not let walls, ceilings, floors become seen as component parts of each other? . . . You may see the appearance in the surface of your hand contrasted with the articulation of the bony structure itself. This ideal, profound in its architectural implications . . . I called . . . continuity.[29]

Wright manifested his vigorous originality early, and by 1900 he had arrived at a style entirely his own. In his work during the first decade of the 20th century, his cross-axial plan and his fabric of continuous roof planes and screens defined a new American domestic architecture.

**ROBIE HOUSE** Wright fully expressed these elements and concepts in the Robie House (FIG. 29-45), built between 1907 and 1909. Like other buildings in the Chicago area Wright designed at about the same time, he called this home a "prairie house." Wright conceived the long, sweeping, ground-hugging lines, unconfined by abrupt wall limits, as reaching out toward and capturing the expansiveness of the Midwest's great flatlands. Abandoning all symmetry, he eliminated a facade, extended the roofs far beyond the walls, and all but concealed the entrance. Wright filled the house's "wandering" plan (FIG. 29-46) with intricately joined spaces (some large and open, others closed), grouped freely around a great central fireplace. (He believed strongly in the hearth's age-old domestic significance.) Wright designed enclosed patios, overhanging roofs, and strip windows to provide unexpected light sources and glimpses of the outdoors as the inhabitants moved through the interior space. These elements, together with the open ground plan, created a sense of space in motion, inside and out. Wright matched his new and fundamental interior spatial arrangement in his exterior treatment. For example, the flow of interior space determined the sharp angular placement of exterior walls.

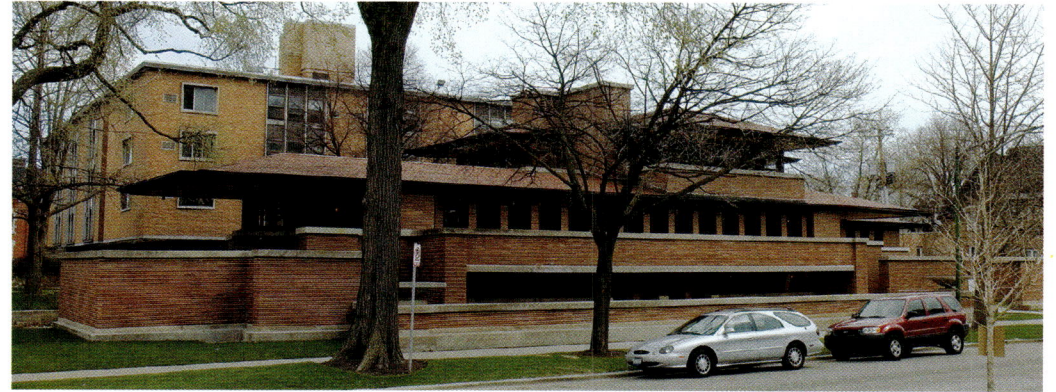

29-45 FRANK LLOYD WRIGHT, Robie House (looking northeast), Chicago, Illinois, 1907–1909.

The Robie House is an example of Wright's "architecture of democracy," in which free individuals move within a "free" space—a nonsymmetrical design interacting spatially with its natural surroundings.

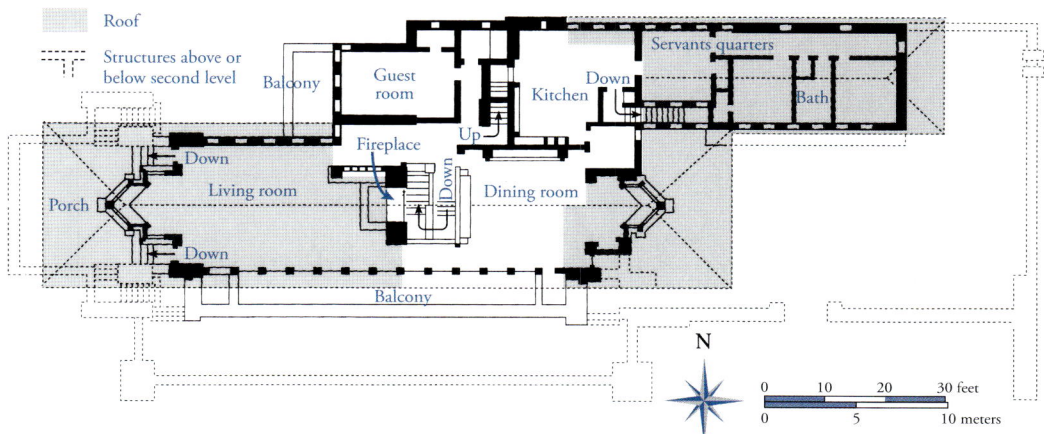

29-46 FRANK LLOYD WRIGHT, plan of the second (main) level of the Robie House, Chicago, Illinois, 1907–1909.

Typical of Wright's "prairie houses," the Robie House has a bold "wandering" asymmetrical plan with intricately joined open and closed spaces grouped freely around a great central fireplace.

**ART DECO** Although Adolf Loos (FIG. 29-33) had strongly condemned ornamentation in the design of buildings, popular taste still favored decoration as an important element in architecture. *Art Deco* was a movement in the 1920s and 1930s whose adherents sought to upgrade industrial design in competition with "fine art." Proponents wanted to work new materials into decorative patterns that could be either machined or handcrafted and could, to a degree, reflect the simplifying trend in architecture. A remote descendant of Art Nouveau, Art Deco acquired its name at the Exposition des Arts Décoratifs et Industriels Modernes (Exposition of Modern Decorative and Industrial Arts), held in Paris in 1925. Art Deco had universal application—to buildings, interiors, furniture, utensils, jewelry, fashions, illustration, and commercial products of every sort. Art Deco products have a "streamlined," elongated symmetrical aspect. Simple flat shapes alternate with shallow volumes in hard patterns. Derived from nature, these simple forms are inherently aerodynamic, making them technologically efficient (because of their reduced resistance as they move through air or water) as well as aesthetically pleasing. Designers adopted streamlined designs for trains and cars, and the popular appeal of these designs led to their use in an array of objects, from machines to consumer products.

Art Deco's exemplary masterpiece is the stainless-steel spire of the Chrysler Building (FIG. **29-47**) in New York City, designed by WILLIAM VAN ALEN (1882–1954). The building and spire are

29-47 WILLIAM VAN ALEN, Art Deco spire of the Chrysler Building (looking south), New York, New York, 1928–1930. ◼◀

The Chrysler Building's stainless steel spire epitomizes Art Deco architecture. The skyscraper's glittering crown of diminishing fan shapes has a streamlined form popular during the 1920s.

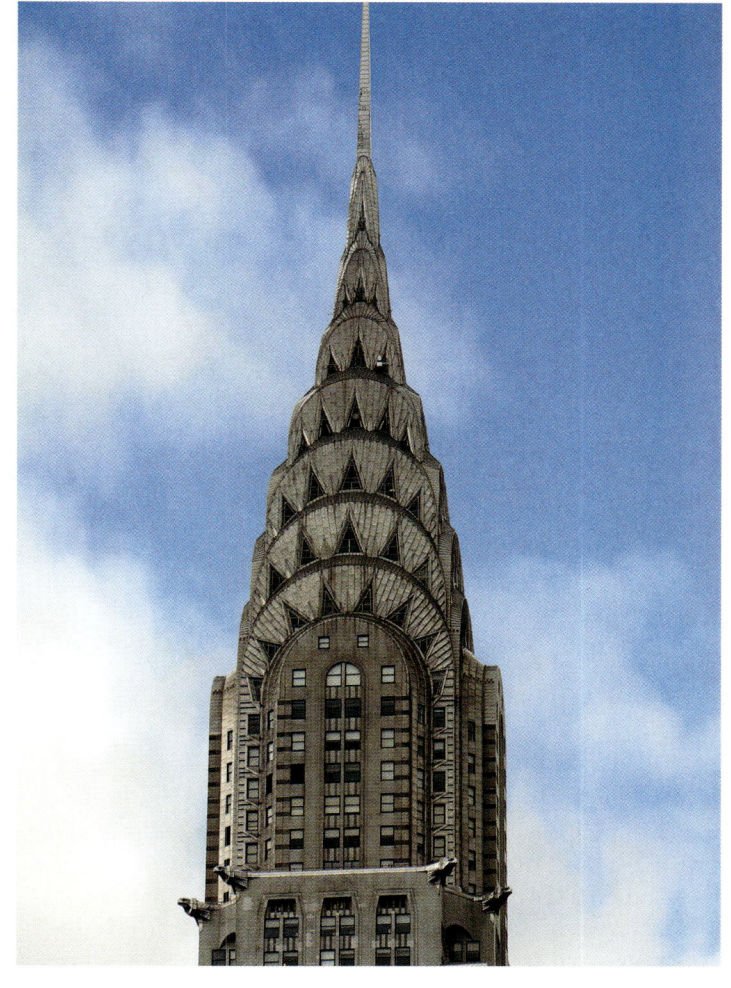

monuments to the fabulous 1920s, when American millionaires and corporations competed with one another to raise the tallest skyscrapers in the biggest cities. Built up of diminishing fan shapes, the spire glitters triumphantly in the sky, a resplendent crown honoring the business achievements of the great auto manufacturer. As a temple of commerce, the Chrysler Building celebrated the principles and success of American business before the onset of the Great Depression.

# EUROPE, 1920 TO 1945

Because World War I was fought entirely on European soil, European artists experienced its devastating effects to a much greater degree than did American artists. The war had a profound effect on Europe's geopolitical terrain, on individual and national psyches, and on the art of the 1920s and 1930s.

## Neue Sachlichkeit

In Germany, World War I gave rise to an artistic movement called *Neue Sachlichkeit* (New Objectivity). All of the artists associated with Neue Sachlichkeit served, at some point, in the German army. Their military experiences deeply influenced their worldviews and informed their art. "New Objectivity" captures the group's aim—

to present a clear-eyed, direct, and honest image of the war and its effects.

**GEORGE GROSZ** One of the Neue Sachlichkeit artists was GEORGE GROSZ (1893–1958), who was, for a time, associated with the Dada group in Berlin. Grosz observed the onset of World War I with horrified fascination that soon turned to anger and frustration. He reported:

> Of course, there was a kind of mass enthusiasm at the start. But this intoxication soon evaporated, leaving a huge vacuum. . . . And then after a few years when everything bogged down, when we were defeated, when everything went to pieces, all that remained, at least for me and most of my friends, were disgust and horror.[30]

The largest canvas Grosz ever painted—*The Eclipse of the Sun* (FIG. **29-48**)—does not depict the Great War itself, but, as are many of his other paintings and drawings (FIG. **29-48A**), it is a stinging indictment of the militarism and capitalism he believed were the root causes of the global conflict. The painting takes its name from the large red German coin at the upper left blocking the sun and signifying capitalism has

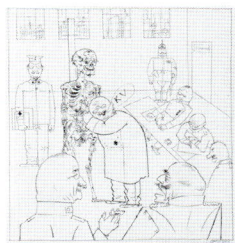

**29-48A** GROSZ, *Fit for Active Service*, 1916–1917.

brought darkness to the world. Also at the top are burning buildings. At the lower right are a skull and bones. Filling the rest of the canvas are the agents of this destruction seated at a table seen at a sharp angle from above. The main figure is the president of Germany, Paul von Hindenburg (r. 1925–1934), who wears his army uniform and war medals. His bloody sword is on the table before him, and on his head is the laurel wreath of victory. He presides over a meeting with four headless ministers—men who act on his orders without question. Grosz, however, also portrayed the president as a puppet leader. A wealthy industrialist wearing a top hat whispers instructions in von Hindenburg's ear. The painting is also a commentary on the gullibility of the public, personified here as a donkey who eats newspapers, that is, as a mindless creature who swallows the propagandistic lies promoted by the government- and business-friendly press.

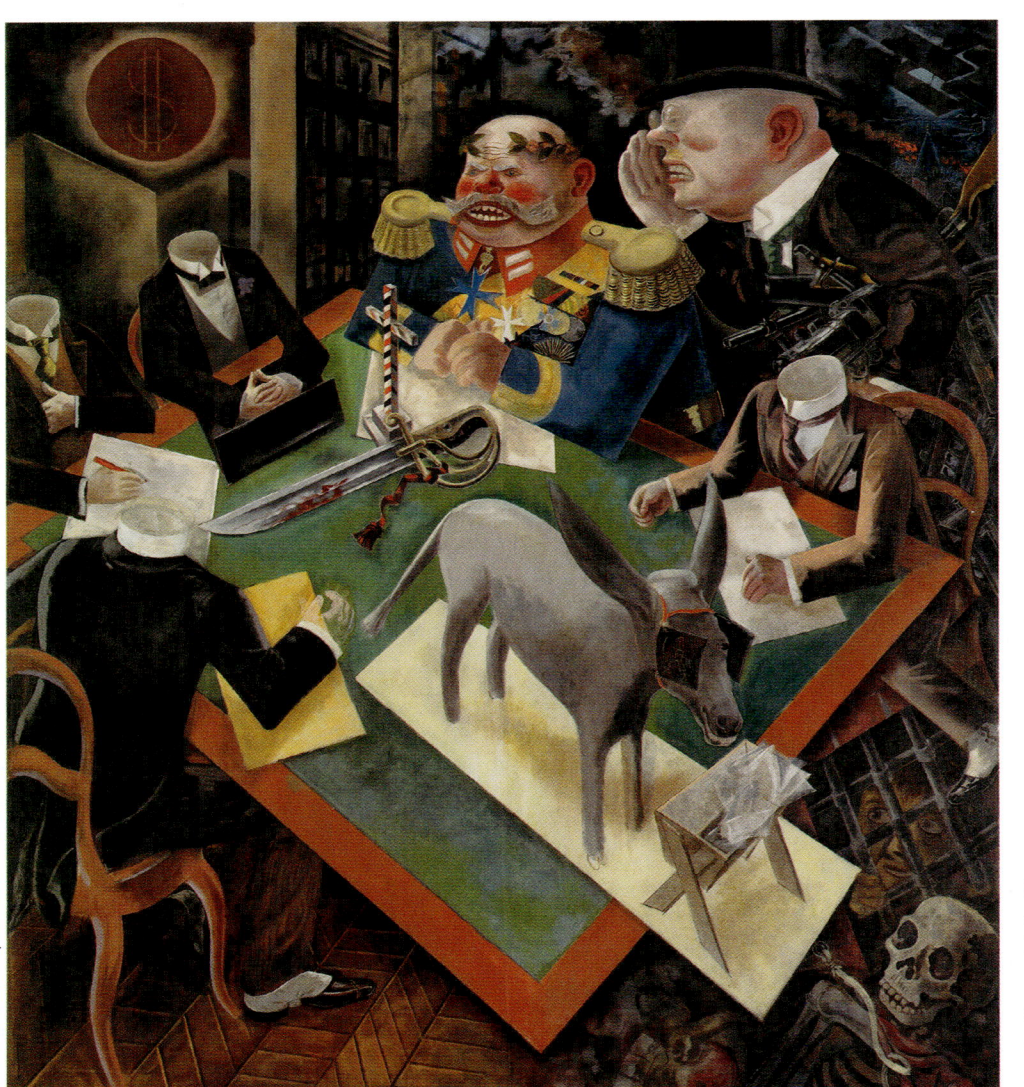

**29-48** GEORGE GROSZ, *The Eclipse of the Sun*, 1926. Oil on canvas, 6′ 9⅝″ × 5′ 11⅞″. Heckscher Museum of Art, Huntington.

In Grosz's indictment of militarism and capitalism, an industrialist whispers instructions in the ear of the uniformed president of Germany, who meets with four of his headless ministers.

1 ft.

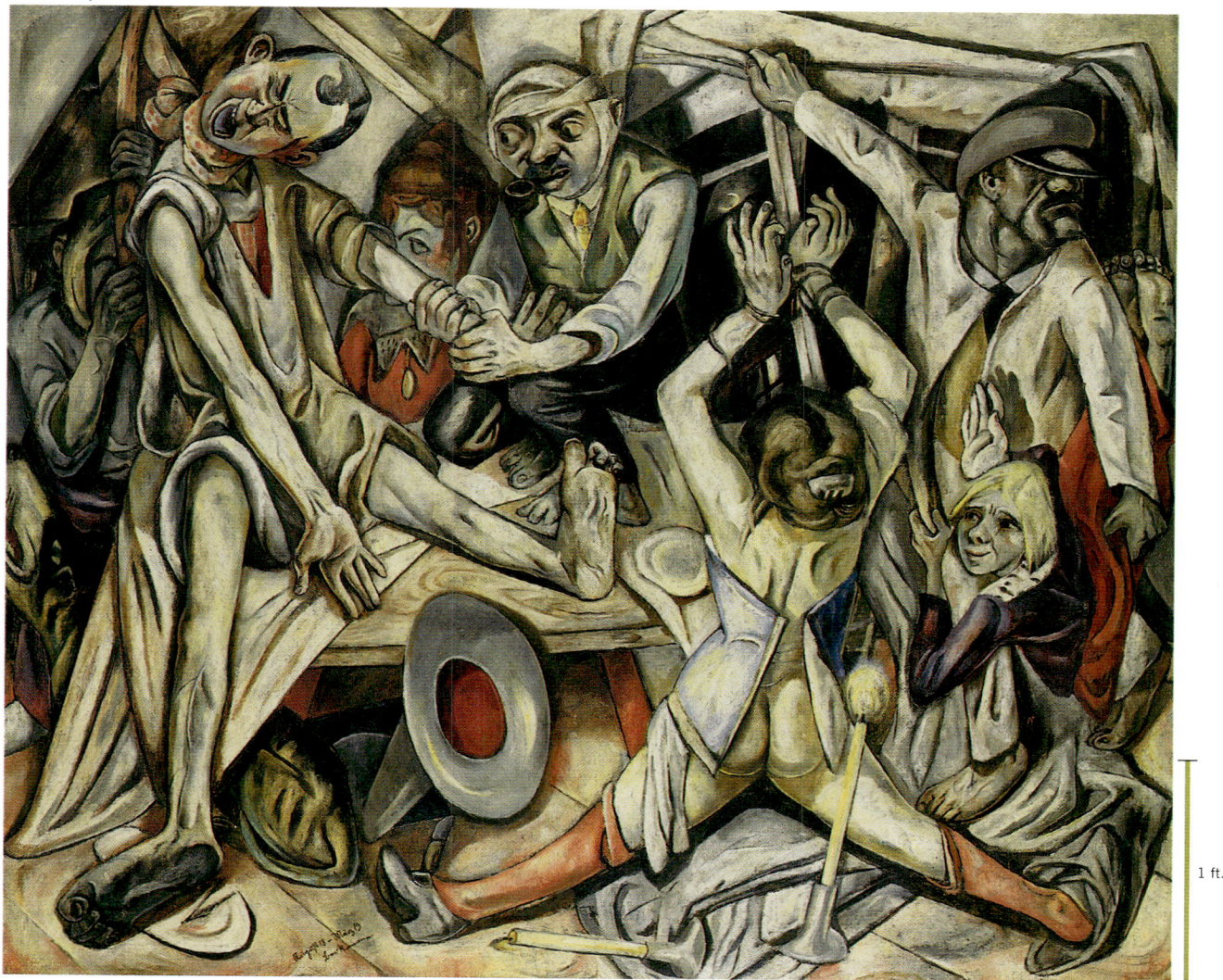

**29-49** Max Beckmann, *Night,* 1918–1919. Oil on canvas, 4′ 4⅜″ × 5′ ¼″. Kunstsammlung Nordrhein-Westfalen, Düsseldorf.

Beckmann's treatment of forms and space in *Night* matched his view of the brutality of early-20th-century society. Objects seem dislocated and contorted, and the space appears buckled and illogical.

**MAX BECKMANN** Another major German artist who enlisted in the German army and initially rationalized the Great War was Max Beckmann (1884–1950). He believed the chaos would lead to a better society, but over time the massive loss of life and widespread destruction increasingly disillusioned him. Soon his work began to emphasize the horrors of war and of a society he saw descending into madness. His disturbing view of society is evident in *Night* (FIG. **29-49**), which depicts a cramped room three intruders have forcefully invaded. A bound woman, apparently raped, is splayed across the foreground of the painting. Her husband appears on the left. One of the intruders hangs him, while another one twists his left arm out of its socket. An unidentified woman cowers in the background. On the far right, the third intruder prepares to flee with the child.

Although this image does not depict a war scene, the wrenching brutality and violence pervading the home are searing and horrifying comments on society's condition. Beckmann also injected a personal reference by using himself, his wife, and his son as the models for the three family members. The stilted angularity of the figures and the roughness of the paint surface contribute to the image's savageness. In addition, the artist's treatment of forms and space reflects the world's violence. Objects seem dislocated and contorted, and the

space appears buckled and illogical. For example, the woman's hands are bound to the window opening from the room's back wall, but her body appears to hang vertically, rather than lying across the plane of the intervening table.

**OTTO DIX** The third artist most closely associated with Neue Sachlichkeit was Otto Dix (1891–1959). Having served as both a machine gunner and an aerial observer, Dix was well acquainted with war's effects. As did Grosz and Beckmann, Dix initially tried to find redeeming value in the apocalyptic event: "The war was a horrible thing, but there was something tremendous about it, too. . . . You have to have seen human beings in this unleashed state to know what human nature is. . . . I need to experience all the depths of life for myself, that's why I go out, and that's why I volunteered."[31] This idea of experiencing the "depths of life" stemmed from Dix's interest in the philosophy of Friedrich Nietzsche (1844–1900). In particular, Dix avidly read Nietzsche's *The Joyous Science,* deriving from it a belief in life's cyclical nature—procreation and death, building up and tearing down, and growth and decay.

As the war progressed, however, Dix's faith in the potential improvement of society dissipated, and he began to produce

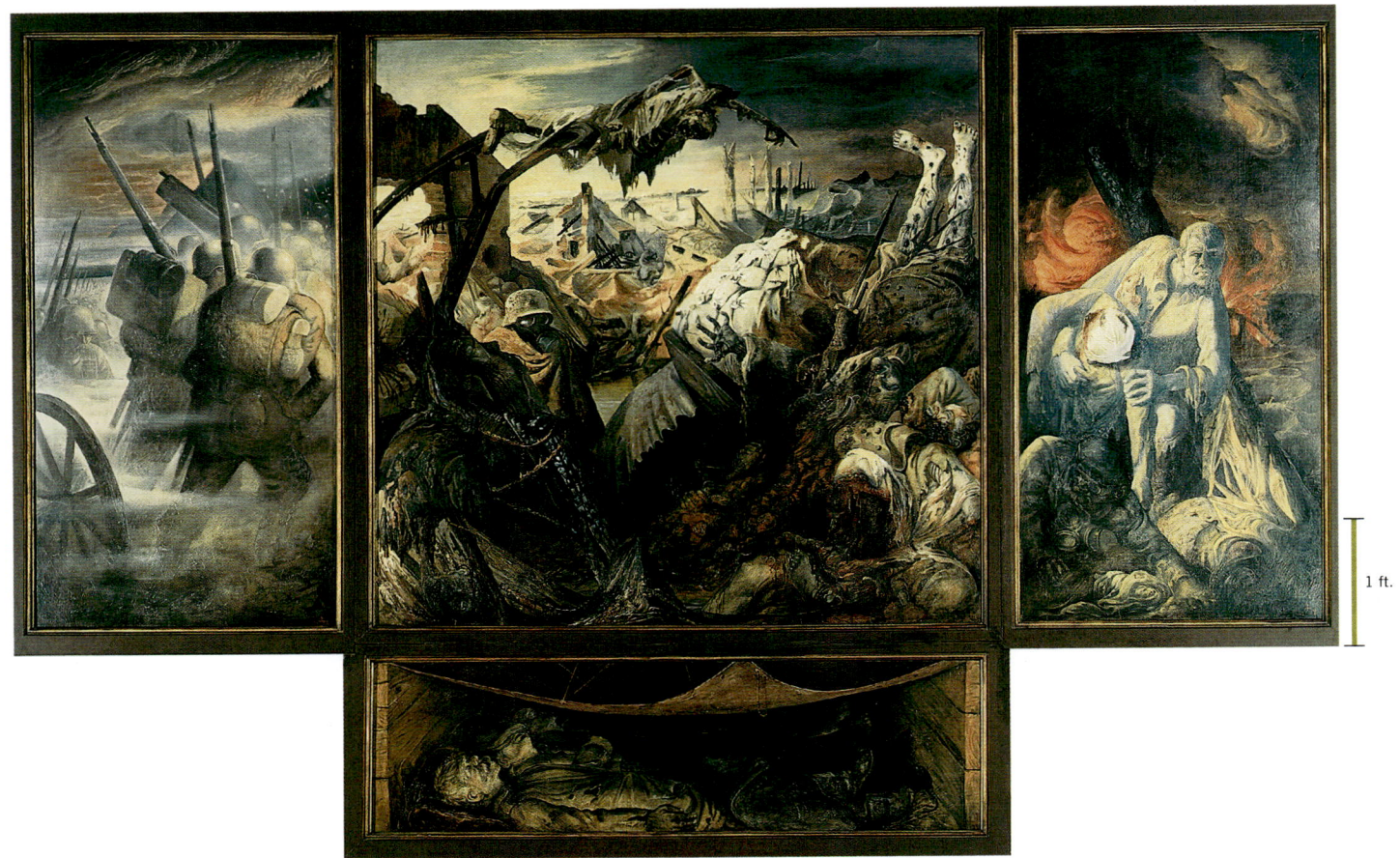

1 ft.

**29-50** Otto Dix, *Der Krieg* (*The War*), 1929–1932. Oil and tempera on wood, 6′ 8⅓″ × 13′ 4¾″. Staatliche Kunstsammlungen, Gemäldegalerie Neue Meister, Dresden.

In this triptych recalling earlier altarpieces, Dix captured the panoramic devastation war inflicts on the terrain and on humans. He depicted himself as a soldier dragging a comrade to safety.

unflinchingly direct and provocative artworks. His triptych titled *Der Krieg* (*The War*; FIG. **29-50**) vividly captures the panoramic devastation war inflicts, both on the terrain and on humans. In the left panel, armed and uniformed soldiers march off into the distance. Dix graphically displayed the horrific results in the center and right panels, where mangled bodies, many riddled with bullet holes, are scattered throughout the eerily lit apocalyptic landscape. As if to emphasize the intensely personal nature of this scene, the artist painted himself into the right panel as the ghostly but determined soldier who drags a comrade to safety. In the bottom panel, in a coffinlike bunker, lie soldiers asleep—or perhaps dead. Dix significantly chose to present this sequence of images in the format of an altarpiece, and the work recalls triptychs such as Matthias Grünewald's *Isenheim Altarpiece* (FIG. 23-2). However, Dix's "altarpiece" presents a bleaker outlook than Grünewald's. The hope of salvation extended to viewers of the *Isenheim Altarpiece* through Christ's eventual resurrection is absent from *Der Krieg*. As did his fellow Neue Sachlichkeit artists, Dix felt compelled to lay bare the realities of his time, which the war's violence dominated. Even years later, Dix still maintained:

> You have to see things the way they are. You have to be able to say yes to the human manifestations that exist and will always exist. That doesn't mean saying yes to war, but to a fate that approaches you under certain conditions and in which you have to prove yourself. Abnormal situations bring out all the depravity, the bestiality of human beings. . . . I portrayed states, states that the war brought about, and the results of war, as states.[32]

**ERNST BARLACH** A work more spiritual in its expression is the *War Monument* (FIG. **29-51**), which the German sculptor ERNST BARLACH (1870–1938) created for the cathedral in his hometown of Güstrow in 1927. Working often in wood, Barlach sculpted single figures usually dressed in flowing robes and portrayed in strong, simple poses embodying deep human emotions and experiences such as grief, vigilance, or self-comfort. Barlach's works combine sharp, smoothly planed forms with intense expression. The cast-bronze hovering figure of his *War Monument* is one of the poignant memorials of World War I. Unlike traditional war memorials depicting heroic military figures, often engaged in battle, the hauntingly symbolic figure Barlach created speaks to the experience of all caught in the conflict of war. The floating human form, suspended above a tomb inscribed with the dates 1914–1918 (and later also 1939–1945), suggests a dying soul at the moment when it is about to awaken to everlasting life—the theme of death and transfiguration. The rigid economy of surfaces concentrates attention on the simple but expressive head. So powerful was this sculpture the Nazis had it removed from the cathedral in 1937 and melted it down for ammunition. Luckily, a friend hid another version Barlach made. A Protestant parish in Cologne purchased it, and bronze workers made a new cast of the figure for the Güstrow cathedral.

## Surrealism

The exuberantly aggressive momentum of the Dada movement that emerged during World War I lasted for only a short time. By 1924, with the publication in France of the *First Surrealist Manifesto*,

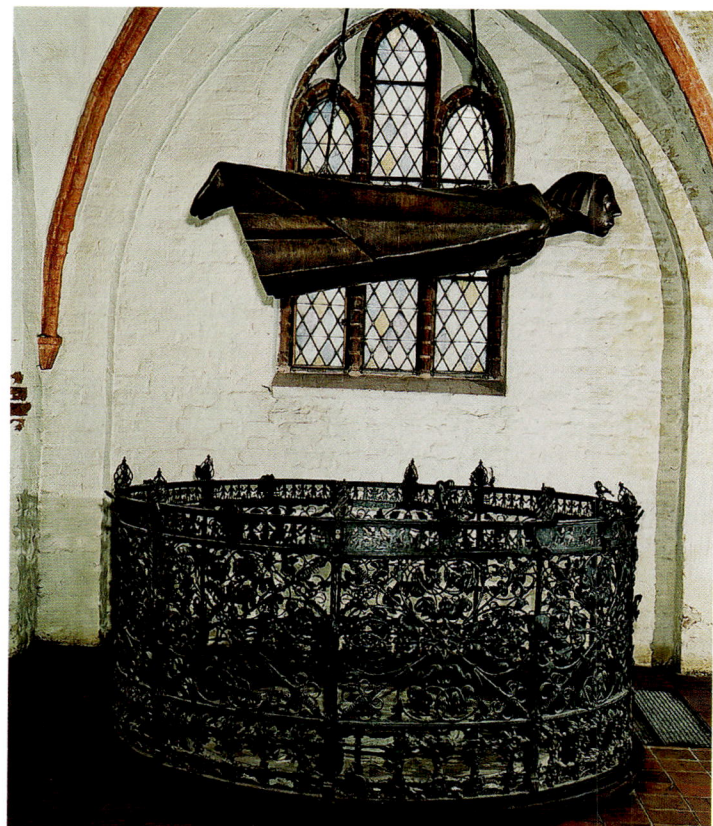

**29-51** ERNST BARLACH, *War Monument*, Güstrow Cathedral, Güstrow, Germany, 1927. Bronze.

In this World War I memorial, which the Nazis melted down for ammunition, a human form floating above a tomb suggests a dying soul at the moment it is about to awaken to everlasting life.

most of the artists associated with Dada joined the *Surrealism* movement and its determined exploration of ways to express in art the world of dreams and the unconscious. Not surprisingly, the Surrealists incorporated many of the Dadaists' improvisational techniques. They believed these methods important for engaging the elements of fantasy and activating the unconscious forces deep within every human being. The Surrealists sought to explore the inner world of the psyche, the realm of fantasy and the unconscious. Inspired in part by the ideas of the psychoanalysts Sigmund Freud and Carl Jung, the Surrealists had a special interest in the nature of dreams. They viewed dreams as occurring at the level connecting all human consciousness and as constituting the arena in which people could move beyond their environment's constricting forces to reengage with the deeper selves society had long suppressed. In the words of André Breton, one of the leading Surrealist thinkers:

> Surrealism is based on the belief in the superior reality of certain forms of association heretofore neglected, in the omnipotence of dreams, in the undirected play of thought. . . . I believe in the future resolution of the states of dream and reality, in appearance so contradictory, in a sort of absolute reality, or surreality.[33]

Thus, the Surrealists' dominant motivation was to bring the aspects of outer and inner "reality" together into a single position, in much the same way life's seemingly unrelated fragments combine in the vivid world of dreams. The projection in visible form of this new conception required new techniques of pictorial construction. The Surrealists adapted some Dada devices and invented new

methods such as automatic writing (spontaneous writing using free association), not so much to reveal a world without meaning as to provoke reactions closely related to subconscious experience.

Surrealism developed along two lines. In *Naturalistic Surrealism,* artists presented recognizable scenes that seem to have metamorphosed into a dream or nightmare image. The artists Salvador Dalí (FIG. 29-55) and René Magritte (FIGS. 29-56 and 29-56A) were the most famous practitioners of this variant of Surrealism. In contrast, some artists gravitated toward an interest in *Biomorphic Surrealism*. In Biomorphic (life forms) Surrealism, *automatism*—the creation of art without conscious control—predominated. Biomorphic Surrealists such as Joan Miró (FIG. 29-58) produced largely abstract compositions, although the imagery sometimes suggests organisms or natural forms.

**GIORGIO DE CHIRICO** The widely recognized precursor of Surrealism was the Italian painter GIORGIO DE CHIRICO (1888–1978). De Chirico's emphatically ambiguous paintings of cityscapes are the most famous examples of a movement called *Pittura Metafisica,* or Metaphysical Painting. Returning to Italy after studying in Munich, de Chirico found hidden reality revealed through strange juxtapositions, such as those seen on late autumn afternoons, when the long shadows of the setting sun transformed vast open squares and silent public monuments into what the painter called "metaphysical towns." De Chirico translated this vision into paint in works such as *The Song of Love* (FIG. 29-52), a dreamlike scene set in the deserted piazza of an Italian town. A huge marble head—a fragment of the

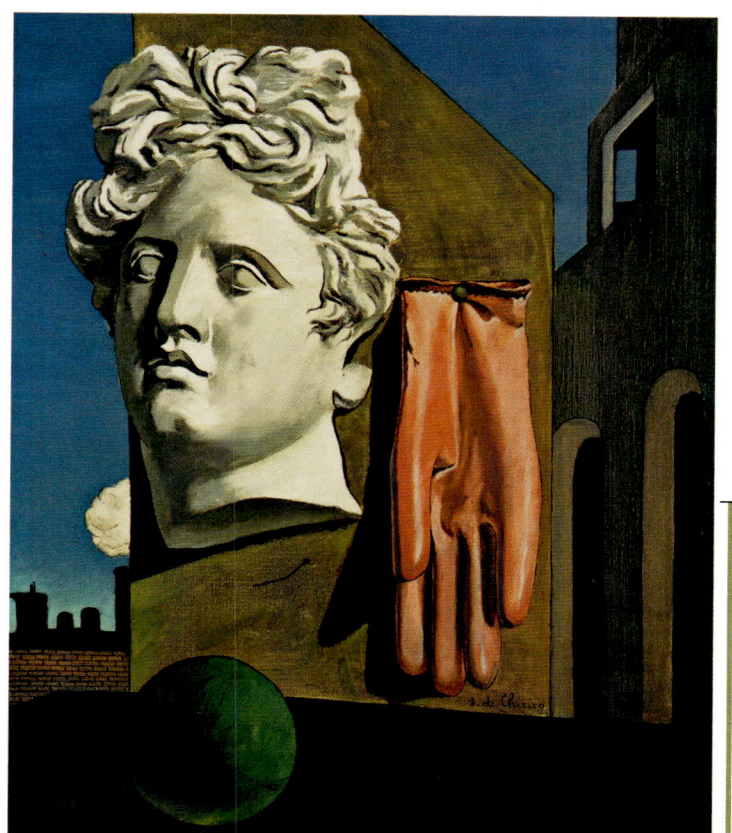

1 ft.

**29-52** GIORGIO DE CHIRICO, *The Song of Love,* 1914. Oil on canvas, 2′ 4¾″ × 1′ 11⅜″. Museum of Modern Art, New York (Nelson A. Rockefeller bequest).

De Chirico's Metaphysical Painting movement was a precursor of Surrealism. Here, a classical head of Apollo floats mysteriously next to a gigantic red glove in a deserted, shadow-filled Italian city square.

famous *Apollo Belvedere* in the Vatican—is suspended in midair above a large green ball. To the right is a gigantic red glove nailed to a wall. The buildings and the three over-life-size objects cast shadows that direct the viewer's eye to the left and to a locomotive puffing smoke—a favorite Futurist motif, here shown in slow motion and incongruously placed near the central square. The choice of the term *metaphysical* to describe de Chirico's paintings suggests these images transcend their physical appearances. *The Song of Love,* for all of its clarity and simplicity, takes on a rather sinister air. The sense of strangeness de Chirico could conjure with familiar objects and scenes recalls Nietzsche's "foreboding that underneath this reality in which we live and have our being, another and altogether different reality lies concealed."[34]

Reproductions of De Chirico's paintings appeared in periodicals almost as soon as he completed them, and his works quickly influenced artists outside Italy, including both the Dadaists and, later, the Surrealists. The incongruities in his work intrigued the Dadaists, whereas the eerie mood and visionary quality of paintings such as *The Song of Love* excited and inspired Surrealist artists who sought to portray the world of dreams.

**MAX ERNST** Originally a Dada activist in Germany, MAX ERNST (1891–1976) became one of the early adherents of the Surrealist circle André Breton anchored. As a child living in a small community near Cologne, Ernst had found his existence fantastic and filled with marvels. In autobiographical notes, written mostly in the third person, he said of his birth: "Max Ernst had his first contact with the world of sense on the 2nd April 1891 at 9:45 a.m., when he emerged from the egg which his mother had laid in an eagle's nest and which the bird had incubated for seven years."[35] Ernst's service in the German army during World War I swept away his early success as an Expressionist. In his own words:

> Max Ernst died on 1st August 1914. He returned to life on 11th November 1918, a young man who wanted to become a magician and find the central myth of his age. From time to time he consulted the eagle which had guarded the egg of his prenatal existence. The bird's advice can be detected in his work.[36]

Before joining the Surrealists, Ernst explored every means to achieve the sense of the psychic in his art. As other Dadaists did, Ernst set out to incorporate found objects and chance into his works, often combining fragments of images he had cut from old books, magazines, and prints to form one hallucinatory collage. He also began making paintings that shared the mysterious dreamlike effect of his collages.

In 1920, Ernst met Breton, who instantly recognized the German artist's affinity with the Surrealist group. In 1922, Ernst moved to Paris, where he painted *Two Children Are Threatened by a Nightingale* (FIG. **29-53**). In it, Ernst displayed a private dream challenging the post-Renaissance idea that a painting should resemble a window looking into a "real" scene rendered illusionistically three-dimensional through mathematical perspective. He painted the landscape, the distant city, and the tiny flying bird in conventional fashion, following all the established rules of linear and atmospheric perspective. The three sketchily rendered figures, however, clearly belong to a dream world, and the literally three-dimensional miniature gate, the odd button knob, and the strange closed building "violate" the bulky frame's space. Additional dislocation occurs in the traditional museum identification label, which Ernst displaced into a cutaway part of the frame. Handwritten, it announces the work's title (taken from a poem Ernst wrote before he painted this), adding another note of irrational mystery.

As is true of many Surrealist works, the title, *Two Children Are Threatened by a Nightingale,* is ambiguous and relates uneasily to what the spectator sees. The viewer must struggle to decipher connections between the image and the words. When Surrealists (and Dadaists and Metaphysical artists before them) used puzzling titles, they intended the seeming contradiction between title and picture to knock the audience off balance with all expectations challenged. Much of the impact of Surrealist works begins with the viewer's sudden awareness of the incongruity and absurdity of what the artist pictured. These were precisely the qualities that subjected the Dadaists and

1 ft.

**29-53** MAX ERNST, *Two Children Are Threatened by a Nightingale,* 1924. Oil on wood with wood construction, 2′ 3½″ × 1′ 10½″ × 4½″. Museum of Modern Art, New York.

In this early Surrealist painting with an intentionally ambiguous title, Ernst used traditional perspective to represent the setting, but the three sketchily rendered figures belong to a dream world.

## Degenerate Art

Although avant-garde artists often had to endure public ridicule both in Europe and America (see "The Armory Show," page 863), they suffered outright political persecution in Germany in the 1930s and 1940s. The most dramatic example of this persecution was the infamous "Entartete Kunst" (Degenerate Art) exhibition Adolf Hitler (1889–1945) and the Nazis mounted in 1937.

Hitler aspired to become an artist himself and produced numerous drawings and paintings reflecting his firm belief that 19th-century realistic genre painting represented the zenith of Aryan art development. Accordingly, Hitler denigrated anything that did not conform to that standard—in particular, avant-garde art. Turning his criticism into action, Hitler ordered the confiscation of more than 16,000 artworks he considered "degenerate." To publicize his condemnation of this art, he ordered his minister for public enlightenment and propaganda, Joseph Goebbels (1897–1945), to organize a massive exhibition of this "degenerate art." Hitler designated as degenerate those artworks that "insult German feeling, or destroy or confuse natural form, or simply reveal an absence of adequate manual and artistic skill."* The term *degenerate* also had other specific connotations at the time. The Nazis used it to identify supposedly inferior racial, sexual, and moral types. Hitler's order to Goebbels to target 20th-century avant-garde art for inclusion in the Entartete Kunst exhibition aimed to impress on the public the general inferiority of the artists producing this work. To make that point all the more dramatic, Hitler ordered the organization of another exhibition, the Grosse Deutsche Kunstausstellung (Great German Art Exhibition), which ran concurrently and presented an extensive array of Nazi-approved conservative art.

Entartete Kunst opened in Munich on July 19, 1937, and included more than 650 paintings, sculptures, prints, and books. The exhibition was immensely popular. Roughly 20,000 viewers visited the show daily. By the end of its four-month run, it had attracted more than two million viewers, and nearly a million more viewed it as it traveled through Germany and Austria. Among the 112 artists whose works the Nazis presented for ridicule were Ernst Barlach, Max Beckmann, Otto Dix, Max Ernst, George Grosz, Vassily Kandinsky, Ernst Kirchner, Paul Klee, Wilhelm Lehmbruck, Franz Marc, Emil Nolde, and Kurt Schwitters. In a memorable photograph (FIG. 29-54) taken during Hitler's preview visit to the exhibition on July 16, 1937, the Nazi leader pauses in front of the Dada wall. Behind him are works by Schwitters, Klee, and Kandinsky, which the organizers deliberately hung askew on the wall. (They subsequently straightened them for the duration of the exhibition.)

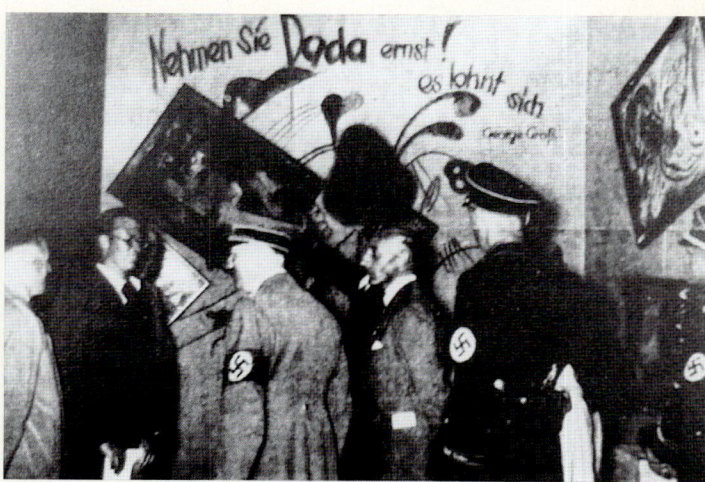

**29-54** Adolf Hitler, accompanied by Nazi commission members, including photographer Heinrich Hoffmann, Wolfgang Willrich, Walter Hansen, and painter Adolf Ziegler, viewing the "Entartete Kunst" show on July 16, 1937.

For Hitler's visit, the curators deliberately hung askew the works of Kandinsky, Klee, and Schwitters. In Nazi Germany, no modernist artist was safe from persecution, and many fled the country.

In Germany in the 1930s and 1940s, in the face of Nazi persecution, artists committed to pursuing avant-garde ideas required courage and a resoluteness that extended beyond issues of aesthetics and beyond the confines of the art world. No modernist artist was safe from Hitler's attack. (Only six of the artists in the exhibition were Jewish.) For example, despite his status as a charter member of the Nazi party, Emil Nolde received particularly harsh treatment. The Nazis confiscated more than 1,000 of Nolde's works from German museums and included 27 of them in the exhibition, more than for almost any other artist. Max Beckmann and his wife fled to Amsterdam on the opening day of the Entartete Kunst exhibit, never to return to their homeland. Ernst Kirchner responded to the stress of Nazi pressure by destroying all his woodblocks and burning many of his works. A year later, in 1938, he committed suicide.

*Stephanie Barron, *"Degenerate Art": The Fate of the Avant-Garde in Nazi Germany* (Los Angeles: Los Angeles County Museum of Art, 1991), 19.

---

Surrealists to public condemnation and, in Germany under Adolf Hitler (1889–1945), to governmental persecution (see "Degenerate Art," above, and FIG. 29-54).

**SALVADOR DALÍ** The Surrealists' exploration of the human psyche and dreams reached new heights in the works of Spanish-born SALVADOR DALÍ (1904–1989). In his paintings, sculptures, jewelry, and designs for furniture and movies, Dalí probed a deeply erotic dimension, studying the writings of Richard von Krafft-Ebing (1840–1902) and Sigmund Freud, and inventing what he called the "paranoiac-critical method" to assist his creative process. As he described it, in his painting he aimed "to materialize the images of concrete irrationality with the most imperialistic fury of precision . . . in order that the world of imagination and of concrete irrationality may be as objectively evident . . . as that of the exterior world of phenomenal reality."[37]

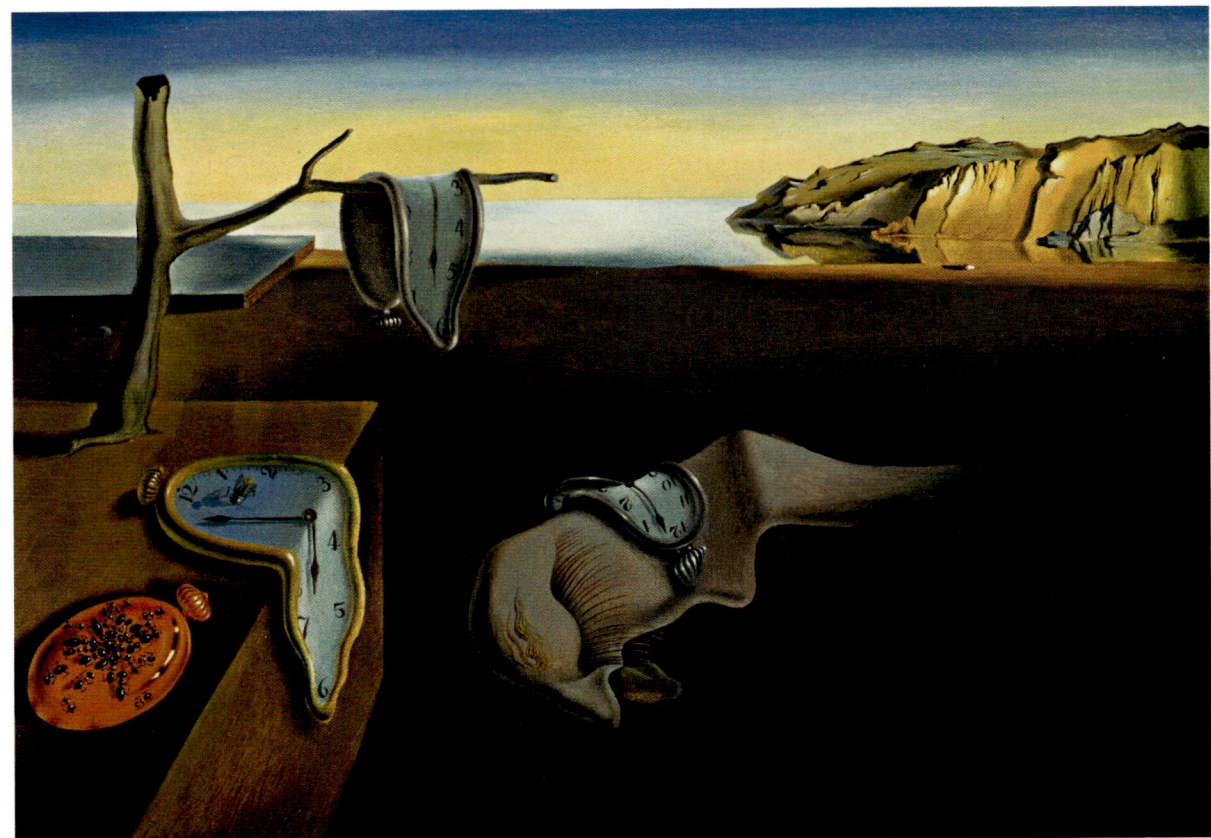

1 in.

In *The Persistence of Memory* (FIG. **29-55**), Dalí created a haunting allegory of empty space where time has ended. An eerie, never-setting sun illuminates the barren landscape. An amorphous creature draped with a limp pocket watch sleeps in the foreground. Another watch hangs from the branch of a dead tree springing unexpectedly from a blocky architectural form. A third watch hangs half over the edge of the rectangular form, beside a small timepiece resting dial-down on the block's surface. Ants swarm mysteriously over the small watch, while a fly walks along the face of its large neighbor, almost as if this assembly of watches were decaying organic life—soft and sticky. Dalí rendered every detail of this dreamscape with precise control, striving to make the world of his paintings convincingly real—in his words, to make the irrational concrete.

**RENÉ MAGRITTE** The Belgian painter RENÉ MAGRITTE (1898–1967) encountered the work of Giorgio de Chirico (FIG. 29-52) in 1922. The Italian artist's disquieting combinations of motifs rendered in a realistic manner deeply impressed the younger Belgian artist, who produced his first Surrealist painting, *The Lost Jockey,* in 1926. The next year Magritte moved to Paris, where he joined the intellectual circle of André Breton and remained in France until 1930. In 1929, Magritte published an important essay in the Surrealist journal *La revolution surréaliste* in which he discussed the disjunction between objects, pictures of objects, and names of objects and pictures. The essay explains the intellectual basis for *The Treachery (or Perfidy) of Images* (FIG. **29-56**), in which Magritte presented a meticulously rendered *trompe l'oeil* depiction of a briar pipe. The caption beneath the image, however, contradicts what seems obvious: "Ceci n'est pas une pipe" ("This is not a pipe"). The discrepancy between image and caption clearly challenges the assumptions underlying the reading of visual art. As is true of the other Surrealists' work, Magritte's paintings for example, *The False Mirror* (FIG. **29-56A**), wreak havoc on the viewer's reliance on the conscious and the rational.

1 ft.

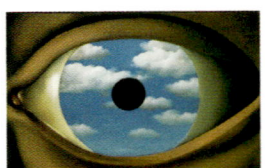

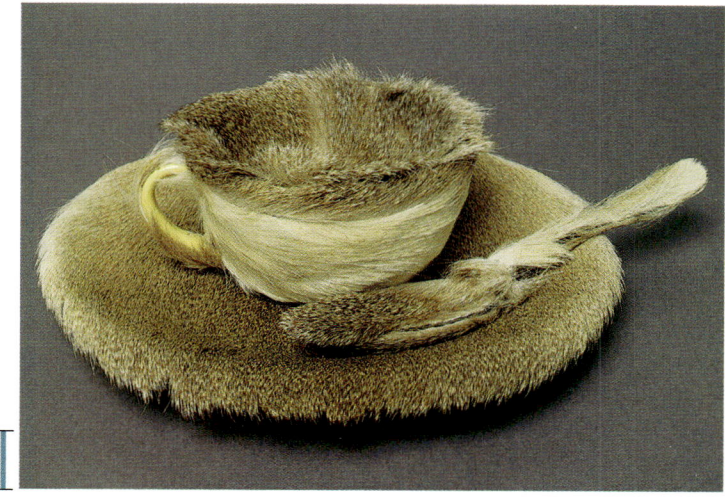

1 in.

**29-57** MERET OPPENHEIM, *Object* (*Le Déjeuner en fourrure*), 1936. Fur-covered cup, 4⅜″ diameter; saucer, 9⅜″ diameter; spoon, 8″ long. Museum of Modern Art, New York.

The Surrealists loved the concrete tangibility of sculpture, which made their art even more disquieting. Oppenheim's functional fur-covered object captures the Surrealist flair for magical transformation.

**MERET OPPENHEIM** Sculpture especially appealed to the Surrealists because its concrete tangibility made their art all the more disquieting. *Object* (FIG. **29-57**), also called *Le Déjeuner en fourrure* (*Luncheon in Fur*), by Swiss artist MERET OPPENHEIM (1913–1985) captures the incongruity, humor, visual appeal, and, often, eroticism characterizing Surrealism. The artist presented a fur-lined teacup inspired by a conversation she had with Picasso.

After admiring a bracelet Oppenheim had made from a piece of brass covered with fur, Picasso noted anything might be covered with fur. When her tea grew cold, Oppenheim responded to Picasso's comment by ordering "un peu plus de fourrure" (a little more fur), and the sculpture had its genesis. *Object* takes on an anthropomorphic quality, animated by the quirky combination of the fur with a functional object. Further, the sculpture captures the Surrealist flair for alchemical, seemingly magical or mystical, transformation. It incorporates a sensuality and eroticism (seen here in the seductively soft, tactile fur lining the concave form) that are also components of much of Surrealist art.

**JOAN MIRÓ** Like the Dadaists, the Surrealists used many methods to free the creative process from reliance on the kind of conscious control they believed society had shaped too much. Dalí used his paranoiac-critical approach to encourage the free play of association as he worked. Other Surrealists used automatism and various types of planned "accidents" to provoke reactions closely related to subconscious experience. Dalí's older countryman JOAN MIRÓ (1893–1983) was a master of this approach. Although Miró resisted formal association with any movement or group, including the Surrealists, André Breton identified him as "the most Surrealist of us all."[38] From the beginning, Miró's work contained an element of fantasy and hallucination. After Surrealist poets in Paris introduced him to the use of chance in the creation of art, the young Spaniard devised a new painting method that enabled him to create works such as *Painting* (FIG. **29-58**). Miró began this painting by making a scattered collage composition with assembled fragments cut from a catalog for machinery. The shapes in the collage became motifs the artist freely reshaped on the canvas to create black silhouettes—solid or in outline, with dramatic accents of white and vermilion. They suggest, in the painting, a host of amoebic organisms or constellations in outer space floating in an immaterial background space filled with soft reds, blues, and greens.

Miró described his creative process as a switching back and forth between unconscious and conscious image-making: "Rather than setting out to paint something, I begin painting and as I paint the picture begins to assert itself, or suggest itself under my brush. The form becomes a sign for a woman or a bird as I work. . . . The first stage is free, unconscious. . . . The second stage is carefully calculated."[39] Even the artist could not always explain the meanings of pictures such as *Painting*. They are, in the truest sense, spontaneous and intuitive expressions of the little-understood, submerged unconscious part of life.

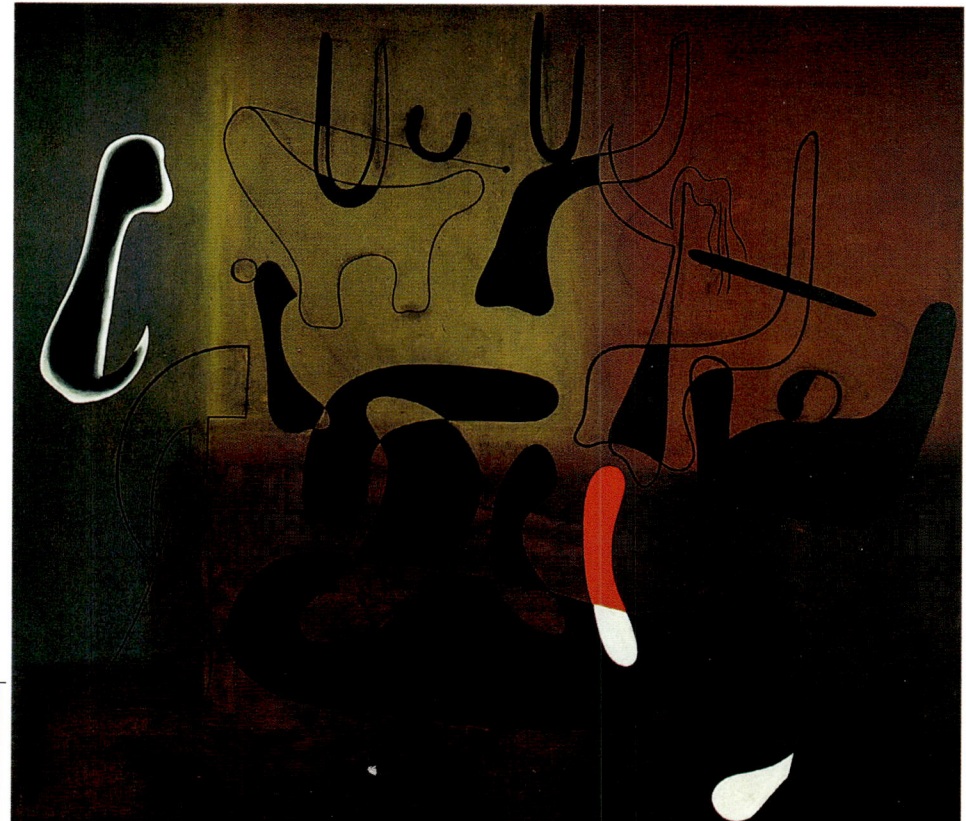

1 ft.

**29-58** JOAN MIRÓ, *Painting,* 1933. Oil on canvas, 5′ 8″ × 6′ 5″. Museum of Modern Art, New York (Loula D. Lasker bequest by exchange). ◼◂

Miró promoted automatism, the creation of art without conscious control. He began this painting with a scattered collage and then added forms suggesting floating amoebic organisms.

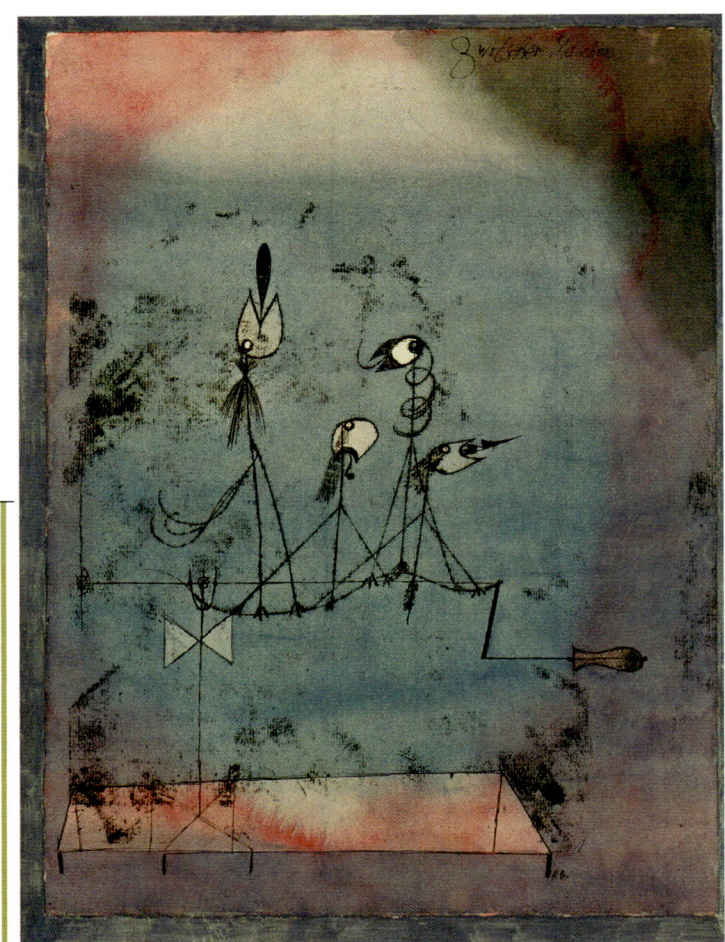

**29-59** PAUL KLEE, *Twittering Machine,* 1922. Watercolor and pen and ink, on oil transfer drawing on paper, mounted on cardboard, 2′ 1″ × 1′ 7″. Museum of Modern Art, New York. ▪◀

Although based on forms in the tangible world easily read as birds, Klee's *Twittering Machine* is a fanciful vision of a mysterious world presented in a simplified, almost childlike manner.

**PAUL KLEE** Perhaps the most inventive artist using fantasy images to represent the nonvisible world was the Swiss-German painter PAUL KLEE (1879–1940). Like Miró, he shunned formal association with groups such as the Dadaists and Surrealists but pursued their interest in the subconscious. Klee sought clues to humanity's deeper nature in primitive shapes and symbols. Like Jung, Klee seems to have accepted the existence of a collective unconscious that reveals itself in archaic signs and patterns and is everywhere evident in the art of "primitive" cultures (see "Primitivism," page 846). The son of a professional musician and himself an accomplished violinist, Klee thought of painting as similar to music in its ability to express feelings through color, form, and line. In 1920, Klee set down his "creative credo," which reads in part:

> Art does not reproduce the visible; rather it makes visible. . . . The formal elements of graphic art are dot, line, plane, and space—the last three charged with energy of various kinds. . . . Formerly we used to represent things visible on earth, things we either liked to look at or would have liked to see. Today we reveal the reality that is behind visible things.[40]

To penetrate the reality behind visible things, Klee studied nature avidly, taking special interest in analyzing processes of growth and change. He coded these studies in diagrammatic form

in notebooks. The root of his work was thus nature, but nature filtered through his mind. Upon starting an image, he would allow the pencil or brush to lead him until an image emerged, to which he would then respond to complete the idea.

*Twittering Machine* (FIG. **29-59**) reveals Klee's fanciful vision. The painting, although based on forms in the tangible world easily read as birds, is far from illusionistic. Klee presented the scene in a simplified, almost childlike manner, imbuing the work with a poetic lyricism. The inclusion of a crank-driven mechanism added a touch of whimsy. The small size of Klee's works enhances their impact. A viewer must draw near to decipher the delicately rendered forms and enter his mysterious dream world. Perhaps no other artist of the 20th century matched Klee's subtlety as he deftly created a world of ambiguity and understatement that draws each viewer into finding a unique interpretation of the work.

Also associated with the Surrealists was WIFREDO LAM (1902–1982), a Cuban painter who studied in Madrid and Paris and whose work (FIG. **29-59A**) was greatly influenced by Picasso. It was Picasso who introduced Lam to Braque, Breton, and other avant-garde artists and critics.

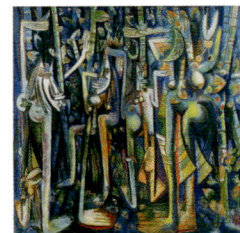

**29-59A** LAM, *The Jungle,* 1943.

## De Stijl

The utopian spirit and ideals of the Suprematists and Constructivists (FIGS. 29-30 and 29-31) in Russia were shared in western Europe by a group of young Dutch artists. They formed a new movement in 1917 and began publishing a magazine, calling both movement and magazine *De Stijl* (*The Style*). The group's cofounders were the painters Piet Mondrian (FIG. 29-60) and Theo van Doesburg (1883–1931). In addition to promoting utopian ideals, De Stijl artists believed in the birth of a new age in the wake of World War I. They felt it was a time of balance between individual and universal values, when the machine would assure ease of living. In their first manifesto of De Stijl, the artists declared: "There is an old and a new consciousness of time. The old is connected with the individual. The new is connected with the universal."[41] The goal, according to van Doesburg and architect Cor van Eesteren (1897–1988), was a total integration of art and life:

> We must realize that life and art are no longer separate domains. That is why the "idea" of "art" as an illusion separate from real life must disappear. The word "Art" no longer means anything to us. In its place we demand the construction of our environment in accordance with creative laws based upon a fixed principle. These laws, following those of economics, mathematics, technique, sanitation, etc., are leading to a new, plastic unity.[42]

**PIET MONDRIAN** Toward this goal of integration, PIET MONDRIAN (1872–1944) created a new style based on a single ideal principle. The choice of the term *De Stijl* reflected Mondrian's confidence that this style—*the* style—revealed the underlying eternal structure of existence. Accordingly, De Stijl artists reduced their artistic vocabulary to simple geometric elements. Time spent in Paris, just before World War I, introduced Mondrian to Cubism and other modes of abstraction. However, as his attraction to theological writings grew, Mondrian sought to purge his art of every overt reference to individual objects in the external world. He initially favored the teachings of theosophy, a tradition basing knowledge of nature and the human condition on knowledge of the divine nature or spiritual powers. (His fellow theosophist Vassily Kandinsky pursued a similar path.) Mondrian, however, quickly abandoned the strictures of

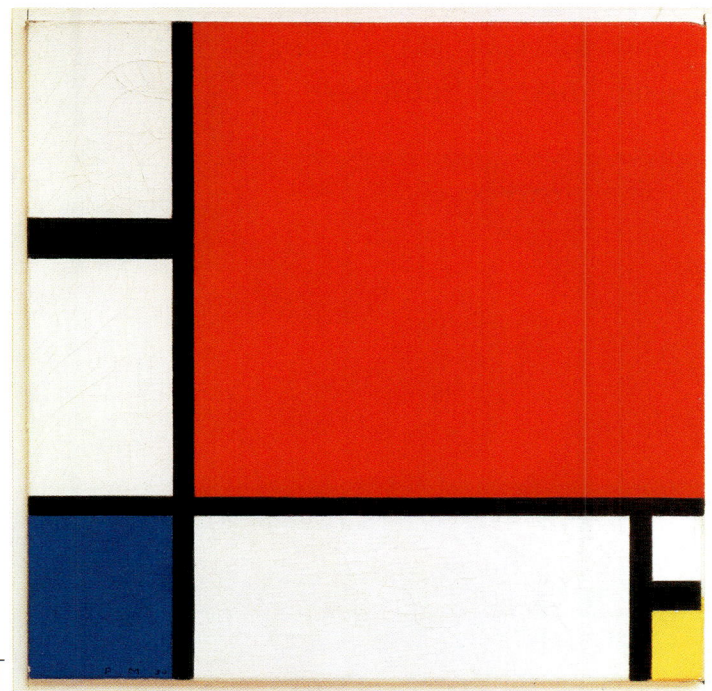

**29-60** PIET MONDRIAN, *Composition with Red, Blue, and Yellow*, 1930. Oil on canvas, 1′ 6⅛″ × 1′ 6⅛″. Kunsthaus, Zürich. © Mondrian/Holtzman Trust c/o HCR International, VA, USA. ◼◀

Mondrian's "pure plastic" paintings consist of primary colors locked into a grid of intersecting vertical and horizontal lines. By altering the grid patterns, he created a dynamic tension.

theosophy and turned toward a conception of nonobjective design—"pure plastic art"—that he believed expressed universal reality. He articulated his credo with great eloquence in 1914:

> What first captivated us does not captivate us afterward (like toys). If one has loved the surface of things for a long time, later on one will look for something more. . . . The interior of things shows through the surface; thus as we look at the surface the inner image is formed in our soul. It is this inner image that should be represented. For the natural surface of things is beautiful, but the imitation of it is without life. . . . Art is higher than reality and has no direct relation to reality. . . . To approach the spiritual in art, one will make as little use as possible of reality, because reality is opposed to the spiritual. . . . [W]e find ourselves in the presence of an abstract art. Art should be above reality, otherwise it would have no value for man.[43]

Mondrian soon moved beyond Cubism because he felt "Cubism did not accept the logical consequences of its own discoveries; it was not developing towards its own goal, the expression of pure plastics."[44] Caught by the outbreak of hostilities while on a visit to Holland, Mondrian remained there during World War I, developing his theories for what he called *Neoplasticism*—the new "pure plastic art." He believed all great art had polar but coexistent goals, the attempt to create "universal beauty" and the desire for "aesthetic expression of oneself."[45] The first goal is objective in nature, whereas the second is subjective, existing within the individual's mind and heart. To create a universal expression, an artist must communicate "a real equation of the universal and the individual."[46]

To express this vision, Mondrian eventually limited his formal vocabulary to the three primary colors (red, yellow, and blue), the three primary values (black, white, and gray), and the two primary directions (horizontal and vertical). Basing his ideas on a combination of teachings, he concluded primary colors and values are the

purest colors and therefore are the perfect tools to help an artist construct a harmonious composition. Using this system, he created numerous paintings locking color planes into a grid of intersecting vertical and horizontal lines, as in *Composition with Red, Blue, and Yellow* (FIG. **29-60**). In each of these paintings, Mondrian altered the grid patterns and the size and placement of the color planes to create an internal cohesion and harmony. This did not mean inertia. Rather, Mondrian worked to maintain a dynamic tension in his paintings from the size and position of lines, shapes, and colors.

## Sculpture

It was impossible for early-20th-century artists to ignore the increasingly intrusive expansion of mechanization and growth of technology. However, not all artists embraced these developments, as had the Futurists. In contrast, many artists attempted to overcome the predominance of mechanization in society by immersing themselves in a search for the organic and natural.

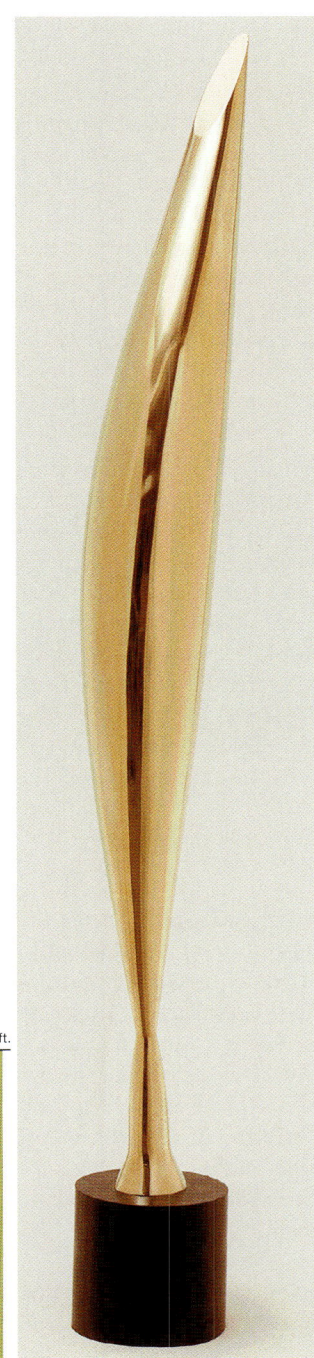

1 ft.

**CONSTANTIN BRANCUSI** One artist who was eager to produce works emphasizing the natural or organic was Romanian sculptor CONSTANTIN BRANCUSI (1876–1957). Brancusi sought to move beyond surface appearances to capture the essence or spirit of the object depicted (see "Brancusi, Hepworth, and Moore on Abstract Sculpture," page 882) in rhythmic, elegant sculptures. The softly curving surfaces and ovoid form of his sculptures refer, directly or indirectly, to the cycle of life. *Bird in Space* (FIG. **29-61**) is not a literal depiction of a bird, nor does his *Newborn* (FIG. **29-61A**) mimic a real baby's head. The abstract form of both works is the final result of a long process. For *Bird in Space,* Brancusi started with the image of a bird at rest with its wings folded at its sides and ended with a gently

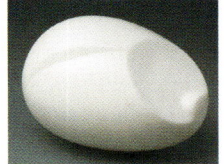

**29-61A** BRANCUSI, *The Newborn,* 1915.

**29-61** CONSTANTIN BRANCUSI, *Bird in Space,* 1924. Bronze, 4′ 2 5/16″ high. Philadelphia Museum of Art, Philadelphia (Louise and Walter Arensberg Collection, 1950). ◼◀

Although not a literal depiction of a bird, Brancusi's softly curving light-reflecting abstract sculpture in polished bronze suggests a bird about to soar in free flight through the heavens.

## Brancusi, Hepworth, and Moore on Abstract Sculpture

Many early-20th-century sculptors rejected the notion that reproducing the physical world of nature was the purpose of sculpture. Instead, they championed abstraction as the sculptor's proper goal. Among those who not only produced enduring masterpieces of abstract sculpture but also wrote eloquently about the theoretical basis of their work were Constantin Brancusi (FIG. 29-61), Barbara Hepworth (FIG. 29-62), and Henry Moore (FIG. 29-63). Some excerpts from their writings on sculpture illustrate their commitment to abstraction as their guiding principle.

**Constantin Brancusi** Simplicity is not an objective in art, but one achieves simplicity despite oneself by entering into the real sense of things.* . . . What is real is not the external form but the essence of things. Starting from this truth it is impossible for anyone to express anything essentially real by imitating its exterior surface.†

**Barbara Hepworth** The forms which have had special meaning for me since childhood have been the standing form (which is the translation of my feeling towards the human being standing in landscape); the two forms (which is the tender relationship of one living thing beside another); and the closed form, such as the oval, spherical, or pierced form (sometimes incorporating colour) which translates for me the association and meaning of gesture in the landscape. . . . In all these shapes the translation of what one feels about man and nature must be conveyed by the sculptor in terms of mass, inner tension, and rhythm, scale in relation to our human size, and the quality of surface which speaks through our hands and eyes.‡

**Henry Moore** Since the Gothic, European sculpture had become overgrown with moss, weeds—all sorts of surface excrescences which completely concealed shape. It has been Brancusi's special mission to get rid of this overgrowth, and to make us once more shape-conscious. To do this he has had to concentrate on very simple direct shapes . . . Abstract qualities of design are essential to the value of a work . . . Because a work does not aim at reproducing natural appearances, it is not, therefore, an escape from life—but may be a penetration into reality. . . . My sculpture is becoming less representational, less an outward visual copy . . . but only because I believe that in this way I can present the

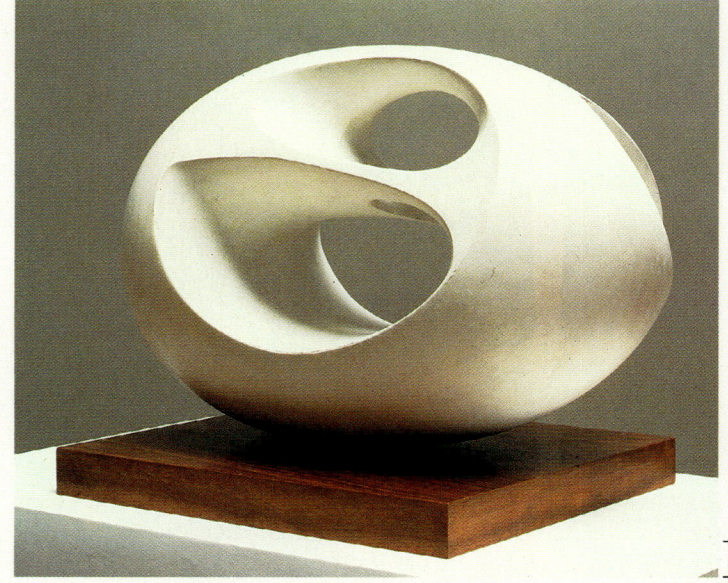

**29-62** BARBARA HEPWORTH, *Oval Sculpture* (*No. 2*), 1943, cast 1958, plaster, $11\frac{1}{4}''$ × 1' $4\frac{1}{4}''$ × 10″. Tate.

Hepworth's major contribution to the history of sculpture was the introduction of the hole, or negative space, as an abstract element that is as integral and important to the sculpture as its mass.

human psychological content of my work with greatest directness and intensity.§

*Quoted in Herschel B. Chipp, *Theories of Modern Art: A Source Book by Artists and Critics* (Berkeley and Los Angeles: University of California Press, 1968), 364–365.
†Quoted in George Heard Hamilton, *Painting and Sculpture in Europe, 1880–1940,* 6th ed. (New Haven, Conn.: Yale University Press, 1993), 426.
‡Barbara Hepworth, *A Pictorial Autobiography* (London: Tate Gallery, 1978), 9, 53.
§Quoted in Robert L. Herbert, *Modern Artists on Art,* 2d ed. (Mineola, N.Y.: Dover, 2000), 173–179.

curving columnar form sharply tapered at each end. Despite the abstraction, the sculpture retains the suggestion of a bird about to soar in free flight through the heavens. The highly reflective surface of the polished bronze does not allow the viewer's eye to linger on the sculpture itself (as do, for example, Rodin's agitated and textured surfaces; FIGS. 28-32, 28-32A, and 28-33). Instead, the eye follows the gleaming reflection along the delicate curves right off the tip of the work, thereby inducing a feeling of flight. Brancusi stated, "All my life I have sought the essence of flight. Don't look for mysteries. I give you pure joy. Look at the sculptures until you see them. Those nearest to God have seen them."[47]

**BARBARA HEPWORTH** In England, BARBARA HEPWORTH (1903–1975) developed her own kind of essential sculptural form,

combining pristine shape with a sense of organic vitality. She sought a sculptural idiom that would express her sense both of nature and the landscape and of the person who is in and observes nature (see "Brancusi, Hepworth, and Moore," above). By 1929, Hepworth arrived at a breakthrough that evolved into an enduring and commanding element in her work from that point on. It represents her major contribution to the history of sculpture: the use of the hole, or void. Earlier sculptors, such as Archipenko (FIG. 29-20) had experimented with sculptural voids, but Hepworth introduced holes in her sculptures as abstract elements. The holes do not represent anything specific. They are simply negative space, but are as integral and important to the sculptures as their mass. *Oval Sculpture* (*No. 2*) is a plaster cast (FIG. **29-62**) of an earlier wood sculpture Hepworth carved in 1943. Pierced in four places, the work is as

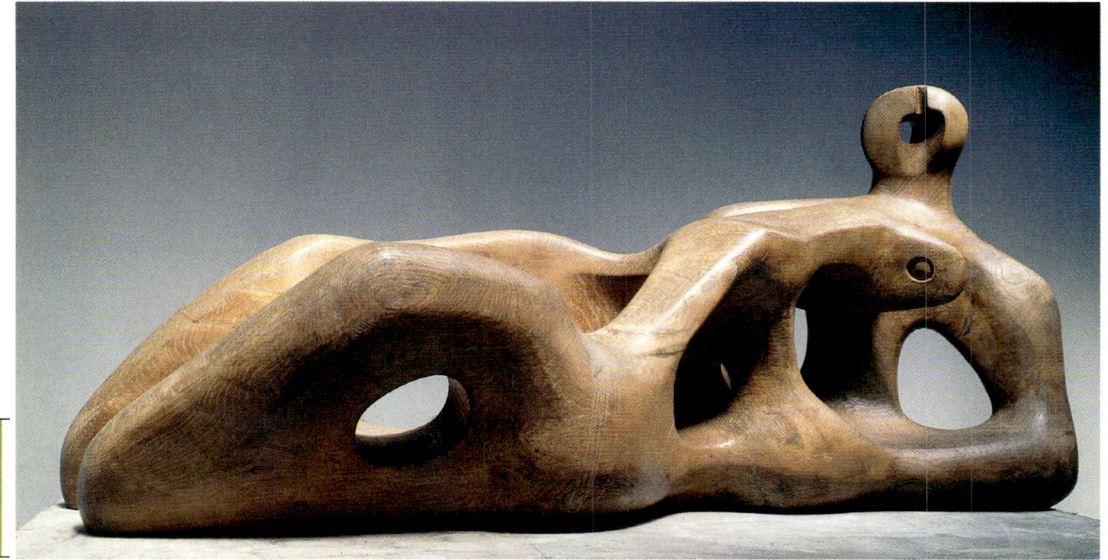

1 ft.

The reclining female figure was a major theme in Moore's sculptures. Inspired by a Mexican chacmool, he simplified and abstracted the body form in a way that recalls Biomorphic Surrealism.

much defined by the smooth, curving holes as by the volume of white plaster. Like the forms in all of Hepworth's mature works, those in *Oval Sculpture* are basic and universal, expressing a sense of eternity's timelessness.

**HENRY MOORE** Fellow Briton Henry Moore (1898–1986) shared Hepworth's interest in the hole, or void, as an important element in sculptural design, but his sculptures, such as *Reclining Figure* (FIG. **29-63**), although abstracted, always remain recognizable. This statue is one of a long series of reclining female nudes inspired originally by a photograph Moore acquired of a *chacmool* (FIG. 18-17) from pre-Columbian Mexico. Moore believed the simple and massive shapes of his statues expressed a universal truth beyond the physical world (see "Brancusi, Hepworth, and Moore," page 882).

*Reclining Figure* is also characteristic of Moore's work in exploiting the natural beauty of different materials—here, elm. Moore maintained every "material has its own individual qualities" and these qualities could play a role in the creative process: "It is only when the sculptor works direct, when there is an active relationship with his material, that the material can take its part in the shaping of an idea."[48] Accordingly, the contours of *Reclining Figure* follow the grain of the wood. The abstracted shapes suggest Surrealist biomorphic forms (FIG. 29-58), but Moore's recumbent woman is also a powerful earth mother whose undulant forms and hollows suggest nurturing human energy. Similarly, the body shapes evoke the contours of the Yorkshire hills of Moore's childhood and the wind-polished surfaces of weathered wood and stone. Moore heightened the allusions to landscape and to Surrealist organic forms in his work by interplaying mass and void, based on the intriguing qualities of cavities in nature. For Moore, the hole was not an abstract shape. It represented "the mysterious fascination of caves in hillsides and cliffs."[49] *Reclining Figure* combines the organic vocabulary central to Moore's philosophy—bone shapes, eroded rocks, and geologic formations—to communicate the human form's fluidity, dynamism, and evocative nature.

**VERA MUKHINA** Not all European sculptors of this period pursued abstraction, however. *The Worker and the Collective Farm Worker* (FIG. **29-64**) by Russian artist Vera Mukhina (1889–1963) presents a vivid contrast with the work of Brancusi, Hepworth, and Moore. Produced in 1937 for the International Exposition

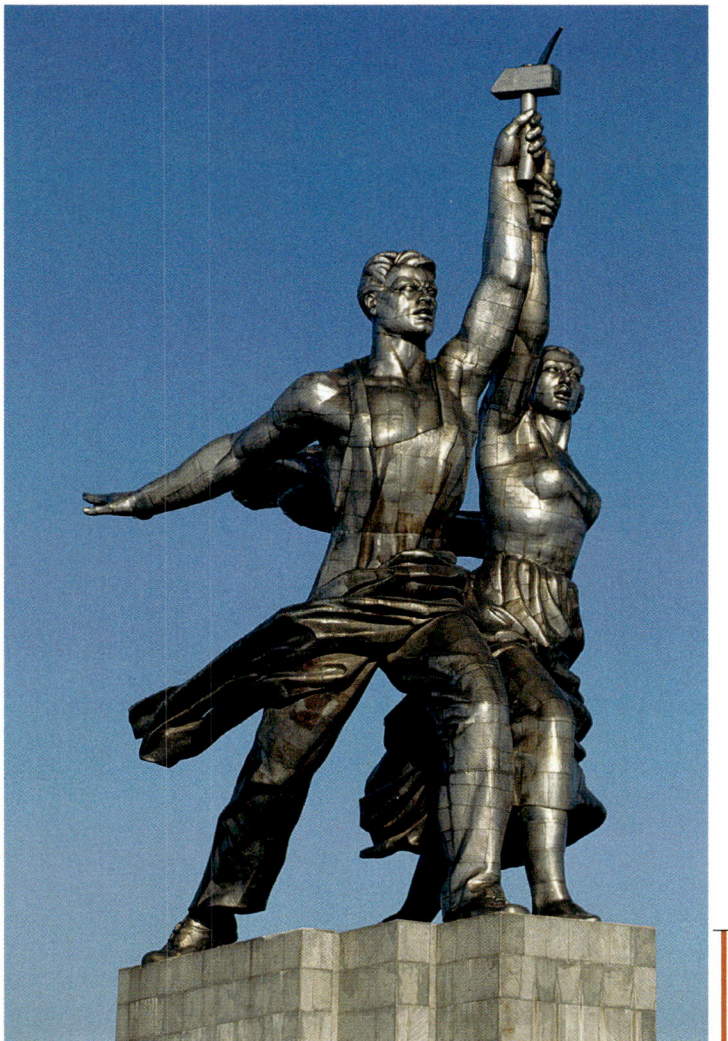

10 ft.

**29-64** Vera Mukhina, *The Worker and the Collective Farm Worker*, Soviet Pavilion, Paris Exposition, 1937. Stainless steel, 78′ high. © Estate of Vera Mukhina/RAO, Moscow/VAGA, New York.

In contrast to contemporaneous abstract sculpture, Mukhina's realistic representation of a male factory worker and a female farm worker glorified the communal labor of the Soviet people.

in Paris—the same venue in which Picasso displayed *Guernica* (FIG. 29-18)—Mukhina's monumental stainless-steel sculpture glorifies the communal labor of the Soviet people. Whereas Picasso employed Cubist abstraction to convey the horror of wartime bombing, Mukhina relied on realism to represent exemplars of the Soviet citizenry. Her sculpture, which stood on the top of the Soviet Pavilion at the exposition, depicts a male factory worker, holding aloft the tool of his trade, the hammer. Alongside him is a female farm worker, raising her sickle to the sky. The juxtaposed hammer and sickle at the apex of the sculpture replicate their appearance on the Soviet flag. Mukhina augmented the heroic tenor of the work by emphasizing the solidity of the figures, who stride forward with their clothes blowing dramatically behind them. Mukhina had studied in Paris and was familiar with abstraction, especially Cubism, but felt a commitment to realism produced the most powerful sculpture. The Soviet government officially approved this realist style and Mukhina earned high praise for her sculpture. Indeed, Russian citizens celebrated the work as a national symbol for decades.

## Architecture

As in the opening decades of the century, developments in European architecture after World War I closely paralleled the stylistic and theoretical concerns of painters and sculptors.

**GERRIT THOMAS RIETVELD**  The ideas Piet Mondrian, Theo van Doesburg, and De Stijl artists advanced found their architectural equivalent in the designs of GERRIT THOMAS RIETVELD (1888–1964). His Schröder House (FIG. **29-65**) in Utrecht, built in 1924, perfectly expresses van Doesburg's definition of De Stijl architecture:

> The new architecture is anti-cubic, i.e., it does not strive to contain the different functional space cells in a single closed cube, but it throws the functional space (as well as canopy planes, balcony volumes, etc.) out from the centre of the cube, so that height, width, and depth plus time become a completely new plastic expression in open spaces. . . . The plastic architect . . . has to construct in the new field, time-space.[50]

The main living rooms of the Schröder House are on the second floor, with more private rooms on the ground floor. However, Rietveld's house has an open plan and a relationship to nature more like the houses of American architect Frank Lloyd Wright (FIGS. 29-45 and 29-46). Rietveld designed the entire second floor with sliding partitions that can be closed to define separate rooms or pushed back to create one open space broken into units only by the furniture arrangement. This shifting quality appears also on the outside, where railings, free-floating walls, and long rectangular windows give the effect of cubic units breaking up before the viewer's eyes. Rectangular planes seem to slide across each other on the Schröder House facade like movable panels, making this structure a kind of three-dimensional projection of the rigid but carefully proportioned flat color rectangles in Mondrian's paintings (FIG. 29-60).

**WALTER GROPIUS**  De Stijl architects not only developed an appealing simplified geometric style but also promoted the notion art should be thoroughly incorporated into living environments. As Mondrian had insisted, "[A]rt and life are *one;* art and life are both expressions of truth."[51] In Germany, WALTER GROPIUS (1883–1969) developed a particular vision of "total architecture." He made this concept the foundation of not only his own work but also the work of generations of pupils under his influence at a school called the *Bauhaus* (see "Walter Gropius and the Bauhaus," page 885).

The building Gropius designed for the Bauhaus in 1925 after the school relocated to Dessau was the Bauhaus's architectural manifesto. The Dessau Bauhaus consisted of workshop and class areas, a dining room, a theater, a gymnasium, a wing with studio apartments, and an enclosed two-story bridge housing administrative offices. Of the major wings, the most dramatic was the Shop Block (FIG. **29-66**). Three stories tall, the Shop Block housed a printing shop and dye works facility, in addition to other work areas. The builders constructed the skeleton of reinforced concrete but set these supports well back, sheathing the entire structure in glass, creating a streamlined and light effect. This design's simplicity followed Gropius's dictum that architecture should avoid "all romantic embellishment and whimsy." Further, he realized the "economy in the use of space" articulated in his list of Bauhaus principles in his interior layout of the Shop Block, which consisted of large areas of free-flowing undivided space. Gropius believed this kind of spatial organization encouraged interaction and the sharing of ideas.

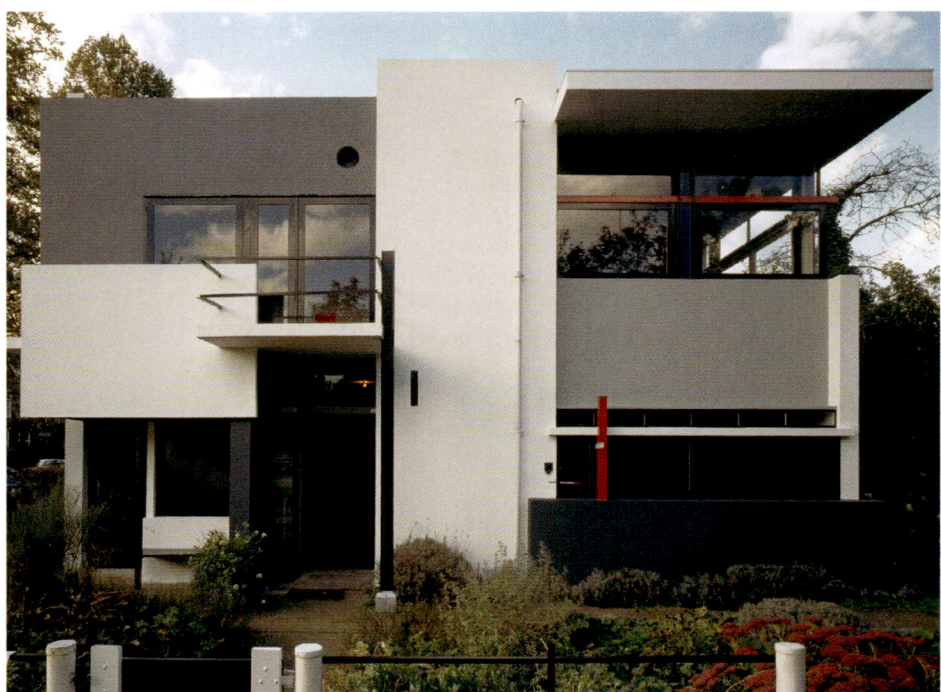

**29-65**  GERRIT THOMAS RIETVELD, Schröder House (looking northwest), Utrecht, the Netherlands, 1924.

The De Stijl Schröder House has an open plan and an exterior that is a kind of three-dimensional projection of the carefully proportioned flat color rectangles in Mondrian's paintings (FIG. 29-60).

## Walter Gropius and the Bauhaus

In 1919, Walter Gropius became the director of the Weimar School of Arts and Crafts in Germany, founded in 1906. Under Gropius, the school assumed a new name—Das Staatliche Bauhaus (State School of Building). Gropius's goal was to train artists, architects, and designers to accept and anticipate 20th-century needs. He developed an extensive curriculum based on certain principles set forth in a formal Bauhaus *Manifesto* published in April 1919.

### BAUHAUS MANIFESTO

The first principle Gropius staunchly advocated in the 1919 manifesto was the importance of strong basic design (including principles of composition, two- and three-dimensionality, and color theory) and craftsmanship as fundamental to good art and architecture. He asserted there was no essential difference between the artist and the craftsperson.

> The Bauhaus strives to coordinate all creative effort, to achieve, in a new architecture, the unification of all training in art and design. The ultimate, if distant, goal of the Bauhaus is the collective work of art—the Building—in which no barriers exist between the structural and the decorative arts.*

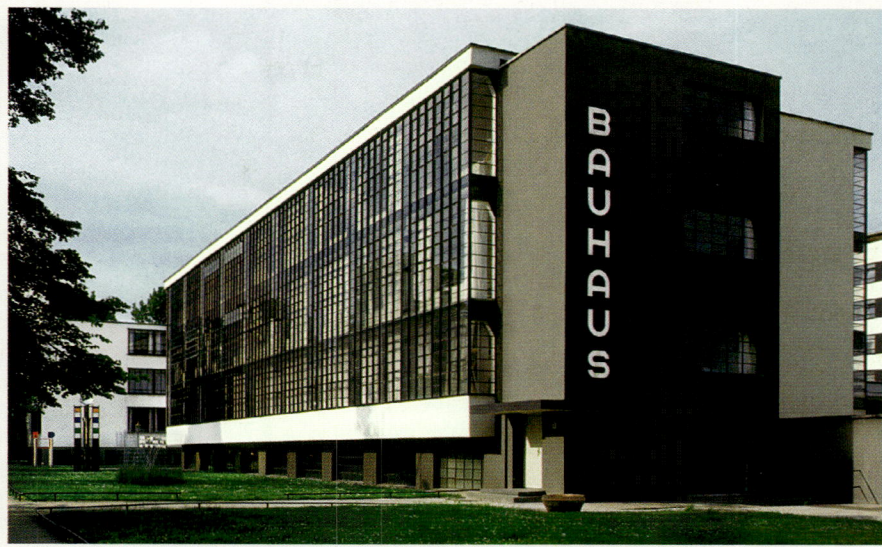

**29-66** WALTER GROPIUS, Shop Block (looking northeast), the Bauhaus, Dessau, Germany, 1925–1926.

Gropius constructed this Bauhaus building by sheathing a reinforced concrete skeleton in glass. The design followed his dictum that architecture should avoid "all romantic embellishment and whimsy."

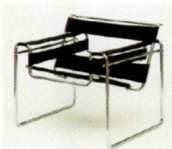

**29-66A** BREUER, Wassily chair, 1925.

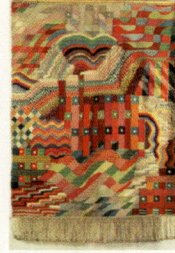

**29-66B** STÖLZL, Gobelin tapestry, 1927–1928.

To encourage the elimination of those boundaries that traditionally separated art from architecture and art from craft, the Bauhaus offered courses in a wide range of artistic disciplines. These included carpentry, furniture design (by MARCEL BREUER [1902–1981]; FIG. **29-66A**), weaving (by GUNTA STÖLZL [1897–1983]; FIG. **29-66B**), pottery, bookbinding, metalwork, stained glass, mural painting, stage design, and advertising and typography, in addition to painting, sculpture, and architecture. Both a technical instructor and a "teacher of form"—an artist—taught in each department. Among the teachers Gropius hired were Vassily Kandinsky (FIG. 29-7) and Paul Klee (FIG. 29-59).

In addition, because Gropius wanted the Bauhaus to produce graduates who could design progressive environments that satisfied 20th-century needs, he emphasized thorough knowledge of machine-age technologies and materials. He felt that to produce truly successful designs, the artist-architect-craftsperson had to understand industry and mass production. Ultimately, Gropius hoped for a marriage between art and industry—a synthesis of design and production. As did the De Stijl movement, the Bauhaus philosophy had its roots in utopian principles. Gropius's declaration reveals the idealism of the entire Bauhaus enterprise:

> Let us collectively desire, conceive, and create the new building of the future, which will be everything in one structure: architecture and sculpture and painting, which, from the million hands of craftsmen, will one day rise towards heaven as the crystalline symbol of a new and coming faith.†

In its reference to a unity of workers, this statement also reveals the undercurrent of socialism present in Germany at the time.

### BAUHAUS IN DESSAU

After encountering increasing hostility from a new government elected in 1924, the Bauhaus moved north from Weimar to Dessau (FIG. 29-66) in early 1925. By this time, the Bauhaus program had matured. In a new statement, Gropius listed the school's goals more clearly:

- A decidedly positive attitude to the living environment of vehicles and machines
- The organic shaping of things in accordance with their own current laws, avoiding all romantic embellishment and whimsy
- Restriction of basic forms and colors to what is typical and universally intelligible
- Simplicity in complexity, economy in the use of space, materials, time, and money‡

*Quoted in Charles Harrison and Paul Wood, eds., *Art in Theory, 1900–2000: An Anthology of Changing Ideas,* 2d ed. (Oxford: Blackwell, 2003), 311.
†Translated by Charles W. Haxthausen, in Barry Bergdoll, ed., *Bauhaus 1919–1933* (New York: Museum of Modern Art, 2009), 64.
‡Quoted in John Willett, *Art and Politics in the Weimar Period: The New Sobriety, 1917–1933* (New York: Da Capo Press, 1978), 119.

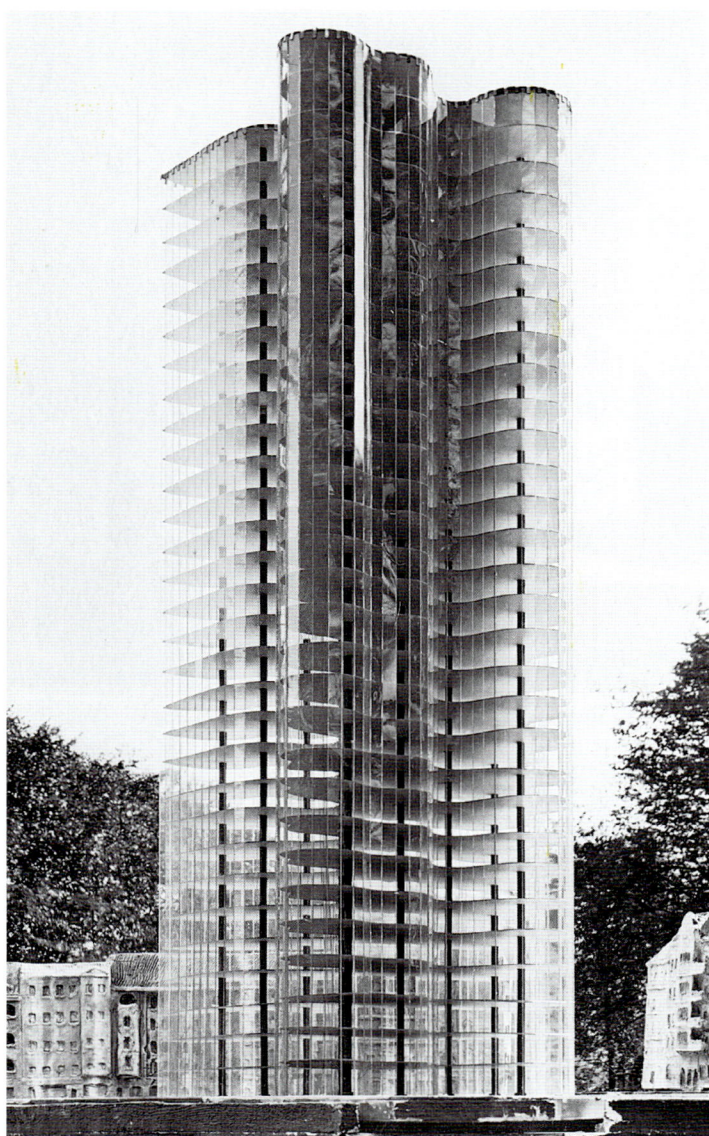

**29-67** LUDWIG MIES VAN DER ROHE, model for a glass skyscraper, Berlin, Germany, 1922 (no longer extant).

In this technically and aesthetically adventurous design, the architect whose motto was "less is more" proposed a transparent building that revealed its cantilevered floor planes and thin supports.

**LUDWIG MIES VAN DER ROHE** In 1928, Gropius left the Bauhaus, and LUDWIG MIES VAN DER ROHE (1886–1969) eventually took over the directorship, moving the school to Berlin. Taking as his motto "less is more" and calling his architecture "skin and bones," the new Bauhaus director had already fully formed his aesthetic when he conceived the model (FIG. **29-67**) for a glass skyscraper building in 1921. In the glass model, which was on display at the first Bauhaus exhibition in 1923, three irregularly shaped towers flow outward from a central court designed to hold a lobby, a porter's room, and a community center. Two cylindrical entrance shafts rise at the ends of the court, each containing elevators, stairways, and toilets. Wholly transparent, the perimeter walls reveal the regular horizontal patterning of the cantilevered floor planes and their thin vertical supporting elements. The bold use of glass sheathing and inset supports was, at the time, technically and aesthetically adventurous. The weblike delicacy of the lines of the

model, as well as the illusion of movement created by reflection and by light changes seen through the glass, appealed to many other architects. A few years later, Gropius pursued it in his design for the Bauhaus building (FIG. 29-66) in Dessau. The legacy of Mies van der Rohe's design can be seen in the glass-and-steel skyscrapers found in major cities throughout the world today.

**END OF THE BAUHAUS** One of Hitler's first acts after coming to power was to close the Bauhaus in 1933. During its 14-year existence, the beleaguered school graduated fewer than 500 students, yet it achieved legendary status. Its phenomenal influence extended beyond painting, sculpture, and architecture to interior design, graphic design, and advertising. Moreover, art schools everywhere began to structure their curricula in line with the program the Bauhaus pioneered. The numerous Bauhaus instructors who fled Nazi Germany disseminated the school's philosophy and aesthetic. Many Bauhaus members came to the United States. Gropius and Breuer (FIG. 29-66A) ended up at Harvard University. Mies van der Rohe moved to Chicago and taught there.

**LE CORBUSIER** The simple geometric aesthetic developed by Gropius and Mies van der Rohe became known as the *International style* because of its widespread popularity. The first and purest exponent of this style was the Swiss architect Charles-Edouard Jeanneret, who adopted his maternal grandfather's name— LE CORBUSIER (1887–1965). Trained in Paris and Berlin, he was also a painter, but Le Corbusier had the greatest influence as an architect and theorist on modern architecture. As such, he applied himself to designing a functional living space, which he described as a "machine for living."[52]

Le Corbusier maintained the basic physical and psychological needs of every human being were sun, space, and vegetation combined with controlled temperature, good ventilation, and insulation against harmful and undesired noise. He also advocated basing dwelling designs on human scale, because the house is humankind's assertion within nature. All these qualities characterize Le Corbusier's Villa Savoye (FIG. **29-68**), located at Poissy-sur-Seine near Paris. The country house sits at the center of a large plot of land cleared of trees and shrubs, but windows on all sides and the villa's roof-terrace provide the residents with broad views of the surrounding landscape. Several colors appear on the exterior—originally, a dark-green base, cream walls, and a rose-and-blue windscreen on top. They were a deliberate analogy for the colors in the machine-inspired Purist style of painting (FIG. 29-22) Le Corbusier practiced.

A cube of lightly enclosed and deeply penetrated space, the Villa Savoye has only a partially confined ground floor (containing, originally, a three-car garage, bedrooms, a bathroom, and utility rooms, and today a ticket counter and small gift shop for visitors). Much of the house's interior is open space, with thin columns supporting the main living floor and the roof garden area. The major living rooms in the Villa Savoye are on the second floor, wrapping around an open central court. Strip windows running along the membranelike exterior walls provide illumination to the rooms as well as views out to nature. From the second floor court, a ramp leads up to the roof-terrace and an interior garden protected by a curving windbreak along the north side.

The Villa Savoye has no traditional facade. The ostensible approach to the house does not define an entrance. Visitors must walk around and through the house to comprehend its layout, which incorporates several changes of direction and spiral staircases. Spaces and masses interpenetrate so fluidly that inside and outside space intermingle. The machine-planed smoothness of the unadorned

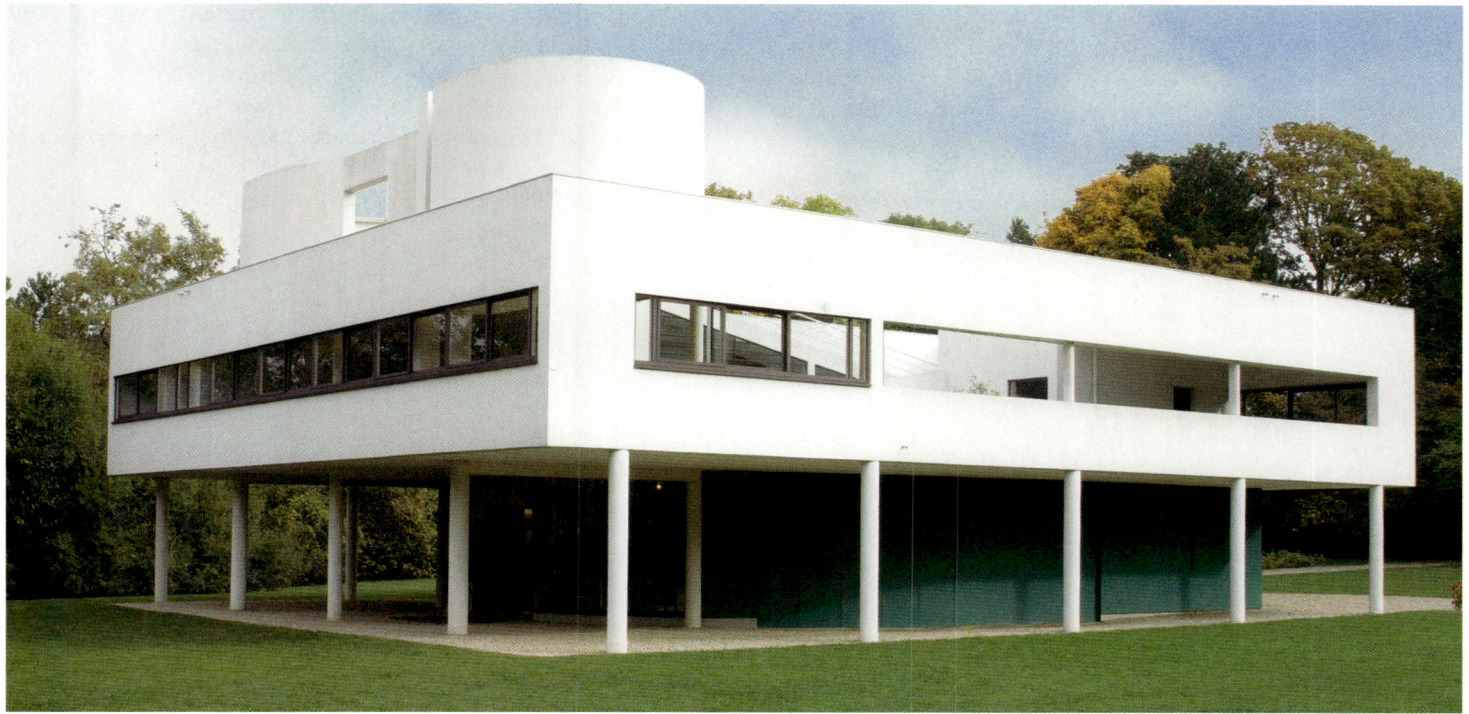

**29-68** LE CORBUSIER, Villa Savoye (looking southeast), Poissy-sur-Seine, France, 1929. ◼◄

Steel and ferroconcrete made it possible for Le Corbusier to invert the traditional practice of placing light architectural elements above heavy ones and to eliminate weight-bearing walls on the ground story.

surfaces, the slender ribbons of continuous windows, and the buoyant lightness of the whole fabric—all combine to reverse the effect of traditional country houses (FIG. 22-28). By placing heavy elements above and light ones below, and by refusing to enclose the ground story of the Villa Savoye with masonry walls, Le Corbusier inverted traditional design practice. This openness, made possible by the use of steel and ferroconcrete as construction materials, makes the "load" of the Villa Savoye's upper stories appear to hover lightly on the slender columnar supports.

**MARSEILLES AND CHANDIGARH** Le Corbusier designed the Villa Savoye as a private home, but as did De Stijl architects, he dreamed of extending his ideas of the house as a "machine for living" to designs for efficient and humane cities. He saw great cities as spiritual workshops and he proposed to correct the deficiencies in existing cities caused by poor traffic circulation, inadequate living units, and the lack of space for recreation and exercise. He proposed replacing traditional cities with three types of new communities. Vertical cities would house workers and the business and service industries. Linear-industrial cities would run as belts along the routes between the vertical cities and would serve as centers for the people and processes involved in manufacturing. Finally, separate centers would be constructed for people involved in intensive agricultural activity. Le Corbusier's cities would provide for human cultural needs in addition to serving every person's physical, mental, and emotional comfort needs.

Later in his career, Le Corbusier designed a few vertical cities, most notably the Unité d'Habitation in Marseilles (1945–1952). He also created the master plan for the entire city of Chandigarh, the capital city of the Punjab, India (1950–1957). He ended his career with a personal expressive style in his design of the Chapel of Notre Dame du Haut (FIG. 30-40) at Ronchamp, France.

# UNITED STATES AND MEXICO, 1930 TO 1945

In the 1930s, much of the Western world was plunged into the Great Depression, which had a particularly acute effect in the United States. The decade following the catastrophic stock market crash of October 1929 dramatically changed the nation, and artists were among the millions of economic victims. The limited art market virtually disappeared, and museums curtailed both their purchases and exhibition schedules. Many artists sought financial support from the federal government, which established numerous programs to provide relief, assist recovery, and promote reform. Among the programs supporting artists were the Treasury Relief Art Project, founded in 1934 to commission art for federal buildings, and the Works Progress Administration (WPA), founded in 1935 to relieve widespread unemployment. Under the WPA, varied activities of the Federal Art Project paid artists, writers, and theater people a regular wage in exchange for work in their professions.

Despite the economic hardships facing artists during the Great Depression, the United States became a haven for European painters, sculptors, and architects seeking to escape from Hitler and the Nazis. Among those who abandoned their homelands for America during the years leading up to World War II in search of freedom from political and religious persecution and a more hospitable environment for their art were Léger, Lipchitz, Beckmann, Grosz, Ernst, and Dalí. This influx of European artists was as significant a factor in exposing American artists to modernist European art as was the Armory Show of 1913 (see "The Armory Show," page 863).

A complementary factor was the desire on the part of American museums to demonstrate their familiarity and connection with the most progressive European art by mounting exhibitions centered on the latest European artistic developments. In 1938, for example, the City Art Museum of Saint Louis presented an exhibition of Beckmann's work, and the Art Institute of Chicago organized *George Grosz: A Survey of His Art from 1918–1938.* This interest in exhibiting the work of persecuted artists driven from their homelands also had political overtones. In the highly charged atmosphere of the late 1930s leading to the onset of World War II, Americans often perceived support for these artists and their work as support for freedom and democracy. In 1942, Alfred H. Barr Jr. (1902–1981), the director of the Museum of Modern Art, stated:

> Among the freedoms which the Nazis have destroyed, none has been more cynically perverted, more brutally stamped upon, than the Freedom of Art. For not only must the artist of Nazi Germany bow to political tyranny, he must also conform to the personal taste of that great art connoisseur, Adolf Hitler. . . . But German artists of spirit and integrity have refused to conform. They have gone into exile or slipped into anxious obscurity. . . . Their paintings and sculptures, too, have been hidden or exiled. . . . But in free countries they can still be seen, can still bear witness to the survival of a free German culture.[53]

Despite this moral support for exiled artists, once the United States formally entered the war, Germany officially became the enemy. It became much more difficult for the American art world to promote German artists, however persecuted. Many émigré artists, including Léger, Grosz, Ernst, and Dalí, returned to Europe after the war ended. Their collective presence in the United States until then, however, was critical for the development of American art.

## Painting

Although the political, social, and economic developments of the 1930s and 1940s brought many modernist European artists to the United States, the leading American painters of this period were primarily figural artists who had only a limited interest in abstract composition.

**BEN SHAHN** Born in Lithuania, BEN SHAHN (1898–1969) came to the United States in 1906 and trained as a lithographer before broadening the media in which he worked to include easel painting, photography, and murals. He focused on the lives of ordinary people and the injustices often done to them by the structure of an impersonal, bureaucratic society. In the early 1930s, he completed a cycle of 23 paintings and prints inspired by the trial and execution of the two Italian anarchists Nicola Sacco and Bartolomeo Vanzetti. Accused of killing two men in a holdup in 1920 in South Braintree, Massachusetts, the Italians were convicted in a trial many people thought resulted in a grave miscarriage of justice. Shahn felt he had found in this story a subject the equal of any in Western art history: "Suddenly I realized . . . I was living through another crucifixion."[54] Basing many of the works in this cycle on newspaper photographs of the events, Shahn devised a style that adapted his knowledge of Synthetic Cubism and his training in commercial art to an emotionally expressive use of flat, intense color in figural compositions filled with sharp, dry, angular forms. He called the major work in the series *The Passion of Sacco and Vanzetti* (FIG. I-6), drawing a parallel to Christ's Passion. This tall, narrow painting condenses the narrative in terms of both time and space. The two executed men lie in coffins at the bottom of the composition. Presiding over them are the three members of the commission chaired by Harvard University president A. Laurence Lowell, who declared the original trial fair and cleared the way for the executions to take place. A framed portrait of Judge Webster Thayer, who handed down the initial sentence, hangs on the wall of a simplified government building. The gray pallor of the dead men, the stylized mask-faces of the mock-pious mourning commissioners, and the sanctimonious, distant judge all contribute to the mood of anguished commentary making this image one of Shahn's most powerful works.

**EDWARD HOPPER** Trained as a commercial artist, EDWARD HOPPER (1882–1967) studied painting and printmaking in New York and then in Paris. When he returned to the United States, he concentrated on scenes of contemporary American city and

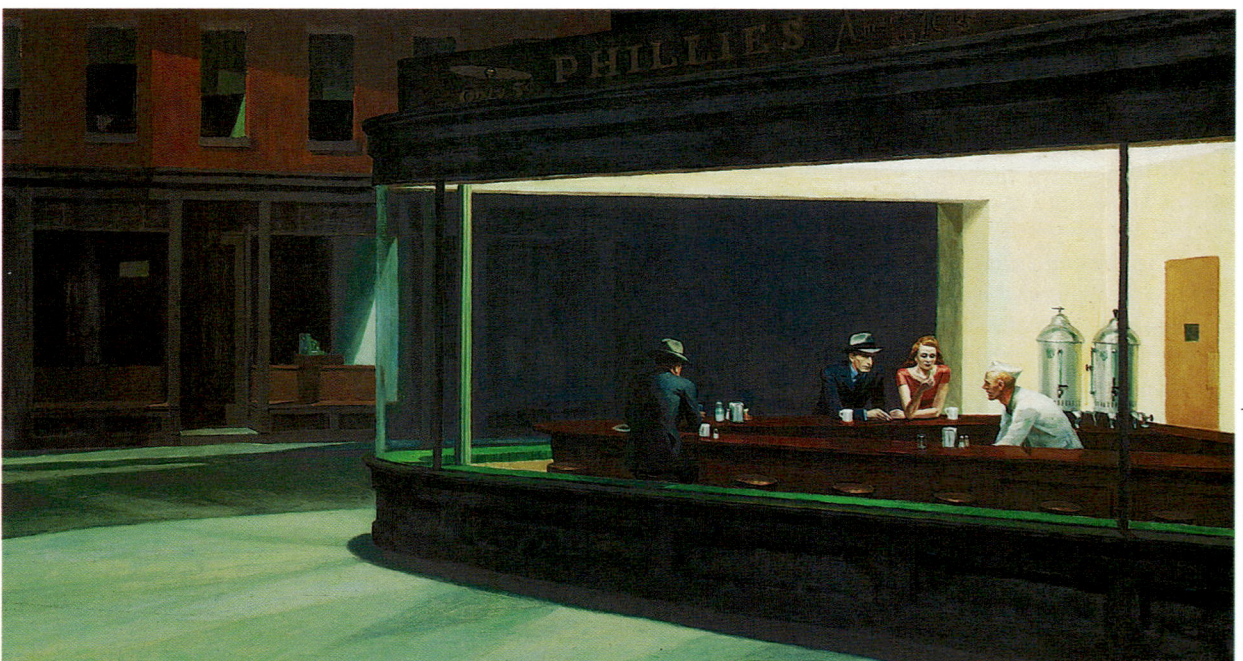

**29-69** EDWARD HOPPER, *Nighthawks,* 1942. Oil on canvas, 2′ 6″ × 4′ 8 11/16″. Art Institute of Chicago, Chicago (Friends of American Art Collection).

The seeming indifference of Hopper's characters to one another, and the echoing spaces surrounding them, evoke the overwhelming loneliness and isolation of Depression-era life in the United States.

1 ft.

country life. His paintings depict buildings, streets, and landscapes that are curiously muted, still, and filled with empty spaces, evoking the national mind-set during the Depression era. Hopper did not paint historically specific scenes. He took as his subject the more generalized theme of the overwhelming loneliness and echoing isolation of modern life in the United States. In his paintings, motion is stopped and time suspended.

From the darkened streets outside a restaurant in Hopper's *Nighthawks* (FIG. 29-69), the viewer glimpses the lighted interior through huge plate-glass windows, which lend the inner space the paradoxical sense of being both a safe refuge and a vulnerable place for the three customers and the man behind the counter. The seeming indifference of Hopper's characters to one another as well as the echoing spaces surrounding them evoke the pervasive loneliness of modern humans. In *Nighthawks* and other works, Hopper created a Realist vision recalling that of 19th-century artists such as Thomas Eakins (FIG. 27-36) and Henry Ossawa Tanner (FIG. 27-38), but in keeping with more recent trends in painting, he simplified the shapes, moving toward abstraction.

**JACOB LAWRENCE**  African American artist JACOB LAWRENCE (1917–2000) moved to Harlem, New York, in 1927 while still a boy. There, he came under the spell of the African art and the African American history he found in lectures and exhibitions and in the special programs sponsored by the 135th Street branch of the New York Public Library, which had outstanding collections of African American art and archival data. Inspired by the politically oriented art of Goya (FIG. 27-11), Daumier (FIG. 27-29), and Orozco (FIG. 29-73), and influenced by the many artists and writers of the Harlem Renaissance whom he met, including Aaron Douglas (FIGS. 29-40 and 29-40A), Lawrence found his subjects in the everyday life of Harlem and in African American history.

In 1941, Lawrence began a 60-painting series titled *The Migration of the Negro* in which he defined his vision of the continuing African American struggle against discrimination. Unlike his earlier historical paintings depicting important figures in American history, such as the abolitionists Frederick Douglass and Harriet Tubman, this series called attention to a contemporaneous event—the ongoing exodus of black labor from the southern United States. Disillusioned with their lives in the South, hundreds of thousands of African Americans migrated north in the years following World War I, seeking improved economic opportunities and a more hospitable political and social environment. But the conditions African Americans encountered both during their migration and in the North were often as difficult and discriminatory as those they had left behind in the South, as Lawrence knew from his own experience:

> I was part of the migration, as was my family, my mother, my sister, and my brother. . . . I grew up hearing tales about people "coming up," another family arriving. . . . I didn't realize what was happening until about the middle of the 1930s, and that's when the *Migration* series began to take form in my mind.[55]

Lawrence's *Migration* paintings provide numerous vignettes capturing the experiences of the African Americans who had moved to the North. Often, a sense of the bleakness and degradation of their new life dominates the images. *No. 49* (FIG. 29-70) of this series bears the caption "They also found discrimination in the North although it was much different from that which they had known in the South." Lawrence depicted a blatantly segregated dining room with a barrier running down the room's center separating

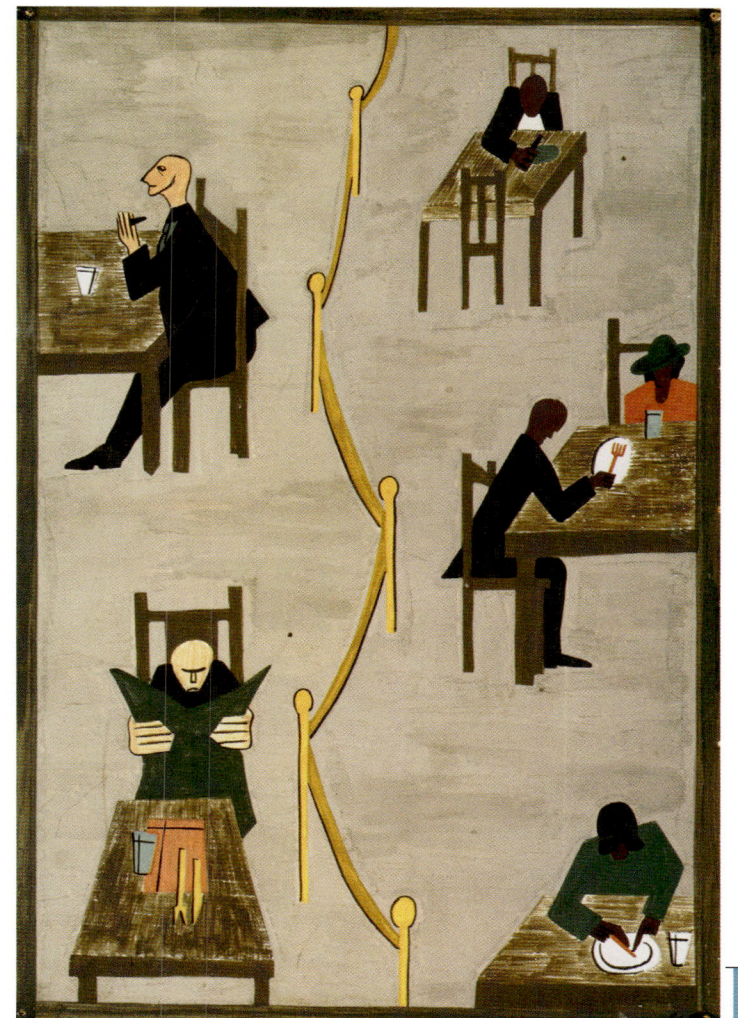

**29-70**  JACOB LAWRENCE, *No. 49* from *The Migration of the Negro,* 1940–1941. Tempera on Masonite, 1′ 6″ × 1′. Phillips Collection, Washington, D.C.

The 49th in a series of 60 paintings documenting African American life in the North, Lawrence's depiction of a segregated dining room underscored that the migrants had not left discrimination behind.

the whites on the left from the African Americans on the right. To ensure a continuity and visual integrity among all 60 paintings, Lawrence interpreted his themes systematically in rhythmic arrangements of bold, flat, and strongly colored shapes. His style drew equally from his interest in the push-pull effects of Cubist space and his memories of the patterns made by the colored scatter rugs brightening the floors of his childhood homes. He unified the narrative with a consistent palette of bluish green, orange, yellow, and grayish brown throughout the entire series.

**GRANT WOOD**  Although many American artists, such as the Precisionists (FIGS. 29-41 and 29-42), preferred to depict the city or rapidly developing technological advances, others avoided subjects tied to modern life. At a 1931 arts conference, GRANT WOOD (1891–1942) announced a new movement developing in the Midwest, known as *Regionalism,* which he described as focused on American subjects and as standing in reaction to the modernist abstraction of Europe and New York. Four years later, Wood published an essay titled "Revolt against the City" that underscored their new focus.

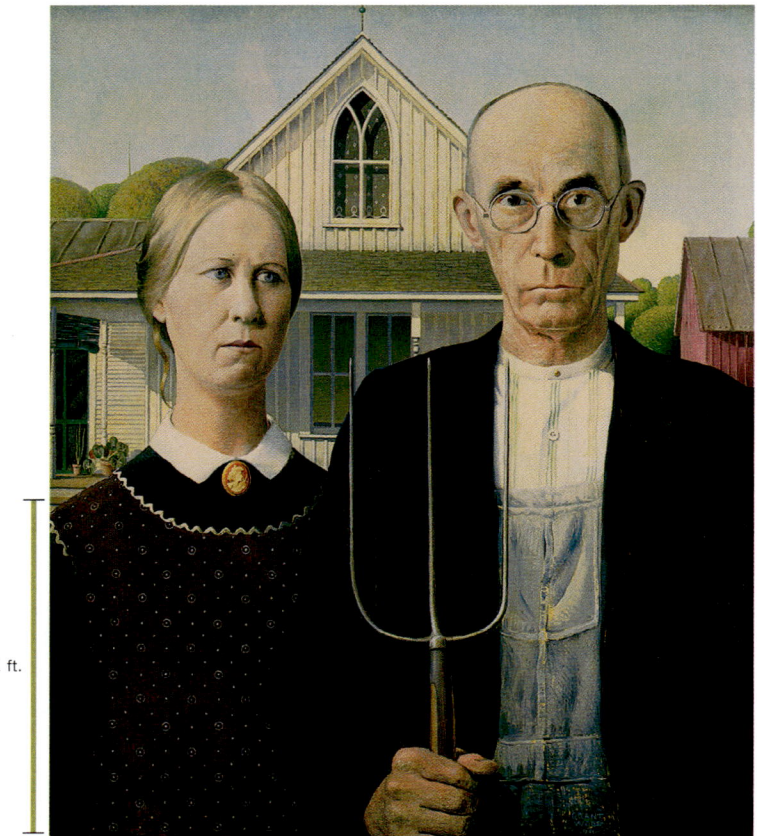

1 ft.

**29-71** GRANT WOOD, *American Gothic,* 1930. Oil on beaverboard, 2′ 5$\frac{7}{8}$″ × 2′ $\frac{7}{8}$″. Art Institute of Chicago, Chicago (Friends of American Art Collection). ◼◀

In reaction to modernist abstract painting, the Midwestern Regionalism movement focused on American subjects. Wood's painting of an Iowa farmer and his daughter became an American icon.

Wood and the Regionalists, sometimes referred to as the American Scene Painters, turned their attention instead to rural life as America's cultural backbone. Wood's paintings, for example, portray the people of rural Iowa, where he was born and raised.

The work that catapulted Wood to national prominence was *American Gothic* (FIG. **29-71**), which became an American icon. The artist depicted a farmer and his spinster daughter standing in front of a neat house with a small *lancet* window, a motif originating in Gothic architecture and associated with churches and religious piety. The man and woman wear traditional attire. He appears in worn overalls and she in an apron trimmed with rickrack. The dour expression on both faces gives the painting a severe quality, which Wood enhanced with his meticulous brushwork. The public and professional critics agreed *American Gothic* was "quaint, humorous, and AMERICAN" and embodied "strength, dignity, fortitude, resoluteness, integrity," qualities that represented the true spirit of America.[56]

Wood's Regionalist vision involved more than his subjects. It extended to a rejection of avant-garde styles in favor of a clearly readable, Realist style. Surely this approach appealed to many people alienated by the increasing presence of abstraction in art. However, despite the accolades this painting received, it also attracted criticism. Not everyone saw the painting as a sympathetic portrayal of Midwestern life. Indeed, some Iowans considered the depiction of life in their state insulting. In addition, despite the seemingly reportorial nature of *American Gothic,* some viewed it as a political statement—one of staunch nationalism. In light of the problematic

nationalism in Germany at the time, many observers found Wood's nationalistic attitude disturbing. Nonetheless, during the Great Depression, Regionalist paintings had a popular appeal because they often projected a reassuring image of America's heartland. The public saw Regionalism as a means of coping with the national crisis through a search for cultural roots. Thus, people deemed acceptable any nostalgia implicit in Regionalist paintings or mythologies these works perpetuated because they served a larger purpose.

**THOMAS HART BENTON** Another major Regionalist artist was THOMAS HART BENTON (1889–1975). Whereas Wood focused his attention on Iowa, Benton turned to scenes from his native Missouri. He produced one of his major works, a series of murals titled *A Social History of the State of Missouri,* in 1936 for the Missouri State Capitol. The murals depict a collection of images from the state's historic and legendary past, such as primitive agriculture, horse trading, a vigilante lynching, and an old-fashioned political meeting. Other scenes portray the mining industry, grain elevators, Native Americans, and family life. One segment, *Pioneer Days and Early Settlers* (FIG. **29-72**), shows a white man using whisky as a bartering tool with a Native American (*left*), along with scenes documenting the building of Missouri (*right*). Part documentary and part invention, Benton's images include both positive and negative aspects of Missouri's history, as these examples illustrate. Although the public perceived the Regionalists as dedicated to glorifying Midwestern life, that was not their aim. Indeed, Grant Wood observed, "Your true regionalist is not a mere eulogist; he may even be a severe critic."[57] Benton, like Wood, championed a visually accessible style, but he developed a highly personal aesthetic that included complex compositions, a fluidity of imagery, and simplified figures depicted with a rubbery distortion.

**JOSÉ CLEMENTE OROZCO** During the period between the two world wars, several Mexican painters achieved international renown for their work both in Mexico and the United States. The eldest of the three was JOSÉ CLEMENTE OROZCO (1883–1949), one of a group of Mexican artists determined to base their art on the indigenous history and culture existing in Mexico before Europeans arrived. The movement these artists formed was part of the idealistic rethinking of society that occurred in conjunction with the Mexican Revolution (1910–1920) and the lingering political turmoil of the 1920s. Among the projects these politically motivated artists undertook were vast mural cycles placed in public buildings to dramatize and validate the history of Mexico's native peoples. Orozco worked on one of the first major cycles, painted in 1922 on the walls of the National Training School in Mexico City. He carried the ideas of this mural revolution to the United States, completing many commissions for wall paintings between 1927 and 1934. From 1932 to 1934, he painted a major mural cycle in the Baker Library at Dartmouth College in New Hampshire. The college let Orozco choose the subject, and he designed 14 large panels and 10 smaller ones that together formed a panoramic and symbolic history of ancient and modern Mexico. The murals recount Mexican history from the early mythic days of the feathered-serpent god Quetzalcoatl (see Chapters 18 and 35) to a contemporary and bitterly satiric vision of modern education.

The imagery in panel 16, *Epic of American Civilization: Hispano-America* (FIG. **29-73**), revolves around the monumental figure of a heroic Mexican peasant armed to participate in the Mexican Revolution. Looming on either side of him are mounds crammed with symbolic figures of his oppressors—bankers, government soldiers, officials, gangsters, and the rich. Money-grubbers empty huge bags of gold coins at the incorruptible peon's feet, cannons threaten him,

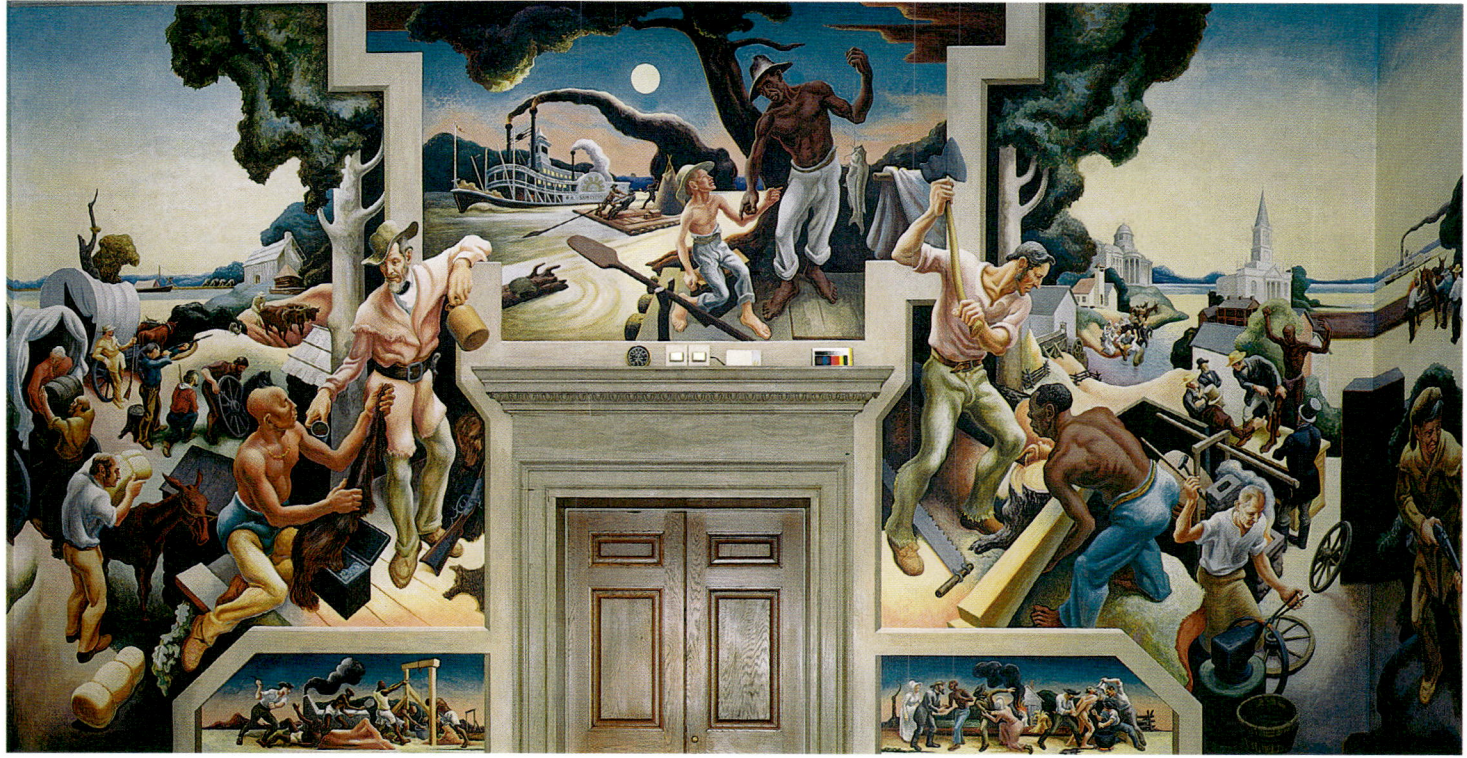

**29-72** THOMAS HART BENTON, *Pioneer Days and Early Settlers,* fresco in the State Capitol, Jefferson City, Missouri, 1936. © T. H. Benton and R. P. Benton Testamentary Trusts/UMB Bank Trustee/Licensed by VAGA, New York.

Benton's mural for Missouri's State Capitol is one of the major Regionalist artworks. Part documentary and part invention, the images include both positive and negative aspects of state history.

and a general bedecked with medals raises a dagger to stab him in the back. Orozco's training as an architect gave him a sense of the framed wall surface, which he easily commanded, projecting his clearly defined figures onto the solid mural plane in monumental scale. In addition, Orozco's early experience as a maker of politi-cal prints and as a newspaper artist had taught him the rhetorical strength of graphic brevity, which he used here to assure his alle-gory could be read easily. His special merging of the graphic and mural media effects gives his work an originality and force rarely seen in mural painting after the Renaissance and Baroque periods.

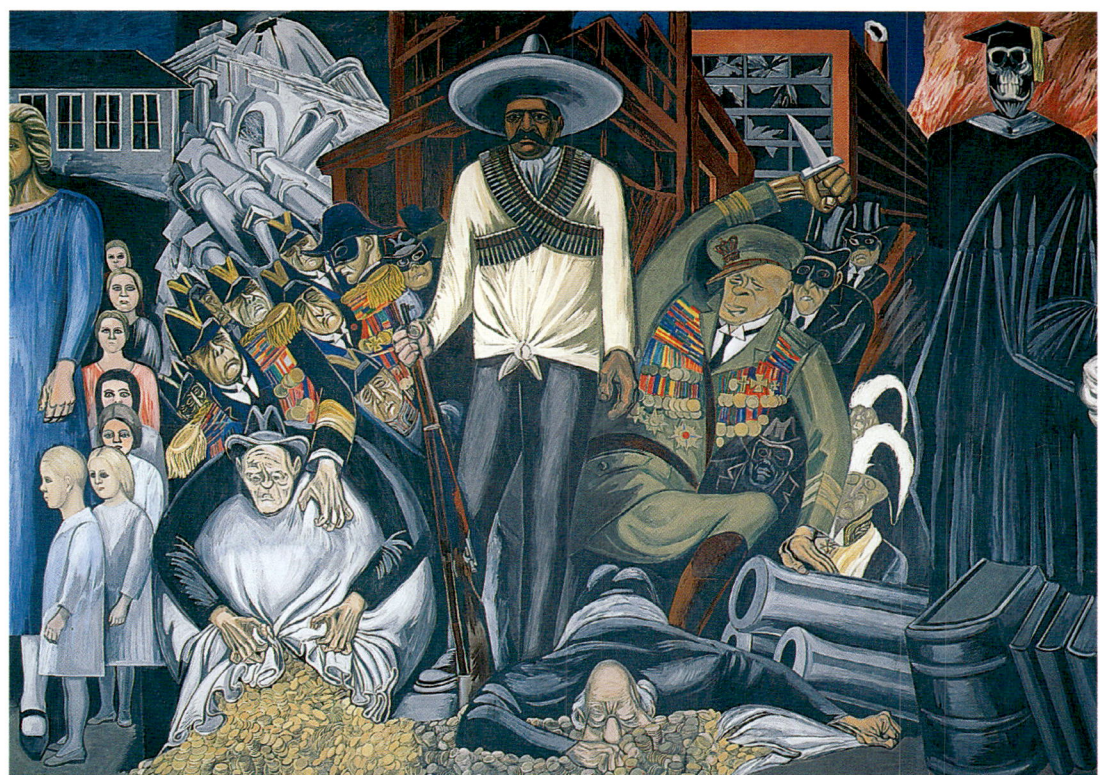

**29-73** JOSÉ CLEMENTE OROZCO, *Epic of American Civilization: Hispano-America* (panel 16), fresco in Baker Memorial Library, Dartmouth College, Hanover, New Hampshire, ca. 1932–1934.

One of 24 panels depicting the history of Mexico from ancient times, this scene focuses on a heroic peasant soldier of the Mexican Revolution surrounded by symbolic figures of his oppressors.

United States and Mexico, 1930 to 1945    **891**

# Rivera on Art for the People

Diego Rivera was an avid proponent of a social and political role for art in the lives of common people and wrote passionately about the proper goals for an artist—goals he fully met in his own murals depicting Mexican history (FIG. 29-74). Rivera's views stand in sharp contrast to the growing interest in abstraction on the part of many early-20th-century painters and sculptors.

Art has always been employed by the different social classes who hold the balance of power as one instrument of domination—hence, as a political instrument. One can analyze epoch after epoch—from the stone age to our own day—and see that there is no form of art which does not also play an essential political role. . . . What is it then that we really need? . . . An art with revolution as its subject: because the principal interest in the worker's life has to be touched first. It is necessary that he find aesthetic satisfaction and the highest pleasure appareled in the essential interest of his life. . . . The subject is to the painter what the rails are to a locomotive. He cannot do without it. In fact, when he refuses to seek or accept a subject, his own plastic methods and his own aesthetic theories become his subject instead. . . . [H]e himself becomes the subject of his work. He becomes nothing but an illustrator of his own state of mind . . . That is the deception practiced under the name of "Pure Art."*

*Quoted in Robert Goldwater and Marco Treves, eds., *Artists on Art from the XIV to the XX Century* (New York: Pantheon, 1945), 475–477.

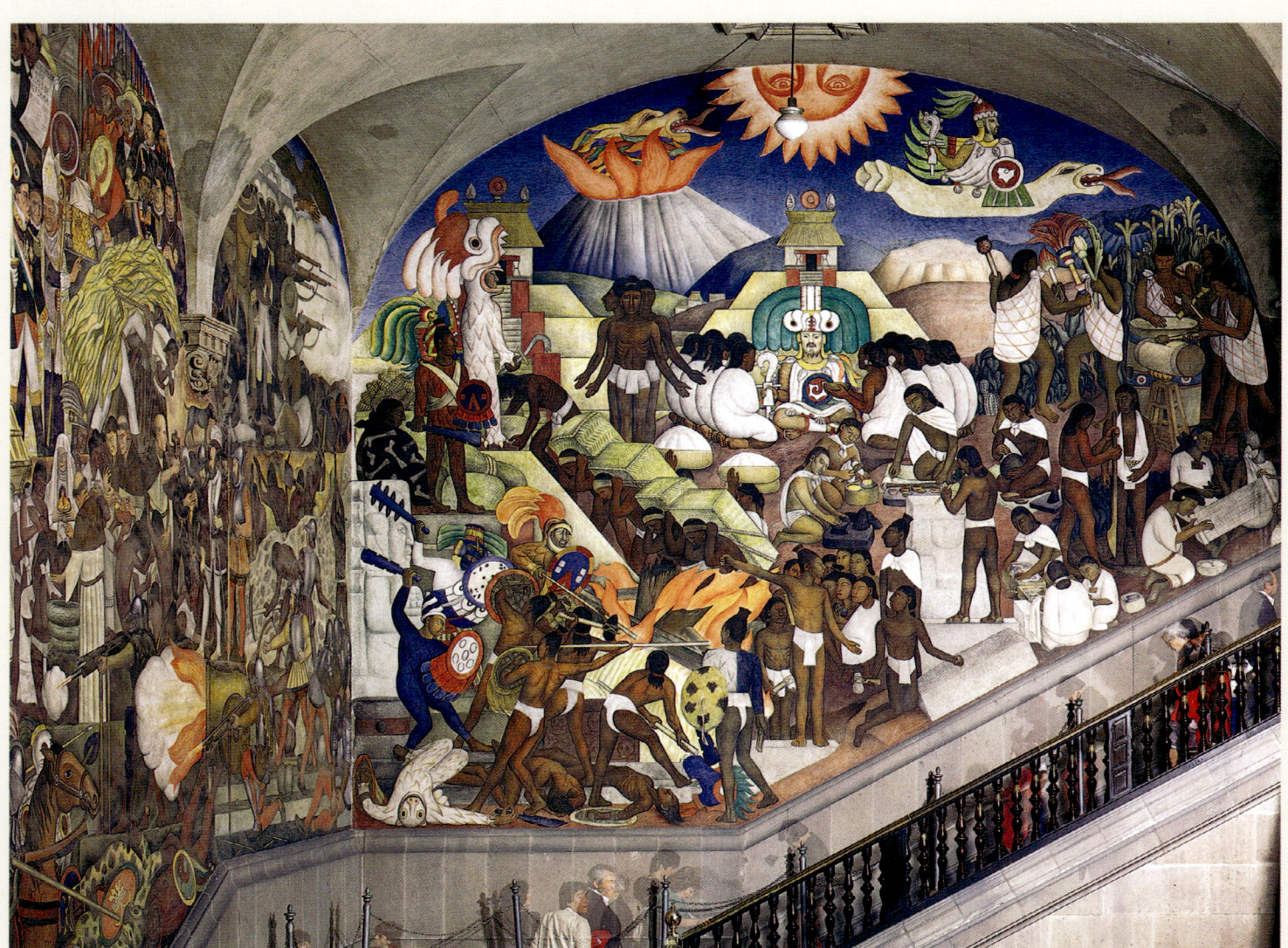

**29-74** DIEGO RIVERA, *Ancient Mexico,* detail of *History of Mexico,* fresco in the Palacio Nacional, Mexico City, 1929–1935.

A staunch Marxist, Rivera painted vast mural cycles in public buildings to dramatize the history of his native land. This fresco depicts the conflicts between indigenous Mexicans and Spanish colonizers.

**DIEGO RIVERA** A second Mexican who received great acclaim for his murals, both in Mexico and in the United States was DIEGO RIVERA (1886–1957). A staunch Marxist, Rivera strove to develop an art that served his people's needs (see "Rivera on Art for the People," page 892). Toward that end, he sought to create a national Mexican style focusing on Mexico's history and also incorporating a popular, generally accessible aesthetic in keeping with the socialist spirit of the Mexican Revolution. Rivera produced numerous large murals in public buildings, among them a series lining the staircase of the National Palace in Mexico City. In these images, painted between 1929 and 1935, he depicted scenes from Mexico's history, of which *Ancient Mexico* (FIG. **29-74**) is one. This section of the mural represents the conflicts between the indigenous people and the Spanish colonizers. Rivera included portraits of important figures in Mexican history, especially those involved in the struggle for Mexican independence. Although the composition is complex, the simple monumental shapes and areas of bold color make the story easily legible.

**FRIDA KAHLO** Born to a Mexican mother and German father, the painter FRIDA KAHLO (1907–1954), who married Diego Rivera, used the details of her life as powerful symbols for the psychological pain of human existence. Art historians often consider Kahlo a Surrealist due to the psychic, autobiographical issues she dealt with in her art. Indeed, André Breton himself deemed her

a Natural Surrealist. (The work of her older contemporary, RUFINO TAMAYO [1899–1991; FIG. **29-74A**] has also been compared to Natural Surrealism.) Kahlo herself, however, rejected any association with the Surrealists. She began painting seriously as a young student, during convalescence from an accident that tragically left her in constant pain. Her life became a heroic and tumultuous battle for survival against illness and stormy personal relationships.

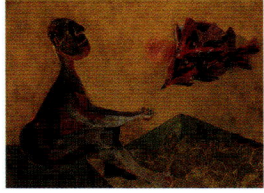

29-74A TAMAYO, *Friend of the Birds,* 1944.

Typical of her long series of unflinching self-portraits is *The Two Fridas* (FIG. **29-75**), one of the few large-scale canvases Kahlo ever produced. The twin figures sit side by side on a low bench in a barren landscape under a stormy sky. The figures suggest different sides of the artist's personality, inextricably linked by the clasped hands and by the thin artery stretching between them, joining their exposed hearts. The artery ends on one side in surgical forceps and on the other in a miniature portrait of her husband as a child. Her deeply personal paintings touch sensual and psychological memories in her audience.

To read Kahlo's paintings solely as autobiographical overlooks the powerful political dimension of her art. Kahlo was deeply nationalistic and committed to her Mexican heritage. Politically active, she joined the Communist Party in 1920 and participated in public political protests. *The Two Fridas* incorporates Kahlo's commentary on the struggle facing Mexicans in the early 20th century in defining their national cultural identity. The Frida on the right (representing indigenous culture) appears in a Tehuana dress, the traditional costume of Zapotec women from the Isthmus of Tehuantepec, whereas the Frida on the left (representing imperialist forces) wears a European-style white lace dress. The heart, depicted here in such dramatic fashion, was an important symbol in the art of the Aztecs, whom Mexican nationalists idealized as the last independent rulers of their land. Thus *The Two Fridas* represents both Kahlo's personal struggles and the struggles of her homeland.

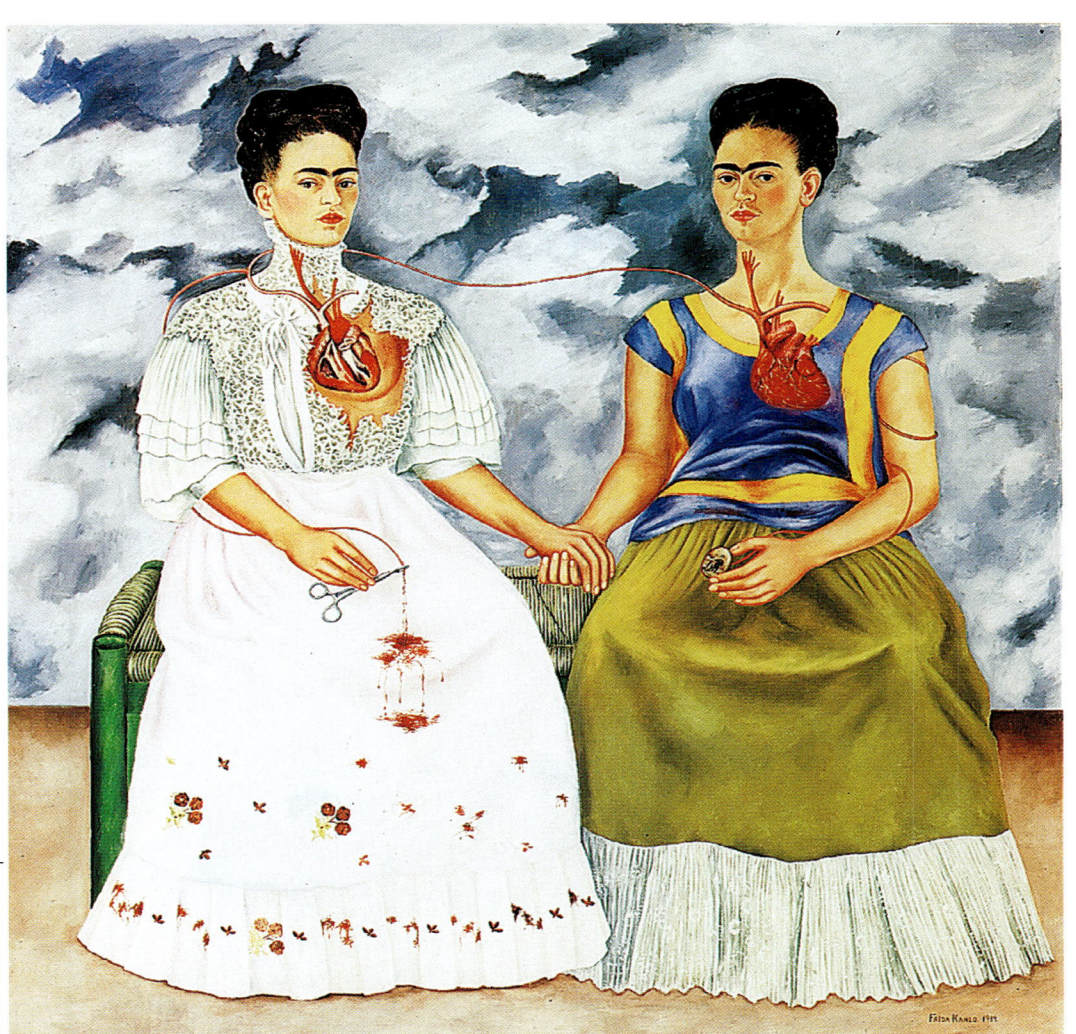

1 ft.

**29-75** FRIDA KAHLO, *The Two Fridas,* 1939. Oil on canvas, 5′ 7″ × 5′ 7″. Museo de Arte Moderno, Mexico City.

Kahlo's deeply personal paintings touch sensual and psychological memories in her audience. Here, twin self-portraits linked by clasped hands and a common artery suggest two sides of her personality.

# Photography

Frida Kahlo is the most famous female artist of her generation, but other women achieved prominence in the arts, especially the photographers Dorothea Lange and Margaret Bourke-White.

**DOROTHEA LANGE** One of the most important programs the U.S. government initiated during the 1930s was the Resettlement Administration (RA), better known by its later name, the Farm Security Administration. The RA oversaw emergency aid programs for farm families struggling to survive the Great Depression. The RA hired DOROTHEA LANGE (1895–1965) in 1936, and dispatched her to document the deplorable living conditions of the rural poor. At the end of an assignment photographing migratory pea pickers in California, Lange stopped at a camp in Nipomo and found the migrant workers there starving because the crops had frozen in the fields. Among the pictures Lange made on this occasion was *Migrant Mother, Nipomo Valley* (FIG. **29-76**), in which she captured the mixture of strength and worry in the raised hand and careworn face of a young mother, who holds a baby on her lap. Two older children cling to their mother trustfully while turning their faces away from the camera. Lange described how she got the picture:

> [I] saw and approached the hungry and desperate mother, as if drawn by a magnet. I do not remember how I explained my presence or my camera to her, but I remember she asked me no questions. I made five exposures, working closer and closer from the same direction. . . . There she sat in that lean-to tent with her children huddled around her, and she seemed to know that my pictures might help her, and so she helped me.[58]

Within days after Lange's photograph appeared in a San Francisco newspaper, people rushed food to Nipomo to feed the hungry workers.

**MARGARET BOURKE-WHITE** Almost 10 years younger than Dorothea Lange, MARGARET BOURKE-WHITE (1904–1971) also made her reputation as a photojournalist in Depression-era America. She was the first staff photographer Henry Luce (1898–1967) hired to furnish illustrations for the magazines in his publishing empire. Beginning in 1929, Bourke-White worked for *Fortune,* then for *Life* when Luce launched the famous newsweekly in 1936. During her long career, she photographed Midwestern farmers in their drought-stricken fields, impoverished Southern sharecroppers, black gold miners in South Africa, the Nazi concentration camp at Buchenwald, and the Korean War.

Bourke-White's most famous photographs, however, were not of people or events but of the triumphs of 20th-century engineering, many of which appeared in Luce's magazines and served to instill pride in an American public severely lacking in confidence during the Depression. She photographed the Chrysler Building (FIG. 29-47) while it was under construction in New York, attracting media attention for her daring balancing act on steel girders high above the pavement. She also achieved renown as the first woman to fly a combat mission when she was an official U.S. Air Force photographer during World War II.

For the first issue of *Life* (November 23, 1936), Bourke-White not only provided the cover photograph (FIG. **29-77**) of *Fort Peck Dam,*

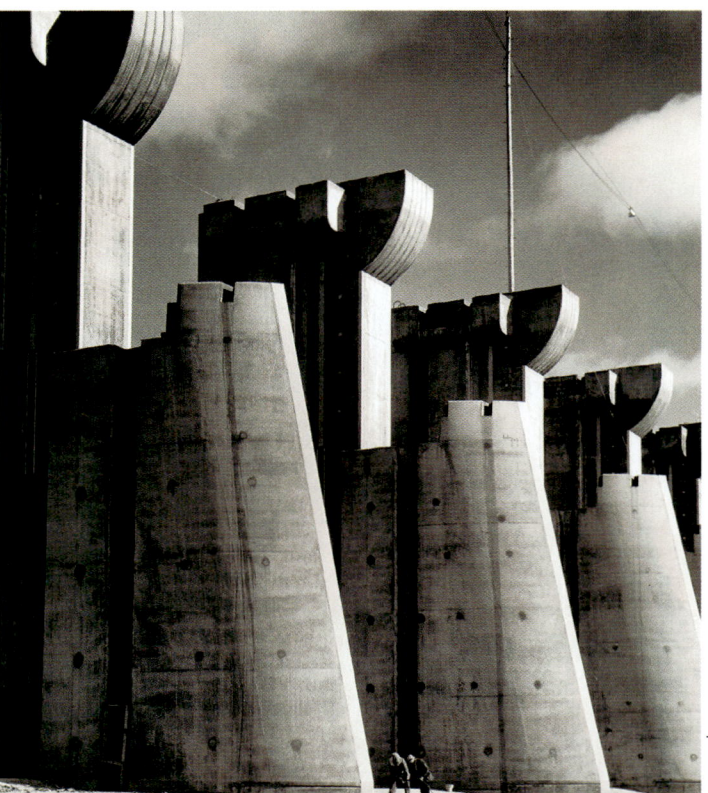

1 in.

**29-76** DOROTHEA LANGE, *Migrant Mother, Nipomo Valley,* 1935. Gelatin silver print, 1′ 1″ × 9″. Oakland Museum of California, Oakland (gift of Paul S. Taylor). ◼◀

While documenting the lives of migratory farm workers during the Depression, Lange made this unforgettable photograph of a mother in which she captured the woman's strength and worry.

1 in.

**29-77** MARGARET BOURKE-WHITE, *Fort Peck Dam, Montana,* 1936. Gelatin silver print, 1′ 1″ × 10½″. Metropolitan Museum of Art, New York (gift of Ford Motor Company and John C. Waddell, 1987).

Bourke-White's dramatic photograph of Fort Peck Dam graced the cover of the first issue of *Life* magazine and celebrated the achievements of modern industry at the height of the Great Depression.

## The Museum of Modern Art and the Avant-Garde

Established in 1929, the Museum of Modern Art (MoMA) in New York City owes its existence to a trio of women—Lillie P. Bliss, Mary Quinn Sullivan, and Abby Aldrich Rockefeller (see "Art 'Matronage' in the United States," page 865)—who saw the need for a museum to collect and exhibit modernist art. Together they founded MoMA, which quickly became the most influential museum of modern art in the world. Their success was extraordinary considering the skepticism and hostility greeting modernist art at the time of the museum's inception. Indeed, in the 1920s and 1930s, few American museums exhibited any late-19th- and 20th-century art.

In its quest to expose the public to the energy and challenge of modernist, particularly avant-garde, art, MoMA developed unique and progressive exhibitions. Among those the museum mounted during the early years of its existence were *Cubism and Abstract Art* and *Fantastic Art, Dada, Surrealism* (1936). Two other noteworthy shows were *American Sources of Modern Art* (*Aztec, Maya, Inca*) in 1933 and *African Negro Art* in 1935, both among the first exhibitions to deal with "primitive" artifacts in artistic rather than anthropological terms (see "Primitivism and Colonialism," page 846).

The organization of MoMA's administrative structure and the scope of the museum's early activities were also remarkable. MoMA's first director, Alfred H. Barr Jr., insisted on establishing departments not only for painting and sculpture but also for photography, prints and drawing, architecture, and the decorative arts. He developed a library of books on modern art and a film library, both of which have become world-class collections, as well as an extensive publishing program.

It is the museum's art collection, however, that has drawn the most attention. By cultivating an influential group of patrons, MoMA has developed an extensive and enviable collection of late-19th- and 20th-century art. The museum boasts such important works as van Gogh's *Starry Night* (FIG. 28-18), Picasso's *Les Demoi-*

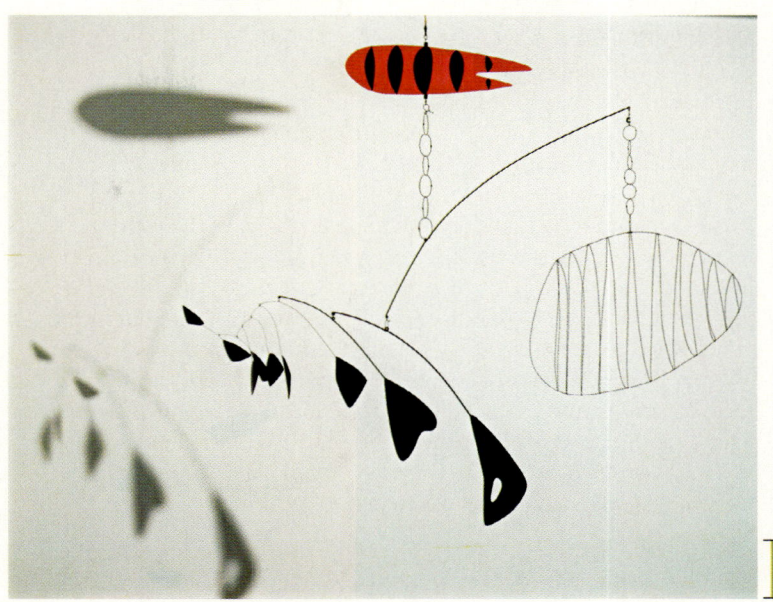

**29-78** ALEXANDER CALDER, *Lobster Trap and Fish Tail*, 1939. Painted sheet aluminum and steel wire, 8′ 6″ × 9′ 6″. Museum of Modern Art, New York.

Using his thorough knowledge of engineering to combine nonobjective organic forms and motion, Calder created a new kind of sculpture—the mobile—that expressed nature's innate dynamism.

*selles d'Avignon* (FIG. 29-12), and Dalí's *The Persistence of Memory* (FIG. 29-55), as well as many others illustrated in this book, including 22 in this chapter alone. MoMA has also served as an art patron itself. For example, in 1939, just a decade after the institution's founding, it commissioned Alexander Calder to produce the mobile *Lobster Trap and Fish Tail* (FIG. 29-78).

---

*Montana,* but also wrote and illustrated with 16 additional photographs the lead story on the town of New Deal, home to the workers who constructed the dam during the depths of the Depression. Fort Peck Dam was at the time the largest earth-filled dam in the world. Bourke-White photographed its towers (designed to conjure a crenellated medieval fortress) at a sharp angle from below to communicate the dam's soaring height, underscoring the immense scale by including two dwarfed figures of men in the foreground. The tight framing, which shuts out all of the landscape and much of the sky, transforms the dam into an almost-abstract composition, a kind of still life, like Edward Weston's peppers (FIG. 29-44). Bourke-White's photographs celebrate modern industry as heir to the architectural achievements of the ancient world's great civilizations, and bear comparison with the paintings of Charles Demuth (FIG. 29-41).

## Sculpture

In striking contrast to the leading American painters and photographers of the 1930s, the most renowned sculptor of this period rose to international prominence because of his contributions to the development of abstract art.

**ALEXANDER CALDER** The son and grandson of sculptors, ALEXANDER CALDER (1898–1976) initially studied mechanical engineering. Fascinated all his life by motion, he explored movement in relationship to three-dimensional form in much of his work. As a young artist in Paris in the late 1920s, Calder invented a circus full of wire-based miniature performers he activated into analogues of the motion of their real-life counterparts. After a visit to Piet Mondrian's studio in the early 1930s, Calder set out to put the Dutch painter's brightly colored rectangular shapes (FIG. 29-60) into motion. (Marcel Duchamp, intrigued by Calder's early motorized and hand-cranked examples of moving abstract pieces, named them *mobiles*.) Calder's engineering skills soon helped him to fashion a series of balanced structures hanging from rods, wires, and colorful, organically shaped plates. This new kind of sculpture, which combined nonobjective organic forms and motion, succeeded in expressing the innate dynamism of the natural world.

An early Calder mobile is *Lobster Trap and Fish Tail* (FIG. **29-78**), which the artist created in 1939 under a commission from the Museum of Modern Art in New York City for the stairwell of the museum's new building on West 53rd Street (see "The

Perched on a rocky hillside over a waterfall, Wright's Fallingwater has long sweeping lines, unconfined by abrupt wall limits, reaching out and capturing the expansiveness of the natural environment.

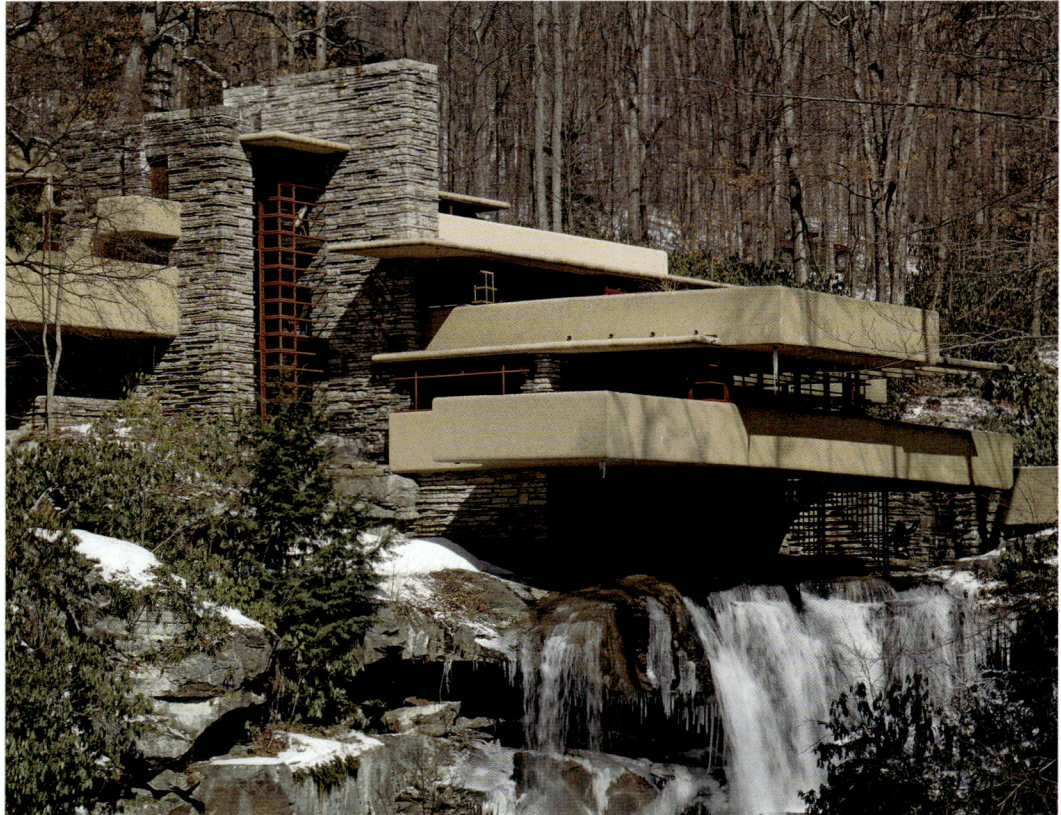

Museum of Modern Art and the Avant-Garde," page 895). Calder carefully planned each nonmechanized mobile so any air current would set the parts moving to create a constantly shifting dance in space. Mondrian's studio may have provided the initial inspiration for the mobiles, but their organic shapes resemble those in Joan Miró's Surrealist paintings (FIG. 29-58). Indeed, viewers can read Calder's forms as either geometric or organic. Geometrically, the lines suggest circuitry and rigging, and the shapes derive from circles and ovoid forms. Organically, the lines suggest nerve axons, and the shapes resemble cells, leaves, fins, wings, and other bioforms.

## Architecture

The most influential American architect of the 1930s, as during the opening decades of the century, was the ever-inventive Frank Lloyd Wright.

FALLINGWATER Wright's universally acclaimed masterpiece of this period is the Kaufmann House (FIG. 29-79), which he designed as a weekend retreat at Bear Run, Pennsylvania, for Pittsburgh department store magnate Edgar Kaufmann Sr. Perched on a rocky hillside over a small waterfall, the house, nicknamed Fallingwater, has become an icon of modernist architectural design. In keeping with his commitment to an "architecture of democracy," Wright sought to find a way to incorporate the structure fully into its site in order to ensure a fluid, dynamic exchange between the interior of the house and the natural environment outside. Rather than build the house overlooking or next to the waterfall, Wright decided to build it over the waterfall, because he believed the inhabitants would become desensitized to the waterfall's presence and power if they merely overlooked it. In Fallingwater, Wright took the blocky masses characterizing his earlier Robie House (FIGS. 29-45 and 29-46) and extended them in all four directions. To take ad-

vantage of the location, he designed a series of terraces that extend on three levels from a central core structure. The contrast in textures among concrete, painted metal, and natural stones in the house's terraces and walls enlivens its shapes, as does Wright's use of full-length strip windows to create a stunning interweaving of interior and exterior space.

The implied message of Wright's new architecture was space, not mass—a space designed to fit the patron's life and enclosed and divided as required. Wright took special pains to meet his clients' requirements, often designing all the accessories of a house (including, in at least one case, gowns for his client's wife). In the late 1930s, he acted on a cherished dream to provide good architectural design for less prosperous people by adapting the ideas of his prairie houses (see page 870) to plans for smaller, less expensive dwellings with neither attics nor basements. These residences, known as *Usonian* houses (for "United States of North America"), became templates for suburban housing developments in the post–World War II housing boom.

The publication of Wright's plans brought him a measure of fame in Europe, especially in Holland and Germany. The issuance in Berlin in 1910 of a portfolio of his work and an exhibition of his designs the following year stimulated younger architects to adopt some of his ideas about open plans that afforded clients freedom. Some 40 years before his career ended, his work was already of revolutionary significance. Mies van der Rohe wrote in 1940: "[The] dynamic impulse from [Wright's] work invigorated a whole generation. His influence was strongly felt even when it was not actually visible."[59]

Frank Lloyd Wright's influence in Europe was exceptional, however, for any American artist before World War II. But in the decades following that global conflict, American painters, sculptors, and architects often took the lead in establishing new styles artists elsewhere quickly emulated. This new preeminence of the United States in the arts is the subject of Chapter 30.

# MODERNISM IN EUROPE AND AMERICA, 1900 TO 1945

## EUROPE 1900 to 1920

▌ In the early 1900s, avant-garde artists searched for new definitions of art in a changed world. Matisse and the Fauves used bold colors as the primary means of conveying feeling. German Expressionist paintings featured clashing colors, disquieting figures, and perspective distortions.

▌ Pablo Picasso and Georges Braque radically challenged prevailing artistic conventions with Cubism, in which artists dissect forms and place them in interaction with the space around them.

▌ The Futurists focused on motion in time and space in their effort to create paintings and sculptures that captured the dynamic quality of modern life. The Dadaists celebrated the spontaneous and intuitive, exploring the role of chance in art and often incorporating found objects in their works.

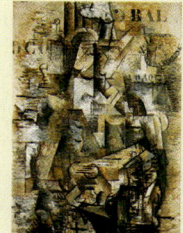

Braque, *The Portuguese,* 1911

## UNITED STATES 1900 to 1930

▌ The Armory Show of 1913 introduced avant-garde European art to American artists. Man Ray, for example, embraced Dada's fondness for chance and the displacement of ordinary items, and Stuart Davis adopted the Cubist interest in fragmented form.

▌ The Harlem Renaissance brought African American artists to the forefront, including Aaron Douglas, whose paintings drew on Cubist principles. Charles Demuth, Georgia O'Keeffe, and the Precisionists used European modernist techniques to celebrate contemporary American subjects.

▌ Photography emerged as an important American art form in the work of Alfred Stieglitz and Edward Weston, who emphasized the careful arrangement of forms and patterns of light and dark.

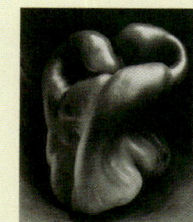

Weston, *Pepper No. 30,* 1930

## EUROPE 1920 to 1945

▌ World War I gave rise to the Neue Sachlichkeit movement in Germany. "New Objectivity" artists depicted the horrors of war and explored the themes of death and transfiguration.

▌ The Surrealists investigated ways to express in art the world of dreams and the unconscious. Natural Surrealists aimed for "concrete irrationality" in their naturalistic paintings of dreamlike scenes. Biomorphic Surrealists experimented with automatism and employed abstract imagery.

▌ Many European modernists pursued utopian ideals. The Suprematists developed an abstract style to express pure feeling. The Constructivists used nonobjective forms to suggest the nature of space-time. De Stijl artists reduced their formal vocabulary to simple geometric forms in their search for "pure plastic art."

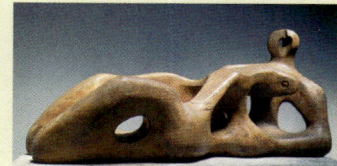

Moore, *Reclining Figure,* 1939

▌ Brancusi, Hepworth, Moore, and other sculptors increasingly turned to abstraction, often emphasizing voids as well as masses in their work.

▌ The Bauhaus in Germany promoted the vision of "total architecture," which called for the integration of all the arts in constructing modern living environments. Bauhaus buildings were simple glass and steel designs devoid of "romantic embellishment and whimsy." In France, Le Corbusier used modern construction materials to build "machines for living"—simple houses with open plans and unadorned surfaces.

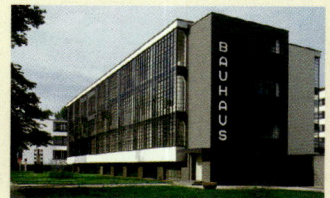

Gropius, Bauhaus, Dessau, 1925–1926

## UNITED STATES AND MEXICO 1930 to 1945

▌ Although Alexander Calder created abstract works between the wars, other American artists favored figural art. Lange and Shahn chronicled social injustice. Hopper explored the loneliness of life in the Depression era. Lawrence recorded the struggle of African Americans. Wood depicted life in rural Iowa.

▌ Mexican artists Orozco and Rivera painted epic mural cycles of the history of Mexico. Kahlo's powerful paintings explored the human psyche and were frequently autobiographical.

▌ The leading American architect of the first half of the 20th century was Frank Lloyd Wright, who promoted the "architecture of democracy," in which free individuals move in a "free" space.

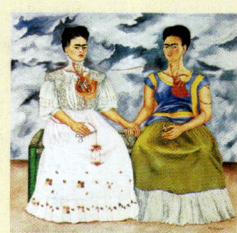

Kahlo, *The Two Fridas,* 1939

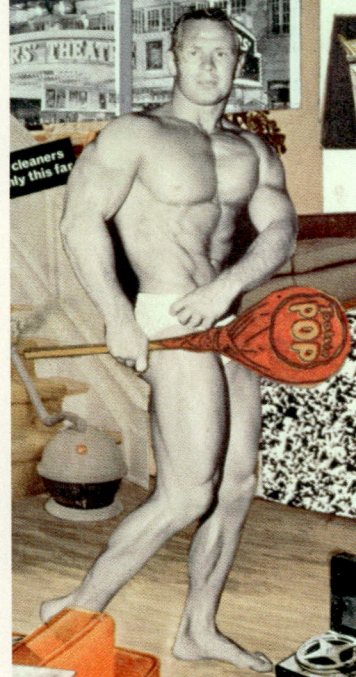

Toying with mass-media imagery typifies British Pop Art. The central motif in Hamilton's modern home is the body builder Charles Atlas, who holds a Tootsie Pop in place of a weightlifter's barbell.

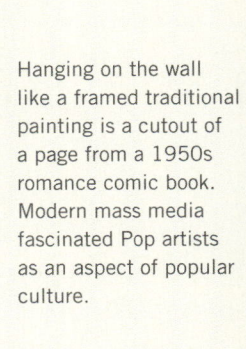

Hanging on the wall like a framed traditional painting is a cutout of a page from a 1950s romance comic book. Modern mass media fascinated Pop artists as an aspect of popular culture.

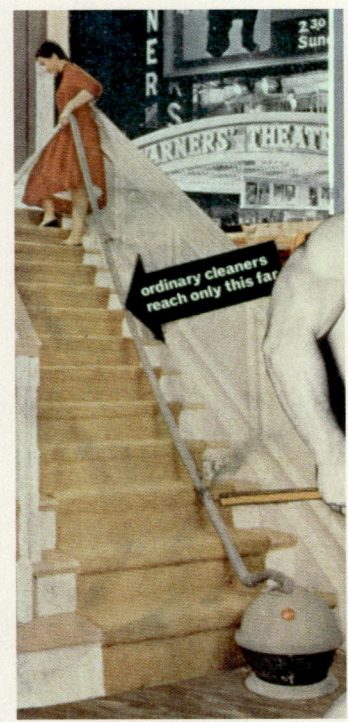

The fantasy interior in Hamilton's collage reflects the values of modern consumer culture. The figures and objects cut from glossy magazines include an advertisement for Hoover vacuum cleaners.

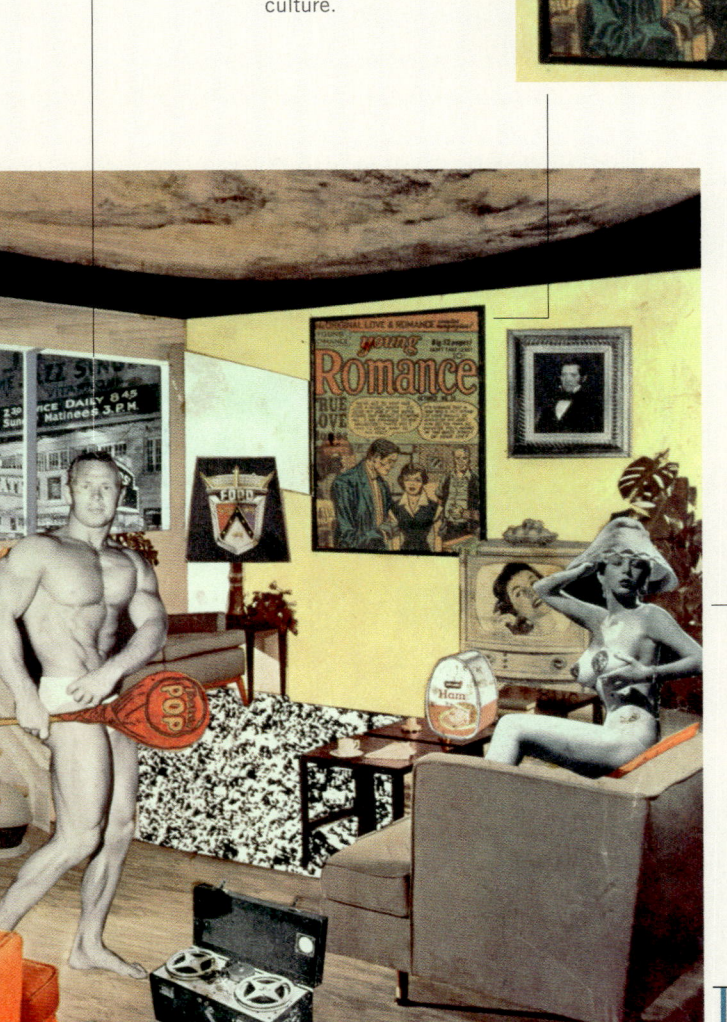

1 in.

**30-1** RICHARD HAMILTON, *Just What Is It That Makes Today's Homes So Different, So Appealing?* 1956. Collage, $10\frac{1}{4}'' \times 9\frac{3}{4}''$. Kunsthalle Tübingen, Tübingen.

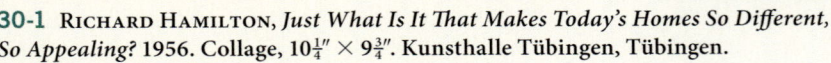

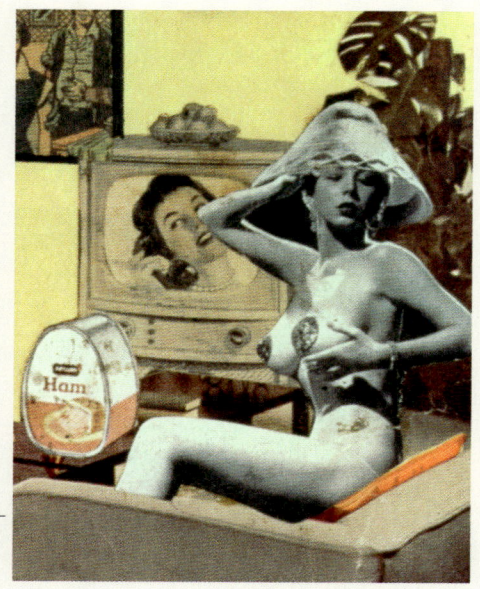

Also included in Hamilton's "appealing" modern home are a television, a can of Armour ham, and a photograph taken from a "girlie magazine" to stimulate speculation about society's values.

# 30

# MODERNISM AND POSTMODERNISM IN EUROPE AND AMERICA, 1945 TO 1980

FRAMING THE ERA

## ART AND CONSUMER CULTURE

The interest in abstraction that emerged so forcefully in avant-garde artistic circles during the first half of the 20th century gained even greater momentum in the decades after the end of World War II. However, a reaction to pure formalism in painting and sculpture also set in. The artists of the *Pop Art* movement reintroduced all of the devices the postwar abstractionists had purged from their artworks. Pop artists revived the tools traditionally used to convey meaning in art, such as signs, symbols, metaphors, allusions, illusions, and figural imagery. They not only embraced representation but also firmly grounded their art in the consumer culture and mass media of the postwar period, thereby making it much more accessible and understandable to the average person. Indeed, the name "Pop Art"—credited to the British art critic Lawrence Alloway (1926–1990)—is short for "popular art" and referred to the popular mass culture and familiar imagery of the contemporary urban environment.

Art historians trace the roots of Pop Art to the young British artists, architects, and writers who formed the Independent Group at the Institute of Contemporary Art in London in the early 1950s. They sought to initiate fresh thinking in art, in part by sharing their fascination with the aesthetics and content of such facets of popular culture as advertising, comic books, and movies. In 1956, an Independent Group member, RICHARD HAMILTON (b. 1922), made a small collage, *Just What Is It That Makes Today's Homes So Different, So Appealing?* (FIG. **30-1**), which exemplifies British Pop Art. Trained as an engineering draftsman, exhibition designer, and painter, Hamilton studied the way advertising shapes public attitudes. Long intrigued by Marcel Duchamp's ideas (see Chapter 29), Hamilton consistently combined elements of popular art and fine art, seeing both as belonging to the whole world of visual communication. He created *Just What Is It?* for the poster and catalog of one section of an exhibition titled *This Is Tomorrow*, which included images from Hollywood cinema, science fiction, and the mass media.

The fantasy interior in Hamilton's collage reflects the values of mid-20th-century consumer culture through figures and objects cut from glossy magazines. *Just What Is It?* includes references to mass media (the television, the theater marquee outside the window, the newspaper), to advertising (Hoover vacuum cleaners, Ford cars, Armour hams, Tootsie Pops), and to popular culture (the "girlie magazine," the body builder Charles Atlas, romance comic books). Artworks of this sort stimulated viewers' wide-ranging speculation about society's values. This kind of intellectual toying with mass-media meaning and imagery typified Pop Art both in Europe and America.

# THE AFTERMATH OF WORLD WAR II

World War II, with the global devastation it unleashed on all dimensions of life—political, economic, and psychological—set the stage for the second half of the 20th century. The dropping of atomic bombs by the United States on the Japanese cities of Hiroshima and Nagasaki in 1945 signaled a turning point not only in the war itself but in the geopolitical balance and the nature of international conflict as well. For the postwar generation, nuclear attack became a very real threat. Indeed, the two nuclear superpowers, the United States and the Soviet Union, divided the world into spheres of influence, and each regularly intervened politically, economically, and militarily wherever and whenever it considered its interests to be at stake.

The cessation of global warfare did not bring global peace. On the contrary, regional conflicts erupted throughout the world during the decades after World War II. In 1947, the British left India, which precipitated a murderous Hindu-Muslim war that divided South Asia into two new hostile nations—India and Pakistan. After a bloody civil war, Communists came to power in China in 1949. North Korea invaded South Korea in 1950 and fought a grim war with the United States and its allies. The Soviets brutally suppressed uprisings in their subject nations—East Germany, Poland, Hungary, and Czechoslovakia. The United States intervened in disputes in Central and South America. Almost as soon as many colonized nations of Africa—Kenya, Uganda, Nigeria, Angola, Mozambique, the Sudan, Rwanda, and the Congo—won their independence, civil wars devastated them. In Indonesia, civil war left more than 100,000 dead. Algeria expelled France in 1962 after the French waged a prolonged war with Algeria's Muslim natives. After 15 years of bitter war in Southeast Asia, the United States suffered defeat in Vietnam.

The period from 1945 to 1980 also brought upheaval in the cultural sphere. In the United States, for example, various groups forcefully questioned the status quo. The struggles for civil rights for African Americans, for free speech on university campuses, and for disengagement from the Vietnam War led to a rebellion of the young, who took to the streets in often raucous demonstrations, some with violent repercussions. The prolonged ferment produced a new system of values, a "youth culture," expressed in the radical rejection not only of national policies but often also of the society generating them. Young Americans derided their elders' lifestyles and adopted unconventional dress, manners, habits, and morals deliberately subversive of mainstream social standards. The youth era witnessed the sexual revolution, the widespread use and abuse of drugs, and the development of rock music, then an exclusively youthful art form. Young people "dropped out" of regulated society, embraced alternative belief systems, and rejected Western university curricula as irrelevant.

This counterculture had considerable societal impact. The civil rights movement of the 1960s and later the women's liberation movement of the 1970s reflected the spirit of rebellion, coupled with the rejection of racism and sexism. In keeping with the growing resistance to established authority, women systematically began to challenge the male-dominated culture, which they perceived as having limited their political power and economic opportunities for centuries. Feminists charged that the institutions of Western society, particularly the traditional family unit headed by a patriarch, perpetuated male power and the subordination of women. They further contended that monuments of Western culture—its arts and sciences, as well as its political, social, and economic institutions—masked the realities of male power.

Increasingly, individuals and groups actively sought to combat the inappropriate exercise of power or to change the balance of power. For example, following patterns developed first in the civil rights movement and later in feminism, various ethnic groups and gays and lesbians mounted challenges to discriminatory policies and attitudes. These groups fought for recognition, respect, and legal protection and battled discrimination with political action. In addition, the growing scrutiny in numerous academic fields—cultural studies, literary theory, and colonial and postcolonial studies—of the dynamics and exercise of power also contributed to the dialogue on these issues. As a result of this concern for the dynamics of power, identity (both individual and group) emerged as a potent arena for discussion and action—and as a persistent and compelling subject for painters, sculptors, and photographers.

# PAINTING, SCULPTURE, AND PHOTOGRAPHY

The end of World War II in 1945 left devastated cities, ruptured economies, and governments in chaos throughout Europe. These factors, coupled with the massive loss of life and the indelible horrors of the bombing of Hiroshima and Nagasaki and of the

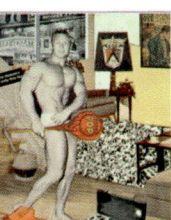

## MODERNISM AND POSTMODERNISM IN EUROPE AND AMERICA, 1945 TO 1980

**1945**    **1960**    **1970**    **1980**

- European Expressionists capture in their paintings and sculptures the revulsion and cynicism that emerged in the wake of World War II
- New York School painters develop Abstract Expressionism, emphasizing form and raw energy over subject matter
- Sleek, geometrically rigid modernist skyscrapers become familiar sights in cities throughout the world

- Post-Painterly Abstractionists reject the passion and texture of action painting and celebrate the flatness of pigment on canvas
- Op artists produce the illusion of motion and depth using only geometric forms
- Minimalists reduce sculpture to basic shapes and emphasize their works' "objecthood"
- Pop artists find inspiration in popular culture and commonplace commercial products
- Superrealists create paintings and sculptures characterized by scrupulous reproduction of the appearance of people and objects
- Performance artists replace traditional stationary artworks with temporal action-artworks

- Artists play a leading role in the feminist movement by promoting women's themes and employing materials traditionally associated with women, such as china and fabric
- Postmodern architects erect complex and eclectic buildings that often incorporate references to historical styles
- Environmental artists redefine what constitutes "art" by manipulating natural materials in monumental earthworks
- Artists increasingly embrace new media—video recorders, computers—as tools for creating artworks

Holocaust, in which six million Jews died at the hands of the Nazis, resulted in a pervasive sense of despair, disillusionment, and skepticism. Although many people (for example, the Futurists in Italy; see Chapter 29) had tried to find redemptive value in World War I, it was nearly impossible to do the same with World War II, coming as it did so soon after the "war to end all wars." Additionally, World War I was largely a European conflict that left roughly 10 million people dead, whereas World War II was a truly global catastrophe, claiming 35 million lives.

## Postwar Expressionism in Europe

The cynicism pervading Europe in the 1940s found voice in existentialism, a philosophy asserting the absurdity of human existence and the impossibility of achieving certitude. Many who embraced existentialism also promoted atheism and questioned the possibility of situating God within a systematic philosophy. Scholars trace the roots of existentialism to the Danish theologian Søren Kierkegaard (1813–1855), but in the postwar period, the writings of French author Jean-Paul Sartre (1905–1980) most clearly captured the existentialist spirit. According to Sartre, if God does not exist, then individuals must constantly struggle in isolation with the anguish of making decisions in a world without absolutes or traditional values. This spirit of pessimism and despair emerged frequently in European art of the immediate postwar period. A brutality or roughness appropriately expressing both the artist's state of mind and the larger cultural sensibility characterized the work of many European sculptors and painters.

**ALBERTO GIACOMETTI** The sculpture of Swiss artist ALBERTO GIACOMETTI (1901–1966) perhaps best expresses the spirit of existentialism. Although Giacometti never claimed he pursued

**30-2** ALBERTO GIACOMETTI, *Man Pointing No. 5,* 1947. Bronze, 5′ 10″ high. Des Moines Art Center, Des Moines (Nathan Emory Coffin Collection).

The writer Jean-Paul Sartre saw Giacometti's thin and virtually featureless sculpted figures as the epitome of existentialist humanity—alienated, solitary, and lost in the world's immensity.

1 ft.

existentialist ideas in his art, his works capture the spirit of that philosophy. Indeed, Sartre, Giacometti's friend, saw the artist's figurative sculptures as the epitome of existentialist humanity—alienated, solitary, and lost in the world's immensity. Giacometti's sculptures of the 1940s, such as *Man Pointing, No. 5* (FIG. **30-2**), are thin, nearly featureless figures with rough, agitated surfaces. Rather than conveying the solidity and mass of conventional bronze sculpture, these severely attenuated figures seem swallowed up by the space surrounding them, imparting a sense of isolation and fragility. Giacometti's evocative, moving sculptures spoke to the pervasive despair that emerged in the aftermath of world war.

**FRANCIS BACON** Although born in Dublin, Ireland, FRANCIS BACON (1910–1992) was the son of a well-to-do Englishman. He spent most of his life in London, where he experienced firsthand the destruction of lives and property the Nazi bombing wrought on the city during World War II. *Painting* (FIG. **30-3**) is Bacon's indictment of humanity and a reflection of war's butchery. The artist presented a compelling and revolting image of a powerful, stocky man with a gaping mouth and a vivid red stain on his upper lip, as if he were a carnivore devouring the raw meat sitting on the railing

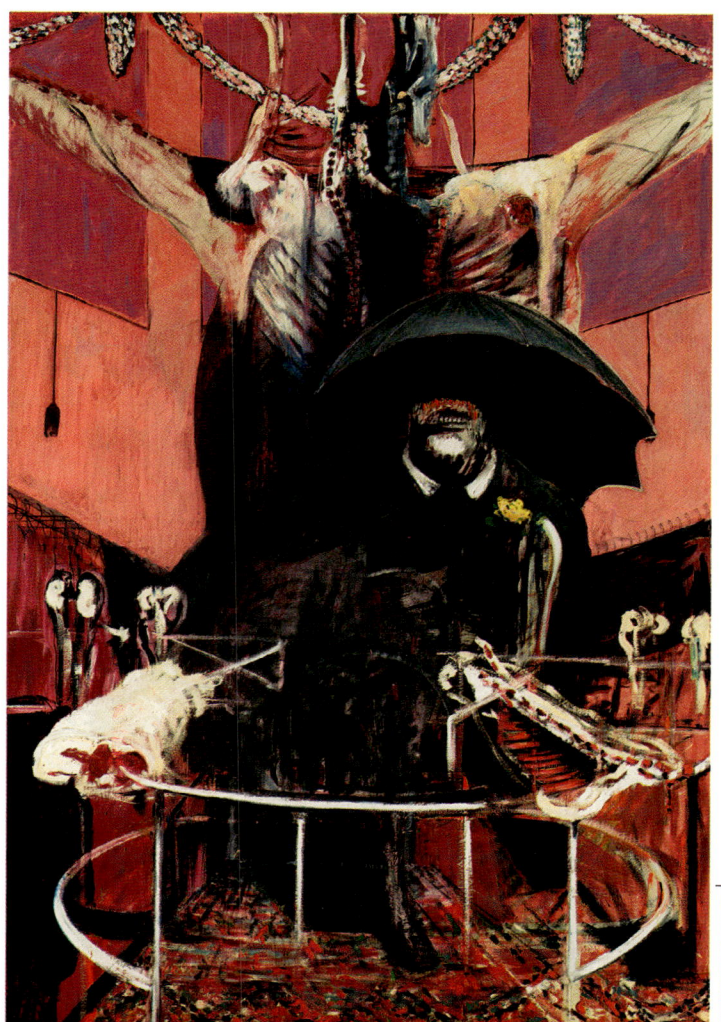

1 ft.

**30-3** FRANCIS BACON, *Painting,* 1946. Oil and pastel on linen, 6′ 5⅞″ × 4′ 4″. Museum of Modern Art, New York.

Painted in the aftermath of World War II, this intentionally revolting image of a powerful figure presiding over a slaughter is Bacon's indictment of humanity and a reflection of war's butchery.

Painting, Sculpture, and Photography　**901**

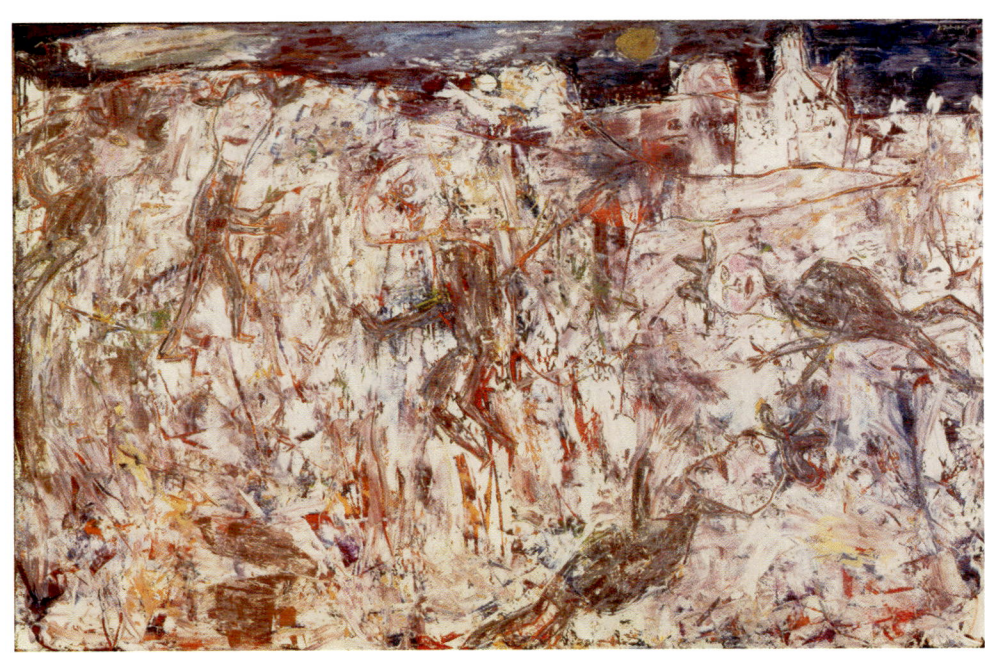

**30-4** Jean Dubuffet, *Vie Inquiète*, 1953. Oil on canvas, 4′ 3″ × 6′ 4″. Tate Modern, London (gift of the artist, 1966).

Dubuffet expressed a tortured vision of the world through thickly encrusted painted surfaces and crude images of the kind children and the insane produce. He called it "art brut"—untaught and coarse art.

1 ft.

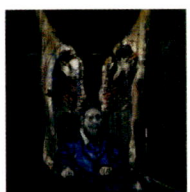

**30-3A** Bacon, *Figure with Meat*, 1954.

surrounding him (compare FIG. 30-3A). Bacon may have based his depiction of this central figure on news photos of similarly dressed European and American officials. The umbrella in particular recalls images of Neville Chamberlain (1869–1940), the wartime British prime minister who frequently appeared in photographs with an umbrella. Bacon added to the visceral impact of the painting by depicting the flayed carcass hanging behind the central figure like a crucified human form. Although the specific sources for the imagery in *Painting* are uncertain, the work is unmistakably "an attempt to remake the violence of reality itself," as Bacon often described his art, based on what he referred to as "the brutality of fact."[1]

**JEAN DUBUFFET** Although less specific, the works of French artist JEAN DUBUFFET (1901–1985) also express a tortured vision of the world through manipulated materials. In works such as *Vie Inquiète* (*Uneasy Life;* FIG. 30-4), Dubuffet first built up an *impasto* (a layer of thickly applied pigment) of plaster, glue, sand, asphalt, and other common materials, over which he painted or incised crude images of the kind produced by children, the insane, and scrawlers of graffiti. Scribblings interspersed with the images heighten the impression of smeared and gashed surfaces of crumbling walls and worn pavements marked by random individuals. Dubuffet believed the art of children, the mentally unbalanced, prisoners, and outcasts was more direct and genuine because those who created it did so unrestrained by conventional standards of art. He promoted "art brut"—untaught and coarse art.

## Abstract Expressionism

In the 1960s, the center of the Western art world shifted from Paris to New York because of the devastation World War II had inflicted across Europe and the resulting influx of émigré artists escaping to the United States. It was in New York that the first major American avant-garde art movement—Abstract Expressionism—emerged. The most important forerunner of the Abstract Expressionists, however, was an Armenian immigrant who arrived in New York in 1924.

**ARSHILE GORKY** Born a Christian in Islamic Turkish Armenia, Vosdanik Manoog Adoian was four years old when his father escaped being drafted into the Turkish army by fleeing the country. His mother died of starvation in her 15-year-old son's arms in a refugee camp for victims of the Turkish campaign of genocide against the Christian minority. The penniless Vosdanik managed in 1920 to make his way to America, where a relative

took him into his home near Boston. Four years later, then a young man, Vosdanik changed his name to ARSHILE GORKY (1904–1948)— "Bitter Achilles" in Russian—and moved to New York City, where he continued the art education he had begun in Boston. In 1948, he hanged himself after an automobile accident robbed him of the use of his right arm. The injury might have been only temporary, but the depressed Gorky thought he would never be able to paint again. In a career lasting only two decades, Gorky contributed significantly to the artistic revolution born in New York. His work is the bridge between the Biomorphic Surrealism of Joan Miró (FIG. 29-58) and the totally abstract canvases of Jackson Pollock (FIG. 30-6).

*Garden in Sochi* (FIG. 30-5), painted in 1943, is the third in a series of canvases with identical titles named after a Black Sea resort but inspired by Gorky's childhood memories of the Garden of Wish Fulfillment in his birthplace. The women of the Armenian village of Khorkom believed their wishes would be granted if they rubbed their bare breasts against a rock in that garden beneath a tree to which they tied torn strips of their clothing. The brightly colored and thinly outlined forms in *Garden in Sochi,* which initially appear to be purely abstract biomorphic shapes, are loose sketches representing, at the left, a bare-breasted woman, and, at the center, a tree trunk with fluttering fabric. At the bottom are two oversized shoes—the Armenian slippers Gorky's father gave his son shortly before abandoning the family.

**CLEMENT GREENBERG** The few traces of representational art in Gorky's work disappeared in *Abstract Expressionism.* As the name suggests, the artists associated with the New York School of Abstract Expressionism produced paintings that are, for the most part, abstract but express the artist's state of mind, with the goal also of striking emotional chords in the viewer. The most important champion of this strict *formalism*—an emphasis on an artwork's visual elements rather than its subject—was the American art critic Clement Greenberg (1909–1994), who wielded considerable influence from the 1940s through the 1970s. Greenberg helped redefine the parameters of modernism by advocating the rejection of illusionism and the exploration of the properties of each artistic medium. So dominant was Greenberg that scholars often refer to the general modernist tenets during this period as Greenbergian formalism.

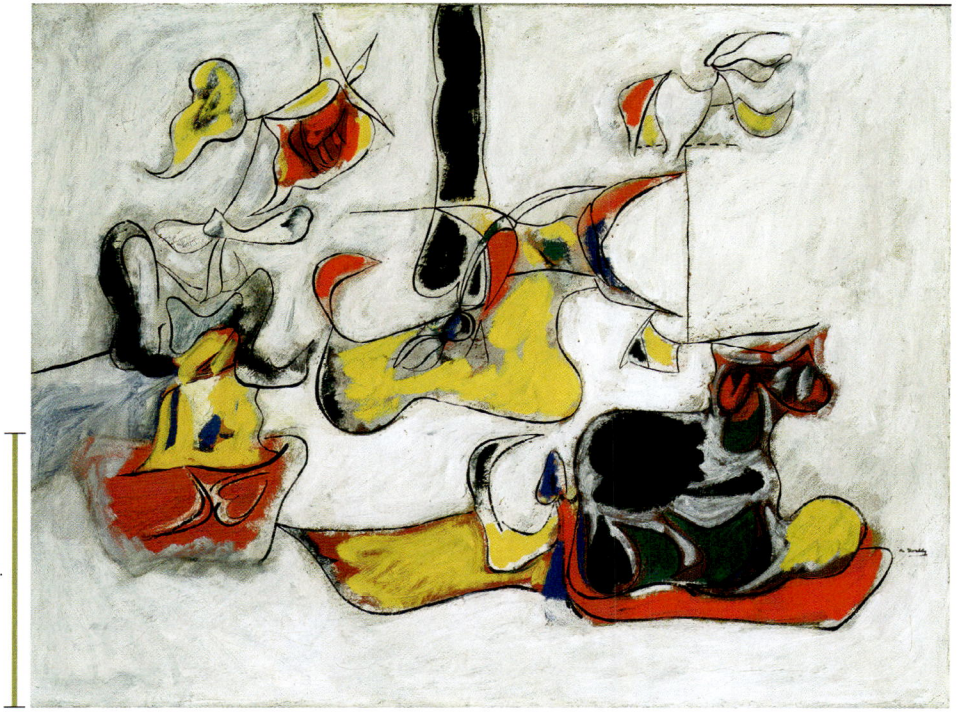

**30-5** ARSHILE GORKY, *Garden in Sochi,* ca. 1943. Oil on canvas, 2′ 7″ × 3′ 3″. Museum of Modern Art, New York (acquired through the Lillie P. Bliss Bequest).

Gorky's paintings of the 1940s, which still incorporate recognizable forms, are the bridge between the Biomorphic Surrealist canvases of Miró and the Abstract Expressionist paintings of Pollock.

Among other things, this means renouncing illusion and explicit subject matter. The arts are to achieve concreteness, "purity," by dealing solely with their respective selves—that is, by becoming "abstract" or nonfigurative.[3]

The Abstract Expressionists turned inward to create, and the resulting works convey a rough spontaneity and palpable energy. The New York School painters wanted the viewer to grasp the content of their art intuitively, in a mental state free from structured thinking. One of the leading painters of this group, Mark Rothko (FIG. 30-10), eloquently wrote:

Although Greenberg modified his complex ideas about art over the years, he consistently expounded certain basic concepts. In particular, Greenberg promoted the idea of artistic purity: "Purity in art consists in the acceptance, willing acceptance, of the limitations of the medium of the specific art."[2] In other words, Greenberg believed artists should strive for a more explicit focus on the properties exclusive to each medium—for example, two-dimensionality or flatness in painting, and three-dimensionality in sculpture.

> It follows that a modernist work of art must try, in principle, to avoid communication with any order of experience not inherent in the most literally and essentially construed nature of its medium.

> We assert man's absolute emotions. We don't need props or legends. We create images whose realities are self evident. Free ourselves from memory, association, nostalgia, legend, myth. Instead of making cathedrals out of Christ, man or life, we make it out of ourselves, out of our own feelings. The image we produce is understood by anyone who looks at it without nostalgic glasses of history.[4]

The Abstract Expressionist movement developed along two lines—*gestural abstraction* and *chromatic abstraction*. The gestural abstractionists relied on the expressiveness of energetically applied pigment. In contrast, the chromatic abstractionists focused on color's emotional resonance.

**JACKSON POLLOCK** The artist whose work best exemplifies gestural abstraction is JACKSON POLLOCK (1912–1956), who developed his signature style in the mid-1940s. By 1950, Pollock had refined his technique and was producing large-scale abstract paintings such as *Number 1, 1950* (*Lavender Mist;* FIG. **30-6**), which consist of rhythmic drips, splatters, and dribbles of paint. The mural-sized fields of energetic skeins of pigment envelop viewers, drawing them into a lacy spider web. Using sticks or brushes, Pollock flung,

**30-6** JACKSON POLLOCK, *Number 1, 1950* (*Lavender Mist*), 1950. Oil, enamel, and aluminum paint on canvas, 7′ 3″ × 9′ 10″. National Gallery of Art, Washington, D.C. (Ailsa Mellon Bruce Fund).

Pollock's paintings emphasize the creative process. His mural-size canvases consist of rhythmic drips, splatters, and dribbles of paint that envelop viewers, drawing them into a lacy spider web.

## Jackson Pollock on Easel and Mural Painting

Jackson Pollock's canvases (FIG. 30-6) constitute a revolution in the art of painting not only because of their purely abstract form but also in the artist's rejection of the centuries-old tradition of applying pigment to stretched canvases supported vertically before the painter on an easel. In two statements Pollock made in 1947, one as part of his application for a Guggenheim Fellowship and one in a published essay, the artist explained the motivations for his new kind of "action painting" and described the tools he used and the way he produced his monumental canvases (FIG. 30-7).

I intend to paint large movable pictures which will function between the easel and mural.... I believe the easel picture to be a dying form, and the tendency of modern feeling is towards the wall picture or mural.*

My painting does not come from the easel. I hardly ever stretch my canvas before painting. I prefer to tack the unstretched canvas to the hard wall or the floor. I need the resistance of a hard surface. On the floor I am more at ease. I feel nearer, more a part of the painting, since this way I can walk around it, work from the four sides and literally be *in* the painting. This is akin to the method of the Indian sand painters of the West [see Chapter 35, page 1032]. I continue to get further away from the usual painter's tools such as easel, palette, brushes, etc. I prefer sticks, trowels, knives and dripping fluid paint or a heavy impasto with sand, broken glass and other foreign matter added. When I am *in* my painting, I'm not aware of what I'm doing.... [T]he painting has a life of its own. I try to let it come through.... The source of my painting is the unconscious.†

**30-7** HANS NAMUTH, Jackson Pollock painting in his studio in Springs, Long Island, New York, 1950. Gelatin silver print, 10″ × 8″. Center for Creative Photography, University of Arizona, Tucson.

"Gestural abstraction" nicely describes Pollock's working technique. Using sticks or brushes, he flung, poured, and dripped paint onto a section of canvas he simply unrolled across his studio floor.

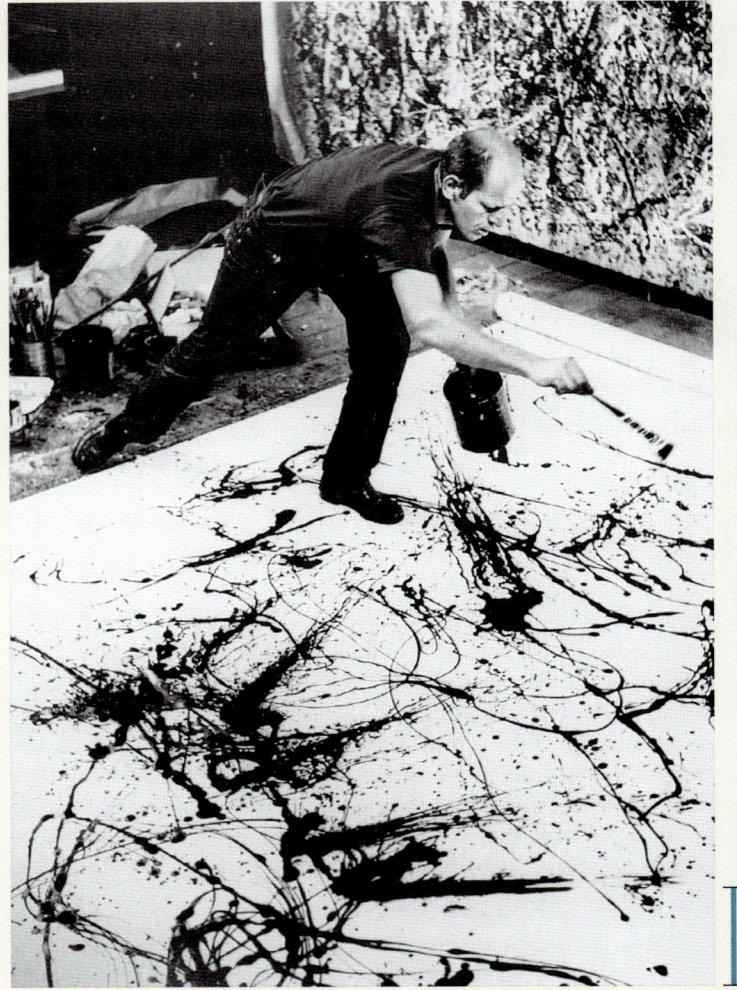

1 in.

*Quoted in Francis V. O'Connor, *Jackson Pollock* (New York: Museum of Modern Art, 1967), 39.
†Ibid., 39-40.

poured, and dripped paint (not only traditional oil paints but aluminum paints and household enamels as well) onto a section of canvas he simply unrolled across his studio floor (FIG. **30-7**). This working method earned Pollock the derisive nickname "Jack the Dripper." Responding to the image as it developed, he created art that was spontaneous yet choreographed. Pollock's painting technique highlights the most significant aspect of gestural abstraction—its emphasis on the creative process. Indeed, Pollock literally immersed himself in the painting during its creation.

Art historians have linked Pollock's ideas about improvisation in the creative process to his interest in what psychiatrist Carl Jung called the collective unconscious. The improvisational nature of Pollock's work and his reliance on the subconscious also have parallels in the "psychic automatism" of Surrealism and the work of Vassily Kandinsky (FIG. 29-7), whom critics described as an Abstract Expressionist as early as 1919. In addition to Pollock's

unique working methods and the expansive scale of his canvases, the lack of a well-defined compositional focus in his paintings significantly departed from conventional easel painting (see "Jackson Pollock on Easel and Mural Painting," above). A towering figure in 20th-century art, Pollock tragically died in a car accident at age 44, cutting short the development of his innovative artistic vision. Surviving him was his wife, LEE KRASNER (1908–1984), whom art historians recognize as a major Abstract Expressionist painter (FIG. **30-7A**), although overshadowed by Pollock during her lifetime.

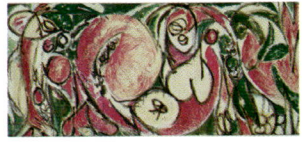

**30-7A** KRASNER, *The Seasons*, 1957.

**WILLEM DE KOONING** Despite the public's skepticism about Pollock's art, other artists enthusiastically pursued similar avenues of expression. Dutch-born WILLEM DE KOONING (1904–1997)

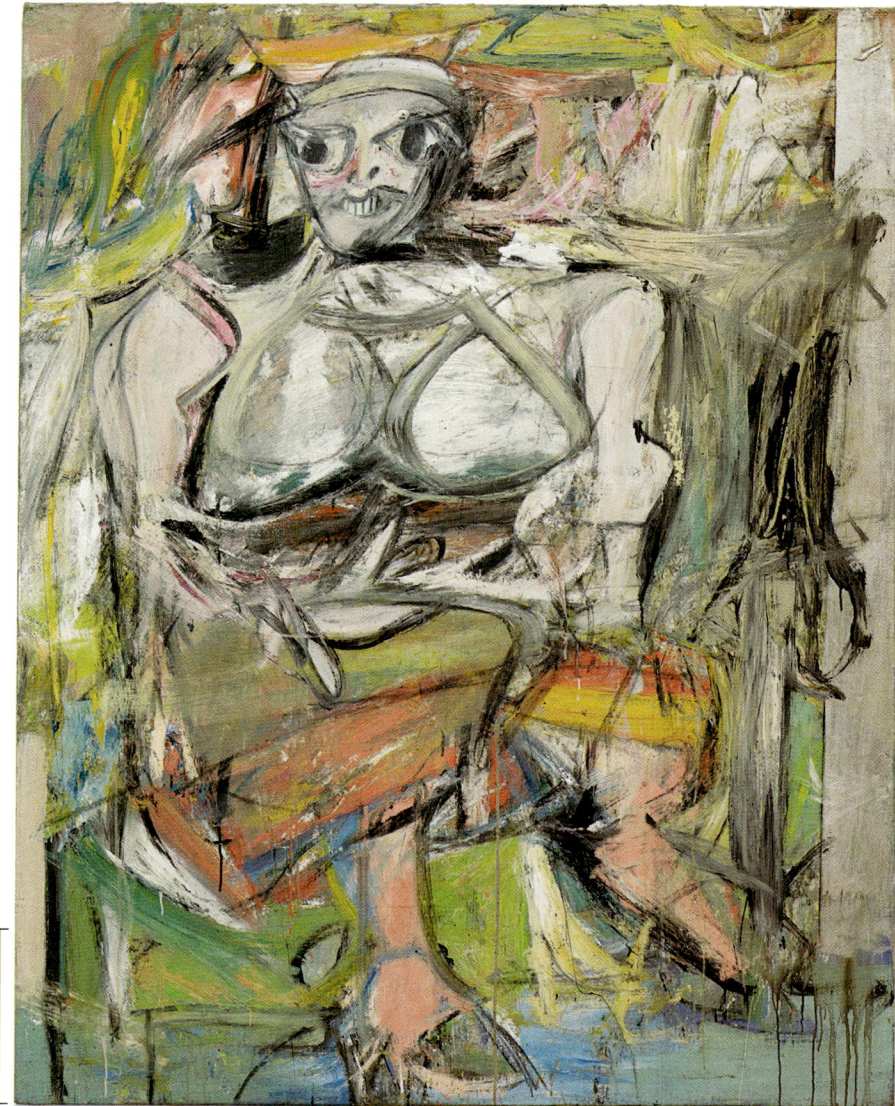

1 ft.

**30-8** WILLEM DE KOONING, *Woman I*, 1950–1952. Oil on canvas, 6′ 3$\frac{7}{8}$″ × 4′ 10″. Museum of Modern Art, New York. ◼◀

Although rooted in figuration, including pictures of female models on advertising billboards, de Kooning's *Woman I* displays the energetic application of pigment typical of gestural abstraction.

In addition to this *Woman* series, de Kooning created nonrepresentational works dominated by huge swaths and splashes of pigment. The images suggest rawness and intensity. His dealer, Sidney Janis (1896–1989), confirmed this impression, recalling de Kooning occasionally brought him paintings with ragged holes in them, the result of overly vigorous painting. Like Pollock, de Kooning was very much "in" his paintings. Vigorous physical interaction between the painter and the canvas led the critic Harold Rosenberg (1906–1978) to describe the work of the New York School as *action painting*. In his influential 1952 article "The American Action Painters," Rosenberg described the attempts of Pollock, de Kooning, and others to get "inside the canvas."

> At a certain moment the canvas began to appear to one American painter after another as an arena in which to act—rather than as a space in which to reproduce, re-design, analyze or "express" an object, actual or imagined. What was to go on the canvas was not a picture but an event. The painter no longer approached his easel with an image in his mind; he went up to it with material in his hand to do something to that other piece of material in front of him. The image would be the result of this encounter.[5]

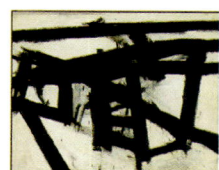

**30-8A** KLINE, *Mahoning*, 1956.

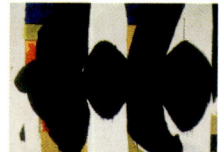

**30-8B** MOTHERWELL, *Elegy to the Spanish Republic*, 1953–1954.

Among the other prominent New York School Abstract Expressionists were Pennsylvania-born FRANZ KLINE (1910–1962), whose predominantly black-and-white paintings (FIG. **30-8A**) resemble Chinese and Japanese calligraphy; ROBERT MOTHERWELL (1915–1991), best known for his series of paintings inspired by the Spanish civil war (FIG. **30-8B**);

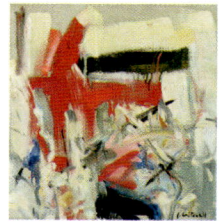

**30-8C** MITCHELL, *Untitled*, ca. 1953–1954.

and JOAN MITCHELL (1925–1992), the leading woman action painter (FIG. **30-8C**) of the 1950s. In the 1970s and later, a new generation of artists, including SUSAN ROTHENBERG (b. 1945; FIG. **30-8D**) reinvigorated Abstract Expressionism in a movement art historians have dubbed *Neo-Expressionism* (see Chapter 31).

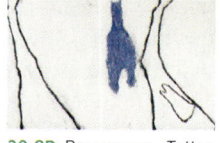

**30-8D** ROTHENBERG, *Tattoo*, 1979. ◼◀

**BARNETT NEWMAN** In contrast to the aggressively energetic images of the gestural abstractionists, the work of the chromatic abstractionists exudes a quieter aesthetic, exemplified by the work of Barnett Newman and Mark Rothko. The emotional resonance of their works derives from their eloquent use of color. In his early paintings, New York native BARNETT NEWMAN (1905–1970) presented organic abstractions inspired by his study of biology and his fascination with Native American art. He soon simplified his

also developed a gestural abstractionist style. Even images such as *Woman I* (FIG. **30-8**), although rooted in figuration, display the sweeping gestural brushstrokes and energetic application of pigment typical of gestural abstraction. Out of the jumbled array of slashing lines and agitated patches of color appears a ferocious-looking woman with staring eyes and ponderous breasts. Her toothy smile, inspired by an ad for Camel cigarettes, seems to devolve into a grimace. Female models on advertising billboards partly inspired *Woman I*, one of a series of images of women, but de Kooning's female forms also suggest fertility figures and a satiric inversion of the traditional image of Venus, goddess of love.

Process was important to de Kooning, as it was to Pollock. Continually working on *Woman I* for almost two years, de Kooning painted an image and then scraped it away the next day and began anew. His wife Elaine, also an accomplished painter, estimated he painted approximately 200 scraped-away images of women on this canvas before settling on the final one.

**30-9** BARNETT NEWMAN, *Vir Heroicus Sublimis*, 1950–1951. Oil on canvas, 7′ 11¾″ × 17′ 9¼″. Museum of Modern Art, New York (gift of Mr. and Mrs. Ben Heller). ◼◂

Newman's canvases consist of a single slightly modulated color field split by "zips" (narrow bands) running from one edge of the painting to the other, energizing the color field and giving it scale.

compositions so that each canvas—for example, the monumental (almost 8 by 18 feet) Latin-titled *Vir Heroicus Sublimis* (*Sublime Heroic Man;* FIG. **30-9**)—consists of a single slightly modulated color field split by narrow bands the artist called "zips," which run from one edge of the painting to the other. As Newman explained it, "The streak was always going through an atmosphere; I kept trying to create a world around it."[6] He did not intend the viewer to perceive the zips as specific entities, separate from the ground, but as accents energizing the field and giving it scale. By simplifying his compositions, Newman increased color's capacity to communicate and to express his feelings about the tragic condition of modern life and the human struggle to survive. He claimed "the artist's problem . . . [is] the idea-complex that makes contact with mystery—of life, of men, of nature, of the hard black chaos that is death, or the grayer, softer chaos that is tragedy."[7] Confronted by one of Newman's grandiose colored canvases, viewers truly feel as if they are in the presence of the epic.

**MARK ROTHKO** The work of MARK ROTHKO (1903–1970) also deals with universal themes. Born in Russia, Rothko moved with his family to the United States when he was 10. His early paintings were figural, but he soon came to believe that references to anything specific in the physical world conflicted with the sublime idea of the universal, supernatural "spirit of myth," which he saw as the core of meaning in art. In a statement cowritten with Newman and artist Adolph Gottlieb (1903–1974), Rothko expressed his beliefs about art:

> We favor the simple expression of the complex thought. We are for the large shape because it has the impact of the unequivocal. . . . We assert that . . . only that subject matter is valid which is tragic and timeless. That is why we profess spiritual kinship with primitive and archaic art.[8]

Rothko's paintings became compositionally simple, and he increasingly focused on color as the primary conveyor of meaning. In works such as *No. 14* (FIG. **30-10**), Rothko created compelling visual experiences consisting of two or three large rectangles of pure color with hazy edges that seem to float on the canvas surface, hovering in front of a colored background. His compositions present shimmering veils of intensely luminous colors that appear to be suspended in front of the canvases. Although the color juxtapositions are visually captivating, Rothko intended them as more than decorative. He saw

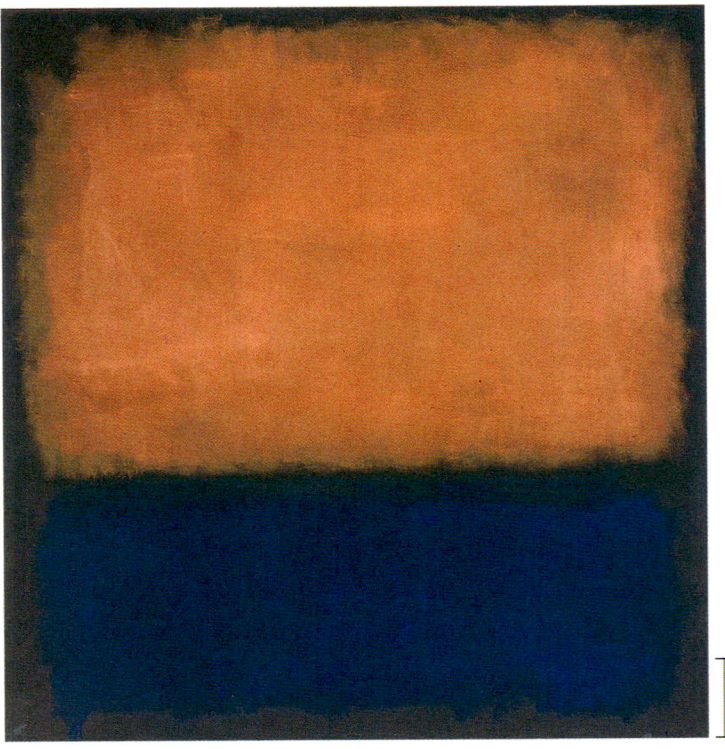

**30-10** MARK ROTHKO, *No. 14*, 1960. Oil on canvas, 9′ 6″ × 8′ 9″. San Francisco Museum of Modern Art, San Francisco (Helen Crocker Russell Fund Purchase).

Rothko's chromatic abstractionist paintings—consisting of hazy rectangles of pure color hovering in front of a colored background—are compositionally simple but compelling visual experiences.

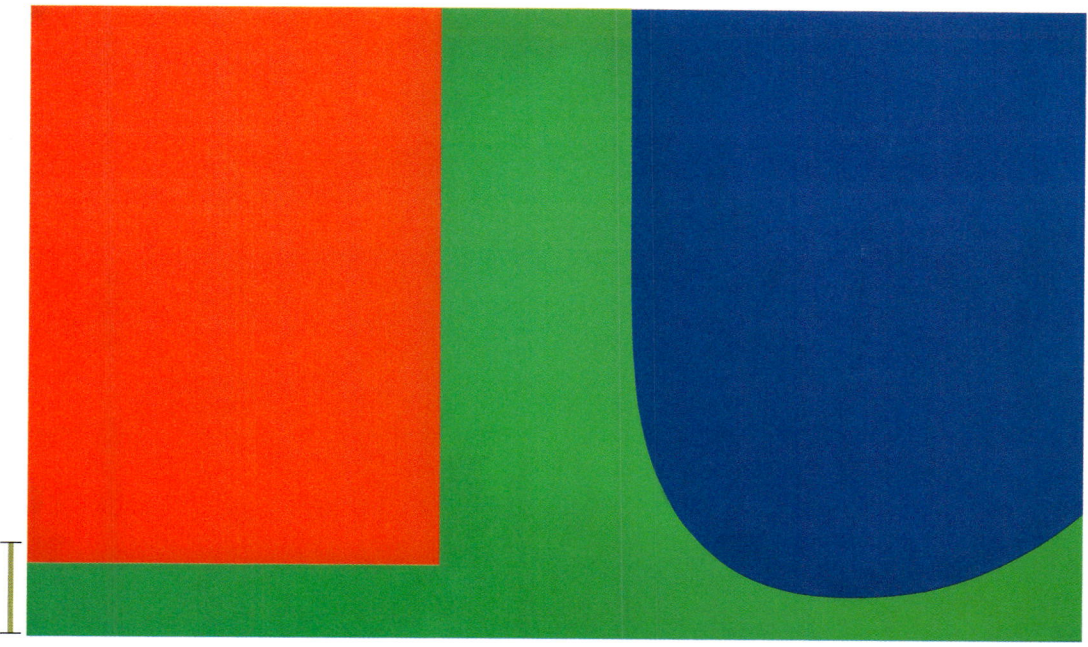

**30-11** ELLSWORTH KELLY, *Red Blue Green*, 1963. Oil on canvas, 6′ 11⅝″ × 11′ 3⅞″. Museum of Contemporary Art, San Diego (gift of Dr. and Mrs. Jack M. Farris).

Hard-edge painting is one variant of Post-Painterly Abstraction. Kelly used razor-sharp edges and clearly delineated areas of color to distill painting to its essential two-dimensional elements.

Post-Painterly Abstraction. Greenberg saw this art as contrasting with "painterly" art, characterized by loose, visible pigment application. Evidence of the artist's hand, so prominent in gestural abstraction, is conspicuously absent in Post-Painterly Abstraction. Greenberg championed this art form because it embodied his idea of purity in art.

color as a doorway to another reality, and insisted color could express "basic human emotions—tragedy, ecstasy, doom. . . . The people who weep before my pictures are having the same religious experience I had when I painted them. And if you, as you say, are moved only by their color relationships, then you miss the point."[9] Like the other Abstract Expressionists, Rothko produced highly evocative paintings reliant on formal elements rather than on specific representational content to elicit emotional responses in the viewer.

## Post-Painterly Abstraction

*Post-Painterly Abstraction,* another postwar American art movement, developed out of Abstract Expressionism. Indeed, many of the artists associated with Post-Painterly Abstraction produced Abstract Expressionist work early in their careers. Yet Post-Painterly Abstraction, a term Clement Greenberg coined, manifests a radically different sensibility from Abstract Expressionism. Whereas Abstract Expressionism conveys a feeling of passion and visceral intensity, a cool, detached rationality emphasizing tighter pictorial control characterizes

**ELLSWORTH KELLY** Attempting to arrive at pure painting, the Post-Painterly Abstractionists distilled painting down to its essential elements, producing spare, elemental images. One of the primary practitioners of one variant of Post-Painterly Abstraction, *hard-edge painting,* was ELLSWORTH KELLY (b. 1923). Born in Newburgh on the Hudson River north of New York City, Kelly studied at the Pratt Institute in Brooklyn and later in Boston and Paris. *Red Blue Green* (FIG. **30-11**) is a characteristic example of his work. With its razor-sharp edges and clearly delineated shapes, the painting is completely abstract and extremely simple in composition. Further, the composition contains no suggestion of the illusion of depth. The color shapes appear resolutely two-dimensional.

**FRANK STELLA** Another artist associated with the hard-edge painters of the 1960s is Massachusetts-born FRANK STELLA (b. 1936). Stella studied history at Princeton University and moved to New York City in 1958, but did not favor the rough, expressive brushwork of the Abstract Expressionists. In works such as *Mas o Menos* (*More or Less;* FIG. **30-12**), Stella eliminated many of the variables associated with painting. His simplified images of thin, evenly spaced pinstripes on colored grounds have no central focus, no painterly or expressive elements, only limited surface modulation, and no tactile quality. His systematic painting illustrates Greenberg's insistence on purity in art. The artist's own famous comment on his work, "What you see is what you see," reinforces the notions that painters interested in producing advanced art must reduce their work to its essential elements and that the viewer must acknowledge a painting is simply pigment on a flat surface.

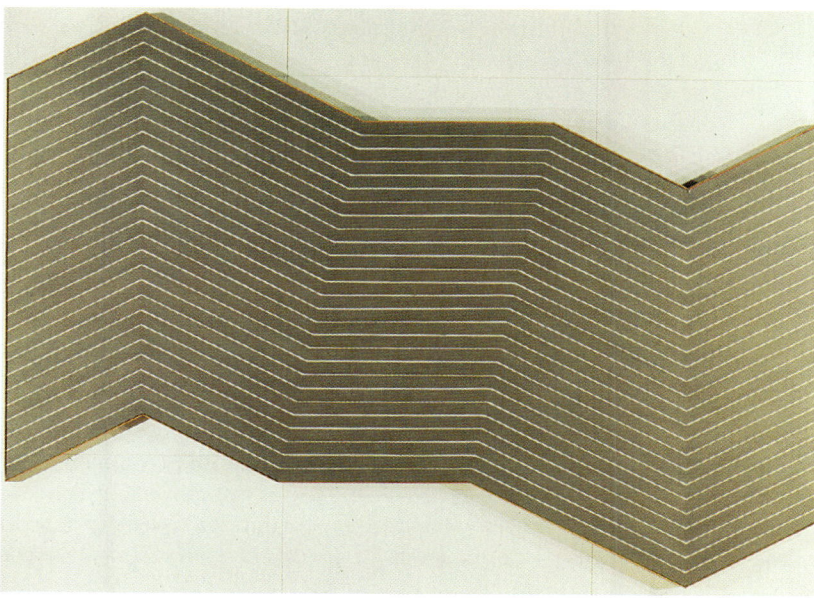

**30-12** FRANK STELLA, *Mas o Menos*, 1964. Metallic powder in acrylic emulsion on canvas, 9′ 10″ × 13′ 8½″. Musée National d'Art Moderne, Centre Georges Pompidou, Paris (purchase 1983 with participation of Scaler Foundation).

Stella tried to achieve purity in painting using evenly spaced pinstripes on colored grounds. His canvases have no central focus, no painterly or expressive elements, and no tactile quality.

# Helen Frankenthaler on Color-Field Painting

Helen Frankenthaler, the daughter of a New York State Supreme Court justice, began her study of art at the Dalton School in New York City under Rufino Tamayo (FIG. 29-74A). She has painted in New York for virtually her entire career. In 1965, the art critic Henry Geldzahler (1935–1994) interviewed Frankenthaler about her work as an abstract painter. In the following excerpt, Frankenthaler described the approach she took to placing color on canvas in *The Bay* (FIG. 30-13) and similar color-field paintings she produced in the early 1960s, and compared her method with the way earlier modernist artists used color in their paintings.

> I will sometimes start a picture feeling "What will happen if I work with three blues and another color, and maybe more or less of the other color than the combined blues?" And very often midway through the picture I have to change the basis of the experience. . . .
>
> When you first saw a Cubist or Impressionist picture there was a whole way of instructing the eye or the subconscious. Dabs of color had to stand for real things; it was an abstraction of a guitar or a hillside. The opposite is going on now. If you have bands of blue, green, and pink, the mind doesn't think sky, grass, and flesh. These are colors and the question is what are they doing with themselves and with each other. Sentiment and nuance are being squeezed out.*

*Henry Geldzahler, "Interview with Helen Frankenthaler," *Artforum* 4, no. 2 (October 1965), 37–38.

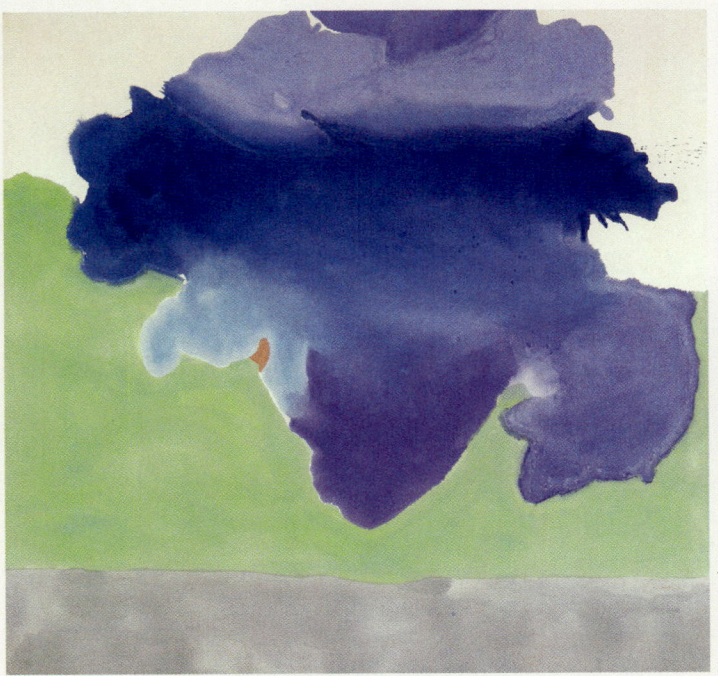

30-13 HELEN FRANKENTHALER, *The Bay*, 1963. Acrylic on canvas, 6′ 8⅞″ × 6′ 9⅞″. Detroit Institute of Arts, Detroit.

Frankenthaler and other color-field painters poured paint onto unprimed canvas, allowing the pigments to soak into the fabric. Their works underscore that a painting is simply pigment on a flat surface.

**HELEN FRANKENTHALER** *Color-field painting,* another variant of Post-Painterly Abstraction, also emphasized painting's basic properties. However, rather than produce sharp, unmodulated shapes as the hard-edge artists had done, the color-field painters poured diluted paint onto unprimed canvas and allowed the pigments to soak in. It is hard to conceive of another painting method resulting in such literal flatness. The images created, such as *The Bay* (FIG. 30-13) by HELEN FRANKENTHALER (b. 1928), appear spontaneous and almost accidental (see "Helen Frankenthaler on Color-Field Painting," above). These works differ from those by Rothko and Newman in that Frankenthaler subordinated the emotional component, so integral to hard-edge painting, in favor of resolving formal problems.

**MORRIS LOUIS** Baltimore native MORRIS LOUIS (1912–1962), who spent most of his career in Washington, D.C., also became a champion of color-field painting. Clement Greenberg, an admirer of Frankenthaler's paintings, took Louis to her studio, where she introduced him to the possibilities presented by the staining technique. Louis used this method of pouring diluted paint onto the surface of unprimed canvas in several series of paintings. *Saraband* (FIG. 30-14) is one of the works in Louis's *Veils* series. By holding up the canvas edges and pouring diluted acrylic resin, Louis created billowy, fluid, transparent shapes running down the length of the

canvas. As did Frankenthaler, Louis reduced painting to the concrete fact of the paint-impregnated material.

**CLYFFORD STILL** Although not a member of the New York School, another American painter whose work art historians usually classify as Post-Painterly Abstraction was CLYFFORD STILL (1904–1980). Born in North Dakota, Still spent most of his career on the West Coast or in Maryland. He is best known for the large series of canvases he titled simply with their dates, underscoring his rejection of the very notion that the purpose of art is to represent places, people, or objects. Nonetheless, Still's paintings remind many viewers of vast landscapes seen from the air. But the artist's canvases make no reference to any forms in nature. His paintings, for example, *1948-C* (FIG. I-2), are pure exercises in the expressive use of color, shape, and texture.

## Op Art

A major artistic movement of the 1960s was *Op Art* (short for *Optical Art*), in which painters sought to produce optical illusions of motion and depth using only geometric forms on two-dimensional surfaces. Among the primary sources of the movement was the work of Josef Albers, whose series of paintings called *Homage to the Square* (FIG. I-11) explored the optical effects of placing different

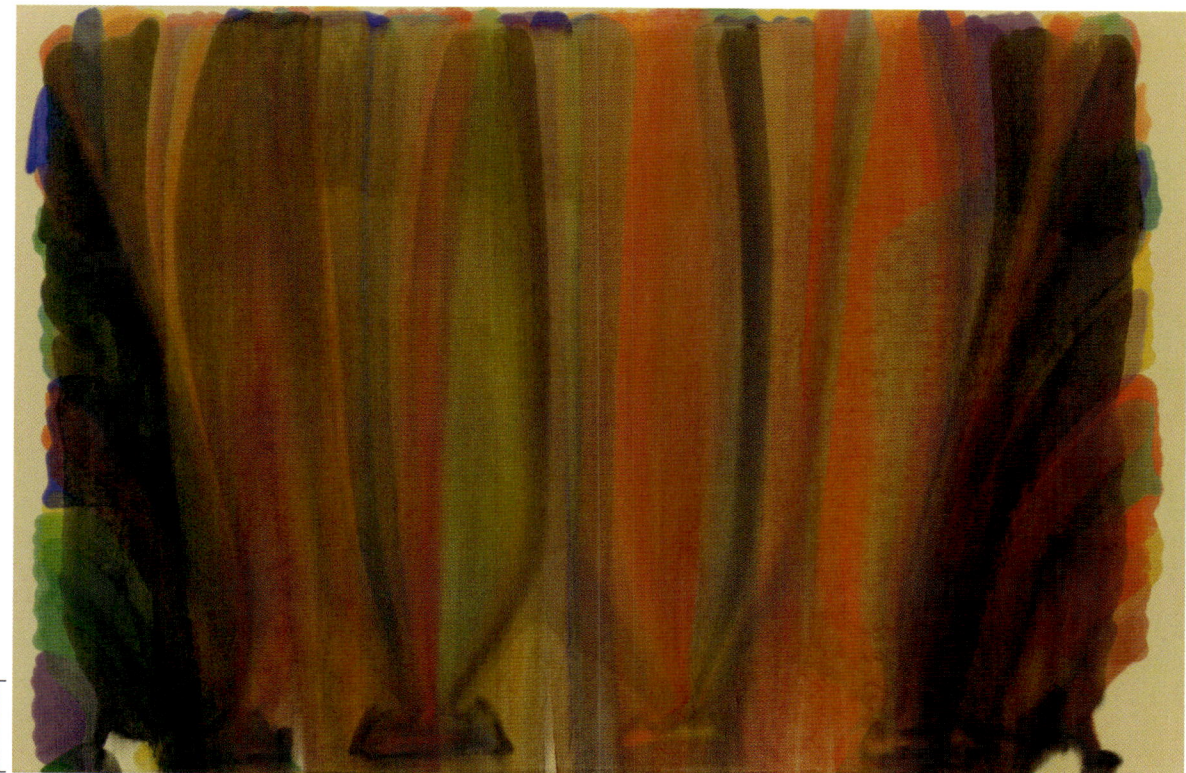

Louis created his color-field paintings by holding up the canvas edges and pouring diluted acrylic resin to produce billowy, fluid, transparent shapes running down the length of the fabric.

1 ft.

colors next to each other. Ultimately, Op Art can be traced to 19th-century theories of color perception and the pointillism of Georges Seurat (see "Pointillism and 19th-Century Color Theory," Chapter 28, page 813, and FIG. 28-16).

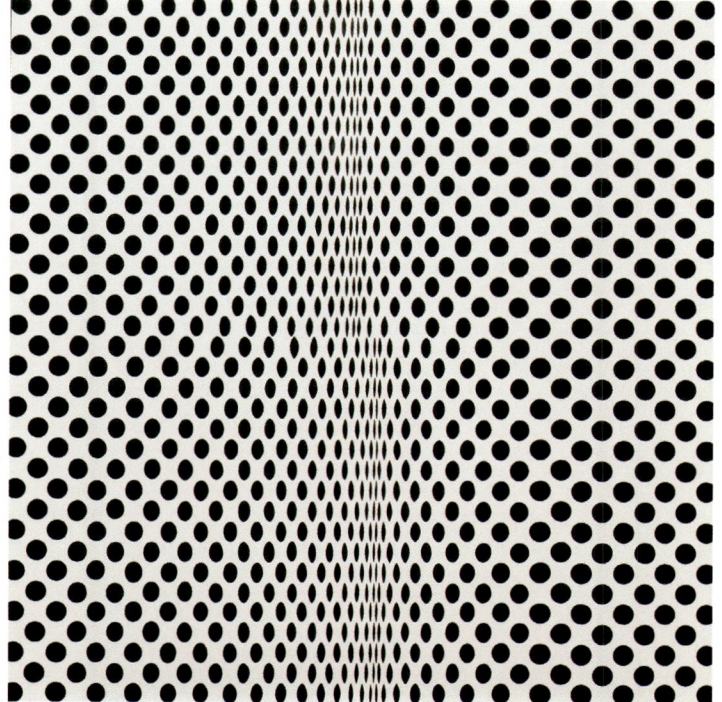

30-15 BRIDGET RILEY, *Fission*, 1963. Tempera on composition board, 2′ 11″ × 2′ 10″. Museum of Modern Art, New York (gift of Philip Johnson).

Op Art paintings create the illusion of motion and depth using only geometric forms. The effect can be disorienting. The pattern of black dots in Riley's *Fission* appears to cave in at the center.

1 ft.

**BRIDGET RILEY** The artist whose name is synonymous with Op Art is the British artist BRIDGET RILEY (b. 1931), who painted in a neo-pointillist manner in the 1950s before developing her signature black-and-white Op Art style. Her paintings, for example, *Fission* (FIG. 30-15) of 1963, came to the public's attention after being featured in the December 1964 issue of *Life* magazine. The publicity unleashed a craze for Op Art designs in clothing. In 1965, the exhibition *The Responsive Eye* at the Museum of Modern Art, which also featured paintings by Ellsworth Kelly and Morris Louis, among others, bestowed an official stamp of approval on the movement.

In *Fission,* Riley filled the canvas with black dots of varied sizes and shapes, creating the illusion of a pulsating surface that caves in at the center (hence the painting's title). The effect on the viewer of Op Art paintings such as *Fission* is disorienting and sometimes disturbing, and some works can even induce motion sickness. Thoroughly modernist in the insistence a painting is a two-dimensional surface covered with pigment and not a representation of any person, object, or place, the Op Art movement nonetheless embraced the Renaissance notion that the painter can create the illusion of depth through perspective.

## Abstraction in Sculpture

Painters were not the only artists interested in Clement Greenberg's formalist ideas. American sculptors also strove to arrive at purity in their medium. While painters worked to emphasize flatness, sculptors, understandably, chose to focus on three-dimensionality as the unique characteristic and inherent limitation of the sculptural idiom.

**DAVID SMITH** After experimenting with a variety of sculptural styles and materials, Indiana-born and Ohio-raised DAVID SMITH (1906–1965) produced metal sculptures that have affinities with the Abstract Expressionist movement in painting. In the

## David Smith on Outdoor Sculpture

From ancient times, sculptors have frequently created statues for display in the open air, whether a portrait of a Roman emperor in a forum or Michelangelo's *David* (FIG. 22-13) in Florence's Piazza della Signoria. But rarely have sculptors taken into consideration the effects of sunlight in the conception of their works. American sculptor David Smith was an exception.

Smith learned to weld in an automobile plant in 1925 and later applied to his art the technical expertise in handling metals he gained from that experience. In addition, working in large scale at the factories helped him visualize the possibilities for monumental metal sculpture. His works, for example, *Cubi XII* (FIG. 30-16), created for display in the open air, lose much of their character in the sterile lighting of a museum.

> I like outdoor sculpture and the most practical thing for outdoor sculpture is stainless steel, and I make them and I polish them in such a way that on a dull day, they take on the dull blue, or the color of the sky in the late afternoon sun, the glow, golden like the rays, the colors of nature. And in a particular sense, I have used atmosphere in a reflective way on the surfaces. They are colored by the sky and the surroundings, the green or blue of water. Some are down by the water and some are by the mountains. They reflect the colors. They are designed for the outdoors.*

*Quoted in Cleve Gray, ed., *David Smith by David Smith* (New York: Holt, Rinehart, and Winston, 1968), 133.

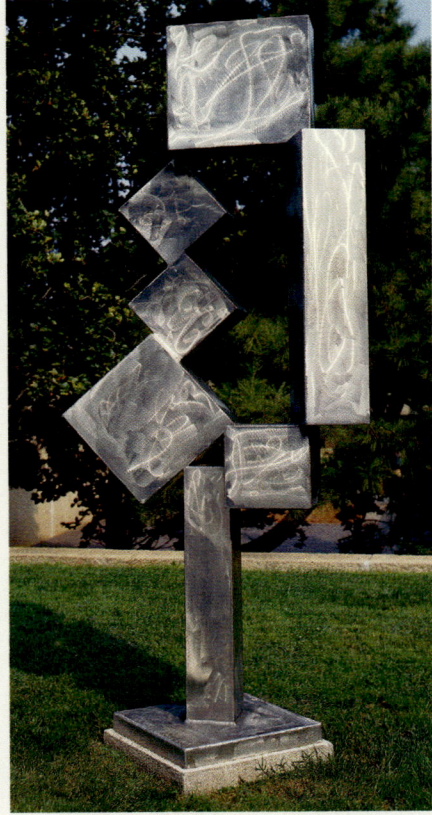

**30-16** DAVID SMITH, *Cubi XII*, 1963. Stainless steel, 9′ 1⅝″ high. Hirshhorn Museum and Sculpture Garden, Smithsonian Institution, Washington, D.C. (gift of the Joseph H. Hirshhorn Foundation, 1972). Art © David Smith, Licensed by VAGA, NY. Photo by Lee Stalsworth, Smithsonian Hirshhorn Museum and Sculpture Garden.

David Smith designed his abstract metal sculptures of simple geometric forms to reflect the natural light and color of their outdoor settings, not the sterile illumination of a museum gallery.

1 ft.

---

1960s he produced a series of monumental works called *Cubi,* designed for display in the open air (see "David Smith on Outdoor Sculpture," above). *Cubi XII* (FIG. **30-16**), a characteristic example, consists of simple geometric forms—cubes and rectangular bars. Made of stainless-steel sections piled on top of one another, often at unstable angles, and then welded together, the *Cubi* sculptures make a striking visual statement. Smith added gestural elements reminiscent of Abstract Expressionism by burnishing the metal with steel wool, producing swirling random-looking patterns that draw attention to the two-dimensionality of the sculptural surface. This treatment, which captures the light hitting the artwork, activates the surface and imparts a texture to his pieces.

**TONY SMITH** A predominantly sculptural movement that emerged in the 1960s among artists seeking Greenbergian purity of form was *Minimalism.* One leading Minimalist was New Jersey native TONY SMITH (1912–1980), who created simple volumetric sculptures such as *Die* (FIG. **30-17**). Minimalist artworks generally lack identifiable subjects, colors, surface textures, and narrative elements, and are perhaps best described simply as three-dimensional objects. By rejecting illusionism and reducing sculpture to basic geometric forms, Smith and other Minimalists emphatically emphasized their art's "objecthood" and concrete tangibility. In so doing, they reduced experience to its most fundamental level, preventing viewers from drawing on assumptions or preconceptions when dealing with the art before them.

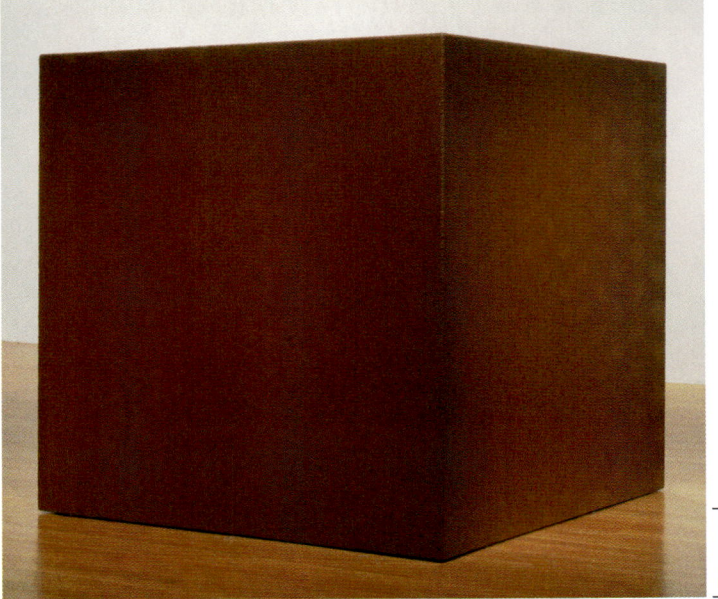

**30-17** TONY SMITH, *Die,* 1962. Steel, 6′ × 6′ × 6′. Museum of Modern Art, New York (gift of Jane Smith in honor of Agnes Gund).

By rejecting illusionism and symbolism and reducing sculpture to basic geometric forms, Minimalist Tony Smith emphasized the "objecthood" and concrete tangibility of his sculptures.

1 ft.

# Donald Judd on Sculpture and Industrial Materials

In a 1965 essay entitled "Specific Objects," the Minimalist sculptor Donald Judd described the advantages of sculpture over painting and the attractions of using industrial materials for his works (FIG. 30-18).

> Three dimensions are real space. That gets rid of the problem of illusionism . . . one of the salient and most objectionable relics of European art. The several limits of painting are no longer present. A work can be as powerful as it can be thought to be. Actual space is intrinsically more powerful and specific than paint on a flat surface. . . . The use of three dimensions makes it possible to see all sorts of materials and colors. Most of [my] work involves new materials, either recent inventions or things not used before in art. Little was done until lately with the wide range of industrial products. . . . Materials vary greatly and are simply materials—formica, aluminum, cold-rolled steel, plexiglas, red and common brass, and so forth. They are specific. If they are used directly, they are more specific. Also, they are usually aggressive. There is an objectivity to the obdurate identity of a material. . . . The form of a work of art and its materials are closely related. In earlier work the structure and the imagery were executed in some neutral and homogeneous material.*

*Donald Judd, *Complete Writings 1959–1975* (New York: New York University Press, 1975), 181–189.

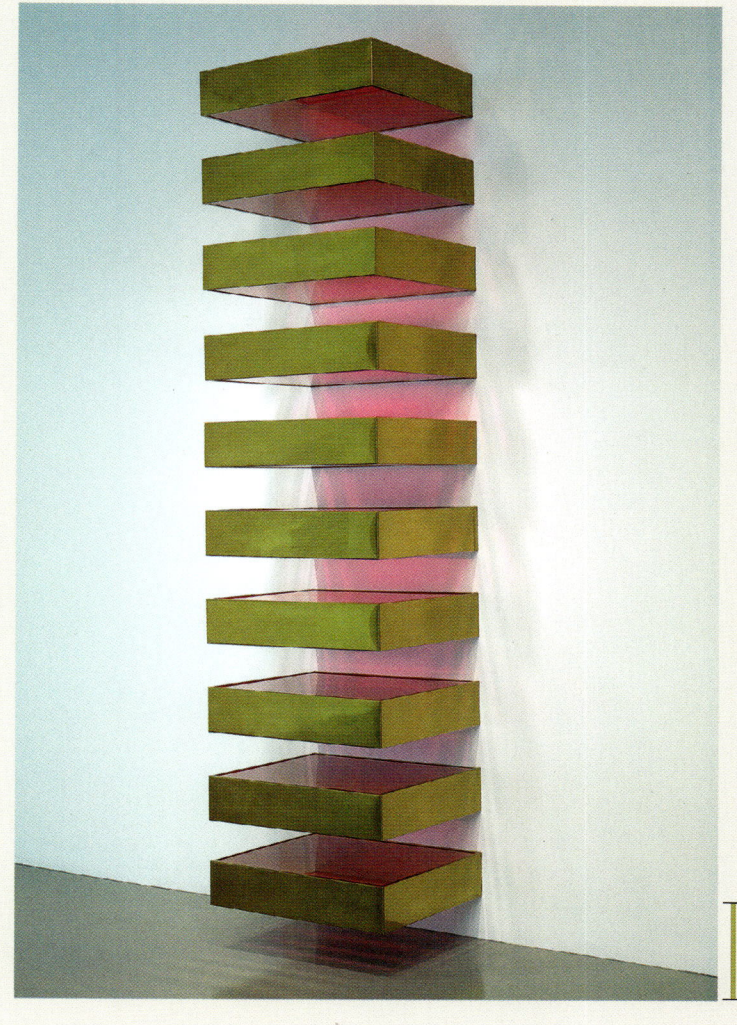

**30-18** DONALD JUDD, *Untitled,* 1969. Brass and colored fluorescent Plexiglas on steel brackets, 10 units, 6⅛″ × 2′ × 2′ 3″ each, with 6″ intervals. Hirshhorn Museum and Sculpture Garden, Smithsonian Institution, Washington, D.C. (gift of Joseph H. Hirshhorn, 1972). © Donald Judd Estate/Licensed by VAGA, New York.

Judd's Minimalist sculpture incorporates boxes fashioned from undisguised industrial materials. The artist used Plexiglas because its translucency gives the viewer access to the work's interior.

1 ft.

**DONALD JUDD** Another Minimalist sculptor, DONALD JUDD (1928–1994), embraced a spare, universal aesthetic corresponding to the core tenets of the movement. Born in Missouri, Judd studied philosophy and art history at Columbia University in New York City, where he produced most of his major works. Judd's determination to arrive at a visual vocabulary devoid of deception or ambiguity propelled him away from representation and toward precise and simple sculpture. For Judd, a work's power derived from its character as a whole and from the specificity of its materials (see "Donald Judd on Sculpture and Industrial Materials," above). *Untitled* (FIG. 30-18) presents basic geometric boxes constructed of brass and red Plexiglas, undisguised by paint or other materials. The artist did not intend the work to be metaphorical or symbolic. It is a straightforward declaration of sculpture's objecthood. Judd used Plexiglas because its translucency enables the viewer access to the interior, thereby rendering the sculpture both open and enclosed. This aspect of the design reflects Judd's desire to banish ambiguity or falseness from his works.

Perhaps surprisingly, despite the ostensible connections between Minimalism and Greenbergian formalism, the critic did not embrace this direction in art:

> Minimal Art remains too much a feat of ideation [the mental formation of ideas], and not enough anything else. Its idea remains an idea, something deduced instead of felt and discovered. The geometrical and modular simplicity may announce and signify the artistically furthest-out, but the fact that the signals are understood for what they want to mean betrays them artistically. There is hardly any aesthetic surprise in Minimal Art. . . . Aesthetic surprise hangs on forever—it is there in Raphael as it is in Pollock—and ideas alone cannot achieve it.[10]

**LOUISE NEVELSON** Although Minimalism was a dominant sculptural trend in the 1960s, many sculptors pursued other styles. Russian-born LOUISE NEVELSON (1899–1988) created sculpture combining a sense of the architectural fragment with the power of Dada and Surrealist found objects to express her personal

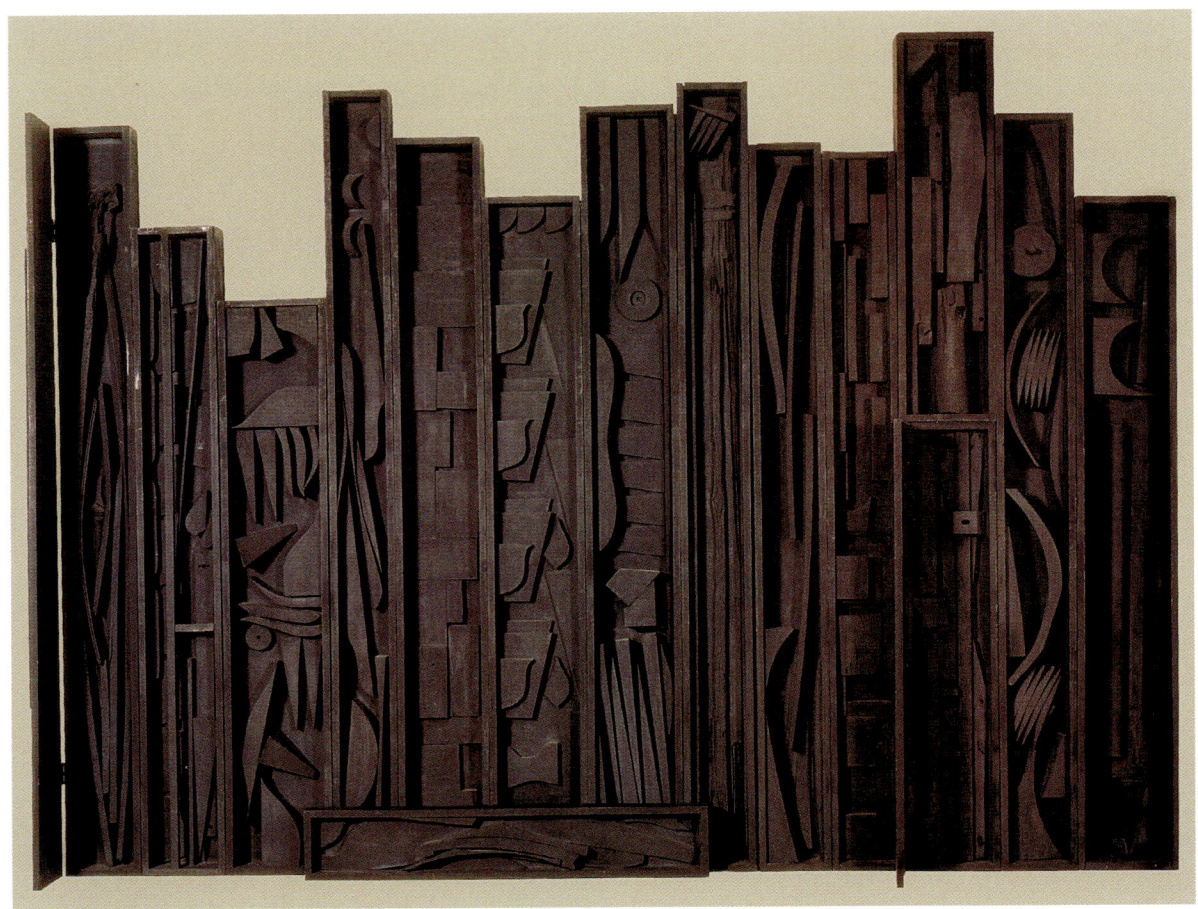

**30-19** LOUISE NEVELSON, *Tropical Garden II,* 1957–1959. Wood painted black, 5′ 11½″ × 10′ 11¾″ × 1′. Musée National d'Art Moderne, Centre Georges Pompidou, Paris.

The monochromatic color scheme unifies the diverse sculpted forms and found objects in Nevelson's "walls" and creates a mysterious field of shapes and shadows suggesting magical environments.

1 ft.

sense of life's underlying significance. Multiplicity of meaning was important to Nevelson. She sought "the in-between place. . . . The dawns and the dusks"[11]—the transitional realm between one state of being and another.

Beginning in the late 1950s, Nevelson assembled sculptures of found wooden objects and forms, enclosing small sculptural compositions in boxes of varied sizes, and joined the boxes to one another to form "walls," which she then painted in a single hue—usually black, white, or gold. This monochromatic color scheme unifies the diverse parts of pieces such as *Tropical Garden II* (FIG. **30-19**) and creates a mysterious field of shapes and shadows. The structures suggest magical environments resembling the treasured secret hideaways dimly remembered from childhood. Yet the boxy frames and the precision of the manufactured found objects create a rough geometric structure the eye roams over freely, lingering on some details. The parts of a Nevelson sculpture and their interrelation recall the *Merz* constructions of Kurt Schwitters (FIG. 29-29). The effect is also rather like viewing the side of an apartment building from a moving elevated train or looking down on a city from the air.

**LOUISE BOURGEOIS** In contrast to the architectural nature of Nevelson's work, a sensuous organic quality recalling the evocative Biomorphic Surrealist forms of Joan Miró (FIG. 29-58) pervades the work of French-American artist LOUISE BOURGEOIS (1911–2010). *Cumul I* (FIG. **30-20**) is a collection of round-headed units huddled, with their heads protruding, within a collective cloak dotted with holes. The units differ in size, and their position within the group lends a distinctive personality to each. Although the shapes remain abstract, they refer strongly to human figures.

Bourgeois used a wide variety of materials in her works, including wood, plaster, latex, and plastics, in addition to alabaster, marble, and bronze. She exploited each material's qualities to suit the expressiveness of the piece.

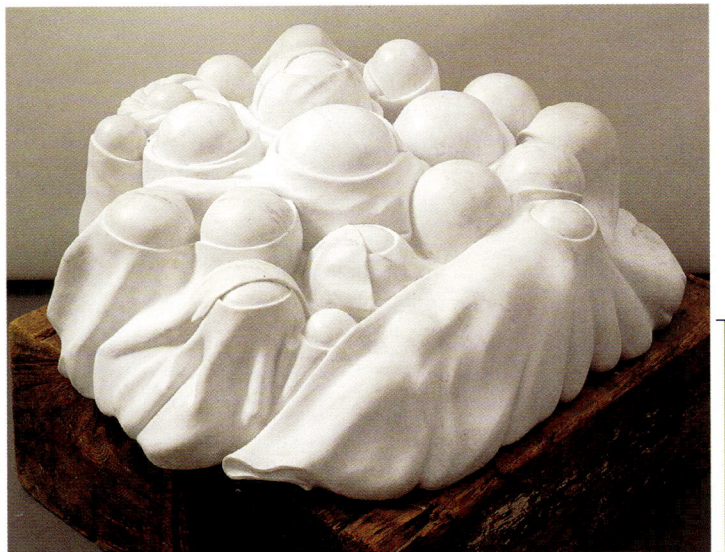

**30-20** LOUISE BOURGEOIS, *Cumul I,* 1969. Marble, 1′ 10⅜″ × 4′ 2″ × 4′. Musée National d'Art Moderne, Centre Georges Pompidou, Paris. © Louise Bourgeois/Licensed by VAGA, New York. ◼◄

Bourgeois's sculptures are made up of sensuous organic forms that recall the Biomorphic Surrealist forms of Miró (FIG. 29-58). Although the shapes remain abstract, they refer strongly to human figures.

1 ft.

In *Cumul I,* the alternating high gloss and matte finish of the marble increases the sensuous distinction between the group of swelling forms and the soft folds swaddling them. As did Barbara Hepworth (FIG. 29-62), Bourgeois connected her sculpture with the body's multiple relationships to landscape: "[My pieces] are anthropomorphic and they are landscape also, since our body could be considered from a topographical point of view, as a land with mounds and valleys and caves and holes."[12] However, Bourgeois's sculptures are more personal and more openly sexual than Hepworth's. *Cumul I* represents perfectly the allusions Bourgeois sought: "There has always been sexual suggestiveness in my work. Sometimes I am totally concerned with female shapes—characters of breasts like clouds—but often I merge the activity—phallic breasts, male and female, active and passive."[13]

**EVA HESSE** A Minimalist in the early part of her career, EVA HESSE (1936–1970) later moved away from the severity characterizing much of Minimal art. She created sculptures that, although spare and simple, have a compelling presence. Using nontraditional sculptural materials such as fiberglass, cord, and latex, Hesse produced sculptures whose pure Minimalist forms appear to crumble, sag, and warp under the pressures of atmospheric force and gravity. Born Jewish in Hitler's Germany, the young Hesse hid with a Christian family when her parents and elder sister had to flee the Nazis.

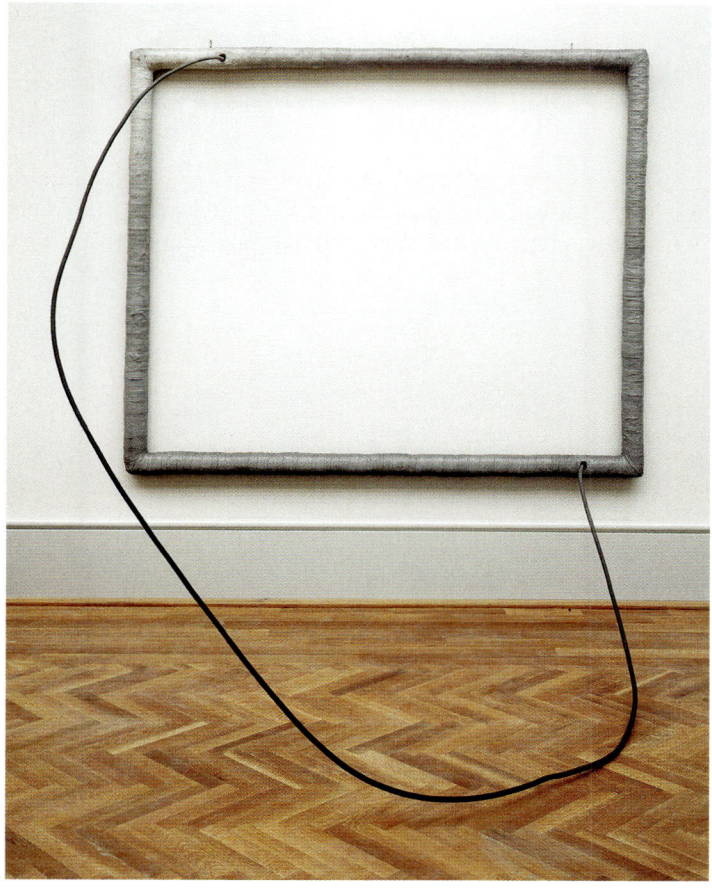

**30-21** EVA HESSE, *Hang-Up,* 1965–1966. Acrylic on cloth over wood and steel, 6′ × 7′ × 6′ 6″. Art Institute of Chicago, Chicago (gift of Arthur Keating and Mr. and Mrs. Edward Morris by exchange).

Hesse created spare and simple sculptures with parts extending into the room. She wanted her works to express the strangeness and absurdity she considered the central conditions of modern life.

She did not reunite with them until the early 1940s, just before her parents divorced. Those extraordinary circumstances helped give her a lasting sense that the central conditions of modern life are strangeness and absurdity. Struggling to express these qualities in her art, Hesse created informal sculptural arrangements with units often hung from the ceiling, propped against the walls, or spilled out along the floor. She said she wanted her pieces to be "non art, non connotative, non anthropomorphic, non geometric, non nothing, everything, but of another kind, vision, sort."[14]

*Hang-Up* (FIG. **30-21**) fulfills these requirements. The piece resembles a carefully made empty frame sprouting a strange feeler extending into the room and doubling back to the frame. Hesse wrote that in this work, for the first time, her "idea of absurdity or extreme feeling came through. . . . [*Hang-Up*] has a kind of depth I don't always achieve and that is the kind of depth or soul or absurdity of life or meaning or feeling or intellect that I want to get."[15] The sculpture possesses a disquieting and touching presence, suggesting the fragility and grandeur of life amid the pressures of the modern age. Hesse was herself a touching and fragile presence in the art world. She died of a brain tumor at age 34.

**ISAMU NOGUCHI** Another sculptor often considered a Minimalist because of pure geometric works such as *Red Cube,* which he created in 1968 for the sidewalk in front of a New York City skyscraper, is Japanese American artist ISAMU NOGUCHI (1904–1988). His work defies easy classification, however, and in sculptures such as *Shodo Shima Stone Study* (FIG. **30-21A**), Noguchi brilliantly wedded Western and Oriental themes and styles.

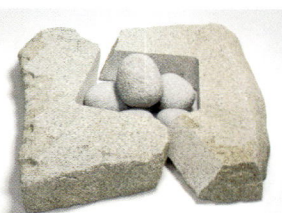

**30-21A** NOGUCHI, *Shodo Shima,* 1978.

## Pop Art

Despite their differences, the Abstract Expressionists, Post-Painterly Abstractionists, Op Art painters, and Minimalist sculptors all adopted an artistic vocabulary of resolute abstraction. Other artists, however, observing that the insular and introspective attitude of the avant-garde had alienated the public, sought to harness the communicative power of art to reach a wide audience. Thus was born the Independent Group in London (FIG. 30-1) and the art movement that came to be known as Pop.

Although Pop Art originated in England, the movement found its greatest articulation and success in the United States, in large part because the more fully matured American consumer culture provided a fertile environment in which the movement flourished through the 1960s. Indeed, Independent Group members claimed their inspiration came from Hollywood, Detroit, and New York's Madison Avenue, paying homage to America's predominance in the realms of mass media, mass production, and advertising.

**JASPER JOHNS** One of the artists pivotal to the early development of American Pop Art was JASPER JOHNS (b. 1930), who grew up in South Carolina and moved to New York City in 1952. Johns sought to draw attention to common objects in the world—what he called things "seen but not looked at."[16] To this end, he did several series of paintings of numbers, alphabets, flags, and maps of the United States—all of which are items people view frequently but rarely scrutinize. He created his first

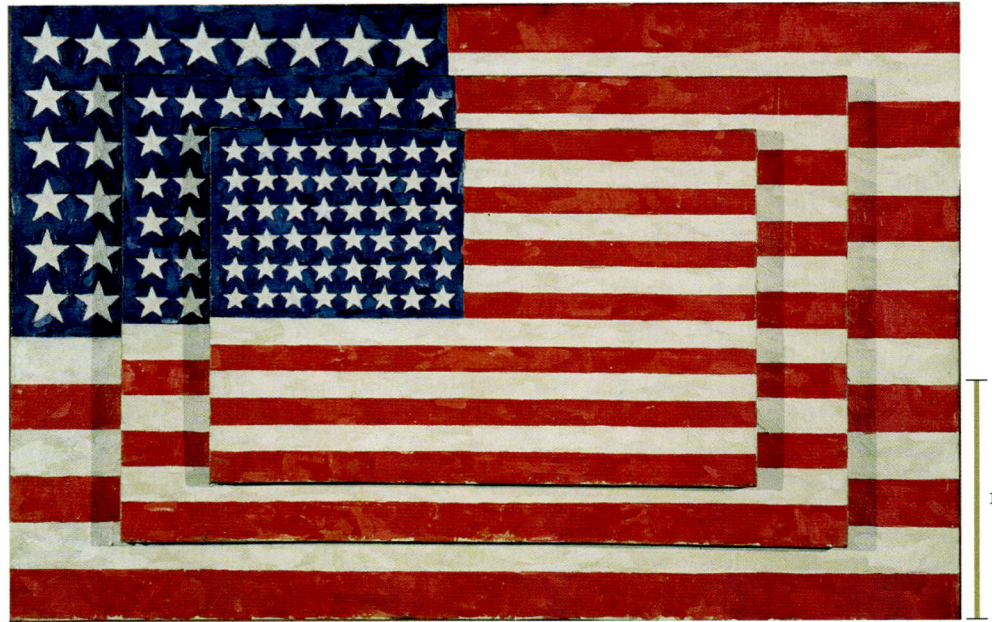

**30-22** Jasper Johns, *Three Flags*, 1958. Encaustic on canvas, 2' 6⅞" × 3' 9½". Whitney Museum of American Art, New York (50th Anniversary Gift of the Gilman Foundation, the Lauder Foundation, and A. Alfred Taubman).

American Pop artist Jasper Johns wanted to draw attention to common objects people view frequently but rarely scrutinize. He made many paintings of targets, flags, numbers, and alphabets.

flag painting in 1954 at the height of the Cold War. Initially labeled a Neo-Dadaist because of the kinship of his works to Marcel Duchamp's readymades (FIG. 29-27), Johns also had strong ties to the Surrealists, especially René Magritte, whose painting of a pipe labeled "This is not a pipe" (FIG. 29-56) is conceptually a forerunner of Johns's flags—for example, *Three Flags* (FIG. 30-22), which could easily carry the label "These are not flags." In fact, when asked why he chose the American flag as a subject, Johns replied he had a dream in which he saw himself painting a flag. The world of dreams was central to Surrealism (see Chapter 29).

In *Three Flags,* Johns painted a trio of overlapping American national banners of decreasing size, with the smallest closest to the viewer, reversing traditional perspective, which calls for diminution of size with distance. Johns drained meaning from the patriotic emblem by reducing it to a repetitive pattern—not the flag itself but three pictures of a flag in one. Nevertheless, the heritage of Abstract Expressionism is still apparent. Although Johns rejected the heroic, highly personalized application of pigment championed by the 1950s action painters, he painted his flags in *encaustic* (liquid wax and dissolved pigment; see "Encaustic Painting," Chapter 7, page 218) mixed with newsprint on three overlapping canvases. His flags thus retain a pronounced surface texture, emphasizing that the viewer is looking at a handmade painting, not a machine-made fabric. The painting, like the flags, is an object, not an illusion of other objects.

**ROBERT RAUSCHENBERG** A close friend of Johns's, Robert Rauschenberg (1925–2008) began using mass-media images in his work in the 1950s. Rauschenberg set out to create works that would be open and indeterminate, and he began by making *combines,* which intersperse painted passages with sculptural elements. Combines are, in a sense, Rauschenberg's personal variation on *assemblages,* artworks constructed from already existing objects. At times, these combines seem to be sculptures with painting incorporated into certain sections. Others seem to be paint-

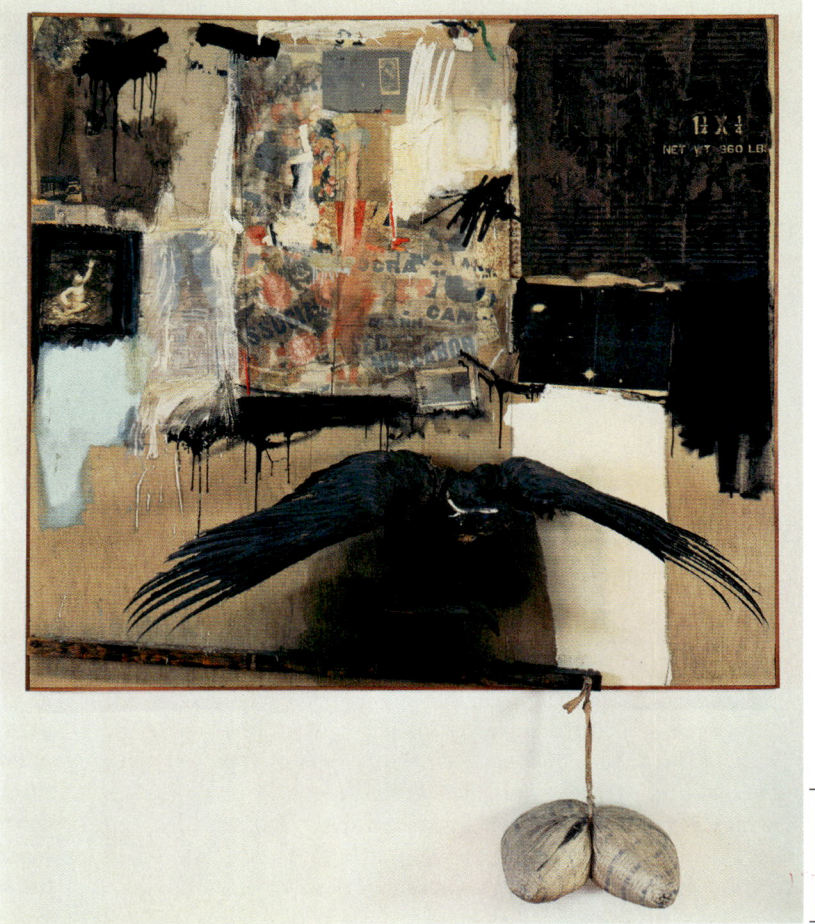

**30-23** Robert Rauschenberg, *Canyon,* 1959. Oil, pencil, paper, fabric, metal, cardboard box, printed paper, printed reproductions, photograph, wood, paint tube, and mirror on canvas, with oil on bald eagle, string, and pillow, 6' 9¾" × 5' 10" × 2'. Sonnabend Collection, New York. © Robert Rauschenberg/ Licensed by VAGA, New York.

Rauschenberg's "combines" intersperse painted passages with sculptural elements. *Canyon* incorporates pigment on canvas with pieces of printed paper, photographs, a pillow, and a stuffed eagle.

## Roy Lichtenstein on Pop Art

In November 1963, Roy Lichtenstein was one of eight painters interviewed for a profile on Pop Art in *Art News*. Gene R. Swenson posed the questions. Some of Lichtenstein's answers follow.

[Pop Art is] the use of commercial art as a subject matter in painting . . . [Pop artists portray] what I think to be the most brazen and threatening characteristics of our culture, things we hate, but which are also so powerful in their impingement on us. . . . I paint directly . . . [without] perspective or shading. It doesn't look like a painting *of* something, it looks like the thing itself. Instead of looking like a painting *of* a billboard . . . Pop art seems to be the actual thing. It is an intensification, a stylistic intensification of the excitement which the subject matter has for me; but the style is . . . cool. One of the things a cartoon does is to express violent emotion and passion in a completely mechanized and removed style. To express this thing in a painterly style would dilute it. . . . Everybody has called Pop Art "American" painting, but it's actually industrial painting. America was hit by industrialism and capitalism harder and sooner . . . I think the meaning of my work is that it's industrial, it's what all the world will soon become. Europe will be the same way, soon, so it won't be American; it will be universal.*

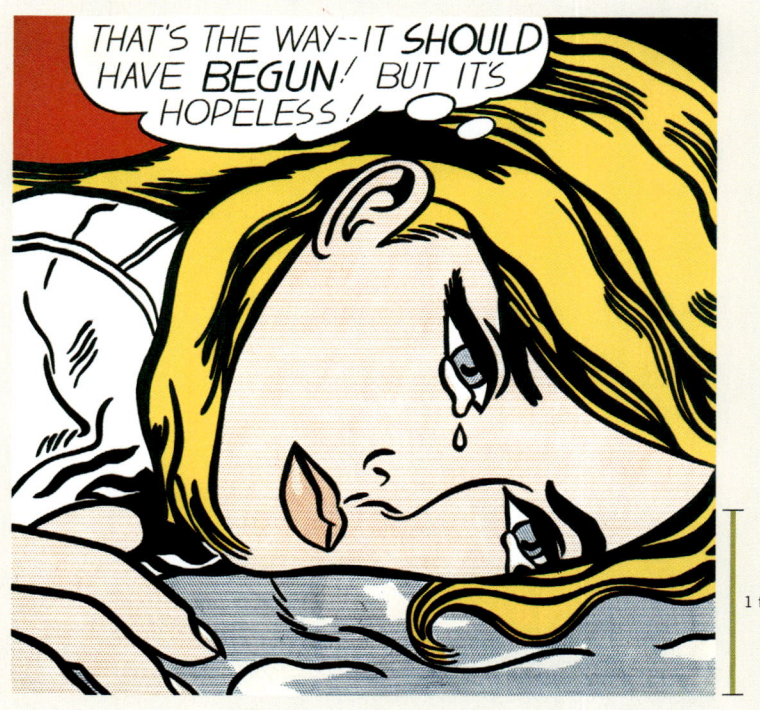

**30-24** Roy Lichtenstein, *Hopeless*, 1963. Oil and synthetic polymer paint on canvas, 3′ 8″ × 3′ 8″. Kunstmuseum Basel, Basel. © Estate of Roy Lichtenstein.

Comic books appealed to Lichtenstein because they were a mainstay of popular culture, meant to be read and discarded. The Pop artist immortalized their images on large canvases.

*G. R. Swenson, "What Is Pop Art? Interviews with Eight Painters," *Art News* 62, no. 7 (November 1963), 25, 64.

---

ings with three-dimensional objects attached to the surface. In the 1950s, assemblages usually contained an array of art reproductions, magazine and newspaper clippings, and passages painted in an Abstract Expressionist style. In the early 1960s, Rauschenberg adopted the commercial medium of *silk-screen printing,* first in black and white and then in color, and began filling entire canvases with appropriated news images and anonymous photographs of city scenes.

*Canyon* (FIG. **30-23**) is typical of his combines. Pieces of printed paper and photographs cover parts of the canvas. Much of the unevenly painted surface consists of pigment roughly applied in a manner reminiscent of de Kooning's work (FIG. 30-8). A stuffed bald eagle attached to the lower part of the combine spreads its wings as if lifting off in flight toward the viewer. Completing the combine, a pillow dangles from a string attached to a wood stick below the eagle. The artist presented the work's components in a jumbled fashion. He tilted or turned some of the images sideways, and each overlays part of another image. The compositional confusion may resemble that of a Dada collage, but the parts of Rauschenberg's combines maintain their individuality more than those, for example, in a Schwitters piece (FIG. 29-29). The eye scans a Rauschenberg canvas much as it might survey the environment on a walk through a city. The various recognizable images and objects seem unrelated and defy a consistent reading, although Rauschenberg chose all the elements of his combines with specific

meanings in mind. For example, Rauschenberg based *Canyon* on a Rembrandt painting of Jupiter in the form of an eagle carrying the boy Ganymede heavenward. The photo in the combine is a reference to the Greek boy, and the hanging bag is a visual pun on his buttocks.

**ROY LICHTENSTEIN** As the Pop Art movement matured, the images became more concrete and tightly controlled. Roy Lichtenstein (1923–1997), who was born in Manhattan not far from Madison Avenue, the center of the American advertising industry, developed an interest in art in elementary school and as a teenager took weekend painting classes at the Parsons School of Design before enrolling at Ohio State University. He served in the army during World War II and was stationed in France, where he was able to visit the Musée du Louvre and Chartres Cathedral. In the late 1950s, however, he turned his attention to commercial art and especially to the comic book as a mainstay of American popular culture (see "Roy Lichtenstein on Pop Art," above).

In paintings such as *Hopeless* (FIG. **30-24**), Lichtenstein excerpted an image from a comic book, a form of entertainment meant to be read and discarded, and immortalized the image on a large canvas. Aside from that modification, Lichtenstein remained remarkably faithful to the original comic-strip image. His subjects were typically the melodramatic scenes that were hallmarks of

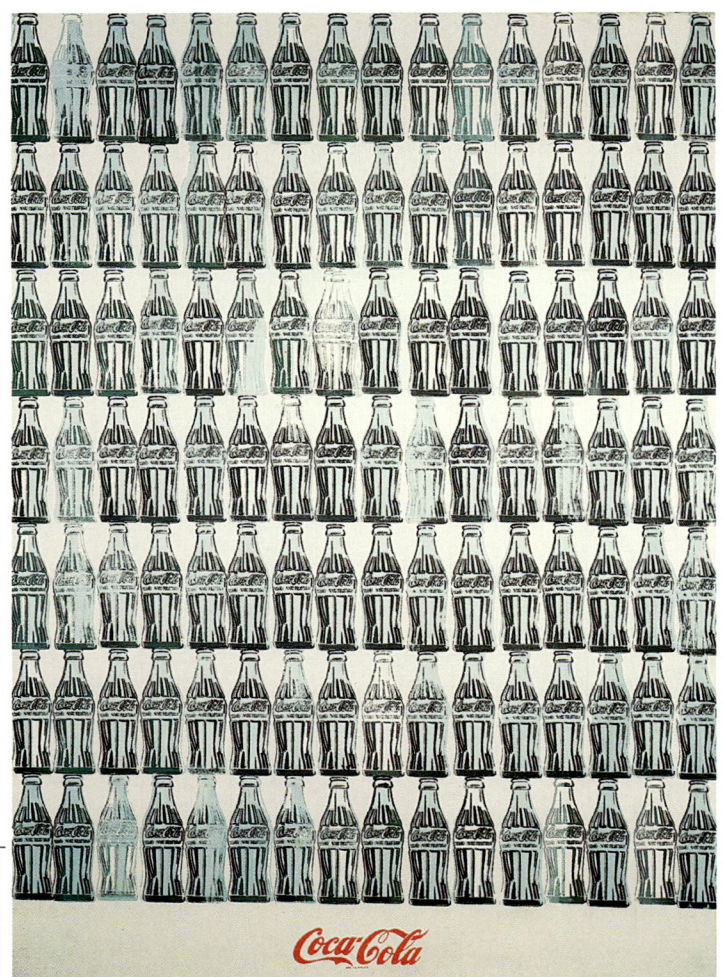

**30-25** ANDY WARHOL, *Green Coca-Cola Bottles,* 1962. Oil on canvas, 6′ 10½″ × 4′ 9″. Whitney Museum of American Art, New York.

Warhol was the quintessential American Pop artist. Here, he selected an icon of mass-produced, consumer culture, and then multiplied it, reflecting Coke's omnipresence in American society.

1 ft.

romance comic books popular at the time and included "balloons" with the words the characters speak. Lichtenstein also used the visual vocabulary of the comic strip, with its dark black outlines and unmodulated color areas, and retained the familiar square dimensions. Moreover, his printing technique, *benday dots,* called attention to the mass-produced derivation of the image. Named after its inventor, the newspaper printer Benjamin Day (1810–1889), the benday-dot system involves the modulation of colors through the placement and size of colored dots. Lichtenstein thus transferred the visual shorthand language of the comic book to the realm of monumental painting.

**ANDY WARHOL** The quintessential American Pop artist was ANDY WARHOL (1928–1987). An early successful career as a commercial artist and illustrator grounded Warhol in the sensibility and

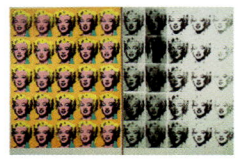

**30-25A** WARHOL, *Marilyn Diptych,* 1962. ▣◀

visual rhetoric of advertising and the mass media. This knowledge proved useful for his Pop artworks, which often depicted icons of mass-produced consumer culture, such as *Green Coca-Cola Bottles* (FIG. **30-25**), and Hollywood celebrities, such as Marilyn Monroe (1926–1962; FIG. **30-25A**). Warhol

favored reassuringly familiar objects and people. He explained his attraction to the ubiquitous curved Coke bottle:

> What's great about this country is that America started the tradition where the richest consumers buy essentially the same things as the poorest. You can be watching TV and see Coca-Cola, and you can know that the President drinks Coke, Liz Taylor drinks Coke, and just think, you can drink Coke, too. A Coke is a Coke and no amount of money can get you a better Coke.[17]

As did other Pop artists, Warhol used a visual vocabulary and a printing method that reinforced the image's connections to consumer culture. The silk-screen technique allowed Warhol to print the image endlessly (although he varied each bottle slightly). The repetition and redundancy of the Coke bottle reflect the saturation of this product in American so-ciety—in homes, at work, literally everywhere, including gas stations, as immortalized by GEORGE SEGAL (1924–2000) in 1963 (FIG. **30-25B**). So immersed was Warhol in a culture of

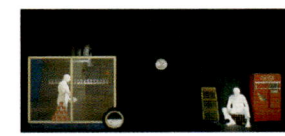

**30-25B** SEGAL, *Gas Station,* 1963.

mass production that he not only produced numerous canvases of the same image but also named his studio "the Factory."

**CLAES OLDENBURG** In the 1960s, CLAES OLDENBURG (b. 1929) also produced Pop artworks that incisively commented on American consumer culture, but his medium was sculpture. The son of a Swedish diplomat who moved to the United States in 1936, Oldenburg attended school in Chicago and graduated from Yale University in 1950. His early works consisted of plaster reliefs of food and clothing items. Oldenburg constructed these sculptures of plaster layered on chicken wire and muslin, painting them with cheap commercial house enamel. In later works, focused on the same subjects, he shifted to large-scale stuffed sculptures of sewn vinyl or canvas, many of which he exhibited in a show he titled *The Store*—an appropriate comment on the function of art as a commodity in a consumer society.

Oldenburg is best known, however, for his mammoth outdoor sculptures. In 1966, a group of graduate students at the Yale School of Architecture, calling themselves the Colossal Keepsake Corporation, raised funds for materials for a giant sculpture that Oldenburg agreed to create (in secret and without a fee) as a gift to his alma mater. The work, *Lipstick (Ascending) on Caterpillar Tracks* (FIG. **30-26**), was Oldenburg's first monumental public sculpture. He installed *Lipstick* on Ascension Day, May 15, 1969, on Beineke Plaza across from the office of the university's president, the site of many raucous protests against the Vietnam War. Oldenburg's characteristic humor emerges unmistakably in the combination of phallic and militaristic imagery, especially in the double irony of the "phallus" being a woman's cosmetic item, and the Caterpillar-type endless-loop metal tracks suggesting not a tractor-earthmover for construction work but a military tank designed for destruction in warfare. *Lipstick* was to be a speaker's platform for protesters, and originally the lipstick tip was a drooping red vinyl balloon the speaker had to inflate, underscoring the sexual innuendo. (Oldenburg once remarked that art collectors preferred nudes, so he produced nude cars, nude telephones, and nude electric plugs to please them.)

Vandalism and exposure to the elements (the original tractor was plywood) caused so much damage to *Lipstick* that it had to be removed and reconstructed in metal and fiberglass. Yale formally accepted the controversial and unsolicited repaired gift in 1974,

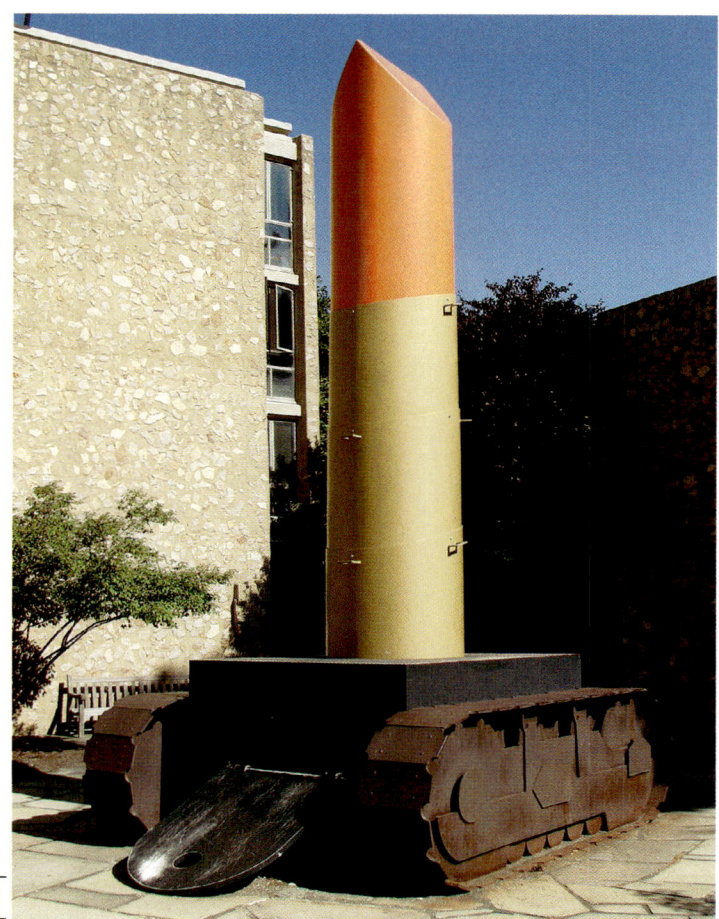

**30-26** CLAES OLDENBURG, *Lipstick (Ascending) on Caterpillar Tracks,* 1969; reworked, 1974. Painted steel, aluminum, and fiberglass, 21′ high. Morse College, Yale University, New Haven (gift of Colossal Keepsake Corporation).

Designed as a speaker's platform for antiwar protesters, *Lipstick* humorously combines phallic and militaristic imagery. Originally the lipstick tip was soft red vinyl and had to be inflated.

when the architectural historian Vincent Scully (b. 1920), then master of Yale's Morse College, offered a permanent home for *Lipstick* in the college courtyard.

Also usually classified as a Pop Art sculptor was French-born NIKI DE SAINT-PHALLE (1930–2002), because her sculptures remind many viewers of dolls and folk art. Her most famous works are the series of polyester statues of women she called *Nanas* (FIG. **30-26A**), oversized, brightly colored sculptures that are feminist commentaries on popular stereotypes of female beauty.

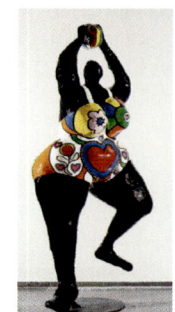

**30-26A** SAINT-PHALLE, *Black Venus,* 1965–1967.

## Superrealism

Like the Pop artists, the artists associated with *Superrealism* sought a form of artistic communication more accessible to the public than the remote, unfamiliar visual language of the Abstract Expressionists, Post-Painterly Abstractionists, and Minimalists. The Superrealists expanded Pop's iconography in both painting and sculpture by making images in the late 1960s and 1970s involving scrupulous fidelity to optical fact. Because many Superrealists used photographs as sources for their imagery, art historians also refer to this postwar art movement as *Photorealism.*

**AUDREY FLACK** One of Superrealism's pioneers was lifelong New Yorker AUDREY FLACK (b. 1931), who studied the history of art at New York University's Institute of Fine Arts after graduating from Yale. Her paintings, such as *Marilyn* (FIG. **30-27**), were not simply technical exercises in recording objects in minute detail but were also conceptual inquiries into the nature of photography and the extent to which photography constructs an understanding of reality. Flack observed: "[Photography is] my whole life, I studied art history, it was always photographs, I never saw the paintings, they were in Europe. . . . Look at TV and at magazines and reproductions, they're all influenced by photo-vision."[18] The photograph's formal

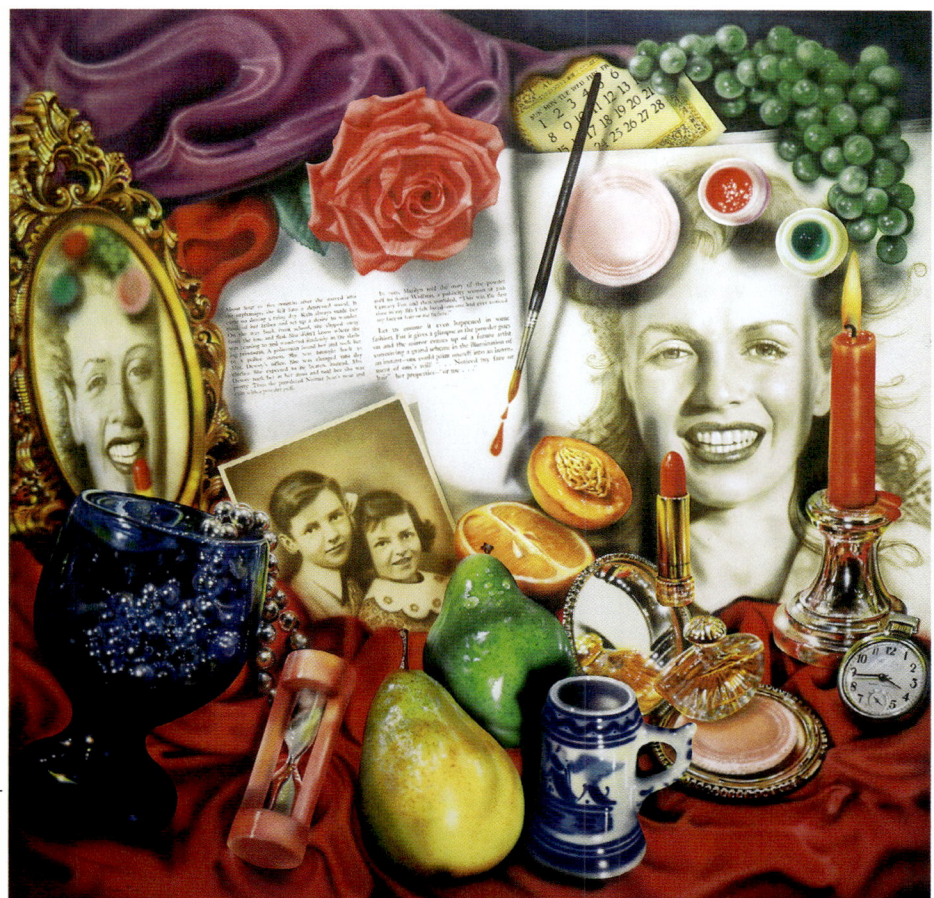

**30-27** AUDREY FLACK, *Marilyn,* 1977. Oil over acrylic on canvas, 8′ × 8′. University of Arizona Museum, Tucson (museum purchase with funds provided by the Edward J. Gallagher Jr. Memorial Fund).

Flack's pioneering Photorealist still lifes record objects with great optical fidelity. *Marilyn* alludes to Dutch vanitas paintings (FIG. 25-1) and incorporates multiple references to the transience of life.

# Chuck Close on Photorealist Portrait Painting

In a widely read 1970 interview in the journal *Artforum,* art critic Cindy Nemser asked Photorealist painter Chuck Close about the scale of his huge portraits (FIG. 30-28) and the relationship of his canvases to the photographs that lie behind them. He answered in part:

> The large scale allows me to deal with information that is overlooked in an eight-by-ten inch photograph . . . My large scale forces the viewer to focus on one area at a time. In that way he is made aware of the blurred areas that are seen with peripheral vision. Normally we never take those peripheral areas into account. When we focus on an area it is sharp. As we turn our attention to adjacent areas they sharpen up too. In my work, the blurred areas don't come into focus, but they are too large to be ignored. . . . In order to . . . make [my painted] information stack up with photographic information, I tried to purge my work of as much of the baggage of traditional portrait painting as I could. To avoid a painterly brush stroke and surface, I use some pretty devious means, such as razor blades, electric drills and airbrushes. I also work as thinly as possible and I don't use white paint as it tends to build up and become chalky and opaque. In fact, in a nine-by-seven foot picture, I only use a couple of tablespoons of black paint to cover the entire canvas.*

*Cindy Nemser, "Chuck Close: Interview with Cindy Nemser," *Artforum* 8, no. 5 (January 1970), 51–55.

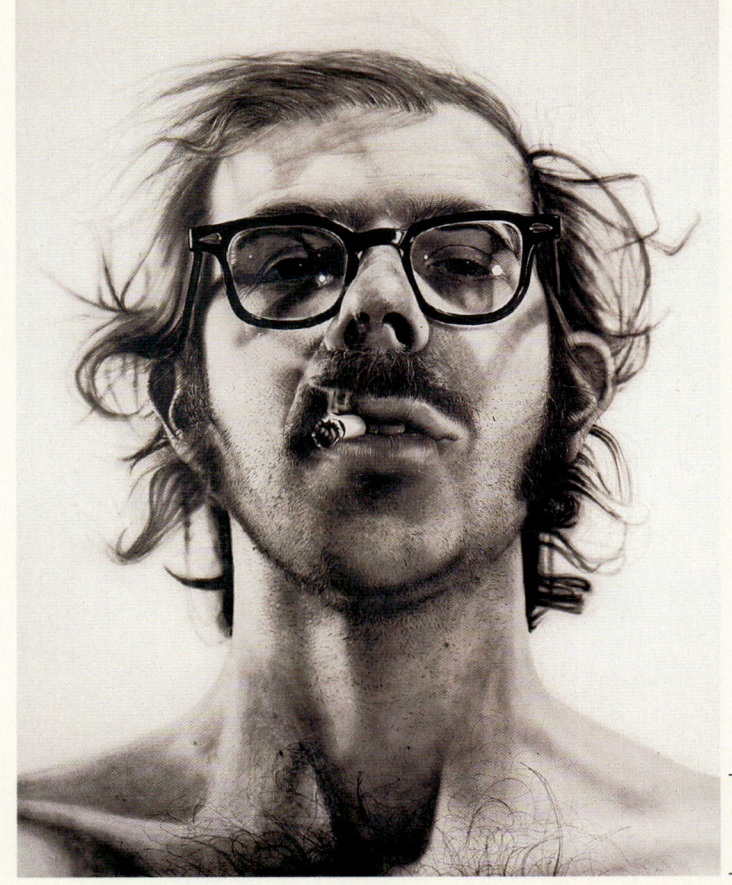

**30-28** CHUCK CLOSE, *Big Self-Portrait,* 1967–1968. Acrylic on canvas, 8′ 11″ × 6′ 11″. Walker Art Center, Minneapolis (Art Center Acquisition Fund, 1969). ◼◄

Close's goal was to translate photographic information into painted information. In his portraits, he deliberately avoided creative compositions, flattering lighting effects, and revealing facial expressions.

1 ft.

---

qualities also intrigued her, and she used photographic techniques by first projecting an image in slide form onto the canvas. By next using an *airbrush* (a device originally designed as a photo-retouching tool that sprays paint with compressed air), Flack could duplicate the smooth gradations of tone and color found in photographs. Most of her paintings are still lifes that present the viewer with a collection of familiar objects painted with great optical fidelity. *Marilyn* is a still life incorporating photographs of the face of famed Hollywood actress Marilyn Monroe. It is a poignant commentary on Monroe's tragic life and differs markedly from Warhol's *Marilyn Diptych* (FIG. 30-25A), which celebrates celebrity and makes no allusion to the death of the glamorous star. Flack's still life includes multiple references to death and alludes to Dutch vanitas paintings (FIG. 25-1). In addition to the black-and-white photographs of a youthful, smiling Monroe, fresh fruit, an hourglass, a burning candle, a watch, and a calendar all refer to the passage of time and the transience of life on earth.

**CHUCK CLOSE** Also usually considered a Superrealist is CHUCK CLOSE (b. 1940), who grew up near Seattle and attended the University of Washington and Yale University. He is best known for his large-scale portraits, such as *Big Self-Portrait* (FIG. **30-28**). However, Close felt his connection to the Photorealists was tenuous, because for him realism, rather than an end in itself, was the result of an intellectually rigorous, systematic approach to painting. He based his paintings of the late 1960s and early 1970s on photographs, and his main goal was to translate photographic information into painted information. Because he aimed simply to record visual information about his subject's appearance, Close deliberately avoided creative compositions, flattering lighting effects, and revealing facial expressions. Not interested in providing great insight into the personalities of those portrayed, Close painted anonymous and generic people, mostly friends. By reducing the variables in his paintings (even their canvas size is a constant 9 by 7 feet), he could focus on employing his methodical presentations of faces, thereby encouraging the viewer to deal with the formal aspects of his works. Indeed, because of the large scale of Close's paintings, careful scrutiny causes the images to dissolve into abstract patterns (see "Chuck Close on Photorealist Portrait Painting," above).

**LUCIAN FREUD** Born in Berlin, LUCIAN FREUD (1922–2011) moved to London with his family in 1933 when Adolph Hitler became German chancellor. The grandson of Sigmund Freud, the painter is best known for his unflattering close-up views of faces in which the sitter seems almost unaware of the painter's presence, and for his portrayals of female and male nudes in foreshortened and often contorted poses. Although Freud always used living

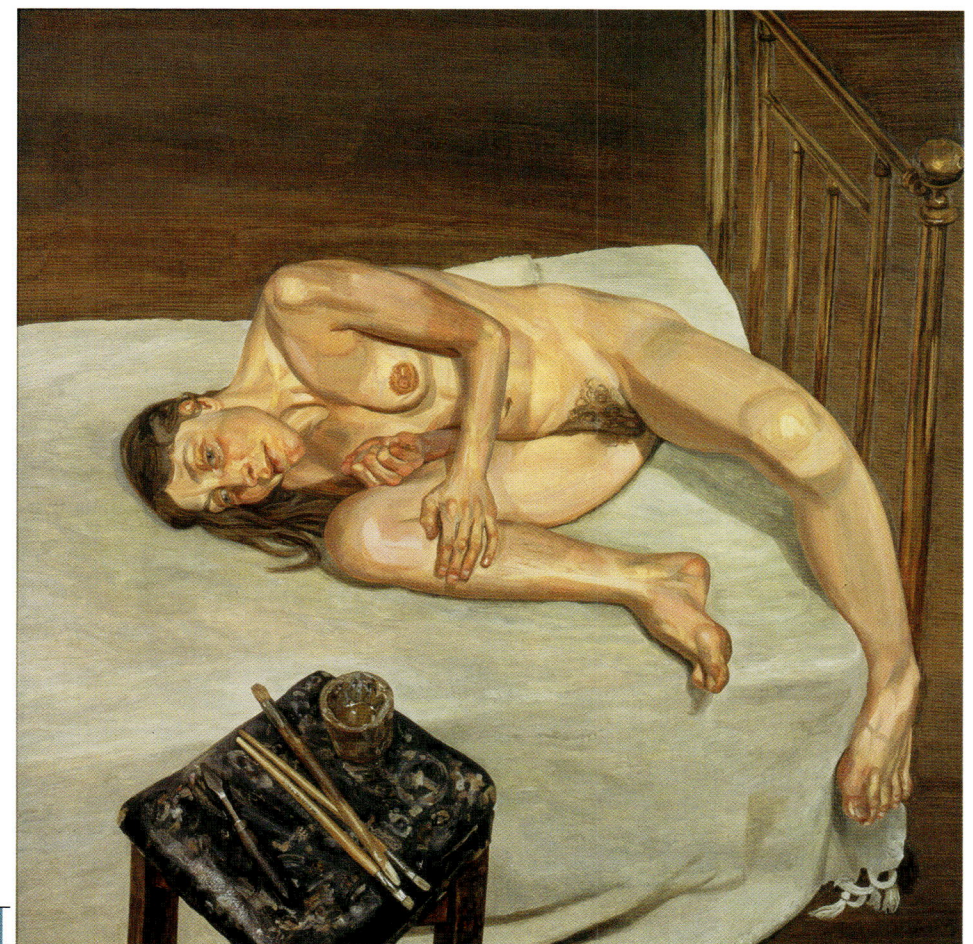

1 in.

30-29 Lucian Freud, *Naked Portrait,* 1972–1973. Oil on canvas, 2′ × 2′. Tate Modern, London.

Freud's brutally realistic portrait of an unnamed woman lying on a bed in an awkward position gives the impression the viewer is an intruder in a private space, but the setting is the artist's studio.

## DUANE HANSON

Not surprisingly, many sculptors also were Superrealists, including Minnesota-born DUANE HANSON (1925–1996), who spent much of his career in southern Florida. Hanson perfected a casting technique that enabled him to create life-size figurative sculptures many viewers mistake at first for real people. Hanson began by making plaster molds from live models and then filled the molds with polyester resin. After the resin hardened, he removed the outer molds and cleaned, painted with an airbrush, and decorated the sculptures with wigs, clothes, and other accessories. These works, such as *Supermarket Shopper* (FIG. 30-30), depict stereotypical average Americans, striking chords with the public specifically because of their familiarity. Hanson explained his choice of imagery:

> The subject matter that I like best deals with the familiar lower- and middle-class American types of today. To me, the resignation, emptiness and loneliness of their existence captures the true reality of life for these people. . . . I want to achieve a certain tough realism which speaks of the fascinating idiosyncrasies of our time.[21]

models whose poses he determined, his paintings convey the impression the artist and the viewer are intruders in a private realm.

In *Naked Portrait* (FIG. 30-29), the viewer observes an unnamed woman lying in an uncomfortable, almost fetal, position at the foot of a bed. Freud depicted her from a sharp angle above and to the left. In the foreground is a small table with the painter's tools on it, revealing that this is not the woman's bedroom but the painter's studio and that the woman is the subject of intense scrutiny by the artist. Freud's models do not have perfect bodies. Some are overweight, and many are well beyond their prime. These are truly "naked portraits" of real people. They break sharply with the Western tradition from Greek antiquity to the Renaissance and into the modern era of depicting idealized Venuses, Eves, and courtesans in graceful and often erotic poses. Freud explained his interest in nudity: "I'm really interested in people as animals. Part of my liking to work from them naked is for that reason. Because I can see more."[19] Regarding the setting of his paintings, Freud observed: "I work from people that interest me, and that I care about and think about, in rooms that I live in and know."[20]

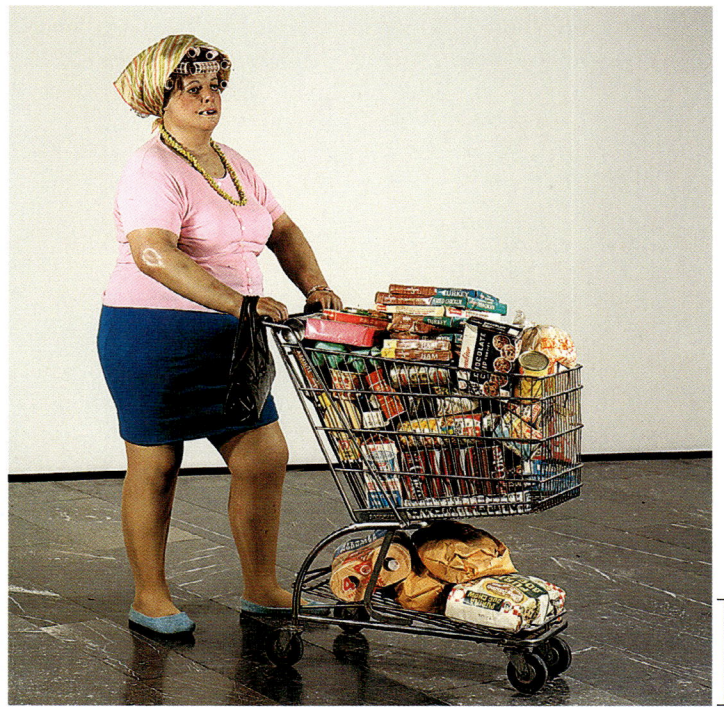

1 ft.

30-30 Duane Hanson, *Supermarket Shopper,* 1970. Polyester resin and fiberglass polychromed in oil, with clothing, steel cart, and groceries, life-size. Nachfolgeinstitut, Neue Galerie, Sammlung Ludwig, Aachen. © Estate of Duane Hanson/Licensed by VAGA, New York.

Hanson used molds from live models to create his Superrealistic life-size painted plaster sculptures. His aim was to capture the emptiness and loneliness of average Americans in familiar settings.

Painting, Sculpture, and Photography **919**

# Photography

Although Superrealist artists admired the ability of photography to reproduce faithfully the appearance of people, objects, and places, photographers themselves used their medium to pursue varied ends. The photographs of Edward Weston (FIGS. 29-44 and 29-44A) and Dorothea Lange (FIG. 29-76) represent the two poles of American photography between the world wars—the art photograph (Weston), which transforms the real into the abstract, and the documentary photograph (Lange), which records people and events directly, without artifice. In the postwar period both approaches to photography continued to flourish.

**DIANE ARBUS** During the 1960s, the most famous photographer of people—with all their blemishes, both physical and psychological—was DIANE ARBUS (1923–1971). New York–born and –educated, Diane Nemerov married Allan Arbus when she was 18 and worked with her husband as a fashion photographer. After their divorce in 1959, Diane chose as her subjects the opposite of the beautiful people with perfect makeup and trendy clothes she had photographed constantly in the 1950s. Her photographs record ordinary people living ordinary lives, people with physical deformities, and people at the margins of society, for example, transvestites—in short, people who rarely were the chosen subjects of professional photographers.

One of Arbus's most memorable photographs (FIG. **30-31**) is of a boy she encountered in New York City's Central Park in 1962 carrying a toy hand grenade. She asked him to stand still and pose

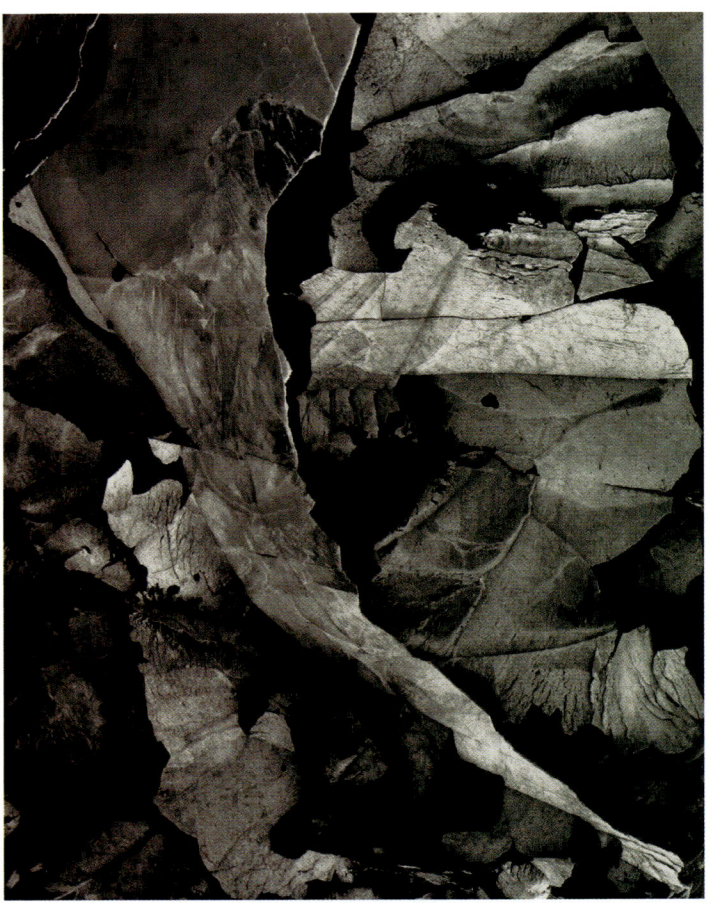

1 in.

**30-32** MINOR WHITE, *Moencopi Strata, Capitol Reef, Utah,* 1962. Gelatin silver print, 1′ $\frac{1}{8}$″ × 9$\frac{1}{4}$″. Museum of Modern Art, New York. © The Minor White Archive, Princeton University.

White's "straight photograph" of a natural rock formation is also an abstract composition of jagged shapes and contrasts of light and dark reminiscent of Abstract Expressionist action paintings.

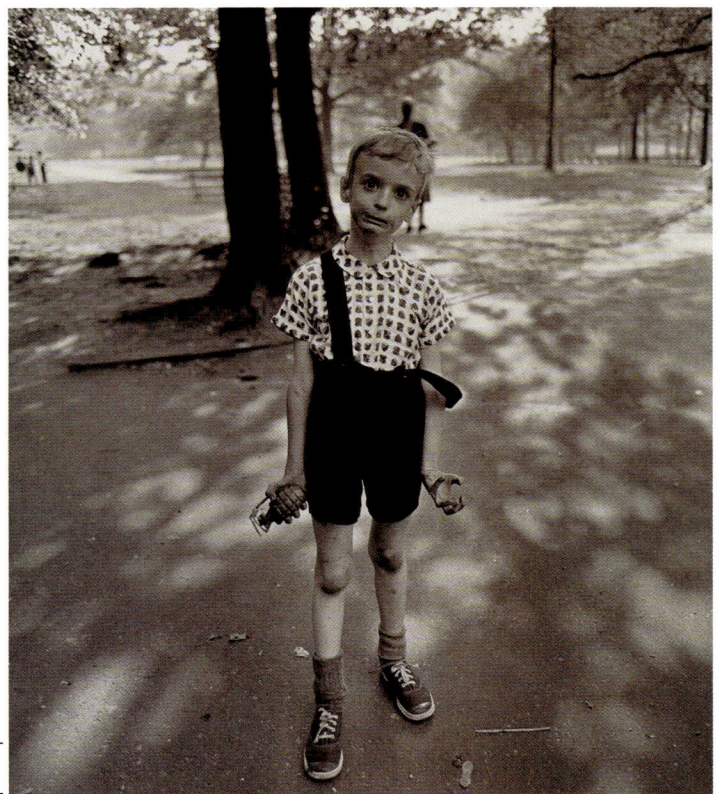

1 in.

**30-31** DIANE ARBUS, *Child with Toy Hand Grenade, New York, New York,* 1962. Gelatin silver print, 7$\frac{1}{4}$″ × 8$\frac{3}{8}$″. The Museum of Modern Art, New York.

Arbus specialized in photographs of people on the margins of society. Her photograph of a boy holding a toy hand grenade in New York's Central Park presents him as a menacing, isolated personality.

for her, and as she moved around him searching for the perfect angle, he became impatient, his body tensed, and his face formed a menacing expression. She snapped the shutter and recorded his peculiar grimace and eerie clawlike left hand. The empty space all around the boy contributes to the sense he is a disturbed personality isolated from society, in contrast to the "normal" family at the top right of the photograph. Arbus's own life was not "picture perfect" either. She committed suicide in 1971.

**MINOR WHITE** Minneapolis native MINOR WHITE (1908–1976) moved to Portland, Oregon, in 1938 and became a photographer for the Works Progress Administration. He served in the United States Army in World War II and then settled in New York City in 1945, where he met Alfred Stieglitz, whose *Equivalent* photographs (FIG. 29-43A) he greatly admired. Deeply influenced by Zen Buddhism (see "Zen Buddhism," Chapter 34, page 1007), White sought to incorporate a mystical element in his own work. His 1962 photograph (FIG. **30-32**) of a rock formation in Utah is a characteristic example. A "straight photograph" in the tradition of Stieglitz and Weston, it is also an abstract composition of jagged shapes and contrasts of light and dark reminiscent of Abstract Expressionist action paintings (FIG. 30-8C). Viewers of *Moencopi Strata, Capitol Reef, Utah* may recognize White's nominal subject as a detail of a landscape, but in his hands nature becomes the springboard for meditation. As one of the founders and the long-

## Judy Chicago on *The Dinner Party*

One of the acknowledged masterpieces of feminist art is Judy Chicago's *The Dinner Party* (FIG. 30-33), which required a team of nearly 400 to create and assemble. In 1979, Chicago published a book explaining the genesis and symbolism of the work.

[By 1974] I had discarded [my original] idea of painting a hundred abstract portraits on plates, each paying tribute to a different historic female figure. . . . In my research I realized over and over again that women's achievements had been left out of history . . . My new idea was to try to symbolize this. . . . [I thought] about putting the plates on a table with silver, glasses, napkins, and tablecloths, and over the next year and a half the concept of *The Dinner Party* slowly evolved. I began to think about the piece as a reinterpretation of the Last Supper from the point of view of women, who, throughout history, had prepared the meals and set the table. In my "Last Supper," however, the women would be the honored guests. Their representation in the form of plates set on the table would

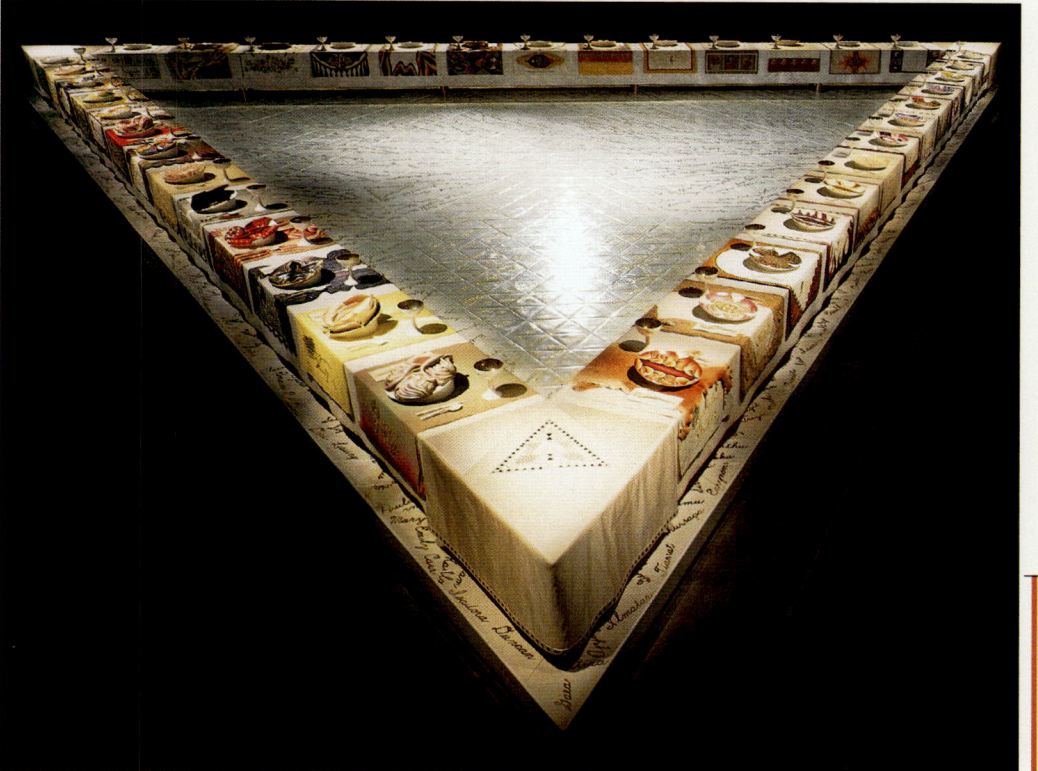

**30-33** JUDY CHICAGO, *The Dinner Party*, 1979. Multimedia, including ceramics and stitchery, 48′ long on each side. The Brooklyn Museum, Brooklyn.

Chicago's *Dinner Party* honors 39 women from antiquity to 20th-century America. The triangular form and the materials—painted china and fabric—are traditionally associated with women.

10 ft.

express the way women had been confined, and the piece would thus reflect both women's achievements and their oppression. . . . My goal with *The Dinner Party* was . . . to forge a new kind of art expressing women's experience . . . [It] seemed appropriate to relate our history through art, particularly through techniques traditionally associated with women—china-painting and needlework.*

*Judy Chicago, "The Dinner Party": *A Symbol of Our Heritage* (Garden City, N.Y.: Anchor Press, 1979), 11–12.

---

time editor (1952–1975) of *Aperture,* the leading art photography magazine of the time, White had a profound influence on the development of the medium in the postwar period.

## Feminist Art

With the renewed interest in representation the Pop artists and Superrealists introduced in the 1960s and 1970s, artists once again began to embrace the persuasive powers of art to communicate with a wide audience. In the 1970s, many artists began to investigate the social dynamics of power and privilege, especially in relation to gender, although racial, ethnic, and sexual orientation issues have also figured prominently in the art of recent decades (see Chapter 31). Women artists played a significant role in the feminist movement, which sought equal rights for women in contemporary society and focused attention on the subservient place of women in societies throughout history. Spearheading the feminist art movement of the 1970s were Judy Chicago (FIG. 30-33) and Miriam Schapiro (FIG. 30-34). Chicago and a group of students at California State University,

Fresno, founded the Feminist Art Program, and Chicago and Schapiro coordinated it at the California Institute of the Arts in Valencia. In 1972, as part of this program, teachers and students joined to create projects such as Womanhouse, an abandoned house in Los Angeles they completely converted into a suite of "environments," each based on a different aspect of women's lives and fantasies.

**JUDY CHICAGO** A major goal of Chicago native Judy Cohen, who took the name JUDY CHICAGO (b. 1939), was to educate the public about women's role in history and the fine arts and to establish a respect for women and their art. Chicago sought to forge a new kind of art expressing women's experiences and to find a way to make that art accessible to a large audience. Inspired early in her career by the work of Barbara Hepworth (FIG. 29-62), Georgia O'Keeffe (FIGS. I-5 and 29-42), and Louise Nevelson (FIG. 30-19), Chicago developed a personal painting style that consciously included abstract organic vaginal images. In the early 1970s, Chicago began planning an ambitious piece, *The Dinner Party* (FIG. **30-33**), using craft techniques (such as china painting and needlework)

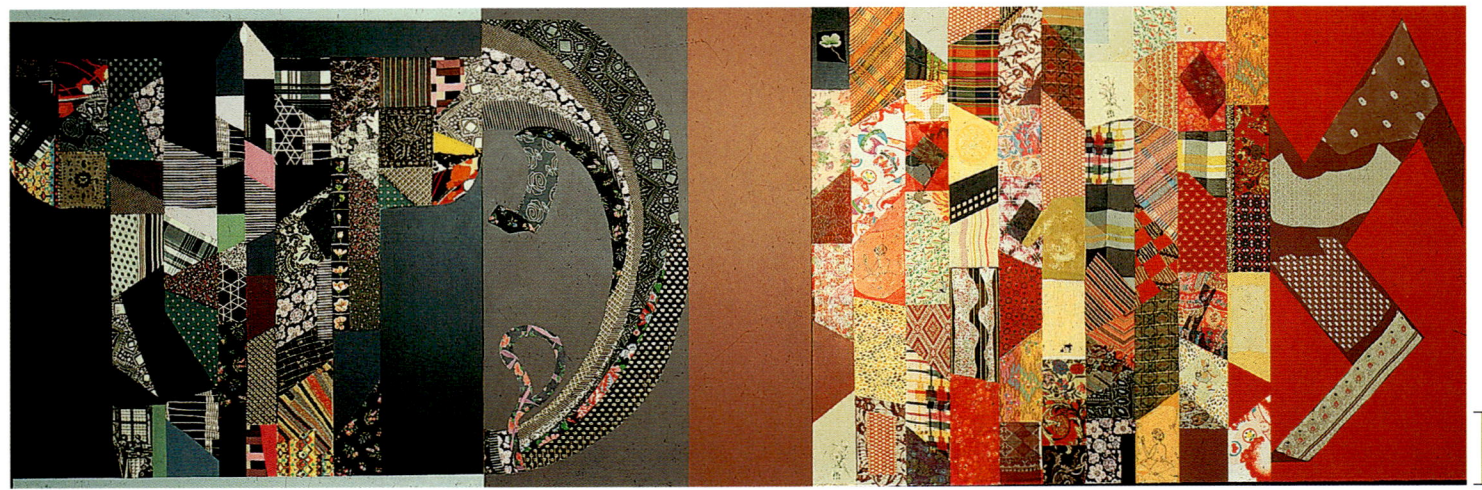

1 ft.

**30-34** MIRIAM SCHAPIRO, *Anatomy of a Kimono* (detail of a 10-panel composition), 1976. Fabric and acrylic on canvas, entire work 6′ 8″ × 52′ 2½″. Collection of Bruno Bischofberger, Zurich.

Schapiro calls her huge sewn collages *femmages* to make the point that women had been doing collages of fabric long before Picasso (FIG. 29-16). This femmage incorporates patterns from Japanese kimonos.

traditionally practiced by women, to celebrate the achievements and contributions women had made throughout history (see "Judy Chicago on *The Dinner Party*," page 921). She originally conceived the work as a feminist *Last Supper* for 13 "honored guests," as in the biblical account of Christ's passion, but at Chicago's table the guests are women instead of men. The number of women in a witches' coven is also 13, and the artist intended her feminist *Dinner Party* additionally to refer to witchcraft and the worship of the Mother Goddess. But because Chicago had uncovered so many worthy women in the course of her research, she tripled the number of guests and placed table settings for 39 women around a triangular table 48 feet long on each side. The triangular form refers to the ancient symbol for both woman and the Goddess. The notion of a dinner party also alludes to women's traditional role as homemakers.

*The Dinner Party* rests on a triangular white tile floor inscribed with the names of 999 additional women of achievement to signify that the accomplishments of the 39 honored guests rest on a foundation other women laid. Among those with place settings at the table are American painter Georgia O'Keeffe, Egyptian pharaoh Hatshepsut (see "Hatshepsut," Chapter 3, page 69), British writer Virginia Woolf, Native American guide Sacagawea, and American suffragist Susan B. Anthony. Each woman's place has identical eating utensils and a goblet but features a unique oversized porcelain plate and a long place mat or table runner covered with imagery reflecting significant facts about that woman's life and culture. The plates range from simple concave shapes with china-painted imagery to dishes whose sculptured three-dimensional designs almost seem to struggle to free themselves. The designs on each plate incorporate both butterfly and vulval motifs—the butterfly as the ancient symbol of liberation and the vulva as the symbol of female sexuality. Each table runner combines traditional needlework techniques, including needlepoint, embroidery, crochet, beading, patchwork, and appliqué. *The Dinner Party* is more than the sum of its parts, however. Of monumental size, as so many great works of public art have been throughout the ages, Chicago's 1979 masterwork provides viewers with a powerful launching point for considering broad feminist concerns.

**MIRIAM SCHAPIRO** After enjoying a thriving career as a hard-edge painter in California in the late 1960s, Toronto-born MIRIAM SCHAPIRO (b. 1923) became fascinated with the hidden metaphors for womanhood she then saw in her abstract paintings. Intrigued by the materials she had used to create a doll's house for her part in Womanhouse, in the 1970s Schapiro began to make huge sewn collages, assembled from fabrics, quilts, buttons, sequins, lace trim, and rickrack collected at antique shows and fairs. She called these works *femmages* to make the point that women had been doing collages using these materials long before Pablo Picasso (FIG. 29-16) introduced them to the art world. *Anatomy of a Kimono* (FIG. 30-34) is one of a series of monumental femmages based on the patterns of Japanese kimonos, fans, and robes. This vast 10-panel composition (more than 52 feet long and almost 7 feet high) repeats the kimono shape in a sumptuous array of fabric fragments.

**CINDY SHERMAN** After studying painting in Buffalo, CINDY SHERMAN (b. 1954) switched to photography as her primary means of expression. She addresses in her work the way much of Western art presents female beauty for the enjoyment of the "male gaze," a primary focus of contemporary feminist theory, which explores gender as a socially constructed concept. Since 1977, Sherman has produced a series of more than 80 black-and-white photographs called *Untitled Film Stills*. She got the idea for the series after examining soft-core pornography magazines and noting the stereotypical ways they depicted women. She decided to produce her own series of photographs, designing, acting in, directing, and photographing the works. In so doing, she took control of her own image and constructed her own identity, a primary feminist concern.

In works from the series, such as *Untitled Film Still #35* (FIG. **30-35**), Sherman appears, often in costume and wig, in a photograph that seems to be a film still. Most of the images in this series recall popular film genres but are sufficiently generic that the viewer cannot relate them to specific movies. Sherman often reveals the constructed nature of these images with the shutter release cable she holds in her hand to take the pictures. (The cord runs across

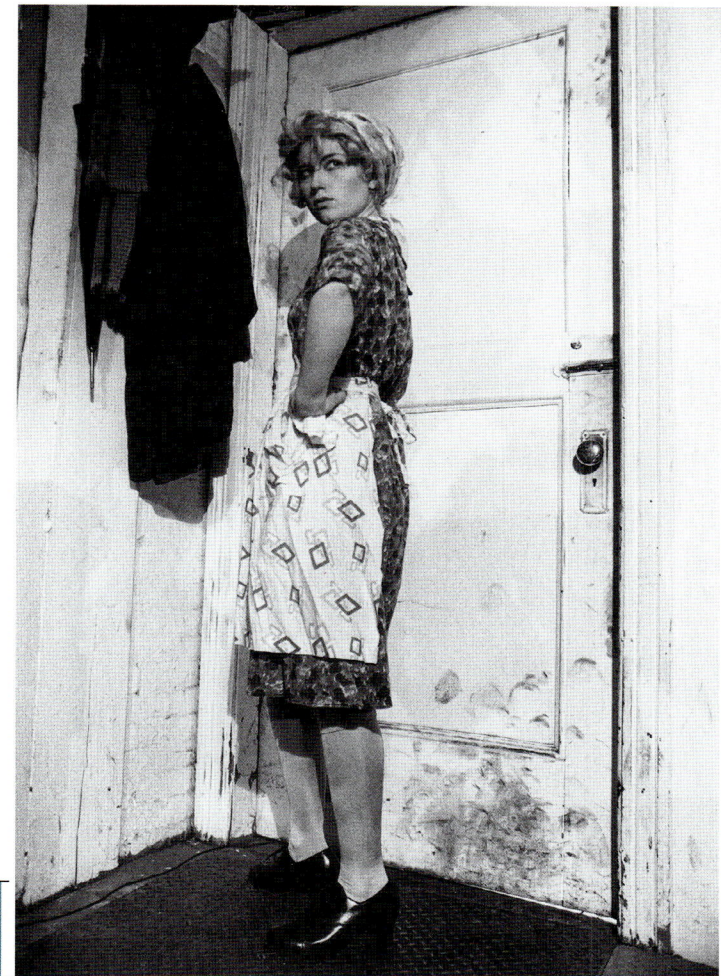

**30-35** CINDY SHERMAN, *Untitled Film Still #35,* 1979. Gelatin silverprint, 10″ × 8″. Private collection. ◼◀

Sherman here assumed a role for one of 80 photographs resembling film stills in which she addressed the way women have been presented in Western art for the enjoyment of the "male gaze."

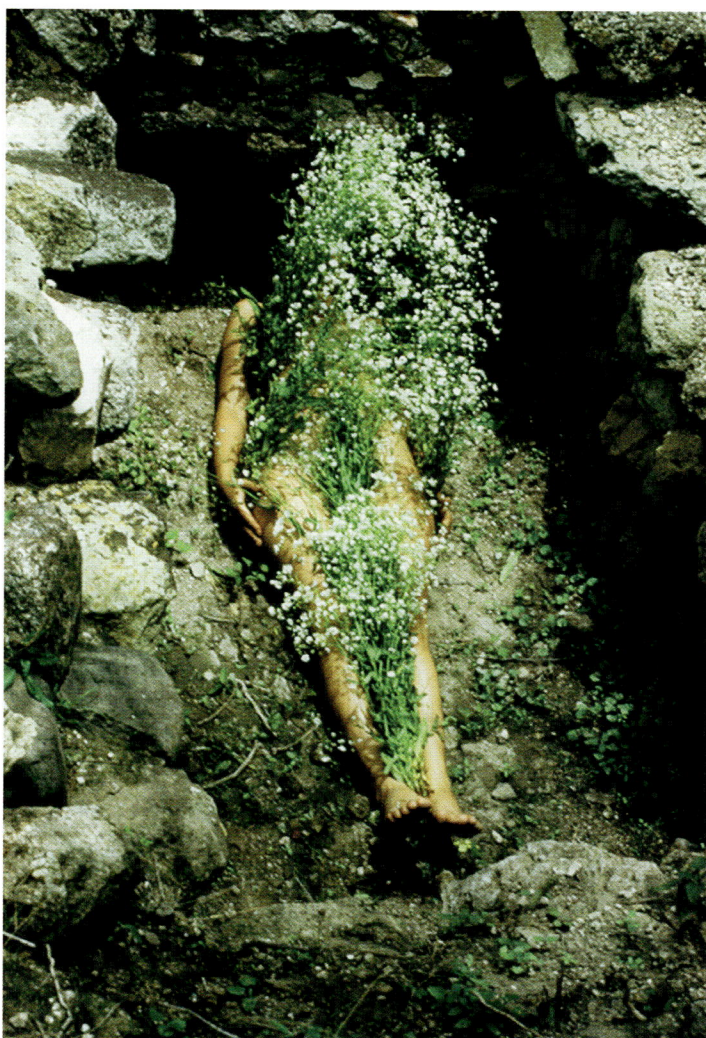

**30-36** ANA MENDIETA, *Flowers on Body,* 1973. Color photograph of earth/body work with flowers, executed at El Yagul, Mexico. Courtesy of the Estate of Ana Mendieta and Galerie Lelong, New York.

In this earth/body sculpture, Mendieta appears covered with flowers in a grave- or womblike cavity to address issues of birth and death, as well as the human connection to the earth.

the floor in *#35.*) Although the artist is still the object of the viewer's gaze in these images, the identity is one she alone chose to assume.

**ANA MENDIETA** Cuban-born artist ANA MENDIETA (1948–1985) also used her body as a component in her artworks. Although gender issues concerned her, Mendieta's art also dealt with issues of spirituality and cultural heritage. The artist's best-known series, *Silueta* (Silhouettes), consists of approximately 200 earth/body works completed between 1973 and 1980. These works represented Mendieta's attempt to carry on, as she described, "a dialogue between the landscape and the female body (based on my own silhouette)."[22]

*Flowers on Body* (FIG. **30-36**) is a documentary photograph of the first of the earth/body sculptures in the *Silueta* series. In this work, Mendieta appears covered with flowers in an earthen, grave- or womblike cavity. Executed at El Yagul, a Mexican archaeological site, the work speaks to the issues of birth and death, the female experience of childbirth, and the human connection to the earth. Objects and locations from nature play an important role in Mendieta's art. She explained the centrality of this connection to nature:

I believe this has been a direct result of my having been torn from my homeland during my adolescence. I am overwhelmed by the feeling of having been cast from the womb (nature). My art is the way I re-establish the bonds that unite me to the universe. It is a return to the maternal source. Through my earth/body sculptures I become one with the earth.[23]

Beyond their sensual, moving presence, Mendieta's works also generate a palpable spiritual force. In longing for her homeland, she sought the cultural understanding and acceptance of the spiritual powers inherent in nature that modern Western societies often seem to reject in favor of scientific and technological developments. Mendieta's art is lyrical and passionate and operates at the intersection of cultural, spiritual, physical, and feminist concerns.

**HANNAH WILKE** Another artist who used her nude body as her medium was New Yorker HANNAH WILKE (1940–1993), who studied art at Temple University. Enlarging images from her mixed media

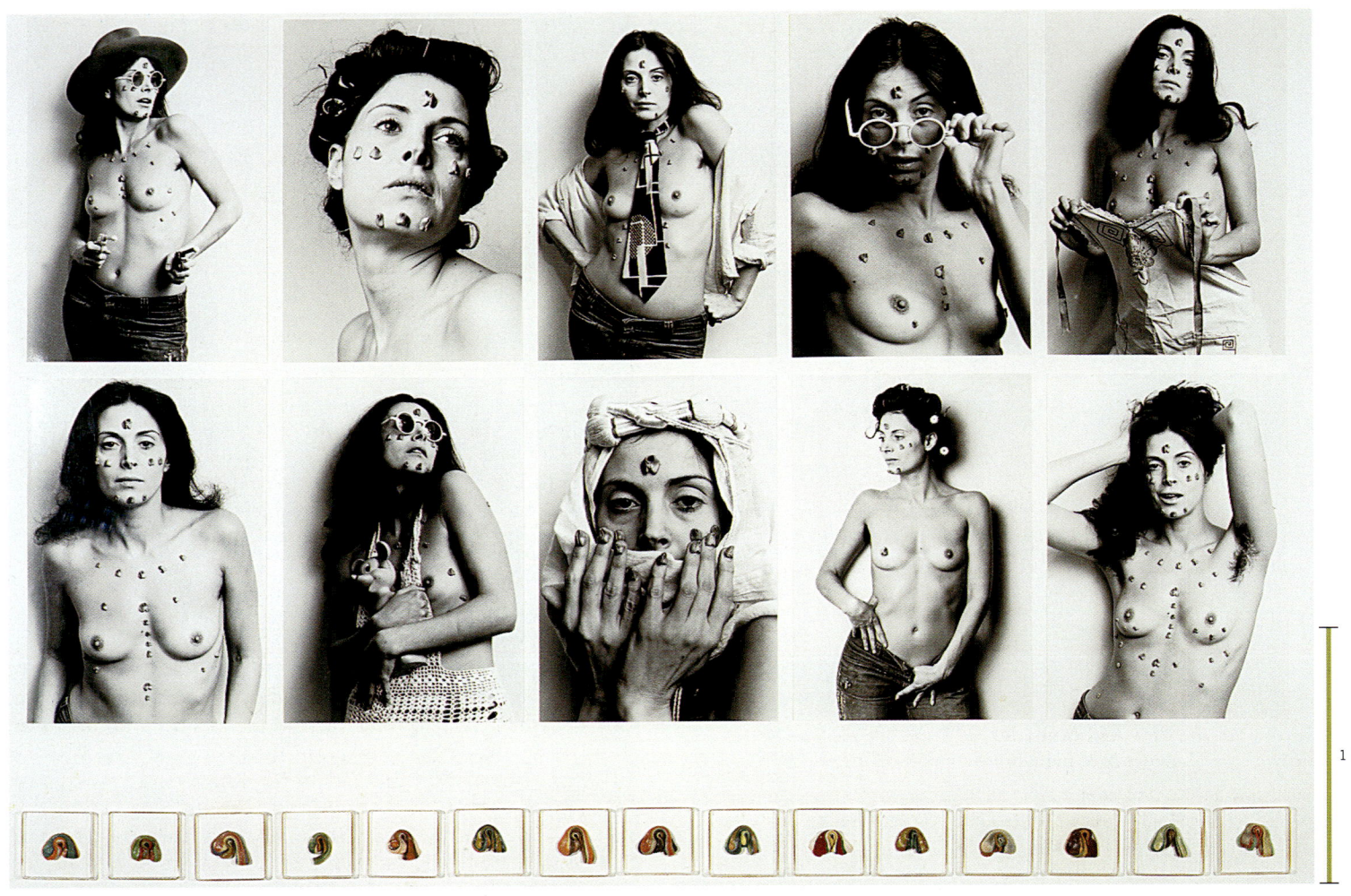

**30-37** HANNAH WILKE, *S.O.S. Starification Object Series,* 1974–1982. 10 black and white photographs and 16 chewing gum sculptures mounted on ragboard, , 3′ 5″ × 4′ 10″ framed. © Marsie, Emanuelle, Damon, and Andrew Scharlatt/Licensed by VAGA, New York, NY. Courtesy Ronald Feldman Fine Arts, New York.

In this photographic series, Wilke posed topless decorated with chewing-gum sculptures of vulvas, which allude to female pleasure, but also to pain, because they resemble scars.

installation of 35 photographs, *S.O.S. Starification Object Series, An Adult Game of Mastication* (FIG. **30-37**), 1974–1975, Wilke, in *S.O.S. Starification Object Series,* 1974–1982, presented images of herself that trigger readings simultaneously metaphorical and real, stereotypical and unique, erotic and disconcerting, and that deal with both pleasure and pain. In these 10 black-and-white photographs, Wilke appears topless. In each, pieces of chewed gum shaped into small vulvas decorate her body. While these tiny vaginal sculptures allude to female pleasure, they also appear as scars, suggesting pain. Ultimately, Wilke hoped women would "take control of and have pride in the sensuality of their own bodies and create a sexuality in their own terms, without deferring to concepts degenerated by culture."[24]

**MAGDALENA ABAKANOWICZ** Not strictly feminist in subject, but created using materials traditionally associated with women, are the sculptures of Polish fiber artist MAGDALENA ABAKANOWICZ (b. 1930). A leader in the exploration of the expressive powers of weaving techniques in large-scale artworks, Abakanowicz gained fame with experimental freestanding figural works expressing the stoic, everyday toughness of the human spirit. For Abakanowicz, fiber materials are deeply symbolic:

I see fiber as the basic element constructing the organic world on our planet, as the greatest mystery of our environment. It is from fiber that all living organisms are built—the tissues of plants and ourselves. . . . Fabric is our covering and our attire. Made with our hands, it is a record of our souls.[25]

Abakanowicz's sculptures are to a great degree reflections of her early life experiences as a member of an aristocratic family disturbed by the dislocations of World War II and its aftermath. Initially attracted to weaving as a medium easily adaptable to the small studio space she had available, Abakanowicz gradually developed huge abstract hangings she called Abakans that suggest organic spaces as well as giant pieces of clothing. She returned to a smaller scale with works based on human forms—*Heads, Seated Figures,* and *Backs*—multiplying each type for exhibition in groups as symbols for the individual in society lost in the crowd yet retaining some distinctiveness.

This impression is especially powerful in *80 Backs* (FIG. **30-38**). Abakanowicz made each piece by pressing layers of natural organic fibers into a plaster mold. Every sculpture depicts the slumping shoulders, back, and arms of a figure of indeterminate sex and

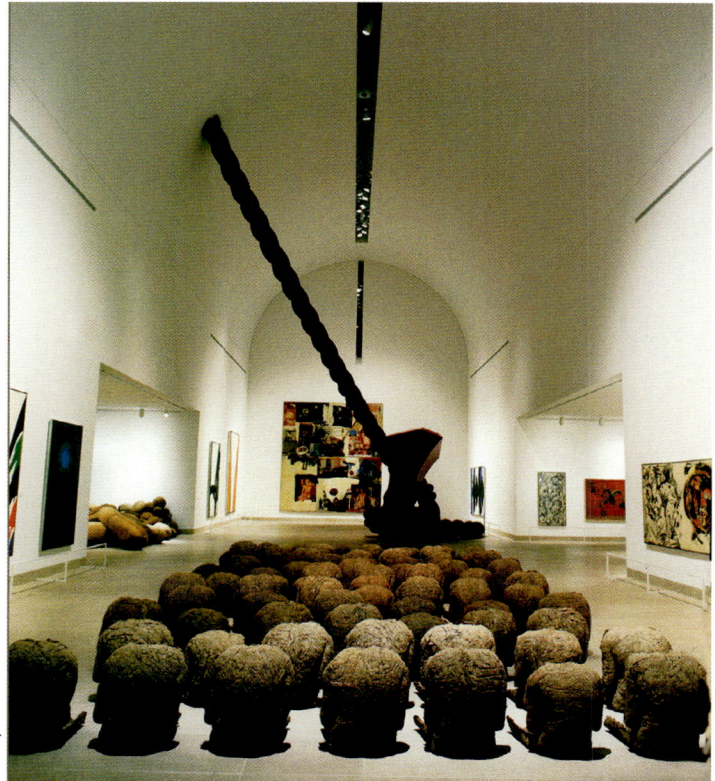

1 ft.

**30-38** Magdalena Abakanowicz, *80 Backs,* 1976–1980. Burlap and resin, each figure 2′ 3″ high. Museum of Modern Art, Dallas.

Polish fiber artist Abakanowicz explored the stoic, everyday toughness of the human spirit in this group of nearly identical sculptures that serve as symbols of distinctive individuals lost in the crowd.

rests legless directly on the floor. The repeated pose of the figures in *80 Backs* suggests meditation, submission, and anticipation. Although made from a single mold, the figures achieve a touching sense of individuality because each assumed a slightly different posture as the material dried and because the artist imprinted a different pattern of fiber texture on each.

# ARCHITECTURE AND SITE-SPECIFIC ART

Some of the most innovative architects of the first half of the 20th century, most notably Frank Lloyd Wright (FIGS. 29-45, 29-46, and 29-79), Ludwig Mies van der Rohe (FIG. 29-67), and Le Corbusier (FIG. 29-68), concluded their long and productive careers in the postwar period. At the same time, younger architects rose to international prominence, some working in the modernist idiom but others taking architectural design in new "postmodern" directions.

## Modernism

In parallel with the progressive movement toward formal abstraction in painting and sculpture in the decades following World War II, modernist architects became increasingly concerned with a formalism stressing simplicity. They articulated this in buildings that retained intriguing organic sculptural qualities, as well as in buildings adhering to a more rigid geometry.

**FRANK LLOYD WRIGHT** The last great building Frank Lloyd Wright designed was the Solomon R. Guggenheim Museum (FIG. **30-39**) in New York City. Using reinforced concrete almost as a sculptor might use resilient clay, Wright, who often described his architecture as "organic," designed a structure inspired by the spiral of a snail's shell. Wright had introduced curves and circles into some of his plans in the 1930s, and as the architectural historian Peter Blake noted, "The spiral was the next logical step; it is the circle brought into the third and fourth dimensions."[26] Inside the building (FIG. 31-44), the shape of the shell expands toward the top, and a winding interior ramp spirals to connect the gallery bays. A skylight strip embedded in the museum's outer wall provides illumination to the ramp, which visitors can stroll up (or down, if they first take an elevator to the top of the building), viewing the artworks displayed along the gently sloping pathway. Thick walls and the solid organic shape give the building, outside and inside, the sense of turning in on itself, and the long interior viewing area opening onto a 90-foot central well of space creates a sheltered environment, secure from the bustling city outside.

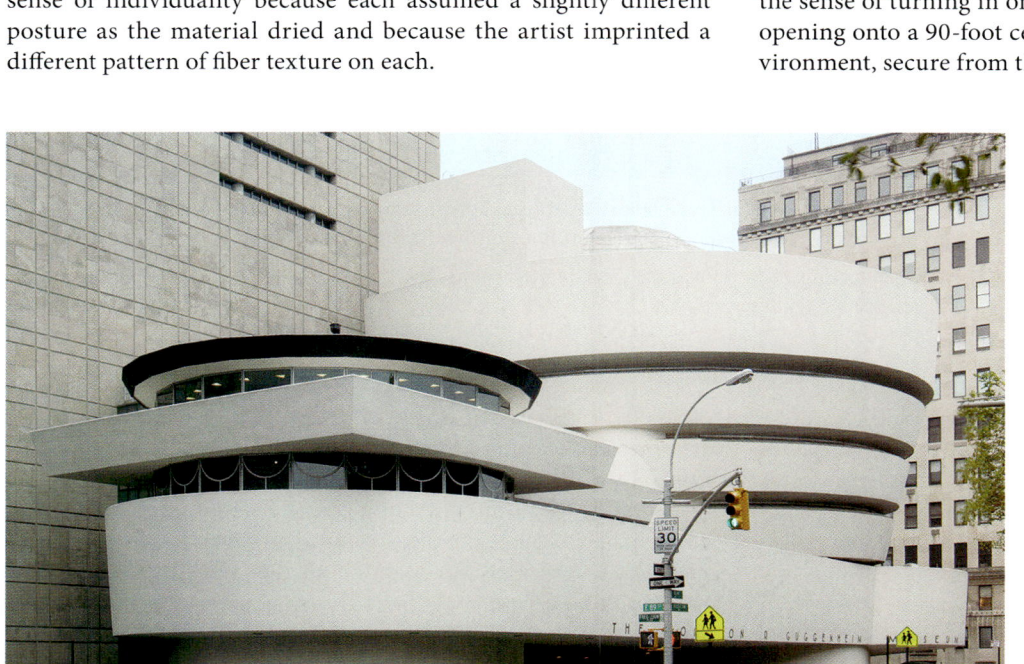

**30-39** Frank Lloyd Wright, **Solomon R. Guggenheim Museum (looking southeast), New York, 1943–1959.** ◼◀

Using reinforced concrete almost as a sculptor might use resilient clay, Wright designed a snail shell–shaped museum with a winding, gently inclined interior ramp for the display of artworks.

**LE CORBUSIER** Compared with his pristine geometric design for Villa Savoye (FIG. 29-68), the organic forms of Le Corbusier's Notre-Dame-du-Haut (FIG. **30-40**) come as a startling surprise. Completed in 1955 at Ronchamp, France, the chapel attests to the boundless creativity of this great architect. A fusion of architecture and sculpture, the small chapel, which replaced a building destroyed in World War II, occupies a pilgrimage site in the Vosges Mountains. The monumental impression of Notre-Dame-du-Haut seen from afar is somewhat deceptive. Although one massive exterior wall (FIG. 30-40, *top*) contains a pulpit facing a spacious outdoor area for large-scale open-air services on holy days, the interior (FIG. 30-40, *bottom*) holds at most 200 people. The intimate scale, stark and heavy walls, and mysterious illumination (jewel tones cast from the deeply recessed stained-glass windows) give this space an aura reminiscent of a sacred cave or a medieval monastery.

Notre-Dame-du-Haut's structure may look free-form to the untrained eye, but Le Corbusier based it, as did the designers of Romanesque and Gothic cathedrals, on an underlying mathematical system. The pilgrimage church has a frame of steel and metal mesh, which the builders sprayed with concrete and painted white, except for two interior private chapel niches with colored walls and the roof, which Le Corbusier wished to have darken naturally with the passage of time. The roof appears to float freely above the worshipers in their pews (FIG. 30-40, *bottom*), intensifying the quality of mystery in the interior space. In reality, a series of nearly invisible blocks holds up the roof. The mystery of the roof's means of support recalls the reaction to Hagia Sophia's miraculously floating dome (FIG. 9-8) a millennium and a half before in Byzantium. Le Corbusier's preliminary sketches for the building indicate he linked the design with the shape of praying hands, with the wings of a dove (representing both peace and the Holy Spirit), and with the prow of a ship (a reminder the term for

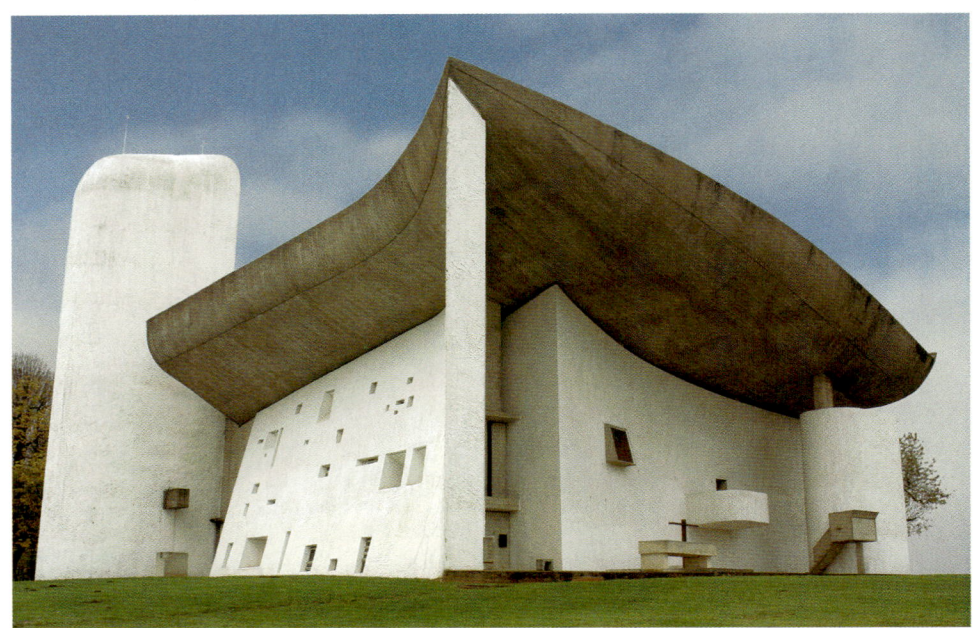

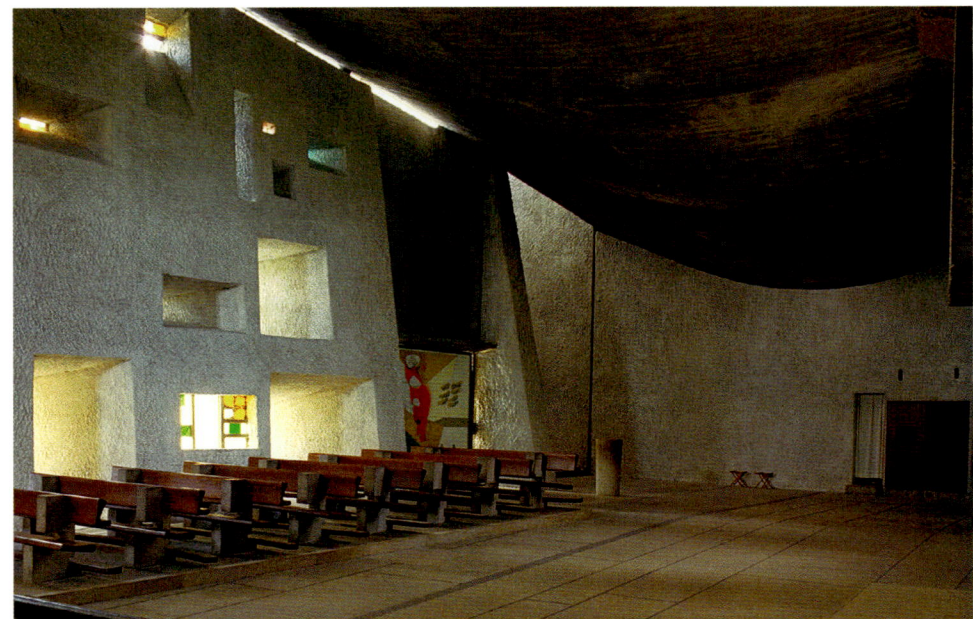

**30-40** LE CORBUSIER, Notre-Dame-du-Haut, Ronchamp, France, 1950–1955. *Top:* exterior looking northwest; *bottom:* interior looking southwest. ◼◀

The organic forms of Le Corbusier's mountaintop chapel at Ronchamp present a fusion of architecture and sculpture. The heavy sprayed concrete walls enclose an intimate and mysteriously lit interior that has the aura of a sacred cave.

the central aisle in a traditional basilican church is *nave*—Latin for "ship"). Le Corbusier hoped that in the mystical interior he created and in the rolling hills around the church, men and women would reflect on the sacred and the natural. No one who has visited Notre-Dame-du-Haut, whether on a bright sunlit day or in a thundering storm, has come away unmoved.

**EERO SAARINEN** Dramatic, sweeping, curvilinear rooflines are also characteristic features of the buildings designed by Finnish-born architect EERO SAARINEN (1910–1961). One of his signature buildings of the late 1950s is the former Trans World Airlines terminal (now the Jet Blue Airways terminal, FIG. **30-41**) at John F.

Kennedy International Airport in New York. The terminal, which Saarinen based on the theme of motion, consists of two immense concrete shells split down the middle and slightly rotated, giving the building a fluid curved outline that fits its corner site. The shells immediately suggest expansive wings and flight. Saarinen also designed everything on the interior, including the furniture, ventilation ducts, and signboards, with this same curvilinear vocabulary in mind.

**JOERN UTZON** Saarinen was responsible for selecting the Danish architect JOERN UTZON (1918–2008) to build the Sydney Opera House (FIG. **30-42**) in Australia. Utzon's design is a bold

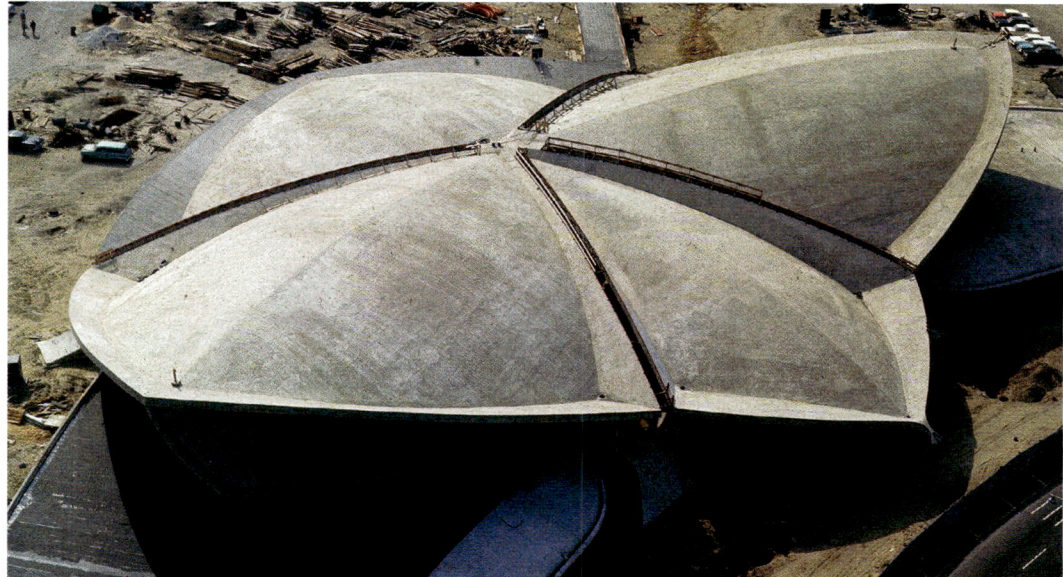

**30-41** Eero Saarinen, Terminal 5 (Jet Blue Airways terminal, formerly the Trans World Airlines terminal; looking southeast), John F. Kennedy International Airport, New York, 1956–1962.

Saarinen based the design for this airline terminal on the theme of motion. The concrete-and-glass building's dramatic, sweeping, curvilinear rooflines suggest expansive wings and flight.

composition of organic forms on a colossal scale. Utzon worked briefly with Frank Lloyd Wright at Taliesin (Wright's Wisconsin residence), and the style of the Sydney Opera House resonates distantly with the graceful curvature of New York's Guggenheim Museum (FIG. 30-39). Clusters of immense concrete shells—the largest is 200 feet tall—rise from massive platforms and soar to delicate peaks. Recalling at first the *ogival* (pointed) shapes of Gothic vaults, the shells also suggest both the buoyancy of seabird wings and the billowing sails of the tall ships of the European settlers who emigrated to Australia in the 18th and 19th centuries. These architectural metaphors are appropriate to the harbor surrounding Bennelong Point, whose bedrock foundations support the building. Utzon's matching of the structure with its site and atmosphere adds to the organic nature of the design.

Though construction of the building began in 1959, completion of the opera house had to wait until 1972, primarily because Utzon's daring design required construction technology not yet developed. Today, the opera house is Sydney's defining symbol, a monument of civic pride that functions as the city's cultural center. In addition to the opera auditorium, the complex houses auxiliary halls and rooms for concerts, the performing arts, motion pictures, lectures, art exhibitions, and conventions.

**MIES VAN DER ROHE** Sculpturesque building design was not the only manifestation of postwar modernist architecture. From the mid-1950s through the 1970s, other architects created massive, sleek, and geometrically rigid buildings. They designed most of these structures following Bauhaus architect Mies van der Rohe's contention

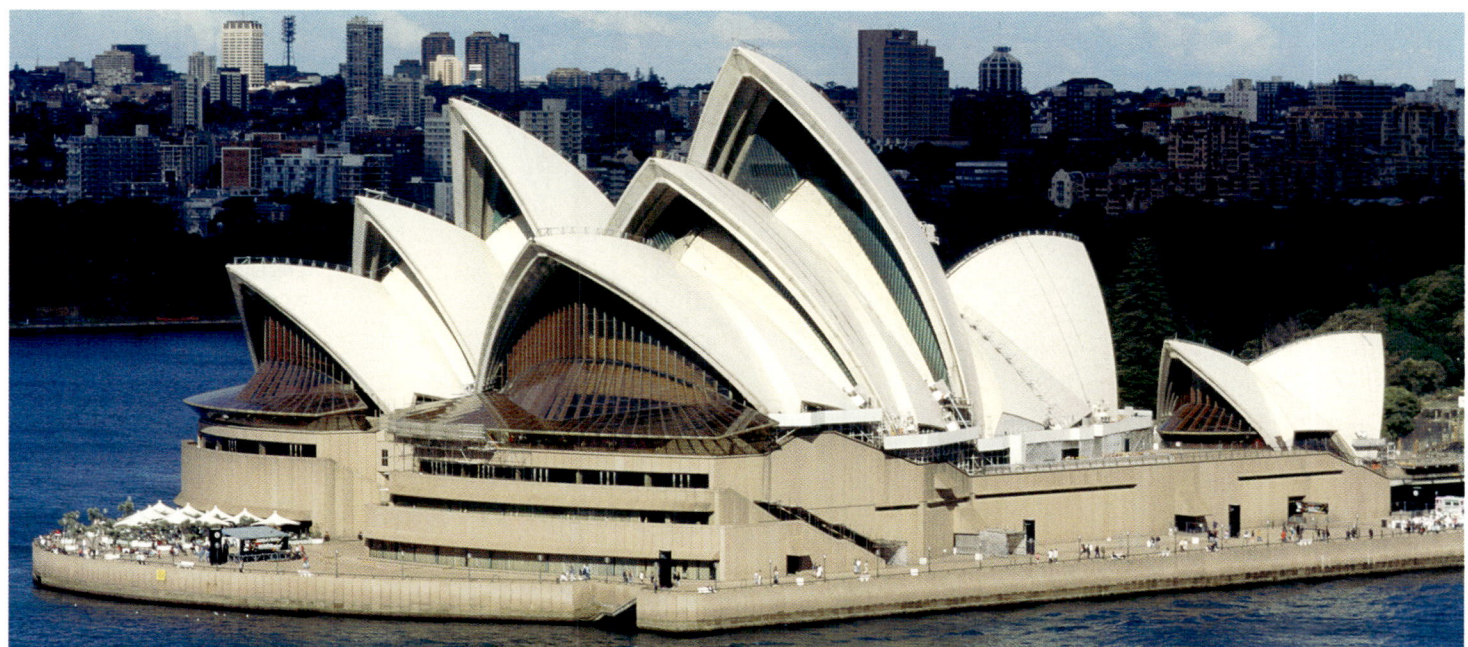

**30-42** Joern Utzon, Sydney Opera House (looking southeast), Sydney, Australia, 1959–1972.

The soaring clusters of concrete shells of Utzon's opera house on an immense platform in Sydney's harbor suggest both the buoyancy of seabird wings and the billowing sails of tall ships.

that "less is more." Many of these more Minimalist designs are powerful, heroic presences in the urban landscape that effectively symbolize the giant corporations often inhabiting them.

The purest example of these corporate skyscrapers is the mid-1950s rectilinear glass-and-bronze Seagram Building (FIG. **30-43**) in Manhattan designed by Mies van der Rohe and American architect Philip Johnson (FIG. 30-46). By this time, the concrete-steel-and-glass towers pioneered by Louis Sullivan (FIGS. 28-40, 28-40A, and 28-41) and carried further by Mies van der Rohe himself (FIG. 29-67) had become a familiar sight in cities throughout the world. Appealing in its structural logic and clarity, the style, easily imitated, quickly became the norm for postwar commercial high-rise buildings. The architects of the Seagram Building deliberately designed it as a thin shaft, leaving the front quarter of its midtown site as an open pedestrian plaza. The tower appears to rise from the pavement on stilts. Glass walls even surround the recessed lobby. The building's recessed structural elements make it appear to have a glass skin, interrupted only by the thin strips of bronze anchoring the windows. The bronze metal and the amber glass windows give the tower a richness found in few of its neighbors. Mies van der Rohe and Johnson carefully planned every detail of the Seagram Building, inside and out, to create an elegant whole. They even designed the interior and exterior lighting to make the edifice an impressive sight both day and night.

**SKIDMORE, OWINGS & MERRILL** The architectural firm SKIDMORE, OWINGS & MERRILL (SOM), perhaps the purest proponent of Miesian-inspired structures, designed a number of these simple rectilinear glass-sheathed buildings, and SOM's success indicates the popularity of this building type. By 1970, the company comprised more than a thousand architects and had offices in New York, Chicago, San Francisco, Portland, and Washington, D.C. In 1974, the firm completed the Sears Tower (FIG. **30-44**), a mammoth corporate building in Chicago. Consisting of nine clustered shafts soaring vertically, this 110-floor building provides offices for more than 12,000 workers. Original plans called for 104 stories, but the architects acquiesced to Sears's insistence on making the building the tallest (measured to the structural top) in the world at the time. The tower's size, coupled with the black

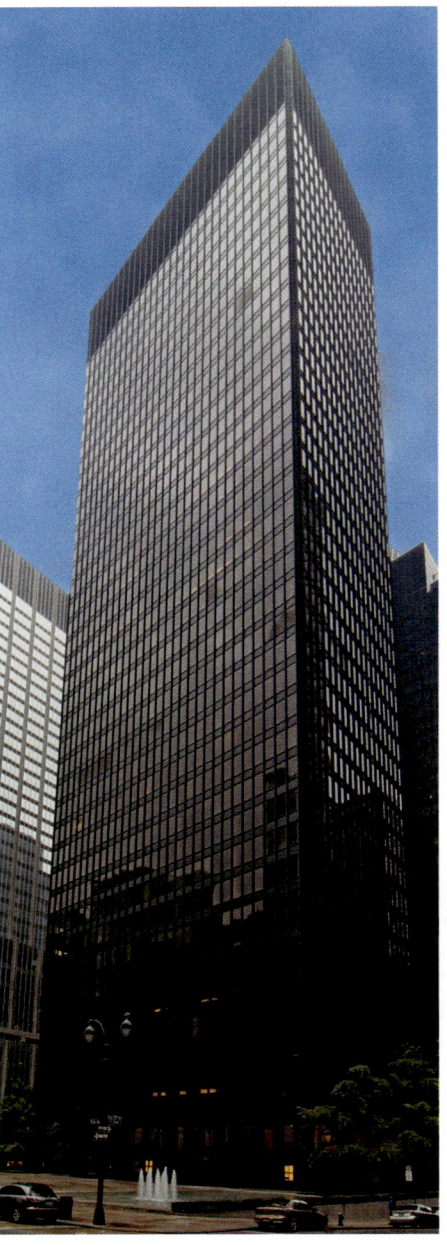

**30-43** LUDWIG MIES VAN DER ROHE and PHILIP JOHNSON, Seagram Building (looking northeast), New York, 1956–1958. ◼◀

Massive, sleek, and geometrically rigid, this modernist skyscraper has a bronze and glass skin masking its concrete-and-steel frame. The giant corporate tower appears to rise from the pavement on stilts.

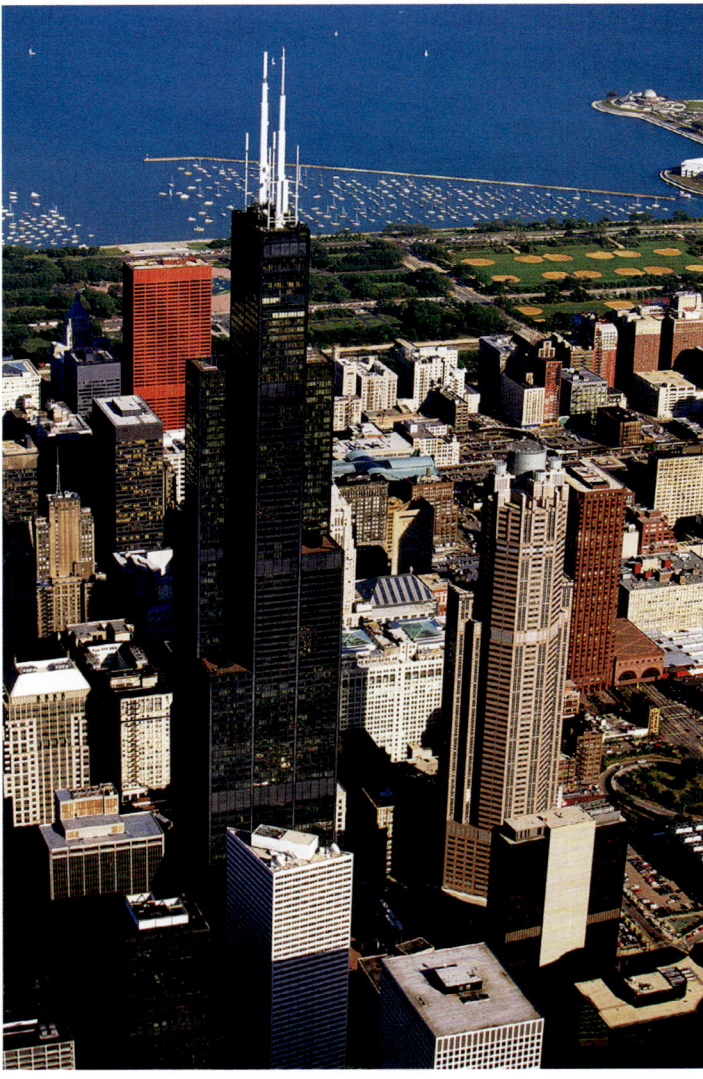

**30-44** SKIDMORE, OWINGS & MERRILL, Willis Tower (formerly Sears Tower; looking east), Chicago, 1974. ◼◀

Consisting of nine black aluminum and smoked glass shafts soaring to 110 stories, the Willis (Sears) Tower dominates Chicago's skyline. It was the world's tallest building at the time of its construction.

aluminum sheathing it and the smoked glass, establish a dominant presence in a city of many corporate skyscrapers—exactly the image Sears executives wanted to project.

## Postmodernism

The restrictiveness of modernist architecture and the impersonality and sterility of many modernist structures eventually led to a rejection of modernism's authority in architecture. Along with the apparent lack of responsiveness to the unique character of the cities and neighborhoods in which modernist architects built their structures, these reactions ushered in *postmodernism,* one of the most dramatic developments in later-20th-century architecture as well as in contemporary painting and sculpture (see Chapter 31). Postmodernism in architecture is not a unified style. It is a widespread cultural phenomenon far more encompassing and accepting than the more rigid confines of modernist practice. In contrast to the simplicity of modernist architecture, the terms most often invoked to describe postmodern architecture are pluralism, complexity, and eclecticism. Whereas the modernist program was reductive, the postmodern vocabulary of the 1970s and 1980s was expansive and inclusive.

Among the first to explore this new direction in architecture were Jane Jacobs (1916–2006) and Robert Venturi (FIG. 30-48). In their influential books *The Death and Life of Great American Cities* (Jacobs, 1961) and *Complexity and Contradiction in Architecture* (Venturi, 1966), Jacobs and Venturi argued that the uniformity and anonymity of modernist architecture (in particular, the corporate skyscrapers dominating many urban skylines) were unsuited to human social interaction and that diversity is the great advantage of urban life. Postmodern architects accepted, indeed embraced, the messy and chaotic nature of big-city life.

When designing these varied buildings, many postmodern architects consciously selected past architectural elements or references and juxtaposed them with contemporary elements or fashioned them of high-tech materials, thereby creating a dialogue between past and present. Postmodern architecture incorporates not only traditional architectural references but references to mass culture and popular imagery as well. This was precisely the "complexity and contradiction" Venturi referred to in the title of his book.

**CHARLES MOORE** A clear example of the eclecticism and the dialogue between traditional and contemporary elements found in postmodern architecture is the Piazza d'Italia (FIG. **30-45**) by American architect CHARLES MOORE (1925–1993), who was educated at the University of Michigan and Princeton University and served as dean of the Yale School of Architecture from 1965 to 1970. Designed in the late 1970s in New Orleans, the Piazza d'Italia is an open plaza dedicated to the city's Italian-American community. Appropriately, Moore selected elements relating specifically to Italian history, all the way back to ancient Roman culture.

Backed up against a contemporary high-rise building and set off from urban traffic patterns, the Piazza d'Italia is accessible to pedestrians from three sides through gateways of varied design. The approaches lead to an open circular area partially formed by short segments of colonnades arranged in staggered concentric arcs, which direct the eye to the focal point of the composition—an *exedra*. This recessed area on a raised platform serves as a *rostrum* (speaker's platform) during the annual festivities of Saint Joseph's Day. Moore inlaid the piazza's pavement with a map of Italy centered on Sicily, from which the majority of the city's Italian families originated. From there, the map's Italian "boot" moves in the direction of the steps that ascend the rostrum and correspond to the Alps.

The piazza's most immediate historical reference is to the Roman forum (FIGS. 7-12 and 7-44). However, its circular form alludes to the ideal geometric figure of the Renaissance (FIGS. 22-3A and 22-21). The irregular placement of the concentrically arranged colonnade fragments inserts a note of instability into the design reminiscent of Mannerism (FIG. 22-55). Illusionistic devices, such as the continuation of the piazza's pavement design (apparently through a building and out into the street), are Baroque in character (FIG. 24-4). Moore incorporated all of the classical orders—most with whimsical modifications. Nevertheless, challenging the piazza's historical character are modern features, such as the stainless-steel columns and capitals, neon collars around the column necks, and neon lights framing various parts of the exedra.

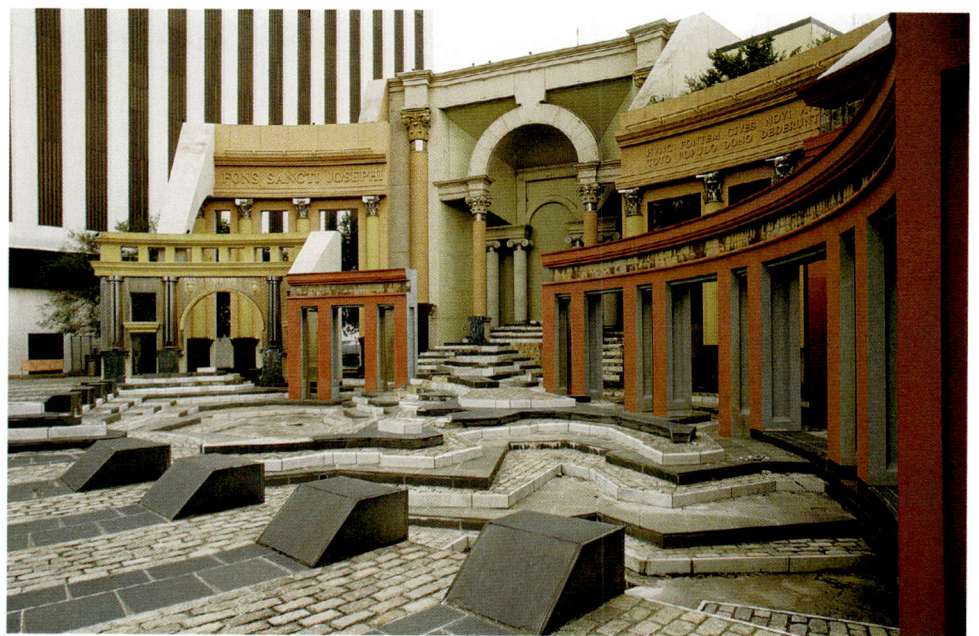

**30-45** CHARLES MOORE, Piazza d'Italia (looking northeast), New Orleans, 1976–1980.

Moore's circular postmodern Italian plaza incorporates elements drawn from ancient Roman architecture with the instability of Mannerist designs and modern stainless-steel columns with neon collars.

## Philip Johnson on Postmodern Architecture

Philip Johnson, who died in 2005 at age 98, had a distinguished career spanning almost the entire 20th century, during which he transformed himself from a modernist closely associated with Mies van der Rohe (FIG. 30-43) into one of the leading postmodernists, whose AT&T (now Sony) Building (FIG. 30-46) in New York City remains an early icon of postmodernism. In the following passages, Johnson commented on his early "Miesian" style and about the incorporation of various historical styles in postmodernist buildings.

> My eyes are set by the Miesian tradition . . . The continuity with my Miesian approach also shows through in my classicism. . . . [But in] 1952, about the same time that my whole generation did, I became very restless. . . . In the last decade there has been such a violent switch that it is almost embarrassing. But it isn't a switch, so much as a centrifugal splintering of architecture, to a degree that I don't think has been seen in the past few hundred years. Perfectly responsible architects build, even in one year, buildings that you cannot believe are done by the same person.*
>
> Structural honesty seems to me one of the bugaboos that we should free ourselves from very quickly. The Greeks with their marble columns imitating wood, and covering up the roofs inside! The Gothic designers with their wooden roofs above to protect their delicate vaulting. And Michelangelo, the greatest architect in history, with his Mannerist column! There is only one absolute today and this is change. There are no rules, surely no certainties in any of the arts. There is only the feeling of a wonderful freedom, of endless possibilities to investigate, of endless past years of historically great buildings to enjoy.†

*Quoted in Paul Heyer, *Architects on Architecture: New Directions in America* (New York: Van Nostrand Reinhold, 1993), 285–286.
†Ibid., 279.

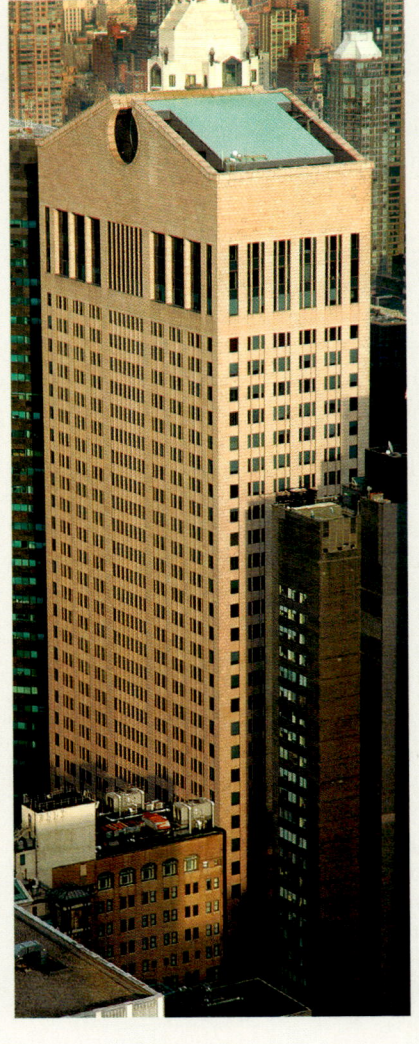

**30-46** PHILIP JOHNSON and JOHN BURGEE (with SIMMONS ARCHITECTS), Sony Building (formerly AT&T Building; looking southwest), New York, 1978–1984.

In a startling shift of style, modernist Johnson (FIG. 30-43) designed this postmodern skyscraper with more granite than glass and with a variation on a classical pediment as the crowning motif.

In sum, Moore designed the Piazza d'Italia as a complex conglomeration of symbolic, historical, and geographic allusions—some overt and others obscure. Although the piazza's specific purpose was to honor the Italian community of New Orleans, its more general purpose was to revitalize an urban area by becoming a focal point and an architectural setting for the social activities of neighborhood residents. Unfortunately, the piazza suffered extensive damage during Hurricane Katrina in 2005.

**PHILIP JOHNSON** Even architects instrumental in the proliferation of the modernist idiom embraced postmodernism. Early in his career, PHILIP JOHNSON (1906–2005), for example, had been a leading proponent of modernism and worked with Mies van der Rohe on the design of the Seagram Building (FIG. 30-43). Johnson even served as director of the Department of Architecture at New York's Museum of Modern Art, the bastion of modernism, in 1930–1934 and 1946–1954. Yet he made one of the most startling shifts of style in 20th-century architecture, eventually moving away from the severe geometric formalism exemplified by the Seagram Building to a classical transformation of it in his AT&T (American Telephone and Telegraph) Building (now the Sony Building, FIG. 30-46) in New York City. Architect JOHN BURGEE (b. 1933) codesigned it with assistance from the firm SIMMONS ARCHITECTS. This structure was influential in turning architectural taste and practice away from modernism and toward postmodernism—from organic "concrete sculpture" and the rigid "glass box" to elaborate shapes, motifs, and silhouettes freely adapted from historical styles (see "Philip Johnson on Postmodern Architecture," above).

The 660-foot-high slab of the former AT&T Building is mostly granite. Johnson reduced the window space to some 30 percent of the structure, in contrast to modernist glass-sheathed skyscrapers. His design of its exterior elevation is classically tripartite, having an arcaded base and arched portal; a tall, shaftlike body segmented by slender *mullions* (vertical elements dividing a window); and a crowning pediment broken by an *orbiculum* (a disklike opening). The arrangement refers to the base, column, and entablature system

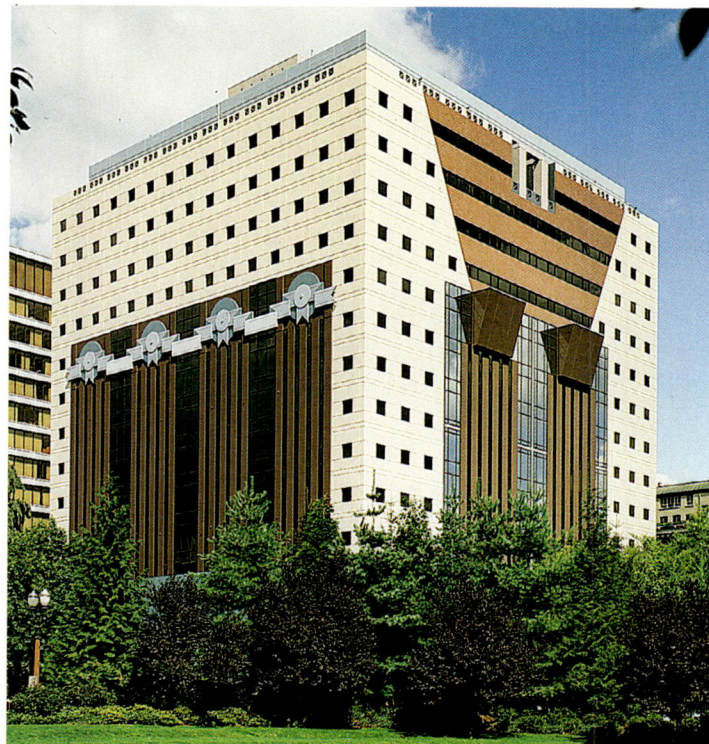

**30-47** MICHAEL GRAVES, Portland Building (looking northwest), Portland, 1980.

In this early example of postmodern architecture, Graves reasserted the horizontality and solidity of the wall. He drew attention to the mural surfaces through polychromy and ornamental motifs.

of classical architecture (FIG. 5-13). More specifically, the pediment, indented by the circular space, resembles the crown of a typical 18th-century Chippendale high chest of drawers. It rises among the monotonously flat-topped glass towers of the New York skyline as an ironic rebuke to the rigid uniformity of modernist architecture.

**MICHAEL GRAVES** Philip Johnson at first endorsed, then disapproved of, a building that rode considerably farther on the wave of postmodernism than did his AT&T tower. The Portland Building (FIG. **30-47**) by Indianapolis-born architect MICHAEL GRAVES (b. 1934) reasserts the wall's horizontality against the verticality of the tall, window-filled shaft. Graves favored the square's solidity and stability, making it the main body of his composition (echoed in the windows), which rests upon a wider base and carries a set-back penthouse crown. Narrow vertical windows tying together seven stories open two paired facades. These support capital-like large hoods on one pair of opposite facades and a frieze of stylized Baroque roundels tied by bands on the other pair. A huge painted keystone motif joins five upper levels on one facade pair, and painted surfaces further define the building's base, body, and penthouse levels.

The modernist purist surely would not welcome the ornamental wall, color painting, or symbolic reference. These features, taken together, raised an even greater storm of criticism than greeted the Sydney Opera House or the AT&T Building. Various critics denounced Graves's Portland Building as "an enlarged jukebox," an "oversized Christmas package," a "marzipan monstrosity," a "histrionic masquerade," and a kind of "pop surrealism." Yet others approvingly noted its classical references as constituting a "symbolic temple" and praised the building as a courageous architectural adventure. Whatever history's verdict will be, the Portland Building, like the AT&T tower, is an early marker of postmodernist innovation that borrowed from the lively, if more-or-less garish, language of pop culture. The night-lit dazzle of entertainment sites such as Las Vegas, and the carnival colors, costumes, and fantasy of theme-park props, all lie behind the Portland Building design, which many critics regard as a vindication of architectural populism against the pretension of modernist elitism.

**ROBERT VENTURI** As coauthor of *Learning from Las Vegas* (1972), Philadelphia native ROBERT VENTURI (b. 1925) codified these ideas about populism and postmodernism. An early example of Venturi's work is the house (FIG. **30-48**) he designed in 1962 for his mother. A fundamental axiom of modernism is that a building's form must arise directly and logically from its function and structure. Against this rule, Venturi asserted form should be separate from function and structure. Thus, the Vanna Venturi house has an

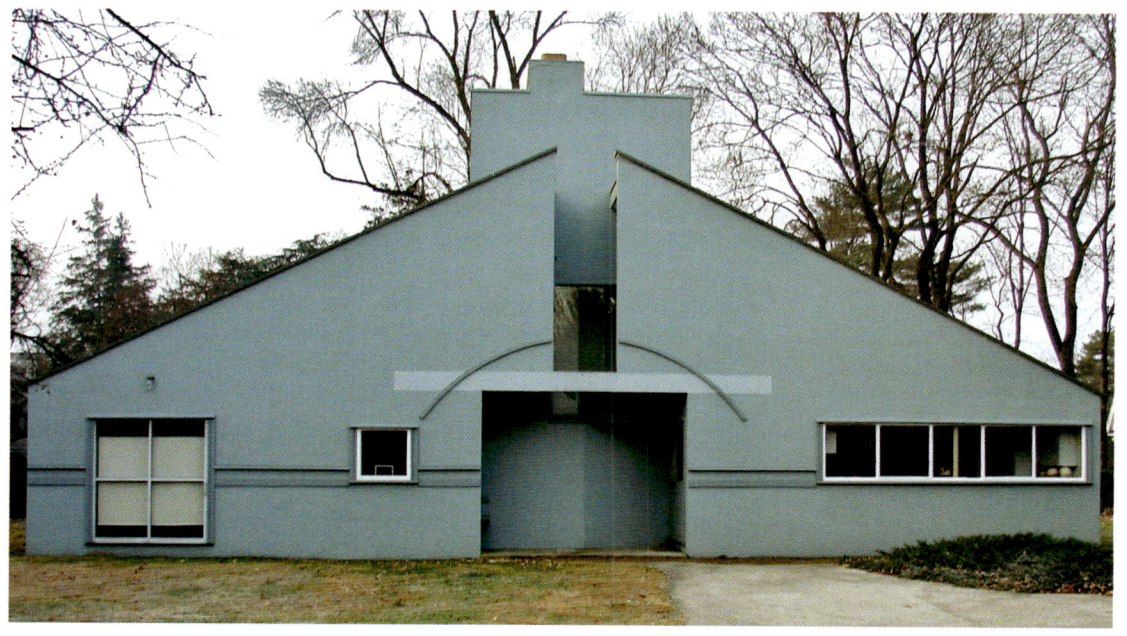

**30-48** ROBERT VENTURI, Vanna Venturi House, Chestnut Hill, Pennsylvania, 1962.

Venturi asserted form should be separate from function and structure. In this house, the facade features an oversized roof recalling a classical temple, but split open at the middle and combined with an arch over the door.

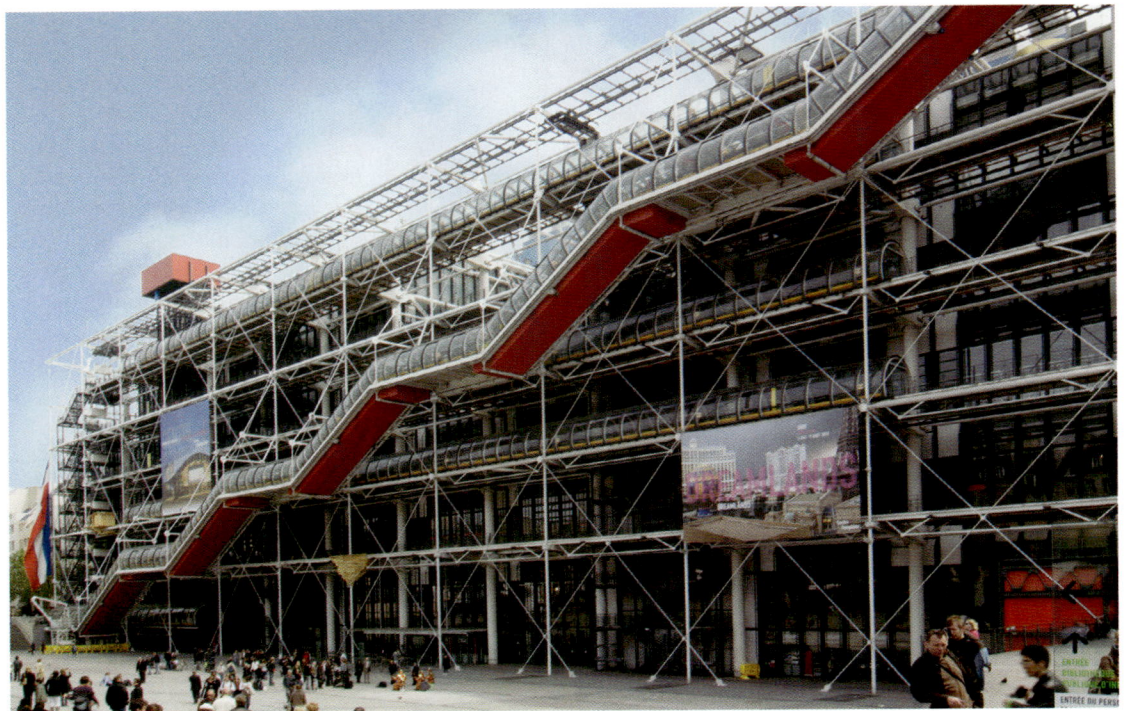

**30-49** RICHARD ROGERS and RENZO PIANO, Centre Georges Pompidou (the "Beaubourg," looking northeast), Paris, France, 1977. ◼◀

The architects fully exposed the anatomy of this six-level building, as in the century-earlier Crystal Palace (FIG. 27-47), and color-coded the internal parts according to function, as in a factory.

oversized gable roof that recalls classical temple design more than domestic architecture. However, the gable has a missing central section, which reveals the house's "chimney" (a penthouse suite). Moreover, Venturi inserted an arch motif over the doorway's lintel, and the placement of the windows violates the symmetry of both classical and modernist design.

**ROGERS AND PIANO** During their short-lived partnership, British architect RICHARD ROGERS (b. 1933) and Italian architect RENZO PIANO (b. 1937) used motifs and techniques from ordinary industrial buildings in their design for the Georges Pompidou National Center of Art and Culture in Paris, known popularly as the "Beaubourg" (FIG. **30-49**). The architects fully exposed the anatomy of this six-level building, which is a kind of updated version of the Crystal Palace (FIG. 27-47), and made its "metabolism" visible. They color-coded pipes, ducts, tubes, and corridors according to function (red for the movement of people, green for water, blue for air-conditioning, and yellow for electricity), much as in a sophisticated factory.

Critics who deplore the Beaubourg's vernacular qualities disparagingly refer to the complex as a "cultural supermarket" and point out that its exposed entrails require excessive maintenance to protect them from the elements. Nevertheless, the building has been immensely popular with visitors since it opened. The flexible interior spaces and the colorful structural body provide a festive environment for the crowds flowing through the building and enjoying its art galleries, industrial design center, library, science and music centers, conference rooms, research and archival facilities, movie theaters, rest areas, and restaurant (which looks down and through the building), as well as dramatic panoramas of Paris from its terrace. The sloping plaza in front of the main entrance has become part of the local scene. Peddlers, street performers, Parisians, and tourists fill this square at almost all hours of the day and night. The kind of secular activity that once occurred in the open spaces in front of cathedral portals now takes place next to a center for culture and popular entertainment.

## Environmental and Site-Specific Art

One of the most exciting developments in postwar art and architecture has been *Environmental Art,* sometimes called *earthworks.* Environmental Art stands at the intersection of architecture and sculpture. It emerged as a major form of artistic expression in the 1960s and includes a wide range of artworks, most of which are *site-specific* (created for a unique location) and in the open air. Many artists associated with the Environmental Art movement also used natural or organic materials, including the land itself. It is no coincidence this art form developed during a period of increased concern for the environment. The ecology movement of the 1960s and 1970s aimed to publicize and combat escalating pollution, depletion of natural resources, and the dangers of toxic waste. The problems of public aesthetics (for example, litter, urban sprawl, and compromised scenic areas) were also at issue. Widespread concern in the United States about the environment led to the passage of the National Environmental Policy Act in 1969 and the creation of the federal Environmental Protection Agency. Environmental artists used their art to call attention to the landscape and, in so doing, were part of this national dialogue.

As an innovative artistic genre challenging traditional assumptions about art making, Environmental Art clearly has an avant-garde, progressive dimension. But as Pop artists did in their time, Environmental artists insist on moving art out of the rarefied atmosphere of museums and galleries and into the public sphere. Most encourage spectator interaction with their works. Ironically, the remote locations of many earthworks have limited public access.

**ROBERT SMITHSON** One of the pioneering Environmental artists was New Jersey–born ROBERT SMITHSON (1938–1973), who used industrial construction equipment to manipulate vast quantities of earth and rock on isolated sites. Smithson's best-known project is *Spiral Jetty* (FIG. **30-50**), a mammoth 1,500-foot-long coil of black basalt, limestone rocks, and earth extending out into Great Salt Lake in Utah. As he was driving by the lake one

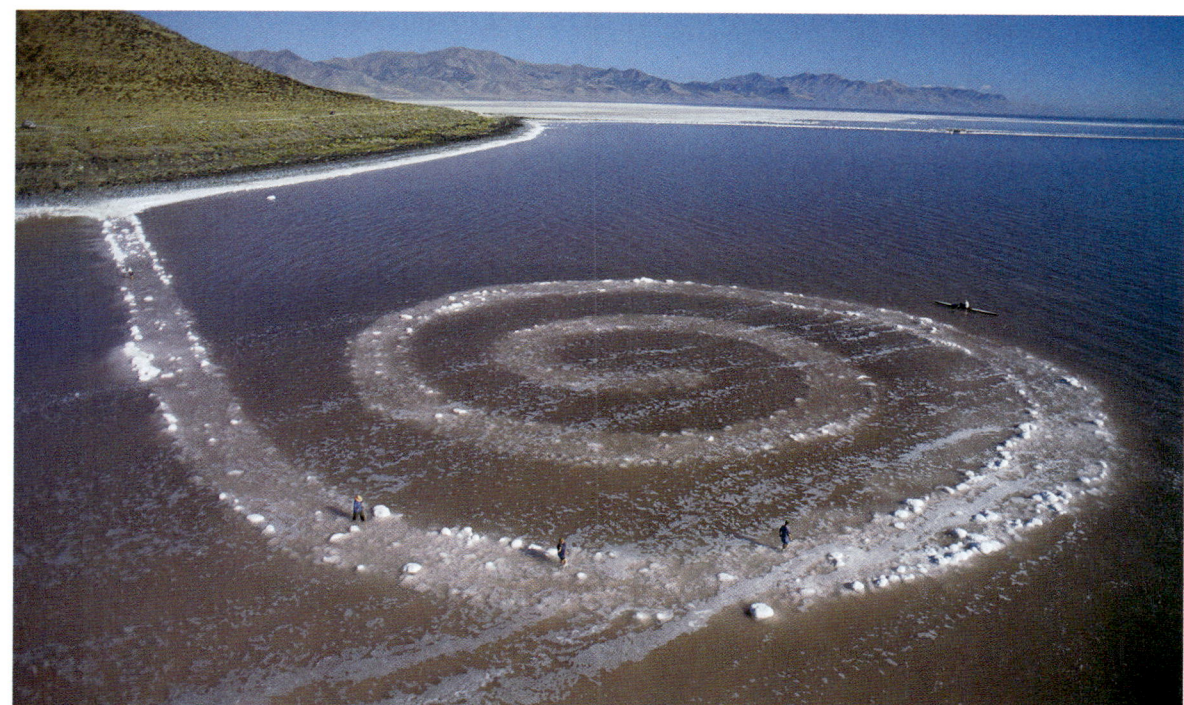

30-50 ROBERT
SMITHSON, *Spiral Jetty*
(looking east), Great
Salt Lake, Utah, 1970.
© Estate of Robert
Smithson/Licensed by
VAGA, New York. ◼◀

Smithson used industrial
equipment to create
environmental artworks
by manipulating earth
and rock. *Spiral Jetty* is
a mammoth coil of black
basalt, limestone, and
earth extending into Great
Salt Lake.

day, Smithson came across some abandoned mining equipment, left there by a company that had tried and failed to extract oil from the site. Smithson saw this as a testament to the enduring power of nature and the inability of humans to conquer it. He decided to create an artwork in the lake that ultimately became a monumental spiral curving out from the shoreline and running 1,500 linear feet into the water. Smithson insisted on designing his work in response to the location itself. He wanted to avoid the arrogance of an artist merely imposing an unrelated concept on the site. The spiral idea grew from Smithson's first impression of the location. Then, while researching Great Salt Lake, Smithson discovered that the molecular structure of the salt crystals coating the rocks at the water's edge is spiral in form.

> As I looked at the site, it reverberated out to the horizons only to suggest an immobile cyclone while flickering light made the entire landscape appear to quake. A dormant earthquake spread into the fluttering stillness, into a spinning sensation without movement. The site was a rotary that enclosed itself in an immense roundness. From that gyrating space emerged the possibility of the Spiral Jetty.[27]

Smithson not only recorded *Spiral Jetty* in photographs, but also filmed its construction in a movie describing the forms and life of the whole site. The photographs and film have become increasingly important, because fluctuations in Great Salt Lake's water level often place *Spiral Jetty* underwater. Smithson tragically died at age 35 in a plane crash while surveying a site for a new earthwork in Amarillo, Texas.

# PERFORMANCE AND CONCEPTUAL ART AND NEW MEDIA

Environmental Art, although a singular artistic phenomenon, typifies postwar developments in the art world in redefining the nature of an "artwork" and expanding the range of works artists and the public at large consider "art." Some of the new types of artworks are the result of the invention of new media, such as computers and video cameras. But the new art forms also reflect avant-garde artists' continued questioning of the status quo.

## Performance Art

An important new artistic genre that emerged in the decades following World War II was *Performance Art*. Performance artists replace traditional stationary artworks with movements, gestures, and sounds performed before an audience, whose members sometimes participate in the performance. The informal and spontaneous events Performance artists staged anticipated the rebellion and youthful exuberance of the 1960s and at first pushed art outside the confines of mainstream art institutions (museums and galleries). Performance Art also served as an antidote to the pretentiousness of most traditional art objects and challenged art's function as a commodity. In the later 1960s, however, museums commissioned performances with increasing frequency, thereby neutralizing much of the subversiveness characteristic of this new art form. Unfortunately, because the earliest Performance artists created their works before the widespread availability of inexpensive handheld video cameras, the only records of their performances are the documentary photographs taken during the events. Photographs are unsatisfying, if invaluable, records because they lack the element of time integral to Performance Art.

**JOHN CAGE** Many of the artists instrumental in the development of Performance Art were students or associates of the charismatic American teacher and composer John Cage (1912–1992). Cage encouraged his students at both the New School for Social Research in New York and Black Mountain College in North Carolina to link their art directly with life. He brought to music composition some of the ideas of Duchamp and of Eastern philosophy. Cage used methods such as chance to avoid the closed structures marking traditional music and, in his view, separating it from the unpredictable and multilayered qualities of daily existence. For

## Carolee Schneemann on Painting, Performance Art, and Art History

Born in Pennsylvania, Carolee Schneemann (FIG. 30-51) studied painting at Bard College and the University of Illinois before settling in New York City in 1962, where she became one of the pioneering Performance artists of the 1960s. In notes she wrote in 1962–1963, Schneemann reflected on the nature of art production and contrasted her kinetic works with more traditional art forms.

> Environments, happenings—concretions—are an extension of my painting-constructions which often have moving (motorized) sections. . . . [But, the] steady exploration and repeated viewing which the eye is required to make with my painting-constructions is reversed in the performance situation where the spectator is overwhelmed with changing recognitions, carried emotionally by a flux of evocative actions and led or held by the specified time sequence which marks the duration of a performance. In this way the audience is actually *visually* more *passive* than when confronting a . . . "still" work . . . With paintings, constructions and sculptures the viewers are able to carry out repeated examinations of the work, to select and vary viewing positions (to walk with the eye), to touch surfaces and to freely indulge responses to areas of color and texture at their chosen speed.*

Readers of this book will also take special interest in Schneemann's 1975 essay entitled "Woman in the Year 2000," in which she envisioned what introductory art history courses would be like at the beginning of the 21st century:

> By the year 2000 [every] young woman will study Art Istory [sic] courses enriched by the inclusion, discovery, and re-evaluation of works by women artists: works (and lives) until recently buried away, willfully destroyed, [or] ignored.†

A comparison between this 14th edition of *Art through the Ages* and editions published in the 1960s and 1970s will immediately reveal the accuracy of Schneemann's prediction.

*Quoted in Bruce McPherson, ed., *More Than "Meat Joy": Complete Performance Works and Selected Writings* (New Paltz, N.Y.: Documentext, 1979), 10–11.
†Ibid., 198.

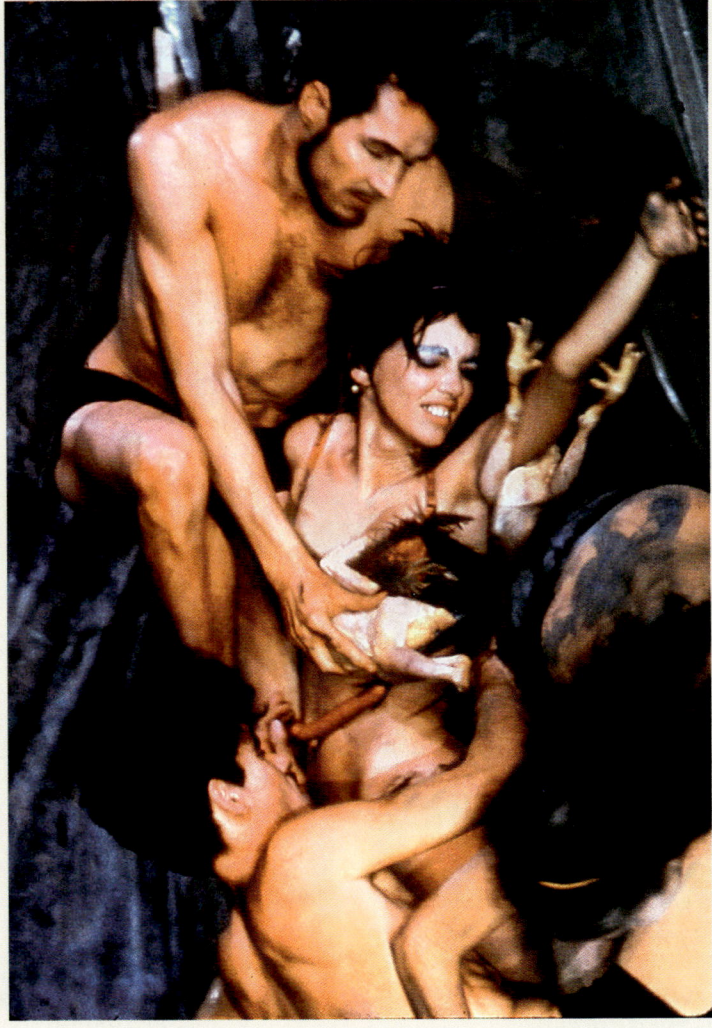

**30-51** CAROLEE SCHNEEMANN, *Meat Joy* (performance at Judson Church, New York City), 1964.

In her performances, Schneemann transformed the nature of Performance Art by introducing a feminist dimension through the use of her body (often nude) to challenge traditional gender roles.

example, the score for one of Cage's piano compositions instructs the performer to appear, sit down at the piano, raise the keyboard cover to mark the beginning of the piece, remain motionless at the instrument for 4 minutes and 33 seconds, and then close the keyboard cover, rise, and bow to signal the end of the work. The "music" would be the unplanned sounds and noises (such as coughs and whispers) emanating from the audience during the "performance."

**ALLAN KAPROW** One of Cage's students in the 1950s was ALLAN KAPROW (1927–2006). Schooled in art history as well as music composition, Kaprow sought to explore the intersection of art and life. He believed, for example, that Jackson Pollock's actions when producing a painting (FIG. 30-7) were more important than the finished painting. This led Kaprow to develop a type of event known as a *Happening*. He described a Happening as

> an assemblage of events performed or perceived in more than one time and place. Its material environments may be constructed, taken over directly from what is available, or altered slightly: just as its activities may be invented or commonplace. A Happening, unlike a stage play, may occur at a supermarket, driving along a highway, under a pile of rags, and in a friend's kitchen, either at once or sequentially. If sequentially, time may extend to more than a year. The Happening is performed according to plan but without rehearsal, audience, or repetition. It is art but seems closer to life.[28]

Happenings were often participatory. One Happening consisted of a constructed setting with partitions on which viewers wrote phrases, while another involved spectators walking on a pile of tires. One of Kaprow's first Happenings, titled *18 Happenings in Six Parts,* took place in 1959 in the Reuben Gallery in New York City. For the event, he divided the gallery space into three sections with translucent plastic sheets. Over the course of the 90-minute piece, performers, including Kaprow's artist friends, bounced balls, read from placards, extended their arms like wings, and played records as slides and lights switched on and off in programmed sequences.

**FLUXUS** Other Cage students interested in the composer's search to find aesthetic potential in the nontraditional and commonplace formed the *Fluxus* group. Eventually expanding to include European and Japanese artists, this group's performances were more theatrical than Happenings. To distinguish their performances from Happenings, the artists associated with Fluxus coined the term *Events* to describe their work. Events focused on single actions, such as turning a light on and off or watching falling snow—what Fluxus artist La Monte Young (b. 1935) called "the theater of the single event."[29] Events usually took place on a stage separating the performers from the audience but without costumes or added decor. Events were not spontaneous. They followed a compositional "score," which, given the restricted nature of these performances, was short.

**CAROLEE SCHNEEMANN** Some artists, notably CAROLEE SCHNEEMANN (b. 1939) in the United States and members of the Concrete Art Association (FIG. 34-17) in Japan, produced artworks integrating painting and performance (see "Carolee Schneemann on Painting, Performance Art, and Art History," page 934). Schneemann's self-described "kinetic theater" radically transformed the nature of Performance Art by introducing a feminist dimension through the use of her body (often nude) to challenge "the psychic territorial power lines by which women were admitted to the Art Stud Club."[30] In her 1964 performance, *Meat Joy* (FIG. **30-51**), Schneemann reveled in the taste, smell, and feel of raw sausages, chickens, and fish.

**JOSEPH BEUYS** The leftist politics of the Fluxus group in the early 1960s strongly influenced German artist JOSEPH BEUYS (1921–1986). Drawing on Happenings and Fluxus, Beuys created actions aimed at illuminating the condition of modern humanity. He wanted to make a new kind of sculptural object that would include "Thinking Forms: how we mould our thoughts or Spoken Forms: how we shape our thoughts into words or Social Sculpture: how we mould and shape the world in which we live."[31]

Beuys's commitment to artworks stimulating thought about art and life derived in part from his experiences as a pilot during the war. After the enemy shot down his plane over the Crimea, nomadic Tatars nursed him back to health by swaddling his body in fat and felt to warm him. Fat and felt thus symbolized healing and regeneration to Beuys, and he incorporated these materials into many of his sculptures and actions, such as *How to Explain Pictures to a Dead Hare* (FIG. **30-52**). This one-person event consisted of stylized actions evoking a sense of mystery and sacred ritual. Beuys appeared in a room hung with his drawings, cradling a dead hare to which he spoke softly. Beuys coated his head with honey covered with gold leaf, creating a shimmering mask. In this manner, he took on the role of the shaman, an individual with special spiritual powers. As a shaman, Beuys believed he was acting to help revolutionize human thought so each human being could become a truly free and creative person.

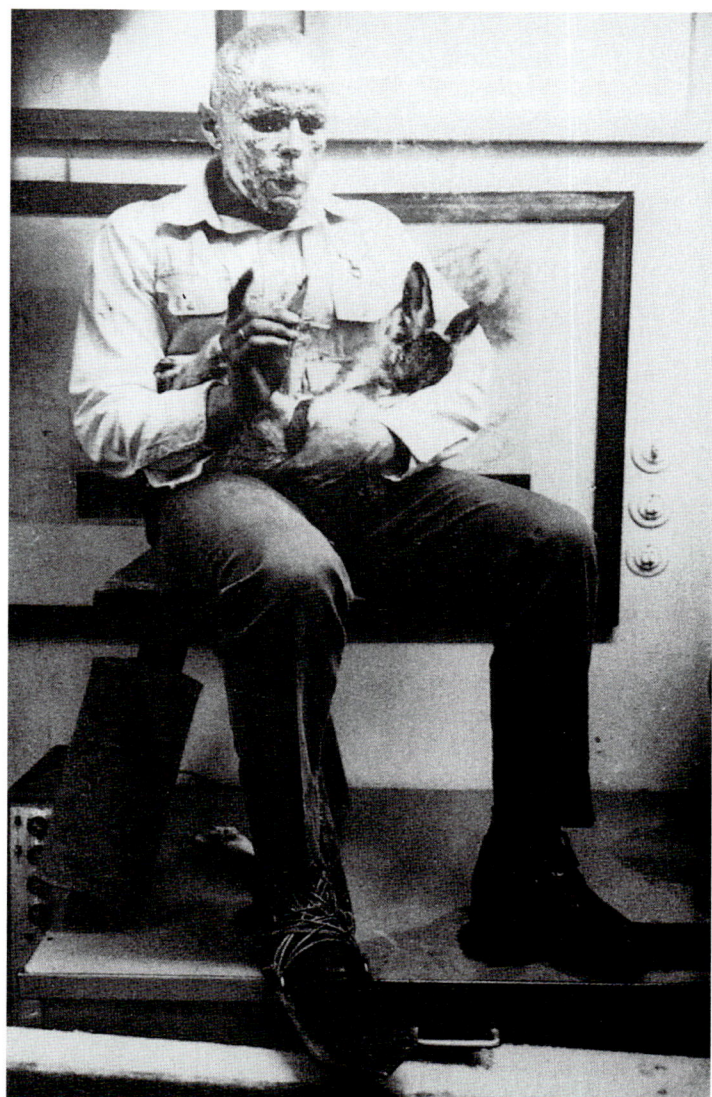

**30-52** JOSEPH BEUYS, *How to Explain Pictures to a Dead Hare* (performance at Schmela Gallery, Düsseldorf), 1965. ◼◀

In this one-person event, Beuys coated his head with honey and gold leaf. Assuming the role of a shaman, he used stylized actions to evoke a sense of mystery and sacred ritual.

**JEAN TINGUELY** The paradoxical notion of destruction as an act of creation surfaces in a number of kinetic artworks, most notably in the sculpture of JEAN TINGUELY (1925–1991). Trained as a painter in his native Switzerland, Tinguely gravitated to motion sculpture. In the 1950s, he made a series of *metamatics,* motor-driven devices that produced instant abstract paintings. He programmed these metamatics electronically to act with an anti-mechanical unpredictability when someone inserted a felt-tipped marking pen into a pincer and pressed a button to initiate the pen's motion across a small sheet of paper clipped to an "easel." Participants in his metamatic demonstrations could use different-colored markers in succession and could stop and start the device to achieve some degree of control over the final image. These operations created a series of small works resembling Abstract Expressionist paintings.

In 1960, Tinguely expanded the scale of his work with a kinetic piece designed to "perform" and then destroy itself in the sculpture garden of the Museum of Modern Art in New York City. He created

Tinguely produced motor-driven devices programmed to make instant abstract paintings. To explore the notion of destruction as an act of creation, he designed this one to perform and then destroy itself.

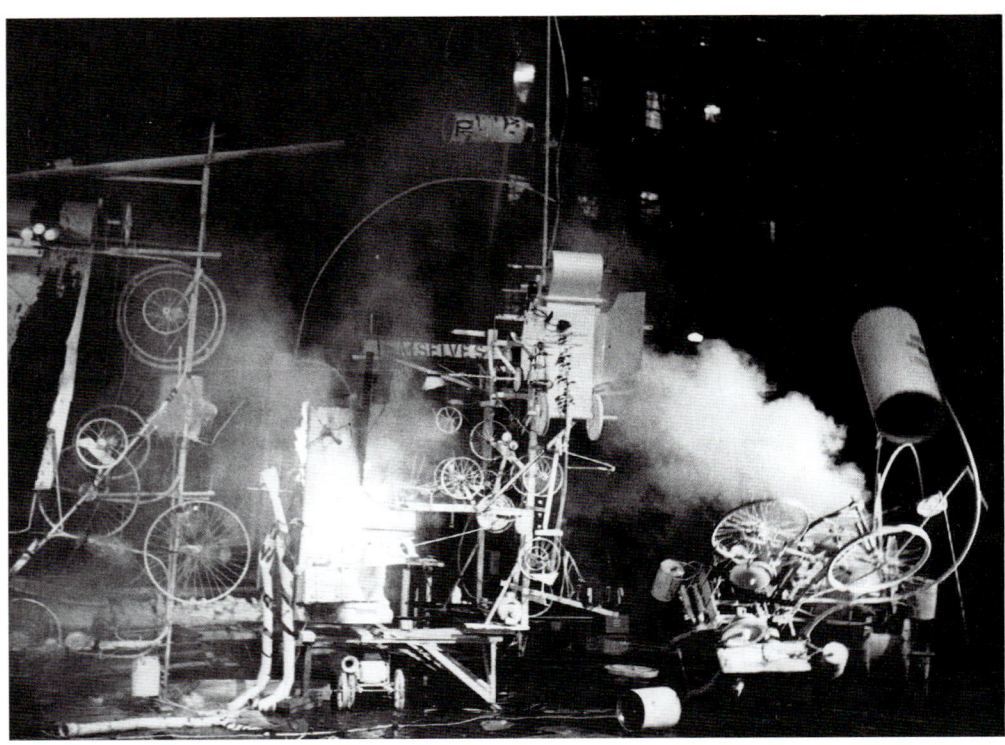

*Homage to New York* (FIG. 30-53) with the aid of engineer Billy Klüver (1927–2004), who helped him scrounge wheels and other moving objects from a dump near Manhattan. The completed structure, painted white for visibility against the dark night sky, included a player piano modified into a metamatic painting machine, a weather balloon that inflated during the performance, vials of colored smoke, and a host of gears, pulleys, wheels, and other found machine parts.

*Homage to New York* premiered (and instantly self-destructed) on March 17, 1960, with the state's governor, Nelson Rockefeller (1908–1979), an array of other distinguished guests, and three television crews in attendance. Once Tinguely turned on the machine, smoke poured from its interior and the piano caught fire. Various parts of the machine broke off and rambled away, while one of the metamatics tried but failed to produce an abstract painting. Finally, Tinguely summoned a firefighter to extinguish the blaze and ensure the demise of his artwork-machine with an ax. Like Tinguely's other kinetic sculptures, *Homage to New York* recalls the satiric Dadaist spirit and the droll import of Klee's *Twittering Machine* (FIG. 29-59). But Tinguely deliberately made the wacky behavior of *Homage to New York* more playful and more endearing. Having been given a freedom of eccentric behavior unprecedented in the mechanical world, Tinguely's creations often seemed to behave with the whimsical individuality of human actors.

## Conceptual Art

The relentless challenges to artistic convention fundamental to the historical avant-garde reached a logical conclusion with *Conceptual Art* in the late 1960s. Conceptual artists maintained that the "artfulness" of art lay in the artist's idea, rather than in its final expression. These artists regarded the idea, or concept, as the defining component of the artwork. Indeed, some Conceptual artists eliminated the object altogether.

**JOSEPH KOSUTH** Born in Toledo, Ohio, and educated at the School of Visual Arts in New York City, JOSEPH KOSUTH (b. 1945) was a major proponent of Conceptual Art.

> Like everyone else I inherited the idea of art as a set of *formal* problems. So when I began to re-think my ideas of art, I had to re-think that thinking process . . . [T]he radical shift, was in changing the idea of art itself. . . . It meant you could have an art work which was that *idea* of an art work, and its formal components weren't important. I felt I had found a way to make art without formal

components being confused for an expressionist composition. The expression was in the idea, not the form—the forms were only a device in the service of the idea.[32]

Kosuth's work operates at the intersection of language and vision, dealing with the relationship between the abstract and the concrete. For example, in *One and Three Chairs* (FIG. 30-54),

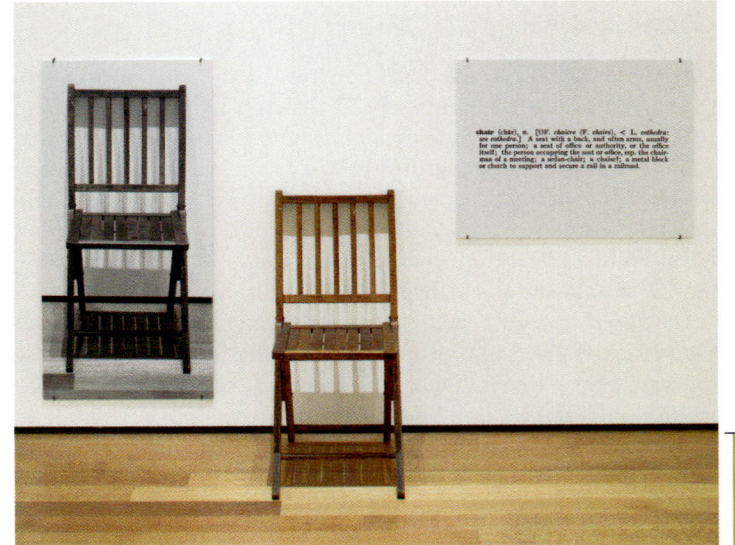

1 ft.

30-54 JOSEPH KOSUTH, *One and Three Chairs,* 1965. Wooden folding chair, photographic copy of a chair, and photographic enlargement of a dictionary definition of a chair; chair, 2' 8⅜" × 1' 2⅞" × 1' 8⅞"; photograph, 3' × 2' ⅛"; text panel, 2' × 2' ⅛". Museum of Modern Art, New York (Larry Aldrich Foundation Fund).

Conceptual artists regard the concept as an artwork's defining component. To portray "chairness," Kosuth juxtaposed a chair, a photograph of the chair, and a dictionary definition of *chair.*

Kosuth juxtaposed a real chair, a full-scale photograph of the same chair, and an enlarged reproduction of a dictionary definition of the word *chair*. By so doing, the Conceptual artist asked viewers to ponder the notion of what constitutes "chairness."

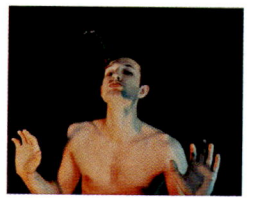

30-55A NAUMAN, *Self-Portrait as Fountain,* 1966–1967.

**BRUCE NAUMAN**  In the mid-1960s in California, Indiana native BRUCE NAUMAN (b. 1941) made his artistic presence known when he abandoned painting and turned to object-making. Since then, his work, produced since 1979 in New Mexico, has been extremely varied. In addition to sculptural pieces constructed from different materials, including neon lights (FIG. 30-55), rubber, fiberglass, and cardboard, he has also produced photographs (FIG. 30-55A), films, videos, books, and large room installations, as well as Performance Art. Nauman's work of the 1960s intersected with that of the Conceptual artists, especially in terms of the philosophical exploration that was the foundation of much of his art, and in his interest in language and wordplay.

*The True Artist Helps the World by Revealing Mystic Truths* (FIG. 30-55) was the first of Nauman's many neon sculptures. He selected neon because he wanted to find a medium that would be identified with a nonartistic function. Determined to discover a way to connect objects with words, he drew on the method outlined in *Philosophical Investigations,* in which the Austrian philosopher Ludwig Wittgenstein (1889–1951) encouraged contradictory and nonsensical arguments. Nauman's neon sculpture spins out an emphatic assertion, which is also the work's title, but as Nauman explained, "[The statement] was kind of a test—like when you say something out loud to see if you believe it. . . . [I]t was on the one hand a totally silly idea and yet, on the other hand, I believed it."[33]

Other Conceptual artists pursued the notion that the idea is a work of art itself by creating works involving invisible materials, such as inert gases, radioactive isotopes, or radio waves. In each case, viewers must base their understanding of the artwork on what they know about the properties of these materials, rather than on any visible empirical data, and must depend on the artist's linguistic description of the work. Ultimately, the Conceptual artists challenged the very premises of artistic production, pushing art's boundaries to a point where no concrete definition of *art* is possible.

## New Media

During the 1960s and 1970s, many avant-garde artists eagerly embraced technologies previously unavailable in their attempt to find new avenues of artistic expression. Among the most popular new media were video recording and computer graphics.

**VIDEO**  Initially, only commercial television studios possessed video equipment, but in the 1960s, with the development of relatively inexpensive portable video recorders and of electronic devices allowing manipulation of recorded video material, artists began to explore in earnest the expressive possibilities of this new technology. In its basic form, video recording involves a special motion-picture camera that captures visible images and translates them into electronic data for display on a video monitor or television screen. Video pictures resemble photographs in the amount of detail they contain, but, like computer graphics, a video image consists of a series of points of light on a grid, giving the impression of soft focus. Viewers looking at television or video art are not aware of the monitor's surface. Instead, fulfilling the ideal of Renaissance artists, they concentrate on the image and look through the glass surface, as through a window, into the "space" beyond. Video images combine the optical realism of photography with the sense that the subjects move in real time in a deep space "inside" the monitor.

**NAM JUNE PAIK**  When video introduced the possibility of manipulating subjects in real time, artists such as Korean-born NAM JUNE PAIK (1932–2006) were eager to work with the medium. Inspired by the ideas of John Cage and after studying music performance, art history, and Eastern philosophy in Korea and Japan, Paik worked with electronic music in Germany in the late 1950s. In 1965, after relocating to New York City, Paik acquired the first inexpensive video recorder sold in Manhattan (the Sony Porta-Pak) and immediately recorded everything he saw out the window of his taxi on the return trip to his studio downtown. Experience acquired as artist-in-residence at television stations WGBH in Boston and WNET in New York allowed him to experiment with the most advanced broadcast video technology.

A grant permitted Paik to collaborate with the gifted Japanese engineer-inventor Shuya Abe (b. 1932) in developing a video synthesizer. This instrument enables artists to manipulate and change the electronic video information in various ways, causing images or parts of images to stretch, shrink, change color, or break up. With the synthesizer, artists can also layer images, inset one image into another, or merge images from various cameras with those from video recorders to make a single visual kaleidoscopic "time-collage." This kind of compositional freedom permitted Paik to

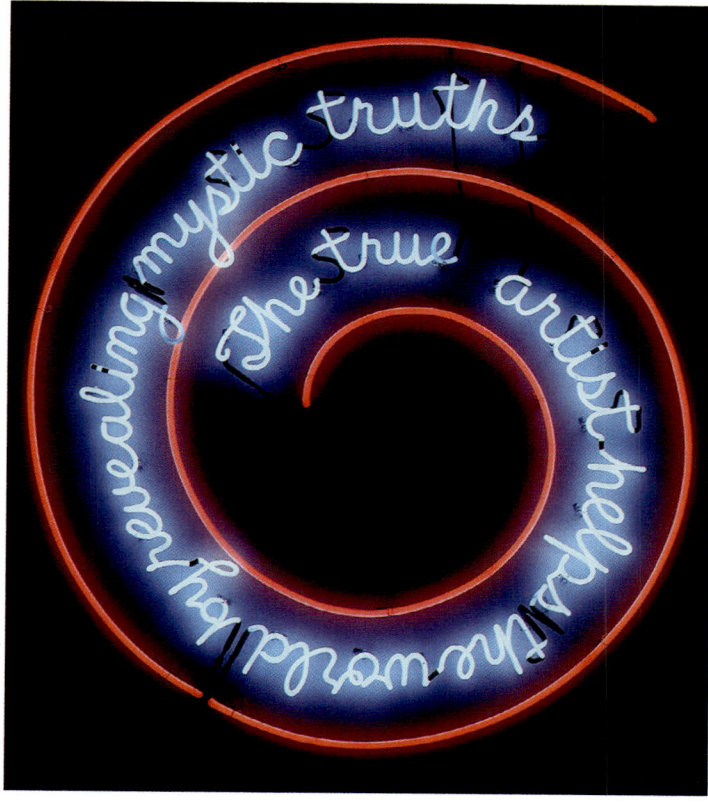

1 ft.

**30-55** BRUCE NAUMAN, *The True Artist Helps the World by Revealing Mystic Truths,* 1967. Neon with glass tubing suspension frame, 4′ 11″ high. Private collection.

Nauman explores his interest in language and wordplay in his art. He described this Conceptual neon sculpture's emphatic assertion as "a totally silly idea," but an idea he believed.

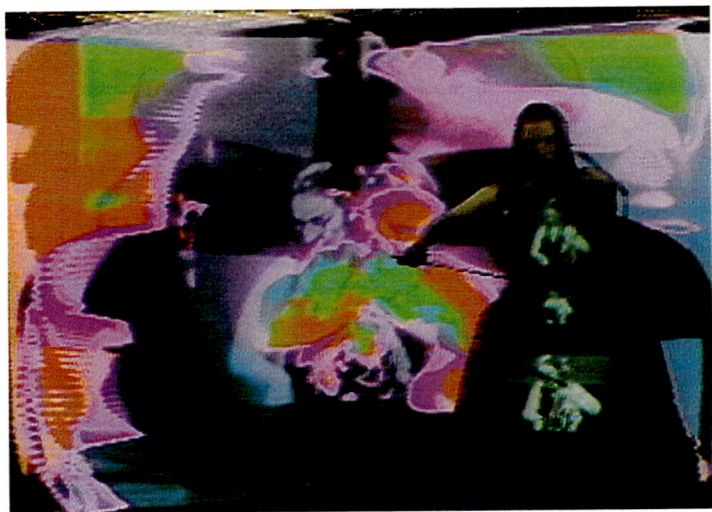

**30-56** Nam June Paik, Video still from *Global Groove*, 1973. $\frac{3}{4}''$ videotape, color, sound, 30 minutes. Collection of the artist. ◼◀

Korean-born video artist Paik's best-known work is a cascade of fragmented sequences of performances and commercials intended as a sample of the rich worldwide television menu of the future.

combine his interests in painting, music, Eastern philosophy, global politics for survival, humanized technology, and cybernetics. Paik called his video works "physical music" and said his musical background enabled him to understand time better than could video artists trained in painting or sculpture.

Paik's best-known video work, *Global Groove* (FIG. **30-56**), combines in quick succession fragmented sequences of female tap dancers, poet Allen Ginsberg (1926–1997) reading his work, a performance by Fluxus artist and cellist Charlotte Moorman (1933–1991) using a man's back as her instrument, Pepsi commercials from Japanese television, Korean drummers, and a shot of the Living Theatre group performing a controversial piece called *Paradise Now*. Commissioned originally for broadcast over the United Nations satellite, the cascade of imagery in *Global Groove* gives viewers a glimpse of the rich worldwide television menu Paik predicted would be available in the future—a prediction that has been fulfilled with the advent of affordable cable and satellite television service.

**COMPUTER GRAPHICS** Perhaps the most promising new medium for creating and manipulating illusionistic three-dimensional forms is computer graphics. This new medium uses light to make images and, like photography, can incorporate specially recorded camera images. Unlike video recording, computer graphic art enables artists to work with wholly invented forms, as painters can. Developed during the 1960s and 1970s, this technology opened up new possibilities for both abstract and figural art. It involves

**30-57** David Em, *Nora,* 1979. Computer-generated color photograph, 1′ 5″ × 1′ 11″. Private collection. ◼◀

Unlike video recording, computer graphic art enables the creation of wholly invented forms, as in painting. Em builds fantastic digital images of imaginary landscapes out of tiny boxes called pixels.

electronic programs dividing the surface of the computer monitor's cathode-ray tube into a grid of tiny boxes called "picture elements," or *pixels*. Artists can electronically address pixels individually to create a design, much as knitting or weaving patterns have a grid matrix as a guide for making a design in fabric. Once created, parts of a computer graphic design can be changed quickly through an electronic program, enabling artists to revise or duplicate shapes in the design and to manipulate at will the color, texture, size, number, and position of any desired detail. Computer graphics pictures appear in luminous color on the cathode-ray tube. The effect suggests a view into a vast world existing inside the tube.

**DAVID EM** One of the pioneering artists working in this electronic painting mode, David Em (b. 1952) uses what he terms *computer imaging* to fashion fantastic imaginary landscapes. These have an eerily believable existence within the "window" of the computer monitor. When he was artist-in-residence at the California Institute of Technology's Jet Propulsion Laboratory, Em created brilliantly colored scenes of alien worlds using the laboratory's advanced computer graphics equipment. He also had access to software programs developed to create computer graphics simulations of NASA's missions in outer space. Creating images with the computer afforded Em great flexibility in manipulating simple geometric shapes—shrinking or enlarging them, stretching or reversing them, repeating them, adding texture to their surfaces, and creating the illusion of light and shadow. In images such as *Nora* (FIG. **30-57**), Em created futuristic geometric versions of Surrealistic dreamscapes whose forms seem familiar and strange at the same time. The illusion of space in these works is immensely vivid and seductive. It almost seems possible to wander through the tubelike foreground "frame" and up the inclined foreground plane or to hop aboard the hovering globe at the lower left for a journey through the strange patterns and textures of this mysterious labyrinthine setting.

**AFTER 1980** The decades following the conclusion of World War II were unparalleled in the history of art through the ages for innovation in form and content and for the development of new media. Those exciting trends have continued unabated since 1980—and with an increasingly international dimension that will be explored in Chapter 31.

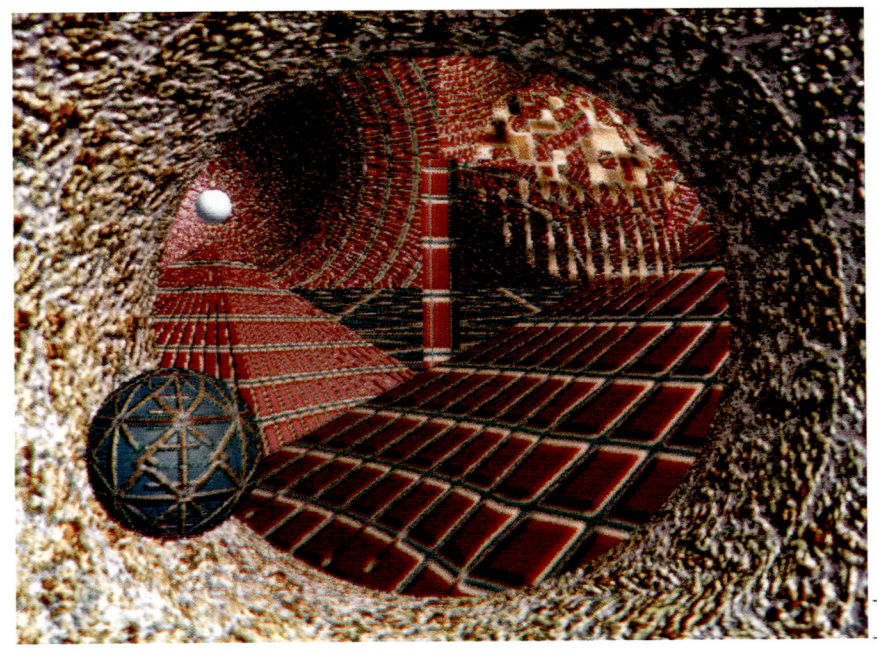

1 in.

# MODERNISM AND POSTMODERNISM IN EUROPE AND AMERICA, 1945 TO 1980

## PAINTING, SCULPTURE, AND PHOTOGRAPHY

▮ The art of the decades following World War II reflects cultural upheaval—the rejection of traditional values, the civil rights and feminist movements, and the new consumer society.

▮ The first major postwar avant-garde art movement was Abstract Expressionism, which championed an artwork's formal elements rather than its subject. Gestural abstractionists, such as Pollock and de Kooning, sought expressiveness through energetically applied pigment. Chromatic abstractionists, such as Rothko, struck emotional chords through large areas of pure color.

▮ Post-Painterly Abstraction promoted a cool rationality in contrast to Abstract Expressionism's passion. Both hard-edge painters, such as Kelly and Stella, and color-field painters, such as Frankenthaler and Louis, pursued purity in art by emphasizing the flatness of pigment on canvas.

▮ Pop artists, such as Johns, Lichtenstein, and Warhol, turned away from abstraction to the representation of subjects grounded in popular culture—flags, comic strips, Coca-Cola bottles—sometimes employing commercial printing techniques.

▮ Riley and other Op artists sought to produce optical illusions of motion and depth using only geometric forms on two-dimensional surfaces.

▮ Superrealists, such as Flack, Close, and Hanson—kindred spirits to Pop artists in many ways—created paintings and sculptures featuring scrupulous fidelity to optical fact.

▮ The leading sculptural movement of this period was Minimalism. Tony Smith and Judd created artworks consisting of simple and unadorned geometric shapes to underscore the "objecthood" of their sculptures.

▮ Arbus and White represent the two poles of photography in the postwar period—documentary photography and art photography.

▮ Many artists pursued social agendas in their work. Postwar feminist artists include Chicago, whose *Dinner Party* honors important women throughout history and features crafts traditionally associated with women; Sherman, who explored the "male gaze" in her photographs resembling film stills; and Mendieta and Wilke, whose bodies were their subjects.

## ARCHITECTURE AND SITE-SPECIFIC ART

▮ Some of the leading early-20th-century modernist architects remained active after 1945. Wright built the snail-shell Guggenheim Museum, Le Corbusier the sculpturesque Notre-Dame-du-Haut, and Mies van der Rohe the Minimalist Seagram skyscraper. Younger architects Saarinen and Utzon designed structures with dramatic curvilinear rooflines.

▮ In contrast to modernist architecture, postmodernist architecture is complex and eclectic and often incorporates references to historical styles. Among the best-known postmodern projects are Moore's Piazza d'Italia and Graves's Portland Building, both of which incorporate classical motifs.

▮ Site-specific art stands at the intersection of architecture and sculpture. Smithson's *Spiral Jetty* is a mammoth coil of natural materials in Utah's Great Salt Lake.

## PERFORMANCE AND CONCEPTUAL ART AND NEW MEDIA

▮ Among the most significant developments in the art world after World War II has been the expansion of the range of works considered "art."

▮ Performance artists, notably Schneemann and Beuys, replace traditional stationary artworks with movements and sounds performed before an audience. Performance Art often addresses the same social and political issues that contemporaneous painters and sculptors explore.

▮ Kosuth and other Conceptual artists believe the "artfulness" of art is in the artist's idea, not the work resulting from the idea.

▮ Paik and others have embraced video recording technology to produce artworks combining images and sounds.

▮ Em was a pioneer in exploring computer graphics as an art form. Unlike video recording, computer art enables artists to work with wholly invented forms, as painters can.

Pollock, *Lavender Mist,* 1950

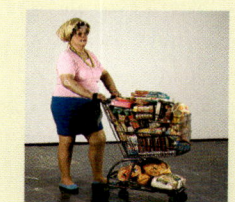
Hanson, *Supermarket Shopper,* 1970

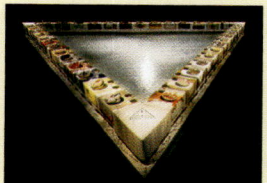
Chicago, *Dinner Party,* 1979

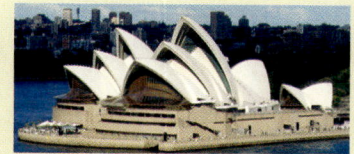
Utzon, Sydney Opera House, 1959–1972

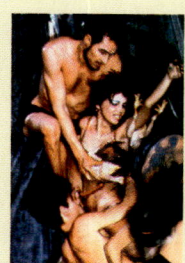
Schneemann, *Meat Joy,* 1964

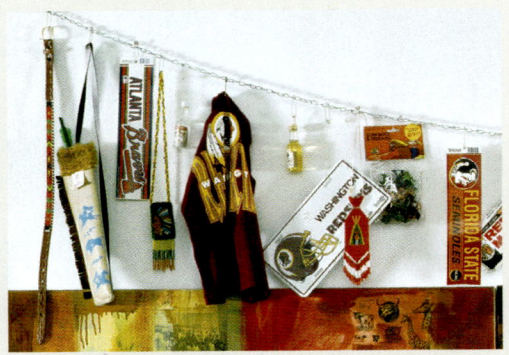

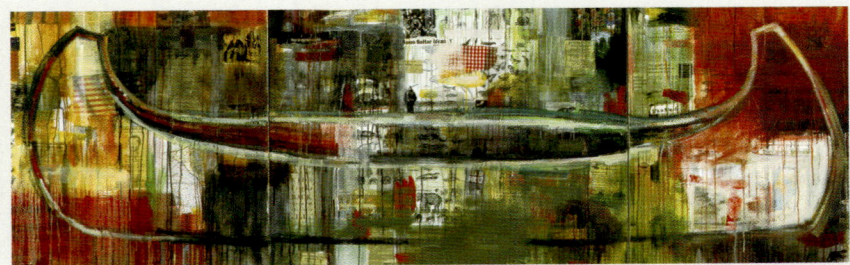

Smith's mixed-media canvases celebrate her Native American identity. Above the painting, as if hung from a clothesline, are cheap trinkets she proposes to trade for the return of confiscated land.

Overlapping the collage and the central motif of the canoe in Smith's anti-Columbus Quincentenary Celebration is dripping red paint, symbolic of the shedding of Native American blood.

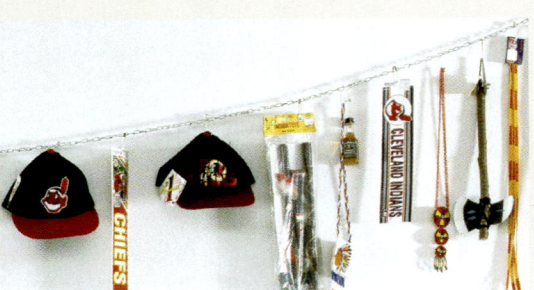

The sports teams represented in *Trade* all have American Indian–derived names, reminding viewers of the vocal opposition to these names and to practices such as the Atlanta Braves' "tomahawk chop."

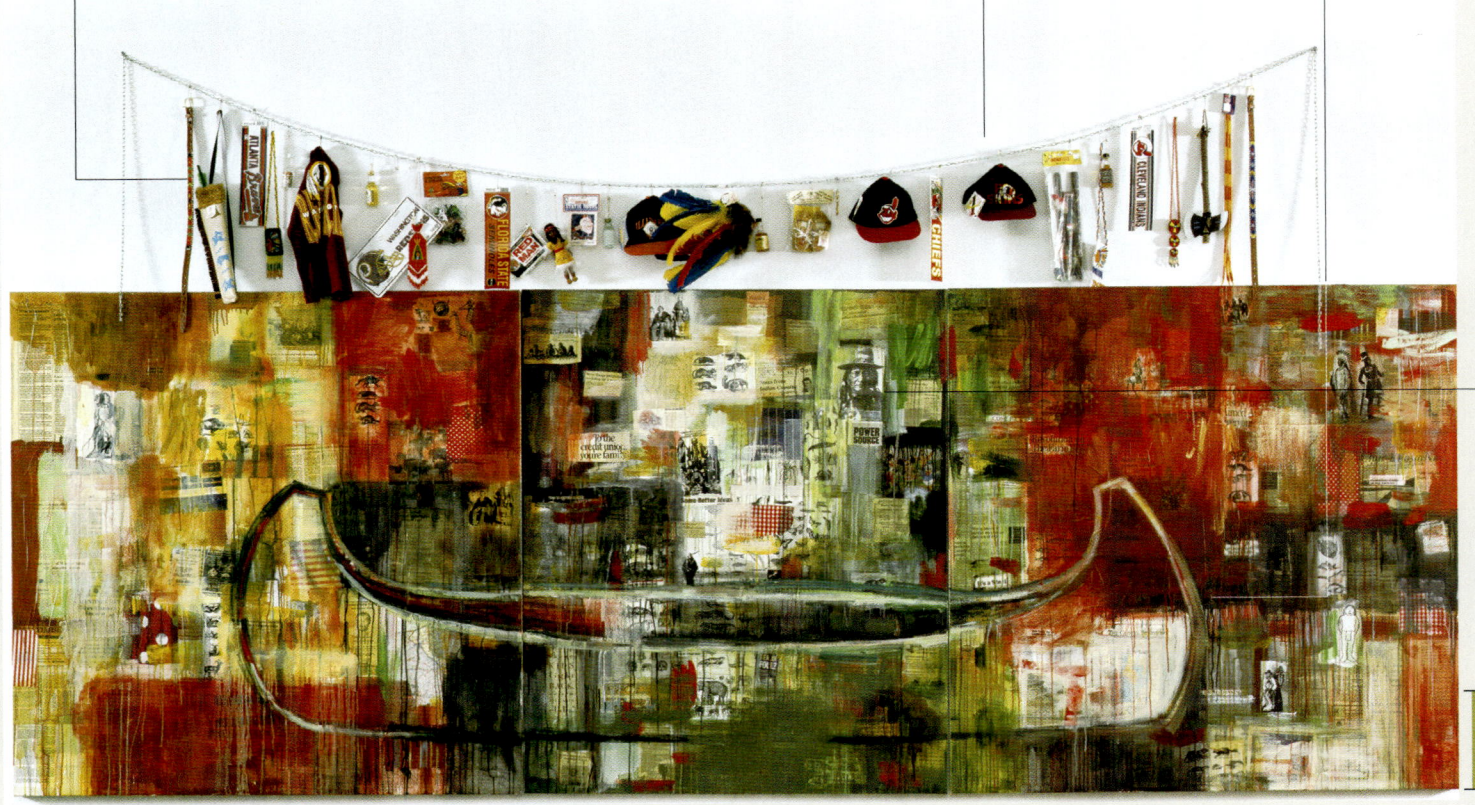

**31-1** JAUNE QUICK-TO-SEE SMITH, *Trade (Gifts for Trading Land with White People)*, 1992. Oil and mixed media on canvas, 5′ × 14′ 2″. Chrysler Museum of Art, Norfolk.

1 ft.

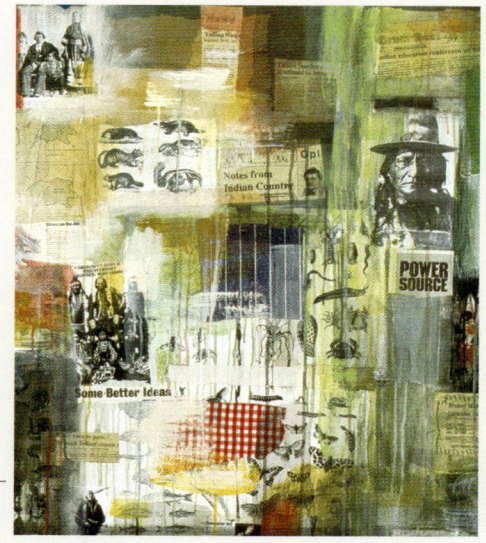

Newspaper clippings chronicle the conquest of Native America by Europeans and include references to the problems facing those living on reservations today—poverty, alcoholism, disease.

# CONTEMPORARY ART WORLDWIDE

## ART AS SOCIOPOLITICAL MESSAGE

Although televisions, cell phones, and the Internet have brought people all over the world closer together than ever before in history, national, ethnic, religious, and racial conflicts are unfortunate and unavoidable facts of contemporary life. Some of the most eloquent voices raised in protest about the major political and social issues of the day have been those of painters and sculptors, who can harness the power of art to amplify the power of the written and spoken word.

JAUNE QUICK-TO-SEE SMITH (b. 1940) is a Native American artist descended from the Shoshone, Salish, and Cree peoples. Raised on the Flatrock Reservation in Montana, she is steeped in the traditional culture of her ancestors, but she trained as an artist in the European-American tradition at Framingham State College in Massachusetts and at the University of New Mexico. Smith's ethnic heritage has always informed her art, however, and her concern about the invisibility of Native American artists has led her to organize exhibitions of their art. Her self-identity has also been the central theme of her mature work as an artist.

In 1992, Smith created what many critics consider her masterpiece: *Trade* (FIG. **31-1**), subtitled *Gifts for Trading Land with White People*. A complex multimedia work of monumental size, *Trade* is Smith's response to what she called "the Quincentenary Non-Celebration," that is, White America's celebration of the 500th anniversary of Christopher Columbus's arrival in what Europeans called the New World. *Trade* combines collage elements and attached objects, reminiscent of a Rauschenberg combine (FIG. 30-23), with energetic brushwork recalling Willem de Kooning's Abstract Expressionist canvases (FIG. 30-8) and clippings from Native American newspapers. The clippings include images chronicling the conquest of Native America by Europeans and references to the problems facing those living on reservations today—poverty, alcoholism, disease. The dripping red paint overlaying the collage with the central motif of the canoe is symbolic of the shedding of Native American blood.

Above the painting, as if hung from a clothesline, is an array of objects. These include Native American artifacts, such as beaded belts and feather headdresses, plastic tomahawks and "Indian princess" dolls, and contemporary sports memorabilia from teams with American Indian–derived names—the Cleveland Indians, Atlanta Braves, and Washington Redskins. The inclusion of these objects reminds viewers of the vocal opposition to the use of these and similar names for high school and college as well as professional sports teams. All the cheap artifacts together also have a deeper significance. As the title indicates and Smith explained:

Why won't you consider trading the land we handed over to you for these silly trinkets that so honor us? Sound like a bad deal? Well, that's the deal you gave us.[1]

# SOCIAL AND POLITICAL ART

Jaune Quick-to-See Smith's *Trade* (FIG. 31-1) is the unique product of the artist's heritage as a Native American who has sought to bridge native and European artistic traditions, but her work parallels that of many other innovative artists of the decades since 1980 in addressing contemporary social and political issues. This focus on the content and meaning of art represents, as did the earlier work of the Pop artists and Superrealists (see Chapter 30), a rejection of modernist formalist doctrine and a desire on the part of artists once again to embrace the persuasive powers of art to communicate with a wide audience.

**POSTMODERNISM** The rejection of the principles underlying modernism is a central element in the diverse phenomenon in art, as in architecture, known as postmodernism (see page 929). No simple definition of *postmodernism* is possible, but it represents the erosion of the boundaries between high culture and popular culture—a separation Clement Greenberg and the modernists had staunchly defended.

For many recent artists, postmodernism involves examining the process by which meaning is generated and the negotiation or dialogue that transpires between viewers and artworks. This kind of examination of the nature of art parallels the literary field of study known as critical theory. Critical theorists view art and architecture, as well as literature and the other humanities, as a culture's intellectual products or "constructs." These constructs unconsciously suppress or conceal the real premises informing the culture, primarily the values of those politically in control. Thus, cultural products function in an ideological capacity, obscuring, for example, racist or sexist attitudes. When revealed by analysis, the facts behind these constructs, according to critical theorists, contribute to a more substantial understanding of artworks, buildings, books, and the overall culture.

Many critical theorists use an analytical strategy called *deconstruction,* after a method developed by French intellectuals in the 1960s and 1970s. In deconstruction theory, all cultural contexts are "texts." Critical theorists who employ this approach seek to uncover—to deconstruct—the facts of power, privilege, and prejudice underlying the practices and institutions of any given culture. In so doing, scholars can reveal the precariousness of structures and systems, such as language and cultural practices, along with the assumptions underlying them.

Critical theorists do not agree upon any single philosophy or analytical method, because in principle they oppose firm definitions.

They do share a healthy suspicion of all traditional truth claims and value standards, all hierarchical authority and institutions. For them, deconstruction means destabilizing established meanings, definitions, and interpretations while encouraging subjectivity and individual differences. Indeed, if there is any common denominator in the art of the decades since 1980, it is precisely the absence of any common denominator. Diversity of style and content and the celebration of individual personalities, backgrounds, and approaches to art are central to the notion of postmodernist art. The art of the 1980s and 1990s and of the opening decades of the 21st century is worldwide in scope, encompasses both abstraction and realism, and addresses a wide range of contemporary social and political issues.

## Social Art: Gender and Sexuality

Many artists who have embraced the postmodern interest in investigating the dynamics of power and privilege have focused on issues of gender and sexuality in the contemporary world.

**BARBARA KRUGER** In the 1970s, some feminist artists, chief among them Cindy Sherman (FIG. 30-35), explored the "male gaze" and the culturally constructed notion of gender in their art. BARBARA KRUGER (b. 1945), who studied at Syracuse University and then at the Parsons School of Design in New York under Diane Arbus (FIG. 30-31), examines similar issues in her photographs. The strategies and techniques of contemporary mass media fascinate Kruger, who was a commercial graphic designer early in her career and the art director of *Mademoiselle* magazine in the late 1960s. In *Untitled* (*Your Gaze Hits the Side of My Face;* FIG. **31-2**), Kruger incorporated the layout techniques magazines and billboards use to sell consumer goods. Although she favored the reassuringly familiar format and look of advertising, Kruger's goal was to subvert the typical use of advertising imagery. She aimed to expose the deceptiveness of the media messages the viewer complacently absorbs. Kruger wanted to undermine the myths—particularly those about women—the media constantly reinforce. Her large (often four by six feet) word-and-photograph collages challenge the cultural attitudes embedded in commercial advertising. She has often used T-shirts, postcards, matchbooks, and billboards to present her work to a wide public audience.

In *Your Gaze,* Kruger overlaid a photograph of a classically beautiful sculpted head of a woman (compare FIG. 5-62A) with a vertical row of text composed of eight words. The words cannot be taken in with a single glance. Reading them is a staccato exercise, with an overlaid cumulative quality that delays understanding and

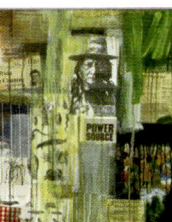

# CONTEMPORARY ART WORLDWIDE

| 1980 | 1990 | 2000 |
|---|---|---|
| ❙ Social and political issues—gender and sexuality; ethnic, religious, and national identity; violence, homelessness, and AIDS—figure prominently in the art of Kruger, Wojnarowicz, Wodiczko, Ringgold, Weems, and many others | ❙ Artworks addressing pressing political and social issues continue to be produced in great numbers by, among others, Quick-to-See Smith, Sikander, Bester, Hammons, and Neshat | ❙ Modern, postmodern, and traditional art forms coexist today in the increasingly interconnected worldwide art scene as artists on all continents work with age-old materials and also experiment with the new media of digital photography, computer graphics, and video |
| ❙ Stirling, Pei, and other postmodern architects incorporate historical references into designs for museums and other public buildings | ❙ Realistic figure painting and sculpture (Kiki Smith, Saville) as well as abstraction (Schnabel, Kiefer, Donovan) remain vital components of the contemporary art scene | |
| ❙ Site-specific artworks by Lin and Serra and exhibitions of the work of Mapplethorpe and Ofili become lightning rods for debate over public financing of art | ❙ Deconstructivism (Behnisch, Gehry, Hadid) and green architecture (Piano) emerge as major architectural movements | |

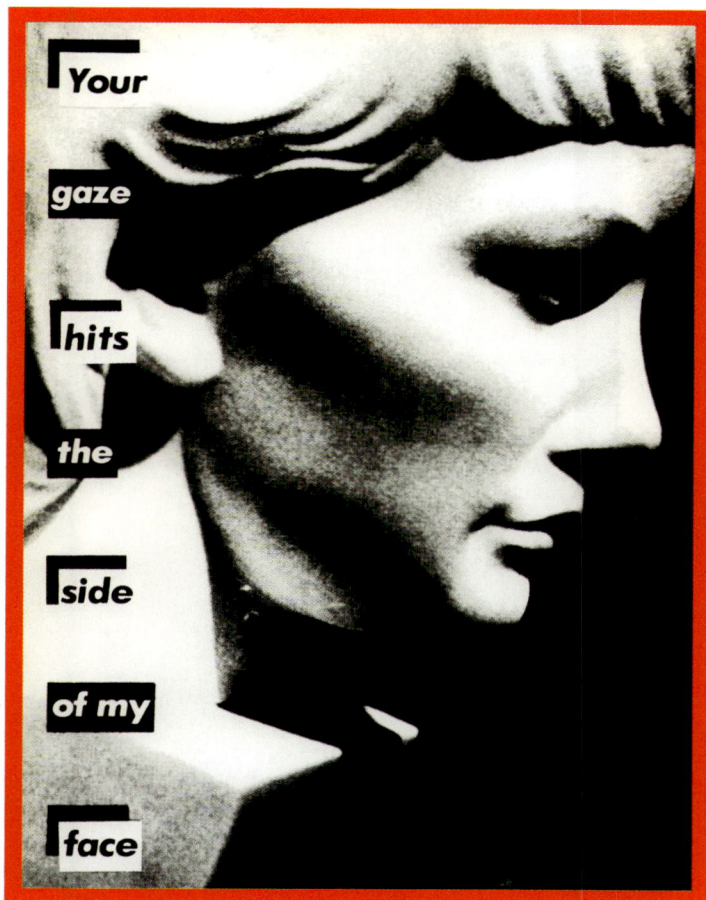

**31-2** Barbara Kruger, *Untitled* (*Your Gaze Hits the Side of My Face*), 1981. Photograph, red painted frame, 4′ 7″ × 3′ 5″. Courtesy Mary Boone Gallery, New York. ▸

Kruger has explored the "male gaze" in her art. Using the layout techniques of mass media, she constructed this word-and-photograph collage to challenge culturally constructed notions of gender.

1 ft.

intensifies the meaning (rather like reading a series of roadside billboards from a speeding car). Kruger's use of text in her work is significant. Many cultural theorists have asserted language is one of the most powerful vehicles for internalizing stereotypes and conditioned roles. Some feminist artists, most notably the GUERRILLA GIRLS (FIG. **31-2A**), have created powerful artworks consisting only of words—presented in a style and format reminiscent of the same kinds of magazine ads Kruger incorporates in her photo-collages.

**THE ADVANTAGES OF BEING A WOMAN ARTIST:**

**31-2A** GUERRILLA GIRLS, *Advantages of Being a Woman Artist,* 1988.

**DAVID WOJNAROWICZ** For many artists, their homosexuality is as important—or even more important—an element of their personal identity as their gender, ethnicity, or race. Beginning in the early 1980s, unwelcome reinforcement for their self-identification came from confronting daily the devastating effects of AIDS (acquired immune deficiency syndrome) in the gay community. Some sculptors and painters responded by producing deeply moving works of art. DAVID WOJNAROWICZ (1955–1992) dropped out of high school in his hometown of Red Bank, New Jersey, and moved to New York City, where he lived on the streets before achieving success as an artist. A gay activist, he watched his lover and many of his friends die of AIDS. He reacted by creating disturbing yet eloquent works about the tragedy of this disease, which eventually claimed his own life. In *When I Put My Hands on Your Body* (FIG. **31-3**), he overlaid a photograph of a pile of skeletal remains with evenly spaced typed commentary communicating his feelings about watching a loved one dying of AIDS. Wojnarowicz movingly describes the effects of AIDS on the human body and soul:

> When I put my hands on your body on your flesh I feel the history of that body. . . . I see the flesh unwrap from the layers of fat and disappear. . . . I see the organs gradually fade into transparency. . . . It makes me weep to feel the history of you of your flesh beneath my hands.

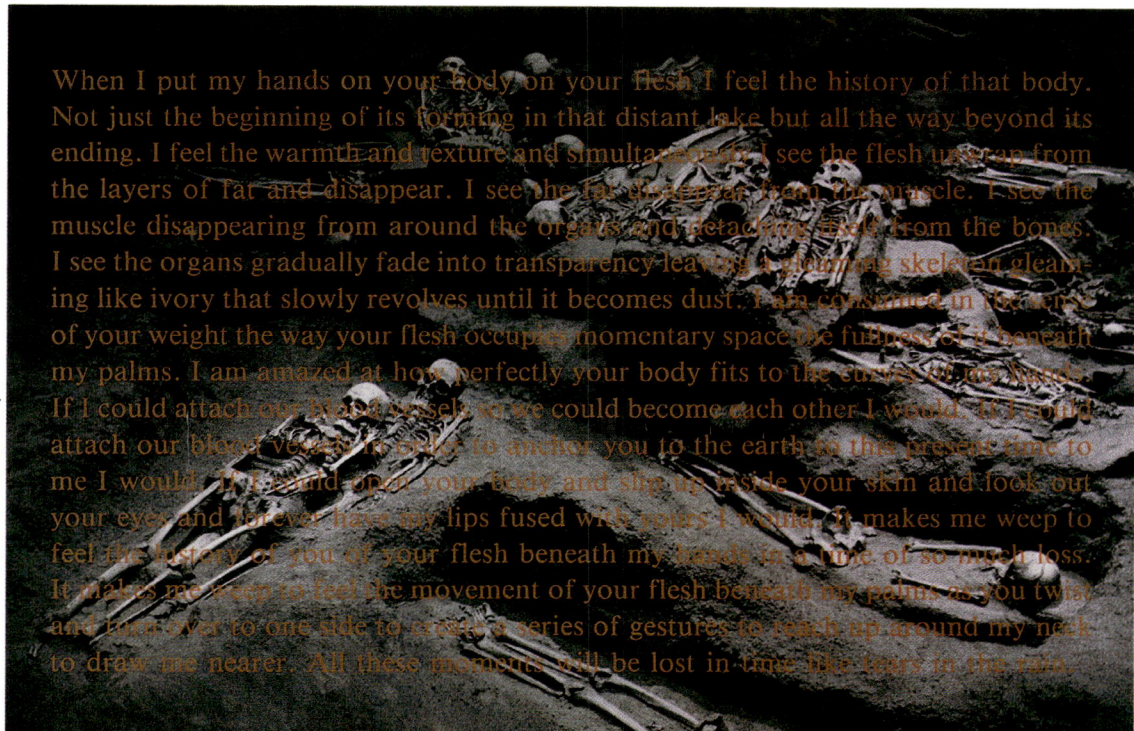

**31-3** DAVID WOJNAROWICZ, *When I Put My Hands on Your Body,* 1990. Gelatin silver print and silk-screened text on museum board, 2′ 2″ × 3′ 2″. Private collection.

In this disturbing yet eloquent print, Wojnarowicz overlaid typed commentary on a photograph of skeletal remains. He movingly communicated his feelings about watching a loved one die of AIDS.

1 ft.

When I put my hands on your body on your flesh I feel the history of that body. Not just the beginning of its forming in that distant lake but all the way beyond its ending. I feel the warmth and texture and simultaneously I see the flesh unwrap from the layers of fat and disappear. I see the fat disappear from the muscle. I see the muscle disappearing from around the organs and detaching itself from the bones. I see the organs gradually fade into transparency leaving a gleaming skeleton gleaming like ivory that slowly revolves until it becomes dust. I am consumed in the sense of your weight the way your flesh occupies momentary space the fullness of it beneath my palms. I am amazed at how perfectly your body fits to the curves of my hands. If I could attach our blood vessels so we could become each other I would. If I could attach our blood vessels in order to anchor you to the earth to this present time to me I would. If I could open your body and slip up inside your skin and look out your eyes and forever have my lips fused with yours I would. It makes me weep to feel the history of you of your flesh beneath my hands in a time of so much loss. It makes me weep to feel the movement of your flesh beneath my palms as you twist and turn over to one side to create a series of gestures to reach up around my neck to draw me nearer. All these moments will be lost in time like tears in the rain.

## Public Funding of Controversial Art

Although art can be beautiful and uplifting, throughout history art has also challenged and offended. Since the early 1980s, a number of heated controversies about art have surfaced in the United States. There have been many calls to remove "offensive" works from public view (see "Richard Serra's *Tilted Arc*," page 967) and, in reaction, accusations of censorship. The central questions in all cases have been whether there are limits to what art can appropriately be exhibited, and whether governmental authorities have the right to monitor and pass judgment on creative endeavors. A related question is whether the acceptability of a work should be a criterion in determining the public funding of art.

Two exhibits in 1989 placed the National Endowment for the Arts (NEA), a U.S. government agency charged with distributing federal funds to support the arts, squarely in the middle of this debate. One of the exhibitions, devoted to recipients of the Awards for the Visual Arts (AVA), took place at the Southeastern Center for Contemporary Art in North Carolina. Among the award winners was Andres Serrano, whose *Piss Christ,* a photograph of a crucifix submerged in urine, sparked an uproar. Responding to this artwork, Reverend Donald Wildmon, an evangelical minister from Mississippi and head of the American Family Association, expressed outrage that this kind of work was in an exhibition funded by the NEA and the Equitable Life Assurance Society (a sponsor of the AVA). He demanded the work be removed and launched a letter-writing campaign that caused Equitable Life to cancel its sponsorship of the awards. To Wildmon and other staunch conservatives, this exhibition, along with *Robert Mapplethorpe: The Perfect Moment,* which included erotic and openly homosexual images of the artist (FIG. 31-4) and others, served as evidence of cultural depravity and immorality. These critics insisted that art of an offensive character should not be funded by government agencies such as the NEA. As a result of media furor over *The Perfect Moment,* the director of the Corcoran Museum of Art decided to cancel the scheduled exhibition of this traveling show. But Dennis Barrie, Director of the Contemporary Arts Center in Cincinnati, chose to mount the show. The government indicted Barrie on charges of obscenity, but a jury acquitted him six months later.

These controversies intensified public criticism of the NEA and its funding practices. The next year, the head of the NEA, John Frohnmayer, vetoed grants for four lesbian, gay, or feminist performance artists—Karen Finley, John Fleck, Holly Hughes, and Tim Miller—who became known as the "NEA Four." Infuriated by what they perceived as overt censorship, the artists filed suit, eventually settling the case and winning reinstatement of their grants. Congress responded by dramatically reducing the NEA's budget, and the agency no longer awards grants or fellowships to individual artists.

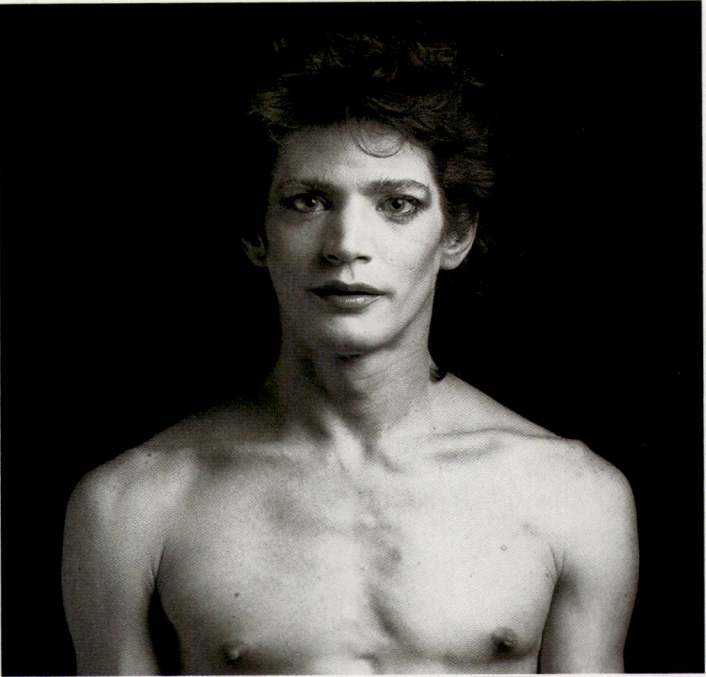

**31-4** ROBERT MAPPLETHORPE, *Self-Portrait,* 1980. Gelatin silver print, 7¾″ × 7¾″. Robert Mapplethorpe Foundation, New York.

Mapplethorpe's *Perfect Moment* show led to a landmark court case on freedom of expression for artists. In this self-portrait, an androgynous Mapplethorpe confronts the viewer with a steady gaze.

Controversies have also erupted on the municipal level. In 1999, Rudolph Giuliani, then mayor of New York, joined a number of individuals and groups protesting the inclusion of several artworks in the exhibition *Sensation: Young British Artists from the Saatchi Collection* at the Brooklyn Museum. Chris Ofili's *The Holy Virgin Mary* (FIG. 31-10), a collage of Mary incorporating cutouts from pornographic magazines and shellacked clumps of elephant dung, became the flashpoint for public furor. Denouncing the show as "sick stuff," the mayor threatened to cut off all city subsidies to the museum.

Art that seeks to unsettle and challenge is critical to the cultural, political, and psychological life of a society. The regularity with which this kind of art raises controversy suggests it operates at the intersection of two competing principles: free speech and artistic expression on the one hand and a reluctance to impose images upon an audience that finds them repugnant or offensive on the other. What these controversies do demonstrate, beyond doubt, is the enduring power of art.

---

Wojnarowicz juxtaposed text with imagery, which, like works by Barbara Kruger (FIG. 31-2) and the Guerrilla Girls (FIG. 31-2A), paralleled the use of both words and images in advertising. The public's familiarity with this format ensured greater receptivity to the artist's message.

**ROBERT MAPPLETHORPE** One brilliant gay artist who became the central figure in a heated debate in the halls of the U.S. Congress as well as among the public at large was ROBERT MAPPLETHORPE (1946–1989). Born in Queens, New York, Mapplethorpe studied drawing, painting, and sculpture at the Pratt

Institute in Brooklyn, but after he purchased a Polaroid camera in 1970, he became increasingly interested in photography. Mapplethorpe's *The Perfect Moment* traveling exhibition, funded in part by the National Endowment for the Arts, featured his photographs of flowers and people, many nude, some depicting children, some homoerotic and sadomasochistic in nature. The show led to a landmark court case in Cincinnati on freedom of expression for artists and prompted new legislation establishing restrictions on government funding of the arts (see "Public Funding of Controversial Art," page 944).

Never at issue was Mapplethorpe's technical mastery of the photographic medium. His gelatin silver prints have glowing textures with rich tonal gradations of black, gray, and white. In many ways, Mapplethorpe was the heir of Edward Weston, whose innovative compositions of still lifes (FIG. 29-44) and nudes (FIG. 29-44A) helped establish photography as an art form on a par with painting and sculpture. What shocked the public was not nudity per se—a traditional subject with roots in antiquity, indeed at the very birth of art during the Old Stone Age (FIGS. 1-5, 1-6, and 1-6A)—but the openly gay character of many of Mapplethorpe's images. *The Perfect Moment* photographs included, in addition to some very graphic images of homosexual men, a series of self-portraits documenting Mapplethorpe's changing appearance almost up until he died from AIDS only months after the show opened in Philadelphia in December 1988. The self-portrait reproduced here (FIG. **31-4**) presents Mapplethorpe as an androgynous young man with long hair and makeup, confronting the viewer with a steady gaze. Mapplethorpe's photographs, like the work of David Wojnarowicz (FIG. 31-3) and other gay and lesbian artists of the time, are inextricably bound with the social upheavals in American society and the struggle for equal rights for women, homosexuals, minorities, and the disabled during the second half of the 20th century.

**SHAHZIA SIKANDER** The struggle for recognition and equal rights has never been confined to the United States, least of all in the present era of instant global communication. In the Muslim world, women and homosexuals face especially difficult challenges, which SHAHZIA SIKANDER (b. 1969) brilliantly addresses in her work. Born in Lahore, Pakistan, and trained at the National College of Arts in the demanding South Asian/Persian art of miniature painting (see "Indian Miniature Painting," Chapter 32, page 979), she earned an MFA from the Rhode Island School of Design and now lives in New York City. So thoroughly immersed in the methods of miniature painting that she makes her own paper, pigments, and squirrel-hair brushes, Sikander nonetheless imbues this traditional art form with contemporary meaning. In *Perilous Order* (FIG. **31-5**), she addresses homosexuality, intolerance, and hypocrisy by portraying a gay friend in the guise of the Mughal emperor Aurangzeb (r. 1658–1707), who was a strict enforcer of Islamic orthodoxy although reputed to be a homosexual. Sikander depicted him framed against a magnificent marbleized background ringed by voluptuous nude Hindu nymphs and behind the shadow of a veiled Hindu goddess. *Perilous Order* thus also incorporates a reference to the tensions between the Muslim and Hindu populations of Pakistan and India today.

# Social Art: Race, Ethnicity, and National Identity

Gender and sexual-orientation issues are by no means the only societal concerns contemporary artists have addressed in their work. Race, ethnicity, and national identity are among the other pressing issues that have given rise to important artworks during the past few decades.

**FAITH RINGGOLD** One of the leading artists addressing issues associated with African American women is Harlem native FAITH RINGGOLD (b. 1930), who studied painting at the City College of New York and taught art education in the New York public schools for 18 years. In the 1960s, Ringgold produced numerous works that provided pointed and incisive commentary on the realities of racial prejudice. She increasingly incorporated references to gender as well and, in the 1970s, turned to fabric as the predominant material in her art. Using fabric enabled Ringgold to make more pointed reference to the domestic sphere, traditionally

1 in.

**31-5** SHAHZIA SIKANDER, *Perilous Order*, 1994–1997. Vegetable color, dry pigment, watercolor, and tea on Wasli paper, $10\frac{1}{2}'' \times 8''$. Whitney Museum of American Art, New York (purchase, with funds from the Drawing Committee).

Imbuing miniature painting with a contemporary message about hypocrisy and intolerance, Sikander portrayed a gay friend as a homosexual Mughal emperor who enforced Muslim orthodoxy.

**31-6** Faith Ringgold, *Who's Afraid of Aunt Jemima?* 1983. Acrylic on canvas with fabric borders, quilted, 7′ 6″ × 6′ 8″. Private collection.

In this quilt, a medium associated with women, Ringgold presented a tribute to her mother that also addresses African American culture and the struggles of women to overcome oppression.

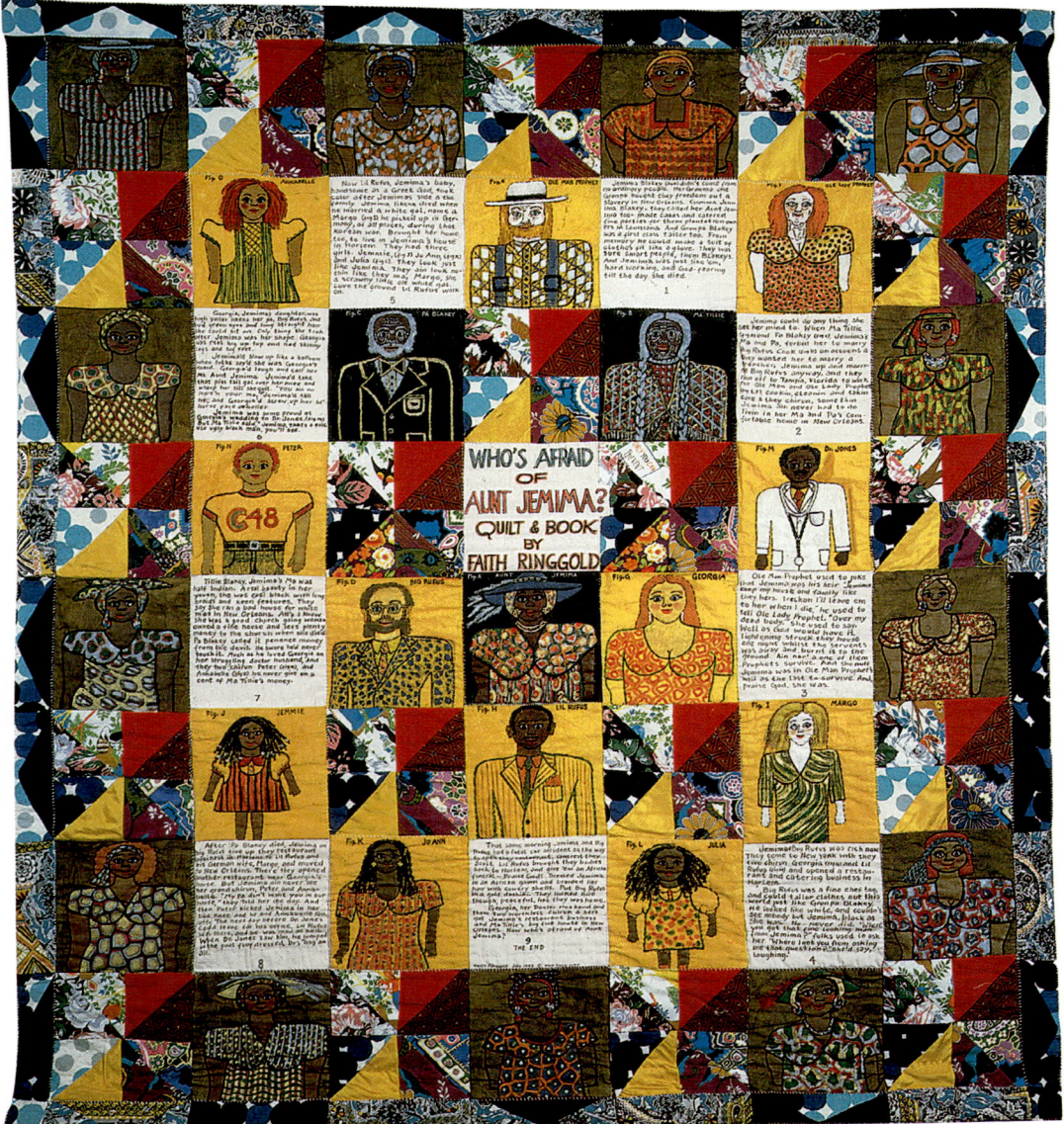

1 ft.

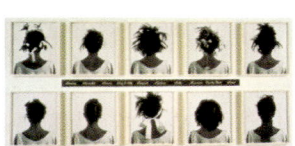

**31-6A** Simpson, *Stereo Styles*, 1988.

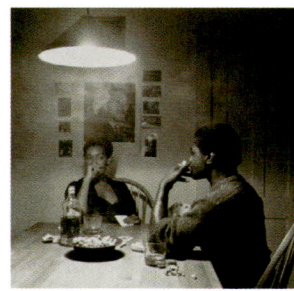

**31-6B** Weems, *Man Smoking/ Malcolm X*, 1990.

associated with women, and to collaborate with her mother, Willi Posey, a fashion designer. After her mother's death in 1981, Ringgold created *Who's Afraid of Aunt Jemima?* (FIG. **31-6**), a quilt composed of dyed, painted, and pieced fabric. A moving tribute to her mother, this "story quilt"—Ringgold's signature art form—merges the personal and the political. Combining words with pictures, as did Barbara Kruger (FIG. 31-2) and David Wojnarowicz (FIG. 31-3), Ringgold incorporates a narrative in her quilt. *Aunt Jemima* tells the witty story of the family of the stereotypical black "mammy" in the mind of the public, but here Jemima is a successful African American businesswoman. Ringgold narrates the story using black dialect interspersed with embroidered portraits and traditional patterned squares. *Aunt Jemima,* while resonating with autobiographical references, also speaks to the larger issues of the history of African American culture and the struggles of women to overcome oppression. Other contemporary feminist artists who have addressed similar racial and social issues are Lorna Simpson (b. 1960; FIG. **31-6A**) and Carrie Mae Weems (b. 1953; FIG. **31-6B**).

**MELVIN EDWARDS** In his art, Californian Melvin Edwards (b. 1937) explores a very different aspect of the black experience in America—the history of collective oppression of African Americans. One of Edwards's major sculptural series focused on the metaphor of lynching to provoke thought about the legacy of racism. His *Lynch Fragments* series, produced over more than three decades beginning in 1963, encompassed more than 150 welded-steel sculptures. Lynching as an artistic theme prompts an immediate and visceral response, conjuring chilling and gruesome images from the past. Edwards sought to extend this emotional resonance further in his art. He constructed the series' relatively small sculptures, such as *Tambo* (FIG. **31-7**), from found metal objects—for example, chains, hooks, hammers, spikes, knife blades, and handcuffs. Although Edwards often intertwined or welded together the individual metal components so as to diminish immediate identification of them, the sculptures still retain a haunting connection to the overall theme. These works refer to a historical act that evokes a

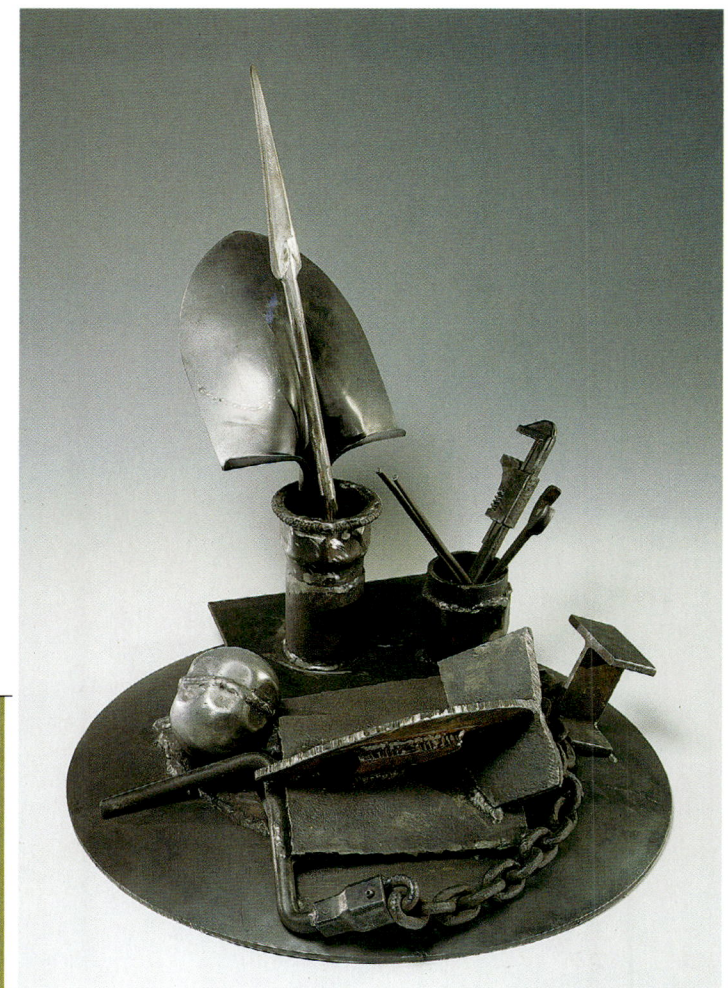

1 ft.

**31-7** MELVIN EDWARDS, *Tambo*, 1993. Welded steel, 2′ 4⅛″ × 2′ 1¼″. Smithsonian American Art Museum, Washington, D.C.

Edwards's welded sculptures of chains, spikes, knife blades, and other found objects allude to the lynching of African Americans and the continuing struggle for civil rights and an end to racism.

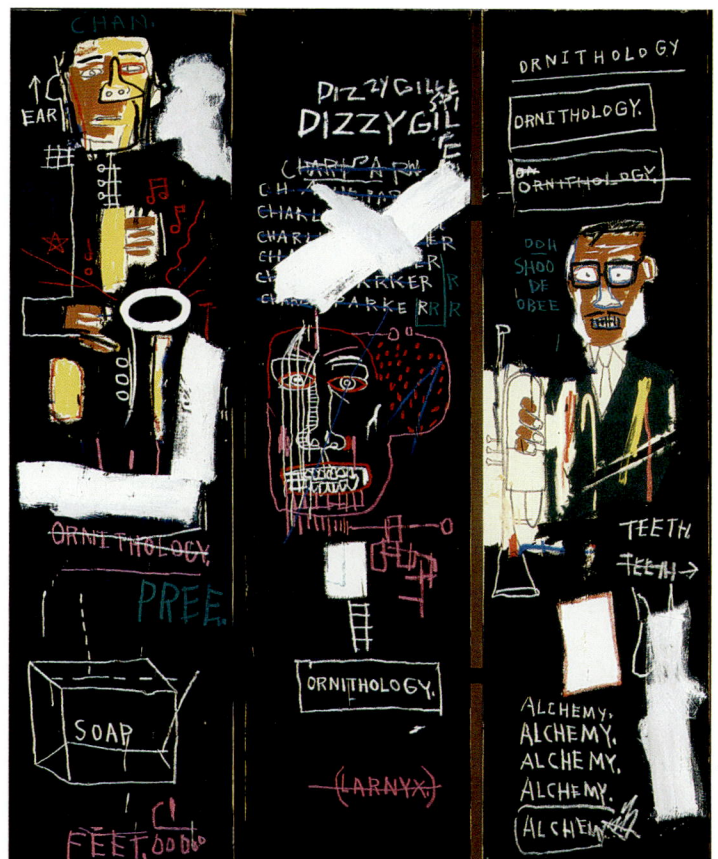

1 ft.

**31-8** JEAN-MICHEL BASQUIAT, *Horn Players,* 1983. Acrylic and oil paintstick on three canvas panels, 8′ × 6′ 3″. Broad Foundation, Santa Monica.

In this tribute to two legendary African American musicians, Basquiat combined bold colors, fractured figures, and graffiti to capture the dynamic rhythms of jazz and the excitement of New York.

collective memory of oppression, but they also speak to the continuing struggle for civil rights and an end to racism. While growing up in Los Angeles, Edwards experienced racial conflict firsthand. Among the metal objects incorporated into his *Lynch Fragments* sculptures are items he found in the streets in the aftermath of the Watts riots in 1965. The inclusion of these found objects imbues his disquieting, haunting works with an even greater intensity.

**JEAN-MICHEL BASQUIAT** The work of JEAN-MICHEL BASQUIAT (1960–1988) focuses on still another facet of the minority cultural experience in America. Born in Brooklyn in a comfortable home—his father was an accountant from Haiti and his mother a black Puerto Rican—Basquiat rebelled against middle-class values, dropped out of school at 17, and took to the streets. He first burst onto the New York art scene as the anonymous author of witty graffiti in Lower Manhattan signed SAMO (a dual reference to the derogatory name *Sambo* for African Americans and to "same old shit"). Basquiat first drew attention as an artist in 1980 when he participated in a group show—the "Times Square Show"—in an abandoned 42nd Street building. Eight years later, after a meteoric rise to fame, he died of a heroin overdose at age 27.

Basquiat was self-taught, both as an artist and about the history of art, but he was not a "primitive." His sophisticated style owes a debt to diverse sources, including the late paintings of Pablo Picasso, Abstract Expressionism, and the "art brut" of Jean Dubuffet (FIG. 30-4). Many of Basquiat's paintings celebrate black heroes, for example, the legendary jazz musicians Charlie "Bird" Parker and Dizzy Gillespie, whom he memorialized in *Horn Players* (FIG. **31-8**). The fractured figures, the bold colors against a black background, and the deliberately scrawled, crossed-out, and misspelled graffiti ("ornithology"—the study of birds—is a pun on Parker's nickname) create a dynamic composition suggesting the rhythms of jazz music and the excitement of the streets of New York, "the city that never sleeps."

**KEHINDE WILEY** Many African American artists have lamented the near-total absence of blacks in Western painting and sculpture, except as servants (compare FIG. 31-13), as well as in histories of Western art until quite recently. Los Angeles native KEHINDE WILEY (b. 1977) set out to correct that discriminatory imbalance. Wiley earned his MFA at Yale University and is currently artist-in-residence at the Studio Museum in Harlem, where he has achieved renown for his large-scale portraits of young urban African American men. Wiley's trademark paintings, however, are reworkings of historically important portraits in which he substitutes

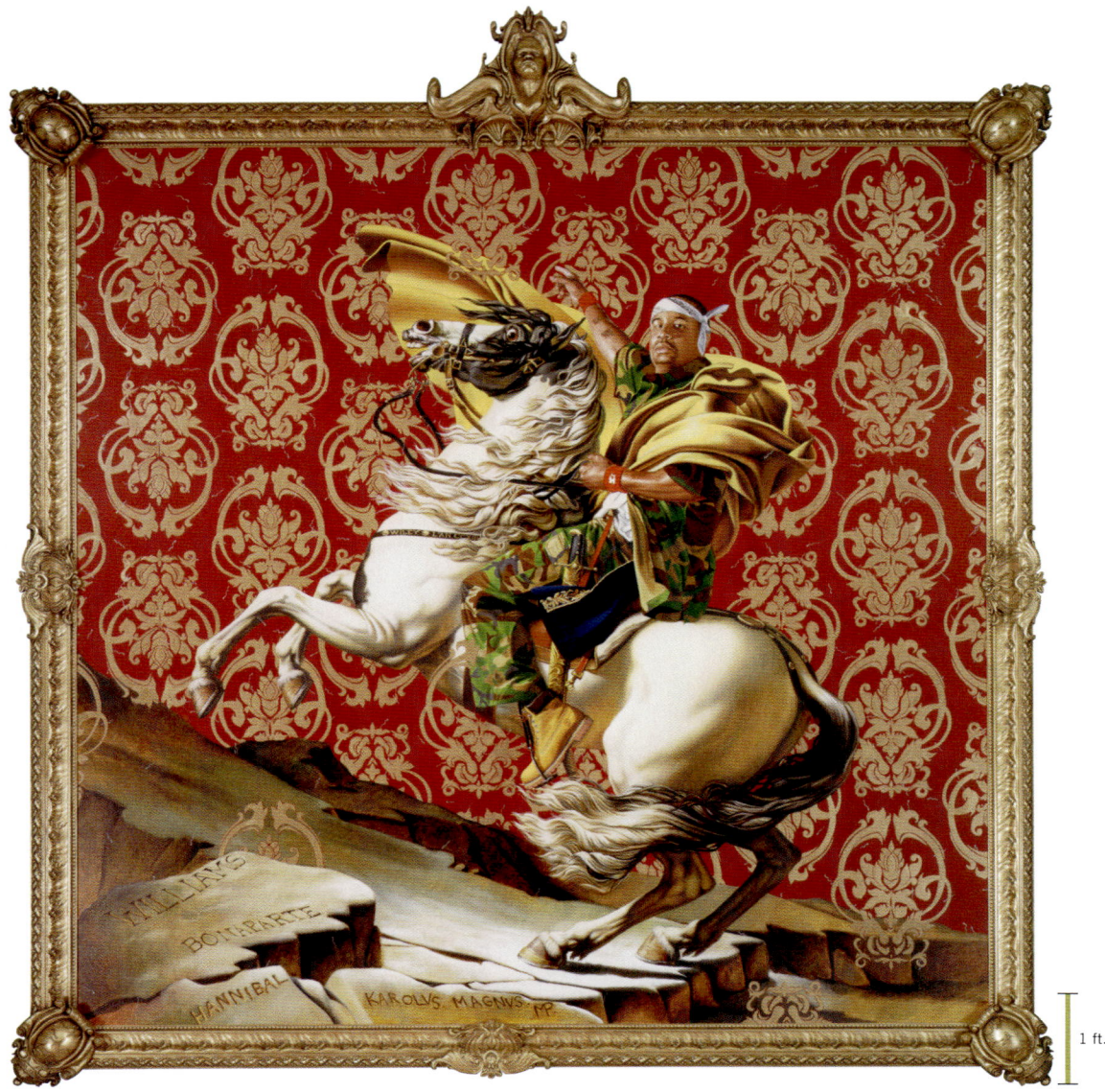

**31-9** KEHINDE WILEY, *Napoleon Leading the Army over the Alps,* 2005. Oil on canvas, 9′ × 9′. Brooklyn Museum, Brooklyn (Collection of Suzi and Andrew B. Cohen).

Wiley's trademark paintings are reworkings of famous portraits (FIG. 27-1A) in which he substitutes young African American men in contemporary dress in order to situate them in "the field of power."

1 ft.

figures of young black men in contemporary dress in order to situate them in what he calls "the field of power." One example is *Napoleon Leading the Army over the Alps* (FIG. **31-9**), based on Jacques-Louis David's painting (FIG. 27-1A) of the same subject. To evoke the era of the original, Wiley presented his portrait of an African American Napoleon on horseback in a gilt wood frame. Although in many details an accurate reproduction of David's canvas, Wiley's version is not a slavish copy. His heroic narrative unfolds against a vibrantly colored ornate wallpaper-like background instead of a dramatic sky—a distinctly modernist reminder to the viewer that this is a painting and not a window onto an Alpine landscape.

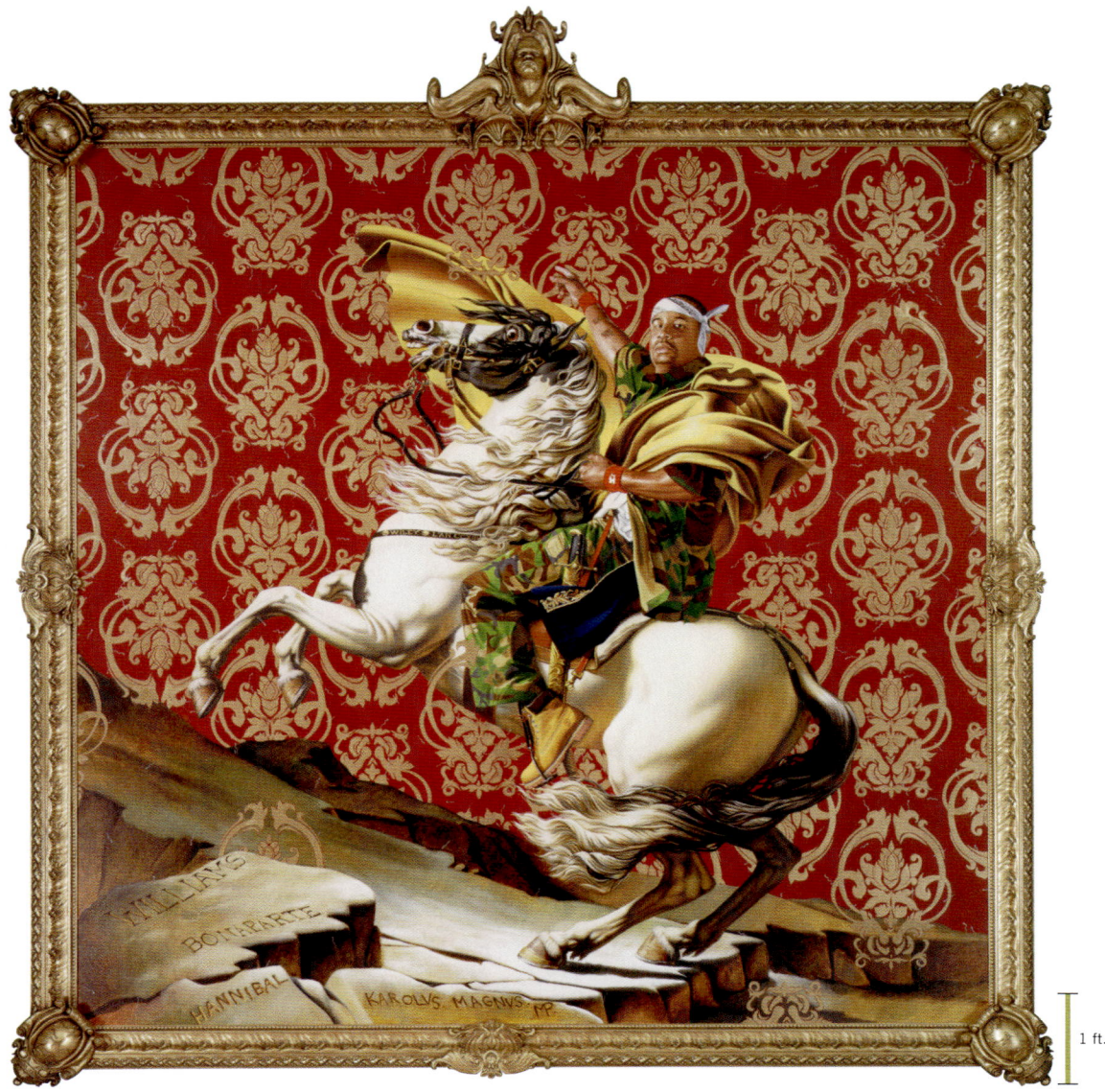

**31-9A** PIULA, *Ta Tele,* 1988. ▶

**CHRIS OFILI** In the global artistic community of the contemporary world, the exploration of personal social, ethnic, and national identity is a universal theme. Three artists who, like Shahzia Sikander (FIG. 31-5), incorporate their national artistic heritages in their work are TRIGO PIULA (b. ca. 1950; FIG. **31-9A**), CHRIS OFILI (b. 1968; FIG. 31-10), and Cliff Whiting (FIG. 31-11).

One theme Ofili has treated is religion, interpreted through the eyes of a British-born Catholic of Nigerian descent. Ofili's *The Holy Virgin Mary* (FIG. **31-10**) depicts Mary in a manner that departs radically from conventional Renaissance representations. Ofili's work presents the Virgin in simplified form, and she appears to float in an indeterminate space. The artist employed brightly colored pigments, applied to the canvas in multiple layers of beadlike dots (inspired by images from ancient caves in Zimbabwe). Surrounding the Virgin are tiny images of genitalia and buttocks cut out from pornographic magazines, which, to the artist, parallel the putti often surrounding Mary in Renaissance paintings. Another reference to Ofili's African heritage surfaces in the clumps of elephant dung—one attached to the Virgin's breast, and two more on which the canvas rests, serving as supports. The dung enabled Ofili to incorporate Africa into his work in a literal way. Still, he wants the viewer to move beyond the cultural associations of the materials and see them in new ways.

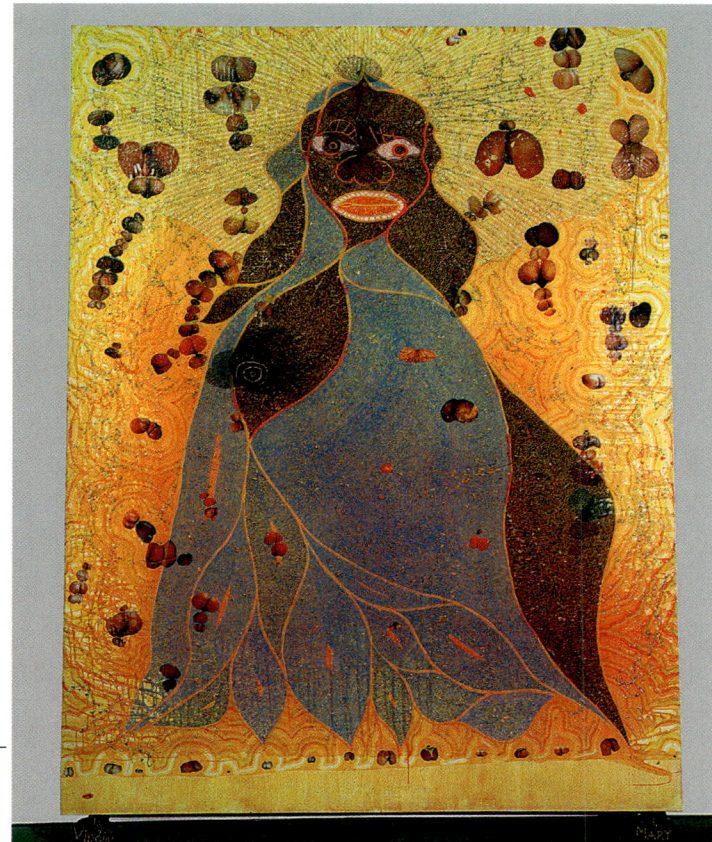

1 ft.

**31-10** CHRIS OFILI, *The Holy Virgin Mary*, 1996. Paper collage, oil paint, glitter, polyester resin, map pins, elephant dung on linen, 7′ 11″ × 5′ 11 5/16″. Saatchi Collection, London.

Ofili, a British-born Catholic of Nigerian descent, represented the Virgin Mary with African elephant dung on one breast and surrounded by genitalia and buttocks. The painting produced a public outcry.

Not surprisingly, *The Holy Virgin Mary* elicited strong reactions. Its inclusion in the *Sensation* exhibition at the Brooklyn Museum in 1999 with other intentionally "sensational" works by young British artists prompted indignant (but unsuccessful) demands for cancellation of the show and countercharges of censorship (see "Public Funding of Controversial Art," page 944).

**CLIFF WHITING** In New Zealand today, some artists draw on their Maori heritage for formal and iconographic inspiration. The historic Maori woodcarving craft (FIGS. 36-1 and 36-19A) brilliantly reemerges in what CLIFF WHITING (TE WHANAU-A-APANUI, b. 1936) calls a "carved mural" (FIG. **31-11**). Whiting's *Tawhiri-Matea* is a masterpiece in the venerable tradition of Oceanic wood sculpture, but it is a work designed for the very modern environment of an exhibition gallery. The artist suggested the wind turbulence with the restless curvature of the main motif and its myriad serrated edges. The 1984 mural depicts events in the Maori creation myth. The central figure, Tawhiri-Matea, god of the winds, wrestles to control the children of the four winds, seen as blue spiral forms. Ra, the sun, energizes the scene from the top left, complemented by Marama, the moon, in the opposite corner. The top right image refers to the primal separation of Ranginui, the Sky Father, and Papatuanuku, the Earth Mother. Spiral koru motifs symbolizing growth and energy flow through the composition. Blue waves and green fronds around Tawhiri suggest his brothers Tangaroa and Tane, gods of the sea and forest.

Whiting is securely at home with the native tradition of form and technique, as well as with the worldwide aesthetic of modern design. Out of the seamless fabric made by uniting both, he feels something new can develop that loses nothing of the power of the old. The artist champions not only the renewal of Maori cultural life and its continuity in art but also the education of the young in the values that made their culture great—values he asks them to perpetuate.

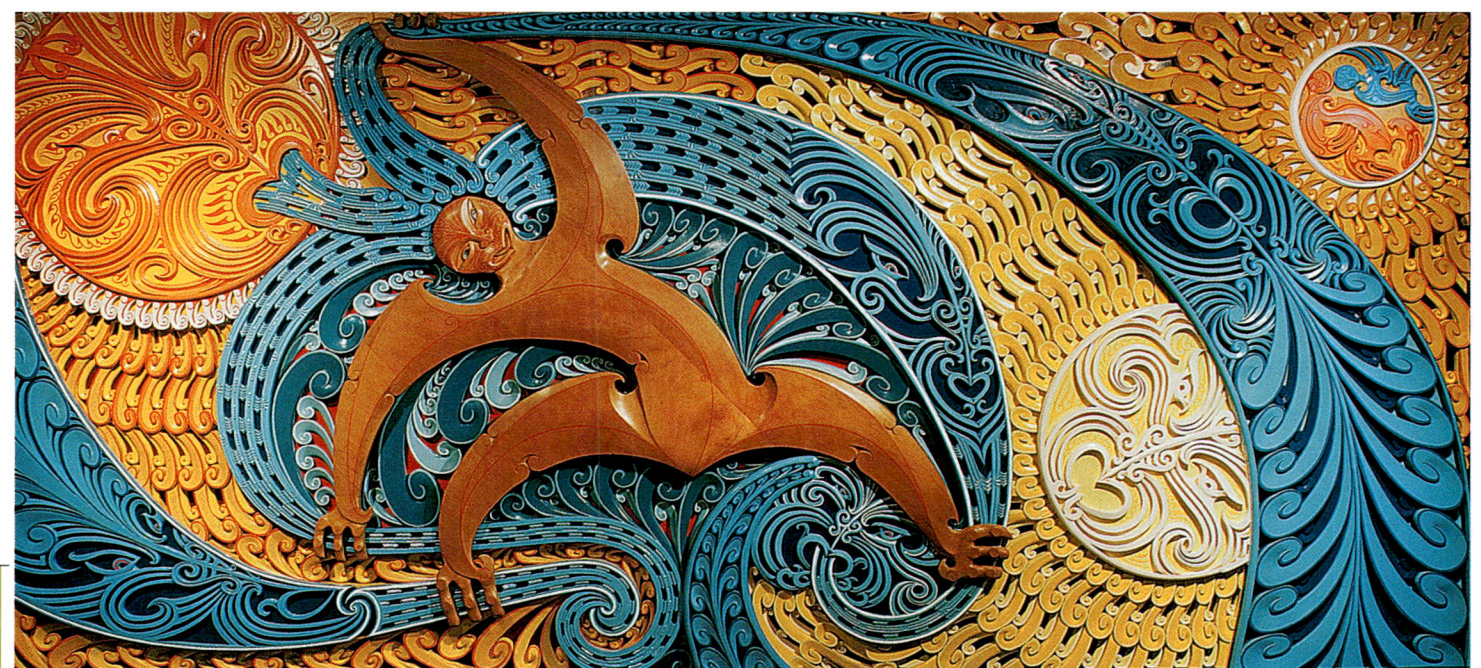

1 ft.

**31-11** CLIFF WHITING (TE WHANAU-A-APANUI), *Tawhiri-Matea* (*God of the Winds*), 1984. Oil on wood and fiberboard, 6′ 4 3/8″ × 11′ 10 3/4″. Meteorological Service of New Zealand, Wellington.

In this carved wooden mural depicting the Maori creation myth, Cliff Whiting revived Oceanic formal and iconographic traditions and techniques. The abstract curvilinear design suggests wind turbulence.

**31-12** WILLIE BESTER, *Homage to Steve Biko,* 1992. Mixed media, 3' 7⅚" × 3' 7⅚". Collection of the artist.

*Homage to Steve Biko* is a tribute to a leader of the Black Liberation movement, which protested apartheid in South Africa. References to the injustice of Biko's death fill this complex painting.

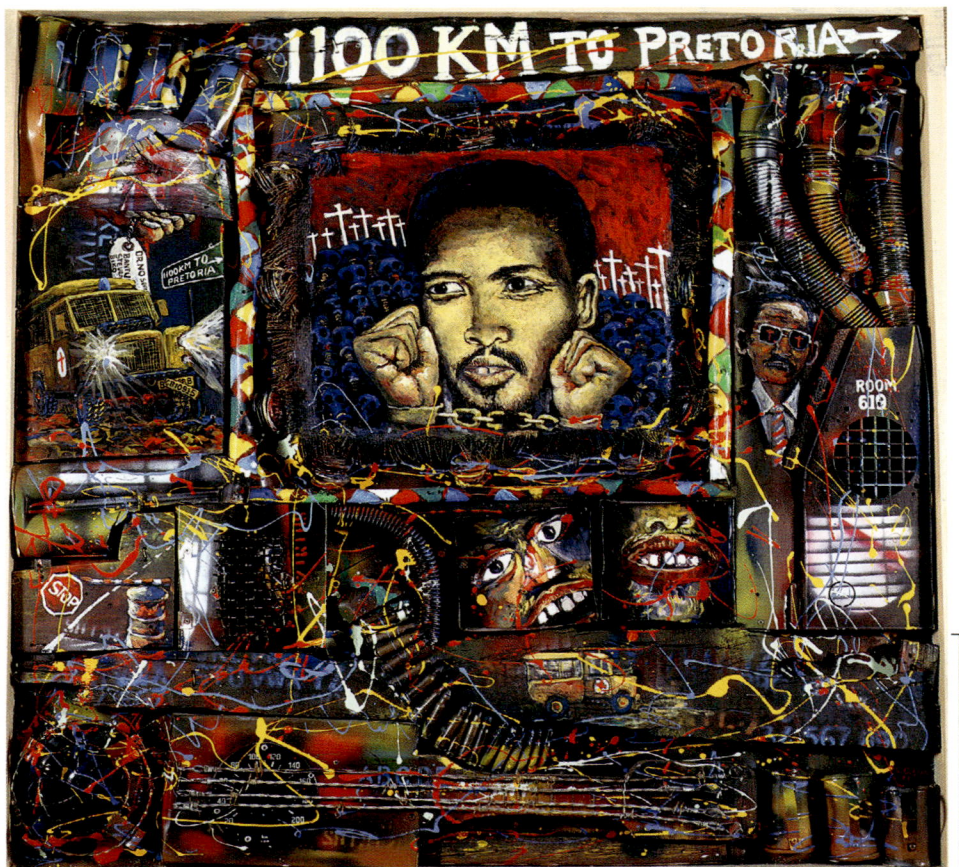

## Political Art

Although almost all of the works discussed thus far are commentaries on contemporary society—seen through the lens of these artists' personal experiences—they do not incorporate references to specific events, nor do they address conditions affecting all people regardless of their gender, race, or national origin, for example, street violence, homelessness, and industrial pollution. Other artists, however, have confronted precisely those aspects of contemporary life in their work.

**WILLIE BESTER** Political oppression in South Africa figures prominently in the paintings of WILLIE BESTER (b. 1956), one of many South African artists who were vocal critics of apartheid (government-sponsored racial separation). Bester's 1992 *Homage to Steve Biko* (FIG. 31-12) is a tribute to the gentle and heroic leader of the South African Black Liberation Movement whom the authorities killed while in detention. The exoneration of the two white doctors in charge of him sparked protests around the world. Bester packed his picture with references to death and injustice. Biko's portrait, at the center, is near another of the police minister, James Kruger, who had Biko transported 1,100 miles to Pretoria in the yellow Land Rover ambulance seen left of center and again beneath Biko's portrait. Bester portrayed Biko with his chained fists raised in the classic worldwide protest gesture. This portrait memorializes both Biko and the many other antiapartheid activists, as indicated by the white graveyard crosses above a blue sea of skulls beside Biko's head. The crosses stand out against a red background, recalling the inferno of burned townships. The stop sign (lower left) seems to mean "stop Kruger," or perhaps "stop apartheid." The tagged foot, as if in a morgue, above the ambulance (to the left) also refers to Biko's death. The red crosses on this vehicle's door and on Kruger's reflective dark glasses repeat, with sad irony, the graveyard crosses.

Blood-red and ambulance-yellow are in fact unifying colors dripped or painted on many parts of the canvas. Writing and numbers, found fragments and signs, both stenciled and painted—favorite Cubist motifs (FIGS. 29-14 and 29-16)—also appear throughout the composition. Numbers refer to dehumanized life under apartheid. Found objects—wire, sticks, cardboard, sheet metal, cans, and other discards—from which the poor construct fragile, impermanent township dwellings, remind viewers of the degraded lives of most South African people of color. The oilcan guitar (bottom center), another recurrent Bester symbol, refers both to the social harmony and joy provided by music and to the control imposed by apartheid policies. The whole composition is rich in texture and dense in its collage combinations of objects, photographs, signs, symbols, and pigment. *Homage to Steve Biko* is a radical and powerful critique of an oppressive sociopolitical system, and it exemplifies the extent to which art can be invoked in the political process.

**DAVID HAMMONS** Racism of all kinds is a central theme of the work of DAVID HAMMONS (b. 1943). Born in Springfield, Illinois, Hammons, an African American, moved to Los Angeles in 1962, where he studied art at the Chouinard and Otis Art Institutes before settling in Harlem in 1974. In his *installations* (artworks creating an artistic environment in a room or gallery), Hammons combines sharp social commentary with beguiling sensory elements to push viewers to confront racism in American society. He created *Public Enemy* (FIG. 31-13) for an exhibition at the Museum of Modern Art in New York in 1991. Hammons enticed viewers to interact with the installation by scattering fragrant autumn leaves on the floor and positioning helium-filled balloons throughout the gallery. The leaves crunched underfoot, and the dangling strings of the balloons gently brushed spectators walking around the installation. Once drawn into the environment, viewers encountered the centerpiece of *Public Enemy*—large black-and-white photographs of a public monument in front of the American Museum of Natural History in New York City depicting President Theodore Roosevelt (1858–1919) triumphantly seated on a horse, flanked by an African American man and a Native American man, both men appearing in the role of servants. Around the edge of the installation, circling the photographs of the monument, were piles of sandbags with both real and toy guns propped on top, aimed at the statue. By selecting evocative found objects and presenting them in a dynamic manner, encouraging viewer interaction, Hammons attracted an audience and then revealed the racism embedded in received cultural heritage and prompted reexamination of American values and cultural emblems.

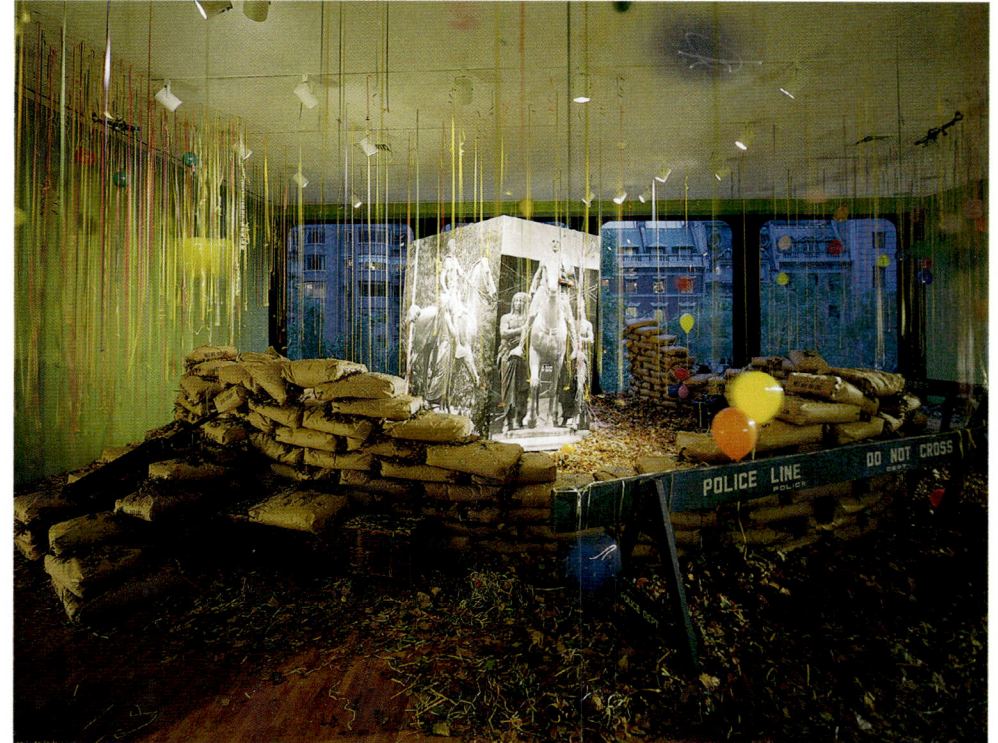

try to visualize the real products of the uses of power.[2]

*Mercenaries IV* (FIG. **31-14**), a canvas rivaling the monumental history paintings of the 19th century in size, presents a mysterious tableau of five tough freelance military professionals willing to fight, for a price, for any political cause. The three clustering at the right side of the canvas react with tense physical gestures to something one of the two other mercenaries standing at the far left is saying. The dark uniforms and skin tones of the four black fighters flatten their figures and make them stand out against the searing dark red background. The slightly modulated background seems to push their forms forward up against the picture plane and becomes an echoing void in the space between the two groups. Golub painted the mercenaries so that the viewer's eye is level with the menacing figures' knees. He placed the men so close to the front plane of the work that the lower edge of the painting cuts off their feet, thereby trapping the viewer in the painting's compressed space. Golub emphasized both the scarred light tones of the white mercenary's skin and the weapons. Modeled with shadow and gleaming highlights, the guns contrast with the harshly scraped, flattened surfaces of the figures. The rawness of the canvas reinforces the rawness of the imagery. Golub often dissolved certain areas with solvent after applying pigment and scraped off applied paint with, among other tools, a meat cleaver. The feeling of peril confronts viewers mercilessly. They become one with all the victims caught in today's political battles.

**LEON GOLUB** During his long and successful career as a painter, LEON GOLUB (1922–2004) expressed a brutal vision of contemporary life. Born in Chicago and trained at the University of Chicago and the Art Institute of Chicago, he is best known for his two series of paintings titled *Assassins* and *Mercenaries*. In these large-scale works on unstretched canvases, anonymous characters inspired by newspaper and magazine photographs participate in atrocious street violence, terrorism, and torture. The paintings have a universal impact because they suggest not specific stories but a condition of being. As Golub observed:

> Through media we are under constant, invasive bombardment of images—from all over—and we often have to take evasive action to avoid discomforting recognitions. . . . The work [of art] should have an edge, veering between what is visually and cognitively acceptable and what might stretch these limits as we encounter or

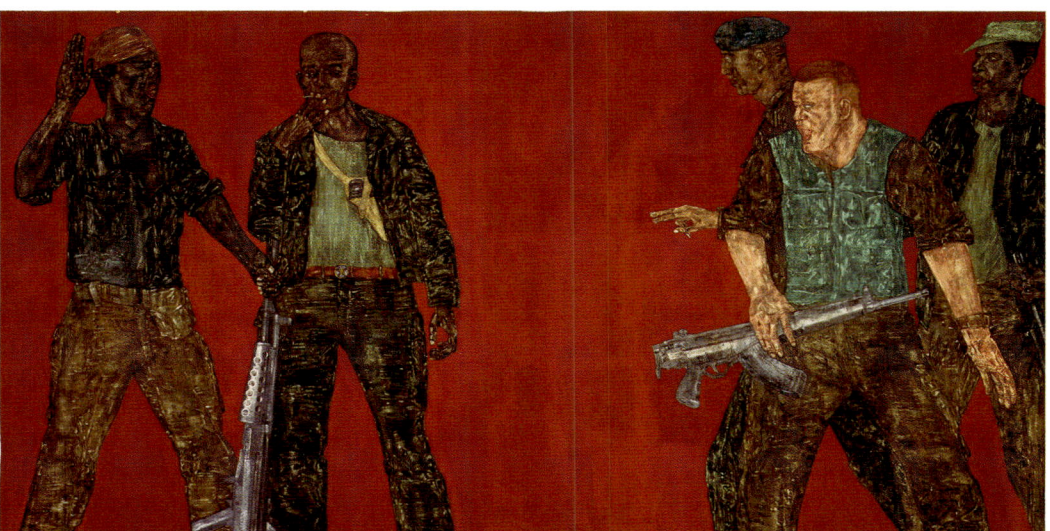

1 ft.

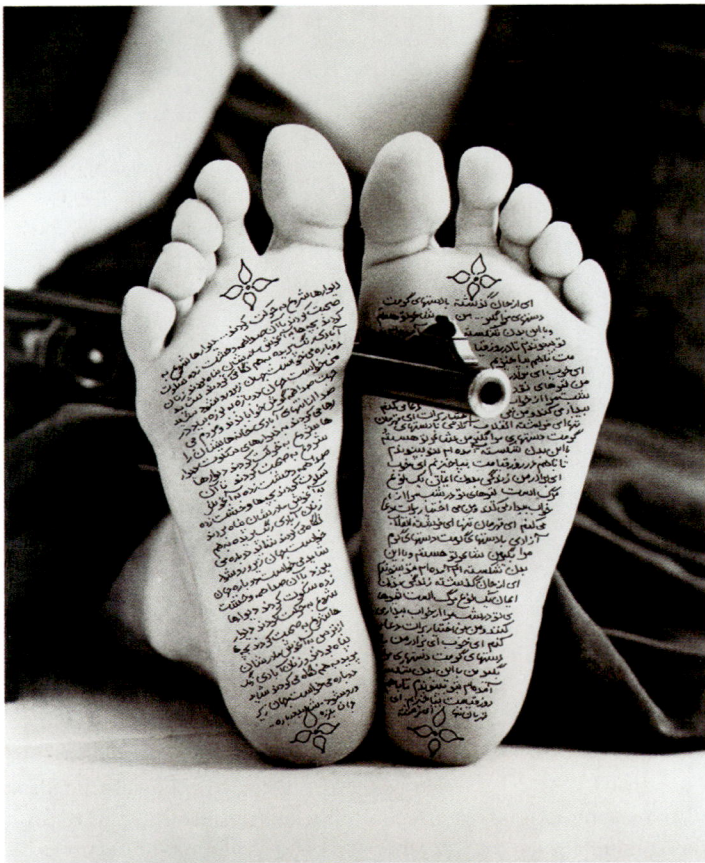

**31-15** SHIRIN NESHAT, *Allegiance and Wakefulness,* 1994. Offset print. Israel Museum, Jerusalem.

Neshat's photographs address the repression of women in postrevolutionary Iran. She poses in traditional veiled garb but wields a rifle and displays militant Farsi poetry on her exposed body parts.

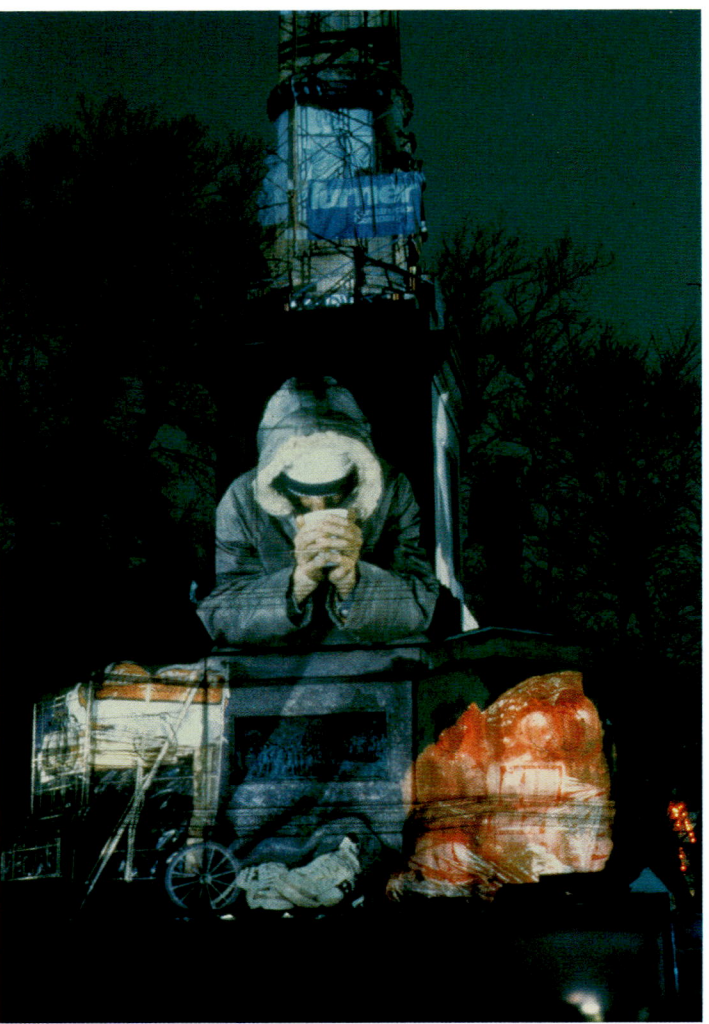

**31-16** KRZYSZTOF WODICZKO, *The Homeless Projection,* 1986. Outdoor slide projection at the Civil War Soldiers and Sailors Monument, Boston. ◼◀

To publicize their plight, Wodiczko projected on the walls of a monument on Boston Common images of homeless people and their plastic bags filled with their few possessions.

**SHIRIN NESHAT** Violence also plays a significant role in the art of SHIRIN NESHAT (b. 1957), who grew up in a Westernized Iranian home and attended a Catholic boarding school in Tehran before leaving her homeland to study art in California, where she earned undergraduate and graduate degrees from the University of California, Berkeley. Today, she lives in New York City and produces films, video, and photographs critical of the fundamentalist Islamic regime in Iran, especially in its treatment of women. Neshat often poses for her photographs wearing a veil—the symbol for her of the repression of Muslim women—and with her face and exposed parts of her body covered with Farsi (Persian) messages. A rifle often figures prominently in the photographs as an emblem of militant feminism, a notion foreign to the Muslim faith. In *Allegiance and Wakefulness* (FIG. **31-15**) from her *Women of Allah* series, the viewer sees only Neshat's feet covered with verses of militant Farsi poetry and the barrel of a rifle.

**KRZYSZTOF WODICZKO** Born in Poland, KRZYSZTOF WODICZKO (b. 1943) focuses on more universal concerns in his art. When working in Canada in 1980, he developed artworks involving outdoor slide images. He projected photographs on specific buildings to expose how civic buildings embody, legitimize, and perpetuate power. When Wodiczko moved to New York City in 1983, the pervasive homelessness troubled him, and he resolved to use his art to publicize this problem. In 1987, he produced *The Home-less Projection* (FIG. **31-16**) as part of a New Year's celebration in Boston. The artist projected images of homeless people on all four sides of the Civil War Soldiers and Sailors Monument on Boston Common. In these photos, the homeless appear flanked by plastic bags filled with their few possessions. At the top of the monument, Wodiczko projected a local condominium construction site, which helped viewers make a connection between urban development and homelessness.

**HANS HAACKE** Some contemporary artists have produced important works exposing the politics of the art world itself, specifically the role of museums and galleries in validating art, the discriminatory policies and politics of these cultural institutions, and the corrupting influence of corporate sponsorship of art exhibitions. German artist HANS HAACKE (b. 1936) has focused his attention on the politics of art museums and how acquisition and exhibition policies affect the public's understanding of art history. The specificity of his works, based on substantial research, makes them stinging indictments of the institutions whose practices he critiques.

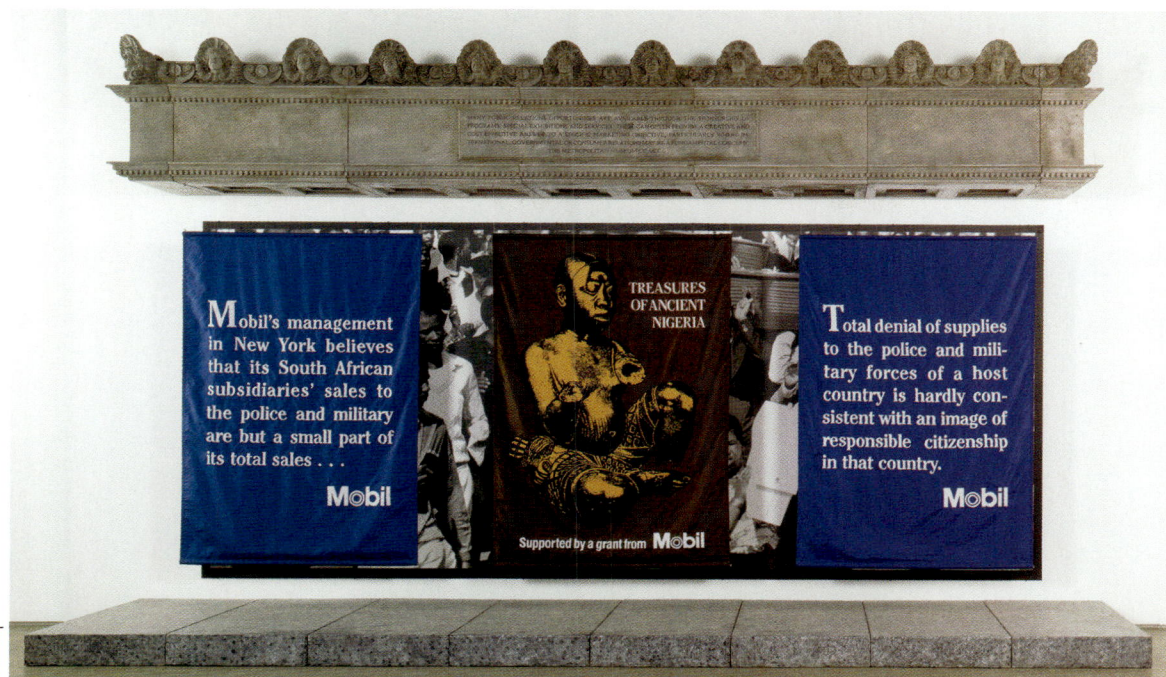

**31-17** Hans Haacke, *MetroMobiltan*, 1985. Fiberglass construction, three banners, and photomural, 11′ 8″ × 20′ × 5′. Musée National d'Art Moderne, Centre Georges Pompidou, Paris.

*MetroMobiltan* focuses attention on the connections between political and economic conditions in South Africa and the conflicted politics of corporate patronage of art exhibitions.

In *MetroMobiltan* (FIG. **31-17**), Haacke illustrated the connection between the realm of art (more specifically, the Metropolitan Museum of Art in New York) and the world of political and economic interests. *MetroMobiltan* is a large sculptural work that includes a photomural of the funeral procession for black victims shot by the South African police at Cross Roads, near Cape Town, on March 16, 1985. This photomural serves as the backdrop for a banner for the 1980 Mobil Oil–sponsored Metropolitan Museum show *Treasures of Ancient Nigeria*. In 1980, Mobil was a principal investor in South Africa, and Haacke's work suggests one major factor in Mobil's sponsorship of this exhibition was that Nigeria is one of the richest oil-producing countries. In 1981, political activists pressured Mobil's board of directors to stop providing oil to the white South African military and police. Printed on the blue banners hanging on either side of *MetroMobiltan* is the official corporate response refusing to comply with this demand. Haacke set the entire tableau in a fiberglass replica of the Metropolitan Museum's entablature. By bringing together these disparate visual and textual elements referring to the museum, Mobil Oil, and Africa, the artist forced viewers to think about the connections among multinational corporations, political and economic conditions in South Africa, and the conflicted politics of corporate patronage of art exhibitions, thereby undermining the public's naive view that cultural institutions are exempt from political and economic concerns.

**XU BING** A different kind of political/cultural commentary has been the hallmark of Xu Bing (b. 1955), a Chongqing, China, native who was forced to work in the countryside with peasants during the Cultural Revolution of 1966 to 1976 under Mao Tse-tung (1893–1976). Xu later studied printmaking in Beijing at the Central Academy of Fine Arts. He moved to the United States in 1990 at the invitation of the University of Wisconsin, where two years earlier he had exhibited his most famous work, a large installation called *A Book from the Sky* (FIG. **31-18**). First exhibited in China and Japan before being installed at Wisconsin's Chazen Museum of Art, the work presents an enormous number of woodblock-printed texts in characters evocative of Chinese writing but invented by the artist.

Producing them required both an intimate knowledge of genuine Chinese characters and extensive training in block carving. Xu's work, however, is no hymn to tradition. Critics have interpreted it both as a stinging critique of the meaninglessness of contemporary political language and as a commentary on the illegibility of the past. Like many works of art, past and present, Eastern and Western, Xu's postmodern masterpiece can be read on many levels.

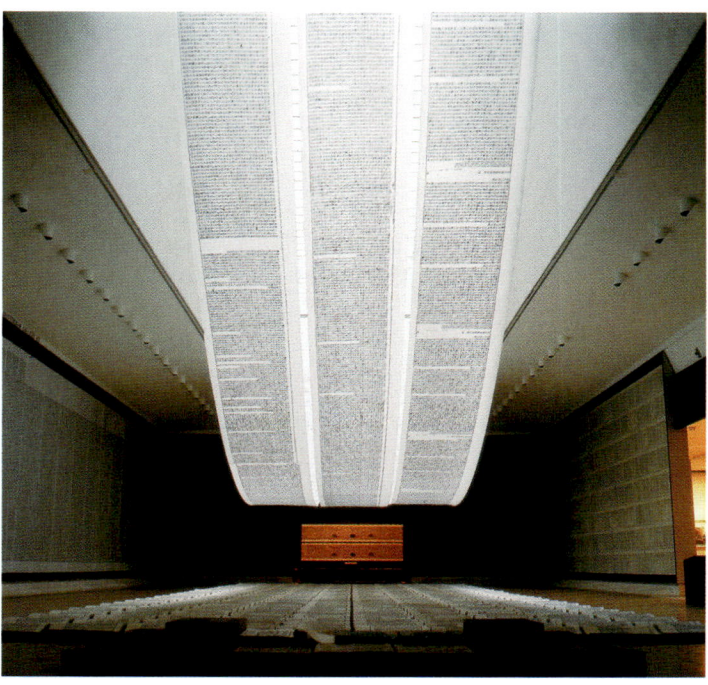

**31-18** Xu Bing, *A Book from the Sky,* 1987. Installation at Chazen Museum of Art, University of Wisconsin, Madison, 1991. Moveable-type prints and books.

Xu trained as a printmaker in Beijing. *A Book from the Sky,* with its invented Chinese woodblock characters, may be a stinging critique of the meaninglessness of contemporary political language.

31-19 EDWARD BURTYNSKY,
*Densified Scrap Metal #3a, Hamilton,
Ontario,* 1997. Dye coupler print,
2′ 2¾″ × 2′ 10⅜″. National Gallery of
Canada, Ottawa (gift of the artist,
1998).

Burtynsky's "manufactured landscapes"
are commentaries on the destructive
effects on the environment of industrial
plants and mines, but his photographs
transform ugliness into beauty.

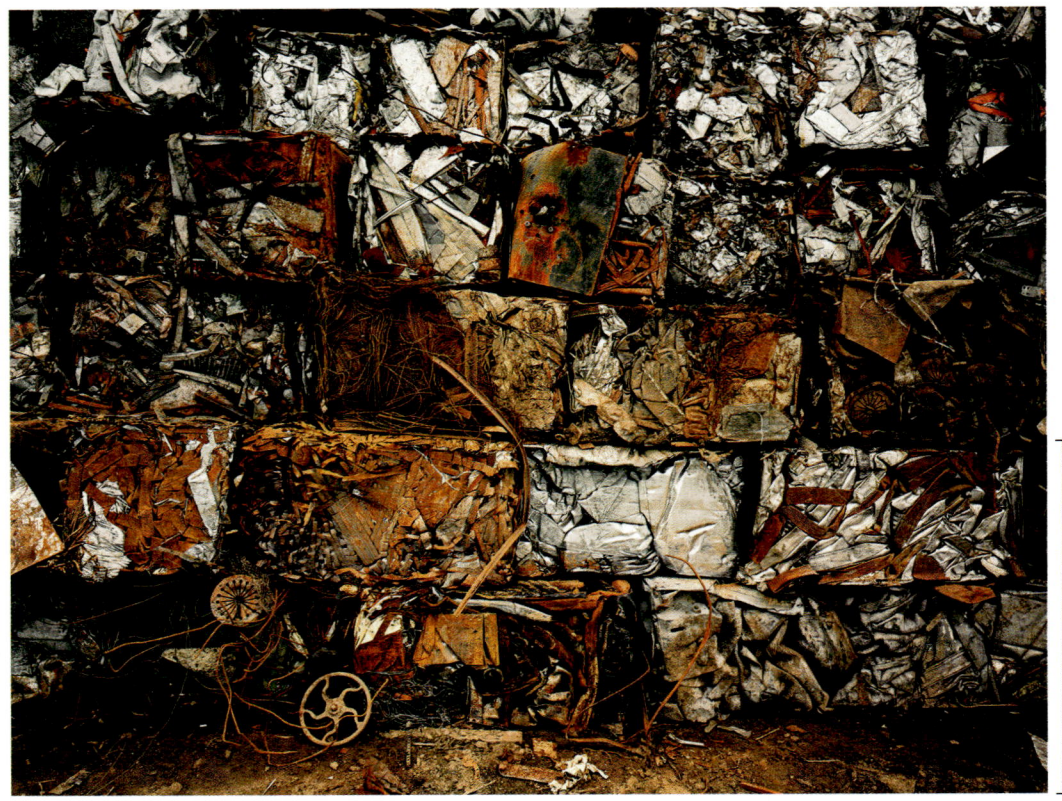

1 ft.

**EDWARD BURTYNSKY** Concern with the destructive effects of industrial plants and mines on the environment has been the motivation for the photographs of "manufactured landscapes" by Canadian EDWARD BURTYNSKY (b. 1955). The son of a Ukrainian immigrant who worked in the General Motors plant in St. Catharines, Ontario, Burtynsky studied photography and graphic design at Ryerson University and Niagara College. He uses a large-format field camera to produce high-resolution negatives of industrial landscapes littered with tires, scrap metal, and industrial refuse. His choice of subjects is itself a negative commentary on modern manufacturing processes, but Burtynsky transforms ugliness into beauty in his color prints. His photograph (FIG. **31-19**) of a Toronto recycling plant from his *Urban Mines* series converts bundles of compressed scrap metal into a striking abstract composition of multicolored rectangles. Burtynsky's work thus merges documentary and fine-art photography and bears comparison with the photographs of Margaret Bourke-White (FIG. 29-76) and Minor White (FIG. 30-32).

# OTHER MOVEMENTS
# AND THEMES

Despite the high visibility of contemporary artists whose work deals with the pressing social and political issues of the world, some critically acclaimed living artists have produced innovative modernist art during the postmodern era. Abstraction remains a valid and compelling approach to painting and sculpture in the 21st century, as does more traditional figural art.

## Abstract Painting and Sculpture

Already in the 1970s, Susan Rothenberg (FIG. 30-8D) had produced monumental "Neo-Expressionist" paintings inspired by German Expressionism and American Abstract Expressionism. Today, sev-

eral important contemporary artists continue to explore this dynamic style.

**JULIAN SCHNABEL** New Yorker JULIAN SCHNABEL (b. 1951), who wrote and directed a 1996 film about fellow artist Jean-Michel Basquiat (FIG. 31-8), has experimented widely with media and materials in his forceful restatements of the premises of Abstract Expressionism. Schnabel's Neo-Expressionist works range from paint on velvet and tarpaulin to a mixture of pigment and fragmented china plates bonded to wood. He has a special interest in the physicality of objects, and by combining broken crockery and paint, as in The Walk Home (FIG. **31-20**), he has found an extension of what paint can do. Superficially, Schnabel's paintings recall the work of the gestural abstractionists, especially the spontaneous drips of Jackson Pollock (FIG. 30-6) and the energetic brushstrokes of Willem de Kooning (FIG. 30-8), but their Abstract Expressionist works lack the thick, mosaiclike texture of Schnabel's canvases. The amalgamation of media brings together painting, mosaic, and low-relief sculpture, and considerably amplifies the expressive impact of his paintings.

**ANSELM KIEFER** Neo-Expressionism was by no means a solely American movement. German artist ANSELM KIEFER (b. 1945), who studied art in Düsseldorf with Joseph Beuys (FIG. 30-52) in the early 1970s, and has lived and worked in Barjac, France, since 1992, has produced some of the most lyrical and engaging works of recent decades. Like Schnabel's canvases, Kiefer's paintings, such as *Nigredo* (FIG. **31-21**), are monumental in scale, recall Abstract Expressionist works, and draw the viewer to their textured surfaces, made more complex by the addition of materials such as straw and lead. It is not merely the impressive physicality of Kiefer's paintings that accounts for the impact of his work, however. His images function on a mythological or metaphorical level as well as on a historically specific one. Kiefer's works of the 1970s and 1980s often involve a reexamination of German history, particularly the painful Nazi era of 1933–1945, and evoke the feeling of despair.

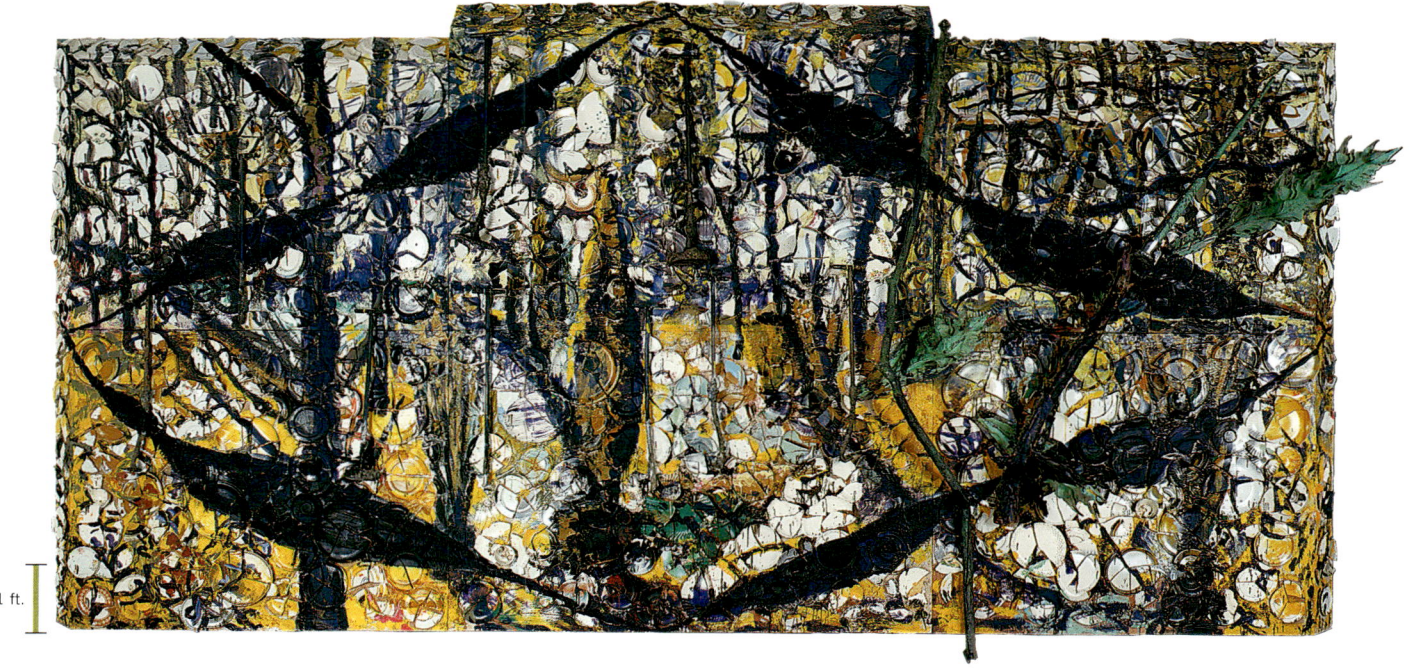

1 ft.

**31-20** JULIAN SCHNABEL, *The Walk Home*, 1984–1985. Oil, plates, copper, bronze, fiberglass, and Bondo on wood, 9′ 3″ × 19′ 4″. Broad Art Foundation and the Pace Gallery, New York. ◼◀

Schnabel's paintings recall the work of the gestural abstractionists, but he employs an amalgamation of media, bringing together painting, mosaic, and low-relief sculpture.

Kiefer believes Germany's participation in World War II and the Holocaust left permanent scars on the souls of the German people and on the souls of all humanity.

*Nigredo* (blackening) pulls the viewer into an expansive landscape depicted using Renaissance perspective principles. This landscape, however, is far from pastoral or carefully cultivated. Rather, it appears bleak and charred. Although it does not make specific reference to the Holocaust, this incinerated landscape indirectly alludes to the horrors of that historical event. More generally, the blackness of the landscape may refer to the notion

of alchemical change or transformation, a concept of great interest to Kiefer. Black is one of the four symbolic colors of the alchemist—a color referencing both death and the molten, chaotic state of substances broken down by fire. Because the alchemist focuses on the transformation of substances, the emphasis on blackness is not absolute, but can also be perceived as part of a process of renewal and redemption. Kiefer thus imbued his work with a deep symbolic meaning that, when combined with the intriguing visual quality of his parched, congealed surfaces, results in paintings of enduring power.

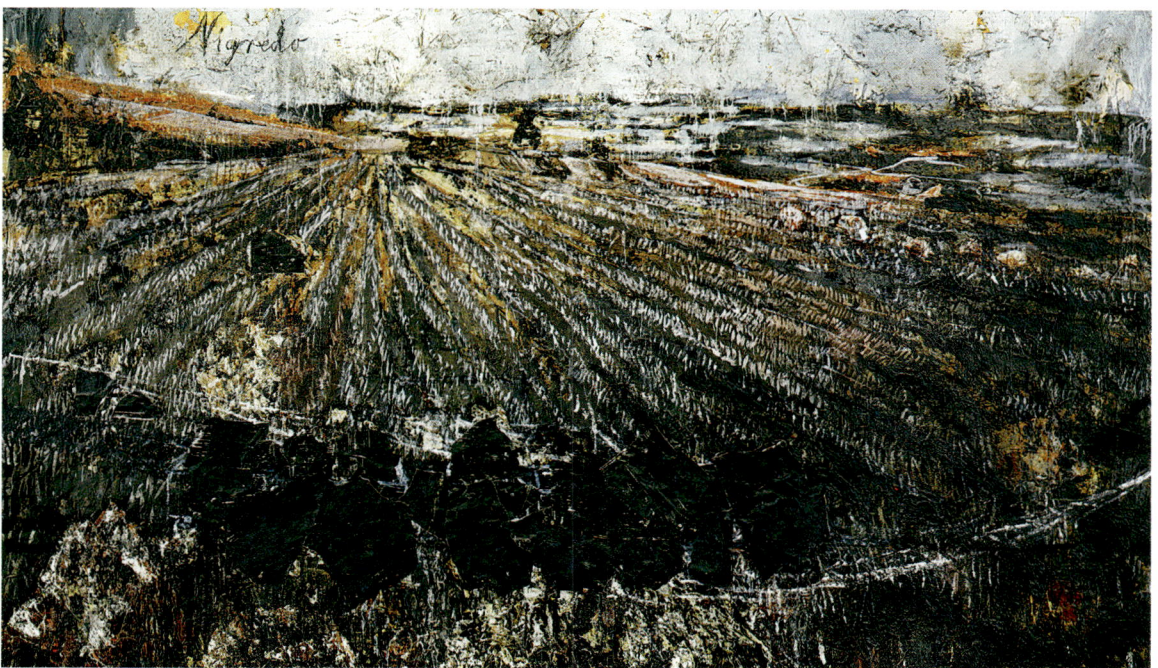

**31-21** ANSELM KIEFER, *Nigredo*, 1984. Oil paint on photosensitized fabric, acrylic emulsion, straw, shellac, relief paint on paper pulled from painted wood, 11′ × 18′. Philadelphia Museum of Art, Philadelphia (gift of Friends of the Philadelphia Museum of Art).

Kiefer's paintings have thickly encrusted surfaces incorporating materials such as straw. Here, the German artist used perspective to pull the viewer into an incinerated landscape alluding to the Holocaust.

1 ft.

Other Movements and Themes **955**

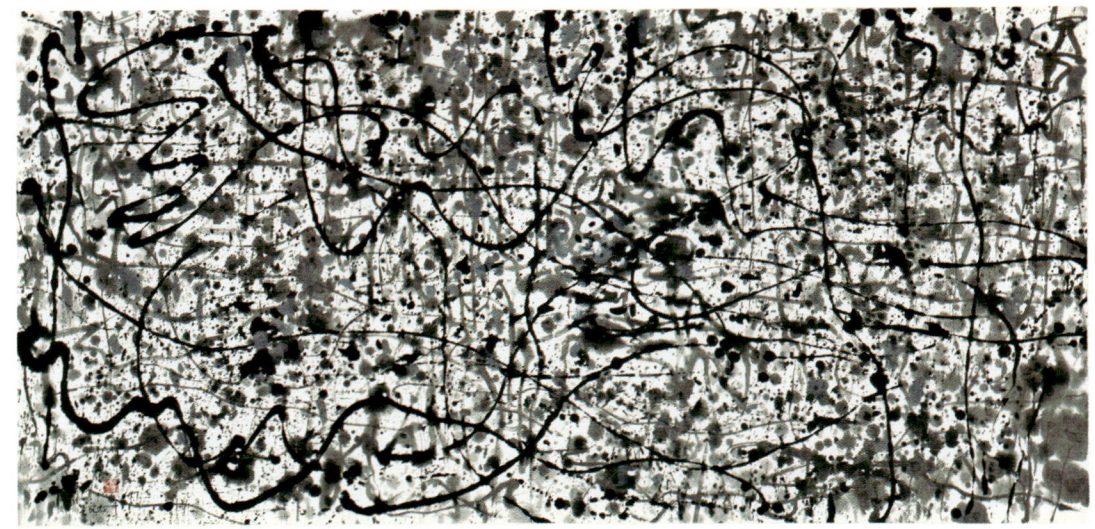

**31-22** Wu Guanzhong, *Wild Vines with Flowers Like Pearls*, 1997. Ink on paper, 2′ 11½″ × 5′ 11″. Singapore Art Museum, Singapore (donation from Wu Guanzhong).

In a brilliant fusion of traditional Chinese subject matter and technique with modern Western Abstract Expressionism, Wu depicted the wild vines of the Yangtze River valley.

**WU GUANZHONG** Abstraction is a still-vital pictorial mode in Asia, where the most innovative artists working in the Neo-Expressionist mode have merged Western and Eastern traditions in their work. WU GUANZHONG (1919–2010) attended the National Art College in Hangzhou, graduating in 1942, and then studied painting in Paris at the École Nationale Supérieure des Beaux-Arts from 1946 to 1950, when he returned to China to take up teaching positions at several prestigious art academies. His early work, reflecting his exposure to the Western tradition, was primarily oil painting on canvas, but in the 1970s he began to embrace the traditional Chinese medium of ink and color on paper, later often restricting his palette only to ink. His mature work, for example, *Wild Vines with Flowers Like Pearls* (FIG. **31-22**), painted in 1997, combines the favored medium and subject matter of the centuries-old *literati* tradition—the 17th-century paintings of Shitao (FIG. 33-15) were important forerunners—with an abstract style strongly influenced by Pollock. American Abstract Expressionist painting was politically impossible to pursue during the Cultural Revolution, when Wu, like Xu Bing (FIG. 31-18), was sentenced to labor on a rural farm because of his refusal to conform to official doctrine.

The inspiration for *Wild Vines,* as for so many of Wu's paintings, was the mountainous landscape and forests of the Yangtze River. The free composition and bold thick brushstrokes brilliantly balance abstract, sweeping, crisscrossing lines with the suggestive shapes of vines and flowers. His work, like that of SONG SU-NAM (b. 1938; FIG. **31-22A**) in Korea and EMILY KAME KNGWARREYE (1910–1996; FIG. **31-22B**) in Australia, represents a highly successful fusion of traditional local and modern Western style and subject matter.

**31-22A** SONG, *Summer Trees,* 1983.

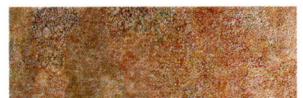

**31-22B** KNGWARREYE, *Untitled,* 1992.

**KIMIO TSUCHIYA** In contemporary Japan, as in China, no single artistic style, medium, or subject dominates, but much of the art produced during the past few decades springs from ideas or beliefs integral to the national culture over many centuries. For example, the Shinto belief in the generative forces in nature and in humankind's position as part of the totality of nature (see "Shinto," Chapter 17, page 479) holds great appeal for contemporary artists such as KIMIO TSUCHIYA (b. 1955), who studied sculpture in London and Tokyo. Tsuchiya is best known for his large-scale sculptures (FIG. **31-23**) constructed of branches or driftwood. Despite their abstract nature, his works assert the life forces found in natural materials, thereby engaging viewers in a consideration of their

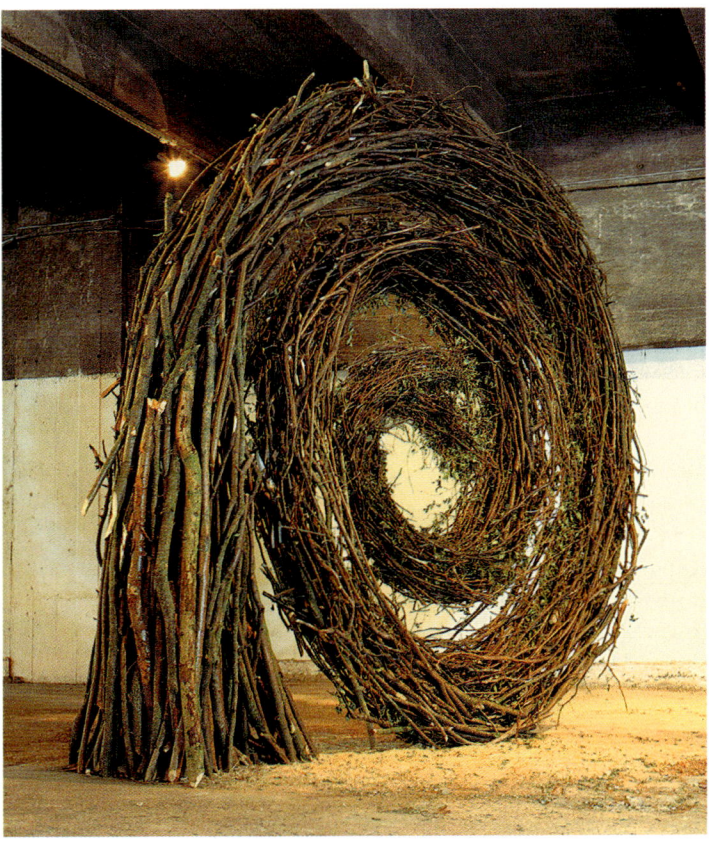

**31-23** KIMIO TSUCHIYA, *Symptom*, 1987. Branches, 13′ 1½″ × 14′ 9⅛″ × 3′ 11¼″. Installation at the exhibition *Jeune Sculpture '87,* Paris 1987.

Tsuchiya's sculptures consist of branches or driftwood, and despite their abstract nature, they assert the life forces found in natural materials. His approach to sculpture reflects ancient Shinto beliefs.

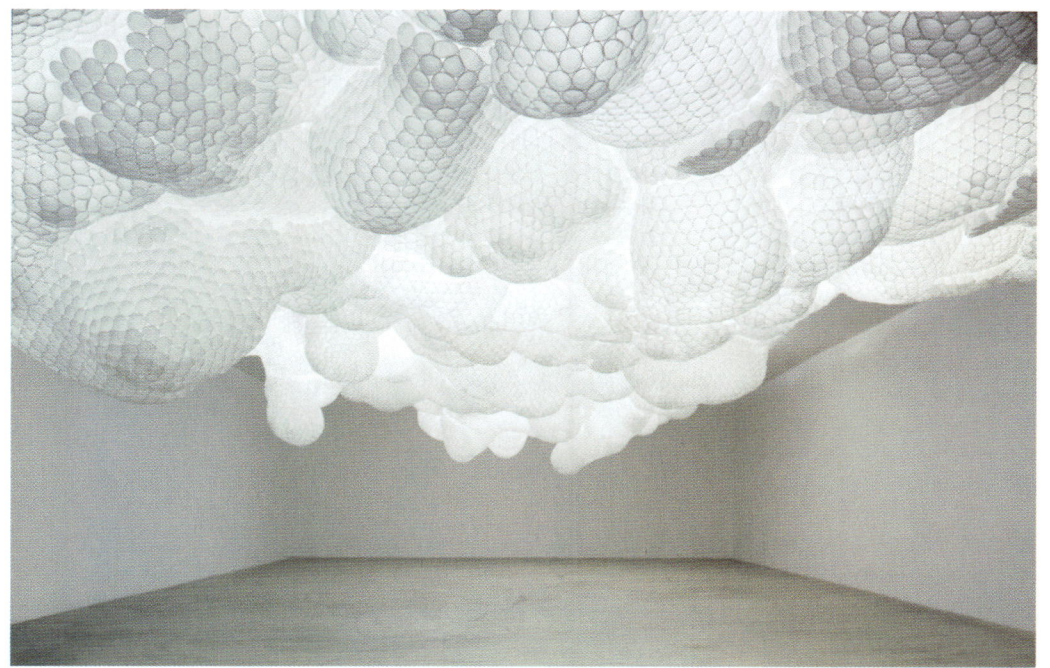

of Egon Schiele (FIG. 29-10), despite the vivid contrast between Schiele's emaciated body and Saville's obesity.

Saville's paintings are a commentary on the contemporary obsession with the lithe bodies of fashion models. In *Branded* (FIG. 31-25), she underscores the dichotomy between the popular notion of a beautiful body and the imperfect bodies of most people by "branding" her body with words inscribed in her flesh—*delicate, decorative, petite*. Art critic Michelle Meagher has described Saville's paintings as embodying a "feminist aesthetics of disgust."[4]

own relationship to nature. Tsuchiya does not specifically invoke Shinto when speaking about his art, but it is clear he has internalized Shinto principles. He identifies as his goal "to bring out and present the life of nature emanating from this energy of trees. . . . It is as though the wood is part of myself, as though the wood has the same kind of life force."[3]

**TARA DONOVAN** Brooklynite TARA DONOVAN (b. 1969) studied at the School of Visual Arts in New York City, the Corcoran College of Art and Design in Washington, D.C., and Virginia Commonwealth University in Richmond. She was the first recipient (in 2005) of the Alexander Calder Foundation's Calder Prize for sculpture. Donovan has won an international reputation for her installations (FIG. 31-24) of large sculptural works composed of thousands of small everyday objects, such as toothpicks, straws, pins, paper plates, plastic cups, and electrical wire. Her abstract sculptures often suggest rolling landscapes, clouds, fungus, and other natural forms, although she seeks in her work not to mimic those forms but to capture nature's dynamic growth. Some of Donovan's installations are unstable and can change shape during the course of an exhibition.

## Figural Painting and Sculpture

Recent decades have brought a revival of interest in figural art, both in painting and sculpture, a trend best exemplified in the earlier postwar period by Lucian Freud (FIG. 30-29), who remains an active and influential painter.

**JENNY SAVILLE** Fellow Briton JENNY SAVILLE (b. 1970) is the leading figure painter in the Freud mold of the younger generation of European and American artists. Born in Cambridge, England, and trained at the Glasgow School of Art in Scotland, Saville lives and paints in an old palace in Palermo, Italy. Her best-known works are over-life-size self-portraits in which she exaggerates the girth of her body and delights in depicting heavy folds of flesh with visible veins in minute detail and from a sharply foreshortened angle, which further distorts the body's proportions. Her nude self-portraits deserve comparison not only with those of Freud but also

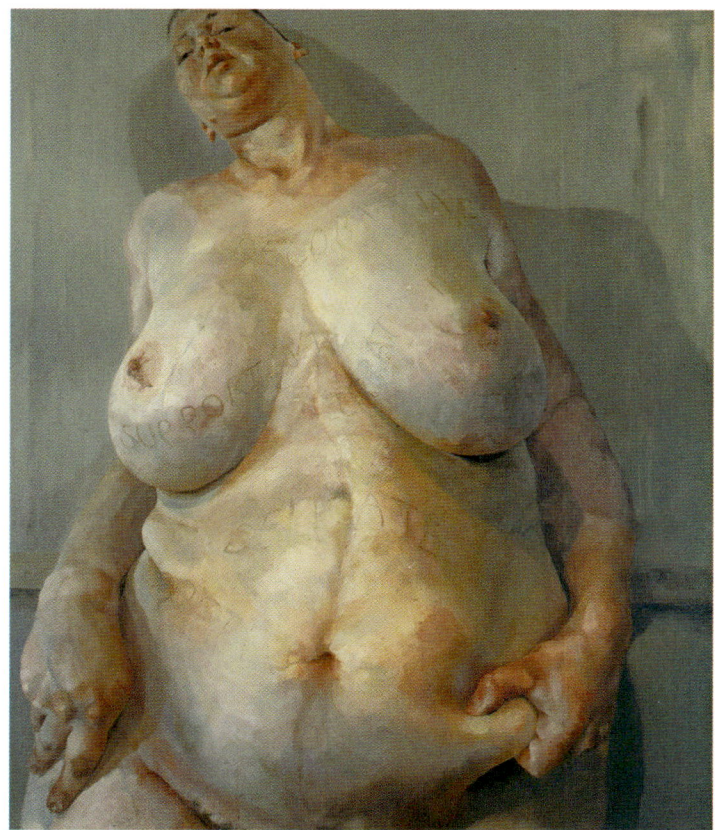

1 ft.

31-25 JENNY SAVILLE, *Branded*, 1992. Oil on canvas, 7' × 6'. Charles Saatchi Collection, London.

**KIKI SMITH** A distinctly unflattering approach to the representation of the human body is also the hallmark of New York–based KIKI SMITH (b. 1954), the daughter of Minimalist sculptor Tony Smith (FIG. 30-17). In her work, Smith has explored the question of who controls the human body, an interest that grew out of her training as an emergency medical service technician. Smith, however, also wants to reveal the socially constructed nature of the body, and she encourages the viewer to consider how external forces shape people's perceptions of their bodies. In works such as *Untitled* (FIG. **31-26**), the artist dramatically departed from conventional representations of the body, both in art and in the media. She suspended two life-size wax figures, one male and one female, both nude, from metal stands. Smith marked each of the sculptures with long white drips—body fluids running from the woman's breasts and down the man's leg. She commented:

> Most of the functions of the body are hidden . . . from society. . . . [W]e separate our bodies from our lives. But, when people are

dying, they are losing control of their bodies. That loss of function can seem humiliating and frightening. But, on the other hand, you can look at it as a kind of liberation of the body. It seems like a nice metaphor—a way to think about the social—that people lose control despite the many agendas of different ideologies in society, which are trying to control the body(ies) . . . medicine, religion, law, etc. Just thinking about control—who has control of the body? . . . Does the mind have control of the body? Does the social?[5]

**JEFF KOONS** The sculptures of JEFF KOONS (b. 1955) form a striking counterpoint to the figural art of Kiki Smith. Trained at the Maryland Institute College of Art in Baltimore, Koons worked early in his career as a commodities broker. He first became prominent in the art world for a series of works in the early 1980s involving the exhibition of everyday commercial products such as vacuum cleaners. Clearly following in the footsteps of Marcel Duchamp (FIG. 29-27), Koons made no attempt to manipulate or

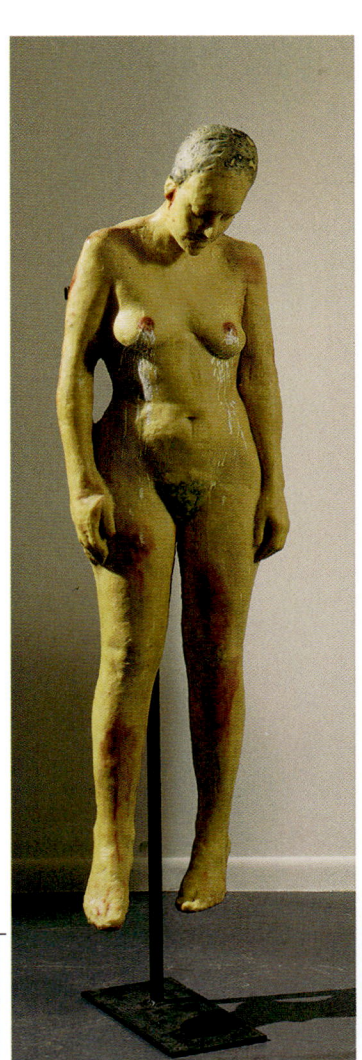
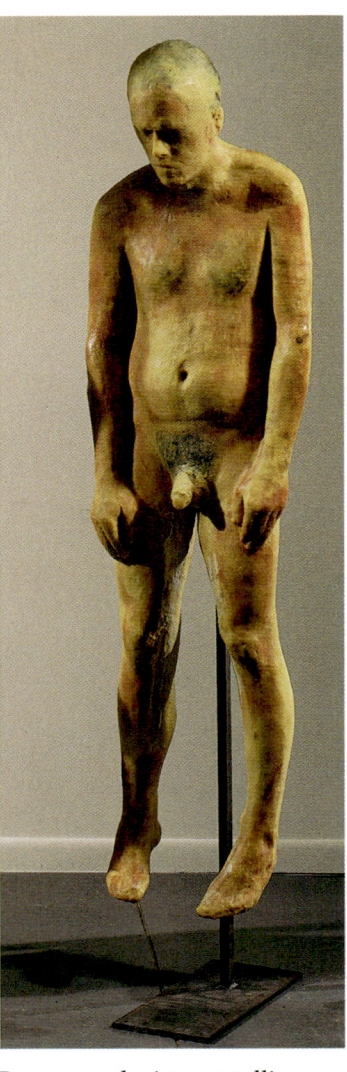

1 ft.

**31-26** KIKI SMITH, *Untitled*, 1990. Beeswax and microcrystalline wax figures on metal stands, female figure installed height 6′ 1½″ and male figure installed height 6′ 5″. Whitney Museum of American Art, New York (purchased with funds from the Painting and Sculpture Committee).

Asking "Who controls the body?" Kiki Smith sculpted two life-size wax figures of a nude man and woman with body fluids running from the woman's breasts and down the man's leg.

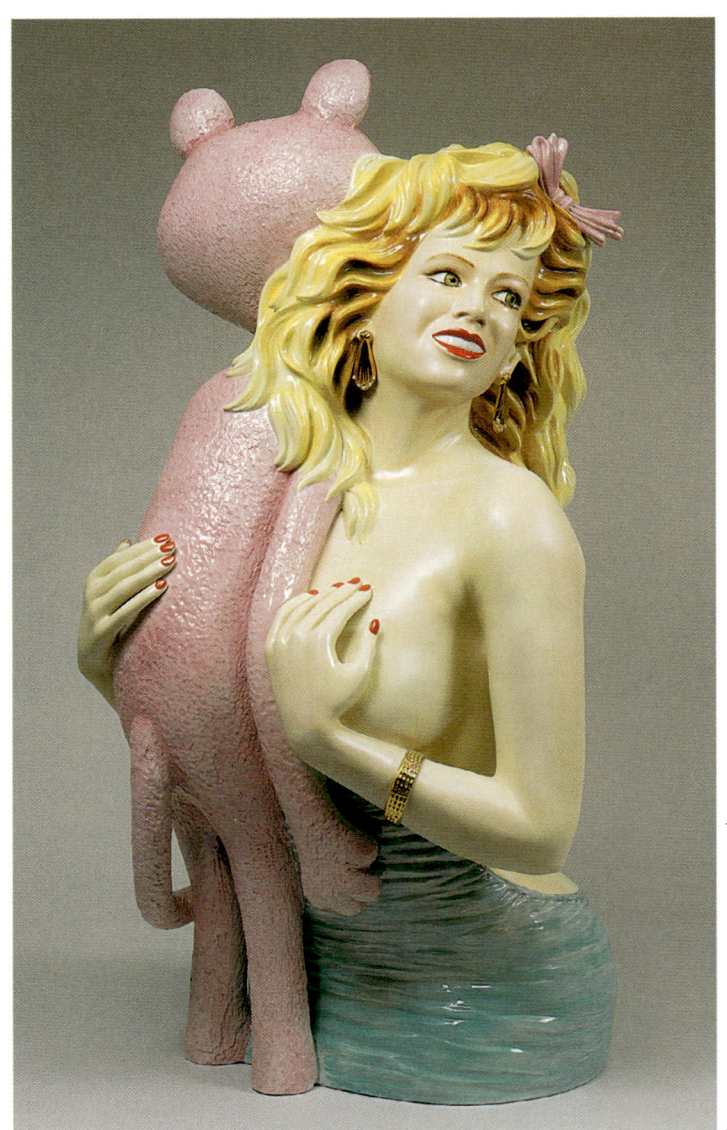

1 ft.

**31-27** JEFF KOONS, *Pink Panther*, 1988. Porcelain, 3′ 5″ high. Museum of Contemporary Art, Chicago (Gerald S. Elliot Collection). ◼◀

Koons creates sculptures highlighting everything he considers wrong with contemporary American consumer culture. In this work, he intertwined a centerfold nude and a cartoon character.

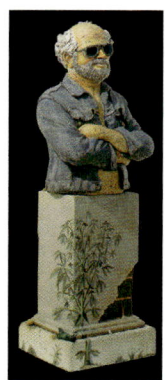

alter the machine-made objects. More recently, he, like Californian ROBERT ARNESON (1930– 1992; FIG. **31-27A**), turned to ceramic sculpture. In *Pink Panther* (FIG. **31-27**), Koons, who divides his time between his hometown of York, Pennsylvania, and New York City, intertwined a magazine centerfold nude with a famous cartoon character. He reinforced the trite and kitschy nature of this imagery by titling the exhibition of which this work was a part *The Banality Show.* Some art critics have argued Koons and his work instruct viewers because both artist and artwork serve as the most visible symbols of everything wrong with contemporary American society. Regardless of whether this is true, Koons's prominence in the art world indicates he has developed an acute understanding of the dynamics of consumer culture.

**MARISOL ESCOBAR** Known simply by her first name, MARISOL ESCOBAR (b. 1930) grew up in a wealthy, widely traveled Venezuelan family. Born in Paris and educated there, in Los Angeles, and in New York City, Marisol first studied painting and drawing, but after discovering Pre-Columbian art in 1951, she pursued a career as a sculptor. Marisol also spent time in Italy, where she developed a deep admiration for Renaissance art.

In the 1960s, Marisol was one of the inner circle of New York Pop artists, and she appeared in two of Andy Warhol's films. Some of her works at that time portrayed prominent public figures, including the Hollywood actor John Wayne and the family of U.S. president John F. Kennedy. Her subjects were always people, however, not the commercial products of consumer culture that fascinated most leading Pop artists and still are prominent in the art of Jeff Koons and others.

Marisol retained her interest in figural sculpture long after Pop Art gave way to other movements. One of her most ambitious works (FIG. **31-28**) is a multimedia three-dimensional version of Leonardo da Vinci's *Last Supper* (FIG. 22-4), including the walls and windows of the dining room in order to replicate the Renaissance master's application of linear perspective. By reproducing the fresco in three dimensions, she transformed it into an object. Marisol's figures are painted wood, with the exception of Christ, whose stone body is the physical and emotional anchor of the composition. In many of her sculptures, the female figures have Marisol's features, and in this tableau she added a seated armless portrait of herself looking at the *Last Supper.* Catholic and deeply religious—as a teenager she emulated martyr saints by inflicting physical harm on herself—Marisol may have wanted to show herself as a witness to Christ's last meal. But more likely her presence here is a tribute to the 16th-century painter. (She also made a sculptural replica of Leonardo's *Madonna and Child with Saint Anne* [FIG. 22-3].)

Marisol's *Self-Portrait Looking at the Last Supper* is a commentary on the artist not only as a creator but also as a viewer of the works of earlier artists, a link in an artistic chain extending back to antiquity. One pervasive element in the work

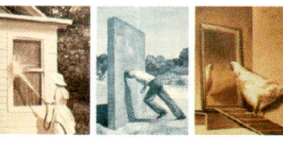

of contemporary artists is a self-consciousness of the postmodern painter or sculptor's position in the continuum of art history. No one better exemplifies that aspect of contemporary art than MARK TANSEY (b. 1949; FIG. **31-28A**).

**KANE KWEI AND PAA JOE** Painted wood sculpture remains a vital artistic medium in Africa, where it has a venerable heritage throughout the continent (see Chapters 19 and 37). Some contemporary African artists have pioneered new forms, however,

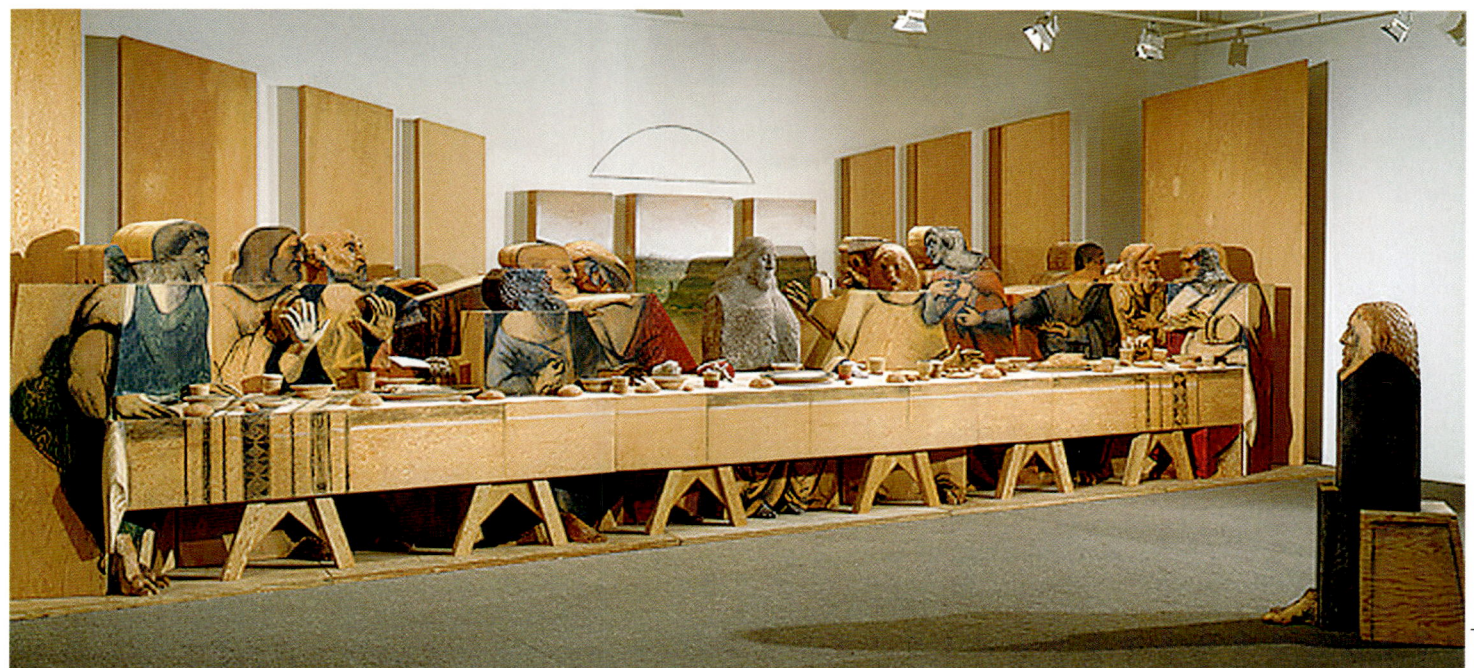

**31-28** MARISOL ESCOBAR, *Self-Portrait Looking at the Last Supper,* 1982–1984. Painted wood, stone, plaster, and aluminum, 10′ 1½″ × 29′ 10″ × 5′ 1″. Metropolitan Museum of Art, New York (gift of Mr. and Mrs. Roberto C. Polo, 1986).

In a tribute to the Renaissance master, Marisol created a sculptural replica of Leonardo's *Last Supper* (FIG. 22-4), transforming the fresco into an object. She is the seated viewer as well as the artist.

1 ft.

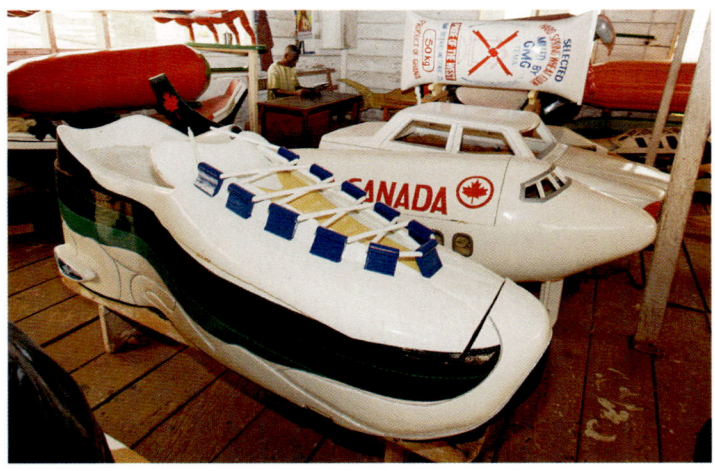

**31-29** PAA JOE, running shoe, airplane, automobile and other coffins inside the artist's showroom in Teshi, Ghana, 2000. Painted wood.

The caskets of Paa Joe take many forms, including items of clothing, airplanes, and automobiles. The forms always relate to the deceased, but many collectors buy the caskets as art objects.

often under the influence of modern Western art movements. Kane Kwei (1922–1992) of the Ga people in urban coastal Ghana created a new kind of wooden casket that brought him both critical acclaim and commercial success. Beginning around 1970, Kwei, trained as a carpenter, created one-of-a-kind coffins crafted to reflect the deceased's life, occupation, or major accomplishments. On commission he made such diverse shapes as a cow, a whale, a bird, a Mercedes Benz, and various local food crops, such as onions and cocoa pods, all pieced together using nails and glue rather than carved. Kwei also created coffins in traditional African leaders' symbolic forms, such as an eagle, an elephant, a leopard, and a stool.

Kwei's sons and his cousin PAA JOE (b. 1944) have carried on his legacy. In a photograph (FIG. **31-29**) shot around 2000 outside Joe's showroom in Teshi, several large caskets are on display, including a running shoe, an airplane, and an automobile. Many of the coffins Kwei and Joe produced never served as burial containers. Collectors and curators purchased them for display in private homes, art galleries, and museums. The coffins' forms, derived from popular culture, strike a familiar chord in the Western world because they recall Pop Art sculptures (FIG. 30-26), which accounts in large part for the international appeal of Kwei and Joe's work.

# ARCHITECTURE AND SITE-SPECIFIC ART

The work of architects and Environmental artists today is as varied as that of contemporary painters and sculptors, but the common denominator in the diversity of contemporary architectural design and site-specific projects is the breaking down of national boundaries, with leading practitioners working in several countries and even on several continents, often simultaneously.

## Architecture

In the late 20th and early 21st century, one of the by-products of the globalization of the world's economy has been that leading architects have received commissions to design buildings far from their home bases. In the rapidly developing emerging markets of Asia, the Middle East, Africa, Latin America, and elsewhere, virtually every architect with an international reputation can list a recent building in Beijing or another urban center on his or her résumé.

**NORMAN FOSTER** Award-winning architect NORMAN FOSTER (b. 1935) began his study of architectural design at the University of Manchester, England. After graduating, he won a fellowship to attend the master's degree program at the Yale School of Architecture, where he met Richard Rogers (FIG. 30-49). The two decided to open a joint architectural firm when they returned to London in 1962, but they established separate practices several years later. Their designs still have much in common, however,

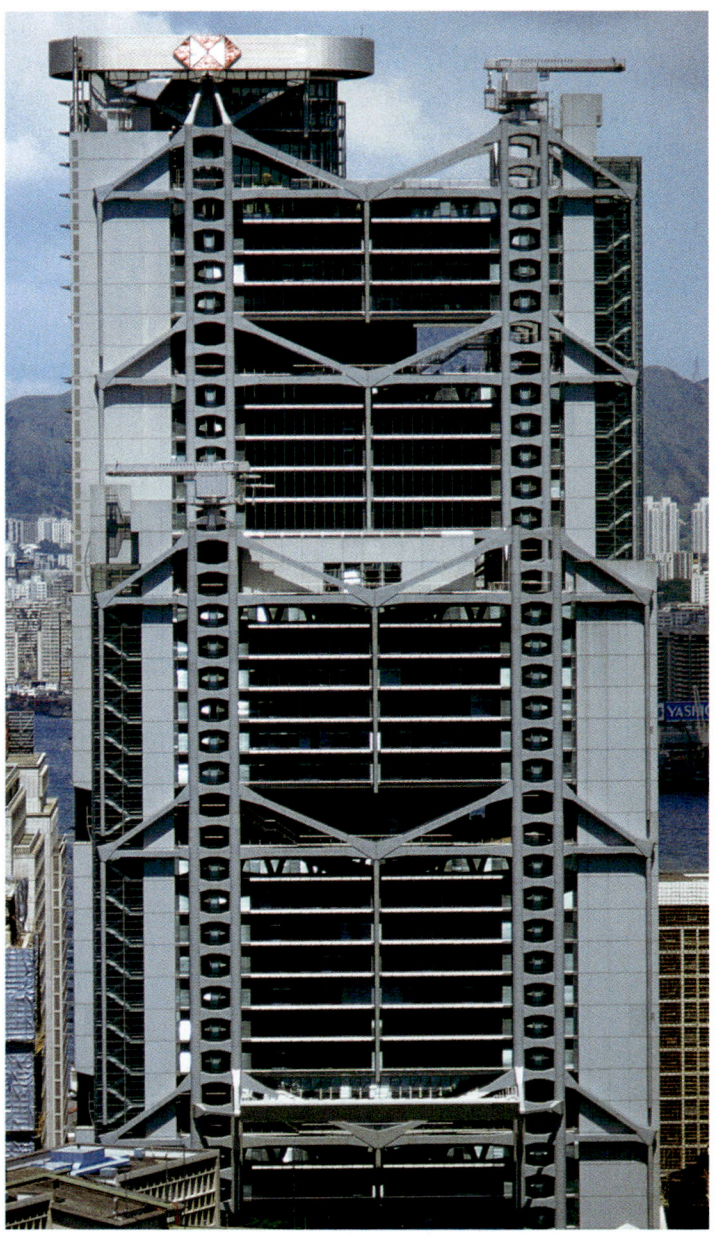

**31-30** NORMAN FOSTER, Hong Kong and Shanghai Bank (looking southwest), Hong Kong, China, 1979–1986.

Foster's High-Tech tower has an exposed steel skeleton featuring floors with uninterrupted working spaces. At the base is a 10-story atrium illuminated by computerized mirrors that reflect sunlight.

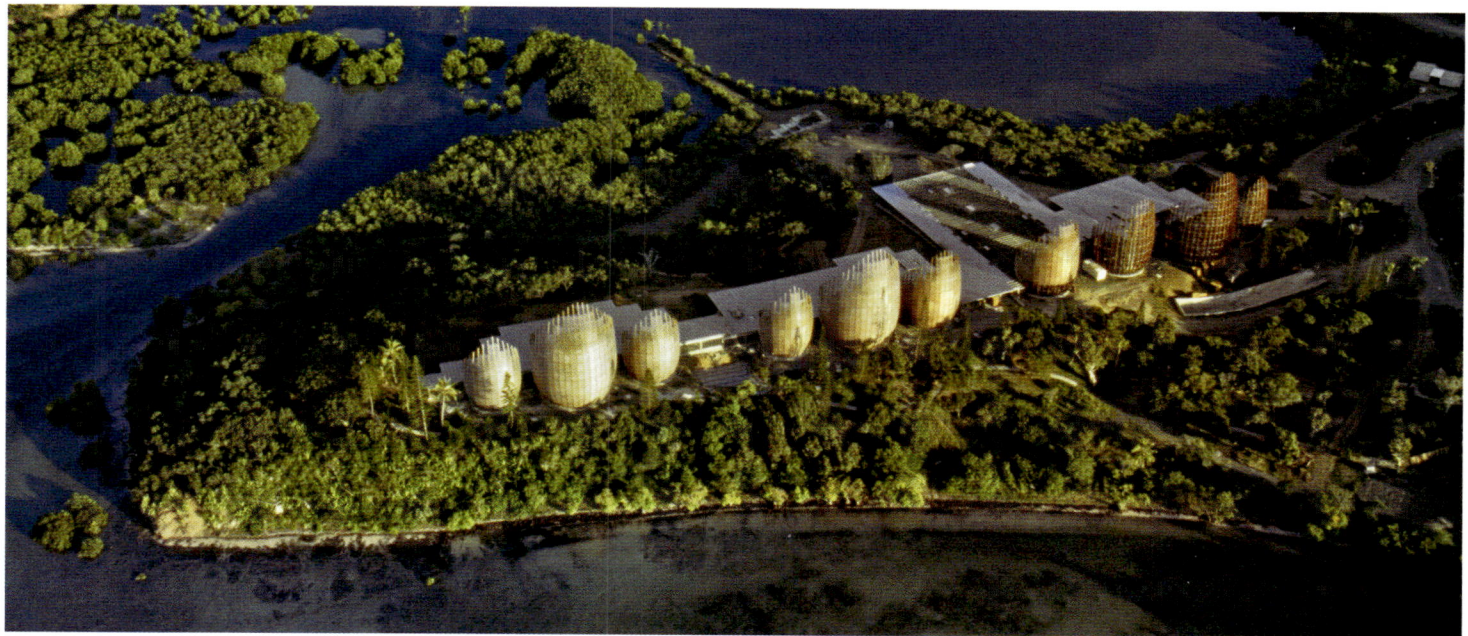

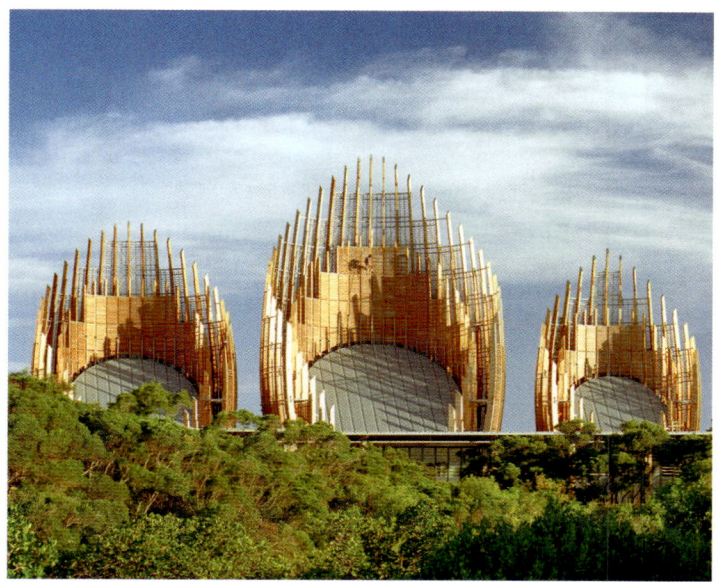

31-31 RENZO PIANO, aerial view (*top;* looking northwest) and three "huts" (*bottom;* looking southeast), Tjibaou Cultural Centre, Noumea, New Caledonia, 1998.

A pioneering example of "green architecture," Piano's complex of 10 bamboo units, based on traditional New Caledonian village huts, has adjustable skylights in the roofs for natural climate control.

because they share a similar outlook. Foster and Rogers are the leading proponents of what critics call *High-Tech* architecture, the roots of which can be traced to Joseph Paxton's mid-19th-century Crystal Palace (FIG. 27-47) in London. High-Tech architects design buildings incorporating the latest innovations in engineering and technology and exposing the structures' component parts. High-Tech architecture is distinct from other postmodern architectural movements in dispensing with all historical references.

Foster's design for the headquarters (FIG. **31-30**) of the Hong Kong and Shanghai Bank Corporation (HSBC), which cost $1 billion to build, exemplifies the High-Tech approach to architecture. The banking tower is as different from Philip Johnson's postmodern AT&T Building (FIG. 30-46) as it is from the modernist glass-and-steel Seagram Building (FIG. 30-43) and Sears Tower (FIG. 30-44). The 47-story Hong Kong skyscraper has an exposed steel skeleton with the elevators and other service elements located in giant piers at the short ends of the building, a design that provides uninterrupted communal working spaces on each cantilevered floor. Foster divided the tower into five horizontal units of six to nine floors

each that he calls "villages," suspended from steel girders resembling bridges. Escalators connect the floors in each village—the floors are related by function—but the elevators stop at only one floor in each community of floors. At the base of the building is a plaza opening onto the neighboring streets. Visitors ascend on escalators from the plaza to a spectacular 10-story, 170-feet-tall atrium bordered by balconies with additional workspaces. What Foster calls "sun scoops"—computerized mirrors on the south side of the building—track the movement of the sun across the Hong Kong sky and reflect the sunlight into the atrium and piazza, flooding the dramatic spaces with light at all hours of the day. Not surprisingly, the roof of this High-Tech skyscraper serves as a landing pad for corporate helicopters.

**GREEN ARCHITECTURE** The harnessing of solar energy as a power source is one of the key features of what critics commonly refer to as *green architecture*—ecologically friendly buildings that use "clean energy" and sustain the natural environment. Green architecture is the most important trend in architectural design in the early 21st century. A pioneer in this field is Renzo Piano, the codesigner with Richard Rogers of the Pompidou Center (FIG. 30-49) in Paris. Piano won an international competition to design the Tjibaou Cultural Centre (FIG. **31-31**, *left*) in Noumea, New Caledonia. Named in honor of the assassinated political leader Jean-Marie Tjibaou (1936–1989), the center consists of 10 beehive-shaped bamboo "huts" nestled in pine trees on a narrow island peninsula in the Pacific Ocean. Rooted in the village architecture of the Kanak people of New Caledonia (see Chapter 36), each unit of Piano's postmodern complex has an adjustable skylight as a roof (FIG. 31-31, *right*) to provide natural—sustainable—climate control. The curved profile of the Tjibaou pavilions also helps the structures withstand the pressure of the hurricane-force winds common in the South Pacific.

Architecture and Site-Specific Art **961**

The roof, walls, and windows of the Deconstructivist Hysolar Institute seem to explode, avoiding any suggestion of stable masses and frustrating viewers' expectations of how a building should look.

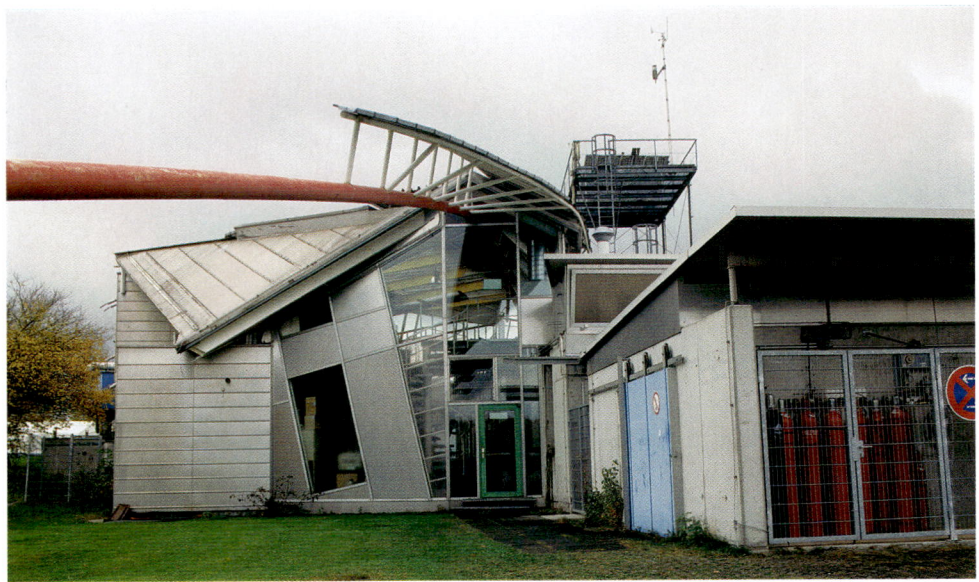

## DECONSTRUCTIVISM

In architecture, as in painting and sculpture, deconstruction as an analytical and design strategy emerged in the 1970s. The name given to this postmodern architectural movement is *Deconstructivism*. Deconstructivist architects attempt to disrupt the conventional categories of architecture and to rupture the viewer's expectations based on them. Destabilization plays a major role in Deconstructivist architecture. Disorder, dissonance, imbalance, asymmetry, irregularity, and unconformity replace their opposites—order, harmony, balance, symmetry, regularity, and clarity. The seemingly haphazardly presented volumes, masses, planes, borders, lighting, locations, directions, spatial relations, as well as the disguised structural facts of Deconstructivist design, challenge the viewer's assumptions about architectural form as it relates to function. According to Deconstructivist principles, the very absence of the stability of traditional categories of architecture in a structure announces a "deconstructed" building.

## GÜNTER BEHNISCH

Audacious in its dissolution of form is the Hysolar Institute (FIG. 31-32) at the University of Stuttgart, Germany, by GÜNTER BEHNISCH (1922–2010). Behnisch, who gained international attention as the architect of the Olympic Park in Munich for the 1972 Olympic Games, designed the institute as part of a joint German–Saudi Arabian research project on the technology of solar energy. In the Hysolar Institute, Behnisch intended to deny the possibility of spatial enclosure altogether, and his apparently chaotic arrangement of the structural units defies easy analysis. The shapes of the roof, walls, and windows seem to explode, avoiding any suggestion of clear, stable masses. Behnisch aggressively played with the traditional concepts of architectural design. The disordered architectural elements of the Hysolar Institute seem precarious and visually threaten to collapse, frustrating the viewer's expectations of how a building should look.

## FRANK GEHRY

The architect most closely identified with Deconstructivist architecture is Canadian FRANK GEHRY (b. 1929). Trained in sculpture, and at different times a collaborator with Donald Judd (FIG. 30-18) and Claes Oldenburg (FIG. 30-26), Gehry works up his designs by constructing models and then cutting them up and arranging the parts until he has a satisfying composition. Among Gehry's most notable projects is the Guggenheim Museum (FIGS. 31-33 and 31-34) in Bilbao, Spain, one

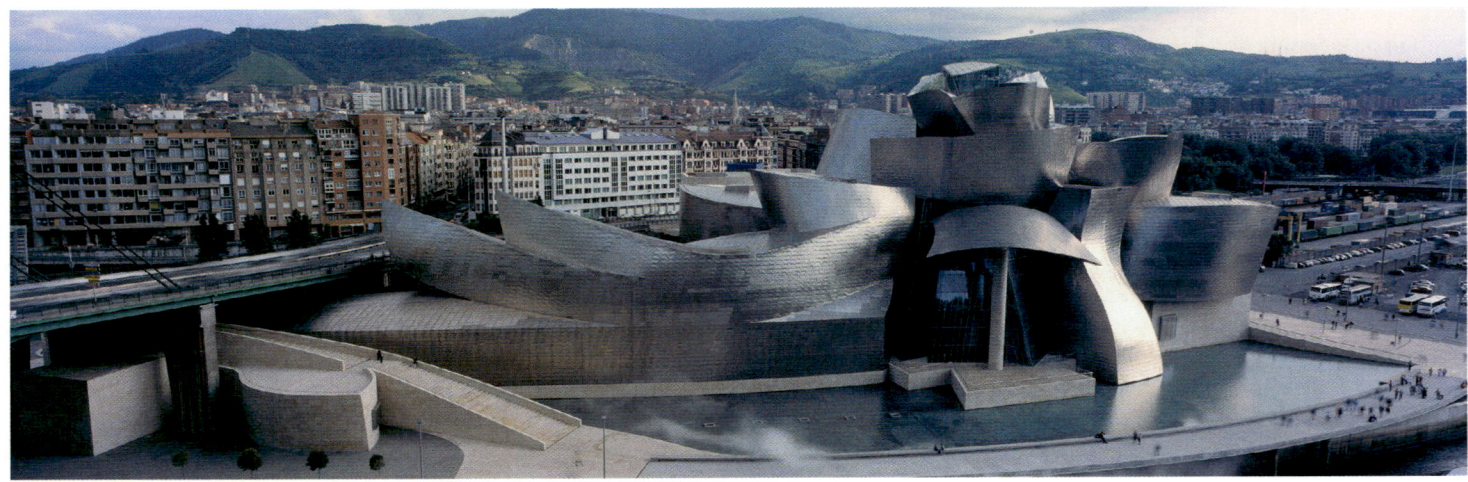

31-33 FRANK GEHRY, Guggenheim Bilbao Museo (looking south), Bilbao, Spain, 1997.

Gehry's limestone-and-titanium Bilbao museum is an immensely dramatic building. Its disorder and seeming randomness of design epitomize Deconstructivist architectural principles.

# Frank Gehry on Architectural Design and Materials

Frank Gehry has been designing buildings since the 1950s, but only in the 1970s did he begin to break away from the rectilinearity of modernist architecture and develop the dramatic sculptural style seen in buildings such as the Guggenheim Museum (FIGS. 31-33 and 31-34) in Bilbao. In 1999, the Deconstructivist architect reflected on his career and his many projects in a book simply titled *Gehry Talks*.

> My early work was rectilinear because you take baby steps. I guess the work has become a kind of sculpture as architecture. . . . I'm a strict modernist in the sense of believing in purity, that you shouldn't decorate. And yet buildings need decoration, because they need scaling elements. They need to be human scale, in my opinion. They can't just be faceless things. That's how some modernism failed.*
>
> They teach materials and methods in architecture school, as a separate course. I'm a craftsman. . . . It seems to me that when you're doing architecture, you're building something out of something. There are social issues, there's context, and then there's how do you make the enclosure and what do you make it with? . . . I explored metal: how it dealt with the light . . . It does beautiful things with light. . . . Flat was a fetish, and everybody was doing that. I found out that I could use metal if I didn't worry about it being flat; I could do it cheaper. It was intuitive. I just went with it. I liked it. Then when I saw it on the building, I loved it. . . . Bilbao . . . [is] titanium. . . . [I] prefer titanium because it's stronger; it's an element, a pure element, and it doesn't oxidize. It stays the same forever. They give a hundred-year guarantee!†

*Milton Friedman, ed., *Gehry Talks: Architecture + Process*, rev. ed. (New York: Universe, 2002), 47–48.
†Ibid., 44, 47.

**31-34 FRANK GEHRY, atrium of the Guggenheim Bilbao Museo, Bilbao, Spain, 1997.**

The glass-walled atrium of the Guggenheim Bilbao Museum soars skyward 165 feet. The asymmetrical and imbalanced screens and vaults flow into one another, creating a sense of disequilibrium.

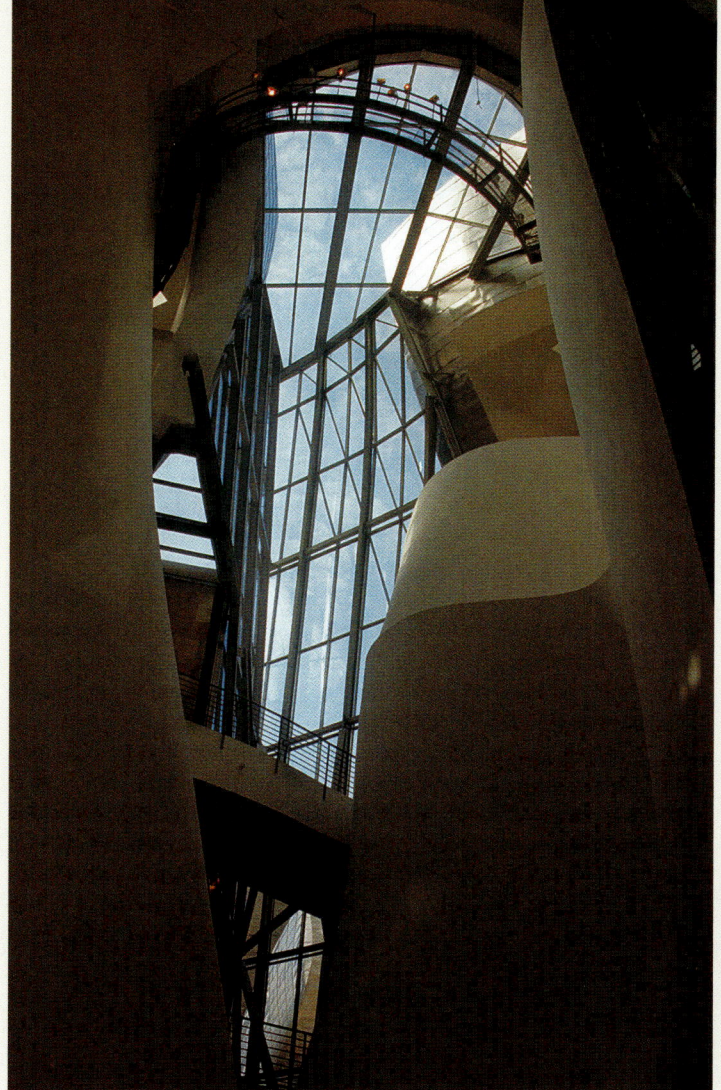

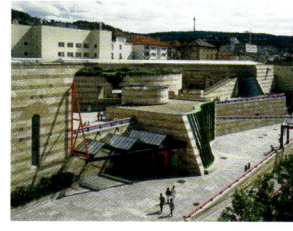

**31-34A** STIRLING, Neue Staatsgalerie, Stuttgart, 1977–1983.

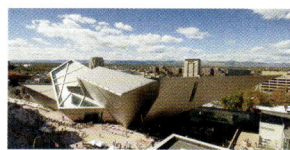

**31-34B** LIBESKIND, Denver Art Museum, 2006.

of several art museum projects of the past few decades as notable for their innovative postmodern architectural designs as for the important art collections they house. These include the Neue Staatsgalerie (FIG. **31-34A**) in Stuttgart, Germany, by British architect JAMES STIRLING (1926–1994); the Denver Art Museum (FIG. **31-34B**) by Polish-born DANIEL LIBESKIND (b. 1946); and the Grande Louvre Pyramide (FIG. 31-36) in Paris.

Gehry's Bilbao museum appears to be a collapsed or collapsing aggregate of units. Visitors approaching the building see a mass of irregular asymmetrical and imbalanced forms whose profiles change dramatically with every shift of the viewer's position. The limestone- and titanium-clad exterior lends a space-age character to the structure and highlights further the unique cluster effect of the many forms (see "Frank Gehry on Architectural Design and Materials," above). A group of organic forms Gehry refers to as a "metallic flower" tops the museum. In the center of the museum, an enormous glass-walled atrium (FIG. 31-34) soars 165 feet above the ground, serving as the focal point for the three levels of galleries radiating from it. The seemingly weightless screens, vaults, and volumes of the interior float and flow into one another, guided only by light and dark cues. The Guggenheim Museum in Bilbao is a profoundly compelling structure. Its disorder, its deceptive randomness of design, and the disequilibrium it prompts in viewers epitomize Deconstructivist principles.

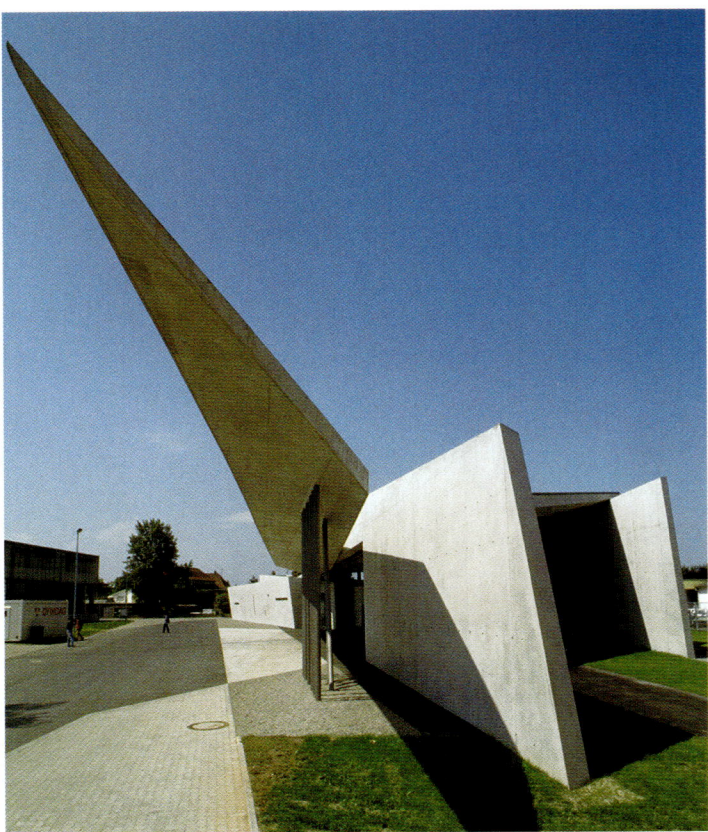

**31-35** ZAHA HADID, **Vitra Fire Station (looking east), Weil-am-Rhein, Germany, 1989–1993.**

Inspired by Suprematism, Hadid employed dynamically arranged, unadorned planes for the Vitra Fire Station. The design suggests the burst of energy of firefighters racing out to extinguish a blaze.

**ZAHA HADID** One of the most innovative living architects is Iraqi Deconstructivist ZAHA HADID (b. 1950). Born in Baghdad, Hadid studied mathematics in Beirut, Lebanon, and architecture in London and has designed buildings in England, Germany, Austria, France, Italy, Spain, and the United States. Deeply influenced by the Suprematist theories and paintings of Kazimir Malevich (FIG. 29-30), who championed the use of pure colors and abstract geometric shapes to express "the supremacy of pure feeling in creative art," Hadid employs unadorned planes in dynamic arrangements that

have an emotional effect upon the viewer. A prime example of her work is the Vitra Fire Station (FIG. **31-35**) in Weil-am-Rhein, Germany, completed in 1993. Composed of layers of reinforced concrete slabs and unframed window panes, the building features a boldly projecting (functionless) "wing" that suggests a burst of energy shooting out from the structure. It expresses the sudden mobilization of the firefighters within the time the alarm sounds and the time they jump into their trucks to race out to extinguish a blaze.

Zaha Hadid is the first woman to win the Pritzker Architecture Prize (in 2004), the architectural equivalent of the Nobel Prize in literature. The first recipient was Philip Johnson in 1979. Other previous winners include Norman Foster, Frank Gehry, Renzo Piano, James Stirling, Joern Utzon, Robert Venturi, and Ieoh Ming Pei.

**IEOH MING PEI** The latest chapter in the long architectural history of the Louvre—the former French royal residence (FIGS. 20-16, 23-14, and 25-25), now one of the world's greatest art museums—is a monumental glass-and-steel pyramid erected in the palace's main courtyard in 1988. Designed by the Chinese-American architect IEOH MING PEI (b. 1917), the Grand Louvre Pyramide (FIG. **31-36**) is the dramatic postmodern entryway to the museum's priceless collections. Although initially controversial because conservative critics considered it a jarring, dissonant intrusion in a hallowed public space left untouched for centuries, Pei's pyramid, like Rogers and Piano's Pompidou Center (FIG. 30-49) a decade before, quickly captured the French public's imagination and admiration.

There are, in fact, four Louvre glass pyramids: the grand central pyramid plus the three small echoes of it bordering the large fountain-filled pool surrounding the glass entryway. Consistent with postmodern aesthetics, Pei turned to the past for inspiration, choosing the quintessential emblem of ancient Egypt (FIG. 3-7), an appropriate choice given the Louvre's rich collection of Egyptian art. But Pei transformed his ancient solid stone models (see "Building the Great Pyramids," Chapter 3, page 62) into a transparent "tent," simultaneously permitting an almost uninterrupted view of the wings of the royal palace courtyard and serving as a skylight for the new underground network of ticket booths, offices, shops, restaurants, and conference rooms he also designed.

## Environmental and Site-Specific Art

When Robert Smithson created *Spiral Jetty* (FIG. 30-50) in Utah's Great Salt Lake in 1970, he was a trailblazer in the new genre of Environmental Art, or earthworks. In recent decades, earthworks

**31-36** IEOH MING PEI, **Grand Louvre Pyramide (looking southwest), Musée du Louvre, Paris, France, 1988.**

Egyptian stone architecture inspired Pei's postmodern entryway to the Louvre, but his glass-and-steel pyramid is a transparent tent serving as a skylight for the underground extension of the old museum.

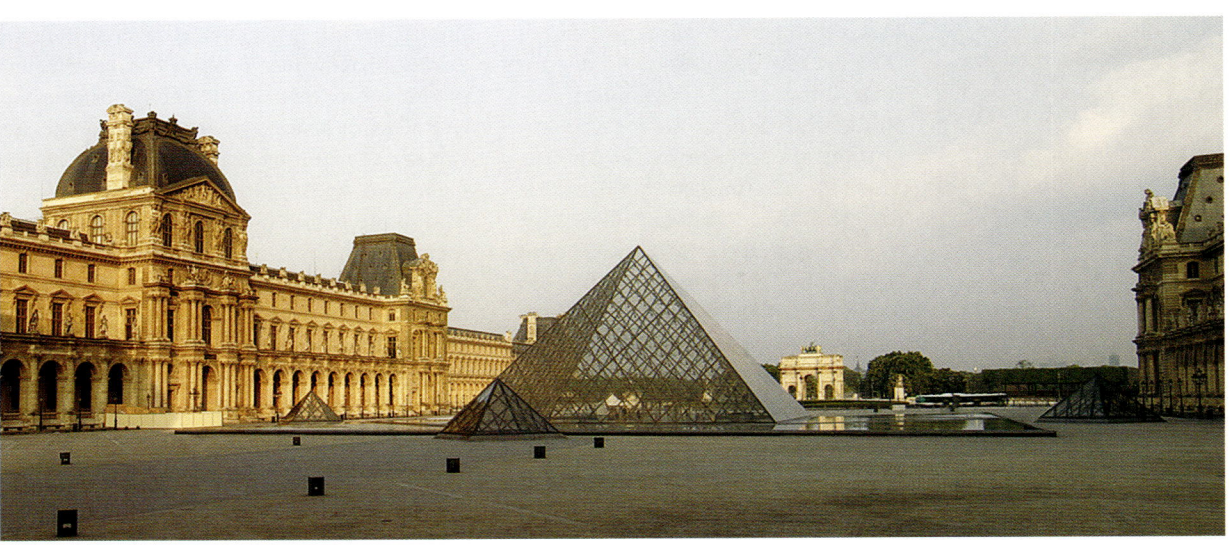

## Maya Lin's Vietnam Veterans Memorial

Maya Lin's design for the Vietnam Veterans Memorial (FIG. 31-37) is, like Minimalist sculptures (FIGS. 30-17 and 30-18), an unadorned geometric form. Yet the monument, despite its serene simplicity, actively engages viewers in a psychological dialogue, rather than standing mute. This dialogue gives visitors the opportunity to explore their feelings about the Vietnam War and perhaps arrive at some sense of closure.

The history of the Vietnam Veterans Memorial provides dramatic testimony to this monument's power. In 1981, a jury of architects, sculptors, and landscape architects selected Lin's design from among 1,400 entries in a blind competition for a memorial to be placed in Constitution Gardens in Washington, D.C. Conceivably, the jury not only found her design compelling but also thought its simplicity would be the least likely to provoke controversy. But when the jury made its selection public, heated debate ensued. Even the wall's color came under attack. One veteran charged that black is "the universal color of shame, sorrow and degradation in all races, all societies worldwide."* But the sharpest protests concerned the form and siting of the monument. Because of the stark contrast between the massive white memorials (the Washington Monument and the Lincoln Memorial) bracketing Lin's sunken wall, some people interpreted her Minimalist design as minimizing the Vietnam War and, by extension, the efforts of those who fought in the conflict. Lin herself, however, described the wall as follows:

> The Vietnam Veterans Memorial is not an object inserted into the earth but a work formed from the act of cutting open the earth and polishing the earth's surface—dematerializing the stone to pare surface, creating an interface between the world of the light and the quieter world beyond the names.[†]

Due to the vocal opposition, a compromise was necessary to ensure the memorial's completion. The Commission of Fine Arts, the federal group overseeing the project, commissioned an additional memorial from artist Frederick Hart (1943–1999) in 1983. This larger-than-life-size realistic bronze sculpture of three soldiers,

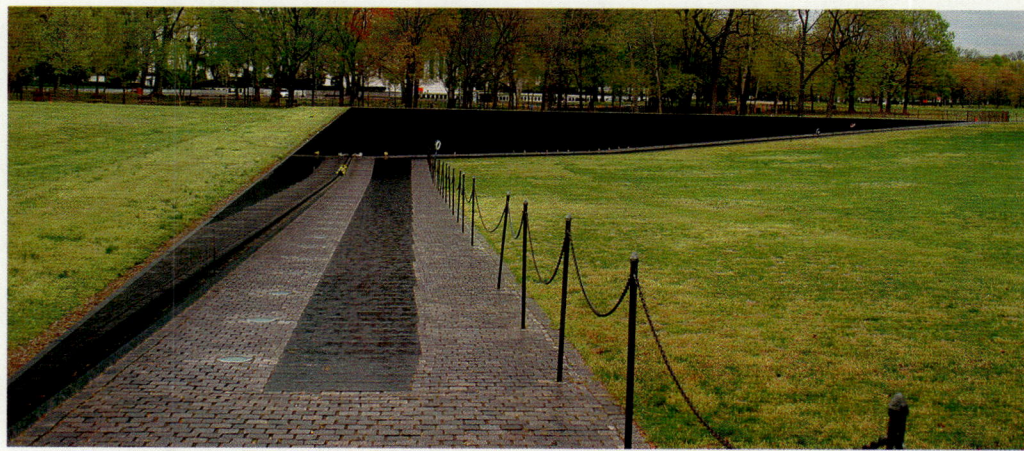

**31-37** MAYA YING LIN, Vietnam Veterans Memorial (looking north), Washington, D.C., 1981–1983.

Like Minimalist sculpture, Lin's memorial to veterans of the Vietnam War is a simple geometric form. Its inscribed polished walls actively engage viewers in a psychological dialogue about the war.

armed and uniformed, now stands approximately 120 feet from Lin's wall. Several years later, a group of nurses, organized as the Vietnam Women's Memorial Project, received approval for a sculpture honoring women's service in the Vietnam War. The seven-foot-tall bronze statue by Glenna Goodacre (b. 1939) depicts three female figures, one cradling a wounded soldier in her arms. Unveiled in 1993, the work occupies a site about 300 feet south of the Lin memorial.

Whether celebrated or condemned, Lin's Vietnam Veterans Memorial generates dramatic responses. Commonly, visitors react very emotionally, even those who know none of the soldiers named on the monument. The polished granite surface prompts individual soul-searching—viewers see themselves reflected among the names. Many visitors leave mementos at the foot of the wall in memory of loved ones they lost in the Vietnam War or make rubbings from the incised names. It can be argued that much of this memorial's power derives from its Minimalist simplicity. Like Minimalist sculpture, it does not dictate response and therefore successfully encourages personal exploration.

*Elizabeth Hess, "A Tale of Two Memorials," *Art in America* 71, no. 4 (April 1983): 122.
†Excerpt from an unpublished 1995 lecture, quoted in Kristine Stiles and Peter Selz, *Theories and Documents of Contemporary Art: A Sourcebook of Artists' Writings* (Berkeley and Los Angeles: University of California Press, 1996), 525.

and other site-specific artworks that bridge the gap between architecture and sculpture have become an established mode of artistic expression. As is true of all other media in the postmodern era, these artworks take a dazzling variety of forms—and some of them have engendered heated controversies.

**MAYA YING LIN** Variously classified as either a work of Minimalist sculpture or architecture is the Vietnam Veterans Memorial (FIG. 31-37) in Washington, D.C., designed in 1981 by MAYA YING LIN

(b. 1959) when she was a 21-year-old student at the Yale School of Architecture. The austere, simple memorial, a V-shaped wall constructed of polished black granite panels, begins at ground level at each end and gradually ascends to a height of 10 feet at the center of the V. Each wing is 246 feet long. Lin set the wall into the landscape, enhancing visitors' awareness of descent as they walk along the wall toward the center. The names of the Vietnam War's 57,939 American casualties (and those missing in action) incised on the memorial's walls, in the order of their deaths, contribute to the monument's dramatic effect.

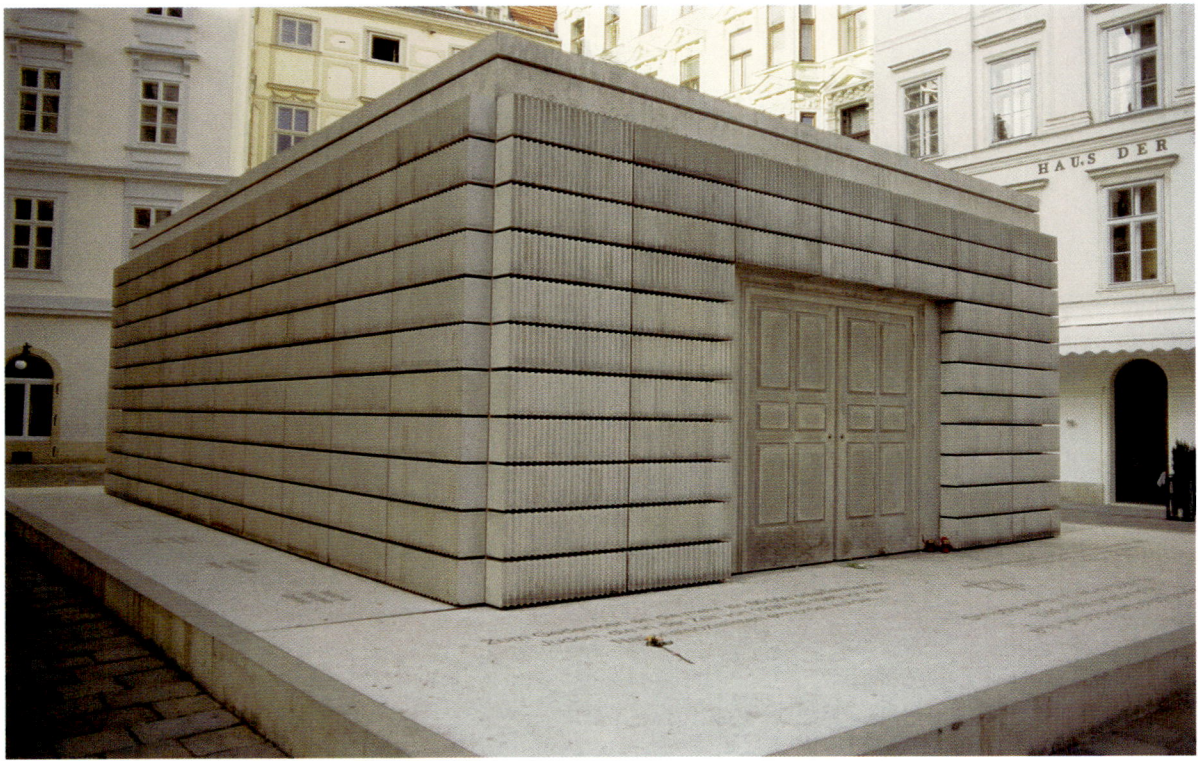

When Lin designed this pristinely simple monument, she gave a great deal of thought to the purpose of war memorials. Her conclusion was a memorial

> should be honest about the reality of war and be for the people who gave their lives. . . . [I] didn't want a static object that people would just look at, but something they could relate to as on a journey, or passage, that would bring each to his own conclusions. . . . I wanted to work with the land and not dominate it. I had an impulse to cut open the earth . . . an initial violence that in time would heal. The grass would grow back, but the cut would remain.[6]

In light of the tragedy of the war, this unpretentious memorial's allusion to a wound and long-lasting scar contributes to its communicative ability (see "Maya Lin's Vietnam Veterans Memorial," page 965).

**RACHEL WHITEREAD** Another controversial memorial commissioned for a specific historical setting is the Viennese Holocaust Memorial by British sculptor RACHEL WHITEREAD (b. 1963). In 1996, the city of Vienna chose Whiteread as the winner of the competition to design a commemorative monument to the 65,000 Austrian Jews who perished at the hands of the Nazis during World War II (FIG. **31-38**). The decision to focus attention on a past most Austrians wished to forget unleashed a controversy that delayed construction of the monument until 2000. Also controversial was the Minimalist severity of Whiteread's massive block of concrete planted in a Baroque square at the heart of the Austrian capital—as was, at least initially, the understated form of Lin's Vietnam monument (FIG. 31-37) juxtaposed with the Washington and Lincoln Monuments in Washington, D.C.

Whiteread modulated the surface of the Holocaust memorial only slightly by depicting in low relief the shapes of two doors and hundreds of identical books on shelves, with the edges of the covers and the pages rather than the spines facing outward. The book motif was a reference both to Jews as the "People of the Book" and to the book burnings that accompanied Jewish persecutions throughout the centuries and under the Nazis. Around the base, Whiteread inscribed the names of Nazi concentration camps in German, Hebrew, and English. The setting for the memorial is Judenplatz (Jewish Square), the site of a synagogue destroyed in 1421. The brutality of the tomblike monument—it cannot be entered, and its shape suggests a prison block—was a visual as well as psychological shock in the beautiful Viennese square. Whiteread's purpose, however, was not to please but to create a memorial that met the jury's charge to "combine dignity with reserve and spark an aesthetic dialogue with the past in a place that is replete with history."

Whiteread had gained fame in 1992 for her monument commemorating the demolition of a working-class neighborhood in East London. *House* took the form of a concrete cast of the space inside the last standing Victorian house on the site. She had also made sculptures of "negative spaces," for example, the space beneath a chair or mattress or sink. In Vienna, she represented the space behind the shelves of a library. In drawing viewers' attention to the voids between and inside objects and buildings, Whiteread pursued in a different way the same goal as Pop Art innovator Jasper Johns (FIG. 30-22), who painted things "seen but not looked at."

**RICHARD SERRA** Also unleashing an emotional public debate, but for different reasons and with a decidedly different outcome, was *Tilted Arc* (FIG. **31-39**) by San Franciscan RICHARD SERRA (b. 1939), who worked in steel mills in California before studying art at Yale. He now lives in New York, where he received a commission in 1979 from the General Services Administration (GSA), the federal agency responsible for overseeing the selection and installation of artworks for government buildings, to install a 120-foot-long, 12-foot-high curved wall of Cor-Ten steel in the plaza in front of the Jacob K. Javits Federal Building in lower Manhattan. He completed the project in 1981. Serra wished *Tilted Arc* to "dislocate or alter the decorative function of the plaza and actively

## Richard Serra's *Tilted Arc*

When Richard Serra installed *Tilted Arc* (FIG. 31-39) in the plaza in front of the Javits Federal Building in New York City in 1981, much of the public immediately responded with hostile criticism. Prompting the chorus of complaints was the uncompromising presence of a Minimalist sculpture bisecting the plaza. Many argued *Tilted Arc* was ugly, attracted graffiti, interfered with the view across the plaza, and prevented use of the plaza for performances or concerts. Due to the sustained barrage of protests and petitions demanding the removal of *Tilted Arc,* the General Services Administration, which had commissioned the sculpture, held a series of public hearings. Afterward, the agency decided to remove Serra's sculpture despite its prior approval of the artist's model. This, understandably, infuriated Serra, who had a legally binding contract acknowledging the site-specific nature of *Tilted Arc.* "To remove the work is to destroy the work," the artist stated.[*]

This episode raised intriguing issues about the nature of public art, including the public reception of experimental art, the artist's responsibilities and rights when executing public commissions, censorship in the arts, and the purpose of public art. If an artwork is on display in a public space outside the relatively private confines of a museum or gallery, do different guidelines apply? As one participant in the *Tilted Arc* saga asked, "Should an artist have the right to impose his values and taste on a public that now rejects his taste and values?"[†] One of the express functions of the historical avant-garde was to challenge convention by rejecting tradition and disrupting the complacency of the viewer. Will placing experimental art in a public place always cause controversy? From Serra's statements, it is clear he intended the sculpture to challenge the public.

Another issue *Tilted Arc* presented involved the rights of the artist, who in this case accused the GSA of censorship. Serra filed a lawsuit against the federal government for infringement of his First Amendment rights and insisted "the artist's work must be uncensored, respected, and tolerated, although deemed abhorrent, or perceived as challenging, or experienced as threatening."[‡] Did removal of the work constitute censorship? A U.S. district court held it did not.

Ultimately, who should decide what artworks are appropriate for the public arena? One artist argued, "We cannot have public art by plebiscite [popular vote]."[§] But to avoid recurrences of the *Tilted Arc* controversy, the GSA changed its procedures and now solicits input from a wide range of civic and neighborhood groups before commissioning public artworks. Despite the removal of *Tilted Arc* (now languishing in storage), the sculpture maintains a powerful presence in all discussions of the aesthetics, politics, and dynamics of public art.

[*]Grace Glueck, "What Part Should the Public Play in Choosing Public Art?" *New York Times,* February 3, 1985, 27.
[†]Calvin Tomkins, "The Art World: Tilted Arc," *New Yorker,* May 20, 1985, 98.
[‡]Ibid., 98–99.
[§]Ibid., 98.

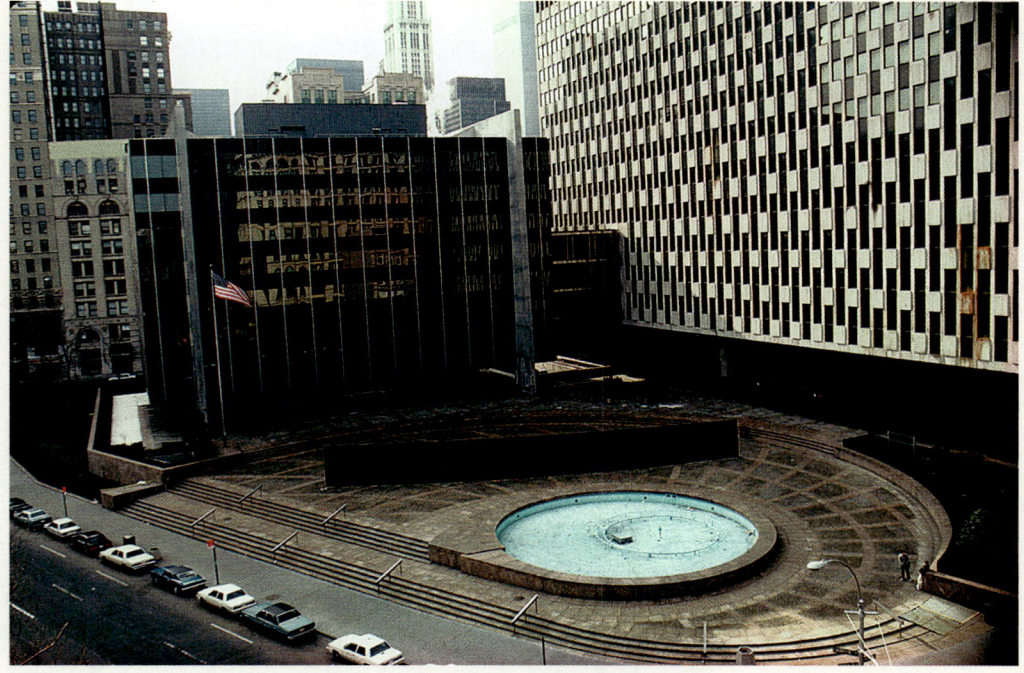

**31-39 RICHARD SERRA,** *Tilted Arc,* **Jacob K. Javits Federal Plaza, New York City, 1981.**

Serra intended his Minimalist *Tilted Arc* to alter the character of an existing public space. He succeeded but unleashed a storm of protest that caused the government to remove the work.

bring people into the sculpture's context."[7] In pursuit of that goal, Serra situated the sculpture so that it bisected and consequently significantly altered the space of the open plaza and interrupted the traffic flow across the square. By creating such a monumental presence in this large public space, Serra succeeded in forcing viewers to reconsider the plaza's physical space as a sculptural form—but only temporarily, because the public forced the sculpture to be removed (see "Richard Serra's *Tilted Arc,*" above).

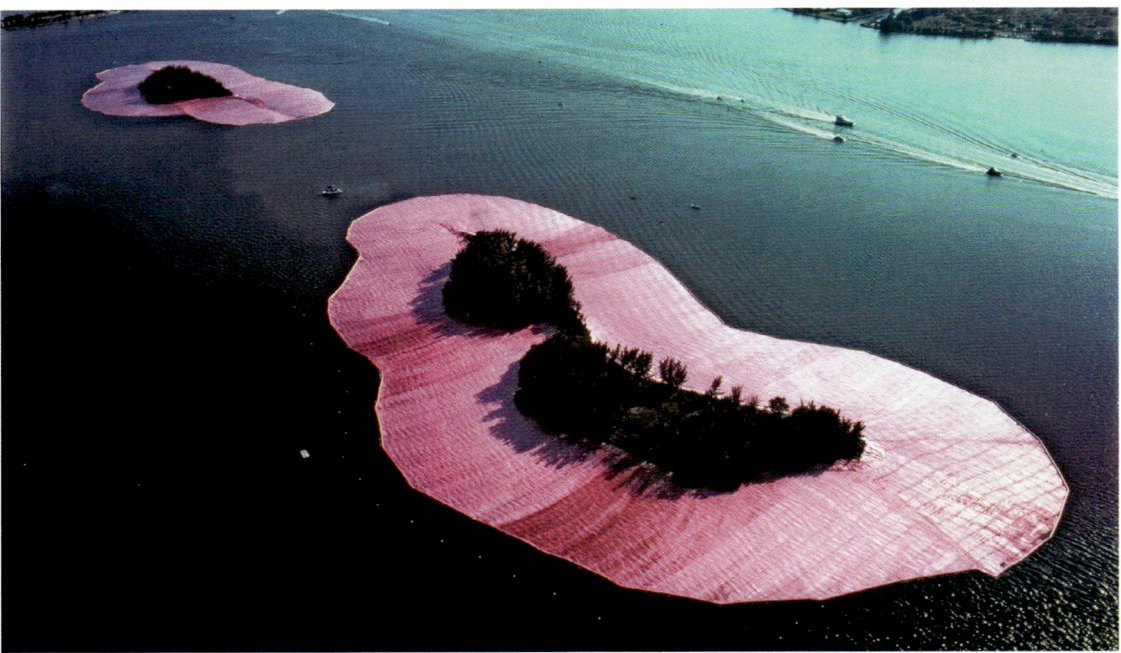

**CHRISTO AND JEANNE-CLAUDE** The most famous Environmental artists of the past few decades are CHRISTO (b. 1935) and his deceased spouse JEANNE-CLAUDE (1935–2009). In their works they sought to intensify the viewer's awareness of the space and features of rural and urban sites. However, rather than physically alter the land itself, as Robert Smithson (FIG. 30-50) often did, Christo and Jeanne-Claude prompted this awareness by temporarily modifying the landscape with cloth. Christo studied art in his native Bulgaria and in Austria. After moving from Vienna to Paris, he began to encase objects in clumsy wrappings, thereby appropriating bits of the real world into the mysterious world of the unopened package whose contents can be dimly seen in silhouette under the wrap.

Starting in 1961, Christo and Jeanne-Claude began to collaborate on large-scale projects normally dealing with the environment itself. For example, in 1969 the couple wrapped more than a million square feet of Australian coastline and in 1972 hung a vast curtain across a valley at Rifle Gap, Colorado. Their projects require years of preparation and research, and scores of meetings with local authorities and interested groups of local citizens. These temporary artworks are usually on view for only a few weeks.

*Surrounded Islands, Biscayne Bay, Miami, Florida, 1980–1983* (FIG. **31-40**), created in Biscayne Bay for two weeks in May 1983, typifies Christo and Jeanne-Claude's work. For this project, they surrounded 11 small artificial islands in the bay (previously created from a dredging project) with 6.5 million square feet of specially fabricated pink polypropylene floating fabric. This Environmental artwork required three years of preparation to obtain the required permits and to assemble the labor force and obtain the $3.2 million needed to complete the project. The artists raised the money by selling Christo's original preparatory drawings, collages, and models of works he created in the 1950s and 1960s. Huge crowds watched as crews removed accumulated trash from the 11 islands (to assure maximum contrast between their dark colors, the pink of the cloth, and the blue of the bay) and then unfurled the fabric "cocoons" to form magical floating "skirts" around each tiny bit of land. Despite the brevity of its existence, *Surrounded Islands* lives on in the host of photographs, films, and books documenting the project.

**ANDY GOLDSWORTHY** The most prominent heir today to the earthworks tradition of Robert Smithson is Environmental artist and photographer ANDY GOLDSWORTHY (b. 1956). Goldsworthy's medium is nature itself—stones, tree roots, leaves, flowers, ice. Because most of his works are ephemeral, the victims of tides, rainstorms, and the changing seasons, he records them in stunning color photographs that are artworks in their own right. Golds-

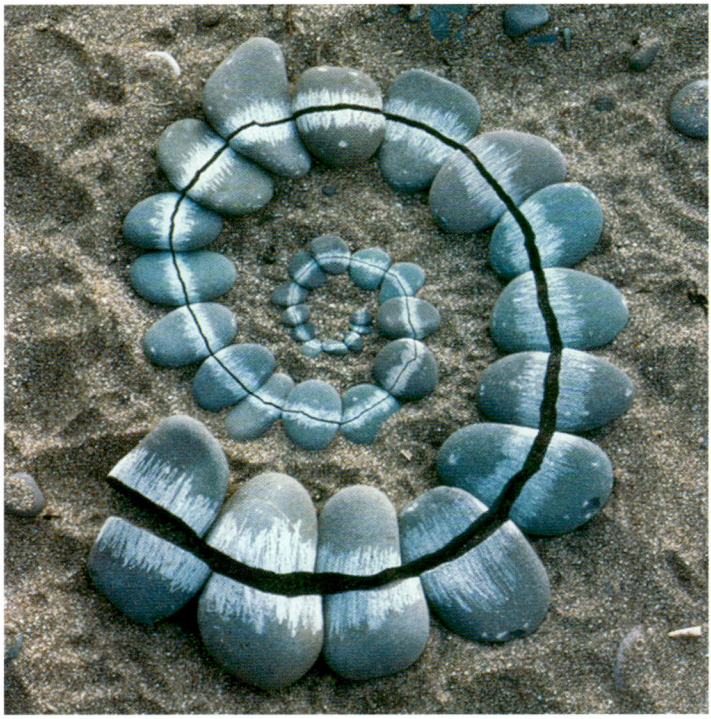

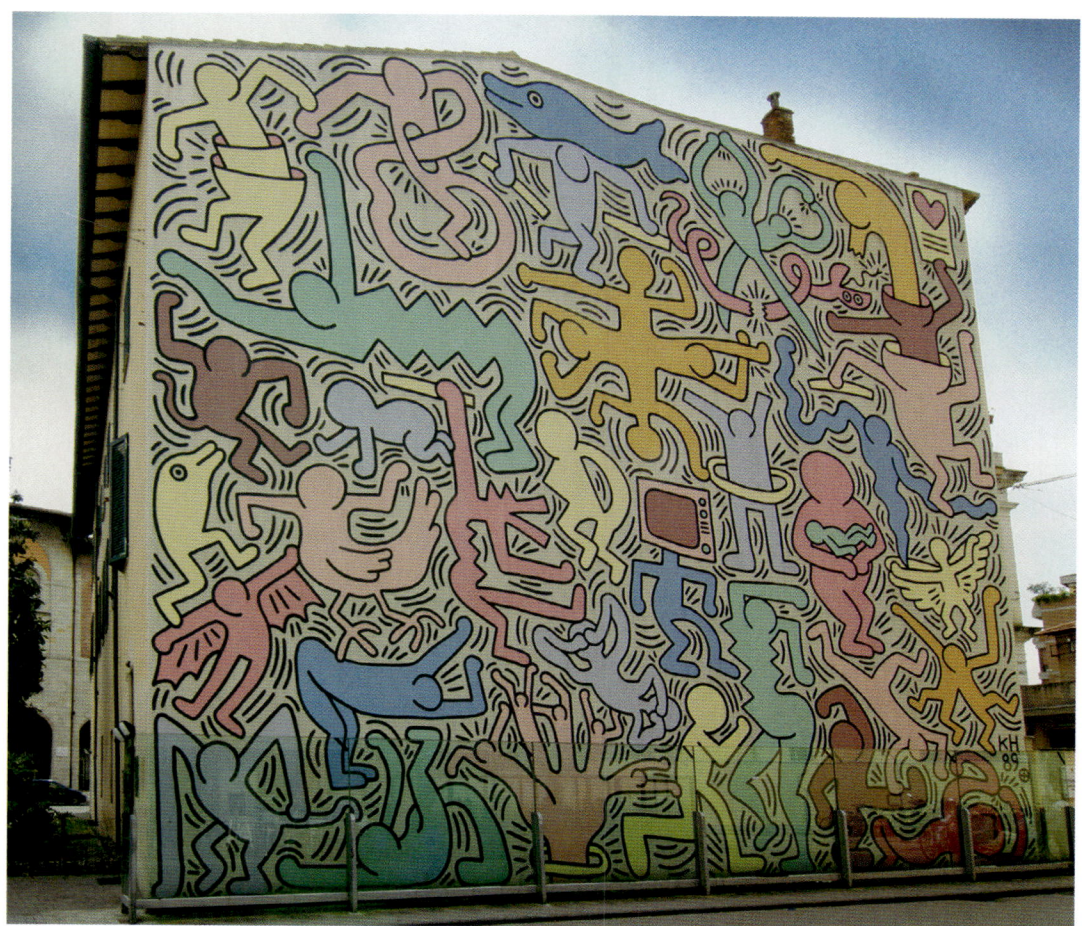

and displayed a genius for marketing himself and his work. In 1986, he parlayed his popularity into a successful business by opening The Pop Shop in the SoHo (South of Houston Street) gallery district of lower Manhattan, where he sold posters, T-shirts, hats, and buttons featuring his universally appealing schematic human and animal figures, especially his two most popular motifs—a crawling baby surrounded by rays and a barking dog.

Haring's last major work was a commission to paint a huge mural at the church of Saint Anthony in Pisa, Italy, a confirmation of his international reputation. *Tuttomondo* (*Everybody*) encapsulates Haring's style (FIG. **31-42**)—bright single-color cavorting figures with black outlines against a matte background. The motifs include a winged man, a figure with a television head, a mother cradling a baby, and a dancing dog. It is a hymn to the joy of life (compare FIG. 29-2A). Haring died of AIDS the next year. He was 31 years old.

# NEW MEDIA

In addition to taking the ancient arts of painting and sculpture in new directions, contemporary artists have continued to explore the expressive possibilities of the various new media developed in the postwar period, especially digital photography, computer graphics, and video.

**ANDREAS GURSKY** German photographer ANDREAS GURSKY (b. 1955) grew up in Düsseldorf, where his father was a commercial photographer. Andreas studied photography at Düsseldorf's Kunstakademie (Academy of Art) and since the mid-1990s has used computer and digital technology to produce gigantic color prints in which he combines and manipulates photographs taken with a wide-angle lens, usually from a high vantage point. The size of his photographs, sometimes almost a dozen feet wide, intentionally rivals 19th-century history paintings. But as was true of Gustave Courbet (FIGS. 27-26 and 27-27) in his day, Gursky's subjects come from everyday life. He records the mundane world of the modern global economy—vast industrial plants, major department stores, hotel lobbies, and stock and commodity exchanges—and transforms the commonplace into striking, almost abstract, compositions. (Compare the photographs of Edward Burtynsky, FIG. 31-19.)

worthy's international reputation has led to commissions in his native England, Scotland (where he now lives), France, Australia, the United States, and Japan, where his work has much in common with the sculptures of Kimio Tsuchiya (FIG. 31-23). Goldsworthy seeks not to transform the landscape in his art but, in his words, to "collaborate with nature."

One of Goldsworthy's most beautiful "collaborations" is also a tribute to Robert Smithson and *Spiral Jetty* (FIG. 30-50). *Cracked Rock Spiral* (FIG. **31-41**), which he created at St. Abbs, Scotland, on June 1, 1985, consists of pebbles Goldsworthy split in two, scratched white around the cracks using another stone, and then arranged in a spiral that grows wider as it coils from its center.

**GRAFFITI AND MURAL PAINTING** Although generally considered a modern phenomenon, the concept of site-specific art is as old as the history of art. Indeed, the earliest known paintings are those covering the walls and ceilings of Paleolithic caves in southern France and northern Spain (see Chapter 1). A contemporary twist on the venerable art of mural painting is the graffiti and graffiti-inspired art of, among others, Jean-Michel Basquiat (FIG. 31-8) and KEITH HARING (1958–1990). Haring grew up in Kutztown, Pennsylvania, attended the School of Visual Arts in New York, and, as did Basquiat, burst onto the New York art scene as a graffiti artist in the city's subway system. The authorities would constantly remove his chalk figures, which he drew on blank black posters awaiting advertisers, and arrested Haring whenever they spotted him at work. However, Haring quickly gained a wide and appreciative audience for his linear cartoon-inspired fantasies, and began to sell paintings to avid collectors. Haring, like Andy Warhol (FIGS. 30-25 and 30-25A), was thoroughly in tune with pop culture

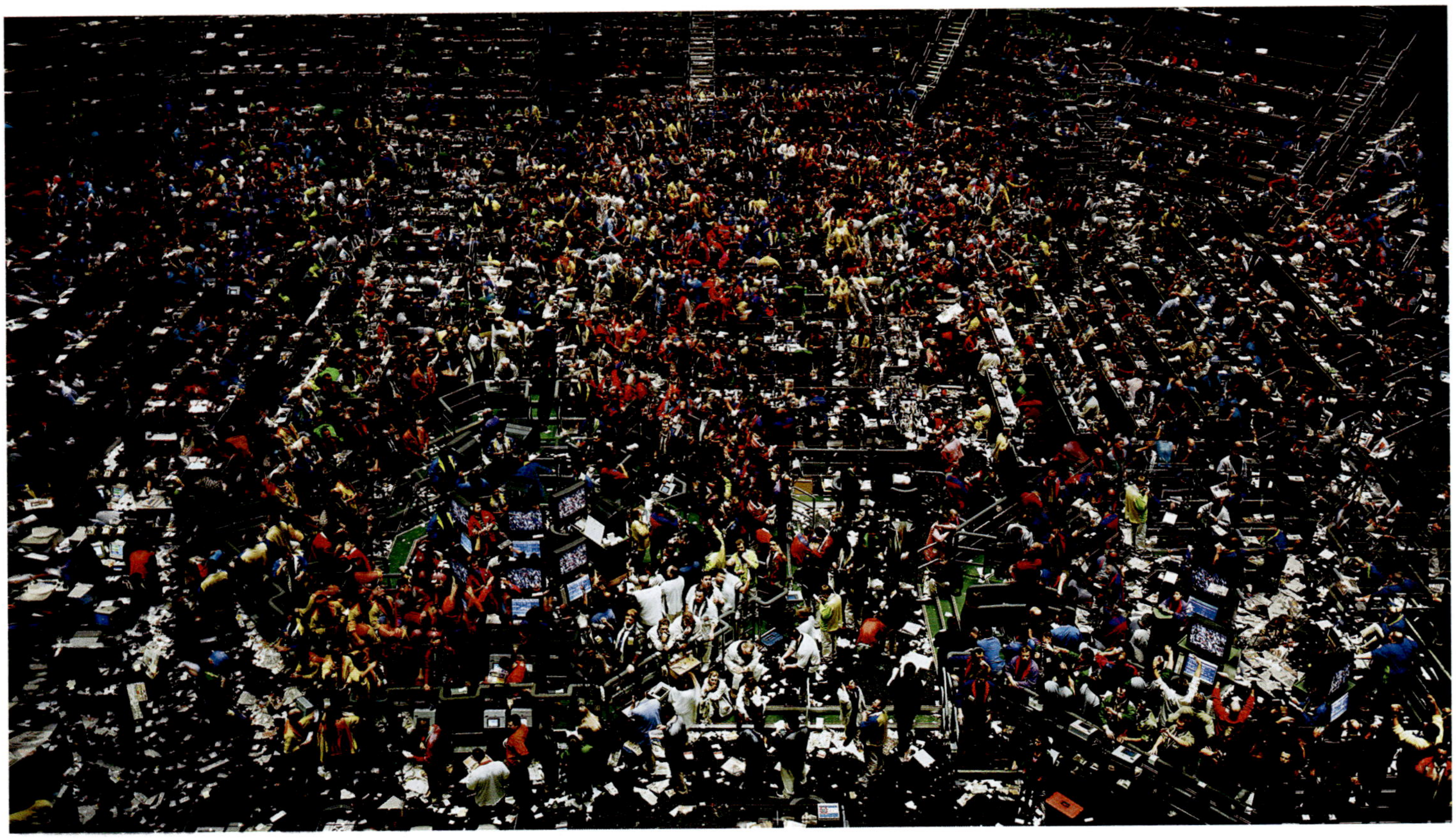

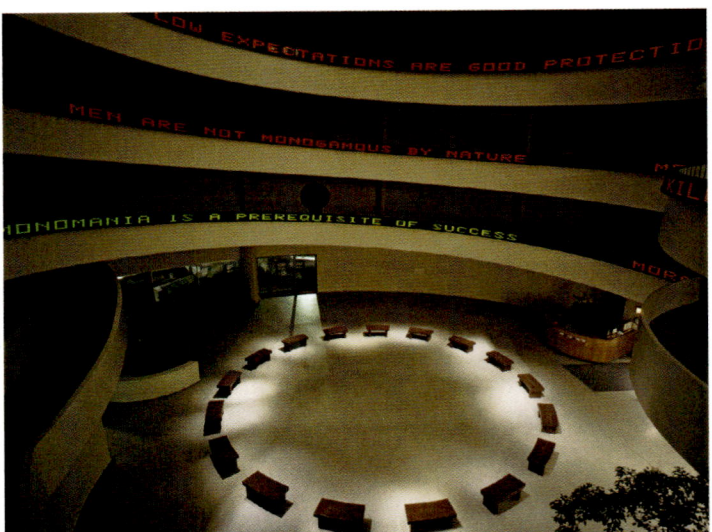

**31-43** ANDREAS GURSKY, *Chicago Board of Trade II,* 1999. C-print, 6′ 9½″ × 11′ 5⅝″. Matthew Marks Gallery, New York.

Gursky manipulates digital photographs to produce vast tableaus depicting characteristic places of the modern global economy. The size of his prints rivals 19th-century history paintings.

Gursky's enormous 1999 print (FIG. **31-43**) documenting the frenzied activity on the main floor of the Chicago Board of Trade is a characteristic example of his work. He took a series of photographs from a gallery, creating a panoramic view of the traders in their brightly colored jackets. He then combined several digital images using commercial photo-editing software to produce a blurred tableau of bodies, desks, computer terminals, and strewn paper in which both mass and color are so evenly distributed as to negate the traditional Renaissance notion of perspective. In using the computer to modify the "objective truth" and spatial recession of "straight photography," Gursky blurs the distinction between painting and photography.

**JENNY HOLZER** Gallipolis, Ohio, native JENNY HOLZER (b. 1950) studied art at Ohio University and the Rhode Island School of Design. In 1990, she became the first woman to represent the United States at the prestigious Venice Biennale art exhibition. Holzer has won renown for several series of artworks using electronic signs, most involving light-emitting diode (LED) technology, and has created light-projection shows worldwide. In 1989, she assembled a major installation at the Solomon R. Guggenheim Museum in New York that included elements from her previous series and consisted of a large continuous LED display spiraling around the interior ramp (FIG. **31-44**) of Frank Lloyd Wright's landmark building (FIG. 30-39). Holzer believes in the communicative power of language, and her installation focused specifically on text. She invented sayings with an authoritative

**31-44** JENNY HOLZER, *Untitled* (selections from *Truisms, Inflammatory Essays, The Living Series, The Survival Series, Under a Rock, Laments,* and *Child Text*), 1989. Extended helical tricolor LED electronic display signboard, 16′ × 162′ × 6′. Installation at the Solomon R. Guggenheim Museum, New York, December 1989–February 1990 (partial gift of the artist, 1989).

Holzer's 1989 installation consisted of electronic signs created using LED technology. The continuous display of texts wound around the Guggenheim Museum's spiral interior ramp.

tone for her LED displays—for example, "Protect me from what I want," "Abuse of power comes as no surprise," and "Romantic love was invented to manipulate women." The statements, which people could read from a distance, were intentionally vague and, in some cases, contradictory.

**ADRIAN PIPER** Video artists, like other artists, pursue diverse goals. ADRIAN PIPER (b. 1948) has used video art to effect social change—in particular, to combat pervasive racism. Born in New York City, she studied art at the School of Visual Arts and philosophy at the City College of New York but now lives in Berlin, Germany. Her videos, such as the installation *Cornered* (FIG. **31-45**), are provocative and confrontational. *Cornered* included a video monitor placed behind an overturned table. Piper appeared on the video monitor, literally cornered behind the table, as she spoke to viewers. Her comments sprang from her experiences as a light-skinned African American woman and from her belief that although overt racism had diminished, subtle and equally damaging forms of bigotry were still rampant. "I'm black," she announces on the 16-minute videotape. "Now let's deal with this social fact and the fact of my stating it together. . . . If you feel that my letting people know that I'm not white is making an unnecessary fuss, you must feel that the right and proper course of action for me to take is to pass for white. Now this kind of thinking presupposes a belief that it's inherently better to be identified as white," she continues. The directness of Piper's art forces viewers to examine their own behaviors and values.

**BILL VIOLA** For much of his artistic career, BILL VIOLA (b. 1951) has also explored the capabilities of digitized imagery, producing many video installations and single-channel works. Often focusing on sensory perception, the pieces not only heighten viewer awareness of the senses but also suggest an exploration into the spiritual realm. Viola, who majored in art and music at Syracuse University, spent years after graduating seriously studying Buddhist, Chris-

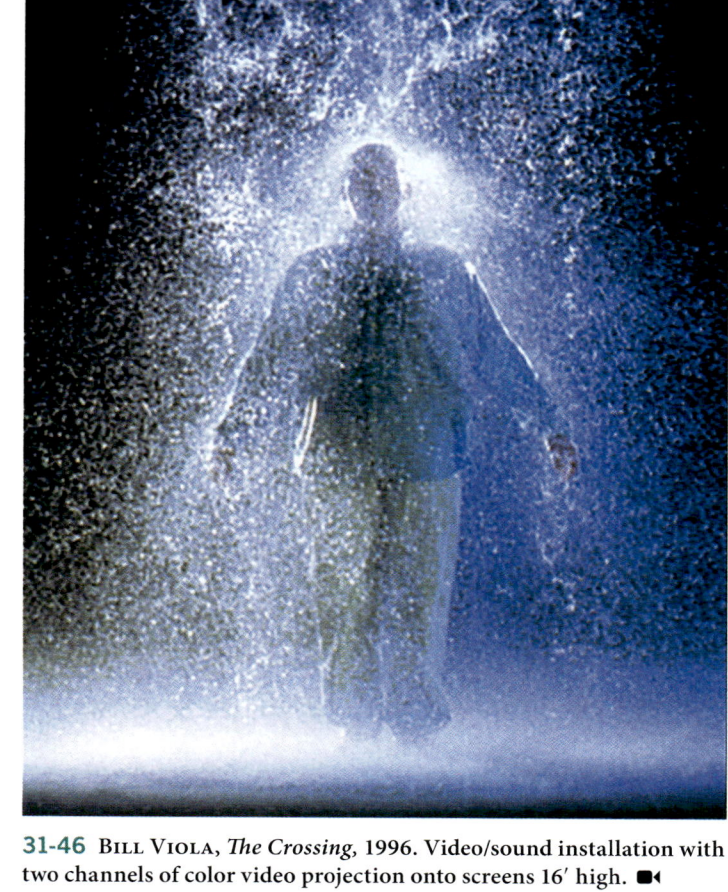

1 ft.

**31-46** BILL VIOLA, *The Crossing*, 1996. Video/sound installation with two channels of color video projection onto screens 16′ high. ◼◀

Viola's video projects use extreme slow motion, contrasts in scale, shifts in focus, mirrored reflections, and staccato editing to create dramatic sensory experiences rooted in tangible reality.

tian, Sufi, and Zen mysticism. Because he fervently believes in art's transformative power and in a spiritual view of human nature, Viola designs works encouraging spectator introspection. His video projects have involved using techniques such as extreme slow motion, contrasts in scale, shifts in focus, mirrored reflections, staccato editing, and multiple or layered screens to achieve dramatic effects.

The power of Viola's work is evident in *The Crossing* (FIG. **31-46**), an installation piece involving two color video channels projected on 16-foot-high screens. The artist either shows the two projections on the front and back of the same screen or on two separate screens in the same installation. In these two companion videos, shown simultaneously on the two screens, a man surrounded in darkness appears, moving closer until he fills the screen. On one screen, drops of water fall from above onto the man's head, while on the other screen, a small fire breaks out at the man's feet. Over the next few minutes, the water and fire increase in intensity until the man disappears in a torrent of water on one screen (FIG. 31-46) and flames consume the man on the other screen. The deafening roar of a raging fire and a torrential downpour accompany these visual images. Eventually, everything subsides and fades into darkness. This installation's elemental nature and its presentation in a dark space immerse viewers in a pure sensory experience very much rooted in tangible reality.

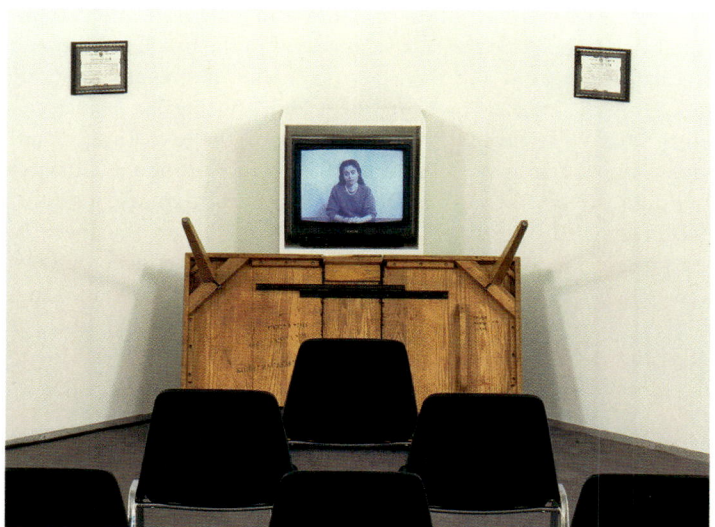

**31-45** ADRIAN PIPER, *Cornered*, 1988. Mixed-media installation of variable size; video monitor, table, and birth certificates. Museum of Contemporary Art, Chicago. ◼◀

In this installation, Piper, a light-skinned African American, appeared on a video monitor, "cornered" behind an overturned table, and made provocative comments about racism and bigotry.

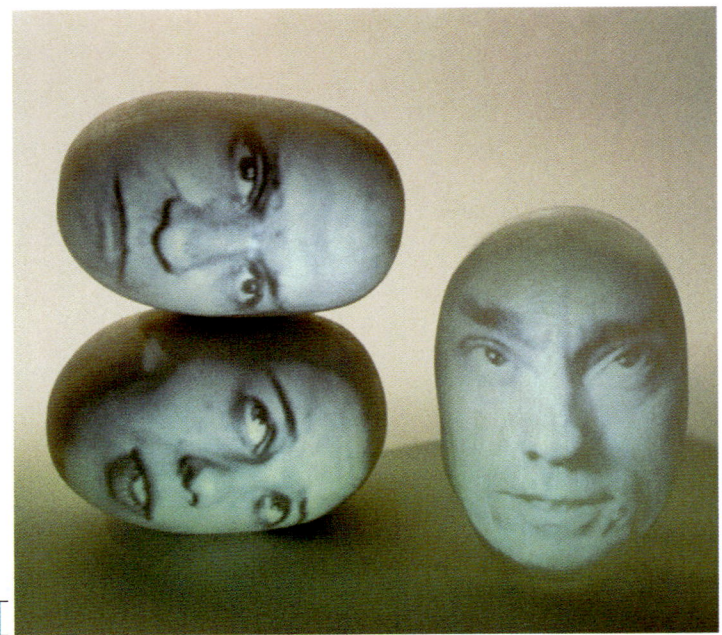

1 in.

**31-47** TONY OURSLER, *Mansheshe*, 1997. Ceramic, glass, video player, videocassette, CPJ-200 video projector, sound, 11″ × 7″ × 8″ each. Courtesy of the artist and Metro Pictures, New York.

Video artist Oursler projects his digital images onto sculptural objects, insinuating them into the "real" world. Here, he projected talking heads onto egg-shaped forms suspended from poles.

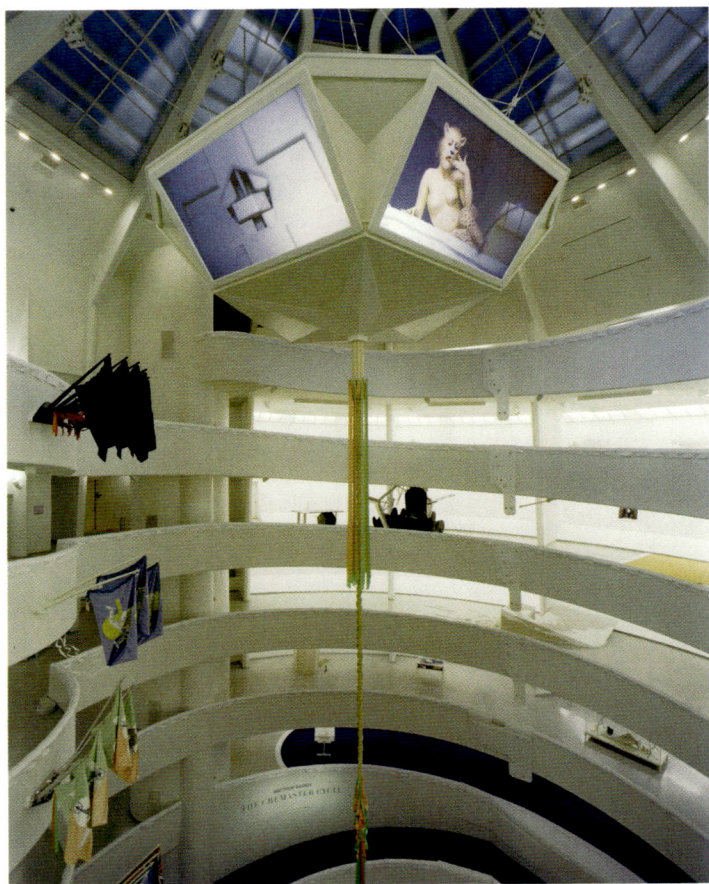

**31-48** MATTHEW BARNEY, *Cremaster* cycle, installation at the Solomon R. Guggenheim Museum, New York, 2003.

Barney's vast multimedia installations of drawings, photographs, sculptures, and videos typify the relaxation at the opening of the 21st century of the traditional boundaries among artistic media.

**TONY OURSLER** Whereas Viola, Piper, and other artists present video and digital imagery to their audiences on familiar flat screens, thus reproducing the format in which we most often come into contact with electronic images, New Yorker TONY OURSLER (b. 1957), who studied art at the California Institute of the Arts, manipulates his images, projecting them onto sculptural objects. This has the effect of taking the images out of the digital world and insinuating them into the "real" world. Accompanied by sound tapes, Oursler's installations, such as *Mansheshe* (FIG. **31-47**), not only engage but often challenge the viewer. In this example, Oursler projected talking heads onto egg-shaped forms suspended from poles. Because the projected images of people look directly at the viewer, the statements they make about religious beliefs, sexual identity, and interpersonal relationships cannot be easily dismissed.

**MATTHEW BARNEY** A major trend in the art world today is the relaxation of the traditional boundaries between artistic media. In fact, many contemporary artists are creating vast and complex multimedia installations combining new and traditional media. One of these artists is MATTHEW BARNEY (b. 1967), who studied art at Yale University. The 2003 installation (FIG. **31-48**) of his epic *Cremaster* cycle (1994–2002) at the Solomon R. Guggenheim Museum in New York typifies the expansive scale of many contemporary works. A multimedia extravaganza involving drawings, photographs, sculptures, videos, films, and performances (presented in videos), the *Cremaster* cycle is a lengthy narrative set in a self-enclosed universe Barney created. The title of the work refers to the cremaster muscle, which controls testicular contractions in response to external stimuli. Barney uses the development of this muscle in the embryonic process of sexual differentiation as the conceptual springboard for the entire *Cremaster* project, in

which he explores the notion of creation in expansive and complicated ways. The cycle's narrative, revealed in the five 35-millimeter feature-length films and the artworks, makes reference to, among other things, a musical revue in Boise, Idaho (where San Francisco–born Barney grew up), the life cycle of bees, the execution of convicted murderer Gary Gilmore, the construction of the Chrysler Building (FIG. 29-47), Celtic mythology, Masonic rituals, a motorcycle race, and a lyric opera set in late-19th-century Budapest. In the installation, Barney tied the artworks together conceptually by a five-channel video piece projected on screens hanging in the Guggenheim's rotunda. Immersion in Barney's constructed world is disorienting and overwhelming and has a force that competes with the immense scale and often frenzied pace of contemporary life.

**WHAT NEXT?** No one knows what the next years and decades will bring, but given the expansive scope of postmodernism, it is certain no single approach to or style of art will dominate. New technologies will undoubtedly continue to redefine what constitutes a "work of art." The universally expanding presence of computers, digital technology, and the Internet may well erode what few conceptual and geographical boundaries remain, and make art and information about art available to virtually everyone, thereby creating a truly global artistic community. As this chapter has revealed, substantial progress has already been made in that direction.

# CONTEMPORARY ART WORLDWIDE

## SOCIAL AND POLITICAL ART

❚ Many contemporary artists use art to address pressing social and political issues and to define their personal identities.

❚ Gender and sexuality are central themes in the work of Barbara Kruger, the Guerrilla Girls, David Wojnarowicz, Robert Mapplethorpe, and Shahzia Sikander. Faith Ringgold, Lorna Simpson, Carrie Mae Weems, Melvin Edwards, Jean-Michel Basquiat, and Kehinde Wiley address issues of concern to African Americans. Jaune Quick-to-See Smith focuses on Native American heritage, Chris Ofili and Trigo Piula on their African roots, and Cliff Whiting on traditional Maori themes.

❚ Other artists have treated political and economic issues: Willie Bester, apartheid in South Africa; David Hammons, racial discrimination; Leon Golub, violence; Shirin Neshat, the challenges facing Muslim women; Krzysztof Wodiczko, the plight of the homeless; and Edward Burtynsky, industrial pollution.

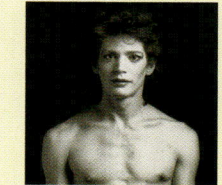

Mapplethorpe, *Self-Portrait,* 1980

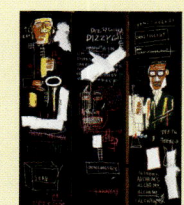

Basquiat, *Horn Players,* 1983

## OTHER MOVEMENTS AND THEMES

❚ Contemporary art encompasses a phenomenal variety of styles ranging from abstraction to brutal realism, both in America and worldwide.

❚ Leading abstract painters and sculptors include Julian Schnabel and Tara Donovan in the United States, Anselm Kiefer in Germany, Emily Kame Kngwarreye in Australia, and Wu Guanzhong, Song Su-nam, and Kimio Tsuchiya in China, Korea, and Japan, respectively.

❚ Among today's best-known figural painters and sculptors are Kiki Smith, Jeff Koons, and Venezuelan Marisol in the United States, and expatriate Englishwoman Jenny Saville in Italy.

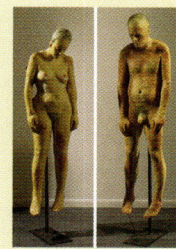

Smith, *Untitled,* 1990

## ARCHITECTURE AND SITE-SPECIFIC ART

❚ Postmodern architecture is as diverse as contemporary painting and sculpture. Leading Hi-Tech architects include Norman Foster and Renzo Piano. Among the major champions of Deconstructivism are Günter Behnisch, Frank Gehry, Daniel Libeskind, and Zaha Hadid.

❚ The monuments designed by Maya Lin, Rachel Whiteread, and Richard Serra bridge the gap between architecture and sculpture, as do the Environmental artworks of Christo and Jean-Claude and of Andy Goldsworthy.

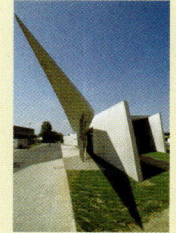

Hadid, Vitra Fire Station, 1989–1993

## NEW MEDIA

❚ Many contemporary artists have harnessed new technologies in their artistic production: Andreas Gursky, digital photography; Jenny Holzer, LED displays; Adrian Piper, Bill Viola, and Tony Oursler, video; and Matthew Barney, complex multimedia installations.

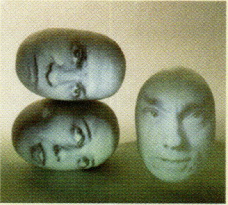

Oursler, *Mansheshe,* 1997

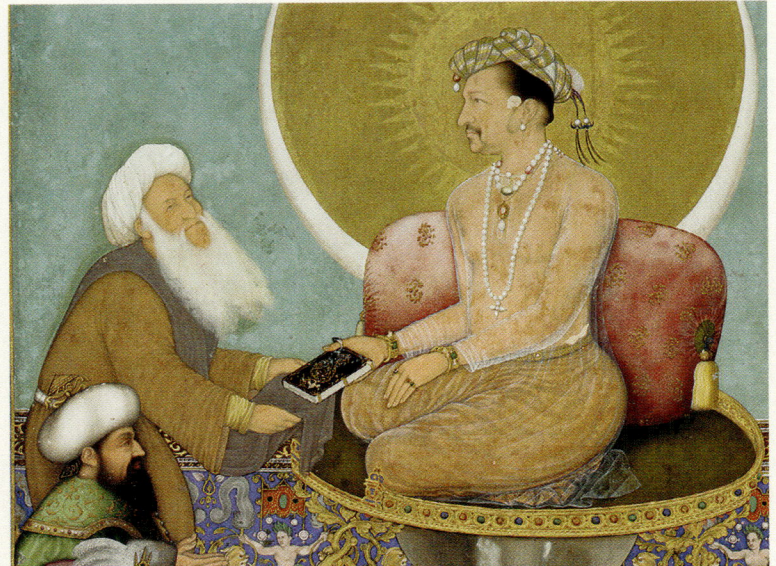

In this allegorical portrait of Emperor Jahangir on an hourglass throne, the Mughal ruler appears with a radiant halo behind him and sits above time, favoring spiritual power over worldly power.

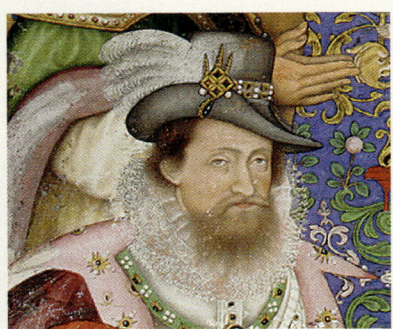

Bichitr included a copy of a portrait of King James I to underscore that the Mughal emperor Jahangir preferred the wisdom of an elder Sufi mystic saint to the counsel of the British monarch.

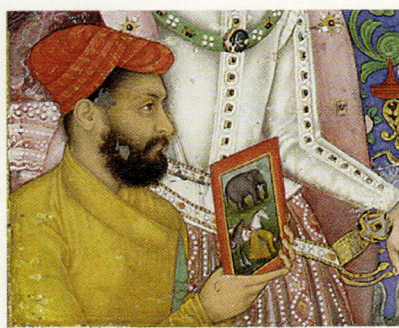

The artist not only signed this painting but inserted a self-portrait. Bichitr bows before Jahangir and holds a painting of two horses and an elephant, costly gifts to the painter from the emperor.

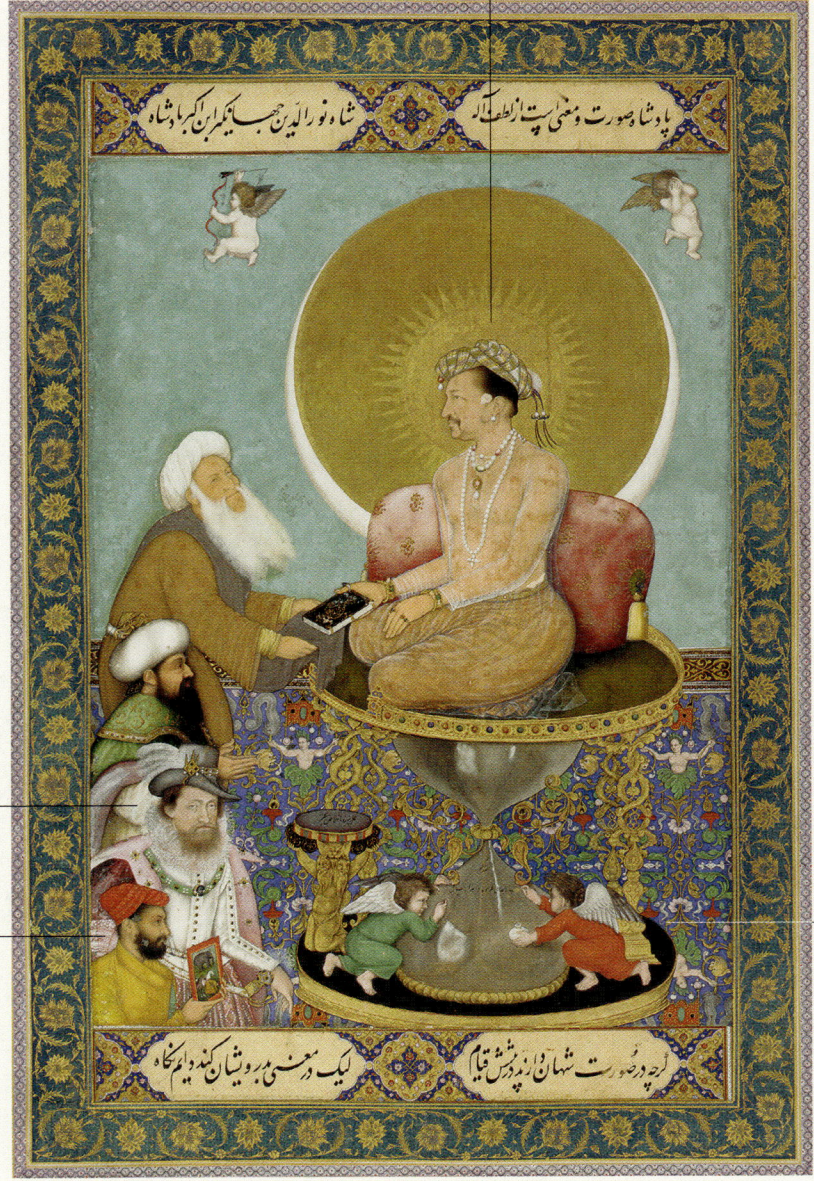

32-1 BICHITR, *Jahangir Preferring a Sufi Shaykh to Kings,* ca. 1615–1618. Opaque watercolor on paper, 1′ 6⅞″ × 1′ 1″. Freer Gallery of Art, Washington, D.C. ◼◣

1 in.

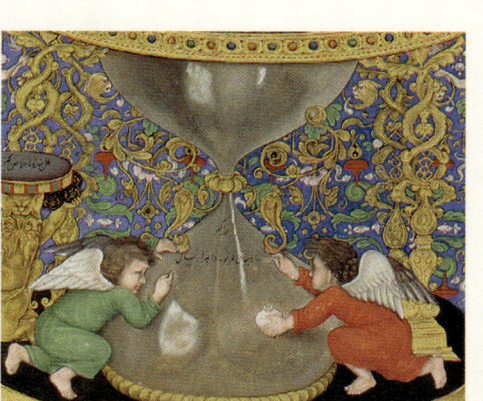

As the sands of time run out, two cupids (clothed, unlike their European prototypes) inscribe Jahangir's hourglass throne with a wish for the Mughal emperor to live a thousand years.

# SOUTH AND SOUTHEAST ASIA, 1200 TO 1980

## PAINTING AT THE MUGHAL IMPERIAL COURT

From the 16th to the 19th century, the most powerful rulers in South Asia were the Mughal emperors. *Mughal,* originally a Western term, means "descended from the Mongols," although the Mughals considered themselves descendants of Timur (r. 1370–1405), the Muslim conqueror whose capital was at Samarkand in Uzbekistan. The Mughal dynasty presided over a cosmopolitan court with refined tastes. British ambassadors and merchants were frequent visitors, and the Mughal emperors acquired many European luxury goods. They were also great admirers of Persian art and maintained an imperial workshop of painters who, in sharp contrast to pre-Mughal artists in India, often signed their works.

The influence of European as well as Persian styles on Mughal painting is evident in the allegorical portrait (FIG. 32-1) BICHITR painted of Jahangir (r. 1605–1627), the great-grandson of the founder of the Mughal Empire. The emperor sits on an hourglass throne. As the sands of time run out, two cupids (clothed, unlike their European models more closely copied at the top of the painting) inscribe the throne with the wish that Jahangir would live a thousand years. Bichitr portrayed his patron as an emperor above time and placed behind Jahangir's head a radiant halo combining a golden sun and a white crescent moon, indicating Jahangir is the center of the universe and its light source. One of the inscriptions on the painting gives the emperor's title as "Light of the Faith."

At the left are four figures. The lowest, both spatially and in the social hierarchy, is the Hindu painter Bichitr himself, wearing a red turban. He holds a painting representing two horses and an elephant, costly gifts to him from Jahangir, and another self-portrait. In the painting-within-the-painting, Bichitr bows deeply before the emperor. In the larger painting, the artist signed his name across the top of the footstool Jahangir uses to step up to his hourglass throne. Thus, the ruler steps on Bichitr's name, further indicating the painter's inferior status.

Above Bichitr is a portrait in full European style (compare FIGS. 23-11, 23-11A, and 23-12) of King James I of England (r. 1603–1625), copied from a painting by John de Critz (ca. 1552–1642) that the English ambassador to the Mughal court had given as a gift to Jahangir. Above the king is a Turkish sultan, a convincing study of physiognomy but probably not a specific portrait. The highest member of the foursome is an elderly Muslim Sufi *shaykh* (mystic saint). Jahangir's father, Akbar, had gone to the mystic to pray for an heir. The current emperor, the answer to Akbar's prayers, presents the holy man with a sumptuous book as a gift. An inscription explains that "although to all appearances kings stand before him, Jahangir looks inwardly toward the dervishes [Islamic holy men]" for guidance. Bichitr's allegorical painting portrays his emperor in both words and pictures as favoring spiritual over worldly power.

# INDIA

Arab armies first appeared in South Asia (MAP 32-1)—at Sindh in present-day Pakistan—in 712, more than 800 years before the founding of the Mughal Empire. With the Arabs came Islam, the new religion that had already spread with astonishing speed from the Arabian peninsula to Syria, Iraq, Iran, Egypt, North Africa, and even southern Spain (see Chapter 10). At first, the *Muslims* (see "Muhammad and Islam," Chapter 10, page 285) established trading settlements in South Asia but did not press deeper into the subcontinent. At the Battle of Tarain in 1192, however, Muhammad of Ghor (Afghanistan) defeated the armies of a confederation of independent states. The Ghorids and other Islamic rulers gradually transformed South Asian society, religion, art, and architecture.

## Sultanate of Delhi

In 1206, Qutb al-Din Aybak, Muhammad of Ghor's general, established the Sultanate of Delhi (1206–1526). On his death in 1211, he passed power to his son Iltutmish (r. 1211–1236), who extended Ghorid rule across northern India.

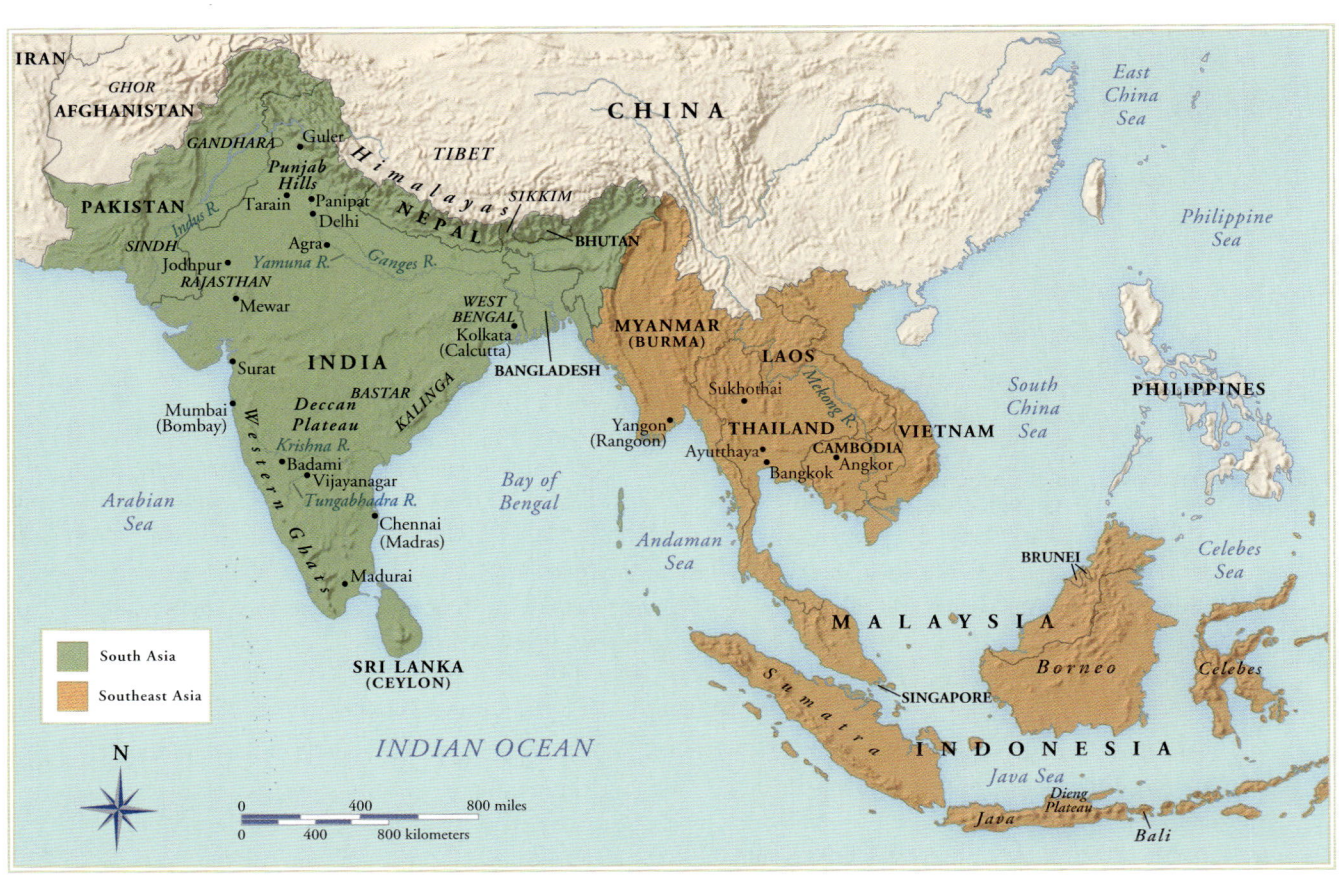

MAP 32-1 South and Southeast Asia, 1200 to 1980.

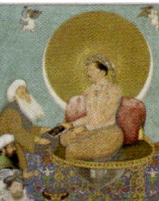

# SOUTH AND SOUTHEAST ASIA, 1200 TO 1980

| 1200 | 1600 | 1900 | 1980 |
|---|---|---|---|

- Arabs establish the Muslim Sultanate of Delhi (1206–1526) and introduce Islamic art and architecture to northern India
- In the south, Hindu kings rule the Vijayanagar Empire (1336–1565) and construct buildings mixing elements of both Hindu and Islamic architecture

- Miniature painting flourishes in the Mughal Empire (1526–1857)
- Muslim builders construct the Taj Mahal at Agra
- Rajput painters in northwestern India produce vividly colored miniature paintings with Hindu subjects
- The southern Nayak dynasty (1529–1736) builds towering Hindu temple precinct gateways decorated with painted stucco sculptures
- Buddhism and Buddhist art and architecture dominate Southeast Asia

- Queen Victoria I of England becomes Empress of India in 1877. European-inspired art and architecture accompany colonial rule
- India and Pakistan achieve independence in 1947. Post–World War II art in South and Southeast Asia is a mix of traditional and Western modernist styles

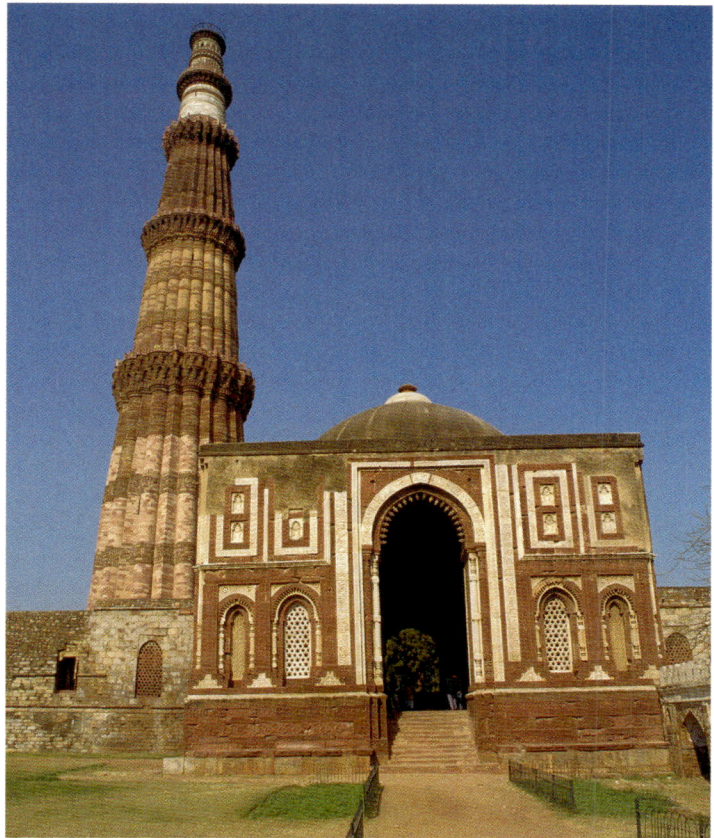

**32-2** Qutb Minar (*left,* looking north), begun early 13th century, and Alai Darvaza (*right*), 1311, Delhi, India. ◼◀

Qutb al-Din Aybak established the Sultanate of Delhi in 1206 and built the city's first mosque to mark the triumph of Islam in northern India. The 238-foot-high Qutb Minar is the world's tallest minaret.

**QUTB MINAR** To mark the triumph of Islam, Qutb al-Din Aybak built a great *congregational mosque* (see "The Mosque," Chapter 10, page 288) at Delhi, in part with pillars taken from Hindu and other temples. He named Delhi's first mosque the Quwwat al-Islam

(Might of Islam) Mosque. During the course of the next century, as the Islamic population of Delhi grew, the *sultans* (Muslim rulers) enlarged the mosque to more than triple its original size. Iltutmish erected the mosque's 238-foot tapering sandstone *minaret,* the Qutb Minar (FIG. **32-2,** *left*)—the tallest extant mosque tower in the world. It is too tall, in fact, to serve the principal function of a minaret—to provide a platform from which to call the Islamic faithful to prayer. Rather, it is a soaring monument to the victory of Islam, engraved with inscriptions in Arabic and Persian proclaiming the minaret casts the shadow of Allah (God) over the conquered Hindu city. Added in 1311, the Alai Darvaza, the entrance pavilion (FIG. 32-2, *right*), is a mix of architectural traditions, combining Islamic *pointed arches,* decorative grills over the windows, and a hemispherical *dome,* with a crowning *finial* recalling the motifs at the top of many Hindu temple towers (see Chapter 15).

## Vijayanagar Empire

While Muslim sultans from Central Asia ruled much of northern India from Delhi, Hindu kings controlled most of central and southern India. The most powerful Hindu dynasty of the era was the Vijayanagar. Established in 1336 by Harihara, a local king, the Vijayanagar Empire (1336–1565) takes its name from Vijayanagara (City of Victory) on the Tungabhadra River. Under the patronage of the royal family, Vijayanagara, located at the junction of several trade routes through Asia, became one of the most magnificent cities in the East. Although the capital lies in ruins today, at its peak ambassadors and travelers from as far away as Italy and Portugal marveled at Vijayanagara's riches. Under its greatest king, Krishnadevaraya (r. 1509–1529), who was also a renowned poet, the Vijayanagar kingdom was a magnet for the learned and cultured from all corners of India.

**LOTUS MAHAL** Vijayanagara's sacred center, built up over two centuries, boasts imposing temples to the Hindu gods in the style of southern India with tall pyramidal *vimanas* (towers) over the *garbha griha,* "the inner sanctuary" (see "Hindu Temples," Chapter 15, page 439). The buildings of the so-called Royal Enclave are more eclectic in character. One example in this prosperous royal city is the two-story monument of uncertain function known as the Lotus Mahal (FIG. **32-3**). The stepped towers crowning the vaulted second-story rooms resemble the pyramidal roofs of southern Indian temple vimanas (FIG. 15-23). But the windows of the upper level as well as the arches of the ground-floor piers have the distinctive multilobed contours of Islamic architecture (FIGS. 10-10 and 10-11). The Lotus Mahal, like the entrance pavilion of Delhi's first mosque (FIG. 32-2, *right*), exemplifies the stylistic crosscurrents typical of much of South Asian art and architecture of the second millennium.

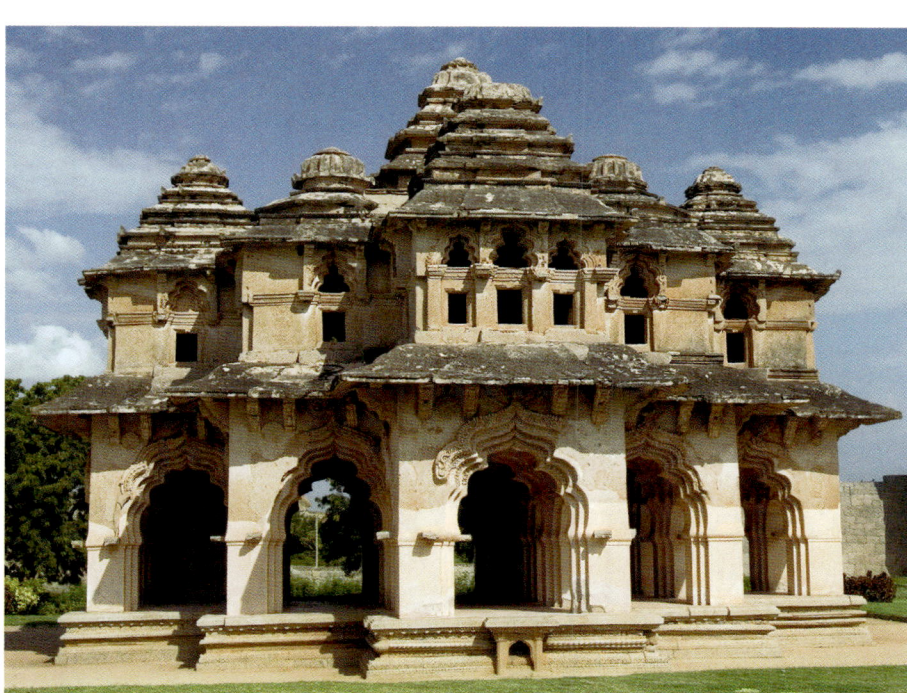

**32-3** Lotus Mahal (looking southwest), Vijayanagara, India, 15th or early 16th century.

The Vijayanagar Empire was the most powerful Hindu kingdom in southern India during the 14th to 16th centuries. The Lotus Mahal is an eclectic mix of Hindu and Islamic architectural elements.

# Mughal Empire

The 16th century was a time of upheaval in South Asia. In 1565, only a generation after Krishnadevaraya, a confederacy of sultanates in the Deccan plateau of central India brought the Vijayanagar Empire of the south to an end. Even earlier, a Muslim prince named Babur had defeated the last of the Ghorid sultans of northern India at the Battle of Panipat. Declaring himself the ruler of India, Babur established the Mughal Empire (1526–1857) at Delhi. In 1527, Babur vanquished the Rajput Hindu kings of Mewar (see page 980). By the time of his death in 1530, Babur headed a vast new empire in India.

**HUMAYUN** The emperor who succeeded Babur was Humayun (r. 1530–1556), but in 1543 the sultan of Gujarat temporarily wrested control of the Mughal Empire. Humayun sought sanctuary in Iran at the court of the Safavid ruler Shah Tahmasp (r. 1524–1576; FIG. 32-5) and remained in exile until 1555. During his years at the Safavid court, the Mughal emperor acquired a taste for Persian illustrated books. Upon his return to power, Humayun brought with him to Delhi two Safavid master painters. Pupils of the renowned Bihzad (FIG. 10-29), they in turn trained a generation of Mughal artists.

**AKBAR THE GREAT** The first great flowering of Mughal art and architecture occurred during the long reign of Humayun's son, Akbar (r. 1556–1605), called the Great, who ascended the throne at age 14. Like his father, Akbar was a great admirer of the narrative paintings (FIG. 10-29) produced at the Safavid court. The young ruler enlarged the number of painters in Humayun's imperial workshop to about a hundred and kept them busy working on a series of ambitious projects. One of these was to illustrate the text of the *Hamzanama*—the story of Hamza, Muhammad's uncle—in some 1,400 large paintings on cloth. The assignment took 15 years to complete.

The illustrated books and engravings that traders, diplomats, and Christian missionaries brought from Europe to India also fascinated Akbar. In 1580, Portuguese Jesuits brought one particularly important source, the eight-volume *Royal Polyglot Bible,* as a gift to Akbar. This massive set of books, printed in Antwerp, contained engravings by several Flemish artists. Akbar immediately set his painters to copying the illustrations.

*AKBARNAMA* Akbar also commissioned Abul Fazl (1551–1602), a member of his court and close friend, to chronicle his life in a great biography, the *Akbarnama* (*History of Akbar*), which the emperor's painters illustrated. One of the full-page illustrations, or so-called *miniatures* (see "Indian Miniature Painting," page 979), in the emperor's personal copy of the *Akbarnama* was a collaborative effort between the painter BASAWAN, who designed and drew the composition, and CHATAR MUNI, who colored it. The painting (FIG. 32-4) depicts the episode of Akbar and Hawai, a wild elephant the 19-year-old ruler mounted and pitted against another ferocious elephant. When the second animal fled in defeat, Hawai, still carrying Akbar, chased it to a pontoon bridge. The enormous weight of the elephants capsized the boats, but Akbar managed to bring Hawai under control and dismount safely. The young ruler viewed the episode as an allegory of his ability to govern—that is, to take charge of an unruly state.

For his pictorial record of that frightening day, Basawan chose the moment of maximum chaos and danger—when the elephants crossed the pontoon bridge, sending boatmen flying into the water. The composition is a bold one, with a very high horizon and two strong diagonal lines formed by the bridge and the shore. Together

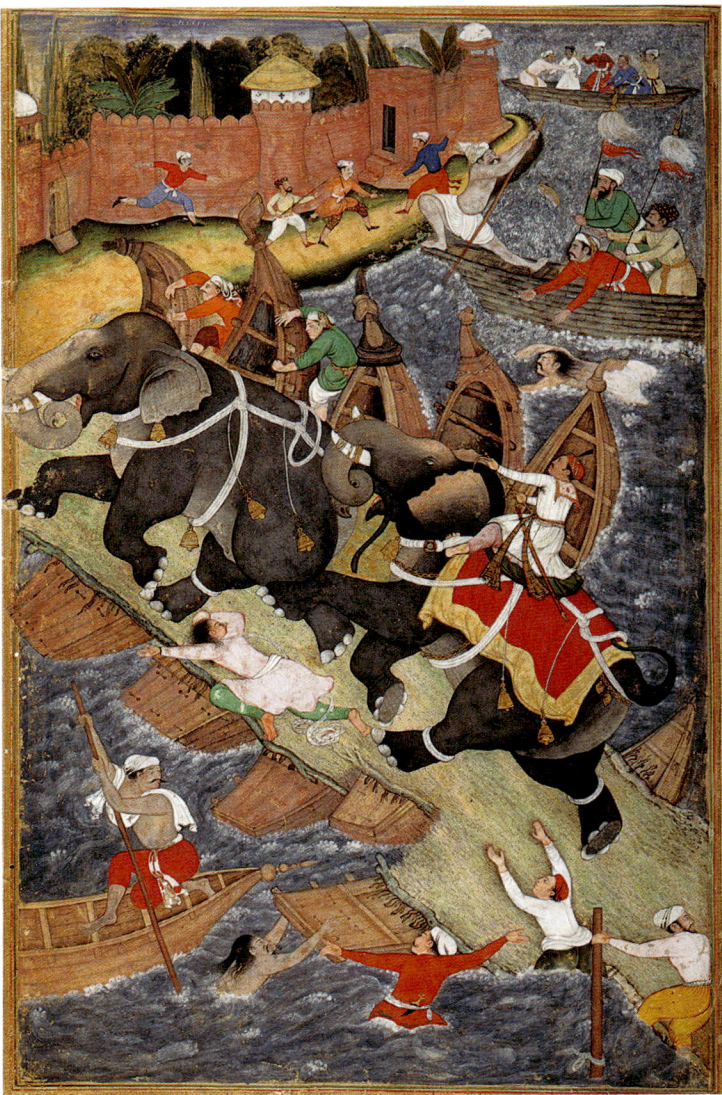

**32-4** BASAWAN and CHATAR MUNI, *Akbar and the Elephant Hawai,* folio 22 from the *Akbarnama* (*History of Akbar*) by Abul Fazl, ca. 1590. Opaque watercolor on paper, $1' 1\frac{7}{8}'' \times 8\frac{3}{4}''$. Victoria & Albert Museum, London.

For this miniature portraying the young emperor Akbar bringing an elephant under control, Basawan chose the moment of maximum danger. The episode is an allegory of Akbar's ability to rule.

these devices tend to flatten out the vista, yet at the same time Basawan created a sense of depth by diminishing the size of the figures in the background. He was also a master of vivid gestures and anecdotal detail. Note especially the bare-chested figure in the foreground clinging to the end of a boat, the figure near the lower right corner with outstretched arms sliding into the water as the bridge sinks, and the oarsman just beyond the bridge who strains to steady his vessel while his three passengers stand up or lean overboard in reaction to the surrounding commotion.

**SAHIFA BANU** Another Mughal miniaturist whose name is known is SAHIFA BANU (active early 17th century), a princess in the court of Jahangir (FIGS. 32-1 and 32-5A) and the most renowned female artist of the Mughal Empire. In one of her miniatures (FIG. 32-5), she paid tribute to Shah Tahmasp of Iran, the great patron of Safavid painting who sent two of his masters to Delhi to train the

# Indian Miniature Painting

Although India had a tradition of mural painting going back to ancient times (see "The Painted Caves of Ajanta," Chapter 15, page 433, and FIG. 15-15), the most popular form of painting under the Mughal emperors (FIGS. 32-1, 32-4, 32-5, and 32-5A) and Rajput kings (FIGS. 32-7 and 32-7A) was miniature painting. Art historians usually call these paintings *miniatures* because of their small size (about the size of a page in this book) compared with paintings on walls, wood panels, or canvas, but the original terminology derives from the red lead (*miniatum*) used as a pigment. The artists who painted the Indian miniatures designed them to be held in the hands, either as illustrations in books or as loose-leaf pages in albums. Owners did not place Indian miniatures in frames and only very rarely hung them on walls.

Indian artists used opaque watercolors and paper (occasionally cotton cloth) to produce their miniatures. The manufacturing and painting of miniatures was a complicated process and required years of training as an apprentice in a workshop. The painters' assistants created pigments by grinding natural materials—minerals such as malachite for green and lapis lazuli for blue; earth ochers for red and yellow; and metallic foil for gold, silver, and copper. They fashioned brushes from bird quills and kitten or baby squirrel hairs. For minute details, the painters used brushes with a single hair.

The artist began the painting process by making a full-size sketch of the composition. The next step was to transfer the sketch onto paper by *pouncing*, or tracing, using thin, transparent gazelle skin placed on top of the drawing and pricking the contours of the design with a pin. Then, with the skin laid on a fresh sheet of fine paper, the painter forced black pigment through the tiny holes, reproducing the outlines of the composition. Painting proper started with the darkening of the outlines with black or reddish brown ink. Painters of miniatures sat on the ground, resting their painting boards on one raised knee. Each pigment color was in a separate half seashell. The paintings usually required several layers of color, with gold always applied last. The final step was to burnish the painted surface. The artists accomplished this by placing the miniature, painted side down, on a hard, smooth surface and stroking the paper with polished agate or crystal.

**32-5** SAHIFA BANU, *Shah Tahmasp Meditating*, early 17th century. Opaque watercolor on paper, figure panel 6″ × 3⅝″. Victoria & Albert Museum, London.

This miniature by one of the few known Mughal women artists depicts the Persian emperor Shah Tahmasp. Two of his court painters went to India to train Mughal imperial book illustrators.

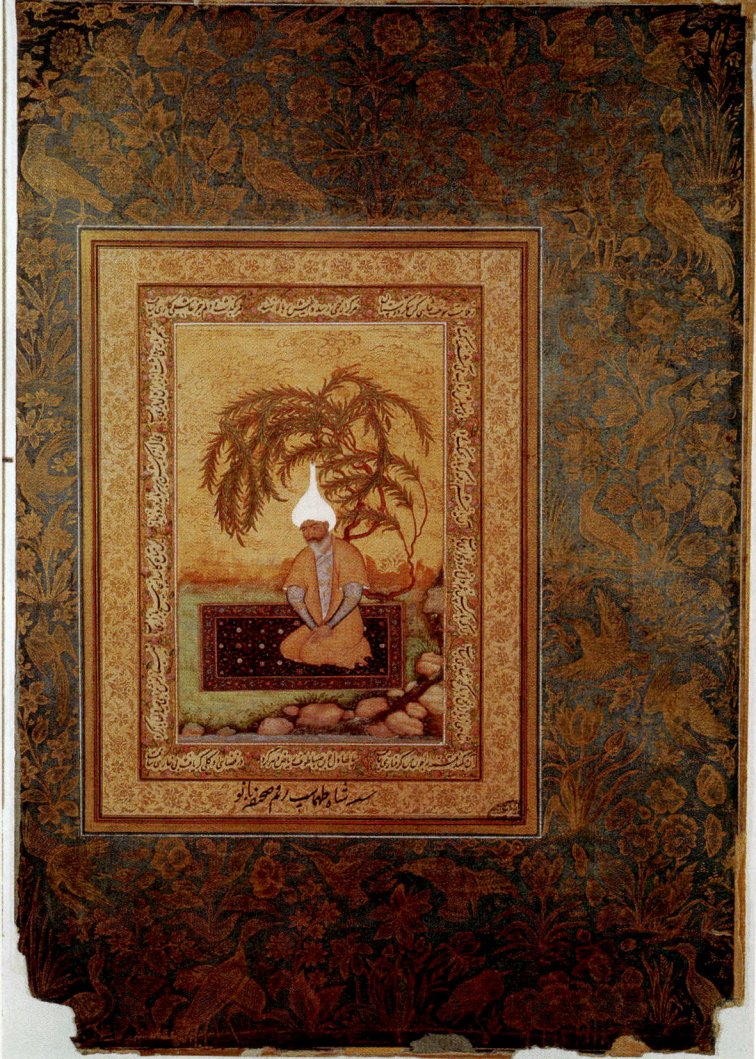

1 in.

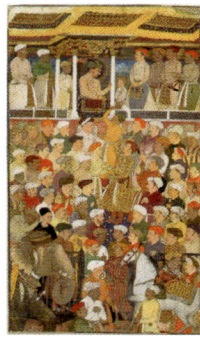

**32-5A** ABDUL HASAN and MANOHAR, *Darbar of Jahangir*, ca. 1620.

early Mughal miniaturists at the court of Humayun. The Safavid ruler sits in meditation on a magnificent Persian carpet at the edge of a stream underneath the windblown branches of a tree. As in other Mughal paintings (FIGS. 32-1, 32-4, and 32-5A)—in sharp contrast to the almost obsessive interest in linear perspective in contemporaneous European painting—the Indian artist combined different viewpoints in the same frame, depicting the shah and the tree seen from eye level, and the carpet, ground, and stream seen from above. This composition enabled the princess to reproduce the intricate design of the woven carpet (compare FIG. 10-27) with pristine clarity and without the distortion that would have resulted from foreshortening the textile patterns. In fact, the miniature itself, with its decorative border, has a textilelike quality and resembles Tahmasp's carpet in both format and proportions. The frame around Banu's portrait of Tahmasp also features elegant calligraphy. Although female painters were rare during the Mughal Empire, many court women were accomplished calligraphers.

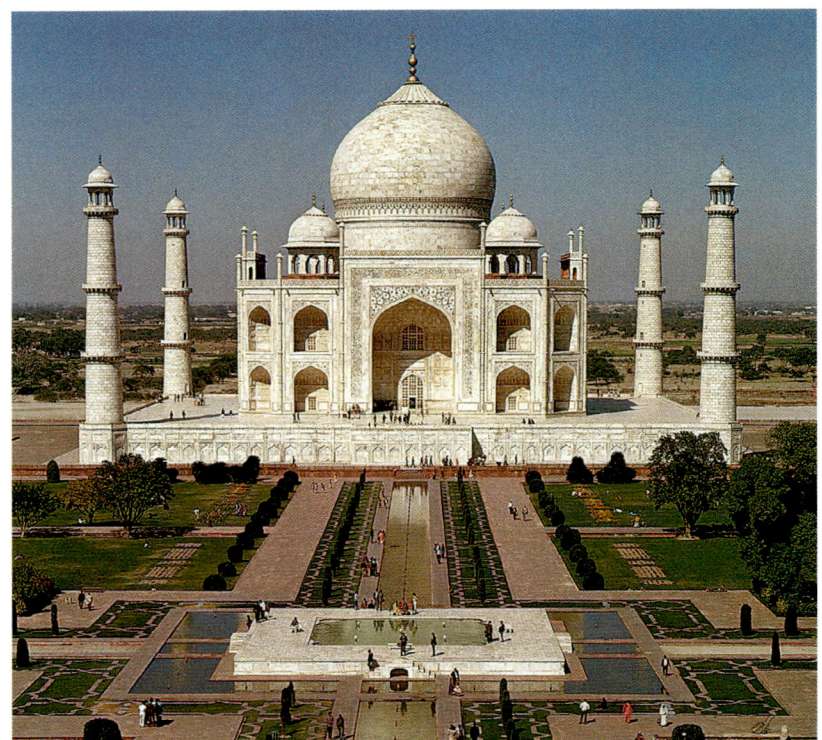

**32-6** Taj Mahal (looking north), Agra, India, 1632–1647. ■◄

This Mughal mausoleum seems to float magically over reflecting pools in a vast garden. The tomb may have been conceived as the throne of God perched above the gardens of Paradise on judgment day.

**TAJ MAHAL** Monumental tombs were not part of either the Hindu or Buddhist traditions but had a long history in Islamic architecture. The Delhi sultans had erected tombs in India, but none could compare in grandeur to the fabled Taj Mahal (FIG. 32-6) at Agra. Shah Jahan (r. 1628–1658), Jahangir's son, built the immense *mausoleum* as a memorial to his favorite wife, Mumtaz Mahal (1593–1631), although it eventually became the ruler's tomb as well. The dome-on-cube shape of the central block has antecedents in earlier Islamic mausoleums (FIGS. 10-8 and 10-22) and other Islamic buildings such as the Alai Darvaza (FIG. 32-2, *right*) at Delhi, but modifications and refinements in the design of the Agra tomb converted the earlier massive structures into an almost weightless vision of glistening white marble. The Agra mausoleum seems to float magically above the tree-lined reflecting pools punctuating the garden leading to it. Reinforcing the illusion of the marble tomb being suspended above water is the absence of any visible means of ascent to the upper platform. A stairway does exist, but the architect intentionally hid it from the view of anyone approaching the memorial.

The Taj Mahal follows the plan of Iranian garden pavilions, except the building stands at one end rather than in the center of the formal garden. The tomb is octagonal in plan and has typically Iranian arcuated niches (FIG. 10-26) on each side. The interplay of shadowy voids with light-reflecting marble walls that seem paper-thin creates an impression of translucency. The pointed arches lead the eye in a sweeping upward movement toward the climactic dome, shaped like a crown (*taj*). Four carefully related minarets and two flanking triple-domed pavilions (not visible in FIG. 32-6) enhance and stabilize the soaring form of the mausoleum. The architect achieved this delicate balance between verticality and horizontality by strictly applying an all-encompassing system of proportions. The Taj Mahal (excluding the minarets) is exactly as wide as it is tall, and the height of its dome is equal to the height of the facade.

Abd al-Hamid Lahori (d. 1654), a court historian who witnessed the construction of the Taj Mahal, compared its minarets with ladders reaching toward Heaven and the surrounding gardens to Paradise. In fact, inscribed on the gateway to the gardens and the walls of the mausoleum are carefully selected excerpts from the Koran confirming the historian's interpretation of the tomb's symbolism. The designer of the Taj Mahal may have conceived the mausoleum as the throne of God perched above the gardens of Paradise on judgment day. The minarets hold up the canopy of that throne. In Islam, the most revered place of burial is beneath the throne of God.

## Hindu Rajput Kingdoms

The Mughal emperors ruled vast territories, but much of northwestern India (present-day Rajasthan) remained under the control of Hindu Rajput (sons of kings) rulers. These small kingdoms, some claiming to have originated well before 1500, had stubbornly resisted Mughal expansion, but even the strongest of them—Mewar—eventually submitted to the Mughal emperors. When Jahangir defeated the Mewari forces in 1615, the Mewari *maharana*

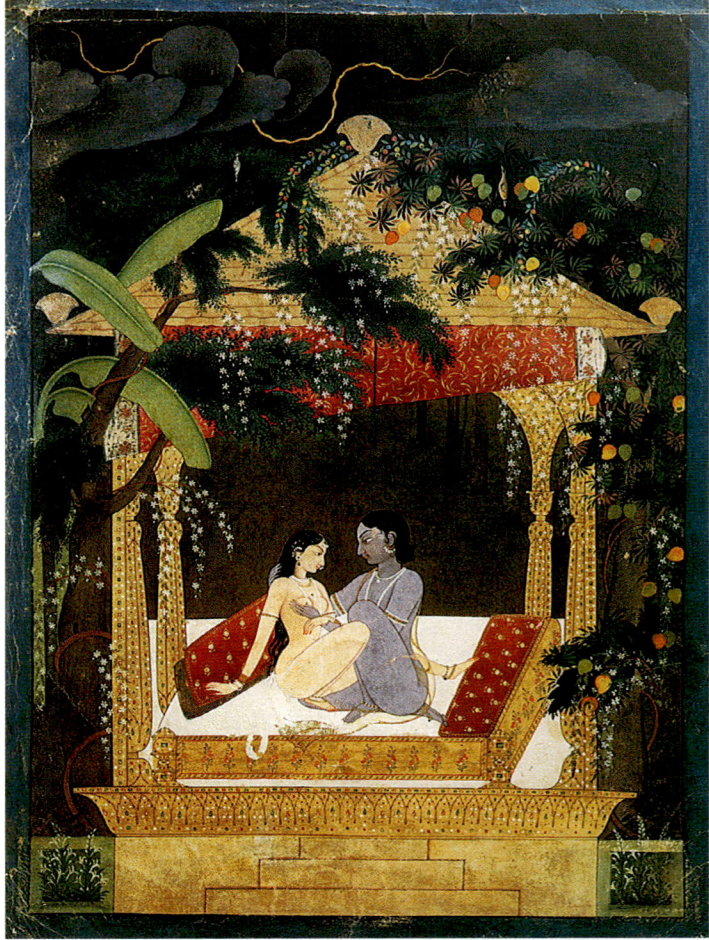

1 in.

**32-7** *Krishna and Radha in a Pavilion,* ca. 1760. Opaque watercolor on paper, $11\frac{1}{8}'' \times 7\frac{3}{4}''$. National Museum, New Delhi.

The love of Krishna, the "Blue God," for Radha is the subject of this colorful, lyrical, and sensual Pahari watercolor. Krishna's love was a model of the devotion paid to the Hindu god Vishnu.

(great king), like the other Rajput rulers, maintained a degree of independence but had to pay tribute to the Mughal treasury until the demise of the Mughal Empire in 1857.

Rajput painting resembles Mughal (and Persian) painting in format and material, but it differs sharply in other respects. Most Rajput artists, for example, worked in anonymity, never inserting self-portraits into their paintings as the Mughal painter Bichitr did in his miniature (FIG. 32-1) of Jahangir sitting on an hourglass throne.

*KRISHNA AND RADHA* One of the most popular subjects for Rajput paintings was the amorous adventures of Krishna, the "Blue God," the most popular of the *avatars,* or incarnations, of the Hindu god Vishnu, who descends to earth to aid mortals (see "Hinduism," Chapter 15, page 435, or page xxxiii in Volume II and Book D). Krishna was a herdsman who spent an idyllic existence tending his cows, playing the flute, and sporting with beautiful herdswomen. His favorite lover was Radha. The 12th-century poet Jayadeva re-

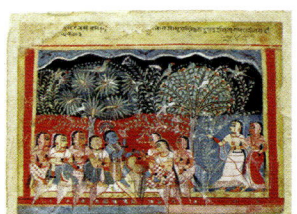

**32-7A** *Krishna and the Gopis,* ca. 1550.

lated the story of Krishna and Radha in the *Gita Govinda* (*Song of the Cowherd*). Their love was a model of the devotion, or *bhakti,* paid to Vishnu. Jayadeva's poem was the source for hundreds of later paintings, including *Krishna and Radha in a Pavilion* (FIG. 32-7) and *Krishna and the Gopis* (FIG. 32-7A).

*Krishna and Radha in a Pavilion* was the work of an artist in the Punjab Hills, probably in the employ of Raja Govardhan Chand

of Guler (r. 1741–1773). The artists producing paintings for the rulers of the Punjab Hill states—referred to collectively as the Pahari School—had a distinctive style. Although Pahari painting owed much to Mughal drawing style, its coloration, lyricism, and sensuality are readily recognizable. In the Krishna and Radha miniature, the lovers sit naked on a bed beneath a jeweled pavilion in a lush garden of ripe mangoes and flowering shrubs. Krishna gently touches Radha's breast while looking directly into her face. Radha shyly averts her gaze. It is night, the time of illicit trysts, and the dark monsoon sky momentarily lights up with a lightning flash indicating the moment's electric passion. Lightning is one of the standard symbols used in Rajput and Pahari miniatures to represent sexual excitement.

## Nayak Dynasty

The Nayakas, governors under the Vijayanagar kings, declared their independence in 1529, and after their former overlords' defeat in 1565 at the hands of the Deccan sultanates, they continued Hindu rule in the far south of India for two centuries (1529–1736).

**GREAT TEMPLE, MADURAI** Construction of some of the largest temple complexes in India occurred under Nayak patronage. The most striking features of these huge complexes are their gateway towers called *gopuras* (FIG. **32-8**), decorated from top to bottom with painted sculptures. After erecting the gopuras, the builders constructed walls to connect them and then built more gopuras, always expanding outward from the center. Each set of gopuras was taller than those of the previous wall circuit. The outermost towers reached colossal size, dwarfing the temples at the heart of the complexes. The tallest gopuras of the Great Temple at Madurai, dedicated to Shiva (under his local name, Sundareshvara, the Handsome One) and his consort Minakshi (the Fish-eyed One), stand about 150 feet tall. Rising in a series of tiers of diminishing size, they culminate in a *barrel-vaulted* roof with finials. The ornamentation is extremely rich, consisting of row after row of brightly painted stucco sculptures representing the vast pantheon of Hindu deities and a host of attendant figures. Reconsecration of the temple occurs at 12-year intervals, at which time the gopura sculptures receive a new coat of paint, which accounts for the vibrancy of their colors today. The Madurai Nayak temple complex also contains large and numerous mandapas, as well

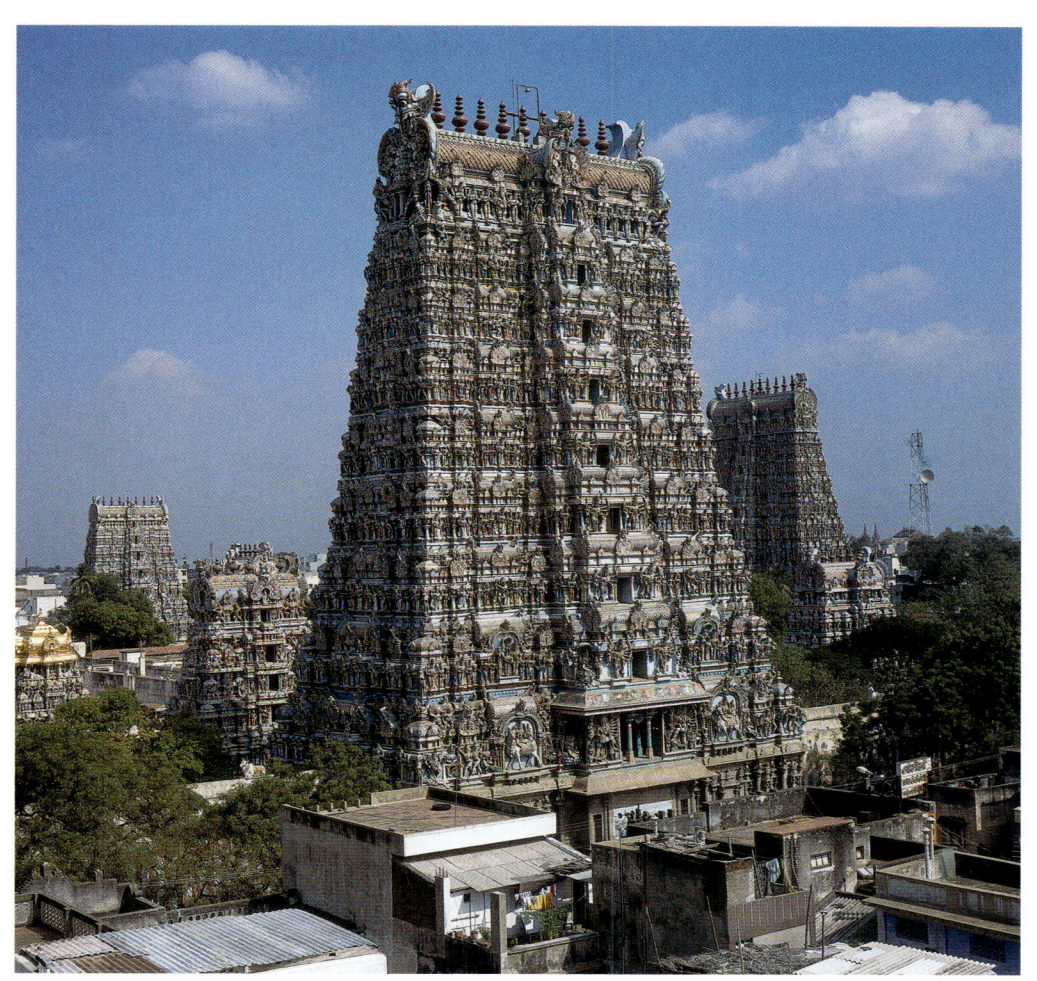

**32-8** Outermost gopuras of the Great Temple (looking southeast), Madurai, India, completed 17th century.

The colossal gateway towers erected during the Nayak dynasty at the Great Temple at Madurai feature brightly painted stucco sculptures representing the vast pantheon of Hindu deities.

as great water tanks worshipers use for ritual bathing. These temples were, and continue to be, almost independent cities, with thousands of pilgrims, merchants, and priests flocking from near and far to the many yearly festivals hosted by the temples.

## The British in India

English merchants first arrived in India toward the end of the 16th century, attracted by the land's spices, gems, and other riches. On December 31, 1599, Queen Elizabeth I (r. 1558–1603) granted a charter to the East India Company, which sought to compete with the Portuguese and Dutch in the lucrative trade with South Asia. The company established a "factory" (trading post) at the port of Surat, approximately 150 miles from Mumbai (Bombay) in western India in 1613. After securing trade privileges with the Mughal emperor Jahangir, the British expanded their factories to Chennai (Madras), Kolkata (Calcutta), and Mumbai by 1661. These outposts gradually spread throughout India, especially after the British defeat of the ruler of Bengal in 1757. By the opening of the 19th century, the East India Company effectively ruled large portions of the subcontinent, and in 1835, the British declared English India's official language. A great rebellion in 1857 persuaded the British Parliament the East India Company could no longer be the agent of British rule. The next year Parliament abolished the company and replaced its governor-general with a viceroy of the crown. Two decades later, in 1877, Queen Victoria (r. 1837–1901) assumed the title Empress of India with sovereignty over all the former Indian states.

**VICTORIA TERMINUS** The British brought the Industrial Revolution and railways to India. One of the most enduring monuments of British rule, still used by millions of travelers, is Victoria Terminus (FIG. **32-9**) in Mumbai, named at the time of its construction for the first British empress of India (but now called Chhatrapati Shivaji Terminus). A British architect, FREDERICK W. STEVENS (1847–1900), was the designer. Construction of the giant railway station began in 1878 and took a decade to complete. Although built of the same local sandstone used for temples and statues throughout India's long history, Victoria Terminus is a European transplant to the subcontinent, the architectural counterpart of colonial rule. Conceived as a cathedral to modernization, the terminus fittingly has an allegorical statue of Progress crowning its tallest dome. Nonetheless, the building's design looks backward, not forward. Inside, passengers gaze up at *groin-vaulted* ceilings and *stained-glass* windows, and the exterior of the station resembles a Western church with a gabled facade and flanking towers. Stevens modeled Victoria Terminus, with its tiers of screened windows, on the architecture of late medieval and Renaissance Venice (FIGS. 14-21 and 21-37A).

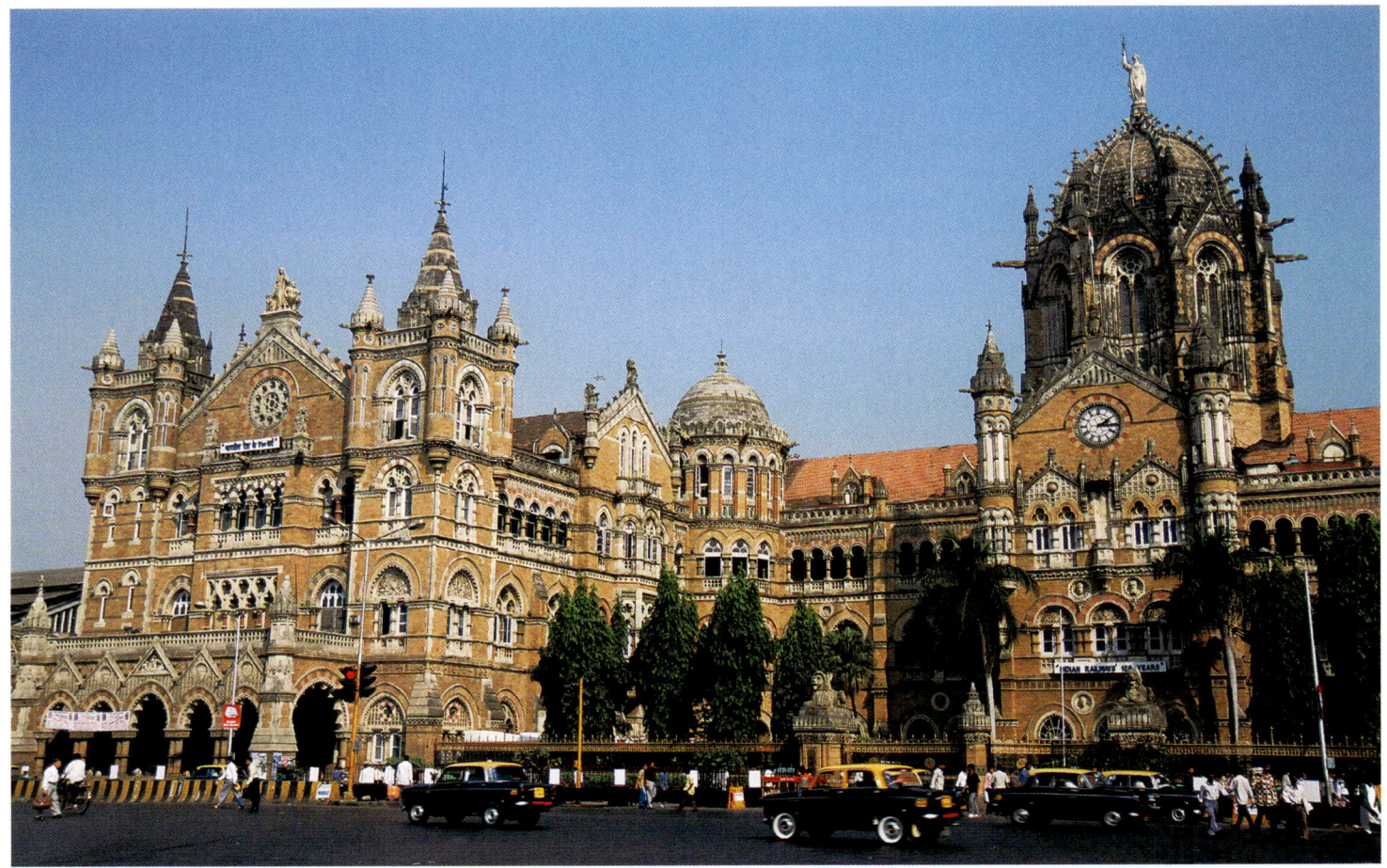

**32-9** FREDERICK W. STEVENS, Victoria Terminus (now Chhatrapati Shivaji Terminus; looking northeast), Mumbai (Bombay), India, 1878–1887.

Victoria Terminus, named after Queen Victoria of England, is a monument to colonial rule. Designed by a British architect, it is a European transplant to India, modeled on late medieval Venetian architecture.

**JASWANT SINGH** With British rulers and modern railways also came British or, more generally, European ideas, but Western culture and religion never supplanted India's own rich traditions. Many Indians, however, readily took on the trappings of European society. When Jaswant Singh, the ruler of Jodhpur (r. 1873–1895) in Rajasthan, sat for his portrait (FIG. **32-10**) around 1880, he chose to sit in an ordinary chair, rather than on a throne, with his arm resting on a simple table with a bouquet and a book on it. In other words, he posed as if he were an ordinary British gentleman in his sitting room. Nevertheless, the painter, an anonymous local artist who had embraced Western style, left no question about Jaswant Singh's regal presence and pride. The ruler's powerful chest and arms, along with the sword and his leather riding boots, indicate his abilities as a warrior and hunter. The curled beard signified fierceness to Indians of that time. The unflinching gaze records the ruler's confidence. Perhaps the two necklaces Jaswant Singh wears best exemplify the combination of his two worlds. One necklace is a bib of huge emeralds and diamonds, the heritage of the wealth and splendor of his family's rule. The other, a wide gold band with a cameo, is the Order of the Star of India, a high honor his British overlords bestowed on him.

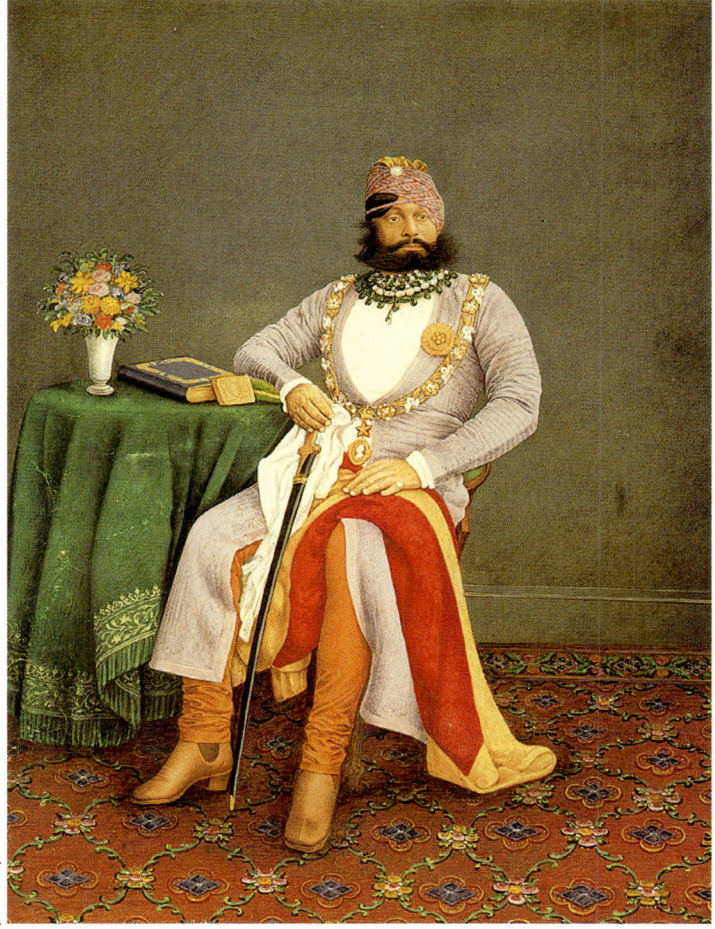

**32-10** *Maharaja Jaswant Singh of Marwar,* **ca. 1880. Opaque watercolor on paper, 1′ 3$\frac{1}{2}$″ × 11$\frac{5}{8}$″. Brooklyn Museum, Brooklyn (gift of Mr. and Mrs. Robert L. Poster).**

Jaswant Singh, the ruler of Jodhpur, had himself portrayed as a British gentleman in his sitting room, but the artist employed the same materials Indian miniature painters had used for centuries.

1 in.

The painter of this portrait worked on the same scale and employed the same materials—opaque watercolor on paper—Indian miniature painters had used for centuries, but the artist copied the ruler's likeness from a photograph. This accounts in large part for the realism of the portrait. Indian artists sometimes even painted directly on top of photographs. Photography arrived in India at an early date. In 1840, just one year after its invention in Paris, the *daguerreotype* (FIG. 27-48) was introduced in Calcutta. Indian artists readily adopted the new medium, not just to produce portraits but also to record landscapes and monuments.

In 19th-century India, however, admiration of Western art and culture was by no means universal. At the end of the century, Abanindranath Tagore (1871–1951) founded a nationalistic art movement, and the opening decades of the 20th century brought ever-louder calls for Indian self-government. Under the leadership of Mahatma Gandhi (1869–1948) and others, India achieved independence in 1947—not, however, as a unified state but as the predominantly Hindu and Muslim nations of India and Pakistan respectively.

## 20th Century

Modern art in India is as multifaceted a phenomenon as modern art is elsewhere in the world. Many traditional artists work at the village level, making images of deities for local use out of inexpensive materials, such as clay, plaster, and papier-mâché. Some urban artists use these same materials to produce elaborate religious tableaux, such as depictions of the goddess Durga killing the buffalo demon for the annual 10-day Durga Festival in Calcutta. Participants in the festival often ornament the tableaux with thousands of colored electric lights. The most popular art form for religious imagery, however, is the brightly colored print, sold for only a few rupees each.

Many contemporary artists, in contrast, create works for the international market. Although many of them received their training in South or Southeast Asia or Japan, others attended schools in Europe or the United States, and some, for example, Shahzia Sikander (FIG. 31-5), now work outside their home countries. They face one of the fundamental quandaries of many contemporary Asian artists—how to identify themselves and situate their work between local and international, traditional and modern, and non-Western and Western cultures.

**MEERA MUKHERJEE** One Indian artist who successfully bridged these two poles of modern Asian art was MEERA MUKHERJEE (1923–1998). Mukherjee studied with European masters in Germany, but when she returned to India, she rejected much of what she had learned in favor of the techniques long employed by traditional sculptors of the Bastar tribe in central India. Mukherjee went to live with Bastar bronze-casters, who had perfected a variation on the classic *lost-wax process* (see "Hollow-Casting Life-Size Bronze Statues," Chapter 5, page 130). Beginning with a rough core of clay, the Bastar sculptors build up what will be the final shape of the statue by placing long threads of beeswax over the core. Then they apply a coat of clay paste to the beeswax and tie up the mold with metal wire. After heating the mold over a charcoal fire, which melts the wax away, they pour liquid bronze into the space once occupied by the wax threads. Large sculptures require many separate molds. The Bastar artists complete their statues by welding together the separately cast sections, usually leaving the seams visible.

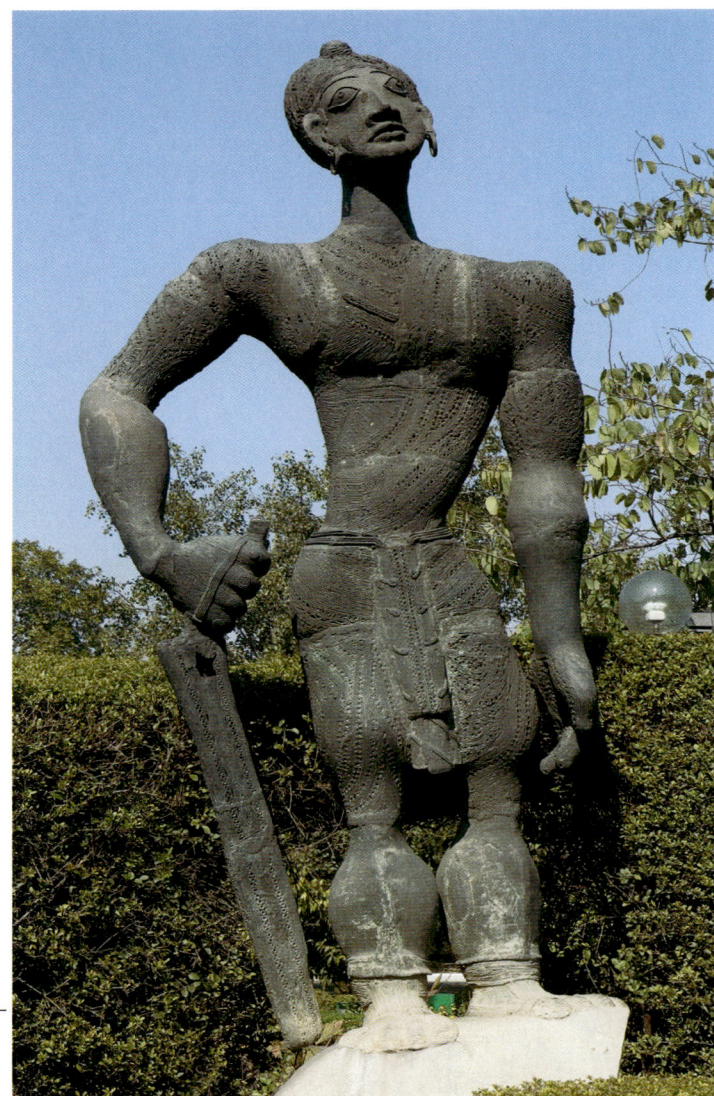

**32-11** MEERA MUKHERJEE, *Ashoka at Kalinga,* 1972. Bronze, 11′ 6¾″ high. Maurya Sheraton Hotel, New Delhi.

Mukherjee combined the Bastar tribe's traditional bronze-casting techniques with the swelling forms of 20th-century European sculpture in this statue of King Ashoka—a pacifist's protest against violence.

Many scholars regard *Ashoka at Kalinga* (FIG. **32-11**) as Mukherjee's greatest work. Twice life-size and assembled from 26 cast-bronze sections, the towering statue combines the intricate surface textures of traditional Bastar work with the expressively swelling abstract forms of some 20th-century European sculpture (FIG. 29-63). Mukherjee chose as her subject the third-century BCE Maurya emperor Ashoka standing on the battlefield at Kalinga. There, Ashoka witnessed more than 100,000 deaths and, shocked by the horrors of the war he had unleashed, rejected violence and adopted Buddhism as the official religion of his empire (see "Ashoka's Conversion to Buddhism," Chapter 15, page 428). Mukherjee conceived her statue as a pacifist protest against political violence in late-20th-century India. By reaching into India's remote history to make a contemporary political statement and by employing the bronze-casting methods of tribal sculptors while molding her forms in a modern idiom, she united her native land's past and present in a single work of great emotive power.

# SOUTHEAST ASIA

India was not alone in experiencing major shifts in political power and religious preferences during the past 800 years. The Khmer of Angkor (see Chapter 15), after reaching the height of their power at the beginning of the 13th century, lost one of their outposts in northern Thailand to their Thai vassals at midcentury. The newly founded Thai kingdoms quickly replaced Angkor as the region's major power, while Theravada Buddhism (see "Buddhism and Buddhist Iconography," Chapter 15, page 427, or page xxxii in Volume II and Book D) became the religion of the entire mainland except Vietnam. The Vietnamese, restricted to the northern region of present-day Vietnam, gained independence in the 10th century after a thousand years of Chinese political and cultural domination. They pushed to the south, ultimately destroying the indigenous Cham culture, which had dominated there for more than a millennium. A similar Burmese drive southward in Myanmar matched the Thai and Vietnamese expansions. All these movements resulted in demographic changes during the second millennium that led to the cultural, political, and artistic transformation of mainland Southeast Asia. A religious shift also occurred in Indonesia. With Islam growing in importance, all of Indonesia except the island of Bali became predominantly Muslim by the 16th century.

## Thailand

Southeast Asians practiced both Buddhism and Hinduism, but by the 13th century, in contrast to developments in India, Hinduism was in decline and Buddhism dominated much of the mainland. Two prominent Buddhist kingdoms came to power in Thailand during the 13th and early 14th centuries. Historians date the beginning of the Sukhothai kingdom to 1292, the year King Ramkhamhaeng (r. 1279–1299) erected a four-sided stele bearing the first inscription written in the Thai language. Sukhothai's political dominance proved to be short-lived, however. Ayuthaya, a city founded in central Thailand in 1350, quickly became the more powerful kingdom and warred sporadically with other states in Southeast Asia until the mid-18th century. Scholars nonetheless regard the Sukhothai period as the golden age of Thai art. In the inscription on his stele, Ramkhamhaeng (Rama the Strong) described Sukhothai as a city of monasteries and many images of the Buddha.

**WALKING BUDDHA** Theravada Buddhism came to Sukhothai from Sri Lanka (see Chapter 15). At the center of the city stood Wat Mahathat, Sukhothai's most important Buddhist monastery. Its *stupa* (mound-shaped Buddhist shrine; see "The Stupa," Chapter 15, page 430) housed a *relic* of the Buddha (*Wat Mahathat* means "Monastery of the Great Relic") and attracted large crowds of pilgrims. Sukhothai's crowning artistic achievement was the development of a type of walking-Buddha statue (FIG. **32-12**) displaying a distinctively Thai approach to body form. The bronze Buddha has broad shoulders and a narrow waist and wears a clinging monk's robe. He strides forward, his right heel off the ground and his left arm raised with the hand held in the do-not-fear *mudra* (gesture) that encourages worshipers to come forward in reverence (see "Buddhism and Buddhist Iconography," Chapter 15, page 427, or page xxxii in Volume II or Book D). A flame leaps from the top of the Buddha's head, and a sharp nose projects from his rounded face. The right arm hangs loosely, seemingly without muscles or joints, and resembles an elephant's trunk. The Sukhothai artists intended the body type to suggest a supernatural being and to express the Buddha's beauty and perfection. Although images in

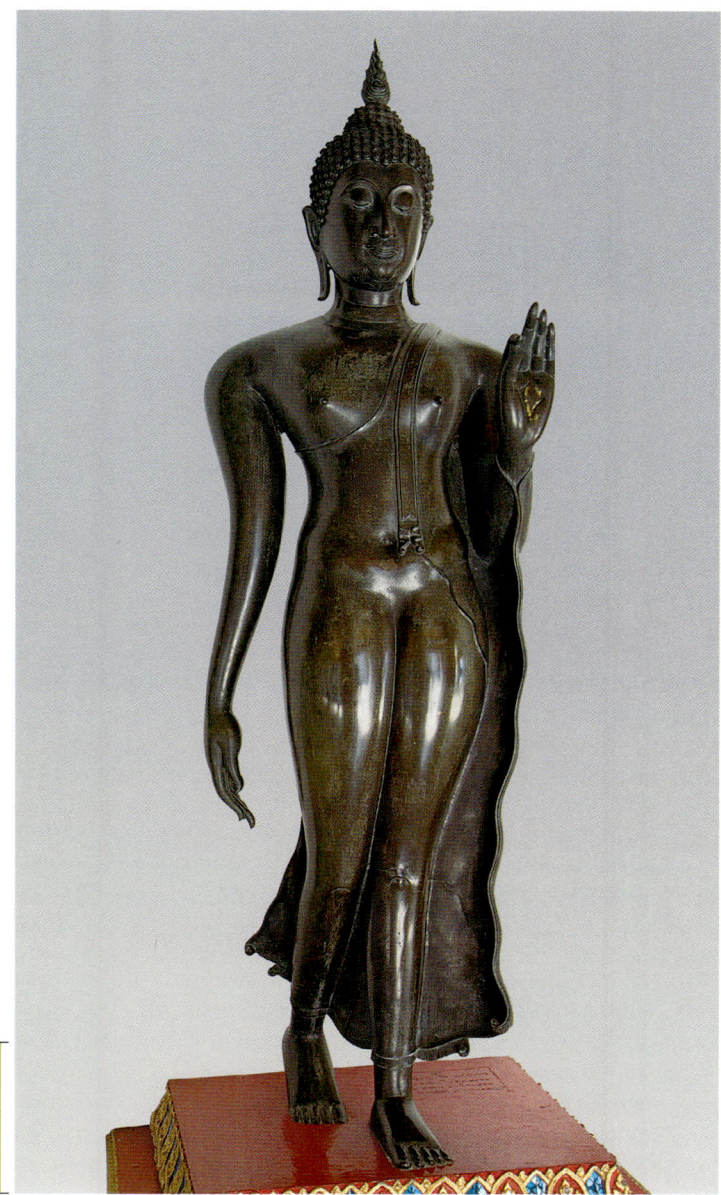

1 ft.

**32-12** Walking Buddha, from Sukhothai, Thailand, 14th century. Bronze, 7′ 2½″ high. Wat Bechamabopit, Bangkok. ◼◀

Walking-Buddha statues are unique to Thailand and display a distinctive approach to human anatomy. The Buddha's body is soft and elastic, and the right arm hangs loosely, like an elephant trunk.

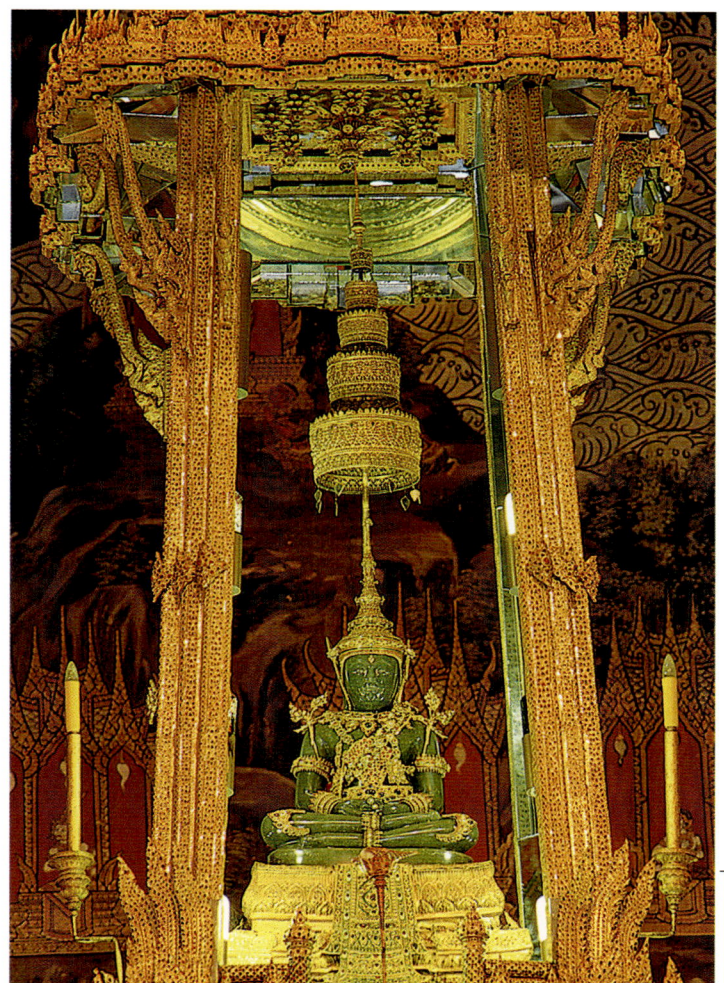

1 ft.

**32-13** *Emerald Buddha,* Emerald Temple, Bangkok, Thailand, 15th century. Jade or jasper, 2′ 6″ high.

The Thai king dresses the *Emerald Buddha,* carved from green jade or jasper, in a monk's robe and a king's robe at different times of the year, underscoring the image's symbolic role as both Buddha and king.

stone exist, the Sukhothai artists handled bronze best, a material well suited to their conception of the Buddha's body as elastic. The Sukhothai walking-Buddha statuary type is unique in Buddhist art.

***EMERALD BUDDHA*** A second distinctive Buddha image from northern Thailand is the *Emerald Buddha* (FIG. **32-13**), housed in the Emerald Temple on the royal palace grounds in Bangkok. The sculpture is small, only 30 inches tall, and conforms to the ancient type of the Buddha seated in meditation in a yogic posture with his legs crossed and his hands in his lap, palms upward (FIG. 15-11). It first appears in historical records in 1434 in northern Thailand, where Buddhist chronicles record its story. The chronicles describe the Buddha image as plaster-encased, and thus no one knew the statue was green stone. A lightning bolt caused

some of the plaster to flake off, disclosing its gemlike nature. Taken by various rulers to a series of cities in northern Thailand and in Laos over the course of more than 300 years, the small image finally reached Bangkok in 1778 in the possession of the founder of the present Thai royal dynasty.

The *Emerald Buddha* is not, in fact, emerald but probably green jade. Nonetheless, its nature as a gemstone gives it a special aura. The Thai believe the gem enables the *chakravartin* (universal king) who possesses the statue to bring the rains. The historical Buddha renounced his secular destiny for the spiritual life, yet his likeness carved from the gem of a universal king enables fulfillment of the Buddha's royal destiny as well. The Buddha is also the universal king. Thus, the combination of the sacred and the secular in the small image explains its symbolic power. The Thai king dresses the *Emerald Buddha* at different times of the year in a monk's robe and a king's robe (in FIG. 32-13 the Buddha wears the royal garment), reflecting the image's dual nature and accentuating its symbolic role as both Buddha and king. The Thai king possessing the image therefore has both religious and secular authority.

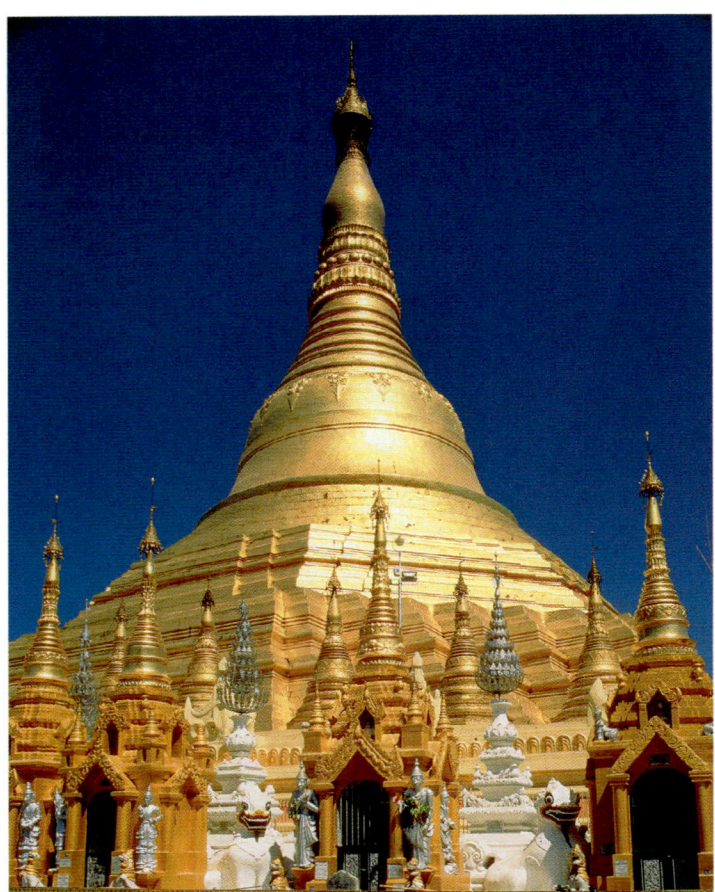

32-14 **Schwedagon Pagoda (looking northeast), Rangoon (Yangon), Myanmar (Burma), 14th century or earlier (rebuilt several times).**

The 344-foot-tall Schwedagon Pagoda houses two of the Buddha's hairs. Silver and jewels and 13,153 gold plates sheathe its exterior. The gold ball at the top is inlaid with 4,351 diamonds.

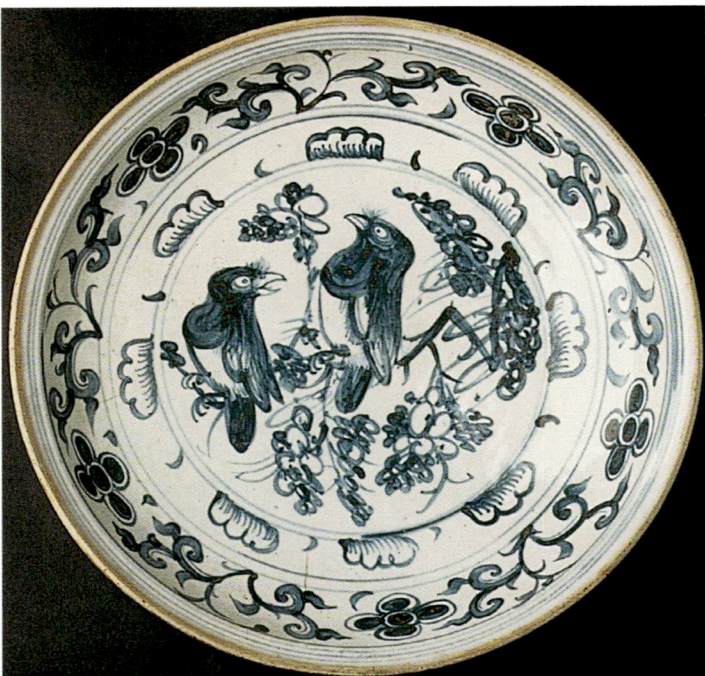

1 in.

32-15 **Dish with two mynah birds on flowering branch, from Vietnam, 16th century. Stoneware painted with underglaze-cobalt, 1′ 2½″ in diameter. Pacific Asia Museum, Pasadena.**

Vietnamese ceramists exported underglaze pottery throughout Southeast Asia and beyond. The spontaneous depiction of mynah birds on this dish contrasts with the formality of Chinese porcelains.

## Myanmar

Myanmar, like Thailand, is overwhelmingly a Theravada Buddhist country today. Important Buddhist monasteries and monuments dot the countryside.

**SCHWEDAGON PAGODA** In Rangoon, an enormous complex of buildings, including shrines filled with Buddha images, has as its centerpiece one of the largest stupas in the world, the Schwedagon Pagoda (FIG. 32-14). (*Pagoda* derives from the Portuguese version of a word for *stupa*.) The Rangoon pagoda houses two of the Buddha's hairs, traditionally said to have been brought to Myanmar by merchants who received them from the Buddha himself. Rebuilt several times, this highly revered stupa is famous for the gold, silver, and jewels encrusting its surface. The Schwedagon Pagoda stands 344 feet high. Covering its upper part are 13,153 plates of gold, each about a foot square. At the very top is a seven-tiered umbrella crowned with a gold ball inlaid with 4,351 diamonds, one of which weighs 76 carats. This great wealth was a gift to the Buddha from the laypeople of Myanmar to earn merit on their path to enlightenment.

## Vietnam

The history of Vietnam is particularly complex, as it reveals both an Indian-related art and culture, broadly similar to those of the rest of Southeast Asia, and a unique and intense relationship with China's art and culture. Vietnam's tradition of fine ceramics is of special interest. The oldest Vietnamese ceramics date to the Han period (206 BCE–220 CE), when the Chinese began to govern the northern area of Vietnam. China directly controlled Vietnam for a thousand years, and early Vietnamese ceramics closely reflected Chinese wares. But during the Ly (1009–1225) and Tran (1225–1400) dynasties, when Vietnam had regained its independence, Vietnamese potters developed an array of ceramic shapes, designs, and *glazes* that brought their wares to the highest levels of quality and creativity.

**UNDERGLAZE CERAMICS** In the 14th century, the Vietnamese began exporting *underglaze* wares modeled on the blue-and-white ceramics first produced in China (see "Chinese Porcelain," Chapter 33, page 992). During the 15th and 16th centuries, the ceramic industry in Vietnam had become the supplier of pottery of varied shapes to an international market extending throughout Southeast Asia and to the Middle East. A 16th-century Vietnamese dish (FIG. 32-15) with two mynah birds on a flowering branch reveals both the potter's debt to China and how the spontaneity, power, and playfulness of Vietnamese painting contrast with the formality of Chinese wares (FIG. 33-5). The artist suggested the foliage with curving and looped lines executed in almost one continuous movement of the brush over the surface. This technique—very different from the more deliberate Chinese habit of lifting the brush after painting a single motif in order to separate the shapes more sharply—facilitated rapid production. Combined with the painter's control, it allowed a fresh and unique design, making Vietnamese pottery attractive to a wide export market.

**CONTEMPORARY ART** In the Buddhist countries of Southeast Asia, some artists continue to produce traditional images of the Buddha, primarily in bronze, for worship in homes, businesses, and temples. But, as in South Asia, many contemporary artists work in an international modernist idiom (see Chapter 31).

# SOUTH AND SOUTHEAST ASIA, 1200 TO 1980

## SULTANATE OF DELHI

▌ After defeating a confederation of South Asian states, Qutb al-Din Aybak (r. 1206–1211) established the Sultanate of Delhi (1206–1526), bringing Muslim rule to northern India and transforming South Asian society, religion, art, and architecture.

▌ To mark the triumph of Islam, the new sultan built Delhi's first mosque—the Might of Islam Mosque—and its 238-foot Qutb Minar, the tallest minaret in the world.

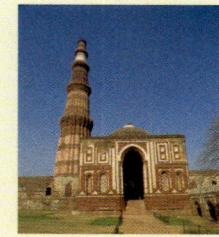

Qutb Minar, Delhi, begun early 13th century

## VIJAYANAGAR EMPIRE

▌ The most powerful Hindu kingdom in southern India when Muslim sultans ruled the north was the Vijayanagar Empire (1336–1565).

▌ Vijayanagar buildings, for example, the Lotus Mahal, display an eclectic mix of Islamic multilobed arches and crowning elements resembling Hindu temple vimanas.

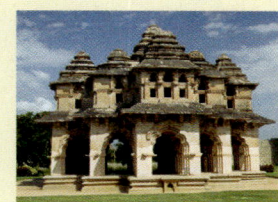

Lotus Mahal, Vijayanagara, 15th or early 16th century

## MUGHAL EMPIRE

▌ Babur (r. 1526–1530) defeated the Delhi sultans in 1526 and established the Mughal Empire (1526–1857).

▌ The first great flowering of Mughal art and architecture occurred under Akbar the Great (r. 1556–1605). The imperial painting workshop continued to produce magnificent illustrated books under his son Jahangir (r. 1605–1627) and his successors. The names of many Mughal miniature painters are known.

▌ Shah Jahan (r. 1628–1658) built the Taj Mahal as a memorial to his favorite wife. The mausoleum may symbolize the throne of God above the gardens of Paradise.

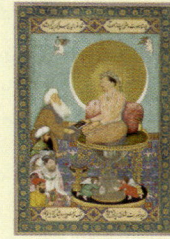

Bichitr, *Jahangir Preferring a Sufi Shaykh to Kings*, ca. 1615–1618

## OTHER SOUTH AND SOUTHEAST ASIAN KINGDOMS

▌ During the Mughal Empire, Hindu Rajput kings ruled much of northwestern India. The coloration and sensuality of Rajput painting distinguish it from the contemporaneous Mughal style.

▌ Between 1529 and 1736, the Hindu Nayak dynasty controlled southern India and erected temple complexes with immense gateway towers (gopuras) decorated with painted stucco sculptures.

▌ In Thailand, Theravada Buddhism was the dominant religion. The Sukhothai walking-Buddha statuary type displays a unique approach to body form as seen, for example, in the Buddha's trunklike right arm.

▌ Myanmar's Schwedagon Pagoda in Rangoon, one of the largest stupas in the world, is encrusted with gold, silver, and jewels.

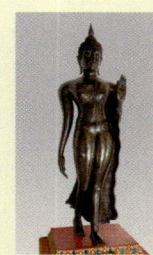

Walking Buddha, from Sikhothai, 14th century

## BRITISH COLONIAL PERIOD TO 1980

▌ Queen Elizabeth I (r. 1558–1603) established the East India Company, which eventually effectively ruled large portions of the subcontinent. In 1877, Queen Victoria I (r. 1837–1901) assumed the title Empress of India. British colonial rule lasted from 1600 to 1947, and Victoria Terminus is its architectural symbol—a European transplant to India capped by an allegorical statue of Progress.

▌ Under the leadership of Mahatma Gandhi (1869–1948), India and Pakistan achieved independence from England in 1947. Post–World War II South Asian art ranges from the traditional to the modern and embraces both native and Western styles.

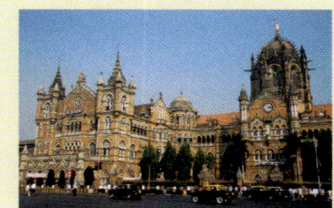

Stevens, Victoria Terminus, Mumbai, 1878–1887

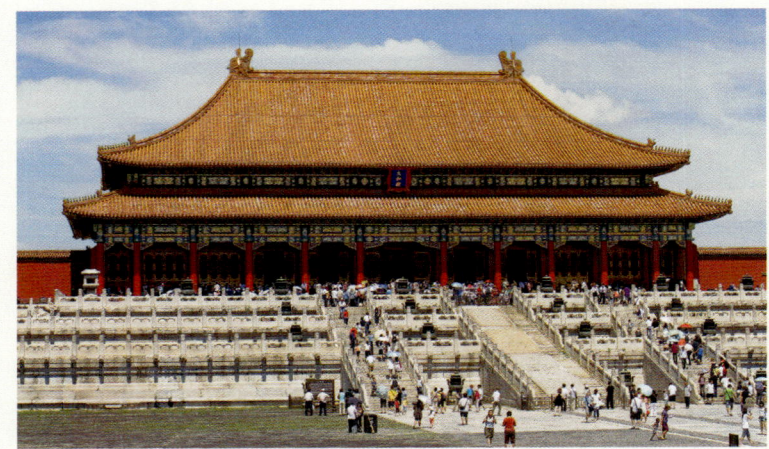

The Hall of Supreme Harmony, the largest wooden building in China, was the climax of the Forbidden City's long north-south axis. It housed the Ming emperor's throne room.

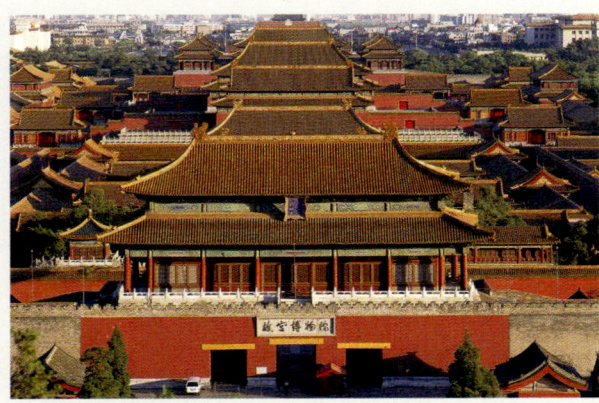

The Forbidden City provided the perfect setting for the rituals surrounding the Ming emperor. Successive gates, such as the Gate of Divine Prowess, regulated access to increasingly restricted areas.

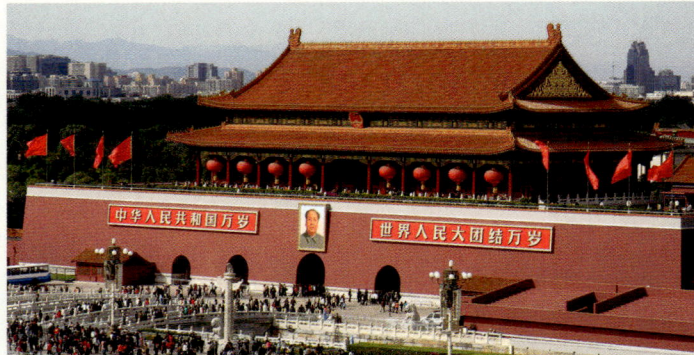

The southern entrance to the Beijing palace complex was the Noon Gate. Only the emperor could walk through the central portal. Those of decreasing rank used the lateral passageways.

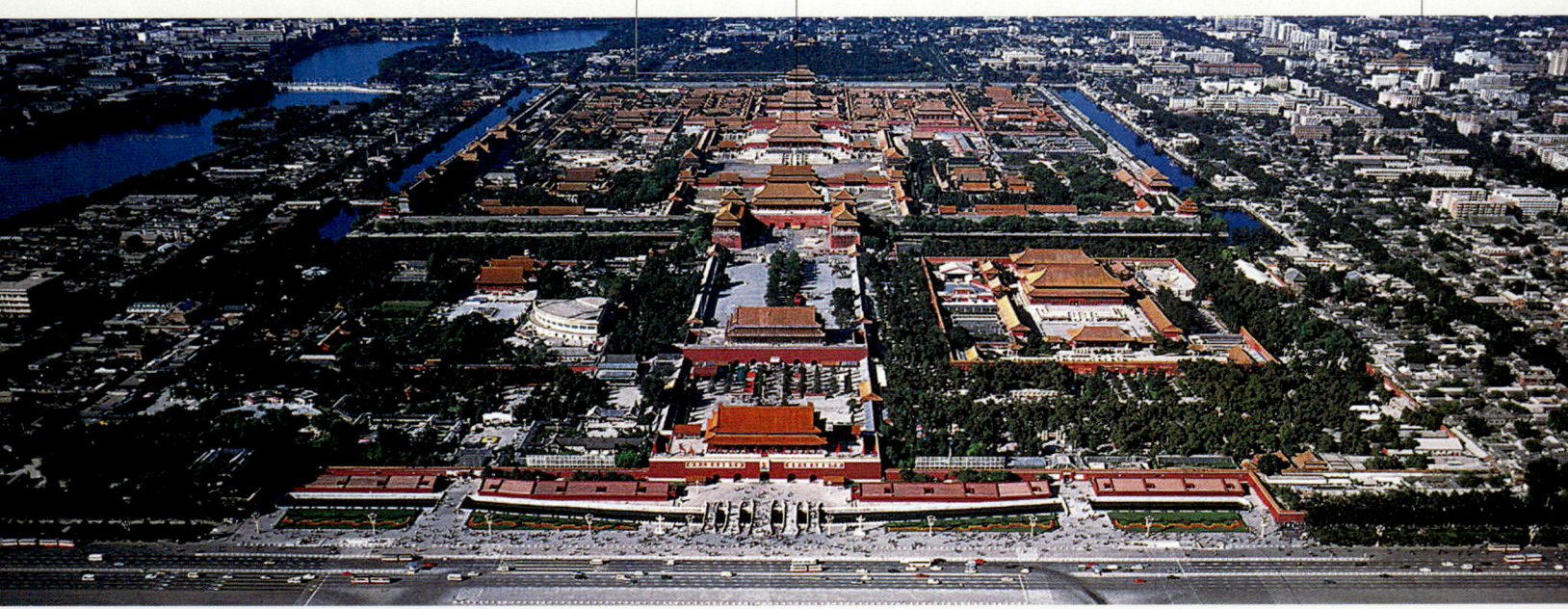

**33-1** Aerial view (looking north) of the Forbidden City, Beijing, China, Ming dynasty, 15th century and later.

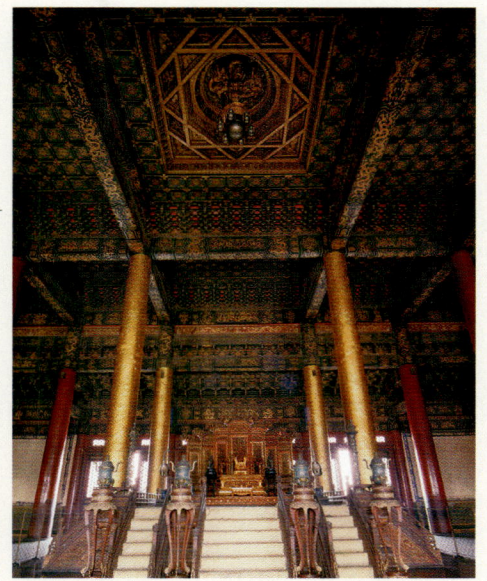

For the columns of the opulently appointed throne room of the Son of Heaven, the Chinese builders had to transport gigantic tree trunks from Sichuan Province down the Yangtze River.

# CHINA AND KOREA, 1279 TO 1980

## THE FORBIDDEN CITY

In 1368, Zhu Yuanzhong led a popular uprising that drove the last Mongol emperor from Beijing. After expelling the foreigners from China, he founded the native Chinese Ming dynasty (r. 1368–1644), proclaiming himself its first emperor under the official name of Hongwu ("Abundantly Martial," r. 1368–1398). The new emperor built his capital at Nanjing (southern capital), but the third Ming emperor, Yongle ("Perpetual Happiness," r. 1403–1424), moved the imperial seat back to Beijing (northern capital). Although Beijing had been home to the Yuan dynasty, Ming architects designed much of the city as well as the imperial palace at its core.

The Ming builders laid out Beijing as three nested walled cities. The outer perimeter wall was 15 miles long and enclosed the walled Imperial City, with a perimeter of 6 miles, and the vast imperial palace compound, the Forbidden City (FIG. **33-1**), surrounded by a 50-yard-wide moat. The name "Forbidden City" dates to 1576 and aptly describes the highly restricted access to the inner compound, where the Ming emperor, the Son of Heaven, resided. The layout of the Forbidden City provided the perfect setting for the elaborate ritual of the imperial court. For example, the entrance gateway to the complex, the Noon Gate, has five portals. Only the emperor could walk through the central doorway. The two entrances to its left and right were reserved for the imperial family and high officials. Others had to use the outermost passageways. Entrance to the Forbidden City proper was through the nearly 40-yard-tall triple-passageway Meridian Gate. Only the emperor and his retinue and foreign ambassadors who had been granted an official audience could pass through the Meridian Gate.

Within the Forbidden City, more gates and a series of courtyards, gardens, temples, and other buildings led eventually to the Hall of Supreme Harmony, in which the emperor, seated on his dragon throne on a high stepped platform, received important visitors. The hall is the largest wooden building in China. For its columns, the Ming builders had to transport gigantic tree trunks from Sichuan Province down the Yangtze River. Perched on an immense platform above marble staircases, the Hall of Supreme Harmony was the climax of a long north-south axis. The fill for the platform consists of the soil and rocks the Ming engineers collected from the excavation of the great moat around the imperial complex.

Beyond that grand reception hall is the even more restricted Inner Court and the Palace of Heavenly Purity—the private living quarters of the emperor and his extended family of wives, concubines, and children. At the northern end of the central axis of the Forbidden City is the Gate of Divine Prowess, through which the palace servants gained access to the complex.

# CHINA

In 1210, the Mongols invaded northern China from Central Asia (MAP 33-1, page 993), opening a new chapter in the history and art of that ancient land (see Chapter 16). Under the dynamic leadership of Genghis Khan (1167–1230), the Mongol armies pushed into China with extraordinary speed. By 1215, the Mongols had destroyed the Jin dynasty's capital at Beijing and taken control of northern China. Two decades later, they attacked the Song dynasty in southern China. It was not until 1279, however, that the last Song emperor fell at the hands of Genghis Khan's grandson, Kublai Khan (1215–1294). Kublai proclaimed himself emperor (r. 1279–1294) of the new Yuan dynasty.

## Yuan Dynasty

During the relatively brief tenure of the Yuan (r. 1279–1368), trade between Europe and Asia increased dramatically. It was no coincidence that Marco Polo (1254–1324), the most famous early European visitor to China, arrived during the reign of Kublai Khan. Part fact and part fable, Marco Polo's chronicle of his travels to and within China was the only eyewitness description of East Asia available in Europe for several centuries. The Venetian's account makes clear he profoundly admired Yuan China. He marveled not only at Kublai Khan's opulent lifestyle and palaces but also at the volume of commercial traffic on the Yangtze River; the splendors of Hangzhou; the use of paper currency, porcelain, and coal; the efficiency of the Chinese postal system; and the hygiene of the

Chinese people. In the early second millennium, China was richer and technologically more advanced than late medieval Europe.

**ZHAO MENGFU** The Mongols were distrustful of the Chinese and very selective in admitting former Southern Song subjects into their administration. In addition, many Chinese loyal to the former emperors refused to collaborate with their new

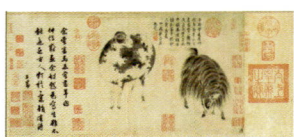

33-1A ZHAO MENGFU, *Sheep and Goat*, ca. 1300. ◼◢

foreign overlords, whom they considered barbarian usurpers. Indeed, most of the great art created during the Yuan dynasty was the work of men and women who refused to play any role in the Mongol court. One artist who did accept an official post under Kublai Khan was ZHAO MENGFU (1254–1322), a descendant of the first Song emperor. A learned man, skilled in both calligraphy and poetry, he won renown as a painter of horses and of landscapes but also painted other subjects (FIG. **33-1A**).

**GUAN DAOSHENG** Zhao's wife, GUAN DAOSHENG (1262–1319), was also a successful painter, calligrapher, and poet. Although she painted a variety of subjects, including Buddhist murals in Yuan temples, Guan became famous for her paintings of bamboo. The plant was a popular subject because it was a symbol of the ideal Chinese gentleman, who bends in adversity but does not break, and because depicting bamboo branches and leaves approximated the cherished art of calligraphy (see "Calligraphy and Inscriptions

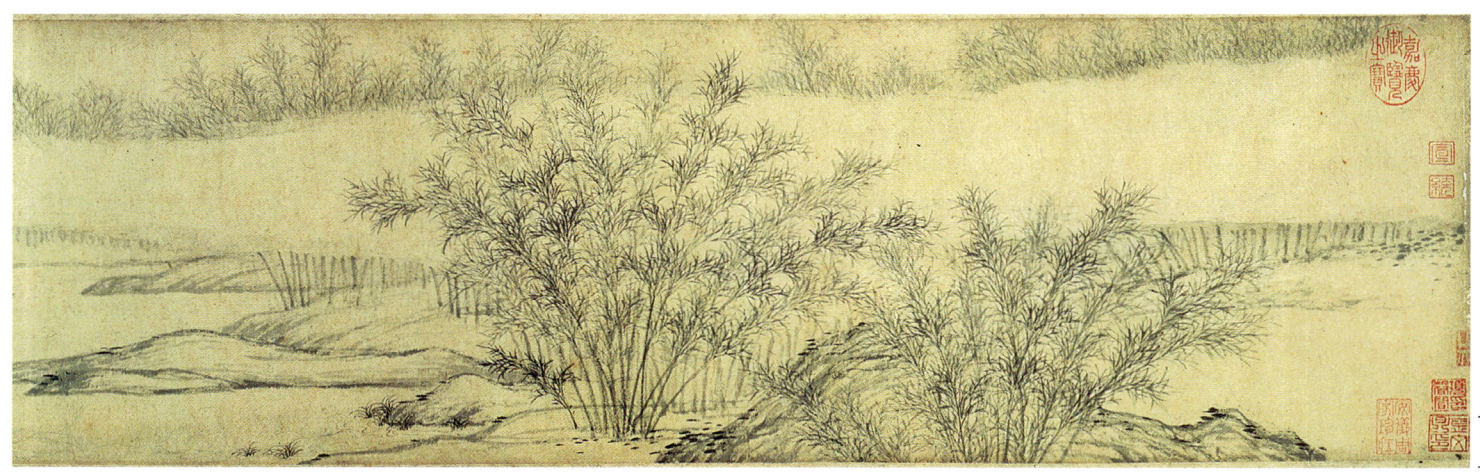

1 in.

**33-2** GUAN DAOSHENG, *Bamboo Groves in Mist and Rain* (detail), Yuan dynasty, 1308. Section of a handscroll, ink on paper, full scroll $9\frac{1}{8}$″ × 3′ $8\frac{7}{8}$″. National Palace Museum, Tabei.

Guan Daosheng was a calligrapher, poet, and painter. She achieved the misty atmosphere in this landscape by using a narrow range of ink tones and blurring the bamboo thickets in the distance.

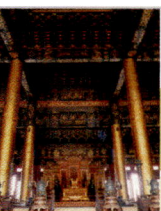

# CHINA AND KOREA, 1279 TO 1980

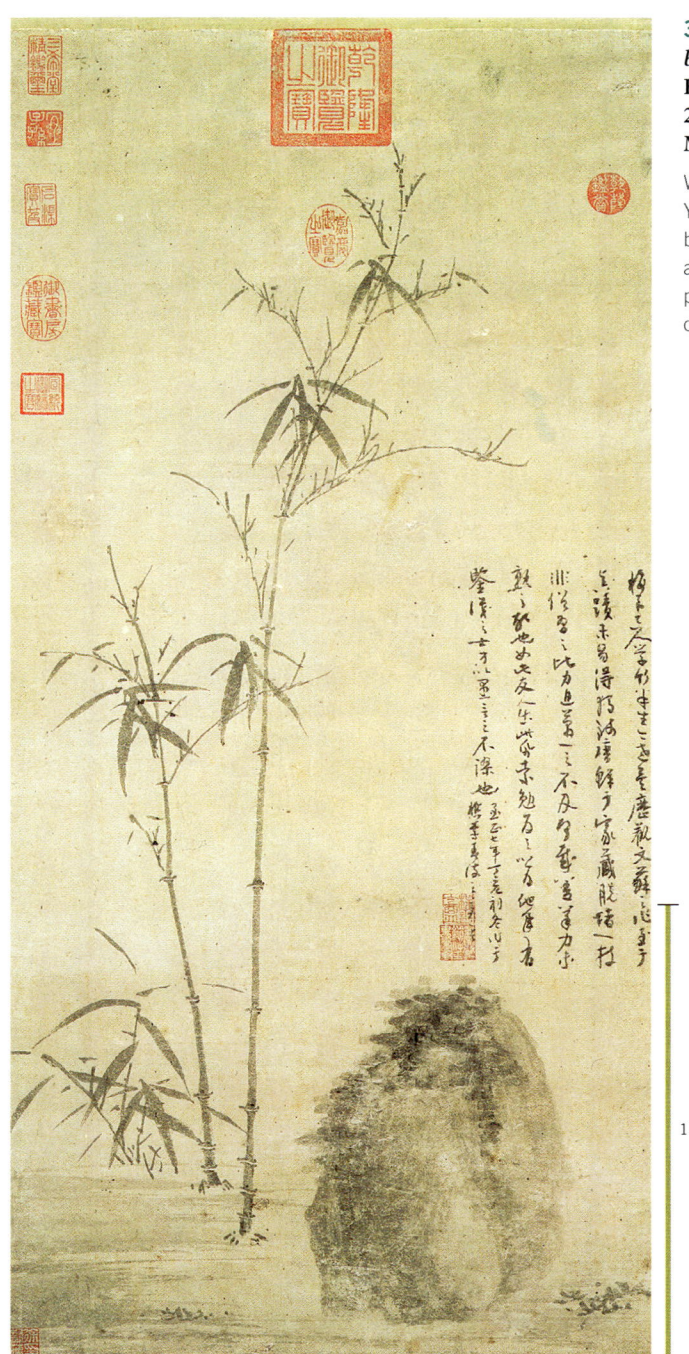

on Chinese Paintings," page 997). *Bamboo Groves in Mist and Rain* (FIG. **33-2**), a *handscroll* (see "Chinese Painting Materials and Formats," Chapter 16, page 459), is one of her best paintings. Guan achieved the misty atmosphere by restricting the ink tones to a narrow range and by blurring the bamboo thickets in the distance, suggesting not only the receding terrain but fog as well.

**WU ZHEN** The Yuan painter Wᴜ Zʜᴇɴ (1280–1354), in stark contrast to Zhao Mengfu and Guan Daosheng, shunned the Mongol court and lived as a hermit, far from the luxurious milieu of the Yuan emperors. He was one of the *literati,* or scholar-artists, who emerged during the Song dynasty. The literati were men and women from prominent families who painted primarily for a small audience of their social peers. Highly educated and steeped in traditional Chinese culture, they cultivated calligraphy, poetry, painting, and other arts as a sign of social status and refined taste. Literati art is usually personal in nature and often shows nostalgia for the past.

Wu Zhen's treatment of the bamboo theme, *Stalks of Bamboo by a Rock* (FIG. **33-3**), differs sharply from Guan's. The artist clearly differentiated the individual bamboo plants and reveled in the abstract patterns the stalks and leaves formed. The bamboo stalks in his *hanging scroll* (see "Chinese Painting Materials and Formats," Chapter 16, page 459) are perfect complements to the calligraphic beauty of the Chinese black characters and red seals so prominently featured on the scroll (see "Calligraphy and Inscriptions," page 997). Both the bamboo and the inscriptions gave Wu Zhen the opportunity to display his proficiency with the brush.

**HUANG GONGWANG** Later artists and critics revered Wu Zhen as one of the Four Great Masters of Yuan painting. The eldest was Hᴜᴀɴɢ Gᴏɴɢᴡᴀɴɢ (1269–1354), a civil servant and a teacher of Daoist philosophy. His *Dwelling in the Fuchun Mountains* (FIG. **33-4**)

1 ft.

**33-4** Hᴜᴀɴɢ Gᴏɴɢᴡᴀɴɢ, *Dwelling in the Fuchun Mountains,* Yuan dynasty, 1347–1350. Section of a handscroll, ink on paper, full scroll 1′ ⅞″ × 20′ 9″. National Palace Museum, Tabei.

In this Yuan handscroll, Huang built up the textured mountains with richly layered wet and dry brushstrokes and ink-wash accents, capturing the landscape's inner structure and momentum.

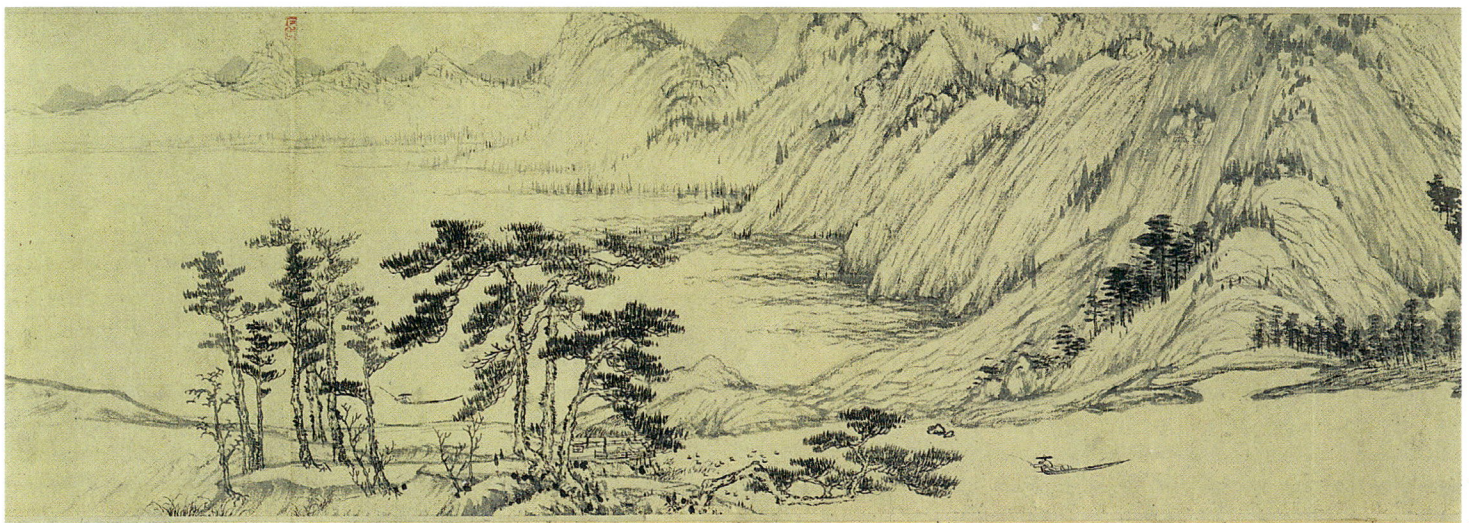

1 in.

China **991**

# Chinese Porcelain

Νo other Chinese art form has achieved such worldwide admiration, inspired such imitation, or penetrated so deeply into everyday life as *porcelain* (FIGS. 33-5 and 33-17). Long imported by China's Asian neighbors as luxury goods and treasures, Chinese porcelains later captured great attention in the West, where potters did not succeed in mastering the production process until the early 18th century.

In China, primitive porcelains emerged during the Tang dynasty (618–906), and mature forms developed in the Song (960–1279). Like *stoneware* (see "Chinese Earthenwares and Stonewares," Chapter 16, page 451), porcelain objects are fired in a kiln at an extremely high temperature (well over 2,000° F) until the clay fully fuses into a dense, hard substance resembling stone or glass. Unlike stoneware, however, ceramists create porcelain from a fine white clay called kaolin mixed with ground petuntse (a type of feldspar). True porcelain is translucent and rings when struck. Its rich, shiny surface resembles jade, a luxurious natural material the Chinese treasured from very early times (see "Chinese Jade," Chapter 16, page 454).

Chinese ceramists often decorate porcelains with colored designs or pictures, working with finely ground minerals suspended in water and a binding agent (such as glue). The minerals change color dramatically in the kiln. The painters apply some mineral colors to the clay surface before the main firing and then apply a clear *glaze* over them. This *underglaze* decoration fully bonds to the piece in the kiln, but because the raw materials must withstand intense heat, Chinese potters could fire only a few colors. The most stable and widely used coloring agents for porcelains are cobalt compounds, which emerge from the kiln as an intense blue (FIG. 33-5). Rarely, ceramists use copper compounds to produce stunning reds by carefully manipulating the kiln's temperature and oxygen content.

To obtain a wider palette, an artist must paint on top of the glaze after firing the work (FIG. 33-17). These *overglaze* colors, or *enamels,* then fuse to the glazed surface in an additional firing at a much lower temperature. Enamels also offer ceramic painters a much brighter palette, with colors ranging from deep browns to brilliant reds and greens, but they do not have the durability of underglaze decoration.

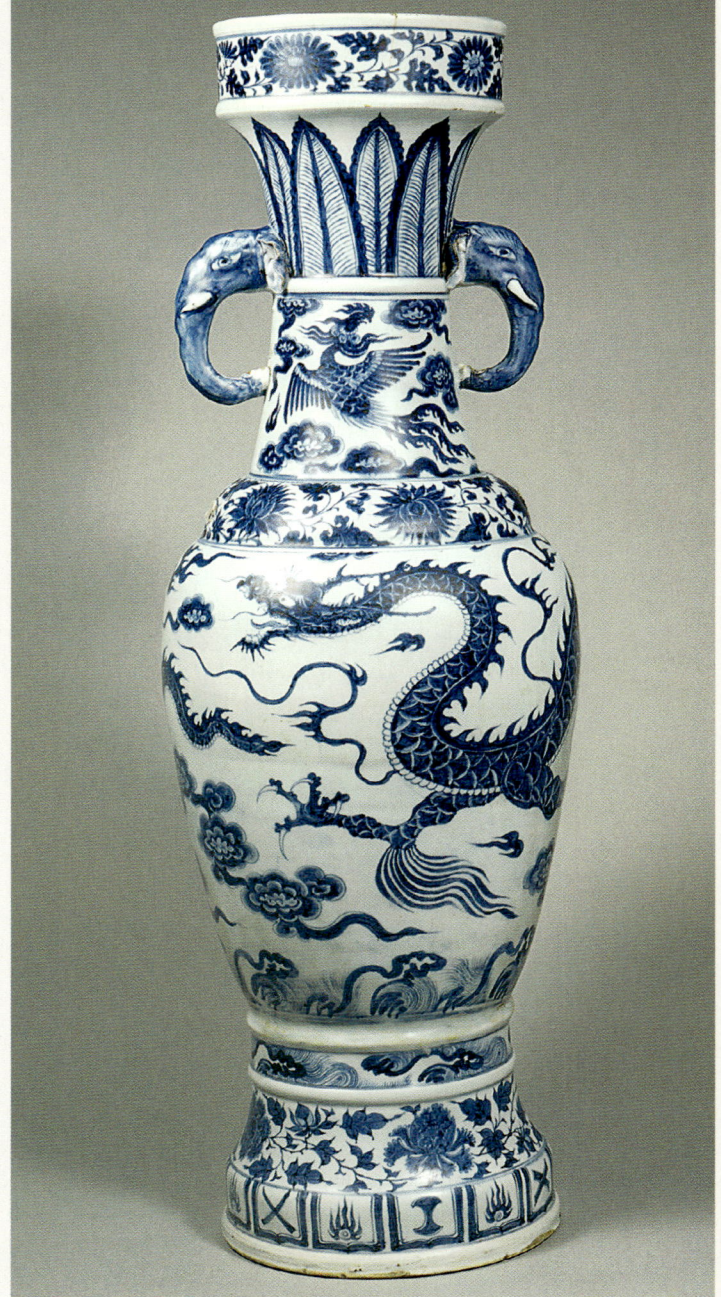

**33-5** Temple vase, Yuan dynasty, 1351. White porcelain with cobalt-blue underglaze, 2′ 1″ × 8⅛″. Percival David Foundation of Chinese Art, London.

This vase is an early example of porcelain with cobalt-blue underglaze decoration. Dragons and phoenixes, symbols of male and female energy, respectively, are the major painted motifs.

1 in.

---

is one of the great works of Yuan literati painting. According to the artist's explanatory inscription at the end of the long handscroll, Huang sketched the full composition in one burst of inspiration, but then added to and modified his painting whenever he felt moved to do so over a period of years. In the detail shown in FIG. 33-4, the painter built up the textured mountains with richly layered brushstrokes, at times interweaving dry brushstrokes and at other times placing dry strokes over wet ones, darker strokes over lighter ones, often with ink-wash accents. The rhythmic play

of brush and ink captures the landscape's inner structure and momentum.

Huang summarized his approach to painting nature in a treatise titled *Secrets of Landscape Painting,* in which he also noted the kinship of ink painting and the art of calligraphy.

In painting each furrow and rock, one should give free rein to the ink allowing it to run unrestrained. . . . [T]oo much detail description will make it look like craftsmanship. . . . For the most part,

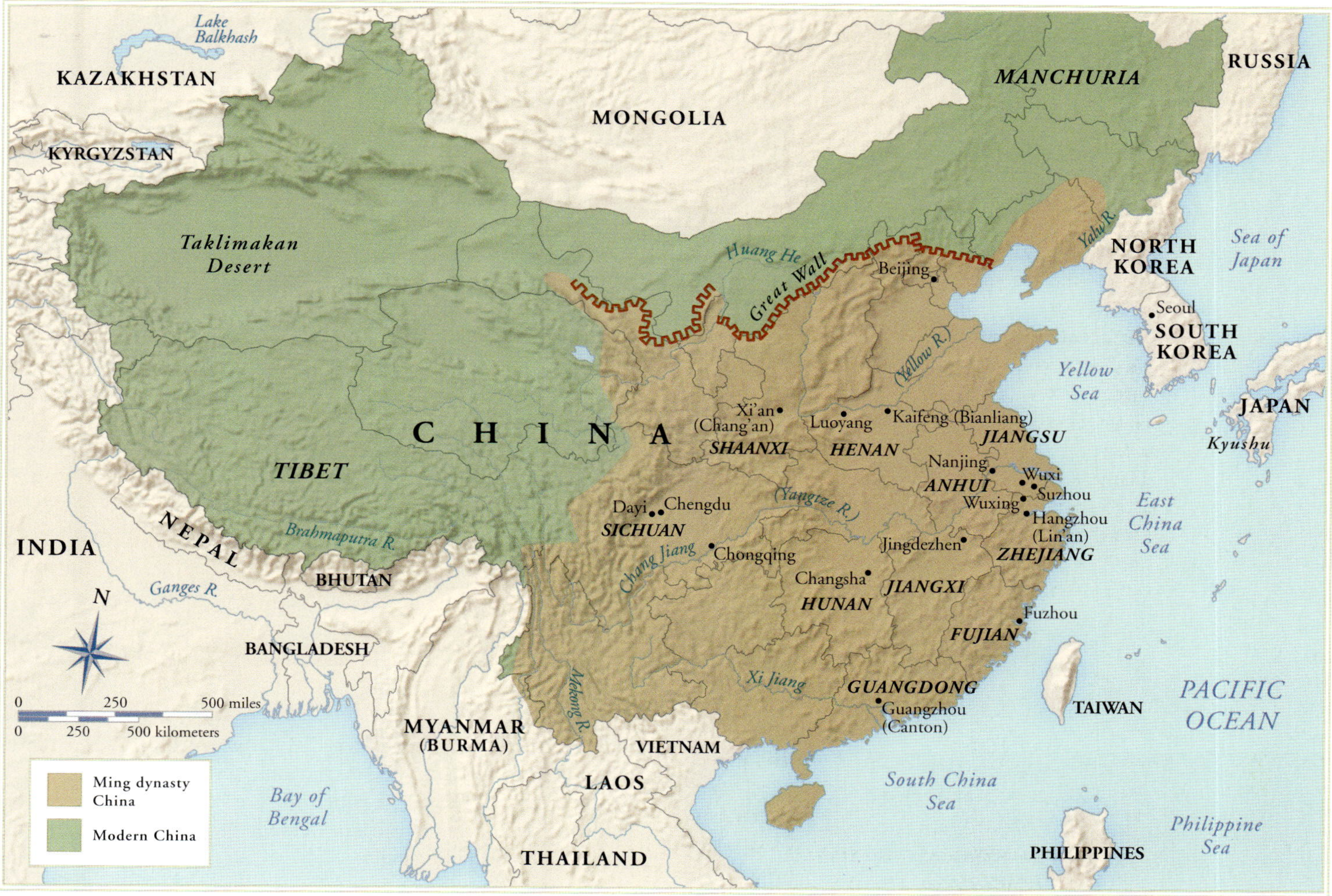

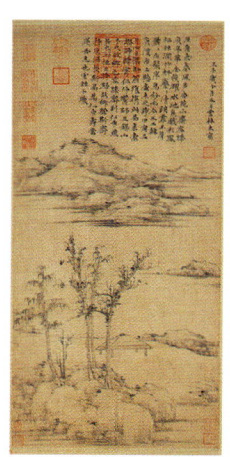

**MAP 33-1** China during the Ming dynasty.

just as in calligraphy, practicing diligently will make mastery perfect.[1]

**NI ZAN AND WANG MENG** Completing the quartet of renowned Yuan masters were two younger artists born in the early 14th century—NI ZAN (1301 or 1306–1374) and WANG MENG (ca. 1308–1385). Both were still active during the early years of the Ming dynasty, when Ni painted his most famous work, *Rongxi Studio* (FIG. **33-4A**), a literati landscape of unsurpassed quality.

**JINGDEZHEN PORCELAIN** By the Yuan period, Chinese potters had extended their mastery to fully developed porcelains, a technically demanding medium (see "Chinese Porcelain," page 992). A tall temple vase (FIG. **33-5**) from the Jingdezhen kilns, which during the Ming dynasty became the official source of porcelains for the court, is one of a nearly identical pair dated by inscription to 1351. The inscription also says the vases, together with an incense burner, composed an altar set donated to a Buddhist temple as a prayer for peace,

**33-4A** NI ZAN, *Rongxi Studio*, 1372.

protection, and prosperity for the donor's family. The vase is one of the earliest dated examples of fine porcelain with cobalt-blue underglaze decoration. The painted decoration consists of bands of floral motifs between broader zones containing auspicious symbols, including phoenixes in the lower part of the neck and dragons (compare FIG. 16-1) on the main body of the vessel, both among clouds. These motifs may suggest the donor's high status or invoke prosperity blessings. Because of their vast power and associations with nobility and prosperity, the dragon and phoenix also symbolize the emperor and empress, respectively, and often appear on objects made for the imperial household. The dragon also may represent *yang,* the Chinese principle of active masculine energy, while the phoenix may represent *yin,* the principle of passive feminine energy.

## Ming Dynasty

The major building project of the Ming emperors who succeeded the Yuan as rulers of China (MAP **33-1**) was the imperial palace complex in Beijing—the Forbidden City (see "The Forbidden City," page 989, and FIG. 33-1). Strictly organized along a north-south axis with traditional wooden buildings featuring curved rooflines (see "Chinese Wooden Construction," Chapter 16, page 457) alternating

China **993**

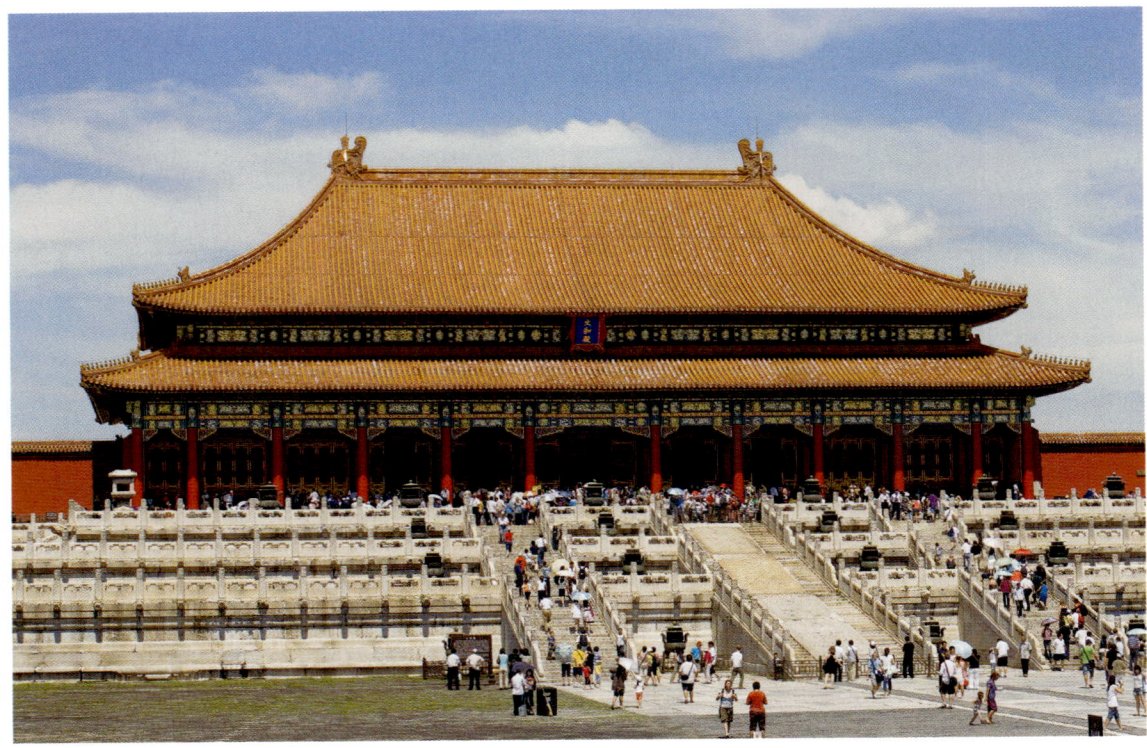

**33-6** Hall of Supreme
Harmony (looking north),
Forbidden City, Beijing,
China, Ming dynasty,
15th century and later.

The Hall of Supreme Harmony
is the largest wooden building
in China. For its gigantic
columns, the Ming builders
had to transport huge tree
trunks down the Yangtze River
from Sichuan Province.

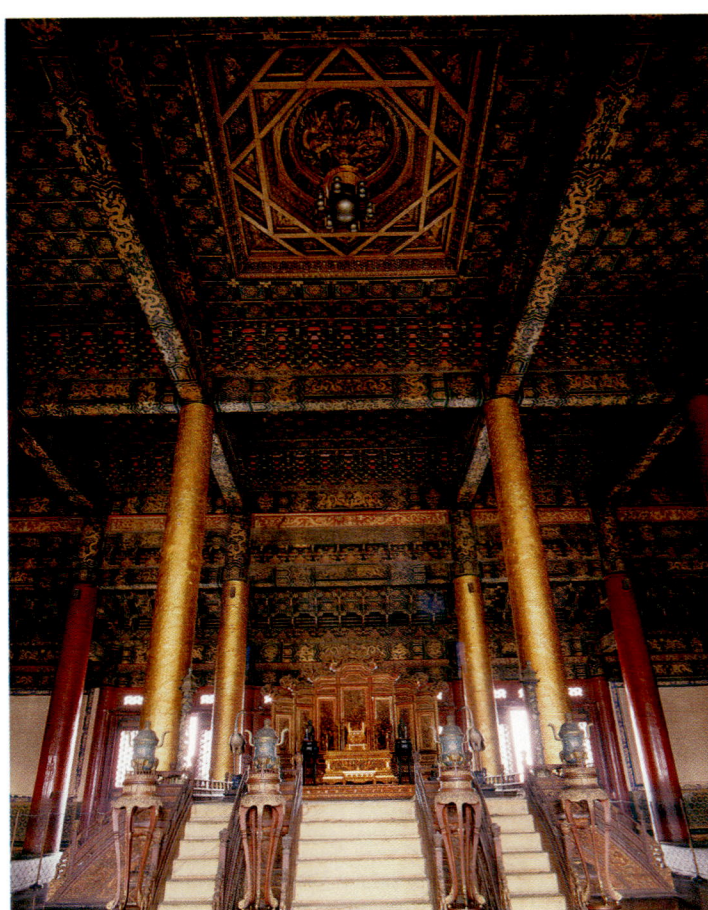

**33-7** Throne room, Hall of Supreme Harmony, Forbidden City,
Beijing, China, Ming dynasty, 15th century and later.

The Ming emperors held official audiences in the opulently appointed
throne room in the Hall of Supreme Harmony. Beyond was the Inner Court,
where the emperor and his extended family resided.

with courtyards, the Forbidden City culminated with the Hall of
Supreme Harmony (FIG. **33-6**) housing the opulently furnished
throne room (FIG. **33-7**) in which the Son of Heaven received official visitors. In front of the hall were bronze statues of a turtle and
a crane, symbols of longevity.

**ORCHARD FACTORY** The Ming court's lavish appetite for
luxury goods to use and display in the imperial palace gave new
impetus to brilliant technical achievement in the decorative arts.
As did the Yuan emperors, the Ming dynasty turned to the Jingdezhen kilns for fine porcelains. For objects in lacquer-covered wood
(see "Lacquered Wood," page 995), their patronage went to a large
workshop in Beijing known today as the Orchard Factory. A table
with drawers (FIG. **33-8**), made between 1426 and 1435, is one of the
workshop's masterpieces. The artist carved floral motifs, along with
the dragon and phoenix imperial emblems, into the thick cinna-
bar-colored lacquer, which had to be built up in numerous layers.

**SHANG XI** At the Ming court, the official painters lived in the
Forbidden City itself, and portraiture of the imperial family was
their major subject. The court artists also depicted historical figures as exemplars of virtue, wisdom, or heroism. An exceptionally
large example of Ming history painting is a hanging scroll painted
by SHANG XI (active ca. 1425–1440) around 1430. *Guan Yu Captures General Pang De* (FIG. **33-9**) represents an episode from China's tumultuous third century (Period of Disunity; see Chapter 16),
whose wars inspired one of the first great Chinese novels, *The Romance of the Three Kingdoms*. Guan Yu was a famed general of the
Wei dynasty (220–280) and a fictional hero in the novel. Shang's
painting depicts the historical Guan, renowned for his loyalty to
his emperor and his military valor, being presented with the captured enemy general Pang De. In the painting, Shang used color to
focus attention on Guan and his attendants, who stand out sharply
from the ink landscape. He also contrasted the victors' armor and
bright garments with the vulnerability of the captive, who has been
stripped almost naked, further heightening his humiliation.

## Lacquered Wood

From ancient times the Chinese used *lacquer* to cover wood. Artisans produced lacquer from the sap of the Asiatic sumac tree, native to central and southern China. When it dries, lacquer cures to great hardness and prevents the wood from decaying. Often colored with mineral pigments, lacquered objects have a lustrous surface that transforms the appearance of natural wood. The earliest examples of lacquered wood to survive in quantity date to the Eastern Zhou period (770–256 BCE).

The first step in producing a lacquered object is to heat and purify the sap. Then the lacquer worker mixes the minerals—carbon black and cinnabar red are the most common—into the sap. To apply the lacquer, the artisan uses a hair brush similar to a calligrapher's or painter's brush, building up the coating one layer at a time. Each coat must dry and be sanded before another layer can be applied. If the artisan builds up a sufficient number of layers, the lacquer can be carved as if it were the wood itself. The lacquer workers in the Orchard Factory in Beijing were master carvers and counted the Ming emperors as major clients for luxurious lacquered furniture. Examples such as the illustrated table (FIG. 33-8)

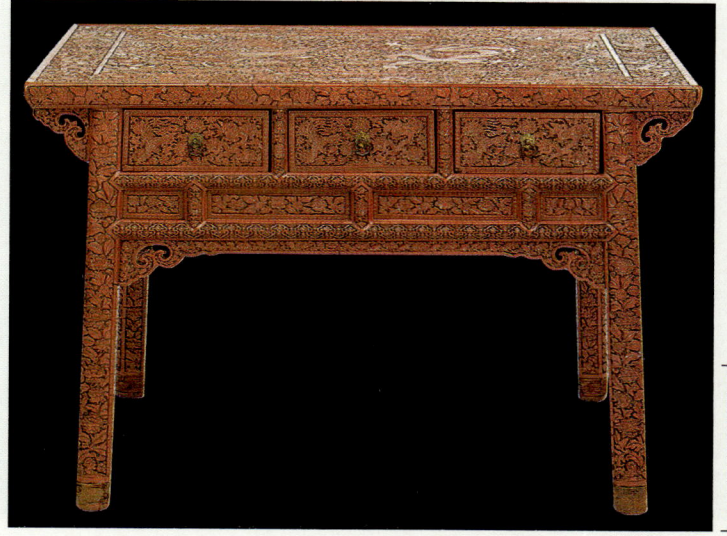

**33-8** Table with drawers, Ming dynasty, ca. 1426–1435. Carved red lacquer on a wood core, 3′ 11″ long. Victoria & Albert Museum, London.

The Orchard Factory was the leading Ming workshop for lacquered wood furniture. The lacquer on this table was thick enough to be carved with floral motifs and the imperial dragon and phoenix.

boast elaborate carving in many layers of lacquer and took a great deal of time as well as skill to produce.

Other techniques for decorating lacquer include inlaying metals and lustrous materials, such as mother-of-pearl, and sprinkling gold powder into the still-wet lacquer. Korean and Japanese (FIG. 34-10) artists also employed these techniques to produce masterful lacquered objects.

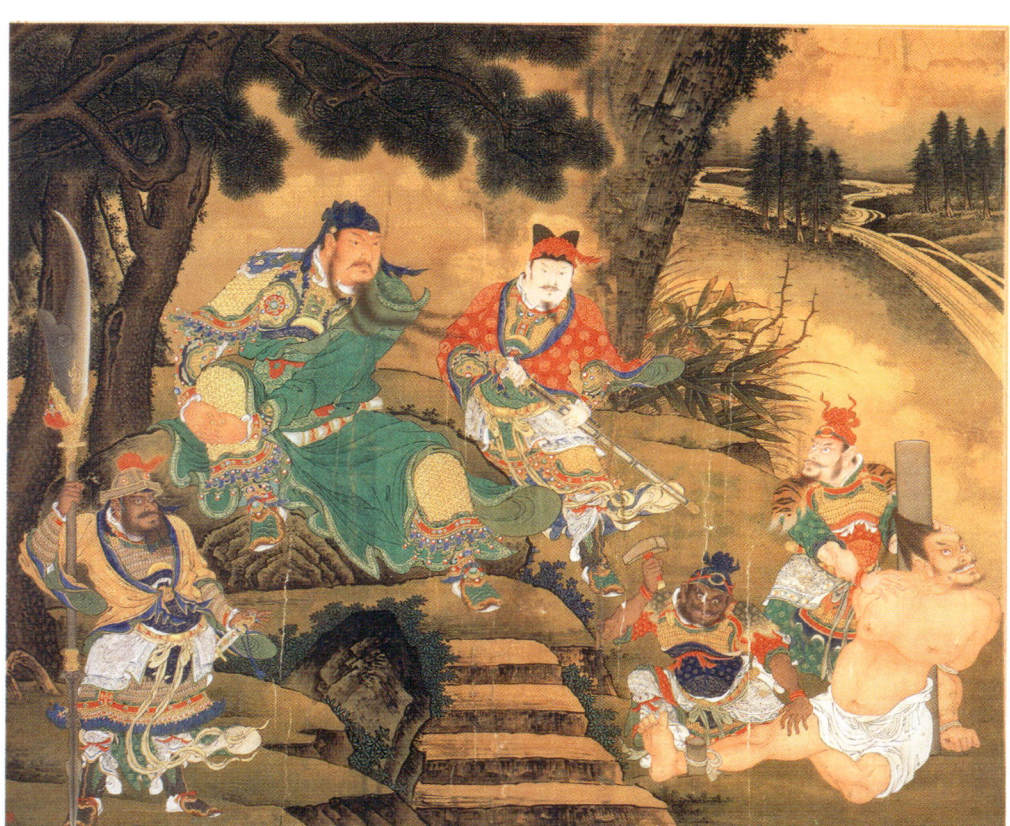

**33-9** SHANG XI, *Guan Yu Captures General Pang De,* Ming dynasty, ca. 1430. Hanging scroll, ink and colors on silk, 6′ 5″ × 7′ 7″. Palace Museum, Beijing. ◖

The official painters of the Ming court lived in the Forbidden City and specialized in portraiture and history painting. This very large scroll celebrates a famed general of the third century.

China   995

**SUZHOU GARDENS** At the opposite architectural pole from the formality and rigid axiality of Ming palace architecture is the Chinese pleasure garden. Several Ming gardens at Suzhou have been meticulously restored, including the huge (almost 54,000 square feet) Wangshi Yuan (Garden of the Master of the Fishing Nets; FIG. **33-10**). Designing a Ming garden was not a matter of cultivating plants in rows or of laying out terraces, flower beds, and avenues in geometric fashion, as was the case in many other cultures (compare, for example, the 17th-century French gardens at Versailles, FIG. 25-26). Instead, Ming gardens are often scenic arrangements of natural and artificial elements intended to reproduce the irregularities of uncultivated nature. Verandas and pavilions rise on pillars above the water, and stone bridges, paths, and causeways encourage wandering through ever-changing vistas of trees, flowers, rocks, and their reflections in the ponds. The typical design is a sequence of carefully contrived visual surprises.

A favorite garden element, fantastic rockwork, is a prominent feature of Liu Yuan (Lingering Garden; FIG. **33-11**) in Suzhou. Workmen dredged the stones from nearby Lake Tai, and then sculptors shaped them to create an even more natural look. The one at the center of FIG. 33-11 is about 20 feet tall and weighs approximately five tons. The Ming gardens of Suzhou were the pleasure retreats of high officials and the landed gentry, sanctuaries where the wealthy could commune with nature in all its representative forms and as an ever-changing and boundless presence. Chinese poets never cease to sing of the restorative effect of gardens on mind and spirit.

**SHEN ZHOU** Just as the formality of Ming official architecture contrasts with the informality of the gardens of Suzhou, the work of Shang Xi (FIG. 33-9) and other professional court painters,

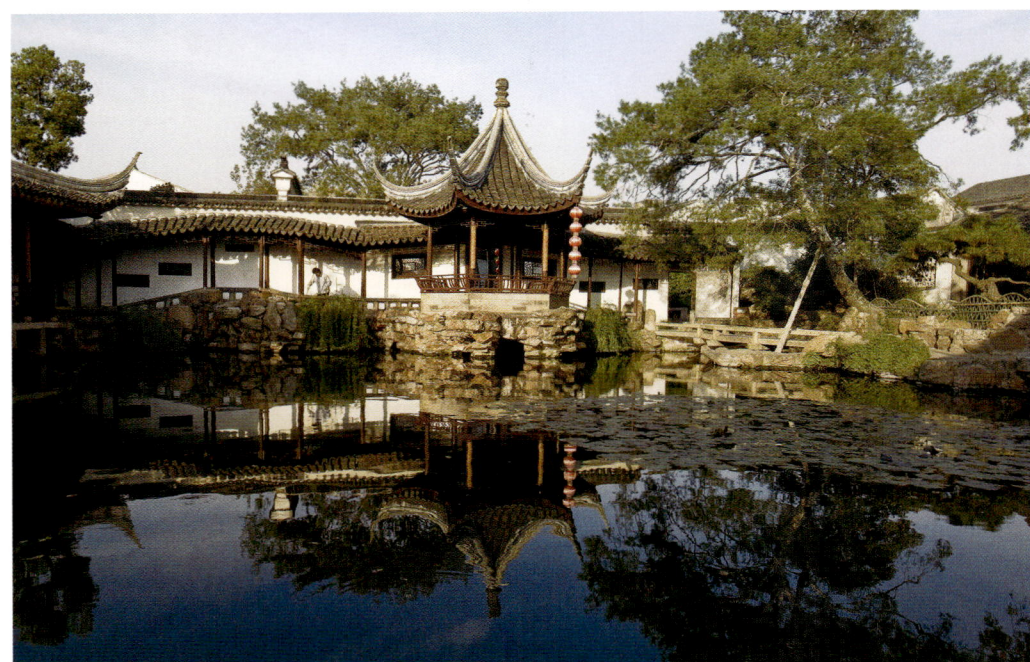

**33-10** Wangshi Yuan (Garden of the Master of the Fishing Nets), Suzhou, China, Ming dynasty, 16th century and later.

Ming gardens are arrangements of natural and artificial elements intended to reproduce the irregularities of nature. This approach to design is the opposite of the formality and axiality of the Ming palace.

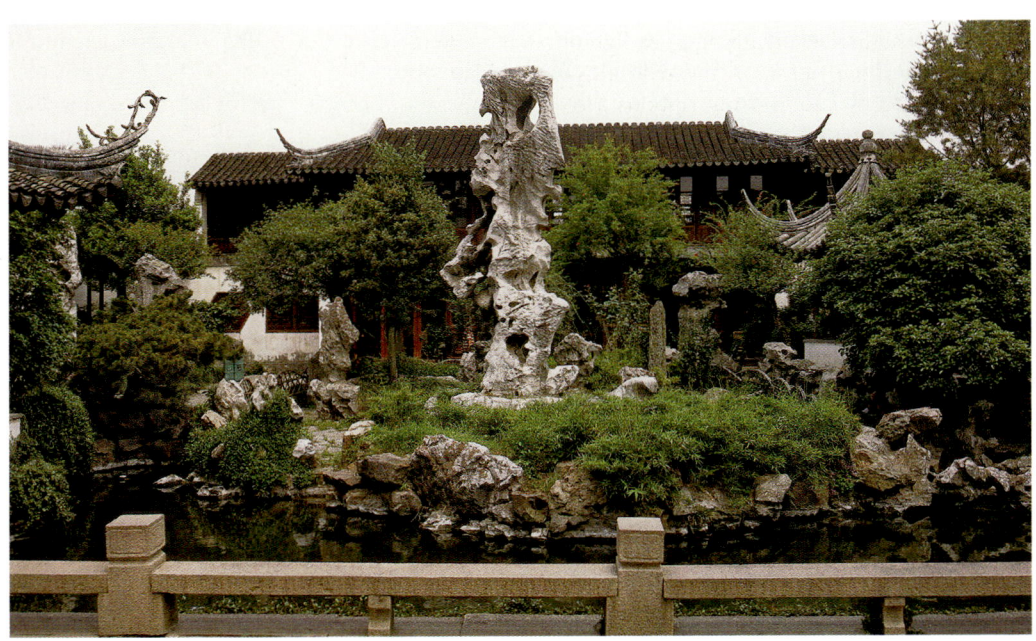

**33-11** Liu Yuan (Lingering Garden), Suzhou, China, Ming dynasty, 16th century and later.

A favorite element of Chinese gardens was fantastic rockwork. For the Lingering Garden, workmen dredged the stones from a nearby lake, and sculptors shaped them to produce an even more natural look.

designed to promote the official Ming ideology, differs sharply in both form and content from the venerable tradition of literati painting, which also flourished during the Ming dynasty. As under the Yuan emperors, Ming literati practiced their art largely independently of court patronage. One of the leading figures was SHEN ZHOU (1427–1509), a master of the Wu School of painting, so called because of the ancient name (Wu) of the city of Suzhou. Shen came from a well-to-do family of scholars and painters and declined an

offer to serve in the Ming bureaucracy in order to concentrate on poetry and painting. *Lofty Mount Lu* (FIG. **33-12**), perhaps his finest hanging scroll, was a birthday gift to one of his teachers. It bears a long poem the artist wrote in the teacher's honor (see "Calligraphy and Inscriptions on Chinese Paintings," page 997). Shen had never seen Mount Lu, but he stated he chose the subject because he wished the lofty mountain peaks to express the grandeur of his teacher's virtue and character. Shen suggested the immense scale of Mount

# Calligraphy and Inscriptions on Chinese Paintings

**M**any Chinese paintings (FIGS. 16-12, 16-16, 16-20, 16-23, 33-1A, 33-3, 33-4A, and 33-12 to 33-14) bear inscriptions, texts written on the same surface as the picture, or *colophons,* texts written on attached pieces of paper or silk. Throughout history, the Chinese have held *calligraphy* (Greek, "beautiful writing") in high esteem—higher, in fact, than painting. Inscriptions appear almost everywhere in China—on buildings and in gardens, on furniture and sculpture. Chinese calligraphy and painting have always been closely connected. Even the primary implements and materials for writing and drawing are the same— a round tapered brush, soot-based ink, and paper or silk. Calligraphy depends for its effects on the controlled vitality of individual brushstrokes and on the dynamic relationships of strokes within a *character* (an elaborate Chinese sign that by itself can represent several words) and even among the characters themselves. Training in calligraphy was a fundamental part of the education and self-cultivation of Chinese scholars and officials, and inscriptions are especially common on literati paintings. Many stylistic variations exist in Chinese calligraphy. At the most formal extreme, each character consists of distinct straight and angular strokes and is separate from the next character. At the other extreme, the characters flow together as cursive abbreviations with many rounded forms.

A long tradition in China links pictures and poetry. Famous poems frequently provided subjects for paintings, and poets composed poems inspired by paintings. Either practice might prompt inscriptions on art, some addressing painted subjects, some praising the painting's quality or the character of the painter or another individual. The Ming literati painter Shen Zhou added a long poem in beautiful Chinese characters to his painting of Mount Lu (FIG. 33-12). The poem praises a beloved teacher. Sometimes inscriptions explain the circumstances of the work. The Yuan painter Guan Daosheng's *Bamboo Groves in Mist and Rain* has two inscriptions (not included in the detail reproduced in FIG. 33-2). One is a dedication to another noblewoman. The other states Guan painted the handscroll "in a boat on the green waves of the lake." Later admirers and owners of paintings frequently inscribed their own appreciative words. The inscriptions are often quite prominent and sometimes compete for the viewer's attention with the painted motifs (FIGS. 33-1A and 33-3).

Painters, inscribers, and even owners usually also added *seal* impressions in red ink (FIGS. 33-2 to 33-4A and 33-12 to 33-16) to identify themselves. With all these textual additions, some paintings that have passed through many collections may seem cluttered to Western viewers. However, the historical importance given to these inscriptions and to the works' ownership history has been and remains a critical aspect of painting appreciation in China.

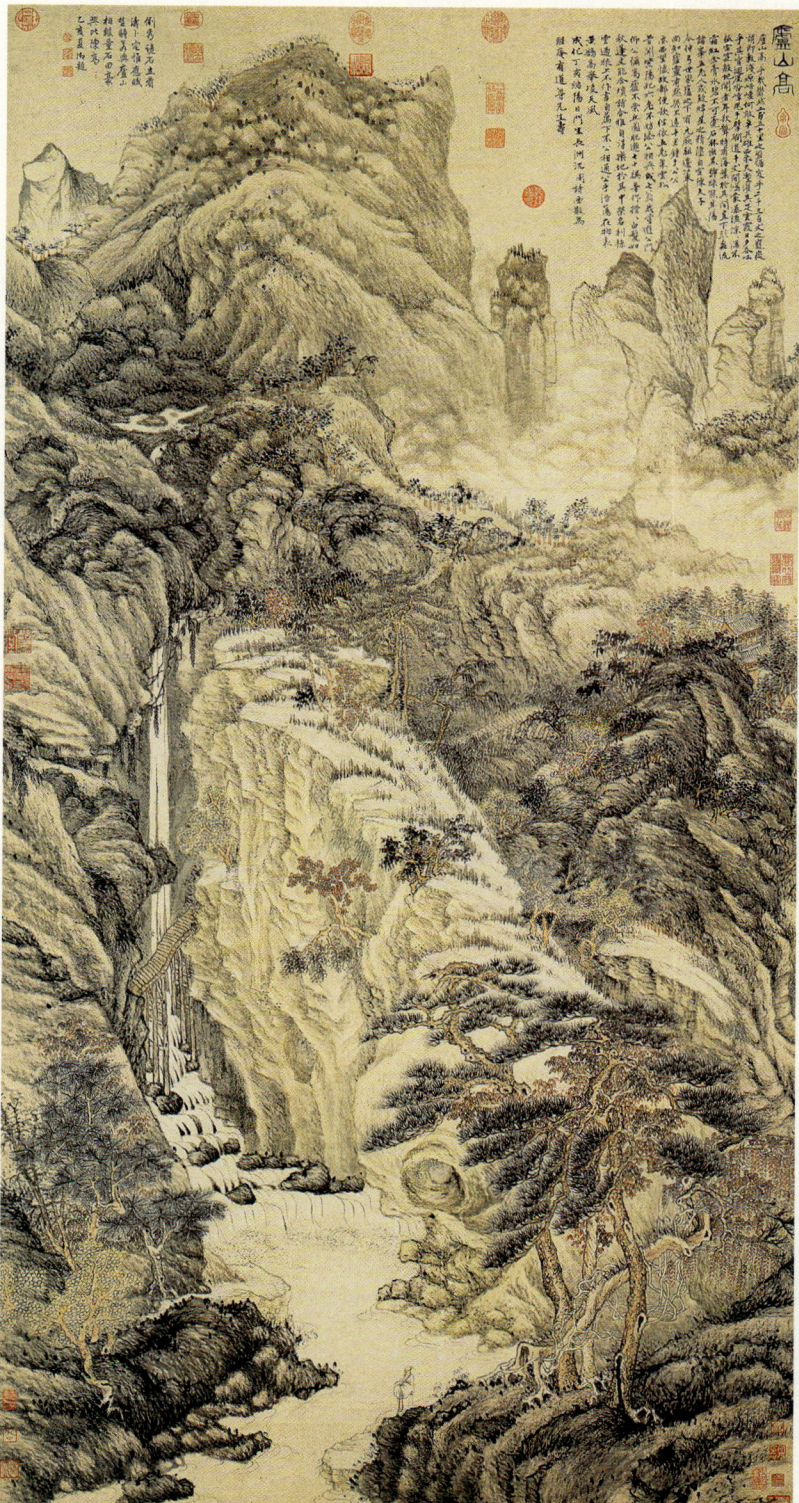

**33-12** SHEN ZHOU, *Lofty Mount Lu,* Ming dynasty, 1467. Hanging scroll, ink and color on paper, 6′ 4¼″ × 3′ 2⅝″. National Palace Museum, Tabei. ◼◂

Inscriptions and seals are essential elements in this hanging scroll, in which Shen used the lofty peaks of Mount Lu to express visually the grandeur of a beloved teacher's virtue and character.

1 ft.

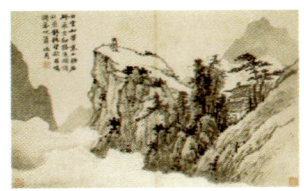

33-12A SHEN ZHOU, *Poet on a Mountaintop*, ca. 1490–1500.

Lu by placing a tiny figure at the bottom center of the painting, sketched in lightly and partly obscured by a rocky outcropping. The composition owes a great deal to Fan Kuan (FIG. 16-19) and other early masters. But, characteristic of literati painting in general, the scroll is in the end a very personal conversation—in pictures and words—between the artist and the teacher it honors. In a later painting (FIG. 33-12A), Shen depicted himself as a poet on a mountaintop, and included a poem he wrote reflecting on the beauty of music and landscape.

**DONG QICHANG** One of the most intriguing and influential literati of the late Ming dynasty was DONG QICHANG (1555–1636), a wealthy landowner and high official who was a poet, calligrapher, and painter. He also amassed a vast collection of Chinese art and achieved great fame as an art critic. In Dong's view, most Chinese landscape painters could be classified as belonging to either the Northern School of precise, academic painting or the Southern School of more subjective, freer painting. "Northern" and "Southern" were not geographic but stylistic labels. Dong chose these names for the two schools because he determined their characteristic styles had parallels in the northern and southern schools of *Chan* Buddhism (see "Chan Buddhism," Chapter 16, page 470). Northern Chan Buddhists were "gradualists" and believed enlightenment could be achieved only after long training. The Southern Chan Buddhists believed enlightenment could come suddenly. Dong's Northern School therefore comprised professional, highly trained court painters. The leading painters of the Southern School were the literati, whose freer and more expressive style Dong judged to be far superior.

Dong's own work—for example, *Dwelling in the Qingbian Mountains* (FIG. 33-13), painted in 1617—belongs to the Southern School he admired so much. Subject and style, as well as the incorporation of a long inscription at the top, immediately reveal his debt to earlier literati painters. But Dong was also an innovator, especially in his treatment of the towering mountains, where shaded masses of rocks alternate with flat, blank bands, flattening the composition and creating highly expressive and abstract patterns. Some critics have called Dong Qichang the first *modernist* painter, because his work foreshadows developments in 19th-century European landscape painting (FIG. 28-21).

**WEN SHU** Landscape painting was the most prestigious artistic subject in Ming China, but artists also painted other subjects, for example, flowers. WEN SHU (1595–1634), the daughter of an aristocratic Suzhou family and the wife of Zhao Jun (d. 1640), descended from Zhao Mengfu and the Song imperial house, was probably the finest flower painter of the Ming era. Her *Carnations and Garden Rock* (FIG. 33-14) is also an example of Chinese arc-shaped fan painting, a format imported from Japan. In this genre, the artist paints on flat paper, but then folds the completed painting and mounts it on sticks to form a fan. The best fan paintings were

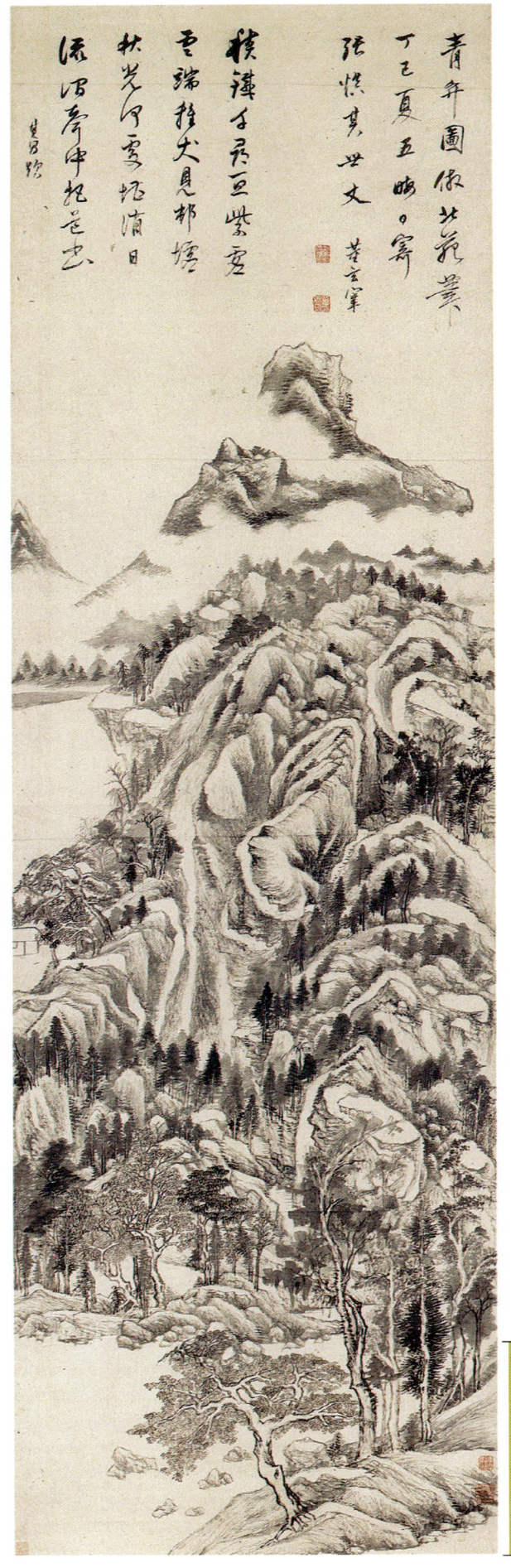

1 ft.

33-13 DONG QICHANG, *Dwelling in the Qingbian Mountains*, Ming dynasty, 1617. Hanging scroll, ink on paper, 7′ 3½″ × 2′ 2½″. Cleveland Museum of Art, Cleveland (Leonard C. Hanna Jr. bequest). ◼◀

Dong Qichang, "the first modernist painter," conceived his landscapes as shaded masses of rocks alternating with blank bands, flattening the composition and creating expressive, abstract patterns.

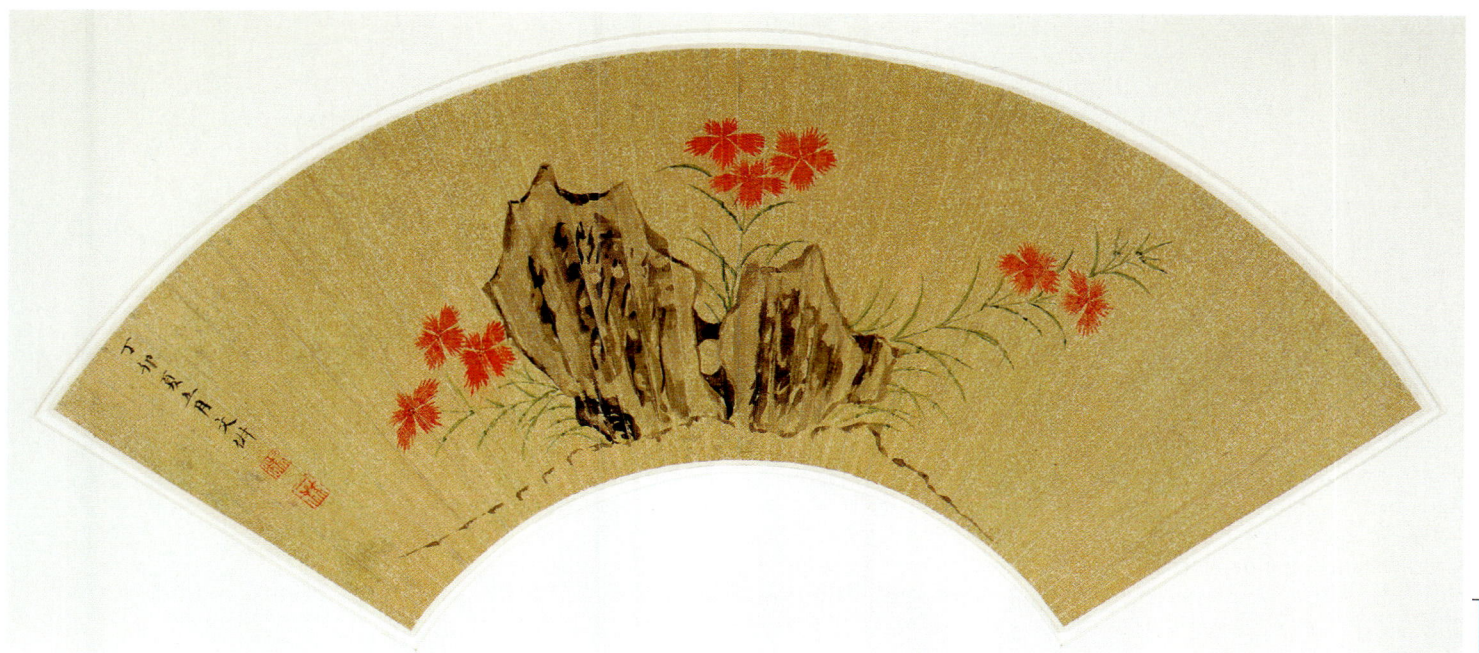

1 in.

**33-14** WEN SHU, *Carnations and Garden Rock*, Ming dynasty, 1627. Fan, ink and colors on gold paper, $6\frac{3}{8}'' \times 1'\ 9\frac{1}{4}''$. Honolulu Academy of Arts, Honolulu (gift of Mr. Robert Allerton).

Wen's depiction of a rock formation and three flower sprays is one of the masterpieces of Ming flower painting. It is also an example of fan painting, a format imported from Japan.

probably never used as fans. Collectors purchased them to store in albums. As in her other flower paintings, Wen focused on a few essential elements, in this instance a central rock formation and three sprays of flowers, and presented them against a plain background. Using delicate brushstrokes and a restricted palette, she brilliantly communicated the fragility of the red flowers, contrasting them with the solidity of the brown rock. The spare composition creates a quiet mood of contemplation.

## Qing Dynasty

The Ming bureaucracy's internal decay permitted another group of invaders, the Manchus of Manchuria, to overrun China in the 17th century. The Qing dynasty (r. 1644–1911) the Manchus established quickly restored effective imperial rule in the north. Southern China remained rebellious until the second Qing emperor, Kangxi ("Lasting Prosperity," r. 1662–1722), succeeded in pacifying all of China. The Manchus adapted themselves to Chinese life and cultivated knowledge of China's arts.

**SHITAO** Traditional literati painting continued to be fashionable among conservative Qing artists, but other painters experimented with extreme effects of massed ink or individualized brushwork patterns. Bold and freely manipulated compositions with a new, expressive force began to appear. A prominent painter in this mode was SHITAO (DAOJI, 1642–1707), a descendant of the Ming imperial family who became a Chan Buddhist monk at age 20. His theoretical writings, most notably his *Sayings on Painting from Monk Bitter Gourd* (his adopted name), called for use of the "single brushstroke" or "primordial line" as the root of all phenomena and representation. Although he carefully studied classical paintings, Shitao opposed mimicking earlier works and believed he could not learn anything from the paintings of others unless he changed them. In *Man in a House beneath a Cliff* (FIG. **33-15**), an *album*

*leaf* (see "Chinese Painting Materials and Formats," Chapter 16, page 459), Shitao surrounded the figure in a hut with vibrant free-floating colored dots and multiple sinuous contour lines. Unlike traditional literati, Shitao did not so much depict the landscape's appearance as animate it, molding the forces running through it.

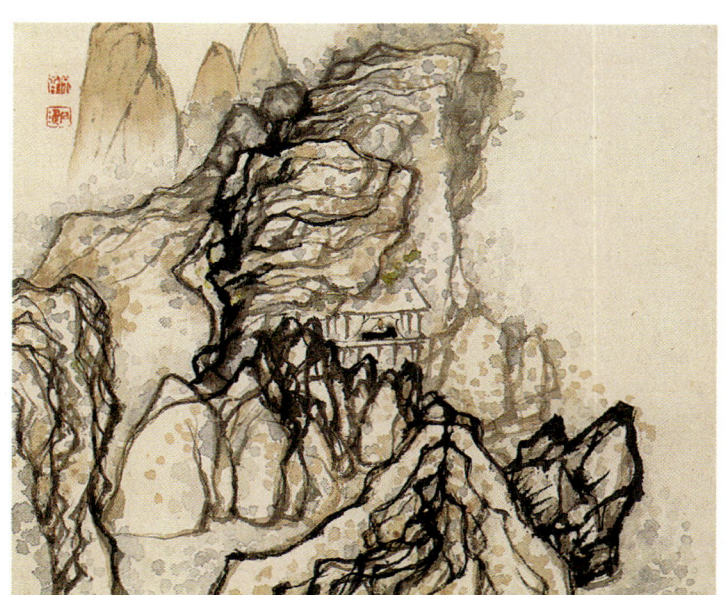

1 in.

**33-15** SHITAO, *Man in a House beneath a Cliff*, Qing dynasty, late 17th century. Album leaf, ink and colors on paper, $9\frac{1}{2}'' \times 11'$. C. C. Wang Collection, New York. ◼◀

Shitao experimented with extreme effects of massed ink and individualized brushwork patterns. In this album leaf, vibrant free-floating colored dots and sinuous contour lines surround a hut.

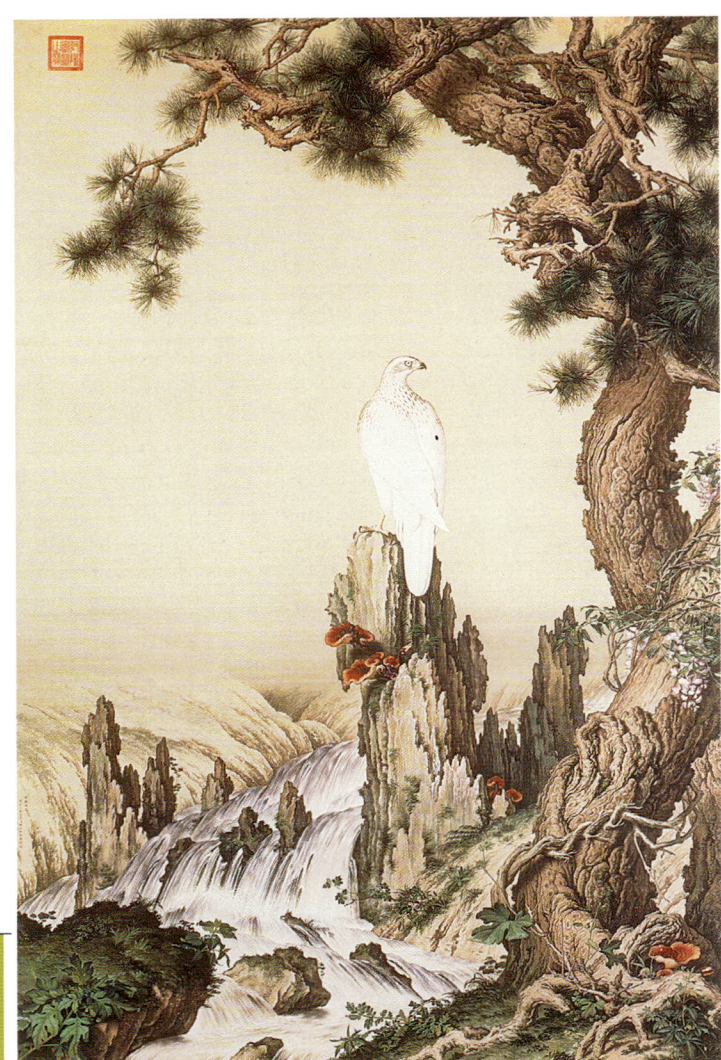

1 ft.

**33-16** GIUSEPPE CASTIGLIONE (LANG SHINING), *Auspicious Objects,* Qing dynasty, 1724. Hanging scroll, ink and colors on silk, 7′ 11¾″ × 5′ 1⅞″. Palace Museum, Beijing.

Castiglione was a Jesuit painter in Qing China who successfully combined European lighting techniques and three-dimensional volume with traditional Chinese literati subjects and compositions.

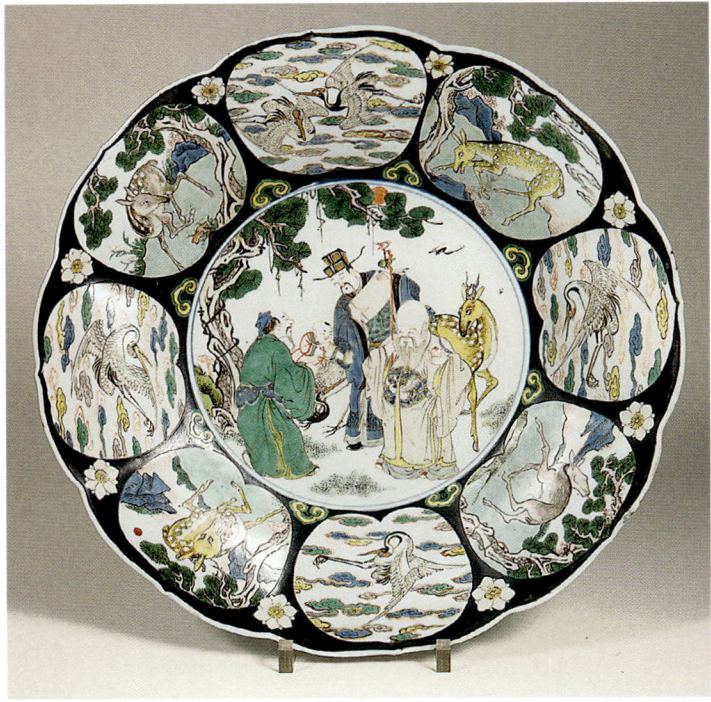

1 in.

**33-17** Dish with lobed rim, Qing dynasty, ca. 1700. White porcelain with multicolored overglaze, 1′ 1⅝″ diameter. Percival David Foundation of Chinese Art, London.

This dish depicting the three star gods of happiness, success, and longevity exemplifies the overglaze porcelain technique in which all the colors come from applying enamels on top of the glaze surface.

**GIUSEPPE CASTIGLIONE** During the Qing dynasty, European Jesuit missionaries were familiar figures at the imperial court. Many of the missionaries were also artists, and they were instrumental in introducing modern European (that is, High Renaissance and Baroque; see Chapters 22 to 25) painting styles to China. The Chinese, while admiring the Europeans' technical virtuosity, found Western style unsatisfactory. Those Jesuit painters who were successful in China adapted their styles to Chinese tastes. The most prominent European artist at the Qing court was GIUSEPPE CASTIGLIONE (1688–1768), who went by the name LANG SHINING in China. *Auspicious Objects* (FIG. **33-16**), which Castiglione painted in 1724 in honor of the birthday of the third Qing emperor, Yongzheng ("Concord and Rectitude," r. 1723–1735), exemplifies his hybrid Italian-Chinese painting style. The Jesuit painter's emphasis on a single source of light, consistently cast shadows, and three-dimensional volume are unmistakably European stylistic concerns. But the impact of Chinese literati painting on the Italian artist is equally evident, especially in the composition of the branches and leaves of the overhanging pine tree and the rock formations in the lower half of the scroll. Above all, the subject is purely Chinese. The white eagle, the pine tree, the rocks, and the red mushroom-like plants (lingzhi) are traditional Chinese symbols. The eagle connotes imperial status, courage, and military achievement. The evergreen pines and the rocks connote long life, which, according to Chinese belief, eating lingzhi will promote. All are fitting motifs for a painting celebrating the birthday of an emperor.

**QING PORCELAIN** Qing potters at the imperial kilns at Jingdezhen continued to expand on Yuan and Ming achievements in developing fine porcelain pieces with underglaze and overglaze decoration—a ceramic technology that gained wide admiration in Europe. The dish with a lobed rim reproduced here (FIG. **33-17**) exemplifies the overglaze technique. All of the colors—black, green, brown, yellow, and even blue—come from applying enamels after the first firing and then firing the dish again at a lower temperature (see "Chinese Porcelain," page 992).

The decoration of the dish reflects important social changes in China. Economic prosperity and the possibility of advancement through success on civil service examinations made it realistic for many more families to hope their sons could achieve wealth and higher social standing. In the center of the dish are Fu, Lu, and Shou, the three star gods of happiness, success, and longevity. The cranes and spotted deer, believed to live to advanced ages, and the pine trees around the rim are all symbols of long life. Artists represented similar themes in the inexpensive woodblock prints produced in great quantities during the Qing era. They were the commoners' equivalent of Castiglione's imperial painting of auspicious symbols (FIG. 33-16).

## People's Republic

The overthrow of the Qing dynasty and the establishment of the Republic of China under the Nationalist Party in 1912 did not bring an end to the traditional themes and modes of Chinese art. But the triumph of Marxism in 1949, when the Communists took control of China and founded the People's Republic, inspired a social realism that broke drastically with the past. The intended purpose of Communist art was to serve the people in the struggle to liberate and elevate the masses.

**YE YUSHAN** In *Rent Collection Courtyard* (FIG. **33-18**), a 1965 tableau 100 yards long and incorporating 114 life-size figures, YE YUSHAN (b. 1935) and a team of sculptors depicted the grim times before the People's Republic. Peasants, worn and bent by toil, bring their taxes (in produce) to the courtyard of their merciless, plundering landlord. The message is clear—this kind of thing must not happen again. Initially, the authorities did not reveal the artists' names. The anonymity of those who depicted the event was significant in itself. The secondary message was that only collective action could effect the transformations the People's Republic sought.

**CHINA TODAY** In the second decade of the 21st century, China is one of the world's great economic powers, and the un-winding of the Cultural Revolution initiated by Mao Zedong (1893–1976) has led to a fruitful artistic exchange between China and the West, with artists such as Xu Bing (FIG. 31-18) and Wu Guanzhong (FIG. 31-22) achieving international reputations. Their works, which can be found in the collections of major museums in Europe and America as well as China, are treated in Chapter 31 in the context of contemporary art worldwide.

# KOREA

The great political, social, religious, and artistic changes that took place in China from the Mongol era to the time of the People's Republic find parallels elsewhere in East Asia, especially in Korea.

## Joseon Dynasty

At the time the Yuan overthrew the Song dynasty, the Goryeo dynasty (918–1392), which had ruled Korea since the downfall of China's Tang dynasty, was still in power (see Chapter 16). The Goryeo kings outlasted the Yuan as well. Toward the end of the Goryeo dynasty, however, the Ming emperors of China attempted to take control of northeastern Korea. General Yi Seonggye repelled them and founded the last Korean dynasty, the Joseon, in 1392. The long rule of the Joseon kings ended only in 1910, when Japan annexed Korea.

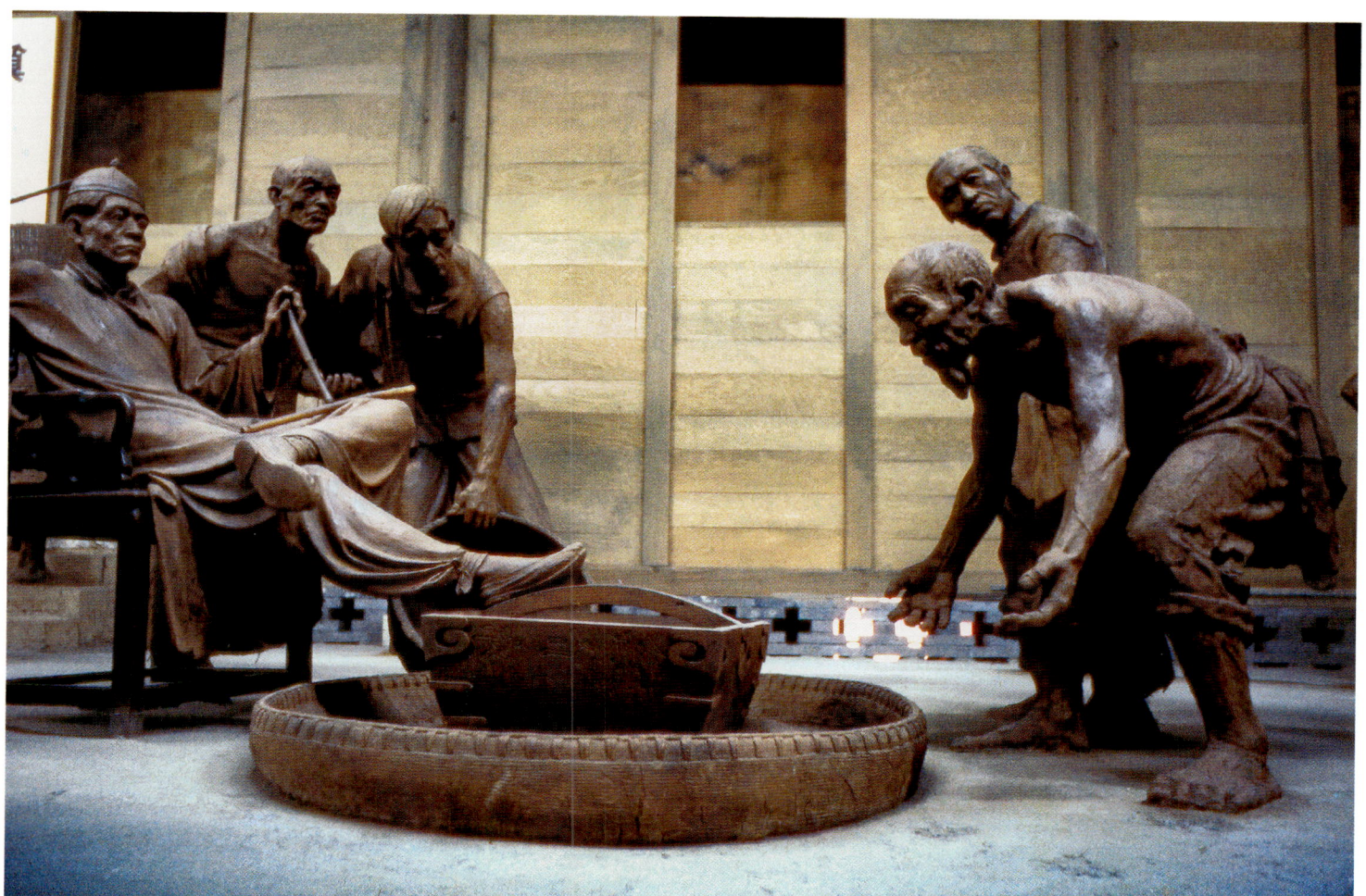

**33-18** YE YUSHAN and others, *Rent Collection Courtyard* (detail of larger tableau), Dayi, China, 1965. Clay, 100 yards long with life-size figures.

In this propagandistic tableau incorporating 114 figures, sculptors depicted the exploitation of peasants by their merciless landlords during the grim times before the Communist takeover of China.

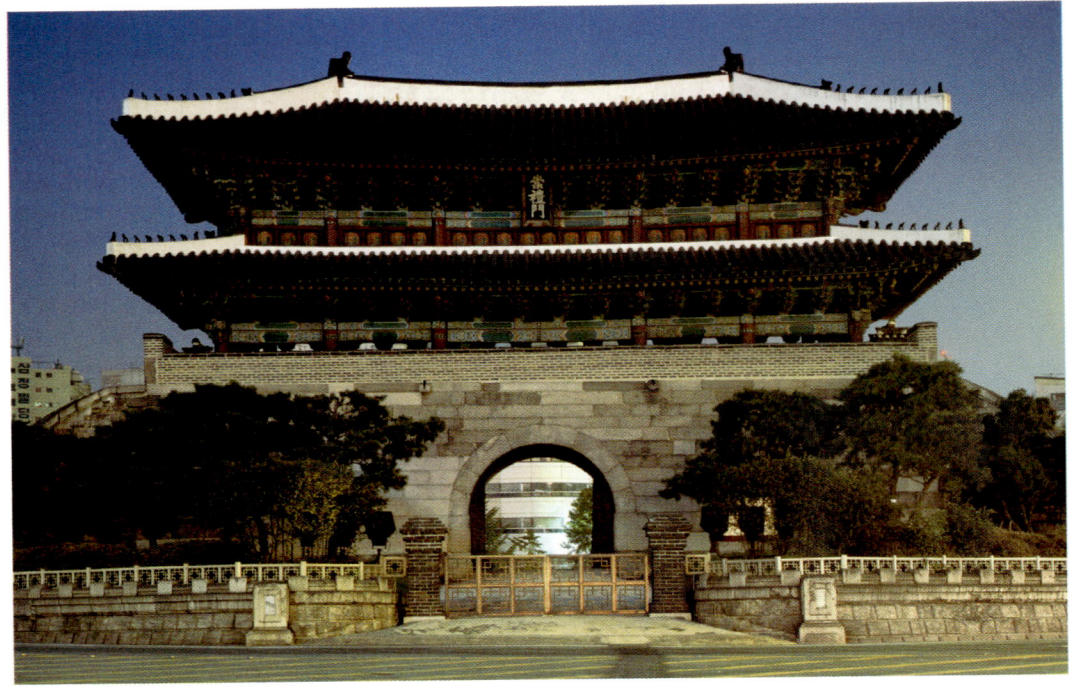

**33-19** Namdaemun, Seoul, South Korea, Joseon dynasty, first built in 1398.

The new Joseon dynasty rulers constructed the south gate to their new capital of Seoul as a symbol of their authority. Namdaemun combines stone foundations with Chinese-style bracketed wooden construction.

**NAMDAEMUN, SEOUL** Public building projects helped give the new Korean state an image of dignity and power. One impressive early monument, built for the new Joseon capital of Seoul, is the city's south gate, or Namdaemun (FIG. **33-19**). It combines the imposing strength of its impressive stone foundations with the sophistication of its intricately bracketed wooden superstructure—the latter regrettably severely damaged by an arson fire in 2008. In East Asia, elaborate gateways, often in a processional series, are a standard element in city designs, as well as royal and sacred compounds, all usually surrounded by walls, as in Beijing's Forbidden City (FIG. 33-1). These gateways served as magnificent symbols of the ruler's authority, as did the triumphal arches of imperial Rome (see Chapter 7).

**JEONG SEON** Over the long course of the Joseon dynasty, Korean painters worked in many different modes and treated the same wide range of subjects seen in Ming and Qing China. One of Korea's most renowned painters was Jeong Seon (1676–1759), a great admirer of Chinese Southern School painting who brought a unique vision to the traditional theme of the mountainous landscape. In *Geumgangsan (Diamond) Mountains* (FIG. **33-20**), he evoked a specific scene, an approach known in Korea as "true view" painting. Using sharper, darker versions of the fibrous brushstrokes most Chinese literati favored, he was able to represent the bright crystalline appearance of the mountains and to emphasize their spiky forms.

## Modern Korea

After its annexation in 1910, Korea remained part of Japan until 1945, when the Western Allies and the Soviet Union took control of the peninsula nation at the end of World War II. Korea was divided into the Democratic People's Republic of Korea (North Korea) and the Republic of Korea (South Korea) in 1948. South Korea soon emerged as a fully industrialized nation, and its artists have had a wide exposure to art styles from around the globe. While some Korean artists continue to work in a traditional East Asian manner, others, for example, Song Su-nam (FIG. 31-22A) have embraced developments in Europe and America. Contemporary Korean art is examined in Chapter 31.

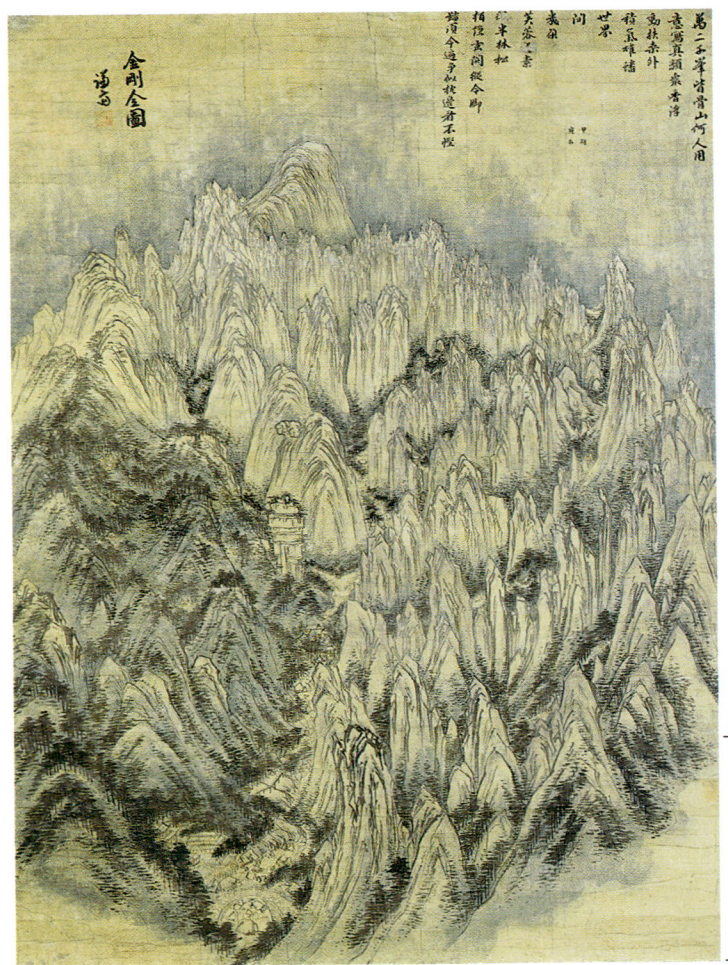

1 ft.

**33-20** JEONG SEON, *Geumgangsan (Diamond) Mountains*, Joseon dynasty, 1734. Hanging scroll, ink and colors on paper, 4′ 3½″ × 1′ 11¼″. Hoam Art Museum, Kyunggi-Do.

In a variation on Chinese literati painting, Jeong Seon used sharp, dark brushstrokes to represent the bright crystalline appearance and spiky forms of the Diamond Mountains.

# CHINA AND KOREA, 1279 TO 1980

## YUAN DYNASTY 1279–1368

▌ The Mongols invaded northern China in 1210 and defeated the last Song emperor in 1279. Under the first Yuan emperor, Kublai Khan, and his successors, China was richer and technologically more advanced than medieval Europe.

▌ Most Chinese artists refused to serve in the Mongol administration, but traditional landscape painting and calligraphy continued to flourish in literati circles during the century of Yuan rule.

▌ The Jingdezhen kilns gained renown for porcelain pottery with cobalt-blue underglaze decoration.

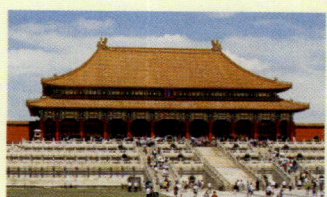

Temple vase,
Yuan dynasty, 1351

## MING DYNASTY 1368–1644

▌ A popular uprising in 1368 drove the last Mongol emperor from Beijing. The new native Ming dynasty expanded the capital and constructed a vast new imperial palace compound, the Forbidden City. Surrounded by a moat and featuring an axial plan, it was the ideal setting for court ritual.

▌ At the opposite architectural pole are the gardens of Suzhou. The Ming designers employed pavilions, bridges, ponds, winding paths, and sculpted rocks to reproduce the irregularities of uncultivated nature.

▌ Ming painting is also diverse, ranging from formal official portrait and history painting to landscape painting. Another subject artists explored was flowers, sometimes painted on fans.

▌ The Orchard Factory satisfied the Ming court's appetite for luxury goods with furniture and other objects in lacquered wood.

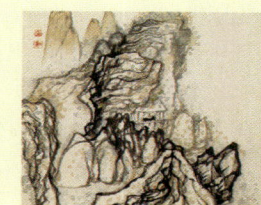

Forbidden City, Beijing,
15th century and later

## QING DYNASTY 1644–1911

▌ In 1644, the Ming dynasty fell to the Manchus, northern invaders who, unlike the Yuan, embraced Chinese art and culture.

▌ Traditional painting styles remained fashionable, but the Qing painter Shitao experimented with extreme effects of massed ink and free brushwork patterns.

▌ Increased contact with Europe brought many Jesuit missionaries to the Qing court. The most prominent Jesuit artist was Guiseppe Castiglione, who developed a hybrid Italian-Chinese painting style.

▌ The Jingdezhen imperial potters developed multicolor porcelains using the overglaze enamel technique.

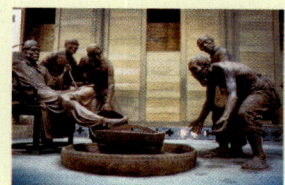

Shitao, *Man in a House
beneath a Cliff*, late 17th century

## MODERN CHINA 1912–1980

▌ The overthrow of the Qing dynasty did not bring a dramatic change in Chinese art, but after the Communists gained control in 1949, state art focused on promoting Marxist ideals. Teams of sculptors produced vast propaganda pieces, such as *Rent Collection Courtyard*.

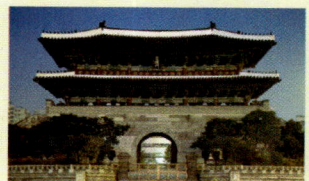

Ye Yushan,
*Rent Collection Courtyard*, 1965

## KOREA 1392–1980

▌ The last Korean dynasty was the Joseon (r. 1392–1910), which established its capital at Seoul and erected impressive public monuments, such as the Namdaemun gate, to serve as symbols of imperial authority.

▌ After the division of Korea into two republics following World War II, South Korea emerged as a modern industrial nation. Some of its artists have brilliantly combined native and international traditions.

Namdaemun, Seoul, 1398

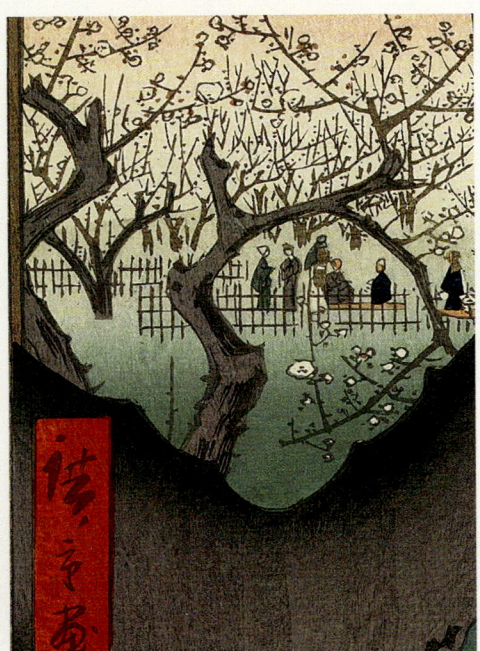

In the 19th century, residents of Edo (modern Tokyo) sought to escape from the noise and pressures of city life to visit places of natural beauty, such as the plum-tree estate at Kameido.

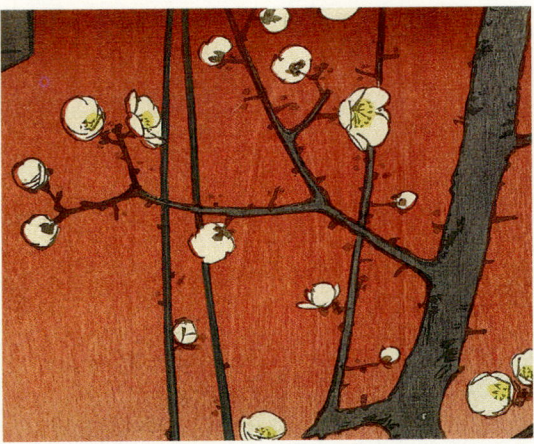

Ando Hiroshige's woodblock print shows only a partial view of the Sleeping Dragon Plum, whose branches spread out in abstract patterns resembling the beloved Japanese art of calligraphy.

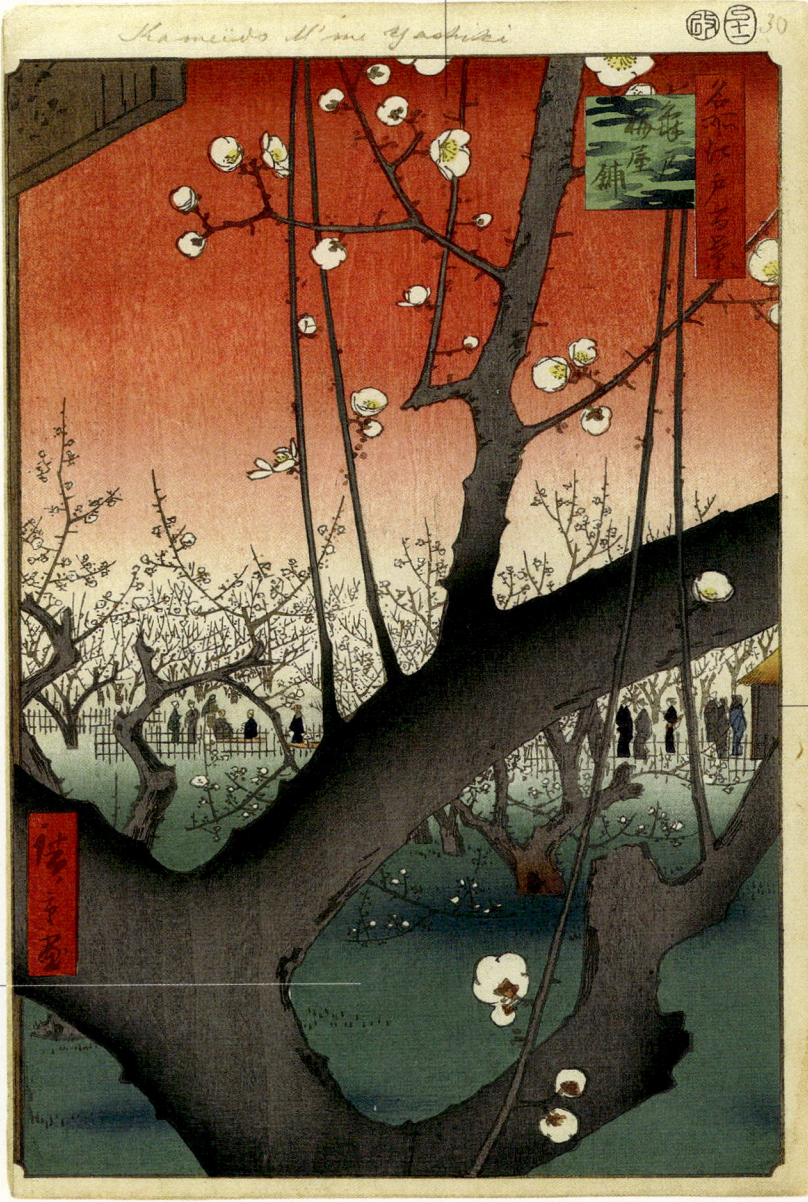

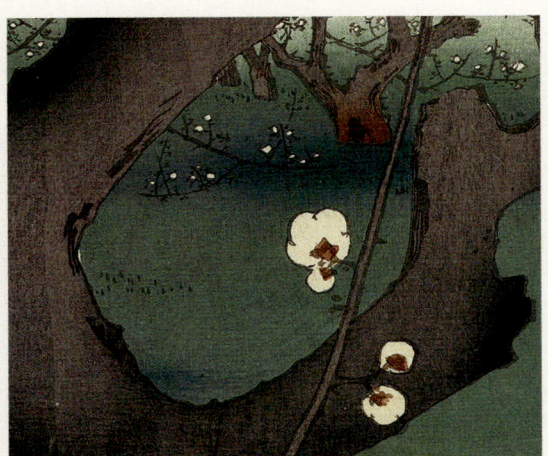

The main attraction of the Kameido estate was the venerable Sleeping Dragon Plum, the most famous tree in Edo, celebrated for its large white blossoms and aromatic fragrance.

1 in.

**34-1** ANDO HIROSHIGE, *Plum Estate, Kameido,* from *One Hundred Famous Views of Edo,* Edo period, 1857. Woodblock print, ink and color on paper, 1′ 1¼″ × 8⅝″. Brooklyn Museum, Brooklyn (gift of Anna Ferris). ◼◀

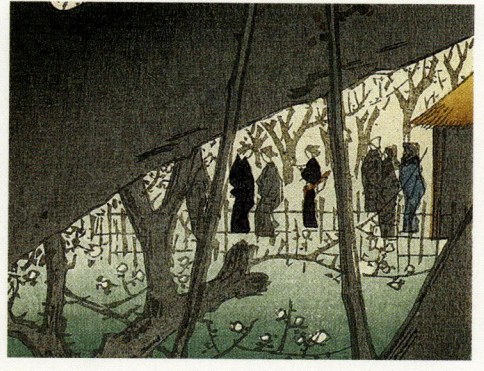

The bold patterns of the Kameido plum tree's limbs seen against the unnaturally colored red sky so dominate the print that the viewer hardly notices the crowd of onlookers behind a fence.

# JAPAN, 1336 TO 1980

## FAMOUS VIEWS OF EDO

Landscape painting—long revered as a major genre of Chinese and Korean painting (see Chapters 16 and 33)—emerged in the 18th century in Japan as an immensely popular subject with the proliferation of inexpensive multicolor woodblock prints (see "Japanese Woodblock Prints," page 1016). Although inspired in part by Dutch landscape engravings imported into Japan at a time when the ruling Tokugawa government was pursuing an isolationist policy (see page 1012), Japanese printmakers radically transformed the compositions and coloration of their Western models.

ANDO HIROSHIGE (1797–1858) and the older Katsushika Hokusai (FIG. 34-13) were the two most renowned Japanese printmakers specializing in landscapes. Hiroshige, born into a wealthy family, decided early on to pursue a career as an artist rather than to follow in his father's footsteps as chief of a fire brigade. In August 1832, he traveled on an official government mission to the emperor in Kyoto and the following year published a series of prints based on sketches he made on that journey—*Fifty-three Stations of the Tokaido Highway*. That collection of views of the countryside along the major roadway on Japan's east coast was an instant success. Many other editions followed, including views of Kyoto (1834) and his last and most ambitious series, published shortly before his death, *One Hundred Famous Views of Edo*.

*Plum Estate, Kameido* (FIG. 34-1), dated "11th Month, 1857," comes from the *Edo* series. The "famous views" are not monuments and buildings but places of leisure and natural beauty where the Japanese sought to escape from the noise and pressures of city life. Many of the sites are Shinto shrines (see "Shinto," Chapter 17, page 479) and Buddhist temples. Others, including the plum orchard of Kameido, were favorite spots to visit at particular times of the year, when their natural beauty was at its peak. The main attraction of the Kameido estate was the Sleeping Dragon Plum, the most famous tree in Edo, celebrated for its large white blossoms and aromatic fragrance. Hiroshige's print shows only a partial view of the venerable tree, with its branches spreading out to touch all sides of the print and forming a bold abstract pattern resembling the beloved art of calligraphy. The pattern of the tree's limbs so dominates the print the viewer hardly notices the crowd of onlookers behind a fence in the background. The unnatural coloration of the red sky enhances the abstract effect, flattening the pictorial space in a manner completely foreign to the Western notion of perspective. It was precisely this quality that fascinated 19th-century European painters who were trying to break free of the Renaissance ideals perpetuated by the official painting academies. One such artist was Vincent van Gogh, who paid tribute to Hiroshige by painting his own version of the Kameido woodblock print (FIG. 28-16B).

# MUROMACHI

In 1185, the Japanese emperor in Kyoto appointed the first *shogun* (military governor) in Kamakura in eastern Japan (MAP **34-1**). Although the imperial family retained its right to reign and, in theory, the shogun managed the country on the ruling emperor's behalf, in reality the emperor lost all governing authority. The Japanese *shogunate* was a political and economic arrangement in which *daimyo* (local lords), the leaders of powerful warrior bands composed of *samurai* (warriors), pledged allegiance to the shogun. These local lords had considerable power over affairs in their domains. The Kamakura shogunate ruled Japan for more than a century but collapsed in 1332. Several years of civil war followed, ending only when Ashikaga Takauji (1305–1358) succeeded in establishing domination of his clan over all of Japan and became the new imperially recognized shogun.

The rise of the Ashikaga clan marked the beginning of the Muromachi period (1336–1573), named after the district in Kyoto in which the Ashikaga shoguns maintained their headquarters. During the Muromachi period, Zen Buddhism (see "Zen Buddhism," page 1007) rose to prominence alongside the older traditions, such as Pure Land and Esoteric Buddhism. Unlike the Pure Land faith, which stressed reliance on the saving power of Amida, the Buddha of the West, Zen emphasized rigorous discipline and personal responsibility. For this reason, Zen held a special attraction for the upper echelons of samurai, whose behavioral codes placed high values on loyalty, courage, and self-control. Further, familiarity with Chinese Zen culture (see "Chan Buddhism," Chapter 16, page 470) carried implications of superior knowledge and refinement, thereby legitimizing the elevated status of the warrior elite.

Zen, however, was not exclusively the religion of Zen monks and highly placed warriors. Aristocrats, merchants, and others studied at and supported Zen temples. Furthermore, those who embraced Zen, including samurai, also generally accepted other Buddhist teachings, especially the ideas of the Pure Land sects. These sects gave much greater attention to the problems of death and salvation. Zen temples stood out not only as religious institutions but also as centers of secular culture, where people could study Chinese art, literature, and learning, which the Japanese imported along with Zen Buddhism. Some Zen monasteries accumulated considerable wealth overseeing trade missions to China.

**SAIHOJI GARDENS** The Saihoji temple gardens (FIG. **34-2**) in Kyoto bear witness to both the continuities and changes mark-

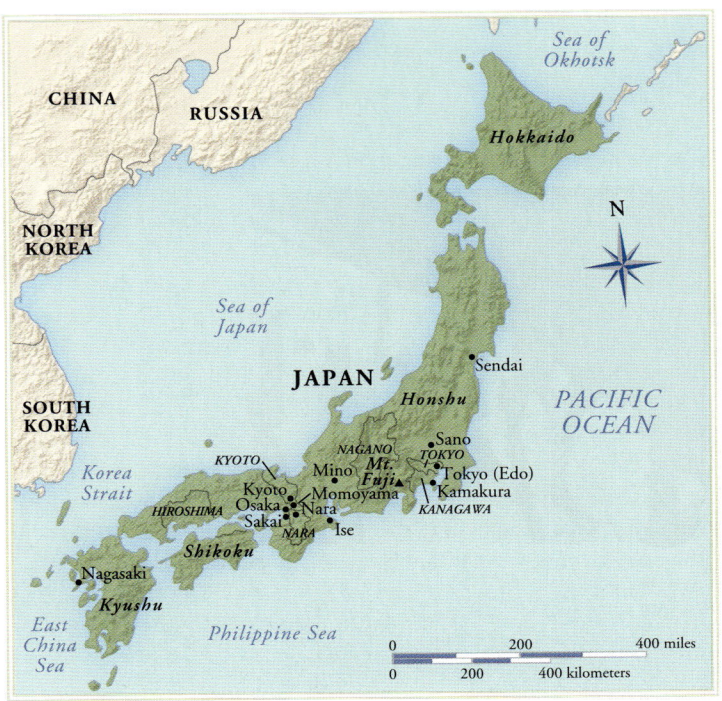

**MAP 34-1** Modern Japan.

ing religious art in the Muromachi period. In the 14th century, this Pure Land temple with its extensive gardens became a Zen institution. However, Zen leaders did not attempt to erase other religious traditions, and the Saihoji gardens in their totality originally included some Pure Land elements even as they served the Zen faith's more meditative needs. In this way, they perfectly echo the complementary roles of these two Buddhist traditions in the Muromachi period, with Pure Land providing a promise of salvation and Zen promoting study and meditation.

Saihoji's lower gardens center on a pond in the shape of the Japanese character for "mind" or "spirit" and are thus a perfect setting for monks to meditate. Today, these gardens are famous for their iridescently green mosses, whose beauty is almost otherworldly. In contrast, arrangements of rocks and sand on the hillsides of the upper garden, especially the dry cascade and pools (FIG. **34-2**), are treasured early examples of Muromachi *karesansui*

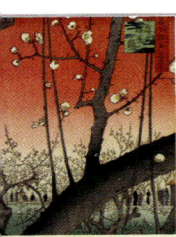

# JAPAN, 1336 TO 1980

| 1336 Muromachi 1573 | Momoyama 1615 | Edo 1868 | Meiji and Showa 1980 |
|---|---|---|---|
| ▌ Zen Buddhist gardens feature dry landscapes<br>▌ Sesshu Toyo produces paintings in the splashed-ink style<br>▌ Kano Motonobu helps establish the Kano School as a virtual Japanese national painting academy | ▌ Japanese shoguns decorate their palatial fortress-castles with painted folding screens featuring lavish use of gold leaf<br>▌ Sen no Rikyu becomes the most renowned master of the Japanese tea ceremony and designs teahouses that foster humility<br>▌ Shino ceramics exemplify the aesthetic principles of wabi and sabi | ▌ The Katsura Imperial Villa at Kyoto sets the standard for Japanese domestic architecture<br>▌ The Rinpa School, named after Ogata Korin, emerges as the major alternative style of painting to the Kano School<br>▌ Japanese woodblock prints depicting the sensual pleasures of Edo's "floating world" reach a wide audience | ▌ European styles and techniques, including oil painting, influence Japanese art after Japan opens its doors to the West<br>▌ Ceramic master Hamada Shoji receives official recognition as a Living National Treasure<br>▌ Kenzo Tange designs the modernist stadiums for the 1964 Olympics in Tokyo |

# Zen Buddhism

*Z*en (*Chan* in Chinese), as a fully developed Buddhist tradition, began filtering into Japan in the 12th century and had its most pervasive influence on Japanese culture starting in the 14th century during the Muromachi period. As in other forms of Buddhism, Zen followers hoped to achieve enlightenment. Zen teachings assert everyone has the potential for enlightenment, but worldly knowledge and mundane thought patterns are barriers to achieving it. Thus, followers must succeed in breaking through the boundaries of everyday perception and logic. This is most often accomplished through meditation. Indeed, the word *zen* means "meditation."

Some Zen schools stress meditation as a long-term practice eventually leading to enlightenment, whereas others stress the benefits of sudden shocks to the worldly mind. One of these shocks is the subject of Kano Motonobu's *Zen Patriarch Xiangyen Zhixian Sweeping with a Broom* (FIG. 34-4), in which the shattering of a fallen roof tile opens the monk's mind. Beyond personal commitment, the guidance of an enlightened Zen teacher is essential to arriving at enlightenment. Years of strict training involving manual labor under the tutelage of this master, coupled with meditation, provide the foundation for a receptive mind. According to Zen beliefs, by cultivating discipline and intense concentration, Buddhists can transcend their ego and release themselves from the shackles of the mundane world. Although Zen is not primarily devotional, followers do pray to specific Buddhas, bodhisattvas, and guardian figures. In general, Zen teachings view mental calm, lack of fear, and spontaneity as signs of a person's advancement on the path to enlightenment.

Zen training for monks takes place at temples, some of which have gardens designed in accord with Zen principles, such as the dry-landscape gardens of Kyoto's Saihoji and Ryoanji temples (FIGS. 34-2 and 34-2A). Zen temples also sometimes served as centers of Chinese learning and handled funeral rites. These temples even embraced many traditional Buddhist observances, such as devotional rituals before images, which had little to do with meditation per se.

As the teachings spread, Zen ideals reverberated throughout Japanese culture. Lay followers as well as Zen monks painted pictures and produced other artworks that appear to reach toward Zen ideals through their subjects and their means of expression. Other cultural practices reflected the widespread appeal of Zen. For example, the tea ceremony (see "The Japanese Tea Ceremony," page 1012), or ritual drinking of tea, as it developed in the 15th and 16th centuries, offered a temporary respite from everyday concerns, a brief visit to a quiet retreat with a meditative atmosphere, such as the Taian teahouse (FIG. 34-7).

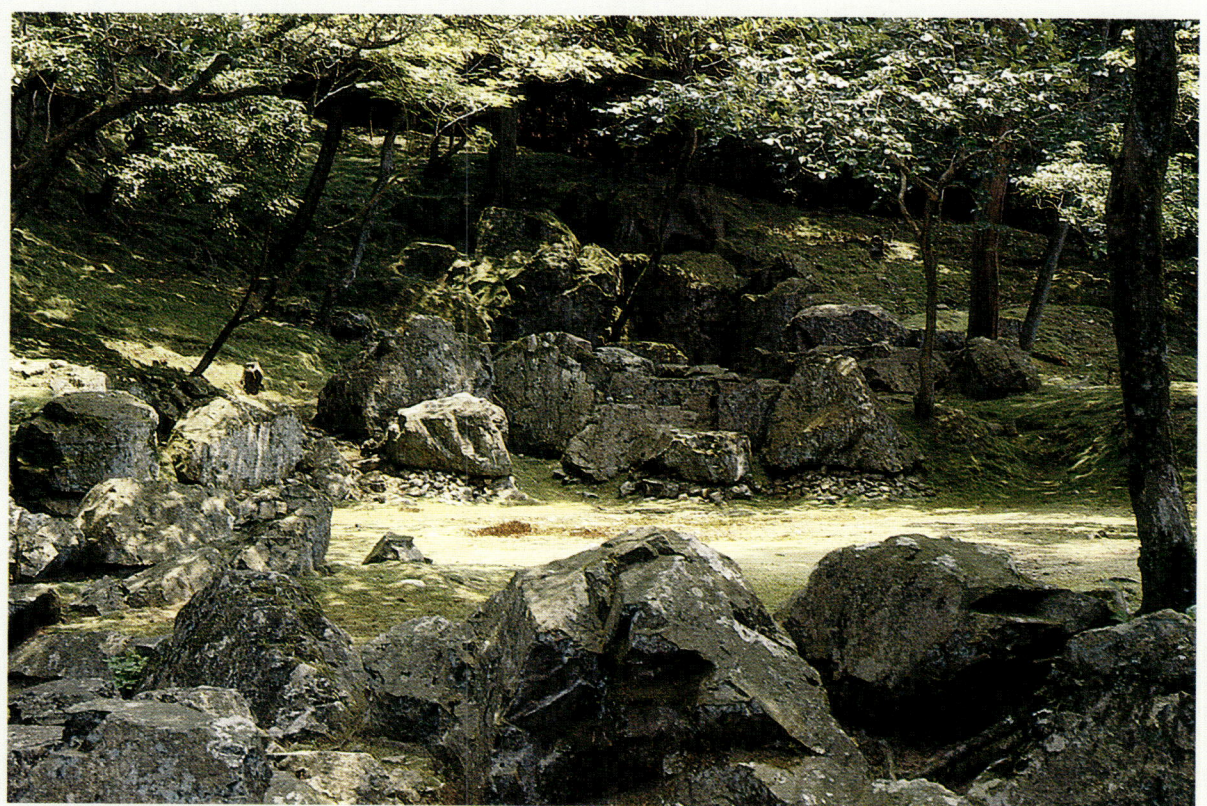

**34-2** Dry cascade and pools, upper garden, Saihoji temple, Kyoto, Japan, modified in Muromachi period, 14th century.

Zen temples often incorporated gardens to facilitate meditation. The upper garden of the Saihoji temple in Kyoto is an early example of Muromachi dry-landscape gardening (karesansui).

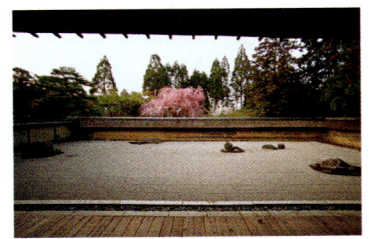

**34-2A** Karesansui garden, Ryoanji, Kyoto, ca. 1488.

(dry-landscape gardening). The designers stacked the rocks to suggest a swift mountain stream rushing over the stones to form pools below. In East Asia, people long considered gazing at dramatic natural scenery highly beneficial to the human spirit. These activities refreshed people worn down from too much contact with daily affairs and helped them reach beyond mundane reality. The dry landscape, or rock garden, became very popular in Japan in the Muromachi period and afterward, especially at Zen temples. In its extreme form, as in the severe, walled Zen garden (FIG. **34-2A**) in Kyoto's Ryoanji temple, a karesansui garden consists purely of artfully arranged rocks on a raked bed of sand.

**SESSHU TOYO** As was common in earlier eras of Japanese history, Muromachi painters usually closely followed Chinese precedents (often arriving by way of Korea), which artists throughout East Asia regarded as part of a shared cultural heritage. Muromachi painting nonetheless displays great variety in both style and subject matter. Indeed, individual masters often worked in different styles, as did the most celebrated Muromachi priest-painter, SESSHU TOYO (1420–1506), one of the few Japanese painters who traveled to China and studied contemporaneous Ming painting. His most dramatic works are in the *splashed-ink* (*haboku*) style, a technique with Chinese roots. The painter of a haboku picture pauses to visualize the image, loads the brush with ink, and then applies primarily broad, rapid strokes, sometimes even dripping the ink onto the paper. The result often hovers at the edge of legibility, without dissolving into sheer abstraction. This balance between spontaneity and a thorough knowledge of the painting tradition gives the pictures their artistic strength. In the haboku landscape illustrated here (FIG. **34-3**), images of mountains, trees, and buildings emerge from the ink-washed surface. Two figures appear in a boat (to the lower right), and the two swift strokes nearby represent the pole and banner of a wine shop.

**KANO MOTONOBU** Representing the opposite pole of Muromachi painting style is the Kano School, which by the 17th century had become virtually a national painting academy. The school flourished until the late 19th century. KANO MOTONOBU (1476–1559) was largely responsible for establishing the Kano style during the Muromachi period. His *Zen Patriarch Xiangyen Zhixian Sweeping with a Broom* (FIG. **34-4**) is one of six panels Motonobu designed as *fusuma* (sliding door paintings) for the abbot's room in the Zen temple complex of Daitokuji in Kyoto. Each panel depicted a different Zen patriarch. The illustrated example, later refashioned as a hanging scroll, represents Xiangyen Zhixian (d. 898) at the moment he achieved enlightenment. Motonobu portrayed the patriarch sweeping the ground near his rustic retreat as a roof tile falls at his feet and shatters. His Zen training is so deep the resonant

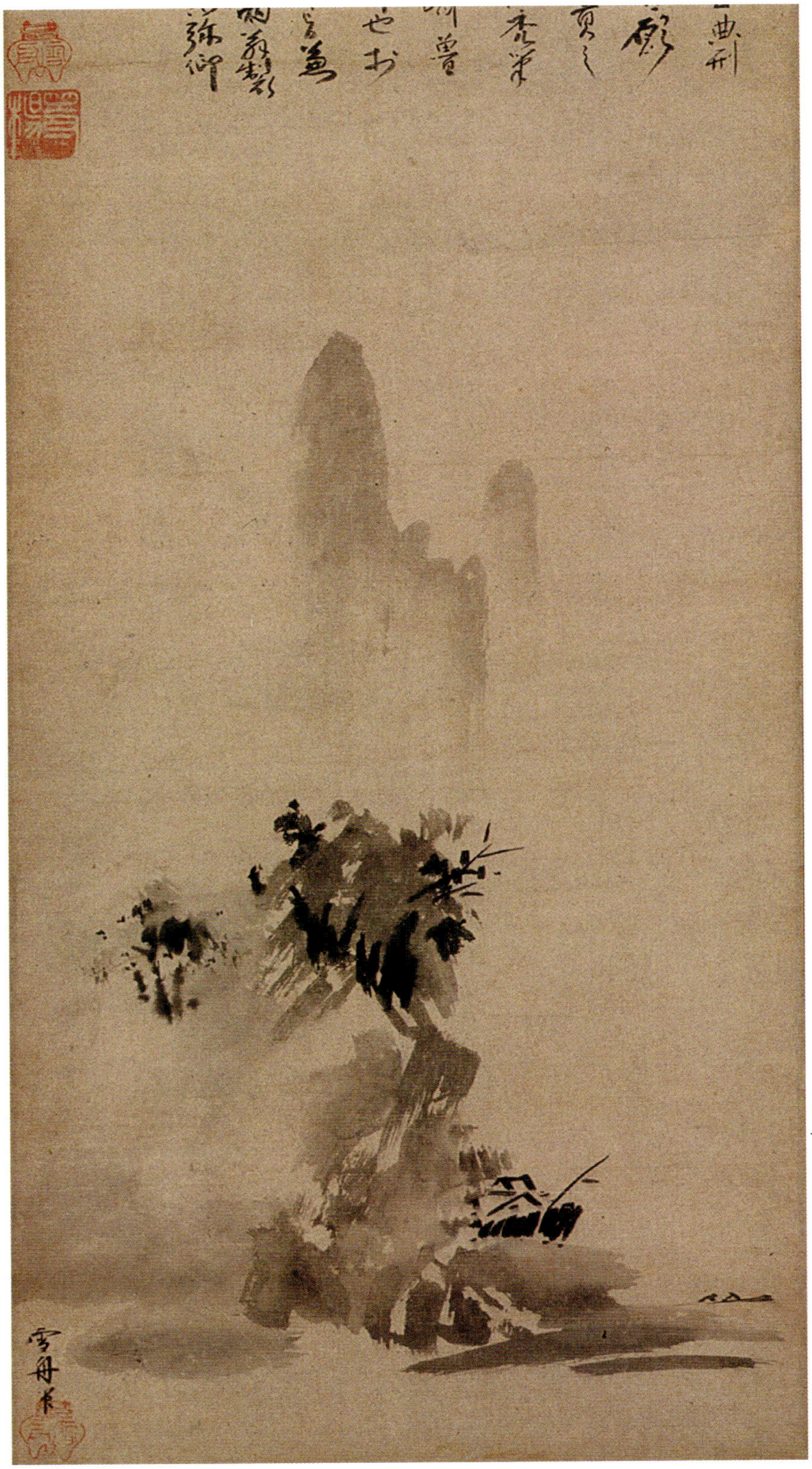

**34-3** SESSHU TOYO, splashed-ink (haboku) landscape, detail of the lower part of a hanging scroll, Muromachi period, 1495. Ink on paper, full scroll 4′ 10¼″ × 1′ 7⅞″; detail 4½″ high. Tokyo National Museum, Tokyo.

In this haboku landscape, the artist applied primarily broad, rapid strokes, sometimes dripping the ink on the paper. The result hovers at the edge of legibility, without dissolving into abstraction.

1 in.

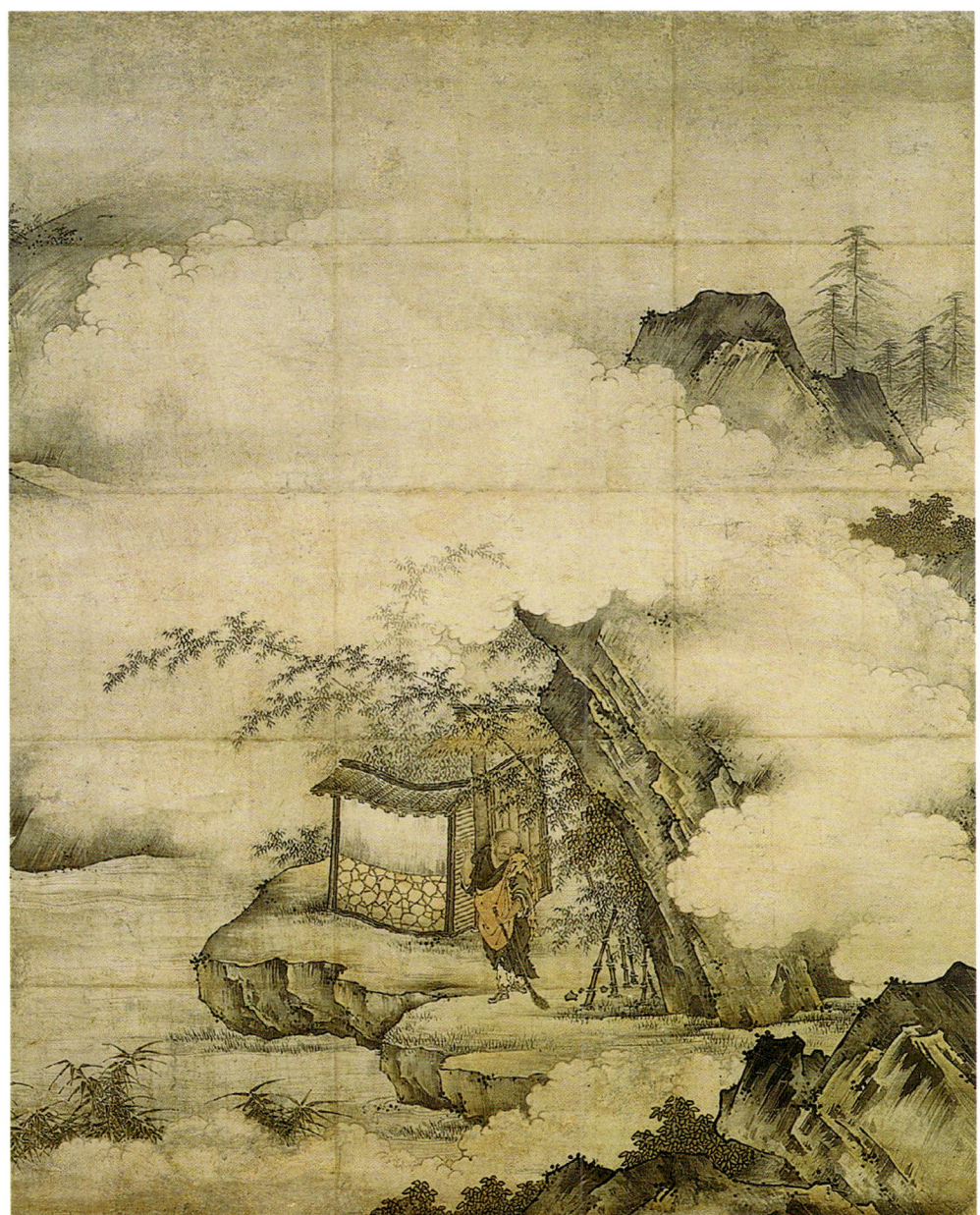

The Kano School represents the opposite pole of Muromachi style from splashed-ink painting. In this scroll depicting a Zen patriarch experiencing enlightenment, bold outlines define the forms.

1 ft.

sound propels the patriarch into an awakening. In contrast to Muromachi splashed-ink painting, Motonobu's work displays exacting precision in applying ink in bold outlines by holding the brush perpendicular to the paper. Thick clouds obscure the mountainous setting and focus the viewer's attention on the sharp, angular rocks, bamboo branches, and modest hut framing the patriarch. Lightly applied colors also draw attention to Xiangyen Zhixian, whom Motonobu showed as having dropped his broom with his right hand as he recoils in astonishment. Although very different in style, the Japanese painting recalls the subject of Liang Kai's Song hanging scroll (FIG. 16-25) representing the Sixth Chan Patriarch's "Chan moment" while chopping bamboo.

# MOMOYAMA

Despite the hierarchical nature of Japanese society during the Muromachi period, the control the Ashikaga shoguns exerted was tenuous and precarious. Ambitious daimyo often seized opportu-

nities to expand their power, sometimes aspiring to become shoguns themselves. By the late 15th century, Japan was experiencing violent confrontations over territory and dominance. In fact, scholars refer to the last century of the Muromachi period as the Era of Warring States, intentionally borrowing the terminology used to describe a much earlier tumultuous period in Chinese history (see Chapter 16). Finally, three successive warlords seized power, and the last succeeded in restoring order and establishing a new and long-lasting shogunate. In 1573, Oda Nobunaga (1534–1582) overthrew the Ashikaga shogunate in Kyoto but was later killed by one of his generals. Toyotomi Hideyoshi (1536–1598) took control of the government after Nobunaga's assassination and ruled until he died of natural causes in 1598. In the struggle following Hideyoshi's death, Tokugawa Ieyasu (1542–1616) emerged victorious and assumed the title of shogun in 1603. Ieyasu continued to face challenges, but by 1615 he had eliminated his last rival and established his clan as the rulers of Japan for two and a half centuries. To reinforce their power, these warlords constructed huge castles

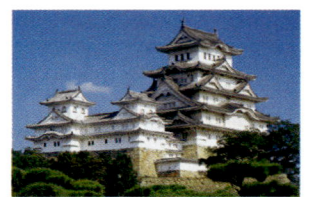
34-4A White Heron Castle, Himeji, begun 1581.

with palatial residences—partly as symbols of their authority and partly as fortresses. An outstanding example is Hideyoshi's White Heron Castle (FIG. 34-4A) at Himeji, west of Osaka. The new era's designation, Momoyama (Peach Blossom Hill), derives from the scenic foliage at another Hideyoshi castle southeast of Kyoto. The Momoyama period (1573–1615), although only a brief interlude between two major shogunates, produced many outstanding artworks.

**KANO EITOKU** Each Momoyama warlord commissioned lavish decorations for the interior of his castle, including paintings, fusuma, and *byobu* (folding screens) in ink, color, and gold leaf. Gold screens had been known since Muromachi times, but Momoyama painters made them even bolder, reducing the number of motifs and often greatly enlarging them against flat, shimmering fields of gold leaf.

The grandson of Motonobu, KANO EITOKU (1543–1590), was the leading painter of murals and screens and received numerous commissions from the powerful Momoyama warlords. So extensive were these commissions (in both scale and number) that Eitoku adopted a painting system developed by his grandfather, which depended on a team of specialized painters to assist him. Unfortunately, little of Eitoku's elaborate work remains because of the subsequent destruction of the ostentatious castles he helped decorate—not surprising in an era marked by power struggles. However, a painting on a six-panel screen, *Chinese Lions* (FIG. 34-5), offers a glimpse of his work's gran-

deur. Possibly created for Toyotomi Hideyoshi, this screen, originally one of a pair, appropriately speaks to the emphasis on militarism so prevalent at the time. The lions Eitoku depicted are ancient Chinese mythological beasts. Appearing in both religious and secular contexts, the lions came to be associated with power and bravery, and are thus fitting imagery for a military leader. Indeed, Chinese lions became an important symbolic motif during the Momoyama period. In Eitoku's painting, the colorful beasts' powerfully muscled bodies, defined and flattened by broad contour lines, stride forward within a gold field and minimal setting elements. The dramatic effect of this work derives in part from its scale—it is more than 7 feet tall and nearly 15 feet long.

**HASEGAWA TOHAKU** Momoyama painters did not work exclusively in the colorful style exemplified by Eitoku's *Chinese Lions*. HASEGAWA TOHAKU (1539–1610) was a leading painter who became familiar with the aesthetics and techniques of Chinese Chan and Japanese Zen painters such as Sesshu Toyo (FIG. 34-3) by studying the art collections of the Daitokuji temple in Kyoto. Tohaku sometimes painted in ink monochrome using loose brushwork with brilliant success, as seen in *Pine Forest* (FIG. 34-6), one of a pair of six-panel byobu. His wet brushstrokes—long and slow, short and quick, dark and pale—present a grove of great pines shrouded in mist. His trees emerge from and recede into the heavy atmosphere, as if the landscape hovers at the edge of formlessness. In Zen terms, the picture suggests the illusory nature of mundane reality while evoking a calm, meditative mood.

**SEN NO RIKYU** A favorite exercise of cultivation and refinement in the Momoyama period was the tea ceremony (see "The Japanese Tea Ceremony," page 1012). In Japan, this important practice

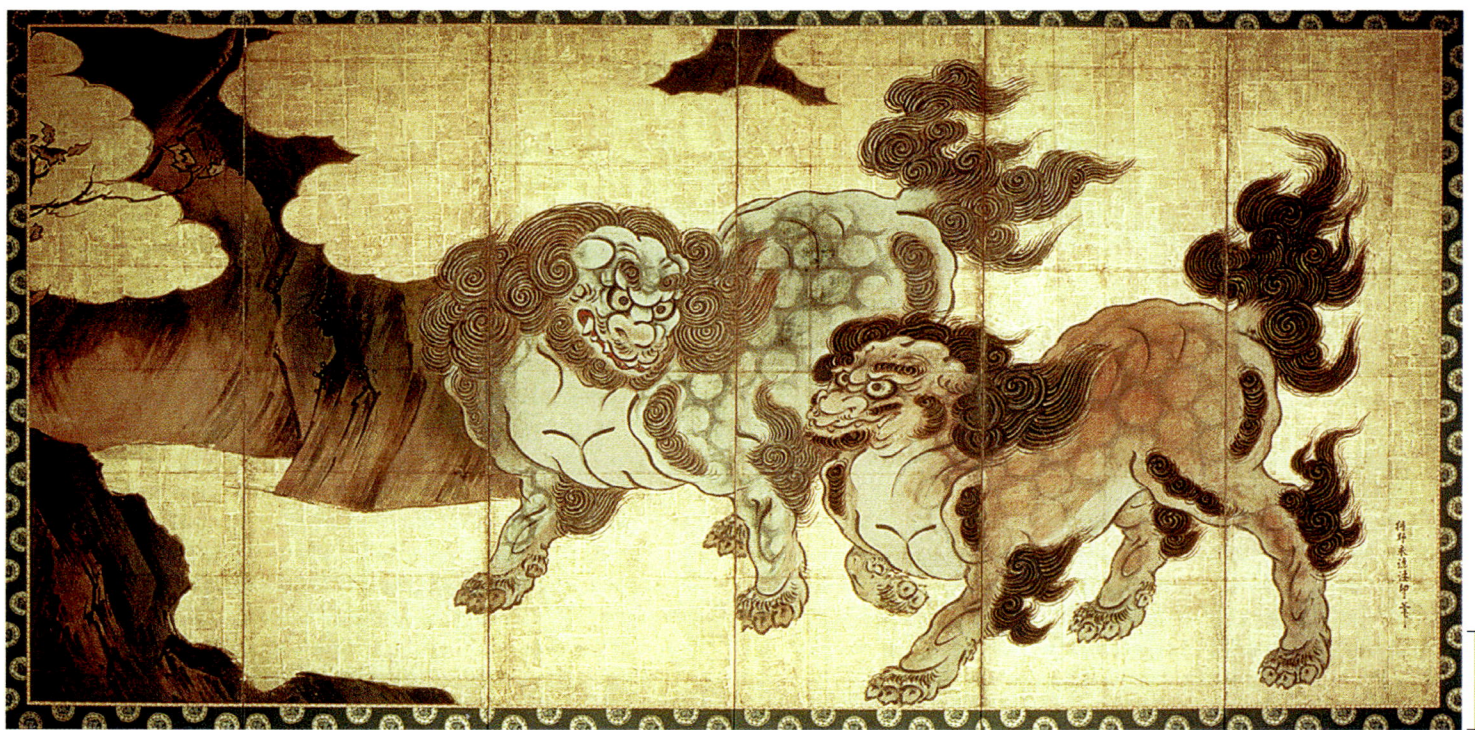

1 ft.

**34-5** KANO EITOKU, *Chinese Lions,* Momoyama period, late 16th century. Six-panel screen, color, ink, and gold-leaf on paper, 7′ 4″ × 14′ 10″. Museum of the Imperial Collections, Tokyo.

Chinese lions were fitting imagery for the castle of a Momoyama warlord because they exemplified power and bravery. Eitoku's huge screen features boldly outlined forms on a gold ground.

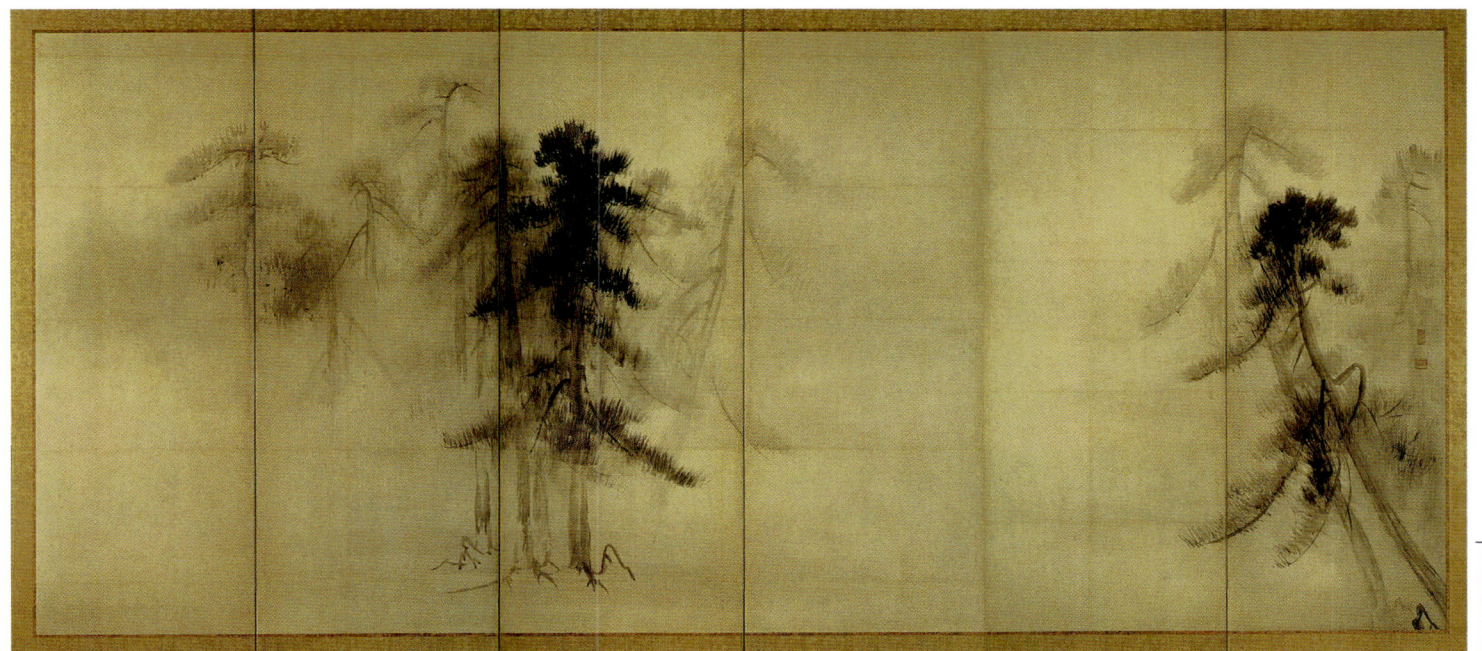

**34-6** HASEGAWA TOHAKU, *Pine Forest,* Momoyama period, late 16th century. One of a pair of six-panel screens, ink on paper, 5′ 1⅜″ × 11′ 4″. Tokyo National Museum, Tokyo.

Tohaku used wet brushstrokes to paint a grove of great pines shrouded in mist. In Zen terms, the six-panel screen suggests the illusory nature of mundane reality while evoking a meditative mood.

1 ft.

eventually came to carry various political and ideological implications. For example, it provided a means for those relatively new to political or economic power to assert authority in the cultural realm. For instance, upon returning from a major military campaign, Toyotomi Hideyoshi held an immense tea ceremony lasting 10 days and open to everyone in Kyoto. The ceremony's political implications became so important that warlords granted or refused their vassals the right to host these rituals.

The most venerated tea master of the Momoyama period was SEN NO RIKYU (1522–1591), who was instrumental in establishing the rituals and aesthetics of the tea ceremony, for example, the manner of entry into a teahouse (crawling on one's hands and knees). Rikyu believed crawling fostered humility and created the impression, however unrealistic, that there was no rank in a teahouse. Rikyu was the designer of the first Japanese teahouse built as an independent structure as opposed to being part of a house. The Taian teahouse (FIG. **34-7**) at the Myokian temple in Kyoto, also attributed to Rikyu, is the oldest in Japan. The interior displays two standard features of Japanese residential architecture of the late Muromachi period—very thick, rigid straw mats called *tatami* (a Heian innovation) and an alcove called a *tokonoma*. The tatami accommodate the traditional Japanese customs of not wearing shoes indoors and of sitting on the floor. They are still features of Japanese homes today. Less common in contemporary houses are tokonoma, which developed as places to hang scrolls of painting or calligraphy and to display other prized objects.

The Taian tokonoma and the tearoom as a whole have unusually dark walls, with earthen plaster covering even some of the square corner posts. The room's dimness and tiny size (about six feet square, the size of two tatami mats) produce a cavelike feel and encourage intimacy among the tea host and guests. The guests enter from the garden outside by crawling through a small sliding door. The means of entrance emphasizes a guest's passage into a ceremonial space set apart from the ordinary world.

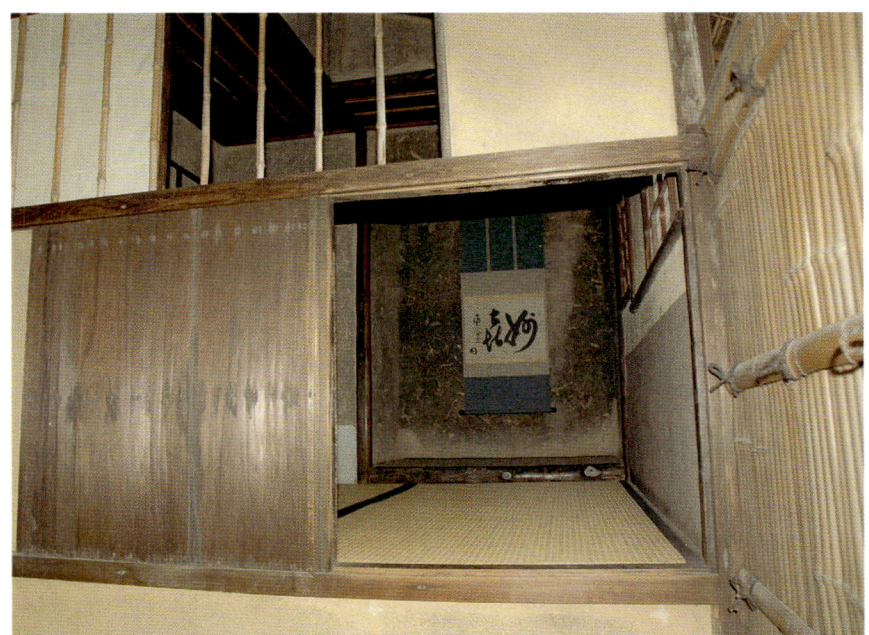

**34-7** SEN NO RIKYU, view into the Taian teahouse, Myokian temple, Kyoto, Japan, Momoyama period, ca. 1582.

The dimness and tiny size of the Taian tearoom and its alcove produce a cavelike feel and encourage intimacy among the host and guests, who must crawl through a small door to enter.

## The Japanese Tea Ceremony

The Japanese tea ceremony involves the ritual preparation, serving, and drinking of green tea. The fundamental practices began in China, but they developed in Japan to a much higher degree of sophistication, peaking in the Momoyama period. Simple forms of the tea ceremony started in Japan in Zen temples as a symbolic withdrawal from the ordinary world to cultivate the mind and spirit. The practices spread to other social groups, especially samurai and, by the late 16th century, wealthy merchants. Until the late Muromachi period, grand tea ceremonies in warrior residences served primarily as an excuse to display treasured collections of Chinese objects, such as porcelains, lacquers, and paintings.

Initially, the Japanese held tea ceremonies in a room or section of a house. As the popularity of tea ceremonies increased, freestanding teahouses (FIG. 34-7) became common. The ceremony involves a sequence of rituals in which both host and guests participate. The host's responsibilities include serving the guests; selecting special utensils, such as water jars (FIG. 34-8) and tea bowls; and determining the tearoom's decoration, which changes according to occasion and season. Acknowledged as having superior aesthetic sensibilities, individuals recognized as master tea-ceremony practitioners (tea masters) advise patrons on the ceremony and acquire students. Tea masters even direct or influence the design of teahouses and

**34-8** Kogan (tea-ceremony water jar), Momoyama period, late 16th century. Shino ware with underglaze design, 7″ high. Hatakeyama Memorial Museum, Tokyo.

The vessels used in the Japanese tea ceremony reflect the concepts of wabi, the aesthetic of refined rusticity, and sabi, the value found in weathered objects, suggesting the tranquility of old age.

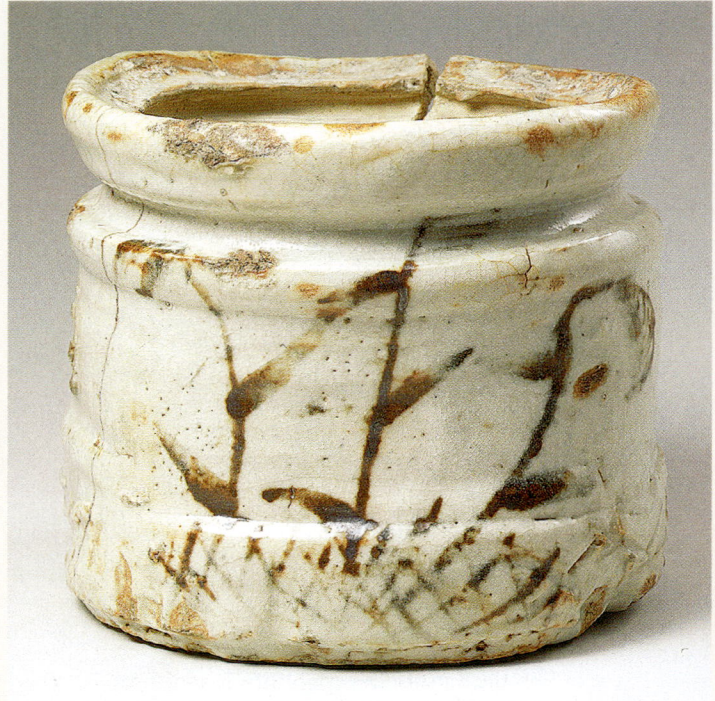

1 in.

tearooms within larger structures (including interiors and gardens), as well as the design of tea utensils. They often make simple bamboo implements and occasionally even ceramic vessels.

---

**SHINO CERAMICS** Sen no Rikyu also was influential in determining the aesthetics of tea-ceremony utensils. In his view, value and refinement lay in character and ability, not in bloodline or rank, and he therefore encouraged the use of tea items whose value was their inherent beauty rather than their monetary worth. Even before Rikyu, in the late 15th century during the Muromachi period, admiration of the technical brilliance of Chinese objects had begun to give way to ever-greater appreciation of the virtues of rustic Korean and Japanese wares. This new aesthetic of refined rusticity, or *wabi,* was consistent with Zen concepts. Wabi suggests austerity and simplicity. Related to wabi and also important as a philosophical and aesthetic principle was *sabi*—the value found in the old and weathered, suggesting the tranquility reached in old age.

Wabi and sabi aesthetics underlie the ceramic vessels produced for the tea ceremony, such as the Shino water jar named *Kogan* (FIG. **34-8**). The name, which means "ancient stream bank," comes from the painted design on the jar's surface as well as from its coarse texture and rough form, both reminiscent of earth cut by water. The term *Shino* generally refers to ceramic wares produced during the late 16th and early 17th centuries in kilns in Mino. Shino vessels typically have rough surfaces and feature heavy glazes containing feldspar. These glazes are predominantly white when fired, but can include pinkish-red or gray hues. The water jar's coarse stoneware body and seemingly casual decoration offer the same sorts of aesthetic and interpretive challenges and opportunities as dry-landscape gardens (FIGS. 34-2 and 34-2A). The jar illustrated here, for example, has a prominent crack in one side and sagging contours (both intentional) to suggest the accidental and natural, qualities essential to the values of wabi and sabi.

# EDO

When Tokugawa Ieyasu consolidated his power in 1615, he abandoned Kyoto, the official capital, and set up his headquarters in Edo (modern Tokyo), initiating the Edo period (1615–1868) of Japanese history and art. The new regime instituted many policies designed to limit severely the pace of social and cultural change in Japan. Fearing destabilization of the social order, the Tokugawa rulers banned Christianity and expelled all Western foreigners except the Dutch. The Tokugawa also instituted Confucian ideas of social stratification and civic responsibility as public policy, and they tried to control the social influence of urban merchants, some of whose wealth far outstripped that of most warrior leaders. However, the population's great expansion in urban centers, the spread of literacy in the cities and beyond, and a growing thirst for knowledge and diversion made for a very lively popular culture not easily subject to tight control.

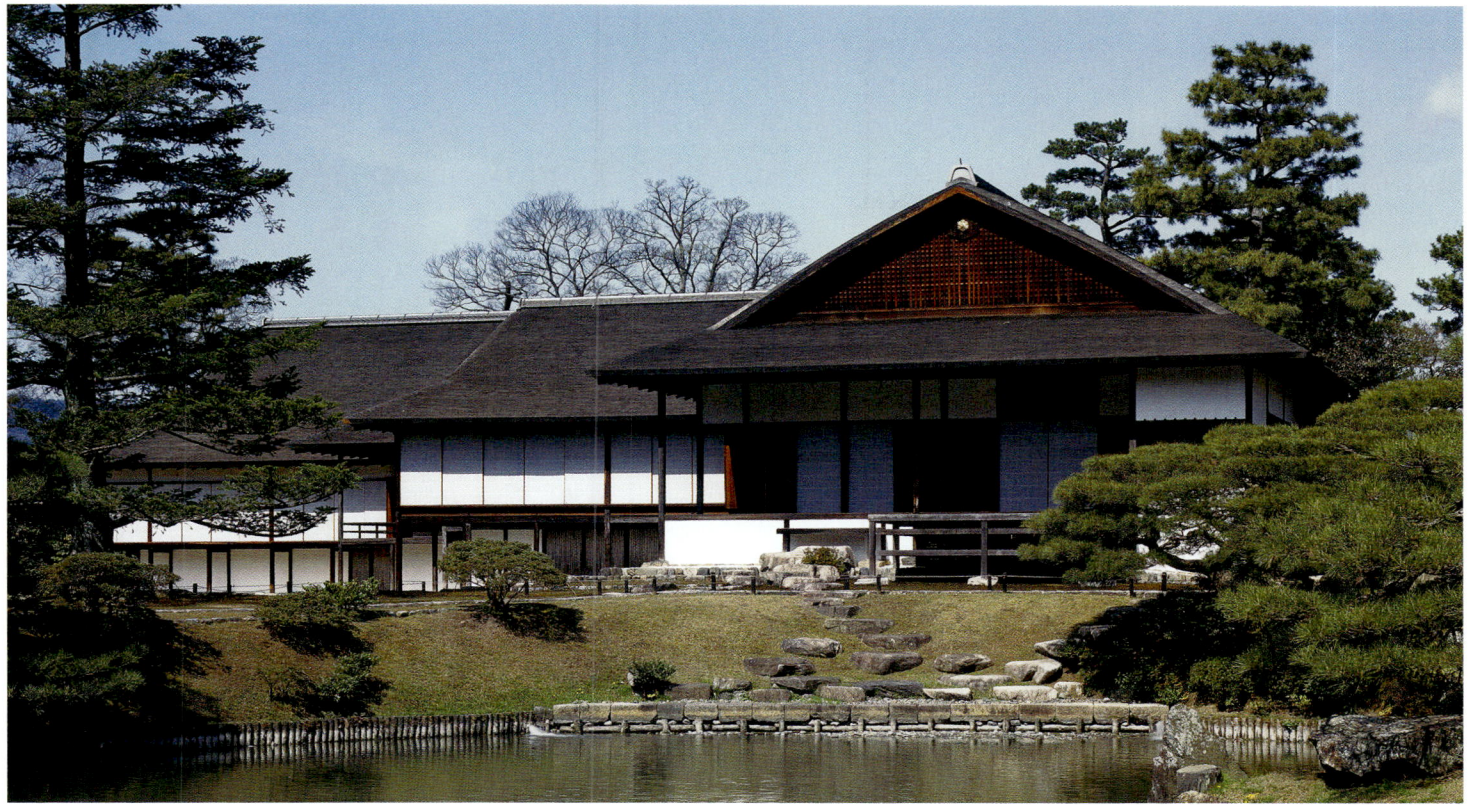

**34-9** East facade of the Katsura Imperial Villa, Kyoto, Japan, Edo period, 1620–1663.

The Katsura Imperial Villa became the standard for Japanese residential architecture. The design relies on subtleties of proportion, color, and texture instead of ornamentation for its aesthetic appeal.

**KATSURA IMPERIAL VILLA** In the Edo period, the imperial court's power remained as it had been for centuries, symbolic and ceremonial, but the court continued to wield influence in matters of taste and culture. For example, for a 50-year period in the 17th century, a princely family developed a modest country retreat into a villa that became the standard for domestic Japanese architecture. Since the early 20th century, it has inspired architects worldwide (FIG. 29-45), even as ordinary living environments in Japan became increasingly Westernized in structure and decor. The Katsura Imperial Villa (FIG. 34-9), built between 1620 and 1663 on the Katsura River southwest of Kyoto, has many features derived from earlier teahouses, such as Rikyu's Taian (FIG. 34-7). However, tea-ceremony aesthetics later retreated from Rikyu's wabi extremes, and the Katsura Villa's designers and carpenters incorporated elements of courtly gracefulness as well.

Ornamentation that disguises structural forms has little place in this architecture's appeal, which relies instead on subtleties of proportion, color, and texture. A variety of textures (stone, wood, tile, plaster) and subdued colors and tonal values enrich the villa's lines, planes, and volumes. Artisans painstakingly rubbed and burnished all surfaces to bring out the natural beauty of their grains and textures. The rooms are not large, but parting or removing the sliding doors between them can create broad rectangular spaces. Perhaps most important, the residents can open the doors to the outside to achieve a harmonious integration of building and garden—one of the primary ideals of Japanese residential architecture.

**RINPA** In painting, the Kano School enjoyed official governmental sponsorship during the Edo period, and its workshops provided paintings to the Tokugawa shoguns and their major vassals.

By the mid-18th century, Kano masters also served as the primary painting teachers for nearly everyone aspiring to a career in the field. Even so, individualist painters and other schools emerged and flourished, working in quite distinct styles.

The earliest major alternative school to emerge in the Edo period, Rinpa, was quite different in nature from the Kano School. It did not have a similar continuity of lineage and training through father and son, master and pupil. Instead, over time, Rinpa aesthetics and principles attracted a variety of individuals as practitioners and champions. Stylistically, Rinpa works feature vivid color and extensive use of gold and silver and often incorporate decorative patterns. The Rinpa School traced its roots to TAWARAYA SOTATSU (d. 1643), an artist who emerged as an important figure during the late Momoyama period, and whose *Waves at Matsushima* (FIG. **34-9A**) is one of the early masterworks of Edo painting. Rinpa, however, takes its first syllable from the last syllable in the name of OGATA KORIN (1658–1716; FIG. I-13). Both Sotatsu and Korin were scions of wealthy merchant families with close connections to the Japanese court. Many Rinpa works incorporate literary themes the nobility favored.

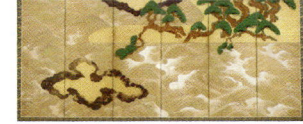

34-9A SOTATSU, *Waves at Matsushima*, ca. 1630.

**HONAMI KOETSU** One of the earliest Rinpa masters was HONAMI KOETSU (1558–1637), the heir of an important family in the ancient capital of Kyoto and a greatly admired calligrapher. He also participated in and produced ceramics for the tea ceremony. Many scholars credit him with overseeing the design of wooden objects with lacquer decoration (see "Lacquered Wood," Chapter 33, page 995), perhaps with the aid of Sotatsu, the proprietor of a

Honami Koetsu, *Boat Bridge*, writing box, Edo period, early 17th century. Lacquered wood with sprinkled gold and lead overlay, $9\frac{1}{2}'' \times 9'' \times 4\frac{3}{8}''$. Tokyo National Museum, Tokyo.

Koetsu's writing box is an early work of the Rinpa School, which drew on ancient traditions of painting and craft decoration to develop a style that collapsed boundaries between the two arts.

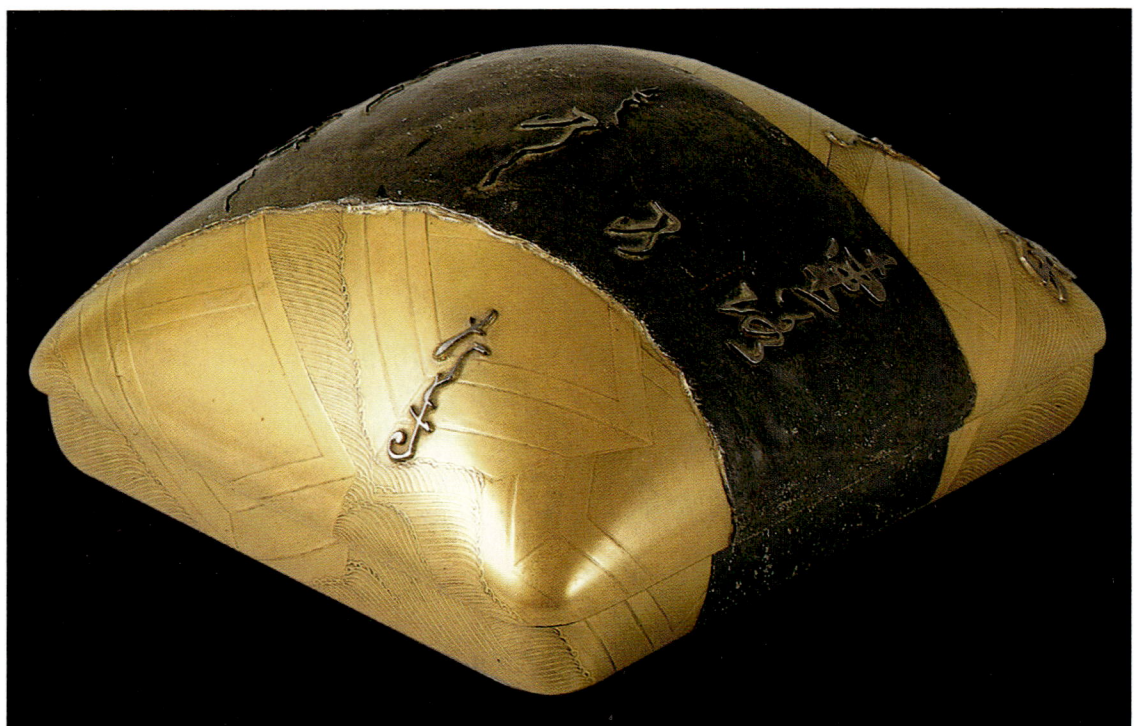

1 in.

fan-painting shop. Scholars know the two drew on ancient traditions of painting and craft decoration to develop a style that collapsed boundaries between the two arts. Paintings, the lacquered surfaces of writing boxes, and ceramics shared motifs and compositions.

In typical Rinpa fashion, Koetsu's *Boat Bridge* writing box (FIG. **34-10**) exhibits motifs drawn from a 10th-century poem about the boat bridge at Sano, in the eastern provinces. The lid presents a subtle, gold-on-gold scene of small boats lined up side by side in the water to support the planks of a temporary bridge. The bridge itself, a lead overlay, forms a band across the lid's convex surface. The raised metallic lines on the water, boats, and bridge are a few Japanese characters from the poem, which describes the experience of crossing a bridge as evoking reflection on life's insecurities. The box also shows the dramatic contrasts of form, texture, and color typifying Rinpa aesthetics, especially the juxtaposition of the bridge's dark metal and the box's brilliant gold surface. The gold decoration comes from careful sprinkling of gold dust in wet lacquer (see "Lacquered Wood," Chapter 33, page 995). Whatever Koetsu's contribution to the design process, specialists well versed in the demanding techniques of metalworking and lacquering produced the writing box.

**LITERATI PAINTING** In the 17th and 18th centuries, Japan's increasingly urban, educated population spurred a cultural and social restlessness among commoners and samurai of lesser rank that the policies of the restrictive Tokugawa could not suppress. People eagerly sought new ideas and images, directing their attention primarily to China, as had happened throughout Japanese history, but also to the West. From each direction, dramatically new ideas about painting emerged.

Starting in the late 17th century, illustrations in printed books and imported paintings of lesser quality brought limited knowledge of Chinese literati painting (see Chapter 33) into Japan. Korea was the essential link at this time between Japan and China, as it was so often in the past. Edo Japan had no official ties with Qing

China but welcomed ambassadors and scholars from Korea. Because of this exposure to Chinese painting, some Edo artists began to emulate Chinese models, although the difference in context resulted in variations. In China, literati were cultured intellectuals whose education and upbringing as landed gentry afforded them positions in the country's governmental bureaucracy. Chinese literati artists were predominantly amateurs and pursued painting as one of the proper functions of an educated and cultivated person. In contrast, although Japanese literati artists acquired a familiarity with and appreciation for Chinese literature, they were mostly professionals, painting to earn a living. Among them, however, were many women, who could more easily work in this painting genre because of its traditional association with amateurism and private intellectual pursuits. Because of the diffused infiltration of Chinese literati painting into Japan, the resulting character of Japanese literati painting was less stylistically defined than in China. Despite the inevitable changes as Chinese ideas disseminated throughout Japan, the newly seen Chinese models were valuable in supporting emerging ideals of self-expression in painting by offering a worthy alternative to the Kano School's standardized repertoire.

**YOSA BUSON** One of the outstanding early representatives of Japanese literati painting was YOSA BUSON (1716–1783). A master writer of *haiku* (the 17-syllable Japanese poetic form very popular from the 17th century on), Buson had a command of literati painting that extended beyond knowledge of Chinese models. His poetic abilities gave rise to a lyricism that pervaded both his haiku and his painting. *Cuckoo Flying over New Verdure* (FIG. **34-11**) exemplifies his fully mature style. He incorporated in this work basic elements of Chinese literati painting by rounding the landscape forms and rendering their soft texture in fine fibrous brushstrokes, and by including dense foliage patterns, but the cuckoo is a motif specific to Japanese poetry and literati painting. Moreover, although Buson imitated the vocabulary of brushstrokes associated with the

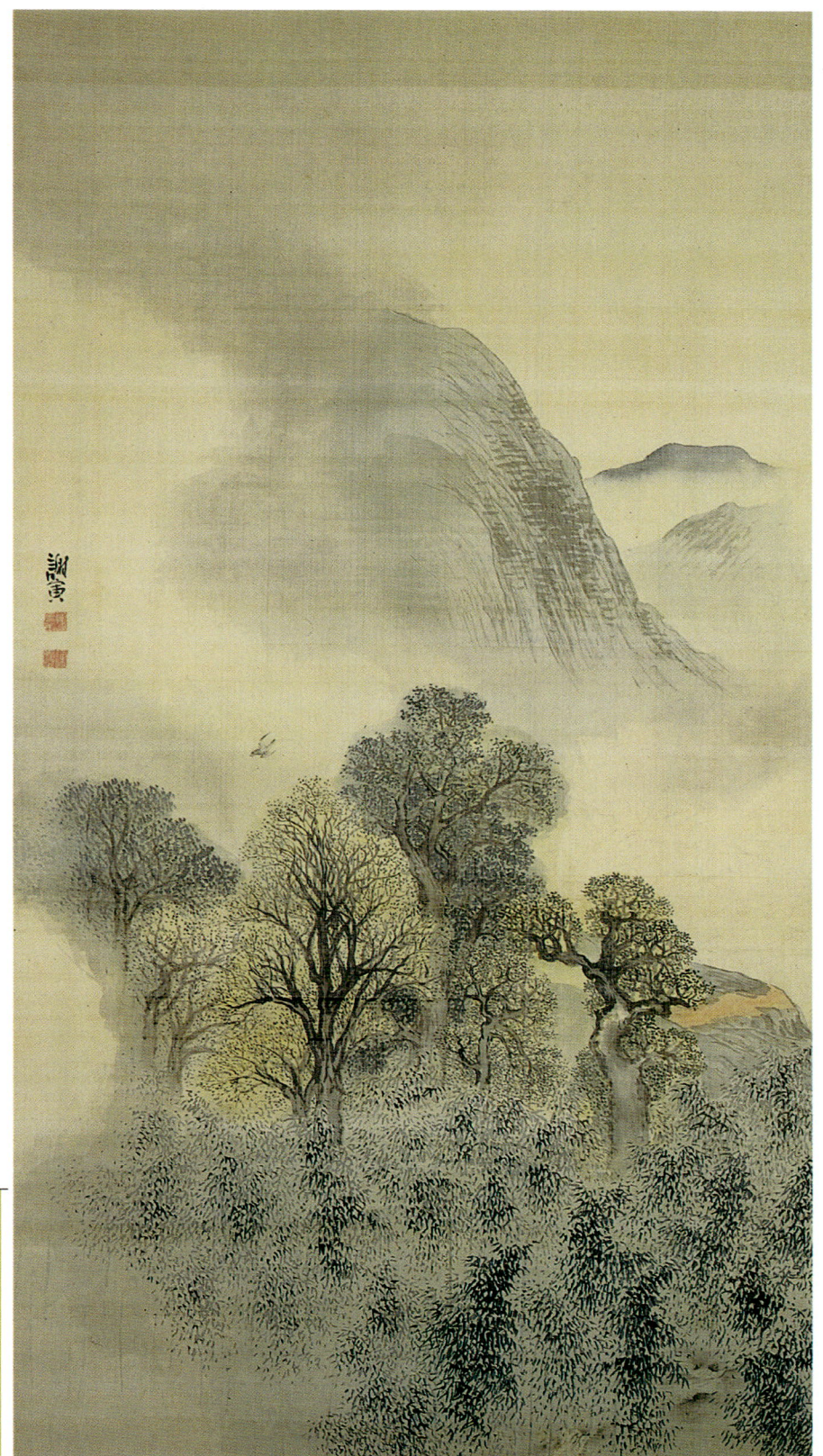

**34-11** Yosa Buson, *Cuckoo Flying over New Verdure*, Edo period, late 18th century. Hanging scroll, ink and color on silk, 5′ $\frac{1}{2}$″ × 2′ 7$\frac{1}{4}$″. Hiraki Ukiyo-e Museum, Yokohama.

A master of haiku poetry, Yosa Buson was a leading Japanese literati painter. Although inspired by Chinese works, he used a distinctive palette of pale colors and bolder, more abstract brushstrokes.

1 ft.

houses found in such locales as Edo's Yoshiwara brothel district. The Tokugawa tried to hold such activities in check, but their efforts were largely in vain, in part because of demographics. The population of Edo during this period included significant numbers of merchants and samurai (whose families remained in their home territories), and both groups were eager to enjoy secular city life. Those of lesser means could partake in these pleasures and amusements vicariously. Rapid developments in the printing industry led to the availability of numerous books and printed images (see "Japanese Woodblock Prints," page 1016), and these could convey the city's delights for a fraction of the cost of direct participation. Taking part in the emerging urban culture involved more than simple physical satisfactions and rowdy entertainments. Many who participated were also admirers of literature, music, and art. The best-known products of this sophisticated counterculture are known as *ukiyo-e*—"pictures of the floating world," a term suggesting the transience of human life and the ephemerality of the material world. The subjects of these paintings and especially prints come mainly from the realms of pleasure, such as the Yoshiwara brothels and the popular theater, but Edo printmakers also frequently depicted beautiful young women in both domestic and public settings (FIGS. 34-12 and 34-12A) and landscapes (FIGS. 34-1 and 34-13).

**SUZUKI HARUNOBU** The urban appetite for ukiyo pleasures and for their depiction in woodblock prints provided fertile ground for many graphic designers to flourish. Consequently, competition among publishing houses led to ever-greater refinement and experimentation in printmaking. One of the most admired and emulated 18th-century designers, SUZUKI HARUNOBU (ca. 1725–1770), played a key role in developing multi-

Chinese literati, his touch was bolder and more abstract, and the gentle palette of pale colors was very much his own.

*UKIYO-E* The growing urbanization in cities such as Osaka, Kyoto, and Edo led to an increase in the pursuit of sensual pleasure and entertainment in the brash popular theaters and the pleasure ticolored prints. Called *nishiki-e* (brocade pictures) because of their sumptuous and brilliant color, these prints, in contrast to most Edo prints, employed the highest-quality paper and costly pigments. Harunobu gained a tremendous advantage over his competitors when he received commissions from members of a poetry club to design limited-edition nishiki-e prints. He transferred much of the

# Japanese Woodblock Prints

During the Edo period, woodblock prints with ukiyo-e themes became enormously popular. Sold in small shops and on the street, an ordinary print went for the price of a bowl of noodles. People with very modest incomes could therefore collect prints in albums or paste them on their walls. A highly efficient production system made this wide distribution of Japanese graphic art possible.

Ukiyo-e artists were generally painters who did not themselves manufacture the prints that made them so famous both in their own time and today. As the designers, they sold drawings to publishers, who in turn oversaw their printing. The publishers also played a role in creating ukiyo-e prints by commissioning specific designs or adapting them before printing. Certainly, the names of both designer and publisher appeared on the final prints.

Unacknowledged in nearly all cases, however, were the individuals who made the prints, the block carvers and printers. Using skills honed since childhood, they worked with both speed and precision for relatively low wages and thus made ukiyo-e prints affordable. The master printmakers were primarily men. Women, especially wives and daughters, often assisted painters and other artists, but few gained separate recognition. Among the exceptions was the daughter of Katsushika Hokusai (FIG. 34-13), Katsushika Oi (1818–1854), who became well known as a painter and probably helped her father with his print designs.

Stylistically, Japanese prints during the Edo period tend to have black outlines separating distinct color areas (FIG. 34-12). This format is a result of the printing process. A master carver pasted painted designs face down on a wooden block. Wetting and gently scraping the thin paper revealed the reversed image to guide the cutting of the block. After the carving, only the outlines of the forms and other elements that would be black in the final print remained raised in relief. The master printer then coated the block with black ink and printed several initial outline prints. These master prints became the guides for carving the other blocks, one for each color used. On each color block, the carver left in relief only the areas to be printed in that color. Even ordinary prints sometimes required up to 20 colors and thus 20 blocks. To print a color, a printer applied the appropriate pigment to a block's raised surface, laid a sheet of paper on it, and rubbed the back of the paper with a smooth flat object. Then another printer would print a different color on the same sheet of paper. Perfect alignment of the paper in each step was critical to prevent overlapping of colors, so the carvers included printing guides in their blocks—an L-shaped ridge in one corner and a straight ridge on one side. The printers could cover small alignment errors with a final printing of the black outlines from the last block.

The materials used in printing varied over time but by the mid-18th century had reached a level of standardization. The blocks were planks of fine-grained hardwood, usually cherry. The best paper came from the white layer beneath the bark of mulberry trees, because its long fibers helped the paper stand up to repeated rubbing on the blocks. The printers used a few mineral pigments but

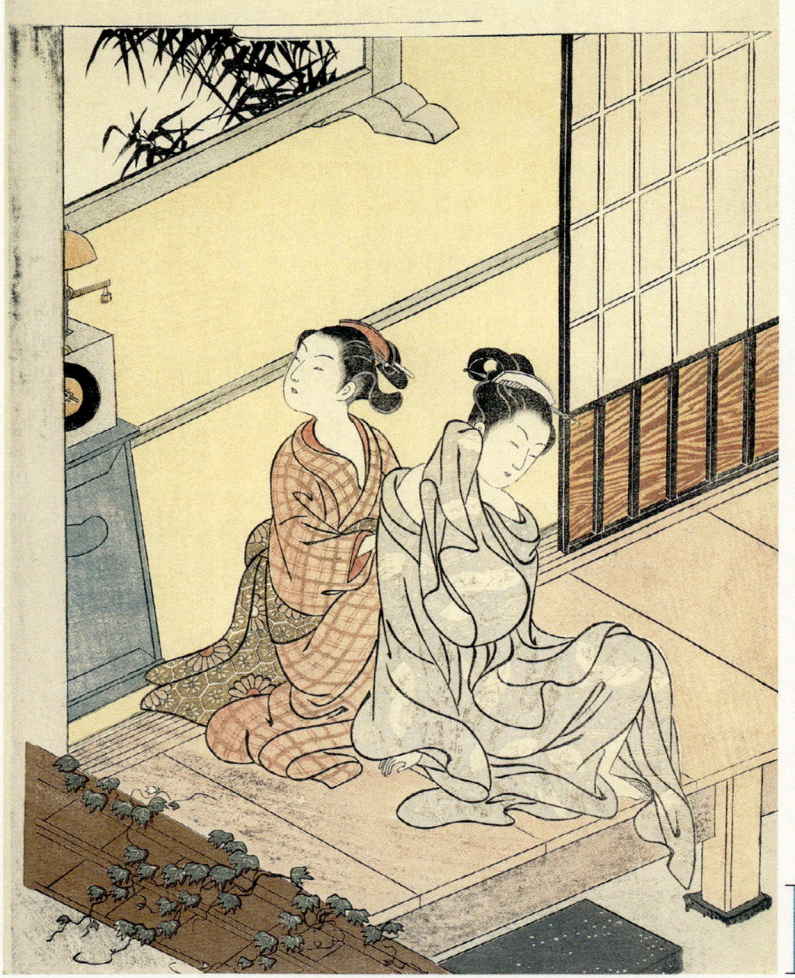

1 in.

**34-12** Suzuki Harunobu, *Evening Bell at the Clock,* from *Eight Views of the Parlor,* Edo period, ca. 1765. Woodblock print, $11\frac{1}{4}" \times 8\frac{1}{2}"$. Art Institute of Chicago, Chicago (Clarence Buckingham Collection). ▶

Harunobu's nishiki-e (brocade pictures) took their name from their costly pigments and paper. The rich color and flatness of the objects, women, and setting in this print exemplify the artist's style.

tended to favor inexpensive dyes made from plants for most colors. As a result, the colors of ukiyo-e prints were and are highly susceptible to fading, especially when exposed to strong light. In the early 19th century, more permanent European synthetic dyes began to enter Japan. The first such color, Prussian blue, appears in Hokusai's *The Great Wave off Kanagawa* (FIG. 34-13).

The popularity of ukiyo-e prints extended to the Western world as well. Their affordability and the ease with which they could be transported facilitated dissemination of the prints, especially throughout Europe. Ukiyo-e prints appear in the backgrounds of a number of Impressionist and Post-Impressionist paintings, attesting to the appeal these works held for Westerners. Some Japanese prints, for example, Ando Hiroshige's *Plum Estate, Kameido* (FIG. 34-1), inspired 19th-century European artists to produce near-copies (see "Japonisme," Chapter 28, page 808, and FIG. 28-16B).

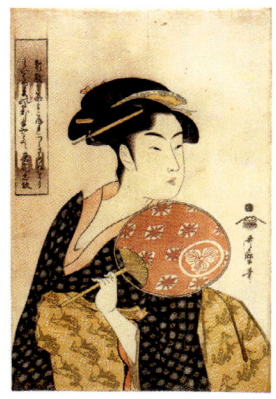

knowledge he derived from nishiki-e to his design of more commercial prints. Harunobu even issued some of the private designs later under his own name for popular consumption.

The sophistication of Harunobu's work is evident in *Evening Bell at the Clock* (FIG. **34-12**), from a series called *Eight Views of the Parlor.* This series draws upon a Chinese series usually titled *Eight Views of the Xiao and Xiang Rivers,* in which each image focuses on a particular time of day or year. In Harunobu's adaptation, beautiful young women—the favorite subject of ukiyo-e master KITAGAWA UTAMARO (1753–1806; FIG. **34-12A**)—and the activities occupying their daily lives became subjects. In *Evening Bell at the Clock,* two young women seen from the typically Japanese elevated viewpoint (compare FIG. 17-14) sit on a veranda. One is drying herself after a bath (compare FIG. 28-12). The viewer gets a privileged glimpse of a private moment. Erotic themes are quite common in ukiyo-e. The bather's companion—her maid—turns to face the chiming clock. Here, the artist has playfully transformed the great temple bell ringing over the waters in the Chinese series into a modern Japanese clock. This image incorporates the refined techniques characteristic of nishiki-e. Further, the flatness of the depicted objects and the rich color recall the traditions of court painting, a comparison many nishiki-e artists openly sought.

**KATSUSHIKA HOKUSAI** Woodblock prints afforded artists great opportunity for experimentation. For example, in producing landscapes, Japanese artists often incorporated Western perspective techniques, although others, Ando Hiroshige (FIG. 34-1) among them, did not. One of the most famous Japanese landscape artists was KATSUSHIKA HOKUSAI (1760–1849). In *The Great Wave off Kanagawa* (FIG. **34-13**), part of a woodblock series called *Thirty-six Views of Mount Fuji,* the huge foreground wave dwarfs the artist's representation of a distant Fuji. This contrast and the whitecaps' ominous fingers magnify the wave's threatening aspect. The men in the trading boats bend low to dig their oars against the rough sea and drive their long low vessels past the danger. Although Hokusai's print draws on Western techniques and incorporates the distinctive European color called Prussian blue, it also engages the Japanese pictorial tradition. Against a background with the low horizon typical of Western painting, Hokusai placed in the foreground the wave's more traditionally flat and powerfully graphic forms.

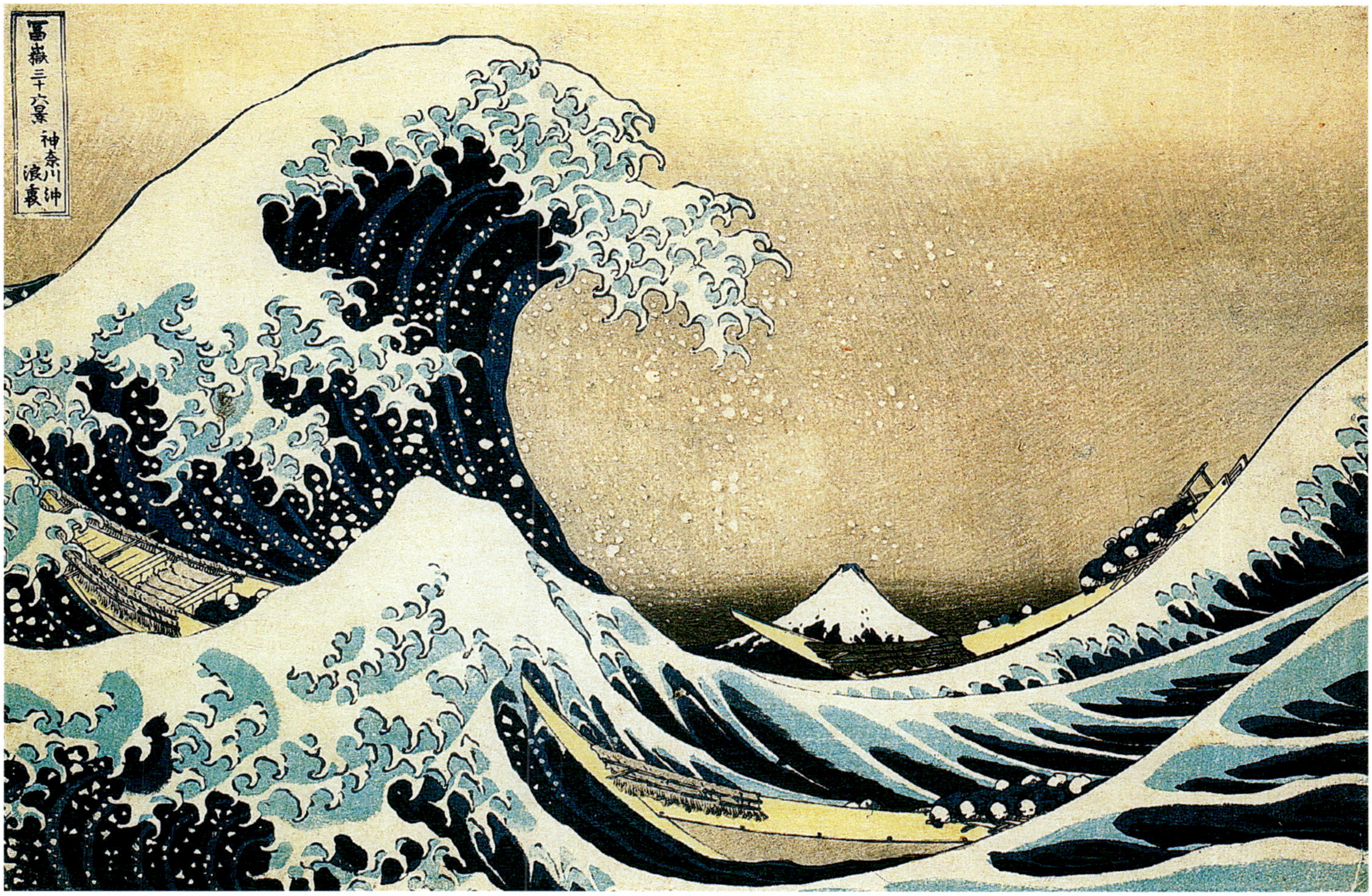

1 in.

**34-13** KATSUSHIKA HOKUSAI, *The Great Wave off Kanagawa,* from *Thirty-six Views of Mount Fuji,* Edo period, ca. 1826–1833. Woodblock print, ink and colors on paper, $9\frac{7}{8}''$ × 1′ $2\frac{3}{4}''$. Museum of Fine Arts, Boston (Bigelow Collection). ◼◀

Adopting the low horizon line typical of Western painting, Hokusai used the traditional flat and powerful graphic forms of Japanese art to depict the threatening wave in the foreground.

# MEIJI AND SHOWA

The Edo period and the rule of the shoguns ended in 1868, when rebellious samurai from provinces far removed from Edo toppled the Tokugawa. Facilitating this revolution was the shogunate's inability to handle the increasing pressure from Western nations for Japan to throw open its doors to the outside world. Although the rebellion restored direct sovereignty to the imperial throne, real power rested with the emperor's cabinet. As a symbol of imperial authority, however, the official name of this new period was Meiji ("Enlightened Rule"; 1868–1912), after the emperor's chosen regnal name.

**TAKAHASHI YUICHI** Oil painting became a major genre in Japan in the late 19th century. Ambitious students studied with Westerners at government schools and during trips abroad. One oil painting highlighting the cultural ferment of the early Meiji period is *Oiran* (*Grand Courtesan*; FIG. 34-14), painted by TAKAHASHI YUICHI (1828–1894). The artist created it for a client nostalgic for vanishing elements of Japanese culture. Ukiyo-e printmakers frequently represented similar grand courtesans of the pleasure quarters. In this painting, however, Takahashi did not portray the courtesan's features in the idealizing manner of ukiyo-e artists but in the more analytical manner of Western portraiture. Yet the painter's more abstract rendering of the garments reflects a very old practice in East Asian portraiture.

**KANO HOGAI** Unbridled enthusiasm for Westernization in some quarters led to resistance and concern over a loss of distinctive Japanese identity in other quarters. Ironically, one of those most eager to preserve "Japaneseness" in the arts was Ernest Fenollosa

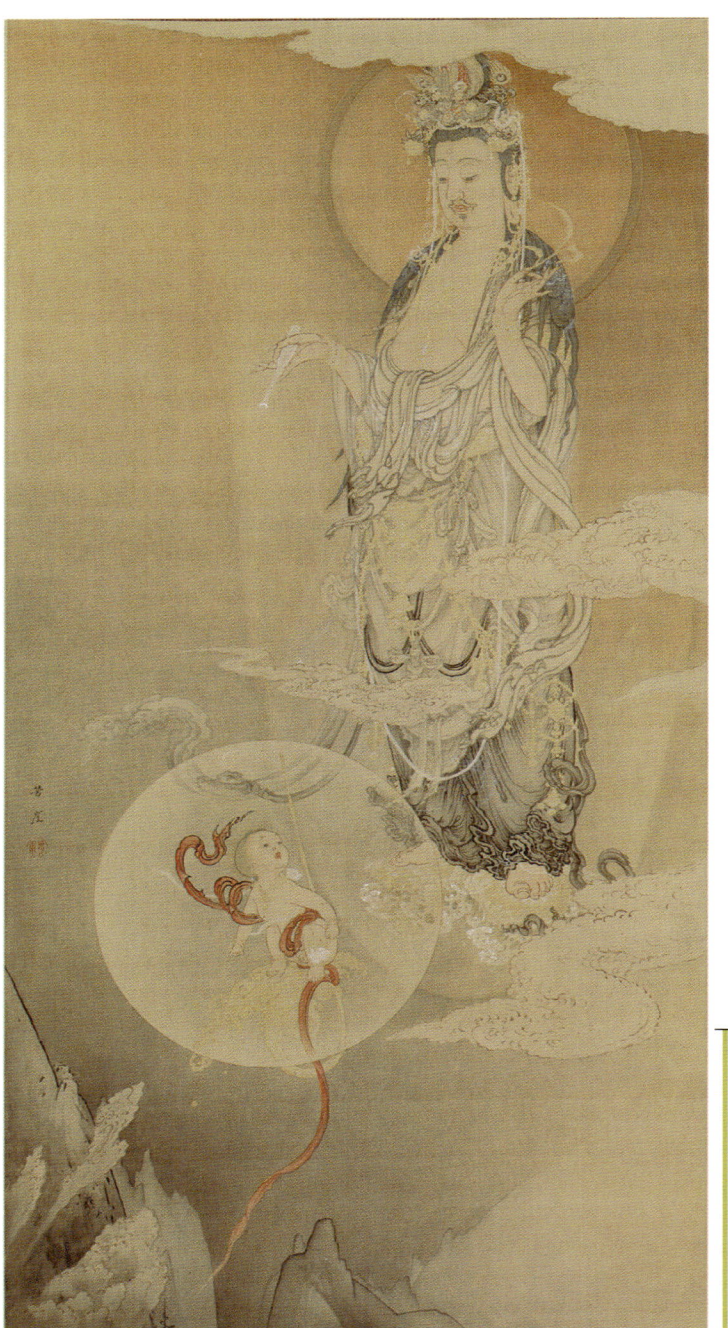

34-14 TAKAHASHI YUICHI, *Oiran* (*Grand Courtesan*), Meiji period, 1872. Oil on canvas, 2′ 6½″ × 1′ 9⅝″. Tokyo National University of Fine Arts and Music, Tokyo.

The subject of Takahashi's *Oiran* and the abstract rendering of the courtesan's garment derive from the ukiyo-e repertoire and traditional Japanese art, but the oil technique is a Western import.

34-15 KANO HOGAI, *Bodhisattva Kannon*, Hanging scroll, ink, color, and gold on silk, 5′ 4¾″ × 2′ 9⅜″. Freer Gallery of Art, Smithsonian Institution, Washington, D.C. (gift of Charles Lang Freer).

In composition, theme, medium, and format, this ink-and-color hanging silk scroll epitomizes the nihonga revival of Japanese subject matter and style, a sharp break from Westernized yoga.

(1853–1908), an American professor of philosophy and political economy at Tokyo Imperial University. He and a former student named Okakura Kakuzo (1862–1913) joined with others in a movement that eventually led to the founding under Okakura's direction of a new academy, the Tokyo School of Fine Arts, dedicated to Japanese arts. Their goal was to make Japanese painting viable in the modern age rather than preserve it as a relic. To this end, they encouraged students to incorporate some Western techniques such as chiaroscuro, perspective, and bright hues in Japanese-style paintings. The name given to the resulting style was *nihonga* (Japanese painting), as opposed to *yoga* (Western painting).

One of the first professors Okakura appointed (although he died before he could take up the position) was KANO HOGAI (1828–1888), who studied painting in Tokyo under the tutelage of a master of the venerable Kano School. Kano had met Fenellosa in 1883, and the American promoted his career and purchased several of his paintings, including *Bodhisattva Kannon* (FIG. **34-15**), later acquired by the American industrialist and art collector Charles Lang Freer (1854–1919). The painting depicts Kannon (Chinese Guanyin; compare FIGS. 16-14A and 16-21A), the mustached but effeminate bodhisattva of infinite compassion, standing on a cloud and pouring drops of the water of wisdom from a small flask upon a newborn suspended in a transparent globe. Fenellosa called the painting *The Creation of Man*. In composition, theme, medium, and format, Kano's ink-and-color silk hanging scroll epitomizes the nihonga style.

**SHOWA** During the Showa period (1926–1989), Japan became increasingly prominent on the world stage in economics, politics, and culture, and played a leading role in World War II. The most tragic consequences of that conflict for Japan were the widespread devastation and loss of life resulting from the atomic bombings of Hiroshima and Nagasaki in 1945. During the succeeding occupation period, the United States imposed new democratic institutions on Japan, with the emperor serving as a ceremonial head of state. Japan's economy rebounded with remarkable speed, and its gross national product became one of the largest in the world. During the past several decades, Japanese artists have also made a mark in the international art world. As they did in earlier times with the art and culture of China and Korea, many Japanese painters, sculptors, and architects internalized Western styles and techniques and incorporated them as a part of Japan's own vital culture. Others, however, shunned Western art forms and worked in more traditional modes.

**HAMADA SHOJI** One modern Japanese art form with ancient roots is ceramics. Many contemporary admirers of folk art are avid collectors of traditional Japanese pottery. A formative figure in Japan's folk art movement, the philosopher Yanagi Soetsu (1889–1961), promoted an ideal of beauty inspired by the Japanese tea ceremony. He argued that true beauty could only be achieved in functional objects made of natural materials by anonymous craftspeople, such as the Shino water jar (FIG. 34-8) discussed earlier. Among the ceramists who produced this type of folk pottery, known as *mingei*, was HAMADA SHOJI

(1894–1978). Although Hamada did espouse Yanagi's selfless ideals, he still gained international fame and in 1955 received official recognition in Japan as a Living National Treasure. Works such as his dish (FIG. **34-16**) with casual slip designs are unsigned, but connoisseurs easily recognize them as his. This kind of stoneware is coarser, darker, and heavier than porcelain and lacks the latter's fine decoration. To those who appreciate simpler, earthier beauty, however, this dish holds great attraction. Hamada's artistic influence extended beyond the production of pots. He traveled to England in 1920 and, along with English potter Bernard Leach (1887–1978), established a community of ceramists committed to the mingei aesthetic. Together, Hamada and Leach expanded international knowledge of Japanese ceramics, and even now, the "Hamada-Leach aesthetic" is part of potters' education worldwide.

**GUTAI** One of the most significant developments in 20th-century art was the emergence of *Performance Art* as a major genre (see Chapter 30), and Japanese artists played a seminal role. Gutai Bijutsu Kyokai (Concrete Art Association) was a group of 18 Japanese artists in Osaka who expanded the principles of *action painting* into the realm of performance—in a sense, taking Jackson Pollock's painting methods (see "Jackson Pollock on Easel and Mural Painting," Chapter 30, page 904, and FIG. 30-7) into a public arena. Led by Jiro Yoshihara (1905–1972), Gutai, founded in 1954, devoted itself to art that combined Japanese traditional practices such as Zen (see "Zen Buddhism," page 1007) with a renewed appreciation for

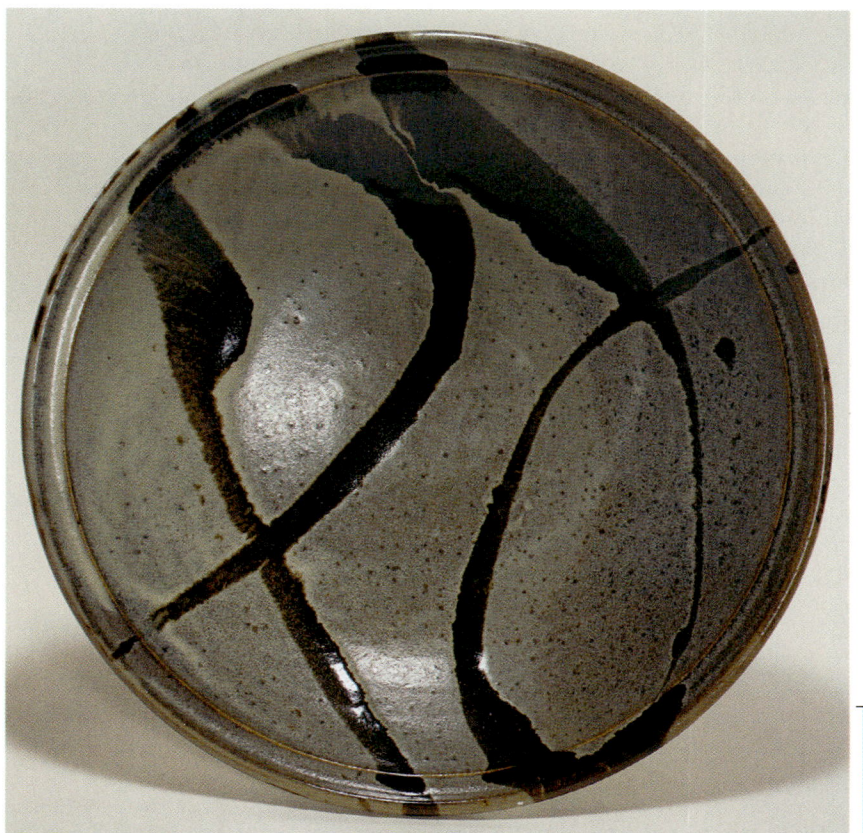

1 in.

**34-16** HAMADA SHOJI, large bowl, Showa period, 1962. Black trails on translucent glaze, $5\frac{7}{8}''$ × 1' $10\frac{1}{2}''$. National Museum of Modern Art, Kyoto.

A leading figure in the modern folk art movement in Japan, Hamada Shoji gained international fame. His unsigned stoneware features casual slip designs and a coarser, darker texture than porcelain.

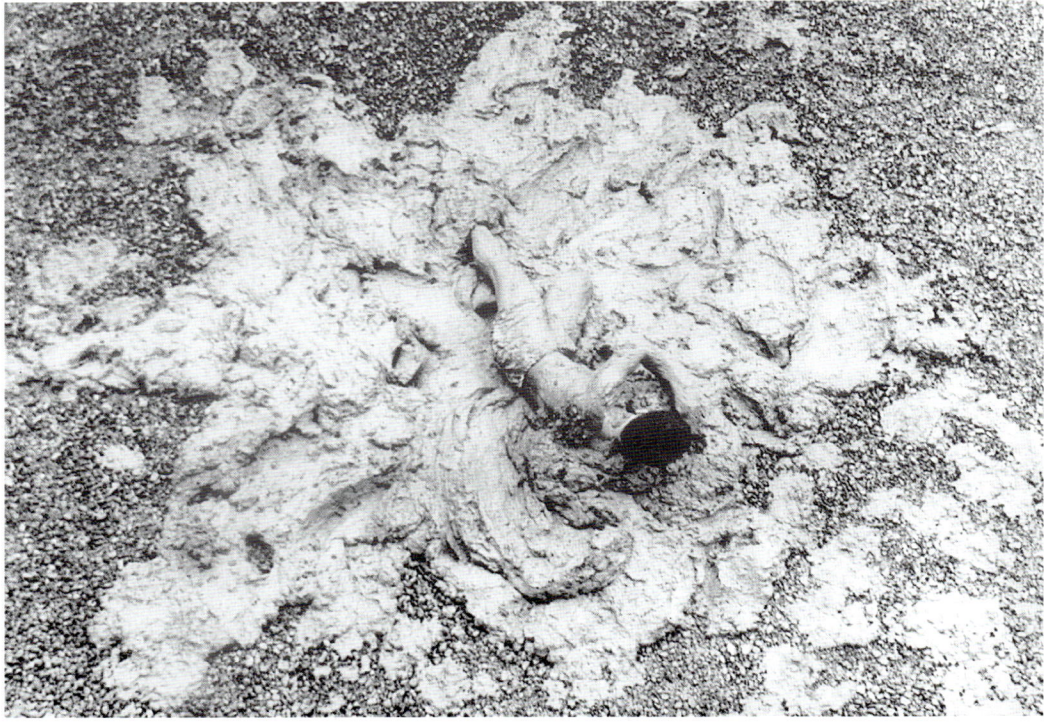

materials. In the *Gutai Art Manifesto,* Yoshihara explained: "Gutai does not alter the material. Gutai imparts life to the material. . . . [T]he human spirit and the material shake hands with each other, but keep their distance."[1] Accordingly, the Gutai group's performances, for example, *Making a Work with His Own Body* (FIG. **34-17**), by KAZUO SHIRAGA (1924–2008), involved actions such as throwing paint balls at blank canvases or wallowing in mud as a means of shaping it. In *Making a Work,* Shiraga used his body to "paint" with mud. The Gutai group disbanded upon Yoshihara's death in 1972, but their work was an important influence on Western performance artists such as Carolee Schneemann (FIG. 30-51).

**KENZO TANGE** In the 20th century, Japanese architecture, especially public and commercial building, underwent rapid transformation along Western lines. In fact, architecture may be the most influential Japanese art form on the world stage today. Japanese architects have made major contributions to both modern and postmodern developments (see Chapters 30 and 31). One of the most daringly experimental architects of the post–World War II period was KENZO TANGE (1913–2005). In his design of the stadiums (FIG. **34-18**) for the 1964 Olympics, he employed a cable suspension system that enabled him to shape steel and concrete into remarkably graceful structures. His attention to both the sculptural qualities of each building's raw concrete form and the fluidity of its spaces allied him with architects worldwide who carried on the legacy of the late style of Le Corbusier (FIG. 30-40) in France. His stadiums thus bear comparison with Joern Utzon's Sydney Opera House (FIG. 30-42).

**CONTEMPORARY ART** In the "global village" the world has become over the past few decades, some Japanese artists have also achieved international renown. The work of Tsuchiya Kimio (FIG. 31-23) and other contemporary Asian sculptors and painters is treated in its worldwide context in Chapter 31.

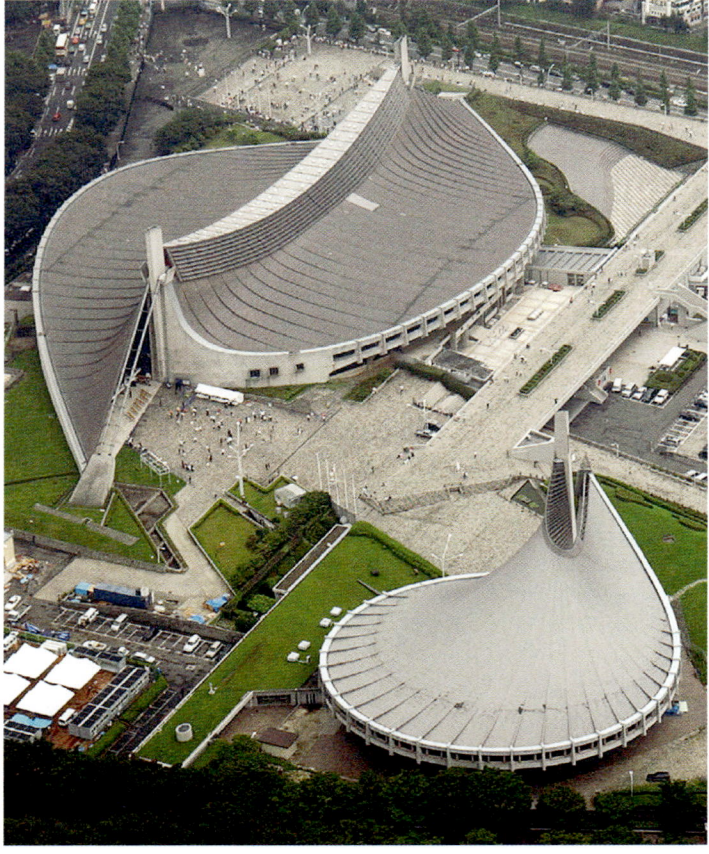

34-18 KENZO TANGE, national indoor Olympic stadiums (looking east), Tokyo, Japan, Showa period, 1961–1964.

Tange was one of the most daring architects of postwar Japan. His Olympic stadiums employ a cable suspension system that enabled him to shape steel and concrete into remarkably graceful structures.

# JAPAN, 1336 TO 1980

## MUROMACHI 1336–1573

▌ The Muromachi period takes its name from the Kyoto district in which the Ashikaga shoguns maintained their headquarters.

▌ At this time, Zen Buddhism rose to prominence in Japan. Zen temples often featured gardens of the karesansui (dry-landscape) type, which facilitated meditation.

▌ Muromachi painting displays great variety in both subject and style. One characteristic technique is the haboku (splashed-ink) style, which has Chinese roots. An early haboku master was Sesshu Toyo.

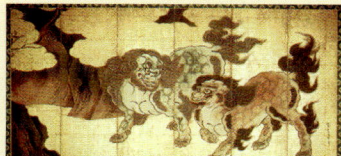

Sesshu Toyo, splashed-ink landscape, 1495

## MOMOYAMA 1573–1615

▌ Three successive warlords dominated this brief but artistically rich interlude between two long-lasting shogunates. The period takes its name from one of the warlord's castles (Momoyama, Peach Blossom Hill) outside Kyoto.

▌ Many of the finest works of this period were commissions from those warlords, including *Chinese Lions* by Kano Eitoku, a six-part folding screen featuring animals considered to be symbols of power and bravery.

▌ During the Momoyama period, the Japanese tea ceremony became an important social ritual. The tea master Sen no Rikyu designed the first teahouse built as an independent structure. The favored tea utensils were rustic Shino wares.

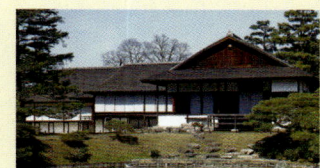

Kano Eitoku, *Chinese Lions,* late 16th century

## EDO 1615–1868

▌ The Edo period began when the shogun Tokugawa Ieyasu (1542–1616) moved his headquarters from Kyoto to Edo (modern Tokyo).

▌ The Katsura Imperial Villa, which relies for its aesthetic appeal on subtleties of proportion, color, and texture instead of ornamentation, set the standard for later Japanese domestic architecture.

▌ The Rinpa School, named for Ogata Korin, emerged as a major alternative school of painting to the Kano School, which had become a virtual national art academy. Rinpa paintings and crafts feature vivid colors and extensive use of gold, as in the *Boat Bridge* writing box by Honami Koetsu.

▌ Growing urbanization in major Japanese cities fostered a lively popular culture focused on sensual pleasure and theatrical entertainment. The best-known products of this sophisticated counterculture are the ukiyo-e woodblock prints of Edo's "floating world" by Suzuki Harunobu and others. The prints feature scenes from brothels and the theater as well as beautiful women in domestic settings.

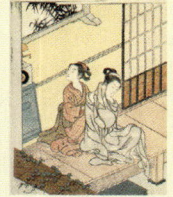

Katsura Imperial Villa, Kyoto, 1620–1663

Suzuki Harunobu, *Evening Bell at the Clock,* ca. 1765

## MEIJI AND SHOWA 1868–1989

▌ The Tokugawa shogunate toppled in 1868, opening the modern era of Japanese history. In art, Western styles and techniques had a great influence, and many Japanese artists incorporated shading and perspective in their works and even produced oil paintings.

▌ In the post–World War II period, many Japanese artists and architects achieved worldwide reputations. Kazuo Shiraga played a seminal role in the development of Performance Art as a major modern genre. Kenzo Tange was a master of creating dramatic shapes using a cable suspension system for his concrete-and-steel buildings.

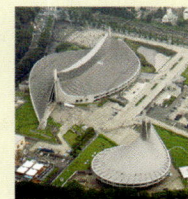

Kenzo Tange, Olympic stadiums, Tokyo, 1961–1964

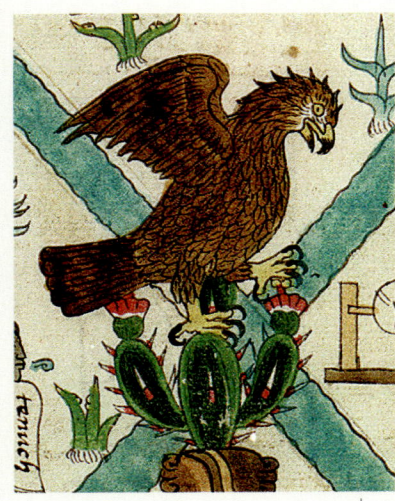

Produced for Charles V, the *Codex Mendoza* recounts the history of the Aztec Empire. The frontispiece represents the legendary landing of the eagle on a cactus and the founding of Tenochtitlán in 1325.

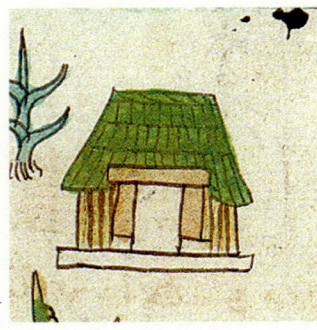

At the heart of Tenochtitlán was the Templo Mayor, a gigantic pyramid surmounted by temples to Huitzilopochtli and Tlaloc, represented in the *Codex Mendoza* in abbreviated form as a single shrine.

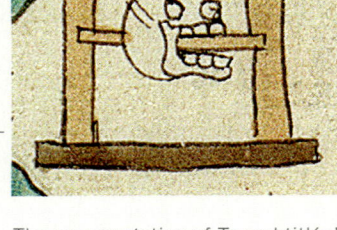

The representation of Tenochtitlán's sacred precinct also includes a rack of skulls of the sacrificial victims the Aztecs threw down the steps of the lofty pyramid after cutting out their hearts.

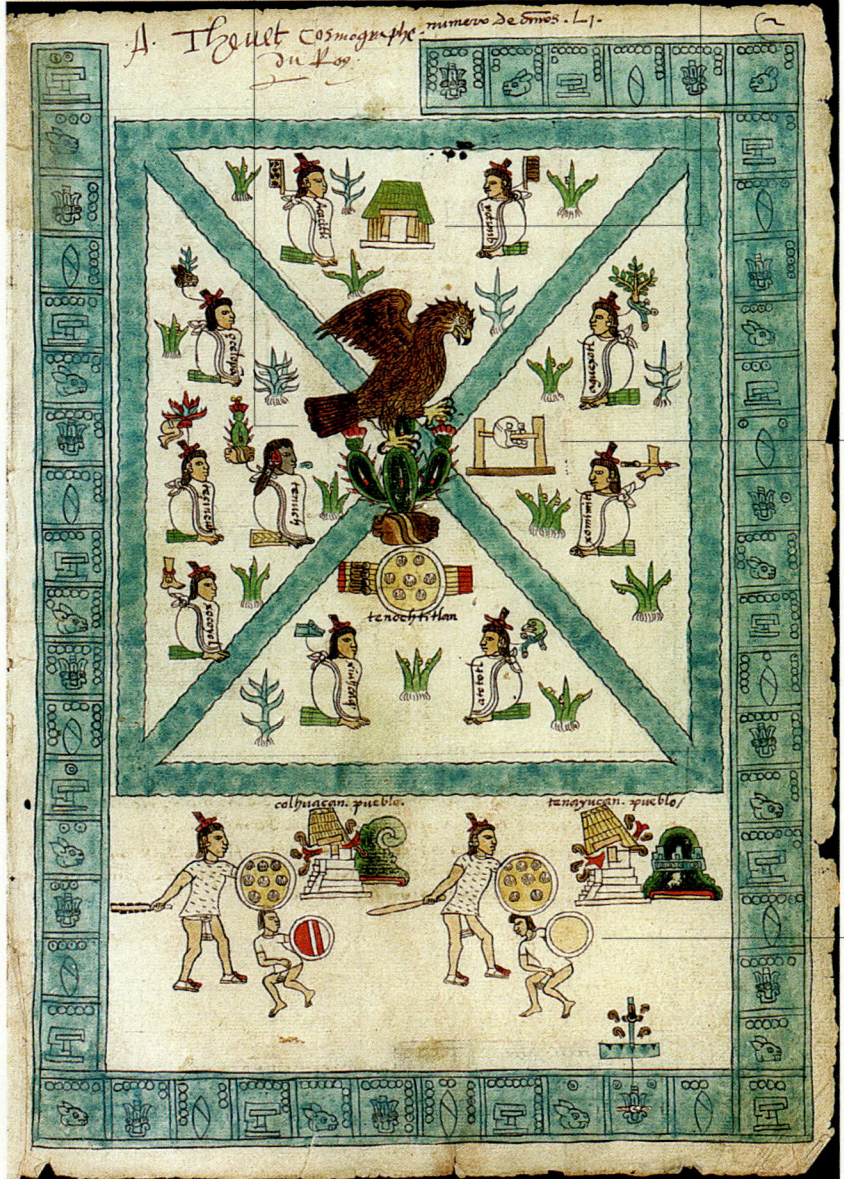

1 in.

**35-1** The founding of Tenochtitlán, folio 2 recto of the *Codex Mendoza,* from Mexico City, Mexico, Aztec, ca. 1540–1542. Ink and color on paper, 1′ $\frac{7}{8}$″ × 8 $\frac{5}{8}$″. Bodleian Library, Oxford University, Oxford.

# NATIVE ARTS OF THE AMERICAS, 1300 TO 1980

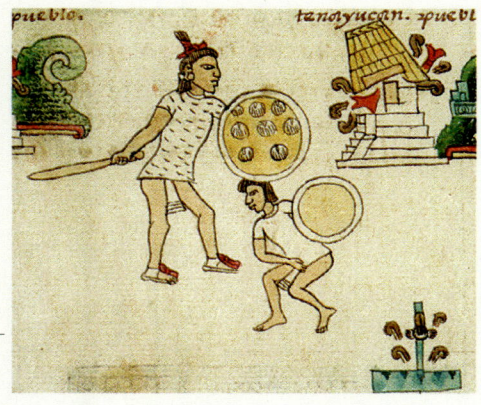

At the bottom of the page, the painter depicted two historical events. Aztec warriors with clubs and shields conquer the cities of Colhuacán and Tenayuca, shown as temple-pyramids set ablaze.

## THE FOUNDING OF TENOCHTITLÁN

When their insatiable quest for gold brought the Spaniards, led by Hernán Cortés, into contact in 1519 with the Aztec Empire in what is today Mexico, they encountered the latest of a series of highly sophisticated indigenous *Mesoamerican* art-producing cultures. Two decades later, the first Spanish viceroy of New Spain, Antonio de Mendoza, commissioned native scribes and painters to produce a remarkable illustrated manuscript (on European paper). The *Codex Mendoza* recounted the history of the empire Cortés had vanquished and included a description of the customs of the people who called themselves Mexica. The book took the form of a *codex* (pl. *codices*)—a bound volume resembling a modern book, in contrast to earlier books in the form of scrolls (*rotulus,* pl. *rotuli*). The intended audience for the *Codex Mendoza* was Charles V of Spain, but the king never saw the manuscript because French pirates intercepted the Spanish ship at sea. Although produced for a Spanish patron, the *Codex Mendoza* closely reflects the format and style of contemporaneous Aztec illustrated manuscripts.

The opening 16 pages of the 71-page codex summarize the 196-year history of the Mexica through the Spanish conquest of 1521. The frontispiece (FIG. **35-1**), with explanatory labels in Aztec *hieroglyphs* and Spanish, represents the founding of the capital city of Tenochtitlán in 1325 on an island in Lake Texcoco (Lake of the Moon). There, according to legend, an eagle landed on a prickly pear cactus, marking the spot where the chief Aztec deity, Huitzilopochtli, instructed the nomadic warriors to settle. The artist depicted the eagle on the cactus (now the central motif on the Mexican flag) at the intersection of two canals, referring to the division of Tenochtitlán into four quarters. At the center of the city—considered the center of the universe—was the sacred precinct archaeologists call the Templo Mayor ("Great Temple," FIG. 35-3), represented in abbreviated form above the eagle as a single temple—one of two surmounting a great pyramid. To the right of the cactus is the rack of skulls of the sacrificial victims whose bodies the Aztec priests threw down the pyramid's steps after cutting out their hearts. The labeled figures seated on reed mats in Tenochtitlán's four quarters are the legendary founders of the city. Below, the painter represented two historical events in stereotypical form. Aztec warriors with clubs and shields conquer two cities, Colhuacán and Tenayuca, shown as temple-pyramids set ablaze. The border contains the hieroglyphs for 51 of the 52 years of one of the recurring cycles of the Aztec calendar system.

Today, Tenochtitlán lies at the heart of densely populated Mexico City. In the early 16th century, the Aztec capital was home to more than 100,000 people. The total population of the area of Mexico the Aztecs dominated was approximately 11 million.

# MESOAMERICA

In the years following the arrival of Christopher Columbus (1451–1506) in the New World in 1492, Spain poured money into expeditions probing the coasts of North and South America, but the Spaniards had little luck finding the wealth they sought. When brief stops on the coast of Yucatán, Mexico, yielded a small but still impressive amount of gold and other precious artifacts, the Spanish governor of Cuba outfitted yet another expedition. Headed by Hernán Cortés (1485–1547), this contingent of explorers was the first to make contact with the great Aztec emperor Moctezuma II (r. 1502–1521) at Tenochtitlán (MAP 35-1). In only two years, with the help of guns, horses, native allies revolting against their Aztec overlords, and perhaps also a smallpox epidemic that had swept across the Caribbean and already thinned the Aztec ranks, Cortés managed to overthrow the vast and rich Aztec Empire. His victory in 1521 opened the door to hordes of Spanish conquistadors seeking their fortunes and to missionaries eager for new converts to Christianity. The ensuing clash of cultures led to a century of turmoil throughout New Spain.

The Aztec Empire of the early 16th century succeeded several other great Mesoamerican civilizations (see Chapter 18). After the fall and destruction of the important central Mexican city of Teotihuacán in the eighth century and the abandonment of the southern Maya sites around 900, new cities arose to take their places. Notable were the Maya city of Chichén Itzá (FIGS. 18-1 and 18-16 to 18-18) in Yucatán and the Toltec capital of Tula (FIG. 18-19), not far from the later seat of Aztec power in Tenochtitlán. Their dominance was relatively short-lived, however. For the early Postclassic period (ca. 900–1200) in Mesoamerica, scholars have less information than for Classic Mesoamerica, but much more evidence exists for the cultures of the late Postclassic period (ca. 1200–1521).

## Mixteca-Puebla

One of the most impressive art-producing peoples of the Postclassic period in Mesoamerica was the Mixtecs, who succeeded the Zapotecs at Monte Albán in southern Mexico after 700. They extended their political sway in Oaxaca by dynastic intermarriage as well as by warfare. The treasures found in the tombs at Monte Albán bear witness to Mixtec wealth, and the quality of these works demonstrates the culture's high level of artistic achievement. The Mixtec were highly skilled goldsmiths and won renown for their work in *mosaic* using turquoise obtained from far-off regions such as present-day New Mexico.

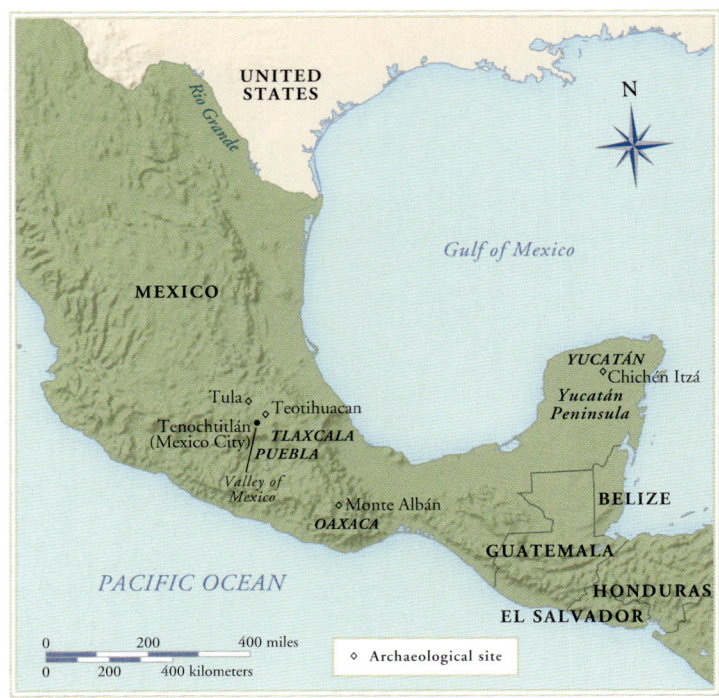

MAP 35-1 Mixteca-Puebla and Aztec sites in Mesoamerica.

*BORGIA CODEX* The peoples of Mesoamerica prized illustrated books, such as the *Codex Mendoza* (FIG. 35-1). The Postclassic Maya were preeminent in the art of writing. Their books—almost all destroyed by the Spanish conquistadors—were precious vehicles for recording history, rituals, astronomical tables, calendar calculations, maps, and trade and tribute accounts. The texts consisted of hieroglyphic columns read from left to right and top to bottom. Miraculously, three pre-conquest Maya books survived the depredations of the Europeans. Bishop Diego de Landa (1524–1579), the author of an invaluable treatise on the Maya of Yucatán, described how the Maya made their books and why so few remain:

> They wrote their books on a long sheet doubled in folds, which was then enclosed between two boards finely ornamented; the writing was on one side and the other, according to the folds. . . . We found a great number of books in these [Mayan] letters and, since they contained nothing but superstitions and falsehoods of the devil, we burned them all, which they took most grievously, and which gave them great pain.[1]

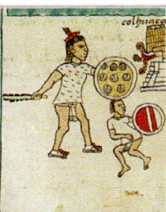

# NATIVE ARTS OF THE AMERICAS, 1300 TO 1980

| 1300 | 1532 | 1800 | 1900 | 1980 |
|---|---|---|---|---|

- Mixteca-Puebla artists produce illustrated codices
- Aztecs build the Templo Mayor at Tenochtitlán and place monumental statues and reliefs in the sacred precinct
- Inka construct 14,000 miles of roads in the Andes and build the city of Machu Picchu and the Temple of the Sun in Cuzco

- Kwakiutl and Tlingit artists carve transformation and war masks
- Great Plains artists fashion elaborate robes and regalia for the elite
- During the reservation period, Native American artists record traditional lifestyles in ledger books

- Many Native American artists continue to practice traditional crafts
- Southwest ceramists develop black-on-black glazed pottery
- Bill Reid carves monumental wood sculptures illustrating traditional Haida themes

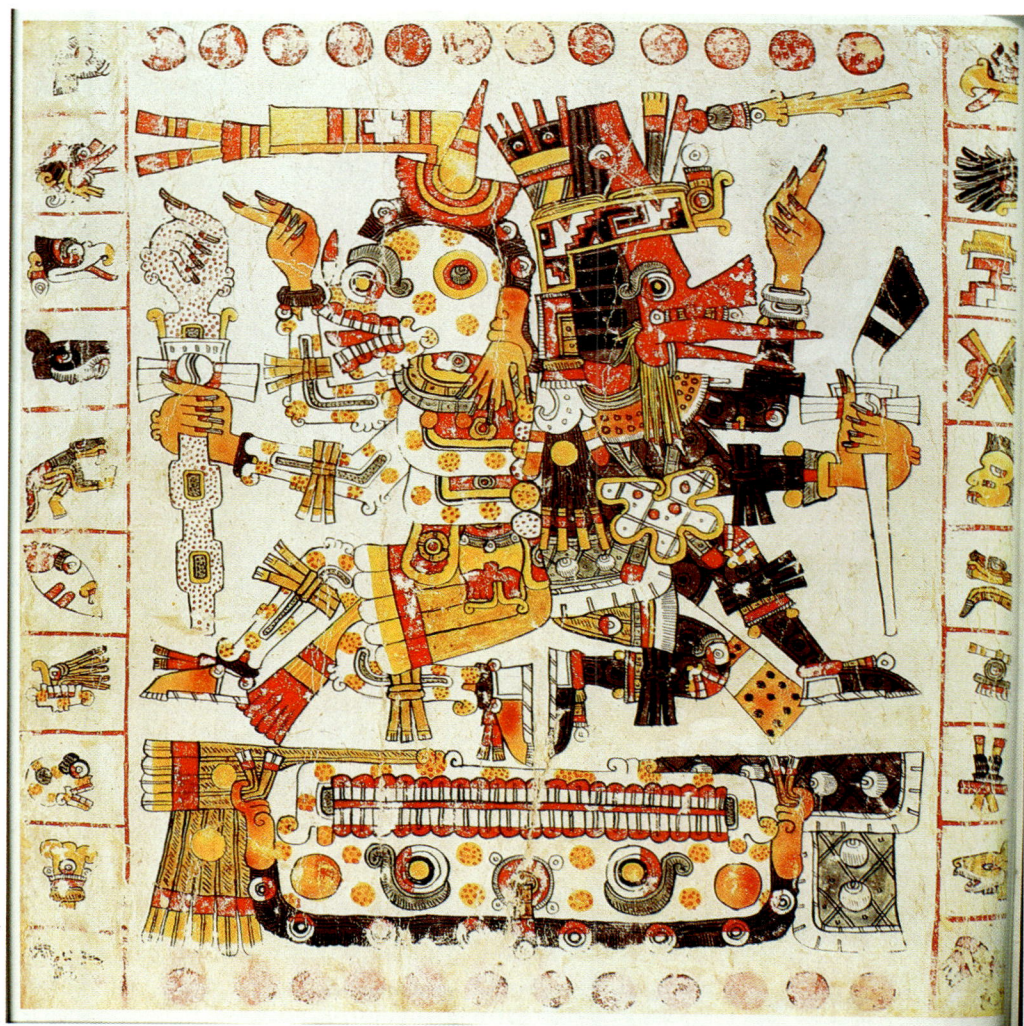

**35-2** Mictlantecuhtli and Quetzalcoatl, folio 56 of the *Borgia Codex,* possibly from Puebla or Tlaxcala, Mexico, Mixteca-Puebla, ca. 1400–1500. Mineral and vegetable pigments on deerskin, $10\frac{5}{8}'' \times 10\frac{3}{8}''$. Facsimile, Biblioteca Apostolica Vaticana, Rome.

One of the rare surviving Mesoamerican books, the Mixteca-Puebla *Borgia Codex* includes this painting depicting the gods of life and death above an inverted skull symbolizing the Underworld.

1 in.

The origins of this calendar, used even today in remote parts of Mexico and Central America, are unknown. Save for the Mixtec genealogical codices, most books painted before and immediately after the Spanish conquest deal with astronomy, calendars, divination, and ritual—with the notable exception of the *Codex Mendoza* (FIG. 35-1), which, as already discussed, records the history of the Aztecs, the greatest Mesoamerican culture at the time Cortés and his compatriots arrived in Mexico.

## Aztec

The Aztecs were a Nahuatl-speaking people who left behind, in the *Codex Mendoza* and elsewhere, a history of their rise to power. Scholars have begun to question the accuracy of that Aztec account, however, and some think it is a mythic construct. According to the traditional history, the destruction of Toltec Tula about 1200 (see Chapter 18) brought a century of anarchy to the Valley of Mexico, the vast highland valley 7,000 feet above sea level now home to sprawling Mexico City. Waves of northern invaders established warring city-states and wrought destruction in the valley. The Aztecs were the last of these conquerors. With astonishing rapidity, they transformed themselves within a few generations from migratory outcasts and serfs to mercenaries for local rulers and then to masters in their own right of the Valley of Mexico's small kingdoms. They began to call themselves Mexica, and, fulfilling a legendary prophecy that they would build a city where they saw an eagle perched on a cactus with a serpent in its mouth, they settled on an island in Lake Texcoco. Their settlement grew into the magnificent city of Tenochtitlán (see "The Founding of Tenochtitlán," page 1023), which in 1519 so amazed the Spaniards.

Recognized by those they subdued as fierce in war and cruel in peace, the Aztecs indeed seemed to glory in battle and in military prowess. They radically changed the social and political situation in Mexico. Subservient groups not only had to submit to Aztec military power but also had to provide victims to be sacrificed to Huitzilopochtli, the hummingbird god of war, and to other Aztec deities (see "Aztec Religion," page 1027). The Mexica practiced bloodletting and human sacrifice to please the gods and sustain the great cycles of the universe. These rites had a long history in Mesoamerica (see Chapter 18). The Aztecs, however, engaged in

In contrast, 10 non-Maya Postclassic books survive, five from Mixtec Oaxaca and five from the Puebla region. Art historians have named the style they represent Mixteca-Puebla, an interesting example of a Mesoamerican style crossing both ethnic and regional boundaries. The Mixteca-Puebla artists painted on long sheets of deerskin, which they first coated with fine white lime plaster and folded into accordion-like pleats to form codices with covers of wood, mosaic, or feathers.

One extensively illustrated book that escaped the Spanish destruction is the *Borgia Codex,* from somewhere in central highland Mexico (possibly the states of Puebla or Tlaxcala). It is the largest and most elaborate of several manuscripts known as the Borgia Group. The page reproduced here (FIG. **35-2**) shows two richly attired and vividly gesticulating gods rendered predominantly in reds and yellows with black outlines. The god of life, the black Quetzalcoatl (depicted here as a masked human rather than in the usual form of a feathered serpent), sits back-to-back with the god of death, the white Mictlantecuhtli. Below them is an inverted skull with a double keyboard of teeth, a symbol of the Underworld (Mictlan), which could be entered through the mouth of a great earth monster. Both figures hold scepters in one hand and gesticulate with the other. The image conveys the inevitable relationship of life and death, an important theme in Mesoamerican art. Some scholars believe the image may also be a kind of writing conveying a specific divinatory meaning. Symbols of the 13 divisions of 20 days in the 260-day Mesoamerican ritual calendar appear in panels in the margins (compare FIG. 35-1).

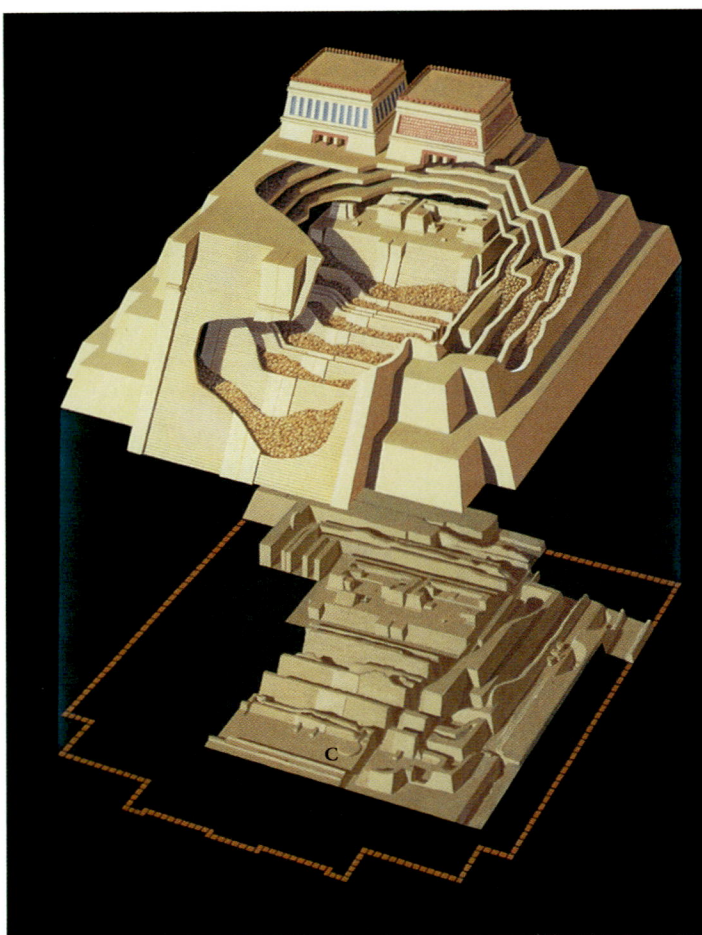

**35-3** Reconstruction drawing with cutaway view of various rebuildings of the Great Temple, Tenochtitlán, Mexico City, Mexico, Aztec, ca. 1400–1500. C = Coyolxauhqui disk (FIG. 35-4).

The Great Temple in the Aztec capital encases successive earlier structures. The latest temple honored the gods Huitzilopochtli and Tlaloc, whose sanctuaries were at the top of a stepped pyramid.

**HUETEOCALLI** In the 1970s, Mexican archaeologists identified the exact location of many of the most important structures within Tenochtitlán's sacred precinct. The excavations in the Zócalo near the city's cathedral have already uncovered impressive remains of architecture and sculpture, most recently a 12-ton *monolithic* (one-piece) relief (FIG. 35-5) discovered in 2006. Additional extraordinary artworks are likely to come to light in the years ahead as excavations continue. The principal building of Tenochtitlán's religious center was the Hueteocalli—the Templo Mayor, or Great Temple (FIG. **35-3**)—a temple-pyramid honoring the Aztec god Huitzilopochtli and the local rain god Tlaloc (see "Aztec Religion," page 1027). Two great staircases originally swept upward from the plaza level to the two sanctuaries at the summit. The Hueteocalli is a remarkable example of *superimposition,* a common trait in Mesoamerican architecture. The excavated structure, composed of seven shells, indicates how earlier walls nested within later ones. (Today, only two of the inner structures remain. The Spaniards destroyed the later ones in the 16th century.) The sacred precinct also contained the temples of other deities, a ball court (see "The Mesoamerican Ball Game," Chapter 18, page 501), a skull rack for the exhibition of the heads of victims killed in sacrificial rites (compare FIG. 35-1, *top right*), and a school for children of the nobility.

Thousands of priests served in Aztec temples. Distinctive hairstyles, clothing, and black body paint identified the priests. Women served as priestesses, particularly in temples dedicated to various earth-mother cults. Bernal Díaz del Castillo recorded his shock upon seeing a group of foul-smelling priests with uncut fingernails, long hair matted with blood, and ears covered in cuts, not realizing they were performing rites in honor of the deities they served, including piercing their skin with cactus spines to draw blood. These priests were the opposite of the "barbarians" the European conquistadors considered them to be. They were, in fact, the most highly educated Aztecs. The European reaction to the customs the conquistadors encountered in the New World has colored popular opinion about Aztec culture ever since. The religious practices that horrified the Spanish conquerors, however, were not unique to the Aztecs but were deeply rooted in earlier Mesoamerican society (see Chapter 18).

**AZTEC SCULPTURE** Given the Aztecs' almost meteoric rise from obscurity to their role as the dominant culture of Mesoamerica, the quality of the art they sponsored is astonishing. Granted, they swiftly appropriated the best artworks and most talented artists of conquered territories, bringing both back to Tenochtitlán. Thus, craftspeople from other areas, such as the Mixtecs of Oaxaca, may have created much of the exquisite pottery, goldwork, and turquoise mosaics the Aztec elite used. Gulf Coast artists probably made the life-size terracotta sculptures of eagle warriors found at the Great Temple. Nonetheless, the Aztecs' sculptural style, developed at the height of their power in the later 15th and early 16th centuries, is unique.

**COYOLXAUHQUI** The Temple of Huitzilopochtli at Tenochtitlán commemorated the god's victory over his sister and 400 brothers, who had plotted to kill their mother, Coatlicue (see "Aztec Religion," page 1027, and FIG. 35-6). The myth signifies the birth of the sun at dawn, a role Huitzilopochtli sometimes assumed, and the sun's battle with the forces of darkness, the stars and moon. Huitzilopochtli killed or chased away his brothers and dismembered the body of his sister, the moon goddess Coyolxauhqui, at Coatepec Mountain near Tula (represented by the pyramid itself). The mythical event is the subject of a huge stone disk (FIG. **35-4**),

human sacrifice on a greater scale than any of their predecessors, even waging special battles, called the "flowery wars," expressly to obtain captives for future sacrifice. It is one of the reasons Cortés found ready allies among the peoples the Aztecs had subjugated.

**TENOCHTITLÁN** The ruins of the Aztec capital, Tenochtitlán, lie directly beneath the center of Mexico City in the Zócalo, the modern city's main square. The Aztecs laid out Tenochtitlán on a grid plan dividing the city into quarters (FIG. 35-1) and wards, reminiscent of Teotihuacán (FIG. 18-5), which, long abandoned, had become a pilgrimage site for the Aztecs. Tenochtitlán's island location required conducting communication and transport via canals and other waterways. Many of the Spaniards thought of Venice in Italy when they saw the city rising from the waters like a radiant vision. Crowded with buildings, plazas, and courtyards, the city also boasted a vast and bustling marketplace. In the words of Bernal Díaz del Castillo (ca. 1495–1585), a soldier who accompanied Cortés when the Spaniards first entered Tenochtitlán, "Some of the soldiers among us who had been in many parts of the world, in Constantinople, and all over Italy, and in Rome, said that so large a marketplace and so full of people, and so well regulated and arranged, they had never beheld before."[2]

## Aztec Religion

The Aztecs saw their world as a flat disk resting on the back of a monstrous earth deity. Tenochtitlán, their capital, was at its center. Hueteocalli, the Great Temple (FIG. 35-3) at the heart of the city, represented the Hill of Coatepec, the sacred Serpent Mountain and reputed birthplace of Huitzilopochtli, and formed the axis passing up to the heavens and down through the Underworld—a concept with parallels in other cultures (see, for example, "The Stupa," Chapter 15, page 430). Each of the four cardinal points had its own god, color, tree, and calendar symbol. The sky consisted of 13 layers, whereas the Underworld had nine. The Aztec Underworld was an unpleasant place where the dead gradually ceased to exist.

Because the Aztecs often adopted the gods of conquered peoples, their pantheon was complex and varied. When the Aztecs arrived in the Valley of Mexico, their own chief god, **Huitzilopochtli** (Hummingbird of the South), a war and sun/fire deity, joined such well-established Mesoamerican gods as the rain and fertility god **Tlaloc** and the feathered serpent **Quetzalcoatl,** who was a benevolent god of life, wind, and learning and culture, as well as the patron of priests. Huitzilopochtli was the son of **Coatlicue** (She of the Serpent Skirt). Coatlicue was also the mother of **Coyolxauhqui** (She of the Golden Bells) and 400 sons, the **Centzon Huitznahua** (Four Hundred Southerners), who, jealous their mother was pregnant with Huitzilopochtli, banded together to murder her. At the moment of her death, she gave birth to Huitzilopochtli, who slaughtered Coyolxauhqui and most of her brothers, then cut his sister's body into pieces and threw it down Coatepec Mountain. Other important Aztec deities were **Mictlantecuhtli** (Lord of the Underworld) and **Tlaltecuhtli** (Lord of the Earth), the earth goddess with a masculine name. As the Aztecs went on to conquer much of Mesoamerica, they appropriated the gods of their subjects, such as **Xipe Totec,** a god of spring fertility and patron of gold workers imported from the Gulf Coast and Oaxaca. Freestanding images of the various gods made of stone (FIG. 35-6), terracotta, wood, and even dough (eaten at the end of rituals) stood in and around their temples. Reliefs (FIGS. 35-4 and 35-5) depicting Aztec deities also adorned the temple complexes.

The Aztecs' ritual cycle was very full, because they celebrated events in two calendars—a sacred calendar of 260 days and a solar calendar of 360 days plus five unlucky and nameless days. The Spanish friars of the 16th century noted the solar calendar dealt largely with agricultural matters. The two Mesoamerican calendars functioned simultaneously, requiring 52 years for the same date to recur in both. A ritual called the New Fire Ceremony commemorated this rare event. The Aztecs broke pots and made new ones for the next period, hid their pregnant women, and extinguished all fires. At midnight on a mountaintop, fire priests took out the heart of a sacrificial victim and with a fire drill renewed the flame in the exposed cavity. Then they set ablaze bundles of sticks representing

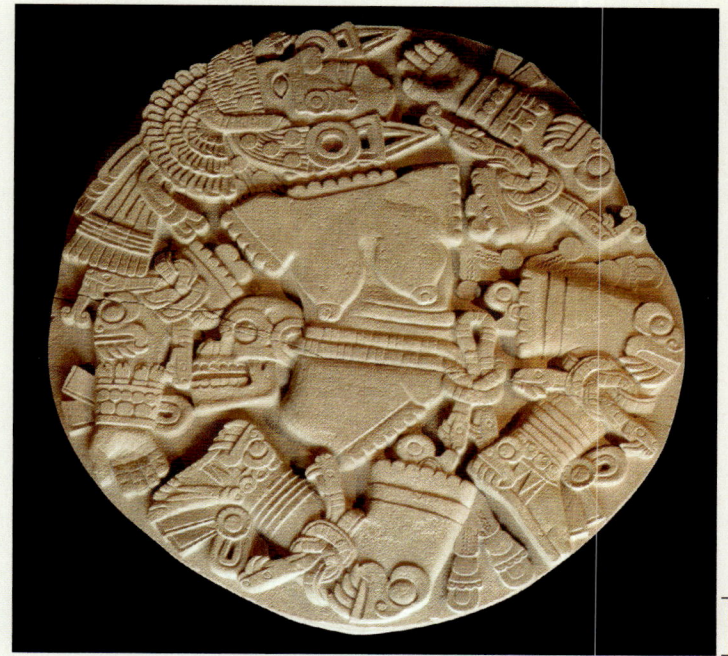

**35-4** Coyolxauhqui, from the Great Temple of Tenochtitlán, Mexico City, Mexico, Aztec, ca. 1469. Stone, diameter 10′ 10″. Museo del Templo Mayor, Mexico City.

The bodies of sacrificed foes the Aztecs hurled down the stairs of the Great Temple landed on this disk, which depicts the segmented body of the moon goddess, Coyolxauhqui, Huitzilopochtli's sister.

1 ft.

the 52 years just passed, ensuring the sun would rise in the morning and another cycle would begin. The Aztecs celebrated the last New Fire Ceremony in 1507.

Most Aztec ceremonies involved the burning of incense. Colorfully attired dancers and actors performed, and musicians played conch-shell trumpets, drums, rattles, rasps, bells, and whistles. Almost every Aztec festival also included human sacrifice. To Tlaloc, the priests offered small children because their tears brought the rains.

Rituals also marked the completion of important religious structures. The dedication of the last major rebuilding of Hueteocalli at Tenochtitlán in 1487, for example, reportedly involved the sacrifice of thousands of captives from recent wars in the Gulf Coast region. Varied offerings have been found within earlier layers of the temple, many representing tribute from subjugated peoples. These include blue-painted stone and ceramic vessels, conch shells, a jaguar skeleton, flint and obsidian knives, and even Mesoamerican "antiques"—carved stone Olmec and Teotihuacán masks made hundreds of years before the Aztec ascendancy.

whose discovery in 1971 set off the ongoing archaeological investigations in the Zócalo. The Aztecs placed the relief at the foot of the staircase leading up to one of Huitzilopochtli's earlier temples on the site. (Cortés and his army never saw the disk because it lay within the outermost shell of the Great Temple.) The relief presents

the image of the murdered and segmented body of Coyolxauhqui. The mythological theme also carried a contemporary political message. The Aztecs sacrificed their conquered enemies at the top of the Great Temple and then hurled their bodies down the temple stairs to land on this stone. The victors thus forced their foes to reenact

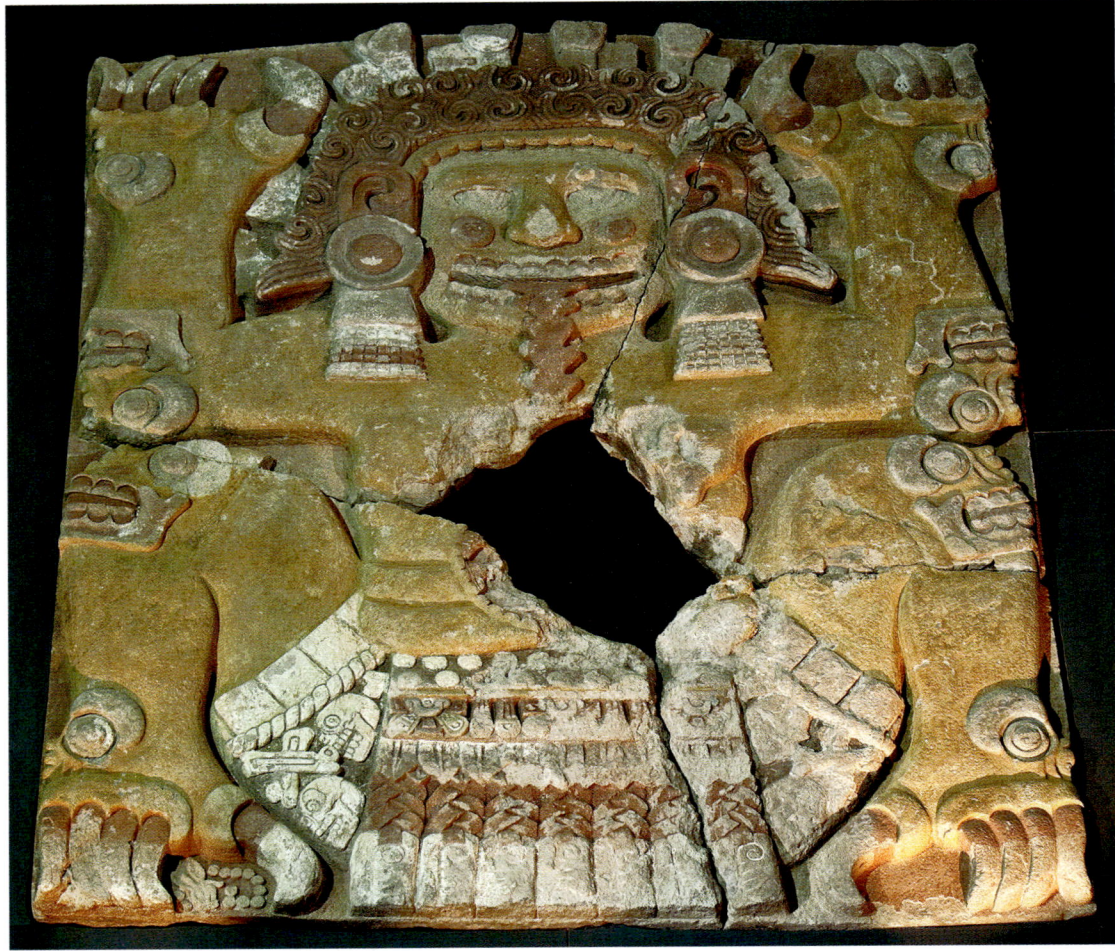

**35-5** Tlaltecuhtli (Earth Lord), from the Great Temple of Tenochtitlán, Mexico City, Mexico, Aztec, 1502. Andesite, painted with mineral colors, 13′ 9″ × 11′ 10½″. Museo del Templo Mayor, Mexico City.

This 12-ton relief depicts Tlaltecuhtli squatting to give birth while drinking her own blood. The slab covered a treasure-filled shaft probably associated with the grave of Emperor Ahuitzotl, who died in 1502.

1 ft.

the horrible fate of the dismembered goddess. The Coyolxauhqui disk is a superb example of art in the service of state ideology. The unforgettable image of the fragmented goddess proclaimed the power of the Mexica over their enemies and the inevitable fate that must befall their foes when defeated. Marvelously composed, the relief has a kind of dreadful beauty. Within the circular space, the design's carefully balanced, richly detailed components have a slow turning rhythm reminiscent of a revolving galaxy. The carving is in low relief, a smoothly even, flat surface raised from a flat ground. It is the sculptural equivalent of the line and flat tone, the figure and neutral ground, characteristic of Mesoamerican painting.

**TLALTECUHTLI** In 2006, Mexican archaeologists uncovered a gigantic pink andesite relief (FIG. **35-5**) painted in ocher, red, blue, white, and black depicting the earth goddess Tlaltecuhtli. The Aztec sculptor depicted the goddess facing the viewer with arms raised, wearing elaborate headgear, and posed in a squatting position to give birth while drinking her own blood. She has claws instead of hands and feet and skulls in place of knees. The relief weighs nearly 12 tons even in its fragmentary state and required at least 200 men to transport it from the quarry at Lake Texcoco to Tenochtitlán. The colossal slab covered a deep shaft at the foot of the north side of the Templo Mayor pyramid. Below, the excavators discovered sacrificial knives, gold bells, two eagles with jade and gold ornaments, and a dog or wolf with a jade necklace and turquoise ear ornaments, as well as 62 species of marine creatures from both the Atlantic and Pacific Oceans—that is, from every corner of the Aztec world. The relief and the treasure-filled shaft are probably associated with the as-yet-unlocated grave of the Aztec emperor Ahuitzotl (r. 1486–1502).

**COATLICUE** In addition to relief carving, the Aztecs produced freestanding statuary. Perhaps the most impressive is the colossal statue (FIG. **35-6**) of the beheaded Coatlicue discovered in 1790 near Mexico City's cathedral. The sculpture's original setting is unknown, but some scholars believe it was one of a group set up at the Great Temple. The main forms are in high relief, the details executed either in low relief or by incising. The overall aspect is of an enormous blocky mass, its ponderous weight looming over awed viewers. From the beheaded goddess's neck writhe two serpents whose heads meet to form a tusked mask. Coatlicue wears a necklace of severed human hands and excised human hearts. The pendant of the necklace is a skull. Entwined snakes form her skirt. From between her legs emerges another serpent, symbolic perhaps of both menses and the male member. Like most Aztec deities, Coatlicue has both masculine and feminine traits. Her hands and feet have great claws, which she uses to tear the human flesh she consumes. All her attributes symbolize sacrificial death. Yet, in Aztec thought, this mother of the gods combined savagery and tenderness, for out of destruction arose new life, a theme seen earlier at Teotihuacán (FIG. 18-7).

**AZTECS AND SPANIARDS** Unfortunately, despite the occasional spectacular find, such as the Tlaltecuhtli monolith (FIG. 35-5), most Aztec and Aztec-sponsored art did not survive the Spanish conquest and the subsequent period of evangelization.

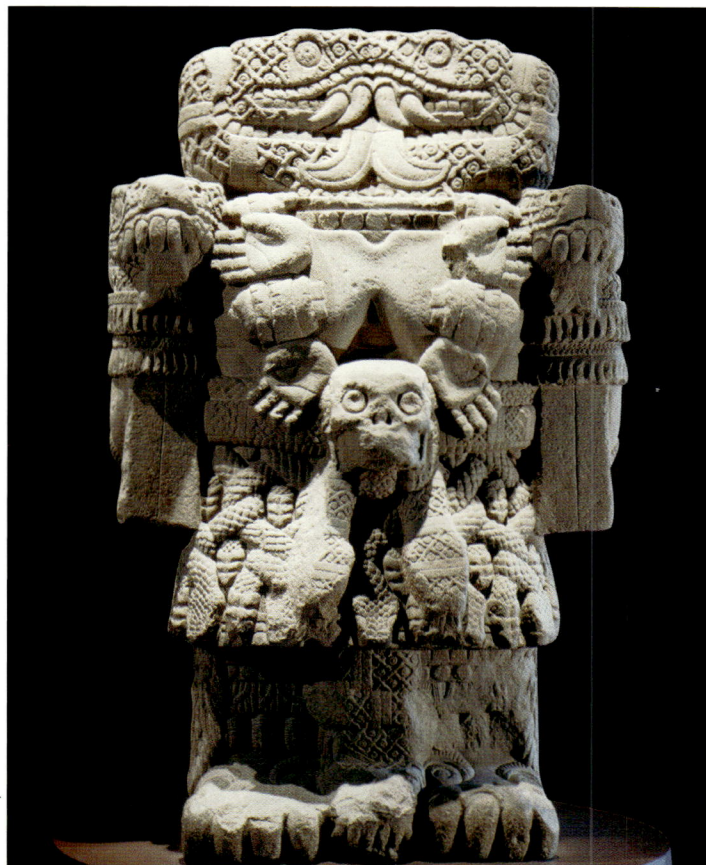

**35-6** Coatlicue, from Tenochtitlán, Mexico City, Mexico, Aztec, ca. 1487–1520. Andesite, 11′ 6″ high. Museo Nacional de Antropología, Mexico City.

This colossal statue may have stood near the Great Temple. The beheaded goddess wears a necklace of human hands and hearts. Entwined snakes form her skirt. All her attributes symbolize sacrificial death.

The conquerors took Aztec gold artifacts back to Spain and melted them down, zealous friars destroyed "idols" and illustrated books, and perishable materials such as textiles and wood largely disappeared. Aztec artisans also fashioned beautifully worked feathered objects and even created mosaic-like images with feathers, an art they put to service for the Catholic Church for a brief time after the Spanish conquest, creating religious pictures and decorating ecclesiastical clothing with the bright feathers of tropical birds.

The Spanish conquerors found it impossible to reconcile the beauty of the great city of Tenochtitlán with what they regarded as its hideous cults. They admired its splendid buildings ablaze with color, its luxuriant and spacious gardens, its sparkling waterways, its teeming markets, and its grandees resplendent in exotic bird feathers. But when Moctezuma II brought Cortés and his entourage into the shrine of Huitzilopochtli's temple, the newcomers started back in horror, recoiling in disgust at the huge statues clotted with dried blood. Cortés was furious. Denouncing Huitzilopochtli as a devil, he proposed to put a high cross above the pyramid and a statue of the Virgin in the sanctuary to exorcise its evil. This proposal came to symbolize the avowed purpose and the historical result of the Spanish conquest of Mesoamerica. The conquistadors venerated the cross and the Virgin, triumphant, in new shrines built on the ruins of the plundered temples of the ancient American gods. In turn, the banner of the Most Catholic King of Spain waved over new atrocities of a European kind.

# SOUTH AMERICA

Late Horizon is the name of the period in the Andes Mountains of Peru and Bolivia (MAP 35-2) corresponding to the end of the late Postclassic period in Mesoamerica. The dominant power in the region at that time was the Inka.

## Inka

The Inka were a small highland group who established themselves in the Cuzco Valley around 1000. In the 15th century, however, they rapidly extended their power until their empire stretched from modern Quito, Ecuador, to central Chile. At the time of the Spanish conquest, the Inka Empire, although barely a century old, was the largest in the world. Expertise in mining and metalwork enabled the Inka to accumulate enormous wealth and to amass the fabled troves of gold and silver the Spanish coveted. An empire as vast and rich as the Inka's required skillful organizational and administrative control. The Inka had rare talent for both. They divided their Andean empire, which they called Tawantinsuyu, the Land of the Four Quarters, into sections and subsections, provinces and communities, whose boundaries all converged on, or radiated from, the capital city of Cuzco.

The Inka aimed at imposing not only political and economic control but also their art style throughout their realm, subjugating local traditions to those of the empire. Control extended even to clothing, which communicated the social status of the person wearing the garment. The Inka wove bands of small squares of various repeated abstract designs into their fabrics. Scholars believe the patterns had political meaning, connoting membership in

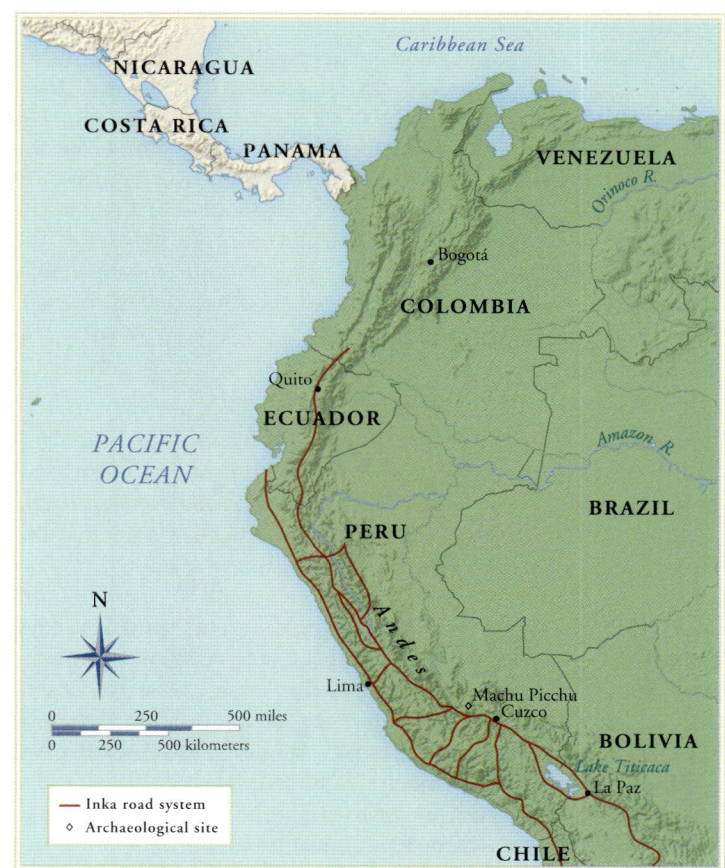

**MAP 35-2** Inka sites in Andean South America.

# Inka Technology

The Inka ruled a vast empire in Andean South America. During the century preceding the Spanish conquest, the Inka Empire probably boasted a population of some 12 million living as much as 3,000 miles apart. To feed their far-flung subjects, the Inka mastered the difficult problems of agriculture in a mountainous region with expert terracing and irrigation. They knitted together their extensive territories with networks of highways and bridges, upgrading more than 14,000 miles of roads, one main highway running through the highlands and another along the coast, with connecting roads linking the two regions. Shunning wheeled vehicles and horses, they used their highway system to move goods by llama herds. They also established a highly efficient, swift communication system of relay runners who carried messages the length of the empire. The Inka emperor in Cuzco could get fresh fish from the coast in only three days. Where the terrain was too steep for a paved flat surface, the Inka built stone steps, and their rope bridges crossed canyons high over impassable rivers. They placed small settlements along the roads no more than a day apart where travelers could rest and obtain supplies for the journey. The terraced cities of the Inka, for example, Machu Picchu (FIG. 35-7) near Cuzco, Peru, are among the engineering wonders of the premodern world.

The Inka never developed a writing system, but they employed a remarkably sophisticated record-keeping system using a device known as the *khipu,* with which they recorded calendar and astronomical information, census and tribute totals, and inventories. For example, the Spaniards noted admiringly that Inka officials always knew exactly how much maize or cloth was in any storeroom in their empire. Not a book or a tablet, the khipu consisted of a main fiber cord and other knotted threads hanging perpendicularly off it. The color and position of each thread, as well as the kind of knot and its location, signified numbers and categories of things, whether people,

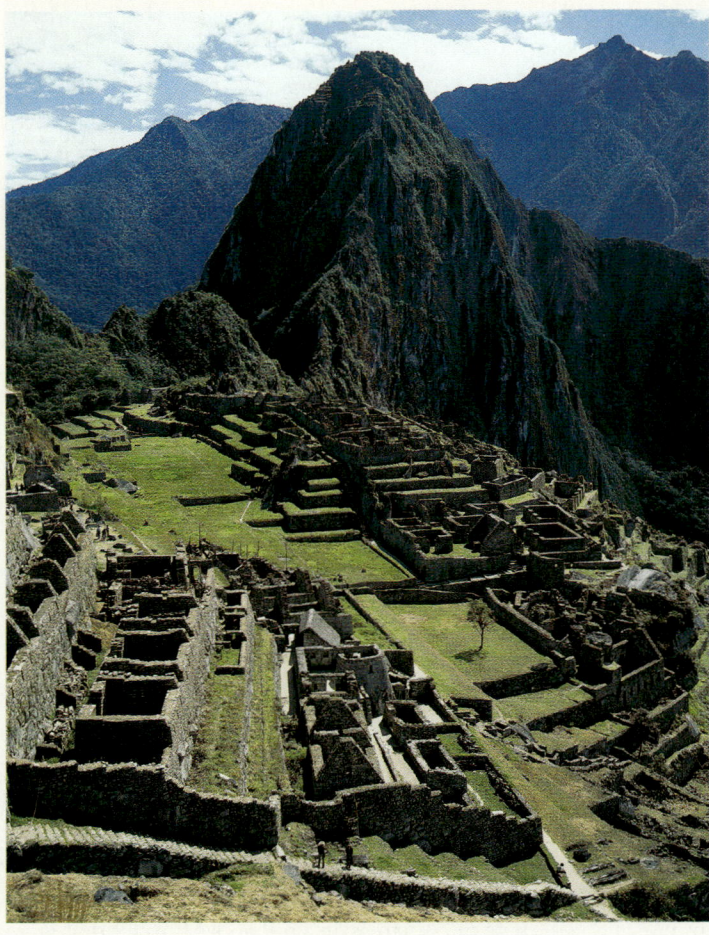

**35-7** Machu Picchu (looking northwest), Peru, Inka, 15th century.

Machu Picchu was the estate of an Inka ruler. Large upright stones echo the contours of nearby sacred peaks. Precisely placed windows and doors facilitated astronomical observations.

llamas, or crops. Studies of khipus have demonstrated the Inka used the decimal system, were familiar with the concept of zero, and could record numbers up to five digits. The Inka census taker or tax collector could easily roll up and carry the khipu, one of the most lightweight and portable "computers" ever invented.

---

particular social groups. The Inka ruler's tunics displayed a full range of abstract motifs, perhaps to indicate his control over all groups. Those the Inka conquered had to wear their characteristic local dress at all times, a practice reflected in the distinctive and varied clothing of today's indigenous Andean peoples.

**MACHU PICCHU** The engineering prowess of the Inka matched their talent for governing (see "Inka Technology," above), and they were gifted architects as well. Although they also worked with adobe, the Inka were supreme masters of shaping and fitting stone. As a militant people, they selected breathtaking, naturally fortified sites and further strengthened them by building various defensive structures. Inka city planning reveals an almost instinctive grasp of the harmonious relationship of architecture to site.

One of the world's most awe-inspiring sights is the Inka city of Machu Picchu (FIG. **35-7**), which perches on a ridge between two

jagged peaks 9,000 feet above sea level. Invisible from the Urubamba River Valley some 1,600 feet below, the site remained unknown to the outside world until Hiram Bingham (1875–1956), an American explorer, discovered it in 1911. In the very heart of the Andes, Machu Picchu is about 50 miles north of Cuzco and, like some of the region's other cities, was the estate of a powerful mid-15th-century Inka ruler. Though relatively small and insignificant compared with its neighbors (its resident population was a little more than a thousand), the city is of great archaeological importance as a rare site left undisturbed since Inka times. The accommodation of its architecture to the landscape is so complete that Machu Picchu seems a natural part of the mountain ranges surrounding it on all sides. The Inka even cut large stones to echo the shapes of the mountain beyond. Terraces spill down the mountainsides and extend even up to the very peak of Huayna Picchu, the great hill just beyond the city's main plaza. The Inka carefully sited buildings so that

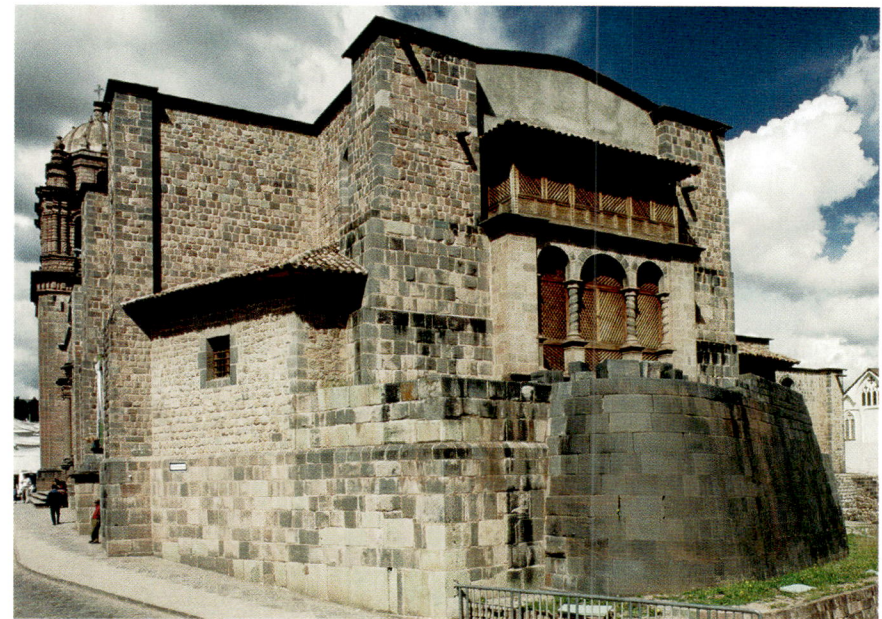
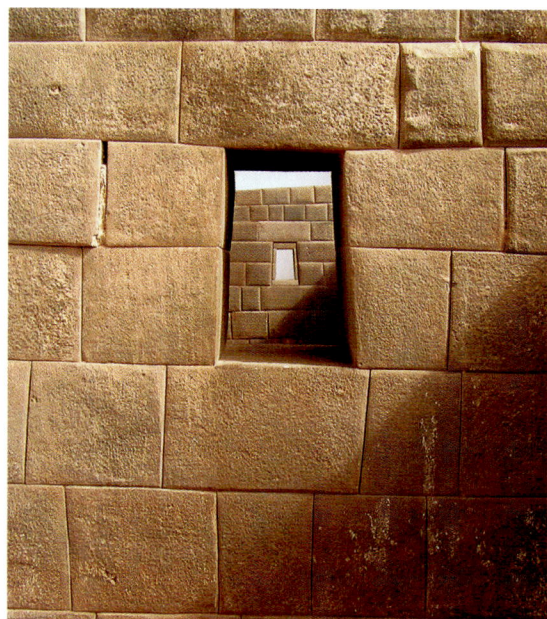

**35-8** Remains of the Temple of the Sun (surmounted by the church of Santo Domingo), Cuzco, Peru, Inka, 15th century. General view of the exterior (*left*) and detail of the interior masonry (*right*).

Perfectly constructed ashlar masonry walls are all that remain of the Temple of the Sun, the most important shrine in the Inka capital. Gold, silver, and emeralds covered the temple's interior walls.

windows and doors framed spectacular views of sacred peaks and facilitated the recording of important astronomical events.

**CUZCO** In the 16th century, the Spanish conquistadors largely destroyed the Inka capital at Cuzco. Consequently, architectural historians have gleaned most of their information about the city from often contradictory Spanish sources rather than from archaeology. Some accounts describe Cuzco's plan as having the shape of a puma, with a great shrine-fortress on a hill above the city representing its head and the southeastern convergence of two rivers forming its tail. Cuzco residents still refer to the river area as "the puma's tail." A great plaza, still the hub of the modern city, nestled below the animal's stomach. The puma was a symbol of Inka royal power.

One Inka building at Cuzco that survives in small part is the Temple of the Sun (FIG. **35-8**), built of *ashlar masonry* (stone blocks fit together without mortar), an ancient construction technique the Inka had mastered. Cuzco masons laid the stones with perfectly joined faces, leaving almost undetectable the lines of separation between blocks. Remarkably, the Inka produced the close joints of their masonry by abrasion alone, grinding the surfaces to a perfect fit. The stonemasons usually laid the blocks in regular horizontal *courses* (FIG. 35-8, *right*). Inka builders were so skilled they could fashion walls with curved surfaces (FIG. 35-8, *left*), their planes as level and continuous as if they were a single form. The surviving walls of the Temple of the Sun are a prime example of this single-form effect. On the exterior, for example, the stones, precisely fitted and polished, form a curving semiparabola. The Inka set the ashlar blocks for flexibility in earthquakes, allowing for a temporary dislocation of the courses, which then return to their original position.

Known to the Spaniards as Coricancha (Golden Enclosure), the Temple of the Sun was the most magnificent of all Inka shrines. The 16th-century Spanish chroniclers wrote in awe of Coricancha's splendor, its interior veneered with sheets of gold, silver, and emeralds and housing life-size statues of silver and gold. Nothing survives,

but some preserved Inka statuettes (FIG. **35-8A**) may suggest the appearance of the lost large-scale statues. Built on the site of the home of Manco Capac, son of the sun god and founder of the Inka dynasty, the Temple of the Sun housed mummies of some of the early rulers. Dedicated to the worship of several Inka deities, including the creator god Viracocha and the gods

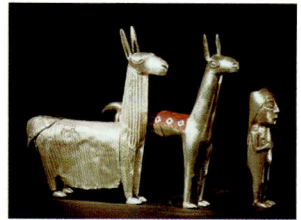

**35-8A** Inka llama, alpaca, and woman, ca. 1475–1532.

of the sun, moon, stars, and the elements, the temple was the center point of a network of radiating sight lines leading to some 350 shrines, which had both calendar and astronomical significance.

**END OF THE INKA** Smallpox spreading south from Spanish-occupied Mesoamerica killed the last Inka emperor and his heir before they ever laid eyes on a Spaniard. The deaths of the emperor and his named successor unleashed a struggle among competing elite families and aided the Europeans in their conquest. In 1532, Francisco Pizarro (1471–1541), the Spanish explorer of the Andes, ambushed the would-be emperor Atawalpa on his way to be crowned at Cuzco after vanquishing his rival half-brother. Although Atawalpa paid a huge ransom of gold and silver, the Spaniards killed him and took control of his vast domain, only a decade after Cortés had defeated the Aztecs in Mexico. Following the murder of Atawalpa, the conquistadors erected the church of Santo Domingo (FIG. 35-8, *left*), in an imported European style, on what remained of the Golden Enclosure. A curved section of Inka wall serves to this day as the foundation for Santo Domingo's *apse*. A violent earthquake in 1950 seriously damaged the colonial building, but the Peruvians rebuilt the church. The two contrasting structures remain standing one atop the other. The Coricancha is therefore of more than architectural and archaeological interest. It is a symbol of the Spanish conquest of the Americas and serves as a composite monument to it.

# NORTH AMERICA

In North America during the centuries preceding the arrival of Europeans, power was much more widely dispersed and the native art and architecture more varied than in Mesoamerica and Andean South America. Three major regions of the United States and Canada are of special interest: the American Southwest, the Northwest Coast (Washington and British Columbia) and Alaska, and the Great Plains (MAP 35-3).

## Southwest

The dominant culture of the American Southwest between 1300 and 1500 was the Ancestral Puebloan (formerly called the Anasazi), the builders of great architectural complexes such as Chaco Canyon and Cliff Palace (FIG. 18-34). The spiritual center of Puebloan life (*pueblo* is Spanish for "urban settlement") was the *kiva*, or male council house, usually decorated with elaborate mural paintings representing deities associated with agricultural fertility. According to their descendants, the present-day Hopi and Zuni, the detail of the Kuaua Pueblo mural shown here (FIG. 35-9) depicts a "lightning man" on the left side. Fish and eagle images (associated with rain) appear on the right side. Seeds, a lightning bolt, and a rainbow stream from the eagle's mouth. All these figures are associated with the fertility of the earth and the life-giving properties of the

seasonal rains, a constant preoccupation of Southwest farmers. The Ancestral Puebloan painter depicted the figures with great economy, using thick black lines, dots, and a restricted palette of black, brown, yellow, and white. The frontal figure of the lightning man seen against a neutral ground makes an immediate visual impact.

**NAVAJO PAINTING** When the first Europeans came into contact with the ancient peoples of the Southwest, they called them "Pueblo Indians." The successors of the Ancestral Puebloan and other Southwest groups, the Pueblo Indians include linguistically diverse but culturally similar peoples such as the Hopi of northern Arizona and the Rio Grande Pueblos of New Mexico. Living among them are the descendants of nomadic hunters who arrived in the Southwest from their homelands in northwestern Canada sometime between 1200 and 1500. These are the Apache and Navajo, who, although culturally quite distinct from the original inhabitants of the Southwest, adopted many features of Pueblo life.

Among these borrowed elements is *sand painting,* which the Navajo learned from the Pueblos but transformed into an extraordinarily complex ritual art form. The temporary sand paintings (also known as *dry paintings*), constructed to the accompaniment of prayers and chants, are an essential part of ceremonies for curing disease. In the healing ceremony, the patient sits in the painting's center to absorb the life-giving powers of the gods and their

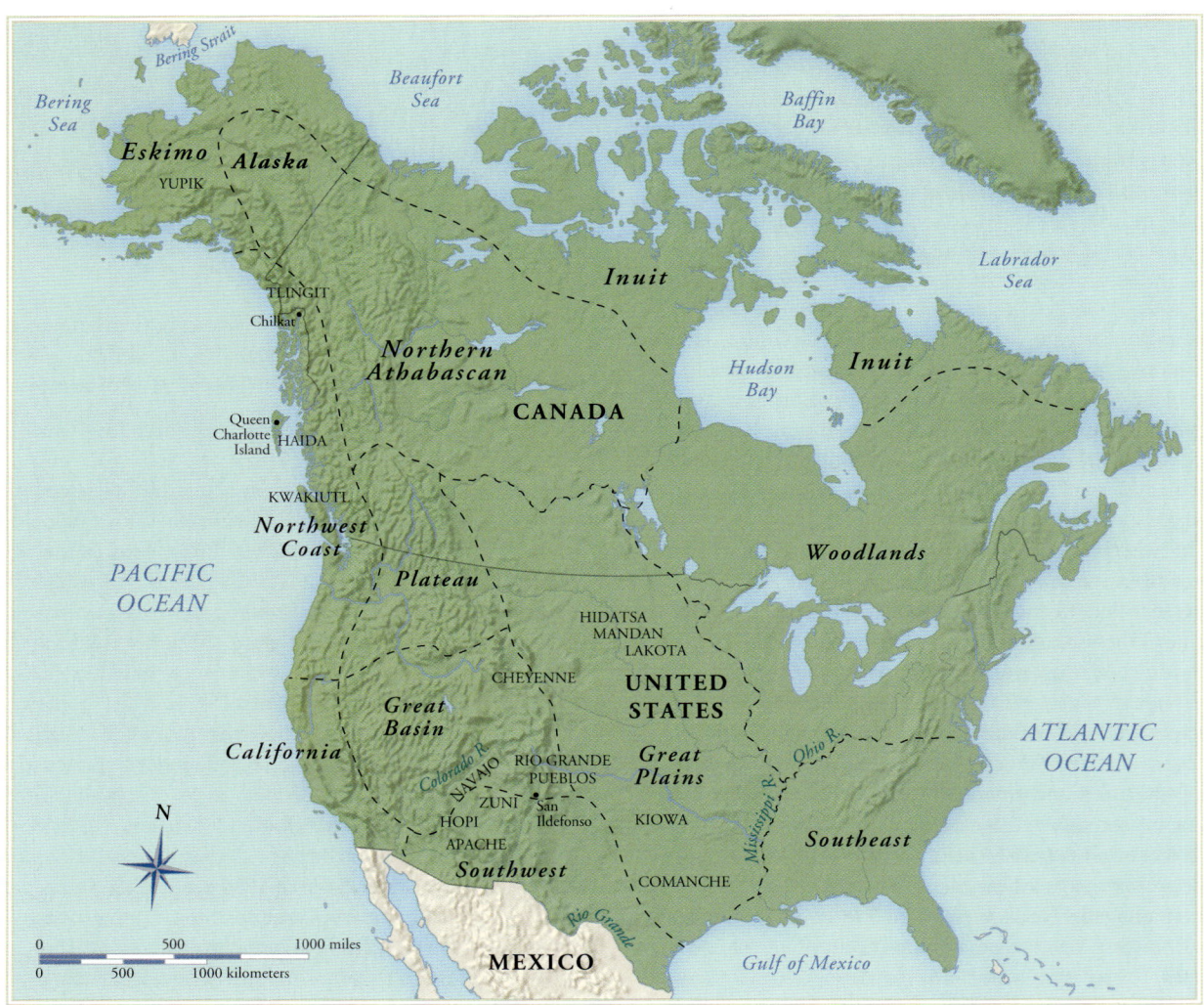

**MAP 35-3** Later Native American sites in North America.

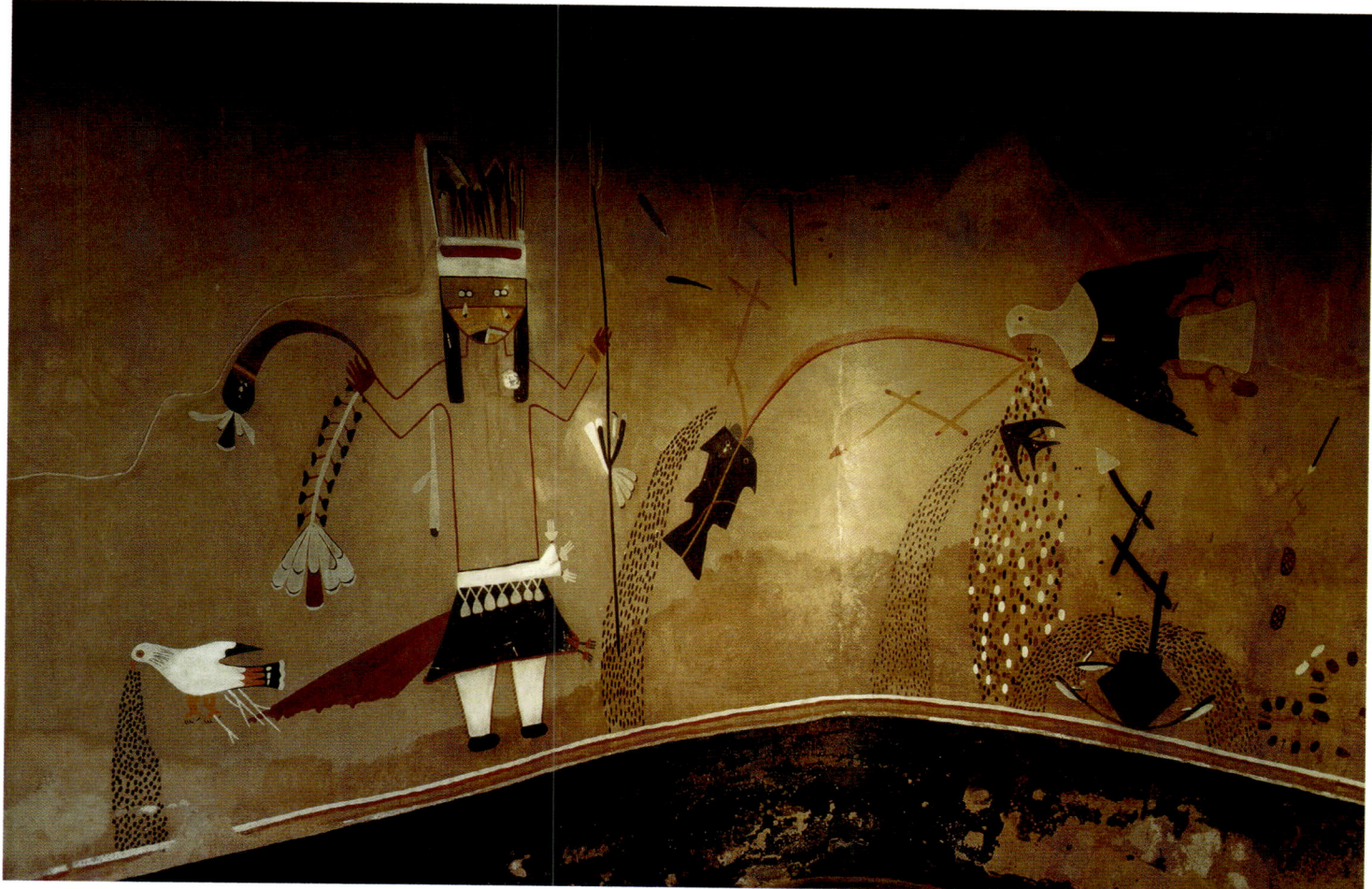

**35-9** Detail of a kiva mural from Kuaua Pueblo (Coronado State Monument), New Mexico, Ancestral Puebloan, late 15th to early 16th century. Interior of the kiva, 18′ × 18′. Museum of New Mexico, Santa Fe.

The kiva, or male council house, was the spiritual center of Puebloan life. Kivas were decorated with mural paintings associated with agricultural fertility. This one depicts a lightning man, fish, birds, and seeds.

representations. The Navajo perform similar rites to assure success in hunting and to promote fertility in human beings and nature alike. The artists who supervise the making of these complex images are religious leaders or "medicine men" (rarely women), thought to have direct contact with the powers of the supernatural world, which they use to help both individuals and the community.

The natural materials used—sand, varicolored powdered stones, corn pollen, and charcoal—play a symbolic role reflecting the Native Americans' preoccupation with the forces of nature. The paintings depict the gods and mythological heroes whose help the Navajo seek. As part of the ritual, the participants destroy the sand paintings, so no models exist. However, the traditional prototypes, passed on from artist to artist, must be adhered to as closely as possible. Mistakes can render the ceremony ineffective. Navajo dry painting is therefore highly stylized. Simple curves, straight lines, right angles, and serial repetition characterize most sand paintings.

Because of the sacred nature of sand paintings, the Navajo do not permit anyone to photograph them. Indeed, the study of Native American art presents special problems for art historians, especially since the passage in November 1990 of the Native American Graves Protection and Repatriation Act (NAGPRA), which, among other provisions, requires any museum receiving federal funding to repatriate sacred Native American objects when requested by a descendant. Native views about what is sacred and what should not

be illustrated in textbooks may lead to the removal in future editions of *Art through the Ages* of some works reproduced in the 14th and earlier editions.

**NAVAJO TEXTILES** By the mid-17th century, the Navajo had learned how to weave from their Hopi and other Pueblo neighbors, quickly adapting to new materials such as sheep's wool and synthetic dyes introduced by Spanish settlers and, later, by Anglo-Americans. They rapidly transformed their wearing blankets into handsome rugs in response to the new market created by the arrival of the railroad and early tourists in the 1880s. Other tribes, including those of the Great Plains, also purchased Navajo textiles, which became famous for their quality (the thread count in a typical Navajo rug is extraordinarily high) as well as the sophistication of their designs. Navajo rugs often incorporate vivid abstract motifs known as "eye dazzlers" and copies of sand paintings (altered slightly to preserve the sacred quality of the impermanent ritual images).

**HOPI KATSINAS** Another art form from the Southwest, the *katsina* figurine, also has deep roots in the area. Katsinas are benevolent supernatural spirits personifying ancestors and natural elements living in mountains and water sources. Humans join their world after death. Among contemporary Pueblo groups, masked dancers ritually impersonate katsinas during yearly festivals

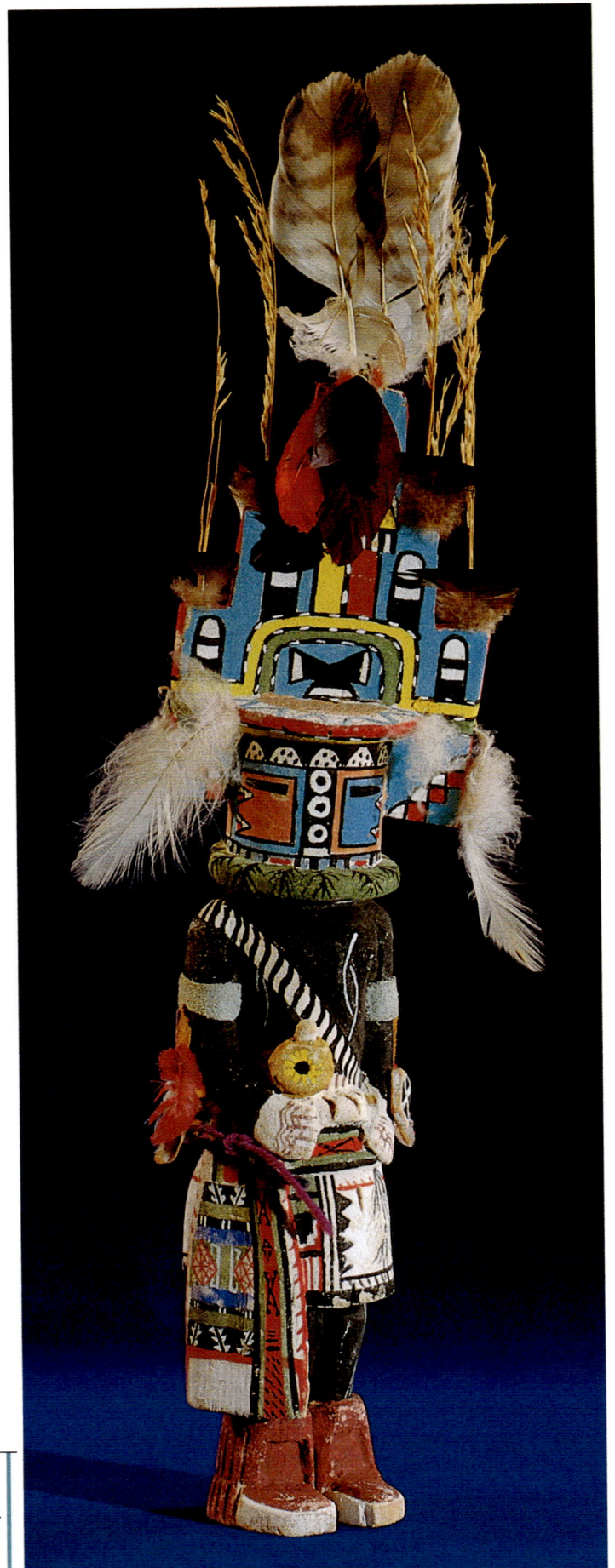

dedicated to rain, fertility, and good hunting. To educate young girls in ritual lore, the Hopi traditionally give them miniature representations of the masked dancers. The Hopi katsina illustrated here (FIG. **35-10**), carved in cottonwood root with added feathers, is the work of OTTO PENTEWA (d. 1963). It represents a rain-bringing deity who wears a mask painted in geometric patterns symbolic of water and agricultural fertility. Topping the mask is a stepped shape signifying thunderclouds and feathers to carry the Hopis' airborne prayers. The origins of the katsina figurines have been lost in time (they even may have developed from carved saints the Spanish introduced during the colonial period). However, the cult is probably very ancient.

**PUEBLO POTTERY** The Southwest has also provided the finest examples of North American pottery. Originally producing utilitarian forms, Southwest potters worked without the potter's wheel and instead coiled shapes of clay they then slipped, polished, and fired. Decorative motifs, often abstract and conventionalized, dealt largely with forces of nature—clouds, wind, and rain. The efforts of San Ildefonso Pueblo potter MARÍA MONTOYA MARTÍNEZ (1887–1980) and her husband Julian Martínez (see "Gender Roles in Native American Art," page 1035) in the early decades of the 20th century revived old techniques to produce forms of striking shape, proportion, and texture. Her black-on-black pieces (FIG. **35-11**) feature matte designs on highly polished surfaces achieved by extensive polishing and special firing in an oxygen-poor atmosphere.

## Northwest Coast and Alaska

The Native Americans of the coasts and islands of northern Washington state, the province of British Columbia in Canada, and southern Alaska have long enjoyed a rich and reliable environment. They fished, hunted sea mammals and game, gathered edible plants, and made their homes, utensils, ritual objects, and even clothing from the region's great cedar forests. Among the numerous groups who make up the Northwest Coast area are the Kwakiutl of southern British Columbia; the Haida, who live on the Queen Charlotte Islands off the coast of the province; and the Tlingit of southern Alaska (MAP 35-3). In the Northwest, a class of professional artists developed, in contrast to the more typical Native American pattern of part-time artists. Working in a highly formalized, subtle style, Northwest Coast artists have produced a wide variety of art objects for centuries: totem poles, masks, rattles, chests, bowls, clothing, charms, and decorated houses and canoes. Some artistic traditions originated as early as 500 BCE, although others developed only after the arrival of Europeans in North America.

**KWAKIUTL AND TLINGIT MASKS** Northwest Coast religious specialists used masks in their healing rituals. Men also wore masks in dramatic public performances during the winter ceremonial season. The animals and mythological creatures represented in masks and a host of other carvings derive from the

**35-10** OTTO PENTEWA, Katsina figurine, New Oraibi, Arizona, Hopi, carved before 1959. Cottonwood root and feathers, 1′ high. Arizona State Museum, University of Arizona, Tucson.

Katsinas are benevolent spirits living in mountains and water sources. This Hopi katsina represents a rain-bringing deity wearing a mask with geometric patterns symbolic of water and agricultural fertility.

# Gender Roles in Native American Art

Although both Native American women and men have created art objects for centuries, they have traditionally worked in different media or at different tasks. Among the Navajo, for example, weavers tend to be women, whereas among the neighboring Hopi the men weave. According to Navajo myth, long ago Spider Woman's husband built her a loom for weaving. In turn, she taught Navajo women how to spin and weave so they might have clothing to wear. Today, young girls learn from their mothers how to work the loom, just as Spider Woman instructed their ancestors, passing along the techniques and designs from one generation to the next.

Among the Pueblos, pottery making normally has been the domain of women. But in response to heavy demand for her wares, María Montoya Martínez, of San Ildefonso Pueblo in New Mexico, coiled, slipped, and burnished her pots, and her husband, Julian, painted the designs. Although they worked in many styles, some based on prehistoric ceramics, around 1918 they invented the black-on-black ware (FIG. 35-11) that made María, and indeed the whole pueblo, famous. The elegant shapes of the pots, as well as the traditional but abstract designs, had affinities with the contemporaneous Art Deco style in architecture (FIG. 29-47) and interior design, and collectors avidly sought (and continue to seek) them. When nonnative buyers suggested she sign her pots to increase their value, María obliged, but in the communal spirit typical of the Pueblos, she also signed her neighbors' names so they might share in her good fortune. María died in 1980, but her descendants continue to garner awards as outstanding potters.

Women also produced the elaborately decorated animal-skin and, later, the trade-cloth clothing of the Woodlands and Plains using moose hair, dyed porcupine quills, and imported beads. Among the Cheyenne, quillworking was a sacred art, and young women worked at learning both proper ritual and correct techniques to obtain membership in the prestigious quillworkers' guild. Women gained the same honor and dignity from creating finely worked utilitarian objects that men earned from warfare. Both women and men painted on tipis and clothing (FIGS. 35-16A, 35-17, and 35-18), with women creating abstract designs (FIG. 35-17) and men working in a more realistic narrative style, often celebrating their exploits in war (FIG. 35-16A) or recording the cultural changes the transfer to reservations brought about.

In the far north, women tended to work with soft materials such as animal skins, whereas men were sculptors of wood masks (FIG. 35-13) among the Alaskan Eskimos and of walrus ivory pieces

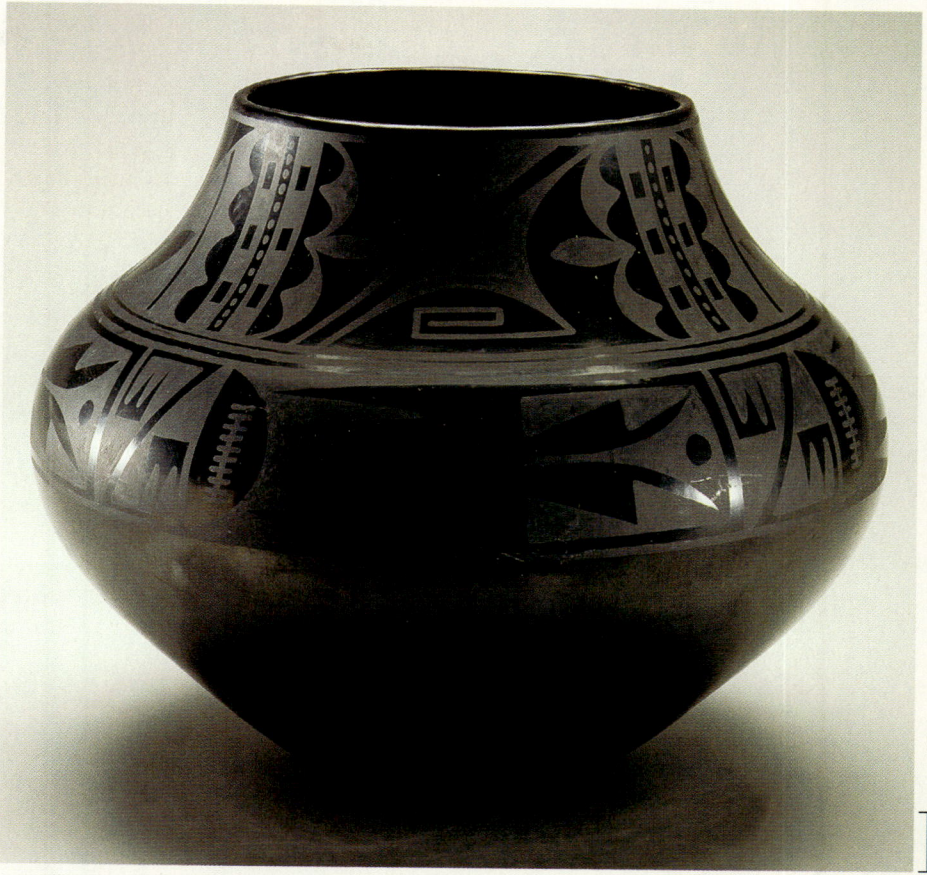

1 in.

**35-11** MARÍA MONTOYA MARTÍNEZ, jar, San Ildefonso Pueblo, New Mexico, ca. 1939. Blackware, $11\frac{1}{8}" \times 1' 1"$. National Museum of Women in the Arts, Washington, D.C. (gift of Wallace and Wilhelmina Hollachy).

Pottery is traditionally a Native American woman's art form. María Montoya Martínez won renown for her black-on-black vessels of striking shapes with matte designs on highly polished surfaces.

(FIG. 18-29) throughout the Arctic. The introduction of printmaking, a foreign medium with no established gender associations, to some Canadian Inuit communities in the 1950s provided both native women and men with a new creative outlet. Printmaking became an important source of economic independence vital to these isolated and once-impoverished settlements. Today, both Inuit women and men make prints, but men still dominate in carving stone sculpture, another new medium also produced for and sold to outsiders.

Throughout North America, indigenous artists continue to work in traditional media, such as ceramics, beadwork, and basketry, marketing their wares through museum shops, galleries, regional art fairs, and, most recently, the Internet. Many also obtain degrees in art and express themselves in European media such as oil painting, often using their art to comment on political, social, and economic issues of central concern to Native Americans (FIG. 31-1).

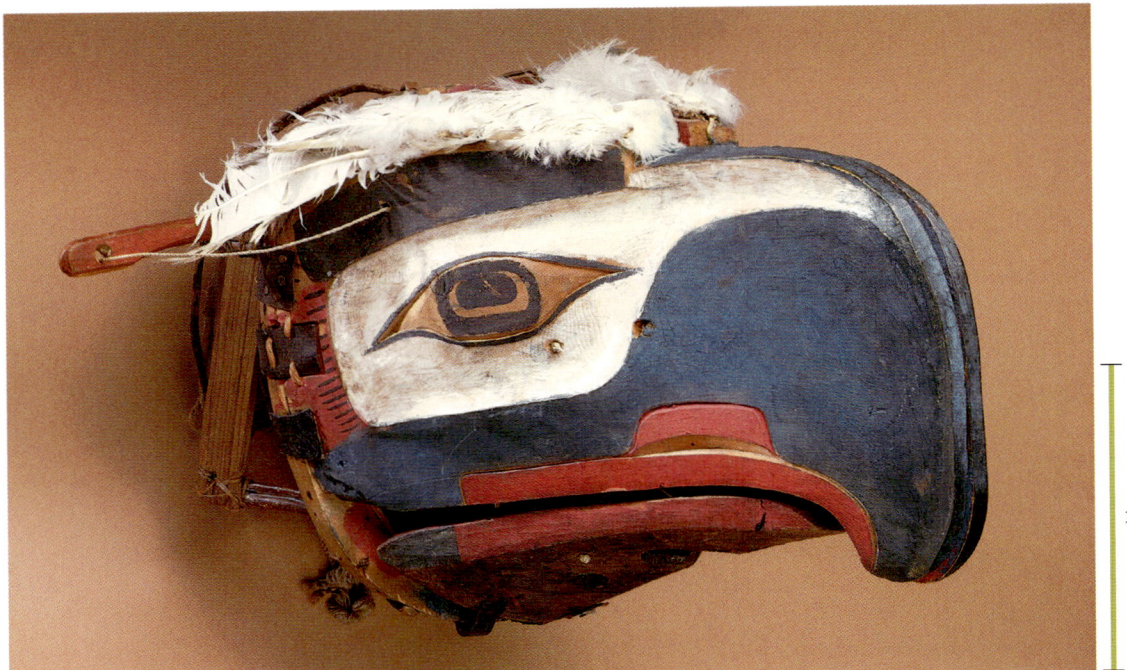

**35-12** Eagle transformation mask, closed (*top*) and open (*bottom*) views, Alert Bay, Canada, Kwakiutl, late 19th century. Wood, feathers, and string, 1′ 10″ × 11″. American Museum of Natural History, New York.

The wearer of this Kwakiutl mask could open and close it rapidly by manipulating hidden strings, magically transforming himself from human to eagle and back again as he danced.

1 ft.

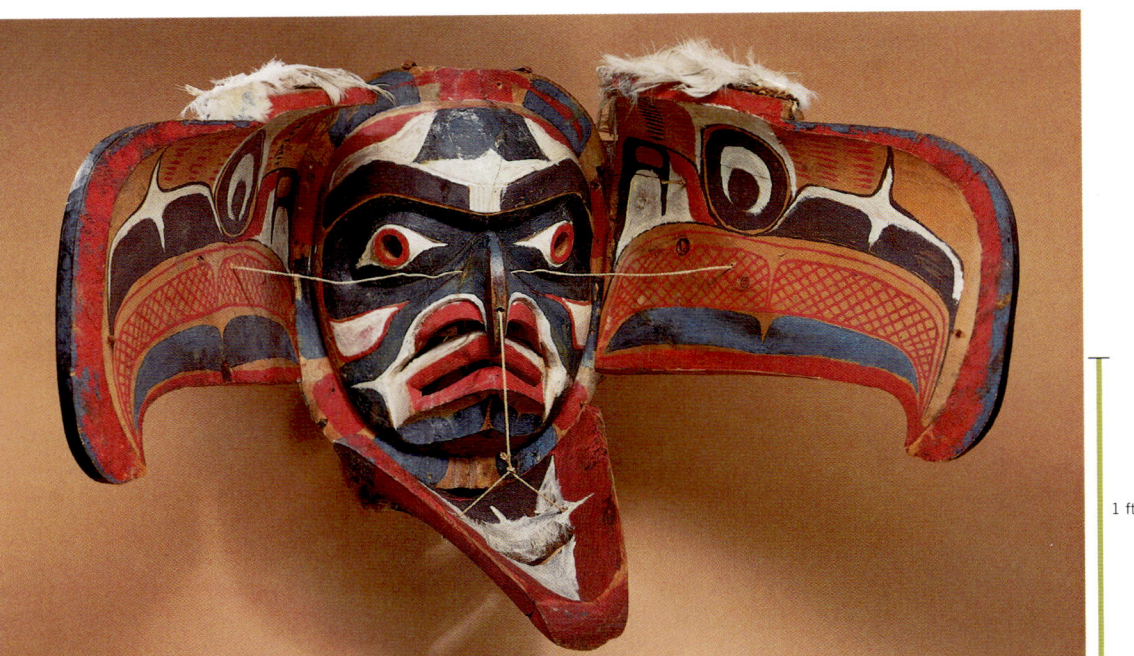

1 ft.

Northwest Coast's rich oral tradition and celebrate the mythological origins and inherited privileges of high-ranking families. The artist who made the Kwakiutl mask illustrated here (FIG. **35-12**) meant it to be seen in flickering firelight, and ingeniously constructed it to open and close rapidly when the wearer manipulated hidden strings. He could thus magically transform himself from human to eagle and back again as he danced. The transformation theme, in myriad forms, is a central aspect of the art and religion of the Americas. The Kwakiutl mask's human aspect also owes its dramatic character to the exaggeration and distortion of facial parts—such as the hooked beaklike nose and flat flaring nostrils—and to the deeply undercut curvilinear depressions, which form strong shadows. In contrast to the carved human face, but painted in the same colors, is the two-dimensional abstract image of the eagle painted on the inside of the outer mask.

The Kwakiutl mask is a refined yet forceful carving typical of the area's more dramatic styles. Others are more subdued, and some, such as a wooden Tlingit war helmet (FIG. **35-13**), are exceedingly naturalistic. Although the helmet mask may be a portrait, it might also represent a supernatural being whose powers enhance the wearer's strength. In either case, the artist surely created its grimacing expression to intimidate the enemy.

**HAIDA TOTEM POLES** Although Northwest Coast arts have a spiritual dimension, they are often more important as expressions of social status. Haida house frontal poles, displaying totemic

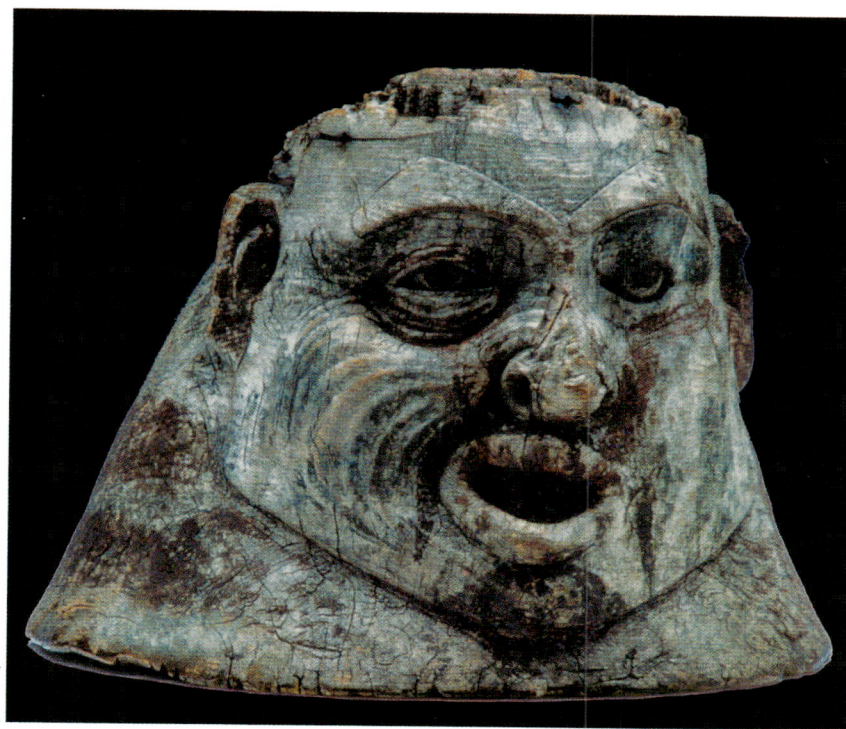

**35-13** War helmet mask, Canada, Tlingit, collected 1888–1893. Wood, 1' high. American Museum of Natural History, New York.

This war helmet mask may be a naturalistic portrait of a Tlingit warrior or a representation of a supernatural being. The carver intended the face's grimacing expression to intimidate enemies.

emblems of clan groups, strikingly express this interest in prestige and family history. Totem poles emerged as a major art form about 300 years ago. The examples in FIG. **35-14** date to the 19th century. They stand today in a reconstructed Haida village BILL REID (1920–1998, Haida) and his assistant DOUG CRANMER (1927–2006, Kwakiutl) completed in 1962. Reid was a master woodcarver who also made monumental sculptures featuring Haida themes, for example, *The Raven and the First Men* (FIG. **35-14A**). Each of the superimposed forms carved on the Haida totem poles represents a crest, an animal, or a supernatural being who fig-

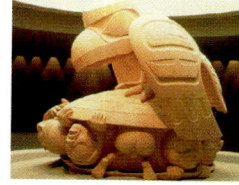

**35-14A** REID, *The Raven and the First Men*, 1978–1980.

ures in the clan's origin story. Additional crests could also be obtained through marriage and trade. The Haida so jealously guarded the right to own and display crests that even warfare could break out over the disputed ownership of a valued crest. In the poles shown, the crests represented include an upside-down dogfish (a small shark), an eagle with a downturned beak, and a killer whale with a crouching human between its snout and its upturned tail flukes. During the 19th century, the Haida erected more poles and made them larger in response to greater competitiveness and the availability of metal tools. The artists carved poles up to 60 feet tall from the trunks of single cedar trees.

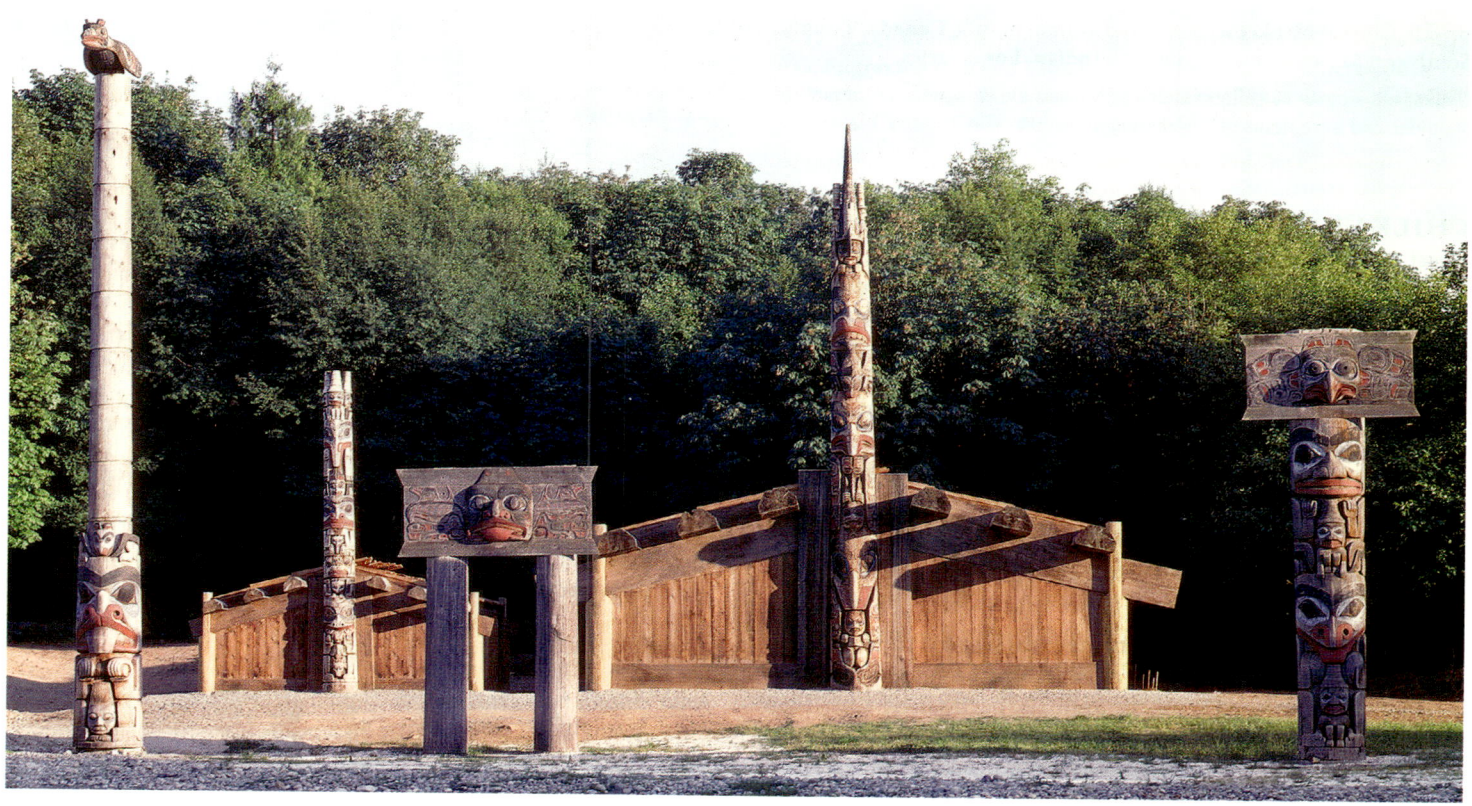

**35-14** BILL REID (Haida), assisted by Doug Cranmer (Namgis), re-creation of a 19th-century Haida village with totem poles, Queen Charlotte Island, Canada, 1962.

Each of the superimposed forms carved on Haida totem poles represents a crest, an animal, or a supernatural being who figures in the clan's origin story. Some Haida poles are 60 feet tall.

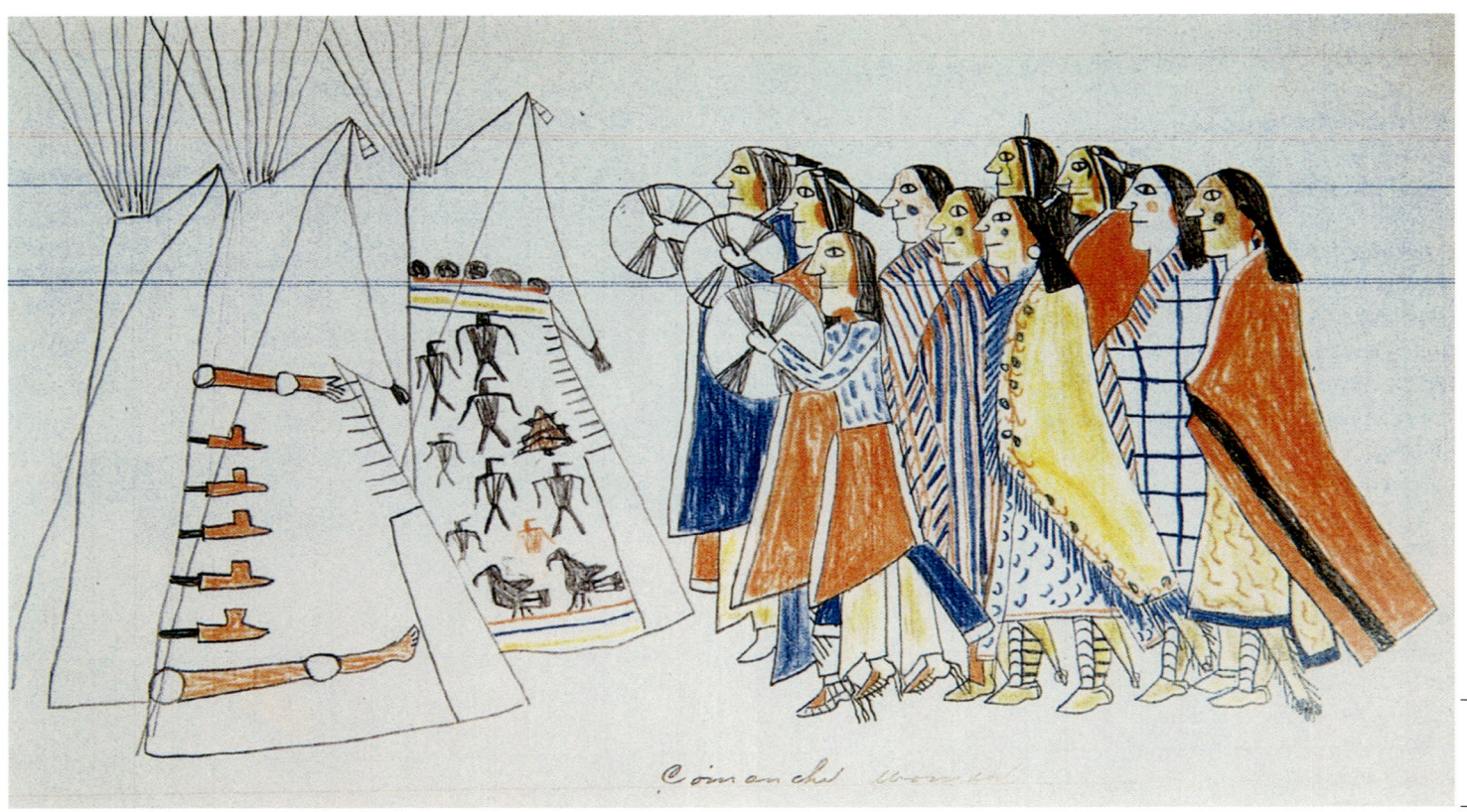

**35-18** Honoring song at painted tipi, in Julian Scott Ledger, Kiowa, 1880. Pencil, ink, and colored pencil, $7\frac{1}{2}'' \times 1'$. Mr. and Mrs. Charles Diker Collection. ◼◂

During the reservation period, some Plains artists recorded their traditional lifestyle in ledger books. This one depicts men and women dancing an honoring song in front of three painted tipis.

rived from personal religious visions. The owners believed the symbolism, the pigments themselves, and added materials, such as feathers, provided them with magical protection and supernatural power.

**LEDGER PAINTINGS** Plains warriors battled incursions into their territory throughout the 19th century. The pursuit of Plains natives culminated in the 1890 slaughter of Lakota participants who had gathered for a ritual known as the Ghost Dance at Wounded Knee Creek, South Dakota. Indeed, from the 1830s on, U.S. troops forcibly removed Native Americans from their homelands and resettled them in other parts of the country. Toward the end of the century, governments confined them to reservations in both the United States and Canada.

During the reservation period, some Plains arts continued to flourish, notably beadwork for the women and painting in ledger books for the men. Traders, the army, and Indian agents had for years provided Plains peoples with pencils and new or discarded ledger books. They, in turn, used them to draw their personal exploits for themselves or for interested Anglo buyers. Sometimes warriors carried them into battle, where U.S. Army opponents retook the ledgers. After confinement to reservations, Plains artists began to record not only their heroic past and vanished lifestyle but also their reactions to their new surroundings, frequently in a

place far from home. These images, often poignant and sometimes humorous, are important native documents of a time of great turmoil and change. In the example shown here (FIG. **35-18**), the work of an unknown Kiowa artist, a group of men and women, possibly Comanches (allies of the Kiowa), appear to dance an honoring song before three tipis, the left forward one painted with red stone pipes and a dismembered leg and arm. The women (in the middle and rear rows) wear the mixture of clothing typical of the late 19th century among the Plains Indians—traditional high leather moccasins, dresses made from calico trade cloth, and (at the far right) a red Hudson's Bay blanket with a black stripe. Although the Plains peoples no longer paint ledger books, beadwork has never completely died out. The ancient art of creating quilled, beaded, and painted clothing has evolved into the elaborate costumes displayed today at competitive dances called *powwows*.

Whether secular and decorative or spiritual and highly symbolic, the diverse styles and forms of Native American art in the United States and Canada have traditionally reflected the indigenous peoples' reliance on and reverence toward the environment they considered it their privilege to inhabit. Today, some Native American artists work in media and styles indistinguishable from those of other contemporary artists worldwide, but in the work of others, for example Jaune Quick-to-See Smith (FIG. 31-1), the Native American experience remains central to their artistic identity.

# NATIVE ARTS OF THE AMERICAS AFTER 1300

## MESOAMERICA

❚ When the first Europeans arrived in the New World, they encountered native peoples with sophisticated civilizations and a long history of art production, including illustrated books. The few surviving pre-conquest books, the *Borgia Codex* among them, provide precious insight into Mesoamerican rituals, science, mythology, and painting style.

❚ The Aztec Empire was the dominant power in Mesoamerica in the centuries before Hernan Cortés overthrew it. Tenochtitlán (Mexico City), the Aztec capital with a population of more than 100,000, was a magnificent island city laid out on a grid plan.

❚ The Great Temple at Tenochtitlán was a towering pyramid encasing several earlier pyramids. Dedicated to the worship of Huitzilopochtli and Tlaloc, it was also the place where the Aztecs sacrificed their enemies and threw their battered bodies down the stone staircase to land on a huge disk with a representation in relief of the dismembered body of the goddess Coyolxauhqui.

❚ In addition to relief carving, Aztec sculptors produced stone statues, some of colossal size, for example, the 11′ 6″ image from Tenochtitlán of the beheaded Coatlicue, who wears a necklace of severed human hands and excised human hearts.

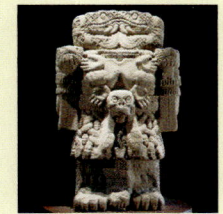

*Borgia Codex,*
ca. 1400–1500

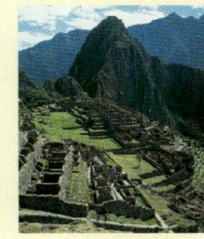

Coatlicue,
ca. 1487–1520

## SOUTH AMERICA

❚ In the 15th century, the Inka Empire, with its capital at Cuzco in present-day Peru, extended from Ecuador to Chile. The Inka were superb engineers and constructed 14,000 miles of roads to exert control over their vast empire. They kept track of inventories, census and tribute totals, and astronomical information using a "computer of strings" called a khipu.

❚ Master architects, the Inka were experts in ashlar masonry construction. The most impressive preserved Inka site is Machu Picchu, the estate of an Inka ruler. Stone terraces spill down the mountainsides, and the buildings have windows and doors designed to frame views of sacred peaks and facilitate the recording of important astronomical events.

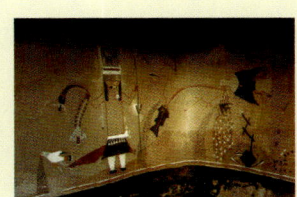

Machu Picchu,
15th century

## NORTH AMERICA

❚ In North America, power was much more widely dispersed and the native art and architecture more varied than in Mesoamerica and Andean South America.

❚ In the American Southwest, the Ancestral Puebloans built urban settlements (pueblos) and decorated their council houses (kivas) with mural paintings. The Navajo produced magnificent textiles and created temporary sand paintings as part of complex rituals. The Hopi carved katsina figurines representing benevolent supernatural spirits. The Pueblo Indian pottery produced by artists such as María Montoya Martínez is among the finest in the world.

❚ On the Northwest Coast, masks played an important role in religious rituals. Some examples can open and close rapidly so the wearer can magically transform himself from human to animal and back again. Haida totem poles sometimes reach 60 feet in height and are carved with superimposed forms representing clan crests, animals, and supernatural beings. Chilkat blankets are the result of a fruitful collaboration between male designers and female weavers.

❚ The peoples of the Great Plains won renown for their magnificent painted buffalo-hide robes, bead necklaces, feather headdresses, and shields. Native American art lived on even after the U.S. government forcibly removed the Plains peoples to reservations. Painted ledger books record their vanished lifestyle, but the production of fine crafts continues to the present day.

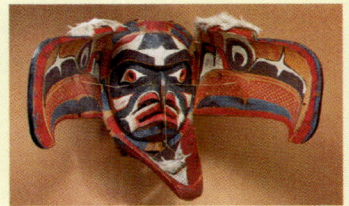

Kiva mural, Kuaua Pueblo,
late 15th to early 16th century

Kwakiutl eagle transformation mask,
late 19th century

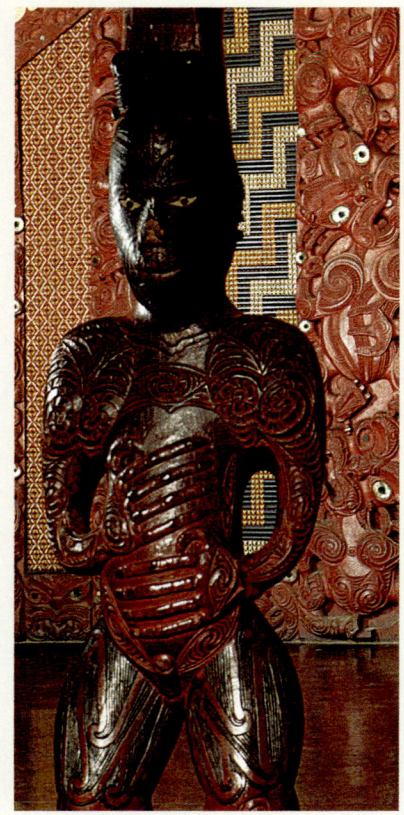

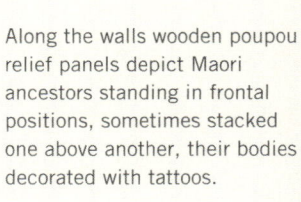

Along the walls wooden poupou relief panels depict Maori ancestors standing in frontal positions, sometimes stacked one above another, their bodies decorated with tattoos.

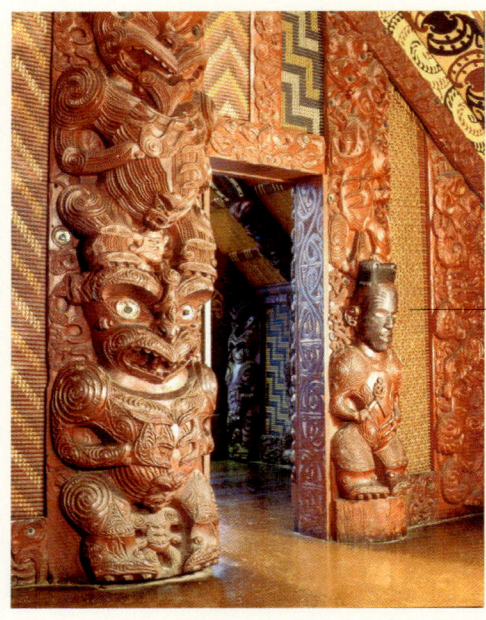

Maori meetinghouses symbolically represent an ancestor's body. Freestanding figures (pou tokomanawa) literally support the ridgepole that is the symbolic spine of the meetinghouse.

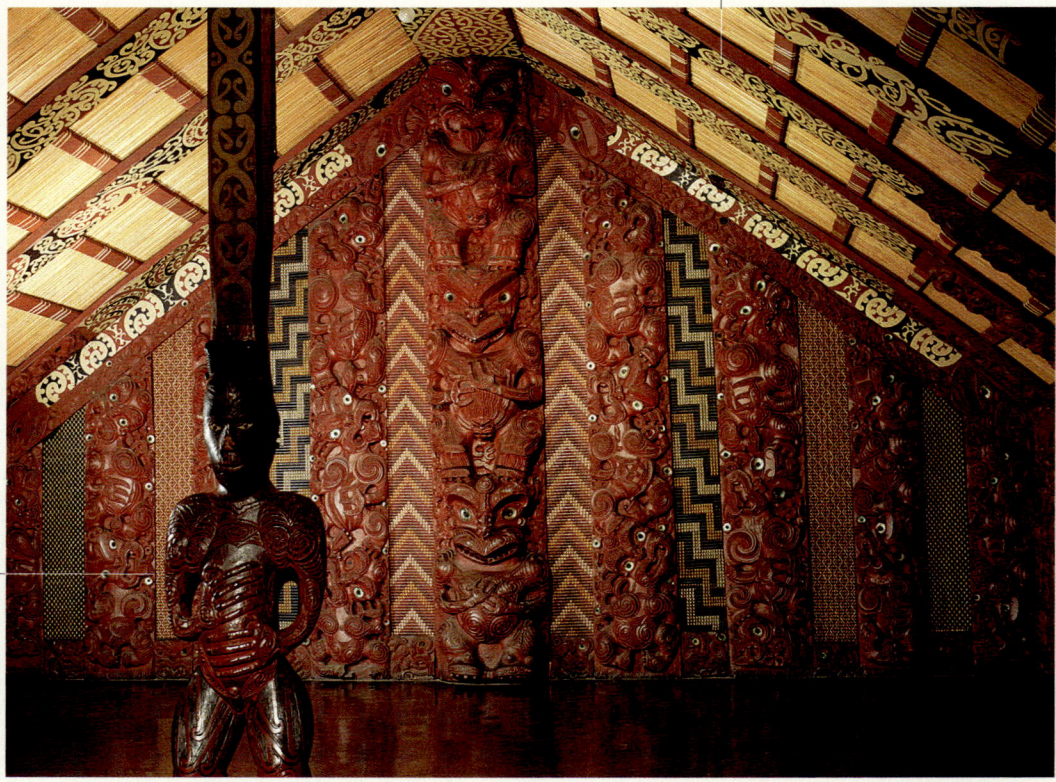

The rafters of a Maori meeting-house are the symbolic ribs of the ancestor's body. The tukutuku panels are the work of female fabric artists, who were not permitted to enter the men's house.

**36-1** RAHARUHI RUKUPO AND OTHERS, interior of Te Hau-ki-Turanga meetinghouse, Poverty Bay, New Zealand, Polynesia, 1842–1845. Reconstructed in the National Museum of New Zealand, Wellington.

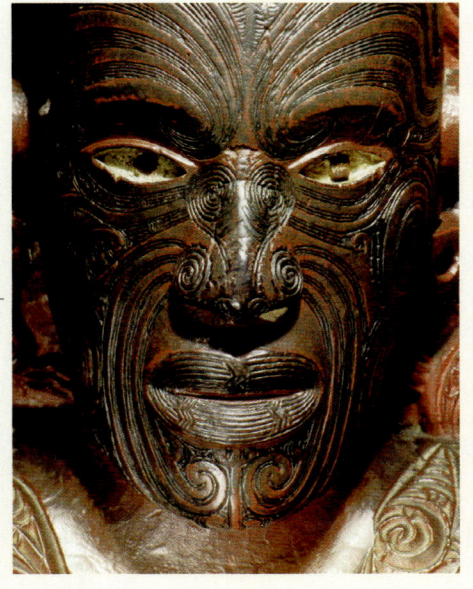

The lead sculptor, Raharuhi Rukupo, who was also chief of the Rongowhakaata tribe, included a self-portrait among the ancestor portraits. His face features an elaborate Maori moko tattoo.

# OCEANIA BEFORE 1980

FRAMING THE ERA

## MAORI MEN'S MEETINGHOUSES

The number and variety of preserved Oceanic artworks are extraordinary, especially in light of the relatively sparse population of this vast region encompassing some 25,000 islands. But in Oceania, as in many non-Western cultures worldwide, artists did not create "artworks" purely for display as aesthetic objects. The art objects Pacific Islanders have produced over the centuries always played important functional roles in religious and communal life. Oceanic art thus cannot be understood apart from its cultural context.

One of the major venues for the display of art in many Oceanic societies was the men's communal house, which itself should be considered a "work of art." A premier example is the Te Hau-ki-Turanga (Spirit of Turanga) meetinghouse (FIG. **36-1**) of the Rongowhakaata tribe at Poverty Bay in New Zealand. RAHARUHI RUKUPO (ca. 1800–1873) and a team of 18 Maori woodcarvers constructed and decorated the building between 1842 and 1845. The Turanga meetinghouse was a place for the male members of the community to assemble in the benevolent presence of their ancestors. The very structure of the building symbolized the body of an ancestor or of the ultimate ancestor, the sky father, with the exterior *barge boards* (the angled boards outlining the house gables) representing his outstretched arms, the *ridgepole* his spine, and the rafters his ribs. Along the walls, relief panels (*poupou*) depict ancestors standing in frontal positions, sometimes stacked one above another, their bodies decorated with tattoos. Freestanding figures (*pou tokomanawa*) comparable to classical caryatids (FIGS. 5-17 and 5-54) literally support the symbolic spine of the ancestral body that is the meetinghouse. The *tukutuku* (stitched lattice panels) between the poupou are the work of female fabric artists, but since women could not enter the meetinghouse, they installed the panels from the outside.

Raharuhi Rukupo was not only a master carver. He was a priest, warrior, and, after the death of his older brother, the chief of the Rongowhakaata. He dedicated the Turanga meetinghouse in honor of his late brother and, as chief, included a self-portrait holding a woodcutter's adze among the ancestor portraits of the poupou. His face features an elaborate *moko tattoo* (see "Tattoo in Polynesia," page 1055). Working in the long-established Maori tradition of woodcarving but using Western metal tools in place of the stone tools their predecessors employed, Rukupo and his assistants were able to complete the meetinghouse in only three years. The house remains the property of the Rongowhakaata tribe but in 1935 was restored and installed in the National Museum of New Zealand at Wellington.

# ISLAND CULTURES OF THE SOUTH PACIFIC

When people think of the South Pacific (MAP **36-1**), images of balmy tropical islands usually come to mind. But the islands of the Pacific Ocean encompass a wide range of habitats. Environments range from the arid deserts of the Australian outback to the tropical rainforests of inland New Guinea and the coral atolls of the Marshall Islands. The region is not only geographically varied but also politically, linguistically, culturally, and artistically diverse.

In 1831, the French explorer Jules Sébastien César Dumont d'Urville (1790–1842) proposed dividing the Pacific Ocean islands into major regions based on general geographical, racial, and linguistic distinctions. Despite its limitations, his division of Oceania into the areas of Melanesia (black islands), Micronesia (small islands), and Polynesia (many islands) continues in use today. Melanesia includes the islands of New Guinea, New Ireland, New Britain, New Caledonia, the Admiralty Islands, and the Solomon Islands, along with other smaller island groups. Micronesia consists primarily of the Caroline, Mariana, Gilbert, and Marshall Islands in the western Pacific. Polynesia covers much of the eastern Pacific and consists of a triangular area defined by the Hawaiian Islands in the north, Rapa Nui (Easter Island) in the east, and Aotearoa (New Zealand) in the southwest.

Although documentary evidence is lacking about Oceanic cultures before the arrival of seafaring Europeans in the early 16th century, archaeologists have determined humans have inhabited the islands for tens of thousands of years. The archaeological evidence indicates different parts of the Pacific experienced distinct migratory waves. The first group arrived during the last Ice Age,

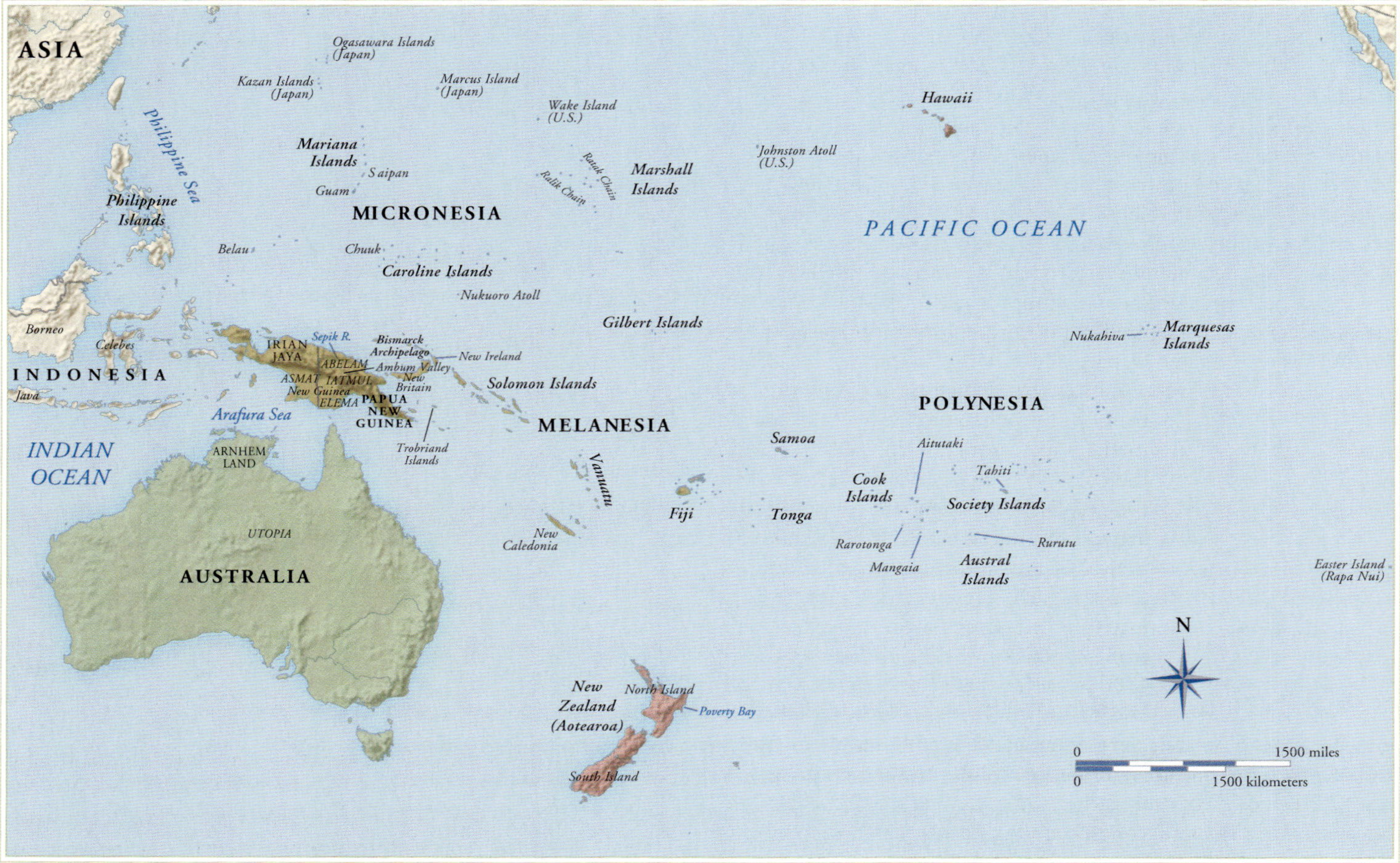

**MAP 36-1** Oceania.

## OCEANIA BEFORE 1980

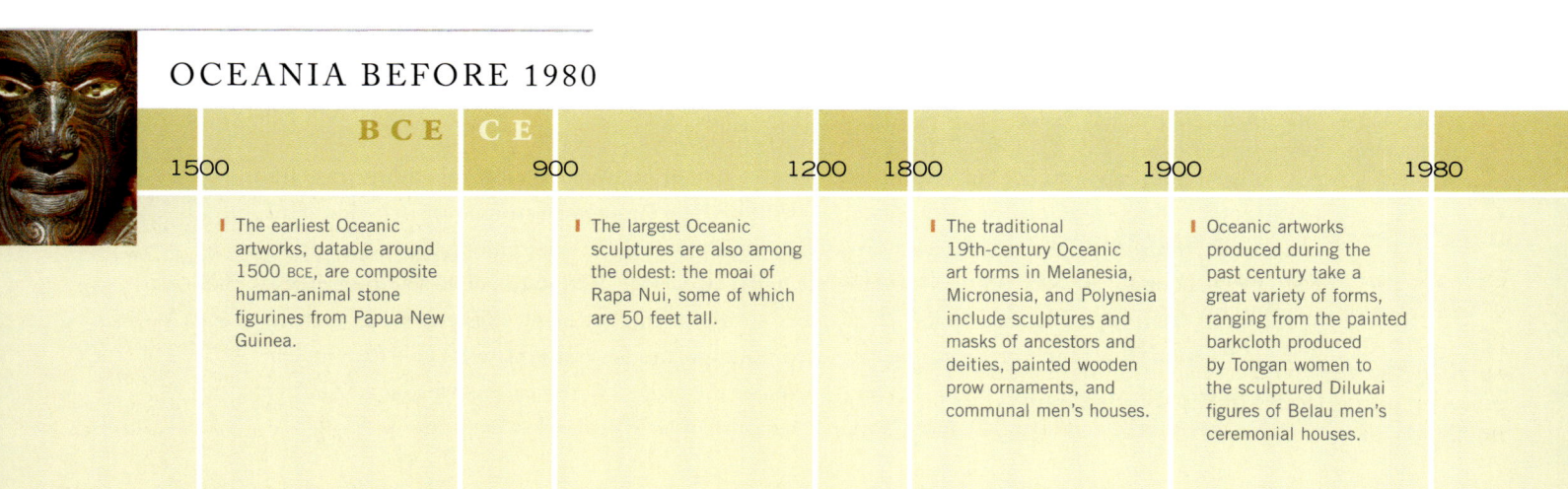

| | BCE | CE | | | | |
|---|---|---|---|---|---|---|
| 1500 | | 900 | 1200 | 1800 | 1900 | 1980 |

- The earliest Oceanic artworks, datable around 1500 BCE, are composite human-animal stone figurines from Papua New Guinea.

- The largest Oceanic sculptures are also among the oldest: the moai of Rapa Nui, some of which are 50 feet tall.

- The traditional 19th-century Oceanic art forms in Melanesia, Micronesia, and Polynesia include sculptures and masks of ancestors and deities, painted wooden prow ornaments, and communal men's houses.

- Oceanic artworks produced during the past century take a great variety of forms, ranging from the painted barkcloth produced by Tongan women to the sculptured Dilukai figures of Belau men's ceremonial houses.

at least 40,000 and perhaps as many as 75,000 years ago, when a large continental shelf extended from Southeast Asia and enabled land access to Australia and New Guinea. After the end of the Ice Age, descendants of these first settlers dispersed to other islands in Melanesia. The most recent migratory wave took place sometime after 3000 BCE and involved peoples of Asian ancestry moving to areas of Micronesia and Polynesia. The last Pacific islands to be settled were those of Polynesia, but habitation of its most far-flung islands—Hawaii, New Zealand, and Easter Island—began no later than 500 to 1000 CE. Because of the expansive chronological span of these migrations, Pacific cultures vary widely. For example, the Aboriginal peoples of Australia speak a language unrelated to any of those of New Guinea, whose languages fall into a distinct but diverse group. In contrast, most of the rest of the Pacific islanders speak languages derived from the Austronesian language family.

These island groups came to Western attention as a result of the extensive exploration and colonization that began in the 16th century and reached its peak in the 19th century. Virtually all of the major Western nations—including Great Britain, France, Spain, Holland, Germany, and the United States—established a presence in the Pacific. Much of the history of Oceania in the 20th century revolved around indigenous peoples' struggles for independence from these colonial powers. Yet colonialism also facilitated an exchange of ideas—not solely the transfer of Western cultural values and technology to the Pacific. Oceanic art, for example, had a strong influence on many Western artists, especially the late-19th-century French painter Paul Gauguin (FIG. 28-20). The "primitive" art of Oceania also inspired many early-20th-century artists (see "Primitivism," Chapter 29, page 846).

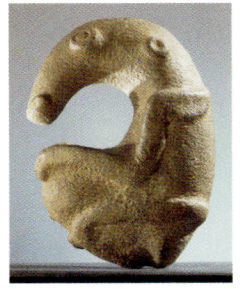

36-1A *Ambum Stone*, Papua New Guinea, ca. 1500 BCE.

This chapter focuses on Oceanic art from the European discovery of the islands in the 16th century until 1980, although the colossal stone statues of Easter Island (FIG. 36-12)—probably the most famous artworks in the South Pacific—predate the arrival of Europeans by several centuries, and the earliest preserved sculptures, for example, the *Ambum Stone* (FIG. 36-1A) from Papua New Guinea, date to around 1500 BCE. Knowledge of early Oceanic art and the history of the Pacific islands in general is unfortunately very incomplete. Traditionally, the transmission of information from one generation to the next in Pacific societies was largely oral, rather than written, and little archival documentation exists. Nonetheless, archaeologists, linguists, anthropologists, ethnologists, and art historians continue to make progress in illuminating the Oceanic past.

# AUSTRALIA AND MELANESIA

The westernmost Oceanic islands are the continent-nation of Australia and New Guinea in Melanesia. Together they dwarf the area of all the other Pacific islands combined.

## Australia

Over the past 40,000 years, the Aboriginal peoples of Australia spread out over the entire continent and adapted to a variety of ecological conditions, ranging from those of tropical and subtropical areas in the north to desert regions in the continent's interior and more temperate locales in the south. European explorers reaching the region in the late 18th and early 19th centuries found the

Aborigines had a special relationship with the land on which they lived. The Aboriginal perception of the world centers on a concept known as the Dreamings—ancestral beings whose spirits pervade the present. All Aborigines identify certain Dreamings as totemic ancestors, and those who share the same Dreamings have social links. The Aborigines call the spiritual domain the Dreamings occupy Dreamtime, which is both a physical space within which the ancestral beings moved in creating the landscape and a psychic space providing Aborigines with cultural, religious, and moral direction. Because of the importance of Dreamings to all aspects of Aboriginal life, native Australian art symbolically links Aborigines with these ancestral spirits. The Aborigines recite creation myths in concert with songs and dances, and many art forms—body painting, carved figures, sacred objects, decorated stones, and rock and bark painting—serve as essential props in these dramatic recreations. Most Aboriginal art is relatively small and portable. As hunters and gatherers in difficult terrain, the Aborigines were generally nomadic peoples, rendering monumental art impractical.

**BARK PAINTING** Bark, widely available in Australia, is portable and lightweight, and bark painting thus became a mainstay of Aboriginal art. Dreamings, mythic narratives (often tracing the movement of various ancestral spirits through the landscape), and sacred places were common subjects. Ancestral spirits pervade the lives of the Aborigines, and these paintings served to give visual form to that presence. Traditionally, an Aborigine could only depict a Dreaming with which the artist had a connection. Thus, specific Aboriginal lineages, clans, or regional groups "owned" individual designs. The bark painting illustrated here (FIG. 36-2) depicts a Dreaming known as Auuenau and comes from Arnhem Land in northern Australia. The artist represented the elongated figure in a style known as "X-ray," which Aboriginal painters used to depict both animal and human forms. In this style, the artist simultaneously depicts the subject's internal organs and exterior appearance. The painting possesses a fluid and dynamic quality, with the X-ray-like figure clearly defined against a solid background.

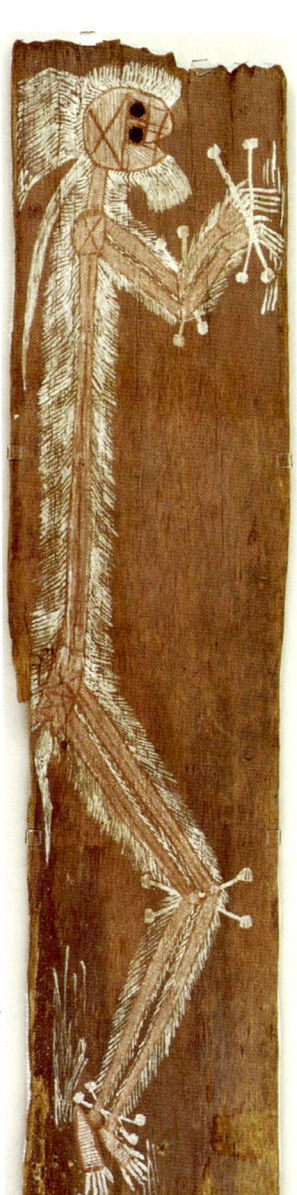

1 ft.

**36-2** Auuenau, from Western Arnhem Land, Australia, 1913. Ochre on bark, 4′ 10$\frac{5}{8}$″ × 1′ 1″. South Australian Museum, Adelaide.

Aboriginal painters frequently depicted Dreamings, ancestral beings whose spirits pervade the present, using the X-ray style that shows both the figure's internal organs and external appearance.

**EMILY KAME KNGWARREYE** Aboriginal artists today retain close ties to the land and the spirits that inhabit it, but some painters, such as EMILY KAME KNGWARREYE (1910–1996), have eliminated figures from their work and produced canvases (for example, FIG. 31-22B) that, superficially at least, resemble American *Abstract Expressionist* paintings (FIG. 30-6).

# New Guinea

Because of its sheer size, New Guinea, the third-largest island in the world, dominates Melanesia. This 309,000-square-mile island consists today of parts of two countries—Irian Jaya, a province of nearby Indonesia, on the island's western end, and Papua New Guinea on the eastern end. New Guinea's inhabitants together speak more than 800 different languages, almost one-quarter of the world's known tongues. Among the Melanesian cultures discussed in this chapter, the Asmat, Iatmul, Elema, and Abelam peoples of New Guinea all speak Papuan-derived languages. Scholars believe they are descendants of the early settlers who came to the island in the remote past. In contrast, the people of New Ireland and the Trobriand Islands are Austronesian speakers and probably descendants of a later wave of Pacific migrants.

Typical Melanesian societies are fairly democratic and relatively unstratified. What political power exists belongs to groups of elder men and, in some areas, elder women. The elders handle the people's affairs in a communal fashion. Within some of these groups, persons of local distinction, known as "Big Men," renowned for their political, economic, and, historically, warrior skills, have accrued power. Because power and position in Melanesia can be earned (within limits), many cultural practices (such as rituals and cults) revolve around the acquisition of knowledge that enables advancement in society. To represent and acknowledge this advancement in rank, Melanesian societies mount elaborate festivals, construct communal meetinghouses, and produce art objects. These cultural products serve to reinforce the social order and maintain social stability. Given the wide diversity in environments and languages, it should come as no surprise that hundreds of art styles flourished on New Guinea alone. Only a sample can be presented here.

**ASMAT** Living along the southwestern coast of New Guinea, the Asmat of Irian Jaya eke out their existence by hunting and gathering the varied flora and fauna found in the mangrove swamps, rivers, and tropical forests. Each Asmat community is in constant competition for limited resources. Historically, the Asmat extended this competitive spirit beyond food and materials to energy and power as well. To increase one's personal energy or spiritual power, one had to take it forcibly from someone else. As a result, warfare and headhunting became central to Asmat culture and art. The Asmat did not believe any death was natural. Death could result only from a direct assault (headhunting or warfare) or sorcery, and it diminished ancestral power. Thus, to restore a balance of spirit power, an enemy's head had to be taken to avenge a death and to add to one's communal spirit power. Headhunting was still common in the 1930s when Europeans established an administrative and missionary presence among the Asmat. As a result of European efforts, headhunting ceased by the 1960s.

When they still practiced headhunting, the Asmat erected *bisj* poles (FIG. **36-3**) that served as a pledge to avenge a relative's death. A man would set up a bisj pole when he could command the support of enough men to undertake a headhunting raid. Carved in one piece from the trunk of a single mangrove tree, bisj poles include superimposed figures of deceased individuals. At the top, ex-

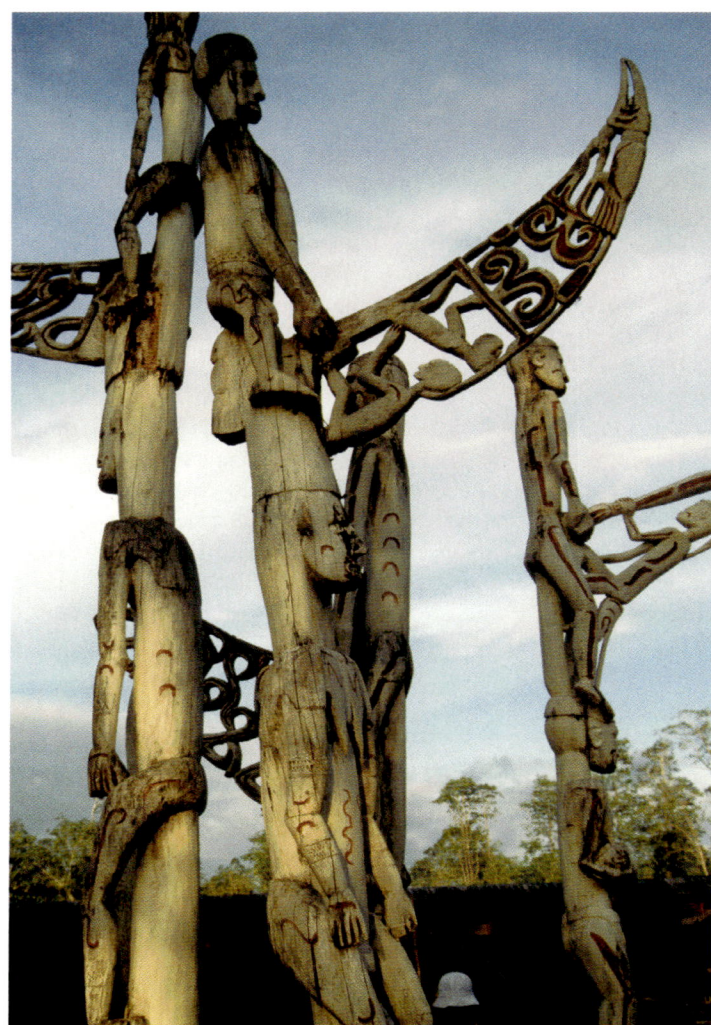

**36-3** Asmat bisj poles, village near Mula, Irian Jaya, Melanesia, mid-20th century, photographed in 2003.

The Asmat carved bisj poles from mangrove tree trunks and erected them before undertaking a headhunting raid. The carved figures represent the relatives whose deaths the hunters must avenge.

tending winglike from the abdomen of the uppermost figure on the bisj pole, is the *cemen,* one of the tree's buttress roots carved into an openwork pattern. All of the decorative elements on the pole related to headhunting and foretold a successful raid. The many animals carved on bisj poles (and in Asmat art in general) are symbols of headhunting. The Asmat see the human body as a tree—the feet and legs as the roots, the torso as the trunk, the arms and hands as the branches, and the head as the fruit. Thus any fruit-eating animal (such as the black king cockatoo, the hornbill, or the flying fox) was symbolic of the headhunter and appeared frequently on bisj poles. Asmat art also often includes representations of the praying mantis. The Asmat consider the female praying mantis's practice of beheading her mate after copulation and then eating him as another form of headhunting. The curvilinear or spiral patterns filling the pierced openwork at the top of the bisj poles can be related to the characteristic curved tail of the cuscus (a fruit-eating mammal) or the tusk of a boar (related to hunting and virility). Once bisj poles were carved, the Asmat placed them on a rack near the community's men's house. After the success of the headhunting expedition, the men discarded the bisj poles and allowed them to rot, because they had served their purpose.

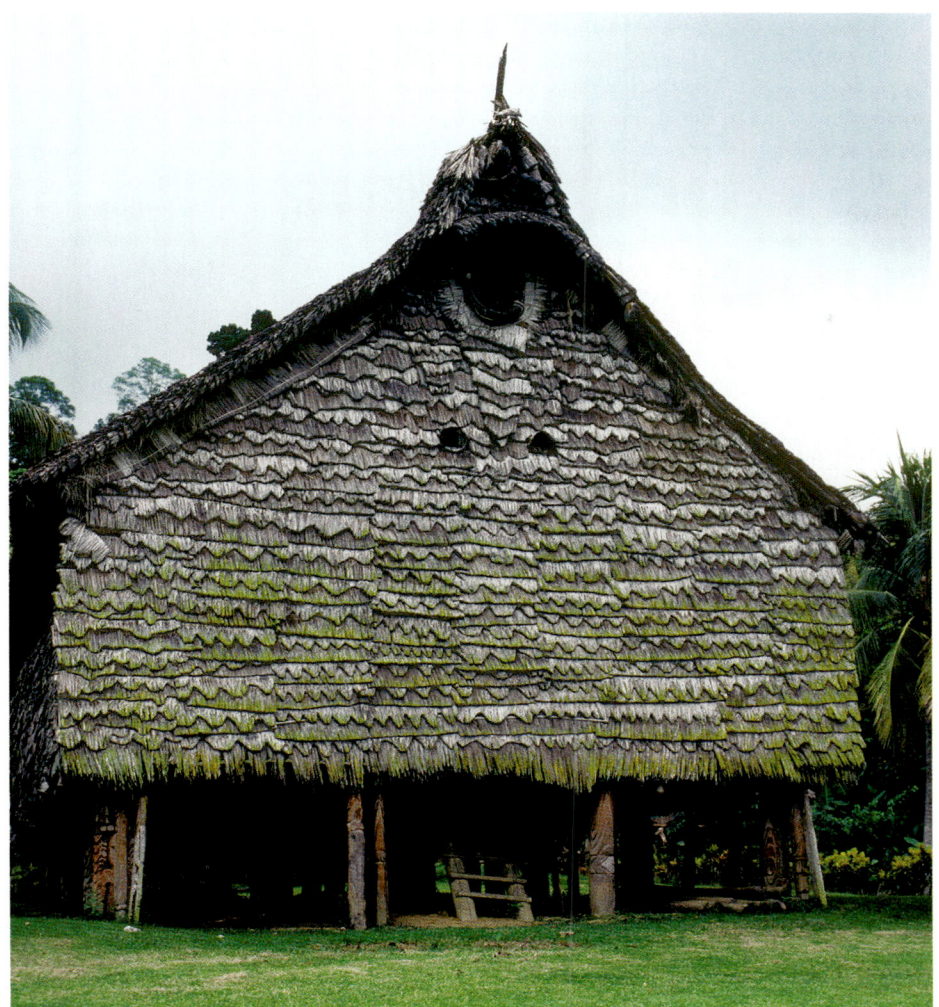

The men's house is the center of Iatmul life. Its distinctive saddle-shaped roof symbolizes the protective mantle of ancestors. The carved decoration includes female ancestors in the birthing position.

on both sides of the house. They topped each roof-support post with large faces representing mythical spirits of the clans. At the top of the two raised spires at each end, birds symbolizing the war spirit of the village men sit above carvings of headhunting victims (on occasion, male ancestors).

The subdivision of the house's interior into parts for each clan reflects the social demographic of the village. Many meetinghouses have three parts—a front, middle, and end—representing the three major clans who built it. These parts have additional subclan divisions, which also have support posts carved with images of mythical male and female ancestors. Beneath the house, each clan keeps large carved slit-gongs to serve as both instruments of communication (for sending drum messages within and between villages) and the voices of ancestral spirits. On the second level of the house, above the horizontal crossbeam beneath the gable, the Iatmul place carved wooden figures symbolizing female clan ancestors, depicted in a birthing position. The Iatmul also keep various types of portable art in their ceremonial houses. These include ancestors' skulls covered with clay modeled to form a likeness of the deceased (a practice similar to one documented thousands of years before in Neolithic Jericho, FIG. 1-14), ceremonial chairs, sacred flutes, hooks for hanging sacred items and food, and several types of masks.

**IATMUL** The Iatmul live along the middle Sepik River in Papua New Guinea in communities based on kinship. Villages include extended families as well as different clans. The social center of every Iatmul village is a massive saddle-shaped men's ceremonial house (FIG. 36-4). In terms of both function and form, the men's house reveals the primacy of the kinship network. The meetinghouse reinforces kinship links by serving as the locale for initiation of local youths for advancement in rank, for men's discussions of community issues, and for ceremonies linked to the Iatmul's ancestors. Because only men can advance in Iatmul society, women and uninitiated boys cannot enter the men's house. In this manner, the Iatmul men control access to knowledge and therefore to power. Given its important political and cultural role, the men's house is appropriately monumental, physically dominating Iatmul villages and dwarfing family houses. Although men's houses are common in New Guinea, those of the Iatmul are the most lavishly decorated.

Traditionally, the house symbolizes the protective mantle of the ancestors and represents an enormous female ancestor. The facade is her face and the rest of the house her body. The Iatmul house and its female ancestral figures symbolize a reenacted death and rebirth when a clan member enters and exits the second story of the building. The gable ends of men's houses are usually covered and include a giant female gable mask, making the ancestral symbolism visible. The interior carvings, however, are normally hidden from view. The Iatmul placed carved images of clan ancestors on the central ridge-support posts and on the roof-support posts

**ELEMA** Central to the culture of the Elema people of Orokolo Bay in the Papuan Gulf was *Hevehe,* an elaborate cycle of ceremonial activities. Conceptualized as the mythical visitation of the water spirits (*ma-hevehe*), the Hevehe cycle involved the production and presentation of large, ornate masks (also called hevehe). The Elema last practiced Hevehe in the 1930s. Primarily organized by the male elders of the village, the cycle was a communal undertaking, and normally took from 10 to 20 years to complete. The duration of the Hevehe and the resources and human labor required reinforced cultural and economic relations and maintained the social structure in which elder male authority dominated.

Throughout the cycle, the Elema held ceremonies to initiate male youths into higher ranks. These ceremonies involved the exchange of wealth (such as pigs and shell ornaments), thereby also serving an economic purpose. The cycle culminated in the display of the finished hevehe masks. Each mask consisted of painted barkcloth (see "Barkcloth," page 1053) stretched around a cane-and-wood frame fitted over the wearer's body. A hevehe mask was normally 9 to 10 feet in height, although extensions often raised the height to as much as 25 feet. Because of its size and intricate design, a hevehe

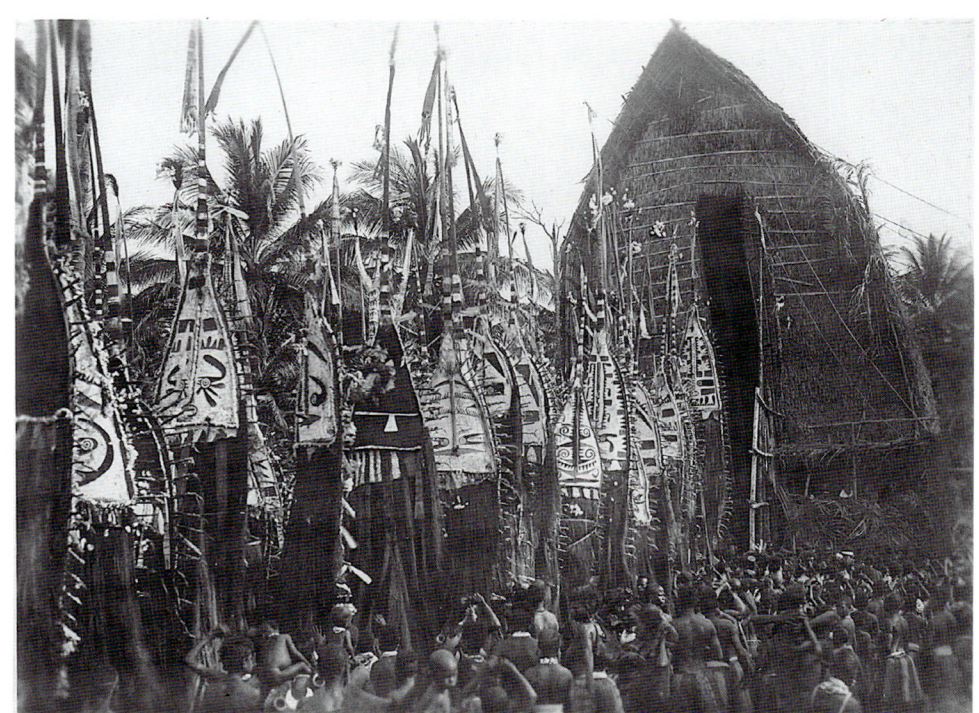

mask required great skill to construct, and only trained men would participate in mask making. Designs were specific to particular clans, and elder men passed them down to the next generation from memory. Each mask represented a female sea spirit, but the decoration of the mask often incorporated designs from local flora and fauna as well.

The final stage of the cycle (FIG. **36-5**) focused on the dramatic appearance of the masks from the *eravo* (men's house). After a procession, men wearing the hevehe mingled with relatives. Upon conclusion of related dancing (often lasting about a month), the Elema ritually killed and then dumped the masks in piles and burned them. This destruction allowed the sea spirits to return to their mythic domain and provided a pretext for commencing the cycle again.

**ABELAM** The art of the Abelam people illustrates how Oceanic art often includes references both to fundamental spiritual beliefs and to basic subsistence. The Abelam are agriculturists living in the hilly regions north of the Sepik River. Relatively isolated, the Abelam received only sporadic visits from foreigners until the 1930s, so little is known about early Abelam history. The principal crop is the yam. Because of the importance of yams to the survival of Abelam society, those who can grow the largest yams achieve power and prestige. Indeed, the Abelam developed a complex yam cult, which involves a series of rites and activities intended to promote the growth of the tubers. Special plantations focus on yam cultivation. Only initiated men who observe strict rules of conduct, including sexual abstinence, can work these fields. The Abelam believe ancestors aid in the growth of yams, and they hold ceremonies to honor these ancestors. Special long yams (distinct from the short yams cultivated for consumption) are on display during these festivities, and the largest (9 to 10 feet long) bear the names of important ancestors. Yam masks (FIG. **36-6**) with cane or wood frames, usually painted red, white, yellow, and black, are an integral part of the ceremonies. The most elaborate masks also incorporate sculpted faces, cassowary feathers, and shell ornaments. They covered the "heads" of the long yams. Humans never wear the yam masks, but the Abelam use the same designs to decorate their bodies for dances, revealing how closely they identify with their principal food source.

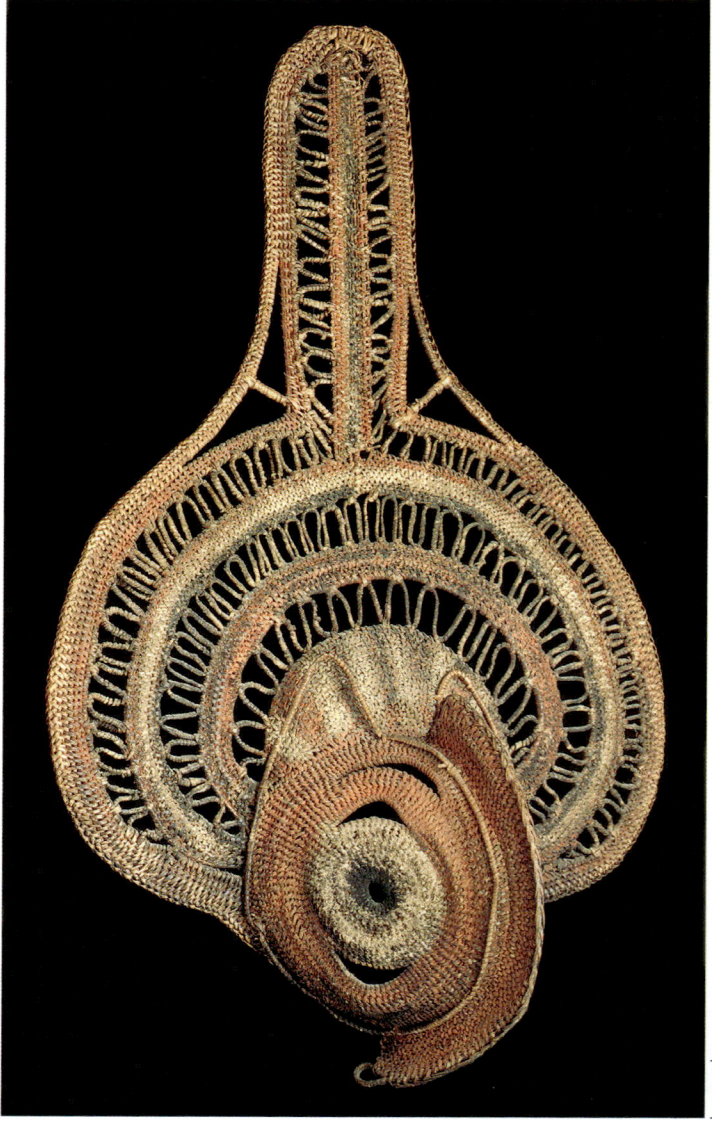

**36-6** Abelam yam mask, from Maprik district, Papua New Guinea, Melanesia, early to mid-20th century. Painted cane, 1′ 6$\frac{9}{10}$″ high. Musée Barbier-Mueller, Geneva.

The Abelam believe their ancestors aid in the growth of their principal crop, the yam. Painted cane yam masks are an important part of the elaborate ceremonies honoring these ancestors.

1 in.

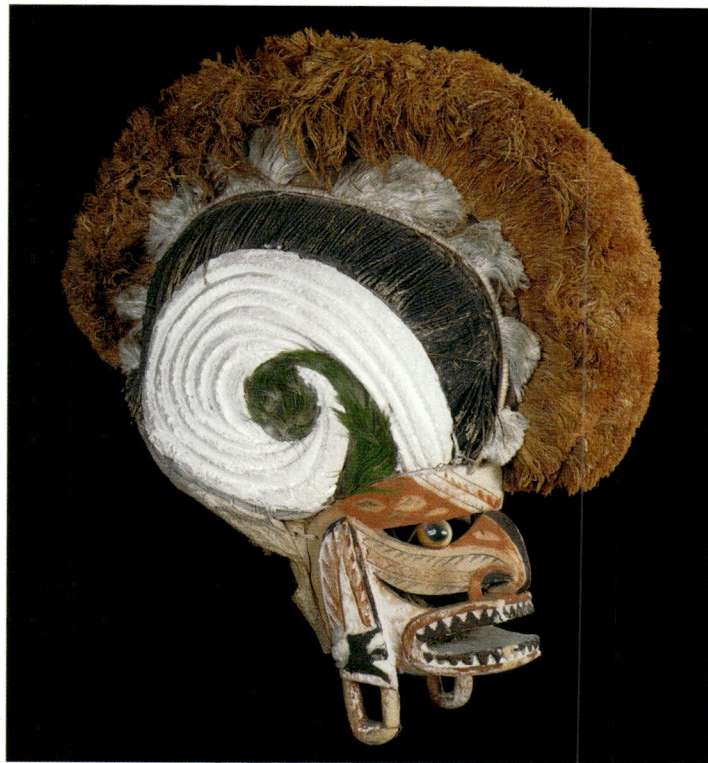

1 in.

**36-7** Tatanua mask, from New Ireland, Papua New Guinea, Melanesia, 19th to 20th centuries. Wood, fiber, shell, lime, and feathers, 1′ 5½″ high. Otago Museum, Dunedin.

In New Ireland, malanggan rites facilitate the transition of the soul from this world to the land of the dead. Dancers wearing tatanua masks representing the deceased play a key role in these ceremonies.

rechanneling of energy from the deceased into the community of the living. In addition to the religious function of malanggan, the extended ceremonies also promote social solidarity and stimulate the economy (as a result of the resources necessary to mount impressive festivities). To educate the younger generation about these practices, malanggan also includes the initiation of young men.

Among the many malanggan carvings produced—masks, figures, poles, friezes, and ornaments—are tatanua masks (FIG. **36-7**). *Tatanua* represent the spirits of specific deceased people. The materials used to make New Ireland tatanua masks are primarily soft wood, vegetable fiber, and rattan. The crested hair, made of fiber, duplicates a hairstyle formerly common among the men. For the eyes, the mask makers insert sea-snail shells. Traditionally, artists paint the masks black, white, yellow, and red—colors the people of New Ireland associate with warfare, magic spells, and violence. Although some masks are display pieces, dancers wear most of them. Rather than destroying their ritual masks after the conclusion of the ceremonies, as some other cultures do, the New Irelanders store them for future use.

## New Ireland and the Trobriand Islands

East of New Guinea but part of the modern nation of Papua New Guinea are New Ireland and the Trobriand Islands, two important Melanesian art centers.

**NEW IRELAND** Mortuary rites and memorial festivals are a central concern of the Austronesian-speaking peoples who live in the northern section of New Ireland. The term *malanggan* refers to both the festivals held in honor of the deceased and the carvings and objects produced for these festivals. Malanggan rites are part of an ancestor cult and are critical in facilitating the transition of the soul from the world of the living to the realm of the dead and the

**TROBRIAND ISLANDS** The various rituals of Oceanic cultures discussed thus far often involve exchanges intended to cement social relationships and reinforce or stimulate the economy. Further, these rituals usually have a spiritual dimension. All of these aspects apply to the practices of the Trobriand Islanders, who live off the coast of the southeastern corner of New Guinea. *Kula*—an exchange of white conus-shell arm ornaments for red chama-shell necklaces—is a characteristic practice of the Trobriand Islanders. Kula exchanges may have originated some 500 years ago. They can be complex, and there is great competition for valuable shell ornaments (determined by aesthetic appeal and exchange history).

Because of the isolation imposed by their island existence, the Trobriand Islanders had to undertake potentially dangerous voyages to participate in kula trading. Appropriately, the Trobrianders lavish a great deal of effort on decorating their large and elaborately carved canoes, which feature ornate prows and splashboards (FIG. **36-8**). To ensure a successful

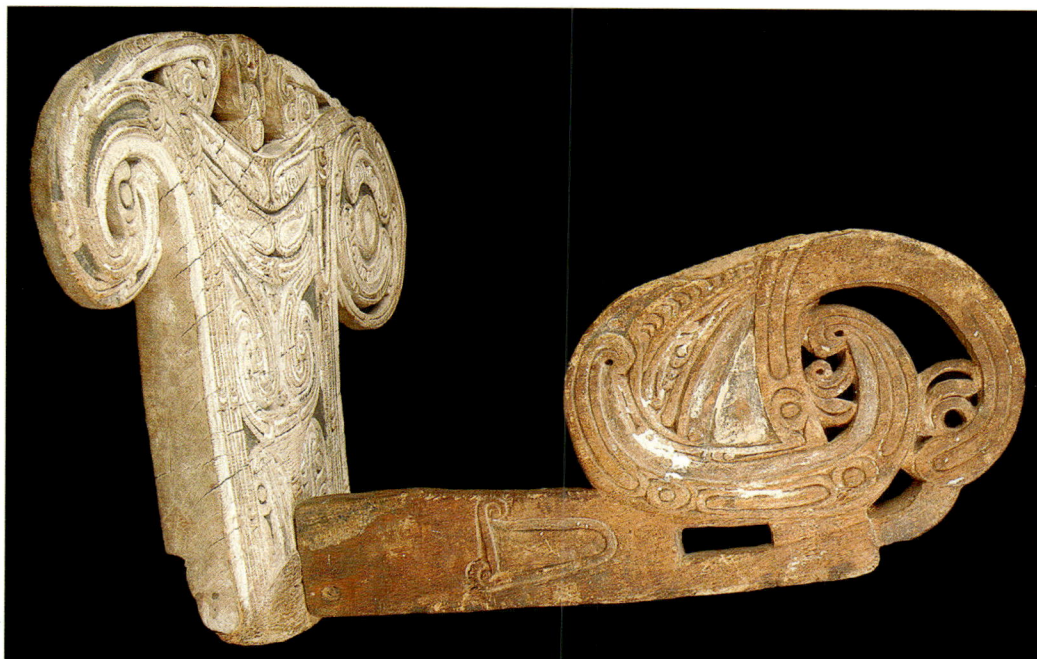

1 in.

**36-8** Canoe prow and splashboard, from Trobriand Islands, Papua New Guinea, Melanesia, 19th to 20th centuries. Wood and paint, 1′ 3½″ high, 1′ 11″ long. Musée du quai Branly, Paris.

To participate in kula exchanges, the Trobriand Islanders had to undertake dangerous sea voyages. They decorated their canoes with abstract human, bird, and serpent motifs referring to sea spirits.

kula expedition, the Trobrianders invoke spells when attaching these prows to the canoes. Human, bird, and serpent motifs—references to sea spirits, ancestors, and totemic animals—appear on the prows and splashboards. Because the sculptors use highly stylized motifs in intricate intertwined curvilinear designs, identification of the specific representations is difficult. In recent decades, the Trobrianders have adapted kula to modern circumstances, largely abandoning canoes for motorboats. The exchanges now facilitate business and political networking.

# MICRONESIA

Some 2,500 islands, most of them tiny, scattered over nearly three million square miles of ocean make up Micronesia, home to about 200,000 people today. The Austronesian-speaking cultures of Micronesia tend to be more socially stratified than those found in New Guinea and other Melanesian areas. Micronesian cultures frequently center on chieftainships with craft and ritual specializations, and their religions include named deities as well as honored ancestors. Life in virtually all Micronesian cultures focuses on seafaring activities—fishing, trading, and long-distance travel in large oceangoing vessels. For this reason, much of the artistic imagery of Micronesia relates to the sea.

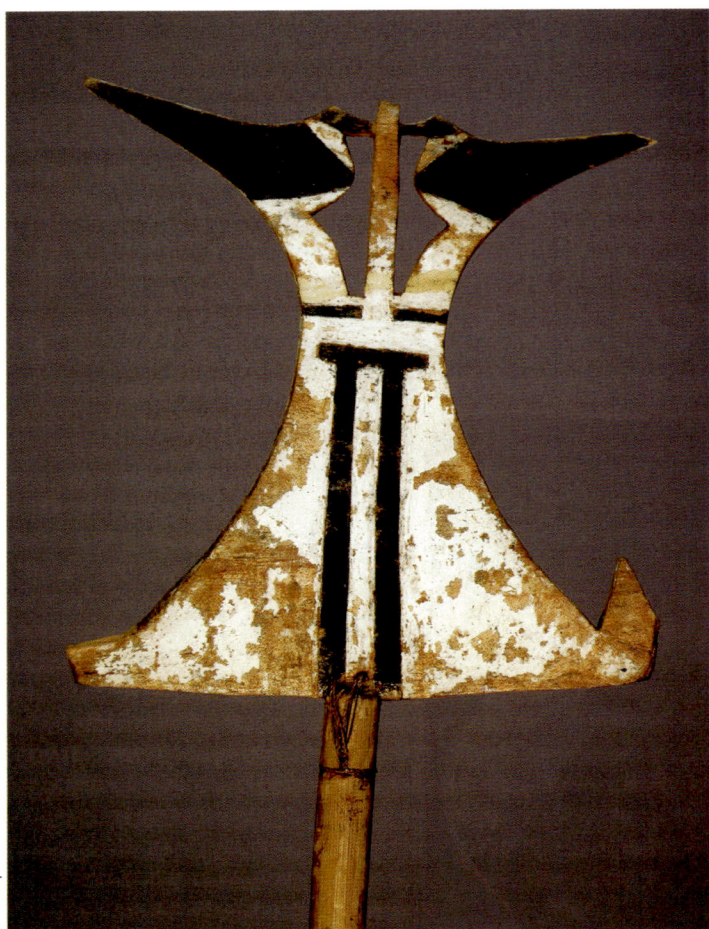

1 in.

**36-9** Canoe prow ornament, from Chuuk, Caroline Islands, Micronesia, late 19th century. Painted wood, birds 11″ × 10⅝″. British Museum, London.

Prow ornaments protected canoe paddlers and could be lowered to signal a peaceful voyage. This Micronesian example may represent facing sea swallows or perhaps a stylized human figure.

## Caroline Islands

The Caroline Islands are the largest island group in Micronesia. The arts of the Caroline Islands include the carving of canoes and the fashioning of charms and images of spirits to protect travelers at sea and for fishing and fertility magic.

**CHUUK** Given the importance of seafaring, it is not surprising many of the most highly skilled artists in the Caroline Islands were master canoe builders. The canoe ornament illustrated here (FIG. 36-9) comes from Chuuk. Carved from a single plank of wood and fastened to the prow of a large, paddled war canoe, the ornament served a decorative purpose but also provided protection on arduous or long voyages. That this and similar ornaments are not permanent parts of the canoes reflects their function. When approaching another vessel, the Micronesian seafarers lowered these ornaments as a signal their voyage was a peaceful one. The Chuuk prow seems at first to be an abstract design but may represent, at the top, two facing sea swallows—creatures capable of navigating long distances. Some scholars, however, think the entire piece represents a stylized human figure, with the "swallows" constituting the arms.

**BELAU** On Belau (formerly Palau) in the Caroline Islands, the islanders put much effort into creating and maintaining elaborately painted men's ceremonial clubhouses called *bai* (FIGS. 36-10 and 36-11). Although the bai was the domain of men, women figured prominently in the clubhouse's imagery, consistent with the important symbolic and social positions women held in Belau culture (see "Women's Roles in Oceania," page 1051). A common element surmounting the main bai entrance was a simple, symmetrical

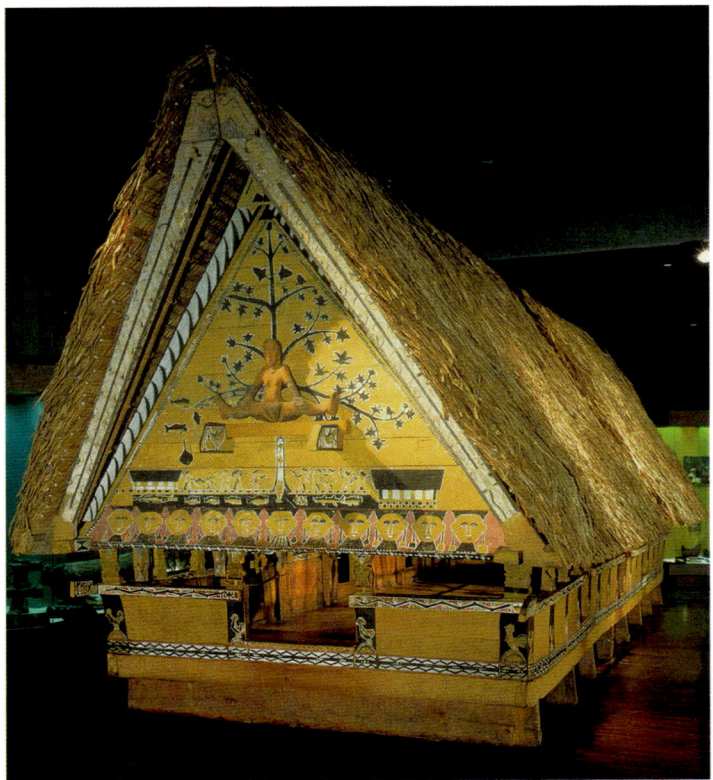

**36-10** Men's ceremonial house, from Belau (Palau), Micronesia, 20th century. Ethnologisches Museum, Staatliche Museen zu Berlin, Berlin.

The Belau men's clubhouses (bai) have extensive carved and painted decorations illustrating important events and myths related to the clan who built the bai. The central motif is a Dilukai (FIG. 36-11).

# Women's Roles in Oceania

Given the prominence of men's houses and the importance of male initiation in so many Oceanic societies, women might appear to be peripheral members of these cultures. Much of the extant material culture—ancestor masks, shields, clubs—seems to corroborate this. In reality, however, women play crucial roles in most Pacific cultures. In addition to their significant contributions through exchange and ritual activities to the maintenance and perpetuation of the social network upon which the stability of village life depends, women are important producers of art.

Historically, women's artistic production has been restricted mainly to forms such as barkcloth, weaving, and pottery. In some cultures in New Guinea, potters were primarily female. Throughout much of Polynesia, women produced barkcloth (see "Tongan Barkcloth," page 1053), which they often dyed and stenciled, and sometimes even perfumed. Women in the Trobriand Islands still make brilliantly dyed skirts of shredded banana fiber that not only are aesthetically beautiful but also serve as a form of wealth, presented symbolically during mortuary rituals.

In most Oceanic cultures, women usually do not use the same adzes and axes male sculptors employ, and they do not work in hard materials, such as wood, stone, bone, or ivory. Further, they do not produce images having religious or spiritual powers or that confer status on their users. Scholars investigating the role of the artist in Oceania have concluded that the reason for these restrictions is a perceived difference in innate power. Because women have the natural power to create and control life, male-dominated societies developed elaborate ritual practices to counteract this female power. By excluding women from participating in these rituals and denying them access to knowledge about specific practices, men derived a political authority that could be perpetuated. It is important to note, however, that even in rituals or activities restricted to men,

women often participate. For example, in the now-defunct Hevehe ceremonial cycle (FIG. 36-5) in Papua New Guinea, women made the fiber skirts for the hevehe masks but feigned ignorance about these sacred objects, because such knowledge was the exclusive privilege of initiated men.

Pacific cultures often acknowledged women's innate power in the depictions of women in Oceanic art. For example, the splayed Dilukai female sculpture (FIG. 36-11) that appears regularly on Palauan bai (men's houses; FIG. 36-10) celebrates women's procreative powers. Often flanked by figures of sexually aroused men, these female figures were surrounded by images of sun disks, trees, and birds. They faced east toward the rising sun and symbolized the sun's gifts to earth as well as human fertility. The Dilukai figure also confers protection upon visitors to the bai, another symbolic acknowledgment of female power. Similar concepts underlie the design of the Iatmul men's house (FIG. 36-4). Conceived as a giant female ancestor, the men's house incorporates women's natural power into the conceptualization of what is normally the most important architectural structure in an Iatmul village. In addition, the Iatmul associate entrance and departure from the men's house with death and rebirth, thereby reinforcing the primacy of fertility and the perception of the men's house as representing a woman's body.

One reason scholars have tended to overlook the active participation of women in all aspects of Oceanic life is that until recently the objects visitors to the Pacific collected were primarily those suggesting aggressive, warring societies. That the majority of these Western travelers were men and therefore had contact predominantly with men no doubt accounts for this pattern of collecting. Recent scholarship has done a great deal to rectify this misperception, thereby revealing the richness of social, artistic, and political activity in the Pacific.

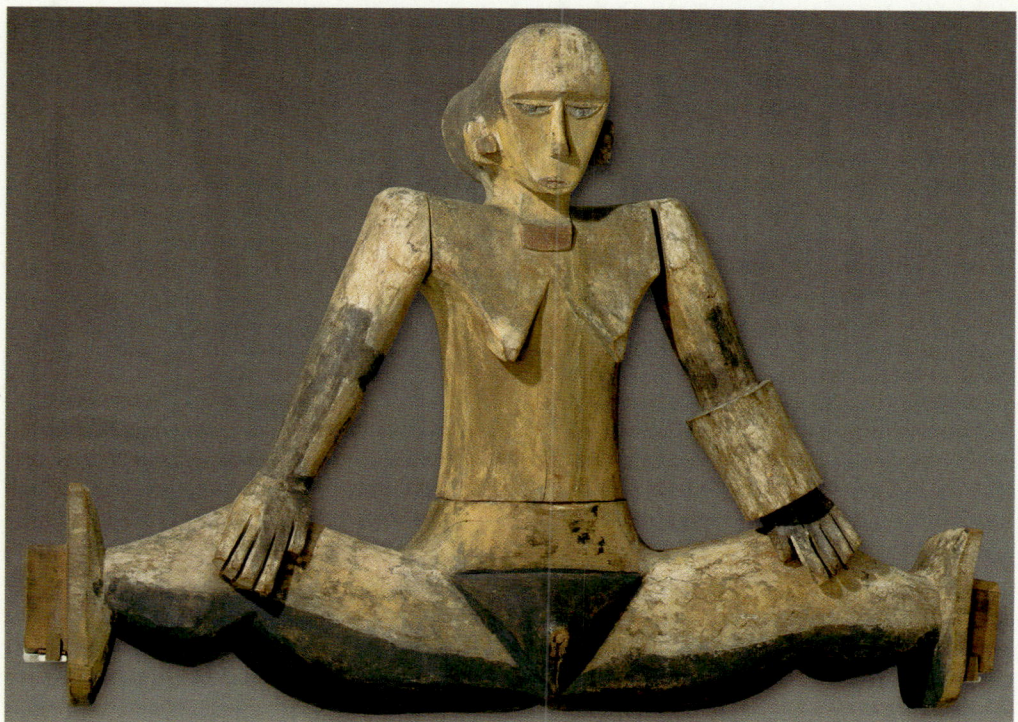

1 ft.

**36-11** Dilukai, from Belau (Palau), Micronesia, late 19th or early 20th century. Wood, paint, and kaolin, 2′ 1⅝″ high. Metropolitan Museum of Art, New York (Michael C. Rockefeller Collection).

Sculpted wooden figures of a splayed female, or Dilukai, commonly appear over the entrance to a Belau bai (FIG. 36-10). The figures served as symbols of fertility and protected the men's house.

wooden sculpture (on occasion, a painting) of a splayed female figure, known as *Dilukai* (FIG. 36-11). She wears jewelry and an armband, emblems of wealth and power, and serves as a symbol of both protection and fertility.

Whereas the Iatmul make their ceremonial houses (FIG. 36-4) by tying, lashing, and weaving different-size posts, trees, saplings, and grasses, the Belau people make the main structure of the bai entirely of worked, fitted, joined, and pegged wooden elements, which enables them to assemble it easily. The Belau bai have steep overhanging roofs decorated with geometric patterns along the roof boards. Skilled artists carve the gable in low relief and paint it with narrative scenes, as well as various abstracted forms of the shell money used traditionally on Belau as currency. These decorated storyboards illustrate important historical events and myths related to the clan who built the bai. Similar carved and painted crossbeams are inside the house. The rooster images along the base of the facade symbolize the rising sun, while the multiple frontal human faces carved and painted above the entrance and on the vertical elements above the rooster images represent a deity called Blellek. He warns women to stay away from the ocean and the bai or he will molest them.

# POLYNESIA

Polynesia was one of the last areas in the world humans settled. Habitation in the western Polynesian islands did not begin until about the end of the first millennium BCE, and in the south not until the first millennium CE. The settlers brought complex sociopolitical and religious institutions with them. Whereas Melanesian societies are fairly egalitarian and advancement in rank is possible, Polynesian societies typically are highly stratified, with power determined by heredity. Indeed, rulers often trace their genealogies directly to the gods of creation. Most Polynesian societies possess elaborate political organizations headed by chiefs and ritual specialists. By the 1800s, some Polynesian cultures (Hawaii and the Society Islands, for example) had evolved into kingdoms. Because of this social hierarchy, historically most Polynesian art belonged to persons of noble or high religious background and served to reinforce their power and prestige. These objects, like their chieftain owners, often possessed *mana,* or spiritual power.

## Rapa Nui (Easter Island)

Some of the earliest datable artworks in Oceania are also the largest. This is especially true of the colossal sculptures of Rapa Nui.

**MOAI** The *moai* (FIG. **36-12**) of Rapa Nui are monumental sculptures as much as 50 feet tall and weighing up to 100 tons. They stand as silent sentinels on stone platforms (*ahu*) marking burial or sacred sites used for religious ceremonies. Most of the moai consist of huge, blocky figures with fairly planar facial features—large staring eyes, strong jaws, straight noses with carefully articulated nostrils, and elongated earlobes. A number of the moai have *pukao*—small red scoria (a local volcanic stone) cylinders that serve as a sort of topknot or hat—atop their heads. Although debate continues,

10 ft.

**36-12**  Row of moai on a stone platform, Rapa Nui (Easter Island), Polynesia, 10th to 12th centuries. Volcanic tuff and red scoria, tallest statues approximately 19′ high. ◼◀

The moai of Rapa Nui are monoliths as much as 50 feet tall. Most scholars believe they portray ancestral chiefs. They stand on platforms marking burials or sites for religious ceremonies.

## Tongan Barkcloth

Tongan barkcloth provides an instructive example of the labor-intensive process of tapa production. At the time of early contact between Europeans and Polynesians in the late 18th and early 19th centuries, ranking women in Tonga made decorated barkcloth (*ngatu*). Today, women's organizations called *kautaha* produce it. The kautaha may have the honorary patronage of ranking women. In Tonga, men plant the paper mulberry tree and harvest it in two to three years. They cut the trees into about 10-foot lengths and allow them to dry for several days. Then the women strip off the outer bark and soak the inner bark in water to prepare it for further processing. They place these soaked inner bark strips over a wooden anvil and repeatedly strike them with a wooden beater until they spread out and flatten. Folding and layering the strips while beating them, a felting process, results in a wider piece of ngatu than the original strips. Afterward, the beaten barkcloth dries and bleaches in the sun.

The next stage of ngatu production involves the placement of the thin, beaten sheets over semicircular boards. The women then fasten embroidered design tablets (*kupesi*—usually produced by men) of coconut-leaf midribs and string patterns to the boards. They transfer the patterns on the design tablets to the outer barkcloth by rubbing. Then the women fill in the lines and patterns by painting, covering the large white spaces with colored figures. The Tongans use brown, red, and black pigments derived from various types of bark, clay, fruits, and soot to create the colored patterns on ngatu. Sheets, rolls, and strips of ngatu play an important role in weddings, funerals, and ceremonial presentations for ranking persons.

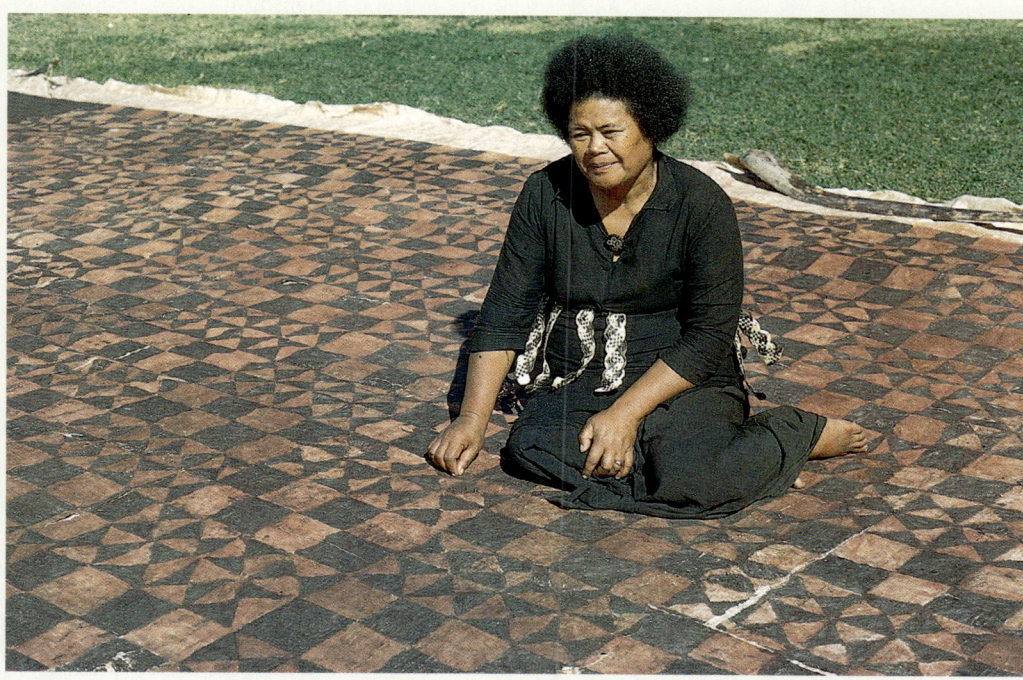

**36-13** MELE SITANI, ngatu with manulua designs, Tonga, Polynesia, 1967. Barkcloth.

In Tonga, the production of decorated barkcloth, or ngatu, involves dyeing, painting, stenciling, and perfuming. Mele Sitani made this one with a two-bird design for the coronation of Tupou IV.

many scholars believe lineage chiefs or their sons erected the moai and the sculptures depict ancestral chiefs. The moai, however, are not individual portraits but generic images the Easter Islanders believed had the ability to accommodate spirits or gods. The statues thus mediate between chiefs and gods, and between the natural and cosmic worlds.

Archaeological surveys have documented nearly 1,000 moai erected on some 250 ahu. Most of the stones are soft volcanic tuff and came from the same quarry at Rano Raraku. Some of the sculptures are red scoria, basalt, or trachyte. After quarrying, the Easter Islanders dragged the moai to the ahu sites, and then positioned them vertically. Given the extraordinary size of these *monoliths*, their production and placement serve as testaments to the achievements of this Polynesian culture. According to one scholar, it would have taken 30 men one year to carve a moai, 90 men two months to transport it from the quarry to the ahu site (often several miles away), and 90 men three months to position it vertically on the platform.

## Tonga

Tonga is the westernmost island group in Polynesia. One of its most distinctive products is barkcloth, which women have traditionally produced throughout Polynesia.

**BARKCLOTH** Artists produce barkcloth from the inner bark of the paper mulberry tree. The finished product goes by various names in Polynesia, but during the 19th century, when the production of barkcloth reached its zenith, *tapa* became the most widely used term. Although the primary use of tapa in Polynesia was for clothing and bedding, in Tonga, large sheets (FIG. **36-13**) were (and still are) produced for exchange (see "Tongan Bark-cloth," page 1053). Barkcloth can also have a spiritual dimension and can serve to confer sanctity upon the object wrapped in it. Appropriately, the Polynesians traditionally wrapped the bodies of high-ranking deceased chiefs in barkcloth.

The use and decoration of tapa have varied over the years. In the 19th century, tapa used for everyday clothing was normally unadorned, whereas tapa used for ceremonial or ritual purposes was dyed, painted, stenciled, and sometimes even perfumed. The designs applied to the tapa differed depending upon the particular island group producing it and the function of the cloth. The production process was complex and time-consuming. Indeed, some Oceanic cultures, such as those of Tahiti and Hawaii, constructed buildings specifically for the beating stage in the production of barkcloth. Tapa production reached its peak in the early 19th century, partly as a result of the interest expressed by Western whalers and missionaries. By the late 19th century, the use of tapa for cloth had been abandoned throughout much of eastern Polynesia, although its use in rituals (for example, as a wrap for corpses of deceased chiefs or as a marker of tabooed sites) continued. Even today, tapa exchanges are still an integral part of funerals and marriage ceremonies, and even the coronation of kings.

The decorated *ngatu* (barkcloth) shown in FIG. 36-13 clearly demonstrates the richness of pattern, subtlety of theme, and variation of geometric forms characteristic of Tongan royal barkcloths. MELE SITANI made this ngatu for the accession ceremony of King Tupou IV (r. 1965–2006) of Tonga. She kneels in the middle of the ngatu, which features triangular patterns known as *manulua*. This pattern results from the intersection of three or four pointed triangles. *Manulua* means "two birds," and the design gives the illusion of two birds flying together. The motif symbolizes chieftain status derived from both parents.

# Marquesas, Austral, and Cook Islands

Even though the Polynesians were skillful navigators, various island groups remained isolated from one another for centuries by the vast distances they would have had to cover in open outriggers. This geographical separation explains the development of distinct regional styles within a recognizable general Polynesian style.

**MARQUESAS ISLANDS** Although Marquesan chiefs trace their right to rule genealogically, the political system before European contact allowed for the acquisition of power by force. As a result, warfare was widespread through the late 19th century. Among the items produced by Marquesan artists were ornaments (FIG. 36-14) that often adorned the hair of warriors. The hollow, cylindrical bone or ivory ornaments (*ivi p'o*) functioned as protective amulets. Warriors wore them until they avenged the death of a kinsman. The ornaments are in the form of *tiki*—carvings of exalted, deified ancestor figures. The large, rounded eyes and wide mouths of the tiki are typically Marquesan, as is the use of a continuous line to outline both the nose, with its wide nostrils, and the oversized eyes.

Another important art form for Marquesan warriors during the 19th century was *tattoo*, which protected the individual, serv-

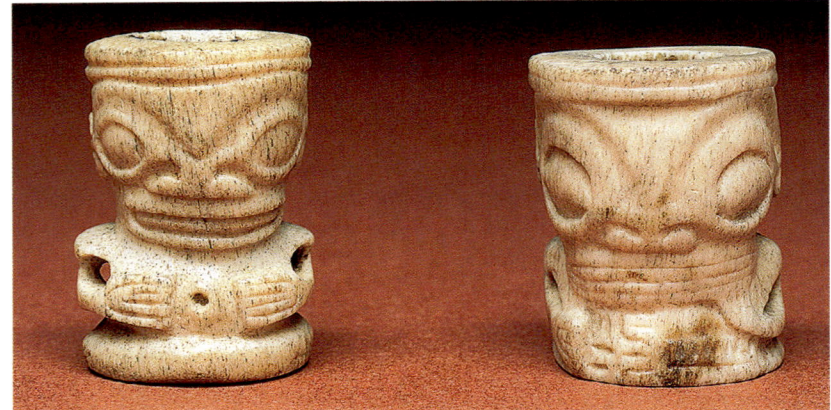

**36-14** Hair ornaments, from the Marquesas Islands, Polynesia, early to mid-19th century. Bone, $1\frac{1}{2}''$ high (*left*), $1\frac{2}{5}''$ high (*right*). University of Pennsylvania Museum of Archaeology and Anthropology, Philadelphia.

These hollow cylindrical bone ornaments representing deified ancestors adorned the hair of Marquesan warriors during the 19th century. The warriors wore them until they avenged the death of a kinsman.

ing in essence as a form of spiritual armor, as did the hair ornaments. Body decoration in general is among the most pervasive art forms found throughout Oceania. Polynesians developed the painful but prestigious art of tattoo more fully than many other Oceanic peoples (see "Tattoo in Polynesia," page 1055), although tattooing also occurred in various parts of Micronesia. In Polynesia, with its hierarchical social structure, nobles and warriors in particular accumulated various tattoo patterns over the years to enhance their status, mana, and personal beauty. Largely as a result of missionary pressure in the 19th century, tattooing virtually disappeared in many Oceanic societies, but some Pacific peoples have revived tattooing as an expression of cultural pride.

An 1813 engraving (FIG. 36-15) depicts a Marquesan warrior from Nukahiva Island covered with elaborate tattoo patterns. The warrior holds a large wooden war club over his right shoulder and carries a decorated water gourd in his left hand. The various tattoo patterns marking his entire body seem to subdivide his body parts into zones on both sides of a line down the center. Some tattoos accentuate joint areas, whereas others separate muscle masses into horizontal and vertical geometric shapes. The warrior also covered his face, hands, and feet with tattoos.

**RURUTU** Deity images with multiple figures attached to their bodies are characteristic of Rurutu in the Austral Islands and of Rarotonga (FIG. 36-15A) and Mangaia in the Cook Islands. These carvings probably represented clan and district ancestors, honored for their protective and procreative powers. Ultimately, the images refer to the creator deities the Polynesians revere for their central role in human fertility.

Rurutu is the northernmost of the Austral Islands in French Polynesia. In August 1821, following an edict of its leaders, the entire population converted to Christianity. As a symbol of their embrace of the new monotheistic religion, the inhabitants presented statues of their gods to the British missionaries stationed on a neighboring island.

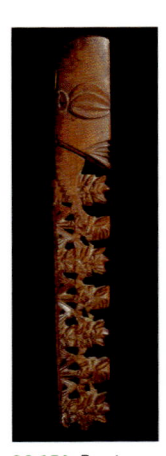

**36-15A** Rarotonga staff god, 19th or early 20th century.

# Tattoo in Polynesia

Throughout Oceanic cultures, as in Africa (see Chapter 37), body decoration was an important means of representing cultural and personal identity. In addition to clothing and ornaments, body adornment most often took the form of tattoo. Although tattooing was a common practice in Micronesia, it was more pervasive in Polynesia. Indeed, the English term *tattoo* is Polynesian in origin, related to the Tahitian, Samoan, and Tongan word *tatau* or *tatu*. In New Zealand, the markings are called *moko*. Within Polynesian cultures, tattoo reached its zenith in the highly stratified societies of New Zealand, the Marquesas Islands, Tahiti, Tonga, Samoa, and Hawaii. Both sexes displayed tattoos. In general, men had more tattoos than women, and the location of tattoos on the body differed. For instance, in New Zealand, the face and buttocks were the primary areas of male tattoo, whereas tattoos appeared on the lips and chin of women.

Historically, tattooing served a variety of functions in Polynesia beyond personal beautification. It indicated status, because the quantity and quality of tattoos often reflected rank. In the Marquesas Islands, for example, tattoos completely covered the bodies of men of high status (FIG. 36-15). Certain patterns could be applied only to ranking individuals, but commoners also had tattoos, generally on a less extensive scale than elite individuals. For identification purposes, slaves had tattoos on their foreheads in Hawaii and on their backs in New Zealand. According to some accounts, victors placed tattoos on defeated warriors. In Polynesia, tattoos often identified clan or familial connections. Tattoos could also serve a protective function by in essence wrapping the body in a spiritual armor. On occasion, tattoos marked significant events. In Hawaii, for example, a tattooed tongue was a sign of grief. The pain the tattooed person endured was a sign of respect for the deceased.

Priests who were specially trained in the art form usually applied the tattoos. Rituals, chants, or ceremonies often accompanied the procedure, which took place in a special structure. Tattooing involves the introduction of black, carbon-based pigment under the skin with the use of a bird-bone tattooing comb or chisel and a mallet. In New Zealand, a distinctive technique emerged for tattooing the face. In a manner similar to Maori woodcarving, a serrated chisel created a groove in the skin to receive pigment, thereby producing a colored line.

Polynesian tattoo designs were predominantly geometric, and affinities with other forms of Polynesian art are evident. For example, the curvilinear patterns found on decorated wall panels (*poupou*) in Maori meetinghouses (FIGS. 36-1 and 36-19A) resemble and make reference to the patterns that predominate in Maori facial moko. Depending on their specific purpose, many tattoos could be "read" or deciphered. For facial tattoos, the Maori generally divided the face into four major, symmetrical zones: the left and right forehead down to the eyes, the left lower face, and the

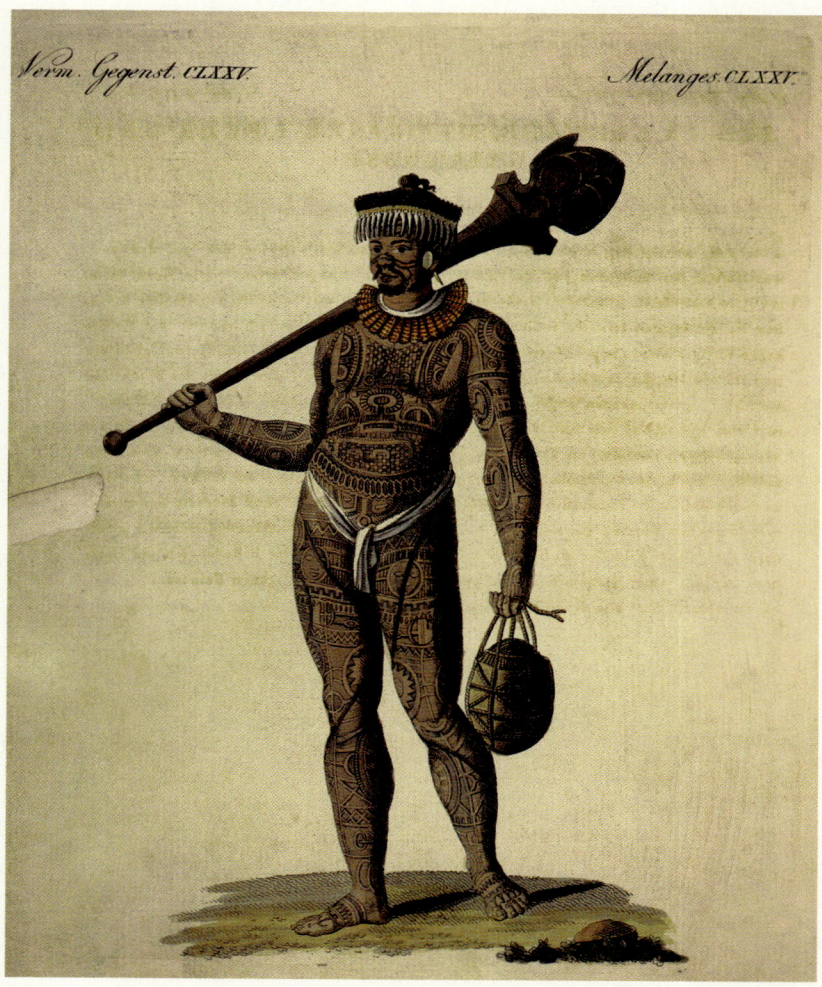

36-15 Tattooed warrior with war club, Nukahiva, Marquesas Islands, Polynesia, early 19th century. Color engraving in Carl Bertuch, *Bilderbuch für Kinder* (Weimar, 1813).

In Polynesia, with its hierarchical social structure, noblemen and warriors accumulated tattoo patterns to enhance their status and beauty. Tattoos wrapped a warrior's body in spiritual armor.

right lower face. The right-hand side conveyed information on the father's rank, tribal affiliations, and social position, whereas the left-hand side provided matrilineal information. Smaller secondary facial zones provided information about the tattooed individual's profession and position in society. Te Pehi Kupe (FIG. I-19) was the chief of the Ngati Toa tribe in the early 19th century. The upward and downward *koru* (unrolled spirals) in the middle of his forehead connote his descent from two paramount tribes. The small design in the center of his forehead documents the extent of his domain—north, south, east, and west. The five double koru in front of his left ear indicate the supreme chief (the highest rank in Maori society) was part of his matrilineal line. The designs on his lower jaw and the anchor-shaped koru nearby reveal Te Pehi Kupe was not only a master carver but descended from master carvers as well.

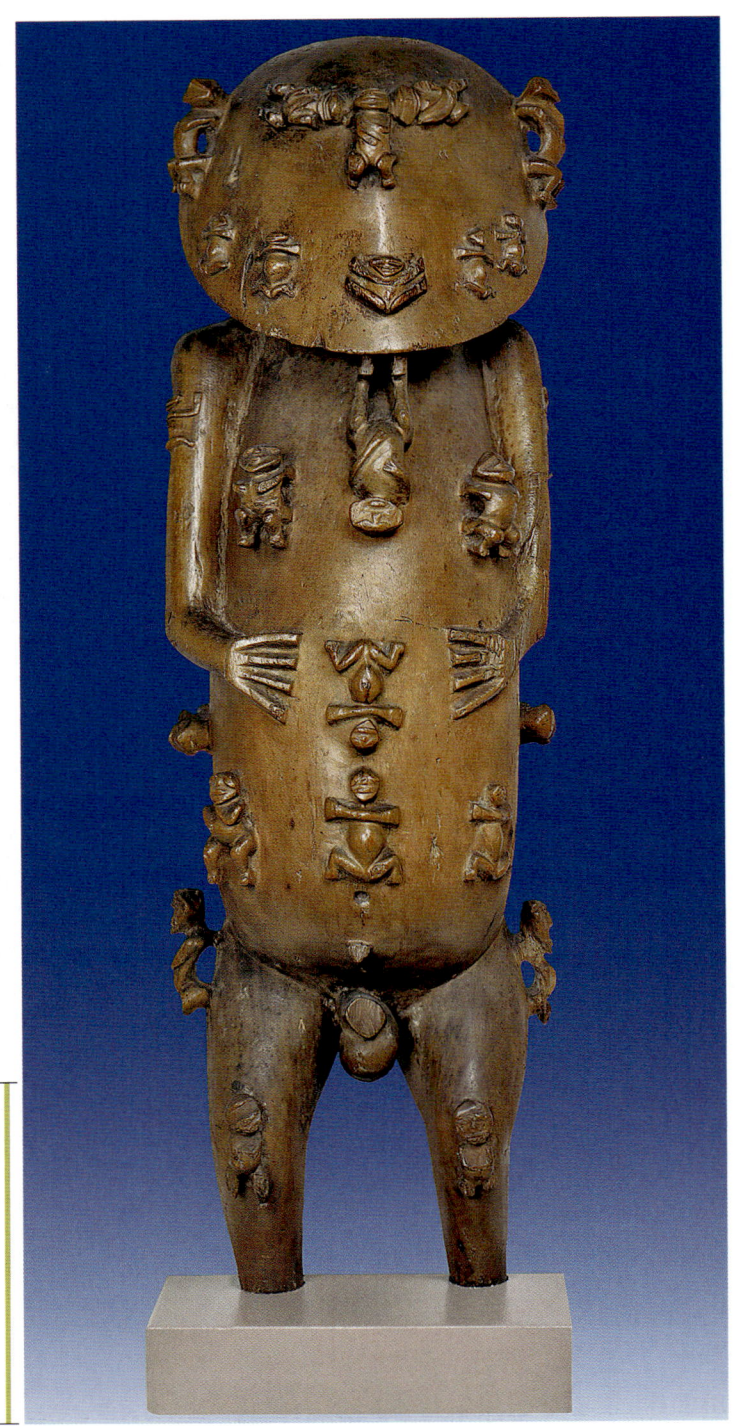

**36-16** A'a, from Rurutu, Austral Islands, Polynesia, late 18th or early 19th century. Wood, 3' 8" high. British Museum, London.

A'a is the chief Rurutu ancestor god. Covering his body—and forming the features of his head—are relief figures of his progeny. A large cavity at the back of the statue held 24 more figures.

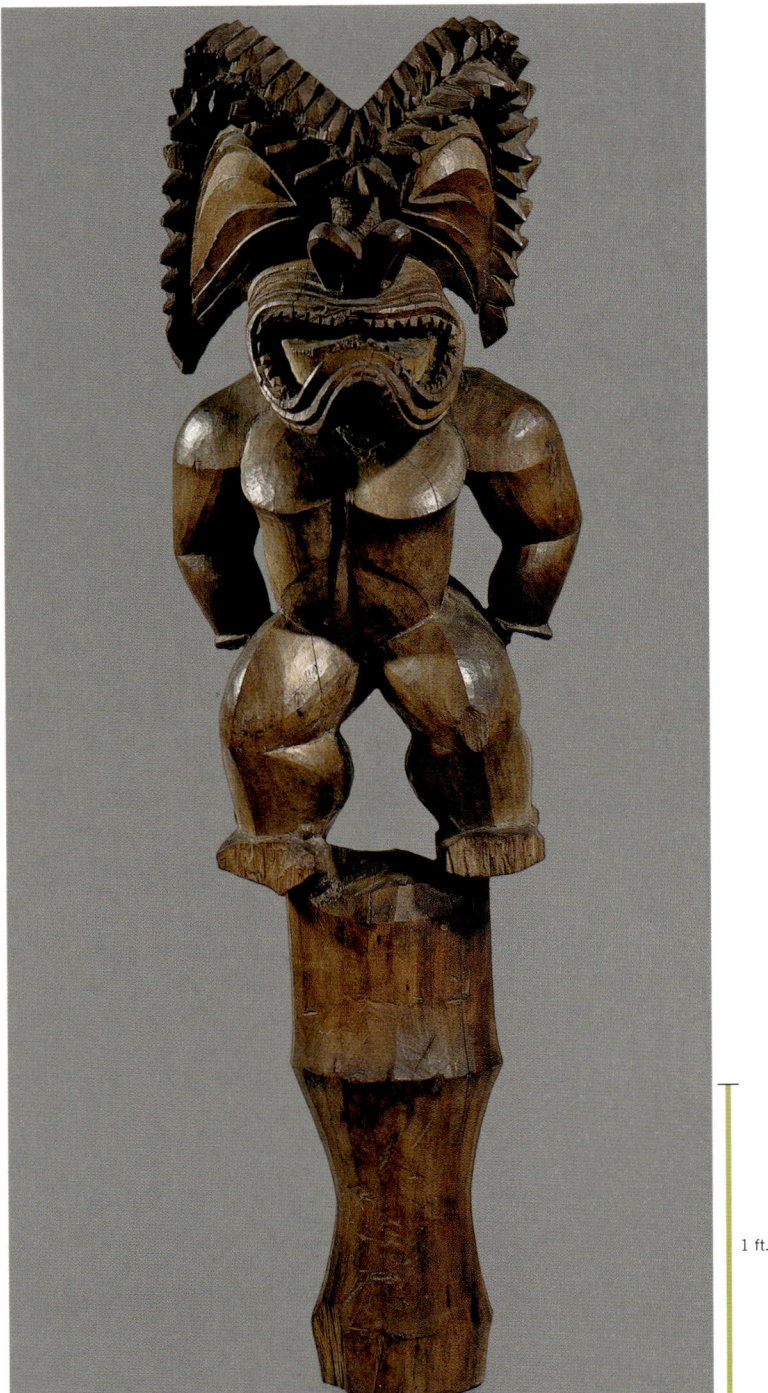

**36-17** Kuka'ilimoku, from Hawaii, Polynesia, late 18th or early 19th century. Wood, 4' 3¼" high. British Museum, London.

This wooden statue of the Hawaiian war god comes from a temple. His muscular body is flexed to attack, and his wide mouth with bared teeth set in a large head conveys aggression and defiance.

The wooden statue illustrated here (FIG. **36-16**), representing the god A'a, was one of those gifts to the London Missionary Society. A'a was the original inhabitant of Rurutu, the ancestor of all its people. He was deified after his death. Distributed over the front and back of the god's body—and forming the eyes, nose, mouth, and ears of the disk-shaped head—are tiny relief figures of the gods and men A'a created. The sculptor depicted them in a variety of positions, including head downward. At the back of the figure is a large cavity that once contained 24 additional miniature figures. The god places his hands on his belly, a gesture that calls attention to the interior compartment holding his progeny.

## Hawaii

The Hawaiians developed the most highly stratified social structure in the Pacific. By 1795, the chief Kamehameha unified the major islands of the Hawaiian archipelago and ascended to the pinnacle

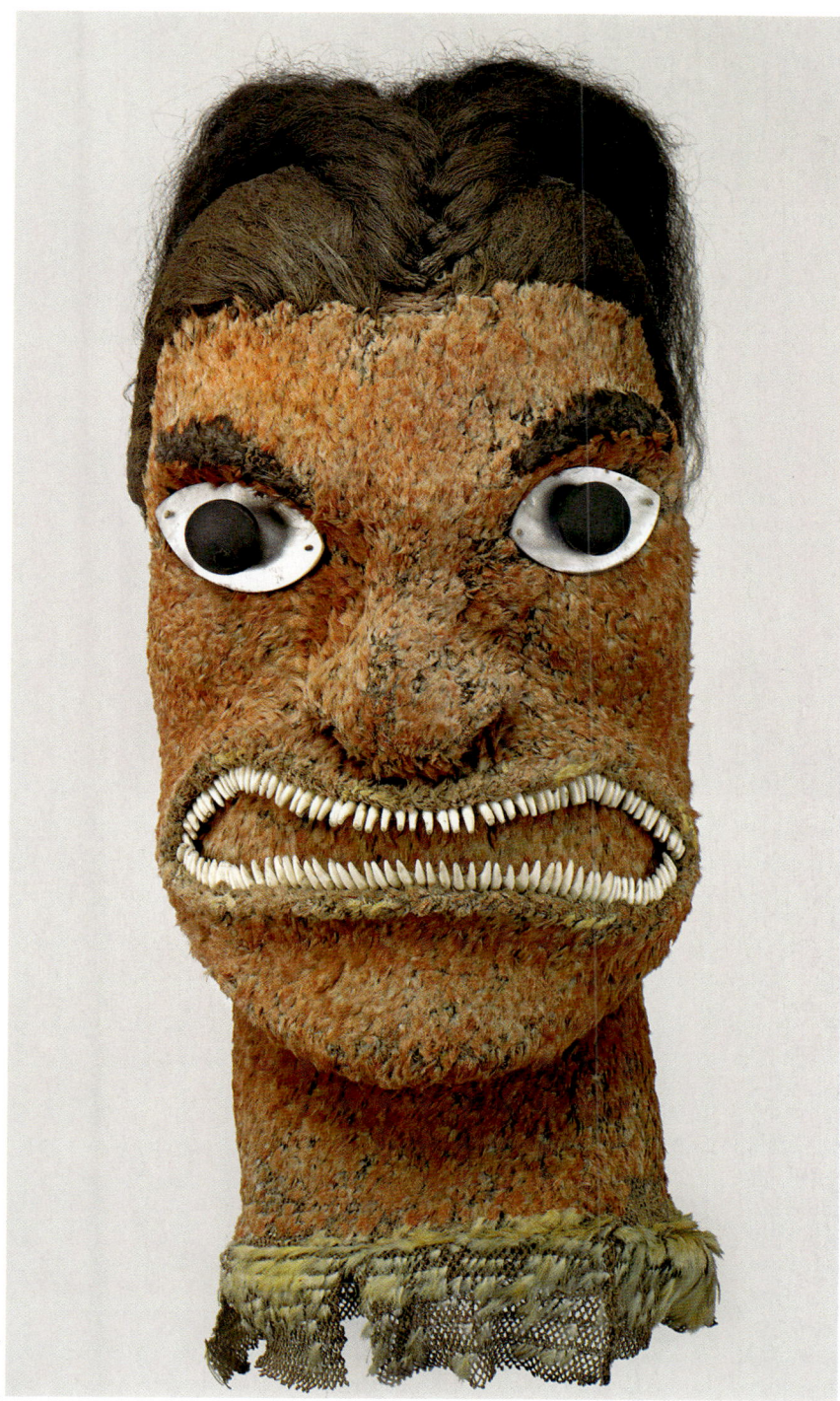

Feather heads of the Hawaiian gods with grimacing mouths, such as this one of Lono with human hair, pearl-shell eyes, and dog's teeth, were mounted on poles and carried in processions and into battle.

1 in.

was endemic—hence the god's importance. Indeed, Kuka'ilimoku served as Kamehameha's special tutelary deity, and the Kuka'ilimoku sculpture illustrated here (FIG. **36-17**) stood in a *heiau* (temple) on the island of Hawaii (Big Island), where Kamehameha I originally ruled before expanding his authority to the entire Hawaiian chain. This late-18th- or early-19th-century Hawaiian wooden temple image, which is more than four feet tall, confronts its audience with a ferocious expression. The war god's head comprises nearly a third of his entire body. His enlarged, angled eyes and wide-open figure-eight-shaped mouth, with its rows of teeth, convey aggression and defiance. His muscular body appears to stand slightly flexed, as if ready to attack. The artist realized this Hawaiian war god's overall athleticism through the full-volumed, faceted treatment of his arms, legs, and the pectoral area of the chest. In addition to sculptures of deities such as this, Hawaiians placed smaller versions of lesser deities and ancestral images in the heiau. Differing styles surface in the various islands of the Hawaiian chain, but the sculptured figures share a tendency toward athleticism and expressive defiance.

**LONO** Hawaiian artists also fashioned images of their gods from rare bird feathers and other natural materials placed over a wickerwork armature. The head illustrated here (FIG. **36-18**), which incorporates pearl shells for eyes as well as human hair and dog's teeth, is one of five heads in the British Museum that Captain James Cook (1728–1779) took back to England after his third voyage to the South Pacific from 1776 to 1779. The Hawaiian feather heads were sacred objects and costly to produce because they incorporated feathers from thousands of birds. The Hawaiians believed their gods had feathers covering their flesh. Feathers therefore connoted prestige, and the feather heads were also thought to be faithful reproductions of the deities' appearance. The Hawaiians mounted the gods' heads on poles, displayed them in religious processions, and carried them as standards into battle. When not in use, they were on exhibit in temples under the care of religious officials.

Although very different in material and overall character, the feather heads of the gods share many iconographical and stylistic traits with Hawaiian full-length wooden statues (FIG. 36-17) of gods, especially the larger-than-life grimacing mouths. Scholars believe the heads with large central crests of feathers represent the war god Kuka'ilimoku. The head in the British Museum instead has a crown of parted human hair and probably depicts Lono, the god of agriculture, fertility, and peace.

of power as King Kamehameha I (r. 1810–1819). The kingdom he established did not endure, however, and Hawaii soon came under American control. The United States annexed Hawaii as a territory in 1898 and eventually conferred statehood on the island group in 1959.

**KUKA'ILIMOKU** As elsewhere in Oceania, the gods were a pervasive presence in Hawaiian society and were part of every person's life, regardless of status. Chiefs in particular invoked them regularly and publicized their genealogical links to the gods to reinforce their right to rule. One of the more prominent Hawaiian deities was Kuka'ilimoku, the war god. As chiefs in the prekingdom years struggled to maintain and expand their control, warfare

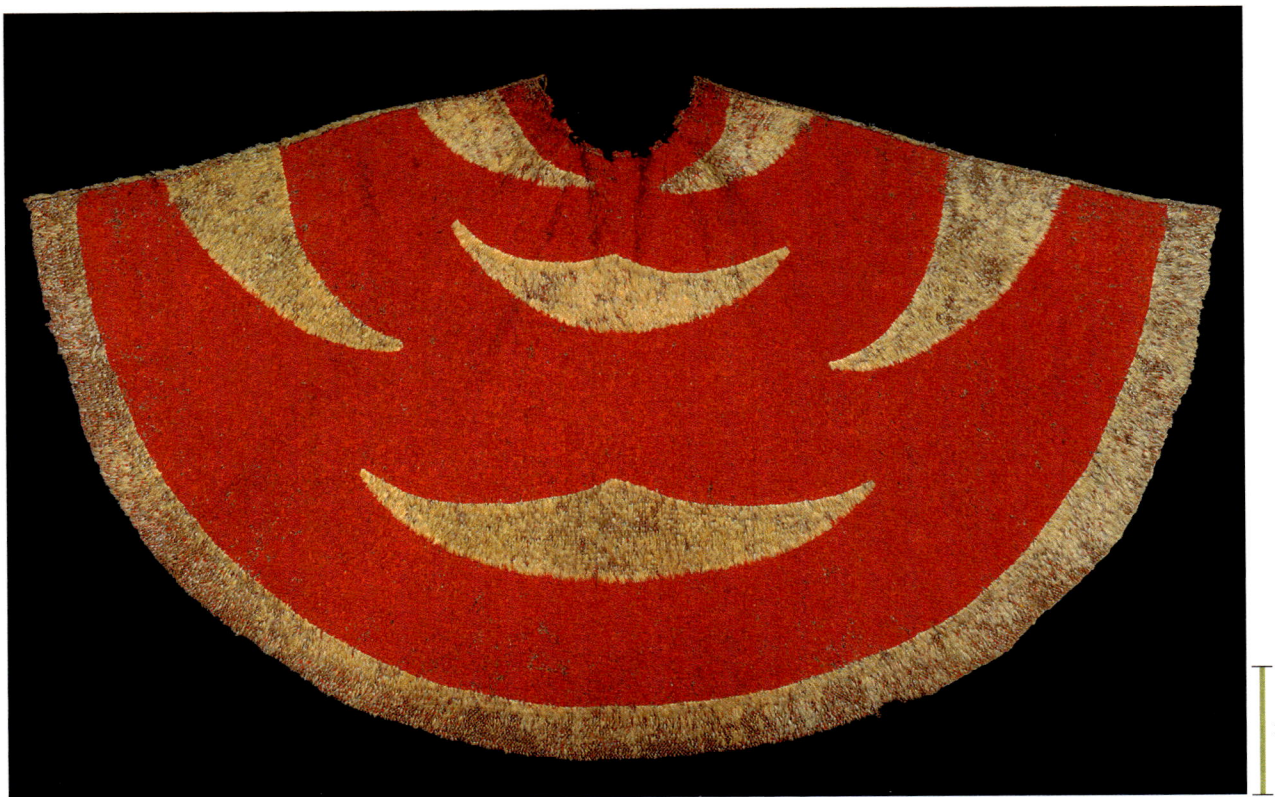

**36-19** Feather cloak, from Hawaii, Polynesia, ca. 1824–1843. Feathers and fiber netting, 4' 8⅓" × 8'. Bishop Pauahi Museum, Honolulu.

Costly Hawaiian feather cloaks ('ahu 'ula) such as this one, which belonged to King Kamehameha III, provided the protection of the gods. Each cloak required the feathers of thousands of birds.

**FEATHER CLOAKS** Because perpetuation of the social structure was crucial to social stability, chiefs' regalia, which visualized and reinforced the hierarchy of Hawaiian society, were a prominent part of artistic production. For example, elegant feather cloaks ('ahu 'ula) such as the early-19th-century example shown here (FIG. **36-19**) belonged to men of high rank. Every aspect of the 'ahu 'ula reflected the status of its wearer. The materials were exceedingly precious, particularly the red and yellow feathers from the 'i 'iwi, 'apapane, 'o 'o, and mamo birds. Some of these birds yield only six or seven suitable feathers, and because a full-length cloak could require up to 500,000 feathers, the resources and labor required to produce a cloak were extraordinary. The cloak also linked its owner to the gods. The Polynesians associated the plaited fiber base for the feathers with deities. Not only did these cloaks confer the protection of the gods on their wearers, but their dense fiber base and feather matting also provided physical protection. The artists who fashioned the cloaks chanted as they worked, believing the power of the sacred chants permeated the fabric lining. The cloak in FIG. 36-19 originally belonged to King Kamehameha III (r. 1824–1854), who gave it to Commodore Lawrence Kearny of the U.S. frigate *Constellation* in 1843 in gratitude for Kearny's assistance during a temporary occupation of Hawaii.

## New Zealand

The Maori of Aotearoa (New Zealand) share many cultural practices with other Polynesian societies. Ancestors and lineage traditionally played an important role, as is evident in the form and decoration of Maori meetinghouses, such as those at Poverty Bay (FIG. 36-1) and at Whakatane (WEPIHA APANUI, lead sculptor; FIG. **36-19A**) and in the design of Maori facial moko (see "Tattoo in Polynesia," page 1055, and FIG. I-19). But as in many other Oceanic cultures, in New Zealand, largely as a result of colonial and missionary intervention in the 18th through 20th centuries, traditional practices were gradually abandoned, and production of many of the art forms illustrated in this chapter ceased. In recent years, however, a new confident cultural awareness has led many Pacific artists to reassert their inherited values with pride and to express them in a resurgence of traditional arts, such as weaving, painting, tattooing, and carving. Today's thriving tourist trade has also contributed to a resurgence of traditional art production.

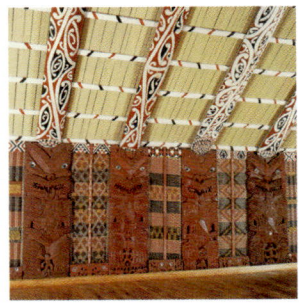

36-19A Mataatua meetinghouse, Maori, 1871–1875.

**CLIFF WHITING** In New Zealand, CLIFF WHITING (TE WHANAU-A-APANUI, b. 1936) and others have carried on the historical Maori woodcarving craft. Whiting has achieved renown for his stunning "carved murals" (FIG. 31-11). He and other artists throughout the Pacific islands have championed not only the renewal of native cultural life and its continuity in art but also the education of the young in the values that made the Pacific cultures great. The preservation of native identity will depend on the success of the next generation in making the traditional Oceanic cultures once again their own.

# OCEANIA BEFORE 1980

## AUSTRALIA AND MELANESIA

▌ The westernmost Oceanic islands have been populated for at least 40,000 years, but most of the preserved art dates to the last several centuries.

▌ The Aboriginal art of Australia focuses on ancestral spirits called Dreamings, whom artists represented in an X-ray style showing the internal organs.

▌ The Asmat of New Guinea avenged a relative's death by headhunting. Before embarking on a raid, they erected bisj poles with carved and painted figures of ancestors and animals.

▌ The center of every Iatmul village was a saddle-shaped ceremonial men's house representing a woman. Images of clan ancestors decorated the interior.

▌ Masks figured prominently in many Melanesian cultures. The Elema celebrated water spirits in the festive cycle called Hevehe, which involved ornate masks up to 25 feet tall. The Abelam fashioned yam masks for rituals revolving around their principal crop. In New Ireland, dancers wore tatanua masks representing the spirits of the deceased.

▌ Seafaring was also a major theme of much Melanesian art. The Trobriand Islanders decorated their canoes with elaborately carved prows and splashboards.

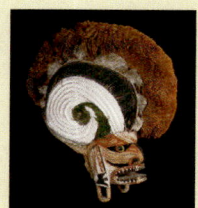

Asmat bisj poles, Irian Jaya, early to mid-20th century

Tatanua mask, Papua New Guinea, 19th to 20th century

## MICRONESIA

▌ The major themes of Melanesian art are also found in Micronesia. For example, in the Caroline Islands, many of the most skilled artists carved and painted wooden prow ornaments for their canoes.

▌ The Micronesian peoples also erected ceremonial men's houses. The bai of Belau are distinctive in having Dilukai figures in the gable of the eastern entrance. The Dilukai is a woman with splayed legs who faces the sun and serves as a symbol of procreation and as a guardian of the house.

Dilukai, Belau, late 19th or early 20th century

## POLYNESIA

▌ Polynesia was one of the last areas of the world humans settled, but the oldest monumental art of Oceania is the series of moai on Rapa Nui (Easter Island). These colossal monolithic sculptures, which stood in rows on stone platforms, probably represent ancestors.

▌ Barkcloth is an important art form in Polynesia even today. The decorated barkcloth, or ngatu, of Tonga was used to wrap the corpses of deceased chiefs and for other ritual purposes, including the coronation of kings.

▌ Body adornment in the form of tattooing was widespread in Polynesia, especially in the Marquesas Islands and New Zealand. Beyond personal beautification, tattoos served to distinguish rank and provided warriors with a kind of spiritual armor.

▌ Meetinghouses played an important role in Polynesian societies, as elsewhere in the Pacific islands. The meetinghouses of the Maori of Aotearoa (New Zealand) are notable for their elaborate ornamentation featuring carved relief panels depicting ancestors.

▌ Images of named gods are common in Polynesia. Wood sculptures from Rurutu represent the chief ancestor god A'a. The Hawaiians erected statues of the war god Kuka'ilimoku in their temples and fashioned images of deities from rare bird feathers. Hawaiian artists also produced elite regalia using feathers, for example, in cloaks worn exclusively by kings and other men of high rank.

Maori meetinghouse, New Zealand, 1842–1845

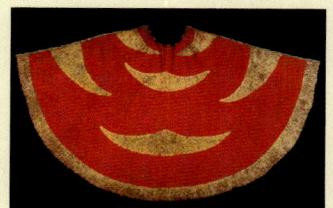

Feather cloak, Hawaii, ca. 1824–1843

The name for these screens
is *nduen fobara* ("foreheads
of the deceased"). The chief's
headdress is in the form of
a 19th-century European
sailing ship, a reference to the
deceased's trading business.

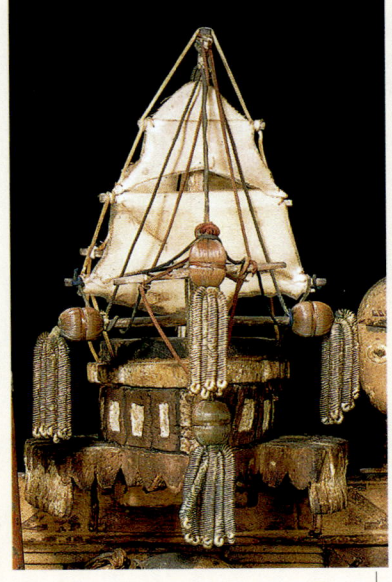

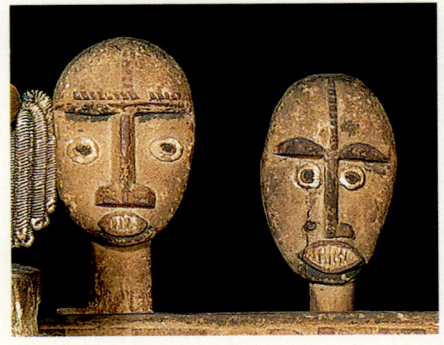

To either side of the chief are
his attendants and, at the top
of the shrine, the heads of his
slaves. Both attendants and
slaves are smaller in size than
the chief, as is appropriate for
their lower rank.

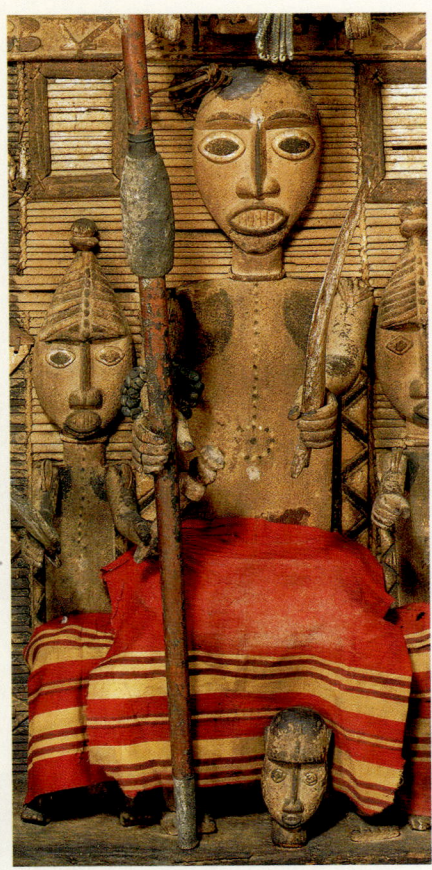

Kalabari Ijaw ancestral screens are
memorials to the chiefs of trading
companies called canoe houses. The
deceased, the central figure holding
a long staff and curved knife, is also
the largest.

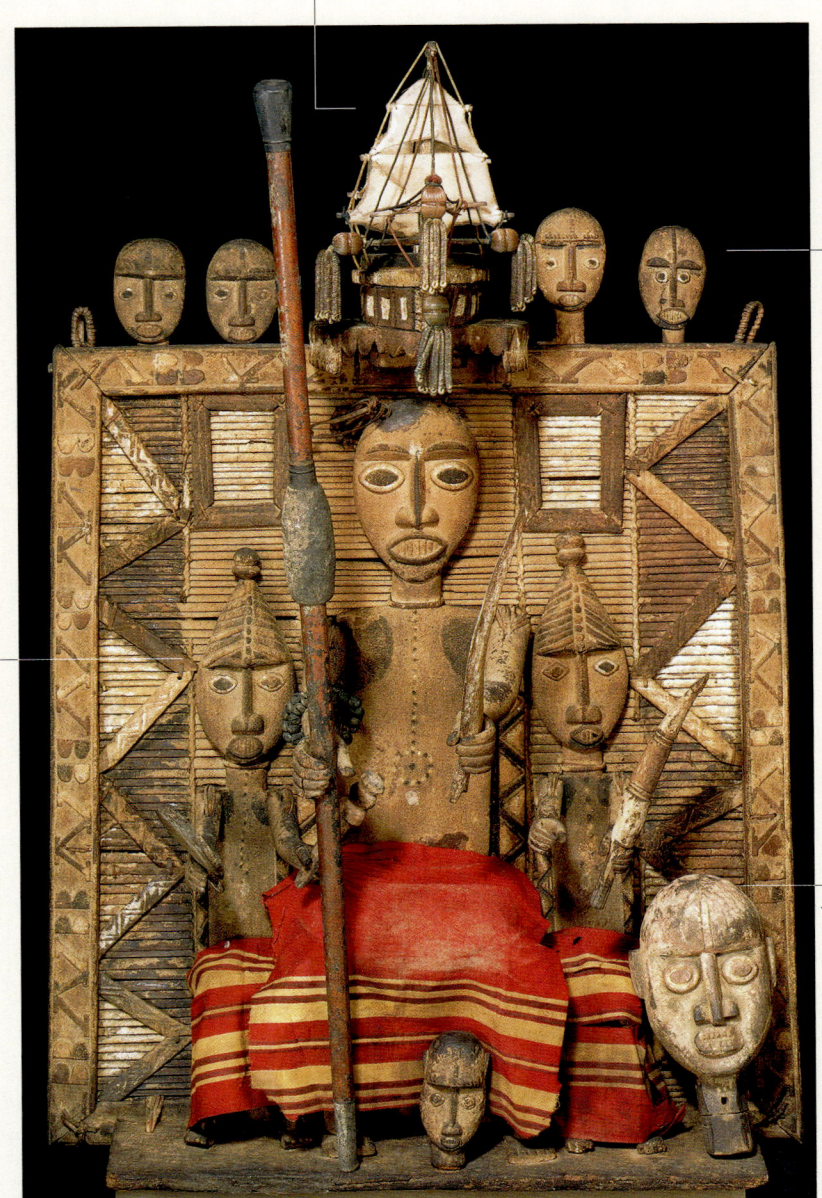

1 ft.

**37-1** Ancestral screen (nduen fobara), Kalabari Ijaw, Nigeria, late 19th century.
Wood, fiber, and cloth, 3′ 9½″ high. British Museum, London.

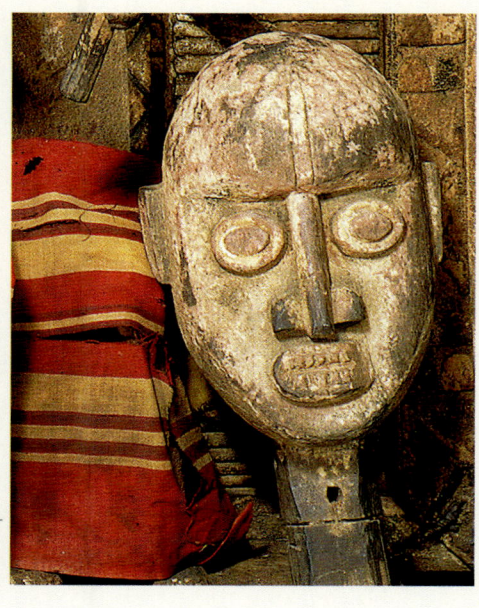

The chief is bare-chested with colorful drapery covering the lower part of his body. At his feet are the heads of conquered rivals, completing the exceptionally rich iconographical program.

# AFRICA, 1800 TO 1980

## KALABARI IJAW ANCESTRAL SCREENS

Throughout the continent, Africans venerate ancestors for the continuing aid they believe they provide the living, including help in maintaining the productivity of the earth for bountiful crop production and ensuring successful hunts. In some African societies, for example, the Fang and Kota, people place the bones of their ancestors in containers guarded by sculptured figures (FIGS. 37-4 and 37-5) in order to protect these treasured relics from theft or harm. In highly stratified societies headed by a monarch, for example, the Benin kingdom, the royal family maintains altars (FIG. 37-13) at which the current king offers animal sacrifices to honor his ancestors and enlist their help in protecting the living and assuring prosperity.

The Kalabari Ijaw peoples have hunted and fished in the eastern delta of the Niger River in present-day Nigeria for several centuries. As in so many other African cultures, Kalabari artists and patrons have lavished attention on memorials to ancestors. Their shrines, however, take a unique form because a cornerstone of the Kalabari economy has long been trade, and trading organizations known locally as "canoe houses" play a central role in Kalabari society. Kalabari ancestor shrines are elaborate screens of wood, fiber, textiles, and other materials. An especially elaborate example (FIG. **37-1**) is the almost four-foot-tall *nduen fobara* (foreheads of the deceased) honoring a former chief of a trading company. The chief's family usually commissioned these memorial screens on or about the one-year anniversary of his death. Displayed in the house in which the chief lived, the screen represents the deceased himself at the center, holding a long silver-tipped staff in his right hand and a curved knife in his left hand. His chest is bare and drapery covers the lower part of his body. His impressive headdress is in the form of a 19th-century European sailing ship, a reference to the chief's successful trading business. Flanking him are his attendants, smaller in size as is appropriate for their lower rank. The heads of his slaves are at the top of the screen and those of his conquered rivals are at the bottom. The hierarchical composition and the stylized rendition of human anatomy and facial features are common in African art, but the richness and complexity of this shrine are exceptional.

Unusual, too, is the way the sculptor created the shrine by assembling it from separately carved sections and then painting it. Most African sculptors fashioned their works from a single block of wood. The carpentry technique employed for the Kalabari screens may be the result of sustained contact with European traders and firsthand knowledge of European woodworking techniques.

# 19TH CENTURY

Africa (MAP **37-1**) was one of the first art-producing regions of the world (see Chapters 1 and 19), but its early history remains largely undocumented. In fact, a generation ago, scholars still often presented African art as if it had no history. For the period treated in this chapter, however, art historians are on firmer ground. Information gleaned from archaeology and field research in Africa (mainly interviews with local people) has provided much more detail on the use, function, and meaning of art objects produced during the past two centuries than for the period before 1800. As in earlier eras, the arts in Africa are integral to a great variety of human situations, and knowledge of these contexts is essential for understanding the artworks. In Africa, art is nearly always an active agent in the lives of its diverse peoples. This chapter presents a sample of characteristic works from different regions of the continent from the early 19th century to 1980. Chapter 31 treats African art of the past few decades in its worldwide context.

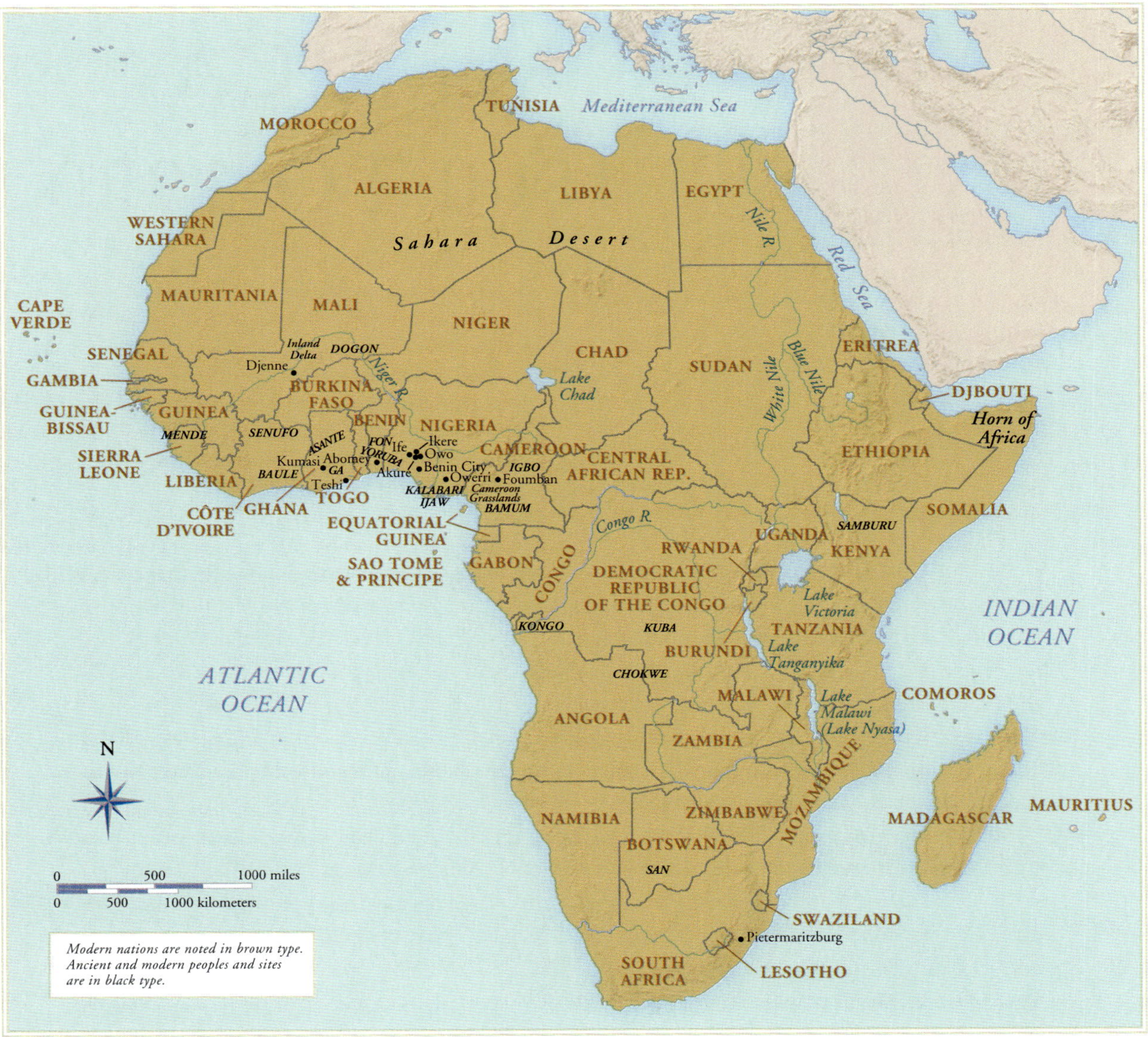

**MAP 37-1** Africa in the early 21st century.

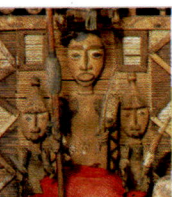

# AFRICA, 1800 TO 1980

| 1800 | 1900 | 1980 |
|---|---|---|

- San rock paintings record contemporaneous events
- Fang, Kota, and Kalabari Ijaw artists produce reliquary guardian figures and memorial screens to venerate ancestors
- Royal arts include the throne of Bamum king Ngansu and Fon king Glele's bocio of the god Gu
- Yombe, Dogon, and Baule sculptors carve wood groups of mother and child or man and woman

- Royal arts continue to flourish in highly stratified societies, such as the Benin kingdom
- The recording of artists' names becomes more common. Osei Bonsu and Ilowe of Ise achieve wide renown as sculptors
- Throughout the continent, African peoples produce elaborate masks to be danced at masquerades
- Personal adornment is a major art form, including body painting, complex coiffures, rich textiles, and the lavish regalia of kings

# San

Rock paintings are among the most ancient arts of Africa (FIGS. 1-3 and 19-2). Yet the tradition also continued well into the historical period. The latest examples date as recently as the 19th century, and some of these depict events involving Europeans. Many examples have been found in South Africa. Some of the most interesting are those produced by the peoples scholars refer to as San, who occupied parts of southwestern Africa in present-day Namibia and Botswana at the time of the earliest European colonization. The San were hunters and gatherers, and their art often centered on the animals they pursued.

**BAMBOO MOUNTAIN** One of the most impressive preserved San rock paintings (FIGS. 37-2 and 37-3), originally about eight feet long but now regrettably in fragments, comes from near the source of the Mzimkhulu River at Bamboo Mountain and dates to the mid-19th century. At that time, the increasing development of colonial ranches and the settlements of African agriculturists had greatly affected the lifestyle and movement patterns of San hunters and gatherers, often displacing them from their ancestral lands. In some regions, the San began to raid local ranches for livestock and horses as an alternate food source. The Bamboo Moun-

tain rock painting probably depicts one of a series of stock raids carried out between about 1838 and 1848. Various South African military and police forces unsuccessfully pursued the San raiders. Poor weather, including frequent rains and fog, added to the difficulty of capturing a people who had lived in the region for many generations and knew its terrain intimately.

Reproduced here are two details of the larger, fragmentary composition. On the right side (not illustrated), two San riders on horses laden with meat drive a large herd of cattle and horses toward a San encampment located left of center (FIG. 37-2) and encircled by an outline. Within the camp are various women and children. To the far left (FIG. 37-3), a single figure (perhaps a diviner or rainmaker) leads an eland, an animal the San considered effective in rainmaking and ancestor rituals, toward the encampment. The similarity of this scene to other rock paintings with spiritual interpretations (a human leading an animal) suggests this may represent a ritual leader in a trance state. The leader calls on rain—brought by the intervention of the sacred eland—to foil the attempts of the government soldiers and police to locate and punish the San raiders. The close correspondence between the painting's imagery and the raids of 1838–1848 adds to the likelihood San painters created this work to record contemporaneous events as well as to facilitate rainmaking.

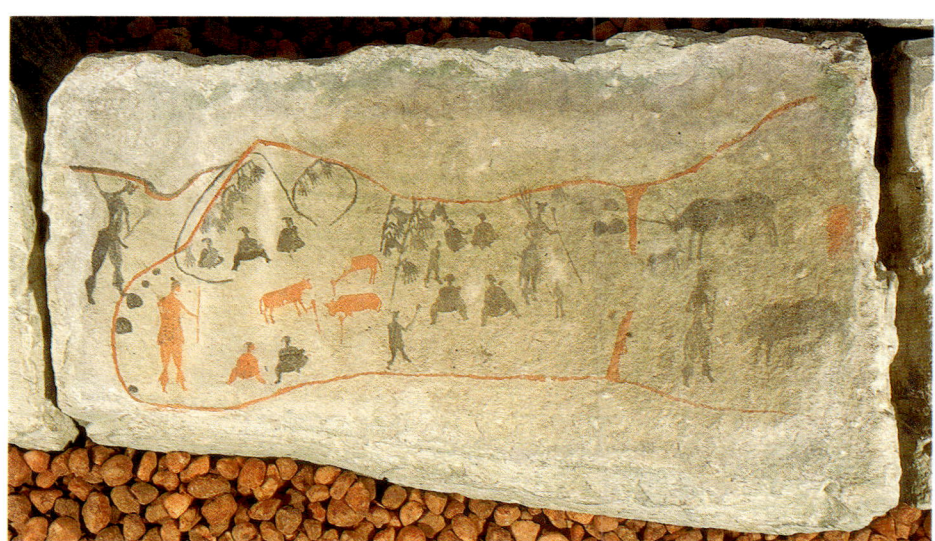

**37-2** Stock raid with cattle, horses, and encampment, rock painting, San, from Bamboo Mountain, South Africa, mid-19th century. Natal Museum, Pietermaritzburg.

Rock paintings are among the most ancient arts in Africa, and the tradition continued into the 19th century. This example depicts the 1838–1848 stock raids by San hunters.

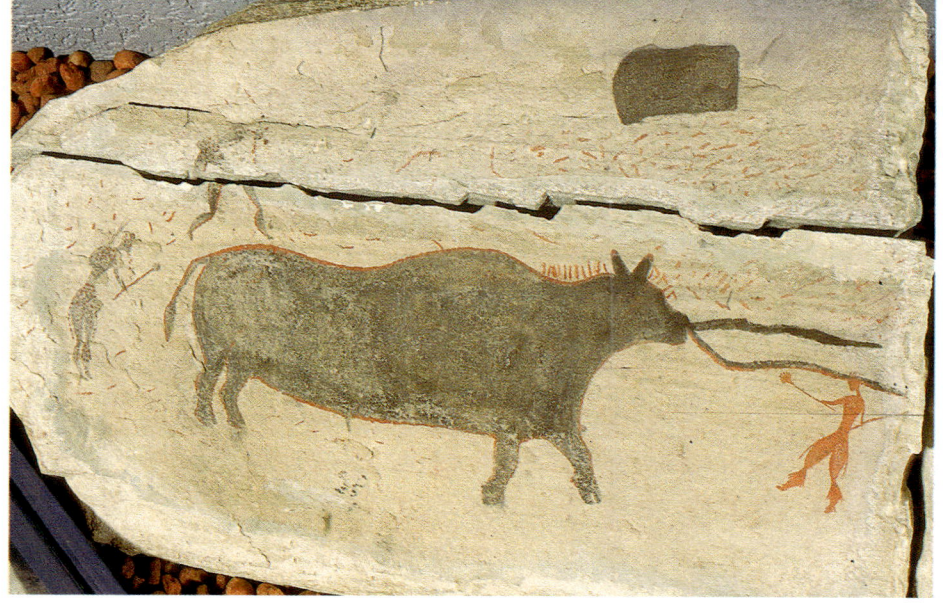

**37-3** Magical "rain animal," rock painting, San, from Bamboo Mountain, South Africa, mid-19th century. Natal Museum, Pietermaritzburg.

Another fragment of the eight-foot-long rock painting from Bamboo Mountain depicts a man, possibly a diviner in a trance, leading an eland, an animal believed to facilitate rainmaking.

## Fang and Kota

Although African works of art are often difficult to date precisely (see "Dating African Art," Chapter 19, page 523), art historians have been able to assign to the 19th century with some confidence a large number of objects that, unlike the Bamboo Mountain rock paintings, lack historical references. These include the Kalabari Ijaw *nduen fobara* (FIG. 37-1) already discussed and the *reliquary* guardian figures of the Fang and several other migratory peoples just south of the equator in Gabon and Cameroon. The reliquary figures play an important role in ancestor worship. Among both the Fang and the peoples scholars usually refer to as Kota in neighboring areas, ancestor veneration takes material form as collections of cranial and other bones (*relics*) gathered in special containers. These portable reliquaries were ideal for African nomadic population groups such as the Fang and Kota.

**FANG BIERI** Stylized carved wood human figures (FIG. 37-4), or in some cases simply heads, protected the Fang relic containers. The sculptors of these Fang guardian figures, or *bieri*, designed them to sit on the edge of cylindrical bark boxes of ancestral bones, ensuring no harm would befall the ancestral spirits. The wood figures are symmetrical, with proportions greatly emphasizing the head, and they feature a rhythmic buildup of forms suggestive of contained power. Particularly striking are the proportions of the bodies of the bieri, which resemble those of an infant, although the muscularity of the figures implies an adult. Scholars believe Fang sculptors chose this combination of traits to suggest the cycle of life, appropriate for an art form connected with the cult of ancestors.

**KOTA MBULU NGULU** The Kota of Gabon also produced reliquary guardian figures, called *mbulu ngulu* (FIG. 37-5), but they differ markedly from the Fang bieri. The Kota figures have severely

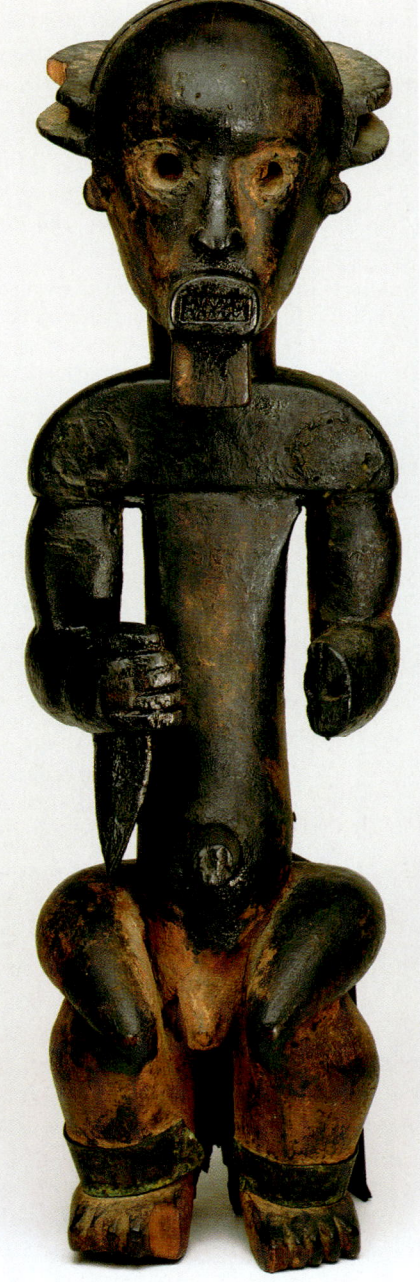

**37-4** Reliquary guardian figure (bieri), Fang, Gabon, late 19th century. Wood, 1′ 8¾″ high. Philadelphia Museum of Art, Philadelphia.

Bieri guard cylindrical bark boxes of Fang ancestor bones (reliquaries). The figures have the bodies of infants and the muscularity of adults, a combination of traits suggesting the cycle of life.

1 in.

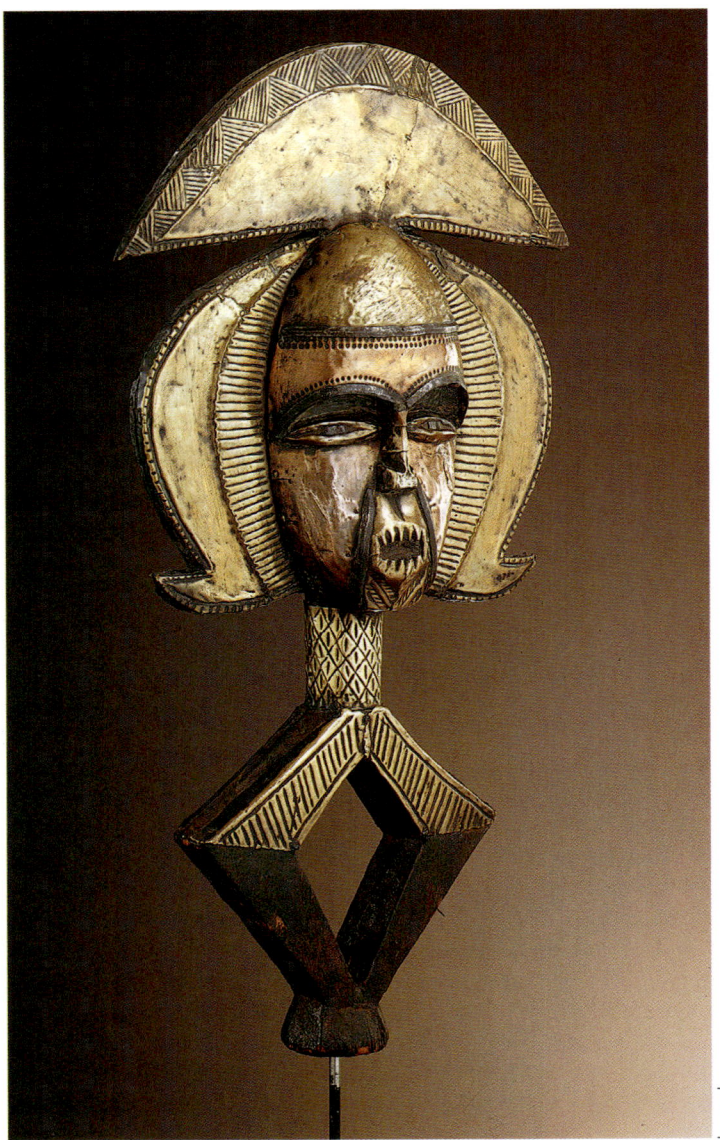

1 in.

**37-5** Reliquary guardian figure (mbulu ngulu), Kota, Gabon, 19th or early 20th century. Wood, copper, iron, and brass, 1′ 9¹⁄₁₆″ high. Musée Barbier-Mueller, Geneva.

Kota guardian figures have large heads and bodies in the form of an open diamond. Polished copper and brass sheets cover the wood forms. The Kota believe gleaming surfaces repel evil.

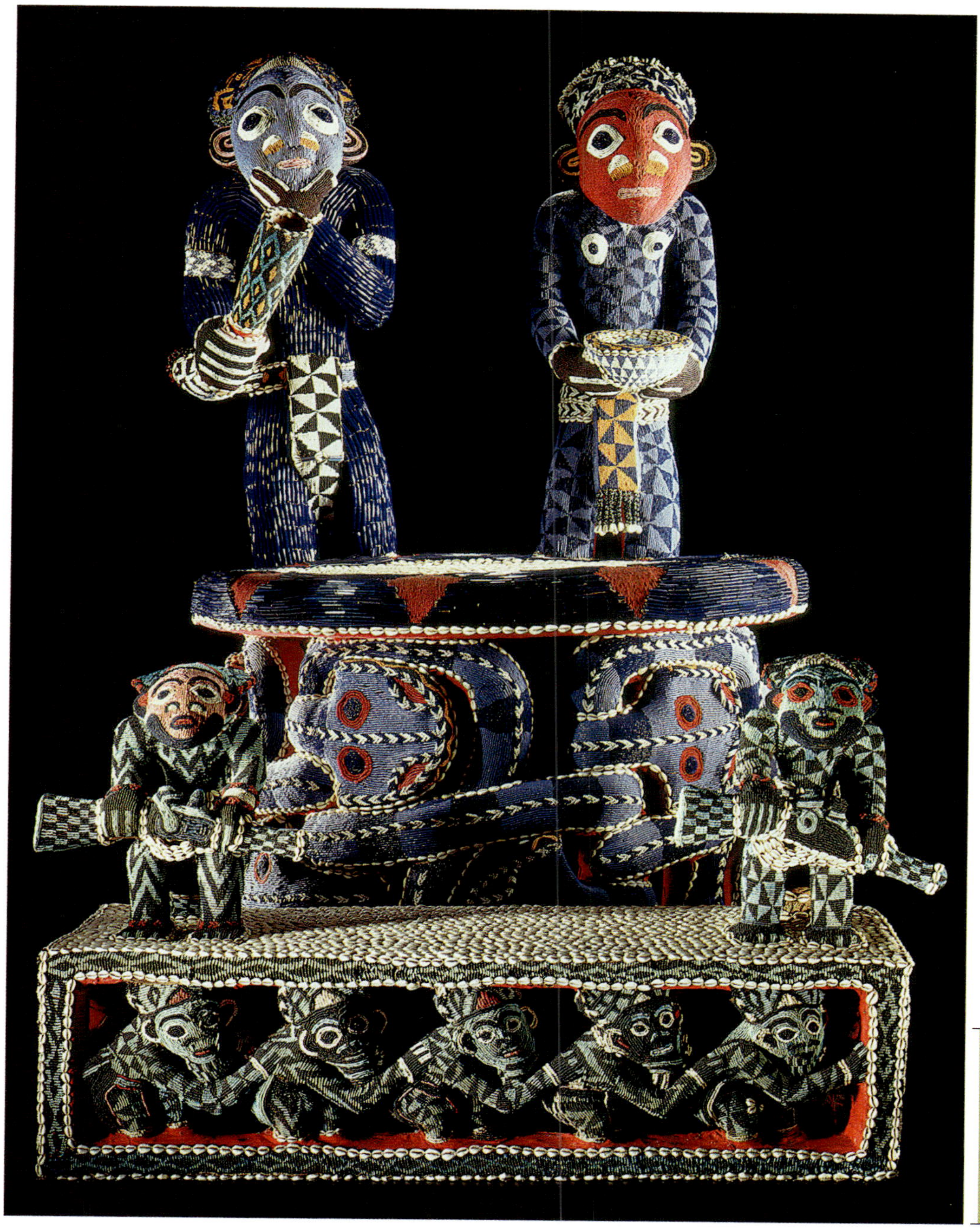

**Throne and footstool of King Nsangu, Bamum, Cameroon, ca. 1870.** Wood, textile, glass beads, and cowrie shells, 5′ 9″ high. Museum für Völkerkunde, Staatliche Museen zu Berlin, Berlin.

King Nsangu's throne features luminous beads and shells and richly colored textiles. The decoration includes intertwining serpents, male and female retainers, and bodyguards with European rifles.

1 ft.

stylized bodies in the form of an open diamond below a wood head. The sculptors of these reliquary guardians covered both the head and the abstract body with strips and sheets of polished copper and brass. The Kota believed the gleaming surfaces repel evil. The simplified heads have hairstyles flattened out laterally above and beside the face. Geometric ridges, borders, and subdivisions add a textured elegance to the shiny forms. The copper alloy on most of these images is reworked sheet brass (or copper wire) taken from brass basins originating in Europe and traded into this area of equatorial Africa in the 18th and 19th centuries. The Kota inserted the lower portion of the image into a basket or box of ancestral relics.

## Bamum

In addition to celebrating ancestors, much African art glorifies living rulers (see "Art and Leadership in Africa," Chapter 19, page 526). In the kingdom of Bamum in present-day Cameroon,

the ruler lived in a palace compound at the capital city of Foumban until its destruction in 1910. Some items of royal regalia survive.

**THRONE OF NSANGU** The royal arts of Bamum make extensive use of richly colored textiles and luminous materials, such as glass beads and cowrie shells. The ultimate status symbol was the king's throne. The throne illustrated here (FIG. **37-6**), a masterpiece of Bamum art, belonged to King Nsangu (r. 1865–1872 and 1885–1887). Intertwining blue and black serpents decorate the cylindrical seat. Above are the figures of two of the king's retainers, perpetually at his service. One, a man, holds the royal drinking horn. The other is a woman holding a serving bowl in her hands. Below are two of the king's bodyguards wielding European rifles. Dancing figures decorate the rectangular footstool. When the king sat on this throne (compare FIG. 37-23), his rich garments complemented the bright colors of his seat, advertising his wealth and power to all who were admitted to his palace.

## Fon

The founding of the Fon kingdom in the present-day Republic of Benin dates to around 1600. Under King Guezo (r. 1818–1858), the Fon became a regional power with an economy based largely on trade in palm oil. In 1900, the French dismantled the kingdom and brought many artworks to Paris, where they inspired several prominent early-20th-century Western artists (see "Primitivism and Colonialism," Chapter 29, page 846).

**KING GLELE** After his first military victory, Guezo's son Glele (r. 1858–1889) commissioned a prisoner of war, AKATI AKPELE KENDO, to make a life-size iron statue (FIG. **37-7**) of a warrior, probably Gu, the Fon god of war and iron, for a battle shrine in Glele's palace at Abomey. This *bocio*, or empowerment figure, was the centerpiece of a circle of iron swords and other weapons set vertically into the ground. The warrior strides forward with swords in both hands, ready to do battle. He wears a crown of miniature weapons and tools on his head. The form of the crown echoes the circle of swords around the statue. The Fon believed the bocio protected their king, and they transported it to the battlefield whenever they set out to fight an enemy force. King Glele's iron warrior is remarkable for its size and for the fact that not only is the patron's name known but so too is the artist's name—a rare instance in Africa before the 20th century (see "African Artists," page 1071).

## Kongo

The Congo River formed the principal transportation route for the peoples of central Africa during the 19th century, fostering cultural exchanges as well as trade, both among Africans and with Europeans.

**YOMBE PFEMBA** Some scholars have suggested the mother-and-child groups (*pfemba*) of the Yombe in the Democratic Republic of Congo may reflect the influence of Christian Madonna-and-Child imagery. The Yombe pfemba are not deities, however, but images of Kongo royalty. One masterful 19th-century example (FIG. **37-8**) represents a woman with a royal cap, chest scarification, and jewelry. The image may commemorate an ancestor or, more likely, a legendary founding clan mother. The Kongo call some of these figures "white chalk," a reference to the medicinal power of white kaolin clay. Diviners own some of them, and others have been used by women's organizations to treat infertility, but the function of this 19th-century pfemba is uncertain.

**NKISI N'KONDI** Among the most distinctive African sculptures of the 19th century are Kongo power figures (*nkisi n'kondi*), such as the statue illustrated here (FIG. **37-9**), which depicts a man bristling with nails and blades. These images, which trained priests consecrated using precise ritual formulas, embodied spirits believed to heal and give life, or sometimes to inflict harm, disease, or even death. Each figure had its specific role, just as it wore particular medicines—here protruding from the abdomen and featuring a large cowrie shell. The Kongo also activated every image differently. Owners appealed to a figure's forces every time they inserted a nail or blade, as if to prod the spirit to do its work. People invoked other spirits by repeating specific chants, by rubbing the images, or by applying special powders. The roles of power figures varied enormously, from curing minor ailments to stimulating crop growth, from punishing thieves to weakening enemies. Very large standing Kongo figures, such as this one, which is nearly four feet tall, had exceptional ascribed powers and aided entire communities. Although benevolent for their owners, the figures stood at the boundary between life and death, and most villagers held them in awe. As

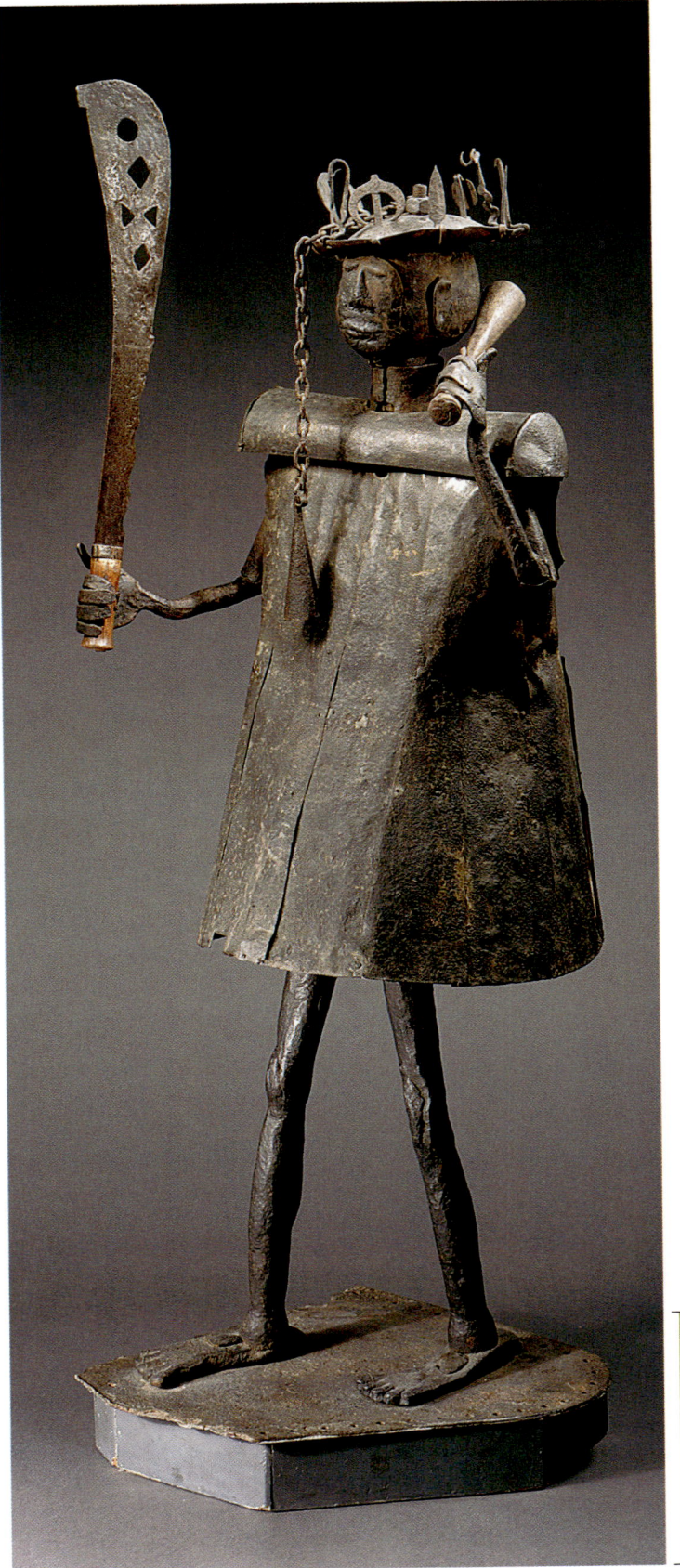

1 ft.

**37-7** AKATI AKPELE KENDO, Warrior figure (Gu?), from the palace of King Glele, Abomey, Fon, Republic of Benin, 1858–1859. Iron, 5′ 5″ high. Musée du quai Branly, Paris.

This bocio, or empowerment figure, probably representing the war god Gu, was the centerpiece of a circle of iron swords. The Fon believed it protected their king, and they set it up on the battlefield.

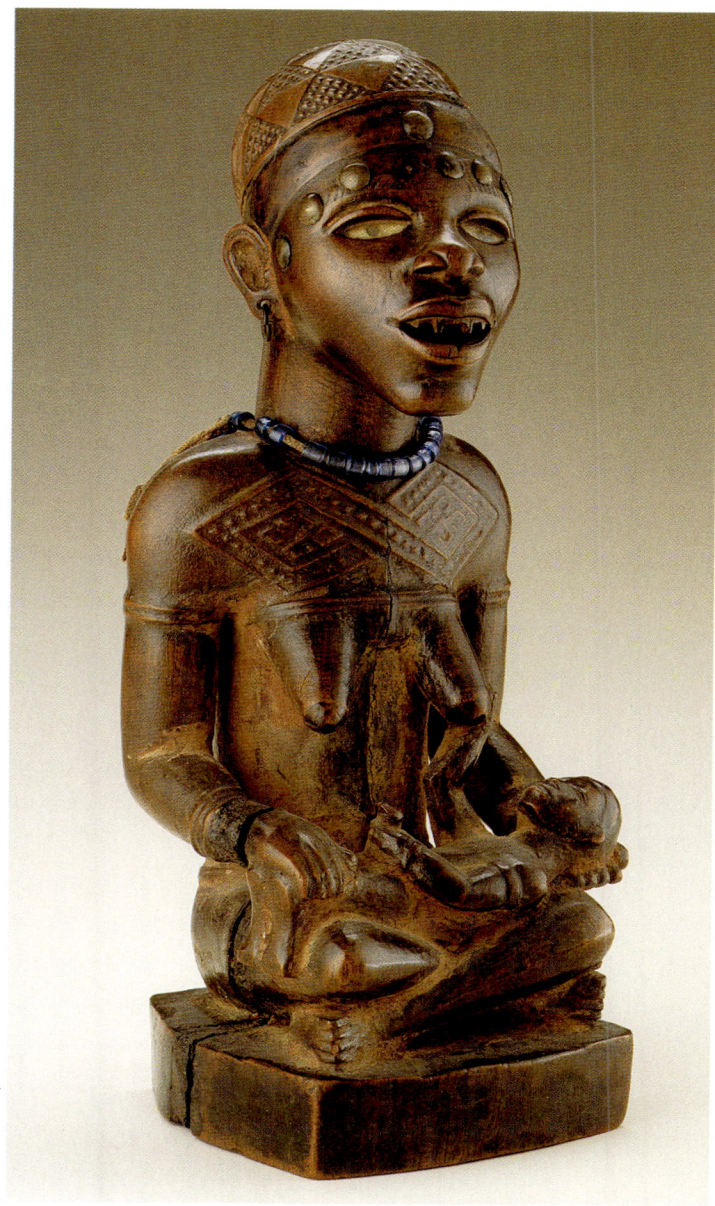

**37-8** Yombe mother and child (pfemba), Kongo, Democratic Republic of Congo, late 19th century. Wood, glass, glass beads, brass tacks, and pigment, 10⅛″ high. National Museum of African Art, Washington, D.C.

The mother in this Yombe group wears a royal cap and jewelry and displays her chest scarification. The image may commemorate an ancestor or, more likely, a legendary founding clan mother.

is true of the Yombe pfemba group (FIG. 37-8), compared with the sculptures of other African peoples, this Kongo figure is relatively naturalistic, although the carver simplified the facial features and magnified the size of the head for emphasis.

## Chokwe

The Chokwe occupy the area of west-central Africa corresponding to parts of northeastern Angola and southwestern Democratic Republic of Congo.

**CHIBINDA ILUNGA** Local legend claims the Chokwe are the descendants of the widely traveled Chibinda Ilunga, who won fame as a hunter. He married a princess named Lueji, who was a

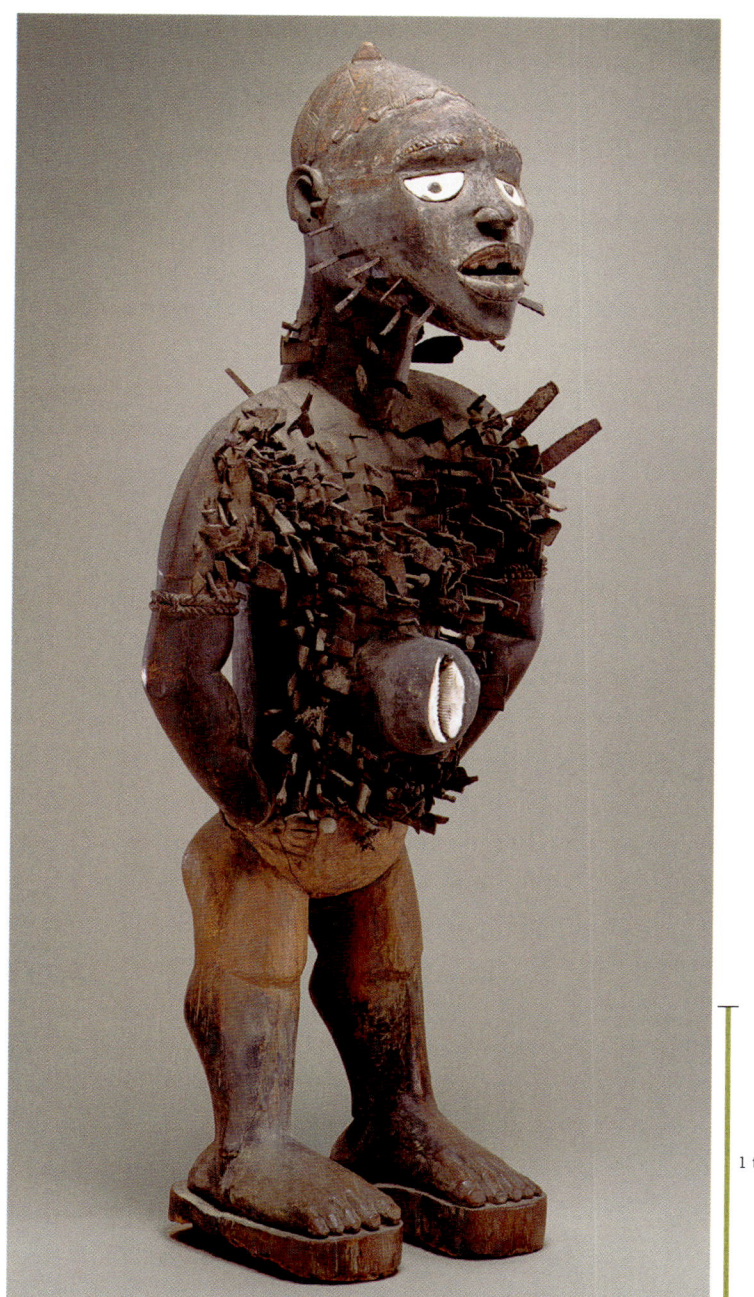

**37-9** Nail figure (nkisi n'kondi), Kongo, from Shiloango River area, Democratic Republic of Congo, ca. 1875–1900. Wood, nails, blades, medicinal materials, and cowrie shell, 3′ 10¾″ high. Detroit Institute of Arts, Detroit.

Only priests using ritual formulas could consecrate Kongo power figures, which embody spirits that can heal or inflict harm. The statue has simplified anatomical forms and an oversized head.

hereditary ruler of one of the kingdoms of the Lunda Empire, an important regional power during the 16th through 19th centuries. Lueji gave Chibinda a sacred bracelet, the basis and symbol of her rule, and he taught the Lunda to be great hunters, enriched the kingdom, and extended its territory. The Chokwe, one of the population groups resulting from that territorial expansion, became skilled elephant hunters and ivory traders. They eventually revolted against the Lunda kings and brought about the collapse of the Lunda Empire in the mid-19th century.

The Chokwe revere Chibinda Ilunga as founder, hunter, and civilizing hero, and he figures prominently in their royal arts. The statue illustrated here (FIG. **37-10**) is one of the finest examples. It shows the legendary hunter-king wearing a chief's barkcloth-and-rattan headdress and holding a staff in his right hand and, in his left hand, a medicine horn containing powerful substances to aid hunters. The sculptor portrayed Chibinda with a muscular body and oversized arms and feet to underscore the hunter's manual dexterity and ability to undertake long journeys. A rare feature of this and other Chokwe figures is the use of human hair for Chibinda's beard.

# Dogon

The Dogon live in the Bandiagara escarpment south of the inland delta region of the great Niger River in what is today Mali. Numbering almost 300,000, spread among hundreds of small villages, the Dogon practice farming as their principal occupation.

**LINKED MAN AND WOMAN** One of the most common themes in African art is the human couple. A Dogon example of exceptional quality is the statue of a linked man and woman reproduced here (FIG. **37-11**). It dates to the early 19th century and is probably a shrine or altar, although contextual information is

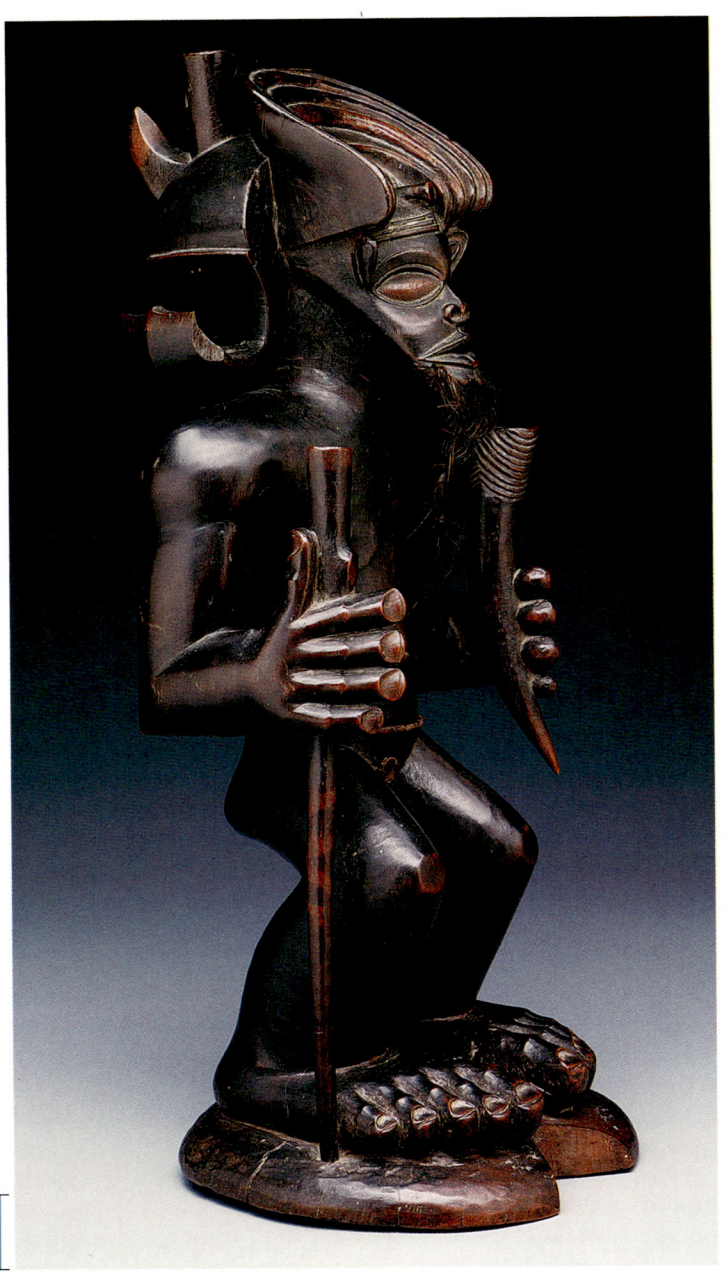

1 in.

**37-10** Chibinda Ilunga, Chokwe, from Angola or Democratic Republic of Congo, late 19th to 20th century. Wood and human hair, 1′ 4″ high. Kimbell Art Museum, Fort Worth.

The Chokwe claim descent from the legendary hunter Chibinda Ilunga, portrayed in art as a muscular man with a chief's headdress, oversized hands and feet, and a beard of human hair.

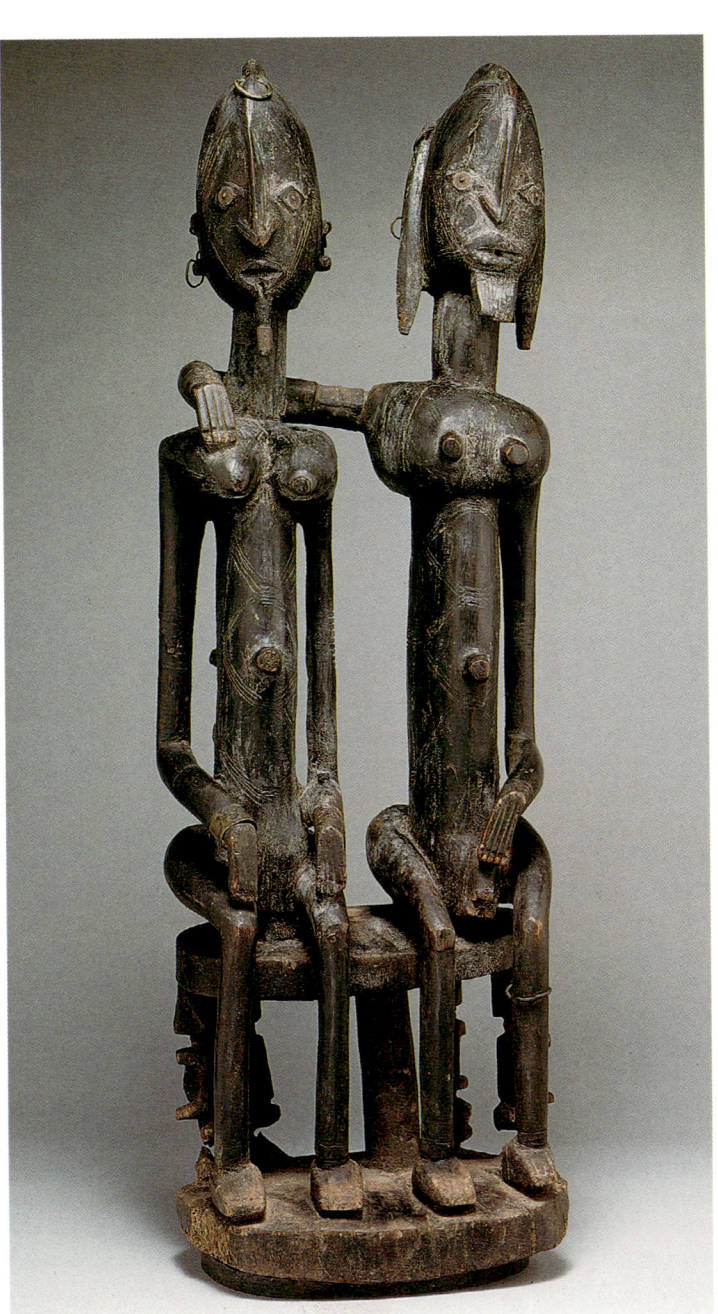

1 in.

**37-11** Seated couple, Dogon, Mali, ca. 1800–1850. Wood, 2′ 4″ high. Metropolitan Museum of Art, New York (gift of Lester Wunderman).

This Dogon carving of a linked man and woman documents gender roles in traditional African society. The protective man wears a quiver on his back. The nurturing woman carries a child on hers.

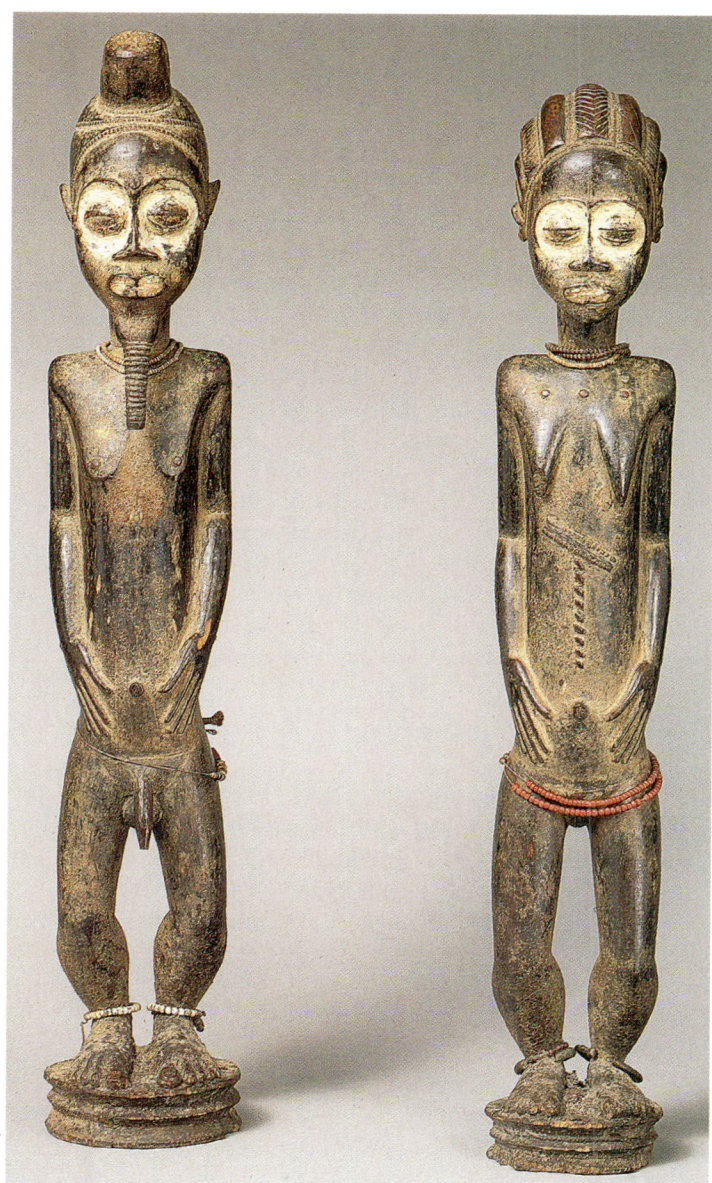

**37-12** Male and female figures, probably bush spirits (*asye usu*), Baule, Côte d'Ivoire, late 19th or early 20th century. Wood, beads, and kaolin, man 1′ 9¾″ high, woman 1′ 8⅝″ high. Metropolitan Museum of Art, New York (Michael C. Rockefeller Memorial Collection, gift of Nelson A. Rockefeller).

In contrast to the Dogon couple (FIG. 37-11), this pair includes many naturalistic aspects of human anatomy, but the sculptor enlarged the necks, calves, and heads, a form of idealization in Baule culture.

carved the Dogon couple (FIG. 37-11) based the forms more on the idea or concept of the human body than on observation of individual heads, torsos, and limbs. The linked body parts are tubes and columns articulated inorganically. The carver reinforced the almost abstract geometry of the overall composition by incising rectilinear and diagonal patterns on the surfaces. The Dogon artist also understood the importance of space, and charged the voids, as well as the sculptural forms, with rhythm and tension.

## Baule

The Baule of present-day Côte d'Ivoire do not have kings, and their societies are relatively egalitarian, especially compared with other highly stratified African population groups, but Baule art encompasses many of the same basic themes seen elsewhere on the continent.

**BUSH SPIRITS** The Baule statues of a man and woman illustrated here (FIG. **37-12**) probably portray bush spirits (*asye usu*). The sculptor most likely carved the pair of wood figures for a trance diviner, a religious specialist who consulted the spirits symbolized by the statues on behalf of clients who were either sick or in some way troubled. In Baule thought, bush spirits are short, horrible-looking, and sometimes deformed creatures, yet Baule sculptors represent them in the form of beautiful, ideal human beings, because ugly figures would offend the spirits and refuse to work for the diviner. Among the Baule, as among many West African peoples, bush or wilderness spirits not only cause difficulties in life but, if properly addressed and placated, also may solve problems or cure sickness. In dance and trance performances—with wood figures and other objects displayed nearby—the diviner can divine, or understand, the will of unseen spirits as well as their needs or prophecies, which the diviner passes on to clients. When not set up outdoors for a performance, the figures and other objects remain in the diviner's house or shrine, where more private consultations take place. In striking contrast to the Dogon sculptor of the seated man and woman (FIG. 37-11), the artist who created this matched pair of Baule male and female images recorded many naturalistic aspects of human anatomy, skillfully translating them into finished sculptural form. At the same time, the sculptor was well aware of creating *waka sran* (people of wood) rather than living beings. Thus, the artist freely exaggerated the length of the figures' necks and the size of their heads and calf muscles, all of which are forms of idealization in Baule culture.

# 20TH CENTURY

The art of Africa during the past 100 years ranges from traditional works depicting age-old African themes to modern works that are international in both content and style (for example, FIGS. 31-9A and 31-12). Both men and women have long been active in African art production, usually specializing in different types of objects (see "Gender Roles in African Art Production," page 1070).

## Benin

Some of the most important 20th-century African artworks come from areas with strong earlier artistic traditions. The kingdom of Benin (see Chapter 19 and FIGS. I-1, 19-1, 19-13, and 19-13A) in present-day Nigeria is a prime example.

**SHRINE OF EWEKE II** In 1897, when the British sacked Benin City, there were still 17 shrines to ancestors in the Benin

lacking. Interpretations vary, but the image vividly documents primary gender roles in traditional African society. The man wears a quiver on his back. The woman carries a child on hers. Thus, the man assumes a protective role as hunter or warrior, the woman a nurturing role. The slightly larger man reaches behind his mate's neck and touches her breast, as if to protect her. His left hand points to his genitalia. Four stylized figures support the stool upon which they sit. They are probably either spirits or ancestors, but the identity of the larger figures is uncertain.

The strong stylization of Dogon sculptures contrasts sharply with the organic, relatively realistic treatment of the human body in Kongo and Chokwe art (FIGS. 37-8 to 37-10). The artist who

# Gender Roles in African Art Production

Until the late 20th century, art production in Africa has been quite rigidly gender-specific. Men have been, and largely still are, ironsmiths and gold and copper-alloy casters. Men were architects, builders, and carvers of both wood and ivory. Women were, and for the most part remain, wall and body painters, calabash decorators, potters, and often clay sculptors, although men make clay figures in some areas. Both men and women work with beads and weave baskets and textiles, with men executing narrow strips (later sewn together) on horizontal looms and women working wider pieces of cloth on vertical looms.

Much African art, however, is collaborative. Men may build a clay wall, for example, but women will normally decorate it. The Igbo people build *mbari* houses (FIG. 37-25)—for ceremonies to honor the earth goddess—that are truly collaborative despite the fact professional male artists model the figures displayed in the houses. Festivals, invoking virtually all the arts, are also collaborative. Masquerades (see "African Masquerades," page 1073) are largely the province of men, yet in some cases women contribute costume elements such as skirts, wrappers, and scarves. Even though women dance masks among the Mende and related peoples (see "Mende Women as Maskers," page 1075), men have always carved the masks themselves.

In late colonial and especially in postcolonial times, earlier gender distinctions in art production began breaking down. Today, women as well as men weave *kente* cloth (FIG. 37-13A), and a number of women are now sculptors in wood, metal, stone, and composite materials. Men are making pottery, once the exclusive prerogative of women. Both women and men make international art forms in urban and university settings, although male artists are more numerous. One well-known Nigerian woman artist, Sokari Douglas Camp (b. 1958), produces welded metal sculptures, sometimes of masqueraders. Douglas Camp is thus doubly unusual. She might find it difficult to do this work in her traditional home in the Niger River delta, but because she lives and works in London, she encounters no adverse response. In the future there will undoubtedly be a further breaking down of restrictive barriers and greater mobility for artists.

royal palace. Today, only one 20th-century altar (FIG. 37-13) remains. According to oral history, it is similar to centuries-earlier versions. With a base of sacred riverbank clay, it is an assemblage of varied materials, objects, and symbols: a central copper-alloy altarpiece depicting a sacred king flanked by members of his entourage, plus copper-alloy heads, each fitted on top with an ivory tusk carved in relief. Behind are wood staffs and metal bells. The heads represent both the kings themselves and, through the durability of the material, the enduring nature of kingship. Their glistening surfaces, seen as red and signaling danger, repel evil forces that might adversely affect the shrine and thus the king and kingdom. Elephant-tusk relief carvings atop the heads commemorate important events and personages in Benin history. Their bleached white color signifies purity and goodness (probably of royal ancestors), and the tusks themselves represent male physical power. The carved wood rattle-staffs standing at the back refer to generations of dynastic ancestors by their bamboolike, segmented forms. The rattle-staffs and the pyramidal copper-alloy bells serve the important function of calling royal ancestral spirits to rituals performed at the altar.

**37-13** Royal ancestral altar of King Eweka II, in the palace in Benin City, Nigeria, photographed in 1970. Clay, copper alloy, wood, and ivory.

This shrine to the heads of royal ancestors is an assemblage of materials, objects, and symbols. By sacrificing animals at this altar, the Benin king annually invokes the collective strength of his ancestors.

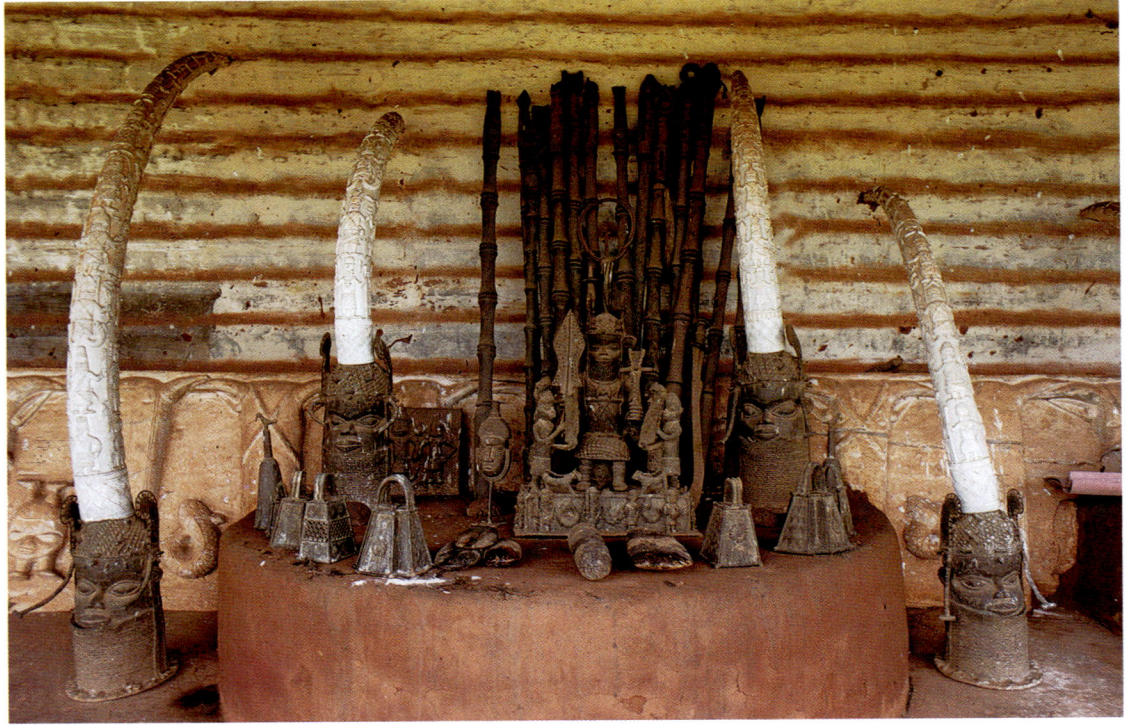

# African Artists and Apprentices

Traditionally, Africans have tended not to exalt artistic individuality as much as Westerners have. Many people, in fact, still consider African art as anonymous, primarily because early researchers rarely asked for artists' names (see "Dating African Art and Identifying African Artists," Chapter 19, page 523). Nonetheless, art historians can recognize many individual hands or styles even when an artist's name has not been recorded. During the past century, art historians and anthropologists have been systematically noting the names and life histories of specific individual artists, many of whom have strong regional reputations. One of the earliest recorded names is that of the mid-19th-century Fon sculptor and metalsmith Akati Akpele Kendo (FIG. 37-7). Two 20th-century artists, renowned even from one kingdom to another, were Osei Bonsu (FIGS. 37-14 and 37-15), based in the Asante capital of Kumasi, and the Yoruba sculptor called Olowe of Ise (FIGS. 37-16 and 37-16A) because he came from the town of Ise. Both artists were master carvers, producing sculptures for kings and commoners alike.

As did other great artists in other places and times, both Bonsu and Olowe had apprentices to assist them for several years while learning their trade. Although there are various kinds of apprenticeship in Africa, novices typically lived with their masters and were household servants as well as assistant carvers. They helped fell trees, carry logs, and rough out basic shapes the master later transformed into finished work. African sculptors typically worked on commission. Sometimes, as in Bonsu's case, patrons traveled to the home of the artist. But other times, even Bonsu moved to the home of a patron for weeks or months while working on a commission. Masters, and in some instances also apprentices, lived and ate in the patron's compound. Olowe, for example, resided with different kings for many months at a time while he carved doors (FIG. 37-16), veranda posts (FIG. 37-16A), and other works for royal families.

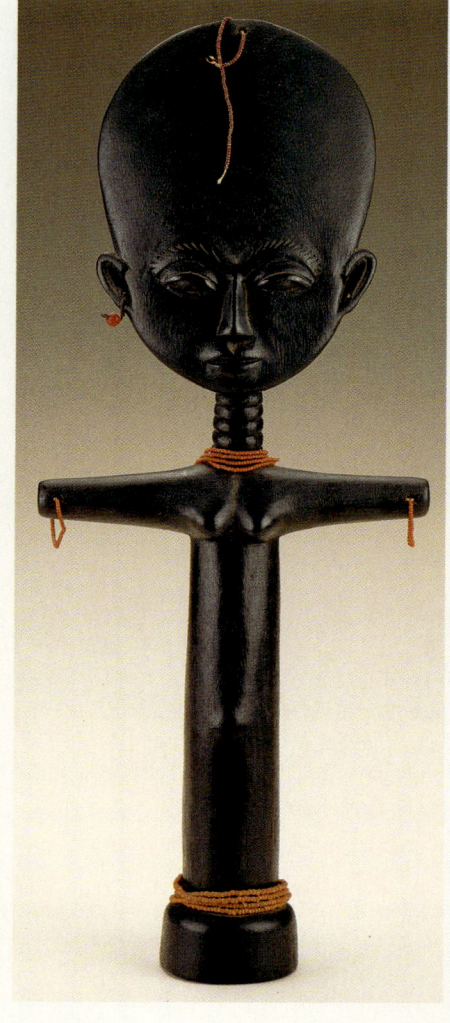

37-14 OSEI BONSU, Akua'ba (Akua's child), Asante, Ghana, ca. 1960. Wood and glass beads, 1' 2½" high. National Museum of African Art, Washington, D.C. (gift of Herbert C. Madison).

Osei Bonsu was one of Africa's leading sculptors. This figure, carried by women hoping to conceive a child, has a flattened face and crosshatched eyebrows, typical features of the artist's style.

1 in.

---

The Benin king's head stands for wisdom, good judgment, and divine guidance for the kingdom. The several heads in the ancestral altar multiply these qualities. By means of animal sacrifices at this site, the living king annually purifies his own head (and being) by invoking the collective strength of his ancestors. Thus the varied objects, symbols, colors, and materials comprising this shrine contribute both visually and ritually to the imaging of royal power, as well as to its history, renewal, and perpetuation. The composition of the shrine, like that of the altar at its center and the mid-18th-century Altar to the Hand and Arm (FIG. 19-1), is hierarchical. At the center of all Benin hierarchies stands the king (FIG. I-1).

## Asante

The Asante of modern Ghana formed a strong confederacy around 1700. They are one of several peoples, including the Baule of Côte d'Ivoire, who speak an Akan dialect. Asante artists work in many media but are probably most famous today for vividly colored and patterned *kente* cloth robes (FIG. 37-13A).

**OSEI BONSU** A common stylistic characteristic of Asante figural art is the preference for conventionalized, flattened heads. Many Akan peoples considered long, slightly flattened foreheads to be emblems of beauty, and mothers gently molded their children's cranial bones to reflect this value. These anatomical features occur in a wooden image of a young girl (FIG. 37-14), or *akua'ba* (Akua's child), carved by OSEI BONSU (1900–1976), one of the 20th century's leading African sculptors (see "African Artists and Apprentices," above). After consecrating a simplified wood akua'ba sculpture at a shrine, a young woman hoping to conceive carried it with her. Once pregnant, she continued to carry the figure to ensure the safe delivery of a healthy and handsome child—among these matrilineal people, preferably a girl. Compared with

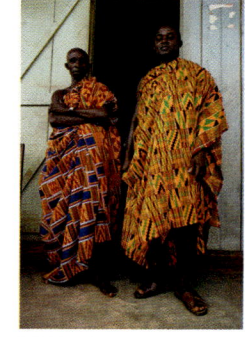

37-13A Asante noblemen in kente cloth robes, 1972.

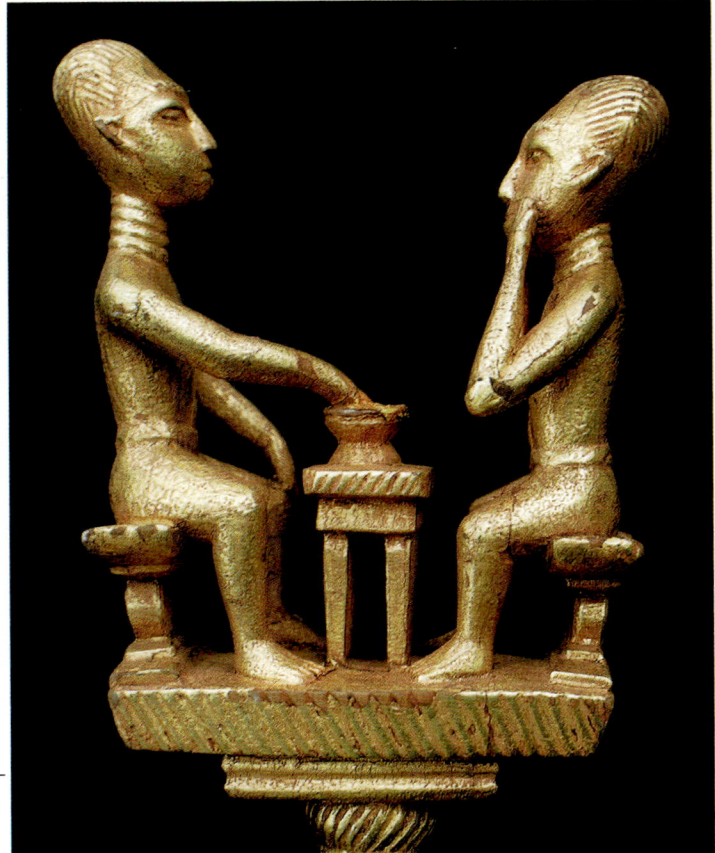

**37-15** OSEI BONSU, two men sitting at a table of food (linguist's staff), Asante, Ghana, mid-20th century. Wood and gold leaf, section shown 10″ high. Collection of the Paramount Chief of Offinso, Asante.

Bonsu carved this gold-covered wood linguist's staff for someone who could speak for the Asante king. At the top are two men sitting at a table of food—a metaphor for the office of the king.

1 in.

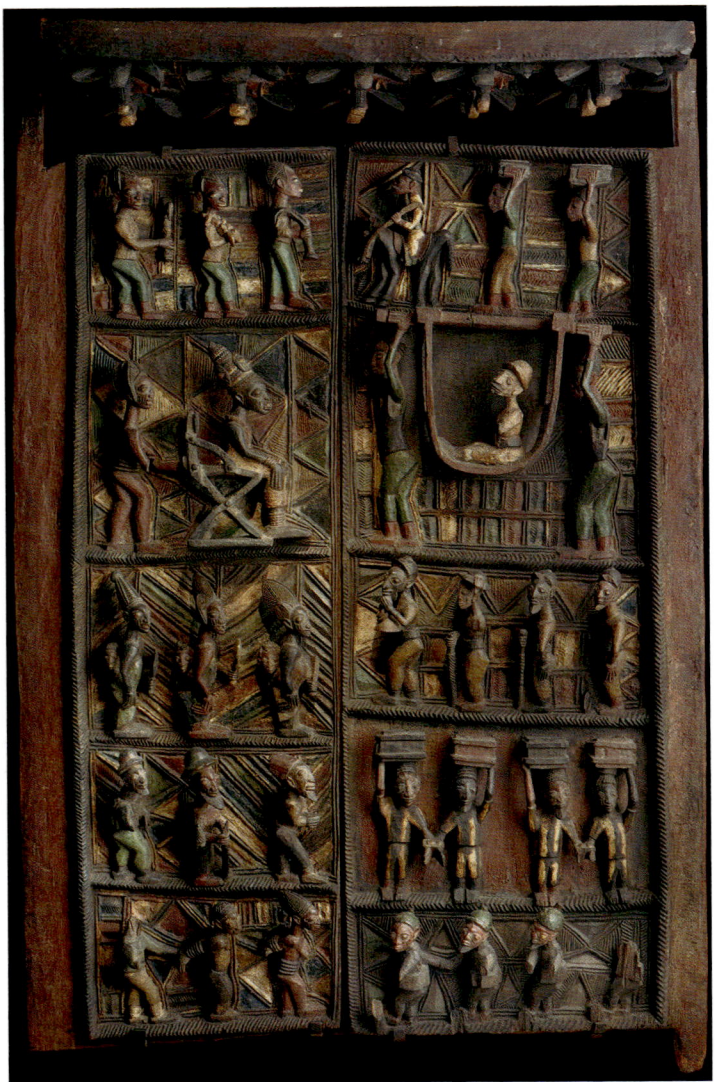

1 ft.

**37-16** OLOWE OF ISE, doors from the shrine of the king's head in the royal palace, Ikere, Yoruba, Nigeria, 1910–1914. Painted wood, 6′ high. British Museum, London.

These masterfully carved and painted doors to the shrine of the king's head in the Ikere palace are the work of Olowe of Ise, one of the few African artists whose name and career have been recorded.

traditional sculptures of this type, the more naturalistic rendering of the face and crosshatched eyebrows in Osei Bonsu's sculpture are distinctive features of his personal style.

**LINGUIST'S STAFF** Bonsu also carved the gold-covered wood sculpture (FIG. **37-15**) depicting two men sitting at a table of food. This object, commonly called a *linguist's staff* because its carrier often speaks for a king or chief, has a related proverb: "Food is for its rightful owner, not for the one who happens to be hungry." Food is a metaphor for the office the king or chief rightfully holds. The "hungry" man lusts for the office. The linguist, who is an important counselor and adviser to the king, might carry this staff to a meeting at which a rival contests the king's title to the stool (his throne, the office). Many hundreds of sculptures from this region have proverbs or other sayings associated with them, which has created a rich verbal tradition relating to the visual arts of the Akan peoples.

## Yoruba

The Yoruba have a long history in southwestern Nigeria and the southern Republic of Benin going back to the founding of Ile-Ife in the 11th century (see Chapter 19). In the 20th century, Yoruba artists were among the most skilled on the continent. One who achieved international recognition was OLOWE OF ISE (ca. 1873–1938).

**OLOWE OF ISE** In 1925, the British Museum acquired directly from the *ogoga* (king) of Ikere (in exchange for a British throne) the elaborately carved and painted doors (FIG. **37-16**) of the shrine of the king's head in his palace in northeastern Yorubaland. At the time, the museum did not inquire about the artist's name. Not until after World War II, when art historians began to document the careers of individual African artists (see "African Artists and Apprentices," page 1071), did the British curators learn the master carver was Olowe of Ise, the most famous Yoruba sculptor of the early 20th century. Kings and aristocrats throughout Yorubaland employed Olowe to carve reliefs, masks, bowls, veranda posts (FIG. **37-16A**), and other works for them, and he traveled widely in

**37-16A** OLOWE OF ISE, veranda post, Akure, 1920s.

# African Masquerades

The art of masquerade has long been a quintessential African expressive form, laden with meaning and of the highest importance culturally. This is so today, but was even more critically true in colonial times and earlier, when African masking societies boasted extensive regulatory and judicial powers. In stateless societies, such as those of the Senufo (FIGS. 37-17 and 37-18), Dogon (FIG. 37-19), and Mende (FIG. 37-20), masks sometimes became so influential they had their own priests and served as power sources or as oracles. Societies empowered maskers to levy fines and to apprehend witches (usually defined as socially destructive people) and criminals, and to judge and punish them. Normally, however—especially today—masks are less threatening and more secular and educational and serve as diversions from the humdrum of daily life. Masked dancers usually embody either ancestors, seen as briefly returning to the human realm, or various nature spirits called upon for their special powers.

The mask, a costume ensemble's focal point, combines with held objects, music, and dance gestures to invoke a specific named character, almost always considered a spirit. A few masked spirits appear by themselves, but more often several characters come out together or in turn. Maskers enact a broad range of human, animal, and fantastic otherworldly behavior that is usually both stimulating and didactic. Masquerades, in fact, vary in function or effect along a continuum from weak spirit power and strong entertainment value to those rarely seen but possessing vast executive powers backed by powerful shrines. Most operate between these extremes, crystallizing varieties of human and animal behavior—caricatured, ordinary, comic, bizarre, serious, or threatening. Such actions inform and affect audience members because of their dramatic staging. It is the purpose of most masquerades to move people, to affect them, to effect change.

Thus, masks and masquerades are mediators—between men and women, youths and elders, initiated and uninitiated, powers of nature and those of human agency, and even life and death. For many groups in West and Central Africa, masking plays (or once played) an active role in the socialization process, especially for men, who control most masks. Maskers carry boys (and, more

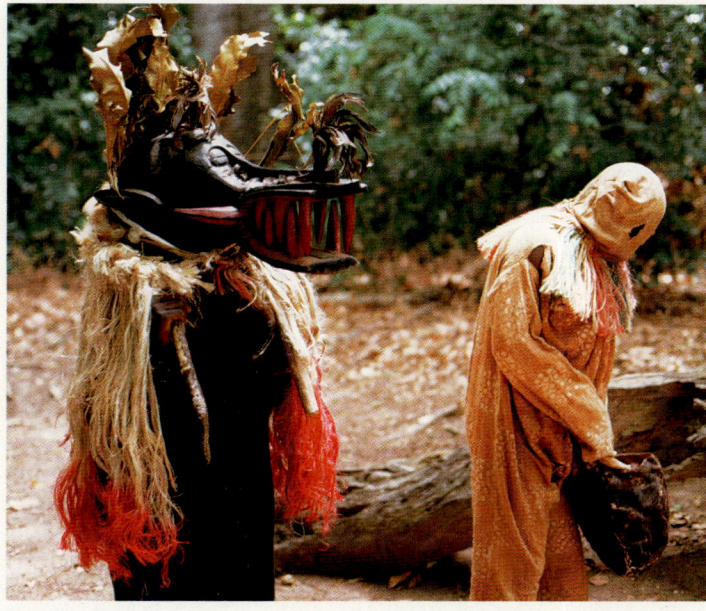

**37-17** Senufo masqueraders, Côte d'Ivoire, photographed ca. 1980–1990. ◼◀

Senufo masqueraders are always men. Their masks often represent composite creatures incarnating both ancestors and bush powers. They fight malevolent spirits with their aggressively powerful forms.

rarely, girls) away from their mothers to bush initiation camps, put them through ordeals and schooling, and welcome them back to society as men months or even years later. A second major role is in aiding the transformation of important deceased persons into productive ancestors who, in their new roles, can bring benefits to the living community. Because most masking cultures are agricultural, it is not surprising Africans often invoke masquerades to increase the productivity of the fields, to stimulate the growth of crops, and later to celebrate the harvest.

---

his homeland to execute those commissions. Between 1910 and 1914 he resided at Ikere while working for the ogoga. The palace shrine doors date from that time.

Departing from convention, Olowe made the two doors of unequal width to accommodate a rare historical narrative in 10 panels in five registers. The reliefs recount the 1897 visit of the representative of the British Empire, Captain Ambrose, commissioner of Ondo province. Litter-bearers carry Ambrose into the palace compound, where the enthroned king, far larger than the British emissary, and his principal wife receive him. The other panels on each door depict the entourage of the two protagonists including, at the left, the king's bodyguards and other wives, and, on the right door, shackled slaves carrying chests. Characteristically for Olowe, the relief is so high some of the figures project as much as six inches from the surface, which has a vividly colored patterned background. Olowe also carved the veranda posts of the courtyard in front of the shrine.

## Senufo

The Senufo of the western Sudan region in what is now northern Côte d'Ivoire have a population today of more than a million. They speak several different languages, sometimes even in the same village. Not surprisingly, there are many different Senufo art forms, including mask-making (FIGS. **37-17** and 37-18) and woodcarving (FIG. **37-17A**), all closely tied to community life.

**MASQUERADES** Senufo men dance many masks (see "African Masquerades," above), mostly in the context of Poro, the main association for socialization and initiation, a protracted process taking nearly 20 years for men to complete. Maskers also perform at funerals and other public spectacles. Large Senufo masks (for example,

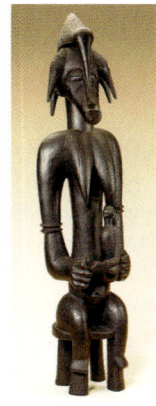

**37-17A** Ancient Mother, Senufo, early 20th century.

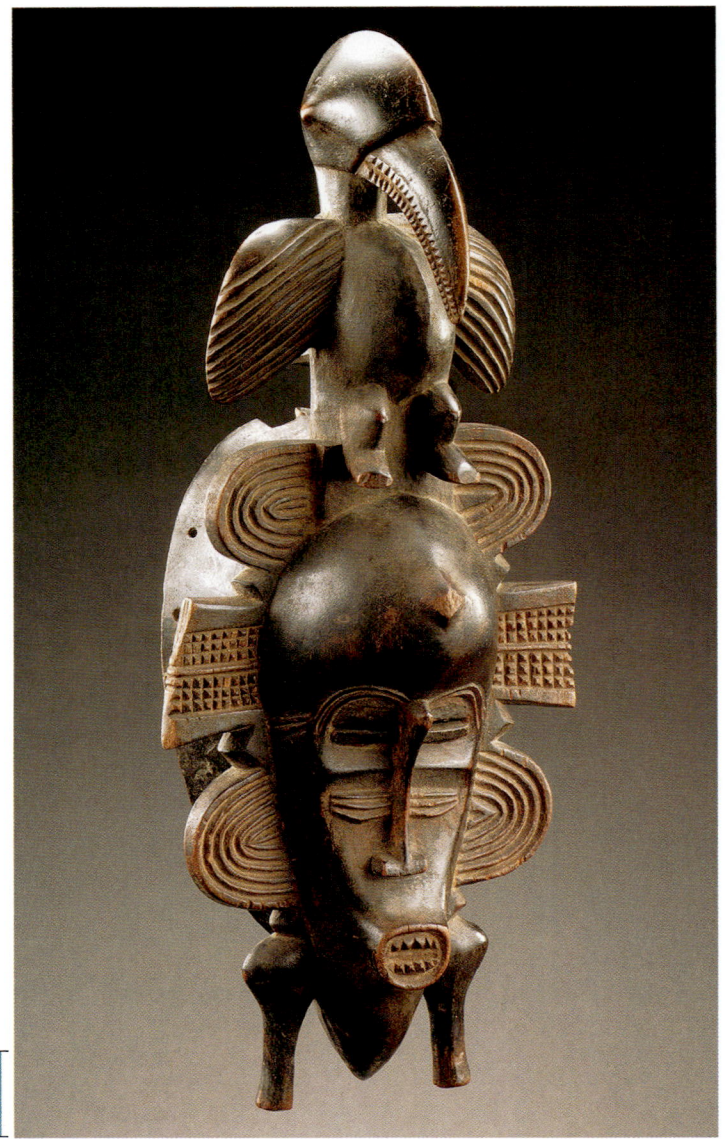

**37-18** "Beautiful Lady" dance mask, Senufo, Côte d'Ivoire, late 20th century. Wood, 1′ $\frac{1}{2}$″ high. Musée Barbier-Mueller, Geneva. ◼◀

Some Senufo men dance female masks such as this one with a hornbill bird rising from the forehead. The female characters are sometimes the wives of the terrorizing male masks (FIG. 37-17).

FIG. 37-17) are composite creatures, combining characteristics of antelope, crocodile, warthog, hyena, and human: sweeping horns, a head, and an open-jawed snout with sharp teeth. These masks incarnate both ancestors and bush powers that combat witchcraft and sorcery, malevolent spirits, and the wandering dead. They are protectors who fight evil with their aggressively powerful forms and their medicines.

At funerals Senufo maskers attend the corpse and help expel the deceased from the village. This is the deceased individual's final transition, a rite of passage parallel to that undergone by all men during their years of Poro socialization, when masks also play a role. When an important person dies, the convergence of several masking groups, as well as the music, dancing, costuming, and feasting of many people, constitute a festive and complex work of art that transcends any one mask or character.

Some men also dance female masks. The most recurrent type has a small face with fine features, several extensions, and varied

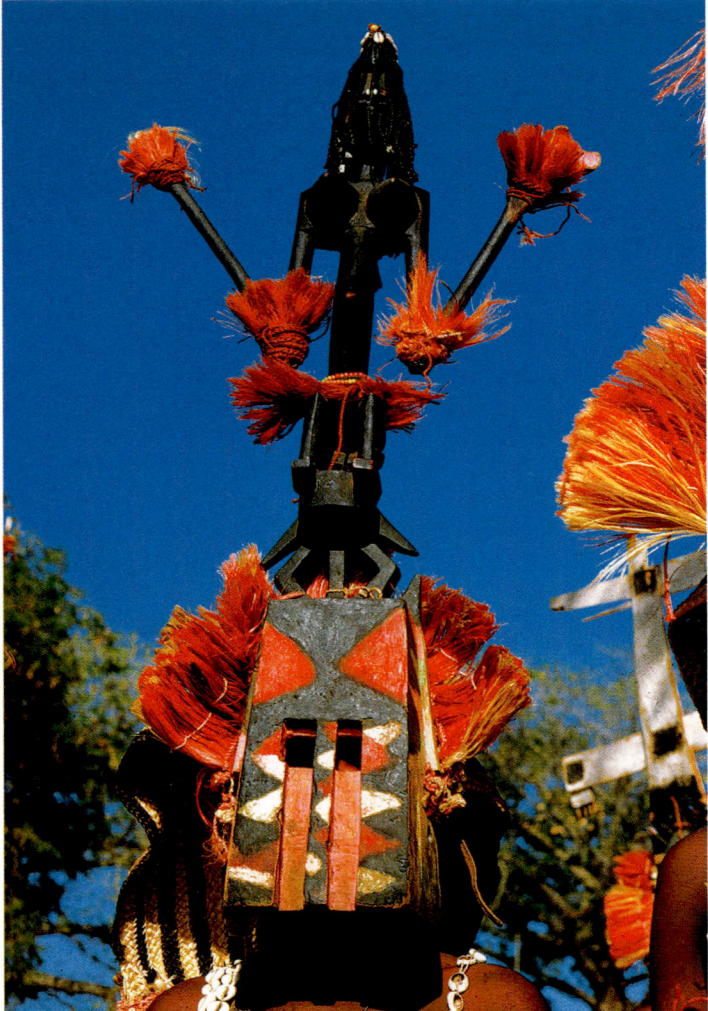

**37-19** Satimbe masquerader, Dogon, Mali, mid- to late 20th century. ◼◀

Satimbe (sister on the head) masks commemorate the legend describing women as the first masqueraders. The mask's crown is a woman with large breasts and sticklike bent arms.

motifs—a hornbill bird in the illustrated example (FIG. **37-18**)—rising from the forehead. The men who dance these feminine characters also wear knitted body suits or trade-cloth costumes to indicate their beauty and their ties with the order and civilization of the village. They may be called "pretty young girl," "beautiful lady," or "wife" of one of the heavy, terrorizing masculine masks (FIG. 37-17) appearing before or after them.

## Dogon

The Dogon (FIG. 37-11) continue to excel at carving wood figures, but many Dogon artists are specialists in fashioning large masks for elaborate cyclical masquerades.

**SATIMBE MASKS** Dogon masquerades dramatize creation legends. These stories say women were the first ancestors to imitate spirit maskers and thus the first human masqueraders. Men later took over the masks, forever barring women from direct involvement with masking processes. A mask called *Satimbe* (FIG. **37-19**), that is, "sister on the head," seems to represent all women and commemorates this legend. Satimbe masks consist of a roughly rectangular covering for the head with narrow rectangular openings

## Mende Women as Maskers

The Mende and neighboring peoples of Sierra Leone, Liberia, and Guinea are distinctive in Africa because the women perform masquerades. The masks (FIG. 37-20) and costumes they wear conceal the women's bodies from the audience attending their performance. The Sande society of the Mende controls the initiation, education, and acculturation of Mende girls. Women leaders who dance the Sande masks serve as priestesses and judges during the three years the women's society controls the ritual calendar (alternating with the men's society in this role), thus serving the community as a whole. Women maskers, who function as initiators, teachers, and mentors, help girl novices with their transformation into educated and marriageable women.

Sande women associate their Sowie masks with water spirits and the color black, which the society, in turn, connects with human skin color and the civilized world. The women wear these helmet masks on top of their heads as headdresses, with black raffia and cloth costumes to hide the wearers' identity during public performances. Elaborate coiffures, shiny black color, dainty triangular-shaped faces with slit eyes, rolls around the neck, and real and carved versions of amulets and various emblems on the top commonly characterize Sowie masks (FIG. 37-20). These symbolize the adult women's roles as wives, mothers, providers for the family, and keepers of medicines for use within the Sande association and the society at large.

Sande members commission the masks from male carvers, with the carver and patron together determining the type of mask needed for a particular societal purpose. The Mende often keep, repair, and reuse masks for many decades, thereby preserving them as models for subsequent generations of carvers.

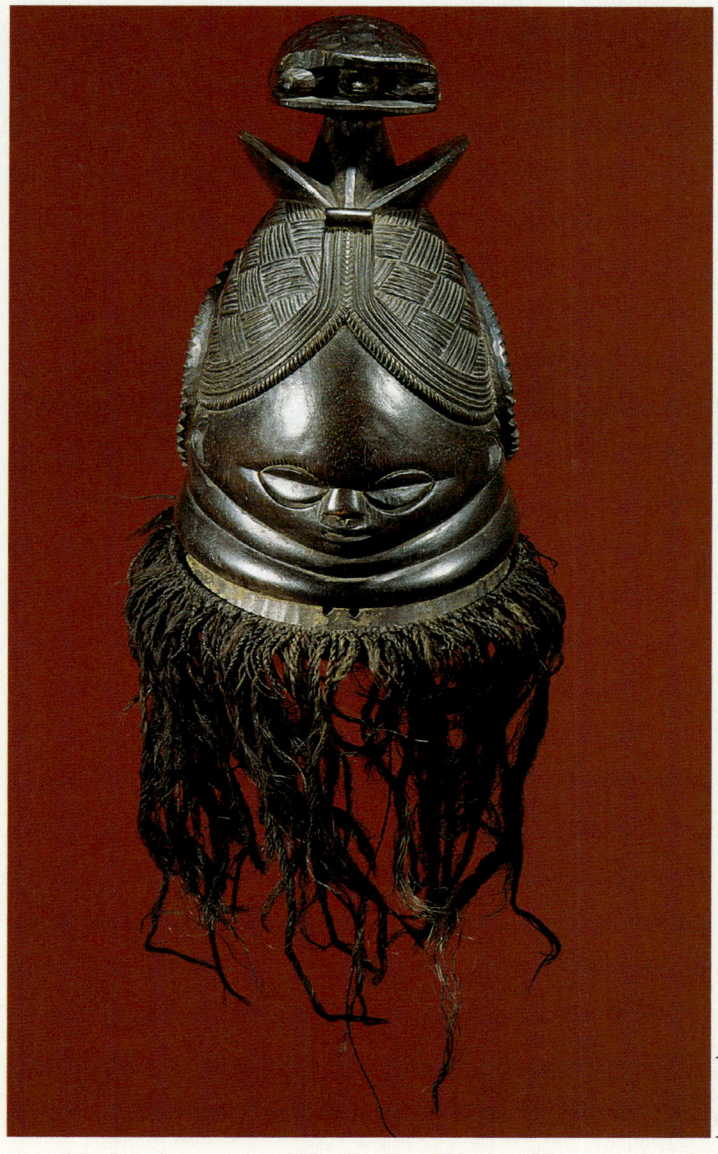

**37-20** Female mask, Mende, Sierra Leone, mid- to late 20th century. Painted wood, 1' 2½" high. Fowler Museum of Cultural History, University of California, Los Angeles (gift of the Wellcome Trust). ◼◀

This Mende mask refers to ideals of female beauty, morality, and behavior. The large forehead signifies wisdom, the neck design beauty and health, and the plaited hair the order of ideal households.

1 in.

for the eyes and a crowning element, much larger than the mask proper, depicting a schematic woman with large protruding breasts and sticklike bent arms. In ceremonies called Dama, held every several years to honor the lives of people who have died since the last Dama, Satimbe is among the dozens of different masked spirit characters escorting dead souls away from the village. The deceased are sent off to the land of the dead where, as ancestors, they will be enjoined to benefit their living descendants and stimulate agricultural productivity.

## Mende

The Mende are farmers who occupy the Atlantic coast of Africa in Sierra Leone. Although men own and perform most masks in Africa, in Mende society women control and dance Sande society masks (see "Mende Women as Maskers," above), while Mende men perform the Poro society masks.

**SOWIE MASKS** The glistening black surface of Mende Sowie masks (FIG. 37-20) evokes female spirits newly emergent from their underwater homes (also symbolized by the turtle on top). The mask and its parts refer to ideals of female beauty, morality, and behavior. A high broad forehead signifies wisdom and success. The neck ridges have multiple meanings. They are signs of beauty, good health, and prosperity and also reference the ripples in the water from which the water spirits emerge. Intricately woven or plaited hair is the essence of harmony and order found in ideal households. A small closed mouth and downcast eyes indicate the silent, serious demeanor expected of recent initiates.

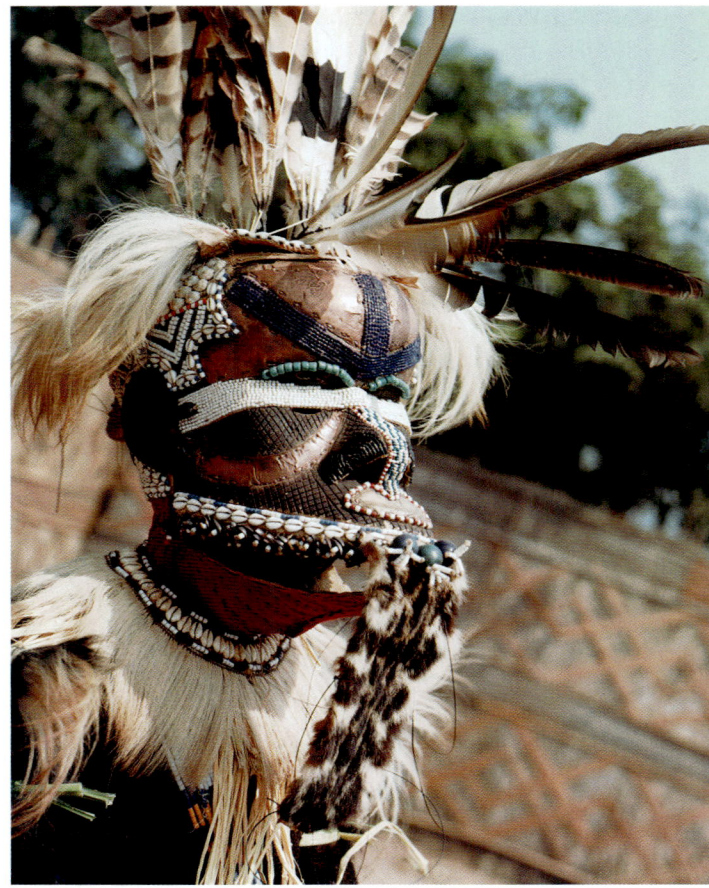

**37-21** Bwoom masquerader, Kuba, Democratic Republic of Congo, photographed ca. 1950.

At Kuba festivals, masqueraders reenact creation legends involving Bwoom, Mwashamboy, and Ngady Amwaash. The first two characters are males who vie for the attention of Ngady, the first female ancestor.

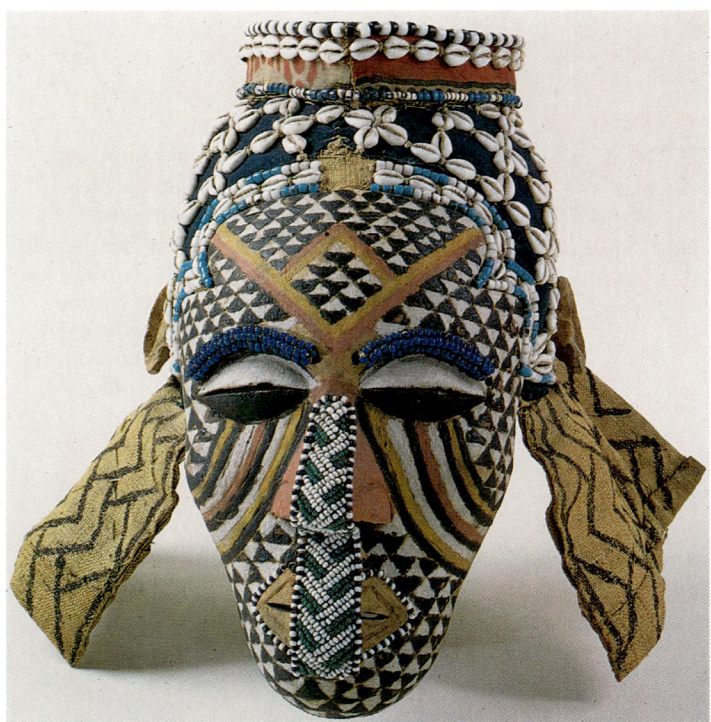

**37-22** Ngady Amwaash mask, Kuba, Democratic Republic of Congo, late 19th or early 20th century. Peabody Museum of Archaeology and Ethnology, Harvard University, Cambridge. ◼◣

Ngady's mask incorporates beads, shells, and feathers in geometric patterns. The stripes on her cheeks are tears from the pain of childbirth after incest with her father, represented by the Mwashamboy mask.

# Kuba

The Kuba have been well established in the Democratic Republic of Congo since at least the 16th century. They represent almost 20 different ethnic groups who all recognize the authority of a single king.

**BWOOM AND NGADY AMWAASH** At the court of Kuba kings, three masks, known as Mwashamboy, Bwoom, and Ngady Amwaash, represent legendary royal ancestors. Mwashamboy symbolizes the founding ancestor, Woot, and embodies the king's supernatural and political powers. Bwoom (FIG. **37-21**), with its bulging forehead, represents a legendary dwarf or pygmy who signifies the indigenous peoples on whom kingship was imposed. Bwoom also vies with Mwashamboy for the attention of the beautiful ancestress, Ngady Amwaash (FIG. **37-22**), who symbolizes both the first woman and all women. On her cheeks are striped tears from the pain of childbirth, and because to procreate, Ngady must commit incest with her father, Woot. These three characters reenact creation stories during royal initiation ceremonies. The masks and their costumes, with elaborate beads, feathers, animal pelts, cowrie shells, cut-pile cloth, and ornamental trappings, as well as geometric patterning, make for a sumptuous display at Kuba festivals.

**KING KOT A-MBWEEKY III** Throughout history, African costumes have been laden with meaning and have projected

messages all members of the society could read. A photograph (FIG. **37-23**) taken in 1970 shows Kuba King Kot a-Mbweeky III (r. 1969–) seated in state before his court, bedecked in a dazzling multimedia costume with many symbolic elements. The king commissioned the costume he wears and now has become art himself. Eagle feathers, leopard skin, cowrie shells, imported beads, raffia, and other materials combine to overload and expand the image of the man, making him larger than life and most certainly a work of art. He is an assemblage. He holds not one but two weapons, symbolic of his military might and underscoring his wealth, dignity, and grandeur. The man, with his regalia, embodies the office of sacred kingship. He is a superior being, in fact and figuratively, raised upon a dais, flanked by ornate drums, with a treasure basket of sacred relics by his left foot. The geometric patterns on the king's costume and nearby objects, and the abundance and redundancy of rich materials, epitomize the opulent style of Kuba court arts.

# Samburu

In addition to wearing masks and costumes on special occasions, people in many rural areas of eastern Africa, including the Samburu in northern Kenya, continue to embellish their own bodies.

**BODY ADORNMENT** The Samburu men and women shown in FIG. **37-24** at a spontaneous dance have distinct styles of personal decoration. Men, particularly warriors who are not yet married, expend hours creating elaborate hairstyles for one another. They paint their bodies with red ocher and wear bracelets, necklaces, and other bands of beaded jewelry made for them by young women. For themselves, women fashion more lavish constellations

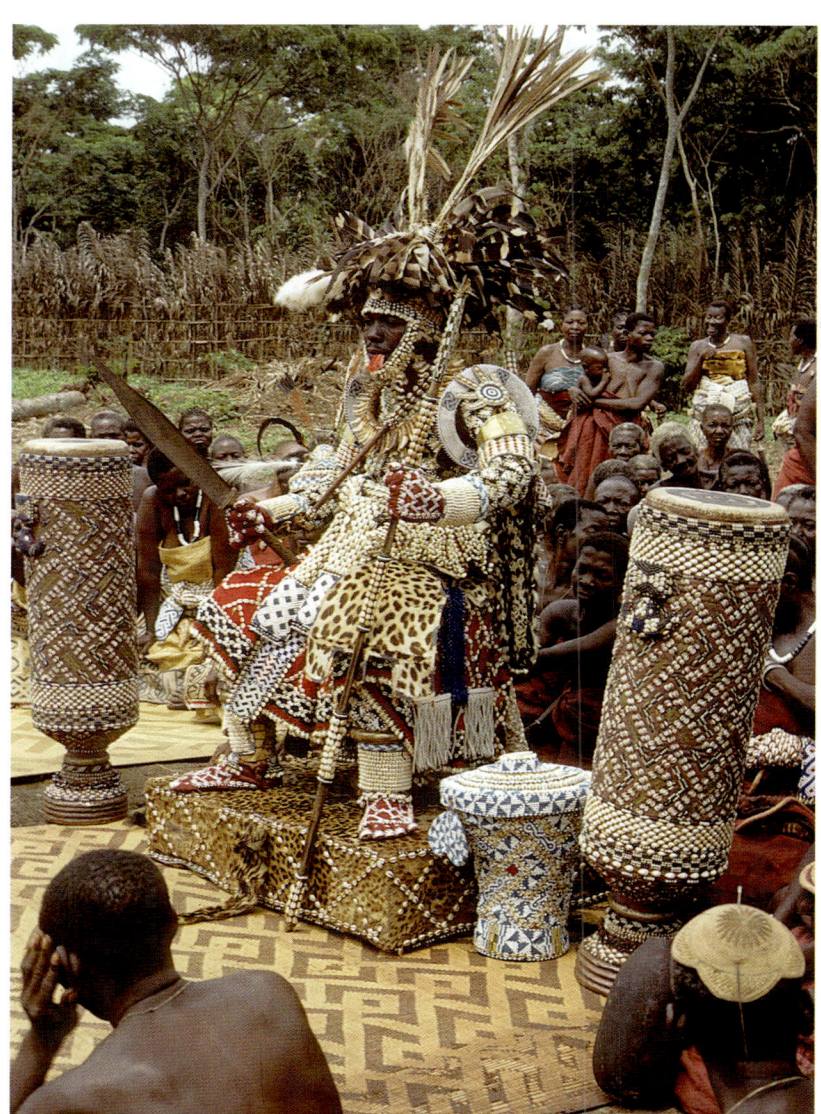

of beaded collars, which they mass around their necks. As if to help separate the genders, women shave their heads and adorn them with beaded headbands. Personal decoration begins in childhood, increasing to become lavish and highly self-conscious in young adulthood and diminishing as people age. Much of the decoration contains coded information—age, marital or initiation status, parentage of a warrior son—that can be read by those who know the codes. Dress ensembles have evolved over time. Different colors and sizes of beads became available, as did plastics and aluminum, and specific fashions have changed, but the overall concept of fine personal adornment—that is, dress raised to the level of art—remains much the same today as it was centuries ago.

# Igbo

The Igbo of the Lower Niger region in present-day Nigeria have a distinguished artistic tradition dating back more than a thousand years (see Chapter 19). The arts still play a vital role in Igbo society today.

**MBARI HOUSES** The powerful nature gods of the Igbo demand about every 50 years that a community build an *mbari* house. The Igbo construct these houses from mud as sacrifices to major deities, often Ala, goddess of the earth. The houses are elaborate unified artistic complexes incorporating numerous unfired clay sculptures and paintings—occasionally more than a hundred in a single mbari house. At Umugote Orishaeze, near Owerri,

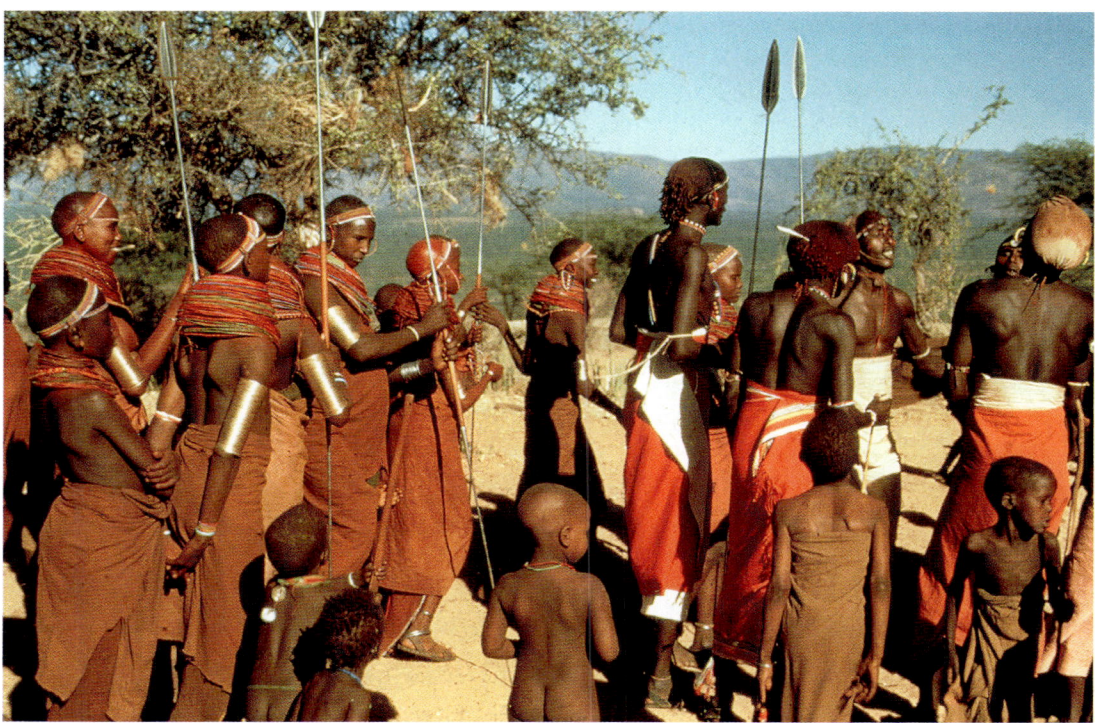

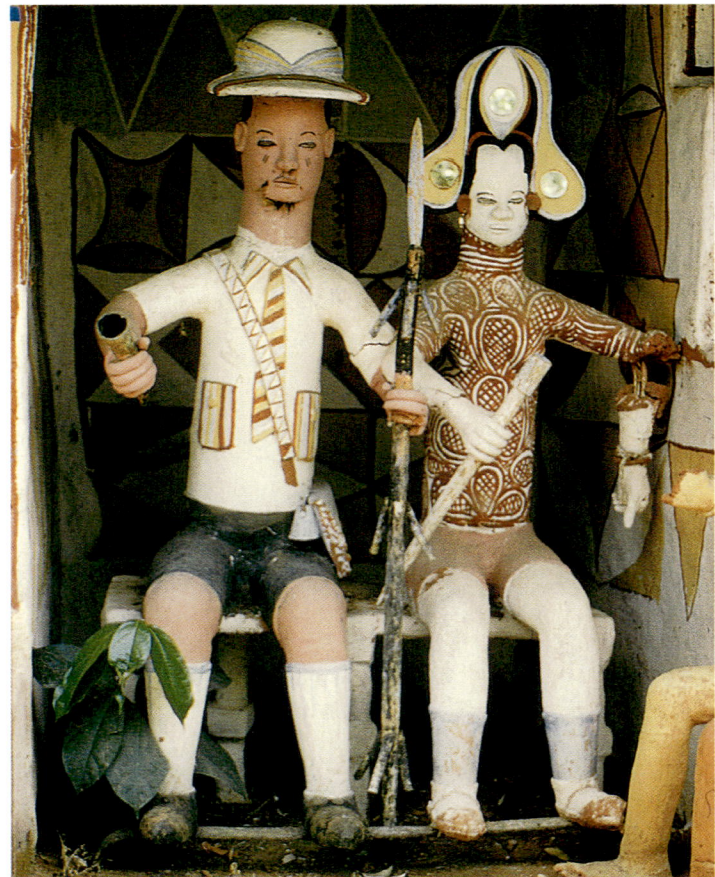

**37-25** Ala and Amadioha, painted clay sculptures in an mbari house, Igbo, Umugote Orishaeze, Nigeria, photographed in 1966.

The Igbo build mud mbari houses to the earth goddess Ala. The painted statues inside this one represent Ala in traditional dress with body paint and the thunder god Amadioha in modern dress.

one mbari house contains, among many others, two sculptures (FIG. **37-25**) depicting Ala and her consort, the thunder god Amadioha. The god wears modern clothing, whereas Ala appears with traditional body paint and a fancy hairstyle. These differing modes of dress relate to Igbo concepts of modernity and tradition, both viewed as positive by the men who control the ritual and art. They allow themselves modern attire but want their women to remain traditional. The artist enlarged and extended the torso, neck, and head of both figures to express their aloofness, dignity, and power. More informally posed figures and groups appear on the other sides of the house, including beautiful, amusing, or frightening figures of animals, humans, and spirits taken from mythology, history, dreams, and everyday life—a kaleidoscope of subjects and meanings. The mbari construction process, veiled in secrecy behind a fence, is a stylized world-renewal ritual. Ceremonies for unveiling the house to public view indicate Ala has accepted the sacrificial offer-

ing (of the mbari) and, for a time at least, will be benevolent. An mbari house never undergoes repair. Instead, the Igbo allow it to disintegrate and return to its source, the earth.

## Contemporary Art

The art forms of contemporary Africa vary immensely and defy easy classification. Those of international character with strong Western influence are discussed in Chapter 31. Others, for example, the Dogon men's house treated here, testify to the continuing vitality of traditional African art in the 21st century.

**DOGON TOGU NA** Traditionalism and modernism unite in the Dogon *togu na,* or "men's house of words." The togu na is so called because men's deliberations vital to community welfare take place under its sheltering roof. The Dogon consider it the "head" and the most important part of the community, and they characterize the togu na with human attributes. The Dogon build the men's houses over time. Earlier posts, such as the central one in the illustrated togu na (FIG. **37-26**), show schematic renderings of legendary female ancestors, similar to stylized ancestral couples (FIG. 37-11) or masked figures (FIG. 37-19). Recent replacement posts display narrative and topical scenes of varied subjects, such as horsemen or hunters or women preparing food, and feature abundant descriptive detail, bright polychrome painting in enamels, and even some writing. Unlike earlier traditional sculptors, the contemporary artists who made these posts want to be recognized, and they are eager to sell their work (other than these posts) to tourists.

**AFRICAN ART TODAY** During the past two centuries and especially in recent decades, the encroachments of Christianity, Islam, Western education, and market economies have led to increasing secularization in all the arts of Africa. Many figures and masks earlier commissioned for shrines or as incarnations of ancestors or spirits are now made mostly for sale to outsiders, essentially as tourist arts. They are also sold in art galleries abroad as collector's items for display. In towns and cities, painted murals and cement sculptures appear frequently, often making implicit comments about modern life. Nonetheless, despite the growing importance of urbanism, most African people still live in rural communities. Traditional values, although under pressure, hold considerable force in villages especially, and some people adhere to spiritual beliefs that uphold traditional art forms. African art remains as varied as the vast continent itself and continues to evolve.

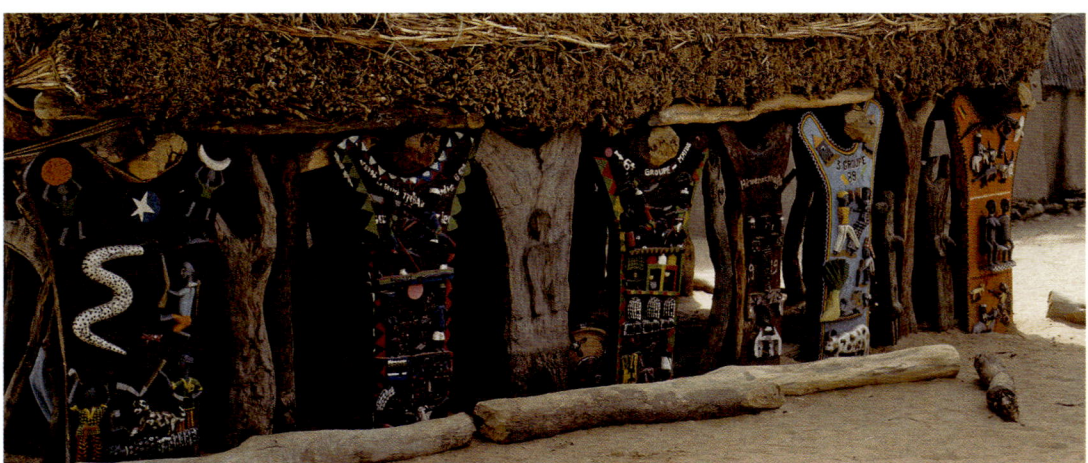

**37-26** Togu na (men's house of words), Dogon, Mali, photographed in 1989.

Dogon men hold their communal deliberations in a togu na. The posts of this one are of varied date. The oldest have traditional carvings, and the newest feature polychrome narrative or topical paintings.

# AFRICA, 1800 TO 1980

## 19TH CENTURY

▮ Most of the traditional forms of African art continued into the 19th century. Among these are sculptures and shrines connected with the veneration of ancestors. Wood or metal-covered wood figures guarded Fang and Kota reliquaries. Especially elaborate are some Kalabari Ijaw screens with figures of a deceased chief, his retainers, and the heads of his slaves and conquered rivals.

▮ The royal arts also flourished in the 19th century. The ultimate status symbol was the ruler's throne, for example the throne of King Nsangu of Bamum, which makes extensive use of richly colored textiles and glass beads, cowrie shells, and other luminous materials.

▮ One of the earliest African artists whose name survives is Akati Akpele Kendo, who worked for the Fon king Glele around 1858, but until the later 20th century, most African art remains anonymous.

▮ Throughout history, African artists have been masters of woodcarving. Especially impressive examples are the Kongo power figures bristling with nails and blades, and the Dogon and Baule sculptures of male and female couples. Although stylistically diverse, most African sculpture exhibits hierarchy of scale, both among figures and within the human body. For example, enlarged heads are common features of African statues.

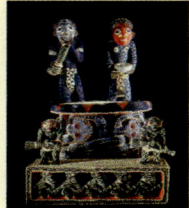

Throne of King Nsangu, Bamum, ca. 1870

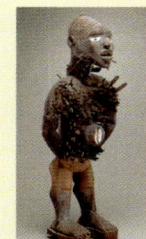

Kongo power figure, ca. 1875–1900

## 20TH CENTURY

▮ As in the 19th century, traditional arts flourished in 20th-century Africa. These include multimedia shrines, such as the ancestral altar of King Eweka II of Benin.

▮ The names of many more individual 20th-century artists are known. Two of the most famous are the Asante sculptor Osei Bonsu and the Yoruba sculptor Olowe of Ise.

▮ Osei Bonsu worked for kings and commoners alike, carving both single figures and groups, sometimes for the linguist's staff of a leader's spokesman. The distinctive features of his style are the flattened faces and crosshatched eyebrows of his figures.

▮ Olowe of Ise won renown for the painted wood doors and multifigure veranda posts he carved for houses and palaces. Elongated bodies and finely textured detail characterize his sculptures, both in relief and in the round.

▮ In Africa, art is nearly always an active agent in the lives of its peoples. A major African art form is the fashioning of masks for festive performances. Masqueraders are almost always men, even when the masks they dance are female, as among the Senufo, Dogon, and Kuba, but in Mende society, women are maskers too.

▮ Africans have also traditionally lavished attention on costume and jewelry and other forms of body adornment such as elaborate coiffures and body painting. The decoration often contains coded information about age, status, and parentage. Royal costumes consisting of animal skins, feathers, shells, beads, and raffia, and symbols of power such as crowns, swords, and scepters make kings seem larger than they really are in life.

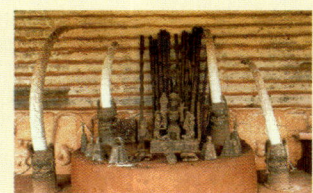

Benin ancestral altar, photographed in 1970

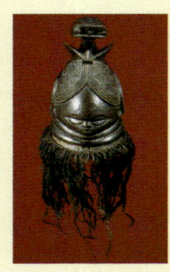

Bonsu, linguist's staff, mid-20th century

Mende female mask, mid- to late 20th century

# NOTES

## Introduction

1. Quoted in George Heard Hamilton, *Painting and Sculpture in Europe, 1880–1940,* 6th ed. (New Haven, Conn.: Yale University Press, 1993), 345.
2. Quoted in *Josef Albers: Homage to the Square* (New York: Museum of Modern Art, 1964), n.p.

## Chapter 2

1. Translated by Françoise Tallon, in Prudence O. Harper et al., *The Royal City of Susa* (New York: Metropolitan Museum of Art, 1991), 132.

## Chapter 3

1. The chronology adopted in this chapter is that of John Baines and Jaromír Malék, *Atlas of Ancient Egypt* (Oxford: Oxford University Press, 1980), 36–37. The division of kingdoms is that of, among others, Mark Lehner, *The Complete Pyramids* (New York: Thames & Hudson, 1997), 89, and David P. Silverman, ed., *Ancient Egypt* (New York: Oxford University Press, 1997), 20–39.
2. Translated by James P. Allen, *The Ancient Egyptian Pyramid Texts* (Atlanta, Ga.: Society of Biblical Literature, 2005), 31.
3. Allen, 57.
4. Allen, 56.

## Chapter 4

1. Homer, *Iliad,* 2.466–649.

## Chapter 5

1. Diodorus Siculus, *Library of History,* 1.91.
2. Pausanias, *Description of Greece,* 5.16.1.
3. Plutarch, *Life of Pericles,* 12.
4. Pliny, *Natural History,* 34.74.
5. Ibid., 36.20.
6. Lucian, *Amores,* 13–14; *Imagines,* 6.
7. Plutarch, *Moralia,* 335A–B. Translated by J. J. Pollitt, *The Art of Ancient Greece: Sources and Documents* (New York: Cambridge University Press, 1990), 99.
8. Pliny, *Natural History,* 35.110.
9. Ibid., 34.88.

## Chapter 7

1. Livy, *History of Rome,* 25.40.1–3.
2. Juvenal, *Satires,* 3.225, 232.

## Chapter 8

1. Translated by Raymond Davis, *The Book of Pontiffs* (Liverpool: Liverpool University Press, 1989), 18–19.

## Chapter 9

1. Paulus Silentiarius, *Descriptio Sanctae Sophiae,* 617–646. Translated by Cyril Mango, *The Art of the Byzantine Empire, 312–1453: Sources and Documents* (reprint of 1972 ed., Toronto: University of Toronto Press, 1986), 85–86.
2. Procopius, *De aedificiis,* 1.1.23ff. Translated by Mango, 74.
3. Paulus Silentiarius, *Descriptio,* 489, 668. Translated by Mango, 83, 86.

4. Translated by Colin Luibheid, *Pseudo-Dionysius: The Complete Works* (New York: Paulist Press, 1987), 68ff.
5. Procopius, 1.1.23ff. Translated by Mango, 75.
6. *Libri Carolini,* 4.2. Translated by Herbert L. Kessler, *Spiritual Seeing: Picturing God's Invisibility in Medieval Art* (Philadelphia: University of Pennsylvania Press, 2000), 119.
7. Nina G. Garsoïan, "Later Byzantium," in John A. Garraty and Peter Gay, eds., *The Columbia History of the World* (New York: Harper & Row, 1972), 453.
8. Garsoïan, 460.

## Chapter 11

1. Translated by Françoise Henry, *The Book of Kells* (New York: Alfred A. Knopf, 1974), 165.
2. *Beowulf,* 3162–3164. Translated by Kevin Crossley-Holland (New York: Farrar, Straus & Giroux, 1968), 119.
3. *Beowulf,* 33.
4. Translated by John W. Williams, in *The Art of Medieval Spain A.D. 500–1200* (New York: Metropolitan Museum of Art, 1993), 156.
5. Translated by Adam S. Cohen, *The Uta Codex* (University Park: Pennsylvania University Press, 2000), 11, 41.

## Chapter 12

1. Translated by Calvin B. Kendall, *The Allegory of the Church: Romanesque Portals and Their Verse Inscriptions* (Toronto: University of Toronto Press, 1998), 207.
2. Translated by John Williams, *A Spanish Apocalypse: The Morgan Beatus Manuscript* (New York: George Braziller, 1991), 223.
3. Translated by Charles P. Parkhurst Jr., in Elizabeth G. Holt, *A Documentary History of Art* (Princeton, N.J.: Princeton University Press, 2d ed., 1981), 1: 18.
4. Translated by Giovanna De Appolonia, Boston University.
5. Bernard of Clairvaux, *Apologia* 12.28. Translated by Conrad Rudolph, *The "Things of Greater Importance": Bernard of Clairvaux's* Apologia *and the Medieval Attitude toward Art* (Philadelphia: University of Pennsylvania Press, 1990), 281, 283.
6. *Rule of Saint Benedict,* 57.1. Translated by Timothy Fry, *The Rule of St. Benedict* (Collegeville, Minn.: Liturgical Press, 1981), 265.

## Chapter 13

1. Giorgio Vasari, "Introduzione alle tre arti del disegno" (1550), ch. 3, in Paul Frankl, *The Gothic: Literary Sources and Interpretation through Eight Centuries* (Princeton, N.J.: Princeton University Press, 1960), 290–291, 859–860.
2. Dante, *Divine Comedy,* Purgatory, 11.81.
3. Translated by Roland Behrendt, *Johannes Trithemius, In Praise of Scribes: De laude scriptorum* (Lawrence, Kansas: Coronado Press, 1974), 71.
4. Frankl, *The Gothic,* 55.

## Chapter 20

1. Francisco de Hollanda, *De pintura antigua* (1548), quoted in Robert Klein and Henri Zerner, *Italian Art, 1500–1600: Sources and Documents* (Englewood Cliffs, N.J.: Prentice-Hall, 1966), 33.

**Chapter 21**

1. Ghiberti, *I commentarii*, II. Quoted in Elizabeth Gilmore Holt, ed., *A Documentary History of Art, I: The Middle Ages and the Renaissance* (Princeton, N.J.: Princeton University Press, 1981), 157–158.
2. Translated by Catherine Enggass, in Howard Saalman, ed., *Antonio Manetti, Life of Brunelleschi* (University Park: Pennsylvania State University Press, 1970), 42.
3. Giorgio Vasari, *Life of Lorenzo Ghiberti.* Translated by Gaston du C. de Vere, ed., *Giorgio Vasari, Lives of the Painters, Sculptors, and Architects* (New York: Knopf, 1996), 1: 304.
4. Ghiberti, *I commentarii*, II. Quoted in Holt, 161.
5. Quoted in H. W. Janson, *The Sculpture of Donatello* (Princeton, N.J.: Princeton University Press, 1965), 154.
6. Vasari, *Life of Masaccio.* Translated by Gaston du C. de Vere, 1: 318.
7. Martial, *Epigrams,* 10.32.

**Chapter 22**

1. Plato, *Ion,* 534. Translated by Benjamin Jowett, *The Dialogues of Plato,* 4th ed., vol. 1 (Oxford: Clarendon Press, 1953), 107–108.
2. Da Vinci to Ludovico Sforza, ca. 1480–1481. In Elizabeth Gilmore Holt, ed., *A Documentary History of Art* (Princeton: Princeton University Press, 1981), I: 274–275.
3. Quoted in Anthony Blunt, *Artistic Theory in Italy, 1450–1600* (London: Oxford University Press, 1964), 34.
4. Quoted in James M. Saslow, *The Poetry of Michelangelo: An Annotated Translation* (New Haven, Conn.: Yale University Press, 1991), 407.
5. Giorgio Vasari, *Lives of the Painters, Sculptors, and Architects.* Translated by Gaston du C. de Vere (New York: Knopf, 1996), 2: 736.
6. Quoted in A. Richard Turner, *Renaissance Florence: The Invention of a New Art* (New York: Abrams, 1997), 163.
7. Quoted in Bruce Boucher, *Andrea Palladio: The Architect in His Time* (New York: Abbeville Press, 1998), 229.
8. Quoted in Robert J. Clements, *Michelangelo's Theory of Art* (New York: New York University Press, 1961), 320.

**Chapter 23**

1. Translated by Erwin Panofsky, in Wolfgang Stechow, *Northern Renaissance Art 1400–1600: Sources and Documents* (Evanston, Ill.: Northwestern University Press, 1989), 123.
2. Translated by Bernhard Erling, in Stechow, 129–130.
3. Giorgio Vasari, *Lives of the Painters, Sculptors, and Architects.* Translated by Gaston du C. de Vere (New York: Knopf, 1996), 2: 863.

**Chapter 24**

1. Filippo Baldinucci, *Vita del Cavaliere Giovanni Lorenzo Bernini* (1681). Translated by Robert Enggass, in Enggass and Jonathan Brown, *Italian and Spanish Art 1600–1750: Sources and Documents* (Evanston, Ill.: Northwestern University Press, 1992), 116.
2. John Milton, *Il Penseroso* (1631, published 1645), 166.

**Chapter 25**

1. Quoted in Julie Berger Hochstrasser, *Still Life and Trade in the Dutch Golden Age* (New Haven, Conn.: Yale University Press, 2007), 16.
2. Translated by Kristin Lohse Belkin, *Rubens* (London: Phaidon, 1998), 47.
3. Albert Blankert, *Johannes Vermeer van Delft 1632–1675* (Utrecht: Spectrum, 1975), 133, no. 51. Translated by Bob Haak, *The Golden Age: Dutch Painters of the Seventeenth Century* (New York: Abrams, 1984), 450.

**Chapter 26**

1. Translated by Robert Goldwater and Marco Treves, eds., *Artists on Art,* 3d ed. (New York: Pantheon Books, 1958), 157.
2. Quoted in Thomas A. Bailey, *The American Pageant: A History of the Republic,* 2d ed. (Boston: Heath, 1961), 280.
3. Translated by Elfriede Heyer and Roger C. Norton, in Charles Harrison, Paul Wood, and Jason Gaiger, eds., *Art in Theory 1648–1815: An Anthology of Changing Ideas* (Oxford: Blackwell, 2000), 451–453.

**Chapter 27**

1. Théophile Gautier, *Histoire de Romantisme* (Paris: Charpentier, 1874), 204.
2. Quoted in Helmut Borsch-Supan, *Caspar David Friedrich* (New York: Braziller, 1974), 7.

3. Translated by Jason Gaiger, in Charles Harrison, Paul Wood, and Jason Gaiger, eds., *Art in Theory 1815–1900: An Anthology of Changing Ideas* (Oxford: Blackwell, 1998), 54.
4. Quoted by Brian Lukacher, in Stephen F. Eisenman, ed., *Nineteenth Century Art: A Critical History* (New York: Thames & Hudson, 2007), 126.
5. Quoted in John W. McCoubrey, *American Art 1700–1960: Sources and Documents* (Upper Saddle River, N.J.: Prentice Hall, 1965), 98.
6. Quoted in Thomas A. Bailey, *The American Pageant: A History of the Republic,* 2d ed. (Boston: Heath, 1961), 280.
7. Quoted in Linda Nochlin, *Realism and Tradition in Art 1848–1900* (Upper Saddle River, N.J.: Prentice Hall, 1966), 42.
8. Quoted in George Heard Hamilton, *Manet and His Critics* (New Haven, Conn.: Yale University Press, 1954), 45.
9. Quoted in Eisenman, ed., *Nineteenth Century Art,* 336.
10. *New York Weekly Tribune,* September 30, 1865.
11. Quoted in Nikolai Cikovsky Jr. and Franklin Kelly, *Winslow Homer* (Washington, D.C.: National Gallery of Art, 1995), 26.
12. Quoted in Lloyd Goodrich, *Thomas Eakins, His Life and Work* (New York: Whitney Museum of American Art, 1933), 51–52.
13. Quoted in Nicholas Pevsner, *An Outline of European Architecture* (Baltimore: Penguin, 1960), 627.
14. Letter from Delaroche to François Arao, quoted in Helmut Gernsheim, *Creative Photography* (New York: Bonanza Books, 1962), 24.
15. Quoted in Naomi Rosenblum, *A World History of Photography,* 4th ed. (New York: Abbeville Press, 2007), 69.
16. Quoted in Kenneth MacGowan, *Behind the Screen* (New York: Delta, 1965), 49.

**Chapter 28**

1. Quoted in Linda Nochlin, *Realism* (Harmondsworth: Penguin, 1971), 28.
2. Clement Greenberg, "Modernist Painting," *Art and Literature,* no. 4 (Spring 1965): 193–194.
3. Quoted in Linda Nochlin, *Impressionism and Post-Impressionism 1874–1904: Sources and Documents* (Englewood Cliffs, N.J.: Prentice Hall, 1966), 35.
4. Translated by Carola Hicks, in Charles Harrison, Paul Wood, and Jason Gaiger, *Art in Theory 1815–1900* (Oxford: Blackwell, 1998), 595.
5. Quoted in John McCoubrey, *American Art 1700–1960: Sources and Documents* (Englewood Cliffs, N.J.: Prentice Hall, 1965), 184.
6. Quoted in Robert Goldwater and Marco Treves, eds., *Artists on Art, from the XIV to the XX Century* (New York: Pantheon, 1945), 322.
7. Ibid., 375.
8. Vincent van Gogh to Theo van Gogh, September 1888, in J. van Gogh–Bonger and V. W. van Gogh, eds., *The Complete Letters of Vincent van Gogh* (Greenwich, Conn.: New York Graphic Society, 1979), 3: 534.
9. Vincent van Gogh to Theo van Gogh, July 16, 1888, in W. H. Auden, ed., *Van Gogh: A Self-Portrait. Letters Revealing His Life as a Painter* (New York: Dutton, 1963), 299.
10. Quoted in Sam Hunter, John Jacobus, and Daniel Wheeler, *Modern Art,* 3d ed. (Upper Saddle River, N.J.: Prentice Hall, 2004), 28.
11. Cézanne to Émile Bernard, March 1904. Quoted in Goldwater and Treves, *Artists on Art,* 363.
12. Cézanne to Émile Bernard, April 15, 1904. Ibid., 363.
13. Translated by Akane Kawakami, in Harrison, Wood, and Gaiger, *Art in Theory,* 1066.
14. Quoted in George Heard Hamilton, *Painting and Sculpture in Europe 1880–1940,* 6th ed. (New Haven, Conn.: Yale University Press, 1993), 124.
15. Quoted in V. Frisch and J. T. Shipley, *Auguste Rodin* (New York: Stokes, 1939), 203.
16. Quoted in Eileen Boris, *Art and Labor: Ruskin, Morris, and the Craftsman Ideal in America* (Philadelphia: Temple University Press, 1986), 7.

**Chapter 29**

1. Quoted in John Elderfield, *The "Wild Beasts": Fauvism and Its Affinities* (New York: Museum of Modern Art, 1976), 29.
2. Translated by Charles Harrison and Paul Wood, eds., *Art in Theory 1900–2000: An Anthology of Changing Ideas* (Oxford: Blackwell, 2003), 65.
3. Quoted in Frederick S. Levine, *The Apocalyptic Vision: The Art of Franz Marc as German Expressionism* (New York: Harper & Row, 1979), 57.
4. Quoted in Sam Hunter, John Jacobus, and Daniel Wheeler, *Modern Art,* rev. 3d ed. (Upper Saddle River, N.J.: Prentice Hall, 2004), 121.

5. Quoted in George Heard Hamilton, *Painting and Sculpture in Europe 1880–1940*, 6th ed. (New Haven, Conn.: Yale University Press, 1993), 246.

6. Ibid., 238.

7. Quoted in Edward Fry, ed., *Cubism* (London: Thames & Hudson, 1966), 112–113.

8. Quoted in Françoise Gilot and Carlton Lake, *Life with Picasso* (New York: McGraw-Hill, 1964), 77.

9. Pablo Picasso, "Statement to Simone Téry," in Harrison and Wood, eds., *Art in Theory 1900–2000*, 649.

10. Quoted in Roland Penrose, *Picasso: His Life and Work*, rev. ed. (New York: Harper & Row, 1971), 311.

11. Filippo Tommaso Marinetti, *The Foundation and Manifesto of Futurism* (*Le Figaro*, February 20, 1909). Translated by Joshua C. Taylor, in Herschel B. Chipp, *Theories of Modern Art: A Source Book by Artists and Critics* (Berkeley and Los Angeles: University of California Press, 1968), 284.

12. Ibid., 286.

13. Quoted in Robert Short, *Dada and Surrealism* (London: Octopus Books, 1980), 18.

14. Quoted in Robert Motherwell, ed., *The Dada Painters and Poets: An Anthology*, 2d ed. (Cambridge, Mass.: Belknap Press of Harvard University, 1989).

15. Hans Richter, *Dada: Art and Anti-Art* (London: Thames & Hudson, 1961), 64–65.

16. Ibid., 57.

17. Quoted in Arturo Schwarz, *The Complete Works of Marcel Duchamp* (London: Thames & Hudson, 1965), 466.

18. Translated by Howard Dearstyne, in Robert L. Herbert, *Modern Artists on Art*, 2d ed. (Mineola, N.Y.: Dover, 2000), 117.

19. Ibid., 124.

20. Translated by Herbert Read and Leslie Martin, quoted in Chipp, *Theories of Modern Art*, 325–330.

21. Quoted in Sam Hunter, *American Art of the 20th Century* (New York: Abrams, 1972), 30.

22. Ibid., 37.

23. Charles C. Eldredge, "The Arrival of European Modernism," *Art in America* 61 (July–August 1973): 35.

24. Quoted in Gail Stavitsky, "Reordering Reality: Precisionist Directions in American Art 1915–1941," in *Precisionism in America 1915–1941: Reordering Reality* (New York: Abrams, 1994), 12.

25. Quoted in Karen Tsujimoto, *Images of America: Precisionist Painting and Modern Photography* (Seattle: University of Washington Press, 1982), 70.

26. Dorothy Norman, *Alfred Stieglitz: An American Seer* (Millerton, N.Y.: Aperture, 1973), 9–10.

27. Ibid., 161.

28. Quoted in Vincent Scully Jr., *Frank Lloyd Wright* (New York: Braziller, 1960), 18.

29. Quoted in Edgar Kauffmann, ed., *Frank Lloyd Wright: An American Architect* (New York: Horizon, 1955), 205, 208.

30. Quoted in Matthias Eberle, *World War I and the Weimar Artists: Dix, Grosz, Beckmann, Schlemmer* (New Haven, Conn.: Yale University Press, 1985), 54.

31. Ibid., 22.

32. Ibid., 42.

33. Quoted in William S. Rubin, *Dada, Surrealism, and Their Heritage* (New York: Museum of Modern Art, 1968), 64.

34. Quoted in Hamilton, *Painting and Sculpture in Europe 1880–1940*, 6th ed. (New Haven, Conn.: Yale University Press, 1993), 392.

35. Quoted in Richter, *Dada*, 155.

36. Ibid., 159.

37. Quoted in Rubin, *Dada, Surrealism*, 111.

38. Quoted in Hunter, Jacobus, and Wheeler, *Modern Art*, 179.

39. Quoted in William S. Rubin, *Miró in the Collection of the Museum of Modern Art* (New York: Museum of Modern Art, 1973), 32.

40. Translated by Norbert Guterman, quoted in Chipp, *Theories of Modern Art*, 182–186.

41. Translated by Nicholas Bullock, quoted in Harrison and Wood, *Art in Theory 1900–2000*, 281.

42. Quoted in Kenneth Frampton, *Modern Architecture: A Critical History*, 4th ed. (New York: Thames & Hudson, 2007), 147.

43. Quoted in Michel Seuphor, *Piet Mondrian: Life and Work* (New York: Abrams, 1956), 117.

44. Piet Mondrian, *Plastic Art and Pure Plastic Art* (1937), quoted in Hamilton, *Painting and Sculpture*, 319.

45. Mondrian, *Plastic Art*, quoted in Chipp, *Theories of Modern Art*, 349.

46. Ibid., 350.

47. Quoted in H. H. Arnason and Peter Kalb, *History of Modern Art*, 5th ed. (Upper Saddle River, N.J.: Prentice Hall, 2004), 154.

48. Quoted in Herbert, *Modern Artists on Art*, 173.

49. Ibid., 177.

50. Quoted in Hans L. Jaffé, comp., *De Stijl* (New York: Abrams, 1971), 185–188.

51. Piet Mondrian, *Dialogue on the New Plastic* (1919). Translated by Harry Holzman and Martin S. James, in Harrison and Wood, *Art in Theory 1900–2000*, 285.

52. Quoted in Wayne Craven, *American Art: History and Culture* (Madison, Wis.: Brown & Benchmark, 2003), 403.

53. Quoted in Vivian Endicott Barnett, "Banned German Art: Reception and Institutional Support of Modern German Art in the United States, 1933–45," in Stephanie Barron, *Exiles and Emigrés: The Flight of European Artists from Hitler* (Los Angeles: Los Angeles County Museum of Art, 1997), 283.

54. Quoted in Frances K. Pohl, *Ben Shahn: New Deal Artist in a Cold War Climate, 1947–1954* (Austin: University of Texas Press, 1989), 159.

55. Quoted in Henry Louis Gates Jr., "New Negroes, Migration, and Cultural Exchange," in Elizabeth Hutton Turner, ed., *Jacob Lawrence: The Migration Series* (Washington, D.C.: Phillips Collection, 1993), 20.

56. Wanda M. Corn, *Grant Wood: The Regionalist Vision* (New Haven, Conn.: Yale University Press, 1983), 131.

57. Quoted in Matthew Baigell, *A Concise History of American Painting and Sculpture* (New York: Harper & Row, 1984), 264.

58. Quoted in Milton Meltzer, *Dorothea Lange: A Photographer's Life* (New York: Farrar, Straus, Giroux, 1978), 133, 220.

59. Quoted in Philip Johnson, *Mies van der Rohe*, rev. ed. (New York: Museum of Modern Art, 1954), 200–201.

**Chapter 30**

1. Dawn Ades and Andrew Forge, *Francis Bacon* (London: Thames & Hudson, 1985), 8; and David Sylvester, *The Brutality of Fact: Interviews with Francis Bacon*, 3d ed. (London: Thames & Hudson, 1987), 182.

2. Clement Greenberg, "Toward a Newer *Laocoon*," *Partisan Review* 7, no. 4 (July–August 1940): 305.

3. Clement Greenberg, "Sculpture in Our Time," *Arts Magazine* 32, no. 9 (June 1956): 22.

4. Marcus Rothko and Adolph Gottlieb, quoted in Edward Alden Jewell, "The Realm of Art: A New Platform and Other Matters: 'Globalism' Pops into View," *New York Times*, June 13, 1943, 9.

5. Reprinted in Harold Rosenberg, *The Tradition of the New* (New York: Horizon, 1959), 25.

6. Quoted in Thomas Hess, *Barnett Newman* (New York: Walker and Company, 1969), 51.

7. Quoted in John P. O'Neill, ed., *Barnett Newman: Selected Writings and Interviews* (New York: Knopf, 1990), 108.

8. Rothko and Gottlieb, "The Realm of Art," 9.

9. Quoted in Selden Rodman, *Conversations with Artists* (New York: Devin-Adair, 1957), 93–94.

10. Clement Greenberg, "Recentness of Sculpture," in Gregory Battcock, ed., *Minimal Art: A Critical Anthology* (New York: Dutton, 1968), 183–184.

11. Louise Nevelson, quoted in John Gordon, *Louise Nevelson* (New York: Praeger, 1967), 12.

12. Quoted in Deborah Wye, *Louise Bourgeois* (New York: Museum of Modern Art, 1982), 22.

13. Ibid., 25.

14. Quoted in Lucy Lippard, *Eva Hesse* (New York: New York University Press, 1976), 165.

15. Ibid., 56.

16. Quoted in Richard Francis, *Jasper Johns* (New York: Abbeville, 1984), 21.

17. Andy Warhol, *The Philosophy of Andy Warhol* (New York: Harcourt Brace Jovanovich, 1975), 100.

18. Quoted in Christine Lindey, *Superrealist Painting and Sculpture* (London: Orbis, 1980), 50.

19. Quoted in Sebastian Smee, *Lucian Freud: Beholding the Animal* (Cologne: Taschen, 2009), 61.

20. Ibid., 7

21. Lindey, *Superrealist Painting,* 130.

22. Quoted in Susanna Torruella Leval, "Recapturing History: The (Un)official Story in Contemporary Latin American Art," *Art Journal* 51, no. 4 (Winter 1992): 74.

23. Ibid.

24. Hannah Wilke, "Visual Prejudice," in *Hannah Wilke: A Retrospective* (Columbia: University of Missouri Press, 1989), 141.

25. Quoted in Mary Jane Jacob, *Magdalena Abakanowicz* (New York: Abbeville, 1982), 94.

26. Peter Blake, *Frank Lloyd Wright* (Harmondsworth: Penguin, 1960), 115.

27. Quoted in Nancy Holt, ed., *The Writings of Robert Smithson* (New York: New York University Press, 1975), 111.

28. Quoted in H. H. Arnason and Peter Kalb, *History of Modern Art,* 5th ed. (Upper Saddle River, N.J.: Prentice Hall, 2004), 489.

29. Quoted in Barbara Haskell, *Blam! The Explosion of Pop, Minimalism, and Performance 1958–1964* (New York: Whitney Museum of American Art), 53.

30. Quoted in Bruce McPherson, ed., *More Than "Meat Joy": Complete Performance Works and Selected Writings* (New Paltz, N.Y.: Documentext, 1979), 52.

31. Quoted in Caroline Tisdall, *Joseph Beuys* (New York: Thames & Hudson, 1979), 6.

32. Quoted in "Joseph Kosuth: Art as Idea as Idea," in Jeanne Siegel, ed., *Artwords: Discourse on the 60s and 70s* (Ann Arbor, Mich.: UMI Research Press, 1985), 221, 225.

33. Quoted in Brenda Richardson, *Bruce Nauman: Neons* (Baltimore: Baltimore Museum of Art, 1982), 20.

**Chapter 31**

1. Quoted in Arlene Hirschfelder, *Artists and Craftspeople* (New York: Facts on File, 1994), 115.

2. Quoted in Richard Marshall and Robert Mapplethorpe, *50 New York Artists* (San Francisco: Chronicle Books, 1986), 448–449.

3. Quoted in Junichi Shiota, *Kimio Tsuchiya, Sculpture 1984–1988* (Tokyo: Morris Gallery, 1988), 3.

4. Michelle Meagher, "Jenny Saville and a Feminist Aesthetics of Disgust," *Hypatia* 18.4 (Fall/Winter 2003), 23–41.

5. Quoted in Donald Hall, *Corporal Politics* (Cambridge: MIT List Visual Arts Center, 1993), 46.

6. Quoted in "Vietnam Memorial: America Remembers," *National Geographic* 167, no. 5 (May 1985): 557.

7. Quoted in Calvin Tomkins, "The Art World: *Tilted Arc,*" *New Yorker,* May 20, 1985, 100.

**Chapter 33**

1. Translated by Wang Youfen. Quoted by Wen C. Fong, in Ouyang Zhongshi, Wen C. Fong et al., *Chinese Calligraphy* (New Haven, Conn.: Yale University Press, 2008), 26.

**Chapter 34**

1. Jiro Yoshihara, "Gutai Art Manifesto" (1956), translated by Reiko Tomii, in *Japanese Art after 1945: Scream against the Sky* (Yokohama: Yokohama Museum of Art, 1994), 370.

**Chapter 35**

1. Diego de Landa, *Yucatan before and after the Conquest,* translated by William Gates (Mineola, N.Y.: Dover, 1978), 13, 82.

2. Bernal Díaz del Castillo, *The Discovery and Conquest of Mexico.* Translated by A. P. Maudslay (New York: Farrar, Straus, Giroux, 1956), 218–219.

# GLOSSARY

**Note:** *Text page references are in parentheses. References to bonus image online essays are in* blue.

**a secco**—Italian, "dried." See *fresco.* (603)

**abacus**—The uppermost portion of the *capital* of a *column,* usually a thin slab. (116)

**abbess**—See *abbey.* (322)

**abbey**—A religious community under the direction of an abbot (for monks) or an abbess (for nuns). (322)

**abbot**—See *abbey.* (322)

**abhaya**—See *mudra.* (427, 984)

**abrasion**—The rubbing or grinding of stone or another material to produce a smooth finish. (64)

**abstract**—Non-representational; forms and colors arranged without reference to the depiction of an object. (5)

**Abstract Expressionism**—The first major American avant-garde movement, Abstract Expressionism emerged in New York City in the 1940s. The artists produced *abstract* paintings that expressed their state of mind and that they hoped would strike emotional chords in viewers. The movement developed along two lines: *gestural abstraction* and *chromatic abstraction.* (902, 1046)

**acropolis**—Greek, "high city." In ancient Greece, usually the site of the city's most important temple(s). (117)

**action painting**—Also called *gestural abstraction.* The kind of *Abstract Expressionism* practiced by Jackson Pollock, in which the emphasis was on the creation process, the artist's gesture in making art. Pollock poured liquid paint in linear webs on his canvases, which he laid out on the floor, thereby physically surrounding himself in the painting during its creation. (905, 1019)

**additive light**—Natural light, or sunlight, the sum of all the wavelengths of the visible *spectrum.* See also *subtractive light.* (7)

**additive sculpture**—A kind of sculpture *technique* in which materials (for example, clay) are built up or "added" to create form. (11)

**adobe**—The clay used to make a kind of sun-dried mud brick of the same name; a building made of such brick. (508, 529)

**aerial perspective**—See *perspective.* (567)

**agora**—An open square or space used for public meetings or business in ancient Greek cities. (138)

**ahu**—A stone platform on which the *moai* of Easter Island stand. Ahu marked burial sites or served ceremonial purposes. (1052)

**'ahu 'ula**—A Hawaiian feather cloak. (1058)

**airbrush**—A tool that uses compressed air to spray paint onto a surface. (918)

**aisle**—The portion of a *basilica* flanking the *nave* and separated from it by a row of *columns* or *piers.* (12, 189, 243)

**akua'ba**—"Akua's child." A Ghanaian image of a young girl. (1071)

**ala (pl. alae)**—One of a pair of rectangular recesses at the back of the *atrium* of a Roman house. (190)

**album leaf**—A painting on a single sheet of paper for a collection stored in an album. (459, 999)

**alchemy**—The study of seemingly magical changes, especially chemical changes. (645)

**altar frontal**—A decorative panel on the front of a church altar. (367)

**altarpiece**—A panel, painted or sculpted, situated above and behind an altar. See also *retable.* (392, 404)

**alternate-support system**—In church architecture, the use of alternating wall supports in the *nave,* usually *piers* and *columns* or *compound piers* of alternating form. (324)

**amalaka**—In Hindu temple design, the large flat disk with ribbed edges surmounting the beehive-shaped tower (*shikara*). (439)

**Amazonomachy**—In Greek mythology, the battle between the Greeks and Amazons. (136)

**ambo**—A church *pulpit* for biblical readings. (392)

**ambulatory**—A covered walkway, outdoors (as in a church *cloister*) or indoors; especially the passageway around the *apse* and the *choir* of a church. In Buddhist architecture, the passageway leading around the *stupa* in a *chaitya hall.* (244, 430)

**amphiprostyle**—A *classical* temple *plan* in which the *columns* are placed across both the front and back but not along the sides. (115)

**amphitheater**—Greek, "double theater." A Roman building type resembling two Greek theaters put together. The Roman amphitheater featured a continuous elliptical *cavea* around a central *arena.* (189, 401)

**amphora**—An ancient Greek two-handled jar used for general storage purposes, usually to hold wine or oil. (110)

**amulet**—An object worn to ward off evil or to aid the wearer. (61)

**Analytic Cubism**—The first phase of *Cubism,* developed jointly by Pablo Picasso and Georges Braque, in which the artists analyzed form from every possible vantage point to combine the various views into one pictorial whole. (847)

**anamorphic image**—A distorted image that must be viewed by some special means (such as a mirror) to be recognized. (656)

**ancien régime**—French, "old order." The term used to describe the political, social, and religious order in France before the Revolution at the end of the 18th century. (736)

**antae**—The molded projecting ends of the walls forming the *pronaos* or *opisthodomos* of an ancient Greek temple. (115)

**ante legem**—Latin, "before the law." In Christian thought, the period before Moses received the Ten Commandments. See also *sub lege.* (392)

**apadana**—The great audience hall in ancient Persian palaces. (51)

**apostle**—Greek, "messenger." One of the 12 disciples of Jesus. (240)

**apotheosis**—Elevated to the rank of gods, or the ascent to heaven. (206, 18-10A)

**apotropaic**—Capable of warding off evil. (118)

**apoxyomenos**—Greek, "athlete scraping oil from his body." (147)

**apse**—A recess, usually semicircular, in the wall of a building, commonly found at the east end of a church. (28, 134, 208, 243, 413, 1031)

**apsidal**—Rounded; *apse*-shaped. (429)

**arcade**—A series of *arches* supported by *piers* or *columns.* (52, 243, 287, 290, 413, 20-4A)

**Arcadian** (adj.)—In Renaissance and later art, depictions of an idyllic place of rural peace and simplicity. Derived from Arcadia, an ancient district of the central Peloponnesos in southern Greece. (625)

**arch**—A curved structural member that spans an opening and is generally composed of wedge-shaped blocks (*voussoirs*) that transmit the downward pressure laterally. See also *thrust.* (48, 12-10A)

**Archaic**—The artistic style of 600–480 BCE in Greece, characterized in part by the use of the *composite view* for painted and *relief* figures and of Egyptian stances for statues. (111)

**Archaic smile**—The smile that appears on all *Archaic* Greek statues from about 570 to 480 BCE. The smile is the Archaic sculptor's way of indicating that the person portrayed is alive. (112)

**architrave**—The *lintel* or lowest division of the *entablature;* also called the epistyle. (116, 640)

**archivolt**—The continuous molding framing an *arch.* In *Romanesque* and *Gothic* architecture, one of the series of concentric bands framing the *tympanum.* (344)

**arcuated**—*Arch*-shaped. (48, 175, 206)

**arena**—In a Roman *amphitheater,* the central area where bloody *gladiatorial* combats and other boisterous events took place. (189)

**armature**—The crossed, or diagonal, *arches* that form the skeletal framework of a *Gothic rib vault.* In sculpture, the framework for a clay form. (11, 368)

**arriccio**—In *fresco* painting, the first layer of rough lime plaster applied to the wall. (408)

**Art Deco**—Descended from *Art Nouveau,* this movement of the 1920s and 1930s sought to upgrade industrial design as a "fine art" and to work new materials into decorative patterns that could be either machined or handcrafted. Characterized by streamlined, elongated, and symmetrical design. (871)

**Art Nouveau**—French, "new art." A late-19th-and early-20th-century art movement whose proponents tried to synthesize all the arts in an effort to create art based on natural forms that could be mass produced by technologies of the industrial age. The movement had other names in other countries: Jugendstil in Austria and Germany, Modernismo in Spain, and Floreale in Italy. (828)

**asceticism**—Self-discipline and self-denial. (427)

**ashlar masonry**—Carefully cut and regularly shaped blocks of stone used in construction, fitted together without mortar. (62, 1031)

**assemblage**—An artwork constructed from already existing objects. (914)

**asye usu**—Baule (Côte d'Ivoire) bush spirits. (1069)

**atlantid**—A male figure that functions as a supporting *column.* See also *caryatid.* (72, 506)

**atlatl**—Spear-thrower, the typical weapon of the Toltecs of ancient Mexico. (506)

**atmospheric perspective**—See *perspective.* (194, 567)

**atrium**—The central reception room of a Roman house that is partly open to the sky. Also the open, *colonnaded* court in front of and attached to a Christian *basilica.* (190, 243, 672)

**attic**—The uppermost story of a building, *triumphal arch,* or city gate. (201)

**attribute**—(n.) The distinctive identifying aspect of a person, for example, an object held, an associated animal, or a mark on the body. (v.) To make an *attribution.* (5)

**attribution**—Assignment of a work to a maker or makers. (6)

**augur**—A Roman priest who determined the will of the gods from the flight of birds and whose attribute is the *lituus.* (165)

**automatism**—In painting, the process of yielding oneself to instinctive motions of the hands after establishing a set of conditions (such as size of paper or medium) within which a work is to be created. (875)

**avant-garde**—French, "advance guard" (in a platoon). Late-19th- and 20th-century artists who emphasized innovation and challenged established convention in their work. Also used as an adjective. (836)

**avatar**—A manifestation of a deity incarnated in some visible form in which the deity performs a sacred function on earth. In Hinduism, an incarnation of a god. (435, 981)

**axial plan**—See *plan.* (72)

**axis mundi**—Latin, "axis of the universe." In South Asia, a tall pillar planted deep in the ground, connecting earth and sky. (15-6A)

**backstrap loom**—A simple Andean loom featuring a belt or backstrap encircling the waist of the seated weaver. (510)

**bai**—An elaborately painted men's ceremonial house on Belau (formerly Palau) in the Caroline Islands of Micronesia. (1050)

**baldacchino**—A canopy on *columns,* frequently built over an altar. The term derives from *baldacco.* (243, 673)

**baldacco**—Italian, "silk from Baghdad." See *baldacchino.* (673)

**baldric**—A sashlike belt worn over one shoulder and across the chest to support a sword. (24-28B)

**baptism**—The Christian bathing ceremony in which an infant or a convert becomes a member of the Christian community. (236)

**baptistery**—In Christian architecture, the building used for *baptism,* usually situated next to a church. Also, the designated area or hall within a church for baptismal rites. (236)

**bar tracery**—See *tracery.* (375)

**baray**—One of the large reservoirs laid out around Cambodian *wats* that served as means of transportation as well as irrigation. A network of canals connected the reservoirs. (444)

**barge boards**—The angled boards that outline the exterior gables of a Maori meetinghouse. (1043)

**Baroque**—The traditional blanket designation for European art from 1600 to 1750. The stylistic term *Baroque,* which describes art that features dramatic theatricality and elaborate ornamentation in contrast to the simplicity and orderly rationality of *Renaissance* art, is most appropriately applied to Italian art of this period. The term derives from *barroco.* (670)

**barrel vault**—See *vault.* (184, 338, 585, 981)

**barroco**—Portuguese, "irregularly shaped pearl." See *Baroque.* (670)

**base**—In ancient Greek architecture, the molded projecting lowest part of *Ionic* and *Corinthian columns.* (*Doric* columns do not have bases.) (51, 116)

**basilica** (adj. **basilican**)—In Roman architecture, a public building for legal and other civic proceedings, rectangular in plan with an entrance usually on a long side. In Christian architecture, a church somewhat resembling the Roman basilica, usually entered from one end and with an *apse* at the other. (189, 413, 583)

**bas-relief**—See *relief.* (12, 820)

**batik**—An Indonesian fabric-dyeing technique using melted wax to form patterns the dye cannot penetrate. (31-22B)

**battlement**—A low parapet at the top of a circuit wall in a fortification. (382, 416)

**Bauhaus**—A *school* of architecture in Germany in the 1920s under the aegis of Walter Gropius, who emphasized the unity of art, architecture, and design. (884)

**bay**—The space between two columns, or one unit in the *nave arcade* of a church; also, the passageway in an *arcuated* gate. (411, 413, 457)

**beam**—A horizontal structural member that carries the load of the superstructure of a building; a timber *lintel.* (457)

**Beaux-Arts**—An architectural *style* of the late 19th and early 20th centuries in France. Based on ideas taught at the École des Beaux-Arts in Paris, the Beaux-Arts style incorporated *classical* principles, such as symmetry in design, and included extensive exterior ornamentation. (789)

**begging bowl**—The bowl Buddhist monks use to collect alms, either money or food. (486)

**belvedere**—Italian, "beautiful view." A building or other structure with a view of a *landscape* or seascape. (623)

**ben-ben**—A pyramidal stone; an emblem of the Egyptian god Re. (57, 61)

**benday dots**—Named after the newspaper printer Benjamin Day, the benday dot system involves the modulation of *colors* through the placement and size of colored dots. (916)

**benedictional**—A Christian religious book containing bishops' blessings. (312)

**bent-axis plan**—A *plan* that incorporates two or more angular changes of direction, characteristic of Sumerian architecture. (33)

**bestiary**—A collection of illustrations of real and imaginary animals. (343)

**bhakti**—In Buddhist thought, the adoration of a personalized deity (*bodhisattva*) as a means of achieving unity with it; love felt by the devotee for the deity. In Hinduism, the devout, selfless direction of all tasks and activities of life to the service of one god. (981)

**Bharat Mata**—Mother India; the female personification of India. (32-10A)

**bhumisparsha**—See *mudra.* (427)

**bi**—In ancient China, jade disks carved as ritual objects for burial with the dead. They were often decorated with piercings that extended entirely through the object, as well as with surface carvings. (453, 454)

**bichrome**—Two-color. (511)

**bieri**—The wooden *reliquary* guardian figures of the Fang in Gabon and Cameroon. (1064)

**bilateral symmetry**—Having the same *forms* on either side of a central axis. (64)

**bilingual vases**—Experimental Greek vases produced for a short time in the late sixth century BCE; one side featured *black-figure* decoration, the other *red-figure*. (121)

**Biomorphic Surrealism**—See *Surrealism*. (875)

**bisj pole**—An elaborately carved pole constructed from the trunk of the mangrove tree. The Asmat people of southwestern New Guinea created bisj poles to indicate their intent to avenge a relative's death. (1046)

**black-figure painting**—In early Greek pottery, the silhouetting of dark figures against a light background of natural, reddish clay, with linear details *incised* through the silhouettes. (111)

**blind arcade**—An *arcade* having no true openings, applied as decoration to a wall surface. (52, 290)

**block statue**—In ancient Egyptian sculpture, a cubic stone image with simplified body parts. (74)

**bocio**—A Fon (Republic of Benin) empowerment figure. (1066)

**bodhisattva**—In Buddhist thought, a potential Buddha who chooses not to achieve enlightenment in order to help save humanity. (427)

**Book of Hours**—A Christian religious book for private devotion containing prayers to be read at specified times of the day. (312)

**boshan**—A Chinese incense burner. (455, 16-6A)

**boss**—A circular knob. (426)

**bottega**—An artist's studio-shop. (569)

**braccia**—Italian, "arm." A unit of measurement; 1 braccia equals 23 inches. (582)

**breakfast piece**—A *still life* that includes bread and fruit. (701)

**breviary**—A Christian religious book of selected daily prayers and Psalms. (312, 386, 550)

**bucranium** (pl. **bucrania**)—Latin, "bovine skull." A common motif in classical architectural ornament. (659, 1-16A)

**Buddha triad**—A three-figure group with a central Buddha flanked on each side by a *bodhisattva*. (475)

**buon fresco**—See *fresco*. (408, 603)

**burgher**—A middle-class citizen. (28-32A)

**burin**—A pointed tool used for *engraving* or *incising*. (556)

**bust**—A freestanding sculpture of the head, shoulders, and chest of a person. (12)

**buttress**—An exterior masonry structure that opposes the lateral *thrust* of an *arch* or a *vault*. A pier buttress is a solid mass of masonry. A flying buttress consists typically of an inclined member carried on an arch or a series of arches and a solid buttress to which it transmits lateral thrust. (184)

**byobu**—Japanese painted folding screens. (1010)

**Byzantine**—The art, territory, history, and culture of the Eastern Christian Empire and its capital of Constantinople (ancient Byzantium). (256)

**caduceus**—In ancient Greek mythology, a magical rod entwined with serpents, the attribute of Hermes (Roman, Mercury), the messenger of the gods. (107, 559)

**caldarium**—The hot-bath section of a Roman bathing establishment. (220)

**caliph(s)**—Islamic rulers, regarded as successors of Muhammad. (285)

**calligrapher**—One who practices *calligraphy*. (294, 466, 997)

**calligraphy**—Greek, "beautiful writing." Handwriting or penmanship, especially elegant writing as a decorative art. (294, 466, 997)

**calotype**—From the Greek *kalos*, "beautiful." A photographic process in which a positive image is made by shining light through a negative image onto a sheet of sensitized paper. (791, 792)

**came**—A lead strip in a *stained-glass* window that joins separate pieces of colored glass. (375)

**camera lucida**—Latin, "lighted room." A device in which a small lens projects the image of an object downward onto a sheet of paper. (791)

**camera obscura**—Latin, "dark room." An ancestor of the modern camera in which a tiny pinhole, acting as a lens, projects an image on a screen, the wall of a room, or the ground-glass wall of a box; used by artists in the 17th, 18th, and early 19th centuries as an aid in drawing from nature. (711)

**campanile**—A bell tower of a church, usually, but not always, freestanding. (350, 416)

**canon**—A rule, for example, of proportion. The ancient Greeks considered beauty to be a matter of "correct" proportion and sought a canon of proportion, for the human figure and for buildings. The fifth-century BCE sculptor Polykleitos wrote the *Canon*, a treatise incorporating his formula for the perfectly proportioned statue. (10, 66)

**canon table**—A concordance, or matching, of the corresponding passages of the four *Gospels* as compiled by Eusebius of Caesarea in the fourth century. (312)

**canonized**—Declared a saint by the Catholic Church. (354, 14-5A)

**canopic jar**—In ancient Egypt, the container in which the organs of the deceased were placed for later burial with the mummy. (61)

**capital**—The uppermost member of a *column*, serving as a transition from the *shaft* to the *lintel*. In *classical* architecture, the form of the capital varies with the *order*. (51, 60, 116, 402, 429)

**Capitolium**—An ancient Roman temple dedicated to the gods Jupiter, Juno, and Minerva. (189)

**capriccio**—Italian, "originality." One of several terms used in Italian *Renaissance* literature to praise the originality and talent of artists. (604)

**caput mundi**—Latin, "head (capital) of the world." (180)

**cardo**—The north-south street in a Roman town, intersecting the *decumanus* at right angles. (189)

**Caroline minuscule**—The alphabet that *Carolingian* scribes perfected, from which the modern English alphabet was developed. (317)

**Carolingian** (adj.)—Pertaining to the empire of Charlemagne (Latin, "Carolus Magnus") and his successors. (317)

**carpet page**—In early medieval manuscripts, a decorative page resembling a textile. (311)

**cartography**—The art of mapmaking. (13-38B)

**cartoon**—In painting, a full-size preliminary drawing from which a painting is made. (408, 602)

**carving**—A *technique* of sculpture in which the artist cuts away material (for example, from a stone block) in order to create a *statue* or a *relief*. (11)

**caryatid**—A female figure that functions as a supporting *column*. See also *atlantid*. (72, 117)

**cassone** (pl. **cassoni**)—A carved chest, often painted or gilded, popular in *Renaissance* Italy for the storing of household clothing. (631)

**castellum**—See *westwork*. (323)

**casting**—A sculptural *technique* in which the artist pours liquid metal, plaster, clay, or another material into a *mold*. When the material dries, the sculptor removes the cast piece from the mold. (11)

**castrum**—A Roman military encampment. (207)

**catacombs**—Subterranean networks of rock-cut galleries and chambers designed as cemeteries for the burial of the dead. (237)

**cathedra**—Latin, "seat." See *cathedral*. (350)

**cathedral**—A bishop's church. The word derives from *cathedra*, referring to the bishop's chair. (350, 412)

**cavea**—Latin, "hollow place or cavity." The seating area in ancient Greek and Roman theaters and *amphitheaters*. (151, 189)

**celadon**—A Chinese-Korean pottery *glaze*, fired in an oxygen-deprived kiln to a characteristic gray-green or pale blue color. (472)

**cella**—The chamber at the center of an ancient temple; in a *classical* temple, the room (Greek, *naos*) in which the *cult statue* usually stood. (33, 115, 618)

**celt**—In Olmec Mexico, an ax-shaped form made of polished jade; generally, a prehistoric metal or stone implement shaped like a chisel or ax head. (494)

**cemen**—The winglike openwork projection at the top of an Asmat *bisj pole*. (1046)

**centaur**—In ancient Greek mythology, a creature with the front or top half of a human and the back or bottom half of a horse. (105)

**centauromachy**—In ancient Greek mythology, the battle between the Greeks and *centaurs*. (120)

**central plan**—See *plan*. (244, 288, 583)

**cestrum**—A small spatula used in *encaustic* painting. (218)

**chacmool**—A *Mesoamerican* statuary type depicting a fallen warrior on his back with a receptacle on his chest for sacrificial offerings. (491, 883)

**chaitya hall**—A South Asian rock-cut temple hall having a votive *stupa* at one end. (429)

**chakra**—The Buddha's wheel, set in motion at Sarnath. (423, 429)

**chakravartin**—In South Asia, the ideal king, the Universal Lord who ruled through goodness. (429, 985)

**Chan**—See *Zen*. (470, 1007)

**chancel arch**—The arch separating the chancel (the *apse* or *choir*) or the *transept* from the *nave* of a basilica or church. (228, 243, 413)

**chantry**—An endowed chapel for the chanting of the mass for the founder of the chapel. (13-42A)

**chaplet**—A metal pin used in hollow-casting to connect the *investment* with the clay core. (130)

**chapter house**—The meeting hall in a *monastery.* (585)

**characters**—In Chinese writing, signs that record spoken words. (450, 997)

**chartreuse**—A Carthusian *monastery.* (537)

**charun**—An Etruscan death demon. (176)

**chasing**—The engraving or embossing of metal. (673)

**chasseur**—French cavalry officer. (27-13A)

**château (**pl. **châteaux)**—French, "castle." A luxurious country residence for French royalty, developed from medieval castles. (657)

**chatra**—See *yasti.* (430)

**cherub**—A chubby winged child angel. (552)

**chiaroscuro**—In drawing or painting, the treatment and use of light and dark, especially the gradations of light that produce the effect of *modeling.* (409)

**chiaroscuro woodcut**—A *woodcut* technique using two blocks of wood instead of one. The printmaker carves and inks one block in the usual way in order to produce a traditional black-and-white print. Then the artist cuts a second block consisting of broad highlights that can be inked in gray or color and printed over the first block's impression. (649)

**chigi**—Decorative extensions of the *rafters* at each end of the roof of a Japanese shrine. (480)

**chimera**—A monster of Greek invention with the head and body of a lion and the tail of a serpent. A second head, that of a goat, grows out of one side of the body. (174)

**chisel**—A tool with a straight blade at one end for cutting and shaping stone or wood. (18)

**chiton**—A Greek tunic, the essential (and often only) garment of both men and women, the other being the *himation,* or mantle. (115)

**choir**—The space reserved for the clergy and singers in the church, usually east of the *transept* but, in some instances, extending into the *nave.* (12, 264)

**Christ**—Savior. (240)

**Christogram**—The three initial letters (chi-rho-iota, or ☧) of Christ's name in Greek, which came to serve as a monogram for Christ. (230, 264, 307)

**chromatic abstraction**—A kind of *Abstract Expressionism* that focuses on the emotional resonance of color, as exemplified by the work of Barnett Newman and Mark Rothko. (903)

**chronology**—In art history, the dating of art objects and buildings. (2)

**chryselephantine**—Fashioned of gold and ivory. (94)

**Cinquecento**—Italian, "500," that is, the 1500s or 16th century. (599)

**circumambulation**—In Buddhist worship, walking around the *stupa* in a clockwise direction, a process intended to bring the worshiper into harmony with the cosmos. (430)

**cire perdue**—See *lost-wax process.* (130, 507, 673, 983)

**cista (**pl. **cistae)**—An Etruscan cylindrical container made of sheet bronze with cast handles and feet, often with elaborately engraved bodies, used for women's toiletry articles. (175)

**city-state**—An independent, self-governing city. (31, 406)

**Classical**—The art and culture of ancient Greece between 480 and 323 BCE. Lowercase *classical* refers more generally to Greco-Roman art and culture. (402)

**clerestory**—The *fenestrated* part of a building that rises above the roofs of the other parts. The oldest known clerestories are Egyptian. In Roman *basilicas* and medieval churches, clerestories are the windows that form the *nave*'s uppermost level below the timber ceiling or the *vaults.* (73, 184, 243, 373, 413, 20-4A)

**cloison**—French, "partition." A cell made of metal wire or a narrow metal strip soldered edge-up to a metal base to hold *enamel,* semiprecious stones, pieces of colored glass, or glass paste fired to resemble sparkling jewels. (310)

**cloisonné**—A decorative metalwork technique employing *cloisons;* also, decorative brickwork in later Byzantine architecture. (271, 310, 817)

**cloister**—A *monastery* courtyard, usually with covered walks or *ambulatories* along its sides. (322, 341, 576)

**cluster pier**—See *compound pier.* (340, 373, 12-4A, 14-12A)

**codex (**pl. **codices)**—Separate pages of *vellum* or *parchment* bound together at one side; the predecessor of the modern book. The codex superseded the *rotulus.* In *Mesoamerica,* a painted and inscribed book on long sheets of bark paper or deerskin coated with fine white plaster and folded into accordion-like pleats. (249, 1023)

**coffer**—A sunken panel, often ornamental, in a *vault* or a ceiling. (210)

**collage**—A composition made by combining on a flat surface various materials, such as newspaper, wallpaper, printed text and illustrations, photographs, and cloth. (8, 835, 850)

**colonnade**—A series or row of *columns,* usually spanned by *lintels.* (70)

**colonnette**—A thin *column.* (194, 290)

**colophon**—An inscription, usually on the last page, giving information about a book's manufacture. In Chinese painting, written texts on attached pieces of paper or silk. (312, 997)

**color**—The value, or tonality, of a color is the degree of its lightness or darkness. The intensity, or saturation, of a color is its purity, its brightness or dullness. See also *primary colors, secondary colors,* and *complementary colors.* (7, 813)

**color-field painting**—A variant of *Post-Painterly Abstraction* in which artists sought to reduce painting to its physical essence by pouring diluted paint onto unprimed canvas and letting these pigments soak into the fabric, as exemplified by the work of Helen Frankenthaler and Morris Louis. (908)

**colorito**—Italian, "colored" or "painted." A term used to describe the application of paint.

Characteristic of the work of 16th-century Venetian artists who emphasized the application of paint as an important element of the creative process. Central Italian artists, in contrast, largely emphasized *disegno*—the careful design preparation based on preliminary drawing. (625)

**colossal order**—An architectural design in which the *columns* or *pilasters* are two or more stories tall. Also called a giant order. (594)

**column**—A vertical, weight-carrying architectural member, circular in cross-*section* and consisting of a *base* (sometimes omitted), a *shaft,* and a *capital.* (10, 51, 402)

**combines**—The name American artist Robert Rauschenberg gave to his *assemblages* of painted passages and sculptural elements. (914)

**commedia dell'arte**—A traditional Italian comic play performed by actors and musicians. (29-19A)

**complementary colors**—Those pairs of *colors,* such as red and green, that together embrace the entire *spectrum.* The complement of one of the three *primary colors* is a mixture of the other two. (7, 813)

**compline**—The last prayer of the day in a *Book of Hours.* (550)

**compose**—See *composition.* (7, 21, 38)

**Composite capital**—A capital combining *Ionic* volutes and *Corinthian* acanthus leaves, first used by the ancient Romans. (206, 587, 21-36A)

**composite view**—A convention of representation in which part of a figure is shown in profile and another part of the same figure is shown frontally; also called twisted perspective. (23, 523)

**composition**—The way in which an artist organizes *forms* in an artwork, either by placing shapes on a flat surface or arranging forms in space. (7, 21, 38)

**compound pier**—A *pier* with a group, or cluster, of attached *shafts,* or *responds,* especially characteristic of *Gothic* architecture. (340, 373, 12-4A, 14-12A)

**Conceptual Art**—An American *avant-garde* art movement of the 1960s whose premise was that the "artfulness" of art lay in the artist's idea rather than its final expression. (936)

**conceptual representation**—The representation of the fundamental distinguishing properties of a person or object, not the way a figure or object appears in space and light at a specific moment. See *composite view.* (35)

**concrete**—A building material invented by the Romans and consisting of various proportions of lime mortar, volcanic sand, water, and small stones. (184)

**condottiere (**pl. **condottieri)**—An Italian mercenary general. (560)

**confraternity**—In Late Antiquity, an association of Christian families pooling funds to purchase property for burial. In late medieval Europe, an organization founded by laypersons who dedicated themselves to strict religious observances. (237, 404)

**congregational mosque**—A city's main *mosque,* designed to accommodate the entire *Muslim* population for the Friday noonday prayer. Also called the great mosque or Friday mosque. (288, 977)

**connoisseur**—An expert in *attributing* artworks to one artist rather than another. More generally, an expert on artistic *style*. (6)

**Constructivism**—An early-20th-century Russian art movement formulated by Naum Gabo, who built up his sculptures piece by piece in space instead of carving or *modeling* them. In this way the sculptor worked with "volume of mass" and "volume of space" as different materials. (860)

**consuls**—In the Roman Republic, the two chief magistrates. (181)

**continuous narration**—The depiction of the same figure more than once in the same space at different stages of a story. (7-44A)

**contour line**—In art, a continuous line defining the outer shape of an object. (7)

**contrapposto**—The disposition of the human figure in which one part is turned in opposition to another part (usually hips and legs one way, shoulders and chest another), creating a counterpositioning of the body about its central axis. Sometimes called "weight shift" because the weight of the body tends to be thrown to one foot, creating tension on one side and relaxation on the other. (129, 564)

**corbel**—A projecting wall member used as a support for some element in the superstructure. Also, *courses* of stone or brick in which each course projects beyond the one beneath it. Two such walls, meeting at the topmost course, create a corbeled *arch* or corbeled *vault*. (416, 640)

**corbeled arch**—An *arch* formed by the piling of stone blocks in horizontal *courses,* cantilevered inward until the blocks meet at a *keystone*. (99)

**corbeled vault**—A *vault* formed by the piling of stone blocks in horizontal *courses,* cantilevered inward until the two walls meet in an *arch*. (27, 99)

**Corinthian capital**—A more ornate form than *Doric* or *Ionic;* it consists of a double row of acanthus leaves from which tendrils and flowers grow, wrapped around a bell-shaped *echinus*. Although this *capital* form is often cited as the distinguishing feature of the Corinthian *order,* no such order exists, in strict terms, but only this type of capital used in the *Ionic* order. (151, 402, 587)

**cornice**—The projecting, crowning member of the *entablature* framing the *pediment;* also, any crowning projection. (116, 586)

**corona civica**—Latin, "civic crown." A Roman honorary wreath worn on the head. (7)

**course**—In masonry construction, a horizontal row of stone blocks. (28, 62, 1031)

**covenant**—In Judaism and Christianity, a binding agreement between God and humans. (561)

**crenel**—See *crenellation*. (382)

**crenellation**—Alternating solid merlons and open crenels in the notched tops of walls, as in *battlements*. (382)

**crossing**—The space in a *cruciform* church formed by the intersection of the *nave* and the *transept*. (246, 323, 14-18A)

**cross-hatching**—See *hatching*. (555)

**cross vault**—See *vault*. (184)

**crossing square**—The area in a church formed by the intersection (*crossing*) of a *nave* and a *transept* of equal width, often used as a standard *module* of interior proportion. (323, 583)

**crossing tower**—The tower over the *crossing* of a church. (246)

**cruciform**—Cross-shaped. (246, 583)

**Crusades**—In medieval Europe, armed pilgrimages aimed at recapturing the Holy Land from the *Muslims*. (346)

**crypt**—A *vaulted* space under part of a building, wholly or partly underground; in churches, normally the portion under an *apse*. (340)

**cubiculum** (pl. **cubicula**)—A small cubicle or bedroom that opened onto the *atrium* of a Roman house. Also, a chamber in an Early Christian *catacomb* that served as a mortuary chapel. (190, 237)

**Cubism**—An early-20th-century art movement that rejected *naturalistic* depictions, preferring *compositions* of shapes and *forms abstracted* from the conventionally perceived world. See also *Analytic Cubism* and *Synthetic Cubism*. (847)

**cuerda seca**—A type of polychrome tilework used in decorating Islamic buildings. (299)

**cuirass**—A military leather breastplate. (186)

**cult statue**—The *statue* of the deity that stood in the *cella* of an ancient temple. (115)

**cuneiform**—Latin, "wedge-shaped." A system of writing used in ancient Mesopotamia, in which wedge-shaped characters were produced by pressing a *stylus* into a soft clay tablet, which was then baked or otherwise allowed to harden. (33)

**cuneus** (pl. **cunei**)—In ancient Greek and Roman theaters and *amphitheaters,* the wedge-shaped section of stone benches separated by stairs. (151)

**cupola**—An exterior architectural feature composed of a *drum* with a shallow cap; a *dome*. (638, 9-32A)

**cutaway**—An architectural drawing that combines an exterior view with an interior view of part of a building. (12, 605)

**Cycladic**—The prehistoric art of the Aegean Islands around Delos, excluding Crete. (87)

**Cyclopean masonry**—A method of stone construction, named after the mythical *Cyclops,* using massive, irregular blocks without mortar, characteristic of the Bronze Age fortifications of Tiryns and other *Mycenaean* sites. (97)

**Cyclops** (pl. **Cyclopes**)—A mythical Greek one-eyed giant. (97)

**cylinder seal**—A cylindrical piece of stone usually about an inch or so in height, decorated with an *incised* design, so that a raised pattern is left when the seal is rolled over soft clay. In the ancient Near East, documents, storage jars, and other important possessions were signed, sealed, and identified in this way. Stamp seals are an earlier, flat form of seal used for similar purposes. (39)

**Dada**—An early-20th-century art movement prompted by a revulsion against the horror of World War I. Dada embraced political anarchy, the irrational, and the intuitive. A disdain for convention, often enlivened by humor or whimsy, is characteristic of the art the Dadaists produced. (835, 856)

**Daedalic**—The Greek *Orientalizing* sculptural style of the seventh century BCE named after the legendary artist Daedalus. (111)

**daguerreotype**—A photograph made by an early method on a plate of chemically treated metal; developed by Louis J. M. Daguerre. (791, 792, 983)

**daimyo**—Local lords who controlled small regions and owed obeisance to the *shogun* in the Japanese *shogunate* system. (1006)

**damnatio memoriae**—The Roman decree condemning those who ran afoul of the Senate. Those who suffered damnatio memoriae had their memorials demolished and their names erased from public inscriptions. (206, 219)

**darbar**—The official audience of a *Mughal* emperor. (32-5A)

**darshan**—In Hindu worship, seeing images of the divinity and being seen by the divinity. (435)

**De Stijl**—Dutch, "the style." An early-20th-century art movement (and magazine), founded by Piet Mondrian and Theo van Doesburg, whose members promoted utopian ideals and developed a simplified geometric style. (880)

**deconstruction**—An analytical strategy developed in the late 20th century according to which all cultural "constructs" (art, architecture, literature) are "texts." People can read these texts in a variety of ways, but they cannot arrive at fixed or uniform meanings. Any interpretation can be valid, and readings differ from time to time, place to place, and person to person. For those employing this approach, deconstruction means destabilizing established meanings and interpretations while encouraging subjectivity and individual differences. (942)

**Deconstructivism**—An architectural *style* using *deconstruction* as an analytical strategy. Deconstructivist architects attempt to disorient the observer by disrupting the conventional categories of architecture. The haphazard presentation of *volumes, masses, planes,* lighting, and so forth challenges the viewer's assumptions about *form* as it relates to function. (962)

**decumanus**—The east-west street in a Roman town, intersecting the *cardo* at right angles. (189)

**decursio**—The ritual circling of a Roman funerary pyre. (215)

**Deësis**—Greek, "supplication." An image of Christ flanked by the figures of the Virgin Mary and John the Baptist, who intercede on behalf of humankind. (276)

**demos**—Greek, "the people," from which the word *democracy* is derived. (106)

**demotic**—Late Egyptian writing. (56)

**denarius**—The standard Roman silver coin from which the word *penny* ultimately derives. (187)

**Der Blaue Reiter**—German, "the blue rider." An early-20th-century *German Expressionist* art movement founded by Vassily Kandinsky and Franz Marc. The artists selected the whimsical name because of their mutual interest in the color blue and horses. (841)

**dharma**—In Buddhism, moral law based on the Buddha's teaching. (423, 15-8A)

**dharmachakra**—See *mudra*. (427)

**dhyana**—See *mudra*. (427)

**di sotto in sù**—Italian, "from below upward." A *perspective* view seen from below. (595, 637)

**diagonal rib**—See *rib*. (373)

**diaphragm arch**—A transverse, wall-bearing *arch* that divides a *vault* or a ceiling into compartments, providing a kind of firebreak. (12-27A)

**dictator**—In the Roman Republic, the supreme magistrate with extraordinary powers, appointed during a crisis for a specified period. Julius Caesar eventually became *dictator perpetuo*, dictator for life. (181, 187)

**dictator perpetuo**—See *dictator*. (181, 187)

**Die Brücke**—German, "the bridge." An early-20th-century *German Expressionist* art movement under the leadership of Ernst Ludwig Kirchner. The group thought of itself as the bridge between the old age and the new. (839)

**Dilukai**—A female figure with splayed legs, a common motif over the entrance to a Belau *bai*, serving as both guardian and fertility symbol. (1052)

**dipteral**—See *peristyle*. (115)

**diptych**—A two-paneled painting or *altarpiece*; also, an ancient Roman, Early Christian, or Byzantine hinged writing tablet, often of ivory and carved on the external sides. (251, 540)

**disegno**—Italian, "drawing" and "design." *Renaissance* artists considered drawing to be the external physical manifestation (*disegno esterno*) of an internal intellectual idea of design (*disegno interno*). (604, 625)

**disputatio**—Latin, "logical argument." The philosophical methodology used in *Scholasticism*. (372)

**divine right**—The belief in a king's absolute power as God's will. (714)

**divisionism**—See *pointillism*. (812)

**documentary evidence**—In art history, the examination of written sources in order to determine the date of an artwork, the circumstances of its creation, or the identity of the artist(s) who made it. (2)

**doge**—Duke; a ruler of the Republic of Venice, Italy. (274)

**dome**—A hemispherical *vault*; theoretically, an *arch* rotated on its vertical axis. In *Mycenaean* architecture, domes are beehive-shaped. (99, 184, 977, 14-18A)

**domus**—A Roman private house. (190)

**donor portrait**—A portrait of the individual(s) who commissioned (donated) a religious work, for example, an *altarpiece*, as evidence of devotion. (535)

**Doric**—One of the two systems (or *orders*) invented in ancient Greece for articulating the three units of the elevation of a *classical* building—the platform, the *colonnade*, and the superstructure (*entablature*). The Doric order is characterized by, among other features, *capitals* with funnel-shaped *echinuses*, *columns* without *bases*, and a *frieze* of *triglyphs* and *metopes*. See also *Ionic*. (116, 587, 640)

**doryphoros**—Greek, "spear bearer." (132)

**dotaku**—Ancient Japanese bronze ceremonial bells, usually featuring raised decoration. (477)

**double monastery**—A *monastery* for both monks and nuns. (352)

**dressed masonry**—Stone blocks shaped to the exact dimensions required, with smooth faces for a perfect fit. (62, 586)

**dromos**—The passage leading to a *tholos tomb*. (99)

**drum**—One of the stacked cylindrical stones that form the *shaft* of a *column*. Also, the cylindrical wall that supports a *dome*. (116, 184, 271)

**dry painting**—See *sand painting*. (1032)

**drypoint**—An *engraving* in which the design, instead of being cut into the plate with a *burin*, is scratched into the surface with a hard steel "pencil." See also *etching, intaglio*. (556)

**duomo**—Italian, "cathedral." (417)

**earthenware**—Pottery made of clay that is fired at low temperatures and is slightly porous. Also, clay figurines and statues produced in the same manner. (451)

**earthworks**—See *Environmental Art*. (932)

**eaves**—The lower part of a roof that overhangs the wall. (457)

**echinus**—The convex element of a *capital* directly below the *abacus*. (116)

**écorché**—The representation of a nude body as if without skin. (582)

**edition**—A set of impressions taken from a single print surface. (556)

**effigy mounds**—Ceremonial mounds built in the shape of animals or birds by native North American peoples. (517)

**elevation**—In architecture, a head-on view of an external or internal wall, showing its features and often other elements that would be visible beyond or before the wall. (12, 413)

**emblema**—The central framed figural panel of a *mosaic* floor. (149)

**embroidery**—The technique of sewing threads onto a finished ground to form contrasting designs. Stem stitching employs short overlapping strands of thread to form jagged lines. Laid-and-couched work creates solid blocks of color. (362, 449, 510)

**emir**—A Muslim ruler. (293)

**empiricism**—The search for knowledge based on observation and direct experience. (775)

**enamel**—A decorative coating, usually colored, fused onto the surface of metal, glass, or ceramics. (301, 992, 28-24A)

**encaustic**—A painting *technique* in which pigment is mixed with melted wax and applied to the surface while the mixture is hot. (111, 218, 914)

**engaged column**—A half-round *column* attached to a wall. See also *pilaster*. (60, 290, 340, 588)

**engraving**—The process of *incising* a design in hard material, often a metal plate (usually copper); also, the *print* or impression made from such a plate. (555, 556)

**Enlightenment**—The Western philosophy based on empirical evidence that dominated the 18th century. The Enlightenment was a new way of thinking critically about the world and about humankind, independently of religion, myth, or tradition. (727)

**en plein air**—See *plein air*. (798, 799, 801, 805, 806, 28-2A, 28-7A)

**ensi**—A Sumerian ruler. (36)

**entablature**—The part of a building above the *columns* and below the roof. The entablature has three parts: *architrave, frieze*, and *pediment*. (116)

**entasis**—The convex profile (an apparent swelling) in the *shaft* of a *column*. (118)

**Environmental Art**—An American art form that emerged in the 1960s. Often using the land itself as their material, Environmental artists construct monuments of great scale and minimal form. Permanent or impermanent, these works transform some section of the environment, calling attention both to the land itself and to the hand of the artist. Sometimes referred to as earthworks. (932)

**eravo**—A ceremonial men's meetinghouse constructed by the Elema people in New Guinea. (1048)

**escutcheon**—An emblem bearing a coat of arms. (628)

**etching**—A kind of *engraving* in which the design is *incised* in a layer of wax or varnish on a metal plate. The parts of the plate left exposed are then etched (slightly eaten away) by the acid in which the plate is immersed after incising. See also *drypoint, intaglio*. (556)

**Eucharist**—In Christianity, the partaking of the bread and wine, which believers hold to be either Christ himself or symbolic of him. (241, 538)

**evangelist**—One of the four authors (Matthew, Mark, Luke, John) of the New Testament *Gospels*. (314)

**Events**—See *Fluxus*. (935)

**exedra**—Recessed area, usually semicircular. (196, 929)

**exemplum virtutis**—Latin, "example or model of virtue." (746)

**Expressionism** (adj. **Expressionist**)—Twentieth-century art that is the result of the artist's unique inner or personal vision and that often has an emotional dimension. Expressionism contrasts with art focused on visually describing the empirical world. (839)

**facade**—Usually, the front of a building; also, the other sides when they are emphasized architecturally. (52, 412)

**faience**—A low-fired opaque glasslike silicate. (94)

**fan vault**—See *vault*. (391)

**fantasia**—Italian, "imagination." One of several terms used in Italian *Renaissance* literature to praise the originality and talent of artists. (604)

**fasces**—A bundle of rods with an ax attached, representing an emblem of authority in ancient Rome. (752)

**fauces**—Latin, "jaws." In a Roman house, the narrow foyer leading to the *atrium*. (190)

**Fauves**—French, "wild beasts." See *Fauvism*. (836)

**Fauvism**—An early-20th-century art movement led by Henri Matisse. For the Fauves, *color* became the formal element most responsible for pictorial coherence and the primary conveyor of meaning. (836)

**Favrile**—A type of leaded stained glass patented by Louis Comfort Tiffany in the late 19th century. (28-36B)

**femmages**—The name American artist Miriam Schapiro gave to her sewn *collages,* assembled from fabrics, quilts, buttons, sequins, lace trim, and rickrack collected at antique shows and fairs. (922)

**femme fatale**—French, "fatal woman." A destructive temptress of men. (820)

**femme savante**—French, "learned woman." The term used to describe the cultured hostesses of *Rococo* salons. (729)

**fenestra coeli**—Latin, "window to Heaven." (688)

**fenestrated**—Having windows. (184)

**fenestration**—The arrangement of the windows of a building. (184)

**fête galante**—French, "amorous festival." A type of *Rococo* painting depicting the outdoor amusements of French upper-class society. (732, 733)

**feudalism**—The medieval political, social, and economic system held together by the relationship between landholding *liege lords* and the *vassals* who were granted tenure of a portion of their land and in turn swore allegiance to the liege lord. (334, 536)

**fibula** (pl. **fibulae**)—A decorative pin, usually used to fasten garments. (167, 309)

**fin-de-siècle**—French, "end of the century." A period in Western cultural history from the end of the 19th century until just before World War I, when decadence and indulgence masked anxiety about an uncertain future. (823)

**findspot**—Place where an artifact was found; *provenance.* (18)

**finial**—A crowning ornament. (294, 541, 977)

**First Style mural**—The earliest style of Roman *mural* painting. Also called the Masonry style, because the aim of the artist was to imitate, using painted *stucco relief,* the appearance of costly marble panels. (191)

**Flamboyant**—A Late French *Gothic* style of architecture superseding the *Rayonnant* style and named for the flamelike appearance of its pointed bar *tracery.* (381)

**flashing**—In making *stained-glass* windows, fusing one layer of colored glass to another to produce a greater range of *colors.* (375)

**fleur-de-lis**—A three-petaled iris flower; the royal flower of France. (376, 388, 698)

**Floreale**—See *Art Nouveau.* (828)

**florin**—The denomination of gold coin of *Renaissance* Florence that became an international currency for trade. (417)

**flute** or **fluting**—Vertical channeling, roughly semicircular in cross-*section* and used principally on *columns* and *pilasters.* (51, 68, 116, 3-5A)

**Fluxus**—A group of American, European, and Japanese artists of the 1960s who created *Performance Art.* Their performances, or Events, often focused on single actions, such as turning a light on and off or watching falling snow, and were more theatrical than *Happenings.* (935)

**flying buttress**—See *buttress.* (12, 372, 373, 20-4A)

**folio**—A page of a manuscript or book. (248, 249)

**fons vitae**—Latin, "fountain of life." A symbolic fountain of everlasting life. (538)

**foreshortening**—The use of *perspective* to represent in art the apparent visual contraction of an object that extends back in space at an angle to the perpendicular plane of sight. (10, 44, 123, 401)

**form**—In art, an object's shape and structure, either in two dimensions (for example, a figure painted on a surface) or in three dimensions (such as a *statue*). (7)

**formal analysis**—The visual analysis of artistic *form.* (7)

**formalism**—Strict adherence to, or dependence on, stylized shapes and methods of *composition.* An emphasis on an artwork's visual elements rather than its subject. (902)

**forum**—The public square of an ancient Roman city. (189)

**Fourth Style mural**—In Roman *mural* painting, the Fourth Style marks a return to architectural *illusionism,* but the architectural vistas of the Fourth Style are irrational fantasies. (194)

**freedmen, freedwomen**—In ancient and medieval society, men and women who had been freed from servitude, as opposed to having been born free. (187)

**freestanding sculpture**—See *sculpture in the round.* (12, 18)

**fresco**—Painting on lime plaster, either dry (dry fresco, or fresco secco) or wet (true, or buon, fresco). In the latter method, the pigments are mixed with water and become chemically bound to the freshly laid lime plaster. Also, a painting executed in either method. (408, 409, 502)

**fresco secco**—See *fresco.* (74, 408, 603)

**Friday mosque**—See *congregational mosque.* (288)

**frieze**—The part of the *entablature* between the *architrave* and the *cornice;* also, any sculptured or painted band in a building. See *register.* (31, 116)

**frigidarium**—The cold-bath section of a Roman bathing establishment. (220)

**furta sacra**—Latin, "holy theft." (336)

**fusuma**—Japanese painted sliding-door panels. (1008)

**Futurism**—An early-20th-century Italian art movement that championed war as a cleansing agent and that celebrated the speed and dynamism of modern technology. (853)

**garbha griha**—Hindi, "womb chamber." In Hindu temples, the *cella,* the holy inner sanctum often housing the god's image or *symbol.* (439, 977)

**genius**—Latin, "spirit." In art, the personified spirit of a person or place. (22-52A)

**genre**—A *style* or category of art; also, a kind of painting that realistically depicts scenes from everyday life. (5, 551, 660)

**Geometric**—The *style* of Greek art during the ninth and eighth centuries BCE, characterized by *abstract* geometric ornament and schematic figures. (108)

**German Expressionism**—An early-20th-century regional Expressionist movement. (839)

**gesso**—Plaster mixed with a binding material, used as the base coat for paintings on wood panels. (545)

**gestural abstraction**—Also known as *action painting.* A kind of *abstract* painting in which the gesture, or act of painting, is seen as the subject of art. Its most renowned proponent was Jackson Pollock. See also *Abstract Expressionism.* (903)

**giant order**—See *colossal order.* (594)

**gigantomachy**—In ancient Greek mythology, the battle between gods and giants. (118, 22-54A)

**giornata** (pl. **giornate**)—Italian, "day." The section of plaster that a *fresco* painter expects to complete in one session. (408)

**gladiator**—An ancient Roman professional fighter, usually a slave, who competed in an *amphitheater.* (203)

**glaze**—A vitreous coating applied to pottery to seal and decorate the surface; it may be colored, transparent, or opaque, and glossy or *matte.* In *oil painting,* a thin, transparent, or semitransparent layer applied over a *color* to alter it slightly. (110, 451, 539, 583, 986, 992)

**glazier**—A glassworker. (375)

**Gobelin tapestry**—A *tapestry* produced on a vertical loom using a weaving *technique* in which no *weft* threads extend the full width of the fabric. (29-66B)

**gold leaf**—Gold beaten into tissue-paper-thin sheets that then can be applied to surfaces. (405)

**gopis**—South Asian herdswomen. (32-7A)

**gopuras**—The massive, ornamented entrance gateway towers of southern Indian temple compounds. (981)

**gorget**—A neck pendant, usually made of shell. (517)

**gorgon**—In ancient Greek mythology, a hideous female demon with snake hair. Medusa, the most famous gorgon, was capable of turning anyone who gazed at her into stone. (118)

**Gospels**—The four New Testament books that relate the life and teachings of Jesus. (312)

**Gothic**—Originally a derogatory term named after the Goths, used to describe the history, culture, and art of western Europe in the 12th to 14th centuries. Typically divided into periods designated Early (1140–1194), High (1194–1300), and Late (1300–1500). (365)

**Gothic Revival**—See *Neo-Gothic.* (788)

**gouache**—A painting *medium* consisting of watercolor mixed with gum. (843)

**Grand Manner portraiture**—A type of 18th-century portrait painting designed to communicate a person's grace and class through certain standardized conventions, such as the large scale of the figure relative to the canvas, the controlled pose, the *landscape* setting, and the low *horizon line.* (742)

**granulation**—A decorative technique in which tiny metal balls (granules) are fused to a metal surface. (167)

**graver**—An *engraving* tool. See also *burin.* (556)

**great mosque**—See *congregational mosque.* (288)

**Greek cross**—A cross with four arms of equal length. (271, 620, 676)

**green architecture**—Ecologically friendly architectural design using clean energy to sustain the natural environment. (961)

**griffin**—An eagle-headed winged lion. (51, 99, 4-9B, 10-5B)

**grisaille**—A *monochrome* painting done mainly in neutral grays to simulate sculpture. (409, 614, 13-36A, 20-8A)

**groin**—The edge formed by the intersection of two barrel *vaults.* (184)

**groin vault**—See *vault.* (184, 340, 350, 982, 14-12A)

**ground line**—In paintings and *reliefs,* a painted or carved baseline on which figures appear to stand. (20, 31)

**guang**—An ancient Chinese covered vessel, often in animal form, holding wine, water, grain, or meat for sacrificial rites. (452)

**guild**—An association of merchants, craftspersons, or scholars in medieval and *Renaissance* Europe. (366, 410)

**haboku**—In Japanese art, a loose and rapidly executed painting *style* in which the ink seems to have been applied by flinging or splashing it onto the paper. (1008)

**Hadith**—The words and exemplary deeds of the Prophet Muhammad. (285)

**haiku**—A 17-syllable Japanese poetic form. (1014)

**halberd**—A combination spear and battle-ax. (626)

**hall church**—See *Hallenkirche.* (348)

**Hallenkirche**—German, "hall church." A church design favored in Germany, but also used elsewhere, in which the *aisles* rise to the same height as the *nave.* (396)

**handscroll**—In Asian art, a horizontal painted scroll that is unrolled right to left, section by section, and often used to present illustrated religious texts or *landscapes.* (459, 991)

**hanging scroll**—In Asian art, a vertical scroll hung on a wall with pictures mounted or painted directly on it. (459, 991)

**haniwa**—Sculpted fired pottery cylinders, modeled in human, animal, or other forms and placed on Japanese *tumuli* of the Kofun period. (478)

**Happenings**—A term coined by American artist Allan Kaprow in the 1960s to describe loosely structured performances, whose creators were trying to suggest the aesthetic and dynamic qualities of everyday life; as actions, rather than objects, Happenings incorporate the fourth dimension (time). (934)

**hard-edge painting**—A variant of *Post-Painterly Abstraction* that rigidly excluded all reference to gesture and incorporated smooth knife-edge geometric forms to express the notion that painting should be reduced to its visual components. (907)

**harmika**—In Buddhist architecture, a stone fence or railing that encloses an area surmounting the *dome* of a *stupa* that represents one of the Buddhist heavens; from the center arises the *yasti.* (430)

**harpies**—Mythological creatures of the underworld. (22-8A)

**haruspex (pl. haruspices)**—An Etruscan priest who foretells events by studying animal livers. (6-13A)

**hatching**—A series of closely spaced drawn or *engraved* parallel lines. Cross-hatching employs sets of lines placed at right angles. (555)

**head cluster**—An abbreviated way of representing a crowd by painting or carving many heads close together, usually with too few bodies for the number of heads. (246)

**heiau**—A Hawaiian temple. (1057)

**Helladic**—The prehistoric art of the Greek mainland (*Hellas* in Greek). (87)

**Hellas**—The ancient name of Greece. (106)

**Hellenes (adj. Hellenic)**—The name the ancient Greeks called themselves as the people of *Hellas.* (106)

**Hellenistic**—The term given to the art and culture of the roughly three centuries between the death of Alexander the Great in 323 BCE and the death of Queen Cleopatra in 30 BCE, when Egypt became a Roman province. (153)

**henge**—An arrangement of *megalithic* stones in a circle, often surrounded by a ditch. (28)

**heraldic composition**—A *composition* that is symmetrical on either side of a central figure. (38)

**herm**—A bust on a quadrangular *pillar.* (133)

**Hevehe**—An elaborate cycle of ceremonial activities performed by the Elema people of the Papuan Gulf region of New Guinea. Also, the large, ornate masks produced for and presented during these ceremonies. (1047)

**Hiberno-Saxon**—An art *style* that flourished in the *monasteries* of the British Isles in the early Middle Ages. Also called Insular. (311)

**hierarchy of scale**—An artistic convention in which greater size indicates greater importance. (11, 31, 14-16A)

**hieroglyphic**—A system of writing using *symbols* or pictures. (55, 493)

**high relief**—See *relief.* (12, 65)

**High-Tech**—A contemporary architectural *style* calling for buildings that incorporate the latest innovations in engineering and technology and expose the structures' component parts. (961)

**Hijra**—The flight of Muhammad from Mecca to Medina in 622, the year from which Islam dates its beginnings. (285)

**himation**—An ancient Greek mantle worn by men and women over the *chiton* and draped in various ways. (115)

**Hippodamian plan**—A city *plan* devised by Hippodamos of Miletos ca. 466 BCE, in which a strict grid was imposed on a site, regardless of the terrain, so that all streets would meet at right angles. (154)

**hiragana**—A phonetic cursive script developed in Japan from Chinese *characters;* it came to be the primary script for Japanese court poetry. (484, 17-13B)

**historiated**—Ornamented with representations, such as plants, animals, or human figures, that have a narrative—as distinct from a purely decorative—function. (342)

**hokkyo**—Japanese, "bridge of the law." The third-highest rank among Buddhist monks. (34-9A)

**hookah**—A Moroccan water pipe. (27-17A)

**horizon line**—See *perspective.* (567)

**hôtel**—French, "town house." (728)

**hubris**—Greek, "arrogant pride." (143)

**hue**—The name of a *color.* See also *primary colors, secondary colors,* and *complementary colors.* (7, 813)

**humanism**—In the *Renaissance,* an emphasis on education and on expanding knowledge (especially of *classical* antiquity), the exploration of individual potential and a desire to excel, and a commitment to civic responsibility and moral duty. (407)

**hydria**—An ancient Greek three-handled water pitcher. (145)

**hypaethral**—A building having no *pediment* or roof, open to the sky. (154)

**hypostyle hall**—A hall with a roof supported by *columns.* (73, 288, 289)

**icon**—A portrait or image; especially in Byzantine churches, a panel with a painting of sacred personages that are objects of veneration. In the visual arts, a painting, a piece of sculpture, or even a building regarded as an object of veneration. (268, 269, 405)

**iconoclasm**—The destruction of religious or sacred images. In Byzantium, the period from 726 to 843 when there was an imperial ban on such images. The destroyers of images were known as iconoclasts. Those who opposed such a ban were known as iconophiles. (257, 269, 543, 652)

**iconoclast**—See *iconoclasm.* (257, 269, 543, 652)

**iconography**—Greek, the "writing of images." The term refers both to the content, or subject, of an artwork and to the study of content in art. It also includes the study of the symbolic, often religious, meaning of objects, persons, or events depicted in works of art. (5)

**iconophile**—See *iconoclasm.* (269)

**iconostasis**—Greek, "icon stand." In Byzantine churches, a screen or a partition, with doors and many tiers of *icons,* separating the sanctuary from the main body of the church. (279)

**ikegobo**—A Benin royal shrine. (520, 521)

**illuminated manuscript**—A luxurious handmade book with painted illustrations and decorations. (249, 405)

**illusionism (adj. illusionistic)**—The representation of the three-dimensional world on a two-dimensional surface in a manner that creates the illusion that the person, object, or place represented is three-dimensional. See also *perspective.* (8)

**imagines**—In ancient Rome, wax portraits of ancestors. (185, 196, 200)

**imam**—In Islam, the leader of collective worship. (288)

**impasto**—A layer of thickly applied pigment. (632, 902)

**imperator**—Latin, "commander in chief," from which the word *emperor* derives. (197)

**impluvium**—In a Roman house, the basin located in the *atrium* that collected rainwater. (190)

**impost block**—The uppermost block of a wall or *pier* beneath the *springing* of an *arch.* (21-31A)

**Impressionism**—A late-19th-century art movement that sought to capture a fleeting moment, thereby conveying the elusiveness and impermanence of images and conditions. (799)

**in antis**—In ancient Greek architecture, the area between the *antae.* (115)

**incise**—To cut into a surface with a sharp instrument; also, a method of decoration, especially on metal and pottery. (556)

**incrustation**—Wall decoration consisting of bright panels of different *colors*. (202, 355)

**incubus**—A demon believed in medieval times to prey, often sexually, on sleeping women. (762)

**indulgence**—A religious pardon for a sin committed. (374, 616, 652)

**ingegno**—Italian, "innate talent." One of several terms used in Italian *Renaissance* literature to praise the originality and talent of artists. (604)

**installation**—An artwork that creates an artistic environment in a room or gallery. (950, 30-25B)

**insula** (pl. **insulae**)—In Roman architecture, a multistory apartment house, usually made of brick-faced *concrete;* also refers to an entire city block. (213)

**Insular**—See *Hiberno-Saxon*. (311)

**intaglio**—A graphic technique in which the design is *incised,* or scratched, on a metal plate, either manually (*engraving, drypoint*) or chemically (*etching*). The incised lines of the design take the ink, making this the reverse of the *woodcut* technique. (556)

**intensity**—See *color*. (7)

**interaxial** or **intercolumniation**—The distance between the center of the lowest *drum* of a *column* and the center of the next. (135)

**intercolumniation**—See *interaxial*. (135)

**internal evidence**—In art history, the examination of what an artwork represents (people, clothing, hairstyles, and so on) in order to determine its date. Also, the examination of the *style* of an artwork to identify the artist who created it. (3)

**International style**—A *style* of 14th- and 15th-century painting begun by Simone Martini, who adapted the French *Gothic* manner to Sienese art fused with influences from northern Europe. This style appealed to the aristocracy because of its brilliant *color*, lavish costumes, intricate ornamentation, and themes involving splendid processions of knights and ladies. Also, a style of 20th-century architecture associated with Le Corbusier, whose elegance of design came to influence the look of modern office buildings and skyscrapers. (413, 886)

**intonaco**—In *fresco* painting, the last layer of smooth lime plaster applied to the wall; the painting layer. (408)

**invenzione**—Italian, "invention." One of several terms used in Italian *Renaissance* literature to praise the originality and talent of artists. (604)

**investment**—In hollow-casting, the final clay *mold* applied to the exterior of the wax model. (130)

**Ionic**—One of the two systems (or *orders*) invented in ancient Greece for articulating the three units of the elevation of a *classical* building: the platform, the *colonnade*, and the superstructure (*entablature*). The Ionic order is characterized by, among other features, *volutes, capitals, columns* with *bases,* and an uninterrupted *frieze*. (116, 587)

**iron-wire lines**—In ancient Chinese painting, thin brush lines suggesting tensile strength. (459, 482)

**ivi p'o**—Hollow, cylindrical bone or ivory ornaments produced in the Marquesas Islands (Polynesia). (1054)

**iwan**—In Islamic architecture, a *vaulted* rectangular recess opening onto a courtyard. (52, 288)

**iy'oba**—Benin queen mother. (532, 19-13A)

**jambs**—In architecture, the side posts of a doorway. (344)

**Japonisme**—The French fascination with all things Japanese. Japonisme emerged in the second half of the 19th century. (808)

**jataka**—Tales of the past lives of the Buddha. See also *sutra*. (430)

**joined-wood technique**—A Japanese sculptural *technique* in which a statue is assembled from multiple wood blocks, each hollowed out to make the pieces lighter. (17-13A)

**jomon**—Japanese, "cord markings." A type of Japanese ceramic technique characterized by ropelike markings. (476)

**Jugendstil**—See *Art Nouveau*. (828)

**junzi**—Chinese, "superior person" or "gentleman." A person who is a model of Confucian behavior. (463)

**ka**—In ancient Egypt, the immortal human life force. (57, 61)

**Kaaba**—Arabic, "cube." A small cubical building in Mecca, the Islamic world's symbolic center. (285)

**kami**—Shinto deities or spirits, believed in Japan to exist in nature (mountains, waterfalls) and in charismatic people. (479)

**karesansui**—Japanese dry-landscape gardening. (1006)

**karma**—In Vedic religions (see *Veda*), the ethical consequences of a person's life, which determine his or her fate. (427)

**katsina**—An art form of Native Americans of the Southwest, the katsina doll represents benevolent supernatural spirits (katsinas) living in mountains and water sources. (1033)

**katsuogi**—Wooden logs placed at right angles to the *ridgepole* of a Japanese shrine to hold the thatched roof in place. (480)

**kautaha**—Women's organizations in Tonga (Polynesia) that produce barkcloth. (1053)

**keep**—A fortified tower in a castle that served as a place of last refuge. (383)

**kente**—Brightly colored patterned cloth woven by Asante men on horizontal looms in long narrow strips sewn together to form *toga*-like robes. (1070, 1071, 37-13A)

**keystone**—See *voussoir*. (175, 344, 640)

**khan**—An Ottoman lord, or *sultan*. (10-23A)

**khipu**—Andean record-keeping device consisting of numerous knotted strings hanging from a main cord; the strings signified, by position and *color,* numbers and categories of things. (1030)

**king's gallery**—The band of *statues* running the full width of the *facade* of a *Gothic cathedral* directly above the *rose window*. (379, 380)

**kiva**—A square or circular underground structure that is the spiritual and ceremonial center of Pueblo Indian life. (518, 1032)

**kline** (pl. **klinai**)—A couch or funerary bed. A type of *sarcophagus* with a reclining portrait of the deceased on its lid. (217)

**kodo**—The lecture hall in a Japanese Buddhist temple complex. (475)

**Kogan**—The name of a distinctive type of *Shino* water jar. (1012)

**kondo**—Japanese, "golden hall." The main hall for worship in a Japanese Buddhist temple complex. The kondo contained *statues* of the Buddha and the *bodhisattvas* to whom the temple was dedicated. (475)

**Koran**—Islam's sacred book, composed of *surahs* (chapters) divided into verses. (285)

**kore** (pl. **korai**)—Greek, "young woman." An *Archaic* Greek *statue* of a young woman. (111)

**koru**—An unrolled spiral design used by the Maori of New Zealand in their *tattoos*. (1055)

**kouros** (pl. **kouroi**)—Greek, "young man." An *Archaic* Greek *statue* of a young man. (112)

**krater**—An ancient Greek wide-mouthed bowl for mixing wine and water. (102)

**Kufic**—An early form of Arabic script, characterized by angularity, with the uprights forming almost right angles with the baseline. (294)

**kula**—An exchange of white conus-shell arm ornaments and red chama-shell necklaces that takes place among the Trobriand Islanders of Papua New Guinea. (1049)

**kupesi**—Embroidered design tablets used by Tonga (Polynesia) women in the production of barkcloth. (1053)

**kylix**—An ancient Greek drinking cup with a wide bowl and two horizontal handles. (5-23A)

**labrys**—Minoan double-ax. (90)

**labyrinth**—Maze. The English word derives from the mazelike plan of the *Minoan* palace at Knossos. (90)

**lacquer**—A varnishlike substance made from the sap of the Asiatic sumac tree, used to decorate wood and other organic materials. Often colored with mineral pigments, lacquer cures to great hardness and has a lustrous surface. (453, 995)

**laid-and-couched work**—See *embroidery*. (362)

**lakshana**—One of the distinguishing marks of the Buddha. The lakshanas include the *urna* and *ushnisha*. (427)

**lalitasana**—In Buddhist iconography, the body pose with one leg folded and the other hanging down, indicating relaxation. (460)

**lamassu**—Assyrian guardian in the form of a man-headed winged bull. (46)

**lancet**—In *Gothic* architecture, a tall narrow window ending in a *pointed arch*. (370, 373, 890, 14-5A, 27-43A)

**landscape**—A picture showing natural scenery, without narrative content. (5, 27, 416)

**Landschaft**—German, "landscape." (662)

**lateral section**—See *section*. (12)

**laudatio**—Latin, "essay of praise." (570)

**leading**—In the manufacture of *stained-glass* windows, the joining of colored glass pieces using lead *cames*. (375)

**lectionary**—A book containing passages from the *Gospels,* arranged in the sequence that they are to be read during the celebration of religious services, including the *Mass,* throughout the year. (312)

**lekythos** (pl. **lekythoi**)—A flask containing perfumed oil; lekythoi were often placed in Greek graves as offerings to the deceased. (142)

**libation**—The pouring of liquid as part of a religious ritual. (36)

**liege lord**—In *feudalism,* a landowner who grants tenure of a portion of his land to a *vassal*. (334)

**line**—The extension of a point along a path, made concrete in art by drawing on or chiseling into a *plane*. (7)

**linear perspective**—See *perspective*. (192, 565, 567)

**linga**—In Hindu art, the depiction of Shiva as a phallus or cosmic *pillar*. (435)

**linguist's staff**—In Africa, a staff carried by a person authorized to speak for a king or chief. (1072)

**lintel**—A horizontal *beam* used to span an opening. (73, 99, 344)

**literati**—In China, talented amateur painters and scholars from the landed gentry. (956, 991, 31-22A, 33-1A)

**lithograph**—See *lithography*. (778)

**lithography**—A printmaking technique in which the artist uses an oil-based crayon to draw directly on a stone plate and then wipes water onto the stone. When ink is rolled onto the plate, it adheres only to the drawing. The *print* produced by this method is a lithograph. (778)

**liturgy** (adj. **liturgical**)—The official ritual of public worship. (242)

**lituus**—The curved staff carried by an *augur*. (165)

**local color**—An object's true *color* in white light. (801)

**loculi**—Openings in the walls of *catacombs* to receive the dead. (237)

**loggia**—A gallery with an open *arcade* or a *colonnade* on one or both sides. (576, 14-19A)

**lohan**—A Buddhist holy person who has achieved enlightenment and *nirvana* by suppression of all desire for earthly things. (468)

**longitudinal plan**—See *plan*. (243)

**longitudinal section**—See *section*. (12)

**lost-wax (cire perdue) process**—A bronze-*casting* method in which a figure is modeled in wax and covered with clay; the whole is fired, melting away the wax (French, *cire perdue*) and hardening the clay, which then becomes a *mold* for molten metal. (130, 507, 673, 983)

**low relief**—See *relief*. (12)

**lunette**—A semicircular area (with the flat side down) in a wall over a door, niche, or window; also, a painting or *relief* with a semicircular frame. (237, 344, 551, 7-54A)

**lux nova**—Latin, "new light." Abbot Suger's term for the light that enters a *Gothic* church through *stained-glass* windows. (369, 375)

**machicolated gallery**—A gallery in a defensive tower with holes in the floor to allow stones or hot liquids to be dumped on enemies below. (416)

**madrasa**—An Islamic theological college adjoining and often containing a *mosque*. (296)

**maebyeong**—A Korean vase similar to the Chinese *meiping*. (472)

**magus** (pl. **magi**)—One of the three wise men from the East who presented gifts to the infant Jesus. (240)

**ma-hevehe**—Mythical Oceanic water spirits. The Elema people of New Guinea believed these spirits visited their villages. (1047)

**malanggan**—Festivals held in honor of the deceased in New Ireland (Papua New Guinea). Also, the carvings and objects produced for these festivals. (1049)

**mana**—In Polynesia, spiritual power. (1052)

**mandala**—Sanskrit term for the sacred diagram of the universe; Japanese, mandara. (430, 439, 483)

**mandapa**—*Pillared* hall of a Hindu temple. (439)

**mandara**—See *mandala*. (430, 439, 483)

**mandorla**—An almond-shaped *nimbus* surrounding the figure of Christ or other sacred figure. In Buddhist Japan, a lotus-petal-shaped nimbus. (267, 460)

**maniera**—Italian, "style" or "manner." See *Mannerism*. (632, 682)

**maniera greca**—Italian, "Greek manner." The Italo-*Byzantine* painting *style* of the 13th century. (404, 14-7A)

**Mannerism**—A *style* of later *Renaissance* art that emphasized "artifice," often involving contrived imagery not derived directly from nature. Such artworks showed a self-conscious stylization involving complexity, caprice, fantasy, and polish. Mannerist architecture tended to flout the *classical* rules of order, stability, and symmetry, sometimes to the point of parody. (632)

**manor**—In *feudalism*, the estate of a *liege lord*. (334)

**mantra**—Sanskrit term for the ritual words or syllables recited in *Shingon* Buddhism. (483)

**manulua**—Triangular patterns based on the form of two birds, common in Tongan *tapa* designs. (1054)

**maqsura**—In some *mosques*, a screened area in front of the *mihrab* reserved for a ruler. (283, 288)

**martyr**—A person who chooses to die rather than deny his or her religious belief. See also *saint*. (237)

**martyrium**—A shrine to a Christian *martyr*. (274, 619)

**Masonry Style**—See *First Style mural*. (191)

**mass**—The bulk, density, and weight of matter in *space*. (8)

**Mass**—The Catholic and Orthodox ritual in which believers understand that Christ's redeeming sacrifice on the cross is repeated when the priest consecrates the bread and wine in the *Eucharist*. (241)

**mastaba**—Arabic, "bench." An ancient Egyptian rectangular brick or stone structure with sloping sides erected over a subterranean tomb chamber connected with the outside by a shaft. (58)

**matins**—In Christianity, early morning prayers. (550, 13-36A)

**matte**—In painting, pottery, and photography, a dull finish. (538)

**maulstick**—A stick used to steady the hand while painting. (661)

**mausoleum**—A monumental tomb. The name derives from the mid-fourth-century BCE tomb of Mausolos at Halikarnassos, one of the Seven Wonders of the ancient world. (225, 537, 980)

**mbari**—A ceremonial Igbo (Nigeria) house built about every 50 years in honor of the earth goddess Ala. (1070, 1077)

**mbulu ngulu**—The wood-and-metal *reliquary* guardian figures of the Kota of Gabon. (1064)

**meander**—An ornament, usually in bands but also covering broad surfaces, consisting of interlocking geometric motifs. An ornamental pattern of contiguous straight lines joined usually at right angles. (108)

**medium** (pl. **media**)—The material (for example, marble, bronze, clay, *fresco*) in which an artist works; also, in painting, the vehicle (usually liquid) that carries the pigment. (7)

**megalith** (adj. **megalithic**)—Greek, "great stone." A large, roughly hewn stone used in the construction of monumental prehistoric structures. (27)

**megaron**—The large reception hall and throne room in a *Mycenaean* palace, fronted by an open, two-*columned* porch. (97)

**meiping**—A Chinese vase of a high-shouldered shape; the *sgraffito technique* was used in decorating such vases. (467, 472)

**mela medica**—Italian, "medicinal apples" (oranges). The emblem of the Medici family of *Renaissance* Florence. (580)

**memento mori**—Latin, "reminder of death." In painting, a reminder of human mortality, usually represented by a skull. (695, 26-7A, 30-25B)

**mendicants**—In medieval Europe, friars belonging to the Franciscan and Dominican orders, who renounced all worldly goods, lived by contributions of laypersons (the word *mendicant* means "beggar"), and devoted themselves to preaching, teaching, and doing good works. (385, 404)

**menorah**—In antiquity, the Jewish sacred seven-branched candelabrum. (207)

**merlon**—See *crenellation*. (382)

**Mesoamerica**—The region that comprises Mexico, Guatemala, Belize, Honduras, and the Pacific coast of El Salvador. (492, 1023)

**Mesolithic**—The "middle" Stone Age, between the *Paleolithic* and the *Neolithic* ages. (16)

**Messiah**—The savior of the Jews prophesied in Hebrew scripture. Christians believe that Jesus of Nazareth was the Messiah. (240)

**metamatics**—The name Swiss artist Jean Tinguely gave to the motor-driven devices he constructed to produce instant abstract paintings. (935)

**metope**—The square panel between the *triglyphs* in a *Doric frieze*, often sculpted in *relief*. (116)

**mihrab**—A semicircular niche set into the *qibla* wall of a *mosque*. (287, 288)

**minaret**—A distinctive feature of *mosque* architecture, a tower from which the faithful are called to worship. (134, 261, 287, 288, 977)

**minbar**—In a *mosque*, the *pulpit* on which the *imam* stands. (287, 288)

**mingei**—A type of modern Japanese folk pottery. (1019)

**miniatures**—Small individual Indian paintings intended to be held in the hand and viewed by one or two individuals at one time. (978, 979, 28-24A)

**Minimalism**—A predominantly sculptural American trend of the 1960s characterized by works featuring a severe reduction of *form*, often to single, homogeneous units. (910)

**Minoan**—The prehistoric art of Crete, named after the legendary King Minos of Knossos. (87)

**Minotaur**—The mythical beast, half man and half bull, that inhabited the *labyrinth* of the *Minoan* palace at Knossos. (86)

**Miraj**—The ascension of the Prophet Muhammad to Heaven. (286)

**mithuna**—In South Asian art, a male-female couple embracing or engaged in sexual intercourse. (431)

**moai**—Large, blocky figural stone sculptures found on Rapa Nui (Easter Island) in Polynesia. (1052)

**mobile**—A kind of sculpture, invented by Alexander Calder, combining nonobjective organic forms and motion in balanced structures hanging from rods, wires, and colored, organically shaped plates. (895)

**modeling**—The shaping or fashioning of three-dimensional forms in a soft material, such as clay; also, the gradations of light and shade reflected from the surfaces of matter in space, or the illusion of such gradations produced by alterations of value in a drawing, painting, or print. (113, 145, 146)

**modernism**—A movement in Western art that developed in the second half of the 19th century and sought to capture the images and sensibilities of the age. Modernist art goes beyond simply dealing with the present and involves the artist's critical examination of the premises of art itself. (801, 998)

**Modernismo**—See *Art Nouveau.* (828)

**module** (adj. **modular**)—A basic unit of which the dimensions of the major parts of a work are multiples. The principle is used in sculpture and other art forms, but it is most often employed in architecture, where the module may be the dimensions of an important part of a building, such as the diameter of a *column.* (10, 323, 457, 582)

**moko**—The form of tattooing practiced by the Maori of New Zealand. (1055)

**moksha**—See *nirvana.* (427, 435)

**mold**—A hollow form for *casting.* (11)

**molding**—In architecture, a continuous, narrow surface (projecting or recessed, plain or ornamented) designed to break up a surface, to accent, or to decorate. (82)

**monastery**—A group of buildings in which monks live together, set apart from the secular community of a town. (267, 537)

**monastic**—Relating to life in a *monastery.* (267, 404, 537)

**monastic order**—An organization of monks living according to the same rules, for example, the Benedictine, Franciscan, and Dominican orders. (404)

**monochrome** (adj. **monochromatic**)—One color. (194, 705)

**monolith** (adj. **monolithic**)—A stone *column shaft* that is all in one piece (not composed of *drums*); a large, single block or piece of stone used in *megalithic* structures. Also, a colossal statue carved from a single piece of stone. (116, 428)

**monotheism**—The worship of one all-powerful god. (233)

**moralized Bible**—A heavily illustrated Bible, each page pairing paintings of Old and New Testament episodes with explanations of their moral significance. (385)

**mortise-and-tenon system**—See *tenon.* (480)

**mortuary temple**—In Egyptian architecture, a temple erected for the worship of a deceased *pharaoh.* (62)

**mosaic**—Patterns or pictures made by embedding small pieces (*tesserae*) of stone or glass in cement on surfaces such as walls and floors; also, the *technique* of making such works. (245, 1024, 28-24A)

**mosaic tilework**—An Islamic decorative *technique* in which large ceramic panels are fired, cut into smaller pieces, and set in plaster. (299)

**moschophoros**—Greek, "calf bearer." (112)

**mosque**—The Islamic building for collective worship. From the Arabic word *masjid,* meaning a "place for bowing down." (261, 288)

**Mozarabic**—Referring to the Christian culture of northern Spain during the time Islamic *caliphs* ruled southern Spain. (316)

**mudra**—In Buddhist and Hindu iconography, a stylized and symbolic hand gesture. The dhyana (meditation) mudra consists of the right hand over the left, palms upward, in the lap. In the bhumisparsha (earth-touching) mudra, the right hand reaches down to the ground, calling the earth to witness the Buddha's enlightenment. The dharmachakra (Wheel of the Law, or teaching) mudra is a two-handed gesture with right thumb and index finger forming a circle. The abhaya (do not fear) mudra, with the right hand up, palm outward, is a gesture of protection or blessing. (427)

**Mughal**—"Descended from the Mongols." The Muslim rulers of India, 1526–1857. (975)

**Muhaqqaq**—A cursive style of Islamic *calligraphy.* (300)

**mullion**—A vertical member that divides a window or that separates one window from another. (381, 930)

**mummification**—A *technique* used by ancient Egyptians to preserve human bodies so that they may serve as the eternal home of the immortal *ka.* (61)

**muqarnas**—Stucco decorations of Islamic buildings in which stalactite-like forms break a structure's solidity. (274, 296, 9-27A)

**mural**—A wall painting. (22, 407, 408, 409)

**Muslim**—A believer in Islam. (976)

**Mycenaean**—The prehistoric art of the Late *Helladic* period in Greece, named after the citadel of Mycenae. (87)

**mystery play**—A dramatic enactment of the holy mysteries of the Christian faith performed at church portals and in city squares. (409, 538, 12-35A)

**mystic marriage**—A spiritual marriage of a woman with Christ. (549)

**Nabis**—Hebrew, "prophet." A group of *Symbolist* painters influenced by Paul Gauguin. (819)

**naos**—See *cella.* (33, 115, 618)

**narthex**—A porch or vestibule of a church, generally *colonnaded* or *arcaded* and preceding the *nave.* (243)

**natatio**—The swimming pool in a Roman bathing establishment. (220)

**naturalism**—The style of painted or sculptured representation based on close observation of the natural world that was at the core of the *classical* tradition. (401)

**Naturalistic Surrealism**—See *Surrealism.* (875)

**nave**—The central area of an ancient Roman *basilica* or of a church, demarcated from *aisles* by *piers* or *columns.* (189, 243, 413, 20-4A)

**nave arcade**—In *basilica* architecture, the series of *arches* supported by *piers* or *columns* separating the *nave* from the *aisles.* (373)

**nduen fobara**—A Kalabari Ijaw (Nigeria) ancestral screen in honor of a deceased chief of a trading house. (1060, 1061)

**necropolis**—Greek, "city of the dead." A large burial area or cemetery. (58, 171)

**nembutsu**—The six-syllable Japanese prayer professing faith in the compassion of Amida Buddha. (488)

**nemes**—In ancient Egypt, the linen headdress worn by the *pharaoh,* with the *uraeus* cobra of kingship on the front. (64)

**Neoclassicism**—A *style* of art and architecture that emerged in the late 18th century as part of a general revival of interest in *classical* cultures. Neoclassical artists adopted themes and styles from ancient Greece and Rome. (745)

**Neo-Expressionism**—An art movement that emerged in the 1970s and that reflects artists' interest in the expressive capability of art, seen earlier in *German Expressionism* and *Abstract Expressionism.* (905, 30-8D)

**Neo-Gothic**—The revival of the *Gothic style* in architecture, especially in the 19th century. (788)

**Neolithic**—The "new" Stone Age. (16)

**Neoplasticism**—The Dutch artist Piet Mondrian's theory of "pure plastic art," an ideal balance between the universal and the individual using an abstract formal vocabulary. (881)

**Neue Sachlichkeit**—German, "new objectivity." An art movement that grew directly out of the World War I experiences of a group of German artists who sought to show the horrors of the war and its effects. (872)

**ngatu**—Decorated *tapa* made by women in Tonga. (1053, 1054)

**niello**—A black metallic alloy. (100)

**nihonga**—A 19th-century Japanese painting style that incorporated some Western techniques in Japanese-style painting, as opposed to *yoga* (Western painting). (1019)

**nimbus**—A halo or aureole appearing around the head of a holy figure to signify divinity. (248, 441)

**nio**—A Japanese guardian figure. (17-17A)

**nipote**—Italian, "nephew." (21-41A)

**nirvana**—In Buddhism and Hinduism, a blissful state brought about by absorption of the individual soul or consciousness into the supreme spirit. Also called moksha. (423, 427)

**nishiki-e**—Japanese, "brocade pictures." Japanese polychrome *woodcut prints* valued for their sumptuous colors. (1015)

**nkisi n'kondi**—A power figure carved by the Kongo people of the Democratic Republic of Congo. Such images embodied spirits believed to heal and give life or to be capable of inflicting harm or death. (1066)

**nomarch**—Egyptian, "great/overlord." A regional governor during the Middle Kingdom. (3-16A)

**Nun**—In ancient Egypt, the primeval waters from which the creator god emerged. (57)

**nymphs**—In *classical* mythology, female divinities of springs, caves, and woods. (107)

**oba**—An African sacred king. (521, 19-13A)

**oculus** (pl. **oculi**)—Latin, "eye." The round central opening of a *dome*. Also, a small round window in a *Gothic cathedral*. (184, 202, 373, 14-6A, 21-31A)

**odalisque**—A woman in a Turkish harem. (761)

**ogee arch**—An *arch* composed of two double-curving lines meeting at a point. (420, 13-42A)

**ogive** (adj. **ogival**)—The diagonal *rib* of a *Gothic vault;* a pointed, or Gothic, *arch*. (369, 402, 927, 21-31A)

**Ogoga**—A Yoruba king. (1072)

**oil painting**—A painting *technique* using oil-based pigments that rose to prominence in northern Europe in the 15th century and is now the standard medium for painting on canvas. (538)

**oni**—An African ruler. (527)

**Op Art**—An artistic movement of the 1960s in which painters sought to produce optical illusions of motion and depth using only geometric forms on two-dimensional surfaces. (908)

**opere francigeno**—See *opus francigenum*. (366, 389)

**opisthodomos**—In ancient Greek architecture, a porch at the rear of a temple, set against the blank back wall of the *cella*. (115)

**optical mixture**—The visual effect of juxtaposed *complementary colors*. (813)

**optical representation**—The representation of people and objects seen from a fixed viewpoint. (35)

**opus francigenum**—Latin, "French work." Architecture in the *style* of *Gothic* France; *opere francigeno* (adj.), "in the French manner." (366, 389)

**opus modernum**—Latin, "modern work." The late medieval term for *Gothic* art and architecture. Also called *opus francigenum*. (365, 373, 389)

**opus reticulatum**—An ancient Roman method of facing *concrete* walls with lozenge-shaped bricks or stones to achieve a netlike ornamental surface pattern. (11-19A)

**oracle**—A prophetic message. (5-17A)

**orant**—In Early Christian art, a figure with both arms raised in the ancient gesture of prayer. (238)

**oratory**—The church of a Christian *monastery*. (267)

**orbiculum**—A disklike opening. (930)

**orchestra**—Greek, "dancing place." In ancient Greek theaters, the circular piece of earth with a hard and level surface on which the performance took place. (151)

**order**—In *classical* architecture, a *style* represented by a characteristic design of the *columns* and *entablature*. See also *superimposed orders*. (116)

**Orientalizing**—The early phase of *Archaic* Greek art (seventh century BCE), so named because of the adoption of forms and motifs from the ancient Near East and Egypt. See also *Daedalic*. (109)

**Orphism**—A form of *Cubism* developed by the French painter Robert Delaunay in which color plays an important role. (848)

**orrery**—A mechanical model of the solar system demonstrating how the planets revolve around the sun. (727)

**orthogonal**—A line imagined to be behind and perpendicular to the picture *plane;* the orthogonals in a painting appear to recede toward a *vanishing point* on the horizon. (547, 567)

**orthogonal plan**—The imposition of a strict grid *plan* on a site, regardless of the terrain, so that all streets meet at right angles. See also *Hippodamian plan*. (154)

**Ottonian** (adj.)—Pertaining to the empire of Otto I and his successors. (324)

**overglaze**—In *porcelain* decoration, the technique of applying mineral colors over the *glaze* after the work has been fired. The overglaze colors, or *enamels,* fuse to the glazed surface in a second firing at a much lower temperature than the main firing. See also *underglaze*. (992)

**oxidizing**—The first phase of the ancient Greek ceramic firing process, which turned both the pot and the clay *slip* red. During the second (reducing) phase, the oxygen supply into the kiln was shut off, and both pot and slip turned black. In the final (reoxidizing) phase, the pot's coarser material reabsorbed oxygen and became red again, whereas the smoother slip did not and remained black. (110)

**pagoda**—An East Asian tower, usually associated with a Buddhist temple, having a multiplicity of winged *eaves;* thought to be derived from the Indian *stupa*. (467, 986)

**pala**—A panel placed behind and over the altar in a church. (9-26A)

**palaestra**—An ancient Greek and Roman exercise area, usually framed by a *colonnade*. In Greece, the palaestra was an independent building; in Rome, palaestras were also frequently incorporated into a bathing complex. (133, 220)

**Paleolithic**—The "old" Stone Age, during which humankind produced the first sculptures and paintings. (16, 522)

**palette**—A thin board with a thumb hole at one end on which an artist lays and mixes *colors;* any surface so used. Also, the colors or kinds of colors characteristically used by an artist. In ancient Egypt, a slate slab used for preparing makeup. (20, 55)

**palette knife**—A flat tool used to scrape paint off the *palette*. Artists sometimes also use the palette knife in place of a brush to apply paint directly to the canvas. (777)

**Pantokrator**—Greek, "ruler of all." Christ as ruler and judge. (272)

**papier collé**—French, "stuck paper." See *collage*. (850)

**papyrus**—A plant native to Egypt and adjacent lands used to make paperlike writing material; also, the material or any writing on it. (56, 249)

**parade helmet**—A masklike helmet worn by Roman soldiers on special ceremonial occasions. (336)

**parallel hatching**—See *hatching*. (555)

**parapet**—A low, protective wall along the edge of a balcony, roof, or bastion. (416)

**parchment**—Lambskin prepared as a surface for painting or writing. (249, 604)

**parekklesion**—The side chapel in a Byzantine church. (279)

**parinirvana**—Image of the reclining Buddha, a position often interpreted as representing his death. (427)

**parthenos**—Greek, "virgin." The epithet of Athena, the virgin goddess. (107)

**passage grave**—A prehistoric tomb with a long stone corridor leading to a burial chamber covered by a great *tumulus*. (27)

**Passional**—A Christian book containing the lives of *saints*. (312)

**Passover**—The annual feast celebrating the release of the Jews from bondage to the *pharaohs* of Egypt. (240)

**pastel**—A powdery paste of pigment and gum used for making crayons; also, the pastel crayons themselves. (809)

**paten**—A large shallow bowl or plate for the bread used in the *Eucharist*. (264)

**patrician**—A Roman freeborn landowner. (181)

**patron**—The person or entity that pays an artist to produce individual artworks or employs an artist on a continuing basis. (6)

**pebble mosaic**—A *mosaic* made of irregularly shaped stones of various *colors*. (149, 245)

**pectoral**—An ornament on the chest. (167)

**pediment**—In *classical* architecture, the triangular space (gable) at the end of a building, formed by the ends of the sloping roof above the *colonnade;* also, an ornamental feature having this shape. (105, 116, 582)

**pendant**—The large hanging terminal element of a *Gothic* fan vault. (391)

**pendentive**—A concave, triangular section of a hemisphere, four of which provide the transition from a square area to the circular base of a covering *dome*. Although pendentives appear to be hanging (pendant) from the dome, they in fact support it. (262, 585, 614)

**Pentateuch**—The first five books of the Old Testament. (235, 312)

**peplos** (pl. **peploi**)—A simple, long belted garment of wool worn by women in ancient Greece. (114)

**Performance Art**—An American *avant-garde* art trend of the 1960s that made time an integral element of art. It produced works in which movements, gestures, and sounds of persons communicating with an audience replace physical objects. Documentary photographs are generally the only evidence remaining after these events. See also *Happenings*. (993, 1019)

**period style**—See *style*. (3)

**peripteral**—See *peristyle*. (115)

**peristyle**—In *classical* architecture, a *colonnade* all around the *cella* and its porch(es). A peripteral colonnade consists of a single row of *columns* on all sides; a dipteral colonnade has a double row all around. (115, 190)

**Perpendicular**—A Late English *Gothic style* of architecture distinguished by the pronounced verticality of its decorative details. (391)

**personal style**—See *style*. (4)

**personification**—An *abstract* idea represented in bodily form. (5)

**perspective**—A method of presenting an illusion of the three-dimensional world on a two-dimensional surface. In linear perspective, the most common type, all parallel lines or surface edges converge on one, two, or three vanishing points located with reference to the eye level of the viewer (the horizon line of the picture), and associated objects are rendered smaller the farther from the viewer they are intended to seem. Atmospheric, or aerial, perspective creates the illusion of distance by the greater diminution of color intensity, the shift in color toward an almost neutral blue, and the blurring of contours as the intended distance between eye and object increases. (8, 409, 547, 565, 567)

**pfemba**—A Yombe (Democratic Republic of Congo) mother-and-child group. (1066)

**pharaoh** (adj. **pharaonic**)—An ancient Egyptian king. (55)

**phersu**—A masked man who appears in scenes of Etruscan funerary games. (165)

**philosophe**—French, "thinker, philosopher." The term applied to French intellectuals of the *Enlightenment.* (736)

**Phoibos**—Greek, "radiant." The epithet of the Greek god Apollo. (107)

**photomontage**—A *composition* made by pasting together pictures or parts of pictures, especially photographs. See also *collage.* (835)

**Photorealism**—See *Superrealism.* (917)

**physical evidence**—In art history, the examination of the materials used to produce an artwork in order to determine its date. (2)

**piano nobile**—Italian, "noble floor." The main (second) floor of a building. (21-37A)

**piazza**—Italian, "plaza." (672)

**pictograph**—A picture, usually stylized, that represents an idea; also, writing using such means; also, painting on rock. See also *hieroglyphic.* (32)

**Picturesque garden**—An "unordered" garden designed in accord with the *Enlightenment* taste for the natural. (750)

**pier**—A vertical, freestanding masonry support. (12, 72, 184)

**Pietà**—A painted or sculpted representation of the Virgin Mary mourning over the body of the dead Christ. (241, 396, 544, 842)

**pilaster**—A flat, rectangular, vertical member projecting from a wall of which it forms a part. It usually has a *base* and a *capital* and is often *fluted.* (175, 575)

**pillar**—Usually a weight-carrying member, such as a *pier* or a *column;* sometimes an isolated, freestanding structure used for commemorative purposes. (71, 72)

**pinakotheke**—Greek, "picture gallery." An ancient Greek building for the display of paintings on wood panels. (139)

**pinnacle**—In *Gothic* churches, a sharply pointed ornament capping the *piers* or flying *buttresses;* also used on church *facades.* (373, 411, 413, 27-43A)

**Pittura Metafisica**—Italian, "metaphysical painting." An early-20th-century Italian art movement led by Giorgio de Chirico, whose work conveys an eerie mood and visionary quality. (875)

**pixels**—Shortened form of "picture elements." The tiny boxes that make up digital images displayed on a computer monitor. (938)

**plan**—The horizontal arrangement of the parts of a building or of the buildings and streets of a city or town, or a drawing or diagram showing such an arrangement. In an axial plan, the parts of a building are organized longitudinally, or along a given axis; in a central plan, the parts of the structure are of equal or almost equal dimensions around the center. (12)

**plane**—A flat surface. (7)

**plate tracery**—See *tracery.* (375)

**Plateresque**—A style of Spanish architecture characterized by elaborate decoration based on *Gothic,* Italian *Renaissance,* and Islamic sources; derived from the Spanish word *platero,* meaning "silversmith." (664)

**platero**—See *Plateresque.* (664)

**plebeian**—The Roman social class that included small farmers, merchants, and freed slaves. (181)

**plein air**—An approach to painting very popular among the *Impressionists,* in which an artist sketches outdoors to achieve a quick impression of light, air, and color. The artist then takes the sketches to the studio for reworking into more finished works of art. (798, 799, 801, 805, 806, 28-2A, 28-7A)

**poesia**—A term describing "poetic" art, notably Venetian *Renaissance* painting, which emphasizes the lyrical and sensual. (626)

**pointed arch**—A narrow *arch* of pointed profile, in contrast to a semicircular arch. (3, 368, 402, 420, 977, 12-10A, 21-31A)

**pointillism**—A system of painting devised by the 19th-century French painter Georges Seurat. The artist separates *color* into its component parts and then applies the component colors to the canvas in tiny dots (points). The image becomes comprehensible only from a distance, when the viewer's eyes optically blend the pigment dots. Sometimes referred to as divisionism. (812)

**polis** (pl. **poleis**)—An independent *city-state* in ancient Greece. (106)

**polyptych**—An *altarpiece* composed of more than three sections. (538)

**polytheism**—The belief in multiple gods. (233)

**pontifex maximus**—Latin, "chief priest." The high priest of the Roman state religion, often the emperor himself. (197)

**Pop Art**—A term coined by British art critic Lawrence Alloway to refer to art, first appearing in the 1950s, that incorporated elements from consumer culture, the mass media, and popular culture, such as images from motion pictures and advertising. (899)

**porcelain**—Extremely fine, hard, white ceramic. Unlike *stoneware,* porcelain is made from a fine white clay called kaolin mixed with ground petuntse, a type of feldspar. True porcelain is translucent and rings when struck. (451, 992)

**portico**—A roofed *colonnade;* also an entrance porch. (154, 576)

**positivism**—A Western philosophical model that promoted science as the mind's highest achievement. (775)

**post-and-lintel system**—A system of construction in which two posts support a *lintel.* (28)

**Post-Impressionism**—The term used to describe the stylistically heterogeneous work of the group of late-19th-century painters in France, including van Gogh, Gauguin, Seurat, and Cézanne, who more systematically examined the properties and expressive qualities of *line,* pattern, *form,* and *color* than the *Impressionists* did. (811)

**postmodernism**—A reaction against *modernist formalism,* seen as elitist. Far more encompassing and accepting than the more rigid confines of modernist practice, postmodernism offers something for everyone by accommodating a wide range of *styles,* subjects, and formats, from traditional easel painting to *installation* and from *abstraction* to *illusionistic* scenes. Postmodern art often includes irony or reveals a self-conscious awareness on the part of the artist of art-making processes or the workings of the art world. (929)

**Post-Painterly Abstraction**—An American art movement that emerged in the 1960s and was characterized by a cool, detached rationality emphasizing tighter pictorial control. See also *color-field painting* and *hard-edge painting.* (907)

**pou tokomanawa**—A sculpture of an ancestor that supports a *ridgepole* of a Maori (New Zealand) meetinghouse. (1043)

**pouncing**—The method of transferring a sketch onto paper or a wall by tracing, using thin paper or transparent gazelle skin placed on top of the sketch, pricking the contours of the design into the skin or paper with a pin, placing the skin or paper on the surface to be painted, and forcing black pigment through the holes. (482, 979, 32-5A)

**poupou**—A decorated wall panel in a Maori (New Zealand) meetinghouse. (1043, 1055)

**Poussiniste**—A member of the French Royal Academy of Painting and Sculpture during the early 18th century who followed Nicolas Poussin in insisting that *form* was the most important element of painting. See also *Rubéniste.* (733)

**powwow**—A traditional Native American ceremony featuring dancing in quilled, beaded, and painted costumes. (1040)

**prasada**—In Hindu worship, food that becomes sacred by first being given to a god. (441)

**Precisionism**—An American art movement of the 1920s and 1930s. The Precisionists concentrated on portraying man-made environments in a clear and concise manner to express the beauty of perfect and precise machine forms. (867)

**pre-Columbian** (adj.)—The cultures that flourished in the Western Hemisphere before the arrival of Christopher Columbus and the beginning of European contact and conquest. (492)

**predella**—The narrow ledge on which an *altarpiece* rests on an altar. (411)

**prefiguration**—In Early Christian art, the depiction of Old Testament persons and events as prophetic forerunners of Christ and New Testament events. (238, 547, 561)

**primary colors**—Red, yellow, and blue—the *colors* from which all other colors may be derived. (7, 813)

**primitivism**—The incorporation in early-20th-century Western art of stylistic elements from the artifacts of Africa, Oceania, and the native peoples of the Americas. (845, 846)

**princeps**—Latin, "first citizen." The title Augustus and his successors as Roman emperor used to distinguish themselves from Hellenistic monarchs. (197)

**print**—An artwork on paper, usually produced in multiple impressions. (556)

**Productivism**—An art movement that emerged in the Soviet Union after the Russian Revolution; its members believed that artists must direct art toward creating products for the new society. (860)

**pronaos**—The space, or porch, in front of the *cella*, or naos, of an ancient Greek temple. (115)

**proportion**—The relationship in size of the parts of persons, buildings, or objects, often based on a *module*. (10)

**proscenium**—The part of a theatrical stage in front of the curtain. (675)

**prostyle**—A *classical* temple *plan* in which the *columns* are only in front of the *cella* and not on the sides or back. (115)

**protome**—The head, forelegs, and part of the body of an animal. (51)

**provenance**—Origin or source; *findspot*. (3)

**psalter**—A book containing the Psalms. (312, 550)

**pseudoperipteral**—In Roman architecture, a pseudoperipteral temple has a series of engaged *columns* all around the sides and back of the *cella* to give the appearance of a *peripteral colonnade*. (182)

**pueblo**—A communal multistoried dwelling made of stone or *adobe* brick by the Native Americans of the Southwest. Uppercase *Pueblo* refers to various groups that occupied such dwellings. (518, 1032)

**pukao**—A small red scoria cylinder serving as a topknot or hat on Easter Island *moai*. (1052)

**pulpit**—A raised platform in a church or *mosque* on which a priest or *imam* stands while leading the religious service. (402)

**pulque**—An intoxicating drink, similar to tequila, consumed during *Mesoamerican* religious rituals. (18-7A)

**punchwork**—Tooled decorative work in *gold leaf*. (412)

**Purism**—An early-20th-century art movement that embraced the "machine aesthetic" and sought purity of *form* in the clean functional lines of industrial machinery. (853)

**purlins**—Horizontal *beams* in a roof structure, parallel to the *ridgepoles*, resting on the main *rafters* and giving support to the secondary rafters. (457)

**putto** (pl. **putti**)—A cherubic young boy. (570)

**pylon**—The wide entrance gateway of an Egyptian temple, characterized by its sloping walls. (72)

**pyxis** (pl. **pyxides**)—A cylindrical container with a hemispherical lid. (293)

**qibla**—The direction (toward Mecca) Muslims face when praying. (288, 289, 529)

**quadrant arch**—An *arch* whose curve extends for one-quarter of a circle's circumference. (359)

**quadrifrons**—Latin, "four-fronted." An *arch* with four equal *facades* and four *arcuated bays*. (23-14A)

**quadro riportato**—A ceiling design in which painted scenes are arranged in panels that re-semble framed pictures transferred to the surface of a shallow, curved *vault*. (680)

**quatrefoil**—A shape or plan in which the parts assume the form of a cloverleaf. (419)

**Quattrocento**—Italian, "400," that is, the 1400s or 15th century. (559)

**quoins**—The large, sometimes *rusticated*, usually slightly projecting stones that often form the corners of the exterior walls of masonry buildings. (621)

**radiating chapels**—In medieval churches, chapels for the display of *relics* that opened directly onto the *ambulatory* and the *transept*. (337)

**radiocarbon dating**—A method of measuring the decay rate of carbon isotopes in organic matter to determine the age of organic materials such as wood and fiber. (22, 523)

**rafters**—The sloping supporting timber planks that run from the *ridgepole* of a roof to its edge. (457)

**raking cornice**—The *cornice* on the sloping sides of a *pediment*. (116)

**ramparts**—Defensive wall circuits. (382)

**ratha**—Small, freestanding Hindu temple *carved* from a huge boulder. (437)

**Rayograph**—A photograph produced without a camera by placing objects on photographic paper and then exposing the paper to light; named for the American artist Man Ray. (864)

**Rayonnant**—The "radiant" style of *Gothic* architecture, dominant in the second half of the 13th century and associated with the French royal court of Louis IX at Paris. (381)

**Realism**—A movement that emerged in mid-19th-century France. Realist artists represented the subject matter of everyday life (especially subjects that previously had been considered inappropriate for depiction) in a relatively *naturalistic* mode. (775)

**red-figure painting**—In later Greek pottery, the silhouetting of red figures against a black background, with painted linear details; the reverse of *black-figure painting*. (121)

**reducing**—See *oxidizing*. (110)

**refectory**—The dining hall of a Christian *monastery*. (267, 576)

**regional style**—See *style*. (3)

**Regionalism**—A 20th-century American art movement that portrayed American rural life in a clearly readable, *Realist* style. Major Regionalists include Grant Wood and Thomas Hart Benton. (889)

**register**—One of a series of superimposed bands or *friezes* in a pictorial narrative, or the particular levels on which motifs are placed. (31)

**relics**—The body parts, clothing, or objects associated with a holy figure, such as the Buddha or Christ or a Christian *saint*. (243, 336, 984, 1064)

**relief**—In sculpture, figures projecting from a background of which they are part. The degree of relief is designated high, low (bas), or sunken. In the last, the artist cuts the design into the surface so that the highest projecting parts of the image are no higher than the surface itself. See also *repoussé*. (556)

**relief sculpture**—See *relief*. (12, 18)

**relieving triangle**—In *Mycenaean* architecture, the triangular opening above the *lintel* that serves to lighten the weight to be carried by the lintel itself. (99)

**reliquary**—A container for holding *relics*. (328, 334, 336, 430, 1064)

**ren**—Chinese, "human-heartedness." The quality that the ideal Confucian *junzi* possesses. (463)

**Renaissance**—French, "rebirth." The term used to describe the history, culture, and art of 14th- through 16th-century western Europe during which artists consciously revived the *classical* style. (401, 406)

**renovatio**—Latin, "renewal." During the *Carolingian* period, Charlemagne sought to revive the culture of ancient Rome (renovatio imperi Romani). (317, 318, 402)

**reoxidizing**—See *oxidizing*. (110)

**repoussé**—Formed in *relief* by beating a metal plate from the back, leaving the impression on the face. The metal sheet is hammered into a hollow *mold* of wood or some other pliable material and finished with a *graver*. See also *relief*. (100, 248, 320, 354, 2-26A)

**respond**—An engaged *column*, *pilaster*, or similar element that either projects from a *compound pier* or some other supporting device or is bonded to a wall and carries one end of an *arch*. (373)

**retable**—An architectural screen or wall above and behind an altar, usually containing painting, sculpture, or other decorations. See also *altarpiece*. (538)

**revetment**—In architecture, a wall covering or facing. (184, 418)

**rhyton**—A pouring vessel. (51)

**rib**—A relatively slender, molded masonry *arch* that projects from a surface. In *Gothic* architecture, the ribs form the framework of the *vaulting*. A diagonal rib is one of the ribs that form the X of a *groin vault*. A transverse rib crosses the *nave* or aisle at a 90° angle. (12, 351, 21-31A)

**rib vault**—A *vault* in which the diagonal and transverse *ribs* compose a structural skeleton that partially supports the masonry *web* between them. (351, 368, 14-5A)

**ridgepole**—The *beam* running the length of a building below the peak of the gabled roof.

**rocaille**—See *Rococo*. (117, 480, 1043)

**Rococo**—A style, primarily of interior design, that appeared in France around 1700. Rococo interiors featured lavish decoration, including small sculptures, ornamental mirrors, easel paintings, *tapestries*, *reliefs*, wall paintings, and elegant furniture. The term Rococo derived from the French word *rocaille* (pebble) and referred to the small stones and shells used to decorate grotto interiors. (728)

**Romanesque**—"Roman-like." A term used to describe the history, culture, and art of medieval western Europe from ca. 1050 to ca. 1200. (333, 413, 588)

**Romanticism**—A Western cultural phenomenon, beginning around 1750 and ending about 1850, that gave precedence to feeling and imagination over reason and thought. More narrowly, the art movement that flourished from about 1800 to 1840. (762)

**roof comb**—The elaborately sculpted vertical projection surmounting a Maya temple-pyramid. (500)

**rose window**—A circular *stained-glass* window. (412, 13-3A)

**rostrum**—Speaker's platform. (929)

**rotulus**—The manuscript scroll used by Egyptians, Greeks, Etruscans, and Romans; predecessor of the *codex*. (249, 1023)

**rotunda**—The circular area under a *dome;* also a domed round building. (472, 538)

**roundel**—See *tondo*. (219, 585, 10-15A)

**rubbing**—An impression of a relief made by placing paper over the surface and rubbing with a pencil or crayon. (456)

**Rubéniste**—A member of the French Royal Academy of Painting and Sculpture during the early 18th century who followed Peter Paul Rubens in insisting that *color* was the most important element of painting. See also *Poussiniste*. (733)

**rusticate (n. rustication)**—To give a rustic appearance by roughening the surfaces and beveling the edges of stone blocks to emphasize the joints between them. Rustication is a technique employed in ancient Roman architecture, and was also popular during the *Renaissance,* especially for stone *courses* at the ground-floor level. (201, 586)

**sabi**—Japanese; the value found in the old and weathered, suggesting the tranquility reached in old age. (1012)

**sacra conversazione**—Italian, "holy conversation." A style of *altarpiece* painting popular after the middle of the 15th century, in which *saints* from different epochs are joined in a unified space and seem to be conversing either with one another or with the audience. (624)

**sacra rappresentazione (pl. sacre rappresentazioni)**—Italian, "holy representation." A more elaborate version of a *mystery play* performed for a lay audience by a *confraternity*. (409)

**sacramentary**—A Christian religious book incorporating the prayers priests recite during *Mass*. (312)

**saint**—From the Latin word *sanctus,* meaning "made holy by God." Applied to persons who suffered and died for their Christian faith or who merited reverence for their Christian devotion while alive. In the Roman Catholic Church, a worthy deceased Catholic who is canonized by the pope. (237, 402)

**Saint-Simonianism**—An early-19th-century utopian movement that emphasized the education and enfranchisement of women. (779)

**sakkos**—The tunic worn by a Byzantine priest. (9-35A)

**saltimbanque**—An itinerant circus performer. (29-11A)

**Samarqand ware**—A type of Islamic pottery produced in Samarqand and Nishapur in which the ceramists formed the shape of the vessel from dark pink clay and then immersed it in a tub of white slip, over which they painted ornamental or *calligraphic* decoration and which they sealed with a transparent glaze before firing. (294)

**samsara**—In Hindu belief, the rebirth of the soul into a succession of lives. (427, 435)

**samurai**—Medieval Japanese warriors. (1006)

**sand painting**—A temporary painting *technique* using sand, varicolored powdered stones, corn pollen, and charcoal. Sand paintings, also called dry paintings, are integral parts of sacred Navajo rituals. (1032)

**sangha**—The Buddhist *monastic* order. (15-8A)

**sarcophagus (pl. sarcophagi)**—Greek, "consumer of flesh." A coffin, usually of stone. (402, 449)

**Satimbe**—"Sister on the head." A Dogon (Mali) mask representing all women. (1074)

**saturation**—See *color*. (7, 813)

**satyr**—A Greek mythological follower of Dionysos having a man's upper body, a goat's hindquarters and horns, and a horse's ears and tail. (159, 27-33A)

**saz**—Ottoman design of sinuous curved leaves and complex blossoms, a Turkish term recalling an enchanted forest. (10-27A)

**scarab**—An Egyptian gem in the shape of a beetle. (61)

**scarification**—Decorative markings on the human body made by cutting or piercing the flesh to create scars. (525)

**Scholasticism**—The *Gothic* school of philosophy in which scholars applied Aristotle's system of rational inquiry to the interpretation of religious belief. (372)

**school**—A chronological and stylistic classification of works of art with a stipulation of place. (6)

**screen facade**—A *facade* that does not correspond to the structure of the building behind it. (12-11A)

**scriptorium (pl. scriptoria)**—The writing studio of a *monastery*. (311)

**scudi**—Italian, "shields." A coin denomination in 17th-century Italy. (684)

**sculpture in the round**—Freestanding figures, *carved* or *modeled* in three dimensions. (12, 18)

**seal**—In Asian painting, a stamp affixed to a painting to identify the artist, the *calligrapher,* or the owner. See also *cylinder seals*. (997)

**secco**—Italian, "dry." See also *fresco*. (408, 603)

**Second Style mural**—The style of Roman *mural* painting in which the aim was to dissolve the confining walls of a room and replace them with the illusion of a three-dimensional world constructed in the artist's imagination. (192)

**secondary colors**—Orange, green, and purple, obtained by mixing pairs of *primary colors* (red, yellow, blue). (7, 813)

**section**—In architecture, a diagram or representation of a part of a structure or building along an imaginary *plane* that passes through it vertically. Drawings showing a theoretical slice across a structure's width are lateral sections. Those cutting through a building's length are longitudinal sections. See also *elevation* and *cutaway*. (12)

**sedes sapientiae**—Latin, "throne of wisdom." A Romanesque sculptural type depicting the Virgin Mary with the Christ Child in her lap. (349)

**segmental pediment**—A *pediment* with a curved instead of a triangular *cornice*. (621)

**senate**—Latin senatus, "council of elders." The Senate was the main legislative body in Roman constitutional government. (181)

**serdab**—A small concealed chamber in an Egyptian *mastaba* for the *statue* of the deceased. (58)

**Severe Style**—The Early *Classical* style of Greek sculpture, ca. 480–450 BCE. (128)

**sexpartite vault**—See *vault*. (358)

**sfumato**—Italian, "smoky." A smokelike haziness that subtly softens outlines in painting; particularly applied to the paintings of Leonardo da Vinci and Correggio. (539, 604)

**sgrafitto**—A Chinese ceramic technique in which the design is *incised* through a colored *slip*. (467)

**shaft**—The tall, cylindrical part of a *column* between the *capital* and the *base*. (51, 116, 373)

**shakti**—In Hinduism, the female power of the deity Devi (or Goddess), which animates the matter of the cosmos. (435)

**shaykh**—An Islamic mystic *saint*. (975)

**sherd**—A fragmentary piece of a broken ceramic vessel. (476)

**shikara**—The beehive-shaped tower of a northern-style Hindu temple. (439)

**Shingon**—The primary form of Buddhism in Japan through the mid-10th century. Lowercase *shingon* is the Japanese term for the words or syllables recited in Buddhist rituals. (483)

**Shino**—Japanese ceramic wares produced during the late 16th and early 17th centuries in kilns in Mino. (1012)

**shogun**—In 12th- through 19th-century Japan, a military governor who managed the country on behalf of a figurehead emperor. (486, 1006)

**shogunate**—The Japanese military government of the 12th through 19th centuries. (486, 1006)

**sibyl**—A Greco-Roman mythological prophetess. (540)

**signoria**—The governing body in the Republic of Florence. (563)

**silentiary**—An usher responsible for maintaining silence in the *Byzantine* imperial palace in Constantinople. (261)

**silk-screen printing**—An industrial printing *technique* that creates a sharp-edged image by pressing ink through a design on silk or a similar tightly woven porous fabric stretched tight on a frame. (915)

**silverpoint**—A *stylus* made of silver, used in drawing in the 14th and 15th centuries because of the fine *line* it produced and the sharp point it maintained. (545, 604)

**Simultanéisme**—Robert Delaunay's version of *Cubism* in which he created spatial effects and kaleidoscopic movement solely through color contrasts; also known as *Orphism*. (848)

**simultaneous contrasts**—The phenomenon of juxtaposed *colors* affecting the eye's reception of each, as when a painter places dark green next to light green, making the former appear even darker and the latter even lighter. See also *successive contrasts*. (813)

**sinopia**—A burnt-orange pigment used in *fresco* painting to transfer a *cartoon* to the *arriccio* before the artist paints the plaster. (408)

**siren**—In ancient Greek mythology, a creature that was part bird and part woman. (110)

**sistrum**—An Egyptian percussion instrument or rattle. (95)

**site-specific art**—Art created for a specific location. See also *Environmental Art*. (932)

**skene**—Greek, "stage." The stage of a *classical* theater. (151)

**skenographia**—Greek, "scene painting"; the Greek term for *perspective* painting. (193)

**skiagraphia**—Greek, "shadow painting." The Greek term for shading, said to have been invented by Apollodoros, an Athenian painter of the fifth century BCE. (149)

**slip**—A mixture of fine clay and water used in ceramic decoration. (110, 451)

**solidus** (pl. **solidi**)—A Byzantine gold coin. (263)

**space**—In art history, both the actual area an object occupies or a building encloses, and the *illusionistic* representation of space in painting and sculpture. (8)

**spandrel**—The roughly triangular space enclosed by the curves of adjacent *arches* and a horizontal member connecting their vertexes; also, the space enclosed by the curve of an *arch* and an enclosing right angle. The area between the arch proper and the framing *columns* and *entablature*. (206)

**spectrum**—The range or band of visible colors in natural light. (7)

**sphinx**—A mythical Egyptian beast with the body of a lion and the head of a human. (63)

**splashed-ink painting**—See *haboku*. (1008)

**springing**—The lowest stone of an *arch,* resting on the *impost block.* In *Gothic* vaulting, the lowest stone of a diagonal or transverse *rib.* (340, 373)

**squinch**—An architectural device used as a transition from a square to a polygonal or circular base for a *dome.* It may be composed of *lintels, corbels,* or *arches.* (262)

**stained glass**—In *Gothic* architecture, the colored glass used for windows. (12, 373, 375, 982)

**stamp seal**—See *cylinder seal.* (39)

**stanza** (pl. **stanze**)—Italian, "room." (606)

**statue**—A three-dimensional sculpture. (12)

**stave**—A wedge-shaped timber; vertically placed staves embellish the architectural features of a building. (311)

**stele** (pl. **stelae**)—A *carved* stone slab used to mark graves or to commemorate historical events. (36, 499)

**stem stitching**—See *embroidery.* (362)

**stigmata**—In Christian art, the wounds Christ received at his crucifixion that miraculously appear on the body of a *saint.* (405)

**still life**—A picture depicting an arrangement of inanimate objects. (5, 196, 687)

**stoa**—In ancient Greek architecture, an open building with a roof supported by a row of *columns* parallel to the back wall. A covered colonnade or *portico.* (154)

**Stoic**—A philosophical school of ancient Greece, named after the *stoas* in which the philosophers met. (154)

**stoneware**—Pottery fired at high temperatures to produce a stonelike hardness and density. (451, 992)

**strategos**—Greek, "general." (133)

**stretcher bar**—One of a set of wooden bars used to stretch canvas to provide a taut surface for painting. (543)

**strigil**—A tool ancient Greek athletes used to scrape oil from their bodies after exercising. (147)

**stringcourse**—A raised horizontal *molding,* or band, in masonry. Its principal use is ornamental but it usually reflects interior structure. (586, 11-19A)

**strut**—A timber plank or other structural member used as a support in a building. Also a short section of marble used to support an arm or leg in a *statue.* (457)

**stucco**—A type of plaster used as a coating on exterior and interior walls. Also used as a sculptural *medium.* (182)

**stupa**—A large, mound-shaped Buddhist shrine. (429, 430, 984, 986)

**style**—A distinctive artistic manner. Period style is the characteristic style of a specific time. Regional style is the style of a particular geographical area. Personal style is an individual artist's unique manner. (3)

**stylistic evidence**—In art history, the examination of the *style* of an artwork in order to determine its date or the identity of the artist. (3)

**stylobate**—The uppermost course of the platform of a *classical* Greek temple, which supports the *columns.* (116, 618)

**stylus**—A needlelike tool used in *engraving* and *incising;* also, an ancient writing instrument used to inscribe clay or wax tablets. (33, 196, 545, 556, 604)

**sub gracia**—Latin, "under grace." In Christian thought, the period after the coming of Christ. (392)

**sub lege**—Latin, "under the law." In Christian thought, the period after Moses received the Ten Commandments and before the coming of Christ. See also *sub gracia.* (392)

**subtractive light**—The painter's light in art; the light reflected from pigments and objects. See also *additive light.* (7)

**subtractive sculpture**—A kind of sculpture technique in which materials are taken away from the original mass; *carving.* (11, 64)

**successive contrasts**—The phenomenon of colored afterimages. When a person looks intently at a *color* (green, for example) and then shifts to a white area, the fatigued eye momentarily perceives the *complementary color* (red). See also *simultaneous contrasts.* (813)

**sultan**—A *Muslim* ruler. (292, 977)

**sunken relief**—See *relief.* (73)

**Sunnah**—The collection of the Prophet Muhammad's moral sayings and descriptions of his deeds. (285)

**superimposed orders**—*Orders* of architecture that are placed one above another in an *arcaded* or *colonnaded* building, usually in the following sequence: *Doric* (the first story), *Ionic,* and *Corinthian.* Superimposed orders are found in later Greek architecture and were used widely by Roman and *Renaissance* builders. (204)

**superimposition**—In *Mesoamerican* architecture, the erection of a new structure on top of, and incorporating, an earlier structure; the nesting of a series of buildings inside each other. (1026)

**Superrealism**—A *school* of painting and sculpture of the 1960s and 1970s that emphasized producing artworks based on scrupulous fidelity to optical fact. The Superrealist painters were also called Photorealists because many used photographs as sources for their imagery. (917)

**Suprematism**—A type of art formulated by Kazimir Malevich to convey his belief that the supreme reality in the world is pure feeling, which attaches to no object and thus calls for new, nonobjective forms in art—shapes not related to objects in the visible world. (859)

**surah**—A chapter of the *Koran,* divided into verses. (285)

**Surrealism**—A successor to *Dada,* Surrealism incorporated the improvisational nature of its predecessor into its exploration of the ways to express in art the world of dreams and the unconscious. Biomorphic Surrealists, such as Joan Miró, produced largely *abstract compositions. Naturalistic* Surrealists, notably Salvador Dalí, presented recognizable scenes transformed into a dream or nightmare image. (875)

**sutra**—In Buddhism, an account of a sermon by or a dialogue involving the Buddha. A scriptural account of the Buddha. See also *jataka.* (480)

**symbol**—An image that stands for another image or encapsulates an idea. (5)

**Symbolism**—A late-19th-century movement based on the idea that the artist was not an imitator of nature but a creator who transformed the facts of nature into a *symbol* of the inner experience of that fact. (819)

**symmetria**—Greek, "commensurability of parts." Polykleitos's treatise on his *canon* of proportions incorporated the principle of symmetria. (135)

**symposium**—An ancient Greek banquet attended solely by men (and female servants and prostitutes). (108)

**Synthetic Cubism**—A later phase of *Cubism,* in which paintings and drawings were constructed from objects and shapes cut from paper or other materials to represent parts of a subject, in order to engage the viewer with pictorial issues, such as figuration, realism, and abstraction. (848)

**taberna**—In Roman architecture, a single-room shop usually covered by a barrel *vault.* (209)

**tablero**—See *talud-tablero construction.* (496)

**tablinum**—The study or office in a Roman house. (190)

**taj**—Arabic and Persian, "crown." (980)

**talud-tablero construction**—The alternation of sloping (talud) and vertical (tablero) rubble layers, characteristic of Teotihuacan architecture in Mesoamerica. (496)

**tapa**—Barkcloth made particularly in Polynesia. Tapa is often dyed, painted, stenciled, and sometimes perfumed. (1053)

**tapestry**—A weaving *technique* in which the *weft* threads are packed densely over the *warp* threads so that the designs are woven directly into the fabric. (362, 513, 730)

**tatami**—The traditional woven straw mat used for floor covering in Japanese architecture. (1011)

**tatanua**—In New Ireland (Papua New Guinea), the spirits of the dead. (1049)

**tatau**—See *tattoo.* (1054)

**tattoo**—A permanent design on the skin produced using indelible dyes. The term derives from the Tahitian, Samoan, and Tongan word *tatau* or *tatu.* (1054)

**tatu**—See *tattoo.* (1054)

**technique**—The processes artists employ to create *form,* as well as the distinctive, personal ways in which they handle their materials and tools. (7)

**tempera**—A *technique* of painting using pigment mixed with egg yolk, glue, or casein; also, the *medium* itself. (219, 404, 502, 538, 539)

**templon**—The columnar screen separating the sanctuary from the main body of a *Byzantine* church. (277)

**tenebrism**—Painting in the "shadowy manner," using violent contrasts of light and dark, as in the work of Caravaggio. The term derives from *tenebroso.* (683)

**tenebroso**—Italian, "shadowy." See *tenebrism.* (683)

**tenon**—A projection on the end of a piece of wood that is inserted into a corresponding hole (mortise) in another piece of wood to form a joint. (480)

**tephra**—The volcanic ash produced by the eruption on the *Cycladic* island of Thera. (92)

**tepidarium**—The warm-bath section of a Roman bathing establishment. (220)

**terminus ante quem**—Latin, "point [date] before which." (2)

**terminus post quem**—Latin, "point [date] after which." (2)

**terracotta**—Hard-baked clay, used for sculpture and as a building material. It may be *glazed* or painted. (90, 414)

**tessera** (pl. **tesserae**)—Greek, "cube." A tiny stone or piece of glass cut to the desired shape and size for use in forming a *mosaic.* (150, 245, 291, 299)

**tetrarch**—One of four corulers. (224)

**tetrarchy**—Greek, "rule by four." A type of Roman government established in the late third century CE by Diocletian in an attempt to foster order by sharing power with potential rivals. (224)

**texture**—The quality of a surface (rough, smooth, hard, soft, shiny, dull) as revealed by light. In represented texture, a painter depicts an object as having a certain texture even though the pigment is the real texture. (8)

**theatron**—Greek, "place for seeing." In ancient Greek theaters, the slope overlooking the *orchestra* on which the spectators sat. (151)

**Theotokos**—Greek, "she who bore God." The Virgin Mary, the mother of Jesus. (245, 267)

**thermoluminescence**—A method of dating by measuring amounts of radiation found within the clay of ceramic or sculptural forms, as well as in the clay cores from metal castings. (523)

**Third Style mural**—In Roman *mural* painting, the style in which delicate linear fantasies were sketched on predominantly *monochromatic* backgrounds. (194)

**tholos** (pl. **tholoi**)—A temple with a circular plan. Also, the burial chamber of a *tholos tomb.* (99, 151, 618)

**tholos tomb**—In *Mycenaean* architecture, a beehive-shaped tomb with a circular plan. (99)

**thrust**—The outward force exerted by an *arch* or a *vault* that must be counterbalanced by a *buttress.* (184, 21-31A)

**tiki**—A Marquesas Islands (Polynesia) three-dimensional carving of an exalted, deified ancestor figure. (1054)

**toga**—The garment worn by an ancient Roman male citizen. (176)

**togu na**—"House of words." A Dogon (Mali) men's house, where deliberations vital to community welfare take place. (1078)

**tokonoma**—A shallow alcove in a Japanese room, which is used for decoration, such as a painting or stylized flower arrangement. (1011)

**tonality**—See *color.* (7)

**tondo** (pl. **tondi**)—A circular painting or *relief* sculpture. (219, 585, 10-15A)

**Torah**—The Hebrew religious scroll containing the *Pentateuch.* (235)

**torana**—Gateway in the stone fence around a *stupa,* located at the cardinal points of the compass. (430, 15-8A)

**torque**—The distinctive necklace worn by the Gauls. (156)

**tracery**—Ornamental stonework for holding *stained glass* in place, characteristic of *Gothic cathedrals.* In plate tracery, the glass fills only the "punched holes" in the heavy ornamental stonework. In bar tracery, the stained-glass windows fill almost the entire opening, and the stonework is unobtrusive. (373, 414)

**tramezzo**—A screen placed across the *nave* of a church to separate the clergy from the lay audience. (14-6A)

**transept**—The part of a church with an axis that crosses the *nave* at a right angle. (243, 564, 14-5A)

**transubstantiation**—The transformation of the Eucharistic bread and wine into the body and blood of Christ. (24-18A)

**transverse arch**—An *arch* separating one *vaulted bay* from the next. (340)

**transverse barrel vault**—In medieval architecture, a semicylindrical *vault* oriented at a 90° angle to the *nave* of a church. (12-10A)

**transverse rib**—See *rib.* (373)

**treasury**—In ancient Greece, a small building set up for the safe storage of *votive offerings.* (119)

**trefoil**—A cloverlike ornament or symbol with stylized leaves in groups of three. (425)

**trefoil arch**—A triple-lobed arch. (402)

**tribune**—In church architecture, a gallery over the inner *aisle* flanking the *nave.* (337)

**triclinium**—The dining room of a Roman house. (190, 6-9A)

**trident**—The three-pronged pitchfork associated with the ancient Greek sea god Poseidon (Roman, Neptune). (107, 435)

**triforium**—In a *Gothic cathedral,* the *blind arcaded* gallery below the *clerestory;* occasionally, the *arcades* are filled with *stained glass.* (370, 373, 20-4A)

**triglyph**—A triple projecting, grooved member of a *Doric frieze* that alternates with *metopes.* (116, 640)

**trilithon**—A pair of *monoliths* topped with a *lintel;* found in *megalithic* structures. (28)

**Trinity**—In Christianity, God the Father, his son Jesus Christ, and the Holy Spirit. (240)

**tripod**—An ancient Greek deep bowl on a tall three-legged stand. (5-17A)

**triptych**—A three-paneled painting, ivory plaque, or *altarpiece.* Also, a small, portable shrine with hinged wings used for private devotion. (275, 392, 415)

**triratna**—A tripartite symbol of the three jewels of Buddhism—the Buddha himself, his *dharma,* and the *sangha.* (15-8A)

**triumphal arch**—In Roman architecture, a freestanding *arch* commemorating an important event, such as a military victory or the opening of a new road. (205, 575)

**trompe l'oeil**—French, "fools the eye." A form of *illusionistic* painting that aims to deceive viewers into believing they are seeing real objects rather than a representation of those objects. (595, 24-14A)

**true fresco**—See *fresco.* (408, 409, 502)

**trumeau**—In church architecture, the *pillar* or center post supporting the *lintel* in the middle of the doorway. (344, 20-2A)

**tubicen**—Latin, "trumpet player." (157)

**tughra**—The official signature of an Ottoman emperor. (10-23A)

**tukutuku**—A stitched lattice panel found in a Maori (New Zealand) meetinghouse. (1043)

**tumulus** (pl. **tumuli**)—Latin, "burial mound." In Etruscan architecture, tumuli cover one or more subterranean multichambered tombs cut out of the local tufa (limestone). Also characteristic of the Japanese Kofun period of the third and fourth centuries. (27, 170, 309, 478)

**tunnel vault**—See *vault.* (12, 52, 184, 338, 585, 981)

**turris**—See *westwork.* (323)

**Tuscan column**—The standard type of Etruscan *column.* It resembles ancient Greek *Doric* columns but is made of wood, is unfluted, and has a *base.* Also a popular motif in *Renaissance* and *Baroque* architecture. (168, 587, 618)

**twisted perspective**—See *composite view.* (23, 523)

**tympanum** (pl. **tympana**)—The space enclosed by a *lintel* and an *arch* over a doorway. (344, 538, 590, 14-12A)

**typology**—In Christian theology, the recognition of concordances between events, especially between episodes in the Old and New Testaments. (238)

**ukiyo-e**—Japanese, "pictures of the floating world." During the Edo period, *woodcut prints* depicting brothels, popular entertainment, and beautiful women. (1015, 28-16B)

**underglaze**—In *porcelain* decoration, the *technique* of applying mineral colors to the surface before the main firing, followed by an application of clear *glaze.* See also *overglaze.* (986, 992)

**Upanishads**—South Asian religious texts of ca. 800–500 BCE that introduced the concepts of *samsara, karma,* and *moksha.* (427)

**uraeus**—An Egyptian cobra; one of the emblems of *pharaonic* kingship. (63)

**urna**—A whorl of hair, represented as a dot, between the brows; one of the *lakshanas* of the Buddha. (427)

**ushabti**—In ancient Egypt, a figurine placed in a tomb to act as a servant to the deceased in the afterlife. (61)

**ushnisha**—A knot of hair on the top of the head; one of the *lakshanas* of the Buddha. (427)

**Usonian**—Frank Lloyd Wright's term for the inexpensive houses he designed for ordinary people. *Usonian* derives from "United States of North America." (896)

**valley temple**—The temple closest to the Nile River associated with each of the Great Pyramids at Gizeh in ancient Egypt. (62)

**value**—See *color*. (7, 813)

**vanishing point**—See *perspective*. (547, 567)

**vanitas**—Latin, "vanity." A term describing paintings (particularly 17th-century Dutch *still lifes*) that include references to death. (695, 23-3A, 26-7A)

**vanth**—An Etruscan female winged demon of death. (176)

**vassal**—In *feudalism*, a person who swears allegiance to a *liege lord* and renders him military service in return for tenure of a portion of the lord's land. (334)

**vault** (adj. **vaulted**)—A masonry roof or ceiling constructed on the *arch* principle, or a concrete roof of the same shape. A barrel (or tunnel) vault, semicylindrical in cross-*section*, is in effect a deep arch or an uninterrupted series of arches, one behind the other, over an oblong space. A quadrant vault is a half-barrel vault. A groin (or cross) vault is formed at the point at which two barrel vaults intersect at right angles. In a ribbed vault, there is a framework of *ribs* or arches under the intersections of the vaulting sections. A sexpartite vault is one whose ribs divide the vault into six compartments. A fan vault is a vault characteristic of English *Perpendicular Gothic* architecture, in which radiating ribs form a fanlike pattern. (12, 52)

**vaulting web**—See *web*. (373)

**Veda**—Sanskrit, "knowledge." One of four second-millennium BCE South Asian compilations of religious learning. (427)

**veduta** (pl. **vedute**)—Italian, "scenic view." (744)

**velarium**—In a Roman *amphitheater,* the cloth awning that could be rolled down from the top of the *cavea* to shield spectators from sun or rain. (190)

**vellum**—Calfskin prepared as a surface for writing or painting. (249, 604)

**venationes**—Ancient Roman wild animal hunts staged in an *amphitheater.* (203)

**veristic**—True to natural appearance; super-realistic. (185)

**vihara**—A Buddhist *monastery,* often cut into a hill. (429)

**vimana**—A pyramidal tower over the *garbha griha* of a Hindu temple of the southern style. (438, 439, 977)

**vita**—Italian, "life." Also, the title of a biography. (682)

**vita contemplativa**—Latin, "contemplative life." The secluded spiritual life of monks and nuns. (342)

**vizier**—An Egyptian pharaoh's chief administrator. (3-11B)

**volume**—The *space* that *mass* organizes, divides, or encloses. (8)

**volute**—A spiral, scroll-like form characteristic of the ancient Greek *Ionic* and the Roman *Composite capital.* (51, 116)

**votive offering**—A gift of gratitude to a deity. (35)

**voussoir**—A wedge-shaped stone block used in the construction of a true *arch.* The central voussoir, which sets the arch, is called the keystone. (175, 344, 640)

**wabi**—A 16th-century Japanese art style characterized by refined rusticity and an appreciation of simplicity and austerity. (1012)

**wainscoting**—Paneling on the lower part of interior walls. (827)

**waka sran**—"People of wood." Baule (Côte d'Ivoire) wooden figural sculptures. (1069)

**warp**—The vertical threads of a loom or cloth. (510)

**wat**—A Buddhist *monastery* in Cambodia. (443)

**web**—The masonry blocks that fill the area between the *ribs* of a *groin vault.* Also called vaulting web. (368)

**wedjat**—The eye of the Egyptian falcon-god Horus, a powerful *amulet.* (57, 61)

**weft**—The horizontal threads of a loom or cloth. (510)

**weld**—To join metal parts by heating, as in assembling the separate parts of a *statue* made by *casting.* (11)

**were-jaguar**—A composite human-jaguar; a common motif in Olmec art. (494)

**westwork**—German, "western entrance structure." The *facade* and towers at the western end of a medieval church, principally in Germany. In contemporaneous documents the westwork is called a castellum (Latin, "castle" or "fortress") or turris ("tower"). (323)

**wet-plate photography**—An early photographic process in which the photographic plate is exposed, developed, and fixed while wet. (792)

**white-ground painting**—An ancient Greek vase-painting *technique* in which the pot was first covered with a *slip* of very fine white clay, over which black *glaze* was used to outline figures, and diluted brown, purple, red, and white were used to color them. (142)

**woodcut**—A wooden block on the surface of which those parts not intended to *print* are cut away to a slight depth, leaving the design raised; also, the printed impression made with such a block. (554, 556)

**yaksha** (m.), **yakshi** (f.)—Lesser local male and female Buddhist and Hindu divinities. Yakshis are goddesses associated with fertility and vegetation. Yakshas, the male equivalent of yakshis, are often represented as fleshy but powerful males. (430, 432, 15-6B)

**yamato-e**—Also known as native-style painting, a purely Japanese style that often involved colorful, decorative representations of Japanese narratives or *landscapes.* (485)

**yang**—In Chinese cosmology, the principle of active masculine energy, which permeates the universe in varying proportions with yin, the principle of passive feminine energy. (463)

**yasti**—In Buddhist architecture, the mast or pole that arises from the dome of the *stupa* and its *harmika* and symbolizes the axis of the universe; it is adorned with a series of chatras (stone disks). (430)

**yin**—See *yang.* (463)

**yoga**—A method for controlling the body and relaxing the mind used in later Indian religions to yoke, or unite, the practitioner to the divine. (426)

**yosegi**—Japanese *joined-wood technique.* (17-13A)

**Zen**—A Japanese Buddhist sect and its doctrine, emphasizing enlightenment through intuition and introspection rather than the study of scripture. In Chinese, Chan. (470, 1007)

**ziggurat**—In ancient Mesopotamian architecture, a monumental platform for a temple. (33, 289)

**zoopraxiscope**—A device invented by Eadweard Muybridge in the 19th century to project sequences of still photographic images; a predecessor of the modern motion-picture projector. (796)

# BIBLIOGRAPHY

*This list of books is very selective but comprehensive enough to satisfy the reading interests of the beginning art history student and general reader. Significantly expanded from the previous edition, the 14th edition bibliography can also serve as the basis for undergraduate research papers. The resources listed range from works that are valuable primarily for their reproductions to those that are scholarly surveys of schools and periods or monographs on individual artists. The emphasis is on recent in-print books and on books likely to be found in college and municipal libraries. No entries for periodical articles appear, but the bibliography begins with a list of some of the major journals that publish art historical scholarship in English.*

## Selected Periodicals

*African Arts*
*American Art*
*American Indian Art*
*American Journal of Archaeology*
*Antiquity*
*Archaeology*
*Archives of American Art*
*Archives of Asian Art*
*Ars Orientalis*
*Art Bulletin*
*Art History*
*Art in America*
*Art Journal*
*Artforum International*
*Artnews*
*Burlington Magazine*
*Gesta*
*History of Photography*
*Journal of Egyptian Archaeology*
*Journal of Roman Archaeology*
*Journal of the Society of Architectural Historians*
*Journal of the Warburg and Courtauld Institutes*
*Latin American Antiquity*
*October*
*Oxford Art Journal*
*Women's Art Journal*

## General Studies

Baxandall, Michael. *Patterns of Intention: On the Historical Explanation of Pictures.* New Haven, Conn.: Yale University Press, 1985.

Bindman, David, ed. *The Thames & Hudson Encyclopedia of British Art.* London: Thames & Hudson, 1988.

Boström, Antonia. *The Encyclopedia of Sculpture.* 3 vols. London: Routledge, 2003.

Broude, Norma, and Mary D. Garrard, eds. *The Expanding Discourse: Feminism and Art History.* New York: Harper Collins, 1992.

Bryson, Norman. *Vision and Painting: The Logic of the Gaze.* New Haven, Conn.: Yale University Press, 1983.

Bryson, Norman, Michael Ann Holly, and Keith Moxey. *Visual Theory: Painting and Interpretation.* New York: Cambridge University Press, 1991.

Burden, Ernest. *Illustrated Dictionary of Architecture.* 2d ed. New York: McGraw-Hill, 2002.

Büttner, Nils. *Landscape Painting: A History.* New York: Abbeville, 2006.

Carrier, David. *A World Art History and Its Objects.* University Park: Pennsylvania State University Press, 2009.

Chadwick, Whitney. *Women, Art, and Society.* 4th ed. New York: Thames & Hudson, 2007.

Cheetham, Mark A., Michael Ann Holly, and Keith Moxey, eds. *The Subjects of Art History: Historical Objects in Contemporary Perspective.* New York: Cambridge University Press, 1998.

Chilvers, Ian, and Harold Osborne, eds. *The Oxford Dictionary of Art.* 3d ed. New York: Oxford University Press, 2004.

Corbin, George A. *Native Arts of North America, Africa, and the South Pacific: An Introduction.* New York: Harper Collins, 1988.

Crouch, Dora P., and June G. Johnson. *Traditions in Architecture: Africa, America, Asia, and Oceania.* New York: Oxford University Press, 2000.

Curl, James Stevens. *Oxford Dictionary of Architecture and Landscape Architecture.* 2d ed. New York: Oxford University Press, 2006.

Duby, Georges, ed. *Sculpture: From Antiquity to the Present.* 2 vols. Cologne: Taschen, 1999.

*Encyclopedia of World Art.* 17 vols. New York: McGraw-Hill, 1959–1987.

Fielding, Mantle. *Dictionary of American Painters, Sculptors, and Engravers.* 2d ed. Poughkeepsie, N.Y.: Apollo, 1986.

Fine, Sylvia Honig. *Women and Art: A History of Women Painters and Sculptors from the Renaissance to the 20th Century.* Rev. ed. Montclair, N.J.: Alanheld & Schram, 1978.

Fleming, John, Hugh Honour, and Nikolaus Pevsner. *The Penguin Dictionary of Architecture and Landscape Architecture.* 5th ed. New York: Penguin, 2000.

Frazier, Nancy. *The Penguin Concise Dictionary of Art History.* New York: Penguin, 2000.

Freedberg, David. *The Power of Images: Studies in the History and Theory of Response.* Chicago: University of Chicago Press, 1989.

Gaze, Delia., ed. *Dictionary of Women Artists.* 2 vols. London: Routledge, 1997.

Hall, James. *Dictionary of Subjects and Symbols in Art.* 2d ed. Boulder, Colo.: Westview, 2008.

Harris, Anne Sutherland, and Linda Nochlin. *Women Artists: 1550–1950.* Los Angeles: Los Angeles County Museum of Art; New York: Knopf, 1977.

Hauser, Arnold. *The Sociology of Art.* Chicago: University of Chicago Press, 1982.

Hults, Linda C. *The Print in the Western World: An Introductory History.* Madison: University of Wisconsin Press, 1996.

Kemp, Martin. *The Science of Art: Optical Themes in Western Art from Brunelleschi to Seurat.* New Haven, Conn.: Yale University Press, 1990.

Kostof, Spiro, and Gregory Castillo. *A History of Architecture: Settings and Rituals.* 2d ed. Oxford: Oxford University Press, 1995.

Kultermann, Udo. *The History of Art History.* New York: Abaris, 1993.

Lucie-Smith, Edward. *The Thames & Hudson Dictionary of Art Terms.* 2d ed. New York: Thames & Hudson, 2004.

Moffett, Marian, Michael Fazio, and Lawrence Wadehouse. *A World History of Architecture.* Boston: McGraw-Hill, 2004.

Morgan, Anne Lee. *Oxford Dictionary of American Art and Artists.* New York: Oxford University Press, 2008.

Murray, Peter, and Linda Murray. *A Dictionary of Art and Artists.* 7th ed. New York: Penguin, 1998.

Nelson, Robert S., and Richard Shiff, eds. *Critical Terms for Art History.* Chicago: University of Chicago Press, 1996.

Pazanelli, Roberta, ed. *The Color of Life: Polychromy in Sculpture from Antiquity to the Present.* Los Angeles: J. Paul Getty Museum, 2008.

Penny, Nicholas. *The Materials of Sculpture.* New Haven, Conn.: Yale University Press, 1993.

Pevsner, Nikolaus. *A History of Building Types.* London: Thames & Hudson, 1987. Reprint of 1979 ed.

———. *An Outline of European Architecture.* 8th ed. Baltimore: Penguin, 1974.

Pierce, James Smith. *From Abacus to Zeus: A Handbook of Art History.* 7th ed. Upper Saddle River, N.J.: Pearson Prentice Hall, 1998.

Placzek, Adolf K., ed. *Macmillan Encyclopedia of Architects.* 4 vols. New York: Macmillan, 1982.

Podro, Michael. *The Critical Historians of Art.* New Haven, Conn.: Yale University Press, 1982.

Pollock, Griselda. *Vision and Difference: Femininity, Feminism, and Histories of Art.* London: Routledge, 1988.

Pregill, Philip, and Nancy Volkman. *Landscapes in History: Design and Planning in the Eastern and Western Traditions.* 2d ed. Hoboken, N.J.: Wiley, 1999.

Preziosi, Donald, ed. *The Art of Art History: A Critical Anthology.* New York: Oxford University Press, 1998.

Read, Herbert. *The Thames & Hudson Dictionary of Art and Artists.* Rev. ed. New York: Thames & Hudson, 1994.

Reid, Jane D. *The Oxford Guide to Classical Mythology in the Arts 1300–1990s.* 2 vols. New York: Oxford University Press, 1993.

Rogers, Elizabeth Barlow. *Landscape Design: A Cultural and Architectural History.* New York: Abrams, 2001.

Roth, Leland M. *Understanding Architecture: Its Elements, History, and Meaning.* 2d ed. Boulder, Colo.: Westview, 2006.

Schama, Simon. *The Power of Art.* New York: Ecco, 2006.

Slatkin, Wendy. *Women Artists in History: From Antiquity to the 20th Century.* 4th ed. Upper Saddle River, N.J.: Prentice Hall, 2000.

Steer, John, and Antony White. *Atlas of Western Art History: Artists, Sites, and Monuments from Ancient Greece to the Modern Age.* New York: Facts on File, 1994.

Stratton, Arthur. *The Orders of Architecture: Greek, Roman, and Renaissance.* London: Studio, 1986.

Summers, David. *Real Spaces: World Art History and the Rise of Western Modernism.* London: Phaidon, 2003.

Sutton, Ian. *Western Architecture: From Ancient Greece to the Present.* New York: Thames & Hudson, 1999.

Trachtenberg, Marvin, and Isabelle Hyman. *Architecture, from Prehistory to Post-Modernism.* 2d ed. Upper Saddle River, N.J.: Prentice Hall, 2003.

Turner, Jane, ed. *The Dictionary of Art.* 34 vols. New ed. New York: Oxford University Press, 2003.

Watkin, David. *A History of Western Architecture.* 4th ed. London: Laurence King, 2010.

West, Shearer. *Portraiture.* New York: Oxford University Press, 2004.

Wittkower, Rudolf. *Sculpture Processes and Principles.* New York: Harper & Row, 1977.

Wren, Linnea H., and Janine M. Carter, eds. *Perspectives on Western Art: Source Documents and Readings from the Ancient Near East through the Middle Ages.* New York: Harper & Row, 1987.

Zijlmans, Kitty, and Wilfried van Damme, eds. *World Art Studies: Exploring Concepts and Approaches.* Amsterdam: Valiz, 2008.

### Ancient Art, General

Aruz, Joan, and Ronald Wallenfels, eds. *Art of the First Cities: The Third Millennium BC from the Mediterranean to the Indus.* New York: Metropolitan Museum of Art, 2003.

Beard, Mary, and John Henderson. *Classical Art: From Greece to Rome.* New York: Oxford University Press, 2001.

Boardman, John. *The World of Ancient Art.* London: Thames & Hudson, 2006.

———, ed. *The Oxford History of Classical Art.* New York: Oxford University Press, 1997.

Chitham, Robert. *The Classical Orders of Architecture.* 2d ed. Boston: Architectural Press, 2005.

Clayton, Peter A., and Martin J. Price, eds. *The Seven Wonders of the Ancient World.* New York: Routledge, 1988.

Connolly, Peter, and Hazel Dodge. *The Ancient City: Life in Classical Athens and Rome.* New York: Oxford University Press, 1998.

De Grummond, Nancy Thomson, ed. *An Encyclopedia of the History of Classical Archaeology.* 2 vols. Westport, Conn.: Greenwood, 1996.

Dunbabin, Katherine. *Mosaics of the Greek and Roman World.* New York: Cambridge University Press, 1999.

Gates, Charles. *Ancient Cities: The Archaeology of Urban Life in the Ancient Near East and Egypt, Greece, and Rome.* London: Routledge, 2003.

Grossman, Janet Burnett. *Looking at Greek and Roman Sculpture in Stone: A Guide to Terms, Styles, and Techniques.* Los Angeles: J. Paul Getty Museum, 2003.

Kampen, Natalie B., ed. *Sexuality in Ancient Art.* New York: Cambridge University Press, 1996.

*Lexicon Iconographicum Mythologiae Classicae.* 10 vols. Zurich: Artemis, 1981–1999.

Ling, Roger. *Ancient Mosaics.* Princeton, N.J.: Princeton University Press, 1998.

Lloyd, Seton, and Hans Wolfgang Muller. *Ancient Architecture: Mesopotamia, Egypt, Crete.* New York: Electa/Rizzoli, 1980.

Oliphant, Margaret. *The Atlas of the Ancient World: Charting the Great Civilizations of the Past.* New York: Simon & Schuster, 1992.

Onians, John. *Classical Art and the Cultures of Greece and Rome.* New Haven, Conn.: Yale University Press, 1999.

Renfrew, Colin, and Paul G. Bahn. *Archaeology: Theories, Methods, and Practices.* London: Thames & Hudson, 1991.

Stillwell, Richard, William L. MacDonald, and Marian H. McAllister, eds. *The Princeton Encyclopedia of Classical Sites.* Princeton, N.J.: Princeton University Press, 1976.

Trigger, Bruce. *Understanding Early Civilizations: A Comparative Study.* New York: Cambridge University Press, 2003.

Ward-Perkins, John B. *Cities of Ancient Greece and Italy: Planning in Classical Antiquity.* Rev. ed. New York: Braziller, 1987.

Wolf, Walther. *The Origins of Western Art: Egypt, Mesopotamia, the Aegean.* New York: Universe, 1989.

### Chapter 1: Art before History

Aujoulat, Norbert. *Lascaux: Movement, Space, and Time.* New York: Abrams, 2005.

Bahn, Paul G. *The Cambridge Illustrated History of Prehistoric Art.* New York: Cambridge University Press, 1998.

———. *Cave Art: A Guide to the Decorated Ice Age Caves of Europe.* London: Frances Lincoln, 2007.

Bahn, Paul G., and Jean Vertut. *Journey through the Ice Age.* Berkeley: University of California Press, 1997.

Beltrán, Antonio, ed. *The Cave of Altamira.* New York: Abrams, 1999.

Berhgaus, Guner. *New Perspectives on Prehistoric Art.* Westport, Conn.: Praeger, 2004.

Burl, Aubrey. *Great Stone Circles.* New Haven, Conn.: Yale University Press, 1999.

Chauvet, Jean-Marie, Eliette Brunel Deschamps, and Christian Hillaire. *Dawn of Art: The Chauvet Cave.* New York: Abrams, 1996.

Chippindale, Christopher. *Stonehenge Complete.* 3d ed. New York: Thames & Hudson, 2004.

Clottes, Jean. *Cave Art.* London: Phaidon, 2008.

———. *Chauvet Cave: The Art of Earliest Times.* Salt Lake City: University of Utah Press, 2003.

Cunliffe, Barry, ed. *The Oxford Illustrated Prehistory of Europe.* New York: Oxford University Press, 2001.

Guthrie, R. Dale. *The Nature of Paleolithic Art.* Chicago: University of Chicago Press, 2005.

Hodder, Ian. *The Leopard's Tale: Revealing the Mysteries of Çatalhöyük.* London: Thames & Hudson, 2006.

Kenyon, Kathleen M. *Digging up Jericho.* New York: Praeger, 1974.

Leroi-Gourhan, André. *The Dawn of European Art: An Introduction to Paleolithic Cave Painting.* Cambridge: Cambridge University Press, 1982.

Marshack, Alexander. *The Roots of Civilization: The Cognitive Beginnings of Man's First Art, Symbol and Notation.* 2d ed. Wakefield, R.I.: Moyer Bell, 1991.

Pfeiffer, John E. *The Creative Explosion: An Inquiry into the Origins of Art and Religion.* New York: Harper & Row, 1982.

Renfrew, Colin, ed. *British Prehistory: A New Outline.* London: Noyes, 1975.

Ruspoli, Mario. *The Cave of Lascaux: The Final Photographs.* New York: Abrams, 1987.

Scarre, Chris. *Exploring Prehistoric Europe.* New York: Oxford University Press, 1998.

Wainwright, Geoffrey. *The Henge Monuments: Ceremony and Society in Prehistoric Britain.* London: Thames & Hudson, 1990.

White, Randall. *Prehistoric Art: The Symbolic Journey of Humankind.* New York: Abrams, 2003.

### Chapter 2: Mesopotamia and Persia

Akurgal, Ekrem. *Art of the Hittites.* New York: Abrams, 1962.

Allen, Lindsay. *The Persian Empire.* Chicago: University of Chicago Press, 2005.

Amiet, Pierre. *Art of the Ancient Near East.* New York: Abrams, 1980.

Ascalone, Enrico. *Mesopotamia: Assyrians, Sumerians, Babylonians.* Berkeley and Los Angeles: University of California Press, 2007.

Bahrani, Zainab. *The Graven Image: Representation in Babylonia and Assyria.* Philadelphia: University of Pennsylvania Press, 2003.

Bienkowski, Piotr, and Alan Millard, eds. *Dictionary of the Ancient Near East.* Philadelphia: University of Pennsylvania Press, 2000.

Collins, Paul. *Assyrian Palace Sculptures.* Austin: University of Texas Press, 2008.

Collon, Dominique. *Ancient Near Eastern Art.* Berkeley: University of California Press, 1995.

———. *First Impressions: Cylinder Seals in the Ancient Near East.* 2d ed. London: British Museum, 1993.

———. *Near Eastern Seals.* Berkeley: University of California Press, 1990.

Crawford, Harriet. *Sumer and the Sumerians.* 2d ed. New York: Cambridge University Press, 2004.

Curatola, Giovanni, ed. *The Art and Architecture of Mesopotamia.* New York: Abbeville, 2007.

Curtis, John E. *Ancient Persia.* Cambridge, Mass.: Harvard University Press, 1990.

Curtis, John E., and Julian E. Reade. *Art and Empire: Treasures from Assyria in the British Museum.* New York: Metropolitan Museum of Art, 1995.

Curtis, John E., and Nigel Tallis, eds. *Forgotten Empire: The World of Ancient Persia.* Berkeley: University of California Press, 2005.

Finkel, Irving L., and Michael J. Seymour, eds. *Babylon.* New York: Oxford University Press, 2008.

Foster, Benjamin R., and Karen Polinger Foster. *Civilizations of Ancient Iraq.* Princeton, N.J.: Princeton University Press, 2009.

Frankfort, Henri. *The Art and Architecture of the Ancient Orient.* 5th ed. New Haven, Conn.: Yale University Press, 1996.

Ghirshman, Roman. *The Arts of Ancient Iran: From Its Origins to the Time of Alexander the Great.* New York: Golden, 1964.

———. *Persian Art: The Parthian and Sassanian Dynasties, 249 BC–AD 651.* New York: Golden, 1962.

Gunter, Ann C., ed. *Investigating Artistic Environments in the Ancient Near East.* Washington, D.C.: Arthur M. Sackler Gallery, 1990.

Harper, Prudence O., Joan Aruz, and Françoise Tallon, eds. *The Royal City of Susa: Ancient Near Eastern Treasures in the Louvre.* New York: Metropolitan Museum of Art, 1992.

Leick, Gwendolyn. *Mesopotamia: The Invention of the City*. New York: Penguin, 2003.

Lloyd, Seton. *The Archaeology of Mesopotamia: From the Old Stone Age to the Persian Conquest*. London: Thames & Hudson, 1984.

Macqueen, James G. *The Hittites and Their Contemporaries in Asia Minor*. Rev. ed. New York: Thames & Hudson, 1986.

Meyers, Eric M., ed. *The Oxford Encyclopedia of Archaeology in the Near East*. 5 vols. New York: Oxford University Press, 1997.

Moortgat, Anton. *The Art of Ancient Mesopotamia*. New York: Phaidon, 1969.

Oates, Joan. *Babylon*. Rev. ed. London: Thames & Hudson, 1986.

Parrot, André. *The Arts of Assyria*. New York: Golden, 1961.

———. *Sumer: The Dawn of Art*. New York: Golden, 1961.

Porada, Edith. *Man and Images in the Ancient Near East*. Wakefield, R.I.: Moyer Bell, 1995.

Porada, Edith, and Robert H. Dyson. *The Art of Ancient Iran: Pre-Islamic Cultures*. Rev. ed. New York: Greystone, 1969.

Postgate, J. Nicholas. *Early Mesopotamia: Society and Economy at the Dawn of History*. London: Routledge, 1992.

Potts, Daniel T. *The Archaeology of Elam: Formation and Transformation of an Ancient Iranian State*. New York: Cambridge University Press, 1999.

Reade, Julian E. *Assyrian Sculpture*. Cambridge, Mass.: Harvard University Press, 1999.

———. *Mesopotamia*. Cambridge, Mass.: Harvard University Press, 1991.

Roaf, Michael. *Cultural Atlas of Mesopotamia and the Ancient Near East*. New York: Facts on File, 1990.

Russell, John M. *Sennacherib's Palace without Rival at Nineveh*. Chicago: University of Chicago Press, 1991.

Saggs, H.W.F. *Babylonians*. London: British Museum, 1995.

Sasson, Jack M., ed. *Civilizations of the Ancient Near East*. 4 vols. New York: Scribner, 1995.

Snell, Daniel C. *Life in the Ancient Near East: 3100–332 BC*. New Haven, Conn.: Yale University Press, 1997.

Strommenger, Eva, and Max Hirmer. *5,000 Years of the Art of Mesopotamia*. New York: Abrams, 1964.

Van de Mieroop, Marc. *The Ancient Mesopotamian City*. New York: Oxford University Press, 1997.

Zettler, Richard L., and Lee Horne. *Treasures from the Royal Tombs of Ur*. Philadelphia: University of Pennsylvania Museum of Archaeology and Anthropology, 1998.

## Chapter 3: Egypt under the Pharaohs

Allen, James P., ed., *Egyptian Art in the Age of the Pyramids*. New York: Abrams, 1999.

Arnold, Dieter. *Building in Egypt: Pharaonic Stone Masonry*. New York: Oxford University Press, 1991.

Arnold, Dorothea. *The Royal Women of Amarna*. New York: Metropolitan Museum of Art, 1996.

———. *When the Pyramids Were Built: Egyptian Art of the Old Kingdom*. New York: Rizzoli, 1996.

Baines, John, and Jaromír Málek. *Atlas of Ancient Egypt*. New York: Facts on File, 1980.

Bard, Kathryn A. *An Introduction to the Archaeology of Ancient Egypt*. Oxford: Blackwell, 2007.

———, ed. *Encyclopedia of the Archaeology of Ancient Egypt*. London: Routledge, 1999.

Bianchi, Robert S. *Cleopatra's Egypt: Age of the Ptolemies*. Brooklyn: Brooklyn Museum, 1988.

———. *Splendors of Ancient Egypt from the Egyptian Museum, Cairo*. London: Booth-Clibborn, 1996.

Capel, Anne K., and Glenn E. Markoe, eds. *Mistress of the House, Mistress of Heaven: Women in Ancient Egypt*. New York: Hudson Hills, 1996.

D'Auria, Sue, Peter Lacovara, and Catharine H. Roehrig. *Mummies and Magic: The Funerary Arts of Ancient Egypt*. Boston: Museum of Fine Arts, 1988.

Davis, Whitney. *The Canonical Tradition in Ancient Egyptian Art*. New York: Cambridge University Press, 1989.

Dodson, Aidam, and Salima Ikram. *The Tomb in Ancient Egypt*. New York: Thames & Hudson, 2008.

Hawass, Zahi. *Valley of the Golden Mummies*. New York: Abrams, 2000.

Ikram, Salima, and Aidan Dodson. *The Mummy in Ancient Egypt: Equipping the Dead for Eternity*. New York: Thames & Hudson, 1998.

Kemp, Barry J. *Ancient Egypt: Anatomy of a Civilization*. 2d ed. New York: Routledge, 2006.

Kozloff, Arielle P., and Betsy M. Bryan. *Egypt's Dazzling Sun: Amenhotep III and His World*. Cleveland: Cleveland Museum of Art, 1992.

Lange, Kurt, and Max Hirmer. *Egypt: Architecture, Sculpture, and Painting in Three Thousand Years*. 4th ed. London: Phaidon, 1968.

Lehner, Mark. *The Complete Pyramids: Solving the Ancient Mysteries*. New York: Thames & Hudson, 1997.

Mahdy, Christine, ed. *The World of the Pharaohs: A Complete Guide to Ancient Egypt*. London: Thames & Hudson, 1990.

O'Neill, John P., ed. *Egyptian Art in the Age of the Pyramids*. New York: Abrams, 1999.

Málek, Jaromír. *Egypt: 4,000 Years of Art*. New York: Phaidon, 2003.

———. *Egyptian Art*. London: Phaidon, 1999.

———, ed. *Egypt: Ancient Culture, Modern Land*. Norman: University of Oklahoma Press, 1993.

Redford, Donald B. *Akhenaton, the Heretic King*. Princeton, N.J.: Princeton University Press, 1984.

———, ed. *The Oxford Encyclopedia of Ancient Egypt*. 3 vols. New York: Oxford University Press, 2001.

Reeves, C. Nicholas. *The Complete Tutankhamun: The King, the Tomb, the Royal Treasure*. London: Thames & Hudson, 1990.

Robins, Gay. *The Art of Ancient Egypt*. Rev. ed. Cambridge, Mass.: Harvard University Press, 2008.

———. *Egyptian Painting and Relief*. Aylesbury: Shire, 1986.

———. *Proportion and Style in Ancient Egyptian Art*. Austin: University of Texas Press, 1994.

———. *Women in Ancient Egypt*. London: British Museum, 1993.

Romer, John. *Valley of the Kings: Exploring the Tombs of the Pharaohs*. New York: Holt, 1994.

Russmann, Edna R. *Egyptian Sculpture: Cairo and Luxor*. Austin: University of Texas Press, 1989.

Schäfer, Heinrich. *Principles of Egyptian Art*. Rev. ed. Oxford: Clarendon, 1986.

Schulz, Regina, and Matthias Seidel, eds. *Egypt: The World of the Pharaohs*. Cologne: Könemann, 1999.

Shafer, Byron E., ed. *Temples of Ancient Egypt*. Ithaca, N.Y.: Cornell University Press, 1997.

Shaw, Ian, and Paul Nicholson. *The Dictionary of Ancient Egypt*. London: British Museum, 1995.

Silverman, David P., ed. *Ancient Egypt*. New York: Oxford University Press, 1997.

Smith, William Stevenson, and William Kelly Simpson. *The Art and Architecture of Ancient Egypt*. Rev. ed. New Haven, Conn.: Yale University Press, 1998.

Tiradritti, Francesco. *Egyptian Wall Paintings*. New York: Abbeville, 2008.

Weeks, Kent R. *The Treasures of Luxor and the Valley of the Kings*. Vercelli: White Star, 2005.

———, ed. *Valley of the Kings*. Vercelli: White Star, 2001.

Wildung, Dietrich. *Egypt: From Prehistory to the Romans*. Cologne: Taschen, 1997.

## Chapter 4: The Prehistoric Aegean

Andreadaki-Vlazaki, Maria, ed. *From the Land of the Labyrinth: Minoan Crete 3000–1100 B.C.* New York: Alexander S. Onassis Public Benefit Foundation, 2008.

Barber, R.L.N. *The Cyclades in the Bronze Age*. Iowa City: University of Iowa Press, 1987.

Betancourt, Philip P. *A History of Minoan Pottery*. Princeton, N.J.: Princeton University Press, 1965.

———. *Introduction to Aegean Art*. New York: Institute for Aegean Prehistory, 2007.

Cadogan, Gerald. *Palaces of Minoan Crete*. London: Methuen, 1980.

Castleden, Rodney. *Mycenaeans*. London: Routledge, 2005.

Chadwick, John. *The Mycenaean World*. New York: Cambridge University Press, 1976.

Cullen, Tracey, ed. *Aegean Prehistory: A Review*. Boston: Archaeological Institute of America, 2001.

Demargne, Pierre. *The Birth of Greek Art*. New York: Golden, 1964.

Dickinson, Oliver P.T.K. *The Aegean Bronze Age*. New York: Cambridge University Press, 1994.

Doumas, Christos. *Thera, Pompeii of the Ancient Aegean: Excavations at Akrotiri, 1967–1979*. New York: Thames & Hudson, 1983.

———. *The Wall-Paintings of Thera*. Athens: Thera Foundation, 1992.

Fitton, J. Lesley. *Cycladic Art*. 2d ed. Cambridge, Mass.: Harvard University Press, 1999.

———. *The Discovery of the Greek Bronze Age*. London: British Museum, 1995.

Forsyth, Phyllis Young. *Thera in the Bronze Age*. New York: Peter Lang, 1997.

Getz-Preziosi, Patricia. *Sculptors of the Cyclades: Individual and Tradition in the Third Millennium BC*. Ann Arbor: University of Michigan Press, 1987.

Graham, James W. *The Palaces of Crete*. Princeton, N.J.: Princeton University Press, 1987.

Hampe, Roland, and Erika Simon. *The Birth of Greek Art: From the Mycenaean to the Archaic Period*. New York: Oxford University Press, 1981.

Higgins, Reynold. *Minoan and Mycenaean Art*. Rev. ed. New York: Thames & Hudson, 1997.

Hood, Sinclair. *The Arts in Prehistoric Greece*. New Haven, Conn.: Yale University Press, 1992.

Immerwahr, Sarah A. *Aegean Painting in the Bronze Age*. University Park: Pennsylvania State University Press, 1990.

MacGillivray, J. A. *Minotaur: Sir Arthur Evans and the Archaeology of the Minoan Myth*. New York: Hill and Wang, 2000.

Marinatos, Nanno. *Art and Religion in Thera: Reconstructing a Bronze Age Society*. Athens: Mathioulakis, 1984.

Marinatos, Spyridon, and Max Hirmer. *Crete and Mycenae*. London: Thames & Hudson, 1960.

McDonald, William A., and Carol G. Thomas. *Progress into the Past: The Rediscovery of Mycenaean Civilization*. 2d ed. Bloomington: Indiana University Press, 1990.

Preziosi, Donald, and Louise A. Hitchcock. *Aegean Art and Architecture*. New York: Oxford University Press, 1999.

Schofield, Louise. *The Mycenaeans*. London: British Museum, 2007.

Shelmerdine, Cynthia W., ed. *The Cambridge Companion to the Aegean Bronze Age*. New York: Cambridge University Press, 2008.

Taylour, Lord William. *The Mycenaeans*. London: Thames & Hudson, 1990.

Vermeule, Emily. *Greece in the Bronze Age*. Chicago: University of Chicago Press, 1972.

Warren, Peter. *The Aegean Civilisations from Ancient Crete to Mycenae.* 2d ed. Oxford: Elsevier-Phaidon, 1989.

### Chapter 5: Ancient Greece

Arias, Paolo. *A History of One Thousand Years of Greek Vase Painting.* New York: Abrams, 1962.

Ashmole, Bernard. *Architect and Sculptor in Classical Greece.* New York: New York University Press, 1972.

Barletta, Barbara A. *The Origins of the Greek Architectural Orders.* New York: Cambridge University Press, 2001.

Berve, Helmut, Gottfried Gruben, and Max Hirmer. *Greek Temples, Theatres, and Shrines.* New York: Abrams, 1963.

Biers, William. *The Archaeology of Greece: An Introduction.* 2d ed. Ithaca, N.Y.: Cornell University Press, 1996.

Boardman, John. *Athenian Black Figure Vases.* Rev. ed. New York: Thames & Hudson, 1991.

——. *Athenian Red Figure Vases: The Archaic Period.* New York: Thames & Hudson, 1988.

——. *Athenian Red Figure Vases: The Classical Period.* New York: Thames & Hudson, 1989.

——. *Early Greek Vase Painting, 11th–6th Centuries BC.* New York: Thames & Hudson, 1998.

——. *Greek Sculpture: The Archaic Period.* Rev. ed. New York: Thames & Hudson, 1985.

——. *Greek Sculpture: The Classical Period.* New York: Thames & Hudson, 1987.

——. *Greek Sculpture: The Late Classical Period and Sculpture in Colonies and Overseas.* New York: Thames & Hudson, 1995.

——. *The Parthenon and Its Sculpture.* Austin: University of Texas Press, 1985.

Camp, John M. *The Archaeology of Athens.* New Haven, Conn.: Yale University Press, 2001.

Carpenter, Thomas H. *Art and Myth in Ancient Greece.* New York: Thames & Hudson, 1991.

Charbonneaux, Jean, Roland Martin, and François Villard. *Archaic Greek Art.* New York: Braziller, 1971.

——. *Classical Greek Art.* New York: Braziller, 1972.

——. *Hellenistic Art.* New York: Braziller, 1973.

Clark, Andrew J., Maya Elston, and Mary Louise Hart. *Understanding Greek Vases: A Guide to Terms, Styles, and Techniques.* Los Angeles: J. Paul Getty Museum, 2002.

Cohen, Beth, ed. *The Colors of Clay: Special Techniques in Athenian Vases.* Los Angeles: J. Paul Getty Museum, 2006.

Coldstream, J. Nicholas. *Geometric Greece.* New York: St. Martin's, 1977.

Coulton, J. J. *Ancient Greek Architects at Work.* Ithaca, N.Y.: Cornell University Press, 1982.

Donohue, A. A. *Greek Sculpture and the Problem of Description.* New York: Cambridge University Press, 2005.

Fullerton, Mark D. *Greek Art.* New York: Cambridge University Press, 2000.

Haynes, Denys E. L. *The Technique of Greek Bronze Statuary.* Mainz: von Zabern, 1992.

Houser, Caroline. *Greek Monumental Bronze Sculpture.* New York: Vendome, 1983.

Hurwit, Jeffrey M. *The Acropolis in the Age of Pericles.* New York: Cambridge University Press, 2004.

——. *The Art and Culture of Early Greece, 1100–480 BC.* Ithaca, N.Y.: Cornell University Press, 1985.

——. *The Athenian Acropolis: History, Mythology, and Archaeology from the Neolithic Era to the Present.* New York: Cambridge University Press, 1999.

Jenkins, Ian. *Greek Architecture and Its Sculpture.* Cambridge, Mass.: Harvard University Press, 2006.

——. *The Parthenon Frieze.* Austin: University of Texas Press, 1994.

Lawrence, Arnold W., and R. A. Tomlinson. *Greek Architecture.* Rev. ed. New Haven, Conn.: Yale University Press, 1996.

Martin, Roland. *Greek Architecture: Architecture of Crete, Greece, and the Greek World.* New York: Electa/Rizzoli, 1988.

Mattusch, Carol C. *Classical Bronzes: The Art and Craft of Greek and Roman Statuary.* Ithaca, N.Y.: Cornell University Press, 1996.

——. *Greek Bronze Statuary from the Beginnings through the Fifth Century BC.* Ithaca, N.Y.: Cornell University Press, 1988.

Mee, Christopher. *Greek Archaeology.* Hoboken, N.J.: Wiley-Blackwell, 2011.

Mee, Christopher, and Tony Spawforth. *Greece: An Oxford Archaeological Guide.* New York: Oxford University Press, 2001.

Morris, Sarah P. *Daidalos and the Origins of Greek Art.* Princeton, N.J.: Princeton University Press, 1992.

Neer, Richard T. *The Emergence of the Classical Style in Greek Sculpture.* Chicago: University of Chicago Press, 2010.

Osborne, Robin. *Archaic and Classical Greek Art.* New York: Oxford University Press, 1998.

Palagia, Olga. *The Pediments of the Parthenon.* Leiden: E. J. Brill, 1993.

——, ed. *Greek Sculpture: Functions, Materials, and Techniques in the Archaic and Classical Periods.* New York: Cambridge University Press, 2006.

Palagia, Olga, and Jerome J. Pollitt. *Personal Styles in Greek Sculpture.* New York: Cambridge University Press, 1996.

Pedley, John Griffiths. *Greek Art and Archaeology.* 4th ed. Upper Saddle River, N.J.: Prentice Hall, 2007.

——. *Sanctuaries and the Sacred in the Ancient Greek World.* New York: Cambridge University Press, 2005.

Petrakos, Vasileios. *Great Moments in Greek Archaeology.* Los Angeles: J. Paul Getty Museum, 2007.

Pollitt, Jerome J. *Art and Experience in Classical Greece.* New York: Cambridge University Press, 1972.

——. *Art in the Hellenistic Age.* New York: Cambridge University Press, 1986.

——. *The Art of Ancient Greece: Sources and Documents.* 2d ed. New York: Cambridge University Press, 1990.

Pugliese Carratelli, G. *The Greek World: Art and Civilization in Magna Graecia and Sicily.* New York: Rizzoli, 1996.

Reeder, Ellen D., ed. *Pandora: Women in Classical Greece.* Baltimore: Walters Art Gallery, 1995.

Rhodes, Robin F. *Architecture and Meaning on the Athenian Acropolis.* New York: Cambridge University Press, 1995.

Richter, Gisela M. *The Portraits of the Greeks.* Rev. ed. by R.R.R. Smith. Ithaca, N.Y.: Cornell University Press, 1984.

Ridgway, Brunilde S. *The Archaic Style in Greek Sculpture.* 2d ed. Chicago: Ares, 1993.

——. *Fifth-Century Styles in Greek Sculpture.* Princeton, N.J.: Princeton University Press, 1981.

——. *Fourth-Century Styles in Greek Sculpture.* Madison: University of Wisconsin Press, 1997.

——. *Hellenistic Sculpture I: The Styles of ca. 331–200 BC.* Madison: University of Wisconsin Press, 1990.

——. *Hellenistic Sculpture II: The Styles of ca. 200–100 BC.* Madison: University of Wisconsin Press, 2000.

——. *Prayers in Stone: Greek Architectural Sculpture.* Berkeley: University of California Press, 1999.

——. *Roman Copies of Greek Sculpture: The Problem of the Originals.* Ann Arbor: University of Michigan Press, 1984.

——. *The Severe Style in Greek Sculpture.* Princeton, N.J.: Princeton University Press, 1970.

Robertson, Martin. *The Art of Vase-Painting in Classical Athens.* New York: Cambridge University Press, 1992.

——. *A History of Greek Art.* Rev. ed. 2 vols. New York: Cambridge University Press, 1986.

——. *A Shorter History of Greek Art.* New York: Cambridge University Press, 1981.

Shapiro, H. Alan. *Art and Cult in Athens under the Tyrants.* Mainz: von Zabern, 1989.

——. *Myth into Art: Poet and Painter in Classical Greece.* New York: Routledge, 1994.

Smith, R.R.R. *Hellenistic Sculpture.* New York: Thames & Hudson, 1991.

Spawforth, Tony. *The Complete Greek Temples.* London, Thames & Hudson, 2006.

Spivey, Nigel. *Greek Art.* London: Phaidon, 1997.

Stansbury-O'Donnell, Mark D. *Pictorial Narrative in Ancient Greek Art.* New York: Cambridge University Press, 1999.

Stewart, Andrew. *Art, Desire, and the Body in Ancient Greece.* New York: Cambridge University Press, 1997.

——. *Classical Greece and the Birth of Western Art.* New York: Cambridge University Press, 2008.

——. *Greek Sculpture: An Exploration.* 2 vols. New Haven, Conn.: Yale University Press, 1990.

Whitley, James. *The Archaeology of Ancient Greece.* New York: Cambridge University Press, 2001.

Wycherley, Richard E. *How the Greeks Built Cities.* New York: Norton, 1976.

### Chapter 6: The Etruscans

Banti, Luisa. *The Etruscan Cities and Their Culture.* Berkeley: University of California Press, 1973.

Barker, Graeme, and Tom Rasmussen. *The Etruscans.* Oxford: Blackwell, 1998.

Boethius, Axel. *Etruscan and Early Roman Architecture.* 2d ed. New Haven, Conn.: Yale University Press, 1978.

Bonfante, Larissa, ed. *Etruscan Life and Afterlife: A Handbook of Etruscan Studies.* Detroit: Wayne State University Press, 1986.

Brendel, Otto J. *Etruscan Art.* 2d ed. New Haven, Conn.: Yale University Press, 1995.

Cristofani, Mauro. *The Etruscans: A New Investigation.* London: Orbis, 1979.

De Grummond, Nancy Thomson. *Etruscan Myth, Sacred History, and Legend.* Philadelphia: University of Pennsylvania Museum, 2006.

Haynes, Sybille. *Etruscan Civilization: A Cultural History.* Los Angeles: J. Paul Getty Museum, 2000.

Heurgon, Jacques. *Daily Life of the Etruscans.* London: Weidenfeld & Nicolson, 1964.

Pallottino, Massimo. *The Etruscans.* Harmondsworth: Penguin, 1978.

Richardson, Emeline. *The Etruscans: Their Art and Civilization.* Rev. ed. Chicago: University of Chicago Press, 1976.

Ridgway, David, and Francesca Ridgway, eds. *Italy before the Romans.* New York: Academic, 1979.

Spivey, Nigel. *Etruscan Art.* New York: Thames & Hudson, 1997.

Spivey, Nigel, and Simon Stoddart. *Etruscan Italy: An Archaeological History.* London: Batsford, 1990.

Sprenger, Maja, Gilda Bartoloni, and Max Hirmer. *The Etruscans: Their History, Art, and Architecture.* New York: Abrams, 1983.

Steingräber, Stephan. *Abundance of Life: Etruscan Wall Painting.* Los Angeles: J. Paul Getty Museum, 2006.

Torelli, Mario, ed. *The Etruscans.* New York: Rizzoli, 2001.

## Chapter 7: The Roman Empire

Aldrete, Gregory S. *Daily Life in the Roman City: Rome, Pompeii, and Ostia.* Westport, Conn.: Greenwood, 2004.

Anderson, James C., Jr. *Roman Architecture and Society.* Baltimore: Johns Hopkins University Press, 1997.

Andreae, Bernard. *The Art of Rome.* New York: Abrams, 1977.

Barton, Ian M., ed. *Roman Domestic Buildings.* Exeter: University of Exeter Press, 1996.

———. *Roman Public Buildings.* 2d ed. Exeter: University of Exeter Press, 1995.

Bianchi Bandinelli, Ranuccio. *Rome: The Center of Power: Roman Art to AD 200.* New York: Braziller, 1970.

———. *Rome: The Late Empire: Roman Art AD 200–400.* New York: Braziller, 1971.

Brendel, Otto J. *Prolegomena to the Study of Roman Art.* New Haven, Conn.: Yale University Press, 1979.

Claridge, Amanda. *Rome: An Oxford Archaeological Guide.* 2d ed. New York: Oxford University Press, 2010.

Clarke, John R. *The Houses of Roman Italy, 100 BC–AD 250.* Berkeley: University of California Press, 1991.

Coarelli, Filippo. *Rome and Environs: An Archaeological Guide.* Berkeley and Los Angeles: University of California Press, 2007.

Cornell, Tim, and John Matthews. *Atlas of the Roman World.* New York: Facts on File, 1982.

D'Ambra, Eve. *Roman Art.* New York: Cambridge University Press, 1998.

———, ed. *Roman Art in Context.* Upper Saddle River, N.J.: Prentice Hall, 1994.

Dobbins, John J., and Pedar W. Foss, eds. *The World of Pompeii.* London: Routledge, 2007.

Dyson, Stephen L. *Rome: A Living Portrait of an Ancient City.* Baltimore: Johns Hopkins University Press, 2010.

Gazda, Elaine K., ed. *Roman Art in the Private Sphere.* Ann Arbor: University of Michigan Press, 1991.

Grant, Michael. *Cities of Vesuvius: Pompeii and Herculaneum.* Harmondsworth: Penguin, 1976.

Hannestad, Niels. *Roman Art and Imperial Policy.* Aarhus: Aarhus University Press, 1986.

Henig, Martin, ed. *A Handbook of Roman Art.* Ithaca, N.Y.: Cornell University Press, 1983.

Kent, John P. C., and Max Hirmer. *Roman Coins.* New York: Abrams, 1978.

Kleiner, Diana E. E. *Roman Sculpture.* New Haven, Conn.: Yale University Press, 1992.

Kleiner, Diana E. E., and Susan B. Matheson, eds. *I Claudia: Women in Ancient Rome.* New Haven, Conn.: Yale University Art Gallery, 1996.

Kleiner, Fred S. *A History of Roman Art.* Enhanced ed. Belmont, Calif.: Wadsworth, 2010.

Kraus, Theodor. *Pompeii and Herculaneum: The Living Cities of the Dead.* New York: Abrams, 1975.

Lancaster, Lynne. *Concrete Vaulted Construction in Imperial Rome.* New York: Cambridge University Press, 2006.

Ling, Roger. *Roman Painting.* New York: Cambridge University Press, 1991.

L'Orange, Hans Peter. *The Roman Empire: Art Forms and Civic Life.* New York: Rizzoli, 1985.

MacCormack, Sabine G. *Art and Ceremony in Late Antiquity.* Berkeley: University of California Press, 1981.

MacDonald, William L. *The Architecture of the Roman Empire I: An Introductory Study.* Rev. ed. New Haven, Conn.: Yale University Press, 1982.

———. *The Architecture of the Roman Empire II: An Urban Appraisal.* New Haven, Conn.: Yale University Press, 1986.

———. *The Pantheon: Design, Meaning, and Progeny.* Cambridge, Mass.: Harvard University Press, 1976.

Mattusch, Carol C., ed. *Pompeii and the Roman Villa: Art and Culture around the Bay of Naples.* New York: Thames & Hudson, 2008.

Mazzoleni, Donatella. *Domus: Wall Painting in the Roman House.* Los Angeles: J. Paul Getty Museum, 2004.

McKay, Alexander G. *Houses, Villas, and Palaces in the Roman World.* Ithaca, N.Y.: Cornell University Press, 1975.

Nash, Ernest. *Pictorial Dictionary of Ancient Rome.* 2d ed. 2 vols. New York: Praeger, 1962.

Pollitt, Jerome J. *The Art of Rome, 753 BC–AD 337: Sources and Documents.* Rev. ed. New York: Cambridge University Press, 1983.

Richardson, Lawrence, Jr. *A New Topographical Dictionary of Ancient Rome.* Baltimore: Johns Hopkins University Press, 1992.

———. *Pompeii: An Architectural History.* Baltimore: Johns Hopkins University Press, 1988.

Sear, Frank. *Roman Architecture.* Rev. ed. Ithaca, N.Y.: Cornell University Press, 1989.

Stambaugh, John E. *The Ancient Roman City.* Baltimore: Johns Hopkins University Press, 1988.

Stamper, John W. *The Architecture of Roman Temples: The Republic to the Middle Empire.* New York: Cambridge University Press, 2005.

Stewart, Peter. *The Social History of Roman Art.* New York: Cambridge University Press, 2008.

Taylor, Rabun. *Roman Builders.* New York: Cambridge University Press, 2003.

Toynbee, Jocelyn M. C. *Death and Burial in the Roman World.* London: Thames & Hudson, 1971.

Wallace-Hadrill, Andrew. *Herculaneum: Past and Future.* London: Frances Lincoln, 2011.

———. *Houses and Society in Pompeii and Herculaneum.* Princeton, N.J.: Princeton University Press, 1994.

Ward-Perkins, John B. *Roman Architecture.* New York: Electa/Rizzoli, 1988.

———. *Roman Imperial Architecture.* 2d ed. New Haven, Conn.: Yale University Press, 1981.

Wilson-Jones, Mark. *Principles of Roman Architecture.* New Haven, Conn.: Yale University Press, 2000.

Wood, Susan. *Roman Portrait Sculpture AD 217–260.* Leiden: E. J. Brill, 1986.

Yegül, Fikret. *Baths and Bathing in Classical Antiquity.* Cambridge, Mass.: MIT Press, 1992.

Zanker, Paul. *Pompeii: Public and Private Life.* Cambridge, Mass.: Harvard University Press, 1998.

———. *The Power of Images in the Age of Augustus.* Ann Arbor: University of Michigan Press, 1988.

———. *Roman Art.* Los Angeles: J. Paul Getty Museum, 2010.

## Chapter 8: Late Antiquity

Bowersock, G. W., Peter Brown, and Oleg Grabar, eds. *Late Antiquity: A Guide to the Postclassical World.* Cambridge, Mass.: Harvard University Press, 1998.

Brody, Lisa R., and Gail L. Hoffman, eds. *Dura Europos: Crossroads of Antiquity.* Chestnut Hill, Mass.: McMullen Museum of Art, Boston College, 2010.

Cioffarelli, Ada. *Guide to the Catacombs of Rome and Its Surroundings.* Rome: Bonsignori, 2000.

Elsner, Jas'. *Art and the Roman Viewer: The Transformation of Art from the Pagan World to Christianity.* New York: Cambridge University Press, 1995.

———. *Imperial Rome and Christian Triumph.* New York: Oxford University Press, 1998.

Fine, Steven. *Art and Judaism in the Greco-Roman World: Toward a New Jewish Archaeology.* New York: Cambridge University Press, 2005.

Finney, Paul Corby. *The Invisible God: The Earliest Christians on Art.* New York: Oxford University Press, 1994.

Grabar, André. *The Beginnings of Christian Art, 200–395.* London: Thames & Hudson, 1967.

———. *Christian Iconography.* Princeton, N.J.: Princeton University Press, 1980.

Gutmann, Joseph. *Sacred Images: Studies in Jewish Art from Antiquity to the Middle Ages.* Northampton, Mass.: Variorum, 1989.

Janes, Dominic. *God and Gold in Late Antiquity.* New York: Cambridge University Press, 1998.

Jensen, Robin Margaret. *Understanding Early Christian Art.* New York: Routledge, 2000.

Koch, Guntram. *Early Christian Art and Architecture.* London: SCM, 1996.

Krautheimer, Richard. *Rome, Profile of a City: 312–1308.* Princeton, N.J.: Princeton University Press, 1980.

Krautheimer, Richard, and Slobodan Ćurčić. *Early Christian and Byzantine Architecture.* 4th ed. New Haven, Conn.: Yale University Press, 1986.

Lowden, John. *Early Christian and Byzantine Art.* London: Phaidon, 1997.

Mathews, Thomas P. *The Clash of Gods: A Reinterpretation of Early Christian Art.* Rev. ed. Princeton, N.J.: Princeton University Press, 1999.

Milburn, Robert. *Early Christian Art and Architecture.* Berkeley: University of California Press, 1988.

Nicolai, Vincenzo Fiocchi, Fabrizio Bisconti, and Danilo Mazzoleni. *The Christian Catacombs of Rome: History, Decoration, Inscriptions.* Regensburg: Schnell & Steiner, 2006.

Perkins, Ann Louise. *The Art of Dura-Europos.* Oxford: Clarendon, 1973.

Poeschke, Joachim. *Italian Mosaics, 300–1300.* New York: Abbeville, 2010.

Rutgers, Leonard V. *Subterranean Rome: In Search of the Roots of Christianity in the Catacombs of the Eternal City.* Leuven: Peeters, 2000.

Spier, Jeffrey, ed. *Picturing the Bible: The Earliest Christian Art.* New Haven, Conn.: Yale University Press, 2007.

Volbach, Wolfgang, and Max Hirmer. *Early Christian Art.* New York: Abrams, 1962.

Webb, Matilda. *The Churches and Catacombs of Early Christian Rome: A Comprehensive Guide.* Brighton: Sussex Academic Press, 2001.

Webster, Leslie, and Michelle Brown, eds. *The Transformation of the Roman World, AD 400–900.* Berkeley: University of California Press, 1997.

Weitzmann, Kurt. *Late Antique and Early Christian Book Illumination.* New York: Braziller, 1977.

———, ed. *Age of Spirituality: Late Antique and Early Christian Art, Third to Seventh Century.* New York: Metropolitan Museum of Art, 1979.

## Chapter 9: Byzantium

Barber, Charles. *Figure and Likeness: On the Limits of Representation in Byzantine Iconoclasm.* Princeton, N.J.: Princeton University Press, 2002.

Borsook, Eve. *Messages in Mosaic: The Royal Programmes of Norman Sicily.* Oxford: Clarendon, 1990.

Cormack, Robin. *Byzantine Art.* New York: Oxford University Press, 2000.

———. *Icons.* Cambridge, Mass.: Harvard University Press, 2007.

———. *Painting the Soul: Icons, Death Masks, and Shrouds.* London: Reaktion, 1997.

———. *Writing in Gold: Byzantine Society and Its Icons.* New York: Oxford University Press, 1985.

Cormack, Robin, and Maria Vassiliki. *Byzantium, 330–1453.* London: Royal Academy of Arts, 2008.

Cutler, Anthony. *The Hand of the Master: Craftsmanship, Ivory, and Society in Byzantium, 9th–11th Centuries.* Princeton, N.J.: Princeton University Press, 1994.

Deliyannis, Deborah Mauskopf. *Ravenna in Late Antiquity.* New York: Cambridge University Press, 2010.

Demus, Otto. *The Mosaic Decoration of San Marco, Venice.* Chicago: University of Chicago Press, 1990.

Evans, Helen C. *Byzantium: Faith and Power (1261–1557).* New York: Metropolitan Museum of Art, 2004.

Evans, Helen C., and William D. Wixom, eds. *The Glory of Byzantium: Art and Culture of the Middle Byzantine Era AD 843–1261.* New York: Metropolitan Museum of Art, 1997.

Freely, John. *Byzantine Monuments of Istanbul.* New York: Cambridge University Press, 2004.

Grabar, André. *The Golden Age of Justinian: From the Death of Theodosius to the Rise of Islam.* New York: Odyssey, 1967.

Grabar, André, and Manolis Chatzidakis. *Greek Mosaics of the Byzantine Period.* New York: New American Library, 1964.

Kleinbauer, W. Eugene. *Hagia Sophia.* London: Scala, 2004.

Lowden, John. *Early Christian and Byzantine Art.* London: Phaidon, 1997.

Maguire, Eunice Dauterman, and Henry Maguire. *Other Icons: Art and Power in Byzantine Secular Culture.* Princeton, N.J.: Princeton University Press, 2007.

Maguire, Henry. *Art and Eloquence in Byzantium.* Princeton, N.J.: Princeton University Press, 1981.

———. *The Icons of Their Bodies: Saints and Their Images in Byzantium.* Princeton, N.J.: Princeton University Press, 1996.

Mainstone, Rowland J. *Hagia Sophia: Architecture, Structure, and Liturgy of Justinian's Great Church.* 2d ed. New York: Thames & Hudson, 2001.

Mango, Cyril. *Art of the Byzantine Empire, 312–1453: Sources and Documents.* Toronto: University of Toronto Press, 1986. Reprint of 1972 ed.

———. *Byzantine Architecture.* New York: Electa/Rizzoli, 1985.

Mark, Robert, and Ahmet S. Cakmak, eds. *Hagia Sophia from the Age of Justinian to the Present.* New York: Cambridge University Press, 1992.

Mathews, Thomas F. *Byzantium: From Antiquity to the Renaissance.* New York: Abrams, 1998.

McClanan, Anne. *Representations of Early Byzantine Empresses: Image and Empire.* New York: Palgrave Macmillan, 2002.

Ousterhout, Robert. *Master Builders of Byzantium.* Princeton, N.J.: Princeton University Press, 2000.

Pelikan, Jaroslav. *Imago Dei: The Byzantine Apologia for Icons.* Princeton, N.J.: Princeton University Press, 1990.

Poeschke, Joachim. *Italian Mosaics, 300–1300.* New York: Abbeville, 2010.

Rodley, Lyn. *Byzantine Art and Architecture: An Introduction.* New York: Cambridge University Press, 1994.

Von Simson, Otto G. *Sacred Fortress: Byzantine Art and Statecraft in Ravenna.* Princeton, N.J.: Princeton University Press, 1986.

Weitzmann, Kurt. *The Icon.* New York: Dorset, 1987.

———. *Illustrations in Roll and Codex.* Princeton, N.J.: Princeton University Press, 1970.

## Chapter 10: The Islamic World

Allan, James, and Sheila R. Canby. *Hunt for Paradise: Court Arts of Safavid Iran 1501–76.* Geneva: Skira, 2004.

Atil, Esin. *The Age of Sultan Suleyman the Magnificent.* Washington, D.C.: National Gallery of Art, 1987.

Baker, Patricia L. *Islam and the Religious Arts.* London: Continuum, 2004.

———. *Islamic Textiles.* London: British Museum, 1995.

Blair, Sheila S., and Jonathan Bloom. *The Art and Architecture of Islam 1250–1800.* New Haven, Conn.: Yale University Press, 1994.

Bloom, Jonathan M., and Sheila S. Blair. *The Grove Encyclopedia of Islamic Art and Architecture.* New York: Oxford University Press, 2009.

———. *Islamic Arts.* London: Phaidon, 1997.

Brend, Barbara. *Islamic Art.* Cambridge, Mass.: Harvard University Press, 1991.

Canby, Sheila R. *Persian Painting.* London: British Museum, 1993.

Dodds, Jerrilynn D., ed. *Al-Andalus: The Art of Islamic Spain.* New York: Metropolitan Museum of Art, 1992.

Ettinghausen, Richard, Oleg Grabar, and Marilyn Jenkins-Madina. *The Art and Architecture of Islam, 650–1250.* Rev. ed. New Haven, Conn.: Yale University Press, 2001.

Ferrier, Ronald W., ed. *The Arts of Persia.* New Haven, Conn.: Yale University Press, 1989.

Frishman, Martin, and Hasan-Uddin Khan. *The Mosque: History, Architectural Development, and Regional Diversity.* New York: Thames & Hudson, 1994.

Goodwin, Godfrey. *A History of Ottoman Architecture.* 2d ed. New York: Thames & Hudson, 1987.

Grabar, Oleg. *The Alhambra.* Cambridge, Mass.: Harvard University Press, 1978.

———. *The Formation of Islamic Art.* Rev. ed. New Haven, Conn.: Yale University Press, 1987.

———. *Islamic Visual Culture, 1100–1800.* New York: Ashgate, 2006.

Grube, Ernst J. *Architecture of the Islamic World: Its History and Social Meaning.* 2d ed. New York: Thames & Hudson, 1984.

Hattstein, Markus, and Peter Delius, eds. *Islam: Art and Architecture.* Cologne: Könemann, 2000.

Hillenbrand, Robert. *Islamic Architecture: Form, Function, Meaning.* Edinburgh: Edinburgh University Press, 1994.

———. *Islamic Art and Architecture.* New York: Thames & Hudson, 1999.

Irwin, Robert. *The Alhambra.* Cambridge, Mass.: Harvard University Press, 2004.

———. *Islamic Art in Context: Art, Architecture, and the Literary World.* New York: Abrams, 1997.

Michell, George, ed. *Architecture of the Islamic World.* New York: Thames & Hudson, 1978.

Necipoglu, Gulru. *The Age of Sinan: Architectural Culture in the Ottoman Empire.* Princeton, N.J.: Princeton University Press, 2005.

Petruccioli, Attilio, and Khalil K. Pirani, eds. *Understanding Islamic Architecture.* London: Routledge, 2002.

Porter, Venetia. *Islamic Tiles.* London: British Museum, 1995.

Robinson, Frank. *Atlas of the Islamic World.* Oxford: Equinox, 1982.

Schimmel, Annemarie. *Calligraphy and Islamic Culture.* New York: New York University Press, 1984.

Stierlin, Henri. *Islam I: Early Architecture from Baghdad to Cordoba.* Cologne: Taschen, 1996.

———. *Islamic Art and Architecture from Isfahan to the Taj Mahal.* New York: Thames & Hudson, 2002.

Tadgell, Christopher. *Four Caliphates: The Formation and Development of the Islamic Tradition.* London: Ellipsis, 1998.

Ward, Rachel M. *Islamic Metalwork.* New York: Thames & Hudson, 1993.

Welch, Anthony. *Calligraphy in the Arts of the Islamic World.* Austin: University of Texas Press, 1979.

## Medieval Art, General

Alexander, Jonathan J. G. *Medieval Illuminators and Their Methods of Work.* New Haven, Conn.: Yale University Press, 1992.

*The Art of Medieval Spain, AD 500–1200.* New York: Metropolitan Museum of Art, 1993.

Benton, Janetta Rebold. *Art of the Middle Ages.* New York: Thames & Hudson, 2002.

Binski, Paul. *Painters (Medieval Craftsmen).* Toronto: University of Toronto Press, 1991.

Calkins, Robert G. *Illuminated Books of the Middle Ages.* Ithaca, N.Y.: Cornell University Press, 1983.

———. *Medieval Architecture in Western Europe: From AD 300 to 1500.* New York: Oxford University Press, 1998.

Coldstream, Nicola. *Masons and Sculptors (Medieval Craftsmen).* Toronto: University of Toronto Press, 1991.

———. *Medieval Architecture.* New York: Oxford University Press, 2002.

Cross, Frank L., and Livingstone, Elizabeth A., eds. *The Oxford Dictionary of the Christian Church.* 3d ed. New York: Oxford University Press, 1997.

De Hamel, Christopher. *A History of Illuminated Manuscripts.* Oxford: Phaidon, 1986.

———. *Scribes and Illuminators (Medieval Craftsmen).* Toronto: University of Toronto Press, 1992.

Doig, Allan. *Liturgy and Architecture: From the Early Church to the Middle Ages.* New York: Ashgate, 2008.

Holcomb, Melanie, ed. *Pen and Parchment: Drawing in the Middle Ages.* New York: Metropolitan Museum of Art, 2009.

Kessler, Herbert L. *Seeing Medieval Art.* Toronto: Broadview, 2004.

———. *Spiritual Seeing: Picturing God's Invisibility in Medieval Art.* Philadelphia: University of Pennsylvania Press, 2000.

Lasko, Peter. *Ars Sacra, 800–1200.* 2d ed. New Haven, Conn.: Yale University Press, 1994.

Murray, Peter, and Linda Murray. *The Oxford Companion to Christian Art and Architecture.* New York: Oxford University Press, 1996.

Pelikan, Jaroslav. *Mary through the Centuries: Her Place in the History of Culture.* New Haven, Conn.: Yale University Press, 1996.

Prache, Anne. *Cathedrals of Europe.* Ithaca, N.Y.: Cornell University Press, 1999.

Raguin, Virginia Chieffo. *Stained Glass from Its Origins to the Present.* New York: Abrams, 2003.

Ross, Leslie. *Medieval Art: A Topical Dictionary.* Westport, Conn.: Greenwood, 1996.

Schütz, Bernard. *Great Cathedrals.* New York: Abrams, 2002.

Sekules, Veronica. *Medieval Art.* New York: Oxford University Press, 2001.

Snyder, James, Henry Luttikhuizen, and Dorothy Verkerk. *Art of the Middle Ages.* 2d ed. Upper Saddle River, N.J.: Prentice Hall, 2006.

Stokstad, Marilyn. *Medieval Art.* 2d ed. Boulder, Colo.: Westview, 2004.

Tasker, Edward G. *Encyclopedia of Medieval Church Art.* London: Batsford, 1993.

## Chapter 11: Early Medieval Europe

Alexander, Jonathan J. G. *Insular Manuscripts, Sixth to the Ninth Century.* London: Miller, 1978.

*The Art of Medieval Spain, AD 500–1200.* New York: Metropolitan Museum of Art, 1993.

Backhouse, Janet, D. H. Turner, and Leslie Webster, eds. *The Golden Age of Anglo-Saxon Art, 966–1066.* Bloomington: Indiana University Press, 1984.

Bandmann, Günter. *Early Medieval Architecture as Bearer of Meaning.* New York: Columbia University Press, 2005.

Barral i Altet, Xavier. *The Early Middle Ages: From Late Antiquity to AD 1000.* Cologne: Taschen, 1997.

Brown, Katharine Reynolds, Dafydd Kidd, and Charles T. Little, eds. *From Attila to Charlemagne.* New York: Metropolitan Museum of Art, 2000.

Brown, Michelle P. *The Lindisfarne Gospels: Society, Spirituality, and the Scribe.* Toronto: University of Toronto Press, 2003.

Carver, Martin. *Sutton Hoo: A Seventh-Century Princely Burial Ground and Its Context.* London: British Museum, 2005.

Collins, Roger. *Early Medieval Europe, 300–1000.* New York: St. Martin's, 1991.

Conant, Kenneth J. *Carolingian and Romanesque Architecture, 800–1200.* 4th ed. New Haven, Conn.: Yale University Press, 1992.

Davis-Weyer, Caecilia. *Early Medieval Art, 300–1150: Sources and Documents.* Toronto: University of Toronto Press, 1986. Reprint of 1971 ed.

Diebold, William J. *Word and Image: An Introduction to Early Medieval Art.* Boulder, Colo.: Westview Press, 2000.

Dodwell, Charles R. *Anglo-Saxon Art: A New Perspective.* Ithaca, N.Y.: Cornell University Press, 1982.

———. *The Pictorial Arts of the West, 800–1200.* New Haven, Conn.: Yale University Press, 1993.

Farr, Carol. *The Book of Kells: Its Function and Audience.* London: British Library, 1997.

Harbison, Peter. *The Golden Age of Irish Art: The Medieval Achievement 600–1200.* New York: Thames & Hudson, 1999.

Henderson, George. *From Durrow to Kells: The Insular Gospel-Books, 650–800.* London: Thames & Hudson, 1987.

Hubert, Jean, Jean Porcher, and Wolfgang Fritz Volbach. *The Carolingian Renaissance.* New York: Braziller, 1970.

———. *Europe of the Invasions.* New York: Braziller, 1969.

Mayr-Harting, Henry. *Ottonian Book Illumination: An Historical Study.* 2 vols. London: Miller, 1991–1993.

McClendon, Charles. *The Origins of Medieval Architecture: Building in Europe, AD 600–900.* New Haven, Conn.: Yale University Press, 2005.

Megaw, Ruth, and John Vincent Megaw. *Celtic Art: From Its Beginning to the Book of Kells.* New York: Thames & Hudson, 1989.

Mütherich, Florentine, and Joachim E. Gaehde. *Carolingian Painting.* New York: Braziller, 1976.

Nees, Lawrence J. *Early Medieval Art.* New York: Oxford University Press, 2002.

Nordenfalk, Carl. *Celtic and Anglo-Saxon Painting: Book Illumination in the British Isles, 600–800.* New York: Braziller, 1977.

O'Brien, Jacqueline, and Peter Harbison. *Ancient Ireland: From Prehistory to the Middle Ages.* New York: Oxford University Press, 2000.

Richardson, Hilary, and John Scarry. *An Introduction to Irish High Crosses.* Dublin: Mercier, 1990.

Stalley, Roger. *Early Medieval Architecture.* New York: Oxford University Press, 1999.

Wilson, David M. *From Viking to Crusader: Scandinavia and Europe 800–1200.* New York: Rizzoli, 1992.

Wilson, David M., and Ole Klindt-Jensen. *Viking Art.* 2d ed. Minneapolis: University of Minnesota Press, 1980.

### Chapter 12: Romanesque Europe

Armi, C. Edson. *Masons and Sculptors in Romanesque Burgundy: The New Aesthetics of Cluny III.* 2 vols. University Park: Pennsylvania State University Press, 1983.

Ashley, Kathleen, and Marilyn Deegan. *Being a Pilgrim: Art and Ritual on the Medieval Routes to Santiago.* Burlington, Vt.: Lund Humphries, 2009.

Bagnoli, Martina, Holger A. Kleiner, C. Griffith Mann, and James Robinson, eds. *Treasures of Heaven: Saints, Relics, and Devotion in Medieval Europe.* New Haven, Conn.: Yale University Press: 2010.

Barral i Altet, Xavier. *The Romanesque: Towns, Cathedrals, and Monasteries.* Cologne: Taschen, 1998.

Burnett, Charles, and Peter Dronke. *Hildegard of Bingen: The Context of Her Thought and Art.* London: Warburg Institute, 1998.

Cahn, Walter. *Romanesque Bible Illumination.* Ithaca, N.Y.: Cornell University Press, 1982.

———. *Romanesque Manuscripts: The Twelfth Century.* 2 vols. London: Miller, 1998.

Conant, Kenneth J. *Carolingian and Romanesque Architecture, 800–1200.* 4th ed. New Haven, Conn.: Yale University Press, 1992.

Demus, Otto. *Romanesque Mural Painting.* New York: Thames & Hudson, 1970.

Dodwell, Charles R. *The Pictorial Arts of the West, 800–1200.* New Haven, Conn.: Yale University Press, 1993.

Fergusson, Peter. *Architecture of Solitude: Cistercian Abbeys in Twelfth-Century Europe.* Princeton, N.J.: Princeton University Press, 1984.

Grape, Wolfgang. *The Bayeux Tapestry: Monument to a Norman Triumph.* New York: Prestel, 1994.

Hearn, Millard F. *Romanesque Sculpture: The Revival of Monumental Stone Sculpture in the Eleventh and Twelfth Centuries.* Ithaca, N.Y.: Cornell University Press, 1981.

Hourihane, Colum, ed. *Romanesque Art and Thought in the Twelfth Century.* Princeton, N.J.: Index of Christian Art, 2008.

Kahn, Deborah, ed. *The Romanesque Frieze and Its Spectator.* London: Miller, 1992.

Kubach, Hans E. *Romanesque Architecture.* New York: Electa, 1988.

Male, Émile. *Religious Art in France: The Twelfth Century.* Rev. ed. Princeton, N.J.: Princeton University Press, 1978.

Minne-Sève, Viviane, and Hervé Kergall. *Romanesque and Gothic France: Architecture and Sculpture.* New York: Abrams, 2000.

Nichols, Stephen G. *Romanesque Signs: Early Medieval Narrative and Iconography.* New Haven, Conn.: Yale University Press, 1983.

Nordenfalk, Carl. *Early Medieval Book Illumination.* New York: Rizzoli, 1988.

Petzold, Andreas. *Romanesque Art.* New York: Abrams, 1995.

Schapiro, Meyer. *The Sculpture of Moissac.* New York: Thames & Hudson, 1985.

Seidel, Linda. *Legends in Limestone: Lazarus, Gislebertus, and the Cathedral of Autun.* Chicago: University of Chicago Press, 1999.

Stalley, Roger. *Early Medieval Architecture.* New York: Oxford University Press, 1999.

Tate, Robert B., and Marcus Tate. *The Pilgrim Route to Santiago.* Oxford: Phaidon, 1987.

Toman, Rolf, ed. *Romanesque: Architecture, Sculpture, Painting.* Cologne: Könemann, 1997.

Wilson, David M. *The Bayeux Tapestry: The Complete Tapestry in Color.* New York: Thames & Hudson, 2004.

Zarnecki, George, Janet Holt, and Tristram Holland, eds. *English Romanesque Art, 1066–1200.* London: Weidenfeld & Nicolson, 1984.

### Chapter 13: Gothic Europe

Barnes, Carl F. *The Portfolio of Villard de Honnecourt.* New York: Ashgate, 2009.

Binski, Paul. *Becket's Crown: Art and Imagination in Gothic England, 1170–1300.* New Haven, Conn.: Yale University Press, 2004.

Bony, Jean. *The English Decorated Style: Gothic Architecture Transformed, 1250–1350.* Ithaca, N.Y.: Cornell University Press, 1979.

———. *French Gothic Architecture of the Twelfth and Thirteenth Centuries.* Berkeley: University of California Press, 1983.

Branner, Robert. *Manuscript Painting in Paris during the Reign of St. Louis.* Berkeley: University of California Press, 1977.

———. *St. Louis and the Court Style in Gothic Architecture.* London: Zwemmer, 1965.

———, ed. *Chartres Cathedral.* New York: Norton, 1969.

Brown, Sarah, and David O'Connor. *Glass-Painters (Medieval Craftsmen).* Toronto: University of Toronto Press, 1991.

Camille, Michael. *Gothic Art: Glorious Visions.* New York: Abrams, 1996.

———. *The Gothic Idol: Ideology and Image-Making in Medieval Art.* New York: Cambridge University Press, 1989.

Courtenay, Lynn T., ed. *The Engineering of Medieval Cathedrals.* Aldershot: Scolar, 1997.

Crosby, Sumner McKnight. *The Royal Abbey of Saint-Denis from Its Beginnings to the Death of Suger, 475–1151.* New Haven, Conn.: Yale University Press, 1987.

Erlande-Brandenburg, Alain. *The Cathedral: The Social and Architectural Dynamics of Construction.* New York: Cambridge University Press, 1994.

———. *Gothic Art.* New York: Abrams, 1989.

Favier, Jean. *The World of Chartres.* New York: Abrams, 1990.

Fitchen, John. *The Construction of Gothic Cathedrals: A Study of Medieval Vault Erection.* Chicago: University of Chicago Press, 1981.

Frankl, Paul. *The Gothic: Literary Sources and Interpretations through Eight Centuries.* Princeton, N.J.: Princeton University Press, 1960.

Frankl, Paul, and Paul Crossley. *Gothic Architecture.* New Haven, Conn.: Yale University Press, 2000.

Frisch, Teresa G. *Gothic Art 1140–c. 1450: Sources and Documents.* Toronto: University of Toronto Press, 1987. Reprint of 1971 ed.

Gerson, Paula, ed. *Abbot Suger and Saint-Denis.* New York: Metropolitan Museum of Art, 1986.

Givens, Jean A. *Observation and Image-Making in Gothic Art.* New York: Cambridge University Press, 2004.

Grodecki, Louis. *Gothic Architecture.* New York: Electa/Rizzoli, 1985.

Grodecki, Louis, and Catherine Brisac. *Gothic Stained Glass, 1200–1300.* Ithaca, N.Y.: Cornell University Press, 1985.

Jantzen, Hans. *High Gothic: The Classic Cathedrals of Chartres, Reims, Amiens.* Princeton, N.J.: Princeton University Press, 1984.

Male, Émile. *Religious Art in France: The Thirteenth Century.* Rev. ed. Princeton, N.J.: Princeton University Press, 1984.

Minne-Sève, Viviane, and Hervé Kergall. *Romanesque and Gothic France: Architecture and Sculpture.* New York: Abrams, 2000.

Nussbaum, Norbert. *German Gothic Church Architecture.* New Haven, Conn.: Yale University Press, 2000.

Panofsky, Erwin. *Abbot Suger on the Abbey Church of St. Denis and Its Art Treasures.* 2d ed. Princeton, N.J.: Princeton University Press, 1979.

Radding, Charles M., and William W. Clark. *Medieval Architecture, Medieval Learning.* New Haven, Conn.: Yale University Press, 1992.

Recht, Roland. *Believing and Seeing: The Art of Gothic Cathedrals.* Chicago: University of Chicago Press, 1999.

Rudolph, Conrad. *Artistic Change at St-Denis: Abbot Suger's Program and the Early Twelfth-Century Controversy over Art.* Princeton, N.J.: Princeton University Press, 1990.

Sauerländer, Willibald, and Max Hirmer. *Gothic Sculpture in France, 1140–1270.* New York: Abrams, 1973.

Scott, Robert A. *The Gothic Enterprise: A Guide to Understanding the Medieval Cathedral.* Berkeley and Los Angeles: University of California Press, 2003.

Simson, Otto G. von. *The Gothic Cathedral: Origins of Gothic Architecture and the Medieval Concept of Order.* 3d ed. Princeton, N.J.: Princeton University Press, 1988.

Toman, Rolf, ed. *The Art of Gothic: Architecture, Sculpture, Painting.* Cologne: Könemann, 1999.

Williamson, Paul. *Gothic Sculpture, 1140–1300.* New Haven, Conn.: Yale University Press, 1995.

Wilson, Christopher. *The Gothic Cathedral: The Architecture of the Great Church, 1130–1530.* London: Thames & Hudson, 1990.

### Chapter 14: Late Medieval Italy

Bomford, David. *Art in the Making: Italian Painting before 1400.* London: National Gallery, 1989.

Borsook, Eve, and Fiorelli Superbi Gioffredi. *Italian Altarpieces 1250–1550: Function and Design.* Oxford: Clarendon, 1994.

Bourdua, Louise. *The Franciscans and Art Patronage in Late Medieval Italy.* New York: Cambridge University Press, 2004.

Cole, Bruce. *Sienese Painting: From Its Origins to the Fifteenth Century.* New York: Harper Collins, 1987.

Derbes, Anne. *Picturing the Passion in Late Medieval Italy: Narrative Painting, Franciscan Ideologies, and the Levant.* New York: Cambridge University Press, 1996.

Derbes, Anne, and Mark Sandona, eds. *The Cambridge Companion to Giotto.* New York: Cambridge University Press, 2004.

Hills, Paul. *The Light of Early Italian Painting.* New Haven, Conn.: Yale University Press, 1987.

Maginnis, Hayden B. J. *Painting in the Age of Giotto: A Historical Reevaluation.* University Park: Pennsylvania State University Press, 1997.

———. *The World of the Early Sienese Painter.* University Park: Pennsylvania State University Press, 2001.

Meiss, Millard. *Painting in Florence and Siena after the Black Death.* Princeton, N.J.: Princeton University Press, 1976.

Moskowitz, Anita Fiderer. *Italian Gothic Sculpture, c. 1250–c. 1400.* Cambridge: Cambridge University Press, 2001.

———. *Nicola & Giovanni Pisano: The Pulpits: Pious Devotion, Pious Diversion.* London: Harvey Miller, 3005.

Norman, Diana, ed. *Siena, Florence, and Padua: Art, Society, and Religion 1280–1400.* New Haven, Conn.: Yale University Press, 1995.

Poeschke, Joachim. *Italian Frescoes: The Age of Giotto, 1280–1400.* New York: Abbeville, 2005.

Pope-Hennessy, John. *Italian Gothic Sculpture.* 3d ed. Oxford: Phaidon, 1986.

Stubblebine, James H. *Duccio di Buoninsegna and His School.* Princeton, N.J.: Princeton University Press, 1979.

White, John. *Art and Architecture in Italy: 1250–1400.* 3d ed. New Haven, Conn.: Yale University Press, 1993.

———. *Duccio: Tuscan Art and the Medieval Workshop.* London: Thames & Hudson, 1979.

### Asian Art, General

Béguin, Giles. *Buddhist Art. An Historical and Cultural Journey.* Bangkok: River Books, 2009.

Brown, Rebecca M., and Deborah S. Hutton. *Asian Art (Blackwell Anthologies in Art History).* Malden, Mass.: Blackwell, 2006.

Leidy, Denise Patry. *The Art of Buddhism: An Introduction to Its History and Meaning.* Boston: Shambhala, 2008.

McArthur, Meher. *The Arts of Asia: Materials, Techniques, Styles.* New York: Thames & Hudson, 2005.

### Chapter 15: South and Southeast Asia before 1200

Asher, Frederick M. *The Art of Eastern India, 300–800.* Minneapolis: University of Minnesota Press, 1980.

Behl, Benoy K. *The Ajanta Caves: Ancient Paintings of Buddhist India.* New York: Thames & Hudson, 2005.

Blurton, T. Richard. *Hindu Art.* Cambridge, Mass.: Harvard University Press, 1993.

Chaturachinda, Gwyneth, Sunanda Krishnamurty, and Pauline W. Tabtiang. *Dictionary of South and Southeast Asian Art.* Chiang Mai, Thailand: Silkworm Books, 2000.

Chihara, Daigoro. *Hindu-Buddhist Architecture in Southeast Asia.* Leiden: E. J. Brill, 1996.

Craven, Roy C. *Indian Art: A Concise History.* Rev. ed. London: Thames & Hudson, 1997.

Dehejia, Vidya. *The Body Adorned: Dissolving Boundaries between Sacred and Profane in India's Art.* New York: Columbia University Press, 2009.

———. *Early Buddhist Rock Temples.* Ithaca, N.Y.: Cornell University Press, 1972.

———. *Indian Art.* London: Phaidon, 1997.

Desai, Vishakha N., and Darielle Mason. *Gods, Guardians, and Lovers: Temple Sculptures from North India AD 700–1200.* New York: Asia Society Galleries, 1993.

Dhavalikar, Madhukar Keshav. *Ellora.* New York: Oxford University Press, 2003.

*Encyclopedia of Indian Temple Architecture.* 8 vols. New Delhi: American Institute of Indian Studies; Philadelphia: University of Pennsylvania Press, 1983–1996.

Fisher, Robert E. *Buddhist Art and Architecture.* New York: Thames & Hudson, 1993.

Frederic, Louis. *Borobudur.* New York: Abbeville, 1996.

Gopinatha Rao, T. A. *Elements of Hindu Iconography.* 2d ed. 4 vols. New York: Paragon, 1968.

Hardy, Adam. *The Temple Architecture of India.* Chichester: Wiley, 2007.

Harle, James C. *The Art and Architecture of the Indian Subcontinent.* 2d ed. New Haven, Conn.: Yale University Press, 1994.

Huntington, Susan L., and John C. Huntington. *The Art of Ancient India: Buddhist, Hindu, Jain.* New York: Weatherhill, 1985.

Jacques, Claude. *The Khmer Empire: Cities and Sanctuaries from the 5th to the 13th Century.* Bangkok: River Books, 2007.

Jacques, Claude, and Michael Freeman. *Angkor: Cities and Temples.* Bangkok: River Books, 1997.

Jessup, Helen Ibbitson. *Art & Architecture of Cambodia.* New York: Thames & Hudson, 2004.

Jessup, Helen Ibbitson, and Thierry Zephir, eds. *Sculpture of Angkor and Ancient Cambodia: Millennium of Glory.* Washington, D.C.: National Gallery of Art, 1997.

Kerlogue, Fiona. *Arts of Southeast Asia.* New York: Thames & Hudson, 2004.

McIntosh, Jane R. *A Peaceful Realm: The Rise and Fall of the Indus Civilization.* Boulder, Colo.: Westview, 2002.

Michell, George. *Elephanta.* Mumbai: India Book House, 2002.

———. *Hindu Art and Architecture.* New York: Thames & Hudson, 2000.

———. *The Hindu Temple: An Introduction to Its Meaning and Forms.* Chicago: University of Chicago Press, 1988.

Mitter, Partha. *Indian Art.* New York: Oxford University Press, 2001.

Possehl, Gregory L. *The Indus Civilization: A Contemporary Perspective.* Lanham, Md.: AltaMira, 2002.

Rawson, Phillip. *The Art of Southeast Asia.* New York: Thames & Hudson, 1990.

Seth, Mira. *Indian Painting: The Great Mural Tradition.* New York: Harry N. Abrams, 2006.

Srinivasan, Doris Meth. *Many Heads, Arms, and Eyes: Origin, Meaning, and Form of Multiplicity in Indian Art.* Leiden: E. J. Brill, 1997.

Stierlin, Henri. *Hindu India from Khajuraho to the Temple City of Madurai.* Cologne: Taschen, 1998.

Williams, Joanna G. *The Art of Gupta India: Empire and Province.* Princeton, N.J.: Princeton University Press, 1982.

### Chapter 16: China and Korea to 1279

Bush, Susan, and Shio-yen Shih. *Early Chinese Texts on Painting.* Cambridge, Mass.: Harvard University Press, 1985.

Cahill, James. *The Painter's Practice: How Artists Lived and Worked in Traditional China.* New York: Columbia University Press, 1994.

Clunas, Craig. *Art in China.* New York: Oxford University Press, 1997.

Fahr-Becker, Gabriele, ed. *The Art of East Asia.* Cologne: Könemann, 1999.

Fisher, Robert E. *Buddhist Art and Architecture.* New York: Thames & Hudson, 1993.

Fong, Wen C. *Beyond Representation: Chinese Painting and Calligraphy, 8th–14th Century.* New Haven, Conn.: Yale University Press, 1992.

———. *The Great Bronze Age of China: An Exhibition from the People's Republic of China.* New York: Metropolitan Museum of Art, 1980.

Fong, Wen C., and James C. Y. Watt. *Preserving the Past: Treasures from the National Palace Museum, Taipei.* New York: Metropolitan Museum of Art, 1996.

Fraser, Sarah Elizabeth. *Performing the Visual: The Practice of Buddhist Wall Painting in China and Central Asia, 618–960.* Palo Alto: Stanford University Press, 2004.

Howard, Angela Falco, Li Song, Wu Hong, and Yang Hong. *Chinese Sculpture.* New Haven, Conn.: Yale University Press, 2006.

Kim, Kumja Paik. *Goryeo Dynasty: Korea's Age of Enlightenment, 918–1392.* San Francisco: Asian Art Museum, 2003.

Kim, Lena. *Buddhist Sculpture of Korea.* Elizabeth, N.J.: Hollym, 2007.

Lee, Hui-Shu. *Empresses, Art, and Agency in Song Dynasty China.* Seattle: University of Washington Press, 2010.

Li, Chu-tsing, ed. *Artists and Patrons: Some Social and Economic Aspects of Chinese Painting.* Lawrence, Kans.: Kress Department of Art History, in cooperation with Indiana University Press, 1989.

Little, Stephen, and Shawn Eichman. *Taoism and the Arts of China.* Chicago: Art Institute of Chicago, 2000.

Murck, Alfreda. *Poetry and Painting in Song China: The Subtle Art of Dissent.* Cambridge, Mass.: Harvard University Press, 2000.

Nelson, Sarah Milledge. *The Archaeology of Korea.* New York: Cambridge University Press, 1993.

Pak, Youngsook, and Roderick Whitfield. *Earthenware and Celadon (Handbook of Korean Art).* London: Laurence King, 2003.

———. *Buddhist Sculpture (Handbook of Korean Art).* London: Laurence King, 2003.

Portal, Jane. *Korea: Art and Archaeology.* New York: Thames & Hudson, 2000.

Powers, Martin J. *Art and Political Expression in Early China.* New Haven, Conn.: Yale University Press, 1991.

Rawson, Jessica. *Ancient China: Art and Archaeology.* New York: Harper & Row, 1980.

———, ed. *The British Museum Book of Chinese Art.* New York: Thames & Hudson, 1992.

Sickman, Laurence, and Alexander C. Soper. *The Art and Architecture of China.* 3d ed. New Haven, Conn.: Yale University Press, 1992.

Silbergeld, Jerome. *Chinese Painting Style: Media, Methods, and Principles of Form.* Seattle and London: University of Washington Press, 1982.

Steinhardt, Nancy S., ed. *Chinese Architecture.* New Haven, Conn.: Yale University Press, 2002.

Sullivan, Michael. *The Arts of China.* 5th ed. Berkeley: University of California Press, 2009.

———. *The Birth of Landscape Painting.* Berkeley: University of California Press, 1962.

Thorp, Robert L., and Richard Ellis Vinograd. *Chinese Art and Culture.* New York: Abrams, 2001.

Vainker, S. J. *Chinese Pottery and Porcelain: From Prehistory to the Present.* New York: Braziller, 1991.

Watson, William. *The Arts of China to AD 900.* New Haven, Conn.: Yale University Press, 1995.

———. *The Arts of China 900–1620.* New Haven, Conn.: Yale University Press, 2000.

Weidner, Marsha, ed. *Flowering in the Shadows: Women in the History of Chinese and Japanese Painting.* Honolulu: University of Hawaii Press, 1990.

Whitfield, Roderick. *Dictionary of Korean Art and Archaeology.* Elizabeth, N.J.: Hollym, 2004.

Whitfield, Roger, and Anne Farrer. *Caves of the Thousand Buddhas: Chinese Art of the Silk Route.* New York: Braziller, 1990.

Whitfield, Roderick, Susan Whitfield, and Neville Agnew. *Cave Temples of Dunhuang: Art and History on the Silk Road.* Los Angeles: J. Paul Getty Museum, 2000.

———. *Cave Temples of Mogao: Art and History on the Silk Road.* Los Angeles: J. Paul Getty Museum, 2000.

Wu, Hung. *Monumentality in Early Chinese Art.* Palo Alto, Calif.: Stanford University Press, 1996.

———. *The Wu Liang Shrine: The Ideology of Early Chinese Pictorial Art.* Palo Alto, Calif.: Stanford University Press, 1989.

Xin, Yang, Nie Chongzheng, Lang Shaojun, Richard M. Barnhart, James Cahill, and Hung Wu. *Three Thousand Years of Chinese Painting.* New Haven, Conn.: Yale University Press, 1997.

Zhiyan, Li, Virginia L. Bower, and He Li. *Chinese Ceramics: From the Paleolithic Period through the Qing Dyansty.* New Haven, Conn.: Yale University Press, 2010.

## Chapter 17: Japan before 1333

Aikens, C. Melvin, and Takayama Higuchi. *Prehistory of Japan.* New York: Academic, 1982.

Coaldrake, William H. *Architecture and Authority in Japan.* London: Routledge, 1996.

Elisseeff, Danielle, and Vadime Elisseeff. *Art of Japan.* Translated by I. Mark Paris. New York: Abrams, 1985.

Kidder, J. Edward, Jr. *The Art of Japan.* New York: Park Lane, 1985.

Kurata, Bunsaku. *Horyu-ji: Temple of the Exalted Law.* Translated by W. Chie Ishibashi. New York: Japan Society, 1981.

Mason, Penelope. *History of Japanese Art.* 2d ed. New York: Abrams, 2004.

Mizoguchi, Koji. *An Archaeological History of Japan: 30,000 B.C. to A.D. 700.* Philadelphia, University of Pennsylvania Press, 2002.

Murase, Miyeko. *The Tale of Genji: Legends and Paintings.* New York: Braziller, 2001.

Nishi, Kazuo, and Kazuo Hozumi. *What Is Japanese Architecture?* Translated by H. Mack Horton. New York: Kodansha International, 1985.

Nishikawa, Kyotaro, and Emily Sano. *The Great Age of Japanese Buddhist Sculpture AD 600–1300.* Fort Worth, Tex.: Kimbell Art Museum, 1982.

Noma, Seiroku. *The Arts of Japan: Ancient and Medieval.* New York: Kodansha, 1966.

Okudaira, Hideo. *Narrative Picture Scrolls.* Adapted by Elizabeth ten Grotenhuis. New York: Weatherhill, 1973.

Pearson, Richard J. *Ancient Japan.* New York: Braziller, 1992.

Pearson, Richard J., Gina Lee Barnes, and Karl L. Hutterer, eds. *Windows on the Japanese Past.* Ann Arbor: Center for Japanese Studies, University of Michigan, 1986.

Rosenfield, John M. *Japanese Art of the Heian Period, 794–1185.* New York: Asia Society, 1967.

Shimizu, Yoshiaki, ed. *The Shaping of Daimyo Culture 1185–1868.* Washington, D.C.: National Gallery of Art, 1988.

Stanley-Baker, Joan. *Japanese Art.* Rev. ed. New York: Thames & Hudson, 2000.

Suzuki, Kakichi. *Early Buddhist Architecture in Japan.* Translated and adapted by Mary Neighbor Parent and Nancy Shatzman Steinhardt. New York: Kodansha International, 1980.

Ten Grotenhuis, Elizabeth. *Japanese Mandalas: Representations of Sacred Geography.* Honolulu: University of Hawaii Press, 1999.

Weidner, Marsha, ed. *Flowering in the Shadows: Women in the History of Chinese and Japanese Painting.* Honolulu: University of Hawaii Press, 1990.

## Chapter 18: Native Arts of the Americas before 1300

Alva, Walter, and Christopher Donnan. *Royal Tombs of Sipán.* Los Angeles: Fowler Museum of Cultural History, 1993.

Andrews, E. Wyllys, and William L. Fash, eds. *Copán: The History of an Ancient Maya Kingdom.* Santa Fe, N.M.: School of American Research, 2005.

Benson, Elizabeth P., and Beatriz de la Fuente, eds. *Olmec Art of Ancient Mexico.* Washington, D.C.: National Gallery of Art, 1996.

Berlo, Janet Catherine, ed. *Art, Ideology, and the City of Teotihuacan.* Washington, D.C.: Dumbarton Oaks, 1992.

Berlo, Janet Catherine, and Ruth B. Phillips. *Native North American Art.* New York: Oxford University Press, 1998.

Berrin, Kathleen, and Virginia M. Fields. *Olmec: Colossal Masterworks of Ancient Mexico.* New Haven, Conn.: Yale University Press, 2010.

Berrin, Kathleen, ed. *The Spirit of Ancient Peru: Treasures from the Museo Arqueologico Rafael Larco Herrera.* San Francisco: Fine Arts Museums of San Francisco, 1997.

Bourget, Steve, and Kimberly L. Jones, eds. *The Art and Archaeology of the Moche: An Ancient Andean Society of the Peruvian North Coast.* Austin: University of Texas Press, 2008.

Brody, J. J., and Rina Swentzell. *To Touch the Past: The Painted Pottery of the Mimbres People.* New York: Hudson Hills, 1996.

Brose, David. *Ancient Art of the American Woodland Indians.* New York: Abrams, 1985.

Bruhns, Karen O. *Ancient South America.* New York: Cambridge University Press, 1994.

Burger, Richard. *Chavín and the Origins of Andean Civilization.* New York: Thames & Hudson, 1992.

Carrasco, David. *The Oxford Encyclopedia of Mesoamerican Cultures: The Civilizations of Mexico and Central America.* New York: Oxford University Press, 2001.

Clark, John E., and Mary E. Pye, eds. *Olmec Art and Archaeology in Mesoamerica.* Washington, D.C.: National Gallery of Art, 2000.

Coe, Michael D. *The Maya.* 8th ed. New York: Thames & Hudson, 2011.

———. *Mexico: From the Olmecs to the Aztecs.* 6th ed. New York: Thames & Hudson, 2008.

Conklin, William J., and Jeffrey Quilter, eds. *Chavín: Art, Architecture, and Culture.* Los Angeles: Cotsen Institute of Archaeology, 2008.

Cordell, Linda S. *Ancient Pueblo Peoples.* Washington, D.C.: Smithsonian Institution, 1994.

Donnan, Christopher. *Moche Portraits from Ancient Peru.* Austin: University of Texas Press, 2003.

Fagan, Brian. *Ancient North America: The Archaeology of a Continent.* 4th ed. New York: Thames & Hudson, 2005.

———. *The First North Americans.* New York: Thames & Hudson, 2011.

Fash, William. *Scribes, Warriors, and Kings: The City of Copan and the Ancient Maya.* New York: Thames & Hudson, 1991.

Feest, Christian F. *Native Arts of North America.* 2d ed. New York: Thames & Hudson, 1992.

Foster, Michael S., and Shirley Gorenstein, eds. *Greater Mesoamerica: The Archaeology of West and Northwest Mexico.* Salt Lake City: University of Utah Press, 2000.

Grube, Nikolai, ed. *Maya: Divine Kings of the Rain Forest.* Cologne: Könemann, 2000.

Janusek, John Wayne. *Ancient Tiwanaku.* New York: Cambridge University Press, 2008.

Kolata, Alan. *The Tiwanaku: Portrait of an Andean Civilization.* Cambridge: Blackwell, 1993.

Kubler, George. *The Art and Architecture of Ancient America: The Mexican, Maya, and Andean Peoples.* 3d ed. New Haven, Conn.: Yale University Press, 1992.

Marken, Damien B., ed. *Palenque: Recent Investigations at the Classic Maya Center.* Lanham, Md.: Altamira, 2007.

Miller, Mary Ellen. *The Art of Mesoamerica, from Olmec to Aztec.* 4th ed. New York: Thames & Hudson, 2006.

———. *Maya Art and Architecture.* New York: Thames & Hudson, 1999.

Miller, Mary Ellen, and Karl Taube. *The Gods and Symbols of Ancient Mexico and the Maya: An Illustrated Dictionary of Mesoamerican Religion.* New York: Thames & Hudson, 1993.

Milner, George R. *The Moundbuilders: Ancient Peoples of Eastern North America.* New York: Thames & Hudson, 2004.

Morris, Craig, and Adriana von Hagen. *The Inka Empire and Its Andean Origins.* New York: Abbeville, 1993.

Nabokov, Peter, and Robert Easton. *Native American Architecture.* New York: Oxford University Press, 1989.

Pasztory, Esther. *Pre-Columbian Art.* New York: Cambridge University Press, 1998.

———. *Teotihuacan: An Experiment in Living.* Norman: University of Oklahoma Press, 1997.

Paul, Anne. *Paracas Ritual Attire: Symbols of Authority in Ancient Peru.* Norman: University of Oklahoma Press, 1990.

Penney, David, and George C. Longfish. *Native American Art.* Hong Kong: Hugh Lauter Levin and Associates, 1994.

Pillsbury, Joanne, ed. *Moche Art and Archaeology in Ancient Peru.* Washington, D.C.: National Gallery of Art, 2005.

Pool, Christopher A. *Olmec Archaeology and Early Mesoamerica.* New York: Cambridge University Press, 2007.

Rohm, Arthur H., and William M. Ferguson. *Puebloan Ruins of the Southwest.* Albuquerque: University of New Mexico Press, 2006.

Schele, Linda, and Peter Mathews. *The Code of Kings: The Language of Seven Sacred Maya Temples and Tombs.* New York: Scribner, 1998.

Schele, Linda, and Mary E. Miller. *The Blood of Kings: Dynasty and Ritual in Maya Art.* Fort Worth, Tex.: Kimbell Art Museum, 1986.

Schmidt, Peter, Mercedes de la Garza, and Enrique Nalda, eds. *Maya.* New York: Rizzoli, 1998.

Sharer, Robert J., and Loa P. Traxler. *The Ancient Maya.* 6th ed. Palo Alto: Stanford University Press, 2006.

Silverman, Helaine, and William H. Isbell, eds. *Handbook of South American Archaeology.* New York: Springer, 2008.

Stone-Miller, Rebecca. *Art of the Andes from Chavín to Inca.* 2d ed. New York: Thames & Hudson, 2002.

———. *To Weave for the Sun: Ancient Andean Textiles.* New York: Thames & Hudson, 1994.

Townsend, Richard F., ed. *Ancient West Mexico.* Chicago: Art Institute of Chicago, 1998.

Von Hagen, Adriana, and Craig Morris. *The Cities of the Ancient Andes.* New York: Thames & Hudson, 1998.

Wardwell, Allen. *Ancient Eskimo Ivories of the Bering Strait.* New York: Rizzoli, 1986.

Whiteford, Andrew H., Stewart Peckham, and Kate Peck Kent. *I Am Here: Two Thousand Years of Southwest Indian Arts and Crafts.* Santa Fe: Museum of New Mexico Press, 1989.

### Chapter 19: Africa before 1800

Bacquart, Jean-Baptiste. *The Tribal Arts of Africa.* New York: Thames & Hudson, 2002.

Bassani, Ezio. *Arts of Africa: 7,000 Years of African Art.* Milan: Skira, 2005.

Ben-Amos, Paula. *The Art of Benin.* New York: Thames & Hudson, 1980.

Berzock, Kathleen Bickford. *Benin: Royal Arts of a West African Kingdom.* Chicago: Art Institute of Chicago, 2008.

Blier, Suzanne P. *Royal Arts of Africa: The Majesty of Form.* New York: Abrams, 1998.

Campbell, Alec, and David Coulson. *African Rock Art: Paintings and Engravings on Stone.* New York: Abrams, 2001.

Connah, Graham. *African Civilizations.* 2d ed. Cambridge: Cambridge University Press, 2001.

Coulson, David, and Alec Campbell. *African Rock Art: Painting and Engravings on Stone.* New York: Abrams, 2001.

Dewey, William J. *Legacies of Stone: Zimbabwe Past and Present.* Tervuren: Royal Museum for Central Africa, 1997.

Drewal, Henry J., John Pemberton, and Rowland Abiodun. *Yoruba: Nine Centuries of African Art and Thought.* New York: Center for African Art, in association with Abrams, 1989.

Drewal, Henry John, and Enid Schildkrout. *Dynasty and Divinity: Ife Art in Ancient Nigeria.* Seattle: University of Washington Press, 2010.

Eyo, Ekpo, and Frank Willett. *Treasures of Ancient Nigeria.* New York: Knopf, 1980.

Fagg, Bernard. *Nok Terracottas.* Lagos: Ethnographica, 1977.

Garlake, Peter. *Early Art and Architecture of Africa.* Oxford: Oxford University Press, 2002.

———. *Great Zimbabwe.* London: Thames & Hudson, 1973.

Grunne, Bernard de. *The Birth of Art in Africa: Nok Statuary in Nigeria.* Paris: Biro, 1998.

Huffman, Thomas N. *Snakes and Crocodiles: Power and Symbolism in Ancient Zimbabwe.* Johannesburg: Witwatersrand University Press, 1996.

Lajoux, Jean-Dominique. *The Rock Paintings of Tassili.* Cleveland: World Publishing, 1963.

Le Quellec, Jean-Loïc. *Rock Art in Africa: Mythology and Legend.* Paris: Flammarion, 2004.

Perani, Judith, and Fred T. Smith. *The Visual Arts of Africa: Gender, Power, and Life Cycle Rituals.* Englewood Cliffs, N.J.: Prentice Hall, 1998.

Phillips, Tom, ed. *Africa, the Art of a Continent.* New York: Prestel, 1995.

Phillipson, D. W. *African Archaeology.* 3d ed. New York: Cambridge University Press, 2005.

———. *Ancient Ethiopia: Aksum, Its Antecedents and Successors.* London: British Museum Press, 1998.

Schädler, Karl-Ferdinand. *Earth and Ore: 2,500 Years of African Art in Terra-Cotta and Metal.* Munich: Panterra Verlag, 1997.

Shaw, Thurstan. *Nigeria: Its Archaeology and Early History.* London: Thames & Hudson, 1978.

———. *Unearthing Igbo-Ukwu: Archaeological Discoveries in Eastern Nigeria.* New York: Oxford University Press, 1977.

Visonà, Monica B., ed. *A History of Art in Africa.* 2d ed. Englewood Cliffs, N.J.: Prentice Hall, 2007.

Willett, Frank. *Ife in the History of West African Sculpture.* New York: McGraw-Hill, 1967.

### Renaissance Art, General

Adams, Laurie Schneider. *Italian Renaissance Art.* Boulder, Colo.: Westview, 2001.

Andrés, Glenn M., John M. Hunisak, and Richard Turner. *The Art of Florence.* 2 vols. New York: Abbeville, 1988.

Campbell, Gordon. *The Grove Encyclopedia of Northern Renaissance Art.* New York: Oxford University Press, 2009.

———. *Renaissance Art and Architecture.* New York: Oxford University Press, 2005.

Campbell, Lorne. *Renaissance Portraits: European Portrait-Painting in the Fourteenth, Fifteenth, and Sixteenth Centuries.* New Haven, Conn.: Yale University Press, 1990.

Christian, Kathleen, and David J. Drogin, eds. *Patronage and Italian Renaissance Sculpture.* Burlington, Vt.: Ashgate, 2010.

Cole, Bruce. *Italian Art, 1250–1550: The Relation of Renaissance Art to Life and Society.* New York: Harper & Row, 1987.

———. *The Renaissance Artist at Work: From Pisano to Titian.* New York: Harper Collins, 1983.

Cranston, Jodi. *The Poetics of Portraiture in the Italian Renaissance.* New York: Cambridge University Press, 2000.

Frommel, Christoph Luitpold. *The Architecture of the Italian Renaissance.* London: Thames & Hudson, 2007.

Furlotti, Barbara, and Guido Rebecchini. *The Art of Mantua: Power and Patronage in the Renaissance.* Los Angeles: J. Paul Getty Museum, 2008.

Hall, Marcia B. *Color and Meaning: Practice and Theory in Renaissance Painting.* Cambridge: Cambridge University Press, 1992.

Hartt, Frederick, and David G. Wilkins. *History of Italian Renaissance Art.* 7th ed. Upper Saddle River, N.J.: Prentice Hall, 2010.

Haskell, Francis, and Nicholas Penny. *Taste and the Antique: The Lure of Classical Sculpture 1500–1900.* New Haven, Conn.: Yale University Press, 1981.

Kent, F. W., and Patricia Simons, eds. *Patronage, Art, and Society in Renaissance Italy.* Canberra: Humanities Research Centre and Clarendon Press, 1987.

King, Catherine E. *Renaissance Women Patrons: Wives and Widows in Italy, c. 1300–1550.* Manchester: Manchester University Press, 1998.

Levey, Michael. *Florence: A Portrait.* Cambridge, Mass.: Harvard University Press, 1998.

Lubbock, Jules. *Storytelling in Christian Art from Giotto to Donatello.* New Haven, Conn.: Yale University Press, 2006.

Paoletti, John T., and Gary M. Radke. *Art, Power, and Patronage in Renaissance Italy.* Upper Saddle River, N.J.: Prentice Hall, 2005.

Partridge, Loren. *Art of Renaissance Florence, 1400–1600.* Berkeley and Los Angeles: University of California Press, 2009.

Pope-Hennessy, John. *Introduction to Italian Sculpture.* 3d ed. 3 vols. New York: Phaidon, 1986.

Richardson, Carol M., Kim W. Woods, and Michael W. Franklin, eds. *Renaissance Art Reconsidered: An Anthology of Primary Sources.* Malden, Mass.: Blackwell, 2007.

Smith, Jeffrey Chipps. *The Northern Renaissance.* New York: Phaidon, 2004.

Snyder, James, Larry Silver, and Henry Luttikhuizen. *Northern Renaissance Art: Painting, Sculpture, the Graphic Arts from 1350 to 1575.* Upper Saddle River, N.J.: Prentice Hall, 2005.

Strinati, Claudio, and Pomeroy, Jordana. *Italian Women Artists from Renaissance to Baroque.* Milan: Skira, 2007.

Thomson, David. *Renaissance Architecture: Critics, Patrons, and Luxury.* Manchester: Manchester University Press, 1993.

Tinagli, Paola. *Women in Italian Renaissance Art: Gender, Representation, Identity.* Manchester: Manchester University Press, 1997.

Wittkower, Rudolf. *Architectural Principles in the Age of Humanism.* 4th ed. London: Academy, 1988.

Woods, Kim W. *Making Renaissance Art.* New Haven, Conn.: Yale University Press, 2007.

———. *Viewing Renaissance Art.* New Haven, Conn.: Yale University Press, 2007.

Woods-Marsden, Joanna. *Renaissance Self-Portraiture: The Visual Construction of Identity and the Social Status of the Artist.* New Haven, Conn.: Yale University Press, 1998.

### Chapter 20: Late Medieval and Early Renaissance Art in Northern Europe

Ainsworth, Maryan W., and Maximiliaan P. J. Martens. *Petrus Christus, Renaissance Master of Bruges.* New York: Metropolitan Museum of Art, 1994.

*Art from the Court of Burgundy: The Patronage of Philip the Bold and John the Fearless 1364–1419.* Cleveland: Cleveland Museum of Art, 2004.

Baxandall, Michael. *The Limewood Sculptors of Renaissance Germany.* New Haven, Conn.: Yale University Press, 1980.

Borchert, Till-Holger. *Age of Van Eyck: The Mediterranean World and Early Netherlandish Painting, 1430–1530.* New York: Thames & Hudson, 2002.

Brinkmann, Bodo. *Konrad Witz.* Ostfildern: Hatje Cantz, 2011.

Campbell, Lorne. *The Fifteenth-Century Netherlandish Schools.* London: National Gallery Publications, 1998.

———. *Van der Weyden.* London: Chaucer, 2004.

Châtelet, Albert. *Early Dutch Painting.* New York: Konecky, 1988.

Friedlander, Max J. *Early Netherlandish Painting.* 14 vols. New York: Praeger/Phaidon, 1967–1976.

———. *From Van Eyck to Bruegel.* 3d ed. Ithaca, N.Y.: Cornell University Press, 1981.

Harbison, Craig. *The Mirror of the Artist: Northern Renaissance Art in Its Historical Context.* New York: Abrams, 1995.

Jacobs, Lynn F. *Early Netherlandish Carved Altarpieces, 1380–1550: Medieval Tastes and Mass Marketing.* Cambridge: Cambridge University Press, 1998.

Kemperdick, Stephan. *Rogier van der Weyden.* Cologne: H. F. Ullmann, 2007.

Kemperdick, Stephan, and Jocen Sander, eds. *The Master of Flémalle and Rogier van der Weyden.* Ostfildern: Hatje Cantz, 2009.

Lane, Barbara G. *The Altar and the Altarpiece: Sacramental Themes in Early Netherlandish Painting.* New York: Harper & Row, 1984.

Meiss, Millard. *French Painting in the Time of Jean de Berry: The Limbourgs and Their Contemporaries.* New York: Braziller, 1974.

Michiels, Alfred. *Hans Memling.* London: Parkstone, 2008.

Müller, Theodor. *Sculpture in the Netherlands, Germany, France, and Spain: 1400–1500.* New Haven, Conn.: Yale University Press, 1986.

Nash, Susie. *Northern Renaissance Art.* New York: Oxford University Press, 2008.

Pächt, Otto. *Early Netherlandish Painting from Rogier van der Wayden to Gerard David.* New York: Harvey Miller, 1997.

Panofsky, Erwin. *Early Netherlandish Painting: Its Origins and Character.* 2 vols. Cambridge, Mass.: Harvard University Press, 1966.

Parshall, Peter, ed. *The Woodcut in Fifteenth-Century Europe.* New Haven, Conn.: Yale University Press, 2009.

Parshall, Peter, and Rainer Schoch. *Origins of European Printmaking: Fifteenth-Century Woodcuts and Their Public.* New Haven, Conn.: Yale University Press, 2005.

Prevenier, Walter, and Wim Blockmans. *The Burgundian Netherlands.* Cambridge: Cambridge University Press, 1986.

Tomlinson, Amanda. *Van Eyck.* London: Chaucer, 2007.

Wolfthal, Diane. *The Beginnings of Netherlandish Canvas Painting, 1400–1530.* New York: Cambridge University Press, 1989.

### Chapter 21: The Renaissance in Quattrocento Italy

Ahl, Diane Cole. *Fra Angelico.* New York: Phaidon, 2008.

———, ed. *The Cambridge Companion to Masaccio.* New York: Cambridge University Press, 2002.

Ames-Lewis, Francis. *Drawing in Early Renaissance Italy.* 2d ed. New Haven, Conn.: Yale University Press, 2000.

———. *The Intellectual Life of the Early Renaissance Artist.* New Haven, Conn.: Yale University Press, 2000.

Baxandall, Michael. *Painting and Experience in Fifteenth-Century Italy: A Primer in the Social History of Pictorial Style.* 2d ed. New York: Oxford University Press, 1988.

Bober, Phyllis Pray, and Ruth Rubinstein. *Renaissance Artists and Antique Sculpture: A Handbook of Sources.* Oxford: Oxford University Press, 1986.

Borsook, Eve. *The Mural Painters of Tuscany.* New York: Oxford University Press, 1981.

Cole, Alison. *Virtue and Magnificence: Art of the Italian Renaissance Courts.* New York: Abrams, 1995.

Cole, Bruce. *Masaccio and the Art of Early Renaissance Florence.* Bloomington: Indiana University Press, 1980.

Dempsey, Charles. *The Portrayal of Love: Botticelli's* Primavera *and Humanist Culture at the Time of Lorenzo the Magnificent.* Princeton, N.J.: Princeton University Press, 1992.

Edgerton, Samuel Y., Jr. *The Heritage of Giotto's Geometry: Art and Science on the Eve of the Scientific Revolution.* Ithaca, N.Y.: Cornell University Press, 1991.

———. *The Renaissance Rediscovery of Linear Perspective.* New York: Harper & Row, 1976.

Gilbert, Creighton, ed. *Italian Art 1400–1500: Sources and Documents.* Evanston, Ill.: Northwestern University Press, 1992.

Goldthwaite, Richard A. *The Building of Renaissance Florence: An Economic and Social History.* Baltimore: Johns Hopkins University Press, 1980.

Goy, Richard J. *Building Renaissance Venice: Patrons, Architects, and Builders c. 1430–1500.* New Haven, Conn.: Yale University Press, 2006.

Heydenreich, Ludwig H. *Architecture in Italy, 1400–1500.* 2d ed. New Haven, Conn.: Yale University Press, 1996.

Hollingsworth, Mary. *Patronage in Renaissance Italy: From 1400 to the Early Sixteenth Century.* Baltimore: Johns Hopkins University Press, 1994.

Holmes, Megan. *Fra Filippo Lippi: The Carmelite Painter.* New Haven, Conn.: Yale University Press, 1999.

Kemp, Martin. *Behind the Picture: Art and Evidence in the Italian Renaissance.* New Haven, Conn.: Yale University Press, 1997.

Kempers, Bram. *Painting, Power, and Patronage: The Rise of the Professional Artist in the Italian Renaissance.* London: Penguin, 1992.

Kent, Dale. *Cosimo de' Medici and the Florentine Renaissance: The Patron's Oeuvre.* New Haven, Conn.: Yale University Press, 2000.

Lieberman, Ralph. *Renaissance Architecture in Venice.* New York: Abbeville, 1982.

Lindow, James R. *The Renaissance Palace in Florence: Magnificence and Splendour in Fifteenth-Century Italy.* Burlington Vt.: Ashgate, 2007.

Manca, Joseph. *Andrea Mantegna and the Italian Renaissance.* New York: Parkstone, 2006.

McAndrew, John. *Venetian Architecture of the Early Renaissance.* Cambridge, Mass.: MIT Press, 1980.

Murray, Peter. *Renaissance Architecture.* New York: Electa/Rizzoli, 1985.

Olson, Roberta J. M. *Italian Renaissance Sculpture.* London: Thames & Hudson, 1992.

Osborne, June. *Urbino: The Story of a Renaissance City.* Chicago: University of Chicago Press, 2003.

Poeschke, Joachim. *Donatello and His World: Sculpture of the Italian Renaissance.* New York: Abrams, 1993.

Radke, Gary M., ed. *The Gates of Paradise: Lorenzo Ghiberti's Renaissance Masterpiece.* New Haven, Conn.: Yale University Press, 2007.

Seymour, Charles. *Sculpture in Italy: 1400–1500.* New Haven, Conn.: Yale University Press, 1992.

Turner, A. Richard. *Renaissance Florence: The Invention of a New Art.* New York: Abrams, 1997.

Wackernagel, Martin. *The World of the Florentine Renaissance Artist: Projects and Patrons, Workshops and Art Market.* Princeton, N.J.: Princeton University Press, 1981.

Welch, Evelyn. *Art and Society in Italy 1350–1500.* Oxford: Oxford University Press, 1997.

White, John. *The Birth and Rebirth of Pictorial Space.* 3d ed. Boston: Faber & Faber, 1987.

Wright, Alison. *The Pollaiuolo Brothers: The Arts of Florence and Rome.* New Haven, Conn.: Yale University Press, 2005.

Zöllner, Frank. *Sandro Botticelli.* New ed. New York: Prestel, 2009.

### Chapter 22: Renaissance and Mannerism in Cinquecento Italy

Beltramini, Guido, and Howard Burns. *Palladio.* London: Royal Academy, 2008.

Blunt, Anthony. *Artistic Theory in Italy, 1450–1600.* London: Oxford University Press, 1975.

Brambilla Barcilon, Pinnin. *Leonardo: The Last Supper.* Chicago: University of Chicago Press, 2001.

Brock, Maurice. *Bronzino.* Paris: Flammarion, 2002.

Brown, David Alan, and Sylvia Ferino-Pagden, eds. *Bellini, Giorgione, Titian, and the Renaissance of Venetian Painting.* New Haven, Conn.: Yale University Press, 2006.

Brown, Patricia Fortini. *Art and Life in Renaissance Venice.* New York: Abrams, 1997.

Cole, Bruce. *Titian and Venetian Painting, 1450–1590.* Boulder, Colo.: Westview, 2000.

Cooper, Tracy E. *Palladio's Venice: Architecture and Society in a Renaissance Republic.* New Haven, Conn.: Yale University Press, 2005.

Cranston, Jodi. *The Muddled Mirror: Materiality and Figuration in Titian's Later Paintings.* University Park, Pa.: Pennsylvania State University Press, 2010.

Dal Pozzolo, Enrico. *Giorgione.* Milan: Motta, 2010.

De Vecchi, Pierluigi. *Raphael.* New York: Abbeville, 2002.

Ekserdjian, David. *Correggio.* New Haven, Conn.: Yale University Press, 1997.

———. *Parmigianino.* New Haven, Conn.: Yale University Press, 2006.

Falomir, Miguel, ed. *Tintoretto.* Madrid: Museo Nacional del Prado, 2007.

Ferino-Pagden, Sylvia, and Giovanna Nepi Scirè. *Giorgione: Myth and Enigma.* Milan: Skira, 2004.

Franklin, David. *Painting in Renaissance Florence, 1500–1550.* New Haven, Conn.: Yale University Press, 2001.

Freedberg, Sydney J. *Painting in Italy: 1500–1600.* 3d ed. New Haven, Conn.: Yale University Press, 1993.

Goffen, Rona. *Piety and Patronage in Renaissance Venice: Bellini, Titian, and the Franciscans.* New Haven, Conn.: Yale University Press, 1986.

———. *Renaissance Rivals: Michelangelo, Leonardo, Raphael, Titian.* New Haven, Conn.: Yale University Press, 2002.

Hall, Marcia B. *After Raphael: Painting in Central Italy in the Sixteenth Century.* Cambridge: Cambridge University Press, 1999.

———. *Rome.* Artistic Centers of the Italian Renaissance. New York: Cambridge University Press, 2005.

———. *The Sacred Image in the Age of Art: Titian, Tintoretto, Barocci, El Greco, Caravaggio.* New Haven, Conn.: Yale University Press, 2011.

———, ed. *The Cambridge Companion to Raphael.* New York: Cambridge University Press, 2005.

Hollingsworth, Mary. *Patronage in Sixteenth Century Italy.* London: John Murray, 1996.

Holt, Elizabeth Gilmore, ed. *A Documentary History of Art. Vol. 2, Michelangelo and the Mannerists.* Rev. ed. Princeton, N.J.: Princeton University Press, 1982.

Humfrey, Peter. *Painting in Renaissance Venice.* New Haven, Conn.: Yale University Press, 1995.

———. *Titian.* London: Phaidon, 2007.

Huse, Norbert, and Wolfgang Wolters. *The Art of Renaissance Venice: Architecture, Sculpture, and Painting.* Chicago: University of Chicago Press, 1990.

Ilchman, Frederick, ed. *Titian, Tintoretto, Veronese: Rivals in Renaissance Venice.* Boston: Museum of Fine Arts, 2009.

Kliemann, Julian-Matthias, and Michael Rohlmann. *Italian Frescoes: High Renaissance and Mannerism, 1510–1600.* New York: Abbeville, 2004.

Levey, Michael. *High Renaissance.* New York: Viking Penguin, 1978.

Lotz, Wolfgang. *Architecture in Italy, 1500–1600.* 2d ed. New Haven, Conn.: Yale University Press, 1995.

Meilman, Patricia, ed. *The Cambridge Companion to Titian.* New York: Cambridge University Press, 2004.

Nichols, Tom. *Tintoretto: Tradition and Identity.* London: Reaktion, 2004.

Partridge, Loren. *The Art of Renaissance Rome.* New York: Abrams, 1996.

Pietrangeli, Carlo, André Chastel, John Shearman, John O'Malley, S.J., Pierluigi de Vecchi, Michael Hirst, Fabrizio Mancinelli, Gianluigi Colalucci, and Franco Bernbei. *The Sistine Chapel: The Art, the History, and the Restoration*. New York: Harmony, 1986.

Pilliod, Elizabeth. *Pontormo, Bronzino, Allori: A Genealogy of Florentine Art*. New Haven, Conn.: Yale University Press, 2001.

Pope-Hennessy, John. *Italian High Renaissance and Baroque Sculpture*. 3d ed. 3 vols. Oxford: Phaidon, 1986.

Rosand, David. *Painting in Cinquecento Venice: Titian, Veronese, Tintoretto*. New Haven, Conn.: Yale University Press, 1982.

Rowe, Colin, and Leon Satkowski. *Italian Architecture of the 16th Century*. New York: Princeton Architectural Press, 2002.

Shearman, John K. G. *Mannerism*. Baltimore: Penguin, 1978.

———. *Only Connect . . . Art and the Spectator in the Italian Renaissance*. Princeton, N.J.: Princeton University Press, 1990.

Summers, David. *Michelangelo and the Language of Art*. Princeton, N.J.: Princeton University Press, 1981.

Talvacchia, Bette. *Raphael*. London: Phaidon, 2007.

Tronzo, William, ed. *St. Peter's in the Vatican*. New York: Cambridge University Press, 2005.

Wilde, Johannes. *Venetian Art from Bellini to Titian*. Oxford: Clarendon, 1981.

Williams, Robert. *Art, Theory, and Culture in Sixteenth-Century Italy: From Techne to Metatechne*. New York: Cambridge University Press, 1997.

Zöllner, Frank. *Leonardo da Vinci: The Complete Paintings and Drawings*. Cologne: Taschen, 2007.

### Chapter 23: High Renaissance and Mannerism in Northern Europe and Spain

Ainsworth, Maryan W. *Man, Myth, and Sensual Pleasures: Jan Gossart's Renaissance. The Complete Works*. New York: Metropolitan Museum of Art, 2010.

Bartrum, Giulia, ed. *Albrecht Dürer and His Legacy: The Graphic Work of a Renaissance Artist*. Princeton, N. J.: Princeton University Press, 2003.

Bätschmann, Oskar, and Pascal Griener. *Hans Holbein*. Princeton, N. J.: Princeton University Press, 1997.

Blunt, Anthony. *Art and Architecture in France, 1500–1700*. Rev. ed. New Haven, Conn.: Yale University Press, 1999.

Brinkmann, Bodo, ed. *Cranach*. London: Royal Academy of Arts, 2008.

Buck, Stephanie, and Jochen Sander. *Hans Holbein the Younger: Painter at the Court of Henry VIII*. New York: Thames & Hudson, 2004.

Chapius, Julien. *Tilman Riemenschneider: Master Sculptor of the Late Middle Ages*. Washington, D.C.: National Gallery of Art, 1999.

Chastel, André. *French Art: The Renaissance, 1430–1620*. Paris: Flammarion, 1995.

Davies, David, and John H. Elliott. *El Greco*. London: National Gallery, 2003.

Dixon, Laurinda. *Bosch*. New York: Phaidon, 2003.

Farago, Claire, ed. *Reframing the Renaissance: Visual Culture in Europe and Latin America, 1450–1650*. New Haven, Conn.: Yale University Press, 1995.

Foister, Susan. *Holbein and England*. New Haven, Conn.: Paul Mellon Centre for British Art, 2005.

Gibson, W. S. *"Mirror of the Earth": The World Landscape in Sixteenth-Century Flemish Painting*. Princeton, N.J.: Princeton University Press, 1989.

Harbison, Craig. *The Mirror of the Artist: Northern Renaissance Art in Its Historical Context*. New York: Abrams, 1995.

Koerner, Joseph Leo. *The Reformation of the Image*. Chicago: University of Chicago Press, 2004.

Landau, David, and Peter Parshall. *The Renaissance Print: 1470–1550*. New Haven, Conn.: Yale University Press, 1994.

Price, David Hotchkiss. *Albrecht Dürer's Renaissance: Humanism, Reformation, and the Art of Faith*. Ann Arbor: University of Michigan Press, 2003.

Roberts-Jones, Philippe, and Françoise Roberts-Jones. *Pieter Bruegel*. New York: Abrams, 2002.

Silver, Larry. *Hieronymous Bosch*. New York: Abbeville, 2006.

Smith, Jeffrey C. *German Sculpture of the Later Renaissance, c. 1520–1580: Art in an Age of Uncertainty*. Princeton, N.J.: Princeton University Press, 1993.

Stechow, Wolfgang. *Northern Renaissance Art, 1400–1600: Sources and Documents*. Evanston, Ill.: Northwestern University Press, 1989.

Zerner, Henri. *Renaissance Art in France: The Invention of Classicism*. Paris: Flammarion, 2003.

### Baroque Art, General

Blunt, Anthony, ed. *Baroque and Rococo: Architecture and Decoration*. Cambridge: Harper & Row, 1982.

Harris, Ann Sutherland. *Seventeenth-Century Art & Architecture*. Upper Saddle River, N.J.: Prentice Hall, 2005.

Harrison, Charles, Paul Wood, and Jason Gaiger, eds. *Art in Theory, 1648–1815: An Anthology of Changing Ideas*. Oxford: Blackwell, 2000.

Held, Julius, and Donald Posner. *17th- and 18th-Century Art: Baroque Painting, Sculpture, Architecture*. New York: Abrams, 1971.

Lagerlöf, Margaretha R. *Ideal Landscape: Annibale Carracci, Nicolas Poussin, and Claude Lorrain*. New Haven, Conn.: Yale University Press, 1990.

Lawrence, Cynthia, ed. *Women and Art in Early Modern Europe: Patrons, Collectors, and Connoisseurs*. University Park: Pennsylvania State University Press, 1997.

Lemerle, Frédérique, and Yves Pauwels. *Baroque Architecture, 1600–1750*. Paris: Flammarion, 2008.

Minor, Vernon Hyde. *Baroque & Rococo: Art & Culture*. New York, Abrams, 1999.

Norberg-Schulz, Christian. *Baroque Architecture*. New York: Rizzoli, 1986.

———. *Late Baroque and Rococo Architecture*. New York: Electa/Rizzoli, 1985.

Toman, Rolf. *Baroque: Architecture, Sculpture, Painting*. Cologne: Könemann, 1998.

### Chapter 24: The Baroque in Italy and Spain

Bissel, R. Ward. *Artemisia Gentileschi and the Authority of Art*. University Park: Pennsylvania State University Press, 1999.

Brown, Jonathan. *The Golden Age of Painting in Spain*. New Haven, Conn.: Yale University Press, 1991.

———. *Velázquez: Painter and Courtier*. New Haven, Conn.: Yale University Press, 1988.

Christiansen, Keith, and Judith W. Mann. *Orazio and Artemisia Gentileschi*. New York: Metropolitan Museum of Art, 2001.

Enggass, Robert, and Jonathan Brown. *Italy and Spain, 1600–1750: Sources and Documents*. Upper Saddle River, N.J.: Prentice Hall, 1970.

Freedberg, Sydney J. *Circa 1600: A Revolution of Style in Italian Painting*. Cambridge, Mass.: Harvard University Press, 1983.

Fried, Michael. *The Moment of Caravaggio*. Princeton, N.J.: Princeton University Press, 2010.

Haskell, Francis. *Patrons and Painters: A Study in the Relations between Italian Art and Society in the Age of the Baroque*. Rev. ed. New Haven, Conn.: Yale University Press, 1980.

Krautheimer, Richard. *The Rome of Alexander VII, 1655–1677*. Princeton, N.J.: Princeton University Press, 1985.

Montagu, Jennifer. *Roman Baroque Sculpture: The Industry of Art*. New Haven, Conn.: Yale University Press, 1989.

Puglisi, Catherine. *Caravaggio*. London: Phaidon, 2000.

Schroth, Sarah, and Ronni Baer. *El Greco to Velazquez: Art during the Reign of Philip III*. Boston: Museum of Fine Arts, 2008.

Strinati, Claudio, and Pomeroy, Jordana. *Italian Women Artists from Renaissance to Baroque*. Milan: Skira, 2007.

Tomlinson, Janis. *From El Greco to Goya: Painting in Spain 1561–1828*. Upper Saddle Ridge, N.J.: Prentice Hall, 1997.

Tronzo, William, ed. *St. Peter's in the Vatican*. New York: Cambridge University Press, 2005.

Varriano, John. *Caravaggio: The Art of Realism*. University Park: Pennsylvania University Press, 2006.

———. *Italian Baroque and Rococo Architecture*. New York: Oxford University Press, 1986.

Wittkower, Rudolf. *Art and Architecture in Italy 1600–1750*. 6th ed. 3 vols. Revised by Joseph Connors and Jennifer Montagu. New Haven, Conn.: Yale University Press, 1999.

### Chapter 25: The Baroque in Northern Europe

Alpers, Svetlana. *The Art of Describing: Dutch Art in the Seventeenth Century*. Chicago: University of Chicago Press, 1984.

———. *The Making of Rubens*. New Haven, Conn.: Yale University Press, 1995.

———. *Rembrandt's Enterprise: The Studio and the Market*. Chicago: University of Chicago Press, 1988.

Belkin, Kristin Lohse. *Rubens*. London: Phaidon, 1998.

Biesboer, Pieter, Martina Brunner-Bulst, Henry D. Gregory, and Christian Klemm. *Pieter Claesz: Master of Haarlem Still Life*. Zwolle: Waanders, 2005.

Blunt, Anthony. *Art and Architecture in France, 1500–1700*. Rev. ed. New Haven, Conn.: Yale University Press, 1999.

Brown, Christopher. *Scenes of Everyday Life: Dutch Genre Painting of the Seventeenth Century*. London: Faber & Faber, 1984.

Bryson, Norman. *Word and Image: French Painting of the Ancien Régime*. Cambridge: Cambridge University Press, 1981.

Carr, Dawson W., ed. *Velázquez*. London: National Gallery, 2006.

Chapman, Perry. *Rembrandt's Self-Portraits: A Study in 17th-Century Identity*. Princeton, N.J.: Princeton University Press, 1990.

Chastel, André. *French Art: The Ancien Régime, 1620–1775*. New York: Flammarion, 1996.

Chong, Alan, and Wouter Kloek. *Still-Life Paintings from the Netherlands, 1550–1720*. Zwolle: Waanders, 1999.

Franits, Wayne. *Dutch Seventeenth-Century Genre Painting: Its Stylistic and Thematic Evolution*. New Haven, Conn.: Yale University Press, 2008.

———. *Looking at Seventeenth-Century Dutch Art: Realism Reconsidered*. Cambridge: Cambridge University Press, 1997.

———, ed. *The Cambridge Companion to Vermeer*. New York: Cambridge University Press, 2001.

Haak, Bob. *The Golden Age: Dutch Painters of the Seventeenth Century*. New York: Abrams, 1984.

Hochstrasser, Julie Berger. *Still Life and Trade in the Dutch Golden Age*. New Haven, Conn.: Yale University Press, 2007.

Keazor, Henry. *Nicholas Poussin, 1594–1665*. Cologne: Taschen, 2007.

Kiers, Judikje, and Fieke Tissink. *Golden Age of Dutch Art: Painting, Sculpture, Decorative Art.* New York: Thames & Hudson, 2000.

Liedtke, Walter. *Vermeer: The Complete Paintings.* Antwerp: Ludion, 2008.

———. *A View of Delft: Vermeer and His Contemporaries.* Zwolle: Wanders, 2000.

Mérot, Alain. *French Painting in the Seventeenth Century.* New Haven, Conn.: Yale University Press, 1995.

Muller, Sheila D., ed. *Dutch Art: An Encyclopedia.* New York: Garland, 1997.

North, Michael. *Art and Commerce in the Dutch Golden Age.* New Haven, Conn.: Yale University Press, 1997.

Olson, Todd P. *Poussin and France.* New Haven, Conn.: Yale University Press, 2000.

Rosenberg, Jakob, Seymour Slive, and E. H. ter Kuile. *Dutch Art and Architecture, 1600–1800.* New Haven, Conn.: Yale University Press, 1979.

Schama, Simon. *The Embarrassment of Riches: An Interpretation of Dutch Culture in the Golden Age.* Berkeley: University of California Press, 1988.

Schroth, Sarah, and Ronni Baer, eds. *El Greco to Velázquez: Art during the Reign of Philip III.* Boston: Museum of Fine Arts, 2008.

Slatkes, Leonard J., and Wayne Franits. *The Paintings of Hendrick ter Brugghen 1588–1629: Catalogue Raisonné.* Philadelphia: John Benjamins, 2007.

Stechow, Wolfgang. *Dutch Landscape Painting of the 17th Century.* 3d ed. Oxford: Phaidon, 1981.

Summerson, John. *Inigo Jones.* New Haven, Conn.: Yale University Press, 2000.

Vlieghe, Hans. *Flemish Art and Architecture, 1585–1700.* New Haven, Conn.: Yale University Press, 1998.

Westermann, Mariët. *Rembrandt.* London: Phaidon, 2000.

———. *A Worldly Art: The Dutch Republic 1585–1718.* New Haven, Conn.: Yale University Press, 1996.

Zega, Andres, and Bernd H. Dams. *Palaces of the Sun King: Versailles, Trianon, Marly: The Châteaux of Louis XIV.* New York: Rizzoli, 2002.

Zell, Michael. *Reframing Rembrandt: Jews and the Christian Image in Seventeenth-Century Amsterdam.* Berkeley: University of California Press, 2002.

### Chapter 26: Rococo to Neoclassicism: The 18th Century in Europe and America

Beddington, Charles. *Venice: Canaletto and His Rivals.* London: National Gallery, 2010.

Bermingham, Ann. *Landscape and Ideology: The English Rustic Tradition, 1740–1850.* Berkeley: University of California Press, 1986.

Boime, Albert. *Art in the Age of Revolution, 1750–1800.* Chicago: University of Chicago Press, 1987.

Bowron, Edgar Peters, and Joseph J. Rishel, eds. *Art in Rome in the Eighteenth Century.* Philadelphia: Philadelphia Museum of Art, 2000.

Braham, Allan. *The Architecture of the French Enlightenment.* Berkeley: University of California Press, 1980.

Brion, Marcel. *Art of the Romantic Era: Romanticism, Classicism, Realism.* New York: Praeger, 1966.

Conisbee, Philip. *Painting in Eighteenth-Century France.* Ithaca, N.Y.: Phaidon/Cornell University Press, 1981.

Craske, Matthew. *Art in Europe, 1700–1830: A History of the Visual Arts in an Era of Unprecedented Urban Economic Growth.* New York: Oxford University Press, 1997.

Crow, Thomas E. *Painters and Public Life in Eighteenth-Century Paris.* New Haven, Conn.: Yale University Press, 1985.

Gaunt, W. *The Great Century of British Painting: Hogarth to Turner.* New York: Phaidon, 1971.

Goodman, Elise, ed. *Art and Culture in the Eighteenth Century: New Dimensions and Multiple Perspectives.* Newark: University of Delaware Press, 2001.

Harrison, Charles, Paul Wood, and Jason Gaiger, eds. *Art in Theory, 1648–1815: An Anthology of Changing Ideas.* Oxford: Blackwell, 2000.

Hedley, Jo. *François Boucher: Seductive Visions.* London: Wallace Collection, 2004.

Herrmann, Luke. *British Landscape Painting of the Eighteenth Century.* New York: Oxford University Press, 1974.

Honour, Hugh. *Neo-Classicism.* Harmondsworth: Penguin, 1968.

Irwin, David. *Neoclassicism.* London: Phaidon, 1997.

Jarrassé, Dominique. *18th-Century French Painting.* Paris: Terrail, 1999.

Kalnein, Wend Graf, and Michael Levey. *Art and Architecture of the Eighteenth Century in France.* New York: Viking/Pelican, 1973.

Lee, Simon. *David.* London: Phaidon, 1999.

Levey, Michael. *Rococo to Revolution: Major Trends in Eighteenth-Century Painting.* London: Thames & Hudson, 1966.

Rosenblum, Robert. *Transformations in Late Eighteenth-Century Art.* Princeton, N.J.: Princeton University Press, 1970.

Roston, Murray. *Changing Perspectives in Literature and the Visual Arts, 1650–1820.* Princeton, N.J.: Princeton University Press, 1990.

Rykwert, Joseph. *The First Moderns: Architects of the Eighteenth Century.* Cambridge, Mass.: MIT Press, 1983.

Stillman, Damie. *English Neo-Classical Architecture.* 2 vols. London: Zwemmer, 1988.

Waterhouse, Ellis Kirkham. *Painting in Britain: 1530–1790.* 4th ed. New Haven, Conn.: Yale University Press, 1979.

Wilton, Andrew. *The Swagger Portrait: Grand Manner Portraiture in Britain from Van Dyck to Augustus John, 1630–1930.* London: Tate Gallery, 1992.

### 19th and 20th Centuries, General

Arnason, H. H., and Peter Kalb. *History of Modern Art: Painting, Sculpture, Architecture, Photography.* 6th ed. Upper Saddle River, N.J.: Prentice Hall, 2009.

Ashton, Dore. *Twentieth-Century Artists on Art.* New York: Pantheon Books, 1985.

Barnitz, Jacueline. *Twentieth-Century Art of Latin America.* Austin: University of Texas Press, 2001.

Brettell, Richard R. *Modern Art, 1851–1929: Capitalism and Representation.* New York: Oxford University Press, 1999.

Brown, Milton, Sam Hunter, and John Jacobus. *American Art: Painting, Sculpture, Architecture, Decorative Arts, Photography.* New York: Abrams, 1979.

Burnham, Jack. *Beyond Modern Sculpture: The Effects of Science and Technology on the Sculpture of This Century.* New York: Braziller, 1968.

Butler, Cornelia, and Alexandra Schwartz, eds. *Modern Women: Women Artists at the Museum of Modern Art.* New York: Museum of Modern Art, 2010.

Chipp, Herschel B. *Theories of Modern Art.* Berkeley: University of California Press, 1968.

Chu, Petra ten-Doesschate. *Nineteenth-Century European Art.* 2d ed. Upper Saddle River, N.J.: Prentice Hall, 2006.

Coke, Van Deren. *The Painter and the Photograph from Delacroix to Warhol.* Rev. ed. Albuquerque: University of New Mexico Press, 1972.

Colquhoun, Alan. *Modern Architecture.* New York: Oxford University Press, 2002.

Craven, Wayne. *American Art: History and Culture.* Rev. ed. New York: McGraw-Hill, 2002.

Dennis, Rafael Cardoso, and Colin Trodd, eds. *Art and the Academy in the Nineteenth Century.* New Brunswick, N.J.: Rutgers University Press, 2000.

Doordan, Dennis P. *Twentieth-Century Architecture.* New York: Abrams, 2002.

Doss, Erika. *Twentieth-Century American Art.* New York: Oxford University Press, 2002.

Driskell, David C. *Two Centuries of Black American Art.* Los Angeles: Los Angeles County Museum of Art; New York: Knopf, 1976.

Eisenmann, Stephen F., ed. *Nineteenth-Century Art: A Critical History.* 4th ed. New York: Thames & Hudson, 2011.

Elsen, Albert. *Origins of Modern Sculpture.* New York: Braziller, 1974.

Facos, Michelle. *An Introduction to Nineteenth-Century Art.* New York: Routledge, 2011.

Foster, Hal, Rosalind Krauss, Yve-Alain Bois, and Benjamin H. D. Buchloh. *Art since 1900: Modernism, Antimodernism, Postmodernism.* New York: Thames & Hudson, 2004.

Frampton, Kenneth. *Modern Architecture: A Critical History.* 4th ed. New York: Thames & Hudson, 2007.

Frascina, Francis, and Charles Harrison, eds. *Modern Art and Modernism: A Critical Anthology.* New York: Harper & Row, 1982.

Giedion, Siegfried. *Space, Time, and Architecture: The Growth of a New Tradition.* 4th ed. Cambridge, Mass.: Harvard University Press, 1965.

Goldwater, Robert, and Marco Treves, eds. *Artists on Art.* 3d ed. New York: Pantheon, 1958.

Greenough, Sarah, Joel Snyder, David Travis, and Colin Westerbeck. *On the Art of Fixing a Shadow: One Hundred and Fifty Years of Photography.* Washington, D.C.: National Gallery of Art; Chicago: Art Institute of Chicago, 1989.

Hamilton, George H. *Painting and Sculpture in Europe, 1880–1940.* 6th ed. New Haven, Conn.: Yale University Press, 1993.

Harrison, Charles, and Paul Wood. *Art in Theory, 1900–2000: An Anthology of Changing Ideas.* Oxford: Blackwell, 2003.

Herbert, Robert L., ed. *Modern Artists on Art.* Upper Saddle River, N.J.: Prentice Hall, 1971.

Hertz, Richard, and Norman M. Klein, eds. *Twentieth-Century Art Theory: Urbanism, Politics, and Mass Culture.* Englewood Cliffs, N.J.: Prentice Hall, 1990.

Heyer, Paul. *Architects on Architecture: New Directions in America.* New York: Van Nostrand Reinhold, 1993.

Hills, Patricia. *Modern Art in the USA: Issues and Controversies of the 20th Century.* Upper Saddle River, N.J.: Prentice Hall, 2000.

Hitchcock, Henry-Russell. *Architecture: Nineteenth and Twentieth Centuries.* 4th ed. New Haven, Conn.: Yale University Press, 1977.

Hunter, Sam, John Jacobus, and Daniel Wheeler. *Modern Art: Painting, Sculpture, Architecture, Photography.* Rev. 3d ed. Upper Saddle River, N.J.: Prentice Hall, 2004.

Janson, Horst W. *19th-Century Sculpture.* New York: Abrams, 1985.

Jencks, Charles. *Modern Movements in Architecture.* Garden City, N.Y.: Anchor; Doubleday, 1973.

Kaufmann, Edgar, Jr., ed. *The Rise of an American Architecture.* New York: Metropolitan Museum of Art; Praeger, 1970.

Krauss, Rosalind E. *The Originality of the Avant-Garde and Other Modernist Myths.* Cambridge, Mass.: MIT Press, 1985.

———. *Passages in Modern Sculpture.* Cambridge, Mass.: MIT Press, 1981.

Lewis, Samella S. *African American Art and Artists.* Rev. ed. Berkeley: University of California Press, 1994.

Licht, Fred. *Sculpture, Nineteenth and Twentieth Centuries.* Greenwich, Conn.: New York Graphic Society, 1967.

Marien, Mary Warner. *Photography: A Cultural History.* 3d ed. Upper Saddle River, N.J.: Prentice Hall, 2011.

Mason, Jerry, ed. *International Center of Photography Encyclopedia of Photography.* New York: Crown, 1984.

McCoubrey, John W. *American Art, 1700–1960: Sources and Documents.* Englewood Cliffs, N.J.: Prentice Hall, 1965.

Newhall, Beaumont. *The History of Photography.* New York: Museum of Modern Art, 1982.

Osborne, Harold. *The Oxford Companion to Twentieth-Century Art.* New York: Oxford University Press, 1981.

Pohl, Frances K. *Framing America: A Social History of American Art.* 2d ed. New York: Thames & Hudson, 2008.

Rose, Barbara. *American Art since 1900.* Rev. ed. New York: Praeger, 1975.

Rosenblum, Naomi. *A World History of Photography.* 4th ed. New York: Abbeville, 2007.

Rosenblum, Robert. *Modern Painting and the Northern Romantic Tradition: Friedrich to Rothko.* New York: Harper & Row, 1975.

Rosenblum, Robert, and Horst W. Janson. *19th-Century Art.* Rev. ed. Upper Saddle River, N.J.: Prentice Hall, 2005.

Ross, Stephen David, ed. *Art and Its Significance: An Anthology of Aesthetic Theory.* Albany: State University of New York Press, 1987.

Russell, John. *The Meanings of Modern Art.* New York: Museum of Modern Art; Thames & Hudson, 1981.

Scully, Vincent. *Modern Architecture.* Rev. ed. New York: Braziller, 1974.

Spalding, Francis. *British Art since 1900.* London: Thames & Hudson, 1986.

Spencer, Harold. *American Art: Readings from the Colonial Era to the Present.* New York: Scribner, 1980.

Steinberg, Leo. *Other Criteria: Confrontations with 20th-Century Art.* New York: Oxford University Press, 1972.

Szarkowski, John. *Photography until Now.* New York: Museum of Modern Art, 1989.

Upton, Dell. *Architecture in the United States.* Oxford: Oxford University Press, 1998.

Weaver, Mike. *The Art of Photography: 1839–1989.* New Haven, Conn.: Yale University Press, 1989.

Whiffen, Marcus, and Frederick Koeper. *American Architecture, 1607–1976.* Cambridge, Mass.: MIT Press, 1983.

Wilmerding, John. *American Art.* Harmondsworth: Penguin, 1976.

Wilson, Simon. *Holbein to Hockney: A History of British Art.* London: Tate Gallery & Bodley Head, 1979.

### Chapter 27: Romanticism, Realism, Photography: Europe and America, 1800 to 1870

Amic, Sylvain, et al. *Gustave Courbet.* Ostfildern: Hatje Cantz, 2008.

Bartoli, Damien, and Frederick C. Ross. *William Bouguereau.* 2 vols. New York: Antique Collectors' Club, 2010.

Bellenger, Sylvain. *Girodet, 1767–1824.* Paris: Gallimard, 2005.

Bergdoll, Barry. *European Architecture 1750–1890.* New York: Oxford University Press, 2000.

Boime, Albert. *The Academy and French Painting in the 19th Century.* London: Phaidon, 1971.

———. *Art in the Age of Bonapartism, 1800–1815.* Chicago: University of Chicago Press, 1990.

Bordes, Philippe. *Jacques-Louis David: Empire to Exile.* New Haven, Conn.: Yale University Press, 2007.

Brown, David Blayney. *Romanticism.* New York: Phaidon, 2001.

Bryson, Norman. *Tradition and Desire: From David to Delacroix.* New York: Cambridge University Press, 1984.

Burns, Sarah, and John Davis. *American Art to 1900: A Documentary History.* Berkeley and Los Angeles: University of California Press, 2009.

Clark, T. J. *The Absolute Bourgeois: Artists and Politics in France, 1848–1851.* London: Thames & Hudson, 1973.

———. *Image of the People: Gustave Courbet and the 1848 Revolution.* London: Thames & Hudson, 1973.

———. *The Painting of Modern Life: Paris in the Art of Manet and His Followers.* Princeton, N.J.: Princeton University Press, 1984.

Clay, Jean. *Romanticism.* New York: Phaidon, 1981.

Eitner, Lorenz. *Neoclassicism and Romanticism, 1750–1850: An Anthology of Sources and Documents.* New York: Harper & Row, 1989.

Fried, Michael. *Courbet's Realism.* Chicago: University of Chicago Press, 1982.

———. *Manet's Modernism, or, The Face of Painting in the 1860s.* Chicago: University of Chicago Press, 1996.

Hilton, Timothy. *The Pre-Raphaelites.* New York: Oxford University Press, 1970.

Hofmann, Werner. *Caspar David Friedrich.* New York: Thames & Hudson, 2001.

———. *Goya.* New York: Thames & Hudson, 2003.

Holt, Elizabeth Gilmore, ed. *From the Classicists to the Impressionists: A Documentary History of Art and Architecture in the Nineteenth Century.* Garden City, N.J.: Anchor Books; Doubleday, 1966.

Honour, Hugh. *Romanticism.* New York: Harper & Row, 1979.

Koerner, Joseph Leo. *Caspar David Friedrich and the Subject of Landscape.* 2d ed. London: Reaktion, 2009.

Krell, Alain. *Manet and the Painters of Contemporary Life.* London: Thames & Hudson, 1996.

Kroeber, Karl. *British Romantic Art.* Berkeley: University of California Press, 1986.

Le Men, Ségolène. *Courbet.* New York: Abbeville, 2008.

Lewis, Michael J. *The Gothic Revival.* New York: Thames & Hudson, 2002.

Licht, Fred. *Goya.* New York: Abbeville, 2001.

Mainardi, Patricia. *Art and Politics of the Second Empire: The Universal Expositions of 1855 and 1867.* New Haven, Conn.: Yale University Press, 1987.

———. *The End of the Salon: Art and the State in the Early Third Republic.* Cambridge: Cambridge University Press, 1993.

Middleton, Robin. *Architecture of the Nineteenth Century.* London: Phaidon, 2003.

Middleton, Robin, and David Watkin. *Neoclassical and 19th-Century Architecture.* 2 vols. New York: Electa/Rizzoli, 1987.

Needham, Gerald. *19th-Century Realist Art.* New York: Harper & Row, 1988.

Nochlin, Linda. *Realism and Tradition in Art, 1848–1900: Sources and Documents.* Upper Saddle River, N.J.: Prentice Hall, 1966.

Novak, Barbara. *American Painting of the Nineteenth Century: Realism and the American Experience.* New York: Harper & Row, 1979.

Novak, Barbara. *Nature and Culture: American Landscape and Painting, 1825–1875.* 3d ed. New York: Oxford University Press, 2007.

*Nature and Culture: American Landscape and Painting, 1825–1875.* 3d ed. New York: Oxford University Press, 2007.

Novotny, Fritz. *Painting and Sculpture in Europe, 1780–1880.* 3d ed. New Haven, Conn.: Yale University Press, 1988.

Porterfield, Todd. *The Allure of Empire: Art in the Service of French Imperialism 1798–1836.* Princeton, N.J.: Princeton University Press, 1998.

Rosen, Charles, and Henri Zerner. *Romanticism and Realism: The Mythology of Nineteenth-Century Art.* New York: Viking, 1984.

Rubin, James Henry. *Courbet.* London: Phaidon, 1997.

———. *Manet: Initial M, Hand and Eye.* Paris: Flammarion, 2010.

Shelton, Andrew Carrington. *Ingres.* London: Phaidon, 2008.

Sloane, Joseph C. *French Painting between the Past and the Present: Artists, Critics, and Traditions from 1848 to 1870.* Princeton, N.J.: Princeton University Press, 1973.

Symmons, Sarah. *Goya.* London: Phaidon, 1998.

Taylor, Joshua, ed. *Nineteenth-Century Theories of Art.* Berkeley: University of California Press, 1987.

Tillier, Betrand, et al. *Gustave Courbet.* New York: Metropolitan Museum of Art, 2008.

Toman, Rolf, ed. *Neoclassicism and Romanticism: Architecture, Sculpture, Painting, Drawings, 1750–1848.* Cologne: Könemann, 2000.

Vaughn, William. *German Romantic Painting.* New Haven, Conn.: Yale University Press, 1980.

Wolf, Bryan Jay. *Romantic Revision: Culture and Consciousness in Nineteenth-Century American Painting and Literature.* Chicago: University of Chicago Press, 1986.

Wood, Christopher. *The Pre-Raphaelites.* New York: Viking, 1981.

### Chapter 28: Impressionism, Post-Impressionism, Symbolism: Europe and America, 1870 to 1900

Baal-Teshuva, Jacob. *Louis Comfort Tiffany.* Cologne: Taschen, 2008.

Bergdoll, Barry. *European Architecture 1750–1890.* New York: Oxford University Press, 2000.

Bryson, Norman. *Tradition and Desire: From David to Delacroix.* New York: Cambridge University Press, 1984.

Calloway, Stephen. *Aubrey Beardsley.* New York: Harry N. Abrams, 1998.

Clark, T. J. *The Painting of Modern Life: Paris in the Art of Manet and His Followers.* Princeton, N.J.: Princeton University Press, 1984.

Cogeval, Guy, ed. *Claude Monet, 1840–1926.* Paris: Réunion des Musées Nationaux, 2010.

Distel, Anne. *Renoir.* New York: Abbeville, 2010.

Eitner, Lorenz. *Neoclassicism and Romanticism, 1750–1850: An Anthology of Sources and Documents.* New York: Harper & Row, 1989.

Facos, Michelle. *Symbolism in Context.* Berkeley: University of California Press, 2009.

Hauptmann, Jodi. *Beyond the Visible: The Art of Odilon Redon.* New York: Museum of Modern Art, 2005.

Loyrette, Henri, Sebastien Allard, and Laurence Des Cars. *Nineteenth Century French Art: From Romanticism to Impressionism, Post-Impressionism, and Art Nouveau.* Paris: Flammarion, 2007.

Masson, Raphaël, and Véronique Mattiussi. *Rodin.* Paris: Flammarion, 2004.

McShine, Kynaston, ed. *Edvard Munch: The Modern Life of the Soul.* New York: Museum of Modern Art, 2006.

Middleton, Robin. *Architecture of the Nineteenth Century.* London: Phaidon, 2003.

Middleton, Robin, and David Watkin. *Neoclassical and 19th-Century Architecture.* 2 vols. New York: Electa/Rizzoli, 1987.

Pfeiffer, Ingrid, et al. *Women Impressionists.* Ostfildern: Hatje Cantz, 2008.

Swinbourne, Anna. *James Ensor.* New York: Museum of Modern Art, 2009.

Thomson, Belinda, ed. *Gauguin: Maker of Myth*. London: Tate, 2010.

Zerbst, Rainer. *Gaudí: The Complete Buildings*. Cologne: Taschen, 2005.

### Chapter 29: Modernism in Europe and America, 1900 to 1945

Antliff, Mark. *Cultural Politics and the Parisian Avant-Garde*. Princeton, N.J.: Princeton University Press, 1993.

Antliff, Mark, and Patricia Leighten. *Cubism and Culture*. New York: Thames & Hudson, 2001.

Arnaldo, Javier, and Max Hollein. *Kirchner*. Ostfildern: Hatje Cantz, 2010.

Baigell, Matthew. *The American Scene: American Painting of the 1930s*. New York: Praeger, 1974.

Barr, Alfred H., Jr. *Cubism and Abstract Art: Painting, Sculpture, Constructions, Photography, Architecture, Industrial Arts, Theatre, Films, Posters, Typography*. Cambridge, Mass.: Belknap, 1986.

Barron, Stephanie. *Exiles and Emigrés: The Flight of European Artists from Hitler*. Los Angeles: Los Angeles County Museum of Art, 1997.

———, ed. *Degenerate Art: The Fate of the Avant-Garde in Nazi Germany*. Los Angeles: Los Angeles County Museum of Art, 1991.

Bayer, Herbert, Walter Gropius, and Ise Gropius. *Bauhaus, 1919–1928*. New York: Museum of Modern Art, 1975.

Bearden, Romare, and Harry Henderson. *A History of African-American Artists from 1792 to the Present*. New York: Pantheon, 1993.

Bergdoll, Barry. *Bauhaus 1919–1933*. New York: Museum of Modern Art, 2009.

Bouvet, Vincent, and Gérard Durozoi. *Paris between the Wars 1919–1939: Art, Life & Culture*. New York: Vendome, 2010.

Breton, André. *Surrealism and Painting*. New York: Harper & Row, 1972.

Brown, Milton. *Story of the Armory Show: The 1913 Exhibition That Changed American Art*. 2d ed. New York: Abbeville, 1988.

Campbell, Mary Schmidt, David C. Driskell, David Lewis Levering, and Deborah Willis Ryan. *Harlem Renaissance: Art of Black America*. New York: Studio Museum in Harlem; Abrams, 1987.

Cowling, Elizabeth, ed. *Picasso: Challenging the Past*. London: National Gallery, 2011.

Cox, Neil. *Cubism*. London: Phaidon, 2000.

Curtis, Penelope. *Sculpture 1900–1945*. New York: Oxford University Press, 1999.

Curtis, William J. R. *Modern Architecture since 1900*. Upper Saddle River, N.J.: Prentice Hall, 1996.

Davidson, Abraham A. *Early American Modernist Painting, 1910–1935*. New York: Harper & Row, 1981.

Dietrich, Dorothea, ed. *Dada: Zurich, Berlin, Hannover, Cologne, New York, Paris*. Washington, D.C.: National Gallery, 2008.

Du Pont, Diana C. *Tamayo: A Modern Icon Reinterpreted*. Santa Barbara, Calif.: Santa Barbara Museum of Art, 2007.

Eberle, Matthias. *World War I and the Weimar Artists: Dix, Grosz, Beckmann, Schlemmer*. New Haven, Conn.: Yale University Press, 1985.

Edwards, Steve, and Paul Wood, eds. *Art of the Avant-Gardes*. New Haven, Conn.: Yale University Press, 2004.

Elderfield, John. *The "Wild Beasts": Fauvism and Its Affinities*. New York: Museum of Modern Art, 1976.

Fer, Briony, David Batchelor, and Paul Wood. *Realism, Rationalism, Surrealism: Art between the Wars*. New Haven, Conn.: Yale University Press, 1993.

Friedman, Mildred, ed. *De Stijl, 1917–1931: Visions of Utopia*. Minneapolis: Walker Art Center; New York: Abbeville, 1982.

Gale, Matthew. *Dada and Surrealism*. London: Phaidon, 1997.

Goldberg, Rose Lee. *Performance: Live Art 1909 to the Present*. New York: Abrams, 1979.

Golding, John. *Cubism: A History and an Analysis, 1907–1914*. Cambridge, Mass.: Belknap, 1988.

Gordon, Donald E. *Expressionism: Art and Idea*. New Haven, Conn.: Yale University Press, 1987.

Harrison, Charles, Francis Frascina, and Gil Perry. *Primitivism, Cubism, Abstraction: The Early Twentieth Century*. New Haven, Conn.: Yale University Press, 1993.

Herbert, James D. *Fauve Painting: The Making of Cultural Politics*. New Haven, Conn.: Yale University Press, 1992.

Herrera, Hayden, ed. *Frida Kahlo*. Minneapolis: Walker Art Center, 2007.

Hills, Patricia. *Painting Harlem Modern: The Art of Jacob Lawrence*. Berkeley and Los Angeles: University of California Press, 2009.

Hitchcock, Henry-Russell, and Philip Johnson. *The International Style*. New York: Norton, 1995.

Hurlburt, Laurance P. *The Mexican Muralists in the United States*. Albuquerque: University of New Mexico Press, 1989.

Jaffé, Hans L. C. *De Stijl, 1917–1931: The Dutch Contribution to Modern Art*. Cambridge, Mass.: Belknap, 1986.

Krauss, Rosalind. *The Originality of the Avant-Garde and Other Modernist Myths*. Cambridge, Mass.: MIT Press, 1986.

Kuspit, Donald. *The Cult of the Avant-Garde Artist*. Cambridge: Cambridge University Press, 1993.

Lloyd, Jill. *German Expressionism: Primitivism and Modernity*. New Haven, Conn.: Yale University Press, 1991.

Lodder, Christina. *Russian Constructivism*. New Haven, Conn.: Yale University Press, 1983.

Lozano, Luis Martin, and Juan Coronel Rivera. *Diego Rivera: The Complete Murals*. Cologne: Taschen, 2008.

Martin, Marianne W. *Futurist Art and Theory*. Oxford: Clarendon, 1968.

Motherwell, Robert, ed. *The Dada Painters and Poets: An Anthology*. 2d ed. Boston: Hall, 1981.

Mundy, Jennifer. *Duchamp, Man Ray, Picabia*. London: Tate, 2008.

Orvell, Miles. *American Photography*. New York: Oxford University Press, 2003.

Peters, Olaf. *Otto Dix*. New York: Prestel, 2010.

Rhodes, Colin. *Primitivism and Modern Art*. New York: Thames & Hudson, 1994.

Richter, Hans. *Dada: Art and Anti-Art*. London: Thames & Hudson, 1961.

Rochfort, Desmond. *Mexican Muralists: Orozco, Rivera, Siqueiros*. San Francisco: Chronicle, 1998.

Rosenblum, Robert. *Cubism and Twentieth-Century Art*. Rev. ed. New York: Abrams, 1984.

Rubin, William S. *Dada and Surrealist Art*. New York: Abrams, 1968.

———, ed. *Pablo Picasso: A Retrospective*. New York: Museum of Modern Art; Boston: New York Graphic Society, 1980.

———. *"Primitivism" in 20th-Century Art: Affinity of the Tribal and the Modern*. 2 vols. New York: Museum of Modern Art, 1984.

Selz, Peter. *German Expressionist Painting*. Berkeley: University of California Press, 1974. Reprint of 1957 edition.

Silver, Kenneth E. *Esprit de Corps: The Art of the Parisian Avant-Garde and the First World War, 1914–1925*. Princeton, N.J.: Princeton University Press, 1989.

Smith, Terry. *Making the Modern: Industry, Art, and Design in America*. Chicago: University of Chicago Press, 1993.

Stott, William. *Documentary Expression and Thirties America*. New York: Oxford University Press, 1973.

Taylor, Joshua C. *Futurism*. New York: Museum of Modern Art, 1961.

Taylor, Michael R., ed. *Arshile Gorky: A Retrospective*. New Haven, Conn.: Yale University Press, 2009.

Terraroli, Valerio, ed. *Art of the Twentieth Century, 1900–1919: The Avant-Garde Movements*. Milan: Skira, 2006.

———. *Art of the Twentieth Century, 1920–1945: The Artistic Culture between the Wars*. Milan: Skira, 2006.

Tisdall, Caroline, and Angelo Bozzola. *Futurism*. New York: Oxford University Press, 1978.

Trachtenberg, Alan. *Reading American Photographs: Images as History—Mathew Brady to Walker Evans*. New York: Hill and Wang, 1989.

Troyen, Carol, ed. *Edward Hopper*. Boston: Museum of Fine Arts, 2007.

Tsujimoto, Karen. *Images of America: Precisionist Painting and Modern Photography*. Seattle: University of Washington Press, 1982.

Tucker, William. *Early Modern Sculpture*. New York: Oxford University Press, 1974.

Vogt, Paul. *Expressionism: German Painting, 1905–1920*. New York: Abrams, 1980.

Weiss, Jeffrey S. *The Popular Culture of Modern Art: Picasso, Duchamp, and Avant-Gardism*. New Haven, Conn.: Yale University Press, 1994.

Whitford, Frank. *Bauhaus*. New York: Thames & Hudson, 1984.

### Chapter 30: Modernism and Postmodernism in Europe and America, 1945 to 1980

Alloway, Lawrence. *American Pop Art*. New York: Whitney Museum of American Art; Macmillan, 1974.

———. *Topics in American Art since 1945*. New York: Norton, 1975.

Altshuler, Bruce. *Isamu Noguchi*. New York: Abbeville, 1994.

Anfam, David. *Abstract Expressionism*. New York: Thames & Hudson, 1990.

Archer, Michael. *Art since 1960*. New ed. New York: Thames & Hudson, 2002.

Ashton, Dore. *American Art since 1945*. New York: Oxford University Press, 1983.

———. *The New York School: A Cultural Reckoning*. Harmondsworth: Penguin, 1979.

Ballantyne, Andrew, ed. *Architectures: Modernism and After*. Malden, Mass: Blackwell, 2004.

Battcock, Gregory, ed. *Idea Art: A Critical Anthology*. New York: Dutton, 1973.

———. *Minimal Art: A Critical Anthology*. New York: Studio Vista, 1969.

———. *The New Art: A Critical Anthology*. New York: Dutton, 1973.

———. *New Artists Video: A Critical Anthology*. New York: Dutton, 1978.

Battcock, Gregory, and Robert Nickas, eds. *The Art of Performance: A Critical Anthology*. New York: Dutton, 1984.

Beardsley, John, and Jane Livingston. *Hispanic Art in the United States: Thirty Contemporary Painters and Sculptors*. Houston: Museum of Fine Arts; New York: Abbeville, 1987.

Beardsley, Richard. *Earthworks and Beyond: Contemporary Art in the Landscape*. New York: Abbeville, 1984.

Broude, Norma, and Mary D. Garrard. *The Power of Feminist Art: The American Movement of the 1970s, History and Impact*. New York: Abrams, 1994.

Bürger, Peter. *Theory of the Avant-Garde*. Minneapolis: University of Minnesota Press, 1984.

Butler, Cornelia H., ed. *WACK! Art and the Feminist Revolution*. Cambridge, Mass.: MIT Press, 2007.

Causey, Andrew. *Sculpture since 1945*. New York: Oxford University Press, 1998.

Caws, Mary Ann. *Robert Motherwell*. New York: Columbia University Press, 1996.

Cockcroft, Eva, John Weber, and James Cockcroft. *Toward a People's Art*. New York: Dutton, 1977.

Cohn, Marjorie, and Eliza Rathbone. *Mark Rothko*. Ostfildern: Hatje Cantz, 2001.

Crow, Thomas. *The Rise of the Sixties: American and European Art in the Era of Dissent*. New Haven, Conn.: Yale University Press, 2005.

Finch, Christopher. *Chuck Close: Work*. New York: Prestel, 2010.

Frascina, Francis, ed. *Pollock and After: The Critical Debate*. New York: Harper & Row, 1985.

Gale, Matthew, ed. *Francis Bacon*. New York: Rizzoli, 2009.

Gaugh, Harry F. *Franz Kline*. New York: Abbeville, 1994.

Geldzahler, Henry. *New York Painting and Sculpture, 1940–1970*. New York: Dutton, 1969.

Godfrey, Tony. *Conceptual Art*. London: Phaidon, 1998.

Goldberg, Rose Lee. *Performance Art: From Futurism to the Present*. Rev. ed. New York: Abrams, 1988.

Goldhagen, Sarah Williams, and Réjean Legault. *Anxious Modernisms: Experimentation in Postwar Architectural Culture*. Cambridge, Mass.: MIT Press, 2002.

Goodman, Cynthia. *Digital Visions: Computers and Art*. New York: Abrams, 1987.

Goodyear, Frank H., Jr. *Contemporary American Realism since 1960*. Boston: New York Graphic Society, 1981.

Gouma-Peterson, Thalia. *Miriam Schapiro: Shaping the Fragments of Art and Life*. New York: Abrams, 2000.

Green, Jonathan. *American Photography: A Critical History 1945 to the Present*. New York: Abrams, 1984.

Greenberg, Clement. *Clement Greenberg: The Collected Essays and Criticism*. Edited by J. O'Brien. 4 vols. Chicago: University of Chicago Press, 1986–1993.

Grundberg, Andy. *Photography and Art: Interactions since 1945*. New York: Abbeville, 1987.

Guilbaut, Serge. *How New York Stole the Idea of Modern Art*. Chicago: University of Chicago Press, 1983.

Hays, K. Michael, and Carol Burns, eds. *Thinking the Present: Recent American Architecture*. New York: Princeton Architectural, 1990.

Henri, Adrian. *Total Art: Environments, Happenings, and Performance*. New York: Oxford University Press, 1974.

Hobbs, Robert. *Lee Krasner*. New York: Abbeville, 1993.

Hoffman, Katherine. *Explorations: The Visual Arts since 1945*. New York: Harper Collins, 1991.

Hopkins, David. *After Modern Art, 1945–2000*. New York: Oxford University Press, 2000.

Hughes, Robert. *The Shock of the New*. New York: Knopf, 1981.

Hunter, Sam. *An American Renaissance: Painting and Sculpture since 1940*. New York: Abbeville, 1986.

Jacobs, Jane. *The Death and Life of Great American Cities*. New York: Random House, 1961.

Jacobus, John. *Twentieth-Century Architecture: The Middle Years, 1940–1964*. New York: Praeger, 1966.

Jencks, Charles. *The Language of Post-Modern Architecture*. 6th ed. New York: Rizzoli, 1991.

———. *What Is Post-Modernism?* 3d ed. London: Academy Editions, 1989.

Johnson, Ellen H., ed. *American Artists on Art from 1940 to 1980*. Boulder, Colo.: Westview, 1982.

Joselit, David. *American Art since 1945*. New York: Thames & Hudson, 2003.

Kaprow, Allan. *Assemblage, Environments, and Happenings*. New York: Abrams, 1966.

Kirby, Michael. *Happenings*. New York: Dutton, 1966.

Kotz, Mary Lynn. *Rauschenberg: Art and Life*. New York: Abrams, 2004.

Kramer, Hilton. *The Age of the Avant-Garde: An Art Chronicle of 1956–1972*. New York: Farrar, Straus & Giroux, 1973.

Leja, Michael. *Reframing Abstract Expressionism: Subjectivity and Painting in the 1940s*. New Haven, Conn.: Yale University Press, 1993.

Lippard, Lucy R. *Mixed Blessings: New Art in a Multicultural America*. New York: Pantheon, 1990.

———. *Pop Art*. New York: Praeger, 1966.

———, ed. *From the Center: Feminist Essays on Women's Art*. New York: Dutton, 1976.

———. *Six Years: The Dematerialization of the Art Object from 1966 to 1972*. New York: Praeger, 1973.

Livingston, Jane, ed. *The Paintings of Joan Mitchell*. New York: Whitney Museum of American Art, 2002.

Lovejoy, Margot. *Postmodern Currents: Art and Artists in the Age of the Electronic Media*. Ann Arbor, Mich.: UMI Research Press, 1989.

Lucie-Smith, Edward. *Art Now*. Edison, N.J.: Wellfleet, 1989.

———. *Movements in Art since 1945*. New ed. New York: Thames & Hudson, 2001.

Mamiya, Christin J. *Pop Art and Consumer Culture: American Super Market*. Austin: University of Texas Press, 1992.

Marder, Tod A. *The Critical Edge: Controversy in Recent American Architecture*. New Brunswick, N.J.: Rutgers University Press, 1980.

———. *An International Survey of Recent Painting and Sculpture*. New York: Museum of Modern Art, 1984.

Mercurio, Gianni. *Lichtenstein: Meditations on Art*. Milan: Skira, 2010.

Meyer, Ursula. *Conceptual Art*. New York: Dutton, 1972.

Mitchell, William J. *The Reconfigured Eye: Visual Truth in the Post-Photographic Era*. Cambridge, Mass.: MIT Press, 1992.

Morris, Francis, ed. *Louise Bourgeois*. New York: Rizzoli, 2008.

Polcari, Stephen. *Abstract Expressionism and the Modern Experience*. Cambridge: Cambridge University Press, 1991.

Popper, Frank. *Origins and Development of Kinetic Art*. Translated by Stephen Bann. Greenwich, Conn.: New York Graphic Society, 1968.

Price, Jonathan. *Video Visions: A Medium Discovers Itself*. New York: New American Library, 1977.

Reichardt, Jasia, ed. *Cybernetics, Art, and Ideas*. Greenwich, Conn.: New York Graphics Society, 1971.

Robbins, Corinne. *The Pluralist Era: American Art, 1968–1981*. New York: Harper & Row, 1984.

Rorimer, Anne. *New Art in the 60s and 70s: Redefining Reality*. New York: Thames & Hudson, 2001.

Rosen, Randy, and Catherine C. Brawer, eds. *Making Their Mark: Women Artists Move into the Mainstream, 1970–1985*. New York: Abbeville, 1989.

Rosenberg, Harold. *The Tradition of the New*. New York: Horizon, 1959.

Rush, Michael. *New Media in Art*. 2d ed. New York: Thames & Hudson, 2005.

Russell, John, and Suzi Gablik. *Pop Art Redefined*. New York: Praeger, 1969.

Sandford, Mariellen R., ed. *Happenings and Other Acts*. New York: Routledge, 1995.

Sandler, Irving. *Art of the Postmodern Era*. New York: Harper Collins, 1996.

———. *The Triumph of American Painting: A History of Abstract Expressionism*. New York: Praeger, 1970.

Sayre, Henry M. *The Object of Performance: The American Avant-Garde since 1970*. Chicago: University of Chicago Press, 1989.

Schneider, Ira, and Beryl Korot. *Video Art: An Anthology*. New York: Harcourt Brace Jovanovich, 1976.

Shapiro, David, and Cecile Shapiro. *Abstract Expressionism: A Critical Record*. New York: Cambridge University Press, 1990.

Shiff, Richard. *Barnett Newman: A Catalogue Raisonné*. New Haven, Conn.: Yale University Press, 2004.

Sims, Lowery Stokes. *Wifredo Lam and the International Avant-Garde, 1923–1982*. Austin, Tex.: University of Texas Press, 2002.

Smagula, Howard. *Currents: Contemporary Directions in the Visual Arts*. 2d ed. Upper Saddle River, N.J.: Prentice Hall, 1989.

Smee, Sebastian. *Lucian Freud: Beholding the Animal*. Cologne: Taschen, 2009.

Sonfist, Alan, ed. *Art in the Landscape: A Critical Anthology of Environmental Art*. New York: Dutton, 1983.

Sontag, Susan. *On Photography*. New York: Farrar, Straus & Giroux, 1973.

Stiles, Kristine, and Peter Selz. *Theories and Documents of Contemporary Art: A Sourcebook of Artists' Writings*. Berkeley and Los Angeles: University of California Press, 1996.

Taylor, Brendon. *Contemporary Art: Art since 1970*. Upper Saddle River, N.J.: Prentice Hall, 2005.

Terraroli, Valerio, ed. *Art of the Twentieth Century, 1946–1968: The Birth of Contemporary Art*. Milan: Skira, 2007.

Tuchman, Maurice. *American Sculpture of the Sixties*. Los Angeles: Los Angeles County Museum of Art, 1967.

Varnedoe, Kirk. *Pictures of Nothing: Abstract Art since Pollock*. Princeton: Princeton University Press, 2006.

Venturi, Robert. *Complexity and Contradiction in Architecture*. New York: Museum of Modern Art, 1966.

Venturi, Robert, Denise Scott-Brown, and Steven Isehour. *Learning from Las Vegas*. Cambridge, Mass.: MIT Press, 1972.

Waldman, Diane. *Collage, Assemblage, and the Found Object*. New York: Abrams, 1992.

Wallis, Brian, ed. *Art after Modernism: Rethinking Representation*. New York: New Museum of Contemporary Art in association with David R. Godine, 1984.

Wheeler, Daniel. *Art since Mid-Century: 1945 to the Present*. Upper Saddle River, N.J.: Prentice Hall, 1991.

Wood, Paul. *Modernism in Dispute: Art since the Forties*. New Haven, Conn.: Yale University Press, 1993.

**Chapter 31: Contemporary Art Worldwide**

Buchhart, Dieter, et al., *Jean-Michel Basquiat*. Ostfildern: Hatje Cantz, 2010.

Butler, Cornelia H., and Lisa Gabrielle Mark. *WACK!: Art and the Feminist Revolution*. Cambridge, Mass.: MIT Press, 2007.

Celent, Germano. *Anselm Kiefer*. Milan: Skira, 2007.

Chilvers, Ian, and John Glaves-Smith. *Oxford Dictionary of Modern and Contemporary Art*. 2d ed. New York: Oxford University Press, 2009.

Cook, Peter. *New Spirit in Architecture*. New York: Rizzoli, 1990.

Cummings, P. *Dictionary of Contemporary American Artists*. 6th ed. New York: St. Martin's, 1994.

Deepwell, K., ed. *New Feminist Art*. Manchester: Manchester University Press, 1994.

Enwezor, Okwui, and Chika Okeke-Agulu. *Contemporary African Art since 1980*. Bologna: Damiani, 2009.

Ferguson, Russell, ed. *Discourses: Conversations in Postmodern Art and Culture*. Cambridge, Mass.: MIT Press, 1990.

Fineberg, Jonathan. *Art since 1940: Strategies of Being*. 2d ed. Upper Saddle River, N.J.: Prentice Hall, 2000.

Galassi, Peter. *Andreas Gursky.* New York: Museum of Modern Art, 2001.

Ghirardo, Diane. *Architecture after Modernism.* New York: Thames & Hudson, 1996.

Goldsworthy, Andy. *Andy Goldsworthy: A Collaboration with Nature.* New York: Abrams, 1990.

Heartney, Eleanor, Helaine Posner, Nancy Princenthal, and Sue Scott. *After the Revolution: Women Who Transformed Contemporary Art.* New York: Prestel, 2007.

Hertz, Richard, ed. *Theories of Contemporary Art.* 2d ed. Upper Saddle River, N.J.: Prentice Hall, 1993.

Hopkins, David. *After Modern Art, 1945–2000.* New York: Oxford University Press, 2000.

Jencks, Charles. *The New Paradigm in Architecture: The Language of Post-Modernism.* New Haven, Conn.: Yale University Press, 2002.

Jodidio, Philip. *100 Contemporary Architects.* Cologne: Taschen, 2008.

Kasfir, Sidney Littlefield. *Contemporary African Art.* New York: Thames & Hudson, 1999.

Kolossa, Alexandra. *Keith Haring 1958–1990: A Life for Art.* Cologne: Taschen, 2009.

Kotz, Mary Lunn. *Rauschenberg: Art and Life.* New York: Abrams, 2004.

Lippard, Lucy R. *Mixed Blessings: New Art in a Multicultural America.* New York: Pantheon, 1990.

Mullins, Charlotte. *Painting People: Figure Painting Today.* New York: Thames & Hudson, 2008.

Nesbitt, Judith, ed. *Chris Ofili.* London: Tate, 2010.

Norris, Christopher, and Andrew Benjamin. *What Is Deconstruction?* New York: St. Martin's, 1988.

Paul, Christiane. *Digital Art.* 2d ed. New York: Thames & Hudson, 2008.

Pauli, Lori, ed. *Manufactured Landscapes: The Photographs of Edward Burtynsky.* New Haven, Conn.: Yale University Press, 2003.

Perry, Gill, and Paul Wood. *Themes in Contemporary Art.* New Haven, Conn.: Yale University Press, 2004.

Raskin, David. *Donald Judd.* New Haven, Conn.: Yale University Press, 2010.

Risatti, Howard, ed. *Postmodern Perspectives: Issues in Contemporary Art.* Upper Saddle River, N.J.: Prentice Hall, 1990.

Sandler, Irving. *Art of the Postmodern Era.* New York: Harper Collins, 1996.

Smith, Terry. *What Is Contemporary Art?* Chicago: University of Chicago Press, 2009.

Sollins, Susan, ed. *Art: 21 (Art in the Twenty-first Century).* 5 vols. New York: Abrams, 2001–2009.

Stiles, Kristine, and Peter Selz. *Theories and Documents of Contemporary Art: A Sourcebook of Artists' Writings.* Berkeley and Los Angeles: University of California Press, 1996.

Taylor, Brendon. *Contemporary Art: Art since 1970.* Upper Saddle River, N.J.: Prentice Hall, 2005.

Terraroli, Valerio, ed. *Art of the Twentieth Century, 1969–1999: Neo-avant-gardes, Postmodern and Global Art.* Milan: Skira, 2009.

Wands, Bruce. *Art of the Digital Age.* New York: Thames & Hudson, 2007.

Warren, Lynne. *Jeff Koons.* New Haven, Conn.: Yale University Press, 2008.

Wines, James. *Green Architecture.* Cologne: Taschen, 2008.

### Asian Art, General

Brown, Rebecca M., and Deborah S. Hutton. *Asian Art (Blackwell Anthologies in Art History).* Malden, Mass.: Blackwell, 2006.

Clark, John. *Modern Asian Art.* Honolulu: University of Hawaii Press, 1998.

McArthur, Meher. *The Arts of Asia: Materials, Techniques, Styles.* New York: Thames & Hudson, 2005.

### Chapter 32: South and Southeast Asia, 1200 to 1980

Asher, Catherine B. *Architecture of Mughal India.* New York: Cambridge University Press, 1992.

Beach, Milo Cleveland. *Mughal and Rajput Painting.* Cambridge: Cambridge University Press, 1992.

Blurton, T. Richard. *Hindu Art.* Cambridge, Mass.: Harvard University Press, 1993.

Chaturachinda, Gwyneth, Sunanda Krishnamurty, and Pauline W. Tabtiang. *Dictionary of South and Southeast Asian Art.* Chiang Mai, Thailand: Silkworm Books, 2000.

Craven, Roy C. *Indian Art: A Concise History.* Rev. ed. London: Thames & Hudson, 1997.

Dallapiccola, Anna Libera, ed. *Vijayanagara: City and Empire.* 2 vols. Stuttgart: Steiner, 1985.

Dehejia, Vidya. *Indian Art.* London: Phaidon, 1997.

*Encyclopedia of Indian Temple Architecture.* 8 vols. New Delhi: American Institute of Indian Studies; Philadelphia: University of Pennsylvania Press, 1983–1996.

Girard-Geslan, Maud, ed. *Art of Southeast Asia.* New York: Abrams, 1998.

Harle, James C. *The Art and Architecture of the Indian Subcontinent.* 2d ed. New Haven, Conn.: Yale University Press, 1994.

Huntington, Susan L., and John C. Huntington. *The Art of Ancient India: Buddhist, Hindu, Jain.* New York: Weatherhill, 1985.

Lambah, Abha Narian, and Alka Patel, eds. *The Architecture of the Indian Sultanates.* Mumbai: Marg, 2006.

Michell, George. *Architecture and Art of Southern India: Vijayanagara and the Successor States, 1350–1750.* Cambridge: Cambridge University Press, 1995.

———. *Hindu Art and Architecture.* New York: Thames & Hudson, 2000.

———. *The Hindu Temple: An Introduction to Its Meaning and Forms.* Chicago: University of Chicago Press, 1988.

Mitter, Partha. *Indian Art.* New York: Oxford University Press, 2001.

Pal, Pratapaditya, ed. *Master Artists of the Imperial Mughal Court.* Mumbai: Marg, 1991.

Rawson, Phillip. *The Art of Southeast Asia.* New York: Thames & Hudson, 1990.

Schimmel, Annemarie. *The Empire of the Great Mughals: History, Art, and Culture.* London: Reaktion, 2006.

Stadtner, Donald M. *The Art of Burma: New Studies.* Mumbai: Marg, 1999.

Stevenson, John, and John Guy, eds. *Vietnamese Ceramics: A Separate Tradition.* Chicago: Art Media Resources, 1997.

Stierlin, Henri. *Hindu India from Khajuraho to the Temple City of Madurai.* Cologne: Taschen, 1998.

Stronge, Susan. *Painting for the Mughal Emperor: The Art of the Book, 1560–1660.* London: Victoria & Albert Museum, 2002.

Tingley, Nancy, ed. *Arts of Ancient Viet Nam: From River Plain to Open Sea.* Houston: Museum of Fine Arts, 2009.

Verna, Som Prakash. *Painting the Mughal Experience.* New York: Oxford University Press, 2005.

Welch, Stuart Cary. *Imperial Mughal Painting.* New York: Braziller, 1978.

———. *India: Art and Culture 1300–1900.* New York: Metropolitan Museum of Art, 1985.

### Chapter 33: China and Korea, 1279 to 1980

Andrews, Julia Frances, and Kuiyi Shen. *A Century in Crisis: Modernity and Tradition in the Art of Twentieth-Century China.* New York: Guggenheim Museum, 1998.

Barnhart, Richard M. *Painters of the Great Ming: The Imperial Court and the Zhe School.* Dallas: Dallas Museum of Art, 1993.

Cahill, James. *The Painter's Practice: How Artists Lived and Worked in Traditional China.* New York: Columbia University Press, 1994.

Clunas, Craig. *Art in China.* New York: Oxford University Press, 1997.

———. *Pictures and Visuality in Early Modern China.* Princeton: Princeton University Press, 1997.

Fahr-Becker, Gabriele, ed. *The Art of East Asia.* Cologne: Könemann, 1999.

Fisher, Robert E. *Buddhist Art and Architecture.* New York: Thames & Hudson, 1993.

Fong, Wen C., and James C. Y. Watt. *Preserving the Past: Treasures from the National Palace Museum, Taipei.* New York: Metropolitan Museum of Art, 1996.

Hearn, Maxwell K. *How to Read Chinese Paintings.* New York: Metropolitan Museum of Art, 2008.

Howard, Angela Falco, Li Song, Wu Hong, and Yang Hong. *Chinese Sculpture.* New Haven, Conn.: Yale University Press, 2006.

Laing, Ellen Johnston. *The Winking Owl: Art in the People's Republic of China.* Berkeley: University of California Press, 1989.

Li, Chu-tsing, ed. *Artists and Patrons: Some Social and Economic Aspects of Chinese Painting.* Lawrence, Kans.: Kress Department of Art History in cooperation with Indiana University Press, 1989.

Li, He, and Michael Knight. *Power and Glory: Court Arts of China's Ming Dynasty.* San Francisco: Asian Art Museum, 2008.

Marks, Andreas. *Japanese Woodblock Prints: Artists, Publishers, and Masterworks: 1680–1900.* North Clarendon, Vt.: Tuttle, 2010.

Nakata, Yujiro, ed. *Chinese Calligraphy.* New York: Weatherhill, 1983.

Portal, Jane. *Korea: Art and Archaeology.* New York: Thames & Hudson, 2000.

Rawson, Jessica, ed. *The British Museum Book of Chinese Art.* New York: Thames & Hudson, 1992.

Sickman, Laurence, and Alexander C. Soper. *The Art and Architecture of China.* 3d ed. New Haven, Conn.: Yale University Press, 1992.

Silbergeld, Jerome. *Chinese Painting Style: Media, Methods, and Principles of Form.* Seattle: University of Washington Press, 1982.

Steinhardt, Nancy S., ed. *Chinese Architecture.* New Haven, Conn.: Yale University Press, 2002.

Sullivan, Michael. *Art and Artists of Twentieth-Century China.* Berkeley: University of California Press, 1996.

———. *The Arts of China.* 5th ed. Berkeley: University of California Press, 2009.

Thorp, Robert L. *Son of Heaven: Imperial Arts of China.* Seattle: Son of Heaven, 1988.

Thorp, Robert L., and Richard Ellis Vinograd. *Chinese Art and Culture.* New York: Abrams, 2001.

Vainker, S. J. *Chinese Pottery and Porcelain: From Prehistory to the Present.* London: Braziller, 1991.

Watson, William. *The Arts of China 900–1260.* New Haven, Conn.: Yale University Press, 2000.

———. *The Arts of China after 1260.* New Haven, Conn.: Yale University Press, 2007.

Watt, James C. Y., ed. *The World of Khubiliai Khan: Chinese Art in the Yuan Dynasty.* New York: Metropolitan Museum of Art, 2010.

Weidner, Marsha, ed. *Flowering in the Shadows: Women in the History of Chinese and Japanese Painting.* Honolulu: University of Hawaii Press, 1990.

———. *Views from Jade Terrace: Chinese Women Artists 1300–1912.* Indianapolis: Indianapolis Museum of Art, 1988.

Xin, Yang, Nie Chongzheng, Lang Shaojun, Richard M. Barnhart, James Cahill, and Wu Hung. *Three Thousand Years of Chinese Painting*. New Haven, Conn.: Yale University Press, 1997.

Zhiyan, Li, Virginia L. Bower, and He Li. *Chinese Ceramics: From the Paleolithic Period through the Qing Dyansty*. New Haven, Conn.: Yale University Press, 2010.

Zhongshi, Ouyang, Wen C. Fong, et al. *Chinese Calligraphy*. New Haven, Conn.: Yale University Press, 2008.

### Chapter 34: Japan, 1336 to 1980

Addiss, Stephen. *The Art of Zen*. New York: Abrams, 1989.

Baekeland, Frederick. *Imperial Japan: The Art of the Meiji Era (1868–1912)*. Ithaca, N.Y.: Herbert F. Johnson Museum of Art, 1980.

Brown, Kendall. *The Politics of Reclusion: Painting and Power in Muromachi Japan*. Honolulu: University of Hawaii Press, 1997.

Cahill, James. *Scholar Painters of Japan*. New York: Asia Society, 1972.

Calza, Gian Carlo. *Ukiyo-e*. New York: Phaidon, 2005.

Coaldrake, William H. *Architecture and Authority in Japan*. London: Routledge, 1996.

Fontein, Jan, and Money L. Hickman. *Zen Painting and Calligraphy*. Greenwich, Conn.: New York Graphic Society, 1970.

Guth, Christine. *Art of Edo Japan: The Artist and the City, 1615–1868*. New York: Abrams, 1996.

Hickman, Money L., John T. Carpenter, Bruce A. Coats, Christine Guth, Andrew J. Pekarik, John M. Rosenfield, and Nicole C. Rousmaniere. *Japan's Golden Age: Momoyama*. New Haven, Conn.: Yale University Press, 1996.

Kawakita, Michiaki. *Modern Currents in Japanese Art*. Translated by Charles E. Terry. New York: Weatherhill, 1974.

Kidder, J. Edward, Jr. *The Art of Japan*. New York: Park Lane, 1985.

Lane, Richard. *Images from the Floating World: The Japanese Print*. New York: Dorset, 1978.

Mason, Penelope. *History of Japanese Art*. 2d ed. New York: Abrams, 2004.

Meech, Julia, and Jane Oliver. *Designed for Pleasure: The World of Edo Japan in Prints and Drawings, 1680–1860*. Seattle: University of Washington Press, 2008.

Munroe, Alexandra. *Japanese Art after 1945: Scream against the Sky*. New York: Abrams, 1994.

Nishi, Kazuo, and Kazuo Hozumi. *What Is Japanese Architecture?* Translated by H. Mack Horton. New York: Kodansha International, 1985.

Ohki, Sadak. *Tea Culture of Japan*. New Haven, Conn.: Yale University Press, 2009.

Sanford, James H., William R. LaFleur, and Masatoshi Nagatomi. *Flowing Traces: Buddhism in the Literary and Visual Arts of Japan*. Princeton, N.J.: Princeton University Press, 1992.

Shimizu, Yoshiaki, ed. *Japan: The Shaping of Daimyo Culture, 1185–1868*. Washington, D.C.: National Gallery of Art, 1988.

Singer, Robert T. *Edo: Art in Japan 1615–1868*. Washington, D.C.: National Gallery of Art, 1998.

Stanley-Baker, Joan. *Japanese Art*. Rev. ed. New York: Thames & Hudson, 2000.

Stewart, David B. *The Making of a Modern Japanese Architecture, 1868 to the Present*. New York: Kodansha International, 1988.

Tiampo, Ming. *Gutai: Decentering Modernism*. Chicago: University of Chicago Press, 2011.

### Chapter 35: Native Arts of the Americas, 1300 to 1980

Bawden, Garth. *Moche*. Oxford: Blackwell, 1999.

Berlo, Janet Catherine, ed. *Plains Indian Drawings 1865–1935*. New York: Abrams, 1996.

Berlo, Janet Catherine, and Ruth B. Phillips. *Native North American Art*. New York: Oxford University Press, 1998.

Boone, Elizabeth. *The Aztec World*. Washington, D.C.: Smithsonian Institution Press, 1994.

Bruhns, Karen O. *Ancient South America*. New York: Cambridge University Press, 1994.

Burger, Richard L., and Lucy C. Salaza, eds. *Machu Picchu: Unveiling the Mystery of the Incas*. New Haven, Conn.: Yale University Press, 2004.

Coe, Michael D. *The Maya*. 7th ed. New York: Thames & Hudson, 2005.

———. *Mexico: From the Olmecs to the Aztecs*. 5th ed. New York: Thames & Hudson, 2002.

D'Altroy, Terence N. *The Incas*. New ed. Oxford: Blackwell, 2003.

Davies, Nigel. *The Ancient Kingdoms of Peru*. New York: Penguin, 1997.

Feest, Christian F. *Native Arts of North America*. 2d ed. New York: Thames & Hudson, 1992.

Fienup-Riordan, Ann. *The Living Tradition of Yup'ik Masks*. Seattle: University of Washington Press, 1996.

Fitzhugh, William W., and Aron Crowell, eds. *Crossroads of Continents: Cultures of Siberia and Alaska*. Washington, D.C.: Smithsonian Institution Press, 1988.

Gasparini, Graziano, and Luise Margolies. *Inca Architecture*. Bloomington: Indiana University Press, 1980.

Hill, Tom, and Richard W. Hill, Sr., eds. *Creation's Journey: Native American Identity and Belief*. Washington, D.C.: Smithsonian Institution Press, 1994.

Jonaitis, Aldona. *Art of the Northwest Coast*. Seattle: University of Washington Press, 2006.

Kubler, George. *The Art and Architecture of Ancient America: The Mexican, Maya, and Andean Peoples*. 3d ed. New Haven, Conn.: Yale University Press, 1992.

Malpass, Michael A. *Daily Life in the Inca Empire*. Westport, Conn.: Greenwood, 1996.

Mathews, Zena, and Aldona Jonaitis, eds. *Native North American Art History*. Palo Alto, Calif.: Peek, 1982.

Matos, Eduardo M. *The Great Temple of the Aztecs: Treasures of Tenochtitlan*. New York: Thames & Hudson, 1988.

Maurer, Evan M. *Visions of the People: A Pictorial History of Plains Indian Life*. Seattle: University of Washington Press, 1992.

McEwan, Gordon F. *The Incas: New Perspectives*. Santa Barbara, Calif.: ABC-CLIO, 2006.

Miller, Mary Ellen. *The Art of Mesoamerica, from Olmec to Aztec*. 4th ed. New York: Thames & Hudson, 2006.

Miller, Mary, and Karl Taube. *An Illustrated Dictionary of the Gods and Symbols of Ancient Mexico and the Maya*. New York: Thames & Hudson, 1993.

Minelli, Laura Laurencich. *The Inca World*. Norman: University of Oklahoma Press, 2000.

Morris, Craig, and Adriana von Hagen. *The Incas*. New York: Thames & Hudson, 2011.

———. *The Inka Empire and Its Andean Origins*. New York: Abbeville, 1993.

Moseley, Michael E. *The Incas and Their Ancestors: The Archaeology of Peru*. Rev. ed. New York: Thames & Hudson, 2001.

Nabokov, Peter, and Robert Easton. *Native American Architecture*. New York: Oxford University Press, 1989.

Pasztory, Esther. *Aztec Art*. New York: Abrams, 1983.

———. *Pre-Columbian Art*. New York: Cambridge University Press, 1998.

Penney, David W. *North American Indian Art*. New York: Thames & Hudson, 2004.

Phillips, Ruth B. *Trading Identities: The Souvenir in Native North American Art*. Seattle: University of Washington Press, 1998.

Samuel, Cheryl. *The Chilkat Dancing Blanket*. Norman: University of Oklahoma Press, 1982.

Schaafsma, Polly, ed. *Kachinas in the Pueblo World*. Albuquerque: University of New Mexico Press, 1994.

Silverman, Helaine. *The Nasca*. Oxford: Blackwell, 2002.

———, ed. *Andean Archaeology*. Oxford: Blackwell, 2004.

Smith, Michael Ernest. *The Aztecs*. 2d ed. Oxford: Blackwell, 2003.

Stewart, Hilary. *Looking at Totem Poles*. Seattle: University of Washington Press, 1993.

Townsend, Richard F. *The Aztecs*. 2d ed. New York: Thames & Hudson, 2000.

Von Hagen, Adriana, and Craig Morris. *The Cities of the Ancient Andes*. New York: Thames & Hudson, 1998.

Wardwell, Allen. *Tangible Visions: Northwest Coast Indian Shamanism and Its Art*. New York: Monacelli, 1996.

Washburn, Dorothy. *Living in Balance: The Universe of the Hopi, Zuni, Navajo, and Apache*. Philadelphia: University Museum, 1995.

Weaver, Muriel Porter. *The Aztecs, Mayas, and Their Predecessors*. 3d ed. San Diego: Academic, 1993.

Wright, Robin K. *Northern Haida Master Carvers*. Seattle: University of Washington Press, 2001.

Wyman, Leland C. *Southwest Indian Drypainting*. Albuquerque: University of New Mexico Press, 1983.

### Chapter 36: Oceania before 1980

Caruana, Wally. *Aboriginal Art*. 2d ed. New York: Thames & Hudson, 2003.

Cox, J. Halley, and William H. Davenport. *Hawaiian Sculpture*. Rev. ed. Honolulu: University of Hawaii Press, 1988.

D'Alleva, Anne. *Arts of the Pacific Islands*. New York: Abrams, 1998.

Ellis, Juniper. *Tattooing the World. Pacific Designs in Print & Skin*. New York: Columbia University Press, 2008.

Feldman, Jerome, and Donald H. Rubinstein. *The Art of Micronesia*. Honolulu: University of Hawaii Art Gallery, 1986.

Greub, Suzanne, ed. *Authority and Ornament: Art of the Sepik River, Papua New Guinea*. Basel: Tribal Art Centre, 1985.

Hanson, Allan, and Louise Hanson, eds. *Art and Identity in Oceania*. Honolulu: University of Hawaii Press, 1990.

Kaeppler, Adrienne L., Christian Kaufmann, and Douglas Newton. *Oceanic Art*. New York: Abrams, 1997.

Kjellgren, Eric. *Oceania: Art of the Pacific Islands in the Metropolitan Museum of Art*. New York: Metropolitan Museum of Art, 2007.

Kjellgren, Eric, and Carol Ivory. *Adorning the World: Art of the Marquesas Islands*. New York: Metropolitan Museum of Art, 2005.

Kooijman, Simon. *Tapa in Polynesia*. Honolulu: Bishop Museum Press, 1972.

Lilley, Ian, ed. *Archaeology of Oceania: Australia and the Pacific Islands*. Malden, Mass: Blackwell, 2006.

Mead, Sidney Moko, ed. *Te Maori: Maori Art from New Zealand Collections*. New York: Abrams in association with the American Federation of Arts, 1984.

Morphy, Howard. *Aboriginal Art.* London: Phaidon, 1998.

Rainbird, Paul. *The Archaeology of Micronesia.* New York: Cambridge University Press, 2004.

Sayers, Andrew. *Australian Art.* New York: Oxford University Press, 2001.

Schneebaum, Tobias. *Embodied Spirits: Ritual Carvings of the Asmat.* Salem, Mass.: Peabody Museum of Salem, 1990.

Smidt, Dirk, ed. *Asmat Art: Woodcarvings of Southwest New Guinea.* New York: Braziller in association with Rijksmuseum voor Volkenkunde, Leiden, 1993.

Starzecka, Dorota, ed. *Maori Art and Culture.* Chicago: Art Media Resources, 1996.

Sutton, Peter, ed. *Dreamings: The Art of Aboriginal Australia.* New York: Braziller in association with the Asia Society Galleries, 1988.

Thomas, Nicholas. *Oceanic Art.* London: Thames & Hudson, 1995.

### Chapter 37: Africa, 1800 to 1980

Abiodun, Roland, Henry J. Drewal, and John Pemberton III, eds. *The Yoruba Artist: New Theoretical Perspectives on African Arts.* Washington, D.C.: Smithsonian Institution Press, 1994.

Bassani, Ezio. *Arts of Africa: 7,000 Years of African Art.* Milan: Skira, 2005.

Binkley, David A., and Patricia Darish. *Kuba.* Milan: 5 Continents, 2009.

Blier, Suzanne P. *The Royal Arts of Africa.* New York: Abrams, 1998.

Boyer, Alain-Michel. *Baule.* Milan: 5 Continents, 2007.

Cole, Herbert M. *Icons: Ideals and Power in the Art of Africa.* Washington, D.C.: National Museum of African Art, Smithsonian Institution, 1989.

———, ed. *I Am Not Myself: The Art of African Masquerade.* Los Angeles: UCLA Fowler Museum of Cultural History, 1985.

Cole, Herbert M., and Chike C. Aniakor. *Igbo Art: Community and Cosmos.* Los Angeles: UCLA Fowler Museum of Cultural History, 1984.

Fraser, Douglas F., and Herbert M. Cole, eds. *African Art and Leadership.* Madison: University of Wisconsin Press, 1972.

Geary, Christraud M. *Bamum.* Milan: 5 Continents, 2011.

———. *Things of the Palace: A Catalogue of the Bamum Palace Museum in Foumban (Cameroon).* Weisbaden: Franz Steiner Verlag, 1983.

Glaze, Anita J. *Art and Death in a Senufo Village.* Bloomington: Indiana University Press, 1981.

Kasfir, Sidney L. *Contemporary African Art.* London: Thames & Hudson, 1999.

———. *West African Masks and Cultural Systems.* Tervuren: Musée Royal de l'Afrique Centrale, 1988.

Magnin, Andre, with Jacques Soulillou. *Contemporary Art of Africa.* New York: Abrams, 1996.

Nooter, Mary H. *Secrecy: African Art That Conceals and Reveals.* New York: Museum for African Art, 1993.

Oguibe, Olu, and Okwui Enwezor, eds. *Reading the Contemporary: African Art from Theory to the Marketplace.* London: Institute of International Visual Arts, 1999.

Perani, Judith, and Fred T. Smith. *The Visual Arts of Africa: Gender, Power, and Life Cycle Rituals.* Upper Saddle River, N.J.: Prentice Hall, 1998.

Perrois, Louis. *Fang.* Milan: 5 Continents, 2008.

Phillips, Ruth B. *Representing Women: Sande Masquerades of the Mende of Sierra Leone.* Los Angeles: UCLA Fowler Museum of Cultural History, 1995.

Plankensteiner, Barbara. *Benin.* Milan: 5 Continents, 2010.

Sieber, Roy, and Roslyn A. Walker. *African Art in the Cycle of Life.* Washington, D.C.: Smithsonian Institution Press, 1987.

Stepan, Peter. *Spirits Speak: A Celebration of African Masks.* Munich: Prestel, 2005.

Thompson, Robert F., and Joseph Cornet. *The Four Moments of the Sun: Kongo Art in Two Worlds.* Washington, D.C.: National Gallery of Art, 1981.

Vinnicombe, Patricia. *People of the Eland: Rock Paintings of the Drakensberg Bushmen as a Reflection of Their Life and Thought.* Pietermaritzburg: University of Natal Press, 1976.

Visonà, Monica B., ed. *A History of Art in Africa.* 2d ed. Englewood Cliffs, N.J.: Prentice Hall, 2007.

Vogel, Susan M. *Baule: African Art, Western Eyes.* New Haven, Conn.: Yale University Press, 1997.

———, ed. *Africa Explores: Twentieth-Century African Art.* New York: Te Neues, 1990.

Walker, Roslyn A. *Olowe of Ise: A Yoruba Sculptor to Kings.* Washington, D.C.: National Museum of African Art, 1998.

Wastiau, Boris. *Chokwe.* Milan: 5 Continents, 2008.

# CREDITS

**1124   Credits**

**16-7:** Far Eastern Seminar Collection, Princeton University Art Museum.; **16-8:** The Nelson-Atkins Museum of Art, Kansas City, Missouri. Purchase, Nelson Trust, 33-521. Photo: Robert Newcombe.; **16-9:** The Nelson-Atkins Museum of Art, Kansas City, Missouri. Purchase, Nelson Trust; **16-11:** © Asian Art Museum of San Francisco, The Avery Brundage Collectio; **16-12:** © The Trustees of the British Museum/Art Resource, NY; **16-13:** © Réunion des Musées Nationaux/Art Resource, NY; **16-13A:** © Wolfgang Kaehler/Corbis; **16-13B:** Photograph @ 2011 Museum of Fine Arts, Boston. 22.47; **16-14:** © TAO Images Limited/PhotoLibrary; **16-14A:** © Trustees of the British Museum; **16-15:** Cultural Relics Publishing House, Beijing.; **16-16:** Photograph © 2011 Museum of Fine Arts, Boston; **16-17:** © Inmagine; **16-18:** © Victoria & Albert Museum, London/Art Resource, NY; **16-19:** The Art Archive/National Palace Museum Taiwan/Picture Desk; **16-20:** Cultural Relics Publishing House, Beijing.; **16-21:** Asian Art Museum of San Francisco, The Avery Brundage Collection; **16-21A:** Nelson-Atkins Museum of Art; **16-22a:** © Bruno Barbier/PhotoLibrary; **16-23:** Collection of the National Palace Museum; **16-23A:** Xia Gui, Chinese, act. 1180-1224. Also known as: Hsia Kuei, Chinese, act. 1180-1224. Twelve Views of Landscape (Shan-shui shih-erh-ching), Southern Song Dynasty (1127-1279). Handscroll, ink on silk. 11 inches x 7 feet 6 3/4 inches (27.94 x 230.51 cm). Purchase: William Rockhill Nelson Trust, 32-159/2; **16-24:** Photograph © 2011 Museum of Fine Arts, Boston; **16-25:** Toyko National Museum. Image ©TNM Image Archives. Source: http://TnmArchives.jp; **16-26:** © DeA Picture Library/Art Resource, NY; **16-27:** National Museum of Korea; **16-28:** © Archivo Iconografico, S.A./Corbis; **16-29:** © Philadelphia Museum of Art/Corbis; **UNF 16-2:** © Chu Yong/PhotoLibrary; **UNF 16-3:** © Réunion des Musées Nationaux/Art Resource, NY; **UNF 16-4:** Photograph © 2011 Museum of Fine Arts, Boston; **UNF 16-5:** © Bruno Barbier/PhotoLibrary; **UNF 16-1:** Asian Art Museum of San Francisco, The Avery Brundage Collection.

**Chapter 17—Opener:** © Fotosearch/Photolibrary; **(detail 1):** © Robert Harding Picture Library/SuperStock; **(detail 2):** Iberfoto/The Image Works; **(detail 3):** Iberfoto/The Image Works; **(detail 4):** Horyuji, Nara. Photo: Benrido; **timeline:** Iberfoto/The Image Works; **17-2:** Toyko National Museum. Image ©TNM Image Archives.; **17-3:** Toyko National Museum. Image ©TNM Image Archives.; **17-4:** Georg Gerster/Photo Researchers, Inc.; **17-5:** Toyko National Museum. Image ©TNM Image Archives.; **17-6:** Jingu-Shicho, Mie; **17-7:** Iberfoto/The Image Works; **17-8:** Yakushiji Temple, Nara.; **17-9:** Iberfoto/The Image Works; **17-10:** Horyuji, Nara. Photo:Benrido; **17-11:** © Sakamoto Photo Research Laboratory/Corbis; **17-12:** Kyoogokokuji (Toji), Kyoto; **17-13:** © All Creation/PhotoLibrary; **17-13A:** © Francesco Venturi/Corbis; **17-13B:** Freer Gallery of Art, Smithsonian Institution, Washington, D.C.; **17-14:** The Gotoh Art Museum, Tokyo.; **17-15:** Chogosonshiji Temple, Nara, Japan; **17-16:** Todaiji, Nara; **17-17:** Asanuma Photo Studio Co.,Ltd, with permission from the Rokuharamitsuji-Temple, Kyoto; **17-17A:** Todaiji Temple; **17-18:** Photograph @ 2011 Museum of Fine Arts, Boston; **17-19:** Zenrin-ji Temple; **UNF 17-01:** Toyko National Museum. Image ©TNM Image Archives.; **UNF 17-2:** Georg Gerster/Photo Researchers, Inc.; **UNF 17-3:** Iberfoto/The Image Works; **UNF 17-4:** The Gotoh Art Museum, Tokyo.; **UNF 17-5:** Todaiji, Nara.

**Chapter 18—Opener:** © Yann Arthus-Bertrand/Corbis; **(detail 1):** © Yann Arthus-Bertrand/Corbis; **(detail 2):** © Yann Arthus-Bertrand/Corbis; **(detail 3):** © DeA Picture Library/Art Resource, NY; **(detail 4):** © Scala/Art Resource, NY; **timeline:** © Yann Arthus-Bertrand/Corbis; **18-2:** © JTB Photo/PhotoLibrary; **18-3:** © Erich Lessing/Art Resource, NY; **18-4:** © Museum Associates/LACMA/Art Resource, NY; **18-5:** © Georg Gerster/Photo Researchers, Inc.; **18-6:** © Gianni Dagli Orti/Corbis; **18-7:** © Richard Maschmeyer/age fotostock; **18-7A:** Image © The Cleveland Museum of Art (1963.252); **18-8:** Sean Sprague/The Image Works; **18-9:** © Stuart Westmorland/PhotoLibrary; **18-10:** © Yoshio Tomii Photo Studio/PhotoLibrary; **18-10A:** © Mel Longhurst/PhotoLibrary; **18-11:** akg-images/François Guénet; **18-12:** 207 Peabody Museum of Archaeology and Ethnology , Harvard University; **18-13:** © Dumbarton Oaks Pre-Columbian Collection, Washington, D.C.; **18-14:** The British Museum/HIP/The Image Works; **18-15:** © Danny Lehman/Corbis; **18-16:** © Yann Arthus-Bertrand/Corbis; **18-17:** © Scala/Art Resource, NY; **18-18:** © DeA Picture Library/Art Resource, NY; **18-19:** © Jonathan Blair/Corbis; **18-20:** Image copyright © The Metropolitan Museum of Art; **18-21:** © Bildarchiv Steffens Henri Stierlin/The Bridgeman Art Library; **18-22:** Photograph @ 2011 Museum of Fine Arts, Boston; **18-23:** Photography © The Art Institute of Chicago; **18-24:** © SGM SGM/PhotoLibrary; **18-25:** © Nathan Benn/Corbis; **18-26:** Copyright © 2011 by Robert Frerck and Odyssey Productions, Inc.; **18-27:** © Hubert Stadler/Corbis; **18-28:** © National Museum of Archaeology, Anthropology, and History of Peru; **18-29:** © Werner Forman/Corbis; **18-30:** Ohio Historical Society; **18-30A:** © Michael S. Lewis/Encyclopedia/Corbis; **18-31:** © Tony Linck/SuperStock; **18-32:** © Werner Forman/Art Resource, NY; **18-33:** Photography © The Art Institute of Chicago; **18-33A:** © Richard A. Cooke/Encyclopedia/Corbis; **18-34:** © Mark Newman/PhotoLibrary; **UNF 18-01:** © JTB Photo/PhotoLibrary; **UNF 18-2:** © Yoshio Tomii Photo Studio/PhotoLibrary; **UNF 18-3:** SGM SGM/PhotoLibrary; **UNF 18-4:** © National Museum of Archaeology, Anthropology, and History of Peru; **UNF 18-5:** © Mark Newman/PhotoLibrary.

**Chapter 19—Opener:** © The Trustees of the British Museum/Art Resource, NY; **timeline:** © The Trustees of the British Museum/Art Resource, NY; **19-2:** Jean-Dominique Lajoux; **Map 19-1:** © Cengage Learning; **19-3:** Photograph ©1980 Dirk Bakker; **19-4:** Artwork in the Social History Collection ofthe Izlko Museums. Image courtesy of Izlko Museums; **19-4A:** © Dirk Bakker; **19-5:** Photograph ©1980 Dirk Bakker; **19-6:** Photograph ©1980 Dirk Bakker; **19-6A:** Ancient Art and Architecture Collection Ltd./The Bridgeman Art Library International; **19-7:** © Scala/Art Resource, NY; **19-8:** Photograph by Franko Khoury, National Museum of African Art, Smithsonian Institution, Museum purchase, 86-12-1; **19-9:** © Yann Arthus-Bertrand/Corbis; **19-10:** © Gavin Hellier/Robert Harding World Imagery/Getty Images; **19-11:** © Vanderhurst/Robert Harding World Imagery/Getty Images; **19-12:** © Colin Hoskins/Alamy; **19-13:** Image copyright © The Metropolitan Museum of Art/Art Resource, NY; **19-13A:** © Werner Forman/Art Resource, NY; **19-14:** Museo Nazionale Preistorico e Etnografico Luigi Pigorini, Rome.;

**UNF 19-01:** Jean-Dominique Lajoux; **UNF 19-2:** Photograph ©1980 Dirk Bakker; **UNF 19-3:** Photograph ©1980 Dirk Bakker; **UNF 19-4:** Yann Arthus-Bertrand/Corbis; **UNF 19-5:** © The Trustees of the British Museum/Art Resource, NY.

**Chapter 20—Opener:** Image copyright © The Metropolitan Museum of Art/Art Resource, NY; **Map 20-1:** © Cengage Learning; **timeline:** Image copyright © The Metropolitan Museum of Art/Art Resource, NY; **timeline:** Image copyright © The Metropolitan Museum of Art/Art Resource, NY; **20-2:** © Erich Lessing/Art Resource, NY; **20-2A:** © Jonathan Poore/Cengage Learning; **20-3a:** © Erich Lessing/Art Resource, NY; **20-3b:** © Erich Lessing/Art Resource, NY; **20-4:** © Scala/Art Resource, NY; **20-5A:** Bildarchiv Preussischer Kulturbesitz/Art Resource, NY; **20-5:** © Erich Lessing/Art Resource, NY; **20-6:** © Erich Lessing/Art Resource, NY; **20-7:** Copyright © National Gallery, London; **20-8:** © Erich Lessing/Art Resource, NY; **20-8A:** © Jonathan Poore/Cengage Learning; **20-9:** Photograph © 208 Museum of Fine Arts, Boston; **20-9A:** Copyright © 1999 Board of Trustees, National Gallery of Art, Washington, D.C.; **20-10:** Image copyright © The Metropolitan Museum of Art/Art Resource, NY; **20-11A_a** © Giraudon/Art Resource, NY; **20-11:** The Art Archive/St Peters Church Louvain/Picture Desk; **20-11A_b** © Scala/Art Resource, NY.; **20-12:** © Scala/Art Resource, NY; **20-13:** © Erich Lessing/Art Resource, NY; **20-14:** © Erich Lessing/Art Resource, NY; **20-14A:** Image copyright © The Metropolitan Museum of Art/Art Resource, NY; **20-14B:** Image copyright © The Metropolitan Museum of Art/Art Resource, NY; **20-15:** © Réunion des Musées Nationaux/Art Resource, NY; **20-16:** © Réunion des Musées Nationaux/Art Resource, NY; **20-16A:** The Art Archive/Osterreichisches National Bibliothek Vienna/Eileen Tweedy/Picture Desk; **20-17a:** © Bildarchiv Preussischer Kulturbesitz/Art Resource, NY; **20-17b:** © Scala/Art Resource, NY; **20-18:** Musee d'Art et d'Histoire, Geneva; **20-18A:** Photo Credit: © Erich Lessing/Art Resource, NY; **20-19:** © Erich Lessing/Art Resource, NY; **20-20A:** John Rylands University Library, University of Manchester, Manchester.; **20-20:** © Erich Lessing/Art Resource, NY; **20-21:** © Historical Picture Archive/Corbis; **20-22:** © Scala/Art Resource, NY; **UNF 20-01:** © Erich Lessing/Art Resource, NY; **UNF 20-2:** Image copyright © The Metropolitan Museum of Art/Art Resource, NY; **UNF 20-3:** © Erich Lessing/Art Resource, NY; **UNF 20-4:** © Réunion des Musées Nationaux/Art Resource, NY; **UNF 20-5:** Historical Picture Archive/CORBIS.

**Chapter 21—Opener:** © Scala/Art Resource, NY; **timeline:** © Scala/Art Resource, NY; **Map 21-1:** © Cengage Learning; **21-2:** © Erich Lessing/Art Resource, NY; **21-3:** © Erich Lessing/Art Resource, NY; **21-4, 21-5, 21-6, 21-7, 21-8:** © Jonathan Poore/Cengage Learning; **21-9:** © Scala/Art Resource, NY; **21-10:** © Jonathan Poore/Cengage Learning; **21-12:** © Scala/Art Resource, NY; **21-12A:** akg-images/Rabatti - Domingie; **21-13:** © Scala/Art Resource, NY; **21-14:** © Scala/Art Resource, NY; **21-15:** © Jonathan Poore/Cengage Learning; **21-16:** Elio Ciol/Corbis; **21-17:** © 2010 Fred Kleiner; **21-18:** © Erich Lessing/Art Resource, NY; **21-19:** © Scala/Art Resource, NY; **21-20:** Canali Photobank, Italy; **21-21:** © Erich Lessing/Art Resource, NY; **21-22:** Canali Photobank, Italy; **21-23:** © Scala/Art Resource, NY; **21-24:** Canali Photobank, Italy; **21-25:** © Scala/Art Resource, NY; **21-25A:** © Nicolo Orsi Battaglini/Art Resource, NY; **21-26:** © Scala/Art Resource, NY; **21-27:** © The Bridgeman Art Library; **21-28:** © National Gallery, London/Art Resource, NY; **21-29:** Summerfield Press Ltd.; **21-29A:** akg-images/Rabatti - Domingie; **21-30:** Image copyright © The Metropolitan Museum of Art/Art Resource, NY; **21-30A, 21-31:** © Jonathan Poore/Cengage Learning; **21-32:** © Alinari/Art Resource, NY; **21-32A:** © The Bridgeman Art Library; **21-33:** © Cengage Learning; **21-35:** © Cengage Learning; **21-34, 21-36, 21-36A, 21-37, 21-39, 21-40:** © Jonathan Poore/Cengage Learning; **21-37A:** © 2010 Fred Kleiner; **21-41:** © Scala/Art Resource, Inc.; **21-41A:** © Scala/Art Resource, NY; **21-42:** © Scala/Art Resource, NY; **21-43A:** © Scala/Art Resource, NY; **21-43:** © Scala/Ministero per i Beni e le Attività culturali/Art Resource, NY; **21-44:** © Scala/Art Resource, NY; **21-45:** © Alinari/Art Resource, NY; **21-46:** © Cengage Learning; **21-47:** Canali Photobank, Italy; **21-48:** © Scala/Art Resource, NY; **21-49:** © Scala/Art Resource, NY; **21-49A:** © Alinari/The Bridgeman Art Library; **21-50:** © Erich Lessing/Art Resource, NY; **UNF 21-01:** © Scala/Art Resource, NY; **UNF 21-2:** © Erich Lessing/Art Resource, NY; **UNF 21-3:** © Jonathan Poore/Cengage Learning; **UNF 21-4:** © Scala/Ministero per i Beni e le Attività culturali/Art Resource, NY; **UNF 21-5:** © Alinari/Art Resource, NY.

**Chapter 22—Opener:** Canali Photobank; **(detail 1):** Photo Vatican Museums; **(detail 2):** Bracchietti-Zigrosi/Vatican Museums; **(detail 3):** Vatican Museums and Galleries, Vatican City, Italy/The Bridgeman Art Library International; **(detail 4):** akg-images/Electa; **timeline:** akg-images/Electa; **22-2:** © Erich Lessing/Art Resource, NY; **22-3:** The Art Archive/National Gallery London/Eileen Tweedy/Picture Desk; **22-4:** © Alinari/Art Resource, NY; **22-3A:** © Scala/Art Resource, NY; **22-5:** © Réunion des Musées Nationaux/Art Resource, NY; **22-6:** Collection @ 2011 Her Majesty Queen Elizabeth II; **22-6A:** Bibliothèque de l'Institut de France/© Réunion des Musées Nationaux/Art Resource, NY; **22-7:** © Erich Lessing/Art Resource, NY; **22-8:** © Erich Lessing/Art Resource, NY; **22-8A:** Scala/Art Resource, NY; **22-9:** © M. Sarri 1983/Photo Vatican Museums; **22-10:** © Scala/Ministero per i Beni e le Attività culturali/Art Resource, NY; **22-10A:** © Erich Lessing/Art Resource, NY; **22-11:** © Scala/Art Resource, NY; **22-12:** © Araldo de Luca/CORBIS; **22-13:** © Arte & Immagini srl/Corbis; **22-14:** © Scala/Art Resource, NY; **22-15:** © Scala/Art Resource, NY; **22-16:** © Scala/Art Resource, NY; **22-17:** Photo Vatican Museums; **22-18:** © Bracchietti-Zigrosi/Vatican Museums; **22-18A:** Vatican Museums and Galleries, Vatican City, Italy/The Bridgeman Art Library International; **22-18B_1:** Vatican Museums and Galleries, Vatican City, Italy/The Bridgeman Art Library International; **22-19:** akg-images/Electa; **22-20:** © Erich Lessing/Art Resource, NY; **22-21:** © Scala/Art Resource, NY; **22-22:** © Cengage Learning; **22-23:** © The Trustees of the British Museum/Art Resource, NY; **22-24:** © Cengage Learning; **22-25:** © Guido Alberto Rossi/Photolibrary; **22-26:** © Alinari Archives/Corbis; **22-26A:** © Guido Alberto Rossi/Photolibrary; **22-27:** © Alinari Archives/Corbis; **22-28:** © Mark Edward Smith/Photolibrary; **22-29:** © Cengage Learning; **22-30:** © 2010 Fred Kleiner; **22-30A:** © Scala/Art Resource, NY; **22-31:** © John Heseltine/Corbis; **22-31A:** © The Frick Collection, NY. 1915.1.3; **22-32:** © Scala/Art Resource, NY; **22-33:** © 1999 Board of Trustees, National Gallery of Art,

Artwork © Jenny Saville; **31-26:** Photo © Whitney Museum of American Art, © Kiki Smith; **31-27:** Museum of Contemporary Art, Chicago © Jeff Koons; **31-27A:** Art © Estate of Robert Arneson/Licensed by VAGA, NY Photo: San Francisco Museum of Modern Art; **31-27A:** Art © Estate of Robert Arneson/Licensed by VAGA, New York, NY. Photo: San Francisco Museum of Modern Art; **31-28:** Art © Marisol Escobar/ Licensed by VAGA, New York, NY; **31-29:** © Johan Gerrits; **31-28A:** Mark Tansey, courtesy Gagosian Gallery, NY; **31-30:** © Martin Jones; Ecoscene/CORBIS; **31-31a:** © John Gollings/Arcaid/Corbis; **31-31b:** © John Gollings/Arcaid/Corbis; **31-32:** Photo Saskia Cultural Documentation; **31-33:** © Santiago Yaniz/Photolibrary; **31-34:** © Jacques Pavlovsky/Sygma/CORBIS; **31-34A:** Arcaid.co.uk; **31-35:** akg-images/ Hilbich; **31-36:** © Jonathan Poore/Cengage Learning; **31-36:** The Denver Art Museum; **31-37:** Kokyat Choong/The Image Works; **31-38:** Robert O'Dea/akg-images; **31-39:** © 2011 Richard Serra/Artists Rights Society (ARS), NY. Photo © Burt Roberts, courtesy of Harriet Senie; **31-40:** Wolfgang Volz ©1983 Christo; **31-41:** © Andy Goldsworthy Courtesy Galerie Lelong, New York; **31-42:** © Jonathan Poore/Cengage Learning; **31-43:** © 2011 ANDREAS GURSKY. Licensed by Artist's Rights Society (ARS) New York.; **31-44:** © 2011 Jenny Holzer/Artists Rights Society (ARS), NY. photograph by David Heald © The Solomon R. Guggenheim Foundation; **31-45:** Adrian Piper Research Archive; **31-46:** Bill Viola, photo: Kira Perov; **31-47:** Tony Oursler, courtesy of the artist and Metro Pictures, NY.; **31-48:** Photograph by David Heald © The Solomon R. Guggenheim Foundation, NY; **UNF 31-01:** Self-Portrait, 1980 © Copyright The Robert Mapplethorpe Foundation. Courtesy Art + Commerce; **UNF 31-2:** © 2011 Estate of Jean-Michel Basquiat/ADAGP, Paris/Artists Rights Society (ARS), New York. Photography: Douglas M. Parker Studio, Los Angeles. Image courtesy of The Broad Art Foundation, Santa Monica; **UNF 31-3:** Photo © Whitney Museum of American Art, © Kiki Smith; **UNF 31-4:** akg-images/Hilbich; **UNF 31-5:** Tony Oursler, courtesy of the artist and Metro Pictures, NY.

**Chapter 32—Opener:** Freer Gallery of Art, Smithsonian Institution, Washington, D.C., Purchase, F1942.15a; **Map 32-1:** © Cengage Learning; **timeline:** Freer Gallery of Art, Smithsonian Institution, Washington, D.C., Purchase, F1942.15a; **32-2:** © Robert Harding/Photolibrary; **32-3:** © V Muthuraman/India Picture RM/Photolibrary; **32-4:** © Victoria & Albert Museum, London/Art Resource, NY; **32-5:** © Victoria & Albert Museum, London/Art Resource, NY; **32-5A:** Photograph © 2011 Museum of Fine Arts, Boston.14.654; **32-6:** © Kevin R. Morris/Documentary Value/Corbis; **32-7:** National Museum, New Delhi; **32-7A:** Courtesy of the Trustees of the Chhatrapati Shivaji Maharaj Vastu Sangrahalaya formerly Prince of Wales Museum of Western India, Mumbai. Not to be reproduced without prior permission of the Trustees; **32-8:** © ml-foto ml-foto/Photolibrary; **32-9:** © Tony Waltham/Robert Harding Picture Library; **32-10:** The Brooklyn Museum of Art, 87.234.6; **32-11:** © Dr. Ronald V. Wiedenhoeft/Saskia, Ltd; **32-12:** © Stuart Westmorland; **32-13:** © Luca Tettoni Photography; **32-14:** © Ladislav Janicek/Bridge/Corbis; **32-15:** Pacific Asia Museum Collection, gift of Hon. and Mrs. Jack Lydman, Museum No. 1991.47.34; **UNF 32-01:** © Robert Harding/Photolibrary; **UNF 32-2:** © V Muthuraman/India Picture RM/Photolibrary; **UNF 32-3:** Freer Gallery of Art, Smithsonian Institution, Washington, D.C., Purchase, F1942.15a; **UNF 32-4:** © Stuart Westmorland; **UNF 32-5:** © Tony Waltham/Robert Harding Picture Library.

**Chapter 33—Opener:** © photos12.com/Panorama Stock; **(detail 1):** © Best View Stock/Photolibrary; **(detail 2):** © View Stock/Photolibrary; **(detail 3):** © Best View Stock/Photolibrary; **(detail 4):** © Alfred Ko/CORBIS; **33-01A:** Freer Gallery of Art, Smithsonian Institution, Washington, D.C.; **33-2:** Collection of the National Palace Museum, Taiwan, Republic of China; **timeline:** © photos12.com/Panorama Stock; **33-3:** Collection of the National Palace Museum, Taiwan, Republic of China; **33-4:** Collection of the National Palace Museum, Taiwan, Republic of China; **33-5:** Percival David Foundation of Chinese Art, B614; **33-4A:** Collection of the National Palace Museum, Taiwan, Republic of China; **Map 33-1:** © Cengage Learning; **33-6:** © Best View Stock/Photolibrary; **33-7:** © Alfred Ko/CORBIS; **33-8:** © Victoria & Albert Museum/Art Resource, NY; **33-9:** Cultural Relics Publishing House, Beijing; **33-10:** © Michael DeFreitas/Robert Harding Travel/Photolibrary; **33-11:** © Mauritius/Photolibrary; **33-12:** Collection of the National Palace Museum, Taiwan, Republic of China; **33-12A:** Nelson-Atkins Museum of Art, Kansas City; **33-13:** Photo copyright © Cleveland Museum of Art, Cleveland; **33-14:** Gift of Mr. Robert Allerton, 1957 (236.1), photo copyright © Honolulu Academy of Arts; **33-15:** John Taylor Photography, C. C. Wang Family Collection, NY; **33-16:** Cultural Relics Publishing House, Beijing; **33-17:** Percival David Foundation of Chinese Art, A821; **33-18:** © Audrey R. Topping; **33-19:** © JTB Photo/Photolibrary; **33-20:** Hoam Art Museum, Kyunggi-Do; **UNF 33-01:** Percival David Foundation of Chinese Art, B614; **UNF 33-2:** © Best View Stock/Photolibrary; **UNF 33-3:** John Taylor Photography, C. C. Wang Family Collection, NY; **UNF 33-4:** © Audrey R.Topping; **UNF 33-5:** © JTB Photo/Photolibrary.

**Chapter 34—Opener:** Museum photograph © 206 The Brooklyn Museum. 30.1478.30; **Map 34-1:** © Cengage Learning; **timeline:** Museum photograph © 206 The Brooklyn Museum. 30.1478.30; **34-2:** Patricia J. Graham; **34-2A:** © Michael S. Yamashita/Documentary Value/Corbis; **34-3:** TNM Image Archives, Source: http// TNMArchives.jp/; **34-4:** TNM Image Archives, Source: http//TNMArchives.jp/; **34-5:** © Sakamoto Photo Research Laboratory/Corbis; **34-4A:** © Steve Vidler/SuperStock; **34-6:** TNM Image Archives, Source: http//TNMArchives.jp/; **34-7:** Photograph by Oyamazaki Town Office. Haga Library/Lebrecht Music and Arts Photo Library; **34-8:** The Hatakeyama Memorial Museum of Fine Art, Tokyo; **34-9:** Lebrecht Music and Arts Photo Library; **34-9A:** Smithsonian Freer Gallery of Art and Arthur M. Sackler Gallery; **34-10:** TNM Image Archives, Source: http//TNMArchives.jp/; **34-11:** Photo copyright © Hiraki Ukiyo-e Museum, Yokohama; **34-12:** Photography © The Art Institute of Chicago1925.243; **34-12A:** © Erich Lessing/Art Resource, NY; **34-13:** Photograph © 2011 Museum of Fine Arts, Boston 11.17652; **34-14:** Tokyo National University of Fine Arts and Music; **34-15:** Freer Gallery of Art, Smithsonian Institution, Washington, D.C., Purchase, F192.225; **34-16:** © Hamada Shoji, Mashiko Reference Collection. Photo: © National Museum of Modern Art, Kyoto; **34-17:** Copyright : Fujiko Shiraga and the former members of the Gutai Art Association Courtesy: Ashiya City Museum of Art and History; **34-18:** © AP Photo/Kyodo News; **UNF 34-01:** TNM Image Archives, Source: http//TNMArchives.jp/; **UNF 34-2:** © Sakamoto Photo Research Laboratory/Corbis; **UNF 34-3:** Lebrecht Music and Arts Photo Library; **UNF 34-4:** 1925.243, Photography © The Art Institute of Chicago; **UNF 34-5:** © AP Photo/Kyodo News.

**Chapter 35—Opener:** The Bodleian Libraries, University of Oxford. Shelfmark: MS. Arch. Selden. A.1, fol. 2r; **Map 35-1:** © Cengage Learning; **timeline:** The Bodleian Libraries, University of Oxford. Shelfmark: MS. Arch. Selden. A.1, fol. 2r; **35-2:** Private Collection/Jean-Pierre Courau/The Bridgeman Art Library International; **35-3:** adapted from an image by Ned Seidler/National Geographic Society; **35-4:** © Gianni Dagli Orti/CORBIS; **35-5:** © Ronaldo Schemidt/AFP/Getty Images; **35-6:** © Gianni Dagli Orti/The Picture Desk Limited/Corbis; **Map 35-2:** © Cengage Learning; **35-7:** © G. Dagli Orti/De Agostini Picture Library/Learning Pictures; **35-8:** left © Michael Freeman/Encyclopedia/CORBIS; **35-8:** right © Milton Keiles; **35-8A:** © American Museum of Natural History, New York, USA/The Bridgeman Art Library; **Map 35-3:** © Cengage Learning; **35-9:** © Ira Block/National Geographic/Getty Images; **35-10:** Arizona State Museum, University of Arizona, photo W. McLennan; **35-11:** Photo © National Museum of Women in the Arts; **35-12a:** American Museum of Natural History, New York; **35-12b:** American Museum of Natural History, New York.; **35-13:** Photo © American Museum of Natural History, NY; **35-14:** Museum of Anthropology at the University of British Columbia, photo W. McLennan; **35-14A:** The Art Archive/ Neil Setchfield/Picture Desk; **35-15:** Southwest Museum of the American Indian Collection, Autry National Center; 761.G.33; **35-16:** © The Metropolitan Museum of Art/Art Resource, NY; **35-16A:** Peabody Museum of Archaeology, Harvard University, Cambridge.; **35-17:** he Art Archive/Gift of Clara S Peck/Buffalo Bill Historical Center, Cody, Wyoming/21.69.37/Picture Desk; **35-18:** Collection of Mr. and Mrs. Charles Diker; **UNF 35-01:** Private Collection/Jean-Pierre Courau/The Bridgeman Art Library International; **UNF 35-2:** © Gianni Dagli Orti/The Picture Desk Limited/Corbis; **UNF 35-3:** © G. Dagli Orti/De Agostini Picture Library/Learning Pictures; **UNF 35-4:** © Ira Block/National Geographic/Getty Images; **UNF 35-5:** American Museum of Natural History, New York.

**Chapter 36—Opener (bottom):** © Werner Forman/Art Resource, NY; **(detail 1):** © Werner Forman/Art Resource, NY; **(detail 2):** © Tara Hunt; **(detail 3):** © Werner Forman/Art Resource, NY; **(detail 4):** © Werner Forman/Art Resource, NY; **Map 36-1:** © Cengage Learning; **timeline:** © Werner Forman/Art Resource, NY; **36-01A:** © Werner Forman/Art Resource, NY; **36-2:** Reproduced courtesy Museum of Victoria; **36-3:** © Yoko Aziz/Alamy; **36-4:** © NHPA/Photoshot; **36-7:** Copyright © Otago Museum, Dunedin, New Zealand, D45.179; **36-5:** AA353/3/22 Vyse Collection. F. E. Williams, photographer, South Australian Museum Archives; **36-6:** abm-Archives Barbier-Mueller, photographer Wolfgang Pulfer; **36-8:** © Scala/Art Resource, NY; **36-9:** © Trustees of the British Museum/Art Resource, NY; **36-10:** © Bildarchiv Preussischer Kulturbesitz/Art Resource, NY; **36-11:** © The Metropolitan Museum of Art/Art Resource, NY; **36-12:** © Wolfgang Kaehler/CORBIS; **36-13:** Adrienne Kaeppler; **36-14:** Photo © University of Pennsylvania Museum/153195; **36-15A:** Reproduced by permission of the University of Cambridge Museum of Archaeology & Anthropology, E 1895.158; **36-15:** akg-images; **36-16:** © The Trustees of the British Museum/Art Resource, NY; **36-17:** © Heritage Images/The British Museum; **36-18:** © The Trustees of the British Museum/Art Resource, NY; **36-19:** Photo Bishop Museum, Honolulu; **36-19A:** Copyright © Otago Museum, Dunedin, New Zealand; **UNF 36-2:** Otago Museum, Dunedin, New Zealand; **UNF 36-3:** © The Metropolitan Museum of Art/Art Resource, NY; **UNF 36-4:** Werner Forman/Value Art/Corbis; **UNF 36-5:** Photo Bishop Museum, Honolulu.

**Chapter 37—Opener:** © The Trustees of the British Museum/Art Resource, NY; **Map 37-1:** © Cengage Learning; **timeline:** © The Trustees of the British Museum/Art Resource, NY; **37-2:** Natal Museum, Pietermaritzburg, South Africa; **37-3:** Natal Museum, Pietermaritzburg, South Africa; **37-4:** © Art Resource, NY; **37-5:** abm-Archives Barbier-Mueller; **37-6:** © Bildarchiv Preussischer Kulturbesitz/Art Resource, NY; **37-7:** © Musee du Quai Branly/© Scala/Art Resource, NY; **37-8:** Photograph by Franko Khoury. National Museum of African Art, Smithsonian Institution; **37-9:** Detroit Institute of Arts, USA/Founders Society Purchase Eleanor Clay Ford Fund for African Art/The Bridgeman Art Library International; **37-10:** © Werner Forman/Art Resource, NY; **37-11:** © The Metropolitan Museum of Art/Art Resource, NY; **37-12:** The Metropolitan Museum of Art/Art Resource, NY; **37-13:** Photo by Eliot Elisofon, 1970. Image no. EEPA EECL 7590. Eliot Elisofon Photographic Archives. National Museum of African Art, Smithsonian Institution; **37-13A:** © Owen Franken/Encyclopedia/Corbis; **37-14:** Photograph by Franko Khoury. National Museum of African Art, Smithsonian Institution"; **37-15:** © Herbert M. Cole; **37-16:** © Trustees of the British Museum, London; **37-16A:** Denver Art Museum Collection: Funds from 1996 Collectors' Choice and partial gift of Valerie Franklin; **37-17:** © Fulvio Roiter/Corbis; **37-17A:** Photograph by Franko Khoury. National Museum of African Art, Smithsonian Institution; **37-18:** Musée Barbier-Mueller, Geneva.; **37-19:** © Charles & Josette Lenars/ CORBIS; **37-20:** Fowler Museum at UCLA, photo: Don Cole; **37-21:** © Otto Lang/ CORBIS; **37-22:** 2011 Peabody Museum, Harvard University 17-41-50/B198 T762.1; **37-23:** Photograph by Eliot Elisofon, 1971, EEPA EECL 2139, Eliot Elisofon Photographic Archives, National Museum of African Art, Smithsonian Institution; **37-24:** © Herbert M. Cole; **37-25:** © Herbert M. Cole; **37-26:** photograph by Philip L. Ravenhill, 1989, EEPA 1989-6346, Eliot Elisofon Photographic Archives, National Museum of African Art, Smithsonian Institution; **UNF 37-01:** © Bildarchiv Preussischer Kulturbesitz/Art Resource, NY; **UNF 37-2:** © Detroit Institute of Arts, USA/The Bridgeman Art Library International; **UNF 37-3:** Photo by Eliot Elisofon, 1970. Image no. EEPA EECL 7590. Eliot Elisofon Photographic Archives. National Museum of African Art, Smithsonian Institution; **UNF 37-4:** © Herbert M. Cole; **UNF 37-5:** Fowler Museum at UCLA, photo: Don Cole.

# MUSEUM INDEX

**Note:** *Figure numbers in* blue *indicate bonus images.*

# SUBJECT INDEX

**Notes:**
- *Page numbers in italics indicate illustrations.*
- *Page numbers in italics followed by* b *indicate bonus images in the text.*
- *Page numbers in italics followed by* map *indicate maps.*
- *Figure numbers in* blue *indicate bonus images.*

in Greek Orientalizing period art, 110, 5-6B

in Han dynasty Chinese art, 449, 456

in Hiberno-Saxon art, 312, 313

in Hittite art, 2-18B

and Islamic art, 287, 293, 301, 303–304, 10-5B, 10-15A

in Italian Quattrocento Renaissance art, 573

in Japanese art, 1010

in Mesolithic art, 16

in Mexican interwar Modernist art, 29-74A

in Native North American art, 35-16A

in Neo-Babylonian art, 49, 2-18B

in Neolithic art, 16

in Northern European High Renaissance/ Mannerist art, 651

in Oceanic art, 1046

in Paleolithic art, 14–15, 16–17, 19, 20–21, 1-12A

in Persian art, 51, 2-26A

in Realist art, 779–780

in South Asian art, 426, 436, 15-6A, 15-22B

in Sumerian art, 31, 31cap, 35, 38–39

*See also* composite animal-human figures

*Annals of Ulster,* 307

Anne (queen of England), 26-1A

Anne, Saint, 579

*Annunciation,* Church of the Virgin Peribleptos, Ohrid (icon), 279–280, *280*

*Annunciation, Hours of Jeanne d'Evreux* (Pucelle), 13-36A

*Annunciation, Nativity, and Adoration of Shepherds,* pulpit, Sant'Andrea, Pistoia (Giovanni Pisano), 403–404, *403*

*Annunciation, Nativity, and Adoration of the Shepherds,* baptistery pulpit, Pisa (Nicola Pisano), 403, *403,* 415

*Annunciation,* Reims Cathedral (sculpture), 380, *380,* 386

*Annunciation,* San Marco, Florence (Fra Angelico), 576, *576,* 579

*Annunciation* altarpiece, Siena Cathedral (Martini and Memmi), 413–415, *413*

Annunciation to Mary, 240

in Burgundian/Flemish late medieval/ early Renaissance art, 534, 535, 538, 539, 540, 20-4A

in Gothic art, 380, 386, 13-36A

in Italian 13th century art, 413–415

in Italian late medieval art, 403–404

in Italian Quattrocento Renaissance art, 576

in Late Byzantine art, 280

in Ottonian art, 326

in Symbolist art, 824

Annunciation to the Shepherds, 240, 329–330, 548

antae, 115, 142

Antaios, 122

ante legem, 392

Anthemius of Tralles. *See* Hagia Sophia

Anthony, Saint, 647, 20-8A

Anthony, Susan B., 922

antiapartheid movement, 950

*Antipater of Sidon, 49

*Antiquities of Athens* (Stuart and Revett), 749–750, 26-28A

Antonello da Messina, 624

Antonine period, 215–218, 7-59A

*See also* Roman High Empire art

Antoninus Pius (Roman emperor), 215–216, 222

Anu (Mesopotamian deity), 33, 34

Anubis (Egyptian deity), 57, 80, 7-62A

Anyang (China): guang (bronze vessel), 452

apadana, 50, 51

Apanui, Wepiha: Mataatua meetinghouse, Whakatane, 1058, *1058b,* 36-19A

*Aperture* magazine, 920

Aphaia, 123–124

Aphrodite (Venus) (Greek/Roman deity), 107

in Flemish Baroque art, 25-1A

in Greek Early/High Classical period art, 137, 138

in Greek Late Classical period art, 145

in Hellenistic period Greek art, 158–159, 5-83A

in Italian Cinquecento Renaissance art, 625, 628, 629, 631

in Italian Mannerist art, 634

in Italian Quattrocento Renaissance art, 558, 559, 581

in Napoleonic era art, 758–759

in Northern European High Renaissance/ Mannerist art, 654

*Aphrodite (Venus de Milo)* (Alexander of Antioch-on-the-Meander) (sculpture), 158–159, *158,* 759

*Aphrodite, Eros, and Pan,* Delos (sculpture), *158b,* 159, 5-83A

*Aphrodite of Knidos* (Praxiteles), 145, *145,* 159, 581, 654, 5-62A, 5-83A

Apocalypse, 314, 333, 348

*See also* Last Judgment

Apollinaire, Guillaume, 844, 847, 29-19A

Apollinaris, Saint, 266, 267

Apollo (Greek/Roman deity), 107

in Baroque art, 717, 24-6A

and Early Christian art, 8-13A

Etruscan counterpart, 167

in Greek Archaic period art, 119

in Greek early/high Classical period art, 126, 127, 5-32A

in Greek Orientalizing period art, 109–110

*Apollo 11 Cave* (Namibia): animal facing left (painting), 16–17, *17*

Apollo, Temple of Zeus east pediment, Olympia (sculpture), 126, *127,* 128

*Apollo and Daphne* (Bernini), 674–675, *674b,* 24-6A

*Apollo Belvedere,* 24-6A

*Apollo of Veii* (Apulu) (sculpture), 168–169, *168*

Apollodoros (Athenian painter), 149

Apollodorus of Damascus

Forum of Trajan, 178, 208, *208,* 326

Markets of Trajan, Rome, 209, *209,* 228

*Apologia* (Justin Martyr), 239

apostles, 240

in Byzantine art, 275

in Early Christian art, 8-17A

in French/Spanish Romanesque art, 346, 348, 12-8B

in Hiberno-Saxon art, 314

in Italian Quattrocento Renaissance art, 585

*See also* four evangelists

apotheosis, 206, 215, 216, 735, 760, 761, 7-40A, 18-10A

*Apotheosis of Antoninus Pius and Faustina,* Column of Antoninus Pius, Rome (relief sculpture), 215, *215,* 216

*Apotheosis of Homer* (Ingres), 760, *761*

*Apotheosis of the Pisani Family,* Villa Pisani, Stra (Tiepolo), 735, *735*

Apotheosis of Titus, relief panel, Arch of Titus, Rome, 206, *206b,* 7-40A

apotropaic, 118

apoxyomenos, 147

*Apoxyomenos (Scraper)* (Lysippos of Sikyon), 147, *147*

*The Apparition* (Moreau), 820, *820*

apprenticeship, 414, 545, 1071

apses, 134

in Early Christian architecture, 243, 8-19A

in Italian 13th century architecture, 14-5A

in Italian 14th century architecture, 413

in Neolithic architecture, 28

in Roman architecture, 208

in Spanish art in the Americas, 1031

in Visigothic architecture, 316

apsidal, 429

Apulia (Italy): Artist painting a marble statue of Herakles (vase painting), *146b,* 5-63A

Apulu (Etruscan deity), 167, 168–169

*Apulu (Apollo of Veii)* (sculpture), 168–169, *168*

aqueducts, 201, 831

Aquinas. *See* Thomas Aquinas, Saint

Ara Pacis Augustae (Altar of Augustan Peace), Rome, 199–200, *199, 199, 200,* 207, 264–265

Arbus, Diane

*Child with Toy Hand Grenade in Central Park,* 920, *920*

Kruger and, 942

Arc de Triomphe, Paris (Chalgrin), 770, *770*

arcades

in Early Christian architecture, 243

in French/Spanish Romanesque architecture, 12-4A, 12-11A

in Gothic architecture, 364, 368, 370, 373, 374, 20-4A

in Islamic architecture, 287, 290

in Italian 13th century architecture, 14-6A

in Italian 14th century architecture, 413, 14-18A

in Italian Cinquecento Renaissance architecture, 22-30A

in Italian Quattrocento Renaissance architecture, 582

in Italian Romanesque architecture, 355

in late 19th century art European and American architecture, 831

in Northern European High Renaissance/ Mannerist architecture, 658

in Persian architecture, 52

Arcadian art, 625, 733

Arcadius (Byzantine emperor), 246, 256

Arch of Constantine, Rome, 226–227, *226, 227,* 235, 589, 7-48A, 11-19A

Arch of Septimius Severus, Lepcis Magna, 220, 221, 235

Arch of Titus, Rome, 205–207, *205, 206,* 220, 7-40A

Arch of Trajan, Benevento, 208, *208b,* 7-44A, 7-44B

archaeology

Aegean, 85, 86–87, 92

Africa, 523, 527

Americas, 491, 492, 493, 508, 512, 514

and the art market, 88

China, 450, 452, 453, 454–455

Egypt, 56

Japan, 476

Mesopotamia, 32

Pompeii/Herculaneum, 745

Archaic period Etruscan art, 164, 165, 167–172, 177, 6-7A, 6-9A

Archaic period Greek art. *See* Greek Archaic period art

Archaic smile, 112, 124

Archangel Michael, Saint Mark's, Venice (icon), *274b,* 9-26B

archer, Djenne (sculpture), *528,* 529

The archer Yi(?) and a reception in a mansion, Wu family shrines, Jiaxiang (rubbing of relief sculpture), *456,* 457

*Archers of Saint Hadrian* (Hals), 704, *704,* 706

arches, 97

in Carolingian architecture, 11-19A

chancel, 228, 243, 413, 12-4A

diaphragm, 12-27A

in early Islamic architecture, 282, 283, 290–291

in Etruscan architecture, 175

in French/Spanish Romanesque architecture, 12-8A, 12-10A, 12-11A

in Gothic architecture, 368, *368,* 374, 398, 13-13A, 13-38A, 13-42A

in Italian 13th century architecture, 14-6A

in Italian 14th century architecture, 420, 14-18B

in Italian Cinquecento Renaissance art, 621, 22-30A

in Italian late medieval architecture, 402

in Italian Quattrocento Renaissance architecture, 586, 586–587, 594, 21-31A

in Italian Romanesque architecture, 12-27A

in later Islamic architecture, 295

in Neo-Babylonian architecture, 48, 49

in Neo-Gothic architecture, 27-43A

ogee, 420, 13-42A

quadrant, 359, 373, 12-7B

in Roman Early Empire architecture, 204, 205–207

in Roman Late Empire architecture, 226–227

trefoil, 402, 14-18B

in Visigothic architecture, 316

*See also* arcades; corbel vaulting; pointed arches; transverse arches

Archipenko, Aleksandr

and Hepworth, 882

*Woman Combing Her Hair,* 852, *852,* 853

*Architectonic Painting,* 1916-1917 (Popova), 860, *860b,* 29-30A

**Architectural Basics boxes**

Chinese wooden construction, 457

Corinthian capitals, 152

Doric and Ionic orders, 116

Gothic cathedrals, 373

Great Pyramids, 62

Greek temple plans, 115, *115*

Hindu temples, 439

mosques, 288

pendentives and squinches, 262

rib vaulting, 368

Roman concrete construction, 184

Roman houses, 190

Romanesque church portals, 344

stupas, 430

architectural drawings, 12, *12*

architecture

18th century, 728, 737, 748–751, 26-1A, 26-27A

African, 529–530, 1078

Andean South American, 508, 512–513, 1030–1031

Baroque. *See* Baroque architecture

Beaux-Arts, 789

Byzantine. *See* Byzantine architecture

Carolingian, 320–324, 11-19A

Chinese. *See* Chinese architecture

contemporary, 960–964, 965–966, 973, 31-34A, 31-34B

drawings, 12, *12*

early 19th century European and American, 787–791, 797, 27-46A

Early Christian. *See* Early Christian architecture

Egyptian. *See* Egyptian architecture

and the Enlightenment, 737

Etruscan, 167–168, 170–172, 175, 6-7A, 6-9A

Gothic. *See* Gothic architecture

Greek. *See* Greek architecture

Hiberno-Saxon high crosses, 315

High Renaissance/Mannerist, 657–658, 664–665, 23-23A

Islamic, 282, 283, 285–286, 289–292, 295–300, 10-5A

Italian 13th century, 3–4, 402, 14-5A, 14-6A

Italian 14th century, 412–413, 415–416, 417–419, 420, 14-12A, 14-18A, 14-18B, 14-19A

Italian Cinquecento Renaissance, 605, 618–624, 22-6A, 22-26A, 22-30A

Italian Mannerist, 640–642

Italian Quattrocento Renaissance, 582–588, 593–594, 21-31A, 21-32A, 21-37A

Japanese. *See* Japanese architecture

Korean, 471–472, 1002

late 19th century art European and American, 828, 829–832, 833, 28-36A, 28-40A

Late Antique, 236, 237

Mesoamerican, 490, 491, 495–497, 499, 500, 504–506, 1026, 18-10A

Mesopotamian, 33–34, 42, 46, 48, 49, 2-18B, 2-20A

Minoan, 89–90

Modernist, 860–861, 870–872, 884–887, 896, 925–929

Mycenaean, 96–99, 115, 170, 184, 244, 4-18A, 4-22A, 5-6A

Napoleonic era, 758, 759

Native North American, 515, 518, 1037, 18-30A, 18-33A

Neolithic, 24–25, 27, 28, 450–451, 1-16A, 1-19A

Dancing Shiva, Badami (cave sculpture), 435–436, *435*

Dante Alighieri, 384, 406, 412, 560, 760

*Daodejing (The Way and Its Power)* (Laozi), 463

Daoism, 454, 458, 463, 465, 16-6A

Daphni (Greece): Church of the Dormition, 272–273, *272, 272*, 9-25A

Daphnis of Miletos: Temple of Apollo, Didyma, 153–154, *153*

Dapper, Olfert, 19-13A

*Darbar of Jahangir, Tuzuk-i Jahangiri (Memoirs of Jahangir)* (Abul Hasan and Manohar), *979b*, 32-5A

darbars, 32-5A

Darby, Abraham, III: iron bridge, Coalbrookdale, 737, *737*

Darius I (king of Persia), 50, 52

Darius III (king of Persia), 49, 150

darshan, 435

Darwin, Charles, 800

Dashizhi, 16-13B

dating (of art). *See* chronology

Datong (China): Yungang Grottoes, 461, *461b*, 16-13A

*The Daughters of Edward Darley Boit* (Sargent), 784, *784*

Daumier, Honoré
   *Nadar Raising Photography to the Height of Art*, 794, *794*
   *Rue Transnonain*, 778, *779*
   *Third-Class Carriage*, 779, *779*

*David* (Bernini), 674–675, *674*

*David* (Donatello), Medici palace, Florence, 568, *568*, 611, 674, 675

*David* (Donatello), town hall, Florence, 568

*David* (Michelangelo Buonarroti), 611, *611*, 674, 675

*David* (Verrocchio), 569, *569*, 611, 674, 675

David, Jacques-Louis
   *Coronation of Napoleon*, 757–758, *757*
   *Death of Marat*, 748, *748*
   *Napoleon Crossing the Saint-Bernard Pass*, 757, *757b*, 948, 27-1A, 27-13A
   *Oath of the Horatii*, 728, 747–748, *747*, 755, 757–758, 760
   on public art, 747
   and Rude, 770
   students of, 759

*David before Saul*, Belleville Breviary, 387–388, *387*

*David Composing the Psalms*, Paris Psalter, 276–277, *277*

Davies, Arthur B., 844, 863

Davis, Stuart: *Lucky Strike*, *866*, 867

Day, Benjamin, 916

Dayi (China): *Rent Collection Courtyard* (Ye Yushan and others), 1001, *1001*

de Chirico, Giorgio
   and Magritte, 878
   *Melancholy and Mystery of a Street*, 875–876, *875*

*De imitatione statuarum* (Rubens), 698

de Kooning, Willem, 904–905
   contemporary art and, 941
   and Kline, 30-8A
   and Mitchell, 30-8C
   Schnabel and, 954
   *Woman 1*, 905, *905*

*De materia medica* (Dioscorides), 258, 268, 9-3A

*De occulta philosophia* (Agrippa of Nettesheim), 651

De Stijl, 880–881, 884

*De vita triplici* (Ficino), 651

de Zayas, Marius, 849

death
   in African art, 1066
   in Baroque art, 688, 695, 718, 25-18A
   in Burgundian/Flemish late medieval/early Renaissance art, 20-8A
   in contemporary art, 950
   in early 19th century European and American photography, 793
   in Italian 14th century art, 419–420
   in Mesoamerican art, 502, 1025, 1028
   in Northern European High Renaissance/Mannerist art, 656, 23-3A, 23-5A

   in Pop Art, 30-25B
   in Pre-Raphaelite art, 786–787
   in Realist art, 777, 779, 783
   in Rococo art, 26-7A
   in Romantic art, 766, 771–772
   in Surrealist art, 918
   *See also* funerary customs

*Death and Assumption of the Virgin*, altar of the Virgin Mary, church of Saint Mary, Kraków (Stoss), 554, *554*

*The Death and Life of Great American Cities* (Jacobs), 929

*Death and the Maiden* (Baldung Grien), *649b*, 23-3A

death mask, tomb of Tutankhamen, Thebes, 78, *79*, 100

*Death of General Wolfe* (West), 742, *743*

*Death of Marat* (David), 748, *748*

*Death of Sardanapalus* (Delacroix), 47–48, 766–767, *767*, 826

death of Sarpedon (Euphronios and Euxitheos), Greppe Sant'Angelo (vase painting), *122b*, 5-22A

*Death of the Buddha (Parinirvana)*, Gal Vihara (sculpture), *442*, 443

*Death of the Virgin*, Strasbourg Cathedral (relief sculpture), 393–394, *393*

*Decameron* (Boccaccio), 406

*Decline and Fall of the Roman Empire* (Gibbon), 746

deconstruction theory, 942

Deconstructivism, 962–963, 31-34B

decumanus, 189

decursio, 215, *215*, 216

decursio, Column of Antoninus Pius, Rome (relief sculpture), 215, *215*, 216

deer hunt mural, Çatal Höyük (cave painting), 26, *26*, 35, 3-1A

Deësis, 276

Degas, Edgar
   and Japonisme, 808, 28-16B
   and Morisot, 28-7A
   and photography, 791, 796, 809
   and Picasso, 29-11A
   *The Rehearsal*, 807–808, *807*, 809
   and Toulouse-Lautrec, 811, 28-15A
   *The Tub*, 808, *808*, 809

Degenerate Art (Entartete Kunst) exhibition, Germany, 877

Deir el-Bahri (Egypt)
   Hatshepsut mortuary temple, 69–71, *69, 70*, 73
   Hatshepsut with offering jars (sculpture), 70–71, *70*

deities. *See* religion and mythology

*Le Déjeuner sur l'Herbe (Luncheon on the Grass)* (Manet), 780–781, *781*, 801, 802, 28-22A

Del Monte, Francesco Maria Bourbon, 681, 24-17A

Delacroix, Eugène, 47–48, 761
   *Death of Sardanapalus*, 47–48, 766–767, *767*, 826
   *Liberty Leading the People*, 768, *768*, 770
   and Moreau, 28-24A
   on Morocco, 769
   and photography, 791
   and Rude, 770
   *Scenes from the Massacre at Chios*, 767, *767b*, 27-15A
   *Tiger Hunt*, 768, 769, *769*
   *Women of Algiers in Their Apartment*, 768, *768b*, 27-17A

Delaroche, Paul, 791

Delaunay, Robert
   *Champs de Mars (The Red Tower)*, 848, *848b*, 29-15A
   and Futurism, 854
   *Homage to Blériot*, 848, *848*

Delaunay, Sonia, 848

Delaware residence (Venturi, Rauch, and Brown), 931–932, *931*

Delhi (India)
   Alai Darvaza, 977, *977*
   Qutb Minar, 977, *977*
   Quwwat al-Islam Mosque, 977

Delhi sultanate, 441, 976–977, 987

Delian League, 133, 137

Delivery of the Keys to Peter, 240, 567, 589–590, 22-18B

della Porta, Giacomo: Il Gesù (Church of Jesus), Rome, 641–642, *642*, 671, 686, *686*

della Robbia, Andrea: roundels, Ospedale degli Innocenti (Foundling Hospital), Florence, 583, 585, 21-36A

della Robbia, Giovanni, 585

della Robbia, Girolamo, 585

della Robbia, Luca: *Madonna and Child*, Or San Michele, 585, *585b*, 21-36A

della Rovere, Marco Vigerio, 614

Delos (Greece): Aphrodite, Eros, and Pan (sculpture), *158b*, 159, 5-83A

Delphi (Greece)
   charioteer (dedicated by Polyzalos of Gela) (sculpture), 130–131, *130*
   Sanctuary of Apollo, 119, *119b*, 5-17A
   Siphnian Treasury, 119, *119*, 141, 156
   tholos (Theodoros of Phokaia), 151–152, *151*

Demeter (Ceres) (Greek/Roman deity), 101, 107

*Les Demoiselles d'Avignon* (Picasso), 845, *845*, 847, 28-22A, 29-2A, 29-11A, 29-22A, 29-59A

demos, 106

*Demosthenes* (Polyeuktos) (sculpture), 160–161, *161*

demotic, 56

Demuth, Charles, 895
   *My Egypt*, 868, *868*

denarius, 186, 187

denarius with portrait of Julius Caesar (coin), *186*, 187

Denial of Peter, 241

Denis (Dionysius), Saint, 366

*Densified Scrap Metal #3A, Toronto, Ontario* (Burtynsky), 954, *954*

Denver Art Museum (Libeskind), 963, *963b*, 31-34B

Deogarh (India): Vishnu Temple, 436–437, *436, 437*

*Departure of the Volunteers of 1792 (La Marseillaise)*, Arc de Triomphe, Paris (Rude), 770, *770*

Deposition (of the body of Jesus from the Cross), 241, 544–545, 617–618

*Deposition* (Rogier van der Weyden), 544–545, *544*

Der Blaue Reiter (artist group), 841–842, 866

Derain, André
   and the Armory Show, 863
   *The Dance*, 839, *839*
   and Dove, 864
   *Mountains at Collioure*, *839b*, 29-4A

Derbyshire (England): Kedleston House (Adam), 745

Descartes, René, 718, 736

Descent into Limbo, 241
   *See also* Anastasis

*Descent of the Ganges River*, Mamallapuram (relief sculpture), 438, *438b*, 15-22A

Desiderius (abbot of Montecassino), 12-27B

Dessau (Germany): Bauhaus (Gropius), 884, *885*, 886

Devi (Hindu deity), 435

*Devi Mahatmya*, 438

dharma, 423, 15-8A

dharmachakra mudra (wheel-turning mudra), 427, 443

dhyana mudra (meditation mudra), 427, 431, 458–459, 16-13A

di sotto in sù, 595, 637

diagonal ribs, 373

Diana. *See* Artemis

diaphragm arches, 12-27A

Díaz del Castillo, Bernal, 1026

Dickens, Charles, 778

dictator (dictator perpetuo), 181, 187

Didarganj (India): Yakshi with fly whisk (sculpture), 429, *429b*, 15-6B

Diderot, Denis, 736, 738, 759

Didyma (Turkey): Temple of Apollo (Paionios of Ephesos and Daphnis of Miletos), 153–154, *153*

*Die* (Smith), 910, *910*

Die Brücke, 839–840

digital photography, 792, 969–970

Dijon (France): Chartreuse de Champmol (Drouet de Dammartin), 537–538, *537*, 20-2A

Dilukai, 1051, 1052

Dilukai, Belau, *1051*

*The Dinner Party* (Chicago), 921–922, *921*

Dio Cassius, 203, 212

Diocletian (Roman emperor), 224–225, 236

Diocletian, palace of, Split, 224–225, *225*, 244, 356, 745, 8-19A, 10-5A

Diodorus Siculus, 111

Diogenes, 607

Dione (Greek deity), 107, 137

Dionysiac mystery frieze, Villa of the Mysteries, Pompeii (fresco), 192, *192*, 207

Dionysios of Berytos, 5-83A

Dionysius (Denis), Saint, 366

Dionysius of Halicarnassus, 166

Dionysos (Bacchus) (Greek/Roman deity), 107
   in Early Christian art, 244, 245
   in Greek art, 137, 144, 146, 151
   in Italian Cinquecento Renaissance art, 625, 628, 629
   in Late Antique art, 252
   in Roman art, 192

Diorama, 792

diorite carvings, 42, 64

Dioscurides (gem cutter), 248

Dioskorides (physician), 258, 268, 9-3A

dipteral colonnades, 115, 154

*Diptych of Martin van Nieuwenhove* (Memling), 549, *549*

Diptych of the Nicomachi and Symmachi (ivory carving), 252, *252*

diptychs, 251, 540

Dipylon Painter: Geometric amphora with mourning scene, Athens, 108, *108b*, 5-2A

disegno, 604, 625
   *See also* drawings

dish with Arabic proverb, Nishapur, 294, *295*

dish with lobed rim, Qing dynasty, 1000, *1000*

dish with two mynah birds on flowering branch, Vietnam, 986, *986*

*Diskobolos (Discus Thrower)* (Myron), 131–132, *131*, 617–618, 674

disputatio, 372

Dispute in the Temple, 240

*Distant View of Dordrecht, with a Milkmaid and Four Cows, and Other Figures (The "Large Dort")* (Cuyp), 710, *710*

distribution of largesse, Arch of Constantine, Rome (relief sculpture), 227, *227*

*Divine Comedy* (Dante), 384, 406, 560

*The Divine Names* (Pseudo-Dionysius), 262

divine right, 714

divisionism. *See* pointillism

Dix, Otto, 873–874, 877
   *Der Krieg*, 874, *874*

Djenne (Mali)
   archer (sculpture), *528*, 529
   Great Mosque, 288, 529, *529*
   *See also* Djenne art

Djenne art, 529, 533

Djoser (pharoah of Egypt), 58, 59, 60, 3-5A

Djoser mortuary precinct, Saqqara, 58, *58b*, 59, 60, *60*, 68, 3-5A

do not fear mudra (abhaya mudra), 427, 432–433, 480, 984, 15-11A, 16-13B

documentary evidence, 2

documentary photography, 794–795, 894–895, 954

Doge's Palace, Venice, 420, *420*, 637, 22-30A

doges, 274

Dogon art, 1068–1069, 1073, 1074–1075, 1078

Dome of the Rock, Jerusalem, 285–287, *285, 286*, 294, 299, 300, 346

Domenico Contarini (doge of Venice), 274

Domenico Veneziano, 405

domes
   in 18th century European and American architecture, 748–749

*Last Judgment,* Sistine Chapel (Michelangelo Buonarroti), *598,* 616, *616,* 754, 755, 826, 22-18B, 22-54A
*Last Judgment Altarpiece,* Hôtel-Dieu (Rogier van der Weyden), 544, *544b,* 20-8A
last judgment of Hunefer, Thebes (scroll), 80, *80*
Last Supper, 241
   in Burgundian/Flemish late medieval/ early Renaissance art, 538, 546–547
   in contemporary art, 959
   in feminist art, 922
   in Italian Cinquecento Renaissance art, 602, 603, 628, 637, 959
   in Italian Mannerist art, 636–637
   in Italian Quattrocento Renaissance art, 576, 577
   *See also* Eucharist
*Last Supper* (Tintoretto), 636–637, *636*
*Last Supper, Altarpiece of the Holy Sacrament,* Saint Peter's, Louvain (Bouts), 546–547, *547*
*Last Supper,* Sant'Apollonia, Florence (Andrea del Castagno), 576, *577*
*Last Supper,* Santa Maria delle Grazie (Leonardo da Vinci), *602,* 603, 628, 637, 959
late 19th century European and American art, *800map*
   architecture, 828, 829–832, 833, 28-36A, 28-40A
   Art Nouveau, 823, 828–829, 861, 28-27A, 28-40B
   Arts and Crafts movement, 808, 823, 827–828, 840
   Post-Impressionist, 811–819, 829, 833, 28-15A, 28-16A, 28-16B, 29-4A
   sculpture, 824–827, 833, 28-31A, 28-32A, 28-33A
   societal contexts, 799, 800–801, 806, 827
   Symbolist, 819–824, 826, 829, 833, 28-24A, 28-26A, 28-27A
   timeline, 800
   *See also* Impressionism
late 20th century European and American art, 898–939
   Abstract Expressionism. *See* Abstract Expressionism
   and Cézanne, 28-22A
   Conceptual Art, 936–937, 30-55A
   Environmental Art, 932–933
   Expressionism, 901–902, 30-3A
   feminist art, 921–925, 30-26A
   Modernist architecture, 925–929
   new media, 937–938
   Op Art, 8, 908–909
   Performance Art, 933–936, 30-55A
   photography, 920
   Pop Art, 898, 899, 913–917, 959, 960, 30-25A, 30-25B, 30-26A
   Post-Painterly Abstraction, 1, 2, 907–908, 31-22A
   postmodernist architecture, 929–933
   societal contexts, 900–901
   Superrealism, 917–919
   timeline, 900
   and Turner, 773
Late Antique art, 220, 232–253, *234map*
   Dura-Europos, 234–236
   Jewish art, 235–236, 237
   luxury arts, 248–252
   societal contexts, 234–235
   timeline, 234
   *See also* Roman Late Empire art
Late Byzantine art, 278–280, 281, 9-35A
Late Gothic style, 381–382, 383–384, 391, 398, 13-42A
Late Renaissance, 600
   *See also* Italian Cinquecento Renaissance art
later Islamic art, 294–304
   architecture, 295–300
   books, 302–303
   calligraphy, 300, 301, 10-23A
   luxury arts, 300–304
   sculpture, 295
   societal contexts, 294–295
   tilework, 299–300

lateral sections, 12
Latrobe, Benjamin: U.S. Capitol, Washington, D.C., 750–751
laudatio, 570
Laurentian Library, Florence (Michelangelo Buonarroti), 640–641, *641*
Lauriya Nandangarh (India): lion pillar, 429, *429b,* 15-6A
Laussel (France): woman holding a bison horn (relief sculpture), 18–19, *19,* 1-6A
*Law and Gospel* (Cranach), 653, *653*
Lawrence: D. H., 165
Lawrence, Jacob: *The Migration of the Negro* series, 889, *889*
Lawrence, Saint, 247
Le Brun, Charles
   east facade, Louvre, Paris, *714,* 715, 724
   Galerie des Glaces, palace of Versailles, 716, *716,* 730
   palace of Versailles, 715, 716
Le Corbusier
   Chandigarh urban planning, 887
   Notre-Dame-du-Haut, Ronchamp, 887, 926, *926*
   and Purism, 853
   Tange and, 1020
   Unité d'Habitation, Marseilles, 887
   Villa Savoye, Poissy-sur-Seine, 886–887, *887*
Le Nain, Louis: *Family of Country People,* 721–722, *721*
Le Nôtre, André: park, palace of Versailles, *715,* 716, 750
Le Plongeon, Augustus, 506
Le Tuc D'Audoubert (France): two bison reliefs, 19, *19*
Le Vau, Louis: east facade, Louvre, Paris, *714,* 715, 724
Leach, Bernard, 1019
leading, 375
League of Cambrai, 622
Leaning Tower of Pisa, *354,* 355
Leclerc, Georges-Louis, 736
lectionaries, 312
*Lectionary of Henry II,* 329–330, *330*
LED technology, 970–971
ledger paintings, 1040
Leenhof, Ferdinand, 780
Legalism, 454
*Legend of the True Cross,* San Francesco, Arezzo (Piero della Francesca), 578, *578b,* 21-24A
*Legenda Maior* (Saint Bonaventura), 14-5B
*Legends of Mount Shigi* (handscroll), 485–486, *486*
Léger, Fernand, 887, 888
   *Ballet Mécanique,* 853
   *The City,* 853, *853*
   and Futurism, 854
   *Three Women (Le Grand Déjeuner),* 853b, 29-22A
   Legrand, Paul: *Hidatsa Warrior Pehriska-Ruhpa (Two Ravens)* (Bodmer) (engraving), 1039
Lehmbruck, Wilhelm, 863, 877
   *Seated Youth,* 843, *843b,* 29-10A
   Leibl, Wilhelm, 785
   *Three Women in a Village Church,* 782, *782*
Leibnitz, Gottfried Wilhelm von, 736
lekythos/lekythoi, 142, 142–143
Lemoyne, Jean-Baptiste: Salon De La Princesse, Hôtel de Soubise, Paris, 729–730, *729*
Lenin, Vladimir, 835, 859
Leo III (Byzantine emperor), 257, 270
Leo III (Pope), 317
Leo X (Pope), 607–608, 613
León (Spain): Cathedral of Santa María, 389, *389b,* 13-38A
Leonardo da Vinci, 601–605
   and Andrea del Sarto, 22-8A
   cartoon for *Madonna and Child with Saint Anne and the Infant Saint John,* 602–603, *602,* 959
   and Correggio, 638
   and Dürer, 649, 23-4A, 23-5A
   *The Fetus and Lining of the Uterus,* 604, 605

   and Francis I, 605, 657
   and human figure, 582
   and humanism, 560
   *Last Supper,* Santa Maria delle Grazie, *602,* 603, 628, 637, 959
   life of, 601
   *Madonna of the Rocks,* 567, 601–602, *601,* 604
   *Mona Lisa,* 567, 603–604, *603,* 856, 857, 21-29A, 22-10A, 29-27A
   name of, 405
   painting techniques, 539
   on painting vs. sculpture, 609
   project for a central-plan church, 605, *605b,* 22-6A
   and Raphael, 605, 606
   *Treatise on Painting,* 609
   *Vitruvian Man,* 603b, 22-3A
Lepcis Magna (Libya): Arch of Septimius Severus, 220, *220,* 235
Les Vingts, 821–822
Lescot, Pierre: Louvre, Paris, 658, *658,* 715, 23-14A
Lespinasse, Julie de, 729
Leto/Latona (Greek deity), 107
*The Letter* (Vermeer), 712, *712b,* 25-20A
*Letter from a Seer* (Rimbaud), 819
Lewis, Edmonia: *Forever Free,* 785–786, *785*
Lewis and Clark expedition, 35-16A
Leyster, Judith: *Self-Portrait,* 705, *705*
Liang Kai, 468
   *Sixth Chan Patriarch Chopping Bamboo,* 469–470, *469,* 1009
Liao dynasty Chinese art, 467–468, 473, 16-21A
libations, 36, 41
*Liber pontificalis* (Book of the Pontiffs), 243
*Liberty Leading the People* (Delacroix), 768, *768,* 770
Libeskind, Daniel
   Denver Art Museum, 963, *963b,* 31-34B
   World Trade Center reconstruction proposal, 31-34B
Libon of Elis: Temple of Zeus, Olympia, 125–126, *126, 127,* 128, 5-32A
Library of San Marco, Venice (Sansovino), *623b,* 22-30A
*Il Libro dell'Arte (The Handbook of Art)* (Cennini), 414, 539, 573
Lichtenstein, Roy
   *Drowning Girl,* 915–916, *915*
   on Pop Art, 915
Licinius, 225–226
liege lord, 334
life and death of Buddha, Gandhara (frieze), *422,* 423
*Life* magazine, 894–895, 909
*Life of Jesus, Maestà* altarpiece, Siena Cathedral (Duccio), *411,* 412, *412,* 14-8B
*Life of Phocion* (Plutarch), 25-32A
light
   in 18th century European and American art, 26-11A
   in Burgundian/Flemish late medieval/ early Renaissance art, 20-4A
   in Byzantine architecture, 272, 274, 376
   in Cubism, 847
   in Dutch Baroque art, 702, 706, 707, 708, 711, 712, 25-13A, 25-18B
   in early Byzantine architecture, 261–262
   in Early Christian architecture, 243
   in French Baroque art, 721, 722
   in Gothic architecture, 365, 367, 368–369, 374, 375, 376, 378, 398, 13-3A, 13-23A
   in Greek Late Classical period art, 150
   in Impressionist art, 801, 803, 806, 28-2A
   in Italian 14th century art, 409, 14-7A
   in Italian Baroque art, 682–683
   in Italian Cinquecento Renaissance art, 602, 624
   in Italian Mannerist art, 637
   in Italian Quattrocento Renaissance art, 573, 574, 21-43A
   in Napoleonic era art, 755
   in Post-Impressionist art, 28-15A
   in Realist art, 780, 785
   in Rococo architecture, 730, 731
   in Roman architecture, 210

   in Romanesque architecture, 348, 350, 351, 358
   in Romantic art, 764
   in Spanish Baroque art, 688, 689, 692
light muqarnas, 296
*Lima Tapestry,* Wari, 510, 513, *513*
Limbourg brothers (Pol, Herman, Jean), 20-15A
*Les Très Riches Heures du Duc de Berry,* 550–551, *550, 551*
Lin, Maya Ying: Vietnam Veterans Memorial, Washington, D.C., 965–966, *965*
*Lindau Gospels,* 319–320, *320,* 328–329
Lindisfare Monastery, 310, 311
*Lindisfarne Gospels,* 312–315, *313, 314,* 318
line, 7
Linear A and B, 87
linear perspective, 192–193, 565, 566–568, 567, 720
   *See also* perspective
linga, 435, 436, 439, 15-22B
Lingering Garden (Liu Yuan), Suzhou, 996, *996*
linguist's staff, 1072
Linnaeus, Carolus, 736
lintel of Temple A, Prinias, 5-6B
lintels, 73, 99, 212–213, 344, 5-6B, 12-8A
Lintong (China): Army of the First Emperor of Qin, 454–455, *455*
*Lion and Tiger Hunt* (Rubens), 25-1A
Lion Gate, Hattusa, *45b,* 2-18B
Lion Gate, Mycenae, *98,* 99, 101, 4-18A
*Lion Hunt* (Rubens), 10, *10,* 697, 25-1A
lion hunt, Hadrianic tondo, *210b,* 7-48A
lion pillar, Lauriya Nandangarh, 429, *429b,* 15-6A
lion pillar, Sarnath, *428,* 429
Lipchitz, Jacques, 852, 887
   *Bather, 852b,* 29-20A
Lippi, Filippino, 577
Lippi, Fra Filippo, 581
   *Madonna and Child with Angels,* 577–578, *577,* 604
*Lipstick (Ascending) on Caterpillar Tracks* (Oldenburg), 916–917, *917*
Lisbon (Portugal): Santa Maria Divina Providencia (Guarini), 24-14A
Liszt, Franz, 767
literati
   and contemporary art, 956, 31-22A
   Edo period Japanese, 1014–1015
   Ming dynasty Chinese, 996, 998, 33-12A
   Qing dynasty Chinese, 999, 1000
   Yuan dynasty Chinese, 991–993, 33-1A, 33-4A
literature
   and 18th century European and American art, 740
   Akkadian, 41
   and Chinese art, 994, 997, 33-12A
   and humanism, 560
   and Italian late medieval art, 406, 412
   and Japanese art, 484–485, 486, 487, 17-13B, 34-9A
   and late 19th century art European and American sculpture, 824
   and Modernism, 844, 853, 867
   and Neoclassical art, 760
   and Pre-Raphaelite art, 786
   and Realism, 777, 778
   and Romanesque art, 336
   and Romanticism, 766, 767
   and South Asian art, 981
   Sumerian, 33
   and Symbolist art, 819
   *See also* books
lithograph of the Crystal Palace (Martinet), *790*
lithography, 778, 794, 28-15A
liturgy, 242, 262–263, 276, 312, 550–551, 13-42A
   *See also* Eucharist
lituus, 165
Liu Sheng (prince), 16-6A
Liu Yuan (Lingering Garden), Suzhou, 996, *996*
*Lives of the Most Eminent Painters, Sculptors, and Architects* (Vasari), 407

Monet, Claude *(continued)*
   *Sailboats on the Seine, Argenteuil,* 799
   *Saint-Lazare Train Station,* 803–804, *803*
   and salons, 802
*Money-Changer and His Wife* (Massys),
   659–660, *660*
Mongols, 295, 472, 990
Monk's Mound, Cahokia, 515, *515b,* 18-30A
monochrome
   in Dutch Baroque art, 705
   in late 20th century European and
      American art, 912
   in Pompeian/Vesuvius area art, 194
   in Roman art, 194
monolith with bird and crocodile, Great
   Zimbabwe (sculpture), 531, *531*
monolithic columns, 116, 428–429
monoliths, 531, 1053
   *See also* monolithic columns
Monophysite heresy, 258, 270
monotheism, 233, 235, 285
Monreale cathedral, 275, *275,* 348, 9-26A
Monroe, Marilyn, 916, 917–918, 30-25A
*Mont Sainte-Victoire* (Cézanne), 817–818, *817*
Monte Albán (Mexico), 504, 1024
Montejo the Younger, Francisco, 23-23A
Monterozzi necropolis, Tarquinia, 164, *164,*
   165, 171–172, *172, 173,* 6-9A
Monticello, near Charlottesville (Jefferson),
   750, *751*
*Monument to the Third International*
   (Tatlin), 860–861, *861*
Moore, Charles: Piazza d'Italia, New
   Orleans, 929–930, *929*
Moore, Henry
   on abstract sculpture, 882
   *Reclining Figure,* 883, *883*
Moorish art. *See* Islamic art
*Moralia in Job* (Saint Gregory), 347–348, *347*
moralized Bibles, 384–386
More, Thomas, 647, 23-11A
Moreau, Gustave, 28-26A
   *The Apparition,* 820, *820*
   *Jupiter and Semele, 820b,* 28-24A
   *Morgan Madonna,* 349, *349*
Morisot, Berthe
   *Summer's Day,* 805, *805b,* 28-7A
   *Villa at the Seaside,* 805, *805*
Morozov, Ivan, 844, 858
Morris, William, 808, 840
   Green Dining Room, South Kensington
      Museum, 827, *827*
mortise-and-tenon system, 480
mortuary precinct of Djoser, Saqqara, 58,
   *58b,* 59, 60, 68, 3-5A
mortuary temples, 62
   Djoser mortuary precinct, Saqqara, 58,
      60, 68, 3-5A
   Great Pyramid complex, 62
   Hatshepsut mortuary temple, Deir
      el-Bahri, 69–71, 73
mosaic tilework, 299–300
mosaics, 28-24A
   Early Byzantine, 254, 255, 264–268
   Early Christian, 244–245, 245, 247–248,
      8-13A, 8-17A, 8-19A
   Greek Late Classical period, 149, 150–151,
      196, 214, 654
   Islamic, 287, 291, 299–300
   Mesoamerican, 504, 1024
   Middle Byzantine, 270–271, 272–274,
      275, 9-25A, 9-27A
   Roman, 196, 214
moschophoros, 112
Moses, 33, 360, 8-10A, 22-32A, 23-15A
*Moses,* tomb of Julius II (Michelangelo
   Buonarroti), 360, 612–613, *612*
*Moses Expounding the Law, Bury Bible*
   (Master Hugo), 360, *360*
mosque lamp of Sayf al-Din Tuquztimur,
   301, *301*
mosque lamps, 301
Mosque of Selim II, Edirne (Sinan the
   Great), 298, *298,* 299
mosques, 261, 287, 288, 290–292, 297, 10-5A
   *See also* great mosques; specific mosques
*Mother India (Bharat Mata)* (Tagore), *983b,*
   32-10A

Mother of God, 245, 267, 280, 380
   modern mother as, 824
   *See also* Theotokos; Virgin Mary
*Mother of the Gracchi (Cornelia Presenting
   Her Children as Her Treasures)*
   (Kauffmann), 746–747, *746*
Motherwell, Robert, 905
   *Elegy to the Spanish Republic, Spanish
      Elegies* series, *905b,* 30-8B
motion pictures, 796, 855, 30-3A
Motonobu: *Zen Patriarch Xiangyen
   Zhixian Sweeping with a Broom,* 1007,
   1008–1009, *1009*
*Le Moulin de la Galette* (Renoir), 806, *806*
Mount Sinai (Egypt): monastery of Saint
   Catherine, 267–268, *267,* 269, *269,* 270,
   277, 279, 9-18A
Mount Vesuvius, eruption of, 188, 745
   *See also* Pompeian/Vesuvius area art
Mount Wutai (China): Foguang Si (Buddha
   Radiance Temple), 462, *462b,* 16-15A
*Mountains at Collioure* (Derain), *839b,* 29-4A
*Mouth of Hell, Winchester Psalter,* 12-35A
Mozarabic art, 316
*Mrs. Richard Brinsley Sheridan*
   (Gainsborough), 741–742, *741*
Mshatta (Jordan): Umayyad palace, 287,
   *287b,* 10-5A, 10-5B
mudras, 427
   abhaya mudra, 427, 432–433, 480, 984,
      15-11A, 16-13B
   bhumisparsha mudra, 427
   dharmachakra mudra, 427, 443
   dhyana mudra, 427, 431, 458–459, 16-13A
   in Shingon, 483
Mughal Empire art, 294–295, 302, 945, 974,
   975, 978–980, 981, 987, 32-5A
Muhammad, 284, 285, 289–290
Muhammad V (sultan of Granada), 295
Muhammad ibn al-Zayn: basin *(Baptistère
   de Saint Louis),* 303–304, *303*
Muhammad of Ghor, 294, 976
Muhaqqaq, 300
Mukherjee, Meera, 983–984
   *Ashoka at Kalinga,* 984, *984*
Mukhina, Vera: *The Worker and the
   Collective Farmworker,* 883–884, *883*
mullions, 381, 930
Mumbai (India): Victoria Terminus
   (Chhatrapati Shivaji Terminus)
   (Stevens), 982, *982*
mummification, 61, 78, 218, 7-62A
mummy portrait of a priest of Serapis,
   Hawara (encaustic painting), 218
mummy portrait of a young woman, Hawara
   (encaustic painting), *218b,* 7-62B
mummy portrait of Artemidorus, Hawara
   (encaustic painting), 218, *218b, 218,*
   7-62A
mummy portraits, 218, 7-62A, 7-62B
Munch, Edvard
   and Schiele, 843
   *The Scream,* 822, *823,* 840, 30-3A
Mundy, Peter, 695
Munich (Germany)
   Amalienburg, 730, *730*
   Olympic Park (Behnisch), 962
muqarnas, 274, 296, 297, 9-27A
mural painting
   Byzantine, 9-25A
   Chinese, 462, 16-14A
   contemporary, 969
   Early Christian, 237–239, 8-5A, 8-6A
   Egyptian, 56–57, *57b,* 58, 74–75, 3-1A,
      3-11B
   Greek, 144, 149–150, 191
   Italian 13th century, 407, 14-5A, 14-5B
   Italian 14th century, 400, 401, 408, 409,
      416–417, 419–420, 14-8A, 14-8B
   Italian Quattrocento Renaissance,
      574–576, 578–579, 589–590, 594–596,
      21-24A, 21-41A, 21-49A
   Italian Romanesque, 12-27B
   Japanese, 17-13A
   Late Antique Jewish, 235–236
   Mesoamerican, 497–498, 18-7A
   Mesopotamian, 46, 47, 2-18A
   Mexican interwar Modernist, 890–891

Minoan, 90–93
Native North American, 1032, 1033
Ottonian, 11-23A
Pompeian/Vesuvius area, 189–190,
   191–195, 196, 197, 248, 7-25A, 7-25B
prehistoric, 22, 26–27
Roman High Empire, 7-54A
Romanesque, 348
   *See also* cave paintings
Murasaki Shikubu: *Tale of Genji,* 484–485,
   *485,* 486, 487
Murillo, Bartolomé Esteban: *Immaculate
   Conception of the Escoria,* 688, *688b,*
   24-25A
Muromachi period Japanese art, 1006,
   1008–1009, 1021
Musée Africain, Marseilles, 846
Musée d'Ethnographie du Trocadéro, Paris,
   846
Musée Permanent des Colonies, Paris, 846
Museum für Völkerkunde, Berlin, 846
Museum of Modern Art (MoMA), New York,
   865, 895, 909, 930
museums: Greek forerunner of, 139
music
   and American Modernism, 867
   and contemporary art, 937, 947
   and new media, 937
   and Performance Art, 933–934
   and Rococo architecture, 731
   and Romanticism, 767
   and Symbolist art, 28-24A
   *See also* musical instruments
musical instruments, 38–39, 88
*Musicians* (Caravaggio), 681, *681b,* 24-17A
musicians and dancers, tomb of Nebamun,
   Thebes (mural), 75
Muslims, 976
   *See also* Islam; Islamic art
Mut (Egyptian deity), 57, 3-24A
Muybridge, Eadweard, 784
   *Horse Galloping,* 796, *796,* 825
*My Egypt* (Demuth), 868, *868*
Myanmar art (Burmese art), 443, 986,
   15-28A
Mycenae (Greece)
   female head (sculpture), 101, *101*
   funerary mask, Grave Circle A, 100, *100*
   Grave Circle A, 99–100, *99b,* 100, 4-22A,
      4-23A
   inlaid dagger blade with lion hunt, 100,
      *100,* 4-23A
   Lion Gate, 98, 99, 101, 4-18A
   Treasury of Atreus, 98, 99, *99,* 170, 184
   two goddesses(?) and a child (sculpture),
      100–101, *101*
   *Warrior Vase,* 102, *102*
   *See also* Mycenaean art
Mycenaean art, 95–102
   and archaeology, 85, 86, 87
   architecture, 96–99, 115, 170, 184, 244,
      4-18A, 4-22A, 5-6A
   ivory carvings, 100–101
   metalwork, 99–100, 4-23A
   sculpture, 98, 99, 101–102
   societal contexts, 95
   vase painting, 102
Myokian temple, Kyoto (Sen no Rikyu), 1011,
   *1011*
Myron: *Diskobolos (Discus Thrower),* 131–132,
   *131,* 617–618, 674
mystery plays, 409, 538, 548, 12-35A
mystic marriage, 549
mythology. *See* religion and mythology

## N

the Nabis, 819
Nabu (Mesopotamian deity), 34, 48
Nadar (Gaspar-Félix Tournachon), 792,
   793–794
   *Eugène Delacroix,* 794, *794*
*Nadar Raising Photography to the Height of
   Art* (Daumier), 794, *794*
nail figure (nkisi n'kondi), Kongo
   (sculpture), 1066–1067, *1067*
*Naked Portrait* (Freud), 919, *919*
Namdaemun, Seoul, 1002, *1002*

Namuth, Hans: Jackson Pollock painting
   in his studio in Springs, Long Island,
   New York, *904*
*Nanas* series (Saint-Phalle), 917, *917b,* 30-26A
Nandi (bull), 435, 436, 15-22B
Nanna (Mesopotamian deity), 34, 41
Nanni di Banco: *Four Crowned Saints,* Or
   San Michele, 563, *563*
naos. *See* cella
Napir-Asu (queen of Elam), 45
Napoleon III (emperor of France), 802, 804
*Napoleon at the Plague House at Jaffa* (Gros),
   754, 755, 760, 766, 27-15A
Napoleon Bonaparte, 56, 755, 757, 764, 27-1A,
   27-4A, 27-5A
   *See also* Napoleonic era art
*Napoleon Crossing the Saint-Bernard Pass*
   (David), 757, *757b,* 948, 27-1A, 27-13A
*Napoleon Leading the Army over the Alps*
   (Wiley), 948, *948*
*Napoleon on His Imperial Throne* (Ingres),
   758, *758b,* 27-2A
Napoleonic era art, 754, 756–761, *756map,*
   797, 27-2A
   and Romanticism, 755, 759, 27-1A, 27-5A
   societal contexts, 756–757
   timeline, 756
Nara (Japan): Todaiji, 482–483, *482,* 486
Nara period Japanese art, 474, 475, 481–483,
   489
Nara Prefecture (Japan)
   Horyuji temple, *474,* 475, 480, *480,* 481–
      482, *481, 482*
   Yakushi triad, Yakushiji, 481, *481*
Naram-Sin (king of Akkad), 40, 41
Naram-Sin victory stele, Susa, *40,* 41, 44, 47
Narmer (pharaoh of Egypt), 54, 55, 57
narrative art
   18th century European and American,
      739, 740–741, 747–748
   African, 1073
   Akkadian, 40, 41
   Baroque, 692
   Burgundian/Flemish late medieval/early
      Renaissance, 20-11A
   contemporary art, 946
   early Christian, 249–250, 251–252, 8-21A
   early medieval, 319, 326–327, 11-15A
   Egyptian, 55, 58, 66, 78
   Gothic, 369–370, 377, 13-3A
   Greek Archaic period, 118, 119, 120,
      122–123
   Greek Early/High Classical period, 104,
      105, 126, 128, 143
   Greek Geometric period, 109, 128
   Greek late Classical period, 150–151
   Hellenistic period Greek, 156
   Italian 14th century, 409, 412, 14-8A
   Italian Cinquecento Renaissance art,
      614–615
   Italian late medieval, 405
   Italian Quattrocento Renaissance, 565,
      566–568, 21-24A
   Japanese, 488
   Late Antique Jewish, 235
   Mycenaean, 102, 4-23A
   Native North American, 35-16A
   Neolithic, 27
   Paleolithic, 22, 23
   Pompeian/Vesuvius area, 192
   Roman, 179, 187, 206–207, 208, 7-44A
   Romanesque, 356, 361–362, 12-8B, 12-11A
   Romantic, 764, 765–767
   South Asian, 422, 423, 426, 432, 436, 438,
      978, 15-22A
   Sumerian, 30, 31, 35, 36, 37, 38
narthex, 243, 264, 350, 8-19A
Nasca art, 510–511
Nasca Plain (Peru): hummingbird, 511, *511*
Nash, John: Royal Pavilion, Brighton,
   788–789, *789*
al-Nasir Muhammad, 301
Nasrid dynasty, 295
natatio, 220
National Endowment for the Arts (NEA)
   (U.S.A.), 944, 945
national identity in contemporary art, 945,
   948–949, 973, 31-10A

Porch of the Confessors, Chartres Cathedral, *377b*, 13-18A
Porta Maggiore, Rome, 201, *201, 22-30A*
Porta Marzia, Perugia, 175, *175,* 204–205
portals, 344–346, 369–370, 377, 380, *12-14A, 13-3A, 13-18A*
*See also* jambs
porticos, 154, 576
Portinari, Tommaso, 547–548, *20-14A*
*Portinari Altarpiece* (Hugo van der Goes), 547–548, *547*
Portland Building, Portland, Oregon (Graves), 931, *931*
portrait bust of a Flavian woman, Rome, 205, *205*
portrait bust of Commodus as Hercules, 217, *217b, 7-59A*
portrait bust of Hadrian, 210, *210*
portrait bust of Livia, Arsinoe (sculpture), 198–199, *198*
portrait bust of Philip the Arabian, 222, *222b, 7-68A*
portrait bust of Trajan Decius, 221–222, *221*
portrait medals, *21-29A*
*Portrait of a German Officer* (Hartley), 866, *866, 29-48A*
portrait of a husband and wife, House VII,2,6, Pompeii, 196, *197*
*Portrait of a Lady* (Rogier van der Weyden), *546b, 20-9A*
*Portrait of a Noblewoman* (Fontana), *630b, 22-40A*
portrait of a Roman general, Sanctuary of Hercules, Tivoli (sculpture), 186–187, *186*
*Portrait of a Young Man with a Book* (Bronzino), *634b, 22-46A*
portrait of an Akkadian king, Nineveh, 40–41, *40*
portrait of Augustus as general, Primaporta (sculpture), 198, *198,* 354
*Portrait of Te Pehi Kupe* (Sylvester), 13, *13*
*Portrait of the Artist's Sisters and Brother* (Anguissola), 635, *635*
portrait of Vespasian (sculpture), *204,* 205
portrait statue of the priest Kuya preaching (Kosho), 487, *487*
portrait statue of the priest Shunjobo Chogen, 486, *486*
portraits of the four tetrarchs (sculpture), 224, *225*
portraiture
    in 18th century European and American art, 739–740, 741–743, 751–752, *26-15A, 26-23A*
    in African art, 527–528, *19-6A, 19-13A*
    in Andean South American art, 511
    in Burgundian/Flemish late medieval/early Renaissance art, 538, 541–543, 548, 549, *20-2A, 20-9A, 20-14A*
    in Byzantine art, 259, *9-26A*
    in Carolingian art, 317
    in Chinese art, 449, 994
    in Dutch Baroque art, 704, 705, 706, 707, 708, *25-15A*
    in early 19th century European and American photography, 793–794, 795
    in Egyptian Amarna period art, 76–77
    in Egyptian first millenium BCE art, 80–81
    in Egyptian Middle Kingdom art, 67–68, *3-16A*
    in Egyptian New Kingdom art, 70–71, 74
    in Egyptian Old Kingdom art, 64–66, 67–68, *3-11B, 3-13A, 3-13B*
    in Egyptian post-Amarna period art, 78
    in El Greco's art, 665
    in Flemish Baroque art, 701
    in French Baroque art, 714–715
    in French late medieval/early Renaissance art, 552
    in Gothic art, 370, 394–395, 396
    in Greek art, 133–134, 160–161
    and humanism, 560
    in Italian Cinquecento Renaissance art, 603–604, 614, 630, 631, *22-10A, 22-40A*
    in Italian Mannerist art, 634–635, *22-46A*

    in Italian Quattrocento Renaissance art, 563, 570, 571, 579–580, 590, 592
    in Japanese art, 486, 487–488, 1018
    in late 20th century European and American art, 920
    in Mesoamerican art, 493–494
    in Mesopotamian art, 40–41, 43
    in Napoleonic era art, 758–759, *27-1A, 27-2A, 27-4A, 27-5A*
    in Northern European High Renaissance/Mannerist art, 656, 657, 661–662, *23-11A*
    in Northern European late medieval/early Renaissance art, 535
    and patronage, 6
    in Pompeian/Vesuvius area art, 196, 197, *7-25A, 7-25B*
    in Pre-Raphaelite art, 787–788
    in Realist art, 777
    in Roman Early Empire art, 197–199, 200, 204, 205
    in Roman High Empire art, 210, 216–217, 218, *7-59A, 7-62A, 7-62B*
    in Roman Late Empire art, 219–220, 221–222, 224, 225, 227–228, 230, *7-64A, 7-68A*
    in Roman Republic art, 185–187, *7-10A, 7-11A*
    in Romantic art, 766, *27-10A*
    in South Asian art, 974, 975, 983, *32-5A*
    in Spanish Baroque art, 689, 690, *24-28B*
    *See also* donor portraits
*The Portuguese* (Braque), 847–848, *847*
Portunus (Roman deity), 182
Poseidon (Neptune) (Greek/Roman deity), 107, 137, 140
positivism, 775
post-and-lintel system, 28, *97*
post-Amarna period Egyptian art, 78–80
Postclassic Mesoamerican art, 490, 491, 504–507, 1024–1025
post-Gupta period art (South Asia), 435–437, 447
Post-Impressionist, 811–819, 833
    and Art Nouveau, 829
    Cézanne, 817–819, *28-22A*
    and Derain, *29-4A*
    Gauguin, 815–817
    Seurat, 812
    Toulouse-Lautrec, 811, *28-15A*
    van Gogh, 812–815, *28-16A, 28-16B*
    postmodernism
    architecture, 929–933, 961, 962–963, 964, *31-34A*
    *See also* contemporary art
Post-Painterly Abstraction, 1, 2, 907–908, *31-22A*
*The Potato Eaters* (van Gogh), 813, *813b, 28-16A*
potters' wheels, 93, 110
pottery. *See* ceramics
pou tokomanawa, 1043
pouncing, 482, 979, *32-5A*
poupou, 1043, 1055
Poussin, Nicolas, 717, 733
    *Burial of Phocion,* 720, *720b, 25-32A*
    *Et in Arcadia Ego,* 718, 719, *719*
    *Landscape with Saint John on Patmos,* 720, *720*
    in Napoleonic era art, 760
    notes for a treatise on painting, 718, 719
Poussinistes, 733, 766
Poverty Bay (New Zealand): Te Hau-ki-Turanga meetinghouse, Poverty Bay (Rukupo and others), *1042,* 1043
powwows, 1040
Pozzo, Fra Andrea
    *Glorification of Saint Ignatius,* Sant'Ignazio, Rome, 686, *687*
    and Tiepolo, 735
Prabhutaratna Buddha, 460–461
Prague (Czech Republic): Saint Vitus Cathedral, 366
Prakhon Chai (Thailand): Bodhisattva Maitreya (sculpture), *443b, 15-29A*
prasada, 441
Prasat Andet (Cambodia): Harihara (sculpture), 443–444, *443*

Praxiteles, 149, 218
    *Aphrodite of Knidos,* 145, *145,* 159, 581, 654, *5-62A, 5-83A*
    and Donatello, 568
    followers of, 145–146, *5-62A*
    and Napoleonic era art, *27-5A*
    on painting, *5-63A*
    Praxiteles(?): Hermes and the infant Dionysos (sculpture), 145–146, *146*
Precisionism, 867–869
Preclassic period Mesoamerican art, 494–495
pre-Columbian civilizations, 492
    *See also* Native American art
predellas, 411
Predynastic period Egyptian art, 10, *54–55, 55–60,* 83, *3-1A, 3-5A*
prefiguration, 238, 547, 561
prehistoric art, 14–29
    Aegean. *See* Aegean art.
    African, 16–17, 522–524, 533
    Neolithic, 23–28, 29, *1-16A, 1-19A*
    Paleolithic, 14, 15, 16–23, 29, 522, *1-5A, 1-6A, 1-12A*
    sites, *17map*
    timeline, 16
Premonstratensian order, *12-23A*
Pre-Raphaelite art, 786, *786–787,* 794
Presentation in the Temple, 240, 538, 539
presentation of captives to Lord Chan Muwan, Bonampak (mural), 502, *502*
presentation of offerings to Inanna (*Warka Vase*), Uruk, 35, *35*
Priam (king of Troy), 118
Priene (Turkey): urban planning, 154, *154*
priest(?) performing a bloodletting rite, Teotihuacán (mural), *497b, 18-7A*
Primaporta (Italy): Villa of Livia, 193–194, *193*
primary colors, 7, 813
Primaticcio, Francesco, 657
*Primavera* (Botticelli), *558,* 559, 581
primitivism, 1045, 1066
    and European interwar Modernism, 880
    and German Expressionism, 840, *29-6A*
    and looting, 523
    and the Museum of Modern Art, New York, 895
    and Picasso, 844–845, 847, 851
    societal contexts, 846
princeps, 197, *7-44B*
Prinias (Crete): Temple A, 111, *111b,* 115, *5-6A, 5-6B*
printing press, 554, 560
printmaking, 536, 556
    18th century European and American, 740, 741
    Baroque, 703, 708–709, 722
    and drawing, 604
    German Expressionist, 842, 843
    Holy Roman Empire late medieval/early Renaissance, 554–556, *20-21A*
    Italian Quattrocento Renaissance, 581–582
    Native North American, 1035
    Northern European High Renaissance/Mannerist, 649–651, 653, *23-5A*
    Pop Art, 915–916
    Post-Impressionist, *28-15A*
    Realist, 778–779, 780, 794
    Romantic, 763–764
    *See also* woodblock prints; woodcuts
Pritchard, Thomas F.: iron bridge, Coalbrookdale, 737, *737*
procession of the imperial family, Ara Pacis Augustae, Rome (relief sculpture), 200, *200*
Procopius of Caesarea, 259, 262
Productivism, 860–861
project for a central-plan church (Leonardo da Vinci), 605, *605b, 22-6A*
*Prometheus Bound* (Rubens), *25-13A*
pronaos, 115
propaganda. *See* art as political tool
proportion, 10–11
    in Egyptian art, 64
    in Etruscan architecture, 167
    in Greek Archaic period architecture, 115, 117, 118

    in Greek Early/High Classical period architecture, 104, 105, 134–136, 154
    in Greek Early/High Classical period art, 132
    in Greek Late Classical period architecture, 151
    in Islamic architecture, 299
    in Italian Cinquecento Renaissance architecture, *22-6A*
    in Italian Quattrocento Renaissance architecture, 584, 586, 588, 594
    in Roman architecture, 201
    in South Asian architecture, 980
    *See also* hierarchy of scale; modules
Propylaia (Mnesikles), Athens, 134, 138–139, *139*
proscenium, 675
prostyle, 115
Protestant Reformation, 646, 656–657
    and Books of Hours, 551
    and Counter-Reformation, 616, 617, 637, 641, 646, 670, 672, 686
    and Dürer, 652
    and Italian Baroque art, 670
    and Netherlands High Renaissance/Mannerist art, 659
    and visual imagery, 652–654
protomes, 50, 51
*Protrepticus* (Clement of Alexandria), *8-13A*
provenance, 3
*Psalter of Saint Louis,* 386, *386*
psalters, 312, 386, 550
Pseudo-Dionysius, 262
pseudoperipteral temples, 182, 200–201, 205
Ptah (Egyptian deity), 58
Ptolemy XIII (king of Egypt), 82
Pu-abi (queen/lady of Ur), 38, 39, 41
public art, 965–967
*Public Enemy* (Hammons), 950–951, *951*
Pucelle, Jean
    *Belleville Breviary,* 387–388, *387,* 550
    *Hours of Jeanne d'Evreux,* 387, *387b,* 550, *13-36A*
Pueblo art, 1033–1034
Pueblo Bonito, Chaco Canyon, 518, *518b,* 1032, *18-33A*
pueblos, 518, 1032
Pugin, Augustus Welby Northmore
    Houses of Parliament, London, 788, *788, 26-27A*
    *True Principles of Pointed or Christian Architecture,* 788, *27-43A*
pukao, 1052
pulpit, Sant'Andrea, Pistoia (Giovanni Pisano), 403–404, *403*
pulpits, 402
pulque, *18-7A*
punchwork, 412, 414
Pupienus (Roman emperor), *7-64A*
Pure Land Buddhism
    in China, 427, 462, *16-13B, 16-14A*
    in Japan, 481, 482, 483–484, 487, 488, 1006, *17-13A*
Purgatory, 584
Purism, 853, *29-22A*
purlins, 457, *16-15A*
purse cover, Sutton Hoo ship burial, *309,* 310
Purvis de Chavannes, Pierre
    and Matisse, *29-2A*
    *Sacred Grove,* 819–820, *819*
pylon temples, 72–73, 82, *3-1A, 3-24A*
pylons, 72, 73, 82, *3-24A*
    *See also* pylon temples
Pylos (Greece): Palace of Nestor, *97b, 4-18A*
Pyramid of the Moon, Teotihuacán, *495,* 496, 497, *29-74A*
Pyramid of the Niches, El Tajín, 504, *504*
Pyramid of the Sun, Teotihuacán, *495,* 496–497, *29-74A*
Pyramid Texts, 61
pyramids
    Egyptian Old Kingdom, 60–62, 72, 73
    Mesoamerican, 495, 496–497, 504, *29-74A*
    stepped, 58, 59, 496
Pythagoras, 132, 607

Tegea (Greece): Temple of Athena Alea (Skopas of Paros), 5-64A
tempera painting
  in Italian 13th century art, 404–405
  in Italian 14th century art, 407–408, 411–412, 413–415, 14-10A
  in Italian Cinquecento Renaissance art, 602, 22-32A
  in Italian Quattrocento Renaissance art, 572, 573, 577–578, 579–580, 581, 591, 592, 21-29A
  in Late Antique Jewish art, 235
  in Mesoamerican art, 502
  vs. oil painting, 538, 539
  in Roman art, 219
  *See also* mural painting; painting
*The Tempest* (Giorgione da Castelfranco), 626–627, *626*, 666
Tempietto, Rome (Bramante), 618–619, *618*, 623, 22-6A
Temple A, Prinias, 111, *111b*, 115, 5-6A, 5-6B
Temple of Aphaia, Aegina, 123–124, *123*, *124, 125*, 126
Temple of Apollo, Didyma (Paionios of Ephesos and Daphnis of Miletos), 153–154, *153*
Temple of Artemis, Corfu, 118, *118*, 124
Temple of Artemis, Ephesos, 49
Temple of Athena Alea (Skopas of Paros), Tegea, 5-64A
Temple of Athena Nike (Kallikrates), Athens, 134, 141, *141*, 152
Temple of Fortuna Virilis (Temple of Portunus), Rome, 182, *182*
Temple of Geshtinanna, Girsu, 43
Temple of Hera, Olympia, 115, 146
Temple of Hera I ("Basilica"), Paestum, 117–118, *117*, 123, 135
Temple of Hera II or Apollo, Paestum, 125–126, *126*
Temple of Horus, Edfu, 82, *82*, 3-1A
Temple of Jupiter Optimus Maximus, Capitoline Hill, Rome (Vulca of Veii), 168, 181
Temple of Portunus (Temple of Fortuna Virilis), Rome, 182, *182*
Temple of Quetzalcoatl, Teotihuacán, *496*, 497
Temple of Ramses II, Abu Simbel, 71–72, *71*
Temple of the Giant Jaguar, Tikal, 500, *500*
Temple of the Inscriptions, Palenque, 500, *500b*, 18-10A
Temple of the Sun, Cuzco, 1031, *1031*
Temple of Venus, Baalbek, 224, *224*, 225, 748, 750
Temple of Vesta(?), Tivoli, 183, *183*
Temple of Zeus, Olympia (Libon of Elis), 125–126, *126, 127*, 128, 146–147, 148, 5-32A
Templo Mayor (Great Temple), Tenochtitlán, *1022*, 1023, 1026–1028, *1026, 1027, 1028*
templon, 277
*Temptation of Saint Anthony* (Grünewald), 647, *648*
Tendai Buddhism, 483
tenebrism, 682–683, *683*, 698
tenebroso. *See* tenebrism
Tenochtitlán (Mexico), *1022*, 1024, 1025
  Coatlicue (sculpture), 1028, *1029*
  Coyolxauhqui (relief sculpture), 1026–1028, *1027*
  Templo Mayor (Great Temple), *1022*, 1023, 1026–1028, *1026, 1027, 1028*
  Tlaltecuhtli (relief sculpture), 1028, *1028*
tenons. *See* mortise-and-tenon system
Teotihuacán (Mexico), 491
  architecture, 495–497, *495, 496*
  Aztecs and, 496, 1026
  and ball games, 501
  destruction of, 504, 1024
  and Modernist art, 29-74A
  murals, 497–498, 18-7A
  Tetitla apartment complex, *497*, 498
tephra, 92
tepidarium, 220
ter Brugghen, Hendrick, 723
  *Calling of Saint Matthew*, 702, *702*
Teresa of Avila, Saint, 675, 688

Terminal 5, John F. Kennedy International Airport, New York (Saarinen), 926, *927*
terminus ante quem, 2
terminus post quem, 2
terracotta
  in African art, 524, 525, 528, 529
  in Chinese art, 451, 454–455
  in Etruscan art, 168, 169, 181
  in Intermediate Area Native American art, 507
  in Italian 14th century art, 414
  in Italian Quattrocento Renaissance art, 583, 585, 21-36A
  in Minoan architecture, 90
  in Roman art, 214–215
terribilità, 599
tesserae, 150, 245, 291, 299
tetrarchs, 224
  *See also* tetrarchy
tetrarchy, 224–225
textiles
  African, 1070, 1071, 37-13A
  Andean South American, 509, 510, 513, 1029–1030
  Bauhaus, 29-66B
  Chinese, 448, 449, 458, 10-15A, 16-14A
  contemporary, 945–946
  early Islamic, 10-15A
  in feminist art, 922, 924–925
  and Italian 14th century art, 412
  Japanese, 483
  Late Byzantine, 9-35A
  later Islamic, 300–301, 10-27A
  Native North American, 1033
  Norman Romanesque, 361–362
  Oceanic, 1042, 1043, 1047, 1051, 1053–1054, 1058
texture, 8
Thai art, 443, 984–985, 15-29A
Thangmar of Heidelberg, 324–325
Thanjavur (India): Rajarajeshvara Temple, 438, *439*, 15-22B
*The Thankful Poor* (Tanner), 784–785, *785*
The Eight (artist group), 862
theater of Epidauros (Polykleitos the Younger), 151, *151*
theatron, 151
Thebes (Egypt), 69
  first millenium BCE, 80–81
  funerary chapel of Rekhmire, *64b*, 3-11B
  Senmut with Princess Nefrura (sculpture), 74, *74*
  tomb of Hunefer, 80, *80*
  tomb of Nebamun, 74–75, *75*
  tomb of Tutankhamen, 78, *78, 79*, 100
  Valley of the Kings, 72
  *See also* Luxor
Thebes (Greece): *Mantiklos Apollo* (sculpture), 109–110, *109*, 112
Theodora (Byzantine empress, wife of Justinian), 254, 255, 264, 265, 266, 275, 309
Theodora (Byzantine empress, wife of Theophilos), 270, 273
Theodora and attendants, San Vitale, Ravenna (mosaic), *254*, 255, 264, 265, 266, 275, 309
Theodore, Saint, 268, 269, 377
Theodoric (king of the Ostrogoths), 246, 247, 263, 308, 317
Theodoros of Phokaia: tholos, Delphi, 151–152, *151*
Theodosius I (Roman emperor), 246, 256
Theodulf of Orléans, 265, 317
*Theogony (Genealogy of the Gods)* (Hesiod), 107
Theophanu, 328
Theopompus, 169
theosophy, 841, 880
Theotokos
  in Early Byzantine art, 267, 268–270, *269*
  in Early Christian art, 245
  in Gothic art, 370, 396
  in Middle Byzantine art, 270–271, *271*, *275, 275*, 276, 277
  western European version, 349
  *See also* Virgin and Child; Virgin Mary
Thera (Cyclades), 87, 91–92, 194

Theravada Buddhism, 427, 446, 984, 15-28A
thermoluminescence, 523
Theseion, Athens, 26-28A
Theseus (king of Athens), 89–90, 120, 137, 5-17A
Thessaloniki (Greece)
  Hagios Georgios (Church of Saint George), 248, *248b*, 257, 8-17A, 8-19A
  Saint Catherine, 278, *278b*, 9-32A
Thierry of Chartres, 369
*The Thinker, Gates of Hell* (Rodin), 826, *826*
Third Dynasty of Ur, 42, 43
*Third of May* (Goya), 764, *764, 779*, 855
Third Style, 194
Third Style wall painting, Villa of Agrippa Postumus, Boscotrecase, 194, *194*
*Third-Class Carriage* (Daumier), 779, *779*
*The Thirteen Emperors* (Yan Liben), 462, *463*
Thirty Years' War (1618–1648), 687, 696, 700, 722
*Thirty-six Views of Mount Fuji* series (Hokusai), 1016, 1017, *1017*
tholos, Delphi (Theodoros of Phokaia), 151–152, *151*
tholos tombs, 98, 99, 170, 244
tholos/tholoi, 99, 151, 183, 184, 618
Thomas, Saint, 241, 12-8B
Thomas Aquinas, Saint, 372
Thomas de Cormont: Amiens Cathedral, *371*, 375, 377–379, *377, 377, 379*, 396, 418, 13-38A
Thoth (Egyptian deity), 57, 61
*Three Angels* (Rublyev), 280, *280*
*Three Flags* (Johns), 914, *914*
Three goddesses (Hestia, Dione, and Aphrodite?), Parthenon east pediment, Athens (sculpture), 137, *137*, 602–603
Three Kingdoms period (Korea), 470–471
Three Marys at the Tomb, 241
*Three Musicians* (Picasso), 851, *851b*, 29-19A
three revelers (Euthymides), Vulci (vase painting), 123, *123*
*The Three Shades, Gates of Hell* (Rodin), 826, *826*
*Three Women (Le Grand Déjeuner)* (Léger), *853b*, 29-22A
*Three Women in a Village Church* (Leibl), 782, *782*
throne and footstool of King Nsangu, Bamum, 1065, *1065*
Throne of Maximianus (ivory furniture), 264, *264b*, 9-14A
thrust, 184, 21-31A
Thutmose (sculptor): Nefertiti, 76–77, *77*, 78
Thutmose I (pharaoh of Egypt), 70, 72
Thutmose II (pharaoh of Egypt), 69
Thutmose III (pharaoh of Egypt), 69, 70, 73, 3-11B
Ti, mastaba of, Saqqara, 66, *66, 67*, 74
Ti watching a hippopotamus hunt, mastaba of Ti, Saqqara (relief sculpture), 66, *66*
Tiberius (Roman emperor), 162
Tiepolo, Giambattista
  *Apotheosis of the Pisani Family*, Villa Pisani, Stra, 735, *735*
  Kaisersaal (Imperial Hall), Residenz (Episcopal Palace), Würzburg, 731, *731b*, 26-5A
Tiffany, Louis Comfort: water lily table lamp, 829, *829b*, 28-36B
*Tiger Hunt* (Delacroix), 768, 769, *769*
Tikal (Guatemala)
  Temple of the Giant Jaguar, 500, *500*
  urban planning, 500
tiki, 1054
tilework, 299–300, 34-5A
*Tilted Arc*, New York (Serra), 944, 966–967, *967*
timelines
  18th century European and American art, 728
  Aegean art, 86
  African art, 522, 1062
  Byzantine Empire, 256
  Chinese/Korean art, 450, 990
  contemporary art, 942
  early 19th century European and American art, 756

  early medieval European art, 308
  Egyptian art, 56
  Etruscan art, 166
  Gothic art, 366
  Greece, 106
  Islamic art, 284
  Italian Baroque art, 670
  Italian Cinquecento Renaissance/Mannerism art, 600
  Italian late medieval art, 402
  Italian Quattrocento Renaissance art, 560
  Japanese art, 476, 1006
  late 19th century art European and American art, 800
  late 20th century European and American art, 900
  Late Antique art, 234
  Mesopotamian art, 32
  Modernism, 836
  Native American art, 492, 1024
  Northern European Baroque art, 696
  Northern European High Renaissance/Mannerist art, 646
  Northern European late medieval/early Renaissance art, 536
  Oceanic art, 1044
  Persian art, 32
  prehistoric art, 16
  Roman art, 180
  Romanesque art, 334
  South Asian art, 424, 976
Timgad, Algeria, 207, *207*
Timur (Tamerlane), 302, 975
Timurid dynasty, 302, 305
Tinguely, Jean: *Homage to New York*, 935–936, *936*
Tinia (Etruscan deity), 167, 168
Tintoretto (Jacopo Robusti), 665, 666
  *Last Supper*, 636–637, *636*
Tiryns (Greece): citadel, 96–97, *96, 97*
Titans, 107
Titian (Tiziano Vecelli)
  *Assumption of the Virgin*, 627, *627*
  and Carracci, 681
  and El Greco, 665
  *Feast of the Gods*, 625, *625*, 626, 628
  *Isabella d'Este*, 630, *630*, 631, 22-40A
  *Madonna of the Pesaro Family*, 628, *628*
  and Matisse, 29-2A
  *Meeting of Bacchus and Ariadne*, 628, *629*
  Palma il Giovane on, 631
  *Pastoral Symphony*, *626*, 627, 780
  *Pietà*, 631–632, *631*
  and Poussin, 718
  and Rousseau, 28-26A
  and Rubens, 697
  and Tintoretto, 636
  *Venus of Urbino*, 628, *629*, 631
Titus (Roman emperor), 203, 204, 205, 236, 286
Tivoli (Italy)
  Hadrian's Villa, 212–213, *212*
  Temple of Vesta(?), 183, *183*
Tiwanaku (Bolivia): Gateway of the Sun, 512–513, *512*
Tiwanaku art, 512–513
Tiye (queen of Egypt), 77
Tiye, Ghurab (sculpture), 77, *77*
Tjibaou Cultural Centre, Noumea (Piano), 961, *961*
Tlaloc (Aztec deity), 1026, 1027
Tlaltecuhtli (Aztec deity), 1027, 1028
Tlaltecuhtli, Great Temple of Tenochtitlán (relief sculpture), 1028, *1028*
Tlingit art, 1036, 1037, 1038
Todaiji, Nara, 482–483, *482*, 486, 17-17A
togas, 176
togu na, 1078
Tohaku: *Pine Forest*, 1010, *1011*
tokonoma, 1011
Tokugawa Ieyasu (shogun), 1009, 1012, 34-5A
Tokugawa shogunate. *See* Edo period Japanese art
Tokyo (Japan): Olympic stadiums (Tange), 1020, *1020*
Toltecs, 506, 1024, 1025
*Tom Jones* (Fielding), 740

*Vishnu Asleep on the Serpent Ananta,* Vishnu Temple, Deogarh (relief sculpture), 436–437, *437*

*Vishnu Lying on the Cosmic Ocean,* Mebon Temple (sculpture), 444, *444*

Vishnu Temple, Deogarh, 436–437, *436, 437*

Vishvanatha Temple, Khajuraho, 438, *439,* 440, *440,* 444

Visigothic art, 282, 291, 315–316

Visigoths, 246, 290, 308

*Vision after the Sermon (Jacob Wrestling with the Angel)* (Gauguin), 815–817, *815*

Visitation, 240, 380, 393, 538, 539

*Visitation,* Reims Cathedral (sculpture), 380, *380,* 393

*Vita* (Bellori), 682

vita contemplativa, 342

Vitalis, Saint, 255

Vitra Fire Station, Weil-am-Rhein (Hadid), 964, *964*

*Vitruvian Man* (Leonardo da Vinci), *603b,* 22-3A

Vitruvius, 135, 152, 167, 586, 588, 603, 622, 650–651, 22-6A

*Vitruvius Britannicus* (Campbell), 749

viziers, 3-11B

*Vladimir Virgin,* 277, *277*

Vollard, Ambroise, 811, 844

Voltaire (François Marie Arouet), 736, 760, 767

volume, 8

volutes, 51, 116, 152

votive disk of Enheduanna, Ur, 41, *41*

votive offerings

in Etruscan art, 174

in Greek art, 109, 112, 114, 115, 119, 5-17A

in Mesopotamian art, 35–36, 41, 43, 45, 2-6A

voussoirs, 175, 344, 640

Voutier, Olivier, 27-15A

Vulca of Veii: Temple of Jupiter Optimus Maximus, Capitoline Hill, Rome, 168, 169

Vulcan. *See* Hephaistos

Vulci (Italy)

Achilles and Ajax playing a dice game (Exekias) (vase painting), 120–121, *121*

Achilles killing Penthesilea (Exekias) (vase painting), *120b,* 5-20A

Hermes bringing the infant Dionysos to Papposilenos (Phiale Painter) (vase painting), 144, *144,* 146

sarcophagus of Ramtha Visnai and Arnth Tetnies, Ponte Rotto necropolis, *176b,* 6-15A

three revelers (Euthymides) (vase painting), 123, *123*

Vyd, Joducus, 540

## W

wabi, 1012

Wagner, Richard, 28-24A

wainscoting, 827

Wainwright Building, St. Louis (Sullivan), 832, *832b,* 28-40A

waist pendate of a queen mother, Benin, 531–532, *531*

waka sran, 1069

al-Walid (Umayyad caliph), 287

*The Walk Home* (Schnabel), 954, *955*

Walking Buddha, Sukhothai (sculpture), 984–985, *985*

*Walking Man* (Rodin), 825–827, *825*

wall tombs: Italian Quattrocento Renaissance, 570

Wallace, Alfred Russell, 800

Walpole, Horace

*The Castle of Otranto: A Gothic Story,* 26-27A

Strawberry Hill, Twickenham, 749, *749b,* 26-27A

*Wanderer above a Sea of Mist* (Friedrich), 771, *771*

Wang Meng, 993

*Wangshi Yuan (Garden of the Master of the Fishing Nets),* Suzhou, 996, *996*

war helmet mask, Tlingit, 1036, *1037*

*War Monument* (Barlach), 874, *875*

warfare

in Egyptian art, 78, 79, 82

in Greek Archaic period art, 119, 120

in Greek Early/High Classical period art, 126, 128, 136, 137

in Greek Late Classical period art, 150–151

in Mesopotamian art, 36, 37, 38, 40, 41, 46–47

in Mycenaean art, 102

in Roman art, 178, 179, 208

Warhol, Andy

*Green Coca-Cola Bottles,* 916, *916*

Haring and, 969

*Marilyn Diptych,* 916, *916b,* 918, 30-25A

Wari art, 510, 513

*Warka Vase* (presentation of offerings to Inanna), Uruk, 35, *35*

warp, 510

Warring States period (China), 453, 454, 463

warrior, sea off Riace (sculpture), 129–130, *129,* 160

warrior figure (Gu?) (Kendo) (sculpture), 1066, *1066*

warrior seated at his tomb (Reed Painter), Eretria (vase painting), *143b,* 5-58A

warrior taking leave of his wife (Achilles Painter), Eretria (vase painting), 142–143, *143*

*Warrior Vase,* Mycenae, 102, *102*

Washing of the Disciples' Feet, 241, 11-29A

Washington, D.C. (U.S.A.): U.S. Capitol (Latrobe), 750–751

Washington, George, 751–752

Wassily chair (Breuer), *885b,* 29-66A

Wat Mahathat, Sukhothai, 984

*Water Carrier of Seville* (Velázquez), 689, *689*

water lily table lamp (Tiffany), 829, *829b,* 28-36B

waterworn pebble resembling a human face, Makapansgat, 16, *16*

wats, 443

Watteau, Antoine

and Gainsborough, 741

*L'Indifférent,* 732–733, *732*

*Pilgrimage to Cythera,* 728, *732,* 733, 25-1A

*Signboard of Gersaint,* 733, *733b,* 26-7A

*Waves at Matsushima* (Korin), 8–9, 9

*Waves at Matsushima, Matsushima Screens* (Tawaraya Sotatsu), 1013, *1013b,* 34-9A

weary Herakles (Farnese Hercules) (Lysippos of Sikyon), 148, *148*

weaving. *See* textiles

webs, 368, 373

Wedgwood, Josiah, 727, 745, 26-11A

wedjat, 57, 61

Weems, Carrie Mae, 946

*Untitled (Man Smoking/Malcolm X), Kitchen Table* series, *946b,* 31-6B

weft, 510

Weil-am-Rhein (Germany): Vitra Fire Station (Hadid), 964, *964*

Weissenau passional (Rufillus), 353, *353b,* 12-23A

welding, 11

*Well of Moses,* Chartreuse de Champmol (Sluter), 537–538, *537*

Wen Shu: *Carnations and Garden Rock,* 998–999, *999*

Wencheng (Chinese emperor), 16-13A

were-jaguars, 494

Wernher (provost of Klosterneuburg), 13-44A

West, Benjamin: *Death of General Wolfe,* 742, *743*

Westminster Abbey, London, 362, 391, *391,* 13-42A, 26-27A

Weston, Edward, 920, 945

*Nude,* 870, *870b,* 29-44A

*Pepper No. 30,* 870, *870,* 895

westworks, 323, 323–324, 357, 11-19B

wet-plate photography, 792, 795cap

Whakatane (New Zealand): Mataatua meetinghouse (Apanui), 1058, *1058b,* 36-19A

wheel-turning mudra (dharmachakra mudra), 427, 443

*When I Put My Hands on Your Body* (Wojnarowicz), 943–944, *943*

*Where Do We Come From? What Are We? Where Are We Going?* (Gauguin), 816, *816,* 817

Whistler, James Abbott McNeill, 808, 862

on "artistic arrangements," 810

*Nocturne in Black and Gold (The Falling Rocket),* 810, *810*

White, Minor, 954

*Moencopi Strata, Capitol Reef, Utah,* 920, *920*

White Heron Castle (Shirasagi), Himeji, 1010, *1010b,* 34-5A

White Monks (Cistercian order), 322, 343, 12-10A

White Temple and ziggurat, Uruk, 33, *33,* 34

white-ground painting, 142–143, 144, 5-58A

Whiteread, Rachel

Holocaust Memorial, Vienna, 966, *966*

*House,* 966

Whiting, Cliff (Te Whanau-A-Apanui), 1058

*Tawhiri-Matea (God of the Winds),* 949, *949*

Whitman, Walt, 783

Whitney, Gertrude Vanderbilt, 865

Whitney Museum of American Art, New York, 865

*Who's Afraid of Aunt Jemima?* (Ringgold), 946, *946*

Wibald (abbot of Stavelot), 354–355

Wieskirche (Church of the Meadow), near Füssen (Zimmermann), 731, *731b,* 26-5B

*Wild Vines with Flowers Like Pearls* (Wu), 956, *956*

Wilde, Oscar, 28-27A

Wildmon, Donald, 944

Wiley, Kehinde, 947–948

*Napoleon Leading the Army over the Alps,* 948, *948*

Wilhelm IV (duke of Bavaria), 654

Wiligelmo, 359

*Creation and Temptation of Adam and Eve,* 356, *356,* 12-23A

Wilke, Hannah: *S.O.S.-Starification Object Series,* 923–924, *924*

Willendorf (Austria): nude woman *(Venus of Willendorf),* 18, *18,* 25, 30-26A

William II Rufus (king of England), 275

William Durandus (bishop of Mende), 375

William of Normandy (William the Conqueror), 357, 361

William of Sens, 339

William the Pious (duke of Aquitaine), 341

Willis Tower (Sears Tower), Chicago (Skidmore, Owings, and Merrill), 928–929, *928,* 961

*Winchester Psalter,* 360, *360b,* 12-35A, 13-38B

Winckelmann, Johann Joachim, 746, 26-23A

windows

in Gothic architecture, 372, 398

in Islamic architecture, 296

in Italian 13th century architecture, 14-5A

lancets, 370, 373, 376–377, 383, 391, 398, 890, 14-5A, 27-43A

in late 20th century European and American architecture, 920, 931

in Northern European High Renaissance/Mannerist art, 658

oculi, 184, 202, 210, 372, 373, 383, 14-6A, 21-31A

in Roman architecture, 184, 228, 229

in Romanesque architecture, 351

*See also* clerestories; fenestration; stained-glass windows

witchcraft, 649

*Witches' Sabbath* (Baldung Grien), 649, *649*

Wittgenstein, Ludwig, 937

Witz, Konrad: *Altarpiece of Saint Peter,* Cathedral of Saint Peter, Geneva, 552–553, *553*

Wodiczko, Krzysztof: *The Homeless Projection,* 952, *952*

Wojnarowicz, David, 945, 946

*When I Put My Hands on Your Body,* 943–944, *943*

Wolgemut, Michel, 649

illustrator of *Nuremberg Chronicle* (Koberger), 554–555, *555,* 556

*Woman 1* (de Kooning), 905, *905*

*Woman Combing Her Hair* (Archipenko), 852, *852,* 853

*Woman Combing Her Hair* (González), 852–853, *852*

*Woman Holding a Balance* (Vermeer), 711, *711*

woman holding a bison horn, Laussel (relief sculpture), 18–19, *19,* 1-6A

"Woman in the Year 2000" (Schneemann), 934

woman sacrificing at an altar, Diptych of the Nicomachi and Symmachi (ivory carving), 252, *252*

*Woman with Dead Child* (Kollwitz), 842, *843*

Woman with stylus and writing tablet ("Sappho"), Pompeii (fresco), *196b,* 7-25A

*Woman with the Hat* (Matisse), 837, *837,* 844

Womanhouse, 921, 922

*Women Artists, 1550–1950* exhibit, 684

women as subjects

in Cycladic art, 87

in Egyptian New Kingdom art, 75

in Greek Archaic period art, 5-23A

in Paleolithic art, 18, 1-6A

*See also specific works of art*

*Women of Algiers in Their Apartment* (Delacroix), 768, *768b,* 27-17A

*Women of Allah* series (Neshat), 952, *952*

*The Women Regents of the Old Men's Home at Haarlem* (Hals), 705, *705*

women's roles in society

and Abstract Expressionism, 30-8C

Africa, 1070, 1074, 1075

Baroque era, 684, 705

Byzantine empresses, 266, 273

and contemporary art, 942–943, 31-2A

early 19th century, 786

early 20th century, 835

early medieval Europe, 316

Egypt, 69, 70–71, 77

Etruscans, 169, 6-9A

femmes savants, 729

Gothic Europe, 386

Greece, 108, 142, 169

Japan, 485, 1014

late 19th century, 805, 809

late medieval/early Renaissance Flanders, 545

Mesopotamia, 41, 44

Modernist era, 865

Native North America, 517, 1035

Oceania, 1042, 1043, 1050, 1051, 1053

precolonial Africa, 524

Renaissance, 414, 630, 661, 662

Romanesque era, 352

and Saint-Simonianism, 779

Schneeman on, 934

South Asia, 979

*See also* feminist art; women as subjects; *specific women*

Wood, Grant, 889–890

*American Gothic,* 890, *890*

woodblock prints

Chinese, 1000

Japanese, 808, 809, 1004, 1005, 1015, 1016, 1017, 28-15A, 28-16B, 34-12A

woodcuts, 6, 554–555, 556, 649–651, 653, 20-21A, 23-5A

*See also* woodblock prints

Woodlands Native American art, 514–517, 1035, 18-30A

Woodstock (England): Blenheim Palace (Vanbrugh and Hawksmoor), 728, *728b,* 26-1A, 26-5A

Woolf, Virginia, 922

Woolley, Leonard, 32, 37

Worcestershire (England): Hagley Park, 750, *750b,* 26-28A

Wordsworth, William, 767

*The Worker and the Collective Farmworker* (Mukhina), 883–884, *883*

Works Progress Administration (WPA) (U.S.A.), 887

World Trade Center reconstruction proposal (Libeskind), 31-34B
World War I
    and American Modernism, 866
    and Cubism, 848
    and Dada, 835, 856, 29-27A
    and Futurism, 855
    and German Expressionism, 839, 842, 29-10A
    and Neue Sachlichkeit, 872, 873–874
    and Surrealism, 876
World War II, 396, 900–901, 955, 1019, 21-49A
Wren, Christopher: Saint Paul's Cathedral, London, 724, 724, 26-1A
Wright, Frank Lloyd, 832, 884
    Kaufmann House (Fallingwater), Bear Run, 896, 896
    Robie House, Chicago, 870, 871, 896
    Solomon R. Guggenheim Museum, New York, 925, 925, 927, 970
Wright of Derby, Joseph, 744
    An Experiment on a Bird in the Air-Pump, 737b, 26-11A
    A Philosopher Giving a Lecture at the Orrery, 726, 727
writing
    Carolingian, 317
    Chinese, 450, 997
    Japanese, 484
    Sumerian, 32–33
    See also calligraphy
writing boxes, 1014
**Written Sources boxes**
    Apollodorus of Damascus, 212
    artists' guilds, 410
    Ashoka, 428
    Babylon, 49
    Bellori, 682
    Bernard of Clairvaux on cloister sculpture, 342
    Byzantine emperors, 259
    Counter-Reformation Italy, 617
    Diderot, 738
    Domus Aurea (Golden House), 202
    Etruscan art in Rome, 168
    femmes savants, 729
    Gudea (ensi of Lagash), 43
    Mount Vesuvius, 188
    Polykleitos, 132

Sinan the Great, 298
stone vaulting, 339
Suger (abbot of Saint-Denis), 367
Xie He's Six Canons, 460
Wrongful Beheading of the Count (Bouts), 546b, 20-11A
wrought iron, 28-36A
Wu (Chinese emperor), 463
Wu family shrines, Jiaxiang, 455–456, 456
Wu Guanzhong, 1001
    Wild Vines with Flowers Like Pearls, 956, 956
Wu School of Chinese painting, 996, 997, 998
Wu Zetian (Chinese empress), 461, 464
Wu Zhen: Stalks of Bamboo by a Rock, 991, 991
Wunmonije compound, Ile-Ife, 19-6A
Würzburg (Germany): Residenz (Episcopal Palace) (Neumann), 731, 731b, 26-5A
Wuwei (China): flying horse, tomb of Governor-General Zhang (sculpture), 456, 456
Wuzong (Chinese emperor), 462

## X

X-ray style, 1045
Xerxes (king of Persia), 50, 125, 2-26A
Xia dynasty (China), 452
Xia Gui: Twelve Views from a Thatched Hut, 468b, 16-23A
Xiangyen Zhiaxian, 1008–1009
Xie He, 460
Xipe Totec (Mesoamerican deity), 1027
Xiuwi (China): meiping vase, 466, 467
Xu Bing, 956, 1001
    A Book from the Sky, 953, 953
Xuan (Chinese emperor), 462

## Y

yakshas, 432
yakshi holding a fly whisk, Didarganj (sculpture), 429, 429b, 15-6B
yakshis, 429, 430, 432, 15-6B, 15-8A
Yakushi (Bhaisajyaguru Buddha), 481
Yakushi triad, Yakushiji, Nara Prefecture (sculpture), 481, 481
yamato-e, 485
Yan Liben, 460, 462
    The Thirteen Emperors, 462, 463
Yanagi Soetsu, 1019

yang, 463
Yang (Chinese empress), 468
Yangon. See Rangoon
Yangshao Culture vases, 451, 451
Yaroslav the Wise (prince of Russia), 9-25A
yasti, 430
Yaxchilán (Mexico): Shield Jaguar and Lady Xoc (relief sculpture), 503, 503
Yayoi period Japanese art, 477, 489
Ye Yushan: Rent Collection Courtyard, 1001, 1001
Yi Seonggye, 1001
yin, 463
Yingxian (China): Foguang Si Pagoda, 467–468, 467
yoga (meditative practice), 426
yoga (Western painting), 1019
Yombe mother and child (pfemba) (sculpture), 1066, 1067, 1067
Yongle (Chinese emperor), 989
Yongtai (Tang princess), 462, 464
Yongzheng (Chinese emperor), 1000
Yoruba, 1072–1073, 37-16A
Yosa Buson. See Buson
yosegi (joined-wood technique), 17-13A, 17-17A
Yoshihara, Jiro, 1019
    Gutai Art Manifesto, 1020
Young, La Monte, 935
young god(?), Palaikastro (sculpture), 94–95, 94
Young Man Holding a Medal of Cosimo de' Medici (Botticelli), 21-29A
youth diving, Tomb of the Diver, Paestum (fresco), 144, 172
Yuan dynasty art, 990–993, 1003, 33-1A, 33-4A
Yuan dynasty Chinese art, 990–993, 1003, 33-1A, 33-4A
Yungang Grottoes, Datong, 461, 461b, 16-13A
Yupik art, 1038, 1039

## Z

Zapotecs, 493, 496, 504, 1024
Zen Buddhism, 470, 920, 1006, 1007, 1008, 1012, 1019, 34-2A
Zen Patriarch Xiangyen Zhixian Sweeping with a Broom (Motonobu), 1007, 1008–1009, 1009
Zeno, 154

Zeus (Jupiter) (Greek/Roman deity), 107
    in Etruscan art, 167, 168, 175
    in Greek art, 118, 126, 131
    and Pompeian/Vesuvius area architecture, 189
    in Roman art, 7-40A
    in Symbolist art, 28-24A
    Zeus (or Poseidon?), sea off Cape Artemision (sculpture), 131, 131
Zeus, Olympia (Phidias), 49, 27-2A
Zhao dynasty Chinese art, 458–459
Zhao Kuangyin (Chinese emperor), 465
Zhao Mengfu, 990
    Sheep and Goat, 990b, 33-1A
    Zhou dynasty Chinese art, 453, 457, 473
Zhou Jichang: Lohans Giving Alms to Beggars, 468, 469
Zhuangzi, 463
ziggurat, Babylon, 34, 48, 49
ziggurat, Ur, 42, 42
ziggurats, 33–34
    Babylon, 34, 48, 49
    Dur Sharrukin (Khorsabad), 2-20A
    and early Islamic architecture, 289
    vs. stepped pyramids, 58
    Ur, 42, 42
    White Temple and ziggurat, Uruk, 33–34
Zimmermann, Dominikus: Wieskirche (Church of the Meadow), near Füssen, 731, 731b, 26-5B
Zimmermann, Johann Baptist: frescoes and stuccoes, Wieskirche (Church of the Meadow), near Füssen, 26-5B
Zimri-Lim, investiture of, palace, Mari (mural), 43, 43b, 44, 45, 46, 2-18A
Zoe Porphyrogenita (Byzantine empress), 273–274, 275
Zola, Émile, 778
zoomorphic forms. See animals
zoopraxiscope, 796
Zuan di Franza, 21-37A
Zuccari, Federico, 604
Zurbarán, Francisco de: Saint Serapion, 688–689, 689
Zwingli, Ulrich, 653–654